THE COMPACT EDITION
OF THE OXFORD
ENGLISH DICTIONARY

THE COMPACT EDITION OF THE OXFORD ENGLISH DICTIONARY

COMPLETE TEXT
REPRODUCED MICROGRAPHICALLY

VOLUME II
P–Z

SUPPLEMENT AND BIBLIOGRAPHY

OXFORD UNIVERSITY PRESS

Oxford University Press, Walton Street, Oxford OX2 6DP

OXFORD LONDON GLASGOW
NEW YORK TORONTO MELBOURNE WELLINGTON
KUALA LUMPUR SINGAPORE JAKARTA HONG KONG TOKYO
DELHI BOMBAY CALCUTTA MADRAS KARACHI
IBADAN NAIROBI DAR ES SALAAM CAPE TOWN

First Published 1971
Reprinted 1972, 1974, 1977, 1979, 1980

Printed in the United States of America

PUBLISHERS' NOTE

For the suggestion of this latest edition of the Oxford English Dictionary in compact form the publishers are indebted to Mr. Albert Boni of Readex Microprint Corporation whose Compact Editions of the British Museum Catalogue and other reference works pioneered this method of publication.

PREFACE TO THE SUPPLEMENT

IN the Indenture drawn up in 1879 between the Philological Society and the Delegates of the Oxford University Press it was provided that

The Delegates may also at any time, and from time to time, prepare and publish a Supplement or Supplements to the principal Dictionary, on the same terms and in the same manner and form as the said Principal Dictionary, provided that such Supplement or Supplements shall not occupy more than 2,000 pages in all, except with the consent in writing of the Society.

From the earliest days of the publication of the Dictionary this provision has been kept in view not only by members of the Dictionary staff but also by a certain number of the regular 'readers' outside who have maintained a continuous flow of contributions to the material from which the work was being compiled; moreover, communications of corrections and additions have been constantly sent in by many interested users of the published work. Consequently, when 'the Principal Dictionary' was completed in 1928, a great body of quotations had been amassed with a view to a Supplement on a grand scale, which should not only treat the new words and new meanings that had come into being during the publication of the successive sections—the dates of which range from 1 February 1884 to 19 April 1928—but should also correct and amplify the evidence for what was already in print. It was soon discovered, however, that such a Supplement, if it were to be at all a worthy and adequate addition to the main work, would demand intensive researches by experienced workers extending over many years. This could not be contemplated, and it was therefore resolved to produce a supplementary volume the scope of which would be in the main restricted to the treatment of those accessions of words and senses which had taken place during the preceding fifty years. To this limitation there were to be two principal exceptions: items of modern origin and present currency that had been either intentionally or accidentally omitted would be included, and account would be taken of earlier evidence for American uses, which Sir William Craigie was in a position to supply. Temporary or casual uses would be recognized only in so far as they marked stages in the recent history of scientific discovery, invention, or fashion, or illustrated the progress of thought, usage, or custom during the half-century under review. A few important corrections or amplifications of existing definitions have been introduced under the necessity of bringing the work into line with recent research.

The chief characteristics of the vocabulary set forth in this volume are sufficiently obvious on a cursory examination: on the technical side, it exhibits the great enlargement of the terminology of the arts and sciences—biochemistry, wireless telegraphy and telephony, mechanical transport, aerial locomotion, psycho-analysis, the cinema, to name a few outstanding subjects; on the purely linguistic side, there is the varied development of colloquial idiom and slang, to which the United States of America have made a large contribution, but in which the British dominions and dependencies also have a conspicuous share. As in the main work, there has been continually present the problem of the inclusion or omission of the more esoteric scientific terms and of the many foreign words reflecting the widened interest in the conditions and customs of remote countries, and it cannot be hoped or pretended that this problem has been solved in every instance with infallible discretion. In one respect this Supplement has gone somewhat beyond the limits of the main Dictionary, namely, in its more generous inclusion of proper names; but, even so, these have not been admitted unless they have some allusive interest or are important for some linguistic, literary, or historical reason. The arrangement of the articles is simple and straightforward and needs no explanation. It is necessary merely to state that an asterisk preceding a word in small capitals indicates an article to be found in the Supplement.

The matter comprised within the 866 pages of this Supplement, extensive though it is, represents only a restricted selection from a specially prepared basis of material from which a much larger volume might have been produced, and which itself was extracted from a collection of closely-packed slips occupying some 75 linear feet of shelving. This original mass had been sorted and made available for use by Miss I. B. Hutchen and Mr. A. Pallemaerts (a Belgian refugee) before the work on the main Dictionary was concluded. A considerable part of the modern material selected from this for immediate use in the preparation of the Supplement had been contributed by such enthusiastic collectors as the late Dr. F. J. Furnivall and the late Rev. W. B. R. Wilson (of Dollar)—both of whom had specialized in newspaper and magazine literature—and the Rev. H. E. G. Rope, a former member of the Dictionary staff. It was evident, however, that many of the quotations in those invaluable collections could not be

used as first-hand evidence, and that the necessary researches by the staff in sifting and completing the data would need to be supplemented from outside. To this end dated lists of desiderata were compiled and published in *The Periodical*, the organ of the Oxford University Press. Many volunteers responded and many thousands of quotations were obtained by this means. Among the most prolific contributors have been the Rev. T. G. Phillips (Isle of Man), Dr. Max Born (Berlin), and Mr. Edvard Giese, Mag. Art. (Copenhagen); Mr. A. J. Fowler and Mrs. A. J. Jenkinson were specially engaged to read modern literature and technical works; others who have made noteworthy contributions or have maintained a continuous interest in the collection of evidence are: the Rev. J. B. Johnston, Mr. Falconer Madan, Mr. H. J. R. Murray, and Dr. E. H. Sugden, whose names appear among the earliest lists of contributors to the main work; Mr. C. W. Adams, Dr. F. A. Bather, Mr. H. Bayles, Mr. E. S. Brown, Dr. R. W. Chapman, Miss M. B. Cruickshank, the late Rev. Dr. W. Cruickshank, the Rev. F. G. Ellerton, Mr. C. A. Exley (Chicago, Ill.), Mr. David Freeman, Mr. Louis N. Feipel (Brooklyn, N.Y.), Mr. E. V. Gatenby (Fukushima, Japan), Mr. H. W. Horwill, Mr. E. W. Hulme (formerly of the Patent Office), Mr. A. Lewis, Mr. G. G. Loane, Professor W. S. Mackie (Capetown), Professor H. L. Savage (Princeton, N.J.), Dr. A. B. A. Scott, Mr. W. B. Shaw, Mr. K. Sisam, Dr. L. J. Spencer (British Museum, Natural History), Mr. E. V. Stocks (University Library, Durham), Mr. L. R. M. Strachan, Dr. A. E. H. Swaen (Amsterdam), Mr. M. Venkanah (Maharajah's College, Vizianagram, India), Mr. J. M. Watt, Miss E. G. Withycombe. By the courtesy of Professor J. H. G. Grattan, a collection of colloquialisms from the volumes of *Punch* made by a pupil, Mr. K. Foster, was placed at the disposal of the Editors, and this has proved of great service. The voluminous War collections of the late Dr. Andrew Clark have been accessible in the Bodleian Library, where, as heretofore, the editorial staff has enjoyed liberal accommodation. In some of the earlier letters valuable additions to the American material were made by Mr. Albert Matthews from his own extensive collections.

Mr. H. F. Rutter and Mrs. E. A. Coulson have read the 'first proof' and have contributed useful suggestions as well as quotations. For some of the earlier letters of the alphabet Dr. E. H. Lendon rendered valuable service in verification and research at the British Museum.

It has often been necessary to have recourse to specialists for information on technical matters, and they have invariably responded in the most generous manner. Grateful acknowledgement of assistance is due to: Sir Richard Burn, Mr. R. P. Dewhurst, Mr. G. R. Driver, the late Professor Nevill Forbes, Dr. J. K. Fotheringham, Mr. R. F. Harrod, Dr. J. G. Milne, Dr. N. V. Sidgwick, Professor F. Soddy, Sir Ernest Swinton, and Professor F. W. Thomas, of Oxford; Sir Arthur Eddington and Dr. J. Chadwick, of Cambridge; Mr. N. B. Jopson and Mr. D. Subotić, of the University of London; Professor A. Findlay, Dr. A. E. M. Geddes, Dr. J. F. Tocher, and Dr. N. T. Walker, of Aberdeen; Mr. L. G. Carr Laughton, Lord Passfield, Lord Riddell, Mr. Martin Shaw, Col. H. R. H. Southam, and Mr. M. H. Spielmann; the Librarian of the India Office, the Superintendent of the Kew Observatory, the Directors and staffs of the Natural History Museum and the Royal Botanic Gardens, the Printer to the University of Oxford, and the Secretary of the Zoological Society; the editors of *The Evening News*, *The Field*, *The Sketch*, and *The Stock Exchange Gazette*; and many business houses which have supplied particular information about proprietary terms.

Thanks are due to Dr. W. D. Simpson, Librarian of King's College, Aberdeen, who kindly provided facilities for the preparation of N and O.

The editorial responsibility has been shared as follows: A–K, S, and T have been allotted to Dr. C. T. Onions, L–R and U–Z to Sir William Craigie, who has also directed for the whole alphabet the assembling and treatment of the earlier, and most of the later, evidence for American usage. Dr. Onions has been assisted throughout by five members of the old Dictionary staff, Mr. Walter Worrall, Mr. W. J. Lewis, Mr. F. J. Sweatman, M.A. Oxon., Mr. J. W. Birt, and Mrs. L. F. Powell, and for longer or shorter periods by Mr. A. T. Maling, M.A. Camb., Hon. M.A. Oxon., Miss R. A. N. R. Murray, Miss E. S. Bradley, Miss E. V. V. Clark, M.A. Oxon., Mrs. A. S. C. Ross (Miss E. S. Olszewska), B.A. Leeds, Miss Evelyn A. Lee, B.A. Leeds, and Mr. J. L. N. O'Loughlin, B.A. Oxon. Sir William Craigie was assisted for a considerable period by Mr. H. J. Bayliss, in part also by Mr. G. Watson and Mr. M. M. Mathews. The letters supervised by him were prepared for the printer by Mr. J. M. Wyllie, M.A. Aberd., assisted by Mr. Bayliss, Mrs. Heseltine, and Miss Dorothy E. Marshall.

KEY TO THE PRONUNCIATION.

I. CONSONANTS.

b, d, f, k, l, m, n, p, t, v, z *have their usual values.*

g as in *go* (gō^u).
h ... *ho!* (hō^u).
r ... *run* (rɒn), *terrier* (teriəɹ).
ɹ ... *her* (həɹ), *farther* (fāɹðəɹ).
s ... *see* (sī), *cess* (ses).
w ... *wen* (wen).
hw ... *when* (hwen).
y ... *yes* (yes).

þ as in *thin* (þin), *bath* (baþ).
ð ... *then* (ðen), *bathe* (bēⁱð).
ʃ ... *shop* (ʃǫp), *dish* (diʃ).
tʃ ... *chop* (tʃǫp), *ditch* (ditʃ).
ʒ ... *vision* (vi·ʒən), *déjeuner* (deʒöne).
dʒ ... *judge* (dʒɒdʒ).
ŋ ... *singing* (si·ŋiŋ), *think* (þiŋk).
ŋg ... *finger* (fiŋgəɹ).

(FOREIGN.)
ñ as in *French nasal*, *environ* (añvirọñ).
lʸ ... It. *seraglio* (serā·lʸo).
nʸ ... It. *signore* (sinʸō·re).
χ ... Ger. *ach* (aχ), Sc. *loch* (lǫχ, lǫχʷ).
χʸ ... Ger. *ich* (iχʸ), Sc. *nicht* (nèχʸt).
γ ... Ger. *sagen* (zā·γĕn).
γʸ ... Ger. *legen*, *regnen* (lē·γʸĕn, rē·γʸnĕn)

II. VOWELS.

ORDINARY.
a as in Fr. *à la mode* (a la mǫdʼ).
ai ... *aye* = *yes* (ai), *Isaiah* (əizai·ă).
æ ... *man* (mæn).
ɑ ... *pass* (pɑs), *chant* (tʃɑnt).
ɑu ... *loud* (lɑud), *now* (nɑu).
ɒ ... *cut* (kɒt), *son* (sɒn).
e ... *yet* (yet), *ten* (ten).
e ... *survey sb.* (sɒ̄·ɹve), Fr. *attaché* (ataʃe).
‖ę ... Fr. *chef* (ʃęf).
ə ... *ever* (evəɹ), *nation* (nēⁱ·ʃən).
əi ... *I*, *eye*, (əi), *bind* (bəind).
‖ə ... Fr. *eau de vie* (ō də vīʼ).
i ... *sit* (sit), *mystic* (mistik).
i ... *Psyche* (səi·ki), *react* (ri₁æ·kt).
o ... *achor* (ēⁱ·koɹ), *morality* (moræ·lĭti).
oi ... *oil* (oil), *boy* (boi).
o ... *hero* (hīᵊ·ro), *zoology* (zo₁ǫlŏdʒi).
ǫ ... *what* (hwǫt), *watch* (wǫtʃ).
ǫ, ǭ* ... *got* (gǫt), *soft* (sǭft).
‖ö ... Ger. *Köln* (köln).
‖ö ... Fr. *peu* (pö).
u ... *full* (ful), *book* (buk).
iu ... *duration* (diurēⁱ·ʃən).
u ... *unto* (ɒ·ntu), *frugality* (fru-).
iu ... *Matthew* (mæ·þiu), *virtue* (vɒ̄·ɹtiu).
‖ü ... Ger. *Müller* (mü·lĕr).
‖ü ... Fr. *dune* (dün).
ᵊ (see Īᵊ, ēᵊ, ōᵊ, ūᵊ)
ⁱ, ᵘ (see ēⁱ, ōᵘ) } see Vol. I, p. xxiv, note 3.
ʼ as in *able* (ēⁱbʼl), *eaten* (ītʼn) = voice-glide.

LONG.
ā as in *alms* (āmz), *bar* (bāɹ).
ɒ̄ ... *curl* (kɒ̄ɹl), *fur* (fɒ̄ɹ).
ē (ēᵊ)... *there* (ðēᵊɹ), *pear*, *pare* (pēᵊɹ).
ē (ēⁱ)... *rein*, *rain* (rēⁱn), *they* (ðēⁱ).
ę̄ ... Fr. *faire* (fę̄rʼ).
ə̄ ... *fir* (fə̄ɹ), *fern* (fə̄ɹn), *earth* (ə̄ɹþ).
ī (īᵊ)... *bier* (bīᵊɹ), *clear* (klīᵊɹ).
ī ... *thief* (þīf), *see* (sī).
ō (ōᵊ)... *boar*, *bore* (bōᵊɹ), *glory* (glōᵊ·ri).
ō (ōᵘ)... *so*, *sow* (sōᵘ), *soul* (sōᵘl).
ǭ ... *walk* (wǭk), *wart* (wǭɹt).
ǭ ... *short* (ʃǭɹt), *thorn* (þǭɹn).
‖ȫ ... Fr. *coeur* (kȫr).
‖ȫ ... Ger. *Göthe* (gȫtĕ), Fr. *jeûne* (ʒȫn).
ū (ūᵊ).. *poor* (pūᵊɹ), *moorish* (mūᵊ·riʃ).
iū, ⁱū ... *pure* (piūᵊɹ), *lure* (lⁱūᵊɹ).
ū ... *two moons* (tū mūnz).
iū, ⁱū ... *few* (fiū), *lute* (lⁱūt).
‖ǖ ... Ger. *grün* (grǖn), Fr. *jus* (ʒǖ).

OBSCURE.
ă as in *amœba* (ămī·bă).
ǣ ... *accept* (ǣkse·pt), *maniac* (mēⁱ·niǣk).
ɒ̆ ... *datum* (dēⁱ·tɒ̆m).
ĕ ... *moment* (mōᵘ·mĕnt), *several* (se·vĕrăl).
ĕ ... *separate* (*adj.*) (se·părĕt).
ė ... *added* (æ·dėd), *estate* (ėstēⁱ·t).
ĭ ... *vanity* (væ·nĭti).
ĭ ... *remain* (rĭmēⁱ·n), *believe* (bĭlī·v).
ŏ ... *theory* (þī·ŏri).
ŏ ... *violet* (vəi·ŏlėt), *parody* (pæ·rŏdi).
ǫ̆ ... *authority* (ǫ̆þǫ·rĭti).
ǫ̆ ... *connect* (kǫ̆ne·kt), *amazon* (æ·măzǫ̆n).
iŭ, ⁱŭ verdure (vɒ̄·ɹdiŭɹ), *measure* (me·ʒⁱŭɹ).
ŭ ... *altogether* (ǭltŭge·ðəɹ).
iŭ ... *circular* (sɒ̄·ɹkiŭlăɹ).

* ǭ the *o* in *soft*, of medial or doubtful length.

‖ Only in foreign (or earlier English) words.

In the ETYMOLOGY,

OE. *e*, *o*, representing an earlier *a*, are distinguished as *ę*, *ǫ* (having the phonetic value of *ę* and *ǫ*, or *ǫ*, above); as in *ęnde* from *andi* (OHG. *anti*, Goth. *andei-s*), *mǫnn* from *mann*, *ǫn* from *an*.

LIST OF ABBREVIATIONS, SIGNS, &c.

a. [in Etymol.] ...	= adoption of, adopted from.
a (as *a* 1300)	= *ante*, before.
a., *adj.*, adj.	= adjective.
absol., absol.	= absolutely.
abst.	= abstract.
acc.	= accusative.
ad. [in Etymol.]...	= adaptation of.
adv., adv.	= adverb.
advb.	= adverbial, -ly.
AF., AFr.	= Anglo-French.
Anat.	= in Anatomy.
Antiq.	= in Antiquities.
aphet.	= aphetic, aphetized.
app.	= apparently.
Arab.	= Arabic.
Arch.	= in Architecture.
arch.	= archaic.
Archæol.	= in Archæology.
assoc.	= association.
Astr.	= in Astronomy.
Astrol.	= in Astrology.
attrib.	= attributive, -ly.
bef.	= before.
Biol.	= in Biology.
Boh.	= Bohemian.
Bot.	= in Botany.
Build.	= in Building.
c (as *c* 1300)	= *circa*, about.
c. (as 13th c.)......	= century.
Cat.	= Catalan.
catachr.	= catachrestically.
Cf., cf.	= *confer*, compare.
Chem.	= in Chemistry.
cl. L.	= classical Latin.
cogn. w.	= cognate with.
collect.	= collective, -ly.
colloq.	= colloquially.
comb.	= combined, -ing.
Comb.	= Combinations.
Comm.	= in commercial usage.
comp.	= compound, composition.
compl.	= complement.
Conch.	= in Conchology
concr.	= concretely.
conj.	= conjunction.
cons.	= consonant.
Const., *Const.* ...	= Construction, construed with.
Cryst.	= in Crystallography.
(D.)	= in Davies (Supp. Eng. Glossary).
Da.	= Danish.
dat.	= dative.
def.	= definite.
deriv.	= derivative, -ation.
dial., *dial.*	= dialect, -al.
Dict.	= Dictionary.
dim.	= diminutive.
Du.	= Dutch.
Eccl.	= in ecclesiastical usage.
ellipt.	= elliptical, -ly.
e. midl.	= east midland (dialect).
Eng.	= English.
Ent.	= in Entomology.
erron.	= erroneous, -ly.
esp., esp.	= especially.
etym.	= etymology.
euphem.	= euphemistically.
exc.	= except.
f. [in Etymol.] ...	= formed on.
f. (in subordinate entries)	= form of.
fem. (*rarely* f.) ...	= feminine.
fig.	= figurative, -ly.
F., Fr.	= French.
freq.	= frequently.
Fris.	= Frisian.
G., Ger.	= German.
Gael.	= Gaelic.
gen.	= genitive.
gen.	= general, -ly.
gen. sign.	= general signification.
Geol.	= in Geology.
Geom.	= in Geometry.
Goth.	= Gothic (= Mœso-Gothic).
Gr.	= Greek.
Gram.	= in Grammar.
Heb.	= Hebrew.
Her.	= in Heraldry.
Herb.	= with herbalists.
Hort.	= in Horticulture.
imp.	= Imperative.
impers.	= impersonal.
impf.	= imperfect.
ind.	= Indicative.
indef.	= indefinite.
inf.	= Infinitive.
infl.	= influenced.
int.	= interjection.
intr.	= intransitive.
It.	= Italian.
J., (J.)	= Johnson (quotation from).
(Jam.)	= in Jamieson, Scottish Dict.
(Jod.)	= Jodrell (quoted from).
L.	= Latin.
(L.)(in quotations)	= Latham's edn. of Todd's Johnson.
lang.	= language.
LG.	= Low German.
lit.	= literal, -ly.
Lith.	= Lithuanian.
LXX.	= Septuagint.
Mal.	= Malay.
masc. (*rarely* m.)	= masculine.
Math.	= in Mathematics.
ME.	= Middle English.
Med.	= in Medicine.
med.L.	= mediæval Latin.
Mech.	= in Mechanics.
Metaph.	= in Metaphysics.
MHG.	= Middle High German.
midl.	= midland (dialect).
Mil.	= in military usage.
Min.	= in Mineralogy.
mod.	= modern.
Mus.	= in Music.
(N.)	= Nares (quoted from).
n. of action........	= noun of action.
n. of agent	= noun of agent.
Nat. Hist.	= in Natural History.
Naut.	= in nautical language.
neut. (*rarely* n.)	= neuter.
NF., NFr.	= Northern French.
N. O.	= Natural Order.
nom.	= nominative.
north.	= northern (dialect).
N. T.	= New Testament.
Numism.	= in Numismatics.
obj.	= object.
Obs., *obs.*, obs. ...	= obsolete.
occas.	= occasional, -ly.
OE.	= Old English (= Anglo-Saxon).
OF., OFr.	= Old French.
OFris.	= Old Frisian.
OHG.	= Old High German.
OIr.	= Old Irish.
ON.	= Old Norse (Old Icelandic).
ONF.	= Old Northern French.
Opt.	= in Optics.
Ornith.	= in Ornithology.
OS.	= Old Saxon.
OSl.	= Old Slavonic.
O. T.	= Old Testament.
OTeut.	= Original Teutonic.
orig.	= original, -ly.
Palæont.	= in Palæontology.
pa. pple.	= passive or past participle.
pass.	= passive, -ly.
pa. t.	= past tense.
Path.	= in Pathology.
perh.	= perhaps.
Pers.	= Persian.
pers.	= person, -al.
pf.	= perfect.
Pg.	= Portuguese.
Philol.	= in Philology.
phonet.	= phonetic, -ally.
phr.	= phrase.
Phren.	= in Phrenology.
Phys.	= in Physiology.
pl., *pl.*	= plural.
poet.	= poetic.
pop.	= popular, -ly.
ppl. a., ppl. adj....	= participial adjective.
pple.	= participle.
Pr.	= Provençal.
prec.	= preceding (word or article).
pref.	= prefix.
prep.	= preposition.
pres.	= present.
Prim. sign.	= Primary signification.
priv.	= privative.
prob.	= probably.
pron.	= pronoun.
pronunc.	= pronunciation.
prop.	= properly.
Pros.	= in Prosody.
pr. pple.	= present participle.
Psych.	= in Psychology.
q.v.	= *quod vide*, which see.
(R.)	= in Richardson's Dict.
R. C. Ch.	= Roman Catholic Church.
refash.	= refashioned, -ing.
refl., refl.	= reflexive.
reg.	= regular.
repr.	= representative, representing.
Rhet.	= in Rhetoric.
Rom.	= Romanic, Romance.
sb., *sb.*	= substantive.
Sc.	= Scotch.
sc.	= *scilicet*, understand or supply.
sing.	= singular.
Skr.	= Sanskrit.
Slav.	= Slavonic.
Sp.	= Spanish.
sp.	= spelling.
spec.	= specifically.
subj.	= subject, subjunctive.
subord. cl.	= subordinate clause.
subseq.	= subsequently.
subst.	= substantively.
suff.	= suffix.
superl.	= superlative.
Surg.	= in Surgery.
Sw.	= Swedish.
s.w.	= south western (dialect).
T. (T.)	= in Todd's Johnson.
techn.	= technical, -ly.
Theol.	= in Theology.
tr.	= translation of.
trans.	= transitive.
transf.	= transferred sense.
Trig.	= in Trigonometry.
Typog.	= in Typography.
ult.	= ultimate, -ly.
unkn.	= unknown.
U.S.	= United States.
v., vb.	= verb.
v. str., or *w.*	= verb strong, or weak.
vbl. sb.	= verbal substantive.
var.	= variant of.
wd.	= word.
WGer.	= West Germanic.
w.midl.	= west midland (dialect).
WS.	= West Saxon.
(Y.)	= in Col. Yule's Glossary.
Zool.	= in Zoology.

Before a word or sense.
† = obsolete.
‖ = not naturalized.

In the quotations.
* sometimes points out the word illustrated.

In the list of Forms.
1 = before 1100.
2 = 12th c. (1100 to 1200).
3 = 13th c. (1200 to 1300).
5–7 = 15th to 17th century. (See General Explanations, Vol. I, p. xx.)

In the Etymol.
* indicates a word or form not actually found, but of which the existence is inferred.
:— = extant representative, or regular phonetic descendant of.

The printing of a word in SMALL CAPITALS indicates that further information will be found under the word so referred to.

THE COMPACT EDITION
OF THE OXFORD
ENGLISH DICTIONARY

P.

P the sixteenth letter of the alphabet in English and other modern languages, was the fifteenth in the ancient Roman alphabet, corresponding in position and value to the Greek *Pi*, Π, Π, earlier Γ, Γ, originally written from right to left ᒣ, and identical with the Phenician and general Semitic *Pe*, forms of which were ᒣ, ᒣ. During its whole known history the letter has represented the same consonantal sound, viz. the labial *tenuis*, or lip unvoiced stop, to which the corresponding sonant or voiced stop is B, and the nasal, M. In English, the simple *p* has always this sound; but it is sometimes silent, as initially in the combinations *pn-*, *ps-*, *pt-* (representing Greek πν-, ψ-, πτ-), and medially between *m* and another consonant, as in *Hampstead*, *Hampton*, *Sampson*, *Thompson*, *Dempster*, *Tompkins*, where it is not etymological, but has the function of indicating for the preceding *m* the short and semi-sonant value which *m* naturally has before pronounced *p*: cf. *Simpson*, *crimson* (si·msən, kri·mz'n), with *wimple*, *wimble*. In words from Latin, such as *exempt*, *tempt*, *peremptory*, *assumpsit*, *consumptive*, *redemption*, and some others, as *Humpty-Dumpty*, where the *p* is (so far as English is concerned) etymological or consciously derivational, there is generally in careful utterance an intention to pronounce it, resulting in an incomplete *p*, which we indicate thus temᵖt, ride·mᵖʃən; but, in rapid or careless utterance, the *p* disappears, just as in *Ham(p)ton*, *Thom(p)son*.

The digraph PH, *ph*, is used, in continuation of Latin usage, to transliterate the Greek letter Φ, φ, the phonetic value of which is now identical with that of F. The words beginning with PH have thus the same relation to the P words proper that those in CH have to the C words; that is, they constitute an alien group, which, only for alphabetical convenience, occupy a place in the midst of the P words proper, between Pe- and Pi-.

Original P in Germanic or Teutonic represents an Indo-European B. But, *initially*, B was of rare occurrence in Indo-European, and it is not certain that any of the words in which it so occurred were retained in Teutonic, where initial P was consequently very rare. Of the OE. words in P, a few were apparently Common West Germanic, a very few, Common Teutonic; of many of the remainder the origin is quite obscure, but the majority were manifestly adoptions within the historical period from other languages, chiefly from Latin. Notwithstanding these extraneous additions, P remained the smallest initial letter (the exotic K, Q, not being counted) in the Old English or Anglo-Saxon vocabulary, occupying less than half the space of I, and little more than two-thirds of that of Y. Its relation to the other mutes, C (= K) and T, and to its own sonant B, is seen by the pages which these occupy in Toller's edition of Bosworth's Anglo-Saxon Dictionary, which are C 50, T 64, B 78, P 8½ pages. P might be expected to comprise a correspondingly small part of the modern English vocabulary; on the contrary, it is actually the third largest initial, being surpassed only by S and C, with which it forms a triad of gigantic letters, which include nearly a third of all the words in the dictionary. This result is mainly owing to the vast accessions from Greek, Latin, and the modern Romanic languages (chiefly, of course, from French), and especially to the enormous number of words formed with the Latin prefixes *per-*, *post-*, *pre-*, *pro-*, and the Greek *para-*, *peri-*, *pro-*, along with the PH group already referred to. But, besides these, P has received great additions, not only in later times from Oriental, African, American, and other remote languages, but, during the Middle English and Modern periods alike, of a multitude of common, familiar, or lower-class words from sources which cannot be traced, often apparently from fresh word-formation. P thus presents probably a greater number of unsolved etymological problems than any other letter.

I. 1. The letter (pī). Plural Ps, P's, p's (pīz).

attrib. as *p-language*, a language which preserves original *p*, or substitutes it for other sounds, as Greek which has πεντέ against L. *quinque*, or Welsh which has *pedwar* against OIr. *cethir*, from **qetwer*, L. *quatuor*.

c1000 [see B]. 1530 PALSGR. 33 The sounding of this consonant *P*. *P* in all thynges followeth the generall rules.. without any manner exception. *Ibid.* 21 Excepte *ps* whiche they sounde but *s*, sayeng for *psálme*, *psaltére*, *salme*, *saltere*. 15.. HEYWOOD (*title*) The playe called the foure P. A new and very mery enterlude of A Palmer. A Pardoner. A Poticary. A Pedler. 1573-80 BARET *Alv.* s.v., This letter p seemeth both by his name and forme to be of kind to b, and as it were a b turned vpside downe. 1601 SHAKS. *Twel. N.* II. v. 97 By my life this is my Ladies hand.. thus makes shee her great *P's*. 1612 DEKKER *If it be not good* Wks. 1873 III. 329 Three Pees haue peppered me, The Punck, the Pot, and Pipe of smoake. 1863 A. M. BELL *Princ. Speech* 161 With reference to the letter *P*, we observe, that it is not made by the conjunction of the lips, but by their separation; and this of course implies previous contact. 1892 *Blackw. Mag.* Mar. 409 The inability of Syrian lips to pronounce the letter P. 1892 JOHNSTON *Place Names Scotl.* 224 Windisch and Stokes' Classification of Celtic languages... The *p* group, Welsh, Pictish, Cornish, &c. 1900 *Contemp. Rev.* Feb. 272 Greek may be called a *p*-language, Germanic a *q*-language.

2. Used, like the other letters, to indicate serial order, as in the 'signatures' of the sheets of a book, the Batteries of the Horse Artillery, etc.

3. P and Q. a. *To be P and Q* (*Pee and Kew*). According to Bound *Provincialisms* as quoted in Eng. Dial. Dict., this was used in 1876 in Shropsh. and Herefordsh. in the sense 'to be of prime quality'.

1612 ROWLANDS *Knave of Harts* (Hunterian Cl.) 20 Bring in a quart of Maligo, right true: And looke, you Rogue, that it be Pee and Kew.

b. *To mind one's P's and Q's* (*peas and cues*), to be careful or particular as to one's words or behaviour. So *to be on* (*in*) *one's P's and Q's*.

1779 MRS. H. COWLEY *Who's the Dupe?* I. i, You must mind your *P's* and *Q's* with him, I can tell you. ?1800 W. B. RHODES *Bomb. Fur.* iv. 30 My sword I well can use So mind your P's and Q's. a1825 FORBY *Voc. E. Anglia* 266 'Mind your p's and q's', q.d. 'be nicely observant of your language and behaviour'. 1866 G. MACDONALD *Ann. Q. Neighb.* x. (1878) 181 Well, I thought it wasn't a time to mind ones peas and cues exactly. 1893 W. S. GILBERT *Utopia* I, He minds his P's and Q's,—And keeps himself respectable.

a1814 *Apollo's Choice* II. ii. in *Mod. Brit. Drama* IV. 208, I must be on my P's and Q's here, or I shall get my neck into a halter. 1888 C. BLATHERWICK *Uncle Pierce* i, He was rather on his p's and q's. 1893 W. A. SHEE *My Contemp.* vi. 149 In a well-dressed crowd you are in your p's and q's.

c. *One's P's and Q's*, put for 'one's letters'.

1820 COMBE *Consol.* I. 30 And I full five-and-twenty year Have always been school-master here; And almost all you know and see, Have learn'd their *P's* and *Qs* from me.

[*Note.* As to the origin of these nothing has been ascertained. An obvious suggestion is that b. (for which the evidence does not go far back) refers to the difficulty which a child beginning to read has in distinguishing the tailed letters p and q; others have conjectured some cryptic reference to the words *peculiar*, or *particular*. There is no necessary connexion between b. and a., which belongs to an earlier date. In a still earlier passage from Dekker 1602, 'Now thou art in thy *pee* and *cue*', *pee* means the coat so called (see PEE *sb.*), and *cue* app. either *queue*, or CUE *sb.*² sense 3 or 4; but there may have been a punning allusion to the expressions here considered, if they were then current.]

II. Abbreviations. P. = various proper names, as Peter, Paul, etc.; P., p. = past, post: P (*Chem.*) = Phosphorus; P (*chess*) = pawn; P (*Mechanics*) = pressure; p- (*Chem.*) = para-; p. = page; *p* (*Music*) = *piano*, softly; p. (in a ship's log) = passing showers; Π (i.e. Greek *pi*) (*Math.*) continued product; π (*Math.*) = *pi*, the ratio of the circumference to the diameter of a circle, the incommensurable quantity 3·14159265...; Pa. (*U.S.*) = Pennsylvania; P. and O., P. & O. = Peninsular and Oriental Steam Navigation Co.; P.A. = Post Adjutant; Pb (*Chem.*) = *plumbum*, lead; P.C. = Police Constable, Privy Councillor; Pd (*Chem.*) = Palladium; P.M., p.m. = *post meridiem*, afternoon; P.O. = post office; P.P. = parish priest; p.p. *per procurationem*, by proxy; *pp* or *ppp* (*Music*) = *pianissimo*, very softly; P.P.C. (written on cards, etc.) = *pour prendre congé*, to take leave; p.p.i. = policy sufficient proof of interest; P.R.A. = President of the Royal Academy of Art; P.R.S. = President of the Royal Society; P.S. = *post scriptum*, postscript; P.S.A. = Pleasant Sunday Afternoon; Pt. (*Chem.*) = Platinum; pt. = part, pint; P.T.O., p.t.o., = please turn over.

1666 HOOK in *Phil. Trans.* 242 March 28th 3h. p.m. 1682 *Grew's Anat. Plants* (Order Roy. Soc.), Chr. Wren P.R.S. 1809-12 MAR. EDGEWORTH *Absentee* xvi, I shall make my *finale*, and shall thus leave a verbal P.P.C. 1833 MARRYAT *P. Simple* lxv, The..count announced his departure by a P.P.C. c1850 *Rudim. Navig.* (Weale) 14 With the astronomical day it is always P.M. 1880 *Standard* 15 May 5/3 The trim mates of P. and O. liners. 1892 MRS. CLIFFORD *Aunt Anne* I. iii. 59 She fancied him on board a P. and O. 1895 KENNEDY in *Law Times Rep.* LXXII. 861/1 All these 'disbursements' policies were p.p.i. or 'honour' policies—policies, that is to say, wherein it was stipulated that the policy should be deemed sufficient proof of interest. 1899 *Daily News* 27 Nov. 8/3 The P.S.A.—or, to give it the full title, the Pleasant Sunday Afternoon—movement has now become pretty well known. 1900 PERKIN & KIPPING *Organic Chem.* 316 The most usual course in the case of the di-derivatives is to employ the terms ortho-, meta-, and para-, or simply *o*, *m*, and *p*., para-nitrophenol or *p*-nitrophenol.

P, variant of PEE *Obs.*, short coat, pea-jacket.

Pa (pā). A childish short form of 'papa'. Hence **Pa** *v. trans. nonce-wd.*, to address as 'pa'.

1811 L. M. HAWKINS *C'tess & Gertrude* (1812) II. 219 The elder sat down [to the piano-forte] and.. answered 'Yes, Pa', to every thing that Pa said. 1823 E. MOOR *Suffolk Words*, *Pa*, an abbreviation of pa-pa. Pretty general perhaps. It is sometimes rather comic to hear a great chuckle-headed lout—*paa*-ing his father—or *maa*-ing his mother. 1829 *Censor* 225 These exhibitions, affording wonderous delight to affectionate *Pas* and *Mas*. 1880 MISS BRADDON *Barbara* vi, With the exception of that decayed female, I have never seen a mortal in pa's offices.

Pa, var. PAH *sb.* **Paa**, var. ME. Po, peacock.

Paage, obs. var. PEAGE, toll paid by passengers.

Paal(e, obs. forms of PALE *a.*

Paalstab, -staff, -stave, var. of PALSTAFF.

Paame, obs. form of PALM, name of a game.

Paan: see PAGNE cloth, PANE.

Paarche, Paarform, Paark, Paart, obs. ff. PARCH, PERFORM, PARK, PART.

Paas, Paast, obs. ff. PACE, PASCH, PASTE.

‖ **Paauw** (pāu). *S. Africa.* Also 9 **paow**. [Du. *paauw* peacock.] The name applied generally in S. Africa to species of Bustard.

1850 R. G. CUMMING *Hunter's Life S. Afr.* (1902) 18/2, I.. perceived a large paow or bustard walking on the plain before me. 1879 A. FORBES in *Daily News* 28 June 5/7 Among the game of the veldt is a noble bird called a paauw—a species of wild turkey. *Ibid.*, The paauw combines the flavours of the grouse and the turkey. 1894 NEWTON *Dict. Birds* 683.

Pab, Sc. dial. var. of POB, refuse of flax.

Pabble (pæ·b'l). *v. Sc.* [Echoic.] *intr.* To make a sound like that of boiling liquid.

1832 J. WILSON in *Blackw. Mag.* XXXI. 879 The hissing, and the fizzing, and the pabbling of the great pan in which the basted trouts are writhing. 1834 — *Ibid.* XXXV. 789 We hear them pabbling in the pan.

‖ **Pabouch** (pābū·ʃ). Also 7 **paboutch**. [See BABOUCHE, PAPOOSH.] A heelless Oriental slipper.

1687 A. LOVELL tr. *Thevenot's Trav.* I. 30 The heel.. is shod with a piece of Iron made purposely half-round, and these Shoes they call Paboutches. 1813 MOORE *Post-bag* ii. 64 All sorts of dulimans and pouches, With sashes, turbans, and pabouches. 1824 SCOTT *St. Ronan's* xxx, I always drink my coffee as soon as my feet are in my pabouches; it's the way all over the East.

† **Pa·bular**, *a. Obs. rare*⁻⁰. [ad L. *pābulār-is*, f. *pābulum* fodder: see -AR¹.] = next.

1656 BLOUNT *Glossogr.*, *Pabular*, *Pabulous*, pertaining to fodder, Provender, forrage. [So in PHILLIPS, BAILEY, etc.]

Pabulary (pæ·biŭlări), *a.* [ad. L. *pābulāri-us* having to do with fodder: see prec. and -ARY.] Of or pertaining to pabulum, fodder, or aliment.

1835 J. S. FORSYTH (*title*) A Dictionary of Diet, being a Practical Treatise on all Pabulary and Nutritive Substances. 1839 G. RAYMOND in *New Monthly Mag.* LVII. 409 His gleanings had done.. credit to his pabulary diligence.

Pabulation (pæbiŭlē¹·ʃən). *rare*⁻⁰. [ad. L. *pābulātiōn-em*, n. of action from *pābulārī* to eat fodder, seek for food, forage.] (See quots.)

1623 COCKERAM, *Pabulation*, grasing, feeding. [So in BAILEY.] 1755 JOHNSON, *Pabulation*, the act of feeding or procuring provender. 1846 WORCESTER, *Pabulation*, act of feeding, fodder. 1864 in WEBSTER.

† **Pa·bulatory**, *a. Obs. rare*⁻⁰. [ad. L. *pābulātōri-us*, f. *pābulātōr-em* fodderer, forager: see -ORY.] Of or pertaining to pabulation.

1656 BLOUNT *Glossogr.*, *Pabulatory*, the same [with *Pabular*, *Pabulous*]. [So in BAILEY.]

Pabulous (pæ·biŭləs), *a. rare.* [f. late L. *pābulōs-us* abounding in *pābulum* fodder: see -OUS.] Abounding in or affording pabulum or food.

1646 SIR T. BROWNE *Pseud. Ep.* III. xxi. 160 Wee doubt the common conceit, which affirmeth that aire is the pabulous supply of fire. 1755 JOHNSON, *Pabulous*.., affording aliment.

‖ **Pabulum** (pæ·biŭlŏm). [L. *pābulum* food, nourishment, fodder, f. stem *pā-* of *pā-sc-ĕre* (*pā-vi*) to feed.] Anything taken in by an animal or plant to maintain life and growth; food, aliment.

nutriment. More usually said of the 'food' of plants, or of animal organs or organisms; rarely in reference to higher animals.

1733 TULL *Horse-Hoeing Husb.* i. 7 Roots must search out and fetch themselves all the *Pabulum* of a Plant. 1813 SIR H. DAVY *Agric. Chem.* i. (1814) 18 No one principle affords the *pabulum* of vegetable life. 1826 KIRBY & SP. *Entomol.* xliv. IV. 216 Affording a pabulum to these animals. 1845 TODD & BOWMAN *Phys. Anat.* I. 43 The blood is the immediate pabulum of the tissues. 1860 MAURY *Phys. Geog. Sea* x. § 493 The rivers bring down and pour into the sea continually the pabulum which those organisms require.

b. That which supports or 'feeds' fire.

1678 CUDWORTH *Intell. Syst.* I. i. 46 Fire.. needs a *Pabulum* to prey upon, doth not continue alwaies one and the same Numerical Substance. 1744 BERKELEY *Siris* § 197 Oil, air, or any other thing that vulgarly passeth for a pabulum or food of that element [fire]. 1860 FARRAR *Orig. Lang.* v. 105 A necessary pabulum of combustion.

c. *fig.* That which nourishes and sustains the mind or soul; food for thought.

1765 STERNE *Tr. Shandy* VII. xxxi, Such a story affords more *pabulum* to the brain, than all the Frusts, and Crusts, and Rusts of antiquity. 1819 CRABBE *T. of Hall* x. 393 An age.. when tales of love Form the sweet pabulum our hearts approve. 1888 M. ROBERTSON *Lombard St. Myst.* iii, To furnish.. more pabulum for reflection and rumination.

Pac, pack (pæk). [Origin uncertain. Thought by some to have been North American Indian; others suggest a Frenchified spelling of Eng. *pack*; but it is not easy to connect it with any sense of PACK *sb.*¹] A moccasin having a sole turned up and sewed on the upper; also applied to a heavy felt half-boot, worn by lumberers in winter.

1875 KNIGHT *Dict. Mech.* s.v., The *pac*, as used by the Indians of the Six Nations, for instance, was made of hide boiled in tallow and wax; or of tawed hide subsequently stuffed with tallow or wax. 1893 *Scribner's Mag.* June 715 Loggers' Footgear [Figures of] India-rubber brogan. Old-fashioned boot-pack. Modern rubber-soled boot-pack. Buckskin and leather moccasin.

Paca (pæ·kă). *Zool.* [a. Pg. and Sp. *paca*, a. Tupi *paca*, the native name (in Guarani, *paig*). Gabriel Soares in his *Noticias do Brazil* 1587 spells it (in Pg.) *pagua*, Claude d'Abbeville *Mission en Maragnan* (1614) 251, has (in Fr.) *pac*.] A genus (*Cœlogenys*) of large dasyproctid rodents, nocturnal in habit, native to Central and South America; the common species (*Cœlogenys paca*) is called also the *spotted cavy* and *water hare*.

[1648 MARCGRAVE *Hist. Nat. Brasil.* II. 224 Paca Brasiliensibus, cuniculi etiam est species.] 1657 S. CLARKE *Geog. Descript.* 179 Their Pacas are like Pigs, their flesh is pleasant. 1796 STEDMAN *Surinam* II. xxii. 152 The Paca, or Spotted Cavey, called in Surinam the Aquatic Hare. 1871 *Routledge's Ev. Boy's Ann.* Sept. 517 When pacas and otters are in question, an Indian will do anything to kill them.

Pacable (pē¹·kăb'l), *a.* [ad. L. *pācābil-is*, f. *pācāre* to appease, pacify, f. *pāx*, *pāc-em* peace.] Capable of being pacified or appeased; placable.

a1834 COLERIDGE *Church & State* (1839) 166 Reasonable men are easily satisfied: would they were as numerous as they are pacable! 1860 THACKERAY *Round. Papers* vi. *Screens in Din. Rooms*, That last Roundabout Paper.. was written in a pacable and not unchristian frame of mind.

Pacadile, bad form of PICKADILL.

† **Pa·cal**, *a. Obs. rare.* [ad. L. *pācāl-is* peaceful.]

1656 BLOUNT *Glossogr.*, *Pacal*.., that brings or signifies peace, peaceable. 1730-6 in BAILEY (folio).

Pacan, pacane, obs. forms of PECAN.

† **Pa·cate**, *a. Obs.* [ad. L. *pācāt-us*, pa. pple. of *pāc-āre* to make peaceful, quiet, pacify.] Pacified, brought into a state of peace and calm, tranquil.

1644 J. GOODWIN *Innoc. Triumph.* (1645) 40 How pacate, flourishing, and free from disturbance this State hath been. a1652 J. SMITH *Sel. Disc.* VII. i. (1821) 309 A pacate, humble, and self-denying mind. 1681 H. MORE *Exp. Dan.* vii, A man of a pacate mind and quick understanding.

Hence † **Pa·cately** *adv.*, quietly; † **Pa·cateness**, the state of being 'pacate' or peaceful.

a1652 J. SMITH *Sel. Disc.* vi. 220 A gentle vocal air, such a one as breathed in the day-time more pacately. 1666 BP. REYNOLDS *Serm. in Westm. Abb.* 7 Nov. 13 This pacateness and serenity of Soul. 1681 H. MORE *Exp. Dan.* i. 10 There was not that pacateness nor tranquillity in the Medo-Persian Empire that there was in the Babylonian.

† **Paca·ted**, *ppl. a. Obs.* [f. as prec. + -ED.]

1727 BAILEY vol. II, *Pacated*,.. appeased, made peaceable. Hence in ASH and mod. Dicts.

Pacation (păkē¹·ʃən). [ad. L. *pācātiōn-em*, n. of action from *pāc-āre*: see PACATE *a.*] The action of pacifying or tranquillizing; the condition of being peaceful and tranquil; pacification.

1658 PHILLIPS, *Pacation*, a stilling or appeasing. 1730-6 BAILEY (folio). 1820 COLERIDGE in *Lit. Rem.* (1839) IV. 152 It was this that.. prevented the pacation of Ireland.

† **Pa·cative**, *a. Obs. rare.* [f. L. *pācāt-*, ppl. stem of *pāc-āre*: see -ATIVE.] Stilling, sedative.

1684 tr. *Bonet's Merc. Compit.* xix. 752 The pacative vertue of Vitriol [seems extended] to the effervescent bile.

‖ **Pacay** (pakai·, pækē¹·). Also **Paccay**. [a. Peruv. *pacay*, in Sp. *pacaya*.] A Peruvian leguminous tree (*Inga Feuillei*) of sub-order *Mimoseæ*, cultivated for its large white pods, which are esteemed as an article of food. Also applied to a tree of the genus *Prosopis*.

[1748 *Earthquake of Peru* iii. 210 The.. Pacayas.. are there very plentiful.] 1866 *Treas. Bot.*, *Inga Feuillei*, a native of Peru, is cultivated in the gardens about Lima, where the inhabitants call it Pacay. 1880 C. R. MARKHAM *Peruv. Bark* xvi. 167 The paccay (*Mimosa Inga*), with its cottony fruit, was drooping over the bubbling waves.

Paccage, Paccan, obs. ff. PACKAGE, PECAN.

Pacche, obs. form of PATCH, PASH *v.*

Pacchionian (pækiō¹·niăn), *a. Anat.* [f. the name of the Italian anatomist Pacchioni (1665–1726) + -AN.] Of or described by Pacchioni.

Pacchionian body, corpuscle, gland, granulation, one of the granular enlargements or outgrowths of the arachnoid membrane of the brain in the neighbourhood of the longitudinal sinus; *P. depression, fossa, line*, a depression on the inner surface of the skull for the reception of the Pacchionian bodies.

1811 HOOPER *Med. Dict.*, *Pacchionian glands*. 1839-47 TODD *Cycl. Anat.* III. 644/1 The Pacchionian bodies are found principally along the edge of the great hemispheres of the brain. 1845 TODD & BOWMAN *Phys. Anat.* I. 255 The Pacchionian glands or bodies are whitish granules, composed of an albuminous material. 1893 *Syd. Soc. Lex.* s.v., They increase in size as the years advance, passing through holes in the dura mater and projecting into the sinus or lying in the Pacchionian fossæ of the skull bones.

Paccioli, variant of PATCHOULI, the perfume.

Pace (pē¹s), *sb.*¹ Forms: 3-5 **pas**, 4-5 **paas**, **pass(e**, 4-7 **pase**, 5 **pasce**, 5-6 *Sc.* **pais(s**, 6 *Sc.* **paice**, 4- **pace**. [ME. a. OF. *pas*:—L. *passum* (nom. *passus*) a step, pace, lit. a stretch (of the leg), f. *pass-*, ppl. stem of *pandĕre* to stretch, extend.]

I. A step, and derived senses.

1. A single separate movement made by the leg in walking, running, or dancing; a step.

13.. *Coer de L.* 536, I bad hym ryde forth hys wey,.. Ageyn he com be another pas. a1375 *Lay Folks Mass Bk.* App. iv. 105 Eueri fote þat þou gas þyn Angel poynteþ hit vch a pas. c1400 MAUNDEV. (1839) xvi. 174 Summe.. at euery thrydde pas þat þei gon.. þei knelen. 1489 CAXTON *Faytes of A.* I. xvi. 47 [They] shal marche paas by paas. 1593 SHAKS. *Lucr.* 1391 Pale cowards, marching on with trembling paces. 1634 [see PACE *v.* 1 d]. 1667 MILTON *P. L.* x. 589 Behind her Death Close following pace for pace. 1832 TENNYSON *Lady of Shalott* III. v, She made three paces thro' the room.

† **b.** *fig.* A 'step' in any process or proceeding.

[1450-1530 *Myrr. our Ladye* 227 Her fete she suffered neuer to moue one pase, but yf she dyscussed fyrste what profyte shulde come therof.] a1628 PRESTON *New Cov.* (1634) 210 We are not to be judged by a few actions, and a few paces, but by the constant tenor of our life. a1698 TEMPLE (J.), The first pace necessary for his majesty to make, is to fall into confidence with Spain.

2. The space traversed by one step; hence as a vague measure of distance.

1382 WYCLIF 2 *Sam.* vi. 13 And whanne thei hadden stied ouer, that baren the arke of the Lord, sexe paas, thei offreden an oxe and a wether. 1485 CAXTON *Chas. Gt.* 69 Olyuer.. came a foure paas nyghe vnto Fyerabras. 1587 FLEMING *Contn. Holinshed* III. 1332/1 On his left hand somewhat more than halfe a pase beneath him. 1667 MILTON *P. L.* VI. 193 Ten paces huge He back recoild. 1703 MAUNDRELL *Journ. Jerus.* (1732) 106 Five hundred and seventy of my paces in length. 1879 *Cassell's Technic. Educ.* IV. 92/2 In many cases the pace of the surveyor is used for determining distances.

3. A definite but varying measure of length or distance; sometimes reckoned as the distance from where one foot is set down to where the other is set down (about 2½ feet), as the *military pace*; sometimes as that between successive stationary positions of the same foot (about 5 feet), as the *geometrical pace*.

13.. *K. Alis.* 7804 An c. pas is hygh the wal. 1398 TREVISA *Barth. De P. R.* XIX. cxxix. (1495) 937 The pace conteyneth fyue fete and the perche enleuen pace and ten fete. c1400 MAUNDEV. (Roxb.) xi. 46 A c. pascez þeine.. es þe charnell of þe hospitale. 1555 EDEN *Decades* 323 To measure the earth by furlonges, pases and feete. 1692 *Capt. Smith's Seaman's Gram.* II. xxvi. 135 (At one deg. of Mounture) she conveyed her Shot 1125 Feet, or 225 Paces. 1756-7 tr. *Keysler's Trav.* (1760) II. 282 An open walk of an hundred and eight paces in length leads to the fountain. 1841 LEVER *C. O'Malley* vi. (The Man for Galway), To kiss your wife, Or take your life At ten or fifteen paces. 1842 BRANDE *Dict. Sci.* etc. s.v., The ancient Roman pace.. was five Roman feet,.. hence the pace was about 58·1 English inches, and the Roman mile, the '*mille passus*', equal to 1614 yards.

II. The action of stepping, and derived senses.

4. The action, or (usually) manner, of stepping, in walking or running; gait, step, walk, way of walking or progression. (See also 7.)

1297 R. GLOUC. (Rolls) 5635 For some meschaunce of þe king he made so glad pas. c1386 CHAUCER *Miller's T.* 555 And Absolon gooth forth a sory pas. 1422 tr. *Secreta Secret.*, *Priv. Priv.* 235 Whoso hath the Paas large and slow, he is wyse and wel spedynge. 1513 DOUGLAS *Æneis* II. xi. 76 Litle Iulus.. With vnmeit paiss his fader fast followand. c1586 C'TESS PEMBROKE *Ps.* L. vii, But loe, thou see'st I march another pace. 1697 DRYDEN *Virg. Georg.* III. 708 Late to lag behind, with truant pace. 1769 SIR W. JONES *Palace Fortune* Poems (1777) 20 Now came an aged sire with trembling pace. 1840 DICKENS *Old C. Shop* i, The little creature accommodating her pace to mine. 1851 LONGF. *Gold. Leg.* III. *Nativity* II. i, I steal with quiet pace, My pitcher at the well to fill.

† **b.** Course, way (in walking or running). *Obs.*

13.. *Cursor M.* 19076 (Edinb.) To þe tempil he sped his pas. 1390 GOWER *Conf.* III. 6 Wherof mi limes ben so dull, I mai unethes gon the pas [*rime* was]. c1460 *Towneley Myst.* xxviii. 364 To Ierusalem take we the pace. 1608 TOPSELL *Serpents* (1658) 770 It is a small creature to see to, keeping on the pace very fearfully. 1657 HOWELL *Londinop.* 87 We will direct our pace downward now. 1727 GAY *Fables* I. xvii, In vain the dog pursu'd his pace.

† **c.** *transf.* and *fig.* Movement, motion; manner of going on. (Cf. 7 b.)

c1386 CHAUCER *Man of Law's T.* 208 O fieble Moone vnhappy been thy paas [*v. r.* pas]. 1603 T. WILSON in Ellis *Orig. Lett.* Ser. II. III. 201 Our English affayres goe on with a smooth pace and a smilinge countenance. c1611 CHAPMAN *Iliad* I. 394 The Pow'r whose pace doth move The round earth, heav'n's great Queen, and Pallas.

† **5.** A walking pace, walking (as distinguished from running, etc.). *Obs.*

a1300 *Cursor M.* 15392 (Cott.) Fra þan he ran him ilk fote, ne yode he noght þe pas, til he com him til þat in. *Ibid.* 15872 (Cott.) His hend þai band and ledd him forth A-trott and noght þe pas [so *Gött.*; *Fairf.* & *Trin.* a pas]. c1386 CHAUCER *Can. Yeom. Prol.* & *T.* 22 His hat heeng at his bak doun by a laas ffor he hadde riden moore than trot or paas. 1390 GOWER *Conf.* III. 41 Withinne his chambre.. He goth now doun nou up fulofte, Walkende a pass.

6. Any one of the various gaits or manners of stepping of a horse, mule, etc., esp. when trained. Also *fig.*, esp. in such phr. as *to put through his paces*, referring to the various accomplishments or actions of which a person or thing is capable.

1589 R. HARVEY *Pl. Perc.* (1590) 5 A horse may ouer reach in a true pace. 1600 SHAKS. *A. Y. L.* III. ii. 327 Time trauels in diuers paces, with diuers persons: Ile tell you who Time ambles withall, who Time trots withal, who Time gallops withal, and who he stands stil withall. 1667 *Lond. Gaz.* No. 200/4 A dark brown Gelding.. having all his paces. 1713 *Ibid.* No. 5127/12 Stoln or stray'd.., a brown bay Gelding,.. his Pace, Trot and Gallop. 1727-41 CHAMBERS *Cycl.* s.v., The natural paces of a horse are three, *viz.* the walk, trot, and gallop: to which may be added an amble; because some horses have it naturally. 1766 GOLDSM. *Vic. W.* xiv, I had.. put my horse through all his paces,.. at last a chapman approached. 1856 EMERSON *Eng. Traits*, *Voy. Eng.*, The captain affirmed that the ship would show us in time all her paces. 1871 B. TAYLOR *Faust* (1875) II. I. vii. 81, I see she means to put him through his paces.

b. A particular gait of the horse (or other quadruped); usually identified with *amble*, but now sometimes used as equivalent to *rack* (cf. PACE *v.* 3).

1663 BUTLER *Hud.* I. ii. 46 They rode, but Authors having not Determin'd whether Pace or Trot... We leave it, and go on. 1727-41 CHAMBERS *Cycl.*, *Pace* is more particularly understood of that easy low motion wherein the horse raises the two feet of the same side at a time; called also *amble*. 1840 BLAINE *Encycl. Rur. Sports* § 1036 The walk may be irregular, though laterally conducted, as we see in the walk of the pace, which, if expedited, produces the amble. 18.. STRICKLAND FREEMAN *ibid.*, The poise being altered by the will of the horse, the off fore [leg] seemed to begin, and not to be succeeded by the off hind-foot being set down at the same time after it, as in the walk of the pace. 1885 *Field* 17 Oct., Col. Dodge's definition of a rack is that it is half-way between a pace and a trot.

III. Rate of movement, etc.

7. Rate of stepping; rate of progression (of a person or animal); speed in walking or running. Usually with qualifying adj. (Cf. also 4.)

c1290 *S. Eng. Leg.* I. 393/15 Þis best orn with gret pas. c1330 R. BRUNNE *Chron. Wace* (Rolls) 3515 Ne go swyþer þan softe paas. c1489 CAXTON *Sonnes of Aymon* xiv. 315 He sette hymselfe for to goo the waye so gret pase that no horse cowde not haue waloped so fast. a1533 LD. BERNERS *Huon* lv. 185 The horse wold nother trot nor galop but go styll his owne pase. 1642 FULLER *Holy & Prof. St.* III. xxi. 211 Their ordinary pace is a race. 1693 DRYDEN *Juvenal* x. (1697) 246 The Beggar Sings,.. and never mends his pace. 1743 J. DAVIDSON *Æneid* VII. 185 Set forward with quick pace. 1863 GEO. ELIOT *Romola* xx, He quickened his pace, and took up new threads of talk.

b. *transf.* and *fig.* Rate of movement in general, or of action figured as movement; speed, velocity.

c1430 LYDG. *Min. Poems* (Percy Soc.) 216 Fro silver wellys.. Comethe cristal water rennyng a gret pas. 1599 SHAKS. *Much Ado* III. iv. 93 What pace is this that thy tongue keepes. *Mar.* Not a false gallop. 1659 *Burton's Diary* (1828) IV. 357 If they go the pace of their ancestors, I would tell them plainly they would not sit long. 1788 FRANKLIN *Autobiog.* Wks. 1840 I. 223 While we stood there the ship mended her pace. 1835 URE *Philos. Manuf.* 29 Had British industry not been aided by Watt's invention, it must have gone on with a retarding pace, in consequence of the increasing cost of motive power.

c. *Pace of the table* (Billiards), *of the wicket* (Cricket): the degree of elasticity of the cushions, or of the ground, as affecting the velocity of motion of the ball. (Cf. FAST *a.* 9.)

1873 BENNETT & CAVENDISH *Billiards* 77 The pace of the table makes a material difference in the strength with which this stroke should be played. 1897 *Daily News* 1 Nov. 7/2 He took four hours and fifty minutes to get his runs, and said that the extreme pace of the wicket bothered him.

8. Phrases. **a.** *To keep* († *hold*) *pace*: to maintain the same speed of movement; to advance at an equal rate; to keep up *with*. (*lit.* and *fig.*)

1590 SHAKS. *Mids. N.* III. ii. 445 My legs can keepe no pace with my desires. 1601 HOLLAND *Pliny* I. 350 Lions and Camels only.. keep pace in their march, foot by foot, that is to say, they never set their left foot before their right, nor ouer-reach with it. 1647 WARD *Simp. Cobler* 61 Who have held pace.. with you in our evill wayes. 1762 GOLDSM. *Cit. W.* xv, His luxuries kept pace with the affluence of his fortune. 1776 ADAM SMITH *W. N.* II. iv. (1869) I. 359 The interest of money, keeping pace always with the profits of stock. 1782 MISS BURNEY *Cecilia* v. xii, [He] walked so fast that they could hardly keep pace with him. 1876 GRANT *Burgh Sch. Scotl.* II. xiii. 355 Boys.. found incapable of keeping pace with the rest of their fellows.

b. *To go the pace*: to go along at great speed; *fig.* to proceed with reckless vigour of action; to indulge in dissipation; to 'go it'. *To set the pace*: to fix or regulate the speed.

1829 *Sporting Mag.* XXIV. 47 The hounds went the pace over the heath towards Lymington. 1854 in *Brasenose Ale* 126 Each man will say you made them go the pace. 1866 MRS. HENRY WOOD *St. Martin's Eve* xxi, He went the pace.. as other young men do.

IV. Special senses.

9. A step of a stair or the like; a part of a floor raised by a step; a stage, platform. Cf. FOOT-PACE 2, HALPACE.

a1300 *Cursor M.* 9948 (Cott.) A tron of iuor graid.. Climband vp wit seuen pass [*v. rr.* pas, pace]. 1535 *Hampton Court Accts.*, 104 fote of hardston rought pase, for the steppes in the Quere. 1845 PARKER *Gloss. Archit.* (ed. 4) I. 267 *Pace*, a broad step, or slightly raised space about a tomb, etc.; a portion of a floor slightly raised above the general level.

† **10.** A passage, narrow way; esp. **a.** a pass between mountains, rocks, bogs, woods, etc.; **b.** a narrow channel at sea, a strait. *Obs.*

a1300 *Cursor M.* 23735 We agh be bun at bide to pass þe pase þat es sa herd. 1377 LANGL. *P. Pl.* B. XIV. 300 3e, þorw þe pas of altoun Pouerte my3te passe with-oute peril of robbynge. 1470-85 MALORY *Arthur* VII. ix, Thou shalt not passe a paas here that is called the paas perillous. a1578 LINDESAY (Pitscottie) *Chron. Scot.* (S. T. S.) I. 368 [He] pullit wpe saillis and came stoutlie throw the pace of Calies. 1590 SPENSER *F. Q.* III. i. 19 She forward went, As lay her iourney, through that perlous Pace. a1604 HANMER *Chron. Irel.* (1633) 1 Making paces thorow woods and thickets. 1612 *Stat. Irel.* (1765) I. 444 The high-ways and cashes and paces and passages throughout the woods of this kingdom. 1617 MORYSON *Itin.* II. 81 He caused.. the woods to be cut downe on both sides of the Pace.

† **11. a.** In a church: A passage between the seats. **b.** *Middle pace*: the nave; *of one pace*, of a nave only. *Obs.*

1499 *Will of J. Robert* (Somerset Ho.), To be buried in the myddell pace before the high crosse. 1507 *Will of Cornell* (ibid.), In the pace ayenst saint Kateryn Chapell dore. 1518 *Will of Hopkynson* (ibid.), The middill pase of the church. 1772 MUILMAN *Hist. Essex* VI. 164 The church consists of a middle pace and two aysles, but the chancel hath only a north aysle, all leaded. 1828 J. HUNTER *South Yorkshire* I. 84 The church is of one pace, with a tower at the west end. *Ibid.* 89.

† **12.** A passage (in a narrative or other writing); a section, division, chapter, canto, etc. *Obs.*

a1300 *Cursor M.* 18583 Nu haf yee herd be tald þe pas, Hu þat he harud hell and ras. c1400 *Destr. Troy* 663 The lady.. Past to hir priue chamber: & here a pas endis. 14.. *ABC Poem on Passion* 44 in *Pol., Rel. & L. P.* 245 Lystyn a lytyl pas. 1621 T. WILLIAMSON tr. *Goulart's Wise Vieillard* 24 Philosophers haue vsed to diuide old age as it were into certaine spaces, paces, or progresses.

† **13.** A 'company' or herd of asses. *Obs.*

1486 *Bk. St. Albans* F vj b, A Pase of Assis. 1688 R. HOLME *Armoury* II. 132/1 A company of.. Asses [is] a Pace.

14. *attrib.* and *Comb.*, as *pace-goer*, *-setter*; **pace-aisle, pace-board** (cf. senses 9, 11); **pace-stick**, a stick used to measure (military) paces. See PACE-MAKER.

1877 LEE *Gloss. Liturg. Terms*, **Pace-aisle*, the ambulatory round the back of a high altar. **Pace-board*, a platform of wood before an altar. 1870 MEADE *New Zealand* 328 A pair of legs which looked like *pace-goers by land or water. 1895 *Westm. Gaz.* 25 Nov. 2/2 With Mr. Redmond as *pace-setter, there will, we may be sure, be a lively competition between him, Mr. Dillon, and Mr. Healy. 1833 *Regul. Instr. Cavalry* I. 16 The *pace stick must be used to measure.. his step. 1876 ALBEMARLE 50 *Yrs. Life* II. 219 Drill-sergeants followed them everywhere, to prove by the pace-stick whether they had accomplished the regulation number of inches at each stride.

Pace (pē¹s), *sb.*² *Sc.* and *north. dial.* Also 5 (9) **paas**, 5-6 **pase**, *Sc.* **payce, paiss**. [In 15th c. *paas* from earlier *pask*; cf. northern *as*, *ass*, from *ask*, ASH *sb.*², etc. In Washington Irving perh. from Du. *paasch*, pronounced *paas*.] Easter, Easter-tide; = PASCH. **Pace eggs**, *dial.* **paste-eggs** (LG. *paaschey*, F. *œufs de pâques*) Easter eggs; hence *pace-egger*, *-egging*: see Eng. Dial. Dict.

c1425 WYNTOUN *Chron.* VIII. i. 3 The sextene day efftyr Pase. c1440 *York Myst.* xxvii. 4 Here will I holde.. The feeste of Paas. 1500-20 DUNBAR *Poems* xxxvi. 19 And nevir is glaid at 3ule nor Paiss. 1530 PALSGR. 805 At Pace, *a Pasques*. 1568 *Durham Depos.* (Surtees) 87 He wold stand up upon paysunday. c1570 *Ibid.* 239 Upon Pase monday was a twelmonth last past. 1579 G. GILPIN tr. *Rabbotem's Bee-Hive Rom. Ch.* ii. (1580) 15 Holy ashes, holy paceegges, & flames, palmes and palme boughes. 1611 COTGR. s.v. *Pasque*, *Oeufs de Pasques*, Paste-egges. 1809 W. IRVING *Knickerb.* VII. ii, There was a great cracking of eggs at Paas or Easter. 1872 HARDWICK *Trad. Lanc.* 73 [They] sallied forth during Easterweek 'a pace-egging' as it was termed. 1876 *Prayer Bk. Interleaved* 117 The custom of asking for Pace.. eggs.

† **b.** Extended, like med.L. *pascha* (see Du Cange) to other great church festivals, e.g. Christmas. (Cf. OF. *pasque de Noël*, Sp. *pascua de Natividad* or simply *Pascua*.) *Obs.*

c1450 *St. Cuthbert* (Surtees) 3393 Done solempnite of pace.

Pace (pē¹s), *v.* Also 6-7 **pase**. [f. PACE *sb.*¹]

1. *intr.* To move with paces or steps; to walk with a slow, steady, or regular pace: to step along.

1513 DOUGLAS *Æneis* XII. Prol. 161 The payntit povne, pasand with plomys gym, Kest vp his taill. 1570 LEVINS *Manip.* 7/3 To Pace, *gradi*. 1587 GREENE *Euphues his Censure* Wks. (Grosart) VI. 164 Hector pazing hand in hand with Achilles, Troilus with Vlisses. 1611 SHAKS. *Wint. T.* IV. iii. 120, I will euen take my leaue of you, & pace softly towards my Kinsmans. 1769 GRAY *Install. Ode* 35 Pacing forth With solemn steps and slow. 1814 CARY *Dante, Inf.* XXIV. 11 There paces to and fro, wailing his lot, As a discomfited and helpless man.

b. *transf.* and *fig.* To proceed or advance in speech or action.

1611 SHAKS. *Wint. T.* IV. i. 23, I.. with speed so pace To speake of Perdita. 1639 W. SCLATER *Worthy Commun.* 49 Let not the moone pace over the Zodaick oftner.. then we performe, if possible, our course this way.

c. Also *to pace it*. (See IT 9.)

1597 BP. HALL *Sat.* I. vi. 8 The nimble dactyls striving to out-go, The drawling spondees pacing it below. 1652 PEYTON *Catastr. Ho. Stuarts* (1731) 23 Charles insted of pacing it, ran violently to destroy his subjects.

d. *trans.* with cognate or adverbial object.

1598 SHAKS. *Merch. V.* II. vi. 12 Where is the horse that doth vntread againe His tedious measures with the vnbated fire, That he did pace them first? 1634 *Documents agst. Prynne* (Camden) 20 Soe many paces as a man paceth in daunceinge soe manye steppes hee is forward to hell. 1849 MACAULAY *Hist. Eng.* ix. II. 438 Sentinels paced the rounds day and night.

e. With *away*: To spend (time) in pacing.

1820 KEATS *Hyperion* I. 194 He paced away the pleasant hours of ease.

2. *trans.* To traverse with paces or steps; to walk with measured pace along (a path) or about (a place); hence, To measure by pacing.

1571 DIGGES *Pantom.* II. xi. N j b, You maye.. measure euery side, and line.. as exactely as with corde, or pole, ye should paynfully pase it ouer. 1693 in *Hearne's Collect.* (O. H. S.) III. 342, I paced it, and found it to bee 70 of my Paces in Length. 1791 MRS. RADCLIFFE *Rom. Forest* v, Louis was pacing the room in apparent agitation. 1801 SOUTHEY *Thalaba* V. *note*, It.. is, as far as I could judge by my pacing it, a large quarter of a league. 1878 *Masque Poets* 195 She rose and paced the room like one distracted.

3. *intr.* Of a horse, etc.: To move with the gait called a pace (see PACE *sb.*¹ 6 b): (*a*) to amble; (*b*) in recent use (chiefly *U. S.*), to rack (RACK *v.*⁴).

1614 B. JONSON *Barth. Fair* II. Wks. (Rtldg.) 317/2 I'll.. have thy pasterns well roll'd, and thou shalt pace again by to-morrow. c1620 Z. BOYD *Zion's Flowers* (1855) 137 Men for a space pace in prosperity, But at the last trot hard in misery. 1673 *Lond. Gaz.* No. 819/4 Stolen.. one Bay Mare.. paces naturally. 1677 *Ibid.* No. 1222/4 A Sorrel Chesnut Gelding.. walks well, paces little, but trotteth high. 1709 *Ibid.* No. 4543/4 Stray'd or stoln.. a Sorrel Gelding.. does not pace. 1833 HT. MARTINEAU *Manch. Strike* 42 The procession.. overtook Mr. W.,.. pacing to business on his gray pony. 1895 *Funk's Stand. Dict.*, *Pace*, to move, as a horse, at the pace, by lifting the feet on the same side synchronously. 1903 *Daily Mail* 11 Mar., A horse trots when his off fore and near hind legs strike the ground simultaneously, and he paces when the legs of a side move in unison, like those of two riders on a tandem cycle.

b. *trans.* (With cognate or adverbial object.)

1607 MARKHAM *Caval.* (1617) 148 In this ring you shall exercise your horse.. making him pace it, and doe his changes first uppon foote pace onely; when he can pace them perfitely, then you shall make him trott. *Ibid.* 152 You may begin with the two distinct or several rings, which after he have pac'd, trotted and gallopped, then.. stop.

4. *trans.* To train (a horse) to pace; to exercise in pacing. Also *fig.*

1603 SHAKS. *Meas. for M.* IV. iii. 137. 1606 — *Ant. & Cl.* II. ii. 64 The third oth' world is yours, which with a Snaffle, You may pace easie, but not such a wife. 1607 MARKHAM *Caval.* II. (1617) 82 You must then leaue exercising him in any lesson.. and onely pace or trott him fairely forth right. 1724 *Lond. Gaz.* No. 6258/3 A bay Mare,.. lately paced.

5. To set the pace for (a rider, boat's crew, etc.) in racing or training for a race.

1886 *N. Y. Herald* in *Cyclist* 3 Nov. 82/1 Crocker was paced by Woodside, Rowe and Hender on bicycles. 1893 *Westm. Gaz.* 22 Mar. 5/3 Oxford had the advantage of the assistance of a Thames Rowing Club eight to pace them.

¶ **6.** A corruption of or blunder for PARSE. *Obs.* (Showing that *pace* was pronounced as *pass*.)

1594 LYLY *Moth. Bomb.* I. iii, I am no Latinist Cand. you must conster it. *Can.* So I will and pace it too: thou shalt be acquainted with case, gender, and number.

Pace, an early (14-15th c.) spelling of PASS *v.*

Pacebil, obs. form of PEACEABLE *a.*

Paced (pē¹st), *a.* [f. PACE *sb.* and *v.* + -ED.]

1. Having a (specified) pace, gait, or rate of walking or going: chiefly in parasynthetic comb.

1583 GREENE *Mamillia* II. Wks. (Rtldg.) 316/1 Dames now-a-days.. Pac'd in print, brave lofty looks, not us'd with the vestals. 1594 J. DICKENSON *Arisbas* (1878) 78 An high-pac'd Muse, treading a lofty march. c1611 CHAPMAN *Iliad* XIII. 24 His brazen-footed steeds, All golden-maned, and paced with wings. 16.. DRYDEN (J.), Revenge is sure, though sometimes slowly pac'd. 1899 *Academy* 15 July 60/2 The best of life comes to the even-paced.

2. Traversed or measured by pacing.

1869 LD. LYTTON *Orval* 169 The primly-paced saloons of Art and Science. 1882 FLOYER *Unexpl. Baluchistan* 177 Hills, each with a paced base of from half a mile to a mile.

3. *Racing.* Having the pace set by a pace-maker.

1899 *Daily News* 8 Apr. 8/6 The National Cyclists' Union.. forbade all riders holding its licences.. to attempt a paced ride of any description on the road.

Pace-gard, -guard, var. PASSE-GARDE.

Pace-maker. [PACE *sb.*¹]

1. A rider (boat's crew, etc.) who makes or sets the pace for another in racing or training for a race.

1884 *Pall Mall G.* 29 Mar. 2/2 The same scratch-crew acted as pace-maker for both the university eights. 1891 *Ibid.* 6 Aug. 1/3 To establish a record for a mile without pace-makers, in order that comparisons may be drawn between the times of an unassisted rider and one paced. 1900 *Field* 8 Sept. 384/1 The value of the pacemaker as a mere leader who set a racing pace.. was lost sight of when his utility as a wind-shield became recognized.

2. An apparatus fixed to a bicycle to indicate when the rider is going at the required pace.

1896 *Godey's Mag.* Apr. 377/1 On the same lines is a pace-maker that can be set at any desired rate... While this rate is maintained, it rings a bell.

Pacement, obs. form of PASSEMENT.

Pacer (pē¹·sər). [Agent-n. from PACE *v.*]

1. *gen.* One who paces; one who walks with measured step; one who traverses or measures (a path, distance, etc.) by pacing.

1835 L. HUNT *Capt. Sword* ii, Pacer of highway and piercer of ford. 1886 DOWDEN *Shelley* II. 510 The pacers on the terrace descried a strange sail rounding the point.

2. A horse that paces, or whose ordinary gait is a pace: see PACE *sb.*¹ 6 b, *v.* 3.

a1661 FULLER *Worthies*, *Huntington.* (1662) 51 It is given to thorough-paced-Naggs, that amble naturally, to trip much whilest artificial pacers goe surest on foot. 1708 J. CHAMBERLAYNE *St. Gt. Brit.* I. I. iv. (1737) 32 Your New England Pads are esteemed as the swiftest Pacers. 1740 BAYNARD *Health* (ed. 6) 31 Be your horse a pacer, or a trotter. 1809 W. IRVING *Knickerb.* V. vi, He entered New-Amsterdam as a conqueror, mounted on a Naraganset pacer. 1817 *Sporting Mag.* L. 25 The parson of the parish.. mounts the old pacer. 1829 *Sporting Mag.* XXIII. 266 The Narraganset pacer is extinct. 1884 E. EGGLESTON in *Century Mag.* Jan. 445/1 The awkward but 'prodigiously' rapid natural amble of the American pacer. 1900 *Field* June. A pacer.. canters with his hind legs, and trots with his fore legs.

b. One who trains a horse to pace; a trainer.

1656 EARL MONM. tr. *Boccalini's Advts. fr. Parnass.* I. xli. (1674) 54 Coults might not put Tramels upon their Pacers.

3. *Racing.* = PACE-MAKER 1.

1893 *Pall Mall G.* 10 July 10/2 In the contest of Saturday the riders were permitted to have pacemakers; but the innovation was not entirely successful, the competitors several times overrunning the pacer.

4. *colloq.* Anything that goes at a great pace.

1890 *Cent. Dict.* 1901 FARMER *Slang*.

Pacha, Pachalik, var. ff. PASHA, PASHALIC.

Pachche, pache, obs. ff. PATCH. **Pache**, obs. var. PASCHE, Easter. **Pachemia** = *pachyhæmia* s.v. PACHY-.

Pachent, obs. form of PAGEANT.

‖ **Pachisi** (patʃī·si). Also 8 **pacheess**; 9 **pachchisi** (erron. *parchesi*, *-chisi*). [a. Hindī *pach(ch)īsī*, lit. 'of *pach(ch)is*', i.e. twenty-five.] A four-handed game played in India, on a cruciform board or (more often) cloth, with six cowries for dice: so named from the highest throw, which is twenty-five. (A simplified form is known in Europe as *ludo*.)

1800 *Asiatic Ann. Reg.*, *Misc. Tracts* 314/2 In one square court the pavement is worked with squares, in the manner of the cloth used by the Indians for playing the game called Pacheess. 1867 A. F. BELLASIS in E. Falkener *Games Anc. & Orient.* (1892) 258 There is a gigantic pachishee board at the palace at Agra where the squares are inlaid with marble on a terrace. 1892 KIPLING & BALESTIER *Naulahka* 78 It seemed to him no extraordinary mark of court favour to play pachisi with the King. 1892 E. FALKENER *Games Anc. & Orient.* 257 Pachisi is the national game of India.

Pachnolite (pæ·knŏləit). *Min.* [Named 1863, f. Gr. πάχνη hoar-frost + -LITE.] Hydrous fluoride of aluminium, calcium, and sodium, occurring on cryolite in small white crystals.

1866 *Amer. Jrnl. Sci.* XLI. 199 Knop has named the new species Pachnolite. 1868 DANA *Min.* (ed. 5) 129 Found with pachnolite on the cryolite of Greenland.

Pachometer (păkǫ·mĭtər). *Physics.* = Pachymeter: see PACHY-.

1857 MAYNE *Expos. Lex.*, An instrument invented by Benoit for measuring the thickness of the glass of mirrors: a pachometer. 1875 in KNIGHT *Dict. Mech.*

Pachy- (pæ·ki, păki·), before a vowel also **pach-**, combining form of Gr. παχύ-ς 'thick, large, massive', used in the formation of zoological, botanical, and pathological terms: ‖ **Pachyæ·mia** = *pachyhæmia*. ‖ **Pachyblepharosis** (-blefărōᵘ·sis) *Path.* [Gr. βλέφαρον eyelid], chronic inflammatory thickening of the eyelid (Mayne *Expos. Lex.* 1857). **Pachycardian** (-kā·rdiăn) *a. Zool.* [Gr. καρδία heart], of or belonging to the *Pachycardia*, or main body of the vertebrates having a thick muscular heart; *sb.*, a vertebrate of this group. **Pachycarpous** (-kā·rpəs) *a. Bot.* [Gr. καρπός fruit], having large thick fruit (Mayne 1857). **Pachycephalic** (-sĭfæ·lik) *a.* [Gr. κεφαλ-ή head], having a very thick skull, exhibiting pachycephaly. **Pachycephaline** (-se·fălain) *a. Ornith.*, of or pertaining to the *Pachycephalinæ*, the thick-heads or thick-headed shrikes. **Pachycephalous** (-se·făləs) *a.* = *pachycephalic*; spec., of or pertaining to the *Pachycephala*, a division of parasitic Crustacea or fish-lice. **Pachycephaly** (-se·făli), thickness of the skull. **Pachycholic** (-kǫ·lik) *a. Path.* [Gr. χολή bile], relating to *pachycholia* or morbid thickness of the bile (Mayne 1857). **Pachydac·tyl, -yle** (-dæ·ktil) *a. Zool.* [Gr. δάκτυλος finger], having thick fleshy digits; *sb.*, an animal with thick toes (Webster 1864). **Pachydactylous** *a.* [-OUS], = prec. *a.* ‖ **Pachyde·rmia** *Path.* [Gr. δέρμα skin], thickening of the skin; hence **Pachyde·rmial** *a.* **Pachyemy** = *pachyhæmia*; so *pachyemic*, *pachyemous*, adjs. (Mayne 1857). **Pachyglo·ssal** *a. Zool.* [Gr. γλῶσσα tongue], of or pertaining to the *Pachyglossæ*, lizards with short or thick fleshy tongues, or the *Pachyglossi*, a tribe of Parrots; so **Pachyglo·ssate**. **Pachyglo·ssous** *a.*, thick-tongued (Mayne 1857). **Pachygnathous** (păki·gnăþəs) *a.* [Gr. γνάθ-ος jaw], thick-jawed (*Cent. Dict.*). ‖ **Pachyhæ·mia** [Gr. αἷμα blood], thickness of the blood; so **Pachyhæ·mic** *a.*, relating to pachyhæmia. **Pachyhæ·mous** *a.*, having thick blood (*Syd. Soc. Lex.* 1893). ‖ **Pachyhyme·nia, Pachyme·nia** *Path.* [Gr. ὑμήν membrane], thickening of the skin; hence **Pachyme·nic, -hyme·nic** *a.*, thick-skinned (Mayne 1857). ‖ **Pachylo·sis** (also **pachu-**): see quot. **Pachymeningitis** (-menindʒəi·tis) *Path.* [MENINGITIS], inflammation of the dura mater of the central nervous system, cerebral or spinal. ‖ **Pachyme·ninx** (-mī·niŋks) [Gr. μῆνιγξ membrane], the dura mater (*Syd. Soc. Lex.* 1893). **Pachymeter** (păki·mĭtər) [-METER] (also **pacho-**), an instrument for measuring the thickness of glass, metal plates, paper, etc. **Pachyodont** (pæ·kiŏdǫnt) *a.* [Gr. ὀδούς, ὀδόντ- tooth], having massive teeth. **Pachyo·pterous** = *pachypterous*. **Pachyote** (pæ·ki,ōᵘt) *a.* [Gr. οὖς, ὠτ- ear], having thick leathery ears; *sb.*, a thick-eared bat, of genus *Pachyotus*; so **Pachyo·tous** *a.* (*Syd. Soc. Lex.* 1893). **Pachyphyllous** (-fi·ləs) *a. Bot.* [Gr. φύλλον leaf], having thick leaves (Mayne). **Pachypod** (pæ·kipǫd), **Pachypodous** (păki·pŏdəs) *adjs.* [Gr. πούς, ποδ- foot], having a large thick foot. **Pachypterous** (păki·ptərəs) *a.* [Gr. πτερόν wing, feather], having thick wings or fins, as an insect, a bat, or a fish. **Pachyrhynchous** (-ri·ŋkəs) *a.* [Gr. παχύρρυγχος, f. ῥύγχος snout], having a large thick bill. **Pachysaurian** (-sǫ·riăn), a thick-skinned saurian. **Pachystichous** (păki·stikəs), *a. Bot.* [Gr. στίχ-ος row, line], thick-sided, applied only to cells (*Treas. Bot.* 1866). **Pachytrichous** (-i·trikəs), *a.* [Gr. θρίξ, τριχ- hair], having thick hair (Mayne 1857).

1878 BARTLEY tr. *Topinard's Anthrop.* v. 177 *Pachycephalic, skull with thick hypertrophied parietes. 1858 HITCHCOCK *Ichnol. Mass.* 81 We should infer a larger number of *pachydactylous than leptodactylous animals to have made the tracks. 1897 *Allbutt's Syst. Med.* IV. 832 Chronic inflammation of the mucous membrane of the larynx.. may exist with the *pachydermial affection. 1893 *Syd. Soc. Lex.*, **Pachulosis*,.. Sir Erasmus Wilson's term for a skin disease in which there is hypertrophy of the epidermis. 1866 A. FLINT *Princ. Med.* (1880) 693 Acute *pachymeningitis is always suppurative, and is chiefly of surgical interest. 1899 *Allbutt's Syst. Med.* VI. 854 A certain degree of compression of the cord is caused by pachymeningitis. 1884 KNIGHT *Dict. Mech.* Suppl., **Pachymeter*, a Viennese instrument which determines the thickness of paper to the 1-1000th of an inch. 1842 BRANDE *Dict. Sci.* etc., **Pachyotes*,.. the name of a family of bats,.. including those which have thick external ears. 1854 WEBSTER, *Pachyote*. 1857 MAYNE *Expos. Lex.*, *Pachypodus*,.. applied by Gray to an Order [of molluscs] corresponding to the *Conchifera Crassipedes* of Lamarck: *pachypodous. 1881 FREWER tr. *Holub's 7 Yrs. S. Africa* I. 140 In the abdomen of this *pachysaurian there is found a collection of lobulated fatty matter.

Pachyderm (pæ·kidə̄m), *sb.* and *a.* [a. F. *pachyderme* sb. (Cuvier 1797), ad. Gr. παχύδερμ-ος thick-skinned, f. παχύ-ς thick + δέρμα skin. In a general sense, *pachuderme* adj. occurs casually in Fr. c1600 (Hatz.-Darm.).]

A. *sb. Zool.* A thick-skinned quadruped; spec. one of the *Pachydermata* of Cuvier.

1838 *Penny Cycl.* XII. 415/2 That the quadruped under consideration [Hyrax] is a true Pachyderm. 1853 KANE *Grinnell Exp.* xx. (1856) 160 That marine pachyderm, the tusky walrus. 1880 HAUGHTON *Phys. Geog.* ii. 53 England was inhabited by herbivorous pachyderms.. previous to the elevation of the east and west chain.

b. *fig.* Cf. PACHYDERMATOUS 2.

1867 GARFIELD in *Century Mag.* (1884) Jan. 417/2 Like all politicians he seems to have become a pachyderm. 1894 W. T. STEAD in *Review of Rev.* (Amer. ed.) Apr. 428 To shrink from the rude shocks and jars which tough pachyderms bear with unruffled composure.

B. *adj. Zool.* = PACHYDERMATOUS *a.*

1868 *Nat. Encycl.* I. 821 *Anthracotherium*, a fossil genus of pachyderm mammals.

Hence **Pachyde·rmal, Pachyde·rmic**, *adjs. Zool.*

1847 ANSTED *Anc. World* ix. 197 The gigantic living pachydermal mammals, such as the elephant, rhinoceros, and hippopotamus. 1838 *Penny Cycl.* XII. 416/2 The general balance of resemblance.. is strongly in favour of the Pachydermic relationship of the animal. 1840 *Ibid.* XVII. 151/2 These and other Pachydermic forms.

‖ **Pachydermata** (pækidə̄·rmătă), *sb. pl. Zool.* [mod.L., f. Gr. παχύ-ς thick + δέρμα, δέρματ- skin.] An order of Mammalia in Cuvier's system of classification, consisting of the hoofed or ungulate

quadrupeds which do not chew the cud, as the elephant, rhinoceros, hippopotamus, hyrax, horse. Disused by recent zoologists; its constituents being distributed into various orders.

1823 BUCKLAND *Reliq. Diluv.* 37 It is foreign to the habits of the hyæna to prey on the larger pachydermata. 1847 YOUATT *Horse* v. 107 The horse does not ruminate, and therefore belongs to the order pachydermata.

Pachyde·rmatocele. *Path.* [f. as prec. + Gr. κήλη tumour.] A tumour arising from hypertrophy of the corium and subcutaneous areolar tissue.

1854 V. MOTT in *Med.-Chirurg. Trans.* Ser. II. XIX. 155 (*title*) On a peculiar form of tumour of the skin, denominated 'Pachydermatocele'. 1900 *Lancet* 2 June 1593/2.

Pachyde·rmatoid, *a.* [See -OID.] Akin to the *Pachydermata*.

1882 in OGILVIE.

Pachydermatous (pækidə̄·rmătəs), *a.* [f. PACHYDERMATA + -OUS.]

1. Of or belonging to the *Pachydermata*.

1823 BUCKLAND *Reliq. Diluv.* 18 Teeth of the larger pachydermatous animals are not abundant. 1874 WOOD *Nat. Hist.* 245 The last on the list of the pachydermatous animals is the well-known Hippopotamus, or River Horse.

2. *fig.* Thick-skinned; not sensitive to rebuff, ridicule, or abuse; not easily affected by outside influences.

1854 LOWELL *Keats* Prose Wks. 1890 I. 229 A man cannot have a sensuous nature and be pachydermatous at the same time. a1876 M. COLLINS *Th. in Garden* (1880) II. 299, I doubt whether the poet might not find better employment than lashing pachydermatous fools.

Hence **Pachyde·rmatously** *adv.*, **Pachyde·rmatousness.**

1854 WOOD *Anim. Life* (1855) 367 [An animal] of whose pachydermatousness, if we may coin such a word, there is no doubt. This is the Giraffe, whose hide is more than an inch in thickness. 1865 MORLEY *Mod. Characteristics* 35 The conditions of social and intellectual pachydermatousness are in themselves equally wonderful. 1900 *Westm. Gaz.* 1 Oct. 11/3 By being able pachydermatously to withstand the protests to which we have referred.

Pachydermia, -dermial: see PACHY-.

Pachyde·rmoid, *a.* = PACHYDERMATOID.

1856 KANE *Arct. Expl.* II. i. 16 The frost-tempered junks of this pachydermoid amphibian [walrus]. 1877 LE CONTE *Elem. Geol.* III. (1879) 547 The Diprotodon.. a pachydermoid Kangaroo as big as a rhinoceros.

Pachydermous (pækidə̄·rməs), *a. rare.* [f. as PACHYDERM + -OUS.] Thick-skinned, pachydermatous. **b.** *Bot.* Thick-coated.

1836 *Encycl. Brit.* (ed. 7) XIV. 146/2 The removal of the genus Equus.. would enable us to simplify our definition of the pachydermous tribes.

Pachyglossal to **Pachymeter**: see PACHY-.

Pachyntic (păki·ntik), *a. Med.* [ad. Gr. παχυντικ-ός of thickening quality, f. παχύν-ειν to thicken.] **a.** Having the power of thickening the bodily fluids. **b.** Fleshy, fat.

1890 BILLINGS *Nat. Med. Dict.* 1893 *Syd. Soc. Lex.*

Pachyodont to **Pachytrichous**: see PACHY-.

Pachytic (păki·tik), *a. Med.* [f. Gr. παχύτ-ης thickness + -IC.] = prec.

1857 MAYNE *Expos. Lex.*, *Pachyticus*,.. of or belonging to *Pachytes*: pachytic. 1890 J. S. BILLINGS *Nat. Med. Dict.* II. 276 Pachytic.. 1 Thick, obese, 2 Pachyntic.

Paci, obs. inf. of PASS *v.*

Paciable, -ibil, obs. forms of PEACEABLE.

Pacience, -ent, etc., obs. ff. PATIENCE, -ENT.

† **Paci·ferous**, *a. Obs.* [f. L. *pācifer* peace-bringing + -OUS.] Peace-bringing. Hence † **Paci·ferousness.**

1656 BLOUNT *Glossogr.*, *Paciferous*. 1727 BAILEY vol. II, *Paciferousness*,.. peace bringing quality.

Pacifiable (pæ·sifəi,ăb'l), *a.* [f. PACIFY + -ABLE.] Capable of being pacified or appeased.

1618 T. ADAMS *Fool & his Sport* Wks. 1861 I. 251 The conscience.. is not pacifiable whiles sin is within to vex it.

Pacific (păsi·fik), *a.* and *sb.* [ad. L. *pācific-us* peace-making, peaceful, f. *pāx*, *pāc-em* peace; see -FIC: perh. through F. *pacifique*, *-ficque* (15th c. in Godef. *Compl.*).]

A. *adj.* **1.** Making, or tending to the making of, peace; leading to peace or reconciliation; conciliatory, appeasing.

a1548 HALL *Chron.*, *Edw. IV* 248 b, Sore lamentyng.. that I did not performe and finally consumate, suche pollitique diuises.. in my long life and paciffique prosperitie. 1581 MULCASTER *Positions* xxxix. (1887) 214 He appointed the pacificque, and friendly Embassages. 1667 MILTON *P. L.* XI. 860 An Olive leafe he brings, pacific signe. 1786 W. THOMSON *Watson's Philip III* (1839) 275 The marquis of Spinola.. had strenuously supported the pacific counsels of Prince Albert at the court of Madrid. 1855 MILMAN *Lat. Chr.* III. vii. (1864) II. 135 The pacific influence which Gregory obtained in this momentous crisis.

2. Of peaceful disposition or character, not belligerent, peaceable.

1641 J. JACKSON *True Evang. T.* III. 189 See whether is more pacifique and charitable, and by consequent whether is the more Euangelicall. 1751 JOHNSON *Rambler* No. 185 ¶ 10 This pacifick and harmless temper. 1774 J. ADAMS in *Fam. Lett.* (1876) 40, I saw the tears gush into the eyes of the old grave pacific Quakers. 1879 DIXON *Windsor* II. xii. 132 In the end he brought them to a more pacific view.

3. Characterized by peace or calm, peaceful, at peace; calm, tranquil, quiet.

1633 T. JAMES *Voy.* lv, Pacificke and open Seas. 1865 CARLYLE *Fredk. Gt.* XVIII. xii. (1872) VIII. 26 The road has hitherto been mainly pacific.

b. *Pacific Ocean*, *Sea*, the 'Great Ocean' stretching between America on the east and Asia on the west; so called by Magellan, because found to be relatively free from violent storms.

[1555 EDEN *Decades* 220 The sayde sea cauled *Pacificum* that is peaceable.] 1660 F. BROOKE tr. *Le Blanc's Trav.* 332 The great pacifick gulph, which may be said one of the calmest Seas of the world. 1777 ROBERTSON *Hist. Amer.* v. Wks. 1826, VI. 19 They enjoyed an uninterrupted course of fair weather, with such favourable winds, that Magellan bestow'd on that ocean the name of Pacific.

4. phr. '*Pacific iron*, an iron band round a lower yard-arm into which the boom-iron screws' (*Cent. Dict.* 1890). † *Pacific Letters* (also *Letters Pacifical* = L. *literæ pacificæ*, Gr. ἐπιστολαὶ εἰρηνικαί), orig. letters of commendation to the church in another city or country recommending the bearer as one in peace and communion with the Church; later, esp. letters recommending the bearer to the alms of the faithful.

1709 J. JOHNSON *Clergym. Vade M.* II. 85 Let no foreigner be received without pacifick letters. *Note.* *Pacifick Letters* were those given to any whether bishop, clergyman, or layman on any occasion he had to travel to another city. 1725 tr. *Dupin's Eccl. Hist. 17th C.* I. v. II. 69 By Letters pacifick, we understand, those which the Bishops gave to the Poor who were unjustly oppress'd or had need of Relief.

B. *sb.*

† **1. a.** *pl.* Peace-offerings [rendering L. *pācifica*.] **b.** An offer or overture of peace, an Eirenicon. *Obs.*

1609 BIBLE (Douay) *Ezek.* xlv. 15 One ramme of a flocke of two hundred.. for holocaust, and for pacifiques. 1687 *Let. from Country* 10 If.. she persists obstinately to refuse this national Paciffick; the Dissenters, I hope, will consider their honest Interest.

2. The Pacific Ocean.

a1821 KEATS *Sonn.*, *On first looking into Chapman's Homer* 12 Like stout Cortez, when with eagle eyes He stared at the Pacific. 1855 MAURY *Phys. Geog. Sea* § 54 The Atlantic is the most stormy sea in the world, the Pacific the most tranquil. 1894 *Westm. Gaz.* 4 Dec. 8/1 Because Keats made a mistake, is the real discoverer to be defrauded to all time? The Pacific was discovered September 26, 1513, by Vasco Nuñez de Balboa.

b. *attrib.* 'of the Pacific Ocean', as *Pacific slope*, *State*. Comb., as *Pacificwards*.

1855 MAURY *Phys. Geog. Sea* § 276 The great chain [of mountains] that skirts the Pacific coast. *Ibid.* § 283 On the Pacific [Aleutian] islands there is an uninterrupted rain-fall during the entire winter. *Ibid.* § 355 The dry season on the Pacific slopes. 1897 *Daily News* 30 Dec. 6/5 Russia's progress Pacificwards. 1902 WEBSTER, *Pacific slope*, that part of North America.. lying west of the continental divide.

Hence **Paci·ficness** (Bailey vol. II, 1727).

† **Paci·ficable**, *a. Obs.* [f. L. *pācificā-re* to pacify + -BLE.] = PACIFIABLE.

1621 BP. HALL *Heaven upon Earth* § 4 The conscience is not pacificable, while sinne is within to vex it.

Pacifical (păsi·fikăl), *a.* [f. L. *pācific-us* (see PACIFIC) + -AL.] Of pacific or peaceful nature; peaceable. *Letters pacifical*: see PACIFIC *a.* 4.

c1485 *Digby Myst.* (1882) III. 1593 Bed hyr axke of his good be weyys pacyfycal. 1609 *Ev. Woman in Hum.* I. i. in Bullen *O. Pl.* IV, Sir, be pacificall, the fellowe was possest with some critique frenzie. 1876 G. MEREDITH *Beauch. Career* I. xiii. 197 He had to think of what was due to his pacifical disposition. 1883 *Canons of Antioch* vii. in Fulton *Index Canonum* 237 No stranger shall be received without letters pacifical.

Paci·fically, *adv.* [f. prec. + -LY².] In a pacific manner; peacefully, peaceably.

1793 *Residence in France* (1797) I. 231 A few dragoons have arranged the business very pacifically. 1865 CARLYLE *Fredk. Gt.* IV. x. (1872) II. 33 Friedrich Wilhelm's first step, of course, was to remonstrate pacifically.

Pacificate (păsi·fikeⁱt), *v.* [f. L. *pācificāt-*, ppl. stem of *pācificāre* to make peace, to pacify.]

† **1.** *intr.* To make peace (*with*). *Obs. rare.*

1646 *Unhappy Game at Scotch & Eng.* 22 What is this other then to pacificate with him without their joynt advice and consent?

2. *trans.* To give peace to, to pacify.

1827 SOUTHEY *Hist. Penins. War* II. 388 He would now pacificate Roncal and the vallies of Aragon. 1865 CARLYLE *Fredk. Gt.* XIV. v. (1872) V. 222 There is one ready method of pacificating Germany. 1884 SIR C. WARREN *Memorandum on Bechuanaland* 29 Oct., The object.. is to remove the filibusters from Bechuanaland, to pacificate the territory.

Hence **Paci·ficated** *ppl. a.*

1885 *Manch. Exam.* 14 Feb. 5/1 To make it [Khartoum] the capital of a pacificated or subjugated Soudan.

Pacification (pæsifikē¹·ʃən). [a. F. *pacification* (15th c. in Hatz.-Darm.), ad. L. *pācificātiōn-em*, n. of action from *pācificāre* to pacify.] The action or fact of pacifying or appeasing; the condition of being pacified; appeasement, conciliation.

Edict of Pacification, an ordinance or decree enacted by a prince or state to put an end to strife or discontent; esp. in *French hist.*, one of the royal edicts in the 16th century granting concessions to the Protestants; e.g. those issued in 1563, 1570, and the Edict of Nantes in 1598.

1490 CAXTON *Eneydos* xxi. 77 That the swete wyndes shalle putte hemselfe vp in pacyfycacion of the see. a1548 HALL *Chron.*, *Hen. VI* 158 To begyn a shorte pacificacion in so long a broyle. 1573 E. VARAMUND *Rep. Outrages France* in *Harl. Misc.* (Malh.) I, The King.. gave his faith, that he would for ever most sacredly and faithfully observe his

Pacificator, agent-n. from *pacificare* to pacify. Cf. F. *pacificateur* (1300 in Godef. *Compl.*) One who pacifies or brings to a state of peace; a peace-maker.

Pacificatory, *a*. [ad. L. *pācificātōri-us*, f. *pacificator*: see prec. and -ORY.] Tending to make peace.

Pacificity. *rare*. [f. PACIFIC + -ITY.] The quality of being pacific, pacific character.

Pacificous, *a*. *Obs.* [See -OUS.] = PACIFIC.

Pacifier (pæ·sifaiəɹ). [f. PACIFY + -ER¹.] One who or that which pacifies or appeases.

Pacify (pæ·sifəi), *v*. [a. F. *pacifie-r* (15th c. in Littré, OF. *pacefier* 1390 in Godef.), ad. L. *pācificāre*, f. *pācificus* peaceful: see -FY.]

1. *trans.* To allay the anger, excitement or agitation (of a person): to calm, quiet; to assuage.

b. To calm or appease (passion, etc.).

2. To bring or reduce to a state of peace; to calm, quiet; a strife, contention, rebellion, etc.

b. To settle (a dispute, etc.).

3. *intr.* To become peaceful.

Pacing (pēi·siŋ), *vbl. sb.* [as PACE v.]

Pacinian (pǎsi·niæn), *a*. [f. name of the Italian anatomist Pacini (1812–1883) + -AN.] Of or described by Pacini.

Packed (pækt), *ppl. a*.

Package (pæ·kēdʒ). Also ⁷ *paccage*. [f. PACK v.¹ + -AGE.]

Packer¹ (pæ·kəɹ). Also ⁵ *pakker*, -our. [f. PACK v.¹ + -ER¹.] One who packs.

Packing (pæ·kiŋ), *vbl. sb.* [f. PACK v.¹ + -ING¹.]

Packing. (Top of first column) ...

Pacock, north. form of *pocock*, PEACOCK.

†Pacolet. *Obs.* Name of a dwarf in the old romance of *Valentine and Orson*, said to have made a magical horse of wood by which he could instantly convey himself to any desired place. Hence allusively, esp. in *Pacolet's horse* (cf. *le cheval de Pacolet*), and *Pacolet* for a swift steed.

Pacquet, obs. form of PACKET.

Pact, *sb.* [a. OF. *pact* (14th c.), later *pacte* (in OF. also *pait, pec, pag, pt, pai*), a. L. *pactum* agreement, covenant, neuter sb. f. *pactus*, pa. pple. of *pac-isc-ere* to agree, covenant, f. ...] ...

Pactional ... *Chiefly Sc.* ...

Packwax: see PAXWAX.

‖Paco [Sp.] ... also **pacos** [Sp. *paco*, a Quichua *paco*, the native name in Peru.] ...

Pactorial [cf. *pactorial*] ...

Pad (pæd). *sb.*[1] ... Also 4-6 *padde*, 7-8 *padd*. ...

Pad (pæd). *sb.*[2] ... [ad.L. type *Pactorius*: — next] ...

Pad (pæd), *v.*[1] [Related to PAD *sb.*[2]: cf. LG. and E.Fris. *padden* = OHG. *pfadōn*, OE. *pæðan*, to tread, go along (a path). Also LG. (Bremisch. Wtterb.) *padjen* to run with short steps: said of children] ...

Pad (pæd), *v.*[2] ... To travel on foot, to walk; to tramp ...

Padder (pæ·dɑ). *sb.*[1] Also 7 *padde*. [f. PAD *v.*[2] + -ER[1].] ...

Padding, *vbl. sb.* [f. PAD *v.* + -ING[1].] 1. The action of PAD *v.*, in its various senses. ...

Paddle (pædl), *sb.*[1] Also 5 *padel*, *pedyll*. [Origin obscure: see also PADDLE, PATTLE.] ...

Paddle (pædl), *v.*[1] Also 7 *paddel*. [app. f. PADDLE *sb.*[1]: cf. Du. *peddelen*, ...] ...

Paddle ... *Sb.* ... [Origin obscure; the form is dim. and frequentative.] ...

I. *intr.* To move or move the feet about in mud or shallow water; to wade about in play or for pleasure; to dabble with the feet, or the feet and hands, in shallow water. ...

2. *intr.* To play or dabble idly or fondly (*in, on, with, or about something*) with the fingers; to toy. ...

II. **1.** *intr.* To walk with short, unsteady, or uncertain steps, like those of a child; to toddle. ...

2. *intr.* To walk or paddle along. ...

3. *trans.* To trifle away, waste, squander. ...

Paddle, *sb.* ... [f. PADDLE *vb.*]
I. 1. *intr.* To move on the water by means of paddles, as in a canoe. Also said of the canoe.

Paddle ... [a Canoe ...turned adrift, by which means he paddled by some ...]

II. trans. To row with oars lightly or gently ... technically applied to the rowing of a racing crew when not exerting their full power. ...

b. *trans.* To convey with paddles; also, to transport (a person) in a canoe. ...

III. **3.** *trans.* To beat (a person) with a paddle or the like; to "spank," "smack." ...

Paddle-beam, -boat, -box, -crab, etc. : see PADDLE *sb.* **Paddle-cock** : see PADDOCK.
Paddled (*pæ'd'ld*), *a.* [f. PADDLE *sb.* + -ED.] Furnished with paddles.

Paddler (*pæ'dlə*). [f. PADDLE *v.* + -ER.] One who of what paddles or dabbles in mire or shallow water. ...

Paddler ... [f. PADDLE *sb.* + -ER.]
1. One who paddles a canoe or the like.

Paddle-steamer, etc. : see PADDLE *sb.*
Paddle-wheel ... **1.** — PADDLE *sb.* 1.

Paddle-wheel. A wheel used for propelling a boat or ship; as originally tried, consisting of or having a series of paddles or paddle-like spokes inserted in an axle, drum, or wheel, whence came, but eventually, having floats or paddle-boards fitted ...

Paddock (*pæ'dək*), *sb.* ... **I.** A small field or enclosure; usually a plot of pasture-land adjoining or near a house or stable. ...

2. In the Australian Colonies, the general term for any field, or piece of land enclosed by a fence, irrespective of size, whether in pasture or tillage. ...

Paddock (*pæ'dək*), *sb.* ... [Also Sc. 9 **poddock**, 9 **puddock**.] **1.** A frog. Obs. *exc. Sc. and north. dial.*

2. A toad. Obs. *exc. Sc. and north. dial.*

Paddock, paddok, -pad, paddie, northern forms of PADDOCK, frog, toad ; so **paddo-pipe**, ...
Paddock-stool. [f. PAD *sb.* 1 + dimin. suffix -OCK.] **a.** A frog. Obs. **b.** A toad, *Sc.* 9 **poddock**, 9-9 **puddock**.

Paddock-stone, -stool, etc. : see TOAD-STONE, TOADSTOOL.

Pad'dock, *v.* **1.** *trans.* To enclose or fence in (a sheep-run, etc.) (*Australia*). **b.** To shut up or enclose in or as in a paddock. ...

Paddy (*pæ'di*), *sb.* ... [a. Malay *padi* rice in the straw, in Javanese and other Malay langs. *pārī*. The identity of this with Canarese *batta, bhatta* rice in the husk, whence the *batta, batty* of early authors, is uncertain.] **1.** Rice in the straw, or (in commerce) in the husk. ...

Paddy (*pæ'di*), *sb.* [Irish pet-form of *Padraig* or *Patrick.*] **1.** A nickname for an Irishman. ...

Paddle ...

Paddy-whack, -wack. *colloq.* [f. PADDY *sb.* 3.] ...

Padle ... **Padishah** ...

Padone ...

Padrone (*pădrō'ne*). ... [It.: cf. med.L. *padro, patrono, patron*; see PATRON.] An Italian term meaning, primarily, Patron, master; applied to the Prime Minister of the Papal Curia (*Cardinal Patron*); To the master of a trading-vessel in the Mediterranean; To an Italian labour-contractor, an employer of street musicians, beggar-children, etc.; d. the proprietor of an inn or hotel. ...

Padua ... **Paduan** ...

Pæan, variant of PÆON.

Pæan ... **1.** ... A song of praise, triumph, joy, or exultation. ...

Pædo-, pedo- (*pī'do, pe'do*), combining form of Gr. παῖς, παιδ- boy, child, an element in several words, scientific and technical, of which the most important will be found in their alphabetical places.

Pædobaptism (*pī'dobæptiz'm*). Also **pedo-**. [f. PÆDO- + BAPTISM; cf. mod.L. *pædobaptismus* (17th c.).] The baptism of infants or young children.

Pædonomy ...

Pædotribe ...

Pagan (*pē'gən*), *sb.* and *a.* ... [ad. L. *pāgān-us* villager, rustic; in Christian L. (Tertullian, Augustine) 'heathen' as opposed to Christian or Jewish.] ...

A. *sb.* **1.** One of a nation or community which does not hold the true religion, or does not worship the true God; a heathen. ...

Pæon (*pī'ən*), *sb.* ... [ad. L. *pæōn*, a. Gr. παίων.] **Prosody.** Also 7-8 **pæan**. ... A metrical foot of four syllables, one long and three short, named, according to the position of the long syllable, a first, second, third or fourth **pæon**. ...

Pæony, *Paganism*, etc.

Paganish ... **Paganism** ... **Paganize** ... **Paganly** ...

Paganically *adv.* ...

Paganish, a. [f. PAGAN + -ISH[1].]

Paga-no-christian, a. and sb.

Pagano-christianism: so Pagano-christianize v.

Pagantry (pē'găntri).

Paganity (păgæ'nĭti).

Paganism (pē'gănĭz'm). [ad. eccles. L. pāgānismus (Augustine), f. pāgānus PAGAN: see -ISM.] Cf. F. paganisme (16th in Cotgr.)

1. The religious belief and practices of pagans; the condition of being a pagan; paganism.

2. fig. or allusively. Pagan character or quality; the moral condition of pagans.

3. A pagan or heathenish feature, rite, or custom.

Paganize (pē'gănəiz). Also med.L. pāganizāre: see PAGAN and -IZE.

1. trans. To make pagan; to give a pagan character or form to.

2. intr. To become pagan; to act as a pagan.

Hence **Pa'ganized** ppl. a., **Pa'ganizing** vbl. sb. and ppl. a.; **Paganiza'tion**, the action of paganizing or fact of being paganized; **Pa'ganizer**, one who paganizes.

Paganly (pē'gănli), adv. [f. PAGAN a. + -LY[2].] In a pagan manner or degree; like a pagan.

Page (pēdʒ), sb.[1] Also 5 page, 6 St. pege, 9a. OF. page n. it. paggio, med.L. pagius (c 1300, Du Cange): cf. Sp. page, Pg. pagem in same sense.

1. †1. A boy, youth, lad. Obs.

†2. A male person of the 'lower orders,' or of low condition or manners; a term of contempt and sometimes of opprobrium; cf. KNAVE 1, 3. Obs.

3. A boy or lad employed as a servant or attendant; hence, a male servant of the lowest grade in his line of service, corresponding to an apprentice in trade; one whose part it is to assist and learn from an upper or more experienced servant or officer.

4. A boy or youth employed as a personal attendant of a person of rank.

5. A youth employed as the personal attendant of a person of rank.

6. A clip or other contrivance, for holding up a woman's skirt in walking.

II. Transferred uses.

II.

Page (pēdʒ), sb.[2] [a. F. page:—L. pāgina.]

1. trans. To put consecutive numbers upon the pages (of a book, manuscript, etc.); to paginate.

Page (pēdʒ), v.[1] [f. PAGE sb.[1]] a. trans. To wait on, attend, or follow, like a page. b. To page it; to act as page.

Page (pēdʒ), v.[2] [f. PAGE sb.[2]]

Full page, a page containing its full complement of printed matter.

Pageant (pæ'dʒĕnt, pā'-). sb. Forms: a. 4-6 pagyn, (6 pagen, -aon, padgin-100, padgeion, Sc. padg(e-ane, -yan), 6-7 pageyn. β. 5 pagend (-padand-end, pagand, paiande, pageant, pagant, pagiant, -iant, pacenn, pachent), 5-6 pagent, (pagaunt, -iaunt), pais(u)nt, -aunt, 6- padgand), 6-7 pageond, pais(u)nt, -aunt, 6- padgand, 6-7 pageant.

Pa'gehood. [-HOOD.] The state or condition of being a page. b. The personality of a page.

Page (pēdʒ), v.[3] [+ PAGE sb.[2] + -SHIP.] On pages (papers, blank books, etc.)

Pa'gery (pē'dʒəri). [f. PAGE sb.[1] + -RY.] The office or position of a page; service as a page.

Pa'geship (pē'dʒʃĭp). [f. PAGE sb.[1] + -SHIP.]

Pageant, pageyond, obs. forms of PAGEANT.

†**Pa'ggle**, v. Obs. [Deriv. uncertain.] intr.

Pagh, obs. variant of PAH int.

Pa'gina (pæ'dʒĭnă), obs. sb. ff. PAGEANT.

Pa'ginal, a. Obs. [f. PAGE sb.[2] + -AL.] Of or pertaining to a page or pages.

Pa'ginal (pæ'dʒĭnăl), a. [ad. L. pāginālis]

Paginate (pæ'dʒĭneit), v. [f. L. pāgina + -ATE[3].] trans. To mark or number the pages (of a book); to page.

Pagina'tion (pædʒĭneiʃən).

Pa'gine. Obs. Also 4-6 pagyn, 4 pagen (5 pagens). [ad. F. pagine, etc.]

†**Paging**, vbl. sb. Obs. [f. PAGE v.[1]]

Paging, vbl. sb.[2] [f. PAGE v.[2]]

Pagod (pē'gŏd). [f. PAGE sb.[2] + -OD.]

Pagodom (pē'gŏdəm). [f. PAGOD + -DOM.]

Pagoda (păgō'dă). sb. Forms: 6-7 pagode, pagado, 6 pagodo, pagoda.

Pagoda-tree.

Pagoda'di-tree.

Pagodite (pæ'gŏdəit). Min. [f. PAGODA + -ITE.]

Pagodo, obs. form of PAGODA.

Pagri, variant of PUGGREE.

Paguma (păgū'mă), Zool.

Pagurian (pægjū'rĭăn). Zool.

Pagynd, obs. form of PAGEANT.

Pah, int.

Pah (pā), sb. [Maori pā.]

Pahi (pā'hi), sb.

Pahlavi, var. PEHLEVI.

Paid (pēd), ppl. a.

†**Paigle** (pē'g'l), sb.[1] Also 6 paygell, paygle, 7 peagle, peggle, 8-9 pagil, 9 dial. paigle, pagle, peggle, teggall: see E. D. D.

Paik (pēk), sb. Sc. and north. dial.

Paik (pēk), v. Sc. and north. dial. [See prec.]

Pail (pēl), sb. Forms: 4-7 payle, 5 pale, (payelle), 6-7 paile, 6- pail. [OE. pægel.]

Pail (pēl), v.

Paila, var. PAYLA.

Paillette (pa'let). [Fr.]

Pailful (pēl'ful), sb.

Pain ...

PAIN

Pain (pən), sb.¹ Forms: 3–6 **peine**, 3–7 **peyne**, 4–6 **pein**, **peyn**, 4–7 **paine**, **payne**, 4– **pain**.

1. Suffering as inflicted for a crime or offence; punishment; penalty; a fine.

2. A small piece of gold or silver foil, mother-of-pearl, or some glittering material, used to ornament a woman's dress; a spangle.

Painful (pən·fŭl), a. Forms: see PAIN sb.¹

PAINT

Paint (pənt), v.

1. To put a coat or colouring upon.

2. That with which anything is painted.

Painted (pən·tĕd), ppl. a.

PAINTER.

(b) any species of the N. American genus *Castilleia*, having bracts more brilliant and showy than the flowers; painted finch, 'one of several names of *Passerina* or *Cyanospiza*, the nonpareil, the indigo-bird, or the lazuli-bird; so called from their brilliant and varied colors'; painted grass, the striped variety of *Phalaris arundinacea*, Lady's laces; painted ground: see *quot.*; painted hyæna = HYENA-DOG (*Lycaon pictus*); painted lady, (a) a species of butterfly (*Vanessa* or *Pyrameis cardui*) of orange-red colour, spotted with black and white; (b) a party-coloured variety of Pink or *Dianthus*; (c) also *painted lady-pea*, a variegated species of *Lathyrus*, esp. of the Sweet Pea; painted longspur, a North American bird; *Centrophanes pictus* (Coues *Key N. Amer. Birds* (1884) 358); painted mischief (1792), poker cards; painted quail, a name applied to several birds allied to the quail, esp. to those of the genus *Excalfactoria*; painted snipe: see *quot.* 1896; painted tortoise, turtle, an American mud-turtle (*Chrysemys picta*) brilliantly marked on the under surface with red and yellow.

1839 Newton *Dict. Birds* 493 The ..gaudy "Painted Bunting or Nonpareil. 1839 *Kelly of Purth* I. 106/1 Kn la "Chaumbre du Peyne. 1890-1 *Dict.* 103 b Chamaune Blanch espece de Chaumbe Peyne. 1 1543 in Parker *Dom. Archit.* III. 79 The pavement chamber & payntede chambre. 1694 Introduction of the Parliament in the Painted Chamber. 1875 STUBBS *Const. Hist.* III. xviii. 119 He [Hen. VI] had been brought into the painted Chamber to preside at the opening of parliament. 1486 Bk. *St. Albans* Cij b in Sig.b (Jam.) 'painful cloth cum pictura S. Antonii. 1545 *Test. Ebor.* (Surtees) V. 75 A payntid clothe wt Christe and ij thefes upon it. 1 1547–1564 *Test Cloth* 26 al. 3. 1587 WITHBRING *Brit. Plants* (ed. 2) II. 651 Barberry, "Painted-cups. 1866 *Treas. Bot.* Painted-cup, an American name for *Castilleia.* 1730 MORTIMER in *Phil. Trans.* XXXVI. 491 Fritipilla tricolor, the "painted Finch ... it's Head and Neck are blue; its Back green, and the Belly red. 1797 GERARDE *Herbal* ii. 175 §. 2. 21 Usually of our English women. , called Ladies laces, or "Painted grass. 1884 MILLER *Plant-n.*, Painted Grass. 1881 *Standard* 7 Oct. 9/1 Designs which remind the ancient spectator of that portion of the old Fleet Prison once known as the "painted ground, because of the vivid illustrations that distinguished it. 1850 Mrs *House-wife* set *ff.* xiii. 100 Called the "Painted Honey Eater on account of its variety of its colouring. Its scientific name is *Entomophila picta*. 1753 *Chambers Cycl. Supp.*, *Painted-lady*, a term for a particular sort of carnations, the flowers of which have all their petals red or purple on the out side, and white underneath. ...

Painter. (pē'ntəɹ). *Naut.* Also 5-9 paynter, 7-9 penter. [Derivation uncertain. Connexion with PANTER *n.*2, net, snare, F. *pantière*, has been conjectured; but no corroborative evidence has been found. Cf. PAINT *v.*2

...

Painter.1 Forms: 4-5 peynto *or*, peynteur, peyntoure, -ore, 4-5 paynter, 5 paintour, payntoure, peyntewer, panter, 5-6 payntour, peynter, 5-7 paynter, 6-7 penter, painter, peinter), 5- painter. [ME. ... a. A.F. *peinture* = OF. *peinteor*, -tor (regimen-cas of *peintre* = Pr. *pintor*, Sp., Pg. *pintor*, It. *pittore*):—Com. Romanic *pinctōr-em*, for L. *pinctōr-em*, *pictor-em*, agent-n. from *pingĕre* to PAINT. In 15–16th c., the ending was conformed to the *-er* of native agent-nouns.] One who paints.

1. An artist who represents or depicts objects on a surface in colours; one who paints pictures.

PAIR.

Pair, Paiþ, sb.2 Also pep (Jam.), 7ar. of Pep.] The stone of a cherry, sloe, plum, or other stone fruit; an orange pip, etc. The *paips*, a game played by schoolboys with cherry-stones.

Pair, Paiþ, sb.1 Forms: 3-5 peire, peyre, 4-7 paire, payre, (4-7 paiere), 4-5 payr, 5 peyr, (peyor, payir, 5-6 par, parre, paire, peere), 4-5 paiþ, (ME. a. F. *paire*:—L. *pāria*, neut. pl. taken as sing. fem.] A pair of; a number of things which are...

...

Palace, *sb.* [OED]

Palace gate.

Palace Court, pa'lace-court. [= Court ...]

Palaced (pæ'lăst), *a.* [f. PALACE *sb.*[1] *and* v. + -ED.] Having a palace, or palaces; living in a palace.

Palacious, *a.* Obs. ... [f. L. *pāla* shovel] + -OUS.]

Palæ-, paleo- (pæ'ljo, p@'li@), *before* a vowel usually **palæ-, paleo-**, combining form of Gr. παλαιός ancient, used in various scientific words ...

Palæarctic, -aarctic, -ward, see -WARD.

Palæ-, paleo- (pæ'ljo, p@'li@), ...

Paladin (pæ'lădin). [ad. F. *paladin*, ...]

Palæo- before a vowel.

Palæechini.

Palætiology.

Palæography, paleo- (pæ·lji·ŏgrăfi, pēˈli·-).

Palæotypography, paleo- (-taipŏgrăfi). [f. PALÆO- + TYPOGRAPHY.]

Palæotypographist, -graphi-, -pher.

Palæstral, pale·stral (see prec.), *a.*

Palæstric, -estrie (pălĕˈstrik, -ˈestrik), *a.*

Palæstriste, -trian.

Palæstra, pale·stra (pălĕˈstra), *sb.*

Palankeen, palanquin (pælănkīˈn, -kwīˈn). Forms: ... **palankeen**, etc.

Palatable (pæˈlătăb'l), *a.* [f. PALATE *sb.* + -ABLE.]

Palatableness, Palatably.

Palate (pæˈlăt), *sb.* [ad. L. *palātum* palate.]

Palate, palated.

Palatial (pălēiˈshăl), *a.*

Palatic (palǣ'tik), a. (sb.) rare. [f. L. palātum PALATE + -IC.] Of or belonging to the palate; palatal. 'b. sb. = PALATAL B. 2.

Palatial (palǣi'ʃăl), a. Belonging to a palatinate.

Palatiform (palǣ'tifǫrm), a. Enlon. [f. L. palātum + -FORM.] Applied to the tongue of an insect when closely united to the under surface of the labium.

Palatinal (plæ'tĭnăl), a. [f. PALATINE a.1 + -AL.] Belonging to a palatinate. Also °at.

Palatinate (plæ'tĭnĭt), sb.

Palatinate (plǽ'tĭnǣt), v. and a.

Palatine (plæ'tĭn, -ǫin), a.1 and sb.1

Palatine (pæ'lǣtǫin, -in), a.2 and sb.2

Palaver (plă'vāl, pǫ'lǣ'vāl), sb.

Palaver, v. Also 8 palaver, 9 dial.

Pale (pēl), sb.1 Also 5 pal, payll, 6 pale, 6–7 pall, 6–7 paille, paile. [– It. pa., pg. palis.]

Palatineship. rare.

Palatinoid.

Palatist.

Palative.

Palato-, comb. form of L. palātum.

Palato-dental (Phonetics) a.

Palato-glossal a.

Palato-glossus.

Palato-maxillary a.

Palato-pharyngeal (Anat.) a.

Palato-pharyngeus.

Palato-pterygoid a.

Palato-pterygo-quadrate a.

Palatoquadrate a.

Palatory a.

Pale (pēl), a.

Pale, v.1

Pale, v.2

Pale-faced a.

Pale, v.3

Paled, a.

Paleaceous a.

Paleate a.

Paled.

Palely, adv.

Paleness.

Paless, **Paleser**, var. PALIS, PALISER Obs.

Palestra, etc. = PALAESTRA, etc.

Palet, obs. f. PALLET, PALATE.

Palette (pæ'lĕt). Forms: 7–9 pallet (7–8 pallat), 8 palette, 9 (sense 2) palette. [a. F. palette (OF which the painter's sense of many senses).]

Palette-knife. A thin flexible blade of steel fitted with a handle, of various forms, used for mixing and tempering colours.

PALEW.

mixing colours on a palette, for distributing printing-ink on a surface, and similar purposes.

Palew, _v._ Obs. Also **palewe**. [app. a derivative of PALE _a._] Int. the nature of for formation in obscure. The later authors give simply to follow Recorde] Light or pale _vb_.flow.

Paley, variant of PALY _a._

Paleyce, **-eyse**, obs. ff. PALACE; var. PALIS _Obs._

Palfrenier (pælfrenēr), _sb._ _arch._ Forms: 5 palfrenayer, &c. [_a._ F. _palfrenier_ (1350 in Godef.)]

Palfrey (pɔ̄lfri, pæ̇l-). Forms: 2-4 palefrai, -frei, -fray, 3-4 palfra, 4-6 -frai, 4-7 -fray, 4-7 palfrey. [a. OF. _palefrei_, -_frey_, -_fre_, _freie_, _fraye_, 6 paulfrey, pawlfre, 7-9 palfrey. A saddle-horse for ordinary riding as distinguished from a war-horse; _esp._ a small saddle-horse for ladies.

Palfreyed (pɔ̄lfrid), _ppl. a._ Furnished with, or carried on, a palfrey.

Pali, _sb._ and _a._ Also **Páli**, **Pâli**. [Short for _páli-bhāsā_, i.e. language of the canonical texts (as opposed to 'commentary'), f. _páli_ line, canon ... _bhāsā_ language.]

Paliard, **Palice**, obs. ff. PALLIARD, PALACE, PALM.

Palify, **Palij**, obs. f. PALLIFY, PALACE.

Palikar (pæ̇likā). Also **palicar**.

Paliform (pæ̇lifɔ̄m), _a._ _Zool._ [f. L. _pálus_ stake, etc. +-(I-)FORM.] Resembling, or having the form of, a palus.

Palilalia (pælilēliǎ), _sb._ _Zool._ Obs. [f. L. _pálus_ stake +-ADO.]

Palilogy, palillogy (pæ̇li-lō̇dʒi). _Rhet._ Also in Gr. and L. forms.

Palimbacchius (pæ̇limbæ̇kiǎs). _Pros._ [L., ad. Gr. παλιμβάκχιος, f. πάλιν back, backwards + βακχεῖος BACCHIUS.] A metrical foot consisting of two long and one short syllable; a reversed bacchius: —ANTIBACCHIUS. Also **Palimbaˈcchic**.

Palimpsest (pæ̇limpsest). _sb._ and _a._ Forms: 7-8 in L. or Gr. form.

Palindrome (pæ̇lindrōm). [ad. Gr. παλίνδρομος running back again] A word, verse, or sentence that reads the same backwards or forwards.

Palindromic (pælindrō̇mik), _a._ Also **palindrome**.

Palinal (pæ̇linǎl), _a._ _Physiol._

Paling, _vbl. sb.[1]_ [f. PALE _v.[1]_ + -ING [1].] The action of becoming or turning pale.

Paling, _vbl. sb.[2]_ [f. PALE _v.[2]_ + -ING [2].] The action of constructing a fence, or of enclosing a place, with pales; fencing.

Paling, _ppl. a.[1]_ [f. PALE _v.[1]_ + -ING[1].] Enclosing, surrounding.

Paling, _ppl. a.[2]_ [f. PALE _v.[2]_ + -ING [2].] Becoming or turning pale.

Palingenesia (pælindʒinīziǎ). [med. L. (1691 in Du Cange), a. Gr. παλιγγενεσία new birth, regeneration, f. πάλιν again + γένεσις birth, origination.] = PALINGENESY.

Palingenesy (pælindʒinisi). [Gr. πάλιν again + γένεσις birth, origination : a modern compound on Greek analogy : see prec.] = PALINGENESY.

Palingenetic (pælindʒinetik), _a._ [f. PALIN-GENESIS: see GENETIC.] Of or belonging to, or characterized by, palingenesis (sense 2 b). Hence **Palingeneˈtically**, _adv._

Palingnostic, _a._ _Obs._ [a. obs. F. _palintocie_, ad. L. _palinnocium_ reckoning of money.] (See quot.)

Palinode (pæ̇linōd). Also **palinody**, _obs._ rare or _Obs._ Also 6-7 -odie; and in L. form palinodia (pæ̇linō̇diǎ). [a. F. _palinodie_ (16th c. in Hatzf.), or ad. L. _palinodia_.]

Palinodial (pæ̇linō̇diǎl), _a._ [f. PALINODE + -IAL.] Of or belonging to a palinode or recantation.

Palinodic (pæ̇linō̇dik), _a._ _Gr. Pros._ [ad. Gr. παλινῳδικός: see PALINODY and -IC.]

Palinody: see PALINODE.

Palis, _sb._ Obs. Forms: 4 palios, 5 pales, palisse, palys, paleis, palpse, palyce, 5-6 palis, 7-9 palisse. [a. F. _palis_, OF. also _paleis_, _paleiz_ (1297), _paleys_, _palès_, _palèts_, repr. a popular or med.L. _pálicium_, sb. neuter, from _pális_ stake, pale.]

Palisade (pæ̇lisēd), _sb._ Also 6 pal(l)isado, 7 palizad, palisado, 7-8 palli-sadoe (-, L. de Hatz.-Darm.), f. _palissier_ to enclose with pales, etc. Also **Palissado**.

Palindial, _a._ _Obs._ [f. as prec. + -AL.] Making or conjuring a 'palinode' or recantation.

Palinodic (pæ̇linō̇dik), _a._ _Gr. Pros._ Applied to verse in palinodic metre; _spec._ of an ode in which the parts of a palinode are similarly disposed.

Palindromic, _a._ _Obs._ rare—1. [ad. Gr. παλινδρομικός.]

Palinodist (pæ̇linōdist), rare—1. The author of a palinode.

PALISADE.

Palisade (pæ̇lisēd), _v._ Also **palissade**, **palizade**, **palizado**. [f. PALISADE _sb._, or ad. F. _palissader_.] trans. To furnish, surround, enclose, or fortify with a palisade or palisades; to fence in. Also _absol._ and _fig._

Palisadoing, **-sado**, obs. var. PALISADE.

Palisado, obs. form of PALISADE _v._

Palisander (pæ̇lisæ̇ndə). _Obs._ [ad. F. _palissandre_ = PALISANDER.]

Paliser, **Palisser**. _Obs._ Also **paliser**, **palesser**, **paer**. [f. PALIS sb. + -ER [1].] A maker of palings or palisades.

Palish (pēlish), _a._ [f. PALE _a._ + -ISH[1].] Somewhat pale.

Paliure (pæ̇liūr). [ad. L. _paliūrus_, a. Gr. Πaλίουρος (Theophrastus).] Name of a thorny shrub.

Palizado, obs. form of _pabke_, PACK _sb._[1]

Palkee, **palki** (pɔ̄lki). _East Ind._ Also 7 pallakee, pallekiˈe. [Hindi +PALANKEEN.]

Pall (pɔ̄l). _sb.[1]_ Forms: 1 pæll, 1-5 pall, 3 peal, 3-5 palle, 3-7 paul, paule, 5 5c paule, 5 7 pale, 6 paule, pawl(e, _Sc._ paill. [OE. _pæll_, ... cogn. with L. _pallium_ covering.]

Pall (pɔ̄l). _sb.[2]_ Also 6-7, paul. [app. aphetic from APPAL, to. which the early senses ... cogn. with PALE _a._]

Pall (pɔ̄l), _v.[1]_ Obs. rare. [Origin obscure.] 1. _trans._ To beat, strike, knock (down).

Pall (pɔ̄l), _v.[2]_ [f. PALL _sb.[1]_] 1. _trans._ To cover with or as with a cloth; to drape with a pall.

Palla (pæ̇llǎ). [L., fem. related to _pallium_.] 1. _Rom. Antiq._ A loose outer garment or wrap worn out of doors by women (sometimes by men).

Pallaˈdian, _a._ [f. L. _Pallad-, Pallas_, Gr. Παλλάς + -AN.] Of, belonging to, or according to the wisdom of Pallas (Athene); hence pertaining to wisdom, knowledge, or study.

Palladian (pǎlēdiǎn), _a.[2]_ [f. name of the Italian architect Andrea Palladio (1518-80), who imitated the ancient Roman architecture.] Pertaining to, or in the style of, Andrea Palladio.

Pallaˈdianism, _sb._ The Palladian school or style of architecture.

Palladic (pǎlæ̇dik), _a._ _Chem._ [f. PALLAD-IUM + -IC.] Applied to compounds of palladium.

Palladious (pǎlēdiǎs), _a._ _Chem._ [f. PALLADIUM + -OUS.] Of or pertaining to palladium; containing a small proportion of the metal than those called palladic.

Palladium (pǎlēdiǎm), _sb.[1]_ [a. L. _palladium_, Gr. Παλλάδιον.] 1. A statue of Pallas on which the safety of Troy was supposed to depend; hence, anything on which the safety of a nation, etc. depends.

Palladium (pǎlēdiǎm), _sb.[2]_ _Chem._ [mod.L. (Wollaston, 1803), named after the asteroid _Pallas_.] A rare metallic element.

Palladiferous, _a._ [f. PALLADIUM + -FEROUS.] Containing or yielding palladium.

Palladine, -yne, obs. forms of PALADIN.

Palladio- (pălā'diŏ-), combining form of PALLADIUM q.v., in names of certain compounds.

Palladium (pălā'diŏm). [a. mod.L., f. *Pallas*: cf. prec.]

Palladium. The image of the goddess Pallas, in the citadel of Troy, on the safety of the city was supposed to depend, reputed to have been thence brought to Rome.

2. *transf. and fig.* Anything on which the safety of a nation, institution, privilege, etc. is believed to depend; a safeguard, protecting institution.

Pallā'dium [a. mod.L., f. *Pallas*: cf. prec.]

Pallah (pæ'la). Also **palla, paala, pala, phala, phaala.** [ad. Zulu *im-pala*.] An antelope (*Æpyceros melampus*) inhabiting parts of S. Africa.

Palladio-, -ade, -e, obs. forms of PALACE.

Palladiade, -ade, obs. f. PALISADO, -ADE.

Pallall (păla'l). Sc. and *north. dial.* Also **pallalls, palall, pallally, pallalies, pallaly, pally-ully.**

Palladine, -yne, obs. forms of PALATINE.

Palle, obs. form of PALL, PALY, PALE.

Palled (pŏld), *ppl. a.* [f. PALL v.1 + -ED.]

†1. Enfeebled, weakened, impaired. *Obs.*

2. Of fermented liquor, etc.: That has lost its briskness or freshness; flat, stale, vapid. *arch.*

3. Inadapted to pleasant tastes or impressions; satiated, cloyed, disgusted.

Palled (pŏld, *poet. -ed*), *ppl. a.* [f. PALL v.2 (or *pl. n.* -ers.)]

† Pa'llen, *a. Obs.* [OE. *pællen, pyllen*, f. *pæl*, PALL sb.1 + *-en*.] Made of rich cloth; in early use, 'of purple'.

Pallen, obs. form of PALSY.

Pallenkeen, -kine, Pallentine, obs. forms of PALACE.

Pallescent (pale'sent), *a.* [ad. L. *pallescent-em*, pr. pple. of *pallescere*, f. *pallescere*.]

Pallet (pæ'let), *sb.1* [a. F. *palette*, dim. of *pale* spade, shovel, blade, etc., a word of many senses, spec of which in English retain the form PALETTE, q.v.]

†2. *Naut.* See quots. *Obs.* (It is not certain where this belongs; some place it under the next.)

† Pa'llen, *a. Obs.*

Pallet (pæ'let), *sb.2* [a. F. *paillet*, -ete, paillette, 5-6 palette, 6 pallat, 5, 6 (9 *Sc.*) pallet, (7 *ad.* L. OF. *palet*, dim. of *pal* stake.)]

†1. A mattress; a small, poor, or mean bed or couch.

2. Of fermented liquor, etc.: That has lost its briskness.

†2. Of armour for the head, a head-piece (*usually of leather*). *Obs.*

3. A flat board, plate, or disk; e.g. the blade of an oar, the front of a paddle-wheel. *Obs.*

4. The head, pate. Now only *Sc.*

Pallet (pæ'let), *sb.3* Also 8 palet, pallat, (8-9 palate). [a. F. *palette*, dim. of *pale* spade, shovel, blade, etc., a word of many senses, spec of which in English retain the form PALETTE, q.v.]

1. A wooden instrument consisting of a flat blade or plate, with a handle attached; *spec.* that used, in various forms, by potters and others for shaping their work.

2. *Watch-m. & Horol.* See quots. Also **7 palett.**

Pallet, *sb.4* Also 7 palate, OF. *paellete* (Gloss. de Salins, 13-14th c.), dim. of *paele* shallow pan (- L. *patella*.) A vessel of a definite measure used to receive the blood in blood-letting.

† Pallet, *sb.5 Obs.* [a. F. *palette*, OF. *paellete* (Gloss. de Salins, 13-14th c.), dim. of *paele* shallow pan (-L. *patella*.)]

† Pallet, *v. Obs. rare.* [a. OF. *palet* (13-14th c. in Godef.), dim. of *pale* PALL sb.1]

Pallet, obs. form of PALETTE, PALATE.

Palleting, obs. form of PALLETING.

Palli (pæ'li), *sb.* [native name.]

Pallia, pl. of PALLIUM.

Palliament (pæ'liăment), *sb.* [f. L. *palliment-um*, f. *palliare* to cloak.] A robe, gown: in quots., the white gown of a candidate for the Roman consulship.

Palliard (pæ'ljard), *sb.* and *a.* Forms: 5 payllard, 6-7 paliard, 5-7 palyard, 7-9 paillard, 6-7 palliard. [a. F. *paillard*, f. *paille* straw, f. *paille* straw: see -ARD.] A professional beggar or vagabond (who sleeps on the straw in barns and outhouses); *transf.* a low or dissolute knave; a lewd fellow, a lecher, a debauchee.

Palliard, *a.* Lecherous, unchaste.

Palliardise (pæ'ljardaiz), *sb.* Also 6-9 -ize, 6 -ice. [a. F. *paillardise*, f. *paillard*: see prec. + -ISE.] Lewdness, fornication.

Palliardy, *sb. Obs. rare.* [f. *palliard* + -Y.] = prec.

Palliate (pæ'liēt), *ppl. a.* [f. prec. + -ED.] Cloaked; having its natural nature concealed.

†2. Of a cure: Superficial or temporary. *Obs.*

Palliate (pæ'liēt), *v.* [f. L. *palliāt-*, ppl. stem of *palliāre* to cloak, f. *pallium* cloak: see PALL sb.3]

†1. *trans.* To cover with or as with a cloak; to cloak, shelter; to invest. Also *fig. Obs.*

2. *fig.* To hide, conceal, disguise. *Obs. or arch.*

3. To alleviate the symptoms of a disease without curing it; to relieve superficially or temporarily; to mitigate the sufferings of; to ease.

4. To disguise or colour the real enormity of (an offence) by favourable representations or excuses; to represent (an evil) as less than it really is.

Palliated (pæ'liētĕd), *ppl. a.* [f. prec. + -ED.]

1. *Zool.* Cloaked; having a pallium.

Palliating (pæ'liētiŋ), *ppl. a.* [f. as prec. + -ING.] That palliates; in the senses of the vb.

Palliation (pæliē'ʃŏn), *sb.* [ad. med.L. *palliation-em*, n. of action f. *palliare*: see PALLIATE *v.* and -ATION.]

1. The action of palliating; the cloaking or concealing (of an act, etc.); that which serves to conceal or hide; a cloak, covering. *Obs.*

2. The action of disguising or seeking to make less conspicuous, the enormity (of a crime, etc.) by excuses and apologies; extenuation; excuse; often in phrase *in palliation of*.

3. The alleviation of the symptoms and incidents of disease without curing it; hence *gen.* alleviation, mitigation, temporary relief.

Palliative (pæ'liătiv), *a.* and *sb.* [a. F. *palliatif*, -*ive* (13-14th c. in Littré), f. type *palliativus*: see PALLIATE and -IVE.]

A. *adj.* 1. Serving to cloak or conceal. *Obs.*

2. Serving to relieve (disease) temporarily, or to mitigate or alleviate (pain or other evil).

B. *sb.* Something that palliates.

Palliator (pæ'liētō.1). One who palliates or alleges extenuating considerations; an extenuator.

Pallid (pæ'lid), *a.* [ad. L. *pallid-us*, f. *pallēre* to be pale.] Pale, wan; pale; *esp.* lacking the warmth of a healthy complexion; faint or feeble in colour, wan, pale.

Pallidity (pæli'diti). The state or condition of being pallid; paleness.

Pallidly (pæ'lidli), *adv.* [f. as prec. + -LY2.] In a pallid manner.

Pallidness (pæ'lidnes). The condition or quality of being pallid.

Pallio- (pæliŏ-), combining form of PALLIUM, used in zoological terms relating to the pallium or mantle of a mollusc, etc.; as **Palliobranchiate** (-bræ'ŋkiĕt), *a.*, belonging to the *Palliobranchiata* or *Brachiopoda*, the tubes of the mantle being supposed to be branchia or gills; **Palliocardinal** (-kā.1dinăl), *a.*, pertaining to the mantle and the viscero-pericardial sac of a cephalopod.

Pallid (pæ'lid), *a.* Also 6-7 paled. [ad. L. *pallid-us*.]

Palliment (pæ'liment), *sb. Obs.* Also 7 pally-.

Pallin, variant of PALING.

Palling, obs. Sc. form of PAVILION.

Pallinode = PALINODE.

Pallion (pæ'liŏn), *sb.* Forms: 6-9 pallion, 7 palion, 9 palyan. [app. var. of PALLET sb.1, or a deriv. of PALL sb.1]

Pallium (pæ'liŏm), *sb.* Pl. **-lia.** [L. *pallium*: see PALL sb.3]

1. *Antiq.* The Latin name for the large rectangular cloak or mantle worn by men, chiefly among the Greeks; *esp.* by philosophers, and by ascetics and others in the early Christian Church. (= Gr. ἱμάτιον.)

2. *Eccl.* The woollen vestment conferred upon archbishops in the Latin Church.

3. *Zool.* The investing fold or MANTLE of a mollusc (or of a brachiopod).

4. *Meteor.* A sheet of cirro-stratus cloud uniformly covering the whole sky.

Pallmall = PALL-MALL.

Pall-mall (pæl·mæl). Also 6-7 palle-maille, 7 pallemaile, paille-maille, -maill, pale-maille, 7-9 pell mell, a. obs. F. *palemaille, pallemaille, palmaile, palemail, palmail, 7-9 pell mail. [a. obs. F. *palemaille*, -*maile* (15th c.), n. f. *palle*, PALL sb.1 + *maille* mallet.]

1. A game in which the players drove a boxwood ball with a mallet through an iron ring suspended at the end of a long alley; the place or ground where this game was played.

Pallone (palō'ne). [It. *pallone*, aug. of *palla* ball.] An Italian game, somewhat resembling tennis, played with a large ball struck with a cylindrical wooden guard, worn over the hand and wrist.

Pallor (pæ'lŏ.1), *sb.* Also 6-7 paller, 9 pallour. [L. *pallor*.] Paleness.

Palm (pām), *sb.1* Also 4-6 *pa.*, palme, 9 *dial.* paum. [OE. *palm* masc., *palma* fem., and *palme* fem., MHG. *palme* fem. and masc., ON. *pálmi* masc., all a. L. *palma* palm-tree, also the palm of the hand, expanded hand.]

1. Any tree or shrub of the Natural Order *Palmæ* or *Palmaceæ*, a large family of monocotyledons, widely distributed in warm climates, chiefly within the tropics, remarkable for their ornamental forms and various usefulness to man.

Palm (pām), *sb.2* Also 4-6 *pa.*, palme, 9 *dial.* paum. [a. F. *paume*, ad. L. *palma* palm of the hand.]

1. The inner surface of the hand between the wrist and the fingers.

2. *Her.* emblematically (of Victory, triumph), superme honour or excellence; prize; *esp.* in such phrases as *to bear the palm, yield the palm*, etc.

Palm, *v.* Also **paume.** [f. PALM sb.2]

Palma (pæ'lma), *sb.* Also **palm,** g. *dial.* paum. [OE. *palma*, ad. L. *palma*, palm of hand.]

[Dense Oxford English Dictionary text in multiple columns; entries include: **Palm**, **Palma Christi**, **Palmaceous**, **Palmar**, **Palmary**, **Palmate**, **Palmated**, **Palmately**, **Palmatifid**, **Palm-cross**, **Palmed**, **Palmelloid**, **Palmeous**, **Palmer**, **Palmer-worm**, **Palmery**, **Palmette**, **Palmetto**, **Palmful**, **Palmi-**, **Palmic**, **Palmiform**, **Palmiferous**, **Palmification**, **Palming**, **Palmist**, **Palmister**, **Palmistry**, **Palmitate**, **Palmitic**, **Palmitin**, **Palmite**, **Palm-oil**, **Palmoscopy**.*]*

Palm sack: see SACK *sb.*

Palm Sunday. The Sunday next before Easter, observed in commemoration of Christ's triumphal entry into Jerusalem; in the medieval church, and still in the Roman, Greek, and other churches, by processions in which branches of palm or (in northern regions) other trees (*see* PALM *sb.* 1 4.) are carried.

Palm-tree (pāˑm|trī). A tree of the order *Palmaceae* or the genus *Palma*: see PALM *sb.* 1.

Palmy (pāˑmi), *a.* [f. PALM *sb.* 1 + -Y.] 1. Containing or abounding in palms; of or pertaining to a palm or palms; palm-like. Chiefly *poet.*

2. *fig.* Bearing or worthy to 'bear the palm', triumphant, flourishing; esp. in *palmy state* (a Shakespearian phrase), *palmy days.*

Palmyra (pælmaiˑră). Forms: 7 palmero, 8 palmeira, palmira, 9 palmyra. [Formerly *palmeira*, a. Pg. *palmeira* (It. *palmera*) palm-tree: f. L. *palma* PALM.]

Palmyra (palmaiˑră), *a.* [ad. mod.L. *Palmyra.*] A sea-worm of the genus *Palmyra* of marine polychaetous annelids.

†Palolo (pălōˑlo). [Native name in Samoa and Tonga.] A nereid worm (*Palolo viridis*), abundant in some parts of the Pacific, and esteemed as food by the natives.

†Palour. Obs. Also 6-8 palour. [ad. F. *palourde*—late pop. L. *pelorida*, for cl. L. *pelōris*, -idem, a. Gr. πελωρίς.] A bivalve shell-fish; a kind of cockle or mussel.

Palp (palp), *sb.* [ad. F. *palpe* or L. *palpus.*] = PALPUS.

Palpability (pælpabiˑliti). [f. next + -ITY. Cf. F. *palpabilité.*] The quality of being palpable; *concr.* a palpable person or thing.

Palpable (pæˑlpab'l), *a.* (*adv.*) Also 6-8bil, -yble. [ad. late L. *palpābilis* (Orosius), f. *palpāre*: see PALP v. and L. *-bilis* (see *-BLE*).]

1. That can be touched, felt, or handled; apprehensible by the sense of touch; tangible, sensible.

2. *transf.* Readily perceived by some one of the senses, esp. the sight, hearing, etc.; perceptible; plainly observable, noticeable, evident.

3. *fig.* Easily perceived; open to recognition; plain, evident, apparent, obvious, manifest.

Palpableness (pæˑlpab'lnes). [f. prec. + -NESS.] The quality or fact of being palpable.

Palpably (pæˑlpabli), *adv.* [f. as prec. + -LY.] In a palpable manner; so as to be felt, plainly seen, observed, etc.; clearly, obviously, manifestly.

†Palped, *ppl. a. Obs.* [f. PALP v. + -ED.] In mod.Dicts.

Palpebra (pæˑlpibră), *Anat.* [L.] An eyelid.

Palpebral (pæˑlpibral), *a.* [ad. L. *palpebrālis,* f. *palpebra* eyelid + -AL. Cf. F. *palpébral* (1741 in Hatz.-Darm.).] Of or pertaining to the eyelids.

Palpebrate (pæˑlpibrĕt), *a. rare.* [ad.mod.L. *palpebrātus,* f. *palpebra* eyelid.] Furnished with eyelids.

Palpebre, *Obs. rare⁻¹.* [a. obs. F. *palpebre* (15th c. in Godef.), ad. L. *palpebra.*] An eyelid.

Palpebrous, *a. rare.* [f. L. *palpebra* eyelid + -OUS.] (See quots.)

Palpate (pæˑlpĕt), *v.* [f. L. *palpāt-,* ppl. stem of *palpāre* to move frequently and quickly, tremble, throb, feq. of *palpēre* PALP v. Cf. F. *palper* (16th c. in Godef. comp.).]

Palpation (pælpēiˑʃən). [ad. L. *palpātiōn-em,* n. of action f. *palpāre*: see PALPATE v.]

Palped, *a.* [ad. mod.L. *palpātus.*] Furnished with palps.

Palpiger (pæˑlpidʒəɹ), *Entom.* [mod. f. L. *palpus* palp, carrier.] The part of the labium of an insect which bears the labial palpi.

Palpigerous (pælpiˑdʒĕrəs), *a.* [f. as prec. + -OUS.] Furnished with palpi or feelers.

Palpitant (pæˑlpitant), *a.* [ad. F. *palpitant* (1419 in Hatz.-Darm.), or L. *palpitant-,* ppl. stem of *palpitāre*: see next.] Palpitating, throbbing.

Palpitate (pæˑlpitĕt), *v.* [f. L. *palpitāt-,* ppl. stem of *palpitāre* to move frequently and quickly, tremble, throb, freq. of *palpāre* PALP v.]

1. *intr.* To pulsate or beat rapidly and strongly, as the result of exercise, strong emotion, or as a symptom of disease; said of the heart, and transf. of the body or its members; to throb.

2. To pulsate rapidly or throb.

Palpitating, *ppl. a.* [f. prec. + -ING.] That palpitates; throbbing, quivering.

Palpitation (pælpitēiˑʃən). [ad. F. *palpitation* (1538), or ad. L. *palpitātiōn-em,* n. of action f. *palpitāre*: see PALPITATE v.] The action of palpitating.

Palsical (po·lzikal), *a. Obs.* [f. PALSY *sb.* + -ICAL.] Of or pertaining to the palsy.

Palsied (po·lzid), *ppl. a.* [f. PALSY v.] Affected with palsy, paralysed; *fig.* deprived of muscular energy or action.

Palsy (po·lzi), *sb.* Forms: 3-6 parlesie, etc. [a. OF. *paralesie,* var. of *paralisie,* etc. f. L. *paralysis* PARALYSIS.]

1. A disease of the nervous system, characterized by impairment or suspension of muscular action or sensation.

Palsy (po·lzi), *v.* [f. prec. *sb.*] 1. *trans.* To affect with palsy, or paralyse.

Palstave (po·lstĕv). *Archæol.* Also -staff, -paalstave, -paalstab. [ad. Da. *paalstav*: Icel. *pálstafr*, f. *páll* hoe or spade + *stafr* stave, staff.] A form or celt of bronze or other metal, shaped so as to fit into a split handle, instead of having a socket into which the handle fitted.

Palster (po·lstəɹ), *sb.* = MD. and Du. *palster* stick with iron spike, pilgrim's staff; cf. OF. *palstr, palster* spike—?OTeut. *pal-stro-* 'stick with a thorn' (Franck); cf. MLG. *palte,* LG. *palt, palter,* palt, Sw. *palta* tatter, splinter.] A pilgrim's staff.

Palsy (po·lzi), *v.¹* [f. PALSY *sb.*] 1. *trans.* To affect with palsy, or paralyse.

Palt, *sb. Obs.* [f. PALT v.] —by-form of PELT *sb.* The phonetic change is unexplained.

Palt, *v.² Obs.* Also 6 pault. [by-form of PELT v. *q.v.*] 1. *trans.* To pelt with missiles.

Palter (po·ltəɹ), *v.* [f. as PALT v.² + -ER¹.]

1. *trans.* To speak indistinctly or idly; to say or recite in an indistinct tone; to mumble, babble, *obs.*

2. *intr.* To shift, shuffle, equivocate, prevaricate, in statement or dealing; to deal crookedly or evasively; to play fast and loose, use trickery. Usually *const.* with.

3. *intr.* To trifle, act without decision or purpose, or in a trifling manner; to trifle *with.*

Palterer (po·ltərəɹ). [f. PALTER v. + -ER¹.] One who palters; an equivocator; a shuffler; one who plays fast and loose; a huckster; a trifler (*with serious matters*).

Paltering, *vbl. sb.* [f. PALTER v. + -ING¹.] The action of the verb PALTER: equivocation, shuffling, playing fast and loose, trifling (*with serious matters*).

Paltering, *ppl. a.* Also 6 paltring, 6-7 pault(e)ring. [f. PALTER v. + -ING².] That palters; shuffling, trifling, worthless, despicable, paltry.

Palterly, *adv. Obs. rare⁻¹.* In 7 paul-. [irreg. f. PALTER v. + -LY.] In a paltering manner, worthlessly, shiftily, trickily.

Palting, *ppl. a. Obs. exc. dial.* Also 6 paulting. [f. PALT v. + -ING².] Trifling, worthless, paltry.

Paltock (po·ltɒk), *sb. Obs.* Also 4-6 paltok, paltocke, 7-8 paltry. [Appears in 16th c. nearly with prec. sb., of which it may be an attrib. use, as in *trumpery sb.* and adj.]

Paltriness (po·ltrines). [f. PALTRY a. + -NESS.] The quality or state of being paltry.

Paltry (po·ltri), *a.* (*sb.*). Now only *dial.* Also 6 paultry, paltery, 6-7 paltrie; see also PELTRY. [f. *palt,* in mod. dial. *paltry* or *peltry* worthless stuff, trash; cf. LG. *paltrig,* palterig ragged, torn, f. dial. Ger. *palter,* -ern rag, MLG. *palter, palter, palter* + rag.]

Palude, *Obs. rare.* [a. OF. *palude* (also *palu,* palud), ad. L. *palūs, palūd-em,* marsh.] A swamp, fen, marsh.

Paludal (pæl(i)ū·dal, pæˑl(i)ūdal), *a.* [f. L. *palūs, palūd-em* marsh + -AL.] Of or pertaining to marshes; malarial.

Paludament (pæl(i)ū·dament). [ad. L. *palūdāmentum.*] A military cloak worn by a Roman general and chief officers; a herald's coat.

Paludina (pæl(i)ūdaiˑnă), *a.* [mod.L. fem. of *palūdinus,* f. *palūs, palūd-em* marsh.] A genus of fresh-water gastropod molluscs, also called *pond-snails.*

Paludine (pæˑl(i)ūdain, -in), *a.* [ad. mod.L. *palūdinus:* see prec. and -INE.] Of or pertaining to a marsh or fen; produced by or arising from a marsh.

Paludose, *a. rare.* [ad. L. *palūdōsus,* f. *palūs, palūd-em.*] Abounding in marshes, marshy; produced by or pertaining to marshes.

Paludous (pæˑl(i)ūdəs), *a. rare.* [ad. L. *palūdōsus.*] Of or belonging to marshes.

Palumbine, *a. rare.* Also 5 palumbyne, -is, -us. [ad. L. *palumbīnus.*] Belonging to the wood-pigeon or ring-dove.

Palus (pēiˑləs), *sb.* *Zool.* Also 5 paluche, pl. paluli.

Palustral (pælʌ·stral), *a. rare.* [f. L. *palustr-is* pertaining to a marsh + -AL.] Pertaining to or inhabiting marshes.

Palustrine (pælʌ·strain, -in), *a.* [ad. L. *palustr-is* pertaining to a marsh + -INE.]

PALY.

Palustral -tre, obs. erron. ff. PALÆSTRAL -TRA.

† Paly, *sb.* Obs. Also 5 paley, peply. [a. OF. *paillé* (12th c. in Littré)— L. *palea* chaff.] Chaff.

Paly (pǣ'li), *a.*[1] Chiefly *poet.* Also 6–7 palie, 9 paley. [f. PALE *a.* + -Y[1]. Of a pale kind of aspect; pale, or somewhat pale.

Paly, *a.*[2] Obs. Also 6 palle, palie. [ad. F. *palé*.] *Her.* Divided by vertical lines into an even number of equal stripes of alternate tinctures.

Paly-bendy, divided both palewise and bendwise, i.e. vertically and diagonally, into alternate tinctures. *Paly-pily:*

Pam (pæm), *sb.* St. Albans. [Corresponds in sense to Sc. *Pamphie*, also *Pawmie*, 'a vulgar name given at cards to the knave of clubs' (Jamieson), and f. 7 *pamphile* name of the card game, and of the knave of clubs in (Littré); of which *Pamphie*, *Pawmie*, appear to be abbreviations. F. *pamphile* is, according to Littré, ad. Gr. personal name [Πάμφιλος] 'beloved of all', in L. *Pamphilus*.]

1. The knave of clubs, esp. in the game of five-card loo, in which this card is the highest trump.

PAMPHELET.

them .. bread of angels. 1775 JOHNSON *Let. to Mrs. Thrale* 26 July, After dinner I went to Snowhill; there I was pampered, and had an uneasy night.

b. To over-indulge (a person) in his tastes and likings generally; to bring up daintily; to indulge with what gratifies or delights the senses.

† ib. *intr.* To indulge oneself with food, to feed luxuriously. Obs.

2. *trans.* To indulge (an appetite, etc.) to the full; to gratify with a full repast Of lavish mirth; at night, we were at last.

3. *trans.* To gratify or cloy a part, quot. 1577.

Pampered (pæ'mpəɹd), *ppl. a.* [f. PAMPER v. + -ED.] Over-fed (obs.); luxuriously fed; over-indulged, spoiled by luxury: see the verb.

Pampering, *vbl. sb.* [f. as prec. + -ING[1].] The action of the vb. PAMPER; luxurious feeding; over-indulgence.

Pampero (pæmpēɹⱺ). [Sp. *pampero*, f. *pampa* PAMPAS.] A cold wind which blows from the Andes across the S. American pampas to the Atlantic.

Pamphelet, variant of PAMPHLET.

PAMPHIL.

compared obs. Du. or Fl. *pampoelie* 'mulier crassa'.]

Pamphlet (pæ'mflet), *sb.* Forms: [4 *pamflet*], 4–7 *pamflett*, 6–7 *pamphlet*, *-flett*(e, 5 *pamflet*, *pamphlett*, *paunflet*, *plaun-*; 6–*pamphlet*, (6 *pampelet*, 7 *-let*); *pamplet*, *pamphlette*. [Appears in 14th c. as *panflet* (*panfletus*), English (*panflet*, 15th c. *pamflet*, *pamphlet*); app. a generalized use of *Pamphilet* or *Panflet*, a familiar name of the 12th c. Latin amatory poem or comedy called *Pamphilus*, *seu de Amore* (in OF. *Pamphilet*, a highly popular romance in the 13th c.

I. A small treatise occupying few pages or sheets that would make a loose, composed and (*a*) written, or (*b*, since c. 1500) printed, and issued as a separate work; always (at least in later use) unbound, with or without paper covers.

PAMPHIL.

in the rapidity with which the stories or scurrilous libels which passed under this name were issued.

The pamphlet fever, occasionally a few months past, now burst forth. 1899 in the British Museum.

PAMPINATION.

Pampleteer (pæmfletēɹ'), *sb.* Also 7 -etteer, -etere, -etier, 7-8 -etier. [f. PAMPHLET *sb.* + -EER. I. A writer of pamphlets; the author of a pamphlet. (Often contemptuous.)

Pamphleteer, *v.* [f. prec. *sb.*] *intr.* To write and issue pamphlets. Chiefly in Pamphleteering.

† Pamphleter. Obs. 1. Pref. o The Jesuitical Soloernation of a Foot-Soldier's Pamphleteer.

† Pamphiler. Obs. Also 7 -etter. [f. PAMPHLET + -ER[1]. 1. Pref. sb.] A writer of a pamphlet.

PAMPHLETER.

Pamphlian, variant of PAMPHAGIA.

Pamphract, (pæ'mfrækt), *a., adv.* Obs. Completely covered or protected, as with a coat of mail.

† Pamphy'sic(al, *a.* Obs. *nonce-wd.* [f. Gr. πᾶν all .. φύσις nature.] Of or concerning all nature.

Pamphysical (pæmfi'zikⱥl), *a.* [f. as prec. + *-al*.] Comprehending material nature as the source of all phenomena.

Pampination. Obs. rare. [ad. L. *pampinātiōn-em*, n. of action f. *pampināre* to prune off tendrils, f. *pampinus* tendril, young shoot, vine-tendril.]

PAMPINATE.

Pampiniform (pæmpi'nifoɹm), *a.* *Anat.* [ad. L. *pampini-* + -(i)FORM, in mod.F. *pampiniforme*.] Curled like a vine-tendril; applied esp. to a convoluted plexus of veins proceeding from the testis or ovary (also called *spermatic* or *ovarian plexus*).

Pampre (pæ'mpəɹ). [F., ad. L. *pampinus*.] An ornament or decoration representing vine-leaves and grape-clusters.

PAN.

Pan (pæn), *sb.*[1] The name of a Greek rural deity, represented as having the head,

arms, and chest of a man, while his lower parts were those of a goat, of which he sometimes also bore the horns and ears.

PAN.

being searched several.. on a few copper coins.

Pan (pæn), *v.*[2] *Sc. and a. dial.* [Derivation uncertain.]

1. *trans.* To wash (gold-bearing gravel, sand, etc.) in a pan, in order to separate by washing out the lighter particles.

[The body of this page consists of densely-set Oxford English Dictionary entries in multiple columns. Headwords include, in order:]

Pan-Ionian, **Pan-Io'nic**, **Pan-Israelitish**, **Pan-Latinist**, **Pan-Orthodox**, **Pan-Protestant**, **Pan-Saxon**, **Pan-Teu·to·nic**, **Pan-Teutonism**

Pan-Io'xian, **Pan-po'pism**, **Pan-po'ptic**, **Panpsychism**, **Pan-Satanism**, **Pansclavism**

Panace (pa'nacē), **Panacea** (pænăsī·a), **Panacean**, **Panache** (pănă·ʃ), **Pan-African**, **Pan-Africander**, **Pan-American**, **Pan-Anglican**, **Panarchy**, **Panaret**, **Panarthritis**, **Panary**, **Panathenæa**

Panathenaic, **Pan-athletic**, **Pan-Britannic**, **Pancake**, **Pan-Celtic**, **Panchart**, **Pancake-bell**, **Pancratical**, **Pancratiast**, **Pancratist**, **Pancratium**, **Pancreas**, **Pancreatic**, **Pancreatin**, **Pancreatitis**, **Pancreatoid**, **Pancosmism**, **Pancosmist**, **Pand**, **Pandean**, **Pandanus**, **Pandaram**, **Pandation**, **Pandean**

PANDECT.

Pandect (pæ'ndekt), *sb.* [ad. F. *pandecte*, ad. L. *pandecta* or *-tēs*, a. Gr. πανδέκτης an all-receiver; esp. in pl. L. *pandecta*, Gr. *πανδέκται* in same sense.]

1. *pl.* (*rarely sing.*) A compendium in fifty books of Roman civil law made by order of the Emperor Justinian in the sixth century, systematizing opinions of eminent jurists, to which the Emperor gave the force of law.

2. (*sing.*) A treatise covering the whole of a subject; a complete treatise or digest.

Hence **Pande'ctist**, one skilled in the Pandects.

Pandect, variant of PANDY *sb.*[2]

‖ Pandemia (pændī'mĭă), also anglicized **Pa'ndemy** [mod. L. f. Gr. *πανδημία* the whole, *πᾶν-* being of or belonging to the whole people, public, general.] = PANDEMIA *sb.*

Pandemian (pændī'niăn), *a.* [f. Gr. *δῆμε*-or of pertaining to all the people + -AN.] Vulgar, popular, human; = PANDEMIC *a.*

Pandemic (pændē'mik), *a.* and *sb.* [f. Gr. *πάνδημε*-of or belonging to all the people, public, + -IC.]

A. *adj.* **1.** General, universal. *esp.* Of a disease: Prevalent over the whole of a continent, or over the whole world.

2. Of or pertaining to vulgar or sensual love.

B. *sb.* A pandemic disease.

Pandemonic (pændīmo'nik), *a.* [f. next.] Of, pertaining to, or characteristic of, or like that of, Pandemonium: esp. of or like that of demons.

‖ Pandemonium (pændĭmō'nĭŏm), *sb.* Also **-nion**.

1. The abode of all the demons; a place represented by Milton as the capital of Hell, containing the council-chamber of the Evil Spirits; in common use, the infernal regions.

2. *transf.* A place regarded as resembling Pandemonium: A centre or head-quarters of vice or wickedness, a haunt of wickedness. **b.** A place or gathering of wild lawless license, confusion, and uproar.

Pandemy: see PANDEMIA.

Pan-denominational, etc.: see PAN-1.

Pander (pæ'ndaɹ), *sb.* Also **-ar**, **-er**, **6-7 pandare, peandar**. [Properly *pandar*, orig. *Pandare*, Eng. or A.Fr. form of L. *Pandarus*, Gr. *Πάνδαρος*, a proper name used by Boccaccio (in form *Pandaro*), and after him by Chaucer in *Troilus and Criseyde*, as that of the man fabled to have procured for Troilus the love and good graces of Chryseis, name and character being alike of mediæval invention: see Skeat *Chaucer* II. Introd. liii-iv. The later spelling *pander* is due, no doubt, to association with agent-sbs. and freq. vbs. in -ER.]

1. As proper name.

‖ Pandiculated, *a.* *Obs. rare.* [f. as prec. + -IZE, *intr.* To act the pander. Hence **Pa'ndicating** vbl. sb. and *ppl. a.*

Panderess (pæ'ndĕres). Now *rare.* Also **-ress**, **-as**. [f. PANDER *sb.* + -ESS.] A female pander, a bawd.

Panderism (pæ'ndĕrĭz'm). Also **pandar-**. [f. PANDER *sb.* + -ISM.] The practice or habit of a pander; systematic pandering.

‖ Panderize, *v.* *Obs.* Also *pandar-*. [f. as prec. + -IZE.] *intr.* To act the pander.

Panderly, *a.* *Obs.* or *arch.* [f. as prec. + -LY.] Of the nature of or befitting a pander.

Pandermite (pæ'ndŏɹmait), *Min.* [Named 1877, from Panderma in Asia Minor: see -ITE.] A variety of Priceite.

‖ Panderous, *a.* *Obs.* Also 6 **-drous**, **7-darous**. [f. PANDER *sb.* + -OUS.] Of the nature of or characterizing a pander.

Panderous: see PANDEROUS.

Pandership. *rare.* [f. as prec. + -SHIP.] The function or trade of a pander.

Pan-destruction, -diabolism: see PAN-2.

Pandiculated, *a.* *rare.* [f. L. *pandicul-us* to stretch oneself, f. *pandĕre* to stretch.] 'Stretched out, opened, extended' (J., 1775).

Pandiculation (pændĭkiu'leɪʃən), [n. of action from L. *pandiculāri*: see prec.] The restless movement, consisting in the extension of the legs, the raising and stretching of the arms, and the throwing back of the head and trunk, accompanied by yawning; it occurs before and after sleeping, also in certain nervous affections, as hysteria, and at the accession of a fit of ague. Sometimes loosely used for 'yawning'.

Pandion (pæ'ndĭŏn), *Ornith.* [f. L. *Pandion*, Gr. *Πανδίων* (see def.) in Mythology the father of Procne and Philomela.] Of or belonging to the genus *Pandion* or ospreys.

Pandit, variant of PUNDIT.

Pandle (pæ'ndl). Also 8 **pandell** [Origin unascertained; app. the source of Leach's generic name *Pandalus*, a local name of the shrimp; applied by some writers to an allied crustacean, perhaps *Pandalus annulicornis*, Leach.]

1. In *pl.* The name borne by a local force organized in 1741 by Baron Trenck on his own estate to oppose to Croats in the service of Austria.

Pandoor, pandore (pæ'ndōɹ). Also **pandur**. [- f. *pandour*, Ger. *pandur*; a.f. Serbo-croatian *pandūr*, a constable, bailiff, beadle, commoner, or catchpole; a mounted policeman or guardian of the public peace; a watcher of fields and vineyards', having also in earlier times the duty of guarding the frontier districts from the inroads of the Turks. For ulterior etymology see Note below. The sense in which the word became known in Western Europe is involved in the history of Trenck's body of pandours.]

1. In *pl.* The name borne by a local force organized in 1741 by Baron Trenck on his own estate to oppose to Croats in the service of Austria, mercenaries, warriors and robbers.

Pandour, Pandoor (pæ'ndūɹ). See PANDOOR.

Pandora (pændō'ră). = PANDORE.

Pandore (pændō'ɹ). Also 7-8 **pandure** (8 pandola), 9 pandoura, pandur. [a. It. *pandora* (also *pandura*), F. *pandore*, *pandore*, ad. L. *pandūra*, a. Gr. πανδοῦρα, a musical instrument the invention of which was attributed to Pan.] A stringed musical instrument of the cither type, the same as the BANDORE.

Pandore, -oos, obs. forms of PANDORE.

Pandour, variant spelling of PANDOOR.

Pandrist. *Obs. rare.* [f. L. *pandūra*.]

Pandy (pæ'ndi). *sb.*[1] *Chiefly Sc.* [perhaps f. L. *pande*(imper.) 'stretch out the palm with a leather strap or *ferule*, ferule, or rod, while the schoolmaster says 'Pande manum', i.e. 'hold out your hand'!] *Sc.* and north. A blow on the extended palm with a leather strap or *tawse*, ferule, or rod, given as a punishment to schoolboys; = PALMY *sb.*

Pandy, *v.* But if *for little rough* lash. I hear that thus a pandy gets. *Sc.* and north. *v.trans.* To punish by striking on the palm of the hand with a cane or ferule, as a punishment; to cane.

Pandy, *sb.*[2] *Anglo-Ind.* Also **-ee**. [According to Yule, from the surname *Pande*, title of a *fot* or subdivisional branch of the Brahmins of the Upper Province, which was very common among the high-caste sepoys of the Bengal army. One of those bearing the surname was *Mangal Pande*, the first man to mutiny in the 34th Regiment.] A mutinous sepoy (in the language in the Indian Mutiny of 1857-9.)

Pan-dynamism, etc.: see PAN-2.

Pane (pēn). Forms: 4-5 **pan**, 6 **paene**, **paan**, **pein**, 6-7 **payn**, 6-8 **pane**. [a. F. *pan*, earlier *pane*, = Pr., Sp., pan, It. *panno*, acc. of *pannus* cloth, piece of cloth.]

1. A piece of cloth; any distinct portion of a garment, a lap, a skirt. *Obs.*

2. A side, face, or surface of anything.

3. A section or length of a wall or fence. *Obs.*

II. A piece, portion, or side of anything.

III. A division of a window, and derived uses.

Pane, *sb.*[2] *Obs.* Also 4-5 **paan**, 6 **payn**. [ME. a. OF. *panne*, pane, penne, *pene*, etc. (Cotgr. *panne* a skin, fell, or hide) = Pr. *pena*, med. L. *penna*, Mod. F. *panne*.] A kind of cloth of burr-stone of which a mill-stone is constructed.

II. A flat side, face, or surface of any object having several sides.

III. A division of a window, and derived uses.

‖ Panegyric (pænĭdʒı'rĭk). *sb.* and *a.* [a. F. *panégyrique* (16th c.), ad. L. *panēgyric-us* public, of or for a general assembly, festive; *sb. panēgyricum* a panegyric or public eulogy, orig. adj., a. Gr. πανηγυρικός fit for a public assembly or festival, f. πανήγυρις.]

A. *sb.* **1.** A public speech or writing in praise of some person, thing, or achievement; a laudatory discourse, a formal or elaborate encomium or eulogy.

B. *a.* **1.** Of the nature of a panegyric or eulogy; publicly or elaborately expressing praise or commendation; eulogistic, encomiastic, laudatory.

Panegyrical, *a.* [as prec. + -AL.]

‖ 1. Of the nature of a general assembly.

2. Of the nature of a panegyric or eulogy; publicly or elaborately expressing praise or commendation; eulogistic, encomiastic.

Panegyrically, *adv.* In or by an elaborate eulogy; by way of panegyric.

Panegyricize, *v.* [f. PANEGYRIC + -IZE.] *intr.* To compose or utter a panegyric, to write a panegyric.

Panegyrics, *sb. pl.* See PANEGYRIC.

Panegyris (pænĕgı'ris). *Gr. Antiq.* = PANEGYRY.

Panegyrist (pænĕdʒı'rist). [f. as PANEGYRIZE + -IST.]

Panegyrize (pænĕdʒaraiz), *v.* [ad. Gr. πανηγυρίζειν to celebrate or attend a public festival.]

1. *trans.* To pronounce or write a panegyric or elaborate eulogy on; to speak or write in praise of; to eulogize.

2. *intr.* To compose or utter panegyrics.

Hence **Panegyrized** *ppl. a.*, **Panegyrizing** *ppl. adj.*

Panegyry (pæ'nĕdʒiri). *Obs.* Also **-ie**. [repr. L. *panēgyris*, Gr. πανήγυρις.]

Panel (pæ'nĕl), *sb.*[1] Forms: 3- **panel**; 4-6 **panell**, -6 **-yll**, -**3ell**, -**ele**, **pannule**, **penelle**), 5-8 **pannel**, (6-8 **pannell**, 6-9 **-el**), **panel**. [ME. a. OF. *panel* piece of cloth, saddle-cushion, piece (of anything), etc., mod. F. *panneau* = Pr. *panel*, It. *pannello*, dim. of *pannus* cloth.]

1. A piece of cloth, and connected uses.

2. A piece of cloth placed under the saddle to protect the horse's back from being galled (obs.); now, the pad or stuffed lining of a saddle employed for this purpose.

3. In more general sense: A small piece of anything. *Obs.*

6. *Scots Law.* In the phrase *on* or *upon the panel* = upon (his, one's) trial. Also, in later use, in the panel, etc.

Panel, *sb.*[2] Forms: 3- **panel**; see PANEL *sb.*[1] A compartment of a wainscot, door, shutter, side of a carriage, etc., consisting of a thinner piece of board or other material, normally rectangular, set in the general framework.

‖ 7. The general context or 'compartment' or section of a fence or railing; a hurdle.

Panel, *v.*

1. *trans.* To furnish or fit with a panel or panels; to furnish with a saddle.

2. *Sc. Law.* To enter (a name) in a panel; to accuse, indict.

'panels' between them. 1880 ZAEHNSDORF *Bookbinding* 179 Panel mitred in gold, with title and small corners.. Small tail panel with date. 1903 *Studio* Aug. 175 A solid outer binding with an inlaid..panel in the centre to contain coats-of-arms..amid a framework of gold tooling.

d. A piece of stuff of different kind or colour, laid or inserted lengthwise in the skirt of a woman's dress; also, the portion of the original material enclosed between two such pieces. (*b*) A panel-shaped piece of embroidery or appliqué work for insertion in any drapery.

1839 *John Bull* 2 Mar. 149/3 The skirt, of grey silk, had panels of dark grey velvet, on which a design of feathers was embroidered in silver. 1899 W. G. P. TOWNSEND *Embroidery* iv. 43 Design for an appliqué panel,..Worked in the Windermere linens, in blues and green. *Ibid.*, Design for..a long panel for the back of a settee. 1903 *Westm. Gaz.* 19 Feb. 4/2 On the skirt these [flatly stitched inverted pleats] are set about five or six inches apart, except in the front, where a wider space is left to give a panel effect..a space amounting to about twelve inches.

e. *fig.* Something resembling a panel in shape and relation to the surrounding space.

1902 A. E. W. MASON *Four Feathers* xviii. 174 Through the open window the moon threw a broad panel of silver upon the floor of the room.

10. †**a.** A window-pane. *Obs.* **b.** A compartment in a stained glass window, containing a separate subject.

1727–41 CHAMBERS *Cycl.* s.v., Hence also Panels, or panes of glass, are compartments or pieces of glass of various figures, square, hexagonal, etc. 1873–5 JAS. FOWLER in *Yks. Arch. Jrnl.* III. 199 The arrangement is a succession of panels, each containing a subject. 1891 J. T. FOWLER *Ibid.* XI. 499 This panel certainly does not belong to the window.

11. *Coal-mining.* **a.** A piece of coal left uncut in a mine. **b.** A compartment or division of a mine separated from the rest by thick masses or pillars of coal.

1747 HOOSON *Miner's Dict.*, *Pannell*, a small Piece of Whole that is left uncut, either to support some Weight from falling, or else..left, because it is..not worth the cutting. *Ibid.* Kiij, Huttrill [is] any hard Pannel in a Vein or Pipe..bound up and crossil'd by mixt Stuff, as Chirts, Chats, Tufts, Caukes, or Kevills. 1847 E. CRESY *Encycl. Civ. Eng.* I. 695 Panel work..is performed by dividing the mine into panels, separated by walls of coal from 40 to 50 yards in thickness. 1882 R. L. GALLOWAY *Hist. Coal Mining* xv. 149 It occurred to Mr. Buddle [c1810] that a great improvement..might be effected by dividing a colliery, in the course of the first working, into districts, or panels, surrounded on all sides by barriers of solid coal.

12. *Gardening.* A compartment of some design in carpet-bedding.

1805 REPTON *Landscape Gard.* 185 The pannel..may be removed in winter. 1892 *Gard. Chron.* 27 Aug. 243/3 These need frequent thinning out and clipping into shape, so as to confine each colour to its own panel or boundary-line, so as to properly define and preserve the character of the several designs.

13. A compartment or division of a pavement.

1883 *Daily News* 21 Sept. 5/3 A 'panel' of karri wood has been laid opposite the West Strand Post Office, where the wear and tear is exceedingly heavy.

IV. A thin board, etc., such as might form a panel in sense 9.

14. A thin wooden board used as a surface for oil painting; also, a painting on such a board.

1709 PRIOR *Protogenes & Apelles* 59 He [Apelles] gave the Panel to the Maid. 1765 H. WALPOLE *Otranto* ii. (1798) 32, I am not in love with a coloured panel. 1821 CRAIG *Lect. Drawing* ii. 117 It was the custom of the first practitioners in this process, to cover the pannels of their pictures with grounds of thin plaster. 1859 GULLICK & TIMBS *Paint.* 217 For small cabinet pictures, panels of well-seasoned mahogany are prepared. 1875 FORTNUM *Majolica* iii. 26 Were they even painted in oil on panel.

b. A large size of photograph, of a height much greater than its width. Chiefly *attrib.*

1888 *Lady* 25 Oct. 374/3 Some of the most delightful panel screens for photographs I ever set eyes on. *Ibid.*, The two-fold..with..sufficient space for panel portraits. 1891 *Pall Mall G.* 14 May 6/1 The panel photo is..as much part of the ceremony of presentation as, in the courtly times of Sir Joshua Reynolds, a few sittings at his studio in Leicester-square were part of the business of a fashionable marriage.

15. A board used by a baker, tailor, etc.

1612 in *Naworth Househ. Bks.* (Surtees) 42 A pannell for the baker. 1658 J. JONES tr. *Ovid's Ibis* 120 Dominus Dumbsick that leaps from the pannel to the pulpit.

V. Unclassed senses.

16. (See quot.)

1802 STOCQUELER *Milit. Encycl.*, *Pannels*, in artillery, are the carriages which carry mortars and their beds upon a march.

17. *Mining.* (See quot.)

1858 SIMMONDS *Dict. Trade*, *Panel*,..in mining, a heap of ore dressed and ready for sale. 1881 RAYMOND *Mining Gloss.*, *Panel.* 1. A heap of dressed ore.

18. (See quot.)

1894 *Northumbld. Gloss.*, *Panels*, the several strata composing a bed of stratified rock: chiefly used with reference to the bands of a limestone, as 'Blue limestone with strong panels'.

19. (See quot.) (A rendering of Fr. *panneau*, perh. never actually in Eng. use: cf. PANE *sb.*[1] 5.)

1727–41 CHAMBERS *Cycl.* s.v., Pannel in masonry, denotes one of the faces of a hewn stone.

VI. 20. *attrib.* and *Comb.*, as *panel-cupboard*, *-ledge*, *-maker*, *-opener*, *-painting*, *-picture*, *-sleeve*, *-saw*; *panel-backed*, *-bodied*, *-lined* adjs.; **panel-den** = *panel-house*; **panel-furring**, a furring to which the external panels of a railway-carriage are fastened; **panel-game**, stealing in a panel-house (*Cent. Dict.* 1890); **panel-house**, a brothel in which the walls have sliding panels for the purpose of robbery; **panel-plane**, 'a long stocked plane having a handle or toat' (Knight *Dict. Mech.* 1875); **panel-planer**, (*a*) a machine for thinning the edges of panels so as to fit into the grooves in the stiles; (*b*) = *panel-raiser*; **panel-raiser**, a machine for forming a raised panel on a board by working away the surrounding surface; **panel-strip**, a strip of wood or metal to cover the joint between a post and a panel or between two panels in a railway-carriage; **panel-thief**, a thief in a panel-house; so **panel-thieving** *sb.*; **panel-truss**, a truss having timbers or bars arranged in rectangular divisions diagonally braced; **panel-wheel**, a wheel which cuts a groove with a flat bottom and sloping or bevelled sides. See also PANEL-WORK.

1835 *Court Mag.* VI. 10/2 Mark the perfectly self-complacent air with which he sits in his quiet *pannel-bodied Tilbury. 1895 CLIVE HOLLAND *Jap. Wife* (ed. 11) 63 She goes to a *panel cupboard, where we keep our..English biscuits. 1860 BARTLETT *Dict. Amer.* (ed. 3), **Panel-house*, or **Panel-den*, a house of prostitution and theft combined. 1901 *Academy* 5 Oct. 293/2 On the *panel-ledge stands an unframed sketch. 1591 PERCIVALL *Sp. Dict.*, *Atbardero*, a *pannell maker, *Clitellarius.* 1896 *Westm. Gaz.* 24 Oct. 4/1 [A] collection of burglar's tools, including a fine brace and centre-bit, and a 'patent *panel-opener', shaped much like the common or domestic tin-opener, but on a larger scale. 1890 W. J. GORDON *Foundry* 157 Trucks do not want upholstering or glazing or *panel-painting. 1880 LITTLEDALE *Plain Reas.* vii. 16 We should disprove the genuineness of a *panel picture declared to be four hundred years old, if we showed it to be painted on mahogany. 1873 J. RICHARDS *Wood-working Factories* 182 To these standard planes may be added a *panel, plough, and right and left rebate planes. 1875 KNIGHT *Dict. Mech.* 1602/1 A double-head *panel-raiser, working upon two edges of the board at once. 1812–16 J. SMITH *Panorama Sc. & Art* I. 106 The *pannel-saw..is used for cutting very thin boards in any direction which may be required. 1825 J. NICHOLSON *Operat. Mechanic* 584 The panel-saw, either for cross-cutting, or cutting very thin boards longitudinally. 1884 *Daily News* 27 Oct. 2/1 The sleeves are of a different material from the other portions...The brocade of which these long *panel sleeves are ..made deserves description. 1860 BARTLETT *Dict. Amer.* (ed. 3), **Panel-thief*, a thief, who..enters the room by a secret opening, and abstracts [the victim's] money, watch, etc. 1868 M. H. SMITH *Sunshine & Shad. N. York* 306 She was one of the most notorious panel-thieves in New York. 1707–12 MORTIMER *Husb.* (1721) II. 202 Those Walls which are built *Pannel-wise, with square Pillars at equal distance,.. look much handsomer.

†**Pa·nel**, *sb.*[2] *Obs.* [Origin obscure: treated by some as a sense of prec.] The fundament or lower part of the alimentary canal of a hawk.

c1575 *Perf. Bk. Kepinge Sparhawkes* (1886) 7 Meates wch endew sonest and maketh the hardest panell are best. *Ibid.* 26 Tokens of Wormes. Straying sodayuly on the fyste,.. champpinge wt her beake, offeringe her beake ofte to the panell, mutes smotty [etc.]. 1611 COTGR., *Brayeul*, the parts, or feathers, about a hawkes fundament, called by our Faulconers the brayle in a short-wingd, and the pannell in a long-wingd, hauke. 1678 PHILLIPS (ed. 4), *Pannel*, in Faulconry, is the Pipe next to the Fundament of the Hawk, there she digesteth her meat from her body.

Panel (pæ·nĕl), *v.* [f. PANEL *sb.*[1]]

I. 1. *trans.* To empanel (a jury).

1451 *Paston Lett.* I. 208 The Shereff wille panell gentylmen to aquyte the Lorde, and jowroures to aquyte his men. 1530 PALSGR. 652/1, I panell a quest of men after the lawes of Englande. 1599 MASSINGER, etc. *Old Law* v. i, The jury's panell'd, and the verdict given Ere he appears.

II. 2. *Sc. Law.* To bring to trial; to indict.

1576 *Reg. Privy Council Scot.* Ser. I. II. 567 That the cuntre men arreistit..may..certanelie knaw at quhat day to be pannellit. 1660 DICKSON *Serm. Isa.* xli. 14–15 Writ. 1845 I. 138 Thou art a rotten hypocrite, thou hast never pannelled thyself before God's tribunal for sin. 1721 WODROW *Ch. Hist.* III. viii. (1830) IV. 124 Some country women were pannelled for being helpful to the wife of one of the persons alleged to have been concerned. 1814 SCOTT *Wav.* lxvi, He ..was soon to be panelled for his life.

III. †**3.** To furnish (a saddle) with a panel or pad. *Obs. rare.*

1508 *Acc. Ld. High Treas. Scot.* IV. 135 For grathing of foure sadilles, new pannalit.

4. To put a panel on (a beast, esp. a mule or ass); to saddle with a panel.

1530 PALSGR. 652/1 Panell my horse, I wyll ryde to market. 1742 JARVIS *Quix.* I. IV. xlvii. (1885) 257 They ordered him to saddle Rozinante and pannel the ass. 1881 DUFFIELD *Don Quix.* I. 144 Don Quixote..ordered Sancho to saddle and pannel at once.

IV. 5. To fit or furnish (a room, wall, etc.) with panels; to adorn with panels.

1633 *Wilmslow Churchw. Acc.* in Earwaker *East Cheshire* (1877) I. 108 Paid for pannelling the churche in the toppe. 17.. PENNANT (T.), A very handsome bridge, the battlements neatly pannelled with stone. 1823 P. NICHOLSON *Pract. Build.* 192 Where the principal stairs were constructed of wood, it was customary to panel the soffit. 1890 W. J. GORDON *Foundry* 73 We look into the saloon, which the cabinetmakers are panelling with satin-wood.

6. To fit or place as a panel in its frame.

1832 LYTTON *Eugene A.* I. v, A few old pictures were panelled in the open wainscot. 1858 — *What will he do?* I. vi, Panelled in wood that had once been painted blue.

7. To ornament (a skirt or piece of drapery) with a panel or panels: see PANEL *sb.*[1] 9 d.

1901 *Westm. Gaz.* 11 July 3/1 A lace flounce might border a skirt of net, or..the lace might panel a skirt of net.

8. *Telegr.* To arrange (wires) in parallels.

1890 in *Cent. Dict.*

Panel, dial. form of PARNEL.

†**Panele.** *Obs.* Also 6–7 panell, pannel, 7–8 penele, 8 paneel, panial. [a. Sp. *panela*; cf. Ger. *panelle*.] Brown unpurified sugar from the Antilles.

1562 BULLEYN *Bk. Simples* 72 Although Suger can not bee simply made, from the panell, or sande whiche cometh from the Cane. 1598 in *Acts Privy Council* N.S. XXII. 465, 9 chests of sugar muscovathes..10 chests of sugar pannels. 1657 R. LIGON *Barbadoes* (1673) 91 They make Peneles, a kind of Sugar somewhat inferiour to the Muscavado. 1712 tr. *Pomet's Hist. Drugs* I. 56 A Sort of duskish, pale-grey Sugar called Paneels. 1740 *Hist. Jamaica* 229 Muscovadoes and Panial Sugar, 6s. per Hundred. 1774 *Ann. Reg.* 215/1 Molasses, syrups, paneles,..from the British plantations.

Paneless (pē¹·nlĕs), *a.* [f. PANE *sb.*[1] + -LESS.] Of a window: Having no panes, lacking panes.

a1763 SHENSTONE *Economy* III. 111 The shifts enormous that in vain he forms To patch his paneless window. 1886 W. J. TUCKER *E. Europe* 220 To keep out the cold by fastening our towels securely across the paneless window.

Panellation (pænĕlē¹·ʃən). [n. of action f. med. (Anglo-) L. *pannellāre*, f. *pannellus* PANEL *sb.*[1] 4, 5.] The empanelling of a jury.

a1695 WOOD *Hist. Univ. Oxf.* (1796) II. 9 They in the said pannellation did put Rich. Wotton..and other privileged persons, which were not wont anciently to be impannelled. 1848 in WHARTON *Law Lex.*

Panelled, paneled (pæ·nĕld), *ppl. a.* [f. PANEL *v.* + -ED.]

1. *Sc. Law.* Brought to the bar, put on trial.

1636 W. SCOT *Apol. Narr.* (1846) 153 Many were unknown to the pannelled.

2. Fitted or made with panels; divided into panels or decorative compartments.

1760–72 H. BROOKE *Fool of Qual.* (1809) IV. 123 A folding door of pannelled looking-glass. 1819 SHELLEY *Lett.* Pr. Wks. 1888 II. 285 Within this arch are two panelled alto relievos. 1902 BESANT *Five Yrs.' Tryst* 95 The dark panelled old room that they called Oliver Cromwell's Library.

Panelling, paneling (pæ·nĕliŋ). [f. PANEL *sb.* + -ING[1].]

1. Wood or other material made into panels, panels collectively, panel-work.

1824 SCOTT *Redgauntlet* ch. v, The very old wainscot which composed the floor and the panelling of the room. 1851 LAYARD *Pop. Acc. Discov. Nineveh* xiii. 343 This alabaster, cut into slabs, served as a kind of panelling to the walls of sun-dried bricks. 1875 W. S. HAYWARD *Love agst. World* i. The oak paneling, of a sombre but rich brown.

2. *Mining.* (See PANEL *sb.*[1] 11.)

1900 *Daily News* 26 Nov. 2/1 Ground..opened out and drained preparatory for panelling.

Pa·nel-work.

1. Work in wood, stone, etc., consisting of or containing panels; *esp.* panelled woodwork.

1874 PARKER *Gothic Archit.* I. vi. 105 The windows frequently appear to be only openings in the panel-work. 1886 WILLIS & CLARK *Cambridge* II. 510 The spaces between the windows..are decorated with panelwork.

2. The working of a mine by division into panels.

1847 E. CRESY *Encycl. Civ. Eng.* I. 695 Panel work was introduced, fifty years ago. [See PANEL *sb.*[1] 11.] 1882 GALLOWAY *Hist. Coal Mining* xv. 149 Panel-work..was first introduced [at Wallsend] in the year 1810.

So **Panel-working.**

1883 GRESLEY *Gloss. Coal-mining*, *Panel-working*, a system of working coal seams..in the North of England.

Panemye: see PAYNIMY *Obs.* **Panence**, obs. f. PENANCE. **Paner, -ere**, obs. ff. PANNIER.

Panes, obs. f. *pence*, pl. of PENNY.

Panentheism, Pan-eulogism: see PAN- 2.

Paneter, -tre, -trie, obs. ff. PANTER *sb.*[1], PANTRY.

Panewes, -3es, obs. ff. *pennies*, pl. of PENNY.

Pa·n-fish. *U.S.* [f. PAN *sb.*[1] + FISH *sb.*[1]]

1. A fish suitable for frying whole in a pan.

1890 in *Cent. Dict.* 1894 *Outing* (U.S.) XXIII. 403/2 The cat-fish, also a good pan-fish. 1899 B. W. GREEN *Virginia Word-bk.*

2. A name for the king-crab (*Limulus*), from its supposed resemblance to a saucepan. (*Cent. Dict.*)

Panful (pæ·nful). [f. PAN *sb.*[1] + -FUL.] The quantity that fills a pan.

1874 RAYMOND *Statist. Mines & Mining* 319, I preferred to calculate upon the result of 40 panfuls worked by rocker. 1887 I. R. *Lady's Ranche Life Montana* 167, I often used to take a panful of salt, and get the whole band round me. 1894 *Outing* (U.S.) XXIII. 356/2 A panful of water.

Pang (pæŋ), *sb.* Also 6–7 pangue. [*Pang* sb. and vb., are known only after 1500, the vb. being exemplified first (which may be accidental). Origin uncertain.

It has been suggested that *pang* sb. was a phonetically-lightened variant of an earlier *prang* (cf. *speech*, OE. *spræc*, where however *three* consonants came together), and thus identical with a word occurring twice as *pronge* a 1450, and once as *prange* c 1530, app. in the same sense as *pang*: see below. These have naturally been viewed as fig. uses of PRONG *sb.*, a stabbing or piercing point; the difficulty is that this has not been found in the literal sense till much later (1567), and is not frequent before 1600.

1447 BOKENHAM *Seyntys* (Roxb.) 151 As thow the prongys of deth dede streyn Here hert root. a1450 *Cov. Myst.* (Shaks. Soc.) 287 These prongys myn herte asondyr thei do rende. c1530 *Crt. of Love* 1150 The prange of loue so straineth them to crie.]

1. A brief keen spasm of pain which appears suddenly to pierce or shoot through the body or any part of it; a shooting pain.

In 16th c. chiefly in 'pangs of death'; also 'of childbirth'.

1526 *Pilgr. Perf.* (W. de W. 1531) 242 b, In the pange & distresse of deth. 1530 PALSGR. 251/2 Pangcs of dethe, *les traictz de mort.* a1548 HALL *Chron.*, *Edw. IV* 250 The pangues and fittes of his sickenes. c1586 C'TESS PEMBROKE *Ps.* XLVIII. ii, The wife, whose wofull care The panges of child bed findes. 1601 F. GODWIN *Bps. of Eng.* 338 This man being very olde, died in a pang. 1603 SHAKS. *Meas. for M.* III. i. 80 The poore Beetle that we treade vpon In corporall sufferance, finds a pang as great, As when a Giant dies. 1609 BIBLE (Douay) *2 Kings* xxii. 5 The pangues of death have compassed me. 1611 BIBLE *Isa.* xxvi. 17 Like as a woman with childe..is in paine, and cryeth out in her pangs. 1709 STEELE *Tatler* No. 27 ¶ 2 The Man in the Pangs of the Stone, Gout, or any acute Distemper. 1833 HT. MARTINEAU *Cinnamon & Pearls* vii. 118 The pang which shot through her yesterday. 1851 CARPENTER *Man. Phys.* (ed. 2) 288 The attempt to allay the pangs of hunger by filling the stomach with non-nutritious substances.

2. *fig.* A sudden sharp mental pain or feeling of intense mental anguish.

1570 DEE *Math. Pref.* 1, I am in no little pang of perplexitie. 1590 SPENSER *F. Q.* II. i. 48 The bitter pangs that doth your heart infest. 1601 SHAKS. *Twel. N.* II. iv. 94 Say that some Lady..Hath for your loue as great a pang of heart As you haue for Oliuia. 1687 DRYDEN *Hind & P.* III. 287 O sharp convulsive pangs of agonizing pride! 1749 SMOLLETT *Regicide* I. iii, Keen are the pangs Of hapless love. 1808 SCOTT *Marm.* III. xiii, High minds, of native pride or force, Most deeply feel thy pangs, Remorse! 1877 BLACK *Green Past.* xxxviii. (1878) 303 Cheerfully and without a pang sacrifice the dollars you have paid.

†**3.** A sudden access of keen feeling or emotion of any kind; a sudden transitory fit. *Obs.*

1542 UDALL *Erasm. Apoph.* 117 b, This pangue or guierie of love dooeth especially..invade & possesse suche persones. 1548 UDALL, etc. *Erasm. Par. Luke* iv. 54 There bee in vs certayne affeccionate pangues of nature, whiche we are not able to cast awaye from vs. 1565 JEWEL *Def. Apol.* Wks. (Parker Soc.) III. 392 O, what a merry pang was this, M. Harding! 1642 ROGERS *Naaman* 6 Only to amuse their minds, and stirre up pangs of affection. 1643 TRAPP *Comm. Gen.* xix. 32 [He] does that in a drunken pang. 1693 *Humours Town* 138 Among their Fits of Devotion they shall have such Amorous Pangs for Heav'n, that one wou'd think [etc.]. a1694 TILLOTSON *Serm.* (1743) VIII. 3417 Galen..when he had anatomized man's body, and carefully surveyed the frame of it..fell into a pang of devotion and wrote a hymn to his Creator.

Pang (pæŋ), *a.* *Sc.* [cf. PANG *v.*[2]] Packed tight, stuffed, crammed. Also *pang-full.*

c1560 A. SCOTT *Poems* (S. T. S.) ii. 178 Thair avaitis fyld vp all the feild, Thay wer so fow and pang With drafe. 1807 RUICKBIE *Wayside Cottager* 110 (E.D.D.) The bench is fill'd, the house is pang. 1895 CROCKETT *Men of Moss Hags* 367 A rude man, and pang full of oaths.

b. Tight, compactly framed.

1813 HOGG *Queen's Wake* (1871) 27 Sae pang was our pearily prow Quhan we cudna speil the brow of the wavis We needilit them through below.

Pang (pæŋ), *v.*[1] Now *rare.* [See PANG *sb.*] *trans.* To afflict with pangs; to pierce or penetrate with acute physical or mental pain. Also *absol.*

c1502 *Joseph Arim.* (E. E. T. S.) 47/323 His chylde in the pestylence was in Ieopardy, And sore panged. a1529 SKELTON *P. Sparowe* 44 What heuynesse dyd me pange. a1548 HALL *Chron.*, *Hen. VII* 3 b, By the tormentyng..of which sicknes, men were so..peynfully pangued. 1598 FLORIO, *Accorare*, to pang or pinch at the hart. 1613 SHAKS. *Hen. VIII*, II. iii. 15 'Tis a sufferance, panging As soule and bodies seuering. 1748 SMOLLETT *Rod. Rand.* (1817) II. lii. 377 The news of your misfortune panged me to the very intrails. 1838 *Fraser's Mag.* XVIII. 531 May the mortal stroke Be balanced well, and pang not.

†**b.** To move by any sudden feeling. *Obs.*

1613 PURCHAS *Pilgrimage* (1614) 526 Heere the kindehearted Iesuit is panged with a fit of Charitie to yoke the Lutherans with them.

Hence **Pa·nged** *ppl. a.*, **Pa·nging** *vbl. sb.*

1827 HOOD *Mids. Fairies* lxxviii, Like a pang'd nightingale, it made him pause. 1876 C. WELLS *Joseph & Brethren* I. vi, But he is dead, and I am left to mourn, And tire on panged recollection. 1863 LD. LYTTON *Ring Amasis* I. I. II. ii. 124 Never shall the panging of your spirits be at rest.

Pang (pæŋ), *v.*[2] *Sc.* and *north. dial.* [Origin uncertain: perhaps onomatopœic.

Identity with Goth. *praggan*, i.e. *prangan* to press, with loss of *r*, has been suggested.]

trans. To pack tight, fill by pressure, stuff, cram.

1637 RUTHERFORD *Lett.* 14 July (1671) 9 Hell will be empty ..and heaven panged full. 1718 RAMSAY *Christ's Kirk Gr.* III. iii, As fou 's the house could pang. 1785 BURNS *Holy Fair* xix, It pangs us fou o' Knowledge. 1824 SCOTT *Wav.* lxiv, The auld gudeman o' Corse-Cleugh has panged it wi' a kemple o' strae amaist. 1825 BROCKETT *N. C. Gloss.*, *Pang*, to fill, to stuff. 1899 *Speaker* 4 Feb. 157 Men whose minds are panged with the lore of old Scotland.

Pangene (pæ·ndʒīn). *Biol.* Also pangen. [f. Gr. παν- all + stem of γένος race, offspring, γεν- to beget: cf. next.] De Vries's name for a (supposed) primary constituent unit of a germ-cell.

1899 J. A. THOMSON *Sci. Life* xi. 146 The theory of 'Pangenes' advocated by De Vries in 1889..incorporates the distinctively modern conception of germinal continuity. *Ibid.* 153 To these hypothetical units numerous names have been given—biophors, pangenes, idiosomes [etc.].

Pangenesis (pæn,dʒe·nĕsis). *Biol.* [f. Gr. παν-, PAN- all + γένεσις birth: see -GENESIS.] The name given by Darwin to his hypothesis, advanced to explain the phenomena of heredity, that every separate unit or cell of an organism reproduces itself by contributing its share to the germ or bud of the future offspring. See quot. 1868.

1868 DARWIN *Anim. & Pl.* II. 359, I venture to advance the hypothesis of *Pangenesis*, which implies that the whole organization, in the sense of every separate atom or unit, reproduces itself. Hence ovules and pollen-grains—the fertilized seed or egg, as well as buds—include or consist of a multitude of germs thrown off from each separate atom of the organism. 1869 F. GALTON *Hered. Genius* 363. 1870 TYNDALL *Sci. Use Imag.* in *Lect. & Ess.* (1903) 72/2 He [Mr. Darwin] has drawn heavily upon time in his development of species, and he has drawn adventurously upon matter in his theory of pangenesis. According to this theory, a germ, already microscopic, is a world of minor germs. 1877 HUXLEY *Anat. Inv. Anim.* i. 40. 1892 J. A. THOMSON *Outlines Zool.* 65 This hypothesis has been repeatedly modified, but, except in the general sense that the body may influence its reproductive cells, 'pangenesis' is discredited by most biologists.

b. *Intracellular pangenesis*: see quot.

1900 GOULD *Dict. Med. Biol.*, *Intracellular Pangenesis*, the origin of ultimate vital principles (pangenes, gemmules, biophors) within the cell.

Pangene·tic, *a.* [See prec. and -GENETIC.] Of or pertaining to pangenesis: see quot.

1875 *Contemp. Rev.* XXVII. 90 We cannot understand how colloid bodies, such as the Pangenetic gemmules must be, could pass freely through membranes. 1899 THOMSON *Sci. Life* xvi. 217 Maupertuis..distinctly stated a pangenetic theory of heredity.

Hence **Pangene·tically** *adv.*

1890 C. L. MORGAN *Anim. Life & Intell.* (1891) 134 [It] is (pangenetically) due to the fact that it takes some time for the modified gemmules to accumulate.

Pange·nic, *a.* = PANGENETIC.

1900 *Brit. Med. Jrnl.* No. 2046. 636 The one [point of view] was known as the 'pangenic theory' of Darwin.

Pangeometry (pændʒi,ǫ·mĕtri). [f. PAN- all + GEOMETRY.] Geometry extended to space of more than three dimensions; universal geometry.

So **Pangeo·meter**; **Pa:ngeome·trical** *a.*

1882 J. B. STALLO *Concepts Mod. Physics* 216 The peculiar tenets of pangeometry. *Ibid.* (1883) 214 The pangeometers erect a transcendental structure on empirical foundations. *Ibid.* 208 *note*, The connection of Gauss's metageometrical or (to use the expression of Lobatschewski) pangeometrical views with his investigations respecting the geometrical interpretation of imaginary quantities.

Pan-German (pæn,dʒə·ɹmăn), *a.* and *sb.* [f. PAN- 1 + GERMAN: cf. Ger. *Alldeutscher*.]

A. *adj.* Of or pertaining to all Germans, or to the union of all Germans in one political state.

1892 *Daily News* 27 Feb. 5/2 The present difficulty is not Prussian merely; it is Pan-German. The riots in Vienna are just as serious as those in Berlin. 1902 *Q. Rev.* July 155 The Pan-German ideal, as presented by the lyric poets of the Liberation. *Ibid.* 160 The Pan-German League.. was founded in 1894.

B. *sb.* An advocate of Pan-Germanism.

1899 *Daily News* 26 Oct. 3/4 The Pan-Germans and Anti-Semites at Hamburg. 1901 *Scotsman* 28 Feb. 7/5 The radical Czechs, by making speeches in their own tongue, caused the Pan-Germans to raise a protest.

So **Pan-Germa·nic** *a.*, Pan-German; **Pan-Ge·rmanism**, the notion or principle of the comprehension of all German peoples in an extended Germany; **Pan-Ge·rmany**, a Germany including all German peoples.

1900 tr. *von Bülow* in *Westm. Gaz.* 13 Dec. 2/2 There are laurels of higher worth than those which the Pan-Germanic League has to bestow. 1882 *Times* 30 Mar. 5/4 The Clericals..will no more tolerate Pan-germanism than the Poles Pan-slavism. 1882 *Echo* 29 Aug. 1/5 In order to oppose and neutralize the advancing aggression of 'Pan-Germanism'. 1902 *Q. Rev.* July 152 It is only quite recently that the term *Alldeutschtum* was coined..or the foreign equivalent Pan-Germanism..supplied. *Ibid.* 161 What the Pan-German League wants is..a 'Greater Germany', or as the exponents of this idea would say, a 'Pan-Germany'.

Pangermic, -germism: see PAN- 2.

[**Pangetive** (in Lodge's *Poore Mans Talent*, Hunterian Cl., 60), error for PUNGITIVE.]

Pa·ngful, *a. rare.* [f. PANG *sb.* + -FUL.] Full of pangs, sorrowful.

1748 RICHARDSON *Clarissa* (1811) VII. 224 He bowed his head upon his pangful bosom. 1897 *Chicago Advance* 5 Aug. 178/3 [To live] far from home..is as pangful to him as to an absent school-boy.

Pang-full: see PANG *a.*

Pangless (pæ·ŋlĕs), *a.* [f. PANG *sb.* + -LESS.] Without a pang.

1811 BYRON *To Thyrza* iv, Death for thee Prepared a light and pangless dart. 1879 E. ARNOLD *Lt. Asia* 4 So brought she forth her child Pangless.

Hence **Pa·nglessly** *adv.*

1877 PATMORE *Unknown Eros* Proem, The furiously gibbering corse Shakes, panglessly convuls'd, and sightless stares.

Pa·ng-like, *a.* [f. PANG *sb.* + -LIKE.] Like or befitting a pang.

a1586 SIDNEY *Arcadia* IV. (1629) 412 With pang-like grones and gastly turning of his eyes, immediately all his limmes stiffened, and his eyes fixed.

Pangolin (pæŋgō·lin). Also 9 pen-. [a. Malay ڤڠݢولڠ *peng-gōling* roller, f. *peng-* denominative + *gōling* to roll, in reference to its power of rolling itself up. The Malays distinguish *peng-gōling sisik* scaly pengolin, from *peng-gōling rambut* hairy pangolin (Marsden).] An edentate mammal of the genus *Manis*, of tropical Asia and Africa, the greater part of whose body is covered with horny scales; a scaly ant-eater. The name originally belongs to *Manis Javanicus*, a native of Java, etc.; but has been extended to Indian and African species, of which there are several.

[1734 SEBA *Thesaur. Rer. Natural.* I. 88 Javanensibus et aliis populis orientalibus *Panggoeling*, quae vox *Convolutorem* notat.] 1774 GOLDSM. *Nat. Hist.* (1862) I. vi. 468 The Pangolin, which has been usually called the *scaly lizard*, ..is about three or four feet long. 1822 SIR T. S. RAFFLES in *Trans. Linn. Soc.* XIII. 249 Pangolin Sisik or Tangiling ..of Sumatra. 1840 *Penny Cycl.* XVII. 188 The Pangolins are slow in motion, and live on worms and insects, especially termites and ants. 1893 SELOUS *Trav. S. E. Africa* 108 The curious ant-eaters (earth pigs and pangolins) are probably relics of an earlier fauna.

†**Pangony, -ie.** *Obs.* [ad. L. *pangōni-us* (Pliny), a. Gr. παγγώνιος, i.e. all-angled.] Name of an unidentified precious stone mentioned by Pliny: in 18th c. employed by some as a class-name.

1658 PHILLIPS, *Pangonie*,..a kinde of precious stone, so called from its multitudes of Angles. 1692 COLES, *Pangonie*, ..a precious stone with very many corners. 1753 CHAMBERS *Cycl. Suppl.*, *Pangonia*,..The bodies of this genus are single-pointed, or imperfect crystals, composed of dodecangular or twelve-planed columns, terminated by twelve-planed pyramids, and the whole body, therefore, made up of twenty four planes. Of this genus there are only three known species: 1. A brownish-white one, with a long pyramid. This is found in Silesia and Bohemia;..and is esteemed a very valuable crystal.

Pan-Gothic to **Pangymnasticon**: see PAN-.

†**Pa·nguts.** *Obs.* [app. f. PAN- all + *guts*.]

1617 MINSHEU *Ductor*, *A Panguts*,..an vnweldie Drossel nothing but guts. 1658 PHILLIPS, *A Panguts* (as it were all guts), a drossel, a gorbelly, an unwieldy fellow. 1704 COCKER, *Pangut*, or *Paunchgut*, a huge fat bellied fellow. 1775 ASH, *Panguts* (s. a low word), a fat hulky lazy fellow.

‖**Panha·gia.** *rare. Gr. Ch.* Also Panagia. [a. Gr. παναγία, fem. of πανάγιος all-holy.] A title of the Virgin Mary in the Orthodox Eastern Church; the All-holy.

[1686 B. RANDOLPH *Pres. St. Morea* 13 Many People came from the City of Zant to pay their devotions to the *Panaija* there.] 1775 R. CHANDLER *Trav. Greece* (1825) II. 59 The picture of the Panagia, or Virgin Mary, in Mosaic, on the cieling of the recess. 1866 FELTON *Anc. & Mod. Gr.* I. II. iii. 314 The Parthenon which had been converted into a church of the Panhagia, or Blessed Virgin. 1903 G. F. ABBOTT in *Daily Chron.* 16 June 3/1 A small table..placed under the lamp which burns in front of the icon of the Panhagia.

Panhandle (pæ·n,hæ:nd'l). [f. PAN *sb.*[1] + HANDLE.] The handle of a pan; hence in *U. S.* a denomination for a narrow prolongation of a State or Territory extending between two others, e.g. the Panhandle of West Virginia. Also *attrib.*

1888 *Missouri Republican* (U.S.) 24 Feb. (Farmer *Americanisms*), The Panhandle of Texas offers desirable homes to a million of people, at a nominal price. 1890 *Cent. Dict.* s.v., The Panhandle of Idaho; the Panhandle of West Virginia, projecting northward between Pennsylvania and Ohio.

Panharmonic (pænhaɹmǫ·nik), *a.* [f. PAN- all + HARMONIC: cf. next.] **a.** Adapted to all the 'harmonies' or musical modes. **b.** Universally harmonic, harmonizing with all.

1875 JOWETT *Plato* (ed. 2) III. 274 We shall not want multiplicity of notes or a panharmonic scale. 1886 FARRAR *Hist. Interpretation* iv. 236 St. Augustine..demanded that all interpretation should be panharmonic.

So **Panharmo·nicon**, a mechanical musical instrument of the orchestrion type, invented by J. N. Maelzel in 1800.

1848 J. H. NEWMAN *Loss & Gain* III. x. 381 The whole congregation was as though one vast instrument or Panharmonicon, moving all together. 1879 *Grove's Dict. Mus.* II. 194 Maelzel..devoted himself to constructing an automaton instrument of flutes, trumpets, drums, cymbals, triangle, and strings struck by hammers...His next machine was the Panharmonicon,..with clarinets, violins and cellos added.

†**Panharmony** (pænhā·ɹmŏni). *Obs.* [f. PAN- + HARMONY; after Gr. παναρμόνιος all-harmonious.] Universal or general harmony.

1651 COLLIER tr. *Comenius' Patterne Univ. Knowl.* 52 Pansophy by its owne desirable Panarmony, or generall agreement will be fit and convenient.

Panhellenic (pæn,helī·nik, -e·nik), *a.* [f. PAN- 1 + HELLENIC; after Gr. πανέλληνιος of or pertaining to all the Greeks, πανέλληνες all the Hellenes, the united Greeks.] Of, concerning, or representing all men of Greek race (including in ancient times the Greek colonies in Asia, Sicily, Italy, etc.; in modern times, the Greeks living in the Turkish dominions, in Crete, etc.).

1847 GROTE *Greece* II. xlvii, The schemes of Periclês were ..eminently Pan-Hellenic. 1853 *Ibid.* lxxii, Athens had never had the power of organizing any such generous Panhellenic combination.

Panhellenism (pænhe·lĕniz'm). [f. PAN- 1 + HELLENISM, or Gr. πανέλληνες + -ISM: see prec.] The idea or plan of a political union of all Greeks; the Panhellenic spirit and aims.

1860 ('Remembered in spoken use in Oxford' (Prof. Bywater)). 1874 FISKE *Outl. Cosmic Philos.* II. xviii. II. 205 The struggle between the higher and the lower patriotism,—between the two feelings known to the Greeks as Panhellenism and Autonomism. 1884 J. T. BENT in *Macm. Mag.* Oct. 429/2 A secret society which was the backbone of Panhellenism.

So **Panhe·llenist**, one who favours Panhellenism.

1882 in OGILVIE *Imper. Dict.* 1900 *Pilot* 2 Sept. 263/1 There is an aloofness that lies deeper down in his [the Cretan's] nature than any pan-Hellenist piety.

Panhidrosis to **Panhysterectomy**: see PAN-.

Panial, variant of PANELE *Obs.*

Panic (pæ·nik), *sb.*[1] Also 5–6 -yk(e, 6–7 -ik(e, -ike, 6–9 -ick; 6 pannycke, 9 -ick. [ad. L. *pānicum*, in It. *panico*, F. *panic*.] A grass or gramineous plant: originally applied to *Panicum italicum* of Linnæus (*Setaria italica* of later botanists), otherwise called Italian Millet, largely cultivated in Southern Europe, etc.; also extended to other species of the genus *Panicum* and its subgenera, many of which are cultivated in different parts of the world as cereal grains.

Panicum is a very extensive genus; Steudel describes 850 species, grouped under eighteen sections, many of these being distinct genera with other authors (*Treas. Bot.*).

c1420 *Pallad. on Husb.* iv. 50 Panyk & mylde in hoot & drie is As now. 1555 EDEN *Decades* 260 Of Moscouia ..the fieldes beare..also mylle and panyke whiche the Italians caule Melica. 1562 TURNER *Herbal* II. 76 b, Panic is a kynde of pulses, and in lykenes lyke vnto millet. 1597 GERARDE *Herbal* I. lvi. 78 There be sundrie sorts of Panick. *Ibid.*, The Panick of India groweth vp like Millet. 1610 W. FOLKINGHAM *Art of Survey* I. vii. 14 Saffron, Millet, Panick, Amilcorne, Spelt-corn, Garences. 1732 ARBUTHNOT *Rules of Diet* I. 251 Panick, aperient, boil'd in milk.. 1814 SOUTHEY *Roderick* Wks. 1838 IX. 378 *note*, ..it took a loaf..made of pannick and of rye. 1852 [illegible] *Nestorians* I. 214 Three kinds of millet or pannick make the bread-flour in general use.

b. *attrib.* and *Comb.*, as *panic-bread*, *-seed*; **panic-grass**, any grassy species of *Panicum*, as *P.* (*Echinochloa*) *Crus-galli*, a weed of cultivated or waste ground in England.

1591 PERCIVALL *Sp. Dict.*, *Panojo*, pannycke seede, *Panicula.* 1668 WILKINS *Real Char.* II. iv. 73 Panic-Grass. 1797 W. JOHNSTON tr. *Beckmann's Invent.* II. 248 *note*, The slender spiked cock's foot panic-grass, *panicum sanguinale.* 1814 SOUTHEY *Roderick* Wks. 1838 IX. 399 *note*, The Goths..eat only of the panick bread, as he had been told. 1835 HOOKER *Brit. Flora* I. 43 *Panicum Crus-galli*, Loose Panick-grass.

Panic (pæ·nik), *a.* and *sb.*[2] Forms: 7- panic; also 7 -ique, -ik, 7–8 -ick, pannick, -ic. [a. F. *panique* adj. (15th c. in Littré) = It. *panico* (Florio); ad. Gr. πανικός adj. of or for Pan, groundless (fear), πανικόν neut. sb. panic terror, a panic.

'Sounds heard by night on mountains and in vallies were attributed to Pan, and hence he was reputed to be the cause of any sudden and groundless fear' (Liddell and Scott). Stories more or less elaborated, accounting for the origin of the expression, are found in Plutarch's *Lives* (Langhorne's tr. (1879) II. 701/2), Polyænus' *Stratagems* (written c160 A.D.; tr. *Greece* III. ix.), etc.]

A. *adj.* (Now often viewed as attrib. use of B.)

1. In *panic fear, terror*, etc.: Such as was attributed to the action of the god Pan: = B. 2.

1603 HOLLAND *Plutarch's Mor.* 425 Sudden foolish frights, without any certeine cause, which they call *Panique Terrors.* *Ibid.* 1293 All sudden tumults and troubles of the multitude and common people, be called Panique affrights. 1647 WARD *Simp. Cobler* 11, I hope my feares are but panick. 1665 SIR T. HERBERT *Trav.* (1677) 241 That great Army.. were put into that pannick fear that they were shamefully put to flight. 1700 DRYDEN *Fables*, *Cock & Fox* 731 Ran Cow and Calf and family of hogs, In panique horror of pursuing dogs. 1770 LANGHORNE *Plutarch* (1879) II. 701/2 A panic fear ran through the camp. 1850 MERIVALE *Rom. Emp.* (1865) II. xiv. 134 A sound of panic dread to the populations of Italy.

b. Of the nature of or resulting from a panic; exhibiting unreasoning, groundless, or excessive fear.

1741 in *Johnson's Debates Parl.* (1787) I. 386 The tumults of ambition in one place, and a panic stillness in another. 1865 *Rothelan* II. III. vii. 70 He cried, with a shrill and panic voice, for Shebak.

†**2.** Of noise, etc.: Such as was attributed to Pan.

a1661 HOLYDAY *Juvenal* 120 Which..they thought to be prevented by making a loud and panick noise with brass kettels.

†**3.** Universal, general. *Obs. nonce-use.*

a1661 FULLER *Worthies* xxiv. (1662) 77 Seeing sometimes a panick silence herein.

4. (cap.) Of or pertaining to the god Pan: as, Bacchic and Panic figures. 1890 in *Cent. Dict.*

B. *sb.*[2] [= mod. F. *une panique*.]

†**1.** Contagious emotion such as was ascribed to the influence of Pan. *Obs.*

1627 tr. *Bacon's Life & Death* (1651) 15 Seeing Pan was their God, we may conceive, that all Things about them were Panicks [L. *Panica* adj.], and vaine, and subject to.. 1708 SHAFTESB. *Charact.* (1711) I. I. ii. 15 We may.. call that Passion Pannick which is rais'd in a Multitude, and convey'd by Aspect, or as it were by Contact or Sympathy. *Ibid.* 16 There are many Pannicks in Mankind, besides merely that of Fear. And thus is Religion also Pannick.

2. (= *panic fear, terror*, etc.; see A. 1): A sudden and excessive feeling of alarm or fear, usually affecting a body of persons, originating in some real or supposed danger vaguely apprehended, and leading to extravagant or injudicious efforts to secure safety. (With and without *a* and *pl.*)

1708 SHAFTESB. *Charact.* (1711) I. I. ii. 15 The Uncertainty of what they fear'd made their Fear get greater...And this was what in after-times men call'd a Pannick. 1709 STEELE *Tatler* No. 18 ¶ 6 The Approach of a Peace strikes a Pannick thro' our Armies, tho' that of a Battle could never do it. 1818 JAS. MILL *Brit. India* II. IV. viii. 277 The General.. fulfilled the fondest wishes of Hyder, by taking the panic, and running away from the army. 1856 KANE *Arct. Expl.* II. xii. 123 Parental instinct was mastered by panic. 1867 FREEMAN *Norm. Conq.* I. v. 375 An unaccountable panic seized on all men. 1879 FROUDE *Cæsar* xxii. 382 Cæsar's soldiers were seized with panic.

b. *spec.* A condition of widespread apprehension in relation to financial and commercial matters, arising in a time of monetary difficulty or crisis, and leading to hasty and violent measures to secure immunity from possible loss, the tendency of which is to cause financial disaster.

1757 HARRIS *Coins* 31 No alteration can be made in the standard of money without..producing..distrusts and panics. 1826 C. KNIGHT *Pop. Hist. Eng.* VIII. xi. 195 This pecuniary crisis [in 1825]..universally obtained the name of 'The Panic'. 1826 T. ATTWOOD 27 Feb. in *Life* viii. (1885) 104 Smith, Payn and Smith, and Barclays have had last week very sharp runs upon them. In many Country Towns also these pleasant 'panics' have prevailed. 1863 FAWCETT *Pol. Econ.* III. xi. (1876) 442 Commercial panics are caused by a reckless employment of credit.

3. *attrib.* and *Comb.* **a.** *attrib.* Of or pertaining to a panic or panics; resulting from panic.

1884 GIFFEN in *Pall Mall G.* 29 Dec. 4/1 The appreciation ..was one not to be regarded with a panic feeling. 1894 *Daily News* 12 July 5/1 The Bill,..as a pure panic measure, must stand or fall by the general estimate of the gravity of the circumstances which have given rise to it.

b. *Comb.* (often not distinctly separable from attrib. use), as *panic-cry*, *-cure*, *-dread*, *-flight*, *-master*; *panic-driven*, *-like*, *-pale*, *-stunned* adjs.; **panic-monger**, one who endeavours to bring about or foster a panic, esp. on a political, social, or financial question; an alarmist: a term of opprobrium; hence **panic-mongering**; **panic-stricken**, **-struck** *a.*, stricken with panic; so **panic-strike** *v.*

1873 BURTON *Hist. Scot.* VI. lxxii. 301 The old *panic-cry about a Scots invasion. 1806–7 J. BERESFORD *Miseries Hum. Life* (1826) II. xviii, When he has..scattered your whole party in a *panic-flight. 1877 RAYMOND *Statist. Mines & Mining* 227 This produced a *panic-like consternation. 1793 H. WALPOLE *Lett., to Miss Berrys* 7 Oct. (1846) VI. 494 The *panic-master-general. 1849 COBDEN *Speeches* 8 Those wicked alarmists and *panic-mongers whom I will never forgive. 1894 LD. WOLSELEY *Life Marlborough* II. 14 Sunderland succeeded in pursuading James that Lewis XIV's warnings were those of the 'panic-monger'. 1886 *Times* 30 Mar. 12/1 This *panicmongering has had the effect of suggesting strikes and rioting. 1883 G. MEREDITH *Poems & Lyrics* 143 How bold when skies are blue; When black winds churn the deep, how *panic-pale. 1798 LADY HUNTER in *Jrnl. Sir M. Hunter* (1894) 122 Our formidable appearance *panic-struck them, and they were moving off. 1898 HENDERSON *Stonewall Jackson* I. xi. 448 They need only a movement on the flank to panic-strike them. 1814 SOUTHEY *Roderick* xxv, The Moors, confused and captainless, And *panic-stricken, vainly seek to escape The inevitable fate. 1859 W. COLLINS *Q. of Hearts* (1875) 19 Owen and I looked at one another in panic-stricken silence. 1848 BUCKLEY *Iliad* 130 A panic-struck and turbulent council. 1791 COWPER *Iliad* XVI. 983 *Panic-stunn'd he stood.

Hence **Pa·nic** *v. trans.*, to affect with panic (*nonce-wd.*); **Pa·nicful** *a.*, 'full of panic, fearful'.

1827 HOOD *Hero & Leander* xliii, The crew..Struck pale and panick'd by the billows' roar. 1846 WORCESTER, *Panicful* (cites C. B. Brown).

Panical (pæ·nikăl), *a. rare.* [f. as prec. + -AL.]

1. = PANIC *a.* 1.

1605 CAMDEN *Rem.*, *Poems* 7 Chaucer our English Homer in the description of the sodaine stirre and Panicall feare when Chanteclere the cocke was caried away by Reynold the Foxe. 1890 CLARK RUSSELL *Shipmate Louise* xx. 128 Was ever panical terror more incomparably suggested?

2. Of or pertaining to the god PAN: = PANIC *a.* 4.

1794 T. TAYLOR *Pausanias' Descr. Greece* III. 235 The Sun produces Angelical, Dæmoniacal, Heroical, Nymphical, Panical, and such-like powers.

Panically (pæ·nikăli), *adv.* [f. prec. + -LY[2].] With panic-like fear.

1882 STEVENSON *Merry Men* v. (1887) 55 Had the sea been a lake of living flames, he could not have shrunk more panically from its touch.

Panicky (pæ·niki), *a. colloq.* [f. PANIC *sb.*[2] + -Y.] Of the nature of, or characterized by a tendency to, panic; subject to panic; unreasonably or excessively apprehensive; said esp. in reference to commercial and financial matters.

1869 *Echo* 12 Oct., Hence the delays, mystification, and consequent panicky results. 1882 *St. James's Gaz.* 13 Feb., Wheat fell on Saturday, and the wheat market is described as being 'panicky'. 1900 *Scotsman* 2 June 8/3 All of a sudden he made a panicky speech in the House of Lords which was held by the panicky newspapers to justify all that they had said.

Panicle[1] (pæ·nik'l). *Bot.* Also 6–9 pannicle. [ad.L. *pānicula* (*-ucula*), dim. of *pānus* a swelling, an ear of millet.] A compound inflorescence, usually of the racemose type, in which some of the pedicels branch again or repeatedly, forming a loose and irregularly spreading cluster, as in oats and many grasses.

1597 GERARDE *Herbal* I. iii. 4 The bushie top, with his long feather-like pannicles do resemble the common Reede. 1792 MARIA RIDDELL *Voy. Madeira* 98 The blossoms are disposed in a panicle, or diffused spike. 1832 *Veg. Subst. Food* 120 When millet is ripe, the panicles are cut off near to the top of the stalk. 1872 OLIVER *Elem. Bot.* I. i. 83 An inflorescence which branches irregularly, like that of Bramble, Horse Chestnut, and most Grasses, is called a panicle.

†**Panicle**[2]. *Obs.* = PANIC *sb.*[1]

1606 PEACHAM *Graphice* (1612) 135 September in his left hand a handful of Millet, Oates and Panicle. 1656 W. D. tr. *Comenius' Gate Lat. Unl.* § 92. 31 Oats, Rice, Millet, Panicle, Beech-wheat. [Johnson's example from Miller is erroneous, M.'s entry is *Panicum*, Panic (etc.).]

Panicle, obs. form of PANNICLE.

Panicled (pæ·nik'ld), *a.* [f. PANICLE[1] + -ED[2].] Arranged in form of a panicle; paniculate; furnished with or bearing a panicle or panicles.

1677 PLOT *Oxfordsh.* 84 Fair panicled corn or bent-grass. 1800 *Asiatic Ann. Reg.*, *Misc. Tr.* 267/1 Flowers panicled about the ends of the branches. 1830 LINDLEY *Nat. Syst. Bot.* 292 Arranged in a spiked, racemed, or panicled manner.

Paniconograph (pænəikǫ·nograf). Also pani·cograph. [f. PAN- + ICONOGRAPH.] (See quot.)

1875 KNIGHT *Dict. Mech.* 1602/1 *Panicograph*, a mode of obtaining printing-plates direct from a subject or transfer by applying it to the face of a plate of zinc, and building up a printing surface in relief corresponding to the design transferred. 1890 *Cent. Dict.*, Paniconograph. 1902 WEBSTER *Suppl.*, *Paniconograph*,..a photozincograph.

So **Pani:conogra·phic, -icogra·phic** *a.*, pertaining or related to paniconography; **Panicono·graphy**, a name given to a process for obtaining printing-plates directly from a design or transfer, by producing the design in relief on a zinc plate; photozincography.

1854 *Chamb. Jrnl.* I. 69 There is a paneiconographic process—a long name, which seems to imply a power of copying or reproducing any or all kinds of engravings. 1890 *Cent. Dict.*, *Paniconographic*, *Paniconography.*

Paniculate (pāni·kiŭlĕt), *a.* [ad. mod. L. *pāniculāt-us*, f. *pānicula* PANICLE[1] + -ATE[2].] Arranged in a panicle; panicled.

1727 BAILEY vol. II. s.v., A Plant is said to be *floribus paniculatis*, i.e. with paniculate Flowers, when it bears a great Number of Flowers standing upon long Foot-Stalks, issuing on all Sides from the middle Stalk. 1760 J. LEE *Introd. Bot.* III. xxi. (1765) 217 *Paniculate*, with the Flowers in Panicles. 1846 DANA *Zooph.* (1848) 578 Incurvate, paniculate in a plane, subtripinnate. 1877–84 F. E. HULME *Wild Fl.* p. vi, The inflorescence paniculate.

Hence **Pani·culately** *adv.*

1870 HOOKER *Stud. Fl.* 306 Scapes..paniculately branched.

Pani·culated, *a. rare.* [See -ED[2].] = prec.

1719 QUINCY *Med. Dict.* (1726) 349/2 Such are call'd Panniculated Plants. 1860 TYAS *Wild Fl.* 117 St. John's wort.—The inflorescence is..branched in paniculated clusters.

Pani·culato-, comb. form of mod.L. *pāniculāt-us*, paniculately, paniculate and —.

1846 DANA *Zooph.* 582 Sparingly ramose, above paniculato-corymbose. *Ibid.* 666 Paniculato-ramose, branches terete.

Panidiomorphic, Panidrosis, etc.: see PAN-.

Panier, variant of PANNIER.

Panifiable, *a. rare*[—1]. [a. F. *panifiable*, f. *panifier*.] Capable of being made into bread.

1849 *Lond. Jrnl.* 10 Mar. 8 An ingenious instrument, called..the *aleurometer*, the purpose of which is to indicate the panifiable properties of wheat flour.

Panification (pænifikē¹·ʃən). [a. F. *panification* (*p. des pommes de terre*, 1781 in Hatz.-Darm.), noun of action f. *panifier* to make into bread.] The making into bread; conversion into the substance of bread, esp. as a chemical process.

1779 *Projects* in *Ann. Reg.* 100/1 It is from this very simple operation that the whole fabrication of potato-bread depends; without it, no panification. 1818 COLEBROOKE *Import Colonial Corn* 129 Whether the panification of the meal of rye or barley..be complete. 1854 *Fraser's Mag.* L. 326 See the blessed idea of Christian communion.. degraded into a mere act of divine panification! 1886 JAGO *Chemistry of Wheat, Flour & Bread* 314 Summing up the changes produced in panification—they are alcoholic fermentation of the sugar, softening and partial peptonising of the albuminoids, and a limited diastasis of the starch by the albuminoids so changed.

†**Pa·nifice.** *Obs. rare.* [ad. L. *pānificium* making of bread, anything baked, f. *pānis* bread. Cf. obs. F. *panifice* 'bread-making,..also bread' (Cotgr.).] (See quot. 1656.)

1656 BLOUNT *Glossogr.*, *Panifice*,..the craft of baking or making Bread; also Bread it self, or a Loaf of Bread. 1657 TOMLINSON *Renou's Disp.* 398 These animalls do not expose their panifice to the injuryes of the aire and Heavens. 1658 in PHILLIPS.

Panigerick(e, -gery, etc., obs. ff. PANEGYRIC, etc.

Panikelle, obs. form of PANNICLE.

Panime, obs. form of PAYNIM.

†**Pa·nion.** *Obs.* Also 6 panyon. [Shortened from COMPANION.] = COMPANION, mate, fellow.

1553 T. WILSON *Rhet.* 50 Whether he be a gamester, an alehouse haunter, or a panion among ruffians. 1581 J. BELL *Haddon's Answ. Osor.* 496 b, Loe here a very pleasaunt panion and Maister of his Arte. 1589 NASHE *Martins Months Minde* Wks. (Grosart) I. 165 These Panions, scorning all modestie, and reiecting al reason. 1592 GREENE *Def. Conny Catching* Wks. (Grosart) XI. 80 He was a kind of Scholastical panyon.

Pan-Ionian, Pan-Ionic: see PAN- 1.

†**Pa·niot.** *Obs. rare.* [a. OF. *paniot* (1282 in Godef.), f. *pan* cloth.] Covering; horse-cloth.

1310 *Acc. Exors T. Bp. of Exeter* (Camden) 6 De iijs. vjd. de iij pecis de panyot debili venditis.

Panisc, panisk (pæ·nisk). *Mythol.* [ad. Gr. πανίσκ-ος, L. *Panisc-us*, dim. of Πάν, PAN *sb.*[2]] A little Pan; an inferior deity representing or attending on Pan. Hence **Pani·sca** as feminine of this.

1604 B. JONSON *Penates*, The Paniskes, and the Siluanes rude. 1850 LEITCH tr. *C. O. Müller's Anc. Art* (ed. 2) § 361. 448 A panisca at the music of Apollo opens her mouth wide. *Ibid.* § 387. 501 A good-natured panisc plucks a thorn from the foot of a satyr.

Panisic (pænəi·sik), *a. nonce-wd.* [f. PAN- all + Gr. ἴσ-ος equal + -IC.] Relating to a social state in which all are equal; = PANTISOCRATIC.

1864 BLACKMORE *Clara Vaughan* lxii, Platonic no doubt, and panisic, but not altogether adapted to double entry. 1887 — *Springhaven* (ed. 4) II. vii. 76 A meek salutation which proved his panisic ideas to be not properly wrought into his system as yet.

Panislam (pæni·slām, -islā·m). [f. PAN- 1 + ISLAM.] All Islam; (the conception of) a union of the Mohammedan world.

1883 *Contemp. Rev.* Jan. 57 Panislam must be crushed by a new crusade.

So **Panislamic, -Islamic** (-islæ·mik, -islā·mik), of or pertaining to all Islam, or to a union of all Mohammedans. **Pani·slamism**, the Panislamic aspiration.

1881 *Times* 22 Dec. 9 Some encouragement being given in Egypt to the Panislamic dreams of the present Sultan. 1883 *Contemp. Rev.* Jan. 62 The phantom of a Panislamic league. 1885 *Encycl. Brit.* XIX. 93/1 The most famous, after the Pan-Islamic pilgrimages, are the great Shiite sanctuaries. 1882 *Echo* 29 Aug. 1/5 In order to oppose the advancing aggression of..'Pan-Islamism'.

Pani·vorous, *a. rare*[—0]. [f. L. *pānis* bread: see -VOROUS.] Devouring or feeding upon bread.

1830 in MAUNDER *Treas. Knowl.* 1848 in CRAIG.

Panjandrum (pæn,dʒæ·ndrŏm). In origin, a nonsense word (simulating compounds of PAN-, and burlesquing a title), occurring in the farrago of nonsense composed by S. Foote to test the memory of old Macklin, who had asserted that he could repeat anything after once hearing it.

1755 FOOTE in *Q. Rev.* (1854) XCV. 516 And there were present the Picninnies, and the Joblillies, and the Garyulies, and the Grand Panjandrum himself, with the little round button at top. 1825 MAR. EDGEWORTH *Harry & Lucy Concl.* II. 153. 1867 F. H. LUDLOW *Little Brother* 39 The little wide-awake, like the Panjandrum 'with the little round button at the top'.

Hence **a.** A mock title for an imaginary or mysterious personage of much power, or a personage of great pretensions: a self-constituted high mightiness or magnifico; a local magnate or official of grand airs; a pompous pretender.

[1825 MAR. EDGEWORTH *Harry & Lucy Concl.* II. 46 He [the gardener] began to praise his carnations...One he called..'The envy of the world, or the great panjandrum'.] a1880 FITZGERALD (Brewer), He was the Great Panjandrum of the place. 1880 BREWER *Reader's Hand-bk. Allusions*, *Panjandrum* (*The Grand*), any village potentate or Brummagem magnate. 1887 *Pall Mall G.* 11 Oct. 1 Wanting to cut a fine figure in high life, as official panjandrums generally do want. 1892 F. HARRISON in *Pall Mall G.* 19 Sept. 4/3, I do not think the future of Ireland can be affected by the utterances of the Panjandrum of Biblical Science and Scotch Presbyterianism. 1896 A. MORRISON *Child of the Jago* 148 A sudden quacksalver, a Panjandrum of philanthropy, who undertook to abolish poverty and sin. 1900 *Pall Mall G.* 16 Feb. 3/2 So will the great British public, even though it may scarcely know what sort of a Panjandrum a Senior Wrangler is.

b. Official and ceremonial fuss or formality.

1883 NASMYTH *Autobiog.* xv. 281, I did not care for all this panjandrum of punctiliousness.

Pank (pæŋk), *v. dial.* *intr.* To pant.

1663 DRYDEN *Wild Gallant* v. iii, We met three or four hugeous ugly devils..that made my heart so panck ever since, as they say! 1746 *Exmoor Scolding* (E. D. S.) 48. 1864 YOUNG *Rabin Hill* 7 (E. D. D.) Jist hark how he do pank an' blow.

†**Pank**, *sb. Obs.* Of uncertain origin and sense.

(The date seems to oppose its being connected with prec. vb., as a collateral form of PANT *sb.*[2])

c1430 LYDG. *Min. Poems* (Percy Soc.) 31 War the sicknesse that called is the pank,..A maladie called *male de flank*, A bocche that nedeth a good cirurgian.

Pankin (pæ·n,kin). Now *dial.* [f. PAN *sb.*[1] + -KIN: cf. PANNIKIN.] A small earthenware pan or jar; also, such a vessel without restriction of size, a pancheon.

1420 *E. E. Wills* (1882) 46 Also ij pankyns & a posnet of a potell. 1533 in Weaver *Wells Wills* (1890) 19 To Aves Philipps, myauntes doughter, a pankyn. 1647–8 *N. Riding Rec.* (1887) V. 9 Presented for stealing an earthen pankin (8d.). 1788 W. MARSHALL *Yorksh.* Gloss. (E.D.S.), *Pankin*, any small earthen jar. 1863 ATKINSON *Stanton Grange* (1864) 231 You get a big pankin,..a large earthenware jar.

Panlogism (pæ·nlodʒiz'm). [ad. mod.L. *panlogismus*, f. Gr. παν- all + λόγος speech, word, reason: see -ISM.] A term formed by J. E. Erdmann (*Deutsche Speculation seit Kant* (1853) II. 853) on the analogy of *pantheismus*, to describe the philosophy of Hegel, as one which holds that only the rational is truly real. (Generally used with an implication of dissent from the position so characterized.) Hence **Panlo·gical, Panlogi·stic** *a.*, pertaining to or of the nature of panlogism.

1871 LEWES *Hist. Philos.* (ed. 4) II. 619 By Erdmann, Hegel's system is happily characterized as Panlogism rather than Pantheism, since, instead of presenting the universe as the evolution of God, he presents it, and God also, as the evolution of the abstract idea. 1872 *Contemp. Rev.* XX. 538 The panlogical system of Hegel. 1893 *Athenæum* 12 Aug. 221/1 In the course of expounding his 'panlogistic' theory. 1902 DEWEY in Baldwin *Dict. Philos.* II. 255/2 *Panlogism*, a term applied to philosophic systems which make thought the absolute—usually to the system of Hegel.

Pan-materialistic, -melodicon, etc.: see PAN- 2.

‖**Panmixia** (pænmi·ksiă). *Biol.* [mod.L., = Ger. *panmixie* (Weismann), f. Gr. παν- all + -μιξία, from μῖξις mixing, mingling; lit. 'universal or general mingling' (*sc.* of ancestral qualities).]

Weismann's term for a supposed promiscuous reproduction of all manner of ancestral qualities or tendencies, consequent on the cessation of natural selection in relation to organs which have become useless or little used, and tending to the degeneration of these organs.

1889 POULTON, etc. tr. *Weismann's Ess. Heredity* 90 This suspension of the preserving influence of natural selection may be termed *Panmixia*, for all individuals can reproduce themselves and thus stamp their characters upon the species, and not only those which are in all respects, or in respect to some single organ, the fittest,..the great variability of most domesticated animals essentially depends upon this principle. 1890 RAY LANKESTER in *Nature* 27 Mar. 487/2 The doctrine of panmixia is this. When there is no longer, owing to changed conditions of life, any use for an organ, it will cease to be the subject of natural selection. Consequently all possible variations..will have (so far as the now lapsed use of the organ is concerned) an equal chance. 1895 MIVART in *Harper's Mag.* Mar., A fortuitous mixture of ancestral tendencies..called panmixia.

Pannach(e, -ashe, Pannada, Pannal(l, obs. ff. PANACHE, PANADA, PANEL *sb.*[1]

‖**Pannade.** *Obs.* [obs. F. *pannade* (Cotgr.), OF. *pennade*, *penade* (15–16th c. in Godef.), whence F. *panader* to strut, caper, curvet. Given by Blount in an entry taken verbally from Cotgrave and repeated in most of the Dicts. to the present day. But app. never in Eng. use.]

[1611 COTGR., *Pannades*, the curvettings, prauncings, or boundings of lustie horses.] 1656 BLOUNT *Glossogr.*, *Pannades* (Fr.), the curvettings, prauncings, or boundings of lusty Horses. 1658–1706 in PHILLIPS. 1721– in BAILEY. 1755 in JOHNSON citing AINSWORTH. Hence in mod. Dicts.

‖**Pa·nnag.** [Heb. פנג *pannag*.] 'Perhaps a kind of confection' (R.V. margin).

1611 BIBLE *Ezek.* xxvii. 17 They traded in thy market wheate of Minnith, and Pannag, and honie, and oyle.

Pannage (pæ·nĕdʒ). Also (4–5 powrage), 6 pannadge, 6–9 panage, (7 pawnage, 7–9 paunage). [a. OF. *pasnage*, 1272 in Godef. (also *paasn-*, *parn-*, *paan-*), *panage* (*paisn-*, *pain-*), *pennage* (Godef.), mod.F. *panage*, in med. L. *pasnāticum*, *pastināticum*:—late L. *pastiōnāticum* (921 in Du Cange), f. *pastiōn-em* feeding, pasturing, from *pascĕre*, *past-um* to feed.]

1. *Law.* **a.** The feeding of swine (or other beasts) in a forest or wood; pasturage for swine; **b.** The right or privilege of pasturing swine in a forest; **c.** The payment made to the owner of a woodland for this right; the profit thus accruing.

[1217 *Charter of Forest* ix, Unusquisque liber homo agistet boscum suum in foresta..et habeat pannagium suum. 1292 BRITTON III. vii. § 5 Et puis soit enquis de mel et de pannage et de pesson des glans des noyz et de autre manere des fructz. 1321–2 *Rolls of Parlt.* I. 388/2 Porcs a pesczer en temps de pestzon..santz doner pasnage. 1347–8 *Ibid.* II. 205/2 En lieu de Disme de Pannage.] 1450 *Ibid.* V. 184/1 All maner of Grauntes..of eny Herbage or Pannage, Fisshyng, Pasture or commyn of Pasture. 1461 *Ibid.* 476/1 A summe of money called custume pannage for Swyne. 1495 *Act 11 Hen. VII*, c. 33 § 10 The office of kepyng of the Parke of Maylewyg..with the Herbage and Pownage of the same. 1523 FITZHERB. *Surv.* viii. (1539) 12 Also it is to be enquered of panage, and herbage. 1598 MANWOOD *Lawes Forest* xii. § 1 (1615) 87/2 The profite of the Mast, which is called Pawnage:..Pawnage is rather the money that is receiued for the Agistment of the Mast, then the Mast, or the Agistment it selfe. 1610 W. FOLKINGHAM *Art of Survey* III. iv. 70 Immunities and Exemptions from Theolonie, Pontage,..Pannage, Passage. 1770 HASTED in *Phil. Trans.* LXI. 165 To afford pannage for so large a number as 1200 hogs. 1878 *Law Rep.* 7 Ch. Div. 562 The Plaintiff..claimed to have..a right of pannage or common of pannage for his swine commonable in the forest. 1880 J. WILLIAMS *Rights of Common* 21 Nuts, acorns, the mast of trees, the right to which is known by the name of pannage.

2. *concr.* Acorns, beech-mast, etc., on which swine feed.

c1374 CHAUCER *Former Age* 7 They eten mast hawes and swych pownage. 1668 WILKINS *Real Char.* II. vi. 171 Mast, Acorn, Pannage. 1713 E. GIBSON *Codex* 706 Acorns.. are the chief of those things, which the ancient Laws call Pannage. 1882 *Athenæum* 19 Aug. 232 Herds of wild ponies and droves of wilder pigs thriving on the pannage. *transf.* 1647 WARD *Simple Cobl.* 28 What usefull supplies the pannage of England would afford other Countries.

Pannam, -um (pæ·nəm). *Thieves' Cant.* Also 7–8 panam. [prob. corrupt form of L. *pānem*, acc. of *pānis* bread, as in the prayer *panem nostrum da nobis hodie*.] Bread.

1567 HARMAN *Caveat* 83 Here followyth their pelting speche...*Pannam*, bread. 1609 DEKKER *Lanthorn & Candlelight* ciij b, If we mawn'd Pannam, lap, or Ruff-peck. 1641 BROME *Jovial Crew* II. Wks. 1873 III. 388 Here's Pannum and Lap, and good Poplars of Yarrum, To fill up the Crib, and to comfort the Quarron. a1700 B. E. *Dict. Cant. Crew*, *Panam*, Bread. 1880 MISS BRADDON *Just as I am* vi. 34 Bits o' mouldy pannam. *attrib.* c1742 in Hone *Every-day Bk.* II. 527 Tickets to be had, for three Megs a Carcass to scran their Pannum-Boxes.

‖**Panne** (pan, pæn). [F. *panne* (15th c. in Littré), earlier *pene*, *penne*, *pane* (13th c.), *pienne* (14th c.) = Pr. *penna*, *pena*, OSp. *peña*, med.L. *panna* (1406 in Du Cange); origin uncertain: see PANE *sb.*[2]] A soft kind of cloth with a long nap, resembling velvet.

1875 KNIGHT *Dict. Mech.*, *Panne*,..worsted plush of French manufacture. 1898 *Daily News* 10 Dec. 6/3 Among the new materials is that called panne, a very silky make of cloth, almost resembling velvet in softness of surface. 1899 *Westm. Gaz.* 18 Sept. 4/1 We see her in a dress of grey panne.

Panne, obs. form of PAN *sb.*[1] and [3].

Pannel, variant of PANEL, PANELE.

[**Pannell**, *v.* Only found in the following passage: app. an error of some kind. Editors have conjectured *spanieled*, *pantl'red*, and *paged*.

1606 SHAKS. *Ant. & Cl.* IV. xii. 21 The hearts That pannelled me at heeles, to whom I gaue Their wishes.]

Pannery (pæ·nəri). [f. PAN *sb.*[1] + -ERY.]

1. The making of salt in pans: see PAN *sb.*[1]

1762 tr. *Busching's Syst. Geog.* V. 470 The pannery here, or the right of salt-works, depends on chancery-writ.

2. *nonce-use.* Pans collectively.

1889 *Pall Mall G.* 30 Apr. 7/2, I asked the manager..what he thought of the new pottery and pannery; he said, 'Not much'.

†**Pa·nnicle.** *Obs.* Also 5 panikelle, pannycele, 5–7 panicle, 6 pannycle, -ickle, -ikell, -icule, 7 -ikle. [a. OF. *panicle*, *pannicle*, ad. L. *panniculus* small piece of cloth, rag, dim. of *pannus* cloth; in mod.F. *pannicule*.]

1. *Anat.* A membrane or membranous structure in an animal body, as the peritoneum, the membranes of the brain, and *esp.* the *panniculus carnosus* (*fleshy pannicle*), a layer of muscular fibres lying just beneath the skin, specially developed in some quadrupeds.

c1400 *Lanfranc's Cirurg.* 27 After hem comeþ panniclis [*Add. MS.* pannyceles]—þat is to seie smal cloop, þat is maad of sutil bredis of senewis, veynes & arteries. *Ibid. marg.* panikelles. *Ibid.*, Þe panicle of þe heed byndiþ seuene boones. 1545 RAYNOLD *Byrth Mankynde* I. (1634) 70 A pannicle springing and growing forth from the right seate of Peritoneum. 1562 BULLEYN *Bulwark*, *Dial. Soarnes* 40 The rimme or pannicule, whiche from out foorthe, covereth the scalpe. 1603 HOLLAND *Plutarch's Mor.* 1337 That all their braines should be contained within one and the same membrane or pannicle. 1641 CRASHAW *Fiscus Papalis* I. iv, Also, there is the very skinne or pannikle that came out of the most holy body of the Virgin Mary, which her sonne Jesus Christ our Lord, in his birth, brought with him. 1656 BLOUNT *Glossogr.* s.v., The fleshy Pannicle. c1720 W. GIBSON *Farrier's Guide* I. i. (1738) 5 Underneath the Skin is placed the fleshy Pannicle, which is Muscular. [1871 DARWIN *Desc. Man* I. i. 19 The power which many animals, especially horses, possess of moving or twitching their skin..is effected by the panniculus carnosus.]

¶ **b.** App. misused as = brain-pan, skull.

1590 SPENSER *F. Q.* III. v. 23 He..Smote him so rudely on the Pannikell, That to the chin he clefte his head in twaine.

2. *Bot.* A membranous covering in plants, as the scales investing a leaf-bud.

1671 GREW *Anat. Plants* I. iv. § 17 Every Bud, besides its proper Leaves, is covered with divers Leafy Pannicles or Surfoyls. 1736 H. BROOKE *Univ. Beauty* III. 403 The flowers' forensic beauties now admire, The impalement, foliation, down, attire, Couch'd in the pannicle or mantling veil.

Pannicle, variant of PANICLE.

†**Panni·cular**, *a. Obs.* [f. L. *pannicul-us*, PANNICLE + -AR.] Of the nature of a 'pannicle'.

1548–77 VICARY *Anat.* ix. (1888) 81 The tayle gutte, whose substance is panniculer.

Panniell, obs. form of PANEL.

Pannier (pæ·niəɹ), *sb.*[1] Forms: 4–7 panyer, 4– panier, 6 pannyer, 6– pannier, (also 4 panyar, payngnier, 4–5 paner, pany3er, 5 panere, -yere, -3er(e, -3ar, -yher, *Sc.* pan3ell, 6 paniar, 7 panniar, -ard, 7–8 panyard, -erd). [ME. *panier*, a. F. *panier* (in 15th c. rarely *pannier*) = Pr. *panier*, Cat. *paner*, It. *paniere*:—L. *pānāri-um* bread-basket, f. *pān-is* bread: see -ARIUM.]

1. A basket; *esp.* one of considerable size for carrying provisions, fish, or other commodities; in later use mostly restricted to those carried by a beast of burden (usually in pairs, one on each side, slung across the back), or on the shoulders of a man or woman.

c1300 *Havelok* 760 Gode paniers dede he make..to beren fish inne. c1358 *Durham Acc. Rolls* (Surtees) 562, j par. de Panyars empt. apud London. c1384 CHAUCER *H. Fame* III. 849 Or maken of these [twigs] panyers. 1426 LYDG. *De Guil. Pilgr.* 21050 Vp-on hyr hed a gret paner. c1440 *Gesta Rom.* I. xc. 414 (Add. MS.) All thofe I solde the þe

Pannierman. [f. PANNIER sb.¹ + MAN.]

Pannier. ... [See below. The name by which the robed waiters at table are known in the Inner Temple.]

Pannier, v. rare. [f. PANNIER sb.¹]

Panniered (pæˈniəd), a. [f. PANNIER sb.¹ + -ED.]

Panning (pæˈniŋ), vbl. sb. [f. PAN v.¹ + -ING.]

Pannikin (pæˈnikin). Also **pannican, pannikin,** a small metal (usually tinned iron) drinking vessel.

Pannikell, obs. form of PANNICLE.

Pannin, variant of PANNAM.

Pannon, **-oun,** obs. forms of PENNON.

Pannonic, a. Of or pertaining to ancient Pannonia.

Pannose (pæˈnəus), a. Bot.

Pannous (pæˈnəs), a. Path.

Pannunculus (pæˈnʌŋkiuləs).

Pannuscorium (pænəsˈkəuriəm).

Panny (pæˈni), a. rare.

Pannicle. Also forms of PANNICLE.

Pannyer, Pannyter, obs. ff. PANNIER, PANTER.

Panoistic, Panolethry: see PAN-².

Panompæan, -ean (pænɒmˈpiːən), a.

Panophia (pæˈnəufiə). Path. Also 9 **panoplia.**

Pannodia, obs. form of PANNICLE.

Panophobia (pænəuˈfəubiə).

Panophthalmia (pænɒfˈθalmiə).

Panophthalmitis (pænɒfθalˈmaitis). [Pan-.] Inflammation of the whole eyeball.

Panoplied (pæˈnəuplid), a. [f. PANOPLY + -ED.] Clad in complete armour.

Panoply (pæˈnəupli), sb. [ad. Gr. πανοπλία complete suit of armour, the 'whole armour' of the πανοπλης.]

Panophia: see PANOPHIA.

Pannoramic, -ical, a. and sb.

Pannon, **-oun,** obs. forms of PENNON.

Panorama (pænəˈrɑːmə, -ˈreiˈmə). [f. Gr. πᾶν all + ὅραμα a view: a name formed by R. Barker c. 1789.]

Panoramic, a. and sb.

Panoramically, adv.

Pannus. [L. pannus cloth.]

Panopathy (pəˈnɒpəθi).

Panoptic (pænˈɒptik), a. [f. Gr. πᾶν all + ὀπτικός seeing + -IC.]

Panoptical (pænˈɒptikəl), a. [as prec. + -AL.]

Panoptican, -con: see PANOPTICON.

Panopticon (pænˈɒptikən).

Panorama: see above.

Pan-. Gr. παν-, the shortened form in which παντο- 'all-' appears before a vowel: see PANTO-.

Panta-, erron. form of PANTO-, in PANTACOSM, PANTALINT, PANTATYPE; also pantagraph, pantastrophic: see PANTAGRAPH, PANTO-.

Pantable, obs. var. PANTOFLE.

Pantacosm (pæˈntəkɒzm).

Pantagamy (pænˈtagəmi).

Pantagruelian (pæntəgruˈiːliən), a.

Pantagruelism (pæntəˈgruːəliz'm).

Pantagruelist (pæntəˈgruːəlist).

Pantagruelize (pæntəˈgruːəlaiz), v.

Pan-Slav (pænˈslɑːv), a. [PAN-.] = next.

Panslavic, Slavic (-slɑːvik), a. [PAN-.]

Panslavism (pænˈslɑːviz'm).

Panslavist (pænˈslɑːvist).

Panslavistic, -Slav-, a.

Pansophic (pænˈsɒfik), a.

Pansophical, a. Hence **Pansophically** adv.

Pansophism (pænˈsɒfiz'm).

Pansophist (pænˈsɒfist).

Pansophy (pænˈsɒfi). Also 7 **-sophie,** 7-8 **pansophia.**

Panspermatism (pænˈspɜːmətiz'm).

Panspermatist (pænˈspɜːmətist). = PANSPERMIST.

Panspermia (pænˈspɜːmiə).

Panspermic (pænˈspɜːmik), a.

Panspermism (pænˈspɜːmiz'm).

Panspermist (pænˈspɜːmist).

Panspermy (pænˈspɜːmi).

Pansy (pæˈnzi). Forms: 5 pensee, 6 pense, 6-7 pansie, 7 pansy, 6-8 pansie, 6-7 panse, paunse, 6-7 pawnce, pawnse, 6-7 pawnse, paunce. [a. F. pensée thought.]

Pant (pont), sb.¹ northern. [Origin unknown: sense 2 suggests Romanic pantem slough, bog.]

Pant (pænt), sb.² [f. PANT v.]

Pant (pænt), v. [f. PANT v.]

Pant-. Gr. παντ-, the shortened form in which παντο-, παντι- appears before a vowel.

Panta-: prec. A **Pantagraphically grave.**

Pantable, **-abstinence, -alogia:** see PANTO-.

Pantacosm (pæntəkɒzm). [Erroneous for pantocosm.] Another name of the instrument called CORMILLARE.

Pantagamy (pænˈtagəmi). [f. Gr. παντο- all + -γαμία, from γάμος marriage.]

Pantagruel (pæntəˈgruːəl), a. and sb.

Pantagruelian (pæntəgruˈiːliən), a.

Pantagruelion (pæntəˈgruːəliən).

Pantagruelism (pæntəˈgruːəliz'm).

Pantaleon (pæntəˈliːən). Also -on, -oin.

breeches. 1667 DRYDEN *Wild Gall.* III. i, I have not yet spoke with the gentleman in the black pantaloons [the Devil]. 1674 BLOUNT *Glossogr.* (ed. 4), *Pantalones*, a sort of Breeches now in fashion, and well known. 1686 tr. *Chardin's Trav. Persia* 87 They [Persians] wear little shirts, that fall down to their knees, and tuck into a streight Pantaloon. 1691 *Satyr agst. French* 6 They taught our Sparks to strut in Pantaloons. 1719 DE FOE *Crusoe* I. xi, The breeches were made of the skin of an old he-goat, whose hair hung down such a length..that, like pantaloons, it reached to the middle of my legs. *a* 1734 NORTH *Lives* (1826) I. 289 [referring to events of *c* 1680], I could not but wonder to see pantaloons and shoulder-knots crowding among the common clowns.

†**b.** Applied to other styles, either historically, or in reference to the dress of the stage character, which, according to quot. 1727–41, was at one time of the nature of 'tights'. *Obs.*

The quot. from Chambers is merely translated from the Fr. *Dictionnaire de Trévoux*, and does not prove English usage. In French the name became associated with the tight garments of the 15–16th c., familiar in the paintings of the Italian artists of the period; but this was nowhere a contemporary application. From this arose the use in c.

1696 PHILLIPS (ed. 5), *Pantaloon*, a sort of Garment formerly worn, consisting of Breeches and Stockings fastned together and both of the same Stuff. 1727–41 CHAMBERS *Cycl.* [from French], *Pantaloon* or *Pantalon*, the name of an ancient garment frequent among our forefathers, consisting of breeches and stockings all of a piece. The denomination comes from the Venetians, who first introduced this habit, and who are called Pantaloni...Also used for the habit or dress these buffoons [in the Italian comedy] usually wear; which is made precisely to the form of their body, and all of a piece from head to foot.

c. A tight-fitting kind of trousers fastened with ribbons or buttons below the calf, or, later, by straps passing under the boots, which were introduced late in the 18th c., and began to supersede knee-breeches. **d.** Hence extended to trousers generally (especially in U.S., where this use may have been independently taken directly from F. *pantalon*, *a* 1800).

1798 [implied in PANTALOONED]. 1804 C. B. BROWN tr. *Volney's View Soil U.S.* 360 He was dressed in the American style; in a blue suit, with round hat and pantaloons. 1806–7 J. BERESFORD *Miseries Hum. Life* (1826) x. lxxxix, Loudly bursting..the fastenings of your braces, and the strings of your pantaloons behind. 1825 *Retrospect. Rev.* XII. 25 *note*, In October 1812, an order was made by St. John's and Trinity College, that every young man who appeared in Hall or Chapel in pantaloons or trowsers, should be considered as absent. 1834 PLANCHÉ *Brit. Costume* 316 Pantaloons and Hessian boots were introduced about the same period [i.e. *c* 1789]. 1855 WHITTIER *Barefoot Boy* 3 With thy turned-up pantaloons, And thy merry whistled tunes. 1857 CHAMBERS *Inform. People* I. 798/1 Pantaloons, which fitted close to the leg, remained in very common use by those persons who had adopted them till about the year 1814, when the wearing of trousers, already introduced into the army, became fashionable. 1858 GEN. P. THOMPSON *Audi Alt.* I. xlviii. 187 British officers, in all the priggery of sash and white pantaloon. 1865 DICKENS *Mut. Fr.* III. xi, Dressed in..pepper and salt pantaloons. 1877 M. M. GRANT *Sun-Maid* viii, His loose shirt hung outside his pantaloons.

e. See quot. and cf. PANTALETTES.

1821 *Ladies' Museum* Feb. (Parisian news), Female children wear pantaloons of merino, with short petticoats of the same. 1881 in Mrs. Power O'Donoghue *Ladies on Horseback* v. 235 [For horsewomen] Pantaloons of chamois leather, buttoning close at the ankles.

4. *attrib.* and *Comb.*, as *pantaloon-like* adj.

1675 PHILLIPS *Theat. Poet.* Pref. **iij, Whether the Trunck-Hose Fancy of Queen Elizabeth's days or the Pantaloon Genius of ours be best. *a* 1822 SHELLEY *Devil* xvi. 4 Could make his pantaloon seams start. 1858 SIMMONDS *Dict. Trade*, *Pantaloon Stuff*, material for men's trousers. 1892 SIR J. C. BROWNE in *Pall Mall G.* 5 May 7/1, I should describe them as pantaloon-like girls, for many of them had a stooping gait and withered appearance, shrunk shanks, and spectacles on nose.

Pantalooned (-lūˑnd), *a.* [f. prec. + -ED 2.] Wearing pantaloons; having pantaloons on; trousered.

1798 CHARLOTTE SMITH *Yng. Philos.* I. 27 He..was pantalooned and waistcoated after the very newest fashion. 1801 in *Spirit Pub. Jrnls.* V. 233 No more the pantaloon'd, unpowder'd spark, Displays his figure in the dusty Park. 1857 READE *Course of True Love* II. iv. 160 These pantalooned females practise a reserve, compared with which the modesty of Europe is masculine impudence.

Pantaloo·nery. [f. as prec. + -ERY.]

1. The performance of a pantaloon in the pantomime.

1821 LAMB *Elia* Ser. I. *My First Play*, The clownery and pantaloonery of these pantomimes have clean passed out of my head. 1855 *Times* 2 Apr., The difficulties of Clownery and Pantaloonery had yet to be surmounted. *fig.* 1885 *Society* Nov. 11/1 At last that pantaloonery is 'over'.

2. 'Materials for pantaloons' (Webster 1864); trouserings.

Pantaloo·ning, *vbl. sb. rare.* [f. PANTALOON + -ING 1: cf. *tailoring, colonelling.*] Playing the part of Pantaloon.

1861 MAYHEW *Lond. Labour* III. 121 He has given up clowning, and taken to pantalooning instead. 1862 *All Year Round* 13 Sept. 12 Pantalooning is bad for a man's spirits, bad for his manners, bad for his opinion of himself.

Pantameter, -morph, etc.: see PANTOMETER, PANTO-.

†**Pantap,** an abbreviation of *pantaple*, PANTOFLE.

1570 LEVINS *Manip.* 27/28 Pantap, *callopodium*

Pantaphel, -ap(p)le, obs. corrupt ff. PANTOFLE.

†**Panta·rbe.** *Obs.* [a. OF. *pantarbe* (Cotgr. 1611), ad. Gr. παντάρβη some kind of precious stone.] A precious stone fabled to act as a magnet to gold: the stone of the sun.

1587 T. UNDERDOWN *Heliodorus' Æthiop. Hist.* 54 The stoane is a Pantarbe, of secrete vertue. 1647 TRAPP *Comm.* 1 *Pet.* ii. 4 *And precious.* Far beyond that most orient and excellent stone *Pantarbe*, celebrated by Philostratus. 1694 MOTTEUX *Rabelais* v. xliii. 201 That Carbuncle alone would have darken'd the Pantharb of Joachas the Indian Magician. 1753 CHAMBERS *Cycl. Supp.*, *Pantarbe*,..an imaginary stone, the virtues of which were similar to those of the magnet; but exerted upon gold as those of the loadstone upon iron.

†**Pa·ntarch.** *Obs. rare.* [a. F. *pantarche*, *-arque* (Rabelais), erron. form of *pancarte* PANCART.] A paper; a general chart.

1694 MOTTEUX *Rabelais, Pantag. Prognost.* To Rdr., I have tumbled over and over all the Pantarchs of the Heavens, calculated the Quadrates of the Moon.

†**Pa·ntas, pa·ntais.** ? *Obs.* Also 6 panties, 7 -asse, -ise, 8 -ess. [a. F. *pantais, -ois*, from *pantoiser*, earlier *pantaisier, -teisier* to PANT.] A pulmonary disease of hawks; also applied to the 'yellows' in cattle.

1577 B. GOOGE *Heresbach's Husb.* (1586) 134 b, If he haue the Panties he will pant much, and shake in the Flanke. 1611 COTGR., *Pantois*, short wind, pursinesse;..in Hawkes we call it, the Pantais. 1614 MARKHAM *Cheap Husb.* II. xliv. (1668) 84 The Pantas is a very faint disease, and maketh a Beast to sweat, shake and pant much. 1688 R. HOLME *Armoury* II. 237/2 (Diseases in Hawks) The *Pantas*, or Asina: a Disease in the Breast, which causeth shortness of breath, or hinders the drawing of breath, called also the Pantise. 1741 *Compl. Fam.-Piece* III. 476 Of the Yellows in a Cow or Bullock, which some call the Pantess. 1847–78 HALLIWELL, *Pantas.*

Pantascope, erron. f. PANTOSCOPE.

†**Pa·ntatype.** *Obs.* [f. Gr. πάντα *pl.* 'all things' + TYPE; but the etymological form is PANTOTYPE.] The name given by Charles, Earl Stanhope, 1803, to a system of 'universal type-printing' projected by him.

1803 A. WILSON *Let. to Authors*, etc., Aug. (in *Collectanea* (O. H. S.) III. 377) Earl Stanhope has lately purchased the two important Secrets of Pantatype Printing and of Stereotype Printing, in order to give them to the Public. Pantatype Printing means universal type printing; being applicable to all subjects. 1896 H. HART *Stanhope & Oxford Press* (ibid. 411) What then was Pantatype? My own opinion is that..Ld. Stanhope thought he saw his way to a wide-spread adoption of what we now call 'process' work..Hard metal relief blocks [were to be used] in place of wood-cuts; intaglio engravings were to be copied and turned into relief blocks by the processes of Gengembre and others.

Pantechnic (pæn,te·knik), *a. rare.* [f. Gr. παν- all + τεχνικός belonging to the arts.] Of, pertaining to, or comprehending all the arts.

1848 LOWELL *Biglow Papers, Notices Indep. Press*, Then do I perceive..the advantages of a pancratic or pantechnic education.

Pantechnicon (pæn,te·knikǫn). [f. Gr. παν- all + τεχνικόν, neut. of τεχνικός: see prec.] A word, invented as the name of a bazaar of all kinds of artistic work, which has (through the fortune of the building) come to be applied to a large warehouse for storing furniture, and also to be colloquially used as short for *pantechnicon van*, a furniture-removing van.

1830 *Mech. Mag.* XV. 393 Pantechnicon [Heading of Article, describing the building, in Motcomb Street, Belgrave Square, which was originally intended for a bazaar, and was afterwards converted into a warehouse for storing furniture]. 1848 THACKERAY *Van. Fair* lxi, The rich furniture and effects,..rolled away in several enormous vans to the Pantechnicon, where they were to lie until Georgy's majority. 1865 DICKENS *Mut. Fr.* I. ii, He would have come home in matting from the Pantechnicon. 1876 JOS. IRVING *Ann. Our Time, Suppl.* (ed. 2) 155/2, 1874 [Feb.] 13.—The Pantechnicon, in Motcomb Street,..used as a repository for furniture and all kinds of goods, destroyed by fire, together with its valuable contents. 1891 *Pall Mall G.* 31 Aug. 2/3 The friends..who sent pantechnicons and heavy waggons doubtless meant well.

b. The attempt to reconcile the use with the etymology has given the following:

1842 BRANDE *Dict. Sci.* etc., *Pantechnicon*, signifies a place in which..every species of workmanship is collected and exposed for sale. The large building near Belgrave Square is an excellent specimen of this modern invention. 1845 FORD *Handbk. Spain* II. 731 The rest of the Peninsula considers them [the shops of Madrid] to be the magazine, the Pantechnicon of the universe.

c. *attrib.*, as *pantechnicon-driver, -van.*

1892 *Daily Chron.* 28 Apr. 9/1 Situation wanted in household removals in pantechnicon vans. 1897 MARY KINGSLEY *W. Africa* vii. 142 When you are an unsophisticated cannibal Fan you don't require a pantechnicon van to stow away your one or two mushroom-shaped stools, knives, and cooking-pots, and a calabash or so. 1902 *Daily Chron.* 28 Apr. 11/3 Pantechnicon Driver required; smart.

Panteen, -ein, var. forms of PANTINE.

Pantel, -ell(e, obs. forms of PANTLE.

Pantelegraph, -telephone: see PAN- 2.

Pante·llerite. *Min.* [Named by Förstner from *Pantelleria*, an island between Sicily and Tunis.] A mineral found at Pantelleria, intermediate in composition between dacite and liparite, and more or less trachytic in character.

1890 in *Cent. Dict.*

Panteloun, -own, obs. ff. PANTALOON.

[**Pantener,** a freq. misreading of PAUTENER.]

Panteon(e, obs. forms of PANTHEON.

†**Pa·nter** 1. *Obs.* (exc. *Hist.*) Forms: α. 3 paniter, 3–4 -eter, 4 -yter, -ytere; β. 4- panter, (4 painter, 5 pant(t)ere, -yr). [ME. *paneter*, etc., a. AF. *paneter* = F. *panetier* (12th c. in Hatz.-Darm.) = Pr. *paneter*, Sp. *panadero*, It. *panatiere*, in med.L. *pāna-, pānetārius, -terius*, baker (cf. OF. *paneter* to bake bread), f. L. *pān-em*, It. *pane*, Sp. *pan*, bread.] A word originally meaning 'baker', but in ME. usually applied to the officer of a household who supplied the bread and had charge of the pantry (an office now merged in that of butler); the controller of the bread in a large establishment.

α. 1297 R. GLOUC. (Rolls) 3868 He ȝef..þat lond of aungeo kaye is paneter [*v. rr.* panyter, panter]. *Ibid.* (Rolls) 9034, & is paniter & is chamberlein & is botiler al so. 1393 LANGL. *P. Pl.* C. XVII. 151 Pacience is hus paneter and payn to pouerte fyndeþ. *c* 1450–60 *Bp. Grossetest's Househ. Stat.* in *Babees Bk.* 330 Command the panytere with youre brede, & the botelare with wyne and ale, come to-gedur afore ȝou at the tabulle. 1496 *Acc. Ld. High Treas. Scot.* I. 305 Item, to the cuke and the panetare in Methven..xiiijs.

β. 14.. *Metr. Voc.* in Wr.-Wülcker 624/8 *Arthocopus*, botelere, bakere *uel* panttere. *c* 1450 *Bk. Curtasye* 667 in *Babees Bk.* 322 Þenne comes þe pantere with loues thre. *c* 1460 J. RUSSELL *Bk. Nurture* ibid. 66 If thou be admitted in any offyce, as Butler or Panter,—in some places they are both one. *c* 1530 TINDALE *Jonas* Prol. C iv, Though all the bred be committed vn to the panter. 1580 HOLLYBAND *Treas. Fr. Tong, Vn Panetier*, a Panter. [1851 TURNER *Dom. Archit.* I. iv. 137 The Pantry..was superintended by the panter or pannetier.]

Pa·nter 2. *Obs.* exc. *dial.* Also 4 paunter, 5 pantire, -yr, 5–6 -ere, (6 panther). [ME. a. OF. *panter* 'tendicula, lacum' (13th c. in Godef.); cf. F. *pantière* (Cotgr. '*panthiere*, a great swoope-net or drawing-net') = It. *pantiera* 'a kind of tramell or fowling net' (Florio), in med.L. *panthēra* (Du Cange) 'a species of net with which ducks are taken'; L. *panthēra* hunting-net, Gr. πανθήρα large net, f. πᾶν all + θήρ wild beast, θηρᾶν to hunt.] A fowling net, a fowler's snare; a net, snare, trap, noose. Also *fig.*

c 1325 *Poem Times Edw. II* 457 in *Pol. Songs* (Camden) 344 Pride hath in his paunter kauht the heie and the lowe. *c* 1325 *Metr. Hom.* 69 Als a fouler Tas foules wyt gylder and panter. *c* 1380 WYCLIF *Sel. Wks.* III. 200 Ydilnesse is þe develis panter. *c* 1385 CHAUCER *L. G. W.* Prol. 119 The smale foulis..That from the panter..ben skapid. ? *a* 1420 LYDG. *Chorle & Byrde* 77 This birde was trapped, & caught with a pantere. *c* 1440 *Promp. Parv.* 381/2 Pantere, snare for byrdys, *laqueus, pedica.* 1483 [see PANTLE *sb.*]. 1509 BARCLAY *Shyp of Folys* (1874) II. 297 As fysshe or byrde to panter, net or snare. 1530 PALSGR. 251/2 Panther to catche byrdes with, *panneau.* 1652 ASHMOLE *Theat. Chem.* 215 The Byrd was trapped and cawt in a Panter. 1782 ELPHINSTON *Martial* III. xciii. 173 Thy panters, unpropt, are decay'd To nets of Arachne's control. 1900 *E. D. Dict.*, *Panter* (N. E. Lancash.), a snare for birds made of hair.

Panter 3 (pæ·ntəɹ). [f. PANT *v.* + -ER 1.]

1. One who or that which pants.

a 1729 CONGREVE *On Mrs. Arabella Hunt's Singing* ii, Which, warbling mystic sounds, Cements the bleeding panter's wounds. 1823 BYRON *Juan* VII. xxxix, All panters for newspaper praise. 1840 *New Monthly Mag.* LX. 492 Panters after posthumous reputation.

2. *slang.* The heart. (Partly a pun upon 'hart'.)

a 1700 B. E. *Dict. Cant. Crew*, *Panter*, a Hart. *c* 1725 *Old Song* in Farmer *Musa Pedestris* (1896) 44 Didst thou know..but half of the smart Which has seized on my panter, since thou didst depart. 1785 GROSE *Dict. Vulg. T.*, *Panter*, a hart, that animal is, in the psalms, said to pant after the fresh water brooks. [*ed.* 1796 *adds*] Also the human heart, which frequently pants in time of danger.

†**3.** (See quot.) *Obs.*

1706 PHILLIPS, *Panter*, the Paunch or Belly; also a Sore or Gall on the Neck of Draught-Beasts.

Panter, obs. form of PAINTER, PANTHER.

Panterer (pæ·ntərəɹ). Now only *Hist.* Also 5–6 -trer. [Expanded form of PANTER 1, as if from *pantry* + -ER: cf. *adulterer, upholsterer*, etc.] = PANTER 1.

14.. *Nom.* in Wr.-Wülcker 684/20 *Hic panterius*, a pantrer. *c* 1420 *Chron. Vilod.* 506 His Panterere to[k] a lofe þo ywys. 1552 HULOET, Pantrer, *Panarius.* *a* 1641 BP. MOUNTAGU *Acts & Mon.* (1642) 427 They meet in the Refectory..where..the Panterer sets bread before them. 1859 PARKER *Dom. Archit.* III. iii. 80 The Cloth being laid, the panterer brought forth the bread. 1883 *Times* (weekly ed.) 6 Apr. 9 Dukes and earls and knights acted as stewards and butlers and panterers, and..haggled for their perquisites of scarlet cloth and wine and candles..like commoner people.

Pan-Teutonic, -Teutonism: see PAN- 1.

Panthan, Pantharb, variants of PANTHEON, PANTARBE.

†**Panthe·an,** *a. Obs.* = next.

1730–6 BAILEY (folio), *Panthean Statues*, statues that represented all or the most considerable of the heathen deities.

Pantheic (pænþī·ik), *a. rare.* [f. PANTHE-UM + -IC.] Of the nature of a pantheum: combining in one figure the symbols or attributes of many different gods.

1818 R. P. KNIGHT *Symbolic Lang.* (1876) 81 Diana..has ..titles and symbols expressive of almost every attribute, whether of creation, preservation, or destruction; as appears from the Pantheic figures of her. *Ibid.* 143 In engravings upon gems,..we often find the forms of the ram, goat, horse, cock, and various others, blended into one, so as to form Pantheic compositions, signifying the various attributes and modes of action of the Deity.

Pantheism (pæ·nþī,iz'm). [mod. f. Gr. παν- all + θεός God + -ISM; app. after PANTHEIST.

Panthéiste and *panthéisme* were used in French in 1712 (F. Benoist *Mélanges* 252, 265) the former app. taken from Toland's English use (see next), the latter formed after it on the ordinary analogy of pairs in *-ist* and *-ism*. Toland does not appear to have used *pantheism*.]

1. The religious belief or philosophical theory that God and the universe are identical (implying a denial of the personality and transcendence of God); the doctrine that God is everything and everything is God.

1732 WATERLAND *Chr. Vind. Charge* 76 Pantheism..and Hobbism are scandalously bad, scarce differing from the broadest Atheism. *a* 1766 J. BROWN *Honour* 176 *note*, That species of atheism commonly called Pantheism. 1823 COLERIDGE *Table-t.* 30 Apr., Pantheism and idolatry naturally end in each other: for all extremes meet. 1848 R. I. WILBERFORCE *Doct. Incarnation* v. (1852) 121 Pantheism, the principle of which is to merge the personality of the moral Governor in the circle of His works.

2. The heathen worship of all the gods.

1837 SIR F. PALGRAVE *Merch. & Friar* i. (1844) 21 The greater portion of the Tartar tribes professed a singular species of Pantheism, respecting all creeds, attached to none. 1861 PEARSON *Early & Mid. Ages Eng.* (1867) I. 18 The spirit of Roman pantheism, which erected a temple to the divinities of all nations.

Pantheist (pæ·nþī,ist). [f. as prec. + -IST. First used by Toland 1705; thence F. *panthéiste*.] One who holds the doctrine of pantheism.

1705 (*title*) Socinianism truly Stated..; to which is prefixt Indifference in Disputes: Recommended by a Pantheist [J. Toland] to an Orthodox Friend. 1705 TOLAND *ibid.* 7 The Pantheists..of which number I profess myself to be one. 1721 BP. HARE *Script. Vind. fr. Misrepr. Bp. Bangor* Pref. 21 Thus prays this *Pantheist* (i.e. the impious author of the *Pantheisticon*) whose impudent Blasphemies loudly call for the Animadversions of the Civil Power. 1750 WARBURTON *Note Pope's Ess. Man* I. 268 We are parts of him, his offspring, as the Greek poet, a pantheist quoted by the Apostle, observes: And the reason is, because a religious theist, and an impious pantheist, both profess to believe the omnipresence of God. 1778 APTHORPE *Preval. Chr.* 223 He is therefore a Spinozist or a philosophic pantheist. 1876 GLADSTONE in *Contemp. Rev.* June 24, I am by no means sure that Dante is not a Pantheist.

Pantheistic (pænþī,i·stik), *a.* [f. as prec. + -IC: cf. Toland's title *Pantheisticon*.]

1. Of or pertaining to pantheists, or pantheism.

[1718 J. TOLAND (*title*) Pantheisticon: sive Formula celebrandæ Sodalitatis Socraticæ.] 1732 WATERLAND *Chr. Vind. Charge* 44 The Pantheistick System..supposes God and Nature, or God and the whole Universe, to be one and the same Substance, one Universal Being; insomuch that Mens Souls are only Modifications of the divine Substance. 1856 SIR B. BRODIE *Psychol. Inq.* I. iv. 118 The pantheistic theory..has descended from the school of Pythagoras to these latter times.

†**2.** = PANTHEIC. *Obs.* (? an error.)

1842 BRANDE *Dict. Sci.* etc., *Pantheistic*,..a term applied to statues and figures.

So **Panthei·stical** *a.* = sense 1; hence **Panthei·stically** *adv.*

1840 THACKERAY *Paris Sk.-bk.* (1872) 176 In this work, the lady asserts her pantheistical doctrine. 1848 *Tait's Mag.* XV. 150 The Creator [is never] pantheistically identified with the works. 1870 DISRAELI *Lothair* xxx. 151 There is that human reason..which insists on being atheistical, or polytheistical, or pantheistical.

Panthelematism, -thelism: see PAN- 2.

Pantheology (pænþī,ǫ·lŏdʒi). [mod. f. Gr. παν-, PAN-, all + THEOLOGY.]

†**1.** The whole sum of theology or divinity. *Obs.*

1656 BLOUNT *Glossogr.*, *Pantheology*, the whole sum of Divinity. 1658 PHILLIPS, *Pantheologie*.

2. A synthetic theology comprehending all deities and all religions.

a 1693 *Urquhart's Rabelais* III. ii. 29 The true Spring and Source of the lively Idea of Pantheology. 1893 *Temple Bar Mag.* XCVII. 69 [His] intimacy with Greek pantheology was scarcely orthodox.

Hence **Pantheo·logist,** one who studies or is versed in pantheology.

1727 BAILEY vol. II, *Pantheologist*, a Student or Writer of universal or a whole Body of Divinity. (So in later Dicts.)

Pantheon (pænþī·ǫn, pæ·nþī,ǫn). Also 4 panteon(e, 6 panthan, -ean, (panthee). [a. L. *panthēon*, *-theum*, a. Gr. πάνθειον a temple consecrated to all the gods (f. παν- all + θεῖος of or sacred to a god, θεός a god). Cf. F. *panthéon*.

The ME. and early mod. Eng. pronunciation (e.g. in Cowley and Bailey's Dict.) was *pa·ntheon*; Johnson has *panthe·on*, which is now the more prevalent in England.]

1. A temple or sacred building dedicated to all the gods, or where images or other memorials of all the deities of a nation are collected; *spec.* that at Rome which was originally built by Agrippa *c* 25 B.C., and being on a circular plan has also been called the *Rotunda*; since A.D. 609 it has served as a Christian church, being known as Santa Maria Rotonda.

?13.. *All Saints* 37 in Herrig's *Archiv* LXXIX. 435 That temple was callyd panteone..Panteone is to sey in greke: 'Of all godis & deuellus eke'. *c* 1350 *All Saints* 37 in Horstm. *Altengl. Leg.* (1881) 143 Panteon þai calde þe name; 'Þe hows of goddes', þat menes þe same. 1549 COVERDALE etc. *Erasm. Par. Rev.* xvi. 25 The firste plage is fallen vpon all ydols and false goddes whiche they had set and packed together in one tempel of Pantheon, that is to saye all goddes. [1585 T. WASHINGTON tr. *Nicholay's Voy.* II. xx. 57 The proportion of the Panthee of Rome.] 1586 SIR E. HOBY *Pol. Disc. Truth* xxx. 140 The Romanes allowed the seruice of all gods, hauing for that ende builded a Temple to all gods called Pantheon. 1588 SHAKS. *Tit. A.* I. i. 242 Lauinia will I make my Empresse..And in the Sacred Panthan her espouse. 1617 MORYSON *Itin.* I. 135 Marcus Agrippa..built this Church, and dedicated it to Jupiter.. and to Ceres, and to all the gods, whereupon it was called *Pantheon*. 1727 BAILEY, *Pan'theon.* 1740 DYER *Ruins of Rome* Poems (1761) 28 Yon venerable dome, Which virtuous Latium, with erroneous aim, Rais'd to her various deities, and nam'd Pantheon. 1860 HAWTHORNE *Marb. Faun* I. (1883) 516 The world has nothing else like the Pantheon.

b. *fig.* 'Temple' or 'shrine of all the gods'.

1596 NASHE *Saffron-Walden* Wks. (Grosart) III. 155 Of this John Thorius..I will speake.., his Church another Pantheon or *Templum omnium deorum*, the absolutest Oracle of all sound deuinitie. 1639 FULLER *Holy War* (1640) 4 Poland, the Pantheon of all religions. 1663 COWLEY *On bk. present. itself to Univ. Libr. Oxf.* I Hail, Learning's Pantheon! Hail the sacred Ark, Where all the World of Science does embarque! 1882 *Athenæum* 30 Dec. 878/1 Scherer..has room in his literary pantheon for every legitimate form of art. 1899 EARL ROSEBERY *Sp. Cromwell* 14 Nov., Everyone, I think..has, in their heart of hearts a Pantheon of their historical demigods..a shrine in which they consecrate the memories of the deaths of the noblest and bravest men.

c. *transf.* A building resembling or compared to the Pantheon at Rome; now, especially, a building serving to honour the illustrious dead of a nation, who are either buried there or have memorials erected to them in it.

The latter use had app. its origin in the church of St. Geneviève in Paris, which in some respects resembles the Pantheon at Rome, and which, both before the Revolution and since, has been used for this purpose, being so renamed at that period.

1713 *Ward's Simp. Cobler* 12 It were..requisite, that the City should repair Pauls..for an English Pantheon, and bestow it upon the Sectaries, freely to assemble in. 1727–41 CHAMBERS *Cycl.* s.v., The chapel of the Escurial, which is the burying place of the kings of Spain, is also a rotondo; and in imitation of that of Rome, is also called pantheon. 1801 [see PANTHEONIZE below]. 1838 *Encycl. Brit.* (ed. 7) XVII. 76/2 The Pantheon, or church of St. Geneviève, is perhaps the most magnificent of the modern edifices in Paris...The west portico bears some resemblance to the Pantheon at Rome. 1855 *London as it is to-day* 29 Westminster Abbey may not inaptly be called the pantheon of the glory of Britain. 1890 *Whitaker's Almanack* 346/2 The French Chamber..decided to transfer the remains of Carnot, Marceau, and Baudin to the Pantheon.

2. A habitation of all the gods; the assemblage of all the gods; the deities of a people collectively.

1550 BALE *Image Both Ch.* xvi. Sel. Wks. (Parker Soc.) 491 The blasphemous Pantheon of Rome once perishing, all other churches of the unfaithful must needs follow soon after in their course. 1806 T. MAURICE *Fall of Mogul* Introd. 15 To that superstitious race the universe is a vast pantheon, filled with intellectual beings of various classes and powers. 1853 MAURICE *Proph. & Kings* xxv. 435 However intricate the relations of the gods may seem to us in the Greek pantheon. 1862 BEVERIDGE *Hist. India* II. IV. ii. 22 The Hindoo pantheon now boasts of being able to muster 330,000,000 deities. 1878 MACLEAR *Celts* ii. (1879) 22 Highest in the Celtic Pantheon was the golden-handed sun.

b. A name for a treatise on all the gods.

1698 [A. TOOKE] (*title of transl.*) The Pantheon, Representing the Fabulous Histories of the Heathen Gods and Most Illustrious Heroes..Written by Fra. Pomey. 1790 (*title*) Bell's New Pantheon, or Historical Dictionary of Gods, Demi-Gods, Heroes, and Fabulous Personages of Antiquity. 1824 WATT *Bibliotheca Brit.* I. s.v. *Stephen Bateman*, Golden Book of Heathen Gods...This work has been considered as one of the first attempts towards a Pantheon, or descriptions of the Heathen Gods.

c. A collection of wax-work models of the gods.

1711 *Spect.* No. 46 Advt., Mr. Penkethman's Wonderful Invention call'd the Pantheon: or, the Temple of the Heathen Gods..The Figures..move their Heads [etc.].

3. Name of a large building in London ('having a dome like the Pantheon'—Walpole, *Let. to Mann* 26 Apr. 1771), opened as a place of public entertainment in 1772: hence allusively.

1772 *Chron.* in *Ann. Reg.* 69 Last night was opened..the much-talked-of receptacle of fashionable pleasure, The Pantheon, to a crouded company. 1774 FOOTE *Cozeners* I. Wks. 1799 II. 146 Expences in attending plays, operas, masquerades, and pantheons. 1768 WESLEY *Wks.* (1872) XI. 158 We are making swift advances toward it [lewdness], by playhouses, masquerades, and pantheons.

4. *attrib.* = Of all the gods or heroes.

1767 H. WALPOLE *Let. to Mann* 30 May, I shall make a solemn dedication of it in my pantheon Chapel.

Hence **Pantheo·nic** *a.*, of the nature of or resembling a pantheon; **Pantheoniza·tion,** admission into the pantheon; **Panthe·onize** *v. trans.*, to admit into the pantheon; to inter in the Pantheon.

1801 *Paris as it was* II. xlviii. 137 Marat..was..pantheonized, that is, interred in the Pantheon. 1804 *Europ. Mag.* XLV. 437/1 The insanity of the people in pantheonizing and dispantheonizing Marat and Mirabeau. 1865 J. H. INGRAHAM *Pillar of Fire* (1872) 223 All these sacred figures decorated this pantheonic portico. 1883 R. BROWN *Eridanus* 4 The formal pantheonization of divinities.

Panther (pæ·nþəɹ). Forms: 3–6 panter, 4–6 pantere, (5 panteere), 5–6 panthere, (7 -ar), 5– panther. [ME. *pantere*, a. OF. *pantère* (Ph. de Thaun, 12th c.), mod.F. *panthère*, ad. L. *panthēra*, ad. Gr. πάνθηρ. (The solitary instance in OE. is merely an alien word from L. or Gr.)

The subjective analysis of the name, as from Gr. παν- all + θήρ beast, gave rise to many fancies and fables: see Ph. de Thaun *Bestiaire* 224, etc.]

1. Another name for the Leopard (*Felis pardus*); popularly applied to large leopards.

As with other exotic animals, the name, handed down from the Latin writers, was known long before the animal; all the early references merely reflect the statements of ancient authors and their mediæval continuators. These statements were long believed to refer to a beast distinct from the leopard; a belief encouraged by there being two Latin names *panthēra* and *pardus*, as to the relation between which the ancient writers themselves were not clear, and by fabulous notions as to the generation of the leopard as a hybrid between the lion and the 'pard', and as to the sweet fragrance fabled to be exhaled by the panther. Down to modern times (cf. quot. 1813) the 'panther' was supposed to be at least a larger and more powerful kind of leopard, a distinction not scientifically tenable.

[*a* 1000 *Panther* 12 (Gr.) Is þæt deor Pandher bi noman haten, þæs þe niðða bearn wisfæste weras on gewritum cyðdan bi þam anstapan.] *c* 1220 *Bestiary* 733 Panter is an wilde der, Is non fairere on werlde her. 1398 TREVISA *Barth. De P. R.* XVIII. lxxxii. (1495) 834 Lyons in Siria ben blacke wyth white speckis and ben lyke to Panteres. *c* 1430 LYDG. *Reas. & Sens.* 6438 In his sheelde, yif ye lyst here, Hath enprented a pantere. 1484 CAXTON *Fables of Æsop* IV. v, Fable of a panthere whiche felle in to a pytte. 1503 S. HAWES *Examp. Virt.* ix. 4 And by a swete smelle I knewe a pantere. 1545 JOYE *Exp. Dan.* vii. 98 The leoparde or spotted panthere..signifieth the kingdom of great Alexander. 1642 ROGERS *Naaman* Ep. Ded. 4 Which (as the Panthars breath..) hath made your name sweet. 1658 PHILLIPS, *Panther*, a kinde of spotted beast, the Leopard, or Libard being the Male, the Panther the Female. 1687 DRYDEN *Hind & P.* II. 228 The Panther's breath was ever famed for sweet. 1813 BINGLEY *Anim. Biog.* I. 261 In his general habits he [the Leopard] resembles the Panther, lying in ambush for prey. 1814 CARY *Dante's Inf.* I. 30 Lo! a panther, nimble, light, And cover'd with a speckled skin, appear'd. 1891 FLOWER & LYDEKKER *Mammals* xi. 515 The attempts to separate a larger and more robust variety, under the name of Panther, from a smaller and more graceful form, to which the name Leopard might properly be restricted, have failed.

fig. 1821 SHELLEY *Hellas* 316 Her slow dogs of war..see The panther, Freedom, fled to her old cover, Amid seas and mountains, and a mightier brood Crouch round.

2. Applied in America to the puma or cougar, *Felis concolor*, also called PAINTER 3; and, sometimes, to the jaguar, *F. onca.*

1730 *N. Jersey Archives* XI. 202 On Monday..was killed ..a monstrous large Panther. 1774 GOLDSM. *Nat. Hist.* I. 146 The jaguar or panther of America. 1808 PIKE *Sources Mississ.* (1810) 66 Saw a very large animal, which, from its leaps, I supposed to have been a panther; but if so, it was twice as large as those on the lower Mississippi. 1822 *Niles' Register* XXII. 304/2 A panther, nine feet long, was lately found dead on the shore of lake Ontario. 1839 *Penny Cycl.* XIII. 434/2 The Jaguar, or American Panther,..is the form of the Leopard found in the New World. It is..the Panther or Great Panther of the furriers. 1843 MARRYAT *M. Violet* xliv. 369 *note*, The puma, or red panther, is also called 'American lion, cougar'. 1894 *Cent. Mag.* Apr. 849 The panther was long called a 'tyger' in the Carolinas, and a 'lyon' elsewhere.

3. *fig.* Applied to a fierce or savage man.

1868 *Sat. Rev.* 18 Jan. 75/2 Even authoresses seem to accept with perfect equanimity the idea that taming the male panther is out of the question.

†**4.** Name of a (?sweet-smelling) drug. *Obs.*

1656 *Acts & Ord. Parl.* c. 20 (Scobell) 464 Drugs called Panther, the pound, £2. 1662 in *Stat. Ireland* (1765) II. 403.

5. *attrib.* and *Comb.*, as *panther-jump, -killing, -springer, -tooth, -tread*; *panther-like, -spotted* adjs.; **panther-cat,** the ocelot (Funk 1895); **panther-cowry,** a spotted cowry, *Cypræa pantherina* of the East Indies (*ibid.*); **panther-lily,** *U.S.*, the Californian lily, *Lilium pardalinum*; **panther-moth,** a collector's name for a European geometrid, *Cidaria unangulata* (*Cent. Dict.* 1890); **panther's bane,** a plant, also called Wolf's bane; **panther-toad,** a South African toad, *Bufo pantherinus* (*Cassell's Encycl. Dict.* 1886); **panther-wood,** a variety of the citron wood or sandarach tree, *Callistris quadrivalvis* (*Cent. Dict.* 1890).

1774 GOLDSM. *Nat. Hist.* (1776) III. 254 An animal of the panther kind. 1857 C. BRONTE *Professor* I. xii. 197 Envy and *panther-like deceit about her mouth. 1884 MILLER *Plant-n.* 78/1 *Panther Lily. 1900 *Field* 23 June 903/3 L[ilium] *superbum*..requires a vegetable soil like the Panther lily. 1820 SHELLEY *Witch of Atlas* xxxviii, Amid The *panther-peopled forests. 1712 tr. *Pomet's Hist. Drugs* I. 39 Wolf or *Panther's bane..is a Root divided by Lumps or Clods. 1593 NASHE *Christ's T.* Wks. (Grosart) IV. 77 Some soules of this *Panther-spotted Ierusalem, may bee extraught to ioy with me. 1898 G. MEREDITH *Odes Fr. Hist.* 48 The smiter, *panther-springer, trapper sly. 1834 *Tait's Mag.* I. 341/2 With *panther-teeth their victim's heart They tear. 1899 *Westm. Gaz.* 9 Feb. 2/1 The cat.. still keeps..the bold, free *panther-tread with which it paced of yore the temple courts of Thebes.

Pantheress (pæ·nþərės). [f. prec. + -ESS.] A female panther.

1862 FROUDE in Sir J. Skelton *Shirley's Table-t.* 127 Mary Stuart..was something between Rachel and a pantheress. 1877 DIXON *Diana, Lady Lyle* II. VII. iv. 201 A pantheress is not armed with a more stealthy foot.

b. *fig.* Applied to a fierce or cruel but beautiful woman. Also *attrib.*

1868 *Sat. Rev.* 18 Jan. 75/1 A heroine of the beautiful pantheress order. 1890 'R. BOLDREWOOD' *Miner's Right* (1899) 43/1 You are just as much carried away by this infernal scoundrel's regular features and soft voice, as that handsome pantheress that he's stolen somewhere.

Pantherine (pæ·nþərəin, -rin), *a.* [ad. L. *panthērīn-us*, f. *panthēra* PANTHER: see -INE 1.] Resembling a panther, spotted like a panther; of, belonging to, or characteristic of a panther.

1656 BLOUNT *Glossogr.*, *Pantherine.* 1753 CHAMBERS *Cycl. Supp.*, Pantherine tables, *pantherinæ mensæ*, among the Romans, tables made of citron wood..had this name from their being spotted after the manner of panthers. 1883 FENN *Eli's Children* (ed. 2) I. I. xix. 314 [She] curled herself gracefully..in a pantherine style in the corner of the carriage. 1890 — *Double Knot* I. i. 73 Marie made a pantherine bound across the room.

Pa·ntherish, *a.* [f. PANTHER + -ISH 1.] Somewhat like, or characteristic of, a panther.

1892 *Blackw. Mag.* CLI. 114/2 Graceful in a lithe, pantherish way. 1895 *Athenæum* 27 July 125/2 A..boneless puppet, at the mercy of any specimen of 'pantherish' grace (there are several panthers) who takes him in hand.

‖**Pantheum** (pænþī·ǫm). Mostly in pl. **panthea.** [late L. *panthēum*, f. Gr. πάνθειος: see PANTHEON. In mod. F. *panthée*.] More fully *signum pantheum*: A statue combining the figures, symbols, or attributes of several deities.

1706 PHILLIPS, *Panthea* or *Signa Panthea.* 1727–41 CHAMBERS *Cycl.*, *Panthea*, Πανθεια, among the ancients were single statues, composed of the figures, or symbols of several different divinities combined. 1730–6 in BAILEY (folio). 1775 ASH, *Pantheum*...A statue adorned with the figures or symbols of the gods. 1838 in *Encycl. Brit.* XVI. 790/2. 1882 FENNELL tr. *Michaelis' Anc. Marbles Gt. Brit.* 628 In the fashion of the *signa panthea* this youth unites in his own person the attributes of various gods..Poseidon.. Apollo..Dionysos..Ares..Eros.

†**Panthne·tist.** *Obs. rare.* [f. Gr. παν- all + θνητός mortal + -IST.] (See quot.)

1660 INGELO *Bentiv. & Ur.* II. (1682) 208, I will premise a few things concerning the Temper and Design of the Panthnetists. [*margin*] Such as think the Soul and Body to perish in Death.

Panthodic (pænþǫ·dik), *a. Physiol. rare.* [f. Gr. παντ(ο- PANTO- + Gr. ὁδός way.] Said of nervous action: Proceeding in all directions from a single point.

1850 MARSHALL HALL *Synops. Diast. Nerv. Syst.* i. § 7 (1852) 13 (*heading*) Panthodic Law of Action of the Vis Nervosa. *Ibid.*, I use the term panthodic in a very emphatic sense; I believe that no spot of the diastaltic system can be excited without telling upon every other. 1853 in DUNGLISON *Med. Lex.* 1893 in *Syd. Soc. Lex.*

Pantible, corrupt form of PANTOFLE.

Pantile (pæ·n,təil). Also 7–9 pan tile, pan-tile, 8 pan-tyle. [f. PAN *sb.* 1 + TILE *sb.* Cf. Du. *dakpan* (Kilian *dack-panne*), lit. roof-pan; Ger. *dachpfanne, pfannenziegel* pan-tile.]

1. A roofing tile transversely curved to an ogee shape, one curve being much larger than the other; when laid on the roof the greater part of their surface forms a concave channel for the descent of water, while one side forms a narrow convex ridge, which overlaps the edge of the adjoining tile.

The name has also been applied to tiles made with a single curve, which were laid edge to edge, on their convex sides, the junction of two edges being covered by another tile laid with its concave side downward; also, improperly, to flat overlapping roofing tiles.

1640 *Charter City London* Table of Rates, Tyles vocat' Pan Tyles or Flaunders Tyles the thousand, ijd. 1703 MOXON *Mech. Exerc.* 240 *Pan-Tiles*, being about thirteen Inches long, with a Nob or Button to hang on the Laths.. The best sort..are called Flemmish Pan-Tiles. 1738 [G. SMITH] *Curious Relations* II. v. 108 Those Leaves..serve instead of Pan-Tiles to cover their Dwellings. 1816 J. SMITH *Panorama Sc. & Art* I. 190 Common tiles for roofs are called pan tiles. 1880 BARING-GOULD *Mehalah* i, A small farm-house..roofed with red pan-tiles. 1881 YOUNG *Every Man his own Mechanic* § 1206. 561 Plain tiles are perfectly flat, while pantiles are curved in form ∾ something after the manner of the letter S.

b. in sing. collectively, or as a material.

1697 DAMPIER *Voy.* (1729) I. 387 The Houses are large, strongly built, and covered with Pan-tile. 1787 *Philip Quarll* 65 Their Houses are..Cover'd with Pantile.

†**c.** Erroneously applied to flat Dutch or Flemish paving tiles, and so to the Parade at Tunbridge Wells which was paved with these. *Obs.*

1774 FOOTE *Cozeners* II. Wks. 1799 II. 171 At Tunbridge.. they have the oddest pantile walk. 1784 H. WALPOLE *Brit. Traveller* 25 (Tunbr. Wells) [The shops] are ranged on one side of a walk called the Pantiles, from its pavement. 1805 MOORE *To Lady H.* I When..Tunbridge saw, upon her Pantiles, The merriest wight of all the kings That ever ruled these gay gallant isles. 1806 *Guide to Watering Pl.* 419 The former [Upper Walk] was once paved with pantiles, raised about four steps above the other.

2. Humorously applied to hard sea biscuit, etc.

1873 *Slang Dict.* s.v., Pantile also means a flat cake with jam on it, given to boys at boarding-schools instead of pudding. 1891 *Labour Commission Gloss.*, *Pantiles*, term used to express the hardness of old sea biscuits ground into meal and then re-baked. 1901 FARMER *Slang*, *Pantile* (nautical) a biscuit.

3. *attrib.* and *Comb.*, as *pantile-roof, -works*; **pantile-lath,** an extra stout lath used for supporting pantiles on a roof.

1776 G. SEMPLE *Building in Water* 66 A nine Foot *Pantile-lath. 1873 E. SPON *Workshop Receipts* Ser. I. 127/1 Laths called by bricklayers double laths, and the larger ones pantile laths. 1837 HOWITT *Rur. Life* II. iv. (1862) 127 A long shed, stone walls and *pantile roof. 1703 *Proclam.* 10 Jan. in *Lond. Gaz.* No. 3879/4 The Brick and *Pantile Works near Tilbury Fort.

†**b.** Applied contemptuously in 18th c. to rural Dissenters' meeting-houses (sometimes, like ordinary cottages, roofed with pantiles), and to those who attended them: see quots. *Obs.*

1715 MRS. CENTLIVRE *Gotham Election* Wks. 1760 III. 163 Mr. Tickup's a good Churchman..none of your occasional Cattle; none of your hellish pantile Crew. *Ibid.* 181 I'll have you hang'd for 't, I will, you Pantile Monster. 1785 GROSE *Dict. Vulg. T.*, *Pantile house* [ed. 1796 *Pantile Shop*], a Presbyterian, or other dissenting meeting house, frequently covered with pantiles.

Hence **Pa·ntiled** *a.*, covered with pantiles; †**Pa·ntiler:** see 3 b.

1778 *Love Feast* 12 Led by the Spirit to John's *pantil'd Roof. 1870 F. R. WILSON *Ch. Lindisfarne* 89 [It] rises over the thatched and pantiled roofs..notably. 1856 MAYHEW *World Lond.* 249 The officers..used to designate the extraordinary religious convicts as '*pantilers'. 1889 DRYSDALE *Hist. Presbyter. Eng.* 443 Their frequenters were in some localities nick-named 'Pantilers', these pantiles forming a substantial yet economical roof.

Pa·n-ti:ling. [f. PANTILE + -ING 1.] The covering of a roof with pantiles; pantiles collectively or in the mass.

1805 R. W. DICKSON *Pract. Agric.* I. 89 Pan-tiling, with small sized deal lath, and sparkled within side. 1825 J. NICHOLSON *Operat. Mechanic* 550 A square of pan-tiling requires 180 tiles, laid at a ten-inch gauge. 1894 *Times* 23 Apr. 13/2 Wood and pantiling and boarded roofs taking the place of brick or stone and slate.

†**Pa·ntine.** *Obs.* Also pantein, -een, -in. [In F. *pantin*, formerly *pantine* ('une jatte de Saxe, une pantine de Boucher', Diderot *Promenade du Sceptique*, 1747–9), which some French etymologists have referred to *Pantin* a village near Paris; but see quot. 1748.] A pasteboard figure of a human being, having the neck, body, and limbs jointed, so as to move when pulled by a thread or wire: a fashionable toy in the middle of the 18th c.

1748 *Lond. Mag.* 271 The ridiculous folly of Panteins [*note.* Paper or pastboard puppets, contriv'd to move in all postures, so call'd from mademoiselle Pantein, one of the marshal Saxe's [ob. 1750] ladies, who is said to be the inventer]. 1749 MRS. DELANY *Life & Corr.* (1861) II. 505 She has begun and almost finished..a set of pantines. 1754 SHEBBEARE *Matrimony* (1766) II. 75 She resembled a Pantine, and wanted nothing but a Whalebone in her Head to give her a Twirl, and flirt her two long Arms into Motion. 1790 *Bystander* 174 Edwin is as much of an actor as a panteen is of a puppet. [1881 BESANT & RICE *Chapl. of Fleet* II. v, Pantines, a ridiculous fashion of paper doll then in vogue as a toy for ladies with nothing to do.]

Panting (pæ·ntiŋ), *vbl. sb.* [f. PANT *v.* + -ING 1.] The action of the verb PANT, in various senses.

c 1440 *Promp. Parv.* 381/2 Pantynge, *anelacio, vel anelatus.* 1580 SIDNEY *Ps.* XLII. i, My soul in panting plaieth, Thirsting on my God to looke. 1647 CLARENDON *Hist. Reb.* I. § 35 The Prince's Journey into Spain, which.. had begot such a terrible panting in the hearts of all good English-men. 1715–20 POPE *Iliad* XVI. 134 His breath, in quick, short pantings, comes and goes. 1837 HAWTHORNE *Twice-told T.* (1851) I. xvi. 251 The horses..heave their glistening sides in short quick pantings.

Pa·nting, *ppl. a.* [f. as prec. + -ING 2.] That pants, in various senses: see PANT *v.*

1572 GASCOIGNE *Dan Bartholomew* Wks. (1587) 91, I feele my panting heart begins to rest. 1616 CHAPMAN *Musæus, Hero & L.* 368 She hugg'd her panting husband. 1718 PRIOR *Power* 172 Frequent for breath his panting bosom heaves. 1828 *Lights & Shades* II. 73 One poor panting girl. 1897 *Allbutt's Syst. Med.* III. 83 The respirations are short and panting.

Hence **Pa·ntingly** *adv.*, in a panting manner; with short quick breaths.

1605 SHAKS. *Lear* IV. iii. 28 (Qo.) Once or twice she heau'd the name of father Pantingly foorth, as if it prest her heart. 1744 ARMSTRONG *Preserv. Health* III. 559 Thick and pantingly The breath was fetch'd. 1892 *Harper's Mag.* July 190/2, 'I came—on the first—train', answered Lois, pantingly.

Pantiple, corrupt form of PANTOFLE.

Pantisocracy (pæntisǫ·krăsi, -əis-). [f. Gr. παντ-, PANTO- all + ἰσοκρατία ISOCRACY.] A form of social organization in which all are equal in rank and social position; a Utopian community in which all are equal and all rule.

1794 SOUTHEY *Let.* 20 Sept. in *Life* I. 221 We preached Pantisocracy and Asphete[r]ism everywhere. 1821 BYRON *Juan* III. xciii, All are not moralists like Southey, when He prated to the world of 'Pantisocrasy'. 1887 DOWDEN *Shelley* I. iv. 135 Southey and Coleridge..had dreamed of pantisocracy on the banks of the Susquehanna.

Pantisocrat (pæntəi·sǒkræt). [f. as prec. after *aristocrat, democrat.*] One who advocates or promotes pantisocracy.

1794 SOUTHEY *Let.* 20 Sept. in *Life* I. 221 It will then be time for you to take leave of the navy, and become acquainted with all our brethren, the pantisocrats. 1895 SAINTSBURY *Ess. Eng. Lit.* Ser. II. 10 It was impossible to start it without money, of which most of the Pantisocrats had none.

So **Pantisocra·tic, Pantisocra·tical** *adjs.*, pertaining to, involving, or upholding pantisocracy; **Pantiso·cratist** = *pantisocrat.*

1794 COLERIDGE *Let.* 18 Sept. in *Life Southey* I. 219 C——, the most excellent, the most *Pantisocratic of aristocrats, has been laughing at me. 1794 SOUTHEY *Let.* 14 Oct. ibid. 222 This Pantisocratic scheme has given me new life. 1887 W. HUNT *Bristol* 186 Here the young poets elaborated their scheme of a pantisocratic settlement on the Susquehanna. 1803 W. TAYLOR in Robberds *Mem.* I. 442 To found a Christian platonical *pantisocratical republic. 1880 DOWDEN *Southey* 39 With such a sum they might both qualify by marriage for membership in the pantisocratical community. 1835 MACAULAY *Ess., Mackintosh's Hist. Rev.* (1843) II. 216 Rushing from one wild extreme to another, out-Paining Paine, out-Castlereaghing Castlereagh, *Pantisocratists, Ultra-Tories, heretics [etc.]. 1883 HALL CAINE *Cobw. Crit.* ii. 37 Coleridge, Southey and Lovell..were all three passionate pantisocratists.

Pantle (pæ·nt'l), *sb.* Now *dial.* Forms: 5 pantelle, 6 -el(l, 9 pantle. [app. an altered form of PANTER 2.] A snare for birds, esp. snipe.

1483 *Cath. Angl.* 268/1 Pantelle stryngе (*A.* A Pantyr), *pedica.* 1552 HULOET, Pantell, setter, or snare, *pedica.* 1856 J. DAVIES *Races* 237 (E.D.D.). 1882 *Lancash. Gloss.*, *Pantle*, a bird-snare made of hair. 1893 J. WATSON *Conf. Poacher* 39 We used to take them [snipe] in pantles made of twisted horsehair. 1897 MACPHERSON *Wild-fowling* 458 (E. D. D.) In South Furness men snare snipe by means of engines locally called pantles.

Pa·ntle, *v. Obs.* exc. *dial.* [f. PANT *v.* with dim. or frequentative ending -LE.] *intr.* To pant.

[1632 ROWLEY *Woman Never Vexed* II. in Hazl. *Dodsley* XII. 128 My heart! O my heart! if it does not go pantle, pantle, pantle..I am no honest woman.] 1652 URQUHART *Jewel* Wks. (1834) 222 The Italian..foamed at the mouth ..and fetched a pantling breath. 1678 COTTON *Scarron.* IV. 142 Although her woful heart did pantle. 1875 PORSON *Quaint Words* 15. 1890 *Glouc. Gloss.*, *Pantle*, to pant. [Also S. Worcestersh. (E. D. D.).]

Pantler (pæ·ntləɹ). Now only *Hist.* [app. an altered form of PANTER 1, PANTERER, ? after *butler.* (Not in French, nor app. in med.L.)] = PANTER 1.

c 1330 R. BRUNNE *Chron.* (1810) 33 The kyng tok þis pantelere, & strangled him right þore. *c* 1440 *Promp. Parv.* 381/2 Pantlere, *panitarius.* 1483 *Cath. Angl.* 268/1 A Pantelere, *vbi* A butlere. 1533 WRIOTHESLEY *Chron.* (1875) I. 21 The Earle of Arondell butler, the Viscount Lisle pantler. 1597 SHAKS. 2 *Hen. IV*, II. iv. 258 Hee would haue made a good Pantler, hee would haue chipp'd Bread well. 1679 BLOUNT *Anc. Tenures* 36 The Mannor..to be held by the service of being Pantler to the Kings..at their Coronations. 1706 *Lond. Gaz.* No. 4252/2 The Butler and the Pantler have taken his Name off the Tables in their Offices. 1842 BARHAM *Ingol. Leg.* Ser. II. *Lay St. Cuthbert*, Pantler and serving-man, henchman and page, Stand sniffing the duck-stuffing (onion and sage).

Panto- (pænto), before a vowel PANT-, repr. Gr. παντο- (παντ-, πανθ-), combining form of πᾶς, πᾶν (stem παντ-) all, already used in ancient Gr. (where often interchangeable with παν- PAN-) in forming adjs. and a few substantives used attrib., as πάνταρχος (Soph.) all-ruling, παντοδαπός of all kinds, παντοκράτωρ almighty, παντοκτίστης creator of all; in later Gr. it became much more frequent. The word παντόμῑμος was adopted in L. as *pantomīmus* and thence came into French and English as *pantomime* before 1600. Otherwise, the formation of words in *panto-* began in the 17th c., and became more frequent in the 19th; but this has not become a living element forming compounds like the cognate PAN- 1 in *Pan-Anglican, Pan-American*, and the like. The chief derivatives of *panto-* appear in their alphabetical places; the following are of minor importance:

†**Panto-chrono·meter:** see quot. †**Panto-de·vil,** *nonce-wd.*, a complete or entire devil. **Pa·ntoganglitis** *Path.*: see quots. **Pa·ntogela·stic, -al** *adjs.* [Gr. γελαστικός risible], all-laughable. **Panto·genous** *a. Min.* [Gr. -γενης born, produced; in F. *pantogène*]: see quots. †**Panto-ia·trical** *a.*, universally healing, all-healing. †**Pa·ntomancer,** a diviner upon all kinds of things. **Pa·ntomorph** (erron. panta-) [Gr. παντόμορφος], that which takes any or all shapes; so **Pantomo·rphic** *a.* (panta-), assuming any or all forms. **Pantopela·gian** *a.* [Gr. πέλαγος sea: cf. F. *pantopélagien* (Littré)], frequenting or inhabiting all seas. †**Pa·ntophile** [F. *pantophile*], a lover of all. **Pantople·thora** *Path.*, general plethora. **Panto·pterous** *a. Zool.* [Gr. πτερόν wing, fin], of or pertaining to the *Pantoptera*, a family of fishes having all fins but the ventral (Mayne *Expos. Lex.* 1857). **Pantothe·rian** *a.* [Gr. θήρα, θηρίον beast], of or pertaining to the *Pantotheria*, an extinct order of American Jurassic mammals; *sb.* a member of this order. ‖**Pantozoo·tia** = *panzooty*: see PAN- 2 (Harris *Dict. Med. Terminol.* 1854–67).

1842 BRANDE *Dict. Sci.* etc., *Pantochronometer, a term recently invented and applied to an instrument which is a combination of the compass, the sun-dial, and the universal time-dial, and performing the offices of all three. 1694 MOTTEUX *Rabelais* v. xiii, Oh you Devils, cry'd Friar Ihon, Proto-Devils, *Panto-Devils, you would wed a Monk, would you? 1857 MAYNE *Expos. Lex.*, **Pantoganglitis*, ..term for inflammation of the *ganglia*, central and peripherical; also for oriental cholera. 1893 *Syd. Soc. Lex.*, *Pantoganglitis*, a term for malignant cholera, introduced on the assumption that it was caused by inflammation of all the sympathetic ganglia. 1808 *Pantogelastical [see PANTOLOGICAL]. 1805–17 R. JAMESON *Char. Min.* (ed. 3) 220 *Pantogenous (pantogene), that is to say, which derives its form from all parts of the crystal, when every edge and angle suffers a decrement. Example, Pantogenous heavy-spar. 1857 MAYNE *Expos. Lex.*, *Pantogenus*, applied by Haüy to crystals in which each edge and each solid angle has undergone a decrease..pantogenous. 1716 M. DAVIES *Athen. Brit.* III. *Diss. Physick* 14 Religiously inclin'd Doctors of the same *Panto-Iatrical Scriptures. 1652 GAULE *Magastrom.* 335 Of astromancers turning *pantomancers, or presaging not onely upon prodigies, but upon every slight occasion, by every vile and vaine means. 1841 SCUDAMORE *Nomencl.*, **Pantamorph*..., that which has all shapes. 1836 SMART, **Pantamorphic*, taking all shapes. 1890 *Cent. Dict.*, Pantomorph, Pantomorphic. 1857 MAYNE *Expos. Lex.*, *Pantopelagian. 1893 *Syd. Soc. Lex.*, *Pantopelagian*, frequenting all seas, or the whole sea; applied by Fleurien to such birds as the albatross and the stormy petrel. 1898 *Allbutt's Syst. Med.* V. 925 'The heart of a pantophile', as Voltaire called that removed from Diderot's body. 1857 MAYNE *Expos. Lex.*, **Pantoplethora*,..universal or general plethora, or fulness of the blood-vessels.

Pantoble, pantocle: see PANTOFLE.

Pantod: see OD 2 b.

Pantofle (pæ·ntǒf'l, pæntǫ·f'l, -tu·f'l). Forms: 5 *Sc.* pantufle, (-uifill), 6 -uffle, 6–7 -afle, -aphel, -of(f)el, -ophle, -ophel, 6– pantofle, -offle, 7–9 pantoufle, 9 -oofle. Also β. 6 pantocle, -acle; pantapple, 7 pantaple, 6–8 pantable, (6 pantiple, 7 -ible, -oble). [a. F. *pantoufle* (1489 in Hatz.-Darm.) = Cat. *plantofa*, Sp. *pantuflo*, Pg. *pantufo*, It. *pantofola, -ufola*; also Ger., Du. *pantoffel* (from It.), Flem. *pattoffel*. Ulterior origin unknown; see Diez and Littré. The English stress on the first syllable facilitated the corruptions *pantaple, pantocle, pantable*, assimilated to words in *-ple, -cle, -ble.* The stress on second syllable follows Fr. and Ger.]

A slipper; formerly applied very variously, app., at one time or another, to every sort of in-door slippers or loose shoes; esp. to the high-heeled cork-soled chopins; also to out-door overshoes or goloshes; and to all manner of Oriental and non-European slippers, sandals, and the like. (In Scottish use from 15th c.; in common Eng. use from *c* 1570 to *c* 1650–60; after that chiefly an alien or historical word.)

1494 *Acc. Ld. High Treas. Scot.* I. 224 Item, to Home the cordinare, for schone, brodykinnis and pantuiffillis tane fra him be Jame Dog. 1497 *Ibid.* 334 Item, for ane par of Franch pantuflis..viij*s*. 1565 COOPER *Thesaurus*, *Baxeæ*, ..a kynde of slippers, or pantofles. 1577 B. GOOGE *Heresbach's Husb.* (1586) 101 Of his [beech's] barke, are made Pantoffels, and Slippers. 1579 GOSSON *Sch. Abuse* (Arb.) 30 The litle crackhalter that carrieth his maisters pantouffles. 1579–80 NORTH *Plutarch* (1895) IV. 22 A payer of pantophles. 1589 PUTTENHAM *Eng. Poesie* I. xv. (Arb.) 49 The actors ..did walke vpon those high corked shoes or pantofles, which now they call in Spaine and Italy *Shoppini*. 1607 R. C[AREW] tr. *Estienne's World of Wonders* 203 The Pope would not entertaine him, except he would..kisse his pantoufle. *c* 1618 FLETCHER *Queen of Corinth* I. ii, [He] takes his oath Upon her Pantoffles. 1624 BURTON *Anat. Mel.* III. ii. I. i. (ed. 2) 356 She..whipped him [Cupid] besides on the bare buttocks with her pantophle. 1636 MASSINGER *Bashf. Lover* v. i, Pray you, let me be your page; I can swear already, Upon your pantofle. 1679 OLDHAM *Sat. Jesuits* Wks. (1686) 44 Spurns to Hell For jearing Holy Toe, and Pantofle. *a* 1715 BURNET *Own Time* (1823) III. IV. 77 [The pope] would give me a private audience abed, to save me the ceremony of the pantoufle. 1767 STERNE *Tr. Shandy* IX. xxi, Nothing..but trunk-hose and pantofles. 1820 SCOTT *Abbot* v, I have been too long the vassal of a pantoufle, and the slave of a silver whistle. *a* 1845 BARHAM *Ingol. Leg.*, *Ld. Thoulouse* vi, *Pantoufles* with bows Each as big as a rose. 1852 THACKERAY *Esmond* I. iii, Great gold clocks to her stockings, and white pantofles with red heels. 1887 ANNA FORBES *Insulinde* i. 9 Indian-looking pantoffles,.. with no upper heels, but very high wooden ones.

β. Corrupt forms. (*Pantable* was exceedingly common from 1580 to *c* 1650.)

a 1568 ASCHAM *Scholem.* I. (Arb.) 84 As it is free..to chose..whether a man lust to weare Shoo or Pantocle. 1571 *Damon & Pithias* in Dodsley *O. P.* I. 215 Even here with a pantacle I wyll you disgrace. 1573–80 BARET *Alv.* P 72 A Pantapple, *vide* Shooe. *a* 1586 SIDNEY *Arcadia* I. (1629) 49 Chafing and swearing by the pantable of Pallace and such other oathes as his rusticall braverie could imagine. 1591 PERCIVALL *Sp. Dict.*, *Calçado de alcorques*, in pantoples, *Crepidatus.* 1596 *Lanc. Wills* III. 2 A payre of pantables and ij payre of slippers. 1602 MARSTON *Ant. & Mel.* II. Wks. 1856 I. 19 By my ladies pantable, I feare I shall live to heare [etc.]. 1676 D'URFEY *Mad. Fickle* v. iii, Out of my doors, by Jacobs Pantible—a Relique of Renown'd memory. 1688 R. HOLME *Armoury* II. 112/2 The Lady Slipper so called from the resemblance the fore-part of the flower hath to a Slipper, or Pantable. 1883 J. PAYNE 1001 *Nights* VI. 291 Except he bring her..another crown and girdle and pantable of gold.

b. Phrase. *To stand* (*be*, etc.) *upon* (*one's*) *pantofles*, i.e. on one's dignity; so *the high pantofle*, etc.

1573 G. HARVEY *Letter-bk.* (Camden) 14 He was now altogither set on his merri pinnes and walkd on his stateli pantocles. 1579 LYLY *Euphues* (Arb.) 47 For the most part they stand so on their pantuffles. 1591 R. TURNBULL *Exp. Epist. James* 171 b, To stand too much vpon our pantiples. 1591 GREENE *2nd Pt. Conny-catch.* Wks. (Grosart) X. 119 Then are they vpon their pantophles, because there is nothing found about them. 1594 CAREW *Huarte's Exam. Wits* xiii. (1596) 224 A Caualiero, who stood much on the pantophles of his gentilitie. 1665 BRATHWAIT *Comment Two Tales* 22 This sets the Carpenter upon his Pantofles. 1685 BUNYAN *Pharisee & Publ.* Wks. (1845) 140 Thou standest upon thy points and pantables, thou wilt not bate God on all of what thy righteousness is worth. *c* 1740 A. ALLEN *MS. Dict.* s.v. *Pantoble*, Pantofle, or Pantoufle, Slippers with high Soles. These, as well as high Heels, making People appear taller, ..gave birth to our Proverb, to stand upon ones Pantables, i. to stand upon high Terms, carry his head Loftily. 1755 H. WALPOLE *Lett.* (1846) III. 156, I could not possibly to-day step out of my high historical pantoufles to tell it you.

†**c.** *Comb.* **Pantofle-shoe** [F. *fer à pantoufle*, or *pantoufle*] = PANTON-*shoe* (for a horse). *Obs.*

1696 HOPE tr. *Solleysel's Parfait Mareschal* I. xl. 131, I have called this shoe the *Panton* or Pantable shoe to distinguish it from those of any other fashion or shape. 1717 *Dict. Rusticum* (ed. 2), *Pantons* or *Pantable-shoes*, a sort of Horse-shoes that serve for narrow and low Heels. 1722 W. GIBSON *Farrier's New Guide* xciv. (ed. 3) 256 The Cure is..to shoe him with Lunets or Half-moon Shoes, or with those Pantofle Shoes describ'd by Solleysell.

Pantogamy: see PANTAGAMY.

Pantoganglitis, -genous, etc.: see PANTO-.

†**Pantoglo·ssical,** *a. Obs. rare*—1. [f. Gr. παντο- all + γλῶσσα tongue + -ICAL.] Of or belonging to all tongues.

1716 M. DAVIES *Athen. Brit.* II. 299 [It] may stand in full Defyance of ever being express'd, even with any Paraphrastical Periphrasis, or any Pantoglossical Mint of Words.

Pantoglot (pæ·ntǫglǫt), *a.* and *sb.* [f. Gr. παντο- all + γλῶσσα, γλῶττα tongue, after *polyglot.*] **a.** *adj.* Knowing or speaking all languages. **b.** *sb.* One who speaks all languages. So **Pantoglo·ttism.**

1848 LOWELL *Biglow P.* Ser. I. ii. Poems 1890 II. 61 This would argue for the pantoglottism of these celestial intelligences. 1895 H. CALLAN *From Clyde to Jordan* ix. 101, I disapprove of a man being a polyglot, or worse, an approach to a pantoglot.

Pantograph (pæ·ntǒgraf). Also *erron.* panta-, panti-, penta-, pento-, pente-. [mod. f. Gr. παντο- PANTO-, all + -γράφος writing, writer. So F. *pentographe* (Bion 1723), *pantographe* (1743 in *Hist. Acad. des Sci.*), the proximate source. Erroneously spelt by Bion and his translator Stone *pento-*, and by Chambers 1727 *penta-* (as if from Gr. πεντα- five); the latter still frequent in commercial and technical use.] An instrument for the mechanical copying of a plan, diagram, pattern, etc., on the same or an enlarged or reduced scale. In 17th c. called *parallelogram.*

It consists of four rods, perforated at uniform distances, and jointed together, two opposite joints being terminal and constant in position, the other two capable of being shifted according to the scale desired; one of the free ends carries a tracing-point, and one of the terminal joints a similar tracing-point; when one of these points is moved over the lines of the diagram, etc., the other traces the copy required.

[1631 C. SCHEINER (*title*) Pantographice, seu Ars Delineandi res quaslibet per parallelogrammum lineare..mobile. 1723 BION *Instr. de Math.* 89 L'instrument..est nommé Pentographe; on le nomme aussi Singe.] 1723 E. STONE tr. *Bion's Math. Instr.* 86 Of the Pentograph, or Parallelogram. 1727–41 CHAMBERS *Cycl.*, *Pentagraph*, an instrument whereby designs, prints, etc. of any kind, may be copied in any proportion;..otherwise called a parallelogram. [1743 *Mach. approuv. par l'Acad. des Sci.* VII. 207 Pantographe, ou singe perfectionné, Par M. Langlois.] 1766 B. MARTIN *Surv. by Goniometer* 18 There remains therefore only the Pantagraph to be described. 1803 HAWKINS *Patent Specif.* No. 2735 Attaching..pencils, etc. to a double pantograph. 1844 G. DODD *Textile Manuf.* vi. 200 An instrument called a pantograph has been introduced for producing an exquisite embroidery on plain silk goods after weaving. 1844 *Mech. Mag.* XL. 92 The Eidograph,..invented about the year 1821..is considered superior in many respects to the Pentograph. 1879 G. PRESCOTT *Sp. Telephone* 303 By using a form of pantograph, Prof. Mayer has obtained magnified tracings on smoked glass. 1897 [see PANTOGRAPHER 2].

attrib. 1875 KNIGHT *Dict. Mech.* s.v. *Pantograph*, The plate is then laid on the curved bed of the pantograph machine. 1895 *Oracle Encycl.* I. 585/2 Patterns are also etched on the rollers with nitric acid, by lines cut..by means of Rigby's pentagraph machine. 1897 *Westm. Gaz.* 26 June 6/3 The pantagraph power-shuttle machine.

b. A device of similar construction for mechanically reducing the cross-head motion of the indicator used for recording the pressure in a steam cylinder.

1893 WHITHAM *Constr. Steam Eng.* 154 A simple form of pantagraph, for use when the indicators are attached to the side of the cylinder. *Ibid.*, Pantagraph motions have been devised for overcoming these defects.

Hence **Pa·ntographing** *vbl. sb.*, the manipulation of a pantograph.

1897 *Sketch* 26 May 181/2 A front girl who must always have had experience in pantagraphing.

Panto·grapher. [f. prec. + -ER 1.]

†**1.** = PANTOGRAPH. *Obs.*

1750 J. HAMMOND (*title*) Practical Surveyor, with Description of Sliding Rule, Universal Dial Pantographer [etc.]. 1774 S. DUNN (*title*) Theory and use of the Pantographer.

2. One who produces patterns, etc., by means of a pantograph.

1897 *Sketch* 26 May 181/2 The pantagrapher follows, or traces, with his pantagraph, the course of the stitches in the sketch of the pattern to be produced. 1897 *Advt. Brit. Embroidery Machine Co.*, The Jacquard producing the pattern and dispensing with the Pantagrapher.

Pantographic (pæntogræ·fik), *a.* Also (in sense 1) erron. penta-, panta-.

1. [f. as prec. + -IC.] Pertaining to or of the nature of a pantograph. In quot. 1759 *fig.* Reproducing copies like the pantograph.

1759 STERNE *Tr. Shandy* I. xxiii, From the honourable devices which the Pentagraphic Brethren of the brush have shewn in taking copies. 1875 KNIGHT *Dict. Mech.* s.v., A system of connected pantographic levers. 1890 W. J. GORDON *Foundry* 175 The prettiest process of all is the pantagraphic one;..The tiny fingers scratching so quietly and humanly the long cylinder of copper once seen will never be forgotten.

2. [f. PANTO- + Gr. γραφικός GRAPHIC.] ?Able to write in every language or character. *nonce-use.*

1801 W. TAYLOR in *Monthly Mag.* XII. 583 The author is polyglottic as the hydra, pantographic as Fry's letter-foundery.

Pantogra·phical, *a.* [See -ICAL.] = prec. 1.

1828 WEBSTER, *Pantographical*, pertaining to [or] performed by a pantograph. 1831 CARLYLE *Germ. Poetry* in *Misc. Ess.* (1872) III. 243 We have no original portrait here, but a pantagraphical reduced copy of some foreign sketches.

Hence **Pantogra·phically** *adv.*: **a.** by means of or in the manner of a pantograph; **b.** in the manner of a general description.

a. 1884 in STORMONTH. **b.** 1890 in *Cent. Dict.*

Pantography (pæntǫ·grăfi). *rare.* [f. Gr. παντο- PANTO-, all + -GRAPHY.]

1. Complete description.

1828 WEBSTER, *Pantography*, general description; view of an entire thing. 1836 SMART, *Pantography*, description of *all*, view of an entire thing. (Also in later Dicts.)

2. The use of the pantograph. (So F. *pantographie* (Littré).) 1890 in *Cent. Dict.*

Panto-iatrical: see PANTO-.

Pantologic (pæntolǫ·dʒik), *a.* Also *erron.* panta-. [f. as PANTOLOGY + -IC.] Of or pertaining to pantology; of universal knowledge.

1858 J. BROWN *Horæ Subs., Educ. through Senses* Ser. I. (1862) 316 We may say of our time in all seriousness, what Sydney Smith said..of the pantologic master of Trinity—Science is our forte; omniscience is our foible.

So **Pantolo·gical** *a.*, dealing with pantology.

1808 (*title*) Fashionable Biography..with a Preface and Notes, Pantological and Pantogelastical. 1852 *Fraser's Mag.* XLV. 175 The development section of the new Pantological Museum. 1868 M. PATTISON *Academ. Org.* v. 266 Still less is the scientific habit generated by the pantological schemes now so much in favour.

Pantology (pæntǫ·lŏdʒi). Also *erron.* panta-. [f. Gr. παντο- PANTO-, all + -λογια -LOGY.] A survey or systematic view of all branches of knowledge; universal knowledge; also, a compendium of universal information.

1819 *Pantologia* IX, *Pantologia, Pantology*, a work of universal instruction, or science: a cyclopædia or encyclopædia. 1822 *Blackw. Mag.* XII. 56 You, North, are undoubtedly a living pantology. 1841 B. PARK (*title*) Pantology, a Systematic Survey of Human Knowledge. 1852 *Fraser's Mag.* XLV. 175 The celebrated Hokus will lecture ..on Pantology.

Hence **Panto·logist,** one who studies or is versed in universal knowledge. (Humorous or sarcastic.)

1840 *Fraser's Mag.* XXII. 148 *Multum legere non multa* is the student's motto—rather disregarded by the pantologists of the day. 1878 *Ibid.* XVII. 533 One more Pantologist—Professor of the Universal.

Pantomancer, etc.: see PANTO-.

Pantometer (pæntǫ·mĭtəɹ). Also *erron.* pantameter. [ad. F. *pantomètre* (1675 Bullet (title) *Usage du pantomètre*), f. Gr. παντο- PANTO-, all + μέτρον measure.] (See quots.)

1696 PHILLIPS (ed. 5), *Pantometer*, an Instrument in Geometry that serves to measure all sorts of Angles, Lengths and Heighths. 1823 CRABB, *Pantometre.* 1867 SMYTH *Sailor's Word-bk.*, *Pantometer*, an instrument for taking angles and elevations, and measuring distances.

b. Applied to other instruments.

a. 'A graduated level' (Gwilt *Archit.* 1842–76). **b.** An instrument for the mechanical production of portraits in profile (*Funk's Stand. Dict.* 1895).

Panto·metry. [f. Gr. παντο- PANTO-, all + Gr. -μετρία measurement.]

†**1.** Universal measurement: see quots. *Obs.*

[1571 DIGGES (*title*) A Geometrical Practise, named Pantometria, diuided into three Bookes, Longimetra, Planimetra, and Stereometria.] 1656 BLOUNT *Glossogr.*, *Pantometrie*, a measuring of all kinde of quantities: It is the title and subject of a Mathematical Book, set forth by one Mr. Digs. 1692 COLES, *Pantometry*, a measuring of all things. 1797 J. DAWES (*title*) Pantometry; or an Attempt to systematize every Branch of Admeasurement.

2. The use of the pantometer. (*Cent. Dict.* 1890.)

Hence **Pantome·tric, Pantome·trical** *adjs.*, of, pertaining to, or dealing with pantometry.

1828 in WEBSTER (both words).

Pantomime (pæ·ntǒmaim), *sb.* (*a.*) [ad. L. *pantomīmus* one who plays a part by dumb show, a ballet-dancer, ad. Gr. παντόμῑμος imitator of all, f. παντο- PANTO-, all + μῖμος mimic. So F. *pantomime* (1570 in Hatz.-Darm.); in Eng. the word was at first used in the L. form.]

PANTOMIME.

1. A Roman actor, who performed in dumb show, representing by mimicry various characters and scenes; hence, generally, a mimic actor; one who represents his meaning by gestures and actions without words; a pantomimist. Now only *Hist.*

2. A kind of dramatic entertainment in which the performers express themselves by gestures to the accompaniment of music, and which may be called a mime ballet.

3. An English dramatic performance, originally consisting of action without speech, but in its further development consisting of a dramatized tale, the dénouement of which is a transformation scene followed by the broad comedy of clown and pantaloon and the dancing of harlequin and columbine. Now a feature of the Christmas holidays.

4. Significant gesture without speech; dumb show.

5. *attrib.* passing into *adj.* Of the nature of pantomime (sense 3); pantomimic.

Pantomime, v.

1. *intr.* To express oneself by dumb show.

2. *trans.* To express or represent by pantomime or dumb show.

Pantomimic, a. Now rare. [See -ICAL.]

1. Of, belonging to, or of the nature of pantomime or dumb show.

2. Characteristic of or like a pantomime, in its quick or sudden transformations.

Pantomimical, a. Now rare.

Pantomimically, adv.

Pantomimist (pæ'ntmimist), sb.

Panton. Sc. (Now local.) Also -s.

Pantophagist (pæntǫ'fǎdʒist). [f. Gr. παντο-φάγος all-devouring + -IST.] A man or animal that devours things of all kinds; an omnivorous eater.

Pantophagous (pæntǫ'fǎgǫs). a.

Pantophagy (pæntǫ'fǎdʒi). sb.

Pantophoby. Obs.

Pantophobia (pæntŏfōʊbiǎ). *Path.*

Pantophobos, a.

Pantopod (pæ'ntǫpǫd). *Zool.*

Pantopragmatic (pæntopragmæ'tik), a. and sb.

Pantoscope (pæ'ntǫskŏʊp). Also *erron.* panta-.

Pantoscopic (pæntǫskǫ'pik), a.

Pantostomate (pæntǫ'stǒmeit), a. *Zool.*

Pantothere (pæ'ntǫθiǎr), sb. *Zool.*

Pantotype (pæ'ntǫtaip). Obs. [L. Panto- + Type.]

PANTRY.

Pantry (pæ'ntri), sb. Forms: a. 3-5 panetrie, 5 panetre; β. 5-6 pantery, 5-7 -trie, 5 pantry, panetry; γ. 6-7 pantrie, 6 pantrey, 7 pantry. 1. A. sb. A pantrie = OF. panetrie bread-room, bread-closet.

2. *attrib.* and *Comb.*, as pantry + coffin, -door, -knife, -linen, -window; pantry-boy, an assistant in the commissariat department or on a passenger ship; pantry-cock, a fancet with upward rising pipe.

Pants (pænts), sb. pl. A vulgar abbreviation of Pantaloons.

Pantun (pæ'ntun). Also erron. (Malay pantum (Devic in Littré Suppl.)) A verse-form in Malay.

PAP.

Pap (pæp), sb.[1] Forms: 5 pappe, 4-6 pappe, 4-7 papp. [Known from 15th c. Corresponds to MLG., LG. pappe, MG. papfe, Ger. pappe.] **1.** Soft or semi-liquid food for infants or invalids, made of bread, meal, etc., moistened with water or milk.

Pap (pæp), sb.[2] Forms: 3-7 pappe, 4-6 papp, 4-7 -(chiefly Sc. 5-6 palp, 6 paup). [Early ME. pappe, corresponds to Du. pap.] **1.** A teat or nipple: a. of a woman's breast (now arch. or northern).

Pap (pæp), v.[1] [f. Pap sb.[1]]

Pap (pæp), v.[2] Sc. and dial.

PAP.

Pap (continued). *b.* The pulp of an apple, esp. when roasted.

PaP, v.[2] *Sc. trans.* To feed with pap; to feed up.

Papa (pǎpā'). Also 8 pappa. a. F. papa.

Papable (pei'pāb'l), a. rare. [f. L. papa pope + -ABLE.]

Papacy (pei'pǎsi). [ad. med. L. papātia (Florence of Worc.) in Du Cange.] **1.** The office or position of pope (the Roman Catholic pope).

2. A parish priest or any member of the lower orders of the clergy in the Orthodox Eastern Church. Also in Gr. Church, papas.

Papal (pei'pǎl), a. [a. OF. papal, F. papal (13th c.) = Sp. papal, etc.] **1.** Of or pertaining to a pope, or to the pope, his dignity or office.

Papally, adv. In a papal manner; by the authority of the pope.

Papain (pǎpei'in). *Chem.*

Papal (pǎpā'l), sb. [a. Papal (1380 in Gower Mirour) or ad. eccl. L. papālis belonging to Papa.]

PAPALLY.

Papal-ine. Obs. [a. F. papaline.]

†Papalin, sb. Obs. [a. F. papalin, It. papalino.]

Papalism (pei'pǎliz'm). [f. Papal + -ISM.]

Papalist (pei'pǎlist). [f. as prec. + -IST. Cf. obs. F. papaliste.] A member of the papal party, an adherent of the papal system.

Papality (pǎpæ'liti). Obs. [a. F. papalité, ad. med.L. papālitas.] **1.** = Papacy.

Papalize (pei'pǎlaiz), v. [f. Papal + -IZE.]

PAPALTY.

†Papalty. Obs. [a. OF. papalté, papaulté (1550 Calvin in Godef. Compl.), mod.F. papauté.] = Papality.

†Papalize Papare Poema.

†2. Adhering to or supporting the pope; belonging to the Church of Rome; popish. Obs.

Papanal. a. *Path.*

Papaphobia (pei'pǎfōʊbiǎ). [f. Papa pope = Gr. -φοβία fear.]

Papa-political, a. *nonce-wd.* Of or pertaining to papal prelates, or prelates who act papally.

†Papal, arch. (Papar-archy.) Papal rule or sovereignty; government by a pope.

†Papary (pei'pǎri), rare. Papal rule or sovereignty; = Papacy.

Papas. Obs. forms of Papa.

Papate (pei'peit). rare. [ad. OF. papat (13th c. in Godef.) or ad. med.L. papātus (Du Cange).]

Papaveraceous (pǎpǎvǎreiʃǎs), a.

Papaverine (pǎpǎ'verīn), sb. *Chem.*

Papaverous (pǎpǎ'verǎs), a.

Papaw (pǎpǎ'). Forms: a. 6-7 papaio, 7-9 papaya, 8 pappaya, papay; papaw; 8 - papaya, 7-9 papah, 7 papah, 7 - papaw.

PAPER.

Pap (continued).

Papelard (pæ'pelǎrd), sb. Also 5 papelard. [a. F. papelard.]

Papelardy, Pape-lardie. [a. F. papelardie.]

Paper (pei'pǎr), sb. Also 3 papir, 4-6 papir, 5 papire, papyr, papire, 5-6 pauper, 5-7 papyre, etc. **1.** A substance composed of fibres interlaced into a compact web, made (usually) from various fibrous materials, as linen and cotton rags, straw, wood, certain grasses, etc., which are macerated into a pulp, dried, and pressed; used chiefly as a material for writing, printing, or drawing on, for wrapping things in, for covering the interior of walls, and for other purposes.

2. (Only in forms papaw, pawpaw.) Name in U.S. for a small N. American tree, Asimina triloba (N. O. Anonaceæ), with dull purple flowers and ovate leaves (papaw-tree); or for its oblong edible fruit, about 3 in. long.

Pap-boat, sb. [f. Pap sb.[1] + Boat sb.]

Supplement, p. 3873; Corrigenda, p. 4092; Spurious words, p. 4093; Books quoted, p. 4094

25 [Buluwayo] well filled with buildings, all single-storeyed, some brick, some tin, some 'paper' (i.e. wire-wove, ready-made in England, sent out in pieces), all with verandahs. *Ibid.* iii. 80 These 'paper' houses are common in Buluwayo—they are really wire-wove, with wooden frames, iron roofs, cardboard walls.

d. In various phrases and connexions, with allusion to writing or drawing; as *to commit to paper*, to write down; *to put pen to paper*, to commence writing, to write. *On paper*: in writing, in print; said esp. of something described or represented in a preliminary sketch or plan, in contrast to the reality; hence = in theory, theoretically.

1582 STANYHURST *Æneis*, etc. (Arb.) 139 But shal I looue the lady, so as Petrarck Laura regarded? In paper her dandling? her person neauer atayning? 1624 CAPT. SMITH *Virginia* IV. 161 All those..are rather things in words and paper then in effect. c1654 DOR. OSBORNE *Lett.* (1903) 146 The fellow thought that putting 'pen to paper' was much better than plain 'writing'. 1771 SMOLLETT *Humph. Cl.* 10 June i, A man may be very entertaining and instructive upon paper..and exceedingly dull in common discourse. 1795 WASHINGTON *Lett.* Writ. 1892 XIII. 64 All this looks very well on paper; but [etc.]. 1865 L. CARROLL *Alice's Adv. Wonderl.* vi. 122 Humpty Dumpty looked doubtful. 'I'd rather see that done on paper', he said. 1888 BURGON *Lives 12 Gd. Men* I. iii. 296 The intention..of committing to paper some recollections of the holy man.

†2. Paper bearing writing; written documents collectively. *Obs.*

1386 CHAUCER *Cook's T.* 40 Vp on a day whan he his papir soghte, that [etc.]. 1393 LANGL. *P. Pl.* C. xiv. 38 The marchante mote nede be lette lenger þen þe messagere; For þe parcels of hus paper and oþer pryuey dettes Wol lette hym, as ich leyve.

3. *Comm.* **a.** Negotiable documents, bills of exchange, etc. collectively. **b.** Paper money or currency as opposed to coin, bank-notes, etc.

a1674 CLARENDON *Hist. Reb.* xvi. § 241 The custom..being to make their payments in Paper by Assignations. 1727–41 CHAMBERS *Cycl.* s.v., I have no money to give you, but only Paper; Paper indeed as good as ready money. 1728 SWIFT *Answ. Memor.* Wks. 1755 V. II. 173 Will foreigners take our bankers paper? 1775 R. MONTGOMERY in Sparks *Corr. Amer. Rev.* (1853) I. 491 It will be necessary to send hard money here..as paper will not yet go down. 1824 BYRON *Juan* XVI. xxii, But rarely seen, like gold compared with paper. 1883 *Manch. Exam.* 14 Dec. 4/1 For three months' bills the terms were..2¾ per cent., but for January paper the rate was stiffer. *Mod.* The bankers will not look at his paper.

4. *slang.* **a.** Free passes of admission to a theatre or other entertainment; *transf.* persons admitted by free passes.

1873 *Routledge's Yng. Gentl. Mag.* Apr. 277/1 The house is filling well without the aid of paper or free tickets. 1885 *St. James's Gaz.* 30 Jan., Another point; I mean the distribution of 'paper', or free admissions. 1888 *Pall Mall G.* 19 May 4/2 How much paper there was in St. James's Hall yesterday we do not know, but the hall, in any case, must have been remuneratively full.

b. *U.S.* Marked cards for sharpers.

1894 MASKELYNE *Sharps & Flats* 43 In America..one may still find 'saloons' which are stocked entirely with this kind of 'paper' as the cards are called.

†5. *Herb paper, water paper*: suggested names for the papyrus plant. *Obs.*

1548 TURNER *Names of Herbes, Papyros*..It maye be called in englishe water paper, or herbe paper.

** Individual singular with *a*, and plural.

(The earliest sense here is 7, the *papers* which first attained to individual distinction being written documents. In 6 also, the specialized b. naturally took precedence of the general sense.)

6. A piece, sheet, or leaf of paper.

1628 EARLE *Microcosm.*, *A Childe*, His Soule is yet a white paper vnscribled with obseruations of the world. 1634 J. BATE *Myst. Nat. & Art* 30 Straine it through a browne paper rowled within a tunnel. 1718 MRS. EALES *Receipt* 5 Let 'em stand all Night in the Pan they are boil'd in, with a Paper laid close to 'em. 1833 J. H. NEWMAN *Arians* I. iii. (1876) 85 The mind is often compared to a tablet or paper...But, in truth, the mind can never resemble a blank paper. 1875 H. C. WOOD *Therap.* (1879) 19 Papers are medicated leaves or sheets of paper for external use.

b. A piece of paper serving as a wrapper or receptacle; often including the contents, a packet done up in paper, a small paper parcel; a paperful; a sheet or card of paper containing pins or needles stuck in it.

1511 GUYLFORDE *Pilgr.* (Camden) 39 The warden..toke a basyn full of folden papres with relyquis in eche of them. 1567 in Hay Fleming *Mary Q. of Scots* (1897) 508 Item xxiiij papir of prenis to the Quenis dule. 1662 J. DAVIES tr. *Mandelslo's Trav.* 227 A paper of Fruits and Conserves for the Desert. 1698 A. BRAND *Emb. Muscovy to China* 82 Two Papers of Thea. a1776 R. JAMES *Dissert. on Fevers* (1778) 48, I gave him half a paper more of the Powder. 1836 DICKENS *Sk. Boz* I. 229 A little basket which..contains a small black bottle and a paper of sandwiches. 1844 — *Mart. Chuz.* xix, Give me the paper of gloves. 1901 *Academy* 17 Aug. 138/1. 'I want a paper of pins'.

c. A curl-paper. (Usually in *pl.*)

1876 MISS BRADDON *J. Haggard's Dau.* ix. 122 Take their hair out of papers.

7. A sheet, leaf, or piece of paper, bearing writing; a document written or printed on paper, as a note, bill, or other legal instrument; in *pl.* written notes, memoranda, letters, official documents, etc. With quot. c1475 cf. F. *être sur les papiers de quelqu'un*, to be in his books, in his debt. † *Papers of concern*: cf. F. *papiers de conséquence, papiers d'affaires.*

[1364–5 *Rolls of Parlt.* II. 287/1 Surmettantz a eux qe sont Dettours, & ce voillent ils prover par lour papirs.] 1389 in *Eng. Gilds* (1870) 5 To kepe wel & trewely alle þe pointz of þis papir. c1475 *Partenay* 4735 Now full merily demene you amonge, For of his paupires strike oute plain be ye! 1590 SPENSER *F. Q.* I. xii. 25 Which he disclosing read thus, as the paper spake. 1682 BUNYAN *Holy War* 203 His name is Pitiless; so he has writ himself in all papers of concern, wherein he has had to do. 1706 MRS. RAY in *Lett. Lit. Men* (Camden) 208 As to my husband's papers I have put them all..into Mr. Dale's hands. 1750 GRAY *Long Story* 66 Papers and books a huge Imbroglio! 1824 J. JOHNSON *Typogr.* II. xvi. 573 Papers printed, by authority of either House of Parliament. 1861 C. KNIGHT *Pop. Hist. Eng.* VII. xxvi. 453 Mr. James Paull..moved for papers, upon which he proposed to ground grave charges against the late governor-general. 1872 YEATS *Growth Comm.* 99 From a state paper of the Doge Moncenigo we learn some particulars of the trade with Italy. 1902 BESANT *Five Yrs. Tryst* 29 'You've signed some paper or other, of course?' 'I've signed a dozen papers'. *Mod.* The honourable gentleman concluded his speech by moving for papers. The Prime Minister promised that papers should be laid on the table of the House.

†b. A note, fastened on the back of a criminal undergoing punishment, specifying his offence. *Obs.*

a1529 SKELTON *Sp. Parrot* 472 So myche papers weryng for ryghte a smalle ex[c]esse. a1548 HALL *Chron., Hen. VIII* 59 He so punyshed periurye with open punyshment & open papers werynge, that in his tyme it was lesse vsed. 1577 KNEWSTUB *Confut.* (1579) 82 b, Allegories, which are H. N. his best witnesses: be as those men who haue heretofore worne papers. 1588 SHAKS. *L. L. L.* IV. iii. 47 Why he comes in like a periure, wearing papers. 1593 — *2 Hen. VI*, II. iv. 31 Led along, Mayl'd vp in shame, with Papers on my back, And follow'd with a Rabble. 1688 R. HOLME *Armoury* III. 310/1 To stand on the Pillory..with Papers of his Offence set on his Back.

†c. *pl.* = STATE-PAPERS, as in *Office of His (Her) Majesty's Papers, Clerk, Keeper, Register of the Papers*; cf. also PAPER-OFFICE a. *Obs.*

Cf. 'Calendar of Documents relating to the History of the State Paper Office' in 30th *Rep. Dep. Kpr.* App. pp. 212–293. The 'Office of Her Majesty's Papers and Records for Business of State and Council' was established in 1578. About 1800 the terms 'papers of state', 'paper-office' etc. became superseded by those of 'State papers', 'State paper office' etc.

1612 in 30th *Rep. Dep. Kpr.* App. 225 The Othe of the Clerke of the Papers for matters of State. 1612 *Indorsement* ibid., A Register of the later Bookes and Papers of English business..delivered into the Office of the Papers at Whitehall, at the death of the Earle of Salisbury, late Lord Treasurer. 1629 SIR T. WILSON *Petition* ibid. 239 Clerk, Keeper and Register of Your Majesty's Papers and Records for business of State and Council. ?1782 *Ibid.* 270 To preserve the Papers of State for the use of the public. 1799 *Ibid.* 287 The King's papers require an arrangement applicable to the dispatch of business.

d. *pl.* The collection of documents which establish the identity, standing, etc., of an envoy, traveller, or other person; the certificates which accompany an officer's application for permission to resign; hence *to send in one's papers*, to resign; (*ship's papers*) the set of documents carried by a ship for the manifestation of her ownership, nationality, destination, etc.

1685–8 in *Black Bk. Admiralty* (1871) I. 29 To examine them well about their lading and likewise their papers and documents. 1794 in *Story's Pract. Prize Courts* (1854) 4 Every ship must be provided with complete and genuine papers. *Ibid.*, If there be false or colourable papers; if any papers be thrown overboard; ..if proper ship's papers are not on board. 1796 PITT *Let.* 2 Nov., I accompanied your memorial with all your papers. 1855 MACAULAY *Hist. Eng.* xx. IV. 473 A fine ship named the Redbridge...Her papers had been made out for Alicant. 1872 *Routledge's Ev. Boy's Ann.* Apr. 302/1, I sent in my papers, packed up my traps, and here I am. 1890 W. E. NORRIS *Misadventure* xvi, He wished him..to send in his papers before his marriage.

e. A set of questions in an examination, usually written or printed on one sheet; also, the written answers to such a set of questions.

1838 ARNOLD in Stanley *Life* (1844) II. 114 The recommendation of the Vice-Chancellor, that the Examinations should be conducted entirely through the medium of printed papers. *Ibid.*, We..know the value of printed papers, and we know also the advantages to be derived from a vivâ voce examination. 1852 BRISTED *5 Years in Eng. Univ.* I. 186 Our best classic had not time to floor the paper. 1859 FARRAR *Julian Home* xi. 131 The papers suited him excellently. 1861 M. BURROWS *Pass & Class* (1866) 21 The Pass papers occupy one day, the Class papers from four to five. *Mod.* I was busy correcting examination papers.

8. = NEWSPAPER, journal.

1642 PR. RUPERT *Declaration* 3 Those impudent unpunished papers cried daily in the streets. 1716 ADDISON *Freeholder* No. 19 ¶ 4 The Examiner was a Paper in the last Reign. 1727–41 CHAMBERS *Cycl.* s.v., We have daily Papers, weekly Papers, morning Papers, evening Papers..political Papers, literary Papers, Papers of entertainment, etc. 1810 LAMB *Let. to Manning* 2 Jan., Coleridge is bringing out a paper in Weekly Numbers, called the *Friend*. 1852 MRS. STOWE *Uncle Tom's C.* xix, She entered the room where St. Clare lay reading his paper. 1883 STEVENSON *Silverado Sq.* 14 The office of the local paper (for the place has a paper—they all have papers).

9. A written or printed essay, dissertation, or article on some particular topic. Now *esp.* A communication read or sent to a learned society.

1665 W. HOLDER *Elem. Speech* 113 A Paper presented to the Royal Society. 1700 T. BROWN *Amusem. Ser. & Com.* 2, I know not what Success these Papers will find in the World. 1754 CHATHAM *Lett. Nephew* iii. 16 Spectators, especially Mr. Addison's papers, to be read very frequently. 1790 *Trans. Soc. Arts* IX. 210 A short paper on the Cinnamon tree. 1882 *Nature* XXV. 351/1 The second paper was..on the system of dredging introduced..on the rivers of France. 1887 *Pall Mall G.* 28 Oct. 3/2 This new theory, on which a paper was read at the late meeting of the British Association.

II. *attrib.* and *Comb.*

10. Simple *attrib.* in special senses, passing into *adj.* **a.** Of paper; made or consisting of paper.

(Also, made of paper of a particular form or kind, as in a *large-paper* copy of a book, a *brown-paper* parcel, an *oiled-paper* bag, etc. See LARGE, etc.)

(Often unnecessarily hyphened to following sb. The hyphen is needed only when the combination itself is used attrib.)

1596 NASHE *Saffron Walden* Wks. (Grosart) III. 173 These Boyes paper-dragons that they let fly with a packthrid in the fields. 1662 J. DAVIES tr. *Olearius' Voy. Ambass.* 236 Certain Cords whereat hung Paper-Lanthorns. 1670 W. CLARKE *Nat. Hist. Nitre* 60 The paper-Bills on the walls..remain'd like the Gold unburn'd. 1707 HEARNE *Collect.* 1 May (O. H. S.) II. 10 The Bp...desires a large-paper Livy. *Ibid.* 2 June 17 A royal paper copy of Mill's N. T. 1708 *Ibid.* 8 Apr. 101, 3 small-paper Livys. 1757 [BURKE] *Europ. Settlem. Amer.* II. 297 Money of credit, which they commonly call paper currency. 1780 COWPER *Table-T.* 385 The inestimable 'Estimate' of Brown Rose like a paper-kite, and charmed the town. 1828 P. CUNNINGHAM *N. S. Wales* (ed. 3) II. 102 Our colonial council has lately committed a great error in prohibiting..all paper issues below one pound. 1849 NOAD *Electricity* 167 A thick paper bag. 1871 KINGSLEY *At Last* v, Paper-nests, ..like those of our tree-wasps at home, hang from the trees. 1875 KNIGHT *Dict. Mech.*, *Paper Collar*, one made from paper in imitation of linen. 1897 MARY KINGSLEY *W. Africa* 477 Seedy young men with the object to carrying paper parcels for fear of being taken for tailors. 1903 *Daily Chron.* 10 July 3/4 Paper-cover issues of scientific and other serious books.

b. *fig.* Like paper; slight, thin, flimsy, frail, feeble (as if made of paper).

1615 CROOKE *Body of Man* 60 The excellent proportion and structure..maketh this Paper-sconce high perill-proofe. a1716 SOUTH *Serm.* IV. iv. 177 What Paper Walls such persons are apt to inclose themselves with. 1730 FIELDING *Rape upon Rape* I. viii, Pox of my paper skull! 1804 COLLINS *Scripscrap* 4 Go patter to paperscull saps, do ye see. 1877 A. H. GREEN *Phys. Geol.* ii. 85 In some very finely laminated rocks as many as 30 or 40 layers may be counted in the thickness of an inch: such beds are..called Paper shales. 1891 *Labour Commission Gloss.*, *Paper Ship*, a ship built of inferior material and badly put together.

c. *fig.* Consisting of, pertaining to, or carried on by means of letters to journals, pamphlets, or books; literary. (Cf. 1 d.)

1592 NASHE *P. Penilesse* Wks. (Grosart) II. 16 So..was this Paper-monster, Pierce Penilesse, begotten. 1592 G. HARVEY *Foure Lett.* iv. Wks. (Grosart) I. 223 Meere Paper-bugs, and inckehorne-pads: or a greate deale worse. 1599 SHAKS. *Much Ado* II. iii. 249 Shall quips and sentences, and these paper bullets of the braine awe a man? 1636 PRYNNE *Unbish. Tim.* (1661) Ep. 22 Books of controversie, and paper-battels. 1641 MILTON *Animadv.* iv. Wks. (1847) 65/1 It will stand long enough against the battery of their paper pellets. 1672 CLARENDON *Ess.* Tracts (1727) 252 It thought it seasonable to discontinue those paper-skirmishes. 1727 W. STUKELEY in *Mem.* (Surtees) I. 199 My retreat secures me from malice and envy and all other kinds of paper-gall. 1761 *Ann. Reg.* 187 A very acrimonious paper war. 1895 C. R. B. BARRETT *Surrey* 80 A life of perpetual paper warfare.

d. Written on paper, in written form; *esp.* existing only 'on paper' (see 1 d) and not in reality; theoretical, hypothetical.

1638 CHILLINGW. *Relig. Prot.* I. Pref. to Auth. 'Charity Maint.' § 18 The paper fortresses of an imaginary Infallibility. 1658–9 *Burton's Diary* (1828) IV. 37 If they have a mind to break in upon a paper law. 1793 SMEATON *Edystone L.* § 122, I determined, from the paper materials that I had..at once to construct the models. 1802 M. CUTLER in *Life*, etc. (1888) II. 74 We see how insignificant the best constructed paper Constitution will prove when opposed to the interests and passions of men. 1854 H. MILLER *Sch. & Schm.* iii. (1857) 50, I remained simply a fictitious or paper cock-fighter. 1872 *Wharton's Law Lex.* (ed. 5), *Paper blockade*, the state of a line of coast proclaimed to be under blockade in time of war, when the naval force on watch is not sufficient. 1882 OGILVIE, *Paper baron, paper lord*, one who holds a title which is not hereditary, or holds it by courtesy. 1893 *Times* 2 May 10/1 Paper profits were divided as if they were real.

11. General Combs.

a. *attrib.* Of, pertaining or relating to, or used for, paper or papers; as *paper-case, -circulation, -clamp, -clip, -colour* (= white), *-excise, -factory, -fibre, -file, market, -merchant, -payment* (sense 3), *-press, -pulp* (see PULP), *-punch, -size, -stuff, -system* (sense 3 in quots.), *trade*, etc.

1679 OATES *Narr. Popish Plot* 48 Who..there drew out of a *Paper-Case a Paper. 1857 HUGHES *Tom Brown* I. viii, A leather paper-case. 1803 *Edin. Rev.* II. 114 The doctrine of unlimited *paper-circulation. 1875 KNIGHT *Dict. Mech.*, **Paper-clamp*, ..for holding newspapers, sheet music, periodicals. *Ibid.*, **Paper-clip*, a clasp for holding papers together. 1888 STEVENSON *Black Arrow* 11 He will turn *paper-colour. 1860 BRIGHT *Sp., Tax bills* 6 July (1876) 497 Persons who were interested in this question of the *paper-excise. 1862 H. MARRYAT *Year in Sweden* II. 400 Next year a *paper-factory will rise. 1871 KINGSLEY *At Last* xvi, The culture of bamboo for *paper-fibre. 1875 KNIGHT *Dict. Mech.*, **Paper-file*, a device to hold letters or other papers in a pack. 1871 KINGSLEY *At Last* xvi, To supply the United States' *paper market. 1600 J. PORY tr. *Leo's Africa* VIII. 307 Next followeth the streete of the *paper-merchants. 1822 COBBETT *Weekly Reg.* 11 May 353 The scheme for making *paper-payments perpetual. 1825 J. NICHOLSON *Operat. Mechanic* 291 The screws employed for *paper-presses are generally formed with such coarse threads, and so rapid a spiral, that the elasticity of the paper is sufficient to force it to run back. 1839 URE *Dict. Arts* 937 The two sheets of *paper pulp thus united are carried forward by the felt over a guide roller. 1900 *Dict. Nat. Biog.* LXI. 146/2 He started a paper-pulp manufactory at Chiswick. 1839 URE *Dict. Arts* 936 [A] sieve is employed to strain the *paper-stuff previously to its being used in the machine. 1803 *Edin. Rev.* II. 105 Dabblers in the *paper-system. 1823 in Cobbett *Rur. Rides* (1885) I. 398 We can have no war, as long as the paper-system lasts.

b. Objective and obj. gen., as *paper-blessing, -saving, -selling, -sparing, -using* adjs.; *paper-colourer, -dauber, -glosser, -holder, -maker, -making, -marbler, -reader, -seller, -sorter, -spiller, -splitting, -tester, -waster.* **c.** Instrumental and parasynthetic, as *paper-bound, -capped, -clothed, -collared, -covered, -mended, -palisaded, -panelled, -patched, -shuttered* adjs. **d.** Similative, etc., as *paper-thick, -white* adjs., *paper-whiteness*; *paper-like* adj.

1597 DRAYTON *Mortimeriados* S ij b, What *paper-blessing Charrecters are you? 1598 E. GILPIN *Skial.* (1878) 5 So euery *paper-clothed post in Poules To thee (Deloney) mourningly doth speake. 1872 *Routledge's Ev. Boy's Ann.* Apr. 261/2 To jump through a *paper-covered hoop. 1682 T. FLATMAN *Heraclitus Ridens* No. 78 (1713) II. 110 We shall ne'er have done, if every whiffling *Paper-dauber must be regarded. 1882 OGILVIE, **Paper-glosser*, a hot-presser for glossing paper or cards; one who gives a smooth surface to paper. 1663 GERBIER *Counsel* 93 *Paper-like walls. 1857 MRS. GATTY *Parables fr. Nat.* (1859) II. 33 Little pieces of his delicate paper-like bark. 1573–80 BARET *Alv.* P 77 A *paper maker, *chartarius*. 1832 BABBAGE *Econ. Manuf.* xxxi. (ed. 3) 320 If the author deals at once with the paper-maker. 1816 SINGER *Hist. Cards* 20 The art of *paper-making not being introduced into England before the reign of Henry VII. 1887 in Moloney *Forestry W. Afr.* 195 We think the West African Colonies specially adapted to the supply of paper-making basts. 1886 CASSELL, **Paper-marbler*, one who marbles or colours paper with veins in imitation of marble for book-binding, paper-hangings, etc. 1726 SWIFT *Adv. to Grub-Street Verse-Writers* iv, Lend these to *paper-sparing Pope. 1691 WOOD *Ath. Oxon.* II. 327 This grand scripturient *paper-spiller..Was strangly tost from post to pillar. 1875 KNIGHT *Dict. Mech.*, **Paper-splitting*, two pieces of muslin are firmly cemented on the sides of the paper and dried. By a pull on each piece the paper is split open. 1655 MRQ. WORCESTER *Cent. Inv.* xliv, A Key..which..hath its Wards and Rose-pipe but *Paper-thick. 1881 H. H. GIBBS *Double Stand.* 67 To supply..a *paper-using country with a required metal. 1682 *Modest Account* 13 For your Lordship to turn *Paper-waster. c1385 CHAUCER *L. G. W.* 1198 *Dido*, Up on a thikke palfrey *paper whit. 1874 R. TYRWHITT *Sketch. Club* 21 You have only the *paper-whiteness to stand for both.

12. Special Combs.: **paper-back**, a book with a paper back or cover; **†paper-bank**, a bank issuing notes; **paper-bark (tree)**, name for *Melaleuca Leucadendron* and species of *Callistemon*, Australian trees, of which the bark peels off in layers; **paper birch** (see BIRCH *sb.* 1 b); **paper-blurrer**, a contemptuous name for an inferior writer; **†paper-board**, pasteboard = BOARD *sb.* 4 (*obs.*); **paper-boy**, a boy employed to sell newspapers; **paper-chase**, the game of hare and hounds (see HARE *sb.* 3 b) when paper is used for the 'scent'; hence *paper-chaser, -chasing* adj.; **†paper-cigar**, a cigarette; **paper-cloth**, (*a*) a kind of cloth faced with paper; (*b*) a fabric made by Polynesians from the inner bark of the paper-mulberry and other trees; **paper-coal**, (*a*) a variety of coal or lignite of the Tertiary period, which splits into thin layers; (*b*) = DYSODYLE; **paper credit** (*Comm.*), 'credit given on the security of any written obligation purporting to represent property' (Wharton *Law Lex.* 1883); 'the term as commonly used includes book-debts, I.O.U.'s, and instruments of credit of all kinds' (Bithell *Counting-ho. Dict.* 1893); **paper-cutter**, (*a*) a paper-knife; (*b*) a machine for cutting the edges of paper; **paper day** (*Law*): see quot.; **paper-faced** *a.*, (*a*) having a face like paper, i.e. thin or pale; (*b*) faced with paper; **paper-fastener**, a metallic contrivance for fastening separate leaves of paper together more conveniently than a pin; **paper-feeder**, a workman or contrivance supplying a printing machine with sheets of paper: cf. FEEDER 8 a and c; **paper-folder**, an instrument for folding paper, as a paper-knife, or the folding-stick used in bookbinding; **paper-gauge, -gage** (*Printing*), = GAUGE *sb.* 12 a; **paper-hornet**, a hornet that makes a papery nest (cf. *paper-wasp*); **paper-hunt** = *paper-chase*; **paper-machine**, a machine for making paper; **paper-man**, a man employed in some way about paper, as a paper-maker, a paper-hanger, etc.; one who sells or supplies papers; **paper-marl**, a kind of marl occurring in thin layers; **paper minister** (*Sc. colloq.*), a minister who reads his sermons; **†paper-moth**, a moth of which the larva devours paper; *fig.* one who is constantly occupied with paper (cf. *bookworm*); **paper-mulberry**, a small tree (*Broussonetia*

papyrifera) allied to the mulberry, from the bark of which paper is made in China and Japan; **paper-muslin**: see quot.; **paper nautilus** = ARGONAUT 2; **†paper paste** [= F. *carton pâte*], *papier mâché*; **paper pholas**, see PHOLAS; **†paper-plant**, papyrus; **†paper-plot**, the plot of a play, etc., drawn up on paper; **paper poplar**: see POPLAR; **paper priest**, ? = *paper minister*; **paper-reed**, the papyrus; **†paper-royal**: see ROYAL; **paper-ruler**, an instrument used for, or person employed in, ruling straight lines on paper, a ruler; **paper-rush**, the papyrus; **paper sailor**, the argonaut or paper nautilus; **paper-shell**, anything with a very thin shell, as a soft-shelled crab; **paper-spar**, a form of calcite occurring in very thin plates (also called *slate-spar*); **†paper-stealth**, literary piracy, plagiarism; **paper-stock**, raw material from which paper is made; **†paper-table**, a sheet or leaf of paper; **paper-tree**, name for various trees and shrubs from which paper is made, as the Chinese *paper-mulberry*, *Daphne cannabina*, *Edgeworthia Gardneri*, and *Trophis aspera*, all of the East Indies; **paper-washing** (*Photogr.*), water in which silver prints have been washed, esp. before toning, which often contains a considerable proportion of silver; **paper-wasp**, a wasp that constructs its nest of a papery substance made from dry wood moistened into a paste; **paper-weight**, a small heavy flat-bottomed object, of stone, metal, glass, etc., often ornamental, intended to be laid upon loose papers to prevent their being removed or disarranged; **paper window**, a window in which paper is used instead of glass; hence **paper-windowed** *a.*; **paper-work**, (*a*) work in paper, a structure made of paper; (*b*) a writing, a literary work; (*c*) the written work of a student in a class or examination; **paper-works**, a set of buildings in which paper is made, a paper-factory, paper-mill; **†paper-worm** = BOOKWORM 2.

1899 R. KIPLING *Stalky* 35 There are a pile of *paper-backs on that shelf. 1796 MORSE *Amer. Geog.* II. 26 Two trading-companies, ..an Insurance company, and a *paper-bank. 1846 STOKES *Discov. Austral.* I. v. 106 The face of the country was covered with specimens of the red and white gum, and *paper bark tree. 1866 *Treas. Bot.* 197 *Callistemon.* ..The outer bark of some of the kinds..peel off in layers, hence the trees are called Paper Bark trees. *Ibid.* 141 The *Paper Birch, *B[etula] papyracea*, so called from the brilliant white colour of the bark of young trees, is an American species. 1581 SIDNEY *Apol. Poetrie* (Arb.) 61, I, that..am admitted into the company of the *Paper-blurrers. 1652–62 HEYLIN *Cosmogr.* III. (1682) 182 Every foolish and idle paper-blurrer. 1852 K. H. DIGBY *Compitum* VI. 269 The conventional, exaggerated effusions of mere paper-blurrers. 1549 *Bk. Com. Prayer* (Colophon), Bounde..in *Paper Boordes. 1876 BESANT & RICE *Gold. Butterfly* v. 38 The *paper-boy was beginning, with the milkman, his round. 1856 DICKENS *Scapegrace* in *Househ. Wds.* XIII. 28/2 What leapers of brooks, what runners in *paper chases! 1884 *Manch. Exam.* 6 Dec. 5/4 There are by-roads and field-paths enough..to satisfy the wants of the *paper chasers. 1884 C. DICKENS *Dict. Lond.* 28/1 There is plenty of cross-country sport promoted by the *paper-chasing clubs. 1833 MARRYAT *P. Simple* xvii, A *paper segar. 1843 [see CIGARETTE]. 1852 DICKENS *Bleak H.* xliii, Walking about..smoking little paper cigars. 1843 HUMBLE *Dict. Geol. & Min.*, **Paper coal*..composed..of a congeries of many kinds of leaves. 1896 CHESTER *Dict. Names Min.*, *Paper-coal*, an early name for dysodile, alluding to the paper-like leaves in which it occurs. a1697 [? POLLEXFEN] *Disc. Trade* A v, *Paper Credit ever was, and will be, necessary for the carrying on of Trade. 1704 *Lond. Gaz.* No. 3991/3 They have set up a sort of Paper Credit at Strasburg, where they pay..in Bills. 1734 POPE *Ep. Bathurst* 39 Blest paper-credit! last and best supply! That lends Corruption lighter wings to fly! 1803 *Edin. Rev.* II. 102 Paper-credit is the visible sign of public credit, and identical with it. 1829 LYTTON *Disowned* xxxv, A pause ensued..Lord Borodaile played with a *paper-cutter. 1901 *Harper's Mag.* CII. 797/1 There he was fitted out with everything he wanted, down to a silver paper-cutter. 1838 CHITTY *Archbold's Pract. Crt. Q. B.* (ed. 6) 101 In each of the courts there are certain days in each term called **Paper Days*, because the court, on those days, hear the causes which have been entered in the paper for argument before they enter upon motions. 1597 SHAKS. *2 Hen. IV*, v. iv. 12 Thou *Paper-fac'd Villaine..Thou thin man. 1892 GREENER *Breech Loader* 174 The wadding used in the shot-gun is of three varieties..3rd, a hard felt paper-faced wad, ..the 'pink edge' or Field wad. 1864 *U. S. Patent Specif.* No. 43,435 A new and useful Legal Cap-*Paper Fastener. 1867 *Patent Specif.* No. 2275 An eyelet and paper fastener combined. 1897 *Daily News* 9 Dec. 7/7 [He] secured the envelope..with a paper-fastener, which he ran through the envelope, doubling over the ends. 1864 LOWELL *Fireside Trav.* 123 A useful old jackknife will buy more than the daintiest..*paper-folder. 1875 KNIGHT *Dict. Mech.*, *Paper-folder*, a bone knife used in folding paper, folding signatures for sewing, and feeding paper from the bank to the press. 1886 *Pop. Sci. Mo.* XXVIII. 642 The positions of the *paper-hornets' nests..are variously asserted to be indicative of a 'hard' or 'open' winter, as they chance to be placed in the upper or lower branches of a tree. 1871 *Routledge's Ev. Boy's Ann.* Jan. 52 Hilton backed up Gordon at the *paper-hunt yesterday. 1839 URE *Dict. Arts* 937 The pulp being diluted to a consistency suitable for the *paper machine, is delivered into a vat. 1619 PURCHAS *Microcosm.* lv. 522 The Printer.., Inke-man, *Paper-man, Corrector. 1753 H. WALPOLE *Lett.* (1846) II. 469, I have..paper-men to scold. 1707–12 MORTIMER *Husb.* (1721) I. 87 *Paper-Marle, which lies near Coals, and [is] like Leaves or Pieces of brown Paper, only 'tis something lighter for Colour. 1854 H. MILLER *Sch. & Schm.* v. (1857) 86 The skin-flint wife of a *paper minister. 1698 FARQUHAR *Love & Bottle* III. i, Are my clothes so coarse, as if they were spun by those lazy spinsters the Muses?..Do my hands look like *paper-moths? 1777 G. FORSTER *Voy. round World* I. 354 Cloth made of the bark of the *paper-mulberry, which we commonly called the cloth-tree. 1872 OLIVER *Elem. Bot.* II. 133 The Paper Mulberry..furnishes to the Polynesian Islanders the useful Tapa cloth, which is fabricated from its fibrous bark. 1864 WEBSTER, **Paper-muslin*, glazed muslin, used for linings, and the like. 1763 W. LEWIS *Comm. Phil. Techn.* 367 This varnish, mixed with ivory-black,..is applied..on the dried *paper paste. 1597 GERARDE *Herbal* I. xxvii. § 4. 37 This kinde of reede, which I haue englished Paper reede, or *Paper plant, is the same..that paper was made of in Egypt. 1628 FORD *Lover's Mel.* III. iii, Enter Palador, Aretus, Corax (with a *paper-plot). 1716 M. DAVIES *Athen. Brit.* II. 56 His Book limited not his design, nor his Paper-Plot his undertakings. 1781 *Reading not Preaching* II. 11 Let our *paper-priests and reading clergy apply this to themselves. 1597 *Paper Reede [see *paper-plant* above]. 1611 BIBLE *Isa.* xix. 7 The paper reeds by the brookes..shall wither. 1727–41 CHAMBERS *Cycl.* s.v. *Paper*, The description given by Pliny of the *Papyrus*, or *Paper-rush. 1884 MILLER *Plant-n.*, Paper-reed, or Paper-rush, of the Nile, or of the Ancients. 1843 HUMBLE *Dict. Geol. & Min.*, *Argonauta*, the *Paper Sailor. 1901 *Daily Chron.* 14 Nov. 3/4 The Argonaut or Paper Sailer..so called from the delicate consistence of its shell. 1890 *Century Dict.* s.v., When the shell has hardened..the *paper-shell [crab] becomes a crackler. 1893 KATE SANBORN *Truthf. Wom. S. California* 132, 190 California paper-shell almond trees. 1647 H. MORE *Song of Soul* I. II. xxxix, The words that he by *paper-stealth had got. 1875 KNIGHT *Dict. Mech.*, **Paper-stock Bleacher*..for expressing the bleaching material from paper-stock, without having recourse to the draining-vat... *Paper-stock Washer*, a machine for cleansing shredded rags preparatory to pulping. 1591 SYLVESTER *Du Bartas* I. v. 908 Blush not (my book)..To bear about upon thy *paper-Tables [F. *paints sur ton blanc papier*], Flies, Butter-flies, Gnats, Bees, and all the rabbles Of other Insects. 1839 URE *Dict. Arts* 940 Processes..in China to make paper with the inner bark of their *paper-tree..or Chinese mulberry. 1884 MILLER *Plant-n.*, Indian Paper-tree, *Daphne cannabina* and *Edgeworthia Gardneri*. *Ibid.*, Paper-tree, of Siam, *Trophis aspera*. 1858 SIMMONDS *Dict. Trade*, **Paper-weight*, a fancy ornament for keeping loose letters or papers on a table or desk from blowing about. 1893 Q. [COUCH] *Delectable Duchy* 283 He spread the plan on the table, with a paper-weight on each corner. 1580 HOLLYBAND *Treas. Fr. Tong*, *Vn Chassis*, a *paper window. 1683 MOXON *Mech. Exerc.*, *Printing* 361 The Journey-men..make every Year new Paper Windows, whether the old will serve again or no. 1889 *Pall Mall G.* 26 Feb. 2/2 We were shown to a clean *paper-windowed room. 1587 HARRISON *England* II. xv. (1877) I. 268 Many goodlie houses..yet they are rather curious to the eie like *paper worke, than substantiall for continuance. 1599 *Broughton's Lett.* ix. 32 Euery later paperwork of yours is but a Tautology of the former. 1898 F. HARRISON in *19th Cent.* Nov. 802 Books are tested, precisely like an undergraduate's paper-work. 1900 *Daily News* 15 Dec. 6/1 The paper work is much above the average, though as yet only the well-educated part of the audience undertakes paper work. 1841 DOUGLAS in *Proc. Berw. Nat. Club* I. No. 9. 246 They reached Mill-Bank *paper-works. 1902 *Westm. Gaz.* 18 Mar. 2/1 The great paper works at Bermondsey, founded in 1803. 1691 WOOD *Ath. Oxon.* II. 316 Prynne..was one of the greatest *paper worms that ever crept into a closet or library.

Paper (pēⁱ·pəɹ), *v.* [f. prec. sb.]

1. *trans.* To write or set down on paper; to write about, describe in writing. Also *absol.* or *intr.* (quot. 1606). Now *rare.*

1594 CAREW *Tasso* (1881) 116 Foorthwith then ech ones name is papered. 1606 WARNER *Alb. Eng.* XIV. To Rdr. (1612) 337 Set is the souereigne Sonne did shine when paperd laste our penne. 1655 *Nicholas Papers* (Camden) II. 341 How farther to deale with them I will not paper with my sence therein. 1865 F. T. BUCKLAND *Curios. Nat. Hist.* Ser. III. (1882) 31 A lady..asked him if he was Robinson Crusoe that Mr. Buckland had papered. 1886 STEVENSON *Kidnapped* 185 I'll have to paper your friend from the lowlands.

2. To enclose in, put *up* in, or cover with paper; to stick (pins, etc.) in a sheet or card of paper.

1599 [see PAPERED]. 1683 MOXON *Mech. Ex.*, *Print.* xxi. ¶ 2 The Boy Papers up each sort in a Cartridge by it self. 1718 MRS. EALES *Receipt* 6 Put 'em in Pots or Glasses, paper 'em close. 1832 BABBAGE *Econ. Manuf.* xix. (ed. 3) 183 A woman gains about 1s. 6d. per day by papering [pins]. 1871 *3rd Rep. Dep. Kpr. Irel.* 33 The following, being unsuitable for the cartons, have been papered and indorsed.

3. To stick paper upon (a wall, etc.); to furnish or decorate (a room) with paper-hangings. (In quot. 1774 the thing stuck on is the subject of the vb.)

1774 *Westm. Mag.* II. 95 Bills plaister posts, songs paper ev'ry wall. 1775 ASH, *Paper*, to adorn with paper, to furnish with paper hangings. 1823 J. BADCOCK *Dom. Amusem.* 170 Walls..may be papered immediately. 1884 G. ALLEN *Philistia* I. 164 I've had my room papered again since you saw it last.

b. To line with paper.

1683 MOXON *Mech. Exerc.*, *Printing* xxii. ¶ 1 Of Papering and Laying the Case. *Ibid.*, The other sides of the Box, he Papers so smooth and tight.

c. *Bookbinding.* To paste the end-papers and fly-leaves at the beginning and end of (a volume) before putting on the cover.

1875 *Ure's Dict. Arts* I. 423 The books..having been..'folded, collated, placed and sewn', and afterwards 'papered'.

d. *To paper out*: to exclude by papering.

1855 MRS. H. A. ROPES *Six Months Kansas* (1856) 87 We must paper out the cold wind.

4. To supply or furnish with paper.

1883 *N. Y. Even. Post* 13 May, The paper-manufactures are able to paper the country for a year in..less than a year. 1890 *Sat. Rev.* 10 May 583/1 Two stately volumes, very handsomely printed, papered, and otherwise got up.

b. *slang.* To fill (a theatre, etc.) by means of free passes: see PAPER *sb.* 4 a.

1879 WEBSTER *Suppl.* s.v., The house is well papered to-night. 1885 *Punch* 31 Jan. 53/2 When on the first night of a new piece the house is badly 'papered', the effect is likely to be fatal. 1897 W. C. HAZLITT *Four Gen. Lit. Fam.* I. III. i. 229 The modern practice of papering the theatres was comparatively unknown.

5. To treat in any way with paper, *e.g.* to smooth with sand-paper.

1875 *Carpentry & Join.* 144 This will scrape down the surface of the wood until it is ready for 'papering', i.e. being further smoothed by glass or sand paper.

†Pa·per-book. *Obs.* [f. PAPER *sb.* + BOOK.]

1. A book of blank paper to write in.

1548 ELYOT *Dict.* s.v. *Codex*, *Cartacens codex*, a paper booke. a1568 ASCHAM *Scholem.* I. (Arb.) 26 After this, the childe must take a paper booke, and sitting..by him self, let him translate into Englishe his former lesson. 1642 HOWELL *For. Trav.* (Arb.) 23 In reading hee must couch in a faire Alphabetique paper-book the notablest occurences. 1747 CHESTERF. *Lett.* (1774) I. xc. 266 To take memorandums of such things in a paper book. 1751 EARL ORRERY *Remarks Swift* (1752) 129 On his birth-day..I sent him a paper-book, finely bound.

2. *Law.* A copy of the demurrer book which contains the pleadings on both sides in an action, when the issue is one of law, not of fact.

1768 BLACKSTONE *Comm.* III. xxi. 317 Copies thereof, called paper-books, are delivered to the judges to peruse. 1796 *Mod. Gulliver* 152 Pleas and paper books conclude this term. 1818 CRUISE *Digest* (ed. 2) II. 472 He had compared the case of Smith *v.* Parker in the report, with the paper-book, which was delivered to one of the Judges who then sat upon the bench. 1872 *Wharton's Law Lex.* (ed. 5), *Paper book*, the issue in law, etc., upon special pleadings, formerly made up by the clerk of the papers..an officer for that purpose, but now by the plaintiff's attorney or agent.

Papered (pēⁱ·pəɹd), *ppl. a.* [f. PAPER *v.* + -ED [1].] Covered, lined, decorated, etc., with paper.

1599 T. M[OUFET] *Silkwormes* 56 Their papred boord whereon they take repast. 1785 PEACOCK in *Phil. Trans.* LXXV. 368 Slip the papered board..into the recess. 1810 CRABBE *Borough* xviii. 307 There mark the fractured door and paper'd pane. 1869 E. A. PARKES *Pract. Hygiene* (ed. 3) 127 The ordinary plastered and papered walls.

Paperer (pēⁱ·pərəɹ). [f. as prec. + -ER [1].] One who papers (see the verb); *spec.* one who papers a room, a paper-hanger; one who fixes pins in paper, as the final process in their manufacture.

1844 MRS. CARLYLE *Lett.* I. 292 The painter, preparatory to the paperer,..has kept me expecting him till now. 1875 *Ure's Dict. Arts* III. 580 The pins are then taken to the paperers, who are each seated in front of a bench.

Pa·perful. [-FUL 2.] As much as fills a paper.

1722 DE FOE *Col. Jack* (1840) 45 There was a great deal in it [a bag of money], and among it a paper-full by itself.

Pa·per-hanger. A man whose business it is to cover or decorate the walls of rooms, etc., with paper-hangings.

1809–12 MAR. EDGEWORTH *Vivian* xii, The vulgar present, full of upholsterers and paper hangers,..pressed upon his attention with importunate claims. 1901 *J. Black's Carp. & Build., Home Handicr.* 42 It is more general to pass the paperhanger's brush down it first and follow this by applying a paperhanger's roller.

Pa·per-hanging.

1. *pl.* Paper, usually printed in ornamental designs, used for covering and adorning the walls of a room, etc. (so called as taking the place of the cloth hangings formerly used); wall-paper. Rarely in *sing.* A piece or length of wall-paper.

1693 *Lond. Gaz.* No. 2899/4 At the Warehouse for New-fashion'd Hangings,..are made and sold strong Paper-Hangings,..at Three-Pence..per Yard. 1759 SYMMER in *Phil. Trans.* LI. 365, I was surprised to find it..sticking against the paper-hangings of my room. 1867 SMILES *Huguenots Eng.* vi. (1880) 101 The art of printing paper-hangings was introduced by some artizans from Rouen.

2. The decorating of a room with wall-paper.

Mod. An expert in paper-hanging.

Paperie, obs. Sc. form of POPERY.

Paperiness (pēⁱ·pərinès). [f. PAPERY *a.* + -NESS.] Papery quality.

1890 *Athenæum* 26 Apr. 537/3 When he has rid his surfaces of a certain dryness and 'paperiness'.

Papering (pēⁱ·pəriŋ), *vbl. sb.* [-ING [1].] The action of the verb PAPER; covering or decoration with paper. **b.** *concr.* Paper with which the walls of a room are covered, paper-hangings.

1825 *Greenhouse Comp.* I. 248 The most suitable colours..for the temporary painting, chalking, or papering. 1843 MRS. CARLYLE *Lett.* I. 203 Your modest allowance for painting and papering. 1883 *Harper's Mag.* Feb. 365/1 This room remains in its original state, with the exception of the papering.

Pa·per-knife. A knife of ivory, bone, wood, or other substance, used to cut paper along a fold, esp. to cut open the leaves of an uncut book.

1806–7 J. BERESFORD *Miseries Hum. Life* (1826) VIII. iii, Being reduced to make a paper-knife of your finger. 1848 THACKERAY *Lett.* 28 July, A paper-knife with a Mother of pearl blade. 1889 BESANT *Bell St. Paul's* II. 137 Standing thoughtfully at a table, playing with a paper-knife.

Hence **Pa·per-knife** *v.*, to cut with a paper-knife.

1898 *Academy* 17 Sept. 267/2 A fresh batch of publications ..has reached us. The first to be paper-knifed was *The Meaning of Education.*

Pa·per-mi·ll. A mill in which paper is made.

1498 *Privy Purse Exp. Hen. VII* 25 May (in Bentley *Excerpta* (1831) 117), For a rewarde yeven at the paper mylne, 16s. 8d. 1545 ELYOT, *Chartariæ officinæ*, paper mylles. 1593 SHAKS. *2 Hen. VI*, IV. vii. 41. a1658 CLEVELAND *Pet. Poem* 64 Where Scholars Teeth are their own Paper-mills. 1707 J. STEVENS tr. *Quevedo's Com. Wks.* (1709) 227 As the Rag-women do for the Paper-Mills. 1825 J. NICHOLSON *Operat. Mechanic* 370 A very large and capital paper-mill, at Maidstone, in Kent, which is the principal seat of the paper trade in England. 1875 *Ure's Dict. Arts* III. 482 Paper-mills, moved by water-power, were in operation in Tuscany at the commencement of the 14th century.

Hence **Pa·per-miller**, a man who works in a paper-mill.

1865 DICKENS *Mut. Fr.* IV. vi, No jealous paper-miller.

Pa·per mo·ney. [PAPER *sb.* 1, 3.] Negotiable documents used instead of money, esp. bank-notes, passing unquestioned from hand to hand; more strictly, a paper currency, which by the law of the country represents money and is a legal tender.

[Cf. c1400 MAUNDEV. (Roxb.) xxv. 117 He [the Grete Caan] makez na monee bot owþer of lether or of papire.]

1691 C. MATHER *Consid. Bills Credit* in A. M. Davis *Tracts* (1902) 13, I therefore cannot a little wonder at the great indiscretion of our Countrymen who Refuse to accept that, which they call Paper-Mony, as pay of equal value with the best Spanish Silver. a1697 [? POLLEXFEN] *Disc. Trade* A 5 We have improved Paper Credit, and turn'd it into Paper-Money, by giving Notes and Bills the privilege of a new Specie of Coin, and using them for making of most great payments. *Ibid.* A. 4 For promoting the sending of Silver Money abroad, and using Paper Money at home. 1735 BERKELEY *Querist* § 219 Whether the abuse of banks and paper-money is a just objection against the use thereof? 1776 ADAM SMITH *W. N.* II. ii. (1869) I. 291 There are several different sorts of paper money; but the circulating notes of banks and bankers are the species which is best known. 1821 in Cobbett *Rur. Rides* (1885) I. 35 The desolating and damnable system of paper-money. 1880 BON. PRICE in *Fraser's Mag.* May 669 What is real paper money? The answer is, banknotes. They are written promises by a bank or Government to pay a certain quantity of coin to the bearer on demand.

attrib. 1740 W. DOUGLAS *Disc. Curr. Brit. Plant. Amer.* 19 We see..in our Paper Money Colonies, the Currencies have incredibly depreciated from Sterling. 1823 in Cobbett *Rur. Rides* (1885) I. 268 To put an end to the gains of the paper-money people. 1828 P. CUNNINGHAM *N. S. Wales* (ed. 3) II. 93 [Each] has charged about the same paper-money price for his articles.

Papern (pēⁱ·pəɹn), *a.* Now *dial.* [f. PAPER *sb.* + -EN [4].] Of paper.

1616 J. LANE *Cont. Sqr.'s T.* v. 441 With deedles wordes ..papern shott. *Ibid.* VII. 542 But kinge Cambuscan noold spend manie shott on papern-gunners barrelles (waxinge hott). [Now common in s. w. dial. Hampsh. to Cornw., e.g. 'papern shoes', 'a paperen bag': see Eng. Dial. Dict.]

†Paper-office. *Obs.* An office or place where documents were kept: cf. PAPER *sb.* 7. **a.** The older name for the STATE PAPER *Office*; spec. the place near Whitehall where the state papers used to be kept. **b.** A place attached to the King's (Queen's) Bench where legal documents were kept.

1637 WOTTON *Will*, Item I leave his said Majesty all the Papers..that perchance his Majesty will think fit to be preserved in his Paper-Office. 1670 EVELYN *Diary* 21 Oct., Mr. Jos. Williamson, Master of the Paper Office. 1704 J. HARRIS *Lex. Techn.* I. s.v., All..Letters of Intelligence, and many other Publick Papers communicated to the King's Council, or the two Secretaries of State, are afterwards transmitted to the Paper-Office, wherein they are all disposed in a place of good Security and Convenience within the King's Royal Palace. 1707 *Chamberlayne's St. Eng.* III. 692 The Custos Brevium, Nisi Prius, and the Paper Offices, are in the Queen's-Bench Office in the Temple. 1707 in Hearne *Collect.* 9 Aug. (O. H. S.) II. 32 The Keeper of ye Paper-Office at Whitehall. ?1782 in *30th Rep. Dep. Kpr.* App. 270 Paper Office, Application for the old office adjoining to Whitehall Chapel.

Pa·per-stai·ner. [STAINER, f. STAIN *v.*]

1. One who stains or colours paper. Humorously used for an author, esp. an inferior author.

1596 NASHE *Saffron Walden* Wks. (Grosart) III. 42 Let anie man but finde mee meate and drinke..while I am playing the paper stainer. 1771 *Gentl. Mag.* XLI. 201 The whole tribe of Paper-stainers, from the sleek Divine, to the more active Devil at the Printing Office. 1887 *Pall Mall G.* 10 Sept. 3/1 The..author..lacks something of the true poet, but rises far above the mere purposeless paper-stainer.

2. A maker of paper-hangings.

1756 MOUNSEY in *Phil. Trans.* L. 19 Mr. Butler, a paper-stainer, trying to make some discoveries for the better fixing of colours. 1819 *P. O. Lond. Direct.* 353 Vincent & Co., Paper-stainers. 1902 *Westm. Gaz.* 3 Oct. 4/3 The wife of a paper-stainer.

Papery (pēⁱ·pəri), *a.* [f. PAPER *sb.* + -Y.] Of the consistence of paper; resembling paper; thin or flimsy in texture.

1627 MAY *Lucan* IV. (1631) 5 So the Ægyptians saile with woven boates Of papery rushes. 1648 HERRICK *Hesper.*, *Oberon's Feast*, The hornes of papyrie butterflies. 1853 SEEMAN in *Pharmac. Jrnl.* XIII. 385 Texture from coriaceous to papery. 1900 *Daily News* 12 May 6/5 China silks ..look meagre and papery except when they are of the best.

[**Papescent**, error for PAPPESCENT in J. and subseq. Dicts.]

Papess (pēⁱ·pès). [ad. F. *papesse* (1567 in Hatz.-Darm.), It. *papessa* 'a shee-pope, a pope-lone' (Florio), med.L. *papissa*, f. *pāpa*: see -ESS [1].] A female pope; = POPESS.

Historically used of the alleged Pope Joan 853–55.

1620 BP. HALL *Hon. Mar. Clergy* II. ix. 196 Was the Historie of that their monstrous Papesse of our making? 1678 R. BARCLAY *Apol. Quakers* x. § 10. 294 *note*, Onuphrius annotations upon this Papess (or Popess). 1866 BARING-GOULD *Cur. Myths Mid. Ages, Antichr. & Pope Joan* 170 She is commonly called the Papess Joan.

‖Papeterie (papetrī·). [F., = paper-manufacture, paper-trade, stationery-case, f. *papetier* paper-maker, paper-merchant, in med.L. *papeterius* (1414 in Hatz.-Darm.) irreg. deriv. of *papier* paper.] A case or box, usually ornamental, for paper and other writing materials; a stationery-case.

1847 in WEBSTER. 1880 *Print. Trades Jrnl.* No. 31. 13 A combination of desk, papeterie, and dispatch-box.

†Pa·pey. *Obs.* Also pappey. [app. a deriv. of L. *pāpa* pope.] A fraternity of priests in Aldgate ward, London, or their residence.

1598 STOW *Surv.* 110 Then come you to the Pappey, a proper house, wherein sometime was kept a Fraternitie, or brotherhood of S. Charitie, and S. Iohn Euangelist, called the Papey, for poore impotent Priestes, (for in some language Priestes are called Papes) founded in the yeare 1430. 1790 PENNANT *London* (1813) 607.

Papey, obs. form of PAPAW.

†Pa·p-hawk. *Obs. rare*⁻¹. [f. PAP *sb.*[1] + HAWK.] A child at the breast, a suckling.

c1450 *Cov. Myst.* (Shaks. Soc.) 179 Popetys and pap-hawkes I [Herod] xal puttyn in peyne With my spere prevyn, pychyn, and to-pende.

Paphian (pēⁱ·fiăn), *a.* and *sb.* [f. L. *Paphi-us* adj. (f. *Paphos*) + -AN.] **A.** *adj.*

1. Of or belonging to Paphos, a city of Cyprus sacred to Aphrodite or Venus (the *Paphian Goddess, Paphian Queen*).

c1614 SIR W. MURE *Dido & Æneas* II. 753 The Paphyen Queen such brood did never beare. 1879 FARRAR *St. Paul* (1883) 403 The orgies of the Paphian goddess.

2. *transf.* Pertaining to love; *esp.* pertaining to, or devoted to, unlawful sexual indulgence; belonging to the class of prostitutes.

1656 BLOUNT *Glossogr.* s.v., Hence..Paphian fire or shot [is taken] for the fire or Arrows of Love. 1742 YOUNG *Night Thoughts* VIII. 994. 1812 BYRON *Ch. Har.* I. vii, Now Paphian girls were known to sing and smile. 1879 E. WALFORD *Londoniana* I. 27 The Paphian sisterhood.

B. *sb.* **1.** An inhabitant or native of Paphos.

2. A devotee of the Paphian Venus; a prostitute.

1811 BYRON *Hints fr. Horace* 690 In turns she'll seem a Paphian or a prude. 1828 P. CUNNINGHAM *N. S. Wales* (ed. 3) II. 270 A miraculously converted Paphian.

Pap-holy: see POPEHOLY.

Paphood (pæ·phud). *nonce-wd.* [f. PAP *sb.*[2] + -HOOD.] Infancy.

1837 *Fraser's Mag.* XV. 576 Betrothed to thee as thy 'little wife' since the days of paphood.

Papiay, obs. form of POPINJAY.

†Papi·colist. *Obs. rare.* [f. L. *pāpa* pope + *-cola* worshipper + -IST.] A 'worshipper of the pope', a papist. So **Papi·colar** *a.*

1633 T. ADAMS *Exp. 2 Peter* i. 17 The word Trinity, say our papicolists, is not found in the Scriptures. 1644 *Speculum Impietatis* 19 The Romish Papicolists are in arms. c1810 COLERIDGE in *Lit. Rem.* (1838) III. 364 As a German would have expressed himself, ..'a-not-of-the-Roman-Catholic-Papicolar-polemics-unmerited, sneer'.

‖Papier mâché (papye maʃe). Also with hyphen, and with simple *a* in *mache*, which is also found variously misspelt. [a. F. *papier* paper, *mâché* chewed, pa. pple. of *mâcher*:—L. *masticāre* to chew. (See below.)]

A substance consisting of paper-pulp or paper reduced to a pulp (often mixed with other substances), and shaped by moulding; used for boxes, jars, trays, various fancy articles, etc.; finer kinds consist of sheets of paper pasted together.

1753 MRS. DELANY *Life & Corr.* (1861) III. 262 The ceiling ornamenting with *papier-machée*. 1758 [R. DOSSIE] *Handmaid to Arts* III. iv. § 1. 407 Paper..is rarely made the subject of japanning till it is converted into *papier maché*. 1759 *Compl. Lett. Writer* (ed. 6) 229 A beautiful and exquisitely carved and gilt chariot of papier mashé. 1766 T. MARTYN *Connoisseur* No. 91 Some large and elegant Jars and Vases in *Papier macheé*. 1816 TINGRY *Varnisher's Guide* (ed. 2) xi, Colouring articles made of papier maché. 1879 G. PRESCOTT *Sp. Telephone* 305 Thin sheets of papier-maché.

b. *attrib.* (usually = made of papier mâché).

1753 MRS. DELANY *Life & Corr.* (1861) III. 260 A *papier-machée* ceiling. 1777 SIR A. I. ELTON in *Burke's Corr.* (1844) II. 137 A *papier-maché* snuff-box. 1899 *Daily News* 26 June 8/4 The foundry room, wherein the papier-mâché moulds, or matrices, receive the boiling lead and turn out complete castings of pages of type.

[*Note.* Although composed of French words, the name *papier mâché* appears not to be of French origin; it is not recognized in the French Dictionaries of the Académie, Littré, or Hatz.-Darm. (except in the sense of 'chewed paper', *papier mouillé*, and figurative uses of this: see Littré). The term is not in the *Description des Arts et Métiers..par l'Academie des Sciences* of 1761; the *Journal de l'Agriculture, du Commerce*, etc., of Sept. 1778, cites it from an English source, translating from the *Handmaid to Arts* of 1758 (see above); so later French works. It seems to be meant as French for 'mashed paper'. Cf. the instructions for making this substance in Boyle's *Uses of Nat. Things* iv, 'First soak a convenient quantity of whitish paper..then mash it in hot water', etc.]

Papilionaceous (păpiliŏnēⁱ·ʃəs), *a.* Also 7 papill-. [f. mod.L. *papiliōnāceus* (of insects), in F. *papilionacé* (Réaumur 1734); *papiliōnāceæ* (of plants), Ray 1682; f. L. *pāpiliōn-em* butterfly: see -ACEOUS.]

1. Of or pertaining to a butterfly or butterflies; of the nature of a butterfly; belonging to the butterfly tribe. Now *rare* or *Obs.*

1668 WILKINS *Real Char.* II. v. § 2. 126 Papilionaceous Fly. 1713 DERHAM *Phys.-Theol.* IV. xiii. 235 A good though very brief Description of the Papilionaceous Fly. 1771 *Gentl. Mag.* XLI. 401 He takes pleasure to impale for days and weeks the papilionaceous race with corking pins. 1837 T. HOOK *Jack Brag* xviii, Psyche..the lovely lively lady with the papilionaceous wings.

b. *fig.* Having the character of which a butterfly is taken as a type: cf. BUTTERFLY 2.

1832 CARLYLE *Misc.*, *Boswell's Johnson* (1857) III. 91 A bright papilionaceous creature. 1875 MISS BRADDON *Hostages to Fortune* I. i. 37 The women he has admired hitherto belong to the papilionaceous tribe.

2. *Bot.* Applied, from its fancied resemblance to a butterfly, to that form of flower found in most leguminous plants, having an irregular corolla consisting of a large upper petal (the *vexillum* or standard), two lateral petals (the *alæ* or wings), and two narrow lower petals between these (forming the *carina* or keel). Also said of the plant.

1668 WILKINS *Real Char.* II. iv. § 5. 96 Herbs..Papillionaceous: the flower having some resemblance to a Butterfly, as the blooms of Pease or Beans, &c. 1693 *Phil. Trans.* XVII. 766 Many papilionaceous and winged Plants. 1797 HOLCROFT *Stolberg's Trav.* (ed. 2) III. lxxviii. 191, I saw the..tree of Judas, covered with its..red papilionaceous flower. 1876 DARWIN *Cross-fertil.* i. 5 Papilionaceous flowers..offer innumerable curious adaptations for Cross-fertilisation.

Papilionine (păpi·liŏnəin), *a.* *Entom.* [ad. mod.L. *Papiliōnīn-æ* (fem. pl.), f. *papilio* butterfly, in mod. Zool. the name of the typical genus.] Belonging to the subfamily *Papilioninæ* or swallow-tail butterflies.

†Papi·lious, *a.* *Obs. rare*⁻¹. [irreg. f. L. *papilio* butterfly + -OUS.] Allied to the butterfly.

1733 CHEYNE *Eng. Malady* I. x. § 4 (1734) 98 Silk-worms, and the other Insects of the papilious Kind.

‖Papilla (păpi·lă). Pl. -æ. [L., = nipple, dim. of PAPULA swelling, pimple.]

1. *Zool.* and *Anat.* **a.** The nipple of the breast; the mamilla. (*rare* in Eng. use.)

[1398 TREVISA *Barth. De P. R.* v. xxxiv. (Bodl. MS.), Þe tette þe heed of þe pappe hatte papilla in latyne.] 1693 tr. *Blancard's Phys. Dict.* (ed. 2), *Papilla*, a red Excrescency in the middle of the Breast. 1727–41 CHAMBERS *Cycl.* s.v., The lacteal tubes, coming from the several parts of the breasts, terminate in the *Papillæ*.

b. Any minute nipple-like protuberance, usually soft and fleshy, in a part or organ of the body: *e.g.* those on the skin, specially abundant at the tips of the fingers and elsewhere, and constituting the apparatus for the sense of touch (*tactile papillæ*); those on the tongue (*circumvallate, conical, filiform, foliate*, and *fungiform papillæ*), most of which are connected with the sense of taste (*gustatory papillæ*); those at the tips of the Malpighian pyramids in the kidney (*renal papillæ*); those in the embryo which ultimately produce the teeth (*dental papillæ*); and those in various parts of insects and other invertebrates, *esp.* two malodorous organs which can be protruded from the abdomen in certain beetles. *Lachrymal papilla*: a slight protuberance on the edge of the eyelid, traversed by the lachrymal duct. *Optic papilla*: see OPTIC A. 2.

1713 DERHAM *Phys.-Theol.* IV. vi. 144 Mr. Cowper hath..given us very elegant Cuts both of the skin, and the Papillae. 1748 HARTLEY *Observ. Man* I. i. 43 The nervous Papillae which are the immediate Organ in the Senses of Feeling, Taste, and Smell. 1844 CARPENTER *Princ. Hum. Phys.* § 316 The *papillæ*,..are little elevations of the surface of the cutis, easily perceptible by the aid of a lens. 1853 *Ibid.* (ed. 4) § 279 The Dentinal pulp..makes its appearance in the form of a papilla, budding-out from the free surface of a fold or groove of the mucous membrane of the mouth. 1881 MIVART *Cat* 23 Each hair grows from a single dermal papilla only, of which it is the greatly prolonged epidermal covering. 1888 ROLLESTON & JACKSON *Anim. Life* 551 [In *Holothurioidea*] The tube feet are either partially or completely retractile, and furnished with a terminal disc..or they are conical *papillæ* without discs.

c. *Path.* A small papule or pimple.

1797 M. BAILLIE *Morb. Anat.* (1807) 152 Papillæ and pustules, somewhat resembling the small-pox. 1892 *Syd. Soc. Lex.*, *Papilla*..Also, a diminutive of *Papula*.

2. *Bot.* A small fleshy projection upon any part of a plant.

1848 CRAIG, *Papillæ*..in Botany, the minute puncta upon the surface of a leaf; the vesicles on leaves of twigs [etc.]. 1870 HOOKER *Stud. Flora* 37 Pepperwort..*papillæ* scale-like when dry. 1885 GOODALE *Physiol. Bot.* (1892) 153 In the earliest stage of its development the leaf is a mere papilla consisting of nascent cortex..and nascent epidermis.

Papillar (pæ·pilăɹ, păpi·lăɹ), *a.* [ad. mod.L. *papillār-is*: see next.] = next.

1830 R. KNOX *Béclard's Anat.* 143 Small papillar eminences, which are much more distinct upon the denuded dermis, than when seen through the epidermis. 1861 HULME tr. *Moquin-Tandon* II. VI. vi. 306 A case of papillar and vesicular inflammation.

Papillary (pæ·pilări, păpi·lări), *a.* [f. L. *papilla* (see above) + -ARY; cf. F. *papillaire* (1690 in Hatz.-Darm.).] Of the form or nature of a papilla; containing, furnished with, or consisting of papillæ; of, pertaining to, or affecting papillæ.

Papillary body: the papillary layer of the skin. *Papillary muscles*: bundles of muscular fibre springing from the walls of the ventricles of the heart and attached to the *chordæ tendineæ*.

1667 *Phil. Trans.* II. 492 Concerning the Tongue, the same Author [Malpighi] has discovered in it many little Eminences, which he calls Papillary. 1713 DERHAM *Phys.-Theol.* IV. v. (1727) 140 *note*, The outward Cover of the Tongue..under which lie papillary Parts. 1886 FAGGE & PYE-SMITH *Princ. Med.* (ed. 2) II. 613 The papillary layer of the cutis. 1899 *Allbutt's Syst. Med.* VII. 847 Irregular contraction of the papillary muscles.

b. *Bot.* Of the nature of a PAPILLA (sense 2).

1874 LUBBOCK *Wild Flowers* iii. 54 The papillary edge of the summit of the pistil is the stigma.

Papillate (pæ·pilĕt, păpi·lĕt), *a.* [ad. mod.L. *papillāt-us*, f. *papilla*: see -ATE [2] 2.]

1. Furnished or covered with papillæ.

1857 MAYNE *Expos. Lex.*, *Papillatus*..papillate. 1874 E. COUES *Birds N. W.* 629 Two short, obtuse cornua, which are thickly papillate. 1887 W. PHILLIPS *Brit. Discomycetes* 96 Hymenium same colour, papillate, granular.

2. Formed into a papilla, papillary.

1890 in *Cent. Dict.*

Papillated (pæ·pilĕ¹tėd), *a.* [f. as prec. + -ED [1].] = PAPILLATE *a.*

1828 STARK *Elem. Nat. Hist.* II. 69 Branchiæ projecting, in the form of scaly plates, papillated, or like cirri. 1834 McMURTRIE *Cuvier's Anim. Kingd.* 141 The neck invested with a plumeless and papillated skin. 1897 *Allbutt's Syst. Med.* II. 1058 A papillated, or a simple mouth.

Papillectomy. *Surg.* [f. PAPILLA + Gr. ἐκτομή excision.] The excision of papillæ.

1900 *Brit. Med. Jrnl.* 3 Feb. 248 Renal Papillectomy.

Papilliferous (pæpili·fĕrəs), *a.* [f. mod.L. *papillifer*, in F. *papillifère* (Littré), f. *papilla* + *-fer* bearing + -OUS.] Bearing papillæ.

1826 KIRBY & SP. *Entomol.* IV. 351 Cauda..5. Papilliferous (*Papillifera*). When at the last segment but one the tail exerts two soft fleshy organs, which secrete a milky fluid and yield a powerful scent. Ex. *Staphylinus.* 1866 *Treas. Bot.* 844/2 *Papillose, Papilliferous*, covered with minute soft tubercles or excrescences. 1900 *Brit. Med. Jrnl.* 20 Jan. 137 The perforation of papilliferous cysts.

Papilliform (păpi·lifǭɹm), *a.* (*erron.* papillæform.) [f. mod.L. *papilliform-is*, f. as prec. + -FORM.] Of the form of a papilla; nipple-shaped.

1828 STARK *Elem. Nat. Hist.* II. 396 Anus at the posterior extremity, and a papilliform filament near it. 1861 HULME tr. *Moquin-Tandon* II. III. iv. 143 The Leech then draws a small papilliform piece of the skin into its mouth. 1878 BELL *Gegenbaur's Comp. Anat.* 139 A thicker cuticular layer is formed on papilliform processes.

‖Papillitis (pæpiləi·tis). *Path.* [mod.L.: see -ITIS.] Inflammation of the optic papilla.

1892 *Syd. Soc. Lex.* s.v. *Papilla, congestion*, All cases of inflammation of the Optic disc are now usually designated Papillitis. 1899 *Allbutt's Syst. Med.* VII. 657 Attended with headache and a slight degree of papillitis.

‖Papilloma (pæpilōᵘ·mă). *Path.* Pl. **-ata.** [f. PAPILLA + Gr. ending -ωμα, -ōma = formation; cf. CONDYLOMA.] A tumour of the skin or of a mucous membrane, consisting of an overgrown papilla or group of papillæ, usually covered with a layer of thickened epidermis or epithelium; *e.g.* a wart, corn, condyloma, etc.

1866 A. FLINT *Princ. Med.* (1880) 45 A papilloma is composed of papillae, often very large and irregular in shape. 1873 T. H. GREEN *Introd. Pathol.* (ed. 2) 151 The Papillomata are new formations resembling in structure ordinary papillæ, and like these they grow from cutaneous, mucous, or serous surfaces.

Comb. 1897 *Allbutt's Syst. Med.* II. 1122 Papilloma-like growths in cysts. *Ibid.* IV. 837 A papilloma-like mass.

Hence **‖Papillomato·sis**, the formation of a papilloma; **Papillo·matous** *a.*, of, pertaining to, or of the nature of a papilloma.

1872 PEASLEE *Ovar. Tumors* 20 The benign papillomatous or dendritic form of tumor. 1897 *Allbutt's Syst. Med.* IV. 683 A small papillomatous growth. 1899 J. HUTCHINSON *Arch. Surg.* X. No. 38. 182 Family proclivity to cancer and to papillomatosis go together.

Papillose (pæ·pilōᵘs), *a.* [ad. mod.L. *papillōs-us*, f. *papilla*: see -OSE [1].] Full of or beset with papillæ or nipple-like projections.

1752 HILL *Hist. Anim.* 425 The Anas, with a naked papillose face. The Muscovy Duck. 1753 CHAMBERS *Cycl. Supp.* s.v. *Leaf*, *Papillose Leaf*, one whose surface is covered with little roundish protuberances, or vesicles. 1835–6 TODD *Cycl. Anat.* I. 532/1 The tongue..becomes soft and papillose. 1877–84 F. E. HULME *Wild Fl.* p. xvi, Burdock.—Anthers exserted: filaments papillose.

Hence **Papillo·sity**, papillose condition.

1881 WEST in *Jrnl. Bot.* X. No. 220. 115 The papillosity of the upper part of the back of the nerve alone thoroughly distinguishes it.

Papilloso-, used as combining adverbial form of mod.L. *papillōsus* PAPILLOSE, as in **Papillo·so-a·sperate** *a.*, rough with closely set papillæ.

1846 DANA *Zooph.* (1848) 491 Surface of the coralla papilloso-asperate.

Papillote (pæ·pilǫᵘt, -ǫt). Also 8 **papillot**, **papilliot(e**, 8–9 **papillotte**, 9 **papilotte.** [a. F. *papillote* (Mme de Sevigne a1696), app. a verbal sb. from **papilloter*, a supposed deriv. of *papillon* butterfly.] A curl-paper.

1748 H. WALPOLE *Let. to H. S. Conway* 6 Oct., I wish you could see him making squibs of his papillotes. 1778 *Refutation* 19 The wild Devonia still on fashion doats, And turns thy satire into papillotes. 1797 MRS. A. M. BENNETT *Beggar Girl* (1813) III. 169 A papilliot having dropped from madame's tête. 1831 BREWSTER *Nat. Magic* iii. (1833) 42 Her fingers were in active motion among the papillotes.

attrib. 1845 STOCQUELER *Handbk. Brit. India* (1854) 80 A good supply of papillote paper.

Papillous (păpi·ləs), *a.* Now *rare* or *Obs.* [ad. mod.L. *papillōsus*: see -OUS.] = PAPILLOSE.

1718 J. CHAMBERLAYNE *Relig. Philos.* (1730) I. xiv. § 6 The Particles of the Olfactory Matter..must strike with some Force against the Papillous Tegument, to produce the Sense of Smelling. 1822–34 *Good's Study Med.* (ed. 4) IV. 486 Cuticle below the scabs..dotted with papillous apertures, oozing fresh matter.

Papillule (păpi·liŭl). [ad. mod.L. *papillula*, dim. of *papilla*.] A minute papilla; in *Entom.* applied to a small elevation or depression with a minute papilla in the centre. Hence **Papi·llulate** *a.*, beset with papillules.

1826 KIRBY & SP. *Entomol.* IV. 274 *Papillule* (*Papillula*), a tubercle or variole with an elevation in its centre. *Papillulate* (*Papillulata*), beset with many papillules. Ex. Elytra of *Dynastes Hercules* ♀.

†Pa·pin. *Obs.* In 5 papyn. [app. a. F. *papin*, now 'pap for children'. Cf. Sc. *Pappin* 'a sort of batter or paste, generally made of flour and water, used by weavers for dressing their linen warp, or their webs' (Jam.).] A dish composed of milk, flour, and yolks of eggs, sweetened with sugar.

c1430 *Two Cookery-bks.* 9 Papyns.—Take fayre Mylke an Flowre, an drawe it þorw a straynoure, an set it ouer þe fyre, an let it boyle a-whyle [etc.].

Papinga, -gay, -go, -jay, obs. ff. POPINJAY.

Papin's digester: see DIGESTER 4.

†Papion, -oun. *Obs.* [a. OF. *papion*, ad. med.L. *papio, -ōnem*, of unknown origin.] A carnivorous beast used in hunting; app. the cheetah or hunting leopard.

[a1244 JAC DE VITRIACO *Hist. Orient.* (Du Cange), Papiones quos appellant canes silvestres acriores quam lupi. a1375 MAUNDEV. (French text) (Roxb.) v. 14 En Cipre lem chace ouesqe papions, qi semblent leopardz priuez, qi preignont trop bien les bestes sauvages.] c1400 (English text) *ibid.*, In Cipre men huntes with papiouns [*MS. Cott. Tit.* papyouns; *v. rr.* papions, pampeons], þe whilk er lyke to leopards. 1598 HAKLUYT *Voy.* I. 98 (tr. *Itin. fr. Will. de Rubruquis*, 1253) The Tartars..make themselues two gownes..of woolues skins, or Fox skins, or else of Papions [*orig.* de pellibus lupinis, vel vulpibus, vel papionibus].

Papir, papire, obs. forms of PAPER.

Papish (pēⁱ·piʃ), *sb.* and *a.* Now *dial.* [app. f. *pape*, dial. form of POPE (F. *pape*, L. *pāpa*).]

A. *adj.* Papistical, popish. (A hostile epithet.)

1546 GARDINER *Declar. Joye* 21 b, This they wyll aske me. Thow papysshe bysshop and folish lawer, doest thow deny predestination? [*Side note*] They vse the word papish, to stop euery mans mouth withall. 1566 in Peacock *Eng. Ch. Furniture* (1866) 137 The vestments, albs, amesses..that belong to the papishe priste. 1759 DILWORTH *Pope* 148 None but apish and papish brats will heed him. c1817 HOGG *Tales & Sk.* III. 160 The rebel crew, and their papish prince. 1898 CROCKETT *Stand. Bearer* xiv. 118 He had been a Papish priest some-gate in his youth.

B. *sb.* = PAPIST. *dial.* or *illiterate.*

1604 in R. E. C. Waters *Parish Reg. Eng.* (1883) 68 Christian Steevens..was buried by women, for she was a papishe. 1668 DRYDEN *Sir M. Mar-all* IV. i, There are some Papishes, I'll warrant, that lie in wait for my daughter. 1792 MAD. D'ARBLAY *Let. to Mrs. Phillips* Sept., Upon the ..supposition that, being nothing but French papishes, they would never pay. 1802 COLERIDGE *Lett.*, *to T. Wedgwood* (1895) 417 The climate and country are heavenly, the inhabitants Papishes. 1828 *Craven Gloss.* (ed. 2), *Papish*, a papist. 1894 LYTTLE *Betsy Gray* 16 (E. D. D.) Ye ca'd him a Papish an' a rebel.

Pa·pisher. *Obs.* or *dial.* [See -ER [1].] = prec. B.

1823 SCOTT *Peveril* xxi, This plot..that they are pursuing the Papishers about. 1836 J. H. NEWMAN *Lett.* (1891) II. 199 Dr. Wiseman (somewhat coolly) has sent me down two fresh Papishers last night.

Papism (pēⁱ·piz'm). [a. F. *papisme* (1578 in Hatz.-Darm.), f. as next + -ISM.] The papal system; popery; Roman Catholicism.

1550 BALE *Apol.* 83 If all thynges muste be persolued, that hathe bene promysed in papisme. 1553 BECON *Reliq. Rome* (1563) 138 So long as yᵉ Masse endureth, so long shall papisme continue. a1614 P. LILIE *Two Serm.* (1619) 47 Papisme ..is not a total defection, but an aberration, from Christ. 1716 M. DAVIES *Athen. Brit.* II. 381 Invocation of Saints, Church-Ornaments, Priest-Vestments, Altar-Garments, or such like Fundamental Articles of Papism. 1850 H. W. GREVILLE *Diary* (1883) 373 He [Bennet] enters into the whole case of Puseyism,..Papism, his own position.

Papist (pēⁱ·pist). [a. F. *papiste* (1525 in Godef. *Compl.*), or ad. 16th c. L. *pāpista*, f. *pāpa* pope: see -IST.]

1. An adherent of the pope; esp. an advocate of papal supremacy; also, more generally, a member of the Roman Catholic Church; a Roman Catholic or Romanist. (Usually hostile or opprobrious.)

[1521 FISHER *Serm. agst. Luther* Wks. (1876) 344 The popes holynes & his fauourers, whom he [Luther] calleth so often in derisyon papistas, papastros, & papanos, & papenses.] 1534 (*title*) A Litel Treatise ageynst the Mutterynge of some Papistis in Corners. 1657 J. SERGEANT *Schism Dispach't* 656 'Tis clear that all Roman-Catholikes, that is, all Communicants with the Church of Rome or Papists (as they call them) hold the substance of the Pope's Authority.

1699 TANNER 28 Apr. in *Pepys' Diary* (1879) VI. 186 The Papists and other enemies of the Ch. of England. 1781 GIBBON *Decl. & F.* xx. II. 152 *note*, In the beginning of the last century, the Papists of England were only a thirtieth, and the Protestants of France only a fifteenth part of the respective nations. 1891 *Times* 10 Oct. 5/3 In spite of the clamour of the extreme Papists, the Vatican recognized that it had still to look to the Italian Government for protection.

2. *attrib.* or *quasi-adj.* = PAPAL.

1819 LADY MORGAN *Autobiog.* (1859) 277 There, and in the bright hopes that opened to them of getting rid of papist government, it is that Bonaparte is a loss to Europe.

Hence **Pa·pistlike** *a.*; **Pa·pistly** *adv.*

1579 FULKE *Refut. Rastel* 739 To reason from the authoritie of men negatiuely, is Papistlike. 1716 M. DAVIES *Athen. Brit.* III. *Diss. Drama* 29 He was suspected to be a Papist or Papistly affected.

Papi·stic, *a.* (*sb.*) [f. as prec. + -IC; cf. F. *papistique* (16th c. in Littré).]

1. = PAPISTICAL. (Usually hostile.)

1545 JOYE *Exp. Dan.* vii. 108 b, Lykewyse in the papistik chirche, what a multitude & variete is there of laudable in syghte ceremonis. 1624 *Brief Inform. Aff. Palatinate* 49 The Armie of the Papistique League .. did extreamely rauage the low Palatinate. 1774 WARTON *Hist. Poetry* xliv. (1840) III. 130 Service-books for the old papistic worship. 1844 LINGARD *Anglo-Sax. Ch.* (1858) II. xiii. 259 *note*, I do not see why the papistic prelate Dunstan has not as good a claim to the honours of a reformer as either Alfred or Ælfric.

2. *absol.* or *sb.* = PAPIST 1.

1589 *Marprel. Epit.* (1843) 21 The papistics affirming all their traditions to be agreeable..to the word.

Papistical (pāpi·stikăl), *a.* [f. as prec. + -AL.] Of, pertaining to, or of the nature of a papist or papists; adhering to the pope; of, pertaining, or adhering to the Church of Rome and its doctrines, ceremonies, and traditions; popish. Usually hostile or opprobrious. (In quot. 1568 = PAPAL.)

1537 CROMWELL in Merriman *Life & Lett.* 17 July (1902) II. 65 Soo his grace cannot a litle mervayl to here of the papisticall facion that is mayntained in that town. 1568 GRAFTON *Chron.* II. 599 Aspiryng to ascend to the Papisticall Sea. 1654 WHITLOCK *Zootomia* 358 Our Protestant Jesuites..(as well as the Papisticall) care not for converting those Indians that have no Gold. 1767 S. PATERSON *Another Trav.* II. 66 A papistical or a calvinistic saint. 1873 M. COLLINS *Squire Silchester* II. ii. 17 The decorations had become unpopular. Somebody had called them Papistical.

Papi·stically, *adv.* [f. prec. + -LY [2].] In a papistical manner; popishly.

1572 ABP. PARKER *Corr.* (Parker Soc.) 403 Inquire of such unordered persons papistically set. 1655 BAXTER *Quaker Catech.* 30 These Quakers that Pharisaically and Papistically justifie themselves. 1848 J. H. NEWMAN *Loss & Gain* 207 What is called papistically inclined.

†Papi·sticate, *v. Obs. nonce-wd.* [f. PAPISTIC + -ATE [3].] *trans.* To render papistic.

1746 W. HORSLEY *Fool* (1748) II. 67 Though he may not make them Traitors, yet he may Popefy, or Papisticate them.

Papistry (pēⁱ·pistri). [f. PAPIST + -RY.] The doctrine or system of papists; popery; the Roman Catholic religion or faith. (A hostile term.)

15.. *Pore Helpe* in *Skelton's Wks.* (Dyce) I. p. cix, Sayinge it is but papistrie, Yea, fayned and hipocrisy. 1549 *Latimer's 2nd Serm. bef. Edw. VI*, To Rdr. (Arb.) 54 The abolishmente of all papestrie. 1549–62 STERNHOLD & H. *Ps.*, *Come Holy Spirit*, Keepe us from sects and errors all, and from all Papistrie. 1617 MORYSON *Itin.* I. 121 There was now small hope of reducing England to papistry. 1732 NEAL *Hist. Purit.* I. 596 Because Papistry was odious. 1856 WHITTIER *Mary Garvin* xxix, Beholding..The stranger cross his forehead with the sign of Papistrie.

†Pa·pize, *v. Obs.* [f. L. *pāpa* POPE + -IZE.] *intr.* To act or play the pope; to act on the side of the pope or papal system; **b.** *trans.* To render papal or popish. Hence **†Papized** *ppl. a.*, imbued with popery, conformed to the papal system; **†Papizing** *vbl. sb.* and *ppl. a.*, playing the pope; following papal doctrines or practices.

1612 R. CARPENTER *Soules Sent.* 41 It is only an opinion of papizing Paganes. 1629 BRENT tr. *Jewell's Epist.* in *Sarpi's Council Trent*, etc. 854 When we see that nothing is decreed in the Councell, but at the Popes pleasure, why may wee not say that the oracles of the Councels doe Papize? 1639 FULLER *Holy War* III. xxix. (1840) 170 Protestants cut off the authority from all papized writers of that age. 1692 *Scotch Presbyt. Eloq.* (1738) 80 Papising Prelates. a 1843 SOUTHEY *Comm.-pl. Bk.* III. 519 He is accused of Papizing, because he wishes for conciliation.

Paplette, paplote, variants of PAPELOTE *Obs.*

Papolatry (pēⁱpǫ·lătri). *nonce-wd.* [f. L. *pāpa* pope + -LATRY.] Worship of, or excessive reverence for, the pope. So **Papo·latrous** *a.*, characterized by 'papolatry'.

1894 *Contemp. Rev.* Aug. 302 Preachers of papolatry. *Ibid.* 303 The new papolatrous and dogmapoeic movement.

‖Papoose (pāpū·s). Also 7 **pappouse, papouse,** 8–9 **pappoose.** [An Algonquin word: in Narragansett *papoos*, Pequot *pouppous* (i.e. poopoos).] A North-American Indian young child.

1634 W. WOOD *New Eng. Prosp.* (1865) 108 This little Pappouse travells about with his bare footed mother to paddle in the Icie Clammbankes. 1677 I. MATHER *New Eng.* (1864) 197 They thought..to make the English believe those base Papooses were of royal Progeny. 1809 KENDALL *Trav.* I. xiii. 152 From *papoose*, a word by which, as it is said, some of the Indians mean a child. 1865 F. PARKMAN *Champlain* xii. (1875) 348 Naked pappooses screamed and ran. 1890 L. C. D'OYLE *Notches* 28 Strapped in that queer contrivance in which squaws carry their papooses.

b. *Comb.* 1866 *Treas. Bot.* 844/2 *Papoose-root*, the root of *Caulophyllum thalictroides.*

‖Papoosh, papouch(e (păpū·ʃ). Also 7 **papucha,** 9 **papoush**: see also BABOUCHE, PABOUCH. [a. Pers. پاپوش *pāpōsh* (Turkish پابوج *pābutch*) slipper, shoe, f. Pers. پا *pā* foot + پوش *pōsh* covering.] A Turkish or Oriental slipper.

1682 WHELER *Journ. Greece* II. 187 They slip off their Papuchas, or Shoes, when they go in to do their Dévotions. *Ibid.* v. 349 They never wear Papouches, or Slippers, like the Turks. 1835 WILLIS *Pencillings* II. liii. 115 A ragged and decrepit dervish, with his papooshes in his hand. 1847 THACKERAY *Eastern Adv. Fat Contrib.* Wks. 1900 XIII. 621 His pipes, narghilés, yataghans, and papooshes made him a personage of no small importance.

†Pappe, *sb. Obs.* [a. F. *pappe*, ad. L. *pappus*.] = PAPPUS.

1657 TOMLINSON *Renou's Disp.* 356 Flowers, which..wither and turne into pappe or down.

†Pappe, *v. Obs. rare*[−1]. [? Connected with PAP *sb.*[2] and *v.*[1] Cf. It. *pappare* 'to feed with pap' (Florio).] *trans.* To feed, cram, pamper.

? a 1400 in Wright *Rel. Ant.* II. 41 To pappe and pampe her fleische.

Pappescent (pæpe·sĕnt), *a. Bot.* Also *erron.* **papesc-.** [f. L. *papp-us*: see -ESCENT.] Producing a pappus, as composite plants.

1720 BLAIR in *Phil. Trans.* XXXI. 33 The *Esulæ* and *Tithymali* are Carthartick; tho' both these are Lactescent, yet they differ from those which are Pappescent also. 1731 ARBUTHNOT *Aliments* vi. (1735) 211 Cooling, lactescent, papescent Plants, as Cichory, Lettuce, Dandelion. 1732 — *Rules of Diet* 346 Some lactescent papescent Plants as Endive.

Pappet, obs. variant of POPPET, PUPPET.

Pappiferous (pæpi·fĕrəs), *a. Bot. rare*[−0]. [f. L. *papp-us* + -FEROUS.] Bearing a pappus.

1890 in *Cent. Dict.* 1893 in *Syd. Soc. Lex.*

Pappiform (pæ·pifǭım), *a. Bot. rare*[−0]. [f. L. *papp-us* + -FORM.] Having the form of a pappus. 1866 *Treas. Bot.* 844/2.

Papple, dial. var. POPPLE, cockle (weed).

Papponymic (pæponi·mik). *nonce-wd.* [f. Gr. πάππ-os grandfather, after *patronymic*.] (See quot.)

1875 M. A. LOWER *Eng. Surnames* (ed. 4) II. vii. 73 Those who assumed the latter [*Mac*] adopted the father's name or *Patronymic*, while those who took the former [O'], chose the designation of the grandfather, the *Papponymic*.

Pappoose, pappouse, variants of PAPOOSE.

Pappose (pæpōu·s), *a. Bot.* [ad. mod. Bot. L. *papposus* (in 17th c. botanists): see PAPPUS and -OSE.] Furnished with a pappus; of the nature of a pappus, downy.

1691 RAY *Creation* I. (1692) 99 That pappose Plumage growing upon the Tops of some of them [Seeds]. 1703 J. PETIVER in *Phil. Trans.* XXIII. 1422 Above a dozen pappose spikes. 1861 BENTLEY *Man. Bot.* 575 Calyx.. superior, with a membranous or pappose limb.

Pappous (pæ·pəs), *a. Bot.* [See prec. and -OUS.] = prec.

1658 SIR T. BROWNE *Gard. Cyrus* iii. 155 The seeds of many pappous or downy flowers. 1785 MARTYN *Rousseau's Bot.* xxviii. (1794) 430 It consists of pappous or villous hairs. 1806 GALPINE *Brit. Bot.* 409 Salix...Seeds pappous.

‖Pappus (pæ·pŏs). [mod.L., a. Gr. πάππος.] **1.** *Bot.* The downy or feathery appendage on certain fruits, esp. on the achenes or 'seeds' of many *Compositæ*, as thistles, dandelions, etc.; hence extended to the reduced calyx of *Compositæ* generally, whether downy, bristly, scaly, toothed, or membranous.

1704 J. HARRIS *Lex. Techn.* I, *Pappus*, in Botany, is that soft light Down, which grows out of the Seeds of some Plants, such as Thistles, Dandelion, Hawkweed, etc. 1811 A. T. THOMSON *Lond. Disp.* (1818) 405 The capsule is crowned with a feathery pappus. 1866 *Treas. Bot.* 844/2 *Pappus*, the calyx of composites, in which that organ is reduced to a membrane, or scales, or hairs, or a mere rim.

Comb. 1847 W. E. STEELE *Field Bot.* 22 Cal. with a superior membranous or pappus-like limb. 1870 HOOKER *Stud. Flora* 212 Tragopogon..pappus-hairs in many series. *Ibid.* 188 Centaurea nigra..pappus-scales short unequal or O.

2. *Anat.* (See quots.)

1857 MAYNE *Expos. Lex.*, *Pappus. Anat.* Term for the first downy beard of the chin. 1893 *Syd. Soc. Lex.*, *Pappus*. ..Also, the downy hair of the skin and cheeks.

Pappy (pæ·pi), *sb.*[1] [dim. of PAPA.] A child's pet-name for 'father'. Now *rare*.

1763 BICKERSTAFF *Love in Village* 66 Come, be a dear good-natured pappy. 1782 MISS BURNEY *Cecilia* VI. viii, O no, Pappy has a world of business to settle first. 1897 'OUIDA' *Massarenes* xx, Now they were doing the same with poor pappy.

Pappy, *sb.*[2] [dim. of PAP *sb.*[2]] A nursery equivalent of PAP *sb.*[2] (also *dial.* of PAP *sb.*[1]).

1807 E. S. BARRETT *All Talents* 38 A giant sputt'ring pappy from the spoon.

Pappy (pæ·pi), *a.* [f. PAP *sb.*[2] + -Y.] Of the nature or consistence of pap; soft and wet.

1676 WISEMAN *Chirurg. Treat.* v. ix. 386, I saw it [his head] swell'd in severall places: some of the Swellings were big and pappy. 1762 MILLS *Syst. Pract. Husb.* I. 137 A sward of their roots laid over a very pappy mud. 1849 *Blackw. Mag.* LXVI. 103 A pappy potato, salted in the boiling. 1896 *Allbutt's Syst. Med.* I. 402 Bread crumbs and milk in fine pappy condition.

b. *fig.* Feeble in character, 'milk-and-watery'.

1809 W. BLAKE *Descr. Catal.* No. 9 There would soon be an end of proportion and strength, and it would be weak, and pappy, ..and thick-headed, like his own works. 1893 G. ALLEN *Scallywag* I. 67 You..left me to talk half the day to that pappy, sappy, vappy big Englishman.

c. *Comb.*, as *pappy-headed*.

1828 SOUTHEY *Ep. to A. Cunningham*, An honest fellow of the numskull race; And, pappier-headed still, a very goose.

Papre, Papry, obs. forms of PAPER, POPERY.

†Papse. *Obs. rare*[−1]. The name of some game or sport; or perh. *pl.* pranks.

c 1440 *York Myst.* xxix. 358 And sone schall ye see Howe we schall play papse for þe pages prowe.

‖Papula (pæ·piŭlă). Pl. **-æ.** [L., = pustule, pimple, in form a dim. of **papa*, app. from a root *pap-* to swell.]

1. *Path.* = PAPULE 1.

1706 PHILLIPS, *Papula*, a Swelling with many reddish Pimples that eat and spread. 1875 B. MEADOWS *Clin. Observ.* 22 The papulæ remain, a hair plainly seen in the centre of each. 1876 DUHRING *Dis. Skin* 41 Papulæ are circumscribed, solid elevations of the skin, varying in size from a pin-head to a split pea.

2. *Zool.* and *Bot.* = PAPULE 2.

1857 [see PAPULIFEROUS]. 1870 BENTLEY *Man. Bot.* (ed. 2) 58 Those with one secreting cell placed above the level of the epidermis are frequently termed papulæ or papillæ.

Papular (pæ·piŭlăı), *a.* [f. prec. + -AR.] Pertaining to or of the nature of papules or pimples.

1818–20 E. THOMPSON tr. *Cullen's Nosol. Method.* (ed. 3) 321 These papular affections are peculiar to infants. 1879 *St. George's Hosp. Rep.* IX. 221 Administration interfered with by..a papular eruption.

Paplarde, obs. form of PAPELARD.

Pa·pulated, *a.* [f. L. *papula* + -ATE[2] 2 + -ED[1].] Covered with or marked by papules or pimples.

1822–34 *Good's Study Med.* (ed. 4) IV. 463 A harsh papulated or watery rind. 1874–88 W. WILLIAMS *Princ. & Pract. Vet. Med.* (ed. 5) 218 The disappearance of the papulated eruption.

Papulation (pæpiŭlēⁱ·ʃən). [n. of action f. L. *papulāre* to produce *papulæ* or pimples.] The formation of papules or pimples.

1877 ROBERTS *Handbk. Med.* (ed. 3) I. 161 Papulation is deferred till the 7th, 8th, 9th, or 10th day. 1899 *Allbutt's Syst. Med.* VIII. 607 The papulation..is as frequently the consequence of the scratching as its cause.

Papule (pæ·piŭl). [ad. L. *papula*; cf. F. *papule* (1555 in Hatz.-Darm.).]

1. *Path.* A small, solid, somewhat pointed swelling of the skin, usually inflammatory, without suppuration; a pimple.

[1857 MAYNE has only *Papula.*] 1864 W. T. FOX *Skin Dis.* 30 Papules and vesicles may exist in abundance with very little erythema. 1893 *Syd. Soc. Lex.* s. v., The minute anatomy and pathology of papules are very various.

2. *Zool.* and *Bot.* = PAPILLA 1 b, 2.

1872 H. C. WOOD *Fresh-Water Algæ* (1874) 223 Nodules approximate, with their papules applanate.

Papuli·ferous, *a.* [f. L. *papula* + -(I)FEROUS bearing.] Bearing papules; papilliferous.

1857 MAYNE *Expos. Lex.*, *Papuliferus*, *Bot.* Having or bearing papulæ, as the branches, leaves and calyces of the *Mesembryanthemum papuliferum*: papuliferous.

Papulo- (pæ·piulo), used as combining form of PAPULA, PAPULE, in pathological terms, as **Pa·pulo-erythe·ma,** erythema accompanied by papules; hence **Pa·pulo-erythe·matous** *a.*, characterized by papulo-erythema. **Pa·pulo-pu·stular** *a.*, characterized by swellings resembling papules but containing pus. **Pa·pulo-squa·mous** *a.*, characterized by papules covered by scales. **Pa·pulo-ve·sicle,** a swelling resembling a papule, but containing fluid; hence **Pa·pulo-vesi·cular** *a.*, characterized by papulo-vesicles.

1899 *Allbutt's Syst. Med.* VIII. 808 Gyrate patches of erythema or *papulo-erythema. *Ibid.* 697 Preceded by a *papulo-erythematous condition. *Ibid.* 869 A *papulo-pustular skin-affection. 1876 DUHRING *Dis. Skin* 247 Where the process runs into a *papulo-squamous stage. *Ibid.* 67 A great variety of stages of exudation .. giving rise to the papule, *papulo-vesicle, vesicle [etc.]. 1875 B. MEADOWS *Clin. Observ.* 47 An irritable and *papulo-vesicular patch on the back of each hand.

Papulose (pæ·piŭlōᵘs), *a.* [ad. mod.L. *papulōs-us*: see PAPULA and -OSE.] Covered with papules or papillæ; papillose.

1776 J. LEE *Introd. Bot.* Explan. Terms 385 *Papulosum*, papulose, covered with vascular Punctures. 1830 LINDLEY *Nat. Syst. Bot.* 57 Stigmata..papulose, or pencil-formed.

So **Papulo·sity.**

1656 BLOUNT *Glossogr.*, *Papulosity*, fulness of pimples or blisters. 1658 in PHILLIPS.

Papulous (pæ·piŭləs), *a.* [f. as prec. + -OUS.] Covered with or characterized by papules, papulose; of the nature of a papule, papular.

1818–20 E. THOMPSON tr. *Cullen's Nosol. Method.* (ed. 3) 320 The varieties of papulous eruption are comprehended under three genera. 1899 *Allbutt's Syst. Med.* VIII. 606 Among the papulous diseases of the skin.

Papure, obs. form of PAPER.

†Pa·pwort. *Obs.* [f. PAP *sb.*[2] (?) + WORT.] An old name of the herb Mercury.

a 1400–50 *Stockh. Med. MS.* 203 Mercurie or papwourtz or þe more smerewourt: *mercurialis*. 1597 GERARDE *Herbal* App., Papwort is Mercurie.

Papy, obs. form of POPPY.

Papyllardie, variant of PAPELARDY *Obs.*

†Papyr, papyre, anglicized forms of PAPYRUS.

1601 HOLLAND *Pliny* XIII. xi. I. 392 The very bodie..of the Papyr it selfe, serveth very well to twist and weave therwith little boats. 1662 STILLINGFL. *Orig. Sacr.* Ded. 1 Moses, when exposed in an Ark of Nilotick papyre. 1855 BAILEY *Spir. Leg.* in *Mystic*, etc. (ed. 2) 88 Nile born papyr.

Papyr, -e, obs. forms of PAPER.

Papyraceous (pæpirēⁱ·ʃəs), *a. Nat. Hist.* [f. L. *papyr-us* (see PAPER) + -ACEOUS.] Of the consistence or thinness of paper; of the nature of paper; papery.

1752 SIR J. HILL *Hist. Anim.* 169 The violet-purple, papyraceous Solen... It's whole substance is not thicker than that of a sheet of tolerably thick paper. 1824 C. DUBOIS *Epit. Lamarck's Arrangem. Testacea* 142 Shell thin, fragile, and papyraceous. 1836–9 TODD *Cycl. Anat.* II. 156/2 The scapula is..quite papyraceous in some places. 1882 HUXLEY in *Nature* 9 Mar. 437 This papyraceous substance has taken the place of the epidermis.

Papyral (păpəi·răl), *a. nonce-wd.* [f. L. *papyr-us* + -AL.] Made or consisting of paper.

1848 LYTTON *Caxtons* VII. ii, Uncle Jack, whose pocket was never without a wet sheet of some kind,..drew forth a steaming papyral monster.

Papyrian (păpi·riăn), *a.* Also **-ean.** [f. L. *papyrius* of papyrus + -AN.] Pertaining to or composed of papyrus.

1754 DODSLEY *Agric.* Poems (1810) 360/1 And from whence, A second birth, grows the papyrean leaf, A tablet firm, on which the painter-bard Delineates thought. 1836 I. TAYLOR *Phys. Theory Another Life* (1858) 77 An inscription, which heretofore had been committed to a leaf, or papyrian scroll.

Papyriferous (pæpiri·fĕrəs), *a.* [f. L. *papyrifer* papyrus-bearing + -OUS: see -(I)FEROUS.] **a.** Producing or yielding papyrus. **b.** Producing or yielding paper, or a substance resembling or serving as paper.

1656 BLOUNT *Glossogr.*, *Papyriferous*, that bears or brings forth Paper, or the Rush Papyrus. 1857 MAYNE *Expos. Lex.*, *Papyriferus*, *Bot.* Bearing paper...papyriferous. 1866 J. B. ROSE tr. *Ovid's Metam.* 463 To steer To Papyriferous seven-mouth Nile.

Papyrin (pæ·pirin). Also **-ine.** [mod. f. L. *papȳrus* (see PAPER) + -IN[1].] The same as *parchment paper* or *vegetable parchment*: see PARCHMENT.

1860 *Edin. Philos. Jrnl.* N. S. XII. 324 Vegetable parchment.—Papyrine. 1863–72 WATTS *Dict. Chem.* I. 819 Unsized paper plunged..into [dilute] sulphuric acid..and then washed with weak ammonia .. [is] converted .. into a tough substance very much resembling animal parchment...The formation of this remarkable substance was first noticed in 1847, by Messrs. Poumarède and Figuier, who gave to it the name of *Papyrin*. 1864 WEBSTER, *Papyrine.*

Papyrine (păpəi·rin), *a.* [ad. L. *papȳrin-us* of papyrus: see -INE[2].] **a.** Made of papyrus. **b.** Resembling paper (Mayne *Expos. Lex.* 1857).

1816 G. S. FABER *Orig. Pagan Idol.* I. 211 They made a papyrine vessel, which in form represented the head of the deity [Osiris]. 1819 — *Dispensations* (1823) I. 372 The active missionaries..whom the great maritime people..is to send by sea with papyrine volumes.

Papyritious (pæpiri·ʃəs), *a. rare*[−1]. [f. L. *papȳr-us* (see PAPER) + -ITIOUS[1]: cf. L. *cinericius*.] = PAPYRACEOUS.

1840 WESTWOOD *Classif. Insects* II. 206 It is of a white, slender, and papyritious texture.

Papyro-, combining form of Gr. πάπυρος PAPYRUS (also in sense 'paper'): as in **Papyrocracy** (pæpirǫ·krăsi) *nonce-wd.* [-CRACY], government by paper, i. e. by newspapers or literature; **Papyrology** (pæpirǫ·lŏdʒi) [-LOGY], the study of papyri; **Papyrophobia** (păpəi·rofōᵘ·biă) *nonce-wd.* [-PHOBIA], dread of paper; **†Papyro·polist** *Obs. rare*[−0] [Gr. πωλεῖν to sell], a seller of paper; **Papy·rotint**: see quot.; **Papyroxylin** (pæpirǫ·ksilin) [after *pyroxylin*] (see quot.).

1843 *Tait's Mag.* X. 238 A vow..against sparing one drop of blood which the tribunals had once devoted to the altars of the *Papyrocracy. 1898 *Athenæum* 24 Dec. 887/1 In the department of *papyrology; if we may use such a word. 1900 *Ibid.* 3 Feb. 140/3 Papyrology is the Greek study which is devouring all the rest. 1790 BEATTIE *Moral Sci.* I. i. ii. § 320 Of this *papyrophobia .. I was cured long ago. 1656 BLOUNT *Glossogr.*, *Papyropolist..a Seller of Paper. 1897 WALL *Dict. Photogr.* (ed. 7) 435 *Papyrotype, Papyrography*, or **Papyrotint*, modifications of photo-lithography, in which paper is used as material on which the original transfer is made. 1894 BOTTONE *Electr. Instr. Making* (ed. 6) 26 Gun-paper, or *papyroxyline, is paper which has been immersed for a few seconds in a mixture of nitric and sulphuric acids, and then washed in an abundance of water. *Ibid.* 27 If papyroxyline is used, it should be made from stout millboard.

Papyrograph (păpəi·rǫgraf), *sb.* [f. Gr. πάπυρ-os papyrus (see PAPER) + -γραφος -GRAPH.] Name of an apparatus patented (1874) by E. Zuccato for copying documents by chemical agents acting through a porous paper-stencil.

(In quot. 1878 erroneously put for *photo-papyrography*.)

[1876 *Papier-Zeitung* 188 (*title*) Zuccato's Papyrograph.] 1877 *Echo* 22 Oct. 4/1 Besides the old-fashioned carbon paper..we have the papyrograph, the auto-polygraph, the autographic, and various other systems of so-called printing. 1878 ABNEY *Photogr.* (1881) 181 This method has been named by Sir H. James as the papyrograph. It must not be mistaken for another process, used for copying letters or circulars, and known by the same name. 1883 R. HALDANE *Workshop Receipts* Ser. II. 179/2 In the early days of papyrograph printing, a pad, saturated with persulphate of iron, was placed at the back of the stencil.

Hence **Papy·rograph** *v. trans.*, to copy with a papyrograph; **Papyrogra·phic** *a.*, pertaining to or produced by a papyrograph or papyrography.

1848 H. E. STRICKLAND in *Jardine's Contrib. Ornith.* 20 If [a person] adopts the Papyrographic process, he has merely to draw on paper with lithographic chalk instead of a lead pencil, and to send his design .. to an anastatic printer, who will speedily strike off the requisite number of impressions. 1874 *Specif. Zuccato's Patent* No. 1078, I shall .. refer to the paper so prepared .. as papyrographic paper. a 1890 W. R. WARE *Wood-working Tools* (Cent. Dict.), The first draft of these lessons was printed or papyrographed.

Papyrography (pæpirǫ·grăfi). [f. as prec. + -GRAPHY.] A term applied to a process of writing or drawing on paper and transferring the design to a zinc plate whence it is printed.

The name had already been given in French (*papyrographie*) to various transfer processes introduced in 1819, 1822, and 1840 respectively. More recently it has been loosely applied in English to Captn. Abney's papyrotype, etc.

1848 H. E. STRICKLAND in *Jardine's Contrib. Ornith.* 20, I found that drawings made on paper with this [lithographic chalk] could be readily transferred to zinc, and would supply an indefinite number of impressions...This new process, the original design being made on paper, I have distinguished by the name of Papyrography. 1849 P. H. DE LA MOTTE (*title*) Anastatic Printing and Papyrography. 1888 LIETZE *Heliographic Processes* 112 Capt. Abney's Papyrography [= Papyrotype].

b. The process of copying with a papyrograph. In mod. Dicts.

Papyrotype (păpəi·rotəip). [f. PAPYRO- + TYPE.] Name given to a modification of photo-lithography, devised by Captain Abney, in which the picture is first printed on a sensitized gelatin film supported on paper, and afterwards transferred to a lithographic stone or to zinc.

1874 ABNEY *Instr. Photogr.* 122 To make a transfer by Papyrotype. 1892 BROTHERS *Photogr.* 159 A process called Papyrotype was patented by Capt. Abney. [*Specif.* 615 of 1873.]

‖Papyrus (păpəi·rŏs). Pl. **papyri** (-əi·rəi). Also 4–7 **papirus.** [L. *papȳrus*, a. Gr. πάπυρος the paper-rush; also, the writing material prepared from it.]

1. An aquatic plant of the sedge family, the Paper Reed or Paper Rush (*Cyperus Papyrus* or *Papyrus antiquorum*), with a creeping rootstock which sends up stems from 8 to 10 feet high, bearing spikelets of flowers on long stalks in a large cluster at the top; formerly abundant in Egypt, and the source of the writing material used by the ancients (see 2); still found in Abyssinia, Syria, Sicily, etc.

1388 WYCLIF *Isa.* xviii. 2 The lond..that sendith messangeris bi the see, and in vessels of papirus on watris. 1398 TREVISA *Barth. De P. R.* XVII. cxxvi. (Bodl. MS.), Papirus is þe name of a rusche þ[t] is idruyed to tende fuyre & lanterns. 1548 TURNER *Names of Herbes* 60 Papyrus groweth not in Englande, it hath the facion of a greate Docke...It maye be called in englishe water paper; or herbe paper. 1615 SANDYS *Trav.* (1632) 102 The sedgie reeds which grow in the marishes of Ægypt, called formerly Papyri, of which they made paper. 1727–41 CHAMBERS *Cycl.* s.v. *Paper*, Besides Paper, they made sails, ropes, and other naval rigging; as also mats, blankets, clothes, and even ships, of the stalk of the Papyrus. 1827 MOORE *Epicur.* xvi. (1839) 173 Planks..bound rudely together with bands of papyrus. 1865 LIVINGSTONE *Zambesi* iii. 82 The shore..was covered with reeds and papyrus.

2. A substance prepared, in the form of thin sheets, from the stem of the papyrus plant, by laying thin slices or strips of it side by side, with another layer of similar strips crossing them, and usually a third layer again parallel to the first, the whole being then soaked in water, pressed together, and dried; used by the ancient Egyptians, Greeks, Romans, etc., as a material for writing on.

1727–41 CHAMBERS *Cycl.* s.v. *Paper*, Taking the MS. of St. Mark's Gospel at Venice to be written on Egyptian Papyrus. 1824 J. JOHNSON *Typogr.* II. xii. 430 Ancient manuscripts written on Papyrus, both in Greek and Latin. 1834 LYTTON *Pompeii* I. iii. 14 The few rolls of papyrus which the ancients deemed a notable collection of books. 1877 A. B. EDWARDS *Up Nile* xv. 397 These invaluable letters, written on papyrus in the hieratic character.

3. (With pl. *papyri*.) An ancient manuscript or document written on papyrus.

1824 J. JOHNSON *Typogr.* II. xii. 430 The first Papyrus was at length unrolled, and proved to be a Treatise of Music. 1863 LD. LYTTON *Ring Amasis* I. II. i. v. 267 This mummy was accompanied by a papyrus. 1875 SCRIVENER *Lect. Text N. Test.* 20 Those Biblical codices which most resemble the Herculanean papyri.

4. *attrib.* and *Comb.*

1837 SIR J. G. WILKINSON *Anc. Egypt.* viii. III. 62 Purposes to which the papyrus plant is said to have been applied. 1866 LIVINGSTONE *Last Jrnls.* (1873) I. ix. 234 Papyrus roots are hard to the bare feet. 1875 SCRIVENER *Lect. Text N. Test.* 16 The papyrus fragments rescued from the ruins of Herculaneum.

Paquet, -ette, obs. forms of PACKET.

Par (pāı), *sb.*[1] [a. L. *pār* equal, (as sb.) that which is equal, equality. Cf. It. *pare*, Sp., Pg. *par*, F. *pair* equal; It., Ger. *pari*, Pg. *paro*, par of exchange.]

1. Equality of value or standing; an equal footing, a level. Now chiefly in phr. *on* or *upon a par*.

1662 PETTY *Taxes* 26 A natural par between land and labour. 1672 — *Pol. Anat.* (1691) 63 The most important [is] to make a Par and Equation between Lands and Labour, so as to express the Value of any thing by either alone. 1706 PHILLIPS s.v., *To be at Par*, i.e. to be equal. 1710 PALMER *Proverbs* 255 Thus matters were brought to a par, and victory stood hovering o're the illustrious combatants. 1726 SWIFT *Gulliver* I. iii, The rest of the great officers are much upon a par. 1741 MONRO *Anat.* (ed. 3) 16 The Renewal and Waste keeping pretty near *par* in adult middle Age. 1753 A. MURPHY *Gray's-Inn Jrnl.* No. 61 II. 53 It will..set the Ladies upon a Par with the Men. 1761–2 HUME *Hist. Eng.* (1806) III. App. iii. 629 Industry..increased as fast as gold and silver, and kept commodities nearly at a par with money. 1802 H. MARTIN *Helen of Glenross* II. 211 Lord Dorville is almost at par with you. 1832 I. TAYLOR *Saturday Even.* 481 All are to beseem themselves as if all were on a par. 1850 W. IRVING *Goldsmith* xv. 181 Elevated almost to a par with his idol. 1873 BURTON *Hist. Scot.* V. lxiii. 404 Something near to par with what Scotland had to render in return. 1876 MOZLEY *Univ. Serm.* v. 120 The rights of natural society are not to be put upon a par with the rude ideas of early ages.

†b. An equal numerical strength. **†c.** A match, something that is equal or a match *to* another. *Obs.*

1708 SWIFT *Sacr. Test* Wks. 1755 II. I. 130 So many of our [Irish] temporal peers live in England, that the bishops are generally pretty near a par of the [Irish] house. 1711 P. H. *View two last Parlts.* 234 The Tryal of this worthless Tool was made a Par to that of Arch-Bishop Laud's.

2. *Comm.* **a.** The recognized value of the currency of one country in terms of that of another; in full, *par of exchange*: see EXCHANGE *sb.* 4.

1622 MALYNES *Anc. Law-Merch.* 416 The diuersitie of the said Par of Exchanges of thirtie three shillings foure pence for the Low-countreys, and twentie foure shillings nine pence for Hamborough. 1691 LOCKE *Lower. Interest* Wks. 1727 II. 72 The *Par* is a certain Number of Pieces of the Coin of one Country, containing in them an equal Quantity of Silver to that in another Number of Pieces of the Coin of another Country. 1727–41 CHAMBERS *Cycl.* s.v., The Par differs from the course of exchange, in this, that the Par of exchange shews what other nations should allow in exchange; which is certain and fixed, by the intrinsic values of the several species to be exchanged: but the course shews what they will allow in exchange. 1832 MCCULLOCH *Commerc. Dict.* (1852) 579 The thousand circumstances which are daily and hourly affecting the state of debt and credit, prevent the ordinary course of exchange from being almost ever precisely at par. 1838 *Penny Cycl.* X. 108/2 Between two countries making use of the same metal a par may exist; but between two countries one of which makes use of gold and the other of silver an invariable par cannot exist. 1861, 1868 [see EXCHANGE *sb.* 4]. 1861 GOSCHEN *For. Exch.* (1864) 6 If the exchanges were at par—that is to say if the indebtedness of the two countries were equal. 1882 R. BITHELL *Counting-Ho. Dict.* (1893), *Mint Par of Exchange*, the weight of pure gold or silver in a coin of one country, as compared with that in a coin of another.

b. Equality between the market value of stocks, shares, bonds, etc., and the nominal or face value. Chiefly in the expressions *at par*, at the face value; *above par*, at a price above the face value, at a premium; *below par*, at a discount.

1726 SWIFT *Gulliver* I. vi, The exchequer bills would not circulate under nine per cent. below par. 1744 TINDAL *Rapin's Hist. Eng.* III. Contin. 336/1 The credit of the Exchequer notes being thus secured, they daily rose nearer to par. 1755 H. WALPOLE *Let. to J. Chute* 20 Oct., Lottery tickets rise: subsidiary treaties under par—I don't say, no price. 1802 *Edin. Rev.* I. 104 A stock bearing one half per cent. would not find many purchasers at par. 1892 BARN. SMITH & HUDSON *Arithm. for Schools* 304 When the price of £100 stock is £100 in money, the stock is said to be at par.

c. *attrib.* *Par value* = value at par.

1861 GOSCHEN *For. Exch.* 6 Thus those who have the bills to sell are able to obtain more than the actual par value for them. *Ibid.* 48 The limits within which the exchanges may vary..are on the one extreme, the par value, plus the cost of transmission of bullion; on the other extreme the par value, minus this identical sum.

3. An average or normal amount, quality, degree, or condition. *On a par*, on an average.

1778 [W. MARSHALL] *Minutes Agric.* 5 Nov. an. 1775, From five bushels of malt, I find, are brewed, on a par, forty-four gallons of strong, and eighty of small. 1796 W. MARSHALL *W. England* I. 12 Taking the par of years, we may fairly place West Devonshire ten days or a fortnight behind the Midland District. 1805 FORSYTH *Beauties Scot.* (1806) IV. 255 The nominal farms..contain on a par about..ninety acres within the head dike, and about 250 acres of moor or hill lands. 1812 SIR J. SINCLAIR *Syst. Husb. Scot.* I. 382 A very small sacrifice of this sort would bring good clover and rye grass to the par of old turf. 1863 FITZROY *Weather Bk.* 15 *note*, Its [the barometer's] average height being 29·95 inches at the mean sea level in England on the London parallel of latitude; which height may be called 'par' for that level. *attrib.* *Ibid.* 323 The barometer had risen..but not to its normal or par height.

b. *Above* or *below* (*under*) *par*, above or below the average, normal, or usual amount, degree, condition, or quality. So *up to par*.

1767 STERNE *Tr. Shandy* IX. xxiv, For the livre or two above par for your supper and bed. 1778 [W. MARSHALL] *Minutes Agric.* 5 Nov. an. 1775, The last brewing..costs but 5d. a gallon, but it is below par. 1782 MISS BURNEY *Cecilia* II. i, Soon find out if they are above par. 1790 M. CUTLER in *Life*, etc. (1888) I. 461 Some of them [speeches in the House] far below par. 1809 MALKIN *Gil Blas* VII. iv. ⁋ 6 A little below par with respect to your own works in general. 1826 ANNE ROYALL *Sketches* 270 The females appeared to be rather under par, as did some of the other sex. 1886 BARING-

GOULD *Court Royal* xlviii, I think he caught a chill, and being below par he succumbed. 1899 H. SPENCER in *Westm. Gaz.* 20 May 4/3 Thanks for your inquiry. I am about up to par, and not without hope of rising above it presently.

4. *Golf.* The smallest number of strokes in which (without chance or fluke) a round has been finished (on a particular course). Also *attrib.*

1898 *Westm. Gaz.* 30 Mar. 9/2 Comparison between the par value of the different championship courses and the winning scores in the last championship meetings over them. 1900 *Ibid.* 9 Mar. 3/2 The professionals went round in the par of the green—74.

‖Par, *sb.*[2] *Anat.* [L. *pār* equal (see prec.); also, a pair.] A pair, in L. names of the pairs of cranial nerves; chiefly in *par vagum*, lit. 'wandering pair', the two pneumogastric nerves.

1704 J. HARRIS *Lex. Techn.* I, *Par Vagum*, a Pair of Nerves arising below the Auditory ones. 1727–41 CHAMBERS *Cycl.* s. v., *Par Vagum*, or the eighth Pair, is a very notable conjugation of nerves, of the medulla oblongata; thus called from their wide, vague distribution. 1893 *Syd. Soc. Lex.* s. v., *Par vagum nervorum*, the two pneumogastric nerves.

Par (pāı), *sb.*[3] *dial.* [Related to PAR *v.*[1], ME. *parren* (13th c.), and thus possibly going back to a ME. **parre*, and even to an OE. **pearre*, radical form of *pearruc*, PARROCK, q. v.] An enclosure for beasts; also in comb., as *par-yard*: see quots.

1819 RAINBIRD *Agric.* (1849) 297 (Eng. Dial. Dict.). a 1825 FORBY *Voc. E. Anglia*, *Par*, an inclosed place for domestic animals, for calves, perhaps, in particular. *Ibid.*, *Par-yard*, the farm-yard, which is itself well separated and inclosed, and contains *pars* for the many and various animals which inhabit it. 1863 MORTON *Cycl. Agric.*, *Par* (Suff., Norf.), an enclosed place for domestic animals.

Par (pāı), *sb.*[4] *colloq.* A printer's, reporter's, and journalistic abbreviation of *paragraph*.

1879 BLACK *Macleod of D.* xviii. 155 Occasionally a reporter ..will drop into the theatre on his way to the office, and 'do a par.', as they call it. 1891 E. NESBIT in *Longm. Mag.* Oct. 605 A picker-up of unconsidered pars, a reporter. 1891 *Publ. Opin.* 27 Mar. 404/1 Knowing something of the way these pars are worked in the Continental Press. *attrib.* 1892 *Daily News* 2 Feb. 7/2 He had paid..hundreds of pounds for par advertisements in the country papers.

Par, parr, *v.*[1] Now *dial.* [ME. *parren*; app. related to PAR *sb.*[3] *dial.*, and possibly representing an unrecorded OE. **pearrian*: see PARROCK.] *trans.* To enclose, confine; to shut up in an enclosure; to fold, pen, etc.

c 1300 *Havelok* 2439 He bunden him ful swiþe faste, ..Þat he rorede als a bole, Þat he wore parred in an hole, With dogges forto bite and beite. c 1380 WYCLIF *Serm.* Sel. Wks. I. 25 Þin enemyes schulen..parre þee in Jerusalem, as sheep ben parrid in a foold. c 1400 *Ywaine & Gaw.* 3228 Yn al þis [? tyme] was sir Ywayn Ful straitly parred with mekil payn. c 1440 *York Myst.* xxxiii. 33 *Cayphas*. In pynyng payne bees he parred. 1863 W. BARNES *Dorset Dial.*, *Par*, to inclose, shut up.

Par (pāı), *v.*[2] *rare*. [f. PAR *sb.*[1]] *trans.* To equate in value.

1878 *Encycl. Brit.* VIII. 789/2 When two countries par their gold coins, the object is to arrive at a common term, for which value for value will be paid.

‖Par (par, pāı), *prep.* [F. *par*:—L. *per* 'through, by way of, by means of, by'.] A French preposition meaning 'through, by': occurring in Fr. phrases, but never itself adopted as an English word.

1. Occurring in ME., in certain asseverations and adverbial expressions (where it was sometimes confused with OF. *pur*, F. *pour*:—L. *pro* 'for'). Many of these subseq. became obsolete, some continued into later use with change of *par* to *per*, others coalesced in popular use into words: see PERADVENTURE (*par aunter*), PARAMOUNT, PARAVAIL, PARAVAUNT, PARDIE, PERCASE, PERFAY.

†a. Par (per) amour, by way of love, for love's sake: see PARAMOUR *adv.*

†b. Par (per, pur) charite (cheryte, etc.), by or for Christian love, out of charity (chiefly in adjurations): see CHARITY 1. Also **par seinte charite** [OF. (13th c.) *pour sainte charité* (Littré)], for the sake of holy charity.

c 1250 *Hymn Virg.* 19 in *Trin. Coll. Hom.* 258 Bisech þin sune par cherite þat he me sschilde from helle pin. 1297 R. GLOUC. (Rolls) 6972, I nam noȝt wurþi to be þi sone ac par seinte charite..uor ȝif it me. a 1300 *Cursor M.* 20248 (Cott.) Quarfor i prai yuu, parcharite [so *G.*; *F.* for, *Tr.* pur charite]..Yee sai it me and helis noght. c 1330 R. BRUNNE *Chron.* (1810) 97 Anselme..kried, pes per charite. c 1375 *Sc. Leg. Saints* xxx. (*Theodera*) 403, & askit hym parcheryte þat scho mycht þare resawit be. c 1430 *Freemasonry* (Halliw.) 794 Amen! amen! so mot hyt be! Say we so alle per charyte. c 1450 *Guy Warw.* (C.) 4551 Y bydde yow now pur charyte, That body ye delyuyr to mee.

†c. Par ma fay (fey), by my faith. Cf. PERFAY.

c 1300 [see FAY *sb.*[1] 6 b]. 13.. *Cursor M.* 636 (Gött.) Þai were noght schamed par ma fay. c 1435 *Torr. Portugal* 830 Ryght gladly, par ma fay!

†d. Par cœur (ceur), by heart, accurately: see PERQUER(E.

†e. Par chaunce, by chance: see PERCHANCE.

†f. Par (per) compaigny(e, by way of or in company, for company's sake: see COMPANY 1 b.

c 1386 CHAUCER *Miller's T.* 653 To sitten in the roof par compaignye. — *Reeve's T.* 247 The wenche rowteth eek par compaignye. 1390 GOWER *Conf.* III. 218 And tawhte hem hou they sholde ascrie Alle in o vois per compaignie. 1413 *Pilgr. Sowle* IV. xx. (Caxton 1483) 67 Now lete vs steruen here per companye.

†g. Par-entrelignarie [cf. OF. *entrelignеure*, etc. (Godef.)], with interlineation.

1377 LANGL. *P. Pl.* B. XI. 298 A chartre is chalangeable byfor a chief iustice; If false latyne be in þe lettre þe lawe it inpugneth, Or peynted parenterlinarie [or] parceles ouerskipped [1393 C. XIV. 119 Oþer peynted par-entrelignarie].

2. In mod.Eng., in advb. phrases from modern French, often hardly naturalized. Such are PARBLEU, q. v.; †*par complaisance*, by deference or indulgence; †*par derrière*, backward, on the back side, behind; *par éminence*, by way of eminence, pre-eminently; *par exemple*, for example, for instance; *par force* = PERFORCE *adv.*; *par parenthèse*, by way of parenthesis.

1597 J. PAYNE *Royal Exch.* 21 So yt ys par derriere. 1819 H. BUSK *Dessert* 106 And I became a volunteer *par force*. 1878 SIR G. SCOTT *Lect. Mediæv. Archit.* I. 9 Pointed architecture..is not exclusively, but *par eminence*, Christian. 1893 F. ADAMS *New Egypt* 25 A small European force, and one, *par parenthèse*, by no means extraordinary as to its military character.

b. Par excellence [L. *per excellentiam*], by virtue of special excellence or manifest superiority; pre-eminently; by the highest claim or title to the designation; above all others that may be so called.

[1598 TOFTE *Alba* I. (1880) 57 My bright Sunne, renowmd *per Excellence*, Through the illustrious splender of her gleames.] 1695 EARL OF PERTH *Lett.* (Camden) 61 The Santo (which is St. Antonio's church, called il Santo *par excellence*). 1777 in W. Roberts *Mem. Hannah More* (1834) I. 118 The whole house groaned at poor Baldwin, who is reckoned, *par excellence*, the dullest man in it. 1804 *Edin. Rev.* V. 85 Of the class of narratives usually denominated 'anecdotes' *par excellence*, M. Kotzebue has given several that deserve notice. 1873 C. ROBINSON *N. S. Wales* 80 The fashionable quarter par excellence is the east end of the city.

Par-, *prefix*, repr. F. *par-*, L. *per-* (see PAR *prep.*), 'through, thoroughly', occurring in words from F., as PARBOIL, PARDON, PARTERRE, PARVENU; esp. common in ME. in words now obs., or in which *par-* has since been changed to PER- after Latin, as *parceve* PERCEIVE, *parfit* PERFECT, *parfourme* PERFORM, *partene* PERTAIN, etc.

Par, var. PARR *sb.*, young salmon; obs. f. PAIR.

‖Para[1] (pā·rā). Also 8 **parrah, perau.** [Turkish (Pers.) پاره *pārah* piece, portion, morsel; the small coin so called. In F. *para.*] A small Turkish coin, the fortieth part of a piastre, in the 17th and 18th c. of silver, but now of copper, and sunk by successive depreciations till its value is at present (1903) about one-twentieth of a penny.

(In other countries formerly Turkish the para has a greater value.)

1687 A. LOVELL tr. *Thevenot's Trav.* II. 62 The *Piastre Ryal* is worth eight *Chais*, and each *Chai* five *Paras*, and the *Para* four *Aspres*, which are all pieces of Silver. 1704 J. PITTS *Acc. Mohammetans* 68 Three or four *Parrahs*. 1776 R. CHANDLER *Trav. Greece* 123 The [Albanian] girls wear a red skull-cap plated with peraus or Turkish pennies of silver perforated, and ranged like the scales of a fish. 1808 A. PARSONS *Trav.* i. 3 Small fish..sell for a para, or three farthings English for a Turkish *oke*, which is forty-two English ounces. 1858 SIMMONDS *Dict. Trade* s. v., In Greece the para passes for about the third of a penny, and 100 make a drachma. 1880 J. NICHOL *Byron* x. 106 He discarded animal food, and lived .. on toast, vegetables, and cheese, olives and light wine, at the rate of forty paras a day. 1886 *Cassell's Encycl. Dict.* s. v., The Para of Servia is the equivalent of the French centime.

‖Pará[2] (parā·). Name of a seaport on the south estuary of the Amazon, in Brazil. Used *attrib.* in the following:

Pará cress, a composite plant (*Spilanthes oleracea*), cultivated in tropical countries as a salad and pot-herb; **Pará grass,** (*a*) = PIASSAVA; (*b*) a Brazilian forage-grass, *Panicum barbinode*, now cultivated in the Southern United States; **Pará nut** = Brazil-nut: see BRAZIL 4; **Pará rubber,** an india-rubber obtained from the coagulated milky juice of *Hevea brasiliensis* (N. O. *Euphorbiaceæ*), a tree growing on the banks of the Amazon.

1866 *Treas. Bot.* 1083 *Spilanthes*,.. the leaves .. have a singularly pungent taste, which is especially noticeable in the *Para Cress, *S. oleracea*. 1882 *Garden* 30 Sept. 295/3. 1858 SIMMONDS *Dict. Trade*, **Para-grass*, a name for the fibres of the leaves of the *Attalea funifera*. 1858 HOGG *Veg. Kingd.* 759 *Attalea funifera* furnishes that fibre, resembling whalebone, which is now so much used in this country for making brushes and brooms,.. their fibre..is called in commerce *Piassaba fibre*, *Monkey Grass*, or *Para Grass*. 1871 KINGSLEY *At Last* x, The creeping Para grass. 1848 CRAIG, **Para Nut*, the fruit of the tree, Bertholetia excelsa. 1866 *Treas. Bot.* 138 Brazil nuts form a considerable article of export from the port of Para (whence they are sometimes called Para nuts). 1897 *Outing* (U. S.) XXX. 280/1 The crude rubber, which..is the best up-river *Para that the market affords. 1898 *Daily News* 31 Aug. 5/1 The area producing Para rubber extends over 1,000 square miles.

Para-[1] (pærā), before a vowel or *h* usually **par-**, repr. Gr. παρα-, παρ-, combining form of παρά *prep.*, occurring in words already formed in Greek, their adaptations, and derivatives, and in modern words formed on the model of these, and, in certain uses, as a living element, in the formation of technical nomenclature.

As a preposition, Gr. παρά had the sense 'by the side of, beside', whence 'alongside of, by, past, beyond', etc. In composition it had the same senses, with such cognate adverbial ones as 'to one side, aside, amiss, faulty, irregular, disordered, improper, wrong'; also expressing subsidiary relation, alteration, perversion, simulation, etc. These senses also occur in English derivatives: see PARABAPTISM, PARABLE, PARADOX, PARASITE; PARALLEL; PARENTHESIS; PARHELION; PARISH; PAROCHIAL, PARODY, PAROXYSM, etc. Two groups of less usual technical words follow here.

1. Terms (substantival or adjectival) chiefly of Anatomy and Natural History, denoting or relating to an organ or part situated beside or near that denoted by the second element, or standing in some subsidiary relation to it; and of Pathology, denoting diseases affecting such parts, or designating disordered conditions and functions. These last are often Latin in form.

‖Para-anæsthe·sia *Path.*, anæsthesia of both sides of the body, esp. its lower half (Billings 1890). **‖Paracantho·sis** *Path.* [Gr. ἄκανθα prickle + -OSIS], morbid growth of the prickle-cell layer of the skin (*Syd. Soc. Lex.*). **Pa·racarp** *Bot.* [Gr. καρπός fruit], also in L. form **‖paraca·rpium,** Link's term for an aborted ovary. **Parachro·matin** *Biol.*, that portion of the nucleoplasm (differing from the rest in taking a faint stain) which forms the spindle in karyokinesis. **Parachro·matism** *Path.*, 'faulty perception of colours' (*Syd. Soc. Lex.* 1893); colour-blindness. **‖Paracolpi·tis** *Path.* [Gr. κόλπος womb], inflammation of the outside of the vagina. **Paraco·ndyloid** *a.*, applied to a process of the occipital bone adjacent to the condyle. **‖Paracope** (păræ·kopi) [Gr. παρακοπή], delirium of fever; hence **Paraco·pic** *a.* (Billings 1890). **Paracoro·lla** *Bot.*, an appendage to the corolla, as in *Narcissus* (Mayne *Expos. Lex.* 1857). **‖Paracou·sia, paracu·sis** [Gr. ἄκουσις hearing], disordered hearing. **‖Paracye·sis** *Path.* [Gr. κύησις conception], extra-uterine pregnancy. **Pa·racyst,** a subsidiary cyst, esp. in the reproductive organs of certain fungi. **‖Paracysti·tis** *Path.*, inflammation in the *paracystium* or connective tissue round the bladder. **‖Paradeni·tis** *Path.* [Gr. ἀδήν gland], inflammation around a lymphatic gland. **‖Paradi·dymis** = *parepididymis*; hence **Paradi·dymal** *a.* **‖Parafiage·llum** (pl. -a), a small supplementary flagellum in an infusorian; hence **Parafla·gellate** *a.*, provided with a paraflagellum or paraflagella. **Parage·rminal** *a.*, situated alongside of the germen in a seed. **‖Parageusia** (-giū·siă) [Gr. γεῦσις sense of taste], perversion of the sense of taste; also **‖Parageu·sis**; hence **Parageu·sic** *a.* **Paragle·nal** [Gr. γλήνη socket of a joint] *a.*, epithet of the coracoid bone or cartilage in fishes; *sb.*, the coracoid bone or cartilage of a fish. **Parahy·al** *a.* (see quot.). **‖Parahypno·sis,** abnormal sleep, as in hypnotized states or somnambulism. **‖Parakerato·sis** *Path.* [Gr. κεράτό-ω to become horny], skin disease characterized by abnormal development of the horny layer. **‖Parakine·sia** *Path.* [Gr. κίνησις motion], disordered motor function; also **‖Parakine·sis.** **‖Parala·lia** *Path.* [Gr. λαλιά talking, speech], disordered or defective articulation. **†Parala·mpsis** *Path.* [Gr. παράλαμψις, f. λάμψις shining], a pearly-looking opacity of the cornea. **‖Paralere·ma** *Path.* [Gr. παράλήρημα talking nonsense], slight delirium, 'wandering' in speech; also **‖Paralere·sis**; so **Parale·rous** *a.* [Gr. παράληρος talking nonsense], slightly delirious. **‖Parale·xia** *Path.* [Gr. λέξις speaking], a form of sensory aphasia in which one word is read for another; hence **Parale·xic** *a.* **‖Paralge·sia** *Path.* [Gr. ἄλγησις sense of pain], (*a*) disordered sense of pain; (*b*) diminished sensibility to pain. **‖Para·lgia** *Path.* [Gr. ἄλγος pain] sensation akin to pain. **†Parame·nia** *Path.* [Gr. μήν-ες menses], disordered or irregular menstruation (Good 1822–34). **‖Parametri·tis** [Gr. μήτρα uterus], inflammation of the *parametrium* or connective tissue by the side of the uterus; hence **Parametri·tic** *a.*, of, affected with, or pertaining to parametritis. **Paramí·tom(e,** the more fluid part of protoplasm, as distinguished from the denser and reticulated *mitome*. **‖Paramne·sia** [Gr. -μνησις memory], disordered or perverted memory, esp. of the meaning of words. **‖Paramyo·clonus** *Path.* [Gr. μῦ-ς, μυο- muscle + κλόνος tumult], a form of convulsions in symmetrically placed muscles. **Paramy·otone** *Path.* [as prec. +

Gr. τόνος stretching], a nervous disease, characterized by persistent tonic spasm. **‖Parane·ma** (pl. **-mata**) *Bot.* [Gr. νῆμα thread] = PARAPHYSIS; hence **Parane·matic** *a.*, pertaining to a paranema. **Paranephric** (-ne·frik) *a.* [Gr. νεφρός kidney], occurring in the tissue beside the kidneys. **‖Paranephri·tis,** inflammation of the *paranephros* or suprarenal capsule; hence **Paranephri·tic** *a.*, pertaining to or affected with paranephritis. **‖Parapa·resis** *Path.* [Gr. πάρεσις letting go, paralysis], partial paralysis of the lower limbs; hence **Paraparé·tic** *a.* **Parapata·gial** *a.*, pertaining to the *parapatāgium*, a fold of skin between the neck and shoulder in birds. **‖Parapa·thia** *Path.* [Gr. πάθος suffering], moral insanity, pathomania. **Parape·talous** *a. Bot.*, situated at each side of a petal, as stamens. **‖Parapha·sia** *Path.* [cf. APHASIA], disordered speech characterized by the incorrect use of words; hence **Parapha·sic** *a.* **‖Para·phia** *Path.* [Gr. ἁφή sense of touch], disordered tactile sense. **‖Paraphy·llum** *Bot.* [Gr. φύλλον leaf], (*a*) a stipule; (*b*) in certain mosses, a small foliaceous organ between the leaves. **Paraphy·sical** *a.*, subsidiary or collateral to what is physical. **Parapo·lar** *a.*, situated beside a pole, or beside the polar cells, as certain cells in *Dicyemidæ*. **†Para·poplexy** *Path.*, an attack simulating apoplexy, false apoplexy. **‖Paraproctium** *Anat.* [Gr. πρωκτός anus], the connective tissue surrounding the rectum; hence **‖Paraprocti·tis,** inflammation of this. **Parare·ctal** *a.*, situated beside the rectum. **‖Para·rthria** *Path.* [Gr. ἄρθρον joint, ἀρθροῦν to articulate], defective or disordered articulation of speech. **‖Parasalpingi·tis** *Path.* [Gr. σάλπιγξ trumpet, taken in sense 'Fallopian tube'], inflammation of the connective tissue around the Fallopian tube. **Parasecre·tion** *Path.*, abnormal or excessive secretion. **Parasinoi·dal** *a.*, situated beside a sinus, e.g. of the brain. **Paraste·mon** *Bot.* [Gr. στήμων thread, taken as 'stamen'], a stamen-like appendage, a staminodium. **‖Parastre·mma** *Path.* [Gr. στρέμμα twisting], a convulsive spasm, distorting the face. **‖Parasynovi·tis** *Path.*, inflammation of the connective tissue next to the synovial membrane of a joint. **Parasyphili·tic** *a.*, indirectly related to or arising from syphilis. **Parata·rsial** *a.*, pertaining to the *paratarsium* or lateral portion of the tarsus in birds. **Parathyroid** (-þəi·roid), one of several bodies adjacent to the thyroid gland; hence **Parathyroi·dal** *a.*, pertaining to a parathyroid. **Parato·mial** *a.*, situated beside the *tomium* or cutting edge of a bird's bill; pertaining to the *paratomium* or lateral part of the upper jaw in birds. **†Paratri·psis** [Gr. τρίψις rubbing] rubbing; hence **Paratri·ptic** *a.*, pertaining to or effected by rubbing (Billings 1890). **‖Paratro·phia, para·trophy** *Path.* [Gr. τροφή food], disordered nutrition; hence **Paratro·phic** *a.* **‖Paratyphli·tis** *Path.* [Gr. τυφλός blind, taken in sense 'cæcum'], inflammation of the connective tissue next to the cæcum; perityphlitis. **‖Parauche·nium** *Ornith.* [Gr. αὐχήν neck], Illiger's term for the lateral region of the neck. **‖Paravagini·tis** = *paracolpitis*. **Parave·sical** *a.* [L. *vēsīca* bladder], situated beside the bladder. Also PARABASAL, PARACHORDAL, PARAGASTER, PAROTID, etc., q. v.

1889 J. M. DUNCAN *Lect. Dis. Women* xxii. (ed. 4) 171 *Para-colpitis. 1888 *Nature* 19 July 288/2 Paradoxal deafness..the *paracousia of Willis, in which the patient is deaf to words uttered in the silence of a room, but not in a noisy street. 1657 *Physical Dict.*, **Paracousis*, noise in the ears which comes from a præternatural motion of the air which is naturally contained in the ears. 1822–34 *Good's Study Med.* (ed. 4) IV. 123 *Paracyesis. Morbid pregnancy. 1876 tr. *Wagner's Gen. Pathol.* 243 Inflammation of .. the loose adipose and connective tissue of the lower and lateral parts of the urinary bladder .. known as .. *paracystitis. 1885 E. R. LANKESTER in *Encycl. Brit.* XIX. 856/1 With a single anterior large flagellum or sometimes with two additional *paraflagella. 1876 KLEIN in *Q. Jrnl. Microsc. Sci.* XVI. 116 That portion..which is..overhanging the *paragerminal groove. 1899 *Allbutt's Syst. Med.* VIII. 327 *Parageusia is seen in nearly every form of insanity. 1822–34 *Good's Study Med.* (ed. 4) III. 204 *Parageusis. Morbid Taste. 1895 *Athenæum* 16 Mar. 348/3 Dr. Mivart..represented two lateral processes of the basihyal (for which he proposed the name *parahyal processes) as probably distinctive of the whole of the Psittaci. 1899 *Allbutt's Syst. Med.* VIII. 882 Bowen..regards the disease as a *parakeratosis. 1878 tr. *von Ziemssen's Cycl. Med.* XIV. 845 *Paralalia is that affection in which the patient..brings forth a different sound from the one he wishes to utter. *Ibid.* 790 In *paralexia incorrect words are uttered. 1900 *Lancet* 15 Sept. 822/1 On being asked to read aloud from a newspaper..his reading was markedly *paralexic. 1885 LANDOIS & STIRLING *Text-bk. Hum. Physiol.* II. 1097 The term 'cutaneous *paralgia' is applied to..itching, creeping, formication. 1893 A. S. ECCLES *Sciatica* 60 Hyperæsthesia, paralgia, and anæsthesia are also greatly modified. 1889 J. M. DUNCAN *Lect. Dis. Women* xxx. (ed. 4) 244 The frequent occurrence of albuminuria in *parametritic cases. 1874 JONES & SIEV. *Pathol. Anat.* (ed. 2) 758 *Parametritis is.. inflammation by the side of the uterus. 1889 J. M. DUNCAN *Lect. Dis. Women* xxviii. (ed. 4) 225 A very common name for parametritis is pelvic cellulitis. 1888 ROLLESTON & JACKSON *Anim. Life* p. xxi, Protoplasm..as a rule..is more or less vesicular, consisting of a denser substance (mitome) enclosing droplets of a more fluid character (enchylema, *paramitome). 1893 *Syd. Soc. Lex.*, *Paramitom*. 1899 *Allbutt's Syst. Med.* VII. 896 All cases of *paramyoclonus cannot be hysterical. 1892 GOWERS *Man. Dis. Nerv. Syst.* I. 540 Ataxic *paramyotone. 1866 *Treas. Bot.* 845/2 **Paranemata*, the paraphyses of algals and other cryptogams. 1897 *Allbutt's Syst. Med.* IV. 454 *Paranephric cysts. 1857 MAYNE *Expos. Lex.*, *Paranephritis.. *Paranephritic. 1880 GRAY *Struct. Bot.* vi. § 2 (ed. 6) 178 *note*. **Parapetalous*, those stamens which stand at each side of a petal, yet not necessarily before a sepal. 1866 A. FLINT *Princ. Med.* (1880) 657 A difficulty of speech may consist in an inability to use the proper words to express the mental ideas...This difficulty is sometimes distinguished as *paraphasia. 1899 *Allbutt's Syst. Med.* VII. 428 A possible cause of *paraphasic speech. 1863 BERKELEY *Brit. Mosses* Gloss. 312 **Paraphylla*, variously shaped foliaceous or filamentous bodies produced near the leaves, but not at definite points like stipules. 1866 *Treas. Bot.* 845/2 **Paraphyllia*, stipules. 1826 *Blackw. Mag.* XX. 853 Physical or *paraphysical; logical or paralogical; nay, even metaphysical or parametaphysical; nothing comes amiss to a German romancer. 1877 HUXLEY *Anat. Inv. Anim.* xi. 653 Cells of the adjacent part of the body (*parapolar cells). 1893 *Syd. Soc. Lex.*, **Pararectal pouch*, a name sometimes given to the peritoneal pouch on either side of the upper part of the rectum. *Ibid.*, **Parasinoidal spaces*, the spaces in the dura mater..which contain the Pacchionian bodies. 1899 *Brit. Med. Jrnl.* 25 Nov. 1483 Both tabes and general paralysis are *parasyphilitic affections. 1897 *Allbutt's Syst. Med.* III. 314 Certain bodies known as accessory thyroids and *parathyroids. *Ibid.*, *Parathyroidal and thyroidal tissue do not play an equivalent part in preventing the development of the symptoms which follow thyroidectomy. 1835–6 TODD *Cycl. Anat.* I. 60/1 Any process of mis-nutrition or *paratrophia. 1857 MAYNE *Expos. Lex.*, *Paratrophic. 1893 *Syd. Soc. Lex.*, *Paratrophic*, of or belonging to paratrophy. **Paratrophy*, a malnutrition; also, hypertrophy. 1897 *Allbutt's Syst. Med.* III. 879 '*Paratyphlitis' conveyed the same view of the position of the inflammatory changes. 1893 *Syd. Soc. Lex.*, **Paravesical pouch*, the peritoneal pouch on either side of the bladder.

2. In *Chemistry*, *para-* is used to form:

a. Names of substances that are (or have been supposed to be) modifications of those to the names of which *para-* is prefixed, or that have been produced along with or instead of these, or, sometimes, that merely occur with them.

This nomenclature appears to have been first used by Berzelius in 1830 (cf. Poggendorf's *Annalen* XIX. 328, where he introduces *acidum paraphosphoricum* and *paraphosphates*, also *acidum paratartaricum*, *a. parastannicum*).

In some cases the *para-* derivatives are isomers or polymers of the simply-named substance, e.g. *paraldehyde*, *paratoluene*; but in others they are neither isomeric with nor closely related to them, e.g. *naphthalene* $C_{10}H_8$, *paranaphthalene* $C_{14}H_{10}$.

Parabe·nzene (**parabe·nzol**) $(C_6H_6)_n$, a hydrocarbon isomeric with benzene, occurring along with it in light coal oil. **Parabu·xine,** an alkaloid, $C_{24}H_{48}N_2O$, obtained from the bark of the box-tree. **Paracampho·ric** *a.*, in *p. acid*, inactive camphoric acid. **Paraca·rthamin,** a red substance allied to carthamin, contained in the bark of *Cornus sanguinea*, dogwood. **Parace·llulose,** a supposed modification of CELLULOSE, occurring in the cellular tissue and pith of plants. **Paraci·tric** *a.*, in *p. acid* = ACONITIC *acid*. **Paraco·nic** *a.* [ACONIC], in *p. acid*, one of the isomeric acids of constitution $C_5H_6O_4$. **Para·conine,** an artificial variety of CONINE, $C_8H_{15}N$, differing from it in some of its chemical reactions and physical qualities. **Paracre·sol,** one of the toluol alcohols found in urine; hydroxyltoluene. **Para-ellagic** *a.*, in *p. acid* = RUFIGALLIC *acid*. **Parafi·brin,** a supposed modification of fibrin occurring in certain morbid conditions (*Syd. Soc. Lex.*). **Paraforma·ldehyde,** a polymer of formic or methyl aldehyde. **Parafuma·ric** *a.*, in *p. acid* = MALEIC *acid*. **Paralbu·min,** a form of albumin found by Scherer in ovarian cysts. **Paramale·ic** *a.*, in *p. acid* = FUMARIC *acid*. **Parama·lic** *a.*, in *p. acid* = Diglycollic acid, O.2 (CH₂·COOH): see GLYCOLLIC. **Parameco·nic** *a.*, in *p. acid* = COMENIC *acid*. **Paramenispe·rmine,** an alkaloid left as an insoluble residue after the extraction of menispermine, $C_{18}H_{12}NO_2$, of which it is an isomer. **Para·mic** *a.*, in *p. acid*, derived from paramide. **Pa·ramide** = MELLITIMIDE. **Paramo·rphia, paramo·rphine** = THEBAÏNE, $C_{19}H_{21}NO_3$. **Para·mylene** = DECENE, $C_{10}H_{20}$. **Para·mylum, -one,** a carbohydrate closely allied to starch (AMYLUM) of formula $(C_6H_{10}O_5)_n$, found in starch-like granules in *Euglena viridis*, a flagellate infusorian. **Paramyosi·nogen,** a proteid occurring in muscle-plasma. **Parana·phthalene** = ANTHRACENE. **Parani·line,** a polymer of ANILINE, $C_{12}H_{14}N_2$, obtained in long white silky needles. **Para·nthracene,** a crystalline isomeric modification of anthracene: see quot. **Parape·ctic** *a.*, in *p. acid*, $C_{24}H_{34}O_{23}$, an uncrystallizable acid formed from pectic acid or pectin by long boiling, or by the action of pectose. **Parape·ctin,** a neutral substance, $C_{32}H_{48}O_{31}$, derived, as a translucent jelly, from pectin by boiling and precipitating with alcohol. **Parape·ptone,** a substance allied to syntonin, precipitated on neutralizing the action of gastric juice on egg-albumin. **†Paraphospho·ric** *a.*, in *p. acid*, Berzelius's name for pyrophosphoric acid; its salts are **Paraphosphates.** **Parapi·coline,** an oily base, $C_{12}H_{14}N_2$, a polymer of PICOLINE, and formed from it by the action of sodium. **Para·rabin,** a modification of ARABIN, prepared from carrots or beet-root, not yielding sugar on treatment with dilute acids. **Parasa·ccharose,** an isomeric modification of saccharose or cane-sugar, $C_{12}H_{22}O_{11}$, formed by a special fermentation of a solution of sugar-candy: see quot. **Parasa·licyl,** the salicylide of benzoyl, $C_{14}H_{10}O_3$; also called *spirin*. **Paraso·rbic** *a.*, in *parasorbic acid*, an isomer of SORBIC *acid*, $C_6H_8O_2$, a volatile oily liquid obtained from mountain-ash berries. **Parasta·nnic** *a.*, in *p. oxide*, a name given by Berzelius to the calcined form of stannic oxide, which differs in some properties from the ordinary oxide. **Paratarta·ric** *a.*, in *p. acid* (Berzelius, 1830) = RACEMIC *acid*; **Parata·rtramide** = *Racemamide* (see AMIDE 2). **Parato·luene,** an isomer of TOLUENE, C_7H_8, along with which it occurs in light coal-tar oil; also **Parato·luol.** **Paraxa·nthine,** a substance, $C_{11}H_{17}N_9O_4$, having relations with the xanthine group, obtained by Salomon from urine. See also PARABANIC, PARALDEHYDE, etc.

1866–72 WATTS *Dict. Chem.* IV. 340 *Parabenzene .. has a faint alliaceous odour, less pleasant than that of pure benzene. 1857–62 MILLER *Elem. Chem.* (ed. 2) III. 654 *note*, Church found..a hydrocarbon isomeric with benzol which he terms *parabenzol. 1866–72 WATTS *Dict. Chem.* IV. 341 The utricular tissue forming the medullary rays of wood consists of *paracellulose. 1893 *Syd. Soc. Lex.* s. v., Paracellulose..is characterized chemically by being insoluble in Millon's reagent, except after heating to 140° F. for several hours. 1885 LANDOIS & STIRLING *Text-bk. Hum. Physiol.* I. 502 According to Hammarsten, metalbumin is a mixture of *paralbumin and other proteid substance. 1865–72 WATTS *Dict. Chem.* III. 880 *Paramenispermine has the same composition as menispermine. *Ibid.* 873 *Paramide or Mellitimide is a white amorphous powder. *Ibid.* 874 *Paramic acid. 1838 T. THOMSON *Chem. Org. Bodies* 746 This substance was discovered by M. Dumas in 1832, in coal tar, and named by him *paranaphthalin, because from his experiments it appears in its composition to be perfectly identical with naphthalin. c 1865 LETHEBY in *Circ. Sc.* I. 107/1 Finally, a more solid material, named paranaphthaline, distils over. 1883 *Athenæum* 15 Sept. 343/2 Dr. D. Tommasi .. states that if anthracene is dissolved in benzol and exposed to the direct rays of the sun it becomes turbid and deposits crystals. This photogenic substance has been named *paranthracene. 1885 LANDOIS & STIRLING *Text-bk. Hum. Physiol.* I. 331 Identical with Kühne's hemialbuminose and Meissner's *parapeptone. 1877 WATTS *Fownes' Chem.* (ed. 12) I. 327 Intermediate between orthophosphates and metaphosphates, there are at least three distinct classes of salts, the most important of which are the pyrophosphates or *paraphosphates. 1866–72 — *Dict. Chem.* IV. 354 The salts of *parapicoline are for the most part uncrystallizable. 1893 *Syd. Soc. Lex.* s.v., Agar-agar, the Chinese vegetable jelly, is composed of *pararabin. *Ibid.* s.v., *Parasaccharose is more strongly dextro-rotatory than Saccharose. 1857–62 MILLER *Elem. Chem.* (ed. 2) III. 385 This new acid is identical with the *paratartaric or racemic acid. 1885 LANDOIS & STIRLING *Text-bk. Hum. Physiol.* II. 539 The crystalline body *paraxanthin occurs in traces in the urine.

b. (More systematically) Names of isomeric benzene di-derivatives in which the two hydrogen-atoms replaced by another element or radical are symmetrically disposed in the benzene ring, being separated on each side by two other atoms; as 1 and 4 in the ring; e.g. *paradichlorobenzene*, $C_6ClHHClHH$. So *coumaric* (1 : 2) and *paracoumaric* (1 : 4) *acids*, etc. See ORTHO- 2.

As these compound names are formed systematically, and are in number unlimited, it is not necessary to give any list; cf. the following:

1876 *Jrnl. Chem. Soc.* (1) 207 Few chemists employ the terms *para-*, *meta-*, *ortho-*, in any other sense than as denoting 1 : 4, 1 : 3, and 1 : 2 compounds respectively. 1872 WATTS *Dict. Chem.* VI. 198 A second series of bi-derivatives of benzene—the *Para-* series—is produced from dinitrobenzene. From this compound is obtained *para-nitraniline*, which may be converted into para-diazonitrobenzene, and from this may be prepared parachloronitrobenzene, parabromonitrobenzene, and para-iodo-nitrobenzene. These ..may be converted by reducing agents into parachloraniline, parabromaniline, and para-iodaniline. 1889 *Anthony's Photogr. Bull.* II. 270 We have called paradihydroxybenzene [or quinol] *one* of the benzenes, and the prefix *para-* shows which one; there are two others, one of which is *ortho*-dihydroxybenzene, or catechol, and the other *meta*-dihydroxybenzene or resorcinol. There are thus three substances, catechol, resorcinol and quinol, all having the same composition $C_6H_4(HO)_2$ and distinguished from each other by the prefixes *ortho*, *meta*, and *para* attached to dihydroxybenzene.

Para-[2], a. F. *para-*, a. It. *para-*, imperative of vb. *parare* 'to ward or defend, to cover from, to

Supplement, p. 3873; Corrigenda, p. 4092; Spurious words, p. 4093; Books quoted, p. 4094

Paraban (pæˈræbæ·nik), a. *Chem.* [f. PARA- see below.] In *parabanic acid*, a dibasic acid, $CO_2(NH.CO)_2$, produced by the action of nitric acid on uric acid or alloxan: crystallizing in colourless prisms. When boiled with dilute acids, it is converted into oxalic acid and urea, whence it is sometimes called *oxalyl carbamide* or *oxalyl urea*. Hence **Parabanate**, a salt of parabanic acid, as *potassium parabanate*.

Parablast (pæˈræblast). [f. PARA- + Gr. βλαστός sprout, germ: see -BLAST.]

Parable (pæˈræb'l). Forms: 1–5 parabola, also 4–7 -bole, 4–6 -bil(l, 5 -byll, 9 -bile. [ME. a. F. *parabole* (13th c. in Littré), ad. L. *parabola* comparison; in Christian L., allegory, proverb, discourse, speech, talk, a. Gr. παραβολή a placing side by side, comparison, analogy, parable, proverb, f. παρα- beside + βολή casting, putting, a throw.

Parabolic (pærăˈbɒlik), a. [see -ICAL.]

Parabolical (pærăˈbɒlikăl), a. [see -ICAL.]

Parabolanus (pærăbəˈleɪnəs). *Eccl. Hist.*

Parabolaster, *Obs.*

Paraboliform, a. *Geom. rare.*

Parabolist (pæ·răbŏlist). [f. παραβολή PARABLE, PARABOLA + -IST.]

Paraboloid (pæ·ræbɒlɔid). *Geom.*

Paraboloidal (pærăbɒˈlɔidăl), a.

Parabolize (pæ·răbɒlaiz), v.

Parabranchia (pærăˈbræŋkiă). *Zool.*

Parabromalide (pærăˈbroʊmălaid). *Chem.*

Paracentral (pærăˈsentrăl), a.

Paracme (pæˈrækmi). *Path.* [mod.L.]

Paracrostic (pærăˈkrɒstik).

Parade (pəˈreɪd), sb.

Paradiastole (pærədaiˈæstɒli).

Column 1

figure paradiastole in some learned Rhetoricians called a faulty trace of speech, opposing the truth by false marrs and wrong names. **1616** PHILLIPS, *Paradiastole*, a Figure whereby things that seem to have one Import, and shews how much they differ.

Hence † **Paradia'stolary** *a*.

1623 URQUHART *Tymel* Wks. (1834) 291 Figurative expressions... paradoxical, paradiastolary.

Paradigm, -dictyma: see PARA-².

Paradigm (pæˈrædim, -daim). Also 7 -digme. [a. F. *paradigme*, ad. L. *paradigma*, a. Gr. παράδειγμα pattern, example, f. παραδεικνύναι to exhibit beside, show side by side. Formerly also in L. form.]

1. A pattern, exemplar.

1483 CAXTON *Gold. Leg.* 208/1 We now haue some enterpretoir of the parables or paradigmes.

2. *Rhet.* [repr. Gr. παράδειγμα]...

Paradigmatic ... **Paradigmatical** ... **Paradigmatically** *adv.*

Parading (pæˈreidiŋ), *vbl. sb.* [f. PARADE *v.* + -ING¹.] The action of the verb PARADE *v.*

Parading, *ppl. a.* [f. as prec. + -ING².]

Paradisaic, -al: see PARADISIAC.

Column 2

Paradisaic (pærædiˈseiik), *a.* [Arbitrarily f. PARADISE + -AIC.] Of or pertaining to the nature of Paradise; paradisaical.

Paradisal (pærædaiˈzæl), *a.* [f. as prec. + -AL.] Of or pertaining to paradise.

Paradise (ˈpærædais). Forms: 4 parais, paris, -eis, 4-5 paradis, pardis... Also *a*. 2-4 paradis, -4 diis, diizs, 4-8 -ice, (5 peradiis, paradise, -yse, 5-6 -yce, 6 -ise), 5-6 parays, parasse, 5-4 paraays. [Early ME. a. F. *paradis* (also in early semi-popular form *pareis*, *pareis*), ad. L. *paradisus*, a. Gr. παράδεισος park, f. παρά around + δεῖσα to form...]

1. The garden of Eden. Also called *earthly* Paradise.

2. A place like or compared to Paradise; a region of surpassing bliss or delight, of supreme bliss.

3. An Oriental park for pleasure-ground.

4. Heaven, the abode of God and his angels and the final abode of the righteous.

5. A pleasure-garden in general.

6. Sometimes given (perh. orig. in jest) as a distinctive name to a particular apartment.

Paradisiac ... **Paradisiacal** ...

Column 3

†Paradisic ... **Paradisical** (pærædaiˈzaikal), *a.* [f. PARADISE + -ICAL.]

Paradiso ...

Paradisean (pærædaiˈziːən), *a. rare.* [f. med.L. *paradise-us* (f. L. *paradisus*) + -AN; cf. *cerulean*, etc.] Of, pertaining to, or of the nature of Paradise.

Paradisean *Ornith.*, a bird of the family Paradiseidæ.

Paradise (ˈpærædais), *v.* [f. the sb.]

Paradisiacal ...

Paradox (ˈpærædɒks). Also 6-7 -oxe. [ad. (perh. through F. *paradoxe*, 13th c. in Hatz.-Darm.) L. *paradoxum*, neut. of *paradoxus*, a. Gr. παράδοξος contrary to received opinion or expectation, f. παρά past, beyond, contrary to + δόξα opinion.]

1. Of, pertaining to, or of the nature of a received opinion or belief.

2. Belonging to the genus *Paradisea* of the family Paradiseidæ.

Column 4 (bottom left)

Paradox, *v. rare.* [f. prec.]

†1. *intr.* To affect with a paradox, to cause to show a paradox or contradiction. *rare.*

2. To bring or drive by paradox. *rare.*

Paradoxal (pærædɒksæl), *a.* [f. PARADOX *a.* + -AL = PARADOXICAL.]

Paradoxer (ˈpærædɒksə(r)). [f. PARADOX *v.* (or sb.) + -ER¹.] A propounder of paradoxes.

†Paradoxial (pærædɒˈksiæl), *a.* = PARADOXICAL.

Paradoxical (pærædɒksikal), *a.* [See -ICAL.]

1. Of a doctrine, proposition, etc.: Of the nature of a paradox, exhibiting or involving paradox.

2. Contrary to common opinion.

Paradoxically *adv.*

Paradoxicalness *sb.*

Paradoxism ...

Paradoxology ...

Paradoxure (pærædɒksjuə(r)), *a.* and *sb.*

Paradoxurine ...

Column 5

Paraffin (ˈpærəfin). Also -ine, -ffine. [L. *parum* little + *affinis* having affinity; so named by Reichenbach 1830 in reference to its neutral quality and the small affinity it possesses for other bodies.]

1. A colourless (or white), tasteless, inodorous, crystalline, fatty substance, solid at ordinary temperatures (chemically a mixture of hydrocarbons of the series C_nH_{2n+2}), discovered by Reichenbach in 1830; obtained by distillation from wood, coal, peat, petroleum, etc., and used extensively as an illuminant.

Paraffin-flagellate, etc.: see PARA-¹.

Paraffin, *v.* [f. prec.]

Paraffinic ... **Paraffinoid** ...

Column 6

Paraganglion ...

Paragram (ˈpærəgræm), *Biol.* [f. Gr. παρά beside, alongside + γράμμα writing.]

Paragastric (pærəˈgæstrik), *a. Zool.* [f. prec.]

Paragastrula ...

Paraglobulin ...

Paragnathous ...

Paragoge (ˈpærəgoudʒi). [a. L. *paragōgē*, a. Gr. παραγωγή a leading past, in Gram. addition to the end of a syllable; f. παρά past, beyond + ἀγωγή carrying, leading.]

Paragogic (pærəˈgɒdʒik), *a.* [ad. Gr. παραγωγικός.] Having the mandibles of equal length.

Paragonimus ...

Paragraph ...

the paragogic forms. **1887** A. Morel-Fatio in *Encycl. Brit.* XXII. 340/2 The infinitives with *r* paragogic (*virrer*, *veurer*, *plurer*) are not used.

Paragogical (pærăgɔˈdʒikăl), *a.* [f. as prec. + -AL.] = prec.

1688 Hickes *Defence* x. 88 They both read it, and that with prickes & tooke it not to be paragogical. **1842** Milton *Animadv.* i. Wks. (1851) 188 You cite them to appear for certaine Paragogical contempts, before a capricious Pedantie of hot-liver'd Grammarians. **1753** Wesley *Wks.* (1872) XIV. 151 Frequently they [Hebrews] add a letter, a compunction or conferring together; a paragon, a match, a compare, an equal (Florio 1611). Cf. Sp. *paragon* or *paragone* 'an equall, a fit man to match him, one comparable in merit or excellence.

I. I. A pattern or model of excellence, *a.* A person superior in merit or excellence.

1548 Hall *Chron., Hen. V* 3 b, Thys prince was almost the Araknall Pluris, and emongest his predecessors a very **1557** *Tottel's Misc.* (Arb.) 227 But thee was neuer Laura more then one, And her had Petrarke for his paragone. **1597** B. Goode *Heresbach's Husb.* (1586) 168 She was the very Phenix and Paragon of all the Gentlewomen that I euer knewe. **1590** Spenser *Philom.* Wks. (Grosart) XI. 175 The paragon of Italy for honorable grace. **1602** Sidwell *Bury Fair* n, 1 Your ladyship ... has been long held a paragon of perfection. **1645** Potter *Virtuous Villagers* III. 129 He is a paragon of beauty. **1613** Mr. Martineau *Charmed Sea* ix. 133 She will turn out a paragon of a wife. **1871** R. Ellis *Catullus* xxxvii. r The paragon of an equall, a fit man to match him, one chiefly, peerless paragon of the long ilock'd... Ignatius.

b. A thing of supreme excellence.

1601 Holland *Pliny* I. 372 [Magic] is at this day reputed by most nations of the earth, for a paragon or chief of all sciences. **1596** Sh. Hall *Sat.* iv. (1602) 280 We came down to Antwerp, the paragon of Cities. **1647** Lucas *Fox Waters* I. Ded. The diuolued ciuill constitution, that paragon of perfect piety [etc.]. **1855** Runswi *Dr. Antonio* ii. Sir John ... pronounced it to be the paragon of easy chaises.

† 2. A match; a mate, companion; a consort in marriage; a rival, competitor. (Also of a thing, whose paragon we have chosen you to bee. **1590** Spenser *F. Q.* vi. ix. r1, But whom so fittest may behight Your paragon.

Paragon (pæˈrăgɔn), *v.* [f. PARAGON *sb.*: cf. F. *paragonner*, It. *paragonare* to equall, to paragone, to compare' (Florio).]

1. *trans.* To place side by side; to parallel, compare. (*Now archaic or poetic.*)

‡2. To treat of (a matter) in a paragraph. *Obs.* **1770** B. Grose *Lett.* in Nichols *Lit. Anecd.* (1818 c. 1826 a) 1768 a [They] deliver them [reports] to the Griffier or the Clerk, by whom they are to be allowed, that is, Paragraphed to be allowed.

Paragraphic (pærăgrafik), *a.* [f. PARA-GRAPH + -IC.] Of, pertaining to, or of the nature or form of a paragraph.

Paragraphically (pærăgrafikăli), *adv.* In the style of, or by means of, newspaper paragraphs.

Parakeet, paroquet (pæˈrăkiːt, pæroˈkɛt), *sb.* Forms: *a.* 6 parrokets, 7 parroquet, 7–9 perroquet, 7, 8 paraquet, 8 paro-, parroquet, 8, 9 paroquet, parakito, keeto, -chito, chite; *b.* 7 perotito, -chito par'-[abbas: parraketo, parakeet, -chetto, paroqueto, 7, 8 paraquito. 7 7 parakete, parakeet, 7 8 parakite, parra-queet, 9 keet], 8 parakeet, 8 parrokeet.

Parakite (pæˈrăkăit), *sb.* [f. PARA-[prefix] + KITE.] A kind of large kite constructed so as to be inflated by the wind like a parachute, proposed by Simmons in 1873 for military use.

Parallactic (pærălaktik), *a.* [ad. Gr. παραλλακτικός of or by the parallax: see PARALLAX.] Pertaining, relating, or due to parallax.

Parallel (pæˈrălɛl), *a.* and *sb.* and *adv.* Also 6 parallele.

Parallaxis, -kinesis, etc.: see PARA-[prefix].

Parallel (pæˈrălɛl), *v. rare.* [f. PARALLEL *a.* + -ED.]

Parallelepiped (pærălɛlɛˈpipɛd), *sb.* Also 6 parallelepipedon.

Parallelinervous (pærălɛliˈnɜːvəs), *a.* *Bot.* [f. PARALLEL + L. *nervus* nerve + -OUS.]

PARALLELISM.

Parallelism (pærălĕli'z'm), [ad. Gr. παραλληλισμός comparison of parallels, f. παραλληλίζ-ειν to place side by side: see PARALLEL. Cf. F. *parallélisme* (1667) in Dict.-Darm.)].

1. The state or position of being parallel; direction parallel *to* or *with* something. Rarely with *pl.*, a particular instance of this (*quot.* 1753).

b. The state or fact of remaining parallel to itself, *i. e.* of maintaining the same direction; constancy of direction, as of a moving line.

c. *fig.* The quality or character of being parallel (see PARALLEL A. 7); close agreement or course or tendency; similarity in detail; precise correspondence or analogy.

2. An instance of correspondence or analogy; a parallel case, passage, etc. (Usually in *pl.*)

3. *spec.* In rhetoric and construction, of successive clauses or passages, esp. in Hebrew poetry; a sentence or passage exemplifying this.

4. A statement of correspondence or analogy; a comparison, simile = PARALLEL sb. B. 7 *Obs.*

5. Levelling, or condition of being levelled.

Parallelist (pæ'rălĕlist). [f. PARALLEL + -IST.]

Parallelize (pæ'rălĕlaiz), *v.* [ad. Gr. παραλληλίζειν: see PARALLELISM.]

Parallelless, *a.* [see prec.] Without a parallel, unparalleled.

Parallelly (pæ'rălĕli), *adv.* [f. PARALLEL + -LY.] In a parallel manner or direction; so as to be parallel. (*lit. or fig.*)

Parallel-meter. [f. PARALLEL + -METER.] (See quot.)

Parallelogram (pærălĕ'lŏgram), [a. F. *parallélogramme* 1552 in Hatz.-Darm.), ad. L. *parallélogrammum*, a. Gr. παραλληλόγραμμον sb., neut. of παραλληλόγραμμος PARALLEL + γραμμή line.]

1. *Geom.* A four-sided rectilineal figure whose opposite sides are parallel; applied to a rectangle.

2. A thing shaped like the figure described in 1.

Parallelwise, *adv.* ? *Obs.* [f. PARALLEL *a.* + -WISE.] In a parallel manner; parallelly.

Paralian, variant of PARELLING *Obs.*

Paralogic (pærălŏ'djik), *a. rare.* [f. παραλογ- : see PARALOGY) + -IC.] next.

Paralogical, *a.* ? *Obs.* [as prec. + -AL.] Involving or of the nature of paralogism or false reasoning; illogical, unreasonable.

Paralogician (pærălŏdʒi'ʃan). [f. PARA-LOGIC, after logician.] = PARALOGIST.

Paralogism (pæræ'lŏdʒiz'm). [a. F. *paralogisme* (1548 in Hatz.-Darm.), ad. late L. *para-logismus* (Boethius), a. Gr. παραλογισμός, f. παραλογίζεσθαι to reason falsely: see PARALOGIZE and -ISM.]

Paralogist (pæræ'lŏdʒist). [f. PARALOGIZE, after sophist: = PARALOGIST.]

Paralogize (pæræ'lŏdʒaiz), *v.* [f. as prec. + -IZE.]

Paraly- ... **Paralysis** (pæræ'lisis), *sb.* ...

Paralytic (pærăli'tik), *a.* and *sb.*

Parament. [f. L. *parāre* to make ready, prepare, fit out, deck, adorn + -MENT.]

PARAMENTO.

Parameter (pæræ'mĕtər). [mod. L. *parameter*, -metron, f. PARA- + Gr. μέτρον measure.]

Paramese (pæ'rămīz). [a. Gr. παράμεσος the string next the middle, f. παρά beside + μέσος mid.]

Parametritis (pærămĕtrai'tis), *Path.* [f. prec. + -ITIS.]

Paramorph (pæ'rămɔːf). [f. Gr. παρά beside + μορφή form.]

Paramorphism (pærămɔː'fiz'm). [f. as prec. + -ISM.]

Paramount (pæ'rămaunt), *a.* (*sb.*)

Paramour (pæ'rămuːr), *sb.* (and *adv.*)

Paramuthetic (pærămiuθe'tik), *a.*

Paranatellon (pærănăte'lŏn). [a. Gr. παρανατέλλον.]

Parang (pæ'ræŋ). [Malay پارنگ *parang*.]

Paranymphal, *a.*

Parao, obs. form of *prahu,* Proa.

Parapareisto·Parapeptone: *see* Para- 1, 2.

Parapegm (pæ·rapem), *sb.* Gr. *Antiq.* Now usually in Lat. form **parapegma** (pærape·gmă). [ad. L. *parapegma,* pl. *-egmata,* a. Gr. παράπηγμα, *-πήγματα,* a rising fixed beside or near, a tablet, calendar, etc., f. παρα- *beside* + πηγνύναι to fix, fasten.] A tablet set up inscribed with some public information or announcement, as a law, a proclamation, or a calendar of annals or astronomical observations: a canon, rule, or precept; a fixed date or epoch.

Parapet (pæ·rapet). Also 7 *parpet,* 9 *pit.* [a. F. *parapet* (Kabelais 16th c.), or It. *parapetto,* f. Para- *protection,* defence + *petto* breast, L. *pectus* breast.] *Lit.* A defence breast-high, a breastwork.

1. *Mil.* A defence of earth or stone to cover troops from the enemy's observation and fire; in permanent works, a protection against shot, raised on the top of a wall or rampart; in field-works, a bank of earth high enough to screen the defenders and thick enough to resist any shot that is likely to be displaced against it.

Paraph (pæ·raf), *sb.* Also 4-5 *parraf,* 5 *-affe.* [a. F. *parafe, parafe* also 15th c. *paraphe,* 4 *paraffe* or It. *parrafo,* med. L. *paragraphus,* shortened form of *paragraphus: see* Paragraph.]

Paraphernalia, obs. error. f. Paraphernalia.

Paraphonia (pærafōu·niă) [med. L., a. Gr. παραφωνία sounding beside (f. παρα- *beside* + φωνή voice), f. παρα- + *-phony* as in certain harmonies; cf. καφωφωνία *discord.*]

1. Gr. *Mus.* The harmony or concord of fourths and fifths; cf. ANTIPHONY 1 and HOMOPHONY 1 a.

Paraphrase (pæ·rafrēiz), *sb.* Also 6 **perra-paraphras.** [a. F. *paraphrase* (1525 in Hatz.-Darm.), ad. L. *paraphrasis,* a. Gr. παράφρασις, f. παραφράζειν to declare, tell: cf. *phrase* (whence φράζειν to declare, tell).]

1. An expression in other words, usually fuller and clearer, of the sense of any passage or text; a free rendering or amplification of a passage. (Sometimes, by extension, of a musical passage.)

†thus. **1708** Sewel Hist. *Quakers* (1795) I. iii. 285 Such of the family as could make repetitions of sermons, and paraphrase thereupon.

Paraphrenitis (pærăfrinəi·tis). *Path.* [mod. L., a. F. PHRENITIS.] A term for inflammation of the diaphragm, formerly thought to be invariably accompanied by delirium; hence applied to delirium supposed to be so produced.

Paraplegia (pærăplī·dʒiă). *Path.* [mod. L., a. Gr. παραπληγία.]

Parasol (pæ·răsɒl, pærasɒ·l). *sb.* [a. F. *parasol* (1580 in Hatz.-Darm.), ad. It. *parasole,* f. Para- 1 + *sole* sun, L. *sōl-em.*]

1. A light portable screen or canopy carried as a defence from the sun's rays; esp. a small umbrella used by women as a sunshade.

Paraplegic (pærăplī·dʒik, -plī·dʒik), *a.* [ad. Gr. παραπληγικός, f. παραπληγία: see PARAPLEGIA.] Marked by or characteristic of paraplegia; affected with paraplegia.

Parasang (pæ·răsæŋg). *sb.* Also *also* FARSANG. [ad. L. (It., Sp.) *parasanga,* ad. Gr. παρασάγγης, of Persian origin, the corresponding mod. Pers. word being فرسنگ *farsang,* Arab. فرسخ *farsax;* in mod. F. *parasange, farsange.*] A Persian measure of length, usually reckoned as equal to between 3 and 3½ English miles.

Parasite (pæ·răsəit). *sb.* Also 6 *parasyte, parasite,* 6–7 *parasit.* [ad. L. *parasītus,* a. Gr. παράσιτος, one who eats at the table of another, lit. *one who eats beside* or *with another,* f. παρα- *beside* + σῖτος food.]

Parasol ... (a small parasol). ... a small parasol.

Parasphenoid ... and Comp. Anat. ... Zool. and Comp. Anat.

Parastacine ... a. Zool. Crust.

Parastas, Arch. ... In pl. Pilasters, antæ.

Parastatic ... a. rare.

Parasyndesis ...

Parasynthesis ... Philol.

Parasynthetic ... a. Philol.

Parasyntheton ...

Parataxis, Gram.

Parate, Law.

Parathesis, Gram.

Parathetic, a. Gram.

Parathyroid, a. and sb.

Paratitle, Obs. ... [ad. med.L. *paratitla*.] ...

Paratonic, a. Bot.

Paravail, a. ... Law.

Paravaunt, -aunt, etc. Obs.

Paravent, Obs.

Parazonium ...

Parbreak, v. ... trans.

Parbreaking ...

Parbuckle ...

Parc, obs. or alien form of PARK.

Parcel, sb. ... A portion or division of anything.

Parcelled, ppl. a.

Parcel-maker ...

Parcelmeal, adv. ...

Parcelment. ... **Parcel post.** ... **Parcenary.** ... **Parcener.** ... **Parch.** ... **Parchable.** ... **Parchedness.** ... **Parchemin.** ... **Parcher.** ... **Parchment.**

Parching. ... **Parchingly.** ... **Parchment.** ... **Parchment-lace.** ... **Parchmenter.** ... **Parchmentize.** ... **Parchy.** ... **Parcidentate.** ... **Parciloquy.** ... **Parcity.** ... **Parcinery, -iner.** ... **Parclose.** ... **Parda.** ... **Parded.** ... **Pardee.** ... **Pardessus.** ... **Pardie.** ... **Pard.** ... **Pardale.**

Pardine. ... **Pardo.** ... **Pardon.** ... **Pardoner.** ... **Pardonable.** ... **Pardonless.** ... **Pardonization, -ize.** ... **Pardonous.** ... **Pare.** ... **Pared.** ... **Parectasis.** ... **Parecious.** ... **Pareira.** ... **Parel.** ... **Paregal.** ... **Paregmenon.**

Paregoric (pærĕgŏˈrik), a. and sb. Also 8 para-. [ad. late L. *parēgoric-us*, a. Gr. παρηγορικ-ός encouraging, soothing, f. παρηγορέειν to speak in the assembly.]

A. *adj.* Of medicines: Assuaging pain, soothing.

B. *spec.* A medicine to assuage pain, an anodyne.

†Paregorical, a. *Obs.* [See -ICAL.] = prec.

Pareil, a and *sb.* *Obs.* Forms: 5 pareille, -elle, -aylle, parelle, parail, parayl, -le, -lle, 6 pareyl, 7 parall. [a. F. *pareil* adj. and sb., like, equal (12th c. in Hatz.-Darm.) = Pr. *parelh*, It. *pareccio* = equal, match, like (Florio)-late pop.L. *°periculum* dim. of *par* equal.]

Pareira (părē'ra). Pharm. [Sp. *pareira* vine trained against a wall; whence *parreira brava* wild climbing vine, the name given to the Brazilian plant.]

Parelectronomy (pærĭlektrŏˈnŏmĭ). Physiol.

Parel, Parelion: see PARELLION.

Parelle, var. PARRELL, Chem. [f. Bot. L. *parella*, f. parvelle (prec.) med.L. *paratella*, f. parte of a plant.] In *Parellic acid* ($C_6H_4O_5$), obtained from a crustacean lichen, *Lecanora Parella*; also called **Parellin**. Hence **Parella**, a salt of parellic acid.

Parelling, vbl. sb. *Obs.* Also 5 parral, -5-7 parrail. [f. PAREL v. and -ING.] The action of the verb Parel; preparation, equipment, arraying, etc.; also *concr.* equipage, furniture, apparatus (= PAREL sb. 3).

Parement, variant of PARAMENT *Obs.*

Paremptosis. *Rhet.* = Gr. παρέμπτωσις irruption, insertion, f. παρ-, PARA-1 + ἔμβολή throwing in, insertion.] A kind of interruption or anticipation falling in; incidence.] = PAREMBOLE.

Parence, obs. f. PARENCE, pl. of PARENT *sb.*

Parencephalon (pærense·fălǫn), *Anat.*

Parenchyma (părĕ·ŋkĭma), *Anat.* or *proper*

Parenchymatis (-a·tis) *Pathol.*, inflammation of the cerebellum; whence **Parenchymatose** (-a·tōs), *adj.* (of the cerebellum); hernia of the cerebellum; a very rare disease.

Parenchyma, -me (pæˈreŋkim). *Pl.*, *sb.* *something poured in beside*. [= παρέγχυμα, *par-* beside + ἔγχυμα in-fusion.]

Parenchymatous (pærĕŋkiˈmātəs), a. Now *rare*. [f. PARENCHYM + -OUS.] = PARENCHYMATOUS.

Parenchymatosis, *adj.* Of or affecting the parenchyma.

Parenchyma, variant of PARAMENT *Obs.*

Parent (pēˈrĕnt), *sb.* a. OF. *parent* (11th c. in Littré, *pl. parenz, parens*) kinsfolk; also *parent-like* adj. (adv.); *cf.* parent-cell (*Biol.*), a cell from which other cells are derived; a genitor: parent-kernel, the nucleus of the fertilized egg-cell; a cytococcus.

Parenchymal (pærĕ·ŋkĭmăl), a. [f. PARENCHYM + -AL.] Of, pertaining to, or consisting of parenchyma; parenchymatous; **Parenchymatis** *Path.*, inflammation of the parenchyma of an organ.

Parenchymatous (pærĕŋkiˈmātəs), a. [f. PARENCHYMA + -OUS.] Belonging to the parenchyma of an organ; occurring in or affecting the parenchyma.

Parenchymatosis

Parenchyma (pærĕ·ŋkĭma), Embryol.

Parenchymula (pærĕ·ŋkĭmūla), *Embryol.* [mod.L. dim. of PARENCHYMA.] (See quot.)

Parenchyme (pærĕ·ŋkĭm), *Embryol.* [mod.L. dim. of PARENCHYMA.] (See quot.)

Parenesis, Parenetic, etc.

Parent (pēˈrĕnt), sb. a. OF. *parent* (11th c. in Littré, *pl. parenz, parens*) kinsfolk.

1. A person who holds the position or exercises the functions of a parent; a protector, guardian; sometimes applied to a father or mother-in-law.

2. *transf.* A person from whom another springs or is derived; a source, cause, origin.

Parentage (pēˈrĕntĭdȝ), sb. [a. F. *parentage* (12th c. in Littré.)]

1. Exercise of the functions of a parent; parental conduct or treatment.

2. Parents collectively.

3. Derivation or descent from parents, esp. in reference to the particular parent or parents; birth', lineage.

Parental (părĕ·ntăl), a. [ad. L. *parentāl-is* = (ad. L. *parentāl-is*).]

1. Of or pertaining to a parent; characteristic of or resembling a parent; fatherly or motherly.

2. Of the nature of a parent; *fig.* that is the source or origin from which something springs.

Hence **Parentality** (pærĕntæ·litĭ), the state or condition of being a parent; parenthood; **Parentally** *adv.*, in the manner of a parent.

†Parentalia (pærĕntē·lĭa), *pl.* [L. *parentālia* lit. parental things or rites.] Among the ancient Romans, Periodical observances in honour of dead parents or relations; also as title of a work (so L. in Plinius).

Parentation, v. *Obs.* [f. *parentation*.]

Parentele (pæˈrĕntēl), *sb.* *Obs.* [a. OF. *parentele*, ad. L. *parentēla* kindred, f. parent-: see PARENT and -ELE.]

Parentation, *sb.* *Obs.*

Parented, a. *rare.* [as prec. + -ED2.] (In comb.) Having parents (of a specified kind).

Parenteele, *sb.* *Obs.* [a. F. *parentèle* relationship.]

1. Kinship, relationship; kindred.

2. = PARENTAGE 3.

Parenterinnarie, -lignarie: see PAREPIGASTRIC.

Parenthesis (pærĕ·nþĭsĭs). Pl. -theses (-ĭsīz). [med.L., a. Gr. παρένθεσις, f. παρεντιθέναι to put in beside, f. παρ- beside + ἐν in + τιθέναι to put, place. Cf. F. *parenthèse* (15th c.).]

1. An explanatory or qualifying word, clause, or sentence inserted into a passage with which it has not necessarily any grammatical connexion, and from which it is usually marked off by round or square brackets, dashes, or commas.

2. A pair of curved lines or figures resembling these, in printing.

Parenthesize (pærĕ·nþĭsaiz), v. [f. PARENTHESIS + -IZE.] One who introduces a parenthesis.

Parenthesise (pærĕ·nþĭsaiz), v. [f. prec. + -IZE.]

Parenthesis (pærĕ·nþĭsĭs), *sb.*

Parenthetic (pærenþe·tik), a. [ad. med.L., i.e. f. PARA-1 + Gr. ἐνθετικ-ός, f. ἐνθετός, f. ἐντιθέναι: see PARENTHESIS.]

1. Of, pertaining to, or of the nature of a parenthesis; inserted as a parenthesis.

2. Given to the use of parentheses.

Parenthetical (pærenþe·tĭkăl), a.

1. = prec. 1.

2. Given to the use of parentheses.

Parenthetically (pærenþe·tĭkălĭ), adv. [f. prec. + -LY2.] In a parenthetic manner; in a parenthesis; by way of parenthesis or interlude.

Parenthood (pēˈrĕnthŭd), *sb.* [f. PARENT *sb.* + -HOOD.] The state or position of a parent; fatherhood or motherhood.

Parenticide (părĕ·ntĭsaid), *sb.* [f. L. *parent-em* + -CIDE.] *rare.* The murder of a parent.

Parentless, a. [f. PARENT *sb.* + -LESS.] Without parents; fatherless and motherless; orphaned.

Parentship (pēˈrĕntʃĭp), *sb.* [f. as prec. + -SHIP.] The office or position of a parent.

Parepididymis (pærĕpĭdiˈdĭmĭs), *Anat.*

Parepigastric

Parepigastric (pærĕpĭgæ·strik), a. [ad. med.L., f. PARA-1 + Gr. ἐπιγάστρι-ον.] *Anat.* Situated or occurring beside or above the epigastric.

Parepithymia (pærĕpĭþĭˈmĭa), *Path.* [mod.L., f. PARA-1 + Gr. ἐπιθυμία desire.] A mental disorder characterized by perverted desires. Hence **Parepithymic**, a., relating to parepithymia.

Parepitome, sb. *Obs.*

Parer (pēˈrăr), sb. [f. PARE v. + -ER1.] An instrument for paring.

Parergon (pærő·gǫn). Pl. *parerga* (-ga). [L., a. Gr. πάρεργον, f. παρ- beside + ἔργον work.] Something subordinate or accessory to the main work; by-work; ornamental accessory or addition, grace, embellishment.

Parergy (pæˈrĕrdȝĭ), *sb.* *Obs.* [f. as prec.] That which is beside the purpose in hand.

Parethmoid (pærĕþˈmoid), a. *Anat.*

Parfleche (parflě·ʃ), sb. Also -flesh. [app. Canadian Fr.] A hide, usually of a buffalo, deprived of the hair and dried by stretching on a frame; an article made of such hide.

Parget (pāˈdȝĕt), sb. Also 5-7 parget. [f. PARGET v. 1.]

1. Plaster used to daub or coat with; a coarse kind of plaster; spec. Plaster of a finer sort, used in plastering the interior of chimneys, etc.; plaster-work ornamented in relief.

Parget (pāˈdȝĕt), v. Also 5-7 parget, pargit. [ad. OF. *pargeter, porgeter* = to cast or throw over (a surface), to roughcast.]

1. *trans.* To cover or daub with parget or plaster; to plaster (a wall, etc.); to adorn with ornamental plaster-work.

Pargeted (pāˈdȝĕtĕd), ppl. a.

†Pargeter (päːɹdʒɪtəɹ). Obs. Forms: 6 pargetour, 6 -getter, 6 -geter, 7 -gettor, -jetter, 9 -giter, 8 -geter. [orig. pargetour = OF. parjetteur, agent-n. from parjeter: see PARGET.]

1. A plasterer; a whitewasher.

Pargeting (päːɹdʒɪtɪŋ). vbl. sb. [-ING.]
1. The action of PARGET v.; plastering; plastering with (plaster-work); †transf. painting (of the face).

Pargeting, ppl. a. [f. as prec. + -ING².]
That pargets; † that whitewashes¹, glosses or smooths over.

†Pargety, a. Obs. rare. [f. PARGET sb. + -Y.]
Of the nature of plaster, sticky.

Fargo, pargie, var. PORGO, PURGY.

Parhedral (paɹhedrəl), a. rare. [f. Gr. παρά beside, ἕδρα seat + -AL.]

Parhelion (paɹhiːliən). Pl. **parhelia** (-liə), rarely -ions. [ad. L. (errον.) -elia, -helia's), 8 parelium, -helium; also 8-7 parelion, -elios, -helius, pl. -elii, -helii ; 7 parelie. [L. ... parelion, a. Gr. παρήλιον, pl.-λια, f. παρά beside + ἥλιος sun.

Parhomologous (päɹhɒməˈlɒgəs), a. Comp. Anat. [f. PAR-¹ + HOMOLOGOUS.] Applied to parts apparently but not really homologous: see quot.

Parhypate (päɹhiˈpætiː). Also 8 parypate. [a. Gr. παρυπάτη, f. παρά beside + ὑπάτη]

Parial (peˈriəl), a. rare⁻¹. [f. L. pari-equal, in pl. paria par + -AL.] Belonging to or constituting a pair ; quot.

Parian (peˈriən), a. and sb. [f. L. Pari-us of the Cyclades, famed for a white marble highly valued]

†Pariation. Obs. [ad. L. pariātiōn-em, f. pariā-re to make equal, balance.] The action of making equal ; equalization, balancing.

Parich, obs. f. PARISH, PERISH.

Paridigitate (pærɪdɪˈdʒɪteɪt), a. Zool. [f. PARI-, stem of L. par + DIGITATE.] Having an even number of toes on each foot ; artiodactyl.

†Pariety. Obs. rare⁻¹. [ad. L. pariēt-em.] Fellowship, parity.

Paries (peˈriiːz), sb. Pl. **parietes** (pəɹaɪˈiːtiːz). Anat., Nat. Hist., etc. [L. paries wall, partition-wall.]

Parietal (pəˈraɪɪtəl), a. and sb. [a. F. pariétal, ad. L. parietāl-em, f. pariēs, pariet- wall.]

Parietary (pəˈraɪɪtəri). Obs. Forms: ... [F., med.L. parietāria.] The herb pellitory.

Parieto- (pəˈraɪɪtəʊ), used as combining form of PARIES or PARIETAL, in several terms of Anatomy.

Paring (peˈrɪŋ), vbl. sb. [f. PARE v.¹ + -ING¹.]

†Parformal, a. Obs. rare⁻¹. [f. par, parm = forma + -AL.]

Parformity Obs. rare. [med.L.]

†Parity, v. Obs. rare. [a. OF. parifier]

Parity (ˈpærɪti), sb. [ad. L. paritās, f. pār equal ; or a. F. parité.] Equality.

Parilla (pəˈrɪlə). Also **parrilla**. [Sp. parilla.]

Paris (ˈpærɪs). [the name of the capital of France.]

Pari mutuel (pari mütüel). [Fr., = mutual stake or wager.]

Parish. (see next column) ...

Parish (ˈpærɪʃ). Forms: 4 paroche, 4-5 paroch, 4 paroche, 6 parrosh... [a. OF. paroche, paroiche, parosche ... ad. eccl.L. parochia, parœcia, f. Gr. παροικία.]

1. In the United Kingdom, an area of the Colonies, the name of a subdivision of a county.

2. A district, often identical with an original parish, but often having quite different limits, constituted for various purposes of civil government, and thus designated a civil parish.

3. The inhabitants of a parish ; parishioners collectively.

Parish church. Forms: see PARISH, CHURCH, KIRK. The church of a parish.

Parish clerk. An official appointed by the incumbent of a parish to assist in various duties connected with the church and its services.

Parish Council. A council of a parish.

Parishen. Sc. dial. Forms: ... The suffix is obscure: cf. PARISHING.

Parishing. vbl. sb. ... The nature and function of a parish.

Parishional (pəˈrɪʃənəl), a. Obs. Also parrishional.

Parishioner (pəˈrɪʃənəɹ). Forms: ... One of the inhabitants or members of a parish.

Parisian (pəˈrɪziən), a. and sb. [ad. F. parisien, med.L. parisiān-us, f. Paris.] Of or pertaining to Paris ; resembling Paris.

Parisianism. Parisian character, habit, or mode of living.

Parisianly, adv. in a Parisian fashion or manner.

Parisienne (parizjɛn). [F. fem. of prec.] A female Parisian.

Parison (ˈpærɪsən). Rhet. Pl. **parisa.** [Gr.] An even balance in the members of a sentence.

Parison², sb. [Named 1845 after the discoverer, J. J. Paris.] A silvery-white metal.

Top half

Column 1 (PARLIAMENT)

whose Christian name was Praise God, a Leatherseller in Fleet Street. ... the 'great parliament,' chosen in the transport of loyalty which had followed the Restoration. ...

†Parliament, v. rare. [f. prec.] ... 1. intr. To talk, converse; to confer, parley. Obs. ... 2. trans. To assemble, gather together. Obs. ... 3. intr. To attend Parliament; to discharge the duties of a member of Parliament.

†Parliamental, a. Obs. [See -AL.] Of or pertaining to Parliament; parliamentary.

Parliamentarian (pārliamentē·ri·ăn), sb. and a. [f. as PARLIAMENTARY + -AN.]

9. attrib. and Comb. Of or belonging to a or the parliament, sometimes = parliamentary ...

Column 2 (PARLIAMENTARY)

Cancelling...was registrate in the 'Parliament-books of that second session. ...

3. One versed and skilful in parliamentary usages and tactics; a skilled and experienced parliamentary debater.

Parliamentarily, adv. [f. PARLIAMENTARY + -LY.] In a parliamentary way; in accordance with parliamentary procedure; in connexion with parliament.

Parliamentarism (pārliamentarizm). [f. as prec. + -ISM: cf. militarism.] A parliamentary system of government.

Parliamentary (pārlimentəri). Also 7 parlie-, 7-8 parla-. [f. PARLIAMENT or med.L. parliamentarius. + -ARY: cf. med.F. parlementaire.]
1. Of, belonging or relating to a parliament, or to parliament as an institution; of the nature of parliament.
2. Short for parliamentary train: see 2 b above.
3. Of or belonging to the Parliament of Paris.

Parliamenteer (pārlimentīr). Also 7 -ier, 7-8 -eir. [f. PARLIAMENT sb. + -EER.]

Parliamenteer, v. [f. prec. sb.] Rarely used exc. in Parliamenteering vbl. sb.

Column 3 (PARLIAMENTARY)

passengers at a rate not exceeding one penny a mile, which, by Act of Parliament (7 & 8 Vict. c. 85), every railway company is obliged to run daily each way over its system. ...

Parliament-house, Parliament house. The building in which a parliament meets. ...

Parliament-man, parliament man. Now Hist., or dial. Also ǁ parliamentman. 1. A member of the Parliament, orig. of England, also of Scotland and Ireland, later of the United Kingdom; occasionally applied to a member of the House of Lords, but usually, like 'Member of Parliament' now, to a member of the House of Commons.

Column 4 (PARLOUR)

ǁre to speak. Cf. the more usual med.L. locutōrium, I. loqui, locūt-us to speak.]

B. Forms. ...

B. Signification. I. 1. An apartment in a monastery for conversation with persons from outside, or among the inmates. ...

Parlour, sb. Forms ... [a. OF. parleor, parlur ...]

†Parliance, par·leance. Obs. [Altered from PARLANCE after parley.] Parleying, parley.

†Parlier, sb. Obs. rare[-1]. [a. F. parlier ...]

Parling, vbl. sb. [f. PARLE v. + -ING.] The action of the vb. PARLE. a. Speaking, conversing.

Parling, ppl. a. [f. PARLE v. + -ING.] Speaking: parleying.

Parlour, parlor (pā·ləɹ). Forms: 3-5 parlur(e), 4 parlour, 4-5 parlour, etc.

Bottom half

Column 1 (PABLOUR)

3. A room in an inn more private than the tap-room, where people may converse apart. ...

Parlour-maid. A female domestic servant who waits at table in houses where indoor menservants are not kept.

Column 2 (PARNASSIAN)

PERILOUS (ME. = perilous, perilous, parelous), found from 14th c. alongside of the fuller form, but since 17th c. more or less arch. in literary use; common dialectally from Durham to Hampshire.

Parmacety, or **parmasety whale:** The Cachalot, or Sperm-whale.

Parmelia (pɑːmiːliă). Bot. ...

Parmeliaceous (pɑːmilieiʃəs), a. Bot.

Parmenidean (pɑːmenidiăn), a. (sb.)

†Parmentier. Obs. [a. OF. parmentier ...]

†Parmesan (pɑːmizæn), a. and sb. Forms ...

†Paris, parlos. Sb. Obs. rare. Paralysis, palsy.

Parley, Parline, Parly(e)ment, obs. ff. PALSY, PURLOIN, PARLIAMENT. **Parly,** colloquial abbreviation of Parliamentary (train).

Column 3 (PARNASSUS)

Parnassety, is now in some sort effectual for the same things that Parnassy is.
2. In full parnassy whale: The Cachalot, or Sperm-whale.

Parnassian (pɑːnæsiăn), a. and sb. [ad. F. Parnassien ...]

Parnassus (pɑːnæ·səs). Also formerly: 6 Parnase, Parnasus, 7 Parnas. [a. L. Parnāsus, ad. Gr. Παρνᾱσός ...]

Parnel (pɑːnel). Obs. rare. [See 2 parnele.]

Parnellism (pɑːnelizm). [f. -ISM.] The principles or policy of the party of Irish members in the House of Commons led by Charles Stewart Parnell.

Parnellite (pɑːneləit). [-ITE.] A member of this party, a follower of C. S. Parnell.

Paroch, Parnter. Obs. rare[-1]. Perh. a contracted form of PERSON.

Parochia (pəɹoʊkiă). [L.] A parish, a diocese.

Parocho, see PARROCK, PARROKET.

Parode (pæɹoʊd), sb. rare. [ad. Gr. πάροδος ...]

Column 4 (PARODIAL)

the parochialism of great men may not be in some way ...

†Parochian, sb. and a. Obs. Also 4-6 -ien, 5-6 -yen. ...

Parochial (pəɹoʊkiăl), a. (sb.) [ad. med.L. parochiālis ...]

Parochialism (pəɹoʊkiălizm). [See -ISM.]

Parochiality (pəɹoʊkiæliti). [f. PAROCHIAL + -ITY.]

Parochialize (pəɹoʊkiălaiz), v. [f. PAROCHIAL + -IZE.]

Parochially (pəɹoʊkiăli), adv. [f. PAROCHIAL + -LY.]

Parochian, obs. f. PAROCHINE.

Parochin, -ine. Sc. Obs. Also 6 parr-. [var. of PAROCHINE.]

Parochine, -in (pæɹokin). Sc. Obs. Also 6 parr-. A parish.

Parochitis, obs. f. PAROCHISM.

Parode, var. of PARODY sb.

Parodial (pəɹoʊdiăl), a. [f. PARODY + -AL.] Of or belonging to, or of the nature of a parody.

PARODIC.

Parodic, *a.*¹ *Math. Obs. rare.* [f. Gr. παρωδικ-ός passing, f. παρωδεῖν a passing, a passage: see -IC.] Applied to any one of the series of degrees or powers of the unknown or variable below the highest that occurs in an equation.

Parodic, *a.*² [f. *parodie* (1723) in Hatz.-Darm.), f. Gr. παρωδία: see -IST.] The author of a parody.

Parodistic (pærōdi'stik), *a.* [f. *parodist* + -IC.] Of the nature of a parody; that parodizes. So **Parodi'stically** *adv.*

Parodize (pæ'rŏdəiz, -əiz), *v.* [f. PARODY *sb.* + -IZE.] = PARODY *v.* 1.

Parody (pæ'rŏdi), *sb.* [ad. L. *parodia* (ult. ad. Gr. παρωδία a burlesque poem or song, f. παρ- beside, in subsidiary relation, mock-, etc. + ᾠδή song; poem; perh. immed. from L. parodia or F. parodie (1622 in Hatz.-Darm.).]

Parody (pæ'rŏdi), *v.* [f. prec.] *trans.* To compose a parody on (a work or author); to turn into parody; to ridicule (a composition) by imitating it.

Paroke, Parokeet, obs. ff. PARROCK, PARAKEET.

Parol (pærŏ'l, pæ'rŏl). Forms: 5-8 parole, 6 parrall, 6-7 parrel, 7 parroll. [Orig. identical with PAROLE *sb.*]

Parole (pærō'l), *sb.* Also 7 -oll, -oll. [a. mod. F. *parole* (parol) word (prec.), in sense 'formal promise, engagement,' F. *parole* of honour, honourable engagement.]

Parole (pærōʊ'l), *v.* [f. prec.] *trans.* To put (a prisoner) on his parole, to liberate on parole.

Parostosis (pærŏstō'sis), *Anat., Zool., Path.* [f. mod.L.] The formation of bone outside the periosteum, as in the ligament or connective tissue, or the sheaths of blood-vessels.

PAROSTIC. 491 PARPEN. | PARQUET. 492 PARRICIDE.

Parostotic (pærŏstō'tik), *a.* [ad. Gr.] Adjacent to the olivary body of the brain.

Parotic (pærō'tik, -ŏ'tik), *a.* and *sb. Anat.* and *Zool.* [ad. mod.L. παρωτικ-ός, f. Gr. παρ- + οὖς, ὠτ- ear; cf. Gr. οὖς, ὠτ-, krucos of the ear.] Situated beside or near the ear; parotid.

Parotid (pærō'tid), *a.* and *sb.* Also 7-8 -ide. [ad. F. *parotide* (1541), ad. L. *parotid-, parotis* — Gr. παρωτίς, -ίδ-.]

Parotidean (pærŏti'diăn), *a.* [f. prec. + -EAN.] Of or pertaining to the parotid gland.

Parotiditis (pærŏtidəi'tis), *Path.* [irreg. for PAROTITIS.] Inflammation of the parotid gland, or of neighbouring structures: usually constituting the disease called *mumps*. Hence **Parotidi'tic** (-ti'tik), *a.*, pertaining to or affected with parotiditis.

Paroxysmal (pærŏksi'smăl), *a.* [f. prec. + -AL.] Pertaining to or of the nature of a paroxysm; marked by paroxysms; violent, convulsive.

Paroxysmic (pærŏksi'smik), *a. rare.* [f. prec. + -IC.] = PAROXYSMAL.

Paroxysmist (pæ'rŏksizmist). [f. prec. + -IST.] One who attributes certain phenomena to paroxysms or sudden and violent natural convulsions; a catastrophist.

Paroxytone (pærŏ'ksitōn), *a.* and *sb. Gram.* [ad. Gr. παροξύτονος.]

Parpal, perpal, obs. ff. PAIR-ROYAL.

Parpen, parpend, parpent (pā'rpen, -énd, -ént). Forms: 5-8 perpen, 5 perpoynt, 6-8 parpin, 6-9 parpen(e), 9 parpoint, 6-9 parpyn, parpen. [a. OF. *parpain* (1304-1550 in Godef.), F. *parpaing*.]

Parquet (pā'rkĕt, pa'rke), *v.* [a. F. *parquet* sb.] *trans.* To make a parquet floor of (a room); to make or lay with parquetry; to make of inlaid wood-work.

Parquetry (pā'rkĕtri), *sb.* Also 9 -erie. [a. F. *parqueterie* (1676 in Hatz.-Darm.), flooring, wooden mosaic, f. *parqueter*: see prec. and -ERY.]

Parrel, parral (pæ'rĕl), *sb.* 5 perell, 6 parel, 7 parell, parall, (8 parell,) -parrel, 9 parral, parrell. [perh. a. OF. *parail*; of uncertain origin.]

Parricidal (pærisəi'dăl), *a.* [ad. L. *parricidal-is*, f. *parricid-ium*, *parricid-a*.] Of, pertaining to, or of the nature of a parricide; guilty of parricide.

Parricide (pæ'risəid), *sb.*¹ Also 7-8 parri-, 6 parre-, pare-. [ad. F. *parricide* (16th c. in Hatz.-Darm.), ad. L. *parricida* a slayer of a near relative.] One who murders his father or other near relative; also, the murderer of any one whose person is specially sacred.

Parsonage, sb. Forms: see PARSON; also 6 -edge, -ige, 7 -adge. [Altered form, as in pl. of *personage*, a. AF. *personage*, OF. *persone(a)ge*, ecclesiastical dignity or preferment, = late L. *personāticum*, med.L. (from Fr. or Eng.) *personāgium*; see PERSONAGE.]

1. The benefice or living of a parson; a rectory. *Obs. exc. in Law.*

2. = *Parsonage-house.* The house attached to a parson's living, the rector's house. Also, in later use, the house of a vicar, perpetual curate, or other incumbent of a parish or parochial district; sometimes (esp. in U.S. and Colonies) applied to the residence provided for any minister of religion.

†3. The parson's or rector's tithe. *Sc. Obs.*

4. *attrib.*, as *parsonage-garden*, -*house*, -*land*.

Parson-bird. [See PARSON 1.]

A New Zealand bird (*Prosthemadera novæ-zelandiæ*), so called from its dark plumage and white neck-feathers; also called *poe-bird* or *tui*.

Parsondom (pā'ɹsəndɒm). [f. PARSON + -DOM.]

The state or quality of a parson; the domain of parsons, parsons collectively.

Parsone, -elly, obs. ff. PARSON, PERSON, -ALLY.

Parsoned (pā'ɹsənd), *ppl. a.* [f. PARSON + -ED 2.]

1. Made or penned by a parson.
2. Furnished with a parson, as a parish.
3. Married in church or chapel. *colloq.*

Parsoness (pā'ɹsənes), *colloq.* or *hunorous.* [See -ESS 1.] The wife of a parson.

Parsonet. [f. PARSON + -ET.]

A petty or newly-fledged parson.

Parsonic (pɑɹsɒ'nik), *a.* [f. PARSON + -IC.] (after words from Gr.) Of or pertaining to a parson; resembling or characteristic of parsons.

Parsonical (pɑɹsɒ'nikăl), *a.* [f. prec. + -ICAL.] = prec. So **Parsonically** *adv.*, after the manner of a parson.

Parsoning, *vbl. sb.* [f. PARSON + -ING 1.] Acting as a parson; playing the parson's work.

Parsons, obs. variant of PERSON.

Parsuadable, -suasion, obs. ff. PERSUADABLE, -SUASION. **Parsy**, obs. form of PARSEE.

Part (pɑɹt), *sb.* [Forms 1, 3- part; also 4-5 *paars*, (*pard*), 4-6 *pert*, 4-7 *parte*, 6 *part*, 6- *part*.]

I. Portion or division of a whole.

1. That which together with another or others makes up a whole (whether really separated from the rest, or more often only separated in thought); a certain amount, but not all, of any thing or number of things (material or immaterial); any one of the smaller things into which a thing is or may be divided (in reality or in idea); a portion, division, section, element, constituent, fraction, fragment, piece.

2. A portion of an animal body; either definitely, a particular member or organ; or indefinitely, a 'spot', 'place' (cf. 13). Usually *pl.*; often with definitive adj., as *hinder parts*, *inward parts*; also *about*, (*neghers*), = *privy parts*.

3. A component or constituent of some quality or action, considered by itself (and with no stress on its being merely a part); a point, particular, *Hence adsol.* Point; matter, affair; respect (= PARTY *sb.* 3). *Obs.*

†4. A minute portion of matter, a particle. *Obs.*

Part (pɑɹt), *v.* Also 4-5 *pert*, 4-6 *parte*, 5- *part*, 6 *parte*, 4-5 (8-9) *part*, *pl. 5 *part*, (*pert*, -*parte*), 6 (8-9) *parte*. [OE. *part-ian*...]

Partage, sb. [a. F. *partage* — It. *partaggio*, med.L. *partāgium* (13th c. in Du Cange), f. F. *partir*, It. *partire*, to part: see -AGE.] Formerly natural-ized (partage); but, since 18th c., treated as F. (pa'rtaʒ). ('A word merely French'.)

1. The action of dividing; division; partition; esp. division into shares. *Also attrib.*

Partage, obs. form of PARTAKE.

Partakable, **-takeable** (pǎɹtḗi'kăb'l), *a. rare*. [f. next + -ABLE.] Capable of being partaken.

Partake (pǎɹtḗi'k), *v.* Also 6–7 partake, 7 -tack, *pa.* partook (back-formation (after 1590) from PARTAK-ING, PARTAKE-R, which were 16th c. synco-pated forms of the earlier singular combinations *part-taking*, *part-taker*, repr. L. *particeps*, *-cipem*. Cf. *housekeep* vb. from *housekeeping*, *housekeeper*.

1. *trans.* 1. To take a part in, to share in.

Partaking, ppl.

Partan (pǎ'ɹtǎn). Sc. and *north. dial.* Also 6 partane, pertane, 7–9 parten, 9 partin, parton.

Parted, ppl. a.

1. Divided into parts; severed, cloven, divided, as the hair, by a parting.

Parter (pǎ'ɹtəɹ). Now *rare.* [f. PART v. + -ER.] One who or which parts; a divider, separator, distributor, etc.; see the verb.

Partedness (in quot., in sense 5.)

Partenie, **Parteiner**, obs. ff. PARTY, PARTNER.

Parthenian (pǎɹþḗi'nɩ̆ăn), *a. rare.* [ad. Gr. παρθέν-ιος, f. παρθένος virgin.] Of or belonging to a virgin.

Parthenium (pǎɹþḗi'nɩ̆ŏm). *Bot.* [L. *parthenium*, a. Gr. παρθένιον.]

Parthenogenesis (pǎɹþḗnŏdʒe'nḗsĭs). *Biol.* [Gr. παρθένος virgin + γένεσις origin, birth, nativity, GENESIS.] Reproduction without con-course of opposite sexes or union of sexual elements.

Parthenogenetic (pǎɹþḗnŏdʒĭnĕ'tĭk), *a.* [f. prec. + -GENETIC.]

Parthenogenetically, adv.

Parthian (pǎ'ɹþɩ̆ăn), *a.* and *sb.* [See -AN.] *a. adj.* Of or pertaining to Parthia, an ancient kingdom of western Asia.

‖ Parti (parti). [Fr., — party; side, match, resolution taken for oneself.]

1. A marriageable person considered in reference to means or position, or what kind of a 'match' he or she may be.

Parti-, combining form of L. *pars*, *part-em*, PART; as in *parti-partial a.* (*Logic*), applied by Sir W. Hamilton to a proposition in which both terms are partial or particular: *parti-total*, in which one term is particular and the other universal.

Partial (pǎ'ɹʃăl, *sb.* -ɩ̆æl). Forms: 5 parcial, -cyale, 5–6 pryall, -ciall, 6 partyall, 6–7 partiall, (6 Sc. partiall), 6– partial. [a. OF. *parcial* (14th c. in Godef.), F. *partial*, ad. late L. *partiālis* (St. Gregory), f. L. *part-em* part: see -AL.]

1. Inclined emotionally to favour one party in a cause, or one side of the question more than the other (*J.*): unduly favouring one party or side in a suit or controversy, or one set or class of persons rather than another; prejudiced; biased; inter-ested; unfair. (The opposite of *impartial*.)

Partialism (pǎ'ɹʃălɩz'm). [f. PARTIAL a. + -ISM.] A partial theory or view, which does not take into account the whole of the facts or subject.

Partialist (pǎ'ɹʃălĭst). [f. PARTIAL a. + -IST.]

Partiality (pǎɹʃɩæ'lĭtɩ). Forms: 5 par-ciælite, -tee, -cyalite, partyalitee, 6– par-cialite, -tialite, (6 -tiallytie, -tialitie, -tye, -tia, parsealyte, perciallitee, persealytie, etc.), 6– partiality.

Partialize (pǎ'ɹʃălǎiz), *v.* [ad. F. *partialiser* (Amyot 1559), f. *partial* : see PARTIAL and -IZE.]

Partialness. [f. PARTIAL a. + -NESS.] The quality of being partial as opposed to total or universal; incompleteness.

Partible (pǎ'ɹtĭb'l), *a.* [ad. post-cl. L. *parti-bĭlis*, f. *partīri* to part, divide: see -BLE.] Capable of being parted or separated; capable of being divided or distributed among a number; subject to partition; divisible; separable.

Partibility (pǎɹtĭbĭ'lĭtɩ). [f. next: see -ITY.]

Participate (pǎɹtĭ'sĭpǎt), *v.* [f. L. *participāt-*, ppl. stem of *participāre* to partake, f. *particeps*, *-cip-* partaking, a partaker, f. *partis* PART + *-cip-*, weak form of *capĕre* to take.]

Participant (pǎɹtĭ'sĭpănt), *a.* and *sb.* [ad. L. *participant-em*, or F. *participant* (14th–15th c.).]

| PARTICIPATED. | 505 | PARTICLE. | PARTICLE. | 506 | PARTICULAR. |

Participle *sb.*

Participative *a.*

Participator.

Participatory *a.*

Participle *sb.*

Participial *a.* and *sb.*

Participation.

Particle *sb.*

Parti-colour, particolour, *a.* (*sb.*) *Obs.*

Parti-colour, party-colour, *v. Obs. rare.*

Parti-coloured, party-, particoloured *ppl. a.*

Parti-coloured, party, particoloured

Particular (pătĭ·kiŭlăr), *a.* and *sb.* (*adv.*)

| PARTICULAR. | 507 | PARTICULARIST. | PARTICULARISTIC. | 508 | PARTICULARNESS. |

Particularian, *Obs. rare.*

Particularism (pătĭ·kiŭlăriz'm).

Particularist (pătĭ·kiŭlărist).

Particularistic *a.*

Particularity (pătĭkiŭlæ·rĭtĭ).

Particularisation (pătĭkiŭlăraizē·shən).

Particularise, -ize (pătĭ·kiŭlăraiz), *v.*

Particularly *adv.*

Particularment. *Obs. rare.*

Particularness.

Particulate, a. [ad. med. or mod.L. *particulātus* divided into particles: see PART.] Only in scientific use.

Particulate, v. ... [f. ppl. stem of med.L. *particulāre* (ed. late L. *particulātio* division into particles, Mart. Capella c 425), f. *particula* PARTICLE.]

Particule ... [Fr. *particule*.]

Particle ...

Particulate, *adv.* ...

Parting, *vbl. sb.* [f. PART v. + -ING.] The action of the verb PART, partition; the result, or place, of this action; something that parts.

Partison, Partizan ...

Partisan, partizan (pä·tizăn, pätiz·n), *sb.* [a. F. *partisan*, -sanne, -sant, -sāne.]

Partisan, partizan ...

Parting cup. A drinking-cup with two handles on opposite sides...

Partite (pä·tait), *a.* [ad. L. *partīt-us* parted, divided...]

Partition (pärti·ʃən), *sb.* [a. F. *partition* (*particion*)... ad. L. *partītiōn-em* a sharing, dividing, distribution.]

Partition, *v.* [f. PARTITION *sb.*]

Partition-wall. A wall forming a partition...

Partitive (pä·titiv), *a.* and *sb.* [ad. L. *partītīv-us*, f. *partīt-*: see prec.]

Partitively, *adv.* [f. prec. + -LY 2.]

Partitioned, *ppl. a.* [f. PARTITION *sb.* and *v.* + -ED.]

Partition, ...

Partitioner, ...

Partitioning, *vbl. sb.* [f. PARTITION *v.* + -ING 1.]

Partitionment ...

Partlet (pä·tlĕt). Forms: 4-5 Pertelot(e, 5 Partelet, ... [ad. OF. *Pertelote*, a female proper name.] 1. A woman's garment. 2. The hen in Chaucer.

Partly, *adv.* [f. PART *sb.* + -LY 2.] Proportionally.

Partner (pä·tnəɹ), *sb.* Forms: 3-8 partener, ... [app. an altered form of *parcener*...]

Partnerless, *a.* [f. prec. + -LESS.] Without a partner.

Partnership (pä·tnəɹʃip). [f. prec. + -SHIP.]

Partook: see PARTAKE.

Parton, Partan: see PARTAN, PARTNER.

Partonless, obs. f. PARTITIONLESS.

Part-owner. One who owns something in common with another...

Partridge (pä·tridʒ), *sb.* Forms: 4-5 pertriche, ... [ad. OF. *pertis*, *pertris* (Florio), mod. perdrix...]

Partridge.

A. Forms. (The collective *pl.* is often like *sing.*)

α. 3–8 (9 *dial.*) partrich, 4–6 -riche, 5 -eriche, -criche, (partryrych), 5–6 partrych, -riche, -rytche, -ridge, (partrydge, -dryche), 6–7 -ridge, 6 -rydge, -ryge, -rage, etc.; 7 pardrige, 6–9 pardrich, 8 partridge, dern.

β. north, *Eng. and Sc.* 4, 4–6 partryk, (4–5 -ryke, -ricke), 4, 9 -rick. 6, 6 partrick, (4–5 -ryke, 4–6 -rite, 5–6 -ryk, -ryeka, 6 -rek, 6–7 -riok, 6–9 partrick, 8 peartrick).

B. Signification.

1. The name of certain well-known game-birds, specifically the British and Central European species *Perdix cinerea*, also called distinctively *Common* or *Grey Partridge*.

2. fg. A kind of charge for cannons consisting of a number of missiles fired together, similar to langrage or case-shot; also *partridge-shot*: see 3 b.

3. Partridge-berry.

Partridge-berry. Name of two North American plants, and their fruit: a. *Mitchella repens* (N.O. *Cinchonaceae*), a trailing evergreen herb with whitish but insipid scarlet berries; called *partridge-vine*. b. *Gaultheria procumbens* (N.O. *Ericaceae*), the CHECKER-BERRY or WINTER-GREEN, whose red berries furnish food for partridges.

Partridge-wood.

1. A hard red wood, much prized for cabinet work, also used for walking and umbrella sticks, obtained from the W. Indies.

2. A name for the appearance of wood when attacked by the saprophytic fungus *Stereum frustulosum*.

Partschinite (pärtʃinəit). *Min.* [f. Ger. *Partschin*, as named 1847 after Prof. *Partsch* of Vienna + -ITE.]

Partsman. *Sc. Obs.* In 6 partsman, *partis-a-part'*; possessive of PART *sb*.: d *daysman*.

Part-song. [f. PART *sb.* 10 + SONG.]

Parturiant (pätiū·riənt), *a.* [ad. L. *parturient-, -ēns, pr. pple. of parturire* to be in labour, to travail, to be pregnant, desiderative of *parĕre, part-* to bring forth.]

Parturience (pätiū·riəns). [f. prec.: see -ENCE.]

Parturiency (pätiū·riənsi). [f. prec.: see -ENCY.]

Parturient (pätiū·riənt), *a. and sb.* [ad. L. *parturient-, pr. pple. of parturire*: see PARTURIANT.]

Parturiently, *adv.* [f. prec. + -LY².]

Parturifacient (pätiū·rifeɪ·ʃənt), *a. and sb.* [f. L. *parturi-* to travail + *-facient*-.]

Parturious, *a. Obs. rare.* [f. L. *parturi-*: see -OUS.]

Parturiometer (pätiū·riɒ·mitə). [irreg. f. L. *parturi-* + -METER.]

Parturition (pätiūri·ʃən). [ad. L. *parturitiōn-em*, n. of action f. *parturire*: see PARTURIENT.]

1. The action of bringing forth or of being delivered of young; childbirth.

Parturitive (pätiū·ritiv), *a. rare.* [f. ppl. stem of L. *parturire* + -IVE.]

Parturiency. *Obs. rare.*

Party (pä·ti). Forms: 3–7 partye, 3–4 partie, 4–5 parti, (4 perti, 4–5 -tye, -tie, perte), pl. 4 partiis, 4–5 parties, -tyes, (partye, -tye, -tio), 4–7 party, etc.; 6 partie, (6–7 -tie), 7 party (11th c. in Littré)=Pr., Sp. *partida*, It. *partita* lit. a parting, F. *partir* part: see PART *sb*.

I. 1. A division of a whole; a part, portion, share; an aliquot part; a part or member of the body. *Obs.*

II. A company or body of persons.

2. *fg.* Ready to bring forth or produce something.

Party-coat. *Obs.* = PARTI-COAT.

Party-coloured, variegated. *Obs.*

Party-jury. *Obs.* [PARTY *a.* + JURY.]

Party-man.

1. *Mil.* A soldier belonging to, or officer commanding, a party.

Party-wall.

1. A wall between two buildings or parts of one which each of the occupiers has a right to use.

Parvenu (pärvənȳ). [F., pa. pple. of *parvenir*, ... L. *pervenire* to arrive, come through, f. *per* through + *venire* to come.]

Parvanimity (pärvăni·miti). *rare.* [f. L. *parv-us* small + *anim-us* mind + -ITY.] Littleness of mind, meanness; also, an instance of this; a little or ignoble mind, or *ignominity*.

Paruria (pärū·riă). *Path.* [f. Gr. *πᾰρα* beside + *οὖρον* urine.] Disordered micturition.

Parvanimous, *a.* [f. L. *parv-us* small + *anim-us*.] Mean-minded.

Parvenue (pärvənȳ), *sb. (and a.)* An upstart.

Parvis (pärvis). Forms: 4–7 parvis, etc. [a. OF. *parvis* (pervis, mod. F. *parvis*), ... L. *paradisus* PARADISE.]

it off entirely. 1826 Disraeli *Viv. Grey* II. xiv, 'Ah! there is nothing like old families!' remarked Mrs. Million, with all the awkward feelings of a parvenue. 1834 L. Ritchie *Wand. by Seine* 68 The Bonaparte people were parvenus, and clung to all the prestiges of the preceding dynasty. 1848 Thackeray *Van. F.* xxxvi, The ladies their wives, who could not bear the parvenue [Rebecca]. 1891 M. O'Rell *Frenchm. in Amer.* 209 The parvenu is a person who makes strenuous efforts to persuade other people that he is entitled to the position he occupies.

B. *adj.* That has but recently risen to wealth or position; like or characteristic of a parvenu in manners, vulgar display, etc.

1839 Poe *W. Wilson* Wks. 1874 I. 347 A young *parvenu* nobleman. 1879 *Q. Rev.* July 14 Other monarchs had treated the *parvenu* ruler of France with distant arrogance. 1897 *Harper's Mag.* Apr. 746 There was nothing *parvenu* in the penniless lad.

Hence **Parvenu·dom**, the domain of parvenus; **Pa·rvenuism**, the habits or practices of parvenus, parvenu character.

1854 Lowell *Jrnl. Italy* Prose Wks. 1890 I. 205 A Roman column standing near .. satirizes silently their tawdry parvenuism. 1868 W. R. Greg *Lit. & Soc. Judgm.* 280 [A] piece of inflated affectation in the richest style of parvenuism. 1891 *Star* 12 Dec. 4/3 The servile grovelling of parvenudom. 1900 *Westm. Gaz.* 31 Jan. 3/2 How far it is true as a study of Berlin parvenudom, few..could say.

Parvers, obs. form of Perverse *a.*

Parvi- (pā·rvi), comb. form of L. *parvus* small, as in **Parvifo·lious** *a.* (*Bot.* L. *parvifolius*), having small leaves; †**Pa·rvipe·nsion** [L. *pensio* a weighing, cf. phr. *parvi pendĕre* to esteem little], slight estimation; **Parvi·potent** *a.* [Potent], having little power; **Parvipsoas** [Gr. ψόα lumbar muscle], a name applied by Coues to the *psoas parvus* or small psoas muscle; hence **Parvipso·a·tic** *a.*; **Parviro·strate** *a.* [L. *rostrum* beak], having a slender beak; **Parvi·scient** *a.* [L. *scient-em* knowing], knowing little.

1857 Mayne *Expos. Lex.*, *Parvifolius*, having small leaves, ..*parvifolious. 1893 in *Syd. Soc. Lex.* 1675 R. Burthogge *Causa Dei* 44 When we consider in it that Contempt, Scorn, and *Parvipension of God, which does compose it. 1678 Phillips (ed. 4) *List Barbarous Words*, *Parvipension*, a setting litely by, an esteeming at a small rate. 1862 F. Hall *Hindu Philos. Syst.* (1897) 152 The ignorance of a single soul .. keeps it *parviscient, *parvipotent. 1857 Mayne *Expos. Lex.*, *Parvirostris*, having a slender beak,..*parvirostrate. 1884 T. J. Scott in J. M. Reid *Doomed Relig.* 160 Brahma alone .. is neither parviscient nor omniscient.

Parvis (pā·rvis). Also 5 **parvys**, **per-**, **parvyce**, 5–9 *erron.* **parvise**. [a. F. *parvis*, 'place in front of the principal door of a church, particularly of a cathedral, as the Parvis of Notre Dame', in OF. *parevis* (12–13th c. in Hatz.-Darm.), earlier *pareïs* (*paraïs*, *-aÿs*, *parewis*) (Godef.):—L. *paradis-um* Paradise (a name given in the Middle Ages to the atrium or court in front of St. Peter's at Rome, and to the courts before other churches: see Du Cange). From F. also a med.L. form *paravīsus*, *paravīsius*.]

1. The enclosed area or court in front of a building, esp. of a cathedral or church; in some cases, surrounded as a cloister with colonnades or porticoes; whence, sometimes applied to a single portico or colonnade in front of a church, and (in dictionaries) explained as a church-porch.

The parvis of St. Paul's in London was a noted place of resort, esp. for lawyers.

c 1386 Chaucer *Prol.* 310 A Sergeant of the Lawe war & wys That often hadde been at the Parvys. c 1440 *Promp. Parv.* 385/2 Parvyce, *parlatorium*. 1476 J. Paston in *P. Lett.* III. 156, I prey yow as ye se hym at the parvyse and ellys where, calle on hym for the same letter. c 1485 in *Digby Myst.*, *Mor. Wisd.* (1882) 167 At the parvyse I wyll be A' Powlys, be-twyn two and three. 1687 A. Lovell tr. *Thevenot's Trav.* II. 80 Before this Mosque there is a Parvis or Walk of many Angles, and in the middle of it a Bason of Water likewise Polygone. 1706 Phillips, *Parvis*, a Court before a Church-Porch, or any Palace or stately House. 1745 Blomefield *Norfolk* II. 748 In 1300, I find Mention of a Publick School for Children to learn to read and sing, kept in the Parvis of this Church [St. Martin's, Norwich]. 1864 Longf. *Div. Commedia* ii, Canopied with leaves Parvis and portal bloom like trellised bowers. 1875 H. James *Trans. Sk.*, *Rom. Neighb.* 179 It stands perched on a terrace as vast as the parvise of St. Peter's. 1881 *Daily News* 1 Apr. 3/1 Its illuminating power was clearly proved by the two lamps on the parvis of St. Paul's Cathedral. 1886 [see sense 2]. 1895 H. Rashdall *Universities* II. II. xii. § 5. 443 *note*, The word 'Parvis' is used of the Cloister of Notre Dame at Paris, the Palace Yard at Westminster, etc.

¶ **b.** By some 19th c. writers applied in error to 'a room over a church-porch'.

App. originating in a misunderstanding of quot. 1745 above. See *Penny Post* 1868, pp. 159, 213.

1836 Parker *Gloss. Archit.*, *Parvis*, a small room over the porch, formerly used as a school. 1838 *Ibid.* ed. 2 s.v. 1842 Gwilt *Archit.* Gloss., *Parvis*.. It seems also to have signified a room over the church porch, where schools used to be held. 1848 *Rickman's Archit.* p. xlvi, A plain porch.. with a room over it (commonly but erroneously called a parvise). 1852 Hook *Ch. Dict.* (1871) 568. 1856 J. Allen *Liskeard* viii. 120. 1867 *Gwilt's Archit.* (ed. 6) 956 A Norman porch, with an upper story or *parvise*, a chamber which appears to have been variously appropriated. 1881 *Archit. Publ. Soc. Dict.*, *Parvise* or *Parvis*... Modern writers have applied this term, but apparently without any good authority, to a room often found over church porches. 1888 *N. & Q.* 7th Ser. VI. 203/1.

†**2.** A public or academic conference or disputation. (So called from being originally held in the court or portico of a church.) *Obs.*

1496 *Dives & Paup.* (W. de W.) III. vi. 142/1 There [in chirche] they holde theyr peruys of many wronges whiche they thynke to doo. c 1530 More *Answ. Frith* Wks. 841/2 Whan he was a young sophister he would I dare say haue been full sore ashamed so to haue ouerseene himselfe at Oxforde at a peruise. 1579 Fulke *Heskins's Parl.* 296 M. Hesk. will set .. a boy in the Paruis to answere the Bishop. 1706 Phillips, *Parvis*, a Court before a Church-Porch,..whence that Disputation at Oxford, call'd *Disputatio in Parvisiis*. It is also apply'd to the Mooting or Law-Disputes among young Students at the Inns of Court. 1886 H. C. Maxwell Lyte *Univ. Oxford* 205 A 'general sophister'..was required to attend the logical 'variations' that were held 'in the parvise' for at least a year, 'disputing, arguing, and responding' on sophisms...The parvise being a cloister, paved platform, or other open space, immediately adjoining a church. A curious instance of the survival of old names is to be found in the 'testamur'..which is nowadays [down to 1893] issued by the examiners at 'Responsions', to the effect that a successful candidate has answered to the questions of the Masters of the Schools 'in parviso'.

Parvitude (pā·rvitiud). *rare.* [f. L. *parv-us* small, after *magnitude*. (The L. derivative was *parvitās*.)] Littleness, smallness.

1657 Tomlinson *Renou's Disp.* 34 Magnitude, Parvitude, and Number. 1661 Glanvill *Van. Dogm.* 59 Because of its parvitude it cannot reach to the same floor with them. 1788 T. Taylor *Proclus* I. 89 They differ in magnitude and parvitude. 1903 *Edin. Rev.* Jan. 59 A continued preference for the slum .. would confess parvitude in the point of view.

†**b.** An absolutely small or minute thing, an atom. *Obs.*

1653 H. More *Conject. Cabbal.* (1713) 189 These perfect Parvitudes .. which are so infinitely subtile, that no Touch can perceive them. 1659 — *Immort. Soul* II. i. 115 By a meer point of Matter I doe not mean a meer Mathematicall point, but a perfect Parvitude, or the least reality of which Matter can consist. 1678 Cudworth *Intell. Syst.* I. v. 777 To suppose Incorporeal Substances, Unextended and Indivisible, is to make them Absolute Parvitudes.

†**Pa·rvity.** *Obs.* [ad. L. *parvitās* smallness, f. *parv-us* small: see -ity.] = prec.

1620 Venner *Via Recta* viii. 190 Through parvity of exercise .. many crude .. humours are bred. 1650 Bulwer *Anthropomet.* i. 4 Such a kind of turbinated figure represents a certain parvitie. 1691 Ray *Creation* I. (1692) 159 But what are these for their fineness and parvity?

Parvoline (pā·rvŏlain). *Chem.* [f. L. *parv-us* small, little + *-oline*, after *quinoline*.] A ptomaine $C_9H_{13}N$, $=C_5H_2N(CH_3)_2(C_2H_5)$ dimethylethylpyridine, obtained as an oily liquid with a disagreeable odour, from decaying mackerel and horse flesh, and also from certain shales and bituminous coals.

1855 Grev. Williams in *Q. Jrnl. Chem. Soc.* VII. 106, I propose to assign it the name of Parvoline in allusion to its small volatility as compared with its associated bases. c 1865 Letheby in *Circ. Sc.* I. 118/2 Of the alkaline matters there are leucoline,..and parvoline ($C^{18}H^{13}N$). 1887 A. M. Brown *Anim. Alkal.* 31 Parvoline $C^9H^{13}N$.—This was the first ptomaine chemically analysed and defined. It was discovered by MM. Gautier and Etard in the putrefactive products of the mackerel and horse flesh.

Parvule (pā·rviul). *U.S.* [f. L. *parvul-us*, *-um* very small, dim. of *parvus* small.] (See quot.)

1890 in *Cent. Dict.* 1893 *Syd. Soc. Lex.*, *Parvules*, an American speciality, similar in all respects to 'granules'; made up with a fixed, but very small, quantity of some active drug.

Parwanah, -wanna, variants of Purwannah.

Parwynke, obs. form of Periwinkle[1].

†**Pary**, *v.* *Obs. rare.* [ad. F. *parier* or L. *pariāre*, to be equal, to tally, f. *pār*, *par-em* equal.]

1. *intr.* To tally.

1716 Bentley *Let. to Abp. Wake* 15 Apr. in Monk *Life* (1833) I. 399 When I came to try Pope Clement's Vulgate, I soon found the Greek of the Alexandrian, and that would by no means pary.

2. *trans.* To bet, stake.

a 1468 Henryson *Practysis of Med.* 84 (Bann. MS.) Sir, minister this medecyne at evin to sum man, And, or pryme be past, my powder I pary, They sall bliss yow or ellis bitterly yow ban.

Pary, obs. f. Parry. **Paryll**, obs. f. Peril. **Parysch(e, parysse, -yzsh**, obs. ff. Parish. **Paryschoon, -shchon**, var. Parishen[1] *Obs.* **Paryse(e**: see Parisis. **Parytory**, obs. f. Parietary *sb.*

‖**Pas** (pā). [F. *pas* step, precedency, etc.]

1. The right of going first; precedence. Phrases, *to dispute, give, take, yield, the pas* [F. *prendre, céder le pas*, etc.] Also *fig.*

1707 *Vulpone* 23 It appears they have always fiercely contended for the *pas* among themselves. 1712 Addison *Spect.* No. 529 ▸ 7 Aristotle would have the latter yield the *Pas* to the former. 1771 Smollett *Humph. Cl.* 8 Nov., My aunt and her paramour took the *pas*. 1848 Thackeray *Bk. Snobs* xvi, He takes the *pas* of dukes. 1885 *Spectator* 22 Aug. 1103/2 It is difficult to give any one portion of it the *pas* of the others.

2. A step in dancing; a kind of dance; mostly in names of special dances, as *Pas de deux*, a dance or figure for two persons; *Pas grave*, a slow or solemn dance; *Pas seul*, a dance or figure for one person.

1775 Sheridan *Rivals* III. iv, Mine are true-born English legs, they don't understand their curst French lingo! their *pas* this, and *pas* that, and *pas* t'other. 1804 Charlotte Smith *Conversations*, etc. I. 140 She .. shewed a new *pas grave*, which her dancing-master had lately introduced. 1819 T. Hope *Anastasius* (1820) I. vii. 136 A *pas-de-deux* which we performed together as a lover and his mistress. 1868 *Daily News* 3 Nov., The father of some 'young phenomenon' of a minor theatre fiddling in an ecstacy of admiration at his little daughter's rehearsal of her '*pas*' before going on. 1870 Miss Bridgman *Rob Lynne* I. viii. 165 Fanny..performed a..*pas de seul* up the garden path.

3. *Pas-de-souris*. (*Fortif.*) [F. lit. 'mouse-steps'.] A staircase from the ravelin to the ditch.

1704 J. Harris *Lex. Techn.* I, *Pas de Souris*. 1859 F. A. Griffiths *Artil. Man.* (1862) 268 *Stairs*, or *Pas de souris*. These steps of masonry are made at the gorges of the several works, and at the salient, and re-entering angles of the counterscarp.

Pas, obs. form of Pace, Pass.

1385 in *3rd Rep. Hist. MSS. Comm.* 410/2 Deferryt tyl his lauchfull day next eftir pas.

Pasan, pasang (pā·zăn, -ăŋ). Also 8 **pazan**, 9 **pazun**, **paseng**. [a. Pers. پازن *pāzan* the mountain goat; erron. analysed as f. *pā* foot + *sang* stone.]

A species of wild goat (*Capra Ægagrus*), found in Western Asia and Crete; the bezoar-goat.

1774 Goldsm. *Nat. Hist.* III. 74 The eighth is called the pazan; or, by some, the bezoar goat. 1834 J. B. Fraser *Persia* xii. 470 Two of the most interesting creatures to be met with in these countries are the .. Pazun (the mountain goat) and the Argali. 1838 *Penny Cycl.* XI. 28/2 Cuvier .. considers the Paseng (*Capra Ægagrus*) to be the parent-stock of all the varieties of the domestic goat. 1893 Lydekker *Horns & Hoofs* 107 The bezoar stone .. is a concretion obtained from the stomach of the pasang.

¶ Mistakenly identified by Buffon (1764, XII. 212) with the oryx or gemsbok, a S. African antelope; the error was formerly followed by some English compilers, and is reproduced in some recent dictionaries.

Pasc, Pasce, obs. ff. Pasch, Pass. **Pascage**, **Pascal**, obs. ff. Pascuage, Paschal, Pascual.

Pascent (pæ·sĕnt), *a.* *rare*[−1]. [ad. L. *pāscent-em*, pr. pple. of *pāscĕre* to feed, graze.] Feeding.

1763 Goldsm. *Misc. Wks.* (1837) II. 538 The pascent creature finds a bed which at once supplies food and protection.

Pasch (pask). Now *arch.* or *Hist.* Forms: 2–4 *pl.* **pasches**, 3 (*Orm.*) **passke**, 3–7 **pasche**, 4–6 **paske**, **pask**, 5, 9 **pasque**, 4– **pasch**, (4 **pasck**, 5 **pasc**, **pasce**, **pache**, **passh**, 5–6 **passe**, 6 **paasse**, *Sc.* 5 **paisch**, 6 **pashe**, **pess**, **peice**, 7 **peace**: see also Pace *sb.*[2]; in L. form, 4, 9 **pascha**). [a. OF. *pasche* (Phil. de Thaun, etc.) and *pasque* (mod.F. *pâque*), ad. L. *pascha*, a. Gr. πάσχα, ad. Heb. פֶּסַח *pesakh*, in Aramaic emphatic state פַּסְחָא *paskhā* a passing over, the Passover; f. פָּסַח *pāsakh* to pass over. The OF. pl. *pasches*:—L. *paschas* (acc. pl.) occurs already in the OE. Chron. *a* 1131. Cognate forms from L. were OS., OFris. *pascha* (MDu. *paeschen*, Du. *paaschen*, MLG. *pasche(n*, LG. *pâschen*, *pâsken*), Icel. *pâskar* (Sw. *påsk*(*a*, Da. *paaske*); the Northern Eng. forms in *paske*, *pask* (whence *pass*, *pace*, etc.), were perh. from Scandinavian. Formerly often *pl.* with *sing.* sense, as in F., Du., LG., Icelandic, etc.]

1. The Jewish feast of the Passover.

c 1200 Ormin 15850 Forr Passke,—ȝiff þu turrnenn willt þatt word till Ennglissh spæche, Þa taccneþþ itt tatt uss birrþ ann Uss flittenn towarrd Criste. c 1250 *Gen. & Ex.* 3157 Ðat niȝt sal ben fest pasche, forð-for, on engle tunge, it be. a 1300 *Cursor M.* 6164 (Cott.) Quat wise þai suld þair paskes [*later MSS.* pask, paske] hald. *Ibid.* 16814+2 If ani man At paschez to ded wore broght. 1382 Wyclif *Exod.* xii. 43 This is the religioun of phask [*Vulg.* phase]; ech alien shal not ete therof. — *Mark* xiv. 14 Wher is my fulfilling [*gloss* or etyng place] where I schal ete pask [1582 *Rhem.* the Pasche] with my disciplis. c 1400 Maundev. (1839) viii. 93 There made our Lord his Pask with his Disciples. c 1440 *York Myst.* xxvii. 29 Þe lambe of Pasc. 1609 Bible (Douay) 1 *Esdras* i. 1 Josias made a Pasch in Ierusalem. 1745 A. Butler *Lives Saints*, *James* 1 May (1847) V. 16 In the second year of Christ's preaching, soon after the Pasch, in the year 31. [1850 Neale *Med. Hymns* (1867) 114 Hail our Pascha, That wast dead!] 1885 *Catholic Dict.* (ed. 3) 284/2 The Churches of Asia Proconsularis .. kept the feast of Passover or Pasch at the same time as the Jews—viz. 14 Nisan.]

2. The Christian festival of Easter. *arch.* or *local*: cf. Pace *sb.*[2] (In ME. often in *pl.* with collective sense = Easter-tide: cf. F. *les Pâques*.)

a 1131 *O. E. Chron.* an. 1122 On þis geare wæs se king Heanri on Cristes mæssan on Norhtwic and on Pasches he weas on Northhamtune. 13.. *Coer de L.* 6475 Hys brother Ihon, Wolde do corowne hym anon, At the Pask. c 1330 R. Brunne *Chron. Wace* (Rolls) 9267 At Londone his Pasches he [Uther] held. 1357 *Lay Folks Catech.* 321 Anes in the yhere, That is at sai, at paskes. c 1450 *Merlin* 104 Sys, we pray yow that the swerde be suffred yet in the ston to Passh. 1481 Caxton *Godeffroy* clxiii. 241 There helde they the feste of ester or pasque, the x day of Apryll. 1535 Lyndesay *Satyre* 2004 And halds me ȝit vnder that same proces, That gart me want the Sacrament at Pasche [*v.r.* pess]. 1557 Tusser 100 *Points Husb.* lxviii, Spare meddowes at shroftide, spare marshes at pashe. 1596 Dalrymple tr. *Leslie's Hist. Scot.* IV. 234 To grant the ryt celebratione of the Pashe. 1638 Chillingw. *Relig. Prot.* I. vi. § 30. 349 Who had assigned the fourteenth of the Moneth of March for the observation of the *Pasche*. 1722 S. Sewall

Diary 21 Dec., They kept not Yule nor Pasch. 1885 *Catholic Dict.* (ed. 3) 284/2 The great majority of Christians celebrated the Pasch on the Sunday after Nisan 14..because on that day Christ rose again.

3. *attrib.* and *Comb.* in many collocations = Easter-, as *pasch-even*, *-lamb*, *-mass*, *-morn*, *-tide*, *-week*. Also Pasch-day, -egg.

c 1200 Ormin 15849 Þa frellsenn þeȝȝ, þatt witt tu wel, Gastlike Passkemesse. a 1300 *Cursor M.* 18617 Þe seuend dai in paske tide, He ras arli, wit-vten bide. 1375 Barbour *Bruce* xv. 101 Quhill the tysday in pask-owk [*v.rr.* payss wouk, Pasche Oulk] On athir half thai trowis tuk. *Ibid.* 105 Apon paske evin all richt To the castell..come schippis xv. c 1460 *Towneley Myst.* xxiii. 666 That Lord that..rose on pasche morne. 1533 Tindale *Supper of Lord* C vj b, I wyll compare circumcision wyth baptysme: and the passe lambe wyth Christes supper. 1605 Sylvester *Du Bartas* II. iii. III. *Law* 583 Th' Israelites, whose doores were markt before, With sacred Pass-Lambs Sacramental gore.

Paschal (pa·skăl), *a.* and *sb.* Also 5–6 **paskal(l**, 6 **pascal(l**, **pascquall**, 8 **pasqual**. [a. F. *pascal* (12th c. in Hatz.-Darm.), ad. late L. *paschāl-is* (Codex Theod.), f. *pascha* Pasch: see -al.]

A. *adj.*

1. Of or pertaining to the Jewish Passover.

Paschal lamb, the lamb slain and eaten at the Passover; applied to Christ, hence also to various symbolic representations of Christ; = Agnus Dei b and c.

c 1430 Lydg. *Hors, Sheep & G.* 1 in *Pol. Rel. & L. Poems* 15 This pascalle Lambe with-owte spott, aile whyte. 1526 Tindale *Mark* xiv. 12 The first daye of swete breed, when they offered the pascal lambe. 1658 Lightfoot *Horæ Hebraicæ* (1859) II. 336 That Judas after the paschal supper ..could make his agreement with the priests, and get his blades..together ready to apprehend our Saviour. a 1714 Sharp *Wks.* (1754) VII. Serm. xii. 223 The paschal feast, from whence our Saviour took his sacrament of the Lord's supper. 1845 H. J. Rose in *Encycl. Metrop.* (1847) II. 891/1 The paschal lamb they called the body of the Passover.

2. Of or pertaining to Easter; used in Easter celebrations.

Paschal candle, a large candle blessed and lighted in the service of Holy Saturday and placed on the gospel side of the altar there to remain till Ascension day.

1432–50 tr. *Higden* (Rolls) V. 377 The grete cicle of the terme Paschalle is finischede or complete in this v[the] yere of Iustinus, whiche is of v.c. yere and xxvij from the passion of Criste, and after Marianus v.c. and lx. yere. 1477–9 in *Rec. St. Mary at Hill* (E. E. T. S.) 92 For makyng of the paschall tapre..weyng xxx lb. 1506 in Glasscock *Rec. St. Michael's Bp. Stortford* (1882) 31 For the paskal sylver at Ester eve. 1519 in Nash *Churchw. Acc. St. Giles, Reading* 6 For mending and scouring of the Pascall causticke. 1653 Jer. Taylor 25 *Serm.* 39 They then thought that when the Paschall taper burn'd, the flames of hell could not burn, till the holy wax was spent. 1670 Blount *Law Dict.*, *Paschal Rents*, are rents or yearly tributes paid by the inferior Clergy to the Bishop or Arch-Deacon at their Easter-Visitation. 1772 Nugent tr. *Hist. Fr. Gerund* I. 61 At the time of confession and pasqual communion. 1875 Lightfoot *Comm. Col.* 56 Polycarp .. visited Rome, hoping to adjust the Paschal controversy.

B. *sb.* Various absolute uses of A. 1 and 2.

1. A great candle lighted at Easter: see A. 2. **b.** A candlestick to hold the same. Cf. Judas 2.

1427 in *Rec. St. Mary at Hill* (E. E. T. S.) 64 A pece of tymbre to þe newe Paschall. *Ibid.*, A dysch of peuter for þe Paskall. 1519 in Nash *Churchw. Acc. St. Giles, Reading* 5 For wax and making of the Pascall. 1590 Munday *Eng. Romayne Life* in *Harl. Misc.* (Malh.) II. 186 After the Iewes..be baptized, they be brought into the church, and there they see the hallowing of the paschall, which is a mightie great wax taper. 1593 in *Rites & Mon. Ch. Durh.* (Surtees 1903) 11 On the height of the s[d] candlestick or pascall of lattine was a fair large flower..wherein did stand a long peece of wood..wheron stood a great long square tap of wax called the pascall. 1826 Hone *Every-day Bk.* I. 436 The paschal or great Easter taper at Westminster Abbey was three hundred pounds' weight. *Ibid.*, The paschal in Durham cathedral was square wax, and reached to within a man's length of the roof.

2. The Passover celebration, Passover supper, or Passover lamb.

1579 Fulke *Heskins's Parl.* 46 He did desire to eat the Pascall of the lawe. 1581 R. Goade in *Confer.* III. (1584) T iij, There was some distance of time betweene the Pascall and the Supper. a 1655 Vines *Lord's Supper* (1677) 16 The Levites killed the paschals. 1670 G. H. *Hist. Cardinals* I. II. 34 To suffer them [Jews]..to Celebrate their Paschal with all possible Solemnity.

†**Pa·schalist.** *Obs. rare*[−1]. [f. prec. + -ist.] An adherent of (the Greek or Roman) Easter.

1641 Milton *Prel. Episc.* Wks. (1851) 89 That which Church Histories report of those East, and Western Paschalists.

†**Pa·sch-day.** *Sc.* and *north. dial.* *Obs.* Forms: see Pasch, Pace *sb.*[2] Easter-day. (Sometimes applied to Good Friday.)

c 1200 Ormin 15552 Forr þatt Judisskenn Passkedaȝȝ þa sholde cumenn newenn. a 1300 *Cursor M.* 13227 (Cott.) Sant ion..was slan in pasch daus [*F.* paske dawes]. 1472 in *Surtees Misc.* (1888) 25 The Lord sall reperell be Passe day. 1596 Dalrymple tr. *Leslie's Hist. Scot.* IV. 227 Anent the celebratione of the Pasche day. a 1670 Spalding *Troub. Chas. I* (1850) I. 262 No preiching nor commvnion..wes vsit and wont, nor yit givin on pash day.

Pasch-egg (pa·sk,eg). *Sc.* and *north. dial.* Forms: see Pasch, Pace *sb.*[2]; also corruptly **paste-egg**. An Easter egg: an egg dyed of various colours, and boiled hard, as an Easter gift.

1579, 1611, etc. [see Pace *sb.*[2]]. 1677 Coles *Eng.-Lat. Dict.*, Pasch-eggs, Eggs given at Easter, *Ovum paschale croceum* or *luteum*. 1777 Brand *Pop. Antiq.* 310 Of Pasche, or as they are commonly called, Paste Eggs. 1825 Brockett *N. C. Gloss.*, *Paste-eggs*. 1847 Mary Howitt *Ballads* 80 And kindly country-women, yet, Their Pasch-eggs ready make, Of divers colours beautiful, To give for Jesus' sake. 1898 *Dublin Rev.* July 153 In France it is, or was until recently, usual to eat the Pasch-egg before any other food was partaken of on Easter Day.

Pasch-flower: see Pasque-flower.

Paschite (pæ·skəit). [f. Gr. πάσχα, Pasch + -ite.] One who observed Easter on the date of the Jewish Passover, the fourteenth of Nisan; a quartodeciman. 1890 in *Cent. Dict.*

Pascible (pæ·sĭb'l), *a.* *rare.* [ad. L. type *pascibilis, f. *pascĕre* to feed: see -ible.] Capable of serving as pasture.

1795 J. Billingsley *Agric. Somerset* (1798) 52 Land.. when pascible for the remaining months, of little value from being overstocked.

Pascioun, Pasck, obs. ff. Passion, Pasch.

Pa·scuage. *rare*[−0]. Also 7 **pascage**. [a. OF. *pascuage* (14th c. in Godef.), ad. late L. *pascuāticum* (med.L. *pascuāgium*), f. L. *pascu-um* pasture, neuter of *pascuus* adj., Pascuous, f. *pascĕre* to feed: see -age.] The grazing of cattle.

1656 Blount *Glossogr.*, *Pascage*, grazing, feeding or pasturing of Cattle. 1848 in Wharton *Law Lex.*

Pascual (pæ·skiuăl), *a.* Also 7 **pascal**. [a. OF. *pascual*, *pascuel*, ad. med.L. *pascuāl-is*, f. *pascu-um* grazing: see -al. Cf. med.L. *pascuale* sb.] Of or pertaining to pastures; growing in pastures.

1656 Blount *Glossogr.*, *Pascal*, feeding here, and there abroad, belonging to pasture. 1863 J. G. Baker *N. Yorks. Stud.* 183 We may employ a series of adjectives such as sylvestral, pratal, pascual, ericetal [etc.]. 1883 A. Fryer in *Jrnl. Bot., Brit. & For.* XXI. 375 No hard and fast line can be drawn between Pascual and Pratal plants.

Pascuant (pæ·skiu,ănt), *a.* *Her.* [f. L. *pascu-um* pasture, grazing + -ant.] Said of deer, oxen, etc. represented as grazing.

c 1828 Berry *Encycl. Herald.* I, *Pascuant*, or *Pasquant* (French *paissant*), is a term used for sheep, cows, &c. when feeding. 1882 Cussans *Her.* vi. (ed. 3) 90 *Pascuant*: Applied to Deer, Oxen, etc., when grazing.

Pascuous (pæ·skiu,əs), *a.* [ad. L. *pascuōs-us* abounding in pasture, f. *pascuum* pasture, grazing: cf. OF. *pascueux*.] = Pascual.

1656 Blount *Glossogr.*, *Pascuous*, serving for pasture, or for feeding, or grazing of Beasts. 1866 *Treas. Bot.*, *Pascuous*, growing in pastures.

Pase, obs. form of Pace, Pass.

Pasement, obs. f. Passement. **Paseng**, var. Pasang. **Paseporte, Pase-tyme, Pas-flower, Pasgarde**: see Passport, Pastime, Pasque-flower, Pass-guard.

Pash (pæʃ), *sb.*[1] *Obs.* exc. *dial.* A head.

1611 Shaks. *Wint. T.* I. ii. 128 Thou want'st a rough pash, & the shoots that I haue, To be full like me. 1674–91 Ray *N. C. Wds.*, *Pash*, 'a mad pash', a mad-brain. *Chesh.* a 1697 Cleland *Poems* 66 Some turning up their gay Mustachoes, And others robbing [i.e. rubbing] their dull pashes. 1719 Ramsay *To Arbuckle* 118, I [wig-maker and poet] theek the out, and line the inside Of mony a douce and witty pash. 1836 J. Struthers *Dychmont* II. 6 Where's Jock Arneil's lang witty pash? [In E. D. D. as *Scotch* and *Cheshire*.]

Pash (pæʃ), *sb.*[2] Now chiefly *dial.* [f. Pash *v.*]

1. A smashing or crushing blow or stroke. *rare.*

1611 Cotgr., *Gourmade*, a cuffe on the mouth, a pash on the nose.

2. A crashing blow or fall; a crash. Now *dial.*

1677 O. Heywood *Diaries*, etc. (1883) III. 190 There was suddenly a pash of a chamber-floore. 1781 J. Hutton *Tour to Caves* (ed. 2) Gloss., *Pash*, a sudden crash. 1828 *Craven Gloss.* (ed. 2), *Pash*. 'I fell wi sike a *pash*.'

3. A heavy fall or dash of rain or snow. *dial.*

1790 Marshall *Midl. Counties* (1796) II. Gloss. (E. D. S.), *Pash* (of rain), a heavy fall of rain. 1828 *Craven Gloss.* (ed. 2), *Pash*. 'We hev hed a sad pash last week'. 1885 *Q. Rev.* Apr. 350 The soil would have been run together like lime by a 'pash' of rain.

4. *transf.* 'The fragments produced by a smash' (E. D. D.), debris; hence, a collection, a medley, a great quantity or number.

1790 Grose *Prov. Gloss.* Suppl., *Pash*, a great many. *North.* 1894 *Sat. Rev.* 14 Apr. 386 (*title of Article*) A Pash of Heraldry.

Pash, *sb.*[3] Aphetic form of Calipash.

1764 Foote *Patron* I. i, Not the meanest member of my corporation but can distinguish the pash from the pee.

Pash (pæʃ), *v.* Also 4 **passche**, 4–6 **pas(s)he**. [app., like many other vbs. in *-ash*, of onomatopœic origin: cf. Bash, Smash. In sense 5 doubtfully related to Sw. dial. *paska*: see Pask.

A much used word (esp. in sense 2) from c 1575 for some 60 years; but now chiefly *dial*: see *Eng. Dial. Dict.*]

1. *trans.* To hurl or throw (something) violently, so as either to break it against something, or smash something with it; to dash. *Obs.* exc. *dial.*

1362 Langl. *P. Pl.* A. v. 16 Piries and Plomtrees weore passchet to þe grounde. 1590 Greene *Orl. Fur.* (1599) 17 As the sonne of Saturne in his wrath Pasht all the mountaines at Typheus head. 1628 Ford *Lover's Mel.* I. i, And in that sorrow, As he was pashing it [the lute] against a tree, I suddenly stept in. 1876 *Mid Yorksh. Gloss.* s. v., To pash a thing is..to hurl or dash it violently, from a short distance.

2. To break or dash (a thing) in pieces or to atoms; to crush or smash by blows.

1377 Langl. *P. Pl.* B. xx. 99 Deth cam dryuende after and al to doust passhed [*v.rr.* paschte, passhte] Kynges & knyȝtes kayseres and popes. c 1540 J. Redford *Mor. Play Wit & Sc.* (Shaks. Soc.) 8 Pash head, pash brayne, The knaves are slayne. 1628 Gaule *Pract. The.* (1629) 9 One should ryse from her Loynes..and push that wily Serpents head. a 1693 *Urquhart's Rabelais* III. xxxiii. 282 It pasheth into pieces the Steel Sword. a 1825 Forby *Voc. E. Anglia*, *Pash*, to beat any thing brittle into small fragments. 1875 Browning *Aristoph. Apol.* 843 Planed and studded club Once more has pashed competitors to dust.

3. To strike or knock violently, usually so as to bruise or smash. Also *absol.*

c 1440 *York Myst.* xlvi. 38 Þei dusshed hym, þei dasshed hym,..Þei pusshed hym, þei passhed hym. 1570–83 Foxe *A. & M.* 295/2 In the meane while the Christians..were pelted and pashed with stones by them which stood aboue. 1606 Shaks. *Tr. & Cr.* II. iii. 213 If I goe to him, with my armed fist, Ile pash him ore the face. 1611 Cotgr., *Gourmé*..cuffed on the mouth, pashed on the nose, or face. 1791 Cowper *Odyss.* XVIII. 119 He his adversary on the neck Pash'd close beneath his ear; he split the bones. 1863 Cowden Clarke *Shaks. Char.* xiv. 362 Never wouldst thou ..have pashed that venerable face with the rude flint-stones.

b. With obj. of cognate meaning.

1602 *How man may chuse good wife* II. iii, *Per Jovem et Junonem!* hoc Shall pash his coxcomb such a knock.

4. To drive *out* by a violent blow, to dash *out* (brains, etc.).

1530 Palsgr. 653/2 He passhed out his braynes with a stone. 1587 Holinshed *Chron.* III. 79/2 They left him [Becket] not till they had cut and pashed out his braines. 1647 H. More *Song of Soul* Quot. xxiv. 199 So may their scattered Brain Pash'd from their cursed Sculls the Pavement stain. 1828 *Craven Gloss.* (ed. 2) s. v., I'll pash thy brains out. 1855 Browning *Childe Roland* xii, 'Tis a brute must walk Pashing their [dock-leaves'] life out.

5. *intr.* Said of the dashing action of sudden heavy rain (now *dial.*); also of that of a wave upon a rock; and of the action of beating or striking water as by the feet of a horse (*rare*).

[With the last of these cf. ME. Pask, to dabble; but this sense does not appear to have come down dialectally, and Browning's use is prob. due to the exigency of rime.]

1589 [see Pashing below]. 1855 Browning *Up at a Villa* vii, There's a fountain to spout and splash!..horses with curling fish-tails, that prance and paddle and pash Round the lady atop in her conch. 1892 Stopf. Brooke *Early Eng. Lit.* II. xvi. 87 The black sea waves pash and push upon it. 1903 in *Eng. Dial. Dict.* s.v., It [the rain] fair pash'd doon. The water was pashing out of the broken spout. The rain came pashing against the windows.

Hence **Pa·shed**, **Pa·shing** *ppl. adjs.*

1589 Nashe *Anat. Absurd.* 24 Y[e] watrie clowdes with pashing showres vncessantlie, sending down their vnreasonable moysture. 1593 — *Christ's T.* (1613) 39. 1606 Shaks. *Tr. & Cr.* v. v. 10 Wauing his beame, Vpon the pashed courses of the Kings. 1828 *Craven Gloss.* (ed. 2), *Pashed*, dashed. 1847 *Bairnsla Ann.* 12 (E. D. D.) Pashin' rain.

‖**Pasha, pacha** (pa·ʃa, păʃā·). Forms: 7–8 **pascha**, 7 **passa**, 9 **pashaw**, **pacha**, 8– **pasha**. [Turkish *pāshā*, generally held to be the same as *bāshā* from *bāsh* head, chief, in some Eastern Turkish dialects *pāsh*. The form with *b* was app. the earlier, being that first adopted in Western languages: see Bashaw.

In Turkish there is no hard-and-fast line between the breath and voice stops; and in the case of *p*, *b*, the confusion is increased by the absence of *p* in Arabic and the occasional replacement of Persian and Turkish *p* by *b* (cf. *papoosh*, *pabouch*, *babouche*, etc): this may have conduced to interchange of *b*, *p*, and survival of the *p* in *pasha*. Some however think *pāshā* and *bāshā* originally distinct words (cf. quot. 1687); Zenker distinguishes *bāshā*, the officer of the Janizaries, from *pāshā*, which is now largely a civil title; but Barbier says that the title, in either form, was under the ancient régime exclusively a military one. The best Turkish scholars think there is no ground for connecting the word in any way with Pers. *pādishah* king or emperor, Turkish *pādishāh* the Sultan.]

A title borne in Turkey by officers of high rank, as military commanders, and governors of provinces. Formerly, esp. in the case of military commanders, written Bashaw.

There are three grades of pashas, formerly distinguished by the number of horse-tails displayed as a symbol in war; the highest grade (of three tails) corresponding to a commanding general, admiral, or governor of equivalent rank; the second (of two tails) to a general of division or vice-admiral, etc.; the third (of one tail) to a general of brigade, rear-admiral, or naval officer of corresponding rank.

[For earlier quotations (1534–1860) see Bashaw.]

1646 Crashaw *Deo Nostro* (1652) 193 The aged Pascha pleads not years, But spies love's dawn, and disappears. 1687 *Lond. Gaz.* No. 2216/2 The Chiaus Bassa is made a Passa, which is a Preferment to his Loss. 1717 Lady M. W. Montagu *Let. to Abbé Conti* 17 May, Every pasha has his Jew, who is his *homme d'affaires*. 1808 A. Parsons *Trav.* i. 4 The price of bread .. is fixed by the pashaw of the province. 1822 Shelley *Hellas* 565 The freedman..has beat back the Pacha of Negropont. 1848 Thackeray *Bk. Snobs* iv, I am like the Pasha of three tails. 1867 Lady Herbert *Cradle L.* i. 3 The rest of the party went on to see the Pacha of Egypt's Palace.

Hence **Pasha-like** *a.*, like or after the manner of a pasha. **Pashadom**, the domain, realm, or estate of pashas.

1849 E. B. Eastwick *Dry Leaves* 172, I .. began to feel quite supreme and Pa-shá-like. 1883 *Pall Mall G.* 24 Nov. 1/2 On the 23rd of October last year I was at Cairo... Pashadom seemed fairly ablaze with decorations and ribbons. 1885 *Manch. Exam.* 24 July 5/3 The Sultan and all pashadom have been filled with growing anxiety and concern.

Pashalic, pachalic (pa·ʃalik, pāʃā·lik), *sb.* (*a.*) Also **-lick**, **-lik**. [Turkish *pāshālik*, from *-lik*, suffix of quality or condition.] The jurisdiction of a pasha; the district governed by a pasha.

1745 Pococke *Descr. of East* II. I. 76 The place of residence of the pasha of this country, on which account it was called the pashalic of Saphet. 1802 *Edin. Rev.* I. 52 A pachalic is divided, for military purposes, into certain districts, called sangiacs, or standards. 1813 Byron *Br. Abydos* II. xv, Abdallah's Pachalick was gain'd. 1894 *Times* 11 Oct. 10/6 In September, 1877, he was appointed Consul for the pashalics of Adana, Aleppo, and Tripoli, residing at Aleppo.

B. as *adj.* Of or pertaining to a pasha.

1863 Woolner *Beautiful Lady* 129 Seizing pachalic power by a swift blow. 1884 *Manch. Exam.* 16 Feb. 4/7 There is to be an end to military exactions and Pashalic oppression [in the Soudan].

†**Pashe.** *Obs.* Also 6 **paishe**. App. short for *passion*, in the asseveration 'for the pashe of God': cf. the full 'for the passion of God', by the same speaker in IV. iii.

a 1553 Udall *Royster D.* IV. iii, Nay for the paishe of God, let me now treate peace. *Ibid.* vii, Backe for the pashe of God, backe sirs. *Ibid.* viii, *R. Royster*. Away, or else die we shall. *M. Mery*. Away for the pashe of our sweete Lord Iesus Christ. *Ibid.* v. v.

Pashe, Pashion, obs. ff. Pasch, Passion.

‖**Pashm** (pæ·ʃm). [Pers. پشم *pashm* wool, down.] The under-fur of hairy quadrupeds in the elevated lands north of the Himalayas, esp. that of the goat, which is the material of Cashmere shawls. So ‖**Pashmina** (pæʃmī·nă) [Pers. *pashmīn* adj., woollen].

1880 Mrs. A. G. F. E. James *Ind. Indust.* xxxi. 364 The *pashm*, or shawl-wool, is a downy substance, growing next to the skin and under the thick hair of those goats found in Thibet and in the elevated lands north of the Himalayas. 1885 Balfour *Cycl. India* III. 154 Pashm and pashmina are specially applied to the fine shawl-wool of Turfan and Changthan. 1893 *R. Nat. Hist.* (ed. Lydekker) I. 7 This under-fur is greatly developed in Mammals of all groups inhabiting Tibet, where it is locally known as 'pashm'; and it is this pashm of the goat of these regions which affords the materials for the celebrated Kashmir shawls.

Pasigraphy (pǎsi·grăfi). [irreg. f. Gr. πᾶσι for all + -graphy.] A name given to a system of writing proposed for universal use, with characters representing ideas instead of words, so as to be (like the ordinary numerals 1, 2, 3, etc.) intelligible to persons of all languages. Applied originally to a system proposed in 1796; subsequently to others having a similar object.

1796 in *Monthly Rev.* XIX. 357 *Pasigraphy*, from πᾶσι to *all* and γράφω *I write*, will not explain the sounds of any known language but the sense of the words of every language, even of that which people have never learnt. 1797 T. Brown in Welsh *Life* i. (1825) 35. 1801 *Sk. Paris as it was* II. xl. 45 It is also in contemplation to teach a blind pupil pasigraphy, or universal language, invented by Demaimieux. 1805 *Med. Jrnl.* XIV. 189 Essay on geological Pasigraphy, or on the manner of representing the phenomena of the stratification of the rocks, by perfectly simple signs. 1870 Bachmaier *Pasigraph. Dict. & Gram.* Introd., Pasigraphy teaches people to communicate with one another in writing by means of numbers, which convey the same ideas in all languages.

Hence **Pa·sigraph** *v. trans.*, to express or represent in pasigraphy; **Pasigra·phic, -ical** *adjs.*, of or pertaining to pasigraphy.

1796 in *Monthly Rev.* XIX. 357 At the end of a very few hours, any intelligent person may pasigraph his own idiom, by consulting the method, characters, and the twelve invariable rules. 1797 W. Taylor in *Monthly Rev.* XXIV. 563 Over each column is stationed one letter of the pasigraphic alphabet. 1804 — in *Crit. Rev.* Ser. III. I. 382 The figures of arithmetic are already pasigraphic. 1839 *Proc. Amer. Philol. Soc.* I. 121 The Chinese alphabet forms a sort of pasigraphic system. 1852 Jerdan *Autobiog.* II. 221. 1870 Bachmaier (*title*) Pasigraphical Dictionary and Grammar.

Pasilaly (pæ·sĭlăli). *rare.* [irreg. f. Gr. πᾶσι for all + -λαλια speaking.] A spoken language for universal use.

1805 W. Taylor in *Ann. Rev.* III. 14 It appears that the Indians have invented, what a recent French writer calls a *pasilaly*, a method of talking to people of all languages, without understanding theirs. 1864 in Webster.

†**Pask**, *v.* *Obs.* [Appears to be cognate with mod.Sw. dial. *paska* to dabble in water (Rietz); cf. Norw. *baska* in same sense: cf. also Pash *v.*, Plash *v.*] *intr.* To dabble or plash (in water).

c 1305 *St. Andrew* 8 in *E. E. P.* (1862) 98 Here nettes gonne forsake And suede him .. Hem was so betere þan to pasken in þe water iwis While oure louerd an vrþe was.

Pask, -e, Pasmain, obs. ff. Pasch, Passement.

†**Pasme.** *Obs. rare.* [a. OF. *pasme* (Godef.) swoon, faint = Pr. *pasme*, Sp., Pg. *pasmo* (and *espasmo*), It. *spasimo*:—L. *spasmus* Spasm, treated as *ex-pasmus*, *pasmus*, and with altered meaning; cf. mod.F. *pâmer* to faint.] A swoon.

1591 Greene *Farew. Folly* Wks. (Grosart) IX. 315 Semyramis no sooner heard of the death of hir husbande, but she fell into a pasme, and was hardly brought to life.

Pasment, -mond, obs. ff. Passement. **Pasnep(pe, -nepe**, obs. ff. Parsnip. **Paspy**, var. Passepied. **Pasque**, var. Pasch, Easter.

Pasque-flower (pa·sk,flau·ə). Forms: α. 6–7 **Passe-**, 7 **Pas-flower**. β. 6– **pasque-**, 7–8 **pasch-flower**. [Orig. *passeflower*, a. F. *passefleur* (1539 R. Estienne) 'a variety of anemone' (Hatz.-Darm.); changed by Gerarde to *pasqueflower*, after *pasque*, Pasch, Easter.] A species of Anemone (*A. Pulsatilla*) growing on chalk downs in England, and elsewhere in Europe, blossoming in April, with bell-shaped purple flowers clothed with silky hairs. Called also *pasque-anemone*.

With distinctive adjuncts the name is applied to other species of Anemone, as the **American Pasque-flower**, *A. patens*, var. *Nuttaliana*; **Japanese P.**, the Autumnal Anemone, *A. Japonica*.

α. 1578 Lyte *Dodoens* III. lxxv. 422 Passeflower or the first Anemone, hath leaves like Coriander. 1597 Gerarde *Herbal* II. lxxiii. 309 Passe flower is called..after the Latin name Pulsatill, or Flawe flower. 1611 Cotgr., *Passe-fleur*, the Passeflower, bastard Anemone, or Windflower. 1651 J. F[reake] *Agrippa's Occ. Philos.* 39 Poisonous things delight in the Plant called Pas-flower. 1658 Phillips, *Passe-flower*, a certain kind of flower, otherwise called Pulsatil.

β. 1597 Gerarde *Herbal* II. lxxiii. 309 They flower for the most part about Easter, which hath mooved me to name it Pasque flower, or Easter flower. 1629 Parkinson *Paradisus* 201 The yellow Pasque flower...Red Pasque flower... White Pasque flower. 1785 Martyn *Rousseau's Bot.* xxi. (1794) 301 The Pasque-flower, so called from its flowering about Easter, .. adorns some of our dry chalky hills, with its beautiful bell-shaped purple flowers. 1854 S. Thomson *Wild Fl.* III. (ed. 4) 175 The pasque-flower, purple anemone.

Pasquil (pæ·skwil), *sb.* Also 6 **pasqual**, 7 **pasquell**. [ad. med.L. *Pasquillus*, ad. It. *Pasquillo*, dim. of *Pasquino*; in F. *Pasquille*: see Pasquin.

The L. form is known as early as 1509: see Pasquin. The Fr. appears in *Les Visions de Pasquille*, 1547 (Ebert).]

†**1.** = Pasquin 1. *Obs.*

1533 Elyot *Wise Man* Proheme A v, For there be Gnathos in Spayne as wel as in Grece, Pasquilles in Englande as welle as in Rome. — *Pasquil the playne* A ij, Pasquille is an olde Romane, but by longe sittinge in the strete, and hering market men chat, he is become rude and homely. 1551 T. Wilson *Logike* (1580) 67 These two verses were written to the Pope, as worthie such a one, and sette upon Pasquillus in Roome. 1609 Dekker *Gulls Horne-bk.* i. (1862) 9 I'm the Pasquil's madcap that will do it. 1616 R. Carpenter *Past. Charge* 66 Making the Pulpit oftentimes a Pasquill to ease their spleenes. 1651 Weldon *Crt. K. Chas.* 205 The Councell Table was growne more like a Pasquil then a grave Senate.

2. A lampoon posted up in a public place; any circulated or published lampoon; a pasquinade.

1542 *St. Papers Hen. VIII*, IX. 12 Here hathe been also after the maner of Rome, a pasqual set up upon Sainct Marques day laste, tantynge thEmperour. 1589 Cooper *Admon.* 56 The Libeller to set out his *Pasquill*, raketh all things. 1612 T. James *Jesuits' Downf.* 38 They blame others for Libells and write vnpriestly Pasquils, and yet write themselues. 1709 Steele *Tatler* No. 92 ▸ 1 All the Pasquils, Lampoons and Libels, we meet with now-a-days. 1865 Wright *Hist. Caricature* xix. 315 The pasquils formed a body of satire which struck indiscriminately at everybody within its range.

3. *attrib.* and *Comb.*, as *pasquil-maker*, *-pulpit*.

c 1643 A. Brome *On Death J. Shute* 35 Nor such as into pasquill pulpits come With thundering non sence, but to beat the drum To civil wars. 1770 Baretti *Journ. Genoa* II. 1 They only put one in mind of the Pasquil-makers of Rome or the Monthly and Critical Reviewers of England.

Hence **Pasqui·llic** *a.*, of the nature of a pasquil.

1833 Carlyle *Misc.* (1872) V. 66 Verse (be it heroic, be it pasquillic).

†**Pa·squil**, *v.* *Obs.* [f. prec. sb.] **a.** *intr.* To compose pasquils. **b.** *trans.* To libel or satirize in a pasquil; to lampoon. So **Pa·squillant** *sb.*, the writer of a pasquil; *adj.* lampooning; **Pa·squiller**, the composer of a pasquil or pasquils.

1621 Burton *Anat. Mel.* I. ii. IV. iv. (1651) 148 Princes .. are grievously vexed with these pasquelling libels and satyrs. 1643 Howell *Twelve Treat.* (1661) 268 In Holland and other places he was pasquill'd at. a 1648 Ld. Herbert *Hen. VIII* (1683) 609 There wanted not some, who took occasion to pasquil it.

1817 Coleridge *Biog. Lit.* (1870) 204 [The character] of a gossip, backbiter and pasquillant. 1833 Carlyle *Misc.* (1872) V. 125 A Pasquillant verse. 1597–8 Bp. Hall *Sat.* v. i. 14 Or Lucile's muse..Or Menips old, or Pasquillers of late. a 1659 Osborn *Luther Vind.* Wks. (1673) 408 This favour ..did so work with him, and the rest of the Pasquillers of the time, that..none used the like Invectives.

Pasquin (pæ·skwin), *sb.* [ult. ad. It. *Pasquino*, in L. *Pasquinus*, F. *Pasquin*.

Pasquino or *Pasquillo* was the name popularly given to a mutilated statue, or piece of ancient statuary, disinterred at Rome in the year 1501, and set up by Cardinal Caraffa at the corner of his palace near the Piazza Navona. Under his patronage, it became the annual custom on St. Mark's Day to 'restore' temporarily and dress up this torso to represent some historical or mythological personage of antiquity; on which occasion professors and students of the newly restored Ancient Learning were wont to salute Pasquin in Latin verses which were usually posted or placed on the statue. In process of time these *pasquinate* or pasquinades tended to become satirical, and the term began to be applied, not only in Rome, but in other countries, to satirical compositions and lampoons, political, ecclesiastical, or personal, the anonymous authors of which often sheltered themselves under the conventional name of Pasquin. According to Mazocchi, in the preface to the printed collection of the *pasquinate* of 1509, the name Pasquino or Pasquillo originated in that of a schoolmaster ('*literator seu magister ludi*') who lived opposite the spot where the statue was found; a later tradition given by Castelvetro, 1558–9, made Pasquino a caustic tailor or shoemaker; another of 1544 calls him a barber. See L. Morandi in *Nuova Antologia* 1889 I. 271, 755, D. Gnoli *ibid.* 1890 I. 51, 275, *Storia di Pasquino*. The latinized form *Pasquillus* was already a 1544 applied both to the author and the pasquinade, in which extended application it was subseq. followed also by *Pasquin*.]

1. The Roman Pasquino (man or statue), on whom pasquinades were fathered; hence, the imaginary personage to whom anonymous lampoons were conventionally ascribed.

1566 (*title*) Pasquine in a Traunce. A Christian and learned Dialogue..Wherunto are added certayne Questions then put forth by Pasquine, to haue beene disputed in the Councell of Trent. 1581 Allen *Apol. Eng. Colleges* 97 b, Neither the Old Comedie, nor Pasquino, nor any ruffian or Carneuall-youth in Rome. 1592 Wotton in *Reliq.* (1685) 680 The Gabell of Sixtus's time, which Pasquin told him of. 1617 Moryson *Itin.* I. 135 At one end of this market place, in a corner of a street opposite to a publike Pallace, is the statua of Pasquin, vpon a wall of a priuate house. 1670 Lassels *Voy. Italy* II. 229 This Pasquin is an old broken statue .. jeering wits set up here, and father upon poore Messer Pasquino, their Satyrical jeasts, called from him, Pasquinades. 1686 Dryden *Addr. Higden* 2 The Grecian wits, who Satire first began, Were pleasant Pasquins on the life of man. a 1797 H. Walpole *Mem. Geo. II*, I. 283 If Pasquin has seen wittier, he never saw more severe or less delicate lampoons. 1885 *Encycl. Brit.* XVIII. 341 The 16th century was indeed Pasquin's palmy time, and in not a few of the rare printed collections of his utterances Protestant polemic ..is mingled. *attrib.* 1582 T. Watson *Centurie of Loue* lxxxi, A Pasquine piller erected in the despite of Loue.

†**2.** = Pasquinade, Pasquil 2. *Obs.*

1611 Florio, *Pasquino*, an old statue in Rome on whom all Satires, Pasquins, rayling rimes or libels are fastned and fathered. 1653 A. Wilson *Jas. I* 53 On him some unhappy Wit vented this Pasquin. 1692 Luttrell *Brief Rel.* (1857) II. 371 Wrote from Rome, the French had caused a pasquin to be fixt reflecting on the pope for conniving at the protestant alliance against his eldest son. a 1745 Swift *Answ. Sheridan* 32 Wks. 1841 I. 761/1 But enough of this poetry Alexandrine; I hope you will not think this a pasquine.

Hence **Pa·squin** *v. trans.* [= It. *pasquinare* (Florio); F. *pasquiner*], to lampoon, pasquinade.

1682 Dryden & Lee *Duke of Guise* Ded., Not .. that any Man delights to see himself pasquin'd and affronted by their inveterate Scriblers.

Pasquinade (pæskwinē·d), *sb.* [ad. It. *pasquinata*: cf. F. *pasquinade*, and see Pasquin and -ade.] A lampoon affixed to some public place; a 'squib', libel, lampoon, or piece of satire generally.

[1592 Wotton in *Reliq.* (1685) 656 A *Pasquinata* set forth against him in form of a Prophesie.] 1658 Phillips, *Pasquinade*, a Satyrical Invective or Libel, savoring of the Pasquin at Rome. 1711 Addison *Spect.* No. 23 ▸ 4 This Pasquinade made a great Noise in Rome. 1760–72 H. Brooke *Fool of Qual.* (1809) III. 136 The very person who ..contrived the honour of the pasquinade on my back this day. 1843 Prescott *Mexico* VII. i. (1864) 411 The white walls of the barracks were covered with epigrams and pasquinades levelled at Cortez. *attrib.* 1858 Borrow *Rom. Rye* I. 10 A pasquinade picture was stuck up at Rome.

Pasquinade (pæskwinē·d), *v.* [f. prec. sb.] *trans.* To satirize or libel in a pasquinade.

1796 *Sporting Mag.* VII. 312 One of the candidates..has already been pasquinaded. 1880 Disraeli *Endym.* i. 5 We dined and voted together, and together pasquinaded our opponents.

Pasquinader (pæskwinē·dəɹ). [f. prec sb. or vb. + -er[1].] **a.** A writer of pasquinades. **b.** (*nonce-use*). A collector of pasquinades.

1862 Burton *Bk. Hunter* (1882) 19 He was not a black-letter man..or a pasquinader. 1888 *N. & Q.* 7th Ser. V. 511/1 Pasquinaders often maintained that the more hidden the allusion the more terrible the import.

†**Pasquina·do.** *Obs. rare*[−1]. [See -ado.] = Pasquinade *sb.*

1600 O. E. *Rep. Libel* III. Pref. 2 His great practise and skill in Pasquinadoes.

Pasqui·nian, *a.* *rare.* [See -ian.] Of, pertaining to, or characteristic of Pasquin; pertaining to a pasquin, satirical.

1796 Burney *Mem. Metastasio* I. 189 You have exhausted all your..friendship, in transports of true Pasquinian passion in my defence.

Pass (pɑs), *sb.*[1] Also 4 **pas**, **pase**, 5 **paas**, 5–6 **passe**. [In ME. *pas*, *paas*, a. F. *pas*:—L. *passus* step, pace, track, trace, etc. Orig. the same word as Pace; in later use often associated with Pass *v.*, and thus in some senses not easily separated from Pass *sb.*[2], F. *passe*.]

I. Obs. senses: = Pace, Passus.

†**1.** Occasional spelling of *pas*, Pace *sb.*[1] (in various senses), q. v.

a 1300 *Cursor M.* 10970, I and mi wijf on ald tas, Of barns er we passed þe pass [*v.r.* pas]. 1375 Barbour *Bruce* VII. 203 Till hym thai ȝeid a full great pass. c 1400 Maundev. (Roxb.) xi. 41 Fra þe kirke of þe sepulcre .. ane aght score passez es þe temple *Domini*. 1615 Chapman *Odyss.* IX. 734 A little pass Beyond our fore-deck from the fall there was.

†**2.** A passage (in a narrative or writing); a canto of a poem, a chapter, section, or division of a book; = Pace *sb.*[1] 12, Passus.

c 1350 *Will. Palerne* 161 Þus passed is þe first pas of þis pris tale. a 1400–50 *Alexander* 2845 Here a passe endes. 1546 Gardiner *Declar. Art. Joye* 27 So as in thys passe of saynt Paule, saynte Chrisostome is verye dylygente to note and conferme vnto vs. 1553 Kennedy *Compend. Tract.* iii, It is to be notit of this pas of Scripture abone rehersit. 1573 *Reg. Privy Council Scot.* Ser. I. II. 275 In quhilk Act, besyde mony utheris passis and claussis,.. it is statute and ordanit [etc.]. 1633 *Sc. Acts Chas. I* (1817) V. 152/1 Dispenssis for ever In all .. heades articles claussis obleisments pointes passis..of the samyn. 1647 N. Bacon *Disc. Govt. Eng.* Prol. ▸ 7 A summary view of the cardinal passes of the government of this Kingdom.

II. A passage.

3. A way or opening by which one passes through a region otherwise obstructed or impassable, or through any natural or artificial barrier. *esp.* **a.** A narrow and difficult or dangerous passage through a mountainous region or over a mountain range; also (less usually) through a forest, marsh, bog, or other impassable ground.

In ME. applied to a road or passage in a wood, over a heath, etc., such as was exposed to ambush, robbery, etc.; in its later application prob. a re-adoption from mod.F. *pas*.

a 1300 *Cursor M.* 2519 Þan he broght þam til a pase [*G.* pas] Þat men cald in Ƿat land temase [*v.r.* themas]. c 1325 *Metr. Hom.* 52 In our gat lis Satenas Wit his felawes, als thef in pas. 1340 Hampole *Pr. Consc.* 1239 Thefs and outlawes,..Þat hald pases, and robbes and reves Men of þat þai have. 1377 Langl. *P. Pl.* B. xiv. 300 Þe sexte is a path of pees: ȝe, þorw þe pas of altoun Pouerte myȝte passe without peril of robbynge. 1390 Gower *Conf.* III. 208 Into the pas whanne he was falle, Thembuisschementz tobrieken alle. 1538 *St. Papers Hen. VIII*, III. 7, I have cut divers pases, and made suche smothe wayes. 1680 Morden *Geog. Rect.*, *Piedmont* (1685) 205 Pignerol .. a Commodious Pass from France to Italy. 1703 Maundrell *Journ. Jerus.* (1732) 35 Having gone thro' a very rugged and uneven Pass. 1806 *Gazetteer Scotl.* (ed. 2) 226 Glentilt; a pass in the Highlands of Athol, famous for..the dangerous road which runs through it. 1810 Scott *Lady of L.* v. iii, The guide, abating of his pace, Led slowly through the pass's jaws. 1833 *Penny Cycl.* I. 388/2 The chief pass of the Lepontian Alps is that of the St. Gothard...The height of the pass is 6890 feet. 1851 Turner *Dom. Archit.* I. 106 The wooded pass of Alton on the borders of Surrey and Hampshire, which was not disafforested until the end of Henry's reign, was a favourite ambush for outlaws, who there awaited the merchants and their trains of sumpter-horses travelling to or from Winchester.

fig. c 1500 *Melusine* 31 But ones as he said he shuld passe the cruell paas of the deth. 1854 Tennyson *Aylmer's F.* 209 But Edith's eager fancy hurried with him Snatch'd thro' the perilous passes of his life.

b. esp. in *Mil.* Such a passage viewed strategically as commanding the entrance into a country or place; hence, by extension, any place which commands or holds the key to such entrance. Also *fig.*, and in various phrases, as *to gain*, *hold*, *keep*, *sell the pass*. †*Pass of arms* [F. *pas d'armes*]: see quot. 1727–41.

1683 Kennett tr. *Erasm. on Folly* 98 They would be able to keep their Pass and fence off all assault of Conviction. 1684 *Scanderbeg Rediv.* v. 108 The City Mohilow on the Dniester, a place of great Importance, as being the pass into Moldavia. a 1704 T. Brown *Sat. agst. Woman* Wks. 1730 I. 56 Thus all the unguarded passes of his mind she'll try. 1727–41 Chambers *Cycl.*, *Pass of arms*, in chivalry, a place which the ancient knights undertook to defend, *e.gr.* a bridge, road, &c. which was not to be passed without fighting the person who kept it. 1751 Johnson *Rambler* No. 165 ▸ 2 The passes of the intellect are barred against her by prejudice and passion. 1774 *Chesterfield's Lett.* I. xvii. 74 Horatius Cocles, who alone defended the pass of a bridge against the whole Tuscan army. 1838 Thirlwall *Greece* V. 283 When Philip reached Thermopylæ, he found the pass strongly guarded. 1897 *Westm. Gaz.* 6 Dec. 7/1 He now warned the men that by accepting the proposal they would be 'selling the pass' for all other trades. 1903 *Daily Chron.* 16 Nov. 5/1 He .. accepted the settlement, and at once fell from his pre-eminence,..being viewed by his followers..as one who had 'sold the pass'.

c. More generally: A way by which to pass or get through; a passage, road, route. Also *fig.*

1608 Chapman *Byron's Trag.* Plays 1873 II. 294 Let your Armie Have the directest passe, it shall goe safe. a 1674 Clarendon *Hist. Reb.* IX. § 92 The force of both counties .. should be drawn to Tiverton, and upon that pass, to fight with the rebels. 1689 Luttrell *Brief Rel.* (1857) I. 617 The Danish horse..are ordered to march for Scotland, being the shortest passe for Ireland. 1787 M. Cutler in *Life*, etc. (1888) II. 395 Through the Sandusky and Scioto lies the most common pass from Canada to the Ohio and Mississippi. 1798 Bloomfield *Farmer's Boy, Spring* 302 [He] Sees every pass secur'd, and fences whole.

fig. 1651 N. Bacon *Disc. Govt. Eng.* II. xvi. (1739) 84 The King and Council seemed to have the sole power .. to open and shut the passes of Trade.

d. A passage across a river; a place at which a river can be crossed by ford, ferry, or, *rarely* a bridge. Now *rare.*

1649–50 Cromwell *Let. to Lenthall* 15 Feb. in *Carlyle*, Desirous to gain a Pass over the Suir; where indeed we had none but by boat, or when the weather served. 1650 *Ibid.* 2 Apr., By which means we have a good pass over the Barrow, and intercourse between Munster and Leinster. a 1661 Fuller *Worthies* (1840) III. 384 The royalists chiefest strength consisted in two passes they possessed over the river of Severn. 1718 Rowe tr. *Lucan* I. 815 To guard the Passes of the German Rhine. 1862 Stanley *Jew. Ch.* (1877) I. iii. 55 The watch-tower of Peniel, which years afterwards guarded the passes of the Jordan.

e. A navigable channel, esp. at a river's mouth, or in a delta.

1698 Fryer *Acc. E. India & P.* 123 The next Morning, with only sending my Servant ashore to acquaint the Rendero, I quitted the Pass. 1704 Addison *Italy* (1733) 56 Passes that lead to the City from the Adriatic. 1758 *Ann. Reg.* 109 The greatest part [of the vessels] escaped by running into the pass of Toulinquet. 1817 J. W. Heustis *Phys. Observ. Topog. & Dis. Louisiana* 23 The main branch of the Mississippi has three mouths, or, as they are called, passes. 1895 J. Winsor *Mississ. Basin* 154 A fort was soon built at the Balize,..on the edge of the Gulf, but which today is nine miles up the pass.

f. Applied to other narrow passages: e.g. in a road or street.

a 1710 Pope *Alley* 2 A narrow pass there is with Houses low. 1712 Steele *Spect.* No. 454 ▸ 4 While he whipped up James-Street, we drove for King-Street, to save the Pass at St. Martin's Lane. *Ibid.* No. 498 ▸ 2 Till he came to the Pass, which is a Military Term the Brothers of the Whip have given the Strait at St. Clement's Church. 1908 *Daily Chron.* 16 Apr. 7/2 How Royal and Coronation processions got through the Pass is a secret which our London forefathers have taken to their graves.

g. A passage or alley in a church. *Sc. dial.*

1871 W. Alexander *Johnny Gibb* xi. (1892) 68 He was going along the pass to shut the door. 1873 Gilmour *Pen-Flk.* 51 (E. D. D.) William M[c]Lerie .. steps noiselessly up the 'pass', asking kindly for each as he slips along.

h. A passage for fish over or past a weir.

1861 *Act* 24 & 25 *Vict.* c. 109 § 23 Any Proprietor of a Fishery with the written Consent of the Home Office may attach to every Dam .. a Fish Pass, of such Form and Dimensions as the Home Office may approve. 1867 *Lond. Rev.* 22 June 696/1 To restore our rivers to their former prolific condition, it is indispensable that salmon-passes should be provided. 1899 *Daily News* 4 May 11/2 In 1863 a salmon pass or ladder was made at Wood Mill, with the result that fish were enabled to ascend into the non-tidal waters.

4. *Mining.* (See quots.)

[May perh. belong to Pass *sb.*[2]]

1671 *Phil. Trans.* VI. 2108 After the Ore is landed,..'tis brought .. and unloaded at the head of the Pass (*i.e.* 2 or 3 bottom-boards with 2 side-boards sloping-wise) in which the Ore slides down into the Coffer. 1710 J. Harris *Lex. Techn.* II. s.v., A Frame of Boards consisting of 2 or 3 bottom Boards and two side ones set slope-wise, thro' which the Ore slides down into the Coffer of the Stamping-Mill, for the Tin-works, is called by the Workmen *the Pass*. 1881 in Raymond *Mining Gloss.*

Pass (pɑs), *sb.*[2] Forms: 4–7 **passe**, (6 **pas**), 7– **pass**. [Partly a. F. *passe*, f. *passer* to pass; partly immed. from Pass *v.* Not always clearly separable from Pass *sb.*[1], with which, since 1600, and occasionally earlier, it has been identified in spelling.]

I. 1. An act or the fact of passing; passage.

[a 1400–50 *Alexander* 2978 Þe pepill of þe palais quen þai his passe [*D.* hym passe] saȝe, Ruschez vp in a res rynnes in-to chambres.] 1599 Shaks. *Hen. V*, II. Chor. 39 Charming the narrow seas To giue you gentle Passe. 1600 W. Watson *Decacordon* (1602) 45 In the passe and repasse out of England into Fraunce. c 1611 Chapman *Iliad* III. 242 Out of his ample breast, he gave his great voice pass. *Ibid.* IV. 406 He went, and safely had his pass Back to Asopus' flood. *Ibid.* XX. 422 One ear it enter'd, and made good his pass to th' other ear. 1647 N. Bacon *Disc. Govt. Eng.* I. xx. (1739) 38 This privilege of Safe Pass being .. ancient and fundamental,..resteth still in force. 1671 Grew *Anat. Plants* ii. § 31 The Sap moving in the Barque, towards the Pith, through the Insertions, thereinto obtains a pass. 1820 J. Cleland *Rise Glasgow* 121 There are four or five hundred passes and repasses in the same period. 1844 D. Welsh *Serm.* 186 How dread must be the pass from the unsubstantial fabric of this earthly state to those abodes.

b. Departure from life, death. Also *fig.*

a 1645 Featly in *Fuller's Abel Rediv.*, *Reynolds* (1867) II. 238 Whose happy pass, agreeable to his godly life, God forbid that any should deplore. 1742 Young *Nt. Th.* III. 134 For Man you smile; Why not smile *at* him too? You share indeed His sudden Pass; but not his constant Pain. 1827 Pollok *Course T.* III, This pass of human thought, This wilderness of intellectual death.

†**2.** (?) Demeanour, 'walk'; (?) course of action.

1555 W. Watreman *Fardle Facions* II. xii. 269 To be honestly appareiled, and accordyngly to vse their passe and conuersacion. 1603 Shaks. *Meas. for M.* v. i. 375 When I perceiue your grace, like powre diuine, Hath look'd vpon my passes.

†**3.** The fact of passing as approved; reputation, estimation; currency. *Obs.*

1598 B. Jonson *Ev. Man. in Hum.* v. i. 442 Or that their slubberd lines haue currant passe, From the fat iudgements of the multitude. 1601 Shaks. *All's Well* II. v. 58, I do know him well, and common speech Giues him a worthy passe.

4. The passing of an examination; *esp.* in a university examination, the attainment of such a standard as satisfies the examiners without entitling the candidate to honours. Often *attrib.*: see 17.

1838 Arnold *Let.* in *Life & Corr.* (1844) II. viii. 127 A pass little *go*, or even great *go*, is surely a ridiculous thing, as all that the University expects of a man after some twelve or fourteen years of schooling and lecturing. 1860 M. Burrows (*title*) Pass and Class: an Oxford Guide-Book through the Courses of Literæ Humaniores, Mathematics, Natural Science, and Law and Modern History. 1874 Burnand *My time* xxxvi. 388 Honours were out of the question, and a pass we most of us obtained. 1882 J. Southward *Pract. Print.* (1884) 199 If, however, there are only three marks or less, there is 'no pass'.

II. That in which the fact of passing is embodied; the condition to or through which anything passes.

†**5.** Event, issue; completion, accomplishment.

[1481: see 6 b.] 1542 Udall *Erasm. Apoph.* I. *Socr.* § 93 n., 38 a, [He] shall easily bryng the same to suche ende, and to such passe and effecte, as he would dooe. 1579 Tomson *Calvin's Serm. Tim.* 287/2 God will bring all to good passe. c 1600 Shaks. *Sonn.* ciii, To no other passe my verses tend Then of your graces and your gifts to tell. 1611 Bible *Transl. Pref.* 11 Wee haue at the length, through the good hand of the Lord vpon vs, brought the worke to that passe that you see. 1649 Milton *Eikon.* ix. 86 By this reckning his consents and his denials come all to one pass.

6. Phrases. (Now somewhat *arch.*)

(Here *to pass* is often regarded as infinitive of the vb.; but see quot. 1549 in a, 1542 in b, and cf. prec.)

a. *To bring to pass* (rarely †*unto pass*): to bring to accomplishment, fulfilment, or realization; to carry out; to accomplish, produce, bring about.

1523 Skelton *Garl. Laurel* 1228 A tratyse he deuysid & browght it to pas, Callid *Speculum Principis*. 1530 Tindale *Gen.* xli. 32 That the thynge is certanly prepared of God, and that God will shortly brynge it to passe. 1538 Starkey *England* II. ii. 195 Thys were a commyn remedy, yf hyt myght be brought to passe. 1539 Bible (Great) *Ps.* xxxvii. 5 Commytte thy waye vnto the Lorde, and put thy trust in hym, & he shall brynge it to passe. 1549 Latimer *1st Serm. bef. Edw. VI* B viij b, Many hath taken in hande to brynge manye thynges vnto passe [*printed* paste]. c 1592 Marlowe *Jew of Malta* v. iii. Doe but bring this to passe which thou pretendest. a 1634 Chapman *Alphonsus* Plays 1873 III. 225 Huge wonders will Alphonsus bring to pass. 1651 Hobbes *Leviath.* II. xxix. 169 They [faith and sanctity] are not Miracles, but brought to passe by education.

b. *To come to pass*: to come to the event or issue; to be carried out, accomplished, or realized; to turn out in the event, to eventuate; to issue, come about. Also, †*to go to pass*. †*To come well to* (*our*) *pass*, *to come evil to pass*, to turn out well (for us), to turn out ill.

1481 Caxton *Reynard* xl. (Arb.) 108 The wulf .. threw the foxe al plat vnder hym, whiche cam hym euyl to passe. [*Leeu's text*, 1479, xli, dat hem seer misuiel]. 1526 Skelton *Magnyf.* 2134 *Magn.* I am Magnyfycence, that somtyme thy mayster was. *Lyb.* What, is the worlde thus come to passe? 1526 Tindale *John* xiii. 19 Nowe tell I you before it come: that when yt is come to passe, ye myght beleve that I am he. a 1533 Ld. Berners *Huon* lxvi. 226 Alas! why dyd not Huon knowe his entente? if he had, the mater had not gone so to passe. 1542 Udall *Erasm. Apoph.* 336 'A man that fleeth will renewe battaill again' is a prouerbiall verse .. by whiche we are warned not .. to be brought in despaire, if some thyng haue not well come to our passe. — in *Lett. Lit. Men* (Camden) 2 If it had succeded and cum to passe accordyng to my request. 1611 Bible *Num.* xi. 23 Thou shalt see now whether my word shall come to pass vnto thee [Coverd. shall be fulfilled in dede], or not. 1662 Stillingfl. *Orig. Sacr.* II. vi. § 5 When therefore any Prophets did foretell things .. and those things did not come to pass, it was a certain evidence of a false Prophet. 1887 Lecky *Eng. in 18th C.* VI. 121 If the projects foreshadowed by De Mauide had come to pass.

c. quasi-*impers.*, with *it*, and subord. clause. To come to be the fact, to come about, to turn out, to happen (esp. in Scriptural lang.).

1526 Tindale *Matt.* xi. 1 And it came to passe when Iesus had ended his preceptes .. he departed thence. 1611 Bible *Gen.* xxii. 1. 1628 Hobbes *Thucyd.* (1822) 49 After this it came to pass that the Athenians and their confederates fought against the Medes. 1712 Addison *Spect.* No. 418 ▸ 3 But how comes it to pass, that we should take delight in being terrified or dejected by a Description. 1796 H. Hunter tr. *St.-Pierre's Stud. Nat.* (1799) III. 44 It comes to pass, that those places only, which are situated in the point of divergence .. experience two tides a day.

7. A position or situation in the course of any affair; *esp.* a position, qualified in some way; a critical position, a juncture, a predicament.

Cf. F. *être en belle passe*, *dans une mauvaise passe*, etc.: see Littré, *Passe* 5. But in Eng. app. sometimes associated with Pass *sb.*[1] as if a fig. use of sense 3 a.

1560 Daus tr. *Sleidane's Comm.* 58 Yet all thynges lyke to come to suche a passe. 1581 Pettie tr. *Guazzo's Civ. Conv.* II. (1586) 49 b, The worlde is come to this passe, that it counteth anie thing to bee lawfull which is delightfull. 1596 Spenser *F. Q.* VI. iii. 14 Him seemed fit that wounded Knight To visite, after this nights perillous passe. 1596 Shaks. *Tam. Shr.* v. ii. 124 Lord let me neuer haue a cause to sigh, Till I be brought to such a sillie passe. 1610 R. Abbott *Old Way* 27 To that desperate passe they are brought by the writings of the authors. 1732 Law *Serious C.* iv. (ed. 2) 66 To such a pass are we now come. 1822 Shelley *Triumph Life* 302 How and by what paths I have been brought To this dread pass. 1833 Ht. Martineau *Fr. Wines & Pol.* vi. 98 Where is the patriotism of bringing things to this pass? 1894 C. N. Robinson *Brit. Fleet* 9 Neglecting, at this critical pass, to secure the maritime approaches to his realm.

†**b.** *To pass.* (?) To (proper) position; in position. [Cf. Du. *te passe*. But see Well *to pass*.]

c 1595 Capt. Wyatt *R. Dudley's Voy. W. Ind.* (Hakl. Soc.) 58 Her ordinance lyinge well to pass, shee went as upright as a church. 1644 Nye *Gunnery* II. (1670) 5 If the first shot had struck under the Mark, then bring the Peece in all points as before to passe.

III. Permission or authorization to pass.

8. 'Permission to go or come anywhere' (J.); *esp.* a written permission to pass into, out of, or through a country or place, or between places within a country; a passport; also, a document authorizing the holder to pass, *e.g.* through the lines of an army; authorization or leave to pass.

1591 Spenser *M. Hubberd* 936 He cast to leave The Court, not asking any passe or leave. 1598 Hakluyt *Voy.* I. 472 They shall haue a letter of passe giuen vnto them. a 1604 Hanmer *Chron. Irel.* (1633) 120 To give him Passe to seek adventures in some forraigne country. 1647 Clarendon *Hist. Reb.* II. § 44 He had given passes to many obscure persons, to go into and return out of that kingdom. 1667 Pepys *Diary* 3 Apr., The Dutch have ordered a passe to be sent for our Commissioners. 1722 De Foe *Plague* (1754) 9 To get Passes and Certificates of Health.. for, without these, there was no being admitted to pass thro' the Towns. 1798 Nelson *Let.* 27 Oct. in Nicolas *Disp.* (1845) III. 163, I am much displeased that you should grant Passes to the Ships of any Power with whom we are at War. 1867 Smyth *Sailor's Word-bk.*, *Pass*, or *Passport*, a permission granted by any state to a vessel, to navigate in some particular sea without molestation. 1900 [see 17 a].

View Soc. Fr. II. lvi. 63 He generally passes the summer in the country. 1859 Geo. Eliot A. Bede xxiv, Those whose lives are passed in humble everyday work. 1860 Thackeray Round. Papers, Lazy Idle Boy (1876) 1, I had occasion to pass a week in the autumn in the little old town of Coire. 1878 J. C. Morison Gibbon 2 The longest period he ever passed at school were two years at Westminster.

†**b.** ? To cause to pass away, dispel. Obs. rare.

1565 Cooper Thesaurus, Acquiescere in re aliqua, ..to take delight and pleasure in: to passe his sorow and phantasies.

II. †45. To carry through its stages, transact; to bring to an end, to accomplish or execute (a matter, a business); to complete (a voyage). Obs.

c 1450 Cov. Myst. 89 We beseche ȝow of ȝoure pacyens, That we pace these materes so lythly away. 1473 Rolls of Parlt. VI. 66/1 In cas all other things were thoroughly passed and concluded betwixt his Highnes and theym. 1596 Shaks. Tam. Shr. iv. iv. 57 Then at my lodging, ..there this night Weele passe the businesse priuately and well. 1602 Marston Antonio's Rev. iv. i, If you but meditate of what is past, And what you plot to passe. 1605 B. Jonson Volpone iii. v, I told his son, brought, hid him here, Where he might hear his father pass the deed. 1748 Anson's Voy. iii. x. 403 The contract being past, it was some satisfaction .. to be certain that his preparations were now going on.

b. To cause or allow (anything proposed) to proceed, esp. after examination or scrutiny; to carry or get carried (a measure in Parliament, a resolution in a meeting); to agree to, declare correct, confirm, sanction, endorse.

1549–62 Sternhold & Hopkins Ps. cxix. iii. 24 They serve in stead of councellours my matters for to passe. 1624 Capt. Smith Virginia 185 The greatest matter passed, was a Proclamation against the spoile of Cahowes. 1666–7 Marvell Corr. Wks. 1872–5 II. 206 His Majesty came yesterday to the Lords' House, and there past five publick Bills. 1669 in 10th Rep. Hist. MSS. Comm. App. v. 104 Severall rectoryes and impropriations .. have been passed into patent in the name of his Grace. 1705 S. Sewall Diary 12 Nov., Brooklin is pass'd to be a Township by the Council. 1707 Watts Hymn, 'Life is the time' vi, There are no acts of pardon pass'd In the cold grave to which we haste. 1799 Jefferson Writ. (1859) IV. 263 Their majority will pass the bill. 1836 Penny Cycl. V. 296/2 Boyle..clearly proved that he passed his accounts in an irregular and dishonest manner. 1863 H. Cox Instit. iii. vi. 663 He was required to pass under the Great Seal the requisite authority to Commissioners. 1868 Freeman Norm. Conq. II. x. 483 They began..to pass decrees in utter defiance of the royal authority. 1878 Montagu Browne Pract. Taxidermy ii. 21, I have submitted the foregoing to a practical birdcatcher, ..and he has 'passed' it as correct. 1885 Law Rep. 29 Ch. Div. 796 A scheme of arrangement passed by the shareholders. 1892 A. S. Wilkins in Bookman Oct. 26/2 He had already passed for the press all the sheets of the present volume.

c. To allow or enable (a person) to pass an examination; to get (him) through.

1833 Marryat P. Simple xxxviii, Come Mr. Simple, stand up again... Don't be afraid, we wish to pass you. 1844 Dickens Mart. Chuz. xxvii, I'll pass you .. I can conscientiously report you a healthy subject. 1889 Nature 18 Apr. 577 His first duty..is to pass his men: and as our systems of examination are at present ordered, the passing is more a question of the facts than of the principles.

†**d.** To allow (something) to pass or go unchecked or without notice; to overlook, excuse, pass over. Obs.

c 1611 Chapman Iliad iii. 114 An old man will consent to pass things past, and what succeeds He looks into. 1768 Woman of Honor II. 212 Pass me this digression. 1802 H. Martin Helen of Glenross I. 247, I tell you, I will not, cannot pass that boy's bravado.

III. 46. To cause to go from one to another; to hand over, hand round, hand, transfer.

1596 Shaks. Tam. Shr. iv. iv. 45 If .. like a Father you will deale with him, And passe my daughter a sufficient dower, The match is made, and all is done. a 1716 South Serm. (1727) IV. 75 When God makes a Man wealthy and potent, he passes a double Obligation upon him. 1824–8 T. Hook Sayings & Doings 221 (Stratm.) Shall I pass you a spoon? 1833 Marryat P. Simple xxvii, Desire the sentry to pass the word for the butcher; I want to speak with him. Ibid. xxxv, Pass the word to reduce the cartridges. 1849 Thackeray Pendennis ii, The intelligence was 'passed round' ..in an instant. a 1901 Besant Five Years' Tryst, etc. (1902) 117 They passed buckets of water from hand to hand.

b. Football, etc. To transfer (the ball) to another player on the same side. Also absol. (sense 27 a). Cf. Pass sb.[2] 12.

c 1865 F. Wood Beeton's Football [Assoc.] Rules 36 No player shall carry the ball, hold it, throw it, pass it to another with his hands, or lift it from the ground with his hands. 1888 Irvine, etc. Football, Laws Rugby 9 It is lawful for any player who has the ball to throw it back towards his own goal, or to pass it back to any player of his own side who is at the time behind him. Ibid. 71 Never pass blindly, and be very chary of passing at all near your own goal. Never throw forward, for it is illegal. 1889 Pall Mall G. 4 Oct. 3/1 Seven years ago hockey was an utterly unscientific game... The Moulsey Club was the first to adopt a passing game. 1900 Fegan, etc. Football etc., Hockey 135 The ball may often be passed as usefully from forwards to halves, or from halves to backs, as in the contrary direction.

c. To put into circulation, give currency to (coin, or the like): esp. used of putting base coin into circulation. Also fig.

1589 Puttenham Eng. Poesie iii. xix. (Arb.) 237 One whom his mistresse burdened with some vnkinde speeches which he had past of her. 1634 Wood New Eng. Prosp. (1865) To Rdr., There hath beene many scandalous and false reports past upon the Countrey. 1802 Mar. Edgeworth Moral T. (1816) I. xix. 155 This bank-note..he was afraid to pass, till all inquiry had blown over. 1864 Daily Tel. 28 Nov., Utterers of base coin have a trick of passing a bad shilling between two good ones.

47. Law. To convey, make over, in legal form or with legal effect.

1587 Ld. Burleigh in Collect. (O. H. S.) I. 204 You passe ..a lease to the Ladie Stafford. 1690 Locke Govt. ii. xvi. § 186 Nor does it at all alter the Case..no more than it excuses the Force, and passes the Right, when I..deliver my Purse myself to a Thief, who demands it with a Pistol at my Breast. 1891 Law Rep. Weekly Notes 201/1 The delivery of the key of a trunk was held to pass the trunk and its contents.

48. To give in pledge (one's word, promise, oath); †to pledge (one's faith, honour, etc.).

1469 Sir J. Paston in Lett. II. 369 Ȝe wryteth in your letter that ye durst not passe your credens. 1528 Wriothesley in Pocock Rec. Ref. I. xli. 79 To pass his promise on such sort..might make much broylery. 1588 Shaks. L. L. L. i. i. 49 Your oath is past, to passe away from these. 1601 — Twel. N. i. v. 86 Sir Toby will be sworn that I am no Fox, but he wil not passe his word for two pence that you are no Foole. 1724 De Foe Mem. Cavalier i. 114 He [King of Sweden] had passed his Honour to the Norembergers, that he would not leave them. 1837 Keble Chr. Y. 2 Sun. Lent viii, That Name, by which Thy faithful oath is past. 1855 Macaulay Hist. Eng. xiii. III. 329 Half the sum was raised, ..and Dundee is said to have passed his word for the remainder. 1896 Edith Thompson in Monthly Packet Christm. No. 97 He had passed his word of honour.. that he would report himself at the fort of Haraf.

†**b.** To give or tender (a vote). Obs.

1642 G. Mountagu in Buccleuch MSS. (Hist. MSS. Comm.) I. 298 These are the votes.., which passed shall be published in a Declaration to the kingdom. 1685 in Picton L'pool Munic. Rec. (1883) I. 266 Everie person .. shall .. passe his vote when required, .. the towne clerke shall .. proceed from person to person till the whole Councell have passed their votes.

IV. †49. To send forth or out, to emit. To pass the ghost: to give up the ghost, to die. Obs. rare.

c 1400 Destr. Troy 8216 Tha he gird to the ground & the gost past. 1602 Marston Antonio's Rev. ii. iii, Here is a vent to passe my sighes. 1621 Quarles Argalus & P. (1678) 46 She past a sigh, and said, O ask not who.

50. To discharge from the body by excretion.

1698 Sir R. Sibbald in Phil. Trans. XX. 266 He hath past none by the Yard since he past these the other way. 1799 Med. Jrnl. II. 264 She passes her stools naturally. 1822–34 Good's Study Med. (ed. 4) I. 192 He..was incapable of passing a motion by any means. 1899 Cagney tr. Jaksch's Clin. Diagnosis vii. (ed. 4) 292 Hairs have been known to be passed with this fluid.

†**51.** To discharge (a volley). Obs.

1681 Lond. Gaz. No. 1628/1 One of them..shooting a-head and passing his Broad-side, ..fell a stern, by her Lee side.

52. To give utterance or expression to; to utter, pronounce (speech, criticism, censure); rarely, to put (a question). Sometimes, to exchange (words).

1615 Chapman Odyss. i. 274 On him again the grey-eyed Maid did pass This kind reply. 1617 Moryson Itin. ii. 38 Tyrone..saluted his Lordship standing on the other banke, and there they passed many speeches. 1654 tr. Scudery's Curia Pol. 35 To passe a censure, or to whisper seditiously against the Actions of Princes. 1694 Atterbury Serm. (1726) I. 186 A Way of exposing Things sacred and serious, by passing a bold Jest upon them. a 1698 South Serm. III. i. 30 By all this (it seems) our Saviour was only teaching those about Him, how to pass Complements upon Almighty God. 1828 Scott F. M. Perth xi, No man shall brook life after he has passed an affront on Douglas. 1875 Jowett Plato (ed. 2) V. 6 They are dissatisfied with the free criticisms which the Athenian passes upon the laws of Minos.

b. To utter or pronounce judicially. (Cf. 21, 22.)

1590 Shaks. Com. Err. i. i. 148 Thou art adiudged to the death, And passed sentence may not be recal'd. 1600 — A. Y. L. iii. iii. 86 Firm and irreuocable is my doombe, Which I haue past vpon her. 1700 Dryden Palamon & Arcite i. 266 If our doom be past in bonds to lie. 1820 W. Irving Sketch Bk. II. 265 When sentence of death was passed upon him. 1894 Hall Caine Manxman vi. viii, The Deemster in the half-lit court was passing sentence.

c. In various phrases, as to pass the time of day (dial. or colloq.), to exchange salutations or gossip in passing; so, to pass (a) good morning, the good day, the compliments of the day.

1836 A. A. Parker Trip to West 165 Two Indians..halted within a few rods of us, stared a moment, and then civilly passed the time of day. 1875 Sussex Gloss. s.v. Time of Day, 'I doānt know any more of him than just to pass the time o' day'. 1882 B. Harte Flip iii, 'Dropping in to pass the time of day' with her father. 1890 L. C. D'Oyle Notches 180 She had simply passed him a pleasant 'Good morning'. 1894 Outing (U. S.) XXIV. 10/1 Nothing has happened to prevent my passing the compliments of the day with Mrs. Crombie.

V. †53. Fencing. To make or execute (a thrust).

1598 Shaks. Merry W. ii. iii. 26 To see thee fight, to see thee foigne, to .. see thee passe thy puncto, thy stock, thy reuerse, thy distance, thy montant.

54. To perform the pass on a pack of cards: see Pass sb.[2] 10.

1884 St. James's Gaz. 5 Dec. 5/2 [To] prevent him from watching the operator too closely when engaged in 'readying' and 'passing' the cards. Ibid., Striking feats of dexterous 'readying' and 'passing' which his companion performed.

D. With prepositions and adverbs.

I. With prepositions.

Pass (intrans., trans., or causal) may be followed by any preposition of motion or direction, with its object, both words having their own senses. Sometimes the prep. appears to be more closely united with the verb, so as to form with it a verbal phrase, often expressible by a single verb with its object. Thus pass across = cross, traverse, pass down = descend, pass into = enter, pass up = ascend, etc. Of these, the following are the more important:

Pass at —. See 23 c.

55. Pass beyond —. a. See simple senses and Beyond prep.

b. To pass the limits of, exceed, transcend.

1819 Keats Lamia ii. 32 His spirit pass'd beyond its golden bourn Into the noisy world. 1875 Jowett Plato (ed. 2) IV. 257 No effort of reflection will enable us to pass beyond the limits of our own faculties.

56. Pass by —.

†**a.** To go through or by way of. Obs.

13.. K. Alis. 1320 Anon they..Passith by Tire, and by Cidoyne, ..Alle til they come to Babiloyne. 1390 Gower Conf. III. 63 Wher as sche passeth be the strete. a 1548 Hall Chron., Hen. VIII 61 [They] assaute the Alyens as they passed by the stretes. 1573–80 Baret Alv. P 162 As we came to this Citie, we passed by Lions, where we soiourned two daies.

b. To go past; to pass; = 28.

13.. K. Alis. 6658 Heo passeden by a quenes lond, That lette Candace, Y undurstond. c 1386 Chaucer Merch. T. 340 Thanne sholde he se ful many a figure pace By his Mirour. 1481 Caxton Reynard xxiii. (Arb.) 54, I supposed to haue passed by hym peasibly toward this feste. 1550 Crowley Epigr. 34 b, As he paste by a pasture most pleasaunte to se. 1606 Shaks. Tr. & Cr. iii. iii. 39 Please it our Generall to passe strangely by him, As if he were forgot. 1711 Addison Spect. No. 63 ⁋ 6, I heard several double Rhymes as I passed by them. 1850 S. Dobell Roman, Chamouni, If Thou.. hast..passed by The sleeping savage dreadful still in sleep.

c. To pass without stopping, or without notice; to take no notice of, disregard, omit: see 61 c.

Pass for —. See 5, 23. Pass into —. See 7.

Pass of —. See 10, 10 c, 23 b.

Pass on —. See 5 c, 21 b, c, 24.

57. Pass over —.

a. To cross above or on the surface of (a sea, river, or expanse); to cross, to traverse; = 30.

c 1275 Lay. 1341 Seyles drawe to toppe, leten lade þane wind, passi ouer bieres. 1297 R. Glouc. (Rolls) 228 Suþþe he ssulde mani lond over passi & wende. a 1300 Cursor M. 10120 Do me to passe þe dikes [v.r. diches] ouer. c 1325 Lai le Freine 141 The maide .. passed ouer a wild heth. c 1400 Melayne 878 To Charls now will I torne agayne þat passes ouer Mountayne & playne. c 1440 Promp. Parv. 376/2 Pacyn ovyr, transgredior. 1600 Shaks. A. Y. L. v. iii. 19 It was a Louer, and his lasse, ..That o're the greene corne feild did passe. 1600 J. Pory tr. Leo's Africa Introd. 39 A man must beware how he passe ouer deepe riuers with them. fig. 1887 Bowen Virg. Æneid ii. 281 O'er thy people and city, alas! what sorrows have passed. Mod. A change passed over his countenance.

b. To pass the hand over.

1805 Southey Madoc in W. xiv, He took a harp..and passing o'er its chords Made music. 1879 Sir E. Arnold Lt. Asia iii. (1883) 52 So sigh we, passing o'er the solemn strings.

†**c.** trans. To spend (time); = sense 44. Obs.

1390 Gower Conf. III. 64 The queene..passeth over thilke nyht, Til it was on the morwe liht. 1548 Udall, etc. Erasm. Par. Matt. i. 20 So that the reste of the life be passed ouer after the rule of Christ. 1577 F. de L'isle's Legendarie A viij, He neuer medled with matters of estate but passed ouer his time in pleasure. 1662 J. Davies tr. Olearius' Voy. Ambass. 198 Many times he pass'd over the Winter therein.

d. To pass a thing without dwelling upon it, or without notice or remark, to omit: see 67 e.

58. Pass through —.

a. To go from side to side of, to cross, traverse.

a 1300 Cursor M. 6265 Þe see on aiþer side þam stod, ..Til þai war passed thoru þat flod. 1375 Barbour Bruce xvi. 319 That he wes passit throu all Irland Fra end till end. c 1385 Chaucer L. G. W. 746 Thisbe, And with a soun as softe as ony shryfte They lete here wordis thour the clift pace. 1526 Pilgr. Perf. (W. de W. 1531) 12 b, Y people of god passynge through the same see drye fote. 1530 Palsgr. 653/2 He shall passe thorowe fyre and water or he get it. 1613 Purchas Pilgrimage (1614) 62 Not cause their children to passe through the fire. 1709 Steele Tatler No. 44 ⁋ 4 On Saturday last he passed through Staines. 1885 Leudesdorf Cremona's Proj. Geom. 237 If two conics which are inscribed in a given quadrilateral pass through a given point. fig. 1639 T. Brugis tr. Camus' Mor. Relat. 318 All the Idea's which passe thorow our mindes. 1722 Wollaston Relig. Nat. i. 11 Abimelek gave greater credit to that information which passed through his eye.

b. In reference to times, stages, states, conditions, processes, actions, experiences, etc.

c 1330 Sir Beues (MS. A.) 1635 Erst þow schelt pase þour3 min hond And þour3 Morgelay, my gode brond! 1362 Langl. P. Pl. A. viii. 11 [Thei] Han pardoun þorw Purgatorie to passen ful sone. 1604 E. G[rimstone] D'Acosta's Hist. Indies iv. iv. 211 Golde which hath often passed through the fire, keepes his colour. 1660 F. Brooke tr. Le Blanc's Trav. 128 Men having passed thorough all sorts of animals at last became Gods. 1711 Addison Spect. No. 115 ⁋ 5 How many Hands must they pass through before they are fit for Use? 1747 Gentl. Mag. XVII. 325 Having pass'd thro' his Degrees in Arts, he became domestick Chaplain to Dr Tho. Smith. 1865 R. W. Dale Jew. Temp. xxi. (1877) 233 We..are passing through times of speculative unbelief.

c. To make or force a passage through; to penetrate; to pierce through; to shoot through, send a shot through.

14.. in Tundale's Vis. (1843) 133 And thorow thi sowle schall a scharp swyrd pace. 1412–20 Lydg. Chron. Troy iv. xxx, For he felte thorugh his herte pace The persyng stremys of hir eyen two. c 1470 Gol. & Gaw. 708 Throw platis of polist steill thair poyntis can pase. 1530 Palsgr. 654/2 He passed thorowe his harnesse and his bodye at one shotte, il transpassa son harnoys et son corps a vng traict. Mod. The bullet passed through his shoulder.

fig. 1638 Junius Paint. Ancients 211 No man is able to passe through the secrets of Art, ..unlesse he first overcome the pompe of vaine glorie.

d. causal. To cause (a thing) to pass or go through; to put, thrust, or impel through.

1530 Palsgr. 654/2, I passe thorowe, as spyce..thorowe a sarce, or pepyr thorowe the querne, or meale thorowe a boulter. 1731 Medley Kolben's Cape G. Hope II. 67 The ground becomes frequently so hard, that twenty oxen are not sufficient to pass a plough through it. 1853 Soyer Pantroph. 288 Take a flour sieve, and pass the cheese through it. 1857 Borrow Rom. Rye xxxix, The principal component parts were burnt wine and rosemary, passed through an alembic. 1885 Law Rep. 15 Q. B. D. 316 A catch..which prevented the pin, when passed through a slit, from repassing. 1898 Florence Montgomery Tony 20 Passing his arm through the strap of the window. 1899 Allbutt's Syst. Med. VIII. 848 The preparations being much reduced in virulence by passing the culture through rabbits. Mod. A dragoon passed his sword through him.

Pass upon —. See 5 c, 21 c.

†**59. Pass with —:** to have done with, take no notice of. Obs. rare.

1641 Nicholas Papers (Camden) 27 Neither have they gratifyed the kinge with the release of the lo. Montrosse or with the passing with the Ea. of Traquaire.

II. With adverbs.

60. Pass away. a. See simple senses and Away adv. **b.** intr. Of persons: To depart; also, to get or break away (as from restraint).

a 1425 Cursor M. 12175 (Trin.) Somme oþere vnswere shaltou say Ar I passe from þe away. c 1430 Syr Tryam. 317 The quene passyd awey & fledd On fote. 1590 Spenser F. Q. i. vi. 48 But, when he saw the Damsell passe away, He left his stond, and her pursewd apace. 1879 E. Arnold Lt. Asia iv. (1883) 88 But that ox-king .. Trampled the warders down, and passed away.

c. intr. To die, expire.

c 1375 Lay Folks Mass Bk. (MS. B) 112 God lord graunt.. rest and pese þat lastis ay to cristen soules passed away. 1806 Southey Lett. (ed. Warter) I. 366 Immediately as he uttered the words he passed away. 1892 Law Times XCII. 144/2 Mr. Richard Williams..passed away on the 21st ult., at the great age of ninety years.

d. intr. Of time: To elapse, come to an end.

a 1425 Cursor M. 20858 (Trin.) Tyme passeþ faste awey. 1711 Addison Spect. No. 93 ⁋ 2 The Moments that are to pass away before the happy Meeting. 1847 Marryat Childr. N. Forest iv, Thus passed the winter away so rapidly, that [etc.].

e. intr. Of things: To pass out of existence, come to an end, cease to be, be dissolved, perish.

13.. S. Paula in Horstm. Altengl. Leg. (1878) 4/1 Precious stones þat wiþ þis world and eorþe here Passen awey al in fere. 1539 Bible (Great) 2 Pet. iii. 10 The heauens shall passe awaye. 1557 N. T. (Genev.) Matt. xxiv. 35 Heauen and earth shall passe awaye [Wyclif passe, Tindale perisshe], but my wordes shal not passe awaye. 1814 Southey Ode War Amer. xiii, Dominion passeth like a cloud away. 1845 M. Pattison Ess. (1889) I. 26 His anger passed away. 1856 Froude Hist. Eng. (1858) I. i. 59 All the..convictions of the old world were passing away, never to return. 1884 Manch. Exam. 20 May 5/2 The fears of a general crisis are passing away.

f. trans. To spend (time, etc.); to while away, to pass: emphatic of 44.

c 1550 Lusty Juventus in Hazl. Dodsley II. 46 What shall I do now to pass away the day? 1560 Daus tr. Sleidane's Comm. 139 Going than to Wittemberge, they passed away the rest of the wynter there. 1594 Shaks. Rich. III, i. i. 25 Why I..Haue no delight to passe away the time. 1665 Earl Dorset Song Written at Sea vii, To pass our tedious hours away. 1712 Addison Spect. No. 106 ⁋ 1 An Invitation..to pass away a Month with him in the Country. 1848 Thackeray Lett. 12 Aug., One day is passed away here very like its defunct predecessor.

†**g.** To transfer away; to relinquish, surrender (rights, etc.); to convey away (property). Obs.

1651 Hobbes Leviath. ii. xxi. 111 What Rights we passe away, when we make a Common-wealth. 1690 Locke Govt. ii. viii. § 116 Because our Fathers or Progenitors passed away their natural Liberty. a 1692 Pollexfen Disc. Trade (1697) 28 A Man that is to pass away Lands, or Goods. 1781 Cowper Hope 11 Riches are passed away from hand to hand.

61. Pass by.

a. intr. To go or proceed past; to move on without stopping; to flow past.

c 1430 Syr Tryam. 278 There the quene schulde passe by. 1568 Grafton Chron. II. 301 The Englishmen passed by without anye approchyng. 1611 Bible Lam. i. 12 Is it nothing to you, all ye that passe by? 1712 Steele Spect. No. 398 ⁋ 1 He saw Robin the Porter..passing by. 1799 Southey Ruined Cottage Wks. 1838 III. 32 The countrymen..leaning o'er the bridge, ..would all look up When she pass'd by. 1850 Tennyson In Mem. xix, There twice a day the Severn fills; The salt sea-water passes by.

b. fig. and in reference to time.

c 1386 Chaucer Man of Law's T. 1026 But I lete all his storie passen by, Of Custance is my tale specially. a 1821 Keats Sonn., Human Seasons, To let fair things Pass by unheeded, as a threshold brook. 1885 Manch. Weekly Times 20 June 5/5 A generation would pass by before the adversaries..would find their way back to power.

c. trans. To go past (a thing or person) without stopping, or without taking notice; to fail to notice, to overlook; to omit; to take no notice of, dismiss from consideration, disregard, ignore; = pass over, 67 e, f.

When the object is a sb., it usually comes after by, so that the construction can be analysed as that of an intrans. vb. with a preposition and its object, as in to pass by his eldest son; cf. to pass him by.

[a 1300 Cursor M. 15634 Quer i sal þis calice drinc, or i sal pass þar-bi?] 1560 Bible (Genev.) Prov. xix. 11 His glorie is to passe by an offence. 1611 Ld. T. Howard in Harington's Nugæ Ant. (ed. Park 1804) I. 393 He was overcharged with confusion, and passed by admiring the dressing of the horse. 1641 T. Williamson tr. Goulart's Wise Vieillard 77 Better to wink at, and passe by an injurie. 1658–9 in Burton's Diary (1828) IV. 3, I would hear him first, and then pass it by... He must come as a delinquent on his knees. 1677 Horneck Gt. Law Consid. v. (1704) 297 These observables are passed by as things out of his element. 1869 J. Martineau Ess. II. 76 Instances.. which legislation passes by in silence. 1869 Freeman Norm. Conq. III. xiii. 278 That Eadward might rightly pass by an incompetent minor. 1871 R. H. Hutton Ess. (1877) I. 71, I pass them by with the remark.

62. Pass forth.

a. intr. To go out or away (arch.). † To pass forth of use, to go out of use, become obsolete (obs.).

1297 R. Glouc. (Rolls) 2910 He sey þe contreys as he passede vorþ & destrued & bar in eche half. c 1394 P. Pl. Crede 96 Leue nouȝt on þo losels but let hem forþ pasen. 1530 Palsgr. 654/1, I passe forthe, I go forthe, as an armye whan it is removynge, or a company by fore a great estate. 1565 Reg. Privy Council Scot. I. 332 Understanding the priviligis of the Scottis merchantis..to decay and pas furth of use in the partis of Flanderis. 1596 Spenser F. Q. vi. iii. 16 He passed forth with her in faire array.

†**b.** To go forward, advance, go on, continue.

c 1386 Chaucer Miller's T. 134 This passeth forth..fro day to day..this Absolon So woweth hire. c 1450 St. Cuthbert (Surtees) 7505 He was wele paste forthe in age. 1568 Grafton Chron. II. 391 The yongest..say their opinions first, and so passe fourth in order vntill it come to the highest.

†**c.** trans. To spend or pass (time). Obs.

1509 Hawes Past. Pleas. xvi. (Percy Soc.) 73 She wyll wyth love her grene flouryng age Passe forth in joye, pleasure, & courage. 1552 Huloet, Passe forth the day or tyme, agitare diem, exigere tempus. 1573–80 Baret Alv. P 158, I will passe forth this day by little and little [paulatim hunc producam diem] with sipping and drinking.

63. Pass in. trans. To hand in (e.g. a cheque to a bank). To pass in one's cheques, to die (slang).

1872 'Mark Twain' Roughing It 332 (Farmer) One of the boys has passed in his checks, and we want to give him a good send-off. 1894 H. Nisbet Bush Girl's Rom. 108 The best thing I can do for you is to give you a cheque of my own made payable to yourself at sight, with an introduction to the bank as well, and I will pass in the form myself next time I am down there. 1900 W. Lond. Observ. 4 May 3/7, I see that young M. has passed in his checks.

64. Pass off.

a. intr. To go off or disappear gradually: said of sensations, physical conditions, moisture, etc.

1845 Budd Dis. Liver 266 In the presence of some medicines that pass off in the bile. 1861 Headland Med. Handbk. 160 Remittent fever instead of intermitting at distinct periods, passes off after a variable time, and then recurs. Mod. After a little the feeling of faintness passed off. The hydrogen unites with the oxygen to form water, which passes off in steam. The smell of the paint will pass off in a few days.

b. intr. Of a proceeding: To be carried through and completed (with more or less success).

1886 Times 23 Nov. 9 In every sense the festival passed off as its promoters must have desired. 1891 Leeds Merc. 2 May 6/3 The Labour Demonstrations throughout Europe yesterday passed off on the whole more peaceably than was anticipated. Mod. How did the wedding pass off? Everything passed off very well.

c. trans. To put into circulation, or dispose of (esp. deceptively); to palm off; to impose.

1799 Han. More Fem. Educ. (ed. 4) I. 297 They might be tempted to pass off for their own what they pick up from others. 1857 Borrow Rom. Rye xvii, And other customers came in, who..also passed off their jokes upon me. Ibid. xli, [He] sometimes shortened money, and at other times passed off what had been shortened by other gentry. 1865 M. Arnold Ess. Crit. ii. 65 Trying to pass off their wares as excellent. 1884 Law Times Rep. LI. 222/2 The applicants ..pass off their goods for those of the Baron de Geer.

d. To cause (a person) to be accepted in some false character; esp. refl. (with for or as), to give oneself out as what one is not, to pretend to be.

1809 Malkin Gil Blas v. i. ⁋ 12 He passed himself off for my servant. Ibid. ⁋ 18 The insolence of this scoundrel who fancies to pass me off for a highwayman. 1871 Smiles Charac. vi. (1876) 181 He does not seek to pass himself off as richer than he is. 1885 H. Conway Family Affair I, A child still young enough to be passed off as a child in arms.

e. To ward off or adroitly put aside (a remark, etc.) without seriously meeting it; to parry.

1890 A. Gissing Village Hampden III. xi. 238 The young man passed off lightly all such reference.

65. Pass on.

a. intr. See simple senses and On adv.; esp. to proceed on one's way, in one's course, in one's discourse or writing; to continue one's course; to proceed or advance, as a transaction or progressive state; to pass, as time.

a 1300 Cursor M. 17288 + 395 Þe day is passed on, ne farrer may þou wyn. 1470–85 Malory Arthur xviii. xx, Soo this paste on alle that wynter with alle manere of huntynge and haukyng. 1573–80 Baret Alv. P 163 The more time that passed on, the more [etc.]. 1611 Bible Gen. xviii. 5, I will fetch a morsell of bread; and comfort ye your hearts, after that ye shall passe on. 1626 C. Potter tr. Sarpi's Hist. Quarrels 46 The Pope spake all this with so great heat, that the Ambassador did not judge fit at that time to passe on further. 1634 Milton Comus 430 Yea there, where very desolation dwels.. She may pass on with unblench't majesty. 1842 Tennyson 'Come not when I am dead' ii, Pass on, weak heart, and leave me where I lie. 1899 Allbutt's Syst. Med. VII. 651 The optic neuritis is passing on to post-neuritic atrophy. Mod. Pass on, please, and do not obstruct the way. The preacher passes on to his second head. But we have said enough on this point; we pass on.

b. trans. To send or hand (anything) to the next member of a series.

1791 'G. Gambado' Ann. Horsem. xvii. (1809) 130 No Vagrants past on. 1877 Spurgeon Serm. XXIII. 357 Getting rid of a case by saving your own pocket and passing the applicant on to another. Mod. Please read this and pass it on.

66. Pass out.

a. intr. See simple senses and Out adv.; chiefly, to go out through a passage. To pass out of, to issue from, leave; to pass out of sight, to go beyond the reach of sight.

13.. K. Alis. 6246 Ther no schal schip out passe. c 1375 Cursor M. 12127 (Fairf.) How lange þi life sal laste or þou passe out of þis werde. a 1425 Ibid. 17350 (Trin.) Þei sent aspies also aboute þat he shulde not passen oute. 1574 tr. Marlorat's Apocalips 3 That he should passe out of Asia into Macedonia. a 1711 Ken Art. Visit. Wks. (1838) 492 When any one is passing out of this life. 1833 Keble Serm. (1848) I. 147 He may..pass out of this world, before he see any abatement in the triumph of disorder and irreligion. 1842 Tennyson Locksley Hall 34 Love .. Smote the chord of Self, that, trembling, pass'd in music out of sight.

†**b.** trans. To spend the whole of (a time).

1603 Knolles Hist. Turks (1621) 55 The poore Sultan utterly discouraged, returned againe to Constantinople, and there..passed out the rest of his dayes.

67. Pass over.

a. intr. To go across; to cross to the other or opposite side. In Chemistry, said of the volatilized substances which pass from the retort in distillation, and are condensed in the receiver.

a 1330 Otuel 707 Ouer þe brugge þei wenten ifeere, ..& þo þei ouer passed were, Such auntres þei funden þere. 1611 Bible Deut. iii. 18 Ye shall passe ouer armed before your brethren the children of Israel. 1641 French Distill. vi. (1651) 196 Adde the tartarizated quintessence, yet so that.. that passe over with it. 1849 Macaulay Hist. Eng. v. I. 601 The hope that some of those regiments which he had formerly commanded would pass over to his standard. 1863–72 Watts Dict. Chem. I. 10 That which passes over towards the middle must be redistilled to free it from copper mechanically carried over. 1864–72 Ibid. II. 337 Some organic compounds boil at so low a temperature that, when heated in a retort, they pass over unchanged. 1875 Bennett & Dyer tr. Sachs' Bot. 802 The contents of one of the conjugating cells pass over into the other which remains stationary. 1879 Harlan Eyesight ii. 25 After lining the inner surface of the lids, it [mucous membrane] passes over to the ball, forming a loose fold.

†**b.** intr. Of a period of time: To go by, elapse, be spent, come to an end. Obs.

c 1470 Henry Wallace i. 271 This passit our, quhill diuers dayis war gane. 1659 H. Plumptre Let. in 12th Rep. Hist. MSS. Comm. App. v. 6 Wishing that all your yeares yet to come may passe over with mirth and jollityes.

†**c.** intr. With compl., as to pass over unpunished, to go unpunished. Obs.

1566 Reg. Privy Council Scot. I. 470 Wordis of dishonour ..quhilk aucht nocht to pas owir untryi. and unpuneist.

d. trans. To hand over to another; to transfer.

1560 Daus tr. Sleidane's Comm. 306 b, [They] leauing behinde them no children, passed ouer the gouernment to their yongest brother. 1577 Harrison England ii. xxiii. (1877) i. 355 But then I should exceed the limits of a description. Wherefore I passe it ouer to others [etc.]. 1631 Weever Anc. Fun. Mon. 687 This house..satisfied the said Sir Richard; who thereupon past it ouer to Q. Mary. a 1686 T. Watson Body Divin. (1692) 460 The Covenant of Grace .. by vertue of which God passeth himself over to us to be our God. 1862 Dana Man. Geol. 583 Geology here passes over the continuation of the history of man to Archaeology.

e. To pass (a thing) without touching it, or without remark or notice, esp. in narration; to omit, to skip, to disregard; to ignore the claims of (a person) to promotion, etc., to pass by in selection for a special post or duty.

As in pass by 61 c, when the object is a sb., it usually comes after over, so that the construction can then be analysed as that of an intrans. vb. followed by a preposition with its object; as in the literal he passed over the bridge. Cf. also the vb. Overpass, of which pass over was formerly the decomposed form used in certain verbal constructions.

c 1380 Wyclif Serm. Sel. Wks. II. 226 Paul passiþ over þes two vertues, and praieþ after charite. c 1386 Chaucer Pard. Prol. 17 This is a pitous tale for to heere But natheles passe ouer is no fors. 1526 Skelton Magnyf. 646, I wyll passe ouer the cyrcumstaunce, And shortly shewe you the hole substaunce. 1530 Palsgr. 654/2, I have many mo thynges to saye..but, for faulte of tyme, I passe them over. 1573 G. Harvey Letter-bk. (Camden) 8, I pas mani sutch misusagis over. 1621 Elsing Debates Ho. Lords (Camden) 54 The matter of Yelverton is of such ymportaunce as yt cannot be paste over. 1711 Addison Spect. No. 1 ⁋ 3 As for the rest of my Infancy, I shall pass it over in Silence. 1839 James Gentl. Old Sch. xiv, This gross offence.. was not to be passed over. 1890 W. E. Norris Misadventure viii, He does not think it would be right to pass over his son. 1890 T. W. Reid Monckton-Milnes (1891) I. viii. 360 He had again been disappointed of his..expectation of office, Peel having once more passed him over.

f. To let go unpunished, to overlook (an offence).

1388 Wyclif Prov. xix. 11 His glorie is to passe ouere wickid thingis. 1611 Bible ibid., It is his glory to passe ouer a transgression. 1814 Wellington 16 May in Gurw. Desp. (1838) XII. 21 If conduct such as that .. be passed over, it will be impossible to maintain the necessary discipline of the army. 1877 Spurgeon Serm. XXIII. 662 The sin.. was not to be winked at and passed over as a mere trifle.

†**g.** To surpass = Overpass v. 7.

1390 Gower Conf. II. 264 A goddesse.. what hir liste.. Sche dede, That passeth over manneskinde.

68. Pass through: emphatic of sense 14.

c 1400 Ywaine & Gaw. 15 Thurgh I past, with mekyl payn.

a 1693 South Serm. II. v. 176 His Heart lies open..for all the Sin and Villainy in the World freely to pass through. 1801 Bloomfield Rural T., Fakenham Ghost xi, So long it [the gate] swung That Ghost and all pass'd through. 1832 Tennyson Dream Fair Women 83 Pass freely thro'; the wood is all thine own.

Pass-, the vb.-stem or imper. of Pass v., used in a few combinations, mostly nonce-words: †pa·ss-dice = Passage 15 [cf. It. passa-dieci: see quot. 1598 s.v.]; †pa·ss-man a., surpassing man, superhuman; pa·ss-out a., of a ticket: that enables the holder to pass out and return to a place of entertainment; †pa·ss-praise a., transcending praise, beyond praise.

1805 T. Holcroft Bryan Perdue II. 56 To..idle away.. part of the four and twenty hours at hazard, pass-dice, picquet [etc.]. 1606 Sylvester Du Bartas ii. iv. ii. Magnif. 1254 The passe-man Wisedome of th' Isaacian Prince, A light so bright, set in such eminence. 1894 A. Chevallier Record by Himself 191 An attendant proffering her a pass-out check respectfully asked if she intended to return. 1896 Westm. Gaz. 24 Nov. 1/3 The agitation for pass-out checks at the variety theatres. a 1586 Sidney Astr. & Stella lxxvii, That skin, whose passe-praise hue scornes this poore tearme of white.

Passable (pa·săb'l), a. Also 5–6 -yble, 7 passeable. [a. F. passable (13th c. in Hatz.-Darm.), f. passer to Pass: see -able. Cf. It. passabile. In OF. the word had most of the senses retained in Eng.; mod.F. retains only sense 4.]

1. That may be passed, crossed, or traversed.

1413 Pilgr. Sowle (Caxton) i. iii. (1859) 4 Ryght as the fleyng ayer geuyth place to the flyght of byrdes..right so was al this erthe passyble to spirites. 1527 Knight in Pocock Rec. Ref. I. xxviii. 57 The rivers not being always passable. 1576 Act 18 Eliz. c. 10 § 7 For the better keeping of the Highways passable for her Majesty's People. 1593 R. Harvey Philad. 4 Since Brutes time the Alpes haue been passable enough. 1614 Raleigh Hist. World iii. (1634) 106 To leave at their backs a wood scarce passeable. 1685 Lond. Gaz. No. 2080/3 The Streets were hardly passable. 1722 De Foe Col. Jack (1840) 104 The ford was not passable. 1841 W. Spalding Italy & It. Isl. I. 38 The river is passable for boats..to the Mediterranean, a distance of nearly sixty miles. 1880 Geikie Phys. Geog. iv. 302 The last time that the Thames at London was passable on ice was in 1814.

†**2.** Able to pass or have passage. Obs.

1555 Eden Decades 121 Forasmuche as they [sunbeams] are not passyble in them selues, as doth manyfestly appeare by the snowe lyinge contynually vnmolten vpon certeyne hygh montaynes. 1664 H. More Antid. Idolatry x. 131 So that a Soul otherwise passable of her self would be necessarily drown'd in this one foul Deluge of Guilt. 1745 Hales in Phil. Trans. XLIII. 502 All passable Stones which have lately fallen from the Kidneys into the Bladder, ..might readily and easily be brought out thence. 1762 Dunn ibid. LII. 464 The Sun's rays become passable through such a length of medium.

3. Of money: That may be circulated, that has valid currency, current; of a book: qualified or fit for circulation. Also fig.

1590 Greene Neuer Too Late Wks. (Grosart) VIII. 26 Sterling coyne passable from man to man in way of exchange. 1607 Shaks. Cor. v. ii. 13 The vertue of your name, Is not heere passable. 1674 Hickman Hist. Quinquart. (ed. 2) 196 He would have prevailed with some of them to authorize his Book, that it might have been more passable. 1702 Eng. Theophrast. 188 It is with Men, as it is with false Money; One piece is more or less passable than another, as it happens to have more or less Sense or Starling in the Mixture. 1688 B. W. Richardson Son of Star III. xi. 186 The coin may cease to be of value as a passable thing, as money, but as a relic it must always live.

4. That can pass muster; tolerable, fairly good, fair; moderate, sufficient, presentable.

1489 Caxton Faytes of A. i. xii. 33 Take gode hede that noon be reteyned but he be passable so that noo fawte be in his persone. 1597 Morley Introd. Mus. 122 At that time I thought it excelling, but nowe I feare it will bee found scant passable. 1637 Laud Sp. in Star-Chamb. 14 June 6 Our maine Crime is..that we are Bishops; were we not so, some of us might be as passable as other men. 1748 Richardson Clarissa (1811) I. ii. 8 There were many women deemed passable who were inferior to herself. 1838 Southey Doctor cxlv. (1862) 398 A passable knowledge of living languages. 1893 Times 12 June 4/2 Potatoes appear in eight departments very good, 13 good, 17 satisfactory, 18 passable, six mediocre, and three bad.

†**5.** Passing, transient, ephemeral. Obs. rare⁻¹.

1627–77 Feltham Resolves i. xx. 36 Things acted..are too more retainable, than the passable tones of the tongue.

6. [f. Pass v. 45 b + -able.] Capable of passing or being passed by a deliberating assembly.

1831 Whately in Life (1866) I. 66 It is a task of double difficulty to frame what shall be at once an improvement and passable in Convocation [of Oxford University].

7. quasi-adv. = Passably.

1581 Savile Tacitus, Hist. i. lxxviii. (1591) 43 Things which the .. cares at hande made passable good. 1675 Marvell Wks. (1872–5) II. 431, I have a passable good estate. 1706 E. Ward Wooden World Diss. (1708) 41 But for him, the Ship's Crew would be passable good Christians.

Hence **Pa·ssableness,** the quality of being passable.

1727 Bailey vol. II, Passableness..capableness of being passed. 1779 Wolff Dansk Ord-bog, Temmelighed, mediocrity, passableness. 1834 Blackw. Mag. XXXV. 176 There was a river to cross, the passableness of which was very questionable. 1888 J. Q. Bittinger Hist. Haverhill (N.H.) 191 The roads of Haverhill will average in passableness and comfort with the roads of neighboring towns.

Passable, obs. erroneous form of Passible.

Passably (pa·săbli), adv. [f. Passable a. + -ly[2].] Tolerably, sufficiently well to pass; fairly well, moderately.

a 1610 Healey Theophrastus To Rdr. (1636) I ij b, The French is elegant enough, passably copious, happie in composition. 1741 Richardson Pamela (1824) I. xlix. 379 [She] is mighty pretty, and passably genteel. 1801 Mar. Edgeworth Gd. French Governess Wks. 1832 III. 175 Miss Fanshaw had learned to speak French passably. 1874 Mrs. H. Wood Mast. Greylands xxvii. 315 The night was passably bright.

‖**Passacaglia** (passăkā·lyă). [It., a. Sp. pasacalle (pasăka·lye), f. pasar to pass + calle street; because often played in the streets.] An early kind of dance tune (of Spanish origin) having a movement slower than the Chaconne, generally constructed on a ground bass and written in triple time; also the dance to this.

1659 Howell Vocab. Sect. 50 Giggs, salibrands, chaconas, passingalias, galiards. 1668 Dryden Evening's Love ii. i, Pray let me hear it: I hope it will go to the tune of one of our Passa-calles. 1724 Short Explic. For. Wds. Mus. Bks., Passacaglio, or Passacaille, or Passagillio, is a Kind of Air somewhat like a Chacoone, but of a more slow or graver Movement. 1880 Grove Dict. Mus. II. 660/1 The feature which, in common with the Chaconne, has elevated the Passacaglia above the majority of dance forms, is the construction of the music on a ground bass, generally consisting of a short theme of two, four, or eight bars. 1898 G. B. Shaw Perf. Wagnerite 3 There are passacaglias on ground basses, canons ad hypodiapente.

‖**Passacaille** (pasăkā·y). [a. F. passecaille (Furetière 1690), ad. Sp. pasacalle: see prec.] = prec.

1711 E. Pemberton (title) Essay for the Further Improvement of Dancing, ..to which is added Three Single Dances: a Chacone, a Passacaille, and a Jig. 1862 E. Pauer Programme 8 Mar., The origin of the Passacaille is Spanish.

Passade (păsē·d). rare. [a. F. passade, ad. Pr. passada or It. passata (Sp. pasada), f. passare to Pass: see -ade, -ada, -ata.]

1. Horsemanship. (See quots.)

1656 Blount Glossogr. [from Cotgr.], Passade, .. the manage of a Horse, backward and forward. 1727–41 Chambers Cycl., Passade, in the manage, signifies a turn, or course of a horse backwards or forwards on the same plot of ground; passing or repassing from one end to the other. 1892 B. Hinton Lord's Return 214 The action of Sir Walter was like the passade in the manege, a turn backward, forward, without being able to extricate himself.

†**2.** An alms given to a passer-by. Obs. rare.

1656 Blount Glossogr. [from Cotgr.], Passade, an alms, benevolence or entertainment given by, or to a Passenger. 1658 in Phillips. 1727–41 in Chambers Cycl.

†**3.** = next, 1. Obs. rare.

1706 Phillips, Passade or Passado, a Pass or Thrust in Fencing. 1727–41 in Chambers Cycl.

‖**Passado** (pāsā·do). Obs. [Altered from F. passade, or Sp. pasada, It. passata (both of these also in early use): see prec. and -ado.]

1. Fencing. A forward thrust with the sword, one foot being advanced at the same time.

1588 Shaks. L. L. L. i. ii. 184 The Passado hee [Cupid] respects not, the Duello he regards not. [1595 Saviolo Practise K ij, You may with much sodainenesse make a passata with your lefte foote.] 1598 B. Jonson Ev. Man in Hum. iv. v, I would teach these 19 the special tricks [ed. 1616 rules], as your Punto, your Reverso, your Stoccato, your Imbroccato, your Passado [ed. 1616 passada], your Montanto. 1636 Dekker Wond. Kingd. i. i. Wks. 1873 IV. 222, I have my Passees Sir: and my Passadoes. 1830 James Darnley xv, We'll have no crowd .. to criticise our passados.

attrib. 1648 Merc. Acad. No. 1. 6 After a Passado complement with his Chancellorship.

2. = Passage 13 b.

1606 Sir G. Goosecappe i. iii. in Bullen O. Pl. III. 19, I am sure I past one Passado of Courtship upon her. 1656 Heylin Surv. France 39 In the Passados of their court-ship, they [the French] expresse themselves with much variety of gesture.

3. Way, going, passage. rare.

1599 Nashe Lenten Stuffe (1871) 89 Angelo went off, and all wind instruments blew .. in his passado to the Pope's ordinary or dining-chamber.

Passage (pæ·sėdʒ), sb. [a. F. passage, pasage (11th c. in Hatz.-Darm.) = Pr. passatge, Sp. pasage, It. passaggio, a Romanic formation from passer, passare to Pass: see -age.]

I. The action of passing, and cognate senses.

1. The action of passing; a going or moving onward, across, or past; movement from one place or point to another, or over or through a space or medium; transition, transit.

Const. of (or with possessive) indicating the person or thing that passes; more rarely of = objective genitive.

c 1290 Beket 682 in S. Eng. Leg. I. 126 He wende eft in-to þe se, þe passage for-to fonde. 1390 Gower Conf. I. 233 He wolde .. The passage of the water take. 1526 Pilgr. Perf. (W. de W. 1531) 1 The passage of the chyldren of Israel from Egypte. 1558 Grafton (title) The Passage of our most drad Soveraigne Lady Queen Elyzabeth through the City of London to Westminster. 1582 Stanyhurst Æneis i. (Arb.) 19 Yeeld to the wynds passadge, duck downe theire fleete with a tempest. 1615 W. Lawson Country Housew. Gard. (1626) 4 So as the Water may be staied from passage. 1702 Rowe Tamerl. ii. i. 546 Not far from hence The Captives were to wait the Emperor's Passage. 1768 Ann. Reg. 67 To observe .. the passage of Venus over the sun's disk on the 3d of June 1769. 1869 Tyndall Notes Lect. Light 20 In the passage from one medium to another of a different refractive index, light is always refracted. 1885 Watson & Burbury Math. Th. Electr. & Magn. I. 236 A cell in which no chemical actions can take place on the passage of the current.

b. The passing of people; hence nearly = people passing, passers. rare.

1590 Shaks. Com. Err. iii. i. 99 If by strong hand you offer to breake in Now in the stirring passage of the day. 1604 — Oth. v. i. 37 What hoa? No Watch? No passage? Murther, Murther. 1886 Stevenson Dr. Jekyll 4 Even on Sunday, when it [the street] lay comparatively empty of passage.

c. The 'passing' or extending of a line, string, or the like, from one point to another.

1615 Crooke Body of Man 485 They are like to nerues in their passage, colour and vse. 1831 R. Knox Cloquet's Anat. 247 It divides, after a short passage, into four very distinct bundles.

d. The migration or migratory flight of birds. See also quot. 1879.

1774 Goldsm. Nat. Hist. (1776) V. 267 At the approach of winter, it totally disappears, and its passage can be traced to no other country. 1879 E. D. Radcliffe in Encycl. Brit. IX. 7/2 The line herons take over a tract of country on their way to and from the heronry when procuring food in the breeding season is called a 'passage'.

e. Of passage (= F. de passage): †(a) That passes through a place or state, without continuing in it; transitory. Obs. exc. as in (b) bird of passage, a bird that migrates from one region to another at a particular season and returns at another, a migratory bird (also fig.); so fish of passage.

1673 Temple Ess. Trade Irel. Wks. 1720 I. 120 The poorer Traders, or the young Beginners, or those of Passage. 1727–41 Chambers Cycl. s.v., Birds of Passage... There are also fishes of passage, as herrings, mackerel, etc. 1732 Pope Ep. Cobham 97 In Man, the judgment shoots at flying game, A bird of passage! gone as soon as found. 1797 Holcroft Stolberg's Trav. (ed. 2) III. lxxxiv. 348 The sword fish is a fish of passage. 1879 Miss Braddon Cloven Foot xxviii, I am only in town as a bird of passage.

2. In various fig. senses: Transition from one state or condition to another (spec. from this life to the next, by death); the passing or lapse of time; the going on, course, or progress of events, etc., or of a person through a course of action; a passing in thought or speech from one point, idea, or subject to another. †In passage, in passing, by the way (obs.).

c 1430 Life St. Kath. (1884) 67 Wyth good passage out of thys lyf. 1516 Life St. Bridget in Myrr. our Ladye p. lii, A lytel before hir blessyd passage out of this world. 1579 W. Wilkinson Confut. Familye of Love 52 The bookes of H. N. do make a more easie passage..to the vnderstandyng thereof. 1605 Bacon Adv. Learn. ii. Ded. § 8 These fundamental knowledges have been studied but in passage. 1769 Sir J. Reynolds Disc. ii. (1876) 317 Students .. this day rewarded for their happy passage through the first period. 1830 Lyell Princ. Geol. I. 206 There is a passage between this and ordinary travertin. 1839 Murchison Silur. Syst. i. xxxiv. 450 The passage of the red marl into the lias is here well exposed. 1871 B. Stewart Heat § 85 The passage of bodies from the solid to the liquid state.

†**b.** absol. 'Departure', death. Obs.

1390 Gower Conf. I. 261 Bot ate laste of thi passage Thi deth was to the houndes like. 1507 in Wood Oxford (O.H.S.) III. 116 By pestilence I had my passage. 1602 Shaks. Ham. iii. iii. 86 When he is fit and season'd for his passage. 1693 Humours Town 13 A perpetual Requiem for your Soul before its Passage.

3. Possibility, power, or opportunity of passing; liberty, leave, or right to pass. (lit. and fig.)

c 1330 R. Brunne Chron. (1810) 30 Þei purueied hir passage, And led hir vnto France, spoused forto be. 1417 in Ellis Orig. Lett. Ser. ii. I. 63 That ye oure Chanceller doo make unto thaim soufficeant Writtes of passage. 1589 Greene Menaphon (Arb.) 68 She made passage to her choller in these termes of contempt. 1667 Milton P. L. xi. 122 All approach farr off to fright, And guard all passage to the Tree of Life. 1844 H. H. Wilson Brit. India II. 79 The refusal to give a passage through Nepal to a British force intended to take possession of Lassa.

†**b.** Admission or permission. Obs.

1622 Bp. Hall Contempl., O. T. xvii. vii, He [Solomon] gave not passage onely to the Idolatry of his heathenish wives, but furtherance.

4. A definite passing or travelling from one place to another, by sea, or formerly sometimes by land; a journey; a voyage across the sea from one port to another, a crossing.

a 1300 Cursor M. 19990 Þis it was þe first passage þat þe apostels in parti Mad mang þe folk o paeni. 13.. E. E. Allit. P. C. 97 Þus he passes to þat port, his passage to seche, Fyndez he a fayr schyp to þe fare redy. a 1529 Skelton Sp. Parrot 324 Prepayre yow, Parrot, breuely your passage to take, Of Mercury undyr the trynall aspecte. 1582 Stanyhurst Æneis iii. (Arb.) 87 Foorth we take oure passadge, oure sayles ful winged vp hoysting. 1776 Hist. Eur. in Ann. Reg. 8/2 Nor was the march by land more eligible than the passage by water. 1815 Chron. ibid. 108/1 A vessel is arrived in the Thames from New South Wales after an extraordinarily short passage of less than five months. 1836 Marryat Midsh. Easy xi, He had suffered all the horrors of a passage in a slave ship. 1877 Talmage 50 Serm. 16 You have found a rough passage.

b. Right of transit or conveyance as a passenger, esp. by sea; accommodation of a passenger.

1632 J. Hayward tr. Biondi's Eromena 6 Carasio..having agreed with the mariners for their passage, acquainted therewith Polemiro. 1743 Bulkeley & Cummins Voy. S. Seas 199 That the Governor would give us a Pass, and that we would work for our Passage. 1782 Johnson Let. to Mrs. Thrale 8 June, I have this day taken a passage to Oxford. 1864 Tennyson En. Ard. 646 And clothes they gave him and free passage home.

†**5.** A charge or custom levied upon passengers; a toll. Obs.

[1200 Charter K. John in Reg. S. Osmundi (Rolls) I. 212 Sint quieti..de theolonio, pontagio, passagio.] ? c 1525 Robyn Hode in Child Ballads (1857–9) V. 425 Yet was he never so curteyse a potter, As one peny passage to paye. 1610 W. Folkingham Art of Survey iii. iv. 70 Immunities and Exemptions from Theolonie, Pontage.., Passage, Tranage,.. Cariage, &c. 1710 J. Harris Lex. Techn. II. Passage, Passagium, was a Tribute or Toll paid by Passengers or Travellers for the Repair or Maintenance of some Road or Passage. 1812 Seyer Bristol Charters Engl. 1 My burgesses of Bristol..shall be quit both of toll and passage, and all custom, throughout my whole land. 1883 Picton L'pool Munic. Rec. I. 6 They claim to be quit of.. passage, pontage and lastage.

†**6.** The fact of 'passing current' or being generally accepted, as coins, customs, etc.; currency, general reception. Obs.

1545 Reg. Privy Council Scot. I. 10 Double dukatis.. quhilkis commonly hes course in France for lxxx and xvis. and ar worth samekle to have passage in this realm. 1605 Bacon Adv. Learn. i. v. § 3 As if the multitude..were not ready to give passage rather to that which is popular and superficial. 1644 Digby Nat. Bodies viii. 53, I would.. render this treatise intelligible to euery rationall man.. (among whom I expect it will haue a fairer passage, then among those that are already deepely imbued with other principles).

7. The passing into law of a legislative measure.

1587 Harrison England ii. viii. (1877) i. 178 This is the order of the passage of our lawes. 1668 Marvell Corr. Wks. 1872–5 II. 249 It is a businesse of that weight that I scarce believe it can have a passage this session. 1669–70 Ibid. 311 [The Bill] had but a narrow passage, there being only 100 for it against 99. 1856 C. Beck Age Petronius Arbiter 73 Soon after,. for the precise time of its passage is not known—the lex Furia Caninia was enacted. 1893 Times 2 May 10/1 The passage of any measure resembling this would be a deadly blow at landed property in Ireland.

8. Horsemanship. See quots. (= F. passage.)

1727–41 Chambers Cycl., Passage, in the manage, an action wherein the horse raises two legs together, a hind and a fore leg, in form of St. Andrew's cross; when, setting those two on the ground again, he raises the other two; and thus alternately. 1884 E. L. Anderson Mod. Horseman. ii. xvii. 146 The Passage..is a slow brilliant trot, in which the horse brings each pair of diagonal legs to the ground at exactly the same moment... Usually employed in traversing.

9. Med. An evacuation of the bowels, a 'motion'; also concr.

1778 Pr. of Wales in Buccleuch MSS. (Hist. MSS. Comm.) I. 416 He took medicine three or four times during the day in order to procure a passage. 1809 Med. Jrnl. XXI. 460 He..has been repeatedly from eighteen to twenty-five days without a passage. 1875 H. C. Wood Therap. (1879) 106 Late in the attack the passages are in most cases very light clay-colored, or even whitish.

10. The action of causing something to pass (in various senses: see Pass v.); transmission, transference, etc. rare.

1860 Tyndall Glac. i. ii. 20 As fine as if produced by the passage of a rake. 1890 in Financial News 31 July 1/4 The passage of the preferred dividend by the directors of the St. Louis and San Francisco Railway is regarded as consistent with policy. 1890 Spectator 16 Aug. 197/1 The passage of a great measure has become as difficult to effect as the passage of a cannon-ball through earthworks. 1896 Allbutt's Syst. Med. I. 531 The virulence of many organisms may..be permanently or temporarily increased.. by passing the organisms through a series of animals (a process which is called 'passage'). 1899 Ibid. VI. 73 The unskilful passage of an œsophageal bougie.

II. 11. That by which a person or thing passes or may pass; a way, road, path, route, channel; a mountain pass; an entrance or exit.

Locally a name for a narrow entry or lane in a town, etc., serving as the approach to a row of houses, or as a thoroughfare for foot-passengers; e.g. Norman Passage, St. Helen's Passage (Oxford), All Saints' Passage (Cambridge).

c 1290 Beket 56 in S. Eng. Leg. I. 108 Heo cam to þe se: and redi fond hire passage. a 1300 K. Horn 1323 To kepe þis passage, Fram horn þat is of age. 1340 Hampole Pr. Consc. 1394 Þis world es þe way and passage, Þurgh whilk lyes our pilgrimage. c 1350 Will. Palerne 2139 And loke þat hirde-men wel kepe þe komune passage, And eche brugge þer a-boute þat burnes ouer wende. 1480 Caxton Chron. Eng. ccxxiii. 222 At an hongyng bought of the more in a streit passage. 1540 Act 32 Hen. VIII, c. 41 In any towne or village being a thorowfare or common passage within this realme. 1553 Eden Treat. Newe Ind. (Arb.) 8 Into the frosen sea..and so forth to Cathay (yf any suche passage may be found). 1585 T. Washington tr. Nichola's Voy. i. xxii. 29 Doria..was tarrying for vs at the passage with 5 principal gallies. 1601 R. Johnson Kingd. & Commw. (1603) 6 Inuironed with mountaines which hath fewe and secret passages. 1627–8 in Swayne Sarum Church-w. Acc. (1896) 187 The open passadge in the middell of the Churche. 1725 De Foe Voy. round World (1840) 6 He had already sent one ship..for a new attempt upon the North-West or North-East passages. 1801 Southey Thalaba vi. xiv, Was it the toil of human hands Had hewn a passage in the rock? 1812 Gen. Hist. in Ann. Reg. 137/2 They weighed anchor, and made sail through the passage Taigneuse. 1828 [see Passenger 1]. 1856 Stanley Sinai & Pal. iv. (1858) 217 As the passage of Beth-horon led up to Gibeon, so the passage of Michmash and Ai led up to Bethel. 1897 Allbutt's Syst. Med. IV. 22 Freeing the liver and its bile passages from their injurious presence.

b. spec. A place at which a river or strait is or may be crossed; a crossing; a ford, ferry, or bridge. ? Obs.

c 1330 R. Brunne Chron. Wace (Rolls) 14012 An heremitage Bysyde Chyunoun, at a passage. 1470–85 Malory Arthur vii. vi, There was a grete ryuer and but one passage. 1477 Paston Lett. III. 203 Wherefore my lord hath do brokyn all the passages except Newnham bryge. a 1533 Ld. Berners Huon lii. 176 When I cam to ony passage of water he wolde caste me in his necke..& bere me ouer. 1611 Bible Judg. xii. 6 Then they tooke him, and slewe him at the passages of Iordan. 1779 S. Rudder Gloucestershire 492 In this parish are two ferries over the Severn. The uppermost, or Old Passage, is in the Tything of Aust...The New Passage is at Redwick. 1853 Kane Grinnell Exp. vii. (1856) 50 Its several 'crossings' have been divided into the South, the Middle, and the Northern passages.

c. A way giving access to the various apartments or divisions of a building, or affording communication from one apartment to another; a corridor or gallery; a lobby or hall.

1611 Coryat Crudities 202 At the West end of this glorious Councell hall..there is a passage into another most stately roome. 1663 Gerbier Counsel 23 By convenient passages about or under them. 1707 Mortimer Husb. (1721) I. 371 In Building of Houses long, the use of some Rooms will be lost, in that the more room must be allowed for Entries and Passages. 1722 De Foe Col. Jack (1840) 207, I was in the passage, or entry of the house. 1810 Crabbe Borough xx. 66 Hark to the winds! which through the wide saloon And the long passage send a dismal tune. 1835 G. A. McCall Lett. fr. Frontiers (1868) 280 The house .. was one of those structures called in the West 'two pens and a passage'.

†**12.** ? A means of passing; a vessel or vehicle in which a person or thing may pass; a conveyance. Cf. Carriage. Obs. rare.

1473 Paston Lett. III. 94, I praye yow wrycht ageyn, and sende it by the next passage.

III. 13. Something that 'passes', goes on, takes place, occurs, or is done; an occurrence, incident, event; an act, transaction, proceeding. Obs. or arch. (exc. as in b and c).

1568 Grafton Chron. II. 731 Surely it was a daungerous passage to conuey a prince in a straunge realme, by such a strayte. 1601 Shaks. Twel. N. iii. ii. 77 There is no christian .. can euer beleeue such impossible passages of grosenesse. 1612 Woodall Surg. Mate Wks. (1639) B vj b, Observing the whole passages of the diseased people, considering both when they began to bee sicke, ..what hath been applyed [etc.]. 1624 Dk. Buckhm. in Ellis Orig. Lett. Ser. i. III. 180 [It] will facilitate..those passages of favors, grace, and goodnes which his Majesty hath promised for the ease of the Romaine Catholickes. 1671–2 Sir C. Lyttelton in Hatton Corr. (Camden) 76 There has lately happened a very strange passage upon occasion of [etc.]. 1710 Steele Tatler No. 198 ⁋ 1 Her Life has lately met with Passages very uncommon. a 1741 T. Chalkley Jrnl. an. 1734 Wks. (1751) 265 A remarkable and dismal Passage he related to me. 1820 Lamb Elia Ser. i. Old Benchers, I remember a pleasant passage, of the cook applying to him..for instructions how to write down edge bone of beef. 1866 Kingsley Herew. xvi, The magnificent young Scot sprang to him, .. talked over old passages.

b. Something that passes between two persons mutually; a negotiation; an interchange of communications, confidences, or amorous relations.

1612 N. Field Woman is Weathercock ii. i. in Hazl. Dodsley XI. 33 And such strange passages and mutual vows. 1647 Sprigge Anglia Rediv. iii. vi. (1854) 165 Several passages between the prince and his excellency, and between his excellency and Goring. 1649 Milton Eikon. viii. 68 The King..gives..order to stop all passages between him [the Governor of Hull] and the Parlament. 1845 R. W. Hamilton Pop. Educ. vi. (1846) 138 Would not both parties profit in these passages of confidence? a 1901 Besant Five Years' Tryst, etc. (1902) 108 She was by no means ignorant of certain passages and rumours of passages between Will Stephen and this simple country maid.

c. (Now usually passage of (or at) arms.) An exchange of blows between two combatants, a fight; also fig. a verbal altercation or dispute; an amorous fence or encounter.

1599 B. Jonson Cynthia's Rev. v. ii, You have your passages and imbrocatas in courtship; as the bitter bob in wit. 1613 Two Noble K. v. iv. 114 The conquerd triumphes, The victor has the losse; yet in the passage The gods have beene most equall. 1845 Froude Hist. Eng. (1858) I. iii. 267 Luther..had not forgotten his early passage at arms with the English Defender of the Faith. 1876 Trevelyan Macaulay I. iii. 136 That passage of arms against the champions of the Utilitarian Philosophy. 1879 Stevenson Trav. Cevennes (1886) 12, I returned it to its maker, with whom I had so contumelious a passage that the street outside was crowded..with gossips..listening. 1885 Manch. Exam. 21 Mar. 6/2 The most interesting part of the debate was a smart passage at arms between his Grace and Lord Bramwell.

14. An indefinite portion of a discourse or writing, usually of small or moderate length, taken by itself; a part of a speech or literary work relating to some particular matter.

c 1611 Chapman Iliad ii. Comm. (1865) 57 His interpreters must needs come [short] of him in his strait and deep places, when in his open and fair passages they halt and hang back so. 1686 South Serm. (1697) II. ix. 386, I shall give you the whole Passage in his own Words. 1711 Steele Spect. No. 2 ⁋ 1 He..gained universal Applause by explaining a Passage in the Game-Act. 1802 Mar. Edgeworth Mor. T. (1816) I. xv. 130 To look for the passage in the original author. 1891 Speaker 2 May 533/1 The paper contains brilliant passages, notably an admirable estimate of Gautier.

†**b.** A part of a discourse or writing in which the author passes or turns aside for a time to some other subject; a digression. Obs.

1625 Bacon Ess., Dispatch (Arb.) 247 Prefaces, and Passages, ..and other Speeches of Reference to the Person, are great wasts of Time. 1663 Gerbier Counsel 102 The first discourse, was..intermixt with recreative passages.

†**c.** The 'passing' or utterance of an opinion or the like; a remark, observation (in speech or writing); a phrase, expression. Obs.

a 1649 Winthrop Hist. New Eng. (1853) I. 247 One of the assistants using some pathetical passages of the loss of such a governour in a time of such danger. 1651 W. Lilly (title) Monarchy or No Monarchy in England. Grebner his Prophecy... Passages upon the Life and Death of the late King Charles. a 1657 Bradford Plymouth Plant. (1856) 307, I would..deliver ye truth..as nere as I can, in their owne words and passages. 1660 Trial Regic. 44 Being there, I did observe some Passages fall from the Prisoner at the Bar: the words were to this purpose.

d. Mus. (a) ? orig. A progression from one note to another by intermediate notes (passing-notes); ? hence, A short series of such notes, or of small notes in general; a run or flourish; a figure or phrase. Obs. exc. as applied (rarely) to ornamental runs or flourishes introduced for display. (b) In mod. use (associated with 14): A portion of a composition, of indefinite but moderate length, and forming more or less of a unity.

1674 Playford Skill Mus. i. xi. 39 Observing the same Rule in making the passages of Division by some few Quavers to Notes and to Cadences, not exceeding the Value of half a Semibreve at most. 1727–41 Chambers Cycl., Passage, or Passo, in music, a portion of an air, or tune, consisting of several short notes, as quavers, demi-quavers, etc. lasting one, two, or at most three measures. 1767 Ess. in Ann. Reg. 199/2 The Italians solfa'd our most pathetic airs, without discovering either passage or tune. 1776 Burney Hist. Mus. (1789) I. v. 62 In no one of the seven treatises upon ancient music is a single air or passage of Greek melody come down to us. 1859 Tennyson Lancelot & Elaine 891–2 As a little helpless innocent bird, That has but one plain passage of few notes, Will sing the simple passage o'er and o'er For all an April morning. 1880 C. H. H. Parry in Grove's Dict. Mus. II. 661.

e. In the phraseology of art criticism: A particular part or detail in a picture.

1861 Thornbury Turner I. 142 In the earliest Saxon and Old English MSS. are to be found passages of transparent colour. 1897 Mag. Art Nov. 39 There are passages which represent the original with curious felicity.

f. gen. An indefinite portion of a course of action; an episode. (Cf. 13.) rare.

1848 W. H. Bartlett Egypt to Pal. xiv. (1879) 315 The track to-day was an easy one, and indeed the whole route from Sinai offered no passages of extreme difficulty. 1897 Ld. Tennyson Life Tennyson I. ii. 40 Despite such passages of gloom he worked on.

IV. [The passing or exceeding of ten = It. passa-dieci, F. passe-dix, i.e. pass-ten.]

†**15.** An obsolete game at dice: see quot. 1680.

1426 Lydg. De Guil. Pilgr. 11194 And after pleyn at the merellys, Now at the dees, in my yong age, Bothe at bassard & passage. 1522 World & Child in Hazl. Dodsley I. 266 And then we will with lombards at passage play. 1598 Florio, Passa dieci, a game at dice called passage or aboue ten. 1602 2nd Pt. Return fr. Parnass. Prol. 12 You that knowe what it is to play at primero, or passage. 1680 Cotton Compl. Gamester 119 Passage is a Game at dice to be played at but by two, and it is performed with three Dice. The Caster throws continually till he hath thrown Dubblets under ten, and then he is out and loseth; or Dubblets above ten, and then he passeth and wins. 1739–40 Act 13 Geo. II. c. 19 § 9 A certain game called Passage is now daily practiced and carried on, to the ruin and impoverishment of many of his Majesty's subjects. 1755 Mem. Capt. P. Drake II. xvi. 262, [1740] The Games of Rowly Powly and Passage..all these Games were suppressed by Parliament, and, on severe Penalties, not to be played after the 25th of March 1745.

V. 16. attrib. and Comb. **a.** Used or serving for the passage or conveyance of passengers, esp. across the sea or a river, as passage-barge, -bark, -canoe, -hoy, -ship, -wagon; of transition, transitional, as passage-form, -time; also in other senses, as passage-bell, -gallery (11 c), -work (14 d). **b.** Special combs.: **passage-bed** (Geol.), a stratum showing transition from one formation to another; **passage-bird,** (a) = bird of passage (see 1 e); (b) = passage-hawk; **passage-board,** a board placed between the parts of an organ to make them accessible for tuning or repairs; †**passage-book** = Pass-book 1; †**passage-gelt, -gilt** [see Gelt sb.[2]] = Passage-money; **passage-hawk,** a falcon taken when full-grown, during its 'passage' or migration, for the purpose of training (opp. to eyas); †**passage-house,** a privy; **passage-penny,** a penny charged for passage or fare; **passage-room,** a room serving as a passage to another, or through which one passes to another; †**passage-thermometer** (see quot.). Also Passage-boat, -money, -way.

1804 Europ. Mag. XLV. 443/1 Going from Fontainbleau to Dijon, in the *passage barge. 1865 Reader No. 147. 465/1 The *passage-beds of Herefordshire. 1825 Eng. Life II. 231 The *passage-bell rung loudly. 1852 R. F. Burton Falconry in Valley of Indus iv. 41 Hawks..are of two kinds, the 'eyess' (or nyess), and the '*passage-bird'. 1878 C. Stanford Symb. Christ v. 139 The passage bird is never lost. High over the waves of the Atlantic it strikes a right path to its home a thousand leagues away. 1880 C. A. Edwards Organs (1881) 59 A *passage-board for the use of the tuner. 1816 in Merivale Rep. Cases Chancery I. 535 A book, called a *passage-book, is opened by the bankers, and delivered by them to the customer. 1901 Nature 3 Jan. 234/2

Supplement, p. 3873; Corrigenda, p. 4092; Spurious words, p. 4093; Books quoted, p. 4094

PASSOVER

Passingness. [f. PASSING ppl. a. + -NESS.] Passing quality; transitoriness.

Passing-note. Mus. A note not belonging to the harmony, interposed between two notes essential to it, for the purpose of passing smoothly from one to the other. Sometimes also applied to auxiliary notes (see AUXILIARY a.).

Passion (pæ'ʃən), sb. Also 2-6 -iun, -toun, -yo(u)n, etc. [a. OF. passiun, passion, ad. L. passiōn-em passion.]

I. The suffering of pain.

1. (Now usually with capital) The sufferings of Jesus Christ on the Cross.

2. The sufferings of a martyr, martyrdom.

3. Suffering or affliction generally.

II. The fact or condition of being acted upon or affected by external agency; subjection to external force.

III. An affection of the mind.

b. A painful affection or disorder of the body.

III. Any kind of feeling by which the mind is powerfully affected or moved.

4. An object of love, a beloved person.

Passionate (pæ'ʃənət), a. [ad. med. L. passiōnāt-us.]

Passionately (pæ'ʃənətli), adv.

Passionateness.

Passionist.

Passion-flower.

Passion Sunday. [tr. med. L. Dominica in Passione.]

Passion-tide.

Passion Week. [PASSION sb. 1 + WEEK.]

Passive (pæ'siv), a. and sb. [ad. L. passīv-us.]

Passively, adv.

Passiveness.

Passivity.

Pass-key.

Pass-man.

Pass-master.

Passover (pɑ·s,ouvər). [f. verbal phrase pass over: see PASS v. 67 c.]

1. The name of a Jewish feast, held on the evening of the fourteenth day of the (first) month Nisan, commemorative of the 'passing over' of the houses of the Israelites when the Egyptians were smitten with the death of their firstborn.

Pasteurian (pastoriăn), a.

Pasteurianism (pɒstorˈiǎnizm).

Pasteurism (pɒstorˈizm), sb.

Pasteurize (pɒstorəiz), v.

Pasteurization.

Pasteurizer.

Pastey(e, obs. form of PASTY sb.

Pasticcio (pasˈtitʃjo), sb.

‖ **Pastiche** (pastiʃ). [F.]

Pastil, **pastille** (pɒstil, pastiːl).

Pastille (pastiːl). [a. F. pastille.]

Pasticate, v. trans.

Pastillicate, v.

Pastime (pɑstəim), sb.

Pastime, v.

Pastine, sb.

Pastiness.

Pasting (pɛistiŋ), vbl. sb.

Pastique (pastiːk), sb.

Pastle. Obs. rare.

Pastime. Now rare.

Pastiming, vbl. sb. and ppl. a.

Pastinaceous, a.

Pastinate, ppl. a.

Pastinate, v.

Pastine, sb.

Pastinum.

Pastion (pɑstʃən).

Pasty (pɑsti), a.

Pastler. Obs.

Pastoral (pastoral), a. and sb.

Pastorale (pastorale).

Pastoral-maker, -monger.

Pastoralism.

Pastoralist.

Pastoralize, v.

Pastorally, adv.

Pastorate (pɑstorət).

Pastored, a.

Pastoret.

Pastoric, a.

Pastorious, a.

Pastorling.

Pastorly, a.

Pastorship.

Pastorale (pastorale).

Pastoralism.

Pastorious, a.

Pastram, sb.

Pastry (pɛistri).

Pastry-cook.

Pasturable, a.

Pasturage (pɑstjuredʒ).

Pasturagious, a. Obs. rare.

Pastural, a.

Pasture (pɑstjur), sb.

Pasture, v.

Pasturer.

Pasty (pɑsti), sb.

Pasty (pɛisti), a.

Pat, sb.[1]

Pat, sb.[2]

1852 R. S. Surtees *Sponge's Sp. Tour* (1893) 93 Both volumes richly bound and lettered, with the Jawleyford crests studded down the backs, and an immense pat of arms plastered on the side. 1888 C. F. Woolson in *Harper's Mag.* Oct. 776/1 It was raining..in torrents, with great pats of water coming over, almost like stones.

III. The sound. (Cf. Pad *sb.*⁵)

4. The sound made by striking lightly with something flat; *esp.* that made by a light foot in walking or running; hence, rate of walking or running, pace.

1697 Collier *Ess. Mor. Subj.* i. vi. 219 The least Noise is enough to disturb the Operation of his Brain...The Patt of a shittle Cock, or the creaking of a Jack will do his Business. 1833 T. Hook *Widow & Marquess* vii, Up hill and down hill..all at the same pat. 1889 Mrs. Oliphant *Poor Gentleman* xvi. I. 295 No sound but..the pat of those footsteps which scarcely touched the ground.

b. Reduplicated, to express repetition.

1876 J. Saunders *Lion in Path* xvii, The peculiar wooden-sounding pat-pat of a lady's fashionable boot. 1899 Werner *Capt. of Locusts* 67 The pat-pat of bare feet on the matting.

Pat (pæt), *sb.*² [Abbreviation of the Christian name *Patrick*.] A nickname for an Irishman; cf. Paddy. Hence **Pa·tess**, an Irishwoman.

1825 Scott *Let. to Morritt* 3 Aug. in *Lockhart*, The habit of the more youthful Pats and Patesses is decent and comely. 1857 Hughes *Tom Brown* i. iv, Here's fun! let the Pats have it about the ears.

‖ **Pát, paut** (pāt), *sb.*³ [Hindī *pāt* leaf, indigo plant, jute.] An East Indian name for a. Jute fibre; b. The leafy part of the indigo-plant, as cut off a foot from the ground, and made into bundles for delivery.

1801 *Trans. Soc. Arts* XIX. 235 Specimen of Paper from Paut fibre. 1881 Jas. Paton in *Encycl. Brit.* XIII. 798/2 Importations of the substance [jute] had been made at earlier times under the name of *pât*, an East Indian native term by which the fibre continued to be spoken of in England till the early years of the 19th century.

Pat (pæt), *v.*¹ [Related to Pat *sb.*¹, and perh. directly formed from it in senses 1 and 2.]

†1. *trans.* To cause (something) to strike or hit *upon* any surface; to throw (something) *upon* anything so as to strike it. *Obs. rare.*

1567 Golding *Ovid's Met.* xii. 508 Like haylestones from a tyled house, or as a man should pat Small stones vppon a dromsiets head.

2. To hit, to strike, properly with a flat or blunt implement; also, to drive or impel by so striking, as a ball with the hand. *Obs.* exc. *dial.*

In later use, perh. ironical from 5.

1591 R. Turnbull *Exp. St. James* 196 Thus was the pryde of Goliah resisted, when..David..with his sling stone patted him on the pate. a 1604 Hanmer *Chron. Irel.* (1633) 166 One takes a sticke, and pats the Irish man on the pate, another..pricks him behinde with a pinne. a 1825 *Jew's Daughter* i. in Child *Ballads* v. (1888) 251/1 And all the boys and girls to-day Do play at pat the ball. *Ibid.* ii, They patted it into the Jew's garden. 1886 Elworthy *W. Som. Word-bk.*, *Pat on the poll*, phr., to kill by a blow such as would dislocate the neck.

3. *intr.* To tap or beat lightly (*upon* any surface).

1601 Holland *Pliny* xii. i. 358 To heare the showers of raine to pat drop by drop, and rattle over his head upon the leaves. 1626 Bacon *Sylva* § 63 It is Childrens sport, to proue whether they can rub vpon their Brest with one hand, and pat vpon their Fore-head with another. 1771 Luckombe *Hist. Print.* 447 Patting upon the Face of the Letter where it Hangs, with the Balls of the Fingers. 1861 G. F. Berkeley *Sportsm. W. Prairies* xxi. 349 Asked them who could 'pat' as an accompaniment to a dance and song. 1902 J. S. Phillimore *Poems, Rain at Naples*, On dusty road and tree Drops, kicking up the faint smells where they pat.

4. *trans.* To strike (something) more or less gently with a flat surface, so as to flatten or smooth; to flatten down by such action.

1607 Walkington *Opt. Glass* xii. (1664) 127 The Hyacinth ..patted down to the Earth with suddain drops of Rain. 1676 Worlidge *Cyder* (1691) 67 Cover the loose ground about the tree, and pat it smooth with the back of your spade. 1801 in *Southey's Thalaba* iii. Notes, Wks. 1838 IV. 111 After they have kneaded the cake..they pat it a little. 1901 H. McHugh *John Henry* 48 Clara Jane..patted her hat-pins and grabbed her gloves.

b. *Brickmaking.* To remove the rough edge of (green bricks) with a stamper.

1895 in *Funk's Stand. Dict.*

5. *esp.* To strike or clap gently with the inner surface of the fingers, esp. as an expression of approbation, encouragement, soothing, or sympathy; hence *fig.* to express such feeling to (any one), esp. in *to pat on the back*.

[1668 Dryden *Even. Love* ii. i, We love to get our mistresses ..and let them go a little way; and..to pat them back again.] 1714 Byrom *Phœbe* v. in *Spect.* No. 603 Phœbe..to my dog said, Come hither, poor Fellow, and patted his Head. 1791 R. Cumberland *Observer* No. 143. V. 198 'Brava!' quoth he, patting the neck of his mule. 1813 Mar. Edgeworth *Patron.* xiii, The child patted Caroline's cheek, played with her hair. 1821 *Examiner* 770/1 Thus is the already inflated faction patted up against the irritated majority. 1874 Green *Short Hist.* vii. § 3. 363 She [Elizabeth] patted handsome young squires on the neck when they knelt to kiss her hand. 1884 *Chr. Commw.* 14 Feb. 424/3 We..pat every man on the back who has the courage of his convictions.

6. *intr.* To tap or strike lightly so as to produce a characteristic sound; *esp.* to walk or run with a light step emitting such sound. Cf. Pad *v.*¹ 2. Also reduplicated, *pat-pat*.

1760–72 H. Brooke *Fool of Qual.* (1809) III. 135 A humming of mixed voices, and patting feet was heard. 1767 E. Jerningham *Alisia* ix, She fondly cried—Oh that is he! While patted fast her heart. 1801 Bloomfield *Rural T., Fakenham Ghost* vi, A short quick step she hears Come patting close behind. 1803 Mary Charlton *Wife & Mistress* IV. 91 It makes a body shiver to hear you pat-patting in those tiny slippers. 1889 *Spectator* 2 Nov., A small, white dog pats along..we can hear the beat of the four light paws upon the country-road.

b. *trans.* To beat with light-sounding steps.

1798 Landor *Gebir* vii. 205 When ye heard My feet in childhood pat the palace-floor.

7. The vb. stem used advb. or as an interj.

1681 Otway *Soldiers Fort.* v. i, What's that upon the Stairs?..Hist, hark, pat, pat, pat. 1801 Bloomfield *Rural T., Fakenham Ghost* xiii, Still on, pat, pat, the Goblin went, As it had done before. a 1849 Holmes *Spectre Pig* xxii, Little mincing feet were heard Pat, pat along the floor.

Hence **Pa·tting** *vbl. sb.* and *ppl. a.*

1611 Cotgr., *Marchis*,..a path beaten out by often patting, or treading. 1726–31 Waldron *Descr. Isle Man* (1865) 65 Smiles, pattings on the cheek, and all the marks of a most sincere and tender passion. 1727 Gay *Fables* i. xiii. 22 He stands, To feel the praise of patting hands. 1885 L. Malet *Col. Enderby's Wife* (ed. 3) II. iii. vi. 44 She.. slowly settled her mantle into its place, with sundry dainty pattings and smoothings.

† **Pat**, *v.*² *Obs. nonce-wd.* [f. Pat *adv.*] *trans.* To bring out 'pat'.

1575 R. B. *Appius & Virg.* Bjb, *Mansipulus.* By the gods how vngraciously the vicksen she chatteth. *Mansipula.* And he euen as knauishly my answer he patteth.

Pat (pæt), *adv.* and *a.* Also 6 **patte**, 7 **patt**. [app. closely related to Pat *sb.*¹, *v.*¹: perh. immediately from the vb. stem, as in the expressions *to fall crash, come pop, go bang*, etc. A frequent early use was to *hit pat*, as if to hit with a pat, i. e. with a flat blow; hence with *fall, lie, come*, etc.

The predicative use (sense 2) was in origin adverbial; cf. *to lie pat, come pat, be pat*; but after it had the same function as an adj. in the predicate; hence the transition to the attrib. or adj. use (sense 3), at first after a sb. was easy.]

1. *adv.* In a way that hits, and does not miss its object or aim; in a manner that fits or agrees to a nicety with the purpose or occasion; so as exactly to suit the purpose; appositely, aptly; in the very nick of time, opportunely; so as to be ready for any occasion, readily, promptly.

1578 Whetstone *1st Pt. Promos & Cass.* iv. vi, I chaunst to light on one, Hyt me as pat as a pudding Pope Ione. 1580 Lyly *Euphues* (Arb.) 296 When I heard my Physition so pat to hit my disease. 1581 *Confl. Consc.* ii. iii. in Hazl. *Dodsley* VI. 62, I will pay them home pat. 1589 Nashe *Almond for Parrat* 6 b, Haue not I hit your meaning patte in this comparison? 1592 Greene *Art Conny-Catch.* iii. Wks. (Grosart) X. 151 Seeing things fadge so pat to his purpose. 1595 Nashe *Saffron-Walden* Wks. (Grosart) III. 52 If they will hit the nayle on the head pat. 1602 Shaks. *Ham.* iii. iii. 74 Now I might do it pat, now he is praying. 1639 Fuller *Holy War* iv. xxi. (1840) 218 An unhappy nation whose heads lie pat for every one's hands to hit. 1658 W. Burton *Itin. Anton.* 176 Camden...seems ..to have lighted pat upon the place. 1665–6 Pepys *Diary* 20 Feb., I came just pat to be a godfather. 1733 Swift *On Poetry* 61 And here a simile comes pat in. 1882 Mrs. Riddell *Pr. Wales's Garden-Party* 259 He..had the whole story pat enough.

2. *predicatively*: as *adv.* or *adj.* (as in 1 or 3).

1638 Wilkins *New World* v. (1707) 41 Whose Words are more pat to the purpose. 1656 Sanderson *Serm.* (1689) 80 A passage..very pat to his purpose. 1710 in Hearne *Collect.* 7 Mar. (O. H. S.) II. 355 A Mitre may be pat to his Mind. 1820 W. Irving *Sketch Bk.* II. 124 To tell a rather broad story out of Joe Miller, that was pat to the purpose. 1903 *Sat. Rev.* 17 Oct. 482 He has pat..the denunciations of sacerdotalism with which the same deputed ones will attack the Church of England.

3. *attrib.* or as *adj.* That comes or lies exactly to the purpose; exactly suitable or to the purpose, apposite, apt; ready or suitable for the occasion, opportune. (Said esp. of things spoken.)

1646 J. Hall *Poems, To young Authour*, With phancies queint and gay expressions pat. 1648 'Mercurius Pragmaticus' *Plea for King* 3 Having a pat occasion offered them. a 1677 Barrow *Wks.* (1687) I. Serm. xiv. 195 Sometimes it [facetiousness] lieth in pat allusion to a known story. 1698 Fryer *Acc. E. India & P.* 47 Concerning..these Winds, perhaps some others may give patter Guesses than my self. 1788 Cowper *Pity for Africans* 18 A story so pat, you may think it is coined. 1852 Thackeray *Esmond* iii. ii, Backing his opinion with a score of pat sentences from Greek and Roman authorities.

b. *Pat hand* (in the game of Poker): see quot.

1889 Farmer *Americanisms*, *Pat Hand* (in poker), an original hand not likely to be improved by drawing, such as full, straight, flush, or pairs. 1903 *Architect* 24 Apr., Suppl. 28/2 Anybody's liable to play a pat hand too strong.

Pat, obs. f. Pate; var. Patte; dial. f. Pot; obs. or dial. pa. t. of Put.

Pat-a-cake. The first words of a nursery rime, said or chanted to accompany the action of patting or gently clapping together the child's hands; hence, the game which the nurse plays with the child in doing this.

A usual form of the rime is: 'Pat a cake, pat a cake, baker's man! Bake me a cake as fast as you can, Shape it and prick it, and mark it with [B], And put it in the oven for [Baby] and me!'

1897 Ld. Tennyson *Life Tennyson* I. xviii. 371 [He] would play pat-a-cake with them.

Hence **Pat-a-cake** *v.*, *nonce-wd.*, to superintend or direct any one's action as the nurse does the baby's hands in this game.

1874 Mrs. Whitney *We Girls* ii. 42, I can be contrary. I don't like to be pat-a-caked.

‖ **Pata·che.** Forms: (6 **pataxo**, 6–8 **patacho**), 7–8 **patach, petach, pattache**, 6– **patache**. [F. *patache* (pataʃ), or Sp. *patache* (pätaˑtʃe), in Pg. *patacho*, † *pataxo*, It. *patacchia, patascia, patazzio*, Du. and Ger. *patas*; of uncertain origin.]

† 1. A small ship used for communication between the vessels of a fleet; an advice-boat. *Obs.* exc. *Hist.*

1589 Greene *Span. Masq.* Wks. (Grosart) V. 274 Hee had in his Fleete, of Gallions, Huikes, Pataches, Zabres, Galeasses, and Gallies 130. 1596 in *Cecil Papers* (Hist. MSS. Comm.) VI. 61 By the help of two patachoes which they had with them, they took a small English bark. *Ibid.* 62 Patacheoes. 1598 W. Phillip *Linschoten* 192/2 Other smal ships Pataxos, yᵗ came to serue as messengers from place to place. 1633 T. Stafford *Pac. Hib.* iii. vii. (1821) 551 There was a Spanish patach landed the night before. 1666 *Lond. Gaz.* No. 58/3 A Genouese Petach is arrived here with Oyls. 1704 *Collect. Voy.* (Churchill) III. 729/2, 6 Patache's or Yachts. 1748 *Anson's Voy.* i. iii. 20 A Patache of twenty guns. 1887 R. Welford *Hist. Newcastle* III. 321 The St. Peter, a Spanish patache,..entered the harbour of the Tyne.

2. *transf.* A small kind of public conveyance used in France.

1833 L. Ritchie *Wand. by Loire* 20 Little country carriages ..called pataches (which in general are nothing more than a cart covered with leather, like a cabriolet).

† **Patacoo·n.** *Obs.* Also 6 **patachine**, 7 **patagon**, 7 **pattacoone, -coon**. [a. Sp. *patacon*, in It. *patacone*, also *patacchina*, a. Pg. *patacão*, augment. of *pataca* piece of eight, dollar.] A Portuguese and Spanish silver coin, worth, in the 17th c., about 4s. 8d. English.

1584 in *Hakluyt's Voy.* (1811) II. 411 There is also a sort of silver money, which they call Patachines and is worth 6 Tangas. c 1645 Howell *Lett.* (1650) II. 31 Unless souldiers would be contented to take cloves and peppercorns for patacoons and pistolls. 1665 G. Turnbull *Diary* (S. H. S.) 315 We hired two wagons for 10 patagons. 1679 Oates *Narr. Popish Plot* 5 The Letter..was carried by a special messenger, for which he had 10 Pattacoones. 1749 *Wealth Gt. Britain* 30 The Dutch oblige themselves to pay..800,000 patacoons.

‖ **Patagium** (pætădʒəi·ŏm). *Zool.* Pl. **-ia**. [med.L., from ancient L. *patagium* a gold edging or border on a Roman lady's tunic = Gr. παταγεῖον.] a. A fold of skin or membrane extending along the side of the body of certain flying mammals and reptiles, capable of expansion so as to act as a parachute; the wing-membrane of a bat or similar animal. b. *Ornith.* The fold or integument occupying the angle between the upper arm and the forearm of birds. c. *Entom.* The name for each of a pair of processes or appendages on the pronotum and thorax of certain Lepidoptera.

1826 Kirby & Sp. *Entomol.* III. 368 *Patagia*...Two corneous scales observable in Lepidoptera, fixed on each side of the trunk, just behind the head, and covered with a long tuft of hair. *Ibid.* IV. 381 The patagia or tippets that adorn their evanescent thorax. 1872 Nicholson *Palæont.* 374 An expanded flying membrane or 'patagium'. 1899 *Cambridge Nat. Hist.* VI. 311 The patagia..are of some interest in connection with the question of wing-like appendages on the prothorax of Palæozoic insects, and they have been considered by some writers to be the equivalents of true wings. *Ibid.* 312 These appendages are frequently erroneously called patagia, but have also been called scapulae, pterygodes, paraptera, and shoulder-tufts, or shoulder-lappets.

Hence **Patagial** (pätāˑdʒiăl) *a.*, of, pertaining to, or connected with a patagium; **Pata·giate** *a.*, formed into or furnished with a patagium.

1877 *Science* 5 Aug. 71/1 Dorsal View of the Patagial Muscles of a Woodpecker. 1894 Newton *Dict. Birds* 607 Garrod devoted much labour to the elucidation of these patagial muscles. 1890 *Cent. Dict.*, Patagiate.

† **Pa·tagon.** *Obs.* [a. Sp. *patagon* large clumsy foot.] A member of a tribe of South American Indians, whence Patagonia received its name.

1579 in *Hakluyt's Voy.* (1812) IV. 257. 1605 Sylvester *Du Bartas* ii. iii. iii. *Law* 211 A Pagan (a proud Infidell, A Patagon, that tasted nought so well As Israel's bloud). 1698 Froger *Voy.* 75 The famous Patagons whom some Authors avouch to be eight or ten feet high..: However..the tallest among them was not above six Foot high. 1773 Johnson *Hebrides, Ostig in Sky*, If we have not searched the Magellanick regions, let us however forbear to people them with Patagons. [1871 G. C. Musters *At Home w. Patagonians* 162 Hide overshoes are worn besides, and the footprints thus made are really large enough to convey the idea of giants' feet, and partly explain the term 'Patagon', or large feet, applied to these Indians by the Spanish discoverers.]

Patagon, obs. form of Patacoon.

Patagonian (pætăgōˑniăn), *a.* and *sb.* [See Patagon and -an.]

A. *adj.* Of or pertaining to Patagonia or its inhabitants (see B); hence, formerly, † Gigantic, huge, immense.

1767 *Jrnl. Byron's Voy. rd. World* 24 + 5 The Patagonian system of education is quite gymnastic. 1786 Wolcott (P. Pindar) *Farew. Odes R. Acad.* viii. 26 This year, of picture, Mister West Is quite a Patagonian maker. 1818 Kirby & Sp. *Entomol.* II. 101 Seeing a number of ants carrying off a Patagonian centipede. 1856 Kane *Arct. Expl.* I. xvii. 202 Their numbers were not as great, nor their size as Patagonian as some of us had been disposed to fancy.

B. *sb.* A South American Indian of a race inhabiting southern Patagonia, said to be the tallest known people (their stature, however, being much exaggerated by 17th and 18th c. travellers and romancers); hence *fig.* † a giant, a gigantic specimen.

1767 *Jrnl. Byron's Voy. rd. World* 24 + 15 A petty Patagonian, not seven and a half feet high. 1786 Wolcott (P. Pindar) *Ep. to Boswell* 63 Two huge Patagonian pockets.. Which Patagonians..Would fairly both his Dictionaries hold. 1871 G. C. Musters (*title*) At Home with the Patagonians.

Patail, obs. form of Patel.

Patamar(e, Patan(d: see Pattamar, Patten.

‖ **Patana** (paˑtăna). Also *erron.* **patena, -ina**. [Sinhalese *patana*, f. Skr. *pat* to descend, fall.] A glade in the jungle-covered mountainous districts of Ceylon, usually with sloping sides.

1854 Baker *Rifle & Hound in Ceylon* viii. 218 Instead of taking across the patinas (plains), she [the elk] doubled back to an immense pathless jungle. 1859 Tennent *Ceylon* I. 24 These verdant openings to which the natives have given the name of patenas generally occur about the middle elevation of the hills. 1880 Mrs. E. H. Edwards *Pecari* in *Macm. Mag.* No. 253. 79 In a small store standing alone on the patina.

Patant, obs. f. Patent. **Patararo, -r(r)ero**, obs. var. Pedrero, a small gun.

Patarin, -ene (pæˑtarin, -rīn), *sb.* and *a.* Also 9 **Paterin(e**. [ad. med.L. pl. *Patarīnī, Patarēnī*, F. *Patarin, Paterin* (13th c. in Littré), commonly understood to be derived from *Pattaria*, name of a low quarter of Milan (see Du Cange s. v. *Paterini*), or to be identical with It. *pat(t)arino* 'a Porter or day-labourer, a base mecanicall fellow' (Florio 1611), which had prob. the same origin.]

A. *sb.* A name which began to be applied at Milan in the middle of the 11th century to the deacon Arialdi and his followers who opposed the marriage of priests; also applied in the 12th c. and later to the Albigenses, Cathari, and others; and generally employed as a term of opprobrium, identified with Manichæan, etc.

1727–41 Chambers *Cycl.* s. v. *Albigenses*, They were also known by various other names; as..Arnoldists, Cathari, Patarins, Publicans,..Passagers, etc. 1854 Milman *Lat. Chr.* vi. iii. III. 63 The Lombard Clergy affected to treat their adversaries as Paterines or Manicheans. 1855 *Ibid.* ix. viii. IV. 189 In the twelfth century Manicheism is rampant... Everywhere are Puritans, Paterines, Populars. 1867 H. C. Lea *Sacerdot. Celibacy* 221 The meetings of Landolfo and Arialdo [at Milan 1044] were held in a spot called Pataria, whence they soon became known as Paterins—a term which for centuries continued to be of fearful import as synonymous with Manicheans.

B. *adj.* Of or pertaining to the Patarins.

Hence **Pa·tarinism**, the doctrine of the Patarins.

1854 Milman *Lat. Chr.* vi. iii. III. 84 The lowest rabble, infected with Paterinism,..furtively placed female ornaments in the chambers of priests.

† **Pata·rt.** *Obs.* [a. OF. *patart, patard*, med.L. *patardus, patarus* (Du Cange).] A former coin of Flanders, Picardy, etc.: see quots.

1583 Stocker *Civ. Warres Lowe C.* iii. 85 b, A Proclamation made, that no Butcher shoulde sell a pounde of the best Beefe aboue a patart. 1656 Blount *Glossogr.*, *Patart*, a Low-countrey coyn worth a *Sol tournois*, or the Stiver. 1658 Phillips, *Patart*, a Dutch coin, five whereof amount to six pence. 1727–41 Chambers *Cycl.* s. v. *Coins*, Flemish Coins..those of copper, patards. *Ibid.*, Patard or penny.

‖ **Patas** (patäˑ). [F. *patas*, from a dialect of Senegal.] The red monkey (*Cercopithecus patas*) of West Africa.

1745 *New Collect. Voy.* (Astley) II. 68 The Sieur Brue, on his anchoring at Tuabo [in 1698], found a new kind of monkeys, of so lively a red, that they seemed painted...The Negros call them Patas. 1774 Goldsm. *Nat. Hist.* (1862) I. vii. i. 505. 1790 Bewick *Quadrupeds* (1821) 466 The Patas, or Red Monkey,..inhabits the same country [Guinea, Congo, &c.]. 1893 *Royal Nat. Hist.* (Lydekker) I. 98 The West African patas, or red monkey, from Senegambia.

Patata, obs. f. Batata, Potato.

Patavinity (pætăviˑniti). [ad. L. *patavīnitās*, f. *Patavīn-us* of or pertaining to *Patavium*, now Padua, the birth-place of the Roman historian Livy.] The dialectal characteristics of Patavium or Padua, as shown in Livy's writings; hence *gen.* Provincialism in style; also an instance of this, a provincial word or usage. (Cf. Paduanism.)

1607 R. C[arew] tr. *Estienne's World of Wonders* ¶ iij b, Find Solœcismes in Tullie, and I know not what Patauinitie in Livie. 1661 Blount *Glossogr.* (ed. 2) s. v., Livy was censured by Asinius for Patavinity in his writings, by which was meant that he had too much used the phrases or affectations of Padua, and neglected those of Rome. 1745 H. Walpole *Lett.* (1846) II. 54 None of the critics could make out what Livy's Patavinity is. a 1814 J. Ramsay *Scot. & Scotsmen in 18th C.* (1883) II. xvi. 544 If a few Patavinities in phraseology or pronunciation..escaped them. 1830 Mackintosh *Eth. Philos.* Wks. 1846 I. 140 Such critics as those who exulted over the Patavinity of the Roman historian.

Pataxo, Patayn, obs. ff. Patache, Patten.

Pat-ball (pæˑt,bǭl). [f. Pat *v.*¹ + Ball *sb.*¹] The game of rounders.

1775 S. J. Pratt *Liberal Opin.* vii. (1783) I. 96, I might go home, and play at pat-ball with my sister. 1891 F. W. Newman *Cdl. Newman* 3 We had cricket and rounders,.. patball and trapball,..and multiform games of marbles. 1896 *Westm. Gaz.* 9 May 3/1 Facetious Undergrad (at tennis, to his partner): Our opponent isn't much good at pat-ball, I take it.

Patch (pætʃ), *sb.*¹ Forms: 4 **pacche**, 4–6 **patche**, 5 **pahche, pacch**, 5–6 **pache, pachch(e**, 6– **patch**. [ME. *pacche, patche*, of unascertained origin. If native, its OE. form would be **pæcce*.

Some have conjectured an earlier **platche*, with subsequent loss of *l*, comparing mod.Sc. Platch, q. v., but for this there is no evidence. Ger. dial. *patsche* puddle, mire, 'mess', also instrument of striking, hand, *patschen* to splash, dabble, dash, clap, tap, suits the form but not the sense.]

1. A piece of cloth, leather, wood, metal, or other material put or fastened on to mend a hole or rent in something, or to strengthen a weak place.

1382 Wyclif *Mark* ii. 21 No man seweth a pacche [1388 patche] of rude..clothe to an old clothe. 1426 Lydg. *De Guil. Pilgr.* 17172 A garnement..Wych she werede vp-on hyr bak: Gret noumbre ther-on I tolde Off cloutys and off pachchys olde. 1481 in *Eng. Gilds* (1870) 320 A brasen krocke of ij galons and more, a pache clowted in the brem wᵗ laten. 1595 Shaks. *John* iv. ii. 32 As patches set vpon a little breach, Discredite more..Then did the fault before it was so patch'd. 1675 Hobbes *Odyssey* (1677) 294 A foul coat full of patches. 1787 Jefferson *Writ.* (1859) II. 152 The hole and the patch should be commensurate. 1875 Helps *Ess., Pract. Wisd.* 6 To prefer a good open visible rent to a time-serving patch. 1898 *Sun* 23 Mar. 4/1 The 'patch' included in the 'ordinary [bicycle] outfit' is by no means large enough for an ordinary burst.

b. A piece of court-plaster or the like put over a wound or scar.

1591 Lodge *Catharos* (Hunter. Cl.) 6 Better to weare patches on my cloake, than to beare the patch on my head. 1599 Shaks. *Hen. V*, v. i. 93 Patches will I get vnto these cudgeld scarres. 1875 Hazlitt *Dodsley's Plays* XI. 140 *note*, Feesimple alludes also to the patch on the face of Tearchaps.

c. A pad or piece of cloth worn to protect an injured eye.

1598 Chapman *Blind Beggar* Wks. 1873 I. 10 Though he.. want an eye, Wearing a velvet patch upon the same. 1702 *Lond. Gaz.* No. 3847/4 [He] had a Patch on his right Eye. 1812 H. & J. Smith *Rej. Addr., Fire & Ale* ix, Over the horse's left eye was a patch, To keep it from burning the manger. a 1901 Besant *Five Years' Tryst*, etc. (1902) 221 You can change your face,..put a patch over one eye.

d. A piece of cloth sewn upon a garment as an ornament, badge, etc.

1898 *Daily News* 22 Oct. 6/3 Spots..such as black silk on scarlet velvet, black or coffee-brown on blue, pale blue on green...These 'patches' are now the very height of the fashion. 1900 *Ibid.* 22 Aug. 5/1 One juvenile wearer of the 'patch', belonging to H.M.S. Aurora, was in the thick of the fire carrying messages to and fro.

e. *Not a patch on* (*colloq.*), in no way comparable to, nowhere near.

1860 Reade *Cloister & H.* xxxvii, He is not a patch on you for looks. 1880 Miss Braddon *Just as I am* xii. 85 A fine handsome-looking young man,..but not a patch upon his father. 1880 *Sat. Rev.* 18 Dec. 779 The adventures with savages..and so on, are, to speak familiarly, not a patch upon the adventures which Captain Mayne Reid would have made out of the same materials. 1889 *Westm. Gaz.* 20 Feb. 10/1 We have some strange weather in England..but it is doubtful whether we are a patch upon Australia. On December 6 the thermometer in many places there fell over 40 deg. within six hours.

2. A small piece of black silk or court-plaster, often of fanciful shape, worn on the face either to hide a fault, or, more usually, to show off the complexion by contrast. (Fashionable, esp. among women, in 17th and 18th centuries; cf. Patch-box.)

1592 Lyly *Midas* iii. ii, *Licio.* Take Masticke else. *Pet.* Mastick's a patch. Masticke does many a foole's face catch. 1601 ? Marston *Pasquil & Kath.* v. 220 Blacke patches are worne, Some for pride, some to stay the Rhewme, and Some to hide the scab. 1611 Cotgr., *Moucheron*,..the little blacke patch thats glued by Masticke, etc., on the faces of many. a 1625 Fletcher *Elder Bro.* iii. v, Your black patches you wear variously, Some cut like stars, some in half moons, some lozenges. c 1706 Prior *Phillis's Age* 6 Her patches, paint, and jewels on. 1715 Lady M. W. Montagu *Town Ecl., Saturday* 49 Hours..pass'd in deep debate, How curls should fall, or where a patch to place. 1876 Planché *Cycl. Costume* I. 388. 1897 Rhoscomyl *White Rose Arno* 23 The patch that lent piquancy to the cheek of beauty.

3. A portion of any surface markedly different in appearance or character from what is around it; a large or irregular spot.

1573 Tusser *Husb.* (1878) 118 Reward not thy sheepe (when ye take off his cote) With twitchis and patches, as brode as a grote. 1701 *Lond. Gaz.* No. 3745/4 A Patch near the Flank on the near Side [on a horse]. 1810 *Edin. Rev.* XVII. 196 Those detached and unmeaning patches of different colours, which compose what opticians call an *anamorphosis*. 1873 Hamerton *Intell. Life* ii. i. (1875) 50 The sky will not come right..it is all spots and patches. 1894 Newton *Dict. Birds* 818 The Surf-Duck..with a white patch on the crown and another on the nape.

b. A small piece or area of undefined shape, of ground, or of anything lying or growing on it.

1577 Harrison *England* ii. iv. (1877) i. 98 In..Buckinghamshire..there is a piece of Hartfordshire..this patch is not aboue three miles in length, and two in breadth. 1602 Shaks. *Ham.* iv. iv. 18 We go to gain a little patch of ground That hath in it no profit but the name. 1684 *Contempl. St. Man* ii. iii. (1699) 154 Why doth he content himself with some patch of the Earth, when he may be Lord of the whole Heavens? 1742 Shenstone *Schoolmistress* v, A patch so green, On which the tribe their gambols do display. 1807 Wordsw. *Wh. Doe Ryl.* iv. 66 Like a patch of April snow. 1847 Grote *Greece* ii. xxvi. IV. 35 Patches of cultivable soil. 1894 Howells *Trav. fr. Altruria* 103 The chief crop was hay, with here and there a patch of potatoes or beans.

c. An area of floating pieces of ice, joining and overlapping one another, of more or less circular or polygonal form.

1817 Scoresby *Nat. Hist.* in *Ann. Reg.* 531/1 If it assume a circular or polygonal form, the name of patch is applied. 1820 *Ibid.* ii. 1324 A *patch* is a collection of drift or bay-ice of a circular or polygonal form. In point of magnitude, a pack corresponds with a field, and a patch with a floe. 1850 *Natural Phenomena* 106 If the field [of ice] is broken up into a number of pieces, none of which are more than forty or fifty yards across, the whole is called a *pack*; if the pieces are broad they are called a *patch*; and when long and narrow a *stream*.

d. *Anat.* and *Path.* A small well-defined area of the skin, etc. distinct in colour or appearance.

Peyer's, Peyerian patches, the agminate glands in the small intestine.

1797 *Monthly Mag.* III. 153 In other cases, there are many circular gangrenous patches, on the surface of the intestines. 1809 *Med. Jrnl.* XXI. 132 As the patch expands, the centre of it gradually assumes the natural colour of the skin. 1849–52 Todd *Cycl. Anat.* IV. 839/1 Each Peyerian patch consists of but a single layer of gland-vesicles. 1878 Huxley *Physiogr.* 226 It undergoes a process of division whereby it is converted into the embryonic patch or cicatricula. 1899 *Allbutt's Syst. Med.* VII. 296 A patch of softening was found in each hemisphere.

4. A piece of cloth sewed together with others of varying shape, size, and colour to form patchwork or to adorn a garment.

a 1529 Skelton *Bowge of Courte* 358 His cote was checked with patches rede and blewe. 1560 Daus tr. *Sleidane's Comm.* 424 The other two..had as it were sowed together certen fragmentes and patches. 1628 Earle *Microcosm., Pot-poet* (Arb.) 45 His Verses are like his clothes, miserable Cento's and patches. 1690 Locke *Hum. Und.* iv. xix. (1695) 400 A pie-bald Livery of coarse Patches and borrowed Shreds.

5. A small scrap, piece, or remnant of anything.

a 1529 Skelton *Replyc.* 3 A lytell ragge of rethorike..A pece or a patche of philosophy. 1579 Fulke *Heskins's Parl.* 81 They reade but patches out of other mens notes. 1602 Shaks. *Ham.* iii. iv. 102 A King of shreds and patches. 1633 T. Adams *Exp. 2 Peter* ii. 9 And fills up the time with ..some..patch of poetry. 1782 Mme. D'Arblay *Lett. to Mrs. Thrale* Apr., This letter is written by scraps and patches. 1835 Arnold *Let.* in Stanley *Life & Corr.* (1845) I. 435 Much of ancient history consists apparently of patches put together..without any redaction.

6. Applied to various things suggesting a patch (sense 1) in the way they are fastened, or in shape or size, or otherwise: a. The operculum of a periwinkle; b. A greased piece of cloth, leather, or other material used as the wadding for a rifle-ball; c. 'A projection on the top of the muzzle in some guns, doing away with the effect of dispart in laying' (Smyth *Sailor's Word-bk.* 1867); d. *Printing*: A piece of thin paper used to fill up low places in the impression; = Overlay *sb.* 2; e. 'A small square of thick leather sometimes used in the grinding of small tools to press the work on the stone, in order to protect the fingers from abrasion' (*Cent. Dict.* 1890).

1835 Kirby *Hab. & Inst. Anim.* I. ix. 279 We find the mouth of its [periwinkle's] shell closed by a horny organ called the *patch*. 1835–40 Haliburton *Clockm.* (1862) 439 Something that will go down the throat like a greased patch down a smooth rifle. 1846 Greener *Sci. Gunnery* 375 The use of patches..on the score of protecting the ball, and also cleansing the tube. 1850 R. G. Cumming *Hunter's Life S. Afr.* (1902) 93/2 [These] contained balls and patches, two sharp clasp-knives, a compass, flint and steel.

7. **Patch-up** [f. the phrase *to patch up*: see Patch *v.*] An act of patching up, or repairing in an imperfect fashion.

1819 *Metropolis* III. 178 He is returned from a patch up abroad. 1898 *Westm. Gaz.* 14 Dec. 1/3 We must avoid any speedy patch-up which would bring us to another letter of resignation twelve months hence. 1901 Miss E. Hobhouse *ibid.* 19 June 9/1 It is all only a miserable patch-up on a great ill.

8. *attrib.* and *Comb.*: † **patch-coat**, a patched coat; † **patch-grease**: see quot.; **patch-ice**, pieces of ice overlapping so as to form a patch (Webster 1864); **patch-leather**, leather used in patching; **patch-ornament**, an ornament resembling a patch in shape or otherwise; **patch-polled** *a.*, having a patch of colour on the head, esp. in *patch-polled coot* = Patch-head. Also Patch-box, etc.

1902 *Daily Chron.* 7 Jan. 6/3 The jacket..with two *patch breast pockets with pleats. 1630 Lennard tr. *Charron's Wisd.* i. Pref. (1670) 111 See then how strange and monstrous a *patch-coat man is. 1614 Markham *Cheap Husb.* i. (1668) Table Hard Wds., **Patch-grease*..is that tallow which is gotten from the boyling of Shoo-makers shreads. 1807 P. Gass *Jrnl.* 188 Each man has also a sufficient quantity of *patch-leather. 1878 Jewitt *Ceramic Art* I. ii. 27 These dots are arranged so as to form bands; and in others simply '*patch' ornaments.

Hence **Pa·tchwise** *adv.*, in the manner of a patch.

1832 Austin *Jurispr.* (1879) II. xxxix. 684 Statute law stuck patchwise on a body of judiciary.

Patch (pætʃ), *sb.*² [According to T. Wilson 1553, and Heywood 1562, orig. the name or rather nickname of Cardinal Wolsey's domestic 'fool' or jester, his real surname being *Sexton*.

Supposed by some to have been so called from his patched garb, or patched face; but perh. rather an anglicized form of It. *pazzo* fool. It seems however to have been later associated or taken as identical with Patch *sb.*¹, as in Shakspere's 'patch'd foole'. The following quots. bear on the history of the word:

1553 T. Wilson *Rhet.* (1580) 176 As to call one Patche or Coulson, whom we see to doe a thing foolishly, because these two in their tyme were notable fooles. 1562 J. Heywood *Epigr.* i. xliv. (1867) 106 A saiyng of Patche my lord cardinal's foole. Master Sexten, a parson of knowne wit, As he at my lord Cardinals boord did sit [etc.]. 1590 Shaks. *Mids. N.* iv. i. 215 But man is but a patch'd foole, if he will offer to say, what me-thought I had. (See also Warton *Hist. Poet.* (1840) III. 87; Douce *Illust. Shaks.* I. 258.)]

A domestic fool; a fool or foolish person generally; a clown, dolt, booby. Now only *dial.* or *colloq.* applied to an ill-natured or ill-tempered person, esp. a child. See also Cross-patch.

1549 Chaloner *Erasm. on Folly* Gij, This kynde of men whom commenly ye call fooles, doltes, ideotes, and paches. 1561 Preston *Camhyses* Ej, Hob and Lob, a ye Cuntry patches. 1588 *Marprel. Epist.* (Arb.) 3 M. Bridges was a verie patch and a duns, when he was in Cambridge. 1590 Shaks. *Mids. N.* iii. ii. 9 A crew of patches, rude mechanicals. 1598 Florio, *Pazzo*, a foole; a patch, a madman. 1655 Fuller *Ch. Hist.* iv. i. § 19 (tr. *Gower*) But Jack the mad patch men and houses does snatch. 1830 Scott *Doom of Devorgoil* ii. i, Thou art a foolish patch. 1900 O'Neill *Glens* 30 (E. D. D.) As ugly as need be, the dark little patch.

Patch (pætʃ), *v.* [f. Patch *sb.*¹]

1. *trans.* To put a patch or patches on; of a thing, to serve as a patch to. *Patch up*, to mend or repair in some sort by putting patches on.

1516 [see Patched 1]. 1523 Skelton *Garl. Laurel* 1209 With pitche she patchid her pitcher shuld not crase. 1548 Udall *Erasm. Par. Luke* v. 60 b, He renteth a newe vesture to patche vp an olde. 1602 Shaks. *Ham.* v. i. 239 Oh, that that earth, which kept the world in awe, Should patch a Wall, t'expell the winters flaw. 1774 Goldsm. *Nat. Hist.* (1776) VII. 256 It either makes a new web, or patches up the old one. c 1817 Hogg *Tales & Sk.* III. 77 Why patch up that tawdry gown? 1840 Dickens *Old C. Shop* xv, Windows patched with rags and paper. 1888 F. Hume *Mme. Midas* i. Prol., It had one mast, and a small sail all torn and patched.

b. In pa. pple., said of a person in reference to his clothing, etc.

c 1500 *How Plowm. lerned Patern.* 147 in Hazl. *E. P. P.* I. 214 He was patched, torne, and all to rente. 1597–8 Bp. Hall *Sat.* iv. ii. 9 Himself goes patched like some bare cottyer. 1611 Middleton & Dekker *Roaring Girle* D.'s Plays 1873 III. 214 Zounds I am so patcht vp, she cannot discouer me.

c. To fit (a bullet) with a patch (Patch *sb.*¹ 6 b).

1877 C. Hallock *Sportsman's Gazetteer* 545 If the bullet is the right size and properly patched, the patch will not be torn in putting the cartridge into the chamber.

d. 'To overlay or bring up an impression sheet with pieces of thin paper' (Jacobi *Printers' Vocab.*).

1884 Southward *Pract. Printing* 470 *Patching the Sheet.* 1890 Jacobi *Printing* 175 Where the type stands..low it should be patched up with the very thin set-off paper.

2. To mend, repair, or make whole, in various *fig.* applications. (Usually with *up*, and implying a hasty, clumsy, imperfect, or temporary manner.)

1573–80 Baret *Alv.* P 184 To Patch, or make whole againe: ..to botch: to make amends for that is done amisse. 1597 Shaks. 2 *Hen. IV*, ii. iv. 252 When wilt thou leaue fighting ..and begin to patch vp thine old Body for Heauen? 1601 — *Twel. N.* i. v. 52 Any thing that's mended, is but patch'd: ..sin that amends, is but patcht with vertue. 1706 E. Ward *Wooden World Diss.* (1708) 34 The Surgeon..takes care to patch him up with Speed. 1875 W. S. Hayward *Love agst. World* 40 You'll have to..patch up your quarrel.

3. To make up by joining pieces together as in patchwork; hence, to make up, put together, or frame hastily or insecurely; to botch *up*.

a 1529 Skelton *Poems agst. Garnesche* Wks. 1843 I. 125 The nexte halter ther xall be I bequeth yt hole to the: Soche pelfry thou hast pachchyd. 1563 Man *Musculus' Commonpl.* 40 b, An aparne patched together of figge leaves. 1579 Lodge *Def. Poetry* in G. G. Smith *Eliz. Crit. Ess.* I. 84 Out of what booke patched you out Cicero's Oration? 1650 Fuller *Pisgah* ii. xi. 34 The Samaritans quitted their.. Idols, and patched up a religion amongst themselves. 1726 Leoni *Alberti's Archit.* I. 23/2 Houses, which they patch'd up of Reeds and Bullrushes. 1848 Kingsley *Saint's Trag.* iii. i. 146 Any formal, heartless matrimony Patched up by Court intrigues. 1879 Black *Macleod of D.* xxxii, To patch together a pair of homespun trousers.

4. To put on or in as a patch; to fit (a thing) into something so as to diversify it, as in patchwork. Also *fig.*; often depreciatory.

1549 Coverdale, etc. *Erasm. Par. Gal.* v. 16 b, To haue newe clothe sowed or patched to an olde garmente. 1593 Nashe *Christs T.* Wks. (Grosart) IV. 166 It is so vgly daubed, plaistred, and patcht on. 1662 Gerbier *Princ.* 4 Things Patcht or glewed against a Wall. a 1825 Forby *Voc. E. Anglia* s. v., He patched it upon me, who knew nothing of the matter. 1886 Willis & Clark *Cambridge* I. 19 The present windows have been patched into the wall in such a manner as to make it impossible to trace accurately the original state of it.

b. To join as one patch to another; to piece together.

1630 J. Taylor (Water P.) *Laugh & be fat* Wks. ii. 71/2 Thy person's odd, vnparallel'd, vnmatchd, And yet thy action's to the person patch'd. 1867 Freeman *Norm. Conq.* I. iv. 239 It is just possible to patch the two narratives together.

5. To mark (a surface) as patches of different colour or material do; to diversify or variegate with patches. (Chiefly in passive.)

1595 Shaks. *John* iii. i. 47 If thou..wert grim.. Patch'd with foule Moles, and eye-offending markes. 1711 Addison *Spect.* No. 115 ¶ 6 His Stable-doors are patched with Noses that belonged to Foxes of the Knight's own hunting down. 1774 Pennant *Tour in Scot. in* 1772. 32 Grey rocks patched with moss. 1853 Kane *Grinnell Exp.* xlvi. (1856) 423 The slopes of the hills were heavily patched with snow. 1881 Miss Braddon *Asph.* xxvi. 290 Yellow lamps..patching with faint light an isolated statue, or a pulpit.

b. *intr.* for *refl.* To become coloured in patches.

1896 G. L. Becke *Pacific Tales, Hollis' Debt* (1897) 120 The red, bloated face of the skipper patched and mottled, and his breath came in quick, short gasps.

6. To adorn (a person, the face) with patches.

1674 R. Newcourt in *T. Flatman's Poems* 7 Which like their Misses Patch't and Painted are. 1704 Steele *Lying Lover* iii. (1747) 46 But alas, Madam, who patch'd you today? 1766 Goldsm. *Vic. W.* iv, Their hair plastered with pomatum, their faces patched to taste. 1881 Besant & Rice *Chapl. of Fleet* ii. i. (1883) 123 We now went..with faces patched, to the new church in Queen Square.

b. *intr.* for *refl.*

1702 Farquhar *Inconstant* ii. i, Your ladyship has patched and painted violently. 1729 Law *Serious C.* ii. (1732) 18 She will find it as impossible to patch or paint, as to curse or swear.

7. *intr.* *Patch off*, to come off in patches. *rare.*

1848 Thackeray *Bk. Snobs* vi, The plaster is patching off the..walls.

Patchable (pæˑtʃăb'l), *a. rare.* [f. Patch *v.* + -able.] That can be patched.

1849 Carlyle *Irish Journ.* (1882) Pref. 6 Like a ragged coat; ..not patched or patchable any longer.

Patchaw, obs. variant of Padishah.

Pa·tch-box. [f. Patch *sb.*¹ 2 + Box *sb.*²] A box for holding patches for the face.

1674 *Lond. Gaz.* No. 859/4 Lost.., two silver powder Boxes, and a patch Box. 1712–14 Pope *Rape Lock* iv. 162 Thrice from my trembling hand the patch-box fell. 1758 H. Walpole *Let. to H. S. Conway* 16 June, If they send a patch-box to Lord George Sackville, it will hold all his laurels. 1876 Miss Braddon *J. Haggard's Dau.* xi. 157 The poets of a patch box and powder period.

† **Pa·tchcock, pa·tchock.** *Obs. rare*⁻¹. [Known only in the passage cited; in which also the reading is uncertain. The first element is app. Patch *sb.*¹ (or ?²); the second may be Cock, or the dim. suffix -ock. See note below.]

A term used by Spenser of the degenerate English in Ireland, either in reference to their character and habits, their mongrel breed, or their costume: ? a base or mean fellow, ? a ragamuffin.

1596 Spenser *State Irel.* (Wks. Grosart IX. 104; Globe 636/2), The rest which dwell aboue in Connagh[t] and Munster,..and some in Leinster and Ulster, ar degenerate and growen to be as very Patchcockes [*v. r.* Patchock(e)s] as the wild Irishe.

[The Lambeth MS. 510, which was the copy submitted to the Abp. of Canterbury for licence, dated by Spenser and initialled E. S., from which Grosart prints his text, reads, lf. 39, *Patchcockes*; but three other MSS., B. M. Add. 22022 (printed in the Globe text), Harl. 7388, Camb. Dd. 10. 60 have *Patchockes, -ocks*. Camb. Dd. 14. 28 has *Rakehells*. If the word was *patchockes*, it was perhaps the same as Shakspere's 'very Paiocke', if this is read *pajocke*. Cf. same play iii. iv. 102 'a King of shreds and patches'.]

Patched (pætʃt, pæˑtʃéd), *ppl. a.* [f. Patch *v.* + -ed¹.] In senses corresponding to those of the verb: Mended with patches; made up of pieces as in patchwork; mended, made up, or put together hastily, clumsily, or insecurely. Also *patched-up*.

1516 in *Myrr. our Ladye* (1873) p. l, In dede for very voluntary pouerte..she had broken patchyd sleuys. a 1591 H. Smith *Wks.* (1867) II. 405 Mahomet's religion is a patched religion, mixed partly with Judaism, partly with Gentilism, partly with Papism, partly with Christianism. 1599 Nashe *Lenten Stuffe* (1871) 42 With it..the patchedest leather piltche *laboratho* may dine like a Spanish Duke. 1764 *Mem. G. Psalmanazar* 152 When he..heard my patched up story. 1792 *Anecd. W. Pitt* III. xxxix. 38 Let us have peace,..but let it be honourable, let it be secure. A patched up peace will not do. 1840 R. H. Dana *Bef. Mast* xxxvi, The patched woolen trousers.

b. Adorned or marked with patches.

1667 Pepys *Diary* 1 May, Peggy Pen..with only her husband's pretty sister with her..both patched and very fine, and in much the finest coach in the park. 1855 Kingsley *Westw. Ho!* xxix, A painted, patched, fucused, periwigged, bolstered,..Lamia!

† c. *Patched work* = Patchwork. *Obs.*

1716 M. Davies *Athen. Brit.* III. 51 Such Bitts and Scraps of patcht Work-Citations.

Hence † **Pa·tchedly** *adv.*, in manner of a patch.

1549 Coverdale, etc. *Erasm. Par. Gal.* v. 16 b, Nor can he beare with to haue..olde clothe be patchedlye sowed into a newe.

Patcher (pæˑtʃəɹ). [f. Patch *v.* + -er¹.] One who patches: see the verb. Also *patcher-up*.

1528 Tindale *Wks.* (Parker Soc.) I. 135 He is no patcher; he cannot build on another man's foundation. 1552 Huloet, Bodger, botcher, mender, or patcher of olde garmentes. 1611 Cotgr., *Renoueur de vieilles causes*,..a peecer or patcher vp of ruinous causes. 1694 Motteux *Rabelais* v. (1737) 214 Patchers, Clowters, and Botchers of old trumpery Stuff. 1841 Emerson *Misc., Conservative* (1884) 259 A timid cobbler and patcher. 1875 Jowett *Plato* (ed. 2) I. 295 A mender of old shoes, or patcher up of clothes.

Patchery¹ (pæˑtʃəri). [f. Patch *sb.*¹ or *v.* + -ery.] The action of patching or mending clumsily or hastily; anything made up of pieces or fragments put together; a patchwork (usually *fig.*).

1579 Fulke *Heskins's Parl.* 239 The Greeke Article is so placed, as it can abide no such patcherie. 1623 R. Bernard *Looke beyond Luther* Ep. Ded. 2 A new vpstart Religion, a patcherie of Iudaisme, Paganisme and Heresie. 1702 C. Mather *Magn. Chr.* iii. ii. xxiii. (1852) 467 Vile human inventions..and patcheries sticht into the service of the Lord. 1834 Gen. P. Thompson *Exerc.* (1842) III. 31 Designating such performances as jargon and patchery. 1880 Swinburne *Stud. Shaks.* (ed. 2) App. 232 A thin sample of poetic patchery cobbled up and stitched together.

† **Pa·tchery**². *Obs.* [f. Patch *sb.*² + -ery.] The conduct of a 'patch'; roguery, knavery.

1582 Stanyhurst *Æneis* ii. (Arb.) 64 From the fathers sermons shal such fond patcherye flicker? *Ibid.*, *Conceits* (Arb.) 140 Cleaue toe the sound Castl, flee from thee patcherye Cautl. 1607 Shaks. *Timon* v. i. 99 You heare him cogge, See him dissemble, Know his grosse patchery.

¶ In the following the sense is uncertain.

1553 *Respublica* (Brandl) v. ix. 79 Tis a bagg of Rye in dede: vsiree, periurce, pitcheree, patcherie, pilferie, briberee, snatcherie, catcherie.

Pa·tch-head. A local name in Maine, U.S., for the surf-scoter (*Œdemia perspicillata*), a kind of duck, from the white patches on its head.

1890 in *Cent. Dict.*

Patchiness (pæˑtʃinès). [f. Patchy *a.* + -ness.] Patchy quality or condition.

1862 H. Spencer *First Princ.* ii. xix. § 150 (1875) 407 Irregularities of distribution..would produce that patchiness which distinguishes the heavens. 1887 R. Garnett *Carlyle* vii. 125 Nothing seems to have struck him so much as the general patchiness of the country.

Pa·tching, *vbl. sb.*¹ [f. Patch *v.* + -ing¹.]

1. The action of the verb Patch, in various senses; also, the condition of being patched, or an instance of this. Also *patching-up*.

1526 Skelton *Magnyf.* 452 It is evyll patchynge of that is torne. 1546 J. Heywood *Prov.* (1867) 47 An olde sacke axeth much patchyng. 1691 T. H[ale] *Acc. New Invent.* 98 That patching and botching with Solder that appears upon all the Cast-lead Coverings. 1791 Mrs. Radcliffe *Rom. Forest* ii, A little patching up would make it comfortable enough. 1832 James *H. Masterton* xxiii, The eye detected some rather anomalous patchings and darnings. 1893 *British Printer* 157 Underlay wherever possible, as the less patching there is on the cylinder the less chance is there of wrinkling.

2. The putting of patches on the face by way of adornment.

1656 *Artif. Handsom.* 78 They forbid all painting, patching, and powdering. 1765 Goldsm. *Double Transform.* 40 Skill'd in no other arts was she, But dressing, patching, repartee. 1885 *Trans. Lanc. & Chesh. Antiq. Soc.* III. 35 The custom of patching amongst ladies.

3. The wadding for a bullet (cf. Patch *sb.*¹ 6 b).

1887 E. Eggleston *Graysons* xiii. (1888) 144 Taking a bullet from his pouch, he felt in his pocket for the patching.

4. *Comb.*, as *patching-cloth, -rubber, -work*.

c 1680 *Roxb. Ball.* VII. 468 The Taylor..had patching-work for a whole season. 1896 *Godey's Mag.* (U.S.) Apr. 374/2 A circle of patching-cloth pushed through to the bottom of the tire. 1898 *Sun* 23 Mar. 4/1 Always carry in your tool-bag a fairly large piece of patching rubber.

† **Pa·tching**, *vbl. sb.*² *Obs.* [f. Patch *sb.*² + -ing¹.] The behaviour of a 'patch'; = Patchery².

a 1550 *Image Ipocr.* in *Skelton's Wks.* (1843) II. 446 With peltinge and patchinge, With findinge and fatchinge. 1562 J. Heywood *Prov. & Epigr.* (1867) 171 After catching and snatchyng, Pyllyng and pollyng, we fall..to patchyng.

† **Pa·tching**, *ppl. a.*¹ *Obs.* [f. Patch *sb.*² + -ing².] Acting like a 'patch'; deceiving, knavish.

Hence † **Pa·tchingly** *adv.*, deceitfully.

1570 Foxe *A. & M.* (ed. 2) 1491/2 Others..dyd..dissemblingly and patchingly vse some part of them. 1591 Greene *Disc. Coosnage* Wks. (Grosart) X. 33 These conycatchers..geuing to diuers vile patching shiftes, an honest and godly title. 1641 J. Trapp *Theol. Theol.* iii. 127 Some slippery persons or patching companions. 1647 Ward *Simp. Cobler* (1843) 37, I am not without some contrivalls in my patching braines.

Patching, *ppl. a.*² [f. Patch *v.* + -ing².] That patches or covers with patches.

1855 Browning *Love among Ruins* iv, The patching houseleek's head of blossom winks Through the chinks.

Pa·tch-leaf. Also **putch-, putcha-leaf**. [A part-transl. of Bengālī *pacha-pāt*, f. Bengālī *pāt* leaf.] = Patchouli.

1698 Fryer *Acc. E. India & P.* 209 Goods from Acheen.. Patch Leaf, 1 Bahar Maunds 7 20 Sear. 1886 Yule & Burnell *Anglo-Ind. Gloss.* 517 Patchouli, Patch-leaf, also Putch- and Putcha-leaf.

† **Pa·tchment.** *Obs. rare*⁻¹. [f. Patch *v.* + -ment.] A patchwork.

a 1603 T. Cartwright *Confut. Rhem. N. T.* (1618) 205 A patchment of untruthes.

Patchock: see Patchcock.

Patchouli (pæˑtʃuli, pătʃūˑli). Also 9 **pach-, pāch-, patschouli, patchouly, paccioli**. [a. *patchouli*, 'the vernacular name over the greater part of the Madras Presidency' (Sir G. Birdwood in *Athenæum* 22 Oct. 1898), the elements of which are referred by some to Tamil *pach, pachai-* green and *ilai* leaf: cf. the Bengālī *pacha-pāt* (*pāt* leaf), and Eng. *putcha-leaf*, or Patch-leaf.

The spelling *patchouli* appears to be French, and may have arisen in the French possessions on the Coromandel coast. If there is anything in the conjecture in Hatz.-Darm. that it is a phonetically-spelt adaptation of Eng. *patch-leaf*, this would necessarily carry back the name in Fr. to a period anterior to the earliest Eng. examples. But in French dictionaries it was entered as a neologism by Littré in 1875, and was admitted by the Académie in 1878, long after it was known in English.]

1. An odoriferous plant (*Pogostemon Patchouli*, N.O. *Labiatæ*), native to Silhat, Penang, and the Malay peninsula, the dried leaves of which are used for various purposes in the East; it yields an essential oil, from which the scent (see 2) is derived.

1851 Forbes in *Art Jrnl. Illustr. Catal.* ii. p. vii/1 The ..aromatic herbs, the lavenders and rosemarys, hyssop and peppermints, patchouli and thyme, all yielding volatile oils. 1858 Simmonds *Dict. Trade*, *Patchouly*, an Indian herb. 1856 Watts *Dict. Chem.* IV. 357 Patchouli, Pachupat or Patscha-pat. 1872 *Ibid.* VI. 902 Volatile oil of patschouli gradually deposits a camphor.

2. A penetrating and lasting perfume prepared from this plant.

1845 Alb. Smith *Scattergood Fam.* I. vii, Evening-party odours..patchouli, white-wine vapours, and cut oranges. 1856 C. Hering *Homœop. Dom. Phys.* p. xi, Perfumery, particularly musk, hartshorn, camphor, paccioli. 1866 *Treas. Bot.* 910/2 Ill effects, such as loss of appetite and sleep, nervous attacks, etc., have been ascribed to the excessive employment of Patchouli as a perfume.

3. *attrib.*, as *patchouli camphor, oil*.

1881 Watts *Dict. Chem.* VIII. 1197 *Patchouli camphor*, $C_{15}H_{26}O$..forms regular hexagonal crystals. 1893 *Syd. Soc. Lex.*, *Patchouli oil*,..is a viscid oil, boils at 282°–294° F., and separates out on standing as *Patchouly camphor*.

† **Pa·tch-panel**, *sb.* and *a. Obs.* [f. Patch *v.* + Panel *sb.*¹]

A. *sb.* One who patches panels; ? a jobbing or botching carpenter: an abusive appellation.

1593 G. Harvey *Pierce's Super.* Wks. (Grosart) II. 280 The starkest Patch-pannell of them all, or the grossest hammer-drudge in a county. 1602 Dekker *Satirom.* Wks. 1873 I. 219 [Woman to retired Captain] Hang thee patch-pannell, I am none a thy Charing-Crosse.

B. *adj.* Fit for patching panels or putting into patchwork; of little value as material.

1605 *Wily Beguiled* Prol., Why, noble Cerberus, nothing but patch-pannel stuff, old gallimawfries, and cotten candle eloquence.

Patchwork (pæˑtʃwəɹk). [f. Patch *v.* or *sb.*¹ + Work *sb.*]

1. Work composed of pieces or fragments put together, esp. in a makeshift or incongruous manner; a thing patched up; a medley, jumble. Now often viewed as *fig.* from 2.

a 1692 Pollexfen *Disc. Trade* (1697) A iv, It cannot be expected they should have any effect for common Good, at best, but Patch-work. 1739 *Wks. of Learned* I. 103 He that thinks the Iliad and Odysses the Patchwork of a Beggar's Rhapsodies. 1872 Geo. Eliot *Middlem.* lxxiv, This imperfectly-taught woman, whose phrases and habits were an odd patchwork. 1837 W. S. Pratt in W. Gladden *Parish Probl.* 457 Latin and German hymns—clever patchwork often resembling real poetic creations.

b. Work of patching up: see Patch *v.* 2. *nonce-use.*

1712 Swift *Jrnl. to Stella* 12 Dec., I should ruin myself with endeavouring to mend them,..and I have been too much engaged in patchwork already.

2. *spec.* Work consisting of small pieces of various kinds of cloth, differing in colour and pattern, and sometimes in size and shape, sewed together by the edges, generally with ornamental effect, so as to form one article, as a counterpane, cushion, tea-cosy, etc. *Crazy patchwork*, that in which the pieces are quite irregular in shape and size: cf. Crazy 5.

1726 Swift *Gulliver* i. vi, My clothes..looked like the patch-work made by the ladies in England, only that mine were all of a colour. 1809 W. Irving *Knickerb.* iii. iv, Every woman..wore pockets..fashioned with patch-work into many curious devices. 1872 G. Macdonald *Wilf. Cumb.* I. iii. 17 The bed was covered with an equally charming counterpane of silk patchwork. 1898 Mrs. Alexander *Mammon* xix. 268, I wish, Claude, you would do a little of my crazy patchwork, you work so beautifully.

b. Any surface divided into many small compartments of various shapes and kinds.

1865 E. Burritt *Walk Land's End* 243 A glorious little world of Devonshire scenery, carpeted to the rim with the picturesque patchwork of Devonshire verdure. 1880 Mrs. Parr *Adam & Eve* xii, A patchwork of fields spread out and ran down to the cliffs.

3. *Mining.* (*local.*) See quot.

1897 *Jrnl. R. Agric. Soc.* Mar. 177 The ironstones were formerly dug out in extensive open-air workings [in S. Wales] known as 'patchworks'.

4. *attrib.* a. Made up of miscellaneous pieces or fragments; composed of a combination of odds and ends.

1713 Gay *Guard.* No. 140 ¶ 7 What Horace [*Ars Poet.* ll. 15–16] says of his patch-work poets: 'Purpureus late qui splendeat unus et alter, Assuitur pannus—'. 1814 W. Taylor in *Monthly Rev.* LXXIII. 463 Those second-hand minds and patchwork intellects. 1876 *N. Amer. Rev.* CXXIII. 420 The patchwork rubric of the English church.

b. Made of, or of the nature of patchwork: see 2.

1840 Hood *Kilmansegg, Dream* vi, No patchwork quilt, all seams and scars. 1865 Dickens *Mut. Fr.* i. xv, There was the old patch-work counterpane. 1880 Mrs. Parr *Adam & Eve* i, A low chair with..a patch-work cushion.

5. *Comb.*

1897 Mary Kingsley *W. Africa* 234 Spread with clean calico and adorned with patchwork-covered pillows.

Patchy (pæˑtʃi), *a.*¹ [f. Patch *sb.*¹ + -y.] Abounding in or diversified with patches; consisting of patches or small separate areas or tracts; resembling patchwork in appearance or structure.

1798 *Trans. Soc. Arts* XVI. 185 [A crop] in many places patchy, with intervals of four or five feet without any plants at all. 1845 *Jrnl. R. Agric. Soc.* VI. i. 84 The land is patchy and of different qualities. 1872 Huxley *Phys.* iii. 65 The layer appears patchy or spotted. 1882 *Gardener's Chron.* 4 Mar. 295 A stone or tile edging is certainly preferable to a patchy Box one. 1895 Kegan Paul in *Month* Aug. 458 Such a Life is often patchy and scrappy.

Hence **Pa·tchily** *adv.*, in a patchy manner.

1903 *Daily Mail* 7 Sept. 5/4 Shops..started with some dim idea of being beautiful, have finished by becoming patchily tin.

Patchy, *a.*² *colloq.* or *dial.* [f. Patch *sb.*² + -y.] Of the nature of a 'patch'; cross, ill-tempered, fractious.

1852 Trollope *Orley F.* II. iii. 20 He'll be a bit patchy.. just for a while...To-morrow morning may be he'll be just as sweet as sweet.

Pate¹ (pēˑt). (Also 7, 9 **pat**.) [In common use from c 1300: origin unknown.

Some have conjectured it to be a by-form of *plate*, comparing med.L. *platta* the clerical tonsure, and Du. and Ger. *platte* a shaven or bald head. But evidence is wanting.]

1. The head, the skull: more particularly applied to that part which is usually covered with hair. (In modern use, more or less ludicrous or humorous; not in serious or dignified use.)

c 1305 *Judas* 83 in *E. E. P.* (1862) 109 He smot him wiþ a ston behynde in þe pate þat al þe sculle to-daschte þe brayn ful out þerate. c 1394 *P. Pl. Crede* 839 He miȝte no maistre ben kald (for Crist þat defended), Ne puten no pylion on his pild pate. c 1430 Lydg. *Jack Hare* Min. Poems (Percy Soc.) 54 Now wesseil N. unto thi jousy pate, Unthrift and thou to-gidre be mett. 1535 Coverdale *Ps.* vii. 16 His vnhappynes shall come vpon his owne heade, and his wickednes shall fall vpon his owne pate. 1593 Shaks. 2 *Hen. VI*, v. i. 135 He is a Traitor, let him to the Tower, And chop away that factious pate of his. a 1604 Hanmer *Chron. Irel.* (1809) 325 A foole..gave him such a blow upon the pat, that the blood ran downe his eares. 1626 R. C. *Times' Whistle* iii. 969 Some curle their pates to make their lookes more faire. 1632 Lithgow *Trav.* ix. 396 An Eagle taking his bald pate for a white rocke, let a shell-fish fall on it. 1810 Cock *Strains* I. 136 (E. D. D.) Wi' powdered pats; The auld blue Bonnet's laid aside, They maun ha'e Hats. 1883 *19th Cent.* Dec. 1092 The stubbles are close shaven as a monk's pate.

2. The head as the seat of the intellect; hence put for skill, cleverness, 'brains', and formerly sometimes for a person possessed of such.

1610 Shaks. *Temp.* iv. i. 244 Steale by line and leuell, is an excellent passe of pate. 1614 Sylvester *Bethulia's Rescue* i. 109 The Able-most For Pate, Prowess, Purse. 1627–77 Feltham *Resolves* i. xliii. 70 To lay the plot at first, well; is matter of more pate. 1630 *R. Johnson's Kingd. & Commw.* 39 The greatest Sages of the kingdome,..and the best pates of Spaine. 1717 Prior *Alma* iii. 355 An odd conceit, As ever enter'd Frenchman's pate. c 1730 Young *Ep. to Pope* 65 Each shallow pate, that cannot read your name, Can read your life, and will be proud to blame. 1899 E. J. Chapman *Drama Two Lives, Amph. & Aucid.* 88 Made manifest to meanest pates.

3. The skin of a calf's head.

1687 *Lond. Gaz.* No. 2225/4 Prohibiting the Exportation of all sorts of Linen Rags, Glovers Clippings, Parchment Shreads, Calves-Pates. 1881 *Sci. Amer.* XLIV. 408 [The hide] is sold to the salters with the pates and tails on.

b. In the fur trade, The fur from a black patch on the head of a rabbit or hare.

1878 *Ure's Dict. Arts* IV. 381 At present hare wool is not sorted, but formerly it was divided into *black back, brown back, sides, pate* (useless), *checks* and *tail*, as in the case of rabbit wool.

Pate² (pēˑt). *north. dial.* Also 7 **payte, paite**, 8 **pait**. [Of obscure origin.

Perhaps from prec., in reference to the white top of its head, suggesting a bald pate.]

A badger. Also in *Comb.*, *pate-head*.

1628 *Vestry Bks.* (Surtees) 92 Whosoever shall take any fox, or pate, or badger, in this parish and bring the heade to the church, shall have twelve pence paid by the churchwardens. 1653 *Ibid.* 104 To George Burne for a pate head, 6d. 1718 *Finghall Church-w. Acc.* (MS.), For 3 Pait Head, 1s. 1788 W. Marshall *Yorksh.* II. Gloss. (E. D. S.), *Pait*, a badger. 1883 T. & K. Macquoid *About Yorksh.* 126 The last pate is said to have been killed hereabouts some twenty-eight years ago.

‖ **Pâté** (pāte). Also 8 **patee**. [F. *pâté*:—OF. *pasté*: see Pasty *sb.*, Patty.]

1. A pie, pasty, or patty. *Pâté de foie gras*, pie or pasty of fatted goose liver, Strasburg pie.

1706 Phillips, *Petty Patees*.., a sort of small Pyes made of March-pane, and fill'd with Sweet-meats. 1768 Sterne *Sent. Journ.*, *Le Patissier*, A chevalier de St. Louis selling *patés*. 1813 *Sk. Character* (ed. 2) I. 117, I..sent off the woman with an oyster pâté. 1813 Moore *Post-bag* iii. 4 His pâtés superb—and his cutlets sublime! 1827 Lytton *Pelham* viii, To help myself to the *pâté de foie gras*.

2. *Fortif.* See quot. (Erroneously written *pate*.)

1704 J. Harris *Lex. Techn.* I, *Pate*, in Fortification, is a kind of Platform like what they call an Horseshoe,..generally oval, encompassed only with a Parapet...It is usually erected in Marshy Grounds to cover a Gate of a Town. 1802 James *Milit. Dict.*, *Pate*, Fr.

Paté, patee, -ée, var. Pattée (in Heraldry).

Pated (pēˑtèd), *a.* [f. Pate¹ + -ed².] Having a pate (of a specified kind).

1580 Lyly *Euphues* (Arb.) 439 Grose and dull pated. a 1613 Overbury *A Wife*, etc. (1638) 210 Let him be found never so idle pated. 1736 Toldervy *Hist. 2 Orphans* III. 173 So jealous pated a fellow. 1834 H. Bulwer *France* II. iii. 144 The emptiest-pated of the male creatures that she meets.

Patedelion: see Pedelion.

† **Patefa·ction.** *Obs.* [ad. L. *patefactiōn-em*, n. of action from *patefacĕre* to Patefy.] The action of making open, visible, or known; a disclosing, manifestation, revelation, declaration.

1553 Bale *Vocacyon* in *Harl. Misc.* (Malh.) I. 364 The patefaction of Christe in the gospel. 1633 T. Adams *Exp. 2 Peter* i. 11 The like patefaction was to Peter; he 'saw heaven opened'. 1659 Pearson *Creed* i. ii. 44 God hath also made frequent patefactions of his Deity. a 1703 Burkitt *On N. T., Acts* xiii. 26 By way of patefaction and discovery. 1871 F. Hall *Recent Exempl. False Philol.* 27 And now for—not to shock a clergyman by profanely applying the term revelation,—the new *patefaction*.

† **Pa·tefy**, *v. Obs.* Also 6–7 **-ify**. [ad. L. *patefac-ĕre* to make open, to open, f. *patē-re* to be open + *facĕre* to make: cf. *liquefy*, and see -fy.] *trans.* To make open; to disclose, manifest, reveal to the eye or mind.

1533 Cranmer *Let. to Bp. of Hereford* in *Misc. Writ.* (Parker Soc.) II. 263 When the verity and truth of them shall be patified and made open unto you. 1591 R. Bruce *Serm.* (1843) 282 He hath patefied himself to us by an heavenly light. 1667 Waterhouse *Fire Lond.* 63 Thus God patefies the way to his displeasure. 1788 *Trifler* No. 25. 323 It dimoves every discruciating pain from the stomach, adjuvates digestion, and patefies obstructions.

† **Patel**¹, **-ell(e**. *Obs.* Also 5 -ɜl, 6 **pattle**. [ad. L. *patella* pan, knee-pan, F. *patelle* knee-pan.] 1. A pan, a frying-pan. b. The paten or shallow dish used with the chalice at Communion.

1481 *Durham Acc. Rolls* (Surtees) 97, ij friyng patyls ferr. 1546 *Confut. N. Shaxton* F viij b, Three crosses..one wyth your thombe in your forheade, an other vpon your crowne wyth the patell of the chalice.

2. The patella or knee-pan; also *patel-bone*.

1578 Banister *Hist. Man* i. 35 This Patell was ordained to couer the ioynt betwene the thighe and legge. 1598 Florio, *Rotola del ginocchio*, the whirle bone ordained to cover the ioint of the knee, the cie-bone, ..the pattle-bone.

‖ **Patel**² (pătēl). *East Ind.* Also 9 **patell, -eil, -ail, pattel, potail**. [a. Marāthī *patil*, Hindūstānī *patel*, app. f. Marāthī *pat* 'roll or register' (Yule).] The head-man of a village in India: the title used in the Central and Western Provinces, and frequently in S. India, but not in the Gangetic Provinces.

1802 *Chron.* App. in *Ann. Reg.* 526/2 The potail or killedar of Tirnakull has been hanged. 1816 'Quiz' *Grand Master* vii. 22 All his attempts could not compel The village rascally patel To get him a few fowls and rice. 1885 G. S. Forbes *Wild Life in Canara* 16 Village constables under the potails, or heads of villages. 1894 *Daily News* 4 Sept. 5/2 The patel decoyed him out of his house at night, and hacked him to pieces with a hatchet.

Patelet, variant of Patlet, a ruff.

‖ **Patella** (pătеˑlă). [L. *patella* pan, knee-pan, dim. of *patina* pan, Paten.]

1. *Anat.* A small movable bone, flattened and convex in shape, covering the front of the knee-joint; the knee-pan or knee-cap.

1693 tr. *Blancard's Phys. Dict.* (ed. 2), *Mola, Patella*, or *Rotula*, a round and broad Bone, at the joynting of the Thigh and Leg. 1706 Phillips, *Patella*,..Among Anatomists, the round, broad Bone, at the joynting of the Thigh and Leg; the Whirl-bone of the Knee. 1840 G. V. Ellis *Anat.* 622 On each side of the patella is the condyle of the femur. 1854 Owen *Skel. & Teeth* in *Circ. Sc., Organ. Nat.* I. 252 The patella [of the lion] is well ossified. 1881 Mivart *Cat* 109 The knee-pan, or Patella, is a small bone of an elongated oval shape.

b. *transf.* In insects, the first joint of the coxa.

2. *Archæol.* A small pan or shallow vessel; the vessel so called by the Romans.

[1398 Trevisa *Barth. De P. R.* xix. cxxviii. (1495) nn j/2 *Patella* is a panne as it were an open crocke.] 1851 D. Wilson *Preh. Ann.* (1863) I. iii. 80 Two brass vessels which.. appear to have been Roman Patellae. 1857 Birch *Anc. Pottery* (1858) II. 331 One is a dish, patera, or patella.

3. A natural formation of the form of a shallow pan. a. In animals: A cup-like formation; a cotyle. b. In plants: see quot.

1671 *Phil. Trans.* VI. 2165, I have often observed on Plumb trees and Cherry trees; also on the Vine and Cherry-Laurel certain patellae or flat Husks containing worms.

4. *Zool.* A genus of Mollusca, containing the common limpet.

1753 in Chambers *Cycl. Supp.*

Patella·ceous, *a. Zool.* Allied to the limpet.

1857 in Mayne *Expos. Lex.*

Patellar (pætеˑlăɹ, pătеˑlăɹ), *a.* [f. Patella + -ar¹. Cf. F. *patellaire* (Littré).] Of or pertaining to the patella or knee-pan.

1886 in *Cassell's Encycl. Dict.* 1893 A. S. Eccles *Sciatica* 25 Some writers on sciatica have mentioned the absence of the patellar reflex as occurring in this malady. 1897 *Allbutt's Syst. Med.* II. 367 The physiological deep reflex called the 'knee-jerk' or 'patellar reflex' is sometimes exaggerated. 1899 *Ibid.* VI. 707 The patellar tendon reactions were lost.

Patellaric (pætĕlæˑrik), *a. Chem.* [f. mod. Bot. L. *Patellāria* a genus of lichens, deriv. of *patella*: see above.] In *Patellaric acid*, an acid ($C_{17}H_{20}O_{10}$) obtained by Weigelt from the lichen *Patellaria scruposa*.

Supplement, p. 3873; Corrigenda, p. 4092; Spurious words, p. 4093; Books quoted, p. 4094

Patellate (pæ'telæt), a. [Latellla + -ate.] Furnished with, or formed into or like, a patella.

Patelliform (pæteliform), a. [ad. mod.L. patelliformis, f. patella: see -form.] Having the form of a patella; shaped like a shallow pan, knee-pan, or limpet-shell.

Patelline (pæ'telæin), a. Zool. [L. Patella, in Zool. *limpet* + -ine.] Of or pertaining to the Patellidae or limpets.

Patelloid (-oid), Conch., a. of the form of a patella, limpet-shaped; sb. a patelloid shell.

Patellula [mod.L. dim. of patella.] A small patella; one of the sucking disks or caps on the tarsus of water-beetles.

Patellulate a., furnished with or formed into a patellula.

Paten (pæ'ten). Forms: 1. patera, 4-9 patin, 5 patyn, 5-6 patyn, 5-7 patent, 5-8 paten, 5-9 patene, 7-9 -ine, 9 paten. [ME. *patene*, *patin*, etc.]

1. The plate or shallow dish, usually circular and of silver, on which the bread is laid at the celebration of the Eucharist.

2. *gen.* A shallow dish or plate.

3. A thin circular plate of metal; anything resembling or suggesting this.

Patency (pē'tēnsi). [f. L. patent-em: see -ency.]
1. The state or condition of being open or exposed to view; openness; manifestness, obviousness.
2. The condition of being open, expanded, or unobstructed, as a passage.

Patener (pæ'tēnər). [ad. L. patenārius, f. patena Paten: see -er.] An acolyte who held up the empty paten during a part of High Mass.

Patent (pē'tent, pæ'tent). a. Also 5 patent, 5-8 patent, 6 patent, paytent, paten, 6-7 patten. [In branch I, a. F. patent, ad. L. patent-em open, lying open, pr. pple. of patēre to lie open, exp. in *lettres patentes*.]

I. 1. In *letters patent* (Lat. *litterae patentes*, Fr. *lettres patentes*, 15-18th c., *letters patent*); also, in 14th c., *lettre patent*: An open letter or document.

II. a. Open as a door, gate, or aperture, so as to allow free passage.

b. Anat. Open, unobstructed.

2. a. Anatomical: certificate or licence generally; esp. a health certificate. Obs.

b. Comm. A sort of royal ship.

2. a. To license to manufacture, sell, or deal in an article or commodity.

b. To protect the inventor of.

3. A process or invention which has been patented.

7. Open to view, exposed to sight; exposed to the mental view; clear, plain, evident, manifest.

8. Elliptically for some patent commodity.

Patentable (pæ'tentab'l), a. [f. Patent + -able.]

Patentee (pætentī'). [f. Patent sb. + -ee.] One to whom a patent is granted.

Patently (pē'tentli, pæ'-), adv. Openly, obviously, evidently.

Patentor (pē'tentər). [f. Patent + -or.] One who grants a patent; a patentee.

Pater (pē'tər). [L.] Father.

Paterfamilias (pē'tərfəmi'liæs). [L. *paterfamilias* the father or head of a household.]
1. *Rom. Law.* The head of a family.
2. The (male) head of a family.

Paternal (pætə'nəl), a. [f. L. patern-us + -al.]
Of or pertaining to a father; fatherly.

Paternalism (pætə'nəliz'm). The principle and practice of paternal administration.

Paternalistic (pətəːnəli'stik), a. Of or relating to paternalism.

Paternally (pætə'nəli), adv.

Paternity (pætə'nĭti). [a. F. *paternité*.]
1. The quality or condition of being a father.

Paternoster (pæ'tərnɒ'stər). [L.]
1. The Lord's Prayer, esp. in the Latin version.

Paternostered a.

Paternosterer a maker of paternosters or rosaries.

Pateroon, **pateroon**, obs. forms of Patroon.

Paterastrophia (pənɪ'ʃroʊfiə). nonce-wd.

Paternostrophe (pænɪ'strɒfi). nonce-wd.

Patero, **pateero**, obs. forms of Pedrero.

Patessing, var. Patising Obs., bargaining.

Patesy, obs. form of Patois.

Path (pæθ), sb. Pl. **paths**. [Common Teut.]

Pathetic (pæθe'tik), a. Also 6-7 pathetique, -ik. [ad. late L. *pathētic-us*, Gr. παθητικός.]
1. Producing an effect upon the emotions; moving, stirring, affecting.
2. Affecting the tender emotions.

PATHETICAL.

pathetick blows. 1755 Young *Centaur* v. Wks. 1757 IV. 241 Nerves...joins my pathetic wish.

+ 3. Causing a physical sensation or affection; affecting the bodily senses. *Obs. rare.*
1632 R. Mason *Let.* in Butler's *Feminine Monarchie*... The stern, lock, heaves, and trust hurt are of such various...pathetique qualities.

4. Pertaining or relating to the passions or emotions of the mind. (In early use applied to bodily movements expressive of emotion.)

+b. *absol.* or as *sb.*

5. *absol.* The pathetic; that which is pathetic; pathetic quality, expression, or feeling.

Pathetically (pə'θetikăli), *adv.* [f. prec. + -LY².] In a pathetic manner.

1. So as to excite passion or emotion; movingly, affectingly.

2. With passion or strong emotion; passionately, vehemently; feelingly, earnestly. *Obs.*

Pathetism (pæ'θetiz'm), *sb.* ?*Obs.* [f. Gr. πάθος + -ISM.] A name for mesmerism or animal magnetism. So **pa'thetist**, a mesmerist.

Pathic (pæ'θik), *sb.* and *a.* Now rare or *Obs.*

A. *sb.* **1.** A man or boy upon whom sodomy is practised; a catamite.

2. One who suffers or undergoes something.

B. *adj.* **1.** That is the subject of sodomy; being, or pertaining to, a catamite.

2. Undergoing something, passive; pathic.

3. Pertaining to suffering or disease; morbid.

Hence **Patheticism** (pə'θetis'm), the practice of a pathic.

† Pathing, *vbl. sb. Obs.* [f. PATH *v.* + -ING¹.] Paving.

Pathless (pɑ·θlės), *a.* [f. PATH *sb.* + -LESS.] Having no path through or across it; destitute of paths; untrodden, trackless. Also *fig.*

Patlet (pæ·tlet), *sb.* *Obs.*
A little or diminutive path.

† Pathment, (*Sc. Obs.* Also 4 payth-, 4-5 paith-, 5 pathe-, 6 paithe-, paithment. [app. an alteration of *pavment* (*pament, payment*) after *path*, due to similarity of sound and association of meaning: cf. PATH *v.* 4.] = PAVEMENT (*Sc.*)

PATHOGENY.

most pathetically.

Patho- (pæ'þo, pá'þo·), repr. Gr. comb. form of πάθος suffering, disease, etc. (see PATHOS), used in scientific and technical terms, for the most important of which see their alphabetical places.

Pa·tho-anato·mical, *a.* pertaining to morbid anatomy. **Pathobiolo·gical**, *a.* relating to living organisms (e.g. bacteria) which cause disease; so **Pa·tho'biologist**, one who studies these. **Pa·thogermic**, *a.* pertaining to or of the nature of a pathogerm. **Patho·graphy**, *sb.* or *a.* description of disease.

Pathicate, *v. nonce-wd.* [f. PATHIC + -ATE³; cf. authenticate.] To make pathetic.

† Pathicly *adv.* *Obs. rare.* [as prec. + -LY².]
Pathetic quality or character.

Pathetism (pæ'þetiz'm). ?*Obs.* [f. Gr. πάθος + -ISM.]

Pathogen (pæ'þodʒen). Also *-gene*. [f. PATHO- + Gr. -γενής born.] A microccocus or bacterium that produces disease.

Pathogenesis (pæþodʒe'nesis). *Med.* and *Path.* [f. PATHO- + GENESIS.] Production or development of disease; the process or manner of origination of a disease or bodily affection. Also **Pathogeny** (-dʒeneai), pathogenesis of diseases. So **Pathogene·tic** (-dʒine'tik), **Pathogenous** (-dʒe'nus) *adjs.*, producing, or relating to the production, of disease or bodily affection; hence **Pathoge'nically** (-dʒeni'atli), quality or capacity of producing disease.

PATHOGNOMIC.

Pathogerm, *-germic*: see PATHO-.

Pathognomic (pæþogno·mik), *a.* [f. PATHOGNOMY +10 παθογνωμικός in Gr. is said to be 'a false form'.]

1. Of or pertaining to pathognomy, or to the signs and expression of the passions or feelings.

2. In relation to the passions or emotions. *rare.*

Pathognomonic (pæþognomo·nik), *a.* [f. PATHOGNOMY + -IC.]

1. *Med.* and *Path.* Specifically characteristic of a particular disease.

2. *gen.* Serving to characterize or distinguish.

Pathologic (pæþolo·dʒik), *a.* [as prec. + -AL¹.]
Pertaining to pathology.

Pathologically (-kăli), *adv.* [f. prec. + -LY².]

In relation to pathology, or to its subject-matter, disease.

PATIBULARY.

Body is molested, 1873 Tennyson *Love & Duty* he Shall sharpen pathos blight in.

3. In reference to art, esp. ancient Greek art: as opposed to the permanent or 'ethos' or ETHOS 2.

Pathway (pɑ·þwē¹), *sb.* [PATH + WAY.]

1. A way that constitutes or serves as a path; a way or along which one may walk or go; a path, track, way. (Often *fig.*)

2. *attrib.* and *Comb.*

Pathologist (pæþo·lodʒist), *sb.* [f. PATHOLOGY + -IST.] One versed in pathology; a student of or writer upon diseases.

Pathology (pæþo·lodʒi). [ad. mod. or med.L. *pathologia*, f. Gr. παθο-, PATHO- + -λογία, -LOGY: see -LOGY.]

1. The science or study of disease; that department of medical science, or of physiology, which treats of the causes and nature of diseases, or abnormal bodily affections or conditions.

2. *sb. a.* a pathognomonic sign or symptom.

Pathos (pē·þos). [a. Gr. πάθος suffering, f. πάθειν (root παθ-) to suffer.]

1. That quality in speech, writing, music, or artistic representation or *transf.* in events, circumstances, persons, etc.) which excites a feeling of pity or sadness; power of stirring tender or melancholy emotion; pathetic or affecting character or influence.

2. A pathetic expression or utterance. *rare.*

Pathologically, *adv.* [f. prec. + -LY²]

In relation to pathology, or to its subject-matter, disease.

PATIBULATE

So **Pati·bulate** *v. trans.* [cf. L. *patibulāt-* pa.ppl. stem of *patibulāre*] To hang. *humorous nonce-wd.*

Patience (pē·ʃens), *sb.* 4-6 paci-, 4-6 pacy-, *-ence*, also 6 -aitience. [ME. a. OF. *patience, pacience* (12th c.), ad. L. *patientia*, f. *patient-*: see -ENCE.]

1. The practice or quality of patience.

The suffering or enduring (of pain, trouble, or evil) with calmness and composure; the quality or capacity of so suffering or enduring.

2. Forbearance, longsuffering, longanimity under provocation of any kind; *esp.* forbearance or bearing with others, their faults, limitations, etc.

3. Quiet and self-possessed waiting for something; the quality of expecting long without discontent.

4. The calm abiding of the issue of time, processes, etc.; quiet and self-possessed waiting for something; the quality of expecting long without discontent.

Patience, *v. rare.* [f. prec.]

† 1. *trans.* To endure with patience, make patient; *refl.* to be patient, have patience. Cf. PATIENT *v.* 1.

2. *intr.* To have or exercise patience.

Patience-dock, *sb.* = prec.; = PATIENCE-DOCK.

Patient (pē·ʃent), *sb.* and *a.* Forms: 4-6 paci-, 4-7 paci-, 6- patient, *passient* (13-14th c.), later *patient*. [a. OF. *pacient, passient* (12th c.), ad. L. *patient-, patiens*, pr. pple. of *patī* to suffer.]

A. *adj.*

1. Bearing or enduring (pain, affliction, trouble, or evil of any kind) with composure, without discontent or complaint; having the quality or capacity of so bearing; exercising or possessing patience.

2. *a.* Slow to anger; long-suffering; forbearing.

3. One who is under medical treatment for the cure of some disease or wound; one of the sick persons whom a medical man attends; an inmate of an infirmary or hospital.

B. *sb.*

1. A sufferer; one who suffers patiently. Now *rare.*

Patonce, a. *Her.* [Of uncertain origin: app. first in lablach, wrongly attributed to Harding (who has *cross patté*); perh. a mistaken use of F. *croix potencée*; see POTENCE.] In *cross patonce*, a cross with its arms usually ending in a curved form from the centre, having ends somewhat like those of the cross fleury.

Patonce, obs. So. form of PATTERN.

†Patoun, Obs. rare. [Origin and meaning uncertain. Possibly = F. *pâton* lump or bolus of dough, pellet of paste to feed chickens, f. *pâte* paste.

†Patrasson, var. PATTERSON.

†Patration. Obs. rare⁻¹. [ad. L. *patrātiōn-em*, n. of action from *patrāre* to accomplish, effect.]

Patre, Patrel, Patremoyne, Patriak, obs. ff. FATHER, PETREL, PATRIMONY, PATRIARCH.

Patrial (peɪˈtriəl), a. (*sb.*) rare. [f. L. type *patriāl-is*, in obs. F. *patrial*, -el (16th c. in Godef.), f. *patria*, f. L. *patria* fatherland.]

Patriarch (peɪˈtriɑːk), *sb.* Also 3-4 -ere, 3-7 -ark, -4 -oke, 5-6 -arche, 4-7 -arke, -arck(e; 4-6 patry-. [ME. = OF. *patriarche* (Tertull.), ad. Gr. *πατριάρχης* chief of head of a family, clan = *ἀρχεν* to rule, *ἄρχειν*.]

Patriarchal (peɪtriˈɑːkəl), a.

Patriarchalism (peɪtriˈɑːkəlɪzm). [See -ISM.]

Patriarchate (peɪtriˈɑːkeɪt), *sb.* [ad. med.L. *patriarchātus*, f. *patriarcha*; cf. -ATE²]

Patriarchdom (peɪtriˈɑːkdəm), rare. [-DOM.]

Patriarchess (peɪtriˈɑːkes). rare. [ad.med.L. *patriarchissa* (Du Cange), OF. *patriarchesse*, -esse, var (Godef.).]

Patrician (pəˈtriʃən), a. (*sb.*) and a¹. [a. F. *patricien*, f. L. *patrici-us*, f. *patr-, pater* father.]

Patrician, a² rare. [f. L. *Patrici-us*, proper name (see PATRICK) + -AN.]

Patriciate (pəˈtriʃiət). [ad. med.L. *patriciātus*.]

Patricidal (pætrɪˈsaɪdəl), a. [f. next + -AL.]

Patricide (ˈpætrɪsaɪd¹). rare. [f. L. *patricīd-a*, *patri-cīd-ium.*]

Patricide². rare. [ad. L. type *patricīdium*.]

Patrick. [From the Christian name *Patrick = L. Patricius*, name of the patron saint of Ireland. Cf. *Paddy*, *Pat*.] An Irish catholic.

Patrick, So. dial. variant of PARTRIDGE.

Patrico (ˈpætrɪkəʊ). *Vagabonds' Cant.* Also 6 *patrico*(e), *pater-*, *patter-*, *patring* cove.

Patrimonial (pætrɪˈməʊniəl), a. [ad. F. *patrimonial*, late L. *patrimōniāl-is*.]

Patrimony (ˈpætrɪməni). Forms: 4 *patri-moyne*, *patrimoigne*, 4-5 -moygne, 4-7 patrimonie, -ye, 5- patrymony, (5-7 patri-monie, 6-7 patrimonye); 6- patrimony.

Patrin (ˈpætrɪn). *Gipsy Cant.* Also *patteran*.

Patriot (ˈpeɪtriət, ˈpætriət). Also 6-7 -ote. [a. F. *patriote* (15th c. in Hatz.-Darm.), ad. late L. *patriōta*, Gr. *πατριώτης*.]

Patriotess (ˈpeɪtriətes). [See -ESS.] A female patriot.

Patriotic (pætriˈɒtɪk), a. [a. F. *patriotique* (Rabelais, 1690s), ad. late L. *patriōticus* (Cassiodorus), a. Gr. *πατριωτικός*.]

Patriotical (pætriˈɒtɪkəl), a. [f. prec. + -AL.]

Patriotism (ˈpeɪtriətɪzm, ˈpæt-). [a. F. *patriotisme* (1750 in Hatz.-Darm.), f. *patriote* PATRIOT.]

Patristic (pəˈtrɪstɪk), a. and *sb.* [a. F. *patristique*, ad. (mod.L. *patristicus*), f. *patr-, pater* father.]

Patristical (pəˈtrɪstɪkəl), a. [f. prec. + -AL.]

Patristics (pəˈtrɪstɪks). [See -ICS.]

Patrix (ˈpeɪtrɪks). [f. *patr-, pater* father.]

Patrocinate, v. Obs. [f. L. *patrōcināt-*, ppl. stem of *patrōcinārī* to defend.]

Patrocination. Obs. [n. of action f. prec.]

Patrocinate². Obs. rare. [ad. L. *patrōcinium*.]

Patrocinium. rare.

Patrol (pəˈtrəʊl), *sb.* [a. F. *patrouille*, earlier *patrouille*, f. *patrouiller*.]

Patrol ...

Patrology ...

Patron ...

Patronate ...

Patroness ...

Patronise, -ize, Patrouille, -roul, Patroun ...

Patroon ...

Patronize ...

Patrony ...

Patronymic ...

Patroon ...

Patruel ...

Patten ...

Patter ...

PATTER. ... **PATTERN.** ... **PATTERNY.**

Patter'd, tried in a court of justice; a man who has undergone that ordeal, is said to have *pattered.*

Patter (pæ·tə1), *sb.*[f. PATTER *v.*] The action or fact of pattering; a quick succession of pats, taps, or similar slight sounds.

Patter (pæ·tə1), *v.*1 Forms: 4–5 pater(e, 6 pattur, (St. *ir*), 6– *er.* [f. PATER + PATERER = Paternoster: from the rapid and mechanical way in which the Latin prayers were often repeated.]

1. *intr.* To repeat the Paternoster or other prayer, esp. in a rapid, mechanical, or indistinct fashion: to mumble or mutter one's prayers.

2. *trans.* To say over, repeat, or recite (prayers, charms. etc.) in a rapid mechanical manner.

3. *intr.* To talk rapidly, fluently, or glibly, without much regard to sense or matter; to chatter, jabber; to prattle.

Patter (pæ·tə1), *v.*2 [Dim. and frequent of PAT *v.*1: see -ER 5.]

1. *intr.* To make a rapid succession of pats, taps, or slight sounding strokes, such as those of rain-drops against a window-pane; often referring mainly to the sound produced.

2. *intr.* To run with a rapid succession of short quick sounding steps.

3. *trans.* (*causal.*) To come to come or fall with a rapid succession of short sharp sounding strokes.

Pattern, Patteran, var. PATARA, PATRIN.

Patteraro(e, var. PEDRERO, a small gun.

Patterer (pæ·tərə1). One who patters. a. One who says paternosters, or mechanically repeats prayers, formulæ, etc.

Pattern (pæ·tə1n), *sb.* Forms: 4–8 patron, (5 patroun, 4–6 patrone), 8 6 patrone, 6–7 •erne, •ern, patterne, 6–7 patern, 6 patten (ME. *patron,* a. F. *patron,* which still means both 'patron' and 'pattern' in 16th c. *patron,* with patrone, evidently began to be pronounced (pat'rn, pa·tən) as in *-pattern,* patron, paterne, pattern, pattern.

Pattern (pæ·tə1n), *v.* Also 6–7 patern, paterne. [f. prec.]

Pa·tulent, *a. rare.* [app. f. L. *patul-* spreading, PATULOUS, with ending as in *patent.*] Open, expanded, gaping.

†Pa·tulcate, *v. Obs. rare−0.* [f. ppl. stem of med. or mod.L. *patulicāre* to open, spread out, f. *patul-us* PATULOUS.] Hence †**Patulca·tion.**

Pa·tulous, *a.* [f. L. *patul-us* + -OUS.]

1. Smallness of number; fewness; a small number.

2. Smallness of quantity; scantiness.

Patu·lous (pæ·tiŭləs), *a.* [f. L. *patul-us* + -OUS.]

Paughty, paughty (pȯ·ti), *a. Sc.* Also *pauchty.* [Origin unknown.] Haughty, proud; saucy, insolent, impertinent.

Paugie, paugy (pȯ·gi). *local U.S.* Also **paughie, porgy.** [From the ending of the Narragansett Indian name *mishcuppauog,* pl. *mishcup*; see PORGY.]

†Paul, *sb.*1 *Obs. rare.* Variant of PAW *sb.*1

Paul, pawl (pȯl), *sb.*2 Naut.

Pauldron, another form of POULDRON, a piece of armour covering the shoulder, a shoulder-plate.

Paulfrey, obs. form of PALFREY.

Paulian (pȯ·liǎn), *sb.* and *a.* [f. L. *Paul-us* Paul: cf. *Christian.*] Ch. Hist.

Paulician (pǭli·ʃǐǎn), *sb.* and *a. Ch. Hist.* [ad. L. *Paulician-us*, Gr. *Παυλικιανοί* pl., of disputed origin, thought by some to refer to PAUL.]

Pauldron (pȯ·ldrǒn). ...

Paul (pȯl). ...

Paulet, Paulette. ...

Pauline (pȯ·lǎin), *a.* and *sb.* Also 8 *-in.* [ad. L. *Paulīnus,* f. *Paul-us* PAUL.] A. *adj.* Of, pertaining to, or characteristic of St. Paul, his writings, or his doctrines.

Pauline (pȯ·lǎin), *sb.*2 ...

Paulinism (pȯ·liniz'm). The doctrine or theology of St. Paul, Pauline theology. Hence **Pau·linist,** an adherent of St. Paul or his theology; **Pau·linistic** *a.,* of or pertaining to a Paulinist or Paulinism.

Pau·linize, *v. intr.,* to follow the doctrine of St. Paul; *trans.,* to make Pauline, imbue with Paulinism.

Paulist (pȯ·list), *sb.* (*a.*) Ch. Hist.

Paulownia (pǭlō·niǎ). Bot. [mod.L. (*Siebold,* 1838), named after Anna Paulowna, daughter of the Tsar Paul I.] A genus of tropical and East Asian climbing shrubs (N.O. *Sapindaceae*).

Paunce (pȯns, pǭns). Also 4 *paunse,* 6 *pance.* [var. of *panche,* the paunch; also in sense 'the fashion of precut doublet or garment, etc.' see PANCE.]

Pauncer, pauncher. Obs. In 5 pancere, pauchere, paurchaere (pau-). 6 pauntcher, pa(w)ncheare. [a. OF. pancier, panichère (also pancier mod.); f. pance, paunch, mod. L. pancera; MLL. panticer, panicer (Ger. panzer), MHG. panzier, etc. (bauplier, f. OF. pance, panche, now panse, it. pancia PAUNCH sb.)]

1. Part of the armour of the 14th and 15th centuries, which covered the lower part of the body ...

Paunch (pɒnʃ, pānʃ), sb. Forms: 4-6 panche, paunche, paunho, 4-8 panch, 5 pawnche, pownche), 6- paunch. Also Sc. and north. dial. 6 penche, painche, 8-9 ponsh, 9 pansch, paunch. [ME. a ONF. panche or OF. pance, now panse = Pr. panca, Cat. panxa, Sp. panza, It. pancia:—L. Rom. type *pantica, L. L. pantex, *pantic-em paunch, belly.]

1. The belly, abdomen; the stomach, as the receptacle of food. (= Belly sb. 5.)

Pauncy, variant of PAUNCHY.

Paund, obs. form of PAWN sb.[?]
Paune, obs. form of PAWN.
Paunod, obs. form of PAWNED.
Paunfet, Paunflet.
Paunse, -ie, Paunst, obs. ff. PANSY, PAST.
Paunyse, oyse, obs. forms of PANSY.

Pauper (pɒ·pəɹ), sb. [a. L. pauper poor: its English use originated in the legal phrase in forma pauperis, in the form or character of a poor man or woman: see sense 1.]

1. A poor person.

Pause (pɔz), sb. Forms: 5 pawse, 6 pause. [ad. F. pause (14th c. in Littré) ... or L. pausa, a. Gr. παῦσις cessation, stopping.]

1. A temporary rest or cessation ...

Pautener (pɔ·tənəɹ), sb. Obs. Also 4-5 pawtener, pautenere, 6 pawtenar, pautnar. [a. OF. pautonnier (1419 in Godef.), a pune, 'a deboshed, scurvie, paltrie, varlet, scrip, curse.]

A small bag, a wallet, scrip, purse.

Pavage (pē[.]), sb. [ad. med. L. paviāticum, f. pavāre to PAVE.]

1. The laying or paving of a street, road, etc.

Pave (pēv), v. [ad. F. paver (14th c. in Littré) = Pr. pavar:—L. pavāre to beat, ram down, tread down.]

1. To cover with a pavement.

Pavement (pē·vmənt), sb. Forms: a. 3- pavement, 3-5 pave-, 4-5 pavi-, 5-6 -mente. [a. OF. pavement (13th c. in Littré) = Pr. paviment, it. pavimento, ad. L. pavimentum a beaten or rammed floor, f. pavīre to beat, etc.]

1. A piece of paved work, a paved surface ...

Pavilion (pavi·lyən), sb. Forms: 3 pavilloun, 4 pavylon, pavylloun, etc. [a. OF. pavillon, paveillon (12th c. in Littré) = Pr. pabalho, It. padiglione:—L. pāpiliōn-em a butterfly, a tent.]

1. A tent ...

PAVILION.

Pavilion (pă·vi·lyăn), *v.* [f. prec. sb.]

1. *trans.* To set or place in or as in a pavilion; to encanopy.

2. *K. Alis.* 2038 Davies full is all redeyne.

Pavin, variant of PAVAN.

Paving (pēi·viŋ), *vbl. sb.* [-ING¹.] The action of the vb. PAVE; *concr.* the product of this action, a pavement; the material of which a pavement is composed.

Paving-stone. A stone prepared for paving.

Paving-tile. A tile used for paving floors, yards, courts, foot-pavements, etc., often glazed, and sometimes bearing an ornamental design on it.

Pavion, obs. form of PAVAN.

Pavious, -ior (pēi·viăs). Forms: 8-9 pavior, (pavyer), 7- -ior, -iour. [f. PAVE *v.*; the later form *paviour, -ior*, was an alteration (perh. after *savior*) of earlier *paver, -yer*, which again appears to have been altered from PAVER, after other sbs. in -IER, q.v.]

1. One who paves or lays pavements.

2. A soldier bearing a pavis. *Obs. rare.*

3. A screen of pavises; a pavisade; any screen of shelter used in fighting.

PAVIS.

Pavis, pavise (pæ·vis), *v.* *Obs.* [f. prec. sb.]

Pavisade, pavesado (pævisēi·dŏ). Now *Hist.* Also 6-8 pavissade, (5-...), pavesade, pavescade.

†Pavisa·do, pavesa·do. *Obs.* Forms: 8 pavisado, -esado; 7-8 -esado.

Paviser (pæ·vizəɹ) *Obs. rare⁻¹.*

Pavois, -e, variants of PAVIS.

Pavon, pavone (pæ·vŏn), *v.* *Obs. rare⁻¹.*

†Pavone (pă·vŏn). *Obs. rare⁻¹.* [ad. It.]

Pavonian (păvŏu·niăn), *a.* [L. *pāvo,* peacock + -IAN: cf. F. *pavonien*.]

Pavonine (pæ·vŏnəin), *a.* [ad. L. *pāvōnīnus.*]

Pavoncello *Obs. rare⁻¹.*

Pavy (pēi·vi), *sb.* [? *pervis.*]

Pavyor, Pavyour, Pavyse, obs. ff. of PAVIOUR, PAVIS.

Paw (pɔ), *sb.*¹ Forms: 4-5 powe, 4-6 pawe, 5-6 *pl.* powes, 6-7 pawe, etc.

Paw (pɔ), *v.*¹ [f. prec.]

PAW.

Pawage, *Pawnage.* [a. F. PAVAGE, PAWNAGE.]

Pawed (pɔd), *a. rare.* [f. PAW *sb.*¹ + -ED².]

Pawer (pɔ·əɹ). One who, or that which paws.

Pawky (pɔ·ki), *a.* *Sc. and north. dial.*

Pawl (pɔl), *sb.* [Derivation unknown.] Trick, artifice, cunning device.

Pawl (pɔl), *sb.* *Sc. and north. dial.* 6 **palk** (?**paik**). [Derivation unknown.]

Pawn (pɔn), *sb.*¹ Forms: 5-6 (8) paun, 6 paune, 6- *sc. and N.* paund, pand, 6-7- pawn, -e. [a. OF. *paun* (rarely *pand, pant*) 'pledge, security, surety'; also 'booty, plunder, spoils taken from the enemy'.]

Pawn (pɔn), *sb.*² Forms: 5-6 (8) paun, 6 paune, 6- *sc.* and *N.* paund, pand, 7- pawn. [a. OF. *paon, pan, peon* (Godef.), *pan* (Pr. *pau, pabo, paon*) foot-soldier, pawn at chess.]

Pawn (pɔn), *sb.*³ *Chiefly Hist.* [f. PAWN *sb.*¹]

Pawn (pɔn), *v.*¹ [f. PAWN *sb.*¹]

Pawn (pɔn), *v.*² *Obs. rare.* [Erroneous back-formation from PAWNAGE; perh. an error of Spelman.]

Pawn, obs. form of PEAN, PEEN, PAWN.

PAWN.

Pawnable (pɔ·năb'l), *a.* [f. PAWN *v.*¹ + -ABLE.] That can be pawned.

Pawnage (pɔ·nḗdʒ), *rare.* [f. PAWN *v.*¹ + -AGE.]

Pawnbroker (pɔ·n|brŏukəɹ). One engaged in the business of lending money upon interest on the security of personal property pawned or pledged.

Pawnbroking (pɔ·n|brŏukiŋ), *vbl. sb.* [f. prec.: see -ING¹.] The action or business of a pawnbroker; the occupation of lending money on the security of articles pawned.

Pawnee (pɔnī·). [f. PAWN *v.*¹ + -EE.] The person with whom something is deposited as a pawn or pledge.

Pawner (pɔ·nəɹ). Also (in legal works) -or. [f. PAWN *v.*¹ + -ER¹.] One who pawns; one who deposits something as a pledge, or a pawnbroker.

Pawnor: see PAWNER.

Pawnshop (pɔ·n|ʃɒp). [f. PAWN *sb.*² + SHOP.]

PAXBRED.

Pawtenar, -er, pawtnere, var. PAUTENER *sb.*²

Paw-waw, variant of POWWOW.

Pax (pæks). Also 6 pex. [a. L. *pax* peace, in Christian L. also the kiss of peace.]

Pax, *Eccl.*

Paxbred (pæ·ksbred). Forms: 4 paxbred³, -brede, -bred, 6 bredd. [f. PAX¹ + BRED [?].]

Paxilla (pæksi'lä). *Zool.* Pl. -æ. [mod.L., from classical L. *paxillus* small stake, peg.] A pillarlike pedicel in echinoderms, surmounted by a tuft of minute calcified spinelets attached to the integument.

Paxillary, *a. Obs.* Erroneous form of BASILARY, applied to the sphenoid bone.

Paxilliferous, *a.* Having the body furnished with paxillæ.

Paxillose, *a. Geol.* Resembling a small stake.

Paxillus (pæksi'lŏs). *Zool.* [L. *paxillus* small stake, peg.] = PAXILLA.

Pay, *sb.*

Pay, *v.*

Payability (pe¹äbi'liti), *sb. rare.* [f. PAYABLE + -ITY.]

Payable (pe¹äb'l), *a.* [f. PAY *v.* + -ABLE.]

Payance, *obs. form of* PAYANCE.

Pay-day.

Payee (pe²i¹), *sb.*

Payen, obs. form of PAYNIM, PAGAN.

Payer (pe¹²ĕr), *sb.*

Payify, *v.*

Payment (pe¹mĕnt), *sb.*

Paymaster.

Payan, obs. or alien form of PAYNIM.

Payse, *obs. form of* PEISE *Obs.*

Payto, **Paytner**, **Paytent**.

Pea (pī). [A new singular evolved from the earlier sing. pl. *pease*, by writing this as a plural inflexion.]

Pea, sb.

Pea-bird, **pee-bird**. A local name for the Wryneck, from its note.

Peace (pīs), sb.

I. Freedom from, or cessation of, war or hostilities; the condition of a nation or community in which it is not at war with another.

2. Freedom from civil commotion and disorder; public order and security.

3. Freedom from disturbance or perturbation (esp. as a condition in which an individual person is); quiet, tranquillity, undisturbed state. Also emphasized as *peace and quiet(ness)*.

4. Freedom from quarrels or dissension between individuals; a state of friendliness; concord, amity.

5. Freedom from mental or spiritual disturbance or conflict arising from passion, sense of guilt, etc.; calmness of mind.

6. Absence of noise, movement, or activity; stillness, quiet; inertness.

7. In generalized sense including several of the preceding.

II. Phrases.

Peace, v.

Peaceable (pīsăb'l), a. (sb., adv.)

Peaceableness.

Peaceably, adv.

Peaceful (pīsfŭl), a.

Peacefully, adv.

Peacefulness.

Peace-keeper. One who keeps or maintains the peace.

Peacemaker.

Peace-breaker. One who breaks or violates the peace.

Peaceful, a.

Pea-comb (see Comb).

Pea-corn.

Peacenestle, sb. form of PINEAPPLE.

Peace-monger.

Peace-offering.

Peace-officer. A civil officer appointed to preserve the public peace, as a constable.

Peach (pīch), sb.[1] Forms: 4 peche, 5 peshe, peshe, peske, peak), 6 peache.

1. The fruit of the *Amygdalus persica*, a large drupe, usually round, of a velvety colour, flushed with red, with downy skin, highly flavoured sweet pulp, and rough furrowed stone enclosing the seed.

2. Applied to other edible fruits resembling the peach, or to the plants producing them.

Peach, sb.

Peach-blow. [See BLOW sb.]

Peacher (pī′tʃər), rare.

Peachery (pī′tʃəri). [f. PEACH sb.]

Peach-pick. [f. PEA + CHICK.]

Peachify (pī′tʃifai), nonce-wd.

Peachiness (pī′tʃines).

Peachlet, nonce-wd.

Peachment, Obt. rare.

Peach-tree. The tree Amygdalus persica.

Peachwort (pī′tʃwort).

Peachy (pī′tʃi).

Peach-bloom.

Peach-blossom.

Pea-coat. [f. PEA-jacket.] = PEA-JACKET.

Peacock (pī′kŏk), sb.

Peacockery (pī′kŏkəri).

Peacock-fish. A European labroid fish.

Peacockishly, nonce-wd.

Peacockishness.

Peacock-iris.

Peacockly, a. and adv. Obs.

Peacock's feather, peacock feather.

Peafowl (pī′faul).

Peag (pēg), sb.

Pea-jacket. Also 8 pay-, 9 pea-, P-jacket.

Peak (pīk), sb.¹

Peage, Obs.

Peagle, Peagoose; see PEAGLE, PEA-GOOSE.

Peahen (pī′hen).

Peak, sb.²

Peak (pīk), v.¹

Peaked (pī′ked), ppl. a.

Peak, sb.³ Also 6 peke, peoke, peaks, 6-7 peake.

Peak, v.² Also 7 pike, 7-8 peek.

Peak, v.³ Naut.

Peak, adv. (sb.) Naut.

Peaked (pīkt, pī′ked), ppl. a.

Peake-goose, **pea-goose**. Obs. Also 6 peok-, 7 pa-goose.

Peaking (pī'kiŋ), ppl. a. Now dial. Also 7-9 peaking.

Peakish (pī'kiʃ), a.1

Peakward, adv.

Peaky (pī'ki), a.1

Peaky, var. form of PECKY a.

Peal (pīl). Forms: 4-6 pele, 5 peell, peyll, 5-6 peel(e, 6 peyle, pelle, 6-7 (peale), 6- peal. [ME. *pele*; in sense 1, aphetic of APPEAL.]

Peal (pīl), v.1

Peale, obs. form of PALE.

Pea-ler. Obs. exc. dial.

Pealite (pī'ləit).

Peall, **Pealok**, **Pealt**, obs. ff. PELL sb.

Pean (pīn). [Origin uncertain.]

Peanut (pī'nʌt).

Peance, variant of PENANCE.

Pea-pod. Plural PEASE-COD.

Peon, variant of PEON.

Pea-pod [PEA + POD].

Pear (pɛə̂r). Forms: 1 pera, peru, 4-6 pere, 5 peyre, 5 poyre, 7 peare, 6- pear.

Pearand.

Peare, obs. form of PEER, PIERCE.

Pearch, obs. form of PARCH, PIERCE.

Pearie, obs. form of PERRY, pear-tree.

Pearce, variant of PIERCE.

Pearle, obs. form of PERCH, PEARL.

Pearl (pɜːl), sb.1 Forms: 4-6 perle, peerle, 5 porl, (perell, -ill, perrel), 5 peirl(e, perl(e, perle(s, 6-7 perle, pearle, 6- pearl. [ME. *perle*.]

Pearl (pɜːl), sb.2

Pearl (pɜːl), sb.3

Pearl (pɜːl), v.1

Pearl, v.2

Pearl, v.3

Pearl, v.4

Pearlaceous, occasional var. PEARLACEOUS.

Pearl-ash (pɜː'læʃ).

Pearl-barley [Cf. PEARL sb.1].

Pearl-diver. One who dives for pearls.

PEARLED.

Pearled (pǎld, poet. pǔrlĕd), ppl.a.[1] [f. PEARL sb.[1] and v.[1] + -ED.]

1. Furnished, set, or adorned with pearls; composed of or fitted with pearl or nacre. Chiefly poet.

2. Formed into pearly drops; be-dewprinkled.

3. Formed into small roundel grains; granulated.

4. In boiling of sugar for confectionery: Brought to the degree called 'pearl'; are quots. and PEARL sb.[1] 13.

Pearling (pǎˈliŋ), vbl. sb. St. and north. dial.

Pearling (pǔˈliŋ), vbl. sb.[1] [f. PEARL v.[1] + -ING[1].]
1. Forming pearls or pearl-like drops. Obs.
2. Fishing for pearls.

Pearlish (pǔˈliʃ), a. [f. PEARL sb.[1] + -ISH[1].] Slightly pearl-coloured or pearl-like.

Pearlite (pǔˈlait). [f. PEARL sb.[1] + -ITE[1].]
1. Min. Variant form of PERLITE, PEARL-STONE.
2. Metallurgy.

Pearl-fisher.

So **Pearl-fishery**, the occupation or industry of fishing for pearls. Is the place where this is carried on, with all its apparatus. **Pearl-fishing** = pearl-fishery a.; also attrib.

Pearlet, rare. 6 perlett, 9 pearl-let.

Pearl-fisher.

Pearl-grass.

Pearl-oyster. A pearl-bearing bivalve mollusc of the family Aviculidæ; spec. Meleagrina margaritifera of the Indian seas.

Pearl-shell.

Pearmain (pĕrˈmain, pǔˈmain). Forms: 5 parmayn, parmeyne, 6-7 pearemain, 6-7 pearmain, (7 pear-, peair-, pair-, pare-, peer-maine, -main, -mayn, 7-9 pearman.

Hence **Pearl-sheller**, one who fishes for pearl-shells.

Pearlwort sb.

Pearl-stone.

Pearlwort.

Pearly (pǎˈli), a. (adv., sb.) [f. PEARL[1] + -Y.]
1. Round and lustrous like a pearl; as a dewdrop, etc.
2. Like pearl in appearance or lustre.
3. Abounding in, having, or bearing pearls.
4. Of the clear greyish- or bluish-white colour of pearl.
5. fg. Exceedingly precious (like a precious pearl).

Pease.

PEAT.

Peasant (peˈzǎnt), sb. Forms: 6 paissaunt, 6 paisaunte, paisant, paysaunt, peasaint, -aunt, peasaunt, 5-7 paysant, peasan, -aunt, 6-8 paisan, 6 paysan, -yne, peyzan, 7 paisan. peasant, 8 paisan.
1. The tree which produces pears.
2. The wood of this tree; pear-tree wood.

Peasant. Obs. rare.

Peasantly (peˈzǎntli), a. Now rare or Obs. Of, characteristic of a peasant or peasantry.

Peasantry (peˈzǎntri). [f. PEASANT sb. + -RY.]
1. Peasants collectively; a body of peasants.

Pearmonger.

PEASE.

Pease (pīz), sb. Forms: 1 pise (poes), 1-4[?] pyse, 4 peoes, 4 pheos, pese, 5 pes (5-8 peis, peas), 6-8 pease, 7-9 peaze, peaze, 6-8 pea, pl. pease, peasyn, (paysen), 6-8 13 peason, peasen, peosen, peasyn, 8-9 peas, peesys, 7-6 peas (as in frag.), [OE. pise, pl. pisan...]

PEAT.

Peat (pīt), sb.[1]
1. Vegetable matter decomposed by water and partially carbonized by chemical change, often forming bogs or 'mosses' of large extent, where it is dug or cut out, and 'made' into peats (in b).
2. A piece or mass of this, cut out for fuel.

Peasen, Peason, forms of PEASE.

Peaseweep: see PEEWEEP.

Pea-soup. Also peas-soup.
Pea-soupy a.

Peastone (pīˈstəʊn). [f. PEA[1] + STONE sb.] A variety of limestone consisting of large rounded grains like peas; also called PISOLITE.

Peat. Obs. or dial. Also PEAT-, PET[3] q.v.

Peaty (pīˈti), a. [f. PEAT sb.[1] + -Y.] Of the nature of peat; abounding in peat.

Peasy (pīˈzi), a. [f. PEASE sb. + -Y.]
2. a. Of the size of peas. **b.** Of the appearance, colour, etc. of pease or pea-meal.

Peat-moss. [f. PEAT[1] + MOSS.]

Peat-reek. [f. PEAT[1] + REEK sb.], smoke.

PEA-VINE.

Pea-vine. U.S. [f. PEA[1] + VINE sb.] The vine or climbing stem, with foliage, of the pea-plant, or of any plant of the leguminous kind.

PECTINACEOUS.

Hence **Pectinaceous** (-ǝʃɒs) *a.*, related to or containing pectin.

Pectinal (pɛ·ktinăl), *a.* (*sb.*) † *Obs.* ...

Pectinate (pɛ·ktineit), *a.* (*sb.*) ...

Pectinated (pɛ·ktineited), *ppl. a.* ...

Pectinately, *adv.* ...

Pectination (pektinei·ʃən). ...

Pectineal (pekti·nĭăl), *a.* ...

Pectines, pl. of PECTEN.

Pectinibranch (-bræŋk), ...

Pectinite (pɛ·ktin‌əit). *Zool.* ...

Pectinoid (pɛ·ktin‌oid), *a. Zool.* ...

Pectinous (pɛ·ktinɒs), *a.* [f. PECTIN + -OUS.] ...

Pectite (pɛ·kt‌əit), *Zool.* ...

Pectize (pɛ·kt‌əiz), *v.* ...

Pectolite (pɛ·ktolɒit). *Min.* ...

Pectoral (pɛ·ktorăl), *sb.* and *a.* ...

Pectoralist. ...

Pectorally, *adv.* ...

Pectoriloquial (pektorilou·kwĭăl), ...

Pectoriloquy (pektori·lokwi). ...

Pectose (pɛ·ktous). *Chem.* ...

Pectosic (pekto·sik), *a.* ...

Pectous (pɛ·ktɒs), *a. Chem.* ...

Pectunculate (pektɒ·ŋkĭŭleit), *a. Entom.* ...

Pectuncle (pɛ·ktɒŋk'l). *Obs.* ...

Pecul, variant of PICUL, *Obs.*

Peculate (pɛ·kĭŭleit), *v.* ...

Peculation (pekĭŭlei·ʃən). ...

Peculator (pɛ·kĭŭleitor). ...

Peculiar (pĭkĭū·ljăr), *a.* and *sb.* ...

PECULIAR.

Peculiarism. *Obs.* ...

Peculiarity (pĭkĭūliæ·riti). ...

Peculiarize (pĭkĭū·ljər‌əiz), *v.* ...

Peculiarly (pĭkĭū·ljərli), *adv.* ...

Peculiarness. ...

Peculium (pĭkĭū·lĭɒm). ...

Pecuniarily (pĭkĭū·niărili), *adv.* ...

Pecuniary (pĭkĭū·niări), *a.* and *sb.* ...

Pecunious (pĭkĭū·niɒs), *a.* ...

Peculiate, *v. Obs. rare.* ...

Peculious, *a. Obs. rare.* ...

Peculium (pĭkĭū·lĭɒm). ...

Pecunious, *a.* ...

Pecuniosity. ...

Ped. Abbreviation of PEDESTRIAN. *Slang.* ...

Pedage (pē·dedʒ). *Obs. Law. Hist.* ...

Pedagogic (pedǎgɔ·dʒik), *a.* and *sb.* ...

Pedagogical (pedǎgɔ·dʒikăl), *a.* ...

Pedagogically, *adv.* ...

Pedagogism, pedagoguism (pē·dǎgɔgiz'm). ...

Pedagogue (pe·dǎgɔg), *sb.* ...

Pedagogy (pe·dǎgɔdʒi, -gɔgi). ...

Pedal (pē·dăl), *a.* ...

Pedal (pē·dăl), *sb.* ...

Pedal (pē·dăl, pī·dăl), *a.* [ad. L. *pedāli-is* of pertaining to the foot, of the size or dimension of a foot, f. *pēs, ped-em* foot + -AL.]

Pedal (pē·dăl), *sb.* [f. prec. *a.*] 1. *Mus.* To play upon the pedals of an organ.

Pedaller (pedăl·ĕr), *sb.*

Pedant (pĕ·dănt), *sb.* [a. F. *pédant* (1566 in Hatz.-Darm.), or its source It. *pedante* teacher, schoolmaster, pedant.] 1. = PEDAGOGUE.

Pedantic (pĭdæ·ntik), *a.* = PEDANTICAL.

Pedantical (pĭdæ·ntikăl), *a.*

Pedantically, *adv.* [f. PEDANTICAL + -LY.] In a pedantic manner; with pedantry.

Pedanticly, *adv.* = PEDANTICALLY.

Pedanticness. So **Peda·nticness.**

Pedantism (pĕ·dăntiz'm), *sb.*

Pedantize (pĕ·dăntəiz), *v.*

Pedantocracy (pedăntŏ·krăsi). [f. PEDANT + -OCRACY.]

Pedantry (pĕ·dăntri). [ad. It. *pedanteria* (used by Sidney), f. *pedante* PEDANT.]

Pedary (pĕ·dări), *a.* and *sb.* Rom. Antiq. [ad. L. *pedāri-us.*]

Pedate (pĕ·dĕt), *a.* Nat. Hist. [ad. L. *pedāt-us.*]

Peddle (pe·d'l), *v.* [Of obscure history.]

Pedder (pe·dĕr). Now Sc. and dial. [repr. OE. *peoddere, pedder.*]

Peddling, *ppl. a.* [See PEDDLE *v.* + -ING².]

Pede (pīd), *sb.* [f. L. *pēs, ped-em* foot.]

Pedee.

Pedestal (pe·děstăl), *sb.*

Pedestrial (pĭde·striăl), *a.*

Pedestrian (pĭde·striăn), *a.* and *sb.* [f. L. *pedester, pedestr-is* + -AN.]

Pedestrianate, *v.*

Pedestrianism (pĭde·striăniz'm).

Pedestrianize, *v.*

Pedetic, *a.*

Pedial (pī·diăl), *a.*

Pedicel (pe·disĕl). Also 7 **pedicil**. [f. mod. L. *pedicell-us.*]

Pedicellaria (pĕdisělæ·riă), *sb. pl. Zool.*

Pedicellate (pĕdi·sĕlĕt), *a.*

Pedicle (pe·dik'l), *sb. Nat. Hist., etc.* [ad. L. *pediculus.*]

Pedicular (pĭdi·kiŭlăr), *a.* [ad. L. *pedicular-is.*]

Pedicule.

Pediculate (pĭdi·kiŭlĕt), *a.*

Pediculous (pĭdi·kiŭlŏs), *a.*

Pediculosis (pĭdikiŭlŏ·sis). *Path.*

Pediculous (pi-diˈkiŭləs), a. [ad. L. *pediculōs-us*, f. *pedicŭl-us* louse.] Infested with lice; lousy; also, of or pertaining to a louse, or characterized by lice (= PEDICULAR).

Pedicure (pe'dikiūr), v. [f. prec. sb.] To care or treat (the feet) by the removal of corns, etc. Hence **Pe'dicuring** *vbl. sb.*

Pedicure (pe'dikiūr), sb. [a. F. *pédicure*; [1781 in Hatz.-Darm.], f. L. *ped-*, *pedi-* foot + *curāre* to take care of.]
1. One whose business is the surgical care and treatment of the feet; a chiropodist.
2. The surgical treatment of the feet, esp. in the removal or cure of corns, bunions, and the like.

So **Pe'dicurism**, the practice or art of a pedicure; **Pe'dicurist** = PEDICURE 1.

Pedicurist (pe'dikiūrist). [f. prec. + -IST.]

Pedicel, Pediment, obs. ff. PEDEE, PEDIMENT.

Pediferous (pĭdi'ferəs), a. *Zool.* and *Bot.* [f. mod. L. *pedifer* (f. *ped-*, *pedi-* foot + *-fer* bearing) + -OUS.] Having feet or foot-like parts; pedigerous.

Pediform (pe'dĭfōrm), a. [f. L. type *pedi-formis*, f. *ped-*, *pedi-* foot + *-form* (see -FORM).] Having the form of a foot; said chiefly of the organs of insects.

Pedigerous (pĭdi'dʒerəs), a. [f. mod.L. type *pedĭger* (f. L. *ped-*, *pedi-* foot + *-ger* carrying) + -OUS.] Bearing feet or legs.

Pedigree (pe'digrī), sb. Forms: see below.

Pedimanous (pĭdi'mănəs), a. *Zool.* [f. mod.L. *pedimānus*: see next.] Having feet like hands.

Pedimane (pe'dĭmān). *Zool.* [ad. mod.L. *pedimān-us*, f. *ped-*, *pedi-* foot + *manus* hand.] A pedimanous quadruped: see next.

Pediment (pe'dĭmənt). Forms: 4-7 periment, peri-, perriment. 8. 7 pede-, peda-, 8 pedie-, pidement, 7 pediment. [An alteration of *periment*, *perriment*, said to be a workman's term, and "corrupt English"; of obscure origin: see earlier below.]

Pedimental (pedĭme'ntal), a. [f. PEDIMENT + -AL.]
1. Of or pertaining to a pediment, of the nature of a pediment.

Pedimented (pe'dĭmentĕd), a. [as prec. + -ED.] Having a pediment; formed with or made like a pediment.

Pediment, another form of PEDOMETER. Hence **Pedime'tric**, **Pedi'metry**.

Pedion (pe'dion). *Cryst.* Pl. **pedia**. [a. Gr. *πεδίον* a plain, a flat surface.]

Pedionomite (pedio'nŏmait), *rare*. [f. Gr. *πεδίον* plain-dweller + -ITE.] An inhabitant of a plain, a dweller in a plain.

Pedipalp (pe'dĭpalp), *Zool.* Also in L. form **pedipalpus**, pl. -i. [f. mod.L. *Pedipalpi*, *-palpus* (F. Cuvier, 1806), f. *ped-*, *pedi-* foot + *palpus* feeler, PALP.]

Pedipalpous (pedĭpa'lpəs), a.

Pedipalpus, pedipalp.

Pedometric (pedŏme'trik), a. [f. PEDOMETER + -IC.] Of or pertaining to a pedometer.

Pedometrical (pedŏme'trikal), a. = prec.

Pedomotive (pedŏmō'tiv), a. [f. *pedo-* for *pedi-* + MOTIVE.] Actuated by the foot or feet; worked by the pressure of the foot.

Pedomotor (pe'dŏmōtər). [erron. f. *pedo-* for + MOTOR.] A contrivance or device for the application of the foot as the driving power in a machine, as a treadle, pedal, etc.; esp. a pedo-motive vehicle, as a bicycle, etc.

Pedoplenral = PLEUROPEDAL (a ganglion in mollusca).

Pedotrophic, etc.: see PÆDO-.

Pedrail (pe'drāl), sb. Mexico and south-western U.S. A rough and rocky tract, esp. of lava. Also attrib.

Pedrero (pĕdre'rō). Now *Hist.* Forms: 4-6 pedrera, 8 peter-, petrera, 7 petrero, 7 petrara, peterera, petarero, 8-9 pet(e)rero. 7-9 petrero, 8-9 pe'(a)ro-, pederero, pat(e)rero, patararo, patterero. [Sp. *pedrero* a stone-throwing engine (in Cange), from *pedrero* to throw stones: many corruptions of the original, the latter ones being influenced by PETER.]

Peduncle (pĭdʌ'nk'l), sb. *Nat. Hist.* [ad. mod.L. *pedunculus* footstalk (Linnæus *Philos. Bot.* § 82 D, *Pedunculus*, truncus partialis elevans Fructificationem nec folia), dim. of *ped-em* foot.]
1. *Bot.* The stalk of a flower or of a cluster of flowers or fruits; the primary or main stalk, or one of the general stalks, of an inflorescence.

Peduncular (pĭdʌ'nk'lər), a. *Nat. Hist.* [ad. mod.L. *peduncul-aris*; see above and -AR.] Of or pertaining to a peduncle (in any sense).

Pedunculate (pĭdʌ'nk'ûlĕt), a. *Nat. Hist.* [ad. mod.L. *pedunculāt-us*, f. *pedunculus* (see -ATE).] Furnished with or having a peduncle; supported by a peduncle; stalked.

Pedunculated (pĭdʌ'nk'ûlĕtĕd), ppl. a. = prec.

Pedunculation (pĭdʌ'nk'ûlē'ʃən). [f. as prec. + -ATION.] The formation of a peduncle; the condition of being pedunculate.

Pedwardes, obs. form of PETARDS.

Pee, sb.[1] *dial.* Also pea. [f. Echoic.] *intr.* To peak in a thin piping voice; to peep, squeak; to utter the slightest sound.

Pee, sb.[2] *dial.* The birds (sandpiping), cries uttered behind the evening.

Peek (pīk), v.[1] [cf. PEEP v.[1].] *intr.* To peak in a thin piping voice; to peep, squeak; to utter the slightest sound.

Peek (pīk), v.[2] Also 6-7 peke. [prob. a var. of PEEP v.] *intr.* To look out, or peep.

Peekie = see PEAK sb.[1] **Peeky**, var. PEAKY a.[2]

Peel (pīl), sb.[1] Forms: 5-7 peele, 5-7 pele, (5 peile), 6 pel, (6 peile), 6-7 peele, 7-9 peel. [a. OF. *pel* stake, pale; now *pieu*; see PALE sb.]

Peel (pīl), sb.[2] Also 6-7 peele, 7 peill. See also PILL sb.[1] A collateral form of the earlier PILE sb.

Peel (pīl), sb.[3] Forms: 5 (poell), 4-5 pele, -yn, 5-6 (5-9. Sc.) pele, 6 peele, piel, 6-8 (9. Sc.) pele, peele. [Known a 1300 in latinized form *pēlum* (later *comburium*), *pēl-*; in AF., pel, later L. pel; whence 14-16th c. Sc. *pele*. In sense 1 = OF. *pel*, *pele* (mod.F. *pieu*): see *pel-*; in L. ME. *pel*, *pele*, whence 15-16th c. Sc. *pele*.]

Peel (pīl), sb.[4] [ad. F. *pelle*.] A baker's shovel, a long flat board on which bread is placed in the oven and from which it is withdrawn.

Peel (pīl), v.[1] Forms: (3 peelien), 4-5 pele, -yn, 5-6 (5. Sc.) pele, 6 peele, piel, 6-9 peal, 9 dial. peel, pill. [In senses 1-3 a. OF. *peler*, *piller*, etc. to strip off hair, to skin.]
I. To despoil.
1. *trans.* To plunder, pillage, spoil, rifle, strip (of possessions (a person or place); = PILL v.[1].]

PEEL. 613 **PEELING.** | **PEELING.** 614 **PEEP.**

Peel, v.[2] sc.

Peeled (pīld), ppl. a.

Peeler (pīˈləɹ).

Peeler[2], local.

Pel-gallio: see PILGARLIC.

Peeling (pīˈliŋ), vbl. sb.

Peeling, ppl. a.

Peelite (pīˈlait).

Peen, pene, v. Obs. exc. dial.

Peen, pene, sb. Obs. exc. dial.

Peeoy (pīˈoi).

Peep, v.[1]

Peep, sb.[1]

Peep, v.[2]

Peep, sb.[2]

Peenge, v. dial.

PEEP-ARM. 615 **PEER.** | **PEER.** 616 **PEERSHIP.**

Peep-arm.

Peepal: see P'a PUL.

Peep-bo (pīˈp·bō), collog.

Peeper (pīˈpəɹ).

Peeper[2] (pīˈpəɹ).

Peep-hole (pīˈp·hōl).

Peeping, vbl. sb.

Peeping, ppl. a.

Peep-of-day.

Peep-show (pīˈp·ʃō).

Peepul (pīˈpul), sb.

Peepy (pīˈpi), a. dial. and collog.

Peer (pīɹ), sb.[1]

Peer, sb.[2]

Peer, v.[1]

Peer, v.[2]

Peer, v.[3]

Peer, obs. f. PEAR sb., PIER.

Peerage (pīˈredʒ).

Peerdom (pīˈɹdəm).

Peerdom, obs. form of PERCH.

Peere, obs. form of PEAR sb., PIER.

Peeress (pīˈres).

Peering (pīˈriŋ), ppl. a.

Peerless (pīˈles), a.

Peerly, adv. rare. Also peerlich.

Peership (pīˈʃip).

Peery, **Peert**, obs. forms of PEAT, PEERT.

Peewit, **Peeweet**, var. PEWIT.

Peevish, a. ...

Peg (peg), sb. ...

Peg (peg), v. ...

Pegged ...

Pegger ...

Pegging ...

Peggle ...

Peggy ...

Peggy-mast ...

Pegless ...

Pegman ...

Peg-top ...

Peignoir ...

Peine ...

Peinture ...

Peirameter ...

Peisage ...

Peisant ...

Peise ...

Peise, Peize, *v. Obs. exc. dial.* Forms: 4–7 peise, peyse, peyce, 5 peyaso, 5–6 paas, 5–7 paise, 6 payse, (peaco), *Sc.* paisse, 6–7 pease, peaze, peyse, pease, poase, peese. [ME. *prise*, *repr.* the stem-stressed form of OF. *peiser* (3rd sing. pres. *peise*) = Pr. *pesar*, *pezar*, Sp. *pesar*, It. *pesare* :—L. *pēnsāre* to weigh, freq. of *pendĕre* to weigh. In later Eng. often became *poise*, and this vocalization was sometimes extended to the inf., etc., e.g. *poiser*, *poisen*, *poisar* …

…

Peitrel, peytrel, poitrel, *sb. Obs.* Forms: 4 (?) peytral, 4–5 -elle, 4–7 -el, 5 peitrel, 6 petrell, 7 poitrel, 6 peytrell.

Peisy, *a. Obs.* In 7 poisie. [f. PEISE *sb.* + -Y.] Weighty, heavy.

Pejorate, *v. Obs. rare.* [f. L. *pejōrāt-*, ppl. stem of *pejōrāre* to make worse, f. *pejor-em* worse.]

Pejoration (pīdʒ̣oˈreıʃən), [ad. med.L. *pejōrātiōn-em*, n. of action from *pejōrāre*: see prec.]

Pejorative, *a.* (*sb.*) [a. F. *péjoratif*, -*ive*, f. L. *pejōrāre*: see PEJORATE.]

Pekan (pekæn) [Canadian Fr. *pékan*, ad. Abnaki (Eastern Algonkin) *pékané* (Rasles).]

Pekoe (ˈpiːkoʊ, ˈpekoʊ) [From Chinese: in Amoy dialect *pak-ho*, in Cantonese *pak-ho*; from *pek, pak* = Mandarin *peh, pai* white + *ho*, Mandarin *hao* down, hair.]

Pela, pé-la (pēˈlaː) [Chinese *pai, pe-*, *peh-white* + *wax*.] The white wax obtained in China from the wax insect (*Coccus pela* or *sinensis*).

Pelade (pelaˈd) [F. *pelade* (16th c. in Littré), disease that causes falling off of down or hair, f. *peler* to deprive of hair.]

Pelage (pelædʒ, F. *pelage* (16th c. in Littré), hair, wool, or fur of an animal, in reference to its kind or colour, f. OF. *peil, poil* hair, wool, down.]

Pelagial, *a.* (*sb.*) [f. pelagi-us, Gr. πελαγι-ος of the sea + -AL.] Of or belonging to the open sea. *= PELAGIAN a.* 1, b.

Pelagian, *a.* and *sb.*[1] [f. L. *pelagi-us* (see PELAGIC) + -AN.]

Pelagian, *a.* and *sb.*[2] [ad. med.L. *Pelagiānus*, f. *Pelagius*, latinized form of Morgan, which signifies the sea.]

Pelagic, *a.* [ad. L. *pelagic-us*, a. Gr. πελαγικός.]

Pelagianism (pelagianiz'm), [f. PELAGIAN a.[2] + -ISM.] The doctrine of Pelagius and his followers.

Pelagic acid [f. *pelagic* + ACID.]

Pelagicite, [f. *pelagi-us* + -ITE.] *Min.*

Pelargonic, *a. Chem.* [f. mod.L. *Pelargonium* + -IC.]

Pelargonium (pelɑːˈgoʊniəm). *Bot.* [mod.L.]

Pelaw, Polch, variants of PILAW, PILCH.

Peldon [of obscure origin.]

Pele, obs. form of PEAL, PIEL, PILL.

Pelecoan, obs. form of PELICAN.

Pe'lecoaine, *a. Ornith.* [f. L. *pelican-us* PELICAN + -INE[1].] Of or pertaining to the genus *Pelecanus* of birds.

Peleoid (p'le·oid), *a.* and *sb. Geom.*

Pelecypod (pele·sipod), *a.* and *sb. Zool.*

Pelerine (ˈpɛlərɪn). *Also* 9 pellerine. [a. F. *pèlerine* PILGRIM.]

Pelf, *sb.* Obs. exc. dial. Forms: 4 pelf, 4–5 pelfe.

Pelican (ˈpɛlɪkən). Forms: 1 pellican, 3–8 -cane, 5 -kane, 6 -kan, 7 pelican.

Pelagra, var. of PELLAGRA.

Pellar, sb. dial. (Cornwall). [?f. PELL v. + -AR sb.¹ -ER¹.] An exorcist; a wizard, conjurer.

Pellar, var. PILLAR.

Pellard, Obs. rare. [f. PELL sb.² + -ARD.] A kind of cloak or tunic: see quots.

Pellatory, Pellitari, var. PELLITORY, PELLETER.

Pelle, obs. f. PALL, PEAL, PEALER, PILLAR; var. PELLET, Pellora, var. PELURE¹ Obs.

Pellet (pe·let), sb.¹ Forms: 4–5 pelet, (5 -ette), pelote, (5 -yt), pale, 6 pellette, -ott, -otte, (6 -ot), -et, 6– pellet. [a. F. pelote (11th c.) = Pr., Sp. pelota, Pg. pelota, It. pillotta = med. L. pilotta, a deriv. of L. pila, L. pila ball.]

1. Any globe, ball, or spherical body, usually one of small size; a ball of some plastic or soft substance, esp. of medicine or food, a bolus, a pill.

2. A ball, usually of stone, used as a missile during the 14th and 15th centuries, and shot from mangonels, mortars, etc.; a cannon-ball; a later use, a bullet; now applied to small shot.

3. Her. A roundel sable — GUNSTONE 2.

4. A circular boss or raised part, rounded or flat, in coins or decorative work.

Pellet, sb.² Her. [f. PELLET sb.¹] Charged with pellets; pelleted.

Pellian (pe·liæn), a. Math. [f. name of John Pell, an English mathematician (1610–85):] Belonging to a particular kind of indeterminate equation: see quot.

Pellibranchiate (pelibræŋ·kiæt), a. (sb.) Zool. Belonging to the Pellibranchia.

Pelliceous (peli·ʃəs), a. rare—¹. [f. L. pelliceus, -us made of skin + -OUS.] Of the nature of a thin skin, membrane, or pellicle.

Pellicle (pe·lik'l). Also 7 cycle, pel(l)ikel. [ad. L. pellicula small or thin skin, dim. of pell-is skin.] A small or thin skin; a fine sheet or layer of some substance; either covering a surface or (less usually) enclosing a cavity; a membrane, cuticle, film. Chiefly in scientific use, and applied to natural formations, as a thin membrane in an animal or plant body, a fine scum on a liquid, etc.

Pellicled, ppl. a. [f. PELLET v. or sb.¹ + -ED.] Marked or charged with (heraldic) pellets.

Pellicular (peli·kiŭlar), a. [ad. mod.L. pellicular-is, f. pellicula PELLICLE: see -AR.] Of, pertaining to, or of the nature of a pellicle; having or characterized by a pellicle; membranous, filmy.

Pellitory¹ (pe·litəri). Forms: 6 peli-, pely-, pellatory, pellytorie, 7 pele-, pillitorie, -tore, (7 pillitorie, 7 zarie. 6– pellitory. [Found first in 16th c.: partly (in sense 1) an alteration of the earlier peletre, pellitry, PELLETER¹] with changed suffix; partly (in sense 3) an alteration of parietarie, paritaire. L. parietaria... by dissimilation of r = L. parietem wall.]

Pellitory², Pelletory. Obs. rare. [ad. mod.L. pelliteria, Pellitory of Spaine.]

Pell-mell (pe·lme·l), adv. Also 6 pelle meale, peale-meale, 6–7 pel mell, pel-mel, pele mele, peale-meale, (8 peale mesle), 6–9 pell mell (7 pell-mell), pelle-mele, 8–9 pêle mêle. [a. F. pêle-mêle, in OF. pesle mesle (13th c.), pelle-mesle (14th c.), also mesle-pesle, mesle-mesle, hurly-burly. First element mêle for earlier mesle, the stem of the vb. mesler, mêler to mingle, MELL: second element pêle for earlier pesle, pile shovel, or peel pan, as if mixed together with a shovel, or in a pan.]

1. With disorderly or confused mingling; in a confused medley; together in disorder, without any order; in mingled confusion, promiscuously.

b. Without discrimination, indiscriminately; in the mass. Obs.

Pellucid (peliū·sid), a. (sb.) [ad. L. pellucid-us, perlucid-us, f. pellucēre, perlucēre to shine through: cf. lucidus, L. lucēre to shine. Frequent in scientific and literary use, but not colloquial.]

1. Having the property of transmitting, or allowing the passage of, light; translucent, transparent; clear. Also fig.

2. Clear to the eye or other sense; easily seen or understood; clear in style or expression.

Pellucidity (peliŭsi·diti). [f. as next + -ITY.] The quality or condition of being pellucid; transparency or clearness; limpidity. Also fig.

Pellucidly, adv. [f. PELLUCID + -LY².] In a pellucid manner.

Pellucidness. [f. as prec. + -NESS.] Pellucid quality, pellucidity.

Pelt-ack, -ock, Sc. [app. f. PELLET sb. + -OCK.] A ball.

Pelly melly, obs. forms of PELL-MELL.

Pellyson, variant of PELISSON Obs.

Pelly, Pellytorie, obs. f. PELLET, PELLITORY.

Pelmatogram, rare—⁰. [f. Gr. πελματο- sole of the foot + -GRAM.] A foot-print.

Pelma, obs. f. PELM.

Pelma-tozoa (pelmătozō·a), sb. pl. Zool. [mod. L. Pelmatozoa, neut. pl. (f. Gr. πελματο- (see prec.) + ζῷον animal).]

Pelmel, Pelmele, obs. forms of PELL-MELL.

Pelo-, combining form of Gr. πηλός clay, mud, occurring in a few rarely used scientific words, chiefly zoological.

Pelo, Pelor, obs. var. PILAU, PILOUR.

Pelorin, a. (sb.) [a. F. pèlerin, bald, hairless.] Bald, hairless: used in Spanish America of nearly hairless races of animals there developed.

Pelorella [dim. of PELORIA.]

Pelora, Pelore, obs. var. PILAU, PILOUR.

Peloria (pelō·ria). Bot. [mod. L. (H. Rose, 1846), f. Pelor, name of the mythical son of Tantalus; see -IA.]

Peloric (pelo·rik), a. Bot. [f. prec. + -IC.] Of or pertaining to peloria.

Pelorism (pe·loriz'm) = peloria.

Pelorize (pe·loraiz) v. trans., to affect with peloria.

Pelorization.

Pelota (pelō·ta). [Sp. pelota ball, augmentative of pila = L. pila ball: cf. PELLET.] A game of Basque origin, somewhat resembling tennis or rackets, played in a large court with a ball.

Pelotin, Peloton, see PLATOON.

Pelour, obs. f. PEALER, PEELER, PILLAR; var. PELURE Obs. Pelows, obs. f. PILLOW, PILAU.

Pelrinage: see PELRINAGE.

Pelsy, -e. Now dial. [f. dial. pelse (also palse) refuse, trash + -Y.] Of little value, trashy.

Pelt (pelt), sb.¹ Also 7 peault. Appears early in 13th c. Evidently related to PELT sb.³, but actual formation obscure.

1. The skin of a sheep or goat with short wool on; also, the raw or undressed skin of a fur-bearing animal; a fell.

2. The beating of rain or snow; a pelting storm.

3. spec. A raw skin of a sheep, goat, or other animal stripped of its wool or fur; the commercial name for a skin in this state before tanning.

4. An outburst of temper, a rage. Cf. PELT v.²6.

Pelt, sb.² Now only dial. [app. a parallel form to pellet, found in mod.Eng. dial. in several senses, and assumed as the stem of PELT v.]

Pelt, v.¹ [Known from end of 15th century: origin uncertain.]

1. trans. To strike with many or repeated blows now, in Standard Eng. with something thrown); to assail with missiles.

b. To strike, as by something thrown.

2. intr. To strike, fall, or beat, as hail, rain, etc.

Pelt, sb.³ = PELT sb.¹ 6.

Pelta (pe·lta). Pl. peltae (-tī). [L. pelta, a. Gr. πέλτη, a small light shield or buckler.]

1. Antiq. A small light shield or buckler used by the ancient Greeks, Romans, etc.

2. transf. and fig.

Peltast (pe·ltæst). Gr. Antiq. [ad. Gr. πελταστής, f. πέλτη PELTA.] One of a body of soldiers in ancient Greece armed with the pelta.

Peltate (pe·lteit), a. Bot. [ad. mod.L. peltat-us, f. pelta PELTA: see -ATE².] Shield-shaped; usually of a leaf: Having the petiole joined to the under-surface of the blade at or near the middle (instead of at the base or end); hence, said of other stalked parts having similar attachment.

Pelta-ti-, Pelta-to-, used in combining forms of L. peltatus PELTATE, as in Peltatifid (-tā·tifid) divided in a peltate manner.

Pelter, sb.¹ [f. PELT v.¹ + -ER¹.]

1. One who pelts or assails with missiles.

Pelter, sb.² Obs. rare—¹. [f. PELT sb.¹ + -ER¹.] A dealer in skins or pelts.

Peltifolious, a. Bot. [f. pelta + -foli- leaf + -OUS.] Having peltate leaves.

Peltiform, a. [f. pelta + -FORM.] Shield-shaped.

Peltinerved, a. Bot. [f. pelta + NERVED.] Of a leaf: having the nerves radiating from the centre as in a peltate leaf.

Pelting, vbl. sb.¹ [f. PELT v.¹ + -ING¹.] The action of PELT v.¹; beating with missiles, etc.

Pelting, ppl. a.¹ [f. PELT v.¹ + -ING².] That pelts.

Pelting, *ppl. a.*

Peltish, *a. rare.*

Peltless, *a. rare.*

Peltogaster.

Peltoid, *a.*

Peltry, *sb.*

Peltry, *sb.*

Pelu, *sb.*

Pelure.

Pelvi-, combining form.

Pelviform, *a.*

Pelvimeter.

Pelvis.

Pelvic, *a.*

Pembroke.

Pemblico.

Pemmican.

Pemmicanize, *v.*

Pemphigoid, *a.*

Pemphigous, *a.*

Pemphigus.

Pemphix.

Pemptarchic.

Pen, *sb.*

Pen, *sb.*

Pen, *sb.*

Pen, *v.*

Pen, *v.*

Pen, *sb.*

Penal, *a.*

Penalize, *v.*

Penally, *adv.*

Penance, *sb.*

Penancel, *sb.*

Penanced.

Penancy.

Penang.

Penates.

Penceid.

Penal, *a.*

Penality.

Penance, *sb.*

Penance.

1. Ecclesiastical punishment, chiefly adjudged to the sin of fornication.

b. Suffering after death as a punishment for sins; the sufferings of purgatory, or the like.

3. transf. In various allusions to sense 2; in later use often coinciding with sense 4.

4. Poor fare, sorry cheer; as of one fasting or doing penance; to take penance, 'to take pot-luck'. Obs. rare.

†4. Pain, suffering, distress, sorrow, vexation. Obs.

†5. Punishment. Obs.

d. attrib. and Comb., in penance-doing sb. and adj., -fire, -gold, -pain, -sheet, -time.

Penance, v. trans. To subject to penance; to impose a penance; to discipline, chastise.

Hence **Penancing** vbl. sb.

Penanceless, a. rare. [f. PENANCE sb. + -LESS.] Without doing or undergoing penance.

Penancer. Obs. [a. OF. penean-, penancier, in both senses (13th c. in Godef.), ad. med.L. penitentiari-us (Du Cange): see PENITENTIARY.]

1. One who imposes penance; spec. a priest specially appointed to hear confession and impose penance in extraordinary cases, a penitentiary.

2. One undergoing penance. rare—⁰.

Penancy. Obs. rare. Also ponancy. Punishment; suffering (after death).

Pen and ink, pen-and-ink, phr.

a. Hit. The instruments of writing: see PEN sb.2 and INK sb. (Hyphened when this helps the sense.)

b. attrib. or as adj.

†Penard. Obs. rare—¹. A crooked pen-and-ink outline of a great turtle.

2. Short for pen-and-ink drawing: see 1.

3. As adj. (properly hyphened.)

1. Using pen and ink; occupied in writing; clerkly. Now rare or Obs.

2. Done, made, or executed with pen and ink; usually of a drawing or sketch; also, done or described in writing.

Penal, v. trans. and intr. (with hyphens): Using or carrying a pen and inkhorn, engaged in writing, clerkly; learned, pedantic (cf. INKHORN 2).

Pen and inkhorn, **Pen-and-inkhorn** clerk. Intermediate forms are seen in the OF. dial. pannecel, pannechel, paignichel, pengnecel, penechiel, penicillus, pencillus (Du Cange), indicating a phonetic series penecel, pencel, penso- or penicel, penecil. Passing through (as adj.) -il, -eill, etc.

Penang, var. PINANG, areca-nut or -tree.

Penang lawyer: see LAWYER 4.

Penannular (pīnæˈniūlᵃr), a. [Penn-, nearly, almost + ANNULAR.] Nearly annular; of the form of an almost complete ring; circular with a small part of the circumference wanting.

†Penant. Obs. Also -aunt-e. [ME. a. OF. penant, earlier penaunt:—late L. pænitent-em PENITENT (by which penant was superseded c 1500).] A penitent; one doing penance; in last quot., one suffering in purgatory.

St. Gregory 944 in Herrig's Archiv LVII. 69 Penaunt he semed wel of lijf.

For fals penantes men zal ham lok.

Thys maketh me to thowpe and dare That I am lyke a pore penaunce, In-to be blise of paradyse.

Penarious, a. Obs. rare—⁰. [f. L. penari-us of or pertaining to victuals, f. pen-us provision.]

†Penary. Obs. rare. Also ponary. [ad. L. penari-um store-house, f. pen-us provisions.] Pertaining to punishment, penal.

Penate. [ad. L. Penātis pl., perh. f. penus innermost part of a house, or penes within.] In ancient Roman mythology, the guardian deities of the household and of the state, who were worshipped in the interior of every dwelling-house; often coupled with Lares (see LAR); household gods. Also penātēs.

Penche, obs. f. PAUNCH sb. f. PINCH.

†Penchant (pᾱnʃⁿ), sb. [F. penchant, sb. use of pr. pple. of pencher to slope, incline = Pr. pensar, pensar:—L. type *pendicare from pendēre to hang.] A (strong or habitual) inclination; a favourable bias; liking.

Penchute (penˈtʃūt), sb. rare—⁰. [f. PEN sb.2 + -CHUTE.] = PENTROUGH.

Penchute (penˈʃȳt), sb. rare—¹. [f. PEN sb.2 + -CHUTE.] A trough containing water for the use of a somewhat conjoint fountain.

Pencil, Pencill: see PERIWIG, PENCEL.

Pencil (penˈsil). Forms: 4–7 pencel, 5–6 ponsel, pinselle, 6 (-)pensille, penselle, pinsel, pinsell, -ell, 6 pensil, -ill, 6– pencil, &c.

1. A painter's brush of camel's hair, fitch, sable, or other fine hair, gathered into a quill; one of small and fine make, suitable for delicate work. Now arch.

b. Formerly associated to a large brush, e.g. for spreading varnish, etc.

2. A thin cylinder or strip of such substance enclosed in a cylinder or strip of wood, used for writing, drawing, etc.; a black-lead (plumbago or graphite) or slate pencil.

b. In Scot. and north of Engl. spec. = Slate-pencil. Hence, a fine clay-slate or other laminated shale, of which slate-pencils are made.

Pencil. A kind of crayon or pencil-like stick of colouring matter, for tinting the eye-brows, eye-lashes, or lips, for theatrical or cosmetic purposes (eyebrow-pencil, lip pencil, etc.).

II. 3. A small tuft of hairs, bristles, or the like, springing from or close to a point in a surface. Now in Nat. Hist.

4. Optics. A set of rays converging to or diverging from a single point, or such number of them as may fall upon any surface or be considered collectively.

b. The particular form of this in painting, put for the painter's art, skill, or style; and transferred to word-painting or descriptive skill. Cf. BRUSH sb.2 2 b.

Pencil (penˈsil), v. [f. prec. sb.]

1. trans. To paint with a 'pencil' or brush (obs. or arch.); now, usually, to colour, tint, or mark with or as with a black-lead pencil.

b. To depict or represent with the pencil or brush; transf. to depict or paint in words (obs.); also (in later use), to outline, sketch, or delineate, in pencil.

2. To restrict or mark by pencil-lines.

3. trans. To treat or 'paint' (a wound, etc.) with something applied with a fine brush.

4. trans. To form into pencils (of light).

Penciller, -iler. [f. PENCIL v. + -ER¹.]

1. One who pencils; a draughtsman, a writer; spec. in Calico-printing, an artist who painted in part of the design, before the introduction of blocks.

2. Racing slang. A bookmaker's clerk.

3. A reporter. rare.

Pencilling, -iling, vbl. sb. [f. PENCIL v. + -ING¹.]

1. The action of the vb. PENCIL in various senses; esp. fine colouring or drawing; also transf. the fine tinting or marking of natural objects resembling that executed by a pencil.

2. concr. A drawing or sketch with a pencil; fig. a literary sketch or portrait.

Pencillipen, -cyon, obs. forms of PENSION.

Pen-clerk = A clerk whose stewardship extended merely to the use of the pen (as distinguished from clerk = clergyman or scholar); a clerk, a secretary; also fig.

Pencil-case (penˈsilˌkɛ²s). A holder for the reception of a pencil or pencil-lead (or of a similar slender stick of prepared aniline, etc.), usually of metal, and sometimes highly ornamented; also, a case of wood, leather, etc., for keeping pencils of any kind in.

Pencilled, ppl. a. [f. PENCIL v. + -ED¹.]

I. 1. Marked or furnished with a pencil.

2. Painted with a 'pencil' or fine brush; depicted with or as with a 'pencil'; now, usually, drawn or sketched 'in pencil'.

3. Marked with or as with a pencil; delicately marked or streaked with fine concentric lines (instead of masses) of colour or shading.

4. Written with a pencil.

Pencraft (penˈkrɑft). The craft or art of the pen; the occupation of, or skill in, writing; the business of a writer, writing, penmanship, authorship.

Pend, sb.1 [a. OF. pende:—L. pendita:—pendēre to hang. But in some cases aphetic f. append, APPEND v.] Obs.

1. To hang, to append.

b. intr. To belong; to depend. Also fig. (now dial.). 'To pen up, depend.'

c. intr. To be pendent, in suspense; to remain undecided.

Pend, sb.2 Sc. dial. Also 6 pent, pent-, pented; also 5 pent. [Aphetic f. append, APPEND v.¹, Cf. apendice.] 1. intr. To belong; pertain (to). b. trans. To hang.

†Pend, v.3 [app. a. F. pendre:—late L. pendēre to hang. But in some cases aphetic f. append, APPEND v.¹] 1. To hang.

2. To depend. &c. (now dial.)

Pendace, Sc. Obs. Also 6 pentace, -ace. [perh. f. PEND.]

Pendale-hanging (app.?)

Pendant (penˈdant), sb. [a. F. pendant, sb. use of pr. pple. of pendre to hang: cf. PENDANT a.] 1. Forms: 4-6 pendaunte, (4-5 -aunt), 5-6 -awnt, 6-7 pendannt, -ant, 5- pendant, -ent; 6 pendaint. L. = F. pendant = pente, slope.

I. 1. Slope, declivity, inclination (of a hill, etc.).

2. A loose hanging part of anything, usually of an ornamental character, as a knob, bead, tassel, etc.; now, chiefly, an ornament of some precious metal or stone, attached to a bracelet, necklace, etc.

b. A similar object in the form of a jewel, hanging from the ear.

c. spec. The pendant part of an ear-ring, an ear-pendant; a drop.

d. A drop; a pendent ornament.

II. Something that hangs or is suspended.

3. Naut. A short swallow-tailed pennant flown as the distinctive mark of a commodore's ship in a squadron.

Pendant (penˈdant), a. [a. F. pendant, pr. pple. of pendre.]

Penetrative (pe'nĭtrắtĭv), a. [ad. med.L. *penĕtrātīv-us*, f. ppl. stem of L. *penetrāre*: see -ATIVE.] Having the quality of penetrating.

1. Having the quality of piercing, entering, or making its way into anything; *spec.* Having the property of entering through the senses, or of keenly affecting the sense organs; sharp, pungent.

Penetrator (pe'nĭtrātŏr). [a. late L. *penetrātor*, agent-n. from *penetrāre*: see PENETRATE and -OR.] One who penetrates (*lit.* or *fig.*).

Penetrie, -y, *obs. ff. PANTRY*.

Pen-feather (pe'n-feðar). [f. PEN *sb.*[2] + FEATHER.]

1. A quill-feather of a bird's wing.

Pen-feathered, *ppl. a.* [f. PEN *sb.*[2] + -ED.]

Penfold, obs. form of PINFOLD.

Penful (pe'nful), *sb.* [f. PEN *sb.*[2] + -FUL.] The quantity (of ink) taken up by a pen at one dip.

Penguin (pe'ngwin, pengwin). Also 6-7 pengwin, *-wyn,* -gven, 7 -guine, (8 pin-).

Pen-gun. *Sc.* [f. PEN *sb.*[2] + GUN *sb.*] A toy air-gun made from a quill.

Penholder (pe'nhōˌldər). [f. PEN *sb.*[2] + HOLDER.]

Penial (pe'nĭăl), *a. Anat.* [f. PENIS + -AL.] Belonging to or connected with the penis.

†Penible, *a. Obs.* Forms: 4-5 penyble, 4-5 peyn, penyble; 5pein-, 7penible. [a. F. *penible*.]

Penibly, *adv. Obs.* Forms: 4-5 peynibly, -ably. [f. prec.]

Penicil (pe'nisǐl). *Nat. Hist.* [L. *penicillus* small brush.]

Penicillate (penisi'lǎt), *a. Nat. Hist.* [f. L. *pænicill-us* (see prec.) + -ATE.]

Penicilliform (penisi'lĭfōrm), *a.* [ad. mod.L. *penicilliform-is*, f. *penicill-us*: see -FORM.]

‖Penicillium (penisi'lĭŭm). *Bot.* [mod.L.]

Peninsula (pĭni'nsiŭlă), *sb.* [L. *pæninsula, f. pæne* almost + *insula* island.]

Peninsular (pĭni'nsiŭlăr), *a. (sb.).* [f. *peninsul-a* + -AR.]

Peninsulate (pĭni'nsiŭlǎt), *v.* [f. PENINSULA + -ATE.] To make into a peninsula.

Penis (pī'nis). Pl. **penes** (pī'nīz). [L.]

Penitence (pe'nĭtĕns). Also 4-5 penytence, (7 penni-). [a. F. *penitence* (11th c. in Littré), ad. L. *pænitentia.*]

Penitencer (pe'nĭtĕnsər). [a. OF. *penitencier*.] In the mediæval Church, a priest appointed to hear confession, assign penance, and give absolution in extraordinary cases.

Penitency (pe'nĭtĕnsĭ). *arch.* [f. as prec.: see -ENCY.] The quality or condition of being penitent.

Penitent (pe'nĭtĕnt), *a. and sb.* Also 4-5 penysaunt, 4-6 penytent. [a. OF. *penitent* (13th c. in Littré).]

Penitential (penĭte'nʃăl), *a. and sb.* Also 5-7 -nci-, 7 poeni-, penni-. [ad. med.L. *pænitentiālis*: see -AL.]

Penitentiary (penĭte'nʃărĭ), *a. and sb.* Also 5-7 -nci-, 7 poeni-, penni-. [ad. med.L. *pænitentiāri-us*.]

Penitently, *adv.* [f. PENITENT *a.* + -LY[2].] In a penitent manner, contritely.

Penitentness, *rare.* [f. as prec.] = PENITENCE.

†Penitive, *a. Obs. rare*[-1]. Punitive, penal.

Penitote, obsolete f. PERIDOT, *q.v.*

Penitude, *rare.* [f. L. *plēnus* full + -TUDE.]

Penk, orig. form of PINK *sb.*[3] a minnow.

Penknife (pe'nnaif). Pl. -knives (-naivz). [f. PEN *sb.*[2] + KNIFE.]

Penman (pe'nmăn). Pl. **penmen** (pe'nmĕn). [f. PEN *sb.*[2] + MAN.]

Penmanship (pe'nmănʃip). [f. prec. + -SHIP.]

Penna (pe'nă). *Ornith.* [L. *penna* feather.]

Pennache, **-ed**, obs. forms of PANACHE.

Pennaceous (pe'nā·ʃəs), *a. rare.* [f. L. *penna* feather + -ACEOUS.]

Supplement, p. 3873; Corrigenda, p. 4092; Spurious words, p. 4093; Books quoted, p. 4094

†Pennage. Obs. rare. [a. F. pennage (Amyot, 16th c.), f. penne plume: see -AGE.] = PLUMAGE.

Pennal, obs. form of PENNILL.

Pennal² (penæl). (Ger. pennal pen-case, school-boy, a med.L. pennale pen-case, f. penna pen.) Formerly, in German Protestant Universities, a slang name for a freshman, from their carrying about with them their pen-cases for use at lectures.

Hence **Pennalism** [Ger. and mod.L. pennalismus], an oppressive system of fagging practised upon freshmen in German Universities in the 17th century.

Pennance, -ans, obs. forms of PENANCE.

Pennant¹ (penant). [app. a compromise between PENDANT and PENNON, representing the usual nautical pronunciation of these words, of which it is now the most usual form.]

Pennated (pe·nēted), a. Now rare. [f. as prec. + -ATE².]

Penner¹ (penal). = PEN³ + -ER¹.] One who pens or words a writing, document, statement, etc.

Penner² (penal). Obs. exc. dial. Also -ur. [? f. PEN sb.²]

Penned (pend, poet. pe·ned), a. [f. PEN sb.²]

Penni (penni). [Welsh.] usually in pl.

Pennied (penid), a. [f. PENNY + -ED².]

Penniferous (peni·ferəs), a. Nat. Hist. [f. L. penni-fer + -OUS.]

Penniform (pe·nifom), a. [f. L. penna feather.]

Penning, vbl. sb.² [f. PEN v.² + -ING².]

Penninite (pe·ninəit). Min. [Named from Pennine + -ITE¹.]

Pennirved (pe·ninəvd), a. Bot. [f. L. penni-, comb. form of penna feather + NERVE + -ED².]

Pennisome, a. Obs. ? nonce-wd. [f. PENNY + -SOME.]

Penniston, obs. form of PENISTONE.

Pennite, obs. form of PENNET.

Pennon (penən). Forms: 4-8 penon, 4-7 penoun, 4-9 pennon, 5-7 pynoun, etc. [ME. penon, OF. penon, OCat. pano, It. pennone.]

Pennoned (penənd), a. [f. PENNON + -ED².]

Penny (peni). Forms: sing. 1 pening, penig, etc.

Penny. [OE. pening, penig, peneg, cogn. w. OFris. panning, penning.]

I. Illustration of forms.

1. Sing. a. 1 pending, pening, -ine, peninge.

2. Pl. a. 1 peningas, pending-, -as.

B. Signification.

I. Original senses.

1. An English coin of the value of ¹⁄₁₂ of a shilling, or ²⁄₄₀ of a pound; originally and for many centuries of silver, in later times of copper, now (since 1860) of bronze.

2. With prefixed numerals, etc.

3. A coin: applied with a defining or descriptive adjunct to various coins of the British Isles, of distinct origin from the ordinary penny. Now Hist.

4. Used as a general or vague word for a piece of money; hence, a sum of money, money.

II. Phrases and Proverbs.

III. Transferred uses: chiefly elliptical.

IV. Attrib. and Comb.

Penny-grass. [f. PENNY + GRASS.] Popular name of three different plants: a. Navelwort or Wall Pennywort, *Cotyledon Umbilicus*; b. Marsh Pennywort, *Hydrocotyle vulgaris* (in both cases from the round leaves); c. Yellow-rattle, *Rhinanthus Crista-galli* (from the coins).

Penny-father. *Obs.* [f. PENNY + FATHER.] A man who is too careful of his pence; an old miser, a niggard, skinflint, penurious fellow.

†**Penny-prick.** *Obs.* An old game of which the nature is uncertain.

Penny-rent. *Obs.* [See RENT.] Rent paid (or received) in money; annual (or periodical) payment in cash; income in money, revenue.

Penny-rot. *Obs.* [See Rot *sb.*] A name for Marsh Pennywort, from its round leaves, and supposed of causing rot in sheep.

Penny post, penny-post. [See Post *sb.*] An organization for the conveyance of letters or packets at an ordinary charge of a penny each.

Penny-a-line. [The phrase (*a*) *penny a line* used attrib.] Of writing or a writer: Paid at the rate of a penny a line: of cheap and superficial literary ability. (Cf. PENNY-A-LINER.)

Penny-a-liner. [f. as prec. + -ER.] A writer for newspaper or journal who is paid at a penny a line, or at a low rate (usually implying inferior quality).

Penny-a-line-r *v. trans.* (*nonce-wd.*), to write at a penny a line; to review in the style of a penny-a-liner (see next).

Penny-stone. *Obs.* form of PEN, PENNY.

1. *Sc.* and *north.* A flat round stone used as a quoit; also, the game played with these.

2. A kind of ironstone, occurring in nodules, found in the Coalbrookdale coalfield, in Shropshire.

Pennystone, *Obs.* form of PENISTONE.

Penny-weight. [f. PENNY + WEIGHT.] A measure of weight, equal to 24 grains, $\frac{1}{20}$ of an ounce Troy, or $\frac{1}{480}$ of a Troy pound; ... Abbreviated *dwt.*

Pennyroyal. [pen/iróial]. Forms: pennyroyal, etc. A species of mint (*Mentha Pulegium*), with small leaves and prostrate habit; formerly much cultivated and esteemed for its supposed medicinal virtues.

Penny-wise, *adj. phr. or a.* [cf. PENNY.] Wise or prudent in regard to pence; careful (*esp. over-careful*) in small matters; usually in phr. *penny-wise and pound-foolish*, thrifty in small matters while careless or wasteful in large ones.

Pennyroyal-tree, *Satureia viminea* (*Treas. Bot.*, 1866); pennyroyal-water, a liquor distilled from the leaves of pennyroyal, formerly used in medicine.

Pennywort. [f. PENNY + WORT.] Name for several plants with rounded leaves.
1. (Distinctively *Wall Pennywort*.) [Umbilicus *or* Cotyledon Umbilicus, N.O. Crassulaceae], a common plant in the west of England and Wales.

Pennywort *or Water Pennywort*, *Hydrocotyle vulgaris*, ... an umbelliferous herb with rounded peltate leaves, growing in marshy places.

Pennyworth (pe'nipwurθ, -wʉrθ, *or* penpmurθ). Forms: a. 1 penis weorð, peninga-wurð, 4 paneworþ, 4-5 peni-, 6-7 penni-, -8 penny-, 5-6 penni-worth, (etc., 6 penyworth, penner'th, penn'worth, 8-9 pennorth). [f. PENNY + WORTH.]
1. The amount of anything which may be bought for a penny; as much as is worth a penny.

Penology (pīnǭ'lǒdʒi). [f. PENO- (L. *poena* penalty, f. *poena* penalty, punishment + -LOGY.] The scientific study of the punishment and prevention of crime; the science of prison and reformatory management.

Penolological, [f. as prec. + -ICAL.] Of or pertaining to penology.

Penologist (pīnǭ'lǒdʒist). [f. PENOLOGY + -IST.] One who studies or is versed in penology.

Penso (pēn'sō). *nonce-wd.* [f. PENSIVE.]

Penserous (pen'sēro), *a. sb.* [From the title of Milton's poem *Il Penseroso* (1632), a. obs. It. *penseroso* (1578 in Tasso *Dialeghi*), now *pensieroso* (Florio 1598), f. *pensiere* thought.] Melancholy, brooding, melancholy.

Penseroso (pensērō'sō), *sb.*

Penship. *rare*−1. [f. PEN *sb.*2 + SHIP.] Use of the pen; writing. ('PENMANSHIP.)

Pensile (pen'sil, -sail), *a.* (*sb.*) [ad. L. *pensilis*, f. *pens-* ppl. stem of *pendēre* to hang.] 1. Suspended from above, hanging down, pendent.

Pensility. [f. PENSILE + -ITY.] The quality of being pensile; hanging position.

Pensively, -ill, *var.* PENCEL; obs. ff. PENCIL.

Pension (pen'ʃən). Forms: 4-6 pension, -cioun, -cion, -cyon, -syon, etc. [a. F. *pension* (12th c. in Hatz.-Darm.), ad. L. *pensiōn-em* payment, rent, f. *pens-*, ppl. stem of *pendēre* to weigh, pay.]

1. A payment, a tribute, tax, charge, or rent (*obs.*)

4. An annuity or other periodical payment made by a government, a company, or an employer of labour, in consideration of past services or of the relinquishment of rights, claims, or emoluments.

b. A sum of money paid periodically to a person.

Pension (ponsyón'), *sb.* [Fr.] A boarding-house; a continental establishment providing board and lodging; ...

Pension, *v.* [f. PENSION *sb.*] *trans.* To grant a pension to; to dismiss or retire with a pension.

Pensionary. [ad. med.L. *pensionarius*.] ... The title of the chief magistrate of certain towns in Holland.

Pentametered, *ppl. a.* written in pentameters.

Penta-metrize *v. trans.*, to make into, or like, a pentameter.

Pentandria (pentǎ'ndrĭă), *Bot.* [mod.L.] *Bot.* The general name of the parasitism of the pentaschion series.

Pentane (pĕ'ntĕn), *Chem.* [f. Gr. πέντε five + -ANE]

Pentangular *a.* [f. as prec. + *angular*.] Having five angles or angular points.

Pentapetalous (-pĕ'tălŏs) *a.* Having five petals.

Pentaploid, *Biol.*

Pentapolis (pentă'pŏlĭs), [L. a. Gr. πεντάπολις.] A confederacy or group of five towns.

Pentaptote *a.*

Pentarch *a. Bot.*

Pentarchy (pĕ'ntărkĭ). Also *2 erron.* pempt-. A government by five rulers.

Pentateuch (pĕ'ntătěūk). [ad. Lat. form *pentateuch-us.*] The first five books of the Old Testament (Genesis, Exodus, Leviticus, Numbers, and Deuteronomy).

Pentateuchal (pentătěū'kăl) *a.*

Pentstyle (pĕ'ntstăĭl), *a. sb. Arch.*

Pentasyllable (pentăsĭ'lăb'l) a. and *sb.* having five syllables.

Pentathlon (pentă'θlŏn). *Gr. Antiq.* An athletic contest consisting of five exercises.

Pentathionic (pentăθĭŏ'nĭk), *a. Chem.*

Pentacle (pĕ'ntăk'l), *a. sb.*

Penthemimer (penθĭmĭ'mĕr). *sb. Gr. & Rom. Antiq.* Hence **Penthemi'meral**, *a.*

Penthouse (pĕ'nthous), *sb.* Also **8 pentice, pentis.**

Pent-roof (pĕ'ntrūf). A sloping roof.

Penthouse *v.*

Pentile: see PANTILE.

Penult (pĕ'nŭlt, pěnŭ'lt). [Originally an abbreviated way of writing the word PENULTIMA.] The last syllable but one.

Pentyl (pĕ'ntĭl), *Chem.*

Pentode *Electr.*

Penultim *a.* and *sb. Obs.*

Penultima (pěnŭ'ltĭmă), *n. and sb. Lat.* properly *penultima,* fem. of *penultimus.*

Penultimate (pěnŭ'ltĭměĭt), *a. and sb.*

Penumbra (pěnŭ'mbră), *n.* [mod.L. (Kepler, 1604), f. PENE-, L. *paene* almost + *umbra* shadow.]

Penumbral (pěnŭ'mbrăl), *a.*

Penurious (pěnĭū'rĭŏs), *a.*

Penuriously, *adv.*

Penuriousness.

Penury (pĕ'nĭūrĭ). Poverty, want, scantness.

Peon (pī'ŏn, pĕ'ŏn). [a. Sp. & Pg. *peão,* *peon,* f. late L. *pedōn-em* foot-soldier.]

Peony, **Peonage**, variant of PEAN.

PEPPER-AND-SALT

Peonage ... [f. prec. + -AGE.] The work or service of a peon; the system of having or using peons or enslaved debtors.

Peonism (pī'ŏnĭz'm). [f. PEON + -ISM.] = PEONAGE.

Peony. Forms: a. 1 peonie. β. 3 pyone, (pioine), 4 piane, 4–5 pione, 5 pyon, -onye, pionye, peony, 6–9 pioney, 6–7 pionie, peonie, 6–9 piony, 7 peiony, peonie, 8 peony, 7– peony. ... A plant (or flower) of the genus Paeonia (N.O. Ranunculaceae), comprising stout herbs, or rarely shrubs, with large handsome globular flowers of various shades of red and white, often becoming double under cultivation.

People (pī'p'l). sb. Forms: a. 3–6 peple; (3–5 pepel, -il, -ul, 5–6 -ill, 5–6 -yll; 6 Sc. peiple, 5 peopel, -ull); 7 peeple, 6 (pepple, -yll, -ull); 4–5 pupile. β. 4–5 peple, 6 -ille, 5–6 (Rolls of Parlt.) Pr. poble, poeble, 5p. puible, ... 1. A body of persons composing a community, tribe, race, or nation; = FOLK 1.

c. People. v. [f. People sb.] trans. To fill or stock (with persons or inhabitants).

Peopleless, a. [f. People sb. + -LESS.] Having no people or population; uninhabited.

Peopler (pī'plǝr). [f. People v. + -ER¹.] One who peoples or causes the peopling of a country; a colonizer; an inhabitant.

Peopling (pī'plĭŋ), vbl. sb. [f. prec. + -ING¹.] The action of the vb. PEOPLE; settling with or occupation by people or inhabitants.

Pepper (pe'pǝr), sb. Forms: 1 piper, pipor, 4 peper, 4–6 pepre, 6–9 peper, 6– pepper. ... A well-known pungent condiment, derived from species of Piper and allied genera (see 2), used from ancient times for flavouring, and acting as a digestive.

Pepper, v. [f. prec. sb.] 1. trans. To sprinkle with pepper; to flavour or season with pepper; to treat with pepper.

Pepper-and-salt. A kind of cloth made of dark- and light-coloured wool woven together, the result being of black and white, dark grey and light grey, or the like; cloth of mingled colours.

Pepper-box.

2. Name for the American plant called 'harbinger of spring' (*Erigenia bulbosa*); from the colour-contrast of its white petals and dark anthers. *U.S.*

Pepper-box.

1. A small box, usually cylindrical, with a perforated lid, used for sprinkling powdered pepper.

b. In allusive expressions. (Cf. PEPPER *sb.* 4.)

c. *transf.* Applied contemptuously to a small cylindrical turret or cupola.

Pepper-caster, castor. [See CASTOR².]

1. A small vessel with a perforated top, usually one of the castors of a cruet-stand, for sprinkling pepper at table.

2. *transf.* & *fig.*

b. *†Of* peppercorns colour; dusky black.

Peppercorn (pe'pəɪkɔɪn). Forms: see PEPPER, f. PEPPER *sb.* + CORN *sb.*¹ 5.

1. The dried berry of Black Pepper.

2. *fig.* Applied to anything of very small value or importance.

b. Formerly often, and still sometimes, stipulated for as a quit-rent or nominal rent: see *quit*.

3. Formerly *attrib.*, now *Comb.*

Pepperer (pe'pərəɪ). *sb.* [In 1, 1 PEPPER *sb.* + -ER¹.] **1.** A dealer in pepper and spices; a grocer.

Pepperidge (pe'pərdʒ). Also *-age*; see also PIPERIDGE.

1. A variant of PIPERIDGE, local English name of the barberry.

2. The Black Gum, Sour Gum, or Tupelo, a North American tree of the genus *Nyssa*, having very tough wood.

Pepper-grass. Any species of *Lepidium*, as *L. sativum*, common garden-cress; from the pungent taste.

Peppering, *ppl. a.* [See -ING².]

Pepperish (pe'pəriʃ), *a.* [-ISH¹.]

Peppermint (pe'pəɪmint). [f. PEPPER + MINT *sb.*¹: app. after EAU.]

1. A species or subspecies of mint (*Mentha piperita*), cultivated for its essential oil (*oil of peppermint*: see 2).

Pepper-tree. **1.** An evergreen tree or shrub of S. America, *Schinus Molle* (N.O. *Anacardiaceæ*).

Pepper-water.

Pepperwood. Name given to several trees having pungent or aromatic wood or bark.

Pepperwort. [See WORT.]

Peppery (pe'pəri), *a.* [f. PEPPER + -Y.]

Pepsin (pe'psin). Also formerly *-ine*. [mod. (Schwann 1836), Poggendorff *Annalen* XXXVIII. 358), f. Gr. πέψις digestion.]

Peptic (pe'ptik), *a.* and *sb.* [ad. Gr. πεπτικός, f. πέπτειν to digest.]

Peptone (pe'ptoʊn). *Chem.* [a. Ger. *pepton* (C. G. Lehmann, 1849, in *Ber. Sächs. Gesellsch.* f. Wissensch. *Math.-Phys.* Cl. I. 115).]

Peptonize (pe'ptonaiz). *trans.* To convert (a protein) into a peptone.

Peptotoxin (peptoʊ'tɒksin). [f. PEPTO(NE + TOXIN.] A poisonous alkaloid.

Per (pɜɹ), *prep.* Latin (Ital. and Old French) preposition, meaning 'through, by means of'; in med.L. and Fr. also in a distributive sense = 'for every'.

4. per contra [It.], on the opposite side (of an account, etc.); on the other hand; as a set-off.

5. per annum (So much) by the year, every year.

6. per centum, per cent (So much) by the hundred; in the hundred.

7. per procuration (commonly abbreviated *per proc.*, *per pro.*, *p.p.*; sometimes *as per procuration*): by procuration, by the action of a procurator or official agent, by proxy or deputy.

8. per saltum, by a leap, at one bound, without intermediate steps, all at once. (Rarely *attrib.*)

9. per se, by or in itself (himself, herself, themselves); intrinsically, essentially, without reference to anything (or any one) else.

†b. Formerly used in naming a letter which by itself forms a word (*cf. per se se in A per se A*, O per se O, etc.); or a symbol which by itself stands for a word (*and per se and* = AMPERSAND); hence allusively: see A, I, O (the letters).

PER- prefix, repr. L. *per-*, *per* prep.

Peract (pe'rakt), *v.* Now *rare*. [f. L. *peract-*, ppl. stem of *peragere* to perform, accomplish, f. *per-* (PER- 1) + *agere* to drive, do.] *trans.* To practise, perform, accomplish, carry out.

Peradventure (perad'ventjəɹ, -vɛn-), *adv.* and accent(*††*), [a. OF. *per aventure*, *par aventure*, by chance. On the one side this was syncopated to *par-, paraunter, peraunter*; on the other, the form began in 15th c. to be conformed to L. spelling as *peradventure*, which in 16th c. superseded the earlier forms.]

A. Illustration of Forms.

B. Signification.

Peragrate (pe'ragreit), *v.* Now *rare*. [f. L. *peragrat-*, ppl. stem of *peragrare* to travel through.]

Peragration (pe'ragreijən). *Now rare.* [f. PERAGRATE: see prec.] The action of peragrating; a travelling through or traversing.

Peral (pɛ'rəl), *n.* The South American fish, the peral.

Peramble (pe'ræmbl), *v.* [f. next: cf. PREAMBLE.] A place for walking in; an ambulatory, cloister.

†Peramble, v. Obs. Also 6-bal, 6-7 -buie. [f. L. *perambulāre* (see PERAMBULATE), conformed to AMBLE v.] To walk about, to perambulate (*trans.* and *intr.*); also *fig.* to wander, ramble.

Perambulant (pĕrǣ mbȯlănt), a. *rare*. [ad. L. *perambulant-em*, pr. pple. of *perambulāre* (see PERAMBULATE).] Perambulating, strolling, itinerant.

†Perambulate, ppl. a. Obs. In 6 -at. [ad. L. *perambulāt-us*, pa. pple.] Perambulated.

Perambulate (pĕrǣ mbȯlēit), v. [f. L. *perambulāt-*, ppl. stem of *perambulāre* to walk through, all over : *ambulāre* to walk : see -ATE[3].]

Perambulation (pĕrǣmbȯlēi·ʃən), sb. [a. AF. *perambulation*, med.L. *perambulātiōn-*.]

Perambulator (pĕrǣ·mbȯlēitə(r)), sb. [f. prec. + -OR[2].]

†Perambulatory, sb. Obs. [f. L. *perambulatōri-um*.]

Perambulatory, a. [f. L. *perambulātōri-us*.]

†Perameles (pĕrǎmī·līz), Zool. [mod.L. (G. St. Hilaire) f. Gr. παρα beside, + L. *mēles*, *mēlis* a marten or badger.]

Peramble — see PARAMOUNT, etc.

Peranof, **Peramour** : see PARAMOUNT, etc.

Peranter, obs. variant of PERADVENTURE.

Perantique (pĕrǎntī·k), a. *nonce-wd.*

Perarate, var. PERARATION.

†Perbreak, -brake, v. Obs. Forms: 4-6 perdrake (4 pore-), 6 5c. perbraik. [f. PER- 2 c + BREAK v.[1].]

†Perbreak, sb. Obs. [f. prec.]

Perbreaker. *Obs.* [f. prec.]

Percale (pĕrkǣ·l, pə(r)kǣ·l). Forms: 7-8 percalla, -callia, cambric, 8 - percale. [a. F. *percale*; cf. Pers. *pargālah* a rag.]

Percaline (pɜ̄·rkəlīn, -lĭn). [a. F. *percaline*, dim. of *percale* : see prec.]

Percarbide (pǎ(r)ǎ·bid). *Chem.* [f. PER- 5 + CARBIDE.]

Perceant (pɜ̄·rsĭǎnt), a. [a. OF. *perceant*, pr. pple. of *percer* to pierce.]

Percavel, **Perceval** : see PARCEL, PERCEVAL.

Perceivance (pĕrsī·văns). *Obs. exc. dial.* [f. PERCEIVE v. + -ANCE.]

Perceive (pĕrsī·v), v. Forms: 4-7 perceyve, -ceive, -ceave, 4-6 perceve, etc. [a. OF. *perçeivre*, *parçoivre* (stressed stem *perceiv-*, *parceiv-*), f. L. *percipĕre* to take wholly, etc.]

Perceived (pĕrsī·vd), ppl. a. [f. prec. + -ED[1].]

Perceiver (pĕrsī·və(r)). [f. PERCEIVE v. + -ER[1].]

Perceiving (pĕrsī·viŋ), vbl. sb. [f. PERCEIVE v. + -ING[1].]

Perceiving, ppl. a. [f. as prec. + -ING[2].]

Percel, obs. form of PARCEL.

Percent, **per cent** (pər se·nt), phr. (sb.) Usually with full-stop (*per cent.*), as f. an abbreviation of L. *per centum*, which is the form used in Acts of Parliament and most legal documents.

Percentage (pəse·ntĕdʒ). [f. prec. + -AGE.]

Percentile (pəse·ntəil, -ĭl). *a.* and *sb.* [f. PER CENT + -ILE.]

Perceptibility (pərse·ptibi·lĭti). [f. next : see -ITY. Cf. F. *perceptibilité* (Diderot, 18th c.).]

Perceptible (pərse·ptib'l), a. [ad. late L. *perceptibil-is* (Cassiod., Boeth.), f. *percip-ĕre* to PERCEIVE: see -BLE. Cf. OF., mod.F. *perceptible*.]

Perceptibly (pərse·ptibli), adv. [f. prec. + -LY[2].]

Perception (pəse·pʃən). *Also* 5 -sepion, -ceptioune. [In earlier senses, a. OF. *perception*, *percepcion* (13th c. in Littré) in later senses, ad. L. *perceptiōn-em*, n. of action from *percipĕre* to take, receive, PERCEIVE.]

Perceptional (pəse·pʃənăl), a. [f. prec. + -AL[1].]

Perceptive (pəse·ptiv), a. [f. L. *percept-*, ppl. stem of *percipĕre* + -IVE.]

Perceptively (pəse·ptivli), adv. [f. prec. + -LY[2].]

Perceptivity (pərse·ptiv·ĭti). [f. prec. + -ITY.]

Percepto-, combining form from L. *percept-um* etc.

Perceptual (pəse·ptiǔǎl), a. [f. L. type *perceptu-s* + -AL[1].]

Percevance, var. of PERCEIVANCE.

Perceve, **Percevaunce**, -ceyve, etc. f. PER- SEVERE, PERCEIVE.

Perch (pɜ̄rtʃ), sb.[1] Forms: 4-6 perche, 7-8 pearch, 7- perch. [a. F. *perche* (Pliny), cf. Gr. πέρκη ; cf. salmon PERCH.] A common spiny-finned freshwater fish (*Perca fluviatilis*) of Europe and the British Isles, the flesh of which is used as food.

Perch (pɑːtʃ), sb.¹ ...

Perch, sb.²

Perchance (pɑːˈtʃɑːns), adv. (a.) arch.

Perché, obs. form of PERCH, PIERCE.

Perched (pɑːtʃt), ppl. a.

Percher (ˈpɜːtʃə(r)). A person or animal that perches.

Percheron (ˈpɜːtʃərɒn). [Fr. adj.]

Perchers, obs. form of PURCHASE.

Perching, vbl. sb.

Perching, ppl. a.

Perchloric, **perchloro-**.

Perchloride (pɜːˈklɔːraɪd).

Percid (ˈpɜːsɪd), a. and sb.

Percipience (pɜːˈsɪpɪəns).

Percipiency.

Percipient (pɜːˈsɪpɪənt), a. and sb.

Percnopterus.

Percoid (ˈpɜːkɔɪd), a. and sb.

Percolate (ˈpɜːkəleɪt), v.

Percolation (pɜːkəˈleɪʃən).

Percolative (ˈpɜːkəleɪtɪv), a.

Percolator (ˈpɜːkəleɪtə(r)).

Percomorph, **-oid**.

Percomorphous adj.

Percontation.

Percurrent (pɜːˈkʌrənt), a.

Percursory (pɜːˈkɜːsərɪ), a.

Percuss (pɜːˈkʌs), v.

Percussion (pɜːˈkʌʃən).

Percussive (pɔ:kɹˈsiv), a. (sb.) [f. L. percuss-, ppl. stem of percutĕre (see PERCUSS) + -IVE.] Having the property of striking; of, pertaining to, characterized by, or connected with percussion.

Percussor (pɔ:kɹˈsɔɹ), [a. L. percussor a striker, agent-n. from percutĕre: see PERCUSS.] One who or that which percusses or strikes; spec. an instrument for medical percussion; a percussion-hammer.

Percutaneous (pɔ:kiutˈeiniəs), a. [f. L. per cutem through the skin + -aneous, after cutaneous: cf. circumforaneous, subterraneous.] Made, done, or effected through the skin. Hence **Percuta·neously** adv., through the skin.

Percute, v. [ad. L. percutĕre, f. per + quatĕre to shake.] To strike; to beat. Hence **Percu·tient** a., striking, percussive; as sb., a striking agent.

Percutient (pɔ:kiuˈʃient), a. and sb. [ad. L. percutient-em, pr. pple. of percutĕre to strike through, etc.: see PERCUSS.] A. adj. Striking, percussive. B. sb. Something that strikes; the striking agent or body.

Perdifoil, perdifol, a. (Anglicized f.) A plant which usually loses its leaves; a deciduous plant. So † **Perdifo·lious** a., perennial.

Perdigon, variant of PERDIGON Obs.

Perdie, erroneous form of PRODIGY Obs.

Perdigwena, variant of PERDIGON Obs.

Perdix The Latin word for 'partridge' retained in the Douay Bible, and used in Ornithology as a generic name: see PARTRIDGE, PERDICINE.

Perdon(e, obs. form of PARDON.

Perdricide, a partridge-killer; in quots. appositive = Partridge-killing.

Perdrigon (pɛɹdigon). (Also 6 perdregon, 7 perdigon.) [a. F. perdrigon (Littré), in 16th c. perdigone, in Cotgr. perdigouu, in Pr. perdigon, perdigoun, properly 'young partridge'.]

Perdu (pɛɹdiu·, pɜˈɹdiu, ‖ pɛɹdy), a. and sb. [Also 7 pur-due; par-, perdieu, -dew.] [a. F. perdu 'lost, perished' (fem. perdue)... A. adj. (or sb. pple.)

Perdurable, a. [a. OF. par-, perdurable (12th c. in Godef.)... The mod. word is a new formation from perdurable]

Perdurance, Perdureli, a strong stubborn enmity.

Perduellion (pɜ:diuˈelliən). Rom. and Sc. Law. [ad. L. perduellion-em, f. perduellis: see PERDUELLION.] Hostility against the state or government; treason.

Perdure, v. intr. Obs. To last; to endure continuously.

Peregrinate (peˈregrineit), v. [f. L. peregrīnat-, ppl. stem of peregrīnārī to sojourn or travel abroad, f. peregrīn-us foreign, a foreigner: see PEREGRINE. Cf. F. pérégriner, Sp. peregrinar.] To travel from place to place; to sojourn in foreign countries.

Peregrinator (peˈregrineitɔɹ). Now only affected. [a. L. peregrīnātor, agent-n. from peregrīnārī to PEREGRINATE.] One who peregrinates; a traveller in foreign lands, or (loosely) from place to place; a pilgrim; a wanderer.

Peregrination (peregrineiˈʃən). [a. F. pérégrination (14th c. in Littré), or ad. L. peregrīnātiōn-em, n. of action from peregrīnārī to PEREGRINATE. Cf. It. peregrinazione, Sp. peregrinacion.]

Peregrine, peregrin (peˈregrin), a. and sb. [ad. L. peregrīn-us coming from foreign parts, foreign, a foreigner, f. pereger that is abroad, on a journey, peregrē abroad, to or from foreign parts, f. per through + ager field, territory, land, country.]

Peregrinity (peregriˈniti). [ad. F. pérégrinité (Rabelais 16th c.), or ad. L. peregrīnitās the condition of being a foreigner or alien, etc.]

4. **Peregrine falcon** (also 4-5 fawcon peregryn(e, 6 fawcon pelegryne, and see B. 3): a typical species of falcon (Falco peregrinus) of very wide distribution, and formerly held in the greatest esteem for hawking.

Peremptor, a. (sb.) Sc. Obs. Forms: 6 peremptor. [ad. L. peremptor, f. perimĕre to destroy.]

Peremptorily (peˈremptɔrili), adv. [f. PEREMPTORY + -LY.] In a peremptory manner; so as to preclude debate, dispute, or refusal.

Peremptoriness (peˈremptɔrines). [f. as prec. + -NESS.] The quality or character of being peremptory; positiveness, absoluteness; conclusiveness, imperativeness, assurance, dogmatism, imperiousness; fixed determination.

Peremptory (peˈremptɔri), a. (sb.) Also 6-7 peremptorie. [a. AF. peremptorie, F. péremptoire (14th c. in Hatz.-Darm.).]

Peremptory. ... (Of a contention, claim, etc.)

... By a peremptory order; without fail. *Obs.* ...

... **Perendinate** (pĕrĕndi·nāt), *v.* [f. ppl. stem of med.L. *perendinārī* ...] *intr.* To put off to the day after to-morrow; to defer.

Peremptorily. ...

Perennial, *a.* and *sb.*

Perennially, *adv.*

Perennibranch (pĕrĕ·nibæŋk), *a.* and *sb.*

Perennibranchiate, *a.*

Perennity.

Perfect, *a.* (*sb.* and *adv.*)

Perfected.

Perfectedly.

Perfecter.

Perfectibilian, Perfectibilist.

Perfectibilitarian.

Perfectibility.

Perfectible.

Perfection.

Perfectional.

Perfectionate, *v.*

Perfectionated ... **Perfectionating** ...

Perfectionation, vbl. sb. [n. of action from prec. + -ATION.] The action of bringing to perfection, perfecting; the fact of being made perfect.

Perfectioner.

Perfectioning, vbl. sb. [f. PERFECTION v. + -ING.]

Perfectionism. [after PERFECTIONIST + -ISM.] A system or doctrine of religious, moral, social, or political perfection; esp. the theory that moral perfection can be or has been attained by man; spec. the system of the Perfectionists of Oneida Creek, N.Y.

Perfectionist. [f. PERFECTION + -IST.]

Perfective (pǝ̄fe·ktiv), a. (sb.) Now rare. [ad. L. type *perfectīvus (perh. in mod.L.: cf. It. perfettivo, Sp. perfectivo): see PERFECT v. and -IVE.]

Perfectly (pǝ̄·fektli), adv.— Forms: see PERFECT a. [f. PERFECT a. + -LY.] In a perfect manner or degree.

Perfector (pǝ̄fe·ktǝr). [a. L. perfector, agent-n. from perficĕre to accomplish, etc.: see PERFECT.]

†Perfectorious, a. Obs. rare⁻¹.

†Perfectory, a. Obs. rare⁻¹. [L. perfectōri-us.]

Perfectress. [f. PERFECTOR + -ESS.]

Perfectuation. Obs. rare⁻¹.

Perfectuous, a. Obs. rare.

Perfervent, a. rare. [f. PER- + FERVENT.]

Perfervid (pǝ̄fǝ̄·vid), a. mod.L. perfervid-us, f. PER- + fervidus FERVID.]

Perfervidity. Obs. rare.

Perfervour, Perfervidness, also **Perfervent**, perfervid quality.

Perficient (pǝ̄fi·ʃ(i)ent), a. [ad. L. perficient-em, pr. pple. of perficĕre to complete, accomplish: see PERFECT a.]

Perfix, v. Obs.

Perfixed, perfixt ppl. a.

†Perfidiance Obs. rare⁻¹.

Perfidious (pǝ̄fi·diǝs), a. [ad. L. perfidiōsus, f. perfidia PERFIDY.] Of persons.

Perfidiously, adv.

Perfidiousness.

Perfidy (pǝ̄·fidi). Also 6 -ie. [ad. L. perfidia, or a. F. perfidie (16th c. in Godef. Compl.).]

†Perfit, Perfite, obs. forms of PERFECT.

Perfix ...

Perflable, a. Obs. [L. perflābilis.]

Perflate, v. Now rare. [f. L. perflāt-, ppl. stem of perflāre to blow through, ventilate.]

Perflation (pǝ̄flē·ʃǝn). [ad. late L. perflātiōn-em, n. of action from perflāre: see prec.]

Perforable.

Perforant (pǝ̄·fǝrant), a. [ad. L. perforant-em, pr. pple. of perforāre to PERFORATE.] Perforating.

Perforate (pǝ̄·fǝrēt), v. [f. L. perforāt-, ppl. stem of perforāre.]

Perforated ppl. a.

Perforating ppl. a.

Perforation (pǝ̄fǝrē·ʃǝn). [ad. late L. perforātiōn-em, n. of action from perforāre.]

Perforative.

Perforator (pǝ̄·fǝrētǝr). [agent-n. in L. form, from perforāre to PERFORATE.]

Perforatory, a.

Perforce (pǝ̄fǝ̄·s), adv., sb. — Forms: 4 par force, 4-5 parforce, 6- perforce. [ME. a. OF. par force, by force.]

Perform (pǝ̄fǝ̄·m), v. — Forms: 4-5 parfourne, perfourne, 5- perform, 4-5 par-, perfourme, 5 parfourmy, 4 parfourm. [ME. a. OF. parfourmer, parfourmen, parfourmen.]

Performable (pǝ̄fǝ̄·mǎb'l), a. [f. PERFORM v. + -ABLE.] Capable of being performed.

Performance (continued)

An issue no lesse performable then reasonable. — **Performancer** *Obs.*, one who goes through a performance, a performer. — **Performant** *Obs.*

Performation *Obs.* [f. *Perform* or *Af. performer*: see -ation.] The action of performing; = Performance (in its various early senses).

1. The carrying out of a command, duty, purpose, promise, etc.; execution, discharge, fulfilment. Often antithetical to *promise*.

2. The accomplishment, execution, carrying out, working out of anything ordered or undertaken; the doing of any action or work; working action. (personal or mechanical.)

Performer (pəɹfɔˑɹməɹ). [f. Perform + -er [1].] One who (or that which) performs.

1. One who carries out or fulfils a promise, undertaking, etc.; one who executes or does an action or piece of work; an agent, doer, worker.

2. One who performs a part in a play, a piece of music, athletic exercises, tricks, etc., as a public exhibition of art or skill; one who gives or takes part in a performance or public entertainment; an actor, player, singer, etc.

Performing, *vbl. sb.* [f. Perform + -ing [1].] The action of the verb Perform, in various senses.

Perfume (pəɹfiūˑm), *sb.* Also 6 par-. [a. F. *parfum* (1528) in Caumont *Voy. en Jérusalem* 131: *pasuit*/*parfumée*, f. *parfumer* to perfume: see next.]

1. *a. orig.* The odorous fumes or vapour given off by the burning of any substance, esp. by such as emit an agreeable odour, an incense.

2. *spec.* Applied to animals trained to perform dogs, and performing leopards are common enough in the show business.

Perfusion (pəɹfiūˑʒən), *sb.* [ad. late L. *perfusiōn-em*, n. of action from *perfundere*: see Perfuse.]

Perfuse (pəɹfiūˑz), *v.* [f. L. *perfūs-*, ppl. stem (see Perfuse) + -ive.]

Perfunctorate *Obs. rare.* — **Perfunctura** *obs. rare* [ad. med.L. type *perfunctūra*, f. *perfunctus*: see Perfunctory.]

Perfurnish *v. Obs.* Chiefly *Sc.* and north. dial. [f. Per- + Furnish.]

Pergameneous, etc.

Perhaps (pəɹhæˑps), *adv.* (*sb.*) Also 5 per happous (?), 6 perhapis, perhaps. In vulgar or careless speech often shortened to *p'raps* (praps).

Perhibit, *v. Obs.* [f. L. *perhibēre* to hold out, ascribe, etc., f. Per- + *habēre* to have, hold.]

Peri-, *prefix*, repr. Gr. περι-, around, about, round about, of place and time.

Perigynous ... Name introduced by Link for a structure surrounding the ovary. In current use: a. A membranous sac, investing the ovary in the Sedges (*Carex*); the utriculus. b. A part of the leafy investment of the female organs of mosses.

Perigyny (pĕrī′dʒini), *sb.* [f. Gr. περί around + γυνή wife, female, pistil] ... The condition of being perigynous.

Perihelion (perihī′liŏn), *Astr.* Also 7-8 **-ium**. Pl. **-ia**. ... That point in the orbit of a planet, comet, or other heavenly body, at which it is nearest to the sun. Opp. to APHELION.

Perihepatic · **-hepatitis**: see PERI- a, c.

Perihermenial (perihɜ′mĕniăl), *a.* [f. Gr. περι- around + ἑρμηνεία interpretation] Pertaining to or characteristic of Aristotle's treatise Περὶ ἑρμηνείας.

Peri-intestinal ... see PERI- a, c.

Perijove (per′idʒouv), *Astr.* [f. PERI- + Jove-m Jupiter, after perigee, perihelion] That point in the orbit of any one of Jupiter's satellites at which it is nearest to Jupiter.

Peril (per′il), *sb.* Forms: 3- peril; also 3-5 perile, -yl, 4-6le, 4-5 -ille, -yle, -elle, 4-6 -el, 4-7 -ill, 5 -aill, -eil, -eyl(l, 5-6 -ylle, -ayle; 5-7 -ill, -yll; 4-6 -aril, etc., 5-7 parel, -ell, pearl, 6 -eanll, pearell. [a. F. peril (10th c. in Littré) = Pr. perilh, Cat. peril, Sp. peligro, It. periglio, periculum.]

1. The position or condition of being imminently exposed to the chance of injury, loss, or destruction; risk, jeopardy, danger.

b. Const. (*at*) of that which is exposed to danger (with life); (*to*) of the evil fate that threatens ...

c. *trans.* To put in peril, expose to danger ...

†c. *Without the peril of* (so the dangerous) reach or power of ...

Perilla (peri′la), *sb.* [mod.L. (Linnæus, 1764); origin unknown.] A genus of Labiates, natives of eastern Asia; esp. *P. ocimoides*, grown as a half-hardy ornamental plant on account of its deep-purple leaves.

Perilous (per′ilăs), *a.* (*adv.*) Forms: see PERIL, and cf. PARLOUS. [a. AF. *perillous* = OF. *perillos, -eus*, mod.F. *périlleux* ...]

1. Fraught with peril; causing or occasioning great danger; full of risk; dangerous; hazardous.

Perilously (per′ilăsli), *adv.* [f. prec. + -LY2] In a manner involving peril ; very dangerously.

Perilousness (per′ilăsnĕs), *sb.* ... The quality of being perilous: dangerousness.

Perilymph (per′ilimf), *sb.* [f. PERI- + LYMPH.] The clear fluid contained within the osseous labyrinth of the internal ear, and surrounding the membranous labyrinth. (Distinguished from ENDOLYMPH.)

Perilymphatic, a. [In 1, f PERILYMPH + -ATIC; in 2, f. PERI- + LYMPHATIC.]

Perimeter (perim′ĭtĕr), *sb.* [a. L. *perimetros*, a. Gr. περίμετρος, f. περί around + μέτρον measure.]

1. Measurement or extent.

2. *Geom.* The continuous line or form constituting the boundary of a closed geometrical figure (of rectilineal), or of any area or surface; circumference, periphery, outline.

Perimetric (perimet′rik), *a.* [f. Gr. περίμετρος : cf. diametric.] ... Pertaining to a perimeter or circumference.

Perimetritis (perimĭtrī′tis), *sb.* ... Inflammation of the perimetrium or tissue surrounding the uterus.

Perinæum, perinœum (perinī′ŏm), *Anat.* [a. med.L. *perinæum*, Gr. περίναιον, περίνεον.]

Period (pī′rĭŏd), *sb.* Forms: 5 peryod, paryode, 6 peryode, periode, 6- period: see below. [a. F. *période* (14th c. in Hatz.-Darm.) ... a. L. *periodus*, a. Gr. περίοδος, lit. going round, way round, circuit, revolution, cycle of years, periodic recurrence, course, recurring fit of disease, rounded period ...]

I. A course or extent of time.

1. The time during which anything runs its course; time of duration.

Period (*cont.*) ... marked by the recurrence of astronomical coincidences (e.g. the changes of the moon falling on the same days of the solar year), used as a unit in chronology; e.g. the Callippic, Dionysian, Julian, Metonic period.

d. *The period*: the time in question or under consideration; *esp.* the present day: cf. DAY *sb.* 13 *b* (*b*).

II. Completion, end of a course.

III. A completed or rounded sentence; *Rhetoric, Music, etc.*

Periodate, per-iodate (pər,aɪ′ŏdĕt), *sb.* [f. PERIODIC + -ATE.] *Chem.* A salt of periodic acid.

Period, v. [f. prec. *sb.*]

Periodic acid, H_2IO_4, an acid containing a larger proportion of oxygen than iodic acid.

Periodic (pĭrĭŏd′ik), *a.¹* [a. F. *périodique* (14th c. in Hatz.-Darm.), ad. L. *periodicus* (Pliny), a. Gr. περιοδικός recurring at certain intervals, f. περίοδος PERIOD.]

1. Of, pertaining, or proper to the revolution of a heavenly body in its orbit; *as*, *periodic motion*, *time*.

2. Characterized by periods; recurring at regular intervals; *spec.* in *Path.* having regularly recurring symptoms; *as*, *periodic fever*. Often loosely, Recurring or reappearing at intervals; intermittent.

Periodical, a. (*sb.*) [f. PERIODIC + -AL.]

Periodically (pĭrĭŏd′ikăli), *adv.* [f. prec. + -LY2]

Periosteous ... see PERIOSTEUM.

PERIOSTEUM

† **Periosteum** (periɒˈstiˌəm). *Anat.* Also 6–7 -icm, 7-ion. [mod.L., for ancient L. *periostēon* (Cœlius Aurelianus 5 420), a. Gr. περιόστεον, neut. of περιόστεος adj. 'round the bones', f. περί round + ὀστέον bone. In F. *périoste* (Paré 16th c.).] The dense fibro-vascular membrane which envelops the bones (except where they are covered by cartilage), and from the inner (vascular) layer of which bone-substance is produced.

Periosteal, **Periosteous**, **Periosteitis**, **Periostitis**, **Periostracum**, **Periostracal**.

Periotic (periˈɒtik), *a.* [f. Gr. περί around + οὖς, ὠτ- the ear.] *Anat.* Of the ear. Surrounding the ear.

Periovular, **Peripatetic**, **Peripatetical**, **Peripateticism**, **Peripateticize**.

PERIPHERALLY

Peripatize, **Peripatus**, **Peripeteia**, **Peripetia**, **Peripheral**, **Peripheria**, **Peripheric**, **Peripherical**, **Periphery**, **Peripherous**, **Peripherally**, **Peripherad**, **Peripheraxial**.

PERIPHERE

Periphere, **Peripheral**, **Peripheria**, **Periphery**, **Periphrase**, **Periphrasis**, **Periphrastic**, **Periphrastical**, **Periphery**, **Periplast**, **Periplus**.

PERIPLUS

Periphyll, **Periplasm**, **Periplast**, **Periplus**.

PERIPNEUMONIA

Peripneumony (periˌnjuːˈmɒni), **peripneumonia** (-ˈməʊniə). *Path.* Now rare or *Obs.* [f. *peripneumon-* + -IA.]

Periscii, **Periscian**, **Periscope**, **Periscopic**, **Periscopism**, **Periscopy**, **Perish**, **Perishability**, **Perishable**, **Perishableness**, **Perished**, **Perisher**, **Perishing**, **Perishment**, **Perisperm**, **Perisome**, **Perispome**, **Perisporangium**, **Perispore**, **Perissad**, **Perissodactyl**, **Perissodactyle**.

PERISH

Perish (ˈperiʃ), *v.* Forms 4–5 *perisse-en*, (3–4, -y 3′), 4-5 *perisch*, (-*yche*, -e), -ysche, 4-5 *perisse*, 5 *perysse*, 6 *perrysshe*, 6 *perysche* (*-sche*), 5-6 *peris*, etc.

1. *intr.* To come to a violent, sudden, or untimely end; to suffer destruction; to lose its life, cease to exist, be cut off.

Perishability, **Perishable**, **Perishableness**, **Perished**, **Perisher**, **Perishing**, **Perishment**.

PERISSODACTYL

Perisperm, **Perispome**, **Perisporangium**, **Perispore**, **Perissad**, **Perissodactyl**, **Perissodactyle**.

Perissology, *Rhet.* †*Obs.* [ad. late L. *perissologīa*, f. Gr. περισσολογία, f. περισσολόγος redundant + λόγος speech.] Redundancy or superfluity of speech; use of more words than are necessary; pleonasm.

†**Perissomerous**, *a.* [f. mod.L. *perissomerus*, f. Gr. περισσόμερος.] Having an unusual number of parts.

Perissosyllabic (peri·sosila·bik), *a.* [f. Gr. περισσοσύλλαβος.] Having a syllable over.

†**Peristalith.** [irreg. f. Gr. περιστά standing round + λίθος stone.] A ring or row of standing stones surrounding a burial-mound, or the like.

‡**Peristalsis** (peristæ·lsis), *sb.* [mod. L., repr. Gr. περίσταλσις, f. περιστέλλειν.] Peristaltic movement; see next.

Peristaltic (peristæ·ltik), *a.* *Physiol.* [ad. Gr. περισταλτικός.]

Peristaphyline (peristæ·filəin), *a.* *Anat.* [ad. mod.L. *peristaphylīnus*, f. Gr. περὶ around + σταφυλή uvula.]

Peristeronic (peristĕrŏ·nik), *a.* [app. f. Gr. περιστερών a dove-cot.] Pertaining to or concerned with pigeons.

Peristeromorph (peri·stĕrŏmǫf). *Ornith.* [f. mod.L. *peristeromorphus*, f. Gr. περιστερά pigeon + μορφή form.]

Peristeropod (peri·stĕrŏpǫd). *Ornith.* [f. ... Gr. περιστερά pigeon, and πο-, πούς foot.]

Peristerophily. The breeding of pigeons.

Peristome (peri·stōm), *sb.* Also in L. forms *peristoma* (pl. -ata), *peristomium* (pl. -ia). —F. *péristome* (18..), ad. mod.L. *peristoma* ... Gr. περὶ around + στόμα mouth; altered by Ehrhart (1787) to *peristomium*, after *pericarpium*, etc.]

Peristomal (peri·stōmal), *a.*, belonging to the peristome.

Peristyle (peri·stail), *sb.* (*a.*) *Arch.* Also 7–9 in L. form **peristy·lium**, 9 in L. form **peri·stylon.** [f. F. *péristyle* (1554 in Hatz.-Darm.), or ad. L. *peristylium*, or its source **peri·stylon**, Gr. περίστυλον.]

Peritheca·rpium *Bot.* Obs.

†**Perithecium** (periþī·siŏm). *Bot.* Pl. **-ia.** [Person (1790), f. Gr. περὶ around + θήκη case.]

Perithelium, -thoracic: see PERI- a, b.

†**Perition.** *Obs.* rare⁻¹. [n. of action from L. *perīre* to perish.] Perishing, destruction, annihilation.

Peritoneum (peritōnē·ŏm), *a.* *Min.* [f. Gr. περὶ around + τοῦ cut, cutting.] (See quot.)

Peritomy (peri·tŏmi). *Surg.* [ad. Gr. περιτομή circumcision, f. περὶ around + τομή cutting.]

Peritonæal, -eal (peritŏnī·al), *a.* [f. next + -AL.] Of, pertaining to, situated in, or affecting the peritoneum.

‡**Peritoneo·scope** (peritŏnī·ŏskōp), *sb.*

Peritoneum, -næum (peritŏnī·ŏm). *Anat.* Also *peritonæum*, *peritonaeum*. [L., a. Gr. περιτόναιον.]

Peritrichan (peri·trikăn), *a.* and *sb. Zool.*

Peritrichic, Peritrichous (peri·trikəs), *a.*

Peritrochium (peritrŏ·kiŏm). *Mech.* [mod. L., a. Gr. περιτρόχιον a wheel (see prec.).] A wheel constituting part of the mechanical power called the wheel-and-axle.

Peritropal (peri·trŏpal), *a.* *Bot.* rare.

Peritrophic (peritrŏ·fik), *a. Entom.* [ad. F. *péritrophique*, f. Gr. περὶ around + τροφή food.]

Peritropous (peri·trŏpəs), *a.*

Peritype (peri·təip). *rare.*

‡**Periuterine** (periū·tĕrəin), *a. Anat.*

‡**Periwig** (peri·wig), *sb.* Also †**perwyke**, **perwyg**, **perwicke**, etc. [A corruption of PERUKE.] An artificial imitation of a head of hair (or part of one); worn formerly, first by women and then by men, as a fashionable decoration.

Periwig (peri·wig), *v.* To dress, cover, or conceal with, or as with, a periwig.

Periwigged (peri·wigd), *ppl. a.* [f. prec. sb. and vb. + -ED.] Wearing or having on a periwig.

Periwinkle, periwink, *sb.* vars. PERIWIG.

Periwinkle (peri·wiŋk'l). Forms: *a.* 1 peruincæ, 2–3 pervenke, 4 parvenke, -uink, pervink(e, -vynke, 4 5 venke -uesik(e, -vinke, 5 -vynke. 8-9 ... A plant of the genus *Vinca* N.O. (*Apocynaceæ*), esp. of the two European species, *V. minor* and *V. major*, the Lesser and Greater Periwinkle, evergreen trailing sub-shrubs with light blue starry flowers, varying in *V. minor* with pure white.

Periwinkle, *sb.* variant of PERIWIG *sb.*

Perjink (pəɹdʒi·ŋk), *a.* *Sc.* Also 9 **prejink, per-, prejinct.** [Origin unknown. The word has the form of a F. or L. derivative; Jam. suggests a F. **perjoint* or L. **perjunctus*; but these words, even if they existed, would hardly give the sense.] Exact, precise, minutely accurate; prim, neat.

Perjinkety, *a. Sc.* To appear finical. **Perjink**, *sb.* *Sc.* Also 9 **perjinct.** ... Exact, precise; minutely accurate. **Perjinkly,** *adv.* With minute accuracy.

Perjournet, *v. Obs.* rare⁻¹. [f. PER- + *journet*.] To pass through.

†**Perjourney**, *v. Obs.* rare⁻¹. To travel, to journey.

Perjured (pə·ɹdʒəɹd), *ppl. a.* [pa. pple. of the intrans. vb. (1. (one) that has perjured himself) betokens or expresses perjury; forsworn.

Perjure (pə·ɹdʒəɹ), *v.* Also 5–6 per- perjur, 6 -jur, -jure. [a. F. *perjurer* (13th c.), or ad. L. *perjūrāre* to swear falsely, f. PER- + *jūrāre* to swear.]

Perjurer (pə·ɹdʒərəɹ). Also 6 **perjurour.** One who commits perjury; one who has perjured himself.

Perjury (pə·ɹdʒəri), *sb.* Also 5 par-, 6 **perjurie**, 7 **perjurye.** Also 7 **par-.** [ad. L. *perjūrium*, f. *perjūrus* PERJUROUS.]

Perjuredly, *adv.* in the manner of one perjured.

Perjurement (pə·ɹdʒəɹmənt). *Obs.* (a. OF. *perjurement*).

Perjurious (pəɹdʒuə·riəs), *a.* †*Perjurous.* *Obs.* [ad. L. *perjūriōsus.*]

Perjuriously, *adv.* In a perjurious manner; with perjury.

Perjurous (pə·ɹdʒuərəs), *a. Obs.* [ad. L. *perjūrus.*] = PERJURIOUS.

†**Perjuroussness,** *sb. Obs.* The quality of being perjurious.

Perk, Perce, *sb.* and term for a bracket.

Perk (pəɹk), *v.*[1] Also 6 **perke**, 7 **pearke, pirke, 7–8 perk.** To carry oneself in a smart, brisk, or jaunty manner; to assume or have a lively, self-assertive, or self-conceited attitude or air.

Perk (pəɹk), *sb.*[2] [var. of PEARCH.] A perch, a pole used to support a clothes-line.

Perk (pəɹk), *v.*[2] To prick, turn over the perk: see PERCH *sb.*[2]

Perk (pəɹk), *sb.*[3] Also 5 pyrk, 6 pirke, perke, 6–7 perck, 7 peark, peerk, peerk, 7–8 perk, perick. A parallel to PERCH *sb.*[2]; chiefly in northern and Irish use, and East Anglian use.

Perk, perke, obs. or dial. forms of PARK.

Perkily (pɔ̄·kili), adv. In a perky manner; self-assertively, with self-importance: 'cockily': perkly.

Perkin (pɔ̄·kin). [? PERR a. + -KIN: cf. PERKINESS.]

I. With up: To recover from depression or sickness; to recover liveliness. dial.

II. trans. 2. To make spruce or smart, to smarten; to prank, to trim, as a bird does its plumage. Also with up, out.

3. To raise briskly or smartly, to prick up; to hold up smartly or self-assertively; to thrust or poke out. Also refl. To perk oneself.

Perk, v.² Now dial. Also 6-7 **pearke.**
I. Collateral form of PERCH v.¹, chiefly northern and E. Anglian. Cf. NF. perquer = F. percher. Its later use sometimes approaches PERK v.¹

Perkish (pɔ̄·kiʃ), a. [f. PERK a. + -ISH.]

Perkness, rare. [f. PERK a. + -NESS.]

Perky (pɔ̄·ki), a. [f. PERK v.¹ a. + -Y.]

Perl, obs. form of PEARL.

Perlaceous (pɔilā·ʃəs), a. [f. med.L. and Rom. perla PEARL + -ACEOUS.] Resembling pearl in appearance; pearly, nacreous.

Perlament, obs. form of PARLIAMENT.

Perlarian (pɔ̄lā·riān), a. [f. med.L. perlāria, f. generic name perla.] Of or pertaining to the genus Perla or family Perlidæ, or stone-flies. Obs. rare⁻¹.

Perla·rious, a.¹ rare⁻¹. = PERLACEOUS.

Perla·rious, a.² rare⁻¹. = PERLARIAN.

†Parlasent, pā·rlement, obs. form of PARLIAMENT.

†Perlate, Perla·ted, a.¹ Chem. Obs. [ad. mod.L. perlāt-um, f. perla PEARL: see quot. 1802.]

Perle (pɔ̄l). [Norm., L., F. perl; cf. PEARL sb. 1.] A pellet: see quot. 1893.

Perlement, obs. form of PARLIAMENT.

†Permain, -maine, -mayn, etc. forms of PEARMAIN.

Perlid, obs. form of PERILOUS.

†Perli·brate, v. Obs. rare⁻¹. [f. ppl. stem of L. perlībrāre, f. PER- + lībrāre, f. lībra balance.] To weigh exactly. So **Perli·bration.**

†Perlo·cution (pɔ̄ilokiū·ʃən), Obs. rare⁻¹. [ad. L. perlocūtiōn-em, n. of action from perloquī to speak out.] The action of speaking out; utterance, elocution.

†Perlu·strate, v. Sc. Obs. [f. perlustrāt-, ppl. stem of L. perlustrāre to traverse, to view all over.] To travel through and view all over; to survey thoroughly.

Perlustration (pɔ̄lʌstrēi·ʃən), Obs. exc. in techn. use. [n. of action f. prec.: cf. L. lustrātio.] The action of perlustrating; a going round and viewing or surveying thoroughly.

†b. fig. The action of going through and examining a document; esp. the inspection of correspondence while passing through the post.

2. A written order giving permission to do something, a warrant, a licence; esp. one permitting the landing or removal of dutiable or excisable goods.

Permanency. [f. as next + -ANCY.]

Permanganate (pɔ̄mæ·ŋgănēt). Chem. [f. as next: see -ATE⁴.] A salt of permanganic acid, as potassium permanganate or $KMnO_4$.

Permanganic (pɔ̄mæŋgæ·nik), a. Chem. [f. PER- 5 b + MANGANIC.] In permanganic acid, $HMnO_4$, obtained from manganese.

†Permana·bly, adv. Obs. rare⁻¹. [prob. for permaneably, ad. L. permanābiliter.]

Permanence (pɔ̄·mănens). [a. F. permanence (13th c. in Godef.).]

Permanency (pɔ̄·mănensi), a. (sb.) [ad. L. permanent-em, pr. pple of permanēre to stay to the end, f. PER- 1, 2 + manēre to stay; perh. through F. permanent (14th c. in Godef.).]

Permanently (pɔ̄·mănentli), adv. In a permanent manner; so as to last or continue; lastingly, enduringly; for ever.

Permansion (pɔ̄mæ·nʃən), Obs. rare⁻¹. [ad. L. permansiōn-em, n. of action f. permanēre to stay to the end.]

Permanganate of Potash.

Permeability (pɔ̄mĭăbi·lĭti). [f. PERMEABLE + -ITY: in F. perméabilité (1625 in Hatz.-Darm.).] The quality or condition of being permeable; capability of being permeated; perviousness.

Permeable (pɔ̄·mĭăb'l), a. [ad. L. permeābilis, f. permeāre: see PERMEATE + -BLE. Cf. F. perméable (1587 in Hatz.-Darm.).]

Permeably, adv.

Permeance (pɔ̄·mĭăns). [f. as next + -ANCE.]

Permeant (pɔ̄·mĭănt), a. [ad. L. permeant-em, pr. pple of permeāre.]

Permeate (pɔ̄·mĭēt), v. [f. L. permeāt-, ppl. stem of permeāre to pass through, f. PER- 1 + meāre to go, pass.]

Permeating, ppl. a.

Permeation (pɔ̄mĭēi·ʃən), [n. of action f. prec.: see -ATION.]

Permeative (pɔ̄·mĭēitiv), ppl. a. [f. permeate + -IVE.] Having the quality of permeating; penetrative, pervasive.

Permian (pɔ̄·miăn), a. (sb.) Geol. [Named by Sir R. Murchison (1841), from the province of Perm in Eastern Russia, where these strata are extensively developed: see -IAN.]

Permillage (pɔ̄mi·led3), rare. [f. PER- + mille, F. mille, thousand + -AGE, after PERCENTAGE.]

Permiscible (pɔ̄mi·sib'l), a. [ad. med.L. permiscibilis, f. permiscēre: see PERMIX.]

†Permi·scible, a. [f. PER- 4 and MIRIFIC.]

†Permi·scuous, a. Obs. rare⁻¹. [f. L. permiscu-us + -OUS.]

Permissible (pɔ̄mi·sib'l), a. [a. OF. permissible (13th c. in Godef.) = It. permissibile, prob. ad. med.L. permissibilis.]

Permissibly, adv.

Permission (pɔ̄mi·ʃən). [ad. L. permissiōn-em, n. of action from permittere to PERMIT. Cf. F. permission (1539 in R. Estienne), It. permissione.]

1. The action of permitting or giving leave; allowance; liberty or licence granted to do something; leave.

Permissionaire (pɔ̄miʃənē·ə), [f. prec. + -KD2.] Having permission granted; doing something by permission.

Permissive (pɔ̄mi·siv), a. (sb.) [a. OF. permissif, -ive, f. L. permiss-: cf. permittere to PERMIT + -IVE.]

1. Having the quality of permitting or giving permission; that allows something to be done or to happen; not forbidding or hindering.

Permissively, adv.

Permissiveness.

Permit (pɔ̄mi·t), v. [ad. L. permittere, f. PER- 1, 2 + mittere to let go, let loose, send: perh. after F. permettre (14th c.).]

1. trans. With the action or fact as object: To admit or allow the doing or occurrence of; to give leave or opportunity for. With simple obj., obj. cl., or inf.; sometimes also with indirect obj.

2. With the agent, etc. as direct object: To allow, give leave to (a person or thing) to do (something); sometimes, With inf. act or pass. (rarely without inf.); sometimes ellipt. with simple obj.

Permit (pɔ̄·mit), sb. [f. prec.]

Permittable, = PERMITTIBLE.

Permittance, [f. PERMIT v. + -ANCE.]

†Permittee (pɔ̄mite·). [f. PERMIT v. + -EE¹.] A person to whom something is (formally) permitted; the recipient or holder of a permit.

Permitter (pɔ̄mi·təɹ). [f. as prec. + -ER¹.] One who permits or allows.

Permittible (pɔ̄mi·tib'l), a. [f. PERMIT v. + -IBLE.] = PERMISSIBLE.

Permittivity.

Permix (pɔ̄mi·ks), v. [Back-formation from permixt, permixed, ppl. a.; cf. COMMIX, MIX.] trans. To mix thoroughly, mingle. (See next.)

†Permi·xable, a., capable of being 'permixed'.

†Permixed, permixt, ppl. a. [orig. ad. L. permixt-us, pa. pple of permiscēre to mix; afterwards treated as pa. pple of PERMIX.]

Permixtion, -mixture, obs. ff. PERMISTION, PERMIXTURE.

Permutability (pɔ̄miūtăbi·liti). [f. next + -ITY.] The quality or condition of being permutable. a. Changeableness, mutability. b. Interchangeableness.

Permutable (pɔ̄miū·tăb'l), a. [a. F. permutable (13th c.), ad. L. permūtābilis, f. permūtāre to PERMUTE + -ABLE.] That may be permuted.

Permutably, adv.

Permutableness; Permutably adv.

Permutant (pɔ̄miū·tănt), Math. [f. permūtant-em, pr. pple of permūtāre: see PERMUTE and -ANT¹.]

Permutate (pɔ̄·miūtēit), v. [f. L. permūtāt-, ppl. stem of permūtāre.]

Permutation (pɔ̄miūtēi·ʃən), [a. OF. permutation, ad. L. permūtātiōn-em, n. of action f. permūtāre to PERMUTE.]

Permute (pɔ̄miū·t), v. [ad. L. permūtāre, f. PER- 1, 2 + mūtāre to change; cf. F. permuter (14th c.).]

Permuter. *Math.* To subject to permutation; to alter the order or to re-arrange in a different order. (Cf. PERMUTATION 3 b.)

Hence **Permuter**, one who permutes.

Pern (pə̄ɹn), *sb.* [ad. mod.L. *pernis* (Cuvier 1817), an erroneous adaptation of Gr. πέρνης name of a kind of hawk.] A bird of the genus *Pernis*; the HONEY-BUZZARD.

† Pern (pə̄ɹn), *v.* *Obs.* trans. To deal with after the manner of Dr. Perne, Master of Peterhouse, Cambridge, 1554–80, who changed his opinions adroitly; to change (a profession, creed, etc.) for some ulterior end.

Hence **† Perning**.

† Pernable, *a.* *Obs.* [a. AF. *pernable* = OF. *prenable* (13th c. in Wace), f. *pern-* = *pren-*, stem of *prendre* to take.] Proper to be taken or caught.

Pernancy (pə̄ɹnænsi). *Law.* Also 7 *purnancie.* [f. as prec. + -ANCY.] *Law.* The action of taking into possession; receipt, as of rents, tithes, etc.

† Pernegate, *v.* *Obs.* [f. ppl. stem of L. *pernegāre* to deny altogether, f. PER- + *negāre* to deny.] To deny absolutely; to deny flatly or stoutly. Hence **† Pernegātion**, absolute denial.

† Pernel. variant of PARNEL, wanton young woman; applied in ridicule to an effeminate man.

† Pernal, variant of PARNEL.

Pernavigate (pə̄ɹnævi·gét), *v.* *Obs.* [f. L. *per-* + *nāvigāre* to NAVIGATE.] *trans.* To sail through; to steer one's course through. Also *fig.*

† Pernegate, *v.* *Obs.* [f. ppl. stem of L. *pernegāre*.]

Pernicious, *a.* Also 6–7 *per-nicious.* [ad. L. *perniciōs-us* destructive, baneful, ruinous, f. *perniciēs* destruction, ruin, death, f. PER- 2 + *nex, necis* death, destruction.] 1. Having the quality of destroying; tending to destroy, kill, or injure; destructive, ruinous; fatal.

2. Pernicious *anæmia*, a disease which advances to a fatal termination without interruption. *Pernicious fever*, that which proves dangerous or fatal at an early stage.

3. That harbours evil designs; wicked; villanous. Now *rare* or *Obs.*

Pernicious-ly, *adv.* In a pernicious manner; destructively, ruinously; wickedly.

Pernici·ousness. The quality of being pernicious.

Pernickety (pə̄ɹni·kéti), *a.* Also *persnickety.* [Of obscure origin; originally Scotch and perh. north. Eng.] Over-fastidious, precise; requiring precise or particular attention to minute or trifling particularities.

Pernicity (pə̄ɹni·siti), *sb.* *Obs.* [ad. L. *pernicitās*, f. *pernix, pernic-* swift.] Swiftness, celerity.

Pernoctation (pə̄ɹnɔktéʃ·ən), *sb.* The action of passing or spending the night, esp. in *Eccl.* use, spending the night in vigil; an all-night vigil.

Peroneal (pérɔni·al), *a.* [f. mod.L. *peroneus*, a. Gr. περόνη the fibula, pin.] *Anat.* Of or pertaining to the fibula.

Peroneo- (pérɔni·o-), comb. form of mod.L. *peronëus*, *-ēus*, PERONEAL, forming adjs. applied to ligaments, muscles, etc. connected with the fibula and some other part denoted by the second element.

Peroneus (pérɔni·ns), *sb.* [mod.L. (prop. adj., sc. *musculus* muscle), f. PERONE.] *Anat.* Name given to various muscles connected with the fibula.

Peronium (pérɔni·ŏm), *sb.* *Zool.* [f. mod.L. from Gr. περόνη pin, fibula.]

Peronospora (pérɔnɔ·spɔra), *Bot.* [mod.L., f. Gr. περόνη pin, and σπορά seed, SPORE.] A genus of minute parasitic fungi.

Perorate (pérɔ·rét), *v.* *intr.* To perorate, make a peroration.

Peroration (pérɔréʃ·ən), *sb.* 1. The concluding part of an oration, speech, or written discourse, in which the speaker or writer sums up and commends to his audience with force or earnestness the matter which he has placed before them; hence, any rhetorical conclusion to a speech, and reflect.

Perpend (pə̄ɹpénd), *v.* *arch.* [ad. L. *perpendere* to weigh carefully, ponder, consider, f. PER- 2 + *pendere* to weigh, pay, ponder.]

Perpendicular (pə̄ɹpéndi·kiuläɹ), *a.* and *sb.* [ad. L. *perpendiculāris*, f. *perpendiculum* plumb-line, plummet.]

Perpendicularity (pə̄ɹpéndikiulæ·riti), *sb.* [f. PERPENDICULAR + -ITY.] The quality or state of being perpendicular.

Perpendicularly, *adv.* In a perpendicular manner.

Perpendi·cularness. *rare.* [f. as prec. + -NESS.]

Perpension. *Obs. rare.* [ad. L. *perpensiōn-em*, f. *perpens-*, ppl. stem of *perpendere* to weigh or consider carefully, freq. of *perpendere* to PERPEND.]

† Perpensed, *a.* *Obs. rare.* [ad. L. *perpens-us*, pa. pple. of *perpendere*.]

† Perpensity. *Obs. rare.* [ad. L. *perpensitās*.]

Perpession. *Obs. rare.* [ad. L. *perpessiōn-em*, f. *perpess-*, ppl. stem of *perpeti* to endure, suffer, PASSION.]

† Perpetration, *sb.* 1. Endurance of suffering.

Perpetrate, *v.* *rare.* [f. L. *perpetrāt-*, ppl. stem of *perpetrāre* to perpetrate.]

Perpetrate (pə̄ɹpétrét), *v.* [f. L. *perpetrāt-*, ppl. stem of *perpetrāre* to perform, achieve, commit, f. PER- + *patrāre* to bring to pass, effect.]

Perpetration (pə̄ɹpétréʃ·ən), *sb.* The action of perpetrating or performing (an evil deed).

Perpetrator (pə̄ɹpétrétəɹ), *sb.* [a. L. *perpetrātor*, agent-n. from *perpetrāre* to PERPETRATE.] One who perpetrates or commits (an evil deed).

Perpetratrix (pə̄ɹpétrétriks), *sb.* [a. L. *perpetrātrix*.] A female perpetrator.

† Perpetre, *v.* *Obs. rare.* [a. F. *perpétrer* (14th c.), ad. L. *perpetrāre.*] *trans.* To perpetrate.

Perpetuable (pə̄ɹpétiuäb'l), *a.* *rare.* [f. L. *perpetu-* + -ABLE.] Capable of being perpetuated.

Perpetual (pə̄ɹpétiuäl), *a.* (*adv.* and *sb.*). [ad. OF. *perpetuel* (13th c., mod.F. *perpétuel*), ad. L. *perpetuālis*, f. *perpetu-us* continuous, unbroken, permanent.]

Perpetually, *adv.* In a perpetual manner.

Perpetualness. *rare.* [f. prec. + -NESS.]

Perpetuance. *Obs.* [f. PERPETU(ATE + -ANCE.]

Perpetuate (pə̄ɹpétiuét), *v.* [f. L. *perpetuāt-*, ppl. stem of *perpetuāre* to make perpetual.]

Perpetuation (pə̄ɹpétiuéʃ·ən), *sb.* [ad. med.L. *perpetuātiōn-em*.]

Perpetuity (pə̄ɹpétiū·iti), *sb.* [ad. OF. *perpetuité* (mod.F. *perpétuité*), ad. L. *perpetuitās.*]

Perpetuator (pəpētiu̯ə·tər). [Agent-n. from PERPETUATE v.: see -OR.] One who perpetuates.

Perpetuity (pə̄pptiu̯·ĭti). [ME. *perpetuite*, a. F. *perpétuité* (13th c. in Littré) = Pr. *perpetuitat*, Sp. *perpetuidad*, It. *perpetuità*; ad. L. *perpetuitāt-em*, f. *perpetuus*: see PERPETUAL and -ITY.]

1. The quality or state of being perpetual; endless or indefinite duration or existence.

2. A perpetual possession, tenure, or position.

Law. Of an estate: The quality or condition of being inalienable perpetually, or for a period beyond certain limits fixed, or conceived as being fixed, by the general law; an estate so restricted or perpetuated.

3. A perpetual annuity. Hence, The amount or number of years' purchase required to buy a perpetual annuity.

Perpetuon (pəpətiu̯·ən), *v.* Obs. rare.

Perpetuum, in *perpetuum mobile*.

Perpeyn, perpin (in Masonry): see PARPEN.

Perpla·cid, *a.* L. rare.

Perplea·d, *v.* Obs. rare.

Perple·x, *a.* [ad. L. *perplex*-us involved, confused, intricate, f. PER- + *plexus* interwoven.]

Perple·x, *v.* [f. prec.]

1. *trans.* To fill (a person) with uncertainty as to the nature or treatment of a thing by reason of its involved or intricate character.

2. Of things: intricate, and hence difficult to unravel or clear up; involved, tangled.

Perplexed (pəple·kst), *ppl. a.*

Perplexedly (pəple·ksedli), *adv.*

Perplexedness (pəple·ksednes).

Perplex·er. rare.

Perple·xful, *a.* Obs. rare.

Perple·xing, *ppl. a.*

Perple·xable, *a.* [ad. L. *perplexābilis*.]

Perple·xion. L. rare.

Perple·xity. [a. F. *perplexité* (14th c. in Godef. Compl.)]

Perple·xive, *a.* L. rare.

Perple·xly, *adv.* rare.

Perple·xment. [f. PERPLEX v. + -MENT.]

Perpolished, *ppl. a.* Obs. rare.

Perporter, *v.* Obs. rare.

Perpotation. Obs. rare.

Perprise, Perprision = PURPRISE, etc.

Perpu·re, *v.* Obs.

Perpu·sill, *a.* L. rare.

Perpu·rify, *v.*

Perquire, *v.* Obs. rare.

Perquisite (pə̄·kwizit). Also 5, 7 perquisite (7 -it). [ad. L. *perquīsī-tum*, neut. pa. pple. of *perquīrĕre*.]

Perqui·sitive, *a.* Obs. rare.

Perquisition (pə̄kwizi·ʃən).

Perquisitor (pə̄·kwizitər).

Perqui·situm, *n.* rare.

Perradial, *a.* Zool.

Perradius (pəřə́idiə̆s).

Perradiate, *v.*

Perreda·de (pəpl·dōid), *n.*

Perron (peř·n, pe·ron).

Perrosin. Obs.

Perrotation, *n.* [L. PER- + -ATION.]

Perrotine (peř·tin).

Perruque, Perruquier, var. PERUKE, etc.

Perry, pery, pirie. Forms.

Perscrutation (pə̄skrūtēi·ʃən).

Perscrutator, *n.*

Persecute (pə̄·sěkiūt), *v.*

Persecuting, *ppl. a.*

Persecution (pə̄siki·ūʃən).

Persecutor (pə̄·sĕkiūtər).

Persaife, -saive, obs. forms of PERCEIVE.

Persall, Persall. [f. PER- + SALT.]

Persant, var. PERSEANT.

Persaunt, Obs. form of PARSE.

Persea. Bot. [a. L., a. Gr. περσέα.]

Persecuted (pə̄·sĕkiūtĕd), *ppl. a.*

Persecutee. ... One who is persecuted.

Persecution (pɜːsiˈkjuːʃən). ...

1. The action of persecuting or pursuing with enmity and malignity; *esp.* the infliction of death, torture, or penalties for adherence to a religious belief or an opinion such as is, with a view to the repression or extirpation of it; the fact of being persecuted; an instance of this.

2. A particular state or period of systematic infliction of punishment directed against the professors of a (religious) belief; as, the ten persecutions of the Christians under the Roman Empire, the Marian persecution, etc.

3. *transf.* Persistent or continued injury or annoyance from any source; sometimes humorously applied to the annoying importunity of advisers, beggars, suitors, etc.

Persecutory. ... *a.* ... Given to persecution; serving or relating to persecution.

Persecutress. A female persecutor.

Persecutrix, fem. of *persecutor.*

Persecutive ... Of or pertaining to perse.

Persic ... Of or pertaining to PARSEE.

Perseid ... *Astron.* ...

Perseity ... *Metaph.* ...

Persevere (pɜːsɪˈvɪə). ... [ad. mod. L. *perseverāre*] ...

Perseverance (pɜːsɪˈvɪərəns). ...

Perseverant (pɜːsɪˈvɪərənt), *a.* ...

Perseveratingly ...

Perseveration ...

Perseveringly (pɜːsɪˈvɪərɪŋlɪ), *adv.* ...

Persevering (pɜːsɪˈvɪərɪŋ), *ppl. a.* ...

Persian (pɜːʃən, -ʒən), *a. and sb.* ...

1. Of or pertaining to Persia, its inhabitants or language.

2. In the specific names of productions, natural or artificial, found in or imported from Persia, or attributed to that country or its people; e.g. *Persian carpet, cat, cyclamen, iris, jasmine, lilac, poplar, ranunculus,* etc.

Persic. ...

Persicary (pɜːsɪˈkɛərɪ). *Herb.* [med. or mod. L. *Persicāria*] ...

Persico, **Persicot** ... [a. F. ...] A kind of cordial prepared by macerating the kernels of peaches, apricots, etc., in spirit.

Persimmon (pɜːˈsɪmən). ...

Persis ...

Persiennes (pɜːsɪˈɛnz, F ...) *sb. pl.* ...

Persism ...

Persiflage (pɜːsɪˈflɑːʒ). ...

Persist (pɜːˈsɪst), *v.* [ad. L. *persistere*] ...

Persiflate ...

Persister ...

Persistency (pɜːˈsɪstənsɪ). ...

1. The quality of persisting or being persistent; firmness or obstinacy in adhering to a course, purpose, or opinion; also = PERSISTENCE 1.

Persistent (pɜːˈsɪstənt), *a.* [ad. L. *persistent-em,* ...] ...

1. Persisting or continuing firmly in some action, course, or pursuit, against opposition or remonstrance, or in spite of failure.

Person (pɜːsən, pɜːˈsn), *sb.* Forms: ...

1. An individual human being; a man, woman, or child. (In earliest use, The human being acting in some capacity, personal agent or actor, person concerned.)

Persistingly, *adv.* ...

Persisting, *ppl. a.* ...

Persistive, *a.* [f. PERSIST *v.* + -IVE] ...

Persistless, *a.* ...

Persistiveness ...

Persive, obs. form of PERCEIVE.

Perske, obs. Sc. form of (?) PARCH *v.*

Perso-, combining form of *Persian.*

Persolve, *v.* ...

Persolution, *sb.* ...

Person. ...

PERSON.

VII. *Zool.* Each individual of a compound or 'colonial' organism, having a more or less independent life, and often specialized in form or function; a zooid.

VIII. *Phrases and Comb.*

10. In one's (own) *person*, formerly also *in* (one's) *proper person* [... in *propriâ personâ*]; † *a.* = in person (see 11). *Obs.* b. In one's own character (not as representing another); see sense 1.

11. *In person*: with *or* by one's own action or bodily presence; personally; oneself.

12. *In the person of* (in *his or her person*).

1. In the character of, as the representative of, as personally representing. See sense 1.

(a) personally represented by.

13. To accept (*take*), respect (*behold*, *look* upon with favour, to favour, to show partiality, esp. on personal or improper grounds. (*Scriptural*.)

14. *Comb.*

† **Person.** *Obs.* *rare.* [f. prec.: cf. late L. *persōnāre* to represent.] = PERSONATE *v.* 5.

Persona (pəɹsóʊnæ). The Latin word for PERSON, q.v., used in certain phrases.

1. *Persona grata* [late L.], an acceptable person or personage; originally applied to a diplomatic representative who is personally acceptable to the personage to whom he is accredited.

2. *In propria persona*: see *In Lat. prep.*

Personable (pəɹsʊnæbl), *a.* [f. PERSON *sb.* + -ABLE: cf. 16th c. F. *personnable*.]

1. Having a well-formed person or body; well-made, handsome; good-looking, comely, presentable. (Now chiefly in literary use.)

† 2. *Law.* Having the status of a legal person (PERSON 6), and as such competent to maintain a plea in court, or to take anything granted or given. *Obs.*

† 3. Personable in figure or appearance; of note. (Originally always with *great* or the like qualification, which in the 19th c. began to be implied in calling any one 'a personage'.)

B. *sb.* † **1.** A personal being or person. *Obs.*

2. Things belonging to an individual person; personal matters or things. † *spec.* Personal goods or property, personalty.

2. *pl.* The Personals of the Nation belong not to this Empire.

Personable. *adv.* (Obs.) [f. prec. + -LY²] Like a personable person.

2. = PERSONALLY. [Cf. OF. *personnablement*—*personnellement.*]

Personage (pəɹsʊnedʒ). [a. OF. *personage*, (*F. personnage*) or a personage, etc.] mod. F. *personnage* a personage.

† 1. A representation or figure of a person; an image or effigy; a statue or portrait. *Obs.*

2. A person of rank or distinction; a man or woman (whose status the speaker does not know, or does not desire to specify).

3. Personal identity; personality, individual self.

4. The quality of being a person or persons; personality. *Obs.*

† 2. The body of a person; chiefly with reference to appearance, stature, etc.; bodily frame, personal appearance.

† 3. A person (man or woman) of high rank, distinction, consideration, or importance; a personage.

PERSONAL.

† **Personage**, obs. form of PERSONAGE.

Personal (pəɹsənæl), *a.* (*sb.*) Also 4-5 -el, etc. 6 personnal [a. OF. *personal* (12th c. in Hatz.-Darm.), —*al* (mod.F. -*nnel*), ad. L. *persōnāl-is* of or pertaining to a person (in Law or Gram.), f. *persōna* PERSON; see -AL.]

1. Of, pertaining to, concerning, or affecting the individual person or self (as opposed, variously, to other persons, the general community, etc., or to one's office, rank, or other external circumstances); individual; private; one's own. Rarely in reference to an animal (quot. 1796).

c. Having oneself as object; directed to oneself.

d. *transf.* Making a personal remark, reflection, or attack; addicted to such remarks, etc.

2. Done, made, performed, held, etc. in person: involving the actual or immediate presence or action of the individual person himself (as opposed to a substitute, deputy, messenger, etc.). Of a reciprocal action or relation, Carried on or subsisting between individual persons directly.

3. Of or pertaining to one's person, body, or figure; bodily; as an action or quality. † *Personal oath* (see CORPORAL *a.* 3).

b. as something affecting or having reference to one's person or body.

4. Of or pertaining to persons or characters of a drama (*dramatis personæ*), or of a dramatic poem, story, etc.; also one of the actors on the stage of history.

† b. Present or engaged in person. *Obs.*

B. *sb.* † 1. A personal being or person. *Obs.*

2. *pl.* Personal matters, private affairs.

3. Something personal; a personal remark. U.S.

† 3. Having an individual body; personal. Also *in pl.* in same sense.

4. Bodily parts in general; body, person.

2. As a person; in the form or character of an individual person.

PERSONAR.

Personar. *obs.* Sc. form of PARCENER.

Personate, *a.* [ad. L. *persōnāt-us* masked, feigned, f. *persōna* mask.]

1. Personated, feigned, pretended; counterfeit. *Obs.*

Personally (pəɹsənæli), *adv.* [f. PERSONAL *a.* + -LY²]

1. In the way of personal presence or action; in (by) himself, themselves, etc.

2. Of the nature of a person, personal; embodied in a person, impersonated. *Obs.*

PERSONIFICATION.

employed by a candidate at an election to detect attempted personation of voters.

Personative (pəɹsóʊnětɪv), *a.* *rare.* [f. as PERSONATE *v.* + -IVE.] Having the quality of personating; involving dramatic personation.

Personator (pəɹsóʊnětəɹ). Also 7 -er. [agent-n. from PERSONATE *v.*: suffix *-or*, Eng. *-er*.]

1. One who personates (in various senses).

Personed (pəɹsənd), *a.* [f. PERSON *sb.* + -ED.]

1. United in one person or substance. *Obs.*

Personification (pəɹsɒnɪfɪkéɪʃən). [f. next vb. + -ATION: cf. F. *personnification*.]

1. Attribution of personal form, nature, or characteristics; the representation of a thing or abstraction as a person; esp. as a rhetorical figure or species of metaphor. Also in *art*, the representation of a thing or abstraction by a human figure.

2. The dramatic representation of a character.

3. *concr.* A person or thing that represents some other, dramatically or in the way of pretence; the embodiment of some quality, idea, or abstraction, in a real person (or other abstraction); usually applied to the actual person (or thing) as embodying the quality, etc.; exemplifying it in a striking manner or degree.

Personified (pə̄·ɹsɔnǝifəid), ppl. a. [f. Personify + -ed[1].]

1. Represented, spoken of, or figured as a person.

Personifier (pə̄·ɹsɔnifǝiɑ̌ɹ). [f. as prec. + -er[1].] One who personifies. b. One who personates or acts the part of another.

Personify (pə̄·ɹsɔnifǝi), v. [app. a. F. personnifier: see Person and -fy.]

1. trans. To figure or represent (a thing or abstraction) as a person; to attribute a personal nature or personal characteristics to, by way of metaphor, in thought, or esp. in speech or writing; in art, to symbolize by a figure in human form.

2. To embody (a quality, etc.) in one's person or self; to be an embodiment or concrete type of; to exemplify in a typical manner; to impersonate.

3. To make or turn into a person; to give a human form or nature to. (Cf. Personize 2.)

4. To assume the person of, to personate. rare.

Hence **Personifying** vbl. sb. and ppl. a.

Personise, v.: see Personize.

Personize (pə̄·ɹsɔnǝiz), v. †Obs. [f. Person or L. persōna + -ize.]

1. intr. To assume a character; to act a part.

2. trans. To represent as a person; to personify.

Hence **Personiza·tion**, rare—°, the action of personizing; impersonation.

Personne, obs. form of Parson, Person.

Personned (pɛɹsǫnd), ppl. a. [f. mod.F., sb. use of personné adj., personal, as contrasted with matériel material, e.g. le matériel et le personnel d'une armée. In earlier use anglicized: see Personal B. 4.] The body of persons engaged in any service or employment, esp. in a public institution, as an army, navy, hospital, etc.; the human as distinct from the matériel or material equipment (of an institution, undertaking, etc.).

Personship. rare. [f. Person sb. + -ship.] Personality, individuality.

Perspective. Obs. [ad. L. perspectīva.]

1. † 1. The science of sight; optics. (Also in pl.)

† 2. An optical instrument for looking through or viewing objects with: a spy-glass, magnifying-glass, telescope, etc. Also fig., esp. in such phrases as to look through the wrong end of the perspective = to look upon something as smaller or of less consequence than it is. Obs.

† 3. trans. The appearance presented by visible objects, in regard to relative position, apparent distance, etc.

II. 4. The art or science of drawing solid objects on a plane surface so that the drawing produces the same impression of apparent relative positions and magnitudes, or of distance, as do the actual objects when viewed from a particular point. (Formerly also pl. in same sense.)

Perspective (pə̄ɹspe·ktiv), sb. and a. [ad. L. perspectīva (sc. ars), the science of optics, fem. of perspectīvus: see next; cf. F. La perspective (14th c.).]

1. † 1. The science of sight: optics. (Also in pl.)

† 2. An optical instrument for looking through viewing objects with: a spy-glass, magnifying-glass, telescope, etc.

Perspectived (-tivd), a.: placed or drawn in perspective, without regard to perspective (in quot. fig.); **Perspective·less**, a., devoid of perspective.

Perspectivist (pə̄ɹspe·ktivist), one who treats of perspective.

Perspectograph (pə̄ɹspe·ktǫgraf). [f. L. perspect-, pple. stem (see Perspective) + -graph.] An instrument for the mechanical drawing of objects in perspective (Francis Dict. Arts, 1842).

Perspicacious (pəɹspikē·ʃəs), a. [f. L. perspicāci-, -cax, having the power of seeing through, sharp-sighted, f. perspicĕre + -ous.] Of clear or penetrating sight; clear-sighted.

Perspicacity (pə̄ɹspikæ·siti). [a. F. perspicacité (16th c. in Hatz.-Darm.).]

Perspicacity (pə̄ɹspikæ·siti). [ad. L. perspicācitāt-, perspicācitas: see prec. and -ITY.]

Perspicil (pə̄·ɹspisil). Obs. [ad. mod.L. perspicillum, telescope, f. L. perspicĕre.] An optical glass; a telescope or microscope.

Perspicuate (pə̄ɹspi·kiu̯ē̆t), v. rare. [f. L. perspicāt-, ppl. stem of perspicĕre.] trans. To make clear or evident.

Perspicuity (pə̄ɹspikiū·iti). [ad. L. perspicuitāt-, -tas: see next and -ITY.]

Perspicuous (pə̄ɹspi·kiu̯əs), a. [f. L. perspicuus transparent, clear, evident (f. perspicĕre to see through) + -ous.]

Perspirable (pə̄ɹspǝi·rǎb'l), a. (sb.). [f. Perspire + -able.]

Perspiration (pə̄ɹspirē·ʃən). [a. F. perspiration, n. of action from perspirer to Perspire.]

Perspirative (pə̄ɹspǝi·rǎtiv), a. [f. L. perspirāt-: see Perspire + -ive.] Promoting or subservient to perspiration.

Perspiratory (pə̄ɹspǝi·rǎtǫri), a. [f. L. perspirāt- (see prec.) + -ory[2].]

Perspire (pə̄ɹspǝi·ɹ), v. [ad. L. perspīrā-re, etymologically, to breathe through (f. Per-1 + spīrāre to breathe); but in ancient L. used only in the senses 'to perspire, blow', 'to blow constantly' of the winds.]

Perspirer (pə̄ɹspǝi·rǎɹ). One who perspires.

Perstand, v. Obs. rare. A confusion of persist and understand.

Perstringe (pə̄ɹstri·ndʒ), v. [ad. L. perstring-ĕre to bind tightly, draw together, graze, rub, blunt, make dull, touch slightly, glance at, touch or wound slightly with words, censure, reprimand.]

Persuade (pə̄ɹswē·d), v. [ad. L. persuādēre to persuade, f. per- thoroughly + suādēre to advise, recommend, urge.]

Persuade ... *v.*

Persuader.

Persuading, *vbl. sb.*

Persuasible, *a.*

Persuasibleness.

Persuasibility.

Persuasion.

Persuasive, *a.* and *sb.*

Persuasively, *adv.*

Persuasiveness.

Persuasory, *a.*

Persulphate.

Persulphide.

Persulphocyanate.

Persulphuret.

Persulphuric, *a.*

Persultation.

Perswade, *v.*, obs. form of PERSUADE.

Pertain, *v.*

Pertainment.

Pertake, *v.*

Perter, *a.*

Perterebration.

Perthite.

Perti, pertie, obs. forms of PARTY.

Pertical, *a.*

Pertinacious, *a.*

Pertinaciously, *adv.*

Pertinaciousness.

Pertinacity.

Pertinate, *a.* Obs.

Pertinence.

Pertinency.

Pertinent, *a.* and *sb.*

Pertinently, *adv.*

Pertingent.

Pertish, *a.*

Pertly, *adv.*

Pertness.

Pertransient, *a.*

Pertransire.

† Pertransition, a passing through, traversing. *Obs. rare*—

Pertre, -ite, f. PLANTRÉE. **Pertrick, -trich(e, -trick, -trix, -trik**, etc. obs. ff. PARTRIDGE.

† Perturable, *a.* *Obs.* Chiefly Sc. In 5–6 perturble, 6 -trubil, -troubil. [a. OF. perturbable, f. L. perturbāre: see PERTURB.] To the -turble form (L. type *perturbābilis*), cf. Disturble.

‡ Pertroublance, mental disturbance, perturbation. *Obs. rare.*—

Perturb (pərtȫ·ıb), *v.* [a. OF. perturber, -turber (14th c. in Godef.), ad. L. perturbāre, f. per + turbāre to disturb, confuse.]

1. *trans.* To disturb greatly (physically or externally); to cause disorder or irregularity in; to unsettle, confuse, derange, throw into confusion.

2. To disturb greatly (mentally), to trouble in mind, to agitate.

Perturbable, *a.* [f. PERTURB v. + -ABLE.] Liable to be perturbed. Hence **Perturbability.**

† Pertu·rbance, *Obs.* [a. OF. *perturbance*, f. *perturber* to PERTURB: see -ANCE.]

Perturbancy, *rare.* = prec.

Perturbant, *a.* and *sb. rare.* [ad. L. *perturbant-em*, ppl. pple. of *perturbāre* to PERTURB.]

Perturbate (see next), *v.* [f. L. *perturbāt-*, ppl. stem of *perturbāre*: see PERTURB.]

Perturbation (pə̄ɪtərbē·ıʃən), *sb.* OF. *perturbation* (14th c. in Littré), ad. L. *perturbātiōn-em*, n. of action f. *perturbāre* to PERTURB.

1. The action of perturbing: the fact or condition of being perturbed; disturbance, disorder, commotion; mental agitation or disquietude; trouble.

2. Perturbed or disturbed condition.

3. Disturbance of the regular order or course; irregular variation.

4. A cause or factor of disturbance or agitation.

Perturbational, *a.* [f. prec. + -AL.] Of, pertaining to, or of the nature of perturbation.

Perturbatious, *a.* [See -OUS.] Causing perturbation.

Perturbative, *a.* [a. late L. *perturbātīv-us*, f. *perturbāt-*: see prec.] Causing or characterized by perturbation.

Perturbator, (pə̄ɪtərbē·ıtəɪ). [a. L. *perturbātor*, agent-n. f. *perturbāre*.] A disturber, troubler.

Perturbatory, *a.* [f. PERTURBATE v. + -ORY.]

Perturbatrix, *Obs.* rare. A female perturbator or disturber.

Perturbed, *ppl. a.* Disquieted, agitated, restless; confused, deranged.

Perturbedly, *adv.* In a perturbed manner; confusedly, distractedly.

Perturber (pə̄ɪtȫ·ıbəɪ). A disturber, troubler.

Perturbing, *vbl. sb.* The action of PERTURB v. Also *attrib.*

Perturbing, *ppl. a.* That perturbs or troubles.

Perturment, *rare.* [f. PERTURB v. + -MENT.]

Pertusate, *a.* *Bot. rare.* [L. *pertūsus* + -ATE.] 'Pierced at the apex.' (Webster 1879.)

Pertuse (pətūs·), *a.* Late. [L. *pertūs-us*, pa. pple. of *pertundere* to punch or bore into a hole, f. per + tundere to beat.]

Pertused, *a.* [f. prec. + -ED.] Wearing a peruke, having a perule on.

Pertusion (pətū·ʒən). *rare.* [f. L. *pertūs-*: see prec.]

Perukier, (perūkī·ɪ). *rare.* [Anglicized form of F. *perruquier*.] A wig-maker. Hence **Perukier·ship** (*nonce-wd.*), the office or art of a wig-maker.

Pertussis (pərtȫ·sıs). *Path.* [mod.L., f. PER- + *tussis* cough.] = HOOPING-COUGH.

Peruke (perū·k). *sb.* Forms: 6–7 peruke, 6–9 perrucq, 7 perruk, -ooke, perwike, 6 perruqe, 7 peruke, 6 peruque, peruque. See also other early forms under PERI-WIG.

Perukeless, *a.* without a peruke.

Perula (pe·rŭla), *sb.* *Bot.* [mod.L., f. PERULE.]

Perule (pe·riūl), *sb.* *Bot.* [ad. F. *perule*, Littré, ad. L. *perula*, having a perule.]

Perusable (pərū·zăb'l), *a.* [f. PERUSE v. + -ABLE.] Capable of being perused.

Perusal (pərū·zăl). *sb.* [f. PERUSE v. + -AL.]

1. Survey, examination, scrutiny.

2. The action of reading through or carefully through any book, etc.

Peruse (pərū·z), *v.* [f. PER- 1 + USE v.; perh. repr. AFr. *per-user.*]

1. *trans.* To use up; to wear out by use.

†2. To go through (a series of things or persons) so as to deal with one after another; to handle, deal with, describe, or examine (a number of things) one by one. *Obs.*

Perusing, *vbl. sb.* The action of the verb PERUSE.

Peruvian (perū·vı̆ăn), *a.* (*sb.*) [f. mod.L. *Peruvia*, Latinized name of the country + -AN.]

Peruvin (perū·vin), *sb.* *Chem.* [f. PERUVI- + -IN 1.] An alcohol (C_nH_nO) distilled from the balsam of Peru.

Pervade (pərvē·d), *v.* [ad. L. *pervādĕre* to go or come through, pass or spread through, f. PER- + *vādĕre* to go, walk.]

1. *trans.* To pass through; to flow or extend through; to traverse.

2. To extend or diffuse itself throughout; to spread through or into every part of; to permeate, saturate.

Pervenke, obs. form of PERIWINKLE 1.

Perverse (pərvȫ·ɪs), *a.* [a. F. *pervers*, -e, ad. L. *perversus* turned the wrong way, awry, perverse, pa. pple. of *pervertĕre* to turn about, subvert, PERVERT.]

Pervert (pərvȫ·ɪt), *v.* [a. OF. *pervertir* (12th c.), ad. L. *pervertĕre* to overturn, overthrow, turn the wrong way, corrupt, f. PER- + *vertĕre* to turn.]

Perversion (pərvȫ·ɪʃən). [ad. L. *perversiōn-em*, n. of action f. *pervertĕre* to PERVERT: cf. F. *perversion* (16th c. in Littré and Hatz.-Darm.).]

Perversity (pərvȫ·ɪsǐtǐ). [a. F. *perversité*, ad. L. *perversität-em*, f. *perversus*: see PERVERSE *a.*]

Perversive (pərvȫ·ɪsǐv), *a.* [f. L. *perversus* + -IVE.]

Pervert (pȫ·ɪvəɪt), *sb.* [app. absolute use of prec., with shifted stress: cf. CONVERT *sb.*] One who has been perverted.

Pervertive (pərvȫ·ɪtǐv), *a.* *Obs.* [f. PERVERT *v.* + -IVE.]

Pervicacious (pȫːɪvǐkē·ʃəs), *a.* Now *rare.* [f. L. *pervicāci-*, *pervicax* stubborn + -OUS.]

Pervigilate, *v.* [f. PERVIGIL + -ATE.]

So ǁ Pervigilation *Obs.* [L. *pervigilātiō*, a watching through the night, keeping of vigil.]

Pervious, -vinā̆e, -āïe, obs. ff. PERIWINKLE.

Pervious (pɜˑɹviəs), *a.* [f. L. *pervi-us* that has a way or passage through (f. PER- 1 + *via* way) + -OUS ; in L. *pervia*.]

1. Allowing of passage through; passable; affording passage or entrance; lying open (*to*).

2. *Anat.* A foetile part or organ; a base of support; a peduncle.

3. *Prot.* A name for each of the two quatrains forming the first part of a sonnet.

Pervious, variant of PERVIOUS *Obs.*

Perviousness, [f. prec. + -NESS.] The quality of being pervious; penetrability.

Pervise [Pervise-, editorial and dictionary error for *pervise*, PERUSE.

Pervise, obs. form of PARVIS.

Pervulgate, *v. rare.* [f. ppl. stem of L. *pervulgā-re* to make publicly known.] *trans.* To make public, make known.

Perwanna, -wanno, etc. var. PURWANNAH.

Perwick(e, -winke, -wynke, -wynke, obs. ff. PERIWINKLE.

Pery, -ie, obs. ff. PERRY 1, PIRRIE.

Peryng, *ppl. a. Obs.* [f. *pere*, PEAR v. + -ING 2] Appearing.

Peryngate, var. PERIGNATE *Obs.*

Peryt, variant of PERER *Obs.*, pear-tree.

Peryshing, obs. form of PERISHING.

Peryte, obs. form of PERIDE, PIERCE.

Perywig, Perywinke, obs. forms of PERIWIG, PERIWINKLE.

ǁ **Pes** (pîz) Pl. **pedes** (pɛˑdiz) [The L. word *pēs* foot, used technically in Comparative Anatomy, Botany, etc.]

1. *Comp. Anat.* The terminal segment of the

hind limb of a vertebrate animal, corresponding to the human foot. Opposed to MANUS hand.

2. *Bot.* A foottile part or organ ; a base of support ; a peduncle.

Pes, obs. form of PEACE, PEASE, PIECE.

ǁ **Pesable, a.** *Obs.* Also *-ABLE.* [a. OF. *pesable,* f. *peser* to weigh, PEISE : see -ABLE.] Capable of being weighed ; in equi., Weighed ; evenly balanced.

Pesade (pᵻzaˑd), [F. *pesade,* altered (under influence of *peser* to poise) from earlier *posade* (1579 in Hatz.-Darm.), ad. It. *posata,* lit. *pause, resting, *posate* arrests which a horse doth make in advancing his forepart.

ǁ **Pesame** (peˑsame). *Obs.* [Sp. phrase *peso me* 'it grieves me,' hence as sb.] A compliment of condolence.

ǁ Pesane, -sane, obs. variant of PISANE.

Pesant, *Obs. rare.* [f. F. *pesant* (11th c. in OF.) pr. pple. of *peser* to weigh,] PEISE ; also as sb. 'weight'.

1. The amount that a thing weighs ; weight.

2. *Pesant,* obs. f. PEASANT ; var. PESANE.

ǁ Pesanter, -ture, *Obs. rare.* [f. *pesanteur* (12th c. in Littre), f. *pesant* : see F. PESANT.] Heaviness, weight.

ǁ Pesaunt, var. PESANT *Obs.*, sb.

ǁ Pesaunt, var. PESANT *Obs.*, sb. 2.

Pesayne, obs. variant of PISANE.

Pescod, -code, -codde, obs. ff. PEASECOD.

Pese, var. PEISE, PEASE, PIECE sb. and v. ; obs. pl. of PEASE. *Pesod, Pesode,* obs. f. of PEASANT.

Peseta (peseˑta). [Sp., dim of *peso* weight ; cf. *peta* Spanish dollar.] A modern Spanish silver coin, equivalent to the French franc and Italian lira ; now (since Oct. 1868) the unit of value in Spain. It is divided into 100 centimos.

Pesewk, obs. form of PEASWEEK.

Pesh(kash [Pers. پيشکش *pēshkash* first drawn, first fruits, tribute, f. *pēsh* before, in front + *kash* drawing.]

Peso (peˑso). Also 6 peaso, 7 peso. [Sp. *peso,* lit. weight.]

Simple' or 'Plain.' The name given to the principal version of the Old and New Testaments in the ancient Syriac tongue, sometimes styled the Syriac Vulgate.

ǁ Peshwa (pɛˑʃwa). Forms : 7 peshua, 8 paish-, -o peish, peshwa...

ǁ Peso, obs. exc. dial. [Derivation obscure : cf. BASS sb.2 ; and PASSOCK.] A hassock or cushion to rest the feet on, or to kneel on, esp. in church.

Pess, -ent, obs. ff. PACE sb.2, PEACE sb.

Pessary (peˑsāri). [ad. med.L. *pessārium,* L. *pessi-um,* ad. a Gr. πεσσός (pl. πεσσά, as if from *πεσσιον*), an oval stone used in playing a game like draughts ; hence, a medicated plug, as later.]

ǁ Pesme, *Med. Obs.* (?)

Peson (peˑsɒn). [a. F. *peson,* a balance weight on a spindle, the balance from the end of a balance, a weighing instrument with fixed counterpoise and movable fulcrum ; deriv. of OF. *peser* to weigh. f. L. *pensum* weight.] A kind of weighing-machine : see sense 1847, and cf. AUNCEL.

Peson, -ob. ff. PEASON ; pl. of PEASE.

Pesse, var. PEASE sb.

Pessimism (peˑsimiz'm). [f. as prec. + -ISM ; cf. F. *pessimisme* (1835 in *Dict. Acad.*)]

Pessimist (peˑsimist), *sb.* (*a.*) [f. as prec. + -IST.]

Pessimistic (pesimiˑstik), *a.* [f. prec. + -IC.]

Pessimistical (pesimiˑstikăl), *a.* [f. prec. + -AL.]

Pessulate, obs. form of PESTILATE.

ǁ Pessoneer, Pessonner, variant of PERSONER *Obs.*

Pessonry, variant of PERSONRY *Obs.*

Pessimum (peˑsiməm). [mod. f. L. *pessimum,* lowest.]

Pesson, obs. form of PEASEN, pl. of PEASE.

Peso (peˑso).

Pest (pest). [a. F. *peste* (R. Estienne 1539), ad. L. *pest-is* plague, pestilence, contagious disease.]

Pestel, obs. form of PISTOL *Obs.*

Pesterer (peˑstərəɹ). [f. PESTER v. + -ER 1] One who pesters : see the verb.

Pestering, *vbl. sb.* [f. PESTER v. + -ING 1] The action of the verb PESTER, in various senses.

Pestering, *ppl. a.* [f. as prec. + -ING 2] That pesters, in various senses of the vb.

Pesteronn (peˑstɛrɒn), *a.* Also 6 **pestorous.** Having the quality of pestering ; cumbersome ; troublesome.

Pestilence (peˑstilens). [a. F. *pestilence,* ad. L. *pestilentia,* sb. of condition f. *pestilent-em* : see PESTILENT sb. -ENCE.]

ǁ Pestis, *a. Obs. rare.* [ad. L. *pesti-fer* plague-bearing, f. *pestis* plague + *-fer* bearing.]

Pestiferous (pestiˑferəs). [f. L. *pestifer-us* plague-bringing, *pesti-* plague + *-fer-* + -OUS.]

Pestify, *v. Obs. rare.* [f. PEST + -FY.]

Pestilent (peˑstilent), *a.* [a. F. *pestilent* or ad. L. *pestilent-em,* unwholesome, noxious.]

Pestle (peˑs'l, peˑst'l), *sb.* Also 7 *pastle.* [ME. a. OF. *pestel, -til* = It. *pestello* L. *pistill-um* pounder, pestle, f. *pist-,* *pinsĕre* to pound, bray, crush.]

Supplement, p. 3873 ; Corrigenda, p. 4092 ; Spurious words, p. 4093 ; Books quoted, p. 4094.

2145

PESTLE.

8. The leg of certain animals, used for food, *esp.* the ham or haunch of the pig (occasionally, the foreleg); also, the knuckle. Now *dial.*

Pestle, *v.* [f. OF. *pesteler* to bray, pound, f. *pestel*: see prec.]

1. *trans.* To beat, pound, or triturate, with or as with a pestle. Also *fig.*

2. *intr.* To use or work with a pestle.

Pestling, *vbl. sb.*

Pestuous, *a.* [f. Pester.]

Pet, *sb.*[1] Also 6 *pette*, 8 *pett*. [Origin-ally Sc. and north. Eng.; of unknown origin. It. *pet* and Gael. *peata* are from Eng.]

1. Any animal that is domesticated or tamed and kept as a favourite, or treated with indulgence and fondness; *esp.* applied to 'a lamb' (or kid) 'taken into the house, and brought up by hand, a cade lamb' (Johnson). The latter is the ordinary literal sense in Sc. and north. Eng.

2. *transf.* A person, *esp.* a child, that is treated with special kindness or favour; a darling, favourite. Also *transf.* of a thing.

Pet, *sb.*[2] [prec.]

1. A fit of offended ill-humour or peevishness from this cause; now usually implying one of a slight or childish kind.

Pet, *v.*[1] [f. Pet *sb.*[1]]

Pet, *v.*[2] [f. Pet *sb.*[2]]

PETALINE.

Pet, **Petach**, obs. forms of Peat, Pit, Patache.

Petal (petăl). *Bot.* [= F. *pétale*, ad. mod.L. *petal-um*, in Fabio Colonna 1649 (Hatz.-Darm.); in ancient L. in sense 'metal plate', a. Gr. πέταλον thin plate, lamina, leaf, neuter of πέταλος *adj.* outspread, f. root *πετ-* to spread.]

1. *Bot.* Each of the divisions (modified leaves) of the corolla of a flower (see Corolla 2), *esp.* when separate. (Strictly, distinguished from the *sepals* or leaves of the calyx, but often including these when coloured or petaloid.)

Petaled, **petalled** (petăld), *a.* [f. Petal + -ED.] Furnished or adorned with or as with petals; having petals.

Petaliferous (petălĭfērəs), *a.* [f. mod.L. *petalum* + -FEROUS.] Bearing or having petals.

Petaliform (petalĭfōrm), *a.* [f. as prec. + -FORM.] Having the form of a petal; petaloid.

Petaline (petălĭn), *a.* [ad. mod.L. *petal-in-us*, f. L. *petal-um* PETAL: see -INE.] Pertaining to a petal; situated on a petal; consisting of petals; resembling a petal, petaloid.

PETALISM.

Petalism (petălĭz'm). *Anc. Hist.* [ad. Gr. πεταλισμός, f. πεταλίζειν: see Petal and -ISM.] A method of temporary banishment (for five years) practised in ancient Syracuse, in imitation of the Ostracism of Athens, but effected by writing the name of the person on an olive-leaf.

Petalite (petălăit). *Min.* [mod. (d'Andrada, 1800). f. Gr. πέταλον leaf + -ITE.] A silicate of aluminium and lithium, occurring in whitish or greyish masses having leaf-like cleavage.

Petalless, **petalless** (petăl-lĕs), *a.* [f. Petal + -LESS.] Destitute of petals; apetalous.

Petaly (petălĭ), *a.* *nonce-wd.* [f. as prec. + -Y.] Having or resembling petals.

Petalocerous (petălŏsērəs), *a.* *Entom.* [f. mod.L. *Petalocera*, neut. pl. of *petalocer-us* (f. Gr. πέταλον leaf + κέρας horn) + -OUS.]

Petaloid (petăloid), *a.* [f. Petal + -OID.] Having the form, appearance, or texture of a petal; petal-like.

Petaliferous [repeated] = Petaliferous.

Petalism (petălĭz'm), *a. rare.* [f. Petal + -ISM.]

Petalody (petălŏdĭ). *Bot.* [f. Gr. πεταλώδης leaf-like, f. πέταλον leaf: see -ODE.] The condition of having other organs or parts of the flower modified into the form of petals.

Petalody [repeated]

PETER-PENNY.

Peter, *sb.*[1] [f. Peter *sb.*[1]] *trans.* To apply oneself.

Peter, *v.*[2] *slang* or *collog.* [Origin unknown.]

1. *trans.* To cease, stop, leave off, *slang.*

2. *intr.* Peter *out*: to give out, U.S. *Mining collog.*;

2. Applied to the voluntary contributions of Roman Catholic peoples to the papal treasury since 1860.

†Peter-see-me. Obs. Also Peter-as-meeno-so-meea. (†) -semine. (A corruption of *Pedro Ximenes*, the name of a celebrated Spanish grape.)

Peter-boat. [app. f. Peter *sb.* + Boat: cf. *Petermen*.] Local name (chiefly on the Thames and adjacent coasts) for a decked fishing-boat.

Peterman. [f. Peter *sb.* + -MAN.]

1. A fisherman; formerly, app. one who practised the Galilean fishery.

2. Combinations of Peter's (= St.) Peter's barge, bark, boat, ship, alluvive names for the Christian or Catholic Church; † St. Peter's-corn, the single-grained wheat, *Triticum monococcum* (Linn.); † Peter's cress, a name for Samphire: see quot.; (St.) Peter's fish, a name given to several fishes (as the John Dory, the haddock, etc.) having a mark on each side near the pectoral fin, affirmed in legend to have been made by St. Peter's thumb and finger when he caught the fish for the tribute-money (Matt. xvii. 27); Peter's penny = PETER-PENNY.

PETER-SEE-ME.

Peter-penny, **Peter's pence**. [U.st. in pl. Peter-pence, Peter's pence.]

1. *Hist.* An annual tax or tribute of a penny from each householder having land of a certain value, paid before the Reformation to the papal see at Rome; also, a similar voluntary contribution of Northern lands.

Hence **Peter-kin**, **Peterling** *nonce-wds.*

PETIT.

Petit, *a.* [a. F. *petit* (11th c.) = Pr. *petit*, Sp. *petit*, Pg. *pequeno* small; of obscure origin.]

1. Small; = PETTY *a.*

Petit, *adv.*

Petition, *sb.* [a. F. *pétition*, ad. L. *petītiōn-em*, n. of action f. *petĕre* to seek.]

Petite (pĕtiˑt, petīt), *a.* [F. *petite*, fem. of *petit* small: see PETIT *a.*]

1. Of a woman or girl: Little, of small stature or size, tiny.

2. Now, of a woman or girl: Little, of small stature or size, tiny.

Petit de degree, *etc.* Cross, former of PEDIGREE.

Petitioners (pĕtiˑʃən|z). [f. PETITE −NESS.]

‖**Petitio** (pĕtiˑʃio, piˑtīˑʃiˌo). [L.: see next.]

‖**Petitio indiciarum**, *Law* = IMPARLANCE 2.

‖**Petitio principii** (prinˑsipiˌəi)

Petition (pĕtiˑʃən), *sb.* [a. F. *pétition*, ad. L. *petītiōn-em*, n. of action f. *petĕre* to seek, ask, beg.]

1. The action of formally asking, begging, supplicating, or humbly requesting; esp. in phr. *to make petition*, to ask, supplicate, or formally beg.

2. A supplication or prayer; an entreaty; *esp.* a solemn and humble petition to the Deity, or to a superior or superior; also, one of the clauses of a prayer, *e. g.* of the Lord's prayer.

4. *Law.* **a.** *Petition of right*: an ancient Common Law remedy against the Crown for obtaining possession or restitution of real or personal property.

b. A formal application in writing made to a court (a) for judicial action concerning the matter of a suit then pending before it (formerly called a *cause petition*)

5. *Math.* A postulate; an axiom. *Obs.*

+6. *Petition and Advice* (*Eng. Hist.*): the Remonstrance presented by Parliament to Cromwell on 4 Apr. 1657.

Petitioner (pĕtiˑʃənəɹ). [f. PETITION *sb.* + −ER.]

Petition, *v.* [f. PETITION *sb.*]

1. *trans.* To address or present a petition to; to make a humble request or supplication to.

Petitional (pĕtiˑʃənăl), *a.* [f. PETITION *sb.* + −AL.] Of, pertaining to, or of the nature of a petition.

Petitionarily (pĕtiˑʃənarili), *adv. rare.* In a petitionary manner: (in quot. 1646) by way of *petitio principii* or unproved assumption.

Petitionary (pĕtiˑʃənari), *a.* [ad. med.L. *petītiōnāri-us*, f. *petītiōn-em* PETITION: see −ARY¹.]

1. Of the nature of, consisting of, containing or characteristic of a petition.

Petitionate, *v. Obs. rare.* [f. L. *petītiōn-*]

Petitioner (pĕtiˑʃənəɹ). [f. PETITION *sb.* + −ER.]

Petitor (peˑtitəɹ). *Obs. rare.* [L. *petitor*, n. of agent f. *petĕre* to seek, ask, aim at.] A seeker, applicant, candidate.

Petitory (peˑtitəri), *a.* (*sb.*) [ad. late L. *petītōri-us*, f. *petītor*: see prec. and −ORY.]

‖**Petit maître** (pĕtiˑ mɛ̄ˑtr). [Fr., lit. little master.] An effeminate man; a dandy, fop, coxcomb.

Petitioning, *vbl. sb.* [f. PETITION *v.* + −ING¹.]

Petitioning, *ppl. a.* [f. as prec. + −ING².]

‖**Petit pâté** (pĕtiˑ pɑ̄ˑtā). A small patty or pie.

Petkin, **Petling**, some diminutives of PET.

Petong, obs. form of PAKTONG.

Petoria, **petovies**, obs. Sc. forms of PITEOUS.

‖**Petralogy**, *etc.*, error for PETROLOGY.

Petrarchal (pĕtrāˑɹkˌăl), *a.* [f. Petrarch, It. *Petrarca*]

Petrarchan (pĕtrāˑɹkăn), *a.* (also as *sb.* = *Petrarchist*)

Petrarchism (pĕtrāˑɹkiz'm). [f. Petrarch + −ISM.]

Petre (peˑtəɹ). Also 7 *peeter*, 7−9 *peter*. [f. *petra*, Gr. *mature* rock.]

1. = SALTPETRE.

Petrel (peˑtrel). Also 7 *pitteral*, 8 *pittrel*, *petrill*, *pettrel*, 9 *pettrel*. [Occurs in 1676 as *pitteral*, in 1703 spelt *peteral* by Dampier, who says that the name was derived from that of St. Peter: see quot.]

Petrescent (pĕtreˑsənt), *a. †Obs.* [f. L. *petra* stone + −ESCENT.] Becoming converted into stone or petrified; hardening.

Petrescence (pĕtreˑsəns). [f. prec.]

Petric (peˑtrik), *a.* Now *rare.* [f. L. *petra*, Gr. *μετρα* stone: see −IC.]

Petricola (pĕtriˑkŏla), *n. Zool.* [mod. L. *petricola* (L. *petra* rock + *col-ĕre* to inhabit) + −OUS: as *saxicolous*: lithodomous.]

Petrie, var. PEITREL *Obs.*

Petrifaction (pĕtrifæˑkʃən). [f. PETRIFY, after *satisfaction*, *stupefaction*, *etc.*, as if from an etymological form *petrifact-*, etc.]

1. The action of petrifying, or condition of being petrified; conversion into stone or stony substance.

Petrifactive (pĕtrifæˑktiv), *a.* [f. prec. + −IVE.] Having the power of petrifying.

Petrifiable (peˑtrifəiab'l), *a.* [f. PETRIFY + −ABLE.] Capable of being petrified.

Petrific (pĕtriˑfik), *a.* Now *rare.* [f. L. *petri-* (PETRI-) + L. *-ficus* making: see −FIC.]

Petrificate (pĕtriˑfikˌeit), *v. Obs. rare.* [f. L. *petrificāt-*, ppl. stem of *petrificāre*.] = PETRIFY.

Petrification (pĕtrifikeiˑʃən). Now *rare.* [a. F. *petrification* (1564), or f. as PETRIFY.]

Petrify (peˑtrifəi), *v.* [a. F. *pétrifier* (16th c. in Littré), f. L. *petra* stone (Gr. *μετρα*) + *-ficāre* (−FY).]

1. *trans.* To convert into stone or stony substance; to turn (an organic body) into a stony concretion by replacing its original substance with stone.

Petrified (peˑtrifəid), *ppl. a.* [f. PETRIFY *v.*]

Petrine (pīˑtrain), *a.* [f. L. *Petr-us* Peter + −INE¹.]

Petro- (peˑtro), properly combining form of Gr. *πέτρος* stone or *πέτρα* rock, as in PETROGLYPH, −GRAPH, *etc.* In *Anat.* used to form adjectives descriptive of parts connected with the petrous portion of the temporal bone and some other part indicated by the second element (most of which may also be used *ellipt.* as substantives): as **Petro-occiˑpital**, **Petro-occipital** (petrooˑksipital), **Petropharyˑngeal**, **Petrosphenoid**, **-sphenoiˑdal**, **Petro-squaˑmo**al, **-squaˑmous**, *etc.*

Petrogenesis (pĕtrodʒeˑnĭsis).

Petroglyph (peˑtrogˌlif). [ad. mod.F. *pétroglyphe*, f. Gr. *πέτρα* rock + *γλυφή* carving.] A rock-carving (usually prehistoric).

Petrographer (pĕtrɒˑgrăfəɹ).

Petrographical (pĕtrogræˑfikˌăl), *a.* [f. as PETROGRAPHY + −ICAL.]

Petrography (pĕtrɒˑgrăfi). [In 7 erron.; f. PETRO- + −GRAPHY.]

Petrol (peˑtrɒl, peˑtrol), *sb.* [a. F. *pétrole*, ad. med.L. *petroleum* PETROLEUM, q. v.]

Petrolene (peˑtrolīn). *Chem.* [f. PETROL(EUM + −ENE.]

Petroleum (pĕtrōuˑleˌəm). [a. med.L. *petroleum*, f. L. *petra* rock + *oleum* oil.]

Petrolean (pĕtrōuˑleˌăn), *a.* nonce-wd. [f. PETROLEUM.]

Petroleous (pǐtrō·lǐəs), a. [f. PETROLE-UM + -OUS.] Abounding in or containing petroleum.

Petroleum (pǐtrō·lǐəm). Also 6–8 -eum. [a. med.L. petroleum, f. L. petra rock + oleum oil.] A natural oil, varying from light yellow to dark brown or black, occurring in rocks or on the surface of water in various parts of the world; in modern times of great economic importance, esp. as a source of oils for illumination and mechanical power; rock-oil.

Petroliferous (petrŏlifərəs), a. [f. PETRO-LEUM + -FEROUS, -FEROUS, q. v.] Producing or yielding petroleum.

Petrolin (pe·trŏlin). Also erron. -ine. [f. PETROLEUM or PETROL + -IN.] Christian's name for a substance obtained by him from Rangoon petroleum, identical with paraffin.

Petrolist. [f. PETROL-EUM + -IST.] = Petroleur.

Petrolize (pe·trŏləiz), v. [f. PETROL-EUM + -IZE.] 1. trans. To set on fire by means of petroleum; cf. Pétroleur, Pétroleuse.

Petrology (pǐtrŏ·lŏdʒi). [f. Gr. πέτρα rock + -OLOGY: orig. formed erron. as petralogy.] That branch of geology which deals with the origin, structure, and composition of rocks.

Petro-maniacal see Petro-.

Petromyzon (petromoi·zŏn). Ichth. [mod. L. (Linnæus, 1735), f. Gr. πέτρα rock, μύζειν to suck.]

† Petrone. Obs. rare⁻¹. [a. L. petro, petron-, stone; cf. petronel.] Rocky, stony.

Petroselinum (pe·trŏsǐloi·nŏm), n. [L. petro-selin-um, a. Gr. πετροσέλινον rock-parsley, f. πέτρα rock + σέλινον parsley.] Of or related to parsley.

Petroleuse (pe·trŏlŏiz). Obs. [mod.L., f. petro- stone or petra + selin flint, pebble.]

† Petrose, a. Obs. rare⁻¹. [a. L. petrōs-us, a. L. petrōsus rocky.]

Petrosilex (pe·trŏsoi·leks), n. [f. petro-silex, a. L. petrosilicem rock-flint.]

Petrostearin. [Petro-stearine, a solid luminous material of which certain kinds of candles are made.]

Petticoat (pe·tikōt). Also 5–7 pettycote.

Pettifog (pe·tifŏg), v. [Back-formation from PETTIFOGGER.]

Pettifogger (pe·tifŏgə(r)). 1. A legal practitioner of inferior status, who gets up or conducts petty cases.

Pettifogging (pe·tifŏgiŋ), vbl. sb. and ppl. a.

Pettifoggery (pe·tifŏgəri).

Pettifogulize (pe·tifŏgiŭləiz), v. nonce-wd. [f. PETTIFOG.]

Pettily (pe·tili), adv. [f. PETTY a. + -LY².]

Pettiness (pe·tinis). [f. PETTY a. + -NESS.]

Pettish (pe·tiʃ), a. [f. PET sb.¹ + -ISH.]

Petting (pe·tiŋ), vbl. sb. and ppl. a.

Pettitoes (pe·titōz), sb. pl.

Petto (pe·tō, It.). [It.] In one's own breast or thoughts; in contemplation; undisclosed.

Petty (pe·ti), a. (sb.) Forms: 4–7 petty.

1. trans. To pet, fondle, indulge.

Petty officer. [PETTY a. 3.]

Petty captain, pe'tticanon.

Pettycoite, -cote, obs. forms of PETTICOAT.

Pettyfog, pettigod.

Petty-island.

Petulancy.

Petulant.

Petulate.

Petulcous.

Petun (pɪtūn, petūn). Obs. Forms 6-8 petun, 7 pitun, 7 — petun.

Petunia (pɪtiū·nia). Bot.

Petunse (pɪtū·ns).

Petunset.

Peucedanin.

Peucedanum (piūse·dănŏm), Bot.

Peun, obs. form of POON, PUNE.

Peur'e, obs. forms of POOR, PURE.

Pew (piū). sb.1 Forms: 4 puwe, 5 pywe, pewe, 5-7 pewe, 5-9 pue, 7 piew (6, 9- pew. [Late M.E. puwe, pywe, app. orig. identical in form with OF. puye, piue, parapet, balustrade, balcony:—L. podia, pl. of podium.]

Pew, sb.2

Pewage (piū·ĕdʒ).

Pewe, obs. form of PAY, PEW.

Pewes, Pewse, obs. forms of PEASE.

Pewet, var. PEWIT.

Pew-fellow.

Pewful.

Pew-gall.

Pew-glede.

Pewit, pewiit (pī·wĭt, pĭwĭt). Forms: a. 6 pewitt, 6-7 pewit, 8, 9 peewit, 8-9 pewet. Echoic.

Pewl, obs. form of PULE.

Pew-leading, Pew-opener.

Pewless (piū·les), a. [f. PEW sb.1 + -LESS.]

Pewne, Pewpe, Pewre, obs. ff. PAWN sb.1, POUR, PURE.

Pew-rent.

Pewt, Pewtar, obs. forms of PUT, PEWTER.

Pewter (piū·təa). Forms: 4-5 pewtre, 4-6 peuter, 4- pewter (also 5 peautry, peawtre, 6 peuter, 6 poutre, 7 pewtre.)

Pewterer (piū·təəə).

Pewter-wort.

Pewtery (piū·təri).

Pewtrell, variant of PEITREL Obs.

Pewtyll, Obs.

Pfennig (pfe·nĭg), sb. Forms: 6-8 pfenig, -ing (6-9 fennig, 8 phenning, 9 pfennig, pfennige). [G. pfennig:—WGer.]

PH, a consonantal digraph, having usually the phonetic value of F. It was the combination used by the Romans to represent the Greek letter φ, or φ as named φί, *Phi*. This letter, cognate with Skr. *bh* (and so with Germanic *b*), was in early Greek written ΠΗ, and was in a real aspirated *p*; it was subsequently often written ΦΗ, φ, and had then *p-oi*, nearly the same sound as German *pf*; but by the second century B.C. it had sunk into a simple sound, prob. the *bilabial* spirant (the sound made in blowing through the lips), as the Roman F was dentilabial, like mod. Eng. *f*, the Romans in earlier times represented the Greek φ not by F, but by PH; in the time of the Emperor Severus, however, the two began to be confused, and from *c* 400 were treated as identical. This in late popular and mediæval Latin, and in the Romanic languages, *f* was often substituted, as it is now regularly in Italian and Spanish (e.g. *fantasia*, *filosofia*, *filippo*, *fotografico*). This was also the case to a great extent in Old French, and in Old and early Middle English (see PHARISEE, PHILISTER, PHANTOM, PHEASANT); but here, under the influence of the Latin forms, most words so written were subsequently altered back to *ph*, the preponderance of which is particularly notable in Gower. Exceptionally *ph* remains in mod. *f* as in *fancy* (= *phantasy*), *fantastic*. In all modern words of Greek derivation which begin with *ph*, as in *phrase*, *phial*, the sound-value of *f* alone is used.

Phacoscope (fæ'kŏskŏp). Also phako-. [f. Gr. φακός lens + -SCOPE.] An apparatus for observing the changes in form of the crystalline lens of the eye in accommodation to objects at different distances.

Phaëton (feɪ'əton, fæ'e-ŏn). [L. *Phaëtōn*, Gr. φαέθων, the tale of Scheria (Corcyra) = son] One of the inhabitants of Scheria, noted for their luxury; hence (= L. *Phæax*, Horace), a gourmand.

Phaeism (fiɪ'zm). Biol. [f. Gr. φαι-ός dusky, which calls short of melanism.]

Phaenogam, phe- (fiɪ'nŏgæm). Bot. [f. mod. L. *phænogamus*, sc. vegetabilia (Willdenow 1804), f. Gr. φαίνειν to show, appear.]

Phaenogamia, phe- (fiɪnŏgeɪ'mɪə). Bot. [mod. L. *phænogamia*, f. Gr. φαίνειν to show + γάμος marriage, sexual union.]

Phaenogamic, phe- (fiɪnŏgæ'mɪk), a. Bot.

Phaenogamous, phe- (fiɪnŏ'gaməs), a. Bot.

Phaenology, Phaenomenon: see PHENO-.

Phaenozygous (fiɪnŏzaɪ'gəs), a. Anthropol. Also pheno-.

Phaeophyll (fiɪ'ŏfɪl). Bot.

Phaeodarian (fiɪŏdeɪ'rɪən), a. and sb. Zool.

Phaeophyll (fiɪ'ŏfɪl). Bot.

Phæton: see PHAETON.

Phagocyte (fæ'gŏsaɪt). Physiol. [mod. f. Metschnikoff (cf. φαγο-eating, devouring + -CYTE.] A leucocyte (white blood-corpuscle or lymph-corpuscle) which, under certain conditions, has the power of absorbing and destroying pathogenic microbes by a process of intracellular ingestion, and thus of guarding the system against infection.

Hence **Phagocytal** (-saɪtăl), **Phagocytic** (-sɪ'tɪk), adjs., pertaining to, or having the nature or function of, a phagocyte; **Phagocytism** (pr. ʒə-saɪ'tɪ'zm), **Phagocytosis** (fæ'gŏsaɪtoʊ'sɪs), the action of phagocytes; the absorption and destruction of pathogenic microbes by phagocytes; **Phagocytoblast**, the embryonic form of a phagocyte.

Phalanster (fæ'lænstə). [ad.F. *phalanstère*, a word coined by its founder Fourier; f. L. *phalanx* + (apparently) *monastère* monastery.]

Phalansterian (fælănsteɪ'rɪən), a. and sb.

Phalansterism (fæ'lænstərɪzm). Also **Phalansterianism**; **Phalansterist** = phalansterian; **sb.** a member of the system of phalansteries.

Phalanstery (fæ'lænstərɪ). [Anglicized form of F. *phalanstère*.] In Fourier's scheme for the reorganization of society, a building or set of buildings occupied by a *phalanx* or socialistic community; hence, such a community itself, numbering about 1800 persons, living together as one family, and holding property in common.

Phalanx (fæ'læŋks). Pl. phalanxes, phalanges (fælæ'ndʒiɪz). Also † falanx, phalanx, -ynx, -ynx. [a. L. *phalanx*, a. Gr. φάλαγξ.]

Phalarism (fæ'lərɪzm). Obs. Also † phalerism.

Phalarope (fæ'lərŏp). [a. F. *phalarope*, f. Gr. φαλαρίς coot + πούς foot.]

Phalera (fæ'lərə). Roman Antiq. Pl. phalerae. [L. *phalera*, a. Gr. φάλαρα.]

Phalerate (fæ'lərət), a. Obs.

Pha'lerate, a. Obs. In 8 phalerate. [ad. L. *phalerātus*.]

Phalangid (fælæ'ndʒɪd). Zool.

Phallus (fæ'ləs). Pl. -i. [L. *phallus*, a. Gr. φαλλός penis.]

Phallism (fæ'lɪzm). Also † phalism.

Phallic (fæ'lɪk), a. [f. Gr. φαλλικός.]

Phallicism (fæ'lɪsɪzm).

Phallin (fæ'lɪn). Chem. and Path.

Phanar (fænaːr). Turkish *fanar*, a. Gr. φανάριον lantern.]

Phanerogam (fæ'nərŏgæm). Bot. [F. *phanérogame* or mod.L. *phanerogamus*.]

Phanerogamia (fænərŏgeɪ'mɪə). Bot.

Phanerogamic (fænərŏgæ'mɪk), a. Bot.

Phanerogamous (fænərŏ'gaməs), a. Bot.

Hence **Phanariot** (fænaˈrɪot). [ad.mod.Gr. φαναριώτης; a resident in the Phanar quarter of Constantinople, one of the class of Greek officials residing there.]

Phanerocarpous, a. Bot.

Phanerocephalous, a.

Phancie, -y, obs. forms of FANCY.

Phangle, obs. erron. form of FANGLE.

Phansigar (fæ'nsɪgaːr). [Hindi *phānsīgar* strangler, noose-man, f. *phānsī* noose.] An East Indian professional robber and assassin, one of a gang who strangled and robbed travellers and others; a thug.

Phantascope (fæ'ntəskŏp). [f. irreg. f. Gr. φαντά- visible, evident + -SCOPE.]

Phantasm (fæ'ntæzm). Forms: 4-5 fantasme, fantum, fantosme, fantome, etc. [ad. L. *phantasma*, a. Gr. φάντασμα.]

Phantasma (fæntæ'zmə). [L. and eccl. Gr. φάντασμα, cf. φαντασία.]

Phantastic, obs. form of FANTASTIC.

Phantasma (fæntæ'zmă). Also 2 fantame. Pl. -as, -ata (7 -aes). [a. It. *fantasma* = L. *phantasma*, a. Gr. φάντασμα appearance, mere appearance, phantom, image, f. φαντάζειν to make visible, present to (or as to) the eye.]

Phantasmagoria (fæntæzmăgō'riă). [f. Gr. φάντασμα PHANTASM + (?) ἀγορά assembly, place of assembly.]

Phantasmagoric (-ō'rik), a. [f. prec. + -IC.]

Phantasmagorical (-ō'rikăl), a.

Phantasmagory (fæntæ'zmăgŏri). [Cf. F.]

Phantasmal (fæntæ'zmăl), a. [f. PHANTASM + -AL.]

Phantasmally, adv. [prec. + -LY.]

Phantasmascope (-skōp). rare.

Phantasmatic (fæntæzmæ'tik), a. Eccl. Hist.

Phantasmatical, a. Obs.

Phantasmatography. rare.

Phantasmist. rare.

Phantom (fæ'ntŏm). Forms: 4-7 fantosme, -osum, 4-6 -ume, -ome, -ima, -umme, -on, fantum, 4-5 fantosn, fantome; 8-6 phantome, (7 -ôm(e), 7-8 phantôme, 7 phantum. [ME. fantosme, fantome, a. OF. fantosme.]

Phantomatic, a.

Phantomize, v. rare.

Phantomry. rare.

Phantomnation, error for *phantom nation*.

Phantomy, a. rare.

Pharaoh (fē'rō). Also Pharaon, Pharaon, Pharo. [a. L. Pharaō.]

Pharaonic (fēărŏ'nik), a.

Phantoscope (fæ'ntŏskōp). [f. Gr. φαντός visible + -SCOPE. Cf. PHANTASCOPE.]

Pharbitin (fār'bitin). Chem.

Pharology (fărŏ'lŏdʒi). error. pharonology.

Phare (fē'ar). [a. F. phare (1553 in Hatz.-Darm.), ad. L. pharus, a. Gr. φάρος: see PHAROS.]

Pharian (fē'ăriăn), a. poet. [ad. L. Pharius.]

Pharis, pl. of *pharie*, obs. form of FAIRY.

Pharisaic (færisē'ik), a. [ad. L. Pharisai-us (Jerome), a. Gr. φαρισαϊκ-ός, f. φαρισαῖ-ος: see PHARISEE.]

Pharisaical, a. prec. + -AL.

Pharisaically, adv.

Pharisaicalness.

Pharisaism (færisēizm). [f. as prec. + -ISM.]

Pharisaize, v.

Pharisean (færisī'ăn), a.

Pharisee (fæ'risī). Forms: 1 farisēus, etc.

Pharisee, v. trans.

Pharmaceutic (fārmăsiū'tik), a. [as prec. + -IC.]

Pharmaceutical (fārmăsiū'tikăl), a.

Pharmaceutist. [irreg. f. Gr. φαρμακευτής (see above) + -IST.]

Pharmacist (fā'rmăsist). [f. PHARMACY + -IST.]

Pharmaco- combining form of Gr. φάρμακον drug.

Pharmacodynamic, a. Obs.

Pharmacognosis, Obs.

Pharmacognosy.

Pharmacognostic, a.

Pharmacography. [Gr. φάρμακον + -γραφία.]

Pharmacolite (fā'rmăkŏlait). Min.

Pharmacology (fārmăkŏ'lŏdʒi). [mod.L. pharmacologia (W. Harris 1683): see PHARMACO- + -LOGY.]

Pharmacological (-lŏ'dʒikăl), a.

Pharmacologist.

Pharmacon (fā'rmăkŏn). [Gr. φάρμακον.]

Pharmacopoeia (fārmăkŏpī'ă). Also 7 -pea.

Pharmacopoeial, a.

Pharmacopoeian, a. and sb. rare.

Pharmacopoean, a. Obs.

Pharmacopolist (fārmăkŏ'pŏlist). Now rare.

Pharmacosiderite (fārmăkŏsi'dĕrait). Min.

Pharos (fē'rŏs). Also 6-7 (9) pharus, 7 pharo, -oe, (var.) faro, 7 pharos.

Pharyngal (fări'ŋgăl), a. [f. Gr. φάρυγγ-, PHARYNX + -AL.]

| PHARYNGEAL. | 769 | PHASIANID. | PHASIANINE. | 770 | PHEASANT-EYED. |

Pharyngeal. ... **Pharyngalgia** ... **Pharyngo-** ... **Pharyngectomy** ... **Pharyngic** ... **Pharyngitis** ... **Pharyngo-** ... **Pharynx** ... **Pharyngography** ... **Pharyngo-laryngeal** ... **Pharyngological** ... **Pharyngonasal** ... **Pharyngo-oesophageal** ... **Pharyngoplegia** ... **Pharyngoscope** ... **Pharyngoscopy** ...

Phascogale ... **Phascolome** ... **Phase** ... **Phasianid** ...

Phasianidae ... **Phasianine** ... **Phasis** ... **Phaseolus** ... **Phasma** ...

Pheasant ... **Pheasant-eyed** ...

| PHEASANTRY. | 771 | PHENOL. | PHENOLIC. | 772 | PHENOMETHOL. |

Pheasantry ... **Pheasant's eye** ... **Pheasant-shell** ... **Pheer** ... **Pheere** ... **Phellandrene** ... **Phellem** ... **Phello-** ... **Phellogen** ... **Phellonic** ... **Phenacetin** ... **Phenacite** ... **Phenakistoscope** ... **Phenazine** ... **Phenol** ... **Phenolic** ... **Phenological** ... **Phenology** ... **Phenologist** ... **Phenomenal** ... **Phenomenalism** ... **Phenomenalist** ... **Phenomenalize** ... **Phenomenally** ... **Phenomenon** ... **Phenomenalist** ... **Phenomenology** ... **Phenomenological** ... **Phenomenon** ... **Phenomethol** ...

Phenose (*fī́nōs*). Chem. [f. PHEN- + -OSE.] A sweetish amorphous deliquescent compound formed by the action of hypochlorous acid on benzene, and having the general formula $C_6H_{12}O_6$ or the carbohydrates.

Phenyl (*fḗnil*, *fĕ́nil*). Chem. [f. PHEN- + -YL, lit. 'radical of benzene (*phene*)'.]
1. The monovalent organic radical C_6H_5.
2. *attrib.* and *Comb.*, as phenyl acetate, carbonate, cyanide, ether, ketones, oxide, phosphate, sulphide; phenyl compounds, derivatives, etc.; phenyl-blue, chemical-anilo-phenylimide of quinone; phenyl-brown, a colouring matter, possessing explosive properties.

Phenyl-acetic = ACETANILIDE. **Phenyl-a-** ... **Phen′ic acid** ...

Phenacetin ...

Phene (*fēn*), obs. form of FERETRAE.

Phenike, obs. form of PHENE.

Phew (*fiū*, *fū*), *int.* (*v.*, *sb.*) Also 7 *pheut*, *pfew*, 8 *pfeu*, 9 *phugh*: see also PHO, PHOO. [Representing the action of puffing or blowing away with the lips.]

Phiala, obs. form of FIOLE.

Phial (*fai′ăl*), *sb.* Forms: *a.* 4 *fiol*, 4–5 *fyole*, 5 *fyolle*, *fialle*, 6 *fyol*, 7 *fiole*. *β.* 4 *phiole*, 6–8 *phiall*. See also VIAL. [ME. *a.* F. *fiole* (12th c. in Hatz.-Darm.), *also phiole* (13th c. in Cotgr. *fiole*, *phiole* = Pr. *fiola*, It. *fiala*, late L. *phiala*, *Gr.* φιάλη a broad flat vessel.]

Phiala, obs. form of FIOLE.

Philadelphian (*filădé′lfiăn*), *a.* and *sb.* [f. Gr. φιλαδελφία brotherly love (f. φιλάδελφος loving one's brother or sister, f. PHILO- + ἀδελφός brother, ἀδελφή sister) + -AN.]

Philadelphianism (from sense 2).

Philadelphite (*filădé′lfait*). *Min.* [Named 1880, from Philadelphia in Pennsylvania.]

Philander (*filæ′ndər*), *sb.* [ad. Gr. φίλανδρος adj., loving or fond of men.]

Philandering, *vbl. sb.*

Philanthrope (*fi′lănθrōp*), *sb.* [ad. F. *philanthrope*, ad. Gr. φιλάνθρωπος.] = PHILANTHROPIST.

Philanthropic (*filănθrɔ′pik*), *a.* [ad. Gr. φιλανθρωπικός, or ad. F. *philanthropique*.]

Philanthropical ... **Philanthropically** ...

Philanthropist (*filæ′nθrōpist*). [f. Gr. φιλάνθρωπος + -IST.]

Philanthropy (*filæ′nθrōpi*). Also 7 in L. form philanthropia. [ad. late L. *philanthrōpia* (in earlier Eng. use, *a.* Gr. φιλανθρωπία love to mankind, f. φιλάνθρωπος.]

Philanthropinism [ad. Ger. *philanthropinismus*], the educational system of the philanthropine.

Philanthropist ...

Philanthropism (*filæ′nθrōpizm*). [f. as next + -ISM.] The profession or practice of philanthropy; a philanthropic theory or system.

Philaster, obs. form of FILACER.

Philately (*filæ′tǝli*). [ad. F. *philatélie*, f. Gr. φιλ-, PHILO- + ἀτέλεια freedom from tax or charge, ἀτελεία exemption from payment (f. ἀτελής not paying toll, f. ἀ- priv. + τέλος toll, tax). Proposed by M. Herpin, a postage-stamp collector, in *Le Collectionneur de Timbres-poste* (15 Nov. 1864).]

Philhellene (*filhé′lēn*), *a.* and *sb.* Also -en. [ad. Gr. φιλέλλην, f. φίλος loving the Greeks, f. φιλ-, PHILO- + Ἕλλην Hellene.]

Philhellenic *a.* **Philhellenism** *b.*

Philhellenist ...

Philibeg, var. FILIBEG.

Philip (*fi′lip*). Also 5 phelyp, 7 phillip. [A personal name; in F. *Philippe*, *Philibert*, etc.]

Philippic (*filí′pik*), *sb.* and *a.* [ad. L. *Philippicus*, *a.* Gr. Φιλιππικός, f. Φίλιππος Philip (of Macedon).] 1. Name for the orations of Demosthenes against Philip king of Macedon in defence of Athenian liberty.

Philippize (*fi′lipāiz*), *v.* [ad. Gr. φιλιππίζειν, f. φίλιππος, f. Φίλιππος Philip (of Macedon).]

Philippized ...

Philippist (*fi′lipist*). A follower of Philip Melanchthon.

Philistia (*filí′stiă*), *sb.* Also 9 Phillistia. [a. L. *Philistia*, *Philistiim*, *Philistini* ...]

Philistine (*fi′listain*, -tin, filí′stin), *sb.* and *a.* Forms: *a.* 4 (Philistien, Palisten, -estine), 4–6 Philistyne, 6–9 Philistine. *β.* 6–7 Philistim (-ijn, -ine, -time), 7 thim, -time. See also PHILISTEE, PHILISTER.

Philistinism (*fi′listinizm*, *fi′listiniz'm*). [f. PHILISTINE + -ISM.]

Phillis, **Phillyrea**, **Phillibeg**, **Phillupine** ...

Philippize ...

Phillis (*fi′lis*), *sb.* Also 9 Phyllis. [a. L. *Phyllis*, a girl's name in Virgil, Horace, etc., *a.* Gr. Φυλλίς.]

Phillis *v.* (*nonce-wd.*) *trans.*, to address in pastoral letters.

Phillyga, var. PHILLYREA, PILLY.

Phillygenin (fili'rdʒīnin). *Chem.* [f. PHILLYRIN with ending of *salicinin*.] A resinous crystallizable substance (C₂₄H₃₄O₉), polymeric with sali-genin, obtained from phillyrin by boiling with hydrochloric acid, or by lactic fermentation.

Phillyrea, var. PHILLYREA.

† Phillyrea (fili'riă, filirrā). *Bot.* Also 7 phill.rea, phyl(l)area, phyllies, 7-8 phyl-lerea, phillirea, 8 phyll(y)rea, -rea, phillarea, anglicized forms: 7-8 philery, phillery, (8 milleroy). [Bot. L. *phyllyrea* (Tournefort); Linnæus *Philos. Bot.* 175), erroneous form; Gr. *φιλύρεα* (Theophr.), app. a deriv. of *φιλύρα* linden tree. There are many erroneous spellings in *phyll-* and *phyl-*.]

A genus of ornamental evergreen shrubs (N.O. *Oleaceæ*), natives of the Mediterranean region and the East, with opposite leaves and inconspicuous greenish-white flowers in axillary clusters; also called *jasmine-box* or *mock thorn*. P. *latifolia* is considered to be the Phillyrea of Dioscorides and Theophrastus.

Phillyrin (fili'rin). *Chem.* [f. prec. + -IN.] A white crystallizable bitter substance (C₂₇H₃₄O₁₁) obtained from the bark of *Phillyrea latifolia*.

Philo-, before a vowel (or *h*) usually **phil-** (fil), repr. Gr. *φιλο-*, *φιλ-*, combining form from root of *φίλος* friend, loving, *φιλεῖν* to love (cf. *φίλο-*, *φιλο-*, from *φίλε-ειν* to hate, *μισεῖν* hate, hatred).

Philochristian, *a.* [f. PHILO- + CHRISTIAN + -AN + -IAN.]

Philocynic (-sinik) (Gr. *κύων*, *κυν-* dog) loving dogs.

Philocyny (-kini) loving of dogs.

Philodemic (-demik) [Gr. *φιλόδημος*, f. *δῆμος* the people], loving the people.

Philodendron [f. Gr. *φιλόδενδρον* tree-loving, f. *δένδρον* tree], a lover of trees.

Philogenet

Philology (fīlɔ'lodʒi). *Now rare* or *Obs.*

Philoprogenitive (fīlǎprodʒɛ'nitiv), *a.* [irreg. f. PHILO- + L. *progenit*-, stem of *progignere* to beget + -IVE.]

Philomath (fi'lomæþ). *Now rare*. [ad. Gr. *φιλομαθής*, f. PHILO- + *μαθ-*, stem of *μανθάνειν* to learn.]

Philomathic (filomæþik), *a.* [f. *philomathique*.]

Philomathy (filɔ'məþi).

Philomel (fi'lomel).

Philomela (filomī'lǎ).

Philopater. *Obs. rare.* [ad. Gr. *φιλοπάτωρ* loving one's father, or *φιλοπάτρης* loving one's fatherland.]

Philopolity (-po'liti).

Philoprogenity (-dʒɛ'niti).

Philosopher (filɔ'sofǝr). Forms: α *philosophre*, β *philesophre*, γ *philisofre* 4-5 *philosophre*. β *filosofer*, *filsofur*, *filozophur*.

Philosophership (filɔ'sofǝrʃip). [f. as prec. + -SHIP.]

Philosophastering *ppl. a.*

Philosophastry (-æstri).

Philosopheme (-sofīm).

Philosopher's stone.

Philosophess (filɔ'sofes). [f. PHILOSOPHER + -ESS.]

Philosophiant. *Obs.* [ad. *philosophant*.]

Philosophic (filosɔ'fik), *a.* (*sb.*) [ad. *φιλοσοφικός*]

† Philosophiant. *Obs.*

Philosophical (filosɔ'fikǎl), *a.*

1. B - PHILOSOPHICAL 1; scientific.

(Upper half — dictionary columns, headwords in reading order)

Philosophically, adv.

Philosophicalness.

Philosophism (filŏs′ŏm). [a. F. *philosophisme*.]

Philosophist (filŏs′ŏfist).

Philosophistic, **Philosophistical**, a.

Philosophize (filŏs′ŏfəiz), v.

Philosophizer.

Philosophling.

Philosophy (filŏs′ŏfi).

Philosopho- combining form.

Philosopho-bia. [f. Gr. φιλοσοφο- + -PHOBIA.]

Philosophoracy. [f. as prec. + -CRACY.]

Philosopheress.

Philosophule, nonce-wd.

Philosophism.

Philo-xenist (filŏ-).

Philter, philtre, sb.

Philtre, philter, v.

(Lower half — dictionary columns, headwords in reading order)

Phiz.

Phiz, phizz, sb. Also ff. FIZZ.

Pho, int. Also PHOH.

Phob-

Phoca, Phoco-.

Phleb-, before a consonant PHLEBO-.

Phlebectasia.

Phlebitis.

Phlebo-.

Phlebogram.

Phlebolite, Phlebolith.

Phlebotomist.

Phlebotomize.

Phlebotomy.

Phlegm (flem), sb.

Phlegmagogue (fleg′magŏg).

Phlegmasia.

Phlegmatic (flegmæ′tik), a.

Phlegmon.

Phlogistic (flŏdʒis′tik), a.

Phlogiston.

Phlogisticate ...

Phlogistion ...

Phlogiston (Chem.) ...

Phlogogenetic, a. Path. Producing inflammation. Also **Phlogogenic**.

Phlogogenous, a.

Phlogosis (Path.) ...

Phlome. Obs. rare.

Phlox (Bot.) ...

Phloxin (Chem.)

Phloridzin, **Phlorizin** (Chem.)

Phloretin (Chem.)

Phloramine (Chem.)

Phloroglucin (Chem.)

Phlorone (Chem.)

Phlorol (Chem.)

Pho, phoh, int. rare.

Phobanthropy ...

phobia, **-phobia** ...

Phobism ...

Phlyctena, -ena (Path.)

Phlyctenula ...

Phlyzacium (Path.)

Phocacean (Zool.)

Phocodont (Zool.)

Phocomelus (Teratology)

Phœbe ...

Phœbus ...

Phœnician ...

Phœnicopter (Zool.)

Phœnicopterid ...

Phœnicopterous, a.

Phœnigm ...

Phœnix, **phenix** ...

Phœnix (Bot.)

Phœnicin ...

Pholas (Zool.)

Pholad, Pholade ...

Pholas ...

Pholcid (Zool.)

Pholcoid ...

Pholerite (Min.)

Pholidolite (Min.)

Pholidolite ...

Pholidota (Zool.)

Pholque (Zool.)

Phonal ...

Phonasthenia ...

Phonate, v.

Phonation (Physiol.)

Phonatory, a.

Phonautograph ...

Phonautogram ...

Phone ...

Phoneidoscope ...

Phonetic, a. and sb.

Phonetician ...

Phonetics ...

Phonetism ...

Phonetist ...

Phonic, a.

Phonetization ...

Phonetize, v.

Phoneme ...

Phonematic ...

Phonics ...

Phono- ...

Phonogram ...

Phonograph ...

Phonology ...

Phonorganum ...

Supplement, p. 3873; Corrigenda, p. 4092; Spurious words, p. 4093; Books quoted, p. 4094

Phonocamptic ... Obs. rare.

Phonogram ... [f. Phono- + -gram.]

Phonograph ...

Phonographer ... [f. Phonography + -er.]

Phonographic ... [f. as prec. + -ic. So Graphic.]

Phonographically, adv. In a phonographic manner.

Phonography ...

Phonographist ...

Phonometer ...

Phonometric ...

Phonophorous ...

Phonoscope ...

Phonolite (Dana). [f. Phono- + -lite.]

Phonolitic ...

Phonology ...

Phonometer ...

-phore ...

Phormium ...

Phoronis ...

Phoronomic ...

Phoronomy ...

Phosgene ...

Phosgenite ...

Phosphide ...

Phosphine ...

Phosphinic ...

Phosphide ...

Phosphite ...

Phospho- ...

Phosphate ...

Phosphoretted ...

Phosphoric ...

Phosphorite ...

Phosphorism ...

Phosphorite ...

Phosphorograph ...

Phosphoroscope ...

Phosphorous ...

Phosphorus ...

Phosphuranylite. Min. Hydrous phosphate of uranium, as a yellow pulverulent incrustation.

†Pho·sphure. *Chem. Obs.* Also 8 phosphur. [a. F. *phosphure* (*Nomencl. Chimique* 1787).]

Phosphuret, -ted (fɔ·sfiuret). *Chem.* Also phosphor-. [f. prec. + -ED.] Combined chemically with phosphorus.

Phosphuret·ted, -eted (fɔ·sfiureted). Combined chemically with phosphorus.

†Phosphu·rize. *Path.* = Phosphorize.

Phosphyl (fɔ·sfil). *Chem.* [f. Phosph- + -yl.] The univalent radical PO₂.

Phosy (fəu·si), *a. colloq.* Also foasy. [f. Phos-]

Photal (fəu·tal), *a.* = Photic.

Phota, *Obs.* Also 9 foota.

Photal.

Photelectric: see Photo-electric.

Photic (fəu·tik), *a. rare.* [f. Gr. φῶς, φωτ- light + -ic.]

Photi·on.

Photism (fəu·tiz'm). *Psychics.*

Photi·nian.

Photinism.

Photism.

Photo (fəu·to). 1. Colloquial abbreviation of Photograph.

2. Colloquial (technical) abbreviation for Photographic.

Photo- (fəu·to), combining form of Gr. φῶς, φωτ- light.

1. Words in *photo-* simply denotes 'light'.

2. Words in which *photo-* indicates connexion with photography.

Photo-aquatint : see quots.

Photo-biblio·graphy, description of books by the aid of photography.

Photo·ceramic *a.*

Photo·chromatic (fɔ·tokromæ·tik), *a.* [f. Photo- + Chromatic.]

Photochromy.

Photochronograph (fɔ·tokrɒ·nograf). [Photo- + Chronograph, or (in *a.*) from the Gr. elements of this.]

Photochronography.

Photo-electric, *a.* Also photelectric. [f. Photo- + Electric.]

Photo-engra·ving. [Photo- + Engraving.]

Photo-engrave, *v. trans.*; **Photo-engraver**.

Photo-galvanic, *a.* [f. Photo- + Galvanic.] = Photo-galvanographic.

Photo-galvanography, a process of obtaining from a galvanic plate or paper.

Photo-galvanograph, a print thus formed.

Photogastroscope, -gelatin: see Photo-.

Photogen (fəu·todʒen). [f. Gr. φῶς, φωτ- light + -gen.] 1. Name for a kind of paraffin oil.

Photogene (fəu·todʒiːn). [mod. f. Gr. type *φωτογενής* light-produced.]

Photogenetic (fɔ·todʒenetik), *a. rare.* [f. Photo- + Genetic.]

Photogenic (fɔ·todʒenik), *a.* [f. as Photogenous + -ic.]

Photogenous (fotɒ·dʒinəs) *a.* [f. as prec. + -ous.]

Photoglyph (fəu·toglif). [Gr. γλυφ-.]

Photoglyphy, Photoglyptic *adj.*

Photography, Photolithy, the art or process.

Photograph (fəu·tograf), *sb.* [f. prec. sb.]

1. *trans.* To take a photograph of.

Photographable (fɔ·tografəb'l), *a.* [f. prec. + -ABLE.] Capable of being photographed.

Photography (fotɒ·grafi). [f. Gr. φῶς light + -GRAPHY.]

Photogravure (fɔtograviuə·r), *sb.* [F.]

Photographer (fotɒ·grafər).

Photographic (fɔtogræ·fik), *a.*

Photographist (fotɒ·grafist).

Photograveur, Photograver, an artist in photogravure.

Photograph·ic, *a.*

Photoheliograph (fɔtohiː·liograf).

Photolith (fəu·toliθ), *Photolitho*, abbreviations of Photolithograph.

Photolithograph.

Photolithographer.

Photolithographic.

Photolithotype: see Photo-.

Photology (fotɒ·lodʒi). *rare.* [f. Gr. φῶς light + -LOGY.] The science of light.

Photologist.

Photomagnetograph.

Photo-magnetic, *a.*

Photomapper to **Photo-metallography**: see Photo-.

Photo-mecha·nical, *a.*

Photometer (fotɒ·mitər). [f. Photo- + -METER.]

Photometric (fɔtometrik), *a.* [f. as Photometry + -ic.]

ments..on the relative light of the principal stars. 1875 Bennett & Dyer Sachs' Bot. 663.

So **Photome·trical** *a.*, dealing with photometry; made or measured by a photometer; = **Photome·trically** *adv.*, according to photometry, by means of a photometer; **Photometrician** (-i·ʃăn), **Photometrist** (-ǫ·mĕtrist), one who practises photometry.

1833 Herschel *Astron.* xii. 375 A numerical estimate, grounded on precise 'photometrical experiments, of the apparent brightness of each star. 1864 *Daily Tel.* 16 Sept., The photometrical standard of gas-light] is more than twice as high in many places than it is in London. 1854 Brewster *More Worlds* v. 95 In measuring 'photometrically the light of these three different structures. 1889 *Athenæum* 16 June 766/2 Method of determining the magnitudes of stars photometrically. 1870 Proctor *Other Worlds* v. 143 The estimates of Zöllner, the eminent *photometrician, serve to show..that Jupiter sends more light to us..than a planet of equal size and constituted like Mars, the moon, or the earth, could possibly reflect to us if placed where Jupiter is. 1887 W. R. Bowditch *Coal Gas* iii. 67 The best way for a *photometrist to be certain of his instrument is to test them himself.

Photometry (fo̍tǫ·mĕtri). [ad. mod.L. *photometria* (1760), f. Gr. φωτ-, φῶς light, Photo- + -μετρία measuring, -metry.] Measurement of light; comparison of the intensity of light from different sources; the use of a photometer.

[1760 Lambert *Photometria* [illegible]] 1845 R. Watt *Biblioth. Brit.* v. *J. H. Lambert*, Photometry. [illegible] 1859 *Encycl. Brit.* (ed. 8) [illegible] *Dissert.* 637/2 The eighteenth century created a new branch of optical science (photometry) [illegible] 1896 G. F. Chambers *Astron.* vi. i. 480 The subject of the photometry of stars..has received but little attention from practical astronomers.

Photo-mezzotype: see Photo- 2.

Photomicrograph (fǭ·to,mai·krǒgraf). [f. Photo- 2 + Gr. μικρό-ς small, Micro- + -graph: cf. Micrograph.] A photograph of a microscopic object on a magnified scale. So **Photomi·crogram** in same sense; **Photomicro·grapher**, one who takes photomicrographs; **Pho·tomicrogra·phic** *a.*, pertaining to photomicrography; used for taking photomicrographs; **Pho·tomicro·graphy**, the art of obtaining photographs of microscopic objects on a magnified scale.

1858 G. Shadbolt in *Sutton's Photogr. Notes* III. 208 The word microphotograph originated, I believe, with myself, and is applied, I think correctly, to very small photographs, not to photographs of small objects, which would more correctly be photomicrographs. 1862 *Catal. Internat. Exhib.* II. xiv. 53 A photo-micrographic camera..for taking photographs of..microscopic objects. 1865 *Chambers's Encycl.* VII. 510/2 Photo-Micrography consists in the enlargement of microscopic objects, by means of the microscope, and the projection of the enlarged image on a sensitive collodion film. 1866 J. J. Woodward *Amer. Jrnl. Sci.* Ser. II. XLII. 190 The paper..is illustrated by photomicrographs reproduced by photolithography. 1870 R. J. Fowler in *Eng. Mech.* 4 Feb. 501/3 By uniting the photomicrographic object glass..with the eyepiece.., the apparatus becomes a dioptric compound microscope. 1889 *Anthony's Photogr. Bull.* II. 156 The admitted advantage which Photomicrography offers to the microscopist for recording the images seen under the microscope. 1893 *Brit. Med. Jrnl.* 26 Aug. 487 Illustrated by..photomicrographs of affected nerves. 1896 *Nature* 24 Sept. 490/1 Excellent stained preparations of bacteria, taken by..well-known photomicrographers. 1903 *Nation* (N. Y.) 21 May 417/1 It would have been better..to keep the photomicrograms and the delineations of the trunk-bark separate.

Pho:tomicrosco·pic, *a.* [Photo- 2.] Produced on a microscopic scale by photography.

1870 *Daily News* 7 Dec., The thousands..of private photomicroscopic telegrams from all parts of the country brought in [to Paris] by pigeon post.

Photo-nephograph to **Photophobe**: see Photo- 1, 2.

‖ **Photophobia** (fǭuto͡ifōu·biă). *Path.* Also anglicized **-phoby**. [mod.L., f. Gr. φῶς light, Photo- + -phobia.] Dread of or shrinking from light, esp. as a symptom of diseases of the eyes.

1799 Hooper *Dict. Med.*, *Photophobia*, such an intolerance of light, that the eye, or rather the retina, can scarcely bear its irritating rays. 1858 Mayne *Expos. Lex.*, *Photophobia*, ..photophoby. 1869 G. Lawson *Dis. Eye* (1874) 15 The lids are then red, swollen, and spasmodically closed, from the excessive photophobia. 1899 *Allbutt's Syst. Med.* VIII. 908 The retina [in albinos] is unprotected, and there is consequent photophobia.

Hence **Photophobic** (-fǫ·bik) *a.*, pertaining to or affected with photophobia; dreading light; ‖ **Pho:tophobophthalmia** (-fǫbǫfþæ·lmia) [mod. L.], ophthalmia attended with photophobia.

1842 Dunglison *Med. Lex.*, Photophobophthalmia. 1858 Mayne *Expos. Lex.*, *Photophobicus*, of or belonging to Photophobia: photophobic. *Ibid.*, Ophthalmy, with excessive intolerance of the light: photophobophthalmy. 1878 T. Bryant *Pract. Surg.* I. 89 The affection is attended with photophobic pain about the orbit and sclerotic injection.

Photophone (fǭu·tofōun). [f. Gr. φῶς light, Photo- + -φωνος sounding, sounder, φωνή voice, sound.] Any apparatus in which sounds are transmitted by light; *esp.* that invented by A. Graham Bell and Sumner Tainter in 1880, by means of which sound-vibrations are conveyed to a distance by means of a beam of light reflected from a mirror and received upon a sensitive selenium cell by means of which the sounds are reproduced. See Radiophone.

1880 A. Graham Bell in *Jrnl. Franklin Inst.* CX. 246 We have named the apparatus for the production and reproduction of sound in this way 'The Photophone', because an ordinary beam of light contains the rays which are operative. 1880 *Athenæum* 25 Sept. 405/1 The sensibility of the metal selenium to the action of the solar spectrum recommends it as the most favourable substance for use in the 'photophone', as the new instrument is called. 1889 Preece & Maier *Telephone* 304 Bell and Sumner Tainter have constructed an apparatus, to which they gave the name of 'photophone', which enabled them to reproduce at a distance..the sounds of articulate speech by means of light. [illegible]

Hence **Photophonic** (-fǫ·nik) *a.*, pertaining to or produced by the photophone; **Photophony** (fotǫ·fŏni), the use of the photophone; the conveyance of sound-vibrations by means of light.

1880 A. Graham Bell in *Athenæum* 11 Dec. 747/3 (*title of paper*) On Methods of preparing Selenium and other Substances for Photophonic Experiments. 1880 S. P. Thompson in *Nature* 17 Feb. 365/1 An elegant series of researches in photophony. 1880 *Nature* 26 Feb. 377/1 Yielding radiophonic and photophonic sounds when illuminated by intermittent beams of different kinds.

Photophore (fǭu·tofōəɹ). [mod. ad. Gr. φωτοφόρος light-bearing or -bringing: see Photo- and -phore.] a. An apparatus with an electric light, used for examination of internal organs of the body and for other purposes.

1883 *Athenæum* 22 Dec. 773/3 Mr. J. Mayall, jun., exhibited the Helot-Trouvé electric photophore, which had been recommended as an excellent illuminant for microscopical purposes. 1893 *Syd. Soc. Lex.*, *Photophore*, the name for an electric light for use in laryngoscopy, adapted to a forehead-band, so as to be reflected by the laryngoscopic mirror into the mouth and throat under examination.

2. A luminiferous organ in certain animals.

1898 *Nature* 23 June LVIII. 192/1 The new bathybial fish from Lord Howe Island, ..*Æthoprora perspicillata*, ..distinguished..by the presence of a pair of supernumerary photophores between the upper angle of the eye and the ante-orbital.

Photophosphorescent to **-salt**: see Photo-.

Photoscope (fōu·tǒskoup). [f. Photo- + -scope.] **a.** A means of examining light, e. g. for purposes of analysis. **b.** An instrument for measuring the intensity of light by means of the varying electrical resistance of some substance sensitive to light, such as selenium. **c.** (See quot. 1896.) **d.** [with *photo-* taken as = *photograph*.] A lens or apparatus with lenses, through which photographs are viewed.

1872 tr. *Schellen's Spectr. Anal.* xli. 230 The solar spectrum is the most perfect photoscope that in the present state of science can be imagined. 1875 Knight *Dict. Mech.* 1690/1 *Photoscope*, an instrument or apparatus for exhibiting photographs. 1896 *Current Hist.* (Buffalo) VI. 16 An instrument called a 'photoscope'..to examine certain internal parts of the human body..with the aid of sunlight only.

Photoscopic (-skǫ·pik), *a.* [f. as prec. + -ic.] **a.** Pertaining to the examination of light. **b.** Belonging to a photoscope.

1872 tr. *Schellen's Spectr. Anal.* xli. 230, I..recommend to the scientific investigator a camera obscura specially adapted to these photoscopic observations.

Photo-sculptural to **-spectroscopy**: see Photo- 2.

Photosphere (fōu·tǒsfīəɹ). [f. Photo- + Gr. σφαῖρα ball, Sphere.]

1. A sphere or orb of light, radiance, or glory. (In mod. use only as *fig.* from 2.)

1664 H. More *Myst. Iniq.*, *Apol.* iii. § 15. 503 Though..Christ be surrounded with Gleams and Raies of inaccessible Light and Glory, which envelop his Body, ..yet if any mortal could get within this so refulgent Photosphere (as I may so call it) or Orb of glory and brightness [etc.]. 1878 Symonds *Shelley* v. 97 The central motive of *Laon and Cythna* is surrounded by so radiant a photosphere of imagery and eloquence that it is difficult to fix our gaze upon it. 1891 T. Hardy *Tess* II. xiv, Her hopes mingled with the sunshine in an ideal photosphere which surrounded her as she bounded along the soft south wind.

2. *Astron.* The luminous envelope of the sun (or a star), from which its light and heat radiate.

1848 Herschel *Ess.* (1857) 287 A self-luminous nebulous matter, of a vaporous or gaseous nature, of which these photospheres, and, perhaps, some entire nebulæ, may consist. 1861 W. Fairbairn *Addr. Brit. Assoc.*, The remarkable discoveries of Kirchoff and Bunsen require us to believe that a solid or liquid photosphere is seen through an atmosphere containing iron, sodium, lithium, and other metals in a vaporous condition. 1893 Sir R. Ball *Story of Sun* 137 That envelope of glowing clouds surrounding the Sun which we call the photosphere.

Photospheric (fǭutosfe·rik), *a.* *Astron.* [f. prec. + -ic.] Of or pertaining to the photosphere.

1865 *Reader* 7 Jan. 16/3 Photospheric clouds affecting forms reminding one of the flocculent mass of an incandescent metal, in suspension in a liquid. 1878 Newcomb *Pop. Astron.* iii. ii. 266 Above the photospheric layer [of the sun] lies an atmosphere of a very complex nature. 1893 Sir R. Ball *Story of Sun* 196 The selective absorption of photospheric light.

Photo-sulphate to **-tachometry**: see Photo-.

Phototactic (fǭutotæ·ktik), *a.* *Biol.* [f. Gr. φῶς light, Photo- 1 + τακτικ-ός fit for ordering or arranging.] Of cells or organisms: Characterized by arranging themselves in some particular way under the influence of light.

1885 *Encycl. Brit.* XIX. 62/1 Protoplasmic masses which respond to the directive action of light are said to be 'phototactic'. 1901 G. N. Calkins *Protozoa* 296 The most phototactic forms are the flagellated cells.

So ‖ **Photota·xis** *Biol.* [mod.L., f. Gr. τάξις arrangement], spontaneous arrangement of cells or small organisms under the influence of light.

1893 in *Athenæum* 16 Sept. 375/3. 1901 G. N. Calkins *Protozoa* 296 Light as well as heat rays frequently have a similar directive effect upon Protozoa, a phenomenon called *phototaxis* by Strasburger. 1901 *Brit. Med. Jrnl.* 4 May 1070 The phototaxis of certain algæ.

Phototelegraphy to **-tint**: see Photo-.

‖ **Phototonus** (fotǫ·tŏnŏs). *Bot.* [mod.L., f. Gr. φῶς, φωτο- light (see Photo-) + τόνος tension, Tone.] Name given by Sachs to the normal condition of sensitiveness to light in leaves and other organs, maintained by continued exposure to light, as opposed to the rigidity induced by long exposure to darkness. Hence **Phototonic** (fǭutotǫ·nik) *a.*, exhibiting phototonus; sensitive to light.

1875 Bennett & Dyer tr. *Sachs' Bot.* 678 The power of movement in plants is lost when they have remained in the dark for a considerable time..; in other words, they become rigid by long exposure to darkness..; the exposure to light must continue for a considerable time..before the motile condition which I have termed 'Phototonus' is restored. *Ibid.* 790 Changes in the intensity of the light produce the same effect as irritants, but only on healthy phototonic plants; leaves which have become rigid from exposure to the dark show no irritability to variations in its intensity until they have again become phototonic from long-continued exposure to light.

Photo-trichroma·tic, *a.* [f. Photo- 2 + Trichromatic.] Of or pertaining to three colours used in colour-photography, or to colour-photography in which three colours are used.

1896 C. G. Zander (*title*) Photo-trichromatic printing. 1904 *Westm. Gaz.* 2 May 9/3 The photo-trichromatic inks of commerce are not optically the true complements of the red, violet, and green, which are the primary colour sensations.

Phototropic (fǭutotrǫ·pik), *a.* *Bot.* [f. Photo- + Gr. -τρόπος turning + -ic: cf. Gr. τροπικός of or pertaining to turning.] Bending or turning under the influence of light: a more accurate substitute for Heliotropic. So **Phototro·pically** *adv.*, **Photo·tropism**.

1899 C. B. Davenport *Exper. Morphol.* ii. 437 Effect of Light upon the Direction of Growth—Phototropism. [*Note.*] On some accounts it is unfortunate to accept this word rather than the older, more familiar term 'heliotropism'; but..the latter is obviously unfitted to our broader view of the subject. *Ibid.* 438 Aquatic plants..are only very slightly phototropic. *Ibid.* 440 Etiolated willow shoots, upon which ..the more strongly refractive rays only act phototropically. 1900 *Nature* 4 Jan. 219/1 The comparative effects of flash light and steady light in producing phototropism in seedling plants.

Phototype (fǭu·tǒtəip), *sb.* [f. Gr. φῶς light, Photo- + -type.] A plate or block for printing from, produced by a photographic process, or by a combination of photography with etching or some mechanical process; also, the process by which such a plate is produced, or a picture, etc., printed from it. Formerly, name of a process of carbon printing invented by M. Joubert. Also *attrib.*

1859 *Sat. Rev.* 26 Feb. 242/1 The term Phototypes being reserved for such as yield impressions that may be taken off from a flat surface by a mechanical method of printing, analogous to that of the lithographer or of the anastatic printer. 1867 *Athenæum* 20 July 90/1 The process generally employed has been that of lithography from the phototype. 1881 *Nation* (N. Y.) XXXII. 441 A phototype portrait of the late Thomas A. Scott. 1888 *Academy* 16 June 405/1 The phototypes are frequently too dark and sombre. 1902 Wall *Dict. Photogr.* 503 *Phototype*, a mechanical printing process in which a gelatine film itself is used to print from.

Hence **Pho·totype** *v. trans.*, to reproduce (a picture, MS., etc.) by means of phototypy; **Phototypic** (-ti·pik) *a.*, pertaining to or of the nature of a phototype; **Phototy·pically** *adv.*, by means of a phototype; **Pho·totypist**, a maker of phototypes; **Pho·totypy**, the art or process of making phototypes.

1859 *Sat. Rev.* 22 Jan. 98/1 Each of the phototypic methods at present before the world..seeks to attain this object by acting upon one and the same fundamental chemical fact. *Ibid.*, Various processes of photoglyphy and phototypy. 1887 *Sci. Amer.* 17 Dec. 385/1 A combined albumen and asphalt process of phototypy. 1888 *Athenæum* 11 Aug. 198/3 May Prof. Bruun and his editor, his phototypist and his subscribers, live for ever. 1891 *Chicago Advance* 16 July, Phototypically. *Mod.* The MS. is being phototyped.

Phototypography (fǭutotəipǫ·grăfi). [f. Photo- + Typography.] Printing from an engraving in relief produced by a photo-mechanical process. Hence **Phototypographic** (fǭu,to,tipǫgræ·fik) *a.*, of, pertaining to, or of the nature of phototypography.

1890 *Cent. Dict.*, *Phototypographic*. 1892 Woodbury *Encycl. Phot.* 540 Phototype..is now applied to a method of Collotype or Albertype printing and to blocks produced by any photo-typographic process. *Ibid.*, *Photo-typography*, a general term applied..to a large number of processes in which printing surfaces are made by the aid of light.

Photovitrotype to **-xylography**: see Photo-.

Photozinc (fǭu·tozink), **Photozi·nco**, abbrev. of Photozincographic *a.*

1884 *Athenæum* 19 Jan. 88/3 From the Ordnance Survey photozinc facsimile of the original charter. 1892 Woodbury *Encycl. Phot.* 540 Photo-zinco Engraving = Photo-zincography.

Photozincography (fǭu:to,zinkǫ·grăfi). [f. Photo- + Zinc + -graphy.] The art or process of producing by photographic methods a design on a zinc plate from which prints can be taken (analogous to Photolithography). Hence **Photozi·ncograph** *sb.*, a plate, or a picture or facsimile, produced by photozincography; **Photozi·ncograph** *v. trans.*, to produce or copy by photozincography; **Pho·tozincogra·phic, -ical** *adjs.*, of or pertaining to, of the nature of, or produced by photozincography.

1860 (Feb. 4) Sir H. James *Rep. Progr. Ordnance Survey* 6 (Parl. Papers XXIII. 400) We have also tried a method.. by which the reduced print is in a state to be at once transferred to stone or zinc, from which any number of copies can be taken, as in ordinary lithographic or zincographic printing...I have called this new method Photo-zincography. 1860 — *Photo-zincography* 5 By the term Photo-Zincography is meant..the art of producing a photographic facsimile of any subject, such as a manuscript, a map, or line engraving, and transferring the photograph to zinc, thereby obtaining the power of multiplying copies in the same manner as is done from a drawing on a lithographic stone, or on a zinc plate. 1861 (*title*) Domesday Book: Cornwall. Photo-Zincographed..at the Ordnance Survey Office, Southampton. 1862 Scott & James *Photo-zincography* Pref. 4 This was the first Photo-zincograph ever taken here or elsewhere. *Ibid.* 1 The Photo-zincographic and Analogous Processes practised at the Ordnance Survey Office, Southampton. 1865 *Pall Mall G.* 4 Aug. 11/1 With large photo-zincographical plates prepared at Southampton under the superintendence of Sir Henry James. 1866 *Contemp. Rev.* III. 520 The reproduction of facsimiles by the photo-zincographic process. 1877 *Reg. Privy Council Scot.* I. Introd. 50 The process of photozincography is available. 1895 *Q. Rev.* Jan. 56 The sheets..are photozincographed.

Photozi·ncotype. [f. Photo- + Zincotype.] A plate for printing from, produced by photozincography. So **Photozincotypy** (-zi·ŋkotəipi), printing from photozincotypes; photozincography.

1886 *Sci. Amer.* 24 July 49/2 (*heading*) Photo-zincotypy and other Photographic Printing Methods for the Printing Press...In place of wood cuts, photo-zincotypes are very often used.

‖ **Photuria** (fotiūə·riă) *Path.* [mod.L., f. Gr. φῶς, φωτ- light + οὖρον urine.] Phosphorescence of the urine (Dunglison *Med. Lex.* 1853).

‖ **Photuris** (fotiūə·ris). *Entom.* [mod.L., f. Gr. φῶς, φωτ- light + οὐρά tail.] A genus of American coleopterous fire-flies of the *Lampyridæ* or glowworm family; *esp.* the common firefly or lightning-bug of the eastern United States (*P. pennsylvanica*).

1883 C. F. Holder in *Harper's Mag.* Jan. 190/2 In the foliage..the brilliant green light of the photuris appears.

‖ **Phragma** (fræ·gmă). *Nat. Hist.* Pl. **-ata.** Rarely anglicized as **phragm.** [mod.L., a. Gr. φράγμα, -ματ- fence; in mod.F. *phragme* (Littré).] A partition, septum: *spec.* **a.** *Entom.* A transverse partition separating the prothorax from the mesothorax, found in some insects, as the Mole-cricket.

1826 Kirby & Sp. *Entomol.* III. xxxiii. 368 Phragma (the Phragm). The Septum that closes the posterior orifice of the Prothorax in Gryllotalpa. *Ibid.* xxxv. 582 The phragm, or septum of the prothorax is most conspicuous in the mole-cricket (Gryllotalpa), in which it is a hairy ligament attached to the inside of the upper and lateral margins of the base of that part: inclining inwards, it forms the cavity which receives the mesothorax.

b. *Bot.* See quot. 1866.

1830 Lindley *Nat. Syst. Bot.* 136 Tribulus has the fruit separating into spiny nuts, with transverse phragmata. 1863 J. H. Balfour *Man. Bot.* § 447. 1866 *Treas. Bot.*, *Phragma*, a spurious dissepiment in fruits, i. e. one which is not formed by the sides of carpels; a partition, of whatever kind.

Hence **Phragma·tic** *a.* (see quot.).

1858 Mayne *Expos. Lex.*, *Phragmaticus*, ..applied to cattle, etc., which suffer from colic or obstruction of the bowels: phragmatic.

Phra·gmocone. *Zool.* Also *erron.* phragma-. [f. Gr. φραγμό-ς fence (or φραγμο- = φραγματο-: see prec., and cf. σπερμο-) + κῶνος Cone.] The conical chambered internal skeleton of a fossil belemnite; also, by extension, the corresponding spiral or otherwise-shaped part in other fossil cephalopods.

1847 *Nat. Encycl.* I. 141 (*Actinocamax*) The species..had no true alveolar cavity or phragmacone. 1851–6 Woodward *Mollusca* 48 Its phragmocone is but the representative of the calcareous axis (or splanchno-skeleton) of a coral. 1862 Dana *Man. Geol.* 451 [In Belemnites] a small chambered cone, called the phragmocone..which has a siphuncle. 1888 Rolleston & Jackson *Anim. Life* 457 The chambered shell ..known in *Belemnitidae* as 'phragmacone'.

Hence **Phragmoco·nic** *a.*, of, pertaining to, or of the nature of the phragmocone of a belemnite.

1890 in *Cent. Dict.*

Phragmo·phorous, *a.* *Zool.* [ult. f. Gr. φραγμο- (see prec.) + -φόρος bearing + -ous.] Having a phragmocone; belonging to the *Phragmophora*, a section of decacerous cephalopods, having a phragmocone. 1890 in *Cent. Dict.*

Phraisse, var. Phairs, obs. Sc. f. Farce *sb.*[2]

Phrampell, obs. form of Frampold.

Phrantic, -ick, obs. forms of Frantic.

Phrasal (frēi·zăl), *a.* [f. Phrase + -al.] Of the nature of or consisting of a phrase.

1871 Earle *Philol. Eng. Tongue* § 445 Often we see that we are obliged to translate a flexional Greek adverb by a phrasal English one. *Ibid.* § 529 A third series..are the phrasal prepositions, consisting of more than one word.

Phrase (frēiz), *sb.* Also 6 in form **phrasis**; 6 **phraze, phrais**; *Sc.* (chiefly in sense 4) 7–9 **frase**, 8–9 **fraise**, 8 **fraze.** [ad. late L. *phrasis*, a. Gr. φράσις speech, way of speaking, phraseology, f. φράζ-ειν to point out, indicate, declare, tell; possibly through F. *phrase* (which however is not cited before Montaigne *c* 1575), also *frase*; so It., Sp. *frase*, OSp., Pg. *phrase*; Du., Ger. *phrase.*]

1. Manner or style of expression, esp. that peculiar to a language, author, literary work, etc.; characteristic mode of expression; diction, phraseology, language.

1530 Palsgr. Introd. 39 Of the differences of phrasys betwene our tong and the frenche tong...The phrasys of our tong and theyrs differeth chefely in thre thynges. 1535 Joye *Apol. Tindale* (Arb.) 38 Yt is the comon phrase of scripture to saye *spiritus sanctificationis pro spiritu sancto* [etc.]. 1540–1 Elyot *Image Gov.* Pref. (1556) 3 Conforme the stile thereof with the Phrase of our Englishe. 1573 Tusser *Husb.* (1878) 207 From Paules I went, to Eaton sent, To learn streight waies the latin phraies. 1579 Lyly *Euphues* (Arb.) 137 So I would have abiect and base phrase eschewed. 1593 Drayton *Eclogues* iv. 19 These men..press into the learned troop With filed Phraze to dignifie their Name. *a* 1600 Montgomerie *Sonn.* xliv, 3it, as I dar, my deutie sall be done With more affectione nor with formall phrais. *a* 1654 Selden *Table-T.* (Arb.) 20 The Bible is rather translated into English Words, than into English Phrase. The Hebraisms are kept, and the Phrase of that Language is kept. 1774 Warton *Hist. Eng. Poetry* vi. (1840) II. 6 Adam Davie writes in a less intelligible phrase than many ..antient bards. 1812 J. Wilson *Isle Palms* iv. 619 Her Mary tells in simple phrase Of wildest perils in former days. 1882 A. W. Ward *Dickens* vii. 205 The supreme felicity of phrase in which he has no equal.

2. A small group or collocation of words expressing a single notion, or entering with some degree of unity into the structure of a sentence; an expression; esp. one in some way peculiar to or characteristic of a language, dialect, author, book, etc.; an idiomatic expression.

1530 Palsgr. Introd. 42 The table of verbes where all suche phrasys be set out at the length. *Ibid.* 814/2 Whan all is doone and sayd, *pour tout potaige*, a phrasis. 1551 T. Wilson *Logike* (1580) 64 b, By the mistaking of wordes, or by false vnderstanding of phrases. 1613 Purchas *Pilgrimage* I. xi. (1614) 59 The liquid pitch floateth on the top of the water, like clouted creame, to vse his owne phrase. 1662 *Bk. Com. Prayer* Pref., Some words or phrases of ancient usage. 1697 W. Pope *Bp. S. Ward* 104 My lord, I might bear you in hand; a western frase, signifying to delay or keep in expectation. 1812 Southey *Omniana* II. 13 This phrase, *a priori*, is in common most grossly misunderstood. 1875 Helps *Ess.*, *Advice* 50 'If I were you' is a phrase often on our lips. 1878 Bosw. Smith *Carthage* 334 The phrase 'it would have been', is a dangerous phrase to use in the study of history.

† **b.** Applied to a single word. *Obs.*

1597 Shaks. *2 Hen. IV*, iii. ii. 79 Accommodated, it comes of *Accommodo*: very good, a good Phrase. 1598 Shaks. *Merry W.* i. iii. 33 Conuay: the wise it call: Steale? foh: a fico for the phrase. 1699 Cotes tr. *Dupin's Hist. O. & N. Test.* I. i. i. 3 St. Jerom is one of the first who absolutely us'd the Phrase of *Canon* to denote the Catalogue of the Sacred Books.

c. *Grammatical Analysis*: see quot. 1865.

1852 Morell *Anal. Sent.* § 17 The predicate may be extended in various ways:—1. By an adverb, or an adverbial phrase. 1865 Dalgleish *Gram. Anal.* 15 A phrase is a combination of words without a predicate; a clause is a term of a sentence containing a predicate within itself, as *Phrase*, spring returning; *Clause*, when spring returns. 1904 C. T. Onions *Adv. Eng. Syntax* 13 Adverb-equivalents: (1) A Phrase formed with a Preposition—He hunts *in the woods*. ..(4) A Clause—*When you come*, I will tell you. *Ibid.* 15 Two or more Sentences, Clauses, Phrases, or Single Words, linked together by one of the Conjunctions *and, but, or, nor, for*, are called co-ordinate..[as] A youth *to fortune* and *to fame* unknown; *To be* or *not to be*—that is the question.

3. A peculiar or characteristic combination of words used to express an idea, sentiment, or the like in an effective manner; a short, pithy, or telling expression; sometimes, a meaningless, trite, or high-sounding form of words.

1579 W. Wilkinson *Confut. Familye of Loue* 1 b, These be their sweete and amiable wordes, and lovely phrases. 1588 Shaks. *L. L. L.* i. i. 166 A man in all the worlds new fashion planted, That hath a mint of phrases in his braine. 1641 J. Jackson *True Evang. T.* i. 19 Thus man degrades himselfe, and (according to the phrase, *Apoc.* 19. 20) receives ..the mark of the beast. 1780 Cowper *Let. to Hill* 16 Mar., To use the phrase of all who ever wrote upon the state of Europe, the political horizon is dark indeed. 1816 Scott *Bl. Dwarf* ii, Greyhounds..who were wont, in his own phrase, to fear neither dog nor devil. 1841 D'Israeli *Amen. Lit.* (1867) 578 The phrase was tossed about till it bore no certain meaning. 1879 Froude *Cæsar* xii. 164 He called him, in the Senate, 'the saviour of the world'. Cicero was delighted with the phrase. 1899 *Daily News* 20 July 6/4 Humanity is the slave of phrase, and the phrase, 'Integrity of the Turkish Empire', is as much a matter of course to the English as 'Britannia rules the waves'.

4. *Sc.* and *north. dial.* Exclamatory or exaggerated talk; an outburst of words, whether in wonder, admiration, boastfulness, praise or flattery; 'gush'; esp. in *to make* (*a*) *phrase*, to express one's feelings in an exclamatory way, to 'gush', to make much ado about a person or thing (sometimes implying mere talk); *to make muckle* or *little phrase about*, to talk or express one's feelings much or little about.

1725 Ramsay *Gentle Sheph.* i. ii, He may indeed, for ten or fifteen days Mak muckle o' ye, with an unco fraise. *Ibid.* v. iii, I ne'er was good at speaking a' my days, Or ever lov'd to make o'er great a frase. 1768 Ross *Helenore* iii. 105 Gin that's the gate, we need na mak gryte fraze. 1816 Scott *Antiq.* xxxiv, An honest lad that likit you weel, though he made little phrase about it. 1901 G. Douglas *House w. Green Shutters* 175 He made a great phrase with me.

5. *Mus.* Any (comparatively) short passage, forming a more or less independent member of a longer passage or 'sentence', or of a whole piece or movement.

1789 Burney *Hist. Mus.* IV. 27 More forms or phrases of musical recitation still in use, may be found in Peri and Caccini, than in Monteverde. 1866 Engel *Nat. Mus.* iii. 82 A phrase extends over about two bars, and usually contains two or more motives, but sometimes only one. 1871 B. Taylor *Faust* (1875) I. Notes 228 In the overture to *Don Giovanni* a certain musical phrase occurs which is not repeated till the finale. 1880 Sir C. H. Parry in Grove *Dict. Mus.* II. 706/1 The complete divisions are generally called periods, and the lesser divisions phrases. The word is not and can hardly be used with much exactness and uniformity.

6. *Fencing.* A continuous passage in an assault without any cessation of attack and defence.

Common in mod. French, and occasionally used by recent Eng. writers on Fencing. (Sir F. Pollock.)

7. *attrib.* and *Comb.*, as *phrase-coiner, -composition, -compound, -Latin, -repeater, -type*; **phrase-book**, a book containing a collection of idiomatic phrases used in a language, with their explanation or translation; also *attrib.*; † **phrase-like** *adv.*, phrase by phrase; **phrase-maker**, a maker of telling or fine-sounding phrases; **phrase-mark**, a sign in musical notation to indicate the proper phrasing: see sense 5; **phrase-monger**, one who deals in or is addicted to fine-sounding phrases; so **phrase-mongering, -mongery.** Also Phraseman.

1600 Nashe *Summer's last Will* Wks. (Grosart) VI. 149 Hang copies, flye out *phrase books, let pennes be turnd to picktooths. 1723 [see *phrase-Latin*]. 1898 *Westm. Gaz.* 11 Oct. 2/1 You must have a phrase-book knowledge of the language. 1901 *Daily Chron.* 17 May 3/2 Professional *phrase-coiners. 1902 Greenough & Kittredge *Words* 70 *Phrase-composition..is alike active in slang and in law-abiding speech. *Ibid.* 188 Native *phrase-compounds are *beside*, ..*betimes*, ..*undershot*, *overlord* [etc.]. 1723 S. Morland *Spec. Dict. Eng. & Lat.* 5 There have..been some Phrase Books put out into the World, and esteemed as a Supplement to Dictionarys..'Twas my Father's Opinion, that to these we owe the Introduction of a thing call'd *Phrase-Latin. 1549 W. Baldwin (*title*) The Canticles or Balades of Salomon, *phraselyke declared in Englysh Metres. 1822 T. Mitchell *Aristoph.* I. 291 This *phrase-maker Hath ta'en thy very senses. 1901 *Academy* 23 Mar. 247 All the characters are phrase-makers and epigrammatists. 1815 *Zeluca* III. 149 The ineffable little old *phrase-monger. 1877 Morley *Crit. Misc.* Ser. ii. 122 If Robespierre had been a statesman instead of a phrase-monger, he had a clear course. 1879 F. Harrison *Choice Bks.* iii. (1886) 73 The jackanapes *phrasemongering of some Osric of the day. 1830 *Examiner* 598/2 We have commenced with his *phrase-mongery, and from it we shall proceed to some specimens of his philosophy.

Phrase, *v.* Also 6–7 **frase.** [f. prec. sb. Cf. F. *phraser* (1755 in Hatz.-Darm.).]

1. *intr.* To employ a phrase or phrases.

a 1550 *Image Hypocr.* iii. 475 in *Skelton's Wks.* (1843) II. 439 Thoughe ye glose and frase Till your eyes dase. 1888 [see Phrasing *ppl. a.*].

2. *trans.* To put into words; to find expression for; to express in words or a phrase, esp. in a peculiar, distinctive, or telling phraseology; to word, express. *To phrase it*, to express the thing, to 'put it'.

1570 Foxe *A. & M.* (ed. 2) 55/2 Clement..who..was adioyned with Paule..dyd phrase them ['Epistle to the Hebrues'] in his style, and maner. 1625 Bp. Mountagu *App. Caesar* 64 So Ezechiel phraseth it. *a* 1652 J. Smith *Sel. Disc.* vi. 205 The Seventy..have much varied the manner of phrasing things from the original. 1701 Rowe *Amb. Step-Moth.* iii. ii, Nor can I phrase my speech in apt Expression, To tell how much I love and honour you. 1771 Johnson *Let. to Mrs. Thrale* 7 July, He has had, as he phrased it, 'a matter of four wives'. 1879 H. George *Progr. & Pov.* x. v. (1883) 388 The free spirit of the Mosaic law.. inspired their poets with strains that yet phrase the highest exaltations of thought.

3. To describe (a person or thing) by a name, designation, or descriptive phrase; to call, designate; † to signify.

1585–7 T. Rogers 39 *Art.* (Parker Soc.) 230 The papists.. phrase the preachers to be uncircumcised Philistines. 1613 Shaks. *Hen. VIII*, i. i. 34 When these Sunnes (For so they phrase 'em). 1614 Camden *Rem.* (ed. 2) 205 To poore man ne priest the penny frases nothing. Men giue God aie the least, they feast him with a farthing. 1636 Prynne *Unbish. Tim.* 36 The Scripture..never phrasing him a Bishop, nor giving him that Title. 1858 Bushnell *Nat. & Supernat.* iv. (1864) 105 Phrasing the conduct and doings of men. 1902 Kipling in Monkshood & Gamble *Life* 49 He is supremely original: which makes it quite difficult to phrase him comparatively.

4. with *adv.* To do (a thing) *away*, do (a person) *out of*, etc., by phrases or talk.

a 1718 Penn *Tracts* Wks. 1726 I. 471 If People will be phrased out of their Religion they may. 1830 *Examiner* 81/1 The Monarch is not permitted to phrase away his people's troubles.

5. *intr.* *Sc.* To 'make a phrase' (prec. 4), to talk exaggeratedly or 'gushingly', esp. in appreciation or praise. Also *trans.* To make much of in words.

1786 Burns *Ep. to G. Hamilton* 3 May, To phrase you and praise you, Ye ken your laureate scorns. 1808 J. Mayne *Siller Gun* iv, In vain his heralds fleech'd and phrased.

6. *trans.* *Mus.* To divide or mark off into phrases, esp. in execution: to perform according to the phrases. Also *absol.* (See also Phrasing *vbl. sb.* 2.)

1796 Burney *Mem. Metastasio* II. 332 The air should be phrased and symmetric. 1896 *Peterson Mag.* VI. 279/1 She phrases naturally and her intonation is admirable.

Phrased (frēizd), *a.* [f. Phrase *sb.* or *v.* + -ed.] Expressed in phrases, worded; characterized by phrases (of a specified kind).

1557 North *Gueuara's Diall Pr.* Prol. A ij b, Suche, so straunge, and high phrased was the matter whiche he talked of. 1886 A. W. Tuer in *Pall Mall G.* 8 Oct. 2/2 The quaintly phrased advertisements are genuine.

Phra·seless, *a.* [f. Phrase *sb.* + -less.] Without a phrase or phrases; in quot. app. 'which there is no phrase to describe'; but cf. 'his speechless hand' in *Coriol.* v. i. 67 (Schmidt).

1597 Shaks. *Lover's Compl.* 225 O, then, aduance of yours that phraseles hand, Whose white weighes downe the airy scale of praise.

Phraseman (frēi·zmæn). [f. Phrase *sb.* + Man.] A man successful in making or using telling phrases; a phrase-monger.

1798 Coleridge *Fears in Solitude* 111 The poor wretch.. Becomes a fluent phraseman. 1814 Cary *Dante, Paradise* viii. 153 Ye..of the fluent phraseman make your King.

Phraseogram (frēi·ziǒgræm). [irreg. f. Gr. φράσις + -gram: see Phraseology.] A written character or symbol representing a phrase; *spec.* in phonography or other shorthand system, a conventional combination of signs or letters standing for a phrase.

1847 I. Pitman *Man. Phonogr.* (ed. 8) 63 An extensive list of phraseograms is given in the 'Reporter'. 1868 *Ibid.* 15 *Phraseogram*, a combination of shorthand letters representing a phrase or sentence. 1895 W. E. A. Axon in W. Andrews *Curious Ch. Customs* 251 There are phraseograms for 'in the name of the Lord', 'wherefore said the psalmist', etc.

Phraseograph (frēi·ziǒgraf). *Shorthand.* [f. as prec. + -graph.] A phrase for which there is a phraseogram. So **Phraseogra·phic** *a.*, of the nature of a phraseogram, written in phraseography. **Phraseo·graphy** [see -graphy], **a.** the representation of phrases or sentences by abbreviated characters in writing, esp. in systems of shorthand; the use of phraseograms; **b.** written phraseology.

1845 I. Pitman *Man. Phonogr.* 52 Phraseography. To promote expedition..the advanced phonographer may join two or more words together, and thus sometimes express a phrase without removing the pen. 1847 *Ibid.* (ed. 8) 64 It is not safe to write the phrase, *I cannot*, as a phraseograph. 1881 — *Phonographic Phrase Bk.* Pref., With very little practice..the phraseographic combinations are found to be quite as legible as the ordinary Phonography. 1888 — *Man. Phonogr.* 11 *Phraseograph*, a phrase that is written without lifting the pen. 1899 *Pall Mall Mag.* Feb. 198 The..task of rendering it [the chorography] into modern phraseography.

Phraseolo·gic, *a.* *rare.* [f. Phraseology (or its mod.L. orig.) + -ic.] = next, 2.

1828–32 in Webster.

Phraseological (frēi:zi,ǒlǫ·dʒikăl), *a.* Also 8 phrasio-. [f. as prec. + -al.]

1. Using phrases or peculiar expressions; expressed in a special phrase or phrases.

1664 H. More *Myst. Iniq.* To Rdr., A Rude, uncivil, uncharitable, phraseological Form of railing against such Things or Persons as are..Sacred. 1748 Richardson *Clarissa* (1811) VII. lxxxi. 341 He said, in his phraseological way, that one story was good till another was heard. 1877 Black *Green Past.* viii, Her father professed an elaborate phraseological love for her.

2. Of or pertaining to phraseology; dealing with phrases, or with the phraseology of a language, etc., or that peculiar to an author or work.

1664 Gouldman (*title*) A Copious Dictionary..With.. Etymological Derivations, Philological Observations, and Phraseological Explications. 1694 *Lond. Gaz.* No. 3037/4 Phraseological Books..published. 1716 M. Davies *Athen. Brit.* III. 3 Jacobus Billius's Greek Phrasiological Collection. 1850 Adler *Fauriel's Prov. Poetry* viii. 157 The correction of a barbarism or phraseological vice. 1899 H. G. Graham *Soc. Life Scot. in 18th C.* (1901) viii. i. 26 *note*, A phraseological peculiarity of these tracts.

Phraseolo·gically, *adv.* [f. prec. + -ly [2].] In a phraseological way; with the use of a phrase.

1867 *Nation* (N. Y.) 3 Jan. 9/1 When the verb *faire* is used phraseologically with a substantive. 1884 *W. Chester* (Pa.) *Local News* XII. No. 44. 3 Phraseologically speaking, it is a 'cold day' when our Justices of the Peace don't have a scene at their offices.

Phraseologist (frēizi,ǫ·lǒdʒist). [f. next + -ist.] **a.** One who treats of phraseology. **b.** A maker or user of phrases; one who uses striking or sounding phrases, esp. in an indiscriminate manner; a phrase-monger.

1713 Berkeley *Guardian* No. 39 ¶ 14 The author..is but a mere phraseologist. 1727 Bailey vol. II, *Phraseologist*, an Explainer of elegant Expressions in a Language. 1809 W. Irving *Knickerb.* iv. i. (1849) 201 To borrow a favorite ..appellation of modern phraseologists. 1899 in *Westm. Gaz.* 18 May 3/2 There is something..which in time perverts its advocate into a mere phraseologist.

Phraseology (frēizi,ǫ·lŏdʒi). [ad. mod.L. *phraseologia*, Gr. φρασεολογία, erroneously formed by M. Neander (see quot.) from Gr. φράσις + -λογια, -logy; the correct Gr. form (used in mod. Gr.) is φρασιολογία *phrasiology*: cf. φυσιολογία physiology, etc.

Neander appears to have had in his mind the genitive case φράσεως; and the erroneous form has perh. been perpetuated in Eng. under the influence of *phrase*.]

† **1.** A collection or handbook of the phrases or idioms of a language; a phrase-book. *Obs.*

[1558 M. Neander (*title*) ΦΡΑΣΕΟΛΟΓΙΑ ΙΣΟΚΡΑΤΙΚΗ ΕΛΛΗΝ ΚΟΛΑΤΙΝΗ. Phraseologia Isocratis Græcolatina: id est, Phraseon siue locutionum, elegantiarumue Isocraticarum Loci, seu Indices. 1681 W. Robertson (*title*) Phraseologia generalis...A Full, Large, and General Phrase Book.] 1776 Baretti (*title*) Easy Phraseology, for the use of young Ladies who intend to learn the colloquial part of the Italian Language.

2. The choice or arrangement of words and phrases in the expression of ideas; manner or style of expression; the particular form of speech or diction which characterizes a writer, literary production, language, etc.

1664 H. More *Myst. Iniq.*, *Apol.* iv. § 6 The Conclusions or Phraseologies of the School-Divines touching this Point. 1669 Gale *Crt. Gentiles* i. iii. x. 96 Such is the incomparable Majestie of the Scripture stile, and Phraseologie. 1714 *Spectator* No. 616 ¶ 1 That ridiculous Phraseology, which is so much in Fashion among the Pretenders to Humour and Pleasantry. 1771 Burke *Corr.* (1844) I. 254 Men, according to their habits and professions, have a phraseology of their own. 1857–8 Sears *Athan.* 6 Religious phraseologies from which religious ideas have been expunged. 1875 Jowett *Plato* IV. 130 Parmenides..is the founder..in modern phraseology, of metaphysics and logic.

† **3.** (See quots.) *Obs. rare*—[0].

1670 Blount *Glossogr.* (ed. 3), *Phraseology*, a speaking of Phrases, or of the proper form of Speech. 1678 Phillips (ed. 4), *Phraseology*, (Greek) a Discourse of Phrases, or an uttering of Phrases in common Speech.

† **4.** *Mus.* Arrangement of phrases. *Obs.*

1789 Burney *Hist. Mus.* IV. 571 The want of symmetry in the phraseology of his melodies.

Phraser (frēi·zəɹ). [f. Phrase *v.* + -er [1]. Cf. F. *phraseur* (18th c. in Hatz.-Darm.).] One who uses phrases, or expresses himself in a peculiar or striking manner; a phrase-monger.

1637 J. Williams *Holy Table* 212 According to this English Phraser. 1878 J. Thomson *Plenip. Key* 19 And though he speaketh much,—beyond demur, No phraser, but a trusty messenger. 1879 G. Meredith *Egoist* v, Like all rapid phrasers, Mrs. Mountstuart detested the analysis of her sentence.

† **Phra·sical**, *a.* *Obs. rare*—[1]. [f. Gr. φράσ-ις Phrase *sb.* + -ical.] Of the nature of a phrase; idiomatic.

1615 T. Adams *Eng. Sickn.* Wks. 1861 I. 395 'Daughter of my people'..This is an abstractive phrase..Here it is phrasical, and therefore not to be forced.

† **Phra·sify**, *v.* *Obs.* [f. L. *phrasi-s* Phrase *sb.*: see -fy.] *intr.* To use a phrase.

1633 Ames *Agst. Cerem.* ii. 267 That which the Def. neglected, the Rejoynder taketh to supplie, *least we should bragge*, as it pleaseth him to phrasifie. 1674 Hickman *Hist. Quinquart.* (ed. 2) 191 To disgrace the Calvinists, by calling them Gospellers; For thus he phrasifieth.

Phra·siness. *colloq.* [f. Phrasy + -ness.] The quality of being of the nature of a phrase: see Phrase *sb.* 3; proneness to use phrases.

1891 *Review of Rev.* 14 Apr. 376/1 The Germans are heartily sick of the phrasiness of their ruler. 1896 W. W. Peyton in *Contemp. Rev.* June 837, I use the word 'communication' of design to release the idea of communion from religious phrasiness.

Phrasing (frēi·ziŋ), *vbl. sb.* [f. Phrase *v.* + -ing [1].]

1. The action of the vb. Phrase; manner or style of verbal expression; phraseology, wording.

1611 Bible *Transl. Pref.* 11 Wee haue not tyed ourselues to an vniformitie of phrasing, or to an identity of words. 1741 Richardson *Pamela* (1824) I. iv. 238 He says, in his usual way of phrasing, that he'll make it as easy to you as a glove. 1887 Saintsbury *Hist. Elizab. Lit.* ix. (1890) 325 Milton..mixes the extremest vernacular with the most exquisite and scholarly phrasing.

2. *Mus.* The rendering of musical phrases. Also *attrib.* as *phrasing slur*, a slur indicating the proper phrasing.

1880 Sir H. Parry in Grove *Dict. Mus.* II. 706/2 Just as the intelligent reading of a literary composition depends upon two things, accentuation and punctuation, so does musical phrasing depend on the relative strength of the sounds, and upon their connection with or separation from each other. 1886 *Academy* 17 July 48/3 He aroused the sympathy and interest of his audience by his soft and liquid tone, his neat playing, and by his delicate and finished phrasing. 1898 *Westm. Gaz.* 29 Dec. 3/2 Where it has seemed desirable, phrasing slurs have been added.

Phra·sing, *ppl. a.* [f. as prec. + -ing [2].] That phrases; using phrases; in *Sc.*, loudly or exaggeratedly expressing one's feelings or sentiments.

1785 Burns *To W. Simpson* ii, In sic phraisin terms ye've penn'd it, I scarce excuse ye. 1888 Stevenson *Across the Plains*, *Beggars* iv. (1892) 268 A..tale of some worthless, phrasing Frenchman.

Phrasy (frēi·zi), *a.* *colloq.* Also erron. **phrasey.** [f. Phrase + -y.] Abounding in phrases; characterized by great use of phrases.

1849 *Ecclesiologist* IX. 125 They resemble what is familiarly known as a piece of phrasy Latin. 1871 *Daily News* 11 Mar., The document smacks overmuch of the phrasey, and is less redolent of the vigorous than of the lachrymose.

Phrator (frēi·tǫɹ). [a. Gr. φράτωρ another form of φράτηρ clansman: cognate with Skr. *bhrātā*, Zend *bhrātar*, L. *frāter*, Goth. *brōþar* Brother.] A member of a Grecian phratry; also *transf.* a fellow-clansman.

1847 Grote *Greece* ii. x. III. 87 If a man was murdered, first his near relations, next his gennêtes and phrators, were both allowed and required to prosecute the crime at law. 1881 L. H. Morgan *N. Amer. Ethnol.* IV. 11 To preserve some degree of equality in the number of phrators in each.

Phratriac (frēi·triæk), *a.* *rare.* [ad. Gr. φρατριακ-ός, f. φρατρία Phratry: see -ac.] = next.

1884 *Athenæum* 21 June 795/3 In Attica there were also two great organizations, one based originally on locality, and another whose sole qualification was that of birth—the demotic and the phratriac.

Phratric (frēi·trik), *a.* [ad. Gr. φρατρικ-ός, f. φρᾱτρ-α = φρατρία Phratry + -ic.] Of or pertaining to a phratry or clan; consisting of phratries.

1847 Grote *Greece* ii. x. III. 75 The phratric union, binding together several gentes, was less intimate [than the gentile union]. 1881 L. H. Morgan *Contrib. N. Amer. Ethnol.* IV. 11 The phratric organization has existed among the Iroquois from time immemorial.

Phratry (frēi·tri). [ad. Gr. φρατρία, f. φράτηρ: see Phrator. In F. *phratrie* (Littré).]

1. *Ancient Gr. Hist.* A politico-religious division of the people, which took its first rise from the ties of blood and kinship; in Athens, each of the three subdivisions into which the phyle was divided; a clan.

[1753 Chambers *Cycl. Supp.*, *Phratriarchus*, among the Athenians, a magistrate that presided over the phratria, or third part of a tribe. He had the same power over the phratria, that the phylarchus had over the tribe.] 1833 Thirlwall in *Philol. Museum* II. 307 The desire of the higher classes to keep aloof from the rustics.., who had been admitted into the phratries. 1875 Jowett *Plato* (ed. 2) I. 231 A family Zeus, and a Zeus guardian of the phratry. [1884 *Athenæum* 21 June 795/3 No deme coincided with a phratria or with any subdivision of a phratria.]

2. *transf.* Applied to tribal or kinship divisions existing among primitive races, as the Indians of North America, aborigines of Australia, etc.

1876 L. H. Morgan in *N. Amer. Rev.* CXXIII. 65 It is.. ..probable..that the Mound-Builders were organized in gentes, phratries, and tribes. 1882 H. Spencer *Pol. Inst.* 549 Not only where descent in the male line has been established, but also where the system of descent through females continues, this development of the family into *gens*, phratry, and tribe is found. 1891 Westermarck *Hist. Hum. Marriage* (1894) 298 The Seneca tribe of the Iroquois was divided into two 'phratries', or divisions intermediate between the tribe and the clan.

† **Phrayes**, obs. illit. form of Froise, Fraise.

1685 *Oldbury Parish Reg.* in *Blakeway MS.* (Bodl.) 3. 72, 2 gamon of Bacon and phrayes made of ye egges.

Phreatic (fri,æ·tik), *a.* [f. Gr. φρέαρ, φρέατ- well, cistern + -ic.] Of or pertaining to a well: applied to water from deep wells.

1892–3 *14th Rep. U. S. Geol. Surv.* ii. 16 'Phreatic water'. [*Note*] This term was coined by Hay, in the course of the recent artesian and underflow investigation.., as a convenient designation for 'underground waters which can be, or which it is hoped may be, reached by wells or other subground works'.

‖ **Phren** (frīn). Pl. **phrenes** (frī·nīz). [mod. L., a. Gr. φρήν midriff, in pl. φρένες parts about the heart, breast; heart, mind, will.]

1. *Anat.* The diaphragm; the upper part of the abdomen: anciently supposed to be the seat of the mind.

1706 Phillips, *Phrenes*, ..the Membranes about the Heart; also the Diaphragm or Midriff. 1893 *Syd. Soc. Lex.*, *Phren*, .. the diaphragm; also, the epigastrium.

2. *Philos.* The seat of the intellect, feelings, and will; the mind.

Phrenalgia: see Phreno-.

† **Phrene·siac**, *a.* *Obs.* [f. Gr. φρένησις (see next), taken as = φρενησία (cf. It. *frenesia*) + -ac.] = Phrenetic *a.* 1.

1814 Scott *Wav.* xliii, Like an hypochondriac person, or, as Burton's Anatomia hath it, a phrenesiac or lethargic patient.

‖ **Phrenesis** (frĭnī·sis). *Path.* [L. *phrenēsis* delirium, a. late Gr. φρένησις, f. φρήν, φρεν-: see next, and cf. Frenzy.] = Phrenitis.

1547 Boorde *Brev. Health* lvii. 26 In the head may be many infirmities, as the Apoplexie, the Scotomy, the Megrym, the Sood, the Phrenyses [1598 phrenises]. 1551 Ascham *Let.* 18 May, Wks. 1865 I. ii. 288 The prince of Spain..is this day fallen sore sick of a phrenesis. 1561 Hollybush *Hom. Apothec.* 5 An apostemacion in the braynes of some litle skinnes, that enuiron the braynes, the same are called Phrenesis. 1800 Lamb *Let. to Manning* 27 Dec., At last George Dyer's phrenesis has come to a crisis; he is raging and furiously mad.

Phrenetic (frĭne·tik), *a.* (*sb.*) Forms: *α.* 4 **frenetyk**, 4–6 **-ike**; 5 **frena-**, 6 **frenetyke, -ik**, 6–7 **-ick**, 7 **frenitick**, 9 **frenetic.** *β.* 6 **phrenetike**, 6–7 **-ique**, 7 **-icke**, 7–8 **-ick**, 9 **-itic**, 7– **phrenetic.** [a. OF. *frenetike* (*Dial. S. Greg.* 12–13th c.), ad. L. *phrenēticus*, a. late Gr. φρενητικός (Epict.), for φρενιτικός afflicted with φρενῖτις delirium, f. φρήν, φρεν- heart, mind. Formerly stressed *phre·netic*, whence Phrentic, Frantic.]

† **1.** Of persons: Delirious; mentally deranged; insane; crazy: = Frantic *a.* 1. *Obs.*

α. *c* 1374 Chaucer *Troylus* v. 206 (Camps.) And in his browes frenetyk [*v. r.* frentyk] and madde He cursed Ioue, Appollo, and ek Cupide. 1377 Langl. *P. Pl.* B. x. 6 To flatereres or to folis þat frantyk [*v. r.* frenetike] ben of wittes. 1483 Caxton *Gold. Leg.* 193/1 Saynt marcial heled one that was frenatyke. 1596 Dalrymple tr. *Leslie's Hist. Scot.* viii. 84 Donald and quha with him appeiret frenetik.

β. 1558 Knox *First Blast* (Arb.) 11 The foolishe, madde and phrenetike shal gouerne the discrete. 1651 Hobbes *Leviath.* iii. xxxiv. 215 Those that became Phrenetique, Lunatique, or Epileptique. 1751 Lavington *Enthus. Meth. & Papists* iii. (1754) 139 They [Persons bit by the Tarantula] are Phrenetic and delirious. 1778 *Phil. Trans.* LXVIII. 206 All that survived..were to the highest degree phrenetic and outrageous.

2. *transf.* Affected with excessive excitement or enthusiasm, esp. in religious matters; furious; frantic; fanatic. Cf. Frantic *a.* 2.

α. *c* 1540 tr. *Pol. Verg. Eng. Hist.* (Camden) I. 107 This.. restrained the rude raginge of the frenetick Scotts. 1657 Hawke *Killing is M.* 40 The foolish dictates of such frenetick Impostor. 1819 Wiffen *Aonian Hours* (1820) 109 Frenetic zealots. 1882 *Pall Mall G.* 27 Oct. 1 Some of the more frenetic of the franc-tireurs of Liberalism.

fig. 1872 Browning *Fifine* v, How the pennon from its dome, Frenetic to be free, makes one red stretch for home!

β. 1565 Calfhill *Answ. Treat. Crosse* 23 It is to be feared greatly, least their arise some phrenetike persons, which will bragge and boast..that they be Prophetes. 1650 Ingelo *Bentiv. & Ur.* v. 138 He esteems Prophetick Visions only as Dreams of phrenetick men. 1858 *Times* 4 Nov. 6/4 The chivalrous and phrenetic Montbar, whose name was a cry to hush infants. 1878 J. P. Newman in *N. Amer. Rev.* CXXVII. 321 When inspired, their individuality was intact. They [sacred writers] were never..phrenetic.

3. † **a.** Of a disease: Consisting of or attended by delirium or temporary madness: = Frantic *a.* 3 a. *Obs.* **b.** Of actions, etc.: Insane; erratic; passionate: = Frantic *a.* 3 b.

α. *a* 1529 Skelton *Agst. ven. Tongues* viii. 10 Ye are so full of vertibilite, And of frenetyke folabilite. 1641 Milton *Ch. Govt.* ii. iii. 50 Sometimes he shuts up [the man] as in frenetick, or infectious diseases. 1816 Keatinge *Trav.* (1817) I. 198 [Of Mohammedanism] Its frenetic might, enthusiasm, too, evaporating in the diffusion of conquest. 1895 Marie Corelli *Sorrows Satan* 378 They run up the gamut of baffled passion to the pitch of frenetic hysteria.

β. 1595 Daniel *Civ. Wars* iv. v, Impotent, By means of his Phreneticque maladie. 1615 H. Crooke *Body of Man* 139 Rending the membranes, cause all our motions to be head-strong and giddy, our sensations phrenetick and mad. 1754 O. in *Connoisseur* No. 28. ¶ 1 Tom Dare-Devil..was carried off last week by a phrenetic fever. 1815 Mary A. Schimmelpenninck *Demolit. Monast. Port Royal* III. 268 He struck every one who approached him, with the most phrenitic violence. 1860 T. Martin *Horace*, *Odes* i. xvi, Clashing again And again their wild cymbals, such fervour phrenetic.

¶ **4.** *Catachrestic* for Phrenic *a.* 1.

1704 J. Harris *Lex. Techn.* I, *Phrenetick Nerves*, are those which are called also *Stomachick*..These descend between the Membranes of the *Mediastinum*, and send forth Branches into them. 1706 in Phillips.

B. as *sb.* A madman: = Frantic *sb.*

α. 1693–4 Molineux *Let.* 17 Feb. in *Locke's Lett.* (1708) 75 How comes it to pass that want of consciousness cannot be proved for a drunkard as well as for a frenitick? 1837 Carlyle *Fr. Rev.* III. i. iv, All men's minds may go mad, and 'believe him', as the frenetic will do, 'because it is impossible'.

β. [1607 Marston *What you will* ii. i, A company of odd phreneteci Did eate my youth.] 1612 Selden *Illustr. Drayton's Poly-olb.* xvii, [They] made this poore King.. euen as a Phrenetique, comit what posterity receiues now amongst the worst actions..of Princes. 1695 Woodward *Nat. Hist. Earth* ii. (1723) 99 A common Fold of Phreneticks and Bedlams. 1881 W. R. Smith *Old Test. in Jew. Ch.* x. 281 The visions of poor phrenetics.

Hence **Phrene·ticness**, madness (Bailey vol. II, 1727).

† **Phrene·tical**, *a.* *Obs.* Also 6 **phræ-**, 6–7 **fre-.** [f. as prec. + -al.]

1. = Phrenetic *a.* 1 and 2.

1588 J. Harvey *Disc. Probl.* 34 Do they not..proceede from some odde vaine phantasticall, or phreneticall braines? 1663 Bp. Patrick *Parab. Pilgr.* (1673) 122 Dæmoniacks and phrenetical people. 1674 Owen *Holy Spirit* (1693) 195 Some Persons Phrenetical and Enthusiastical, whose Madness is manifest to all.

2. = Phrenetic *a.* 3.

a 1548 Hall *Chron.*, *Hen. V* 63 b, Thether came Isabell, the Frenche Quene, because the kyng her husband was fallen into his old freneticall desease. 1602 T. Fitzherbert *Apol.* 62 The phantastical or rather phrenetical opinions of these new fangled fellowes. 1696 Bp. Patrick *Comm. Exod.* x. 170 Another raving fit or phrenetical symptom.

Phrenetically (frĭne·tikăli), *adv.* [f. prec. + -ly [2].] In a frenzy; frantically.

1837 Carlyle *Fr. Rev.* II. ii. ii, If all mobs are properly frenzies, and work frenetically with mad fits of hot and of cold. 1898 *Westm. Gaz.* 14 Jan. 3/1 We welcome his sober prose and phrenetically applaud his common sense.

Phreniatric (frenai,æ·trik), *a.* [f. Gr. φρήν, φρεν- mind + Iatric.] Of or pertaining to the treatment of mental disease. In mod. Dicts.

Phrenic (fre·nik), *a.* (*sb.*) [ad. mod.L. *phrenicus* or a. F. *phrénique* (1690 in Hatz.-Darm.), f. Gr. φρήν, φρεν- diaphragm, mind: see -ic.]

1. *Anat.* and *Path.* Of, pertaining to, or affecting the diaphragm; diaphragmatic.

1704 J. Harris *Lex. Techn.* I, *Phrenick Vessels*, are the Veins and Arteries that run through the Diaphragm, Mediastinum, and Pericardium. 1741 Monro *Anat. Nerves* (ed. 3) 10 Press one or both the phrenic Nerves. 1832 J. Thomson *W. Cullen* I. 441 The Phrenic or Epigastric Centre. 1842 E. Wilson *Anat. Vade M.* 350 The Phrenic veins return the blood from the ramifications of the phrenic arteries. 1899 *Allbutt's Syst. Med.* VI. 649 Phrenic neuritis.

† **2.** Of or relating to the mind; mental. *Obs.*

1835–6 Todd *Cycl. Anat.* I. 126/2 The nerves of animal, or, better, of phrenic life. 1838 *Fraser's Mag.* XVII. 27 The Theosophs were right in separating entirely the mind from the soul, in considering them..as different principles, as the physic and the phrenic. 1847 Medwin *Shelley* I. 149 Two sorts of dreams, the Phrenic and the Psychic.

B. *sb.* (absolute use of A.)

1. *Anat.* Short for *phrenic nerve*.

1776 Cruikshank in *Phil. Trans.* LXXXV. 187 The possibility of having divided only one of the phrenics. 1881 Mivart *Cat* 209 It gives off a long and very slender branch, called the superior phrenic.

2. *Med.* A remedy or medicine for mental disease.

1853 Dunglison *Med. Lex.*, *Phrenica*, diseases affecting the intellect...Also remedies that affect the mental faculties —Phrenics.

3. *pl.* **Phrenics**: That branch of science which relates to the mind; psychology.

1841 R. Park *Pantology* ii. iii. (1847) 82 We would apply the term Phrenics to Mental Philosophy; or to that branch of knowledge, which treats of the faculties of the human mind, and their laws of action. 1893 *Syd. Soc. Lex.*, *Phrenics* ..also metaphysics.

‖ **Phreni·cula.** *Path.* [mod.L., f. as prec. + dim. suffix: see -cule.]

1799 M. Underwood *Dis. Children* (ed. 4) I. 282 What he [i.e. Dr. Paterson] calls a phrenicula, or diminutive species of phrenitis. 1893 *Syd. Soc. Lex.*, *Phrenicula*, term used by Rust for Brain-fever.

Phrenism (fre·niz'm). [f. Gr. φρήν, φρεν- mind + -ism.] Thought-force: see quot.

1871 Cope *Origin of Fittest* v. (1887) 205, I discard the use of the term 'Vital Force', what was originally understood by that term being a complex of distinct ideas. The *Vital forces* are (nerve-force) *Neurism*, (growth-force) *Bathmism*, and (thought-force) *Phrenism*.

Phrenitic (frĭni·tik), *a.* *Path.* [ad. Gr. φρενιτικ-ός, f. φρενῖτ-ις Phrenitis: see -ic.] Affected with or suffering from phrenitis; subject to fits of delirium or madness.

1771 T. Percival *Ess.* (1777) I. 24 He indulged his phrenitic patients in the use of wine. 1838 *Encycl. Brit.* (ed. 7) XVII. 453/2 *Phrenitic*, a term used to denote those who, without being absolutely mad, are subject to such strong sallies of imagination as in some measure pervert their judgment. 1893 *Syd. Soc. Lex.*, *Phrenitic*, belonging to phrenitis.

† **Phreni·tion.** *Obs. rare.* [irreg. f. Phrenitis.] Frenzy; rage.

1642 H. More *Song of Soul* i. iii. viii, The fourth of furious fashion Phrenition hight, fraught with impatiencies.

‖ **Phrenitis** (frĭnəi·tis). *Path.* [Late L. *phrenītis*, a. Gr. φρενῖτις delirium, f. φρήν, φρεν- mind + -itis. Cf. F. *phrénite.*] Inflammation of the brain or of its membranes, attended with delirium and fever; brain fever.

1621 Burton *Anat. Mel.* i. i. i. iv, *Phrenitis*, ..is a disease of the mind, with a continual madness or dotage, ..or else an inflammation of the brain. 1684 Boyle *Porousn. Anim. & Solid Bod.* iii. 28 Oftentimes the matter, ..being discharged upon some internal parts of the Head, produces a Delirium or Phrenitis. 1842 Brewster *Mart. Sc.* iii. ii. (1856) 187 His wife was seized with fever, epilepsy and phrenitis.

Phreno-, before a vowel **phren-**, a. Gr. φρενο- (combining form of φρήν, stem φρεν-, midriff, mind), an element of Greek compounds, and of modern scientific and technical words, usually in sense of 'the mind, mental faculties'.

Phrena·lgia [Gr. ἄλγος pain], acute mental distress; psychalgia; melancholia. **Phrenoco·lic** *a.* [Gr. κόλον Colon [1]], pertaining to both the diaphragm and the colon, as in *phrenocolic* (also *pleurocolic*) *ligament* (*Syd. Soc. Lex.* 1893). **Phrenoga·stric** *a.* *Anat.* as in *phrenogastric ligament*, = Gastrophrenic *a.* (Mayne *Expos. Lex.* 1858, *Syd. Soc. Lex.*). **Phre·nogram**, the curve or tracing made by the phrenograph (Webster 1902). **Phre·nograph**, (*a*) an instrument for recording the movements of the diaphragm in respiration; (*b*) a phrenological description or 'chart' of a person's mental characteristics. **Phreno·graphy**, the observation and description of phenomena in comparative psychology. **Phreno-hy·pnotism** (see quot. and Hypnotism). **Phreno-ma·gnetism**, the excitation of the phrenological organs by magnetic influence; hence **Phreno-magne·tic** *a.* **Phreno-me·smerism**, the excitation of the powers of the brain by mesmeric influence. **Phrenonarco·sis** [Gr. νάρκωσις a benumbing], Schultz's term for a dulling of the senses or intellect; a state of stupor (Mayne, *Syd. Soc. Lex.*). **Phreno·nomy** [Gr. -νομια distribution, management], the deductive and predictive part of comparative psychology. **Phrenopara·lysis** = *phrenoplegy* (*Syd. Soc. Lex.*). **Phreno·pathy** [-pathy] disease of the mind; so **Phrenopa·thic** *a.* **Phrenophysio·gnomist**, one skilled in phrenophysiognomy. **Phrenophysio·gnomy**, a combination of phrenology and physiognomy. **Phre·noplegy** [Gr. φρενοπλήξ, -πληγ- stricken in mind, f. πληγή stroke], sudden failing of the mind; disturbance of mental balance (Mayne, *Syd. Soc. Lex.*). **Phrenosple·nic** *a.* *Anat.*, of or pertaining to the diaphragm and the spleen (Mayne, *Syd. Soc. Lex.*).

1890 Billings *Nat. Med. Dict.*, *Phrenalgia. 1899 *Allbutt's Syst. Med.* VIII. 361 Melancholia and Hypochondriasis, Syn[onyms]—In the older English writers Lypemania and Phrenalgia. 1893 *Syd. Soc. Lex.*, *Phrenograph..Rosenthal's lever..he used it to demonstrate the stoppage of those movements produced by faradisation of the cut end of the vagus nerve. 1896 *Voice* (N.Y.) 13 Feb. 6/6 A phrenograph of a famous French actress, lately in this city. 1881 *Smithson. Inst. Rep.* 501 Observing and descriptive stage...*Phrenography...Inductive and classifying stage...Phrenology... Deductive and predictive stage...Phrenonomy. 1896 *Cosmopolitan* XX. 368/2 Adding to the magnetizer's equipment the extravagant doctrine of *phreno-hypnotism: the excitation of the phrenological organs by pressing various points on the heads of hypnotized subjects. 1845 G. Moore *Power of Soul over Body* (1846) 161 Assuming all that is related of *phreno-magnetism and neurypnology to be true. 1854 Huxley *Lay Serm.* v. (1870) 99 The simple physiological phænomena known as spirit-rapping, table-turning, phreno-magnetism. 1855 Smedley, etc. *Occult Sc.* 240 *note*, It was not necessary to resort to *phreno-mesmerism. 1858 Mayne *Expos. Lex.*, *Phreno-Magnetism*, *Phreno-Mesmerism*, terms for a combination of two assumed branches of science embracing the rationalities of Phrenology and more questionable pretensions of Mesmerism. 1881 *Phrenonomy [see *phrenography*]. 1858 Mayne *Expos. Lex.*, *Phrenopathia*, ..*phrenopathy. 1899 *Allbutt's Syst. Med.* VIII. 197 The various types and classes of the phrenopathies. 1892 Miss A. J. Oppenheim in *Daily News* 4 Aug. 6/6 A scientific *phreno-physiognomist...To explain *phreno-physiognomy from a scientific point of view.

† **Phreno·loger.** *Obs.* [f. Phrenolog-y + -er [1].] One who practises phrenology, a phrenologist.

1846 in Worcester (citing *Phren. Jrnl.*). 1849 H. Miller *Footpr. Creat.* xiv. (1874) 265 Low-minded materialists and shallow phrenologers.

Phrenologic (frenǒlǫ·dʒik), *a.* *rare.* [f. as prec. + -ic. In mod.F. *phrénologique.*] Of or belonging to phrenology.

1821 *Joseph the Book-Man* 12 For learned Phrenologic lore Were needful such a man t' explore. *a* 1845 Hood *Craniology* iii, These men I say, make quick appliance And close, to phrenologic science.

Phrenological (frenǒlǫ·dʒikăl), *a.* [f. as prec. + -al.] Of or pertaining to phrenology; connected with or relating to phrenology.

1823 (*title*) Phrenological Journal. 1836–7 Sir W. Hamilton *Metaph.* I. App. ii, When I publish the results [of my enquiry] they will disprove a hundred times over all the phrenological assertions in regard to the cerebellum. 1870 Dickens *E. Drood* xvii, As to the phrenological formation of the backs of their heads.

Hence **Phrenolo·gically** *adv.*

1838 E. FitzGerald *Lett.* (1889) I. 44 Phrenologically speaking, he must be fully and equally furnished with the bumps of ideality and causality. 1846 Poe *G. Bush* Wks. 1864 III. 23 The forehead, phrenologically, indicates causality and comparison, with deficient ideality.

Phrenologist (frĭnǫ·lŏdʒist). [f. Phrenolog-y + -ist. In mod.F. *phrénologiste* (1875 in Littré).] One skilled in phrenology.

1815 T. Forster in *Pamphleteer* V. 222 The Phrenologist admits an arrangement of certain organs, which gives us free-will. 1850 Kingsley *Alt. Locke* i, Call it..conformation of the brain..if you are..a phrenologist. 1876 C. M. Davies *Unorth. Lond.* 33 A collection of heads that would have delighted a phrenologist.

Phrenologize (frĭnǫ·lŏdʒəiz), *v.* [f. as prec. + -ize.]

1. *trans.* To treat or locate phrenologically. **b.** *humorous.* To produce 'bumps' or protuberances (on the head) by blows.

1848 *Blackw. Mag.* LXIII. 262 You emerged with a broken hat, and a head phrenologised by a blacking bottle. 1858 J. W. Donaldson *Lit. Greece* III. 13 He not only made the soul a mere function of the body, but even phrenologized it by placing it in the forehead.

2. To examine or analyse phrenologically.

1860 O. W. Holmes *Prof. Breakf.-t.* viii, It only remained to be phrenologized. 1895 *Daily News* 22 Nov. 4/7 Burns's skull was phrenologised.

Phrenology (frĕnŏ·lŏdʒi). [f. Gr. φρεν-, φρήν mind + -(O)LOGY; lit. 'mental science'; in F. *phrénologie* (Littré 1818, Hatz.-Darm.), Ger. *phrenologie*.] The scientific study or theory of the mental faculties (quots. 1815, 1881); *spec.* and in ordinary use, the theory originated by Gall and Spurzheim, that the mental powers of the individual consist of separate faculties, each of which has its seat and location in a definite region of the surface of the brain, the size or development of which is commensurate with the development of the particular faculty; hence, the study of the external conformation of the cranium as an index to the character and position of these organs, and thus of the degree of development of the various faculties.

Phrenosin ... **Phrenosinic** ...

Phrenetic, **Phrenetical** ...

Phrenitis ...

Phronesis ...

Phrontistery ...

Phrygana ...

Phrygian ...

Phrygianise ...

Phthalic ...

Phthisis (θəi·sis). *sb.* and *a.* Now *rare*. Forms: 4–5 tysyk, tisyk, -ik, -e, 5 tysyke, -ik, 6 tysyke, -ike, tisicke, tisike, 7 tisick, tysick ... A wasting disease of the lungs; pulmonary consumption.

Phthisic ...

Phthisical (θi·zikăl), *a.* Forms: 7 tisisall, phthisicall, 7–8 tisical, 7 -phthisical, 8 phth.; phthisical. [f. prec. + -AL.] Of the nature of or pertaining to phthisis.

Phthongometer ...

Phthore ...

Phthorite ...

Phu ...

Phyco- ...

Phycochrome ...

Phylactery (filæ·ktĕri). Forms: 4 fil-, phila-, 5–6 filatery, 6– phylactery. [a. late L. *phylactērium*, a. Gr. φυλακτήριον ...] A small leathern box containing four texts of Scripture, Deut. vi. 4–9, xi. 13–21, Ex. xiii. 1–10, 11–16, written in Hebrew letters on vellum and, by a literal interpretation of the passages, worn by

Jews during morning prayer on all days except the sabbath, as a reminder of the obligation to keep the law. ...

Phylactoc'matous ...

Phylarch ...

Phyle ...

Phyletic ...

Phylite ...

Phyllary ...

Phyllidiobranchiate ...

Phyllidium ...

Phylliform ...

Phyllirrhoe ...

Phyllite ...

Phyllobranchia ...

Phyllocladous ...

Phylloclade ...

Phyllode ...

Phyllody ...

Phyllophagan ...

Phyllopod ...

Phyllorhine ...

Phyllosiphonic ...

Phylloscopine ...

Phyllula ...

Phyllyrea, **-rea**, obs. forms ff. PHILLYREA.

Phylo-, before a vowel **phyl-**, combining form of Gr. φῦλον race, tribe (see PHYLE, PHYLUM), used in mod. scientific terms, mostly of biology.

Phylogenic, the cycle or whole course of the development of a phylum; hence Phylogenic a.

Phylogenesis (Gerontic) α., of or pertaining to the old age or stage of decay of a race or type of organisms. Phylogeny sb.α. [Gr. γένεσις.]

Phylogenesis (fəilə'dʒenɪsis), Biol.

Phylogenetic (fəilodʒe'netɪk), α.

Phylogenic (fəilə'dʒenɪk), α.

Phylogeny (fəi'lɒdʒəni), Biol.

Phyma (fəi'mə), Path. Pl. **-ata**.

Phymatic, α., of or pertaining to phyma.

Phymatin, Chem.

Phymatosis, Path.

Phymosis, error, form of PHIMOSIS.

Phyngogenae (fəidʒeme'riɒm), Zool. Pl. **-ia**.

Physa (fəi'sə), Zool.

Physagogue, Med.

Physalia (fi'seɪliə), Zool.

Physalite, Min.

Physalis, Bot.

Physeter (fəi'si:tə), Zool.

Phys-harmonica, Mus.

Physianthropy.

Physiatric, α.

Physiatric.

Physalite (fi'zeɪlaɪt), Min.

Physcomitrium, Bot.

Physcomyarium.

Physianthropy.

Physic (fɪ'zɪk), sb.

Physic, v.

Physical (fɪ'zɪkl), α.

Physically, adv.

Physician (fi'zɪʃən), sb.

Physicianer.

Physicianess.

Physicianless.

Physicianly.

Physicianship.

Physicism.

Physicist (fi'zɪsɪst).

Physician.

Physic garden, Obs.

Physico-, combining form of Gr. φυσικός physical.

Physico-astronomical α.

Physico-geographical α.

Physico-logical α.

Physico-mathematical α.

Physico-mechanical α.

Physico-chemical α.

Physico-chemist.

Physico-theology.

Physico-theological α.

Physico-theologist.

Physico-philosophy.

Physico-philosophical α.

Physico-psychical α.

Physics (fi'zɪks).

manifestations of the same fundamental energy. 1900 W. WATSON *Textbk. Physics* 2 We are led to define Physics in its most general aspect as a discussion of the properties of matter and energy. It is, however, usual..to exclude the discussion of those properties of matter which depend simply on the nature of the different forms of matter (Chemistry), as also the properties of matter and energy as related to living things (Biology). The line of demarcation separating Physics and Chemistry has never been very clear, and of late years has practically vanished.

†3. The science of, or a treatise on, medicine. *Obs. rare.*

1626 R. HARRIS *Hezekiah's Recovery* (1630) 33 For the second, Health: great Salomon hath written a Physicke for us. 1785 JEFFERSON *Writ.* (1859) I. 467 When college education is done with..he must cast his eyes (for America) either on Law or Physics.

Physiform (fai·sifǭɹm), *a. Zool.* [f. PHYSA + -FORM.] Having the form of the gastropod PHYSA.

†**Physiner**, a corrupt or erroneous form of PHYSICIANER: cf. PHYSION.

1616 SIR R. BOYLE in *Lismore Papers* (1886) I. 100 Lent Mr. Shea of Kilkenny the phisiner iiij^li x^s.

Physio- (fi·zio), combining element, representing Gr. φυσιο-, f. φύσις nature, as in φυσιογνώμων 'judging of a man's nature', φυσιολόγος discoursing upon nature, φυσιοσκοπεῖν to observe nature; used as a formative with the sense 'nature' or 'natural', as in PHYSIOCRACY, PHYSIOGNOMY, PHYSIOGRAPHY, PHYSIOLOGY, etc.; also in the following less important compounds (in some of which it is treated as an abbreviation of *physiology* or *physiological*): **Phy:sio-che·mical** *a.*, pertaining to physiological chemistry. †**Phy:sioglyphic** [after *hieroglyphic*] (see quot.). **Phy:siogno·stic, Physio·gnosy** [Gr. γνῶσις knowledge] (see quots.). **Phy:siome·dicalism**, the system of 'natural' medicine which uses vegetable drugs, only discarding those which are poisonous (*Syd. Soc. Lex.*); so **Phy:siome·dical** *a.*; **Phy:siome·dicalist**. **Phy:siopa·thic** *a.*, of or pertaining to physiopathy. **Phy:siopatholo·gical** *a.*, of or pertaining to a pathological state influenced by physiology. **Physio·pathy** [Gr. -παθεια, f. πάθος suffering] (see quot.). **Physio·philist** [Gr. φιλεῖν to love], a lover or student of nature. **Phy:siophy·ly** [see PHYLUM] (see quot.). **Phy:siopla·stic** *a.*, formed by nature. **Phy:sioscope** [Gr. -σκόπος viewing] (see quot. 1846). **Physio·scopy**, the rendering of the physical appearances and conditions in a painting. **Phy:sio-sociolo·gical** *a.*, combining physiology and sociology. **Physio·sophy** [Gr. σοφία wisdom], an assumption of knowledge of nature; hence **Phy:sioso·phic** *a.* **Phy·siotype**, a process for taking an impression direct from a flat object, on prepared paper; also an image made by such process. **Phy:sioty·py**, printing from plates made by various processes direct from natural objects; nature-printing.

1887 A. M. BROWN *Anim. Alkal.* 5 The presence of the alkaloid might be owing to *physio-chemical action after death. 1844 UPTON *Physioglyphics* 101 In a literal hieroglyphic, therefore, or what I shall now more aptly term a *physioglyphic, no name must be involved. 1635 PERSON *Varieties* II. 60 The Meteorologians answer not so fully satisfactorie as theirs, who treate of spirits, whom I may well call Physiognosticks. 1811–31 BENTHAM *Logic* App., Wks. 1843 VIII. 284 Natural History..which..may more aptly and expressively, it should seem, be designated by the term *Physiognosy. 1880 C. A. CUTTER *Classif. Nat. Sc.* in *Library Jrnl.* June, A similar word, Fysiognosy..supplies a name which was wanted for the natural sciences collectively. 1885 *Proc. Boston Soc. Nat. Hist.* XXIII. 226 It should consist of three parts or sections, first Statical Geognosy or Physiognosy. 1800 COLERIDGE in C. K. Paul *W. Godwin* (1876) II. 3 Your poetic and *Physiopathic feelings. 1897 *Allbutt's Syst. Med.* III. 777 We cannot even say if it..be of a *physio-pathological character, or a specific germ. 1898 P. MANSON *Trop. Dis.* xxvi. 413 Certain physio-pathological qualities predisposing to the disease may be inherited. 1797–1803 FOSTER in *Life & Corr.* (1846) I. 212 What may be called *physio-pathy, a faculty of pervading all nature with one's own being. 1804 COLERIDGE *Lett., to N. Sharp* (1895) 448, I have met with several genuine Philologists, Philonoists, *Physiophilists, keen hunters after knowledge and science. 1879 tr. *Haeckel's Evol. Man* I. i. 24 *Physiophyly. The tribal history of the functions, or the history of the palæontological development of vital activities. 1811–31 BENTHAM *Logic* App., Wks. 1843 VIII. 284/1 In their *physioplastic state, in the state in which, fashioned by the hand of nature, they [bodies] are found in the bosom of nature. 1846 JOYCE *Sci. Dial., Optics* xxii. 332 What is the opaque microscope?..Very much the same sort of thing as the magic lantern; except that the light, instead of passing through the object, shines upon it, and is reflected off through the lenses, and so onward to the screen...The *physioscope is the same instrument, employed to depict 'the human face'..in colossal dimensions upon the screen. *c* 1865 J. WYLDE in *Circ. Sc.* I. 64/2 The physio-scope is a modification of the magic lantern. 1886–94 H. SPENCER *Autobiog.* II. xlvi. 193 *note*, Under '*physio-copy' I propose to include the rendering of the phenomena of linear perspective, of aerial perspective, of light and shade, and of colour in so far as it is determined not by artistic choice, but by natural conditions. 1904 *Westm. Gaz.* 29 June 2/1 The average medical man cannot afford the leisure for the systematic study of the *physio-sociological problems that lie in his path. 1886 GÜNTHER in *Encycl. Brit.* XX. 437/1 Morphological facts are entirely superseded by fanciful ideas of the vaguest kind of *physiosophy. 1904 *Daily News* 23 June 11 A remarkable invention is..called 'The *Physiotype'. A leaf, piece of lace, or other flat object is pressed upon a piece of prepared paper, but there is no visible mark made; the paper then has a powder..brushed over it, and the structure of the leaf or the pattern of the lace immediately appears in black.

Physiocracy (fiziǫ·krăsi). [ad. F. *physiocratie* (1767 in Hatz.-Darm.): see PHYSIO- and -CRACY.] Government according to natural order; *spec.* the doctrine of the physiocrats.

1875 *Contemp. Rev.* XXV. 882 The doctrine that all wealth is formed out of the materials of the globe may be called Physiocracy. 1895 L. F. WARD in *Forum* (N. Y.) Nov. 304 If we had a pure physiocracy or government of nature, such as prevails among wild animals.

Physiocrat (fi·ziokræt). Also in Fr. form **-crate**. [a. F. *physiocrate*, f. *physiocratie*: see prec. and -CRAT.] One of a school of political economists founded by François Quesnay in France in the 18th c.; they maintained that society should be governed according to an inherent natural order, that the soil is the sole source of wealth and the only proper object of taxation, and that security of property and freedom of industry and exchange are essential: = ECONOMIST 4 c.

1798 W. TAYLOR in *Monthly Mag.* V. 332 About the year 1774, the philosophic sect of Physiocrates was already organized into a political body. 1804 — in *Crit. Rev.* Ser. III. I. 21 The only merit of the *economistes*, or physiocrates, consists in arguing well against legal interference, and legal restraint. 1896 *Athenæum* 19 Sept. 390 Questions..as to the relation of Adam Smith to the physiocrats.

Physiocratic (fi:ziokræ·tik), *a.* [f. as PHYSIOCRAT + -IC.] Of or pertaining to physiocracy or the physiocrats.

1804 W. TAYLOR in *Ann. Rev.* II. 324 Much is said of the theory of the physiocratic sect. 1888 W. L. COURTNEY *J. S. Mill* 96 The physiocratic theory begins with the idea of a *Jus Naturæ*, a simple..and beneficial code established by Nature.

So †**Physiocra·tical** *a. Obs. rare*⁻¹.

1792 A. YOUNG *Trav. France* 141 The *œconomistes*, in their writings, speak much of an experiment he made in their Physiocratical rubbish.

Physiocratism (fiziǫ·krătiz'm). [f. as prec. + -ISM.] 1. = PHYSIOCRACY. 1890 in *Cent. Dict.*

2. In Kant's use, The doctrine that all causality is dependent on nature.

Physiog, humorous colloquial abbreviation of PHYSIOGNOMY (sense 3).

1865 E. C. CLAYTON *Cruel Fortune* I. 145 Glad to behold your distinguished physiog.

Physioge·nesis. *Biol.* [f. as next + Gr. γένεσις GENESIS.] = next, b.

1887 COPE *Primary Factors Org. Evol.* 488 Changes may be effected in the weight, colour, and in functional capacity by temperature, humidity, food, &c., thus exhibiting physiogenesis.

Hence **Phy:siogene·tic** *a.*, of or pertaining to physiogenesis.

Physiogeny (fiziǫ·dʒĭni). [ad. mod.L. *physiogenia*, f. Gr. φυσιο- PHYSIO- + -γένεια -GENY. Cf. Ger. *physiogenie*.] †**a.** The genesis of natural bodies. *Obs.* **b.** *Biol.* The genesis of vital functions; the development or evolution of the functions of living organisms, which are the province of physiology; the science or history of this.

1858 MAYNE *Expos. Lex.*, *Physiogenia*, term for the operations of nature, according to Rumpf, of the formation of bodies from original elements: physiogeny. 1879 tr. *Haeckel's Evol. Man* I. 24 *Physiogeny*, the germ-history of the functions, or the history of the development of vital activities in the individual. *Ibid.* II. 461 So will Physiogeny..make a true recognition of functions possible, by discovering their historic evolution.

Hence **Physiogenic** (-dʒe·nik) *a.*, of the nature of physiogeny.

†**Physio·gnomer.** *Obs.* Forms: 6 **fisnomier, phisnamour, phisiognomier, -yer**, 7– **physiognomer.** [f. PHYSIOGNOMY + -ER¹: cf. *astronomy, astronomer*.] = PHYSIOGNOMIST.

a 1500 P. JOHNSTON *Thre Deid Pollis* 42 This questioun quha can obsolue, lat see, Quhat phisnamour, or perfyt palmester. 1519 HORMAN *Vulg.* 10, I beleue nat the reders of dremes and fisnomiers. 1542 UDALL *Erasm. Apoph.* Table Xij b, Arte and profession of Phisiognomyers. 1586 A. DAY *Eng. Secretary* II. (1625) 55 When a Phisiognomer by chance..came into the forum of Athens, he declared by the view of diuers mens faces, the diuersity of their conditions. 1656 H. MORE *Enthus. Tri.* 35 That Sanguine was the Complexion of David George, the foregoing description of his person will probably intimate to any Physiognomer. 1706 PHILLIPS, *Physiognomer* or *Physiognomist*.

Physiognomic (fiziǫgnǫ·mik, fi ziǫnǫ·mik), *a.* (*sb.*) [ad. late L. *physiognōmic-us* (Fulgentius, *c* 550), corruption of Gr. φυσιογνωμονικ-ός, f. φυσιογνωμονία: see PHYSIOGNOMY and -IC. In OF. *physionomique* (15th c. in Godef. *Compl.*), in mod. F. *physiognomonique* (*Dict. Trévoux* 1732).]

1. Of the nature of physiognomy; relating to the face or form as indicating character; characteristic.

1755 JOHNSON, *Physiognomic*, drawn from the contemplation of the face. 1817 COLERIDGE *Biog. Lit.* II. xxii. 166 The very spirit which gives the physiognomic expression to all the works of nature. 1856 KINGSLEY *Lett.* 26 Feb., It is sad to see how much faults of character seem to depend on physiognomic defects. 1868 *Contemp. Rev.* IX. 75 Currents of thought and feeling which are physiognomic of the atmosphere he lives in.

2. Of, pertaining to, or skilled in physiognomy; 'conversant in contemplation of the face' (J.).

1755 in JOHNSON. 1818 COLERIDGE in *Lit. Rem.* (1836) I. 146 There is great physiognomic tact in Sterne. 1885 COUPLAND *Spirit Goethe's Faust* i. 11 Such physiognomic science [is] lighter than a water-bug.

B. *sb.* (in *pl.*) See quots.

[1693 tr. *Blancard's Phys. Dict.* (ed. 2), *Physiognomica*, Signs whereby we conjecture something by the Countenance.] 1704 J. HARRIS *Lex. Techn.* I, *Physiognomicks*,..a Term used by some Physicians and Naturalists for such Signs as are taken from the Countenance of Persons, to judge of their Dispositions and Temper. 1727–41 in CHAMBERS *Cycl.* 1828 in WEBSTER, and in later Dicts.

Physiogno·mical, *a.* [f. as prec. + -AL.]

1. Pertaining to, dealing with, or skilled in physiognomy; indicative of character.

1588 FRAUNCE *Lawiers Log.* I. viii. 43 b, Divers physionomicall conjectures, as that of Martiall, *Crine ruber, niger ore, brevis pede*. 1644 BULWER *Chirol.* 72 Hence Physiognomicall Philosophers..doe easily discerne the differences. 1830 D'ISRAELI *Chas. I*, III. vi. 113 Had the physiognomical predicter examined the two portraits..he might have augured a happier fate. 1840 CARLYLE *Heroes* iii. (1858) 264 All that a man does is physiognomical of him.

2. Of or pertaining to the face or form (properly) as an index of character, but often used simply in reference to personal appearance. (In quot. 1815 earlier term for *phrenological*.)

1811 LAMB *Danger Confound. Mor. w. Personal Deformity*, To distinguish between that physiognomical deformity which I am willing to grant always accompanies crime, and mere physical ugliness. 1812 R. H. in *Examiner* 28 Dec. 828/1 The analogy..that appears between the physiognomical and intellectual..character. 1815 (*title*) The Physiognomical System of Drs. Gall and Spurzheim, founded on an ..Examination of the Nervous System in general, and of the Brain in particular. [transl. of French ed. 1810] 1861 *Times* 16 Oct., Certain original physiognomical types peculiar to himself.

Hence **Physiogno·mically** *adv.*, in a physiognomical manner; according to the rules of physiognomy; as regards characteristic features.

1608 TOPSELL *Serpents* (1658) 640 The one and other are thus Physiognomically described by the Poet. 1797 COLERIDGE *Wks.* (1893) p. xxxiv. *note*, My eyes, eyebrows, and forehead are physiognomically good. 1854 *Blackw. Mag.* LXXVI. 521 County differed from county physiognomically. 1882 *Academy* 14 Jan. 24/3 A charmingly etched and evidently characteristic portrait..confirms physiognomically the popular estimate of his character.

Physiognomist (fiziǫ·gnŏmist, -ǫ·nŏmist). [a. OF. *physionomiste* (1557 in Godef. *Compl.*), f. *physionomie*: see -IST.] One skilled in physiognomy; one who reads character or disposition (or, formerly, professed to foretell destiny) from the face.

1570 DEE *Math. Pref.* c iv, The Anatomistes will restore to you, some part: The Physiognomistes, some. 1601 HOLLAND *Pliny* XXXV. x. 539 A certaine Physiognomist or teller of fortune. 1788 REID *Active Powers* II. iii. 540 The physiognomist saw, in the features of Socrates, the signatures of many bad dispositions. 1802 MAR. EDGEWORTH *Moral T.* (1816) I. xv. 123 By no means a good physiognomist, much less a good judge of character. 1865 DICKENS *Mut. Fr.* I. ix, Her remarkable powers as a physiognomist.

Hence †**Physiognomi·stic, -ical** *adjs.*, of or pertaining to a physiognomist; †**Physio·gnomistry**, the art or trade of the physiognomist.

1651 BIGGS *New Disp.* § 98 To be seen with Physiognomisticall corporall eyes. 1708 *Brit. Apollo* No. 66. 2/1 We may include Palmistry, Physiognomistry, etc.

Physio·gnomize, *v.* [f. PHYSIOGNOMY + -IZE.]

1. *trans.* To examine or study physiognomically; to deduce the character of from physiognomy.

1660 STANLEY *Hist. Philos.* IX. (1701) 372/1 Before he had physiognomized the man what he were. 1796 SOUTHEY *Lett. to G. C. Bedford* 24 Feb. in *Life* (1849) I. 269, I defy you or Mr. Shandy to physiognomise that man's name rightly. 1809 — *Lett.* (1856) II. 173 That good lady who, as you remember, physiognomised me so luckily for 'a man of sorrow and acquainted with woe'.

†2. To assume the physiognomy or characteristic appearance of. *Obs. rare.*

1653 R. SANDERS *Physiogn.* b j b, Archangel physiognomising the fingers. *Ibid.* b ij, Divers plants physiognomize the horns of Beasts, as Cornop, Plaintain.

Physiognomonic (fiziǫgnǫmǫ·nik), *a.* (*sb.*) *rare.* [ad. med.L. *physiognōmonic-us*, a. Gr. φυσιογνωμονικός adj., f. φυσιογνωμονία: see PHYSIOGNOMY and -IC. In F. *physiognomonique*.] The etymologically correct form for PHYSIOGNOMIC.

1755 JOHNSON, *Physiognomonick* adj. 1798 FERRIAR *Illustr. Sterne* iv. 118 The chapter is concluded by the physiognomonic doctrine of the nose. 1858 MAYNE *Expos. Lex.*, *Physiognōmonica*,..physiognomonics. 1893 in *Syd. Soc. Lex.*

Physiognomonical (fiziǫgnǫmǫ·nikăl), *a.* Now *rare* or *Obs.* [f. as prec. + -AL.] Etymological form for PHYSIOGNOMICAL.

1668 G. C. in *H. More's Div. Dial.* Pref. (1713) 6 In the Character of which Person the Dramatist seems to have been judicious even to Physiognomonical Curiosity. 1737 FIELDING *Tom Thumb* (ed. 3) Pref., Affirmed by our English Physiognominical writers. 1805 T. HOLCROFT *Bryan Perdue* II. 114 Not having yet completed my course of physiognomonical experiments. 1824 *Phil. Mag.* XLIV. 305 Demonstrative Course of Lectures on Drs. Gall and Spurzheim's Physiognomonical System.

Physiognomy (fiziǫ·gnŏmi, -ǫ·nŏmi). Forms: see below. [ME. *fisnomye, fis-, phisonomye*, etc., a. OF. (13th c.) *fis-, phis-, phizonomie, -anomie*, in mod.F. *physionomie* = Pr. *phizonomia*, Sp. *fisonomia*, Pg. *physionomia*, It. *fisio-, fisonomia*, ad. med.L. *phisonomia, physionomia*, *physiognōmia*, ad. Gr. φυσιογνωμονία the judging of a man's nature (by his features), f. φύσις nature (PHYSIO-) + γνώμων, γνωμον- judge, interpreter: wrongly written φυσιογνωμία in Stob. Ecl. (Liddell and Scott), whence the med.L. form. As will be seen, the word shows contraction in all the Romanic langs., and still more in Eng., where in vulgar use it has even been abridged to *physiog., phizog.*, and *phiz*. The pronunciation (fiziǫ·nŏmi) which formerly prevailed (see A. γ, quots. 1783, 1840) is now somewhat old-fashioned.]

A. Illustration of Forms.

α. 4–5 **fysnomye, -namye, fyss-**, 5–6 **fisnamy, phis-, physnomie**, 5–7 **-nomy**, 6 **phis-, phys-, fis-, fys, fiz-, -nomy, -namy (-ye, -ie), phisnami, (-nom, physnome)**, 6–7 (9) **visnomy, -ie**, 7 **fisnomie.**

?*a* 1400 *Morte Arth.* 1114 He feyed his fysnamye with his foule hondez. 1450–80 tr. *Secreta Secret.* 38 The mervelous science of ffysnomye. *c* 1470 HENRYSON *Mor. Fab.* xiii. (*Frog & Mouse*) viii, Ane thrawart will, ane thrawin phisnomy. 1513 BRADSHAW *St. Werburge* I. 2765 His fysnamy restaured to his kynde agayne. 1548 UDALL, etc. *Erasm. Par. Mark* ix. 3 His face, whiche before seemed not to diffre from the common phisnami of others, shone as brighte as the sunne. *a* 1585 MONTGOMERIE *Flyting w. Polwart* 490 With flirting and flyring, their physnome they flype. *a* 1652 BROME *Love-sick Court* v. i, I can read guilty lines Palpably on this villans visnomy. 1660 J. S. *Andromana* IV. v. in Hazl. *Dodsley* XIV. 253 If he have not rogue writ in great letters in's face, I have no physnomy. [1822 LAMB *Elia* Ser. I. *Distant Corr.* (1823) 245 A pun is reflected from a friend's face as from a mirror. Who would consult his sweet visnomy, if the polished surface were two or three minutes..in giving back its copy?]

β. 4–6 **phisonomie**, 5 **phiso-, phizo-, physonomye, (physynomye, fysenamye)**, 6 **vysonamy, visenomy**, 6–7 **phisognomie, -y**, 7 **-gminy.**

1390 GOWER *Conf.* III. 5 Thou scholdest be Phisonomie Be schapen to that maladie Of lovedrunke. *c* 1425 *Seven Sag.* (P.) 1072 The childe couthe of fysenamye That he saw evyl with hys eye. 1489 CAXTON *Faytes of A.* I. x. 27 By the phizonomye of yᵉ yongmen..they knowe whiche were moost able. 1531 TINDALE *Wks.* (Parker Soc.) II. 127 The false prophets do well to paint God after the likeness of their own visenomy. *a* 1562 G. CAVENDISH *Wolsey* (1893) 33 A dosyn of other maskers,..with visors of good proporcion of vysonamy. 1642 S. W. *Parl. Vind. agst. Pr. Rupert* 3 Not new in Phisognomy. 1678 W. STROTHER in *Lauderdale Papers* (1885) III. xciii. 161 We think Welsh was amongst them, by the discription of his phisogminy.

γ. 6– **physiognomy**, (6 **phisionomie, visiognomi**, 6–7 **phisio-, physiognomie**, 6–8 **phisio-**, 7 **visiognomy**).

1569 J. SANFORD tr. *Agrippa's Van. Artes* 50 b, Physiognomie..doth presume that shee is able to finde out..by vewing of the whole bodie, the dispositions of the minde and body. 1660 *A. Durer Revived* 2 The Visiognomy or Circumference of a Face. 1783 JOHNSON *Let. to Mrs. Thrale* 21 Oct., Physiognomy, as it is a Greek word, ought to sound the G; but..G, I think, is sounded in formal, and sunk in familiar language. 1840 A. R. WEBSTER *Oxf. Songs, Town & Gown*, You'll find it bad economy To carry home a tattered gown and battered physiognomy.

B. Signification.

I. 1. The art of judging character and disposition from the features of the face or the form and lineaments of the body generally.

1390 [see A. β]. 1422 tr. *Secreta Secret., Priv. Priv.* 219 One lyght manere and general of Phisnomye is to deme vertues and maneris of man aftyr the conpleccion. *c* 1450 LYDG. & BURGH *Secrees* 2467 The excellent science..I mene phisonomye, Be which thou shalt..knowe disposicion in ech degree and signe, Of al thy peple. 1591 GREENE *Farew. Follie* Wks. (Grosart) IX. 327, I haue not..such assured sight in Phisognomie, as I dare auouch it for truth. 1638 R. BAKER tr. *Balzac's Lett.* (vol. III) 19 The reputation of my skill in Physnomie and Prognosticating. *a* 1720 SHEFFIELD (Dk. Buckhm.) *Wks.* (1753) II. 60 An illustrious exception to all the common rules of Physiognomy. 1853 C. BRONTË *Villette* vii. (1876) 60, I want your opinion. We know your skill in physiognomy...Read that countenance.

†b. *transf.* A judging of the form of a living body from the skeleton. *Obs.*

1658 SIR T. BROWNE *Hydriot.* ii. 30 Since Bones afford..Figure unto the Body, it is no impossible Physiognomy to conjecture at Fleshy Appendencies.

†2. The foretelling of destiny or future fortune from the features and lines of the face, etc.; the fortune so foretold: *loosely*, fortune foretold (or character divined) by astrology. *Obs.*

1531 *Act 22 Hen. VIII*, c. 12 § 4 Physyke, Physnamye, Palmestrye or other craftye scyences wherby they beare the people in hande that they can tell theire destenyes deceases & fortunes. 1577 HARRISON *England* II. x. (1877) I. 220 Roges..practisers of physiognomie and palmestrie, tellers of fortunes [etc.]. 1589 NASHE *Martins Months Mind* Ep. Ded., Wks. (Grosart) I. 146 For that it seemeth you have some skill in Astrologie,..let vs haue a glimpse at the least of the fooles phisnomies. 1651 BAXTER *Inf. Bapt.* 242 According to my little skill in Physiognomy, I hope he may live yet many a yeer.

II. 3. The face or countenance, especially viewed as an index to the mind and character; expression of face; also, the general cast of features, type of face (of a race); vulgarly, the face or countenance (formerly very common, esp. in the α form, now rare).

c 1400 *Beryn* 3196, I knowe wele by thy fisnamy, thy kynd it were to stele. 1555 W. WATREMAN *Fardle Facions* I. iv. 39 Dyuers peoples of sondry phisonomy and shape. 1575 G. HARVEY *Letter-bk.* (Camden) 98 Eies glauncinge, fisnamy smirkinge. 1621 BURTON *Anat. Mel.* III. iii. I. ii. (1651) 605 She did abhorre her husbands phisnomy. 1623–33 FLETCHER & SHIRLEY *Night-Walker* v. i, I haue seen that physiognomy: Were you never in prison? *a* 1718 ROWE *Biter* II. i, That Blow upon your Forehead has decompos'd your Phisiognomy strangely. 1754 RICHARDSON *Grandison* (1781) I. ii. 8 The grace which that people call *Physiognomy*, and we may call Expression. 1856 EMERSON *Eng. Traits, Race* Wks. (Bohn) II. 21 Each religious sect has its physiognomy. The Methodists have acquired a face; the Quakers, a face; the nuns, a face. 1869 TOZER *Highl. Turkey* II. 305 The distinctive Greek physiognomy was no longer to be found.

†b. A representation of a face; a portrait. *Obs.*

1483 CAXTON *Gold. Leg.* 339/2 Oure lord..toke fro the payntour a lynnen clothe and set it upon his vysage and enprynted the very physonomye of his vysage therin. 1587 in Ellis *Orig. Lett.* Ser. I. III. 52 *note*, One little Flower of gold with a frogg thereon, and therein Mounsier his phisnamye. 1603 H. CROSSE *Vertues Commw.* (1878) 130 Apelles would not loose a day without shadowing a phisnomie.

4. *transf.* The general appearance or external features of anything material; e. g. the contour or configuration of a country.

1567 MAPLET *Gr. Forest* 7 Efestides [a kind of stone] is in colour and Phisiognomie verie shamefast and childish. 1819 SHELLEY *Let.* Pr. Wks. 1888 II. 294 Its physiognomy indicates it to be a city, which..yet possesses most amiable qualities. 1830 LYELL *Princ. Geol.* I. 362 The most grand and original feature in the physiognomy of Etna. 1863 HAWTHORNE *Our Old Home* (1879) 159 The old highways..adapted themselves..to the physiognomy of the country.

5. *fig.* The ideal, mental, moral, or political aspect of anything as an indication of its character; characteristic aspect.

a 1680 BUTLER *Rem.* (1759) II. 494 There is a Kind of Physiognomy in the Titles of Books, no less than in the Faces of Men, by which a skilful Observer will as well know what to expect from the one as the other. *c* 1796 T. TWINING *Trav. Amer.* (1894) 91 The moral physiognomy of certain sections of the United States. *a* 1854 H. REED *Lect. Eng. Lit.* iii. (1878) 93 You may discover the physiognomy, that is in speech, as well as in face. 1879 *Echo* No. 3374. 2 The utter change in the political physiognomy of the new Landtag.

Physio·gnotype. [f. PHYSIOGN(OMY + Gr. τύπος impress, print, model.] 'A machine for taking casts and imprints of human faces or countenances' (Worcester).

a 1846 WORCESTER cites *Observer*. 1878 BARTLEY tr. *Topinard's Anthrop.* II. iii. 296 A craniograph, which must have been suggested by the physio[g]notype of Huschke, and reminds one of the circular band used by hatters.

Physiogony (fiziǫ·gŏni). [f. Gr. φύσις nature (see PHYSIO-) + -γονία begetting, production.] The generation or production of nature.

a 1834 COLERIDGE in *Lit. Rem.* (1838) III. 158 Their physiology imbrangled with an inapplicable logic and a misgrowth of..substantiated abstractions; and their physiogony a blank or dream of tradition. 1840 J. H. GREEN *Vital Dynamics* 103 The distinctive..aim..of physiogony is to present the history of Nature as preface and portion of the history of man.

Physiographer (fiziǫ·grăfəɹ). [f. PHYSIOGRAPH-Y + -ER¹.] One versed in physiography; a physical geographer.

1885 *Amer. Jrnl. Sc.* Ser. III. XXX. 261 The same eminent..physiographer, in his paper on the Ocean, remarks [etc.]. 1902 C. LENNOX *J. Chalmers* vi, A belt of very shallow water suggesting to the physiographer that it had once formed part of the continent.

Physiographic (fi:ziogræ·fik), *a.* [f. mod.L. *physiographia* PHYSIOGRAPHY + -IC.] Of or belonging to physiography: cf. next.

1840 J. H. GREEN *Vital Dynamics* 104 The physiographic details which form the main body of these lectures. 1863 DANA *Man. Geol.* 7 Physiographic Geology,—a general survey of the earth's surface-features.

Physiographical (fi:ziogræ·fikăl), *a.* [f. as prec. + -AL.] Dealing with or treating of physiography; pertaining to physiography.

1796 MORSE *Amer. Geog.* II. 56 Other literary societies are formed at Upsala, Gottenburg, &c., and a physiographical one at Lund. 1882 GEIKIE *Text-bk. Geol.* VII. 910 The branch of geological enquiry which deals with the evolution of the existing contours of the dry land is termed Physiographical Geology. 1890 *Q. Rev.* July 88 The Vosges interested him profoundly, but from a purely physiographical point of view.

Physiography (fiziǫ·grăfi). [mod. f. Gr. φύσις nature + -γραφία description, -GRAPHY: cf. F. *physiographie* (1812).]

1. A description of nature, or of natural phenomena or productions generally.

1828–32 WEBSTER, *Physiography*, a description of nature, or the science of natural objects. *Journ. of Science.* *a* 1834 COLERIDGE in *Lit. Rem.* (1838) III. 158 The ignorance of natural science, their physiography scant in fact, and stuffed out with fables. 1840 J. H. GREEN *Vital Dynamics* 101 The office of..Physiography is to enumerate and delineate the effects and products of nature as they appear. 1878 HUXLEY *Physiogr.* Pref. 6, I undertook to deliver twelve lectures on natural phenomena in general; and I borrowed the title of 'Physiography'..for my subject, inasmuch as I wished to draw a clear line of demarcation, both as to matter and method, between it and what is commonly understood by Physical Geography. 1891 E. HULL (*title*) Physiography: an introduction to the Study of Nature.

2. A description of the nature of a particular class of objects (in quot., of minerals).

[1873 ROSENBUSCH (*title*) Mikroskopische Physiographie der petrographisch wichtigen Mineralien.] 1888 J. P. IDDINGS (*title*) Microscopical Physiography of the Rock-making Minerals:..By H. Rosenbusch. Translated and abridged.

3. Physical geography.

1873 J. GEIKIE *Gt. Ice Age* xiii. 176 To restore the physiography of the land during successive stages of the glacial epoch. 1877 — *Elem. Lessons in Phys. Geog.* 3 *note*, This term [physical geography] as here used is synonymous with Physiography, which has been proposed in its stead. 1895 *Educat. Rev.* Nov. 353 Physiography on the other hand treats of the science of earth-sculpture, viewed in the light of systematic processes.

Physiolater (fiziǫ·lătəɹ). [f. as prec. + Gr. -λατρης worshipper.] A worshipper of nature. So **Physio·latry** [-LATRY], nature-worship.

1860 MAX MÜLLER *Hist. Sanskrit Lit.* (ed. 2) Introd. 32 The primæval physiolatry which was common to all the members of the Aryan family. 1879 *Scribner's Mag.* May 145 Physiolatry, or the worship of natural objects of awe, such as rivers, mountains, etc. 1882 L. F. WARD in *Internat. Rev.* May, These modern physiolaters are among the most eminent teachers of science and philosophy.

Physiologer (fiziǫ·lŏdʒəɹ). Now *rare* or *Obs.* Also 7 **phis-**. [f. PHYSIOLOGY (or L. *physiolog-us*, a. Gr. φυσιολόγος, one who discourses on nature, f. φύσις nature + -λόγος -speaking) + -ER¹.]

1. A student or teacher of natural science; *spec.* a philosopher of the Ionic sect.

1598 R. HAYDOCKE tr. *Lomazzo* II. 199 Astrologers, Physiologers, Optickes, Paynters. 1656 BLOUNT *Glossogr.*, *Physiologer*, he that searcheth out, or disputes of Natural things, a Natural Philosopher. 1678 CUDWORTH *Intell. Syst.* 9 Democritus and most of the Physiologers here commit a very great Absurdity, in that they make all Sense to be Touch. *a* 1688 — *Immut. Mor.* (1731) 105 The very same with that which Aristotle imputes to the antient Physiologers as a Paradox, that Black and White were not without the Sight. 1707 *Curios. in Husb. & Gard.* 145 The famous Bacon, and several Physiologers assure, that 'tis easy to have Roses so backward, as not to blow till towards the End of Autumn. 1867 MAURICE *Patriarchs & Lawg.* ii (1877) 53 The belief which a very large body of physiologers, not believers in the Bible, resolutely maintain.

2. = PHYSIOLOGIST 2.

1680 J. AUBREY in *Lett. Eminent Persons* (1813) III. 620 His head was of a mallet forme, approved by the physiologers. 1831 W. GODWIN *Thoughts Man* 8 An important remark, suggested to me many years ago by an eminent physiologer and anatomist. 1838–9 HALLAM *Hist. Lit.* IV. viii. § 36 Willis, a physician at Oxford,..his bold systems have given him a distinguished place among physiologers.

†**Physio·loget.** *Obs.* In 3 **fisiologet.** [dim. (perh. in OF.) f. PHYSIOLOG-US + -ET. Cf. PAMPHLET.] A diminutive or pet appellation for a physiologus or book on natural history.

c 1220 *Bestiary* 307 Ðus it is on boke set ðat man clepeð fisiologet.

Physiologian (fi:ziolōu·dʒiăn). *rare*⁻¹. [f. L. *physiologia* PHYSIOLOGY + -AN: cf. *theologian*.] = PHYSIOLOGIST 2.

1825 BEDDOES *Let.* Sept., Poems (1851) p. xlvii, Blumenbach,..is, I fancy, of the first rank as mineralogist, physiologian, geologist, botanist, natural-historian, and physician.

Physiologic (fi:ziolǫ·dʒik), *a.* [ad. L. *physiologic-us*, a. Gr. φυσιολογικός adj., f. φυσιολόγος: see PHYSIOLOGER and -IC. Cf. F. *physiologique* (G. Budé, 16th c.).]

†1. Of or belonging to natural science. *Obs. rare.*

1669 GALE *Crt. Gentiles* I. Introd. 3 Thales..informed himself touching..the Chaos, and other Physiologic Contemplations. 1677 *Ibid.* II. III. 32 Our Gospel..has availed more to the Knowledge of God than al their Physiologic Contemplations. 1736–44 H. COVENTRY *Lett. Phil. to Hyd.* v. (T.), It may ascertain the true era of physiologic allegory.

2. = PHYSIOLOGICAL 2.

1828 in WEBSTER. 1838 MILLIGEN *Curios. Med. Exp.* (1839) 565 To elucidate obscure parts of physiologic enquiry. 1878 *N. Amer. Rev.* CXXVI. 553 No method is more alluring, in physiologic studies, than this of accurate measurement and description. 1884 J. W. POWELL in *Science* IV. 472/2 In early society, incest laws do not recognize physiologic conditions, but only social conditions.

Physiological (fi:ziolǫ·dʒikăl), *a.* Also 7 **phi-**. [f. as prec. + -AL: see -ICAL.]

†1. Relating to the material universe or to natural science, physical; belonging to the Physiologers as students of nature. *Obs.*

1610 HEALEY *Vives' Comm. St. Aug. Citie of God* v. ix. (1620) 196 This opinion is Physiologicall and imbraced by Alexander, one of Aristotles interpreters. 1662 H. MORE *Def. Philos. Cabbala* App. i. (1712) 114 The Mosaical Philosophy, in the Physiological part thereof, is the same with the Cartesian. 1673 RAY (*title*) Observations Topographical, Moral, and Physiological, made in a Journey through part of the Low Countries, Germany, Italy, and France. 1768–74 TUCKER *Lt. Nat.* (1834) II. 348 The laws of gravitation, attraction, and impulse, and other objects of physiological science. 1809–10 COLERIDGE *Friend* II. x. (1818) III. 188 With these secret schools of physiological theology the mythical poets were doubtless in connection.

2. Pertaining or relating to physiology; relating to the functions and properties of living bodies.

1814 D. STEWART *Philos. Mind* II. iv. vi. 465 One of the most noted physiological works which have lately appeared on the Continent. 1845 G. E. DAY tr. *Simon's Anim. Chem.* I. 100 The General Physiological Chemistry of the Blood. 1861 BENTLEY *Man. Bot.* (1870) 1 Physiological Botany treats of plants, and their organs, in a state of life or action. 1873 RALFE *Phys. Chem.* Introd. 13 The term Physiological Chemistry is generally limited to the study of the chemical phenomena attendant upon the life of Animals. 1880 RICHARDSON in *Med. Temp. Jrnl.* 70 The physiological action of alcohol.

Physiologically (fi:ziolǫ·dʒikăli), *adv.* [f. as prec. + -LY².] In a physiological manner; according to the principles of physiology; from a physiological point of view.

1610 HEALEY *St. Aug. Citie of God* VI. viii. 246 But these things, say they, are all to be interpreted naturally and Phisiologically..as though we..sought Nature, and set God aside. 1775 HUNTER in *Phil. Trans.* LXV. 395 This animal may be considered, both anatomically and physiologically, as divided into two parts. 1874 P. BAYNE in *Contemp. Rev.* Oct. 697 The child..was physiologically a wreck,—damaged irretrievably in body and mind.

Physiologist (fiziǫ·lŏdʒist). [f. PHYSIOLOGY + -IST. Cf. F. *physiologiste* (1757 in Hatz.-Darm.).]

†1. A natural philosopher; a naturalist; = PHYSIOLOGER 1. *Obs.*

1664 POWER *Exp. Philos.* I. 72 The Physiologist also may gather something from the former Observations, touching the nature of Colours. 1677 GALE *Crt. Gentiles* II. III. 31 Socrates..perceiving how much his Predecessors, Thales &c. (who were generally Physiologists) had abused Physics. 1797 *Monthly Mag.* III. 50 Priestley, Black, Cavendish, and Macbride, had opened to physiologists a sort of new creation. 1827 R. P. WARD *De Vere* viii. (ed. 2) 145 Questions..which as they seem to depend upon a particular sort of air, we must leave to physiologists.

2. One versed in animal (or vegetable) physiology; a student or teacher of the science of the functions and properties of organic bodies.

1778 A. REID *Inquiry Suppress. Urine* (M.), The most skilful anatomist and physiologist. 1843 R. J. GRAVES *Syst. Clin. Med.* xxv. 312 This distinguished surgeon and physiologist has done more than all who preceded him to illustrate his subject. 1881 BURDON-SANDERSON in *Nature* 8 Sept. 440/2 The subjects of experiment used by the two last-mentioned physiologists were themselves; the work done was the mountain ascent from Interlaken to the summit of the Faulhorn.

Physio·logize (-dʒəiz), *v.* [f. as prec. + -IZE.]

†1. *intr.* To speculate or reason on nature: to inquire into natural causes and phenomena. *Obs.*

1678 CUDWORTH *Intell. Syst.* Pref. 7 Divers of the Italicks, and particularly Empedocles—before Democritus—physiologized atomically. *Ibid.* I. iii. 120 They who first theologized, did physiologize after this manner. 1730–6 BAILEY (folio) Pref., *Physiologize*, to Study, Discourse or Reason on the Nature of Things.

†2. *trans.* To explain in accordance with physical or natural science. *Obs.*

1678 CUDWORTH *Intell. Syst.* I. iv. 450 Unless we would rather with Macrobius, Physiologize them all Three, and make Minerva to be the Higher Heaven, Jupiter the Middle Ether, and Juno the Lower Air and Earth, all Animated; that is, One God, as acting differently in these Three Regions of the world. 1819 G. S. FABER *Dispensations* (1823) I. 234 Much the same remark is made by Eusebius on the humour of physiologising the religious system of the Egyptians.

3. *intr.* To act the physiologist; to form physiological conclusions or theories. *rare.*

1866 OWEN *Vertebr. Anim.* (L.), The somewhat capricious appearance of the gall-bladder in vegetarian mammals discourages such attempts to physiologize.

Hence **Physio·logising** *vbl. sb.*

1669 GALE *Crt. Gentiles* I. III. i. 17 Al which Poetic Physiologisings were but corrupt imitations of..Moses's description of the Creation.

‖**Physiologus** (fiziǫ·lŏgŏs). [L., a. Gr. φυσιολόγος, natural philosopher (see PHYSIOLOGER): used by Epiphanius as the name of his work on Natural History with moral and theological applications, whence the mediæval use.] A BESTIARY: see quot.

1898 STOPFORD BROOKE *Eng. Lit.* xiii. 203 The three first [Old Eng. poems, the *Whale*, the *Panther*, and the *Partridge*] must be taken together, and form part..of an English *Physiologus*. A *Physiologus* in the literature of the Middle Ages was a collection of descriptions of beasts, birds, or fishes, of their life and habits..each..followed by a religious or moral allegory based on this description.

Physiology (fiziǫ·lŏdʒi). Also 6–7 **phi-**. [ad. L. *physiologia*, a. Gr. φυσιολογία (Arist.), natural philosophy, natural science, f. φυσιολόγ-ος: see PHYSIOLOGER, and -LOGY; perh. immed. a. F. *physiologie* (1547 in Hatz.-Darm.).]

†1. The study and description of natural objects; natural science or natural philosophy; also, a particular system or doctrine of natural science. *Obs.*

1564 *Bauldwin's Mor. Philos.* (Palfr.) II. i. 73 That it may be knowen what they beleued of god, of themselues, and of his workes, all which they them selues call Phisiologie. 1603 HOLLAND *Plutarch's Mor.* 1346 Certeine Epicureans..standing much upon this their goodly and beautifull Physiologie forsooth (as they terme it). 1662 H. MORE *Def. Philos. Cabbala* App. i. (1712) 113 Whence there must be no small affinity betwixt this ancient Moschical, or rather Mosaical Physiology, and the Cartesian Philosophy. 1704 J. HARRIS *Lex. Techn.* I, *Physiology, Physicks*, or Natural Philosophy, is the Science of Natural Bodies. 1797 *Encycl. Brit.* (ed. 3) XVI. 18/1 Re-action, in physiology, the resistance made by all bodies to the action or impulse of others that endeavour to change its state whether of motion or rest.

2. The science of the normal functions and phenomena of living things.

It comprises the two divisions of *animal* and *vegetable physiology*; that part of the former which refers specially to the vital functions in man is called *human physiology*.

[1597 A. M. tr. *Guillemeau's Fr. Chirurg.* 1 b/1 *Physiologia* handelethe and treatethe of the structure and situatione of mans bodye. 1611 COTGR., *Physiologie*,..also..that part of Phisicke which treats of the composition, or structure of mans bodie.] 1615 CROOKE *Body of Man* 289 Amongst the new writers Fernelius the best learned Physitian of them all, in the 7. book of his Phisiologie, proueth that this bloud is not Alimentarie. 1704 J. HARRIS *Lex. Techn.* I, *Physiology*, is by some also accounted a Part of Physick, that teaches the Constitution of the Body so far as it is sound, or in its Natural State; and endeavours to find Reasons for its Functions and Operations, by the Help of Anatomy and Natural Philosophy. 1748 HARTLEY *Observ. Man* I. iv. Concl. 511, I..bring some Arguments from Physiology and Pathology. 1804 ABERNETHY *Surg. Obs.* 244 The anatomy and physiology of the nervous system. 1831 CARLYLE *Sart. Res.* III. vi, A Peasant unacquainted with botanical Physiology. 1831 BREWSTER *Optics* xxxv. 293 This important truth in the physiology of vision. 1860 HUXLEY *Lay Serm.* xii. 284 That part of biological science which deals with form and structure is called Morphology—that which concerns itself with function, Physiology. 1871 tr. *Pouchet's Universe* ix. 482 Hales, whose beautiful experiments laid the foundation of vegetable physiology.

fig. 1876 LOWELL *Among my Bks.* Ser. II. 26 As a contribution to the physiology of genius no other book is to be compared with the *Vita Nuova*. 1903 *Westm. Gaz.* 24 June 3/2 The amateur statistician may know something of the anatomy of commerce, but he knows nothing of what I may call its physiology—its circulating..and..digestive system[s].

†**Physion, phision**, corrupt or erron. forms of PHYSICIAN (perh. only typographical errors).

c 1580 LODGE *Repl. Gosson's Sch. Abuse* (Hunter. Cl.) 5 That they like good Phisions: should so frame their potions. 1611 BIBLE *Transl. Pref.* 3 The Scripture is..a Physions-shop (Saint Basill calleth it).

Physionomy, obs. spelling of PHYSIOGNOMY.

Phy:sio,philo·sophy. [transl. of Ger. *Naturphilosophie*, i. e. philosophy of nature, in the title of Oken's *Lehrbuch der Naturphilosophie* 1808–11, called in the Eng. transl. 'Elements of Physiophilosophy'.] A name for the philosophic system of nature of Oken, who 'aimed at constructing all knowledge *a priori*, and thus setting forth the system of nature in its universal relations'.

1847 TULK tr. *Oken* (*title*) Elements of Physiophilosophy. 1856 R. A. VAUGHAN *Mystics* (1860) II. 254 He [Oken] imagined that he wrote his *Physio-philosophy* in a kind of inspiration. 1887 COPE *Orig. Fittest* 8 The disfavour in which physiophilosophy was held secured to evolution a cold welcome.

Hence **Phy:siophi·losoph, Phy:siophilo·sopher** [= Ger. *Naturphilosoph*], an adherent of the system of Oken; **Phy:siophiloso·phic, -ical** *adjs.*, of or pertaining to this system.

1887 COPE *Orig. Fittest* 8 The *physiophilosophs became extravagant and mistook superficial appearances for realities. 1861 G. MOORE *Lost Tribes* 127 Here..it is that the *physio-philosophers have supposed mankind to have originated. 1865 tr. *Strauss' Life Jesus* I. I. xxx. 247 The allegorical interpretation..applied to Homer and Hesiod in order to extract *physiophilosophical ideas out of the Gods and their histories.

Physique (fizī·k). [a. F. *physique* sb. masc., absolute use of *physique* physical, i. e. that which is physical.] The physical or bodily structure, organization, and development; the characteristic appearance or physical powers (of an individual or a race).

1826 LADY GRANVILLE *Lett.* (1894) I. 384 You must allow that this describes his physique admirably. 1856 EMERSON *Eng. Traits, Manners* Wks. (Bohn) II. 47 So much had the fine physique and the personal vigour of this robust race worked on my imagination. 1864 R. F. BURTON *Dahome* II. 64 The masculine physique of the women enabling them to compete with men in enduring toil, hardships, and privations. 1881 A. G. C. LIDDELL in *Macm. Mag.* XLIV. 478/2 They..had tremendous physiques, though rather fleshy.

Physique, obs. form of PHYSIC.

Physitheism (fi·ziþi,iz'm). [f. Gr. φύσι-ς nature + θεός God + -ISM: cf. *polytheism*.] The deification of the powers or phenomena of nature. So **Phy:sithei·stic** *a.*

1891 J. W. POWELL in *Chautauquan* Dec. 291 (Funk) Physitheism is the theology and religion of the barbaric world. In this religion the weather-producing agents and the phenomena of the weather are personified and deified. 1889 G. MALLERY in *Pop. Sci. Monthly* XXXVI. 208 The prophets tried to pull the Israelites too rapidly through the zoötheistic and physitheistic stages into monotheism.

Phy·sitism. *rare.* [f. Gr. φύσι-ς nature + -ITE + -ISM.] A system of nature-worship.

1885 DUNS in *Proc. Soc. Antiq. Scot.* XIX. 396.

Physiurgic (fizi,ǝ̄·ɹdʒik), *a. rare.* [f. Gr. φύσι-ς nature + ἔργον work + -IC: cf. *theurgic*.] Produced or acted upon solely by nature.

1826 BENTHAM *Chrestom.* 187 Applied to bodies..in their natural, or say physiurgic, state—human art—or say elaboration by human art—has two distinguishable objects. 1843 BOWRING *Introd. Bentham's Wks.* I. 16/2 Natural History and Natural Philosophy are respectively represented by Physiurgic Somatology, and Anthropurgic Somatology.

So **Physiurgosco·pic** *a. rare.*

1816 BENTHAM *Chrestom.* Wks. 1843 VIII. 86 Division of Somatology, or Somatics at large, into *Physiurgic* (Physiurgoscopic) and *Anthropurgic* (Anthropurgoscopic).

Physnamy, -nomy, obs. ff. PHYSIOGNOMY.

Physo- (fəiso), repr. Gr. φυσο-, combining form of Gr. φῦσα bellows, bladder, bubble, in a few Gr. compounds, and in many modern scientific terms. **Physoca·rpous** *a. Bot.* [Gr. καρπός fruit], having an inflated or bladder-like fruit (Mayne *Expos. Lex.* 1858). **Phy·socele** (-sīl), *Path.* [Gr. κήλη tumour], a tumour or hernia distended with gas. **Physograde** (fəi·sǒgrēd), *Zool.* [ad. mod.L. *Physograda*, f. -*gradus* going]. **a.** *adj.* moving by means of a hollow vesicular float or buoy; of or pertaining to the *Physograda*, a group of oceanic hydrozoa furnished with such floating organs; **b.** *sb.* a member of this group; hence **Physo·gradous** *a.* ‖**Physometra** (fəisomī·tră), *Path.* [Gr. μήτρα womb], the presence of gas in the uterus, uterine tympanites. **Physonect** (fəi·sonekt), *Zool.* [Gr. νήκτης a swimmer, f. νήχειν to swim], a member of the *Physonectæ*, a suborder of siphonanthous siphonophores; hence **Physone·ctous** *a.* **Physopod** (fəi·so,pǫd) [Gr. πούς, ποδ- foot], a mollusc of the section *Physopoda* or *Thysanoptera*, rhipidoglossate gastropods, with a sort of sucker on the foot.

1753 CHAMBERS *Cycl. Supp.*, *Physocele, a word used by many authors to express a wind-rupture. 1811 HOOPER *Med. Dict.*, *Physocele*, a species of hernia, whose contents are distended with wind. 1893 in *Syd. Soc. Lex.* 1835–6 TODD *Cycl. Anat.* I. 37/1 The principal organ of locomotion in the *physograda is the air-filled vesicle or bladder. 1858 MAYNE *Expos. Lex.* 957/2 Animals..characterized by their body being provided with an aëriform dilatation of the intestinal canal, serving for a swimming organ: *physogradous. 1822 GOOD *Study Med.* IV. 434 Emphysema uteri. Inflation of the Womb...This is the *physometra of Sauvages and later nosologists. 1875 JONES & SIEV. *Pathol. Anat.* (ed. 2) 759 Physometra is sometimes observed after severe labours. 1890 *Cent. Dict.*, *Physopod.

Physoclist (fəi·soklist), *a.* and *sb. Ichthyol.* [f. mod.L. *Physoclisti* (pl.), f. Gr. φῦσα bladder + -κλειστ-ος shut, closed.] **a.** *adj.* Belonging to the *Physoclisti*, a group of teleost fishes having the duct between the air-bladder and the intestine closed: cf. PHYSOSTOME. **b.** *sb.* A member of this group. So **Physocli·stic, Physocli·stous** *adjs.*, having the air-bladder so closed or cut off.

1887 HEILPRIN *Distrib. Anim.* 303 Both the *physoclist and physostome types appear..very nearly simultaneously in the same deposits. *Ibid.*, The severance of the bladder in the physoclists being the result of the disuse of parts. 1883 LANKESTER in *Encycl. Brit.* XVI. 671/1 The parallel cases [of the secretion of gas] ranging from the Protozoon Arcella to the *Physoclistic Fishes. 1887 COPE *Orig. Fittest* 327 The descent of the *Physoclystous fishes has probably been from Holostean ancestors, both with and without the intervention of Physostomous forms.

Physodin (fəi·sodin). *Chem.* [f. specific name *physōd-ēs* (cf. Gr. φυσοειδής bladder-like) + -IN¹.] A neutral substance ($C_{12}H_{10}O_8$), a white loosely-coherent mass, occurring in a lichen, *Parmelia ceratophylla* or *physodes*.

1866–8 WATTS *Dict. Chem.* IV. 635 Physodin behaves to water like a resin, not being wetted thereby.

‖**Physophora** (fəisǫ·fŏră). *Zool.* [mod.L., f. Gr. φῦσα bladder + -φορος bearing, borne.] A genus of oceanic hydrozoa, the species of which float by means of numerous vesicular organs. So ‖**Physophoræ** *pl.* (sometimes **Physophora**), a suborder or division of *Siphonophora* (an order of *Hydrozoa Craspedota*), having the proximal end modified into a pneumatophore or float; **Physo·phoran** *a.*, of or pertaining to the *Physophoræ*; *sb.*, a member of this division; also **Physophore** (fəi·sŏfōəɹ). ‖**Physopho·ridæ** *pl.*, the family containing the genus *Physophora*; **Physophorous** (fəisǫ·fŏrəs) *a.*, of the nature of the *Physophoræ*, having pneumatophores or swimming-bells (Mayne 1858).

1869 tr. *Pouchet's Universe* (1871) 13 At other times it is owing to..the *Physophora, trailing their tresses all spangled with stars like those of Berenice in the firmament. 1870 HARTWIG *Sea & Wood.* xv, The Hydrostatic Acalephæ, or *Physophoræ..were formerly supposed to be a special class of animals, but have been proved by Sars and other naturalists to be merely alternating generations of the bell-shaped Acalephæ. 1888 ROLLESTON & JACKSON *Anim. Life* 774 In the *Physophores *Forskalia* and *Agalma* the single ovum is arrested in the endoderm, and surrounded by the spadix. 1860 H. SPENCER in *Westm. Rev.* Jan. 103 In the *Physophoridæ, a variety of organs similarly arise by transformation of the budding polypes. 1878 tr. *Gegenbaur's Comp. Anat.* 97 The greater development of these bladders, which in most Physophoridæ are rather small.

‖**Physostigma** (fəisosti·gmă). [mod.L., f. Gr. φῦσα bladder + στίγμα STIGMA.] *Bot.* A genus of leguminous plants, the flower of which has a spiral keel, and a bent style continued into an oblique hood above the stigma; the only species is *P. venenosum*, producing the highly poisonous Calabar bean. Hence, The Calabar bean or its extract as a drug.

1864 *N. Syd. Soc. Year-bk. Med.* 428 Dr. Fraser has used the physostigma internally in cases of erysipelas. 1878 A. HAMILTON *Nerv. Dis.* 118 Physostigma, aconite, and other cardiac sedatives may be mentioned as other anæmiants. 1880 GARROD & BAXTER *Mat. Med.* 322 The..administration of an appropriate dose of physostigma.

Hence †**Physosti·gmia, Physosti·gmine** *Chem.*, the alkaloid $C_{15}H_{21}N_3O_2$, constituting the active principle of the Calabar bean.

1865 *N. Syd. Soc. Year-bk. Med.* 447 Jobst and Hesse..have succeeded in isolating the active principle of the Calabar bean, to which they give the name physostigmin. 1896 *Allbutt's Syst. Med.* I. 228 It is in this way that strychnine and physostigmine respectively stimulate and depress the spinal cord.

Physostome (fəi·sǒstoᵘm), *a.* and *sb. Ichthyol.* [f. mod. L. *Physostomi*, f. Gr. φῦσα bladder + στόμα mouth, -στομος -mouthed.] **a.** *adj.* Belonging to the *Physostomi*, a group of teleost fishes, in which the air-bladder is connected with the alimentary canal by an air-duct: cf. PHYSOCLIST. **b.** *sb.* A member of this group. So **Physosto·matous, Physo·stomous** *a.*, having the air-bladder opening into an air-duct.

1880 GÜNTHER *Fishes* 199 [In] the Cretaceous group..Physostomes and Plectognaths are likewise well represented. 1887 Physostome, Physostomous [see PHYSOCLIST, PHYSOCLISTOUS].

†**Physy**, obs. f. FUSEE², wheel of a watch.

1690 LOCKE *Hum. Und.* III. vi. § 39 Some Watches..are made with four Wheels..some have Strings and Physies, and others none.

Physyk, obs. form of PHYSIC.

Phyt- (fəit, fit), combining form used before a vowel for PHYTO-.

Phytalbu·min, vegetable albumin. **Phyta·lbumose**, a form of albumen occurring in plants. **Phyteco·nomy**, vegetable economy. **Phytœco·logy** [Gr. οἶκος abode: see -LOGY], the science which treats of plants in relation to their environment or habitat; so **Phytœco·logist**.

1899 CAGNEY tr. *Jaksch's Clin. Diagn.* viii. (ed. 4) 405 The products of bacterial life, toxines, and *phytalbumins appear also to play an important part in the process of suppuration. 1890 *Cent. Dict.*, *Phytalbumose. 1897 *Allbutt's Syst. Med.* IV. 520 Ricin and abrin, phytalbumoses obtained from the seed of the castor-oil plant. 1902 *Brit. Med. Jrnl.* No. 2151. 920 The action of some of the phytalbumoses. 1898 *Naturalist* 180 If soils are a factor in its *phyteconomy. 1899 *Pop. Sci. Monthly* Nov. 99 One of the general views of *phytoecology is that the forms of plants are modified to adapt them to the conditions under which they exist. 104 The phytoecologist to-day watches his subject as it grows.

-phyte, a terminal element representing Gr. φυτόν a plant, and denoting a vegetable organism, as *microphyte, protophyte, saprophyte*. See also ZOOPHYTE (= animal plant).

Phytiform (fəi·tifǭɹm, fi·ti-), *a. rare.* [irreg. f. Gr. φυτόν plant + -FORM.] Plant-like, phytoid.

1890 in *Cent. Dict.* 1893 in *Syd. Soc. Lex.*

Phytiphagan, -ous, incorrect forms of PHYTOPHAGAN, -OUS.

Phytivorous (fəiti·vŏrəs, fit-), *a.* Now *rare* or *Obs.* [irreg. f. Gr. φυτόν plant + -VOROUS.] Feeding on plants or vegetable substances.

1668 WILKINS *Real Char.* II. v. § 4. 144 Birds may be distinguished by..their food..into..Carnivorous; feeding chiefly on Flesh. Phytivorous; feeding on Vegetables. 1693 *Phil. Trans.* XVII. 851 All which last are Herbivorous or Phytivorous Animals. 1798 *Ibid.* LXXXVIII. 46, I have not found the uric oxide in the urinary concretions of any phytivorous animal. 1833 MANTELL *Geol. S. E. Eng.* 394 The teeth and jaws of two other phytivorous saurians.

Phyto- (fəi·to, fi·to), combining form of Gr. φυτόν a plant, lit. that which has grown, f. φύειν to produce, pass. and intr. to grow; used in forming scientific words, chiefly botanical.

As the υ in Gr. φυτόν is a short vowel, the etymological pronunciation of *phyt-* in all the following words is (fit); but the general tendency in English to view *y* as a long *i*, as in *my, cry*, etc., has made the (etymologically erroneous) pronunciation (fəit) all but universal: it is adopted in all the pronouncing dictionaries from Walker onward.

Phytobio·logy, the biology of plants; hence **Phytobiolo·gical** *a.* **Phytobranchiate** (-bræ·ŋkiět) *a. Zool.* [see BRANCHIATE], of a group of isopodous crustaceans: having leaf-like gills. **Phytoche·mistry**, the chemistry of plants; so **Phytoche·mical** *a.* †**Phyto·chimy** [F. *chimie* chemistry] = *phytochemistry* (Webster 1847). **Phy·tochlore** [Gr. χλωρός green] = CHLOROPHYLL. **Phy·tochrome** [see CHROME]: see quots. **Phytoco·llite** *Min.* [Gr. κόλλα glue + -ITE¹], name proposed for certain jelly-like hydrocarbons found in peat. **Phytogelin** (-dʒe·lin) [GEL(ATIN) + -IN¹], the gelatinous matter of Algæ (*Treas. Bot.* 1866). **Phytoglyphy** (fəitǫ·glifi, fit-) [Gr. γλυφή: see GLYPH], nature-printing, as originally used for plants; hence **Phytogly·phic** *a.* **Phytoma·nia** *nonce-wd.*, a mania for collecting plants. **Phytomelin** (-me·lin) [Gr. μέλι, L. *mel* honey (in reference to its colour and appearance)] = RUTIN. **Phyto·nomy** [see -NOMY], the science of the laws of plant-growth. **Phy:to,palæonto·logy**, vegetable palæontology, study of fossil plants; hence **Phy:to,palæonto·logist**. **Phy:topatho·logy**, (*a*) the study of the pathology or diseases of plants; (*b*) the pathology of diseases due to vegetable organisms, as fungi; mycology; hence **Phy:to,patholo·gical** *a.*; **Phytopatho·logist**, one versed in phytopathology (a). **Phyto·philous** *a.* [Gr. φίλος friendly], plant-loving: esp. of insects. **Phytophthirian** *Entom.* (-fəiriăn) [Gr. φθείρ louse] **a.** *adj.*, pertaining to the *Phytophthiria* or plant-lice; **b.** *sb.*, a member of this group, a plant-louse. **Phy:to,phylogene·tic** *a.*, relating to the phylogeny of plants. **Phy:tophysio·logy**, vegetable physiology. **Phytosco·pic** *a.* [Gr. σκοπεῖν to view], caused by sight of plants: said of the effect of surrounding vegetation on the colour of a larva. †**Phyto·scopy**: see quot. **Phyto·sophy**, knowledge of plants; botany (Oken). **Phyto·sterin** [Gr. στερεός solid]: see quot. 1881. **Phy·totaxy** [Gr. τάξις arrangement], systematic botany. **Phy:toterato·logy**, vegetable teratology. **Phy:tovite·llin** [L. *vitell-us* yolk], a globulin occurring in many seeds, and agreeing in all its reactions with vitellin from egg-yolk.

1887 *Athenæum* 26 Feb. 292/3 Sir J. Lubbock read the second part of his *phytobiological observations. 1890 *Ibid.* 1 Mar. 278/3 There remains a large collection of memoirs on general botany and *phyto-biology. 1858 MAYNE *Expos. Lex.* 959/1 *Phytochemical. 1846 WORCESTER, *Phytochemistry*, vegetable chemistry. *Philos. Mag.* 1866 WATTS *Dict. Chem.* IV. 636 Phytochemistry, the Chemistry of Plants. The most comprehensive treatise on this subject is that of Rochleder, published at Leipzig in 1854. 1866 *Treas. Bot.*, *Phytochlore*, green colouring matter; chlorophyll. 1893 *Syd. Soc. Lex.*, *Phytochrome*, a name for chlorophyll. 1902 WEBSTER Suppl., *Phytochrome*, yellow pigment of plants. 1881 H. C. LEWIS in *Proc. Amer. Phil. Soc.* XX. 117 *Phytocollite. 1864 WEBSTER, *Phytoglyphic*,..relating to phytoglyphy. *Phytoglyphy*,..the art of printing from nature, by taking impressions from plants or other objects. 1855 E. R. LANKESTER *Macgillivray's Nat. Hist. Dee Side & Braemar* 63 This risk incurred for the mere chance of finding a few rare plants..one can hardly designate it by any other name than *Phytomania. 1866 WATTS *Dict. Chem.* IV. 636 *Phytomelin* or *Plant-yellow*. A name proposed by W. Stein for rutin, on account of its wide diffusion in the vegetable kingdom. 1864 WEBSTER, *Phytonomy. 1883 *Science* 6 Apr. 252 The nature of some impressions described by *phytopaleontologists as remains of fossil Algæ. *Ibid.* 253 The evidence..renders great service to *phytopaleontology. 1886 *Cassell's Encycl. Dict.*, *Phytopathologist. 1893 ELEANOR ORMEROD in *Autobiog. & Corr.* xx. (1904) 218 One of our leading European Phytopathologists. 1864 WEBSTER, *Phytopathology*,..an account of diseases to which plants are liable. 1880 *Nature* 12 Feb. 364/1 On the method and data of *phyto-phylogenetic research. 1854 H. SPENCER in *Brit. Q. Rev.* July 115 Biology, Organosophy, Phytogeny, *Phyto-physiology, Phytology. 1892 POULTON in *Trans. Entom. Soc.* X. 294 The effect cannot be phytophagic in the strict sense of the word, but rather *phytoscopic, inasmuch as the colour of the surface of the leaf rather than its substance acts as the stimulus. 1730–6 BAILEY (folio), *Phytoscopy*,..a viewing and contemplating or considering plants. 1854 H. SPENCER in *Brit. Q. Rev.* July 115 He [Oken] says..'Biology, therefore, divides into Organogeny, *Phyto-sophy, Zoosophy'. 1881 WATTS *Dict. Chem.* VIII. II. 1624 *Phytosterin, $C_{26}H_{44}O$... A neutral substance, identical or homologous with cholesterin, obtained from Calabar beans by extraction with petroleum-ether. 1897 *Naturalist* 47 Various higher alcohols and phytosterin being present therein as bases. 1883 L. F. WARD *Dynamic Sociol.* I. 120 *Phytotaxy. 1898 tr. *Strasburger's Bot.* I. 154 The study of the abnormal development of plants is called *Phytoteratology.

Phytobiology to **-gelin**: see above.

Phytogenesis (fəito,dʒe·nĕsis, fito-). [f. PHYTO- + -GENESIS.] The generation or evolution of plants. So **Phytogene·tic, Phytogene·tical** *adjs.*, of or pertaining to phytogenesis; **Phytogene·tically** *adv.*; also **Phyto·geny** = *phytogenesis*.

1858 MAYNE *Expos. Lex.*, *Phytogenesis*, term by Dupetit-Thouars for germination..phytogenesy. 1882 VINES *Sachs' Bot.* 904 In the latter case we have the end, in the former the beginning of *phytogenetic series. 1881 WILLIAMSON in *Nature* 27 Oct. 607/1 Minute, but *phytogenetically important forms of plant-life. 1854 H. SPENCER in *Brit. Q. Rev.* July 115 Biology, Organosophy, *Phytogeny.

Phytogenic (fəito,dʒe·nik, fito-), *a. Geol.* and *Min. rare.* [f. Gr. φυτόν plant + -GEN 2 + -IC.] Of vegetable origin. So **Phyto·genous** *a. rare.*

1858 MAYNE *Expos. Lex.* 959/2 Under the name of *phytogenous substances*, Haüy has formed an Appendix to the *Combustibilia*, comprehending those of which the origin is evidently vegetable. 1878 LAWRENCE tr. *Cotta's Rocks Class.* 352 Phytogenic deposits are such as consist chiefly of vegetable substances.

Phy:togeo·graphy. [f. PHYTO- + GEOGRAPHY.] The geographical distribution of plants.

1858 in MAYNE *Expos. Lex.* 1881 *Nature* 13 Oct. 556/1 The numerous writings on phytogeography of the late Prof. A. Grisebach. 1896 J. THOMSON *African Explorer* xiv. 343 The phytogeography of Central Africa.

Hence **Phy:togeo·grapher**, one who is versed in phytogeography; **Phy:togeogra·phic, -gra·phical** *adjs.*, of or pertaining to phytogeography, dealing with the geographical distribution of plants.

1889 *Nature* 30 May 98/1 Apart from the value of the work to the systematist and *phytogeographer, it possesses an interest for a wide circle. 1885 W. B. HEMSLEY in *Challenger Rep., Bot.* I. 6 For *phyto-geographical purposes Insular Floras may be divided into three categories based upon their endemic element. 1883 THISELTON DYER in *Nature* 4 Jan. 224/2 A right understanding of the phytogeographical facts of the north temperate flora. 1886 *Athenæum* 5 June 750/2 Phyto-geographical Map of Europe.

Phytoglyphic, -glyphy: see PHYTO-.

†**Phyto·gnomy.** *Obs.* [Formed on the analogy of *physiognomy*, after the mod.L. *Phytognomonica* of J. Baptista Porta (1583): see PHYTO- and GNOMIC.] The alleged art of discovering the qualities of a plant from its appearance; vegetable physiognomy. Hence †**Phytogno·mical** *a.*

[1583 PORTA (*title*) Phytognomonica..in quibus nova facillimaque affertur methodus, qua plantarum..ex prima extimæ faciei inspectione quivis abditas vires assequatur.] 1643 SIR T. BROWNE *Relig. Med.* II. § 2, I hold moreover that there is a Phytognomy, or Physiognomy, not onely of men, but of Plants, and Vegetables. 1646 — *Pseud. Ep.* II. vi. 93 Whoever shall peruse the signatures of Crollius, or rather the Phytognomy of Porta. 1653 R. SANDERS *Physiogn.* b ij, In Phytognomical Physiognomie we may observe certain plants resembling the heads of Animals.

Phytography (fəitǫ·grăfi, fit-). [ad. mod.L. *phytographia*: see PHYTO- and -GRAPHY.]

1. Description of plants; descriptive botany.

[1691 PLUKENET (*title*) Phytographia, seu Stirpium illustrium et minus cognitarum Icones.] 1696 RAY in *Lett. Lit. Men* (Camden) 202, I shall..put down what I find in..Plukenet's Phytography. 1730–6 BAILEY (folio) Pref., *Phytography*,..a Treatise or Physiological Description of Plants and Vegetables. 1835 HENSLOW *Phys. Bot.* Introd. 3 A third..department is styled 'Phytography', in which a full description of plants themselves is given. 1885 GOODALE *Physiol. Bot.* (1892) 3 Phytography or Descriptive Botany.

2. = PHYTOGLYPHY.

Hence **Phyto·grapher**, an expert in or writer on phytography; **Phytogra·phic, Phytogra·phical** *adjs.*, pertaining to phytography.

1890 *Cent. Dict.*, *Phytographer. 1693 *Phil. Trans.* XVII. 618 A new Set of *Phytographic Tables. 1888 *Nature* 5 July 220/1 The introductory narrative..enables a phytographic botanist to apprehend the nature of the country [Afghanistan] and climate. 1828–32 WEBSTER, *Phytographical*, pertaining to the description of plants.

Phytoid (fəi·toid, fit-), *a.* and *sb. rare.* [f. Gr. φυτ-όν plant + -OID. Cf. Gr. φυτώδ-ης plant-like.]

A. *adj.* Plant-like; esp. in *Zool.* of an animal. 1858 in MAYNE *Expos. Lex.*

B. *sb. Bot.* (See quot.)

1852 CARPENTER *Veg. Phys.* § 397 In order to distinguish between the separated buds of plants and animals, those of the former have been called phytoids, and the latter zooids.

‖**Phytolacca** (fəito-, fitolæ·kă). [mod.L. (Tournefort 1700), f. Gr. φυτόν plant + mod.L. *lacca* crimson lake.] *Bot.* The genus of plants including the Pocan, Virginian Poke, Pokeweed, or Red-ink plant (*P. decandra*), and several other tropical or sub-tropical species, chiefly American; also various preparations of the Poke used medicinally. Hence **Phytolaccin** (-læ·ksin) *Chem.*, a neutral crystalline compound obtained from the Virginian Poke.

1753 *Scots Mag.* June 283/2 Give purges..with the phytolacca decoction. 1882 *Garden* 18 Mar. 179/3 Several other Phytolaccas are widely distributed throughout the Tropics. 1864 *N. Syd. Soc. Year-bk. Med.* 441 The dose of the concentrated preparation (phytolaccin).

†**Phy·tolite, phy·tolith.** *Obs.* [f. PHYTO- + -LITE, -LITH. In F. *phytolithe*.] A fossil plant.

1794 SULLIVAN *View Nat.* II. 175 The former are called zoophytes; the latter phytolites. 1849 MURCHISON *Siluria* xvi. 402 The so-called 'transition' and 'grauwacke' phytolites described by various German authors.

Hence †**Phy:tolitho·logy**, vegetable palæontology; †**Phy:tolitho·logist**, a writer on this subject. 1864 in WEBSTER.

Phytological (fəitolǫ·dʒikăl, fito-), *a.* Now *rare.* [f. as PHYTOLOGY: see -LOGICAL. Cf. F. *phytologique*.] Relating to the study of plants; botanical.

1654 GAYTON *Pleas. Notes* III. iii. 79 Priapus..the greatest Herbalist in the World;..This Phutologicall Deitie. 1673 GREW *Anat. Roots* Ep. Ded., The promotion of Phytological Science is one Part of Your Work. 1673 — (*title*) An Idea of a Phytological History propounded. 1833 LYELL *Princ. Geol.* III. 332 The zoological and phytological characters of the same formations were far more persistent than their mineral peculiarities.

Phytologist (fəitǫ·lŏdʒist, fit-). Now *rare.* [f. PHYTOLOGY + -IST.] One versed in phytology; a botanist.

1699 EVELYN *Acetaria* (1729) 138 Charles Hatton Esq. to whom all our Phytologists and Lovers of Horticulture are oblig'd. 1727 BAILEY vol. II, *Phytologist*, a Botanist, one who treats of Plants. 1827 STEUART *Planter's G.* Pref. (1828) 5 If he be a Phytologist of research, or, still more, a Planter of experience. 1881 ROUTLEDGE *Science* ii. 34 There was a botanical garden for the phytologist.

Phytology (fəitǫ·lŏdʒi, fit-). Now *rare.* [ad. mod.L. *phytologia*, f. Gr. φυτόν plant + -λογία: see -LOGY. Cf. F. *phytologie* (d'Holbach 1753).] The science of plants; botany.

[1647 G. DUVAL (*title*) Phytologia; sive, Philosophia Plantarum.] 1658 SIR T. BROWNE *Hydriot.* Ep. Ded. to N. Bacon, We pretend not to multiply vegetable divisions by Quincuncial and Reticulate plants; or erect a new Phytology. 1819 *Pantologia*, *Phytology*, that part of Natural History which treats on plants. 1849 H. MILLER *Footpr. Creat.* xiv. (1874) 264 He calls into court Astronomy, Geology, Phytology and Zoology.

Phytomania, -melin: see PHYTO-.

Supplement, p. 3873; Corrigenda, p. 4092; Spurious words, p. 4093; Books quoted, p. 4094

Phytomer ... *Bot.* = PHYTON.

Phyton ... *Bot.*

Phytonise ... rare. form of PYTHONISE.

Phytonomy ...

Phytopathology ...

Phytophaga ...

Phytophagic ...

Phytophagous ...

Phytophily ...

Phytophthora ...

Phytotomist ...

Phytotomous ...

Pī The name of the Greek letter π (in Gr. πῖ, πῑ): used in *Math.* to express the ratio of the circumference or periphery (περιφέρεια) of a circle to its diameter; see π (the letter) II.

Pi (pai), *sb.* Public School and Univ. slang.

Pia ...

Pia-arachnoid, piara-chnoid. *Anat.*

Piabā ...

Piaba ...

Piacaba see PIASSABA.

Piache ...

Piacle ...

Pia-culary ...

Piacular ...

Piaculous ...

Piaculum ...

Piaffer ...

Piaffe ...

Piage variant of PEAGE.

Pial ... Of or pertaining to the pia mater.

Pia mater ...

Pian ...

Piano (pii-ˈano) ...

Pianino ...

Pianism ...

Pianissimo ...

Pianist A player on the pianoforte.

Pianistic ...

Pianiste ...

Pianist's cramp ...

Pianno ...

Pianoforte A musical instrument of which is usually ascribed to B. Cristofori of Padua ...

Pianofortist One who plays on the pianoforte.

Pianograph ...

Pianola ...

Piano-organ ...

Piano piano adv. Obs.

Pianist var. PIANIST.

Piano-violin ...

Piarachnoid see PIA-ARACHNOID.

Piarist ...

Piaroa ...

Piassaba ...

Piast ...

Piaster, piastre ...

Piastrina ...

Piazza ...

Piazzian ...

Pibal ...

Pibble ...

Pibroch ...

Pic ...

Pica magpie ...

Picamar ...

Picard ...

Picaresque ...

Picarian ...

Picaro ...

Picaroon ...

Picayune (pikˈayūn), *sb.* ...

PICAYUNISH.

Piedmont, now in Fr. 'halfpence, cash, money'; of uncertain origin (Hatz.-Darm.)]

A. *sb.* The name formerly given in Louisiana, Florida, etc., to the smallest half-real, value 6½ cents or 5 pence: now in the U.S. 5-cent piece or other coin of small value; hence *colloq.*, a person or thing considered small, mean, or insignificant.

B. *adj.* Mean, contemptible, paltry.

Picayunish (pikiə'niʃ), *a.* *U.S. colloq.* [f. prec. + -ISH.] Of little value or account, insignificant, paltry, mean. Hence **Pica'yunishness.**

Pi'cadill, pi'cadill. *Obs.* Forms: α. 7 pickadel(l, picadel; picoe, picos-, pickadill, dillʒe; pickedaille; paccoe, pickadillie, pacadile; pickar-, picardil(l). β. 7 picka-, picka-, pecoadillo. γ. 7 pickă-, piccă-, peccă-, pickydilly. [a. Fr. *picadillo* (a 1589 in Godel.)

Picher. one, form of PITCH, PIPE, PYCHE.

Picher, Pichot, obs. forms of PITCHER, PIQUET.

† Pichey (pit'ʃi). *Obs.* Local name in the native name of PIPE. *The Little Armadillo.*

Pichiciego (pitʃiʒ'eʒ). [ad. Sp. *pichi-ciego*, (.(?) Guarani *pichey* (see prec.) + Sp. *ciego* blind.] A small burrowing edentate animal of Chili, *Chlamyphorus truncatus,* allied to the Armadillos; its back and head are covered with a hard leather-like shell attached only along the spine, and clipping abruptly over the haunches.

Pichurim (pit'ʃurim). *Ornith.* The native name

PICIFORM.

a luxuraceous South American tree, *Nectandra Puchury (Laurus Puchurim of Richard).*

Piciform (pi'sifəm), *a.* [ad. mod.L. *Piciformes,* f. *Picus* woodpecker: see -FORM.] Having the form or structure of, or resembling, a woodpecker; of or pertaining to the *Piciformes,* a group of pician birds.

Picine (pai'sain), *a.* *Ornith.* [f. L. *pic-us* woodpecker + -INE.] Of, pertaining to, or allied to the woodpeckers.

Pick (pik), *sb.[1]* Forms: 4 **pikk,** 4–6 **pyk,** 4–8 **pic,** 5 **pikke, pykke,** 6 **piex, pickes,** 6–7 **pikes, 7 pike, 6 picke,** [app. a collateral form, with short vowel, of PIKE *sb.1* (Cf. the collateral forms *pick* and *pike* in PITCH *v.1*.)]

PICK.

10. To open (a lock) with a pointed instrument, a skeleton key, or the like; to open clandestinely.

b. intr. To toy or trifle with food.

† Pick, † picke, obs. forms of PIKE *sb.* and *v.*, PITCH.

Pick, *sb.1* [attrib. use of PICK *sb.* 3.]

I. 1. *trans.* To pierce, penetrate, indent, dig into, or break the surface of (anything) by striking it with something sharp or pointed, as to break up (ground, a road, etc.) with a pick, to indent the surface of (a millstone); † rarely, to hoe. Also *absol.,* to ply the pick, mattock, pickax, etc.

Pick. ... (dictionary entries, OED)

Pick, pick *v.* To break up (ground) with a pick; to extract from the ground by picking; to take up.

Pick *sb.* Also **pykke, pik,** 6-7 **picke,** 6 **pyke.** Now only *dial.* or *techn.*

Pick-a-back *adv.* Also 7-8 **pick-a-back, pick-pack, picky-back.**

Pick- In comb.

Pickage *sb.*

Pickax, pickaxe *sb.*

Picked *ppl. a.*

Picked-hatch *sb.*

Pickeer *v.*

Pickering *vbl. sb.*

Pickerel *sb.*

Picket *sb.*

Picked-devant, pique devant *Obs.*

Picker *sb.*

Pickerel-weed *sb.*

Pickering

PICKET.

...Wellington Gen. Desp. I. 1799 The advanced picquets of the British army were attacked by the enemy. ...picket, sent out to bring in men who have exceeded their leave.

b. A camp-guard, sent out to bring in men who have exceeded their leave.

c. *transf.* and *fig.* A party of watchers or sentinels, an outpost: an outlying host.

5. (usually *pl.*) Applied to men acting in a body or singly who are deputed by a trades-union or the like, to watch men going to work during a strike or in non-union workshops, and to endeavour to dissuade or deter them.

III. *6.* An elongated rifle bullet, with a conoidal front; a conoidal-conical bullet.

IV. *7.* *attrib.* and *Comb.*, as (sense 1) picket-fence, -gate, -machine, -pin, -rope, -strap; (senses 4, 5) picket-duty, -picion, -trench; picket-boat, -launch, -ship, a vessel employed for reconnoitring, or scouting in advance of the fleet, or on a river in military operations; picket-clamp, a clamp for holding fence-pickets while being pointed; picket-guard, an inlying picket, also a picket protecting a position; picket-header, -pointer, a machine for pointing fence-pickets; picket-house, a garrison, the building where a picket is stationed; picket-launch: see picket-boat; picket-line, (a) a tether; (b) a line held by pickets: picket-ship: see picket-boat.

Picket, picketter, obs. forms of Piquet.
Picket-beard. [See Pickel 1 3, Pike v.²]

Picketee, obs. form of Picotee.

Picketing (pi·ketiŋ), *vbl. sb.* [f. Picket v. + -ing¹.]

Pick-fault: see Pick- in comb.

Pickfork. *Obs. exc. dial.* Forms: 3 pie-, 5 pykk-, pik-, pyke-, 6-7 pick, 6 pickeus; 9 *dial.* pike-; *also* pitch-fork. [Origin of the first element obscure: occurring as *pic, pik, pyke,* it appears to be identical with Pick sb.¹, Pike sb.¹, at if a fork with a pike-head...

Pickfork, *obs. dial. Forms:* 3 pie-, ...

Picket, *sb.²* A local name of the tern: cf. **Pictarne.**

PICKING.

Pick-goose: see **Pike-.** **Pickhill:** see **Pickle.**

† Pikeman. *Obs.* Also † peakeman.

b. To tether (a horse, etc.) to a picket or peg fixed in the ground.

Pickiron, pick-iron, obs. forms of **Pickeron.**

Picking, *vbl. sb.¹* [f. Pick v.¹ + -ing¹.]
1. The action of Pick v.¹ in various senses.

2. *Weaving.* The driving of the shuttle to and fro in a loom; *esp. attrib.*, as in a picking peg (obs.) = Picker²; picking cord, lever, motion, shaft, staff, stick, names of parts employed in this action: cf. Picker² b.

2. spec. Stealing, theft; in later use, petty theft, pilfering; *esp.* in *picking and stealing.*

3. The action of pitching or throwing sheaves, etc. Also *attrib.*, as picking-fork, a hay-fork, pitchfork; picking-hole, a window or door aloft in a barn or hayloft, through which hay or sheaves are pitched; a pitch-hole. *north. dial.*

4. a. (See quot.) *pl.* 'Pounded oyster shells for gravel walks' (Simmonds Dict. Trade 1858).

PICKLE.

Pickle (pi·k'l), *sb.¹ Sc.* and *north. dial.* [Origin unknown.]

Pickle (pi·k'l), *sb.²* [f. Pickle v.? Cf. MDu. *pekel* (mod.Ger. *pökel*).]

b. de pickle (*fig.*), kept in preparation for use; *esp.* in phr. *a rod in pickle,* a punishment in reserve, ready to be inflicted on occasion: see Rod.

5. A person, usually a boy, who is always causing trouble: cf. Pickle v.¹ 5, a troublesome or mischievous child: a wild young fellow. *collog.*

Pickle, *v.¹* [f. Pickle *sb.²*]

PICKLED.

b. To deal with in a minute way, to **Piddle** (obs.); see also quot. *a* 1825.

Pickle, obs. var. of **Pightle;** local var. of **Pikel.**

Pickled (pi·k'ld), *ppl. a.¹* [f. Pickle v.¹ + -ed¹.]
1. Preserved in pickle: steeped in some chemical preparation: see Pickle v. 1, 3.

Pickle-herring. Now *rare.* [Found first in Dutch, later in G. and E.]

† Pickled, *ppl. a.²* *Obs.* Also 5 pekeled. [Early variant of Pickled.]

Pickle-herring, a somewhat later pickle-herring; after MLG. or early mod.Du.

Pickler (pi·klər), *sb.* [f. Pickle v.¹]
1. One who pickles a lock; a thief.

2. An instrument for pickling locks.

b. *adj.* Of a lock, easily picked; also *in phr. pick-lock a.²*

Picklock, *sb.³* and *a.³* *Wool Manuf.* [f. Pick v.¹ + Lock sb.] Name for the highest quality of English wool.

Picklesome (pi·k'lsəm), *a.* = notce-tail.

Pickman, [in sense 1, f. Pick sb.¹ + Man.]

Pickman, obs. form of **Pikeman.**

PICKPURSE.

Pick-me-up. *colloq.* [A phrase used as sb.]

† Pick-quarrel. *Obs.* [See Pick-.]
1. One given to picking quarrels; a quarrelsome person.

b. *transf.* and *fig.*

Pickpack: see Pick-a-back; **Pickpenny.**

Pickpocket (pi·kpŏket), *sb.* [f. Pick v.¹ + Pocket: see Pick-.]
1. One who steals from the pockets of others.

2. An instrument for picking pockets.

b. a. or *attrib.*

c. *dial.* Given as a name to various weeds which importunate the land, as Shepherd's Purse, Corn Spurrey, etc.: *cf.* next *a* and seq. Eng. Dial. Dict.

† Pickpurse (pi·kpūrs), *sb.* Also **picke-,** **pyke-** (*dial.*). [f. Pick v.¹ + Purse: see Pick-.]
1. One who steals purses or from purses; a pickpocket.

2. *fig.* A name to various wild plants.

PICK-QUARREL.

Pickwick (pi·kwik), *sb.¹* Name for a cheap kind of cigar.

Pickwick, *a.* [See Pickwickian.]

Pickwickian (pikwi·kiən), *a.*

PICNIC.

Picksy, Sc. and north. dial. var. Pixy.

Pickydilly, Picle: see Piccadill, Pightle.

Picnic (pi·knik), *sb.* Also *3-9* pique-nique, pic-nick, pic-nic, etc. [Occurs (in reference to foreign countries) from 1748, but *app.* not before 1800 as an English institution; ad. F. *pique-nique,* stated by Ménage Dict. Etymol. (1694) to be of recent introduction; *c* 1740.]

1. Originally, a fashionable social entertainment in which each person present contributed a share of the provisions...

2. Pertaining to, or of the nature or character of, a picnic; in earlier use with reference to contributions made by each member of a party; *esp.* as *in phr.* a 'picnic' in the original sense.

Picnicer.

Picnicky, Picnicy.

Picnic (pī'knik), *v.* Inflexions picnicked, picnicking. [f. prec.

Picnicker (pī'knikəl). [f. Picnic *v.* + -er¹.]

Picnickery (pī'knikəri). [f. Picnic *sb.* + -ery.] *a.*

Picnicky (pī'kniki), *a.* *colloq.*

Pico (pī'kə), *sb.* Obs. pico: see Peak 5.2 VI.]

Picoid (pī'koid), *a.* Ornith. [f. mod. L. Pico(idea + -oid.]

Picoline (pī'kolin), *Chem.* [mod. f. L. pix, pic-em pitch + -ol and -ine.]

Pico-passerine (poikəpæ'sərəin), *a.* Ornith.

Picot (pī'kot), *sb.* [F., *picot*, dim. of *pic* peak, point, prick.]

Picote (pikə't), *a.* [F., pa. pple. of *picoter* to peck, etc.: see Picotee.]

Picotee (pikəti·), *sb.* [a. F. *picotée*, f. *picoter*.]

Picotite (pī'kə₂tait). Min. [a. mod. F., named 1812 after Picot, Baron de la Peyrouse (1744–1818).]

Picrate (pī'krét), *sb.* Chem.

Picric (pī'krik), *a.* Chem. [mod. f. Gr. πικρός bitter + -ic.]

Picrite (pī'krait). Min. Also -ite. [mod. f. Gr. πικρός bitter + -ite.]

Picro-, combining form of Gr. πικρός bitter.

Picrotoxin (pikrōto·ksin). Chem. [f. Picro- + Toxin.]

Picryl (pī'kril), *a.* Chem. [f. Gr. πικρός bitter, or immed. f. Picr ic + -yl.] (See quot.)

Pict (pikt), *sb.* [ad. L. *Picti* (pl.).]

Pictarnie, pictarney (pikta·ni), *sb. dial.*

Pictish (pī'ktiʃ), *a.* [f. Pict + -ish.]

Pictland (pī'ktlænd). [f. Pict + Land.]

Pictograph (pī'ktōgraf), *sb.* [f. L. *pict-us* (see Pict) + -graph.]

Pictographic (piktōgræ'fik), *a.* [f. prec. + -ic.]

Pictography (pikto·grafi). [f. as prec. + -graphy.]

Pictorial (pikto·riăl), *a.* [f. late L. *pictori-us* (f. *pictor* a painter) + -al.]

Picturable (pī'ktiŭrăb'l), *a.* [f. Picture *v.* + -able.]

Picturableness.

Pictural, *a.* [f. L. *pictura* Picture + -al.]

Picture (pī'ktiŭr), *sb.* [a. L. *pictūra* painting, etc., f. *pict-*, ppl. stem of *pingĕre* to paint.]

Picture (pī'ktiŭr), *v.* [f. Picture *sb.*]

Pictured (pī'ktiŭrd), *ppl. a.* [f. prec. + -ed¹.]

Picturer. Now *rare.* [f. Picture *v.* + -er¹.]

Picturesque (piktiŭre·sk), *a.* Also 8 picturesk, pictoresque, picturesk. [ad. F. *pittoresque*, or It. *pittoresco*, f. *pittore* painter.]

Picturesquely, *adv.* [f. prec. + -ly².]

Picturesqueness. [f. as prec. + -ness.]

Picture-writing.

Picturing, *vbl. sb.* [f. Picture *v.* + -ing¹.]

Picuculé (pikiūkiū·lě). [a. F. *picucule* (D'Aubenton, a 1780, Plate 621 in Buffon, etc.), name given to

a bird of the genus *Dendrocolaptes*, f. L. *picus* woodpecker + *cuculus* cuckoo.] (See quots.)

1829 GRIFFITHS *Cuvier's Anim. Kingd.*, *Aves* II. 350 Picucule Creeper, Climbing Grackle. *Lath.* 1875 NEWTON in *Encycl. Brit.* III. 743/2 The Picucules [*misspelt* Piculules] (*Dendrocolaptidæ*) with as many genera, and over 200 species. 1894 NEWTON *Dict. Birds*, *Picucule*, a name.. adopted for want of a better, as that of the large Family of *Tracheophonæ*, *Dendrocolaptidæ*, which is so highly characteristic of the Neotropical Region.

‖**Picul** (pi·kǝl). Forms: 6 **pyco**, 6–7 **pico**, 7 **picull**, **peecull**, 7–8 **pecul**, 7–9 **picul**, **picol**, 8–9 **pekul**, 9 **pikul**. [Malay-Javanese *pikul* a man's load (Yule); in Sp. *pico*.] A measure of weight used in China and the East generally, equal to 100 catties, i. e. about 133⅓ lbs. avoirdupois.

1588 PARKE tr. *Mendoza's Hist. China* 367 One pyco of rice. 1598 W. PHILLIP *Linschoten* I. (Hakl. Soc.) I. 149 Every Pico is 66¼ Caetes. 1618 R. COCKS *Diary* (Hakl. Soc.) II. 3. 30 pico silk..30 picull of silk. 1625 PURCHAS *Pilgrims* I. 369 The Peecull, which is one hundred Cattees, making one hundred thirtie pound English subtill. *Ibid.* 390 Foure Peeculls. 1662 J. DAVIES tr. *Mandelslo's Trav.* II. (1669) 106 A hundred Picols of black Lacque, at ten Thails the Picol. 1771 J. R. FORSTER tr. *Osbeck's Voy.* I. 262 A Pekul or Idaam as the Chinese call it. 1838 CAPT. P. P. KING in *Penny Cycl.* XII. 271/1 If each vessel returns with 100 picols of trepang, her cargo will be worth 5000 dollars. 1862 ST. JOHN *Forests Far East* II 31 Obtained two pikuls more of sago. 1883 LITTLE *Yangtse Gorges* 279 The coal is sold for 130 cash..per picul of 133 pounds.

Picule (pi·kiul). *rare*—°. [dim. f. L. *picus* woodpecker.] = next. 1890 in *Cent. Dict.*

Piculet (pi·kiulét). *Ornith.* [f. as prec. + -ET dim.] A bird of the subfamily *Picumninæ*; a small soft-tailed woodpecker.

1849 G. R. GRAY *Genera Birds* II. 432 *Picumninæ* or *Piculets* have the Bill short, straight; the sides compressed towards the tip [etc.]. 1894 NEWTON *Dict. Birds* 720.

[**Pi·cy** (in *Piquet*): see PIQUE *sb.*[2]]

Piddle (pi·d'l), *v.* [Origin obscure. The form is that of a dim. or freq. vb. Cf. the synonymous PEDDLE *v.* 3, PADDLE *v.*[1] 2, 3, PITTLE *v.* Of these the first two seem to be corruptions of *piddle*, erroneously confused with *peddle*, *paddle* in their proper senses. *Pittle* was an inconsiderable variant. (It is questionable if sense 2 here and in PITTLE *v.* are the same word as 1.)

Words corresponding in form and sense are used in some German dial.: viz. Hessian *piddeln* (v. Pfister *Nachtr. z. Vilmar's Idiotikon v. Hessen*, 1886, p. 204); Westerwald *putteln*, *pütteln* (Schmidt *Westerwäld. Idiot.* 1800, p. 138); Jülich and Berg *pötteln* (*ibid.*). The first two, if old, may go back to an orig. **puddlian* or **puddilôn*, which would also give an OE. **pyddlan* and Eng. *piddle*; but the late appearance of the Eng. word, with absence of evidence as to the age of the Ger. dial. forms, leaves their relation doubtful. Even if related, the ulterior etymology (of root **pudd-*) is unknown.]

1. *intr.* To work or act in a trifling, paltry, petty, or insignificant way; to trifle, toy, dally; = PEDDLE *v.* 3. (Always depreciatory.) Now *rare*.

1545 ASCHAM *Toxoph.* (Arb.) 117 Neuer ceasynge piddelynge about your bowe and shaftes whan they be well. 1594 CAREW *Huarte's Exam. Wits* (1616) 182 Such as I haue marked to be good practitioners, do all piddle somewhat in the art of versifying, and raise not vp their contemplation verie high. 1602 — *Cornwall* 65 b, Very few among them make use of that opportunity..for building of shipping, and trafficking in grosse: yet some of the Eastern townes piddle that way. 1606 *Sir G. Goosecappe* II. i. (Bullen *O. Pl.*), My head must devise something, while my feet are pidling thus. a 1619 FLETCHER *Wit without M.* I. ii, She..begins to piddle with Philosophie. 1752 H. WALPOLE *Lett. Mann* (1834) III. 15, I am always piddling about ornaments and improvements for Strawberry-Hill. 1754 *Connoisseur* No. 7 ⁋ 2 During our conversation he was..piddling with her fingers, tapping her cheek, or playing with her hair. 1776 ADAM SMITH *W. N.* IV. vii. (1869) II. 205 Instead of piddling for the little prizes..they might then hope..to draw some of the great prizes. 1828 *Craven Gloss.* (ed. 2), *Piddle*, to be employed in trifles or to do things ineffectually; to take short steps in walking. 1878 BROWNING *Poets Croisic* lxxxviii, Fussily feeble, harmless..Piddling at so-called satire.

b. Said of a bird: To move the bill about, feeling for food in a hole, heap of refuse, etc.

1598 BARCKLEY *Felic. Man* (1631) 225 As he [Mahomet] was preaching..there commeth a Dove flying towards him, and alighteth upon his shoulder, and pidleth in his eare looking for meate, having used her before to feede in his eare for the same purpose. 1651 OGILBY *Æsop* (1665) 63 This [Stork] piddles with his bill While young Sir Reynard did whole Rivers swill. 1799 J. STRUTHERS *To Blackbird* vii, Beware in that caff heap to piddle.

c. To trifle or toy with one's food; to pick at one's food instead of eating heartily.

a 1620 J. DYKE *Sel. Serm.* (1640) 292 Diseases..that make them eate nothing at all, or else they doe but piddle and trifle. 1660 SWINNOCK *Door Salv.* Op. 177 If thou shouldst sit at table and see a man pidling at his meat, picking and chewing. a 1761 CAWTHORN *Poems* (1771) 112 Is there a saint that would not laugh to see The good man pidling with his fricassee? 1785 MRS. MONTAGU in Doran *Lady of last Cent.* xiii. (1873) 330 The lovers sigh'd and look'd..and piddled a little on a gooseberry tart. 1824 BYRON *Juan* XV. lxvi, And 'entremets' to piddle with at hand.

d. *trans.* *Piddle away*, to trifle away.

1760 C. JOHNSTON *Chrysal* (1822) I. 143 A house where she used to piddle away her leisure hours.

2. *intr.* To make water, urinate. *colloq.* or in childish use.

1796 *Grose's Dict. Vulg. T.* (ed. 3), *To Piddle*, to make water: a childish expression. 1836 SMART *Walker's Dict.* (ed. 3), *Piddle*,..this word is now scarcely used except as a child's word in the sense of to make water.

fig. 1871 B. TAYLOR *Faust* (1875) II. IV. i. 232 Fountain jets..There grandly shooting upwards from the middle, While round the sides a thousand spirt and piddle.

Piddle, variant of PIGHTLE.

Piddler (pi·dlǝɹ). [f. PIDDLE *v.* + -ER[1].] One who piddles; a poor ineffectual worker; a dabbler, toyer, trifler: see the verb.

1602 MIDDLETON *Blurt, Master-Constable* II. ii. 129 These flaxen-haired men are such pulers, and such piddlers. a 1625 FLETCHER & MASSINGER *Elder Bro.* IV. iv, I'm but a pidler, A little will serve my turn. 1646 N. B[ARNET] *Regenerate Man's Growth Grace* 42 We are but Pidlers in his service, we can do nothing to any purpose. 1779 J. LOVELL in *J. Adams's Wks* (1854) IX. 490 If this was not the piddler, it might be the oddity of Virginia. 1800 in *Spirit Pub. Jrnls.* IV 360 He was a mere piddler compared to me.

Piddling (pi·dliŋ), *vbl. sb.* [f. as prec. + -ING[1].] The action of PIDDLE *v.*; trifling, toying, etc.

1573 TUSSER *Husb.* (1878) 127 If hops looke browne, go gather them downe. But not in the deaw, for piddling with feaw. 1655 *Clarke Papers* (Camden) III. 37 The French Ambassadour makes a pidling still. 1760 C. JOHNSTON *Chrysal* (1822) I. 87 This dissipated pidling soon gave way to the serious business of the evening. 1816 SCOTT *Old Mort.* xii, No piddling..but that steady and persevering exercise of the jaws which is best learnt by early morning hours.

Pi·ddling, *ppl. a.* [f. as prec. + -ING[2].] Trifling, insignificant, petty, paltry.

1559 AYLMER *Harborowe* Q ij b, You haue the pidlyng Scottes, whiche are alwayes Frenche for their lyues. 1593 G. HARVEY *Pierce's Super.* 14 Pidlinge and driblinge Confuters, that sitt all day buzzing vpon a blunt point, or two. 1675 PRIDEAUX *Lett.* (Camd.) 41 We have two or three small pidleing things printeing here. 1735 POPE *Prol. Sat.* 164 Yet ne'er one sprig of laurel grac'd these ribalds, From slashing Bently down to pidling Tibalds. 1768–74 TUCKER *Lt. Nat.* (1834) II. 342 The man of business has not time for such piddling work. 1827 SCOTT *Chron. Canongate* Introd. i, For the piddling concern of a few shillings. 1866 A. L. PERRY *Elem. Pol. Econ.* (1873) 524 The country is too large for the petty, piddling processes of 'protection'.

Piddock (pi·dǝk). Also **piddick**. [Origin unascertained. It has the form of a dim. in *-ock*.] A bivalve mollusc of the genus *Pholas* or family *Pholadidæ*, which burrow in soft rock, wood, etc.; *esp.* one of the common species, such as *P. dactylus*, with a long ovate shell, which are used for bait.

1851 *Zoologist* IX. 3175 Notes on the Pholas dactylus, or Sussex Piddick. 1868 WOOD *Homes without H.* v. 99 Our next example of the burrowing molluscs is the well known Pholas, popularly called the piddock (*Pholas dactylus*).

Pide, **Pidgeon**, obs. forms of PIED, PIGEON.

Pidgin, pigeon (pi·dʒin, -ǝn). Also **pidjin**, **pidjun**, **pidgeon**. A Chinese corruption of Eng. *business*, used widely for any action, occupation, or affair. Hence **Pidgin-English**, the jargon, consisting chiefly of English words, often corrupted in pronunciation, and arranged according to Chinese idiom, used for intercommunication between the Chinese and Europeans at seaports, etc. in China, the Straits Settlements, etc.; also *transf.* (quot. 1891).

1850 BERNCASTLE *Voy. China* II. 65 The Chinese not being able to pronounce the word 'business', called it 'bigeon', which has degenerated into 'pigeon', so that this word is in constant use. 1859 *All Year Round* I. 20 'Piece of China', A-tye will row you out, because she can speak pigeon English. 1872 A. D. CARLISLE *Round World* x. 106 The dialect..current between Englishmen and Chinamen..goes by the name of Pigeon-English. 1873 *Macm. Mag.* Nov. 45 [Article]. 1876 LELAND *Pidgin English Sing Song* 3 Pidgin is with great ingenuity made expressive of every variety of calling, occupation, or affair. 1876 BESANT & RICE *Gold. Butterfly* xlv, He had a ghost story of his own—an original one in pigeon English. 1891 *Argus* (Melbourne) 7 Nov. 13/4 That ridiculous pigeon-English which the whites have used ..throughout Queensland..as their medium of communication with the blacks. 1901 A. LANG *Magic & Relig.* 37 His rude *lingua franca*, or pidgin English. (See also *N. & Q.* 10th s. V 90/2.)

Pid-pad. [Echoic: cf. PAD *sb.*[5]; the two different vowels suggesting alternation, as in *zigzag*. Cf. PIT-PAT.] Imitation of the dull sound of footsteps.

1900 'HEADON HILL' *Plunder Ship* iii. 31, I..heard the pid-pad of bare feet. *Ibid.* xxiii. 214 There was..a pid-pad of sandals on the deck.

Pidrero, variant of PEDRERO, a small gun.

Pie (pai), *sb.*[1] Also 4–8 **pye**, 5–6 **py**, (6 **pee**). [a. OF. *pie* (13th c. in Littré) = Pr. *piga*, It. *pica*:—L. *pica* magpie.]

1. The bird now more usually called MAGPIE.

a 1250 *Owl & Night.* 126 Þat pie and crowe hit todrowe. 1303 R. BRUNNE *Handl. Synne* 355 Beleue nouȝt yn þe pyys cheteryng. c 1380 WYCLIF *Serm.* Sel. Wks. I. 165 It is a foul þing þat prestis speken as pies. 1398 TREVISA *Barth. De P. R.* XII. i. (Bodl. MS.), Alle foules of rauen kinde as chogghes crowes rokes rauens and pies. a 1450 *Knt. de la Tour* (1868) 22 Ther was a woman that had a pie in a cage. ?c 1475 *Sqr. lowe Degre* 47 (text of Copland c 1550), The woodwale, The pee, and the Popiniaye. a 1548 HALL *Chron.*, *Hen. VI* 85 Pies will chatter and Mice will pepe. 1559 *Mirr. Mag.* (1563) N iv, The Fox descrye the crowes and chateryng Pyen. 1646 J. HALL *Poems* 4 Pies Do ever love to pick at witches eyes. 1713 SWIFT *Salamander* Wks. 1755 III. II. 75 Pyes and daws are often still'd With christian nick-names like a child. 1774 GOLDSM. *Nat. Hist.* (1776) V. 219 Birds of the Pie Kind. 1853 C. BRONTE *Villette* xiii, Chattering like a pie to the best gentleman in Christendom.

2. *fig.* Applied to † **a.** a cunning or wily person: esp. in phr. *wily pie* (*obs.*); **b.** a chattering or saucy person, a 'chatter-pie' (= MAGPIE 2).

[c 1374 CHAUCER *Troylus* III. 478 (527) Dredles it clere was in the wynd From euery pye and euery lette game.] 1542 UDALL *Erasm. Apoph.* 321 b, One Accius..a wylie pye, and a feloe full of shiftes. c 1554 *Interlude of Youth* in Hazl. *Dodsley* II. 22 Ye be a little pretty pye! i-wis, ye go full gingerly. 1563 B. GOOGE *Eglogs* vii. (Arb.) 60 Than cownt you them for chatring Pies Whose tongs must alwayes walke. 1579 FULKE *Heskins's Parl.* 47 Maister Heskins like a wilie Pye, obiecteth this article of the resurrection. 1692 WASHINGTON tr. *Milton's Def. Pop.* M.'s Wks. 1738 I. 523 Salmasius, that French chatt'ring Pye. 1886 MRS. LYNN LINTON *P. Carew* xl, 'She was no more a hussy than you, you bold pie!' said Patty in a fume.

3. With defining words, applied locally to various other birds, usually having black-and-white ('pied') plumage: see quots. (See also SEA-PIE.)

1883 *List Anim. Zool. Soc.* (ed. 8) 283 *Dendrocitta vagabunda*, Wandering Tree-Pie...*D. sinensis*, Chinese Tree-Pie. 1885 SWAINSON *Prov. Names Brit. Birds* 30 Dipper... The white breast and blackish upper plumage have caused it to be called..River pie (Ireland). *Ibid.* 31 British Long-tailed Titmouse..Long-tailed pie. *Ibid.* 47 Great Grey Shrike..Murdering pie. *Ibid.* 209 Black-headed Gull.. Scoulton pie, or Scoulton peewit. 1890 *Cent. Dict.* s. v., The smoky pie, *Psilorhinus morio*.

b. *French pie*, *rain-pie*, *wood-pie*: applied to various species of woodpecker. [Here perh. = OF. *pi* (mod.F. *pic*, but *pivert*, *pi vert* great green woodpecker):—L. *pic-us* woodpecker; if so, really a distinct word. But *French Pie* in quot. 1677 may be the Shrike or Butcher-bird, F. *pie cruelle*, *pie grièche grise*; cf. *murdering pie* above.]

1677 N. COX *Gentl. Recreat.* II. (ed. 2) 161 Of the Short-winged Hawks there are these:..The Sparrow-hawk and Musket, Two sorts of the French Pie. 1783 AINSWORTH *Lat. Dict.* (ed. Morell) II, *Picus*, a woodpecker, a speckt, a hickway, or heighhould; a French pie, a whitwall. 1837–40 MACGILLIVRAY *Hist. Brit. Birds* III. 80 Greater spotted woodpecker..wood-pie, French-pie. 1885 SWAINSON *Prov. Names Brit. Birds* 98 Great Spotted Woodpecker..Wood pie (Staffordshire; Hants)...Lesser Spotted Woodpecker.. Little wood pie (Hants). *Ibid.* 99 Green Woodpecker.. Wood pie (Somerset). *Ibid.* 100 The constant iteration of its cry before rain..gives it the names Rain bird; Rain pie.

4. Applied to a pied or parti-coloured animal (cf. F. *pie* = *cheval pie*, Littré): in quot. to a pied hound. Cf. 5 b.

1869 *Daily News* 7 Aug., A couple of those beautiful lemon pyes, Nosegay and Novelty..just beat the flower of the Brocklesby 'lady pack'.

5. *attrib.* and *Comb.* **a.** In compounds relating to the bird, as *pie-pecked* adj.; † **pie-maggot**, a magpie (= MAGGOT[2]).

1597 J. KING *On Jonas* Ep. Ded. (1618) ⁋ iij b, We all write, learned and vnlearned, crow-poets and py-poetesses. 1601 HOLLAND *Pliny* II. 296 *margin*, The Deuill take thee, or, the Rauens peck out thine eies, or I had rather see thee Pie pekt. 1602 *Contention Liberality & Prodigality* IV. iv. in Hazl. *Dodsley* VIII. 366 O thou vile, ill-favoured, crow-trodden, pye-pecked rout! 1628 LAYTON *Syons Plea* (ed. 2) 21 [The bishops are] Rauens and Pye-Maggots to prey upon the State. a 1652 BROME *Queenes Exchange* v. i. Wks. 1873 III. 537 What are thou..thus Piepickt, Crow-trod, or Sparrow blasted?

b. In compounds denoting 'parti-coloured', 'of various colours' (like the black-and-white plumage of the magpie: cf. PIED 1), as *pie-coated*, *-coloured* adjs. See also PIEBALD.

1630 BRATHWAIT *Eng. Gentlem.* (1641) 11 To display thy pie-coloured flag of vanity. 1813 HOGG *Queen's Wake* 291 The pye-duck sought the depth of the main. 1848 THACKERAY *Bk. Snobs* ii, The liveries of these pie-coated retainers.

c. *Friars of the Pie*: see *Pied friars*, PIED *a.*

Pie (pai), *sb.*[2] Also 4–9 **pye**, 6 **py**, (7 **paye**). [Occurs (in Latin context) in 1303; evidently a well-known popular word in 1362. No related word known outside Eng. (exc. Gaelic *pighe*, from Eng. or Lowland Sc.). Being in form identical with PIE *sb.*[1] (known half a century earlier), it is held by many to have been in some way derived from or connected with that word. See Note below.]

1. A dish composed of meat, fowl, fish, fruit, or vegetables, etc., enclosed in or covered with a layer of paste and baked.

The *pie* appears to have been (*a*) at first of meat or fish; doubtful or undefined uses (*b*) appear in 16th c.; *fruit pies* (also called, esp. in the north of England and Ireland, in Scotland, and often in U. S., *tarts*) appear (*c*) before 1600, the earliest being APPLE-PIE, q.v.

(*a*) 1303 *Bolton Priory Compotus* lf. 68 b, Frumentum expenditum..In pane..pro Priore Celerario et aliis..et in pyis et pastellis per annum 9 qr. 1 bus. di. 1304 *Ibid.* lf. 82 In pane furnato..et in pyes et pastellis, 33 qr. 2 bus. di. 1362 LANGL. *P. Pl.* A. Prol. 104 Cookes and heore knaues cryen 'hote pies, hote! Goode gees and grys, Gowe dyne, Gowe!' c 1386 CHAUCER *Prol.* 384 He koude rooste and sethe and boille [*v.r.* broille] and frye, Maken Mortreux and wel bake a pye. c 1425 *Voc.* in Wr.-Wülcker 662/26 *Hec artocria* [Gr. ἀρτόκρεας bread and meat], a pie *de pundio*. c 1430 *Two Cookery-bks.* 53 Pyez de parez [p. 75 of Parys].—Take and smyte fayre buttys of Porke, and buttys of Vele, to-gederys [etc.]..; þan caste þer-to ʒolkys of Eyroun [etc.]..; þen make fayre past, and cofynnys, & do þer-on; kyuer it, & let bake, & serue forth. c 1440 *Promp. Parv.* 395/2 Pye, pasty, *artocrea*, *pastillulus*. 1512 FABYAN *Will* in *Chron.* (1811) Pref. 9 If it happen the saide obite to fall in Lent, than..for the peces of beeff abovesaid..be ordeyned pyes of elys, or som other goode fysh mete. a 1568 *Nyne Ordour of Knavis* 66 in *Bannatyne Poems* (Hunter. Cl.) 448 He thrawis and he puttis fast at his vly pyiss. 1624 HEYWOOD *Gunaik.* IX. 444 Burnt alive, for killing young infants and salting their flesh and putting them into pyes. 1784 COOK *Third Voy.* IV. xi. II. 495 A pye made in the form of a loaf..inclosed some salmon, highly seasoned with pepper. 1838 DICKENS *Nich. Nick.* vii, It's a pity to cut the pie if you're not hungry..Will you try a bit of the beef?

(*b*) 1530 PALSGR. 254/1 Pye a pasty, *pasté*. a 1568 '*In somer quhen flouris will smell*' 35 in *Bannatyne Poems* (Hunter. Cl.) 410 It is lyk that ye had eitin pyiss, Ye are so sweit. 1577 WHETSTONE *Life Gascoigne* xviii, Spight foule Envies poy-oned pye. 1694 CROWNE *Regulus* II. 12 A man all vertue, like a pye all spice, will not please. c 1710 CELIA FIENNES *Diary* (1888) 242 He weares a great Velvet cap.. like a Turbant or great bowle in forme of a great open pye. 1765 GRAY *Shakespeare* 24 Glorious puddings and immortal pies. a 1839 PRAED *Poems* (1864) II. 58 And lords made love,—and ladies, pies. 1853 SOYER *Pantroph.* 284 All pass away whether they be temples, columns, pyramids, or pies.

(*c*) 1590–1861 [see APPLE-PIE]. 1706 PHILLIPS, *Pie*, a well known Dish of Meat, or Fruit bak'd in Paste. 1864 SALA in *Daily Tel.* 18 Aug., There it is; pumpkin pie, blackberry pie, whortleberry pie, huckleberry pie—pie of all kinds.

b. With defining word, usually denoting the essential ingredient, as *apple-pie*, *eel-pie*, *game-pie*, *meat-pie*, *mince-pie*, *pigeon pie*, *plum-pie*, *pork-pie*, *rhubarb-pie*, *venison-pie*, etc. (see these words); also *Christmas pie* (see CHRISTMAS 4), *French pie* (see quot. 1611), *Périgord pie* (see PÉRIGORD).

1602 *2nd Pt. Ret. fr. Parnass.* V. ii. (Arb.) 66 A black Iack of Beere, and a Christmas Pye. 1611 FLORIO, *Carne ne tegami*, meate stewed between two dishes, which some call a French pie. 1698 in Warrender *Marchmont* (1894) 184 Could pigeon paye. a 1700 B. E. *Dict. Cant. Crew*, *Superstitious-Pies*, Minc'd, or Christmas-Pies, so Nick-nam'd by the Puritans, or Precisians. 1769 MRS. RAFFALD *Eng. Housekpr.* (1778) 155 Send it up hot without a lid, the same way as the French pye. 1798 FRERE & CANNING in *Anti-Jacobin* No. 23. 120 Youthful Horner..Cull'd the dark plum from out his Christmas pye. 1834 SOUTHEY *Doctor* cix. (1848) 266 2 The great goose-pye, which in the Christmas week was always dispatched by the York coach to Bishopsgate Street. 1872 CALVERLEY *Fly Leaves* (1881) 21 But I shrink from thee Arab! Thou eat'st eel-pie.

c. Phr. *To have a finger* († *hand*) *in the pie*: to have a part or share in the doing of something (often implying officious intermeddling). *Cold pie*: see COLD *a.* 19. See also HUMBLE PIE.

1553 *Respublica* (Brandl) I. iii. 105 Bring me in credyte, that my hande be in the pye. 1604 DEKKER *Honest Wh.* Wks. 1873 II. 171 My hand was in the Pye, my Lord, I confesse it. 1613 SHAKS. *Hen. VIII*, I. i. 52 The diuill speed him: No mans Pye is freed From his Ambitious finger. 1649 *Man in Moon* No. 33. 262 We heare Jermyn and the Lord Culpepper had a finger in the pye. 1659, 1885 [see FINGER *sb.* 3 c]. a 1845 MOORE *Fragm. Character* xi, Whatever was the best pye going, In that Ned..had his finger.

2. Applied to something resembling a pie. *Bran-pie*, a tub full of bran with small articles hidden in it to be drawn out at random, at Christmas festivities, etc. See also CLAY-*pie*, DIRT-PIE, MUD-*pie*.

1842 ORDERSON *Creol.* ii. 14 The Jews..still withheld their unleavened pie..a simple crust covering a pretty round sum. 1873 GARDNER *Hist. Jamaica* 199 The governor's purse was called a pie. 1904 *Daily Chron.* 27 Feb. 3/2 The bran-pie..is the receptacle of second-rate presents: gifts not quite showy enough to be displayed upon a Christmas tree.

3. Applied to a collection of things made up into a heap; *spec.* a shallow pit, or heap of potatoes or other roots, covered with straw, earth, etc. for storing and protection from frost; also, a heap of manure stacked for maturing. *local.*

1526 in *Househ. Ord.* (1790) 227 Item, that the Pye of Coales be abridged to the one halfe that theretofore had been served. 1791 *Trans. Soc. Arts* IX. 42 [The potatoes] were taken up, and a large pye made of them, which is laying them in a heap and covering them with straw. 1848 *Jrnl. R. Agric. Soc.* IX. II. 514 Mangolds..stored 'in pies' on the level surface. 1886 *S. W. Linc. Gloss.* s.v., Potatoes or other roots placed in a hole, against the winter,..are said to be 'pied down' or..'in pie'. 1887 *Daily Tel.* 4 Apr. 2 Making 'pies' of the green fodder just as dung pies are made.

4. *fig.* Something to be eagerly appropriated; a prize, a treat; a bribe. *U. S. slang.*

1895 *Outing* (U. S.) XXVI. 436/1 Green dogs are pie for him [the racoon]. 1902 *Westm. Gaz.* 16 June 3/1 Sometimes he is 'pie' for the cartoonist to an unfortunate extent.

5. *attrib.* and *Comb.*, as *pie-baker*, *-eater*, *-feast*, *-gaudy* (GAUDY *sb.* 5), *-maker*, *-meat*, *-pan*, *-paste*, *-plate*, *-shop*, *-tin*; **pie-board**, a board on which pies are made, baked, or carried; **pie-dish**, the deep dish in which a pie is made; **pie-house**, a house at which pies are sold, a pie-shop; **pie-lass**, a girl who sells pies; **pie-plant**, any plant yielding fruit, etc. used for pies; *spec.* (*U. S.*) garden rhubarb; also locally applied to the wild *Rumex hymenosepalus*, which is similarly used (*Cent. Dict.*); † **pie-wife**, **pie-woman**, a woman who sells pies. See also PIE-CRUST, PIEMAN.

1379 in Riley *Memorials* (1868) 432 *Pie bakere. c 1440 *Promp. Parv.* 395/2 Pye baker, *ceregius*. 1594 R. ASHLEY tr. *Loys le Roy* 28 b, Prepared and dressed by Cookes and pybakers. 1709 *Brit. Apollo* II. No. 70. 3/2 The Puny Author who supplies still The Cooks, and on their *Pye-boards lies still. 1844 DICKENS *Mart. Chuz.* xxxix, She tripped downstairs into the kitchen for the flour, then for the pie-board. 1859 JEPHSON *Brittany* iv. 38 Scanty ablutions of the morning in my *pie-dish. 1864 *Soc. Science Rev.* 37 A pie-dish and decanter take the place of jug and bason at the washing stand. 1904 *Daily Chron.* 12 Sept. 4/6 New Englanders, those champion *pie-eaters of the world. c 1550 *Lusty Juventus* in Hazl. *Dodsley* II. 78 Will you go to the *pie-feast? 1659 HEYLIN *Certamen Epist.* 136 The suppressing of so many Gaudies, and *Pie-Gaudies, to the destruction of the hospitality and charity of the noble foundation. 1589 RIDER *Bibl. Schol.* 1017 A *pie house, *artocrearium*. 1836–48 B. D. WALSH *Aristoph.*, *Knights* III. i, Why, that he'll seize on the *pie-lass, And rob her and render her pieless. c 1450 *Dict. Garlande* in Wright *Voc.* 127 *Pastillarii* [gloss] *pye-makyers. 1598 *Epulario* C ij b, Mince it..like *Pie meat. 1847 WEBSTER, **Pie-plant*, *Pie-rhubarb*, the garden rhubarb, used as a substitute for apples in making pies. 1864 LOWELL *Fireside Trav.*, *Cambridge*, His pie plants..blanched under barrels, each in his little hermitage, a vegetable Certosa. 1741 *Compl. Fam.-Piece* I. ii. (ed. 3) 105 Cover your Bason with a *Pye-plate. 1593 NASHE *Four Lett. Confut.* Wks. (Grosart II. 283 To..cozen poore victuallers and *pie-wiues of Doctours cheese and puddinges. 1817 J. EVANS *Excurs Windsor*, etc. 343 An old *Pie-woman carried them provisions, but never saw them.

[*Note.* Prof. Skeat suggests 'from the miscellaneous nature of its (i. e. the dish's) contents' which might recall the black and white or piebald appearance of the bird; others have thought of the habit which the magpie has of picking up and forming accumulations of miscellaneous articles. In this connexion, the similarity between the forms of the words HAGGIS and HAGGESS (F. *agace*, *agasse*) magpie, has also been pointed out. The quotations for the word afford no light, exc. that in one place in a late 14th c. L. poem *Modus cenandi* (Furnivall, *Babees Book*, II. 36) l. 51, 'sint inter fercula pice, Pastilli cum fartulis', appears to mean, 'let there be served between the dishes, pies, pasties' as if the writer identified *pie*, the dish, with *pica* the *pie* or magpie. On the other hand, in two early 14th c. quotations the Eng. word is used in Latin context, as if not identified with *pica*.]

Pie, pye, *sb.*[3] Now only *Hist.* [The Eng. word answering to med.L. *pica*; thus both in L. and Eng. identical in form with the name of the bird: see PIE[1], and PICA[1].]

1. A collection of rules, adopted in the pre-Reformation Church, to show how to deal (under each of the 35 possible variations in the date of Easter) with the concurrence of more than one office on the same day, accurately indicating the manner of commemorating, or of putting off till another time, the Saints' days, etc., occurring in the ever-changing times of Lent, Easter, Whitsuntide, and the Octave of the Trinity. (Cf. Blades *Caxton*, 1882, 240.)

c 1477 CAXTON *Advertisement* (*Broadside*), If it plese ony man spirituel or temporel to bye ony pyes of two and thre comemoracions of salisburi vse enpryntid after the forme of this present lettre whiche ben wel and truly correct, late hym come to westmonester in to the almonesrye at the reed pale and he shal haue them good chepe. 1498 *Will of Thomson* (Somerset Ho.), My boke callid a pie. 1507 *Yatton Churchw. Acc.* (Som. Rec. Soc.) 129 Payd for a Mashoke and a pye. xjᵈ. vi. 1548–9 (Mar.) *Bk. Com. Prayer* Pref., The nombre and hardnes of the rules called the pie, and the manifolde chaunginges of the seruice, was the cause, yᵗ to turne the boke onlye, was so hard and intricate a matter, that many times, there was more busines to fynd out what should be read, then to read it when it was founde out. 1549 *Act 3 & 4 Edw. VI*, c. 10 § 1 All Books called..Manuals, Legends, Pies, Portuasses, Primers..shall be..abolished. a 1568 ASCHAM *Scholem.* II. (Arb.) 136 If he..could turne his Portresse and pie readilie. 1852 HOOK *Ch. Dict.* (1871) 585 The pie was the table used before the Reformation to find out the service for the day. It may be referred to the Greek πίναξ or πινάκιον. But the Latin word is *pica*, which perhaps came from the ignorance of the friars, who have thrust many barbarous words into the liturgies. 1879 MARQUIS OF BUTE tr. *Roman Breviary* I. p xii, As to anything else, see the Chapters of the Pye treating specially of each detail.

b. Hence app. COCK AND PIE, q. v.

† **2.** (Usually **pye book**.) An alphabetical index to rolls and records. *Obs.*

There are 'Pye Books' to Indictments extending as far back as 1660; but there is nothing to show when the term first came into use. It was in use in the Court of King's Bench early in the 18th century. It was also pretty generally used in the Courts of the Palatinate of Lancaster, the Indexes to the Affidavits, Declarations, and Sessional Papers being each styled 'Pye Books' (J. J. Cartwright, Sec. Publ. Rec. Office).

1788 *Chambers' Cycl.* (ed. Rees) s. v., In much the same sense the term was used by officers of civil courts, who called the calendars or alphabetical catalogues directing to the names and things contained in the rolls and records of their courts the Pyes.

Pie (pai), *sb.*[4] *Printing.* Also 7 **py**, 7–9 **pye**, (*U. S.*) **pi**. [Origin obscure: supposed by some to be a transferred use of PIE *sb.*[2], in reference to its miscellaneous contents; others think of PIE *sb.*[3], and the unreadable aspect of a page of the pie.] A mass of type mingled indiscriminately or in confusion, such as results from the breaking down of a forme of type.

1659 HOWELL *Vocab.* li. (Printing terms), A Corrector, a proof, a revise,..pye all sorts of letter mixed, *Correctore*, &c. 1683 MOXON *Mech. Exerc.*, *Printing* 370 Breaking the orderly Succession the Letters stood in, in a Line, Page, or Form, &c. and mingling the Letters together, which mingled Letters is called *Py*. 1771 FRANKLIN *Autobiog.* Wks. 1887 I. 144 Having impos'd my forms..one of them by accident broke, and two pages reduced to pi, I immediately distributed and compos'd it over again before I went to bed. 1845 CARLYLE *Cromwell* I. Introd. ii. 12 This same Dictionary ..gone to pie, as we may call it. 1847 WEBSTER, *Pi* [app. after Franklin]. 1888 J. SOUTHWARD *Pract. Print.* (1884) 80 If composed matter gets..into a state of confusion, it is 'pie'.

b. *transf.* A disintegrated and confused mass; a jumble, medley, confusion, chaos; a 'mess'.

1837 CARLYLE *Fr. Rev.* II. II. iv, Your..Arrangement going all (as the Typographers say of set types, in a similar case) rapidly to pie! 1841 CATLIN *N. Amer. Ind.* II. xli. 53 We were thrown into 'pie' (as printers would say) in an instant of the most appalling alarm. 1870 *Daily News* 30 Nov., It was the merest luck..that the bones of the kings were not made inextricable 'pie' of. 1888 MRS. LYNN LINTON in *Fortn. Rev.* Oct. 532 Witness the 'pie' he made of his finances. 1897 *Spectator* 30 Jan. 162/2 To make pie of the European arrangements for securing peace.

‖ **Pie** (pai), *sb.*[5] Also **pai**, **pi**. [a. Hindī, Marāṭhī, etc. *pā'ī*, from Skr. *pad*, *padī*, quarter, being 'originally, it would seem, the fourth part of an anna, and in fact identical with *pice*' (Yule).] The smallest current Anglo-Indian copper coin, the twelfth part of an anna; before the depreciation of the rupee, about one-eighth of a penny.

1859 LANG *Wand. India* 69 He would tell you the interest due on such sums as three rupees, five annas, and seven pie, for twenty-one days, at forty-one three-fourth per cent. 1879 MRS. A. E. JAMES *Ind. Househ. Managem.* 49 The copper coins—1 anna = 4 pice. 1 pice = 3 pie. 1883 F. M. CRAWFORD *Mr. Isaacs* xii. 261 Several coins, both rupees and pais. 1904 *Mission Field* June 64 The charge of a small fee, six pies (one cent) for the first prescription.

Pie, variant of PEE *Obs.*, kind of coat or jacket.

† **Pie**, *a.* *Obs.* *rare*—[1]. [a. F. *pie*, fem. of OF. *pi*, *pis*, *piu*, *pif*:—L. *pi-us* PIOUS.] Pious.

c 1450 *Mirour Saluacioun* 786 Sho was ouer craft to telle humble pie [*v. r.* mercifull] and devoute.

† **Pie**, *v.*[1] *Obs. nonce-wd.* [f. PIE *sb.*[1]] *trans.* To repeat like a magpie.

1657 J. WATTS *Dipper Sprinkled* 74 Yea, to Pie and Parrat out our Tongues, Degrees, and Learning of the University.

Pie, *v.*[2] *local.* Also **pye**; *vbl. sb.* **pying**. [f. PIE *sb.*[2] 3.] *trans.* To put (potatoes, etc.) in a pit or heap and cover them with straw and earth, for storing and protection from frost.

1791 *Trans. Soc. Arts* IX. 44 Weeding potatoes, getting them up, and pyeing them. 1817–18 COBBETT *Resid. U. S.* (1822) 164 He may pie them [potatoes] in the garden..but he must not open the pie in frosty weather. 1845 *Jrnl. R. Agric. Soc.* V. II. 326 This system of pyeing turnips is a very common one in Norfolk. 1886 [see PIE *sb.*[2] 3].

Pie, *v.*[3] *Printing.* [f. PIE *sb.*[4]] *trans.* To make (type) into 'pie'; to mix or jumble up indiscriminately.

1870 [see PIED[2]]. 1889 *Daily News* 17 June 7 (Advt.), The ..delay..in printing offices, caused by what is technically called 'pyeing'. 1893 *Linotype Company's Prospectus*, In the economy of this machine...To pye matter is impossible. 1903 *Brit. & Col. Printer* 19 Nov. 15/4 Nearly all the cases are empty and those that have anything in are pied.

Pie-annet: see PIANNET.

Piebald (pai·bǫld), *a.* (*sb.*) Forms: 6 **pibald**, **pibauld**, 6–7 **py(-)bald**, 6– **pie(-)ba'd**, 7 **pye(-)bald**, **pyedball**, 7–8 **pye-balled** (**-ball'd**), 8– **pye(-)ball**. [f. PIE *sb.*[1] + BALD *a.* 5: cf. BALL *sb.*[3]] Of two different colours, esp. white and black or other dark colour (like the plumage of a magpie), usually arranged in more or less irregular patches; pied: usually of animals, esp. horses. Loosely used of other colours (cf. SKEWBALD) or of three or more colours; parti-coloured.

1594 BARNFIELD *Aff. Sheph.* I. xxviii, I haue a pie-bald Curre to hunt the Hare. 1610 MARKHAM *Masterp.* I. x. 26 His colour is either a milke white, a yellow dun, a kiteglewd or a pyedball. 1622 MALYNES *Anc. Law-Merch.* 328 Signified by the Pybald horse whereon hee was mounted. 1626 *Faithful Friends* I. i, Millions..lavished in excessive sports, And piebald pageantry. 1676 *Lond. Gaz.* No. 1135/4 A white Gelding..having pye-bald marks on both flanks of bluish colour. 1789 MRS. PIOZZI *Journ. France* II. 20 [At Naples]. Yesterday..shewed me what I knew not had existed—a skew-ball or pyeballed ass. 1802 *Med. Jrnl.* VIII. 97 There are Negroes, (Albinoe-) born white, some are party coloured or pie-bald. 1822–34 *Good's Study Med.* (ed. 4) IV. 542 Individuals thus motley coloured are commonly called pie-ald negroes, or are said to have piebald skins. 1845 DARWIN *Voy. Nat.* xi. (1852) 233 Dusky woods, piebald with snow. 1871 — *Desc. Man* II. xvi. 230 Piebald birds..for instance, the black-necked swan, certain terns, and the common magpie.

b. *fig.* Composed of parts or elements of dissimilar or incongruous kinds; of mixed characters or qualities (always in bad sense); motley, mongrel.

1589 R. HARVEY *Pl. Perc.* (1590) 13 Leaue thrumming thy Pibauld Iestes with Scripture. 1663 BUTLER *Hud.* I. i. 96 A Babylonish Dialect, Which learned Pedants much affect. It was a Parti-colour'd Dress Of patch'd and Pye-ball'd Languages. 1763–5 CHURCHILL *Candidate* 716 Shall hurl his piebald Latin at thy head. 1815 W. H. IRELAND *Scribbleomania* 58 *note*, To produce such a pyebald style of composition. 1878 BAYNE *Purit. Rev.* ii. 27 In the piebald character of the man.

B. *sb.* A piebald animal, esp. horse. **b.** *fig.* A person or thing of mixed character, a 'mongrel'.

1765 FOOTE *Commissary* II. Wks. 1799 II. 26 The right honourable Peer..calls me..Plebeian, and says if we have any children, they will turn out very little better than pyeballs. 1842 TENNYSON *Walking to Mail* 104 As quaint a four-in-hand As you shall see—three pyebalds and a roan.

1845 FORD *Handbk. Spain* I. 53 Strabo..had an idea that Spanish piebalds..changed colour if taken out of Spain.

Hence **Pie·balding**, becoming piebald, development of patches of different colours; **Pie·baldism**, **Pie·baldness**, the quality of being piebald; **Pie·baldly** *adv.*, in a piebald manner, with patches of different colours.

1886 ROMANES in *Life & Lett.* (1896) III. 175 The young ones show no signs of 'piebalding'. 1881 *Standard* 8 Sept. 5/3 Domestication tends to produce irregular colour, or what is commonly called 'piebaldism'. 1613 CAMPION *Relat. Entertainm. Ld. Knowles*, A strawn hat, *piebaldly drest with flowers. 1893 *Sat. Rev.* 8 Apr. 375/2 Glaring *piebaldness. 1899 E. PHILLPOTTS *Human Boy* 120 The piebaldness of the rat was the great feature.

Piece (pīs), *sb.* Forms: 3–7 **pece** (3–5 **pees**, 4 **pise**, 4–5 **pice**, **peis**, 5 **pes**, **peyce**, **peese**, 5–6 **pes(s**, **pesse**); 5– **piece**, (5 **pyece**, 5–8 **peace**, 6 **pease**, **peise**, **peyss**, (*Sc.* **peax**), **pysse**, 6–7 **peece**, 6–8 **peice**). Plural in ME. sometimes the same as the sing. [ME. *pece*, in 15th c. *piece*, a. OF. *pece* (1241 in Godef.), *piece* (Roland, 11th c.), mod.F. *pièce* = Pr. *peça*, *pessa*, Sp. *pieza*, Pg. *peça*, It. *pezza* piece of cloth, rag, beside *pezzo* 'piece' in other senses. The Romanic forms point to late L. types **pettia*, **pettium*: cf. early med.L. *pecia*, *petia*, also *pecium*, *petium*, 'broken piece, fragment', also 'piece of land'. Ulterior origin obscure: see Note below. The sense-development is in many points uncertain, though most of the senses occur also in French: the following arrangement is to a great extent provisional.]

I. In general sense; or followed by *of*.

1. A separate or detached portion, part, bit, or fragment of anything; one of the distinct portions of which anything is composed.

a 1225 *St. Marher.* 122 Þe scourgen [were] smerte & kene; Bi peces þe flesch orn adoun, þe bones were isene. c 1320 *Sir Tristr.* 1086 His swerd brak in þe fiȝt And in morauntes brain Bileued a pece briȝt. a 1450 *Voc.* in Wr.-Wülcker 601/11 *Pecia*, a pece, or lytyl part of a thyng. 1560 DAUS tr. *Sleidane's Comm.* 25 That day..is roosted a whole Oxe.. a piece whereof is serued to the Emperours table. 1570 LEVINS *Manip.* 48/13 A Peece, *pars, partis*. 1605 CAMDEN *Rem.* 189 In delivering of livery and seisin a peece of the earth is taken. 1653 WALTON *Angler* IV. 108, I think the best [rods] are of two pieces. 1713 M. HENRY *Catech. Youth* Wks. 1853 II. 169/1 Gave them a piece of a honeycomb to eat. 1847 CARPENTER *Zool.* § 603 The tegumentary skeleton of Insects, that is to say, the hard skin of these animals... We see in it a great number of pieces, which are sometimes soldered (as it were) together; whilst in other instances they are united by soft portions of the skin. *Ibid.* § 605 The head is formed only by a single piece.

fig. 1821 LAMB *Elia* Ser. I. *Imperfect Sympathies*, They are content with fragments and scattered pieces of Truth.

b. *In pieces*: broken, divided, disintegrated, in fragments: *fig.* divided, at variance. *In*, *into*, † *on*, † *a pieces*: into fragments, asunder. *To take in pieces*: to separate the parts of, to analyse.

1297 R. GLOUC. (Rolls) 375 Is scolle to brec in peces manion. c 1320 *Sir Tristr.* 1456 Eft þat spere tok he; ..It brast on peces þre. 13.. *K. Alis.* 2999 A-two peces he hadde him gurd. c 1380 *Sir Ferumb.* 5591 Þe stede ful doun on peces tweye. 1390 GOWER *Conf.* III. 244 He kut it into pieces twelve. 1393 LANGL. *P. Pl.* C. XXI. 62 *note*, The wal of þe temple to-cleef euene a two peces. c 1400 *Laud Troy Bk.* 10305 Hir beer was rent & torne In pes. c 1400 MAUNDEV. (Roxb.) x. 38 Men..paynd þam to breke þe stane in pecez. 1470–85 MALORY *Arthur* I. xxiii. 71 But the swerd of the knyght smote kyng arthurs swerd in two pyeces. 1480 CAXTON *Chron. Eng.* ccxxiv. 227 Ther man myght see hir baners displayed hakked in to pyeces. 1562 PILKINGTON *Expos. Abdias* Pr. f. 9 The forther that the bowe is drawen, the sooner it flies in pieces. 1600 J. PORY tr. *Leo's Africa* III. 133 The butchers cut their flesh a peeces, and sell it by weight. 1659 *Burton's Diary* (1828) IV. 480 This takes in pieces your whole form. c 1680 HICKERINGILL *Hist. Whiggism* Wks. 1716 I. II. 154 If we offer to tear them apieces. 1687 A. LOVELL tr. *Thevenot's Trav.* I. 169 A fair large Church.. where..the Body of St. Catherine is in pieces. 1754 RICHARDSON *Grandison* IV. iv. 21 We are all in pieces: we were in the midst of a feud, when you arrived. 1761–2 HUME *Hist. Eng.* (1806) IV. lxi. 566 The instrument of government was taken in pieces, and examined, article by article. 1843 MACAULAY *Lays Anc. Rome*, *Virginia* 264 Must I be torn in pieces? 1876 FREEMAN *Norm. Conq.* IV. xvi.i. 193 When they submitted, their army..at once fell in pieces.

c. *To pieces*: into fragments, asunder; also *fig.* *To go* or *come to pieces*: to break up, dissolve, lose cohesion. *To take to pieces*: to separate into its parts. *To hit*, *huff*, *puzzle*, *vex*, etc., *to pieces*: to bring by such action to a state of distraction, disorganization, confusion, or rout.

By omission of *come*, *gone*, *torn*, or other pple., *to pieces* is sometimes = 'in pieces': see quots. 1622, 1690.

c 1290 *S. Eng. Leg.* I. 46/24 And to-brak it al to smale peces. 13.. *Cursor M.* 6542 (Cott.) To pees [*Gött.* etc. in pecis] he þam brak right þar. c 1400 *Land Troy Bk.* 8386, I schal ȝow hewe al to pece. a 1533 LD. BERNERS *Huon* cxvii. 419 Our shyp brast all to pecys. 1622 MASSINGER & DEKKER *Virgin Martyr* II. iii, The smock of her charity is now all to pieces. 1661 BOYLE *Exam.* ii. (1682) 6, I thus take Mr. Hobbs his Argument to pieces. 1690 J. WILSON *Belphegor* IV. i, They [friends] 're all to pieces. 1703 MOXON *Mech. Exerc.* 253 Pulling the Building to pieces after it is begun. 1727 *Philip Quarll* (1816) 73 The flat-bottomed boat..he had taken to-pieces. 1741 RICHARDSON *Pamela* I. 144 She has huffed poor Mr. Williams all to-pieces. 1765 COWPER *Wks.* (1837) XV. 1, I am puzzled to pieces about it. 1832 FR. A. KEMBLE *Jrnl.* in *Rec. of Girlhood* (1878) III. 215, I thought I should have come to pieces in his hands, as the housemaids say of what they break. 1883 R. BUCHANAN *Love me for Ever* I. ii. 28 A large ship had gone to pieces on the Wantle reef. 1890 *Daily News* 11 July 3/6 The Oxonians went all to pieces after passing the post. 1902 *Daily Chron.* 7 Aug. 3/6 To analyse anything implies..the taking it to pieces in a chemical sense.

† **2.** A part *of* a whole, marked off, ideally separated, or considered as distinct; a portion *of* an immaterial thing. (Now superseded by *part*, *portion*.)

1377 LANGL. *P. Pl.* B. XIV. 48 Þanne was it a pece of þe pater-noster, fiat voluntas tua. 1534 MORE *Passion* Wks. 1303/1 That he might steale a peece of the pryce. 1535 JOYE *Apol. Tindale* (Arb.) 24 In the fourthe peise [= paragraph] of his pistle. 1562 *Child-Marriages* 116 Roberte Rile the younger neuer promysid her any pease of the lease of the house where her husband nowe dwellis, nor nothinge els. a 1639 WOTTON in *Reliq.* (1651) 438 One of the most fastidious pieces of my life, as I account, the week of our Annuall Election of Scholers. 1642 ROGERS *Naaman* 182 Now in a word, for the other peece of the question. 1699 WANLEY in *Lett. Lit. Men* (Camden) 292 For other Saxon books, I have copied large pieces of them. 1755 WASHINGTON *Lett.* Writ. 1889 I. 161 After waiting a day and piece in Winchester.

b. A limited portion *of* land, enclosed, marked off by bounds, or viewed as distinct. (An early sense of med.L. *petia*, *petium*.)

a 1450 *Knt. de la Tour* (1868) 88 A man that was called Nabot, the whiche had a good pece of wyne. 1463 in *Bury Wills* (Camden) 31 There is vij acres lond lying..not ferre from Herdwyk wich vij acres lieth in ij pecys. 1535 COVERDALE *Josh.* xxiv. 32 The bones of Ioseph..buried they at Sichem, in the pece of the londe, yᵗ Iacob boughte of the children of Hemor. 1611 BIBLE *Luke* xiv. 18, I haue bought a piece of ground. 1772 *MS. Award, Winterton, Lincs.*, All that other piece or parcel of Ground. 1796 STEDMAN *Surinam* (1813) II. xxix. 367 The planting ground ..is divided into large square pieces. 1808 COL. HAWKER *Diary* (1893) I. 13, I went into a piece of potatoes..without a dog. 1897 J. W. CLARK *Barnwell* Introd. 10 A list of the different pieces of property, with their yearly values.

c. A portion *of* a road, rope, line, linear distance.

1561 T. HOBY tr. *Castiglione's Courtyer* I. K ij b, Accompanienge the Pope a peece of the way. *Mod.* A weak piece in a rope. A piece of the road is now under repair.

d. Phrase. *A piece of one's mind*: something of what one thinks; one's candid opinion; a rebuke, scolding. Cf. BIT *sb.*[2] 4.

1572 SANDYS in Ellis *Orig. Lett.* Ser. II. III. 24 Thus am I bolde to unfolde a peece of my mynde. 1667 DRYDEN *Maiden Queen* II. i, I have told her a piece of my mind already. 1861 MRS. H. WOOD *East Lynne* II. xiii. (1888) 233 The justice was giving her a 'piece of his mind'.

† **e.** *fig.* *A piece of* (*a scholar*, *logician*, *surgeon*, *philosopher*, etc.): somewhat of; 'a bit' of; one who partakes to some extent of the character mentioned. *Obs.* Cf. BIT *sb.*[2] 4.

[1552 ELYOT *Dict.*, *Frustum hominis*, a litle pretie felow, that semeth to be but a peece of a man. Plaut. *Petit bout d'homme: moitié de homme*.] 1581 SIDNEY *Apol. Poetrie* (Arb.) 19 If I had not beene a peece of a Logician before I came to him. 1633 J. CLARKE *Second Praxis* 12 Hoo! would you faine be thought a piece of an Astronomer now? a 1635 NAUNTON *Fragm. Reg.* (Arb.) 57 Being a good piece of a Schollar. 1743 in Howell *State Trials* (1813) XVII. 1172 He is a piece of a surgeon. 1768 STERNE *Sent. Journ.* (1778) I. 101 If I am a piece of a philosopher.

3. A portion or quantity *of* any substance or kind of matter, forming a single (usually small) body or mass; a bit; as 'a piece of lead, granite, ice, bread, dough, cloth, paper'; also, *piece of water*, a small detached sheet of water, a small lake.

Such a 'piece' is, in fact, often a portion of a larger mass, but this is not thought of in the use of the word, the notion being rather that of so much of the substance or material in question forming one body of finite dimensions, which may be either a small or a large piece. It is a separate part or portion of the whole existing stock of the substance.

1362 LANGL. *P. Pl.* A. VII. 297 Mai no peny Ale hem paye, ne no pece of Bacun. 1483 *Cath. Angl.* 272/2 A Pece of leder..or of clathe. 1530 PALSGR. 252/2 Pece of steele. 1535 COVERDALE 1 *Sam.* ii. 36 For a syluer peny and for a pece of bred. c 1595 CAPT. WYATT *R. Dudley's Voy. W. Ind.* (Hakl. Soc.) 26 Our Generall caused our Queenes armes to be drawne on a peece of lead. 1657 AUSTEN *Fruit Trees* I. 43 A hard peece of wood. 1698 NORRIS *Pract. Disc.* (1707) IV. 224 Like a red-hot piece of Iron upon an Anvil. 1769 WESLEY *Jrnl.* 24 Aug., Pieces of water that surround it. 1831 MACAULAY *Civ. Disabilities Jews* Ess. 146 The scrawl of the Jew on the back of a piece of paper.

b. In this sense *piece* is commonly used in *Sc.* without *of* (cf. Ger. *ein Stück Brod*). Cf. BIT *sb.*[2] 9.

1580 J. HAYE in *Cath. Tract.* (S.T.S.) 59 That we adore ane peace bread for God. 1681 COLVIL *Whigs Supplic.* (1751) 106 There a piece of beef, there a piece cheese lyes. 1787 [BEATTIE] *Scoticisms* 73 A piece cheese, bread, &c. 1876 WHITEHEAD *Daft Davie* (1894) 205 (E.D.D.) She had a piece bread and cheese in her pouch. *Mod.* Give me a small piece paper.

c. *Piece of money*, *of gold*, *of silver*: A coin.

1526 TINDALE *Matt.* xxvi. 15 And they apoynted vnto hym [Judas] thyrty peces of syluer [WYCLIF 1382 thritti platis of seluer, 1388 thretti pans of siluer]. a 1533 LD. BERNERS *Huon* xliii. 143 To pay these .iiii. peses of golde yerly. 1540 *Act 32 Hen. VIII*, c. 14 A piece of flemmishe money called an Englyshe. 1560 DAUS tr. *Sleidane's Comm.* 57 b, His Purse..chatcheth vp the other thinkyng to haue a pece of money. 1675 BROOKS *Gold. Key* 302 Look, as the worth and value of many pieces of Silver, is to be found in one piece of Gold. 1726 SWIFT *Gulliver* I. ii, My purse with nine large pieces of gold. 1841 LANE *Arab. Nts.* III. 6, I..amassed three thousand pieces of silver.

d. *Piece of flesh*, applied to a living person, a human being; *piece of goods*, applied humorously or contemptuously to a woman or child. Now *dial.*

1593 *Tell-Troth's N. Y. Gift* (1876) 30 Oh, she is a tall peece of flesh. 1611 SHAKS. *Cymb.* IV. ii. 127 Why should we be tender, To let an arrogant peece of flesh threat vs? a 1759 SIR C. H. WILLIAMS *Song* vii. in Locker *Lyra Eleg.* (1867) 163 This beautiful piece Of Eve's flesh is my niece. 1809 MALKIN *Gil Blas* I. ii. ⁋ 6 She seemed a pretty piece of goods enough. 1895 PINNOCK *Black Country Ann.* (E. D. D.), Her's a nice piece o' goods to be a skule guvness.

e. Of something non-material, as *a piece of poetry*, *of prose*, *of music*.

1601 SHAKS. *Twel. N.* II. iv. 2 Giue me some Musick..that peece of song, That old and Anticke song we heard last night. 1616 B. JONSON *Epigr.* xlv, Here doth lye Ben Ionson his best piece of poetrie. 1852 MRS. STOWE *Uncle Tom's C.* xvi. He sat down to the piano, and rattled a lively piece of music. *Mod.* A piece of nervous prose.

4. A (more or less) definite quantity in which various industrial products are made or put up for sale or use.

a. A length (varying according to the material) in which cloth or other textile fabric is woven; also, a length *of* wall-paper as made (in England, generally 12 yards). Often used *absolutely*: cf. 15 c.

A *piece* of muslin is 10 yards; of calico, 28 yards; of Irish linen, 25 yards; of Hanoverian linen, 100 double ells, or 128 yards. (Simmonds *Dict. Trade* 1858.)

1523 *Act 14 & 15 Hen. VIII*, c. 3 § 7 Every peace of Worstede Sayes or Stamyns to be made withyn any of the said Townes. 1588 *Acc. Bk. W. Wray* in *Antiquary* XXXII. 54 Item j pece tawnye buffing xxs. Item ij pece blacke buffing, xxiijs. 1622 E. MISSELDEN *Free Trade* (ed. 2) 9 Ther they goe at Twelve Gilders eight stivers the piece. 1706 PHILLIPS (ed. Kersey), *Piece*,..a certain Number of Ells or Yards of Cloth, Stuff, Silk, etc. 1711 SHAFTESB. *Charact.* (1737) II. 200 Some of those rich stuffs..with such irregular work, and contrary colours, as look'd ill in the pattern, but mighty natural and well in the piece. 1810 J. T. in *Risdon's Surv. Devon* p. xxvi, The..trade took off..about 35,000 pieces, each piece containing 26 yards. 1844 G. DODD *Textile Manuf.* ii. 48 A 'piece' of cotton cloth varies from twenty-four to forty-seven yards in length, and from twenty-eight to forty inches in width. 1881 YOUNG *Every Man his own Mechanic* § 1639 A 'piece' of English paper is 12 yards long and a piece of French paper about 9 yards.

b. A half-pig *of* lead.

1773 *Gentl. Mag.* XLIII. 63 Blocks of lead..called pigs.. being found too heavy to be easily managed, as they weighed three hundred weight..are now commonly made in Derbyshire into two pieces. 1829 *Glover's Hist. Derby* I. 81 The pieces, or half-pigs of lead are not of any certain weight, though the smelter endeavours..to approach as near to 176½ lbs. as he can.

5. A cask *of* wine or brandy, varying in capacity according to the locality, but generally equivalent to the butt, or to two hogsheads. [Fr. *pièce*.]

c 1490 *Paston Lett.* III. 364, I sen my lady a lytyll pes of Renysch wyne of the best, of x. gallons. 1523 LD. BERNERS *Froiss.* I. ccii. 238 They wanne the good town of Athyen..and there they founde mo than a hundred peces of wyne. 1619 FLETCHER *Mons. Thomas* VIII. x, Home, Launce, and strike a fresh piece of wine; the town's ours. 1687 *Lond. Gaz.* No. 2223/4, 76 Pieces of Conyack Brandy in 32 Lotts. 1705 *Ibid.* No. 4089/3 One hundred and eighty Pipes or Pieces, of double Spanish Brandy. 1839 URE *Dict. Arts* 4 There are tuns which can contain from 12 to 15 pieces of wine. 1840 T. A. TROLLOPE *Summer in Brittany* II. 281 A 'piece' ..of the best brandy, consisting of four hundred bottles, may be purchased at Bordeaux for two hundred and fifty francs. 1895 *Westm. Gaz.* 8 Apr. 3/2 Forty to fifty basketfuls [of grapes] are put upon the press at one time, and yield from ten to twelve pieces of wine.

¶ For the sense 'cup, wine-cup', see PECE *Obs.*

6. A single object or individual forming a unit of a class or collective group, as *a piece of furniture*, *of plate*, *of artillery* or *ordnance*, *of luggage*; † a head of cattle or game (*Sc. obs.*). See also 18.

c 1400 *Destr. Troy* 9504 Syluer and Sarrigold sadly þai grippet,..Pesis of plates plentius mekyll. 1473 SIR J. PASTON in *P. Lett.* III. 102, I most have myn instrumentes hydder, whyche..I praye yow and Berney..to trusse in a pedde. and sende them me hyddre in hast, and a byll ther in how many peces. 1523 EARL SURREY in Ellis *Orig. Lett.* Ser. I. I. 216 Dyvers other good peces of ordynaunce for the feld. 1563 *Reg. Privy Council Scot.* I. 237 Ane brasin pece of artailyerie, ten irn pecis. 1715 *Lond. Gaz.* No. 5336/2 A Piece of Plate of the value of 100 Ducats. 1792 *Gentl. Mag.* 12/2 A statue or a piece of plate require inscriptions very different from a monument. 1832 SOUTHEY *Hist. Penins. War* III. 319 A regiment..succeeded in taking two pieces of cannon. 1837 GORING & PRITCHARD *Microgr.* 62, I can almost always see the shot of a piece of ordnance when I fire it myself. 1886 MARY LINSKILL *Haven under Hill* I. xv. 201 It was a handsome piece of furniture. 1899 *Westm. Gaz.* 15 May 10/1 It handled last year 6,214,447,000 pieces of mail matter. 1899 *Daily News* 12 Sept. 7/5 It had at our ports been deemed sufficient to take about one 'piece' of luggage in five for examination. But when the dynamiters came..the inexorable order went forth that every 'piece' was to be searched.

7. *Piece of work*: **a.** A product of work, a production, a (concrete) work. **b.** A task, difficult business; *fig.* a commotion, ado (*colloq.*).

a. c 1540 HEYWOOD *Four P P.* in Hazl. *Dodsley* I. 363 Here is an eye-tooth of the Great Turk. Whose eyes be once set on this piece of work, May happily lese part of his eyesight. 1568 GRAFTON *Chron.* II. 941 The Kings Chapell at Westminster,..one of the most excellent peeces of worke, wrought in stone, that is in Christendome. 1602 SHAKS. *Ham.* II. ii. 315 What a piece of worke is a man! how Noble in Reason! how infinite in faculty! in forme and mouing how expresse and admirable! 1638 USSHER *Incarnation* (1649) 2 Most admirable peeces of work.

b. 1594 CAREW *Huarte's Exam. Wits* (1616) 103 It were an infinit peece of worke. 1715 tr. *Gregory's Astron.* I. 462 It would be a tedious Piece of Work to take out the two component Parts with their Signs. 1724 DE FOE *Mem. Cavalier* (1840) 76 It would be a long piece of work. 1810 *Sporting Mag.* XXXVI. 262 He kept jawing us, and making a piece of work all the time. 1844 DICKENS *Mart. Chuz.* xxx, What are you making all this piece of work for? 1872 'OUIDA' *Fitz's Election* (ed. Tauchn.) 194 How do you expect to get along..when it's such a piece of work to make you shake hands?

8. An individual instance, exemplification, specimen, or example, *of* any form of action or activity, function, abstract quality, etc.

a. Applied to a concrete thing.

a 1568 ASCHAM *Scholem.* (Arb.) 104 The conference of these two places, conteinyng so excellent a peece of learning, as this is. 1657 SIR W. MURE *Hist.* Wks. (S.T.S.) II. 235, I have adventured to offer this small peace of labour to posteritie. 1664 POWER *Exp. Philos.* I. 58 These puny automata, and exsanguineous pieces of Nature. 1686 tr. *Chardin's Trav. Persia* 398 A..delicate Piece of Architecture. 1705 J. TAYLOR *Journ. Edinb.* (1903) 71 A noble Monument of its former Grandeur, being one of the finest pieces of ruin in the Kingdom. 1723 T. THOMAS in *Portland Papers* VI. (Hist. MSS. Comm.) 74, I think it is the worst piece of portrait that ever in my life I saw. 1869 GOULBURN *Purs. Holiness* Pref. 7 A piece of religious literature.

b. Applied to an abstract thing.

1570 FOXE *A. & M.* (ed. 2) 2279/1 What a peece of Gods tender prouidence was shewed of late vpon our English brethren and countrey men. a 1586 SIDNEY *Arcadia* I. (1622) 51 Making a peece of reverence unto him. 1601 R. JOHNSON *Kingd. & Commw.* (1603) 211 They want the use of footmen, to whom these peeces of service doe properly belong. 1656 EARL MONM. tr. *Boccalini's Advts. fr. Parnass.* I. lxv. (1674) 84 It being an hateful piece of petulancy to envy great Princes. 1691 RAY *Creation* I. (1692) 112 Eminent pieces of Self-denial. 1748 *Anson's Voy.* III. x. 407 It would have been a piece of imprudence. 1832 HT. MARTINEAU *Hill & Valley* xiii. 123 Some fresh piece of bad news. 1876 TREVELYAN *Macaulay* I. iii. 139 A rare piece of luck. 1884 SIR F. NORTH in *Law Times Rep.* 22 Mar. 122/2 Another piece of carelessness on the part of the auctioneer.

† **c.** Applied to a person in whom some quality is exemplified or realized. *Obs.*

1623 FLETCHER *Rule a Wife* III. v, The master of this little piece of mischief. a 1635 NAUNTON *Fragm. Reg.* (Arb.) 38 Sir Nicholas Bacon, An arch-piece of Wit and Wisdom. 1648 GOODWIN in Jenkyn *Blind Guide* i. 6 Green-head, young peece of presumption, Prelaticall peece of Presbytery,..swelling peece of vanity. 1712 ARBUTHNOT *John Bull* III. i, One of your affected curt'sying pieces of formality. 1778 MISS BURNEY *Evelina* (1791) II. xxx. 182 As to the little Louisa, tis such a pretty piece of languor.

II. Absolute uses (elliptical, contextual, or conventional), without *of* and specification of the substance, etc.

9. A person, a personage, an individual. *arch.* and *dial.* **a.** Applied to a man.

In early use often = One of a multitude, army, or company; in 17th c. tending to be dyslogistic: cf. b.

1297 R. GLOUC. (Rolls) 7314 He at stod vpe þe brugge mid an ax alone,..A stalwarde pece þat was, nou god cuþe is soule loue. a 1300 *Cursor M.* 11058 Til Ion were born, a wel god pece. c 1330 R. BRUNNE *Chron. Wace* (Rolls) 156 In his buke has Dares demed, Both of Troie & of Grece, whatkyns schappe was ilka pece. c 1400 *Laud Troy Bk.* 4446 That fel faire for men of Grece, Thei hadde elles dyed euery pece. 1614 B. JONSON *Bart. Fair* I. iv, Hee is another manner of peece then you think for. 1651 ISAACKSON in *Fuller's Abel Rediv.*, *Andrewes* (1867) II. 161 King James ..selecting him as his choicest piece, to vindicate his regality. 1673 KIRKMAN *Unlucky Citizen* 171 She having so untoward a piece to her Husband, was undone by him. 1692 WOOD *Ath. Oxon.* II. 179 Say & Sele was a seriously subtil piece. 1736 CHANDLER *Hist. Persec.* 346 Bancroft.. was, as the historian calls him, a sturdy Piece. 1746 in *Leisure Hour* (1880) 117 An old nasty grunting bishop.. who plagues me out of my life, he is such a formal piece.

b. Applied to a woman or girl.

Now mostly with depreciatory attribute.

13.. *E. E. Allit. P.* A. 192 A precios pyece in perlez pyȝt. 1567 TURBERV. *Ovid's Epist.* 157 b, Faire Helena, that passing peece. 1576 FLEMING *Panopl. Epist.* 441 Stately, proude, and disdainefull peeces. 1613 SHAKS. *Hen. VIII*, V. v. 27 All Princely Graces That mould vp such a mighty Piece as this is [Queen Elizabeth]. 1621 BURTON *Anat. Mel.* I. ii. IV. i. (1651) 143 A waspish cholerick slut, a crazed peece. 1668 SEDLEY *Mulb. Gard.* III. ii, She is a tender Piece. 1668 R. L'ESTRANGE *Fables*, *Life Æsop* 5 Xanthus having a kind of a Nice froward Piece to his wife. 1783 WOLCOTT (P. Pindar) *Odes to Roy. Acad.* vi, Think of the Sage, who wanted a fine piece. *Mod. dial.* She is a forward piece.

10. a. A piece of armour; † esp. in the phrase *armed at* (*of*) *all pieces*, at all points, completely [F. *armé de toutes pièces*] (*obs.*). Also in comb., as *head-piece*, *shoulder-piece*, *thigh-piece*, etc.

c 1400 *Destr. Troy* 181 Knightes, Armyt at all peses, able to were. *Ibid.* 12878 Armet at all pes. c 1500 *Melusine* 248 Thenne toke he his armures & armed hym of al pieces. 1600 HOLLAND *Livy* XXXI. 799 The regiment of the footmen.. came but slowly forward, by reason they were heavily armed at all peeces. 1635 J. HAYWARD tr. *Biondi's Banish'd Virg.* 157 Deadora..arming herself at all peics, ranne to the prore.

† **b.** A fortified place, fortress, stronghold. *Obs.*

1525 *St. Papers Hen. VIII*, I. 160 The demaundes made by Monsʳ. de Buren for the Duchie of Burgon, and diverse other gret peaces in Fraunce. 1527 *Ibid.* 187 With the revocacion of tharmye, and rendicion of Genes, and other peces, whiche the Frenche King shulde rendre. 1568 GRAFTON *Chron.* II. 83 He receyued agaìne all the holdes and peeces which his father had lost. 1570–6 LAMBARDE *Peramb. Kent* (1826) 136 They set wide open their gates, and made a sudden sallie out of the peece. 1602 WARNER *Alb. Eng.* X. lviii. (1612) 254 This Guise bereft vs Calice, and in France our Peeces all. 1673 RAY *Journ. Low C.* 3 Ostend..is most regularly and exactly fortified, so that it seemed to us one of the strongest Pieces in all the Low-Countries. 1721 STRYPE *Eccl. Mem.* II. II. v. 288 A commission..to repair..to the town of Calais and to certain other pieces on that side of the seas.

† **c.** A sailing or rowing vessel. *Obs.*

1545 *St. Papers Hen. VIII*, I. 809 Capitaynes and leaders of His Highnes rowyng peces. 1675 *Lond. Gaz.* No. 1004/1 To go and see the Royal James,..and several other pieces built by Commissioner Deane.

11. A weapon for shooting, fire-arm. **a.** A piece of artillery; a cannon, gun.

a 1550 *Sir A. Barton* in *Surtees Misc.* (1888) 68 He hath three-score peece on ether side. 1565 *Reg. Privy Council Scot.* I. 360 To mak bullettis for small pecis. 1585 T. WASHINGTON tr. *Nicholay's Voy.* II. xxiv. 65 b, Diuers great and little peeces aswell of brasse as of yron. 1600 FAIRFAX *Tasso* IX. liv, So from a piece two chained bullets flie. 1669 STURMY *Mariner's Mag.* V. xii. 67 To know what Shot and Powder is meet for every Piece. 1706 PHILLIPS, *Pieces*, (in Warlike Affairs) signify Cannon or great Guns, as Battering-Pieces which are us'd at Sieges..: Field-pieces. 1875 CLERY *Min. Tactics* x. (1877) 123 Part of the attacking force should be directed against the covering party and part against the pieces.

b. A portable fire-arm, hand-gun; as a musket, carbine, pistol, fowling-piece.

1581 STYWARD *Mart. Discip.* I. 44 Such must haue..a good and sufficient peece, flaske, touch bore, pouder, shot, &c. 1590 SIR J. SMYTH *Disc. Weapons* 42 *margin*, The inuention of artillery, powder, shot, and small peeces of fire was not first in Germanie. 1591 G. FLETCHER *Russe Commw.* (Hakl. Soc.) 76 The stocke of his piece is not made caliever wise but..somewhat like a fowling piece. 1603 KNOLLES *Hist. Turks* (1621) 332 Taught to handle all manner of weapons, but especially the bow, the peece, and the Scimetar. 1704 *Lond. Gaz.* No. 4044/3 Our Grenadiers..put their Bayonets in the Muzzles of their Pieces. 1788 PRIESTLEY *Lect. Hist.* V. lx. 475 Considering how many arrows might be drawn before one piece could have been loaded and discharged. 1855 MACAULAY *Hist. Eng.* xvi. III. 674 Five hundred grenadiers rushed..to the counterscarp, fired their pieces, and threw their grenades. 1870 E. PEACOCK *Ralph Skirl.* III. 254 He knelt on one knee, and levelled his piece direct at William's head.

† **c.** A crossbow. *Obs.*

1590 *Nottingham Rec.* IV. 60 Quod dictus Fabianus non sagittabit in aliquo le peece ad aliquam rem vivam. 1598 DALLINGTON *Meth. Trav.* (1606) T iv b, The Crossebowe... Once in a yere, there is in each city a shooting with the Peeces at a Popingay of wood. *Ibid.* T v, By this practise., he groweth more ready and perfit in the vse of his Peece.

12. Each of the pieces of wood, ivory, etc., also called 'men', with which chess is played; technically restricted to the superior 'men' ('pieces of honour', 'dignified pieces'), as distinguished from the pawns. Also extended to those with which draughts, backgammon, etc., are played. [So It. *pezzo*, Sp. *pieza*, F. *pièce*.]

In the Continental use of the word, traces of its restriction in chess to the eight superior 'men' are found already in the 16th c.

[1497 LUCENA *Arte de Axedres* A j b, Sabiendo como juega cada pieza. c 1570 *B. M. Add. MS.* 28710 lf. 360 a, Todas las piecas y peones salvo el Rey.] 1562 ROWBOTHUM *Play Cheasts* A iv, The principle is to knowe the pieces, to wit, the name, the number, and the seat of euery one. As for the fashion of the pieces, that is according to the fantasie of the workman. 1591 FLORIO *Sec. Frutes* 262 A. Doth it please you then to play at the chesse..? *S.* Order your peeces. a 1649 DRUMM. OF HAWTH. *Fam. Epist.* Wks. (1711) 146 In this case they [pawns] are surrogated in those void rooms of the pieces of honour, which, because they suffered themselves to be taken, were removed off the board. 1688 R. HOLME *Armoury* III. xvi. (Roxb.) 67/1 What peice or man soeuer of your owne you touch or lift from its place, you must play it for that draught where you can. 1778 C. JONES *Hoyle's Games Impr.* 139 If..you find a Prospect of Success, rush on boldly and sacrifice a Piece or two. 1788 *Chambers' Cycl.* (ed. Rees) s. v. *Chess*, In this game each player had eight dignified pieces..and also eight pawns...These pieces are distinguished by being painted in white and black colours. 1797 *Encycl. Brit.* (ed. 3) s. v. *Chess*, In order to begin the game, the pawns must be moved before the pieces. 1870 HARDY & WARE *Mod. Hoyle*, *Chess* 37 Eight pieces of different denominations and powers, and eight Pawns, are allotted to each competitor... The pieces are named..King, Queen, Bishop, Knight, Rook. *Ibid.*, *Draughts* 139 The antagonist can insist on this being done or huff the piece. 1898 CULIN *Chess & Playing Cards* 836 Set of thirty-two domino pieces of teak wood. *Ibid.* 841 *Jeu de l'Oie*..the pieces are moved according to the throw.

13. A piece of money (see 3 c); a coin. Often with defining word, as *seven-shilling piece*, *crown piece*, *threepenny piece*, *twopenny piece*, *penny piece*, *five-franc piece*, etc.

1575 *Reg. Privy Council Scot.* II. 455 To be payit all in half merk pecis. 1617 MORYSON *Itin.* I. 289 They coyne any peece, of which they can make gayne. 1642 ROGERS *Naaman* 106 He must be a foole who really can satisfie himselfe in counters as if they were peeces. 1658 WOOD *Life* (O. H. S.) I. 241 A peice of p(ope) Jo(hn) the 23, and also a French peice. 1710 *Lond. Gaz.* No. 4748/4 A Queen Elizabeth Piece of 35s. 1711 HEARNE *Collect.* (O. H. S.) III. 102 The Gold Piece found in St. Gyles's Field. 1788 PRIESTLEY *Lect. Hist.* III. xvi. 134 These pieces were not called *farthings*, but *farthing tokens*. 1845 FORD *Handbk. Spain* I. 5 The value..of any individual piece is very uncertain.

† **b.** *spec.* Popularly applied to an English gold coin; orig. to the *unite* of James I, and afterwards to the sovereign, and guinea, as the one or other was the current coin. Hence *half-piece*. *Obs.*

The *Unite* was issued in 1604 as = 20 shillings; but was raised in 1612 to 22 shillings.

1616 B. JONSON *Devil an Ass* I. i. 5 I'll warrant you for halfe a piece. *Ibid.* III. iii. 83 What is't? a hundred pound? ..No, th' Harpey, now, stands on a hundred pieces. 1618 FEATLY *Clavis Myst.* xxxii. (1636) 426 All our crownes and soveraines, and pieces, and halfe pieces, and duckatts and double duckatts are currant but to the brim of the grave. 1659–60 PEPYS *Diary* 14 Mar., Here I got half-a piece of a person of Mr. Wright's recommending to my Lord to be Preacher of the Speaker frigate. a 1700 B. E. *Dict. Cant. Crew*, *Job*, a Guinea, Twenty Shillings, or a Piece. 1706 ESTCOURT *Fair Examp.* III. i. 34 Fifty Pieces are 50 Pound, 50 Shillings, and 50 Six-pences: I know what they are well enough, and you too. 1727–41 CHAMBERS *Cycl.* s. v. *Coin*, Guinea, or piece.

c. *Piece of eight*, the Spanish dollar, or *peso*, of the value of 8 *reals*, or about 4*s.* 6*d.* It was marked with the figure 8.

1610 B. JONSON *Alch.* III. iii. 15 Round trunkes, Furnish'd with pistolets, and pieces of eight. 1670 NARBOROUGH *Jrnl.* in *Acc. Sev. Late Voy.* I. (1694) 97 The Spaniards..paid for what things they bought in good Pillar pieces of Eight. 1679 OLDHAM *Sat. upon Jesuits* ii, Strange!..What charity pieces of eight produce. 1706 PHILLIPS, *Piece of Eight* or *Piece of eight Ryals*, a Spanish Coin; of which there are several sorts. 1748 *Earthquake of Peru* i. 9 His annual Allowance is 7,000 Pieces of Eight. 1882 ARBER *Garner* V. 227 *note*, *Peso*..was the monetary Unit of Central America; afterwards known as the Piece of Eight, and is the Mexican dollar of the present day.

14. A portion of time or space. Now *dial.*

a. A portion or space of time; *esp.* a short space of time; a while.

(Occurs in OF. in 13th c., and in AF. in Britton II. iii. § 12 Cum il avera esté graunt pece en seisine.)

a 1300 *Cursor M.* 7063 Þe wer lasted sa lang a pece. 14.. in *Pol. Rel. & L. Poems* (1866) 245 About þis a pece I wyl spede, þat I myth þis lettrys rede. 1825 BROCKETT *N. C. Gloss.*, *Piece*, a little while. 'Stay a piece and then aw will'. c 1825 in *N. & Q.* 9th Ser. III. 330 A piece back, three tides came up the Trent on one day.

† **b.** Here probably belongs *o pece*, *opece*, *opese* (*a peace*), in *still opece* (erron. *still a peace*), continually, continuously, constantly: see STILL *adv.* *Obs.*

c 1440 *Generydes* 1385 He wold not leve, butt stille alway opece Dede all that he cowde to hunt Generydes. *Ibid.* 3391 And euer more in prayours still opese, Vnto the tyme she knew it shuld goo. *Ibid.* 5254 Haue here a ryng and kepe it still opece, To the tyme that ye come onto Clarionas. 1555 W. WATREMAN *Fardle Facions* II. xii. 294 How she from thre yeres of age..remained ther [in the temple] seruing God stil a peace.

c. A portion of the way or distance between two points; a short distance. *dial.*

1612 BRINSLEY *Lud. Lit.* 230 By practice, euery day going a piece, and oft reading ouer and ouer, they will grow very much, to your great ioy. c 1730 BURT *Lett. N. Scotl.* (1818) I. 151 He told us we must go west a piece..and then incline to the north. 1760–72 H. BROOKE *Fool of Qual.* (1809) III. 59 Then I would run a piece off,..and again I would delay, and stop. c 1817 HOGG *Tales & Sk.* V. 231 I'll make my brother Adam carry it piece about with you. 1852 MRS. STOWE *Uncle Tom's C.* vii, I've walked quite a piece to-day, in hopes to get to the ferry.

15. A (small) portion of some specific substance.

a. A small portion, scrap, or cutting, of cloth, leather, or the like; esp. as used to repair a hole or tear: a patch. Cf. PIECE *v.* 1.

c 1380 WYCLIF *Wks.* (1880) 41 Þei may pese hem [cloþis] aȝen or cloute hem of sacchis & oþere pecis. 1433 *Rolls of Parlt.* IV. 452/1 The same Clothe to be sold for a remenaunt, or for a pece and nat for a Clothe. [1526 TINDALE *Matt.* ix. 16 Noo man peceth an olde garment with a pece [ἐπίβλημα, *commissuram*, WYCL. medlynge, clout] off newe cloothe.]

b. Short for 'piece of bread' (with or without butter, etc.); *spec.* such a piece eaten by itself, not as part of a regular meal. *Sc.* and *Eng. dial.* (Northumb. to Shropsh., and Cornwall).

1787 A. SHIRREFS *Bess & Jamie* IV. i, Neither tak' her siller nor a piece. 1881 GREGOR *Folk-Lore* 93 Pieces, however, were ordinarily given. 1883 *Daily News* 12 Dec. 2/6 On one occasion defendant gave her a bit of bridecake, on another a jelly piece. 1893 STEVENSON *Catriona* xvi. 185, I..took the road again on foot, with the piece in my hand and munching as I went. 1898 *Westm. Gaz.* 14 Dec. 2/1 When they get off at mid-day to eat their 'piece', there is talking and laughing among the field workers. 1903 *Eng. Dial. Dict.* (Wigtown), A dry piece is plain loaf bread or oat cake, without butter, jam, or treacle. *Ibid.* (Cornwall), If a child tells you she had 'nothing but a piece all day', you know she means bread and butter.

c. A length of cloth, wall-paper, etc.: see 4 a.

d. *Whaling.* A section or chunk of blubber, more fully called *blanket-piece*.

e. *Bookbinding.* A tablet of leather which fills a panel on the back of a book, and receives the title (*lettering-piece*).

f. *Malting.* A quantity of grain steeped and spread out at one time: = FLOOR *sb.*[1] 6 b.

1832 W. CHAMPION *Maltster's Guide* 43 The turning of his floors or pieces. 1876 WYLLIE in *Encycl. Brit.* IV. 268/2 It is of importance to the maltster that the law allows him to sprinkle water over the 'pieces' on the floor.

g. pl. *pieces*. An inferior quality of crystallized sugar obtained in the manufacture of crystals and crushed sugar.

Supplement, p. 3873; Corrigenda, p. 4092; Spurious words, p. 4093; Books quoted, p. 4094

1867 *Produce Markets Rev.* 13 July 161/1 The character of the Pieces Sugar made in London retrogrades rather than improves as a whole. 1875 *Ure's Dict. Arts* III. 948 The first crystallisation is called 'crushed' and the second 'pieces', the drainage from which goes by the name of 'syrup'. 1884 *West. Morn. News* 4 Sept. 6/5 Sugar.. London pieces, rather quiet, steady.

16. A separate article or item of baggage or property in transit. (Chiefly *U.S.*)

1809 A. Henry *Trav.* 15 The freight of a canoe..consists in sixty pieces, or packages, of merchandize, of the weight of from ninety to a hundred pounds each. *Ibid.* 24 The method of carrying the packages, or pieces, as they are called, is the same with that of the Indian women. 1890 Cooley, etc. *Railways Amer.* 253 The cases in which pieces go astray are astonishingly rare. 1899 *Westm. Gaz.* 15 May 10/1 The postal establishment of the United States..handles more pieces, employs more men, spends more money..than any other human organisation, public or private.

17. A production, specimen of handicraft, work of art; a contrivance; = *piece of work* (7 a). *Obs.* in general sense. See also Masterpiece.

1604 E. G[rimstone] *D'Acosta's Hist. Indies* v. viii. 349 They buried with them much wealth, as golde, silver, stones, ..bracelets of gold, and other rich peeces. 1626 B. Jonson *Staple of N.* v. i, It were a piece Worthy my night-cap, and the Gowne I weare, A Picklockes name in Law. 1643 Sir T. Browne *Relig. Med.* i. § 15 Ruder heads stand amazed at those prodigious pieces of Nature, Whales, Elephants, Dromidaries and Camels. 1650 Baxter *Saints' R.* i. vii. (1662) 121 Surely were it not for Eternity, I should think man a silly piece. 1697 Dampier *Voy.* (1729) I. 517 He busied himself in making a Chest..he was as proud of it as if it had been the rarest piece in the World. 1698 A. Brand *Emb. Muscovy to China* 71 Several rare pieces made at Augsburgh, that moved by the help of Clock-work.

b. A painting, a picture; † a portrait.

1574 *Appius & Virginia* in Hazl. *Dodsley* IV. 125 O fond Apelles, prattling fool, why boasteth thou so much, The famous't piece thou mad'st in Greece? 1594 Plat *Jewell-Ho.* iii. 51 To refresh the colours of olde peeces that bee wrought in oyle. 1662–3 Pepys *Diary* 27 Feb., There is also a very excellent piece of the King, done by Holbein. 1697 tr. *C'tess D'Aunoy's Trav.* (1706) 173, I was all alone in my apartment, busie in painting a small Piece. 1770 Langhorne *Plutarch* (1879) I. 183/1 The painter valued himself upon the celerity and ease with which he dispatched his pieces. 1853 Lytton *My Novel* i. xii, The walls..were thickly covered, chiefly with family pictures:..now and then some Dutch fair, or battle-piece. 1861 M. Pattison *Ess.* (1889) I. 45 Among the portraits which hung above were two allegorical pieces by Master Hans Holbein.

† c. A piece of statuary or sculpture. *Obs.*

1579 Fulke *Confut. Sanders* 634, I do so honour auncient images, that I make as great account of a peece of Nero,.. as I do of Constantius. 1629 Maxwell tr. *Herodian* (1635) 61 Most of the fairest Peeces in all the Citie, perisht in these flames.

d. A literary composition, in prose or verse, generally short.

1533 More *Debell. Salem* Pref., Wks. 930/1 Vnto one little piece, one greate cunning man had made a long aunswere, of twelue whole shetes of paper. 1643 Sir T. Browne *Relig. Med.* i. § 20 That Villain and Secretary of Hell, that composed that miscreant piece *Of the Three Impostors*. 1691 Ray *Creation* i. (1692) 32 There is a Posthumous piece extant, imputed to Cartes. 1710 Shaftesb. *Advice Author* iii, That exteriour Proportion and Symmetry of Composition, which constitutes a legitimate Piece. 1775 Johnson *Let. to Mrs. Thrale* 22 May, I am not sorry that you read Boswell's journal. Is it not a merry piece? 1824 J. Johnson *Typogr.* I. 529 He printed most of Archbishop Cranmer's pieces. 1878 Browning *Poets Croisic* xxix, A poet also, author of a piece Printed and published.

e. A drama, a play.

1643 Sir T. Browne *Relig. Med.* i. § 47 In the last scene, all the Actors must enter to compleat and make up the Catastrophe of this great peece. 1779 Sheridan *Critic* i. i, On the first night of a new piece they always fill the house with orders to support it. 1851 Thackeray *Eng. Hum.* v. (1876) 315 To supply himself with [money]..he began to write theatrical pieces. 1867 Freeman *Norm. Conq.* I. iv. 252 Arnulf, as usual, appears as the villain of the piece. 1885 *Bath Herald* 17 Jan. 3/2 The usage was to engage stars for the run of the piece.

f. A musical composition, usually short, either independent or forming an individual part of a larger work.

1825 J. Neal *Bro. Jonathan* I. 95 Nobody can bear to hear..a favourite piece over and over again the same night. 1856 *Amy Carlton* 208 Amy..played the piece that she was learning. 1880 in Grove *Dict. Mus.* II. 751 *Piece*. This word ..has since the end of the last century been applied to instrumental musical compositions as a general and untechnical term.

III. Phrases. (See also 1 b, c, 2 d, 10 a, 14 b.)

18. *A piece, the piece, each* (Sc. *ilk*) or *every piece*: each piece of a number of pieces; each unit of a number, set, or company; each of them or these: esp. in stating the share or price of each unit or individual member (see sense 6). Hence, *adverbially*, Apiece, q.v., *the piece, per piece*. [F. *la pièce*.]

Apiece can still be said of persons as well as things (so *the piece* in Sc. and north dial.).

a 1400–50 *Alexander* 5474 Lamprays of west Twa hundreth pond ay a pece. c 1483 Caxton *Dialogues* 47 The good candelmaker Gyueth foure talow candellis For one peny the pece [F. *le piece*]. 1489 *Acta Audit.* (1839) 131/1, xiij. horss and meris, price of þe pece xl.s. 1529 in *Wills Doctors Commons* (Camden) 18, xiij^{ti} peerles at iiijd. the peace. 1530 Tindale *Answ. More* Wks. (1573) 267/1 The Pope.. set vp in Rome a stewes of xx. or xxx. thousand whores, taking of euery pece tribute yearly. 1533 *Test. Ebor.* (Surtees) VI. 35, xijd. a peice. 1553 *Reg. Privy Council Scot.* I. 150 Thai had payit ane grott for the heid off ilk peax [of cattle] for thair poindlaw. 1566 *Ibid.* 493 The soum of ten markis for ilk pece of xxv. oxin. 1600 J. Pory tr. *Leo's Africa* vii. 289 Horses..sold againe for fortie and sometimes for fiftie ducates a piece. 1637 in *Bury Wills* (Camden) 169, I giue..John Mount and John Muske xs. peece, Margaret Texall xxs. 1660 *Act 12 Chas. II*, c. 4 Sched. s.v. *Bowes*, Bowes, vocat. stone-bowes of steel, the piece x.s. a 1670 Spalding *Troub. Chas. I* (1850) I. 81 The bischopis had causit imprint thir bookis..and sould haue gottin fra ilk minister four pundis for the peice. 1686 tr. *Chardin's Trav. Persia* 355 Sold for five hunder'd Crowns a piece. a 1692 Pollexfen *Disc. Trade* (1697) A vij b, Fat Oxen were often sold at 6s. per piece. 1797 *Statist. Acc. Scot.* XIX. 48 A fine of a cow the piece [= each person]. *Mod. Sc.* He gae them twa shillin' the piece for helpin' him.

19. *By the piece*: at a rate of so much for a definite amount or quantity; according to the amount done. *On the piece*: at piece-work.

1703 T. N. *City & C. Purchaser* 23 These Posts are..made by the Piece, viz. 1d...per Post. 1807 Southey in Robberds *Mem. W. Taylor* II. 209, I think such work is good enough to be paid by the piece. 1859 Jephson *Brittany* iii. 23, I could not ascertain whether they worked by the day or by the piece. 1879 *Print. Trades Jrnl.* xxix. 40 An employer is not bound to provide constant work for a man on the piece. 1885 *Times* (weekly ed.) 9 Oct. 3/2 Most pottery workers are paid by 'piece'.

20. *In* or *of one piece*: consisting of a single or undivided piece or mass.

[1535 Coverdale *Exod.* xxxvii. 22 The knoppes & braunches ..were all one pece of fyne beaten golde.] 1585 T. Washington tr. *Nicholay's Voy.* ii. xvi. 50 [An] obelisquie of coloured stone all of one peece 50. cubits high. 1825 J. Nicholson *Operat. Mechanic* 317 The whole is cast in one piece in bell-metal. 1864 Longf. in *Life* (1891) III. 32 Finished to-day the revision and copying..the translation of the *Purgatorio*, so as to have it all of one piece with the rest. 1885 Bible (R.V.) *Exod.* xxxvii. 8 Of one piece with the mercy-seat made he the cherubim at the two ends thereof.

21. *Of a piece*: of one piece, in one mass (= 20); often *fig.* of one and the same kind or quality; uniform, consistent; in agreement, harmony, or keeping. [F. *tout d'une pièce*.]

1632 Massinger *City Madam* i. iii, I have seen and heard all..and wish heartily You were all of a piece. 1639 N. N. tr. *Du Bosq's Compl. Wom.* ii. 23 Those Nations who make their Doublet and Shirt all of a peece. 1644 Digby *Nat. Bodies* xii. § 3. 102 To moue all of a piece. 1663 Butler *Hud.* i. ii. 448 He and his Horse were of a Piece, One Spirit did inform them both. 1700 Dryden *Pref. Fables* Wks. (Globe) 503 He writes not always of a piece, but sometimes mingles trivial things with those of greater moment. 1726 Swift *Gulliver* i. ii, One of them was covered, and seemed all of a piece. 1809 Mar. Edgeworth *Absentee* vi, After all, things were not of a piece. 1812 Col. Hawker *Diary* (1893) I. 51 The harness..second-hand, one horse in plated, another in brass harness, and, in short, all of a piece.

b. *Of a piece with.*

1665 Boyle *Occas. Refl.* iv. ii. (1848) 176 None appear'd more of a piece with the Earth than he. 1711 Addison *Spect.* No. 256 ¶ 3 It is not of a Piece with the rest of his Character. 1849 Macaulay *Hist. Eng.* ii. I. 233 All their proceedings were of a piece with this demand.

† c. *O pece, opece, opese*: see 14 b.

22. *Piece by piece* († *piece and piece*, Sc. obs.): one piece or part after another in succession; a piece at a time, piecemeal, little by little, gradually. [F. *pièce à pièce*.]

1560 Bible (Genev.) *Ezek.* xxiv. 6 Bring it out piece by piece. 1621 Quarles *Argalus & P.* (1678) 115 Peece by peece they dropt upon the ground. 1719 De Foe *Crusoe* i. 65 Had the calm Weather held I should have brought away the whole Ship Piece by Piece. 1877 Spurgeon *Serm.* XXIII. 208 The great architect unrolls his drawings piece by piece.

1533 Bellenden *Livy* iii. iii. (S.T.S.) I. 252 Fra thens þe pepill began Ilk day pece & pece to convalesce in þare bodyis fra all maledyis. a 1584 Montgomerie *Cherrie & Slae* 273, I felt My hart within my bosome melt, And pece and pece decay. 1681 Colvil *Whigs Supplic.* (1751) 121 Then piece and piece they dropt away, As ripe plumbs in a rainy day. 1721 *Wodrow Corr.* (1843) II. 550 Piece and piece as your leisure allows, pray send me what hath been remarkable as to religion and learning this last year.

IV. 23. *attrib.* and *Comb.*: **piece-compositor**, a compositor who is paid by the piece; **piece-dyed** *a.*, of cloth, dyed after it is woven; so **piece-dyeing**; **piece-fraction**, in *Typog.* (see quot.); **piece-hall**, an exchange where cloth is sold by the piece; **piece-knife** (see quot.); **piece-labour**, labour paid by the piece; **piece-looker**, an inspector of cloth woven in definite lengths; **piece-maker, -man** = Piece-worker; **piece-market**, the market for cloth sold by the piece; **piece-master**, a middleman who acts between the employer and the employed in the giving out of piece-work; † **piece-money**, money distributed to recipients at so much apiece; **piece-mould**, in *Sculpture*, a plaster-of-Paris mould, removed in pieces, and then fitted together; also, a mould consisting of separate pieces of metal, etc., which are fitted and beaten together upon the model; **piece-patch**, a piece inserted as a patch; **piece-patched** *a.*, patched up; **piece-payment**, payment by the piece; **piece-price**, a price paid for piece-work; **piece-rate**, rate of payment for piece-work; **piece-stuff**, lumber or timber in pieces; **piece-trade**, the trade in pieces of cloth; **piece-velvet**, velvet made in the piece of various widths (as distinguished from narrow ribbon-velvet, etc.); **piece-wage**, a wage paid by the piece of work. See also Piece-broker, -goods, etc.

1897 *Westm. Gaz.* 6 July 10/1 It took time, and time to the piece compositor..means bread. 1844 G. Dodd *Textile Manuf.* iii. 97 The wool being always dyed either in the state of wool, before spinning, or after being woven. This gives rise to the distinction between 'wool-dyed' cloth and '*piece-dyed' cloth. 1898 *Westm. Gaz.* 13 Dec. 8/1 The Bradford *piece-dyeing trade. 1900 De Vinne *Pract. Typogr.* 174 *Piece fractions, or split fractions in two pieces, or on two bodies, are not proper parts of the font, and are sold in separate fonts at higher rates. 1844 G. Dodd *Textile Manuf.* iv. 119 Instead of having a cloth-hall or a *piece-hall of its own, its productions are sent to one or other of those two towns for sale at the piece-halls. 1849 C. Brontë *Shirley* iv, The tradesman in the Piece Hall, i.e. the Cloth Exchange. 1833 J. Holland *Manuf. Metal* II. 17 The *piece-knives, or sportsmans' knives, as those complex articles containing saws, lancets, phlemes, gun-screw, punches, large and small blades, &c. used to be called. 1866 Rogers *Agric. & Prices* I. xv. 252 For the most part day labour. The other two are *piece labour. 1867 *Address to J. Bright* in *Morn. Star* 28 Jan., J. Moloney, *piece looker. 1895 *Daily News* 13 Mar. 3/1 To obtain a piecework statement to be based upon a *piecemaker's average. *Ibid.* 11 Mar. 3/3 The Union notice to the *piece-men being circulated. 1883 *Ibid.* 28 Sept. 2/7 The *piece market is without material alteration. 1851 Mayhew *Lond. Labour* II. 256 The abolition of the middleman, whether 'sweater', '*piece master', 'lumper' or what not, coming between the employer and employed. 1890 *Pall Mall G.* 11 Mar. 7/1 The present sweating piece-master system. 1610 *MS. Acc. St. John's Hosp., Canterb.*, Item payd in *pesse mony xvijs. vjd. 1642 *Ibid.*, Payed to 38 brothers and sisters for peesmoney xixs. 1895 *Daily News* 20 June 6/3 A *piece-mould is made upon the statue itself, and from this a hollow wax statue is cast. 1880 *Plain Hints Needlework* 27 A straight stitch 6 or 8 threads deep on each *piece-patch and material. a 1625 Fletcher *Bloody Bro.* ii. i, This *piece-patcht friendship, This rear'd-up reconcilement on a billow. 1903 *Daily Chron.* 11 July 3/7 London daily newspapers are..produced on a *piece payment system. 1895 *Westm. Gaz.* 21 Mar. 2/2 The question which underlies all surface disputes is that of fixing *piece-prices for the new machinery which is being introduced into the trade. 1892 *Pall Mall G.* 27 July 1/2 A reduction in the *piece-rates per ton at certain furnaces. 1881 *Chicago Times* 14 May, The cargo..consisting of short length *piece-stuff. 1891 *Times* 5 Oct. 4/3 There is no change to note in the *piece trade. 1872 Howells *Wedd. Journ.* (1892) 246 The *piece-velvets and the linens smote her to the heart. 1879 Mrs. A. E. James *Ind. Househ. Managem.* 17 Buy also some piece-velvet, silk, ribbon, flowers, feathers, net,..bonnet and cap wire. 1900 *Fabian News* Sept. 28/2 This 'log'..is 'a remarkable effort to adjust a *piece-wage rate on a time-wage basis'.

24. *Piece* is often the second element in a combination, in various senses, e.g. *back-piece, base-piece, bodice-piece, breech-piece, catch-piece, ear-piece, eye-piece, franc-piece, head-piece, penny-piece*, etc. See the first element.

Hence (*rare* or *nonce-wds.*) **Pie·celess** *a.*, without pieces or parts; **Pie·cely** *adv.*, in pieces; **Pie·cewise** *adv.*, by pieces.

a 1631 Donne *To C'tess Bedford* Poems (1650) 181 In those poore types of God (round circles) so Religions types the peecelesse centers flow. 1552 Huloet, Piecelye, or in pieces, *concise, frustatim*. 1674 N. Fairfax *Bulk & Selv.* 107 Whether wholewise or piece-wise?

[*Note.* L. *Pecia*, in sense of 'fragment', occurs in the Salic Law (a 596. MSS. 5 and 6, c 800) lx, (Ibi iiii Fustes alninos super caput suum frangere debet et illos in quattuor pecias [*earlier and later recensions* partes] per quattuor angulos iactare debet); *petia, petium*, in sense 'piece of land', appear in Muratori *Ant. Ital.* A.D. 730 'et alia petia', 757 'uno petio de terra' (Diez); see also many later med.L. instances in Du Cange. The ulterior source has been the subject of much research: see Diez s.v. *Pezza*; Scheler, Littré, Hatz.-Darm. s.v. *Pièce*; Körting s.v. *pett-* (7106); Thurneysen s.v. *Pezza*. The prevalent opinion is that late pop.L. **pettia, -ium*, were derived from a Brythonic stem *pett(i)-*, represented by Breton *pez* a piece, Welsh and Cornish *peth* a part, cognate with proto-Celtic **quett(i)-*, whence **cotti-*, in OIr. *cuit*, genitive *cota*, mod. Gaelic *cuid* part, share; but there are many difficulties. A very frequent early sense in OF. was that of 'portion or space of time' (see Godef.) = 14 above. The sense 'person', found so early in Eng., is not met with in French till late in 16th c.]

Piece (pīs), *v.* [f. prec. sb.]

I. 1. *trans.* To mend, repair, make whole, or complete by adding a piece or pieces; to patch.

c 1380 Wyclif *Wks.* (1880) 41 Þei may pese hem aȝen or cloute hem of sacchis & oþere pecis. c 1440 *Promp. Parv.* 388/2 Pecyn, or set pecys to a thynge, or clowtyn, *repecio*, .. *sarcio, reficio*. 1530 Palsgr. 655/1, I pece a thyng, I sette on a pece.. If it be broken it muste be peced, *sil est rompu il le fault piecer*. 1596 Shaks. *Tam. Shr.* iii. ii. 63 Petruchio is comming..with..one girth sixe times peec'd, and a womans Crupper..heere and there peec'd with pack-thred. 1601 *Vestry Bks.* (Surtees) 135 For picing a bell clapper that brake when Andrew Hawkins was buried, xijd. 1775 Mme. D'Arblay *Early Diary* 28 Feb., She was piecing a blue and white tissue with a large patch of black silk! 1884 *Harper's Mag.* July 306 It's nothin' but play, piecin' quilts.

b. *fig.*

1606 Shaks. *Ant. & Cl.* i. v. 45, I will peece Her opulent Throne, with Kingdomes. 1633 P. Fletcher *Purple Isl.* i. i, To paint the world, and piece the length'ning day.

2. To join, unite or put together, so as to form one piece; to mend (something broken) by joining the pieces; also *absol.* in spinning, to join or piece up threads, to work as a Piecer.

1483 *Cath. Angl.* 272/2 To Pece, *assuere*. 1559 *Ludlow Churchw. Acc.* (Camden) 90 Payd for a rope to pysse the

lyttelle belle rope. 1637 Suckling *Aglaura* v. i, There is no piecing Tulips to their stalks When they are once divorc'd by a rude hand. 1793 Smeaton *Edystone L.* § 138, I found the seamen..employed in piecing the ground cable, which..had again parted. 1819 *Evidence fr. Rep. Committee Ho. Lords*, 'How do they get their breakfast and afternoon meal?' '..When the machinery is moving, they eat it as they are piecing'. 1859 Mrs. Gaskell *Round the Sofa* 35, I cannot piece the leg as the doctor can.

b. *fig.* To put together, join, unite; *refl.* to join oneself *to*, unite *with*.

1579 W. Wilkinson *Confut. Familye of Loue* Ep. Ded. *iij b, To peece vnto themselues this their broken Religion. 1632 B. Jonson *Magn. Lady* iii. i, *Item*. I heard they were out. *Nee*. But they are pieced, and put together again. 1652–62 Heylin *Cosmogr.* iii. (1673) 5/2 This Prusias, when the Romans became so considerable..pieced himself with them. 1656 — *Surv. France* 214 She hath peeced her self to the strongest side of the State. 1681 Dryden *Abs. & Achit.* i. 661 His judgment yet his memory did excel, Which pieced his wondrous evidence so well. 1879 G. Meredith *Egoist* xxiv, Piecing fragments of empty signification.

† 3. *intr.* To unite, come together, assemble; to come to an agreement, agree; to join on. *Obs.*

1622 Bacon *Hen. VII* 23 It pieced better and followed more close and handsomely vpon the bruit of Plantagenet's escape. 1625 — *Ess., Innovations* (Arb.) 526 New Things peece not so well. 1636 Sir H. Wotton in *Lismore Papers* Ser. ii. (1888) III. 260 Owre Schoole Annually breaketh vp two weekes before Whitsontyde and peeceth agayne a fortnight after. 1692 R. L'Estrange *Josephus, Antiq.* xvi. viii. (1733) 434 Telling him..that things would mend in Time, and Friends piece again, if they could but come to.. a fair Understanding.

II. In combination with adverbs.

4. Piece in. a. *trans.* To join in, add by insertion; † **b.** *intr.* to join in (in action), unite (*obs.*).

a 1656 Hales *Gold. Rem.* i. (1673) 247 He that can comply, and peice in with all occasions, and make an easie forfeiture of his honesty. 1724 De Foe *Mem. Cavalier* ii. 187 The.. Officers..pieced in some Troops with those Regiments.

5. Piece on. *trans.* and *intr.* To fit on (as the corresponding piece).

1849 H. Miller *Footpr. Creat.* iv. (1874) 45 The super-occipital bone..pieces on to the superior frontal. 1869 Freeman *Norm. Conq.* III. xii. 218 It is so hard to fix the date of the event, or to piece it on in any way to the undoubted facts of the history, that [etc.].

6. Piece out. *trans.* To complete, eke out, extend, or enlarge by the addition of a piece.

1589 Puttenham *Eng. Poesie* ii. xiv. (Arb.) 138 Ye may note..how much better some bissillable becommeth to peece out an other longer foote then another word doth. 1639 Fuller *Holy War* iv. xxix. (1840) 232 Like a cordial given to a dying man, which doth piece out his life. 1643 Sir T. Browne *Relig. Med.* i. § 18 He..pieces out the defect of one by the excess of the other. 1728 Young *Love Fame* v. 436 The motion of her lips, and meaning eye, Piece out the idea her faint words deny. 1858 Hawthorne *Fr. & It. Note-Bks.* I. 133 The old Pons Emilius..has recently been pieced out by connecting a suspension bridge with the old piers.

7. Piece together. *trans.* To join together, combine (pieces or fragments) into a whole; to make up of pieces so combined.

1589 Puttenham *Eng. Poesie* iii. ix. (Arb.) 168 To peece many words together to make of them one entire, much more significatiue than the single word. 1618 Bolton *Florus* (1636) 235 Himselfe..peeceth together no lesse an army than the former mad-man. 1687 A. Lovell tr. *Thevenot's Trav.* i. 134 Cut out of the natural Rock..though it seem to be of five Stones pieced together one upon another. 1865 Merivale *Rom. Emp.* VIII. lxiii. 65 Our account of his exploits..must be..pieced imperfectly together.

8. Piece up. *trans.* To make up (esp. that which is broken); to repair by uniting the pieces, parts, or parties; to patch up.

1586 A. Day *Eng. Secretary* i. (1625) 75 Let these..constraine thee..whilst there is yet but one craze..in the touchstone of thy reputation, piece it vp & new flourish again by a great excellency. 1625 Bacon *Ess., Unity Relig.* (Arb.) 429 When it is peeced vp, vpon a direct Admission of Contraries. 1630 *R. Johnson's Kingd. & Commw.* 368 All being now piec't up betweene them. c 1645 Howell *Lett.* I. iv. xx. (1650) 124 'Tis thought the French King will peece him up again with new recruits. 1794 Burke *Corr.* (1844) IV. 213 They will of course endeavour to piece up their own broken connexions in England. 1884 *Pall Mall G.* 20 Nov. 3/2 Arranging, disposing, and piecing up these fragments.

b. *intr.* To make up matters, come to an arrangement.

1654 Earl Monm. tr. *Bentivoglio's Warrs Flanders* 212 By all means it was necessary to piece up with Alanson.

‖ **Pièce** (pyęs). The French for 'piece'; occurring in French phrases, more or less in current Eng. use.

a. A document used as evidence; esp. in *pièce justificative*, a document serving as proof of an allegation; a justification of an assertion.

1789 Han. More in W. Roberts *Mem.* (1834) II. iii. iv. 160 You will think me a great brute and savage..till you have read my *pièce justificative*.

b. *Pièce de résistance* (pyęs də rezistãs): the most substantial dish in a repast; also *fig.* the chief item in a collection, group, or series; in quot. 1860, used for 'a means of resistance'.

[1797 Burke *Regic. Peace* iv. Wks. IX. 7 Our appetite demands a *piece of resistance*.] 1839 Lockhart *Scott* xix. III. 214 *note*, In answer to her host's apology for his *piece de resistance*. 1840 Thackeray *Misc. Ess., Pict. Rhapsody* (1885) 184 To supply the picture-lover with the *pièces de résistance* of the feast. 1860 Jowett in *Essays & Reviews* 335 This authorized text is a *pièce de résistance* against innovation. 1893 *Outing* (U.S.) XXII. 149/2 The *pièce de résistance* of the entire ride lies between Poughkeepsie and Yonkers.

Piece-broker. (See quot. 1756.)

1697 *Lond. Gaz.* No. 3304/3 One Gawen Hardy.., Piece-Broker, was.. Indicted for Felony.., for paying and putting off Counterfeit Milled Money. 1720 Strype *Stow's Surv.* II. iv. vii. 118/2 Hollowel Street..a Place inhabited by divers Salesmen and Piece-Brokers. 1756 Rolt *Dict. Trade*, *Piece-broker*, is a shopkeeper in London, who buys the shreds and remnants of all materials that go through the hands of the taylor, and sells them again to such persons as want them for mending cloaths; being generally decayed taylors, or some cunning men who have crept into the secrets of the trade. 1770 *Chron.* in *Ann. Reg.* 143/2 Mr. Muzere, aged 90, many years an eminent piece-broker, who never trusted any money out at interest, but put it into an iron chest. 1858 Simmonds *Dict. Trade*, *Piece-broker* [as in Rolt].

Pieced (pīst), *ppl. a.* [f. Piece *v.* + -ed[1].]

1. Composed or made up of pieces joined together.

1420 in *E. E. Wills* (1882) 42 To Robard Leget my pesid Bowe. [*Ibid.*, A Bowe wyth-owte pecis.] 1569 *Wills & Inv. N. C.* (Surtees) I. 305 Also I gyue to ffrancis walker my peaced bowe. 1601 Sir W. Cornwallis *Ess.* ii. xxvii. (1631) 21 A pieced stuffe of divers colours of divers ragges. 1785 Sarah Fielding *Ophelia* II. vi, To descend..down a pieced ladder, appeared..terrible. 1851 Ruskin *Stones Ven.* I. viii. § 11 A larger number of solid and perfect small shafts, or a less number of pieced and cemented large ones.

2. Mended, patched, made up. Also *fig.*

1542–3 Brinklow *Lament.* 6 b, Is Christ a peced God, or a patched Redeamer? 1609 B. Jonson *Sil. Wom.* i. i, A poxe of her autumnall face, her peec'd beautie. 1617 Moryson *Itin.* i. 4 Three Marble pillars..one of them is peeced for one foot.

3. With adverbs: see Piece *v.* II.

1635–56 Cowley *Davideis* i. 313 The infected King..started back at piec'd up shapes, which fear And his distracted Fancy painted there. 1901 *Daily Chron.* 16 Oct. 3/3 A mere pieced-together book.

Piece goods, *sb. pl.* Textile fabrics, such as calico, shirtings, mull, etc., woven in recognized lengths (see Piece *sb.* 4 a) for sale; a term formerly applied to Indian and other Oriental fabrics exported to Europe, but now chiefly applied to Lancashire cotton goods exported to the East.

1665 *Lond. Gaz.* No. 12/1 A Fregat of the Eastern Squadron, hath sent in a Vessel laden with Wax, Pitch, Tar, and Piece-goods. 1722 *Ibid.* No. 6045/9 All Piece Goods, as Bays, Cloaths, Stuffs, or any other Manufactury. 1785 in Seton-Karr *Select. Calcutta Gaz.* (1864) I. 82 That the Captains and Officers of all ships that shall sail from any part of India, after receiving notice hereof, shall be allowed to bring eight thousand pieces of piece-goods, and no more. 1817 Jas. Mill *Brit. India* I. i. iii 45 *note*, Piece goods is the term..chiefly employed by the Company and their agents to denote the muslins and wove goods of India and China in general. 1844 G. Dodd *Textile Manuf.* i. 36 The cotton yarn is woven into piece-goods either by the hand-loom or the power-loom. 1886 Yule & Burnell *Anglo-Ind. Gloss.* s.v., Lancashire..has recently procured the abolition of the small import duty on English piece-goods in India. 1898 *Westm. Gaz.* 8 Oct. 6/3 Combination of the worsted piece-goods dyers.

Pie·ce-lace. Lace made in broad pieces, which can be cut and used like cloth.

1702 *Lond. Gaz.* No. 3806/8 A new Piece-Lace Head.., and a loop'd Flanders Lace Head. 1899 *Westm. Gaz.* 16 Mar. 3/1 Some amazingly good imitations of Irish lace— ..being but a few shillings per yard—for piece lace, that is. 1901 *Ibid.* 12 July 3/1 These coats are made mainly from piece laces with lace flouncing rippling round the edge.

Piecemeal (pī·smīl), *adv.* (*sb.*, *a.*) Forms: see Piece *sb.* and Meal *sb.*[2] [ME. f. *pece*, Piece + *-mēle*, -meal. Taking the place of OE. *styccemǣlum*; *pece-mēle* being a later word has not the OE. form in *-mǣlum*, nor an early ME. in *-mēlen*. The later amplification *by pece-mele* follows other words in *-mele* with *be, by* (e.g. Dropmeal, Flockmeal, Footmeal, Heapmeal), and introduces the quasi-sb. use B. The example in *-s* (1 β) was prob. due to the plural notion rather than an instance of the adverbial genitive.]

1. One part or piece at a time; piece by piece, gradually, by degrees; separately, by pieces.

1297 R. Glouc. (Rolls) 5624 Þat folc to drou þat traytour, ech lime pece mele. c 1440 *Jacob's Well* 151 Þei etyn a man noȝt al hole, but pece-mele. 1513 More *Rich. III* (1883) 85 Miles Forest at sainct Martens pecemele [*a* 1548 Hall *Chron., Rich. III* 28 by pece meale] rotted awaye. 1579 Tomson *Calvin's Serm. Tim.* 125/1 Now it remaineth that we looke peecemeale vnto these wordes. 1617 Moryson *Itin.* i. 5 The stone couering him is compassed with a grate, least it should bee broken and carried away peece-meale by Passengers. 1773 Burke *Corr.* (1844) I. 423 The business will be done covertly and piecemeal. 1865 Kingsley *Herew.* xvii, He means to conquer England piece-meal. 1885 Sir J. Pearson in *Law Rep.* 29 Ch. Div. 453 A party is not allowed to bring his case before the Court piecemeal.

β. 1698 Norris *Pract. Disc.* IV. 424 To have taken him Piecemeals, Paragraph by Paragraph, and to have consider'd every single Objection distinctly.

b. With *by* (rarely *in*). (Transitional to B.)

1545 Raynold *Byrth Mankynde* 100 Lette it be cut out by pese mele. 1566 Drant *Horace* To Rdr. 3, I..haue dispatched it by piece meale, or inche meale. 1692 Washington tr. *Milton's Def. Pop.* Pref., Wks. 1851 VIII. 5, I am forced to write by piece-meal, and break off almost every hour. 1693 W. Freke *Sel. Ess.* xix. 114 They that can bear Pedantry in Piece-meal, will be even sick when they peruse his Masse of it. 1796 Jefferson *Writ.* (1859) IV. 130 It is better to do the whole work once for all, than to be recurring to it by piece-meal. 1868 E. Edwards *Ralegh* I. viii. 129 After previous alienations by piecemeal.

† c. *In piecemeal*: piece by piece, in detail. (Cf. B.) *Obs.*

1561 T. Hoby tr. *Castiglione's Courtyer* iii. (1577) R v, To reason thus in peecemeale of these rules..were a taking of an infinite matter in hand. *Ibid.* iv. V iij b, [To] vnderstand in peecemeale whatsoeuer belongeth to hys people.

2. Piece from piece; into or in pieces or fragments: with *break, tear, cut*, etc.

1570 Googe *Pop. Kingd.* i. (1880) 7 Who rather will be peecemeale torne than once their prince forsake. c 1580 Sidney *Ps.* ii. 21 Bruse Thou shalt and peecemeale breake These men like potshards weake. 1664 Butler *Hud.* ii. i. 751 I'll be torn piece-meal by a Horse, E'er I'll take you for better or worse. 1712 E. Cooke *Voy. S. Sea* 75 Hewing them Piece-meal, and delighting in their Blood. 1826 Scott *Woodst.* viii, To be now pulled asunder, broken piecemeal and reduced.

† b. With *in*. *Obs.* (Cf. B.)

1577 Stanyhurst *Descr. Irel.* in *Holinshed* (1808) VI. 40 The fishmongers were forced to hacke it in gobbets, and so to carrie it in peecemeale throughout the countrie. c 1590 Marlowe *Faust.* xiii. 69 Revolt, or I'll in piece-meal tear thy flesh. 1704 Swift *T. Tub* ix. 178 Is any Student tearing his Straw in piece-meal, Swearing and Blaspheming?

† B. quasi-*sb.* (with *pl.*) A small piece, portion, or fragment; chiefly in phrase *by piecemeals*, also *at, in, into piecemeals*. *Obs.*

1577 Whetstone *Life Gascoigne* xxviii, By peece meales care so wrought me vnder foot. 1612 Woodall *Surg. Mate* Wks. (1653) 268 *Buccellatio* is dividing into gobbets, or by peece-meals. 1616 J. Maitland in *Scot. Hist. Soc. Misc.* (1904) 171 He choosit rather to blame, tax and charge my father..in hidlings and at peece-male. 1642 T. Goodwin *Zerubbabels Enc.* 17 That..perfection of light which the Apostolicall times had..by piece-meals and degrees. 1651 R. Vaughan in *Ussher's Lett.* (1686) 562 To register any thing to the purpose..that I could come by, (some few piecemeals excepted). 1657 W. Rand tr. *Gassendi's Life Peiresc* ii. 294 Being torn into piece-meale-. 1762 Sterne *Tr. Shandy* V. iii, Those are falling..by piece-meal- to decay.

C. *adj.* (*attrib.* use of the adv.). Consisting or done in pieces or by instalments; done bit by bit.

1600 Rowlands *Lett. Humours Blood* vi. 75 A pox of peecemeale drinking. 1713 Derham *Phys. Theol.* To Rdr., None..have done it otherwise than in a transient, piecemeal Manner. 1768–74 Tucker *Lt. Nat.* (1834) I. 640 What tortures and piecemeal executions have not been practised by tyrants and persecutors. 1831 J. W. Croker in *Croker Papers* 9 Oct., Giving no opinion on piecemeal reform. 1871 Freeman *Norm. Conq.* IV. xviii. 184 Our history just at this time has to be put together in so piecemeal a way.

Pie·cemeal, *v.* Now *rare*. [f. prec.] *trans.* To divide or distribute piecemeal; to dismember. Hence **Pie·cemealing** *vbl. sb.*

1611 Cotgr., *Emmenuiser*, to make small, to peecemeale, to reduce into little parcels, or peeces. *Ibid.*, *Parcelé*, peecemealed; cut, or made, into parcels. 1632 Heywood *1st Pt. Iron Age* v. i. Wks. 1874 III. 338 My seuen-fold Targe With thousand gashes peece-meald from mine arme. 1655 Gurnall *Chr. in Arm.* i. 20 The glory of the work shall not be crumbled, and piece-mealed out, some to God, and some to the Creature. a 1700 *Oxford Laureat* in Johnson *L. P., Walden*, Had he ta'en the whole ode, as he took it piece mealing, They had fin'd him but ten-pence at most. 1718 *Entertainer* No. 21. 144 The Piece-meal'd Quarters..exposed to the four Corners of the Earth. 1749 Fielding *Tom Jones* xiii. i, The heavy, unread, folio lump, which long had dozed on the dusty shelf, piece-mealed into numbers, runs nimbly through the nation. 1853 *Tait's Mag.* XX. 259 The division, the piece-mealing of Germany, is the strength of Russia.

† Pie·cemealwise, *adv.* *Obs. rare*[−1]. [See -wise.] = Piecemeal 1.

1594 Carew *Tasso* (1881) 78 The Christians force peecemale-wise to impair.

Piecen (pī·s'n), *v.* *local* or *techn.* [f. Piece *sb.* + -en[5] 2.] *trans.* To join, to piece; chiefly, to join broken threads or ends in spinning.

1835 Ure *Philos. Manuf.* 180 The children have..to piecen their slubbing ends with double rapidity. *Ibid.* 223 With the covers has been also introduced a new method of piecening or joining on any end.., namely, by splicing it to the adjoining roving. 1844 G. Dodd *Textile Manuf.* i. 18 The plan of 'piecening', by which time is saved in spinning cotton. 1887 *19th Cent.* Dec. 820 The building..has been piecened and enlarged from time to time.

Piecener (pī·s'nəɹ). [f. prec. + -er[1].] One who pieces or piecens; a piecer; *spec.*, a child or young person employed in a spinning-mill to keep the frames filled with rovings, and to join together the ends of threads which break while being spun or wound; formerly, also, to join the cardings or slivers for the slubber, a work now done by machinery: see Piecer 2.

1835 Ure *Philos. Manuf.* 178 The cardings..are taken up by the children, called pieceners, from the nature of their work, being to piece or join those porous rolls together, to fit them for being drawn into a continuous thread. 1839 Mrs. F. Trollope *M. Armstrong* I. viii. 191 *note*, The children whose duty it is to walk backwards and forwards before the reels, on which the cotton, silk, or worsted is wound, for the purpose of joining the threads when they break, are called piecers, or pieceners. 1843 *Penny Cycl.* XXVII. 552/1 A child, called a 'piecener', takes the cardings from the carding machine...The pieceners are employed and paid by the slubber.

Piecer (pī·səɹ). [f. Piece *v.* + -er[1].]

1. *generally.* One who pieces; a patcher.

1836 L. Hunt in *New Monthly Mag.* XLVIII. 70 Fancy's the wealth of wealth, the toiler's hope, The poor man's

piecer-out. 1841 *Blackw. Mag.* L. 155 The English are blunderers here, piecers and patch-workers. 1858 Gladstone *Homer* I. 46 The piecers, who say that there were originally a number of Iliadic or Odyssean songs, afterwards made up into the poems such as we now have them.

2. *spec.* In a spinning-mill: see Piecener.

1825 J. Nicholson *Operat. Mechanic* 384 The pieces are joined by children, called piecers, who are in attendance on each mule, to join any yarn that may be broken in the act of stretching or twisting. 1833 Ht. Martineau *Manch. Strike* i. 3 You earn as much as a piecer as some do at a hand-loom. 1857 Livingstone *Trav.* Introd. 3, I was put into the factory as a 'piecer'. 1891 *Labour Commission Gloss.*, *Piecers*, assistants to the mule spinner or minder, with the special duty of keeping the frames filled with 'rovings'. They derive their name from their work of piecing up the broken threads.

Piece-work (pī·s,wɒɹk). Work done and paid for by the piece: see Piece *sb.* 19.

1795 Washington *Let.* Writ. 1892 XIII. 58 The new have gone more into the execution of it by contracts, and piece work. 1830 *Cumb. Farm Rep.* 60 in *Libr. Usef. Knowl., Husb.* III, Labourers are easily obtained here, either for piece-work or by the day. 1878 Jevons *Prim. Pol. Econ.* viii. 74 Some trades-unions endeavour to prevent their members from earning wages by piece-work.

attrib. 1890 *Daily News* 1 Nov. 3/2 This is one of the last of the piece-work jobs in Victoria Dock under the agreement of last November.

Hence **Pie·ce-wo:rker**, a workman who does piece-work, or is paid according to the amount done.

1884 *Harper's Mag.* Sept. 625/1 With a piece-worker, time is literally money. 1891 *Times* 7 Oct. 4/6 Piece-workers are supposed to earn, on the average, from one-fourth to one-third more than their rating.

Piecing (pī·siŋ), *vbl. sb.* [f. Piece *v.* + -ing[1].] The action of the verb Piece; patching, mending or completing by joining pieces.

1399 Langl. *Rich. Redeles* iii. 168 Ffor þei ffor þe pesinge paieth pens ten duble That þe clothe costened. 1545 Ascham *Toxoph.* (Arb.) 127 Peecynge of a shafte with brasell and holie..is to make the ende compasse heauy. 1649 Bp. Hall *Cases Consc.* iv. ii. Wks. 1863 VII. 374 The piecing up of these domestick breaches betwixt husband and wife. a 1680 Butler *Rem.* (1759) II. 303 Rhime is like Lace, that serves excellently well to hide the Piecing and Coarsness of a bad Stuff. 1771 Luckombe *Hist. Print.* 281 Piecing of Rules is often attended with considerable trouble. 1835 Ure *Philos. Manuf.* 312 The pieceing is soon over, as the carriage does not stop an instant at the frame. 1884 *Athenæum* 1 Nov. 562/3 An infinite piecing of minute facts.

b. *attrib.* and *Comb.*

1545 *Rates of Customs* c iij, Pesing threde the dossen pound xiiis. iiiid. 1594 *Acc.-Bk. W. Wray* in *Antiquary* XXXII. 347, ili. pecinge thred, iis. vjd. 1640 in Entick *London* (1766) II. 170 Whited brown or pieceing thread. 1881 Jacobi *Printer's Vocab.* 100 *Piecing leads* in wide measures of type the leads required are usually pieced.

Piecrust (pai·krɒst). [f. Pie *sb.*[2] + Crust.] The baked paste forming the crust of a pie.

1582 Hester *Secr. Phiorav.* iii. liii. 75 Ye shall not eate.. Butter, Milke, Cheese, or Pie crustes, or suche like thynges. 1626 B. Jonson *Staple of N.* ii. i, One that..preserues himselfe, Like an old hoary Rat, with mouldy pye-crust. 1817 Scott in Lockhart *Life* (1837) IV. 98 The posts, which are as cross as pye-crust, have occasioned some delay. 1869 *Hazlitt's Eng. Prov.* 320 Promises are like pie-crust, made to be broken.

b. *fig.* (in reference to hardness or dryness).

1869 Blackmore *Lorna D.* xlii, I will work it out by myself, you pie-crusts. 1872 Baker *Nile Tribut.* xviii. 322 The dry season baked it into a pie-crust.

c. *attrib.*; proverbially and humorously of promises lightly broken (see quot. 1869 above), as *piecrust pledge, promise*; of the colour of piecrust, as *piecrust hair, straw*.

1739 'R. Bull' tr. *Dedekindus' Grobianus* 162 Then all the Vengeance of the Gods invoke, In Case this Pye-crust Promise should be broke. 1888 *Pall Mall G.* 7 Dec. 11/1 Having laid to Mr. Smith's charges another piecrust pledge. 1889 W. S. Gilbert *Foggerty's Fairy*, etc. (1892) 98 The pie-crust hair had not been placed in mourning.

Pied (paid), *ppl. a.*[1] Also 6–7 **pide**, 6–8 **pyed**, 7 **py'd**, **pyde**, (6 *Sc.* **pyet**). [As if pa. pple. of a verb *pie*, f. Pie *sb.*[1]: see -ed.]

Parti-coloured; originally, black and white like a magpie; hence, of any two colours, esp. of white blotched with another colour; also of three or more colours in patches or blotches. Also, wearing a parti-coloured dress.

1382 [see c]. 1509 Hawes *Past. Pleas.* xxix. (Percy Soc.) 134 With a hood, a bell,..and a bagge; In a pyed cote he rode brygge a bragge. 1575 *Brieff Disc. Troubles Franckford* (1846) 203 To weare the pied coate off a foole. 1588 Shaks. *L. L. L.* v. ii. 904 Dasies pied, and Violets blew, And Cuckow-buds of yellow hew. 1596 — *Merch. V.* i. iii. 80 That all the eanelings which were Streakt and pied Should fall as Iacobs hier. 1611 Cotgr., *Pecile*, a pide, or skude colour of a horse. 1627 Drayton *Nymphidia* xviii, The wing of a pyde Butterflee. 1652 Gaule *Magastrom.* 366 In a town within the territories of Brunswick, they had hired a pyed piper to conjure away all the rats and mice, that much infested him. [Cf. quot. c 1645 in f.] 1665 Sir T. Herbert *Trav.* (1677) 16 Zebræ or Pide-horses. 1774 Lambert in *Phil. Trans.* LXVI. 493 The bullock is pyed, white and red. 1839 Youatt *Horse* 376 The pied horse is one that has distinct spots or patches of different colours, but almost invariably of white with some other colour. 1841 Catlin *N. Amer. Ind.* II. xli. 58 Others [horses] were pied, containing a variety of colours on the same animal.

b. Construed as *pa. pple.* = variegated.

1632 Milton *L'Allegro* 75 Meadows trim with Daisies pide, Shallow Brooks, and Rivers wide. 1671 Marten in *Acc. Sev. late Voy.* ii. (1694) 79 In the middle, they are white pyed with black. 1853 G. Johnston *Nat. Hist. E. Bord.* I. 122 A garment pied with daisies, and buttercups, and dandelions. 1887 Bowen *Virg. Æneid* v. 566 A Thracian courser with white all dappled and pied.

† c. *Pied Friars, Friars of the Pie*: orig. name of a small order of friars: see quot. 1904; in *P. Pl. Crede* app. applied to the Carmelites or White Friars (whose dress was a brown tunic and a white cloak): see Skeat *Student's Pastime* § 53. *Pied Monk*, a Bernardine or Cistercian, from their white tunic and large black scapular. *Obs.* exc. *Hist.*

1382 in *Pol. Poems* (Rolls) I. 262 With an O and an I, fuerunt pyed freres; Quomodo mutati sunt rogo dicat Pers. [c 1394 *P. Pl. Crede* 65 Sikerli y can nouȝt fynden, who hem first founded, But þe foles foundeden hem-self, freres of the Pye. c 1440 Walsingham *Hist. Angl.* (Rolls) I. 182 Cadaver..in quodam veteri cœmeterio, quod fuerat quondam Fratrum quos 'Freres Pyes' veteres appellabant,..projecerunt.] 1530 Palsgr. 254/1 Pyed monke, *barnardin*. 1537 Wriothesley *Chron.* (Camden) I. 63 An Abbott condam of Fountens, of the order of pyed monkes. 1904 Gasquet *Eng. Monast. Life* xi. 242 Pied Friars, or Fratres de Pica, ..had but one house in England, at Norwich, and..were obliged by the Council of Lyons [1245] to join one or other of the four great mendicant Orders.

d. In the specific names of many birds and other animals characterized by variegated colouring; as **Pied antelope** = Bontebok; **pied blackbird**, any Asiatic thrush of the genus *Turdulus* (Webster 1890); **pied brant** = Harlequin *brant*; **pied duck**, the extinct *Somateria labradoria*; **pied finch**, the chaffinch, *Fringilla cœlebs*: cf. Piefinch; **pied flycatcher** (*Muscicapa atricapilla*); **pied goose** = Magpie *goose*; **pied grallina**, the Magpie Lark of Australia (*Grallina australis* or *picata*); **pied hyena**, the spotted hyena (*H. crocuta*); **pied hornbill**, species of *Anthracoceros*; **pied kingfisher**, *Ceryle rudis*, a native of India and Africa; **pied seal**, the Mediterranean Seal (*Monachus albiventer*); **pied starling**, an extinct starling of Réunion (*Fregilupus varius*); **pied wagtail**, the common Wagtail (*Motacilla lugubris*); **pied wigeon**, (*a*) the Garganey (*Anas querquedula*); (*b*) the Golden-eye (*Clangula glaucion*); (*c*) the Goosander (*Mergus merganser*) (Swainson *Prov. Names Birds* 1885); **pied wolf**, a pied variety of the American wolf.

1899 *Cambr. Nat. Hist.* IX. 119 The extinct '*Pied Duck'..was black, with white head, neck, chest [etc.]. 1898 Morris *Austral Eng.*, *Magpie-Goose*..called also *Swan-goose*, and *Pied-goose*. 1865 W. Boyd *Swartzen* 72 Robes of striped or *pied hyena. 1901 *Nature* 10 Jan. 254/2 A notable loss is the handsome crested *pied starling..which is believed to have become extinct about the middle of the [19th] century. 1837 Gould in *Mag. Nat. Hist.* N.S. I. 460, I was..surprised to find that the sprightly and *pied wagtail..could not be referred to any described species.

e. *fig.*

1600 B. Jonson *Underwoods, Misc. P.* xxiii, Not wearing moods, as gallants do a fashion, In these pied times. 1635 [Glapthorne] *Lady Mother* i. iii. in Bullen *O. Pl.* II. 120 Noe speckld serpent weares More spotts than her pide honor. 1658 Osborn *Adv. Son* ii. Pref. (1673) K v, Py'd and contaminated constructions. *Ibid.* 166 This pied Goddess [Fortune].

f. *Comb.* (parasynthetic), as *pied-billed, -coated, -coloured, -faced, -winged*, etc.

1595 Chapman *Coronet Mistr. Philos.* vi, The Protean rages Of pied-faced fashion. 1634 S. R. *Noble Soldier* ii. i. in Bullen *O. Pl.* I. 276 These pide-winged Butterflyes. c 1645 Howell *Lett.* I. vi. xlix. (1650) 241 The said Town of Hamelen was annoyed with Rats and Mice; and it chanc'd, that a Pied-coated Piper came thither. 1709 Strype *Ann. Ref.* I. xxiii. 236 Eighteen great horses, all of them pyed coloured. 1888 Trumbull *Bird Names* 82 *note*, The Pied-billed Grebe..familiar to us all.

Pied (paid), *ppl. a.*[2] *rare.* [f. Pie *v.*[3] + -ed[1].] Converted into printers' pie; mixed up, confused.

1870 *Daily News* 2 Oct., Since then matters stand as above described, in a curiously pied condition.

Piedestal(l, -istal, piedstal, -stoole, obs. ff. Pedestal.

Piedly (pai·dli), *adv. rare.* [f. Pied *a.*[1] + -ly[2].] In a pied manner; in clothes of divers colours.

1545 Brinklow *Compl.* xxiv. (1874) 70 How pyedly goo thei lyke mommers, disgysed from the common peple.

Piedment, obs. form of Pediment.

Piedmontite (pī·dmɒntait, pyē·m-). *Min.* [Named 1853, f. *Piedmont* (It. *Piemonte*, lit. Mountain-foot), its locality + -ite 2 b.] A brownish red or reddish black silicate of aluminium, iron, manganese, and calcium, resembling epidote; often called manganese epidote.

1854 Dana *Min.* Index, Piedmontite. 1894 *Min. Mag.* X. 261 In the rhyolites the manganese-epidote, Piedmontite, is widely distributed.

Piedness (pai·dnės). [f. Pied *a.* + -ness.] The quality of being pied; or parti-coloured.

1600 Hakluyt *Voy* III. 269 For their likenesse and vniformity in roundnesse, orientnesse, and pidenesse of many excellent colours. 1635 Heywood *Hierarch.* iii. 142 Superfluous Fare and Pydenesse in Attyre. 1843 *Tait's Mag.* X. 617 By what process goose-berries may be made gigantic, and piccotees enriched with piedness.

Pie-dog: see Pye-dog.

‖ **Piedouche** (pyedūʃ). [F. *piédouche*, ad. It. *pieduccio*, dim. of *piede* foot.] A small pedestal.

1704 J. Harris *Lex. Techn.* I, *Piedouche*, in Architecture, is a little Square Base smoothed, and wrought with Mouldings, which serves to support a Bust or Statue drawn half way, or any small Figure in Relief. 1727–41 in Chambers *Cycl.*, and in mod. Dicts.

‖ **Piedra** (pye·drā). *Path.* [Sp. *piedra* stone:—L. *petra*.] An epiphytic affection of the hair, prevalent in certain parts of Colombia, in S. America.

1895 *Westm. Gaz.* 20 May 8/1 Dr. Unna recognised the disease as 'piedra', which is chiefly met with in Colombia. 1898 P. Manson *Trop. Diseases* xxxvii. 587 Piedra is supposed by some to be induced by the mucilaginous hair applications in vogue among the Colombians.

‖ **Piedroit** (pyedrwa). *Arch.* [F. *pied droit*, lit. 'straight foot', the vertical wall supporting an arch, also as below.] A square pier or pillar attached to a wall, which differs from a pilaster in having neither base nor capital.

1696 Phillips (ed. 5), *Piedroit* [ed. 1706 *Pied-droit*], a square Pillar, that is partly within the Wall. 1704 J. Harris *Lex. Techn.* I, *Pied-droit*, in Architecture, is a Square Pillar, differing from a Pillaster in this respect, that it hath no Base nor Capital: It is taken also for part of the Jaumbs of a Door or Window. 1723 Chambers tr. *Le Clerc's Treat. Archit.* I. 38 Cornices which terminate the Piedroits of Portico's.

Piefinch (pai·finʃ). [f. Pie *sb.*[1] 5 b + Finch.] A local name of the chaffinch.

1848 *Zoologist* VI. 2191 In Warwickshire, as elsewhere,.. the chaffinch [is] a 'piefinch'.

Piejamah, variant of Pyjama.

Piel (pīl). *Sc.* 'An iron wedge for boring stones' (Jamieson, 1808). (North of Scotl.)

1858 in Simmonds *Dict. Trade*. Hence 1864 in Webster, etc.

Piel, Pielage, Pieled, Pieler, pieller, obs. ff. Peel, Pillage, Piled, Peeled, Peeler[1].

Pieless (pai·lės), *a.* [f. Pie *sb.*[2] + -less.] Without a pie; having no pies.

1836–48 Walsh *Aristoph., Knights* iii. i, Why, that he'll seize on the pie-lass, And rob her and render her pieless. 1901 *Daily News* 9 Mar. 5/1 We think we would sooner pay our money..and go pieless.

Pielet (pai·lėt). [See -let.] A small pie.

1881 Wilmington in *Delaware Morn. News* IV. No. 44. 2 It..was too much like a dinner in tarts and pielets. 1896 *Westm. Gaz.* 24 Dec. 2/3 Extend to it the caution you bestow on pielets of mince and puddings of plums.

† Pielf, variant of Pelf *v.* *Obs.*, to pilfer.

1542 Udall *Erasm. Apoph.* 105 A poore sely folle that hath percase pielfed away tenne grotes. *Ibid.* 126 The one partie had pielfed, or embesleed awaye a thyng of the others.

Piemag (pai·mæg). [f. Pie *sb.*[1] + Mag *sb.*[2]] A local name of the Magpie.

1885 Swainson *Prov. Names Birds* 75–6 Magpie..Pye Mag (Hundred of Lonsdale). Pie nanny, do.

Pieman (pai·mæn). A man who makes pies for sale; a vendor of pies.

c 1820 *Nursery Rime*, Simple Simon Met a Pyeman, Going to the Fair; Says Simple Simon To the Pyeman, Let me taste your ware. 1823 *Blackw. Mag.* XIV. 508 The flying pieman ceases his call. 1865 *Sat. Rev.* 12 Aug. 204/2 Beware of cheap cook-shops and itinerant piemen.

Piement, -mento, var. of Piment, Pimento.

Piend (pīnd). *Arch. local.* [Origin unascertained.] The edge or angle formed by the meeting of two surfaces. Also *attrib.*, as *piend check, joint, rafter, stone, tree*.

1842–76 Gwilt *Archit.* Gloss., *Piend*, an arris; a salient angle; a hip. It is a northern appellation. *Ibid.*, *Piend Check*, the rebate formed on the piend or angle at the bottom of the riser of a stone step of a stair, to catch upon the angle formed at the top of the under step. 1881 *Archit. Publ. Soc. Dict.*, *Pien, Peind* or *Piend*, a term used in the south-west districts of Scotland, being the hip rafter of a roof. It is sometimes called 'pien-tree'. *Pien stone*, the stone covering the rafter in continuation of the ridge stones.

Piend, dial. form of Peen *sb.*

1882 in Ogilvie.

Pienet (pai·nėt). *local.* [A deriv. of Pie *sb.*[1]: perh. the same as Piannet.]

1. A name of the sea-pie or oyster-catcher.

1833 *G. Montagu's Ornith. Dict.* 351 Oyster-catcher.. provincial, Pienet, Olive. 1885 Swainson *Prov. Names Birds* 188 Pienet.

2. A local form of Piannet, the magpie.

1900 in *Eng. Dial. Dict.* s.v. *Pianet*, Pienet, *W. Yorksh.*

Piep, obs. form of Peep *v.*[1]

Piepowder (pai·paudəɹ), *a.* and *sb.* Forms: 3 (*adj.*) **pepoudrous, -rus**, *Sc.* **piepowdrous, pipouderous, -rus, pipuderous**, 5 **pypoudrus**; (*sb.*) 4 **pipoudre**, 5–6 **pepowder**, 5–9 **pipowder**, 6 **pipoulder**, 6–8 **pye(-)powder**, 7 **pye-poulder, -pouldre, pi-, pie-, pypouder, pypoudre**, 7–8 **py(-)powder**, 7– **pie(-)powder**, 8– **pie(-)poudre**. [Anglo-Fr. had in 13th c. *piepuldrus, -pouldrous, -poudrous* = F. *pied-poudreux* adj., sing. and pl., = med.(Anglo-)L. *pede-pulverōsus* dusty of foot, dusty-footed, also as sb., a dusty-footed man, a Dustyfoot, a wayfarer, itinerant merchant, etc.; found also in 15th c. English, and in 15–16th c. Scottish versions of the Burgh Laws. ME. had *pie-poudres, pie-powders* sb. pl., wayfarers, esp. in the designation *Court of Piepowders* = Court of wayfarers or travelling traders, whence through the attrib. use in *Piepowder Court* came the less correct *Court of Piepowder*.]

1. (*Piepoudrous*, etc.) *adj.* 'Dusty-footed'; wayfaring, itinerant; *absol.* as *sb. sing.* and *pl.* = 2.

1220–1 *Liber Albus* (Rolls) I. 67 Terminare querelas transeuntium per villam qui moram non poterunt facere, qui dicuntur *pepoudrous*. a 1267 Bracton v. i. vi. § 6 (Rolls) 126–7 Propter personas qui celerem habere debent justitiam, sicut sunt mercatores quibus exibetur justitia pepoudrous [*v.r.* pepoudrus]. a 1300 *Leges Burg.* xxix. in *Stat. Scotl.* I. App. v. 361 De placito inter piepoudrous [*Skene*, pede pulverosum et alios]. Si quis extraneus mercator..vagans qui vocatur piepowdrous [*Skene*, piepouldreux] hoc est anglice dustifute [tr. a 1500 Ony stranger man merchand..beand vagabund in þe contre þe quhilk is callit pipouderus]. *Ibid.* xxxi. *ibid.* 362 Burgenses qui sunt mercatores et pedepuluerosi [tr. Burges or merchandis or pipouderous]. a 1436 *Domesday Ipswich* in *Black Bk. Admir.* (Rolls) II. 23 The plees be twixe straunge folk that men clepeth pypoudrus, shuldene ben pleted from day to day. 1609 Skene *Reg. Maj., Burrow Lawes* 136 Ane stranger merchand..vaigand fra ane place to ane other, quha therefore is called *pied-puldreux*, or dustifute.

† 2. (*Piepowder*) *sb.* A travelling man, a wayfarer, *esp.* an itinerant merchant or trader. Chiefly used in *Court of Piepowders*, a summary court formerly held at fairs and markets to administer justice among itinerant dealers and others temporarily present.

1399 Langl. *Rich. Redeles* iii. 319 To ben of conceill ffor causis þat in þe court hangid, And pledid pipoudris alle manere pleyntis. 1477 *Rolls of Parlt.* VI. 187 To iche of the same Feyres is of right perteynyng a Court of Pepowders. 1531 *Dial. on Laws Eng.* i. vii. (1638) 13 To every fair and market is incident..a Court of Pipowders. 1614 B. Jonson *Bart. Fair* ii. i, Many are the yeerely enormities of this Fayre, in whose Courts of Pye-pouldres I haue had the honour during the three dayes sometimes to sit as Iudge. 1658 Phillips, *Piepouders Court* [ed. 1678 *Pie-Powders* Court; 1706 *Pie-Powder Court*]. a 1735 Arbuthnot *John Bull* ii. xvi, Dost think, that John Bull will be tried by Piepowders?

b. *attrib.* and *sb. sing.* esp. in *Piepowder Court*, *Court of Piepowder* = *Court of Piepowders* (in 2).

1574 in *10th Rep. Hist. MSS. Comm.* App. v. 335 That the citie, by auncient usage have a Pipoulder Courte, commonly called the Courte of Delyverannce, for thexpedition of strangers. 1631 Brathwait *Whimzies, Pedlar* 138 His pypouder court is his onely terror. 1664 Butler *Hud.* ii. ii. 306 To..Have its Proceedings disallow'd, or Allow'd, at fancy of Py-powder. 1671 F. Phillips *Reg. Necess.* 180 The Steward of the Sheriffs Turn, or a Leet, or of a Court of Piepowder. 1768 Blackstone *Comm.* III. iv. 32 The lowest, and at the same time the most expeditious, court of justice known to the law of England is the court of *piepoudre, curia pedis pulverizati*. a 1797 H. Walpole *Geo. II* (1847) II. iii. 113 Such poor little shifts and evasions might do in a pie-poudre court. 1881 *Newcastle Proclam. of Fair* in *Antiquary* Oct. 180/2 Notice is Hereby Further Given, That a Court of Piepowder will be holden during the time of this Fair, that is to say, one in the forenoon, another in the afternoon. 1896 *Daily News* 21 July 8/3 The government of the town [Hemel Hempstead] at present ostensibly rests in a Bailiff, Bailiff's Committee, and Court of Pie Poudre, though in reality in the Parish and District Councils.

† Pier[1]. *Obs. rare.* [a. OF. *piere, pierre* stone:—L. *petra*, Gr. πέτρα rock.] A stone: in *fraunche pier*, F. *franche pierre*, Freestone; *precious pier*, F. *pierre précieuse*, precious stone.

a 1400–50 *Alexander* 4356 Ne nouthire housing we haue, ay quils we here duell Bot at is fetid of flesch & of na fraunche piers. *Ibid.* 5270 Onycles & orfrays & orient perles ..with þire precious piers of paradise stremes.

Pier[2] (pīəɹ). Forms: 2–4 **per**, 4–8 **pere**, 5–8 **peer**, (6 **piere, pyre, pyerre**), 6–7 **peere, peir, pire**, (8 **peor**), 6– **pier**. [In 12th c. *per*, rendering med.L. *pera* (prob. *pēra*), of unknown origin.

It was suggested by Lambard, Spelman, and Du Cange, that *pera* was derived from OF. *piere* or L. *petra* stone, but this satisfies neither the phonetics nor the signification. There is an OF. (Picard and Flamand) word *pire* (rarely *piere* Godef.), meaning a breakwater or barricade of piles, a weir on a river, a boom defending a harbour, which might perh. have given the sense, but it is difficult to equate the form with *pēra* and *pēr*.]

1. One of the supports of the spans of a bridge, whether arched or otherwise formed.

(Appears in 12th c. and then not till end of 14th; examples not numerous till 17th c.)

c 1150 *Rochester Bridge-bote Charter* in Birch *Cart. Sax.* III. 657 Primum ejusdem civitatis episcopus incipit operari in orientali brachio [pontis] primam peram de terra; deinde tres virgatas planeas ponere, & tres sulinas .i. tres magnas trabes supponere...Secunda pera pertinet ad gillingeham & de cætham [etc.]. *Ibid.* 653 [*OE. version*] Æreſt þære burge biscop fæhð on þone earm to wercene þa land peran & þreo gyrda to þillianne, & iii sylla to lyccanne...Ðonne seo oþer per gebyrað to gyllingeham & to Cætham [etc.; nine examples of *per*]. c 1380 *Sir Ferumb.* 1682 Sixty pers [*error for* arches, F. *xxx ars*] þar buþ þar-on þat buth grete & rounde. *Ibid.* 1684 Oppon ech pere þar stent a tour [F. *x bretesques y a, chascune sor piler*] enbataild wyþ queynte engynne. c 1440 *Promp. Parv.* 394/1 Pere, or pyle of a brygge, or other fundament, *pila*. 1624 Wotton *Archit.* in *Reliq.* (1651) 238 Pilasters must not be..too Dwarfish and grosse, lest they imitate the Piles and Peers of Bridges. 1718 Rowe tr. *Lucan* iv. 24 A stable Bridge runs cross from Side to Side,..And jutting Peers the wint'ry Floods abide. 1756–7 tr. *Keysler's Trav* (1760) III. 133 The harbour of Puzzuolo..is formed by fourteen piers, or pilasters, rising above the surface of the water, which were anciently joined together by arches. 1761 *Brit. Mag.* II. 333 Tuesday, June 23. The first stone of the first pier of Black-Friars bridge, was laid. a 1842 Arnold *Later Hist. Rome* (1846) II. xii. 419 The emperor Hadrianus..took away all the upper part of the bridge, and left merely the piers standing. 1866 Brande & Cox *Dict. Sc.* II. 902/2 An abutment pier in a bridge is that next the shore; and, generally, this is made of a greater mass than the intermediate piers.

2. A solid structure of stone, or of earth faced with piles, extending into the sea or a tidal river to protect or partially enclose a harbour and form a landing-place for vessels; a breakwater, a mole; in modern times, also of iron or wood, open beneath and supported on columns or piles, forming a pleasure promenade and place of resort, or combining this purpose with that of a landing-place; also, a projecting landing-stage or jetty on the bank of a river or lake, as the piers on the Thames in London.

[1390 *Pat. Roll* 14 *Rich. II*, ii. m. 44 Concessimus vobis in auxilium construccionis cuiusdam pere per vos iam nouiter pro saluacione et defensione nauium et batellorum in Conuerso vocato Crowemere.] 1453 in W. Rye *Cromer* (1889) 56 *note*, [Will of John Bound, leaving] sustentacioni fretisfragii alias vocati le pere viij.s. 1487 *Ibid.*, [Will of Rich. Fenne] emend' le peer [3s 4d]. 1511 *Regist. Mag. Sig. Reg. Scot.* (1882) 764/1 Rex..concessit preposito [etc.] burgi de Edinburgh..le Newhavin..libertate, et spatio, ad edificandum et prolungandum munitionem, viz. le pere et bulwark ejusdem. 1515 *Aberdeen Regr.* (1844) 94 To the reparatioun and biggin of thar common peir and key. 1530 *Test. Ebor.* (Surtees) V. 300 (*Will of J. Ledum, Whitby*) Also to the peir, if it go furthwardes, xls. 1530–1 in *Chron. Calais* (Camden) 123 Also the pere that standeth in the Fishers gapp, must be new made. 1545 *Act 37 Hen. VIII*, c. 14 (Preamble) Shippes Bootes and Vesselles..within the Key or Peere in the Haven of Scardburghe. 1546 *Reg. Privy Council Scot.* I. 39 To pass to the mercat croces of Edinburgh..Quenisferrie, pere and schore of Leith, Dunde,.. and uthair places neidfull. 1551 in W. Rye *Cromer* (1889) 57 The same Inhabytantes hathe..defended the same by makyng of grete peeres. 1559 *Acts Privy Council* (1893) VII. 82 Sent to Dovour to vieu..the state of the blacke Bulwerke and pyerre there. 1559 *Contn. Fabyan's Chron.* vii. 706 The toune of Lithe also, and the hauen and pire destroied. 1572 Bossewell *Armorie* ii. 65 The mole or pere whiche Alexander the great had caused to bee made agaynste the citie of Tyre. 1582 N. Lichefield tr. *Castanheda's Conq. E. Ind.* i. x. 26 b, There is a certain Piere or recife wheron the sea doth beat. 1610 B. Jonson *Alch.* iii. iii, Our Castle, our cinque-Port, Our Douer pire. 1626 Bacon *Sylva* § 658 Timber..some are best for..Peers, that are sometimes Wet and some-times dry. 1656 Blount *Glossogr.*, *Peere*,..seems properly to be a Fortress made against the force of the Sea. 1677 Otway *Cheats of Scapin* ii. i, We went to walk upon the Pier. 1708 J. C. *Compl. Collier* (1845) 52 There wants a Peor, as at Whitby and Burlington. 1781 Perry *Daggenh. Breach* 33 He then resolv'd to square and compleat his Jetties, or Peers. 1726 Leoni *Alberti's Archit.* II. 121 To carry out a Pier into the Sea in order to fortifie a Port. 1823 Lady Granville *Lett.* (1894) I. 239, I have been all the morning on the Chain Pier [Brighton], which is delicious. 1852 Mrs. Carlyle *Lett.* II. 160 They..offered to land us at any pier we liked. 1884 Pae *Eustace* 119 The boats to be at the pier at noon.

transf. 1774 Goldsm. *Nat. Hist.* (1776) IV. 161 This [beaver] dam, or pier, is often four score or an hundred feet long, and ten or twelve feet thick at the base. 1853 Phillips *Rivers Yorks.* iv. 143 Nature has run out immoveable piers of hard lias shale with a long deep channel between them.

† b. *transf.* A haven. *Obs.*

a 1552 Leland *Itin.* (1711) II. 60 [This] makith the Fascion of an Havenet, or Pere, whither Shippelettes sumtime resorte for socour. *Ibid.* III. 9 The Pere [at Pendinas] is sore chokid with Sande. 1600 Holland *Livy* xxviii. vi. 671 It maketh a shew of a double peere or haven [*portus*], opening upon two divers mouths, but in very truth, ther is not a worse harborogh, & a more daungerous rode for ships. 1622 R. Hawkins *Voy. S. Sea* (1847) 239 The cittie..hath also a pere in itselfe for small barkes; at full sea it may have some sixe or seaven foote water, but at low water it is drie. 1721 Perry *Daggenh. Breach* 110 Preventing the rolling of the Beach from choaking up the Entrance into the Peer. *Ibid.* 114 Scowering away the Beach from the Mouth of the Peer.

3. *Arch.* and *Building*. A solid support of masonry or the like designed to sustain vertical pressure: **a.** A square pillar or pilaster; **b.** The solid masonry between doors, windows, or other openings in a wall; **c.** Each of the pillars from which an arch springs; **d.** Each of the pillars or posts of a gate or door; **e.** A solid structure of masonry or ironwork supporting a telescope or other large instrument.

1663 Gerbier *Counsel* 44 So must well proportioned window-cases be,..that the peeres of Brick or Stone between them, will fall to be of a fit width. 1666 *Act 18 & 19 Chas. II*, c. 8 § 6 That there shall be Partie walls and Partie peeres sett out equally on each Builders ground. 1706 Phillips (ed. Kersey), *Peer*..also a solid Wall between two Doors or Windows; also a sort of square Pillar. 1710 J. Harris *Lex. Techn.* II, *Peers*, in Architecture, are a kind of Pilasters or Buttresses for Support, Strength, and sometimes Ornament. 1727 Bradley *Fam. Dict.* s.v. *Greenhouse*, The Front [of a greenhouse] towards the South should be all of Glass,.. there ought to be no Peers of Brick-work, or Timber in the glaz'd Part, for they cast more Shade into the House. 1823 P. Nicholson *Pract. Build.* 291 The mode, now commonly adopted, of constructing arches between piers of stone. 1836 Parker *Gloss. Archit.* (1845) I. 283 *Pier*,..this name is often given to the pillars in Norman and Gothic architecture, but not very correctly. 1842–76 Gwilt *Archit.* § 2734 The composition..of gates and their piers. 1870 F. R. Wilson *Ch. Lindisf.* 140 The Saxon [tower] lay in ruins, save the piers. 1879 Sir G. G. Scott *Lect. Archit.* I. iii. 135 The piers destined to bear several arches divide themselves into as many columns as there are arches. 1883 *Knowledge* 15 June 357/2 To mount to the top of the pier and lubricate..the joints of the giant [telescope].

f. *transf.* and *fig.*

1611 in Gutch *Coll. Cur.* I. 113 By the King's summons to the parliament..as piers and strong rocks in the common-wealth. 1889 J. M. Duncan *Clin. Lect. Dis. Women* xxii. (ed. 4) 188 It lies between the posterior pier of a labium and the adjoining tuber ischii.

† 4. Short for Pier-glass. *Obs. rare.*

1760–72 H. Brooke *Fool of Qual.* (1809) II. 49, I dashed the piers and jars to shivers.

5. *attrib.* and *Comb.*, as (in sense 2) *pier-crane, -fishing, -man, -master, -shed, -warden*; (in sense 3) *pier-mullion, -order, -stone*; *pier-supported* adj.; **pier-arch**, an arch springing from piers; so **pier-arcade**; **pier-cap**, the cap of a gate-pier; **pier-looking-glass, -mirror** = Pier-glass; † **pier-reeve**, the officer in charge of a pier, a pier-master; **pier-table**, a low table or bracket occupying the space between two windows, often under a pier-glass.

1879 Sir G. G. Scott *Lect. Archit.* I. 117 The triforium was united with the *pier-arcade. 1842–76 Gwilt *Archit.* Gloss., **Pier Arch*, an arch springing from a pier. 1843 *Ecclesiologist* II. 51 A single arch of the same breadth as the pier-arch. 1897 *Daily News* 3 June 3/3 Charged..with wilfully damaging a *pier-cap. 1894 *Westm. Gaz.* 22 Oct. 5/3 At South Shields the *pier-crane was washed away. 1745 *De Foe's Eng. Tradesman* xxii. (1841) I. 207 Two large *pier looking-glasses, and one chimney-glass are in the shop. 1897 *Westm. Gaz.* 30 Nov. 5/2 One *pierman.. declared..that last night was the highest tide he had known. 1901 P. M. Johnson in *Archæol. Jrnl.* Mar. 64 The east window consists of two broad lancets divided by a wide *pier-mullion. 1879 Sir G. G. Scott *Lect. Archit.* II. 76 An arch-order may be moulded or otherwise decorated, while the corresponding *pier-order may remain square. 1591 *Replication* in Rye *Cromer* (1889) p. lviii, He was lately *Pereive of the said Peire. *Ibid.* p. lix, Perereves. 1667 Primatt *City & C. Build.* 68 *Peer-stones on both sides the Building, fronting high and principal Streets. 1828–32 Webster, *Pier-table. 1856 Mrs. Hawthorne in *N. Hawthorne & Wife* (1885) II. 90 In front of a golden pier-table over which hung a vast mirror. 1657 in *Sussex Archæol. Coll.* (1862) XIV. 96 That all persons..bring the same [timbers, etc.] unto the *Peere Wardens.

Pierage (pī·rėdʒ). [f. Pier[2] + -age.] **† a.** The use of, or privilege of using, a pier or wharf (*obs.*). **b.** The toll or fee paid for this; wharfage.

c 1599 in J. J. Cartwright *Chapters Hist. Yorks.* (1872) 273 The fees due for anchorage and perage. 1656 Blount *Glossogr.*, *Peerage*, which word may also signifie an Imposition for maintenance of a Sea-peer. 1809 R. Langford *Introd. Trade* 134 *Pierage*, money paid for the use of a pier or wharf. 1894 *Manch. Even. News* 7 Nov. 2/7 Vessels entering the port..will only be charged a moderate pierage.

Pierce (pīəɹs), *v.* Forms: α. 3–6 **perce**, (4 **parse**), 4–6 **perse**, *Sc.* **perss(e**, 5 **peerce, peerse**, 6 *Sc.* **peirs(e, pers, pairse**, 6–7 **pearce, pearse, pierse**, 6–8 **peirce**, 6– **pierce**. β. 4–5 **persche, persshe, perisse, -ische, perisshe, -issche**, 4–6 **perch(e, perish(e**, 5 **pershe, peresche**, 5–6 **perysshe**, 6–7 (9 *dial.*) **pearch**. [a. OF. *percer*, earlier *percier* (11–12th c., also *persier* 13th c.), ONF. *perchier*, mod. Picard *percher*; ulterior etymology uncertain.

Ménage, Diez, Burguy, Hatz.-Darm. take *percer* as:—L. type **pertusiāre*, deriv. of L. *pertundĕre* to thrust or bore through (pa.pple. *pertūsus*, n. of action *pertūsio*), although the contraction *pertusiar, pert'siar, percier* is violent, and there are the full forms F. *pertuiser*, Pr. *pertusar*, It. *pertugiare*. For other conjectures see Littré and Scheler. The β-forms appear to have been confused with those of *perish* v.]

1. *trans.* To penetrate, or run through or into (a substance), as a sharp-pointed instrument does; of an agent: to thrust (anything) through *with* such an instrument; to stab, prick, puncture.

1297 R. Glouc. (Rolls) 9019 Þei it ne percede noȝt þat yre þat blod vaste adoun drou. c 1315 Shoreham *Poems* (E.E.T.S.) i. 2209 Þo hand and fet and al hys lymes I-persed were ine payne. 1375 Barbour *Bruce* xiv. 292 Scottis men ..perssit thar armyng. 1470–85 Malory *Arthur* xvi. viii. 675 Thenne they came to gyders with suche a raundon that they perced their sheldes and their hauberkes. 1526 Tindale *John* xix. 37 They shall loke on hym, whom they pearsed. 1590 Spenser *F. Q.* i. vi. 43 They perst both plate and maile. 1596 Shaks. *1 Hen. IV*, v. iii. 59 If Percy be aliue, Ile pierce him: if he do come in my way. 1727–41 Chambers *Cycl.*, *Piercing*, among farriers.—*To pierce a horse's shoe lean*, is to pierce it too near the edge of the iron.—*To pierce it fat* is to pierce it further in. 1784 Cowper *Task* iii. 201 Pierce my vein, Take of the crimson stream meand'ring there, And catechise it well. 1860 Tyndall *Glac.* i. ix. 62 The mighty Aiguilles piercing the sea of air. *Ibid.* ii. xi. 290, I pierced the ice with the auger, drove in the stake, and descended.

β. 1377 Langl. *P. Pl.* B. xvii. 189 Were þe myddel of myn honde ymaymed or ypersshed [*v.rr.* ypersed, I-perisshed]. c 1380 *Sir Ferumb.* 5301 Þe nayles three, & þe croune. þat perschede cryst on ys passyoune. c 1400 Maundev. (Roxb.) xxi. 94 So þat þe bark be perched; and þan commez oute a licour thikk. c 1500 *Joseph Arim.* (W. de W.) 31 His.. handes & feet peryysshed with the spere & nayles.

absol. c 1380 Wyclif *Wks.* (1880) 288 Men stable in bileue ben a bick walle to turnen aȝen þis þondir þat it persiþ noȝt. 1576 Fleming *Panopl. Epist.* 118 It is..as commendable to pearce to the bone, as to pare the skinne.

fig. 1526 *Pilgr. Perf.* (W. de W. 1531) 256 b, It myght not swage the malyce of the iewes, ne..pearse theyr pryde. 1557 N. T. (Genev.) *1 Tim.* vi. 10 They erred from the faith, and perced them selues throwe with many sorowes.

b. *transf.* and *fig.*; *spec.* said of the penetrating action of cold, etc.

1390 Gower *Conf.* I. 294, I telle him schent, If he mai perce him with his tunge. 1563 *Mirr. Mag., Induct.* 4 With chilling cold had pearst the tender green. 1697

PIERCE.

Pierce, sb. rare.

+Pierce, v. Obs. nonce-wd.

Pierce-, the verb-stem or sb. in comb., as in pierce-brea e, free from perforations...

Pierceable, a.

Pierced, ppl. a.

Pierceless, a.

Piercel, (piers), sb.

Piercer (piʳsəɹ). Forms: 5–6 persour, percer, 5 porsour, -ore, -owre, -owyr, -ure, -ore, parsoure, persechor), 6 persor, -ar, parser, pierser, 6–7 poarcer, 7– piercer. [Orig. f. Anglo-F. perceour, persour = F. perceur.]

Pierceryn, obs. form of Piercing.

Pier-glass, [f. PIER sb.^2 3 + GLASS sb.] A large tall mirror; orig. one fitted to fill up the pier or space between two windows, or over a chimney-piece.

Pierian (pəiˈəɹiæn), a. [f. L. Pierius adj. (f. Pieria, a. Gr. Πιερία) + -AN. So F. Piérien.] 1. Belonging to Pieria, a district in N. Thessaly, the reputed home of the Muses; hence allusively in reference to poetry or learning.

Pier-head. The outward or seaward end of a pier.

Pierrette (pəiˈɹet), sb. [a. F., fem. of next.]

Pierrie, -rye: see PERRIE, jewellery; PIRRIE, a squall.

+Pierrot (pɪˈəɹot). [F. pierrot, dim. of Pierre, a peasant's name, applied to a 'clown' or buffoon.] 1. A typical character in French pantomime.

Pierrot-stone. Obs.

Pieta (pɪˈəta), sb. [It. pietà: — L. pietāt-em PIETY.]

Pietas, obs. f. PIETY.

Piercive, a. Obs. rare. Also 6 peruse. [f. PIERCE v. + -IVE: cf. coercive.] Having the quality of piercing; penetrative.

Pieteously, -tuous, etc.: see PITEOUS, etc.

Piety (pəiˈəti), sb. Forms: 4 (6 S.) piete, 5–7 pietie, 7– piety. [a. OF. piete (12th cent.), ad. L. pietāt-em PIETY.]

Pietism (pəiˈətizm). [ad. Ger. (mod.L.) Pietismus; see PIETIST and -ISM.]

Pietist (pəiˈətist). [ad. Ger. (mod.L.) Pietist; f. PIETY.]

Pietistic (pəiˈətɪstɪk), a. [f. prec. + -IC.]

Pietistical, a.

Pieton, Obs. [OF. piéton foot-soldier, f. L. type *peditōn-em.]

Pietoso, a. [It. pietoso.]

+Pietous, a. Obs. Also 5 pyetous, 6 pittuous, -tous, -teous. [a. OF. pieteus, piteus.]

+Pietranello, Petronello.

Pieu, obs. form of PEW.

+Piezo-, combining form from Gr. πιέζειν to press.

Piezo-electricity.

Piezometer (pəiɪˈzɒmɪtəɹ). [f. piezo- + -meter.] An instrument for measuring the compressibility of water or other liquid under varying pressures.

Piff (pif), int. An imitation of various sounds, as of that made by the swift motion of a bullet through the air.

+Piffero (pɪˈfeɹo). Also 8 fife, 8 phiffero, 8 pyfero, 8 fifre. [It. piffero, a. Sp. pífaro, F. fifre.]

Piffle (pɪˈf'l), v. dial. and slang.

Pig (pig), sb.^1 Forms: 3–7 pigge, 6 pygge, 6–7 pygg, 6 pyge, 5–7 pigg, 9 dial. pygg, 4– pig. [ME. pigge (? OE. *picga, *pigga).]

Pig, sb.^2 [Etymology obscure.]

I. 1. The young of swine; 'a young sow or boar' (J.).

II. Technical uses. 7. An oblong mass of metal, as obtained from the smelting-furnace; an ingot.

III. Proverbial phrases.

10. * a. When the pig is offered, to hold open the poke: to seize upon one's opportunity.

11. In various other phrases and locutions.

12. Special Comb. (of Pig sb.^1):
pig-bird, pig-broth, pig-buyer, etc.

13. attrib. and Comb. (of pig sb.^2):
pig-bed, pig-boat, pig-iron, pig-lead, pig-metal, pig-mould, etc.

Pigmentose, a. [as next + -OSE] = next.

Pigmentous (pigmentəs), a. [f. pigment sb. (pigmentum) + -OUS.] Characterized by presence of pigment; pigmentary.

Pig-metal. [f. PIG sb.1 7 + METAL: cf. SOW-METAL.] Metal, usually iron, in the form of pig.

Pig-rat. [transl. of Telugu *pandikokku.*] The large bandicoot rat of India.

Pigmy: see PYGMY.

Pignerate, -ation: see PIGNORATE, -ATION.

Pignorate, -ation = see PIGNORATE, -ATION.

† Pignolate, pi'niolate. Obs. [a. F. *pignolat*...] A conserve or confection made of pignons or pine-kernels.

Pignon[1]. *?Obs.* [F. *pignon* (pin·oñ) a pine-kernel = Sp. *piñon*, Pg. *pinhão*— late L. type *pīneōnem,* f. *pīnea* pine-cone.] 1. A pine-kernel.

Pignon[2] (pi·nyən). *Arch.* [f. pignon a gable.] ... = PINION sb.2

Pignorate (pi·gnŏrēt), *ppl. a.* [ad. L. *pignerāt-,* ppl. stem of *pignerāre*: see next.] 1. Pawned, pledged. 2. Related to things pledged, pignoratitious.

Pignoration (pignŏrēi·ʃən). *Law.* Also pigner-. [ad. late L. *pignorātiōn-em:* ...] 1. The action of pledging or pawning.

Pignorative (pi·gnŏrātiv), a. [f. L. *pignorāt-:* see PIGNORATE + -IVE.] That gives in pledge; pledging, pawning.

Pig-nut. [f. PIG sb.1 + NUT.] 1. The tuber of *Bunium flexuosum*: = EARTH-NUT 1.

Pigskin. [f. PIG sb.1 + SKIN.] 1. The skin of the pig or hog (called in 18th c. HOGSKIN); tanned leather made of this. Hence in *Sporting slang,* a saddle.

Pigsney, -ny, *arch.* and *dial.* Forms: a. 4 *piggesny,* 4–6 *pigesnye,* 6 *pyggesny,* *pygges nye,* *pigges-ny,* *pigsney,* *pygesnye* ... [ME. *pigges eye* pig's eye.] A term of endearment.

Pigsty. [f. PIG sb.1 + STY.] 1. An enclosure for pigs. 2. *fig.* A dwelling only fit for a pig; a miserable or dirty hovel.

Pig's wash, pigwash. The will of a brewery or kitchen given to pigs.

Pigtail. [f. PIG sb.1 + TAIL.] 1. The hunting of the wild boar with a spear.

Pig-tailed, a. [f. PIGTAIL + -ED[2].] 1. Having a tail in a pig's tail.

Pickery, Pikary, obs. ff. PICKERY.

Pike (pəik), sb.[1] Forms: 1 *pīc,* 3 *pic* ... 1. A pickaxe; a pick used in digging.

Pikeir, variant of PIQUER Obs., a pikeman.

Pikel, pikle (pai·kel), local, dial. Also local pikkel, pickle, pitchell, poikel, -klo. [f. PIKE sb.¹]

Pikeman (pai·kmăn). Plural -men.

Pikelet (pai·klet). Also dial. pikelin.

Pikelet² (pai·klet). A small or young pike.

Pikeman¹ (pai·kmăn). Also (in sense 1) pikesman.

Pikeman² [f. PIKE sb.¹ + MAN sb.¹]

Pike-pole. U.S. [PIKE sb.¹]

Piker¹. Now dial. Also 4-6 pyker, 5-6 ar.

† **Piker**², piquer. Obs.

† **Pikel**², piquer. Obs.

Piker³, slang or dial.

Piker, var. PICARD Obs.

Pikerel, Pikery, obs. ff. PICKEREL, PICKERY.

Pikestaff (pai·kstaf).

Pikeserve, Pikesteed, obs.

Pikestower. Obs.

Pikey¹, Pikey². slang or dial.

Piki, -nance nonce. [f. PICKAX, PICKFAULT.]

Pikit, Pikt, obs. forms of PICKED, PICKET.

† **Pikestower**. Obs.

Pikoise, obs. form of PICKAXE.

Piky (pai·ki), a.¹ + y.

Piky², a. erron. pikey. [f. PIKE sb.¹ + Y.]

Pilaff, -aff, variants of PILAU.

Pilap (pai·lădg). Also 9 pileage.

Pilar, Pilaster, obs. ff. PILLAR.

Pilate (pai·lět), sb.

Pilau, Pilaw (pi·lau, pilǎ·), pilaf.

Pilch (pilʃ). Now dial. Forms 3 pileken.

Pilchard (pi·ltʃărd). Forms: 4-6 pilcher.

† **Pilcher**¹. Obs.

† **Pilcher**², pilchard, the fish.

Pilcrow (pi·lkrou). arch.

Pile (pail), sb.¹ [OE. píl masc. = OLG.]

Pile, obs. form of PILLED. see PILL v.¹

Pilaster (pilă·stăʳ), sb.

Pilastered (pilă·stăʳd), a.

Pilastrade (pilă·strêd).

† **Pilastrel**. Obs.

Pilaster, dim. of pilastro PILASTER.

Pilau, pilaw (pi·lau, pilǎ·), pilaf, pilaw.

Pile (pail), sb.² [a. F. pile, ad. L. pīla]

Pile, sb.³ Forms: 5-7 pyle, 7 pile.

† **Pile**, sb.⁴ Obs. Forms: 4 pyle, 5 pyl.

† **Pile**, sb.⁵ Obs.

Pile (pail), sb.⁶ Also 4-6 pyle.

Pile (pail), sb.⁷ Also 4-7 pyle.

† **Pile**, sb.⁸ Obs. Forms: 4-6 pyle, 5 pyl.

Pile (pail), v.¹ [ad. L. pīlum]

Pile (pail), v.² [f. PILE sb.⁶]

Pile (pail), v.³ [f. PILE sb.⁷]

Pileate. *(continued)* ... Pileaster ... Pileate, *a.* ... Pileated, *ppl. a.* ... Pileiform ... Pilement ... Pileole, Pileolus ... Pileous, Pilose ... Piler ... Pilework ... Pileum ... Pileus ...

Pilfer, *v.* ... To plunder, steal; *spec.* (in later use), to commit petty theft.

Pilferer. One who pilfers.

Pilfering, *vbl. sb.* and *ppl. a.* Pilferingly, *adv.*

Pilfery, *Obs.* ...

Pilgaric, *Obs.* ...

Pilgarlic, **pilgarlick** ...

Pilgrim, *sb.* Forms: 2–4 pilegrim, pelegrim, 3 pilgrim, pelgrim, 4–6 pilgrime, pelgrime, 4–7 pilgrime, 5–6 pylgryme, -grome, 6 pyl- pylgryme, pilgram; 6 pilgrim, *sc.* pelerin, *etc.* pilgrim.

 1. One who travels from place to place; a person on a journey; a wayfarer; a traveller; a wanderer; a sojourner.

 2. One who journeys (usually a long distance) to some sacred place, as an act of religious devotion; one who makes a pilgrimage.

 b. *U.S.* and *Colonial.* A new-comer, a recent immigrant.

Pilgrim *(continued).* ... Pilgrim Fathers ... pilgrim-bottle, pilgrim's bottle ... pilgrim-salve ...

Pilgrimage, *sb.* Forms: 3 pelrimage, pilegrim-, pilgrim-, 4 pylegrim-, pylgrym-, pilgrymage, -grymage, pilgrimage, 5–6 pylgrymage ...

 1. A journey made by a pilgrim; a journey (usually of considerable duration) made to some sacred place, as an act of religious devotion.

 b. *transf.* and *gen.* A journey; a travelling about; peregrination.

Pilgrimage, *v.* ... To go on a pilgrimage.

Pilgrimager. ...

Pilgrimer, *rare.* ...

Pilgrimess. A female pilgrim.

Pilgrimize, *v.* ...

Pilgrim-like. ...

Piligerous, *a.* Bearing hair, clothed with hair.

Piliferous, *a.* Bearing or tipped with a hair.

Piliform, *a.* Having the form of a hair, hair-like.

Piling, *vbl. sb.* [f. PILE *v.*[1] + -ING[1].] The action of forming into a pile or piles; heaping up, building up in a regular pile.

 b. *attrib.* and *Comb.*, as piling furnace, swivel.

Piling, *vbl. sb.*[2] [f. PILE *sb.*[4] + -ING[1].] The action of driving piles; the driving of piles.

Piline, *sb.* ...

Pill, *sb.*[1] Forms: 4 pylle, 5 pylle, 6 pylle, pil, 6–7 pille, 6– pill. [a. OE. *pyl*, *pyll*... related to PILE *sb.*[1]] A small ball or globular mass of medicinal substance, made up of a size convenient to be swallowed.

Pill, *sb.*[2] ...

Pill, *v.*[1] [f. prec.] *trans.* To plunder, rifle, pillage, spoil; to commit depredation or extortion upon; to despoil.

 b. *intr.* To plunder, rob, pillage, or extort.

PILL. (continued)

II. To decorticate, etc. To strip of the skin, rind, or integument, as an orange, apple, potato, garlic, etc.; a tree of its bark, etc.: to remove the peel of. Rarely const. *of* (that which is stript off).

Pill (pil), *sb.*

Pilla, obs. form of PILLAU.

Pillage (pi·lēdʒ), *sb.*

Pillage (pi·lēdʒ), *v.*

Pillager (pi·lēdʒəɹ). One who pillages; a plunderer.

Pillar (pi·ləɹ), *sb.*

10. *Conch.* The central axis of a spiral shell; the modiolus or columella.

11. *Phrase.* *From pillar to post*, originally *from post to pillar*: from one party or place of appeal or resource to another; hither and thither, to and fro: implying weariness, worry, and harassment.

12. *attrib.* and *Comb.*

Pillar (pi·ləɹ), *v.*

Pillar-box. A hollow pillar about five feet high, erected in a public place, containing a letter-box or receptacle for posting letters.

Pillared (pi·ləɹd), *ppl. a.*

Pillaret (pi·ləɹet). A little pillar. Also *fig.*

Pillar-saint. = STYLITE.

Pillarist (pi·ləɹist).

Pillas, Pillez, obs. forms of PILLERY.

Pillary, obs. form of PILLORY.

Pillar-wise, *adv.* In the manner or fashion of a pillar.

Pillas, *sb.* A Cornish dialect name for naked oats.

Pill-box (pi·lbɒks).

Pillbox-maker.

Pile, var. of PILE *sb.*

+ Pilled, *ppl. a.* arch. and dial.

Pillen, obs. form of PILLION.

Piller (pi·ləɹ), *sb.* One who pills; a robber, plunderer; a spoiler.

Pillerie, -ery, obs. forms of PILLORY.

Pillery (pi·ləɹi), *sb.* and *a.*

Pillie, Pilluck, all north. dial., = Norw. dial. *pill* (Aasen) penis: cf. Cock *sb.* 20.

Pillicock.

Pilliver, obs. Sc. and north. dial. = PILLOW.

Pillie, *sb.* pilleis, obs. Sc. form of PULLEY.

Pilliwinkes: see PILLIWINKS.

Pilling, *vbl. sb.*

Pilling, *vbl. sb.* The action of PILL *v.* in its various senses.

Pillion (pi·lyən). Forms: 4 pylion, 5 pyllyon, pelyone, pillyon, 4-6 pillion, 4-7 pilion, pillion, pyllion, pillon. A light saddle.

Pillioned (pi·lyənd), *ppl. a.*

Pillion-pad.

Pill-machine, Pill-nettle, etc.: see PILL *sb.*

Pillock, obs. form of PILLOCK.

Pillon, obs. form of PILLION.

Pillor, obs. Also 7 *own*, -*er*, 8-*or*.

Pillorise (pi·ləɹaiz), *v.* [f. PILLORY + -IZE: or a. Fr. *pilloriser*] = next.

Pillorize (pi·ləɹaiz), *v.* [f. PILLORY + -IZE.]

Pillory (pi·ləɹi), *sb.* Forms: 3-4 pillori, 3-7 pillorie, -orye, -ory, etc.

Pillory (pi·ləɹi), *v.*

Pilluck, Pilwinkes, etc.: see PILLIE, PILLIWINKS.

Pilliwinks (pi·liwiŋks). An instrument of torture for squeezing the fingers; supposed to resemble the thumbkins or thumb-screw.

PILLORY. 865 PILLOW. 866 PILOT.

PILORY.

Pilosity (pilŏsĭ·tĭ). [L. type *pilōsitās, f. pilōsus hairy, PILOSE: see -ITY.] The quality or state of being hairy, hairiness.

Piloso-, used as combining form of L. pilōsus hairy, Pilose, as in Piloso-fimbriate a., fringed with soft hairs; Piloso-hispid a., having somewhat stiff hairs.

Pilot (pəi·lət), sb. Also 6 pilotte, pylotte, -lett, -late, 6-7 pilote, pylote, 6 8 pilot. [a. F. pilot, pillotte (1529 in Hatz.-Darm.), pillot (1520), mod.F. pilote, a. It. pilota, med.It. piloto, pedota (Florio), pedota (Du Cange; Gette des Cisp. 1292 p. 291), supposed to be altered, perh. by popular etymology, from It. pedota (Florio), pedota (Du Cange; Gette des Cisp...

Pilocarpine (pailŏkā·pəin). Chem. [f. mod.L. Pilocarpus, generic name in Bot. (f. Gr. πῖλος wool, felt + καρπός fruit) + -INE[5].] A white crystalline or amorphous alkaloid, $C_{11}H_{16}N_2O_2$, obtained from the leaves of Jaborandi, Pilocarpus pinnatifolius (or other species), used in pharmacy.

Pilose (pəi·lōs), a. [ad. L. pilōs-us hairy. Cf. -OSE.] Covered with hair, esp. with soft flexible hair; hairy; pilous.

Pilosity see Pilosity.

Pilous (pəi·ləs), a. [f. L. pil-us hair + -OUS.] Hairy; = PILOSE.

Pilot (pəi·lət), v. [f. prec.] trans. To conduct as a pilot; to direct the course of (a vessel) through difficult or dangerous waters; to steer, guide.

PILT.

PILOT.

Pea-jacket; pilot-flag = pilot-jack; pilot-flame = pilot-light; pilot-frame, a low truck supported the fore-part of a locomotive engine...

PIMENTO. 868

Piment (pəi·ment). Obs. Also 3-5 (8) piment, piment, 4-6 pyment, 4-6 (8) pyment, pymente. [a. OF. piment (written 12th c. pimenz), Sp. pimiento, pimienta (scented unguent; in med.L. spiced drink, bastard...

Pimento (pəime·nto). [ad. Sp. pimienta, pimiento = Pg. pimenta, pepper (generally), repr. L. pigmenta pl. of pigmentum, in med.L. spiced drink, bastard-pepper: see PIGMENT.]

Pimlico (pi·mlĭkŏ). [Origin unknown.]

Pimlico. [Echoic from the cry of the bird.] † **1.** Variant of PIMLICO. Obs. The Australian friar-bird: see FRIAR 2b 6.

Pimp (pimp), sb.[1] [Origin obscure.]

Generally thought to be in some way related to 16th c. F. *pimper*-n., *pe-pple*, *pimper*al or *seducing* in outward appearance or dress, *pimpescocte* a pretentious woman (Hatzf.)...

Pimp, sb.[2] dial. A name in London and the southern counties for a small faggot or bundle of firewood.

Pimp, v.[1] [f. PIMP sb.[1]]

1. intr. To act as pimp or pander; to pander.

Pimlico[2] (pimliko). [Echoic from the cry of the bird.]

Pimpel, variant of PIPPLE v.

† **Pi-mper**, v.[1] dial. In b 6 pimp-. [Attenuated from *pamper*.] trans. I. To pamper, coddle.

† **Pimper**, v.[2] rare. [Cf. early mod. Du. *pimperen* to blink, look through half-shut eyes (Kilian).] intr. (?) To blink.

Pimpernel (pimpanel). Forms: α. 5 pimpernelle, -nell), 4-6 pympper-(-ir-, -yr-)-nol, -nel, -nele, -nell(e, -nyll, 6-7 pimpernoll, 6 pimpernel, (6-8 pimpernall), 8 pimpernill. 8-(in senses 1, 2) pimpinell, 9 -ol. [a OF. *pimper-nelle*, *pimpernelle*, earlier *pimprenelle* (12th c.)...]

Pimpernol. Obs. [- OF. *pimpernol*, *-nean*, 'a broad-nosed variety of the common eel' (G. A. Boulanger), 'a grig, scaffling, spitchcocke, fenow Eele' (Cotgr.)...]

Pimping, vbl. sb. and ppl. a.: see PIMP v.

Pimple (pimp'l), sb. Forms: 4 pimpe, 6 pymple, pimpel, 6-7 (9 dial.) pumple. [Origin unknown : connexion with 1. *papula* or *pupula* the skin con- jectured...]

1. A small solid rounded tumour of the skin, usually inflammatory, without, or rarely with, purulent or pustular...

Pimple, v. rare. [f. prec. sb.] **1.** trans. To raise pimples upon ; to spot or deface with pimples (in quot. fig.). b. intr. To become pimply. Hence **Pimpling** vbl. sb. and ppl. a.

Pimpled (pimp'ld), a. [f. prec. sb. or vb. + -ED.] Having, or characterized by, pimples.

Pimple-stone: see PIMBLE-. † **Pimpling**: see PIPPLING ppl. a. **Pimple-toe**: see PIMPILLO.

Pimply (pimpli), a. [f. PIMPLE sb. + -Y.] Full of pimples ; covered or spotted with pimples.

Pimpillo, -owe, var. PIMPILLOW Obs., the prickly pear.

Pimping, vbl. sb. and ppl. a.: see PIMP v.

Pin (pin), sb.[1] Forms: α. 1 pinne, pinn, 5-6 pyn, (5 penne, pyne, 6 pynn, pine), 6-8 pin, pun. [Late OE. *pinn*, a common Low Ger. word: MLG., LG. *pinne*...]

I. A primary sense: = *peg*.

1. A small piece of wood, metal, or other solid substance, of cylindrical or similar shape, often tapering or pointed, used for some one of various purposes, as to fasten or hold together parts of a structure, to hang something upon, to stop up a hole, or as a part of mechanism to convey or check motion ; a peg.

Pin, sb.[2] local. [Origin obscure: perh. connected with PIN v.] **1.** The middle place in a tandem team of three horses.

Pin, sb.[3] Chess. [In PIN v. 5 b.] The act of pinning, the fact of being pinned.

Pin (pin), v.[1] Forms: see the sbs. [In branch I. f. PIN sb.[1] In branch II., perh. worn down from PIND v., but blending with I. in the sense 'fasten'.]

I. To transfix, fix, attach, confine, with a pin.

1. trans. To fasten (things or parts of a thing) together, or one thing to another ...

†Piña (pī'nǎ). Also 6 pinna, 6- pina. [S. Amer. Sp. *piña* (formerly *pinna*), Pg. *pinha* pine-apple, orig. pine-cone, pine-nut (ad. L. *pinea*.)

†1. (Spelt *pina, pinna, pinna*.) The pine-apple.

2. Pine-apple leaf fibres (Simmonds *Dict. Trade* 1858) ; a fine fabric made of this, usually called piña-cloth, piña-muslin, pine-apple cloth.

Pinace, obs. form of PINNACE.

Pinaces (pīnǎ'sēz). *n. rare.* [f. mod.Bot.

1. *Pinaceæ* the pine family.

†Pina-cloth. Obs. rare⁻¹. Characters unknown: the *quoc* corresponds probably with the first under PIQUET M.]

Pinacle, obs. form of PINNACLE.

Pinacocyte (pinǎ'kosǎit). *Zool.* [f. Gr. πίναξ, πίνακ- tablet + -CYTE.]

†Pinacoid (pī'nǎkoid). Obs. rare.

Pinacoid, pinakoid (pī'nǎkoid). *a.* and *sb.* *Cryst.* [f. Gr. πίναξ, πίνακ- slab : see -OID.]

Pinacolin (pinǎ'kolin). *Chem.* [f. next +

Pinacone (pī'nǎkōn). *Chem.* [f. Gr. πίναξ tablet + -ONE.]

†Pinacotheca as pī'nǎkoθēkǎ). Also anglicized as pī·nacothe·k (-ǒk). [L. *pinacotheca* (Varro).

†Pincette (pɛ̃set). *Obs.* Also 6 pynsettes. [a. F. *pincette* (Cotgr.)

Pinbe (pɔi'n). *Chem.* [f. PIN-IC + -ATE⁴.]

Pinax (pī'næks). *Pl.* pinaces (pī'nǎsēz). [a. Gr. πίναξ board, plank, tablet, picture.]

Pin-ball (pin'bǎl). *U.S.* [f. PIN *sb.*¹ + BALL *sb.*¹]

Pin-ba·sket. *local.*

Pin-before, *obs. rare⁻¹.* [f. PIN *v.*¹ + BEFORE.]

Pin-case.

†Pince. Obs. [Variant of PINCH *sb.*; perh. immed. a. F. *pince*.]

Pincel, obs. variant of PENCIL, PENCILLER.

Pince-nes (pɛ̃s·ne). *F. pince-nez, lit.* pinch-nose, nip-nose.]

Pincer (pi'nsǎr). *v.* [f. PINCERS.] *trans.* To nip or pinch with pincers ; to torture or wring with or as with pincers.

†Pincern. Obs. rare⁻¹. [ad. late med.L. *pincerna*, a. late L. *pincerna* cup-bearer, prop. a wine-mixer, f. *misco* to drink + *expírocum* to mix : cf. OF. *bincerne* a butler.] A cup-bearer.

Pincers (pi'nsǎrz). *sb. pl.* Rarely (exc. in comb.) in sing. form pincer (pi'nsǎr). Forms : 4-6 pynceoure, 4-5 pyncourz, -soura, 6-7 pinsons, -80es, pinsars, 6-7 -so3-6, pincers.

Pinch ; cf. OF. *pincheure* pincers, tongs, *pincair* (= *pincer*) pincers. See also PINSON 7.]

1. A tool for tightly grasping or nipping anything, consisting of two limbs pivoted together, forming a pair of jaws with a pair of handles or levers by which they can be pressed tightly together.

2. An organ (or pair of organs), in various animals, resembling pincers, and used for grasping or tearing ; as the claws of crustaceans, the incisor teeth of a horse, etc.

3. *Comb.*, as *pincer-grip* ; *pincer-like adj.*

Pincette (pɛ̃se't). Also 6 pynset(te, 6-7 pincet. [F. *pincette* small pincers, dim. of *pince* a pair of pincers.]

Pinch (pinʃ). *sb.* Forms : see next. [f. PINCH *v.*]

1. An act of pinching ; the compression between the finger and thumb or two opposing surfaces ; a nip, a squeeze ; †a seizure with the teeth, a bite (obs.).

2. Pressure, stress (usually of want, misfortune, or the like) ; difficulty, hardship.

3. The origin or pang of pinching ; compression between the teeth or lips ; sharp censure.

Pinch (pinʃ), *v.* Forms : 4-6 pinche, 5 pynche, (4-5 pinche, 6 pyntche, pynshe, pench(e, 5c. 5c. pinche, 7 pynch.) 6- pinch. 8 ONF. *pinchier* (= OF. *pincier*.

Pinchbeck (pi'nʃbek). *sb.*² [Named after the inventor Christopher Pinchbeck, a watch-maker in Fleet Street, London (died 1732), orig. a place-name ; there is a village so named near Spalding.] Hence *fig.* Pinchbeckiness. †Pinchbeckism.

Pinche (pinʃ). Also 8 pinch. [F. ; cf. Sp. *pincho* (also in Eng. use.) A South American species of marmoset (*Midas œdipus*). Also *attrib.*

Pinched (pinʃt). *ppl. a.*

†Pincher. Obs. [f. PINCH *v.* + -ER¹.]

Pinching (pi'nʃiŋ), *ppl. a.* (*adv.*) [f. PINCH *v.* + -ING².]

Pinching (pi'nʃiŋ), *vbl. sb.* [f. PINCH *v.* + -ING¹.]

†Pinchpenny. Obs. [f. PINCH *v.* + PENNY.]

Pincushion (pi'nkuʃǎn). [f. PIN *sb.*¹ + CUSHION.]

PINFOLD

PINE (pəin), *sb.*¹ *Obs.* or *arch.* Forms: [Early ME. *pine*—OE. *pín, píne, a.* L. *pœna* punishment, pain (see Pogatscher § 130–134). Cf. OS. *pína*, (MD. *pîne*, Du. *pijn*), OHG. *pína* (MHG. *pîne, pîn*, G. *pein*), ON. *pína*, Da. *pine*, Sw. *pina*, all from Latin. L. *pœna* introduced into Teut. and Celtic with Christianity, and in sense 'torment of hell.'…]

† 1. Punishment; suffering inflicted as punishment, torment, torture; *spec.* the penal sufferings of hell or of purgatory.

b. Mental suffering; grief, sorrow, trouble or anguish.

Pine (pəin), *sb.*² Forms: 1 pin, 4– pine also 4 pynn, 4–5 pyne, 5–7 pyn. [OE. *pín, ad.* L. *pínus a* pine-tree, in MF. *f. pin.*]

1. A tree of the genus *Pinus*, or of various allied coniferous genera; comprising trees, mostly of large size, with evergreen needle-shaped leaves, of which many species afford valuable timber, tar, turpentine and some have edible seeds.

PINE. 879 **PINE-APPLE.** **PINEATE.** 880 **PINFOLD.**

Pine-apple (pəinˌæp'l), *sb.* Forms: 1 pin-æppel, 4– pine-apple… [PINE *sb.*² + APPLE.]

1. The fruit of the pine-tree; a pine-cone.

2. The plant which bears this, *Ananas sativa*, a native of tropical South America.

Pinge (pindȝ), *sb.* and *v.* Echoic: cf. PING *sb.*]

Pingle (pi·ŋ'l), *sb.*[1] *Sc.* [f. PINGLE *v.*]

Pingle (pi·ŋ'l), *sb.*[2] *Sc.* [Of uncertain origin: cf. PIGHTLE.] A small enclosed piece of land; a paddock, a close.

Pingle (pi·ŋ'l), *v.*[1] *Sc.* Struggle with difficulties; strenuous exertion.

Pingle (pi·ŋ'l), *v.*[2] *Sc.* To press hard in a contest, to trouble, worry.

Pingle (pi·ŋ'l), *sb.*[3] *Sc.* [Origin unknown.] A small pan or cooking-pot of tinned iron, having a long handle. Also *pingle-pan*.

Ping (piŋ), *sb.* Also reduplicated. [Echoic.]

Ping (piŋ), *v.* [Echoic: cf. PING *sb.*]

Pingler. *Obs.* [f. prec. II + -ER[1].]

Pin-gout, *sb.* see PIN *sb.*[1] 18.

Ping-pong (pi·ŋ'pɒŋ), *sb.* [Echoic. Cf. PING *sb.*] A parlour game resembling lawn-tennis.

Ping-pong *v. intr.*, to play ping-pong; **Ping-ponger** (pi·ŋ'pɒŋəɹ), a ping-pong player or enthusiast.

Pin-grass, **-ground**: see PIN *sb.*[1] 18.

Pinguecula, incorrect form of PINGUICULA.

Pinguescence (piŋgwe·sens), *sb.* [ad. L. *pinguescent-em*, ppl. pple. of *pinguēscĕre* to grow fat, f. *pinguis* fat: see -ENCE.] Becoming or growing fat, fattening; fleshiness.

Pinguescent (piŋgwe·sent), *a.* [ad. L. *pinguescent-em*: see prec.] Becoming or growing fat, fleshy.

Pinguedinous (piŋgwī·dinəs), *a.* [f. L. *pinguēdin-, pinguēdo* fatness + -OUS.] Of the nature of or resembling fat.

Pinguefy (pi·ŋgwifai), *v.* Now *rare*. Also 6-9 erron. pinguify.

Pinguescence, erron. form of PENGUIN.

Pinguicula (piŋgwi·kiŭla), [ad. L. to represent Ger. *fettkraut* or butterwort.] *Bot.* A genus of small stemless insectivorous bog plants.

Pinguid (pi·ŋgwid), *a.* [ad. L. *pinguis* fat.] Fat, unctuous, greasy, oily; of soil: rich, fertile.

Pinguidinous, *a.* [f. L. *pinguēdin-*: see prec.] Fatty.

Pinguin, obs. form of PENGUIN.

Pinguinitescent (piŋgwinite·sent), *a.* [f. *pingui-* + NITESCENT.]

Pinguite (pi·ŋgwait), *sb.* [ad. G. *pinguit*.] *Min.* A hydrous silicate of aluminium and potassium.

Pinguitude (pi·ŋgwitiūd), *sb.* [ad. L. *pinguitūdin-, pinguitūdo* fatness.] Fatness.

Pin-head, *sb.* see PIN *sb.*[1] 18. The head of a pin, a pin's head.

Pin-hole (pi·nhōul), *sb.* see PIN *sb.*[1] 18.

Piniferous (pini·fərəs), *a.* [f. L. *pīni-, pīnus* PINE + -FEROUS.] Bearing or producing pine-trees.

Piniform (pi·nifɔɹm), *a.* Having the form of a pine-cone.

Pining (pai·niŋ), *vbl. sb.* [f. PINE *v.*[1] + -ING[1].]

Pining (pai·niŋ), *ppl. a.* [f. PINE *v.*[1] + -ING[2].]

Pinic (pai·nik), *a.* *Chem.* [ad. F. *pinique*, f. *pin* PINE: see -IC.]

Pinicoline (paini·kəlain), *a.* *Zool. rare*. Living or growing on pine-trees.

Pinicolous (paini·kələs), *a.* [f. as prec. + -OUS.] Living or growing among pine-woods.

Pinite (pi·nait, pai-), *sb.*[1] *Min.* [Named (Ger. *Pinit*) by A. Breithaupt, 1829, f. L. *pinguis* fat: see -ITE[2].] An olive-green hydrated silicate of alumina.

Pinite (pai·nait), *sb.*[2] *Chem.* [f. F. *pinite*, f. *pinus* PINE-tree.]

Pinivorous (paini·vərəs), *a.* [f. L. *pīni-, pīnus* pine + -VOROUS.] That feeds on pine-trees.

Pinjane (pi·ndʒein). Also pinjeen. [Manx - Gael. *binnjeen*. Ir. *binidean* rennet.] 'Curds and whey' (E. D. D.).

Pink (piŋk), **penk** (peŋk). Forms: 4- 5 pink, 7 penck, pencke. Also 8 pynk. A name applied to several small fish.

Pink (piŋk), *sb.*[2] *Chem.* [f. prec.] *Zool.* A young of the salmon; a minnow.

Pink (piŋk), *sb.*[3] Now chiefly *Hist.* Forms: 5-7 pinck, 6 pyncke, 6-7 pincke, 7 pink, 6-9 pink. [app. a. MDu. *pincke, pinke*, name of a small sea-going ship, also a fishing-boat.] A ship with a narrow stern.

†Pinnace, *sb.*[4] [Etymology obscure.] A kind of small ship.

Pink (piŋk), *sb.*[5] [The general name of various species of *Dianthus* (N.O. *Caryophyllaceae*), esp. of *D. plumarius*, a favourite garden plant. Also the colour of this flower: a pale red or rose colour.]

PINION. 883 PINIPICRIN. PINITE. 884 PINK.

Pinion (pi·njən), *sb.*[1] [a. OF. *pignon*, *pinion*, in Froissart a lance in pl. 'wing feathers, wings, feathers', a collateral form of OF. *pennon, pennne* (also 'feather of an arrow', and 'streamer, pennon').]

Pinion (pi·njən), *sb.*[2] *Mech.* [ad. mod.F. *pignon* in same sense MOD.F. *pignon* latch-piece (see 2), the teeth of a wheel being compared to the crenellations of battlements.]

Pinion (pi·njən), *sb.*[3] *Obs.* exc. *dial.* Also 6 pynion, 4 pynyon. [a. OF. *pignon*, *piñon*, *piñon* (Godef.), mod.F. *pignon* in same sense, Romanic augmentative of L. *pinus* battlement, pinnacle.] A battlement, pinnacle.

Pinion (pi·njən), *v.* [f. PINION *sb.*[1]]

Pinioned (pi·njənd), *ppl. a.* [f. PINION *sb.*[1] + -ED[1], or PINION *v.* + -ED[1].]

Pin-iron (pi·naiəɹn), *sb.* Also pinirn. Woollen Manuf. An iron used in the combing process.

Pinic, var. of PINIC.

Pinion-leaf ... (various sub-entries)

Pinionless, *a.* *rare*[1]. [f. PINION *sb.*[1] + -LESS.] Without pinions; wingless.

Pinipicrin (painipi·krin), *sb.* *Chem.* [f. L. *pīni-, pīnus* pine + Gr. πικρός bitter + -IN[1].] A bitter substance.

Pink (piŋk), *a.* [f. PINK *sb.*[5]] 1. Of the colour of the flower called *pink*; pale red or rose colour.

Pink, sb. [Echoic.] 1. An imitation of the note of the chaffinch (often reduplicated, *pink-pink*); hence *transf.*, a local name of the bird itself.

Pink, a.[1] and sb.[4] Obs. or dial. [Of obscure history.] a. adj. used chiefly in *pink eye*, † *pink nye*, where it seems to be related to Du. *pink oeghen*: see PINK n.[2]; the sb. is used more widely in Sc.: cf. Du. *pink* the little finger, also a young bullock, a steer; pointing to an original sense 'something small.'

Pink (piŋk), v.[1] Forms: 4-6 pynke, 6 pynk, pyncke, 6-7 pinke, pincke, 6-8 pinck, 6 wick.

1. *intr.* To make holes; to prick, thrust, stab. Now *rare* (or only as dial.). Obs. or D. as a person.

2. *trans.* To pierce, prick, or stab with any pointed weapon or instrument.

3. To ornament (cloth, leather, or the like) by cutting or punching eyelet-holes, figures, letters, etc.

4. To cut or puncture the skin as an adornment; to tattoo.

Pinkeen (piŋkī·n), *dial.* A little minnow; *fig.* a very diminutive or insignificant person.

Pinken (piŋ·kən), v. *rare.* [f. PINK a.[2] + -EN.] *intr.* To become pink.

Pink (piŋk), sb.[3] Obs. exc. dial. Forms: 6 pynke, 6-7 pinck, pinke, 7- pink. [-Du. *pinke* to steer in the eyes (Kilian 1678), to wick.]

Pinker (piŋ·kər), v. [freq. of PINK v.[1]] *intr.* To twinkle.

Pink (piŋk), v.[2] [app. echoic.] *intr.* To trickle, drip; also, to make a tinkling sound in dripping. Hence **Pink** sb.[5] a drop, also the sound made by a drop.

Pinked (piŋkt), *ppl. a.* [f. PINK v.[1] + -ED.] 1. Pierced, pricked, wounded; also, tattooed.

2. Of cloth, leather, etc.: having perforations, or (later) cut edges; slashed, scalloped.

Pink-eye (piŋk·əi), sb.[1] (Also *pink-for potato*.) A variety of potato having pink eyes or buds.

2. A contagious fever or influenza in the horse.

3. An Australian species of duck (see quot.).

Pink-eyed (piŋk·əid), a.[1] Obs. exc. dial. 1. Having small, narrow, or half-closed eyes; also, squint-eyed.

2. Of a pink or rosy colour.

Pinkie, pinky (piŋ·ki), sb.[1] and a.[3] Chiefly Sc. [Either f. PINK a.[2], or the orig. form of that word.] a. The smallest finger.

2. adj. Small, diminutive; tiny; in general sense, a childish word.

Pinkerton (piŋ·kərtən). [From the name of Allan Pinkerton, who organized a body of detectives in the U.S. in 1850.] a. *attrib.* Applied to the semi-official detective force originally organized and controlled by Allan Pinkerton. b. *sb.* A member of this force.

Pinkish (piŋ·kiʃ), a.[1] [f. PINK a.[2] + -ISH.] Somewhat pink; having a shade of pink.

Pinkly (piŋ·kli), adv.[1] [f. PINK a.[2] + -LY[2].] With a pink hue.

Pinkness (piŋ·knes). [f. PINK a.[2] + -NESS.] The quality or state of being pink; pink colour.

Pinkster (piŋ·kstər). U.S. (N.Y.) Also **pingster, pinxter**. [Du. *pinxter* (now *pinkster*), MDu., Ger. *pfingsten* (= OHG. *fimfchusti* Goth. *paintekoste*) Whitsuntide.]

Pinky (piŋ·ki), a.[2] [f. PINK sb.[3] + -Y[1].] Abounding in pinks, or resembling a pink.

Pinless (pin·les), a. [-LESS.] Without a pin or pins.

Pin-money (pin·mʌni), sb. 3 + MONEY: see quots. 1542-1640. [Cf. F. *épingles*, in Littré, sense 2.] An annual sum allotted for the personal expenses in dress, etc.; *esp.* such an allowance in money.

Pinna (pi·nă). Zool. [L. *pinna*, variant of *pina* (Cic., Plin.), a Gr. πίννα (also πίνα, πίνη), in same sense.] A genus of bivalve molluscs, having a large silky byssus or 'beard.'

Pinna. Pl. -ae (formerly also -as). [mod.L., use of L. *pinna* a feather, wing, fin, etc.] 1. *Anat.* The 'wing' of the ear, the broad upper part of the external ear; also applied to the whole external ear.

2. Each lateral cartilage of the nose. — ALA 1.

3. *Zool.* A feather, or one of the feathers of a wing.

Pinnacle (pi·năk'l), sb. Forms: 4-6 pynakle, 4-7 pinnacle, 6 -nakle, 5-6 pynnacle, 6- pinnacle. [a. OF. *pinacle*, ad. late L. *pinnāculum.*] 1. A turret, or one of a number of turrets, usually terminating in a pyramid or cone, crowning a buttress, angle of a parapet, or other portion of a building.

Pinnacle (pi·năk'l), v. [f. prec. sb.] 1. *trans.* To set or as on a pinnacle; *in quot.* 1846, to rear as a pinnacle.

Pinnacled (pi·năk'ld), *ppl. a.* [PINNACLE] Having or furnished with pinnacles or peaks.

Pinnaculate (pi·năk·iūlit), a. Obs. [f. PINNACLE + -ATE[2].]

Pinnage (pi·nedʒ). Obs. [f. PIN sb.[1] + -AGE.] 1. The action of impounding cattle. 2. The fee for impounding.

Pinnal (pi·năl). Sc. form of PINNACLE.

Pinnate (pi·net), a. [ad. L. *pinnātus* feathered, winged, f. *pinna* feather, wing.] 1. Resembling a feather; having lateral parts or branches on each side of a common axis, like the vanes of a feather.

Pinnated (pi·netid), a. = prec. 1.

Pinnately (pi·netli), adv. In a pinnate manner or form; so as to form pinnae.

Pinnation (pinē·ʃən). Bot. and Ornith. The quality or state of being pinnate; also, a formation or division into pinnae.

Pinnato- (pi·năto-), occasional advb. combining form of L. *pinnātus* PINNATE, or (DENTATE) pinnate, with toothed leaflets: **Pinna·to-pe·ctinate** a. [PECTINATE].

Pinner[1] (pi·nər). [f. PIN v. + -ER[1].] 1. A coif with two long flaps, one on each side, pinned on and hanging down, worn by women in the 17th and 18th centuries.

Pinner[2]. Now local. [Another form of PINNER[1] or PIN v.] An officer whose duty it is to impound stray beasts; a pinder.

Pinner[3]. [f. PIN v.[1] + -ER[1].] One who or that which pins.

PIP. 893 **PIPE.** **PIPE.** 894 **PIPE.**

PIPE. 895 **PIPE.** **PIPE.** 896 **PIPER.**

2. Popular name of several kinds of fish. A species of gurnard, *Trigla lyra*; so called from the sound it makes when caught. †b.

Piper. [f. PIPE *sb.*[1] or *v.*[1] + -ER[1].] **1.** (?) A workman who lays or repairs pipes; a plumber. *Obs.*

b. One who smokes tobacco in a pipe. Now *rare*.

Piperaceous, *a.* [f. Bot. L. *Piperaceæ* + -OUS.] †**a.** Of the nature of pepper; pungent. *Obs.* **b.** Belonging to the Natural Order *Piperaceæ*, the pepper tribe (typical genus *Piper*).

Piperic (pipe'rik), *a. Chem.* [f. L. *piper* pepper + -IC.] Pertaining to or derived from pepper; in *piperic acid*, an acid ($C_{12}H_{10}O_4$) obtained by boiling piperine with potash.

Piperide, variant of PIPERIDE.

Piperidine (pipe'ridəin), *Chem.* [mod. f. L. C$_5$H$_{11}$N] produced by the action of alkalis on piperine.

Piperine (pi'pərin), *sb.* [f. L. *piper*.] *Chem.* An alkaloid ($C_{17}H_{19}NO_3$) obtained from species of pepper (*Piper nigrum* and *P. longum*).

Piperno, variant of PEPERINO.

Pipe-roll. [f. PIPE *sb.*[1] + ROLL *sb.*] The Great Roll of the Exchequer.

Pipe-work. [f. PIPE *sb.* + WORK *sb.*]

Pipe-stapple. *Sc.* and *north. dial.* Also **-staple, -stopple.**

Pipette (pipe't), *sb.* [a. F. *pipette*, dim. of *pipe* PIPE *sb.*[1] See -ETTE.] A pipe or tube of small calibre, and of various forms, used esp. in chemistry or in scientific experiments) to transfer or measure small quantities of a liquid or gas.

Piperivorous (pipe'rivərəs), *a. rare⁻⁰.* [f. mod. L. *piper* pepper + *-vorus* devouring.] Feeding on pepper, as a bird.

Piperly, *a. rare⁻¹.*

Pipery, variant of PEPERINO.

Pipi. **1.** A hard red clay or soft stone used by the American Indians for tobacco-pipes: see CATLINITE. **b.** *Maori.* Name of a shell-fish.

Pipient, *a. rare.* [ad. L. *pipient-, -ens*, pr. pple. of *pipire* to cheep.] Piping or chirping like a chicken or young bird.

Piping, *vbl. sb.* [f. PIPE *v.*[1] + -ING[1].] The action of PIPE *v.*[1] **1.** Playing on a pipe; the music of pipes or wind-instruments.

Piping, *ppl. a.* [f. PIPE *v.*[1] + -ING[2].] That is piping; characterized by piping.

Pipistrelle, -el (pipistre'l), *sb.* [a. F. *pipistrelle*.] A small species of bat, *Vespertilio pipistrellus*.

Pipit (pi'pit). Also 8 pippet, -it, 9 pipet. [prob. imitative of the bird's note.] Name of various small birds of the family *Motacillidæ*.

Pippin. **1.** The seed of certain fruits; others: cf. PIP *sb.*

Pipple (pi'p'l), *v. Obs.* Also 6 pypple (pimpel).

Pipple-stone, [Echoic.] A representation of the sound of a Mauser rifle.

Pippy (pi'pi), *a.* [f. PIP *sb.*[1] and *b.*[1] + -Y[1].] Full of pips.

Piquant (pi'kant), *a.* [a. F. *piquant*, pr. pple. of *piquer* to prick, sting.] **1.** Agreeably pungent or sharp of taste; sharp, stinging.

Piquancy (pi'kansi). Also 7 piqu-. [f. PIQUANT + -CY.] **1.** Sharpness, severity. *Obs.*

Pique (pīk), *sb.*[1] [a. F. *pique*, f. *piquer*.] **1.** A feeling of anger, resentment, or ill-will, resulting from some slight or injury, esp. such as wounds one's pride or vanity; offence taken.

Pique (pīk), *v.*[1] [f. prec. or a. F. *piquer*.] **1.** *trans.* To excite the feelings of; to excite anger, resentment, or enmity; to irritate, to offend by wounding pride or vanity.

Piqué (pi'kē), *sb.* **Comb. Piqué work**: a kind of decorative needlework.

Piquet (pike't). Forms: 6-7 picket, pick-et, 7 pickett, picquet, -quette, 7- piquet. [a. F. *piquet*.] A card-game played by two persons with a pack of 32 cards.

Piqueur (pikö'r). Also anglicized as PICKER.

Pirace, *v. Obs. rare.* [Abnormal formation f. PIRACY.]

Piracy (pai'rəsi). [med. L. *piratia*, a. Gr. πειρατεία, f. πειρατής PIRATE.] **1.** The practice or crime of robbery and depredation on the sea or navigable rivers, etc.

Piragua, variant of PERAI, S. American fish.

Pirameter, variant spelling of PEIRAMETER.

Piramidig, var. obs. f. PYRAMID.

Piramidig (pi·rămidig). [Echoic, after the bird's call.] A name given in the W. Indies to a bird's-nest bird...

Pirastic,k, variant of PEIRASTIC.

Pirate (pai·rĕt), sb. Also 5-8 pyrat·e, 6 pyraote, pirote, -atte, 6-7 pyrote, pyra, 7 pyrat. [ad. L. pīrāta, a Gr. πειρατής, f. πειρᾶν to attempt, attack, assault. Cf. F. pirate (1448 in Hatz.-Darm.), Sp. Pg., It. pirata. Du. piraat.]

1. One who roves and plunders on the sea, navigable rivers, etc., or cruises about for that purpose; a sea-robber...

Pirate (pai·rĕt), v. Also 7 pyrate.

1. *intr.* To practise piracy; to plunder...

Pirateer, obs. form of PRIVATEER.

Piratery (pai·rətəri), rare. Also piratry.

Piratic (pairæ·tik), a. [ad. L. pīrāticus, a Gr. πειρατικός.] Of or pertaining to a pirate or piracy...

Piratical (pairæ·tikăl), a. [f. as prec. + -AL.]

Piratically, adv. [f. prec. + -LY.] In a piratical manner; by piracy.

Piratism, var. [f. PIRATE sb. + -ISM.]

Piratize, v. Obs. rare⁻⁰.

Piraya, variant of PERAI, PIRANHA.

Pirol, obs. form of PEROL (?).

Pire, v. Obs. exc. dial. Also 9 pyre. [ME. *piren*, identical in form and sense with LG. (in Brem. Wbch.) and EFris. *pīren*, of unknown origin...

Pirie, obs. form of PEAR, PEARY.

Pirl, sb. [? var. PURL sb. and v.]

Pirl, v.

Pirlie, pirlie-, variants of PORLICE.

Pirliewinkle = PILLIWINKS.

‖ **Pirn**, sb. Obs. rare⁻¹. [app. metathesis of prin, prene, PREEN, a pin.] A pointed twig or branch.

‖ **Pirn** (pərn, pirn), sb. Chiefly north and Sc. Dial. Also 5-8 pyrn, etc.: see quots.

Piraya (pirai·ă), variant of PERAI, PIRANHA.

Pirok, obs. form of PERK 2.

Pirn (pərn), v. Obs. exc. dial. Also 9 pyrne.

Pirnie, pirny (pə·rni), a. and sb. Sc. [app. related to prec. sb. and to PIRN sb. sense 4.]

Pirnie, pirny (pə·rni), sb.² Diminutive of PIRN sb.²

Pirogue (piro·g). Also 7 pyrage, pyrogua, 8-9 periroga, 9 perogua, periogua, perogue. See also PIRAGUA.

Pirol, obs. form of PEROL.

Pirr, sb. Sc. Also pirro, purro. [Onomatopoeic.]

Pirr, v. Sc. [Onomatopoeic: goes with PIRR sb.¹]

Pirre, obs. var. pirre.

Pirrie, var. PERRIE Obs.; jewellery; var. PIRR sb.²

Pirrikick, Pirritie, obs. ff. PYRRHIC, PYRITE.

Pirrie, pirry (pi·ri). Now only dial. Forms: 5-6 pyrry, pyrie, 5-7 pery, 6 pyrry, -ye, -ie, pirie, pierie, pierrie, perrys, -e, 6-7 pirry, perry 9 -ie, and dial. perry ; also n. parry, -y. [Of unknown origin.]

Pirate, obs. f. PIRATE (Cotgr.); cf. PIDDOCK.

Pirotte, obs. form of PIRATE.

Pirouette (pirue·t), sb. Also 8 pi-, pyroet.

Pirouette (pirue·t), v. [f. F. pirouetter, f.

Pirow, Pirrow, variant of PERROW Obs.

Pirry, variant of PERRY 1 Obs., pear-tree.

Pirwike, -wycke, obs. ff. PERUKE, PERIWIG.

Pirwinkle, obs. ff. PERIWINKLE (? the mollusc).

Pиry, var. PERRY, PERRY 1; obs. f. PERRY 2.

Pisa (pai·ză). Name of a city in Italy.

Pis aller (pīzale). [F., lit. 'go worst.']

Pisan, variant of PEshCUSM, an offering.

Piscary (pi·skări), sb. rare. [ad. L. piscārius a fisherman ; a fishmonger.]

Piscation (piskē·ʃən). rare. [ad. L. piscātiōn-em, n. of action f. piscāri to fish, f. piscis a fish.] Fishing.

Piscatology (piskătɔ·lədʒi). rare.

Piscator (piskē·tɔɹ), [L. = a fisher.]

Piscatorial (piskătɔ·riăl), a. [f. L. piscātōri-us + -AL.] Of or pertaining to fishermen or fishing.

Piscatorially, adv.

Piscatory (pi·skătəri), a. [ad. L. piscātōri-us, f. piscātor.] Of or pertaining to fishermen or fishing; of fishers.

Pisang (pi·sæŋ). Also 7 pisan, pisang, pysangh. [Malay *písang*.] The Malay name of the Banana.

Piscary (pi·skări), sb. Also 7 piscary, -ie.

Pisciculture (pi·sikʌltjuɹ). [f. L. pisci-, piscis a fish + CULTURE.] The rearing of fish by artificial means.

Pisciculturist (pisikʌ·ltjuɹist).

Piscifauna (pisifɔ·nă).

Pisciform (pi·sifɔɹm), a. [f. L. pisci- + -FORM.] Having the form of a fish.

Piscina (pisai·nă), sb. Pl. -æ, -as. [L. piscīna a fishpond, bathing-pool, tank, f. piscis a fish.]

Piscine (pi·sin, -ain), a. [f. L. piscīn-us, f. piscis fish.] Of or pertaining to fish; fish-like.

Piscivorous (pisi·vərəs), a. [f. L. type *pisci-vor-us* (f. piscis fish + vorāre devour) + -OUS.] Fish-eating.

Pise, Pisé (pī·ze), sb. Also 8 pisay.

Pisgah (pi·zgă). Name of a mountain east of Jordan, whence Moses was allowed to view the Promised Land...

PISH.

Pish, *int.* An exclamation expressing contempt, impatience, or disgust.

Pish, *v.* [prec.]
1. *intr.* To say 'pish.' Often with *at.*

Hence **Pishing** *vbl. sb.*; also **Pisher**, one who pishes.

Pish, var. form of PISS.

Pishamin (piʃ'amin). Another form of PERSIMMON.

Pishogue, *sb. fig. Irish.* Also pishrogue, pishrogue, *sb. fig.* Sorcery, witchcraft; a spell, incantation, charm.

Pishmew, var. form of PISMIRE.

Pisidiid (pisi'diid). *Zool.* A member of the *Pisidiidæ*, a family of bivalve gastropod molluscs, typified by the genus *Pisidium*.

Pisiform (pai'sifɔːm, pi'-), *a.* (*sb.*) [ad. –FORM.]

Pisk, var. form of PISMIRE.

Pinkle, pisky, var. PIXY. Pisle, obs. f. PIZZLE.

Pismire (pi'smaiə). *Obs. exc. dial.* Forms:

b. *transf.*, and in various allusive and proverbial uses.

Pisser. [f. PISS v. + -ER[1].] One who pisses.

Pissing, *vbl. sb.* Not now in polite use.

Piss (pis), *sb.* Not now in polite use. Forms:

Piss (pis), *v.* Not now in polite use. Forms:

Pissabed (pi'səbed). *Obs. exc. dial.* [f. PISS v. + ABED.] Also in various dialects. A name for the dandelion.

Piss-ant. [f. PISS *sb.* + ANT.] cf. PISMIRE.

Pissasphalt (pi'səsfælt). Also in L (or Gr. L.) forms *pissasphaltum, -um, -os.* [ad. L. *pissasphalt-us* (Plin.), a. Gr. πισσάσφαλτος.]

Piss-a-prophet. *Obs. rare⁻¹.* Suppression (or retention) of urine.

Pist, *sb.*: see PISTE[1].

Pistacho (pistaː'tʃo, -tʃoˑ, -tʃi, -təˑʃ). Forms:

Pistacite (pi'stəsait). *Min.* [ad. Ger. *pistazit* (A. G. Werner, 1803), f. PISTACIA + -ITE.]

Pistacia (pistaː'ʃiə). *Bot.* [mod. L. *pistacia* tree (Pallad.), f. Gr. πιστακη.]

Pistaren (pistaˑrən). Also 8 pistereen, 9 -areen. [app. a popular formation from *peseta.*]

Pist, *sb.*: see PISTE[1].

Piste (pist), *pist* (pist). *F. piste* = It. *pista, pesta,* [a. F. piste, ad. It. *pesta, pista* (= Sp. *pista*), beaten track or trail, f. *pistare* to pound, stamp, f. pist-ppa. pple. of *pinsēre* to pound, crush.]

Pistia (pi'stiə). *Bot.* [mod. L. (Linn.)]

PISTIC.

Pistic (pi'stik), *a.* [ad. L. *pistic-us* (Vulg.), a. Gr. πιστικός perhaps 'genuine, pure', f. πίστις faith; but see quot. 1882.]

Pistil (pi'stil). *Bot.* [a. F. *pistil* (1690), ad. mod. L. *pistillum* PESTLE.] = PISTILLUM.

Pistilliferous (pistili'fərəs), *a. Bot.* [f. PISTILLUM + -FEROUS.]

Pistilligerous (-dʒərəs), *a. rare.* [f. PISTILLUM + -GEROUS.] Productive of or fertile in pistils.

Pistilline (pi'stilain), *a.* [f. Bot. L. *pistill-um* + -INE[1].] = PISTILLARY.

Pistillody (pi'stilodi). *Bot.* [mod. L. *pistill-um* + -ODY.]

Pistillogy. *erron. piste-logy.* [f. Gr. σληρ- + faith = court + religious belief.]

Pistillum (pi'stiləm). *Bot.* Forms. [a. L. *pistillum* (also *pistillus*), f. root of *pistus* pounded (see PESTLE).]

Pistil, var. PESTLE, PISTOL.

Pistle, *sb.* *Obs.* Forms: 1 pistol, 2-6 pistel, 4 pistol, etc.

Pistol (pi'stəl), *sb.* Also 6 pistolet, 6-7 pistoll, 7 pistole, etc.

Hence † **Pi'stole** (*nonce-wd.*) *trans.*, to write an epistle upon, assail with an epistle, satirize.

Pistler, Pistler, obs. f. PISTLE, EPISTLER.

Pistol, var. of PISTLE *sb.*

Pistol (pi'stəl), *v.* Also 6 pistole, 6-7 pistoll, 7 pistole. [f. PISTOL *sb.*]

Pistolade (pistoleː'd). *Obs.* [a. F. *pistolade.*]

Pistole (pistoˑl). *Obs.* Also 6 pistol, pystole, 6-7 pistoll. [a. F. *pistole* (16th c. in Hatz.-Darm.)]

Pistoleer, -ier (pistoli'ə). [a. F. *pistolier.*]

Pistolet (pi'stolet). *Obs.* [a. OF. *pistolet.*]

Pistolgraph (pi'stolgraf). Also pistolograph.

Pistolless. *Obs. rare.* [f. PISTOL + -LESS.]

Pistole (pistoˑl). *Obs.* Also pistol.

Pistoleer, -ier, var. PISTOLEER.

Pistoler (pi'stoleə). *Obs. rare.* [f. PISTOLE *sb.*]

Pistolet, -er. [var. of PISTOLET[1].]

Pistolo-. [ad. med.L. *pistolet.*]

Piston (pi'stən). Also 7 piston, 8 pistone. [a. F. *piston* (16th c. in Hatz.-Darm.), ad. It. *pistone,* var. of *pestone* great pestle, runner, augm. from stem *pist-* pound (see PESTLE).]

PISTOR.

Pistor (pĭstŏr). *Obs.* [L.] A baker.

Pistoria (pĭstōˈrĭă), *Obs.* [It.] A kind of dagger.

Pistol (pĭstŏl), *sb.* Forms: see below. [a. F. *pistole*, *pistolet* a. G. *pistole*.]

Pit (pit), *sb.¹* Forms: see below. [OE. *pytt*, ME. *putt*, *put*, *pet*, *pit* = OFris. *pet*, OS. *putti*, MLG., MDu. *putte*, LG. *putt*, OHG. *pfuzzi*, *pfuzza*, MHG., Ger. *pfütze* ; also ON. *pyttr* (from OE) ; all repr. a L. *puteus*.

A. Illustration of Forms.

B. Signification.

1. A hole or cavity in the ground, formed either by digging or by some natural process.

2. A hole dug or sunk in the ground for water; a well, a water-hole ; a pond, pool. *Obs.* or merged in 1.

3. A hole dug in the ground for a dead body; a grave. *Obs.* or *dial.*

II. † 8. A hollow or cavity in any vessel. *Obs.*

9. A hollow or indentation in an animal or plant body, or in any surface.

10. That part of the auditorium of a theatre which is on the floor of the house.

11. A place set apart for cock-fighting.

12. U.S.A. part of the floor of an Exchange appropriated to a special branch of business.

13. The framework supporting the pivoted yoke of a swinging bell in a belfry.

Pit, *sb.²* *U.S.* (and *Eng. dial.*) [app. a. Du. *pit*, early mod. and late MDu. *pitte* kernel, pip, radically agreeing with OE. *pȳða* marrow, PITH.] The stone of a stone-fruit.

Pit, *v.* [f. PIT *sb.¹*]

1. *trans.* To put or cast into a pit; to inter, bury.

2. To set (cocks, dogs, pugilists, etc.) to fight for sport, prop. in a 'pit' or enclosure.

3. To pit against (a person): to oppose to another.

4. To make hollows or depressions in; to mark with small scars or spots, as those left on the skin after small-pox.

PITCH

Pitch (pitʃ), *sb.¹* Forms: 1–2 pic; 5 pyth, 5–6 pych, 5 peche; 5–6 piche, pytche, pyche (5 peche), 5–6 piche, pytche, 6– pitch.

Pitch (pitʃ), *sb.²* Forms: 1–2 pic; 3–4 piche, 4–5 pich, pych, 5 pitche, 6– pitch.

Pitch, *v.¹* [f. PITCH *sb.²*]

Pitch, *v.²*

Pita (pīˈtă). Also 7 *peet*, 8–9 *pito*, 9 *pittee*. [ad. F. *pita*, or Sp. *pita* Also *pita-fibre*, *-flax*.]

Pitch. sb.² Forms: 3–4 piche, 4–5 piche, pecche, 5–6 pytche (6 pydche, 6–pight, † pecsho). Pa.t. and pp. pile, pitched, pight: see below. [ME. piche, v. Pa.t. pight, also pa.pple., pt. tenses of CLITCH, STITCH.]

Pitched, ppl.a.¹ [f. PITCH v.¹]

Pitch-back. v. [PITCH sb.¹ + v.¹ + BACK adv.]

Pitch-blende. Min. [ad. Ger. pechblende.] Native oxide of uranium.

Pitch-block: see PITCH sb.¹ 26.

Pitch-board. Obs. rare⁻¹.

Pitch-bottle. sb. ...

Pitch-boltery, etc.: see PITCH sb.¹

Pitch-brand.

Pitch-button.

Pitch-cap. sb. [f. PITCH sb.¹ 24.]

Pitch-chain, -diameter: see PITCH sb.¹ 26.

Pitch-circle, -coal: see PITCH sb.¹

Pitch-dark. a.

Pitched, ppl.a.² Also sb.² pykked, 6 piki... [PITCH sb.¹ + ED²]

Pitcher. sb.¹ Forms: 3–5 picher, 4–6 pycher (5–ere), 6 pyochar, (5–are), 6 pitcher, pytcher, pitchard, 5–picher, pytchar; 6–pitcher. [a. OF. pichier, pechier, picher (mod.F. pichet, pichier, pecher, pichier); etc.]

Pitcher. sb.² [f. PITCH v.¹]

Pitcher-ful. [PITCHER¹ + -FUL.]

Pitcher-man.

Pitcher-plant. [PITCHER¹ + PLANT sb.]

Pitchering. vbl.sb. [f. PITCHER + -ING¹.]

Pitch-faced. a. PITCH sb.¹ 26.

Pitch-farthing.

Pitch-fir: see PITCH sb.¹

Pitchfork. sb. Forms: 5 picheforke, 5 pycheforke, pytche-, pitche-, 6–pitchfork. [Also (in earlier use) PICKFORK.]

Pitchfork, sb.²

Pitchfork, v.
1. trans.
2. fig.

Pitch-hole¹

Pitch-hole²

Pitchiness, [f. Pitchy + -ness.]

Pitching, vbl. sb. [f. Pitch v.¹ + -ing¹.]
1.
2.
3.
4.
5.
6.
7.
8.
9.
10. Brewing.
11.

Pitching-bar ... : see Pitching vbl. sb.

Pitching, ppl. a.

Pitch-kettle, sb.

Pitch-in-the-hole

Pitch-knot, -ladle, -like: see Pitch sb.¹ 26.

Pitchlongs, adv. Obs. rare.

Pitch-mark, -mineral, -opal, etc.

Pitch-pine, sb.

Pitch-pipe, sb.

Pitch-plaster, sb.

Pitch-point ... : see Pitch sb.¹ 26.

Pitchpoll, -pole, sb., adv., dial.

Pitchpoll, -pole, v. intr.

Pitch-pot, etc.: see Pitch sb.¹

Pitch-resin, -rosin. Obs.

Pitch-speeched, -stain: see Pitch sb.¹

Pitchstone (pitʃstōn).

Pitch-tree: see Pitch sb.¹ + Tree sb.¹

Pitch-wheel: see Pitch sb.¹ 26.

Pitch-wine: see Pitch sb.¹

Pitchwork (pitʃwəɹk). [f. Pitch sb.²]

Pitchy (pitʃi), a. (adv.) [f. Pitch sb.¹ + -y.]
1.
2.
3.
b.

Pite, obs. var. pight, pa. pple. of Pitch v.; obs.

Piteous (pi·tiǝs), a. [ME. pitous, -e, OF. (12th c.) pitos, (13th c.) piteus...]
1.
2.
3.
4.
b.

† **Piteous**, adv. Obs.

† **Piteously**, adv.
1. With pity; piously, devoutly. Obs.
2. With pity; compassionately, mercifully, kindly.
3. In a manner that excites pity to see or hear; so as to call for or deserve pity; lamentably, grievously, sadly; pitiably.

† **Piteousness**.

Pitfall, sb. [f. Pit sb.¹ + Fall sb.²]
†1. A trap for the capture of birds in which a trap-door or the like falls over a cavity or hollow. Obs.
2.
b.
3. fig.

Pitfall, v.
1. To set with traps or pitfalls.
2. To entrap, ensnare. Also fig.

Pit-fold, sb.

+ **Pit-hold**, sb.

Pith (piθ), sb. [OE. piþa...]
1.
2.
3.
b.
4.
5.
6.

Pith, v.
1.
2.
b.

Pith-ball

Pithecanthrope (pi·θĕkănθrōp). Also in Latin form **Pithecanthropus**.

Pithecanthropic (pìθĕkănθrō·pik), a.

Pithecanthropoid (-poid), a.

Pithecanthropus: see Pithecanthrope.

Pithecian (piθē·siǎn), a. Zool. [ad. F. pithécien...]

Pithecoid (pi·θĭkoid), a.

Pithecological (-kǫ·lǫdʒǐkǎl), a. nonce-wd.

Pithful (pi·θful), a. [f. Pith sb. + -ful.]

Pithily (pi·θĭli), adv. [f. Pithy + -ly².]

† **Pithiness** (pi·θines). [f. Pithy a. + -ness.]

† **Pithless** (pi·θles), a. [f. Pith sb. + -less.]

Pithole

Pithos (pi·θǫs). [Gr.] A large wide-mouthed earthenware jar of spherical form, used for holding wine, oil, food, etc.

Pithsome (pi·θsǝm), a.

Pithy (pi·θi), a. [f. Pith sb. + -y¹.]
1. Consisting of or the nature of pith; abounding in or full of pith.
2.
3.
b.

Pitiable (pi·tĭǎb'l), a. [ad. F. pitiable.]
1. Deserving, worthy of, or standing in need of pity; exciting pity; lamentable.
2. Contemptible, miserable. = Pitiful 4.

Pitiableness.

Pitiably (pi·tĭǎbli), adv.

Pitied (pi·tid), ppl. a. [f. Pity v. + -ed¹.]

Pitier (pi·tiǝɹ). [f. Pity v. + -er¹.] One who pities.

Pitiful (pi·tiful), a. [f. Pity sb. + -ful.]
1. Characterized by piety; pious. Obs.
2. Full of or characterized by pity; compassionate, merciful, tender.
3. Exciting or fitted to excite pity; pitiable, deplorable, lamentable. (Usually, now always, of actions, conditions, sights, cries, or the like; formerly also of persons.)
4. Full of contempt or significance; paltry and insignificant; exciting pitying contempt; miserably insignificant or trifling; despicable, mean.

Pitifully (pi·tifuli), adv.
1. With compassion; compassionately, mercifully.
2. Piteously, pitiably.
3. Contemptibly, meanly, meagrely.

Pitifulness (pɪ'tɪfʊlnɛs). [f. PITIFUL + -NESS.]
The quality of being PITIFUL, q.v.

Pitifulsome, obs. variant of PITIFUL.

Pitikin, pittikins, dim. of PITY, after bodikins, in *Ods pittikins:* see On 1 2.

Pitiless (pɪ'tɪlɛs). a. [f. PITY sb. + -LESS.]
1. Without pity or compassion; showing no pity; merciless.

2. Receiving no pity; unpitied. *Obs. rare.*

Pitilessly adv.; **Pitilessness.**

Pitill : see PITTEL. **Pitle,** var PIGHTLE.

Pitless (pɪ'tlɛs). a. rare. [f. PIT sb.1 + -LESS.]
Having no pit : i.e. square, said of a theatre.

Pit-maker, etc.

Pitman (pɪ'tmæn). [f. PIT sb.1 + MAN sb.1]
1. The digger of a pit or common grave. *Obs.*

2. A man who works in a pit or mine, esp. a coal-mine; a collier.

3. *(transf. from sense 2.)* In machinery, the rod connecting a rotating with a reciprocating part, and communicating motion from one to the other.

Pit-mouth: see PIT sb.1 Pito, var of PITA.

Pitot, *Obs. rare.* [Origin obscure : cf. PIDDOCK.] app. A razor-shell.

Pitous, -tee, obs. var. of PITEOUS, PITEOUSNESS.

Pitpan. (pɪt'pæn). Also 9 pittpan.
A long flat-bottomed boat hollowed out of the trunk of a tree, used in Central America; a dugout.

Pit-pat: see PIT-A-PAT.

Pit-saw, -sawyer, -stone, etc.: see PIT sb.1

Pitta (pɪ'tæ). Ornith. [mod.L., a Telugu *pitta* meaning small, a pet.] Name of a genus of passerine birds, type of the family *Pittidæ*, the Ant-thrushes of the Old World, species of which inhabit China, India, and Australia, and one, *P. angolensis*, the W. Coast of Africa.

Pittacal (pɪ'tækæl). Chem. Also -cal.
A blue solid substance obtained from the high-boiling portions of wood-tar.

Pittance (pɪ'tæns). Forms: 3-6 pittauno, 4-6 (8)-ance, (4-6 pyt(t)-, pet-, -anc, -auns,) 4-5 pittans, (5 pittauns,) 6 pitance, pittans, [ME] *pitauntce*, *pitance*, *petance*, pity, ad. L., type *pietantia.*
1. A pious donation or bequest to a religious house or order, to provide an additional allowance of food, wine, etc., at particular festivals, or on the anniversary of the benefactor's death, in consideration of masses; hence, the allowance or dole itself; also, the anniversary service. Also *fg.* Now only *Hist.*

† Pittance (v.), *Obs.*
To give a (small) pittance to; to allowance.

Pittancer (pɪ'tænsər). *Obs. exc. Hist.* Forms: see PITTANCE sb. 3, etc.
An officer in a religious house having the duty of distributing the pittances.

† Pittancery (pɪ'tænsərɪ). *Obs. rare.* [f. prec. + -ERY.]
The office of the pittancer of a convent; the estate belonging to this office.

Pit-mark, -martin, etc.: see PIT sb.1 14.

Pit-mirk, a. Sc. and *north. dial.* [f. PIT sb.1 + MIRK a.] As dark as a pit (or as the pit).

Pit-mouth: see PIT sb.1 Pito, var of PITA.

Pitman, obs. humorous synforc of EPITOME.

Pitou, *Obs. rare.* *Manche, de coulume,* the Pitot; a long, and round shell-fish.

Pitous, -tee, obs. var. of PITEOUS, PITEOUSNESS.

Pit : see PIT, var. of PITA, var. of PITTA.

Pit, sb. Also 4 pitte. 5 Pitt sb.
1. A charitable gift or allowance of food or drink; a scanty meal; square portion or diet.

2. A small allowance or portion of food and drink; a scanty meal; square portion or diet.

3. An allowance, remuneration, or stipend, by way of livelihood. Usually connoting its scanty amount or bare sufficiency.

4. In allowance, remuneration, or stipend, by way of livelihood.

5. Matched against each other : see PIT 1 3.

† Pittel, pitill. *Obs.* Forms: 7 pittel, pittal, 7 pitell (d.) pittle, piddle, pickle).
A bird of prey; app. the Marsh Harrier.

Pitted (pɪ'tɛd), ppl. a.
1. Having pits or small depressions on the surface; marked or spotted with pits; † dimpled; *spec.* in *Bot.* of cells, vessels, etc.

2. Also, marked with small-pox; pock-marked.

Pitter (pɪ'tər). *U.S.* [f. PIT sb.2 + -ER 1.]
A one who removes the pits or stones from fruit.

Pitter (pɪ'tər), v. *rare.* [Echoic, with frequentative form : cf. PATTER v., TWITTER v.]
To make a rapid repetition of a monosyllabic sound in quality approaching short *i*, as in the sound made by the grasshopper, or by a thin stream of water running over stones.

Pittite (pɪ'taɪt), sb. *Obs.* [f. PIT sb. + -ITE 1.] One who occupies a seat in the pit of a theatre.

Pittle, v. *Obs. exc. dial.* Also 6 pitel. [var. of PIDDLE v.]

† Pit-tie-pa tie, a. *Obs. rare.—1* [Redupl. of pretty.] Rather pretty.

Pitter-patter, sb. (adv.) [Reduplicated from PATTER sb.1 and *v.,* implying rhythmic repetition.]
1. Rapid repetition of words; sometimes applied to rapid and mechanical repetition of prayers. Cf. PATTER sb.1

Pitter-patter, v. [f. prec.]
1. *intr.* To patter or repeat in a rapid mechanical way. Cf. PATTER v.1

Pitter-pat-ter, v. [f. prec. sb.]

Pitting (pɪ'tɪŋ), vbl. sb.
The action of the verb PIT, or the result of this.

Pitting, *Obs.* variant of PITYING.

Pittite : see PITTITE.

Pittey, pittite : see PITTI.

Pittie : see PITTY.

Pittol, obs. f. PISTOL.

Pitto (pɪ'tɔ). Forms: 7 poitou, 8 potoe, putto, 9 pito, pitt, pittu, 9d. Dahom *apity.*

Pittosporum (pɪtɔ'spɔrəm). Bot. [mod.L.]

Pitty-pat, v., -pat, sb.: see PIT-A-PAT.

Pituitary (pɪtjuː'ɪtərɪ), a. and sb. [ad. L. *pituītārius.*]

Pituite (pɪ'tjuːaɪt). *Obs.* [ad. L. *pituīta.*]

Pituri (pɪ'tjʊrɪ). Also pitchery, pitcheri, pitchiri, pitury.
[Native name.] The native name of a kind of plant (*Duboisia Hopwoodii*).

Piturine. [f. prec. + -INE 5.]

Pitviper, -water, -work, etc.: see PIT 1 14.

Pity (pɪ'tɪ), sb. Forms: 2-3 pite, pyte, 4-5 pitee, 3 pitte, 5-6 pytie, (-yte,) 3-7 (5-6-7e,) 6-pity. 8-9 (5-6) pitte, (-7e) pittie, 4-6 pytie, 7-8 pitty, -ie. See also PIETY. [ME]
1. The quality of being pitiful; the disposition to mercy or compassion; clemency, mercy, mildness, tenderness. *(To merged in next.)*

2. A feeling or emotion of tenderness aroused by the suffering, distress, or misfortune of another, and prompting a desire for its relief; compassion, sympathy.

Pity (pɪ'tɪ), v. Forms: see prec. [f. prec.]
1. *trans.* To feel pity for; to commiserate.

2. To move to pity.

Pityriasis (pɪtɪ'raɪəsɪs). [mod.L., a. Gr.]
1. Path. A condition of the skin characterized by the formation and falling off of branny patches of small bran-like scales, without inflammation; *spec.* formation of dandruff or scurf.

Pityroid (pɪ'tɪrɔɪd), a. rare. [f. Gr.]
Resembling bran; bran-like.

Pity (pɪ'tɪ), v.
1. *trans.* To feel pity for; to compassionate.

Piiútabe, -isabe, obs. forms of PEEVISH.

Pit-a. *Obs. rare.*

Pivot (pɪ'vət), sb. Also 7 pivat, 8 pevot, povet(t.) [a. F. *pivot* (12th c. in Hatz.-Darm.)]
1. A short shaft or pin, usually of metal and pointed, forming the fulcrum or centre on which something turns or oscillates; as the pin of a hinge, the end of an axle or spindle, or the actor on which the hands of a timepiece turn; a pintle.

Pivot, v. [f. prec.]
1. *trans.* To furnish with, mount on, or attach by means of, a pivot or pivots.

2. *intr.* To turn on or about (chiefly *local*), as a pivot; to move as on a pivot.

Pivotal (pɪ'vətəl), a. [f. prec. + -AL 1.] Of, pertaining to, or of the nature of, or constituting a pivot; forming that on which anything turns or depends; central, cardinal.

Pivoted (pɪ'vətɛd), ppl. a. [f. PIVOT sb. + -ED 2.]

Piwarree (pɪwæ'riː). Forms: 8 piwaree, 9 warri, -4, is- pawarl. [Carib of Guiana.] An intoxicating beverage made from cassava, used by the natives of tropical America.

Pix, Pixis : see PYX, PYXIS.

Pixwer, var of PAX-WAX.

Pix, obs. f. PIECE.

Pixie, pixy : see PIXY.

Pixy (pɪ'ksɪ). Also 7 pixie, pixey, pixye. [Origin obscure.]
In local folk-lore a name for a supposed supernatural being akin to a fairy.

Pixy-led, a.

Pixy-ring, pixy-stool : see PIXY.

Piya, *Obs.*

Pizazz : see PIZZAZZ.

Piz (pɪz). *Obs. exc. dial.* [app. syncopated f. PIZZLE.]

Pizzazz, Pizazz : var. forms.

Pizzicato (pɪtsɪ'kɑːtoʊ). [It., prop. pa. pple. of *pizzicare* to pinch, twitch (a string).]
In music, directing that the string of a violin, etc., is to be plucked with the finger instead of played with the bow.

on a violin or the like by plucking the string with the finger instead of using the bow. (Abbrev. *pizz.*)
1880 P. David in Grove *Dict. Mus.* II. 760/1 Playing a pizzicato accompaniment to a tune played with the bow. 1884 *Athenæum* 5 Dec. 740/1 Violas and violoncellos play pizzicato throughout.

B. *sb.* A note or passage played in this way.
1845 E. Holmes *Mozart* 119 When they heard me accompany the Pizzicato on the keys. 1885 P. David in Grove *Dict. Mus.* IV. 295 Who copied with more or less success.. his pizzicatos with the left hand.

Pizzle (pi·z'l). Now *dial.* or *vulgar.* Forms: α. 6 **peezel, peisill,** 7 **peezle,** 8 **pesil;** β. 6 **pys(s)ell,** 6–7 **pissel(l,** 7 **pisle, pisell, pizle, pizell,** 7– **pizzle.** [Occurs from early 16th c. = Flem. *pēzel*, LG. *pesel*, dim. of OLG. *pēsa sinew, whence MLG. *pēse*, MDu. *pēze*, Du. *pees* sinew, string, pizzle. Cf. also MDu. *peserick* sinew, string, whip of bull's hide, pizzle, Du. *pezerik, peesrik*, MLG. *peserik*, LG. (and Ger. dial.) *peserick* pizzle.] The penis of an animal; often that of a bull, used as a flogging instrument (see Bull *sb.*¹ 11 b).
1523 Fitzherb. *Husb.* § 56 Thoughe he [an ox].. be broken, both of tayle and pysell, yet wyll he fede. 1544 Phaer *Regim. Lyfe* (1560) H vj b, Take the peisill of an harte, and drie it into pouder. 1577 B. Googe *Heresbach's Husb.* (1586) 127 Take the peezel of a Stagge, burne it, and make it in pouder. 1599–1737 Bulls pissell, etc. [see Bull *sb.*¹ 11 b]. 1693 *Phil. Trans.* XVII. 976 Of the Whale's Pizzle, and its Use in Physick. 1710 Addison *Tatler* No. 216 ⁋ 13. 1814 Scott *Let. Southey* 17 June in *Lockhart*, The wholesome discipline of a bull's pizzle and strait-jacket.

Plaas, obs. form of Place.

Placability (plǣkăbi·lĭti, plæk-). [ad. L. *plācābilitās*, f. *plācābilis* Placable: see -ity. Cf. obs. F. *placabilité* (1577 in Godef.)] The quality or character of being placable; readiness to be appeased or to forgive; mildness of disposition.
1531 Elyot *Gov.* II. vi. Placabilitie is no litle part of benignitie. *a* 1620 Moryson *Itin.* IV. IV. i. (1903) 290 All writers commend the Germans.. for Modesty, Integrity, Constancy, Placability, Equity, and for Gravity, but somewhat inclyning to the vice of Dullnes. 1741 Middleton *Cicero* II. xii. 505 He declared nothing to be more.. worthy of a great man, than placability. 1839 James *Louis XIV*, IV. 62 He would endure with dignified placability much irritating opposition.

Placable (plǣ·kăb'l, plæ·kăb'l), *a.* [ME. a. OF. *placable*, ad. L. *plācābilis*, f. *plācāre* to appease: see -ble.]
†**1.** Pleasing, agreeable. *Obs.*
c 1400 *Mirour Saluacioun* 723 Marie was body and sawle perfitely placable. *c* 1540 Boorde *The boke for to Lerne* A iij b, It may be placable to the iyes of all men to se. 1542 — *Dyetary* ii. (1870) 234 That it may be placable to the eyes of all men to se and to beholde.
2. Capable of being, or easy to be, appeased or pacified; mild, gentle, forgiving.
1586 A. Day *Eng. Secretary* II. (1625) 93 To thy Enemies thou art placable. 1667 Milton *P. L.* XI. 151 Since I sought By Prayer th' offended Deitie to appease,.. Methought I saw him placable and mild. 1741 Richardson *Pamela* II. 166 My Pamela is very placable. 1819 J. W. Croker in *C. Papers* 15 Sept., Tories are placable people. 1876 Bancroft *Hist. U. S.* IV. xxv. 6 Though irritable, he was placable, and at heart was truly loyal.
†**b.** *transf.* (of a thing). *Obs.*
1609 Bible (Douay) *Isa.* lx. 7 They shal be offered upon my placable altar.
†**3.** Peaceable, quiet. (*Catachrestic.*)
1611 Speed *Hist. Gt. Brit.* VIII. iii. (1623) 400 Being at length.. surfeited with glory,..he resolved on a more placable course of life. 1841 D'Israeli *Amen. Lit.* (1867) 130 The civil wars.. soon drew off the minds of men from the placable innovators of language. 1858 Hawthorne *Fr. & It. Note-Bks.* I. 259 The wind blew in momentary gusts, and then became more placable.

Pla·cableness. [f. prec. + -ness.] The quality of being placable; placability.
1678 Cudworth *Serm., 1 Cor.* xv. 57 (1676) 72 A sensible Demonstration..of God's..Placableness and Reconcileableness to sinners returning to obedience. 1741 Richardson *Pamela* (1824) I. xv. 256 That softness of nature, and placableness of disposition, which he holds to be the greatest merit in our sex. 1896 *Current Hist.* (Buffalo, N.Y.) VI. 417 They had gained a grace of placableness.

Placably, *adv.* [f. as prec. + -ly².] In a placable manner.
1829 James *Louis XIV*, IV. 317 He..heard patiently and placably complaints of himself and of his government. 1861 Geo. Eliot *Silas M.* iii, 'Ay, ay', said Dunstan, very placably, 'you do me justice, I see'.

Placad, obs. Sc. form of Placard.

‖ **Placage** (plăkā·ʒ). [Fr., f. *plaquer* to plate, veneer, cover (with plaster, stone, etc.), f. *plaque* a plate, slab: see Plaque and -age.] The facing of walls with thin slabs of marble or the like, or with stucco or plaster.
1774 *Projects* in *Ann. Reg.* 115/2 He likewise employed the same kind of cement for the placage of a subterraneous vault. 1862 *Ecclesiologist* XXIII. 32 The cost of a simple placage.

Placard (plæ·kāɹd, plăkā·ɹd), *sb.* Forms: α. 5 **placquart, plakart, -ert,** 6 **plagart,** 6–9 **placart,** 7 **plachart,** 7–8 **placaert,** 8 **playcart.** β. 5– **placard,** (6 **placarde, plakard, plackerd, plakerde, plagard(e, placbard(e;** 6–7 **placcard(e,** 6–9 **plackard(e).** γ. 6 **placcat, -att,** 7 **placat,** 7–8 **placaet,** 7 **placate,** 8 **placaat,** *Sc.* **placad.** [a. OF. *plackart* (1410), *pla(c)quar(d, placard, -art* in the same senses, mod.F. *placard*, f. OF. *plaquier* (mod.F. *plaquer*) to plate, lay flat, plaster, etc., ad. MFlem. *placken* (Du. *plakken*) to plaster, coat with something sticky: see -ard. The OF. *plackart* was taken into Du. as *plackaert, plakaet, plakkaat*, whence app. the 16–17th c. Eng. forms *placaert, placaet, placcat*, etc.; also Ger., Da. *plakat*. See also Placcate, Placket².]

I. An official or public document.
†**1.** A formal document (originally) authenticated by a thin seal affixed to its surface. *Hist.*
Cf. F. *sceau plaqué* seal affixed to the surface of a document.
†**a.** Such a document issued by a competent authority, authorizing or permitting a person to do something; a warrant, licence, permit, letters patent. *Obs.*
†*Letters of placard*, a letter under seal.
1482 in Rymer *Fœdera* (1711) XII. 164/1 Certain Letters in Pauper sealed in Placquart wise with a grete rownde Seale in Rede Wex. 1495 *Act 11 Hen. VII*, c. 33 § 12 Lettres of Placardys made to the same John, of thoffice of Constablisshippe of the Castell of Ludlowe. 1501 in *Yorks. Archæol. Soc., Record Ser.* XVII. 196, I received from the Kingges grace a plagarde. 1503–4 *Act 19 Hen. VII*, c. 4 The Kynges speciall licens undre his placarde signed & sealede wyth his pryve seale. 1530 *Clerical Subsidies* (P. R. O. 64/299 B), The kinges moost honorable lettres of placcarde dated under his signet. 1538 Starkey *England* I. iv. 102 Ther be few lawys and statutys,..but, by placardys and lycence opteynyd of the prynce, they are broken and abrogate. 1573 Tusser *Husb.* (1878) 206 For sundrie men, had piagards then, Such childe to take. 1601 R. Johnson *Kingd. & Commw.* 141 Neither doth he suffer other ships to saile in those seas, without a speciall placard signed with his owne hand. 1652–62 Heylin *Cosmogr.* III. (1682) 226 So cautelous, that without his Placard no stranger can have Ingress into his Dominions. 1726 Ayliffe *Parergon* 341 Religious Houses cannot acquire real Estates by way of Legacy .. without the Princes [Charles V.'s] Placart or Licence.
fig. *a* 1555 Bradford *Wks.* (Parker Soc.) I. 60 Have we a placard that God will do nothing to us? 1642 Fuller *Holy & Prof. St.* III. xiii. 183 Others .. [think] that Christianity gives us a placard to use these Sports.
†**b.** An edict, ordinance, proclamation, official announcement. *Obs. exc. Hist.*
c 1528 Wolsey in Fiddes *Life* II. (1726) 62 You count none assurance by treaties, plakards, proclamations or articles. 1591 *Acts Privy Council* (1900) XXI. 90 An open placard to al Maiors, Sherives, Justices of Peace, Baylifes, Constables, &c. *c* 1645 Howell *Lett.* II. 25 All Placarts or Edicts are publish'd in his name. 1665 *Lond. Gaz.* No. 2/3 A strict Placcard against Duels throughout all the Provinces. 1756 *Gentl. Mag.* XXVI. 363 On the 21st of last month was published a placart or declaration. 1768 (*title*) General Wolfe's Instructions to Young Officers,..and a Placart to the Canadians. 1855 Motley *Dutch Rep.* I. i. 114 Charles [V.] introduced and organised a papal inquisition, side by side with those terrible 'placards' of his invention [1550].
c. esp. in 17th c., A decree or ordinance of the States General or other competent authority in the Netherlands. In this sense often spelt *placaert, placaet, placaat*, after Du. *placaet* (now *plakkaat*).
1589 in 3rd *Rep. Hist. MSS. Comm.* 283/2 A commission to proceed with the States in requiring their justification of such points of their placart as concern my Lord Willoughby. 1654 Whitelocke *Jrnl. Swed. Emb.* (1772) II. 45 The queen had sent unto the states to repeale that placart. 1738 *Observ. Brit. Wool* title-p., A Playcart or Proclamation for preserving the Woollen Manufactures in Flanders. 1748 *Whitehall Evening-Post* No. 363 Rotterdam, June 14. A Placart, suspending the Execution of the three Placarts published last Year in relation to the French Trade, was issued.
1589 *Ancaster Papers*, O. S. 13 May (R. R. O.), [Draft of Ld. Willoughby's Defence against] slaunders by a placcat. 1601 Wheeler *Treat. Comm.* 41 Those foresaid Placates, Edictes and Prohibitions, made against the English. 1678 Marvell *Growth Popery* 13 For revoking their Placaets against Wine, Brandy, and French Manufactures. 1688 Luttrell *Brief Rel.* (1857) I. 433 The states have ordered a placaet promising a reward of 1000 guilders. 1706 Phillips, *Placaert* or *Placaet*, (Dutch) a Proclamation or Ordinance, by the States of Holland.
2. A notice, or other document, written or printed on one side of a single sheet, to be posted up or otherwise publicly displayed; a bill, a poster.
1560 Daus tr. *Sleidane's Comm.* 112 Persecution at Paris, by reason of certen placardes. 1567 in Calderwood *Hist. Kirk* (1843) II. 352 Bruited and calumniated by placats presentlie affixed on publick places of the burgh of Edinburgh. 1701 *Lond. Gaz.* No. 3752/7 A Placart was affixed last night on the Doors of our Cathedral [Cologne], in Answer to that which was lately published by the Chapter. 1706 Phillips, *Placard*,..a Libel or abusive Writing, posted up or dispersed abroad. *c* 1730 Burt *Lett. N. Scotl.* (1818) I. 66 A bill to let you know there is a single room to let is called a placard. 1818 Cobbett *Pol. Reg.* XXXIII. 338 A placard..was published to call the attention of the people to the intended meeting. 1838 Dickens *Nich. Nick.* xvi, In the window hung a long and tempting array of written placards, announcing vacant places. 1885 *Daily Tel.* 3 Oct. 5/7 Flaring posters and placards of many hues.
II. A thin plate of armour, etc.
†**3. a.** A piece of armour; a breast- or backplate; esp. an additional plate of steel, iron, etc., worn over or under the cuirass: = Placcate 1. *Obs.*
1481–90 *Howard Househ. Bks.* (Roxb.) 274 In a gardviande, a peir brigandines, a plakart, ij. bavieres. 1503 Hawes *Examp. Virt.* xi. 7 Fyrst she my legge harneys sette on And after my plackerd of grete ryches. *a* 1548 Hall *Chron., Hen. IV* 12 Some had the helme, the visere, the two baviers & the two plackardes..curiously graven. 1552 Huloet, Placard or breast plate, *thorax*. 1625 Markham *Sould. Accid.* 39 Some .. would .. adde a Placcard to cover the brestplate. 1630 Capt. Smith *Trav. & Adv.* 13 Their Pistolls was the next, which marked Smith upon the placard; but the next shot the Turke was..wounded. 1826 Hor. Smith *Tor Hill* (1838) I. 41 Sir Giles hastily pulled down his vizor, and clasped it to the plackard.
†**b.** An article of dress, sometimes richly embroidered, app. worn by both sexes in the 15th and 16th c., beneath an open coat or gown. *Obs.*
1483 *Wardr. Acc.* in Grose *Antiq. Rep.* (1807) I. 41 A plakert maade of half a yard and half a quarter of blac velvet. 1529 *Will of J. Ap Jonkyng* (Somerset Ho.), My doblet of lether wᵗ sleves & plagard of Russet velvet. *a* 1548 Hall *Chron., Hen. VIII* 2 b, His iacket or cote of raised gold, the placard embrowdered with Diamondes, Rubies, Emeraudes, great Pearles, and other rich stones.
†**4.** = Placket² 2–4. *Obs.*
1589 Rider *Bibl. Schol.* 1095 A Placarde, the fore part of a womans peticote, *gremialarium, thorax.* 1589 [? Nashe] *Almond for Parrat* 4 She will carrie a Martin in her plackarde in despite of the proudest of them all. *c* 1590 Greene *Fr. Bacon* i. 111 For fear of the cut-purse, on a sudden she'll swap thee into her plackerd.
†**5.** (See quot.) *Obs.* (Perh. only French.)
1727–41 Chambers *Cycl.*, *Placard*, in architecture, denotes the decoration of the door of [an] apartment; consisting of a chambranle, crowned with its frieze or gorge, and a corniche sometimes supported by consoles. So 1765 in Croker *Dict. Arts.* 1823 Crabb *Technol. Dict.*
6. *attrib.* and *Comb.*: **placard-man, -bearer,** one who walks about the streets bearing an advertisement; *placard-wise* adv.
1482 Placquart wise [see 1]. 1846 *Ecclesiologist* V. 47 It is no worse to convert an Angel into a link-boy than into a placard-man. 1895 *Daily News* 5 Dec. 7/7 Interesting to placard collectors of all countries. 1899 Knapp *Life G. Borrow* I. 275 He employed placard-bearers to walk about the streets exhibiting his flaming advertisements.

Placard (plăkā·ɹd, plæ·kāɹd), *v.* [f. prec. sb.: cf. F. *placarder.*]
1. *trans.* To affix or set up placards on or in (a wall, window, town, etc.).
1813 *Stamford News* in *Examiner* 8 Mar. 148/1 Meetings were convened, walls placarded, and hand-bills distributed. 1868 Milman *St. Paul's* vi. 124 The pillars were placarded with advertisements. 1884 *Manch. Exam.* 8 May 5/2 The town is already placarded with huge posters.
2. To make public, make known, advertise (something) by means of placards; to post, expose, or display (a poster, inscription, etc.) as a placard.
1818 Todd, *Placard*, to notify publickly: in colloquial language, to post. 1826 Scott *Jrnl.* 10 Mar., It would be exactly placarding me in a private and confidential manner. 1836 Lytton *Athens* (1837) I. 351 The prytanes always placarded in some public place a programme of the matters on which the people were to consult. 1838 Dickens *Nich. Nick.* xxiv, Bills..were placarded on all the walls. 1854 H. Ainsworth *John Law* IV. ii, The parliament..placarded written copies on the walls.
Hence **Placarded** *ppl. a.*; **Placarding** *vbl. sb.*
1830 *Gentl. Mag.* Nov. 456/1 In Paris..no further rioting or placarding has taken place. *a* 1845 Hood *T. Trumpet* xxix, By chalking on walls, or placarding on vans. 1861 Ludlow in *Macm. Mag.* III. 320 Workers have been brought together on a placarded offer of employment.

Placardee·r. *nonce-wd.* [See -eer.] = next.
1821 *Blackw. Mag.* IX. 34 A motley band of printers, editors, pamphlet paragraph and placardeers.

Placarder (plăkā·ɹdəɹ, plæ·kāɹdəɹ). [f. Placard *v.* + -er¹.] One who puts up placards.
1825 *Examiner* 17/2 M'Donnell then asked for the name of some private placarder. 1837 Carlyle *Fr. Rev.* (1872) III. I. i. 8 Then Durosoy, Royalist Placarder,..went rejoicing.

Pla·cate, *a.* *Obs. rare.* [ad. L. *plācāt-us* appeased, pa. pple. of *plācāre*: see next.] Composed; placid.
1662 Gurnall *Chr. in Arm.* verse 18 II. v. (1669) 446/2 When are you more placable and serene? 1675 Brooks *Gold. Key* Wks. 1867 V. 138 *Animo tam tranquillo*.., with as placate, serene and tranquil a mind.

Placate (plǣ·keɪt, plæ·keɪt, plăkē¹·t), *v.* [f. L. *plācāt-*, ppl. stem of *plācāre* to appease: see -ate³.] *trans.* To render friendly or favourable (one who is hostile or offended); to pacify, conciliate; to propitiate.
1678 Cudworth *Intell. Syst.* I. iv. § 31. 476 Therefore is He always Propitiated and Placated both First and Last. 1792 J. Townsend *Journ. Spain* (1792) III. 14 Solicitous to placate an offended deity. 1836 J. Gilbert *Chr. Atonem.* vi. (1852) 170 Such satisfaction is not really placating anger, not appeasing a personal passion. 1868 Edwards *Ralegh* I. xiii. 249 Nottingham .. wrote earnestly to Essex, trying to placate him. 1894 Knight *Garrick* vi. 97 A victory so complete..failed to placate the indignant young actress.
Hence **Placated** *ppl. a.*; also **Placater** (*U. S.*), one who placates.
1735 D. Forbes *Th. Relig.* (1747) 10 To approach, and rely on the protection and beneficence of a placated Deity. 1867 Ludlow *Little Briggs & I* 223 The stern but placated bosoms of Barker and Moodle. 1894 *Nation* (N. Y.) 22 Mar. 205/2 What the Americans call a 'placater'. He 'placates' opposing interests as Thurlow Weed used to do. 1894 *19th Cent.* Oct. 495 The successful placater brings into line men who are apparently irreconcilable.

Placation (plăkē¹·ʃən). [a. obs. F. *placation* (16th c. in Godef.), ad. L. *plācātiōn-em*, n. of action from *plācāre*: see prec. and -ation.] The action of

placating; appeasing, pacifying; conciliation, propitiation. With *a* and *pl.* a propitiatory action.
1589 Puttenham *Eng. Poesie* I. iii. (Arb.) 23 Sacrifices of placation, with inuocations and worship. *Ibid.* III. iv. 159 Many more like vsurped Latine and French words: as *Methode, methodicall, placation.* 1609 Bible (Douay) *1 Macc.* i. 47 Holocausts and sacrifices, and placations to be made in the temple of God. 1830 J. Douglas *Truths Relig.* v. (1832) 222 Such terms as atonement, placation, expiation. 1884 Traill *New Lucian* 109 The Supreme Being is not so savage and childish as to need placation by the steam of victims.

Placatory (plǣ·kătəri, plæ·k-), *a.* [ad. L. *plācātōri-us* appeasing, propitiatory (Tert.), f. *plācāre* to appease: see -ory.] Tending or calculated to placate or appease; conciliatory; propitiatory.
a 1640 Jackson *Creed* XI. xxxix. § 5 Some gods the heathens honoured with placatory sacrifices. 1799–1805 S. Turner *Anglo-Sax.* (1830) I. II. App. iii. 132 [He] made a placatory offering of two wax lights and nine pieces of money. 1862 Lytton *Str. Story* I. 110 A reply which seemed .. both dignified and placatory.

Placcard(e, placcat(t, obs. ff. Placard.

Pla·ccate. *Obs.* exc. *Hist.* Also 8 **plaquet,** 9 **placate.** [app. a variant of Placard (in sense 3): cf. the γ forms there. See also Placket² 1.]
1. A piece of armour consisting of a plate of steel or iron worn over the cuirass: = Placard *sb.* 3 a. Also, a leather jacket or doublet lined with strips of steel, worn under the outer armour.
1632 J. Cruso *Milit. Instr. Cavallerie* (Fairholt), [A breast and back] caliver proof by addition of the placcate. 1688 R. Holme *Armoury* III. xix. (Roxb.) 166/2 They.. haue vnder their Armour a good Buffe coate, or a Placcate or an under brest plate to make them caliver proofe. 1783 Grose *Milit. Antiq.* (1801) II. 252 The breastpiece [of the cuirass] was occasionally strengthened by an additional plate called a plaquet. 1869 Boutell *Arms & Armour* x. (1874) 204 The plates..placed in front of the shoulders were *placates*; but when the shoulders were covered by the reinforce-plates, they were distinguished as *pauldrons*.
†**2.** = Placket². *Obs.*
1588 Shaks. *L. L. L.* III. i. 186 Don Cupid, Regent of Loue-rimes, Lord of folded armes,..Dread Prince of Placcats, King of Codpeeces.
†**3.** See Placard *sb.* 1 c. *Obs.*

Place (plē¹s), *sb.* Forms: (1 Northumb. **plæce, plætse, plæse**); 3– **place,** (3 **plasce,** 3–5 **plasse,** 4 **plass,** 4–6 **plas(e,** 5 **plaas, plays,** 6 **p'eaze**). [ME. *place*, a. F. *place* (11th c.) = Pr. *plassa*, Sp. *plaza*, Pg. *praça*, It. *piazza*, med.L. *placia*:—late L. type *plattia for classical L. *platea*, broad way, open space, ad. Gr. πλατεῖα (sc. ὁδός) broad way. The L. word had been already taken into Old Northumbrian in the form *plæce, plætse*, rendering L. *platea* of the Vulgate; but the history of the current word begins with the adoption of the F. *place* in sense 3, the mod. use in 1 b. being a more recent borrowing from the Romanic langs. From the latter came also MDu. *plaetse*, Du. *plaats*, MHG., Ger. *platz*, MLG. *plas*, LG. *plāts, plātse*, Icel. *plāz* (13th c.), Sw. *plats*, Da. *plads*. Welsh *plâs* is app. from ME. *Place* has superseded OE. *stow* and (largely) *stede*; it answers to F. *lieu*, L. *locus*, as well as to F. *place*, and the senses are thus very numerous and difficult to arrange.
With the doubled *t* of late L. *plattia, cf. the similar phenomenon in *plattus Plat (with which *platea* was prob. associated); also in *pettia Piece, *piccus Pike, *pippa Pipe, etc.]

I. 1. An open space in a city; a square, a market-place. †**a.** Used in OE. to render L. *platea* of the Vulgate.
a 950 *Durham Ritual* (Surtees) 36/7 On plæcum (*in plateis*). *Ibid.* 65/37 In plæcum. *c* 950 *Lindisf. Gosp.* Matt. vi. 5 Ða ðe lufas in somnungum & huommum ðara plæcena..stondes..to ȝebiddanne. — Luke x. 10 Færað on plæcum hire. *c* 975 *Rushw. Gosp.* ibid., Farað on plætsa his.
b. In modern use, forming the second element in the name of a group of houses in a town or city, now or formerly possessing some of the characters (positive or negative) of a square, chiefly that of not being properly a street.
Often used in the name of a small area more or less built around, and lying aside from a street or thoroughfare, or of a short *cul-de-sac* or byway turning out of a main thoroughfare; also, more vaguely given to a short row or 'terrace' of houses which originally stood by themselves on a suburban road; being in fact a ready denomination for any aggregation of houses which cannot be more particularly classed.
Employed in 16th c. to render F. *place* and its Italian, Spanish, and German cognates, in reference to foreign towns, whence introduced in English towns. (But in some cases the name 'Place' has arisen out of sense 4 b, the site being that of a nobleman's or bishop's town-residence, which bore the name, e.g. *Ely Place* in London.)
1585 T. Washington tr. *Nicholay's Voy.* I. viii. 7 b, The places and streetes are so well ordeined. 1653 H. Cogan tr. *Pinto's Trav.* xxiii. 86 They conducted him into a great place before the Town Hall. 1687 A. Lovell tr. *Thevenot's Trav.* I. 10 There are in it many lovely Piazza's, or Places. 1704 *Collect. Voy.* (Churchill) III. 6/1 Being gone to the Great Place to see the Bull-feast. 1796 J. Owen *Trav. Europe* II. 458 Squares, as we improperly call them in England, but which the Germans, as well as the French and Italians, more properly denominate Places. *c* 1813 Byron *Devil's Drive* iii, I have a state-coach in Carlton House, A chariot in Seymour Place. 1849 Macaulay *Hist. Eng.* vii. II. 267 At Rome..on the south of the stately place of Navona. 1883 *Century Mag.* Oct. 859/2 From Washington Square upward began the endless succession of 'places', and of houses in long, monotonous rows.

II. A material space.
2. Space; extension in two (or three) directions; 'room'. *arch.* †*To offer place*, to make way, give way (*obs.*). *Give place*: see 23.
a 1225 *Ancr. R.* 258 He ne uond nout on eorðe so muche place as his luttle licome muhte been ileid on. 1382–1571 [see 23]. 1602 Carew *Cornwall* 75 b, For performing this play, the beholders cast themselves in a ring, which they call, Making a place. 1628 Hobbes *Thucyd.* (1822) 85 When they were come in the city had not place for them all. 1654 tr. *Scudery's Curia Pol.* 169 Nature .. opposeth those things that do resist her, and gently yeilds to those things which courteously offer place. 1683 T. Smith *Observ. Constantinople* in *Misc. Curiosa* (1708) III. 41 There is no place between the Propontis and the walls of the City, except just at the Seraglio-point,..where they have raised .. a battery for Great guns. 1808 Scott *Marm.* I. xii, Place, nobles, for the Falcon-Knight! Room, room, ye gentles gay. 1852 James *Agnes Sorel* (1860) 4 Men with flambeaux in their hands,..calling 'Place! Place!' to clear the way for their master.
b. In generalized sense: Space, extension. (Chiefly *rhetorical*, and in antithesis to *time*.)
a 1631 Donne *Nativitie* to Seest thou, my Soule,..how he Which fils all place, yet none holds him, doth lye? 1655 Stanley *Hist. Philos.* I. (1701) 7/2 That the World is contained in place. This agrees with the definition of place by space. 1755 Gray *Progr. Poesy* III. ii, He pass'd the flaming bounds of Place and Time. 1775 Harris *Philos. Arrangem.* Wks. (1841) 335 *Time*..is continuity, successive in itself, and accumulative of its proper subjects: *place* is continuity, co-existent in itself, and distributive of its proper subjects. 1888 Tennyson *Crossing the Bar* 13 Tho' from out our bourne of Time and Place The flood may bear me far.
3. A particular part of space, of defined or undefined extent, but of definite situation. (= L. *locus*, OE. *stow*.) Sometimes applied to a region or part of the earth's surface.
c 1250 in *Rel. Ant.* I. 22 Heil Marie, ful of grace, þe lavird þich þe in heverilk place. 1297 R. Glouc. (Rolls) 11038 Þe quene..ibured was..In þe quer of hailes an hey in a vair place. *a* 1300 *Cursor M.* 15687 He ras vp o þe place [*Cott.* plasse] Þat he honurd him in. ?*a* 1366 Chaucer *Rom. Rose* 657 In many places were nighingales, Alpes, finches, and wodewales. *c* 1400 *Three Kings Cologne* 31 In summe plaas þe grounde is hiȝere and in summe plaas lowere. 1426 Audelay *Poems* 1 In hel ne purgatore non other place. 14.. *Nom.* in Wr.-Wülcker 736/9 *Hoc confragum*, a plays where the whyrwynd metes. *c* 1440 *Promp. Parv.* 402/2 Place, *locus*. 1535 Coverdale *Ps.* cxli. 4, I haue no place to fle vnto. 1568 Grafton *Chron.* II. 672 At tyme and place conuenient. 1600 J. Pory tr. *Leo's Africa* VI. 278 It is an extreme hot and drie place, bringing foorth no corne at all, but great plenty of dates. 1613 Purchas *Pilgrimage* VI. xiii. 534 Not staying aboue three or foure dayes in a place, as long as the grasse will serue their Camels. 1625 N. Carpenter *Geog. Del.* II. i. (1635) 1 The description of the Terrestriall Globe, so farre forth as it is diuided into places. 1658 *Torments of Hell* in *Phenix* (1708) II. 440 Some say Hell is a local Place, Augustine saith it is not a Place. 1726 Shelvocke *Voy. round World* Pref. 18 The day, hour and place of the sea in which the ship was taken. 1850 Tennyson *In Mem.* cii, We leave the well-beloved place Where first we gazed upon the sky. 1890 Besant *Demoniac* i. 18 Even that is better than to have your shame proclaimed all over the place. 1897 *Westm. Gaz.* 13 Mar. 5/1 The Act expressly declared such betting in any place, whether in or out of an enclosure, to be an illegal practice...They had arrived at the conclusion that any area, covered or uncovered, to which persons were known to resort for the purpose of betting, and where professional bookmakers resorted for the purpose of carrying on their calling, should be held to be 'a place' within the meaning of the statute.
b. The portion of space actually occupied by a person or thing; the position of a body in space, or with reference to other bodies; locality; situation.
1570–6 Lambarde *Peramb. Kent* (1826) 221 There is variance..touching the true place of that building. 1600 Shaks. *A. Y. L.* I. ii. 204 In the world I fil vp a place, which may be better supplied, when I haue made it emptie. 1603 — *Meas. for M.* I. ii. 110 Though you change your place, you neede not change your Trade. 1603 Holland *Plutarch* 815 The Stoicks, and Epicurus doe holde, that there is a difference betweene Voidnesse, Place, and Roome: for Voidnesse (say they) is the solitude or vacuitie of a body: Place, that which is fully occupied and taken up with a body: but Roome or Space, that which is occupied but in part. 1678 Hobbes *Decam.* ii. 17 Then I may define Place to be The precise Space within which the Body is contained. 1690 Locke *Hum. Und.* II. xiii. § 7 We say it hath kept the same Place:..it hath changed its Place. 1706 Phillips s.v., Place is said to be either Absolute or Relative, the former being that Space which any Natural Body takes up or fills: but the latter is the apparent, secondary or sensible Position of such a Body, with respect to other contiguous or adjoyning Bodies. 1777 *Scott. Paraphrases* VII. iv, The trembling earth deserts her place. 1837 Whewell *Hist. Induct. Sc.* (1857) I. 200 The Categories are..substance, quantity, relation, quality, place, time, position, habit, action, passion.
†**c.** Short for 'place of battle', 'field'. *Obs.*
13.. *Sir Beues* (A.) 613 Were ich alse stiþ in plas, Ase euer Gii, me fader, was, I wolde.. Fiȝte wiþ ȝow euerichon. *c* 1330 R. Brunne *Chron. Wace* (Rolls) 16384 Þrytty dukes slayn y þat plas. 1375 Barbour *Bruce* IX. 528 Bot the best of thair company Left ded behynd thame in the plass. 1705 tr. *Bosman's Guinea* 181 That Engagement is very warm which leaves one thousand Men upon the place. [1871 Freeman *Norm. Conq.* IV. xvii. 47 We are inclined to wonder..that every field did not become a local and unrecorded Place of Battle.]
†**d.** *To leave* or *win place*: to lose or gain ground, to retreat or advance. *Obs.*
1375 Barbour *Bruce* XII. 563 Thai wan plass ay mair & mair On thair fais. *Ibid.* XIII. 271 Thai war than in-till sa gret effray That thai left place ay mar & mar.
†**4.** *spec.* A piece or plot of land. *Obs.*
[Med.L. *placea, placia*, from 1215 in Du Cange.]
1337 (March) *Survey* in *Tynemouth Chartulary* lf. 23 b, Idem Robertus tenet unam placeam quæ vocatur *Priores place*, et reddit vj d. *c* 1450 *Godstow Reg.* 106 One place of his tenement in the towne of wycombe, the which conteynyth in lengthe viij. perches and x. fote, and in brede..iiij. perchis, and iiij. fote. *Ibid.* 545 One place of a curtilage lyng in the towne of Shillyngford. 1460 *Cal. Anc. Rec. Dublin* (1889) I. 306 Hit be lawfull to the rent gaderer of the citte to take in all voyd placis of the town that beryt chef rent.
5. a. A portion of space in which people dwell together; a general designation for a city, town, village, hamlet, etc.
13.. *E. E. Allit. P.* A. 1033 As Iohan hym wrytez..Vch pane of þat place had þre ȝatez. *c* 1380 Wyclif *Wks.* (1880) 419 Plasis þat han chirchis approprid. 1458 *Nottingham Rec.* II. 366 Schepley and in odor plassus. *c* 1470 *Gol. & Gaw.* 157 Thare come ane laithles leid air to this place. 1618 J. Taylor (Water P.) *Penniless Pilgr.* (1872) 22, I held on my journey..unto a place called Carling hill. 1626 R. Peeke *Three to One* C ij, I am a Deuonshire-man borne, and Tauestock the place of my once-abiding. 1697 Dryden *Virg. Georg.* III. 17, I..shall.. With Foreign Spoils adorn my native Place. 1704 J. Trapp *Abra-Mule* II. i. 359 The loss of this important Place. 1814 Jane Austen *Mansf. Park* (1870) II. vii, I could not expect to be welcome in such a smart place as that [i. e. Brighton]. 1843 *Penny Cycl.* XXVII. 666/2 Schools at Tours and other places in France. 1866 *Daily Tel.* 10 Jan. 7/4 Hanover is, as the Americans would phrase it, 'quite a place'.
b. A residence, dwelling, house; a seat, mansion, palace; formerly sometimes, a religious house, a convent; also *spec.* the chief residence on an estate; a manor-house; a country-house with its surroundings. Also *place-house* (see 29). (Cf. Welsh *plâs*.)
a 1349 Hampole *Medit. Passion* Wks. 1896 I. 95 Of alle þe housis and prisouns þat þei heelden þee ynne & closid wiþ-ynne in her placis. *c* 1386 Chaucer *Prol.* 607 With grene trees shadwed was his place. 1420 *E. E. Wills* (1882) 53, I wull þat..my brothir [haue] a place in Duffelde,..þat I purchesede. 1463 *Bury Wills* (Camden) 20 The welle werke afore my place. *a* 1548 Hall *Chron., Hen. VIII* 203 b, Ye haue hearde before how the kyng had purchased the Byssh p of Yorkes place. 1561–2 *Reg. Privy Council Scot.* I. 202 The places of freris, as yit standand undemolissit. 1611 Cotgr., *Manoir*, a Mansion, Mannor, or Mannorhouse;..a place, or chiefe dwelling place. 1796 *Statist. Acc. Scot.* XVII. 570 An old tower or castle .. called the old Place of Mochrum. 1806–7 J. Beresford *Miseries Hum. Life* (1826) XVIII. xiv. 181 To be dragged by a soi-disant man of taste through every corner of his new Place, within and without doors. 1891 S. Mostyn *Curatica* 143, I called at your place..last night, but Dan said you had been gone half an hour. 1902 R. Hichens *Londoners* 33 Mitching Dean was Mr. Rodney's place in Hampshire.
†**c.** A fortress, citadel, 'strong place'; a fortified city. *Obs.*
[Med. (Anglo) L. *placea* 1409 in Rymer (Du Cange).]
1575 *Reg. Privy Council Scot.* II 448 The Tour Fortalice and Place of Rosdew. 1670 Lassels *Voy. Italy* II. 375 Palma Nuova in Friuli..is one of the best places in Europe. It hath nine royal bastions [etc.]. 1693 *Mem. Cnt. Teckely* IV. 64 Since it durst afterwards besiege one of their strongest Places. 1704 J. Harris *Lex. Techn.* I, *Place* in Fortification usually signifies the Body of a Fortress. 1819 *Pantologia*, *Place*, in war and fortification, a general name for all kinds of fortresses. 1849 in Craig.
d. A building, apartment, or spot devoted to a specified purpose. (Usually with specification, as *place of amusement, of resort, bathing-place*, etc.)
Another place, in House of Commons phraseology, the other house, the House of Lords. *Place of worship*: see 16.
1530 Palsgr. 255/1 Place where justyce is mynystred, *parlement*. *Ibid.*, Place to bathe one in, *thermes*. 1540–1 Elyot *Image Gov.* 78 Their places of easement ouer the riuer. 1560 Daus tr. *Sleidane's Comm.* 47 b, Colledges and such other places were fyrst founded for the pore. 1617 Moryson *Itin.* I. 3 The Exchange where the Merchants meet is a very pleasant place. 1653 Walton *Angler* i. 2, I know the thatcht house very well: I often..taste a cup of Ale there, for which liquor that place is very remarkable. 1714 Addison *Spect.* No. 556 ⁋ 7 The Coffee-houses have ever since been my chief Places of Resort. 1789 Burke *Sp. Ho. Comm.* 6 Feb., Speeches 1816 III. 394 The present minister, he understood, had been called 'a heaven-born minister' in another place. 1875 Jowett *Plato* (ed. 2) III. 376 A theatre, or a camp, or. some other place of resort. 1901 *Daily Chron.* 29 Oct. 4/6 The Chapter House..is to be, as the Bishop of Southwark said, 'a place of speaking for the wants of the diocese'.
6. A particular part or spot in a body or surface.
1377 Langl. *P. Pl.* B. XIII. 275 He badde a cote of crystendome..Ac it was moled in many places. 1382 Wyclif *2 Kings* v. 11, I wende that he schulde goon oute to me,.. and touche with his hond the place of the lepre, and helen me. *c* 1400 *Destr. Troy* 9477 Paris bend vp his bow.. Waited the wegh in his wit ouer, In what plase of his person to perse. 1600 Shaks. *A. Y. L.* III. iii. 45 The Vicar..hath promis'd to meete me in this place of the Forrest. 1665 Hooke *Microgr.* lv. 214 Eight. legs,..each of them joynted or bendable in eight several places or joynts. 1799 *Med. Jrnl.* I. 23 The blistered place was healing very fast. 1804 Ann Taylor *My Mother* vi, Who..when I fell.. would..Kiss the place to make it well? 1868 *Mag. for Young* Feb. 48 My nephew..taunted him with his companions..and I soon saw that we had touched a sore place. *Mod.* A wet place on the floor. There are two specially difficult places in the ascent.
†**b.** *Chess.* A square on the board. *Obs. rare.*

1560 Rowbothum *Playe Cheastes* B j, The rowes where every one of them are set I wyll name Seates: the other which be emptie I wil name them places or houses indifferently. 1725 Bertin *Chess* 54 White, the king in his own place.
7. A particular part, page, or other point in a book or writing.
c 1340 *Spec. Gy Warw.* 294, I shal ȝou shewe in þis place, What ioie þeih sholen han ifere, þat serueþ god on eorþe here. *c* 1380 Wyclif *Sel. Wks.* II. 104 Crist seiþ in anoþer place þat þe world hatiþ þes apostlis. 1617 Moryson *Itin.* To Rdr., The First Part of this Worke,.. in some obscure places is barren and unpleasant..but in other places I hope you will judge it more pleasant. 1661 Fell *Hammond* 142 His Catalogue had an especial place for sequestred Divines. 1690 Locke *Hum. Und.* II. xiii. § 9 If any one should ask here, what place are the verses..; the use of the idea of place, being to know in what part of the book that story is. 1861 Miss Yonge *Stokesley Secret* xii. 201 They shut up her lesson-books and lost her place. 1881 N. T. (R. V.) *Luke* xx. 37 But that the dead are raised, even Moses shewed, in the place concerning the Bush.
†**b.** A (short) passage in a book or writing, separately considered, or bearing upon some particular subject; a text, extract. *Obs.*
[= L. *locus*; cf. Commonplace.]
1526 *Pilgr. Perf.* (W. de W. 1531) 3 Saynt Gregory exponynge the same place of scripture sayth [etc.]. *c* 1555 Harpsfield *Divorce Hen. VIII* (Camden) 282 The walls were painted..with places of holy Scripture. 1612 Brinsley *Lud. Lit.* viii. (1627) 123 Many places may trouble the best schollers at first sight. 1641 *Vind. Smectymnuus* 142 The last place he bringeth out of Hierome is a most plaine place. 1654 Whitlock *Zootomia* 454 The nimble Perfunctorinesse of some Commentators (that skip over hard Places). 1743 J. Morris *Serm.* vii. 203 They do not understand such places.
†**c.** A subject, a topic: esp. in *Logic* and *Rhet.*: = Locus *sb.*¹ 2. *Obs.*
c 1530 L. Cox *Rhet.* (1899) 45 The places or instrumentes of a symple theme. 1581 Pettie *Guazzo's Civ. Conv.* I. (1586) 5 b, I neuer learned the places from whence arguments are drawen. 1597 Bacon (*title*) Essayes. Religious Meditations. Places of perswasion and disswasion. 1620 T. Granger *Div. Logike* 11 Certaine places, or heads, to which Logicall innention directs vs. 1654 Z. Coke *Logick* 170 The place from Unlike, is either Simple [or] Compound. 1697 tr. *Burgersdicius his Logic* II. xvii. 69 Of Canons belonging to Consentaneous Places, or Places from whence Arguments are drawn...And first of those belonging to the Place of Notation or Etymology; and this has two Canons.
8. In technical uses:
a. *Astron.* The apparent position of a heavenly body on the celestial sphere.
1669 Sturmy *Mariner's Mag.* II. Kalendar 120 Reckoning a Degree for each Day.., you shall have the Place of the Sun exact enough. 1704 J. Harris *Lex. Techn.* I, *Place of the Sun, Star, or Planet*, is the Sign of the Zodiack, and Degree of it, which the Planet is in. 1842 *Penny Cycl.* XXII. 448/1 When observations of a star, made at two different periods, have been cleared of the effects of aberration and refraction, the only difference between the two places ought to be that due to precession and nutation.
†**b.** *Geom.* = Locus *sb.*¹ 3. *Obs. rare.*
1704 J. Harris *Lex. Techn.* I, *Place Geometrick*, is a certain Bound or Extent wherein any Point may serve for the Solution of a Local or Indetermined Problem. *Ibid.*, *Place Simple*, or *Locus ad Lineam rectam*, as the Geometers call it, is when the Point that resolves any Problem is in a Right Line. *Ibid.*, *Place Solid*, is when the Point is in one of the Conick Sections.
†**c.** *Falconry.* The point or pitch attained by a falcon or similar bird of prey before swooping down on its quarry. *Obs.* (or *arch.*, after Shaks.)
1605 Shaks. *Macb.* II. iv. 12 A Faulcon towring in her pride of place. 1636 Massinger *Bashf. Lover* v. ii, Though from An eminent place, to add strength to her wings, And mount her higher. 1806 T. Thornton *Sporting Tour Eng.* viii. (1896) 178 Eagles..can have no speed, except when at their place: then, to be sure, their weight increases the velocity. 1816 Byron *Ch. Har.* III. xviii, In 'pride of place' here last the eagle flew.
d. *Mining.* A drift or level driven from side to side of a wide lode as a beginning of a slide.

III. Position in some scale, order, or series.
9. Position or standing in the social scale, or in any order of estimation or merit; rank, station, whether high or low. **b.** *absol.* High rank or position; dignity.
c 1325 *Deo Gratias* 38 in *E. E. P.* (1862) 129 So pouert haþ my plas. *a* 1586 Sidney *Arcadia* (1627) 237 He holding place and estimation as heire of Arcadia. 1601 R. Johnson *Kingd. & Commw.* (1603) 69 Thirty other Dukes, amongst whome, the Archduke of Austria holdeth the highest place. 1641 Hinde *J. Bruen* xxxvi. 114 A young Gentleman..of great place for his birth and bloud. 1666 Wood *Life* 29 Nov. (O. H. S.) III. 32 Duke of Ormond to keep his old title but to take place in England as duke. 1824 W. Irving *Braceb. Hall* iii. 24 Of late years, since he has risen into place. 1852 Mrs. Stowe *Uncle Tom's C.* xvi, I hold to being kind to servants—but you must make 'em know their place. Eva never does. 1870 Rogers *Hist. Gleanings* Ser. II. 4 Poor men often rose to eminent place. 1876 Gladstone *Glean.* II. 339 We have not attempted to ascertain his [Macaulay's] place among historians. 1893 Ld. Lorne in *Bookman* June 85/2 As an English critic of English literature, his place is in the front rank. *Mod.* To keep inferiors in their proper place.
c. *Racing*, etc.: A position among the placed competitors: see Place *v.* 5 d.
1885 *Daily Tel.* 30 Sept. 5/3 Even a larger sum of money was wagered by the public upon Lonely for a place in the St. Leger. 1885 *Times* 4 June 10/3 Royal Hampton, who was ridden out for a place, was a bad third.
10. *Arith.* The position of a figure in a series, in decimal or similar notation, as indicating its value or denomination: in *pl.* with numeral, often used merely to express the number of figures, esp. after the decimal point in a decimal fraction.
1542 Recorde *Gr. Artes* (1575) 43 A Place is called the seate or roome that a Figure standeth in. 1656 H. Phillips *Purch. Patt.* (1676) 25, I have abreviated this Table to four places [of decimals]. 1706 W. Jones *Syn. Palmar. Matheseos* 6 A Number has so many Places, as there are Figures in it. 1706 — *Introd. Math.* 103 A Figure in the 1st, 2d, 3d, etc. Decimal Place. 1841 *Penny Cycl.* XIX. 186/2 He also calculated the ratio [of π] to 55 decimal places. *Ibid.* 187/1 A manuscript..in which it was carried to 154 places. 1876 Tait *Rec. Adv. Phys. Sc.* ix. (ed. 2) 223 Which contains some thirty-five places of figures.
11. A step or point in the order of progression. Mostly with ordinal numeral or its equivalent (*first, next, last*, etc.) preceded by *in*: *in the first place* = firstly, first in order; etc.
1639 *Act* in *Arch. Maryland* (1883) I. 60 All debts growing due for wine..or other licquors shall be paid in the last place after all other debts are satisfied. 1660 F. Brooke tr. *Le Blanc's Trav.* 325 Two thousand..lost their lives, and the Priests in the first place. 1711 Addison *Spect.* No. 39 ⁋ 7, I must in the next place observe [etc.]. 1888 Bryce *Amer. Commw.* III. lii. 301 In the first place, frost strikes deeper [etc.]...In the next place, the streets are more often disturbed.

IV. Position or situation with reference to its occupation or occupant.
12. A proper, appropriate, or natural place (for the person or thing in question to be in or occupy); sometimes in an ideal or imaginary region. (See also 19 c, d.)
1377 Langl. *P. Pl.* B. XIX. 57 He ȝaf largely alle his lele lyges Places in paradys at her partynge hennes. *c* 1440 *Promp. Parv.* 403/1 Place, or stede, *situs*. 1526 *Pilgr. Perf.* (W. de W. 1531) 2 b, Hath place deputed & assygned to them by god & nature. 1597 A. M. tr. *Guillemeau's Fr. Chirurg.* 4 iv, There is a common prouerbe that all thinges haue theire time, theire place, and theire sayson. 1600 Shaks. *Much Ado* II. i. 48 Heere's no place for you maids. 1711 Addison *Spect.* No. 131 ⁋ 8 The Country is not a Place for a Person of my Temper. 1713 M. Henry *Meekness & Quietn. Spirit* (1822) 147 We are all offenders: and the bar is our place, not the bench. 1802 Wordsw. *To Small Celandine* 6 Long as there are Violets, They will have a place in story. 1849 Macaulay *Hist. Eng.* v. I. 605 But the genius which, at a later period, humbled six marshals of France was not now in its proper place. 1897 Rhoscomyl *White Rose Arno* 305 The two lovers took their places, kneeling on the curb..of the fount.
b. *fig.* A fitting time, point in the order of events; occasion, opportunity.
1382 Wyclif *Heb.* xii. 17 Forsoth he found not place [1539, 1611, 1881, no place] of penaunce. *c* 1400 *Destr. Troy* 5040 Here is plainly no place in þis plit now, Your wille for to wirke. 1413 *Pilgr. Sowle* (Caxton) I. xv. (1859) 17 Repentaunce ne prayer may here no place haue. 1662 Stillingfl. *Orig. Sacr.* I. v. § 7 When the Egyptian Kingdom was first founded, is not here a place to enquire.
c. *fig.* 'Room': reasonable occasion or ground.
1638 R. Baker tr. *Balzac's Lett.* (vol. II.) 17 There will be no place left for calumnie. 1654 Hammond *Fundamentals* 60 There is no place of doubting, but that it was the very same which we now call the Apostles Creed. 1721 Bentley *Proposals for Printing New Test.* 4 In the Sacred Writings there's no place for Conjectures or Emendations.
13. The space which one person occupies by usage, allotment, or right; a seat or accommodation engaged in a public building, conveyance, or the like, a space at table; seat, station, quarters.
1390 Gower *Conf.* III. 125 Janus with his double face In his chaiere hath take his place. 1568 Grafton *Chron.* II. 390 The king..commaunded him to sytte downe againe in his place. 1611 Tourneur *Ath. Trag.* v. ii, In the meane time vouchsafe your place with us. 1768 Mme. D'Arblay *Diary* (1842) IV. 61 Indeed I trembled at these words, and hardly could keep my place. 1806–7 J. Beresford *Miseries Hum. Life* (1826) v. xix, After having fee'd very high for places at Mrs. Siddons's benefit. 1812 Col. Hawker *Diary* (1893) I. 45 Having taken places for Ferrybridge. 1881 Mallock *Rom. 19th C.* I. iii, You must lay another place..as we shall be five dining this evening instead of four. 1884 *Chr. World* 19 June 453/2 Accommodation is provided for 4,670,000 children, showing an increase of 32,000 places.
b. With *possessive* or *of*: The space previously or customarily occupied by some other person or thing; room, stead, lieu; often in phrases *in (the) place of*, instead of, in the room or lieu of, in exchange or substitution for; *to take the place of*, to be substituted for, to stand instead of.
1533 Cromwell in Merriman *Life & Lett.* (1902) I. 353 His highnes is contente that your grace in the lewe and place therof shall haue his letteres patentes of the Justiceshipp of his Forestes. 1566 *Cheque Bk. Chapel Royal* (Camden) 2 Mr. Alsworthe died .. and Robert Greene of Poules sworne in his place. 1591 Shaks. *1 Hen. VI*, IV. iii. 25 O God, that Somerset..were in Talbots place. 1646 Gillespie *Male Audis* 54 For that passage concerning Excommunication its supplying the place of the sword. 1793 Beddoes *Calculus* 23 The pills were now substituted in the place of the solution. 1844 Herschel *Ess.* (1857) 556 In place of immediately entering into business, he continued to reside for some time with his parents. 1849 Macaulay *Hist. Eng.* vi. II. 142 Their places were supplied by men who had no recommendation but their religion. 1875 Jowett *Plato* (ed. 2) V. 27 In the Laws..religion takes the place of philosophy in the regulation of human life. 1885 *Sci. Amer.* 3 Jan. 7/1 The aquamarine contains oxide of iron in the place of oxide of chromium.
14. An office, employment, situation; sometimes *spec.* a government appointment, an office in the service of the crown or state. (Cf. b.)
1558 in Strype *Ann. Ref.* I. App. iv. 5 Such persons..every one, according to his ability to serve in the commonwealth, to be set in place. 1631 J. Done *Polydoron* 17 Hee may well clayme a boat-sons place in Barkleyes Shippe of fooles. 1633 Bp Hall *Hard Texts, N. T.* 81 A Priest, and therefore by his very place professing examples of holinesse and charity. *a* 1661 Fuller *Worthies* I (1662) 17 The Office of Lord Treasurer was ever beheld as a Place of great charge and profit. 1687 in *Magd. Coll. & Jas. II* (O. H. S.) 78 To amove the said Mr. John Hough from the Place of President. 1710 Addison *Tatler* No. 162 ⁋ 1 In my younger Years I used many Endeavours to get a Place at Court. 1714 Swift *Pres. St. Affairs* Wks. 1755 II. I. 208 This general ambition of hunting after places. 1749 Fielding *Tom Jones* VII. viii, Good servants need not want places. 1838 Marryat *Jac. Faithf.* xxxvi, He purchased a patent place, which he still enjoys. 1871 *Punch* 18 Nov. 212/1 Couldn't let you do it, sir. Much as my place's worth. *Mod.* Has he got a place yet? He has got a place in the Custom House. She (a maid-servant) is leaving her place, and going home.
b. Without *a* or *pl.*: Official position, esp. of a minister of state: = Office *sb.* 4 b.
a 1568 Ascham *Scholem.* Pref. (Arb.) 17 The most part were of hir Maiesties most honourable priuie Counsell, and the rest seruing hir in verie good place. 1607–12 Bacon *Ess., Great Place* (Arb.) 278 Men in Great Place, are thrice Seruants: Seruants of the Soueraigne or State; Seruants of Fame; and Seruants of Businesse. 1673 Ray *Journ. Low C.* 25 Twenty four Magistrates...These chuse all Publick Officers out of their own number. Themselves continue in place during life. 1702 *Eng. Theophrast.* 173 Place shows the man; some for the better and some for the worse. 1774 Goldsm. *Retal.* 41 'Twas his fate, unemployed, or in place. 1824 Byron *Juan* XVI. lxxii, He exactly the just medium hit 'Twixt place and patriotism. 1871 Morley *Crit. Misc., Condorcet* Ser. I. (1878) 47 To glut their insatiable craving for place and plunder.
c. The duties of any office or position; (one's) duty or business. Hence †*to perform one's place* (*obs.*).
1652 Milton in *Marvell's Wks.* (Grosart) II. 9 If..I shall need any assistance in the performance of my place. 1655 *Nicholas Papers* (Camden) II. 272 Beinge to ould to performe the place. 1884 W. C. Smith *Kildrostan* 72 She'll think It is her place to keep me company.

V. Phrases. *With other sbs.
15. *Place of arms* [ad. F. *place d'armes*]: **a.** An open space for the assembling of troops.
Provision for various kinds of these, either temporary or permanent, is or was formerly made in the laying out of encamping grounds or fortifications: see quots.
1598 Barret *Theor. Warres* Gloss. 252 Place of armes generall: is the place of assemblie, where the people of warre are ranged in order of battell. 1704 J. Harris *Lex. Techn.* I. s.v., *Place of Arms in a Garrison*, is a large open Spot of Ground in the middle of the City, where the great Streets meet, else between the Ramparts and the Houses, for the Garrison to Rendezvous in, upon any sudden Alarm, or other Occasion. 1724 De Foe *Mem. Cavalier* (1840) 205, I was posted upon a parade, or place of arms. 1727–41 Chambers *Cycl.*, *Place of arms*, in a camp, is a large space at the head of the camp, for the army to be ranged in and drawn up in battalia. 1823 Crabb *Technol. Dict.* s.v., In offensive fortification those lines are called places of arms on parallels which unite the different means of attack. 1853 Stocqueler *Milit. Encycl.*, *Re-entering place of arms* is an enlargement of the covered way of a fortress..; it serves..for assembling troops previously to making sorties.
b. A strongly fortified city or a fortress, used as an arsenal or magazine, or as a place of retreat; also, †a tent at the head of each company where the arms were stored (*obs.*).
1704 J. Harris *Lex. Techn.* I, *Place of Arms*, when taken in the General, is a strong City which is pitch'd upon for the Magazine of an Army. 1708 *Lond. Gaz.* No. 4466/1 It is said the Germans design to make St. Germano .. a Place of Arms. 1768 Simes *Milit. Dict.*, *Place of arms of a camp*, are the belltents, at the head of each company, where they lodge their arms. 1849 Macaulay *Hist. Eng.* ii. I. 190 Dunkirk was..prized..not merely as a place of arms,..but also as a trophy of English valour.
16. *Place of worship* (see 5 d): A place where religious worship is performed; *spec.* a building (or part of one) appropriated to assemblies or meetings for religious worship: a general term comprehending churches, chapels, meeting-houses, synagogues, and other places in which people assemble to worship God.
In 15th c., *place of worship* occurs in the sense 'worshipful place (cf. sense 5 b), house of a person of rank'; in 16th c. in that of 'honourable post or position'. The existing use is app. shortened from 'place (of assembly or meeting) for religious worship', occurring in Statutes, from 1689 onwards, recognizing the public religious worship of Protestant Dissenters, Roman Catholics, and Jews. In these statutes the short form is rare and late (see quots. 1832, 1846).
[1470–85 Malory *Arthur* IV. xiii. 135, I wold fayn be at some place of worship said syr Arthur that I myghte reste me. *Ibid.* VIII. xxv. 310 Hit was neuer the custome of no place of worship..whan a knyghte and a lady asked herberugh, and they to receyue hem & after to destroy them that ben his gestes. 1592 Greene *Upst. Courtier* Wks. (Grosart) XI. 236 The shamelesse vpstart..that hath a hungry eie to spie out,..and a flattering toong to intreat for some void place of worship.]
1689 *Act 1 Will. & Mary* c. 18 § 4 If any Assembly of persons dissenting from the Church of England shall be had in any place for Religious Worship. [*Ibid.*, Except such Persons come to some Congregation or Assembly of Religious Worship allowed or permitted by this Act.] 1791 *Act 31 Geo. III*, c. 32 § 6 If any Assembly of Persons pro-

fessing the Roman Catholic Religion shall be had in any Place for religious Worship. 1812 *Act 52 Geo. III*, c. 155 § 2 (*margin*) Places of Religious Worship certified and registered. 1832 *Act 2 & 3 Will. IV*, c. 115 (*margin*) Roman Catholics to be subject to the same laws as Protestant Dissenters, with respect to Schools and Places of Worship. 1833 *Act 3 & 4 Will. IV*, c. 30 (*title*) An Act to exempt from Poor and Church Rates all Churches, Chapels, and other Places of Religious Worship. 1846 *Act 9 & 10 Vict.* c. 59 § 2 Persons dissenting from the Worship or Doctrines of the United Church of England and Ireland, and usually attending some Place of Worship other than the Established Church. 1853 *Act 16 & 17 Vict.* c. 137 § 62 Any Cathedral or Collegiate Church, or any Building registered as a Place of Meeting for Religious Worship. 1855 *Act 18 & 19 Vict.* c. 81 (*Preamble*) Save as therein excepted with respect to Places of Worship of the Established Church and otherwise.
[1797 *Encycl. Brit.* (ed. 3) XVI. 71/2 *margin*, Of clean and unclean beasts, and the place of worship [in the Mosaic Law].] 1816 J. Wilson *City of Plague* Poems 1825 I. 263 Her soul serene, That like a place of worship aye was husht By day and night. 1857 Mrs. Carlyle *Lett.* II. 334 They had gone every one to her different 'Place of Worship'. 1865 *Pall Mall G.* 29 Dec. 10 St. Mary's [a district church in a town] is a place of worship rather than a church to the minds of the townsmen.
17. *One's heart (lies) in the right place*: see Heart *sb.* 54. *To have a soft place in one's heart for*, to regard affectionately, be well-disposed towards, be fond of.
1809 Malkin *Gil Blas* I. xii. ⁋ 2 God knows if his heart lay in the right place for all that! 1894 Blackmore *Perlycross* 25 Mr. Penniloe had a very soft place in his heart for this young lady.
** With prepositions.
18. From place to place. From one place to another, and so on in succession.
c 1380 Wyclif *Wks.* (1880) 457 Crist wente mekely fro plase to place. 1568 Grafton *Chron.* II. 1361 He pervsed the whole towne.., from place to place. 1711 Addison *Spect.* No. 98 ⁋ 3 This holy Man travelled from Place to Place. *Mod.* Nomads who roam about from place to place in search of pasture for their cattle.
19. In place, etc.: †**a.** Before or without moving away; on the spot; then and there, immediately. So *in the place, on* or *upon the place*. *Obs.*
c 1290 *S. Eng. Leg.* I. 110/138 So þat heo i-cristned was.. and i-spouse in þe place. *a* 1330 *Roland & V.* 504 He toke him in þe plas, & to þe castel he went. *a* 1425 *Cursor M.* 1600 (Trin.) Þis worde he seide anoon in plas. 1600 E. Blount tr. *Conestaggio* 217 To sell them at lowe prices vpon the place. 1665 Temple *Let. to Sir J. Temple* Wks. 1731 II. 4, I told him upon the Place, I would serve his Majesty the best I could in it. 1675 *Lond. Gaz.* No. 1004/3 On the part of the Suedes, 2000 were killed upon the place.
†**b.** In presence, present, at hand, on the spot. So *upon the place*. *Obs.*
a 1425 *Cursor M.* 3078 (Trin.) Archere was he beste in plas. 1590 Spenser *F. Q.* I. v. 36 They all, beholding worldly wights in place, Leave off their worke..To gaze on them. 1670 Marvell *Corr.* Wks. (Grosart) II. 345 Those matters can not be transacted by the Post, but men must be upon the place. 1681 in *Scott. Antiq.* (1901) July 4 Without .. ever acquainting him, albeit he was wpon the place.
c. In its original or proper position; in position; *in situ*; *spec.* in *Geol.*; in *Mining*, applied to a vein or lode situated between fixed rocks.
1560 Daus tr. *Sleidane's Comm.* 108 That the ecclesiasticall iurisdiction remayne in place as it nowe is. 1869 Huxley *Elem. Physiol.* (ed. 3) v. § 20 The liver is invested by a coat of peritoneum, which keeps it in place. 1881 Raymond *Mining Gloss.*, *In place*, ..occupying, relative to surrounding masses, the position that it had when formed. 1884 Knight *Dict. Mech.* Suppl., *Placer*, .. includes all forms of mineral deposits excepting veins in place. 1884 Anna K. Greene *Leavenworth Case* ii. 8 The open piano with its sheet of music held in place by a lady's..fan.
d. *fig.* In his or its proper or fitting position; in one's element, at home; in harmony, timely. (The opposite of *out of place*, 20.)
1897 *Chicago Advance* 4 Feb. 138/2 If Mr. Manss were not a successful pastor, he would be very much in place as a journalist.
e. *In* (some one's) *place*: in (his) position, situation, or circumstances; situated as (he) is.
1735 T. Hill *Zara* II. i. 11 What have I done, .. Beyond, what You wou'd, in my place, have done? 1770 Foote *Lame Lover* III. Wks. 1799 II. 89 What could I do? Put yourself in my place. 1870 Reade (*title*) Put Yourself in his Place.
f. *In (the) place of*, instead of: see 13 b. *In the first, second, next*, etc. *place*: see 11.
20. Out of place. Out of, or not situated in the natural or appropriate position; misplaced; *fig.* unsuitable, unseasonable.
[1551 Robinson tr. *More's Utop.* (1895) 73 Wordes and saynges, brought furth so out of time and place, to make sporte and moue laughter.] 1822 [see Out of, III]. 1853 Maurice *Theol. Ess.* 77 The ordinary methods of controversy are entirely out of place. 1864 Pusey *Lect. Daniel* (1876) 346 The two verses .. are evidently..out of place. 1892 *Law Times* XCII. 158/1 It may not be out of place to examine it here.
*** With verbs.
21. Come in place. †**a.** To come to be, come forth, originate, turn up; to come into notice, appear; to appear, present itself for consideration. Also *become in* (*to*, etc.) *place*. *Obs.*
a 1225 *Leg. Kath.* 1316 Ne funde we nowhwer nan swa deope lereart þat durste sputin wið us; and ȝef he come in place [etc.]. *a* 1300 *Cursor M.* 5589 (Cott.), I sal tell yow of [moyses]..How-gat first he com in place. *Ibid.* 18623 And þus bicome þat oile in place. *Ibid.* 22405 For if sant michel cum to place, to dome befor vr lauerd grace. 1390 Gower *Conf.* II. 84 Hou that metall cam a place. 1579 Tomson *Calvin's Serm. Tim.* 114/2 When yᵉ honour of God commeth in place.
†**b.** To occur, take place. *Obs.*
a 1425 *Cursor M.* 2884 (Trin.) Lecchery..Þe foulest þat euer coom on plas. *Ibid.* 13131 Til a feste day coom in plas.
†**c.** To come into a position (to do something).
c 1450 *Merlin* xxiv. 444 And gladly ther-of wolde thei ben a-venged, yef thei myght come in place.
22. Find place. To find room to dwell or exist, to have being (*in* something).
a 1729 Congreve *To Cynthia* 5 Can Discontent find Place within that Breast? 1839 Yeowell *Anc. Brit. Ch.* x. (1847) 105 Confidence in their own strength found no place in their counsels. 1846 Trench *Mirac.* vi. (1862) 189 And now the solemn awakening finds place.
23. Give place. To make room, make a way, get out of the way; to yield *to*, give way *to*; to be succeeded by: see Give *v.* 47. *arch.* exc. *fig.*
1382, etc. [see Give *v.* 47 a–d]. *c* 1460 *Towneley Myst.* xxiv. 10 Stynt, I say! gyf men place. 1526 *Pilgr. Perf.* (W. de W. 1531) 14 The water deuydyng it selfe, & gyuynge place to them for theyr passage. 1571 R. Edwardes *Damon & Pithias* in Hazl. *Dodsley* IV. 92 Give place; let the prisoner come by; give place. *c* 1595 Capt. Wyatt *R. Dudley's Voy. W. Ind.* (Hakl. Soc.) 35 The Generall gaue place to his earnest suite. *a* 1604 Hanmer *Chron. Irel.* (1809) 165 Hee prudently governed his Church some thirty yeeres, and gave place to nature. 1746–7 Hervey *Medit.* (1818) 211 What was gay..as well as glittering..gives place to an universal gravity. 1871 R. Ellis *Catullus* lxiv. 268 Thessaly's youth gave place to the Gods high-throned in heaven.
24. Have place. a. To have room to exist; to have being or existence (*in, among*, etc. something); to exist; to be situated, have lodgement.
1398 Trevisa *Barth. De P. R.* III. xii. (1495) dj/2 The vertue ..naturalis..hath pryncipall place in the lyuer. 1489 Caxton *Faytes of A.* IV. vii. 247 Yf all sinnes were punyshed in this worlde the Iuges of god shulde haue noo place. 1526 Tindale *John* viii. 37 Ye seke meanes to kyll me be cause my sayinges have no place in you. 1624 Bedell *Lett.* vii. 110 But this..hath no place amongst all your motiues. 1752 Hume *Ess., Remark. Customs* (1817) I. 366 The same law had place in Thebes. 1896 Dk. Argyll *Philos. Belief* 117 The notion..that time..can have no place in Nature except as a mere condition..of human thought.
†**b.** To have or take precedence (also *to have the place*): = 27 c. *Obs.*
1659 *Burton's Diary* (1828) IV. 272 These persons petitioning are dangerous...Safety must have place of all. 1686 Plot *Staffordsh.* 283 The female Sex, which according to the custom of England has always the place.
†**25. Hold place.** To obtain regard, to prevail; = 27 b. (See also 9.)
1513 More *Rich. III* in Grafton *Chron.* (1568) II. 757 If either kind [= nature] or kindnesse had holden place. *Ibid.* 762 If some folkes friendship had not holden better place with the king then any respect of kindred.
26. Make place. †**a.** To make room or space *for*; to give a position, station, or office *to*. *Obs.*
a 1400–50 *Alexander* 2277 (Dubl. MS.) Þen makes þe prince hym a place & prestly hym maches. 1565 T. Stapleton *Fortr. Faith* 113 All mercie shall make place to euery man according to the merit of his workes. 1581 G. Pettie tr. *Guazzo's Civ. Conv.* II. (1586) 56 To furnish himselfe with such good giftes, that he make himself place, be desired, honoured, and esteemed. 1585 T. Washington tr. *Nicholay's Voy.* III. x. 86 b, Making place for al commers.
b. *To make places* (*Change-ringing*): said of two bells which shift their position in successive changes so as to make room, as it were, for another bell which is struck successively before, between, and after them.
1872 Ellacombe *Ch. Bells Devon*, etc. ii. 221 The..terms of the art are enough to frighten an amateur,..Hunting, dodging, snapping, and place making. 1880 C. A. W. Troyte in Grove *Dict. Mus.* I. 334/2 In change-ringing terms the 4th and 5th are said to 'make places'.
27. Take place. †**a.** To take effect, to succeed; to be accomplished or realized. *Obs.* or *arch.*
1460 Capgrave *Chron.* (Rolls) 153 Alisaunder the Pope gaf us leve for to edifie coventis in these places..but there tok no place but Clare and Wodous. 1542 Udall in *Lett. Lit. Men* (Camden) 2, I am..as well contented that my suite hath not taken place. 1600 J. Pory tr. *Leo's Africa* VIII. 304 When the Christian religion began to take place in Egypt. *a* 1766 Mrs. F. Sheridan *Sidney Bidulph* IV. 30 This design can't possibly take place till next winter. 1789 Wesley *Wks.* (1872) IV. 465 His medicine immediately took place. 1825 Knapp & Baldw. *Newgate Cal.* IV. 334/2 Two shots..did not take place.
†**b.** To find acceptance; to have weight or influence. *Obs.*
1535 Joye *Apol. Tindale* (Arb.) 17 These playn testimonyes of the scripture wolde take no place with Tindal. 1665 J. Webb *Stone-Heng* (1725) 33 Then must the Corinthian Column be condemned..if Baldo's Judgment take Place. 1737 Bracken *Farriery Impr.* (1757) II. 134 This Doctrine ..I don't expect will take place with many. *a* 1774 Goldsm. *Hist. Greece* I. 1 Among an unenlightened people every imposture is likely to take place.
†**c.** To take precedence *of*; to go before. (Cf. 9.) *Obs.*
1600 W. Watson *Decacordon* (1602) 10 Whether a Iesuit cobler or schoolemaister, being but a lay brother..ought to take place and go before a secular Priest. 1626 S. D'Ewes in Ellis *Orig. Lett.* Ser. I. III. 219 The Lorde Conway tooke place of all barons. 1711 *Brit. Apollo* III. No. 149. 2/2 Which Woman takes Place? 1721 Bradley *Philos. Acc. Wks. Nat.* 188 After this, the Physick Garden at Oxford takes place in Reputation. 1814 Jane Austen *Mansf. Park* xxiii, Though Miss Crawford is in a manner at home, at the Parsonage, you are not to be taking place of her.
†**d.** To take up or have a position: to be present.
1622 Wither *Mistr. Philarete* G j, Marke, if euer red or white, Any where, gaue such delight, As when they haue taken place In a worthy womans face. 1653 H. More *Antid. Ath.* II. vii. (1712) 61 The Uses indeed of the forenamed Plants..take place so in every Affair of Man.
e. To come into existence, come to pass, happen; to occur (in place or time).
1770 Langhorne *Plutarch* (1879) I. 207/2 These respects being paid, and silence taking place. 1816 Playfair *Nat. Phil.* II. 145 The shadow may reach the earth, and a total eclipse may take place. 1894 A. Robertson *Nuggets*, etc. 217 The police were informed of what had taken place.
f. *To take the place of*: see 13 b.
VI. 28. Short for Place brick.
1843 *Mech. Mag.* XXXIX. 192 The difference between.. stacks and places ten shillings.
VII. 29. *attrib.* and *Comb.*, as *place-description, -disease, -illustration, -name, -poetry*; *place-bound* adj.; esp. in sense 14, as *place-broker, -monger, -mongering, -seeker*; *place-begging, -loving, -proud, -seeking* adjs.; **place act,** the Act of Parliament excluding persons holding office under the crown from sitting in the House of Commons; †**place-being,** the fact of being or dwelling in some particular place, habitat (*obs. rare*); **place betting,** the action of backing a horse or other competitor for a 'place': see 9 c; **place-bill** (cf. *place act*); **place-book,** a blank book for the collection of interesting or valuable literary extracts; = Commonplace-book; **place horse,** a horse which comes in among those placed: see Place *v.* 5 d; **place-house** = Place *sb.* 5 b; †**placelike** *a.*, local; **place-making**: see 26 b; **place-skating** (*U. S.*) = Figure-*skating*; **place-woman,** a female office-holder under government. See also Place brick, Place-holder, Place-hunter, Place-kick, Placeman.
1903 *Westm. Gaz.* 9 Sept. 10/1 The *Place Act, by which holders of places of profit under the Crown are ineligible for the House of Commons. 1567 Maplet *Gr. Forest* 79 Chelidros the Serpent..is in *placebeing, one of those kindes which be doubtfull. For it is now abiding vpon the earth now in the waters. 1885 *Times* 4 June 10/3 *Place Betting. 1742 H. Walpole *Let. to Mann* 8 Apr., The *Place Bill has met with the same fate from the Lords as the Pension Bill and the Triennial Act. 1827 Hallam *Const. Hist.* II. xvi. 617 We owe to this ministry the place-bill of 1743, which .. seems to have had a considerable effect; excluding a great number of inferior officers from the house of commons. *a* 1659 Osborn *Charac.* etc., Wks. (1673) 619 In the *Place-Book of virtue and vice. 1808 Knox & Jebb *Corr.* I. 431 It might be .. useful to keep the plan open for continual increase, in the way of, not a common, but a special place-book. 1647 Fuller *Good Th. in Worse T.* (1841) 132 When we are time-bound, *place-bound, or person-bound so that we cannot compose ourselves to make a large solemn prayer. 1810 *Sporting Mag.* XXXV. 267 Lawyers, and speculators, and *place-brokers. 1892 *Spectator* 16 Jan. 92/1 No writer has left us so many *place-descriptions which can be..identified with actual localities. 1898 P. Manson *Trop. Diseases* xiv. 233 Beriberi, a *place disease like malaria. 1890 *Pall Mall G.* 19 Sept. 7/3 Such an animal..would..be looked upon as a winner, or, at least, a *place horse in a race. 1675 Wycherley *Country Wife* II. i, I hate London: our *place-house in the country is worth a thousand of't. 1674 N. Fairfax *Bulk & Selv.* 85 Still they would bear no *place-like respect. 1839 *Record* 21 Oct., The time serving and *place-loving spirit. 1785 Trusler *Mod. Times* III. 77 Seeing..an advertisement.. from a man who advertised places under government to be disposed of..I..waited on Provider the *place-monger. 1868 Visct. Strangford *Selection* (1869) I. 344 The Athenian bureaucrat or placemonger. 1888 Bryce *Amer. Commw.* I. xxv. 371 A monstrous system of bribery and *place-mongering. 1868 G. Stephens *Runic Mon.* I. p. xvi, *Place names are..found both on Old-Northern and on Scandinavian-runic pieces. 1884 H. Rix in *Gd. Words* June 393/2 Speculating on the origin of place-names. *a* 1619 Fletcher *Wit without M.* III. i, To be *place-proud. 1895 *Outing* (U. S.) XXVII. 206/1 To his mastery of edges and *place-skating he owed his ability to defeat the great skaters of the world. 1817–18 Cobbett *Resid. U. S.* (1822) 257 Sinecure placemen and *placewomen.

Place (plē¹s), *v.* *Pa. t.* and *pple.* **placed** (plē¹st); also 6 *Sc.* **plaait, plaist, placeit,** 6–7 **plast(e;** *pa. pple.* 6 **yplasde.** [f. Place *sb.* So F. *placer* (1606 in Hatz.-Darm.).]
1. *trans.* To put or set in a particular place, position, or situation; to station; to posit; *fig.* to set in some condition, or relation to other things. Often a mere synonym of *put, set*.
1551 T. Wilson *Logike* (1580) 40 This manne is no Rhetoricien, because he can not place his thynges in good order. 1560 Daus tr. *Sleidane's Comm.* 25 The Archebyshoppe of Treuers was placed right ouer against the emperour. *Ibid.* 333 They place this as a generall Rule. 1565 Golding *Cæsar* 29 b, Cesar..taking the towne placed a garryson in it. 1567 Drant *Horace, Epist.* vii. D v, A younge man in a chare At ease yplasde. 1570–6 Lambarde *Peramb. Kent* (1826) 227 A Castle high, and thundring shot, At Quinbroughe is now plaste [*rime* waste]. 1602 in *St. Papers, Dom.* (1870) 226 We delivered the goods...and placed two of our company aboard each ship. 1630 Prynne *Anti-Armin.* 120 It placeth Election..within our owne command. 1663 Gerbier *Counsel* 99 The placing a Gate or Doore. 1703 Moxon *Mech. Exerc.* 167 Placing one Foot of a pair of Compasses on a Plane. 1712 Steele *Spect.*

No. 421 ¶ 2, I was so placed..that I could not avoid hearing. 1800 *Med. Jrnl.* IV. 26 He used to place the patient under a pump, and allow the water to play over him. 1818 CRUISE *Digest* (ed. 2) VI. 568 Thereby placing land out of circulation, during any one life. 1840 LARDNER *Geom.* xii. 153 Three points, however they may be placed, must always lie in the same plane. 1896 *Law Times Rep.* LXXIII. 615/2 To place gatekeepers at level crossings.

b. To put or set (a number of things) in the proper relative places, *i.e.* in order or position: to arrange, dispose, adjust.

1548 UDALL, etc. *Erasm. Par. Acts* 2 In Iohn I haue only placed the texte and diuided the paraphrase. 1553 T. WILSON *Rhet.* (1580) 6 What helpeth it though wee can finde good reasons, and knowe how to place them? 1613 PURCHAS *Pilgrimage* 368 He obtaineth places of honour, which can most fitly place his words. 1638 JUNIUS *Paint. Ancients* 118 Which things..in painting, draw the eyes by their glittering brightnesse, though they be never placed by any art. *a* 1717 POPE *Ep. Jervas* 71 Should the Graces all thy figures place. 1777 SHERIDAN *Sch. Scand.* IV. iii. (Stage direction) Places chairs.

2. To appoint (a person) to a place or post; to put in office; *spec.* to induct to a pastorate.

c 1570 *Schort Summe 1st Bk. Discipl. Ch. Scot.* § 4 Sic as ar preichers alreddie placeit. 1607 SHAKS. *Timon* IV. iii. 35 This yellow Slaue, Will..place Theeues, And giue them Title, knee, and approbation. 1669 STURMY *Mariner's Mag.* I. ii. 16 Placing deserving men according to their merit. 1817 JAS. MILL *Brit. India* II. v. ix. 694 These commissioners were..to have the sole power of placing and displacing all persons in the service of the Company. 1901 *Robert Anderson* ii. 8 When my father was 'placed' as fourth minister of the Relief Church.

b. To find a place or situation for; to arrange for the employment, living, or marriage of; to settle. Sometimes const. †*forth* (obs.), *out*.

1596 DRAYTON *Piers Gaveston* cii, Those in Court we for our purpose plac'd. 1633 BP. HALL *Hard Texts, N.T.* 213 Whether..to keep them at home in an unmarried state, or place them forth in Wedlock. *a* 1652 BROME *Eng. Moor* III. i, At an old wives house in Bow-lane That places Servants. 1751 JOHNSON *Rambler* No. 170 ¶ 6 He had resolved to place me happily in the world. 1847 MARRYAT *Childr. N. Forest* xxv, If I can only place my sisters as I want, Humphrey and I will seek our fortunes. 1889 *Spectator* 21 Sept., Fathers lament..over children whom..they cannot 'place'.

3. To put (a thing) into a suitable or desirable place for some purpose. *spec.* **a.** To put out (money, funds) at interest; to invest. Often with *out*. **b.** To put into the hands of a particular (selected) person or firm (an order for something to be supplied). **c.** To dispose of to a customer. **d.** To arrange for the performance or publication of (a play, literary production, or the like).

1700 FARQUHAR *Constant Couple* I. ii, I suppose twenty or thirty pieces handsomely placed will gain the point. 1713 STEELE *Guard.* No. 2 ¶ 3 Placing money on mortgages. 1765 *Act 5 Geo. III*, c. 26 *Preamble*, With Power to the Trustees..to place out the Money..on Real securities in Scotland. 1858 T. DALTON in *Merc. Marine Mag.* V. 338 The best mode of placing funds at Bangkok. 1889 *Boston (Mass.) Jrnl.* 7 May 2/3 The demand for Florida orange-trees..is..increasing. Many large orders have already been placed for next season. 1893 PEEL *Spen Valley* 342 All orders of the French Government which they needed to place in England. 1901 DABBS in *Westm. Gaz.* 27 Aug. 8/1, I have had six plays 'placed' at a cost to myself in trial matinées of hundreds of pounds. *Ibid.*, A single play placed on the evening bill.

4. *fig.* To put, set, fix, repose (faith, confidence, esteem, etc.) *in* or *on* a particular person or thing.

1601 T. WILLIAMSON tr. *Goulart's Wise Vieillard* 7 How are they to be..pittied, that haue nothing whereon to rest and place their assurance. 1654–66 EARL ORRERY *Parthen.* (1676) 646, I found my passion was unworthily plac't. 1700 H. WANLEY in *Pepys' Diary* (1879) VI. 233 His judgment ..in placing his friendships. 1711 STEELE *Spect.* No. 53 ¶ 3 If our Sex knew always how to place their Esteem justly. 1813 SOUTHEY *Nelson* II. vi. 34 A man, upon whose sagacity..he could place full reliance. 1849 MACAULAY *Hist. Eng.* x. II. 591 No confidence could be placed in any of the twelve Judges.

5. To determine or indicate the place of; to assign a place to. **a.** To assign or refer to a particular locality or set of circumstances; to locate. **b.** To assign a certain rank or station to; to rank, class. **c.** To fix the chronological position of; to date; to fix, determine (a date).

1597 BACON *Coulers Good & Evil Ess.* (Arb.) 139 For sayth he [Cicero], aske a Stoicke which Philosophie is true, he will preferre his owne: Then aske him which approcheth next the truth, he will confesse the Academiques. So..the Epicure..as soone as he hath placed himselfe, he will place the Academiques next him. 1662 STILLINGFL. *Orig. Sacr.* I. i. § 20 Capellus placeth Cadmus in the third year of Othoniel. 1707 *Curios. in Husb. & Gard.* 118 Having excluded them from the Society of Men, he places them among..Beasts. 1732 POPE *Ess. Man* I. 50 Then, in the scale of reas'ning life, 'tis plain, There must be, somewhere, such a rank as Man: And all the question..is..if God has plac'd him wrong? 1885 *Pall Mall G.* 24 Mar. 3/2 Lord Lytton,..learned in American dialects, could no doubt 'place' her particular peculiarities of pronunciation.

d. *Racing.* To state the place or position of (a horse, etc.) among the competitors when passing the winning post, which is usually done officially of the first three only; *to be placed*, to obtain a place among the first three. Also *fig.*

1831 MACAULAY *Ess., Boswell's Johnson* (1887) 180 Boswell is the first of biographers. He has no second. He has distanced all his competitors so decidedly that it is not worth while to place them. Eclipse is first, and the rest nowhere. 1849 ALB. SMITH *Pottleton Leg.* 161 However you start, you'll never be placed. 1863 KINGSLEY *Water Bab.* i, She came in nowhere, and is consequently not placed. 1895 *Daily News* 4 Sept. 7/1 The last-named trio provided the winner and the placed horses.

6. To assign, attribute, impute, ascribe. **a.** To hold (a quality or attribute) to reside or consist *in* something. †**b.** To refer (a fact or circumstance) *to* something as a cause; to 'put down' *to*. *Obs.*

1608 WILLET *Hexapla Exod.* 830 They placed a certaine religion in the shadow of trees. 1631 GOUGE *God's Arrows* III. § 8. 199 They did not place honour or honesty simply in victory. 1697 LOCKE *Repl. to Bp. of Worcester's Answ. to his Let.* 97 Whether..I am..mistaken, in the placing Certainty in the Perception of the Agreement or Dis agreement of Ideas. 1802 MRS. E. PARSONS *Myst. Visit* I. 105 He placed it [her delight] to the ease it would afford her anxiety. 1814 JANE AUSTEN *Mansf. Park* xliv, She..places her disappointment..to her being..less affluent than many of her acquaintance.

7. *Football* (Rugby). To get (a goal) from a place-kick.

1890 *Daily News* 3 Nov. 5/3 A goal placed from a try. 1896 *Field* 8 Feb. 207/1 Thompson placed a goal.

Place, obs. erron. f. *pleas* (pl. of PLEA: see COMMON PLEAS); obs. f. PLEASE.

Placeable (plēⁱ·săb'l), *a. rare.* [f. PLACE *v.* + -ABLE.] Capable of being or liable to be placed.

1802–12 BENTHAM *Ration. Judic. Evid.* (1827) V. 179 The privy seal being placeable and displaceable by the king.

‖**Placebo** (plăsī·bo). Pl. **-os, -oes.** [a. L. *placēbo* (I shall be pleasing or acceptable), 1st sing. fut. ind. of *placēre* to please: also used in OF. in senses 1 and 2.]

1. *Eccl.* In the Latin rite: The name commonly given to Vespers in the Office for the Dead, from the first word of the first antiphon (*Placebo Domino in regione vivorum*, Ps. cxiv. 9, Vulg.).

a 1225 *Ancr. R.* 22 Efter euesong anonriht siggeð ower Placebo. *c* 1380 WYCLIF *Wks.* (1880) 57 Prelatis ben more bounden to his prechynge..þan to seie matynes, masse, euen song, or placebo. *c* 1440 *Jacob's Well* 110 Clerkys seydin Placebo & dirige for his soule. 1535 *Lanc. Wills* (1857) II. 165 Shall synge and say placebo and dirige on nyght. 1874 GREEN *Short Hist.* v. § 5. 248 He..earned a miserable livelihood..by singing placebos and diriges.

†**2.** In allusive phrases: *To sing* (*a*), *play* (*with*), *make, be at the school of placebo*, etc.: to play the sycophant, flatter, be servile or time-serving. *Obs.*

1340 *Ayenb.* 60 Þe uerþe zenne is þet huanne hi alle zingeþ 'Placebo', þet is to zigge: 'mi lhord zayþ zoþ, mi lhord deþ wel'. *c* 1386 CHAUCER *Pars. T.* ¶ 543 Flatereres been the deueles Chapelleyns that syngen euere Placebo. 1483 CAXTON *G. de la Tour* H vb, He ought..not flatere hym ne make the placebo. 1554 KNOX *Godly Let.* A viij b, Nowe they haue bene at the skoole of Placebo, and ther they haue lerned.. to daunse as the deuill lyst to pype. 1583 *Leg. Bp. St. Androis* Prol. 78 Plaing *placebo* into princes faces. 1607–8 BACON *Gen. Naturaliz.* Wks. 1879 I. 467 If any man shall think that I have sung a placebo, for mine own particular, I would have him know that I am not so unseen in the world. 1679 J. P. *Lett. Friend in Country* 3 Where every one would sing a Placebo to the rising Sun [the next Heir to the Crown].

†**3.** A flatterer, sycophant, parasite. (In Chaucer as proper name.) *Obs.*

c 1386 CHAUCER *Merch. T.* 234 Placebo seyde o Ianuarie brother [etc.]. 1426 LYDG. *De Guil. Pilgr.* 22417 Fflateryng ..Somme callen hir Placebo, ffor sche kan maken an Eccho Answere euere ageyn the same. *a* 1572 KNOX *Hist. Ref.* Wks. 1846 I. 37 The Bischop..having his placeboes and jackmen in the toun, buffatted the Freir, and called him Heretick. *a* 1651 CALDERWOOD *Hist. Kirk* (1843) II. 220 Placeboes and flatterers went to court.

4. *Med.* (See quot. 1811.) Also *fig.*

1811 HOOPER *Med. Dict.*, *Placebo*,..an epithet given to any medicine adapted more to please than benefit the patient. 1824 SCOTT *St. Ronan's* xx, There is nothing serious intended—a mere *placebo*—just a divertisement to cheer the spirits, and assist the effect of the waters. 1885–8 FAGGE & PYE-SMITH *Princ. Med.* (ed. 2) I. 205 It is probably a mere placebo, but there is every reason to please as well as cure our patients.

Hence **Placebo·ic** *a. nonce-wd.*, of the nature of a placebo.

1880 A. FLINT *Princ. Med.* 1093 This was given regularly, and became well known..as the 'placeboic remedy' for rheumatism.

Pla·ce-brick. *orig.* A brick made of soft clay, and laid on a prepared 'place' to harden before being burnt: see quot. 1753; *now*, an ordinary stock brick which has been imperfectly burnt, through being on the outward or windward side of the kiln or clamp.

1703 T. N. *City & C. Purchaser* 41 Place-bricks. 1753 CHAMBERS *Cycl. Supp.* s.v. *Brick*, Place-bricks..so called because of a level smooth place just by where they are struck or moulded..where they are left till they are stiff enough to be turned on their edges.., they carry them to stacks,..they are covered with straw on the top, till they are dry enough..to be burnt. 1823 P. NICHOLSON *Pract. Build.* 343 Place-Bricks are too frequently poor and brittle. 1847 SMEATON *Builder's Man.* 19 Place bricks are the refuse of a burning, and are in fact those which have not been perfectly burnt. 1881 YOUNG *Every Man his own Mechanic* § 1155 Prices per 100 at which bricks are quoted: place-bricks, 4*s.* 6*d.*; grey stocks, 5*s.*; red stocks, 6*s.* [etc.].

Placed (plēⁱst), *ppl. a.* [f. PLACE *v.* + -ED[1].] Put or set in a particular position or condition; located, situated; holding place or rank: see the vb. *Placed minister*, a pastor inducted to a charge.

1733 P. LINDSAY *Interest Scot.* 124 Where one placed Minister dies at least three young men are licensed. 1796 *Instr. & Reg. Cavalry* (1813) 75 When the Regiment forms open Column of Divisions, behind a placed Flank Division. 1818 SCOTT *Hrt. Midl.* vi, He was in orders, but was not a placed minister. 1844 P. HARWOOD *Hist. Irish Reb.* 50 Every liberal..motion..was unfailingly crushed by placed and pensioned majorities. 1890 *Daily News* 17 Feb. 3/5 Brownie..finished fifth, Theodolite, the second favourite, alone dividing him from the placed horses. *Ibid.* 3 Nov. 4/7 Blackheath beat the London Scottish by a placed goal to a penalty goal.

†**Pla·ceful**, *a. Obs. nonce-wd.* [f. PLACE *sb.* + -FUL 1.] (?)

1615 CHAPMAN *Odyss.* IX. 134 And in their precinct (Proper and placefull) stood the troughs and pailes, In which he milkt.

Pla·ce-holder. One who holds a place or office. †**a.** One who acts as deputy for another; a lieutenant, substitute, proxy. *Sc. Obs.*

1560 in Calderwood *Hist. Kirk* (1843) II. 13 Committed by the place-holders of the ministrie. 1566 *Reg. Privy Council Scot.* I. 451 His deputtis and place haldaris. *c* 1610 SIR J. MELVIL *Mem.* (1683) 188 The Prince, who is God's place-holder.

b. One who holds office under the government.

1818 MOORE *Fudge Fam. Paris* ii. 105 A youth of parts, Who longs to be a small place-holder. 1848 W. H. KELLY tr. *L. Blanc's Hist. Ten Y.* II. 238 The strength of government..resulted, not from its having some thousands of place-holders..at its disposal, but from the means it possessed of making its will reach everywhere.

So **Pla·ce-holding** *a.*

1830 LD. J. RUSSELL *Select Sp. & Desp.* (1870) I. 296 That corrupt and place-holding Parliament.

Pla·ce-hunter. One who seeks persistently for a place or post in the public service. (With unfavourable connotation: cf. PLACEMAN.)

1713 STEELE *Guard.* No. 29 ¶ 16 The Ionick laugh..is esteemed by judicious place-hunters a more particular mark of distinction than the whisper. 1818 *Examiner* 19 Oct. 666/1 Place-hunters and Fortune-hunters. 1898 BODLEY *France* II. IV. vii. 434 Moderate men who are not place-hunters, and are therefore impartial witnesses.

So **Pla·ce-hunting** *sb.* and *a.*

1823 in W. Cobbett *Rur. Rides* (1885) I. 276 A place-hunting lawyer. 1860 MILL *Repr. Govt.* (1865) 34/2 Place-hunting..is a form of ambition to which the English..are almost strangers. 1898 BODLEY *France* II. III. v. 257 The place-hunting solicitations of constituents.

Pla·ce-kick. *Football.* [f. PLACE *sb.* + KICK *sb.*[1]] (See quot. 1856, and cf. DROP-KICK.) So **Pla·ce-kick** *v.*, **Pla·ce-kicker**, **Pla·ce-kicking.**

1856 *Rules for Football, St. Peter's School, York* ii, A place kick is a kick when the ball is previously placed on the ground..Kick off must be a place kick. *Ibid.* ix, It [the football] is to be place-kicked, and not dropped. 1890 *Pall Mall G.* 20 Oct. 1/3 A try, from which the champion place-kicker..gained a goal. 1892 *Daily News* 17 Oct. 5/1 [He] played for Scotland, and did the place-kicking at the early age of sixteen. 1896 *Westm. Gaz.* 6 Jan. 2/3 This place-kicking record was the least creditable feature of the game.

Placeless (plēⁱ·slės), *a.* [f. PLACE *sb.* + -LESS.]

†**1.** Without a fixed place or home; having no place. *Obs. rare*[—1].

1387 TREVISA *Higden* (Rolls) V. 261 Þanne þe Saxons, strong men of armes, and placelees to wone ynne [L. *Saxonum gens..sedibus vaga*], were i-prayed of þe Britouns forto come in to Bretayne.

2. Not confined to place; not local; not bounded or defined.

1598 SYLVESTER *Du Bartas* II. i. II. *Imposture* 210 Holding a place-less place. 1630 J. TAYLOR (Water P.) *Sculler* Wks. III. 19/2 Such a placelesse place is Purgatory Created by the Pope without God's leaue. *a* 1834 COLERIDGE *Picture* 129 Placeless, as spirits. 1881 FRASER *Berkeley* 212 Our placing and dating intelligence must be inadequate to the placeless and dateless Intellect.

3. Having no stated place or locality.

1644 PRYNNE & WALKER *Fiennes's Trial* 5 With the datelesse, namelesse, placelesse, sealelesse Proclamation inclosed. 1876 D. CAMPBELL *Rational & True Gosp.* xv. 80 Dateless, placeless wonders are not very credible.

4. Having no place or post; out of office or remunerative employment.

1831 *Lincoln Herald* 28 Jan., Placeless walked the pensive Whigs. 1864 *Sat. Rev.* 13 Aug. 220/1 The landless and placeless Irish gentleman.

†**Pla·cely**, *a.* and *adv. Obs.* [f. PLACE *sb.* + -LY.] **a.** *adj.* Of or pertaining to place; local, spatial. **b.** *adv.* Locally, spatially.

a. 1546 COVERDALE *Lord's Supper* Wks. (Parker Soc.) I. 455 Imagining I cannot tell what manner of placely presence. 1674 N. FAIRFAX *Bulk & Selv.* 83 The placing of body between two ghostly beings, would not give them a placely behaviour.

b. 1548 GEST *Pr. Masse* in H. G. Dugdale *Life* (1840) App. I. 86 Christes body be presented in thee bred..not placely as ther placed, spaced, and mesured, but ghostly.

Placeman (plēⁱ·smăn). [f. PLACE *sb.* 13 + MAN *sb.*[1]] One who holds an appointment in the service of the sovereign or state; almost always with depreciatory or hostile connotation: One who is appointed (or who aspires) to such a position from motives of interest, without regard to fitness.

1741 *Protests of Lords* II. 15 A constant majority of placemen meeting under the name of a Parliament to establish grievances instead of redressing them. 1754 HUME *Hist. Eng.* I. xv. 369 The Sherriffs and other placemen had made interest to be elected. 1763 *Brit. Mag.* IV. 235 In 1679 the House of Commons brought in a bill for excluding placemen and pensioners from seats in parliament. 1830 LD. J. RUSSELL *Select Sp. & Desp.* (1870) I. 296 In the first Parliament of George II it is stated that 257 placemen had seats in this House. 1831 *Philad. Record* No. 3443. 4 One of the most disheartening signs of the times is the facility with which the crimes of politicians and placemen are condoned by the people.

Hence **Pla·cemanship**, the position or character of a placeman.

1833 *Fraser's Mag.* VII. 751 When placemanship is combin'd with Whiggery, the combination is..odious.

Placement (plēⁱ·smėnt). [f. PLACE *v.* + -MENT: cf. F. *placement* (d'Aubigné 1616), and *displacement, replacement.*] The action of placing, or fact of being placed; placing, arrangement.

1844 STEPHENS *Bk. Farm* II. 688 A malformation in the placement of its tines. 1854 *Tait's Mag.* XXI. 304, I.. cannot consent to the placement of such a word in our Dictionaries. 1887 *Pop. Sci. Monthly* XXXI. 415/2 In proportion as the placement of the loan disturbs the market value of the commodities. 1897 J. C. ROBINSON in *19th Cent.* Dec. 961 Art treasures..have found their way..to abiding placements from which there can be no return.

†**Pla·cency.** *Obs.* [ad. L. *placentia* (post-class.) suavity, f. *placent-em*: see PLACENT *a.*] The quality of pleasing, pleasantness; disposition to please or gratify.

1639 SALTMARSHE *Policy* 153 Men are naturally prone..to bend in placency towards their superiours humours. 1649 BULWER *Pathomyot.* II. ii. 102 The cause or matter of molestation or placencie.

†**Pla·ceness.** *Obs. rare.* [f. PLACE *sb.* + -NESS.] The quality of having or occupying a place; position, locality.

1674 N. FAIRFAX *Bulk & Selv.* 78 It cannot but harshly be said, that the world has a placeness or whereness at all. *Ibid.* 84 Such a thing as placeness or stowage.

†**Pla·cent**, *sb. Obs. rare.* [ad. L. *placenta* a cake: see PLACENTA.] A flat cake or tablet.

1603 F. HERING *Cert. Rules* (1625) B ij b, Certaine Placents or Amulets confected of Arsenicke. 1617 T. ADAMS *Gen. Pract. Phisicke* (*N. & Q.* 7th Ser. VII. 29), Clarified hony, which must be so hard that you may make small placents or trocisces of it.

Placent (plēⁱ·sėnt), *a. rare.* [ad. L. *placent-em*, pr. pple of *placēre* to please.] Pleasing, gratifying.

1683 E. HOOKER *Pref. Pordage's Mystic Div.* 71 Under the plausibl prætext, placent notion, specious name,..and fair construction of that famous Evangelic Canon.

¶ Misused for: Favourably disposed, propitious.

1898 C. READE in *New Cent.* IV. 501 A winning cause to placent gods is dear.

‖**Placenta** (plăse·ntă). [L. *placenta* cake = Gr. πλακοῦεις, -όεντα, contr. -οῦς, -οῦντα, flat cake, also mallow seed, f. the root πλακ- of πλάξ, πλάκα flat plate. So in It., Sp., Pg., Fr. in sense 1.]

1. *Zool.* and *Anat.* (Originally *placenta uterīna* uterine cake.) The spongy vascular organ, of flattened circular form, to which the fœtus is attached by the umbilical cord, and by means of which it is nourished in the womb, in all the higher mammals, and which is expelled in parturition; the afterbirth. Also applied to a structure having a similar function in other animals, as some viviparous fishes, ascidians, etc.: see quots. 1875, 1888.

1691 RAY *Creation* I. (1692) 65 The *Fœtus*..doth receive Air ..from the maternal Blood in the *Placenta uterina*, or the *Cotyledons*. *Ibid.* 67 The Blood still circulates through the *Cotyledons* or *Placenta*. 1727–41 CHAMBERS *Cycl.* s.v., In women, unless in case of twins, &c. there is but one placenta. 1855 RAMSBOTHAM *Obstetr. Med.* 68 The term placenta was derived from its shape. 1875 C. C. BLAKE *Zool.* Pref., Sharks bring forth their young alive, and nourish them while in the womb by a temporary structure called 'placenta'. 1888 ROLLESTON & JACKSON *Anim. Life* 445 In *Salpa* the developing embryo is nourished by a placenta formed, in part at least, by follicle cells.

2. *Bot.* The part of the carpel to which the ovules are attached; also sometimes applied to a structure which bears the sporangia in certain vascular cryptogams.

1677 GREW *Anat. Fruits* vii. § 5 The Seeds stuck all round about upon the Ambit or Sides of the Case; or upon a great Bed or Placenta within it. 1727 BRADLEY *Fam. Dict.* s.v. *Flower of Parnassus*, A Membranous fruit.. having..one cell full of seeds, fastened to a placenta which is often very square. 1845 LINDLEY *Sch. Bot.* i. (1858) 16 In the inside of the ovary is a space called the *placenta*, on which the young seeds, or *ovules*, originate. 1875 BENNETT & DYER *Sachs' Bot.* 395 The sporangia arise.. from some of the superficial cells of the placenta or part to which the sorus is attached.

Placental (plăse·ntăl), *a.* (*sb.*) [ad. mod.L. *placentāl-is*, f. prec.: see -AL.]

1. *Zool.*, etc. Of or pertaining to the placenta.

Placental murmur, sound, soufflet, the sound made by the blood entering the distended uterine vessels, heard in auscultation during the later months of pregnancy.

1808 BARCLAY *Muscular Motions* 367 From a change of function, placental blood is no longer returned to the liver. 1843 R. J. GRAVES *Syst. Clin. Med.* vii. 84 *note*, No one who has ever heard the placental soufflet. 1876 BRISTOWE *The. & Pract. Med.* (1878) 265 The raw surfaces of wounds or of the placental area. 1893 *Syd. Soc. Lex.*, *P[eriod], placental*, the time occupied in the expulsion of the placenta.

b. Furnished with a placenta; placentate.

1840–45 OWEN *Odontogr.* III. xi. 501 The development of the true molar teeth to their typical number in the placental Mammalia. 1871 DARWIN *Desc. Man* I. vi. 202 The Marsupials stand..below the placental mammals.

2. *Bot.* Pertaining to the placenta (of a plant).

1857 HENFREY *Elem. Bot.* § 227 In Leguminosæ the double placental base is so narrow that the ovules alternate with one another. 1870 HOOKER *Stud. Flora* 259 Ovule.. flanked by a column of placental tissue.

B. *sb. Zool.* A placental mammal.

1854 WEBSTER cites OWEN. 1897 *Pop. Sci. Monthly* Nov. 17 The marsupials..have been gradually supplanted by the more highly organized placentals.

‖**Placentalia** (plæsĕntēⁱ·liă), *sb. pl. Zool.* [mod.L. (L. Bonaparte 1837), neuter pl. of *placentāl-is* adj.: see prec.] Placental mammals; a primary division of Mammalia, comprising those provided with a placenta: contrasted with *Marsupialia* and *Monotremata*. It corresponds to the more recent divisions *Monodelphia* and *Eutheria.*

1842 in BRANDE *Dict. Sci.* etc. 1873 J. GEIKIE *Gt. Ice Age* App. 526.

Hence **Placenta·lian**, **a.** *adj.*, of or pertaining to the *Placentalia*; **b.** *sb.* one of these.

1890 in *Cent. Dict.* 1895 in *Syd. Soc. Lex.*

Placentary (plæ·sĕntări, plăse·ntări), *a.* (*sb.*) [ad. mod.L. *placentāriᵘs*, f. PLACENTA: see -ARY[1]. So F. *placentaire.*] Of, pertaining or relating to the placenta; placental (*Zool.* and *Bot.*). **b.** *Zool.* Of or pertaining to the *Placentalia* or *Placentaria.*

1843–4 *Trans. Linnean Soc.* (1845) XIX. 321 The placentary hypothesis of M. Schleiden. 1848 LINDLEY *Introd. Bot.* (ed. 4) I. 377 Uncertainty in the position of the placentary lines. 1864 WEBSTER s.v., The placentary system of classification. 1895 *Syd. Soc. Lex.*, *Placentary*, belonging, or referring to, the Placenta.

B. *sb. Zool.* A placental mammal.

1890 in *Cent. Dict.*

Placentate (plæ·sĕntēⁱt), *a. Zool.* [ad. mod. L. *placentāt-us*, f. PLACENTA: see -ATE[2].] Having a placenta: = PLACENTAL *a.* 1 b.

1890 in *Cent. Dict.* 1895 in *Syd. Soc. Lex.*

Placentation (plæsĕntēⁱ·ʃən). [a. F. *placentation*, f. PLACENTA: see -ATION.]

1. *Zool.* The formation and disposition of the placenta in the uterus.

1880 HUXLEY in *Times* 25 Dec. 4/1 The non-prehensile pes would separate it from the former, and the placentation from the latter group.

2. *Bot.* The disposition or arrangement of the placenta or placentas in the ovary.

1760 J. LEE *Introd. Bot.* III. xi. (1765) 197 By Placentation is meant the Disposition of the Cotyledons at the Time when the Seed is beginning to grow. 1848 LINDLEY *Introd. Bot.* (ed. 4) I. 389 The placentation of Water-lilies..Broomrapes..and Butomads, is equally at variance with the central theory. 1872 DARWIN *Orig. Spec.* (ed. 6) I. vii. 174 Instances of both marginal and free central placentation.

†**Placentiate**, *v. Obs. nonce-wd.* [f. L. *placĕnt-em* pleasing, suave + -ATE[3]: cf. *differentiate.*] *trans.* To please, satisfy.

1694 MOTTEUX *Rabelais* v. 248 When you're placientated [*sic*], the Fort is won.

Placentiferous (plæsĕnti·fĕrəs), *a. Zool.* and *Bot.* [f. PLACENTA + -FEROUS.] Bearing or having a placenta.

1667 H. OLDENBURG in *Phil. Trans.* II. 512 All Placentiferous Animals (if I may assume this word) he affirms to have three Membranes. 1702 DR. DRAKE in *Phil. Trans.* XXIII. 1236 The one [Uterus] being Glanduliferous, and the other Placentiferous. 1878 MASTERS *Henfrey's Bot.* 300 As though the placentiferous lines were detached.

Placentiform (plăse·ntifǭɹm), *a. Zool.* and *Bot.* [f. PLACENTA + -FORM.] Having the form of a placenta; discoid; cake-shaped.

1858 MAYNE *Expos. Lex.*, *Placentiformis*,..*Bot.* resembling a cake..placentiform. 1861 BENTLEY *Man. Bot.* (1870) 125 When what would be otherwise a napiform root becomes compressed both at its base and apex..it is said to be placentiform. 1895 *Syd. Soc. Lex.*

Placentigerous (plæsĕnti·dʒĕrəs), *a. Zool.* and *Bot.* [f. PLACENTA + -GEROUS.] Bearing a placenta: = PLACENTIFEROUS.

1890 in *Cent. Dict.* 1895 in *Syd. Soc. Lex.*

†**Placentious**, *a. Obs. rare.* [f. L. *placĕntia* suavity, PLACENCY + -OUS.] Pleasing, or disposed to please; complaisant, amiable, agreeable, suave.

a 1661 FULLER *Worthies* III. *York* (1662) 230 A Placentious Person, gaining the goodwill of all. 1683 PETTUS *Fleta Min.* II. 20 Such things as are placentious or pleasing to us.

‖**Placentitis** (plæsĕntai·tis). *Path.* [mod.L., f. PLACENTA + -ITIS.] Inflammation of the placenta.

1844 in DUNGLISON *Med. Lex.* 1849–52 *Todd's Cycl. Anat.* IV. 943/2 Simpson has described an acute and chronic form of placentitis.

Placentoid (plăse·ntoid), *a.* [f. as prec. + -OID.] Resembling a placenta; placentiform.

1890 in *Cent. Dict.* 1895 in *Syd. Soc. Lex.*

Placentophagy (plæsĕntǫ·fădʒi). [f. as prec. + -PHAGY.] The eating of the placenta.

1900 *Brit. Med. Jrnl.* 12 Apr. 909 In certain parts of the Soudan, placentophagy is habitually practised.

Placentule (plăse·ntiul). *Bot.* [ad. mod.L. *placentula*, dim. of PLACENTA: see -ULE.] A small placenta (but in quot. 1826 applied to a cotyledon: cf. COTYLEDON 3).

1677 GREW *Anat. Fruits* v. § 13 A great Parenchymous Boss, which is, as it were, the Bed or Placentula of the Seeds; which lie all over it, as in a Strawberry. 1826 GOOD *Bk. Nat.* (1834) I. 164 The cotyledon appears..necessary for the..growth of the seed, and may hence be denominated its lungs or placentule. 1858 MAYNE *Expos. Lex.*, *Placentula*,..a little placenta: a placentule.

Placer[1] (plēⁱ·səɹ). [f. PLACE *v.* + -ER[1].] One who places, puts, or sets; one who puts in place or arranges; in various technical uses, e.g. in *Bookbinding*, a workman employed in arranging the sheets; in *Pottery*, the workman who puts the ware ready for burning.

1579 SPENSER *Sheph. Cal.* Feb. 164 Thou placer of plants both humble and tall. 1599 *Life Sir T. More* in Wordsw. *Eccl. Biog.* (1853) II. 135 A sorter out and placer of the principall matters in the same [book] contained. 1802 *Sporting Mag.* XX. 56 Setters of broken bones, and placers of dislocations. 1862 T. WRIGHT *Hist. Dom. Manners* viii. 153 An *asséeur*, or placer, took the dishes from the hands of the valets, and arranged them in their places on the table. 1898 C. F. BINNS *Story of Potter* 206 The art of putting the ware ready for burning is called 'placing', and upon the skill of the placer much of the success of the oven depends. 1902 *Daily Chron.* 18 June 10/5 Collaters and Placers wanted.

Placer[2] (plæ·səɹ). *Mining.* (Chiefly *U.S.*) [a. Amer. Sp. *placer* (plaθe·r) 'deposit, shoal', allied to *placel* a sand-bank, f. *plaza* place.]

A deposit of sand, gravel, or earth, in the bed of a stream, or any alluvial or diluvial detritus, containing gold or other valuable minerals in particles; a place where this detritus is washed for gold, etc. Also *fig.*

In U.S. law, *placer* includes all forms of mineral deposits excepting veins in place.

1848 WISLIZENUS *Tour N. Mexico* 24 (Stanf.) The old and the new *Placer*, near Santa Fe, have attracted most attention, and not only gold washes, but some gold mines..are worked there. 1851 APPLETON in *Longfellow's Life* (1891) II. 219 Why it is a Golden Legend..if it be not that it is such a placer of richness. 1856 EMERSON *Eng. Traits, Lit.* Wks. (Bohn) II. 113 Like diggers in California 'prospecting for a placer'. 1858 LOWELL *Study Wind.* (1870) 306 It is a vast placer full of nuggets for the philologist. 1874 RAYMOND *Statist. Mines & Mining* 325 This placer covers an area of perhaps two hundred acres, with probably an average depth of 25 feet of gold-bearing earth.

b. *attrib.* and *Comb.*, as *placer-diggings, -gold, -mine, -miner, -mining.*

1867 MURCHISON *Siluria* xix. (ed. 4) 471 There are placer-workings on rocks containing Jurassic fossils. 1868 ISAB. SAXON *Five Years within Gold. Gate* 84 Almost wholly 'placer' or surface diggings. 1872 RAYMOND *Statist. Mines & Mining* 208 Sixty-one placer-claims..nearly all located in the southern part of the county. 1879 H. GEORGE *Progr. & Pov.* I. iii. (1881) 55 In the early days of California..the placer miner..picked up..his 'wages'..in actual money. 1881 *Lit. World* (Boston U.S.) 21 May 177/1 The Chinaman ..has found it lucrative to continue placer mining where the whites have given it up. 1897 *Daily News* 21 July 5/4 The workings on the Klondyke or Deer River are placer mines, i.e., the earth is dug up and washed with sluices.

Placet (plēⁱ·set). [a. L. *placet* 'it pleases', 3rd sing. pres. ind. of *placēre* to please.]

‖**1.** The Latin for 'it pleases (me or us)'.

The word is part of the form used in the old Universities when a question is put to the vote: 'Placetne vobis, domini doctores? placetne vobis, magistri?' (Does it please you, Doctors? does it please you, Masters?); the answer being 'Placet', or 'Non placet'. The declaration of the vote after a count is in the form, 'Majori parti placet', or 'non placet', as the case may be. It is also in the power of the Vice-Chancellor, or of the Proctors conjointly, to veto any proposal by their 'Non placet', as in quot. 1893.

c 1592 MARLOWE *Massacre Paris* II. vi. Wks. (Rtldg.) 240/1 Whilst I cry placet, like a senator. 1893 LIDDON, etc. *Life Pusey* I. xvi. 378 Amidst a tremendous shout of 'Placet' from the area the decisive formula was uttered, 'Nobis procuratoribus non placet' [Us, the proctors, it pleases not], and the question of the statute was for the time at an end.

2. as *sb.* **a.** The expression of assent or sanction (by this word); formerly, the assent of the temporal power necessary for the publication and execution of an ecclesiastical ordinance.

1589 NASHE *Pref. Greene's Menaphon* (Arb.) 5 Whose placet he accounts the plaudite of his paines. 1593 tr. *Guicciardini's Descr. Low-C.* 21 b, The pope cannot giue a benefice, nor a pardon, nor send a bull into the countrey without the Princes Placet.

b. A vote of assent in a council, or in the congregation or convocation of a university.

1883 *Manch. Exam.* 1 Dec. 4/7 The report..was rejected by 40 non placets to 39 placets. 1905 *Daily News* 6 Mar. 6 'Why should the University be ruled from the country parishes?'..was asked again by the 'placet' party.

†**3.** *erron.* for PLACIT, q.v.

Placfont, erroneous form of PAKTONG.

1893 JOHNSTONE-LAVIS in *Nature* 12 Jan. 257/2 The amplifying lever is composed of fine placfont tubes.. The pendulum bob is a flattened cylinder supported by a placfont wire 1.50 m. long.

Plachart, obs. form of PLACARD.

Placid (plæ·sid), *a.* [ad. L. *placid-us* pleasing, favourable, gentle, mild, calm, f. root of *placēre* to please; see -ID[1]. Cf. F. *placide* (15–16th c.).]

1. Mild, gentle; calm, peaceful; unruffled, tranquil, still, serene.

1626 BACON *Sylva* § 292 It conduceth unto long life, and to the more placid motion of the spirits. 1669 STURMY *Mariner's Mag.* III. i b, To the end the placid Fruits of these my Labours..may be..preserved from the turbulent Storms of discontented Spirits. 1671 MILTON *P. R.* III. 217 That placid aspect and meek regard. 1775 JOHNSON *Lett. to Mrs. Thrale* 21 July, That you sit down placid and content, disposed to enjoy the present. 1832 G. DOWNES *Lett. Cont. Countries* I. 93 The..Valley..of Interlaken..is altogether of a placid, pastoral character. 1850 TENNYSON *In Mem.* ix, Fair ship, that from the Italian shore Sailest the placid ocean-plains. 1871 L. STEPHEN *Playgr. Europe* (1894) x. 251 The male population is distinctly of a placid temperament.

†**b.** Of peaceful disposition towards another; free from anger or wrath. *Obs.*

1663 *Aron-bimn.* 23 To make an atonement, to render him placid and gracious.

†**2.** Pleasing, agreeable, welcome. *Obs. rare.*

1627–77 FELTHAM *Resolves* I. lix. 92 Those things..are made placid or disgustful, as fond Opinion catches them.

3. *Comb.*, as *placid-faced, -mannered*, etc.

1840 DICKENS *Old C. Shop* xiv, A little fat placid-faced old gentleman.

†**Placi·dious**, *a. Obs. rare*[—1]. [irreg. f. PLACID + -IOUS.] = prec.

1607 TOPSELL *Four-f. Beasts* (1658) 125 The Dogs did.. discern betwixt Christians and Turks; for towards the Turks they were most eager, furious, and unappeaseable, but towards Christians, although unknown, most easie, peaceable and placidious.

Placidity (plăsi·diti). [ad. L. *placiditās*, f. *placidus* PLACID: see -ITY. So F. *placidité* (1878 in *Dict. Acad.*).] The quality of being placid; mildness, calmness, tranquillity, peacefulness.

1619 W. SCLATER *Exp. 1 Thess.* (1630) 142 First Meeknesse; secondly Placiditie, as for want of a plainer terme, I am forced to call it. 1766 CHANDLER *Life David* I. ii. 36 He..behaves with the utmost placidity, moderation, and calmness. 1816 G. CRABB *Eng. Synonymes* 187/2 Placidity is more of a natural gift; *serenity* is acquired. 1866 G. MACDONALD *Ann. Q. Neighb.* xix. (1878) 360 All the placidity of his countenance had vanished.

Placidly (plæ·sidli), *adv.* [f. PLACID + -LY[2].] In a placid manner; mildly, calmly, quietly; peacefully, without agitation.

1626 JACKSON *Creed* VIII. xxix. § 11 Hee..sweetly and placidly resigned up his soule into his Father's hands. 1695 WOODWARD *Nat. Hist. Earth* III. i. (1723) 145 It placidly distends the Tubes and Vessels of Vegetables. 1786 tr. *Beckford's Vathek* (1883) 125 How placidly doth he recline his lovely little head! 1877 MRS. FORRESTER *Mignon* I. 24 The two friends are placidly smoking their cigars by the open window.

Placidness (plæ·sidnės). [f. PLACID + -NESS.] The quality of being placid: = PLACIDITY.

1727 BAILEY vol. II, *Placidness*, Peaceableness, Quietness. 1748 RICHARDSON *Clarissa* (1811) II. xlii. 310 To enjoy yourself with your usual placidness, and not to be ruffled. 1898 *Daily News* 15 Nov. 6/1 The British navvy at work amidst an armed camp..plied his vocation with placidness.

Placing (plēⁱ·siŋ), *vbl. sb.* [-ING[1].] The action of the verb PLACE; the condition or mode of being placed; putting, setting, location; position, situation; arrangement, etc.: see the verb.

1549 COVERDALE, etc. *Erasm. Par. 1 Cor.* 34 The diuers placyng and vse [of the members]..apertayneth to the welth of the whole body. 1585 T. WASHINGTON tr. *Nicholay's Voy.* I. xix. 21 b, Hauing wel considered the placing of the campe. 1611 SHAKS. *Cymb.* III. v. 65 Shee being downe, I haue the placing of the British Crowne. 1705 HEARNE *Collect.* 2 Dec. (O. H. S.) I. 111 It stood according to ye old Placing, U. 3. 7. *Jur.* 1723 CHAMBERS tr. *Le Clerc's Treat. Archit.* I. 116 The commodious and agreeable placing of Statues. 1821 GALT *Ann. Parish* xx, More than all my absences..from the time of my placing. 1824 L. MURRAY *Eng. Gram.* (ed. 5) I. 446 The wrong placing of the adverb *only*. 1894 *Daily News* 26 July 3/3 He won the race so easily that little notice need be taken of the placings of the remainder of the field. 1898 [see PLACER 1].

b. *attrib.*, as **placing-house**, the building in a china or earthenware factory where the ware is 'placed' in fire-clay saggers or setters in preparation for being baked.

1881 *Porcelain Works Worcester* 25 The manufactured objects being now ready for baking are taken to the placing house of the biscuit oven.

†**Placit** (plæ·sit). *Obs.* Also **placet.** [ad. L. *placit-um*: see PLACITUM. So It. *placito.*]

1. What is decided or determined upon; an opinion, a judgement; a decision, decree, ordinance.

1605 BACON *Adv. Learn.* II. xxv. § 5 That Secondarie reason..which is grounded upon the placets of God. 1641 J. TRAPP *Theol. Theol.* iii. 125 Those Masters of opinions ..that seek to obtrude upon Gods inheritance their conceits and placits. 1661 GLANVILL *Van. Dogm.* 129 As little in their Power as the placits of destiny. 1738 WARBURTON *Div. Legat.* App. 50 Delivering us the placits of the old philosophers. 1832 J. BREE *St. Herbert's Isle* 70 Oral theorems and placits.

2. A plea, a petition. *rare.*

1822 SCOTT *Nigel* ix, The boon which I am now to ask.. is, that your Majesty would be pleased, on the instant, to look at the placet of Lord Glenvarloch.

†**Pla·citatory**, *a. Obs. rare*[—1]. [f. L. *placitāt-*, ppl. stem of *placitāre* (Plaut.), freq. of *placēre* to please + -ORY[2].] = next.

1569 J. SANFORD tr. *Agrippa's Van. Artes* 164 An other exercise of the lawe, which they terme the Arte Placitatorie, or els Aduocatorie.

†**Pla·citory**, *a. Law. Obs. rare.* [f. med.L. *placit-um* (see below) + -ORY[2].] Relating or pertaining to pleas or pleading.

1690 J. CLAYTON *Reports Chancery* Pref. a j, The art Placitory..is double, first, that in writing upon the Records; ..The other..vocall, which pleads before the Judge to the Jury. 1836 in SMART, and in later Dicts.

‖**Placitum** (plæ·sitǝm). *Obs.* exc. *Hist.* Pl. **placita.** [L., an opinion, determination, maxim, prop. neuter pa. pple. of *placēre* to please; in med L. the sentence of a court, a fine, a trial, a plea.] The decree of a judge, the decision or determination of a public assembly, a court of justice, or the like; hence 'the public assemblies of all degrees of men where the king presided, and where they consulted upon the great affairs of the kingdom' (*Blount's Law Dict.* 1717). Also, in *pl.* the proceedings at such assemblies or courts, debates, trials at law, pleadings or pleas.

1668 HOWE *Bless. Righteous* (1825) 22 The placita or decretals of the Redeemer. 1706 PHILLIPS, *Placitum*, a Sentence of the Court, an Opinion, an Ordinance or Decree; ..In our Common-Law, Placita signifies Pleas or Pleadings; it was also sometimes taken for Penalties or Fines. 1769 ROBERTSON *Chas. V* (1796) I. 269 In a placitum or trial in the presence of Charlemagne. 1794 G. ADAMS *Nat. & Exp. Philos.* II. xxi. 413 If the *placita* of their predecessors were not lost sight of or neglected. 1864 BRYCE *Holy Rom. Emp.* ix. (1889) 138 The *placita* at which these laws were framed or published, would not have been crowded, as of yore, by armed freemen.

Plack[1] (plæk). *Sc.* and *north. dial. Obs.* exc. *Hist.* Forms: 5–7 **plak, plake, plakk**(e, **placke,** 6– **plack.** [prob. a. Flem. *placke, plecke*, a small coin of Brabant and Flanders, current in the 15th c., of varying value, in 17th c. Du. (Hexham) applied to the French *sou*; hence F. *plaque* (1425), *placque, plecque*, med.L. *placca* (1481). Orig. 'flat disk, tablet'; so Flem. *plak*, F. *plaque*. Cf. MLG. *plack*, LG. *plak, plakke* spot, piece, patch, rag, flat piece of land, dug turf; Du. *plak* flat lath for beating, blow, spot, slice; MHG *placke, phlacke* spot, patch, rag. Cf. PLACARD, PLACKET, PLECK.

Cf. 1425 *Journal d'un Bourgeois de Paris*, an. 1425, 355, Buchon. (Godef.) En ce temps couroit une monnoie a Paris, nommee plaques, pour douze deniers parisis, et estoient de par le duc de Bourgogne. See also Du Cange, *Placa, Placca.*]

†**a.** A coin of the Netherlands of the 15th and 16th centuries. *Obs.* **b.** A small billon coin issued by James III of Scotland; also, a small copper coin current in Scotland in the 15th and 16th centuries, worth 4 pennies Scots.

a. 1479 in *Cely Papers* (1900) 20 Item ij docates..xxxiij[s] Item in plakes vj[li]..x[s] fls. 1482 *Ibid.* 126 Item iij plakes.. xxvj[d]. *c* 1483 CAXTON *Dialogues* 17 Thise ben grotes of englond: Suche ther be of flaundres; Plackes and half plackes [*Patards et demi patards*]. 1526 in *L. & P. Hen. VIII*, IV. II. 1149 Double plakks or Carolus shall be current for 4*d.* as now.

b. 1473 *Sc. Acts Jas. III* (1814) II. 105/1 As tuiching þe plakkis & þe new pennyis, þe lordis thinkis þat þe striking of þame be cessit. 1513 DOUGLAS *Æneis* VIII. Prol. 93 Sum penis furth a pan boddum to prent fals plakkis. 1540 *Lanc. Wills* (1857) II. 140 A bende plucke whyche ys in my purse. *a* 1578 LINDESAY (Pitscottie) *Chron. Scot.* (S. T. S.) I. 169 The wyffis wald refuse the said cunzie quhilk was callit ane Couchrinis plak and said to him that it wald be cryit doun. 1583 in Cochran-Patrick *Rec. Coinage Scot.* (1876) I. 159 That all the saides twelf pennie peices babeis and plackes with the thre pennie grottis and half plackes now current salbe brocht in to his hienes cunyehous..and thairof new money to be cunyeit. 1617 MORYSON *Itin.* I. 283 The Scots haue of long time had..Placks, which they esteemed for 4 pence, but 3 of them make an English penny. 1662 RAY *Three Itin.* II. 162 One bodel they call two-pennies; two bodels a plack. *a* 1706 R. SEMPLE *Piper Kilbarchan* ix. At bridals he wan many placks. 1786 CARDONNEL *Numism. Scot.* Pref. 33 The plack is an ideal coin at this present time in Scotland. 1834 H. MILLER *Scenes & Leg.* xix. (1857) 279 After collecting all the placks and boddles of the party (little pieces of copper coin, with the head of Charles II on one side, and the Scotch thistle on the other).

c. In proverbial phrases, as the type of something of very small value; the smallest possible amount; a farthing; a bit; as in *not worth a plack*, utterly worthless: *plack and bawbee, plack and boddle*, in full, every penny, to the last farthing; *two and a plack*, a trifle, a small sum.

a 1550 in *Dunbar's Poems* (S.T.S.) 307 He wald nocht mend thame worth ane plack. 1572 *Satir. Poems Reform.* xxviii. 118 Plaitter nor pois we neuer left ane plak. 1693 *Scotch Presbyt. Eloq.* (1738) 126 I'll hazard twa and a plack. 1787 W. TAYLOR *Scots Poems* 6 Ise frankly own mysel his debtor For plack an' boddle. 1802 R. ANDERSON *Cumberld. Ball.* 31 They pick'd my pocket i' the thrang, And de'il a plack had I. 1814 SCOTT *Wav.* xlix, He wasna a plack the waur. 1820 — *Abbot* vi, I would not Sir Halbert had seen her..for two and a plack.

d. *attrib.* Of the value of or costing a plack.

1560 *Aberdeen Regr.* XXIV. (Jam.), His wyf brewit plakaill. 1567 *Gude & Godlie B.* (S. T. S.) 204 His plak Pardonis, are bot lardonis, Of new fund vanitie. 1824 SCOTT *Redgauntlet* ch. xx, He asked..'Whether he could have a plack-pie'. 1899 *Westm. Gaz.* 28 July 3/3 From ancient times the revenues in Scotch burghs were derived from small imposts, variously called petty customs, plack dues, and so on,..levied on animals and goods entering the burgh.

†**Plack**[2]. *Obs. rare*[—1]. [app. a. F. *plaque.*] = PLACKET[1], q.v. for quot. **Plack**, var. PLAYOCK, toy. **Plackard(e, -erd**, obs. ff. PLACARD.

†**Placket**[1]. *Obs. rare.* [app. a. F. *plaquette* tablet, dim. of *plaque* thin plate.] A plan or map.

1552 T. BARNABE in Strype *Eccl. Mem.* II. II. App. E. 154 He sent me thither [Newhaven = Havre] upon the kings cost; and I drew a plack of yt, and brought yt to hym..my Lord Fitz Williams..better than three or four hours, perviewing the placket.

Placket[2] (plæ·kėt). [Origin obscure. Perh. the same word as *placat*, var. form of PLACARD *sb.*, sense 3 of which coincides with sense 1 here, and may possibly be the origin of the other uses. But the order of the senses is uncertain, and the following is merely provisional.]

†**1.** (?) = PLACCATE 1, PLACARD 3. *Obs. rare.*

1626 CAPT. SMITH *Accid. Yng. Seamen* 16 Braded plackets for brests of defence.

2. An apron or petticoat: hence *transf.* the wearer of a petticoat, a woman. *Obs.* or *arch.*

1606 SHAKS. *Tr. & Cr.* II. iii. 22 The curse dependant on those that warre for a placket. *a* 1625 FLETCHER *Hum. Lieut.* IV. iv, Not half so troublesome as you are to yourself, Sir; Was that brave heart made to pant for a placket? 1661 W. K. *Conf. Charac., Old Holding Hag* (1860) 88 The extent of her placket is alwayes lower than her smock, and that comes but an inch lower than her navel. 1685 CROWNE *Sir C. Nice* II. 13 Eve, the mother of jilts,..pretended to modesty, and fell a making plackets presently. 1711 E. WARD *Quix.* I. 244 Because the Meal from off his Jacket Should not be seen upon her Placket. 1810 SCOTT *Lady of L.* VI. v, Our vicar thus preaches—and why should he not? For the dues of his cure are the placket and pot. 1881 DUFFIELD *Don Quix.* II. 493 A farthingale and placket [Sp. *saboyanas de seda*] instead of her grey petticoat.

3. The opening or slit at the top of a skirt or petticoat, for convenience in putting on and off; also, the slit in a shirt, usually behind.

(Quots. 1605, *c* 1620 are doubtful.)

1605 SHAKS. *Lear* III. iv. 100 Keepe..thy hand out of Plackets. *c* 1620 FLETCHER & MASS. *Lit. Fr. Lawyer* v. ii, Keep thy hand from thy sword, and from thy Laundresse placket. 1706 PHILLIPS, *Placket*, the fore-part of a Woman's Petticoat or Shift. 1719 D'URFEY *Pills* (1872) II. 19 And Madge had a ribbon hung down to her Placket. 1755 SMOLLETT *Quix.* (1803) IV. 104 Teresa Panza..came forth ..with a grey petticoat, so short that it seemed to have been cut close to the placket.

†**b.** Also *sensu obscœno*. *Obs.*

1601 MUNDAY *Downfall Earl Huntington* II. ii. D ij b, And lust doe vncase, From the placket to the pappe. 1673 HICKERINGILL *Gregory Father Greybeard* 230, I got all, to her very plackit. 1709 *Brit. Apollo* II. No. 28. 3/2 She's ..Well pleas'd with her Cull in her Placket.

4. A pocket, esp. that in a woman's skirt.

1663 *Hist. Cromwell* in *Select. Harl. Misc.* (1793) 368 Which instrument of his, as was said, was found in my Lady Lambert's placket. 1820 L. HUNT *Indicator* No. 60 (1822) II. 62 In a placket at her side is an old enamelled watch. *a* 1825 FORBY *Voc. E. Anglia*, *Placket*, a pocket. 1841 CHORLEY *Mus. & Manners* (1844) III. 186 The coupé was occupied by a substantial burgher, with his placket at his side, and his pipe for ever at his mouth. 1868 BROWNING *Ring & Bk.* V. 1155 What meaneth this epistle..I pick from out thy placket and peruse?

5. *Comb.* **placket-hole**, an opening in the outer skirt to give access to the pocket within; also = 3.

1762 STERNE *Tr. Shandy* V. i, Are not trouse, and placket-holes, and pump-handle—and spigots and faucets, in danger still, from the same association? 1880 *Daily Tel.* 29 May, The well-known 'placket hole', which is seldom free from points of escape, and has a trick of gaping wide open to disclose its contents to any curious eye. 1898 *Westm. Gaz.* 17 Mar. 3/2 The concealing of the placket hole is quite an object just now. 1903 *Pilot* 20 June 529/1 The purse dropped through her placket-hole, instead of going into her pocket.

Plackless (plæ·klės), *a. Sc.* [f. PLACK + -LESS.] Without a plack; penniless.

1786 BURNS *Scotch Drink* xvi, Poor plackless devils like mysel'. 1837 R. NICOLL *Poems* (1842) 161 In cottages Where poor folk plackless gae.

Placo- (plæ·ko), before a vowel **plac-**, combining form of Gr. πλάξ, πλακ- a flat plate, tablet, entering into various scientific words. **Placobra·nchid** (-kid) [Gr. βράγχια gills], one of the *Placobranchia*, a division of nudibranchiate gastropods having lamellar gills covering the upper surface of the lobes and back; so **Placobra·nchoid** (-koid) *a.*, resembling or akin to the *Placobranchia*. **Pla·coderm** [Gr. δέρμα skin] *a.*, having the skin encased in broad flat bony plates, as certain fossil fishes; of or belonging to the *Placodermata* or *Placodermi*, an order of Palæozoic fishes having the head and pectoral region thus protected; *sb.* one of the *Placodermata*; so **Placode·rmal, Placode·rmatous** *adjs.*; **Placode·rmoid** *a.*, resembling the placoderms in form or structure. **Pla·codont** [Gr. ὀδούς tooth] *a.*, of or belonging to the *Placodontia*, a division of fossil saurians having thickly-set short flat palatal teeth; *sb.* (also **Placodo·ntid**), a reptile belonging to the *Placodontia*; so **Placodo·ntoid** *a.*, resembling the placodonts in form or structure. **Placoga·noid** [GANOID] *a.*, of or pertaining to the *Placoganoidei*, a division of fossil Devonian fishes, having the head and part of the body protected by large ganoid plates; *sb.*, a fish of the *Placoganoidei*; also **Placoganoi·dean** *a.* and *sb.* **Placo·phoran** [Gr. -φόρος bearing] *a.*, of or pertaining to the *Placophora*, a sub-order of molluscs, sometimes made a primary division, comprising only the CHITONS (*Polyplacophora*); *sb.*, one of the *Placophora*, a chiton; so **Placo·phorous** *a.*

1859–65 PAGE *Geol. Terms* (ed. 2), **Placoderms*,..Dr. Pander's term for the bony-plated or bone-encased fishes of the Old Red Sandstone. 1886 A. WINCHELL *Walks Geol. Field* 239 The placoderm was destined to disappear with the Devonian period. 1889 NICHOLSON & LYDEKKER *Palæont.* (ed. 3) II. 1001 Points in which the Siluroids resemble the *Placodermatous Ganoids. *Ibid.* 921 It has..been suggested..that the 'Placodermoid Ganoids were closely related to the Ascidian Invertebrates. 1859 OWEN in *Encycl. Brit.* (ed. 8) XVII. 124/2 The *placoganoid and ganoid, heterocercal and notochordal fishes of the Devonian. 1852 DANA *Man. Geol.* vii. 276 Placoganoids, having the body covered with plates instead of scales. 1872 W. S. SYMONDS *Rec. Rocks* vii. 254 During the latter part of the Silurian epoch the..Placoganoids make their appearance.

Pla·codine. *Min.* Also **placodite.** [ad. Ger. *plakodin* (A. Breithaupt 1841), f. Gr. πλακώδης flat, cake-like, f. πλάξ, πλακ- tablet, cake.] A name given, on the supposition of its being a native mineral, to an arsenide of nickel, Ni_4As_2, now considered to be a furnace-product.

1856 *Eng. Cycl.* IV. 367/2 Placodine (Arseniuret of Nickel). ..Primary form an oblique rhombic prism. 1886 *Cassell's Encycl. Dict.*, *Placodine, placodite.*

Placoid (plæ·koid), *a.* and *sb. Zool.* [f. Gr. πλάξ, πλακ- flat plate, tablet: see -OID. Cf. F. *Placoïdes*, in mod.L. form *Placoidei*, name given by Agassiz, 1833, to certain fishes, on account of the plate-like appearance of their scales. (The earliest derivative in Eng. was app. *placoidean*.)]

A. *adj.*

1. Having the form of a plate; applied to the horny scales and tubercles of the *Placoidei*: see B.

1842 H. MILLER *O. R. Sandst.* iv. 73 One kind of scale, for instance the Placoid or broad plated scale, is found to characterize all the cartilaginous fishes of Cuvier except the sturgeon. 1870 ROLLESTON *Anim. Life* Introd. 68 The dermal exo-skeleton may take the form of..placoid or spiny dentinal formations. 1880 GÜNTHER *Fishes* 349 Very young individuals possess a series of small 'placoid' spines. 1888 ROLLESTON & JACKSON *Anim. Life* 411 The primitive form [of the exoskeleton] occurs..in the shape of dermal teeth (= placoid scales), similar in structure and development to oral teeth.

2. Having placoid scales; of or pertaining to the *Placoidei*: see B.

1847 *Nat. Encycl.* I. 136 A genus of fossil Placoid fishes. 1851 RICHARDSON *Geol.* (1855) 275 The first order, or Placoid, ..have the skin irregularly covered with plates of enamel, sometimes large, as in the rays, sometimes reduced to small points, as in the sharks. 1880 GÜNTHER *Fishes* 21 The distinctions between..placoid and ganoid fishes are vague.

B. *sb.* A fish of the division *Placoidei*, containing the sharks and rays, distinguished by having the skin protected by irregularly disposed bony scales, sometimes bearing spines.

1854 H. MILLER *Sch. & Schm.* xxi. (1858) 473 The mere detached teeth and spines of placoids. 1873 DAWSON *Earth & Man* v. 96 The Placoids or shark-like fishes.

Hence **Placoi·dal** *a. rare*; **Placoi·dean** *a.* and *sb.*

1836 BUCKLAND *Geol. & Min.* I. xiii. 269 *note*, *Placoidians*. ..Fishes of this Order are characterized by having their skin covered irregularly with plates of enamel [etc.]. *Ibid.* 283 Genera of the first and second orders (Placoidean and Ganoidian)..ceased suddenly. 1845 R. CHAMBERS *Vestiges* (ed. 4) 207 When fishes came, the first forms were those ganoidal and placoidal types which correspond with the early fœtal condition of higher orders. 1849 SMART *Dict.* Suppl., Placoideans.

Placquart, obs. form of PLACARD.

Placque, variant of PLAQUE.

‖**Placula** (plæ·kiŭlă). *Biol.* [mod.L., dim. from Gr. πλάξ, πλακ- tablet, plate.] Name for the embryo of *Calcispongiæ* at that stage in its development when it has the form of a plate or disk. Hence **Pla·cular, Pla·culate** *adjs.*, having the form of a placula.

1884 A. HYATT in *Proc. Boston Soc. Nat. Hist.* XXIII. 89 The primitive differentiation of the placula into two layers is established in what we have designated the diploplacula. *Ibid.* 97 The embryo of Calcispongiæ is also a placula until the same stage. *Ibid.* 150 A full-grown, primitive, placulate form. 1895 *Syd. Soc. Lex.*, *Placular*,..*Placulate.*

Plad, Pladding, obs. ff. PLAID, PLAIDING.

†**Pladding**, ? variant of *platting*, PLAITING.

a 1711 KEN *Damonet* Poet. Wks. 1721 IV. 505 The Garlands are begun of Pladding fine, Our Wedding-clothes are made, which richly shine.

Pladge, obs. Sc. variant of PLEDGE.

Pladman, var. of PLAIDMAN, Highlander.

‖**Plafond** (plafoṅ). *Arch.* Also 7 **platfound,** 7–9 **platfond,** 8 **plaffond.** [F. *plafond* (†*platfond*) a ceiling (1559 in Hatz.-Darm.), f. *plat* flat + *fond* bottom.]

1. A ceiling, either flat or vaulted; usually as enriched with paintings; hence, a painting executed on a ceiling. †*In plafond*: on the ceiling.

1664 EVELYN tr. *Freart's Archit.* II. ix. 110 Also they do rarely well about Platfonds and upon Ground-works. 1670 LASSELLS *Voy. Italy* I. 87 The roof..is all guilt, and set with curious pictures in Platfound. 1705 JOS. TAYLOR *Journ. Edinb.* (1903) 37 The plaffond is handsomely painted. 1714 STEELE *Lover* No. 33 (1723) 192 The whole Plafond or Ceiling. 1801 FUSELI in *Lect. Paint.* ii. (1848) 398 The platfonds, panels, and cupolas, of palaces and temples. 1835 WILLIS *Pencillings* xiii. 102 Naked female figures fill every plafond.

2. (See quots.)

1723 CHAMBERS tr. *Le Clerc's Treat. Archit.* I. 52 The Plafond or Soffit of the Cornice. 1842–76 GWILT *Archit.* Gloss., *Plafond* or *Platfond*,..also the underside of the projection of the larmier of the cornice; generally any soffite.

‖**Plaga** (plēⁱ·gă). *Zool.* [L. *plāga* blow, stroke, wound, stripe, a. Gr. πληγή, Doric πλāγά blow, stroke.] A stripe of colour.

1826 KIRBY & SP. *Entomol.* IV. xlvi. 286 Plaga..A long and large spot. 1895 *Syd. Soc. Lex.*, *Plaga*,..also *Zool.*, a stripe of colour.

Plagal (plēⁱ·găl), *a. Mus.* [ad. med.L. *plagālis* (whence It. *plagale*, F., Ger. *plagal*), f. med. L. *plaga* the plagal mode (Du Cange), app. a back-formation from med.L. *plagius*, a. med. Gr. πλάγιος plagal (πλάγιος ἦχος a plagal mode), in class. Gr. 'oblique', f. πλάγος side. (Cf. Ger. *Seitenton* a plagal mode.)]

a. In *Gregorian Music*, Applied to those ecclesiastical modes which have their sounds comprised between the dominant and its octave, the final being near the middle of the compass. **b.** *Plagal cadence*: that form of perfect cadence in which the chord of the subdominant (major or minor) immediately precedes that of the tonic. In both senses opposed to AUTHENTIC.

1597 MORLEY *Introd. Mus.* Annot., Euery song..which in the middle hath an eight aboue the finall keye, is of an autenticall tune; if not it is a plagall. 1609 DOULAND *Ornith. Microl.* 13 Euery Song in the beginning, rising straight beyond the final Note to a Fift, is Authenticall: but that which fals straight way to a Third, or a Fourth, vnder the finall Key, is *Plagall*. 1796 BURNEY *Mem. Metastasio* III. 197 If you find yourself involved in the difficulties of the Plagal tones, I am not among the Authentic. 1836 *Penny Cycl.* VI. 99/2 There is another kind of Cadence, to which the name *Plagal* is given. 1875 OUSELEY *Harmony* xiii. 154 If the piece is serious and solemn..it is usual, especially in sacred pieces, to add to it a plagal cadence. 1880 ROCKSTRO in Grove *Dict. Mus.* II. 760/2 S. Gregory added to these Modes four others, directly derived from them, and hence called Plagal Modes.

Plagard(e, plagart, obs. forms of PLACARD.

Plagate (plēⁱ·gēⁱt), *a. Zool.* [f. L. *plāga* (see above) + -ATE[1].] Having a plaga or plagæ; marked with a streak or streaks.

1890 in *Cent. Dict.*

†**Plage**[1]. *Obs.* Also 4 **plaag,** 6 **plague.** [a. OF. *plage* region (1290 in Hatz.-Darm.):—late L. *plagia* (see Du Cange) a plain, shore, prop. adj. (*plagia regio*), f. *plaga* a region. So It. *piaggia*.

Hatz.-Darm. take *plage* in the sense 'littoral tract, shore' to represent *plagia*, but in the sense 'region, extent of land' to be a learned formation from *plaga*.]

1. A region, district, clime; sometimes, a zone.

c 1386 CHAUCER *Man of Law's T.* 445 Payens that conquereden al aboute The plages of the North. 1432–50 tr. *Higden* (Rolls) II. 53 The prouince Lindeseience, whiche longede somme tyme to the Marches, dothe diuide Northumbrelonde from that other plage. *a* 1548 HALL *Chron., Hen. VI* 185 King Henry..nesteled and strengthend him and his alyes in the North regions and boreal plage. 1586 MARLOWE *1st Pt. Tamburl.* IV. iv, From the frozen plage of Heaven. 1613 PURCHAS *Pilgrimage* VIII. i. 602 A Plage, plagued with scorching heats.

2. Any one of the four principal directions or quarters of the compass; direction, side.

1382 WYCLIF *Ezek.* vii. 2 Ende cometh vp on the foure plagis, or parties, of the erthe [1388 on foure coostis of the lond]. *c* 1391 CHAUCER *Astrol.* I. § 5 The 4 quarters of thin astrelabie, deuyded after the 4 principals plages or quarters of the firmament. 1432–50 tr. *Higden* (Rolls) I. 115 The mownte off Caluarye is at the northe plage of the mownte of Syon. 1501 DOUGLAS *Pal. Hon.* I. 195 Ane dyn I hard approching..Quhilk mouit fra the plague Septentrionall. 1590 *Serpent of Devis.* C j, A large Commit [= comet] of stremes, whose branches reacht on the fower plagues on the firmament. 1652 J. WRIGHT tr. *Camus' Nat. Paradox* VII. 151 Heavens alter the motion of your Spheares, and thou Sun ..go take thy Resting-place in the Orientall plage.

3. One of the divisions or parts of a church, *esp.* a transept. *rare.*

[*c* 1214 GAUF. DE COLDINGHAM in *Scriptores Tres Dunelm.* (Surtees) 11 *Ad orientalem ejusdem ecclesiæ plagam* [i.e. the triapsidal east end].] 1593 *Rites of Durham* (Surtees 1903) 23 Hee lyeth buryed..in the north plage. *Ibid.* 30 Johne Hemmyngbrowghe..lieth buried in the south plage.

†**Plage**[2]. *Obs. rare*[—1]. Also **plague.** [ad. L. *plaga* net, snare.] A net, snare, toil.

1608 TOPSELL *Serpents* 273 Spyders..hang their threds in ayre aboue, By plages [1658 plagues] vnseene to th' eye of man. [Here *threds* and *plages* seem to be erroneously transposed. The Latin rendered is: Sed liciis hinc densioribus plagas In aere appendunt.]

Plage, obs. form of PLAGUE, PLEDGE.

Plageat, -et, -ette, obs. forms of PLEDGET.

Plager, ? error for *plaget*, PLEDGET, pad, plug.

1656 RIDGLEY *Pract. Physick* 164 Wet the bands and plagers in Oxycratum. *Ibid.* 167 He sprinkled the Plagers with Oxycratum and red wine.

†**Plagia·rian**, *a. Obs. rare.* [f. as PLAGIARY + -AN.] Of or pertaining to plagiaries or man-stealers.

1656 BLOUNT *Glossogr.*, *Plagiarian Law* (*plagiaria lex*), a law made against these men [plagiaries], &c. 1706 PHILLIPS, *Plagiarian*, as The Plagiarian Law; a Law made against Plagiaries.

Plagia·rical, *a. rare.* [f. as PLAGIARY + -ICAL.] = PLAGIARISTIC.

1887 HALLIWELL *Shaks.* (ed. 7) II. 281 Without incurring the smallest risk of a plagiarical imputation.

Plagiarism (plēⁱ·dʒiăriz'm). [f. as PLAGIARY + -ISM.]

1. The action or practice of plagiarizing; the wrongful appropriation or purloining, and publication as one's own, of the ideas, or the expression of the ideas (literary, artistic, musical, mechanical, etc.) of another.

1621 BP. MOUNTAGU *Diatribæ* 23 Were you afraid to bee challenged for plagiarisme? 1716 M. DAVIES *Athen. Brit.* II. To Rdr. 46 A good Plea to any Charge of Plagiarism or Satyrism. 1753 JOHNSON *Adventurer* No. 95 ¶ 9 Nothing.. can be more unjust than to charge an author with plagiarism merely because he..makes his personages act as others in like circumstances have done. 1820 HAZLITT *Lect. Dram. Lit.* 257 If an author is once detected in borrowing, he will be suspected of plagiarism ever after. 1861 BUCKLE *Civiliz.* II. vi. 542 A certain unity of design which is inconsistent with extensive plagiarism.

2. A purloined idea, design, passage, or work.

1797 *Monthly Mag.* III. 260 He found the..song..to be 'a most flagrant plagiarism from Handel'. 1890 MAURICE *Mor. & Met. Philos.* (ed. 2) I. 98 A Thaumaturgist whom they had created..to convince the world that the Christian church was a plagiarism. 1875 JOWETT *Plato* (ed. 2) I. p. xx, They are full of plagiarisms, inappropriately borrowed.

Plagiarist (plēⁱ·dʒiărist). [f. PLAGIARY + -IST.] One who plagiarizes; one who is guilty of plagiarism.

1674 R. GODFREY *Inj. & Ab. Physic* 56 The Author (..I should say the Collector or Plagiarist). 1779 SHERIDAN *Critic* I. i, A dexterous plagiarist..might take out some of the best things in my tragedy, and put them into his own comedy. 1822 HAZLITT *Table-t.* Ser. II. v. (1869) 123 The poorest of all plagiarists, the plagiarists of words. 1866–7 BARING-GOULD *Cur. Myths Mid. Ages, Antichr. & Pope Joan* (1894) 172 The story spread among the mediæval chroniclers, who were great plagiarists.

Hence **Plagiari·stic** *a.*, characteristic of a plagiarist; pertaining to or characterized by plagiarism; whence **Plagiari·stically** *adv.*

1821 WAINEWRIGHT *Ess. & Crit.* (1880) 150 The whole series was cold, commonplace, and plagiaristic. 1823 *Blackw. Mag.* XIII. 93 They..have very unhandsomely and plagiaristically anticipated my own original lucubrations. 1838 *Fraser's Mag.* XVIII. 545 There is risk..in any or all of these plagiaristic devices.

Plagiarize (plēⁱ·dʒiărəiz), *v.* [f. PLAGIARY + -IZE.]

1. *trans.* To practise plagiarism upon; to take and use as one's own the thoughts, writings, or inventions of another. (With the thing, rarely the person, as object.)

1716 M. DAVIES *Athen. Brit.* III. *Diss. Physick* 29 Manto or Daphnes, Tiresias the Priest's Daughter, who writ or paraphras'd in such excellent Strains, some of the..Oracles at the Temple of the Delphians, that they were worth to be plagiariz'd by Homer himself. 1822 *Blackw. Mag.* XII. 783, I do not mean to say that they are plagiarized (let me coin the word, for I do not like to say stolen) from Miss Lee. 1830 TENNYSON *Talking Oak* v, For oft I talk'd with him apart, And told him of my choice, Until he plagiarised a heart, And answer'd with a voice. 1888 G. A. SCHRUMPF in *Athenæum* 25 Feb. 243/2 Mr. Kirby..seeks to create the impression that I plagiarized Ujfalvy.

2. *intr.* To practise or commit plagiarism.

1832 LYTTON *Eugene A.* I. vi, I cannot plagiarise..from any scholastic designs you might have been giving vent to. 1863 *Blackw. Mag.* Sept. 279 Little wits that plagiarise are but pickpockets: great wits that plagiarise are conquerors.

Hence **Plagiariza·tion** = PLAGIARISM 1; **Pla·giarizer** = PLAGIARIST.

1839 *Fraser's Mag.* XX. 413 Plagiarizers..have..stolen their thoughts. 1884 *Athenæum* 3 May 575/3 No direct ..plagiarization from his German model.

Plagiary (plēⁱ·dʒiări), *sb.* and *a.* [ad. L. *plagiārius* one who abducts the child or slave of another, a kidnapper; a seducer; also (Mart. I. 53. 9) a literary thief. Cf. late L. *plagium* kidnapping, *plagiāre* to kidnap. So F. *plagiaire* (16th c.) a plagiarist.]

A. *sb.* †**1.** A kidnapper, a man-stealer. *Obs.*

1613 PURCHAS *Pilgrimage* III. iii. 199 In the time of his.. childhood, he was by some Plagiary stolne away from his friends. 1626 H. KING *Serm. Deliverance* 46 How many be there..that, like Plagiaries, make it their trade to hunt and catch men? 1697 BP. PATRICK *Comm. Exod.* xx. 16 No Israelite would buy him, and therefore such Plagiaries sold him to Men of other Nations.

2. = PLAGIARIST.

1601 B. JONSON *Poetaster* IV. iii, Why? the ditt' is all borrowed; 'tis Horaces: hang him plagiary. 1649 JER. TAYLOR *Gt. Exemp.* I. Ad Sect. viii. 119 He that is a Plagiary of others titles or offices, and dresses himself with their beauties. 1676 LISTER in *Ray's Corr.* (1848) 125, I am glad you have discovered those authors to be plagiaries. 1758 JOHNSON *Idler* No. 85 ¶ 7 Compilers and plagiaries are encouraged, who give us again what we had before. 1855 MACAULAY *Hist. Eng.* xix. IV. 354 Blount was one of the most unscrupulous plagiaries that ever lived.

3. = PLAGIARISM 1; literary theft. [Cf. -ARY B. 1.]

1646 SIR T. BROWNE *Pseud. Ep.* 22 Plagiarie had not its nativitie with printing, but began in times when thefts were difficult. 1688 G. LANGBAINE (*title*) Momus Triumphans: or, the Plagiaries of the English Stage; Expos'd in a catalogue of all the Comedies, Opera's,..&c. 1775 SHERIDAN *Rivals* Pref., My first wish in attempting a play was to avoid every appearance of plagiary. 1880 SWINBURNE *Study Shaks.* 52

Supplement, p. 3873; Corrigenda, p. 4092; Spurious words, p. 4093; Books quoted, p. 4094

Plagiaryship. No parasitic rhymester .. ever uttered a more parrot-like note of plagiarism.

Plagiate, a. and adv. Kidnapping, man-stealing. *rare*.

Plagio-, before a vowel or h **plagi-**, comb. form, repr. Gr. πλάγιο- oblique, slanting, ζ πλάγ-ιον side.

Plagiocephalic, a.

Plagioclase (-klæ˙stik), a. Min. [f. Plagio- + Gr. κλάσις breaking.] Having oblique cleavage.

Plagionite.

Plagiostome.

Plagiostomatous, adj.

Plagiostomous, adj.

Plagiotropic, a. Bot.

Plagiotropism.

Plagium (plēˑdʒi̯ɒm). [L. plagium kidnapping.] Civil Law. Kidnapping, man-stealing.

Plagose (plēgōuˑs), a.

Plagula.

Plague (plēg), sb. [ME. plage, a-4 plaga a stroke. Also -OSE.] Inclined to flog, fond of flogging (corporal punishment).

Plague (plēg), sb. 1. An affliction, calamity, evil, 'scourge'; esp. a visitation of divine anger or justice, a divine punishment; with reference to 'the ten plagues' of Egypt.

2. In weakened sense: Anything causing trouble, annoyance, or vexation.

3. An infectious disease or epidemic attended with which men or beasts are stricken.

4. *esp.* An infectious disease or epidemic attended with which men or beasts are stricken.

Plague (plēg), v. 1. To afflict with plague or calamity.

2. In weakened sense (chiefly *colloq.*): To torment, harass.

Plague-sore.

Plag-spot.

Plaguily (plēˑgili), adv.

Plaguy (plēˑgi), a. (adv.)

Plaice (plēs). Forms: 3–5 plais, 4–5 playce, 4–7 playce, 5 playsze, playse, place, 6 pleise, 6–9 plaise, 4, 6– plaice. [ME. *plaïs* (390 Auson.), a. OF. *plaïs* (390 Auson.), F. plie, Pr. *plais*, med.L. platessa (a 390 Auson.).] A well-known European flat-fish, *Pleuronectes platessa*.

Plaid (plæd, plēd). Forms: 6 pladde, 6–8 plad, 7 pleid, 8 pladdie, (pladd), 8 (dial. 9) plod. [a. Gael. *plaide*, of obscure origin.] 1. A long piece of twilled woollen cloth.

2. A garment consisting of a long piece of twilled woollen cloth.

3. A plaid or tartan fabric.

4. *transf.* A man wearing a plaid; a Highlander.

5. *attrib.* and *comb.*, as plaid cloak, -fold, shawl, trousers; plaid-performed, -wrapped adjs.; plaid bed, a bed draped with plaid or tartan (fashionable in England early in 18th c.); plaidman, a Highlander; plaid-nook (-neuk) Sc., one end of the folded plaid sewn up so as to form a large pouch or pocket.

Plaided (plēˑded), a. Dressed in or wearing a plaid.

Plaidie (plēˑdi), dim. of Plaid. Sc. Also plaiddy, plaiddie.

Plaiding (plēˑdiŋ). Also 6–8 plaiding; 7 pleiding; Sc. 7 pladain, 7–8 plaidine, 8 +plaiding, 8– plaidden; 6 pladden [f. Plaid + -ING 1; cf. *shirting*, etc.] 1. Material for plaid; a twilled woollen cloth; a cloth of a tartan pattern.

Plaidman.

Plaig, plaik, var. of Platock Sc., plaything, toy.

Plaigt, obs. form of Plat sb. and v.

Plain (plēn), sb.1 Forms: see Plain a.1 Of. *plain*—L. *plān-um* a plain, *proj.* neut. of *plān-us* Plain a.1]

1. A tract of country of which the general surface is comparatively flat; an extent of level ground or flat meadow land; applied *spec.* in proper or quasi-proper names) to certain extensive tracts of this character.

2. The horizontal surface of a billiard-table.

Plain (plēn), sb.2 Sc. A wound.

Plain (plēn), v.1 Forms: see Plain a.1 An expression of grief, of discontent; complaint, lamentation = Plaint.

Plain (plēn), v.2 Now dial. [f. Plain a.1] An expression of grief, of discontent; complaint, lamentation = Plaint.

Plain (plēn), v.3 arch. Also 4 playne (playen), 4–6 playn, 4– plain. [a. OF. *plaindre*—L. *plān-gere* flat. In Sc.] 1. To make plain or smooth; to level, flatten.

Plain (plēn), a.1 [In English orig. *plain* (etc.) in all senses, including the geometrical (1 c), where Plain was substituted ε Plane a.]

I. 1. Flat, level, even; free from elevations and depressions.

2. A level or flat surface (of material or matter); esp. a plane.

II. 5. That is clearly what the name expresses; open, manifest, direct, unmistakable; downright, mere, sheer, flat; absolute.

III. 9. Without embellishment, addition, or decorative intent or colouring; unembellished, not ornate; simple, bare, bald (of the hair) worn straight, not curled; (of drawings, lithographs, etc.) not coloured. Also *fig.*

IV. 11. Open in behaviour or disposition; free from duplicity or reserve; guileless, honest, candid, frank.

V. 13. Having no special qualities or pretensions; unexceptional; undistinguished; ordinary.

Plaice (continued)

17. Of ordinary appearance; not beautiful or well-favoured; homely: often used euphemistically for ill-favoured, ugly.

18. *Plain* is emphasized by various comparisons, orig. applicable in particular senses, but afterwards humorously or irrationally applied to others.

VI. Phrases.

+6. Entirely, quite; fully. — CLEAN *adv.* 5.

7. Directly, duer; full. *Obs.*

8. With the adj.: chiefly parasynthetic, as *plain-bodied*, *-clothed*, *-faced*, *-featured*, *-garbed*, etc.; also *plain-looking*. See also PLAIN-HEARTED.

b. With the adv., as *plain-dressing*, *-going*, *-meaning*, *-speaking*, *-steering*. See also PLAIN-DEALER, -SPEAKING, -SPOKEN.

c. Special combs.: *plain-back*, *backs*, *weaver's name for a kind of worsted fabric*; *plain clothes*, *ordinary civil or citizen dress*, *unofficial dress*; *plain-song*; *plain-tile*, *attrib.*, as *plain-knitting-orange*.

Plain *sb.* Obs. Forms: 4-5 plein, 4-6 playne, etc.

Plain *v. arch. or dial.* Forms: 3-6 pleine, 3-7 playne, plaine, 4 pleigh(e, 4-6 playn(e, pleyne, plaine, 3-7 plaign-, 6 plain, (6, 8-9 *dial.* plean, 8-9 *dial.* plean, pleaign), 6 plaine, 7-9 pleyne, 9 pleyne, plainje, -(9s *arch.* and *dial.* plene, plaine, plenje.

Plainant, *a Law. Obs.* [a. F. *plaignant*, pple. of *plaindre*.]

Plain-chant. [a. F. *plain chant*: PLAIN-SONG.] = PLAIN-SONG, CANTO FERMO.

Plain-dealer. [f. PLAIN *a.* + DEALER.]

Plain-dealing, *plain-dealing*, *sb.* [f. PLAIN *a.* + DEALING *vbl. sb.*: cf. DOUBLE-DEALING.]

Plain-dealing, *ppl. a.* [f. PLAIN *a.* + *dealing*, ppl. of DEAL *v.*: cf. prec.]

Plainer (plē'nəz), *sb.* [f. PLAIN *v.* + -ER¹.] *Law.* — COMPLAINANT *sb.* Obs. *b.* A complainer, complainant. Now *dial.*

Plainful (plē'nfūl), *a. arch.* [f. PLAIN *v.* or stem of PLAINT + -FUL 1.]

Plain-hearted, *a.* Now *rare.* [f. *plain heart* + -ED².]

+Plaint. *sb.* Obs. Forms: 4-5 plein, 4-6 playne, playnt, plaint, plaint, etc.

Plainness (plē'nnes). Forms: *a.* 4 playnes, 4-5 playnnes, 4-7 playnnes, 6 plainnesse, playnes, 6 plaines, playnes, pleines. *b.* See PLAIN *a.* and -NESS.

Plain-sailing *sb.* [prob. a popular corruption of PLANE SAILING.]

Plain-song (plē'n-sŋ). *Mus.* [Rendering med. L. *cantus planus*, f. *plain* chant, lit. *canto piano*: see quot. 1795] in sense c.

Plain-speaking, *sb.* and *a.*

Plain-spoken, *ppl. a.*

Plaint (plānt). *Mus.* Forms: *a.* 3-4 pleinte, 5-6 playnte, plainte, (5 plaincte, plaintte, 6 pleint), 3 pleynt, 4-5 plaint, plant. *b.* In ME. two words - *a.* *pleinte*, plainte, *a.* OF. *plainte* in med. L. *plancta* (Du Cange), sb. from fem. pa. pple. of *plang-ère*, (ppl. sens above), to beat the breast.

+Plaintful, *a.* Obs. [f. PLAINT *sb.* + -FUL.]

Plaintie, obs. Sc. form of PLENTEOUS.

Plaintiff (plē'ntif). *a.* Forms: 4-5 plaint-, 4-6 plaintif, 5-6 -if, 7-8 -yfe, -ife, -iffe.

Plaintive (plē'ntiv). *a.* Forms: 4-8 as in PLAINTIFF; 6 -ive.

Plain-work, *plain work*. 1. Work of a plain or simple kind, as distinguished from ornamental or 'fancy' work; plain needlework or sewing.

2. *Masonry.* See quot. 1823.

Plaisance, etc., obs. form of PLEASANCE, etc.

Plaisand, obs. f. PLEASANT.

Plaisant, obs. form of PLEASANT.

Plaisanter (plezanter), *rare.* [obs. F. *plaisanter*.]

Plaister, obs. f. PLASTER.

Plait (plāt), *sb.* Forms: *a.* 5-6 playto, plyghte, 4-5 plyght, 7-8 plaight, plighte, 6-7 plight, 5-9 pleight, 6-9 pleight.

Plait. (plāt, plēt, plīt), *v.* Forms: see prec. *sb.* ; also PLAT *v.*[3], PLEAT *v.*, PLEIT *v.*, PLIGHT *v.*[2] [f. PLAIT *sb.*, where see note on pronunciation.]

1. *trans.* To fold (a woven or other fabric, etc.) to fold flat, to double; to gather in pleats ; …

Plaiter. [f. PLAIT *v.* + -ER[1].] One who or that which plaits.

Plaiting. *vbl. sb.* [f. PLAIT *v.* + -ING[1].] The action of the verb PLAIT.

Plaited, *ppl. a.* [f. PLAIT *v.* + -ED[1].] Folded, doubled, gathered in folds ; furnished with pleats.

Plait, *sb.* Also *plak,* *plakke,* obs. forms of PLACK.

Plan (plæn), *sb.* [a. F. *plan* (1553 in Hatz.-Darm.) a plane (surface), also a ground-plan, subst. use of *plan,* plane adj., flat, plane, 16th c. ad. L. *plān-us* flat …

Plan (plæn), *v.* [f. prec. sb.]
1. *trans.* To make a plan of …

Planar (plē'nǎȷ), *a. Math.* [ad. L. *plānār-is* (Mart. Cap.), f. *plān-us* plane.] …

Planch-board. *Obs.* [f. PLANCH *sb.* + BOARD.] …

Planchard (plæn'ʃǎȷd), *sb. Obs.* …

Planche (plænʃ), *sb. Obs.* …

Plancher (plæn'ʃǝȷ), *sb.* [a. F. *plancher*.] …

Planchery. *Obs. rare.* …

Planchet (plæn'ʃet), *sb.* [a. F. *planchette.*] …

Planchette (plænʃet'), *sb.* [a. F. *planchette* small board, dim. of *planche* PLANK.] …

Planaria (plǎnē'ȷȧ), *Zool.* …

Planarian (-ȷȧn), *a.* and *sb.* …

Planch (plǎnʃ), *sb.* …

Plancier (plæn'sȧȷ), *sb.* …

Plane (plēn), *sb.*[1] Also 6–7 *playne,* *plaine.* …

Plane (plēn), *sb.*[2] Also 6–7 *playne, plaine, plane.* …

Plane (plēn), *sb.*[3] …

Plane (plēn), *a.* …

Plane (plēn), *v.* …

Planeness. *rare.* …

Planer (plē'nǎȷ). …

Planerite (plæ'nĕrəit). *Min.* [Named 1862 after its discoverer D. J. Planer, mine director: see -ITE¹.] A hydrous phosphate of aluminium, allied to wavellite, found in Russia.

Planer-tree. [From the surname of I. J. Planer, a German botanist, whence the genus has its mod.L. name *Planera*.] A small tree (*Planera aquatica*, P. Gmelini, or other species) allied to and resembling the elm, found in moist situations in the Southern United States.

Plane sailing. In 7–8 *plain*. 1. [f. PLANE *a.*¹, formerly *plain*.] In *Navigation*, the art of determining a ship's place on the theory that she is moving on a plane, or that the surface of the earth is plane instead of spherical; navigation by a *plane chart*: see PLANE *sb.* 3.

Planeshear (plæ·nʃiə), planksheer (plæ·ŋkʃiə). Forms: 8 planeshear, -shire, 9 plane-sheer, plankshear, -sheer. [A corruption of PLANCHER *sb.*, by imagined connexion with PLANE, PLANE, and SHEER *sb.*] A continuous planking, covering the timber-heads of a wooden ship, in men-of-war forming a shelf below the gunwale; = *covering-board* (COVERING *vbl. sb.*³ 3); also loosely applied to the gunwale.

Planet (plæ·nĕt), *sb.*¹ Forms: 3–6 planete, (4–6 -ette, 5 -ed, 6 -it, -et, 7 planett's), 6– planet. [ME. a. OF. *planete* (cf. mod.L. *planéta*; cited only in pl. *planetae* — cl. L. *stella errantes*), a Gr. *πλανήτης* wanderer, hence, in pl. (*ἀστέρες*) *πλανῆται* wandering stars, planets. (Another Gr. form was *πλανήτης*, *πλάνης*, *πλανήτος*, in pl. *πλάνητες πλάνητες* *planites*.)]

1. *Old Astron.* A heavenly body distinguished from the fixed stars by having an apparent motion.

planet-book, a book professing to tell fortunes by means of the planets.

Planet (plæ·nĕt), *sb.*²

planets.

Planet, *v.*

Plane-table, *sb.* A surveying instrument used for measuring angles in mapping, consisting of a circular drawing-table mounted horizontally on a tripod, and having an alidade pivoted over its centre.

Plane-table, *v.* To survey with the plane-table.

Plane-tabler.

Plane-tabling.

Plane-tal.

Planetarian, *sb.*

Planetary, *a.* and *sb.* [ad. late L. *planetārius*, prop. adj.: 'belonging to a planet'.]

Planet-struck.

Plane-tree. A tree of the genus *Platanus*.

Planetoid (plæ·nĕtoid).

Plano- combining form of L. *plānus* level, flat, smooth.

Plangorous (plæ'ŋgərəs). *rare.* [f. L. type *plangor-em*: see next and -OUS.] Characterized by loud lamentation.

Plani- combining form of L. *plānus* level, flat, smooth, used chiefly in scientific terms.

Planicaudate (-kǭ·dāt) *a.* *Zool.* [ad. L. *cauda* tail], having a flat tail, as in certain reptiles (Mayne *Expos. Lex.* 1855).

Planiform.

Planifolious.

Planimeter (plæni·mĭtə), *sb.* An instrument for mechanically measuring the area of an irregular plane figure.

Planimetric.

Planimetry (plæni·mĕtri). Also 4 planemetrie, -ye; 8–9 planetry. [Ult. f. L. *planum*, *plani-* + -METRY.]

Planing (plē·niŋ), *vbl. sb.* 1. The action of PLANE *v.*

Planisher.

Planish (plæ·niʃ), *v.*

Planisphere (plæ·nisfiə). Also 4 planisphaere, 7 -sphaere, 7 -sphere, -ephere. [In ME. form *planispherie*, ad. med.L. *plānisphaerium*, f. L. *plānus* flat. Taken *a sphaera* or *aphere*.] A map or chart formed by the projection of a sphere, or part of one, on a plane.

Plank (plæŋk), *sb.* Also 4–5 planke, 4–5 plaunk, 6–7 planke. [ME. *planke*, a. ONF. *planke* = F. *planche*: — L. *planca*, prob. f. root *plak-* of Gr. *πλάξ*, etc.] 1. A long flat piece of smoothed timber, thicker than a BOARD.

Plank, *v.* 1. *trans.* To furnish, lay, floor, or cover with planks. Also with *over.*

Planked, *ppl. a.* [f. PLANK *v.* + -ED.] 1. Furnished, made, floored, or covered with planks.

Plank-board. *Obs.* [f. PLANK *sb.* + BOARD *sb.*] A thick board suitable for flooring and similar purposes.

Planker.

Planking (plæ·ŋkiŋ), *vbl. sb.* [f. as prec. + -ING¹.] The action of PLANK *v.*
1. Furnishing, flooring, or covering with planks.
2. *concr.* Planks in the mass; plank-work; the planks of a structure; *spec.* those forming the outer shell and inner lining of a ship.
3. The lagging or 'cleading' of a steam-cylinder.
4. In technical senses of the verb.

Plankless, *a.* [f. PLANK *sb.* + -LESS.] Having no planks; void or stripped of its planks.

Plankshear, -sheer, variants of PLANESHEAR.

Plankton (plæ·ŋktǫn), *Biol.* [a. Ger. *plankton* (V. Hensen 1887), a. Gr. πλαγκτόν, neut. of πλαγκτός adj., drifting.] A collective name for all the forms of floating or drifting organic life found at various depths in the ocean, or, by extension, in bodies of fresh water. *Also attrib.*

Planktologic(al. *Zool.* [f. PLANO- + Gr. βλαστ- is sprout, shoot.]

Plano-¹ (plæ·no), used as combining form of L. *plānus* flat, smooth, level; in scientific or technical adjectives, denoting (*a*) that is, flattened manner, with modification of a specified form in the direction of a plane, as *plano-compressed*, *-conical*, *-hemispherical*, *subconical*, *orbicular*, *-patellate*, *-rotund*, *-subciliate*; (*b*) a combination of a plane with another surface, esp. plane on one side, and of another surface on the other, as PLANO-CONCAVE, -CONVEX, etc. Also *plano-cylindrical*, plane on one side and half of a cylindrical form on the other; *plano-horizontal*, having a plane horizontal surface or position; *plano-solid*...

Plano-² (plæ·no), before a vowel or â *plan-*, combining form of Gr. πλάνος wandering, used in a few scientific terms : see PLANOBLAST, PLANOGIA, PLANOGAMETE, PLANURIA.

Planoblast (plæ·noblæst), *Zool.* [f. PLANO-² + Gr. βλαστ- is sprout, shoot.]

Plano-concave, *a.* [f. PLANO-¹ + CONCAVE *a.*] Having one surface plane and the opposite one concave, as a lens.

Plano-convex, *a.* [as prec. + CONVEX *a.*] Having one surface plane and the other convex.

Planform.

Planimeter (plænimītər), *Math.* [f. Gr. πλάνη + -METER.]

Planish (plæ·niʃ), *v.* [ad. F. *planir*.]

Planisher.

Planispheric(al.

Planity.

Plank.

Planotomy.

Plant (plānt), *sb.¹* [OE. *plante*, ad. L. *planta*.]
1. A young tree, shrub, or herb newly planted, or intended for planting; a set, cutting, slip; a sapling.
2. A member of the lower of the two series of organized living beings.

Plant (plānt), *v.* [OE. *plantian*, ad. L. *plantāre*, f. *planta* PLANT *sb.¹*]

PLANTAIN. 951 PLANTAIN. PLANTAIN. 952 PLANTATION

Plantable.

Plantage.

Plantain. A plant of the genus *Plantago*.

Plantain. A tree-like tropical herbaceous plant (*Musa paradisiaca*).

Plantal.

Plantar (plæ·ntər), *a. Anat.* [ad. L. *plantāris*.] Of or pertaining to the sole of the foot.

Plantation (plæntēiʃən). [ad. L. *plantātiōn-em*.]

PLANTATION.

Planter. (plɑ'ntɛɹ). [f. PLANT v. + -ER¹.]

Plantule (plæ'ntiʊl). Bot. [ad. mod.F. *plantule*.]

Planting, vbl. sb. [f. PLANT v. + -ING¹.]

Planta-cracy, etc.

Planto-cracy, etc.

Plantivorous (plænti'vɒɹəs).

Plantlet.

Plantling. [f. PLANT sb.¹ + -LING.] A little or young plant; a plantlet.

†Planure. Obs. rare.

Planty (plɑ'nti). Irish Music. Also 8 plangstone, plangsty, plansty.

Plaque (plɑk). [a. F.]

‖Plaquette (plakɛt). [F. dim. of *plaque*.]

Plash (plæʃ), sb.¹ Forms: 1 plæsc, pleos; 4 plasch, 5 plaisshe, plaesshe, 5-6 plasche, plasshe, 5- plash.

Plash, sb.² [a. OF. *plaissie*, *plais(s)ier*, *plais(s)er*.]

Plash, v.¹

Plash, v.²

Plashing, vbl. sb.¹

Plashing, vbl. sb.²

Plashy (plæ'ʃi). [f. PLASH sb.¹ + -Y.]

Plasher, local.

Plash-mill.

Pla'sh-pole.

Plasm (plæ'zm). [ad. late L. *plasma*.]

Plasma (plæ'zmă). [Late and eccl. L. *plasma*.]

Plasmation (plæzmeɪ'ʃən). Obs. rare⁻¹.

PLATEASM. — **PLATER.**

3. To make or beat (metal) into plates. *rare*⁻¹.

†Plateasm. *Obs.* [ad. Gr. πλατειασμός (Quintil.) a broad Doric pronunciation, f. πλατειάζειν to pronounce broadly, f. πλατύς, fem. of πλατύς broad.] [See quot.]

Plateau (plæ·tō). Pl. p'ateaux, -eaus (-ōz). [a. F. *plateau* (earlier *platel*) piece of metal, wood, etc., dim. of *plat*: see PLAT *a.*]

1. *Geog.* An elevated tract of comparatively flat or level land; a table-land.

2. a. An ornamental tray or salver for the table-service. b. In *modern* use.

Plated (plē·ted), *a.* [f. PLATE *sb.* + -ED.]

1. Overlaid, covered, or strengthened with a plate or plates of metal for ornament or defence; (of persons) wearing plate-armour; (of ships, trains, etc.) protected by armour-plates.

2. *transf.* Covered with plates of precious metal or silver.

Plate-mark [f. PLATE *sb.* + MARK *sb.*]

1. A name for the various marks legally impressed

Plateful (plē·tfʊl) [f. PLATE *sb.* + -FUL.]

Plate-glass (plē·tglɑ·s).

Plate-hat to -lap: see PLATE *sb.* 19, 20.

Plate-layer [plē·t,lē·əɹ], *orig.* One who lays, keeps in order, and renews the plates (see PLATE *sb.* 8) on a tramway or railway; hence, a man employed in laying and keeping in order the rails, metals, or permanent way of a railway. So **Pla·te-laying.**

Plate-lead, -leather, etc.: see PLATE *sb.* 20.

Plateless (plē·tlēs), *a.* [f. PLATE *sb.* + -LESS.] Without a plate or plates.

Platelet (plē·tlēt).

Plate-machine, etc.: see PLATE *sb.* 20.

Plate-maker [f. PLATE *sb.* + MAKER.]

Plate-man [f. PLATE *sb.* + MAN.]

Plate-painter to -painter: see PLATE 19, 20.

Plater (plē·təɹ). [f. PLATE *v.* + -ER ¹.]

1. One who coats or plates articles with a film of metal, usually of silver or gold; often in comb., as *electro-plater*. *Obs.*

2. A man who has the custody of silver plate.

Plater, *obs.* form of PLATTER.

Plate-rack : see PLATE *sb.* 20.

Plateresque (platɛɹe·sk), *a.* [ad. Sp. *plateresco,* f. *platero* a silversmith, goldsmith, f. *plata* silver.]

†2. = PATEN ¹ (cf. *etymol.*), sb.

Plate-siform (plē·ti,sīf·ɔɹm), *a.* [f. L. *platessa* place + -form.] Resembling the plaice, or the genus *Platessa,* in form or shape.

Platerope (plē·t,tɹō·p), *sb.* [f. Gr. πλατύς, πλατε- breadth, width + τρόπος turning.]

†Plate-vein. *Obs.* Also 7-9 plat-, 8 plaict-. The cephalic vein in the arm.

†4. a. A plan of action; a scheme, design, device. *Obs.*

Platform (plæ·tfɔɹm), *sb.* (*a.*) Forms: 6 plate-, 6-7 platt-, 6 -plat-; 6-7 -forme, -form. In 6-8 often as two words, or hyphened.

1. a. A plane surface; a plan on the flat.

†2. *Geom.* A plane figure (as a triangle, quadrilateral, circle, etc.); also, a plane surface, a plane, and, in wider sense, any surface. *Obs.*

†3. A plan, design; something intended or planned in a pattern, a model. *Obs.*

PLATFORM. — **PLATINA.**

8. A raised level surface formed with planks, boards, or the like.

a. *generally,* as used for standing, sitting, walking, for seeing or being seen, or for any purpose for which such an arrangement is useful.

b. A horizontal stage or piece of flooring resting on wheels, as in a railway carriage, truck, or tram-car; in the colonies and U.S. *esp.* the open portion of the floor at the end of a railway car.

9. *spec.* A temporary (or sometimes permanent) piece of raised flooring in a hall, or in the open air, from which a speaker addresses his audience, and on which the promoters of a meeting sit; hence, *transf.* or allusively, in reference to public speaking or discussion on a platform, the making of political or other speeches, platform oratory; also, the body of supporters who appear on a platform; as 'an inclination' or 'representative platform.'

Platic (plæ·tik), *a. Astrol.* [ad. late and med.L. *platicus* (Firmicus, 4th c. Period), also late Gr. πλατικός, adv. -κῶς, broad, diffuse, f. πλατύς broad: see -IC.]

Pla·ti-la. *Obs.* Also 7 -illo, 8 -ille (?). [a. Sp. *platilla* 'a sort of Silesia linen'; 7 dim. of *plata* silver.] [See quot. 1848.]

Platin-, occas. form of PLATINO-.

Platina (plæ·tinə), *sb.* [Sp. *platina* = F. *platine,* Pg. *platina,* now rare form of *platino* PLATINUM.]

Platinate (plæ·tinēt), *sb. Chem.* [f. PLATIN-UM + -ATE ¹.] A salt derived from platinic oxide, in which platinum is tetravalent.

Platinate (plæ·tinēt), *v.* [f. PLATIN-UM + -ATE ³.]

Pla·tine. *Weaving. Obs.* [a. F. *platine*: see PLATEN.] A plate-steel: see post.

Platinferous (platini·fɛɹəs), *a.* [f. PLATIN-UM + -I + -FEROUS.] Bearing or yielding platinum.

Plating (plē·tiŋ), *vbl. sb.* [f. PLATE *v.* + -ING ¹.]

a. The action of the verb PLATE in various senses.

b. The making or application of metal plates.

Platinic (plæti·nik), *a. Chem.* [f. PLATIN-UM + -IC.] Of, pertaining to, or derived from platinum; *spec.* applied to compounds in which it exists in its higher valency (cf. PLATINIC).

Platiniferous (platini·fɛɹəs), *a.* [f. PLATIN-UM + -I + -FEROUS.] Bearing or yielding platinum.

Platinize (plæ·tinəiz), *v.* [f. PLATIN-UM + -IZE.] *trans.* To coat with platinum. Hence **Pla·tinized** *ppl. a.,* **Pla·tinizing** *vbl. sb.*

Platinization (platinəize·ʃən). The action or process of platinizing.

Platino- (plæ·tino), combining form of PLATINUM in various Chemical compounds, denoting compounds in which the platinum has its lower valency.

Platinoid (plæ·tinɔid), *a.* and *sb.* [f. PLATIN-UM + -OID.] *adj.* Resembling platinum.

1. *Chem.* Any metal of the class comprising platinum and the more commonly found in association with it and resembling it in several properties, viz. iridium, osmium, palladium, rhodium, and ruthenium. Also called *platinum metal.*

2. Name for an alloy of nickel, zinc, copper, and a little tungsten.

Platinotype (platino·təip).

Platinum (plæ·tinəm), *sb.* [mod.L., altered by Bergman (followed by Davy), from Platina, in conformity with the names of other metals in -um.]

Platitudinal, a. rare. [f. as prec. + -AL.] = PLATITUDINOUS.

Platitudinarian, sb. and a. [f. as prec. + -ARIAN.]

A. sb. One who utters or deals in platitudes.

B. adj. Characterized by platitude; addicted to the use of platitudes.

Hence **Platitudinarianism**.

Platitudinize, v. intr. To utter platitudes. Hence **Platitudinizing**.

Platitudinous, a. [f. as prec. + -OUS.] Characterized by platitude; addicted to the use of platitudes.

Hence **Platitudinously** adv., **Platitudinousness**.

Platitude, sb. [a. F. platitude, f. plat flat.]

Platting, vbl. sb. [f. PLAT v.²]

Platinize, v. [f. platin(um + -IZE.]

Platometry. Obs. rare. [f. as prec. + -METRY.]

Platonian. [f. L. Platōn-, Plato + -IAN.]

Platonic, a. and sb. [ad. L. Platōnicus, a. Gr. Πλατωνικός, f. Πλάτων Plato.]

Platonical, a. Obs. [f. as prec. + -AL.]

Platonically, adv.

Platonicalness.

Platonician. Obs. [ad. F. platonicien.]

Platonicism. rare. [f. PLATONIC + -ISM.]

Platoniciser. Obs. rare⁻¹.

Platonism. [ad. F. Platonisme.]

Platonist. [ad. med. L. platonista.]

Platonistic, a.

Platonize, v. [ad. Gr. πλατωνίζειν.]

Platonizer.

Platoon. [a. F. peloton.]

Plat-roof, sb.

Platted, ppl. a. [f. PLAT v.³ + -ED.]

Platten, v.

Platter, sb.¹ [a. AF. plater.]

Platter-faced, a.

Platting, vbl. sb. [f. PLAT sb.³ + -ING.]

Platy-, combining form of Gr. πλατύς broad, flat.

Platycephaly. [f. Gr. -κέφαλος.]

Platyrhine, **platyrrhine**, a. [ad. Gr. πλατύρρινος.]

Platysma. [mod. L., a. Gr. πλάτυσμα.]

Plaud, v.

Plaudible, a. Obs.

Plaudit, sb.

Plaudite.

Plauditor.

Plausibility.

Plausible, a. [ad. L. plausibilis.]

Plausibleness.

Plausibly, adv.

Platypus. [mod. L., a. Gr. πλατύπους.]

Play, sb.

Plea, *v*. *Sc.* and *north. dial.* Forms: 5 play, pleye, 5-6 pley, 6 plea, 7- plea. [f. PLEA sb.]

Pleach (plitʃ), *v.* Interlacing; intertwining; interlacement of boughs.

Pleach'er, *local*.

†Plead, *sb.* Chiefly *Sc. Obs.* Forms: 3 plaid, 5-6 (*Sc.*) plad, plede, pleid, 6 (*Eng.*) plead, -e, (*Sc.*) plaid. [f. PLEAD *v.*; perh. in part a re-formation of OF. and early ME. *plait*, *plaid*, *plet*; see PLEA *sb.*]

Plead (plīd), *v.* Forms: a. 3-4 plaide(n, plede(n, 4-7 plede (6 pledde), pledde, plidde, pleden, 4-7 Sc. pleid, 6- plead. Pa.t. and ppl. pleaded; contracted 5 pladde, 6 *dial.* plad; 5- pled.

II. Transitive uses.

Pleadable (plī'dăb'l), *a.* Also 5-7 pled-, 6 plaidable, 7 pleadible. [a. AF. *pledable* (1292 Britton); f. PLEAD: see -ABLE.] That may be pleaded.

Pleader (plī'dəɹ), *sb.* Forms: a. 3- plaidour, pleidur, 4-6 pleder, 5 pledour, 6- pleader.

Pleading (plī'diŋ), *vbl. sb.* [f. PLEAD *v.* + -ING[1].] The action of the verb PLEAD.

Plea'ding, *ppl. a.* [f. as prec. + -ING[2].]

†Plea'ful, *a. Obs.*

Plea'sance (plē'zăns). *Obs.* Forms: 4- pleasance, (-aunce; also 4-7 pleasaunce, *Sc.* pleasans, -ance, etc.) [a. F. *plaisance*, f. *plaisant* PLEASANT.]

†Plea'sancy, *Obs.* Also 6 PLEASANCE.

†Plea'sant, *sb.* Also 7 plaisant. [a. F. *plaisant* (16th c.), use of *plaisant* PLEASANT *a.*]

Pleasant (ple'zănt), *a.* (*adv.*) Forms: 4-7 ples-, pleys-, 5-6 plees-, 6 pleas-, 4-7 Sc. pleis- ; 4-5 ar-, 5 ay-, sayant-, 5- plesant, 6 (chiefly *Sc.*) 4-6 pleasand, -ande, (5 -aund, -ond, pleasande, 6 pleis-, pleasand), pleasant.

Pleasantish, *a. rare*. [Intrans. use f. PLEASANT *a*.]

Pleasantly (ple'zăntli), *adv.* [f. PLEASANT *a.* + -LY[2].] In a pleasant manner.

Pleasantness. Also 8-9 plaisanterie. [a. F. *plaisanterie* (16th c., Godef.), f. *plaisanter*, f. *plaisant* PLEASANT, jocose; see -RY.]

Pleasantry (ple'zăntri). Also 8-9 plaisanterie.

Plea'santsome, *a. rare*. [f. PLEASANT *a.* -SOME.]

Please (plīz), *v.* Forms: 4-5 (*Sc.* 6-8) plais(e, 4-6 pleis(e), 4-7 plese, 5-6 pleace, 4-6 ples(e, 5-6 plees, 6- please. [ME. *plaise*, *playse*, *plese*, a. OF. *plaisir*, *plesir* (3 pl. *plese*) = Pr. *plazer*, Sp. *placer*, It. *piacere*, L. *placēre* to be pleasing or agreeable.]

† Please-man. Obs. rare.

Please (plī'zn). [f. PLEASE v.]

Pleasance. Obs. rare.

Pleaship.

Pleasing (plī'ziŋ), vbl. sb.

Pleasing, ppl. a.

Pleasingly, adv.

Pleasingness.

Pleased (plīzd), ppl. a.

Pleasedly (plī'zedli), adv.

Pleasedness.

† Plea-se-God, a. Obs. rare.

Pleasurability.

Pleasurable (ple'ʒürǎb'l), a.

Pleasurableness.

Pleasurably, adv.

Pleasure (ple'ʒür), sb.

Pleasure (ple'ʒür), v.

Pleasureful, a.

Pleasureless, a.

Pleasureless-ness.

Pleasurer.

Pleasure-boat.

Pleasure-ground.

Pleasurehood, nonce-wd.

Pleasure-house.

Pleasureless (ple'ʒürles), a.

Pleasurement.

Pleasure-monger.

Pleasurer (ple'ʒürǎr).

Pleasure-seeker.

† Pleasure-take, v.

Pleasuring (ple'ʒüriŋ), vbl. sb.

Pleasurist.

Pleasurous, nonce-wd.

Pleat (plīt), sb.

Pleb (pleb). slang.

† Pleb-al, a. Obs. rare.

† Pleb-an. Obs. rare.

Phillips, Plebanus.

† Plebania.

Plebanian.

Plebe (plīb).

† Plebe'ial, a. Obs. rare.

Plebeian (plǐbī'ǎn), a. and sb.

Plebe'ious, a. Obs. rare.

† Plebe'ity. Obs. rare.

Plebeianism.

Plebeianize, v.

Plebianize.

Plebeiance.

Plebs.

Plebiscitarian (plébĭsĭtā'riǎn), a. and sb.

Plebiscitary.

Plebi'scitory.

Plebiscite, -it (ple'bĭsĭt).

Plebiscitum.

Plebification.

Pleck.

Plebs (plebz).

Flecked, ppl. a.

Flecken.

Flecore.

Plecopterous, a.

Plectellarian.

Plectine.

Plectrum.

†Plectile, a. Obs. rare. [ad. L. plectil-is plaited, f. plectĕre to plait, weave: see -IL, -ILE.] Plaited, woven.

Plectognath (plek·tǒgnăþ), a. and sb. Ichthyol. [f. mod.L. Plectognathi, f. Gr. πλεκτός twisted + γνάθος jaw.] a. adj. Of or pertaining to the Plectognathi, a suborder of teleostean fishes, having the upper jaw attached to the cranium, and the skeleton imperfectly ossified. b. sb. A fish of this suborder. So **Plectognathism** (-gnă·þiz'm) sb., **Plectognathic** (-gnæ·þik), **Plectognathous** (-ǒgnăþ̇s) adjs.

Plectopteran (plektǒ·ptĕran), a. and sb. Ichthyol.

Plectospondyl (plekto·spǒndil), a. and sb.

Plectre (ple·ktar). rare. [F. plectre] = PLECTRUM.

†Plectron (ple·ktrǒn). Pl. -a. [L., a Gr.]

†Plectrum (ple·ktrŏm). Pl. -a. [L., a Gr. πλῆκτρον anything to strike with, esp. an instrument for striking the lyre.] 1. An instrument, usually of horn, quill, or metal, with which the strings of the cithara or lyre were plucked.

Pled, plede, pledd: see PLEAD sb. and v.

Pledge (pledʒ), sb. Forms: 4-6 plege, plegge, 6 pleg, 5- pledge, plige, pliage, pleage, 7 piog'). [Late M.E. OF. plege (Roland, 1° 1061, and Anglo-F.), pletgge, plo(i)ge, etc., mod.F. pleige: hostage, security f. pop. Frankish L. plevium, plivium, plebium, = 600 in Past. Childeb. & Chlot. 10...]

... *(remainder of dense dictionary columns illegible at resolution)* ...

Pleiococcus, Pleiohippus: see PLIO-.

Pleiomorphy (plai·ǒmǎfi), [f. PLEIO- Gr. μορφή form + -Y.] = PLEOMORPHY.

Pleon-, ...

PLENTEOUSLY.

PLENTEOUSLY.

Plenteous.

Plenteousness.

Plentiful.

Plentifully.

Plentifulness.

Plentify.

Plentily.

Plentious.

Plentitude.

Plentive.

Plenty.

Plenum.

Pleny.

Pleochroic.

Pleochroism.

Pleochroite.

Pleochromatism.

Pleodont.

Pleomorphism.

Pleomorphic.

Pleomorphy.

Pleon.

Pleonasm.

Pleonectic.

Pleonexia.

Pleopod.

Plesi-.

Plesiomorphism.

Plesiosaurus.

Pleura.

Pleurenchyma.

Pleurite.

Pleuritic (pluri·tik), a. Forms: 6 pleurotique, -itique, 7 -etike, 8-9 -otic, (error, 7 plureisik, 8 pleuratik), 7-8 pleuretic, 8 pleuritic. [a. F. pleurétique (OF. pleuritic, -itik), ad. L. pleuriticus, a. Gr. πλευριτικός.]

1. Affected with or suffering from pleurisy.

Pleuritical, a. Obs. [see -ICAL.] = PLEURITIC.

Pleuritis (pluri·tis). Path. [L. pleuritis (Vitr.), a. Gr. πλευρῖτις (Hipp.).] Inflammation of the pleura; more usually called PLEURISY.

Pleuro- (pluə·ro), before a vowel pleur-, combining form of Gr. πλευρά side, PLEURA, πλευρόν rib; used in various scientific terms, chiefly in the senses of 'side' and 'pleura', occasionally in that of 'rib'.

Pleuroblastic (-blæ·stik), a. Bot.

Pleurobranchia (-bræ·ŋkiă)...

Pleurobranchiate, a.

Pleuro-bronchi·tis, Path.

Pleurocarp (plûə·rokâ·p), a.

Pleurocele (-sîl), Zool.

Pleuropericardi·tis...

Pleurotomy, Surg.

Pleurodont (plûə·rodǫnt), a. and sb. Zool.

Pleuroid (plûə·roid), a. Anat.

Pleurolepidal (-lepidăl)...

Pleuron (plûə·rǫn). Anat. and Zool. Pl. pleura.

Pleurotomid, Zool.

Pleuropneumonia (plûə·ronjū·moniă). Path. [mod.L. PLEURO- + PNEUMONIA.] Inflammation involving the pleura and the lung.

Pleurisy, obs. form of PLEURISY.

Pliability (plaiăbi·liti). [f. PLIABLE + -ITY.] The quality or property of being pliable.

Pliable (plai·ăb'l), a. [a. F. pliable (15th c. in Godef.), f. plier to bend, fold.]

1. Easy to be bent or folded; flexible, supple, yielding; readily moulded or shaped, pliant.

Pliableness. [f. prec. + -NESS.] The quality of being pliable; pliability.

Pliably, adv. [f. as prec. + -LY.] In a pliable manner; flexibly; yieldingly, docilely.

Pliades, obs. form of PLEIADES.

†**Pliance.** Obs. rare⁻¹. [f. PLIANT + -ANCE: cf. compliance.] Compliance, yielding.

Pliancy (plai·ănsi). [f. PLIANT: see -ANCY.] The quality of being pliant.

Pliant (plai·ănt), a. [a. F. pliant, pplle. of plier to bend.]

1. Bending; capable of being bent or folded with ease; supple, lithe, flexible; ductile, plastic.

Plica (plai·kă, plaï·kă). Pl. plicae (med.L plica plait, fold, f. plicāre to fold: see PLY.

Plicate (plai·kêt), a. [ad. L. plicātus, pa. pple. of plicāre to fold.]

Plicated, a.

Plicately, adv.

Plicatile (pli·kăt'l), a.

Plicate·ntine...

Plication (plikê·ĭən). [ad. L. plicātiōn-, -ō, n. of action f. plicāre.]

Plier (plai·ə). [f. PLY v. + -ER.]

1. One who plies.

2. In pl. Pincers, usually small, having long jaws mostly with parallel surfaces, sometimes toothed.

Plight (plait), sb.¹ Forms: 1-4 pliht, 4 plihte, 4-6 plite, 4-8 plyte, 5-6 plyght, 6 plyte. [OE. pliht danger, risk.]

Plight (plait), sb.² Now chiefly poet. or rhet. Pl. plights, plyghtes. [a. OF. plite, pliste, pl. of ploit, pleit, PLAIT sb.]

Plight (plait), v.¹ Forms: 1 plihtan, 3-5 plihte. [OE. plihtan, f. pliht PLIGHT sb.¹]

Plight, v.² [f. PLIGHT sb.²]

Plight, *a.* *Obs. rare.* In 3 plihtliche.

† Plightly, *a. Obs. rare.* Perilous, of grave import.

† Plighty, *a.* Full of solds, wrinkled, rugose.

Plim, *v.* To swell, fill out, grow plump.

Plim- mould. The name of S. Plimsoll, M.P. for Derby, whose agitation the Merchant Shipping Act of 1876 was due.

Plinian, *a.* Belonging to or named after Pliny.

Plinth (plinþ). The lower square member of the base of a column.

Pliocene (plai·ŏsīn), *a.* and *sb. Geol.* Also **pliocene**.

Pliocene, *a. Geol.* Also **pliocene**.

Pliohippus (plai·ohi·pŏs). *Palæont.* Also **pleo-**, **pleio-**.

† Pliolophus (plai·ŏlŏfŏs). *Palæont.*

Pliosaurus (plai·osōrŏs). *Palæont.* Also **pleio-**, **plesio-**.

Plisky (pli·ski), *sb.* *a.) Sc. and north. dial.*

Plisky, *v. Obs. rare.*

Plit, *sb. Agric.* [Invented by W. Marshall: see quot. 1778.] A slice of earth turned over by a ploughshare.

Plitch, *v.* = PLYCH.

Plith, obs. f. PLIGHT.

Ploat, *v. north. dial.* = PLOT *sb.*

Ploce (plō·sē). *Rhet.* Also 6 **ploke**, 7 **ploke**.

Plod (plɔd), *sb.*

Plodder (plɔ·də). *Obs.*

Ploddider, *Obs.*

Plodtall.

Ploot, *obs. f.* PLOT.

Plod (plɔd), *v.*

† Plo·dderly, *adv. Obs.*

Plod·ding, *ppl. a.*

Ploo, obs. form of PLOUGH.

Plock, **Plocky**, etc.: see PLOCK, PLOUKY.

Plop (plɔp), *sb.* and *int.* [Echoic: cf. PLUMP.]

Plop, *adv.*

Plop, *v.*

† Ploraband, *a. Obs. rare.*

Floration (plŏrē·ʃən). *rare.*

Plore, *v. Obs. rare.*

Plosh, dial. form of PLASH *sb.*

Plot (plɔt), *sb.*

Plot, *v.*

Plote, *v.* Also 5-7 **plote**, 6-7 **plott**.

Plotful, *a.*

Plotinian (plŏti·nian), *a.* and *sb.*

Plotless (plɔ·tlĕs), *a.* Without a plot or story; having no plot.

† Plotment. *Obs. rare.*

† Plotock. *Obs.* [app. a perversion of *Plute*, in accordance with some popular etymology.]

Plotter, **Plot**: see FLOAT, PLATFORM.

Plotting (plɔ·tiŋ), *vbl. sb.*

Plotting, *ppl. a.*

Plough, plow (plau), *sb.*

2210

PLOUGH. 1005 PLOUGH.

PLOUGH. 1006 PLOUGH.

PLOUGH. 1007 PLOUGH-GEAR.

PLOUGH-GRAITH. 1008 PLOUGH-START.

Plough-stilt, plow-, [f. as prec. + STILT sb.] A plough-handle.

Plough-strake, plow-, Obs. [f. as prec. + STRAKE sb.] A piece of hoop-iron for strengthening or repairing a plough.

Plough-swain, plow-, Obs. [f. as prec. + SWAIN sb.] A ploughman.

Plough-tail, plow-. The rear or handles of a plough. Symbolically, the following of the plough, the place of the farm-labourer, farm-labour; as in *at, to, from the plough-tail.*

Plough-wise, a. [f. PLOUGH sb. + -WISE.] Said of writing, the lines of which run alternately from right to left and from left to right; boustrophedon.

Plough-wright, plow- (plou·rəit), [f. as prec. + WRIGHT.] A maker of ploughs.

Plouk, plook (pluk), sb. Forms: 5 plowke, 6 plouke, plukke, 8c. pluik, 6-7 plouke, 7 plouk-, 9 plook-. [Origin obscure: cf. Sc. *plook,* *pluke* = PIMPLE sb.] A pimple; a lump, knot, bung, tumour, pimple, appears to be from Sc.]

Plouk, variant of PLUCK sb. and v., north. dial.

Plouky, plooky (plu·ki), a. Sc. and north. dial. Forms: 5 plowkky, 6 plowkie, 8 plouckie.

Plounce, obs. form of PLANT.

Plout, Plowt, sb. [f. Ger. *ploudern* rich + -CRACK. The regular romanized form would be *plusio-.*] The rule of the wealthy, plutocracy.

Plout (plöut), v. Sc. and north. dial. Also **plowt.** [Origin obscure: perh. onomatopoeic: cf. PLOUTER.] intr. To fall with a splash or plump; to plunge or splash in water.

Plouter, Plowter, Plotter (plöu·təɹ), v. Sc. and north. dial. Also **plotter, ploiter.**

Plover (plʌ·vəɹ). Forms: 4 pluver, 4-6 pliuer, 4-7 plouer, 5 plouuer, plouuere, 5-6 plouuar, 5-6 plouer, 6 plover, 7 pleuer, 8 plever, pliuer, 7 pliuer.

Plover-page, plover's page. Sc. [f. prec.] The golden plover.

Plow, another spelling of PLOUGH sb.1 and v.

Plowe, plowgh, -e, plowh, -e, ploy(e, obs. ff. PLOUGH.

Plowmip, plowmip, plowine, obs. ff. PLUM.

Ploy (plɔi), sb.1 Obs. 6 ploye. [a. OF. *ploi, plei,* cf. L-ie'te 1. *plica* a fold. Cf. MDu. *plie,* Du. * plooi,* MLG. *ploy* a fold, also PLY.] A ply or fold.

Ploy, sb.1 [In sense 1, f. F. *ployer* —L. *plicāre* MLG. *ployen,* Du. *plooijen.*]

Ploy, v. [In sense 1, perh. back-formation from DEPLOY.]

Pluck, plyck (plʌk), sb. [OE. *plucc* app. a mod.Sc. *pluck,* plic, ME. *plicke, ploke, plokke.*]

Pluck (plʌk), v. Forms: 1 plucian, 4-6 plukke, pluk(e, 4-7 plucke, pluck-. [Common WGer.: cf. MDu. *plocken,* Du. *plukken,* plucke fowls, Sw. *plocka,* Da. *plukke.*]

Pluck. type *plukkōn.* OE. type *plyccé(e)an* (PLITCH) = MDu. *plucken,* Du. *plukken,* LG. *plukken,* MHG., Ger. *pflücken* (not in OHG., and still absent from Oberdeutsch dialects), which indicate an unlatuted type from *plukkjan.*

Pluck, v. 1. *trans.* To pull off (a flower, fruit, leaf, hair, feather, etc.) from where it grows; to pick off or out; to pick, cull, gather.

Pluckage (plʌ·kedʒ), nonce-wd. [f. PLUCK v. + -AGE.] The action or process of plucking.

Plucked (plʌkt), a. colloq. [f. PLUCK sb.3 + -ED.] Having pluck or courage.

Plucker. 1. One who plucks, in various senses. 2. A machine for disentangling and straightening long wool to render it fit for combing.

Pluckerian (plʌke·riən), a. Math. [f. proper name Plücker (see below) + -IAN.]

Pluckily (plʌ·kili), adv. colloq. [f. PLUCKY + -LY.] In a plucky manner; bravely, courageously.

Pluckiness (plʌ·kines), colloq. [f. PLUCKY + -NESS.] The quality of being plucky; pluck.

Plucking (plʌ·kiŋ), vbl. sb. [-ING 1.]

Pluckless (plʌ·kles), a. [f. PLUCK sb.3 + -LESS.] Without pluck; devoid of courage or spirit. Hence **Pluckless·ness.**

Plucky (plʌ·ki), a. colloq. [f. PLUCK sb.3 + -Y.] Characterized by pluck; showing determination to fight or struggle; brave, courageous, spirited.

Pluff (plʌf), sb. (a., int.) Sc. [Echoic. So LG. *pluff,* Du. *plof* interj.; LG. *pluffen,* WFris. *plofje,* to puff, explode.]

Plug (plʌg), sb. [app. a. MDu. and early mod.Du. *plugge* a bung, stopper, Du. *plug,* also MLG., LG. *plugge, plugge,* Sw. *plugg, plugg,* Da. *plög.*]

Plug, v.

Column 1 — PLUG. / 1013

6. Applied to a horse: with various connotations. *U.S.* and *Colonial slang.*

Explained in American Dict. as 'a horse past his prime'; 'an old horse worn down by hard work'; a New Zealander knows it as 'a good sort'; an Australian authority as applied to horses of 15 hands or 15½ of a good steady ambling character, working well but not fast.

7. *attrib.* and *Comb.*, as *plug-hat*, *-bolt*, *-bullet*, *-finisher* (sense 2 f.), *-machine*, *-point*, *-pony* (sense 6), *-shut* (*plug-like* adj.); *plug-apron*, an arbor or mandril in a lathe on which a drill chuck is mounted (*Knight Dict. Mech. Suppl. 1884*); *plug-basin*, a wash-hand basin having a plug-hole for letting the water out; †*plug-basket* (*Brewing*), ? the depression at the bottom of the mash-tun into which the plug drops.

Column 2 — PLUM. / 1013

To supply the necessary telephones and to make plug-holes in the alarm posts.

Plugged (plʌgd), *ppl. a.* [f. PLUG *v.* + -ED[1].] Stopped up, closed, or filled with or as with a plug. Of a shell: Having a plug in place of the fuse.

Plugger (plʌ·gə(r). [f. PLUG *v.* + -ER[1].] One who or that which plugs; *spec.* in *Dentistry*, an instrument for driving in and consolidating the filling material in the cavity of a carious tooth.

Plugging (plʌ·giŋ), *vbl. sb.* [f. PLUG *v.* + -ING[1].]
1. The action of the verb PLUG in various senses.
b. See quot.

Plug (plʌg), *v.* [f. PLUG *sb.*; or immediately a. early mod. Du. *pluggen* (Plantin).]
1. *trans.* To stop, close tightly, or fill (a hole or aperture) with or as with a plug; to drive a plug into. Chiefly with *up*.

Column 3 — PLUM. / 1014

The change of *pv-* to *pl.* is found only in the Teutonic forms, or in med. L. written in England.

1. The fruit of the tree *Prunus domestica*, a roundish fleshy drupe of varying size and colour, covered with a glaucous waxy bloom, and having a somewhat flat pointed stone and sweet pulp.

†**b.** *Phrase*. *The bloom or the blue of the plum:* delicate freshness, charm, *cf.* BLOOM *sb.* 4, 7b.

2. The tree bearing this fruit, *Prunus domestica* (N. O. *Rosaceæ*).

3. With qualifying words. *a.* Applied to many species (and varieties) of the genus *Prunus*:

4. A dried grape or raisin as used for puddings, cakes, etc.

Column 4 — PLUM. / 1014

highly eligible for every good man, i.e. every Plumb.

2. *attrib.* and *Comb.*, as *plum-blossom*, *-bullock*, *-cake*, etc.

Plum, a. Also 6 *plumbe*, 7–9 *plumb*. [apu. L. sense 2.] Now *dial.*
1. Soft and elastic, as a cushion; well-raised and light. *Obs.*

Column 5 (bottom) — PLUMACEOUS. / 1015

clene and pure aier and movde swete humoure and hot for plumynge and holes but drawis and forgeth swete humoure.

Plumaceous (plumei·ʃəs), *a.* [f. L. *plūma* feather + -ACEOUS.]
Feathery, having the character of a contour-feather.

†**Pluma·ciol.** *Med. Obs.* [a. F. *plumachel* (now rare) dial. *f. plumaciolum*, dim. from late L. *plūmaciolum* cushion.]

†**Pluma·cle.** *Obs.* [ad. F. *plumage.*]

Column 6 (bottom) — PLUMB. / 1015

vii.] 26 (Feather-stitch) is not to be confounded with what is called 'plumage-stitch', which... is a version of satin-stitch. *Ibid.* n. 110 The worker adapts... the length of the stitch to the work to be done, directing it also according to the form to be expressed, and so arriving... by way of satin-stitch, at what is called plumage-stitch.

Plumaged (plū·medʒd), *a.* [f. prec. + -ED[2].] Furnished with or as with plumage, feathered; having plumage.

Plumage (plū·medʒ), *v.* rare. [f. prec. + -ED[2].]

Column 7 (bottom) — PLUMB. / 1016

keep the latter in an upright position; a ball or bullet of lead as a missile; a kind of dumb-bell.

II. 2. a. *trans.* To sound (the sea, etc.) with a plummet; to measure (the depth) by sounding.

b. *fig.* To sound the depths of; to fathom, to reach the bottom of.

c. To plumb a track (*U.S. colloq.*), to trace or follow out a road.

III. 3. To render vertical, to adjust or test by a plumb-line. *Obs.* †*fig.*

4. To place vertically above or below.

IV. 5. *trans.* To load or cover with lead.

6. To weight with lead.

Column 8 (bottom) — PLUMBEOUS. / 1016

Plumbagine (plʌmbæ·dʒin), *a.* and *sb.* [See PLUMBAGO.] Of the nature of or pertaining to plumbago or graphite.

Plumbaginous (plʌmbæ·dʒinəs), *a.* [f. L. *plumbāgo, -inem* PLUMBAGO + -OUS.] Of the nature of or containing plumbago.

Plumbago (plʌmbei·go). Also 7 *plumbage*.
1. Min. Black-lead, graphite.

Plumbagol (plʌmbeigɒl), *sb.* A solution of plumbago, black-leaded.

Plumbe·llophane. *Min.* [See PLUMBO-.]

Plumbe·ous, *a.* [f. L. *plumb-um* lead + -EOUS[1].] Resembling lead, leaden.

Plumber (plɐ·məɹ). Forms: 4 plomber, 4-8 plummer, 5 plommer, plumber, plumbas, 5-6 plomer, 5-7 plumer, 6 plommar, Sc. plummair, 5- plumber. [a. OF. *plummier* (1266), plommier, etc., F. *plombier* :— L. *plumbārium* a plumber, f. *plumbum* lead.] An artisan who works in lead, zinc, and tin, fitting in, soldering, and repairing the water and gas pipes, cisterns, boilers, and other work executed in these metals in the construction of a dwelling-house or other building. Originally applied to a man who dealt and worked in lead.

Plumbery (plɐ·məɹi). Also 4 plomerye, 6 plombmery plumery. [ME. a OF. *plommerie* (1304), *plomberie* lead-work, plumber's work; f. *plommier* plumber; in mod.L. *plumbāria*: cf. L. *plumbārius* of or belonging to lead, *plumbārium* a place to keep leaden vessels in.]

Plumbiferous (plʌmbi·fərəs). [f. L. *plumb-um* lead + -FEROUS. Cf. F. *plombifère*.] Containing lead.

Plumbum, or Obs. rare. [L. L. *plumb-um* lead + -INE[1].] Of leaden colour.

Plumbing (plɐ·miŋ), vbl. sb. [f. PLUMB, in various senses; now esp. the work of a plumber.]

Plumby, a. Sc. the presence of lead.

Plumb-line, sb. [L. PLUMB sb.]

Plumbo-, combining form of L. *plumbum* lead, forming chemical and mineralogical terms.

Plume (plūm). Also 6 plome. [a. OF. *plume* :— L. *plūma* a small soft feather, down.]

Plumed (plūmd), ppl. a.

Plumeless (plū·mlɛs), a.

Plumelet (plū·mlɛt), sb.

Plume-like, a.

Plumeous, a.

Plumer.

Plumery (plū·məɹi).

Plumet, obs. form of PLUMMET.

Plumeless (plū·mlɛs), a. Without plums.

Plummet (plɐ·mɛt), sb.

Plummet-block (plɐ·mɛtblɔk), Mech.

Plumminess, a.

Plummy (plɐ·mi), a.

Plump (plɐmp), sb.

Pump *sb.*, found also in LG. *plumpe* and vb. *plumpen* to pump. Perh. one of the cognates with PLUMP v.1 and its congeners, from the plumping or plunging action of the piston. An obsolete by-form of PUMP.

Plump (plǒmp), *sb.*2 Also 5 plumbe, 9 plomp.

1. An act of plumping (see PLUMP v. 1); the fall of a solid body into water, mud, etc., with little or no splash; an act of dropping flat on the ground; an abrupt plunge or heavy fall. *familiar.*

Plump (plǒmp), *a.*1 [A Common LG. verb.-MLG., LG. *plumpen*, MDu., Du. *plompen* to fall or plunge into water with the characteristic sound.]

II. 3. Of full and rounded form; sufficiently fleshy or fat to show no angularity of outline; chubby; having the skin well filled or elastically distended.

Plump, *v.*3 [f. PLUMP *sb.*]

Plump (plǒmp), *int., adv., and a.*2 [app. the onomatopœic stem of PLUMP v.1 used to express the manner of the action, or the echoic imitation of the sound of the act.]

Plump (Mas.) See *Plumper.*

Plumper3. [f. PLUMP *sb.*3 and *v.*] A machine for sowing seed in 'plumps' or clumps.

Plum-pie, *sb.* [f. PLUM *sb.*1 4 + PIE.]

Plumpish, *a. rare.* [f. PLUMP *a.*1 + -ISH.]

Plumply, *adv.*1 [f. PLUMP *a.*1 + -LY1.]

Plumply, *adv.*2 [f. PLUMP *a.*2 + -LY1.]

Plumpness1. [f. PLUMP *a.*1 + -NESS.]

Plumpness2. [f. PLUMP *a.*2 + -NESS.]

Plum-porridge. *Obs.*

Plum-pottage. *Obs.* 7 = prec.

Plum pudding, plum-pudding (plǒm'pu·diŋ). A pudding containing plums.

Plumula. 1023 PLUNDEROUS.

Plumula (plū·miǔla). *Bot.* [L. *plūmūla* (Colum.), dim. of *plūma* PLUME.] = PLUMULE 1.

Plumulaceous (plūmiǔlē·ʃǝs), *a.* [f. L. *plūmula* (see prec.) + -ACEOUS.] Of the nature of or resembling a plumule, downy.

Plumular (plū·miǔlǎr), *a.* [f. L. *plūmula* PLUMULE + -AR.]

Plumularia (plūmiǔlēˑria). *Zool.* [mod.L. f. *plūmula* (see above).] A genus of hydrozoa having a plume-like form.

Plumule (plū·miǔl), *sb.* [ad. L. *plūmula.*]

Plumuliferous (plūmiǔli·fĕrǝs), *a.*

Plumulose (plū·miǔlǒus), *a.* [ad. mod.L. *plūmulōsus,* f. *plūmula*: see -OSE.]

Plumy (plū·mi), *a.* [f. PLUME *sb.* + -Y1.]

Plunder (plǒ·ndǝr), *sb.*

1. The action of plundering or taking as spoil; *spec.* as practised in war or a hostile incursion.

Plunderable, *a.*

Plunder-bund.

†Plunder, *v.*1 [a. Ger. *plündern* (also + *blündern,* late MHG., MLG., plündere(n, *plünnern* (early mod.Du. and Du. *plunderen,* also + plündern).]

Plunderage (plǒ·ndǝredʒ), [f. PLUNDER *sb.*1 + -AGE.]

Plunderer (plǒ·ndǝrǝr). [f. PLUNDER *sb.*1 + -ER1.]

Plunderless, *a. nonce-wd.* [see -LESS.]

Plunderous (plǒ·ndǝrǝs), *a. rare.* [f. PLUNDER *sb.*1 + -OUS.]

Plunge (plǒndʒ), *sb.* [f. PLUNGE v.]

1. *trans.* To put violently, thrust, or cast *into* (or + *in*) a liquid, a penetrable substance, or a cavity; to immerse, submerge; to baptize by immersion.

Plunge (plǒndʒ), *v.* Forms: 4-5 plunge, 6-7 plounge, 6-7 plunge, 7-8 plunge.

Plunger (plǒ·ndʒǝr).

1. A person who plunges.

Plunging.

Plunging, vbl. sb. [-ING.] The action of the verb PLUNGE in various senses; spec. immersion in baptism (obs.).

b. attrib. and Comb., as plunging bath, -hole, -material, -pit; plunging-battery (Electr.), a battery in which the plates may be plunged into or withdrawn from the fluid, when the battery is or is not in use (Knight Dict. Mech. 1875); plunging-siphon, a small tube with open ends, used to draw a small quantity of liquor by plunging it into the bulk, and stopping one end with the finger (Dunglison, 1857).

Plunging, ppl. a. [-ING.] That plunges. a. Of a horse or its action, a wave, a ship, etc.; Diving; rushing or falling forward or downward; pitching; sinking steeply.

b. fig. in various senses: see the verb.

c. Plunging fire, artillery or rifle fire directed downwards from a higher level. Cf. PLUNGE v. 9.

Hence **Plunging** adv.

Plunk, sb. Chiefly dial. [PLUNK v.]

Plunk, v. Chiefly dial. [Imitative.]

Plunge, sb. and v. see PLUNGE.

Plunther. To flounder.

Pluperfect.

Plural, a. and sb. [L. PLURALIS.]

Pluralism.

Pluralist.

Pluralistic.

Plurality.

Pluri-, combining form of L. plus.

Pluries.

Pluriliteral.

Pluripresence.

Plurisy.

Plurative.

Plush, sb. [ad. F. pluche, contracted form of peluche.]

Plushed.

Plushette.

Plushy, a.

Plus, sb. [MINUS.]

Plutocrat.

Plutocracy.

Plutocratic.

Plutology.

Plutomania.

Plutonian.

Plutonic, a. [L. Plūton-, Pluto.]

Plutonism.

Plutonist.

Pluvial.

Pluvialiform. Of or pertaining to rain; rainy; characterized by much rain.

Pluvialine (plē·vian), *a.* *Ornith.* [f. mod. L. *Pluvialis*, the group of the plovers and allied birds, rain-birds, pl. of *pluvialis* rainy, as sb. a plover or rain-bird, whence specific name of the Golden plover, *Charadrius pluvialis* : see 1-2.] Pertaining to a plover, resembling the plover.

Pluviameter, erron. var. PLUVIOMETER.

Pluviam, *a. nonce-wd.* [f. L. *pluvi-a* rainy + -AN.] Rain-giving; rainy (in quot. -L. *Jupiter pluvius*).

Pluviograph (plū·viǒgrȧf). [f. L. *pluvia* rain + -GRAPH.] A self-recording rain-gauge.

Pluviometer (plūviǒ·mītȧ). (Also erron. -iameter.) [f. L. *pluvia* rain + -METER. So F. *pluviomètre* (1788 in Hatz.).] An instrument for measuring the rainfall; a rain-gauge.

Pluvioscope (plū·viǒskǒup). [f. as prec. + -SCOPE.] = PLUVIOMETER.

Pluviose (plū·viǒus). [a. F. *pluviôse.*]

Pluviôse (plüviǒz). rainy; [f. *pluvia* rain : see -OSE.] Rainy, watery. In quot. *fig.*: tearful.

Pluviosity (plūviǒ·sǐtï). *rare.* [f. L. *pluviôs-us* (see prec.) + -ITY.] The quality of being rainy or of giving rain.

Pluvious (plū·viǒs), *a.* [a. OF. *pluvieus* (1245 in Godef.), F. *pluvieux*, or ad. L. *pluviôsus* rainy. Of, pertaining to, or characterized by rain; full of or bearing rain or moisture ; rainy.

Ply (plai), *sb.* Also 6-7 *plie.* [a. F. *pli* (13th c. in Hatz.-Darm.) a fold, bend, altered from OF. *plot* (12th c.), vbl. sb. f. *plier*, later *plier* : see PLY *v.*]

I. A fold; each of the layers or thicknesses produced by folding cloth, etc.; a strand or twist of rope, yarn, or thread.

PLY. PLY. 1030

Pleyadc, var. of PLEIA. **Plyades,** obs. f. PLEIADES. **Plyar, plyer :** see PLIER.

Plyhon. *Surg.* *Obs.* [corruption of PELI-CAN.] (See quot.)

Plying (plai·ïŋ), *vbl. sb.* [f. PLY *v.*² + -ING.] The action of PLY *v.*, in various senses. *attrib.* Plying-place, a place where a porter, hackney-carriage, or boat stands for hire (PLY *v.* 9).

+ Plym, plymme, *v.* *Falconry.* *Obs.* A parallel form of PLUME.

Plymouth Brethren. [See *Brethren* in N. Newman *Lect. & Gain* viii. 297 Where she tell you 90? Not surely to Methodism or Plymouth-brotherhood.

† Plymouth cloak. *Obs. slang.* A cudgel or staff, carried by one who walked in *cuerpo*, and thus facetiously assumed to take the place of a cloak.

† Plymouthism (pli·mǒuthiz'm). [See -ISM.] The system or doctrine of the Plymouth Brethren. So **Ply·mouthist, Ply·mouthite,** an adherent of this body ; also *attrib.*

Pneuma (pniū·mȧ, niū·mȧ). [a. Gr. πνεῦμα wind, breath, spirit, *prop.* that which is blown or breathed, f. πνεῖν to blow, breathe.]

Pneumathæmia (pniūmȧþī·miǎ, niū-). *Path.* [f. Gr. πνεῦμα, πνευματ- (see PNEUMA) + αἷμα blood; cf. *hyperæmia*, etc.] 'The presence of air in a blood vessel' (*Syd. Soc. Lex.* 1895).

Pneumatic (niūmæ·tik), *a.* (*sb.*) [ad. L. *pneumaticus* of or belonging to air or wind (Vitr., Plin.), a. Gr. πνευματικός of, caused by, or of the nature of wind, breath, or spirit. So F. *pneumatique* (1530 in Hatz.-Darm.).]

1. Pertaining to, or acting by means of, wind or air. **a.** Chiefly applied to various mechanical contrivances which operate by pressure or exhaustion of air.

Pneumatic (niūmæ·tik), *sb.* [ad. L. *pneumaticus* of or belonging to air or wind (Vitr., Plin.), a. Gr. πνευματικός.]

Pneumatical (niūmæ·tikȧl), *a.* (*sb.*) Now *rare* or *Obs.*

Pneumaticity (niūmȧti·sǐtï), *rare.* [f. PNEUMATIC + -ITY.] The quality or condition of being pneumatic (in quot., in sense 3 b of the adj.).

Pneumatics (niūmæ·tiks), *sb. pl.* [f. PNEUMATIC *a.*: see -IC 2.]

Pneumatism (niū·mȧtiz'm). [f. Gr. πνευματ- (see PNEUMA) + -ISM.] The doctrine of the pneumatists : see next sb.

Pneumatist (niū·mȧtist). [ad. late L. *pneumatistæ* pl., a. Gr. πνευματισταί.]

Pneumatize (niū·mȧtǝiz), *v.* [ad. Gr. πνευματίζειν.] 1. *trans.* To pass a blast of air through (molten metal) in the process of converting it into steel by the Bessemer process.

Pneumatograph (niūmæ·tǒgrȧf). [f. Gr. πνεῦμα, πνευματ- + -GRAPH.]

Pneumatographic (niūmȧtǒgræ·fik). [f. prec. + next + -IC.]

Pneumatography (niūmȧtǒ·grȧfï). [f. PNEUMATO- + -GRAPHY.]

Pneumatological (niūmȧtǒlǒ·dʒikȧl), *a.* [f. PNEUMATOLOGY + -IC + -AL.]

Pneumatology (niūmȧtǒ·lǒdʒï). [ad. mod.L. *pneumatologia*, f. Gr. πνεῦμα, πνευματ- + -λογία : see -LOGY.]

Pneumatometer (niūmȧtǒ·mītȧ). [f. PNEUMATO- + -METER.] An instrument for measuring the amount of air breathed in or at each inspiration or expiration.

Pneumatophore (niū·mȧtǒfǒǝ). [f. Gr. πνεῦμα, πνευματ-.]

Pneumatosis (niūmȧtǒu·sis). [mod.L., a. Gr. πνευμάτωσις.]

Pneumectomy (niūme·ktǒmï). *Surg.* [f. PNEUM-O- + Gr. ἐκτομή a cutting out.]

Pneumic (pniū·mik, niū·-), a. rare. [f. *pneumique*, etron. for *pneumonique*, f. Gr. πνεύμων lung : see -IC, and cf. PNEUMO-.] Pertaining to the lungs, pulmonary : = PNEUMONIC[1].

Pneumo-, combining form and verbal element, Gr. πνεῦμα wind, spirit, etc. (see PNEUMA), — the fuller form PNEUMATO- (cf. Gr. αἷμα — αἱματο-, etc.), in various scientific terms.

Pneumococcus (pniū·mŏkǫ·kŏs, niū·-). [mod. L. f. PNEUMO- + Gr. κόκκος berry : cf. *micrococcus*.] Name for two different micro-organisms of oval form (Friedländer's and Fränkel's) which have been found in the rusty sputum of pneumonia.

Pneumoderm (pniū·mǫdẽm, niū·-). Zool. [f. PNEUMO- + Gr. δέρμα skin.] A gymnosomatous pteropod of the family *Pneumodermata* (typical genus *Pneumoderma* of Cuvier 1817), having processes of the skin which serve as gills.

Pneumogram (pniū·mǫgræm, niū·-). [f. PNEUMO- + -GRAM.] A tracing taken with the pneumograph (*Syd. Soc. Lex.*) : = PNEUMATOGRAM[1].

Pneumograph (pniū·mǫgraf, niū·-). [f. as prec. + -GRAPH.] An instrument for automatically recording the movements of the chest in respiration ; also called *stethograph*.

Pneumography (pniūmǫ·grafi, niū·-). [f. as prec. + -GRAPHY.] A description of the lungs. b. The recording of the respiratory movements, as by a pneumograph.

Pneumology (pniūmǫ·lǫdʒi, niū·-). rare. [f. PNEUMO- + -LOGY.] A treatise on, or the scientific description or knowledge of, the lungs.

Pneumometer (pniūmǫ·mītǝr, niū·-). [f. PNEUMO- + -METER.] = PNEUMATOMETER.

Pneumonalgia, Pneumonectomy: see PNEUMONO-.

Pneumonia (niūmǭ·niǎ). Path. Also rarely in anglicized form : *pneumony*. [mod. L., a. Gr. πνευμονία (Plat.) inflammation of the lungs, f. πνεύμων, πνεύμονος lung. So F. *pneumonie*.] Inflammation of the substance of the lungs, a disease having many varieties, induced by cold or various other causes.

Pneumonic (niūmǫ·nik), a. and sb. [ad. medical L. *pneumonicus*, a. Gr. πνευμονικός (Plat.), f. πνεύμων, πνεύμονος.] A. adj. 1. Pertaining to the lungs, pulmonary ; now TOBL.
b. A remedy for lung-disease. rare—⁰.

Pneumonitis (pniūmǫnəi·tis, niū·-). Path. [mod. L. f. PNEUMON- + -ITIS.] Inflammation of the lungs, esp. in its more appropriate term, being in conformity with the plan of distinguishing inflammations affecting the parenchyma of the lungs. So F. *pneumonite*.

Pneumono- (pniū·mono, niū·-), before a vowel **pneumon-**, combining form of Gr. πνεύμων, πνεύμονος lung. (Often contracted to PNEUMO-.)
Pneumonalgia (-æ·ldʒiǎ) [Gr. ἄλγος pain], pain in the lung. **Pneumonectomy** = PNEUMECTOMY (*Syd. Soc. Lex.*). **Pneumonocace** (-ǫ·kăsi) [Gr. κακή evil], decay or gangrene of the lung (Mayne Expos. Lex. 1858). **Pneumono·carcinoma** [CARCINOMA], cancer of the lung (Mayne). **Pneumono·ie** = pneumonocele : see PNEUMO- (Dunglison Med. Lex. 1853). **Pneumono·cirrhosis**, cirrhosis of the lung (Mayne). **Pneumo·no·conio·sis** (also -koni-). **Pneumono·lith** (Mayne). **Pneumono·lithiasis** (*Syd. Soc. Lex.*). **Pneumono·meter** [-METER], an instrument for measuring the capacity or strength of the lungs (= PNEUMATOMETER, PNEUMOMETER) (Mayne). **Pneumono·mycosis** [Gr. μύκης fungus], growth of a fungus in the lungs. **Pneumono·phthisis** (-ǫ·ftǒra) a. [Gr. -φάγος eating], bearing or having lungs. **Pneumono·rhagia** (-rǣ·dʒiǎ) = *pneumorrhagia*: see PNEUMO- (Mayne).
Po: for Poo and *pow*.
Poa (pō·ǎ). Bot. [mod. L., a. Gr. πόα grass.] A large genus of grasses widely distributed in temperate and cold regions. **Pneumono·pathy** [-PATHY], any disease of the lungs (Mayne). 1753 in CHAMBERS *Cycl. Suppl.* 1775 MARTYN Rousseau's Bot. xxviii. 437 If... there are four sorts if Poa very common in most meadows. 1785 MARTYN tr. Rousseau's Lett.... mixture of... burnet, and dwarf poa.
b. Comb. **Poa-grass** ('po-grass'), a grass of this genus ; meadow-grass.

Pneumonophorous (pniūmǫ·nǫfǝrǝs, niū·-). Zool. Also **pneumo·tocus**. [f. mod. L. *Pneumóstoca*, *Pneumophóra* (Owen), f. PNEUMO- b + Gr. φορός-bearing, στέγος house.] Belonging to the *Pneumostoca*, or vertebrates that breathe air by means of lungs, and lay eggs, as birds and reptiles.

Pneumo-pericardium, a Path. [f. PNEUMO-b + PERICARDIUM.] Applied to a sound heard in pleurisy, attributed to the friction of the investing... -*pleuropericardial* (see PLEURO-).

Pneumopericarditis, a Path. [mod. L., f. PNEUMO- + PERICARDIUS.] The presence of air or gas in the pericardium ; a **Pneumopericardi·tis**, pneumopericardium accompanied by pericarditis (Billings *Med. Dict.* 1890).

Pneumothorax, a Path. [f. PNEUMO- + THORAX.] The presence of air or gas in the cavity of the thorax, i.e. of the pleura ; usually caused by a wound or by perforation of the lung. Also *pneumatothorax* (see PNEUMATO-).

Pnyx (puks). [ad. Gr. Πνύξ, genitive Πυκνός, probably f. πυκνός packed, crowded.] Name of the public place of assembly in ancient Athens, a semicircular level cut out of the side of a little hill west of the Acropolis.

Po¹, poo. Obs. Forms: a. 1 pāwa, pǎwa, pǎwe, 5 paa, paw. β. 4–5 po, 4–9 poe. OE. *pāwa*—OLG. *pāwo* or MLG. *pāwe*, LG. *pau*, Du. *paa*, OHG. *phāwo* (MHG. *pfāwe*, Ger. *pfau*), both wk. m.; WGer. a. L. *pāwo* peacock. Thence (through *pā̆w*, *pǎue*), ME. northn. *paa*, *pō̆*...

Po², obs. f. POKE v.; to cook (an egg) by dropping it, without the shell, into boiling water.

Po³. Obs. [Origin obscure.] see quot. 1898.

Poach (pōtʃ), v.¹ Forms: 5 pooche, 6-8 poche, potch, 7- poach. [a. OF. *pochier* (13th c. in Godef.), later *pocher* to enclose in a poke or bag, f. *poche* POKE. The Eng. sense were adopted separately... The *o* seems to have been originally short as in Fr.]
1. trans. To cook (an egg) by dropping it, without the shell, into boiling water.

Poach (pōtʃ), v.² [a. OF. *pocher*, in the main a collateral form of POKE v.⁴, q.v.]
I. 1. trans. To push or stir (anything) with the point of a stick, a finger, a foot, etc. ; = POKE v.¹
2. intr. To encroach or trespass (on the lands or rights of another) in order to possess oneself unlawfully or injuriously of something, esp. in order to steal game ; hence, to take game or fish illegally...
II. intr. To tread or trample (land or water).

Poch, obs. f. POACH, POUCH.

Poached (pōtʃt), ppl. a. 1. Cooked in boiling water, without the shell.
Poachy (pōtʃi), a. [f. POACH v.² + -Y.] Of land : Spongy, retentive of moisture, and so liable to be trampled into muddy holes; sodden, swampy.
Poachiness [f. prec. + -NESS.] The condition or quality of being poachy.
Pob, sb.¹ Pod, sb. Also dial. pob. [Origin obscure.] The refuse of flax or (more recently) jute.
Pobbie, obs. or dial. var. of PEBBLE.
Pobs (pobz), sb. pl. dial. Also pobbies. Occas. in sing. [Eng. Dial. Dict.] A dialect and nursery name for porridge, pap, bread and milk.
Pocan (pō·kǎn), sb. U.S. [app. native Indian name.] The Virginian Poke or Poke-weed (*Phytolacca decandra*) : = POKE sb.¹
Pocary, Pochard: see POCHARD, POCHER, etc.

Poacher¹ (pō·tʃǝr), sb. Also potcher. [f. POACH v.² + -ER¹.] 1. One who poaches or trespasses in pursuit of game ; one who takes or kills game unlawfully.
Poacher², a fish of the family *Agonidæ* (but F. *poachard*).
Poaching (pō·tʃiŋ), vbl. sb. [f. POACH v.² + -ING.] 1. The action of POACH v.²

Poachard (pō·tʃǝrd), sb. [f. prec. + -ARD.] Forms: a. 6 pochard, 7- pochard. β. 6-9 pocard, 7 pocker, card, 9 pockard. 7- pokar. [Of uncertain origin : perh. augmentative of OF. and mod.F. *poche* POKE.]

Pock (pok), sb. Forms: 1 poo, 4-6 pokke, 4-5 pocke, 5 poke, 6 & 7c. 6 po, 4-6 pocke. Pl. 1 poccas, 4-6 pokkes, 4 pockes, 6 pokkes ; also 6-7 poxe, 6- pox : see Pox. [OE. *poc*, pocc- pustule, ulcer = MDu., MLG. *pocke*.] A pustule in an eruptive disease; esp. (1300-1514 in Godef.), from LG. *pocke*.
Pock-broken, ppl. a. rare.
Pock-pit, Pock-hole, etc.
Pockwood (pok·wud), sb. Pocock.

Pocket (pǫ·ket), v. [f. POCKET sb.: cf. F. *pocheter* (16th in Godef.).]

1. *trans.* To put into one's pocket. Also with *up*.

13. *Special Comb.*: pocket-borough, a borough of which the parliamentary representation was under the control of one person or family; pocket-burner (*humorous*), a coin in the pocket (in allusion to the saying used of one who cannot keep money, that the coin burns a hole in the pocket); † pocket-cloth, a pocket-handkerchief; pocket-cutter, a thief who cuts pockets; pocket-expenses, small personal outlays; pocket-filled a., having the pockets full, rich; pocket-ilah = ANGLER 1; pocket-hay, pocket-lid, a larget covering a pocket; † pocket-hay, pocket-net: see quot.; † pocket-hoop, a hoop consisting of two parts, one worn on each hip, and serving as a pocket; pocket-judgement: see quots.; pocket-like a., resembling a pocket; pocket-mouse, a rodent of the family *Saccomyidæ*, a pouched mouse; pocket-pistol (see PISTOL); pocket-plum = bladder-plum (BLADDER 10); see quots.; pocket-rat = GOPHER sb.¹ 1; pocket-sheriff: see quots; † pocket-tortoise, a pocket-tortoiseshell comb; pocket veto: see quot. See also POCKET-BOOK, -HANDKERCHIEF, etc.

Pocket-book (pǫ·ket,buk).

1. A small book, adapted to be conveniently carried in the pocket. Now usually two words.

2. A book for notes, memoranda, etc., intended to be carried in the pocket; a note-book; a book-like case of leather or the like, having compartments for papers, bank-notes, bills, etc.

Pocketer. *Obs. rare.* [f. POCKET sb. + -ER.]
A pickpocket.

Pocket-handkerchief (pǫ·ket,hæ·ŋkətʃif).
A handkerchief carried in the pocket.

Pocket-hole (pǫ·ket,hǫul). The opening in a garment through which the hand is put into the pocket.

Pocket-knife (pǫ·ket,naif). A knife with one or more blades which fold into the handle, for carrying in the pocket.

Pocketless (pǫ·ket,les), a. [f. POCKET sb. + -LESS.] Without a pocket; having no pocket.

Pocket-money. Money carried in the pocket for occasional expenses; *esp.* that allowed to those who have no other money under their control, as schoolboys or schoolgirls.

Pocket-picking. 'Picking' of pockets; see PICK v.¹ 5; stealing from the pockets of others.

Pocky (pǫ·ki), a. Now rare. [f. POCK sb. + -Y.]

1. Infected with pox (in quot., with *small* pox).

2. *fig.* and *transf.* Contemptible, mean.

POD. 1039 **PODDED. PODDER.** 1040 **PODOLOGY.**

Pod (pǫd), sb.¹ [A comparatively recent word, found in 18th c. compounds and derivatives late in 17th c. Origin unknown.

Pod (pǫd), v. [f. POD sb.¹]

Podagra (pǫ·dăgră, pŏdē·gră). Med. [L. podagra, a. Gr. ποδάγρα, f. πούς, ποδ- foot + ἄγρα a catching.] Gout in the feet; by extension, gout generally.

Podagral (pǫ·dăgrăl), a. [f. PODAGRA + -AL.] Of or pertaining to gout; gouty.

Podagric (pǫdæ·grik), a. and a. [ad. L. *podagricus*, a. Gr. ποδαγρικός of or pertaining to gout, gouty.]

Podagrous (pǫ·dăgrəs), a. [f. PODAGRA + -OUS.]

Podalgia (pǫdæ·ldʒiă). [mod.L., f. Gr. πούς, ποδ- foot + -αλγία pain.] Pain in the foot, as from gout, rheumatism, or the like.

Podder (pǫ·dər). [f. POD sb.¹ + -ER¹.]

Poddish, poddidge. Now dial. Also 6 poddage, 6-7 podge, 9 dial.

Poddy (pǫ·di), a. colloq. [f. POD sb.¹ + -Y.] Corpulent.

† Pode. Obs. rare. [Var. form of PAD sb.¹] A toad; perh. also applied to other creatures reputed to be venomous; cf. *transf.* in PODAGY.

Podesta (pŏdestā·). Also 6-8 podestate. [It. *podestà*, ad. L. *potestāt-em* power, authority, hence (concr.) magistrate. Cf. POTESTATE.]

Podite (pǫ·dăit). Zool. [f. Gr. πούς, ποδ- foot + -ITE¹.] A leg or ambulatory limb of an arthropod, *esp.* of a crustacean.

Podium (pǫu·diəm). Pl. **podia**. [L. *podium*, an elevated place, balcony, ad. Gr. πόδιον.]

Podley (pǫd·li). Sc. Forms: 6 podlo, 7 poddlo, 7-8 poddy, -ley, 8-9 le, 9 podlie, -ley, podle, 8-9 pudle.

Podo-, before a vowel pod-, a. Gr. ποδο-, combining form of πούς, ποδ- foot.

Podology (pǫdǫ·lŏdʒi). [f. PODO- + -LOGY.] The science which treats of the feet.

Podomancy. ... of the foot; also, a treatise on the foot; so **Podo-logist.** **Podomance** [Gr. μαντεία divination]: divination from signs derived from inspection of the feet (Syd. Soc. Lex. 1895). **Podomancer** = PODO-METER. † **Podometry**: see quots. **Podo-scaph** [Gr. σκάφη boat]: a canoe-shaped float attached to the foot, or a pair of these, for moving on water; also, a water-velocipede, or boat propelled by treadles like a bicycle; hence **Podoscaphor.** **Podo-scopy** = *podomancy.* **Podosomatous** (-sō′-matəs) a., Zool., of or pertaining to the Podosomata or sea-spiders, an order of Arthropoda having long many-jointed legs; syn. with *Pycnogonida.* **Podosperm** Bot. [Gr. σπέρμα seed], the stalk of a seed.

Podophyllum (-fĭl′əm). [mod. L. f. Gr. πόδο- foot + φύλλον leaf.] a. Bot. A genus of *Ranunculaceæ* with two known species, P. peltatum of eastern N. America, and P. Emodi of the Himalayas, having long thick creeping rhizomes, large solitary white flower, &c. b. Pharm.

Podosomatous, **Podosperm**

Podophthalmate (pŏdŏfþăl′mĕt) a. [f. Gr. πούς, πόδ- foot + ὀφθαλμός eye + -ATE 2.] Having the eye at the end of a movable stalk, stalk-eyed; of or pertaining to the stalk-eyed crustaceans. So **Podophtha′lma, -lma′ta**, **-thalma′ta** [mod.L. pl.], an order of Crustacea, including those with eyes set on movable foot-stalks, as crabs and lobsters.

Podophyllous (pŏdŏf′ĭləs), a. [f. Gr. πόδο-, PODO- + φύλλον leaf + -OUS.]

Poem (pō′ĕm). Forms: 5-7 poeme. [a. F. poëme (in Oresme 14th c.), ad. L. poēma (in Plautus), a. Gr. ποίημα (4th c. B.C.), early variant of ποίημα, thing made or created; work, fiction, poetical work; f. ποιεῖν (really variant ποιεῖν) to make. (If ποίημα had been the form introduced, the L. would have been *poïma*.)

1. 'The work of a poet, a metrical composition' (Johnson); 'a work in verse' (Littré); a composition of words expressing facts, thoughts, or feelings in poetical form; a piece of poetry.

Poematic (pōĭmăt′ĭk), a. [ad. Gr. ποιηματικός (Plut.) poetical.] Of the nature of a poem.

Poesis (pōĕs′ĭs, pō-). Obs. [L. poēsis, a. Gr. ποίησις poetry.]

Poesy (pō′ĭzĭ, -sĭ). Forms: 4-5 poysy, 4-6 poesie, poysie, poesy, &c. [a. F. poésie, OF. poesie (12th c.), ad. L. poēsis.]

Poet (pō′ĕt). Forms: 4-5 poete, 4-6 poyet, poyete, poyt, 5-6 poete, poyet, 4-9 poete. [ME. poete, poyete, a. OF. poete (12th c.), ad. L. poēta, a. Gr. ποιητής maker, author, poet; f. ποιεῖν to make, create, compose.]

1. a. One who composes poetry; a writer of poems; an author who writes in verse.

Poet laureate, a poet officially appointed.

Poetaster (pō′ĕtā̆stər). [a. med. or mod.L. *poetaster* (Erasmus, L. 25 Mar. 1521), in It. mod. poetastro, obs. F. poetastre (1603 in Sainte-Palaye): see Poet and -ASTER.] A petty or paltry poet; a writer of poor or trashy verse; a rimester.

Poetastery. **Poetastress.**

Poetess (pō′ĕtĕs). [f. POET + -ESS. So It. poetessa (Florio 1598), F. poétesse (1643 in Hatz.-Darm.), Sp. poetisa, etc.] A female poet; a woman who composes poetry.

Poethood (pō′ĕthŭd). [f. POET + -HOOD.] The position or status of poet; the domain or fraternity of poets.

Poetic (pōĕt′ĭk), a. and sb. Also 6-7 poetique, -ike, 7-8 -ick. [a. F. poétique (16th c. in Littré), ad. L. poēticus, a. Gr. ποιητικός.]

A. adj. 1. Belonging or proper to poets or poetry. In quot. 1610, Fictitious, fabulous.

Poetical (pōĕt′ĭkăl), a. [f. prec. + -AL.] Of, belonging to, or proper to poets or poetry; having the character or qualities of poetry; fictional, imaginary, ideal.

Poeticality (pōĕtĭkăl′ĭtĭ). [f. prec. + -ITY.] The quality of being poetic.

Poetically (pōĕt′ĭkălĭ), adv. [f. prec. + -LY.] In a poetical manner, style, or form; in poetry or in a way suitable to poetry or a poet.

Poeticalness. **Poeticism.** **Poeticize.**

Poetics (pōĕt′ĭks). [See -ICS.] The branch of knowledge that deals with the nature and laws of poetry.

Poeticule (pōĕt′ĭkūl). A petty or insignificant poet.

Poetize (pō′ĕtaiz), v. [a. F. poétiser.] 1. intr. To make poetry; to write poetically; to put into poetry, write poetry about.

Poetly. **Poetomachia.** **Poetress.**

Poetry (pō′ĕtrĭ). Forms: 4-7 poetrie, 5-7 poetry, poesie. [ME. poetrie, a. OF. poeterie, poetrie (13th c.), med.L. poetria, f. L. poēta POET.]

I. 1. The art or work of the poet; poetic composition; the writing of poetry.

quence, of Musick, and of Picture, which are all allowed to make so strong Impressions upon humane Minds. 1779–81 Johnson *L. P., Waller* Wks. II. 267 The essence of poetry is invention; such invention as, by producing something unexpected, surprises and delights... Poetry pleases by exhibiting an idea more grateful to the mind than things themselves afford. 1798 Wordsw. *Lyr. Ballads* (ed. 2) Pref., Poetry is the breath and finer spirit of all knowledge: it is the impassioned expression which is in the countenance of all Science. 1853 Robertson *Serm.* Ser. ii. xx, All Christ's teaching is a Divine Poetry, luxuriant in metaphor, overflowing with truth too large for accurate sentences, truth which only a heart alive can appreciate. *a* 1854 H. Reed *Lect. Brit. Poets* vi. (1857) 220 A strain of prose which is poetry in all but poetry's metrical music. 1885 Watts-Dunton in *Encycl. Brit.* XIX. 257/2 Absolute poetry is the concrete and artistic expression of the human mind in emotional and rhythmical language. 1906 H. B. Yeats *Poems* Pref., Poetry.. is in the last analysis an endeavour to condense as out of the flying vapours of the world an image of human perfection, and for its own and not for the art's sake.

d. Extended (with reference to the etymology) to creative or imaginative art in general. *rare.*

[1815 D. Stewart in *Encycl. Brit., Suppl.* I. 5 *note*, The latitude given by D'Alembert to the meaning of the word *Poetry* is a real and very important improvement on Bacon, who restricts it to fictitious History or Fables... D'Alembert, on the other hand, employs it in its natural signification, as synonymous with *invention* or *creation*.] 1856 Ruskin *Mod. Paint.* III. iv. i. § 15 Painting is properly to be opposed to speaking or writing, but not to poetry. Both painting and speaking are methods of expression. Poetry is the employment of either for the noblest purposes.

4. *pl.* Pieces of poetry; poems collectively. *rare.*

c 1384 Chaucer *H. Fame* iii. 388 Oon seyde Omere was [*v.r.* made] lyes Feynynge in hys Poetries. 1587 Golding *De Mornay* xxiv. (1592) 372 What shall we say then to the Poetries [of our Scriptures], specially of Dauid, considering that he was afore all the Poetries of the Heathen? 1656 Earl Monm. tr. *Boccalini's Advts. fr. Parnass.* 284 Desired that she might see both their Poetries; which after she had perused several times, and duly considered them, she..chose Mauro's *Fava.* 1818 Scott *Rob Roy* xxiii, And this young birkie here,..will his stage-plays and his poetries help him here, d'ye think..?—Will *Tityre tu patulæ*, as they ca' it, tell him where Rashleigh Osbaldistone is? 1886 M. F. Tupper *My Life as Author* 222 If some few have appeared among other poetries in print, they shall not be repeated here.

5. *fig.* Something resembling or compared to poetry; poetical quality, spirit, or feeling.

1816 Keats *Sonn. Grasshopper & Cricket*, The poetry of earth is never dead:..a voice will run..about the new-mown mead; That is the Grasshopper's. 1817 Coleridge *Biog. Lit.* II. xiv. 1 The sudden charm, which accidents of light and shade, which moon-light or sun-set diffused over a known and familiar landscape..these are the poetry of nature. 1846 Mackay *Poems, Railways* 1 'No poetry in railways!' foolish thought Of a dull brain, to no fine music wrought. 1874 Blackie *Self-Cult.* 70 To live poetry, indeed, is always better than to write it.

6. The name given to the sixth, or (reckoning the *Preparatory* as one, the seventh) class from the bottom or third from the top, in English Roman Catholic schools, seminaries, or colleges, on the continent, and subsequently in England. The class so called comes between *Syntax* and *Rhetoric.*

1679 *Trials of White & other Jesuits* 56 *Fall.* I saw him when I was in my Syntax, and now I am in Poetry. 1906 ['Still in use at Stonyhurst, etc.; also at St. Edmund's or Douay College, now located at Woolhampton in Berks.' (Rev. Sir D. O. Hunter Blair, O.S.B.)]

7. *attrib.* and *Comb.*

1798 Wolcott (P. Pindar) *Tales of Hoy* Wks. 1812 IV. 410 He scrawls the chairs and tables over, and walls whenever the poetry-fit is upon him. 1846 Thackeray *L. Blanchard* Wks. 1900 XIII. 477 The young fellow..poetry-stricken, writing dramatic sketches. 1885 *Illustr. Lond. News* 7 Nov. 463/3 The book is one on which every poetry lover should form his own opinion. 1887 Dowden *Transcripts* (1896) 516 The ignominious years of dreaming, poetry-making, and the receiving of wretched praise.

Hence **Po·etryless** *a.*, devoid of poetry.

1854 H. Strickland *Trav. Th.* 28 A soulless, poetryless, utilitarian, money-making Englishman is bad enough.

Poetship (pō^u·ĕtʃip). [f. Poet + -ship.] The position or function of a poet; also with *poss. adj.* as a mock title for a poet.

1781 Cowper *Let. to J. Newton* 25 Aug., Johnson uses the discretion my poetship has allowed him, with much discernment. 1834 Sir J. Stephen in *Sir H. Taylor's Corr.* (1888) 59 Do not let your poetship snort and grow saucy. 1878 Browning *Poets Croisic* l, Fury of favour, Royal Poetship, Prophetship.

Poeuere, poeure, obs. forms of Poor.

Poff, obs. form of Puff.

Poffle (pǫ·f'l). *Sc.* Also **paffle.** [Deriv. obscure: cf. Pightle and the phonetic variations under Hickwall.] A small parcel of land: cf. Pendicle 2 b.

(*Max poffil*, the poffle of Maccus, now Maxpoffle in Roxburghshire, is mentioned in 1317.)

1797 *Statist. Acc. Scot.* XIX. 328 Some places are parcelled out into small poffles or farms, few of which are above 30 acres each. 1818 Scott *Hrt. Midl.* Ded., Disclaiming all intention of purchasing that pendicle or poffle of land called the Carlinescroft. 1901 A. Lang in *Longm. Mag.* Feb. 380 In Spot itself he purchased a poffle or pendicle of land.

†**Poge.** *Obs. rare*⁻¹. [app. repr. It. *appoggio* leaning place, stay, help: cf. *poggio* mounting block:—L. *podium*: see Pew.] Stay, support.

c 1525 Br. Clerke *Let. to Wolsey* in Ellis *Orig. Lett.* Ser. ii. I. 308 His Holynes being excluded frome the belp and poge of other Princes.

Pogge (pǫg). [Origin unascertained.] A name given to certain fishes. **a.** The armed bull-head, *Cottus cataphractus*, having a large broad flat head and sharply tapering body, armed with spines and bony plates. **b.** *Aspidophorus*, an acanthopterygian genus, armed with shield-like scales.

a 1672 Willughby *Ichthyogr.* (1686) Tab. N. 6, 2 Cataphractus supinus Schonfeldij. 3 idem. a Pogge. 1740 R. Brookes *Art of Angling* ii. xxix. 137 The Pogge...is about two Hands breadth in Length. 1753 Chambers *Cycl. Supp.*, *Pogee*, or *Cataphractus*. 1769 Pennant *Zool.* III. 178 The pogge is very common on most of the British coasts. 1823 Crabb *Technol. Dict., Pogge*,...a sort of Bull-Head, the *Cottus cataphractus* of Linnæus, a fish having the head larger than the body. 1856 Gosse *Marine Zool.* ii. 200 *Aspidophorus* (Cuv.). Pogge. Body eight-angled, enclosed in plates; recurved spines on the snout; teeth only on the jaws; lower jaw fringed.

Poggy (pǫ·gi). Also **poggie.** [Origin unknown.] A small arctic whale; supposed to be the young of the common whale, *Balæna mysticetus.*

1874 Scammon *Marine Mamm.* i. v. 60 The whales of this sea [Sea of Okhotsk] are the same species as those of the Arctic; although in the bays is found, in addition, a very small whale called the 'Poggy', which yields but little oil.

Pogh(e: see Poh *int.*, Pough *sb. Obs.*

Poghaden, the menhaden: see Pauhaugen.

‖**Pogoniasis** (pǭ gonai·ăsis). *Phys.* [mod.L., f. Gr. πωγώνι-ον, dim. of πώγων beard + -asis.] Excessive growth of beard; also, growth of beard in a woman.

1842 Dunglison *Med. Lex., Pogoniasis*, a female beard. Also, great strength or quantity of beard. 1895 *Syd. Soc. L.*

Pogo·niate, *a.* [C. Gr. πωγωνιάτης bearded man.] **a.** *Zool.* Bearded. **b.** *Ornith.* Webbed, as a feather.

[1786 *Pogonologia* 19 The emperor Constantine is distinguished by the epithet of Pogonate, which signifies the Bearded.] 1890 in *Cent. Dict.* 1895 in *Syd. Soc. Lex.*

Pogonic (pogǫ·nik), *a.* [f. Gr. πώγων beard + -ic.] Of or pertaining to a beard.

1858 Mayne *Expos. Lex., Pogonicus*, of or belonging to the beard: pogonic.

So **Pogono·logist,** a writer on beards; **Pogono·logy,** a treatise on beards; **Pogono·tomy** [Gr. τομή cutting], the cutting of the beard; **Pogono·trophy** [Gr. τροφή nourishment], cultivation of the beard, beard-growing.

[1786 (*title*) Pogonologia, or a Philosophical Essay on Beards, translated from the French.] 1788 V. Knox *Winter Even.* I. ii. 24 It would not be surprising to see a barber style himself..Pogonologist. 1801 W. Taylor in *Monthly Mag.* XII. 422 Some years ago we had to read the Pogonology. 1861 *Temple Bar Mag.* III. 261 Ten years' experience may have made ourselves a little enthusiastic in favour of pogonotrophy. 1883 Rolleston in *Archæologia* XLVII. 455 There appears to be some necessary correlation between Hippophagy, Pogonotrophy, and perhaps Paganism. 1897 *Columbus* (Ohio) *Dispatch* Jan., Pogonotomy is what the Greeks used to call the gentle art of self-shaving.

‖**Pogrom** (pǒgrǫ·m). [Russian погромъ, devastation, destruction.] An organized massacre in Russia for the destruction or annihilation of any body or class: in the English newspapers (1905–6) chiefly applied to those directed against the Jews.

[1882 *Times* 17 Mar. 3/6 That the 'Pogromen' (riots against the Jews) must be stopped.] 1905 *Daily News* 12 June 5 The only means of combating the 'pogroms' is armed resistance. 1906 *Westm. Gaz.* 21 June 12/1 The Russian word 'pogrom' (pronounced with stress on the final syllable) is generally translated 'desolation, devastation'. The word is related to the Russian words *grom*, thunder, the thunder-clash, and to *g omit*, to thunder, to batter down as with a thunderbolt, to destroy without pity.

Pogy (pō^u·gi). local *U.S.* Also **pogie.** [Contr. from *pauhaugen*.] Local name of the menhaden: see Pauhaugen. *Comb.* **pogy-catcher,** a vessel employed in the menhaden fishery; **pogy-gull,** a sea-gull found near Cape Cod, Massachusetts.

1888 Goode *Amer. Fish* 385 North of Cape Cod the name Pogy is almost universally in use, while in southern New England the fish is known only as the menhaden.

Poh (pō^u), *int.* Also 7–8 **pough,** 8 **pogh,** 9 **po.** An ejaculation of contemptuous rejection. (Cf. Pooh.)

1679 Prance *Narr. Pop. Plot* 13 Pough, Pough, said Sr. Edmundbury, refusing at first to trouble himself. 1708 Mrs. Centlivre *Busie Body* ii. i, *Sir Fran.* For what? *Marpl.* Po'gh, for a hundred Things. *c* 1738 Swift *Lit. Ho. at Castleknock* Wks. 1755 IV. i. 306 Poh! fellow, keep not such a pother. 1787 *Minor* 174 Pogh; thought I, why should I fear a man. 1820 Cobbett *Gram. Eng. Lang.* § 210 Poh! Never think a man either learned or good merely on account of his being called a Doctor. 1824 Galt *Rothelan* i. vii, Po! yours are as the pebble stones on the seashore to the jewels that may be bought in Ghent.

‖**Poi** (poi). Also **poe.** [Hawaiian name.] A dish made in Hawaii from the root of the taro or kalo plant, by grinding, mixing, and allowing it to ferment; also, a dish made from the banana and pandanus fruit. Also *attrib.*

1840 F. D. Bennett *Whaling Voy.* I. 213 They eat it in the form of a paste, or poë. 1877 Lady Brassey *Voy. Sunbeam* (1878) 289 Poi is generally eaten from a bowl placed between two people, by dipping three fingers into it, giving them a twirl round, and then sucking them. 1894 *Outing* (U.S.) XXIII. 392/1 The poi-pudding tasted like fig-pudding and was extremely palatable.

†**Poid,** *a.* (*sb.*) *Sc. Obs.* Also **poyd.** [perh. a. OF. *puit, puet, put*, etc., good for nothing, dirty, evil.] Vicious, evil, vile; as *sb.* a vile person.

1501 Douglas *Pal. Hon.* i. 641 And all the court in haist thair horsis renȝeit. Proclamand loude, quhair is ȝone poid that plenȝeit, Quhilk deith deseruis committand sic dispite. 1513 — *Æneis* iv. Prol. 190 Sic poyd makrellis for Lucifer bene leche.

Poiet, obs. form of Poet.

Poietic (poiˌe·tik), *a. rare.* [ad. Gr. ποιητικ-ός active, effective, f. ποιεῖν to do, make. (So spelt and pronounced to differentiate the sense from *poetic*, of identical origin.)] Creative, formative, productive, active.

1905 *Athenæum* 29 Apr. 519/3 There are four classes in the State: the Poietic, the Kinetic, the Dull, and the Base. 1905 *Edin. Rev.* July 73 As its organisation becomes settled and efficient the State loses its poietic activity.

Poietic, -al, obs. Sc. ff. Poetic, -al.

Poignado, poinado (poinā·do). *Obs.* or *arch.* Also 6 **poineado, poinardo,** 6–7 **poynado,** (7 **poinadoe, -adow, poynedo**). [An alteration of Poniard, app. through *poniardo*: see -ado.] A small dagger; a poniard.

1567 J. Sanford *Epictetus* To Rdr. A iv, A short dagger: which is vsed in the warres, or a Poineado. 1581 Pettie *Guazzo's Civ. Conv.* iii. (1586) 168 Perchance they perswade themselues that their seruaunts can not helpe themselues with their Poignadoes. 1587 *Mirr. Mag., Q. Cordila* xxxviii, Poynadoes all bedyde With blood. 1593 G. Harvey *Pierce's Super.* Wks. (Grosart) II. 226 What will he do..with the tempestuous Engins of his owne wit, that keepeth such a horrible coile with his Schoole fellowes poinardo? 1611 Coryat *Crudities* 408 Duke John his nephew drew his poinado out of his sheath. 1654 R. Codrington tr. *Justine* xxxv. 341 Brennus..did end his life with his Poynedo. 1658 Phillips, *Poinard*, or *Poinado*. 1694 Motteux *Rabelais* v. ix. (1737) 34 Poinadoes, Skenes, Penknives. 1821 Scott *Kenilw.* xxix, A melancholy gallant; who..has his hand on his poignado, and swears death and fury!

Poignance (poi·nāns). *rare.* [f. Poignant: see -ance.] = next.

1782 Elphinston tr. *Martial* iii. ii. 132 To lend the pepper poignance. 1893 A. L. Haddon *What ails the House?* I. 129 Everything that surrounded me..lent poignance to my uneasiness.

Poignancy (poi·nānsi). [f. Poignant: see -ancy.] The quality or fact of being poignant.

1. Pungency of taste or smell. Also *fig.*

1730 Swift *Let. to Gay* 19 Nov., I..sat down quietly at my morsel, adding only..a principle of hatred to all succeeding measures..by way of sauce..; and..one point of conduct in my lady duchess's life has added much poignancy to it. 1786 tr. *Beckford's Vathek* (1868) 50 Aromatic herbs of the most acrid poignancy. 1814 Scott *Chivalry* (1874) 11 Sated with indulgences which soon lose their poignancy.

2. Keenness or sharpness of pain, distress, or grief; also, of pleasure (cf. next, 3 b).

17.. J. Ryland in Spurgeon *Treas. Dav.* Ps. lxxvii. 6 Sometimes this reflection..adds a poignancy to our distress. 1787 J. Barlow *Oration 4th July* 15 The tidings [were] received with a peculiar poignancy of grief. 1885 *Manch. Exam.* 15 June 5/4 The remembrance..gives our regrets a poignancy due to something like personal gratitude.

3. Piercing quality of words, expressions, looks, etc.; sharpness, keenness; piquancy.

a 1688 Villiers (Dk. Buckhm.) *Militant Couple* Wks. (1775) 125 Those words have lost all the poignancy of their signification. 1719 J. Welwood in *Rowe's Lucan* Pref. 36 The first [Virgil] surpasses all in solid strength; the latter [Lucan] excells in vigour and poynancy. 1838 Thirlwall *Greece* III. xviii. 83 Feelings..deeply stung by the poignancy of their wit.

Poignant (poi·nănt), *a.* Forms: 4–6 **poynaunt,** 4–8 **-ant,** 7–8 **poinant,** 7– **poignant,** (5 **pugnaunt, ponȝeand, -yaunt, -yawnt, poygnaunt, poyngnant**). [ME. a. OF. *puignant* (12th c. in Godef.), *poignant* (13th c.), pr. pple. of *poindre*:—L. *pungĕre* to prick, pierce.]

†**1.** Of weapons, or other pointed material objects: Sharp-pointed, piercing. *Obs.*

c 1400 *Rom. Rose* 1879 The God of Love an arowe took; Ful sharp it was and ful pugnaunt. *c* 1470 Henry *Wallace* iii. 141 The Scottis..With ponȝeand speris throuch platis prest of steylle. 1567 Turberv. *Ovid's Epist.* 69 b, Poynant hornes of fell and yrefull bulles. 1624 Gee *Hold Fast* 51 This weapon, being made so poinant and deadly, that it would pearce..reasonable good armour. 1695 J. Edwards *Perfect. Script.* 339 They were dispatch'd themselves by a more poinant stroke.

b. *fig.* Of the eye or look: Piercing, keen.

1787 'G. Gambado' *Acad. Horsemen* (1809) 15 Jeffery was not so slim, or was his eye so poignant. 1820 Miss Mitford in L'Estrange *Life* II. v. 120 Jeffrey has a singular expression—poignant, bitter, piercing—as if his countenance never lit up but at the perception of some weakness in human nature.

2. Sharp, pungent, piquant to the taste or smell.

c 1386 Chaucer *Nun's Pr. T.* 14 Of poynaunt sauce hir neded neuer a deel. *c* 1430 Lydg. & Burgh *Secrees* 1919 Wyn..Ponyaunt, delectable, sharp in savour. *c* 1450 *Douce MS.* 55 (Bodl.) iii, Sesyn hit..so that hit be poynant. 1610 B. Jonson *Alch.* ii. ii, Drest with an exquisite, and poynant sauce. 1728 Young *Love Fame* vi. 44 Those charms are greatest which decline the sight, That makes the banquet poignant and polite. 1864 Hawthorne *Dolliver Rom.* (1879) 61 The rich, poignant perfume spread itself through the air. 1883 Stevenson *Silverado Sq.* 237 A laboratory of poignant scents.

3. Painfully sharp to the physical or mental feelings, as hunger, thirst, a pang, an affront; also said of a state of feeling, as grief, regret, despair.

c 1386 Chaucer *Pars. T.* ₱ 56 And this sorwe..shal been heuy and greuous and ful sharpe and poynant in herte. 1651 N. Bacon *Disc. Govt. Eng.* ii. i. (1739) 3 The last affront was from France, and that..more poinant. 1728 Eliza Heywood *Mme. de Gomez's Belle A.* (1732) II. 10 This final Answer threw the King of Portugal into the most poinant Despair. 1809–10 Coleridge *Friend* (1818) III. 233 Those rare excellencies which make one grief poignant. *a* 1882 Rossetti *Ho. Life* ii, Creature of poignant thirst And exquisite hunger. 1887 Lowell *Democr.*, etc. 48 This pang is made more poignant by exile.

b. Stimulating to the mind, feelings, or passions; pleasantly or delightfully piquant.

1649 G. Daniel *Trinarch., Hen. V*, cccxlvi, Better rellish, [which] in this poynant State Might give an Edge to Witt, at less expence. 1668 H. More *Div. Dial.* ii. viii. (1713) 113 That Delights thereby may become more poinant and triumphant. 1772 Gouv. Morris in Sparks *Life & Writ.* (1832) I. 17 Those poignant joys, which are the lot of the affluent. 1860 Hawthorne *Marb. Faun* xliii, Sensible of a more poignant felicity than he had yet experienced.

4. Of words or expressions: Sharp, stinging; severe; also, pleasantly keen or pointed, piquant.

1542 Udall *Erasm. Apoph.* 270 b, With these sharpe & poynaunte woordes he clene putte awaye yᵉ fearefull trembleyng of all the legions. 1668 Dryden *Dram. Poesy* Ess. (Ker) I. 103 Quick and poynant brevity. 1678 Wycherley *Pl. Dealer* iii. i, Poinant and sower Invectives. 1706 *Reflex. upon Ridicule* 208 Witticisms which you think so delicate and poignant. 1773 Mrs. Chapone *Improv. Mind* (1774) I. v. 157 A witty repartee or a stroke of poignant raillery. 1821 Lamb *Elia* Ser. i. *Mrs. Battle's Opinions on Whist*, Her illustrations were apposite and poignant. 1844 Disraeli *Coningsby* iii. i, Poignant sarcasm.

Poignantly (poi·năntli), *adv.* [f. prec. + -ly ².] In a poignant manner; piercingly, pungently, acutely, keenly.

1794 G. Adams *Nat. & Exp. Philos.* II. xvii. 250 How poignantly this loss [of sight] was felt by our great poet is painfully evident from his own words. 1818 Mrs. Shelley *Frankenst.* xii. (1865) 147 They often..suffered the pangs of hunger very poignantly. 1837–9 Hallam *Hist. Lit.* II. ii. v. § 16. 192 Burlesque poetry, sometimes poignantly satirical. 1871 Ruskin *Fors Clav.* I. iv. 8, I have a piece of red oxide of copper..which grieves me poignantly by losing its colour.

Poignard, variant of Poniard.

†**Poigne** (poin). *Obs. rare.* [a. OF. *poigne*, fem. form parallel to *poing*:—L. *pugn-um* fist.] The closed hand or fist: in phr. *kept in poigne* (fig.).

a 1734 North *Exam.* i. ii. § 139 (1740) 107 The Witnesses, which the Faction kept in Poigne (like false Dice, high and low Fullhams) to be played forth upon Plots, and to make Discoveries as there was Occasion. *Ibid.* ii. v. § 126. 393 The Engineers..determined what was to be communicated,..and what to be kept in Poigne, secret from them.

†**Poignet,** *sb. Obs.* Forms: 5 **ponyet, poinett, punȝet,** 5–6 **poynett,** 6 **poygniet,** 9 **poignet.** [a. F. *poignet* wrist, in 14th c. *poingnet*, OF. *pugnet* (13th c.), deriv. of *poing* fist.]

1. An ornament for the wrist or hand; a wristlet or bracelet.

1402 *Will of Matilda Sweeton* (Fairholt), I par de ponyets de scarlet. 1416 *Maldon, Essex, Court Rolls* (Bundle 10 No. 3), Poynetts, iid. *c* 1440 *Promp. Parv.* 408/2 Ponyet, of a sleue,..*pr manica, mantus.* 1483 Caxton *Gold. Leg.* 44/1 Whan he had seen the ryngis in his susters eeris & her poynettis or armyllis on her hondes. 1530 Palsgr. 256/1 Poygniet for ones sleves, *poignet.* *c* 1540 J. Heywood *Four P. P.* B j b, Theyr bonettes and theyr poynettes. 1575 Laneham *Let.* (1871) 38 Hiz doobled sleeues of blak woorsted, vpon them a payr of poynets of towny Chamblet laced a long the wreast wyth blu threeden points.

¶**2.** *erron.* The handle or hilt of a dagger. (For F. *poignée.*) *rare*⁻¹.

1820 Scott *Monast.* xvi, The *poignet* being of silver exquisitely hatched.

Hence †**Poi·gnet** *v. Obs. trans.*, to put cuffs on (a garment); whence †**Poi·gneting** *vbl. sb.*

1555 T. Marshe *Instit. Gentleman* I vj b, A certayne kyng of Inglande caused his doublet to bee half stocked with foresleues of veluet, called in those dayes, poignetting of a doublet.

Poigniard, Poik: see Poniard, Poke *sb.*¹

Poikilitic (poikili·tik), *a. Geol.* Also **poic-.** [var. of Pœcilitic.] A term formerly applied to the Triassic and Permian systems, as being mainly composed of variegated rocks.

1836 Buckland *Geol. & Min.* II. 38 The word *Pœcilitic* is in sound so like to *Pisolite*, that it may be better to adhere more literally to the Greek root ποικίλος, and apply the common name of *Poikilitic* group to the strata in question. 1846 De la Beche in *Mem. Geol. Surv. Gt. Brit.* I. 239 Poicilitic or New Red Sandstone Series. 1861 *Eng. Wom. Dom. Mag.* III. 59 The reconstruction of the cretaceous, poikilitic, oolitic, or silurian landscape, peopled with revivified Batrachians. 1885 Geikie *Text-Bk. Geol.* (ed. 2) 748 The term 'Poikilitic' was formerly proposed for them, on account of their characteristic mottled appearance.

Poi·kilo-, a formative element from Gr. ποικίλος variegated, various, used in modern scientific terms (in some of which the Latinized form Pœcilo- is preferred):

Poi·kiloblast, Poi·kilocyte, names for red blood-corpuscles of irregular shape, elongated, pyriform, etc. (*Syd. Soc. Lex.*); **Poikilocyto·sis,** the condition of the blood when it contains poikilocytes. **Poikilothe·rmal, Poikilothe·rmic** *adjs.*, said of animals in which the bodily heat varies with the temperature of the environment; cold-blooded.

1897 *Allbutt's Syst. Med.* IV. 578 Irregular forms of red corpuscles which are generally included under the name of *poikilocytes. 1899 Cagney tr. *Jaksch's Clin. Diagn.* i. (ed. 4) 42 Gräber believes that the poikilocytes do not exist in the circulating blood. 1880 A. Flint *Princ. Med.* 62 The name *poikilocytosis has been proposed to designate the condition of blood in which the corpuscles present manifold variations in shape. 1884 tr. *Claus' Zool.* I. 74 Most of the lower animals are *poikilothermic, or, as they have less appropriately been called, cold blooded.

‖**Poil.** *Obs. rare.* [F. *poile, poêle* a stove, OF. *poisle, peisle*:—L. *pēsile, pensile* adj. neut. hung, suspended, f. *pendĕre* to hang.] A furnace, a stove.

1756 in Ellis *Orig. Lett.* Ser. ii. IV. 374 (from Berlin) He would find the ashes in the poil or furnace where they were burnt. *Ibid.* 377 They immediately put them into the poil or furnace, and set fire to them.

Poil, poill, obs. Sc. ff. Pole, Poll.

†**Poile.** *Obs. rare.* [a. F. *poil*:—L. *pil-um* hair.] Down, fine hair.

1746 *Phil. Trans.* XLIV. 180 (transl. fr. French) Its Substance was crumbling..like the Membrane of the Bladder, having a fungous Poile on it.

Poimenic (poime·nik), *a.* and *sb.* [ad. Gr. ποιμενικ-ός relating to a shepherd (ποιμήν): see -ic.]

A. *adj.* Of or pertaining to pastoral care.

1902 in Webster *Suppl.*

B. *sb.* (Chiefly pl. *poimenics.*) Pastoral theology, or the study of it.

1883 W. G. Blaikie *Ministry of Word* 296 Ample treatises on Homiletics, Liturgics, Catechetics and Poimenics. 1892 Schaff *Theol. Propædeut.* Pref. 3 (Funk), I beg the indulgence of the English reader for introducing a uniform terminology in the singular form for the several departments, as Isagogic, Poimenic, Evangelistic.

†**Poin,** *v. Obs.* Also **poyn.** [f. stem *poign-* of OF. *poindre* to pierce, prick:—L. *pungĕre*: cf. *join* from *joindre.*]

1. *trans.* To prick; to harass, annoy.

c 1330 R. Brunne *Chron. Wace* (Rolls) 16218 The power of Cadwalyn was mikel, Penda poyned hym [Oswy] als a prykel.

2. To stitch or sew through and through, to qu lt (cf. Broche *v.*); to ornament with stitching.

13.. *E. E. Allit. P.* A. 217 Pyȝt watz poyned & vche [*ed. Gollancz* pyght and poyned wacz uche] a hemme. 1395 *E. E. Wills* (1882) 6 A keuerlit of selk ypoynet. ?*a* 1400 *Morte Arth.* 2623, I poyne alle his pavelyouns þat to hymselfe pendes, Dyghttes his dowblettez for dukes and erles. *a* 1440 *Sir Degrev.* 1491 Quyltus poyned of that ylk.

3. To thrust (a spear).

c 1400 *Laud Troy Bk.* 14263 Eyther on other her speres poygned, Wel hard to-geder tho thei Ioyned.

Hence †**Poi·ning** *vbl. sb.*, piercing, stitching.

c 1430 *Pilgr. Lyf Manhode* i. cxi. (1869) 59 Ribt as the doublet is maad with poynynges.

Poinado, -ardo: see Poignado.

Po·nard, variant of Poniard.

Poind (see next), *sb. Sc.* [f. Poind *v.*] **a.** An act of poinding, a distraint. **b.** A beast or other chattel poinded. *Dead poind*, a poinded article of goods as opposed to live cattle.

1563–4 *Reg. Privy Council Scot.* I. 259 The poindis takin thairfoir to be restorit to the said George. 1609 Skene *Reg. Maj.* i. 71 Gif ane takes ane poynde for debt, within ane other mans land, without licence of him, or of his Baillie. *Ibid.* [see Poinder]. 1676 Ld. Fountainhall in M. P. Brown *Suppl. Dict. Decis.* (1826) III. 61 Poinded goods,..if they be a dead poind, that puts the creditor poinder to no..expence in keeping it. 1823 N. Carlisle *Topogr. Dict. Scot.* II. s.v. *Priestwick*, Sometimes Points are driven, and executed at the Cross of Priestwick. 1868 J. Salmon *Gowodean* 63 (E. D. D.) Glad to catch him with your poind and horn.

Poind (pīnd, pind), *v. Sc.* Forms: α. 5–7 **pund,** 6 **puind, pwynd.** β. 5–8 **poynd,** 6– **poind.** [Sc. repr. of OE. *pyndan* to enclose, shut in, impound, = Eng. Pind. The *u, ui, wy*, symbolized the vowel (ü), representing, as in Build (*Sc.* büld), an OE. *y*. Of this, *oi* is a 16th c. spelling, retained in the law-courts. The Sc. pronunciation is (pīnd) or (pind: cf. *mither, brither*); (poind), given in dictionaries, is merely founded on the spelling.]

1. *trans.* To distrain upon (a person or his goods); to seize and sell under warrant (the goods of a debtor): = Pind *v.* 2.

α. *a* 1400 *Burgh Laws* iii. (*Sc. Stat.* I), Of punding of upland's men in burgh. 1500 *Exch. Rolls Scotl.* XI. 393 To pund Thomas Fresale for viij li. vij s. vj d. 1531 *Acc. Ld. High Treas. Scotl.* VI. 54 To pas to pwynd the Shereff off Renfrew and utheris for restis of the chakkar. 1604 *Urie Crt.-bk.* (1892) 4 The transgressouris thairof to be punddit preceislie as is aboun wryttin.

β. 1516 *Acc. Ld. High Treas. Scotl.* V. 85 To Dauid Lowry..to poynd xxxiij lordis and lardis absent fra the assis. 1564–5 *Reg. Privy Council Scot.* I. 317 Lettres to be direct to poind..the said complenaris and thair gudis for the soum of thre hundreth pund stirling. 1698 *Min. Baron Crt. of Stitchell* (1905) 132 He was poynding the defender at the instance of James Hoggart. 1786 Burns *Twa Dogs* 98 He'll apprehend them, poind their gear. *a* 1803 *Lament Border Widow* iii. in Child *Ballads* iv. (1886) 429/2 He slew my knight, and poind his gear. 1886 *Act* 49 *Vict.* c. 23 § 3 (2), The right to poind the ground hereinafter provided.

b. *absol.* To distrain.

a. 1500 *Exch. Rolls Scotl.* XI. 457 Falyeing of the said preif the said schiref sal pund for the said thre termes. 1532 *Aberdeen Regr.* (1844) I. 146 Tha ordanit Henry Irvein, bailȝe,..gif neid beis, to cause puind for the same. β. 1545 *Reg. Privy Council Scot.* I. 21 Quhair his officiaris ar deforcit in poynding for the said taxt. 1641 *Ferguson's Sc. Prov.* (1785) § 936 Ye may poind for debt but not for unkindness.

2. To impound (stray cattle, contraband goods, etc.): = Pind 1 b.

[*c* 1450: see Poinder.] 1536 Bellenden *Cron. Scot.* x. xii. (1541) 144/1 All othir beistis that eittis mennis corne or gres salbe poyndit quhil the awnar thairof redres the skaithis. 1637–50 Row *Hist. Kirk* (Wodrow Soc.) 9 What shall poore sillie sheep doe that are poyndit in a fold where there is no meat? 1678 Sir G. Mackenzie *Crim. Laws Scot.* i. xxvi. § ii. (1699) 130 The Customers Officers were about to poynd some unfree goods. 1815 Scott *Guy M.* vii, Their asses were poinded by the ground-officer when left in the plantation.

†**3.** *intr.* To plunder. *Obs. rare.*

c 1425 Wyntoun *Cron.* viii. xliv. 6960 The qwhethir offt ryot wald thai ma To pryk, and poynd, bathe to and fra.

Hence **Poi·nded** *ppl a.*, **Poi·nding** *vbl. sb.* and *ppl. a.*: see also Multiple-*poinding.*

1401 *Aberdeen Regr.* (1844) I. 380 Sa that hym nedit nocht in tyme to cum til mak sic pundyng and namly in our toon. 1540 *Records of Elgin* (New Spald. Cl.) I. 50 The vrangus punding of Robert Dauidsone. 1585 *Reg. Privy Council Scot.* IV. 10 Ane actioun and caus of double-poinding. 1676 Poinded [see Poind *sb.*]. 1678 Sir G. Mackenzie *Crim. Laws Scot.* i. xxvi. § iii. (1699) 131 Poyndings.. cannot be execute after the Sun is set, because a Poynding is a sentence. 1746–7 *Act* 20 *Geo. II*, c. 43 § 28 It shall.. be lawful for the officer executing such poyndings, to carry the goods poynded..to the market cross. 1899 *Scotsman* 6 July, Notes of expenses of carrying through sales under sequestration or poindings, and also..of carrying back poinded or sequestrated effects.

Poi·ndable, *a. Sc.* [f. Poind *v.* + -able.] Liable to be, or capable of being, poinded.

15.. *Aberdeen Regr.* XXV. (Jam.), To seiss geir poindabill quhaireuir he may apprehend the same. 1566 *Reg. Privy Council Scot.* I. 457 Substantious inlandit men, poindabill. 1772 *Weekly Mag.* 25 June 398/1 He has poindable goods.

Poi·nder. *Sc.* Also 5 **pundar,** 9 **-er.** [f. Poind *v.* + -er ¹.] A person, esp. an official, who poinds or distrains goods; also, **b.** 'A person who has the charge of hedges, woods, etc., and who pounds cattle that trespass' (Jam.).

c 1450 Holland *Howlat* 783 The Corn Crake, the pundar at hand, Had pyndit all his pryss horss in a pundfald. 1609 Skene *Reg. Maj.* ii. 12 The poynds..salbe reteined ..in sic ane place pertaining to the poynder..quhere sic poynds or distresse may remaine and be keeped. 1676 [see Poind *sb.*]. 1805 A. Scott *Poems* (1808) 146 The punder's axe, with ruthless rap, Fell'd down their favourite tree. *Ibid.* 147 For sure this tree's enormous trunk Defies the punder's axe. 1816 Scott *Antiq.* xxiv, I'll..get my bit supper frae Ringan the poinder up by. 1886 *Act* 49 *Vict.* c. 23 § 3 (1) Any arrester or poinder..who shall be thus deprived of the benefit of his diligence.

†**Poindfald, poyndfauld,** obs. Sc. ff. Pinfold.

1494 *Acta Audit.* (1839) 185/1 Anent..doune castin of xii Rudis of dik of þe said Samellis landis, and doune castin of the poyndfalt of Akinbar. 1650 in *Spottiswood Misc.* (1844) I. 211 Ther were neuer such a company of bedlames driuin wnto ane poyndfauld as wee.

†**Poindlar, pundler.** *Sc. Obs.* Also 7 **poundler,** 8 **punler.** [A parallel form of Poinder, with changed suffix. Cf. Pantler.] = Poinder.

1533 *Aberdeen Regr.* (1844) I. 149 The prouest, baillȝeis, and counsaill,..ordanit Georg. Annan pvndler of thar kirk yard, and ordanit the pundlene of euery best to be four d. 1583 *Reg. Privy Council Scot.* III. 603 To poind thame, letting thame out for reasonable poindlaris fee, unhoundit, slayne, or hocht. 1673 *Min. Baron Court of Stitchell* (1905) 64 For scandallizing Andro Burn poundler. 1715 Pennecuik *Poems* 52 The trusty Punler of the Newland pease. 1808 Jamieson s.v. *Pundler*, Even of late, a person employed to watch the fields, in order to prevent the grain from being stolen or injured, was called a pundler. *Angus.*

Poineado, Poinred: see Poignado, Poniard.

Poiner, dial. var. of Piner ¹, labourer.

‖**Poinsettia** (poinse·tiă). [mod.L.; named 1836 after the discoverer J. R. Poinsett, American Minister to Mexico.] A Mexican species of Euphorbia, *E.* (*Poinsettia*) *pulcherrima*, formerly made the type of a genus, having large scarlet floral leaves surrounding small greenish-yellow flowers; much cultivated in conservatories as Mexican Flame-leaf and Lobster-flower, called in America Easter-flower or Christmas-flower.

1871 Kingsley *At Last* iv, What is this that hangs over into the road, some fifteen feet in height..? What but the Poinsettia, paltry scions of which..adorn our hothouses and dinner-tables. 1872 Darwin in *Life & Lett.* (1887) III. 170, I have been more than once assured that butterflies like bright colours—for instance, in India the scarlet leaves of Poinsettia. 1883 V. Stuart *Egypt* 3 Over the rubbish ..still waved magnificent poinsettias and oleander trees.

Point (point), *sb.*¹ Forms: 3– **point;** also 3–6 **pointe, poynte,** 4–8 **poynt,** (4 *pl.* **poyne**), 5 **pointt(e, puynt, pynt, pyntte,** 6 **poinct, -e, poynct, -e,** *Sc.* **pwint.** β. 4–5 **pont, -e,** 5–6 **pounte,** 6 **pownt,** 6–9 *Sc.* **pount.** Also **punt:** see Punct. [In origin, two, or perh. three, words. In A., a. F. *point* = Pr. *punt*, Sp., It. *punto*, Pg. *ponto*:—L. *punct-um* that which is pricked, a prick, a minute mark like a prick, a dot, a point in writing, a point in space, a point of time, a small measure, a particular of a discourse, etc.; subst. use of pa. pple. neuter of L. *pungĕre, punct-*, F. *poindre, point* to prick, pierce. In B., a. F. *pointe* = Pr., Sp., It. *punta*, Pg. *ponta*:—Com. Romanic (and med.L.) *puncta* the action of piercing, the piercing part of anything, a sharp or pointed extremity (in med.L. the point of a knife, shoe, foot, promontory, etc.); ppl. sb. fem. from *pungĕre* (parallel to those in *-āta, -ada, -ée*). In C., in some senses, app. an independent derivative, as a noun of action, from F. *poindre*, or *pointer*, or from Eng. Point *v.*¹ In ME., through the loss or non significance of final *-e*, *point* and *pointe* ran together, combining under the same form two senses which in all other langs. are kept apart (e. g. Ger. *punkt, spitze*). Transferred and fig. senses subsequently arose related to both primary notions, so that in senses where there is no corresponding F. *point* or *pointe*, the development is often very difficult to determine. The occasional spellings *pynt, pyntte* prob. indicate a pronunciation formerly prevalent and still dialectal of *oi* as *ī*, *point* being pronounced like *pint*. The β-forms in *pont, pount pownt*, are difficult to place; perh. they ought to be equated with *punt*, and so rather to be included under the by-form Punct.]

A. = F. *point.*

I. A prick, a dot.

†**1.** A minute hole or impression made by pricking; a prick, a puncture. *Obs. rare.*

c 1400 *Lanfranc's Cirurg.* 142 Make a poynt bi þe space of a litil fyngre from þe oon eende of þe wounde, & anoþer poynt at þe oþere eende of þe wounde. *c* 1440 *Promp. Parv.* 406/2 Poynte, *punctus* vel *punctum.* [1826 Kirby & Sp. *Entomol.* IV. 270 A *Point* (*Punctum*), a minute impression upon the surface, but not perforating it.]

2. A minute mark on a surface, of the size or appearance of a fine puncture; a dot, a minute spot or speck; also, anything excessively small or appearing like a speck.

1390 Gower *Conf.* III. 65 Which [Astrolabe] was of fin gold precious With pointz and cercles merveilous. 1600 E. Blount tr. *Conestaggio* 202 Now he only subscribed *Rey*:: pointed with fiue points, called by the Portugals the fiue wounds. 1655 Mrq. Worcester *Cent. Inv.* § 4 This invention..so abbreviated that a point onely sheweth distinctly and significantly any of the 24. Letters. 1732 Law *Serious C.* xiii (ed. 2) 228 As the fix'd Stars..appear but as so many points. 1822–34 *Good's Study Med.* (ed. 4) III. 468 The pupil, instead of being dilated, is contracted to a point. 1848 Stark *Elem. Nat. Hist.* I. 468 Body dotted with numerous red points. 1899 *Allbutt's Syst. Med.* VIII. 550 The lesions begin as minute scaly points in the epidermis.

3. A dot or other small mark used in writing or printing.

a. A punctuation-mark; *esp.* the *full point* or full stop; also extended to the marks of exclamation (!) and interrogation (?); and sometimes to reference-marks, as the asterisk, obelisk, etc.

c 1386 Chaucer *Can. Yeom. Prol. & T.* 927 And þer a poynt, for ended is my tale; God send euery trewe man boote of his bale. 1530 Palsgr. 15 b, A poynt, whether it be suche as the Latins call *punctum planum* thus made . , or with suche as the Latins cal *comma* thus made : , or *virgula* thus made /. 1589 Nashe *Anat. Absurd.* 40 In yᵉ pause of a ful point. 1623 Lisle *Ælfric on O. & N. Test.* ad init., The Saxon vseth our note of Full-point commonly for all other distinctions. 1735 Pope *Prol. Sat.* 161 Commas and points they set exactly right. 1771 Luckombe *Hist. Print.* 258, ¶ The Paragraph. † The Obelisk. ‡ The Double Dagger. ‖ The Parallel. § The Section. * The Asterism. These are the Names and Figures of what Founders reckon among Points, and Printers call References. *Ibid.* 262 He assigned the former Points their proper places..and added the Semicolon..to come in between the Comma and the Colon. 1804 L. Murray *Eng. Gram.* (ed. 5) I. 406 The point of Interrogation, ? The point of Exclamation, !. 1891 *N. & Q.* 7th Ser. XII. 99/2 All abbreviations being uniformly denoted by the full-point.

b. In Semitic alphabets, Any one of the dots, minute strokes, or groups of these, which are placed over, under, or within the letters or consonants, in order to indicate the vowels; in Hebrew also to indicate variation or doubling of the consonant, stress accent, punctuation, etc.; in Arabic and Persian to distinguish consonants otherwise identical in form, as ﻥ *n*, ﺕ *t*, ﺙ *þ*, ﺏ *b*, ﻱ *i*, ﭖ *p*, etc., called *diacritical points.*

1614 Selden *Titles Hon.* 102 The three words haue ouer the Aliphs their point Vashlu. 1620 T. Granger *Div. Logike* 167 They added the points (which wee call vowels). 1668 Wilkins *Real Char.* 365 That Argument..against the Antiquity of the Hebrew Points, or Vowels. 1748 Hartley *Observ. on Man* i. iii. 312 The Manner of writing Hebrew without Points. 1776 J. Richardson *Arab. Gram.* iii. 11 When final..it [ﻳ] has often two points above. *Ibid.*, Like ﻝ and ﻳ..it [ﻱ] is considerably influenced by the vowel points. 1834 *Penny Cycl.* II. 210/1 In it [the Cufic character] the Koran was written, originally without diacritical points and vowels. 1837 G. Phillips *Syriac Gram.* 3 The points of the vowel Zekofo may coalesce with the point of the letter. 1891 A. F. Kirkpatrick *Bk. Psalms* i. Introd. vii. 51 The present elaborate system of vowel marks or 'points', commonly called the 'Massoretic punctuation' or 'vocalisation'.

c. A dot used in writing numbers. (*a*) In decimals, separating the integral from the fractional part; also, placed over a repeating decimal, or over the first and last figures of the period in a circulating decimal. (*b*) A dot or stroke used to separate a line of figures into groups.

1704 [see Decimal *a.* 1 b]. 1797 *Encycl. Brit.* (ed. 3) II. 312/2 Decimals are distinguished by a point, which separates them from integers, if any be prefixed. 1900 *Daily News* 9 June 5/3 Two 'four-point-sevens', ..two naval twelve-pounders.., and two five-inch guns. *Mod.* We read 4·6 as 'four point repeating six'.

4. A dot or mark used in mediæval musical notation (med.L. *punctus* or *punctum*).

a. A mark indicating a tone or sound; corresponding to the modern 'notes'. (Cf. Counterpoint *sb.*¹)

1674 Playford *Skill Mus.* iii. 1 Counterpoint..was the old manner of Composing Parts together, by setting Points or Pricks one against another. 1782 Burney *Hist. Mus.* II. i. 39 Points were first used simple, afterwards with tails.

b. = Dot *sb.*¹ 5 d.

Point of alteration or *duplication*, a dot placed before two short notes in 'perfect' or triple rhythm, to indicate that the second of them is to be reckoned as of twice its ordinary length. *Point of augmentation*, a dot placed after a note in 'imperfect' or duple rhythm, to lengthen it by one half (as in modern music). *Point of division* or *imperfection*, a dot placed between two short notes in 'perfect' rhythm, of which the first is preceded and the second followed by a long note; indicating a division of the rhythm (like the bar in modern music), and rendering the two long notes 'imperfect'. *Point of perfection*, a dot placed in 'perfect' rhythm after a long note which would otherwise be 'imperfect' by position, to indicate that it is to be 'perfect'.

1597 Morley *Introd. Mus.* 12, I pray you say what Prickes or poynts..signifie in singing.

II. 5. A separate or single article, item, or clause in an extended whole (usually an abstract whole, as a course of action, a subject of thought, a discourse, etc.); an individual part, element, or matter, a detail, a particular; sometimes, a detail of nature or character, a particular quality or respect; † an instance (of some quality, etc.).

a 1225 *Ancr. R.* 178 ȝif eni ancre is þet ne veleð none uondunges, swuð drede hire iðet point. *c* 1290 *S. Eng. Leg.* I. 27/30 Fondede in eche pointe to answerien heom wel quoyntliche. *a* 1300 *Cursor M.* 23261 (Cott.) Bot a point es þar þam pines mare, Þan elles al þair oþer fare. *Ibid.* 26092 Þe toþer pont es scrift o muth. 1340 *Ayenb.* 33 And yet eft þer byeþ zix poyns kueade, huerby sleuþe brengeþ man to his ende. 1389 in *Eng. Gilds* (1870) 6 These ben þe poyntz & þe articles ordeyned of the bretheren of seint Katerine. *c* 1394 *P. Pl. Crede* 6 In my paternoster iche poynt after oþer. *c* 1400 *Rule St. Benet* 657 Ther er the pontes of perfite lifyng That nedful er to eld and ȝing. *c* 1400 *Brut* E. E. T. S.) 157 He sent worde..þat þai shulde done out and put awey þat o poynt of restitucion. 1500–20 Dunbar *Poems* xlv. 17 It is ane point of ignorance To lufe in sic distemperance. 1526 Tindale *Jas.* ii. 10 Whosoeuer shall kepe the whole lawe, and yet fayle in one poynt, he is gyltie in all. 1533 Gau *Richt Vay* 55 The ix artikil. I trou that thair is ane halie chris-tine kirk and ane communione of sanctis. Thir ii pwintis ar baith bot ane thing. 1541 *Test. Ebor.* VI. 135 That..this my last will and testament be fulfillid in every poynte. 1641 J. Jackson *True Evang. T.* i. 7, I have prefaced and scholied sufficiently unto the Text, I come now to seek out first the parts, and then the points of it. 1663 Gerbier *Counsel* 49 The censure of the Surveyor, on the point of all the materialls which are brought in. 1702 Norris *Ideal World* i. ii. 74 This is the point upon which the whole reasoning turns. 1784 J. Potter *Virtuous Villagers* II. 23 We shall never agree on these points, so we'll drop them. 1833 Ht. Martineau *Manch. Strike* v. 55 If they had known what poin was in dispute. 1866 G. Macdonald *Ann. Q. Neighb.* v, Is it a point of conscience with you? 1897 J. T. Tomlinson *Prayer Bk., Articles & Hom.* vii. 211 We shall find.. that..he [Cosin] never adopted any one of the 'six points' of modern Ritualism.

†**b.** *To stand* (*up*)*on* (*one's*) *points*, to insist upon details of conduct or manners which one has espoused; to be punctilious or scrupulous. *Obs.*

c 1590 Greene *Fr. Bacon* i. 122 Our country Margret is so coy, And stands so much vpon her honest points, That marriage or no market with the mayd. 1590 Shaks. *Mids. N.* v. i. 118. 1602 B. Jonson *Ev. Man in Hum.* (Qo.) i. ii. 32 He stood vpon poynts with me too. 1685 Bunyan *Pharisee & Publican* Wks. 1861 II. 237 For a man here to stand thus upon his points, it is death.

c. *To Strain* or *Stretch a point*: see the verbs.

III. A minute part or particle of anything; the smallest unit of measurement.

†**6.** The very least or a very small part *of* something; a jot, whit, particle. *Obs.*

a 1300 *Body & Soul* in *Map's Poems* (Camden) 338 O poynt of ore pine to bate in the world ne is no leche. *c* 1450 Lovelich *Grail* lv. 182 Neuere Man On hym Cowde Aspye that Evere he hadde poynt of Meselrye. *c* 1450 *Mirour Saluacioun* 368 Nor neuer hafe felt a poynt of vnhelth, nor sekenesse. 1477 Norton *Ord. Alch.* vii. in Ashm. *Theat. Chem. Brit.* (1652) 104 By one point of excesse all your Warke is shent.

†**b.** *No point* (cf. F. *ne point*): not a bit, not at all, not in the least. *Obs.*

1542 Udall *Erasm. Apoph.* 137 Diogenes esteemed the fruite to bee no poyncte the more polluted. 1588 Shaks. *L. L. L.* ii. i. 190 *Boy.* Will you prick't with your eye? *La. Ro.* No poynt, with my knife. 1610 *Histrio-m.* iii. 266 The Players now are growne so proud, Ten pound a play, or no point Comedy.

†**7.** The smallest or a very small portion of time; a moment, instant. *Obs.*

1382 Wyclif *Isa.* liv. 7 At a poynt in a litil I forsoc thee. 1434 Misyn *Mending Life* 106 In a poynt we lyfe, ȝa les þen a poynt, for [if] all our lyfe to lyfe euerlastynge we wald likkyn, noȝt it is. *a* 1533 Ld. Berners *Gold. Bk. M. Aurel.* (1546) Kkj b, Theyr felicitie hath been but a shorte poynt.

†**8.** *Sensible point*: the least discernible portion of matter or space. *Obs. rare.*

1690 Locke *Hum. Und.* ii. xv. § 9 A sensible Point, meaning thereby the least Particle of Matter or Space we can discern, which is ordinarily about a Minute, and to the sharpest Eyes seldom less than thirty Seconds of a Circle, where the Eye is the Center. 1704 in J. Harris *Lex. Techn.* I.

9. *Mus.* A short strain or snatch of melody; esp. in phr. *point of war*, etc., a short phrase sounded on an instrument as a signal. *arch.*

13.. *E. E. Allit. P.* A. 890 Of þat songe myȝt synge a poynt. 1578 Gosson in T. N. tr. *Conq. W. India* ad fin., When..threatnyng trumpet sounde the poyntes of warre. 1597 Shaks. *2 Hen. IV*, iv. i. 52. 1602 Marston *Ant. & Mel.* iv. Wks. 1856 I. 48 Make me a straine;..Breath me a point that may inforce me weepe. 1814 Scott *Wav.* xlvi, To perform the beautiful and wild point of war. 1867 Morris *Jason* i. 127 His guardian drew The horn from off his neck, and thereon blew A point of hunting known to two or three. 1871 Ruskin *Fors Clav.* viii. (1896) I. 152 Bid him put ghostly trump to lip and breathe a point of war.

b. An important phrase or subject, usually in a contrapuntal composition, esp. in relation to its entry in a particular part; the entry of such a phrase or subject.

1597 Morley *Introd. Mus.* 76 There can bee no point or Fuge taken without a rest. *a* 1646 J. Gregory *Posthuma* (1649) 48 The Contrapunctum figuratum, consisting of Feuges, or maintaining of Points. 1881 in Grove *Dict. Mus.* III. 7 *Points*, a term applied..to the opening notes of the Subject of a Fugue, or other important Motivo, to which it is necessary that the attention of the Performer should be particularly directed.

†**10.** In mediæval measurement of time: The fourth (or according to some, the fifth) part of an hour. (See Atom *sb.* 7.) *Obs.*

1495 *Trevisa's Barth. De P. R.* ix. ix. (W. de W.) 354 An houre conteynyth foure poyntes [*Bodl. MS.* punctes] and a poynt ten momentes. [*Ibid.* xxi. 359 A puncte is the fourth partye of an houre.] 1844 Lingard *Anglo-Sax. Ch.* (1858) II. xi. 138 Twenty-four hours, each of which admits of four different subdivisions, into four points [etc.].

†**11.** The twelfth part of the side or radius of a quadrant, etc.: *spec.* in *Astron.* One of the 24 (or, according to some, 12) equal divisions of the diameter of the sun or moon, by which the degree of obscuration in an eclipse was measured.

c 1391 Chaucer *Astrol.* i. § 12 The skale..that seruith by hise 12 poyntes..of ful many a subtil conclusioun. *c* 1400 in Halliwell *Rara Mathem.* (1841) 59 Þe 12 departynges of aiþer of þo sides are called poyntes, þan es a poynte þe twelft parte of any thyng, namely of ouþer side of þe quadrat in Þe quadrant. 1550 W. Lynne *Carion's Cron.* 252 b, The third Eclipse was of the Moone..the Moone was darkened .xvii. pointes and .xxv. minutes. 1594 Blundevil *Exerc.* iii. i. xv. (1636) 309 The Astronomers do divide the Diameter as well of the Sunne, as of the Moone into 12, and some into 24 parts, which they call points.

12. *Nine* or *eleven points*, usually in the saying 'Possession is nine (*formerly* eleven) points of the law', i. e. is = nine or eleven out of a supposed ten or twelve points (= a vast majority of the points) that may be raised in a legal action. So by hyperbole, *ninety-nine points* (out of a hundred).

1697–8 Watts *Relig. Juv.* (1789) 149 Prejudice and education had eleven points of the law, and it was impossible for arguments to dispossess them. 1809 Malkin *Gil Blas* x. x. ₱ 20 She had possession, and that is nine points of the law. 1863 Reade *Very Hard Cash* xliii, Possession is ninety-nine points of Lunacy law.

13. A unit of count in the score of a game.

1746 Hoyle *Whist* (ed. 6) 69 *Points.* Ten of them make a Game. 1816 Singer *Hist. Cards* 261 *note*, The five is called Towser. The six, Tumbler, which reckon in hand for their respective number of points. 1856 Lt. Col. B. *Whist-player* (1858) 21 The party revoking forfeit three points. 1873 Bennett & 'Cavendish' *Billiards* 14 The game (1200 up) was won by Cook by 117 points. 1895 *Westm. Gaz.* 3 Dec. 7/1 Cumberland scored 14 points [at Football].

b. Hence, *to give points to* [F. *donner, rendre des points*], to allow (a rival) to count so many points at starting, to give odds to; *colloq.* to have the advantage of: so *to gain a point, to get points*, to gain an advantage.

1871 Freeman *Hist. Ess.* Ser. i. xii. 400 The English Minister can often gain a point by dexterous dealing in Parliament. 1881 *Confess. Frivolous Girl* 106, I got more [bouquets] than she did; thereby (to use a bit of slang) getting points on her for the time being. 1883 *American* VI. 333 Any average Eton boy could give points to His Holiness in the matter of Latin verses. 1895 F. E. Trollope *F. Trollope* II. i. 16 She could give points to many younger women and beat them.

c. *spec.* in *Piquet*: The number of cards of the most numerous suit in one's hand after discarding; the number scored by the player who holds the highest number of one suit. See Piquet ¹.

1719 R. Seymour *Court Gamester* 75 He who reckons most in this Manner [either by greater number of cards, or, in case of equality, of Pips, Ace = 11, Court cards 10 each] is said to win the Point. 1727–41 Chambers *Cycl.* s. v. *Piquet*, The carte blance [*sic*] is the first thing that reckons; then the point. 1809 Malkin *Gil Blas* i. xvii. ₱ 3 Point, quint, and quatorze. 1824 Scott *St. Ronan's* xviii, By an infraction of the laws of the game [piquet]..Lord Etherington called a point without showing it.

d. *pl.* Name of a particular game at bowls.

1902 J. A. Manson in *Encycl. Brit.* XXVI. 329/1 (*Bowls*) On Scottish greens the game of Points is occasionally played. ..Three points are scored if the bowl come to rest within one foot of the jack...It is obvious that the Points game demands an ideally perfect green.

14. A unit in appraising the qualities of a competitor, or of an exhibit in a competitive show. Also *fig.*

1777 Sheridan *Sch. Scand.* iv. iii, Charles's imprudence and bad character are great points in my favour. 1867 Trollope *Chron. Barset* I. xxi. 179, I cannot accept it as a point in a clergyman's favour, that he should be opposed to his bishop. 1886 Stevenson *Dr. Jekyll* ii, All these were points against him.

15. A recognized unit in quoting variations in price of stocks, shares, and various commodities, differing in value according to the commodity in question. In *Betting*, a unit in stating fluctuations of the odds.

1814 *Sporting Mag.* XLIII. 54 Betting reduced two points. 1890 *Daily News* 13 Nov. 2/4 Cotton.—Liverpool... 'Futures' advanced 2 points, but the improvement has not been maintained, and prices are now one point below yesterday's closing rates. 1901 *Westm. Gaz.* 4 Oct. 9/3 An important advance in American cotton has set in in Liverpool, the rise at noon to-day being nine points, or one-eighth per pound. 1901 Mary E. Wilkins *Portion Labor* 159 The mining stock dropped fast—a point or more a day. 1902 *Westm. Gaz.* 20 Jan. 11/1 The Brighton dividend is 3½ per cent. on ordinary, preferred, and A stock alike. The price has fallen 3 points.

†**16.** A measure of length, the twelfth part of a French line: cf. Line *sb.*² 16. *Obs.*

1815 J. Smith *Panorama Sc. & Art* I. 472 The smallest no more than one-half of a Paris point, or the 144th part of an inch in diameter..is said to magnify the diameter of an object 2560 times.

b. *Printing.* A unit of measurement for type bodies: in the French or Didot system the seventy-second part of a French inch (i.e. twice the amount of prec.); in the U.S. system slightly smaller (in the proportion of about twelve to thirteen), i.e. ·0138 of an inch.

1890 *Cent. Dict.* s.v., The American point was adopted by the United States Type-Founders' Association in 1883. 1900 H. Hart *Century of Oxford Typog.* 154 The typographical unit is the point. *Ibid.*, Oxford Press Type-bodies ..Nonpareil, 5·68 Didot Points..Brevier, 7·35 Didot Points. 1901 *Westm. Gaz.* 6 Feb. 4/3 The type..must be at least 'eight point', and the lines must be separated by at least two points.

17. In Australian use: A unit in measuring rainfall, the hundredth part (·01) of an inch.

1889 *Australasian* 20 Apr., The following reports have been received:—Brewarrina, 40 points; Bourke, 47 points; ..Ivanhoe, 100 points; Mossgiel, 188 points;..Hillston, 288 points. 1893 *Westm. Gaz.* 17 May 2/1 In the district of the Thompson River there had only been nine points of rain in 15 months. 1895 *Queenslander* 7 Dec. 1061 Rain set in early this morning, ninety-eight points having fallen up to 2.30 p.m.

IV. Something having definite position, without extension; a position in space, time, succession, degree, order, etc.

18. *Geom.* That which is conceived as having position, but not magnitude (as the extremity of a line, or the intersection of two lines).

c 1391 Chaucer *Astrol.* i. § 18 This forseide cenyth is ymagened to ben the verrey point ouer the crowne of thyn heued. 1551 Recorde *Pathw. Knowl.* i. Defin., A Poynt or a Prycke, is named of Geometricians that small and vnsensible shape, whiche hath in it no partes, that is to say: nother length, breadth, nor depth. 1570 Dee *Math. Pref.* *j, A Point is a thing Mathematicall, indiuisible, which may haue a certayne determined situation. 1660 Barrow *Euclid* i. Defin., i. A Point is that which has no part...iii. The ends, or limits, of a line are Points. 1704 J. Harris *Lex. Techn.* I. s.v., If a Point be supposed to be moved any way, it will by its Motion describe a Line. 1828 J. H. Moore *Pract. Navig.* (ed. 20) 11 To draw a Circle through any Three given Points not situated in a right Line. 1866 Brande & Cox *Dict. Sc.*, etc. II. 946/1 It is sometimes convenient to consider a point as an evanescent circle or sphere.

b. In various phrases with *of* (in *Geom., Optics*, and *Perspective*), as *point of contrary flexure, p. of convergence, p. of dispersion, p. of distance, p. of divergence, p. of incidence, p. of inflexion, p. of osculation, p. of reflection, p. of refraction, p. of sight, p. of vision*, etc.: see these words. See also Vanishing *point.*

c. *Astron.*, etc. Applied with qualifying adjs. to special points of the celestial sphere, etc.: see Cardinal, Equinoctial, Solstitial, Vertical.

Cardinal points = Fr. *points cardinaux*; but *the 32 points of the compass* (sense B. 9) = Fr. *pointes de la boussole, ou du compas.*

†**d.** Middle or central point, centre. *Obs. rare.*

1481 Caxton *Myrr.* i. xx. 59 No more than hath the poynt or pricke in the myddle of the most grete compaas that may be. 1614 W. B. *Philosopher's Banquet* (ed. 2) 117 Our Ecclesiasticall writers have thought Iudea to be the middle of the Earth, and Ierusalem the very poynt.

19. A place having definite spatial position but no extent, or of which the position alone is considered; a spot.

13.. *E. E. Allit. P.* C. 68 In þat Cete my saȝes soghe alle aboute, Þat, in þat place at þe poynt, I put in þi hert. *c* 1400 *Destr. Troy* 564 The perlouse pointtes þat passe you behoues. 1568 Grafton *Chron.* II. 698 King Edward.. was not a little troubled..and driuen to seeke the furthest poynt of his witte. 1669 Sturmy *Mariner's Mag.* iv. xi. 178 If you keep a true Account of the Ship's way.., you may at any time have the true Point where the Ship is. 1710 J. Clarke *Rohault's Nat. Phil.* (1729) I. 263 All the Rays which come from any Point of the Object, and fall upon the whole Superficies of the Glass do..enter into the Pupil. 1837 Lady W. de Eresby in C. K. *Sharpe's Corr.* (1888) II. 498 The nearest way from point to point. 1864 Pusey *Lect. Daniel* (1876) 411 Susa was a good point, whence to invade Babylon.

b. *spec.* The spot at which a policeman is stationed. (Cf. Point-duty.)

1888 *Pall Mall G.* 11 Oct. 2/1, I came..in search of a constable: the one on 'point' at Holborn Town Hall could not come.

c. *Hunting. colloq.* A spot to which a straight run is made; hence a straight run from point to point, a cross-country run. Cf. D. 11. *To make his point* (of a fox, etc.) to run straight to a spot aimed at.

1875 Whyte-Melville *Riding Recoll.* (1879) xi. 185 In Leicestershire especially, foxes will make their point with a stiff breeze blowing in their teeth. *Ibid.* xii. 211 A sportsman must..admit that 'ten mile points' over grass with one of the handsomest packs of [stag-]hounds in the world, are most enjoyable. 1883 R. E. Egerton-Warburton *Hunting Songs* (ed. 7) Introd. 36 The increase of..dwellings prevents a fox, headed at every corner, from making straight to his point. 1896 *Westm. Gaz.* 25 Nov. 9/1 The Belvoir hounds made an eight mile point in a little over 45 minutes.

20. *Her.* **a.** One of nine particular spots or places upon a shield, which serve to determine accurately the position a charge is to occupy. **b.** The middle part of the chief or base, as distinguished from the dexter or sinister divisions. **c.** One of a number of horizontal stripes of different tinctures into which a shield may be divided. (See also B. 3 c, D. 4 e.)

c 1394 *P. Pl. Crede* 562 Þe penounes & þe pomels & poyntes of scheldes Wiþ-drawen his deuocion. 1508 Kennedie *Flyting w. Dunbar* 414 A stark gallowis, ane wedy, and a pyn, The hede poynt of thyne elderis armes ar. 1658 Phillips, *Points*, in Heraldry are certain places in an Escutcheon diversly named according to their several positions. 1725 Coats *Dict. Her.* s.v., There are nine principal Points in any Escutcheon...A...the Dexter Chief. B. the..Middle Chief. C. the Sinister Chief. D. the Honour Point. E. the Fesse Point, call'd also the Center. F. the Nombril Point, that is, the Navel Point. G. the Dexter Base. H. the Sinister Base. I. the precise Middle Base. 1865 *Chambers' Encycl.* VII. 626 In order to facilitate the description of a coat-of-arms, it is the practice to suppose the shield to be divided into nine points.

†**21.** One of the squares of a chessboard. *The four points*, the four centre squares. *Obs.*

c 1407 Lydg. *Reson & Sens.* 6044 The vnkouth craft of the tabler And the poyntes of the chekker. *c* 1440 *Gesta Rom.* xxi. 71 (Harl.) The chekir or þe chesse hath viij. poyntes in eche partie. 1474 Caxton *Chesse* 135 The bordeure about is hygher than the squarenes of the poyntes. *a* 1500 *MS. Ashmole* 344 (Bodl.) to This is a fair Jupertie to mate a man in on of the iiij poyntes for it cumyth offt in play.

22. A definite position in a scale of any kind; a position reached in a course (e.g. Dead point); a step, stage, or degree in progress or development, or in increase or decrease; an exact degree of some measurable quality or condition, as temperature (e.g. *boiling-point, dew-point, freezing-point, melting-point*).

a 1425 *Chaucer's Pars. T.* ₱ 847 (Harl. MS.) Whan naturel lawe was in his first [6-*text* right] poynt in paradis. 1526 *Pilgr. Perf.* (W. de W. 1531) 5 b, [This] declareth some poynt of our iourney. 1568 Grafton *Chron.* II. 678 The extreme poynt of decay of his house and estate. 1639 S. Du Verger tr. *Camus' Admir. Events* 206 Her beauty and comely grace..amounted unto a high point. 1747 Freezing Point [Freezing *vbl. sb.* 2]. 1773 Boiling point [Boiling *vbl. sb.* 5]. 1798 Washington *Lett.* Writ. 1891 XII. 177 Differences in political opinions are as unavoidable, as, to a certain point, they may perhaps be necessary. 1871 B. Stewart *Heat* § 89 The melting points of various substances. 1886 Ruskin *Præterita* I. 324, I was brought to the point of trying to learn to sing. 1891 *Law Times* XCII. 93/2 The shares reached their highest point on the 13th June 1890, when they might have been sold for £600.

b. A critical position in the course of affairs; a decisive state of circumstances, a juncture; the precise moment for action, an opportunity. Now only in phrases *when it comes* (*came*) *to the point*, and *at, on, upon the point of* (see D. 1 c, 5).

1375 Barbour *Bruce* vii. 500 In all that tyme schir Amery, ..In carleill lay, his poynt to se. 1489 Caxton *Faytes of A.* ii. xiii. 114 Atte laste he sawe hys poynte whan that his enemyes were wery. *a* 1533 Ld. Berners *Huon* liii. 178 When it cometh to the poynt ther as strokes shold be gyuen. 1612 Br. Hall *Contempl., O. T.* iv. iii, But now, when it comes to the point, 'Who am I?' 1796 Jane Austen *Pride & Prej.* xxvii, Her father..who, when it came to the point, so little liked her going, that he told her to write to him.

23. In time, that which has 'position' but not duration (as the beginning or end of a space of time); the precise time at which anything happens; an instant, moment, as the moment of noon, the moment of death.

a 1400 *R. Brunne's Chron. Wace* (Rolls) 8080 Drecchynge by tymes haue [*Petyt MS.* poyntes haf] þey wrought. *c* 1400 *Apol. Loll.* 28 To ani man in þe poynt of deþ. 1413 *Pilgr. Sowle* (Caxton) ii. xlii. (1859) 47 In this poynt I herde ..a lusty melodye of wonder swete songe. 1653 Holcroft *Procopius* iv. 151 The point of opportunity being past, the greatest endeavours afterward faile. 1737 Whiston *Josephus, Hist.* i. iii. § 5 Four hours..are over already, which point of time renders the prediction impossible. 1833–6 J. H. Newman *Hist. Sk.* (1873) II. iv. ii. 380 There is..no assignable point at which the belief was introduced. 1844 Mrs. Browning *Drama of Exile* Poems 1850 I. 30 Though at the last point of a million years.

b. *At* or *on the point of*: see D. 1 c, 5.

†**24.** A (specified) degree of condition; condition, plight, state, case (good, evil, better, etc.). (Cf. F. *en bon point.*) *Obs.*

1297 R. Glouc. (Rolls) 8868 Engelond & normandie in god point he broȝte. 1340–70 *Alex. & Dind.* 315 To godus pay is our peple in bettur point founde. *c* 1386 Chaucer *Prol.* 200 A lord ful fat and in good poynt. 1481 Caxton *Godeffroy* cxv. 173 The barons toke counseyl..how they myght conteyne them in this greuous poynt in whiche they were. *a* 1533 Ld. Berners *Huon* xcv. 307 She demaundyd of hym yf he were hole and in good poynt. 1563 *Reg. Privy Council Scot.* I. 246 The said kirk is at sik ane point that throw decaying thairof,..the wallis in sindrie partis ar revin. 1685 Evelyn *Mrs. Godolphin* 176 Daniell and his companions..looked fairer and in better point than all the rest. 1732 Pope *Ess. Man* i. 283 Know thy own point..this due degree Of blindness, weakness, Heav'n bestows on thee.

V. Figurative and transferred senses.

†**25.** The highest part or degree; the height, summit, zenith, acme. *Obs.*

13.. *E. E. Allit. P.* B. 1502 In þe poynt of her play he poruayes a mynde. 1576 Fleming *Panopl. Epist.* 17 *margin*, It is the point of folly to shew a will to hurte him, whom thou canst not..by any meanes annoy. 1640 Quarles *Enchirid.* (1641) Ded., Your Highnesse is the Expectation of the present Age, and the Poynt of future Hopes. 1728 Ramsay *Bonny Chirsty* v, This point of a' his wishes, He wadna with set speeches bauk.

26. A distinguishing mark or quality; a distinctive trait or feature; a characteristic.

c 1470 Henryson *Mor. Fab.* v. (*Parl. Beasts*) xxiv, This suddane semblie..Haifand the pointis of ane parliament. *c* 1530 H. Rhodes *Bk. Nurture* 438 in *Babees Bk.* 94 To forbeare in anger is the poynt of a friendly leeche. 1581 J. Bell *Haddon's Answ. Osor.* 449 b, A shyft of subtle sophisters, and not a poynt of sober Divynes. 1604 James I *Counterbl.* (Arb.) 111 It is become..a point of good fellowship..to take a pipe of Tobacco. 1694 Atterbury *Serm., On Prov.* xiv. 6 (1726) I. 184 To be cautious, and upon our Guard, in receiving Doctrines..is a Point of great Prudence. 1889 T. A. Guthrie *Pariah* i. ix, Description was not Lettice's strong point.

b. *spec.* A physical feature in an animal; *esp.* one by which excellence or purity of breed is judged. Hence *transf.* in reference to a person or thing. (Cf. 14.)

1546 J. Heywood *Prov.* (1867) 52 She hath one poynt of a good hauke, she is hardie. 1841 Borrow *Zincali* II. ii. 56 Much better versed in the points of a horse than in points of theology. 1859 G. Meredith *R. Feverel* xxxvii, She seemed to scan his points approvingly. 1894 G. Armatage *Horse* ii. 14 They [American and Canadian horses] are not remarkable for beauty, though not showing any peculiarly unsightly points. *Ibid.* 20 That the race horse should have all his various points in true relative development. *Ibid.* iv. 47 The points essential to a hunter are a lean head and neck [etc.].

27. *The point*: the precise matter in discussion or to be discussed; the essential or important thing. Often in phr. *to come to the point, to keep to the point*, etc.: see also *in point, to the point* (D. 4 d, 6 c).

c 1381 Chaucer *Parl. Foules* 372 But to the poynt, nature held on hire hond A formele egle of shap the gentilleste That euere she a-mong hire werkis fond. *c* 1386 — *Prol.* 790 This is the poynt, to speken short and pleyn. *a* 1533 Ld. Berners *Huon* lxix. 236 Come to y poynt, and vse no more suche langage nor suche serymonyes. 1602 *2nd Pt. Return fr. Parnass.* v. iii. (Arb.) 68 But the point is, I know not how to better myselfe. 1693 Creech in *Dryden's Juvenal* xiii. Argt. (1697) 319 Then coming closer to his Point, he tells him,..The Wicked are severely punish'd by their own Consciences. 1738 tr. *Guazzo's Art Conversation* 12 Let us now come to the Point in Hand. 1791 Mrs. Radcliffe *Rom. Forest* ii, 'Is it impossible for you to speak to the point?' said La Motte. 1868 Helps *Realmah* (1876) 256 Do keep to the point, my excursive friends. 1875 Jowett *Plato* (ed. 2) I. 18 The point is not who said the words, but whether they are true or not.

b. *To make a point of* (= F. *faire un point de*): to treat or regard (something) as essential or indispensable; to make (it) a special object. Usually with vbl. sb. or gerund: formerly also *to make a point to do* something.

a 1778 Goldsmith in Boswell *Johnson* 9 Apr., Whenever I write any thing, the publick make a point to know nothing about it. *a* 1806 Fox *Hist. Jas. II* (1808) 12 The King made no point of adhering to his concessions. 1823 W. Tennant *Cdl. Beaton* iv. iii. 121, I mak a pount to be an e'e-witness o' ilka business o' that sort. 1833 Ht. Martineau *Brooke Farm* vii. 88 Her husband made such a point of his tea that she had little hope of persuading him to give it up. 1868 Freeman *Norm. Conq.* II. App. 581 A former colleague of mine in the Oxford Schools always made a point of describing him as 'William the Purchaser'.

28. That at which one aims, or for which one strives or contends; aim, object, end. Often in phr. *to carry one's point*: see Carry *v.* 17 b.

13.. *De Sancta Anastasia* 86 in Horstmann *Altengl. Leg.* (1881) 26 Þe prynce..Opon a day his poynt wold proue. 1580 Sidney *Ps.* xxxi. vii, They their counsells led All to this point, how my poore life to take. 1607 Shaks. *Cor.* ii. ii. 43

Supplement, p. 3873; Corrigenda, p. 4092; Spurious words, p. 4093; Books quoted, p. 4094

Point-blank, point blæⁿk, a., sb., and adv.

Point-duty. The duty of a police constable stationed at a particular point in a thoroughfare, to regulate the traffic, etc.

Pointed (pointed), ppl. a.[1] and

Pointedness (pointednes). [f. as prec. + -NESS.] The quality of being pointed; chiefly reference to the expression of thought.

Pointel. Now rare. Forms: 3-pointel; also 3 poyntel, 4 poyntele, -til, 4-6 -tell, -6, 4-7 -tel, 6 -tyl[.] Sc. poyntal, 6-7 pointell, -till, 7-8 -til, 7 potail, 7-9 pontel, pontello.

Pointille (pwæⁿtī'yŭ). Also 4 -ment, -ad. [a. F. pointillé, 1. pointiller: see prec.] A method, invented by French impressionist painters, of producing luminous effects by crowding a surface with small spots of various colours, which are blended by the eye.

Pointilling, vbl. sb.

Point-lace. [f. POINT sb.[1] A. 3¹ + LACE sb. 6.]

Pointless (pointles), a.

Pointsman (pointsmæn). 1. A man who has charge of the points on a railway.

Pointy (pointi), a. [f. POINT sb.[1] B. + -Y.] 1. Characteristically or notably pointed.

Point-maker. Obs. A maker of points or laces (for fastening apparel).

Point-making. Obs.

Pointless ...

Pointlet (pointlet). [f. as prec. + -LET.] A small point.

Poise, poiz, sb. Forms: 5 poys, 5-6 poys, 5-7 poyse, 6-7 poyze, 7 poys, 8 poize, 5- poise. [late ME. poys, a Central OF. pois (now poids), from earlier OF. peis, Central poise.]

Point. 1053

Poise (poiz), v. Forms: 5-poise, 5-7 poyse, 6-7 poyze ... [late ME. poise (parallel form to Paise), repr. OF. poiser, peiser, pre-eminence of the stem-stressed forms.]

Point. (point), a.

Pointwise, adv. [f. POINT sb.[1] B. + -WISE.]

Pointways, adv.

POISE

Poised, etc. *a.*, balanced, etc. (in quot. *attrib.*) and *ppl. a.*, balancing, weighing, hovering, etc. (see under **Poise** *v.*)

Poiser. Forms: 5 poisour, 7 poyser, 9 poiser.

Poise, -sure, obs. ff. **Poesy**.

Poison (poi′z'n), *sb.* (*a.*) Forms: 4–7 poysoun, 4–6 poysun, 4–7 poyson, 4–6 poyson, 4–7 puson, *Sc.* and *north. dial.* 7 puso(u)n, puyso(u)n, pwsoune, 6 puasoun (9 *dial.* poason), 7 poisoun, 4 poison, *etc.* [a. OF. (also *mod.F.*) poison, *etc.*]

1. A drink prepared for a special purpose; a medicinal draught; a potion. *Obs.*

2. Any substance which, when introduced into or absorbed by a living organism, destroys life or injures health, irrespective of mechanical means or direct thermal changes.

b. *esp.* A action prepared with a deadly or deleterious agent; also, such an ingredient of a drink or food. *Obs.* or merged in 2.

3. *fig.* Something that has a baneful or corrupting influence.

Poison (poi′z'n), *v.* Forms: see the sb.; also 4 poisone, 5 poysone.

b. *esp.* in names of plants (or parts of them) having poisonous qualities: poison-ash = *poison-sumac*; poison-bag, *Illicium floridanum* (N.O. *Magnoliaceæ*), the leaves of which are reputed poisonous; poison-ivy.

Poisonable (poi′zanăb'l), *a.* [f. prec. + -ABLE.]

Poisoned (poi′z'nd), *ppl. a.* [f. POISON *v.* + -ED.]

1. Of men or animals: Affected with, sickened with, or killed by poison.

Poisonless, *a. rare.* [f. POISON *sb.* + -LESS.]

Poisonly, *adv. Obs. rare⁻.* [f. POISON *a.*]

Poisonment. *Obs. rare.* [f. POISON *v.* + -MENT.] The act of poisoning.

Poisonous (poi′zanas), *a.* [f. POISON *sb.* + -OUS.]

1. Containing or of the nature of poison; having the quality or properties of a poison; venomous.

b. *fig.* Morally destructive or corrupting; conveying an evil influence; malevolent; malignant.

Poisoner (poi′zanar). [f. POISON *v.* + -ER.]

Poisonful, *a. Obs.* [f. POISON *sb.* + -FUL.] Full of or containing poison; poisonous, venomous, deadly, baneful, &c.

Poisoning (poi′zaniŋ), *vbl. sb.* [f. POISON *v.* + -ING.] The action of the verb POISON.

Poisonsome, *a. Obs.* [f. POISON *sb.* + -SOME.] Charged or tainted with poison; poisonous.

Poison-tree.

Poisonwood.

Poisony, *a. Obs. rare.* [f. POISON *sb.* + -Y.]

Poissarde. [F., a low foul-mouthed woman, a market-woman, fem. of *poissard* pickpocket, rogue, f. *poix* pitch + -ARD.] A fishwoman of the lowest class, *esp.* one of the Parisian market-women, who led riots during the first revolution.

Poisson. [F.] = POISON *sb.*

† Poister. *Obs.* [app. a variant of PESTER.]

† Poisure. *Obs. rare.* [f. POISE *v.* + -URE.] Poise, balance.

Poist, obs. *Sc.* form of POST.

† Poistel. *Obs.* Now *Hist.* and *arch.* Forms: 5–6 poystyll, 6 poisterill, 6-8 poistril, 7 -il, poistrel(l, poytrel, 7–9 al, 9–al, [a. OF. *poitral, poitrel*, now with *poitrail* = L. *pectorale* breast-pla'e, PECTORAL.]

† Poitrel, error for POINTEL.

† Poitrinaire (pwatrinɛ·r). [F., f. *poitrine*, chest + -aire—L. -ārius: see -ART.]

† Poivrade (pwavra·d). Also 7–8 poivrade.

† Poivre. [F., = pepper: see PEPPER.]

Pokakila. *a.* [f. POKE *sb.* + -ABLE.] Capable of being poked.

Poke (pōk), *sb.¹* Now chiefly *dial.* Forms: 3(?) 4 poke, 5–7 poke, 6–7 poake, 6–9 *dial.*

6. The stomach of a fish. *colloq.* or *dial.*

Poke (pōk), *sb.²* [app. from an application of prec.]

1. A projecting brim or front of a woman's bonnet or hat.

2. = POKE-BONNET.

Poke, *sb.³* [f. POKE *v.*]

1. An act of poking; a thrust, push, nudge.

b. in *dial.* phrases.

Poke, *sb.⁴* [Of N. American Indian origin.]

1. Some plant smoked by the North American Indians, here called *Indian-tobacco.*

2. A name for American species of *Phytolacca*, *esp. P. decandra*, Virginian Poke, the Green Hellebore or Poke root, *Veratrum viride.*

Poke, *sb.⁵* The small green heron of U.S.

out; poke-round, a going round and poking into places; poke-up, an act of poking or stirring up.

Poke (pōk), *v.¹*

1. *trans.* To thrust or push (anything) with one's hand or arm, the point of a stick, or the like, usually so as to move or stir it.

2. *fig.* To thrust or push (a thing) away, out, in, up, about, from, into (a place) *etc.* To poke through, to thrust through (with a weapon).

Poke-bonnet. [f. POKE *sb.²* or POKE *v.* + BONNET.]

Poked (pōkt), *a.* [f. POKE *sb.¹, ² + -ED².]

Poked (pōkt), *ppl. a.* [f. POKE *v.* + -ED¹.]

Supplement, p. 3873; Corrigenda, p. 4092; Spurious words, p. 4093; Books quoted, p. 4094

Pokeful, sb.[1] Also (Sc.) **pook-puddle**, contr. 8-9 **pook-pud**. [f. POKE sb.[1] + -FUL.]
A bagful, a small sackful.

Poke-lo'ken, pokelo'gan. U.S.
Ojibwa *pakwejigan*. ...

Pokemanteau, variant of POCKMANTEAU.

Po-ke-pudding. Also (Sc.) **9 pook-puddle**, contr. 8-9 **pook-pud.** [f. POKE sb.[1] + PUDDING.]
A pudding made in a poke or bag, a bag-pudding.

Poker (pəʊˈkə(r)), sb.[1] [f. POKE v.[1] + -ER.]
1. An instrument for poking or stirring a fire, consisting of a stiff metal rod, one end of which is fitted with or formed into a handle.

Jew's poker; see quot. 1899.

b. *humorous.* The staff or rod of office carried by a verger, bedell, etc.

Poker, sb.[2] Chiefly U.S. [Origin uncertain. Cf. *Ger. poch, poche, pochen, bockspiel*, a similar bluffing card-game of considerable age...]
A card game, popular in America, a variety of BRAG, played by two or more persons, each of whom, if not bluffed into declaring his hand, bets on the value of it, the player who holds the highest combination of cards as recognized in the game winning the pool.

Poker, sb.[3] a kind of duck. = POCHARD.

Poker, sb.[4] [prob. f. POKER sb.[1]]
1. *trans.* a. To use a poker to; to poke, stir or strike with a poker. b. *Poker-up:* To stiffen up, or make as stiff as a poker, *nonce-use.*

Po'kering *vbl. sb.* ... Also *attrib.*

Po'kerish[1], *a.* U.S. *colloq.* [f. POKER sb.[1] + -ISH.[1]] Fraught with a kind of mysterious dread; ghostly, uncanny.

Poker-work. [f. POKER sb.[1] + WORK sb.]
Artistic work done by burning a design on the surface of white wood with a heated pointed implement.

Poking (pəʊˈkɪŋ), *vbl. sb.* [f. POKE v.[1] + -ING[1].]
1. The action of the vb. POKE; thrusting, pushing; projecting forward.

Po king-stick (-iron). A rod used for stiffening the plaits or ruffs; originally of wood or bone, afterwards of steel so as to be applied hot. *Hist.*

Poking (pəʊˈkɪŋ), *ppl. a.* [f. POKE v.[1] + -ING[2].]
1. Projecting; thrust forward : esp. of the head.

2. Of a person or his work: That pokes or potters; pottering, peddling; hence petty, mean. Of a place : Petty, in size or accommodation; confined, shabby, insignificant.

Poky (pəʊˈkɪ), *sb.* Also *pokey*. [f. POKE v.[1] or POKY *a.*]
1. Of a person, on his life or work : Pottering, peddling; taken up with petty matters or narrow interests.

Poky (pəʊˈkɪ), *a.* Also *pokey*. [f. POKE v.[1] + -Y[1].]

a. Of a place : Petty in size or accommodation; affording scanty room to sit; confined, mean, shabby. = POKING *ppl. a.* 2.

b. Of dress, etc. : Shabby, dowdy.

2. *Cricket.* Inclined to 'poke' when batting.

Poky, var. POLAYN *Obs.*, knee-armour.

Po'kiness.

Poky.[2] Obs.

Polacca[1] (pəʊˈlækə). [It., orig. adj. fem. of *polacco* Polish, ad. Ger. *Polack*, f. Pol. *Polak* a native of Poland.] A Polish dance, a polonaise; also the music for it.

Polacca[2]. = POLACRE.

Polacre (pəʊˈleɪkə(r)), **polacca**[2] (pəʊˈlækə). A three-masted merchant vessel of the Mediterranean. See quot. 1769–70 n.

Polack (pəʊˈlæk), *sb.* Obs. Also 7 Polaque, -ake, -aque, -acke, 7 Polak. [a. Pol. *Polak* a Pole; or a native or inhabitant of Poland; a Pole; in quot. 1609, the king of Poland. So 7 Polakes *Obs.* rare.]

Poland (pəʊˈlənd). Also 6-7 **Poleland.** [POLE sb.[2] + LAND sb. (or perh. ad. Ger. *Polen*, MHG. *Pôlân*, with ending assimilated to *land*).]

Polar (pəʊˈlə(r)), *a.* and *sb.* [ad. med.L. *polaris*, f. *polus* POLE sb.[1]]
1. Pertaining to the poles of a voltaic battery; having positive and negative electricity.

2. *Magn.* Disposing itself in the direction of the poles of the earth; having polarity; of or pertaining to a magnetic pole (see POLE sb.[1])

b. Of animals: Regularly or symmetrically arranged in a definite direction, e.g. like iron filings under the influence of a magnet.

c. *Physics.* As forces : Acting in two opposite directions. (In one of two opposite applications.)

d. *Math.* ...

e. *Geom.* Relating or referred to a pole (see POLE sb.[1]); esp. Reciprocal to a pole of the corresponding curve.

Polar curve, *Polar co-ordinates*, etc.

B. *sb.* ...

POLARCHY. 1063 **POLARIZATION.** **POLARIZE.** 1064 **POLATOUCHE.**

Polarchy, var. POLYARCHY.

b. Directly opposite in character, action, or tendency. ...

+ Po'larchy, *obs.* erron. form for POLYARCHY, government by many, or by a number of persons. So **† Po'larch** *one* of the persons so governing; **† Pola'rchical** *a.*, pertaining to or of the nature of a 'polarchy'; **† Po'larchist**, an advocate of a 'polarchy'.

Polari'metric *a.*, of or pertaining to a polarimeter or polarimetry; **Pola'rimetry**, *n.*, the art or process of measuring or analysing the polarization of light.

Polari'scope (pəʊˈlærɪskəʊp). [f. med.L. *polaris* + -SCOPE.]
An instrument for showing the rotation of light, or viewing objects in polarized light; consisting essentially of two plates or prisms, a *polarizer* and an *analyzer*; made in various forms, simple or complex, according to the special use. Also *attrib.*

Polariscopic (pəʊˌlærɪˈskɒpɪk), *a.* [f. prec. + -IC.] Of or pertaining to the polariscope, or viewed by a polariscope.

Polaristic, *a. rare*[0]. [erron. f. POLARIZE : see -ISTIC.] = POLARIC.

Polaristrobo'meter. [mod.f. med.L. *polaris* + Gr. *στρέφειν* to turn + -METER; devised 1865 by Prof. H. Wild of Zürich.]

Polari'stically.

Polarite (pəʊˈlərɪt). [f. POLAR *a.* + -ITE[1].]
Trade name for an insoluble porous mineral substance, containing about fifty-three per cent. of magnetic oxide of iron, with silica, lime, magnesia, carbon, etc., and having the power of absorbing and giving off oxygen. Used in conjunction with 'Ferrozone' in the so-called 'International' process of sewage treatment. Also *attrib.*

Polarity (pəʊˈlærɪtɪ). [f. POLAR *a.* + -ITY; cf. F. *polarité*, med.L. *polaritas*, 1835 in *Dict. Acad.*] A form tried earlier was POLITY[2].

1. *Magnetism.* The quality or property possessed by certain bodies, as a lodestone or magnetized bar, of turning (when free to move) so as to point with their two extremities to the two (magnetic) poles of the earth; the quality of being polar, or possessing magnetic poles.

2. *gen.* Possession or exhibition of two opposite or contrasted aspects, principles, or tendencies.

Polarizable (pəʊˈlərʌɪzəb(ə)l), *a.* [f. POLARIZE + -ABLE.] Capable of being polarized. Hence **Polarizabi'lity.**

Polarization (pəʊˌlərʌɪˈzeɪʃ(ə)n). [f. POLARIZE : see -ATION; cf. F. *polarisation.*]

I. 1. *Optics.* (*trans.*) A modification of the condition of light or radiant heat, whereby the ray exhibits different properties on different sides, so that the same ray cannot be reflected, transmitted, etc., with the same facility at all azimuths.

Polarize (pəʊˈlərʌɪz), *v.* [ad. F. *polariser* (1811), f. *polaire*, ad. med.L. *polaris* : see POLAR *a.* and -IZE.]

1. *Optics.* *trans.* To modify (light, etc.) so as to give it polarity; to cause (light, radiant heat, etc.) to undergo polarization.

Polarized (pəʊˈlərʌɪzd), *ppl. a.* [f. prec. + -ED.]

Polarizer (pəʊˈlərʌɪzə(r)). [f. as prec. + -ER[1].] One who or that which polarizes; esp. That plate or prism in a polariscope which polarizes the incident ray of light (opp. to *analyzer*).

Polarizing (pəʊˈlərʌɪzɪŋ), *vbl. sb.* [f. as prec. + -ING[1].] The action of the vb. POLARIZE, in various senses. Also *attrib.*

Polarizing, *ppl. a.* [f. as prec. + -ING[2].] That polarizes or produces polarization.

Polarly (pəʊˈləlɪ), *adv.* [f. POLAR *a.* + -LY[2].] In a polar direction, manner, or degree; after the manner of or with reference to poles.

Polatouche (pəʊləˈtuːʃ). *Zool.* [F. *polatouche*, ad. Russ. *полетучий (poletuchii)* flying : cf. *летучка*.]

POLAYN. *Obs.* [OFr. *poleyne*.] The knee. ...

Polay, obs. f. POLLEY, a measure of land.

Polayn, variant of POULAINE, PULLEN *Obs.*, poultry.

Pold, obs. spelling of POLLED.

Poldavy (pǫldǟ·vi), **poldavis** (pǫldǟ·vis). *Now rare.* Forms: 5 poldavy; also 6-7 pole-, 7 pool-, poole-, powle-, 7-8 poll-, poul-; 6 -davy, 7 -dauy, -davys, 9 -davey; pol-davy, 7 -davys, -davies, 6 -davis. [app. f. *Poldavide*, a place on the south side of Douarnenez Bay, on the coast of Brittany. ...]

Polder (pǫ·ldə(r)). *Obs.* or *dial.* [Corruption of *poller*, variant of POLLARD.] A pollard tree. ...

Polder [1] (pǫ·ldə(r)). Also 7 **polther.** [a. Du. *polder*, MDu. *polre, poldere*.] A piece of low-lying land reclaimed from the sea, a lake, or a river, from which it is protected by dikes: so called in the Netherlands; rarely used of similar land in other countries.

Polder, comb. and *attrib.* (as *polder-land*): **polder-man,** a labourer employed in making polders. (All in reference to Holland.)

Pole [1] (pōl), *sb.* Forms of PULLALLE *Obs.*, poultry.

Pole [1] (pōl), *sb.* [Com. Teut.: OE. *pāl* masc. = OFris. *pāl*, MLG., LG. *pāl*, OHG., MHG., *phāl, pfāl*, Ger. *pfahl*), ON. *páll* (Norw. *paale*, Sw. *påle*); ...]

Pole [2] (pōl), *sb.* [a. OFr. *pole, pol*, var. of POILE = L. *polus*, a. Gr. πόλος.]

Pole [3] *sb.* Also 6 Poyle, Poole. [a. Ger. *Pole*, a Polander.]

Poleaxe, pollaxe (pōu·læks), *sb.* Forms: 4-5 pollax, polax, 5 polhax, 5 pollaxe, 6 polax, 7-8 pole-axe. ...

Poleaxe, *v.* To fell with a poleaxe.

Polecat (pōu·lkæt), *sb.* Forms: 4-7 polcat, -kat, -catte, 5-6 pollecat, 8 pole-cat, 6 pule-cat. ...

Polehead, pollhead. Now only *Sc.* and *north. dial.* Forms: 3 pollheade, 6 polled, 9 poll-head. ...

Poleless, *a.* Having no pole.

Poleis, obs. Sc. form of POLISH *v.*

Poleless (pōu·llĕs), *a.* [f. POLE [1] + -LESS.] Having no pole.

Poleman (pōu·lmǎn). [f. POLE [1] + MAN.] A man who uses, carries, or is armed with a pole.

Polemarch (pǫ·lemāɹk). *Anc. Hist.* [ad. Gr. πολέμαρχος, f. πόλεμος war + ἄρχειν to rule.] ...

Polemic (pǫlē·mik), *a.* and *sb.* [ad. med.L. or F. *polémique*, a. Gr. πολεμικός.]

Polemicist (pǫlē·misist). A writer of polemics.

Polemics (pǫlē·miks), *sb. pl.* The art or practice of controversy.

Polemise, -ize (pǫ·lemaiz), *v.* [ad. Gr. πολεμίζειν.] *intr.* To argue or write polemically.

Polemist (pǫ·lemist). [ad. F. *polémiste*.] A writer of polemics; a polemicist.

Polemomania (pǫ·lemomēi·niǎ), *nonce-wd.* [f. Gr. πόλεμος war + MANIA.] Rage for war.

Polemonium (pǫlemōu·niǒm). *Bot.* [mod.L. *Polemonium* (L. *Polemonion*), a. Gr. πολεμώνιον.] A genus of plants. ...

Polemoscope (pǫlē·moskōup). [ad. Gr. πολέμος war + -SCOPE.] An opera-glass or field-glass fitted with a mirror to enable the spectator to view objects not directly before the eye. ...

Polenta (pǫlē·ntǎ). Also *Sc.* **polenty.** [It. *polenta*.] A porridge or pudding made of maize. ...

Poler (pōu·lə(r)). [f. POLE [1] + -ER [1].] A thing that poles.

Pole-star. The star *Ursæ Minoris*, at present about 1¼ distant from the northern pole of the heavens; also called *Polaris, Pole-star*, and *Polaris*.

Polewards (pōu·lwəɹdz), *adv.* and *a.* [f. POLE [2] + -WARDS.] Towards or in the direction of the pole.

Poleward (pōu·lwəɹd), *adv.* and *a.* Toward the pole. ...

Polewig (pōlē'wig). *local.* [See Polliwog.]

1. A tadpole: see Polliwog. 1808 in Ogilvie.

2. The name given by the Thames fishermen to a small fish, the Spotted or Freckled Goby.

Polex, polley (pō'leks), *obs.* forms of Pole-ax.

Poley, polley (pō'li), *a.* Now *dial.* and *Austral.* [f. Pole *sb.*[5] + -y[1].] Hornless; polled.

Poley, poley-mountain : see Poly.

Poleyn, poleyns : see Poly.

Polhode (pō'lhŏd). *Geom.* [mod.f. Gr. πόλος pole + ὁδός way, path (Poinsot 1851).]

Poliad (pō'liăd). *nonce-wd.* [f. Gr. πόλις city + -ad 1, after Oread, etc.] A city nymph.

Poliadic (poliǎ'dik), *a. rare.* [f. Gr. Πολιάς + -ic.]

Polian (pō'liăn), *a.* *Zool.* [f. proper name.]

+Polible, *a. Obs. rare⁻¹.* [f. L. polī-re to polish : see -ible.]

Police (pŏlī's), *sb.* Also 6 polyce, -yse, police. [a. F. *police* (1477 in Godef.), organized government, civil administration, ad.med.L. *politīa* for earlier *policia*, Polity.]

Police station. The office or head-quarters of a local police force, or of a police district.

Police court. A court of summary jurisdiction for the trial or investigation of charges performed by the police.

Police, *ppl. a.* [f. Police *v.* or *sb.* + -ED.] *Orig.* (*pl. list.*)

Policeman (pŏlī'smăn). A member of the police force; a paid constable. *New Policeman.*

Policer (pŏlī'sər). One who polices.

Police office. The head-quarters of the police force in a city or town, at which the police and the City police in London.

Policlinic (pŏlikli'nik), *a.* Also *erron.* polyclinic.

Policy (pŏ'lisi), *sb.*[1] Forms: 4-7 policie, 5 -ecye, 5-6 -icye, -ysye, -icy, 6-7 -esye, -icie.

Policy (pŏ'lisi), *sb.*[1]

I. 1. An organized and established system or form of government or administration of a state or city; a constitution, polity. Now *rare* or *Obs.*

2. An organized state, a commonwealth.

3. *Sc.* Law. Also pl. (treated as sing.)

4. In reference to conduct or action generally: Prudent, expedient, or advantageous procedure.

Policy (pŏ'lisi), *sb.*[2] Also 6 police, 7 -cie, -y. [ad. F. *police* (1371) bill of lading, contract of insurance, etc.]

Poligar (pŏ'ligar). Also 8-9 polygar. [ad. Tamil *pāḷaiyakkāraṉ* the holder of a *pālaiyam*, Pollam.]

Polish (pō'lij), *v.* [a. F. *poliss-*, lengthened stem of *polir* = Pr., Sp. *pulir*, It. *pulire*, ad. L. *polīre*.]

Polish (pō'lij), *sb.* [f. Polish *v.*]

Polish (pŏ'lij), *a.* and *sb.* [f. Pole *sb.*[2] + -ish.] Of or pertaining to Poland or its inhabitants.

Poll-parrot. Poll-parroty, a. or of proper to a parrot.

Poll, sb.³ [An alteration of Moll, a familiar equivalent of Mary: cf. Peg = Meg, Margaret.] A familiar equivalent of the name Mary (as Polly), used as the conventional proper name of any parrot; hence = parrot. So Poll-parrot, also used fig. and attrib., with reference to the parrot's unintelligent repetition of words.

Poll, sb.⁴ [Traditionally explained as ad. Gr. οἱ πολλοί the many, the multitude.] The poll: those students who read for or obtain a 'pass' degree; the pass-man. To go out in the Poll: to come out in the list of those who take a pass degree. † Captain of the Poll: formerly, the highest amongst those who passed without honours.

Poll, v. Forms: 4-5 pollen, 4-6 polle, 5-pol; also 5-7 powle, 6 pol, 6-7 powl, poule, poulle, 6-9 poll, 7-8 pole. Pa. pple. (see Polled) ppl. a. 1. trans. To cut the hair of (a person or animal); to crop, clip, shear; also b. with the head, hair, etc. as object.

Poll, v. To get by extortion or pillage. Obs.

Pollage. Obs. Also 6 pollag. [app. f. Poll v. + -age, after pillage, etc.]

Pollan (pŏˈlăn). East Ang. [ad. Telugu palangi.] A local estate or territory kept by a family.

Pollam (pŏˈlăm). East Ind. [ad. Telugu.]

Pollard (pŏˈlărd). Also 6 pollarde, 6-8 pollerd, 7-ord. [f. Poll v. + -ard.] I. 1. An animal of a kind naturally horned, as an ox or stag, which has cast or lost its horns; also, an ox, sheep, or goat of a hornless variety.

2. A tree which has been polled or cut back.

Polled (pŏld), ppl. a. [f. Poll v. + -ed².] In comb. Having a poll or head of a specified form or appearance, as curly-polled.

Pollen (pŏˈlĕn), sb. [ad. L. pollen, -inem fine flour, fine dust, in sense from mod.L. (Linn.)]

Pollenin. Chem. [f. Pollen + -in.]

Pollened, a. Obs.

Pollen-grain.

Pollen-tube.

Pollency. rare. [ad. L. pollentia.]

Pollent, a. rare. [ad. L. pollent-em.]

Polleniferous, erron. form of Polliniferous.

Pollenize, etc. see Pollinize, etc.

Pollenless, a. [f. Pollen + -less.] Destitute of pollen.

Pollent (pŏˈlĕnt), a. rare. [ad. L. pollent-em.]

Poller (pŏˈlǝr). [f. Poll v. + -er¹.]
† 1. A barber or hair-cutter. Obs.
2. A plunderer, spoiler, extortioner, despoiler.
3. One who votes at an election; a voter.

Pollicar. [f. L. pollex, pollic-, thumb + -ar.]

Pollicate (pŏˈlĭkeit), a. [f. L. pollex, pollic- thumb.]

Pollical (pŏˈlĭkăl), a. Anat. [f. L. pollex, pollic-em + -al.] Of or pertaining to the pollex or thumb.

Pollicitation (polˌlisiteiˈʃǝn). [ad. L. pollicitātiōn-em.]

Pollinar, Pollinarious, etc.

Pollinate.

Pollinctor (polˈlǐŋktǝr). [a. L. pollinctor, agent-n. f. pollingere to wash.]

Pollinic (poˈliniĸ), a.

Polliniferous (poliˈnifěrǝs), a. Also erron.

Pollinium (poˈliniǝm). Bot. Pl. -ia.

Polling (pŏˈliŋ), vbl. sb. [f. Poll v. + -ing¹.]

Pollini·vorous, a. (erron. pollen-) [f. as prec. + L. -vorus devouring + -ous.] Devouring or feeding on pollen.

Po·llinize, pollenize, v. [f. L. pollen, pollin- (directly f. POLLEN) + -IZE.] trans. = POLLINATE.

So **Polliniza·tion** (-ne-) = POLLINATION.

Pollinodial, **Pollinoid**, etc.

Pollinose (pr'li-nōs), a. Bot. [mod.L., f. as prec. + -OSE¹.] Having the surface covered with a fine mealy or powdery substance.

Pollinose (pr'li-nōs), a. Entom. [ad. mod.L. pollinōsus, f. as prec. + -OSE.] (See quot.)

Pollock: see POLLACK.

Poll-tax (pō·ltæks), sb.¹ [f. POLL sb.¹ + TAX sb.] A tax levied on every person; a capitation or head-tax. A later name for POLL-MONEY.

Pollu·cite (po-liū̆sait), sb. Min. [ad. G. pollucit (Breithaupt, 1846), lettering named Pollux (Breithaupt, Castor + Pollux).] Silicate of aluminium and cæsium, found in brilliant transparent colourless crystals.

Pollu·te (poliū·t), v. Also 4-7 polute, 5 polewt. [f. L. pollūt-, ppl. stem of polluěre to soil, defile, f. *por- = pro forth + luěre to wash.]

1. trans. To render ceremonially or morally impure; to impair, violate, or destroy the purity or sanctity of; to profane, desecrate; to soil, corrupt.

2. To make physically impure, foul, or filthy; to dirty, stain, taint, befoul.

Pollu·ted (poliū·téd), ppl. a. [f. prec. + -ED¹.] Defiled, rendered impure or unclean.

Pollu·ter (poliū·tǝr), [f. prec. + -ER¹.] One who pollutes; a defiler; one who profanes.

Pollu·tion (poliū·ʃǝn), Forms: 4 pollucioun, 5-6 polucioun, 5 polucyon, 7 pollution, 6- pollution. [ad. L. pollūtiōn-em defilement, noun of action f. pollūtus to POLLUTE. So F. pollution (14th c. in Hatz.-Darm.).]

1. The action of polluting, or condition of being polluted; defilement; uncleanness or impurity caused by contamination (physical or moral).

2. Ceremonial impurity or defilement; profanation.

3. Seminal emission apart from coition; self-pollution.

Hence **Pollu·tionate** a. [cf. *afectionate, confirmationate*, etc.], charged with (pollution, foul); whence **Pollu·tionately** adv., foully.

Pollu·tive, v. Sc. Obs. [perh. for pollitive, poltive, f. *polther*, L. *poltrire*: see POLLUTE v.] trans. = POLLUTE v.

Pollux (po·lʌks), sb. [a. F. Pollux (Herodotus... during crocodile in Le templi of Jupiter, pollowing In-r, pollowing) and defining every thing in it?

Poly-, comb. form of PULLEY, Polygony, Pollypod, etc. Polygony, etc. Pollytick, Pollywog: see POLITIC, POLLIWOG. Poltmere, Obs., pottmer.

Polo (pō·lo), sb. [a. Balti *polo*: cf. Tibetan *pulu*.]

1. A game of Eastern origin resembling hockey, played on horseback with long-handled clubs and a wooden ball.

polo is hockey on the water.

2. attrib. and Comb., as polo-ball, -match, -player, -playing, -pony, -stick.

Polonian (polō·niǝn), a. and sb. [f. prec. + -AN.]

A. adj. Of Poland: = POLISH a. Obs. or arch.

B. sb. A native of Poland, a Pole, arch.

Polonaise (polone·z), sb. and a. Also 8 polonaise. [a. F. *polonaise*, prop. adj. fem. of *polonais* Polish; lit. a Polish robe or ridingcoat.]

1. A name applied, at various periods from c 1770 onward, to an article of female dress.

2. A slow dance of Polish origin, consisting chiefly of an intricate march, procession, or promenade of the dancers in couples; also, the music which accompanies this dance, or any music written in its peculiar triple rhythm.

Polone, sb. and a. Obs. Also 8 polonese. [ad. F. *polonais* Polish, It. *Polonese*, f. med.L. *Polonia* Poland: see POLE sb.³]

A. sb. 1. = POLONAISE 1. Also apparently applied to the material for this.

2. A native of Poland, a Pole. (Sing. and pl.)

Polony (polō·ni), sb. [prob. corruption of *Bologna*, q.v.] A Bologna sausage, a sausage made of partly cooked pork.

Polony², Also 8 pullony. [Origin uncertain: perh. the same as prec.; perh. corruption of BOLOGNA, q.v.] In *Polony* dressage, a sausage made of partly cooked pork.

Poloron, Polron(d, obs. ff. POLYPODY, POLYDRON.

Polros (po·lros), Cornwall. [a. Corn. *pol-ros*, f. *pul*, Welsh *pwll* pit + *ros*, Welsh *rhos*—L. *rota* wheel.] The pol under a wheel.

Polt, sb. and v. Obs. rare⁻¹. [prop. *poll-shred*.]

Polt (pōlt), sb. Obs. exc. dial. [Origin obscure: in sense 1 it may be a variant of PELT sb.; but cannot easily be connected with *pelt*. It is not certain that sense 2 is the same word.]

1. A blow, a hard rap or knock. Now dial.

2. Polyandry, polygamy. (See quots.)

Poltergeist (pō·ltǝrgaist), sb. [Ger. f. *poltern* noise, uproar + *geist* ghost.] A spirit which makes its presence known by noise, a noisy spirit.

Poltroon (poltrū·n), sb. and a. Forms: 6 pultrowne, poltron, 6-7 poultron, 6-9 poltroon, 7 poultroone, poultran, -oun, 7-9 poltroon, 7- poltroon. [a. F. *poltron* (also in 16th c. *poultron*) 'a knave, rascal ..., a dastard, coward', (Cotgr.), lazie-backs, base idle fellow' (Cotgr.), ad. It. *poltrone* 'a poltron, an idle fellow, a base coward, a lazie, lither or sluggard... one that loves his ease' (Florio), prop. 'one who keeps his bed', f. *poltro* bed.] A craven-hearted fellow, a mean-spirited, worthless wretch; a craven.

Poltroonery (poltrū·nǝri), sb. [f. POLTROON + -ERY.] The behaviour of a poltroon; cowardice; pusillanimity.

Poly-, combining form. 1. General words.

(Continued from preceding page.)

Polyacanthous (-ækǝnθǝs) a. Bot. [Gr. ἄκανθα spine, thorn], having many thorns (Mayne *Expos. Lex.* 1858). **Polyacoustic** a. and sb. [see ACOUSTIC] see quots. **Polya·cron** (pl. -ona or -a), Geom. [Gr. ἄκρον summit], a solid having many vertices or solid angles; a polyhedron (classed according to the number of its vertices). **Polya·ct** (-ækt), **Polyactinal** (-æktinǎl) adjs. [Gr. ἀκτίς, ἀκτίν-, ray], having numerous rays, as a sponge-spicule; multiradiate. **Polya·dantic** (-ædæntik). **Polya·delphous** a. Bot. [see ADELPH], having many glands (Mayne). **Polya·ffected** a. (nonce-wd.), having a multiplicity of affections. **Polya·ngle**, a figure having many angles, a polygon; so **Polya·ngular** a., having many angles, polygonal.

Poly-, combining form. 1. General words.

(Continued from preceding page.)

Polyergic (-ʒ·ɪdʒik) a. [Gr. ἔργον work: cf. κολέργυs hard-working], acting in many ways, having various functions. **Polyethnic** (-e·θnik) a. [Gr. ἔθνος nation], belonging to or containing many nations or races. **Polyfene·stral** a. (nonce-wd.), having, or relating to, more than three dimensions of space. **Polyforgery** (nonce-wd.), the keeping of a number of dogs. **Polygelatin** (-æl), Biol. [Gr. εἶδος appearance, form], metamorphosis in which an organism passes through several different forms in different stages.

(General words.)

Polyprism, Polyprismatic a. Cryst.: see quots. **Polyprotic** (-pro·tik), Chem. [Gr. πρῶτος first], having many acidic hydrogen atoms. **Polyrhizous** (-rai·zǝs) a. Bot. [Gr. ῥίζα root], having many roots or rootlets. **Polysarcous** (-sɑ·rkǝs) a. [Gr. σάρξ, σαρκ-, flesh], having excessive flesh, corpulent.

Polyadelphite (polˌiæˈdelfəit). *Min.* [f. as prec. + -ITE ...] so named as consisting of five different silicates united.] A massive brownish-yellow variety of iron garnet, found in New Jersey.

Polyadenopathy to **Poly-affectioned**: see POLY- 1.

Polyander (pɒliˈændə). *Bot.* = POLYANDRIA.

Polyandria (pɒliˈændriə). [mod.L. *polyandrium*, for earlier POLYANDRIUM. In sense 2, ad. F. *polyandrie* adj., ad. mod.L. *polyandrus* POLYANDROUS. Cf. DIANDRIA.]

Polyandry (pɒliˈændri). [mod. (L. *polyandria*), n. of state from Gr. πολύανδρος, n. of state from πολυ-, POLY- + ἀνήρ man, male), employed by Linnæus (1735) in the sense 'having many stamens or male organs'.]

Polyanth (ˈpɒliænθ), *rare*. Anglicized form of POLYANTHUS.

Polyanthus (pɒliˈænθəs). *Bot.* [a. med. L. *polyanthus*, f. Gr. type *πολύανθος*, f. πολυ-, POLY- + ἄνθος flower.] A collection of the 'flowers' of poetry or other literature, i. e. of choice literary extracts; an anthology.

Polyarch (ˈpɒliɑːk). *rare*[-]. [f. Gr. πολυ-, POLY- + ἀρχή beginning, origin.] Proceeding from many points of origin: said of the primary xylem or woody tissue of a stem or root.

Polyarchal, *a. rare*[-]. [f. as POLYARCHY + -AL.] Having many rulers. So **Polyarchical** *a.* (*rare*), of the nature of or pertaining to a polyarchy (opp. to *monarchical*); **Polyarchist** (*rare*), one who advocates or believes in a polyarchy.

Polyarchy (ˈpɒliɑːki). [ad. Gr. πολυαρχία.] Government of a state or city by many: contrasted with *monarchy*.

Polyatomic (pɒliəˈtɒmik), *a. Chem.* [f.

Polychroite (pɒliˈkrəʊəit). *Chem.* [a. F. *polychroïte* (Chem. 1806), f. Gr. πολύχροο-ος (see POLYCHROIC): see -ITE 2.] Name for the colouring matter of saffron (also called SAFRAGIN).

Polychromy (pɒliˈkrəʊmi), *a.* [ad. F. *polychromie*.] The art of painting or decorating in several colours.

Polychrome (ˈpɒlikrəʊm), *a.* and *sb.* [ad. F. *polychrome*.] **A.** *adj.* Many-coloured; polychromatic. **B.** *sb.* A work of art executed or decorated in several colours.

Polydæmonism (pɒliˈdiːmənɪz'm). [f. POLY- + Gr. δαίμων + -ISM.] A belief in many divinities.

Polydactyl (pɒliˈdæktil), *a.* (*sb.*) Also *-yle*. [a. F. *polydactyle*, ad. Gr. πολυδάκτυλος many-toed.] Having more than the normal number of fingers or toes.

Polydipsia (pɒliˈdipsiə). *Path.* [In 7 anglicized as *poludipsie*.] Gr. type *πολυδιψία*; excessive or morbid thirst. So **F.** *polydipsie*.] Morbidly or abnormally excessive thirst.

Polygamia (pɒliˈgeɪmiə). *Bot.* [mod.L. *Polygamia* (cl. L. *Polygamia* (pɒliˈgeɪmiə), name of the typical genus), f. Gr. πολύγαμος POLYGAMOUS.]

Polygamist, *a.* [f. POLYGAMIA + -OUS.] Belonging to the Linnæan class Polygamia.

Polygamous (pɒˈligəməs), *a.* Also 2 *poligamous*. [f. as next + -OUS.]

Polygamy (pɒˈligəmi). *Also* 6-8 *poli-*. [ad. late L. *polygamia*.]

Polygenistic (pɒlidʒɛˈnɪstɪk), *a.* [f. POLYGENIST + -IC, or ad. *polygeniste*.] Of or pertaining to polygenesis.

Polygenist (pɒˈlidʒənɪst). [app. f. POLYGENY + -IST.]

Polygenous (pŏlýdʒĭnəs), a. [irreg. f. Gr. πολυγεν- or many kinds (f. πολύ-, POLY- + γένος kind) + -OUS: perh. associated with words from L. such as *indigenous*, etc.]

1. *Geol.* composed of various kinds of rocks.

2. *Chem.* in *Eng. Mech.*

Polygeny (pŏlídʒĭni). [f. POLY- + -γενια, γένεια.] **1.** The (theoretical) origination of mankind (or of any species) from several independent pairs of ancestors; *loosely*, the theory of such origination.

Polyglot, var. of POLYGLOT.

Polyglot (pŏ'lĭglŏt), *a.* and *sb.* Also *sp.* polyglott. [ad. F. *polyglotte*, or ad. Gr. πολύγλωττος, πολύγλωσσος many-tongued, f. πολύ- + γλῶττα, γλῶσσα tongue.]

A. *adj.* **1.** Of a person: That speaks or writes many or several languages.

2. Of or relating to many languages; *esp.* of a book or writing: In many or several languages.

3. *sb.* One who speaks or writes several languages.

Polyglottic, *a.* var. POLYGLOT.

Polyglottism. [f. POLYGLOT + -ISM.]

Polyglottist. One versed in many languages.

Polygon (pŏ'lĭgŏn), *sb.* and *a.* Also 7 polygone. [ad. L. *polygōnum*, *polygōnon*, a. Gr. πολύγωνον, prop. neut. of πολύγωνος adj. many-angled, f. πολύ- + γωνία angle.]

A. 1. *Geom.* A figure (usually, a plane rectilineal figure) having many, i.e. (usually) more than four, angles (and sides): a many-sided figure.

Polygonaceous, *a.* [f. POLYGONUM + -ACEOUS.] Belonging to the Natural Order *Polygonaceæ*, of which the typical genus is POLYGONUM.

Polygonal (pŏlĭgŏn'l), *a.* Also 7 polygonal. [f. POLYGON + -AL.] **1.** Having the form of a polygon; having many, i.e. (usually) more than four, angles (and sides); many-sided.

Polygonum (pŏlĭ'gŏnŏm), *sb.* *Bot.* [mod.L. *polygonum* (Scribonius), ad. L. πολύγονον, πολύγονος many-kneed, prop. many-seeded (f. πολύ- + γόνυ knee).]

A large and widely distributed genus of plants, type of the N.O. *Polygonaceæ*.

Polygony, *a.* rare⁻¹. [f. POLY- + γόνυ knee + -ATE²] Having many joints.

Polygraph (pŏ'lĭgrăf). [ad. Gr. πολύγραφος, f. POLYGRAPHY + -IC.] *polygraphy* (Florio) in sense 4.

Polygraphic (pŏlĭgră'fĭk), *a.* [f. POLYGRAPHY + -IC.]

Polygraphy (pŏlĭ'grăfi). [ad. Gr. πολυγραφία.]

Polygyny (pŏlĭ'dʒĭni). [f. POLY- + Gr. γυνή, γυναικ- woman, wife.] That form of polygamy in which one man has several wives at the same time.

Polyhedral (pŏlĭhī'drăl), *a.* [f. POLYHEDRON + -AL.] Of the form of a polyhedron; having many faces or sides, as a solid figure or body.

Polyhedric (pŏlĭhī'drĭk), *a.* = POLYHEDRAL.

Polyhedron (pŏlĭhī'drŏn). [ad. Gr. πολύεδρον, f. πολύ- + ἕδρα seat, base, face.]

Polyhedrous, *a.* Also polyedrous.

Polyhistor (pŏlĭhĭ'stŏr). Also 6 polihistor.

Polymath (pŏ'lĭmăθ). [ad. Gr. πολυμαθής, f. πολύ- + μαθεῖν to learn.] A person of much or varied learning.

Polymathic (pŏlĭmă'θĭk), *a.*

Polymathy (pŏlĭ'măθi).

Polymere (pŏ'lĭmēr). [f. Gr. πολυμερής, f. πολύ- + μέρος part.]

Polymeric (pŏlĭme'rĭk), *a.* [f. as prec.]

Polymerous (pŏlĭ'mĕrəs), *a.*

Polymignite (pŏlĭmĭ'gnīt). *Min.* [f. Gr. πολυμιγής much-mixed + -ITE¹.]

Polymite (pŏ'lĭmīt). *a.* [ad. L. *polymita*, a. Gr. πολύμιτος.]

Polymorph (pŏ'lĭmôrf). [f. POLY- + μορφή form.]

Polymorphic (pŏlĭmô'rfĭk), *a.* [f. as POLYMORPHOUS + -IC.]

Polymorphism (pŏlĭmô'rfĭzm). [f. POLYMORPH + -ISM.]

Polymorphous (pŏlĭmô'rfəs), *a.* [f. Gr. πολύμορφος (f. POLY- + μορφή shape) + -OUS.] multiform

Polynesian (pŏlĭnī'zĭăn), *a.* and *sb.* [f. *Polynesia* + -AN.]

Polynomial (pŏlĭnō'mĭăl), *a.* and *sb.* [f. POLY- + L. *nomen* name.] *Alg.* Consisting of many terms.

Column 1

Polynomialism. [f. prec. + -ISM.] Hence **Poly·no·mialist**, a system of polynomial nomenclature; **Poly·no·mialist**, one who uses or favours polynomial nomenclature.

Polynomic (pǫlinǭmik), a. rare. [f. POLY-NOMIC + -IC.] = POLYNOMIAL A. 1, 2.

Polynomial (pǫlinǭmiăl), a. and sb. [f. POLY- + mod.L. *Polyodon*, -*ont* (Lacépède 1798), generic name, ad. Gr. πολυόδων, -όντ- having many teeth, f. πολύς, POLY- + ὀδών- stem of ὀδούς tooth; so F. *polyodonte*.] **a**. adj. Having many teeth; *spec.* belonging to the genus *Polyodon* or family *Polyodontidæ* of fishes, which in the young state have numerous crowded teeth. **b**. sb. A fish of this genus or family.

Polynym (pǫ·linim). rare. [ad. Gr. πολύ-νυμ-ον: see POLY-.]
1. Each of a number of different words having the same meaning; = SYNONYM. rare or Obs.
2. A scientific name (of a species, etc.) consisting of more than three terms.

Polyonymal, a. = POLYONYMOUS.

Polyonymic (pǫlionimik), a. [f. as prec. + -IC.] Of the nature of a polyonym or name consisting of several words.

Polyonymous (pǫliǫ·nimǫs), a. Also g erron. **-onomous**. [f. Gr. πολυώνυμος having many names (f. πολύς, POLY- + ὄνομα, Æol. ὄνυμα name) + -OUS: cf. *anonymous*.] Having many names or titles; called or known by several different names.

Polyonymy (pǫliǫ·nimi). Also g erron. **-onomy**. [ad. Gr. πολυωνυμία a multitude of names, f. πολυώνυμ-ος: see prec. and -Y.]
1. The use of several different names for the same person or thing; variety of names or titles (esp. in ancient mythology).
2. The use of a designation consisting of several names; the use of scientific names consisting of more than two terms or words, to denote species, varieties, etc., of animals or plants; polynomial nomenclature.

† **Polyopia** (pǫliǫ·pĭă). Path. Also in anglicized form **Poly·opy**, **Poly·opy**. [f. Gr. πολύς, POLY- + ὤψ, ὠπ- eye: cf. *amblyopia*, *diplopia*, *myopia*.] An affection of the eyes in which one object is seen as two or more; multiple vision.

So **Polyo·pia** [Gr. -ωπία, from ὤψ sight] = POLYOPIA.

Column 2

polyparium (pǫlipē·riǫm), pl. -**ia**; erron. sing. **polyparia**, pl. -**iæ**. [ad. mod.L. *polyparium*, f. POLY- + -ARIUM.] The common stem, stock, or supporting structure of a colony of polyps (see POLYP 1 c), to which the individual zooids are attached, usually each in a cell or cavity of its own; also called POLYPIDOM. Cf. POLYPE 1.

Polypean, a. rare. [f. L. *polyp*-us POLYP + -*ean*, after L. adjs. in -*eus*: see -AN.] Pertaining to, or resembling that of, a polyp.

Polyped, a. rare. [f. POLY- 1.

Polypetal, a. and sb. Bot. rare. [f. POLY- + PETAL.] = POLYPETALOUS.

Polypetalous (pǫlipe·tălǫs), a. Bot. [f. mod.L. *polypetal-us* (see prec.): see -OUS.]
1. Bot. Literally, Having many petals; but commonly used for: Having the petals distinct or separate, not coherent or united.

Polyphagia (pǫlifē·dʒiă). Rarely in anglicized form **polyphagy** (pǫli·fădʒi). [mod.L., a. Gr. πολυφαγία, f. πολυφάγος: see POLYPHAGOUS. So F. *polyphagie*.]
1. *Phys.* and *Path.* Excessive eating, or desire for eating; voracious or ravenous appetite, esp. as a morbid symptom.

Polyphagous (pǫli·făgǫs), a. [f. Gr. πολυφάγ-ος (f. see POLYPHAGIA) eating much, voracious; f. POLY- + φαγ- eat: see -PHAGOUS. So F. *polyphage*.] Eating much, voracious; *Zool.* feeding upon various kinds of food.

Polyphagy: see POLYPHAGIA.

Polyphant (pǫ·lifănt). Properly Pollaphant, name of a place between Bodmin and Launceston, whence *polyphant stone*, a kind of Cornish potstone, in colour between greenish and green.

Column 3

Polypharmacy (pǫlifā·rmăsi). Med. [= F. *polypharmacie*: see POLY- and PHARMACY: cf. Gr. πολυφάρμακος knowing or characterized by many drugs or poisons.] The use of many drugs or medicines in the treatment of disease.

So **Polypha·rmacal** a. Obs., 'that hath many medicines' (Blount *Glossogr.* 1656); **Polypha·rmacist**, one who practises polypharmacy.

Polyphase (pǫ·lifēz), a. (sb.) Electr. [f. POLY-+ PHASE 2.] Of many phases: applied to systems of alternating electric currents (magnets, transformers, etc.) in which are employed two, three, or more such currents of identical frequency but differing from one another in phase.

Polypheme (pǫ·lifīm). Also 7 **Polyphem**. [a. F. *Polyphème*, ad. L. POLYPHEMUS.] Name of a Cyclops or one-eyed giant in Homer's *Odyssey*; hence used allusively.

Polyphonic (pǫlifǫ·nik), a. [f. as prec. + -IC.]
1. *Mus.* Composed or arranged for several voices or parts, each having a melody of its own; consisting of a number of melodies combined; contrapuntal; of or pertaining to polyphonic music.

So **Polypho·nical** a. = prec.; **Polyphonism**, **Polyphonist**, **Polyphonous**.

Column 4

Polyphonium (pǫlifǭniǫm), a. [f. Gr. πολύ-φωνος (see POLYPHONE) + -OUS.]
1. POLYPHONIC 2.

Polyphony (pǫli·fǫni). [ad. Gr. πολυφωνία, f. πολύφωνος: see POLYPHONE.]
1. Multiplicity of sounds; = POLYPHONISM 1.

Polyphore (pǫ·lifōˌ). Bot. rare. [f. F. *polyphore* (Richard c 1810), ad. Gr. πολυφόρος bearing much.] Term for a receptacle bearing a number of ovaries, as in the buttercup, strawberry, etc.

Polyphragmon, Obs.

Polyphyletic (pǫlifiˌle·tik), a. [f. Gr. πολυ-φυλετικός of many tribes, f. POLY- + φυλετικός.] Belonging to several tribes or families; originating, as a species, from several independent ancestors or sources; relating to such origination; polygenetic.

Polyphyllous (pǫlifi·lǫs), a. Bot. [f. Gr. πολύφυλλ-ος many-leaved + -OUS.] Properly, Having or consisting of many leaves; usually, Having the (perianth-) leaves separate, not united.

Polypid (pǫ·lipid). Zool. [f. POLYP + -ID.] = POLYPIDE.

Polypidom (pǫli·pidǫm). Zool. [irreg. f. POLYP + -IDOM.] = POLYPARIUM, POLYPDOM.

Polypier (pǫ·lipiˌ), obs. f. POLYPARY.

Polypite (pǫ·lipəit). Zool. [f. POLYP + -ITE.] A fossil polyp.

Polypode, **Polypody**.

Polypore (pǫ·lipōˌr), and sb. [mod. Zool. = POLYPORUS.]

Polypus (pǫ·lipǫs). Forms: 5–8 polipus, 7–9 polypus, etc.

Polysperm, **Polyspermy**.

Polyspore (pǫ·lispōˌr), Bot. [f. POLY- + SPORE.]

Polysporic (pǫlispǫ·rik), a. and sb. [mod. Zool. f. POLYSPORE + -IC.]

Column 5 (lower half)

Polypide (pǫ·lipəid). Zool. [f. POLYP + -ide: cf. -id.] An individual or unit of a compound polyzoan.

Polypier, **Polyplastide**: see POLYP- 1.

Polyplacophora (pǫliplăkǫ·fŏră). Zool. pl. [mod.L., neut. pl. (J. E. Gray, 1821), f. Gr. πολύς, POLY- + πλάξ, πλακο- tablet, plate, etc. + -φορος bearing.] **a.** Belonging to the division *Polyplacophora*, comprising the chitons.

Polypide to **Polyplacophora**: see POLYP- 1.

Polyplastid, -ide, sb. Biol. [f. POLY-+ PLASTID.] An organism consisting of many plastids or cells: opposed to *monoplastid*; also attrib.

Polypod (pǫ·lipǫd), a. and sb. Zool. Also 5 pollypod, 7 poli-, polli-, polypode.

Polyporite (pǫli·pǫrəit), a. Bot. [mod.L. *Polyporites* (Fries 1836–8) (a. Gr. πολύπορος: see next) + -ITE.] Resembling or belonging to *Polyporus*.

Polypodiaceous (pǫlipǭdiē·ʃǫs), a. Bot. [f. mod.L. *Polypodi-um* + -ACEOUS.] Belonging to the Natural Order (or sub-order) *Polypodiaceæ*, comprising the large majority of ferns.

Polypodium (pǫlipǭ·diǫm). Bot. [mod.L. 6 polipodium. (L. [Pliny], a. Gr. πολυπόδιον (Theophr.) a kind of fern, lit. many-footed, f. πολύπους many-footed.]

Polypody (pǫ·lipǫdi). Bot. Forms: 4–5 poly-podi, 5 polipodie, polipody, 5–6 polipodie, 5–7 polypody, 6 polypodie, -pody, -podi, 6 polypody. [ad. L. *polypodium* (Plin.: see prec.).] A fern of the genus *Polypodium*; esp. *P. vulgare*, the Common Polypody, a widely distributed species, growing on moist rocks, old walls, and trees.

Polypome (pǫ·lipǭm). Surg. [f. as prec. (see POLYPUS 2) + Gr. -τομος cutting. (See quot. 1857.)]

Polypous (pǫ·lipǫs), a. [f. POLYP-US + -OUS: or f. *polypus* (see POLYPUS 2) in sense 2.]
1. *Zool.* Pertaining to, or of the nature of, a polyp; also *fig.* like that of a polyp (esp. in reference to its reproduction by budding, as in *Hydra*).

Column 6

+ -AN], a. adj. Belonging to the *Polypomedusæ*, a group of Cœlenterata comprising the *Hydrozoa* and *Actinozoa*. **b.** sb. A cœlenterate belonging to this group.

Polypomorphic (pǫlipŏmǭ·rfik), a. Zool. [f. Gr. πολύπους, -ποδ- + μορφή form + -IC.] Having the form of a polyp, polypiform, polypoid; *spec.* belonging to the *Polypomorpha*, a synonym of *Hydrozoa*. So **Polypomorphous** a.

Polyporite (pǫli·pǫrəit), a. Bot. A fossil resembling a species of *Polyporus* (see next), found in the Welsh coal-measures.

Polyporoid (pǫli·pǫrɔid), a. Bot. [f. next + -OID.] Resembling or belonging to *Polyporus*, a large widely distributed genus of hymenomycetous fungi, growing in the form of projecting shelves or brackets on dead or decaying trees.

Polyporus (pǫli·pǫrǫs), Bot. [mod.L., a. Gr. πολύπορος having many passages (see PORE 20).]

Polypose (pǫ·lipǭs), a. [ad. L. *polypōsus* (Martial in sense 2: see POLYPUS, POSE.)]

Polypragmatic (pǫlipragmæ·tik), a. (sb.) [f. Gr. πολυπράγματος busy about many things, over-busy (f. πολύς, POLY- + πρᾶγμα(τ-) thing done) + -IC.] = POLYPRAGMON. Busy about many affairs (that are not one's own); meddlesome, officious. So **Polypra·gmatist**, a meddlesome person. So **Polypra·gmatism**, officious or over-busy conduct; **Polypra·gmaty**, the state of being over-engaged with business or matters.

Polypragmon (pǫlipra·gmǫn). Obs. rare[−0]. [ad. Gr. πολυπράγμων, see prec.] A meddlesome person, a busybody. So **Polypra·gmon** a. and **Polypra·gmosyne** [Gr. πολυπραγμοσύνη], officiousness.

Column 7

Polyprothetic (pǫliprǫθe·tik), a. [f. POLY- + PROTHETIC.] = POLYSYNTHETIC.

Polyprotodont (pǫliprǭ·tǫdǫnt), a. and sb. Zool. [f. POLY- + πρῶτος first + ὀδούς, ὀδοντ- tooth: see -DONT.] *a.* adj. Having more than two front or incisor teeth in the lower jaw, as the carnivorous and insectivorous marsupials. *b.* sb. A polyprotodont marsupial. (Opp. to DIPROTODONT.) Hence **Polyprotodo·ntia**, a division of the polyprotodonts.

Polyprotodo·ntid (pǫliprǭ·tǫdǫntid). Zool. A member of the polyprotodont marsupials.

Polypsychical (pǫlisəi·kikăl), a. nonce-wd. [f. next + -IC.] Having many souls, many-souled. So **Polypsychical**.

Polypterid, a. Ichthyol. [f. mod.L. *Polypterus* (Geoffroy 1802), generic name, a. Gr. πολύπτερος many-winged (see POLY- and PTERYGIUM) + -ID.] A fish of the family *Polypteridæ* of crossopterygian ganoids.

Polyptote (pǫ·liptǭt), a. and sb. Gram. [ad. Gr. πολύπτωτος, see POLY- and πτῶτος verbal adj. of πίπτειν fall.]

Polyptych (pǫ·liptik). [ad. late L. *polyptych-on*, a. Gr. πολύπτυχον (sc. βιβλίον), neut. of πολύπτυχος having many folds.]

Column 8 (lower right)

Polyschematist (pǫliskēmătist), a. Prosody. [f. Gr. πολυσχημάτιστος 'multiform' (f. verses, composed of various metres.]

Polyscope (pǫ·liskǭp). [f. POLY- + -SCOPE: so F. *polyscope*. Cf. Gr. πολύσκοπος far-seeing.]
1. An optical instrument through which objects appear multiplied; a multiplying-glass; *spec.* (see quot. 1842). Cf. POLYOPTRON.

Polypus (pǫ·lipǫs). Forms: 5–8 polipus, 7–9 polypus, -(-pes, -pous), etc.; 5 polypodes, polipuse. [a. L. *polypūs*, -ī, a Doric or Æolic Gr. πωλύπους, see -πους (see -POD).]

Polysarcia (pǫlisā·rsiă). Path. Also **Polysarcy**. [mod.L., a. Gr. πολυσαρκία fleshiness, corpulence, f. POLY- + σάρξ, σαρκ- flesh.]

Polysarcous (pǫlisā·rkǫs), a. rare. [f. Gr. πολύσαρκ-ος + -OUS.] Excessively fleshy or corpulent.

Polysporangium (pǫlispǫræ·ndʒiǫm), Bot. [f. POLY- + SPORANGIUM.]

Polyspore (pǫ·lispōˌr), Bot. [f. POLY- + SPORE.]

Polysporic (pǫlispǫ·rik), a. Bot. [f. POLY- + SPORIC.] = POLYSPOROUS.

Polysporous (pǫlispǭ·rǫs), a. Bot. [f. POLY- + SPOROUS.] Containing or producing numerous spores.

Polysporous (pŏlĭ-spōrŭs, pŏlĭspō·rŭs), *a.* Bot. and Zool. [f. Gr. πολύσπορος (see POLYSPORE) + -OUS.] Having of or producing numerous spores, as certain cryptogams plants and protozoans.

Polysporous (as prec.).

Polystachous to -stigmous : see POLY-1.

Polystome (pŏ·lĭstōm), *a.* and *sb.* [f. Gr. στόμα mouth.] *A.* *adj.* Having many mouths.

Polystomatous, etc.

Polystomella, **Polystomium** : see POLY-.

Polystomous. Zool.

Polystomum (pŏlĭstō·mŏm).

Polystyle to **Polysulphuretted** : see POLY-.

† **Polysyllabe**. *Obs.*

Polysyllabic (pŏlĭsĭlæ·bĭk), *a.* [f. med.L.]

Polysyllabical *adv.*

Polysyllabically *adv.*

Polysyllabism (pŏlĭ·sĭlăbĭz'm).

Polysyllable (pŏ·lĭsĭlăb'l), *sb.*

Polysynthesis (pŏlĭsĭ·nþĕsĭs). [f. POLY- + SYNTHESIS.]

Polysyndeton. [mod.L., ad. Gr. πολυσύνδετον.]

Polysynthetic (pŏlĭsĭnþĕ·tĭk), *a.* [f. Gr.]

Polysynthetical, *a.*

Polysynthetically *adv.*

Polysynthetism (pŏlĭsĭ·nþĕtĭz'm).

Polytechnic (pŏlĭtĕ·knĭk), *a.* and *sb.* [ad. F. *polytechnique* (École polytechnique, 1795).]

Polytheism (pŏ·lĭþīĭz'm). Also 7 poli-, potu-, (polytheism). [ad. F. *polythéisme* (16th c.), or ad. Gr. πολύθεος : see -ISM.] Belief in, or worship of, many gods (or more than one God).

Polytheist (pŏ·lĭþīĭst), *sb.* [as prec. + -IST. Cf. F. *polythéiste* (1762 in Hatz.-Darm.).] One who believes in or worships many gods (or more than one); a believer in polytheism.

Polytheistic (pŏlĭþīĭ·stĭk), *a.* [f. prec. + -IC: see -ISTIC.] Of, pertaining to, holding, or characterized by polytheism.

Polytheistical, *a.*

Polytheistically *adv.*

Polythalamia. *Zool.*

Polythalamous (pŏlĭþæ·lămŭs), *a.* *Nat. Hist.*

Polythecium (pŏlĭþī·sĭŏm, -þĕ·sĭŏm). Pl. -ia. *Zool.*

Polytheism.

Polythelia (pŏlĭþī·lĭa), *a.*

Polythionic (pŏlĭþīŏ·nĭk), *a.* *Chem.*

Polytocous (pŏlĭ·tŏkŭs), *a.* *Zool.*

Polytomous (pŏlĭ·tŏmŭs), *a.*

Polytomy (pŏlĭ·tŏmĭ).

Polytope.

Polytrich (pŏ·lĭtrĭk). *Obs. rare.* (Erron. politrich.)

Polytrichal (pŏlĭ·trĭkăl), *a.* [f. mod. *polytrichus* (Ehrenberg) (f. Gr. πολύ, etc.)

Polytrichum (pŏlĭ·trĭkŏm).

Polytrochal (pŏlĭ·trŏkăl), *a.* [f. mod. *polytrochus* (f. Gr. πολύ, etc.)

Polytrophic (pŏlĭtrŏ·fĭk), *a.*

Polytropic (pŏlĭtrŏ·pĭk), *a.*

Polytype (pŏ·lĭtaip). *a.* mod.F. *polytype.*

Polytypic (pŏlĭtĭ·pĭk), *a.* [f. Gr. πολύ, POLY-]

Polyvalent (pŏlĭ·vălĕnt), *a.* [Hybrid f. POLY- + VALENT.]

Polyzoan (pŏlĭzō·ăn), *a.* and *sb.* Zool.

Polyzoary (pŏlĭzō·ărĭ). Zool.

Polyzoic (pŏlĭzō·ĭk), *a.*

Polyzoism (pŏlĭzō·ĭz'm), the character of being polyzoic (sense 1).

Polyzomal.

Polyzone (pŏ·lĭzōn). *Goms.*

Polyzonal (pŏlĭzō·năl), *a.* [f. POLY- + ZONAL.]

Polyzoon (pŏlĭzō·ŏn). Zool.

Polyzooid.

Polyzoon, sing. of POLYZOA, q. v.

Polyzoonite (pŏlĭzō·ŏnait). Zool. rare.

† **Poma** (pō·mă). *Anat.*

Pomace (pŏ·mĕs). Also 7 pomace, pomise, pummice, pummace. See also POMMEY.

Pomade (pŏmē·d). *sb.* [-med.L. *pomada*.]

Pomate. See POMATE.

Pomander (pŏmæ·ndăr). *sb.*

Pomate (pŏ·mĕt), *sb.* Also 6 pomato.

Pomatum (pŏmē·tŏm), *sb.* [mod.L. *pōmātum*.]

Pomatic.

Pomatoid (pō·mătoid), *a.* Zool.

Pomatorhine (pō·mătŏrain), *a.* Ornith.

Pome (pōm), *sb.* [a. F. *pomme*, f. L. *poma*.]

Pome-citron.

† **Pomelo** (pŏ·mĕlō). *Obs.* Also in comb.

Pomace (pō·măs), sb. [f. POME.]

Pome-dorry, *Obs.* Also 7 pome-dorree.

Pomegranate (pŏ·mĕgrănĕt, pŏmgrănĕt, -grē·nĕt, pŏ·mgrănĕt). [ME. *poumgarnet*.]

Pomegranate-tree.

Pome-pirk, abbrev. form of POMPERKIN.

Pomeranian (pɒmᵻréɪnɪən), a. (sb.). [f. *Pomerania*, f. *Pomern* of the province, a med.L. *Pomerānia*, f. *Pomern* a Slavonic tribe. (Ger. *Pom-mern*.)] Of or pertaining to Pomerania, a district on the south coast of the Baltic Sea, now a province of Prussia. b. sb. Short for *Pomeranian dog*.

Pomeridian (pɒmᵊrɪdɪən), a. [ad. L. *pōmerīdiānus* (pomerīdiānus), f. *post* after + *merīdiānus* MERIDIAN.] †a. = POSTMERIDIAN a. Obs.

b. *Entom.* Flying in the afternoon, as some lepidopterous insects. 2. *Bot.* Opening or closing in the afternoon, as a flower.

Pomerium, obs. form of POMŒRIUM.

† **Pomeroy.** Obs. Also ʒ pome-roie, pomroy. [app. f. F. *pomme* (OF. *pome*) apple + *roi* king.] An old variety of apple; perh. = king-apple.

† **Pomeroyal,** Obs. Also 6 pome ryall. [app. f. *pomme* (OF. *pome*) apple + *royal* royal.] Some kind of apple, ? the same as POMEROY.

Pomewater. Obs. exc. dial. Also 6–7 pome-water. [app. f. POME + WATER sb.] A large juicy kind of apple.

Pomeys, pomeis (pɔ̄ɪˈmᵻz), sb. pl. *Her.* [app. f. POME + WATER sb.] (Cf. *apple* in sense 7.)

Pomfret (pɒmˈfrᵻt). Also pamflet, pomphlet. [app. derived from Pg. *pampo*, F. *pample*, said to be applied to the same fish. A dim. "*pampfret*" may have become *pamphlet*, *pomphlet*, and *pomfret*.] A fish of the genus *Stromateus*, inhabiting the Indian and Pacific Oceans.

Pomfret-cake (pɒmˈfrᵻt kēik). [f. *Pomfret* (AN. and ME. *Pontfret*, now spelt *Pontefract*), a town in Yorkshire.] A liquorice cake made at Pontefract.

Pomgarnade, -garnat(e, -granat(e, etc., obs. ff. POMEGRANATE.

Pomice, obs. form of POMACE, PUMICE.

Pomiculture (pɒ̄ˈmᵻkʌltᶨər). [f. L. *pōm-um* apple + CULTURE.] The art or practice of fruit-growing. Hence **Pomicul'turist.**

Pomiferous (pɒmɪfərəs), a. [f. L. *pōmifer* (f. *pōmum* apple + *-fer* bearing) + -OUS.] 1. Producing fruit, or specifically apples; esp. in *Bot.*, applied to trees and plants bearing pome or pome-like fruits.

Pomiform (pɒ̄ˈmɪfɔrm), a. [f. L. type *pōmi-formis*, f. *pōmum* fruit, apple : see -FORM.] Having the shape of a pome or apple.

Pomiglion, obs. form of POMMELION.
Pomiœ, Pomiœd, obs. ff. POMEE, PUMICED.
Pomivorous (pɒmɪvɔrəs), a. *nonce-wd.* [f. L. *pōmum* fruit + -VOROUS.] The common boy. The small and unwelcome animal which we so call.

Pomly, variant of POMELY Obs.

Pommade, -do, var. POMADE sb.¹, v.¹ **Pom-made, Pommander, pommaundre,** obs. ff. POMADE, POMMANDER. **Pommage** (pɒ̄ˈmᵻdʒ). Also 6–8 pomage. [Cf. F. *pommage* cider harvest or production, f. F. *pomme* apple + -AGE. In sense 2 perh. a variant of POMACE.] 1. Cider. Obs. rare.

Pomace (pɒmᵻs, pɒmᵻs), or in some other way related to that word.] = POMACE 1.

Pommé (pɒmēi), a. *Her.* [F. *pommé*, pa. pple. of *pommer* to come to a round head, f. *pomme* apple : see POME.] 1. *Heraldry.* A Cross Pommettée is certainly the same above call'd Pommée.

Pommel (pʌmᵊl, formerly pᵿmᵊl), sb. Forms: 4, 4–7 ʒ pomel, -elle, ʒ poomel, 5–6 pomyl, 6 pommell, 6– pommel. [ME. a OF. *pomel*, pummel, -elle, -ele, 6 pommel, etc.] 1. A rounded knob or prominence ; a ball; a round boss, knob, or button. Obs.

† **2. a.** An ornament placed on the summit of a tower, dome, gable, or pillar, at the corners of an altar, etc.; the ornamental top of the pole of a tent, a flag-staff, etc.; a finial.

3. A rounded knob; an ornamental knob generally.

4. The rounded knob, usually of metal, terminating the hilt of a sword, dagger, or the like.

b. The knob on the breech of a muzzle-load-ing cannon.

Pommel, v. Also 6 pomel: see POMMEL.

Pommelion. Obs. Forms 7 pomiglion, pumelion, 9 pommellion, pomelion, pome-melion. [An unexplained extension of POMEL in sense 3; said to be originally a sailors' word.]

Pommelled, pomelled (pʌmᵊld), a. [f. POMMEL sb. + -ED².] Of a sword : Having the pommel of a specified tincture.

Pommette, pometté (pɒmēˈtēi), a. *Her.* [f. F. *pommette,* f. *pomme* apple : see POME.] Terminating in a knob or knobs, as the arms of a cross.

Pommey, obs. form of POMELY Obs. Also **Pommey** (pᵿmᵊl). dial. Also pommy, pumy.

Pomona (pɒmōˈnᵊ). *Rom. Mythol.* [L. *Po-mōna*.] The goddess of fruits and fruit-trees; hence, the fruit-tree of a country, or a treatise on them (cf. *flora*). *Pomona green* : see quot. 1842.

Pommelled, pomelled.

Pomonic (pɒmɒnɪk), a. [f. POMONA + -IC.] Consisting of or pertaining to fruits.

Pomp (pɒmp), sb. Also 4–7 pompe, 5 pumpe. [a. F. *pompe* (13th c. in Du Cange)—L. *pompa*, a. Gr. *πομπή* a sending, a solemn procession, a train, parade, display, pomp, f. *πέμπειν* to send.] **1.** Splendid display or celebration, magnificent show; splendour, magnificence.

b. †spec. An ostentatious display of wealth, etc.

2. A parade or procession.

† 3. A vain or ostentatious display. Obs.

Pomp, v. [f. prec.] *trans.* To feed (any one) luxuriously, feed up. Obs.

Pompano (pɒmˈpᵊnōʊ, pɒmpᵊnōʊ). [Sp. *pámpano*, applied to a stromateoid fish, *Stromateus fiatola*.] 1. One of various W. Indian and N. American fishes, highly esteemed for the table; as in the W. Indies, *Trachynotus carolinus*, a deep-bodied fish with blunt snout.

Pompature, obs. form of POMPOSITY.

Pompe, obs. form of POMP, POMPOM.
Pompettone, obs. form of PUMPION.

Pompholygos (pɒmfɒlᵻgɒs), sb. pl. [as next + -OUS.] Affected with pompholyx. Obs.

Pompholyx (pɒmfɒlɪks), sb. *Path.* [a. Gr. *πομφόλυξ.*] 1. *Chem.* Crude zinc oxide, flowers of zinc.

2. *Path.* A vesicle on the skin; also, an eruption of vesicles, without inflammation or fever, appearing chiefly on the palms of the hands and soles of the feet.

Pompier (pɒmpɪˈēi, *F.* pɔ̃pje), sb. [F.] An engine; = FIRE-ENGINE. Obs.

Pompillion. Obs. [See prec.] A term applied in pharmacy to an ointment.

Pompine, var. next. **Pompinoe,** var. POMPANO.

Pompion, pumpion. Obs. Now rare. Forms: 6–7 pompeon, -ion, 6 pumpion, pumpion (7 pompan), 6– pompion. [Orig. a. obs. F. *pompon* a pumpion.

Pomace (pɒmᵻs, pᵿmᵻs), sb. or in some other way related to that word. = POMACE 1.

Pomme, var. POMMÉ; obs. form of PUMELO.

Pomology (pɒmɒˈlᵊdʒɪ), sb. [ad. mod.L. *pomologia*, f. *pōmum* : see POME and -LOGY. So F. *pomologie* (Littré).] The science and practice of fruit-culture; also, a treatise on fruit-culture.

Pomona (pɒmōˈnᵊ). [see POMONA.]

Pompelmoose, pompelmous, pompelmoos, etc. [ad. Du. *pompelmoes*, some form of POMPELMOUSE.]

Pomperkin. dial. Also 8 pomperkin. [Origin uncertain : ? f. *pous* or *paus*-pear, apple, and -KIN.] A 'small drink' made from refuse apple and water; ciderkin.

Pompey (pɒmpᵻ), v. dial. Also pomphy. [? f. a word of Dickens'.] *trans.* To pamper, indulge.

Pompet, -ett, etc. variant of PUMPET.

Pompier (pɒmpɪər), sb. [French form of POMP + -IER.] A fireman. Hence **Pompier ladder**, a fireman's scaling ladder, having a central pole and cross-bars for rungs, and a hook at the top to attach it to a building, etc.

Pompelmoose, pampelmoose, -musse, etc. [In the Dutch Indies (ʃ 1691).]

Pompeian (pɒmpēˈiən), a. Also 9 Pompeiian (pɒmpēˈiiən). [f. L. *Pompēiānus,* f. *Pompēii* Pompeii.] Of or pertaining to Pompeii, an Italian town, buried by an eruption of Mount Vesuvius in the year 79 A.D., and since 1755 gradually laid bare by excavation.

Pomponeon, obs. form of PUMPION.

Pompon (pɒmˈpɒn, *F.* pɔ̃pɔ̃). Also 8 pong pompon, 9 pumpoon, pompoon. [F. *pompon* (18th c. in Hatz.-Darm.) a tuft, top-knot ; of uncertain origin ; possibly a collective deriv. of *pompe,* POMP. Cf. POMPOON.] 1. A jewel or ornament attached to a long pin; a tuft or bunch of ribbon, velvet, feathers, threads of silk, etc.

Pompoon, var. POMPON.

Pomposity (pɒmpɒsᵻtɪ). [ad. late L. *pompositas* (Isidore).] 1. Pomp, magnificence, stately or ostentatious show. Obs.

Pompous (pɒmpəs), a. Also 5 pompous, 6–ous, 7–8 -ous, 6 -ose, 6–7 -ose, 6–8 -ouse, 5–6 -us, 6–7 -ous, 6–8 -ious. [a. F. *pompeux,* -euse (14th c. in Hatz.-Darm.), or ad. late L. *pompōsus,* f. *pompa* POMP.] 1. Characterized by pomp or stately show; magnificent, splendid ; † processional.

2. Characterized by an exaggerated display of self-importance or dignity; boastful, vainglorious; arrogant; consequential; pretentious.

Pompously, adv.

Pompousness.

Pomum.

Pomyce, **pomya**, obs. forms of PUMICE.

Pon, obs. f. PAN.

Ponaster.

Ponce, slang.

Poncean.

Poncho.

Poncor, Ponchion, obs. ff. PUNCHEON.

Pond.

Pondfish.

Pondage.

†**Ponder**, sb.

Ponder, v.

Ponder, -dre, etc.

Ponderability.

Ponderable.

Ponderal.

Ponderance.

Ponderancy.

†**Ponderate**, ppl. a.

Ponderate, v.

Ponderation.

Ponderer.

Pondering, vbl. sb.

Pondering, ppl. a.

Ponderling.

Ponderment.

Ponderomotive.

Ponderose.

Ponderosity.

Ponderous, a.

Ponderously, adv.

Ponderousness.

Pondfish.

Pondlet.

Pond-lock.

Pondlily.

†**Pondus.**

Ponds.

Pondweed.

Pondy.

†**Pone**, v.

Pone.

Ponency.

Pong.

Pone, -garde, etc.

Ponent.

Poney.

Ponerid.

Ponerology.

Poney, Pony.

Pong.

Pongee.

Pongo.

Poniard, sb.

†**Pont** [1].

Pont [2], obs.

Pontage.

Ponto.

Pons.

Ponsion, ponsone.

Ponsway.

Pont-

Pontal.

Pontic.

Pontifex.

PONTIFF. 1109 **PONTIFICALLY.** **PONTIFICATE.** 1110 **PONTOONER.**

Pontiff

Pontiff (pɒ'ntif). Also 7 -iffe, 7-8 -if. [ad. F. *pontife* (1516), ad. L. *pontif-, pontifex*: see prec.]

1. *Rom. Antiq.* = PONTIFEX 1.

2. A bishop (of the medieval Western church); *spec.* and usually, the bishop of Rome, the pope in full, *sovereign pontiff*).

3. *gen.* A chief or high priest (of any religion).

4. *catachr.* Pertaining to a bridge. (Cf. PONTIFICAL 6.)

† **Pontiffhicary** obs. [irreg. f. med.L. *pontificatio* : see -ACY 3.] = PONTIFICATE 2.

Pontifical (pɒnti'fikăl), *a.* and *sb.* [ad. L. *pontificalis* or F. *pontifical*.]

A. *adj.*

1. Pertaining to a pontiff.

2. Characterized by the pomp, state, dignity, authority, or dogmatic character of a pontiff.

3. Applied to a shade of purple.

4. *catachr.* Pertaining to a bridge.

B. *sb.*

1. *Rom. Antiq.* = PONTIFEX.

Pontificality (pɒntifikæ'liti). [ad. obs. F. *pontificalité* (Godef.), pontifical dignity: see PONTIFICAL and -ITY.]

1. Pontifical office or dignity = the office, state, or dignity of a bishop, esp. of the pope.

Pontificate (pɒnti'fikĕt), *sb.* [ad. L. *pontificatus*, f. *pontific-*, *pontifex*: see PONTIFF and -ATE 1.]

1. The office or dignity of a pontifex: see -ATE 1.

2. = PONTIFICALITY 2.

Pontificate (pɒnti'fikeit), *v.* [f. L. *pontificat-*, ppl. stem of *pontificari*.]

1. *intr.* To perform the functions of a pontiff; to officiate as a bishop, esp. at mass.

Pontifice (pɒ'ntifis). *Obs. rare.* [ad. L. *pontific-, pontifex*; or F. *pontifice*.]

Pontify (pɒ'ntifai), *v.* [f. PONTIFF, ad. med.L. *pontificare*: see PONTIFICATE v.]

Pontil (pɒ'ntil). *Glass-making.* [a. F. *pontil*, *pointil*.]

Pontine (pɒ'ntain), *a.* *Anat.* and *Path.* [f. L. *pont-, pons* bridge + -INE.]

Pontle-vis (pɒ'ntlevis). *Obs.* [a. OF. *ponteleïs*, *pontleïs*.]

Pontoon

Pontonier, -ier [a. F. *pontonnier* (13th c. in Hatz.).]

Ponto (Cards, and Glass-making): see PUNTO.

Pontoneer, -ier [a. F. *pontonnier* (13th c. in Hatz.).]

Pontonage (pɒ'ntɒnedʒ), *sb.* [a. F. *pontonnage* (14th c. in Littré).]

Pontoon (pɒntū'n), *sb.* [ad. F. *ponton* (14th c. in Littré).]

Pontonier see PONTOONER.

Ponton see PONTOON.

Pontoon, -toon (pɒntū'n).

Pontooner see PONTONEER.

PONY. 1111 **POOK.** **POOK.** 1112 **POOL.**

Pony

Pont-tournis, Pont-volant: see PONT 1.

Ponty, variant of PUNTY.

Pony (pəʊ'ni), *sb.* Forms: 7-8 *powny*, 8 *Sc.* *powney*, -ie, 8-9 *poney*, 8- *pony*. [Sc. *powney*, *puni*, (as suggested by Prof. Skeat, 1890) = *pouliney*, ad. OF. *poulenet* a little foal (1444 in Godef., dim. of *poulain, polain* a foal, colt—late L. *pullāmen*, f. L. *pullus* young animal).]

Pooch (pūtʃ). [a. F. POOR; Sc. and ad. F. POUL.]

Poodle (pūd'l). Forms: 6-7 *poude*, 7 *poude*, 7-8 *poud-le*, 8 *pudel*, *poodle*, 8-9 *puddle*. [a. Ger. *pudel*, Du. *poedel*.]

Poodling, pooding, -ynge, obs. ff. PUDDING.

Pood (pūd). [a. Russ. *pud'.*]

Pook, Pool

Pooh (pū, puh), *int.* (1.) Also 7 *puh, poe, pow*, 7-8 *pugh*, 8- *poo*: see POH, POOF. [A 'vocal gesture' expressing the action of puffing or blowing anything away.]

Pooh-pooh (pū'pū'), *v.* [redupl. of prec.] *trans.* To express contempt or disdain for; to make light of; dismiss as unworthy of notice.

Pook (pʊk). *Obs. exc. dial.* [Goes with prec.] *trans.* To heap up; *esp.* to put up (newly mown hay or unsheathed corn) in cocks or pooks (POOK *sb.*)

Pook (pʊk). *Obs. exc. dial.* [Origin uncertain.] *trans.* To pluck, pull, pick, or pinch with the thumb and finger.

Pook (pʊk), *sb.* [A parasitic Sc. *v.t.* Forms: 7 *puik*, 8- *pook*. [a. Du. POOK.]

Pookah, phooka (pū'kə). *Irish folk-lore.* [a. Ir. *púca*, OIr. *púca*; cf. PUCK.]

Pooka (pū'kə). Also POOKA, POOKAW. = prec.

Pool, *sb.* local. [Origin uncertain.] A measure of weight in cooking fresh-water eels.

Pool (pūl). *sb.* [F. *poule* in sense (1676 in Menn. de Sévigné): see Note below.]

1. In certain card games, etc.: The collective amount of the stakes and fines of the players joining in the game.

The sort of pot-hunting known at Wimbledon and elsewhere as Pool, where the value of a bull's-eye is much more considered than the credit of handling with success the Queen of weapons. 1869 *Daily News* 6 July, Pool and other breech-loading firing is made continuous instead of intermittent.

b. *Betting.* The collective stakes of a number of persons who each stake a sum of money on one of the competitors in some contest, the proceeds being divided among the backers of the winner.

1881 [see Pari mutuel].

5. A common fund into or from which all gains or losses of the contributors are paid; hence, a combination of capitalists for united speculative operation in a stock or commodity; a combine.

1872 W. R. Travers in *N. York Herald* 25 Nov. 8/3, I find myself charged by Mr. Jay Gould.. with being interested in a put or pool in Northwestern common with Mr. Drew,..and others. 1884 *Boston* (Mass.) *Jrnl.* 29 Jan. 4/4 Stamford rich men have formed a pool to pay the fines imposed upon them for fast driving. 1906 *Blackw. Mag.* Jan. 146/1 His little history of the fifty-million dollar pool in Union Pacific Preferred Stock showed that it was a 'blind pool', to run for five years.

6. An arrangement between previously competing parties, by which rates or prices are fixed, and business or receipts divided, in order to do away with mutually injurious competition: see quot. 1882. Also *attrib.* Originally *U. S.*

1881 *Chicago Times* 1 June, The marine insurance men are still striving to form a pool, and expect soon to succeed. *Ibid.* 4 June, The company will now compete with the other pool lines leading eastward. *Ibid.* 17 June, The agreement for a reorganization of the south-western freight pool. 1882 Bithell *Counting Ho. Dict.* (1893) 231 The object of a 'pool' is to put an end to the 'war of rates' which breaks out so frequently between two or more competing lines... Sometimes the proceeds of the traffic on competing lines are put into a common fund, and afterwards distributed according to conditions previously agreed on. This is called a 'Financial Pool'. In other cases, arrangements are made for a distribution of the traffic, each line agreeing to accept a specified proportion. This is called a 'Physical Pool'. 1887 *Pall Mall G.* 11 Oct. 12/1 Salt is the latest commodity placed under the control of a pool in the United States... The object of such a pool is 'to keep up the price of salt, and to be able to compete with the foreign manufacturers'.

7. *Fencing.* A contest between teams, in which each member of one side fights each member of the other.

1901 *Oxford Times* 9 Mar. 12/4 What is termed a Poule à l'epée was arranged between teams of six a side, each member of the one team fighting a duel with the six members of the other, in rotation. *Ibid.*, Came out head of the pool, receiving only one hit in his six engagements.

8. *Comb.*, as (in sense 1) *pool-dish, -game*; (sense 3) *pool-ball, -table*; (sense 4 b) *pool-check, -room, -seller, -selling, -ticket*: see also 4 a and 6.

1858 Simmonds *Dict. Trade*, *Pool-balls, ivory balls, 9 or 12 to the set, about 2 inches in diameter, for playing a kind of billiards. 1890 L. C. D'Oyle *Notches* 11, I walked up ter see wot the preacher had giv' him; boys, 'twas nothing but a brass *pool-check. 1878 H. H. Gibbs *Ombre* 19 The Dealer then setting the *pool-dish at his right hand, places in it five points. 1865 *Compl. Domino-Player* 16 Domino *Pool Game..is played by fitting the same numbers together, as in all the games with dominoes, except the matadore. 1887 *Chicago Advance* 13 Oct. 6/1 The betting ..is now mostly done in *pool-rooms. 1892 *Pall Mall G.* 4 May 5/1 Only one or two of the women came out of the pool-room with more money than when they entered it. *Ibid.*, The New York police have steadfastly resisted the efforts of enterprizing '*pool-sellers' to make betting on horse racing as easy for women as for men. 1887 *Daily Tel.* 12 Mar. 5/1 Wagering, or, as it is called on the other side of the Atlantic, *pool-selling. 1860 Hughes *Tom Brown at Oxf.* xxxiii, Tom's good eye and steady hand, and the practice he had had at the..*pool-table, gave him considerable advantage.

[*Note.* In Eng. use this word has undoubtedly from the 18th c. been identified with Pool *sb.*[1]: see quots. 17.., 1766 in sense 1, with their references to the *fish* in the *pool*. But the French use of *poule* for the same thing, with the fact that the French is found earlier, makes it almost certain that the term was taken from Fr., and associated with the Eng. word *pool*. F. *poule* is held to be a sense of *poule* hen, chicken, being perh. at first slang for 'booty, spoil, plunder'. Mme. de Sévigné in a letter of 29 July 1676 uses *poule* exactly in the sense of Eng. *pool*; and in a letter of 30 June 1680 says 'Si Denjean est de ce jeu, il prendra toutes les poules; c'est un aigle', a play upon the sense 'hen'. The Dict. of the Académie, ed. 1, 1694, and that of Furetière, ed. 2, 1701, also explain *poule* almost in the words in which it stands in the Dict. Acad. ed. 7, 1878: 'Poule se dit, à certains jeux, de la quantité d'argent ou de jetons qui résulte de la mise de chacun des joueurs et qui appartient à celui qui gagne le coup. *La poule est grosse. Mettre à la poule. Gagner la poule*'. There is perh. a similar relation between F. *fiche* a fish at cards, and the Eng. 'fish' in the 'pool'.]

Pool (pūl), *v.*[1] [f. Pool *sb.*[1]]

† 1. *intr.* Of land: To be marshy or full of pools. Of water: To form pools, to stand, stagnate. *Obs.*

c 1420 *Pallad. on Husb.* I. 89 Ne poole [*v. r.* pulle; L. *stagnet*] hit not, but goodly playn elonge. 1626 Bacon *Sylva* § 537 On the other side the Water must but Slide, and not stand or Poole.

2. *trans.* In quarrying granite: To sink or make (a hole) for the insertion of a wedge; hence *pool-hole*, a hole made in this process. In coal-mining: To undermine (coal) so as to cause it to fall.

1793 Smeaton *Edystone L.* § 91 Holes or notches, cut (or, as they term it, *pooled*) in the surface of the stone. *Ibid.*, These pool-holes are sunk with the point of a pick. 1816 J. A. Paris *Guide Mounts Bay & Land's End* ii. 45 The method of splitting it [granite] is by applying several wedges to holes cut or (pooled) in the surface of the stone. 1839 Ure *Dict. Arts* 979 The first set [of workmen] curves or pools the coal along the whole line of walls, laying in or pooling at least 3 feet. 1863 *N. Brit. Daily Mail* 5 May, [He] was working at the face of the seam, undermining or pooling the coal so as to bring it down.

Pool (pūl), *v.*[2] [f. Pool *sb.*[2]] *trans.* To throw into a common stock or fund to be distributed according to agreement; to combine (capital or interests) for the common benefit; *spec.* of competing railway companies, etc.: To share or divide (traffic or receipts).

1879 *Daily Chron.* 30 Apr., A diminution in the volume of traffic passing over the line under the arrangements made with competing lines to 'pool', or, as in England would be said, to 'divide' the traffic carried. 1879 H. George *Progr. & Pov.* III. iii. (1881) 166 It is this general averaging, or as we may say, 'pooling' of advantages, which necessarily takes place. 1884 *Pall Mall G.* 2 Aug. 5/1 The arrangement for 'pooling' the Continental traffic of the two companies to Folkestone. 1895 *Westm. Gaz.* 25 Sept. 1/3 The endowed funds of the Church ought to be pooled, equalised, and redistributed according to the work done.

Hence **Pooled** *ppl. a.*; **Pooling** *vbl. sb.*

1884 *American* VII. 229 A pooling combination to regulate prices. 1884 *Pall Mall G.* 30 Apr. 11/1, I don't think this pooling of the [railway] rates will stand. 1888 *Ibid.* 21 Jan. 2/2 Negotiations..with a view of extending the pooled area. 1892 *Nation* (N.Y.) 15 Dec. 446/1 The repeal of the section of the law prohibiting railway pooling.

Pool, dial. f. Pull *v.* **Pool, poole**, obs. ff. Pole, Poll. **Pooler**, var. Poler (sense 1). **Pool-hole**: see Pool *v.*[1] 2.

Pooly (pū·li), *a.* [f. Pool *sb.*[1] + -y.] Resembling a pool; abounding in pools; swampy.

1821 Joanna Baillie *Metr. Leg.*, *Wallace* viii, As angler in the pooly wave. 1822 *Blackw. Mag.* XI. 181 The water struggled onwards through narrow gullets, boiling caldrons, and pooly whirls.

Pooly, obs. f. Pulley. **Poomel**, obs. f. Pommel. **Poomgarnet, -gernett**, obs. ff. Pomegranate. **Poompe**, obs. f. Pump.

‖ **Poon** (pūn). Also 7 **pone**, 9 **puhn, puna, poona, -ay.** [Singhalese *pūna*, Tamil *punnai.*] One of several large East Indian trees of the genus *Calophyllum*, esp. *C. Inophyllum*; also, the timber furnished by these trees, used for masts and spars, and for building purposes. Chiefly *attrib.*, as *poon-mast, -spar, -tree, -wood*; poon-oil, a dark-green thick oil, having a strong scent and bitter taste, expressed from the seeds of *C. Inophyllum* (poon-seed), used in medicine and for burning in lamps.

1699 Dampier *Voy.* II. I. 64 For Masting, the Fir and Pone Trees are the best. 1727 A. Hamilton *New Acc. E. Ind.* I. xxii. 264 There is good Poon Masts, stronger, but heavier than Fir. 1840 *Encycl. Brit.* (ed. 7) XXI. 300/2 Poon is also of two kinds, the dark and the light. It is a wood that answers very well for masts...The Malacca red poon is that of which masts and yards are made. 1858 Simmonds *Dict. Trade*, *Poon-wood*, an Indian wood, .. used for ship-building, for planks, and also for spars. 1880 C. R. Markham *Peruv. Bark* 377 The poon trees .. are chiefly found in Coorg.

‖ **Poonac** (pū·næk). [Tamil *Punnakku*, Singhalese *Punakku.*] The oil-cake or mass left after the oil has been expressed from coco-nut pulp: used as fodder or manure.

1890 in Webster. 1895 in *Funk's Stand. Dict.*

Poonah (pū·nă). Name of an Indian city in the Bombay Presidency; *attrib.* in **Poonah painting**, an artistic process in imitation of oriental work, in which pictures of flowers, birds, etc. were produced on rice (or other thin) paper, by the application of thick body-colour, with little or no shading, and without background: fashionable in England in the early part of the 19th c. So **Poonah brush**, a stumpy round-headed brush used for this; **Poonah paper**, the paper on which it was done; **Poonah-painted** *a.*; **Poonah painter.** (See *N. & Q.* 10th s. VII. 107, 152.)

1821 *Examiner* 272/2 The Poonah taught in a superior style. Ladies instructed in the above Elegant Art. 1822–3 *Pigot & Co.'s Directory*, Cheltenham .. Stanton Mrs., Indian poonah painter, 21 Bath Street. 1829 *Yng. Lady's Bk.* 469 A piece of tracing-paper, of a peculiar manufacture, which is sold at the stationers' shops as Poonah-paper. 1840 Thackeray *Paris Sk.-bk.* (1869) 253 What are called 'mezzotinto' pencil-drawings, 'poonah paintings', and what not. 1859 Sala *Tw. round Clock* (1861) 179 Two pairs of silver grape-scissors, a poonah-painted screen, a papier-mâche work-box. 1889 *Anthony's Photogr. Bull.* II. 48 It may be applied by using a strong hog hair or poonah brush charged with vermilion.

Poonahlite (pū·nălait). *Min.* Also **poona-, punah-.** [f. *Poonah* (*Púna*) in India, where found + -lite.] A variety of Scolecite from Poonah.

1831 H. J. Brooke in *Philos. Mag.* Ser. II. X. 110 *Poonahlite* .. a beautiful variety of apophyllite from Poonah, .. accompanied by some slender crystals, which I at first supposed were mesotype or needle-stone, but which differ from both substances in measurement; the *Poonahlite* being a rhombic prism of 92° 20′. 1866 Watts *Dict. Chem.* IV. 689 Poonahlite. *Ibid.* Index, *Punahlite.*

Poond, -e, obs. ff. Pond, Pound (an enclosure).

‖ **Poonga-oil** (pū·ngă,oil). [f. Tamil *punga* or Malayal(an) *pungam*, name of the plant.] A dark-yellow oil expressed from the seeds of the Kurung, *Pongamia glabra*, and used in India as lamp-oil and as a remedy in skin-diseases; Kurung oil.

1866 *Treas. Bot.* 919/1 In India an oil, called Kurunj, or Poonga oil, is expressed from the seeds. 1890 Billings *Med. Dict.* II. 370/2 Poonga oil is in high repute in India as an application for scabies and other skin diseases.

‖ **Poonghie, phoongyee, phungyi** (pū·ŋgi, pɒ·ndgi). Forms: 8 **pongui**, 9 **phonghi, -gee, phoongee, -gye(e, poongee, -ghee, -ghie, -gy, -gyee.** [Burmese *hpōngyi*, f. *hpōn* glory, *kyi* great.] The name generally given in Burma to a Buddhist priest or monk. Also *attrib.*

1788 F. Magnus tr. *Sonnerat's Voy.* III. 17 Their Priests .. are called Ponguis, and are less informed than the Bramins. 1834 Bp. Bigandet in *Jrnl. Ind. Archip.* IV. 222–3 (Y.) The Talapoins are called by the Burmese Phonghis, which term means 'great glory'. 1879 F. Pollok *Sport Brit. Burmah* II. 7 The poonghee houses or monasteries are splendid. 1897 Ld. Roberts 41 *Yrs. India* lxvi. (1898) 518, I still hear occasionally from one or other of my Poonghie friends. 1899 F. T. Bullen *Log Sea-waif* 302 Yellow-garbed, close-shaven Phoongyees were squatting all over the pavement.

Poop (pūp), *sb.*[1] Forms: 5 **pouppe, pope, poppe**, 5–7 **powpe**, 6 **pupe, pewpe**, 6–7 **poup(e, poope, puppe, pup**, (7 **pub**), 7– **poop.** [ME. a. OF. *pupe, pope* (*c* 1400 in Godef. *Compl.*), F. *poupe* = It. *poppa*, Prov., Sp., Pg. *popa*:—late L. **puppa* for L. *puppis* poop, stern.]

1. The aftermost part of a ship; the stern; also, the aftermost and highest deck, often forming the roof of the cabin built in the stern.

1489 Caxton *Faytes of A.* II. ii. 93 The pouppe whiche is the hindermost partye of the shippe. 1495 *Naval Acc. Hen. VII* (1896) 195 In the poppe of the seid shipp. 1496 *Ibid.* 176 The dekke ovyr the somercastell & the pope. 1497 *Ibid.* 227 The powpe abaft. 1555 Eden *Decades* 203 The highest parte of the Castel of the poope. 1558 Phaer *Æneid* I. A ij b, There fell a sea that made the puppe to yelde. 1566 J. Partridge *Plasidas* 492 The lusty fish begin at paynted pupe to toy. 1573 Twyne *Æneid* X. E e j, She with right hand pup did shoue. 1581 J. Bell *Haddon's Answ. Osor.* 452 The chief prore and pewpe (as the Proverbe is) and shooteanker of their whole Idolatrous Sacrifice. 1606 Shaks. *Ant. & Cl.* II. ii. 197 The Poope was beaten Gold. 1643 Prynne *Sov. Power Parl.* App. 209 Those are equally safe who are in the fore part, as those who are in the puppe. 1674 tr. *Scheffer's Lapland* xxi. 101 Made in the fashion of half a boat having..the poupe of one flat board. 1704 J. Harris *Lex. Techn.* I, *Poop of a Ship*, is the Floor or Deck over the Round-house or Master's Cabbin, being the highest part or uppermost part of her Hull astern. 1776 Mickle tr. *Camoens' Lusiad* 53 High on the poop the skilful master stands. 1868 *Regul. & Ord. Army* § 1305 When the prisoners are on deck, the detachment of Troops is to be on the poop.

† b. *At poop, in (the, one's) poop*, of the wind: Astern. Hence *fig. Obs.*

1567 Golding *Ovid* XII. 148 b, The thousand shippes had wynd at poope. 1588 Hickock tr. *Frederick's Voy.* 31 They goe to Pegu, with the winde in powpe. 1598 Barckley *Felic. Man* (1631) 411 They continue with him so long as the wind bloweth in the poope. 1621 Molle *Camerar. Liv. Libr.* IV. ix. 255 When they saw the wind blew merrily in their poope. 1687 A. Lovell tr. *Thevenot's Trav.* I. 16 We bore away to the starboard..with a Wind in Poop.

c. *transf.* A cabin built on the after part of the quarter-deck; a round-house. *rare.*

1551 *Acts Privy Counc.* (1891) III. 257 The covering of clothe of golde belonging to the captaines cabane or powpe of the Gallie.

† 2. *transf.* The dickey or seat at the back of a coach; the hinder part of a man or animal, the posteriors, rump. *colloq.* or *vulgar. Obs.*

c 1614 Fletcher, etc. *Wit at Sev. Weap.* IV. i, If you.. meet a footman by the way, in orange-tawny ribbands, running before an empty coach, with a buzzard [the bare-headed lackey] i' th' poop on't. *c* 1645 Howell *Lett.* (1650) II. 25 She took a mouthfull of claret, and spouted it into the poope of the hollow bird. 1706 E. Ward *Wooden World Diss.* (1708) 96 While he manages his Whip-staff with one Hand, he scratches his Poop with the other.

3. *attrib.* and *Comb.*, as *poop-cabin, -deck, -end, -ladder, -rail, -staff*; **poop-lantern, -light**, a lantern or light carried at the stern to serve as a signal at night; **poop-royal**, the deck forming the roof of the poop-cabin; a top-gallant-poop.

1851 W. Colton *Deck & Port* i. 16 Another order soon came for the construction of a *poop-cabin. 1840 R. H. Dana *Bef. Mast* xvii, A large, clumsy ship,..with her top-masts stayed forward, and high *poop-deck. 1839 Marryat *Phant. Ship* x, Philip remained on deck by the *poop-ladder. 1727–41 Chambers *Cycl.* s. v. *Ship*, Plate, Hull .. *Poop Lanthorns. 1769 Falconer *Dict. Marine* (1789), *Aiguille de fanal*, an iron crank or brace, used to sustain the poop-lanthorn. 1836 E. Howard *R. Reefer* lvii, We carried .. the customary *poop-light of the commodore. 1867 Smyth *Sailor's Word-bk.*, **Poop-rails*, the stanchions and rail-work in front of the poop. 1769 Falconer *Dict. Marine* (1789), *Dunette sur Dunette*, the *poop-royal. 1800 *Naval Chron.* III. 274 The poop royal, in our present first rates is omitted. 1847 Grote *Greece* II. xxxvi. IV. 472 Kynegeirus..in laying hold on the *poop-staff of one of the vessels, had his hand cut off by an axe.

† **Poop** (pūp), *sb.*[2] *Obs.* Also 6 **poope.** [Echoic, or f. Poop *v.*[1] Cf. LG. *pup, pūp*, Du. *poep* crepitus ventris.] A short blast in a hollow tube, as a wind instrument; a toot; a gulping sound.

a 1553 Udall *Royster D.* II. i. (Arb.) 32 Then to our recorder with toodleloodle poope As the howlet out of the yuie bushe should hoope. *c* 1580 Jefferie *Bugbears* v. vii. in *Archiv Stud. Neu. Spr.* (1897), I taught them thier lerrie, and thier poop to, for their knacking. 1674 Ray *N. C. Words* 37 *Poops*, Gulps in drinking. 1772 *Ann. Reg.* 99/1 When this captain [frog] gives the signal for stopping, you hear a note like *poop* coming from him.

† **Poop**, *sb.*[3] *Obs.* In 6 pope, 7 poope. [Origin unascertained.] Some part of the furniture of a church bell: "perh. the 'stay' by which the swing of a bell is regulated, moving against the 'slider'" (*Gloss.* to work cited for quot. 1625).

1507–8 *Rec. St. Mary at Hill* 264 Item, payd for v bell popys for the bell Ropys xvd. 1625 *Churchw. Acc. St. Mary, Reading* (1893) 137 Paid for a board for the treble poope to save it 11 d. 1631 *Ibid.* 147 Paid to willis for poopes and strapes for the bell this yeire, 9s. 9d.

Poop (pūp), *v.*[1] Forms: 5 **poupe, powpe, pope**, 6– **poop**, (9 *dial.* **pup**). [ME. *poupen*, of echoic origin: cf. MLG., LG. *pūpen*, MDu., Du. *poepen.*] † *intr.* To make an abrupt sound as by blowing a horn; to blow, toot; to gulp in drinking.

c 1386 Chaucer *Nun's Pr. T.* 579 Of bras they broghten bemes and of box Of horn of boon in whiche they blewe and powped [*v.rr.* poupid, pouped, poped]. *c* 1386 — *Manciple's Prol.* 90 And whan he hadde pouped in this horn To the Manciple he took the gourde agayn. 1593 R. Barnes *Parthenophil & P.* Ode xi. in Arb. *Garner* V. 457 The Shepherds poopen in their pipe.

b. (See quots.) *dial.* and *vulgar.*

1721–36 Bailey, *To Poop*, to break Wind backwards softly. 1903 *Eng. Dial. Dict.*, Poop, *v.*, *Cacare*, used of and by children.

† **Poop**, *v.*[2] *Obs.* Forms: 6 **powp(e**, 6–7 **poup(e, poop(e.** [Of obscure derivation: cf. Du. *poep* a clown (Franck).] *trans.* To deceive, cheat, cozen, befool.

1575 *Gamm. Gurton* II. i, But there ich was powpte indeede. 1596 Nashe *Saffron Walden* 134 Wee shall.. trumpe and poope him well enough, if .. he will needes fall a comedizing it. 1608 Shaks. *Per.* IV. ii. 25, I, shee quickly poupt him, she made him roast-meate for wormes. *a* 1650 May *Satyr. Puppy* (1657) 26 My two Gallants, (being poopt of what they enjoyed meerly to feel misery in the losse). 1663 Dryden *Wild Gallant* IV. ii, Hee's poopt too.

Poop (pūp), *v.*[3] *Naut.* [f. Poop *sb.*[1]] *trans.* Of a wave: To break over the stern of (a vessel).

1748 *Anson's Voy.* III. ii. 319 A large tumbling swell threatened to poop us. 1769 Falconer *Dict. Marine* (1789) Llj b, The principal hazards incident to scudding are generally, a pooping sea; the difficulty of steering. 1836 Marryat *Midsh. Easy* xxvi, The frigate was pooped by a tremendous sea, which washed all those who did not hold on down into the waist.

b. *transf.* Of a ship: To receive (a wave) over the stern; to ship (a sea) on the poop.

1894 *Westm. Gaz.* 7 Dec. 5/1 An enormous wave was pooped which demolished the hatchways and flooded the hold with several feet of water. 1898 F. T. Bullen *Cruise Cachalot* xxviii, The supreme test .. is the length of time she will scud before a gale without 'pooping' a sea.

Poope, obs. f. Poop, Pope *sb.*[1]

Pooped (pūpt), *a.* [f. Poop *sb.*[1] + -ed[2].] Having a poop: chiefly in comb. as *high-pooped.*

1879 Beerbohm *Patagonia* i. 7 Magellan dropped anchor there, with his quaint, high-pooped craft. 1897 *Westm. Gaz.* 30 Dec. 1/3 There were soldier sentries .. ready to shoot from the pooped watch-tower [on a convict-ship].

Poope-holy, variant of Pope-holy *Obs.*

Poopet, obs form of Poppet.

† **Poo·p-noddy.** *Obs.* [? f. Poop *v.*[2], to cheat, cozen + Noddy, fool, simpleton, as if = cozen-the-simpleton.] ? = Cony-catcher, Cony-catching. Cf. Noddypoop.

1606 *Wily Beguiled* C j b, I am sure I saw them close together at Poop-noddie, in her Closet. 1616 J. Deacon *Tobacco Tortured* 57 Alas poore Tobacco..thou that hast bene hitherto accompted the Ale-knights armes, the Beere-brewers badge,..the Poope-noddies paramour, the Ruffians reflection.

Poor (pūᵊr), *a.* (*sb.*) Forms: α. 3–5 **pouere** (**povere**), 3–6 **pouer (pover)**, (4 **poeuere, poeure, pouir**), 4–5 **poer, powere**, 5 **poyr**, 5–6 **power**, (6 **poware**). β. 3–5 **poure**, 4–6 **powre, pour.** γ. 3–7 (–9 *dial.*) **pore**, 4–7 **poore**, (6) 7– **poor.** δ. *Sc.* and *north. dial.* 4–6 **pur**, 4–8 **pure**, (4 **puyre**, 5 **pwyr, poyr**, 6 **peur(e, pwir, puire**), 6– **puir**(ü), (9 **peer**). [ME. *pov(e)re, pouere, poure*, a. OF. *povre, -ere, poure*, in mod.F. *pauvre*, dial. *paure, pouvre, poure* = Pr. *paubre, paure*, It. *povero*, Sp., Pg. *pobre*:—L. *pauper*, late L. also *pauper-us*, poor. The mod.Eng. *poor* and Sc. *puir* represent the ME. *pōre*: with mod. vulgar *pore*, cf. *whore* and the pronunciation of *door, floor.*

On account of the ambiguity of the letter *u* and its variant *v* before 1600, it is uncertain whether ME. *pouere, poure, pouer*, meant *pou-* or *pov-*. The phonetic series *pauperem, paupre, paubre, pobre, povre*, shows that *povre* preceded *poure*, which may have been reached in late OF., and is the form in various mod.F. dialects. But the 15th and early 16th c. literary Fr. form was *povre*, artificially spelt in 15th c. *pauvre*, after L. *pauper*, and ME. *pōre* (the source of mod.Eng. *poor*) seems to have been reduced from *povre* like *o'er* from *over*, *lord* from *loverd*. Cf. also Poortith, Porail, Poverty. But some Eng. dialects now have *pour* (paur), which prob. represents ME. *pour* (pūr).]

A. Illustration of Forms.

α. *c* 1205 Lay. 22715 Riche men and pouere. *c* 1300 *Cursor M.* 19775 (Edin.) Wiþ pouir [*v. r.* pouer] widus umbisette. *c* 1375 *Sc. Leg. Saints* vi. (*Thomas*) 453 Vith powere folk. *c* 1380 Wyclif *Wks.* (1880) 69 Be þe peple neuere so poer. *c* 1380 — *Sel. Wks.* III. 518 Poeure nedy men. *c* 1440 *York Myst.* xli. 48 And yf so be that she be power [*rime* honoure]. 1434 Misyn *Mending Life* iii. 110 Blissyd be þai þat ar poyr in spirytt. 1540 *Test. Ebor.* (Surtees) VI. 108 My power frendes and neghbors. 1554–9 in *Songs & Ball.* (1860) 11 Uppone the poware commens.

β. *c* 1200 *Trin. Coll. Hom.* 47 Gif hie was poure. 13.. *Cursor M.* 4375 (Cott.) Leuer es me be pour [*v. rr.* pouer, pore] and lele. *c* 1489 Caxton *Sonnes of Aymon* iv. 117 The foure powre knyghtes. *Ibid.* xviii. 400 He lived like an heremyte a poure liffe. 1535 *Bury Wills* (Camden) 125 The helpe and socour of my pour soule.

γ. *c* 1275 Lay. 22715 Riche and pore. *a* 1400 *Prymer* (1891) 84 [Ps. xl. 17] Forsoþe y am a beggere and poore. 1475 *Bk. Noblesse* (Roxb.) 73 The pore comons. 1536 in *Lett. Suppress. Monasteries* (Camden) 132 Desyuryng you..to be good and gracyus lord unto me synful and poor creatur. 1592 C'tess Shrewsbury in Ellis *Orig. Lett.* Ser. II. III. 165 Against the pore chyld. 1611 Bible *Jas.* ii. 2 A poore man in vile raiment. 1629 Sir W. Mure *True Crucif.* 2587 In soule most pore [*rime* Ore]. 1650 Poor [see B. 1 c]. 1677 Lady Chaworth in *12th Rep. Hist. MSS. Comm.* App. v. 36 To honour my poore house.

δ. 1340 Hampole *Pr. Consc.* 500 Naked we come hider, and bare And pure. *c* 1375 *Sc. Leg. Saints* vi. (*Thomas*) 365 Puyre and riche men elyke. *c* 1470 Henry *Wallace* VIII. 467 Our rewme is pur, waistit be Sotheroun blud. 1483 *Cath. Angl.* 294/1 Pure (*A.* Pwyr). 1533 Gau *Richt Vay* 14 Thair pwir frendis. 1530 *Aberdeen Regr.* (1844) I. 165 Puyr boddeis. 1568 *Satir. Poems Reform.* xlvii. 82 Quhat cummer castis the formest stane..At tha peure winschis. 1802 R. Anderson *Cumberld. Ball.* 43 She..can always feel For peer fwok when distress.

B. Signification.

I. 1. Having few, or no, material possessions; wanting means to procure the comforts, or the necessaries, of life; needy, indigent, destitute; *spec.* (esp. in legal use) so destitute as to be dependent upon gifts or allowances for subsistence. In common use expressing various degrees, from absolute want to straitened circumstances or limited means relatively to station, as 'a poor gentleman', 'a poor professional man, clergyman, scholar, clerk', etc. The opposite of *rich*, or *wealthy*. *Poor people*, the poor as a class: often with connotation of humble rank or station.

c 1200 [see A. β]. *a* 1240 *Sawles Warde* in *Cott. Hom.* 261 Ich iseh þe apostles poure ant lah on eorðe. 13.. *Cursor M.* 13312 (Cott.) To petre þat he pouerest fand, Of all he mad him mast weldand. 1390 Gower *Conf.* III. 155 He wiste wel his pours was povere. 1432–50 tr. *Higden* (Rolls) V. 7 The son of a pover wedowe. 1547–8 in E. Green *Somerset Chantries* (1888) 12 Ther is within the saide paryshe a house of poore people, callyd the spitle howse. 1605 Shaks. *Lear* I. iv. 21 If thou be'st as poore for a subiect, as hee's for a King, thou art poore enough. 1665 Brathwait *Comment Two Tales* 8 This *Poor* hath been an Epithete for Scholars in all Ages. *a* 1687 Petty *Pol. Arith.* Pref., The whole Kingdom grows every day poorer and poorer. 1789 W. Buchan *Dom. Med.* (1790) 23 Mothers of the poorer sort. 1847 C. Bronte *J. Eyre* iv, They are almost like poor people's children!

b. In proverbial comparisons: see Church-mouse, Job *sb.*[4] 1, Rat *sb.*[1] 2 c.

1390 Gower *Conf.* II. 211 To ben for evere til I deie As povere as Job. 1533, etc. [see Job *sb.*[4] 1]. 1782 Miss Burney *Cecilia* IX. iv, See, he's as poor as a rat. 1900 Weyman *Sophia* v, All as poor as rats, and no one better than the other.

c. Of, involving, or characterized by poverty.

13.. *Cursor M.* 13272 (Cott.) Mene men o pour lijf [*Fairf.* men of pouer lode]. *c* 1380 Wyclif *Sel. Wks.* III. 518 Crist wiþ his apostlis lyvede most povere lif. 1650 Fuller *Pisgah* II. vi. 143 Here he [Christ]..had his poor and painfull education, working on his Fathers trade. *a* 1661 — *Worthies* (1662) I. 57 Forced..to take..poor and painful Employments for their Livelyhood. 1816 Scott *Antiq.* xxvii, I'm sorry to see ye in sic a peer state, man.

d. *fig.* (or in generalized sense).

c 1325 *Spec. Gy Warw.* 164 Þouh man haue muche katel .. 3it he may be pore of mod And low of herte. 1390 Gower *Conf.* II. 128 So is he povere, and everemore Him lacketh that he hath ynowh. *c* 1400 Maundev. (Roxb.) xi. 48 Blissed be þai þat er pouer in spirit. 1867 Jean Ingelow *Regret* 12 They are poor That have lost nothing; they are poorer far Who, losing, have forgotten. 1876 C. D. Warner *Wint. Nile* ii. 33 People are poor in proportion as their wants are not gratified.

2. Lacking, ill supplied; having a want or deficiency of some specified (or implied) possession or quality: const. † *of* (obs.), *in.*

1377 Langl. *P. Pl.* B. XIII. 301 Pore of possessioun in purse and in coffre. 1393 *Ibid.* C. XVII. 161 He þat haþ londe and lordshep,..Shal be pourest of power at hus partyng hennes. 14.. *Tundale's Vis.* 22 He hadde ynow3 of all rychesse, But he was pore of all godenesse. 1581 Marbeck *Bk. of Notes* 717 So long as God is not poore of mercie, so long cannot I be poore of merite. 1638 Baker tr. *Balzac's Lett.* (vol. II.) 30 They that are poore in reputation ought to presse up to the trenches. 1842 Macaulay in Trevelyan *Life & Lett.* (1876) II. ix. 109 The English language is not so poor but [etc.]. 1853 E. V. Neale *Anal. Th. & Nat.* 157 Stratified masses, rich in organic remains, though poor in mineral substances.

b. Of soil, ore, etc.: Yielding little, unproductive.

1592 Nashe *P. Penilesse* (Shaks. Soc.) 32 Onely poore England giues him bread for his cake. 1600 E. Blount tr. *Conestaggio* 30 All other delights that poore Iland coulde yeelde. 1604 E. G[rimstone] *D'Acosta's Hist. Indies* IV. v. 218 They cal that [ore] poore which yields least silver. 1765 A. Dickson *Treat. Agric.* (ed. 2) 475 The poor clays require such manures as contain the greatest plenty of the vegetable food. 1813 Sir H. Davy *Agric. Chem.* (1814) 192 Poor and hungry soils. 1877 Raymond *Statist. Mines & Mining* 385 The poor slag contains about 7 ounces of silver and a trace of gold. It is too poor to treat, and is thrown away.

3. In lean or feeble condition from ill feeding.

1539 Bible (Great) *Gen.* xli. 19 Seuen other kyne .. poore [Coverd. thynne] and very euell fauored and leane fleshed. 1600 Holland *Livy* XXI. xl. 415 Their horses, no other than lame jades and poore hidebound hildings. 1697 Dryden *Virg. Georg.* III. 321 Before his Training, keep him poor and low. 1716 Swift *Progr. Poetry* Wks. 1755 III. II. 161 Cackling shews the goose is poor. 1887 Rider Haggard *Jess* xxxi, The horse perished, as 'poor' horses are apt to do.

† b. Out of health, unwell: = Poorly *a. Obs.*

1758 L. Lyon in *Milit. Jrnls.* (1855) 15 Corperal Carpenter was taken poor. *Ibid.* 25 This day at night Leiut. Smith came back and very poor he was. 1758 S. Thompson *Diary* (1896) 12 Our men are very poor, and we scarce could get men for work or for guard.

4. Small in amount; less than is wanted or expected; scanty, insufficient, inadequate.

a 1225 *Ancr. R.* 114 Hwar was euer iȝiuen to eni blodletunge so poure pitaunce? 13.. *Cursor M.* 11307 (Cott.) Pouer gift can sco for him giue þat com in pouert for to liue. 1535 Stewart *Cron. Scot.* (Rolls) II. 239 Schir Modred, his power wes so puir, Into the feild no langar micht induir. 1585 T. Washington tr. *Nicholay's Voy.* I. xv. 16 b, By reason of the poore treasure of the religious.. [the place] coulde not haue bin fortified. 1652 Needham tr. *Selden's Mare Cl.* 493 Every man and maid servant, or Orphan, having any poor stock may venture the same in their Fishing-voiages. 1703 Rowe *Ulyss.* II. i. 850 Death is too poor a Name, for that means Rest. 1849 Macaulay *Hist. Eng.* iii. I. 314 The crop of wheat would be thought poor if it did not exceed twelve millions of quarters.

b. Depreciatively, with a numeral, connoting the smallness of the number or sum.

1596 Shaks. 1 *Hen. IV*, III. iii. 180 One poore peny-worth of Sugar-candie. 1600 — *A. Y. L.* I. i. 2 It was..bequeathed me by will, but poore a thousand Crownes. 1712 Arbuthnot *John Bull* IV. ii, What are twenty-two poor years towards the finishing a Lawsuit? 1737 Bracken *Farriery Impr.* (1757) II. 11 All..he had wagered was poor Thirteen-Pence. 1759 Sterne *Tr. Shandy* II. viii, It is but poor eight miles from Shandy-Hall. 1819 Keats *Isabella* xxvi, A poor three hours' absence.

5. Deficient in the proper or desired quality; of little excellence or value; not worth much; of inferior quality, paltry, 'sorry'; mean, shabby. Usually of abstract things: in reference to material objects, often approaching 1 c.

a 1300 *Cursor M.* 14869 Þis folk.. O littel wijt, o pour resun. 1432–50 tr. *Higden* (Rolls) I. 71 After some men of pover and breve intellecte, and also of lytelle experience. 1551 T. Wilson *Logike* (1580) 62 b, Although it be a poore helpe. 1624 Capt. Smith *Virginia* 51 Such poore bridges, onely made of a few cratches thrust in the o[o]se, and three or four poles laid on them. 1714–15 Hearne *Collect.* (O.H.S.) V. 37 'Twas a poor Discourse. 1719 De Foe *Crusoe* (1840) II. xiii. 264 They made but poor work of it. 1777 Burke *Corr.* (1844) II. 149 The House never made so poor a figure as in the debate on that bill. 1843 Mrs. Carlyle *Lett.* (1883) I. 252 Seditious cries will make a poor battle against cannon. 1888 Bryce *Amer. Commw.* II. lii. 301 The poor paving of the streets and their lack of cleanliness. *Mod.* It was poor consolation to me to know [etc.].

b. Mentally or morally inferior; mean-spirited, sneaking; paltry, despicable, 'small'; wanting in courage, spiritless.

1425 *Paston Lett.* I. 19 So fals, and so pouere,—but he was nevere of my kyn. 1611 Tourneur *Ath. Trag.* II. v, A poore spirit is poorer than a poore purse. 1627 tr. *Bacon's Life & Death* (1651) 17 A Man of a poore Minde, and not valiant. 1685 Earl of Rochester *Valentinian* v. ii, Shall I grow then so poor as to repent? 1796 Nelson in Nicolas *Disp.* (1846) VII. p. lxxxviii, He is a poor creature and more of a Genoese than an Englishman. 1882 Stevenson *New Arab. Nts.*, *Rajah's Diamond*, He seemed altogether a poor and debile being. 1884 *St. James' Gaz.* 12 Jan. 3/1 From the intellectual point of view, there could not be a poorer creature.

c. Slight, insignificant, of little consequence.

1603 Knolles *Hist. Turks* (1621) 1 The glorious Empire of the Turkes,.. hath .. nothing in it more wonderfull or strange, than the poore beginning of itself. 1721 Strype *Eccl. Mem.* III. iv. 38 Henry Earl of Surrey .. for .. the poor crime of assuming somewhat into his coat of arms, was actually beheaded. 1903 Myers *Hum. Personality* I. Each one of those great sciences was in its dim and poor beginning.

d. In modest or apologetic use, said depreciatively of oneself, one's performance, or something belonging to or offered by oneself: Of little worth or pretension; humble, lowly, insignificant.

1423 Jas. I *Kingis Q.* xcix, Vnto 3oure grace lat now ben acceptable My pure request. ? *a* 1500 *Chester Pl.* (E.E.T.S.) 250 Well is me that I may se thy face, here in my house, this poore place! 1585 T. Washington tr. *Nicholay's Voy.* Ep. Ded., To exclude olde men .. is (in my poore conceipt) palpable erronious. 1602 Shaks. *Ham.* I. v. 131 For mine owne poore part, Looke you, Ile goe pray. 1605 Camden *Rem.* Ded. 1 This silly pittifull, and poore Treatise. *a* 1745 Swift (J.), To be without power or distinction, is not, in my poor opinion, a very amiable situation to a person of title. 1814 Wordsw. *Excurs.* III. 118 If from my poor retirement ye had gone Leaving this nook unvisited.

6. Such, or so circumstanced, as to excite one's compassion or pity; unfortunate, hapless. Now chiefly *colloq.*

In many parts of England regularly said of the dead whom one knew; = late, deceased.

c 1275 Lay. 15421 To 3am saide þo þer þe pore king Vortiger. 1390 Gower *Conf.* III. 296 This yonge lord..Al naked in a povere plit. *c* 1400 *Destr. Troy* 9596 Then Deffibus..Pletid vnto Paris with a pore voise. 1484 Caxton *Fables of Æsop* I. iv, Thus was the poure sheep vaynquysshed. 1513 More *Rich. III* in Grafton *Chron.* (1568) II. 776 Going her waye, leaving the poore innocent childe weeping as fast as the mother. *a* 1568 Ascham *Scholem.* (Arb.) 113 If Osorius would leaue of..his ouer rancke rayling against poore Luther. 1577 B. Googe *Heresbach's Husb.* II. (1586) 85 Betwixt the Oke and it [the Olive] there is great hatred .. though you cut downe the Oke, yet the very Rootes poysoneth and killeth the poore Oliue. 1691 J. Wilson *Belphegor* v. iii, Poor comfortless Woman; she's fall'n asleep at last. 1787 Mme. D'Arblay *Diary* 26 Feb., Till his [Boswell's] book of poor Dr. Johnson's life is finished and published. 1834 Medwin *Angler in Wales* II. 347, I often think of poor Leyden's lines. 1857 Mrs. Carlyle *Lett.* (1883) II. 330 He looked dreadfully weak still, poor fellow! 1870 E. Peacock *Ralf Skirl.* III. 82 The poor thing had fallen asleep also. 1886 Elworthy *W. Somerset Word-bk.* s.v., People who are dead are always spoken of as *poor* so-and-so..'You mind the poor old Farmer Follett, that's th' old Farmer George's father you know'. 1887 *How to Make a Saint* viii. 114–15 In common parlance the word 'poor' had by general consent been prefixed to the names of the dead in this country...[They] had been in the habit of speaking of their departed friends as 'poor So-and-so'. *Oxford boatman.* 'When my poor dad was ferryman here'.

II. 7. *absol.* or as *sb.* (almost always in sense 1).

a. *absol.* in *pl.* sense (usually with *the*): poor people as a class; those in necessitous or humble circumstances (often contrasted with *the rich*); *spec.* those dependent upon charitable or parochial relief; paupers.

a 1225 *Leg. Kath.* 50 Poure ba & riche comen þer to-foren him. *c* 1230 *Hali Meid.* 9 Hwen þus is of þe riche, hwat wenes tu of the poure? 13.. *Cursor M.* 4707 Þe wrecche pouer [*Gött.* þe wrecched pore] moght find na fode. 1375 Barbour *Bruce* I. 276 Bath pur, and thai off hey parage. *c* 1475 *Litt. Red Bk. Bristol* (1900) I. 141 Aswell to the power as to the riche. 1526 Tindale *Mark* xiv. 5 It myght have been soolde for more then two houndred pens, and bene geven vnto the povre. 1560 Daus tr. *Sleidane's Comm.* 47 b, Colledges and such other places were fyrst founded for the pore. 1621 Fletcher *Pilgrim* I. i, What poor attend my charity to-day, wench? *a* 1687 Petty *Pol. Arith.* (1690) 80 The poor of France have generally less Wages than in England. 1750 Gray *Elegy* viii, The short and simple annals of the poor. 1795 Burke *Th. Scarcity* Wks. VII. 377 Nothing can be so base and so wicked as the political canting language, 'The labouring poor'. 1864 Tennyson *Northern Farmer, New Style* xii, Taäke my word for it, Sammy, the poor in a loomp is bad. *Mod.* Money left to the poor of the parish.

† b. *sing.* = poor man, poor person. (In quot. 13.., in sense 5 d.) *Obs.*

13.. *E. E. Allit. P.* B. 615 Passe neuer fro þi pouere, 3if I hit pray durst, Er þou haf biden with þi burne & vnder boȝe restted. *c* 1400 *Rom. Rose* 5601 But the povre that recchith nought, Save of his lyflode, in his thought. 1484 Caxton *Fables of Alfonce* iii, I byleue not that this poure may be maculed ne gylty of the blame. *c* 1500 Kennedy *Passion of Christ* 480 Thoucht now I stand dispitit as a pure. 1625 Jackson *Creed* v. xvi. § 6 He had given somewhat to every poore in the Parish.

† c. *sb. pl.* poors. *Obs.*

[1343 *Rolls of Parlt.* II. 136/2 La Lei eit owel Cours entre Poures & Riches.] 1483 Caxton *G. de la Tour* I iv b, Who that receyueth the prophetes the predycatours and the poures he receyueth my owne self. 1556 Lauder *Tractate* 336 Quhilk nother techis ryche nor puris. 15.. *Burgh Rec. Glasgow* I. 395 (Jam. *Suppl.*) Sua that the gude toun nor nane resortand thairto sall be trublit with thair puris.

d. possessive *poor's* (in sing. or pl. sense). Now *rare* exc. *dial.*

c 1412 Hoccleve *De Reg. Princ.* 4893 Þat your hye dygnite.. No desdein haue of þe pores sentence. *a* 1425 *Cursor M.* 19766 (Trin.) To sewe þe pores clo[þing. *a* 1656 Hales *Gold. Rem.* III. *Serm.*, etc. (1673) 16 It is the poors money, and the Talent of thy Lord which thou hidest under the ground. 1844 A. Page *Suppl. Kirby's Suffolk Trav.* 799 The poor's estate comprises a cottage .. and 13 A. 3 R. 7 P. of land. *Sc. dial.* She is now in the Poor's-house.

III. Combinations and Phrases.

8. Qualifying a sb. in special collocations: **poor child**, a pupil at a charity school (Child *sb.* 4); **poor Clares**, an order of nuns (see Clare); **poor debtor** (see Debtor 1 c); **poor preachers, poor priests**, an order of itinerant preaching clergy founded by Wyclif; **poor relation**, a relative or kinsman in humble circumstances (also *transf.*); † **poor Robin** *sb.*, an almanack (from the title of *Poor Robin's Almanack*, first published in 1661 or 1662); *v. intr.* (with *it*), to play the part of 'poor Robin' (? in allusion to *Poor Robin's Jests*, *c* 1669, or one of various works with similar titles); **poor vicar** (see Vicar); **poor white** (see White *sb.*). See also Poor John, Poor man.

1706 'Poor children [see Child *sb.* 4]. 1714 J. Walker *Suff. Clergy* II. 214/2 Educated at Queen's-College in Oxford; where he became successively Poor Child, Taberder, Fellow and Proctor. *c* 1380 in *Wyclif's Wks.* (1880) 245 (*title*) Whi *pore prestis han none benefice. *Ibid.* 248 3it bou3 pore prestis my3ten freliche geten presentacion of lordis to haue benefices wiþ cure of soulis. 1880 F. D. Matthew *ibid.* Pref. 16 Wyclif's aim in instituting the poor priests was to supply the defects of the existing parsons, who too often, after collecting their tithes and dues,..left their flock without preaching or spiritual instruction. 1804 Coleridge *Lett.* II. 475 You sometimes see thirty or forty together of these our *poor relations [monkeys]. 1823 Lamb *Elia* Ser. II. *Poor Relations*, A Poor Relation—is the most irrelevant thing in nature,—a piece of impertinent correspondency,—an odious approximation,—a haunting conscience,—a preposterous shadow, lengthening in the noontide of your prosperity. 1898 *Westm. Gaz.* 16 July 2/1 The discarded ones [clothes]..were not sold. They were bestowed on the Poor Relation. 1682 T. Flatman *Heraclitus Ridens* No. 82 (1713) II. 251, I never *Poor-Robin'd it, I never fasten'd upon any notorious Servant of the City, the Name of Sir Thomas Creswel, upon the score of any private Immoralities. 1716 *Gentlem. Instructed* (ed. 6) 120, She discern'd .. a Feast from a Feria, without the Help of poor Robin.

9. General Combs. a. Attributive (from the absol. or sb. use), Of or for the poor, as *poor-hour, -money, -relief, -school.* b. Objective, as *poor-bettering, -feeding* adjs. c. Parasynthetic and adverbial, as *poor-blooded, -charactered, -clad, -looking, -minded, -sighted* adjs.

1818 Bentham *Ch. Eng.* 90 *note*, The objection, urged against that system.., in the name of the *Poor-bettering Society. 1889 W. F. Rae *Austrian Health Resorts* 71 *Poor-blooded patients may indulge in a little old red wine. 1654 Gataker *Disc. Apol.* 80 He might produce.. a *poor Charactered man, to do something for them. *a* 1586 Sidney *Arcadia* (1622) 82 To heare The *poore-clad truth of loues wrong-ordred lot. 1908 *Westm. Gaz.* 6 Dec. 7/1 Shivering, starving, poor-clad men and boys. 1657 J. Watts *Vind. Ch. Eng.* 265 Is it not to deal our bread unto the hungry, etc., *poor-feeding fasts? 1897 H. Drummond *Ideal Life* 68 The soul-sick had to take their turn like the out-patients at the *poor-hour outside the infirmary. 1622 Dekker & Massinger *Virgin Martyr* II. i, To..give your *poor-minded rascally servants the lie! 1796 J. Benson in *Mem.* (1822) 295 The choice of stewards to manage the *poor-money. 1898 *Dublin Rev.* Jan. 131 Questions of property, capital, labour, and *poor-relief. 1857 G. Oliver *Collect. Hist. Cath. Relig.* in *Cornwall*, etc. 427 He established a *poor-school on the premises. 1901 *Westm. Gaz.* 10 Dec. 3/2 In the poor-schools where the bairns get more warmth .. than anywhere else. 1898 J. D. Rees in *19th Cent.* June 1023 These beasts [elephants] are very *poor sighted, though their noses are extremely good.

10. Special Combs.: † **poor and rich**, name of some game; **poor-chest** = Poor-box; **poor-farm** (*U. S.*), 'a farm maintained at public expense for the housing and support of paupers' (*Cent. Dict.*); **poor-fellow** *v. trans.* (*nonce-wd.*), to address commiseratingly as 'poor fellow' (cf. 6); **poor-master** (*U. S.*), a parish or county officer who superintends the relief and maintenance of paupers; † **poor-tax** (also *poor's tax*), a tax for the relief of the poor, a poor-rate; **poor-thing** *v. trans.* (*nonce-wd.*), to speak of or address as 'poor thing' (cf. *poor-fellow*). See also Poor-book, -box, etc.

1621 J. Taylor (Water P.) *Motto* D iv, At Nouum, Mumchance, mischance,..or at *Poore and rich. 1618 W. Parkes *Curtaine-Dr.* (1876) 67 Hadst thou a gainefull hand a rich *poore-chest. 1889 G. Huntington in *Chicago Advance* 31 Jan., Now don't *poor-fellow me, or imagine that I find life a bore. 1883 *American* VI. 40 When he spares both undertaker and *poor-master further trouble. 18.. *Amer. Mission.* XXXIX. 8 (Cent.) The Agent of the United States to the Sioux Indians was to act as a sort of national poor-master, and deal out rations. 1721 Berkeley *Prev. Ruin Gt. Brit.* Wks. 1871 III. 298 If the *poor-tax..was fixed at a medium in every parish. 1793 *Friendly Address to Poor* 3 The Poor's Tax is much increased in every part of the kingdom. 1860 *New Virginians* II. 9 In my inexperience I '*poor thinged' her from the bottom of my heart.

Poor, *v.* Forms: see prec. adj. [f. Poor *a.* Cf. OF. *pouverir* to impoverish (Froissart).]

† 1. *intr.* To become poor. *Obs. rare.*

c 1375 *Digby MS.* 86 lf. 126/1 Now þou art riche, and now þou pouerest [*rime* couerest].

† 2. *trans.* To make poor, impoverish. *Obs.*

c 1380 Wyclif *Sel. Wks.* I. 216 Þus ben lordis and rewmes poorid. *c* 1450 in *3rd Rep. Hist. MSS. Comm.* (1872) 280/2 Thus is he riched, the kynge pouered. *c* 1470 Henry *Wallace* XI. 43 This land is purd off fud that suld ws beild. *a* 1500 *Priests of Peblis* in Pinkerton *Scot. Poems* (1792) I. 14 Your tennants..ar puird: And, quhan that thay ar puird, than are ye pure.

3. To call 'poor' (Poor *a.* 6). *nonce-use.*

1865 Dickens *Mut. Fr.* I. iv, Miss Lavinia .. put in that she didn't want to be 'poored by pa', or anybody else. 1868 Helps *Realmah* viii. (1869) 227 Don't 'poor' me, Sir. Nobody ever 'poored' me before.

† **Poo·rable**, *a. Obs. rare*[−1]. In 6 **pooreable.** [Anomalous f. Poor *a.* + -able.] Able through poverty, poor enough.

1570 Levins *Manip.* Ep. Ded., His [Huloet's Dict.] is great & costly, this is little & of light price, his for greter students, & them yᵗ are richable to haue it, this is for beginners, & them that are pooreable to haue no better.

† **Poora·lity.** *Obs. rare*[−1]. [f. Poor *a.*, app. after *commonality.*] The poor (collectively).

1536 *Petit. Lincoln Rebels to Hen. VIII* (P. R. O.), Whereby..the pooralitie of your Realme be vnreleuyd.

Pooranic, Pooraun: see Puranic, Purana.

Poorblind, obs. form of Purblind.

† **Poo·r-book.** *Obs.* Also 7 **poor's-book.** A book containing a list of the poor in receipt of parish relief.

1681 [see *poll-book*, Poll *sb.*[1] 10]. 1682 Luttrell *Brief Rel.* (1857) I. 165 Such poor people who goe to conventicles, and not to their parish churches, shall be putt out of the poors book, and have no parish collections. 1819 *Sporting Mag.* IV. 274 It [a parish meeting] was called for the inspection of our poor-book.

Poo·r-box. Also 7–9 **poor's box.** A money-box (esp. in a church) for gifts towards the relief of the poor. Cf. *poor man's box*, Poor man 4.

1621 B. Jonson *Gipsies Metamorph.* Wks. (Rtldg.) 624/2 On Sundays you rob the poor's box with your tabor. 1662 Pepys *Diary* 5 Mar., To the pewterer's, to buy a poore's box, to put my forfeits in, upon breach of my late vows. 1708 *Diss. on Drunkenness* 27 Overseers go to the Tavern and get drunk with the Poor's Box. 1777 Sheridan *Sch. Scand.* II. ii, She draws her mouth till it .. resembles the aperture of a poor's-box. 1851 Mayhew *Lond. Labour* II. 76/2 The magistrates..gave me 2s. out of the poor's-box. 1852 Hook *Ch. Dict.* (1871) 591 In Ireland the Poor Man's Box, or 'poor-box', as it is generally called, is still in use. It is an oval box, half-covered, of copper or wood, with a long handle.

Poorche, obs. f. Porch. **Poore**, obs. f. Pore, Pour, Power; var. Porr *v. Obs.* **Poore-blind**, obs. f. Purblind. **Poorety**, obs. f. Poverty.

† **Poo·rful**, *a. Obs.* In 4 **porful.** [irreg. f. Poor *a.* + -ful. Cf. *direful, fierceful.*] Poor; thoroughly poor.

13.. *Pol. Rel. & L. Poems* 226 Iesu, swete son dere! On porful bed list þou here, And þat me greueþ sore.

Poorge, obs. form of Purge.

† **Poo·rhead.** *Obs.* In 4 **poure-, pouerehede.** [f. Poor *a.* + *hede*, -head.] The condition of being poor; poverty.

1340 *Ayenb.* 130 Huanne þe man..onderstant and knawþ his pourehede, þe vilhede, þe brotelhede of his beringe. *Ibid.* 138 Þe guodes þet byeþ in guode pouerehede.

Poorhouse (pūᵊ·rhaus). A house in which poor people in receipt of public charity are lodged; a workhouse.

1782 *Phil. Trans.* LXXII. 376 Examination of the Poorhouse at Heckingham. 1821 Byron *Occas. Pieces*, *Irish Avatar* xix, And a palace bestow for a poor-house and prison! 1894 Baring-Gould *Kitty Alone* II. 74 The parish officers would interfere, and carry her off to the poor-house.

Poo·rify, *v. nonce-wd.* [f. Poor *a.* + -[i]fy (with pun on *purify*).] *trans.* To make poor.

1711 *Countrey-Man's Let. to Curat* 6 That Prince seem'd calculat rather for Poorifying (pardon the Clench) than Purifying the Church.

Poorish (pūᵊ·riʃ), *a.* [f. as prec. + -ish[1].] Somewhat poor, rather poor (in various senses).

1657 in R. Potts *Liber Cantabr.* (1855) 408 Born of poorish parents. 1766 J. Bartram *Jrnl.* 9 Jan. in W. Stork *Acc. E. Florida* 29 Generally poorish land. 1801 Charlotte Smith *Lett. Solit. Wand.* I. 34 His honour is living, though in a poorish state of health. 1884 H. Collingwood *Under Meteor Flag* 236 It's poorish weather for a fight, I'll allow.

† **Poor-Jack.** *Obs.* = next, 1. Cf. Jack[1] 30 d.

c 1682 J. Collins *Salt & Fishery* 93 The sort of Cod that is caught near the Shore, and on the Coast of Newfoundland and dryed, is called Poor-Jack. 1775 R. Twiss *Trav. Spain & Port.* 267 Salt bacallão, which is like the fish called poor-jack.

Poor Jo·hn, poo·r-john. [f. Poor *a.* + proper name John: cf. prec.]

1. A name for hake (or ? other fish) salted and dried for food; often a type of poor fare. ? *Obs.* exc. *Hist.*

c 1585 T. Cates *Drake's Voy. W. Indies* in *Hakluyt's Voy.* (1905) X. 100 In this ship was great store of dry Newland fish, commonly called with us Poore John. 1592 Shaks. *Rom. & Jul.* I. i. 37. *a* 1612 Harington *Epigr.* II. I, Poore-Iohn, and Apple-pyes are all our fare. 1657 R. Ligon *Barbadoes* (1673) 113 Two barrels of salt Fish, and 500 poor-Johns, which we have from New England. 1695 Congreve *Love for L.* II. vii, I warrant nou he'd rather eat a Pheasant, than a Piece of poor John. 1769 Pennant *Zool.* III. 157 When cured it [the hake] is known by the name of Poor John. 1841 *Mann. & Househ. Exp.* (Roxb.) p. xlii, Salted cod, and hake or Poor John, had been in long esteem as Lenten food.

† b. Applied to a person. *Obs.*

1589 *Pappe w. Hatchet* 29 It is your poore Johns, that with your painted consciences haue coloured the religion of diuers.

2. Name for some sea bird. ? *Obs.*

1775 Dalrymple in *Phil. Trans.* LXVIII. 399 A. M. saw a bird like a booby, but shorter winged and necked, called by sailors, poor John. 1778 *Ibid.* 404 Saw several poor Johns, some sheerwaters, and a young alcatrass.

Poork, Poork poynt, obs. ff. Pork, Porcupine.

Poor-law (pūᵊ·r,lǭ). The law, or system of laws, relating to the support of paupers at the public expense.

1752 T. Alcock (*title*) Observations on the Defects of the Poor Laws. [1758 J. Massie *Plan for Charity-Houses* (title-p.), Considerations relating to the Poor and the Poor's-Laws of England.] 1764 R. Burn (*title*) The History of the Poor Laws. 1818 Cobbett *Pol. Reg.* XXXIII. 165 In these documents..the calamities of the nation have..been traced back to the Poor-Laws. 1838 Lytton *Alice* II. vii, The abuses of the old poor-laws were rife in his neighbourhood.

b. *attrib.*, as *poor-law bill, officer, system*, etc.; **poor-law parish**: see Parish *sb.* 2.

1835 Marryat *Olla Podr.* xi, How the new Poor Law Bill will work remains to be proved. 1857 Kingsley *Two Y. Ago* viii, In the present dependent condition of poor-law medical officers.

Hence **Poo·r-lawism** (*nonce-wd.*), the framing and practical application of poor-laws.

1858 S. G. Osborne in *Times* 12 Nov. 7/4 Something more was wanted than stringent poorlawism.

Poo·rless, *a. rare.* [See -less.] Free from poor people.

1778 *Eng. Gazetteer* (ed. 2) s. v. *Wimborn*, When Harley is hareless, Cranborn whoreless, and Wimborn poorless, the world will be at an end.

Poorliness: see after Poorly *a.*

† **Poo·rling.** *Obs. rare.* [f. Poor *a.* + -ling[1] 1.] A child of poverty, one of the poor.

1581 Mulcaster *Positions* xxxvii. (1887) 147 Be there not as vntoward poorelinges, as there be wanton wealthlinges?

Poorly (pūᵊ·ɹli), *adv.* and *a.* [f. Poor *a.* + -ly[2].] In a poor manner or condition.

A. *adv.* 1. In a state of poverty or indigence; indigently, necessitously. Now somewhat *rare.*

c 1386 Chaucer *Clerk's T.* 157 Poureliche yfostred vp was she. 1483 Caxton *Cato* D iij, Bycause that nature hath created the pourly & al naked. 1588 Greene *Perimedes* 31 Poorely content is better then richlye couetous. 1698 Fryer *Acc. E. India & P.* 121 The Banyans that live poorly and meanly. 1876 S. C. J. Ingham *White Cross* xxxvii, I will use all these ill-gotten gains in doing good, while I live poorly myself.

2. With deficiency of supply, or of some desirable quality; scantily, inadequately, insufficiently, imperfectly, defectively; in mean style, in lowly guise, humbly; in an inferior way, not well, rather badly, with no great success; not highly, with low estimation.

c 1300 *Havelok* 323 And ther-hinne dede hire fede Pourelike in feble wede. *c* 1386 Chaucer *Knt.'s T.* 554 Oonly a Squier..Which was disgised pourely as he was. 1483 Caxton *G. de la Tour* H ij b, The poure wymmen that lay pourely in theyr childbedde. 1552 Latimer *Serm. Luke* ii. 6–7 Rem. (Parker Soc.) 98 His first coming is but very poorly, without any jollity or pomp. 1626 Bacon *Sylva* § 669 If you sow one ground still with..the same kind of grain, as wheat, barley, &c. it will prosper but poorly. *a* 1715 Burnet *Own Time* IV. an. 1686 (1823) III. 98 Their books were poorly but insolently writ. 1748 *Anson's Voy.* III. iii. 320 They knew how poorly she was manned and provided for struggling with so tempestuous a gale. 1823 Southey *Hist. Penins. War* I. 772 From the beginning Sir John Moore had thought..poorly of the Spaniards. 1840 Dickens *Barn. Rudge* iii, Long lines of poorly-lighted streets. 1883 Mrs. F. Mann *Parish of Hilby* xviii. 219 Even now the wives and children came but poorly off.

b. Often with ppl. adj. (to which, when used *attrib.*, it is properly hyphened).

1877 Black *Green Past.* v, A spacious, poorly-furnished chamber. 1894 Sir E. Sullivan *Woman* 19 Male births are more numerous than female births amongst the poorly-fed of the country. 1897 *Westm. Gaz.* 10 Dec. 4/3 The best modes of dealing with poorly-gifted children.

† 3. In a way unworthy of one's position; unhandsomely, meanly, shabbily. *Obs.*

13.. *St. Gregory* (Vernon MS.) 579 Þe penaunt porliche he gret [*Cotton MS.* Gregori wiþ scorn he gret]. 1666 Pepys *Diary* 6 Aug., They told me how poorly my Lord carried himself the other day to his kinswoman, Mrs. Howard, and was displeased because she called him uncle. 1676 Dryden *Aurengz.* v. i, The Gods have poorly robb'd my Virgin Bloom. 1680 Otway *Orphan* II. vii. 738 'Twas poorly done, unworthy of your self. 1723 Steele *Consc. Lovers* II. i, A Man, who poorly left me, to marry an Estate.

4. Piteously, abjectly, humbly; despicably, contemptibly: mean-spiritedly, without courage.

1525 Ld. Berners *Froiss.* II. cxiii. [cix.] 326 To put hymselfe poorely, without any reseruacyon into his obeysaunce and commaundement. 1535 Stewart *Cron. Scot.* (Rolls) I. 64 Out throw the thrang rycht puirlie he flaw. 1649 Milton *Eikon.* xxviii, To set free the minds of Englishmen from longing to return poorly under that captivity of Kings. 1664 Pepys *Diary* 24 Dec., He, instead of opposing..did poorly go on board himself, to ask what De Ruyter would have. *a* 1811 Leyden *Lord Soulis* Poet. Wks. (1875) 82 Young Branxholm peeped, and puirly spake, 'Oh, sic a death is no for me!'

B. *adj.* Chiefly *colloq.* [app. evolved from the *adv.*, through such a use as *to look poorly*: cf. *to look ill.*] In a poor state of health; somewhat ill; unwell, indisposed. (Always *predicative.*)

[1573 Tusser *Husb.* (1878) 79 Some cattle waxe faint, and looke poorely and thin.] 1750 B. Lynde *Diary* (1880) 171 All summer I complaining and poorly, and my eyes troublesome. 1756 Toldervy *Hist. 2 Orphans* III. 201 This quotation caused even Mrs. Nightley to laugh, tho' she was but poorly. 1797 J. Benson in *Mem.* (1822) 304, I have been rather poorly today. 1855 Macaulay *Hist. Eng.* XX. IV. 530 His wife had..been poorly.

Hence **Poo·rliness**, the condition of being poorly; **Poo·rlyish** *a.*, somewhat poorly. Both *rare.*

1847 J. J. Gurney in Braithwaite *Mem.* (1854) I. 323 Notwithstanding my poorliness. 1827 Lamb *Let. to Barton* 28 Aug., I am but poorlyish, and feel myself writing a dull letter.

Poor man.

1. *lit.* A man who is poor (in any sense of the adj.); *esp.* a man who is indigent or needy, or who belongs to the class of the poor.

a 1225 *Ancr. R.* 86 Ase þe þe seið to þe knihte þet robbeð his poure men. *a* 1350 *Cursor M.* 10386 (Gött) To godd he gaue þe lambis to lottis, And to þe pore men þe bole stottis. *c* 1400 Maundev. (Roxb.) xxii. 101 In þat land es na beggar, ne na pouer man. *c* 1450 in Parker *Dom. Archit.* III. 82 Be hit distributed & deportyd to poure men, beggers, syke folke & febell. 1677 Yarranton *Eng. Improv.* 169 But the poor Man is forced many times to buy his Materials he makes his Commodity with, of some of his own Trade.

2. Applied in Banffsh., Aberdeensh., etc., with the local pronunciation *peerman* (pī·rmăn), to a rude device for holding a fir-candle (i.e. a splinter of resinous wood), formerly the ordinary source of artificial light in farm-houses, barns, and cottages. In the times of licensed mendicancy, the duty of holding and attending to the fir-candle was usually imposed upon the 'bedesman' or vagrant 'poor man', who was granted a night's shelter; and it is generally believed that from him the name *peer-man* passed to the mechanical holder.

1866 Gregor *Dialect of Banffsh.* 123 *Peer-man*, a candle-stick for candles made of bog-fir..with a cleft piece of iron into which the candle was fixed. 1870 — *Echo of Olden Time* 20 Light was given either by pieces of bog-fir laid on the fire, or by *fir-can'les*, that is thin splinters of bog-fir, from one to two and a half or three feet long, fixed in a sort of candle-stick called the *peer-man* or *peer-page*. 1880–83 J. Linn in *Trans. Inverness Scientific Soc.* II. 342 It was from this [employment of a mendicant] that the stand on which the fir-candle..was fixed..got its name Peer-Man, Pure-Man, or Puir-Man, these being local pronunciations of Poor Man.

3. *Poor man of mutton* (Sc. colloq.): name for the remains of a shoulder of mutton, consisting mainly of the blade bone, broiled.

1818 Scott *Br. Lamm.* xix, I should like well..to return to my sowens and my poor-man-of-mutton. *Ibid.* (note), I think, landlord..I could eat a morsel of a poor man.

4. Combs. with *poor man's* (or *poor men's*): † **poor man's (men's) box** = Poor-box (*obs.*); **poor man's** Mustard, Parmacety, Pepper, Plaster, Treacle (see these words); **poor man's remedy**, local name for wild valerian, *Valeriana officinalis*; **poor man's salve**, local name for *Scrophularia nodosa* and *S. aquatica* (Britten & Holl.); **poor man's sauce**: see quot.; **poor man's weather-glass**, the pimpernel, *Anagallis arvensis*, from its closing its flowers before rain.

1548–9 (Mar.) *Bk. Com. Prayer*, *Communion*, So many as are disposed, shall offer vnto the *poore mennes boxe. 1560 Daus tr. *Sleidane's Comm.* 70 The rest to be geven to the poore mens boxe. 1657 W. Coles *Adam in Eden* 220 Of Valerian... They never make any pottage or broath for any one that is sick, but they put some of this Herb therein, be the disease what it will, and is called of them, The **Poor Mans Remedy.* 1706 Phillips, **Poor-man's Sauce* or *Carrier's Sauce*, Sauce made of a Shalot, cut very small, with Salt, white Pepper, Vinegar and Oil. 1847 *Nat. Cycl.* I. 661 The Pimpernel, or '*Poor Man's Weather-Glass', so called because its flowers..refuse to expand in rainy weather.

Poorness (pūᵊ·ɹnès). [f. Poor *a.* + -ness.] The quality or condition of being poor; poverty.

† 1. Want of wealth or possessions; indigence. *Obs.* (Now replaced by Poverty.)

c 1275 *Sinners Beware* 113 in *O. E. Misc.* 75 Þe poure may wel mysse Bute he his pouernesse Mid mylde heorte þolye. 1382 Wyclif 1 *Chron.* xxii. 14 Loo! I in my lytyl pornesse haue mad redy before the expenses of the hous of the Lord. *c* 1450 *Godstow Reg.* 71 For powrenesse of his vicariage. 1613 Chapman *Revenge Bussy D'Ambois* I. i, See how small cause..the most poore man [has] to be grieu'd with poorenesse. *a* 1661 Fuller *Worthies* (1662) I. 11 Which See,.. for the poorness thereof, lay Bishopless for three years.

b. *fig.* (Cf. Poor *a.* 1 d.)

1380 *Lay Folks Catech.* 1265 (Lamb. MS.) To schew hem meknesse and porenesse to stoppe pride. 1786 A. Maclean *Christ's Commission* iii. (1846) 129 [The Gospel] enjoins poorness of Spirit.

2. Deficiency in some good constituent; unproductiveness; leanness or want of vigour caused by ill feeding; thinness, scantiness, insufficiency.

1577 B. Googe *Heresbach's Husb.* III. (1586) 142 b, Lacke of good feeding, whereof proceedeth poorenesse, and of poorenesse, skabbes and manginesse. 1626 Bacon *Sylva* § 665 The Poornesse of the Herbs..shew the Poornesse of the Earth. 1782 H. Watson in *Med. Commun.* (1784) I. 89 From the poorness of the blood contained in its vessels. 1883 *Contemp. Rev.* June 904 Exhausted from poorness of diet.

3. Deficiency in some desirable quality; smallness of worth; inferiority, paltriness, meanness. Also (with *pl.*) an instance of this, a paltry or inferior piece of work.

1628 Wither *Brit. Rememb.* v. 1493 Let none the poorenesse of my gifts deride. 1712 Addison *Spect.* No. 285 ¶ 4 Ovid and Lucan have many Poornesses of Expression upon this Account. 1884 *Law Times* 29 Nov. 73/2 The poorness of the accommodation provided for the judges.

b. Want of spirit or courage; paltriness or meanness of character or conduct.

1625 Bacon *Ess.*, *Simulation* (Arb.) 507 A Habit of Dissimulation, is a Hinderance, and a Poorenesse. *a* 1716 South *Serm.* (1744) X. 226 Those indeed .. would, no question, account all refusal of a duel poorness and pusillanimity. 1822 C. Wells *Stories after Nat.* 99 The duke unhorsed the lady, chiding Alfred for his poorness.

Poo·r-rate. Also 8–9 **poor's rate.** A rate or assessment, for the relief or support of the poor.

1602 *Acc. Bk. W. Wray* in *Antiquary* XXXII. 80, ixs. xd...for the pur rait mony. 1782 Miss Burney *Cecilia* IX. iv, I pay the poor's rate, and that's what I call charity enough for any man. 1797 *Monthly Mag.* III. 74 The exorbitant poor-rates with which the public there have been burthened for some time past. 1817 Byron *Beppo* xlix, Poor's rate, Reform, my own, the nation's debt. 1863 H. Cox *Instit.* III. ix. 730 Householders..paying poor-rates and borough-rates.

Poo·r-spi·rited, *a.* Having or showing a poor spirit (cf. quot. 1611 s. v. Poor *a.* 5 b); † having a paltry spirit, low-minded (*obs.*); deficient in spirit or courage, cowardly.

1670 G. H. *Hist. Cardinals* II. II. 170 Certain pittifull and poor-spirited reasons. 1710 Norris *Chr. Prud.* viii. 363 That sottish and poor-spirited Vice, the Vice of Covetousness. 1749 Fielding *Tom Jones* III. v, Master Blifil was generally called a sneaking rascal, a poor-spirited wretch, with other epithets of the like kind. 1860 Geo. Eliot *Mill on Fl.* III. i, Mr. Tulliver would never have asked anything from so poor-spirited a fellow for himself.

Hence **Poo·r-spi·ritedness.**

1662 Gurnall *Chr. in Arm.* verse 19. xiii. § 2 (1669) 515/2 Ye that think it childish and poor-spiritedness to weep at a Sermon. 1898 R. F. Horton *Commandm. Jesus* iv. 50 He does not praise poverty as such, still less does He refer to what we mean by poor-spiritedness.

‖ **Poort** (pōᵊrt). *S. Afr.* [Du. *poort* (pōrt) gate, Port *sb.*[2], in S. Africa, a pass.] A mountain pass.

1834 Pringle *Afr. Sk.* ii. 149 We entered the poort, or gorge of the mountains, through which the River of Baboons issues. 1850 R. G. Cumming *Hunter's Life S. Afr.* (ed. 2) I. 45 This poort, or mountain pass, the terror of waggon-drivers. 1894 B. Mitford *R. Fanning's Quest* xxii, A poort is a pass or defile as distinct from a kloof.

Poort, Poort colyce, obs. ff. Port, Portcullis.

Poortith (pūᵊ·ɹtiþ). *Sc.* and *north. dial.* Forms: 6 **purteth, puirteith**, 6– **puirtith**, 8– **poortith.** [a. OF. *pouer-, poverteit* (12th c. in Littré), *povretet* (1329 in Godef. *Compl.*), *poevreteit* (1466 Ibid.), *povretez* (pl. of *-tet*, 15th c. Ibid.):— L. *paupertāt-em*, accus. of *paupertās* Poverty. The examples cited show the OF. form in *-tet*, surviving almost to the date of the Sc. examples in *-teth.*] The condition of being poor; poverty.

1508 Dunbar *Flyting* 118 Bot now, in winter, for purteth thow art traikit. 1567 *Gude & Godlie B.* (S.T.S.) 73 Extreme puirteith, nor greit ryches, Thow gif me not. 1721 Ramsay *Prospect of Plenty* 199 Curs'd poortith! love and hymen's deadly fae. 1786 Burns *Twa Dogs* 104 They're no sae wretched's ane wad think, Tho' constantly on poortith's brink. *a* 1839 Praed *How Poetry is best paid for* i, Though sorrow reign within his heart, And poortith hold his purse. [In E. D. D. from Shetland to Northumbld. and Cumbld.]

Poorty: see Poverty.

Poo·r-will. [So named in imitation of its disyllabic note: cf. Whip-poor-will.] A bird of the N. American genus *Phalænoptilus*, esp. *P. nuttalli*, common in the Western United States.

1888 Roosevelt in *Century Mag.* Mar. 664/2 At nightfall the poor-wills begin to utter their boding call from the wooded ravines back in the hills; not 'whip-poor-will', as in the East, but with two syllables only. *Ibid.*, A poor-will lit on the floor beside me.

Poory, Poose, Poost, obs. ff. Pory *a.*, Pose, Post. **Pooste**, var. Poustie, power.

Poot (put), *sb.*[1] Now chiefly *north.* A dial. form of Poult, applied not only to chickens and young game birds, but to the young of various other animals, e. g. a small haddock, a young trout.

(In the latter application some would refer it to OE. *pūta* in *ǣle-pūta* eel-pout.)

1512 *Will of J. Barlowe* (Somerset Ho.), Fur of fox pootes. 1616 Surfl. & Markh. *Country Farme* 679 Partridge, pheasant, quaile, raile, poots, and such like. 1688 R. Holme *Armoury* II. 311/1 A Cock [is called] first a Peep, then a Chicken, then a Poot. 1697 *Phil. Trans.* XIX. 573 Found them as big as Poot-Eggs. 1825 Jamieson, *Poot*, this seems to be the same with *Pout*, used to denote a small haddock, *Fife.* 1828 *Craven Gloss.* (ed. 2), *Poot*, a young growse or moor poot. 1890 J. Service *Thir Notandums* i. 5 The lambin' o' the yowes, the cleckin' o' the poots.

Poot, *sb.*[2] *Obs.* [A variant of Pote *sb.*[1]: cf. *poot* Pote *v.*] A stirring rod: see quot.

1683 Moxon *Mech. Exerc.*, *Printing* xviii. ¶ 2 A long strong round Iron Stirring Poot; the Handle of which Stirring Poot is also about two Yards long or more, and the Poot it self almost twice the length of the depth of the Melting Pot.

Poot, poote, var. Pote *v.*; obs. or dial. f. Put *v.*

† **Pooter.** *Obs. rare.* [f. *poot*, Pote *v.* + -er[1].] = Poting-stick, or Poking-stick.

1602 Warner *Alb. Eng.* IX. xlvii. 218 Busks, Perrewigs, Maskes, Plumes of feathers fram'd, Supporters, Posters, Fardingales aboue the Loynes to waire, That be she near so bomle-thin, yet she crosse-like seem's four-squaire.

Poother, obs. or dial. f. Pother, Powder.

Pop (pɒp), *sb.*[1] Forms: see Pop *v.*[1] [Onomatopœic: goes with Pop *v.*[1]]

1. An act of popping. a. A blow, knock, stroke, slap; now, a slight rap or tap. *Obs.* exc. *dial.*

c 1400 *Laud Troy Bk.* 4421 Philomene..3aff him certes suche a poppe, That he fel ouer his hors croppe. *Ibid.* 9300 He hadde lau3t many a pop, For ther was many a strok 3euen. 1483 *Cath. Angl.* 286/2 A Poppe; vbi a strake. 1825 Jamieson, *Pap, pawp*, a blow, a thwack. *Aberd.* 1857 G. Outram *Lyrics* (1887) 137 Ilka pap wi' the shool on the tap o' the mool.

† b. A humorous remark, a joke; cf. Crack *sb.* 5. *Obs. rare.*

a 1550 *Image Hypocr.* I. 51 in *Skelton's Wks.* (1843) II. 420 With your mery poppes: Thus youe make vs sottes, And play with vs boopepe.

2. A short abrupt sound of explosion.

1591 Percivall *Sp. Dict.*, *Buchete*, the cheeke and a pop with the mouth. 1634 T. Johnson tr. *Parey's Wks.* 629 By the only regresse of the extended muscles into themselves.. somewhiles with a noyse or pop. 1855 Chamier *My Travels* II. vi. 91 The common pops of the squibs and crackers. 1876 Geo. Eliot *Dan. Der.* xxxix, I cannot bear people to keep their minds bottled up for the sake of letting them off with a pop.

b. The moment occupied by a pop; *at a pop*, in one instant, suddenly. *dial.* [cf. F. *tout à coup, tout d'un coup.*]

1534 More *Comf. agst. Trib.* II. Wks. 1202/2 At a poppe, down they descende into hell. 1847–78 Halliwell, *Pop*, a short space. *Lanc.* 1903 in *Eng. Dial. Dict.*

3. A shot with a fire-arm. Also *fig.*

Pop (pɒp), *sb.*[2] [app. short for POPPET or POPLET. Cf. also *dim.* F. *poupée*, *poupine*, a pretty little woman (see POPPET).] A term of endearment for a girl or woman; darling; also, a mistress, a kept woman.

Pop (pɒp), *sb.*[3] A local name of the Redwing (*Turdus iliacus*).

Pop (pɒp), *sb.*[4] A colloquial abbreviation of *popular concert*: see POP *sb.*[1]

Hence *Pop*pite, a performer at, or a frequenter of, the popular concerts.

Pop, *sb.*[5] [Said to be so called from L. *popina*, *cook-shop*; the rooms having been orig. in the house of Mrs. Hatton, who kept such a shop'.] At Eton College. The name of a social club and debating society; founded in 1811.

Pop (pɒp), *adv.*[1] Also 5-7 *poppe*, 7-8 *popp*, 9 *dial. pap*, *pawp.* [Onomatopœic: goes with POP *sb.*[1], *int.*, *adv.*]

8. *intr.* To pass, move, go or come promptly, suddenly, unexpectedly (*up*, *down*, *in*, *out*, *between*, etc.).

Pop, *int.* [Cf. POP *v.*1, *adv.*] Usually the verb in combination with a *sb.* or *adv.*, meaning something that pops, or that which pops in some way; rarely the *sb.* or *adv.*: pop-dock, pop-glove, pop-gun (*Digitalis purpurea*); pop-eye, an out-starting, bulging, prominent eye; hence pop-eyed *a.*; pop-in, a drink composed of beer into which a small proportion of whisky or brandy is 'popped'; † pop-mouth, a mouth able to utter an exclamation with a sharp outburst; pop-off, the discharge of fire-arms; pop-out, the act of popping out, as when a cork is drawn; pop-shooter = POPGUNNER; pop-valve = POPPET-VALVE; pop-weed, a provincial name of the Bladderwort.

Popadam (pɒˈpædəm). Also papadom, pappadom. [Tamil *paṭpaḍam*, contr. from *parappu-adam* 'lentil cake' (Vule).] (See quots.)

† Popal, *a.* *Obs. rare*—[1]. [f. POPE + -AL.]

Popas *a.* So POPIAN *a.* = PAPIAN *d.*

Popcorn *U.S.* [f. POP *v.*3 + CORN *sb.*1 § 2: in orig. *popped corn*.] **a.** Maize or Indian corn parched till it bursts open and exposes the white inner part of the grain; 'popped' corn: see Pop *v.*3 § 3. **b.** A variety or sub-species of maize suitable for 'popping'. Also *attrib.*

Pope (pəʊp), *sb.*[1] Forms: 1, 2 *pápa*, 2-6 *pape*, 4-7 *sc. paip*(*e*, 6-7 *paipe*, 7 *sc. popp*, (3-7 POPE. [OE. *pápa*, a. eccl. L. *pápa* (in Juvenal *pāpas*), ad. late Gr. *πάπας*, *πάππας* 'father, bishop' (orig. a child's word) cf. PAPA.)

I. 1. The Bishop of Rome, as head of the Roman Catholic Church.

Pope (pəʊp), *sb.*[2] [f. prec.] **a.** A small blackish freshwater fish of the Perch family; the Ruff. **b.** The Puffin (*Fratercula arctica*). **c.** A bright-coloured American bird.

Pope, *v.* *Obs.* [f. POPE *sb.*1]

Popedomship. *Obs.*

† Popedom. *Obs.*

† Pope-holy, *a.* (*sb.*) *Obs.*

Pope Joan. [After the fabulous female pope Joan.]

Popekin (pəʊpkɪn). *contemptuous.* [See -KIN.] A little or petty pope.

† Popel. *Obs.* Also 4 *popelle*, -ill. *-elle*, 5 *-ell*, -il, -in. [Me. a. OF. *popele*, -ill. -ulle, 5 -elle, -in, -in. [a. of French squirrel.]

Popelican. *Obs.*

† Popelot. *Obs.* Also 4 *popelet*, 5 popelere.

Popelote (pɒpˈləʊt). *Obs. rare*—[1]. [perh. ad. OF. *popelote*.]

Popeler. *Obs.*

† Popeline. *Obs. rare.*

Popelot. *Obs.*

Popeling. *Obs.*

Popery (pəʊpərɪ). [f. POPE *sb.*1 + -ERY.]

Pope's eye.

Pope's head. [From its appearance.]

Pop-holy, variant of POPE-HOLY.

Popish (pəʊpɪʃ), *a.* [f. POPE *sb.*1 + -ISH.]

Popjoy (pɒpdʒɔɪ), *v.*

Popelote *Obs. rare.*

† Popelot *Obs.*

Popeship (pəʊpʃɪp).

† Popify, *v.* *Obs. rare.* [See -FY.]

† Popil, *a. or sb.*

Popinjay (pɒpɪndʒeɪ). Forms: see below. [a. OF. *papegai*, *papejai*, etc.]

Popish, a. [f. POPE sb.1 + -ISH.]
1. Of or pertaining to the pope: papal. Obs.
2. Of or pertaining to popery; or belonging to the Church of Rome (papistical. (In hostile use.)

Hence **Po·pishness**.

Popism (pǒ·piz'm), nonce-wd. [f. POPE + -ISM.]

Popishly, adv. [f. prec. + -LY.]

Popism (pǒ·piz'm), nonce-wd.

Popishness. Now rare. [f. POPISH + -NESS.]

Poplar (pǒ·plǎ). Forms: 4-5 poplere, 4-6 popler, 5 popeler, 5 poplar, 6- poplar.
1. A tree of the genus *Populus*, comprising large trees of rapid growth, natives of temperate regions.

Poplexy, **Poplar-tree**.

Poplin (pǒ·plin), sb.
A woollen or linen fabric in imitation of poplin.

Poplite, a. Obs. rare—1. [irreg. ad. mod.L. *poplites* = see below.]

Poplitead, a. ? Obs.

Poplitead, a. ? Obs.

Poplitic (pǒplī·tik), a. Anat.

Poplitic, **Poplite**.

Popliny, a. Obs. Chiefly Sc.

Poplitical, a. Obs. (erron. -et-).

Poplolly: see POPELY.

Poplot. Obs.

Poplin1 Obs. Also 8 poupelin.

Popify, v.

Poplitic, **Poplite**.

Popolino, sb. Obs. Also popolino.

Poppling.

Popper, v. Obs. rare—1.

Poppering. Obs.

Poppet: see POPPET.

Poppet (pǒ·pet), sb. Forms: 4-5 popet, 5 popett, 6 poppette, 6-8 poppet, 7, 6-9 poppet, 6- poppet.

Poppet-head. Also rarely puppet-head.

Poppied (pǒ·pid), ppl. a. [f. POPPY sb. + -ED2.]
1. Filled or adorned with poppies.

Poppin. Now dial. Also 5 popyn, 6 poppyn.

Popping, vbl. sb.1 [f. POP v.2 + -ING1.]
The action of POP v. in its various senses.

Popping, vbl. sb.2: see after POP v.2

Popple (pǒ·p'l), sb.1 Now dial. and U.S. Forms: (1 popul), 4-5 popil, 5 -ille, -ull, 5-6 popel, -yl(-1, 6-9 popple, 7- popple, (9 dial.)

Popple, sb.2 Now dial. Forms: 5 popel, 5-6 popil, 5-8 popill, 6 popple, 7 poppel, 9 dial.

Popple (pǒ·p'l), v.1 Also 4-6 (6- Sc.) popil.

Popping-crease. Cricket. [f. POPPING vbl. sb.]

Popple (pǒ·p'l), v.2

Poppy (pǒ·pi), sb. Forms: 1 papaeg, 2 popæg, 3 papig, 3-6 popy, 6-7 poppie, 6- poppy.

Poppy-head.

Poppycock. U.S. slang.

Poppy-seed.

Poppy-head.
1. The capsule of the poppy. Also attrib.

Populacy (pǒ·piulǎsi). [? f. POPULACE.]

Popple-wort, **Poppy-wort**.

Populace (pǒ·piulǎs). [a. F. populace (16th c. in Hatz.-Darm.), ad. It. popolaccio, popolazzo 'the grosse, base, vile, common people' (Florio), f. popolo PEOPLE + augm. suffix -accio, -azzo (-L. -aceus).]

Popp-shop. slang. A pawnbroker's shop. Also attrib.

Poppy, sb. app. a kind of nursery appellation for a girl.

Popular (pǒ·piulǎr), a. [ad. L. populāris, f. populus the people, nation, the public.]

Popular, *a.* (*sb.*) Forms: 5–7 popular, 6 *Sc.* -air, 7 -are, 6– popular. [ad. L. *populāri-s* adj. belonging to the people, f. *populus* people. So OF. *populaire*.]

1. *Law.* Affecting, concerning, or open to all or any of the people; public; esp. in *action popular*.

2. Of or pertaining to the common people, or the people as a whole as distinguished from any particular class; constituted or carried on by the people.

b. Of lowly birth; belonging to the commonalty or populace; plebeian. *Obs.*

c. Having characteristics attributed to the common people; low, vulgar, plebeian. *Obs.*

3. Full of people; populous; crowded. *Obs.*

4. Intended for or suited to ordinary people.

5. Studious of, or designed to gain, the favour of the common people.

6. Finding favour with or approved by the people; liked, beloved, or admired by the people, or by people generally.

7. Prevalent or current among, or accepted by, the people generally; common, general.

Popularity (ˌpɒpjʊˈlærɪti). [ad. F. *popularité* (15.. in Hatz.-Darm.), or ad. L. *populāritāt-em*.]

Popularize (ˈpɒpjʊləraɪz), *v.* [f. POPULAR + -IZE. So F. *populariser* (1798 in Dict. Acad.).]

Popularizer. One who popularizes.

Popularly, *adv.* [f. POPULAR + -LY[2].] In a popular manner.

Popularness, *rare.* [f. as prec. + -NESS.]

Populary, *Obs.* [f. L. *populāri-s*: see POPULAR and -ARY[2].]

Populate (ˈpɒpjʊleɪt), *v.* [f. L. late *populāt-* ppl. stem: see POPULATE.]

Population (ˌpɒpjʊˈleɪʃən). [ad. late L. *populātiōn-em* (Sedulius *c* 470) population, multitude.]

Populin (ˈpɒpjʊlɪn). *Chem.* [ad. F. *populine* (Braconnot 1831), f. L. *populus* poplar.]

Populism. [f. as next + -ISM.]

Populist (ˈpɒpjʊlɪst). [f. L. *populus* + -IST.] A member of the People's party.

Populous (ˈpɒpjʊləs), *a.* [ad. L. *populōs-us*, f. *populus* people.]

Populously, *adv.* [f. as prec. + -LY[2].]

Populousness. [f. as prec. + -NESS.] The state or condition of being populous; density of population.

Pop-value, -weed: see POP-.

Pop-visit. [f. POP *v.* + VISIT *sb.*]

Popybine, popyhe, popyn, popyon, popyr, obs. forms of POPINJAY.

Popylyon, variant of POPULEON *Obs.*

Por, var. PORR, a poker, a thrust.

Poraceous, obs. form of PORRACEOUS.

Porail, overwhelle. *Obs.* Forms: 4. 3 poureayl, 3-4 -ail(e, 4-5 -aile, -ayle.

Porate (ˈpɔəreɪt), *a. Zool.* [f. L. *pora* ridge + -ATE[2].] (See quot.) So **Porated** *a.*

Porcate (ˈpɔəkeɪt), *a.* vi. Porcate (Fervefort), ridged, formed in ridges.

Porcelain (ˈpɔəslɪn, -leɪn). Forms: 6 (6 porcellana, 6–7 porcellane, 7 -) porcelaine, (6–7 -ellan, -6–9 -cellaine, 7 -'cline), 8 -cellin, porcelain.

Porcelainize (ˈpɔəslɪnaɪz), *v.* [f. prec. + -IZE.]

Porcelainous (ˌpɔəsˈleɪnəs), *a.* Also 9 **-elanous.** [f. L. *porcellāna* PORCELAIN + -OUS.]

Porcelainy (ˈpɔəslɪnɪ), *a.* [f. as prec. + -Y[1].]

Porcelainite (ˌpɔəsˈleɪnaɪt). *Min.* Also **porcellanite.**

Porcellanous (pɔəˈsɛlənəs), *a.* Also -ious.

Porch (pɔətʃ). Also 3–7 porche, 4 poorche, 6 portche, 7 porth. [a. F. *porche*, :—L. *porticus.*]

Porcine (ˈpɔəsaɪn), *a.* [a. F. *porcin*, -e, or ad. L. *porcīn-us*, f. *porcus* swine.]

Porcipine, obs. form of PORCUPINE.

Porcula (ˈpɔəkjʊlə). [a. mod.L. dim. f. *porcus* swine.]

Porcules, -ier, obs. forms of PORTCULLIS.

Porcupine (ˈpɔəkjʊpaɪn), *sb.* Forms: see below.

1. A rodent quadruped of the genus *Hystrix*.

2. *fig.* Applied allusively to a person.

1594 ? GREENE *Selimus* Wks. (Grosart) XIV. 286 What are the vrchins crept out of their dens, Vnder the conduct of this porcupine? 1606 SHAKS. *Tr. & Cr.* II. i. 27 *Ther.* Thou art proclaim'd a foole... *Aia.* Do not Porpentine, do not; my fingers itch. 1861 FITZ-PATRICK *Life Doyle* (1880) II. 7 This letter to Lord Farnham drew forth a porcupine of pens.

†**3.** Name of a form in which meat was dressed.

1769 MRS. RAFFALD *Eng. Housekpr.* (1778) 89 To make a Porcupine of a Breast of Veal. *Ibid.* 299 To make a cold Porcupine of Beef.

4. Applied to machines or mechanical devices having numerous projecting spikes or teeth; *esp.* an apparatus for heckling flax, worsted, or cotton; a kind of masher used in brewing.

1869 W. MOLYNEUX *Burton-on-Trent* 243 *note*, At some of the breweries the porcupine is supplanted by an instrument known as Steele's Patent Mashing Machine. 1875 KNIGHT *Dict. Mech.*, *Porcupine*, a heckling apparatus for flax; or a cylindrical heckle for worsted yarn. 1891 R. MARSDEN *Cotton Spinning* (ed. 4) 87 The porcupine is another opener, whose chief difference from the willow [etc.].

5. a. = *Porcupine ant-eater*; **b.** = *Porcupine fish*: see 6.

1875 *Melbourne Spectator* 4 Sept. 213/2 The echidna, or native porcupine. 1888 GOODE *Amer. Fishes* 205 In this limpid pool were.. the angel-fish, the parrot fish,.. the porcupine.

6. *attrib.* and *Comb.*, as *porcupine mustachio*, *quill*, *skin*, *tribe*; *porcupine-backed*, *-like* adjs.; **porcupine ant-eater**, an Australian monotremate mammal (*Echidna hystrix*), having spines; **porcupine crab**, a Japanese crab (*Lithodes hystrix*), having spiny carapace and limbs; **porcupine disease**, a malformation of the skin characterized by the growth of spine-like projections (Billings *Med. Dict.*); **porcupine fish**, a fish having the skin covered with spines, as *Diodon hystrix*; a sea-porcupine; **porcupine grass**, name for (*a*) *Triodia irritans* and other species, of Australia, with stiff sharp-pointed leaves; (*b*) *Stipa spartea*, of the western U.S., with long stiff awns; hence **porcupine-grass ant**, an Australian ant (*Hypoclinia flavipes*) which makes its nest round the root of a species of porcupine grass (*Triodia pungens*); **porcupine hair** (*Path.*) = HYSTRICIASIS; **porcupine man** (*Path.*), a man affected with *porcupine disease*; **porcupine roller**, a roller in a spinning-machine, set with projecting spikes (cf. 4); **porcupine skin disease**, = *porcupine disease*; †**porcupine stone**, a hard concretion alleged to be found in the head or body of a porcupine; **porcupine teeth**, the teeth of a contrivance for carding wool; **porcupine-wood**, the wood of the coco palm, which when cut across shows variegated markings like those of a porcupine-quill.

1867 WOOD *Pop. Nat. Hist.* I. 247 Echidna or *Porcupine Ant-eater.—*Echidna Hystrix*. 1899 *Daily News* 10 Apr. 8/2 The duck-billed platypus and the porcupine ant-eater, two of the chief objects of the expedition. 1598 E. GILPIN *Skial.* (1878) 52 Gulfe-brested is he, silent, and profound *Porpentine backed, for he lies on thornes. 1681 GREW *Musæum* I. v. ii. 106 A sort of *Porcupine-Fish. 1773 *Gentl. Mag.* XLIII. 220 From these I will proceed to the exotics,.. the Porcupine Fish, the Porcupine Globe Fish, the Porcupine Bladder Fish. 1885 LADY BRASSEY *The Trades* 407 'Porcupine-fish' (*Chilomycterus reticulatus*), looking.. very much more like hedgehogs swimming about than porcupines. 1880 P. J. HOLDSWORTH *Station-hunting on Warrego*, Rough tufts of bristly grass.. stemmed like quills (and thence termed *porcupine). 1902 *Westm. Gaz.* 2 Apr. 10/2 The desert North of Lake Eyre, where the vegetation consists largely of porcupine grass—a serious obstacle to explorers and useless as fodder. 1822 GOOD *Study Med.* IV. 686 The hystriacis or *porcupine hair of Plenck. 1859 DARWIN *Orig. Spec.* vii. (1878) 201 Monstrosities, such as six-fingered men, *porcupine men. 1603 DEKKER *Wonderfull Yeare* B ij, The quills of his stiffe *Porcupine mustachio. 1664 POWER *Exp. Philos.* I. 5 Her body is.. stuck all over with great black Bristles, like *Porcupine quills, set all in parallel order. 1836 W. IRVING *Astoria* II. 51 A spear or bow decorated with beads, porcupine quills and painted feathers. 1884 W. S. B. MCLAREN *Spinning* (ed. 2) 107 A revolving brush, or star wheel, or *porcupine roller, is placed at H,.. which guides the fibres forward. 1809 A. HENRY *Trav.* 146 The fat of our deer was melted down, and the oil filled six *porcupine-skins. 1899 *Allbutt's Syst. Med.* VIII. 670 *Porcupine skin disease. 1676 *Phil. Trans.* XI. 757 There is another Stone, highly esteem'd, called the *Porcupine stone, which is in the head of this Animal, though sometimes also in its belly. 1845 *Specif. Lister's Patent* No. 11004. 2 Card, or what are known in the trade as '*porcupine teeth' are caused to operate upon wool to comb the same. 1857 HENFREY *Bot.* § 569 The wood of the Cocoa-nut Palms.. (*Porcupine-wood). 1887 MOLONEY *Forestry W. Afr.* 441 The wood is commercially known as Porcupine wood, and is used in India for rafters and ridge poles, house-posts,.. also for spear-handles, walking-sticks, and fancy work.

Hence **Po·rcupine** *v. trans.*, to make like a porcupine; to cause (the hair) to stand on end like a porcupine's quills; **Porcupinish, Po·rcupiny** *adjs.*, resembling or suggesting a porcupine.

1716 M. DAVIES *Athen. Brit.* II. 139 'Tis not call'd Declamation or Invective, or Satyr, but a certain Mediastin Genius, porcupin'd all over with all the three. 1827 *Mirror* II. 37/2 Pull your gills and porcupine your hair. 1829 SOUTHEY *Sir T. More* I. 15, I had now.. a distinct sense of that sort of porcupinish motion over the whole scalp which is so frequently described by the Latin poets. 1857 R. WILLIAMS *Rev. Bp. Ollivant's Charge* 60 You may goad any one, by three years of organised libelling, .. into a porcupinish method of expressing himself. 1890 *Sat. Rev.* 2 Aug. 151/1 A rather porcupiny, and not wholly consistent bundle [of prejudices].

Porcupisce, -pise, obs. forms of PORPOISE.

Porcyon(e, -oun, obs. forms of PORTION.

Pore (pōə̆ɹ), *sb.*[1] Forms: 4–6 **poore**, 6 **powre**, **poure**, 5– **pore**. [a. F. *pore* (*porre*, 1312 in Hatz.-Darm.) = Sp., It. *poro*, ad. L. *porus*, a. Gr. πόρος passage, pore.]

1. A minute opening, orifice, aperture, perforation, or hole (usually, one imperceptible to the unaided eye), through which fluids (rarely solid bodies) pass or may pass. **a.** In an animal body (or substance); esp. applied to those in the skin (the orifices of the ducts of the sweat-glands).

1387 TREVISA *Higden* (Rolls) I. 53 Þe contrarie is of norþeren men, in þe whiche colde wiþ oute stoppeþ smale holes and poorus, and holdeþ the hete wiþ ynne. 1422 tr. *Secreta Secret.*, *Priv. Priv.* 230 Men wyche haue the complexcion hote and stronge, and haue throgh al the body the ouertures large, that clerkys callyth Pores. 1563 HYLL *Art Garden.* (1593) 145 A stopping both of the vaines & poures. 1582 HESTER *Secr. Phiorav.* I. xv. 15 Those.. you shal washe with Aqua vitæ, because it openeth the powres. 1601 B. JONSON *Poetaster* Prol., A freezing sweate Flowes forth at all my pores. 1704 F. FULLER *Med. Gymn.* (1711) 5 A sudden Constriction of the Pores of the Skin. 1822–34 *Good's Study Med.* (ed. 4) I. 271 The articulations are long and narrow, with marginal pores by which it [tape-worm] attaches itself to the intestines. 1858 O. W. HOLMES *Aut. Breakf.-t.* xi, As a hide fills its pores lying seven years in a tan-pit.

b. *fig.* (and in *fig.* expressions), esp. in phrase *at every pore*.

1632 J. HAYWARD tr. *Biondi's Eromena* 53 Their rales.. penetrating through the pores of the heart, made themselves knowen. *a* 1720 SHEFFIELD (Dk. Buckhm.) *Wks.* (1753) I. 13 Love's pow'r can penetrate the hardest hearts; And through the closest pores a passage find. 1847 EMERSON *Repr. Men, Goethe* Wks. (Bohn) I. 388 He sees at every pore. 1865 DICKENS *Mut. Fr.* III. x, I see him chafe and fret at every pore.

c. In a plant (or vegetable substance); as the stomata in the epidermis of leaves, etc., or the small openings in certain anthers and capsules when ripe, for the discharge of the pollen or seeds.

1398 TREVISA *Barth. De P. R.* XVII. i. (Tollem. MS.), Tren wiþ þinne substaunce and nouȝt harde, but ful of holes, and poores. 1634 HABINGTON *Castara* (Arb.) 20 The flowers adore The Deity of her sex, and through each pore Breath forth her glories. 1712 tr. *Pomet's Hist. Drugs* I. 96 A Bark that is adorn'd with Pores like Stars. 1776 WITHERING *Brit. Plants* (1796) III. 761 Leaves.. transparent, with many minute pores. 1861 MISS PRATT *Flower. Pl.* IV. 88 Snapdragon.. capsule.. opening by pores at the top. 1873 E. SPON *Workshop Receipts* Ser. I. 16/1 This coat closes all the pores of the wood, and does not crack or scale off.

d. In inanimate bodies or substances; esp. applied to the minute interstices or spaces between the particles of matter.

1398 TREVISA *Barth. De P. R.* XIX. cxxx. (1495) nn iij/1 For shyrenesse of partyes in suche [*sc.* thynne matere] ben many poores. 1501 DOUGLAS *Pal. Hon.* I. xxvii, The eirth,.. with poris seir Vp drinkis air that mouit is be sound. *c* 1645 HOWELL *Lett.* I. vi. xxxv, The Sun, whose all-searching Beams penetrating the Pores of the Earth, do heat the Waters. 1660 BOYLE *New Exp. Phys. Mech.* xxi. 154 In the Pores or invisible little recesses of Water it self there lie.. many parcels.. of.. Air. 1706 PHILLIPS, *Pores*.. are small void Spaces between the Particles of Matter, of which all Bodies are made up. 1748 H. ELLIS *Hudson's Bay* 223 The Form or Essence of a Magnet.. is supposed to consist in it's being perforated by an infinite Number of parallel Pores. 1830 HERSCHEL *Stud. Nat. Phil.* III. i. 235 Water was forced through the pores (as was said) of a golden ball.

†**e.** In abstract or collective sense. *Obs. rare.*

1756 P. BROWNE *Jamaica* 50 The substances.. are seldom of a very strong texture, though frequently of a fine pore and smooth grain. 1773 HORSLEY in *Phil. Trans.* LXIV. 271 A large proportion of pore, or interspersed vacuity, is sufficient for all purposes.

†**2.** A passage, channel, canal, duct (esp. in an animal body). *Obs. rare.*

c 1400 *Destr. Troy* 8801 Þen [the balm] sewit furth soberly, & sanke fro aboue,.. Passond by poris into þe pure legges. 1541 R. COPLAND *Guydon's Quest. Chirurg.* N iv b, The wayes and poores wherby the vryne passeth from the reynes to the bladder. 1615 H. CROOKE *Body of Man* 138 But this pore of choler is inserted into the small guts, not at their beginning, least the Choler should flye vp into the stomack .. but into the end of the Duodenum.

3. A small point or dot resembling a pore.

1833 HERSCHEL *Astron.* v. 208 Its ground [sun's disk] is finely mottled with an appearance of minute, dark dots, or pores. 1869 PHIPSON tr. *Guillemin's Sun* (1870) 234 It explains neither the faculæ nor the pores nor the curious granulations known as 'willow-leaves'.

4. *attrib.* and *Comb.*, as *pore-area*, *-canal*, *-facet*; *pore-like* adj.; **pore-capsule**: see quot.; **pore-coral**, **pore-stone**, a stone-coral having pores; **pore-sieve**, name for some part of a sponge.

1880 *Nature* XXI. 450/1 Hollow spines with peculiar *pore-areas at their bases. 1878 BELL *Gegenbaur's Comp. Anat.* 111 The number of these *pore-canals (dermo-gastric pores), which have consequently a dermal and gastric orifice, is generally very great. 1877 A. W. BENNETT tr. *Thomé's Bot.* (ed. 6) 149 Some capsules again dehisce by pores, as the poppy.. when they are termed *pore-capsules. 1880 *Nature* XXI. 450/2 The shell has a large opening, as well as scattered *pore-facets. 1887 *Amer. Nat.* XXI. 565 Lateral surfaces with irregular, shallow, *pore-like fossæ. 1887 SOLLAS in *Encycl. Brit.* XXII. 415/2 Section through the cortex of *Cydonium eosaster*,.. showing the *pore-sieve overlying the chone. 1708 *Phil. Trans.* XXVI. 79 The *Pore Stone, or Pore Coral.

†**Pore**, *sb.*[2] *Physiol. Obs. rare.* [ad. Gr. πῶρος callus.] The callus, or matter exuded at the site of the fracture of a broken bone.

[*c* 1400 *Lanfranc's Cirurg.* 48 If þat ilk mater þat is restorid be nyȝ as hard as is þe boon, it is clepid porus sarcoides.] 1543 TRAHERON *Vigo's Chirurg.* (1586) 273 When the bone is hardened and somewhat bound together with the pore called Sarcoides. [1657 *Physical Dict.*, *Poros*, that matter which consolidateth the broken bones within.]

Pore, *sb.*[3] *rare.* [f. PORE *v.*] An act of poring over something; a careful or close examination.

1871 *Daily News* 12 Aug., I brought the book.. and Madge.. and myself shall have many a good pore over it.

†**Pore**, *sb.*[4] *Obs.* (Said to be a Huntsman's term: see quot.)

1630 J. TAYLOR (Water P.) *Navy Land Ships*, *Huntsm. Ship* Wks. I. 93/1 What Necromanticke spells are Rut, Vault, Slot, Pores, and Entryes, Abatures, and Foyles, Frayenstockes,.. and a thousand more such Vtopian fragments of confused Gibberish.

Pore (pōə̆ɹ), *v.* Forms: 4 **pure**, **pouri**, 4–5 **poure**, 5–7 **powre**, 6 **poor**, 6–8 **poar**, 5– **pore**. [ME. *pūren*, *pouren*, *pouri*, of obscure origin. There is no corresp. verb in OF. or OE., though the early ME. forms answer to an OE. **pūrian*. Sense 2 is strikingly identical with the main sense of PEER *v.*[2], PIRE *v.*, both also of obscure origin; but, although an OE. double form **pūrian*, **pȳran* would explain the forms, there is no trace of such a verb in OE. or the cognate languages. The phonology is abnormal; the ME. (pūr-) would normally have given mod. *pour* (pauə̆ɹ), whereas in the 15th c. the form began to be *pore*, *poar* (pōə̆ɹ).]

1. *intr.* **a.** To look intently or fixedly, to gaze (*in*, *on*, *upon*, *at*, *over*); to search *for* or *into* something by gazing. (Often, now always, with admixture of sense b.)

a 1300 *K. Horn* 1092 Aþulf was in þe ture [*v. r.* toure] Abute for to pure [*v. r.* poure] After his comynge. 13.. *K. Alis.* 5799 There he seighen a selcouth folk Al day pouren in the walken. 1340 *Ayenb.* 177 Þe men þet doþ zuo grat payne ham to kembe and to pouri ine sseaweres. *c* 1384 CHAUCER *H. Fame* III. 31 And for to powren [*v. r.* poure] wonder low Yf I koude eny weyes know What maner stoon this roche was. 1553 T. WILSON *Rhet.* (1580) 224 Some pores vpon the grounde as though they sought for pinnes. 1621 QUARLES *Esther* Medit. v. E iv, All Creatures else pore downward to the ground, Man lookes to heauen. 1722 DE FOE *Plague* (1840) 24 No wonder if they who were poring continually at the clouds, saw shapes and figures, representations and appearances. 1834 HT. MARTINEAU *Farrers* iv, Down on his knees, poring over the pavement, to see which way the stones were laid. 1854 MACAULAY *Biog.*, *Johnson* (1867) 82 He would stand poring on the town clock without being able to tell the hour.

b. To look at something (usu. a book) with fixed attention, in the way of study; to read or study earnestly or with steady application; to be absorbed in reading or study. (Const. *on*, *upon*, (now chiefly) *over*; rarely *in*, *into*, or absol.)

c 1386 CHAUCER *Prol.* 185 What sholde he studie and make hym seluen wood Vpon a book in Cloystre alwey to poure [*MS. Lansd.* powre]. *c* 1449 PECOCK *Repr.* I. xvi. 87 Thouȝ ȝe wolden labore, and powre, and dote alle the daies of ȝoure lijf in the Bible aloon. 1594 LYLY *Moth. Bomb.* I. iii, Instead of poaring on a booke, you shall holde the plough. 1610 HOLLAND *Camden's Brit.* Auth. to Rdr., I have pored upon many an old Rowle. 1718 *Free-thinker* No. 37. 271 He rises by Three in the Morning to pore over Mathematicks. 1768 BEATTIE *Minstr.* I. li, Where dark cold-hearted sceptics, creeping, pore Through microscope of metaphysic lore. 1874 L. STEPHEN *Hours in Library* (1892) II. iii. 90 He had pored over their pages till he knew them by heart.

c. To fix one's thoughts earnestly upon something; to meditate, muse, or think intently; to ponder. Const. *on*, *upon*, *over*; rarely with dependent clause (quot. 1856).

1423 JAS. I *Kingis Q.* lxxii, The longe day thus gan I prye and poure, Till phebus endit had his bemes bryght. *a* 1591 H. SMITH *Wks.* (1866) I. 173 So, while he pores and gapes upon it, by little and little the love of it grows more and more in his heart, until at last he hath mind on nothing else. *a* 1628 PRESTON *Saint's Daily Exerc.* (1629) 138 If a man be poring on his wants still. 1722 DE FOE *Moll Flanders* (1840) 64 When he has thought and pored on it. 1856 MRS. BROWNING *Aur. Leigh* I. 348 She had pored for years What sort of woman could be suitable To her sort of hate. 1882 PEBODY *Eng. Journalism* xviii. 137 Dickens.. took himself off.. to Geneva,.. to pore over the story of 'Dombey and Son'.

†**2.** To look with the eyes half shut; to look closely, as a near-sighted person; to peer. *Obs.*

1699 WAFER in *Phil. Trans.* LV. 51 For they see not well in the sun, poring in the clearest day. 1706 PHILLIPS, To *Pore*, to look close, as they do that are short-sighted. 1709 STEELE *Tatler* No. 27 ⁋ 5 Poring with her Eyes half shut at every one she passes by. 1774 FOOTE *Cozeners* I. Wks. 1799 II. 157 He doesn't pore, with his eyes close to the book, like a clerk that reads the first lesson. 1862 THOREAU *Excursions*, *Ch. Night* (1863) 310 Their eyes which are weak and poring.

3. *trans.* To bring or put into some state by poring; in phrase *to pore one's eyes out*, to blind oneself or ruin one's sight by close reading or over-study; to tire (one's eyes) by close reading.

1593 NASHE *Christ's T.* 43 b, I that haue poor'd out myne eyes vpon bookes. 1698 *Phil. Trans.* XX. 455 Old, rusty, Moth eaten Books, upon which a Man may pore his Eyes out before he can read a Word or a Line. 1706 E. WARD *Wooden World Diss.* (1708) 37 He might have.. por'd himself into Stupidity. 1712 SWIFT *Jrnl. to Stella* 7 Aug., I have been poring my eyes all the morning. *a* 1754 FIELDING *Fathers* v. v, Though I have hated books as I do the devil,.. I'll pore my eyes out rather than lose her.

Hence **Po·ring** *vbl. sb.* and *ppl. a.* (whence **Po·ringly** *adv.*).

c 1374 CHAUCER *Troylus* III. 1411 (1460) Dispitous day.. Thi pouryng In wol no where late hem dwelle. *c* 1449 PECOCK *Repr.* I. xvi. 85 Bi her powring in the Bible aloon thei misten leerne. 1594 NASHE *Unfort. Trav.* Wks. (Grosart) V. 120 He that viewd them a farre off, and had not directly stood poaringly ouer them, would haue sworne they had liued. 1615 G. SANDYS *Trav.* 124 Many of the Pilgrims by poaring on hot bricks, do voluntarily perish their sights. 1728 POPE *Dunc.* III. 191 There, dim in clouds, the poreing Scholiasts mark. 1874 L. STEPHEN *Hours in Library* (1892) II. vii. 211 That disposition which.. delights in poring over its own morbid emotions.

Pore, obs. (and dial.) var. of POOR *a.*; obs. f. PORR, POUR, POWER. **Pore(-)blind**, obs. f. PURBLIND.

Pored (pōə̆ɹd), *a.* [f. PORE *sb.*[1] + -ED[2].] In parasynthetic combs.: Having pores (of some kind).

1688 CLAYTON in *Phil. Trans.* XVII. 945 If a Gummous Plant or Tree, that grows low, and close pored, it abounds with acid Spirits,.. if it grow tall, and be open pored, it abounds with a subtile volatile Spirit.

Poreger, obs. form of PORRINGER.

†**Po·relet.** *Obs. nonce-wd.* [f. *pore*, POOR + -LET.] (Rendering L. *pauperculus*, dim. of *pauper* POOR.)] A poor man.

1382 WYCLIF *Isa.* lxvi. 2 To my porelet [1388 a pore man] and contrit in spirit.

‖**Porencephalus, -on** (pōrense·fălŏs, -ŏn). *Path.* [mod.L., f. Gr. πόρος PORE *sb.*[1] + ἐγκέφαλος brain.] A defect of the cerebral hemisphere consisting in the formation (congenital or caused by disease) of a depression or hollow, sometimes communicating with the lateral ventricle. So **Porence·phaly** [ad. mod.L. *porencephalia*] in same sense. Hence **Porencephalic** (porensĭfæ·lik), **Porencephalous** (-se·făləs) *adjs.*, pertaining to, of the nature of, or affected with porencephalus.

1890 BILLINGS *Med. Dict.*, *Porencephalus*.. *Porencephaly*. 1890 *Cent. Dict.*, *Porencephalic*.. *Porencephalous*. 1896 *Allbutt's Syst. Med.* I. 179 Atrophy of the fillet and the posterior column nuclei has resulted from porencephalon of the central convolution of the cortex cerebri. 1899 *Ibid.* VI. 534 Diseases.. which give rise to a porencephalic condition. *Ibid.* VII. 292 Cases of porencephaly.

Porer (pōə̆·rəɹ). [f. PORE *v.* + -ER[1].] One who pores *upon* or *over* something, as a book.

1670 H. STUBBE *Plus Ultra* 69 The Disputative followers of Hippocrates, Aristotle, Galen, those superstitious Porers upon the Writings of the Ancients. 1797 W. TAYLOR in *Monthly Rev.* XXII. 345 The multitudinous porers in black literature. 1892 *Pall Mall G.* 16 Aug. 2/1 The wielder of the spade has outrun the porer over manuscripts.

Poret(e, -ett(e, variants of PORRET *Obs.*

†**Porfe·nd**, *v. Obs. rare*⁻¹. [a. OF. *po(u)rfendre* to cleave completely (*c* 1145 in Godef.), f. *pour* (:—L. *prō* forth), with intensive force + *fendre* :—L. *findĕre* to cleave.] *trans.* To cleave or split through.

c 1489 CAXTON *Blanchardyn* vii. 28 The goode swerde entred in to the brayne porfended, and cloue his hed vnto the chynne.

‖**Po·rfido.** *Obs.* [It.] = PORPHYRY.

1611 SPEED *Hist. Gt. Brit.* IX. xxi. § 134 The pauement .. shall be of Orientall stone: That is to say, of Alabaster, Porfido, Serpentines, and other stones of diuers colours.

Porfil, -e, porfyl, obs. ff. PROFILE, PURFLE.

Porful: see POORFUL. **Porge**, obs. f. PURGE.

Porge (pōə̆ɹdʒ), *v. Jewish Ritual.* [app. f. L. *purgāre* to make (ceremonially) clean, to PURGE.] *trans.* To make (a slaughtered beast) ceremonially clean by drawing out and removing the sinews and veins (esp. from the hinder quarters: cf. Gen. xxxii. 32). Hence **Po·rger**, a man whose business is to do this.

1864 *Times* 4 Aug. Advt., I. I. M... Butcher.. Walworth begs to inform the Jewish Public that he has succeeded in obtaining a qualified killer and porger for himself. *Mod.* (*Notice in Jewish Newspr.*) The licence of Mr. A. B. has been revoked for having sold (to Jewish customers) meat which has not been porged.

Porgo, pargo. [a.Sp. and Pg. *pargo*, app. :—L. *pagrus* a kind of fish.] A fish; the sea bream.

1557 W. TOWRSON in Hakluyt *Voy.* (1589) 113 We found there certain Caruels fishing for Pargoes. 1616 CAPT. SMITH *Descr. New Eng.* 12. 40 or 50 Saile yearely to Cape-blank, to hooke for Porgos, Mullet, and [to] make Puttardo. 1624 — *Virginia* 227 The Duke of Medina receiueth yeerely tribute of the Fishers, for Tunny, Mullit, and Porgos, more then ten thousand pounds. [*a* 1643 SIR W. MONSON *Naval Tracts* VI. (1704) 532/1 Porgus, somewhat like to an over-grown Sea-Bream, but much bigger.] 1688 R. HOLME *Armoury* III. xv. (Roxb.) 40/1 Fish hookes for Porgos, Bonettos or dorados. 1902 JORDAN & EVERMANN *Amer. Food & Game Fishes* 405 The Snappers, or Pargos, genus *Lutjanus*.. species very numerous, Asiatic, American, or African.

Porgy (pǭ·ɹgi). Also 8 **pargie, porgie**, 9 **porgee, -ghee**. See also PAUGIE. [Of obscure and app. various origin; in part = PORGO, PARGO; in part = PAUGIE, q. v.; also corruptly for POGY, q. v. Much vagueness appears to prevail in the use of the name.] A name in U. S. applied, with or without distinctive adjuncts, to various sea-fishes, chiefly N. American species of *Sparidæ* or Sea Breams, but also locally to fishes of other families.

Among the Sparoid fish, applied to **a.** the Braise, *Sparus pagrus* (*Pagrus vulgaris*), of the Mediterranean and N. Atlantic; **b.** *Stenotomus chrysops*, the Scuppaug, Scup, or Paugie, and *S. aculeatus*, the Fair Maid, found along the Atlantic coast of U.S., to the north and south respectively; **c.** *Lagodon rhomboides*, also called Sailor's Choice and Pinfish; **d.** various species of *Calamus* found at Bermuda and near Florida; **e.** one or more species of *Lutjanus*, called also Snapper and Grunt. Among those of other families: **f.** in southern U.S. an ephippioid fish, *Chætodipterus faber*, also known as Moon-fish, Spade-fish, or Angel-fish; **g.** in Florida, the Toad-fish, *Chilomycterus geometricus*; **h.** in California, one of various viviparous perches, as *Ditrema jacksoni* or *Damalichthys argyrosomus*. ¶ **i.** Erron. for POGY, the menhaden.

1725 SLOANE *Jamaica* II. 286 The Pargie. It was taken at Old Harbour, and reckoned very good food. 1734 MORTIMER in *Phil. Trans.* XXXVIII. 317, 16. *Aurata Bahamensis*. The Porgy. It is a good eating Fish. 1848 SCHOMBURGK *Hist. Barbados* 668 *Haemulon heterodon*, porghee grunt.. the peculiar noise which they emit when caught, has given rise to the vernacular name. 1849 H. W. HERBERT *Fish & Fishing U.S.* 280 The colour of the Porgee is a deep brownish black on the head and back. 1883 *Fisheries Exhib. Catal.* (ed. 4) 170 The principal salt-water fishes are:—The Calipeva.. Hog-fish.. Porgee, Grouper, Sun-fish, Grunts, Croakers, and Drummers. 1883 GOODE *Fish. Industries U.S.* 70 Saint Jerome's Creek, Point Lookout, Maryland. A station for the artificial propagation of.. the bandy porgy (*Chætodipterus faber*). 1884 *Ibid.* Sect. I. Plates. Pl. 137 The Margate Fish, Bastard Snapper, or Charleston 'Porgy', *Sparus pagrus*. 1885 C. F. HOLDER *Marvels Anim. Life* 68 I've tossed a dead porgy to one [sword-fish] and seen him knock it up and down. 1888 GOODE *Amer. Fishes* 43 In the North the Sea-Bass occupies the feeding grounds in company with the scuppaug or porgy. *Ibid.* 80 The Red-mouth Grunt, *Diabasis aurolineatus*, is probably the Flannel-mouthed Porgy familiar to Florida fishermen. *Ibid.* 92 About New York, the second syllable of the abbreviated Indian name (*mishcuppauog*) has been lengthened into 'Paugy' or 'Porgy'. *Ibid.* 99 *Lagodon rhomboides*.. in the St. John's River,.. the 'Sailor's Choice' and 'Porgy'. *Ibid.* 100 There are other species known by the name of Porgy.. found in this region, such as *Calamus bajonado* common also at Charleston, where it is called the 'White-boned Porgy', the 'Jolthead Porgy' of Key West, *C. megacephalus*, *C. arctifrons*, the 'Shad Porgy' or 'Grass Porgy' of Key West, and *C. macrops*. *Ibid.* 146 The Moonfish or Spadefish, *Chætodipterus faber*.. at Beaufort N.C. where it is called the Porgee or Porgy... Three-tail Sheepshead and Three-tailed Porgee are names said to have been formerly in use among the New York fishermen. 1897 H. G. CARLETON in *Outing* (U.S.) XXIX. 329/2 Dibbling with a light rod for little porgies and whiting.

‖**Porifera** (pori·fĕră), *sb. pl. Zool.* [mod.L., neut. pl. of *porifer*, f. L. *porus* (a. Gr. πόρος) PORE *sb.*[1] + *-fer* bearing.] The Sponges, reckoned as a class or main division of *Cœlenterata*, characterized by having the body-wall perforated by numerous inhalant pores. Hence **Porifer** (pōə̆·rifəɹ), a member of the *Porifera*, a Sponge; **Pori·feral** *a.* = next; **Pori·feran**, *a.* belonging or relating to the *Porifera*; *sb.* = *porifer*.

1843 CARPENTER *Anim. Phys.* ii. 113 Satisfactory reasons for placing the class of *Porifera*, or the Sponge tribe, in the animal kingdom. 1864 WEBSTER, *Poriferan*, an animal of the group comprising the sponges. 1867 J. HOGG *Microsc.* II. ii. 385 The term *Porifera*.. was applied by Professor Grant to designate the remarkable class of organized beings known as sponges. 1877 HUXLEY *Anat. Inv. Anim.* iii. 113 The fundamental type of Poriferal organisation is to be sought among the Calcispongiæ. *Ibid.* xii. 678 Comparable to Physemarian or Poriferan embryos. 1888 ROLLESTON & JACKSON *Anim. Life* 716 The irregular and continuous growth of a Poriferan. 1890 *Cent. Dict.*, *Poriferan theory*, that theory which considers the tracheæ or tubes of some animals as having a common origin with the incurrent tubes of the *Porifera* or sponges.

Poriferous (pori·fĕrəs), *a.* [f. L. *por-us* PORE *sb.*[1] + -FEROUS: in mod.L. *porifer*.] Bearing or having pores.

1852 DANA *Man. Geol.* iii. 313 The poriferous side of the same. 1870 NICHOLSON *Man. Zool.* 124 The other five double rows of plates alternate regularly with the former, and are termed the 'ambulacral areas' or poriferous zones.

Poriform (pōə̆·rifǭɹm), *a.* [f. as prec. + -FORM.] Having the form of, or resembling, a pore.

1846 DANA *Zooph.* (1848) 706 Minute, poriform cells. 1858 MAYNE *Expos. Lex.*, *Poriformis*,.. having the form of simple pores, as the cellules of certain *polypi*..: poriform.

Poriger, obs. form of PORRINGER.

†**Po·rime.** *Obs. rare*⁻⁰. [ad. Gr. πόριμ-ος able to be passed, practicable, f. πόρος passage.] See quot. and APORIME.

1704 J. HARRIS *Lex. Techn.* I, *Porime*,.. in Geometry, is a Theorem or Proposition so easie to be demonstrated, that 'tis almost self-evident; as, *That a Chord is all of it within the Circle*. Hence 1706 in PHILLIPS. 1727–41 in CHAMBERS *Cycl.* 1730–6 in BAILEY (folio). 1823 in CRABB *Technol. Dict.*; and in mod. Dicts.

†**Po·riness.** *Obs.* [f. PORY + -NESS.] The condition of being 'pory' or porous; porosity; also *concr.* a porous part.

1653 WALTON *Angler* iii. 86 It is reported, there is a fish that hath not any mouth, but lives by taking breath by the poriness of her gils. 1662 J. CHANDLER *Van Helmont's Oriat.* 57 Vapours may be contained in the porinesses or hollow places of the Air. 1676 WISEMAN *Chirurg. Treat.* V. ix. 392, I took off the Dressings, and set the Trepan above the fractured Bone,.. considering withall the Poriness of the Bone below.

Poring, Poringly: see under PORE *v.*

†**Po·rish**, *a.*[1] *Obs. rare*⁻⁰. [f. PORE *v.* + -ISH[1].] Having the character of 'poring' or looking with the eyes half shut (see PORE *v.* 2). Hence †**Po·rishly** *adv. Obs.*

1523 SKELTON *Garl. Laurel* 626 Sum were made peuysshe, porisshly pynk iyde, That euer more after by it they were aspyide. 1530 PALSGR. 840/2 *Porisshly*, as one loketh that can nat se well, *louchement*.

†**Po·rish**, *a.*[2] *Obs.* [f. PORE *sb.*[1] + -ISH[1].] Porous. Hence †**Po·rishness** *Obs.*, porosity.

1652 GAULE *Magastrom.* 119 That the stars are made of an earthy porish matter, much like to that of a pumice stone. 1670 CAPT. J. SMITH *Eng. Improv. Reviv'd* 16 All barren sands are loose and light,.. by reason of their porishness or hollowness.

Porism (pǭ·riz'm, pǫ·r-). *Math.* [ad. L. *porisma*, a. Gr. πόρισμα a deduction from a previous demonstration, a corollary, also a problem, f. πορίζειν to carry, deduce, f. πόρος way. So F. *porisme*.] With the ancient Greek mathematicians, a kind of geometrical proposition, the nature of which has been much disputed; app. one arising during the investigation of some other proposition, either by immediate deduction from it (= COROLLARY *sb.* 1), or by consideration of some special case in which it becomes indeterminate.

The sense indicated by Playfair's definition (quot. 1792) is that now most generally accepted and used; but other widely different definitions have been given.

c 1374 CHAUCER *Boeth.* III. pr. x. 71 (Camb. MS.) Ryht as thyse geometryens whan they han shewyd hyr proposiciouns ben wont to bryngen in thinges þat they clepyn porysmes or declaraciouns of forseyde thinges. Ryht so wole I yeue the heere as a corolarye or a mede of coroune. [*c* 1645 *Enquiry*, etc. in *Harl. Misc.* (Malh.) V. 499 It may be proposed a problem, or porisma, to be considered, whether the souls of brutes are not more than rarefied, or inflamed matter.] 1704 J. HARRIS *Lex. Techn.* I, *Porisme*. Proclus and Pappus define this Geometrical Term to signifie a kind of Theorem, in the form of a Corollary, which is dependant upon, or deduced from some other Theorem already demonstrated. And 'tis commonly used to signifie some General Theorem, which is discovered from finding out some Geometrical Place. 1792 PLAYFAIR in *Trans. Roy. Soc. Edinb.* III. II. 156 There was another subject, that of Porisms, the most intricate and enigmatical of any thing in the ancient geometry. *Ibid.* 170 From this account of the origin of Porisms, it follows, that a Porism may be defined, A proposition affirming the possibility of finding such conditions as will render a certain problem indeterminate, or capable of innumerable solutions. 1795 HUTTON *Math. Dict.* s. v., Pappus says, a Porism is that in which something was proposed to be investigated. 1798 H. BROUGHAM in *Phil. Trans.* LXXXVIII. 383 This is a case of a most general enunciation, which gives rise to an infinite variety of the most curious porisms. 1853 CAYLEY *Coll. Math. Papers* II. 56 Researches on the Porism of the in- and circumscribed triangle. 1855 J. MARTINEAU *Ess.* (1890) I. 434 An epic or song.. may have a human power greater than the Porisms or the Principia. 1887 H. DELEVINGNE in *N. & Q.* 7th Ser. IV. 424/2 Between i. 15 and 16 occurs the first porism or corollary, to the effect that the angles formed by two straight lines at their point of intersection are together equal to four right angles.

Porismatic (pōə̆rizmæ·tik, pǫr-), *a.* [f. Gr. πόρισμα, -ατ- PORISM + -IC.] Pertaining to or of the nature of a porism. So †**Porisma·tical** *a. Obs.* (in quot.) following immediately as a corollary; whence **Porisma·tically** *adv.* (in quot.) as a corollary, by direct inference.

1646 J. HALL *Horæ Vac.* 119 It will Porismatically follow. 1649 J. H. *Motion to Parl. Adv. Learn.* 11 If they be not guided by forcible demonstrations and porismaticall inferences. 1792 PLAYFAIR in *Trans. Roy. Soc. Edinb.* III. II. 190 Another species of impossibility may frequently arise from the porismatic case of a problem. 1886 FARRAR *Hist. Interpr.* vii. 361 The porismatic method consisted in the abstraction of dogmatic results.

Poristic (pori·stik), *a. Math.* [ad. Gr. ποριστικός able to procure, f. πορίζειν: see PORISM.] Relating to a porism, porismatic; having the quality of rendering a determinate problem indeterminate.

1704 J. HARRIS *Lex. Techn.* I, *Poristick Method*, in Mathematicks, is that which determines when, by what way, and how many different ways, a Problem may be resolved. 1890 *Cent. Dict.* s. v., *Poristic points*, a set of points of the number which usually suffice to determine a curve of a given order, but so situated that an indefinite number of such curves can be drawn through them.

So **Pori·stical** *a. rare*⁻⁰.

1828 WEBSTER, *Poristic*, *Poristical*. Hence in later Dicts.

Porite (pōə̆·rəit). *Zool.* [ad. mod.L. generic name *Porītēs* (Lamarck); f. Gr. πορός passage, pore, or ? πῶρ-ος calcareous stone, stalactite: see MADREPORE and -ITE[1].] A coral of the genus *Porites* or family *Poritidæ* of perforate sclerodermatous corals.

1828 WEBSTER, *Porite*, a petrified madrepore. *Dict. Nat. Hist.* 1846 DANA *Zooph.* vii. (1848) 110 The Porites.. graduate into the Astræsporæ, and thence to the Astroites.

Pork[1] (pōə̆ɹk). Forms: 3 **porc**, 5 **poork**, **-e**,

5–7 **porke**, 6 **porcke**, 8 **porck**, 4– **pork**. [a. F. *porc* = Pr. *porc*, It. *porco*, Sp. *puerco* :—L. *porc-us* swine, hog.]

†**1.** A swine, a hog, a pig. Sometimes distinguished from a pig or young swine. *Obs.* or *Hist.*

? *a* 1400 *Morte Arth.* 3122 Poveralle and pastorelles passede one aftyre, With porkes to pasture at the price ȝates. *c* 1400 *Destr. Troy* 3837 Polidarius was pluccid as a porke fat. 1528 PAYNEL *Salerne's Regim.* F j, Porkes of a yere or .ij. olde are better than yonge pygges. 1533 BELLENDEN *Livy* I. ix. (S. T. S.) I. 55 He slew þe pork with ane hevy stane. 1598 STOW *Surv.* (1842) 145/1 There were brought to the slaughter-house.. 34 porks, 3*s.* 8*d.* the piece; 91 pigs, 6*d.* the piece. 1682 J. COLLINS *Salt & Fishery* 83 Very large like Calves,.. and as fat as Porks. [1799 SOUTHEY *Pig* 24 Woe to the young posterity of Pork! Their enemy is at hand. 1887 ROGERS *Agric. & Prices* V. 343 Hogs and porks, the word appearing to be used indifferently, are occasionally found.]

†**b.** Applied opprobriously to an uncultured person. *Obs.*

1645 MILTON *Colast.* Wks. 1851 IV. 358, I mean not to dispute Philosophy with this Pork, who never read any.

2. The flesh of swine used as food; *spec.* the fresh flesh.

c 1290 *S. Eng. Leg.* I. 472/343 Huy nomen with heom into heore schip.. porc, motoun and beof. 1398 TREVISA *Barth. De P. R.* XVIII. vii. (Bodl. MS.) lf. 246 b/1 Boores flesche is more hard and drye.. þan tame porke. *c* 1440 *Promp. Parv.* 409/2 Poork, fleche, *suilla*. 1486 *Bk. St. Albans* C vij, Take a quantyte of poorke and ony [= honey] and butter. 1533 ELYOT *Cast. Helthe* (1539) 27 b, Aboue all kyndes of fleshe in nouryshyng the body, Galene most commendeth porke. 1598 W. PHILLIP *Linschoten* I. iv. 9/1 Porke is there a very costly dish. 1748 E. DARWIN *Let.* in *Life* (1879) 9 We affirm Porck not only to be flesh but a devillish Sort of flesh. 1848 THACKERAY *Bk. Snobs* xxv, Roast ribs of pork.

3. *attrib.* and *Comb.*: simple attrib., as *pork-blubber*, *-chop* (CHOP *sb.*[1] 3 b), *-fat*, *-griskin*, *-sausage*, *-shop*; obj. and obj. gen., as *pork-curer*, *-dealer*, *-eater*, *-packer* (PACKER[1] 2 b), *-packing*, *-pickling*; **pork-butcher**, one who slaughters pigs for sale (BUTCHER *sb.* 1); **pork-fish**, a local name of various American fishes: see quots.; † **pork-hog** = PORKER 1; **pork-pit**, that part of a produce exchange where pork is dealt in. Also FORK-FLESH, etc.

1804 A. WILSON in *Poems & Lit. Prose* (1876) I. 114 We ate some *pork-blubber and bread. 1836–48 B. D. WALSH *Aristoph.*, *Knights* I. iii, We'll observe *pork-butcher's laws. 1858 SIMMONDS *Dict. Trade*, *Pork-chop*, a slice from the rib of a pig. 1872 *Punch* 3 Feb. 46/2 The *menu* consisted of sausages.. and pork-chops. 1844 H. STEPHENS *Bk. Farm* II. 232 *Pork-curers buy from farmers and dealers in the carcass. 1596 SHAKS. *Merch. V.* III. v. 27 If wee grow all to be *porke-eaters, wee shall not shortlie haue a rasher on the coales for money. 1705 (*title*) A Pill for Pork Eaters, or a Scots Lancet for an English Swelling. 1856 KANE *Arct. Expl.* II. xix. 193 Hung a dripping slab of *pork-fat over their lamp-wick. 1734 MORTIMER in *Phil. Trans.* XXXVIII. 315 The *Pork-Fish. The Bahamians esteem this a good Fish. 1888 GOODE *Amer. Fishes* 81 The Norfolk Hog-fish, *Pomodasys fulvomaculatus*,.. is the.. 'Pork-fish' and 'Whiting' at Key West. 1902 WEBSTER Suppl., *Pork-fish*,.. a sparoid fish (*Anisotremus Virginicus*). 1727 *Pork grisking [see GRISKIN]. 1755 J. SHEBBEARE *Lydia* (1769) II. 284 Attending a pork-griskin which the parson had also ordered for their suppers. 1470–85 MALORY *Arthur* VII. i. 214 As fatte.. as a *porke hog. 1884 SIR L. GRIFFIN in *Fortn. Rev.* Jan. 55 Annually, a flight of *pork-packers and successful tradesmen cross the Atlantic. 1905 *Athenæum* 5 Aug. 174/2 In a few days fashionable people, from the peer to the pork-packer, will be rushing to the Highlands. 1892 A. CRAIB *America* 66 *Pork-packing is one of the chief sources of wealth in Illinois, Ohio, and Kentucky. 1890 *Pall Mall G.* 8 May 3/2 A *pork-pickling establishment.. has lately been opened there. 1829 MARRYAT *F. Mildmay* xvi, That fellow is only fit for fly-flapper at a *pork shop!

†**Pork**[2]. *Obs.* [Echoic.] An imitative name for the hoarse croak of the raven: cf. MOREPORK. So †**Pork** *v. intr.*, to croak; hence †**Po·rking** *vbl. sb.*; and (with reduplication expressing repetition) **Pork-porking** *ppl. a.*

1606 SYLVESTER *Du Bartas* II. iv. III. *Schism* 285 From the Mountains nigh The Rav'ns begin with their pork-porking cry. 1640 BROME *Sparagus Gard.* IV. iv, Harke, the Ravens cry porke for him and yet he dyes not. 1655 MOUFET & BENNET *Health's Impr.* 5 They foresee by porking of raven.. when it will raine.

Porke despyne, porkepine, etc., early ff. PORCUPINE. **Porkepes**, obs. form of PORPOISE.

Porker (pōə̆·ɹkəɹ). [f. PORK[1] + -ER[1] 1.]

1. A young hog fattened for pork; also, any swine or pig raised for food.

1657 HEYLIN *Ecclesia Vind.* 181 They sacrificed a swine or porker, with this solemn form. 1670 CAPT. J. SMITH *Eng. Improv. Reviv'd* 195 Beech-mast is very good feeding for Swine to make them Porkers, and for Bacon. 1726 POPE *Odyss.* XVII. 201 Then sheep and goats and bristly porkers bled. 1828 SCOTT *F. M. Perth* ii, As round and full as a six-weeks' porker. 1880 MISS BRADDON *Just as I am* ii, Even the pigs were the aristocracy of the porker tribe. 1884 *St. James' Gaz.* 11 Dec. 12/1 The stock.. consisted of.. bacon hogs and porkers.

†**2.** A sword. *Obs. slang.* (Cf. *pigsticker*, a long-bladed pocket-knife, or sword.)

1688 SHADWELL *Sqr. Alsatia* I. i, The Captain whipt his porker out. *Ibid.* II. *a* 1700 B. E. *Dict. Cant. Crew*, *Porker*, a Sword. 1725 in *New Cant. Dict.*

Porkery (pōə̆·ɹkəri). [f. PORK[1] + -ERY. Cf. ONF. *porkerie*, OF. *porcherie* herd of swine, med. (Anglo-) L. *porcaria*, *porcheria* a piggery.]

1. Swine collectively, stock of swine.

1829 LANDOR *Imag. Conv.*, *Emp. China & Tsing-Ti* Wks. 1853 II. 146/1, I have killed rats as good meat as your Excellencies, and where your Excellencies (pest on such porkery!) dared not come.

2. Stock of pork, bacon, ham, and the like; pork department.

1890 *Balance Sheet of Co-op. Store*, Balance to Profit and Loss Account Bakery.. Porkery.. General.

Porkespine, -pick, etc., obs. ff. PORCUPINE.

Porket (pōə̆·ɹkét). [a. ONF. *porket*, *porquet*, OF. *porchet*, dim. of *porc* PORK[1].] A small or young pig or hog; in mod. dial. use = PORKER 1.

[1312 *Bolton Priory Comp.* 244 b, Preter, vj. bacones de dono Petri de Mytone. Et .ix. porchettos de dono Eue de Landa.] 1554 BRADFORD in Strype *Eccl. Mem.* (1721) III. App. xxix. 82 Nor any liberty or power upon a poor porket have al the devils in hel. 1563–87 FOXE *A. & M.* (1684) III. 277 We are now become Gergesites, that would rather lose Christs than our Porkets. 1697 DRYDEN *Æneid* XII. 257 [He] off'rings to the flaming altars bears—A porket, and a lamb that never suffer'd shears. 1837 WHEELWRIGHT tr. *Aristophanes* II. 139 Bring.. figs to my porkets. 1900 *Oxford Times* 1 Dec. 2 Prizes.. for bacon hogs and porkets.

Pork-flesh. Now *rare*. The flesh of the hog or pig; = PORK[1] 2.

1477 EARL RIVERS (Caxton) *Dictes* 10 He commaunded that porke flesshe and camelys shold be eten. 1563–87 FOXE *A. & M.* (1596) 1417/1 He delighted greatlie in Porke fleshe and Peacockes. 1643 TRAPP *Comm. Gen.* iv. 24 Bring me my pork-flesh. 1904 *Daily Chron.* 4 Aug. 3/3, I almost taste the pork-flesh of Brother Wainwright.

†**Po·rkin.** *Obs.* [f. PORK[1] + -KIN.] = PORKLING.

1570 LEVINS *Manip.* 134/12 A Porkin, *porcellus*. 1575 TURBERV. *Venerie* 206 They will roundely carie a sheepe or gote or a good porkine in their mouths.

†**Po·rkish**, *a. Obs.* [f. PORK[1] + -ISH[1].] Pig-like, swinish.

1554 BALE *Declar. Bonner's Art.* 66 See.. how arrogaunt this porkishe papist is here. 1570 B. GOOGE *Pop. Kingd.* (1880) 10 And rounde about his porkish necke, his Pall of passing price, He casteth on.

Porkling (pōə̆·ɹkliŋ). Also 6–7 **porklin.** [f. PORK[1] + -LING[1].] A little or young pig.

1570 LEVINS *Manip.* 137/31 These be diminutiues, and may be expounded by this signe little, as gosling, or little goose, porkling or little porke. 1577 B. GOOGE *Heresbach's Husb.* III. (1586) 148 b, Twelve hogsties, everie stie conteyning fiftie Porklinges. 1598 FLORIO, *Maranello*, a young pig, or a porklin. 1684 tr. *Agrippa's Van. Arts* lxxxix. 309 The other.. devoured a whole Boar, a hundred Loaves, a Weather, and a Porkling. 1843 *P. Parley's Ann.* IV. 267 The little porkling might have squeezed his way through the palings. 1898 *Blackw. Mag.* Feb. 231/2 A mottled porkling crashed through a little rug of branches.

b. Contemptuously or derisively applied to a person. Also *attrib.*

1542 BECON *Potation for Lent* K viij, The fat Pharise.. the porkelynge Justiciarie, whiche trust in theyr owne righteousnes, are no fytte Gestes for this mooste delicious table. 1550 BALE *Image Both Ch.* II. 92 b, The gloryouse gluttons, and franke fedde porkelynges of that gredye gulfe .. whose God ys their bellye. 1602 *Contention Betw. Liberality & Prodigal.* v. i. in Hazl. *Dodsley* VIII. 369 Come, porkling, come on.

Po·rkman. [f. PORK[1] + MAN *sb.*[1]] A man who sells pork, a dealer in pork.

1764 *Low Life* (ed. 3) 31 Pork-Men busy in their Shops and Cellars. 1859 DICKENS *T. Two Cities* I. v, The butcher and the porkman painted up only the leanest scrags of meat.

†**Po·rknell.** *Obs. rare.* [Arbitrary derivative of PORK[1]: cf. *cracknel*.]

1. One as fat as a pig.

c 1400 *Destr. Troy* 6368 Polidarius, the porknell, and his pere Machaon, Suet with the xvij [batell].

2. Some part of the offal of a sheep.

1596 NASHE *Saffron Walden* 111 No more doth he feed on anie thing when he is at Saffron Walden, but trotters, sheepes porknells, and buttered rootes.

Porkpen, obs. form of PORCUPINE.

†**Pork physic**, for *Poke physic*, old name of Virginian Poke, POKE *sb.*[4] 2 a.

1733 [see POKE *sb.*[4] 2 a]. 1753 CHAMBERS *Cycl. Supp.* App., *Poke*, or *Pork Physic*, the name by which the *Phytolacca* of botanists is sometimes called. 1760 J. LEE *Introd. Bot.* App. 323. 1858 in MAYNE *Expos. Lex.*

Pork-pie·. [f. PORK[1] + PIE *sb.*[2]]

1. A pie of pastry enclosing minced pork.

1732 FIELDING *Miser* III. iii, Let there be.. some dainty fat pork-pye or pasty. 1859 *Eng. Cookery Bk.* 202 A Plain Crust for Pork Pies. 1896 *Cassell's Dict. Cooking* 610 Pork pies are generally made of the trimmings taken from a hog when it is cut up.

2. (In full *pork-pie hat*.) Popularly applied to a hat with a flat crown and a brim turned up all round, worn by women *c* 1855–65, recalling the shape of a deep circular pie; also applied loosely to similar hats worn by men in some countries.

1860 G. A. SPOTTISWOODE in *Vac. Tour.* 98 Pork-pie hats with streaming ribbons. 1863 MRS. H. WOOD *Shadow Ashlydyat* (1878) 329 Charlotte rose.. and carried the pork-pie to the chimney-glass, to settle it on. 1883 LD. R. GOWER *My Remin.* I. x. 173 He [Garibaldi] wore a sort of large pork-pie hat. 1891 *Spectator* 26 Dec. 924/1 The bull-fighter's hat known in England as the 'pork-pie'.

Porkpik, porkpin, obs. ff. PORCUPINE. **Porkpisce**, obs. form of PORPOISE.

†**Po·rkrel.** *Obs. rare*⁻¹. [dim. of PORK[1]: see -REL.] A young swine; a pig.

1688 CLAYTON in *Phil. Trans.* XVIII. 122 Shoats, or Porkrels are their general Food.

Po·rkwood. [f. PORK[1] + WOOD *sb.*] The name of certain trees or shrubs. **a.** A bush or small tree (*Kigellaria capensis*) found in the warmer parts of Africa. **b.** *Pisonia obtusata*, the Pigeon-wood, Beef-wood, or Corkwood of the West Indies and Florida.

1880 *S. Africa* (ed. 3) 127 In these kloofs grow.. the Speckhout or Porkwood.

Porky (pōə̆·ɹki), *a. colloq.* [f. PORK[1] + -Y.] Of, pertaining to, or resembling pork; fleshy, obese.

1852 R. S. SURTEES *Sponge's Sp. Tour* li, Mr. Sponge was a good deal more put out by the incident.. than his porky host. 1866 MRS. RIDDELL *Race for Wealth* xxix, A fat, light-haired, snub-nosed, porky kind of a child. 1890 *Cent. Dict.* s. v., A porky odor permeated the whole place.

Porle, obs. form of PURL.

Pormanton, obs. corrupt f. PORTMANTEAU.

Pornerastic (pǭɹnĕræ·stik), *a.* [f. Gr. πόρνη harlot + ἐραστής lover + -IC.] Addicted to harlotry; whoremongering.

1870 F. HARRISON *Choice Bks.* (1886) 151 We hear nothing of.. those pornerastic habits in high places,.. which are too often thrust before our eyes in fiction.

[**Pornial** (in *Cent. Dict.* and Funk's *Standard Dict.*), a spurious word, due to a misreading or misprint of *primal*.]

Pornocracy (pǫɹnǫ·krăsi). [f. Gr. πόρνη harlot + -CRACY.] Dominating influence of harlots or prostitutes: *spec.* the government of Rome during the first half of the tenth century.

1860 EDERSHEIM tr. *Kurtz's Ch. Hist.* II. § 126. 379 For half a century Theodora.. and her equally infamous daughters,.. filled the See of Peter with their paramours, their sons, and grandsons,.. (the so-called Pornocracy). 1874 DEUTSCH *Remains* 245. 1882–3 *Schaff's Encycl. Relig. Knowl.* I. 484 A century of shameless intrigue and fighting—the period of the Pornocracy.

So **Po·rnocrat**, a member of a pornocracy.

1894 *Contemp. Rev.* Aug. 286 The most licentious and shameless of the Pornocrats.

Pornograph (pǭ·ɹnǒgraf), *sb.* (*a.*) [In sense 1, a. F. *pornographe* pornographer, ad. Gr. πορνογράφ-ος: see next; for sense 2 cf. -GRAPH.]

†**1.** = PORNOGRAPHER. *Obs.*

1877 *Contemp. Rev.* Mar. 562 He would recognize.. the difference between Pheidias and the pornographs.

2. An obscene writing or pictorial illustration.

1890 in *Century Dict.*

B. as *adj.* = PORNOGRAPHIC.

1893 SALTUS *Madam Sapphira* 165 Here the reporter can be as pornograph as the Marquess of Sade, if he knows how.

Pornographer (pǫɹnǫ·grăfəɹ). [f. Gr. πορνογράφ-ος writing of harlots (f. πόρνη harlot + -γραφος writing, writer) + -ER[1].] One who writes of prostitutes or obscene matters; a portrayer of obscene subjects.

1850 LEITCH tr. *C. O. Müller's Anc. Art* § 429 (ed. 2) 619 The pornographers of the later times. 1886 *Lit. World* (U. S.) 1 May 152/1 They call themselves 'naturalists'... but they are in fact only pornographers, and immature, inexperienced, conceited, love-mad youngsters. 1890 *Harper's Mag.* Nov. 904/2 Parisian artistic pornographers.

Pornographic (pǭɹnǒgræ·fik), *a.* [f. as prec. + -IC. So F. *pornographique*.] Of, pertaining to, or of the nature of pornography; dealing in the obscene.

1880 *Guardian* 27 Oct. 1450 The excesses of the [French] press designated as 'pornographic'.. have become such as to compel the authorities to adopt strong measures against them. 1881 SYMONDS *Ital. Renaiss.*, *Ital. Lit.* II. xiv. 365 Pornographic Pamphleteers and Poets. 1894 STEAD *If Christ Came to Chicago* 117 Two booksellers.. whose windows still contain a large and varied collection of pornographic literature.

Pornography (pǫɹnǫ·grăfi). [f. as prec. + -Y. So F. *pornographie*.]

1. (See quot.)

1857 DUNGLISON *Med. Dict.*, *Pornography*, a description of prostitutes or of prostitution, as a matter of public hygiene. 1858 in MAYNE *Expos. Lex.* 1895 in *Syd. Soc. Lex.*

2. Description of the life, manners, etc., of prostitutes and their patrons; hence, the expression or suggestion of obscene or unchaste subjects in literature or art; pornographic literature or art.

1864 WEBSTER, *Pornography*, licentious painting employed to decorate the walls of rooms sacred to bacchanalian orgies, examples of which exist in Pompeii. 1881 *Daily Tel.* No. 8313. 5/4 Pictorial and glyptic 'pornography'.. grew, flourished, declined, and fell with the Second Empire. 1896 MACKAIL *Lat. Lit.* 18 The Casina and the Truculentus [of Plautus] are studies in pornography which only the unflagging animal spirits of the poet can redeem from being disgusting.

So **Porno·graphist**, a writer on pornography.

1893 *Nation* (N. Y.) 3 Aug. 79/2 The 'grossness of the naturalists and the subtleties of the pornographists', to use the words of M. Lavisse, cannot have any other result.

Porodinic (pǫrǒ-, pōə̆rodi·nik), *a. Zool.* [f. Gr. πόρος PORE *sb.*[1] + ὠδίς, ὠδῖν- travail, birth + -IC.] Discharging the genital products by means of a pore; opp. to SCHIZODINIC.

1883 E. R. LANKESTER in *Encycl. Brit.* XVI. 682/1 *note*, Cœlomate animals are, according to this nomenclature, either Schizodinic or Porodinic. The Porodinic group is divisible into Nephrodinic and Idiodinic, in the former the nephridium serving as a pore, in the latter a special (ἴδιος) pore being developed.

Poro·dinous, *a. Geol. rare.* [Improperly f. Ger. *porodine* (Breithaupt 1832) (f. Gr. πωρώδης having the form of stalactite (f. πῶρος hardened stone, stalactite): see -INE[2]) + -OUS. A better form would be *porodine*, like *crystalline*, *hyaline*.] See quot.

1876 A. H. GREEN *Phys. Geology* ii. § 4. 45 *Porodinous* [rocks], or those which have solidified from a gelatinous state. Certain minerals, such as Opal,.. have in all likelihood been formed in this way.

Porogamic (pǫrǒ-, pōə̆rogæ·mik), *a. Bot.* [mod. f. Gr. πόρος PORE *sb.*[1] + γάμ-ος marriage + -IC. (Treub, *Ann. Jardin Bot. de Buitenzorg*, 1891.)] Applied to fertilization in which the pollen-tube enters the ovule by the micropyle, as in most plants: opposed to *chalazogamic*. (Also said of the plant.) So **Po·rogam**, a plant characterized by this mode of fertilization.

1894 *Times* 11 Aug. 11/3 Professor Balfour hesitated to adopt Treub's division into chalazogams and porogams until the limits of the former group were better defined. 1895 OLIVER tr. *Kerner's Nat. Hist. Plants* II. 412 This type of fertilization has been termed chalazogamic in contradistinction to the more usual micropylar or porogamic method.

†**Poro·logy.** *Obs. nonce-wd.* [f. Gr. πόρος PORE *sb.*[1] + -LOGY.] A scientific treatise on, or investigation of, pores or minute openings.

1684 BOYLE *Porousn. Anim. & Solid Bod.* i. 2 If such little things had not escaped the sight of our illustrious Verulam, he would have afforded a good Porology.. among his *Desiderata*.

Porophyllous (pǫrǒ-, pōə̆rofi·ləs), *a. Bot. rare*⁻⁰. [f. mod.L. *porophyllus* (f. Gr. πόρος PORE *sb.*[1] + φύλλον leaf) + -OUS.] (See quot.)

1858 MAYNE *Expos. Lex.*, *Porophyllus*, *Bot.*, having leaves sprinkled with transparent points like pores..: porophyllous.

Poroplastic (pǫrǒ-, pōə̆roplæ·stik), *a.* [f. Gr. πόρος PORE *sb.*[1] + PLASTIC.] Both porous and plastic: applied to a kind of porous felt, plastic when heated, becoming stiff when cold, used for splints and other surgical appliances.

1879 *St. George's Hosp. Rep.* IX. 615 Severer cases.. have had the plaster-of-Paris or 'poro-plastic' jacket applied. 1898 *Westm. Gaz.* 19 July 5/1 An elastic kneecap costs half a crown, a moleskin one five shillings, a leather one five to twenty, and a poroplastic any sum.

‖**Po·ro-po·ro.** *New Zealand.* [Maori name.] A flowering shrub, *Solanum aviculare*, with an edible fruit, called in Australia Kangaroo Apple.

1857 C. HURSTHOUSE *N. Zealand* I. 136 The Poroporo.. is a sodden strawberry flavoured with apple peel. 1872 A. DOMETT *Ranolf* XVIII. vi. 312 Potato-apples of the poroporo tall.

Porose (porōu·s), *a.* [ad. L. type **porōs-us* (in mod.L.); in It. and Sp. *poroso*.] Containing or abounding in pores; porous; now rare exc. in *Zool.*, said of corals of the division *Perforata*, as opposed to the *Aporosa*, and of the sculpture of insects dotted or pitted as if with minute holes.

[*c* 1400: see POROUS.] 1656 BLOUNT *Glossogr.*, *Porose* or *Porous* (*porosus*), full of pores or little holes. *Bacon*. 1697 A. DE LA PRYME *Diary* (Surtees) 147 There is a most delicate fine freestone,.. but so porose.. that, troughs being made of it, it will let the water run out for a year or two. 1715 CHEYNE *Philos. Princ. Relig.* I. (1716) 15 These Porose Bodies must be equally heavy with the most compact ones. 1826 KIRBY & SP. *Entomol.* IV. 270 Porose, beset with many pores. Ex. *Elytra* of most *Apions*.

Hence **Poro·seness** = POROSITY.

1746 ARDERON in *Phil. Trans.* XLIV. 282 *note*, The Nature of these Horns seems.. changed into that of Chalk; only retaining their outward Form, and the Poroseness of their inward Parts.

‖**Porosis** (porōu·sis). *Physiol.* [mod.L., a. Gr. πώρωσις in same sense, f. πωροῦν to form a callus, f. πῶρος PORE *sb.*[2]] The formation of a callus, as in a fractured bone.

1693 tr. *Blancard's Phys. Dict.* (ed. 2), *Porosis*, the breeding of callous Matter. 1706 in PHILLIPS. 1858 in MAYNE *Expos. Lex.*

Porosity (porǫ·sĭti). [ad. med.L. *porōsitās* (Albertus Magnus *a* 1250), f. L. type **porōs-us* POROUS: see -ITY. Cf. F. *porosité*.] The quality or fact of being porous; porous consistence.

1398 TREVISA *Barth. De P. R.* IV. ii. (1495) e v b/1 The porositee of the tree drawyth þe fumosyte from the rynde. 1615 CROOKE *Body of Man* 385 This porosite also makes their vpper face smooth, and bedewed with a kind of slimy moisture. 1796 KIRWAN *Elem. Min.* (ed. 2) I. 231 It is the porosity of this stone that renders it so light. 1872 TYNDALL *Fragm. Sc.* (1879) I. v. 183 In virtue of its extreme porosity, a similar power is possessed by charcoal.

b. *concr.* A porous part or structure; an interstice or pore. (Usually in *pl.*)

1597 A. M. tr. *Guillemeau's Fr. Chirurg.* 9 b/2 The Diploe, that is, the porositye which is betweene them bothe [tables of skull]. 1669 W. SIMPSON *Hydrol. Chym.* 284 Sudden floods filling the porosities and chanels of the superficies of the earth. 1831 R. KNOX *Cloquet's Anat.* 15 Found in the interstices of the laminæ of the compact tissue, and the porosities with which they seem perforated.

Poro·so-, combining form of mod.L. *porōsus* POROSE, as in **poro·so-pu·nctate** *a.*, minutely punctate as if with pores.

1846 DANA *Zooph.* (1848) 416 Interstices smooth, poroso-punctate.

Porostomatous (pǫrǒ-, pōə̆rostǫ·mătəs), *a. Zool.* [f. mod.L. *Porostomata* (f. Gr. πόρο-ς pore + στόμα(τ-) mouth) + -OUS.] Belonging to or having the characters of the *Porostomata*, a group of nudibranchiate gastropods in which the mouth is pore-shaped.

Porotic (porǫ·tik), *a.* and *sb. Med.* ? *Obs. rare*⁻⁰. [ad. mod.L. *pōrōtic-us*, f. Gr. πωρόειν to form a callus, f. πῶρος PORE *sb.*[2]: see -IC.] (See quots.)

1696 PHILLIPS (ed. 5), *Porotick Medicines*, Medicines which by drying, thickning and astringent Qualities turn part of the Nourishment into brawny or callous Matter. 1753 CHAMBERS *Cycl. Supp.*, *Poroticks*, a term used by the antients for such medicines as would consume callus. 1842 DUNGLISON *Med. Lex.*, *Porotic*, a remedy believed to be capable of assisting the formation of callus. 1895 *Syd. Soc. Lex.*

Porotype (pǫrǒ-, pōə̆·rotəip). [mod. f. Gr. πόρος PORE *sb.*[1] + TYPE.] A print made upon prepared paper by exposing an engraving or writing to some gas which penetrates those parts not rendered impervious by the ink, and bleaches or discolours the paper so as to produce a copy of the original, in the same way as light produces a copy from a photographic negative.

1884 KNIGHT *Dict. Mech.* Suppl., *Porotype*, a method of copying engravings. It depends upon the fact that the portion of the face of the print occupied by ink is non-porous.

Porous (pōə̆·rəs), *a.* [= F. *poreux* (14th c. in Hatz.-Darm.), It., Sp. *poroso*, ad. L. type **porōs-us* (in mod.L.), f. *porus* PORE *sb.*[1]: see -OUS.] Full of or abounding in pores; having minute interstices through which water, air, light, etc. may pass.

Porous plaster, a plaster having numerous small holes pierced through it so as to enable it to lie smoothly (*Syd. Soc. Lex.*).

c 1400 *Lanfranc's Cirurg.* 107 It schulde ben more rare & more porous [*v.r.* porose], þat is to seie, more ful of hoolis. 1567 MAPLET *Gr. Forest* 33 It is nothing solide or massie, but much porouse. 1625 N. CARPENTER *Geog. Del.* II. ix. (1635) 153 The Porous and spongy nature of the Earth is apt to drinke in the water of the sea. 1692 BENTLEY *Boyle Lect.* 207 If gold it self be admitted, as it must be, for a porous concrete. 1794 SULLIVAN *View Nat.* I. 359 Light, in its passage, penetrates the porous vacuities. 1879 RUTLEY *Stud. Rocks* i. 5 Questions of water supply hinge mainly on the porous or impervious character of rocks.

b. *fig.*

1642 H. MORE *Song of Soul* III. Pref., Many [arguments] .. go through their more porous and spongy minds without any sensible impression. 1795 COLERIDGE *Plot Discovered* 19 But our minister's.. style is infinitely porous. 1864 CARLYLE *Fredk. Gt.* XVI. vii. (1872) VI. 207 Men are very porous; weighty secrets oozing out of them, like quicksilver through clay jars.

c. Acting or performed by means of pores.

1861 BENTLEY *Man. Bot.* (1870) 302 Porous dehiscence is an irregular kind of dehiscence.

Po·rously, *adv.* [f. prec. + -LY[2].] In a porous manner; with porousness; by means of pores.

1847 in WEBSTER; and in later Dicts.

Po·rousness. [f. as prec. + -NESS.] The quality or condition of being porous; porosity.

1668 WILKINS *Real Char.* II. vii. § 6. 186 Porousness, Spunginess, fungous, sinking, hollow. 1670 CAPT. J. SMITH *Eng. Improv. Reviv'd* 16 Marle.. by its glutinous substance being incorporated with the sand, closes the hollows and porousness thereof. 1775 STRANGE in *Phil. Trans.* LXV. 419 This porousness I also remember to have once before observed. *Mod.* There is a constant evaporation from the surface of the jar, on account of the porousness of the material.

fig. 1904 *Daily News* 6 June 3 Not less striking was the evident porousness of this over seventy-year-old man to fresh conceptions of truth.

b. *concr.* Porous substance or part. *rare.*

1644 DIGBY *Nat. Bodies* IV. § 4. 28 They will forcibly gett into the porousnesse of it, and passe with violence betweene part and part.

Porpaise, -pas(s(e, -pes(s(e, obs. ff. PORPOISE.

Porpan-, porpentine, etc.: see PORCUPINE.

Porpere, obs. form of *purpure*: see PURPLE.

Porphere, -erie, -ier, -ir(e, -iry, -ure, -yr, obs. forms of PORPHYRY.

Porphyr-, porphyro-, repr. Gr. πορφυρ(ο-, comb. stem of πόρφυρα purple, and its derivatives; in Eng. (and other mod. langs.) a formative element, in senses 'purple' and 'porphyry', as in *porphyr-aceous*, *porphyr-ite*, *porphyr-ize*, *porphyrogenetic*, etc.

‖**Porphyra** (pǭ·ɹfĭră). *Bot.* [mod.L. (Agardh), a. Gr. πορφύρα purple.] A small genus of Algæ or Seaweeds, type of the sub-order *Porphyreæ*, with fronds varying in colour from a clear rose to a livid purple. The chief species are *P. laciniata* and *P. vulgaris*, known as Purple Laver.

1849 CRAIG, *Porphyra*, a genus of Algæ: Order, Confervaceæ. 1857 WOOD *Com. Objects Sea-shore* 69 The ulva and porphyra, if intended to be eaten, must be gathered in the winter... The purple laver is said to be much superior to its green companion.

Porphyraceous (pǭɹfĭrē¹·ʃəs), *a.* ? *Obs. rare.* [f. PORPHYR- + -ACEOUS.] Of the nature of or allied to porphyry; porphyritic.

1799 KIRWAN *Geol. Ess.* 207 Charpentier mentions a sort of stone which he calls porphyraceous, though he does not ascribe felspar to it. Hence 1828 in WEBSTER; and in mod. Dicts.

†**Po·rphyrat**, *a. Obs. rare*⁻¹. [f. as prec.: see -ATE[2].] = PORPHYRITIC.

1611 SPEED *Theat. Gt. Brit.* I. xl. 78/1 His ashes bestowed in a little golden potte or vessell of the Porphyrat stone, were carried to Rome.

Porphyrate (pǭ·ɹfĭrĕt). *Chem.* [f. as PORPHYRIC + -ATE[1].] A salt of porphyric acid.

1866 WATTS *Dict. Chem.* IV. 690 The porphyrates explode when heated.

†**Porphyre.** *Obs.* [a. F. *porphyre* (Cotgr. 1611), ad. med.L. *porphyrius*, f. Gr. πορφύρεος purple.] Name applied to a kind of serpent.

[1584 GREENE *Anat. Fort.* Wks. (Grosart) III. 220 He resembleth the serpent *Porphirius*, who is full of poison, but being toothlesse hurteth none but him selfe.] 1608 TOPSELL *Serpents* (1658) 745 Of the Porphyre. There is among the Indians a Serpent about the bignesse of a span or more, which in outward aspect is like to the most beautiful and well coloured Purple. *Ibid.*, Unto this Porphyre I may add the Palmer Serpent.

Porphyre, -ie, obs. forms of PORPHYRY.

†**Porphy·rian**, *a.*[1] *Obs.* [f. med.L. *porphyri-us* (see PORPHYRY) + -AN.] Of, or composed of, porphyry.

1638 SIR T. HERBERT *Trav.* (ed. 2) 62 Foure hundred porphirian pillars. 1687 A. LOVELL tr. *Thevenot's Trav.* I. 124 Many lovely Pillars of Porphyrian Marble.

Porphyrian (pǫɹfi·riăn), *a.*[2] (*sb.*) [ad. L. type **Porphyriānus*, f. *Porphyri-us* (a. Gr. Πορφύριος), proper name (f. πόρφυρ-ος purple) + *-ānus*, -AN.] Of or pertaining to Porphyrius or Porphyry, the Neo-Platonic philosopher and antagonist of Christianity (A.D. 233–*c* 306), or to his doctrines.

Porphyrian scale or *tree*, a definition of *man*, in the form of a kind of genealogical table or tree displaying the series of subaltern genera to which he may be assigned below the summum genus *substance*, and the differentiæ by which each subaltern genus is distinguished within the genus next above it. The 'tree' is frequently used as an example of dichotomy. Its origin is to be found in Porphyry's *Isagoge in Aristotelis Categorias* 2 a 13 seqq. (ed. Brandis). In the diagram the names of the genera occupy the middle column; the positive differentiæ are on the left hand, the negative differentiæ on the right.

Substance
Corporeal — *Incorporeal*
Body
Animate — *Inanimate*
Living
Sensible — *Insensible*
Animal
Rational — *Irrational*
Man
Socrates, Plato, Others.

1593 NASHE *Christ's Teares* Wks. (Grosart) IV. 194 Prosecute with all your authority, these Porphirian deriders. 1656 COWLEY *Misc.*, *Tree of Knowledge* i, That right Porphyrian Tree which did true Logick shew, Each Leaf did learned Notions give, And th' Apples were Demonstrative. 1678 CUDWORTH *Intell. Syst.* 589 Even according to the Porphyrian Theology it self.. the Three Hypostases in the Platonick Trinity, are ὁμοούσιοι, Co-Essential. 1678 NORRIS *Coll. Misc.* (1699) 59 You err, if you think this is he, Tho' seated on the top of the Porphyrian Tree. 1802–12 BENTHAM *Ration. Judic. Evid.* (1827) I. 286 Every step it takes in the region of particulars, whether downwards in the Porphyrian scale, or sideways all round in the field of circumstances affords an additional security.

B. *sb.* A disciple or follower of Porphyry; also called **Porphy·rianist.** [F. *Porphyrien*.]

1678 CUDWORTH *Intell. Syst.* I. iv. 594 The Arians (as Socrates recordeth) were by Constantine called Porphyrianists,.. because Arius and Porphyrius did both of them alike, though upon different grounds, make their Trinity a foundation for creature-worship and idolatry. 1701 tr. *Le Clerc's Prim. Fathers* (1702) 125 In another Letter.. he [Constantine] enjoins the Name of Porphyrus to be given to Arius, and his Followers to be called Porphyrians. 1882–3 *Schaff's Encycl. Relig. Knowl.* I. 640 [Diodorus] combated Platonists and Porphyrians, Manichaeans and Apollinarists.

Porphyric (pǫɹfi·rik), *a.*[1] *Geol. rare.* [f. PORPHYR- + -IC: in mod.F. *porphyrique*.] = PORPHYRITIC.

1824 J. HODGSON in J. Raine *Mem.* (1858) II. 43 The bold red seared line of porphyric hills lying east and west.

Porphyric (pǫɹfi·rik), *a.*[2] *Chem.* [f. Gr. πόρφυρ-os purple + -IC.] In *porphyric acid* ($C_{16}H_{4}N_{2}O_{7}$), obtained, as a yellow crystalline powder, or in minute crystals, by the action of nitric acid on euxanthone, and producing a blood-red colour with ammonium carbonate.

1866 WATTS *Dict. Chem.* IV. 690 Porphyric acid is slightly soluble, with red colour, in pure water; very slightly soluble in cold, more soluble in boiling alcohol.

Porphyrine[1] (pǭ·ɹfĭrĭn). Also 6 **porphurine**, 9 **porphyrin.** [f. as PORPHYRIC *a.*[1] + -INE[4].]

†**1.** = PORPHYRY. *Obs. rare.*

1588 GREENE *Perimedes* Wks. (Grosart) VII. 57 Houses stuffed within with plate and outwardly decked and adorned with such curious worke of porphurine, as nature in them seemeth to be ouerlaboured with arte.

2. *Geol.* A porphyritic rock: see quots.

1811 PINKERTON *Petralogy* I. 88 The Swedish porphyry, already mentioned, approaches nearer to a porphyrin,.. forming the passage from basaltin to porphyry. 1862 DANA *Man. Geol.* 79 Porphyrine. Opaque or nearly so... Consists of feldspar; sometimes quartzose.

Supplement, p. 3873; Corrigenda, p. 4092; Spurious words, p. 4093; Books quoted, p. 4094

PORPHYRINE. 1133 **PORPHYRY.**

Porphyrine[2]. *Chem.* [f. Gr. πορφύρα purple + -INE[2].] An amorphous alkaloid obtained from the bark of an Australian species of *Alstonia* (N. O. *Apocynaceæ*), which exhibits a characteristic red colour with nitric acid.

Porphyrio (pǭfi'riǫ). *Ornith.* Also 7-8 porphir-, -phyrion. L. [porphyrio (Plin.), ad. Gr. πορφυρίων the purple coot.] A name given by the ancients to the purple coot, sultana, or water-hen (see quot. 1894) taken by Brisson, 1760, as name of the genus of Rallidæ including this, distinguished by their deep-blue plumage and scarlet bill and legs, widely distributed in warm and tropical regions.

Porphyrite (pǭ'firǝit). *Min.* Also 6-phirite, 7-phyrit, pherite. [ad. L. *porphyrites* a purple-coloured precious stone in Egypt (Pliny), ad. Gr. πορφυρίτης adj. like purple, n. Also stone of this colour, porphyry, f. πορφύρα purple: see PORPHYRE and -ITE[1]. So mod.F. *porphyrite*, in sense 4.]

Porphyritic (pǭfiri'tik), a. Also 7-etiok. [ad. mod.L. *porphyriticus*, f. L. *porphyrites* PORPHYRITE; so F. *porphyritique*. The classical L. was *porphyritus*.] Of or pertaining to the porphyry or the nature or structure of the porphyry of modern mineralogists; *spec.* containing distinct crystals or crystalline particles embedded in a compact ground-mass.

Porphyrize (pǭ'fǝrǝiz), v. [f. PORPHYRY + -IZE.] *trans.* Obs. rare. q.d. Purple-coloured. Also *ellipt.* as *sb.*: see quot.

Porphyritic (pǭfiri'tik), a. Also 7-etiok.

Porphyrogenetic (pǭfīrǫdʒini'tik), a. [f. PORPHYRO-, PORPHYRO- + GENETIC.] Producing or generating porphyry.

Porphyrogene (pǭ'fīrǝdʒīn), a. Obs. exc. in L. form *porphyrogenitus*, fem. -a. Also 7-genete.

Porphyrogenite.

Porphyroid (pǭ'firoid), sb. (a.) *Geol.* and *Min.* [f. PORPHYR(Y + -OID. So F. *porphyroïde*.] A *sb.* A rock resembling porphyry or of porphyritic structure.

Porphyrous (pǭ'firǝs), a. poet. rare. [f. Gr. πορφύρα purple + -OUS.] Purple.

PORRACEOUS. 1135 **PORRY.**

Porraceous (pǫræ'ʃǝs), a. Also 7-9 erroneous. [L. *porraceus* of or like leeks, leek-green, f. *porrum* leek: see -ACEOUS.] Of the nature or colour of the leek; leek-green.

Porrect (pǫre'kt), v. *Zool.* [ad. L. *porrectus* stretched out, extended: see -porrect.] Stretched out; extended.

Porrect (pǫre'kt), v. [L. *porrect-*, ppl. stem of *porrigĕre* to stretch out in front of oneself, put forth, extend, offer, f. *por- = pro-* forth + *regĕre* to stretch, direct.]

Porrection (pǫre'kʃǝn). [ad. L. *porrection-em*, n. of action f. *porrigĕre*: see prec. So F. *porrection*.]

Porret (pǫre't). Now dial. Forms: *a.* porret, porretto. [a. F. *porrette* dim. L. *porrum* leek.]

Porridge (pǫ'ridʒ), *sb.* Forms: 6 porage, 6-7 edge, 6-8 -age, 6-8 (9 dial.) -age, 7-idg, &c. (9 dial.) -itch, 9 partridge, 8 partige. [Altered form of POTTAGE, PODDISH (cf. PORRINGER).]

Porrigo (pǫrǝi'gǫ). *Path.* [L. *porrīgo* scurf, dandruff.]

Porrige, Porringer.

Porry. *Obs.* [f. PORR(Y sb. + -Y[1].] The portion of the warp lying between the warp-roll or beam and the back of the heddles or harness through which the threads pass.

PORPHYRY. 1134 **PORR.**

Porphyry (pǭ'firi). Forms: *a.* 5 porfurie, -lirye, -lorie, -phyrye, 6-phire, -phyre. 8 purfire, 7-pore, -fure, 6-phure, purphire, -phuer, 6-7-phir, -e, 6-9-phyro, 7-phre, purphire, 7-8-phir, 7-8-phry, 7-phury, purphorie, 8 porphyri, 6-porphyry, -phyrie, -phurie, porphyri. [In Chaucer, in sense 3 *porfurie, -firie*, etc.]

Porpoise (pǭ'pǝs). Forms: *a.* 4-6 porpays, -peys, -poys, 4-6 -pas, 5 -pays, -o, -pyn, 5-6 -pes, 6 -poise, -pos, -pyse, -pyhe, 5-9 -pesse, 7-paise, -piece, -pois, -pos, -puis, -puise, -pise, 7-8 -pass, -pos, -poise, -posse, -porpoisa.

Porporino.

Porpus, -pus, -pysse, pus, obs. ff. PORPOISE.

Porr (pǫr, pǭr), *sb.* Now only dial. Forms: 4-6 porre, 6 pore, 6- port, pore, 9 purr. [ME. *porre* = MDu. *porren*, Du. *porren*, MLG. G. *purren*.]

Porr (pǫr, pǭr), v. Now only dial. [ME. *porren*, MDu. *porren*, Du. *porren*, MLG. G. *purren*.]

PORT. 1136 **PORT.**

Porry, var. POTTAGE.

Porry: see PORRAY, Pors, -e, obs. f. PURSE.

Porselan, -aland, -elin, obs. ff. PORCELAIN.

Porslane, aulaigne, obs. ff. PURSLANE.

Port (pǭrt), *sb.*[1] Also 4-6 porte, 5 portt. [OE. *port* a harbour, port, ad. L. *portus* port, harbour. In ME. reinforced by F. *port* (= Pr. *port*, Sp. *puerto*, It. *porto*) from OF.]

Port (pǭrt), *sb.*[2] Also 3-8 porte, 5 port(e. [a. F. *port*, a. F. *porte*, L. *porta* gate.]

Port (pǭrt), *sb.*[3]

Port (pǭrt), *sb.*[4]

cullis coins of Elizabeth, coined in rivalship of the Spanish king..of different sizes from the crown downwards. 1898 G. B. RAWLINGS *Story Brit. Coinage* 196 They [coins for use of the E. I. C.] are called the 'portcullis-money' from their reverse type.

4. Title of one of the Pursuivants of the English College of Arms, from his badge.

1616 BULLOKAR *Eng. Expos., Percullis*, the name of an office of one of the Pursiuants at armes. 1631 WEEVER *Anc. Fun. Mon.* 682 Segar being Portcullis Pursuiuant of Armes in the yeare 1586. 1656 BLOUNT *Glossogr.* s.v. *Harold*, There be four others called Marshals or Pursuivants at Arms,..those are Blew-mantle, Rouge-cross, Rouge-dragon, and Percullis. 1722 *Lond. Gaz.* No. 6084/5 Portcullis, Pursuivant of Arms. 1905 *Whitaker's Alm.* 157/1 Arms, College of, or Heralds' College...Four Pursuivants... Portcullis, Thomas Morgan Joseph-Watkin.

†5. (?) Name of some room in an inn. *Obs.*

1631 HEYWOOD *Fair Maid of West* I. Wks. 1874 II. 268 Besse, you must fill some wine into the Portcullis, the Gentlemen there will drink none but your drawing. *Ibid.* III. 293 *Enter the Kitchin-maid. Maid.* I pray forsooth, what shall I reckon for the Iolle of Ling in the Port-cullis?

Portcu·llis, *v.* In 7 **portcullice, percullis, purcullise.** [f. prec. sb.] *trans.* To furnish with a portcullis; to close with or as with a portcullis.

1593 SHAKS. *Rich. II*, I. iii. 167 Within my mouth you haue engaol'd my tongue, Doubly percullist with my teeth and lippes. 1611 FLORIO, *Rastellare*..to purcullise. *a* 1640 DAY *Parl. Bees* (1881) 25 *note*, Portcullice up the gates; hees poore and base.

Portcullised (poətkʌ·list), *a.* Also 6 **portcolized, -cullis'd**; *β.* 6. **purculleised**, 7 **percullis'd, percullist**, ?9 **perculaced.** [f. prec. sb. or vb. + -ED.]

1. Furnished with or having a portcullis; closed or barred with or as with a portcullis.

1572 N. ROSCARROCK in Bossewell *Armorie* Prelim. Verses, A hugie building olde, Portcolized and bard with bolts. 1598 DRAYTON *Heroic. Ep., Mortimer to Q. Isabel* 125 And all those Townes..Within their strong port-culliz'd Ports shall lie. 1598 FLORIO, *Cataratto*, purculleised or cataracted. 1611 HEYWOOD *Gold. Age* IV. i. Wks. 1874 III. 58 The rest keep watchfull eye On your percullist entrance. *a* 1763 SHENSTONE *Progr. Taste* II. 118 The stately fort, the turrets tall, Portcullis'd gate, and battled wall. 1861 M. PATTISON *Ess.* (1889) I. 45 A lofty massive front with three fortified and portcullised gateways.

2. *Her.* (See quot.) Cf. PORTCULLIS *sb.* 2.

1828 BERRY *Encycl. Herald.* I. Gloss., *Portcullised*, barred upright and across, after the form of a portcullis, termed also *latticed*. 1882 OGILVIE, *Perculaced*, in *her.* latticed.

Porte (pōᵊɹt). Also 6–8 **port.** [a. F. *porte*, in full *la Sublime Porte* = It. *la Porta Sublima*, transl. Turkish (Arabic) باب عالي *bāb i-ʿāliy*, lit. 'the sublime, high, or lofty gate', the official title of the central office of the Ottoman government, comprising the office of the Grand Vezir, of the Minister of Foreign Affairs, and of the Council of State (Redhouse, *Turkish Lex.* 1890). 'Gate' is supposed to refer to the ancient place of audience, etc., at the gate of the tent, or the king's gate; the attribute 'high' or 'lofty' is not literal, but the honorific attribute of the Turkish government. According to Zenker, the Western application of 'Sublime Porte' to the Turkish government or Ottoman state answers rather to the Turkish *dawlet-i-ʿāliye*, 'the sublime empire or state.'

In the 17th and 18th c., often erroneously taken as referring to the position of Constantinople as a sea-port.]

(In full, *the Sublime* or *Ottoman Porte.*) The Ottoman court at Constantinople; hence *transf.* the Turkish government.

1600 R. C. *Fumée's Hist. Hungary* 248 [Sultan speaks] Send your Ambassadours, as well towards our royall Port, as also to him. 1615 G. SANDYS *Trav.* I. 48 Some Vizers of the Port. *c* 1645 HOWELL *Lett.* (1650) II. 44 He that had bin Ambassadour at the Port to the greatest Monark upon earth. [1671 *Charente's Let. Customs Mauritania* 48 The King of Morocco usually gives audience at the Gate of this Palace, and here, as well as at Constantinople, La Porta signifies the Court or Kings Palace.] 1676 *Lond. Gaz.* No. 1145/1 Articles of Peace concluded between the King of Poland and the Ottoman Port. 1706 PHILLIPS, The *Port*, the Court of the Grand Seignior..at Constantinople. 1721 *Lond. Gaz.* No. 5983/1 Before the Port has had any Account of it. 1747 *Gentl. Mag.* Nov. 530 2 Report of which being made to the sublime Porte, the sultan advanced him to the post of Cadi. 1772 *Hist.* in *Ann. Reg.* 78/2 That haughty capital, which had been named the Porte by way of eminence, from its incomparable naval and commercial situation. 1847 MRS. A. KERR tr. *Ranke's Hist. Servia* 210 A better understanding was in consequence soon established between him [Napoleon] and the Porte. 1836 *Queen's Speech in opening Parlt.*, Under a convention..concluded with the Ottoman Porte, Commissioners have been appointed, on behalf of England and Turkey, to confer with His Highness the Khedive. 1891 *Blackw. Mag.* Oct. 470 The Sublime Porte is a time-honoured institution.

‖**Porte-** (port), Fr. imperative of *porter* to bear, carry; used in combination with a sb. as obj. in numerous compound words in Fr., several of which are more or less used in Eng.; the first element is occasionally anglicized as *port-*; and other words have been formed after these with the second element English (PORT-ELECTRIC, PORT-FIRE, etc.). From French: **Porte-acide** (-asīd), an instrument for the application of an acid to a part of the body. **Porte-aiguille** (-egwīy') [F. *aiguille* needle], a fine forceps for holding a surgical needle; a needle-holder. **Porte-bonheur** (-bonœ̄r) [F. *bonheur* good luck], an amulet, or a trinket worn like an amulet. **Porte-bouquet** (-buke), a bouquet-holder. **Porte-caustique** (-kostīk), also anglicized *port-caustic*, an instrument for applying a caustic. **Porte-feu** (-fö) (*port-feu*) [F. *feu* fire] = PORT-FIRE. **Porte-lumière** (-lümyɛr) [F. *lumière* light], an apparatus consisting of a mirror so arranged as to reflect light in any desired direction: used as a substitute for the heliostat. See also PORTEFEUILLE, etc.

1890 BILLINGS *Med. Dict.*, *Porte-acid, a glass tube through which a platinum wire passes carrying a tuft saturated with the acid to be applied. 1857 DUNGLISON *Dict. Med.*, *Porte-aiguille, an instrument for accurately laying hold of a needle, and giving it greater length. 1895 in *Syd. Soc. Lex.* 1884 G. MOORE *Mummer's Wife* (1887) 206 She had..a little gold *porte-bonheur..she had bought that morning. 1900 *Daily News* 6 Nov. 6/1 Some of them [prizes] were cut chrysanthemums in artistically-carved *porte-bouquets. 1846 BRITTAN tr. *Malgaigne's Man. Oper. Surg.* 274 Preference should always be given to a *porte-caustique like that of Ducamp for the urethra. 1884 M. MACKENZIE *Dis. Throat & Nose* II. 252 An ingenious porte-caustique has been invented by Dr. Fauvel. 1802 JAMES *Milit. Dict.* s.v. *Entonnoir*, the tin-case or *port-feu which is used to convey the priming powder into the touch-hole of a cannon. 1656 BLOUNT *Glossogr.*, *Porte-guidon, an Ensign-bearer to a troop of men at Arms. 1884 *Century Mag.* XXIX. 238/2 This apparatus consisted of a long photometer-box with a *porte lumière at one end.

‖**Porte-cochère** (port,koʃɛr). Also 7–8 (anglicized) **port-cocher.** [F., f. *porte* PORT *sb.*[3] + *cochère*, fem. adj. f. *coche* COACH *sb.*] A gateway for carriages, leading into a court-yard; a carriage-entrance.

1698 W. KING tr. *Sorbière's Journ. Lond.* 3 Divers of the Citizens Houses have Port-cochers [*mispr.* -ezs] to drive in a Coach, or a cart either, and Consequently have Courts within. 1699 M. LISTER *Journ. Paris* 8 All the Houses of Persons of Distinction are built with Port-cochers, that is, wide Gates to drive in a Coach. 1769 *De Foe's Tour Gt. Brit.* (ed. 7) II. 170 Kensington cannot be named without mentioning the King's Palace there:..there are two great Wings built..and a large Port-cocher at the Entrance, with a Postern. 1804 *Edin. Rev.* Apr. 95 The darkness of their court-yards and *portes cocheres*. 1848 THACKERAY *Van. Fair* lxiv, Their carriage stood in the *porte-cochère* of the hotel. 1882 *Century Mag.* XXIV. 843/1 The *porte-cochères*..afford glimpses of..court-yards.

Porte-colis, -cules, etc., obs. ff. PORTCULLIS.

Porte-crayon: see PORT-CRAYON.

Ported, *a. rare.* [f. PORT *sb.*[3] + -ED [2].] Having 'ports' or gates: in comb.

c 1611 CHAPMAN *Iliad* IV. 433 We tooke the seuen-fold ported Thebes, when yet we had not there So great helpe as our fathers had.

Ported (pōᵊ·ɹtėd), *ppl. a.* [f. PORT *v.*[1] + -ED [1].] Of arms: Held in the position of the port: see PORT *sb.*[4] 9 and *v.*[1] 2.

1650 T. BAYLY *Herba Parietis* 51 His own hair, standing stiffe an end, like ported feathers of some porcupine. 1667 MILTON *P. L.* IV. 978 Th' Angelic Squadron bright..began to hemm him round With ported Spears. 1844 *Regul. & Ord. Army* 265 The man or men going on the Post, who, with ported Arms, approach the Sentinels to be relieved.

‖**Portefeuille** (port,fœ·y'). [F., f. PORTE- + *feuille* leaf, sheet; cf. PORTFOLIO.]

1. = PORTFOLIO 1.

1699 M. LISTER *Journ. Paris* 92 He shewed his *Portefeuilles* in Folio, of Red Spanish Leather finely adorned. 1768 in *N. & Q.* 10th Ser. VI. 466/1 Ninety-five capital drawings..in two Russia portefeuilles. 1815 MME. D'ARBLAY *Diary* (1846) VII. 227 Neither..were of any avail, till he condescended to search his portefeuille for a passport.

2. = PORTFOLIO 2.

1792 *Amer. St. Papers, Foreign* (1832) I. 390 (Stanf.) The portefeuille was given to Monsieur Delessart. 1836 LADY H. STANHOPE *Mem.* (1845) I. x. 369 It was not Napoleon that he was so much attached to; it was to him who had the *portefeuille*.

Portegue, var. PORTAGUE *Obs.*

Portekoles, obs. form of PORTCULLIS.

Port-ele·ctric, *a.* [See PORTE-.] Carrying by electricity: applied to a proposed system of electric traction for transmission of parcels, etc.

1890 *Globe* 14 Nov. 3/1 The *Portelectric* car is an air cylinder 10 inches in diameter, 12 feet long, and 350lb. in weight. It runs on two wheels, one above, the other below, along an elevated railroad which supports the..hollow coils.

Portemantue, obs. form of PORTMANTEAU.

‖**Porte-monnaie** (port,mone). Also (in vulgar use) anglicized as **port-money.** [F., f. PORTE- + *monnaie* MONEY.] A flat leathern purse or pocket-book.

1855 THACKERAY *Newcomes* lxxix, Mrs. Mackenzie briskly shut her porte-monnaie. 1878 B. HARTE *Man on Beach* 78, I left my portmoney at home. 1885 C. F. WOOLSON in *Harper's Mag.* Apr. 785/1 A battered porte-monnaie.

Portenans, -aunce, varr. PURTENANCE *Obs.*

Portend (poɹte·nd), *v.*[1] Also 5 **portende**, 6 **pourtende.** [ME. ad. L. *portendĕre* to foretell, presage, archaic form of *protendĕre* to stretch forth, specialized in ritual sense, f. *por-* = *pro-* forth + *tendĕre* to stretch; see PROTEND.]

1. *trans.* To presage as an omen; to foreshow, foreshadow.

1432–50 tr. *Higden* (Rolls) VII. 33 A blasynge sterre was seene in the firmamente, whiche is wonte to portende other a pestilence of provinces other the chaungenge of a realme. 1560 DAUS tr. *Sleidane's Comm.* 285 [They] judged that it did pourtende and signifie some great trouble. 1654 BRAMHALL *Just Vind.* vi. (1661) 146 Like as that single meteor Castor appearing without Pollux portends an unfortunate voyage. 1868 FARRAR *Seekers* II. iv. (1875) 225 The croak of the raven can portend no harm to such a man.

b. By extension: To point to or indicate beforehand; to give warning of, by natural means.

1592 KYD *Sp. Trag.* I. ii, What portends thy cheerful countenance? 1685 EVELYN *Diary* 5 Nov., Bonfires were forbidden on this day; what does this portend! 1756 FRANKLIN in *Phil. Trans.* LV. 188 Small black clouds thus appearing in a clear sky..portend storms, and warn seamen to hand their sails. 1878 BOSW. SMITH *Carthage* 160 Everything portended an early renewal of the conflict.

2. Of a person: To foretell, predict, forecast, prognosticate, as by interpreting an omen. *rare.*

1611 HEYWOOD *Gold. Age* III. i. Wks. 1874 III. 48 What portend you in these hostile sounds Of clamorous warre? 1731 SWIFT *On his Death* 119 Some great misfortune to portend, No enemy can match a friend. 1851 GLADSTONE *Glean.* VI. iii. 2 A fact plain enough to those..who in the moral hemisphere can portend foul weather when 'the sky is red and lowering'.

†3. To signify, symbolize, mean, indicate. *Obs.*

1586 A. DAY *Eng. Secretary* II. (1625) 87 *Antanaclasis*, when we produce a word in a contrary signification to that it commonly portendeth. 1601 SHAKS. *Twel. N.* II. v. 130 What should that Alphabeticall position portend..? Softly, M.O.A.I. 1726 POPE *Odyss.* XIX. 645 The geese (a glutton race) by thee deplored, Portend the suitors fated to my sword. 1782 HAN. MORE *Belshazzar* II. 76 What do the mystic characters portend?

4. *intr.* To utter or give portents. *rare.*

1887 BOWEN *Virg. Eclogue* I. 18 Oft from the holm-oak's hole on the left did a raven portend.

Hence **Porte·nding** *vbl. sb.* and *ppl. a.*; also **†Porte·ndance, †Porte·ndment**, the quality or fact of portending; presage, omen, signification; **Porte·nder**, one who or that which portends.

1644 J. GOODWIN *Fighting agst. God* 22 It is a thing of the saddest consideration under heaven, and of more grievous *portendance unto us. 1657 — *Triers Tried* 5 [It] must needs be of a sad abode and portendance unto the people. 1635 SWAN *Spec. M.* v. § 2 (1643) 125 They have appeared as the *portenders of change in states and kingdomes. 1675 TEONGE *Diary* (1825) 26 An absolute portendor of a prosperous voyage. 1590 WATSON *Eclogue Sir F. Walsingham* 419 For they portending stormie windes surcease, but by *portending cause the hearts content. 1632 LITHGOW *Trav.* x. 459 The portending heauinesse of my presaging soule. 1626 BP. HALL *Contempl., O. T.* xx. ii, Like comets who were never seene without the *portendement of a mischeife. 1634 JACKSON *Creed* VII. vii. § 2 It only argues some deeper insight in ominous forewarnings or portendments.

Portend (poɹte·nd), *v.*[2] [ME. a. OF. *portend-re* to stretch forth, extend, to drape, cover, etc.:—L. *protendĕre* to stretch forth, with pop. L. *por-* for *pro-* forth. See prec. and PROTEND.]

†1. *trans.* To put forward, as authority or excuse; to pretend. *Obs. rare.*

1432–50 tr. *Higden* (Rolls) VIII. 93 William bischop of Hely..oppressede moche the clergy, portendynge the power of the kynge [L. *regis prætendens potestatem*].

2. To stretch forth, to extend, hold out (something). Now *rare* or *Obs.*

1657 TOMLINSON *Renou's Disp.* 678 The Alembick sometimes..portends out of its head..a Pipe. 1782 MICKLE *Q. Emma* III. 298 Spear to spear was now portended, And the yew-bows half were drawn. 1803 *Edwin* I. xii. 192 The fury that marked my brow as I portended my sword over the senseless bodies of my wife and child.

Portent (pōᵊ·ɹtėnt). Also 7 **portend**, and in L. form **portentum.** [ad. L. *portent-um* a portent, sign, omen, monster, marvellous tale (whence also It., Sp., Pg. *portento*, obs. F. *portente*), f. L. *portendĕre* to PORTEND. Orig. stressed *porte·nt*, which came down to 19th c.; but *po·rtent* is found also in 1711. Pope has both.]

1. That which portends or foretells something momentous about to happen, esp. of a calamitous nature; an omen, significant sign or token.

1563–87 FOXE *A. & M.* (1596) 762 (R.) A strange portent and prodigious token from heauen, in the yeare of our Lord 1505. 1596 SHAKS. *1 Hen. IV*, II. iii. 65 O what portents are these? *c* 1611 CHAPMAN *Iliad* II. 268 And there appear'd a huge portent, A Dragon with a bloody skale, horride to sight, and sent To light by great Olympius. 1671 MILTON *P. R.* IV. 491 As false portents, not sent from God, but thee. 1697 DRYDEN *Virg. Past.* I. 22 My Loss by dire Portents the Gods foretold. 1711 POPE *Temp. Fame* 452 Of prodigies and portents seen in air. 1736 S. WESLEY *Hymn*, From whence these dire Portents around, That Earth and Heaven amaze? 1814 SCOTT *Ld. of Isles* VI. xxx, Portents and miracles impeach Our sloth. 1821 BYRON *Sardan.* II. i, Let us think Of what is to be done to justify Thy planets and their portents. 1845 HIRST *Poems* 73 Such portents shook the soul of Rome. 1871 FROUDE in *Devon. Assoc. Trans.* IV. 20 The early records of all nations are full of portents and marvels.

b. The fact or quality of portending; in phr. *of dire* (etc.) *portent*.

1715–20 POPE *Iliad* II. 372 A mighty dragon shot, of dire portent; From Jove himself the dreadful sign was sent.

1865 PARKMAN *Huguenots* iii. (1875) 28 A cloud of black and deadly portent was thickening over France.

c. In weakened sense: A sign of coming weather or other natural phenomena.

1868 HAWTHORNE *Amer. Note-Bks.* (1879) II. 37 Lowering with portents of rain. 1882 'OUIDA' *Maremma* viii, She was not so familiar with the portents of the land.

2. Something considered portentous; a prodigy, wonder, marvel.

1741 MIDDLETON *Cicero* II. x. 422 L. Antony, the portent and disgrace of his species. 1842 MACAULAY *Ess., Fredk. Gt.* (1877) 671 Frederic was not one of these brilliant portents. 1863 GEO. ELIOT *Romola* I, If you talk of portents, what portent can be greater than a pious notary? 1881 M. G. WATKINS in *Academy* 19 Mar. 202 That portent the 'general reader' will find this book entertaining.

3. *Comb.*, as *portent-like* adj. and adv.

1744 HANMER *Shaks. Wks.*, *L. L. L.* V. ii. 67 Portent-like [Hanmer's emendation of *pertaunt-*, *pertlaunt-like* of the Quartos and Folios]. 1747 WARBURTON in *Shaks. Wks.* II. 256 Portent-like, i. e. I would be his fate or destiny, and like a portent hang over, and influence his fortunes.

Hence **†Porte·ntful** *a. Obs.*, portentous.

1633 T. ADAMS *Exp. 2 Peter* iii. 5 There are bred those portentful comets and exhalations, out of which fantastical heads pick fanatical meanings.

†Portenti·fical, *a. Obs. rare*^{—0}. [f. L. *portentificus* (f. *portentum* PORTENT: see -FIC) + -AL.]

1656 BLOUNT *Glossogr.*, *Portentifical*, which worketh wonders, or whereby monstrous and strange things are done.

†Porte·ntion. *Obs. rare.* In 7 **portension.** [ad. med.L. *portentiō-nem* a portent, f. *portendĕre* to PORTEND.] The action of portending; a portent.

1658 SIR T. BROWNE *Pseud. Ep.* VI. xiv. 417 Why although the Red Comets do carry the portensions of Mars, the brightly-white should not be of the Influence of Jupiter or Venus,..is not absurd to doubt.

†Porte·ntive, *a. Obs. rare.* [f. L. *portent-*, ppl. stem of *portendĕre* to PORTEND + -IVE.] Having the quality of portending; = PORTENTOUS 1.

1594 NASHE *Terrors Night* Wks. (Grosart) III. 245 Commonly that [dream] which is portentiue in a King is but a friuolous fancie in a beggar. 1659 FULLER *App. Inj. Innoc.* I. 51* The Portentive Idolls of their Country. 1773 J. ROSS *Fratricide* IV. 9 (MS.) The Heavens Portentive roll'd their thunders o'er his head.

Portentous (poɹte·ntəs), *a.* Also 6 **portentius**, 7–9 **-uous**, 7 **-eous.** [ad. L. *portentōsus*, *-uōsus* (whence also obs. F. *portenteux*, It. *portentoso*), f. *portentum* PORTENT: see -OUS and -UOUS.]

1. Of the nature of a portent; foreboding some extraordinary and (usually) calamitous event; ominous, threatening, warning.

c 1540 tr. *Pol. Verg. Eng. Hist.* (Camden) I. 140 With these portentius thinges albeit he was feared,..yeat, fearinge noe deceite..went forward on his waye. 1573 L. LLOYD *Marrow of Hist.* (1653) 153 Such portentuous miracles then seen in Rome. 1603 HOLLAND *Plutarch's Mor.* 1332 Many portenteous signes were given by terrible tempests. 1611 B. JONSON *Catiline* IV. ii, Stop that portentous mouth. 1641 MILTON *Reform.* II. Wks. 1851 III. 45 Let the Astrologer be dismay'd at the portentous blaze of comets. 1708 *Brit. Apollo* No. 14. 2/1 Actual Bleeding must needs be more Portentuous than a meer Dream. 1727 DE FOE *Syst. Magic* I. iv. (1840) 106 Having foretold the portentous events of the late meteor. 1829 LYTTON *Devereux* I. iii, There is something portentous in this sudden change. 1878 STEWART & TAIT *Unseen Univ.* ii. § 66. 81 The event loses from thenceforth much of its portentous significance.

2. Applied, without any connected sense of augury, to an object exciting wonder, awe, or amazement; marvellous, monstrous, prodigious; hence as an intensive (sometimes *humorous*) = extraordinary.

1553 EDEN *Treat. Newe Ind.* (Arb.) 36 A foure foted beast of monstrous shape..hauinge..beneath his comon belye, an other belye lyke vnto a purse or bagge, in which he kepeth his yonge whelpes...This portentous beast with her three whelpes was broughte to Cimle in Spaine. 1555 — *Decades* 159 A towne of such portentous byggenes. 1607 BP. J. KING *Serm. 5 Nov.* 23 So nefarious, flagitious, portentuous a wickednesse, as this was. 1639 FULLER *Holy War* V. xix. (1840) 275 By such portentous and extravagant numbers. 1695 WOODWARD *Nat. Hist. Earth* III. ii. (1723) 175 Such a Deluge..would require a portentous Quantity of Water. 1790 BURKE *Fr. Rev.* 252 See whether we can discover in their schemes the portentous ability, which may justify these bold undertakers. 1821 CRAIG *Lect. Drawing* i. 4 Since that portentuous period, the wealth of our happy country has..increased. 1823 LOCKHART *Reg. Dalton* II. i, A portentous apple-dumpling. 1877 GLADSTONE *Glean.* IV. xvii. 352 Russia will have to make..a portentous effort, when she is to leap from Constantinople to Calcutta.

Porte·ntously, *adv.* [f. prec. + -LY [2].] In a portentous manner; in a way that portends or foreshadows something unusual; hence (loosely) prodigiously, extraordinarily, astonishingly.

1656 TRAPP *Comm. 2 Thess.* ii. 3 That breathing devil, so portentously, so peerlessly vicious. 1755 WARBURTON *Div. Legat.* (ed. 4) I. II. iv. 246 Creatures, which by a reciprocal translation of the parts to one another, became all portentously deformed. 1816 SCOTT *Antiq.* vii, The distant sea..lay almost portentously still. 1858 BUCKLE *Civiliz.* (1869) II. viii. 468 The de line was portentously rapid. 1872 MORLEY *Voltaire* i. (1886) 9 Portentously significant silence. 1882 HAWTHORNE *Fort. Fool* I. xviii, He would be portentously severe against very trifling shortcomings.

Porteous: see PORTAS. (Common in Sc. legal use.) **Portepyne**, obs. form of PORCUPINE.

Porter (pōᵊ·ɹtəɹ), *sb.*[1] Forms: 3– **porter**; 3–5 **-ere**, 4 **-or**, (6 *Sc.*) **-ar**, 4–5 **-are, -our**, 5 **-eour, -iere**, 6 *Sc.* **-eir.** [ME. and AF. *porter* = OF. *portier* (12th c. in Godef.):—late L. *portārius* door-keeper, f. L. *porta* door: see -ER [2].]

1. One who has charge of a door or gate, esp. at the entrance of a fortified town or of a castle or other large building, a public institution, etc.; a gate-keeper, door-keeper, janitor.

c 1290 *S. Eng. Leg.* I. 382/210 Þat ich moste here porter beo. *a* 1300 *Cursor M.* 10013 At ȝates four er four porters [*v.rr.* -eris, -eres] Þat nathing mai cum in þat ders. 1382 WYCLIF *John* x. 3 To this the porter openeth, and the scheep heeren his vois. *c* 1400 *Apol. Loll.* 35 Þei schal be in my sanctuari huschers, & portars. 1413 *Pilgr. Sowle* (Caxton) I. x. (1859) 7 Peter is porter of heuen and lyeutenant of the souerayn lord in erthe. 1433 *Rolls of Parlt.* IV. 475/2 By the hondis of his Portour of the said Castell. 1530 PALSGR. 257/1 Porter, a kepar of a gate, *portier*. *a* 1631 DONNE *Lett.* (1651) 32 Like a porter in a great house, ever nearest the door, but seldomest abroad. *c* 1720 PRIOR *Wandering Pilgrim* 46 Let him in thy hall but stand, And wear a porter's gown. 1800 *Med. Jrnl.* III. 178 There shall be a resident Apothecary,..a Secretary, a Collector, a Porter, and such other Officers as shall be found necessary. 1885 MORLEY *Crit. Misc.*, *Pattison's Mem.* III. 151 Accomplishments..more fitted for the porter of a workhouse than for the head of a college.

fig. 1377 LANGL. *P. Pl.* B. xx. 296 And made pees porter [*C.* portor, -our] to pynne þe ȝates. *c* 1400 tr. *Secreta Secret.*, *Gov. Lordsh.* 97 Þes v. portours byfore-sayd er þe v. wyttes, þat dwellys yn þe eighen, yn þe eryn, yn þe nese, yn þe tonge, and yn þe hondes. 1423 JAS. I *Kingis Q.* cxxv, I fand, full redy at the ȝate, The maister portare, callit pacience. 1610 T. COLLINS *Mercy* in Farr *S. P. Jas. I* (1848) 357 Mercy's the porter of heauen's pretious dores. 1614 PURCHAS *Pilgrimage* 531 Two mightie Colosses or statues of Lions, were set as porters at the doore. 1668 BP. HOPKINS *Serm., Vanity* (1685) 72 God hath set that grim porter, Death, at the gate.

b. Applied to a watch-dog. **c.** (See quot. 1846.)

c 1420 LYDG. *Assembly of Gods* 37 Cerberus, the porter of hell, with hys cheyne. *a* 1661 FULLER *Worthies, Somerset* (1662) III. 18 [Mastiffs] are not (like Apes) the fooles and jesters, but the useful Servants in a Family, viz. the Porters thereof. 1846 *P. Parley's Ann.* VII. 325 Gamekeepers give various names to rabbits: with them they are warreners, porters, sweethearts, and hedgehogs...The porter's favourite haunt is in gentlemen's pleasure grounds.

†2. *Anat.* (tr. Gr. πυλωρός): The pyloric orifice of the stomach, where it opens into the small intestine. *Obs.*

1594 T. B. *La Primaud. Fr. Acad.* II. 349 It beginneth at the porter of the stomach, and is so seated beside the liuer. 1615 CROOKE *Body of Man* 119 It is called πυλωρὸς or the Porter, commonly the neather orifice.

3. *attrib.* and *Comb.*: **porter's lodge** (†**porter-lodge**), a lodge for the porter at the gate of a castle, park, etc. (formerly a place of corporal punishment for servants and dependants); †**porter-vein**, the *vena portæ* or portal vein (see PORTAL *a.* 2).

1471–2 *Durham Acc. Rolls* (Surtees) 644 Factura muri infra le *Porterloge. 1500–20 DUNBAR *Poems* xlii. 76 Strangenes, quhair that he did ly, Wes brint in to the porter luge. *a* 1592 GREENE *Newes fr. Heaven & Hell* (1593) B j, Wee be not farre from Heauen gates, and if S. Peter should understand of your abuse, I knowe he would commit you both to the Porters Lodge. 1623 MASSINGER *Dk. Milan* III. ii, Fit company only for pages and for footboys That have perused the porter's lodge. 1822 W. IRVING *Sketch Bk., Christmas Eve*, Close adjoining was the porter's lodge. 1899 CROCKETT *Kit Kennedy* 106 Gang doon to the porter-lodge, and wait till I come till ye. 1625 HART *Anat. Ur.* II. viii. 105 But what if such creatures were conueyed..through the mesaraicke veines into the great *porter veine? 1686 A. SNAPE *Anat. Horse* I. ix. 17 A small Vein..called *pylorica* or Porter-vein.

Hence **Po·rter** *v.*[1] *intr.*, to be or act as a porter.

1605 [see DEVIL *sb.* 23 a]. 1627 P. FLETCHER *Locusts* IV. xxviii, Wee'l hold their heart, wee'l porter at their eare.

Porter (pōᵊ·ɹtəɹ), *sb.*[2] Also 4 **portour**, 5 **-oue, -owre.** [ME. *portour*, a. OF. *porteour* (12th c. in Godef.) (mod.F. *-eur*):—L. *portātōr-em*, agent-noun f. L. *portāre* to carry, PORT *v.*[1] The ending *-our* was changed in 16th c. to *-er*: see -ER [2] 3.]

1. A person whose employment is to carry burdens; now *esp.* a servant of a railway company employed to carry luggage at a station (in full, *railway porter*).

†*Porter's ale, beer*: see PORTER *sb.*[3] *Porter's knot*: see KNOT *sb.*[1] 5.

1382 WYCLIF *1 Chron.* xvi. 42 The sonis forsothe of Ydithym he made to ben porters. 1393 LANGL. *P. Pl.* C. VII. 370 A dosen harlotes Of portours and of pykeporses and pylede tob-drawers. 1469 *Cal. Anc. Rec. Dublin* (1889) I. 336 If any of the portoures goo owt with cariage into the contry. 1530 PALSGR. 257/1 Porter of burdens, *crocheteur*. 1650 BULWER *Anthropomet.* 114, I saw a Porter..drink up a Flagon of Beer. 1683 MOXON *Mech. Exerc., Printing* xxi. ¶ 2 About an hundred Pounds weight, viz. a Porters Burthen. 1809 R. LANGFORD *Introd. Trade* 134 Porters,..employed to carry goods or parcels, also persons duly authorised, who attend wharfs for employment in various capacities respecting shipping. 1878 F. S. WILLIAMS *Midl. Railw.* 621 Porters for the passenger department are not accepted if they are less than 5 ft. 8 in. high. 1890 *Daily News* 17 Nov. 5/4 The Fellowship Porters—who must not be confounded with their humbler brethren the 'Ticket Porters' and the 'Tackle Porters'—are an association with a standing that entitles them to a hearing. 1898 *Westm. Gaz.* 15 July 4/2 The porter's rest, which stood so long on the north side of St. Paul's, disappeared at Jubilee time last year. 1901 *Census Schedule, Instruct.*, Porters..should specify the nature of their employment—as Railway Porter. The term Porter should never be used alone.

b. *gen.* and *fig.* One who or that which carries or conveys; a bearer, carrier.

1581 MARBECK *Bk. of Notes* 700 There is no need of porter, of a mediatour or minister, say onely, Lord haue mercie vpon me. 1634 BP. HALL *Contempl., N. T.* IV. xxxii, Simon of Cyrene is forced to be the porter of Thy cross. 1659 T. PECKE *Parnassi Puerp.* 67 The Grecian Tongue, Porter of Wit, and Art. 1817 *Sporting Mag.* L. 231 It enables him [the spaniel] to be a good roader, as it is styled in the south; in the north it is termed a good porter. 1896 *Allbutt's Syst. Med.* I. 868 Ships..are not such good porters of cholera as caravans, armies, hordes of pilgrims and unsanitary travellers.

c. (See quot.)

1607 COWELL *Interpr.*, Porter in the circuit of Iustices, is an officer that carieth a verge or white rodde before the Iustices in Eyre, so called, *a portando virgam*, an. 13 *Ed. I cap.* 24. 1772 *Jacob's Law Dict.* s.v., There is also a porter bearing a verge before the justices of either bench.

2. An appliance for lifting, carrying, or supporting.

†a. A lever. *Obs.*

1538 ELYOT *Dict.*, *Palange*, leauers or porters, wherewith they left and beare tymbre, and suche like thynges of greatte weight. *Palango*.., to beare on leyuars or porters. 1566 WITHALS *Dict.* 32/1.

†b. A supporting structure of timber or stone. (Cf. BEARER 9.) *Obs.*

1591 LODGE *Diogenes* (Hunter. Cl.) 19 He..swore that he would ouerthrowe the porters and bearers, which he practising to doo, the timber fell sodainly in the midst of his sawing.

c. An iron bar attached to a heavy body to be forged, by which it may, when suspended from a crane, be guided beneath the hammer or into the furnace; a porter-rod. Also, a bar from the end of which something (e. g. a knife-blade) is forged. (Knight *Dict. Mech.*)

1794 *Rigging & Seamanship* I. 78 (*Anchor*), *Porter*, a straight bar of iron, about 2 inches square, confined at one end to the end of the shank. 1839 URE *Dict. Arts* 44 The lower part [of an anchor] is left disunited, but has carrier iron bars, or *porters*, as these prolongation rods are commonly called, welded to the extremity of each portion. *Ibid.* 704 The *bloom* or rough ball, from the puddle furnace, is laid and turned about upon it, by means of a rod of iron welded to each of them, called a *porter*. 1875 KNIGHT *Dict. Mech.* s.v., A cross lever fixed to the porter is the means of rotating the forging beneath the hammer.

d. A light carriage with two or three wheels, to hold up from the ground the chain or rope of a steam plough.

1864 *Jrnl. R. Agric. Soc.* XXV. II. 416 The Travelling-porters are intended to carry the implement rope, the outer rope being best carried by the ordinary three-wheel porters.

3. *Weaving.* (*Sc.*) = BEER *sb.*[3]

1814 A. PEDDIE *Manuf., Weaver & Warp. Assist.* (1818) 152 What the Scotch weavers term a Porter, the English term a beer. 1846 G. WHITE *Treat. Weaving* 277 The hundred splits in all kinds of reeds is nominally divided into five equal portions for the sake of calculation, called porters in Scotland and beers in England. 1867 BLACK *Hist. Brechin* xii. 271 A thirty porter or 600 reed is divided into 600 openings in the breadth of 37 inches: 20 of these openings are called a porter. 1894 *Dundee Advertiser* 5 July 4 The new duty of 20 per cent. would also apply to tarpauling up to 11 or 12 porters.

4. *attrib.* and *Comb.*, as *porter-beer* (see PORTER *sb.*[3]), *-clerk*, *-crab* (see quot.), *-guard*, *-riot*, *-rod* (= sense 2 c).

1906 *Daily Chron.* 25 Jan. 6/7 A youth of seventeen, engaged there as *porter-clerk. 1904 *Ibid.* 11 Jan. 3/3 At Patami was obtained the '*porter' crab, which lies in the mud clasping a sea anemone to its back by means of modified legs. 1851 GALLENGA *Italy* 181 Student-plots at Pisa, *porter-riots at Leghorn, and demonstrations at Florence. 1839 URE *Dict. Arts* 44 (*Anchor*) To one end a *porter-rod is fastened, by which the palm is carried and turned round in the fire during the progress of the fabrication.

Hence **Po·rter** *v.*[2] *trans.*, to carry as a porter (sense 1), or by means of a porter or porters (sense 2 d); **Po·rtering**, the work or occupation of a porter.

1609 *Ev. Woman in Hum.* II. i. in Bullen *O. Pl.* IV, At night he shall be portered to our chamber. 1864 *Jrnl. R. Agric. Soc.* XXV. II. 305 It would have been interesting..to have tested the draft of this rope dragging on the surface, against the wire rope properly 'portered'. 1904 *Daily Chron.* 4 July 6/7 Nominally he is a licensed porter,..but he does not do much portering.

Porter (pōᵊ·ɹtəɹ), *sb.*[3] [Short for *porter's ale*, *porter's beer*, or *porter beer* (PORTER *sb.*[2]), app. because orig. made for or chiefly drunk by porters and the lower class of labourers; cf. the early quots.

There is no direct contemporary evidence as to the origin of the name. Statements going back to *c* 1750 attribute the first brewing of the liquor to Ralph Harwood 'at the place afterwards called Doctor's Brewhouse, on the east side of High Street, Shoreditch'; but these statements concern the origin not of the appellation *porter's ale*, *porter's beer*, but of the term *entire*. The probability is that *porter's ale* or *beer* arose as a popular descriptive appellation.]

A kind of beer, of a dark brown colour and bitterish taste, brewed from malt partly charred or browned by drying at a high temperature.

a. 1727 SWIFT *Further Acc. E. Curll* Wks. 1755 III. I. 161 Nursed up on grey peas, bullocks liver, and porters ale. 1734 SWIFT in *Mrs. Delany's Life & Corr.* (1861) I. 502, I cannot make shifts..by starving in scanty lodgings,..as I used to do in London, with port-wine, or perhaps Porter's ale, to save charges! 1745 MORTIMER in *Phil. Trans.* XLIII. 552 Their Urine..as high-coloured as Porter's Beer. 1770 MASSIE *Reas. agst. Tax on Malt* 5 So that every

Person.., must pay more than Three Halfpence for a Pint of Porter-Beer in London.

β. 1739 'R. BULL' tr. *Dedekindus' Grobianus* 139 The Fumes of Porter, Stout, or Home-brew'd Ale. 1743 *Lond. & Country Brew.* III. (ed. 2) 221 Of Brewing Butt-Beer, called Porter. *c* 1750 J. GUTTERIDGE (of Shoreditch) in *Gentl. Mag.* May (1819) 394/2 Harwood, my townsman, he invented first Porter to rival wine, and quench the thirst. Porter,..Whose reputation rises more and more. 1772 *Town & Country Mag.* 117 Hard working people delight in a kind of strong beer called porter, brown, clear, bitter and wholesome. 1781 in Hone *Every-day Bk.* (1827) II. 836 My electors shall have porter at threepence a pot. 1839 URE *Dict. Arts* s.v., At first the essential distinction of porter arose from its wort being made with highly-kilned brown malt. 1846 M'CULLOCH *Acc. Brit. Empire* (1854) I. 757 Breweries..The latter principally produce porter, the favourite beverage of the Londoners.

b. *attrib.* and *Comb.*, as *porter-brewer*, *-brewery*, *-malt*, *-pot*, *-pump*, *-shop*, *yeast*; *porter-coloured*, *-drinking*, *-hued* adjs.; **porter-cup**, a mixed beverage containing porter (see quot.). See also PORTER-HOUSE.

1818 CALVERT in *Parl. Deb.* 1012 It had been proved by those *porter brewers who had been examined before the police committee. 1776 ADAM SMITH *W. N.* V. ii. (1869) II. 486 In the *porter brewery of London, a quarter of malt is commonly brewed into more than two barrels and a half, sometimes into three barrels of porter. 1898 KIPLING in *Morn. Post* 9 Nov. 5/2 Clumps of gorse and heather and the *porter-coloured pools of bog water. 1882 *Barman's Manual* 51 *Porter Cup. Mix, in a tankard, a bottle of porter and an equal quantity of table ale; pour in a glass of brandy and a dessert-spoonful of syrup of ginger; add 3 or 4 lumps of sugar and a nutmeg grated [etc.]. 1851 G. BLYTH *Remin. Mission. Life* II. 121 His *porter-drinking propensities. 1863 *Royal Exchange Assurance* Art. ii, Maltsters (who make no high-dried or *porter malt). 1824 SOUTHEY in *Life* (1849) I. 137 He used to..fling the *porter-pot or the poker at me. 1838 DICKENS *O. Twist* xxvii, A porter-pot and a wine-bottle. 1804 LARWOOD *No Gun Boats* 15 The Caffés of France, and the *Porter Shops of England. *c* 1796 SIR J. DALRYMPLE *Observ. Yeast-cake* 2 London *porter-yeast..is preferred..by the distillers.

Porter *v.*[1], [2]: see PORTER *sb.*[1], [2].

Porter, variant of PORTURE *v. Obs.*

Porterage[1] (pōᵊ·ɹtəredʒ). [f. PORTER *sb.*[2] + -AGE.]

1. The action or work of a porter; carriage or transportation of goods, parcels, etc.; also, the charge for this.

1437–8 in *5th Rep. Hist. MSS. Comm.* 541/1, 5s. 8d. received from the Porters in the Strande, for the porterage of fish this year. 1611 *Lett. E. India Co.* (1896) I. 141 Item for porterage of particulars above to the barque, 03. 13. 1671 L. ROBERTS *Merch. Map Commerce* (ed. 2) 54 Other charges are Boat-hire, Wharfage, Porterage and Ware-house room. 1761 *Chron.* in *Ann. Reg.* 123/2 The carrier had no right to stop the goose for the porterage. 1809 R. LANGFORD *Introd. Trade* 131 *Porterage*, the hire of porters. 1859 TOZER *Highl. Turkey* I. 241 Female porterage is the custom of the country. 1880 *Post Office Guide* 235 When the addressee resides beyond the free delivery, porterage is charged. 1884 *G. W. R. Time Tables* July 83 No charge for porterage..at Holyhead.

†2. Something to be carried, a burden. *Obs. rare.*

1666 J. SMITH *Old Age* (1676) 179 These Porters do now become a porterage themselves, and those parts that were wont to bear the greatest burdens, are now so great a burden.

3. *attrib.* as *porterage fee*, *work*.

1774 *Acts Gen. Assembly Georgia* (1881) 418 For any Porterage Work from the several parts of the Town..to any of the Wharves the like rates. 1895 *Westm. Gaz.* 18 Apr. 7/1 Even the British Commissioner when he journeys to and from Uganda has to employ slave labour for porterage purposes. 1905 *Daily Chron.* 12 Nov. 5/4 A tariff regulating porterage fees.

Porterage[2]. *rare.* [f. PORTER *sb.*[1] + -AGE.] The duty or occupation of a porter or door-keeper.

1763 CHURCHILL *Duellist* II. 161 In rules of Porterage untaught.

Po·rteress: see PORTRESS.

Porter-house. Chiefly *U.S.* [f. PORTER *sb.*[3] + HOUSE *sb.* Cf. *ale-house*.] A house at which porter and other malt liquors are retailed; also, one where steaks, chops, etc. are served, a chop-house.

1800 COBBETT in Polwhele *Trad. & Recoll.* (1826) II. 531 They adjourned from the porter-houses and gin-shops to the cheese-mongers and bakers. 1807–8 W. IRVING *Salmag.* (1824) 236 Those temples of politics, popularity, and smoke, the ward porter-houses. 1858 *N. Y. Tribune* 16 Mar. 3/3 This morning, an altercation took place in the porter-house of Michael Byrne,..between Joseph Kelly..and others.

b. *attrib.*, as *porter-house boy*; **porter-house steak** (*U.S.*), 'a beefsteak consisting of a choice cut of the beef between the sirloin and the tenderloin..: supposed to derive its name from a well-known porter-house in New York' (*Cent. Dict.*).

1807 SOUTHEY *Espriella's Lett.* (1808) I. 67 Then came the porter-house boy for the pewter-pots. 1864 SALA in *Daily Tel.* 27 Sept., The 'tenderloin', the 'porterhouse' steak of America, are infinitely superior to our much-vaunted rump steak. 1902 *Westm. Gaz.* 11 Apr. 6/3 Porterhouse steaks sold for 15c. and now sell for 24c.

Porterlike, *a.* [f. PORTER *sb.*[2] + LIKE *a.*] Like a porter: = PORTERLY *a.*[2]

1598 FLORIO, *Facchinarie*, base, filthie, rascally, porter-like-tricks.

†Porterly, *a.*[1] *Obs. rare*^{—1}. [f. PORTER *sb.*[1] + -LY [1].] Proper to a porter or door-keeper.

1581 J. BELL *Haddon's Answ. Osor.* 397 b, Wherein he promised full remission..in the fullnesse of his Porterly power [= power of the keys].

†Porterly, *a.*[2] and *adv. Obs.* [f. PORTER *sb.*[2]]

A. *adj.* Pertaining to, or characteristic of, a porter (PORTER *sb.*[2]); hence, Rude, vulgar, low.

1603 FLORIO *Montaigne* (1634) 140 Off the stage,..they are base rascals, vagabond abjects, and porterly hirelings. 1673 KIRKMAN *Unlucky Citizen* 108 That Porterly Game of Nine-pins. 1709 *Brit. Apollo* II. No. 48. 2/2 Silly and Porterly Reflections on you. 1765 WESLEY *Jrnl.* 4 Sept., His language was as..foul, and porterly, as ever was heard at Billingsgate.

B. *adv.* In a 'porterly' manner; vulgarly.

1659 TORRIANO, *Facchinésco*, basely, or porterly. 1663 DRYDEN *Wild Gallant* I. i, I was porterly drunk, and that I hate of all things in nature.

Portership[1] (pōᵊ·ɹtəɹʃip). [f. PORTER *sb.*[1] + -SHIP.] The office of porter or door-keeper; also with possessive, as a humorous title.

1450 *Rolls of Parlt.* V. 197/2 Th' office of the Portership of the Castell of Rutland. 1503 *Act 19 Hen. VII*, c. 10 § 7 The office of Porter or Portershipp of the same Castell. 1592 NASHE *P. Penilesse* Wks. (Grosart) II. 95, I commend them..to the protection of your Portership. 1610 T. COCKS *Diary* (1901) 98 Yf Short and he got not through for the patent of the porter-shipp. 1886 LOWELL *Lett.* (1894) II. 349 Content with a portership in the House of the Lord.

Po·rtership[2]. [f. PORTER *sb.*[2] + -SHIP.] The office of a porter or carrier of burdens.

1521 *Maldon, Essex, Liber B.* 57 The tyme yew shall contynewe in the office of portershipp of this towne.

†Portery, portary. *Sc. Obs.* [a. MFl. *porterie*, *-erije*, f. *porter* citizen, burgher, f. *port* town, city: see PORT *sb.*[2]] Citizenship or burghership in a Flemish or Dutch city; the body of citizens collectively; the rights or privileges of a citizen or burgher (in the Netherlands).

(In the quotation referring to Scottish merchants or factors residing in Flanders.)

1565 *Reg. Privy Council Scot.* I. 333 All factouris that ar Scottismen..sall answer to the Conservatour, and nocht allege fra him to thair portary; and gif thai will abyde at thair portary, and nocht obey to the said Conservatour, the Quenis majestie..charges the said Conservatour that he discharge..hir liegis.

Portes s, Po·teur, var. PORTAS, PORTURE *sb.*[1]

Portfire (pōᵊ·ɹtfaiəɹ). [After F. *porte-feu*, in same sense: see PORTE-.] A device used formerly for firing artillery, and now for firing rockets and other fireworks, and for igniting an explosive in mining, etc.; = FUSE, MATCH *sb.*[2] 2.

1647 NYE *Gunnery* IX. 77 For the priming thereof, make a Potfire [*sic*], or Fuse. 1659 STURMY *Mariner's Mag.* V. xiii. 90 Leaving a small hole or a Port-Fire. 1710 J. HARRIS *Lex. Techn.* II, *Portfire*, is a Composition of Meal, Powder, Sulphur and Salt-Peter drove into a Case of Paper, but not very hard; 'tis about 9 or 10 Inches long, and is used to fire Guns and Mortars instead of Match. 1798 CAPT. BERRY in Nicolas *Disp. Nelson* (1845) III. 52 A port fire from L'Orient fell into the main royal of the Alexander. 1859 F. A. GRIFFITHS *Artil. Man.* (1862) 95 Portfires are of four different natures—viz., Common portfires, Percussion portfires, Miners' portfires, and Slow portfires. 1875 KNIGHT *Dict. Mech.* s.v., The *common portfire* is sixteen inches long, and is packed with a composition which burns at the rate of about one inch per minute. The *slow port-fire* consists of paper impregnated with saltpeter and rolled into a solid cylinder about sixteen inches long. It will burn three or four hours.

attrib. 1814 LEWIS & CLARK *Exp. Missouri* (1893) III. 922 Taking a port-fire match from his pocket. 1828 J. M. SPEARMAN *Brit. Gunner* (ed. 2) 331 Portfires...Papers for forming portfire cases. 1875 KNIGHT *Dict. Mech.*, *Portfire Clipper*, a nippers for cutting off the ends of port-fires.

†Port-flask. *Obs. rare.* [See PORTE-.] A belt or attachment for carrying a drinking-flask.

1598 R. BARRET *Theor. Warres* III. i. 34 With his flaske at his girdle, or hanging by a Port-flask, or Flask-leather vpon the right thigh.

Portfolio (port,fōᵊ·lio). Also 8 **porto folio, portefolio, port folio**, 8–9 **port-folio.** [In 18th c. *porto folio*, ad. It. *portafogli*, f. *porta*, imper. of *portare* to carry + *fogli*, leaves, sheets of paper, pl. of *foglio*:—L. *folium* leaf. First element altered after F. *portefeuille*: see PORTE-.]

1. A receptacle or case for keeping loose sheets of paper, prints, drawings, maps, music, or the like; usually in the form of a large book-cover, and sometimes having sheets of paper fixed in it, between which specimens are placed. Also *fig.*

1722 J. RICHARDSON *Statues, etc. Italy* 13 Another Porto Folio, all of Raffaele. 1764 *Chron.* in *Ann. Reg.* 85/1 A porto folio of choice original designs. 1768 FORSTER in *Phil. Trans.* LVIII. 215 More than 3000 MSS. maps and drawings were kept in their portefolios. 1796 *Mod. Gulliver* 53, I tied up my port folio. 1806–7 J. BERESFORD *Miseries Hum. Life* (1826) XII. vii, An huge portfolio of Miss' or Master's early school drawings. 1812 COMBE *Picturesque* XIV. (1813) 113 The Doctor forward stepp'd to shew The wealth of his port-folio. 1838 LYTTON *Alice* I. ix, His servant..placed his portfolios and letter-boxes on the table. 1858 C. W. GOODWIN in *Cambr. Ess.* 246 The compilers did not always confine themselves to the stores of their own portfolios.

2. *spec.* Such a receptacle containing the official documents of a state department; hence *fig.* the office of a minister of state. Orig. said in reference to France and other foreign countries.

1835 ALISON *Hist. Europe* (1849–50) V. xxxii. § 8. 405 The portfolio of the war office was put into the hands of Carnot. 1845 M. PATTISON *Ess.* (1889) I. 2 As the subs of office quit their desks when premiers deliver up their portfolios. 1860 FREEMAN *Hist. Ess.* I. ii. 46 On the other side of the Channel, the Minister bears his portfolio, here the Secretary bears his seal. 1898 *Westm. Gaz.* 10 May 2/2 It seems hard that Lord Salisbury may do with impunity..what would cost Lord Rosebery not merely his windows but his portfolio.

3. *attrib.* and *Comb.*, as *portfolio form*, *-hunter* (cf. *place-hunter*); **portfolio-stand**, a piece of furniture for holding portfolios, drawings, music, etc.

1902 *Daily Chron.* 1 Oct. 3/4 The present monograph will be in *portfolio form, with many illustrations. 1899 *Westm. Gaz.* 13 June 1/2 Falls of Cabinets have become a custom and startle only *Portfolio-hunters. 1887 RUSKIN *Præterita* II. 20 In his *portfolio-stands..were the entire series of the illustrations to Scott, to Byron.

Hence **Portfo·lioed** *a.*, furnished with a portfolio.

1848 *Blackw. Mag.* Aug. 185 All portfolioed, all handbooked..without compassion or conscience. 1892 *Review of Rev.* Jan. 6/2 Bewailing the consequences of portfolioed incapacity.

†Port-glaive. *Obs.* [ad. F. *porte-glaive*: see PORTE- and GLAIVE.] A sword-bearer; a member of the military and religious Order of the Knights Sword-bearers founded 1201 in Livonia.

1656 BLOUNT *Glossogr.*, *Portglaive*, a Sword-bearer. 1725 COATS *Dict. Her.* s.v., Knights of the Order of the Portglaive, or Sword Bearers in Poland, in Latin called *Ensiferi*. 1755 JOHNSON, *Portglave*, a sword bearer.

Port-grave: see PORT-REEVE.

Porth (pōᵊɹþ). *Cornw. dial.* [Corn. and W. *porth*, ad. L. *portus* PORT [1].] A small bay or cove.

1860 *Biog. & Crit. fr. 'The Times'* 245 Romantic coves provincially called Porths. 1880 CHARL. M. MASON *Forty Shires* 301 One of the little lovely inlets, or porths, as they are called, which break every part of the Cornish coast.

Port-hole (pōᵊ·ɹt,hōᵘl). [f. PORT *sb.*[3] + HOLE *sb.*]

1. *Naut.* An aperture in a ship's side; *spec.* formerly one of those through which cannon were pointed; now, one of the apertures for the admission of light and air; = PORT *sb.*[3] 2 b.

1591 PERCIVALL *Sp. Dict.*, *Portañola*, a port-hole, *porta*. *a* 1618 RALEIGH *Royal Navy* 26 Wont to plant great red Port-holes in their broad sides, where they carried no Ordnance at all. 1691 T. H[ALE] *Acc. New Invent.* p. x, So contrived the Port Holes therein, that most of her Guns might point to one Center. 1707 *Lond. Gaz.* No. 4329/5 [They] went through the Port-holes into the Long-boat. 1759 FALCONER 90-*Gun Ship* 41 Full ninety brazen guns her port-holes fill. 1802 *Naval Chron.* VIII. 481 The contrivance of port-holes..is attributed to Descharges, a French ship-builder at Brest, in the reign of Louis the Twelfth. 1892 CLARK RUSSELL *Marriage at Sea* iii, A black steamboat,..her portholes glittering as though the whole length of her was studded with brilliants.

fig. 1602 MARSTON *Antonio's Rev.* II. ii, The port holes Of sheathed spirit are nere corb'd up.

2. *transf.* **a.** An aperture in a wall for shooting through, etc.; an embrasure; **b.** a similar aperture in other structures, e.g. in the door of a furnace.

1644–5 N. DRAKE *Siege Pontefr.* (Surtees) 37 One of our men was looking out of a porthole on the round tower. 1703 MAUNDRELL *Journ. Jerus.* (1721) 19 It has the face of a Castle, being built with portholes for Artillery, instead of Windows. 1753 HANWAY *Trav.* (1762) I. III. xxxiv. 157 This city is inclosed within a wall above a mile in each square, with a great number of regular turrets and port-holes for arrows. 1870 J. ROSKELL in *Eng. Mech.* 18 Feb. 547/2 The 'port holes' are left open.

3. A steam port (PORT *sb.*[3] 4).

1875 in KNIGHT *Dict. Mech.* 1888 HASLUCK *Model Engin. Handybk.* 27 On turning the fly-wheel the crank draws the piston-rod out and inclines the cylinder sideways, bringing the port-hole to the left. *Ibid.* 37 Fig. 29, where the size and position of each port hole may be seen.

4. *attrib.* and *Comb.*, as *port-hole shutter*, *window*.

1766 ENTICK *London* IV. 88 The roof is..enlightened by four port-hole windows. 1892 E. REEVES *Homeward Bound* 95 We now find the advantage of the port-hole shutters.

Porthors, -hos, early forms of PORTAS.

†Portic. *Obs. rare.* Also 7 **portick.** [OE. ad. L. *porticus*: see next; cf. OHG. *pforzih*, etc. Not in ME., where F. *porche* PORCH took its place; re-introduced in 17th c.] A portico, a porch.

a 900 tr. *Bæda's Hist.* III. iii. (1890) 106 Fordon þe þone forecwedenan portic ma ne meahte beon [L. *eo quod praedicta porticus plura capere nequiuit*]. *c* 950 *Lindisf. Gosp.* John x. 23 And ȝe-eade se hælend in temple in portic salamones. *c* 1000 *Ags. Gosp.* John v. 2 Se mere hæfð fif porticas.

1682 WHELER *Journ. Greece* I. 18 It hath on the outside a Portic round it...Each side of the Portick is of Fourteen foot long. *Ibid.* 76 A fine Mosque; whose Portick is supported by Red Marble Pillars.

b. A philosopher of the Porch; a Stoic philosopher. *nonce use.*

a 1644 QUARLES *Funeral Elegies* Poems (1717) 417 Thou dry-brain'd Portick, whose Athenean brest Transcending passion, never was opprest With grief.

Portico (pōᵊ·ɹtiko). Pl. **-oes, -os** (also 7 **-o's**). [a. It. (also Sp., Pg.) *portico*:—L. *porticus* colonnade, arcade, porch, f. *porta* door, gate, PORT *sb.*[3]]

1. *Arch.* A covered ambulatory consisting of a roof supported by columns placed at regular intervals, usually attached as a porch to a building, but sometimes forming a separate structure; a colonnade; †a pergola in a garden (*obs.*).

1605 B. JONSON *Volpone* II. i, I..wont to fix my bank in face of the public Piazza, near the shelter of the Portico to the Procuratia. 1649 EVELYN *Diary* 30 May, His Majesty's statues thrown down at St. Paule's Portico and the Exchange. *a* 1662 HEYLIN *Laud* I. 210 He caused a stately Portico to be erected at the West end of the Church. 1686 BURNET *Trav.* iv. (1750) 233 The Beauty of their Temples, and of the Porticos before them, is amazing. 1706 *Lond. Gaz.* No. 4249/3 Making all sorts of Parterres, Porticoes, Arbours. 1758 JOHNSON *Idler* No. 33 ¶ 27 The porticos where Socrates sat. 1870 BRYANT *Iliad* I. VI. 194 Priam's noble hall, A palace built with graceful porticos. 1886 RUSKIN *Præterita* I. 325 Porticoes should not be carried on the top of arches.

b. *spec.* The Painted Porch at Athens: see PORCH 4; hence *fig.* the Stoic philosophy. Also *allusively*.

1788 GIBBON *Decl. & F.* xliv. IV. 352 From the portico, the Roman civilians learned to live, to reason, and to die. 1825 LAMB *Elia* Ser. II. *Barbara S—*, Poor men's smoky cabins are not always porticoes of moral philosophy. 1837 MACAULAY *Ess., Bacon* (1877) 403 Suppose that Justinian..had called on the last few sages who still haunted the Portico.

2. *transf.* and *fig.*

1720 OZELL *Vertot's Rom. Rep.* I. IV. 228 Two Javelins were fixed in the Earth, and a third fastened across upon the Points of those. All the Æqui..passed under this military Portico. 1727–46 THOMSON *Summer* 1393 Now to the verdant portico of woods..they walk. 1831 CARLYLE in Froude *Life* (1882) II. 226 Now it seems to me as if this life were but the inconsiderable portico of man's existence.

Hence **Po·rticoed** *a.*, furnished with a portico.

1665 J. WEBB *Stone-Heng* (1725) 103 The Temples..were circumalated, or either singly or doubly porticoed about. 1856 MISS MULOCK *J. Halifax* i, The High Street, with the mayor's house..porticoed and grand.

‖**Porticus.** *Obs.* [L.; see prec.] = prec.

1624 B. JONSON *Masque, Neptune's Triumph* Wks. (Rtldg.) 640/2 Till the whole tree become a porticus, Or arched arbour. *a* 1661 HOLYDAY *Juvenal* 146 Their baths..were of a less extent then their porticus or arch'd walks. 1682 SIR T. BROWNE *Chr. Mor.* III. § 21 Sleep not in the Dogma's of the Peripatus, Academy, or Porticus: be a moralist of the mount. 1685 H. MORE *Paralip. Prophet.* xxxii. 289 Porticus's likewise ran through the whole Ground-plot of the Temple.

‖**Portière** (portyɛr). [Fr.:—med.L. *portāria*, prop. fem. sing. of adj. *portārius* belonging to a door or gate; see PORTER *sb.*[1]] A curtain hung over a door or doorway, to prevent draught, to serve as a screen, or for ornament.

1855 THACKERAY *Newcomes* lxiii, What frightful Boucher and Lancret shepherds and shepherdesses leered over the portières! 1881 *Cornh. Mag.* July 50 He drew aside the portière that concealed the door.

attrib. 1893 SALTUS *Madam Sapphira* 83 There was a jostle of portière rings. 1897 *Daily News* 9 Nov. 6/5 A pair of portière curtains, old appliqué embroidery on crimson silk velvet ground.

†Portifo·lium, portyfolyom. *Obs. rare.* Corruption of med.L. *portiforium*, a PORTAS.

1546 BALE *1st Exam. A. Askew* 34 b, Their popish portyfolyoms and maskynge bokes. 1550 — *Image Both Ch.* I. 141 Though they neuer haue Beades, Latine Primers, portifolyomes, nor other signes of hipocrisie.

Po·rtify, *v. nonce-wd.* [f. PORT *sb.*[7]] To convert (claret) into port; in quot. *fig.*

1861 THACKERAY *Round. Papers* xiv, I grant you..that this claret is loaded, as it were; but your desire to *portify* yourself is amiable, is pardonable, is perhaps honourable.

Portigue, -ingue, var. PORTAGUE *Obs.*, gold coin.

Portinance, variant of PURTENANCE *Obs.*

Portingale, -gall, etc., obs. ff. PORTUGAL.

Portion (pōᵊ·ɹʃən), *sb.* Forms: 4 **porciun**, 4–6 **-ion, -ioun** (etc.); 4–5, 7 **portioun**, 7– **ione**, 5– **portion.** [ME. *porcium*, *portion*, a. OF. *porcion*, *portion* (12th c. in Hatz.-Darm.), ad. L. *portiō-nem* share, part, proportion (whence also Prov., Sp. *porcion*, It. *porzione*, Pg. *porção*).]

I. 1. The part (of anything) allotted or belonging to one person; a share. Also *fig.*

a 1300 *Cursor M.* 4716 (Cott.) He salde ilk man his porcion [*v.rr.* -ciun, -cioun]. *c* 1325 *Chron. Eng.* 352 (Ritson) The kyng of Esex wes riche, He hade to ys portion Wylteschire, Barkschyre. 1382 WYCLIF *Luke* xv. 12 Fadir, ȝyue to me the porcioun of substaunce, ethir catel, that byfallith to me. *c* 1400 *Ywaine & Gaw.* 3585 Gif the yonger damysele The half, or els sum porciowne, That sho mai have to warisowne. 1535 COVERDALE *1 Esdras* v. 8 Euery man sought his porcion agayne in Iewry. 1591 SHAKS. *1 Hen. VI*, V. iii. 125, I vnworthy am To woe so faire a Dame to be his wife, And haue no portion in the choice my selfe. 1696 PHILLIPS (ed. 5), *Portion*, a Lot, or Share of any thing that is to be parcell'd out or divided. 1772 *Junius Lett.* lxviii. (1820) 338 The study of the law requires but a moderate portion of abilities. 1847 MRS. A. KERR tr. *Ranke's Hist. Servia* 25 He honourably performed his portion of the compact.

b. A quantity or allowance of food allotted to, or enough for, one person.

1484 CAXTON *Fables of Poge* ii, She dyd brynge to hym [a poor man] his porcion as she was custommed for to doo. 1525 LD. BERNERS *Froiss.* II. ccxxii. [ccxviii.] 691 To close you vp in a castell, and there to be holden vnder subiection, and to lyue by porcion. 1611 BIBLE *Esther* ix. 22 Daies of feasting and ioy, and of sending portions one to another. 1629 WADSWORTH *Pilgr.* iii. 16 Each man hath..brought him..halfe a pound of beefe which they call their portion. *c* 1880 *Newspaper*, The demand, in London alone, for soles [fish] of the size to make one 'portion'.

2. The part or share of an estate given or passing by law to an heir, or to be distributed to him in the settlement of the estate. Also *fig.*

a 1340 HAMPOLE *Psalter* xv. 5 He is porcioun & mede of myn heritage. *c* 1440 *Jacob's Well* 21 In defraude of here wyves & chylderyn, to lettyn hem fro þe porcyoun þat longyth to hem, be ryȝt. 1538 STARKEY *England* I. iv. 113 Inheritarys to a grete porcyon of intaylyd land. 1590 SPENSER *F. Q.* II. ii. 2 Full little weenest thou what sorrows are Left thee for porcion of thy livelyhed. 1642 FULLER *Holy & Prof. St.* V. xix. 437 On whom the earth as their common mother bestowed a grave for a childs portion. 1818 CRUISE *Digest* (ed. 2) II. 21 Sir Joseph Jekyll decreed, that the plaintiffs were entitled to their original portions, as well as to the additional portions given by the will. 1855 MACAULAY *Hist. Eng.* xii. III. 210 On what security..could any man invest his money or give a portion to his children, if he could not rely on positive laws and on the uninterrupted possession of many years?

3. Dowry; a marriage portion. Also *portion-money*. (In quot. 1511 = DOWER 1.)

1511 FABYAN *Will* in *Chron.* (1811) Pref. 7 Also I will that my chalice, wt my ij crewetts and pax of siluer,..whiche before daies I gave to my wif, remayn styll to her, in augmentyng of hir porcion. 1602 WARNER *Alb. Eng.* IX. xlvii. 221 Who loues not for the Person but the Portion loues no whit. 1625 BOSWELL in Ellis *Orig. Lett.* Ser. I. III. 195 Her portion money..is already paying here. 1647 N. BACON *Disc. Govt. Eng.* I. xli. (1739) 64 This custom..[was] from the Latins, who used to give Dower with the man, and receive Portion with the woman. 1726 SWIFT *Gulliver* I. i, I married Mrs. Mary Burton..with whom I received four hundred pounds for a portion. 1861 M. PATTISON *Ess.* (1889) I. 35 Edward, on his side, is to give the moderate portion of 10,000 marks with his daughter.

4. That which is allotted to a person by providence; lot, destiny, fate. †*To lay one's portion with*, to cast in one's lot with (LOT *sb.* 1 e).

a 1325 *Prose Psalter* xlix. [l.] 19 Þou..laid þy porcioun wyþ spouse-breches. *c* 1400 *Apol. Loll.* 51 If ani presume aȝen þis, know he him to haue porcoun wiþ Giezi. 1535 COVERDALE *Job* xx. 29 This is the porcion that yᵉ wicked shal haue of God, and the heretage that he maye loke for of the Lorde. — *Ecclus.* xxv. 19 Yᵉ porcion of the vngodly shal fall vpon her. 1667 MILTON *P. L.* I. 70 Eternal Justice..here their Prison ordain'd In utter darkness, and their portion set. 1709 STEELE *Tatler* No. 54 ¶ 1 When Labour was pronounced to be the Portion of Man. 1851 NEALE *Hymn*, Brief life is here our portion.

II. 5. A part of any whole: = PART *sb.* 1.

1340 HAMPOLE *Pr. Consc.* 8118–20 A day here may be a porcyon Of ane hundreth yhere, als men may se, Alle-if þat porcyon fulle lytylle be. 1387 TREVISA *Higden* (Rolls) I. 99 Þe norþ est portioun of Arabia hatte Saba. 1480 CAXTON *Chron. Eng.* ccxvii. 204, xxx thousand pounde of syluer to be payed within iii yere..euery yere x thousand pound by euyn porcyons. 1633 *Sc. Acts Chas. I* (1817) V. 103/1 That..portioun of the lordshipe of Dumbar boundit meithit and merchit as eftir-followes. 1715 tr. *Gregory's Astron.* (1726) I. 416 Such a Portion of the Ecliptic, as the Sun describes in the mean while by its Annual Motion towards the East. 1831 MACAULAY *Ess., J. Hampden* (1887) 205 Almost every part of this virtuous and blameless life..is a precious and splendid portion of our national history. 1860 TYNDALL *Glac.* I. vii. 48 A portion of the pressure was transmitted laterally.

6. A part of the whole existing stock (of anything); a (limited) quantity or amount; some.

13.. *Coer de L.* 5413 The Sarezynes..cryede, trewes!..To the false Kyng off Fraunse; And he hem grauntyd..For a porcioun off golde. *c* 1386 CHAUCER *Shipman's T.* 56 Toward the toun of Brugges for to fare To byen there a porcion of ware. 1426 in *Surtees Misc.* (1888) 6 He boght of John Lyllyng a porcion of alom. 1526 *Pilgr. Perf.* (W. de W. 1531) 12 b, But grace, ye the leest porcyon of grace,..is sufficyent. 1817 JAS. MILL *Brit. India* III. VI. i. 8 Nujeef Khan, whose talents had..given a portion of stability to the imperial throne. 1838 T. THOMSON *Chem. Org. Bodies* 965 It would not be surprising if a portion of water, so far from being decomposed, were actually formed by the union of its constituents previously existing in the grain.

†7. The action of dividing; division, partition, distribution. *Obs. rare.*

c 1450 *Life St. Cuthbert* (Surtees) 4796 And parted in to twa knyghts hande, Be euen porciounе. 1494 FABYAN *Chron.* VI. cxlix. 136 After yᵉ which porcion, Charlmayne, herynge of the dyuycion & stryfe among the Almayns..sped hym thyther. 1635 SWAN *Spec. M.* (1670) 174 That proportion is quite taken away which God the Creator hath observed in all other things: making them all in number, weight and measure, in an excellent portion and harmony.

Portion (pōᵊ·ɹʃən), *v.* [ad. obs. F. *portionner*, *porcionner* (1339 in Godef.) to apportion, divide into shares (= med.L. *portiōnāre*, 1374 in Du Cange), f. F. *portion* PORTION; see APPORTION.]

1. *trans.* To divide into portions or shares; to assign or distribute in shares, to share *out*; = APPORTION *v.* 2.

c 1330 R. BRUNNE *Chron.* (1810) 51 Þe barons portiond þe lond euen þam bituene. 1725 POPE *Odyss.* VIII. 514 Now each partakes the feast, the wine prepares, Portions the food, and each his portion shares. *a* 1763 SHENSTONE *A Vision* Wks. 1765 II. 87 The journey seemed to be portioned into four distinct stages. 1859 JEPHSON *Brittany* xvi. 254 The petty chiefs among whom the country was portioned out. 1887 BOWEN *Æneid* V. 362 After the races are ended, the prizes portioned as due.

b. To allot or assign to any one as his portion or share; = APPORTION *v.* 1.

1871 BROWNING *Balaustion* 2326 No: it was praise, I portioned thee, Of being good true husband to thy wife! 1904 LD. BURGHCLERE *Virg. Georg.* I. 43 Not that the gods Have portioned them some special gift [L. *quia sit divinitus illis Ingenium*], or fate Bestowed a deeper sense of things to be.

2. To give a portion or dowry to; to dower, endow.

1712 M. HENRY *Commun. w. God* (1822) 365 The Psalmist having given preference to God's favour,..and portioned himself in that, here expresseth his great complacency in the choice he had made. 1838 *Murray's Handbk. N. Germ.* 449 Louis of Arnstein, having no son, married and portioned off his seven daughters, dividing among them a part of his estates. 1855 M. ARNOLD *Balder Dead* 114 That one, long portion'd with his doom of death, Should change his lot, and fill another's life. 1865 DICKENS *Mut. Fr.* III. iv, When I marry with their consent they will portion me most handsomely.

3. To mix in due proportion; = APPORTION *v.* 3.

1811 *Self Instructor* 514 Roman oker..when properly portioned with gum-water.

Hence **Po·rtioned** *ppl. a.*, **Po·rtioning** *vbl. sb.*

1732 POPE *Ep. Bathurst* 267 Him portion'd maids, apprentic'd orphans blest. 1845 S. AUSTIN *Ranke's Hist. Ref.* III. 521 Revenues..consecrated to the portioning of noble young ladies in marriage. 1850 BLACKIE *Æschylus* II. 22 We all must bear our portioned lot.

†Po·rtionable, *a. Obs. rare.* [f. PORTION *sb.* + -ABLE: cf. *proportionable*.] Proportional.

c 1374 CHAUCER *Boeth.* III. met. ix. 68 (Camb. MS.) Thow byndest the elementus by nowmbyres porcionables, þat the colde thinges mowen acorden with the hote thinges.

Portional (pōᵊ·ɹʃənăl), *a. rare.* [ad. late L. *portiōnālis* partial; see PORTION *sb.* and -AL.]

1. Pertaining to or of the nature of a portion or part; partial.

1382 WYCLIF *1 Esdras* viii. 31 These ben the prouostis, after ther kuntres, and porciounelis [*v.r.* porciounel, 1388 porcionel] princehodis [*Vulg.* porcionales principatus] of hem, that with me steyeden vp fro Babiloine. 1662 GUNNING *Lent Fast* 30 Why apply we the 4th, and 6th day of the week to stations? (or meetings for prayer, portional-fasting, and Sacrament). *a* 1670 HACKET *Cent. Serm.* (1675) 247 The Christians should punctually observe a portional abstinence, according to the time of forty days.

2. Of the nature of a portion or dowry.

1683 EVELYN *Mem.* 16 Mar., He [Sir J. Child] lately married his daughter to the eldest son of the Duke of Beaufort,..with £50,000 portional present, and various expectations.

Hence **Po·rtionally** *adv.*, by way of a portion or part; partly, in part. *rare.*

1617 COLLINS *Def. Bp. Ely* I. i. 29 Peter receiued, and receiued for himselfe,..but μερικῶς, not ὁλικῶς, portionally and particularly, not wholly and entirely. 1865 ELIZA METEYARD *J. Wedgwood* I. 330 The 'Brick House and Works' stood on what now forms portionally the site of the Wedgwood Institute.

Po·rtionary. *Obs.* exc. *Hist.* [ad. med.L. *portiōnārius* a canon's deputy in a cathedral, receiving half a prebend (*c* 1200 in Du Cange) (so OF. *porcionaire* 1442 in Godef.): see PORTION *sb.* and -ARY [1].] = PORTIONIST 2.

1548 *Act 2 & 3 Edw. VI*, c. 13 § 3 That all and everie person...shall paye their tythes for thincrease of the saide cattell so goinge in the saide waste or common, to the parson vicar proprietorie porcyonarie owner or other their fermors. 1620 BRENT tr. *Sarpi's Counc. Trent* VIII. (1676) 734 That in Cathedral Churches, all the Canons and Portionaries shall be Priests, Deacons, or Sub-deacons. 1778 *Eng. Gazetteer* (ed. 2) s. v. *Wolverhampton*, In this parish K. Edgar founded a chapel of 8 portionaries, the chief of whom he made patron to them all.

†Po·rtionate, *a. Obs. rare*^{—0}. [ad. med.L. *portiōnātus* provided with a portion.] = PROPORTIONATE. Hence **†Po·rtionately** *adv. Obs. rare*^{—1}, in equal shares, proportionately.

1548 UDALL, etc. *Erasm. Par. John* 115 b, They so deuided the resydue of his garmentes saue his coate..that euery manne had hys parte porcionately.

Portioner (pōᵊ·ɹʃənəɹ). [f. PORTION *sb.* or *v.* + -ER [1], [2]. Cf. med.L. *portiōnārius*.]

I. 1. *Scots Law.* The proprietor of a small piece of land forming a portion of an original forty-merk land, which has been subdivided among co-heirs or otherwise broken up; a small laird.

1552 *Reg. Privy Council Scot.* I. 130 Quhair happinis to be sindrie portioneris of landis within the Schyir, the Scheref sall adjoun the samyn togidder, quhill he mak the fouretie mark land of auld extent. 1569 *Ibid.* 676 Alexander Chalmer portioner of Petty. 1674 in Wodrow *Hist. Suff. Ch. Scot.* (1721) I. 367 Robert Schaw Portioner in Auchmouty [fined] in 49 Pounds. 1791 *Statist. Acc. Scot.* I. 9 There are sixteen greater, and a considerable number (about a hundred) of smaller proprietors, called here Portioners, from their having a small portion of land belonging to them. 1833 *Fraser's Mag.* Oct. 396 My father belonged to that respectable class of landowners termed portioners.

b. *Heir-* or *heiress-portioner*: One of two or more heirs female who succeed to equal portions of a heritage in default of heirs male; or the son or other male representative of such a joint-heiress.

1576 *Reg. Privy Council Scot.* II. 571 Alisoun Dunbar ane of the airis portionaris of the lordschip of Loch and Kilconquhair. 1655 in Z. Boyd *Zion's Flowers* (1855) App. 29/2 We Marion Boyd and Zacharias McCallum aires portionairis to umquhill Mr. Zacharias Boyd. 1765 *Act 5 Geo. III*, c. 26 *Preamble*, The eldest heir female always succeeding without division and excluding heirs portioners. 1886 *Act 49 & 50 Vict.* c. 29 § 19 The eldest of such heirs portioners shall succeed to the tenancy without division.

†2. *Eccl.* = PORTIONIST 2. *Obs.*

1670 BLOUNT *Law Dict.*, *Portioner* (.. *Portionarius*).. where a Parsonage is served by two or sometimes three Ministers alternately..the Ministers are called Portioners, because they have but their Portion or Proportion of the Tythes or Profits of the Living. 1848 WHARTON *Law Lex.*, *Portioner*, a minister, who, together with others, serves a benefice, because he has only a portion of the tithes or profits of the living.

3. *Eng. Law.* One of several persons among

Portionist. [ad. med. L. *portionista* (1499 in Du Cange).] ... **1.** A student in a college, receiving or entitled to a defined portion or allowance of food (whether as a boarder or as recipient of a benefaction). ... **†2.** At St. Andrews, A student who boarded with the principal of the college, and was entitled to his 'commons'. *Obs.* ... **b.** In reference to Merton College, Oxford: A rendering of the Latin term *portionista*, applied to the class of poor scholars usually called *postmasters*. ...

Portionless, *a.* Without a portion; dowerless. ...

†Portitor. *Obs. rare.* [a. med. L. *portitor*, irreg. f. *portā-re*, *port-* to carry.] A door-keeper, a janitor. ...

Portiture, *obs.* form of PORTRAITURE.

†Portimochle. *Obs. rare.* [f. PORTION *sb.*] ... A small portion (of land). ...

Portland¹ ('island' ...). A peninsula or 'island' on the coast of Dorsetshire; *attrib.* in names of natural and artificial products of Portland, or of objects connected with it; as Portland arrowroot, Portland beans; see quots.; Portland cement, a cement resembling *P. stone* in colour ...

Portland²: see next.

Port-last. *Naut. ?Obs.* Also ? portlasse, †lasse, †-9 (*1erms.*) portland. ...

†Portledge. *Naut. Obs.* Forms: 7 portlege, portledge, 7-8 portledge, -lidge, 8 -lege, -ledg, -lage. [Corruption of PORTAGE *sb.*] ...

Portless, *a.* [f. PORT *sb.¹* + -LESS.] Without a port. ...

Portlet. [f. PORT *sb.¹* + -LET.] A small or tiny port; a creek. ...

†Portloke, -like. *Naut.* ... see PORTLY.

Portly, *a.* (*adv.*) Also 6 portely. ... **1.** Of stately appearance and manner; stately, dignified, handsome, majestic; imposing. ... **b.** Now usually connoting 'Large and bulky in person; stout, corpulent.' ...

Portman. Now *obs.* [f. PORT *sb.¹* + MAN *sb.¹* Cf. MD. *portman*.] ... **1.** In OE. use, a citizen of a town, a burgess or *spec.* (after the Conquest) = *capital* or *chief* citizen, one of a select number of citizens, chosen to administer the affairs of a borough. ...

†Portman-mote, -moot. *Obs.* = MOOT *sb.* [OE. *portgemōt.*] The assembly of the portman-mote; the court or common council of the portmen of a borough or town. ...

Portman-mote. Forms: **+ ME. mote**, Moot *sb.* : corresp. to an OE. *portgemōt* ...

†Portman. *Naut.* ... In OE. a citizen of a town, a burgess ...

Portmantle, portmantua, -mantua. *Obs.* = PORTMANTEAU. ...

†Portmantua. *Obs.* ... **1.** A case or bag for carrying clothing and other necessaries when travelling ...

Portment. (*portmĕnt*). *rare.* [f. L. *portā-re*.] ... **1.** Carrying, bearing; behaviour; *porter* to carry. ...

†Portmote. *Obs.* ... Forms: 4 portmote, 4 portmot. = PORTMAN-MOTE. ...

†Portobello in South America ... gave rise to the name of the game. ?A kind of game resembling billiards. ...

†Portoir. *Obs. rare.* [a. F. *portoir* (16th c. in Godef.), f. *porter* des vignes, 'the branch that bears the grapes'.] A bearing branch of a vine. ...

†Portoise. *Naut.* [a. F. ... Origin uncertain.] = PORT-LAST.

Portrait (*pō·ɪtrt̄*). *sb.* Forms: 4-6 portraits, 6-7 -traicts, 6-7 -trait, 7 pourtraict, 7 pourtraite, -trayt, -trayte. ... **1.** A figure drawn, painted, or carved upon a surface to represent some object; a drawing, painting, or other delineation of any object; a picture, design (in general). Now *rare* or *Obs.* ...

Portraiture (*pō·ɪtrātiūr*). Forms: a. 4-5 purtreyture, -treiture, 5 -treture, -treyture, -tretur, -trature, 6-7 portraiture, 8 -portraiture, etc. ... **1.** The action or art of making a portrait of an object by painting, drawing, etc.; delineation in colours or collective sense; *esp.* in *phr. in portraiture* = portrayed, delineated. ...

Portray (*pōȝtrē·*), *v.* Forms: a. 4 purtreye, -traye, 4-5 -trayen, 6 -tray. ... **1.** The action or an instance of portraying; representation of an object by painting, drawing, etc.; delineation in colour or collective sense; *esp.* in *phr. in portraiture* ...

Portray, *sb.* *rare.* Also 7 *pour-*, 7-9 pourtray. [f. PORTRAY *v.*] ... **1.** The act of portraying. ...

Portrayable, *a.* [f. PORTRAY *v.* + -ABLE.] That may be portrayed. ...

Portrayal (*pōɪtrē·al*). [f. PORTRAY *v.* + -AL.] **1.** The action of portraying (or its product); delineation, a picture, portrait. *lit.* and *fig.* Pictorial representation. ...

Portrayer. Also 4-5 *-our.* So *obs.* F. *po(u)rtrayeour* (16th c.) One who portrays; a painter of pictures or portraits; a delineator (*lit.* and *fig.*). ...

Portrayment. *rare.* [f. PORTRAY *v.* + -MENT. Cf. OF. *po*(*u*)*rtraiment.*] The action or result of portraying; portraiture; a portrayal. ...

Portred, *pa. pple.* ... see PORTURE *v.* *Obs.*

Portress, Porteress (*pō·ɪtres*), **porteress** (*pō·ɪteres*). Forms: 4 portres, 6-8 pourtress, 5 portresse. ... A female porter; a woman who acts as porter or door-keeper, *esp.* in a nunnery. ...

†Port-reeve, -greve. *Obs.* [OE. *portgerēfa*, f. *port* town + *gerēfa* reeve, GRAVE *sb.²*] The chief officer of a town or borough. ...

Port-Royal. The name of a convent near Versailles (*Port-Royal des Champs*) in the 17th c. ... **Port-Royalist** (*pōɪt-roi·alist*), an adherent of the community of Port-Royal des Champs. ...

†Port-salut. *Obs. rare.* Forms: 5 port *salut*, in mod.F. *port de salut* ... A port or haven of safety ; 'Haven of safety'; the port or goal one is making for. ...

Port-sale. *Obs.* Forms: 6-8 port-sale, *port salut*. ... Public sale to the highest bidder; sale by auction. ...

†Port-soken. *Old Law.* *Obs.* [f. PORT *sb.¹* + SOKEN.] The jurisdiction of a port or town; *hence, spec.* the district outside a city or borough, over which its jurisdiction extended. ...

Port-town. [PORT *sb.¹*] A market-town or borough; *spec.* a town with a harbour, a seaport. ...

Portuall ... = PORTUARY. ...

Portuary (pōˈtiŭări). *arch.* [A modern formation... var. of **Portas**. Also *attrib.*]

Portugal (pōˈtiŭgăl). Forms: a. 5-6 Portyngale, 6 -gail, gale, Portingaill, 7 -gale, 9 -gal, 6-9 -gaill, 8 -b, 6-7 Portugale, 6-7 Portugall. ... *Portugal*, earlier *Portucal*, ad. med.L. *Portus Cale*, the port of Gale, Oporto, Alfonso, Count of *Portucale*, became the first king of Portugal, Cl. MD. *Portenglie*. The form *Portyngale* is perh. to be compared with *nightingale*; but cf. OF. *Portingalois* Portuguese.]

1. A country in the west of the Iberian peninsula.

2. A native or inhabitant of Portugal; a Portuguese. *Obs.*

3. The Portuguese language. *Obs.*

4. = **Portugal**, the coin. *Obs.*

5. A sweetmeat from Portugal. *Obs. rare¯¹*.

6. a. *attrib.* as *adj.* = **Portuguese** A.

Portulaca (pōˈtiŭlăˈkă). [L. *portulāca* purslain (*P. oleracea*): taken by Tournefort, 1700, as a generic name.] A genus of plants, comprising low succulent herbs bearing white, yellow, red, or purple terminal flowers, expanding only once in direct sunshine; esp. a plant of a cultivated species of this genus.

Portulaca-jack. *Obs.*

Portulan, *portolan*. [a. Ger. *portunal*, a. F. *portunal*... ad. med.L. *portunalis*.]

Portunal. [a. Ger. *portunal*.]

Portunian (pōˈtiŭˈniăn). *Zool.* [f. *Portunus*.]

Portuous, -tous, etc. variants of **Portous**.

Porturate, *ppl. a.* *Sc. Obs. rare¯¹*.

Portus, etc., variants of **Portas**.

Hence Port-winy, smacking of port-wine.

Porty, a. [f. **Port** sb.² + -Y.]

Portyoliom, Portyngale, var. **Portuage** *Obs.*

Port-yowi (pŏˈtyowˈl). *Sc.* Also 9 portule.

Porty, variant of **Portuage** *Obs.*

Porule (pōˈriŭl). *rare.* [f. **Pore** sb.² + -ULE.]

Hence Po'rulous, Po'rulous *adj.*, abounding in minute pores.

Pose, sb.¹ Also 4-5 pose, 5 posse. [Sp., a resting place, an inn, ppl. sb. f. *posar* to lodge: see **Pose** v.¹] A (Spanish) inn or place of accommodation for travellers.

Posage. *Obs. rare.* var. of **Posy**.

Posaume, -aune, etc. variants of **Posaune**.

Posaune (pǒˈzauˈne). Also posaum. [G., a trumpet trombone: — Du. *bazuin*, Du., Sw. *bazun*]

Posca (pǒˈskă). [L.] Also 7 pausa, a wooden pipe, well-closed, which serves to convey the wind from the bellows to the sound-board of the organ.

Posn, variant of **Poison** *Obs.*

Posnet. *Obs.* variant of **Postnet**.

Poson, variant of **Poison** *Obs.*

Pose, sb.² *Obs.* Also 4 poos, 5 poce, poze. A catarrh, cold in the head.

Pose, sb.³ *Obs.* App. a variant of **Posy**, first in the plural, *posies* being taken as *poses*.

Pose, sb.⁴ Now used, often as in *pose plastique*; an attitude, posture of the body, or of a part of the body, esp. one deliberately assumed, or in which a figure is placed for effect, or for artistic purposes.

Pose, v.¹ *rare.* [a. F. *pose* f. *poser* to put, place: see **Pose** v.²] An act of posing.

Pose, v.² [a. F. *poser*...] An attitude or posture of the body, or of a part of the body, esp. one deliberately assumed, or in which a figure is placed for effect, or for artistic purposes.

Pose, v.³ Also 7 poze, 7-9 pose. *trans.* To examine by questioning, question, interrogate: = **Appose** v.¹ 3.

Pose, v.⁴ *Obs.* [a. OF. *pose* a land measure.]

Pose, var. of **Posy**.

Pose, v.¹ *dial.* [f. **Pose** sb.²] *trans.* To hoard, store up money, etc.

Posé (pōˈzā). *Her.* [F., ppl. of *poser* to place.]

Posé, *ppl. a.* Also 8 poser. [Aphetic form of **Apposed**: see **Pose** v.³]

Poser¹. [f. **Pose** v.³ + -ER¹.] One who sets or asks questions; an examiner: = **Apposer** 1.

Poser². [f. **Pose** v.² + -ER¹.] One who poses or attitudinizes: = **Poseur**.

Poseur (pōˈzœr). [F., agent-n. f. *poser* **Pose** v.²] One who practises an affected mental or social attitude; an affected person. The fem. **Poseuse** (pōˈzœz).

Posh, sb.¹ *dial., pash, posh.* *cf.* **Pash** sb.²

Poser³. [f. **Pose** v.²] A puzzle.

Posh, a. *slang.* Smart, stylish, fine.

Posied (pōˈzid), *a.* [f. **Post** v. + -ED¹.]

Posing, Posingly: see **Pose** v.³

Posit (pŏˈzit). *v.* Also 7 -ite. [f. L. *posit-*, ppl. stem of *ponĕre* to place, put, lay down.]

Position (pŏˈziˈʃən). *sb.* Also 6 posycyon, -cion, -cyon, position, 6 L. *position*, ad. L. *positiōn-em* a putting, placing, position; affirmation; theme, subject, etc., n. of action from *pōnĕre* (*posit-um*) to put, place, set.]

1. I. The action of positing; the laying down or statement of a proposition or thesis; affirmation, affirmative assertion. Chiefly in *Logic* and *Philos.*

2. A proposition or thesis laid down or stated; something posited; a statement, assertion, tenet.

3. Arith. A method of finding the value of an unknown quantity by positing or assuming one or more values for it, finding by how much the results differ from the actual data of the problem, and then adjusting the error. Also called *rule of (false) position*, *rule of supposition*, *rule of falsehood*, *rule of trial and error*.

4. The action of positing or placing, esp. in a particular order or arrangement; disposition. *Obs.*

5. The manner in which a body as a whole, or the several parts of it, are disposed or arranged; disposition, posture, attitude.

6. fig. The situation which may metaphorically be compared to, or likened to, a position in space, etc.

II. The place occupied by a thing, or in which it is put; situation, site, station. *In position*, in its (its, etc.) proper or appropriate place; so *out of position*.

III. 10. *attrib.* and *Comb.*, as *position-relation*, *-value*: *position angle* = *angle of position* (7 b); *position-artillery*, heavy field-artillery; *cf. part of position* in 7 b; so *position-battery* (position error, the variation of a watch when laid in certain positions; *position-micrometer*, an apparatus by means of which a gunner is enabled to aim a cannon at an object not visible to him; *position-light*, a light carried by a ship which is in company with others to indicate its course at night; position micrometer: see quot.; *position-piece* (see quot.), *position-piece* who composes short pieces containing definite statements (as in commendation of a person).

b. Phrases.

Position (pŏˈziˈʃən). *v.* [f. prec. sb.]

1. *trans.* To set or place in a particular or appropriate position; to assign a position to.

2. *intr.* To take up one's position; to lay down a position or principle; to posit.

Positional (pŏˈziˈʃənăl). *a.* [f. **Position** sb. + -AL.] Of, pertaining to, or indicating position.

Positive (pŏˈzitiv). *a.* and *sb.* Forms: 4 positif, -tyue, -tyve, 5 -tife, 4-7 -tiue, 5 -tyve, -tyfe, -tytve, 6-7 -tive... positive (4-7 poss-). [ME. *positif*, a. F. *positif* (13th c. in Hatz.-Darm.) characterized by laying down or by being laid down, ad. L. *positīv-us*, in grammar, positive, f. *posit-*: see **Posit** v.]

I. Having relation only to matters of fact.

6. Dealing only with matters of fact and observation; practical, realistic; not speculative or theoretical.

II. Connected with the notion of formal, explicit, or artificially instituted.

7. Formally laid down or imposed; arbitrarily or artificially instituted; proceeding from enactment or custom; conventional; opp. to *natural*.

8. Explicitly laid down; expressed without qualification; admitting no question; stated, explicit, express, definite; emphatic; positively certain.

III. Confident in opinion or assertion; over-sure; positive, dogmatical.

IV. Definite, unrelated, absolute.

V. Having no relation to or comparison with other things; free from qualifications, conditions, or reservations; absolute, unconditional.

B. *sb.*

I. Gram. A positive quantity. *Math.*

II. Photogr. A positive picture.

POSITIVE.

Positivism (pǒ'zitiv'iz'm). [ad. F. *positivisme*: see -ISM.]

Positivist (pǒ'zitivist). [ad. F. *positiviste*: see -IST.] An adherent or supporter of positivism.

Positivistic (pǒzitivi'stik), a. [f. prec. + -IC.] Of the nature of positivism.

Positivity (pǒziti'vĭti), a. [f. positive + -ITY, cf. F. *positivité*, -ité.] The quality, character, or fact of being positive.

Positor (pǒ'zitə). [L. *positor* one who places, agent-n. from *pōnĕre, posit*- to place.]

Positum (pǒ'zitʊm). [L., pa. pple. of *pōnĕre* to place, put, lay.]

Positure. Obs. [a. obs. F. *positure* (1547 in Godef.) ad. L. *positūra* position, posture, f. *pōnĕre, posit*- to place: see POSTURE.]

Posnet (pǒ'snet). Now arch. and dial. Forms: posnet, possynet, &c. A small metal pot or vessel for boiling, having a handle and three feet.

Posologic(al (pǒsolǒ'dʒik(al), a. [f. F. *posologique* (in medical sense): see POSOLOGY + -AL.] Pertaining to posology (in either sense).

Posology (pǒsǒ'lŏdʒi). [a. F. *posologie* (in medical sense), f. Gr. *πόσος* how much + -LOGY.] That department of medicine which relates to the quantities or doses in which drugs should be administered.

Posse (pǒ'si). Also *posset*. [a. L. *posse* to be able, have power, avail, in med.L. as sb., power, armed force (1246 in Du Cange): in scholastic terminology, potentiality, capability of being. In sense 1 short for POSSE COMITATUS.]

Posse comitatus.

Posse comitatus (pǒ'si kŏmitei'təs). [med.L.] The force of the county; the body of men above the age of fifteen in a county (exclusive of peers, clergymen, and infirm persons), whom the sheriff may summon or "raise" to repress a riot or for other purposes; also, a body of men actually so raised and commanded by the sheriff.

Possess (pǒze's), v. [a. OF. *possess-ier* (c1179 in Godef.) f. L. *possess-*, ppl. stem of *possidēre* to possess, pres. through influence of F. *possesseur* POSSESSOR, etc., the regular OF. type of *possidēre* being *possoier, -eir, -eer*.]

Possessed (pǒze'st), *ppl. a.* [f. prec. + -ED.]

Possessedness. [f. prec. + -NESS.]

Possessible, a. rare. Also -able. [f. POSSESS v. + -IBLE.] Capable of being possessed.

Possessing (pǒze'siŋ), *vbl. sb.* [f. POSSESS v. + -ING[1].]

Possessing, *ppl. a.* [f. as prec. + -ING[2].] Having something as a possession; *spec.* having material possessions.

Possession (pǒze'ʃən), *sb.* Forms: 4- possession, 4-6 -ioun, -ione, -yon, (4 -ioune, -yone, 6 -yonn) &c.

Possessionist, *sb.* Possessive, *a.* Possessoress, *rare.* Possessorial, *a. rare.* Possessorship. Possessory, *a. sb.* Possessively, *adv.* Possibilist. Possibility. Possibilitate. Possible, *a. sb.*

Possibly, *adv.* Possident. Possodie, *Sc.* Possum, *U.S.* Possess. Post, *sb.* Post, *sb.* Post, *v.*

POST.

Poste restante ... A direction written upon a letter which is to remain at the post office till called for; in English use, transferred to the department in a post office in which letters for travellers or others not yet applied for.

Posterior, a. ... 1. Later, subsequent in time; opposed to *prior*. 2. Turned towards the hinder side. 3. Coming after in a series or order. 4. Hinder; situated or further back than something else. Opposed to *anterior*.

Posteriority ... 1. The state or quality of being later or subsequent in time. Opposed to *priority*. 2. Inferiority in order, rank, or dignity. 3. *Fortif.* (See quots.)

Posterly, adv. ... In a posterior position; behind; to the rear.

Posterior-form, sb. pl. Obs. ...

Posteriorly, adv. ...

Posteriorac, v. ...

Posterity ... 1. The descendants collectively; all who have proceeded from a person; offspring. 2. A later generation (with plural). Obs.

Postero- ... combining form of Lat. *poster-us* hinder, prefixed to adjectives, chiefly forming anatomical terms.

P. a. anterior, situated in the posterior-external side of the branch and thigh.

Post-eternity, Posteternal, etc.

Post-exilian ...

Post-exist, v. rare ...

Post-existence, rare ...

Postero-terminal, etc.

Posthitis ... Inflammation of the prepuce.

Postho-, for Postero-.

Postholder ... In Dutch colonial administration: A civil official in charge of a trading settlement or post.

Post-hole, sb. A hole made in the ground to receive the foot of a post.

Post-horn ... A horn formerly used by a postman or the guard of a mail-coach, to announce arrival; now often used on pleasure coaches.

Post-horse, sb. A horse kept at a post-house or inn for the use of post-riders, or for hire for the conveyance of travellers.

Post-house, sb. ... 1. A post office. 2. An inn or other house where horses are kept for the use of travellers.

Po'sthumate, a.

Po'sthume, sb.

Posthumous, a. and sb. 1. Born after the death of the father. 2. Published after the death of the author. 3. Arising or continuing after death.

Posthumous-ly, adv.

Posthumous-ness, sb.

Posthumian, sb.

Posthumity, sb. Obs. rare

Postic, a. and sb.

Postical, a.

Postice, sb.

Posticous, a.

Postil, sb. Now only Hist. 1. A note or comment on, or marginal to, a passage of Scripture.

Postil, v. To write comments on, or marginal notes to; to annotate.

Postillation, sb.

Postiller, sb. ... One who postils.

Postilling, vbl. sb.

Postilion, sb. ... One who rides the near horse of the leaders; one who rides post.

Postillism, sb. Obs. rare

Postilment, sb.

Posting, vbl. sb. The action of Post v. in various senses.

Postle, sb. and v. ... aphetic form of *apostle*.

Postless, variant of POSTAL.

Post-like: see POST sb.1

Postliminary, a. [f. L. *post*, *limin-*, threshold + -ARY]

Postliminiar

Postliminiation, -tion. = POSTLIMINIATION.

Postliminiary, a.

Postliminium

Postliminy

Postliminious, a.

Postliminiate, v.

Postliminous

Postliminy

Postman, sb.1

Postman, sb.2

Postmark, sb.

Postmark, v.

Postmaster, sb.1

Postmaster, sb.2

Postmastership, 1.

Postmastership, 2.

Postmaster-general. Pl. postmasters general.

Postmaster-generalship

Postmastress

Postma·stership

Post-median, a.

Postmedial, a.

Post-meridian, a.

Postmeridional, a.

Post meridiem

Post-mistress

Postmillenarian

Postmillennial, a.

Postmillennialism

Postmillennialist

Post mortem, adv., phr.

Post-mortem, a.

Postmundane, a.

Postmortuary, a.

Postmutative

Postnasal, a.

Post-natal, a.

Post-natalist

Postnate, a.

Postnatus, pl. -ti

Post-neuritic, -Nicene: see POST- B. 1.

Post-night. [f. POST sb.2 + NIGHT.]

Post-note. U.S. *Obs. exc. Hist.*

Post-oak. [f. POST sb.1 + OAK.]

Postnuptial, a.

Postobit, sb.

Postobital, a.

Post-obit, a.

Post-obituary

Postomia

Postomie

Post office, post-office

Post-officer. *Obs.*

Postoral, a.

Post-oral, a.

Postorbital, a.

Post-paid, -paper: see POST sb.1

Post-painter, POSTPAINE

Postpalatal, -parietal, etc.: see POST- B. 1

Postparative

Postpartum

To postast, *Obs.*

Postpense

Postpone, v.

Postponable, a.

Postpone, v.

Postponement

Postponence

Postponer

Postpone

Postpontile

Postposit, v.

Postpositive, a.

Postposition

Postpositional, a.

Postpositive, a.

Postpositively, adv.

Postpredicament

Postprandial, a.

Postprandially, adv.

Postpubic

Postpubis

Postpyramidal, a.

Post-pyramidal, a. [f. POST- + PYRAMIDAL.] Subsequent to the building of the Egyptian pyramids.

Post-Raphaelite: see POST- B. 1 b.

†Postverme, a. (sb.) Obs. nonce-wd. L. *postvimus* last, hindmost.] *adverb.* one who is last.

Post-remote: see POST- B. 2. **Post-rider**: see POST- sb.[2] 13.

†Postri-duan, a., Obs. rare⁻⁰. [ad. L. *post-riduan-us*, adj.: see -AN.] Of the next day.

Post-road. A road on which a series of post-houses or stations for post-horses is (or was) established; a road on which mails were carried.

Postrorse, a. [f. mod.L. *postrorsus*, f. POST(R)RO + *versus* turned: cf. AN-TRORSE.] Turned or bent backward; retrorse.

Post-runner. A ' runner ' who acts as a post: see POST sb.[2] 9. Obs.

Postscalene, etc.: see POST-.

Postscriptal, a. [f. POSTSCRIPT + -AL.] Pertaining or relating to a postscript.

Post-scriptum, -scribere to write.

Post-stage, sb. [f. POST sb.[2] + STAGE.]

Postumous: see POSTHUMOUS.

Post-village. [f. POST sb.[2] + VILLAGE.]

Post-wagon. [f. POST sb.[2] + WAGON.]

Postulary, a. and sb. [ad. L. *postulāri-us*, *-um*, pa. pple. of *postulāre*.]

Postulate (pǒ·stiŭlĕt), sb. [ad. L. *postulātum*.]

Postulate (pǒ·stiŭleit), v. [f. ppl. stem of L.]

Postulation (pǒstiŭlē·ʃən). [a. F. *postulation*.]

Postulator (pǒ·stiŭleitəʳ). [a. L. *postulātor*.]

Postulatory (pǒ·stiŭleitəri), a.

Postulatum (pǒstiŭlē·tŏm). Pl. **-a**.

†Postule, sb. Obs.

†Postule, v. Sc. Obs.

†Postume, Obs.

Postural (pǒ·stiŭrăl), a. [f. POSTURE + -AL.] Pertaining or relating to posture or position.

Posture (pǒ·stiŭʳ), sb. [a. F. *posture* (16th c. in Montaigne *Ess.* II.), contr. from earlier L. Sp., Pg. *postura*): see POSTURE.]

Posture (pǒ·stiŭʳ), v. [f. prec. sb.]

Posture-maker.

Posturing vbl. sb.

Posture-master.

Posy (pōu·zi). Forms: see POESY.

Posywise (pōu·ziwaiz).

Pot (pǒt). Forms: -2-8 pott, 4-7 potte, (5 putte), 3- pot. (Also 4-5 poot, 5-9 Sc. pow, mod.Sc. dial. pat, patt.) [Late OE. or early ME. *pott*, cognate with OFris. *pot*, MDu. *pot*(t, Da., Dan. *pot*, MLG. *pot*, pot, LG. *pot*, Sw. *pott*, Icel. *pottr*, ...]

Potable (pōu·tăb'l), a. and sb. [a. F. *potable* (14th c. in Littré), ad. L. *potābilis*.]

Potage, etc.: see POTTAGE.

Potato. The plant *Solanum tuberosum*, a native of the Pacific slopes of South America, introduced into Europe late in the 16th century, and now widely cultivated for its farinaceous tubers.

Pota *v. trans.*, to plant or crop with potatoes.

Pota-toey *a.*, *nonce-wd.*, of the nature of a potato.

Pota-toless *a.*, without potatoes.

Potato-root.

Potatory *a.* [f. POTATOR + -Y.] Of, pertaining to, or given to drinking.

Pot-bellied (pᵏt-be·lid), *a.* Having a pot-belly.

Pot-belly (pᵏt·be·li), *Pot* *sb.* + BELLY. A person who has a pot-belly.

Pot-bound, *a.* [f. POT *sb.*] + BOUND *ppl. a.*] Said of a plant growing in a flower-pot when its roots fill the pot and have no more room to expand.

Pot-boy.

Pot-carrier. A perversion of POTHECARY, i.e. POTTER-CARRIER, POTYCARYAR.

Pot-clip. *north. dial.* [f. POT *sb.* + CLIP *sb.* 2; cf. POT-KILP.] A contrivance for suspending a pot or cauldron having no 'bool', consisting of two iron rods joined together, with hooks at the free ends fo catch hold of the ears or brim of the pot.

Pot-companion. [f. POT *sb.* + COMPANION *sb.*] A companion in drinking; a fellow-toper.

Pot-earth.

Pote, *sb.* form of POOT *sb.*

Pote, *v.* Now *dial.* Forms: 1 potian, 3 pote, 4 po·ten.

Pote, *v.* obs. form of POTE *v.*

Potecarie, *-ary*, variants of POTHECARY.

Potence, **pothen** (pᵏt'n, pᵏʊθ'n). Forms: 4 potamen, potesn, potens. [a. F. *potence*.]

Potenae, obs. form of POTENCY.

Potence ² (pᵏ·tᵉns). *rare.*

Potency (pᵏ·tᵉnsi). [ad. L. *potentia* power.]

Potent (pᵏ·tᵉnt), *a.*¹ and *sb.*² [app. an alteration or variant of F. *potence* POTENCE.]

Potent (pᵏ·tᵉnt), *a.*¹ and *sb.*¹ [a. F. *potent*, ad. L. *potentem*, f. *posse* (*potis esse*) to be powerful or able.]

Potentacy.

Potentate (pᵏ·tᵉntǁt), *sb.* (and *a.*) [a. F. *potentat* (w-stem) potentate.]

Potential (potᵉn·ʃal), *a.* and *sb.*

of actual energy; amongst those of potential energy are those of the mechanical powers of gravitation, elasticity, chemical affinity, statical electricity, and magnetism. 1866 Odling *Anim. Chem.* 71 We may thus render muscular force latent in a stretched bowstring, raised cannon-ball, or other instrument, for any length of time. This latent force is generally spoken of as potential energy, while the active force exertable at any moment by the flying arrow or falling ball constitutes its actual or dynamic energy. 1868 Thomson & Tait *Elem. Dynamics* 74 The *potential energy* of a conservative system, in the configuration which it has at any instant, is the amount of work that its mutual forces perform during the passage of the system from any one chosen configuration to the configuration at the time referred to. 1875 Gangee tr. *Hermann's Elem. Hum. Physiol.* Introd. 1 The human body..is an organism in which, by the chemical change of its constituent parts, *potential* is converted into *kinetic* energy. 1876 Tait *Rec. Adv. Phys. Sc.* (1885) 364 Excellent instances of potential energy are supplied by..the wound up 'weights' of a clock.., by gunpowder, the chemical affinities of whose constituents are called into play by a spark [etc.]. 1881 Maxwell *Electr. & Magn.* (ed. 2) I. 16 To determine the value of the potential energy when the magnet is placed in the field of force expressed by this potential.

B. *sb.* †1. A potential agent, a thing that gives power. *Obs. rare.*

1656 Blount *Glossogr.*, *Potentials*, things apt to breed or give power, strength or ability.

2. That which is possible, opposed to what is actual; a possibility.

1817 Coleridge *Biog. Lit.* I. xii. 245 The *potential* works *in* them, even as the *actual* works on them! 1883 Edersheim *Life Jesus* (ed. 6) I. 634 With this belief our highest thoughts of the potential for humanity..are connected. 1889 J. M. Robertson *Ess. Crit. Method* 92 The faculty..must be held to reach its highest potential, on the side of literature, in the case of personal gift cultivated by a literary life.

3. *Gram.* Short for *Potential mood*: see A. 4.

4. *Physics.* Short for *potential function*: see A. 5 a. Hence, the amount of energy or quantity of work denoted by this, considered as a quality or condition of the matter, electricity, etc., in question. See quots.

('*Potential* as the name of a function was undoubtedly introduced by Gauss in 1840' (G. F. Becker in *Amer. Jrnl. Sci.* 1893, Feb. 97). [Cf. Gauss *Allgem. Lehrsätze d. Quadrats d. Entfernung* Wks. 1877 V. 200 Zur bequemern Handhabung..werden wir uns erlauben dieses *V* mit einer besonderen Benennung zu belegen, und die Grösse das *Potential* der Massen, worauf sie sich bezieht, nennen.])

1828 G. Green *On Applic. Math. Anal.* etc. in *Math. Papers* (1871) 32 This equation is remarkable on account of its simplicity and singularity, seeing that it gives the value of the potential for any point *p'*, within the surface, when *V̄*, its value at the surface itself, is known, together with [etc.]. 1853 Sir W. Thomson in *Philos. Mag.* Ser. iv. V. 288 *note*, The potential at any point in the neighbourhood of or within a charged body is the quantity of work that would be required to bring a unit of positive electricity from an infinite distance to that point if the given distribution of electricity remained unaltered. 1866 R. M. Ferguson *Electr.* (1870) 277 Instead of the word tension, used with reference to the work that can be effected by a charge when openly insulated, or electro-motive force, the word *potential* is now used. 1867 Thomson & Tait *Nat. Philos.* (1883) II. 29. § 483 This function [the potential] was introduced for gravitation by Laplace, but the name was first given to it by Green, who may almost be said to have in 1828 created the theory, as we now have it. *Ibid.* § 485 The *Potential* at any point, due to any attracting or repelling body, or distribution of matter, is the mutual potential energy between it and a unit of matter placed at that point. 1876 Preece & Sivewright *Telegraphy* 5 Potential implies that function of electricity which determines its motion from one point to another. And the difference of potential, which determines the amount of this motion, is called electromotive force. 1879 G. Prescott *Sp. Telephone* 37 The difference..of magnetic potential existing between the diaphragm and the core is increased. 1881 Maxwell *Electr. & Magn.* I. 76 Potential, in electrical science, has the same relation to Electricity that pressure, in Hydrostatics, has to fluid, or that temperature, in Thermodynamics, has to Heat. 1881 Jenkin *Electr.* 51 The effect of contact in producing or maintaining difference of potentials. 1892 *Pall Mall G.* 4 Feb. 6/3 (Mr. Tesla's demonstration.) Currents of these extremely high potentials appear to be absolutely without effect upon the human organism. 1902 Sloane *Stand. Electr. Dict.* (ed. 3), The magnetic potential at any point of a magnetic field expresses the work which would be done by the magnetic forces of the field on a positive unit of magnetism as it moves from that point to an infinite distance therefrom...It is the exact analogue of absolute electric potential.

attrib. 1896 *Academy* 11 Apr. 300/2 The rate of leak..was no greater when the potential difference was 500 volts than when it was 5. 1898 *Engineering Mag.* XVI. 101 'High potential' electrical heat for irons, broilers, chafing dishes, and local applications. *Ibid.* 104 To run an engine dynamo ..to furnish high potential heat and light.

Potentiality (potenʃiæ·lĭti). [ad. med.L. *potentiālitās* (Albertus Magnus, *a* 1250), f. *potentiāl-is*: see prec. and -ity. So F. *potentialité*.]

1. The quality of being powerful or having power: see Potential *a.* 1.

1627 Hakewill *Apol.* i. ii. 70 'Habent aliquid potentialitatis admixtum', as Lyra speakes, they haue some kinde of potentiality (I know not how otherwise to render his word) mixed with them. 1656 Hobbes *Liberty, Necess. & Chance* 266 Nor do I understand what derogation it can be to the Divine perfection, to attribute to it Potentiality, that is (in English) Power. 1820 Coleridge *Lett., Convers.* etc. I. 133, I have the power, the potentiality of walking. 1875 Stubbs *Const. Hist.* II. xvii. 514 An unlimited and unimpaired potentiality of sovereignty.

2. *esp.* The state or quality of possessing latent power or capacity capable of development into activity; possibility of action or active existence: opposed to *actuality*: see Potential *a.* 2.

1625 Jackson *Creed* v. xiv. §10 That potentiality or aptitude which the soul hath to be linked, and made one substance with the body. 1653 H. More *Conject. Cabbal.* (1713) 11 By Earth you are to understand, the Potentiality or Capability of the Existence of the outward Creation. 1781 Johnson Apr. in Boswell, We are not here to sell a parcel of boilers and vats, but the potentiality of growing rich beyond the dreams of avarice. 1855 Bain *Senses & Int.* iii. i. § 37 (1864) 378 The mental conception that we have of empty space, is *scope for movement*, the possibility or potentiality of moving. 1862 Dana *Man. Geol.* 599 Characteristics before only foreshadowed, or existing only in potentiality, come out into full expression.

b. With *a* and *pl.* An instance of this quality; a capacity or possibility, or a condition, thing, or being in which it is embodied.

1668 Howe *Bless. Righteous* (1825) 44 By the former it hath a potentiality, by the latter an habitude in reference thereunto. 1690 Locke *Hum. Und.* ii. xxiii. § 7 (1695) 160 In this looser sense, I crave leave to be understood, when I name any of these Potentialities amongst the simple Ideas, which we recollect in our Minds, when we think of particular Substances. 1855 H. Spencer *Princ. Psychol.* (1872) II. viii. vi. 586 In the joy of liberty regained there are massed together the potentialities and gratifications in general. 1862 — *First Princ.* i. ii. § 11. 33 The self-creation of such a potential universe would involve over again the difficulties here stated—would imply behind this potential universe a more remote potentiality. 1875 *Encycl. Brit.* II. 522/1 The seed is the potentiality of the plant. 1879 Huxley *Hume* iii. 85 The conversion, by unknown causes, of these innate potentialities into actual existences.

3. *Electr.* = Potential *sb.* 4. *rare.*

1898 *Allbutt's Syst. Med.* V. 857 The individual, through whose body there is passing an electric current of not too high potentiality, generally experiences pain.

Potentialize (potenʃălaiz), *v.* [f. Potential + -ize.] *trans.* To make potential, give potentiality to; *spec.* in reference to energy, To convert into a potential condition. Hence **Pote·ntialized** *ppl. a.*, **Pote·ntializing** *vbl. sb.*; **Potentializa·tion**, the action of making potential.

1856 P. Fairbairn *Prophecy* ii. iii. iv. 431 *note*, The six highly potentialized—three times repeated (666) is the utmost that could be assigned him for a symbolical indication of his nature—this is the number of his name. 1865 tr. *Strauss' New Life Jesus* II. ii. lxxix. 273 Neander's attempt to substitute a mere potentialization of the water for vinous properties. 1886 *Amer. Jrnl. Sci.* Ser. iii. XXXI. 120 At the extreme configurations of any simple vibration, the energy of the simple movement is entirely potentialized. 1889 *Nature* 3 Oct. 562/1 With a given metal, there is large potentializing in the first stages of strain, and large dissipation in the final stages.

Potentially (pote·nʃăli), *adv.* [f. Potential *a.* + -ly².]

1. Powerfully, mightily; authoritatively. Now *rare.*

1549 in Foxe *A. & M.* (1583) 1381/2 The wordes of holy scripture doe worke theyr effectes potencially and thorowly by the mighty operation of the spirite of God. 1656 Blount *Glossogr.*, *Potentially*, powerfully, mightily, substantially, effectually. 1878 B. Harte *Man on Beach* ii. 53 'That settles the whole matter then,' said Bessie potentially.

2. In a potential or possible manner or state; in potentiality, possibility, or capability: opposed to *actually.*

c 1430 *Art Nombryng* 15 Seithe Boice in Arsemetrike, that vnyte potencially is al numbre, and none in act. 1597 A. M. tr. *Guillemeau's Fr. Chirurg.* 39 b/2 The matter applyed on the bodye, actuallye combureth or potentiallye, wherfore they are called actuall or potentialle Cauteryes. 1614 Selden *Titles Hon.* Pref. B iv, It's thought, that, in the Seed are alwaies potentially seuerall indiuiduating Qualities deriu'd from diuers of the neere ancestors. 1768–74 Tucker *Lt. Nat.* (1834) I. 292 The doctrine of atoms actually, if not potentially, indivisible. *a* 1822 Shelley *Def. Poetry* Essays & Lett. (Camelot Class.) 29 The first acorn..contained all oaks potentially. 1864 Bowen *Logic* iv. 61 Every Concept must denote some existing object,—existing, that is, either really or potentially.

3. In the potential mood. *rare.*

1861 Dickens *Gt. Expect.* xlv, Imperative mood, present tense: Do not thou go home, let him not go home, let us not go home...Then, potentially: I may not and I cannot go home.

So **Pote·ntialness**, potentiality.

1668 Wilkins *Real Char.* 28 Potentialness, Reversion, may, can. 1727 Bailey vol. II, *Potentialness*, Powerfulness, Efficacy.

Pote·ntiary. *nonce-wd.* [After Plenipotentiary.] One possessing power to act.

1854 Thackeray *Newcomes* xxx, The last great potentiary had arrived who was to take part in the family congress.

Potentiate (pote·nʃiˌeɪt), *v.* [f. L. *potentia* power + -ate³. In quot. 1817 after Ger. *potenzi(e)ren.*]

1. *trans.* To endow with power or potency.

1817 Coleridge *Biog. Lit.* xii. (1882) 135, I have even hazarded the new verb potenziate, with its derivatives, in order to express the combination or transfer of powers. 1820 — in *Lit. Rem.* (1839) IV. 137 Of such exertions..I do not believe a human soul capable, unless substantiated and successively potentiated by an especial divine grace. 1827–48 Hare *Guesses* (1859) 430 The true ideal is the individual, purified and potentiated, the individual freed from everything that is not individual in it.

2. To make possible.

1865 *Englishm. Mag.* Jan. 51 Before a language can arrive at that maturity which potentiates a strict art of composition, it must pass through every intermediate phase from the formless to the regular.

Hence **Pote·ntiated** *ppl. a.*; **Potentia·tion**, the action of potentiating, endowment with power.

a 1834 Coleridge *Notes & Lect.* (1849) I. 94 The energies of intellect..in a rich and more potentiated form. 1840 J. H. Green *Vital Dynamics* 31 That potentiation of living existence, which we name animated. 1847 — *Mental Dynamics* 10 This individuality..which consists in a higher potentiation and happier combination of the human powers. 1851 *N. Brit. Rev.* No. 70. 377 A highly potentiated feeling of human brotherhood.

Po·tentil. *rare.* Anglicized form of next.

1884 Miller *Plant-n.*, Potentil, Marsh, *Potentilla Comarum* (*Comarum palustre*). 1906 *Daily Chron.* 4 May 6/7 Tormentil and potentil are opening in the woods.

‖**Potentilla** (pōtĕnti·lă). *Bot.* [med.L. *potentilla*, f. L. *potens, -ent-em* Potent + dim. *-illa*; applied *a* 1500 to the Garden Valerian or Phu; in 16th c. to *Potentilla anserina*, whence adopted by Linnæus as name of the genus.] An extensive genus of *Rosaceæ*, comprising herbs and under-shrubs, of which the Silverweed, Cinquefoil, and Tormentil are common British species.

[*c* 1300 Simon Januensis, *Amantilla*, potentilla, fu, valleriana idem. *c* 1450 *Alphita* (Anecd. Oxon.) 150 *Portentilla*, amantilla idem. *Ibid.* 69 *Fu*, ualeriana, amantilla, ueneria, portentilla.] 1548 Turner *Names of Herbes* H iv, Potentilla or as some write Potentilla, is named also Tanacetum syluestre..in englishe wylde Tansey. 1578 Lyte *Dodoen.* i. lix. 86. 1706 Phillips, *Potentilla*, (Lat.) wild Tansey or Silver-weed; an Herb so call'd from its admirable Virtues. 1776 Withering *Brit. Plants* (1796) II. 477 Which confirms the opinion of those who maintain that Potentilla and Tormentilla are not distinct genera. 1867 H. Macmillan *Bible Teach.* ii. (1870) 30 Golden *geums* and *potentillas* gleamed like miniature suns. 1883 G. Allen in *Longm. Mag.* 306 The potentillas are a group of very lowly and primitive roses.

Potentiometer (potenʃiǫ·mĭtəɹ). [f. L. *potentia* power (with allusion to Potential *sb.* 4) + -meter.] An instrument for measuring differences of electrical potential.

1881 W. G. Adams in *Nature* 21 Apr. 582 The electrometer or potentiometer method, in which the difference of potential between two points in the circuit with a given resistance between them is directly measured. 1897 W. C. Fisher (*title*) The Potentiometer and its adjuncts. 1906 *Athenæum* 27 Oct. 517/3 The various methods of measuring resistances and a description of the uses of the potentiometer.

†**Potentional**, *a.* *Obs. rare*⁻¹. Erroneous form for Potential.

1651 French *Distill.* v. 162 Then..the earth..did specificate that potentionall salt..into a nitrous salt.

Potentite (pōu·tĕntəit). [f. L. *potent-em* Potent *a.*¹ + -ite¹ 4.] Name of an explosive.

1883 V. D. Majendie in *Standard* 19 Apr. 5/6 Explosives (such as dynamite, blasting gelatine,..tonite, potentite, and detonators). 1884 Knight *Dict. Mech.* Suppl., *Potentite*, an explosive used in the Cumberland and Furness mines.

Po·tentize, *v.* [f. L. *potent-em* powerful + -ize, after G. *potenzi(e)ren* to potentiate.] *trans.* To make potent; *spec.* to develop the power of (a medicine) by trituration or succussion; = Dynamize.

1857 Dunglison *Med. Dict.* s.v. *Dynamic*, By certain processes, called, in the aggregate, dynamization and potentizing, the dynamic powers of a medicine may be set free and developed—as by shaking the bottle in which the article is contained. 1881 J. G. Glover in *Encycl. Brit.* XII. 127/1 The most characteristic feature of Hahnemann's practice—the 'potentizing', 'dynamizing', of medicinal substances. 1892 E. Haughton in *Echo* 1 Sept. 2/5 Some brand-new microbe, alive and kicking, is to be duly distilled and potentised, until a single drop of his juice, squirted under the skin of your bock, will enable you to defy the foul fiend now, henceforth, and for ever.

Potently (pōu·tĕntli), *adv.* [f. Potent *a.*¹ + -ly².] In a potent manner; powerfully, mightily.

1558 Knox *First Blast* (Arb.) 38 With these women, I say, did God worke potentlie. 1613 Shaks. *Hen. VIII*, v. i. 135 You are Potently oppos'd, and with a Malice Of as great Size. 1660 Boyle *New Exp. Phys. Mech.* xvii. 129 The Air having more room..does less potently press upon the subjacent Mercury. 1740 Wesley *Wks.* (1872) I. 265 Idle tales, which they now potently believe. 1884 W. S. Lilly in *Contemp. Rev.* Feb. 261 A new conception..destined most potently to influence the structure of society.

Po·tentness. *rare*⁻⁰. [f. as prec. + -ness.] The quality of being potent; potency; might.

1727 Bailey vol. II, *Potentness*, mightiness, powerfulness.

Po·ter. *rare.* Also 7 -our. [app. f. L. *pōt-āre* to drink, or *pōt-us* drink + -er¹; but cf. Potter *sb.*²] A drinker, a toper.

1657 Howell *Londinop.* 392 They inquire after Potours, Panders, and Bawds. 1900 *Daily News* 13 Jan. 5/7, I fear I have given myself into the hands of the Philistines, whether they be total abstainers or good honest 'poters'.

Potere, obs. form of Pot-ear.

‖**Poterium** (poti·riǫm). *Bot.* [L. *poterium*, a. Gr. ποτήριον drinking-cup, wine-cup; also, name of a shrub. (The mod. application is said in *Treas. Bot.* to refer to the use of the Salad Burnet in flavouring Cool tankard.)] A genus of herbaceous plants of N.O. *Rosaceæ*; Salad Burnet.

1597 Gerarde *Herbal* iii. xxiii. 1148, I haue sowen the seede of Poterion in April which I receiued.., that grew in my garden two yeres togither, and after perished by some mischance. 1706 Phillips, *Poterium*,..a sort of Thistle

1753 Chambers *Cycl. Supp.*, *Poterium*, a word used by many for the prickly pimpernell.

Poteron, variant of Potron *Obs.*

Pote·stal, *a.* *rare.* [irreg. f. next + -al.] Of or pertaining to potestas: see next, 3.

1880 Muirhead *Gaius* iv. § 78 Of opinion that my action is only suspended while the child or slave is in my *potestas*, because I cannot proceed against myself, but that it revives on the potestal relationship coming to an end.

‖**Potestas** (pǫ·testæs). Pl. **potestates** (-ē·tīz). [L. *potestās* power, used in certain connexions.]

†**1.** *Alg.* = Power *sb.*¹ 11. *Obs.*

1656 Hobbes *Six Less.* Wks. 1845 VII. 330 The roots and potestates themselves. 1675 Collins in Rigaud *Corr. Sci. Men* (1841) I. 213 They will both ascend to the 18th potestas of the unknown symbol.

†**2.** Chemical or pharmaceutical power; active principle; = Essence *sb.* 9. *Obs.*

1683 Salmon *Doron Med.* i. 290 That Potestates or Powers of things are as if they were the Nature. 1694 — *Bate's Dispens.* (1713) 152/1 After the same Manner..prepare the Pótestates or Powers of other Vegetable Productions.

3. *Roman Law.* The power or authority of the head of a family over those depending on him; *esp.* parental authority.

1870 Abdy & Walker tr. *Gaius* i. § 109. 35 Whereas both males and females may be in our *potestas*, females alone come into *manus*. 1880 [see Potestal].

†**Po·testate.** *Obs.* Also 5–6 -at. [ad. L. *potestās, ātem* power, a ruler, supreme magistrate. So OF. *potestat* (learned form = pop. *poustee*); It. *podestà*. The pl. *potestates* is uniform with the pl. of *potestas*, and sometimes indistinguishable from it.]

1. A person possessed of power over others; a superior, potentate, ruler, lord.

c 1380 Wyclif *Wks.* (1880) 227 Eche man owiþ to be suget to heiȝere potestatis, þat is to men of heiȝe power. *c* 1380 — *Sel. Wks.* III. 297 Wilt þou not drede þe potestate? *c* 1386 Chaucer *Sompn. T.* 303 Whilom ther was an Irous potestat. *c* 1470 Henryson *Mor. Fab.* vii. (*Lion & Mouse*) xxxvii, Ane prince or empriour, Ane potestate, or ȝit ane king with croun. 1583 Stubbes *Anat. Abus.* i. (1879) 33 Lawfull for the potestates, the nobilitie, the gentrie [etc.]. 1593 G. Harvey *Pierce's Super.* 120 Some Potestats are queint men. *a* 1678 Woodhead *Holy Living* (1688) 29 They always giving a relation, or account..to their superior potestates, or to God.

2. Rendering *potestas* in the Vulgate (Eph. vi. 12, 1 Pet. iii. 22), applied to a spiritual (angelic or demonic) 'power'.

1382 Wyclif *Eph.* vi. 12 Aȝens the princes and potestatis, aȝens gouernours of the world of thes derknessis. 1520 M. Nisbet 1 *Peter* iii. 22 Angels, potestatis, and virtues, ar made subiectis to him. 1542 Becon *Pathw. Prayer* xxv. Lij b, It is no man nor Aungel, but God..whome the angelike potestates do reuerently feare. 1582 N. T. (Rhem.) *Eph.* i. 21 Aboue al Principalitie and Potestate and Power, and Dominion. *c* 1610 *Women Saints* 195 They lyuing with flesh, like vnto the Potestates who want bodies, are not oppressed with the burden of their bodie.

b. *spec.*, in mediæval angelology, a member of the sixth order of angels: see Order *sb.* 5.

1483 Caxton *Gold. Leg.* 255 b/2 The pryncypates armonysed, The potestates harped, Cherubyn and Seraphyn songen louynges and preysynges. 1584 R. Scot *Discov. Witchcr.* xv. viii. (1886) 337 Thrones, dominions, principats, potestats, virtutes, cherubim and seraphim.

3. The chief magistrate in mediæval Italian towns and republics: = Podestà b; *transf.* a chief magistrate in certain Turkish towns.

1456 Sir G. Haye *Law Arms* (S.T.S.) 208 A noble marchand of Paris suld pas before thair Potestate of Florence. 1470–85 Malory *Arthur* v. viii. 174 Whan ye shal come to Rome to the potestate and all the counceylle and Senate. *a* 1548 Hall *Chron.*, *Hen. VIII* 187 Then folowed the potestates & gouernors of the citie [Bologna] all in Crimosyn veluet, & within a myle of the citie there met hym [Charles V] foure and twentie Cardinalles. 1585 T. Washington tr. *Nicholay's Voy.* ii. viii. 41 One of the saide Mahomies is elected and created potestate, and chiefe iustice both ciuil and criminal [of Chios]. 1603 Knolles *Hist. Turks* (1621) 157 The potestate of Pera came by sea also with eight gallies more.

†**4.** A (collective) authority, a governing body, e.g. of a university. *Obs. rare.*

1530 *Let. fr. Venice* 1 July (*MS. Cott. Vit. B. xiii.* 92), They [all the doctors] causyd the Chaunceler of the potestate [of the University of Padua] to set his hande and seale for the approbation of the authorytye off the notarye.

†**5.** Power, authority. *Obs. rare.*

1535 Stewart *Cron. Scot.* (Rolls) I. 110 Trowand thairof that no man dar speik ill, Becaus he is ane prince of potestate.

†**Potesta·tion.** *Obs. rare.* Also 5 -acion. [f. L. *potestās* power + -ation; cf. *gravitation.*] Power, authorization.

c 1485 *Digby Myst.* (1882) ii. 177 The prynces haue gouyn me full potestacion. 1623 Cockeram, *Potestation*, the same that Potencie is.

Potestative (pǫ·testeˌtiv), *a.* [ad. F. *potestatif*, ad. late L. *potestātīvus* adj. (Tert.) denoting or containing power, f. L. *potestāt-em* power + *-īvus*, -ive; cf. *facultative, qualitative*, etc.]

1. Befitting a 'potestate'; having power or authority; authoritative.

1630 Donne *Serm.* xiii. 134 So I might contemplate him in a judiciary posture, in a potestative, a soveraigne posture, sitting [etc.]. 1644 [H. Parker] *Jus Pop.* 56 All commands are not alike binding and Potestative. 1670 Baxter *Cure Ch. Div.* 234 The abuse of the Potestative Primality is Tyranny. 1724 R. Wodrow *Life J. Wodrow* (1828) 66 A probationer only, for order's sake and without any potestative mission.

2. *Potestative condition*, a condition within the power or control of one of the parties concerned.

1652 Warren *Unbelievers* (1654) 17 We do not..make it a potestative uncertain condition. 1671 R. MacWard *True Nonconf.* 328 If we did hold faith, as it is our act to be required as a proper potestative foregoing condition of our acceptance. 1726 Ayliffe *Parergon* 342 Such a Condition ..is said to be a Potestative Condition in respect of a third Person, but a Casual Condition in regard to the Person to whom such Legacy is given. 1818 Colebrooke *Obligations* 12 A potestative or arbitrary condition is that, which makes the execution of the agreement depend on the will of one of the contracting parties, or upon an event which it is in the power of that party to bring about or to prevent. 1853 Whewell *Grotius* II. 43 If the condition under which the thing may come into the power of the promiser be also potestative (such as he himself can bring about or accelerate).

Pote-stick: see Pote *sb.*¹ 3.

†**Pote·stolate.** *Obs. nonce-wd.* ? Humorous dim. of Potestate.

1522 Skelton *Why not to Court* 985 He is suche a grym syer, And suche a potestolate, And suche a potestate.

[**Poteuere, potewer**, scribal errors for *potener*, Pautener, purse. See Skeat *Notes Eng. Etym.* 227.

a 1650 *Sir Degree* 866 in Furniv. *Percy Folio* III. 47 By that sword I know thee heere; The poynt is in my poteuere [*Auchinleck MS.* aumenere]. *a* 1650 *Boy & Mantle* 21 *ibid.* II. 305 He plucked out of his potewer..a pretty mantle.]

‖**Potews.** *Cookery. Obs. rare.* [a. OF. *potaus* (1387–8 in Godef.), **poteus*, pl. of *potel* a little pot, Pottle.] A fancy dish moulded in an earthen pot, which was broken when the contents had become solid.

? *c* 1390 *Form of Cury* § 177 (1780) 80 Potews. Take Pottus of Erþe lytell of half a quart and fyll hem full of fars of pomme dorryes...Whan þey buth ynowȝ, breke þe pottus of erþe & do þe fars on þe spyt & rost hem wel.

Po·t-eye. *Spinning.* [Pot *sb.*¹] (See quot.)

1864 W. S. B. McLaren *Spinning* Gloss., *Pot-eye*, a little cup with a slit in it, set in a spinning frame for the thread to run down, and to avoid friction. 1884 *Ibid.* (ed. 2) 177 On a throstle frame the yarn is first passed through and rubbed against the 'pot-eye' of the wire-board, and then tightly wound round a hard bobbin.

†**Po·t-fish.** *Obs.* Also **pott-.** [ad. Du. *potvisch*, in Ger. *pottfisch*, Da., Swed. *potfisk*; the first element being perh. the same as in obs. Du. *potshoofd* thick-head (Kilian), Flem. *potshoofd* an eel-pout, in reference to the huge head of this whale.] The cachalot or spermaceti whale.

1743 *Phil. Trans.* XLII. 611 In these Seas are Cachelots or Pot-fish, a sort of Whales, their Length 50 to 70 Feet. 1799 W. Tooke *View Russian Emp.* III. 105 The Frozen Ocean..teems with the narwhal, the pott-fish, from whose brain spermaceti is prepared.

Po·t-fi:sher. **a.** = next. **b.** One who fishes merely 'for the pot': cf. Pot-hunter 2.

1890 in *Cent. Dict.*

Po·t-fi:sherman. A fisherman who fishes while floating on the water supported by a pot, into which also he puts the fish when caught: a method practised on some Asiatic rivers.

Potful (pǫ·tful). [f. Pot *sb.*¹ + -ful.] The quantity that fills a pot; as much as a pot holds.

1362 Langl. *P. Pl.* A. vii. 176 A potful of peosun þat pers hedde I-mad [C. ix. 182 A potful of potage þat peersses wyf made]. *c* 1450 *Mankind* 265 in *Macro Plays* 10, I was neuer worth a potfull o wortes, sythyn I was borne. 1646 Sir T. Browne *Pseud. Ep.* ii. v. (1686) 65 A potfull of ashes. 1881 *Scribner's Mag.* XXII. 77 A fire is started..to cook a potful of meat.

†**Pot-gallery.** *Obs.* A 'gallery' of some kind on the banks of the Thames (and perhaps other navigable rivers), which often projected over the water, and was found to be an encroachment.

(Its actual nature and purpose have not been ascertained; the suggestion that it was the outside gallery or balcony of a pot-house overhanging the river (see N. & Q. 31 Aug. 1907, p. 172) appears to be set aside by the recorded dimensions of some 'pot-galleries': see the quots.)

1630 *Sir R. Ducie's Orders* § 20 in R. Griffiths *Conservacy of Thames* (1746) 70 *Item*, That no Person do make or continue any Wharf, Building, Potgallery, or other Purpresture, or Incroachment into, upon, or over any Part of the Soil of the said River. 1684 *Survey of Buildings & Encroachments on Thames* (Bodl. Lib., Gough Maps 46 ff. 42'), On the South Side...1. At Allen's Dye-house a Pott Gallery, 21 ft. E. to W., 12 ft. out into the River, Old. *Ibid.* (lf. 43), On the North Side..3. St Katherines, from Iron Gate towards St Katherines Dock are Pot Galleries, 620 ft. E. to W., 8 and 10 ft. out into the river, Old.

Po·t-ga·rden. A garden of pot-herbs, a kitchen-garden. Also *attrib.*

1511 *MS. Acc. St. John's Hosp., Canterb.*, For dygyng off þe byen grownd in þe pot gardyne. 1519 Horman *Vulg.* 172 The knot-garden serueth for pleasure: the potte garden for profitte. 1642 *MS. Acc. St. John's Hosp., Canterb.*, Mending the locke of the potgarden gate. 1898 *Atlantic Monthly* Apr. 503/1 The cabbage and the cauliflower and most things that grow in a pot-garden are but little known to him who sees them only in the pot or on the plate.

†**Po·t-gun, po·tgun.** *Obs.* Also 6 -gonne, -goon, 6–7 -gunne. [f. Pot *sb.*¹ + Gun *sb.*]

1. A short piece of ordnance with a large bore, a mortar; so called from its shape.

1549 Chaloner *Erasm. on Folly* H iv, Another striken through with a potgonne recouered. 1557 A. Jenkinson *Voy. & Trav.* (Hakl. Soc.) II. 360 They haue..a great many of morter pieces or potguns. 1599 Hakluyt *Voy.* II. i. 81 Then the enemies were warned by the Iewe that wrote letters to them.., that the sayd potgunnes did no harme.

2. = Pop-gun *sb.* 1.

1580 Whitehorne *Ord. Souldiours* (1588) 30 b, One of those potgunnes of elder, that boyes vse to shoote paper and slowes in. 1611 Cotgr., *Caloniere*, a pot-gunne made of a Quill, or Elder sticke. 1660 M. R. *Exact Acc. Receipts* 3, I..wish I had been chang'd into an Elder-tree, to have been cut out into Pot-guns. 1729 Swift *To Dr. Delany on Libels* 14 When first in Print, you see him dread Each Pot-Gun levell'd at his Head. 1801 [see Pop-gun 1].

b. Contemptuously or ludicrously applied to a pistol or similar fire-arm; cf. Pop-gun *sb.* 2.

a 1553 Udall *Royster D.* iv. vii. (Arb.) 75 Once discharge my harquebouse And for my heartes ease, haue once more with my potgoon. *a* 1619 Fletcher, etc. *Kni Malta* iv. iv, How! fright me with your pot-gun? 1659 Shirley *Honoria & Mam.* i. i, When all your liveries go a-feasting By water, with your gally-foist and pot-guns.

3. *fig.* A loud talker, a mere boaster, a braggart; also, an unfounded report.

1623 Webster *Duchess of Malfi* iii. iii, I saw a Dutchman break his pate once For calling him pot-gun. *c* 1626 *Dick of Devon.* i. i. in Bullen *O. Pl.* II. 9, I heard such a report, But had no faith in't: a mere Potgun! 1693 Congreve *Old Bach.* iii. viii, That sign of a man there, that pot-gun charged with wind.

4. *attrib.* and *Comb.*

1624 Ford *Sun's Darling* To Rdr., The First Season. Presents him in the Twilight of his age, Not pot-gun-proof. 1651 W. Jane Εἰκὼν Ἀκλαστος 168 These are potgun preparations for a Civill war. 1691 *New Discov. Old Intreague* xvi, Their Pot-gun Volleys charge Her Royal Ear.

†**Po·t-hanger.** *Obs.* [f. Pot *sb.*¹ + Hanger².] A device for hanging a pot or kettle over the fire; a series of links, a rack, or a bar with a series of holes, on which a pot-hook or crook could be hung at different heights; = Hanger² 4 d. Mostly in *pl.*

1580 Hollyband *Treas. Fr. Tong*, *Cramaillère*, the pot hanger. 1591 Percivall *Sp. Dict.*, *Llares o ollares*, pot-hangers, *ollares catenæ*. 1608 Willet *Hexapla Exod.* 235 They sate by the pot hangers, whereon they vsed to hang their pots. 1617 in W. F. Shaw *Mem. Eastry* (1870) 227 Three brass stupens [stewpans], one payer of pott-hangers. 1642 in *Archives Maryland* (1887) IV. 94, 1 Pot-hanger and potthooks. 1678–84 Littleton *Lat. Dict.*, *Climacter*,..pot-hanger or pot-hooks.

†**Po·t-hangings**, *sb. pl.* *Obs. rare.* **a.** = Pot-clips. **b.** = Pot-hangers.

1521 in *Bury Wills* (Camden) 119 Item a gredyern, and a andern, a payr of poott hangyngs, and frynge pan. 1530 Palsgr. 182 *Vnes ancestes*, a payre of potte hangynges. *Ibid.* 257/1 Potte hangynges, *cremilliere*.

†**Po·t-hangle.** *Obs. rare.* [f. Pot *sb.*¹ + *hangle*, f. Hang *v.* + -le, suffix of the instrument. (*Hangle* occurs otherwise only as var. of Hingle a hinge.)] In *pl.* (const. as *sing.*) = prec. b.

1538 in *Lett. Suppress. Monasteries* (Camden) 267 Item, a fryeng panne and a peyre of pothangles sold to the seyd Scudamour vjd. *Ibid.*, Item, sold to the baylyf of Staff. a pothangles vijd. 1614 *MS. Stratford-on-Avon* (Nares), Item, one pothangles, price ij.s.

Po·t-head. *colloq.* [Pot *sb.*¹] A stupid person. So **Po·t-hea·ded** *a.*, stupid, thick-headed.

1533 More *Apol.* xlvii. Wks. 920/2 These heretikes..some potheaded postles they haue, that wander about ye realme into sondry shyres. 1855 Kingsley *Westw. Ho!* xv, She was too good for a poor pot-head like me.

†**Pothecar(e, -aire.** *Sc.* and *north. Eng. dial.* *Obs.* Also 9 potticar. [Aphetic form of *apothecar*, = F. *apothecaire*, corresp. to Eng. *pothecary*: see next. Hence by phonetic corruption **pot(t)egar*, *potingar*, Pottingar.] An apothecary: = next.

c 1480 Henryson *Test. Cres.* 248 Spycis belangand to the pothecairis [*rime* electuairis = electuaries], With mony hailsum sweit confectioun. *a* 1585 Polwart *Flyting w. Montgomerie* 231 This present from the pothecares [*rimes* wares, saires] Mee think meet to amend thee. 1825 Brockett *N. C. Gloss.*, *Potticar, Potecary, Pothecary*, an apothecary. 1869 *Lonsdale Gloss.*, *Pottiker*, an apothecary.

Pothecary. Now only *dial.* Forms: α. 4–5 potecarie, 4–7 -cary(e, 5 -kary, 6 -cari; 5–6 potycary(e; 6 poticarie, -carye, 6–7 (9 *dial.*) -cary; 7 pottecary, -icary. β. 6–7 pothicary, 7 pothecarie, 7–8 (9 *dial.*) -cary, 8–9 'pothecary. See also prec. Aphetic form of Apothecary, formerly in common use.

c 1386 Chaucer *Pard. T.* 524 (Camb.) And forth he goth no lengere wolde he tarye In-to the toun vn-to a potecarye [so *Corp.*, *Lansd.*, *Harl.*; *Ellesm.*, *Hengw.*, apothecarie; *Petw.* apot-]. 1426 Lydg. *De Guil. Pilgr.* 24210 Sondry lettuaryes Maked at the potycaryes. 1530 Palsgr. 257/1 Potycary that selleth medycins, *apothecayre*. 1551 Turner *Herbal* i. Prol. A iij b, If the potecari..is ignorant in herbes. 1632 Lithgow *Trav.* iii. 98 Abundance of Alloes.., so much esteemed by our Pothecaries. 1668–9 Pepys *Diary* 8 Feb., Going to visit Roger Pepys, at the pothecary's in King's Street. 1720 W. Stukeley in *Mem.* (Surtees) I. 112 A league between a few doctors, poticarys, and surgeons, who play into one anothers hands. 1820 Southey *Devil's Walk* vii, He saw a Pothecary, on a white horse, Ride by on his vocation. *a* 1825 Forby *Voc. E. Anglia*, *Poticary*. 1886 Elworthy *W. Somerset Word-bk.*, *Potecary*, apothecary...Not now of common use..but I have heard it used disparagingly.

b. *attrib.* quasi-*adj.*

1540 *Act 32 Hen. VIII*, c. 40 § 2 Suche poticary wares drugges and stuffes. 1558 Bulleyn *Govt. Health* 111 Who

liueth..so euill as these pothicary men? 1607 Chapman *Bussy D'Ambois* v. i. Plays 1873 II. 90 If I scape Monsieurs Pothecarie Shops. 1614 Markham *Cheap Husb.* To Rdr., Yet have I seene smiths so unprovided of Pothecary simples.

Potheen, variant form of Poteen.

Pothel, ME. variant of *podel*, Puddle.

Pother (pǫ·ðəɹ, pɒ·ðəɹ), *sb.* Forms: α. 7– pother; also (7 powther), 7–9 puther, 7 (9 *dial.*) poother. β. 7– pudder. [Origin unknown: appears early in 17th c. Historically *pother* rimes with *other, brother, mother, smother*, the vowel app. repr. orig. *ŏ*; so the dial. *puther, pudder*. The current pǫ·ðəɹ appears to be a 19th c. literary innovation, after the spelling, and perh. influenced by association with *bother*. The form *pudder* is parallel to the dial. *udder, brudder, mudder, fadder*, etc. in some of which *d*, in others *ð*, is original.

Original identity with Powder, though suggested by the sense 'dust', appears to be phonetically untenable.]

1. A choking smoke or atmosphere of dust. *To kick up a pother*, to raise a choking dust.

α. 1627 Drayton *Nymphidia* lxxxii, The Poke Which out of it sent such a smoke, As ready was them all to choke, So greeuous was the pother. 1637 G. Daniel *Genius of Isle* 138, I, in this smoaking pother, Had sole the want. 1886 *Cheshire Gloss.* s.v. *Poother*, What a poother tha kicks up wi' thi brush! [i.e. in sweeping a room]. 1887 T. Darlington *S. Chesh. Gloss.* s.v., A puff of tobacco smoke directed into a person's face would be a poother. 1833 Baring-Gould *Mrs. Curgenven* xlvi, There be such a pother o' smoke I doubt if that you can see her.

β. 1642 Milton *Apol. Smect.* 4 To lay the dust and pudder in antiquity, which he and his..are wont to raise.

2. Disturbance, commotion, turmoil, bustle; a tumult, uproar; a noise, din. Cf. Dust *sb.*¹ 5.

α. 1591 Sylvester *Ivry* 71 As a Torrent..in his furious Pother Takes Land from som, and giveth more to other. 1607 (1623) Shaks. *Cor.* ii. i. 234 Such a poother, As if that whatsoeuer God, who leades him, Were slyly crept into his humane powers, And gaue him gracefull posture. 1682 N. O. *Boileau's Lutrin* ii. 249 But Oh! these Chanters, Chanons make a Pother, A Dog can't rest, whilst one worries another. 1709 O. Dykes *Eng Prov. & Refl.* (ed. 2) 308 What a Noise and Pother do our Hawkers make in a Hurry about the Streets with their News-Books. *a* 1849 Hor. Smith *Addr. Mummy* x, Didst thou not hear the pother o'er thy head When the great Persian Conqueror, Cambyses Marched armies o'er thy tomb with thundering tread? 1898 F. T. Bullen *Cruise Cachalot* 72 Smiting the sea with his mighty tail, making an almost deafening noise and pother.

β. 1623 *Shaks.'s Wks.*, *Lear* iii. ii. 50 Let the great Goddes, That keepe this dreadfull pudder [*Qq.* 1. 3 thundring; *Qo.* 2 powther] o're our heads, Finde out their enemies now. 1657 Thornley tr. *Longus' Daphnis & Chloe* 189 A busie noise, tumultuous pudder of carriages. 1671 Crowne *Juliana* i. 4 Here's a pudder, ho! see if none of my cups or silver spoons be missing. 1673 in Halliwell *Pal. Anthol.* (1850) 109 'Twas uncivilly done Such a hideous pudder to keep. 1816 Scott *Antiq.* xv, The pony, hearing this pudder over his head, began apparently to think [etc.].

b. *transf.* A verbal commotion, stir, or fuss.

α. 1631 Massinger *Emperor East* iv. v, All this pother for an apple! 1654 Whitlock *Zootomia* 481 When Heathen Authority hath kept all the Puther it can, with their Amphion and Orpheus. 1663 Butler *Hud.* i. i. 32 Some hold the one, and some the other, But, howsoe'er they make a Pother, The difference was so small. 1783 *Trifler* No. 13. 175 Your Sister too would make a pother, She'd never brook to call him Brother. 1850 Blackie *Æschylus* I. Pref. 57 With high-sounding words he will make such a pother.

β. 1609 Bp. W. Barlow *Answ. Nameless Cath.* 23 In this pudder of different opinions, recourse is had to the Great Oracle. 1759 Sterne *Tr. Shandy* II. ii, What a pudder and racket in Councils about οὐσία and ὑπόστασις! 1858 Gen. P. Thompson *Audi Alt.* I. lvii. 223 A mortal pudder has been raised against so harmless a proposal, as that the community should have the relief [etc.].

3. Mental perturbation or tumult; trouble, fuss; display of sorrow or grief.

1641 Milton *Reform.* i. Wks. 1851 III. 3 Being scarr'd.. by the pangs, and gripes of a boyling conscience, all in a pudder shuffles up to himselfe such a God, and such a worship as is most agreeable to remedy his feare. 1656 S. Holland *Zara* (1719) 34 Of Sorrow, making a most grievous puther [*rime* Mother]. 1738 *Gentl. Mag.* VIII. 43/1 Well! if all husbands keep so great a pother, I'll live unmarried—till I get another. 1822 Hazlitt *Table-t.* Ser. ii. vii. (1869) 143 This coil and mighty pudder in the breast.

Pother (pǫ·ðəɹ, pɒ·ðəɹ), *v.* Also 7 pudder, 9 *dial.* puther. [app. f. Pother *sb.*; but sometimes app. associated with Bother *v.*]

1. *trans.* To put into a fuss; to fluster, worry; to confuse, perplex, trouble.

α. 1692 Locke *Educ.* § 72 If at that Time he forces himself to it, he only pothers and wearies himself to no purpose. 1795 Birch *Adopted Child* i. ii, At his old employment, his pencils and his compasses, and I don't know what, pothering his poor little brains. 1860 Emerson *Cond. Life, Wealth* Wks. (Bohn) II. 339 But how can Cockayne..be pothered with fatting oxen? 1904 M. Hewlett *Queen's Quair* ii. x. 324 Sir James all pothered to reply; rare for him.

β. *c* 1698 Locke *Cond. Underst.* § 13 He..will abound in contrary Observations, that can be of no other Use but to perplex and pudder him if he compares them.

b. To get *out* by worrying.

1740 J. Clarke *Educ. Youth* (ed. 3) 167 He must pother the Meaning..out of a Dictionary.

2. *intr.* To make a fuss; to fuss, to worry.

1735 Savage *Progr. Divine* 361 Detach the sense, and pother o'er the text. 1778 *Learning at a Loss* I. 32, I found the old Gentleman..pothering over the Newspaper. 1895 R. Burton in *Forum* (N.Y.) Apr. 251 It is idle to pother with secondary causes when here is the native source.

3. *dial.* To move, pour, or roll in a cloud, as smoke or dust.

Widely used in midland dialects from Yorksh. to Warwick, Leicester, Lincoln: see *Eng. Dial. Dict.* s.v. *Puther*. Hence perh. *pothering* in 19th c. quots. below.

Hence **Po·thering** *vbl. sb.* and *ppl. a.*; also **Pothera·tion** (*nonce-wd.* after *botheration*), stir, turmoil, trouble; **Po·therment**, *dial.* petty trouble.

1690 Locke *Hum. Und.* iv. iii. § 30 That perplexity, puddering, and confusion, which has so much hindred Mens progress in other parts of Knowledge. 1791–1823 D'Israeli *Cur. Lit.* (1866) 269/1 A multitude confused of pothering odours. 1827 Hare *Guesses* Ser. i. (1873) 229 The words of their [Irish] orators are wont to roll out just like so many potatoes..rumbling, and pothering and incoherent. 1855 Robinson *Whitby Gloss.*, *Potherments*, perplexities, troubles. 1901 *Essex Herald* 9 Apr. 2/5 All the potheration had been purposely caused by the master of the house.

Pot-herb (pǫ·tˌhəɹb). [f. Pot *sb.*¹ + Herb.] A herb grown for boiling in the pot; any of the herbs cultivated in a kitchen-garden.

Black pot-herb, White pot-herb, old names for Alexanders (*Smyrnium Olusatrum*) and Corn-salad (*Valerianella olitoria*) respectively. (Gerarde 1597, 243.)

1538 Elyot, *Caulis*...Also an herbe called colewortes. It is somtyme taken for all pot herbes. 1605 *Tryall Chev.* ii. i. in Bullen *O. Pl.* III. 290 E're he do my Lord any wrong, zounds Ile be cut smaller then pot-hearbs. 1644 Evelyn *Diary* 20 Nov., The Circus Maximus, ..one entire heape of rubbish, part of it converted into a garden of pot-herbs. 1855 Macaulay *Hist. Eng.* xix. IV. 369 A spot which seemed to be part of Holland, a straight canal, a terrace, rows of clipped trees, and rectangular beds of flowers and potherbs.

¶**b.** *erron.* = *pot-plant.*

1882 Stevenson *New Arab. Nts.* (1884) 101 Flowering pot-herbs garnished the sills of the..windows.

c. *attrib.* **Pot-herb butterfly**, a N. American species (*Pieris oleracea*), closely allied to the cabbage-butterfly.

1692 Dryden *Cleomenes* iii. i, A people, baser than the beasts they worship; Below their pot-herb gods, that grow in gardens.

Po·thery, *a.* [f. Pother *sb.* + -y.]

1. Choking, stifling; close, sultry; also *transf.*

1696 Whiston *The. Earth* iv. (1722) 365 That Pothery and Sultry..Weather..we usually now feel. 1846 Landor *Imag. Conv.*, *Southey & L.* Wks. 1853 II. 168/2 They [Shakspere's Sonnets] are hot and pothery; there is much condensation, little delicacy.

2. *dial.* Of sheep: Giddy and liable to fall, through water on the brain.

Perh. a different word, related to Potter *v.*

1839 Holloway *Dict. Provinc.*, A sheep which has water on the brain, which causes it to fall down, or move in a very weak, tottering, and uncertain manner, is said to be pothery.

Pot-hole. *Geol.* [f. Pot *sb.*¹ + Hole *sb.*]

1. A deep hole of more or less cylindrical shape; esp. one formed by the wearing away of rock by the rotation of a stone, or a collection of gravel, in an eddy of running water, or in the bed of a glacier.

1839 *Civil Eng. & Arch. Jrnl.* II. 373/1, 8 feet of the workable stone may be considered free from 'allum' or 'pot holes' containing calcareous spar, to which this stone is subject. 1862 Dana *Man. Geol.* 641 The 'Basin' in the Franconia Notch (White Mountains) is a pot-hole in granite, fifteen feet deep and twenty and twenty five feet in its two diameters. 1873 J. Geikie *Gt. Ice Age* (1894) 431 Large pot-holes formed on the bed of a glacier by water plunging down through crevasses. 1878 Huxley *Physiogr.* ix. 134 The grinding action of pebbles, when set in motion by water, is strikingly shown in the formation of potholes.

2. See quot.

1898 *Archæol. Jrnl.* Ser. ii. V. 294 That the manufacture of pottery was carried on in Hayling in former times is shown by the existence of 'pot-holes', i.e. holes from which clay has been taken.

Pot-hook (pǫ·tˌhuk), *sb.* [f. Pot *sb.*¹ + Hook *sb.*]

1. a. A hook suspended over a fireplace, for hanging a pot or kettle on; a crook. **b.** An iron rod (usually curved) with a hook at the end, for lifting a heated pot, stove-lid, etc.

1467 *Maldon, Essex, Court Rolls* (Bundle 43 No. 14), ii. keteles; i. rakke; i par de pottehokes. *c* 1475 *Pict. Voc.* in Wr.-Wülcker 770/14 *Hec capana*, a pothoke. 1530 Palsgr. 257/1 Potte hokes, *unes ancestes*. 1698 Fryer *Acc. E. India & P.* 296 Setting their Earthen or Copper Pots thereon, not hanging them on Pothooks as we do. 1869 Mrs. Stowe *Oldtown* vi. (1870) 56 The great black crane..swung over it, with its multiplicity of pot-hooks and trammels. 1875 Knight *Dict. Mech.*, *Pot-hook*, an S-shaped hook for suspending a culinary vessel from a chimney-crane.

†**c.** *pl.* An instrument of punishment: see quot.

1707 Sloane *Jamaica* I. p. lviii, For running away they put..pottocks about their necks, which are iron rings with two long necks riveted to them. 1740 *Hist. Jamaica* vi. 159 The Chain and Pot-hooks are painted by his own Order in the Picture I spoke of just now. 1751 MacSparran *Diary* (1899) 52 He [a runaway slave in Rhode Island] had wt is called Pothooks put about his Neck.

2. A curved or hooked stroke made in writing; a crooked stroke or character, a scrawl; now usually applied to a hooked stroke, as an element of handwriting, made by children in learning to write. (Often with *hanger*: cf. Hanger² 4 d.)

1611 Cotgr., *Pasté*..a blurre, scraule, pothooke, or ill-favoured whim-wham, in writing. *a* 1625 Fletcher & Mass. *Elder Bro.* i. ii, *Bri.* What have we here? Pot-hooks and Andirons! *And.* I much pity you, it is the Syrian Character, or the Arabick. 1690 Dryden *Don Sebastian* ii. ii, No peeping here, though I long to be spelling her Arabick scrawls and pot-hooks. 1710 Swift *Lett.* (1767) III. 61 You know such a pothook makes a letter; and you know what letter, and so, and so. 1738, 1809 [see Hanger² 4 d]. 1799 B. Thompson *Kotzebue's Stranger* in *Inchbald's Theatre* I. 59 I'll go for his copy-book. He makes his pothooks capitally. 1887 G. R. Sims *Mary Jane's Mem.* 237 She's scrawling pothooks and hangers on a dirty sheet of paper.

†**b.** *attrib.* in reference to crabbed or illegible writing or unintelligible characters. *Obs.*

1674 T. Flatman *To Mr. Austin* 9 No more, than read that dung fork, pothook hand That in Queen's Colledge Library does stand. *a* 1683 J. Oldham *Charact. Old P.* Rem. (1684) 112 Nonsense and the fittest Character to write it in, that Pot-hook-hand the Devil us'd at Oxford. [See *Wood's Life & Times* (O. H. S.) I. 498.]

Hence (*nonce-wds.*) **Po·t-hook** *v. trans.*, to curve into the shape of a pot-hook; **Po·t-hooked** *a.*, having a pot-hook (sense 2); **Po·t-hoo·kery**, making of pot-hooks or scrawls; **Po·t-hooky** *a.*, full of or consisting of pot-hooks, scrawled.

1795 T. Twining in *Parr's Wks.* (1828) VIII. 273 The Professor's conscribillatio is a more illegible..piece of pot-hookery than yours. 1867 *Harper's Mag.* Nov. 793 It was written in a cramped, pot-hooky hand. 1875 Maund in *Alpine Jrnl.* May (1876) 414 After packing myself away as well as I could in the shape of a pot-hook, Martin followed and pot hooked himself alongside me. 1898 Chr. Murray in *Daily News* 27 Jan. 6/2 The Dreyfus letters very commonly have a curious pothooked starting point...They curl upwards at the start. There is nothing of the sort in the *bordereau*.

‖**Pothos** (pōu·pǫs). *Bot.* [mod.L. (Linnæus, 1737), ad. Sinhal. *pótha, pôtr.*] A genus of climbing shrubs (N.O. *Araceæ* or *Orontiaceæ*), natives of Asia, Australia, etc.: some species are cultivated as foliage plants.

1836 Macgillivray tr. *Humboldt's Trav.* xviii. 271 The pothoses, arums, and lianas, furnished so thick a covering that..they were completely sheltered. 1863 Bates *Nat. Amazon* i. (1864) 10 Climbing Pothos plants, with large, glossy, heart-shaped leaves.

Po·t-house. [f. Pot *sb.*¹ + House *sb.*¹]

†**1.** A house where pottery is made. *Obs. rare.*

1697 *Lond. Gaz.* No. 3300/4 A very convenient Brick House to be let, having a Potthouse belonging to it, and a very fine Yard for Washing of Clay. 1761 *Chron.* in *Ann. Reg.* 95/2 A premium to..master of the stone pot-house at Fulham for..making crucibles of British materials.

2. A house where pots of beer and other intoxicants are retailed; an ale-house; a small, unpretentious, or low tavern or public-house.

1724 *Lond. Gaz.* No. 6320/3 A large well built accustomed Pot-House,..known by the Name of the Hermitage Pot-House. 1748 Warton *Panegyr. on Oxford Ale* 27 To pot-house I repair, the sacred haunt, Where, Ale, thy votaries in full resort Hold rites nocturnal. 1861 Hughes *Tom Brown at Oxf.* xii, The paragon of all pothouses; snug little bar with red curtains [etc.]. 1887 Jessopp *Arcady* iii. 92 They were extremely capable men, but they could not keep from the pot-house.

b. *attrib.* Belonging to or characteristic of a pot-house; low, vulgar.

1816 Southey in *Q. Rev.* XVI. 275 The class of men for whom these pot-house epistles are written, read nothing else. 1840 Dickens *Barn. Rudge* xxxvii, Reeking yet with pot-house odours. 1895 Hollingshead *My Lifetime* I. xiii. 124 There was no pot-house bluster about the two combatants.

Pot-hu·nter. [f. Pot *sb.*¹ + Hunter.]

†**1.** An opprobrious appellation: ? a sycophant, a parasite: cf. Barnacle *sb.*² 3 b. *Obs.*

1592 Nashe *Four Lett. Confut.* Wks. (Grosart) II. 242 This indigested Chaos of Doctourship, and greedy pothunter after applause, is an apparant Publican and sinner. 1592 Greene *Blacke Bks. Messenger* Wks. (Grosart) XI. 7 The verser in conny-catching is called the Retriuer And the Barnacle, the pot hunter. 1592 *Admonition Bk. Emm. Coll. Cambr.* in *4th Rep. Hist. MSS. Comm.* 420/1 Mr. Catsby..for saying my Lord [of Routland] hymself was but a child, and that he was maintained by pott-hunters.. was admonished.

2. 'A sportsman who shoots anything he comes across, having more regard to filling his bag than to the rules which regulate the sport' (*Slang Dict.* 1860).

1781 W. Blane *Ess. Hunting* (1788) 102 As arrant a Pot-hunter as ever England bred, that..had not scrupled to kill a Buck or Doe at any season. 1825 *Bull baiting* i. in *Houlston Tracts* I. xxvii. 9 There's nothing a regular Shot would be sooner chafed at than being called a Pot-hunter. 1895 J. G. Millais *Breath fr. Veldt* (1899) 109 My hope is that some traveller..who is something more than a pot-hunter, may..send home to our Museum a series of the common white-quilled black Khoorhan.

3. One who takes part in any contest or competition merely for the sake of winning a prize. (With allusion to Pot *sb.*¹ 1 g.)

1873 *Slang Dict.*, *Pot-hunter*, a man who gives his time up to rowing or punting, or any sort of match in order to win the 'pewters' which are given as prizes. *University*... Now much used in aquatic and athletic circles; and.. applied, in a derogatory sense, to men of good quality who enter themselves in small races they are almost sure to win. 1883 *Pall Mall G.* 7 July 6/1 The increase..in the number of 'pot-hunters', as they are called—an epithet which originated in the early days of the Wimbledon meeting, when prizes were given 'in kind', and not as now in money. 1886 *Cycl. Tour. Club Gaz.* IV. 122 To tempt..many a 'pot-hunter' who follows racing for what he can get out of it.

So **Po·t-hu·nting** *sb.* and *a.* (in senses corresponding to 2 and 3 above).

1808 W. Cobbett in L'Estrange *Friendships Miss Mitford* (1882) I. 43 Rush they go, the pot-hunting crew, into that manor. 1862 *Sat. Rev.* 5 July 7 The sort of pot-hunting known at Wimbledon and elsewhere as Pool, where the value of a bull's-eye is much more considered than the credit of handling with success the Queen of weapons. 1881 Tylor *Anthropology* ix. 210 The quest of food (now often contemptuously called 'pot-hunting') becomes subordinate to the excitement of the chase. 1881 *Gd. Words* XXII. 46/1 Some men are too fond of starring or pothunting at 'sports'. 1893 Sinclair & Henry *Swimming* (Badm. Libr.) 369 Some swimmers seem able..to stand the strain of racing night after night...The rage for pot-hunting is apparently unconquerable.

Potica·ry, obs. variant of Pothecary.

Potichomania (pǫtiʃoˌmēⁱ·niă). Also in Fr. form -manie. [ad. F. *potichomanie*, irreg. f. *potiche* an oriental porcelain vase, also a glass vase coloured in imitation + *-manie*, -mania.] The craze for imitating Japanese or other porcelain by covering the inner surface of glass vessels, etc., with designs on paper or sheet gelatine; the process of doing this.

1855 *Househ. Words* XI. 129 (heading) *Potichomania*. 1855 *Mechanic's Mag.* LXII. 279 *Potichomanie* is the present fashion. 1863 Sala *Capt. Dangerous* ... 7 He..talked about chemistry and Mr. Faraday; taught my wife *potichomanie* and modelling in wax. 1903 *Temple Bar Mag.* Feb. 152 Hence she..cared nothing for wax flowers or potichomania.

‖**Potin** (potæ̃). Also 7 pottain. [F. *potin* (13th c. in Hatz.-Darm., also *potain* 1582 in Godef.), f. *pot* Pot *sb.*¹ + *-in*: cf. -ine⁴.]

1. Old pot-metal (Pot-metal 1, 3).

1601 Holland *Pliny* II. 503 Such pottain or old metall which is ouerworne, and by ordinary occupying and vsing to the hand, bright-shining. 1825 J. Nicholson *Operat. Mechanic* 348 To work all the surface into furrows or grooves, in order that it may retain the substance called the potin, which is to be welded upon one side of the iron, to form the hard matter on which the holes are to be pierced. This potin is nothing but fragments of old cast-iron pots. *Ibid.* 349 It must be repeatedly heated and worked until the potin fixes to the iron. The workman then throws dry powdered clay upon it, in order..to soften the potin.

2. A name for an alloy of tin, copper, lead, and zinc, used in coining by the ancient Gauls.

1853 Humphreys *Coin-Coll. Man.* xi. (1876) 134 Many of the coins are of base metal (potin).

Poting, poting-stick: see Pote *v.*

Potinger, obs. form of Pottinger.

Potion (pōu·ʃən), *sb.* Forms: 4–6 pocion, 5 -oun, (*Sc.* poycion), 5–6 pocyon, 6 potioun, 6– potion. [a. OF. *pocion, potion* (12–13th c. in Hatz.-Darm.), mod.F. *potion*, ad. L. *pōtiō-nem* a drinking, draught, potion, philtre, vbl. sb. f. *pōtāre, pōt-um* to drink.]

1. A dose of liquid medicine or of poison; a draught: see Draught *sb.* 15.

13.. *K. Alis.* 3509 (Bodl. MS.) He dude hym bere to pavylouns, And sauid hym wiþ pociouns. *c* 1375 *Sc. Leg. Saints* vi. (*Thomas*) 481 It is lyk to poycion men takis fore purgacione. 1432–50 tr. *Higden* (Rolls) III. 411 He hadde diede anoon, but that he receyvede a pocion of Philippe his phisicion. 1548–77 Vicary *Anat.* i. (1888) 13 If a man may be cured with Dyet and Pocion, let there not be ministred any Chirurgerie. 1592 Shaks. *Rom. & Jul.* v. iii. 244 Then gaue I her..A sleeping Potion, which so tooke effect As I intended. 1610 Holland *Camden's Brit.* (1637) 370 Bewitched by sorcerie and amorous potions. 1732 Lediard *Sethos* II. vii. 84 To discern the innocent..by trials of fire and potions. 1848 Mrs. Jameson *Sacr. & Leg. Art* (1850) 435 Neither potions nor physicians can do more than postpone the evil hour.

fig. 1577 tr. *Luther's Comm. Gal.* iv. 95 He goeth about to qualify and mitigate his bitter Potion. 1597 Shaks. *2 Hen. IV*, i. ii. 145 Your Lordship may minister the Potion of imprisonment to me. 1631 Heywood *Eng. Eliz.* (1641) 108 The bitter potion of indignity. 1790 Burke *Fr. Rev.* Wks. V. 140 To administer the opiate potion of amnesty.

†**2. a.** A portion of drink; a drink, a draught. **b.** A kind of drink; a beverage. *Obs. rare.*

1526 *Aberdeen Regr.* (1844) I. 115 Inprimis to the iustice ane potioun of wyne; item to my lord chancellar, ane potioun of wyne. 1634 Sir T. Herbert *Trav.* 150 They [Persians] vse another potion, faire water, juice of Lemmons, Sugar, and Roses.

3. *Comb.*, as *potion-monger.*

1894 H. A. Jones in *Daily News* 7 May 6/5 The family friend, rather than the doser and potion-monger.

Potion (pōu·ʃən), *v.* [f. prec. sb. Cf. L. *pōtiōnāre* to give to drink, f. *pōtiōn-em* drinking.] *trans.* To treat or dose with potions; to drug.

1611 Speed *Hist. Gt. Brit.* ix. xi. § 49 Hauing corrupted his Keepers, or..hauing potioned them with a sleepy drinke, [he] escaped out of the Tower of London. 1768 Foote *Devil on 2 Sticks* iii. Wks. 1799 II. 275 Full power ..to pill, bolus, lotion, potion,..and poultice, all persons. 1812 L. Hunt in *Examiner* 25 May 321/1 Puff'd and potion'd up like any bladder.

†**Po·tionate**, *v.* *Obs. rare*⁻⁰. [f. ppl. stem of L. *pōtiōnāre*: see prec. and -ate³.]

1623 Cockeram, *Potionate*, to give a medicine.

‖**Po·tiron.** *Obs.* [F. *potiron* (dial. *potron, poturon*) a kind of large champignon; also, a kind of pumpkin: origin unknown.] A kind of pumpkin: see quots.

1719 London & Wise *Compl. Gard.* 323 Citrules, or Pumpions, Harts Horn Sallet, Potirons, or flat Pumpeons, Parsnips, Leeks, &c. keep their Places nine Months. *Ibid.* 324 Citruls or Pumpions, Potirons or comon Pumpions, Garlick and Shallots.

†**Po·tisuge.** *Obs. humorous nonce-wd.* [f. L. *pōtus* drink (or ? Pot *sb.*¹) + L. *sūgĕre* to suck.] A 'pot-sucker', toper.

1620 Venner *Via Recta* ii. 34 How impudently would our drunken potisuges vaunt themselues.

Po·t-kilp. *north. dial.* [f. Pot *sb.*¹ + Kilp.] = Pot-clip.

1542 *Richmond Wills* (Surtees) 31, ij. pare of pot kylpes, and a pare of tanges, xxd. 1611–12 *Knaresborough Wills* (Surtees) II. 20 A paire of potkilpes. 1828 *Craven Dial.* s.v. *Kelps*, The loose handle of a kale pot is called pot-kelps. 1855 Robinson *Whitby Gloss.*, *Pot kelps*, the loose bow or handle of a porridge-pot.

‖**Potlatch, po·tlach(e.** [Chinook jargon, from Nootka Indian *potlatsh, patlatsh* sb. a gift, vb. to give.] Among some N. American Indians of the Pacific coast: **a.** A gift, a present.

1883 T. Winthrop *Canoe & Saddle* iv. 42 They [Klickatat Indians]..expressed the friendliest sentiments, perhaps with a view to a liberal 'potlatch' of trinkets.

b. A tribal feast at which presents are given and received, given by an aspirant to chiefship.

1884 *San Francisco Chron.* Sept., A potlatch is..a sort of grand reunion and general gathering.., an occasion for the exchanging of big presents. 1890 *Amer. Antiquarian* Mar. 75 On his return he again called the people together and held a big potlatch, giving the Indians what appeared to them at that time great curiosities. 1895 *Westm. Gaz.* 18 July 8/1 In a far-away corner of British Columbia, on the occasion of the last birthday..the Red-skins held a 'potlach' in honour of their Great White Mother. 1907 C. Hill-Tout *Brit. N. Amer.* 52 Occasions of public festivity such as potlatch gatherings.

Hence **Po·tlatching** *sb.*, holding a potlatch.

1896 *Pall Mall Mag.* Sept. 106 After two or three days of feasting and pot-latching.

†**Pot-lead**¹. *Obs.* Used to render F. *gluq*, 'a word used by Schollers of Paris, in derision of an absurd conclusion' (Cotgr. s.v. *Gluc*).

1630 Lennard tr. *Charron's Wisd.* iii. xiv. § 19. 505 If he chance to speake, he entreth into a long discourse of definitions, and diuisions of Aristotle; *ergo* potlead [orig. F. *ergo gluq*].

Pot-lead² (pǫ·tˌled), *sb.* [ad. Du. *potlood* black-lead, f. *pot* Pot *sb.*¹ + *lood* lead.] A name for black-lead or graphite, esp. as used for coating the hulls of racing-yachts below the water-line so as to diminish the friction of the water. Hence **Po·t-lea·d** *v. trans.*, to coat with pot-lead.

1890 in *Cent. Dict.* 1894 *Outing* (U.S.) XXIV. 72/1 The racing shell, used only three times, its bottom pot-leaded, is brought out. *Ibid.* 194/1 Using very fine sandpaper and pot lead till my boat's bottom was beautifully burnished.

Potleg (pǫ·tˌleg). [app. f. Pot *sb.*¹ + Leg.] **a.** (?) The leg or foot of an iron pot. **b.** Broken scraps of cast-iron, used as shot.

1895 *Chambers' Jrnl.* XII. 738/1 Ball or shot they rarely use, but prefer a handful of broken cast-iron potleg, which at close quarters makes a ghastly wound. 1896 *Westm. Gaz.* 15 May 4/3 Their [Matabele] shot consisted of pot-legs, stones, and pieces of iron. 1900 *Longm. Mag.* Dec. 143 When the sergeant raised his officer, ragged potleg was whirring everywhere.

Potler, variant of Poteller *Obs.*

Pot-lid. [f. Pot *sb.*¹ + Lid *sb.*]

1. The lid of a pot.

(When of iron, sometimes used as a warming-pan.)

1403 *Nottingham Rec.* II. 20, j. potlede de ligno. 1530 Palsgr. 257/1 Potlydde for a potte, *couuerlecque*. 1590 Greene *Never too late* ii. (1616) N iv b, To bed man, to bed, and we will haue a warme pot-lid [*ed.* 1590 pot-lid]. 1682 T. Flatman *Heraclitus Ridens* No. 62 (1713) II. 134 It might be, for ought they knew, a Project for altering the Breadth of Pot-lids. 1902 *Daily Chron.* 28 Aug. 3/2 A new hobby..is the collection of small china pot-lids; the covers of those artistic jars which long ago were used for holding shrimp-paste and meats.

2. *Curling.* A stone so played as to rest on the tee.

1853 Walter Watson *Poems & Songs* 63 (E. D. D.). 1885 'J. Strathesk' *More Bits Blinkb.* xiv. 271 His stone landed on the Tee. 'A pat-lid', said Douce Davie. 1893–4 *Caled. Curl. Cl. Ann.* 114 A rare patlid, I fear your play is just owre guid.

3. *Geol.* Popular appellation of a concretion occurring in various sandstones and shales.

1827 Fitton *On Stonesfield-slate* in *Zool. Jrnl.* (1828) III. 416 Concretions of calcareous grit..that form a part of almost every group...These concretions, from a coarse resemblance, are called 'Pot-lids'; and the rock which they consist of,..bears the name of 'Pendle'.

4. *attrib.* **Pot-lid valve**, 'a cap-formed valve which shuts down like a cover upon a port or the end of a pipe'; also, 'the cover of the air-pump of a steam-engine' (Knight *Dict. Mech.* 1875).

†**Po·tling.** *Obs. humorous nonce-wd.* [f. Pot *sb.*¹ + -ling¹.] ? A votary of the pot; a tippler (but cf. Poetling).

1598 B. Jonson *Ev. Man in Hum.* iv. i, You must haue your Poets and your Potlings, your Soldados and Fooalados to follow you vp and down the City.

Pot-liquor (pǫ·tˌlikəɹ). [f. Pot *sb.*¹ + Liquor *sb.*] The liquor in which meat has been boiled; thin broth: see also quot. 1886.

1773 Graves *Spir. Quixote* i. ix, Together with her broth or pot-liquor, he contrived to slip something more substantial into Dorothy's pipkin. 1803 Han. More *Way to Plenty* 56 The pot liquor made such a supply of broth for the sick poor. 1852 Dickens *Bleak Ho.* xxvii, Mrs. Bagnet..sitting with every dish before her; allotting to every portion of pork its own portion of pot-liquor, greens, potatoes, and even mustard! 1886 Elworthy *W. Somerset Word-bk.*, *Pot-liquor*, the water in which vegetables have been boiled; sometimes called green-liquor, when cabbage or other green vegetables have been boiled in it.

Po·t-lu·ck. [f. Pot *sb.*¹ + Luck *sb.*] One's luck or chance as to what may be in the pot, i.e. cooked for a meal: used in reference to a person accepting another's hospitality at a meal without any special preparation having been made for him; chiefly in phr. *to take pot-luck.* Also *transf.*

1592 Nashe *Four Lett. Confut.* Ded., That that pure sanguine complexion of yours may never be famisht with pot-lucke. 1773 Graves *Spir. Quixote* ix. xii, The Gentleman said..he should be very welcome to take pot-luck with him. 1773 Mme. D'Arblay *Early Diary* Sept., If they have any prospect of more sport, they take pot-luck at any cottage. 1883 *Longm. Mag.* July 253 Go home with this man, take pot-luck with him..as one of the family. *attrib.* 1775 Mme. D'Arblay *Early Diary, Let.* Mar., [He] took the same kind of pot-luck company in those days when he was not so shy of London. 1894 J. C. Jeaffreson *Bk. Recoll.* I. xv. 292 A suburban villa, at which he was in the habit of taking pot-luck dinner on Sunday.

Pot-ma·ker. Now *rare.* One who makes pots or pottery; a potter.

1535 Coverdale *1 Chron.* iv. 23 These were potmakers, and dwelt amonge plantes and hedges. 1550 — *Spir. Perle* i. (1560) 3 It is not seeming, that the pot should murmur against the potmaker. 1579–80 North *Plutarch* (1595) 665 He made a herauld proclaime that all potmakers should stand vp on their feete.

†**b.** *spec.* A maker of pots or crucibles for the Mint. *Obs.*

1548 *Privy Council Acts* (1890) II. 177 For a smyth xxs; for a potmaker xxs. 1587 Fleming *Contn. Holinshed* III. 1972/2 William Forleie pot-maker for the mint of the Tower of London. 1647 Haward *Crown Rev.* 23 Pot-maker: Fee, 10. 0. 0.

Potman (pǫ·tmæ̆n). [f. Pot *sb.*¹ + Man *sb.*¹]

†**1.** A man addicted to pots of liquor; a toper.

1589 Nashe *Anat. Absurd.* Wks. (Grosart) I. 45 A man.. if lasciuious, good in some English deuise of verse, to conclude, a passing potman, a passing Poet. 1685 Wood *Life* 23 Nov. (O. H. S.) III. 171 The pot men and juniors carry all before them.

2. A man employed at a public-house to attend to the pots and serve the liquor. (Cf. Pot-boy.)

1846 Worcester, *Potman*,..a servant at a public house. 1851 Mayhew *Lond. Labour* (1862) II. 345 He got a situation as potman to a public-house. 1860 Dickens *Uncomm. Trav.* xiii, The potmen thrust the last brawling drunkards into the street.

3. *dial.* A dealer in earthenware.

1889 in *N. W. Linc. Gloss.* (ed. 2).

Pot-metal (pǫ·tˌmetăl). [f. Pot *sb.*¹]

1. An alloy of lead and copper of which pots were formerly made.

1693 Povey in *Phil. Trans.* XVII. 736 Bell-metal being Copper and Tin, Pot-metal Copper and Lead. About 20 *l.* of Lead is usually put into 100 *l.* of Pot-metal. 1832 Carlyle *Remin.* i. 38 Tinkers also, making pot metal,.. often came upon the scene.

2. Stained glass coloured in the melting-pot, so that the colour pervades the whole substance.

1832 G. R. Porter *Porcelain & Gl.* 290 Small pieces of glass coloured throughout during the process of its original manufacture..called by artists pot metal. 1898 *Daily News* 6 Jan. 6/1 Stained glass is coloured 'in the pot', by means of metallic oxides; hence 'pot metal', as the technical name for this kind of glass. 1899 *Q. Rev.* Jan. 171 In these windows pot-metal glass is used as far as possible for the larger pieces of ruby or other colour.

3. A kind of cast iron suitable for making pots.

1864 Webster, *Pot-metal*...The metal from which iron pots are made, different from common pig iron. 1875 in Knight *Dict. Mech.*

Po·t-net. [f. Pot *sb.*¹ + Net *sb.*¹]

†**1.** A net in which to boil vegetables in a pot with meat; a cabbage-net. *Obs.*

1562 in H. Hall *Soc. Eliz. Age* (1886) App. 158 A brass pot and a potnet. 1599 *Acc. Bk. W. Wray* in *Antiquary* XXXII. 243 A potte nette.

2. ? A fishing-net having the form of a pot. (Cf. *pock-net* s.v. Poke *sb.*¹ 7.) ? *Obs.*

1584 in *Descr. Thames* (1758) 63 Purse Nets, Casting Nets, ..Pot Nets, Barrock Nets at Crooks, Heaving Nets. 1806 Forsyth *Beauties Scotl.* IV. 224 A kind of pot-net, fastened to a long pole,..is used here.

Potok, obs. form of Puttock.

Potoma·nia. [f. Gr. ποτόν drink + -mania.] Morbid craving for drink; dipsomania.

1858 Mayne *Expos. Lex.*, *Potomania*,..drink-madness. 1890 Billings *Med. Dict.*, *Potomania*, dipsomania.

Potometer (potǫ·mĭtəɹ). [f. as prec. + -meter.] An instrument for measuring the amount of water absorbed by a growing plant.

1884 F. Darwin in *Nature* 1 May 7 An ingenious instrument..the Potometer. It is a modification of Sachs' apparatus for determining the amount of water which a cut branch absorbs in a given time. 1895 in *Syd. Soc. Lex.*

‖**Potoo** (potū·). [Echoic; from its cry.] The name given in Jamaica to one of the Nightjars (*Nyctibius jamaicensis*).

1847 Gosse *Birds Jamaica* 42 The Potoo is not unfrequently seen in the evening..soon after sunset on some dead tree or fence-post, or floating by on noiseless wing, like an owl. *Ibid.* 47 The Potoo has become a proverb of ugliness. 1894 in Newton *Dict. Birds.*

Potoquane, *erron.* potaquina. The name of the Sable Antelope, *Hippotragus niger*, among the Southern Bechuanas.

Potoroo, *var.* Potaroo.

Pot-oven.

Potowane.

Pot-paper.

Pot-pie.

Pot-piece.

Pot-plant.

Pot-pourri.

Pot-shop.

Pot-shot.

Potrick.

Pot-stick, *shotten*.

Potrack.

Potron *or* Potrou.

Potrum.

Potsar, *scarfi*, *shard*, *share*, *var.* Potter.

Potstone.

Potsherd.

Pottage.

Pottah.

Pottaine, *var.* Poteen.

Potted.

Potter.

Pottern.

Potteen.

Pottle.

Pottle-pot.

Pottock.

Potto.

Potto.

Pot-tree.

Pot-valiant.

Pot-walloping.

POT-WARE ... POUCE ... POUCH ... POUCHED ... POUCHER ... POUCHFUL ... POUCHLESS

POUCH-MAKER ... POUCH-MOUTH ... POUCH-PENNY ... POUCH-RING ... POUGH ... POUK ... POUL ... POULARD ... POULT

POULT ... POULTER ... POULTERER ... POULTICE ... POULTRY ... POULTRYCIDE ... POUN ... POUNCE

Pounce (pouns), v.[2] *trans.* to seize, as a bird of prey, with the pounces or talons; to swoop down upon and lay hold of suddenly.

Pounced (pounst), *ppl. a.*[1] Having talons like a hawk : usually in comb.

Pounced (pounst), *ppl. a.*[2] Of metal-work : Embossed or chased by way of ornament.

Founcer (pou·nsəɹ). One who or that which pounces; *spec.* a pouncing tool.

Pouncet (pou·nset). [A modern application, deduced from Pouncet-box, used in the same sense.]

Pouncet-box, quasi-*Hist.* [Derived in some way from Pounced *sb.*[2] or *v.*[1] : perh. orig. a misprint for *pounced-box*, i.e. pierced or perforated box.]

Pouncing, *vbl. sb.*[1] [f. Pounce *v.*[1] + -ing[1].] The action of Pounce *v.*[1] in various senses. Also *attrib.*

Pouncing, *vbl. sb.*[2] The action of Pounce *v.*[2, 3, 4]. Pouncing-machine, a machine in hat-making to smooth the nap, the hat-body being caused to rotate against a revolving cylinder of sand-paper.

Pouncing, *ppl. a.*[1] and *sb.*; see Pounce *v.*[1]

Pouncing, *ppl. a.*[2] and *sb.*; see Pounce *v.*[2] and -ing[2].

Pound (pound), *sb.*[1] Forms: 1-4 (Sc. and *n. dial.* -9) pund; pundo; 3-4 pound, (4-6 pounde, powende) pond; *pl.* (4-6 pounde, powende) pound, etc.

Pound (pound), *sb.*[2] Also 5 pown, 7 pun. [f. Pound *sb.*[1]]

Pound (pound), *sb.*[3] Forms: 1-4 (*Sc.* and *n. dial.* -9) pund; 4-6 pond; (4-6 pounde, powende) pound; OE. *pund.* [OE. *pund,* known only in comb. with the ME. period—OE. **pund.*]

Pound (pound), *v.*[1] Forms: 4-5 pownde, 4-9 pownd, 6-7 pound, pownde, 7 powne. [OE. *punian.*]

Pound (pound), *v.*[2] Also 5 pown, 7 pun. [f. Pound *sb.*[2]]

Pound (pound), *v.*[3] Also 5 *Sc.* poind-. [f. Pound *sb.*[2]]

Poundage (pou·ndédʒ), *sb.*[1] Also 5 poundage, 5-7 poundage, 7 powndage. [f. Pound *sb.*[1] + -age; hence med. (Anglo-) L. *pondagium.*]

Poundage (pou·ndédʒ), *sb.*[2] [f. Pound *sb.*[3] + -age.] A payment to the poundkeeper for the impounding and release of cattle.

Pound-breach. Early ME. *pundbreche* (see def.). *Law.* [f. Pound *sb.*[3] + Breach *sb.*]

Pounder (pou·ndəɹ), *sb.*[1] [f. Pound *v.*[1] + -er[1].] One who or that which pounds.

Pounder (pou·ndəɹ), *sb.*[2] [f. Pound *sb.*[1] + -er[1].]

Pounder, *sb.*[3] Also [?] *pinere.* [f. Pound *sb.*[3] + -er[1].] = Pound-keeper, Pinder, Pinner.

Pounded, *ppl. a.*[1] see Pound *v.*[1]

Pounded, *ppl. a.*[2] see Pound *v.*[3]

Pounder ... **Pound** sb.1 ...

III. attrib. and Comb., as pounder pear-pound-pear (? cartridge) ...

+Pouncdar, v. Obs. rare⁻¹. [app. freq. of POUND sb.1] = POUND v.1 ?

Poundalia, obs. form of PINFOLD.

Pound foo'lish, a. Foolish in dealing with large sums: antithetical to PENNY-WISE, v. So **Pound-foolishness, Pound-folly:** see PENNY-WISDOM.

Pound garnett, obs. f. POMEGRANATE.

Pound-house. [f. POUND sb.1 + HOUSE sb.] A building in which the pounding, pulverizing, or crushing of material is done: as part of a glassworks; b. a cider-mill.

Pounding (pou'ndiŋ), vbl. sb.1 [f. POUND v.1 + -ING.] The action of POUND v.1

Pounding, vbl. sb.2 [f. POUND v.3]

Pounding, ppl. a. [f. POUND v.1 + -ING.]

Pound-keeper. [f. POUND sb.1 + KEEPER.]

+Pound-land. Obs. Also pound-.

Poundal (pou'ndal), Sc. Obs. ...

Poundale, var. of PUNDLAR, steelyard.

Pound-law. Sc. Obs. ...

Pound-lien. Sc. Obs. ...

+Pound-lock. Obs. ...

+Poupista. Cookery. Obs. ...

Pour (pǝ⁹r), v. Forms: see below. [ME. pour-en, evidenced early in 14th c.; not in OE, nor in the cognate langs.; source obscure: see Note below.]

I. intr. ...

II. trans. ...

+Pouncdrel. Also a poundrelle. Cf. POUNDER sb.1 and I.

Poundfraune. var. of ...

Pound-weight. sb. (a.) ...

Pound-werte. ...

†Poup, -e, poupge, obs. F. POWEE.

+Poupe. Obs. rare⁻¹. [? Shortened from F.]

†Poupé (pūpē). Obs. [F. poupée baby, doll, puppet, wax figure, plaster cast, etc.]

III. Special uses with adv. or prep. ...

Pour (pǝ⁹r), v.² Also poorie. [f. POUR v.¹]

Pour (pǝ⁹r), v.³ ...

Pourer (pǝ⁹·rǝr), sb. [f. POUR v.¹ + -ER.] A vessel.

†Pour. Also poorie. [f. POUR v.]

Pouring (pǝ⁹·riŋ), vbl. sb. [f. POUR v.¹ + -ING.]

+Pourfile, obs. form of PROFILE, PURFLE.

Pourge, obs. form of PURGE.

Pourie (pǝ⁹·ri). Sc. Also poorie. [f. POUR v.¹]

Pouring (pǝ⁹·riŋ), ppl. a. [f. POUR v.¹ + -ING.] The action of the v. POUR...

Pouring (pǝ⁹·riŋ), vbl. sb., ppl. a. ...

Pour (poor), v. Also pur. In 5 pouryy, 6 ...

+Pourparler (pur'pärlér), v. Obs. Also in anglicized form PURPARLEY, q.v. ...

Pourparley, sb. ...

Pourparty, ...

Pourpoint (pū⁹·point), sb. ...

Pourprise, Pourpays, Pourpensed, obs. ...

Pourpresture, ...

Pourpoint, sb. ...

Pourtraicture, -traiture, etc., obs. ...

Poussette, pousté (pou'sté). Obs. (or Sc. arch.) ...

Poustie, poust, ...

Poury, n. Obs. rare. In 5 poury. [f. POUR v.¹]

Pousse, var. POUZE; obs. f. PULSE.

+Pousse-café (pus-kafé). [F., lit. "push coffee".]

Poussette (pousét'), v. [f. F. poussette, dim. of pousse a push; see -ETTE.]

Poussette, v.² ...

Pout (pout), sb.¹ [f. POUT v.¹] A protrusion of the lips, expressive of pique or annoyance.

Pout (pout), sb.² [OE. *píta in æle-píutan pl., EEL-POUT = MDu. puyt'e, puid, puyde a pout, also F. ...]

+Pout (pout), sb.³ [perh. from POUT sb.² or POUT v.²]

+Pou, a. ...

+Pousse, v. ...

Pout (pout), v.¹ ...

Pout (pout), v.² [Cf. POUT sb.²] intr. To shoot at poults. Hence **Pou'ter,** a sportsman who shoots young partridges or moorfowl; **Pou'ting,** vbl. sb.

Pout, obs. Sc. form of POULT v.

Poutch, obs. form of POUCH.

Pouter (pou'tǝr), sb.¹ [f. POUT v.¹ + -ER¹.]

Poustie, pousté ...

Pout, sb. A kind of small fish; a small kind of whiting, whiting-pout (Morrhua lusca).

Pout-net (pou't,net). Sc. Also 5-6 pol(e-. [Origin obscure.] A small fishing-net of conical form, its mouth framed with wood or iron into a semicircle, the flat edge of which is pushed or drawn along the bottom of a stream by means of a long pole or staff.

+Pout, obs. ...

Pouter (pou'tǝr), sb.² Also 4-6 poute, 5-6 power, 9 powter. [Origin and sense-history obscure.]

Pouther, obs. form of POWDER.

+Poutal, ...

Poutful, a. [f. POUT sb.¹ + -FUL.] Full of pouts; pouting. Hence **Pou'tfulness.**

Pouther (pou'ðǝr), sb. Sc. and north. dial. ...

Pouting (pou'tiŋ), vbl. sb. [f. POUT v.¹ + -ING.] The action of POUT v.¹

Pouting (pou'tiŋ), ppl. a. [f. POUT v.¹ + -ING.]

Pou'tingly, adv. In a pouting manner.

Pouty, a. [f. POUT sb.¹ + -Y.] Given to pouting; sulky.

Poverish ... obs. f. POVERTY.

Poverished, ppl. a., **Po'verishing** vbl. sb. ...

Povert, obs. form of POVERTY.

+Povertous, Obs. rare⁻¹. [f. povert, POVERTY.] Poor.

Poverty (pǝ'vǝrti), sb. Forms: 2-7 poverte, (3 poverete, poure-, poueer-, 4 powerte, poverti, 4-5 pouerte, etc.) [a. OF. poverte, poverté (pouerté, poureté, etc. = Pr. pauretat, Sp. pobredad, It. povertà:—L. paupertāt-em.] The condition or quality (in various degrees) of being poor.

1. The condition of having little or no wealth or material possessions; indigence, destitution, want (in various degrees).

POVERTY.

1209

POWDER.

Poverty-stricken, a. Stricken or afflicted with poverty; suffering from poverty; reduced to great poverty; extremely poor or destitute.

Powder (pau·dəɹ). Forms: 3-6 poudre, 4 pudre, pouder, 4-6 poudyr, pouder, 4 (9-dur), 4-8 pouder, (5-7, -ire, 4-8 poudre), 4-6 poudir, 5-6 pulder (6 -dre, 5c. -dir, -dyr), 5-7 poulder (6 Sc. -der), 6-7 poulder. 8 poulder. [ME. poudre (13th c.) ...]

POWDER.

1210

POWDER.

† powder-shop, a shop for the sale of powder and other cosmetics, a perfumer's shop; powder-spot, a spot on the skin produced by gunpowder.

Powder, v.[1] Also ² powder. [... f. POWDER sb.[1]]

POWDERED.

1211

POWDERED.

Powder, v.[2] colloq. and dial. [f. POWDER sb.[1]] intr. To run, to hurry with impetuosity and rushing speed: said esp. of riders.

Powdered (pau·dəɹd), ppl. a. [f. POWDER v.[1] + -ED[1].]

Powderable (pou·dərăb'l), a. rare. [f. POWDER v.[1] + -ABLE.] Capable of being powdered.

Powder-bag. a. A bag for holding powder.

POWDERER.

1212

POWER.

Power-derous, a. Obs. rare⁻¹. [f. POWER sb.[1]] Apt to crumble to powder.

Supplement, p. 3873; Corrigenda, p. 4092; Spurious words, p. 4093; Books quoted, p. 4094

Poyeoye, Poyet, Poyn. obs. ff. POESY, POET.

†**Poygne, poynyé.** Obs. Forms: 4-5 poygne, poyn̄e, 5c poygne, peruyhe, 5 6c poyghe, poyhne, poygne. 1. Obs. *peigné* or *poignée* — late L. type *pugnāta*, f. *pugnāre* to fight.] A fight, combat, skirmish.

Poynado, Poynard, etc. forms of POIGNADO, POIGNARD.

Poyning's Law. See quot.

Poynson, obs. f. POISON. **Poyra,** var. P-BRAY. **Poyse,** obs. f. POISE. **Poyse,** -see, etc. obs. ff. POESY. **Poynset, poon,** -syt, etc. obs. ff. POISON, etc. Poyte, obs. form of POET.

†**Poyson,** sb. [Native name in Guarani.]

†**Poyon** (poi·ŏn) Obs.

Poyt, obs. f. POOT.

Poyza, Pozze, var. P-BRAY.

Poz (pŏz). colloq. Abbreviation of POSITIVE.]

Poze, Pozed, Pozer, obs. ff. POSE, etc.

†**Pozzolana, pozzuolana** (pŏtsŏ- / pŏtswo-), sb.

Pra, obs. f. I. PRAY, PREY. **Praam, var. PRAM. Prabble,** sb. Obs.

Pracht, variant of PRATCHANT Obs.

†**Pract,** v. Sc. Obs.

Pracm, obs. form of PRESS.

PRACTIC.

x. *leading,* Heyr Turnus and Camylla gan devys Practikis

Practic (præ·ktik), a.

†**b.** As one of the ancient division of Philosophy.

c. An action, deed, work; *pl.* works, doings, deeds, practices; things practical, practical matters.

†**d.** Mode of action or operation; custom, habit, usage; — PRACTISE 2 c. Obs.

†**2.** = PRACTICE d. 2, 4. Obs.

†**3.** That has had experience in any process or course of action; experienced, practised, well-versed, skilled. Obs.

Practic, v. Pr. iii. 7 Right practike was Sir

Practical (præ·ktikăl), a.

I. I. I. Of, pertaining or relating to practice; consisting of or exhibited in practice or action. Opp. to *speculative, theoretical,* or *ideal.*

Practician (prækti·ʃăn), sb.

Practicability (præ·ktikăbi·liti).

Practicable (præ·ktikăb'l), a.

Practical, etc.: see PRACTIC.

Practicalize, v. rare.

Practically (præ·ktikăli), adv.

Practicalness.

Practicant. Obs. rare.

Practicate, v. Obs. rare.

Practice (præ·ktis), sb.

PRACTICE.

I. Simple senses.

1. The action of doing something; performance, execution; working, operation; method of action or working. (In quot. 1553, The bringing about; production.) [*Sic, see PRACTISE, v.*]

2. The habitual doing or carrying on of something; usual, customary or continued action as distinguished from profession, theory, knowledge, etc.; conduct. (See also 9 a, b, 10 b, 11 a.)

3. The doing of something repeatedly or continuously by way of study; exercise in any art, handicraft, etc., for the purpose, or with the result, of attaining proficiency; hence, the practical acquaintance with or experience in a subject or process, so gained. (See also 9 c.)

5. *spec.* The carrying on or exercise of a profession or occupation, esp. of law, surgery, or medicine; the professional work or business of a lawyer or medical man.

Practician (prækti·ʃăn), sb.

†**Practisant.** Obs. rare⁻¹.

Practise (præ·ktiz), v.

1. trans. To perform, do, act, execute, carry on, exercise (any action or process). Now rare, or merged in sense 2.

2. absol. or intr. To exercise oneself with the view of acquiring skill or proficiency; esp. in the performance of music.

6. trans. To exercise (any one) in some action so as to make him proficient in it; to train, drill, instruct.

Practised, ppl. a. [f. PRACTISE v. + -ED.]

1. That has had practice; experienced, expert, skilled, proficient. (See also PRACTISE v. 6 b.)

2. Executed or gone through beforehand in order to acquire proficiency in performance.

†3. Habitually used or frequented; accustomed.

†4. (app.) Plotted against, made the object of conspiracy. Obs. rare⁻¹.

Hence **Practisedness**, the quality or fact of being practised or experienced.

†**Practisement**, Obs. rare⁻¹.

Practiser (præ·ktīsəɹ). Forms: see PRACTISE; 4-5 -our, 5 -owr, -ar, 6 -er, 5-7 -or, -our; 6-9 -ser. [f. PRACTISE v. + -ER.]

Practising, ppl. a. [f. as prec. + -ING.]

1. Exercising a profession, esp. medicine or law; engaged in practice.

2. One who uses artifice or trickery; a schemer, plotter, conspirator. Obs.

Hence **Practitioner** (rare), the practice of a (mere) practitioner; professional action.

Prac·tive, a. (sb.) Obs. [f. stem pract- in PRACTIC + -IVE. (After active, etc.)]

1. Of persons: a. Devoted to practice or action; active; practical.

2. A note containing particulars of a writ which must be filed with the officer of the Court from which the writ issues, by the party asking for the writ, or by his solicitor.

Practively adv. Obs., practically, in practice, actively.

Prad (præd), sb. slang. [By metathesis from Du. paard a horse:—late L. paraverēdus (see PALFREY).] A horse.

†**Prado** (præ·do). [Sp.:—L. prātum meadow.] The proper name of the public park of Madrid, a fashionable promenade; hence sometimes in transferred applications.

Præco·gnitum (prīka·gnĭtŏm). Pl. -a. Also pl. -cognita. [f. præ before + cognitum, neut. pa. pple. of cognoscere to know: see COGNOSCE, PRECOGNITION.]

‖**Præcipe** (prī·sĭpĭ). Law. Also 5 precipe, 6-8 precipe, 7-9 præcipe. [imper. of præcipĕre to admonish, enjoin (see PRECEPT).]

†**Præcordia** (prīkō·ɹdĭă). Gr. ἄκρον pain), pain referred to the precordia.

Præcordial (prīkō·ɹdĭăl), a. and sb. = PRECORDIAL.

†**Præcura·tion** (prīkĭŭreɪ·ʃən), n. [see PRECURATION.]

Prædal to Præbel: see PREDAL, etc.

Præfatio to Prefect: see PREFACE sb. 1.

Præmunire (prīmĭŭneɪ·rĭ). [ellipt. from phrase in the writ, f. L. præmunīre, in med.L. = præmonēre to forewarn, admonish, warn, f. præ, PRE- + 1 + monēre to warn.]

Præmunire (continued).

†**Præmunire real**, -ial, pro- etc. Obs. rare.

‖**Præsepe** (prīsī·pĭ). Astron. [L. præsēpe enclosure, stall, manger, hive, f. præ, PRE- + sæpīre to fence.] The name of a loose cluster of stars, appearing to the naked eye as a nebula, in the constellation Cancer.

‖**Prætexta** (prītɛ·kstă). Rom. Antiq. Also pro-. [L., short for toga prætexta gown bordered or fringed in front; fa. pple. fem. of prætex-ĕre to weave before, fringe, border.]

Prætor, prœtor (prī·tŏɹ). Forms: 5-7 pre-tor, 6 -tour, 5- pretor, 6- prætor. [Early mod.L. prætor = F. préteur, ad. L. prætor, dr-em (contracted from *præitor, lit. one who goes before, f. præ before + īre to go).]

Prætorian, prœtorian (prĭtō·rĭăn), a. and sb. [ad. L. prætōriānus: see PRÆTOR and -AN.]

A. adj. 1. Of, belonging, or pertaining to a Roman prætor, or to the office or functions of one.

2. Of or belonging to the body-guard of a Roman military commander or of the emperor.

Prætorianism, pro- (prĭtō·rĭănĭz'm). [f. PRÆTORIAN + -ISM.] The office of a Roman prætor; the term or prætorianism.

†**Pre·tory, pre·tory**, sb. (a.) Obs. [ME. pretorie, a. OF. pretoire, prevtoire (mod.F. prétoire), ad. L. prætōrium: see PRÆTORIUM.]

Pragmatic (prægmæ·tik), a. and sb. [= F. pragmatique (or, pragmatick, etc., ad. L. pragmaticus skilled in business, esp. law (Cic.), in late L. relating to civil affairs (also sb.), a. Gr. πραγματικός active, business-like, versed in affairs, relating to matter of fact, also sb. a man of business, etc.]

A. adj. 1. Relating to the affairs of a state or community.

Pragmatical (prægmæ·tikăl), a. [f. as prec. + -ICAL.]

1. = PRAGMATIC a. 1.

Pragmaticalness. The quality or character of being pragmatical; †activity; assiduity (obs.); officiousness, meddlesomeness; opinionativeness, dogmatism; practical or utilitarian quality; etc. ... see the adj.

Pragmaticism. rare. 1. = PRAGMATICALNESS. 2. Philos. (Used to designate a specific variety of pragmatism.)

Pragmatism (præ'gmătiz'm). [f. Gr. πρᾶγμα, πραγματ- a deed, act (see PRAGMATIC) + -ISM. Cf. pragmatismus.]
1. Officiousness; pedantry; an instance of this.
2. Matter-of-fact treatment of things; attention to facts.
3. A method of treating history in which the phenomena are considered with reference to their causes, antecedent conditions, and results, and to their practical lessons. Hist.
4. Philos. The doctrine that the whole 'meaning' of a conception expresses itself in practical consequences, either in the shape of conduct to be recommended, or of experiences to be expected...

Pragmatist (præ'gmătist). [f. as prec. + -IST.]
1. A pragmatical person, a busybody.
2. An adherent of the doctrine called pragmatism.

Pragmatize (præ'gmătaiz). [f. Gr. πρᾱγμα + -IZE.]
trans. To represent what is imaginary or subjective as real or actual; to materialize or rationalize (a myth). Hence **Pra'gmatizing** ppl. adj.

Pragmatizer. [f. prec. + -ER.] One who pragmatizes.

Prahm variant of PRAAM, PRAHU, Malay boat.

† Praisarc. Obs. rare. in a PRAYER.

Prairial (præ·riəl, F. preyal). 1793) prairie meadow.] The name for the ninth month of the French revolutionary calendar, extending from May 20 to June 18.

Prairie (prĕə·ri). Forms: 5 prairie... F. prairie = Pr. praderia, Sp. pradería; med.L. *prataria...*] 1. A tract of meadow land: in early use, a grass meadow...

Hence **Prai'ried** a., containing or characterized by prairies; **Prai'riedom**, the prairie region.

Prairie-chicken. The Pinnated Grouse, Cupidonia or Tympanuchus cupido, a gallinaceous bird of N. America.

Prairie-dog. A N. American rodent animal, genus Cynomys, of the squirrel family.

Prairie-hen = PRAIRIE-CHICKEN.

Prairie schooner. U.S. A fanciful name for the large covered wagons used by emigrants in crossing the N. American plains.

Praisable (prĕi·zăb'l), a. Now rare. Also 7-9 praiseable. [f. PRAISE v. + -ABLE.] Deserving of praise; praiseworthy, laudable, commendable. Hence **Prai'sableness**; **Prai'sably** adv.

Praise (prĕiz), sb. Forms: 5 preyse, 6-7 prayse, 4-7 preyse, 4-7 prease, 4-6 prais, 5 prayes... [f. PRAISE v.] 1. The action or act of praising; the expression of approbation or commendation; the worth or excellence of a person or thing; eulogy; laud, laudation.

Praise (prĕiz), v. Forms: 3-6 preise, 3-7 preyse, 4-7 prayse, 5-6 preyse, 6 prease, 4-6 prayse, 6 praise, 6 preayse... [ME. preisen, a. OFr. preisier (preisir) to price, value, prize, praise...] 1. trans. To set a price or value (upon); to rate. Obs. 2. To appraise, value, estimate. Obs. 3. To express approbation, commendation, or admiration of; to commend, extol; to laud.

Praiseful (prĕi'zful), a. 1. Deserving of praise or honour; praiseworthy, laudable. Obs. 2. Full of praise; laudatory, commendatory.

Praiseless (prĕi'zlĕs), a. Without praise or honour; unpraised; undeserving of praise.

Praiser (prĕi'zɹə). [f. PRAISE v. + -ER. Cf. prec.; partly a. OFr. preiseor, F. priseur; preisier, prizer, F. priser: see -ER.]
1. One who appraises; a valuer, appraiser. Obs.
2. One who praises, commends, or extols; a eulogist.

Praising (prĕi'ziŋ), vbl. sb. [f. PRAISE v. + -ING.] The action of the verb PRAISE. Valuing, valuation, appraising. Obs.
1. Commending, commendation; the offering of praise. Also in pl.

Praiseworthy (prĕi'zwə́ŏ̤i), a. [f. PRAISE sb. + WORTHY a. Formerly hyphened or treated as two words.] 1. Worthy or deserving of praise; laudable, commendable. Hence **Prai'seworthily** adv.; **Prai'seworthiness**.

Praising ppl. a. [f. PRAISE v. + -ING[2].] That praises or expresses praise; laudatory.

Hence **Prai'singly** adv., in a praising or laudatory manner; with praise.

Prakrit (prä·krĭt). Also 8-9 Prakriti, Prkrt., Prākrit, Prāçrita. [ad. Skr. prākṛta natural, unrefined, vulgar: opposed to saṃskṛta prepared, refined, polished (Sanskrit).] A general name for those popular languages or dialects of Northern and Central India which existed alongside of or grew out of Sanskrit.

Hence **Prakri'tic** a., pertaining to Prakrit.

Pram (præm). Forms: 6 prame, 7 pram[m]e, 9 pram. [a. Du. praam, MDu. prame, OFris. prām, etc.] A flat-bottomed boat; a ship's boat.

Pram[2] (præm). vulgar or colloq. [See sense 1.] Abbreviation of PERAMBULATOR[2].

Prance (prɑns), v. [ME. praunce, of obscure origin.] 1. intr. Of a horse: To spring or rise from the hind legs; to bound or spring forward in a lively or spirited manner.

Prancer (prɑ·nsə). [f. PRANCE v. + -ER[1].] One who or that which prances. 1. A horse.

Column entries (top)

Prance, *v.* ...

+Prancome, *sb.* ...

Prandial (præ'ndial), *a.* ...

Prang, **Prang-ing**, ...

+Prangle, *v.* ...

Prank, *sb.¹* ...

Prank, *sb.²* ...

+Prank, *v.¹* ...

Prank, *v.²* ...

Pranker.

Pranking, *vbl. sb.*

Pranking, *ppl. a.*

Prankingly, *adv.*

Prankish.

Prankful.

Prankle.

Pranksome.

Prankster.

Pranksomeness.

Pranky.

Prase (preiz), *sb.*

Praseochrome.

Praseocobalt.

Praseodymium.

Praseolite.

Praseophagus.

Prasine, *a.*

Prasinous, *a.*

Prasoid, *a.*

Prasophagy.

Prat, *sb.¹*

Prat, *sb.²*

Prate, *v.*

Prate-apace.

Prateful.

Prately.

Pratement.

Prater.

Pratincole.

Prating, *vbl. sb.*

Prating, *ppl. a.*

Column entries (bottom)

+Prate-rost, *sb.*

Pratey, *a.*

Prati-, ...

Pratical.

Pratincole.

Prating.

Prattle (præ't'l), *v.*

Prattle, *sb.*

Prattle-basket.

Prattle-box.

Prattlement.

Prattler.

Prattling.

Pravity.

Praw, **Prawn.**

Prawle.

Prawn (prɔn), *sb.*

+Prave, *a.*

Praxinoscope.

Praxis.

Praxitelean, *a.*

Pray (prē), *sb.*

Pray, *v.*

Pray. [F. *élément*s Biv, Syr...]

Pray., erron. f. Spray (Douglas *Æneis* (ed. 1553) XII. Prol. 90).

Prayable, *a. Obt.* [f. PRAY...] That may be prayed to or entreated.

Pray. (pr²), *a.² Now dial.* [Deriv. unknown.]

Prayer¹ (prèr). Forms: 3–4 preiere, 3–6 praiere, 4 preire, preyer...

Prayer-bead.

1. One of the beads of a rosary.

2. A seed of the plant *Abrus precatorius*...

Prayer-book.

A book of forms of prayer; *spec.* the Book of Common Prayer, containing the public liturgy of the Church of England.

Prayer-bell. A bell rung to call a household, school, or body of worshippers, to prayer.

Prayerwise, *adv.* [f. PRAYER¹ + -WISE.]

Praying (prè²-ing), *vbl. sb.* [f. PRAY + -ING¹.] The action of the vb. PRAY; prayer, earnest request.

Prayerful (prè²-ŭl), *a.* [-FUL.]

Prayerfully (prè²-ŭli), *adv.*

Prayerfulness, *sb.*

Praying, *vbl. sb.* *nonce-wd.* (contemptuous)

Prayerless, *a.* [f. PRAYER¹ + -LESS.]

Prayer (prā²r), *sb.²* Also (for distinctness) **pray-er.**

Prayer-bead.

Prayer-meeting, a meeting for prayer; a religious meeting for devotion, in which several of those present offer prayer.

Prayer-mill: = next.

Pray-er-mill.

Prayer-wheel. A mechanical aid to substitute for prayer, used especially by the Buddhists of Tibet.

Prayn, obs. form of PRAWN.

Prayne, obs. form of PRAISE.

Pre- (prĭ, prĕ, prē) *prefix*, repr. L. *præ* adv. and prep. (of place, rank, and time) before, in front, in advance.

[Dense etymological and compound-form entries for the prefix *pre-* follow, including numerous hyphenated compounds such as Pre-abdomen, Pre-anal, Pre-artistic, Pre-existence, Pre-natal, Pre-ordain, Pre-scene, Pre-shadow, etc.]

Supplement, p. 3873; Corrigenda, p. 4092; Spurious words, p. 4093; Books quoted, p. 4094

God. 1894 MITCHELL tr. *Harnack's Hist. Dogma* App. i. 319 The pretemporal existence was a matter of certainty. *Ibid.* 322 The old idea of *preterrestrial existence with God. 1866 S. H. HODGSON *Princ. Reform Suffrage* 103 A part of the *prevolitional nature of man.

2. With sbs. or phrases (adj. + sb.), forming *quasi*-adjs. or attributive phrases, usually nonce-words, of obvious meaning; as *pre-advertisement, pre-advertising* (belonging to the days before advertising was usual), *pre-amalgamation, -betrothal, -breakfast, -chloroform, -Christmas, -civilization, -convention, -crusading, -dispersion, -disruption, -dynamite, -Easter, -emancipation, -free-trade, -independence, -inscription, -Islam, -log-rolling, -marriage, -Mutiny, -pneumatic-tire, -police, -portraying, -printing, -railroad, -railway, -Reformation, -remittance, -Renaissance, -settlement, -telegraph, -treaty, -vaccination, -war, -wire*, etc. The use of these appears to have begun about 1860. **b.** with personal names, meaning 'before the time or public work of': e.g. *pre-Augustine, pre-Shakspere, pre-Johnson, pre-Reynolds, pre-Jenner, pre-Gladstone, pre-Chamberlain*, etc.

These combinations are formed at pleasure and without limit: a few illustrations follow in order of date.

1860 THACKERAY *Round. Papers, De Juventute*, We elderly people have lived in that prae-railroad world. *Ibid.*, There will be but ten prae-railroadites left. 1861 J. G. SHEPPARD *Fall of Rome* xiii. 719 Early British, or pre-Augustine Christianity. 1864 *Realm* 22 June 5 The highwayman of our old-fashioned romances and pre-police reports cried, 'Stand and deliver!' as he met you. 1864 LUMLEY *Remin. Opera* 37 Whatever success attended the pre-Easter season. 1856 *Standard* 27 Aug. 4/7 Holders of pre-amalgamation preferences. 1868 A. K. H. BOYD *Less. Mid. Age* 9 Only three dwellings in the city date from pre-reformation days. 1869 *Routledge's Ev. Boy's Ann.* 370 It was not an uncommon event in pre-Davenport days for some mountebank to allow himself to be tied hand and foot. 1876 GEO. ELIOT *Dan. Der.* xxxvi, Old portraits stretching back..to the pre-portraying period. 1886 F. H. DOYLE *Remin.* 26 In the happy predynamite days. 1887 *Pall Mall G.* 5 Jan. 4/1 The simple souls of the pre-log-rolling era. 1889 *Ibid.* 6 Nov. 1/2 In the pre-advertisement era a good newspaper was the exclusive luxury of the rich. 1890 'R. BOLDREWOOD' *Col. Reformer* (1891) 281 This is my ..pre-remittance stage. 1892 J. MACKINNON *Culture in Celtic Scot.* i. v. 51 The Celts carried with them in their wanderings from their predisruption home, a theology. 1894 *Westm. Gaz.* 22 Jan. 3/3 Merivale..wrote in the pre-inscription and the pre-Mommsen period. 1896 CROCKETT *Cleg Kelly* (ed. 2) 92 The men..answering one another in pre-breakfast monosyllables. 1897 *Allbutt's Syst. Med.* II. 184 In Great Britain during prevaccination times, small-pox showed a periodic intensity of prevalence, every three, four, or five years. 1897 *Daily News* 4 Jan. 6/3 The picturesqueness of Cairo in the pre-plaster-of-Paris age. 1898 *Ibid.* 2 Nov. 2/2 A school to whose welfare I am still as much attached as I was when in the golden sixties I enjoyed the happiness of the pre-flogging, pre-bullying era. 1900 *Ibid.* 26 Nov. 8/3 Mr. Tuckwell remembers Oxford in the pre-railway, pre-science, pre-earnestness days. 1902 *Daily Chron.* 1 Sept. 3/4 The attitude taken up by pre-Mutiny officers towards their troops. 1905 *Ibid.* 11 Dec. 3/3 The obvious fact about painting in England in pre-Reynolds days was the indifference to native practitioners.

II. Denoting local position: in which *pre-* = before, in front of, anterior to.

These appear to have arisen since 1825: see PREOCULAR 1826, *predorsal* 1831, *prepigmental* 1835.

These are generally written without the hyphen, which may however be used when it makes the composition clearer, as before a vowel. *Pre-* is usually (prī-), but may be (pri-) when it immediately precedes the main stress, as in *preve·rtebral*.

3. In adjs. (also sometimes used as sbs.), chiefly *Anat.* and *Zool.*, denoting parts or organs situated in front of (or, rarely, in the front part of) other parts or organs: as **Pre-aceta·bular,** in front of the acetabulum or socket of the hip. **Pre-a·nal,** in front of the anus. **Pre-ao·rtic,** in front of the aorta. **Pre-api·cial,** *Conch.*: see quot. **Pre-au·ditory,** in front of the auditory nerve. **Preba·sal,** in front of a base or basal part. **Preba·silar,** in front of a basilar part. **Prebrachial** (-brē·kiăl), in front of the brachium or upper arm; applied to a group of muscles; also to a vein in the wing of some insects. **Prebranchial** (-bræ·ŋkiăl), in front of the gills or branchial region. **Prebronchial** (-brǫ·ŋkiăl), in front of the bronchi or bronchia. **Prebu·ccal** [L. *bucca* cheek], situated in front of the mouth or buccal cavity; = PREORAL. **Preca·rdiac,** in front of or (in *Human Anat.*) above the heart. **Precau·dal,** situated in front of the caudal vertebræ. **Prece·ntral,** anterior to the centre; applied to parts of the brain. **Prece·rebroid,** situated anterior to a cerebroid organ. **Precoccy·geal,** in front of the coccyx. **Preco·ndylar, -oid,** in front of the condyles. **Preco·rneal,** situated on the front of the cornea (*Cent. Dict.* 1890). **Preco·stal,** in front of the ribs. **Precru·cial,** anterior to the crucial sulcus of the brain. **Prede·ntary,** in front of the dentary bone (in some reptiles). **Predi·gital,** noting the two remiges attached to the second phalanx of the second digit. **Predo·rsal,** anterior to the dorsum or dorsal region. **Prege·nital,** in front of the genital aperture or external genital organs (*Cent. Dict.*). **Pregle·noid,** in front of the glenoid fossa: applied to a process of the temporal bone (also *ellipt.* as *sb.*): also **Preglenoi·dal** (*ibid.*). **Prela·bial,** in front of the lips, or a labium (in an insect or crustacean). **Prelu·mbar,** in front of the loins. **Premandi·bular,** in front of the mandible: applied to a bone of the lower jaw in some fishes, reptiles, etc.; also as *sb.* **Prena·sal,** in front of the nose or nasal region; also as *sb.* **Preocci·pital,** in front of the occipital lobe of the brain. **Preœsopha·geal,** in front of the œsophagus, or, in invertebrates, of the œsophageal ring. **Prepa·latal,** in front of the palate; also **Prepa·latine** (*Cent. Dict.*). **Preparocci·pital,** in front of the paroccipital convolution of the brain. **Prepate·llar,** situated above or in front of the patella. **Preperitone·al,** in front of the peritoneum. **Prepigme·ntal,** in front of the pigmental layer of the eye. **Prepitu·itary,** anterior to the pituitary body. **Prepo·ntile,** in front of the *pons Varolii* (PONS 2). **Preprosta·tic,** in front of the prostate gland. **Prepylo·ric,** anterior to the pylorus or small end of the stomach. **Prere·ctal,** in front of the rectum. **Prere·nal,** in front of the kidney. **Presa·cral,** in front of the sacrum. **Presemilu·nar,** in front of the semilunar lobe of the cerebellum. **Prespi·nal:** see quot. **Presubte·rminal,** before a subterminal. **Presy·lvian,** in front of the Sylvian fissure of the cerebrum. **Presymphy·sial,** in front of a symphysis or point of union, usually of the jaw. **Prethora·cic,** in front of the thorax. **Preti·bial,** in front of, or on the front part of, the tibia. **Pretra·cheal,** in front of the trachea or windpipe. **Pretympa·nic,** in front of the tympanum of the ear; also as *sb.* = *pretympanic bone* or *cartilage*. **Preve·rtebral,** in front of the vertebral column. **Preve·sical,** in front of the bladder (*Cent. Dict.*).

1856 *Pre-acetabular [see *postacetabular*, in POST- B. 2]. 1870 ROLLESTON *Anim. Life* 29 The presence of praeacetabular spurs. 1890 *Cent. Dict.*, *Preanal. 1897 *Allbutt's Syst. Med.* II. 1034 The four pairs of pre-anal and three pairs of post-anal papillæ on the tail of the male. 1890 BILLINGS *Med. Dict.*, *Preaortic plexus, aortic plexus. 1858 MAYNE *Expos. Lex.*, *Præapicialis*,..applied to the hinge of a bivalve shell, when, being on the back of the valve, it is before the summit: *preapicial. 1875 HUXLEY & MARTIN *Elem. Biol.* (1883) 187 The *Preauditory nerves are the following. 3. *Motores oculorum* [etc.]. 1890 *Cent. Dict.* s.v., The *prebasal plate of a myriapod. 1858 MAYNE *Expos. Lex.*, *Prebasilar. 1887 COUES & SHUTE, *Prebrachial [group of muscles] (*C.D.*). 1893 E. A. BUTLER *Househ. Insects* 179 The chief difference is in the præbrachial nervure (the third on the disc of the wing towards the tip). 1887 *Trans. Roy. Soc. Edin.* 108 The aperture in the *prebranchial zone is small. 1888 *Encycl. Brit.* XXIII. 611/2 The prebranchial zone, which separates the branchial sac behind from the branchial siphon in front. 1883 *Athenæum* 29 Dec. 870/3 The air-cells of the flamingo, which were shown to..agree with those of storks in having the *præbronchial air-cell much divided. 1858 MAYNE *Expos. Lex.*, *Præbuccalis*,.. applied to a kind of funnel which precedes the mouth..in the Holothuriæ, termed the *prebuccal cavity. 1890 *Cent. Dict.*, *Precardiac. 1895 *Syd. Soc. Lex.*, *Precardiac*, on the cephalic side of, or superior..to, the heart. 1854 MURCHISON *Siluria* x. (1867) 238 A wide expanded *precaudal joint. 1890 BILLINGS *Med. Dict.*, *Præcentral sulcus*,..furrow on convex surface of hemispheres in front of anterior central convolution, running parallel to central sulcus. 1899 *Allbutt's Syst. Med.* VII. 284 The ascending frontal or precentral convolution [of the brain]. 1870 ROLLESTON *Anim. Life* 107 Which has not any separate *præ-cerebroid ganglion frontale developed upon it as in insects. 1893 *Athenæum* 25 Mar. 382/2 The parts of the urostyle and *precoccygeal vertebræ. 1866 OWEN *Anat. Vert.* II. 78 The position..of the *precondylar groove.. helps in the determination of the bird-affinities. *Ibid.* 532 The jugular fossa is distinct from the *precondyloid and carotid foramina. 1854 — *Skel. & Teeth* in *Orr's Circ. Sc.* I. *Org. Nat.* 197 For the insertion of the *precostal ligament. 1885 *Athenæum* 3 Jan. 20/3 A distinct and conspicuous lozenge-shaped patch of brain substance defined by the crucial and *precrucial sulci. 1889 NICHOLSON & LYDEKKER *Palæont.* II. 1155 The mandible [in the Iguanodontidæ], again, presents the peculiar feature of having a horse-shoe-like *predentary bone at the extremity of the symphysis. 1887 WRAY in *Proc. Zool. Soc.* 348 The *predigitals are the only other remiges of the manus which show modifications of any interest. 1831 R. KNOX *Cloquet's Anat.* 772 They..anastomose with those of the heart and lungs, and enter the *predorsal ganglia. 1842 DUNGLISON *Med. Lex.*, *Prædorsal Region* of the vertebral column is the anterior surface of the dorsal region. 1852 DANA *Crust.* I. 24 The anterior portion of the *prælabial plate pertains to the same segment as the second antennæ. 1842 DUNGLISON *Med. Lex.* s.v., The *prelumbar surface of the spinal column is the anterior surface of the lumbar portion. 1854 OWEN *Skel. & Teeth* in *Orr's Circ. Sc.* I. *Org. Nat.* 271 There are three..laniaries at the anterior end of each *premandibular bone. *Ibid.* 273 The exposed portions of the premaxillaries and premandibulars are incased by a complicated dental covering. 1900 MIALL & HAMMOND *Harlequin Fly* vi. 169 The third is the premandibular segment. 1875 HUXLEY & MARTIN *Elem. Biol.* (1883) 170 The lateral angles of this truncated face are produced outwards and forwards into two flattened *præ-nasal processes. 1891 FLOWER & LYDEKKER *Mammals* ix. 282 A peculiar prenasal bone is developed at the anterior extremity of the mesethmoid, which serves to strengthen the cartilaginous snout [in the *Suidæ*]. 1889 *Buck's Handbk. Med. Sc.* VIII. 152/2 *Preoccipital fovea. 1854 OWEN *Skel. & Teeth* in *Orr's Circ. Sc.* I. *Org. Nat.* 208 The *prepalatal or naso-palatal aperture. 1890 BILLINGS *Med. Dict.*, *Prepatellar*, in front of the patella. 1895 in *Syd. Soc. Lex.* 1900 *Lancet* 20 Oct. 1142/1 The 'deep prepatellar bursa'..is surely a misnomer, for the bursa is not prepatellar in the least degree. 1904 *Br. Med. Jrnl.* 3 Dec. 83 *Preperitoneal Fatty Tumours. 1835-6 *Todd's Cycl. Anat.* I. 553/1 We..regard [this layer] ..as constituting a true *prae-pigmental retina. 1839-47 *Ibid.* III 235/2 Certain accessory glands..called..*prepro-static. 1875 HUXLEY & MARTIN *Elem. Biol.* (1877) 132 A short '*pre-pyloric' ossicle which ascends obliquely forwards and is articulated with the anterior edge of the pyloric piece. 1877 HUXLEY *Anat. Inv. Anim.* vi. 319 With this process is articulated, posteriorly, a broad prepyloric ossicle. 1890 BILLINGS *Med. Dict.*, *Prerectal. 1878 BELL tr. *Gegenbaur's Comp. Anat.* 434 The lumbar region contains the *pre-sacral group of vertebræ. 1889 NICHOLSON & LYDEKKER *Palæont.* II. 1056 There are 29 vertebræ, of which 18 are presacral. 1842 DUNGLISON *Med. Lex.*, *Prespinal, that which is situate before the spine. The prespinal surface of the vertebral column is the anterior surface. 1895 MEYRICK *British Lepidoptera* 239 Discal dot beyond median *prae-subterminal not black-marked. 1868 OWEN *Anat. Vert.* III. 137 Cerebral Folds: Sylvian.. *Presylvian..Postsylvian. 1888 *Geol. Soc. Quart. Jrnl.* XLIV. 146 The largest *presymphysial bone recorded in the annals of vertebrate anatomy. 1870 ROLLESTON *Anim. Life* 108 The number..is never made up of the same *pre-thoracic, thoracic, abdominal, and post-abdominal factors. 1842 DUNGLISON *Med. Lex.*, *Pretibial*,..situate before the tibia; as the *ilio-pretibial* and *ischio-pretibial* muscles. 1897 *Allbutt's Syst. Med.* II 457 Diminished tactile sensibility of the pretibial skin area. 1898 *Ibid.* V. 211 The glands most affected are the anterior or *pretracheal. 1854 OWEN *Skel. & Teeth* in *Orr's Circ. Sc.* I. *Org. Nat.* 178 The foremost of the two middle pieces is the '*pretympanic'. 1858 MAYNE *Expos. Lex.*, *Pretympanic*, applied ..to the anterior subdivision of the tympanic pedicle which supports the mandible in fishes. 1880 GÜNTHER *Fishes* iii. 55 The next bone of the series is the pretympanic or metapterygoid, a flat bone forming a bridge towards the pterygoid. 1840 G. V. ELLIS *Anat.* 570 A gangliated portion situated by the side of the vertebral column, and of *prevertebral plexuses.

Pre-abdomen, Pre-accusation, Pre-acetabular: see PRE- A. 4, 2, B. 3.

Preace, obs. by-form of PRESS *sb.*[1] and *v.*[1]

Preach, *sb. colloq.* [f. PREACH *v.*; in quot. 1597 after F. *prêche* m. a Protestant sermon (16th c. in Littré), similarly f. *prêcher* to PREACH.] An act of preaching; a preachment; a discourse.

c1500 *Wyntoun's Cron.* v. 3392 (Wemyss MS.) At Constantinople, quhare he had His duelling and his prechis [*other MSS.* prechynge] maid. 1597 HOOKER *Eccl. Pol.* v. xxviii. § 3 According to this forme of theirs..No Sermon, no Seruice. Which..occasioned the French spitefully to terme Religion in that sort exercised, a meere Preach. 1643 in *7th Rep. Hist. MSS. Comm.* 445 Mr. Henderson immediately after made a thing between a speech and a preach to us. 1838 *Lett. fr. Madras* (1843) 138 [I] took the opportunity of being alone with him to give him a preach, and try to do him a little good. 1870 MRS. WHITNEY *We Girls* vi, I preached a little preach.

Preach (prītʃ), *v.* Forms: 3-6 **preche,** 4 **preyche, preeche,** 4-6 (chiefly *Sc.*) **preiche,** 5-6 **prech,** 6 **preache,** 6- **preach.** [ME. *prechen*, a. F. *prêcher*, OF. *prechier*, syncopated form of *preëchier* (11th c. in Godefroy) from *predichier, ad. L. *prædicāre* to proclaim publicly, announce, in eccl. L. to preach, f. PRÆ- + *dicāre* to proclaim.

The eccl. word *prædicāre* was adopted early in nearly all the Romanic and Teutonic langs., as It. *predicare*, Prov. *prezicar*, Sp., Pg. *predicar*; OSax. *predikôn*, OE. *predician*, OHG. *predigôn*, ON. *prédika*.]

1. *intr.* 'To pronounce a public discourse upon sacred subjects' (J.); to deliver a sermon or religious address (now usually from or on a text of Scripture).

a1225 *Ancr. R.* 70 ȝe ne schulen..preche to none mon.. Seinte Powel uorbead wummen to prechen. a1300 *Cursor M.* 175 Iesu crist..openlik bigan to preche [..*S. F.* preyche]. c1330 R. BRUNNE *Chron.* (1810) 226 Þe pape his bulle sent hider vnto þe legate, & comanded him to preche þorgh alle þe lond. 1387 TREVISA *Higden* (Rolls) V. 215 He hadde i-preched aȝenst wommen þat pleyde aboute þe ymage of Eudoxia. c1425 *Cast. Persev.* 804 in *Macro Plays* 101 Ȝa! whanne þe fox prechyth, kepe wel ȝore gees! 1500-20 DUNBAR *Poems* xiv. 6 Sic pryd with prellattis, so few till preiche and pray. c1532 DU WES *Introd. Fr.* in *Palsgr.* 952 To preache, *prescher*. 1567 *Gude & Godlie B.* (S.T.S.) 45 Till all Creature for to preiche. 1644 MILTON *Areop.* (Arb.) 65 Christ urg'd it as wherewith to justifie himself, that he preacht in publick. 1674 PRIDEAUX *Lett.* (Camden) 6 On Sunday morneing I went to hear on Bayly of Maudlins preach. 1697 M. HENRY *Life P. Henry* Wks. 1853 II. 674/1 He preached over the former part of the Assembly's Catechism, from divers texts; he also preached over Psalm 116. 1763 JOHNSON in *Boswell* 31 July, Sir, a woman preaching is like a dog's walking on his hind legs. It is not done well; but you are surprized to find it done at all. 1853 J. H. NEWMAN *Hist. Sk.* (1873) II. i. iii. 138 The Greek clergy preached against them as heretics.

b. To utter a serious or earnest exhortation, esp. moral or religious; to talk seriously in the way of persuasion or moralizing. Now usually dyslogistic: To give moral or religious advice in an obtrusive or tiresome way.

1523 LD. BERNERS *Froiss.* I. lxxxvii. 110 They were brought to his tent, and there they were so preched to that they tourned to sir Charles parte. 1602 SHAKS. *Ham.* III. iv. 126 His forme and cause conioyn'd, preaching to stones,

Would make them capeable. 1754 RICHARDSON *Grandison* (1810) V. xxv. 168 Let us..when we are called upon to act a great or manly part, preach by action. 1806 METCALFE in Owen *Wellesley's Desp.* (1877) 807 To meet their ambition.. with the language of peace, would be to preach to the roaring ocean to be still. a1834 COLERIDGE in Patmore *Friends & Acquaint.* (1854) I. 89 'Pray, Mr. Lamb, did you ever hear me preach?' 'Damme', said Lamb, 'I never heard you do anything else'. 1875 W. S. HAYWARD *Love agst. World* 45 Why do you preach to me in that manner?

2. *trans.* To proclaim, declare, or set forth by public discourse (the gospel, something sacred or religious). Also with *obj. cl.*

c1290 *S. Eng. Leg.* I. 24/10 To preche cristendom. 1297 R. GLOUC. (Rolls) 1528 Seinte peter..sende seint Marc þe ewangelist in to egypt vor to preche þen gospel þat he adde imaked. 1382 WYCLIF *1 Cor.* i. 23 Forsoth we prechen Crist crucified. 1388 — *Rom.* x. 15 As it is writun Hou faire ben the feet of hem that prechen pees, of hem that prechen good thingis. c1450 *St. Cuthbert* (Surtees) 1826 Cuthbert, sittand at þe borde, Prechid to þaim goddis worde. 1535 COVERDALE *Isa.* lxi. 1 Yᵉ Lorde hath anoynted me, and sent me, to preach good tydinges vnto the poore. 1590 SPENSER *F.Q.* II. x. 53 Joseph of Arimathy, Who brought with him the holy grayle, they say, And preacht the truth. 1651 HOBBES *Leviath.* III. xli. 263 He was to preach unto them, that he was the Messiah. 1864 TENNYSON *Sea Dreams* 21 Not preaching simple Christ to simple men.

b. To set forth or teach (anything) in the way of exhortation; to advocate or inculcate by discourse or writing; to exhort people to (some act or practice). Also with *obj. cl.*

a1340 HAMPOLE *Psalter* cxxi. 8, I prechid pes, þat neghburs & breþere be samynd in charite. c1400 *Rom. Rose* 6181 [To] preche us povert and distresse, And fisshen hem-self greet richesse. 1523 LD. BERNERS *Froiss.* I. 136 [He] preched to theym that they shulde disheryte the erle Loyes. *Ibid.* 752 Than the prelates..began to preche this voiage in maner of a crosey. 1590 SHAKS. *Com. Err.* V. i. 174 My Mʳ preaches patience to him. 1667 MILTON *P. L.* XI. 723 And to them preachd Conversion and Repentance, as to Souls In prison. 1709 PRIOR *Hans Carvel* 47 At first He therefore Preach'd his Wife The Comforts of a Pious Life. 1875 JOWETT *Plato* (ed. 2) V. 47 He practised the lesson..which Hesiod only preached. 1906 MARIE CORELLI *Treas. Heaven* i, Are you resolved to preach copy-book moralities at me?

c. *Preach up*: to extol, commend, or support by preaching; to discourse in praise of. So *preach down*: to decry or oppose by preaching; to discourse against; to put down or silence by preaching.

1644 J. GOODWIN *Danger Fighting agst. God* 10 [He] preacheth error up, and truth downe. 1724 A. COLLINS *Gr. Chr. Relig.* Pref. 56 Preaching down the receiv'd notions both of Jews and Gentiles. 1796 BURNEY *Mem. Metastasio* II. 190 It is easy to preach up fasting, upon a full stomach. 1855 TENNYSON *Maud* I. x. iii, Last week came one to the county town, To preach our poor little army down.

3. To utter or speak publicly, deliver (now only a sermon, a religious or moral discourse).

c1400 *Beryn* 119 Thouȝe it be no grete holynes to prech þis ilk matere, And þat som list not to her it; ȝit [etc.]. c1400 *Destr. Troy* 2207 When Priam hade his prologe preched to ende, Ector hym answarede esely and faire. 1549 (*title*) The fyrste Sermon of Mayster Hughe Latimer, whiche he preached before the Kynges Maiest. 1625 BP. HALL (*title*) A Sermon of publike Thanksgiuing preacht before his Matⁱᵉ. 1706 E. WARD *Wooden World Diss.* (1708) 82 He cooks by the Hour-Glass, as the Parsons preach Sermons. 1715 DE FOE *Fam. Instruct.* I. iii. (1841) I. 58, I had such a lecture preached to me yesterday by..our own youngest child. 1798 COLERIDGE *Fears in Solitude* 65 Words that even yet Might stem destruction, were they wisely preached.

†4. With personal obj. (orig. indirect): To preach to; to address in the way of exhortation (public or private); to exhort, instruct. *Obs.* **a.** on religious subjects; **b.** in any sense.

c1290 *S. Eng. Leg.* I. 89/88 Þis holie man honourede hem þe more, And prechede heom ofte of clannesse. c1290 *Beket* 1932 ibid. 162 Seint thomas..Stod and prechede al þat folk þat mani a man i-sai. 1362 LANGL. *P. Pl.* A. Prol. 56, I Fond þere Freres all þe Foure Ordres, Prechinge þe peple for profyt of heore wombes. c1386 CHAUCER *Frankl. T.* 96 They prechen hire, they telle hire nyght and day That causelees she sleeth hir self allas. a1450 MYRC *Festial* 82 Þys byschop had preched hym all þat he couþe, and fonde hym euer þe lengur þe wors. c1500 *Melusine* xxiv. 196 How, sire knyght,..are ye come hither for to preche vs? 1523 LD. BERNERS *Froiss.* I. 576 The foles & outragious people..sayd howe they were preched inough. 1706 E. WARD *Wooden World Diss.* (1708) 45 He shall preach ye..about giving Cæsar his Due. 1709 [see 2 b].

5. To bring or put by preaching into or out of some specified state; to affect in some way by preaching. (Cf. *preach down* in 2 c.)

1609 B. JONSON *Sil. Wom.* IV. iv, We had a Preacher that would preach folke asleepe still. a1716 SOUTH *Serm.* (1823) IV. 427 He may preach his heart out..., and all to no purpose. a1845 HOOD *Recipe Civiliz.* 88 What reverend bishop.. Could preach horn'd Apis from his temple? 1852 M. ARNOLD *Empedocles* I. ii, These hundred doctors try To preach thee to their school.

Hence **Preached** *ppl. a.*

1854 MARION HARLAND *Alone* ix, It did me more good than the preached sermons I have listened to since. 1891 S. MOSTYN *Curatica* 36 Both the preacher—and the preached—are too weary to do justice to them.

Preachable (prī·tʃăb'l), *a.* In 5 **preche-.** [f. PREACH *v.* + -ABLE: cf. OF. *preëschable*, L. *prædicābil-is*.] Capable of being preached, or preached about or from; affording material for a sermon or religious discourse.

c1449 PECOCK *Repr.* I. xvi. 89 Textis and parabolis and othere precheable processis. 1895 H. R. REYNOLDS *Lamps Temple* vii. 110 It is clearly your duty and function to discern the preachable aspects of theology. 1906 H. VAN DYKE *Manhood, Faith, Courage* xi. 242 Jesus Christ is the foundation of a truly preachable and powerful Gospel.

Preachee (prītʃī·). *nonce-wd.* [f. PREACH *v.* + -EE.] A person preached to; one to whom a sermon or exhortation is addressed.

1806 *Sporting Mag.* XXVIII. 237 The preachee and flogee, in the late assault and battery case. 1864 J. R. GREEN *Lett.* (1901) 141 Preaching implies some common understanding between preacher and preachee.

Preacher (prī·tʃəɹ). Forms: 3-4 **prechur,** (3 **-or,** 4 **-ore, -ure**), 3-6 **prechour,** (4-5 **-oure**), 4 **preychour, preichour** (also 6 *Sc.*), 4-5 (6 *Sc.*) **precheour,** 4-7 **precher,** (5 **-owre,** 6- **ar**), 5-6 **preachour,** 6 *Sc.* **preicheour, -eir, -er,** 6- **preacher.** [ME. *precho(u)r*, a. OF. *prech(e)or*, earlier *preēch(e)or* (13th c. in Godef.), popular ad. L. *prædicātōr-em* a preacher, whence also It. *predicatore*, Prov. *prezicaire*, Sp., Pg. *predicador*: see PREACH *v.* and -ER [2].] One who preaches.

1. One who proclaims or sets forth religious doctrine by public discourse; one who delivers a sermon or sermons; *esp.* one whose occupation or function it is to preach the gospel; a minister of religion; *spec.* one licensed to preach.

a1225 *Ancr. R.* 10 Prelaz & treowe prechures. a1300 *Cursor M.* 20934 (Edin.) He firste was werrayure, eftirward bicom prechure [*v.rr.* -ur, -our, preichour]. c1305 *Edmund Conf.* 314 in *E. E. P.* (1862) 79 þe beste prechour he was iholde þat me ow[h]ar vnderstode. c1325 *Metr. Hom.* Prol. 3 Forthi suld ilke precheour schau The god that Godd hauis gert him knau. 1377 LANGL. *P. Pl.* B. XIX. 226 Prechoures & prestes & prentyce[s] of lawe. c1380 WYCLIF *Wks.* (1880) 23 Þat suche prechoris ben heretikis. c1449 PECOCK *Repr.* I. xvi. 88 A famose and a plesaunt precher to peple in a pulpit. 1530 PALSGR. 34 As a famous preachour. 1548 UDALL, etc. *Erasm. Par. Matt.* iii. 28 That now was the tyme to playe the preacher. 1561-2 *Reg. Privy Council Scot.* I. 202 Sustentatioun of the precheouris and readaris. 1562 in Strype *Ann. Ref.* (1709) I. xxvii. 284 By a preacher is meant such an one as hath preached before his ordinary, and hath his approbation under seal to be a preacher. a1631 DONNE *Serm.* lvii. (1640) 574 A word of the fœminine gender, not Concionator, but Concionatrix, a Shee-Preacher. 1662 PEPYS *Diary* 2 Nov., To church, and there being a lazy preacher I slept out the sermon. a1774 GOLDSM. tr. *Scarron's Com. Romance* (1775) I. 289 While he rehearsed his heroics, they walked cap in hand before him, respecting him like a high-way preacher. 1859-60 J. H. NEWMAN *Hist. Sk.* (1873) III. II. ii. 232 John of Antioch..had been the great preacher of the day. 1899 *Allbutt's Syst. Med.* VI. 887 This [paralysis] gives rise to a peculiar position of the hand which has been named 'the preacher's hand'.

b. One who exhorts earnestly; one who advocates or inculcates something by speech or writing. Also *fig.*

c1386 CHAUCER *Wife's Prol.* 165 Now dame..by god and by seint Iohn Ye been a noble prechour in this cas. 1599 SHAKS. *Hen. V*, IV. i. 9 They are our outward Consciences, And Preachers to vs all. 1706 SWIFT *Th. Various Subj.* Wks. 1841 II. 304/1 No preacher is listened to but Time. 1900 SPIELMANN *Ruskin* 107 The artists welcome him as a writer, and he would be taken for an art-preacher.

c. With *of*: One who preaches (something specified). So *preacher up* (cf. PREACH *v.* 2 c).

1377 LANGL. *P. Pl.* B. XIII. 428 Prechoures of goddes wordes. a1425 *Cursor M.* 21179 (Trin.) Þese were þe apostlis twelue..precheres [*earlier MSS.* speller-] of troube. 1552 ABP. HAMILTON *Catech.* (1884) 6 Precheouris of the word of God. 1611 BIBLE *Transl. Pref.* 4 The first Preachers of the Gospel. 1649 MILTON *Eikon.* xii, We have him still a perpetual preacher of his own virtues. 1860 TYNDALL *Glac.* I. xxii. 158 The precipice to my left was a continual preacher of caution. 1870 LOWELL *Study Wind.* 139 The denouncer of shams, the preacher up of sincerity.

†2. (In full, *friar preacher*.) A name for the order of Dominican friars. Also *preaching friar*: see PREACHING *ppl. a.* Cf. PREDICANT. *Obs.*

1297 R. GLOUC. (Rolls) 10105 Ther after the verste ȝer þe ordre bigan of frere prechors. c1380 WYCLIF *Sel. Wks.* III. 353 Prechouris and Menours seyn þe reverse. c1394 *P. Pl. Crede* 154 Þanne þouȝt y to frayne þe first of þis foure ordirs, And presede to þe prechoures to proven here wille. 1474 CAXTON *Chesse* 130 To the frere prechours an hondred pounde. 1544 tr. *Littleton's Tenures* (1574) 41 b, In the order of fryers mynoures or preachers.

3. *spec.* A name for Solomon as supposed speaker in the Book of Ecclesiastes; hence, that book itself.

1535 COVERDALE *Eccl.* i. 1. 2 These are the wordes of the Preacher, the sonne of Dauid, kynge of Ierusalem. All is but vanite, saieth yᵉ preacher [*Vulg.* dixit Ecclesiastes, WYCLIF seide Ecclesiastes]. 1579 FULKE *Heskins' Parl.* 7 The book of Psalmes, the Preacher, & the song of Salomon.

4. *attrib.* and *Comb.*, chiefly appositive, as *preacher-editor, -musician, -playwright, -saint, -teacher*; also *preacher-like* adj. and adv.; **preacher-in-the-pulpit,** a local N. American name of *Orchis spectabilis*.

1884 MILLER *Plant-n.*, *Orchis spectabilis*, Preacher-in-the-pulpit, Showy Orchis of N. America. 1895 *Westm. Gaz.* 24 July 7/1 He may be described as preacher-teacher to the pitmen. 1900 *Ibid.* 13 Dec. 7/3 If he thought he could help the preacher-editor he would. 1904 R. SMALL *Hist U. P. Congregations* II. 488 [He] returned to preacher life again.

Hence **Prea·cherdom,** the realm or community of preachers, preachers collectively; **Prea·cherless** *a.*, without a preacher; **Prea·cherling,** a petty or inferior preacher; **Prea·cherly** *a.*, of or pertaining to preachers.

1891 *Sat. Rev.* 7 Nov. 516/1 The veriest dumb dog in *preacherdom. 1893 *Boston Mission. Herald* Dec. 526 The converts from *preacherless villages are swept off their feet by the tide of persecution. 1772 NUGENT tr. *Hist. Friar Gerund* II. 27 A certain *preacherling pronounced, or was to pronounce, a funeral oration. 1905 A. LANG in *Longm. Mag.* Aug. 376 Under any despotism, lay or priestly or *preacherly.

Preacheress (prī·tʃərés). [f. PREACHER + -ESS. Cf. OF. *proicheresse* (Godef.).] A female preacher. (Used only for distinction or emphasis.)

1649 ROBERTS *Clavis Bibl.* 365 In the Heb. this word is ..in the Feminine Gender; and so may be translated exactly, The Congregatrix, or the Preacheresse. 1671 H. M. tr. *Erasm. Colloq.* 231 How come we by this preacheress? 1880 FOWLER *Locke* vi. 101 They listened to the famous Quaker preacheress, Rebecca Collier.

Preachership (prī·tʃəɹʃip). [f. as prec. + -SHIP.] The office of a preacher.

a1656 BP. HALL *Specialities in Life* Wks. 1808 I. p. xxxii, By occasion of the public preachership of St. Edmund's Bury then offered me upon good conditions. 1757 WARBURTON *Lett. to Hurd* cxvi. (1809) 259 You have seen by the papers the disposition of the preachership to Dr. Ross. 1855 MACAULAY *Hist. Eng.* xiv. III. 459 Jeremy Collier, who was turned out of the preachership of the Rolls, was a man of a much higher order. 1900 *Westm. Gaz.* 27 Nov. 12/1 To secure a fitting successor to the Rev. T. W. Lupton, who has been Preacher of Gray's Inn for many years...The Preachership has been held by many distinguished men in the past. 1903 M. A. TUCKER in *Eng. Hist. Rev.* Apr. 283 In 1503..the Lady Margaret preachership was founded through the influence of John Fisher, at that time vice-chancellor of the University of Cambridge.

b. With *his, your*, as a humorous title.

1772 NUGENT tr. *Hist. Friar Gerund* I. 483 What does his Preachership mean?

† Prea·chery. *nonce-wd. Obs.* Preaching.

1818 W. TAYLOR *Hist. Surv. Germ. Poetry* (1830) I. 107 A deistical creed..superscribed *Poetæ Kazungali*; that is, *The Poet's Preachery*.

Preachify (prī·tʃifəi), *v. colloq.* [f. PREACH *v.* + -[I]FY: cf. *speechify*.] *intr.* To preach in a factitious or a tedious way; to make a 'preachment'. Often merely contemptuous for *preach*. Hence **Prea·chifying** *vbl. sb.*; also **Prea:chifica·tion.**

1775 S. J. PRATT *Liberal Opin.* liv. (1783) II. 147 He wrote obstinately on,..preachifying, till he piously picked my pocket of above a hundred and fifty guineas. 1828 tr. *Manzoni's Betrothed Lovers* I. vi. 180 When in his preachifying, he fixes his eyes on me, I am afraid that he will shoot out before everybody—those twenty five lira! 1843 LOCKHART in *Croker Papers* (1884) 6 Dec., Alison deserves all anybody can say of his coxcombical pomposity and preachification. 1848 THACKERAY *Van. Fair* x, She has written to say that she won't stand the preachifying. 1869 MISS MULOCK *Woman's Kingd.* II. 137, I am going to preachify in earnest; and..it is about a very serious thing.

Preachiness (prī·tʃinės). *colloq.* [f. PREACHY + -NESS.] The quality of being preachy.

1861 *Illustr. Lond. News* 13 Apr. 336/1 He made a capital speech..notwithstanding the drawback of a slight preachiness—so to speak—of tone. 1892 LOUNSBURY *Stud. Chaucer* I. iv. 478 It is pervaded..by a general flavor of preachiness, not delicate but obtrusive.

Preaching (prī·tʃiŋ), *vbl. sb.* [-ING [1].]

1. The action of the verb PREACH; the delivery of a sermon or public religious discourse; the practice or art of delivering sermons.

c1275 *Passion our Lord* 671 in *O. E. Misc.* 56 We iherden heom heryen in heore preching After vre tunge þen heoueliche kyng. 13.. *Cursor M.* 196 (Gött.) For his preching [*v.r.* sermon] þai him thrett. c1400 MAUNDEV. (1839) xxii. 239 The prechynge of religiouse cristen men. c1440 *York Myst.* xxi. 6 Men are so dull þat my preching Serues of noght. 1532 MORE *Confut. Tindale* Wks. 601/1 They could not beleue it at the preaching of a woman, without any other miracle. 1560 DAUS tr. *Sleidane's Comm.* 60 The preaching of the Gospell. 1673 *True Worsh. God* 45 Preaching is nothing else but Publishing, Declaring, or Pronouncing what is said to be Preached. 1681-6 J. SCOTT *Chr. Life* (1747) III 428 By an immediate miraculous Unction of the Holy Ghost, by which they were inspired with the Gifts of Preaching. 1882 J. PARKER *Apost. Life* I. 96 Apostolic preaching was religious preaching,.. and it kept itself to this one theme—the turning away men from their iniquities.

2. with *a* and *pl.* **a.** The delivering of a sermon; that which is preached, a sermon or discourse; **b.** (chiefly *Sc.*) a public religious service.

c1449 PECOCK *Repr.* 90 For without him Grees goon on out of gree and prechingis rennen arere. 1508 DUNBAR *Tua Mariit Wemen* 71 At playis, and at preichingis, and pilgrimages greit. 1523 FITZHERB. *Husb.* § 155 A preachyng or a sermon is where a conuocacyon or a gatherynge of people on holy dayes..[is] in chirches or other places & tymes set & ordeyned for yᵗ same. 1535 COVERDALE *Jer.* li. 64 Thus farre are yᵉ preachinges of Ieremy. — *Jonah* iii. 2 Preach vnto them the preachinge, which I bade the. a1548 HALL *Chron.*, *Hen. VIII* 135 b, This infamie was spoken in preachynges and euerywhere. c1650 Z. BOYD in *Zion's Flowers* (1855) Introd. 50 There is not a preaching preached but some gracious pickle falleth upon some heart. 1837 HT. MARTINEAU *Soc. Amer.* III. 145 In New England, a vast deal of time is spent in attending preachings, and other religious meetings. 1861 M. PATTISON *Ess.* (1889) I. 48 We find the Germans..attending the preachings in Allhallows.

3. *attrib.* and *Comb.*, as *preaching age, business, place, time, tour, -yard*, etc.; **preaching-cross,**

see quot. 1882; **preaching-station,** a station or fixed place to which a missionary or preacher comes from time to time to hold a religious service. See also PREACHING-HOUSE.

1440-1 *Norwich Sacrist's Roll* (MS.), Pro magnis portis de le prechyngyerd juxta Carnarium. 1549 LATIMER *5th Serm. bef. Edw. VI* (Arb.) 139 *Scala cœli*, is a preachynge matter..and not a massyng matter. 1556 *Chron. Gr. Friars* (Camden) 20 Pecoke..stode at Powlles crosse,..& there he abjuryd & revokyd them in the prechenynge tyme in the presens of the byshoppe of Cauntorbury. 1571 GOLDING *Calvin on Ps.* xxix. 9 To appoint the temple as it were the preaching place of God's glory. 1641 *Arminian Nunnery* 7 By the preaching-place stood the Font. 1686 PLOT *Staffordsh.* 275 He left..30 l3 Sermons..accounted a prodigious number in this preaching age. 1875 W. MᶜILWRAITH *Guide Wigtownshire* 86 A preaching-station in connection with the Reformed Presbyterian Church, Stranraer. 1882 OGILVIE, *Preaching Cross*, a kind of cross formerly erected on a highway or in an open place, at which the monks and others were wont to preach. 1894 HALL CAINE *Manxman* 24 Cæsar returned home from a preaching tour.

Prea·ching, *ppl. a.* [f. PREACH *v.* + -ING [2].] That preaches: see the verb.

Preaching friar, (*spec.*) a Dominican; = PREACHER 2.

1583 STUBBES *Anat. Abus.* II. (1882) 71 Are those preaching prelates, or else reading ministers? c1585 R. BROWNE *Answ. Cartwright* 12 The preaching Minister can not cause them to bee a Church of God. 1650 R. STAPYLTON *Strada's Low C. Warres* II. 35 So that nothing was done to oppose the preaching-men. 1700 TYRRELL *Hist. Eng.* II. 882 The Preaching Friars and Minors exhorted him. 1855 MACAULAY *Hist. Eng.* xii. III. 140 It was known that a preaching friar had been exerting himself to inflame the Irish population of the neighbourhood against the heretics.

Hence **Prea·chingly** *adv.*, in a preaching manner.

1657 J. SERGEANT *Schism Dispach't* Post-Script, Their old method of talking preachingly, quotingly and quibblingly.

Prea·ching-house. [f. PREACHING *vbl. sb.* + HOUSE *sb.*] A house or building devoted to or adapted for preaching; *spec.* Wesley's name for a Methodist place of worship, in frequent use among Methodists in the 18th and early 19th c.

1760 WESLEY *Jrnl.* 16 Sept., I ordered all the windows of the preaching-house to be set open. a1791 — *Wks.* (1830) VIII. 321 Warn them..Against calling..our Houses, 'Meeting-houses': Call them plain preaching-houses, or chapels. 1763 LADY F. GARDINER in Coke & Moore *Wesley* III. ii. (1792) 414, I have never..been at the preaching-house in a morning yet, as they preach so early. 1817 S. DREW *T. Coke* iv. 49 The building of a preaching-house [in New York] was taken into serious consideration. This was..accomplished in the year 1768, being the first Methodist preaching-house that ever presented itself to view in the western world. 1874 MICKLETHWAITE *Mod. Par. Churches* 1 The old preaching-house type of the Georgian period.

† Prea·chman. *Obs. rare.* [f. PREACH *v.* + MAN *sb.*[1]] A man who preaches, a preacher. (Usually *contemptuous*.)

c1645 HOWELL *Lett.* II. xxxiv, Som of our Preachmen are grown dog mad, ther's a worm got into their toungs, as well as their heads. 1677 W. HUBBARD *Narrative* (1865) II. 197 Madockawando..began to demand something for Satisfaction,..not understanding before that his Father was a great Preachman, as they use to call it. 1727-8 in *Reliq. Hearnianæ* (1857) II. 675 She beareth..in a feild of sedition a crop-eared preachman.

Preachment (prī·tʃmĕnt). [ME. *prechement*, a. OF. *prechement*, earlier *preē(s)chement* (12th c. in Godef.), ad. L. *prædicāment-um*, in med.L. a public speech; cf. PREDICAMENT, PREACH *v.*, -MENT.]

1. The fact or action of preaching; delivery of a sermon, or of a discourse or exhortation. Now usually: Obtrusive or wearisome discourse.

c1330 R. BRUNNE *Chron.* (1810) 222 A legate Ottobon þe pape hider sent, To mak þe barons on þorgh his prechement. 13.. *Reinbrun* cviii. in *Guy Warw.* p. 667 Sire, let be þe prechement: Hit is þe meche schame. c1500 *Melusine* xxiv. 196, I take my dysport in your talkyng & prechement. 1600 W. WATSON *Decacordon* (1602) 226 They rose vp presently in armes at Saint Iohns-towne (excited by Knox his preachment). 1660 H. MORE *Myst. Godl.* VI. xiv. 255 How vain a thing is it to make this Man that Angel that preached the Everlasting Gospel, whenas that Angelical Preachment was at least seven or eight hundred years before he lived. 1672 KIRKMAN *Eng. Rogue* II. 247, I..performed my Preachment and Disputation to the general satisfaction of all. 1889 D. HANNAY *Capt. Marryat* viii. 125 It [*Masterman Ready*] is didactic, and yet there is no preachment.

2. With *pl.* The delivery of a sermon; a sermon, discourse, or exhortation. Usually *contemptuous*.

c1400 *Beryn* 1263 Is this a sermon, or a prechement? 1565 T. STAPLETON *Fortr. Faith* 51 b, To folow the preachments of a few apostat friers and monkes. 1602 WARNER *Alb. Eng.* IX. liii. (1612) 238 Making teadious Preachments, of no edifying powre. 1660 MILTON *Brief Notes on Serm.* Wks. 1738 I. 604 The rest of his Preachment is meer groundless Chat. 1742 RICHARDSON *Pamela* III. 263 There were such Preachments against Vanities, and for Self-denials. 1864 J. H. NEWMAN *Apol.* App. 9 This Volume of Sermons then cannot be criticised at all as preachments; they are essays.

Preachy (prī·tʃi), *a. colloq.* [f. PREACH *v.* + -Y.] Inclined to preach; given to preaching; characterized by a preaching style.

1819 MISS MITFORD in L'Estrange *Life* (1870) II. 70 He was a very good man..though abundantly heavy, preachy and prosy. 1859 HOLYOAKE in *Reasoner* 27 Feb. 66/1 The Rev. Mr. M...was a little preachy and complacent. 1890 *Spectator* 15 Mar., It belongs to the class of preachy novels.

Pre-acknow·ledge, *v.* [PRE- A. 1.] *trans.* To acknowledge beforehand or as a preliminary. Hence **Pre-acknow·ledged** *ppl. a.*

1657 J. SERGEANT *Schism Dispach't* 67 A preacknowledged Infallibility strengthen'd by a long Possession. *Ibid.* 655 Had there not been some preacknowledg'd power to ground and countenance such a demand.

Pre-acquaint (prīăkwē·nt), *v.* [PRE- A. 1.] *trans.* To acquaint beforehand, inform previously. Const. *with.* So **Pre-acquai·ntance,** previous acquaintance; **Pre-acquai·nted** *ppl. a.*, having previous acquaintance or knowledge.

1609 B. JONSON *Sil. Wom.* II. v. You haue beene preacquainted with her birth, education [etc.]. 1633 SHIRLEY *Witty Fair One* I. iii, My intention was to pre-acquaint you. a1670 HACKET *Abp. Williams* I. (1693) 75 The Terms of the Common Law..seem Barbarous to the vulgar Ear and had need to be familiariz'd with pre-acquaintance. 1702 STEELE *Funeral* III. i, Leave the care of Lady Charlotte to me; I'll pre-acquaint her, that she may not be frightened. 1751 HARRIS *Hermes* II. i. (1765) 223 From implying an ordinary pre-acquaintance, to presume a kind of general and universal Notoriety. 1775 T. SHERIDAN *Art Reading* 169 We are pre-acquainted with the sounds of the words.

Pre-act (prīæ·kt), *v.* Also 7 **præact.** [PRE- A. 1.] *trans.* and *intr.* To act beforehand. So **Pre-a·cting** *ppl. a.*; **Pre-a·ction,** previous action.

1646 SIR T. BROWNE *Pseud. Ep.* II. ii. 61 An iron..being already informed by the Loadstone and polarily determined by its preaction. 1655 FULLER *Ch. Hist.* XI. ii. § 33 Those [recreations], which, though acted after Evening-Service, must needs be preacted by the fancy..all the day before. 1660 A. SADLER *Subject's Joy* 2 She also (to acheer the King) doth..præsagingly præact his just Inauguration. 1796 C. CALDWELL *Three Phenom. Fever* 10 These phenomena can no more occur, than an effect can..take place without the pre-existence and pre-action of its cause. 1870 PROCTOR *Other Worlds* viii. 179 There is no form of force which is not the representative of some other pre-acting form of force.

† Prea·cuate, *v. Obs. rare*⁻⁰. [irreg. f. L. *præ-acu-ĕre* to sharpen at the end, or to a point (f. PRÆ- before + *acuĕre* to sharpen) + -ATE [3].] (See quot.) So **† Preacua·tion.**

1623 COCKERAM, *Præacuate*, to make very sharpe. *Ibid.* II, Sharpening or whetting, *preacuation*.

Pread, variant of PREDE *sb.* and *v. Obs.*

Pre-adamic (prīădæ·mik), *a.* [f. PRE- B. 1 + ADAMIC.] Anterior to Adam: = next, B. 1.

1846 in WORCESTER citing I. TAYLOR. 1855 BAILEY *Mystic* 54 To him came too from Preadamic kings The shield of power. 1875 E. WHITE *Life in Christ* II. xii. (1878) 133 By geology we have learned that there was a long pre-adamic history of the globe.

Pre-adamite (prīæ·dămait), *sb.* and *a.* Also without hyphen, and with capital A. [ad. mod.L. *præadamīta* (whence also F. *préadamite*): see PRE-B. 1, ADAM, -ITE [1].]

A. *sb.* **1.** One who lived (or one of a race held to have existed) before the time of Adam.

An appellation given by Isaac de la Peyrère in his *Præadamitæ*, 1655, to a race of men, the progenitors of the Gentile peoples, supposed by him to have existed long before Adam, whom he held to be the first parent of the Jews and their kindred only.

1662 STILLINGFL. *Orig. Sacr.* III. iv. § 2 If the report given of things in Scripture bee true, the hypothesis of Præ-Adamites is undoubtedly false. 1775 ADAIR *Amer. Ind.* 11 The wild notion which some have espoused of the North American Indians being Prae-Adamites, or a separate race of men. 1879 tr. *De Quatrefage's Hum. Spec.* 31 The descendants of these Preadamites were identical with the Gentiles.

† 2. A believer in the existence of men before Adam. *Obs.*

1710 STEELE *Tatler* No. 256 ¶ 4 Mr. Bickerstaff..finding Reasons, by some Expressions which the Welshman let fall in asserting the Antiquity of his family, to suspect that the said Welshman was a Præ-adamite. 1768-74 TUCKER *Lt. Nat.* (1834) II. 468 St. John had nothing of the preadamite belonging to him.

¶ 3. ?*erron.* for ADAMITE *sb.*[1] 2.

1709 STEELE *Tatler* No. 69 ¶ 7 Dancing without Clothes on, after the manner of the Præ-Adamites. 1710 STEELE & ADDISON *Tatler* No. 257 ¶ 12 There were written on the Foreheads of these dead Men several hard Words, as Præ-Adamites, Sabbatarians, Camaronians, Muggletonians.

B. *adj.*

1. That existed before Adam; belonging to the time previous to that of Adam; prehuman.

1786 tr. *Beckford's Vathek* (1883) 142 Upon two beds of incorruptible cedar, lay recumbent the fleshless forms of the Preadamite Kings, who had been monarchs of the whole earth. 1836 LANE *Mod. Egypt.* I. x. 283 The Ginn are said to be of præ-adamite origin, an intermediate class of beings between angels and men. 1851 RICHARDSON *Geol.* (1855) 271 The bones of the *Mastodon* and *Megatherium*—those terrestrial giants of the pre-Adamite earth. 1877 DAWSON *Orig. World* xv. 356 Our knowledge of pre-Adamite and present nature.

2. Relating to the time, or to a race, previous to Adam; belonging to the Pre-adamites (sense A. 2).

1882 OGILVIE, *Preadamite, a*...2. Pertaining to the Preadamites: as the preadamite theory.

Hence **Pre-adami·tic, -ical** *adjs.* = PRE-ADAMITE B. 1; **Pre-a·damitism,** the doctrine of the existence of pre-adamite man.

1716 *Gentleman Instr.* II. (ed. 6) 414 Upon what Memorials do you ground the Story of your Præ-adamitical Transactions? 1790 *Monthly Rev.* III. 543 The author adds a vindication of himself from an accusation of Pre-adamitism; ..he insists on it, that, provided he excepts the human species, he may believe rational animals to have existed on the earth before Adam, without being guilty of this terrible heresy. 1799 KIRWAN *Geol. Ess.* 127 These, however, have been by some, ascribed to some fictitious Præadamitick periods. 1865 COL. WISEMAN in *Ess. Relig. & Lit.* Ser. I. 26 How many human skeletons have been announced as found in preadamitic positions! Yet not one has yet been admitted as proved.

Pre-adapt to **Pre-administration:** see PRE- A. 1, 2.

Pre·admi·ssion. [PRE- A. 2.] Admission beforehand: *spec.* the admission of a certain amount of steam into the cylinder of a steam-engine before the end of the back stroke.

1887 J. A. EWING in *Encycl. Brit.* XXII. 501/2 (*Steam-engine*) An effect of lead [i.e. the condition of the valve being to a certain extent open when the piston-stroke begins] is to cause *preadmission*, that is to say, admission before the end of the back stroke. *Ibid.* 502/1 The position of the crank at which preadmission occurs.

Pre·admi·t, *v.* [PRE- A. 1.] *trans.* To admit beforehand. Hence **Pre·admi·tted** *ppl. a.*

1626 DONNE *Serm.* lxviii. 694 He pre-admitted a fearfull apprehension of Death. a1674 CLARENDON *Surv. Leviath.* (1676) 156 Any preadmitted power of the Pope.

Preadmonish (prīădmǫ·niʃ), *v.* [PRE- A. 1.]

1. *trans.* To admonish beforehand, to forewarn.

1649 CANNE *Gold. Rule* 17 Of which thing they were often preadmonished and fore-told by the prophets. 1809-10 COLERIDGE *Friend* (1866) 324 Bacon and Stewart..warn and preadmonish the sincere inquirer. 1822 T. TAYLOR *Apuleius* 311 [He should] pre-admonish him of what ought to be foreknown by him.

† 2. To give previous notice or warning of. *Obs.*

1644 MILTON *Judgm. Bucer* xxx. Wks. 1851 IV. 322 These things thus preadmonisht, let us enquire what the undoubted meaning is of our Saviours words. 1727 BRADLEY *Fam. Dict.* s.v. *Chesnut*, However, the Beams pre-admonish the Fall of a House by their cracking.

Preadmonition (prīædmŏni·ʃən). [PRE- A. 2.] The action, or an act, of preadmonishing; forewarning, premonition.

1652 GAULE *Magastrom.* 129 Men..stick not to accept them..as the preadmonitions of Divine Providence. 1671 FLAMSTEED in Rigaud *Corr. Sci. Men* (1841) II. 120 To continue my annual preadmonitions of the lunar appearances. 1871 M. COLLINS *Mrq. & Merch.* II. iv. 91 Whether dreams are ever preadmonitions is one of the most vexed questions of the psychologists.

† Pre·a·dvertise, *v. Obs.* [f. PRE- A. 1 + ADVERTISE 4.] *trans.* To give previous notice to; to notify or inform beforehand; to forewarn.

1653 H. MORE *Conject. Cabbal.* (1713) 7 Wherefore Adam, being preadvertised by the vision, was presently able to pronounce, This is now bone of my bone, and flesh of my flesh. 1657 W. RAND tr. *Gassendi's Life Peiresc* I. 142 Johannes Bochartus..had already pre-advertized his Majesty thereof. 1675 WOODHEAD, tr. *Paraphr. St. Paul* Pref., It will not be amiss to preadvertise the reader.

Pre·advi·se, *v.* [PRE- A. 1.] *trans.* To advise or warn before.

1670 COTTON *Espernon* I. III. 121 He certainly believ'd, these were the men appointed to kill him, as he had been pre-advis'd. 1845 T. W. COIT *Puritanism* 202 The Puritans had sent Simon Bradstreet and John Norton..to preadvise them of coming storms.

Pre-æstival, -albuminuric: PRE- B. 1 d, c.

Preak, variant of PREKE *Obs.*

Preak, Preakar, obs. Sc. ff. PRICK, PRICKER.

Preallable (prīæ·lăb'l), *a. rare.* Also 9 **præ-.** [a. obs. F. *preallable*, now *préalable* going before, preliminary, f. OF. *preal(l)er* to precede (f. *pre-*, PRE- A. 1 + *aller* to go): see -ABLE; cf. obs. F. *al(l)able* passable (as a road).] Preceding, previous, preliminary. Hence **Prea·llably** *adv.*, previously, beforehand.

1603 FLORIO *Montaigne* I. xxvii. 93 Regular and remisse friendship, wherein so many precautions of a long and preallable conversation, are required. 1652 URQUHART *Jewel* Wks. (1834) 220 There are few..that have not preallably been stung with the tarantula of a preposterous ambition. 1883 H. JUTA tr. *Van der Linden's Instit. Holland* 274 It very often happens that the defendant.. before answering makes one or more preliminary or praeallable applications.

Preamble (prī·æmb'l, prīæ·mb'l), *sb.* [ad. F. *préambule* (13-14 c. in Hatz.-Darm.), ad. med.L. *præambulum* a preamble (whence also It. *preambolo*, Sp., Pg. *preambulo*), prop. neut. sing. of L. *præambulus* adj. (Martial) going before: see next.]

1. A preliminary statement, in speech or writing; an introductory paragraph, section, or clause; a preface, prologue, introduction.

c1386 CHAUCER *Wife's Prol.* 831 Now dame, quod he, so haue I ioye or blis, This is a long preamble of a tale. c1460 *Lydgate's Thebes* (MS. Roy. 18 D. ii, lf. 147 b/1) *Incipit Prologus.* In this preamble shortly is comprihendid A Mery conseyte of Iohn Lydgate, Monke of Bury, declarynge how he aionyde þe sege of Thebes to the mery tallys of Caunterburye. 1542-3 *Act* 34 & 35 *Hen. VIII*, c. 1 New testamentes, with anie suche annotacions or preambles. a1626 BP. ANDREWES *Serm.* (1856) I. 107 Without any exordium or preamble here in the beginning of his Epistle he hits on the point straight. 1745 *De Foe's Eng. Tradesman* (1841) II. xxxii. 43 There needs no preamble or declaration at the head of the leaf what the meaning of the book is. 1882 FARRAR *Early Chr.* II. 29 A man..whose manner it was to say what he had to say without formula or preamble, in the fewest and simplest words.

b. *spec.* An introductory paragraph or part in a statute, deed, or other formal document, setting forth the grounds and intention of it.

1628 COKE *On Litt.* 79 a, The rehearsall or preamble of the statute is..as it were a key to open the understanding thereof. 1630 *R. Johnson's Kingd. & Commw.* 141 These French Lawes are too full of Preambles, Processes, Interims, and Provisoes. 1772 *Junius Lett.* lxviii. (1820) 345 The preamble to the statutes made by the first parliament of Edward the First. 1840 *Penny Cycl.* XVII. 277/1 If the committee allow that the allegations of the preamble have been proved, they proceed to consider the bill clause by clause...There are so many grounds upon which the preamble may fail to be proved..that [etc.]. 1863 H. COX *Instit.* I. ix. 174 Passing of Private Bills...At the close of the general case for the promoters and opponents, the committee usually decide first whether the preamble of the bill has been proved. If they decide that it has not been proved, the bill is in general lost. 1893 *Times* 8 May 9/3 Under the Standing Orders as amended in 1882 the preamble of all public Bills is reserved for consideration in Committee until after the clauses have been dealt with.

c. A (musical) prelude. *poet.*

1667 MILTON *P. L.* III. 367 With Præamble sweet Of charming symphonie they introduce Thir sacred Song. 1832 TENNYSON *Palace of Art* 174 No nightingale delighteth to prolong Her low preamble all alone, More than [etc.].

2. *gen.* A preceding or introductory fact or circumstance; a preliminary; *esp.* one betokening that which follows; a presage, prognostic.

1548 UDALL, etc. *Erasm. Par. Matt.* xxiv. 145 Of those aduersities which I haue recyted, as of certayne preambles and tokens before ye maye gesse, that the tyme is not far of. 1663 BLAIR *Autobiog.* viii. (1848) 107 This was the preamble of the great troubles that after followed. 1686 BURNET *Trav.* iii. (1750) 146 The first Step, without any Preamble or Preparative, is downright Beastliness. 1885 BAIN *Senses & Int.* III. i. § 3 (1864) 336 In writing, the sight of the part last formed is the preamble to what comes next.

Preamble (prīæ·mb'l), *v.* [In branch I, ad. L. *præambulāre* to walk before: see PRE- A. 1 and AMBLE *v.*; in branch II, f. prec. sb.]

I. †1. *intr.* To walk before or in front. *rare*⁻¹.

1402 *Pol. Poems* II. 56 Poerte preamblis to presse afore Anticristis comyng, to sleen the thridde party of men.

† 2. *trans.* To perambulate previously. *Obs.*

1647 WARD *Simp. Cobler* 15 To take a through view of those who have preambled this by-path.

II. 3. a. *trans.* To utter or deliver by way of preamble; to state in a preamble.

1621 [see PREAMBLED below]. 1667 WATERHOUSE *Fire Lond.* 164 All the execrable issues preambled in the Statute.

b. *intr.* To make a preamble or introductory statement.

1641 [see PREAMBLING below]. 1664 PEPYS *Diary* 15 July, Which, put together with what he preambled with yesterday, makes me think that my Lord do truly esteem me still. 1771 T. HULL *Sir W. Harrington* (1797) II. 199 How foolishly I preamble! 1861, 1865 [see PREAMBLING below].

4. *trans.* To make a preamble to; to preface.

1628 FELTHAM *Resolves* II. [I.] xciii. 272 Some will preamble a Tale impertinently.

Hence **Prea·mbled** *ppl. a.*, **Prea·mbling** *vbl. sb.* and *ppl. a.*

1621 BP. MOUNTAGU *Diatribæ* 67 [These] might haue sufficiently manifested the argument, without so long a preambled discourse. 1641 MILTON *Animadv.* Wks. 1851 III. 187 Ere a foot furder we must be content to heare a preambling boast of your valour. 1861 *Temple Bar Mag.* III. 273 The upshot of which preambling is, that I heartily hate writing. 1865 CARLYLE *Fredk. Gt.* XXI. iv. (1872) X. 11 Well,..your account, without farther preambling.

Preambular (prīæ·mbiŭlăɹ), *a.* [f. med. L. *præambul-um* PREAMBLE + -AR; so F. *préambulaire*.] Of, pertaining to, or of the nature of, a preamble; introductory, prefatory, preliminary.

c1645 HOWELL *Lett.* (1650) II. 9, I must begin with the fulfilling of your desire in a preambular way. 1648 *Regall Apology* 13 Their four last modest Bils, only preambulary to a personall Treaty. 1702 *Refl. Case W. Penn* 3 We shall not detain you by any preambular Discourse. 1784 R. BAGE *Barham Downs* I. 351 In the first place it was preambular.

Pre·a·mbulary, *a.* [f. as prec. + -ARY.] = prec.

1659 PEARSON *Creed* xi. 755 These three Evangelicall resuscitations are so many preambulary proofs of the last and generall Resurrection. 1774 BURKE *Amer. Tax.* Wks. II. 363 A description of revenue not yet known in all the comprehensive vocabulary of finance—a preambulary tax. 1882 *Edin. Rev.* July 215 Burke..scoffed at the bill..as a 'preambulary' Bill.

Preambulate (prīæ·mbiŭlēɪt), *v. rare.* [f. L. *præambulāt-*, ppl. stem. of *præambulāre* to walk before: see -ATE [3].]

† 1. *intr.* To walk or go before or in front: = PREAMBLE *v.* 1. *Obs.*

1609 *Ev. Woman in Hum.* II. i. in Bullen *O. Pl.* IV, Being mortally assaild, he did preambulate or walk off. c1660 JORDAN *Poems* §§ iij b, When fierce destruction followes to Hell-gate, Pride doth most commonly preambulate.

2. *intr.* To make a preamble: = PREAMBLE *v.* 3 b.

1608 PARKE *Fal of Babel* 113 Sanders..preambulateth from the matter before he come to it. 1741 RICHARDSON *Pamela* I. 71 But I will no more preambulate. 1903 *Sat. Rev.* 16 May 614 In previous articles I have preambulated somewhat to this effect.

Preambulation (prīæmbiŭlēɪ·ʃən). [Noun of action from prec.: see -ATION.]

1. The making of a preamble; a preamble, preface.

c1385 CHAUCER *Wife's Prol.* 837 Now dame quod he... This is a long preamble of a tale..What spekestow of preambulacioun [*MSS. Harl.* 7334, *Camb.* perambulacioun]. 1623 COCKERAM II, The first Speech of any thing, *exordium*, *preambulation*. 1768 MME. D'ARBLAY *Early Diary* 27 Mar., And now I have done with preambulation. 1805 EMILY CLARK *Banks of Douro* III. 69 Introduced the subject.. after a long preambulation.

2. 'A walking or going before'. *rare*⁻⁰.

1828 in WEBSTER; hence in later Dicts.

Preambulatory (prīæ·mbiŭlătəri), *a.* [f. as PREAMBULATE: see -ORY [2].] Having the character of a preamble; prefatory, preliminary.

1608 T. MORTON *Preamb. Encounter* Pref., A Preambulatory Epistle vnto P. R. 1664 H. MORE *Myst. Iniq., Apol.* 551 To which, without any Preambulatory Ambages, I answer. 1808 BENTHAM *Sc. Reform* 109 Before the Circuit Court; i.e. (as explained in the preambulatory part of this section) 'the Circuit Court of Justiciary by appeal'.

† Pre·a·mbulous, *a. Obs. rare*⁻¹. [f. med.L. *praeambul-um* PREAMBLE + -OUS.] = PREAMBULAR.

1646 SIR T. BROWNE *Pseud. Ep.* I. x. 38 He..destroyeth the principle preambulous unto all beliefe.

Pre-anal: see PRE- B. 3.

Pre-ana·phoral, *a.* [f. PRE- B. 1 d + Gr. ἀναφορά offering.] Preceding the *anaphora* or part of the eucharistic service containing the oblation.

1882-3 *Schaff's Encycl. Relig. Knowl.* II. 1326 That preceding the consecration of the elements (pre-anaphoral) and the *anaphora*, or sacramental service.

Preannounce (prīănau·ns), *v.* [PRE- A. 1.] *trans.* To announce beforehand or previously. Hence **Pre·annou·ncer,** one who pre-announces; **Pre·annou·ncement,** a previous announcement.

1846 WORCESTER, *Pre-announce*, to announce before. *Coleridge.* 1852 C. WORDSW. *Occas. Serm.* Ser. IV. 57 The Prophet Isaiah..pre-announces the rising of the Sun of Righteousness. 1872 W. HANNA *Resurrect. Dead* 78 The preannouncer of a singular alteration. 1880 *Libr. Univ. Knowl.* (N. Y.) IX. 227 The pre-announcement of the betrayal, of Peter's denial.

Pre·antepenu·lt, *a.* [PRE- B. 1 d.] That precedes or stands immediately before the antepenult; the last but three. Also **Pre·antepenu·ltimate** *a.* (in same sense).

1791 WALKER *Dict.*, *Preantepenultimate*, the fourth syllable from the last. 1852 DANA *Crust.* II. 1061 The præantepenult [joint] has the anterior seta as long as the joint.

Pre·anti·cipate, *v. rare.* [PRE- A. 1.] *trans.* To anticipate some time beforehand.

1658 FRANCK *North. Mem.* (1821) 214 Warmth..which suddenly dissolves the snow that falls preanticipating the formation of frost. 1813 SIR R. WILSON *Priv. Diary* II. 275 The approbation pre-anticipated by Lord Aberdeen on this subject, which concerns him so personally.

Pre-antiquity to **-apicial:** PRE- A. 2, B. 3.

Preappoint (prīăpoi·nt), *v.* [PRE- A. 1.] *trans.* To appoint beforehand or previously.

1633 BP. HALL *Hard Texts, N. T.* 179 Those did he preappoint and predestinate to be conformable to the image of his Son. 1768-74 TUCKER *Lt. Nat.* (1834) I. 591 By a long series of causes pre-appointed for that purpose. 1866 CARLYLE *E. Irving* 131, I remember our..visit preappointed for us by Irving.

Hence **Pre·appoi·nted** *ppl. a.*; **Pre·appoi·ntment,** previous appointment, fore-ordination.

a1618 SYLVESTER *Sonn. Mirac. Peace* ix, They both attain By war-like broyls their pre-appointed Reigne. 1654 H. L'ESTRANGE *Chas. I* (1655) 182 April the 13. the Parliament sate according to preappointment. 1827 CARLYLE *Misc.* (1857) I. 33 Whom wealth could not tempt..from their preappointed aims. 1850 R. I. WILBERFORCE *Doctr. Holy Baptism* 147 It is otherwise when we pass from the region of foreknowledge to that of pre-appointment.

Preapprehension (prīæprĭhe·nʃən). [PRE- A. 2.]

1. A conception or idea formed beforehand; a preconceived notion.

1646 SIR T. BROWNE *Pseud. Ep.* II. vi. 93 Such as regarding the clouds, behold them in shapes conformable to preapprehensions. 1677 HALE *Contempl.* II. 90 The pre-apprehensions and Image that the mind makes to it self of them.

2. A preconceived fear of what may happen; fearful anticipation, foreboding.

1633 T. ADAMS *Exp. 2 Peter* iii. 18 The..preapprehension of sickness and death, is an antedating of sickness and death. 1702 C. MATHER *Magn. Chr.* III. I. App. (1852) 343 Under these pre-apprehensions it was his own endeavor to beware of abating his own first love. 1820 J. BROWN *Hist. Brit. Ch.* II. vi. 308 To see the pre-apprehensions of the protestors so fearfully verified.

Pre-apprise to **Pre-aptitude:** PRE- A. 1, 2.

Pre·a·rm, *v. rare.* [PRE- A. 1.] *trans.* To arm beforehand, to fore-arm.

1615 T. ADAMS *Lycanthropy* 2 The great Bishop of our soules..heere..pre-armes them to that entertainment which the Samaritans of the world are likely to give all those whose faces looke towards Jerusalem. 1660 tr. *Amyraldus' Treat. conc. Relig.* Pref. 7 To pre-arm others against its poison.

Prearrange (prīărē·ndʒ), *v.* [PRE- A. 1.] *trans.* To arrange beforehand.

1851 J. MARTINEAU *Stud. Chr.* (1858) 281 A theatre whose scenery is not all pre-arranged. 1896 BARRIE *Marg. Ogilvy* x, A sign, prearranged between us.

So **Pre·arra·nged** *ppl. a.*, arranged beforehand; **Pre·arra·ngement,** action of pre-arranging or fact of being pre-arranged; previous arrangement.

1775 DE LOLME *Eng. Constit.* II. xxi. (1784) 340 By a happy pre-arrangement of things. 1875 POSTE *Gaius* IV. Comm. (ed. 2) 503 Pre-determined conditions, and pre-arranged, pre-capitulated stipulations. *Ibid.* 638 There took place, by prearrangement, a molestation of one of the litigants.

Preas, prease, obs. forms of PRAISE, PRESS *sb.*[1] and *v.*[1] **Preason,** obs. Sc. form of PRISON.

† Pre·a·spect. *Obs. rare.* [PRE- A. 2.] An aspect beforehand, a looking forward.

1635 JACKSON *Creed* VIII. xxxiii. § 8 This law had a special ..pre-aspect unto our Saviour's death upon the crosse.

† Pre·aspe·ction. *Obs. rare.* [f. PRE- A. 2 + ASPECTION.] Previous beholding or knowledge.

1646 SIR T. BROWNE *Pseud. Ep.* IV. xi. 207 To beleeve they [pigmies] should be in the stature of a foot or span, requires the preaspection of such a one as Philetas the Poet in Athenæus, who was faine to fasten lead unto his feet lest the wind should blow him away.

Preassume (prīăsiū·m), *v.* [PRE- A. 1.]

† 1. *trans.* To take previously or beforehand.

1620 VENNER *Via Recta* (1650) 315 Before the meat preassumed be well concocted. 1657 TOMLINSON *Renou's Disp.* 318 If any preassume this, lethal poyson..shall not hurt him.

2. To assume or take for granted beforehand.

1789 T. TAYLOR *Proclus' Comm.* II. 129 It is necessary to pre-assume that a b is equal to c d, in order that the circles may be also equal. 1816 COLERIDGE *Statesm. Man.* (1817) 365 All alike pre-assume, with Mr. Locke, that the mind contains only the relics of the senses.

Preassurance (prīăʃūə·răns). [PRE- A. 2.]

1. An assurance given or received beforehand.

1635 JACKSON *Creed* VIII. xvi. § 2 That great deliverance whereof the first Passover in Egypt was the pledge, or pre-assurance. 1645 *King's Cabinet Open.* in *Select. fr. Harl. Misc.* (1793) 342 The treaty shall be renewed upon.. a pre-assurance, that the rebels will submit to reason.

2. A previous assurance or feeling of certainty in one's own mind; an assured presentiment.

1671 WOODHEAD *St. Teresa* I. Pref. 33 Who have, many times, a pre-assurance, before..their asking, of their obtaining it. 1825 COLERIDGE *Aids Refl.* (1848) I. 287 No pre-assurance common to a whole species does in any instance prove delusive.

Preassure (prīăʃūə·ɹ), *v.* [PRE- A. 1.] *trans.* To assure or make certain beforehand. Hence **Pre·assu·red** *ppl. a.*

1746 W. HORSLEY *Fool* (1748) I. 264 Being pre-assured of his returning Victorious. 1776 BENTHAM *Man. Pol. Econ.* Wks. 1843 III. 37 A preassured stock of the articles of subsistence. 1846 MRS. GORE *Eng. Char.* (1852) 155 Pre-assuring herself by a mysterious missive whom he will be best pleased to meet at her table.

Preast(e, variant of PREST *sb.* and *a. Obs.*

Pre·atta·chment. [PRE- A. 2.] A prior or previous attachment.

1790 *Norman & Bertha* I. 150 Some ill-fated pre-attachment..had seduced her from the paths of duty. 1824 MRS. J. WEST *Alicia de Lacy* I. 318 A pre-attachment was all he dreaded.

Pre·attu·ne, *v.* [PRE- A. 1.] *trans.* To attune beforehand.

1794 COLERIDGE *Lett., to Southey* (1895) 80, I..preattuned my heartstring to tremulous emotion. 1839 BAILEY *Festus* xxviii. (1852) 474 The ear which hears is preattuned in Heaven.

Preaty, etc., obs. forms of PRETTY, etc.

Preaudience (prīǭ·diĕns). [PRE- A. 2.] The right to be heard before another; precedence or relative rank (of lawyers at the Bar).

1768 BLACKSTONE *Comm.* III. iii. 28 A custom has of late years prevailed of granting letters patent of precedence to such barristers, as the crown thinks proper to honour with that mark of distinction: whereby they are entitled to such rank and pre-audience as are assigned in their respective patents. 1815 *Edin. Rev.* XXV. 539 The remarkable contest for precedence which occurred between Lord North and Lord Surry. 1884 *Times* 27 Nov. 9/4 Gradually their [Q.C.'s] right of preaudience under their royal patents accustomed Judges and litigants to look to them as constituting a separate class, like the Serjeants.

Pre-auditory: see PRE- B. 3.

† Pre·au·gurate, *v. Obs.* [f. PRE- A. 1 + L. *augurāre* to augur.] *trans.* To prognosticate.

1635 PERSON *Varieties* II. 66 Seeing Comets portend drouth, they cannot likewise preaugurate inundations.

† Pre·ave·r, *v. Obs.* [PRE- A. 1.] *trans.* To aver or assert beforehand.

1591 SYLVESTER *Du Bartas* I. i. 778 Another, past all hope, doth pre-averr The birth of John, Christ's holy Harbenger.

Pre-a·xal, *a. Anat.* [f. PRE- B. 3 + AX-IS + -AL.] Situated in front of the body-axis; prechordal; pre-axial.

1890 in *Cent. Dict.*

Pre-a·xiad, *adv. Anat.* [f. as next + *-ad*: see DEXTRAD.] In a pre-axial direction, forward; in or towards the front.

1888 W. K. PARKER in *Proceed. Royal Soc.* XLIII. 486 Two well-marked carpals.., one of which—the radiale—lies pre-axiad and slightly proximad of the other. 1895 *Proc. Zool. Soc.* 331 The prezygapophyses..of the other two extend preaxiad more and more.

Pre-a·xial, *a. Anat.* [f. PRE- B. 3 + L. *axis*: cf. AXIAL.] Situated in front of the axis of the body or of a limb. Hence **Pre-a·xially** *adv.*

1872 MIVART *Elem. Anat.* 37 All parts which in man are relatively superior, and in beasts anterior, can be termed pre-axial in all cases. *Ibid.* 52 In the common european Terrapin we find the fourth cervical with its centrum convex pre-axially, and concave post-axially. 1875 SIR W. TURNER in *Encycl. Brit.* I. 819/2 Quite recently the term *pre-axial* has been introduced as equivalent to atlantal, and *post-axial* to sacral. 1899 *Allbutt's Syst. Med.* VIII. 169.

Prebacillary to **-basilar:** PRE- A. 1, B. 1, 3.

† Pre·bea·ring. *Her. Obs.* [f. PRE- A. 1 +

Prebend (pre'bend), *sb.* Also 5–6 -ende, 6 -ente. [a. OF. *provende* (14–15th c. in Littré), in earlier popular forms *provende* (13th c. in Littré), *prevende*, mod. F. *prébende*, ad. med.L. *prebenda*, a pension (Cassiodorus), a daily pittance, an ecclesiastical living, granted, prop. 'things proper to be supplied', neut. pl. gerundive of L. *præbēre* to offer, grant, furnish, supply for *præhibēre* (Plaut.), f. *præ* before, forth + *habēre* to hold.]

1. The portion of the revenues of a cathedral or collegiate church granted to a canon or member of the chapter as his stipend. Also *transf.*

2. The separate portion of land or tithe from which the stipend is furnished; hence a benefice.

3. = PREBENDARY 1.

† Prebendal, *a. Obs. rare⁻¹.*

Prebend, *v.* [f. prec.] *trans.* to give a daily allowance to (a canon).

† Prebendary, *sb.* Obs.

Prebendary (pre'bendari), *sb.* Also 5–6 -arie, med.L. *prebendarius*, f. *prebenda*: see PREBEND.

1. The holder of a prebend; a canon of a cathedral or collegiate church who holds a prebend.

2. = PREBENDARY.

Prebendaryship, the office or benefice of a prebendary; a prebend.

† Prebendate, *v. Obs. rare⁻¹.* [f. *prebendat-*, ppl. stem of med.L. *prebendāre* to endow with a prebend.] *trans.* To present to a prebend.

† Prebender. Obs. [A parallel form of PREBENDAR.]

† Prebendship. Obs. Prebendaryship.

† Preble. Obs. *rare.* [Origin obscure: it has been compared with *pebble*.] Gravel.

Precalculate (prīkæ'lkiuleit), *v.* [See PRE- A. 1.] *trans.* To calculate or reckon beforehand; to forecast. Hence **Precalculated** *ppl. a.*

Precant, *sb. (and a.) Obs. rare.* [ad. L. *præcant-em*, pres. pple. of *precārī* to pray: see PRAY, PRAYER.] One who prays; a pray-er.

Precantation (prīkæntā'ʃən), *n.* of action from L. *præcantāre*: see PRECANT.

Precaria. Feudal Law: see PRECARY *sb.* 3.

Precarious (prīkê'riəs), *a.* [f. L. *precāri-us* obtained by entreaty, depending on the favour of another; hence, uncertain, precarious (f. *prec-em* prayer, entreaty + *-ōus*, -ARY²) + -OUS.]

Precarium. *Rom.* and *Sc. Law.* [L. *precārium* a thing granted or lent upon request at the will and pleasure of the grantor, sb., use of neuter of *precārius* adj.: see PRECARIOUS.]

Precary (pre'kāri), *sb.* arch. [See senses.]

Precaudal (prīkǭ'dal), *a.*

Precaution (prīkǭ'ʃən), *sb.* [a. F. *précaution* (16th c. in Littré), ad. late L. *præcautiōn-em*, n. of action from *præcavēre*: see PRE- A. 1 and CAUTION.]

Precaution, *v.* [a. F. *précautionner* (17th c. in Hatz.-Darm.), f. *précaution* sb.]

Precautional, *a. rare.*

Precautionary, *a.*

Precava (prīkē'va), *sb.*

Precedaneous, *a. Obs.*

Precede (prīsī'd), *v.* Also 5 precede, 6–8 proceed, proceede, proceed. [a. F. *précéder* (14th c. in Littré), ad. L. *præcēdere* to go before, precede, f. *præ* before + *cēdere* to go.]

Precedence (prīsī'dens), *sb.* Also 5 precydence, 5–6 -aidence, 7 -ence. [prob. f. the earlier PRECEDENT *a.*: see -ENCE. Cf. F. *précédence* (16th c. in Littré).]

Precedency (prīsī'densi), *sb.* Also 7 -ie, prec. [f. as prec.: see -ENCY.]

Precedent (pre'sīdent), *sb.* Forms: 4–5 president, -çydent, 5– preced·nt (5–6) pres-, prexy-, 7 prece-, 5–8 presidents (5–6 -e). [a. F. *précédent* subst. use of the adj.: see PRECEDENT ppl. a.]

Precedented (pre'sīdentéd), *ppl. a. rare⁻¹.*

Precedential (presīde'nʃal), *a.* Now *rare.* [f. PRECEDENT *sb.* + -AL.]

Precedentially, *adv.*

Precedently (prīsī'dentli), *adv.* [f. PRECEDENT *a.* + -LY².]

Preceder (prīsī'dər), *sb. rare.* [f. PRECEDE + -ER¹.]

Preceding (prīsī'diŋ), *ppl. a.* [f. PRECEDE + -ING².]

Precel, *v. Obs.* Also 6 *Sc.* precell. [ad. L. *præcellĕre* to (rise above), surpass, excel, f. *præ* + *-cellĕre* to rise higher, to tower: cf. EXCEL.]

Precellence. *Obs.* [ad. late L. *præcellentia*; cf. OF. *precellence* (16th c. in Littré).]

Precellency. *Obs.*

† Precellent, *a. Obs.* [ad. L. *præcellent-em*, pres. pple.]

Precellently, *adv. Obs.*

†Precelling, ppl. a. Obs. Also 6 Sc. and, -end. [f. PRECEL + -ING².] That' precels' or excels; excelling, excellent; surpassing, pre-eminent.

Precent (prĭse·nt), v. [ad. L. praecent-, a. F. prĕcenter. Also 7 Sc.] To lead in singing (a psalm, antiphon, etc.). **†1.** intr. **2.** trans. To lead in singing (a psalm, antiphon, etc.).

†Precen·tion. Obs. rare⁻¹. [ad. L. praecentiōn-em a singing before, a prelude, n. of action (see next.)] A singing before.

Precentor (prĭse·ntǝɹ). Also 7-9 precentor. [a. late L. praecentor a leader in music, precentor, f. L. praecinĕre, -cent- to sing or play before (a person, etc.), also to foretell, f. prae, PRE- + canĕre to sing. So F. précenteur (16th c.), earlier precentre.] One who leads or directs the singing of a choir or congregation; spec. a. in cathedrals of the Old Foundation, a member of the chapter (ranking next to the dean), whose duties as precentor are now commonly discharged by the succentor; b. in those of the New Foundation, one of the minor canons (among whom he usually takes precedence) or a chaplain, who performs the duties in person; c. in churches or chapels in which there is no instrumental accompaniment, the officer who leads congregational singing. Also transf.

Precentorship (prĭse·ntǝɹʃip). [f. prec. + -SHIP.] The office, position, or function of a precentor.

Precentral (prĭse·ntrǎl), a. [Pre- B. 1.]

Precentrix (prĭse·ntriks). [a. med.L. praecentrix, corresp. to praecentor PRECENTOR: see -TRIX.] A female precentor or leader of a choir.

‖Précieuse (presyȫz), sb. (a.) [F., fem. of précieux PRECIOUS (sense 3), used as a popularized in this sense by Molière in Les Précieuses ridicules, 1659, a comedy in which the affectations of the members of a Parisian coterie were satirized.] A woman aiming at or affecting a refined delicacy of language and taste; usually connoting ridiculous over-refinement or over-fastidiousness.

Precious (pre·ʃǝs), a. (adv., sb.) Forms: 3-6 preciouse (3-4 preciuse), 4 precyous, 4-6 precyouse, 4-5 precyos, 5-6 preciows, -ows, -ouse, -ose, -ous, 6 precius, [preciouse]. [ME. a. OF. precios (11th c. in Hatz.-Darm.), mod.F. précieux, ad. L. pretiōsus, f. pretium price, value: see -OUS.]

Precipitant (prĭsi·pitǎnt), a. and sb. [as next: see -ANCE.] 1. Very swift downward or onward movement; headlong fall or speed.

Precipitance (prĭsi·pitǎns). [f. as next: see -ANCE.]

Precipitancy (prĭsi·pitǎnsi). [f. PRECIPITANT: see -ANCY.]

Precipitant (prĭsi·pitǎnt), a. and sb. [ad. L. praecipitant-em, pr. pple. of praecipitāre: see PRECIPITATE v.]

Precipitantly, adv. [f. prec. + -LY².] in a precipitant manner; precipitately.

1. With headlong fall or descent; headlong.

2. With headlong movement; hurryingly, very swiftly, at great speed; suddenly, abruptly.

Precipitantness, rare⁻⁰. [f. prec. + -NESS.] = PRECIPITANCY.

Precipitate, sb. and a. [ad. mod.L. precipitātum a precipitate, sb. use of neut. pa. pple. of L. precipitāre: see PRECIPITATE v.] That which is precipitated; the product of precipitation.

Precipitate, v. [f. L. precipitāre to throw or drive headlong, to fall, be overhasty, f. precceps, -cipitem adj. headforemost, headlong, steep, rapid, violent, etc., f. pre before + caput head: see -ATE³.]

I. 1. trans. To throw down headlong; to hurl or fling down. (Often refl.)

Precipitating, vbl. sb. [f. PRECIPITATE v. + -ING¹.] The action of the verb PRECIPITATE; usually = PRECIPITATION 5. Also attrib.

Precipitating, ppl. a. [f. as prec. + -ING².] That precipitates, in various senses.

Precipitation. [ad. L. precipitātiōn-em, n. of action from precipitāre to PRECIPITATE v.]

I. 1. The action of casting down or falling headlong from a height; a hurling down; the fact of being hurled down; headlong fall or descent.

Precipitative, a. (or its 1 source: see -ATIVE.) Having the quality of precipitating (i.e. in quot., of accelerating motion).

Precipitator. Also -er. [a. late L. precipitātor a destroyer, overthrower: see PRECIPITATE v. and -OR.] One who or that which precipitates.

Precipitine: see PRECIPITIN.

Precipitin. Biol. Chem. [irreg. f. base of PRECIPITATE + -IN².] A substance that causes precipitation from a solution: see quot. 1903.

Precipitious, a. + OUS.] In sense 1 this form is more correct etymologically than PRECIPITOUS.

Precipitiousness. [f. prec. + -NESS.] The quality or character of being precipitious.

Precipitous, a. [ad. mod.F. precipiteux (16th c. in Godef.)—It. Sp., Pg. precipitoso, ad. late L. *precipitōsus, f. preceps, precipit-: see PRECIPICE and -OUS.]

1. + 1. Acting, or done with excessive or undue haste; rash, headlong = PRECIPITATE a.

Precipitously, adv. [f. prec. + -LY².] in a precipitous manner.

1. With headlong onward movement; with a rushing violence = PRECIPITATELY 1.

2. With undue haste; over-hastily, rashly.

Precipitousness. [f. as prec. + -NESS.] The quality of being precipitous.

Précis, sb. [F. précis, sb. use of précis adj., cut short, condensed, Precise.] A concise or abridged statement; a summary; an abstract.

Precise, v. [a. F. préciser to determine exactly, f. précis Precise.] trans. To make precise or definite; to define precisely or exactly; to particularize.

Precise, a. (adv.) Also: 6 precyse, -syse, -sise, 6 precyse, 6-7 precise, 9 Sc. preceese. [— F. précis, -ise (precis), 14-15th c. in Hatz.-Darm.], ad. L. precīsus cut off, abrupt, shortened, pa. pple. of precīdere to cut off (in front), cut short, abridge, f. pre, Pre- & cīd- = cædere to cut.]

1. Definitely or exactly expressed; exactly defined; definite, exact; of a person, definite and exact in statement.

Precisely, adv. Forms: see PRECISE (3-6 erron. perays-). [f. PRECISE a. + -LY².]

Preciseness. [f. PRECISE a. + -NESS.] The quality of being precise.

Precisian (prīˈsiʒan). [f. PRECISE a. + -IAN. after Christian, etc.]

Precisianism. Also 6 erron. -onism. [f. prec. + -ISM.]

Precision (prīˈsiʒən). [ad. F. précision (16th c. in Godef.) or ad. L. precīsiōn-em a cutting off, f. precīs-, ppl. stem of precīdere to cut off beforehand, f. pre, Pre- & cīd- = cædere to cut.]

Precisionist. (Also erron. after precisian) -anist.) [f. PRECISION + -IST.]

Precisive, a. rare. [f. L. precīs-, ppl. stem of precīdere (see PRECISE) + -IVE.]

Preclamate, v. Obs. rare⁻¹. [f. ppl. stem L. preclāmāre to call out beforehand, f. pre, Pre- A. + clāmāre to cry.]

Preclamation, sb. Obs. rare⁻¹. [f. prec.] Previous declaration or proclamation.

Preclara, v. Chiefly Sc. Obs. Also 6 precleir- [ad. L. preclārāre very clear, f. prev, Pre- A. + clārus clear.]

Preclude, v. [ad. L. preclūd-ĕre to close, shut off, impede, f. prev, Pre- A. 4 c + claudĕre to shut.]

Preclusion (prīklūˈʒən). [ad. L. preclūsiōn-em, n. of action f. preclūdĕre: see prec.]

Preclusive (prīklūˈsiv), a. [f. L. preclūs-, ppl. stem of preclūdĕre (see PRECLUDE) + -IVE.]

Precoce, a. rare⁻¹. [a. F. précoce (1690) precocious, ad. L. precōcem: see PRECOCIOUS.]

2. = Precocious 2.

1689 Evelyn *Diary* 27 Jan., I had read of divers forward and precoce youths. 1868 M. Collins *Sweet Anne Page* I. viii. 191 Is he not a trifle too precoce?

B. as *sb.* An early plant; *spec.* = *precoce tulip.*

1699 Evelyn *Acetaria* (1729) 157 The Hot Beds for the raising of those Præcoces. 1721 Mortimer *Husb.* II. 240, I shall begin with the Precoces or early blowing Tulips.

Hence † **Preco·ceness** (precose-), precocity, earliness in flowering or fruiting. *Obs.*

1664 Evelyn *Sylva* 78 As to this extraordinary Precoseness, the like is reported of a certain Walnut-tree, as well as of the famous White-thorn of Glastonbury.

Precocious (prĭkōu·ʃəs), *a.* [f. L. *præcox, -ocem* (Precoce): see -ious.]

1. Of a plant: Flowering or fruiting early; *spec.* bearing blossom before the leaves; also said of the blossoms or fruit.

1650 Sir T. Browne *Pseud. Ep.* II. vi. (ed. 2) 79 Many precocious trees, and such as have their spring in the winter, may be found in most parts of Europe. *a* 1682 — *Tracts* (1684) 72 That there were precocious and early bearing Trees in Judæa, may be illustrated from some expressions in Scripture concerning precocious Figgs. 1872 Oliver *Elem. Bot.* II. 234 A..tree, with..precocious hermaphrodite flowers.

2. *fig.* Of persons: Prematurely developed in some faculty or proclivity.

1678 Cudworth *Intell. Syst.* I. iv. § 21. 388 However it hath been of late so much decried..by..precocious and conceited wits also, as non-sence and impossibility. 1819 Byron *Juan* I. liv, To be precocious Was in her eyes a thing the most atrocious. 1829 Lytton *Devereux* I. v, We were all three.. precocious geniuses. 1868 E. Edwards *Ralegh* I. xv. 299 She was somewhat precocious in love matters.

b. Of, pertaining to, or indicative of precocity or premature development.

1672 Sir T. Browne *Let. Friend* § 28 'Tis superfluous to live unto gray Hairs, when in a precocious Temper we anticipate the Virtues of them. 1827 Macaulay *Machiavelli* Ess. (1887) 36 Untimely decrepitude was the penalty of precocious maturity. *a* 1863 Thackeray *Christmas Bks.* (1872) 19 His 'Love Lays'..were pronounced to be wonderfully precocious for a young gentleman then only thirteen.

c. Of things: Of early development.

1838 Dickens *Nich. Nick.* xx, Youthful misery stalks precocious. 1899 *Allbutt's Syst. Med.* VII. 668 'Specific' phenomena are more commonly observed within a comparatively short time from the date of infection, in which case they are not rightly regarded as 'precocious' symptoms.

3. *Zool.* (See quot.) Contrasted with Serotinous.

1900 *Quekett Microsc. Club Jrnl.* Ser. II. VII. 260 All the social or colonial Radiolarians (Polycyttaria) and most of the Acantharia are precocious, for in them the nucleus divides early in the life history of the cell.

Preco·ciously, *adv.* [f. prec. + -ly 2.] In a precocious manner; with premature development.

1842 Arnold *Hist. Rome* (1843) III. 269 A child in understanding, but with passions precociously vigorous. 1862 Burton *Bk. Hunter* (1863) 82 He took precociously to rhyming; like Pope he lisped in numbers.

Preco·ciousness. [f. as prec. + -ness.] The quality of being precocious; = Precocity.

1681 Manningham *Disc.* 10 To prevent a sawcy precociousness in Learning, [they] invite others to drudge in their methods. 1829 Southey *Sir T. More* (1831) II. 44 And as natural precocity is always to be regarded with fear, so the precociousness which art produces cannot be without its dangers. 1855 Thackeray *Newcomes* liii, Poverty and necessity force this precociousness on the poor little brat.

Precocity (prĭkǫ·sĭti). [ad. F. *précocité* (17th c.), f. L. type **præcocitās*, f. *præcox*: see Precoce.] The quality of being precocious.

1. Of plants: Early flowering or ripeness.

1656 Blount *Glossogr.*, *Precocity*, early ripeness, forwardliness in ripening, over hastiness in ripening. 1875 A. R. Wallace in *Encycl. Brit.* I. 86/2 The grain was very fine and well grown, which gave me the idea to..see if the following year it would preserve its precocity.

2. Early maturity, premature development.

1640 Howell *Dodona's Gr.* 101 Imputing the cause of it [his fall] to a precocitie of Spirit and valour in him. 1682 Sir T. Browne *Chr. Mor.* I. § 25 From such foundations thou may'st be Happy in a Virtuous precocity, and make an early and long walk in Goodness. 1820 Hazlitt *Lect. Dram. Lit.* 140 Their productions..bear the marks of precocity and premature decay. 1879 Gladstone *Glean.* II. vi. 267 In a happy childhood he evinced extreme precocity.

b. *transf.* One in whom this quality is exemplified; a precocious child.

1882 A. Matheson in *Macm. Mag.* XLVI. 488/2 George Eliot's children..They are not impossible cherubs, or wingless fairies, or idealised precocities.

† **Pre-coeta·nean.** *Obs. rare*⁻¹. [f. Pre- A. 2 + Coetanean.] An older contemporary.

a 1661 Fuller *Worthies* (1662) I. 27, I read of Petrarch, (the pre-coetanean of our Chaucer) that he was crowned with a Laurel, in the Capitol.

† **Preco·gitancy.** *Obs. rare.* [f. L. *præcōgitānt-em*, pr. pple. of *præcōgitāre*: see below and -ancy.] Previous cogitation or thought.

c 1635 A. Stafford *Apol.* in *Fem. Glory* (1860) p. xxxiv, Wee speake not to Princes without great study, and precogitancy.

† **Preco·gitate,** *ppl. a. Sc. Obs. rare.* [ad. L. *præcōgitātus*, pa. pple. of *præcōgitāre*: see next.] = Precogitated.

1573 Morton in *Cal. Scott. Papers* (1905) IV. 516 They fund the wind favorable to the executioun of thair precogitat mischeif. 1664 *Judiciary Rec.* (S. H. S.) 101 Francis Crichton without any provocation and forethought felony and precogitate malice drew his sword.

Precogitate (prĭkǫ·dʒiteit), *v.* Now *rare.* [f. L. *præcōgitāt-*, ppl. stem of *præcōgitāre*, f. *præ*, Pre- A. 1 + *cōgitāre* to think, Cogitate: see -ate³.] *trans.* and *intr.* To cogitate, think, or think over beforehand; to consider beforehand, premeditate. Hence **Preco·gitated** *ppl. a.*

1611 Cotgr., *Precogiter*, to precogitate, premeditate, thinke of beforehand. 1639 G. Daniel *Ecclus.* xviii. 62 Precogitate thy vowes; and doe not Say From a fantastick humor, what will rise. *a* 1652 Brome *Mad Couple* III. i. Wks. 1873 I. 56, I must come on her with a little wit though, for which I will precogitate. 1657 Hawke *Killing is M.* Introd. It is Murder in any private Person upon precogitated malice to kill any private Man.

Precogitation (prĭkǫdʒitē¹·ʃən). Now *rare.* [ad. late L. *præcōgitātiōnem*, n. of action f. *præcōgitāre*: see prec. Cf. obs. F. *précogitation* (16th c. in Godef.).] Previous consideration or meditation; a thinking over beforehand.

1596 J. Norden *Progr. Pietie* (1847) 8 We may proceed on in our progress, with this precogitation following. 1658 Sir T. Browne *Gard. Cyrus* v. 200 To spin out our awaking thoughts into the phantasms of sleep, which often continueth præcogitations; making Cables of Cobwebbes and Wildernesses of handsome Groves. 1809–10 Coleridge *Friend* (1866) 315 This purpose may have been itself excited, and this precogitation itself abstracted from the perceived likenesses and differences of the objects to be arranged.

† **Preco·gnit.** *Obs. rare*⁻¹. [ad. L. *præcognitum*, pa. pple. neut. of *præcognōscĕre* to Precognosce.] A preliminary discussion.

1654 Vilvain *Epit. Ess.* Introd. 18 A Compend of Chronography..intended for a previous Precognit to the two insuing Tomes.

Precognition (prĭkǫgni·ʃən). Also 7 præ-. [ad. late L. *præcognitiōnem*, n. of action f. *præcognōscĕre*: see Precognosce; or perh. a. obs. F. *précognition* foreknowledge (15th c. in Godef.).]

1. Antecedent cognition or knowledge; foreknowledge.

1611 Cotgr., *Precognition*, a precognition. *a* 1619 Fotherby *Atheom.* I. viii. § 2 (1622) 56 This præcognition and anticipation of God. 1651 Biggs *New Disp.* § 230 It acts without any precognition of an end. 1678 Gale *Crt. Gentiles* III. 67 God..by his determinate Counsel and precognition delivered his Son to them. 1839 Bailey *Festus* xi. (1852) 136 O Thou!..Whom all the faiths and creeds, and rites of old..In precognition of eternal truth Foreshadowed and foretyped. 1903 Myers *Hum. Personality* I. 31 Here again we find also precognitions which transcend what seems explicable by the foresight of every mind such as we know.

2. *Scots Law.* The preliminary examination of witnesses or persons likely to know about the facts of a case, in order to obtain, with a view to trial, a general knowledge of the available evidence; *esp.* in criminal law, an examination by a procurator-fiscal of those who can give evidence regarding a crime or offence (in older practice conducted by or before a sheriff or other judge ordinary), in order to know whether there is ground for trial and to enable a relevant libel to be prepared; also the statement itself taken down from a witness before the trial.

1661 *Sc. Acts Chas. II* (1820) VII. 22/2 That the mater of fact cannot be so well cleired at a peremptorie dyet befor the Justice without ane precognition and previous tryell of the wholl circumstances of the same. 1720 *Wodrow Corr.* (1843) II. 505 Several are taken up [= apprehended], and lawyers have taken a precognition. 1753 *Stewart's Trial* 33 We have gone thro' this libel with the greatest attention, and have taken a view of the several facts, which, after a precognition of above a thousand witnesses, are set forth to support the charge against the pannel. 1828 Scott *F. M. Perth* vii, The precognition of Simon Glover and Henry Gow would bear out a matter less worthy of belief. 1887 *Law Times* LXXXII. 175/1 Prisoners are not allowed to see the precognitions for the prosecution.

So **Preco·gnitive** *a.*, of the nature of, or giving, foreknowledge.

1903 Myers *Hum. Personality* I. 142. I mean precognitive dreams; pictures or visions in which future events are foretold or depicted.

Precognitum, variant of Pr**æ**cognitum.

Precognizance, erron. f. Preconizance.

Precognizant, -is- (prĭkǫ·gnizănt), *a.* [f. Pre- A. 3 + Cognizant.] Having previous cognizance.

1828–40 Tytler *Hist. Scot.* (1864) III. 404, I shall now state..the evidence upon which I have affirmed..that he [Knox] was precognisant of the intended murder [of Riccio]. 1848 Clough *Bothie* iv, The wary precognisant Piper.

Precognization, erron. f. Preconization.

Precognize (prĭkǫ·gnəiz), *v. rare.* [f. Pre- A. 1 + Cognize.] *trans.* To know beforehand.

1612 Sturtevant *Metallica* 34 Except that the Art.., general to all Arts & inuentions called *Heuretica* be first precognized. 1862 M. Hopkins *Hawaii* 189 He could not ..intuitively precognize the system of Christianity.

Precognosce (prĭkǫgnǫ·s), *v. Sc. Law.* [f. Pre- A. 1 + Cognosce; cf. L. *præcognōscĕre* (rare) to foreknow, foresee.] *trans.* To make a preliminary examination of (witnesses), in order to enable parties to an action to set up their respective pleas and defences, and particularly in criminal suits to enable the libel to be relevantly stated and maintained: cf. Precognition 2.

1753 *Stewart's Trial* 93 The pannel's wife and his children, who, by law, cannot be called as witnesses against him, have been precognosced, or judicially examined, and.. their declarations are proposed to be produced in this trial. 1888 *Daily News* 17 July 5/2 Pending the trial of the accused, the Procurator-Fiscal 'precognosces' witnesses, and collects all available evidence, which is afterwards formulated in a detailed and printed indictment supplied to counsel, jury, and Court officials. 1901 *Scotsman* 2 Mar. 12/3 He respectfully submitted that the defence had no power to precognosce police officers.

Pre-collection, -Columbian, -communicant, etc.: see Pre- A, B.

Pre-commu·nion. [Pre- B. 2.] The part of the Communion office in the Book of Common Prayer which precedes the Communion service proper; the ante-communion service.

1868 Milman *St. Paul's* xvii. 431 There was a full service with the pre-communion.

Precompose (prĭkǫmpōu·z), *v.* [Pre- A. 1.] *trans.* To compose beforehand.

1648 Herrick *Hesper.*, *To Mistr. Amie Potter*, Nature has pre-compos'd us both to love. 1651 H. L'Estrange *Smectymnus-mastix* 30 Every man is best able to know whether his own prayers be precomposed, or of sudden conception. 1799 C. Winter in Jay *Mem. & Lett.* (1843) 27 It is very easy to distinguish them [sermons] which were precomposed, from others which were preached extempore.

Hence **Precompo·sed** *ppl. a.*

1741 *Chr. Liturgy* Pref., Those who pray extempore,.. say, that precomposed Forms stint and restrain the Spirit of God in its Operations. 1861 *Sat. Rev.* 21 Dec. 632 The professional lecturer commonly has a set of precomposed lectures,..any of which he is ready to deliver anywhere on the receipt of his fee.

† **Preconcei·t.** *Obs.* [f. Pre- A. 2 + Conceit *sb.*] A preconceived notion or opinion.

1594 Hooker *Eccl. Pol.* Pref. iii. § 9 Which..through their misfashioned preconceit, appeared unto them no less certayne. 1647 N. Bacon *Disc. Govt. Eng.* I. iii. (1739) 7 God had an eye on all this beyond all reach of pre-conceit of man. 1682 *2nd Plea Nonconf.* 79 Clear from all sinister Pre-conceits, Passion, and Disaffection to Practical..Piety.

† **Preconcei·ted,** *a. Obs. rare.* [In 1, f. Pre- A. + Conceited *ppl. a.* In 2, f. prec. + -ed ².]

1. Conceived beforehand, preconceived.

1600 W. Watson *Decacordon* (1602) 330 No man on earth can tell what gouernment it is they intend to establish,.. when they come to their preconceited monarchie. 1604 Earl Stirling *Aurora* Song ix, Whose sweet-supposed sowers Of preconceited pleasures grieu'd me most.

2. Having a previous conception or notion.

1698 tr. *Fenelon's Maxims Saints* 110 But these two things had only their Origin from Scholastick Philosophy, whereof these Mystical Men were preconceited.

Preconceive (prĭkǫnsī·v), *v.* [Pre- A. 1.] *trans.* To conceive or imagine beforehand; to anticipate in thought.

1597 Bacon *Ess., Coulers Good & Evill* (Arb.) 144 In a dead playne, the way seemeth the longer, because the eye hath preconceyued it shorter then the truth. 1701 Norris *Ideal World* I. i. 37 The great Architect of the world præconceived and foreknew what he would make. 1858 Hawthorne *Fr. & It. Note-Bks.* (1872) I. 55 The Coliseum was very much what I had preconceived it.

Hence **Preconceived** (prĭkǫnsī·vd) *ppl. a.*

1580 *Reg. Privy Council Scot.* III. 291 Upoun preconsavit malice borne aganis hir thir mony yeris begane. *a* 1688 Cudworth *Immut. Mor.* (1731) 205 Anticipated and preconceived Ideas of Regular Lines and Figures. *a* 1704 Locke *Posth. Wks.* (1706) 68 We must..not endeavour to bring things to any præ conceived Notions of our own. 1830 Lyell *Princ. Geol.* (1875) I. II. xvi. 367 Contrary to his preconceived notions. 1875 Jowett *Plato* (ed. 2) I. 114.

Pre-concept (prĭkǫ·nsept). *Psychol.* [f. Pre- A. 2 + Concept *sb.*] A term applied by Romanes to a higher Recept (q. v.), or rudimentary Concept: see quot. 1888.

1888 Romanes *Mental Evolut. Man* ix. 185 Higher Recepts, then, are what may be conveniently termed Preconcepts: they occupy the interval between the receptual life of brute and the earliest dawn of the conceptual life of man. A pre-concept, therefore, is that kind of higher recept which is not to be met with in any brute; but which occurs in the human being after surpassing the brute and before attaining self-consciousness. 1896 *Nat. Science* Dec. 382 From this he argues that there is a logic of recepts in animals, and probably also a logic of preconcepts.

Preconception (prĭkǫnse·pʃən). [f. Pre- A. 2 + Conception; cf. F. *préconception.*] The action of preconceiving; usually (with *a* and *pl.*), a conception or opinion formed and entertained prior to actual knowledge; a prepossession, a prejudice; an anticipation.

1625 Donne *Serm.* lxvi. (1640) 667 God does nothing, Man does nothing well, without these Idea's, these retrospects, this recourse to pre-conceptions, pre-deliberations. 1711 Hickes *Two Treat. Chr. Priesth.* (1847) II. 154 Men biassed by preconceptions. 1744 Harris *Three Treat.* III. (1765) 286 *note*, A Pre-conception is the natural Apprehension of what is general or universal. *a* 1834 Coleridge in *Lit. Rem.* (1836) II. 372–3 To hear an evolving roll, or a succession of leaves, talk continually the language of deliberate reason in a form of continued preconception, Y and Z already possessed, when A was being uttered. 1843 J. Martineau *Chr. Life* (1867) 175 Our preconceptions of wrong and of right. 1867 *Chronicle* 27 July 424 Mr. Longfellow's poetic reputation..establishes a preconception in his favour. 1882 Farrar *Early Chr.* I. 142 Human perversity has darkened the very heavens by looking at them through the medium of its own preconceptions.

Pre-conce·ptional, *a. rare*⁻¹. [Pre- B. 1.] Previous to conception.

1904 *Brit. Med. Jrnl.* 17 Dec. 1644 The first, or preconceptional period of germinal life.

Preco·ncert, *sb.* [f. Pre- A. 2 + Concert *sb.*] A previous concert, agreement, or arrangement.

1748 Richardson *Clarissa* (1811) VI. xlv. 175 A book, which had there not been a preconcert, would not have taken his attention for one moment. 1834 *Blackw. Mag.* XXXV. 395 A medical man being (by preconcert) at hand.

Preconce·rt, *v.* [f. Pre- A. 1 + Concert *v.*] *trans.* To concert or arrange beforehand.

1748 Richardson *Clarissa* (1811) III. vii. 59 The opportunity to effect an escape which they suppose preconcerted. 1828 D'Israeli *Chas. I*, I. vi. 188 With this motive we must suppose them to have preconcerted their plans. 1855 Prince Albert in *Lett. Q. Victoria* (1907) III. 134 How can the Foreign Secretary and Ambassador at Paris..carry on their business, if everything has been privately preconcerted between the Emperor and the English Prime Minister?

Preconce·rted, *ppl. a.* [f. prec. vb. + -ed ¹.] Concerted or agreed upon beforehand.

1766 Blackstone *Comm.* II. viii. 136 Upon preconcerted marriages, and in estates of considerable consequence, tenancy in dower happens very seldom. 1774 Goldsm. *Nat. Hist.* IV. vii. 211 They do not go singly to work, but in large companies and with preconcerted deliberation. 1840 Dickens *Barn. Rudge* lxvii, As though the setting in of night had been their preconcerted signal.

Hence **Preconce·rtedly** *adv.* (Worcester *Dict.* 1846 cites Dr. Allen); **Preconce·rtedness.**

1819 Coleridge in *Lit. Rem.* (1836) II. 168 The rhymes.. well express the preconcertedness of Bolingbroke's scheme.

Preconce·rtion. [irreg. f. Preconcert *v.*, for *preconcertation*: see Concertion.] The action of preconcerting; preconcert.

1846 Worcester cites Dwight. 1880 Mrs. Lynn Linton *Rebel of Family* II. 270 Bois-Duval had come to London without preconcertion as to time.

Precondemn (prĭkǫnde·m), *v.* [f. Pre- A. 1 + Condemn *v.*] *trans.* To condemn beforehand. Hence **Precondemned** (-de·md), **Precondemning** (-de·miŋ) *ppl. adjs.*; **Precondemnation** (-demnē¹·ʃən).

a 1631 Donne *Serm.* (ed. Alford) IV. 220 Not things which make him an unmerciful, a cruel, a precondemning God. 1633 Prynne *Histrio-Mastix* Ep. Ded. *iv, They will quite reject and precondemne them, ere they have once examined them. 1847 Webster, Precondemnation. 1864 *Realm* 30 Mar. 2 The Judge of the Assize Court of Aix.. sate as judge, having precondemned the prisoner in his own mind. 1890 Talmage *Manger to Throne* 537 There stood Jesus..the pre-condemned victim of an ecclesiastical..mob.

Precondition (prĭkǫndi·ʃən). [f. Pre- A. 2 + Condition *sb.*] A prior condition; a condition required to be fulfilled beforehand; a preliminary or precedent stipulation; a pre-requisite.

1825 Coleridge *Aids Refl.* (1848) I. 36 The ground-work and pre-condition of the spiritual state, in which the humanity strives after godliness. 1851 De Quincey *Ld. Carlisle on Pope* Wks. 1859 XIII. 19 Absolute truth and simplicity are demanded by all of us as preconditions to any sympathy with moral expressions of anger or intolerance. 1877 E. Caird *Philos. Kant* I. 165 The idea of God is the precondition of all thought and being.

Precondylar, -condyloid, -confess: see Pre- B. 3, A. 1.

Preconfigure (-fi·giŭɹ), *v.* [f. Pre- A. 1 + Configure *v.*] *trans.* To configure in advance; to conform or adapt in figure beforehand.

1809–10 Coleridge *Friend* (1818) I. 293 It was the aweful power of Law, acting on natures pre-configured to its influences. 1835 J. Harris *Gt. Teacher* (1837) 237 Wherever the Bible comes, it finds our nature preconfigured to many of its truths. 1882–3 *Schaff's Encycl. Relig. Knowl.* III. 1723 The country was preconfigured to its history.

Hence **Preconfigura·tion** *rare*⁻¹.

a 1860 in *Nonconformist*, He sees the preconfiguration of human nature to spiritual truth.

Preconfo·rm, *v.* [f. Pre- A. 1 + Conform *v.*] *trans.* and *intr.* To conform beforehand.

1845 De Quincey *Coleridge & Opium-eating* Wks. 1859 XII. 110 There are..two classes of temperaments as to this terrific drug—those which are, and those which are not preconformed to its power. 1847 — in *Tait's Mag.* XIV. 103 Though the passions..are such..as could not have existed under Paganism; in some respects they condescend and preconform to the stage.

So **Preconfo·rmity**, antecedent conformity.

1825 Coleridge *Aids Refl.* (1848) I. 186 These holy and humanizing spells, in the preconformity to which our very humanity may be said to consist.

† **Preco·nious,** *a. Obs. rare*⁻⁰. [f. L. *præcōni-us* (f. *præcōn-em* crier, herald) + -ous.]

1656 Blount *Glossogr.*, *Preconious*, of or belonging to a Common-cryer; also to praise or commendation.

Preco·nizance. *rare.* In 8 *erron.* **precognizance.** [f. med. L. *præcōnizāre* to Preconize: see -ance.] = Preconization 1.

1730 *St. Trials* I. 367/2 The Lord Steward, after a solemn Precognizance, commanded the Indictments to be certified and brought in.

† **Preco·nizate,** *ppl. a. Obs. rare.* [ad. med.L. *præcōnizāt-us*, pa. pple. of *præcōnizāre* to Preconize.] Summoned by proclamation. (In quots. as pa. pple.)

1529 Hen. VIII *Let.* in Burnet *Hist. Ref.* (1679) I. *Records* II. xxviii. 78 Wherefore she was thrice preconisate, and called eft-soons to return and appear. *c* 1555 Harpsfield *Divorce Hen. VIII* 181 The legates caused her to be thrice preconisate and called eftsoones to return.

Preconization (prĭkǫnaizē¹·ʃən). [ad. med.L. *præcōnizātiō-nem*, n. of action f. *præcōnizāre*, see next; cf. F. *préconisation* (*preconizacion*, 1321).]

1. Public proclamation or announcement. *rare.*

1644 Bp. Hall *Modest Offer* (1660) 10 A publick preconization of lawful warning affixed upon the Cathedral Church door. 1649 — *Cases Consc.* Add. iii. (1654) 399 The Minister in a solemne preconization, called you..then to speake, or for ever after to hold your peace.

2. *spec.* in *R. C. Ch.* The public confirmation of an appointment (as that of a bishop) by the pope.

1692 *Lond. Gaz.* No. 2753/1 The Dispute grew very warm ..when the Pope put a stop to it, by ordering the Preconisation of the said four Bishops to go on in the usual Form. 1882–3 *Schaff's Encycl. Relig. Knowl.* 1886 Preconization ..the act by which the Pope, in the assembly of the cardinals, proclaims new bishops, and assigns them their respective seats.

Preconize (prī·kǫnəiz), *v.* Also præ-. [ad. med.L. *præcōnīzāre*, f. L. *præcōn-em* public crier, herald: see -ize; cf. F. *préconiser* (1321 in Godef.).]

1. *trans.* To proclaim or announce publicly; to publish; to commend or extol publicly, to cry up.

c 1420 *Pallad. on Husb.* XIII. 86 Yet treste y crie Thy laude, and his honour eft preconise. 1803 W. Taylor in *Ann. Rev.* I. 311 Louis 14th, whose reign he preconizes as the happiest period in French history. 1847 *Blackw. Mag.* LXII. 293 [They] had all praeconised their accomplishments to us. 1902 *Contemp. Rev.* Dec. 802 Italian ecclesiastics.. undermining the monarchical principle throughout Italy, ..preconising it in Russia.

b. To call upon publicly, to summon by name.

1863 *Church Instit. Circular* II. 139 The certificates having been read, the Registrar preconized the Bishops mentioned in the return from the Dean of the Province, and the Archbishop then referred to the Vicar-General to report upon the certificates transmitted by them and upon the letters of proxy. 1877 Sir T. Twiss in *Encycl. Brit.* VI. 329/2 The clergy are præconized or summoned by name to appear before the metropolitan or his commissary.

2. *spec.* in *R. C. Ch.* Of the pope: To approve publicly the appointment of (a bishop).

1692 *Lond. Gaz.* No. 2753/1 On Monday last the Pope held a Consistory, wherein the four last preconis'd French Bishops were confirmed. 1706 Phillips, *Preconise*,..to make a Report in the Pope's Consistory, That the Party presented to a Benefice is qualify'd for the same. 1887 *Detroit Free Press* 21 May 2/1 After eighteen months' service in Perugia, Pope Gregory preconized him [Leo XIII] archbishop of Damietta. 1892 *Times* 23 Mar. 5/5 The Pope will preconize Dr. Vaughan at the first consistory held after Easter.

Hence **Pre·conizing** *vbl. sb.*; **Pre·conizer,** one who preconizes.

1703 *Pretended Indep. Lower Ho. Convocation* 40 The great end of Preconizing, is, to know who have incurr'd the Censure due to Contumacy, in not appearing pursuant to Archiepiscopal Summons. 1711 Hickes *Two Treat. Chr. Priesth.* (1847) I. 320 The great disperser and preconizer of it at home and abroad. 1804 W. Taylor in *Ann. Rev.* II. 240 He is commonly the panegyrist of event, the preconizer of destiny, he rows with the stream.

Preconjecture, -connubial, etc.: see Pre- A. 1, 2, B. 1.

Preco·nquer, *v. rare.* [f. Pre- A. 1 + Conquer *v.*] *trans.* To conquer beforehand.

a 1661 Fuller *Worthies, Cornw.* (1662) I. 196 He [the Duke of Medina] resolved it [Mount Edgecombe] for his own possession in the partage of this Kingdome..which they had preconquered in their hopes and expectation.

Pre-co·nqueror, *a.* [Pre- B. 2.] Anterior to (William) the Conqueror. So **Pre-co·nquest** *a.*, preceding the (Norman) Conquest; **Pre-conque·stal, -conque·stual** *a.* [Pre- B. 1], existing in, or belonging to, times preceding the Conquest.

a 1878 Sir G. G. Scott *Lect. Archit.* (1879) II. 59 There were pre-conquestal Norman and post-conquestal Saxon buildings. 1880 *Sat. Rev.* 3 Apr. 439/2 The fact of the town having been a pre-conquestal see no more makes the place a city than it makes the parson a dean. 1889 *Athenæum* 10 Aug. 184/1 Dr. Stubbs..sums up strongly in favour of the antiquity of the Leet and its jury, to which he confidently assigns a pre-conquestual origin. 1900 *Edin. Rev.* July 150 A unique collection of preconquest stones. 1901 *Daily Chron.* 15 July 5/1 Royal lineage in our noble and gentle families is common enough:..most of them derive from the Plantagenet, and not from the pre-Conqueror kings.

Preconscious (prĭkǫ·nʃəs), *a.* [f. Pre- B. 1 + Conscious *a.*] Antecedent to consciousness, or to conscious action of some specified kind.

1870 E. Peacock *Ralf Skirl.* I. 154 A preconscious exercise of the critical faculty. 1874 Carpenter *Ment. Phys.* I. viii. (1879) 352 The Physiological doctrine of 'Unconscious Cerebration', or, in the language of German Psychologists, the 'Preconscious Activity of the Soul'. 1876 Maudsley *Physiol. Mind* vi. 366 The so-called preconscious soul, of which some philosophers have written, is truly the preconscious mental life of the race. 1891 *Antidote* 9 June 180 A yearning which is at present, except in a few cases, all preconscious, but still none the less hopeful.

Preconsider (prĭkǫnsi·dəɹ), *v.* Also 7 præ-. [f. Pre- A. 1 + Consider *v.*] *trans.* To consider beforehand or previously. Hence **Preconsi·dered, Preconsi·dering** *ppl. adjs.*

1647 Clarendon *Contempl. Ps.* Tracts (1727) 393 A stubborn, pertinacious, preconsidered sin. 1670 G. H. *Hist. Cardinals* I. II. 51 They pray not for the Publick, whose interest is alwayes præ-consider'd by our Saviour. 1671 Woodhead *St. Teresa* I. Pref. 18 Not to go to Prayer, without preconsidering whereon to employ it. 1847 Grote *Greece* II. xi. III. 175 The new pro-bouleutic or pre-considering senate consisted of 400 members. 1873 Holland *A. Bonnic.* vi, Playing a part, thoroughly pre-considered. 1879 Froude *Cæsar* ii. 8 The Senate was allowed the privilege of preconsidering intended acts of legislation.

† **Preconsi·derate,** *a. Obs. rare.* [f. Pre- A. 3 + Considerate *a.*] That considers or deliberates beforehand: considerate beforehand.

1598 Barret *Theor. Warres* IV. i. 98 If he be not very preconsiderate in the same, and know well the way, he runneth into these inconveniencies.

Preconsidera·tion. [f. Pre- A. 2 + Consideration.] Previous consideration; consideration beforehand; a preliminary consideration.

1598 Barret *Theor. of Warres* 29 Without preuention, preconsideration, and forecast of such successes. 1656 H. Phillips *Purch. Patt.* (1676) 23 Thus much for these pre-considerations: I shall now set the Tables before you. 1701 Beverley *Apoc. Quest.* 25 A Second most necessary Preconsideration in the Understanding of the Beast. 1858 Sir A. Grant in *Oxford Ess.* 94 Chrysippus said, that 'no ethical subject could be rightly approached except from the preconsideration of entire nature and the ordering of the whole'.

Preconsign (prĭkǫnsəi·n), *v.* [f. Pre- A. 1 + Consign *v.*] *trans.* † **a.** To signify or symbolize beforehand. *Obs.* **b.** To consign or make over in advance (Bailey 1721).

1649 Jer. Taylor *Gt. Exemp.* I. Disc. vi. § 17 St. Cyril calls baptism..'the antitype of the passions of Christ'. It does preconsign the death of Christ, and does the infancy of the work of grace, but not weakly.

Preconsolidate, -constitute, etc.: see Pre- A. 1, 2.

Preconsu·lt, *v.* Now *rare.* [Pre- A. 1.] *trans.* and *intr.* To consult beforehand or previously.

1620 Wotton in *Reliq.* (1672) 527 Intending in the meanwhile to preconsult with his friends. 1651 Howell *Venice* 14 These use to preconsult of generall matters tending to the administration of the Commonwealth..and make relation thereof to the Senat. 1683 Pepys *Corr.* (1841) I. 336 Had my mean advice been preconsulted in it.

So **Preconsulta·tion** [Pre- A. 2], previous consultation; † **Preconsu·ltor** (præ-), one who advises or holds consultation beforehand.

c 1620 Wotton *Election Dk. Venice* in *Reliq.* (1651) 187 During his Election, all Inferiour Tribunals cease, only the Colledge of the Preconsultors (as they term it) is daily open for the hearing of Ambassadours. 1631 in *Crt. & Times Chas. I* (1848) II. 144 What an honour is it to King Charles, that had an ambassador who was a præ-consultor to so lofty an action. 1656 Blount *Glossogr.*, *Preconsultor*, a Pre-adviser; there is a Colledge of these at Venice. 1682 Norris *Hierocles* 85 Add to the other advantages of Preconsultation that it cuts off the causes of uncertain opinions.

Precontai·n, *v. rare.* [f. Pre- A. 1 + Contain *v.*] *trans.* To contain beforehand.

1656 [? J. Sergeant] tr. *T. White's Peripat. Inst.* 283 God is a most Simple Entity, precontaining in one most simple formality, the whole plenitude of Being. 1784 Kirwan in *Phil. Trans.* LXXIV. 162 Fixed air pre-contained in the dephlogisticated.

Precontemplation, -contemporaneous: see Pre- A. 2, B. 1 d.

† **Preconte·st.** *Obs.* [f. Pre- A. 2 + Contest *sb.*¹] A former or previous fellow-witness.

c 1570 in *Durham Depos.* (Surtees) 272 One John Lawson was burying in the barn with the said Agnes brother, her precontest. 1594 *Depos. Bk. Well's Dioc. Reg.* lf. 1 b, Presente then and ther,..this Jurate, and Thomas Jeanes his preconteste.

Pre-contract (prĭkǫ·ntrækt), *sb.* Also 7 præ-. [f. Pre- A. 2 + Contract *sb.*] A pre-existing contract; a contract or agreement previously entered into: **a.** of marriage.

1483 *Rolls of Parlt.* VI. 241/1 Oone Dame Elianor Butteler,..with whome the same King Edward had made a precontracte of matrimonie. 1540 *Act 32 Hen. VIII*, c. 38 (*title*) An act concernyng precontractes of mariages. 1603 Shaks. *Meas. for M.* IV. i. 72 Nor gentle daughter, feare you not at all: He is your husband on a pre-contract. 1657–8 in *Burton's Diary* (1828) II. 337 The law lies very loose as to things that are naturally essential to marriages, as to pre-contracts and dissolving of marriages. 1765 Blackstone *Comm.* I. xv. 434 Of this nature are pre-contract; consanguinity, or relation by blood; and affinity, or relation by marriage. 1878 Stubbs *Const. Hist.* III. xviii. 224 Edward being already bound by a pre-contract of marriage to the lady Eleanor Butler.

b. in general sense.

1610 Donne *Pseudo-martyr* 125 The King of Spaine had very many subiects in that Order, to whom no other Prince pretended any such precontract or interest. 1649 G. Daniel *Trinarch., Hen. IV*, ccclxxiii, They are never safe Who weare their Titles by a Præ-contract In Treason. 1821 Scott *Kenilw.* v, Lawyers..to draw his contracts, his pre-contracts, and his post-contracts, and to find the way to make the most of grants of church lands, and commons, and licenses for monopoly. 1855 Macaulay *Hist. Eng.* xvi. III. 704 The Presbyterian nonjurors..held that their country was under a precontract to the Most High, and could never..enter into any engagement inconsistent with that precontract.

Precontra·ct, *ppl. a. rare. poet.* [f. Pre- A. 1 + Contract *ppl. a.*] Pre-contracted. (Used as *pa. pple.*)

1568 *Satir. Poems Reform.* ix. 205 His mother precontract Was in most solemn wise Unto the King. 1887 Swinburne *Locrine* I. ii. 137 Albeit their hands were precontract By Brute your father dying.

Pre-contract (prĭkǫntræ·kt), *v.* Also 7 præ-. [f. Pre- A. 1 + Contract *v.*]

1. *trans.* **a.** To engage (a person) in a previous contract of marriage; to affiance or betroth beforehand. **b.** To establish (an agreement, etc.) by contract in advance. **c.** To acquire or form (habits, etc.) beforehand. Hence **Pre-contra·cted** *ppl. a.*

1579–80 North *Plutarch* (1676) 639 This Lepida had been pre-contracted unto Metellus Scipio. 1611 Middleton & Dekker *Roaring Girle* D.'s Wks. 1873 III. 209 Deere husband, pardon me, I did dissemble, Told thee I was his precontracted wife. 1631 Vicars *Eng. Hallelujah* Ps. cv. vii, That Cou'nant-good, once præ-contracted To Abraham and Isaacs Seed. 1768–74 Tucker *Lt. Nat.* (1834) I. 613 If they would employ their talents sincerely for the public good, in preference to any private views or favourite schemes or pre-contracted prejudices. 1819 *Life & Death Jas. I of Scot.* 122 Notwithstanding she had been pre-contracted to Frederic, elector palatine of the Rhine. 1856 Froude *Hist. Eng.* I. ii. 167 Nor could a contract with Percy have invalidated her marriage with the king..Percy having been pre-contracted to another person.

2. *intr.* To enter into a contract beforehand; to agree or arrange in advance.

1638 Sir T. Herbert *Trav.* (ed. 2) 88 Having precontracted with Byrambeg and Darab-chawn, to seize him.

Precontrive (prĭkǫntrai·v), *v.* [f. Pre- A. 1 + Contrive *v.*] *trans.* To contrive beforehand. So **Precontri·vance** [Pre- A. 2].

1751 Warburton *Pope's Wks.*, *Ess. Man* III. 295 *note*, When the mind had the will to raise the arm to the head, the body was so pre-contrived, as to raise, at that very moment, the part required. 1840 Carlyle *Heroes* iii. (1858) 265 Shakspeare's Art is not Artifice; the noblest worth of it is not there by plan or precontrivance.

Preconveyance (prĭkǫnvē¹·ăns). [f. Pre- A. 2 + Conveyance *sb.*] A previous or prior conveyance (of property).

1628 *Petit. conc. Recusants* in Rushw. *Hist. Coll.* (1659) I. 517 This mystery of Iniquity patched up of colourable Leases, Contracts, and Preconveyances. 1655 Fuller *Hist. Camb.* (1840) 221 Recusant-patrons, before their conviction, had such sleights, by pre-conveyances to make over their advowsons to others.

† **Precony.** *Obs.* Also in L. form **præconium.** [ad. L. *præcōnium* the office of a public crier, a proclaiming, laudation; sb. use of neut. sing. of *præcōnius* Preconious, f. *præcōn-em* a public crier.] Public commendation; laudation, extolment.

c 1410 Love *Bonavent. Mirr.* viii. (Gibbs MS.), So that here is schewed a grete precony and worthy ensaumple of pouert. 1432–50 tr. *Higden* (Rolls) I. 3 Thei ar to be enhaunsede and exaltede by merite with grete preconyes. 1653 R. G. tr. *Bacon's Hist. Winds* 208 It hath been abused both by false opinions, and false Præconiums.

† **Preco·que,** *a.* (*sb.*) *Obs. rare.* Also 5 *pl.* **precox.** [ad. L. *præcoqu-us* (Columella), occas. equivalent of *præcox* early ripe: see Precoce.] Early ripe. **b.** As *sb.* Applied to an early fig.

1398 Trevisa *Barth. De P. R.* XVII. clxxxi. (Bodl. MS.), Some [grapes] ben precoque..for þei ripeþ sone. *c* 1420 *Pallad. on Husb.* IV. 578 In places passyng cold, hit is most sure Precox [= precoques, L. *præcoqua*] to plaunte; her fruyt they sone enhaunce, Er shoures come.

Precoracoid, *a.* and *sb.* [Pre- B. 3.]

A. *adj.* Situated anterior to the coracoid.

1872 Humphry *Myology* 31 In Menobranch the long precoracoid cartilage lies upon the omo-hyoid.

B. as *sb.* A precoracoid bone or cartilage.

1870 Rolleston *Anim. Life* 39 The prolongation of the more perfectly developed præcoracoids. 1875 Huxley & Martin *Elem. Biol.* (1877) 221 The posterior end articulates with the præcoracoids and the clavicles.

Hence **Precoracoi·dal** *a.* = Precoracoid *a.* So **Preco·raco-** in comb., as *precoraco-brachial*, (a muscle) connecting the precoracoid with the arm.

1872 Humphry *Myology* 33 Precoraco-brachial..arises from the whole of the outer surface of the precoracoid cartilage, with the exception of the marginal part. 1875 Huxley in *Encycl. Brit.* I. 761/2 (*in some copies*) The pectoral arch in the Amphibia is distinguishable into a scapular, a coracoidal, and a præcoracoidal region.

† **Precordiac, præ-,** (*a.*) *sb. Obs.* [irreg. f. Præcordia, perh. after *cardiac.*] = Precordial.

1671 Blagrave *Astrol. Physic* 83 Proceeding from obstructions and distempers of the precordiacks and arteries.

Precordial, præ- (prĭkǭ·ɹdiăl), *a.*¹ (*sb.*) [f. Præcordia + -al.] Situated in front of or about the heart; of or pertaining to the Præcordia.

1562 Bulleyn *Bulwark, Bk. Simples* 1 Against all the aboundance of humours in the breaste or precordiall parts. 1601 Holland *Pliny* XXII. viii. II. 119 For the midriffe and precordial parts, it is very wholsome. *Ibid.* (see Præcordia). 1834 J. Forbes *Laennec's Dis. Chest* (ed. 4) 379 A remitting dyspnœa, attended with dry cough and precordial anxiety. 1842 Dunglison *Med. Lex.* s. v. *Præcordia*, The Præcordial Region is the epigastric region. Also, and more properly, the region of the heart [etc.]. 1880 A. Flint *Princ. Med.* 316 It may be limited to a portion of the præcordial space. 1895 *Syd. Soc. Lex.*, *Præcordial anxiety*, a feeling of anxiety and oppression, with a sensation of constriction of the chest over the præcordial region.

† **B.** *sb.* (absolute use of adj.) *pl.* The precordial parts; the parts in front of or over the heart. *Obs.*

1513 Douglas *Æneis* VII. vii. 14 Amyde hir hart-pypys or precordialis lycht. 1555 Eden *Decades* 66 The naturall heate is not dryuen from the owtewarde partes into the inwarde partes and precordials.

† **Preco·rdial,** *a.*² *Obs. rare.* [f. Pre- A. 6 + Cordial *a.*] Exceedingly cordial; very hearty, warm, or sincere.

1530 Lyndesay *Test. Papyngo* 349 Brether of court, with mynd precordial, To the gret god hartlie I commend 3ow. 1542 Becon *News out of Heaven* Prol. A iv b, Christ sayeth here playnely, that whosoeuer hath an herty & precordial [*ed.* 1560 vnfeigned] loue toward hym, kepeth his commaundementes. 1757 Mrs. Griffith *Lett. Henry & Frances* (1767) III. 273 Mutual Tenderness, or præcordial Sympathy.

b. *fig.* Very comforting or cheering. *Sc. rare*⁻¹.

a 1600 Montgomerie *Misc. Poems* xxxiv. 37 Restore thairfore to glore precordiall My lif from stryf or knyf of Atropus.

Hence † **Preco·rdially** *adv.*, most heartily.

c 1531 Boorde *Let.* in *Introd. Knowl.* (1870) Forewords 47 Venerable faþer, precordyally I commend me vnto yow with thanks. 1534 — in Ellis *Orig. Lett.* Ser. III. II. 299, I humyly and precordyally desyre yor Mastershepp to be good master..to ye faithfull bedmen.

† **Precordium.** *Obs.* An error for Pericardium (confused with Præcordia).

1541 R. Copland *Guydon's Quest. Chirurg.* H j, Wherof is the substaunce of the coueryng of the herte?..It is called precordium, & is of a skynny substaunce, wher to descendeth synewes as vnto other inwarde intraylles.

Precorneal to **-costal**: see Pre- B. 1 d, 3.

† **Precou·rse,** *sb. Obs. rare.* [ad. L. *præcurs-us*: see Precurse *sb.*] Forerunning, anticipation, anticipatory action.

1678 Marvell *Def. J. Howe* Wks. (Grosart) IV. 226 If God do not determine men to such wicked actions by concourse, he doth it..by precourse. 1786 A. Gib *Sacr. Contempl.* III. 470 According to the doctrine of Calvinists, there is a precourse or predetermination of the divine power in respect to every action of the Soul.

Precourse (prĭkōᵊ·ɹs), *v. rare.* [f. L. *præcurs-*, ppl. stem of *præcurrĕre*: see Precurse *v.*] *trans.* To run before, forerun, herald, prognosticate. In quot. 1847 *intr.* To act as a precursor.

1847 *Tait's Mag.* XIV. 643 The precursors are understood to be gentlemen in the transition state towards repeal. Some of them have, however, denied that they can be said to 'precourse' in this form. 1888 Clark Russell *Death Ship* xl, The weighty swells which had precoursed the growth of the storm had run away down the eastern waters.

Pre-creative, -crucial: see Pre- B. 1, 3.

Pre-critical (prĭkri·tikăl), *a.* [Pre- B. 1.] Previous to the critical treatment of a subject; in quot. 1881, previous to the development of Kant's critical philosophy as shown in his 'Critique of Pure Reason'.

1881 *Encycl. Brit.* XIII. 847/2 Belonging to the precritical period of Kant's development. 1892 Montefiore *Hibbert Lect.* ii. 83 Jeroboam's revolt can no longer be estimated as in the pre-critical age.

Precuneus, præ- (prĭkiū·nĭŭs). *Anat.* [f. L. *præ* Pre- B. 3 + Cuneus.] The quadrate lobule of the brain, situated immediately in front of the cuneate lobule. Hence **Precu·neal** *a.*, of or pertaining to the precuneus (*Cent. Dict.* 1890).

1890 in Billings *Med. Dict.* 1893 W. R. Gowers *Man. Dis. Nerv. Syst.* (ed. 2) II. 437 Very rarely softening is limited to the paracentral region or to the precuneus. 1899 *Allbutt's Syst. Med.* VII. 308 We have found that lesion of the gyrus fornicatus, at the point where it passes into the precuneus, caused loss of sensation.

Precurrent (prĭkʋ·rĕnt), *a.* [ad. L. *præcurrens, -entem*, pres. pple. of *præcurrĕre* to run before, precede: see Pre- A. 1 and Current *a.*]

1. Occurring beforehand; forerunning, precursory.

1628 J. Hume *Jewes Deliv.* ii. 29 The precurrent signes of the day of Iudgement. 1799 M. Underwood *Dis. Childr.* (ed. 4) I. 192 An account of the various precurrent symptoms. 1893 *Athenæum* 2 Sept. 310/3 Precurrent symptoms of the transition to some such society.

2. *Anat.* Running or extending forward, i. e. towards the front or head. Opposed to Recurrent.

1890 in *Cent. Dict.*

† **Precu·rrer.** *Obs. rare*⁻¹. [f. **precur*, ad. L. *præcurr-ĕre* (see prec.) + -er ¹.] A forerunner.

1601 Shaks. *Phœnix & Turtle* ii, Thou shriking harbinger, Foule pre-currer of the fiend.

† **Precu·rse,** *sb. Obs. rare*⁻¹. [ad. L. *præcurs-us* a running before, from *præcurrĕre*: see next and Precurrent.] Forerunning, heralding, foretokening. So **Precu·rsal** *a. rare*⁻¹, of or pertaining to a forerunner, precursory.

1602 Shaks. *Ham.* I. i. 121 And even the like precurse of fierce events, As harbingers preceding still the fates. 1817 G. S. Faber *Eight Dissert.* (1845) I. 262 When John began his precursal ministry.

Precurse (prĭkʋ̄·ɹs), *v. rare.* [f. L. *præcurs-*, ppl. stem of *præcurrĕre* (see Precurrent); so F. *précurser* (15th c. in Hatz.-Darm.).] *trans.* To run or occur before; hence, to herald, foretoken, prognosticate. Hence **Precu·rsing** *ppl. a.*

1865 S. Wilberforce *Sp. Missions* (1874) 173 This which we hear whispered there, and see spreading we know not how through the air, is just the precursing atmosphere which comes before his [Antichrist's] advent. 1891 Froude *Erasmus* viii. (1895) 155 You cannot regard heresy and schism and precursing antichrist as trifles.

† **Precu·rsion.** *Obs. rare*⁻¹. [ad. L. *præcursiōn-em* a running before, previous occurrence, n. of action from *præcurrĕre*: see prec.] = Precurse *sb.* Hence † **Precu·rsionary** *a. Obs. rare*⁻¹.

1701 Beverley *Apoc. Quest.* 15 That such a State of Empire, was at the change of that from Pagan to Christian as a Precursion to it. 1839 *Blackw. Mag.* XLV. 217 The landlords not named in the lists of Precursionary proscription were to be regarded popular and unattainted.

Precursive (prĭkʋ̄·ɹsiv), *a.* [f. L. *præcurs-* (see Precurse *v.*) + -ive.] = Precursory.

a 1814 *Sorceress* II. ii. in *New Brit. Theatre* III. 14 Does thy simple mind See the precursive harbingers of woe Like brooding guilt? 1845 *New Statist. Acc. Scot.* XIX. 281 A groundswell precursive of a storm rolls in. 1868 E. Edwards *Ralegh* I. xviii. 362 These rumours were..the precursive shadows which are said to be cast by coming events.

Precursor (prĭkʋ̄·ɹsəɹ). Also 6–7 præ-; 7 -cursoure, -curser. [a. L. *præcursor* forerunner, advanced guard, agent-n. from *præcurrĕre* to run before; cf. F. *précurseur* (15th c.).]

1. One who or that which runs or goes before; a forerunner; *esp.* one who precedes and heralds the approach of another; a harbinger; *spec.* applied to John the Baptist. Also *attrib.*

1504 Lady Margaret tr. *De Imitatione* IV. xvii. 281 The right excellent precursor Iohn Baptyste. 1612 Jas. I in Ellis *Orig. Lett.* Ser. I. III. 106, I knowe this wilbe the more wellcome that it is my præcursoure. 1792 A. Young *Trav. France* I. 179 Abbé Raynal, one of the undoubted precursors of the present revolution in France. 1852 Mrs. Jameson *Leg. Madonna* (1857) 9 The Baptist is here in his character of Precursor. 1856 Miss Mulock *J. Halifax* xxiii, Shame, the precursor of saving penitence. 1869 Dunkin *Midn. Sky* 173 In ancient times Procyon..was called the Precursor Dog. 1871 Tyndall *Fragm. Sc.* (1879) I. ii. 55 That dark radiation, which is the precursor..of their luminous rays.

† **b.** *Irish Politics.* See quots. *Obs.*

1847 *Tait's Mag.* XIV. 643 Conservatives 39, Repealers 37, Whigs 17, Precursors 12. The precursors are understood to be gentlemen in the transition state towards repeal. 1907 *Daily Chron.* 4 Sept. 4/7 Precursor was one of the many names that O'Connell gave to his popular organisations. The 'Precursor Society' meant that it was the precursor of O'Connell's last resource—the Repeal of the Union.

2. One who precedes in some course or office.

1792 Burke in Ellis *Orig. Lett.* Ser. II. IV. 540 Sufferers in one Common Cause, and..our precursors in misfortune. 1835 I. Taylor *Spir. Despot.* vi. 248 There is now no need that we should err as our precursors have done for want of experience. 1879 M. Arnold *Mixed Ess., Guide Eng. Lit.* 202 Cowper..by his genuine love of nature was a precursor of Wordsworth.

Hence † **Precu·rsorism,** the principles and practice of the Irish 'precursors' (see Precursor 1 b).

1839 *John Bull* 29 Apr., Otherwise what need would there be for 'Precursorism' and 'Repeal'? 1839 *Times* 17 Sept., Precursorism has turned out to be utterly hopeless.

Precu·rsorship. [f. prec. + -ship.]

1. The office or function of a precursor.

a 1603 T. Cartwright *Confut. Rhem. N. T.* (1618) 152 The Eremitship of Elias and Iohn Baptist, and likewise of the Precurs[or]ship of Elias. 1892 G. Saintsbury *Misc. Ess.* Pref. 9 Without the faintest intention of giving any fatuous hint of prophecy or precursorship.

2. Antecedence; prior occurrence.

1856 Ruskin *Mod. Paint.* III. IV. xvii. § 21 It depends for its force on the existence of ruins and traditions,..and the precursorship of eventful history. 1867 C. J. Smith *Syn. & Antonyms* s. v. *Antecedence*, Syn...Priority, Precursorship.

Precursory (prĭkʋ̄·ɹsŏri), *a.* (*sb.*) [ad. L. *præcursōrius*: see Precursor and -ory ².] Having the character of a precursor; running before or preceding, esp. as the harbinger or presage of something to follow; preliminary, introductory. Const. *of.*

1599 Sandys *Europæ Spec.* (1632) 125 After the kindling of many precursorie lights of knowledge. 1669 W. Simpson *Hydrol. Chym.* 77 Being a precursory provision to that end. 1796 *Hist.* in *Ann. Reg.* 16/1 Reprobated..as precursory of far greater evils. *a* 1883 D. King in *Mem.* (1885) 357. I cannot regard it [Pentecost] as the precursory advent here designed. 1899 *Allbutt's Syst. Med.* VI. 835 Another symptom which is sometimes precursory of exophthalmic goitre.

B. *sb.* (the adj. used *absol.*) A precursory fact, condition, or symptom; an antecedent.

a 1660 Hammond *Serm. Ezek.* xvi. 30 Wks. 1684 IV. 568 Virtue is the way to Truth: Purity of affections a necessary precursory to depth of knowledge. 1822 Good *Study Med.* II. 692 Yet not unfrequently the blood issues suddenly without any of these precursories.

Precydence, -ent, obs. ff. Precedence, -ent.

Precydent, obs. Sc. variant of President.

† **Pre·dable,** *a. Obs. rare*⁻¹. [ad. med.L. *prædābilis*, f. *prædārī* (see Prede *v.*) + -able.] Liable to be preyed on or seized as prey.

1610 Guillim *Heraldry* III. xx. (1660) 226 Fowles..which are Predable whereof some are Savage some Domesticall. *Ibid.* xxi. 227 From Predable Fowles that are Savage, we come to Fowles Domesticall and home-bred that are delighted with Mens Society.

† **Preda·cean.** *Obs. rare.* [f. *predace-ous*, erron. form of Predacious + -an (after *crustacean*, etc.).] A predacious animal; a bird or beast of prey.

1835 Kirby *Hab. & Inst. Anim.* II. xxiv. 481 The Predaceans and several others, when first born are blind. 1895 *Syd. Soc. Lex.*, *Predacean*, a syn. for *Carnivora*.

Predacious (prĭdē¹·ʃəs), *a.* Also erron. predaceous. [f. L. type **prædāx, -ācem* (cf. It. *predace*: f. L. *prædārī* to prey upon) + -ous: cf. *audacious, voracious, ferocious*: see -acious.]

1. Of animals: Naturally preying upon other animals; subsisting by the capture of living prey; predatory, raptorial.

1713 Derham *Phys.-Theol.* IX. i. (1727) 399 Those are endow'd with Poison, because they are predaceous. 1774

Goldsm. *Nat. Hist.* IV. 22 These snails may be regarded as the predacious tribe among their fellows. 1789 Mrs. Piozzi *Journ. France* II. 195 One predaceous creature caught in the very act of gorging his prey. 1836 W. Irving *Astoria* (1849) 383 They were now in a land of danger, subject to the wide roamings of a predacious tribe. 1877 Coues *Fur Anim.* iii. 61 Strictly carnivorous, predacious, and destructive to many kinds of small Mammals and Birds.

2. Of or pertaining to predatory animals.

1822–34 *Good's Study Med.* (ed. 4) IV. 509 He is as troublesome by his sudden and predacious sallies. 1844 Stephens *Bk. Farm* I. 363 A barrier against the predacious attempts on the stock. 1877 Coues *Fur Anim.* IV. 128 The instincts and predacious habits of the Weasels and Stoats.

Hence **Preda·ciousness** = next.

1904 Branford *Ideals Sc. & Faith* 118 Characterised by, on the one hand, audacity and predaciousness, and on the other by timidity and submission.

Predacity (prĭdæ·sĭti). [f. as prec. + -ty; see -acity.] The quality or fact of being predacious.

1836–9 *Todd's Cycl. Anat.* II. 971/1 Indicatory of predacity of habits in the insect. 1853 *Tait's Mag.* XX. 314 Predacity is the order of the day. Bargains are battles, in which the greatest rogue stands the best chance. 1892 *Q. Rev.* Apr. 493 Thanks to his audacity and his predacity.

† **Pre·dal,** *a. Obs. rare.* [f. L. *præda* prey + -al.] Of or pertaining to plunder; predatory.

1737 Boyse *Olive* i, Sarmatia, laid by prædal Rapine low. *Ibid.* xix, Allur'd, the prædal raven took his flight.

Predamn (prīdæ·m), *v.* Now *rare.* [ad. L. *prædamnāre*: see Pre- A. 1 and Damn *v.*] *trans.* To damn or condemn beforehand.

1624 F. White *Repl. Fisher* 82 The deedes..for which the cities of Sodome and Gomorrha were predamned. 1794 J. Williams *Shrove Tuesday* in *A Cabinet*, etc. 14 Swear we're all predestin'd or predamn'd.

Predamnation (prīdæmnē¹·ʃən). Now *rare.* [ad. late L. *prædamnātiōn-em*, n. of action from *prædamnāre*: see prec.] The action of condemning or condition of being damned beforehand.

1626 J. Yates *Ibis ad Cæsarem* II. 32 As for damnation, predamnation, &c., they are acts of iustice, and not to be thought vpon without sinne. *a* 1711 Ken *Preparatives* Poet. Wks. 1721 IV. 27 'Tis Predamnation to despair, 'Tis Bliss to trust God's tender Care. 1865 W. G. Palgrave *Arabia* I. viii. 367 An adequate idea of predestination, or, to give it a truer name, pre-damnation, held and taught in the school of the Coran.

Predate (prīdē¹·t), *v.* [f. Pre- A. 1 + Date *v.*]

1. *trans.* To date before the actual time; to antedate.

1864 in Webster. 1902 *Edin. Rev.* Apr. 486 The tendency —found in all early as well as modern writings—to pre-date the origin of empire. 1906 *Westm. Gaz.* 9 Jan. 9/3 Mr. Gorst predates the fall of Lord Randolph Churchill.

2. To precede in date, to date before (something).

1889 *N. & Q.* 7th Ser. VII. 436/1 The Bonnington, or Lawday oak, is not a boundary tree, but it predates the times of the Tudors.

† **Preda·tion.** *Obs.* Also 5–6 -acion. [ad. L. *prædātiōn-em* a taking of booty, n. of action f. *prædārī* to plunder: see Prede *v.*] The action of plundering or pillaging; depredation.

c 1460 G. Ashby *Dicta Philos.* 968 On erthe ther is no thing so vnsemyng As a kynge to be in predacion, Or by compulsion to be taking. *a* 1548 Hall *Chron.*, *Hen. VIII* 143 Thys sodain visitacion or predacion, cleane shaued them. [*Margin*] Predacion, that is a robbery. 1664 Evelyn *Sylva* (1679) 20 The good Husbands expected..that the Fruit should improve, as freed from the predations of the Hedge.

† **Predati·tious,** *a. Obs.* [f. L. *prædātīci-us, -itius*, f. *prædārī*, *prædāt-*: see prec. and -itious ¹.] Characterized by plundering or robbing; predatory.

1659 Gauden *Serm.*, etc. (1660) 25 Not predatitious to any, but propitious to all true Saints. 1675 Evelyn *Terra* (1729) 3 Provided no rank Weeds, or predatitious Plants (consummating their Seeds) be suffered to..exhaust it.

† **Predato·rial,** *a. Obs. rare*⁻¹. [f. L. *prædātōri-us* (see Predatory) + -al.] = Predatory.

c 1781 (*title*) Authentic Memoirs..from the Journal of his Predatorial Majesty, the King of the Swindlers.

† **Predato·rious,** *a. Obs.* [f. as next + -ous.] = Predatory (esp. in sense 3).

1640 Gaudyn *Love of Truth* (1641) 21 Interpreting that zeale, which is but naturall passion and choler, an humane, feaverish and prædatorious, not that holy, gentle, and propicious heate of love. 1659 — *Slight Healers* (1660) 56 In complicated diseases..to give check to that, which is most accute, malignant and predatorious of the spirits. *a* 1677 Manton *Serm. Ps. cxix.* 36 xli. Wks. 1872 VI. 379 There is a vital heat necessary to our preservation, and there are unnatural predatorious heats which argue a distemper.

Predatory (pre·dătŏri), *a.* Also 7–8 præ-. [ad. L. *prædātōri-us*, f. *prædātōr-em* a plunderer, agent-n. f. *prædārī*: see Prede *v.* and -ory ².]

1. Of, pertaining to, characterized by, or consisting in plundering, pillaging, or robbery.

1589 Puttenham *Eng. Poesie* I. xviii. (Arb.) 53 So saith Aristotle,..that pasturage was before tillage, or fishing or fowling, or any other predatory art or cheuisance. 1673 Marvell *Reh. Transp.* II. 30 It is a predatory course of life. 1788 Gibbon *Decl. & F.* lxiv. (1869) III. 611 Necessity and revenge might justify his predatory excursions by sea and land. 1803 Wellington in Gurw. *Desp.* (1837) II. 203 The Marhattas have long boasted that they would carry on a predatory war against us. 1878 Maclear *Celts* i. 9 They for a time indulged their predatory instincts unchecked.

2. Addicted to, or living by, plunder; plundering, marauding, thieving: in modern use sometimes applied to the criminal classes of great cities.

1781 Gibbon *Decl. & F.* xxvi. (1869) II. 35 He recalled to their standard his predatory detachments. 1801 Wellington in Gurw. *Desp.* (1837) I. 367 A predatory and formidable race, the Mahrattas. 1841 Macaulay *Ess., W. Hastings* (1887) 638 The principle..is fully expressed by the old motto of one of the great predatory families of Teviotdale, 'Thou shalt want ere I want'.

† **3.** Destructive, consuming, wasteful, deleterious.

1626 Bacon *Sylva* § 299 The Evils that come of Exercise, are:..that it maketh the Spirits more hot and predatory. *Ibid.* § 318 The cause is, for that all exclusion of open air (which is ever predatory) maintaineth the body in his first freshness and moisture. 1686 Plot *Staffordsh.* 32 Some sorts of it [air] being as predatory and wastful of the body, as others again are comfortable and refreshing. *a* 1711 Ken *Hymnotheo* Poet. Wks. 1721 III. 122 If of himself the Patient takes no Care, But runs into the Predatory Air.

4. Of an animal: That preys upon other animals; that is a beast, bird, or other creature of prey; carnivorous. Also, of its organs of capture.

1668 Wilkins *Real Char.* 165, I shall be content to suppose that those Animals which are now Prædatory were so from the beginning. 1861 G. F. Berkeley *Sportsm. W. Prairies* xi. 185 They will fly from a dog or a predatory animal. 1884 Sedgwick *Claus' Text-bk. Zool.* I. 562 The lower lip [of *Libellulidæ*] is modified to form a special predatory apparatus (the mask). *Mod.* The Cicindela is one of the *Geadephaga* or predatory land beetles.

Hence **Predatorily** (pre·dătŏrĭli) *adv.*, in a predatory manner (Webster 1847); **Pre·datoriness,** the quality of being predatory (*Cent. Dict.* 1890).

Predazzite (prĭda·tsəit). *Min.* [ad. G. *predazzit*, named 1843 f. Predazzo, in the Tyrol: see -ite ¹ 2 b.] 'A rock composed of calcite and brucite, long considered a mineral species' (Chester *Names of Minerals*).

1867 Brande & Cox *Dict. Sc.*, etc. III, *Predazzite*, a variety of Bitter Spar mixed with Brucite, which forms mountain masses at Predazzo in the Southern Tyrol. It has a granular structure, and is white with a vitreous lustre on the planes of cleavage.

† **Prede, pread,** *sb. Obs. rare.* Also 6 **preede.** [ad. L. *præda* booty, spoil.] Plunder, spoil, booty, prey.

1538 *St. Papers Hen. VIII*, III. 41 He was constreyned to leave behinde him the spoile and prede he had there takyn. 1542 Udall *Erasm. Apoph.* 186 They..conspired together of all the preade & bootie that thei should geat not to bryng a iote into ye kynges pauilion. 1582 Stanyhurst *Æneis* I. (Arb.) 35 For we hither sayld not,..from their region with prede too gather an heardflock. *Ibid.*, etc. 139 Not a practise honest, nor a preede toe be greatlye recounted.

† **Prede, pread,** *v. Obs. rare.* Also 6 **preid.** [ad. L. *prædārī* to plunder, spoil, f. *præda*: see prec.] **a.** *trans.* To plunder, rob. **b.** *absol.* or *intr.* To seize booty, to plunder. Hence † **Preding, preading,** *vbl. sb.* and *ppl. a.*

1577 Stanyhurst *Descr. Irel.* in *Holinshed* (1587) II. 23/1 The inhabitants being dailie and hourelie molested and preided by their prolling mounteine neighbors. 1600 Holland *Livy* III. vii. 92 To..sit still without preading, in a wast and desart countrey. 1609 — *Amm. Marcell.* XIV. vi. 12 Crewes and troupes of preading brigands. 1632 — *Cyrupædia* 66 Some Chaldees..that live by preading and robbing.

Prede, ME. dial. form of Pride.

Pre-decay: see Pre- A. 2.

Predecease (prīdĭsī·s), *sb.* [f. Pre- A. 2 + Decease *sb.*, after next. Cf. F. *prédécès* (1690 in Hatz.-Darm.).] The decease or death of one person before another.

a 1765 Erskine *Inst. Law Scot.* (1773) III. ix. § 21 Upon the dissolution of a marriage by the predecease of the wife without issue. 1883 *Stubbs' Merc. Circular* 28 Nov. 1046/1 The same right..which the wife formerly had in the husband's [estate] on his predecease. 1888 Ld. Watson in *Law Rep.*, *Ho. Lords* XIII. 381 Her consent had no reference to the rights arising to her next of kin upon her own pre-decease.

Predecease (prīdĭsī·s), *v.* Also 6 præ-. [f. Pre- A. 1 + Decease *v.* Cf. F. *prédécéder* (16th c. in Hatz.-Darm.).] *trans.* To die before (some person, or, rarely, some event).

1593 Shaks. *Lucr.* 1756 If children prædecease progenitours, We are their ofspring and they none of ours. 1828 Scott *Diary* 24 May in *Lockhart*, Burke was under the strange hallucination that his son who predeceased him was a man of greater talents than himself. 1858 Gladstone *Homer* III. 32 Several of the heroes who predeceased the war. 1872 Jacox *Aspects Authorsh.* xxii. 370 How continually do the words predecease (as they say in Scotland) the author of them!

b. *intr.* or *absol.* To die first or before the other.

a 1765 Erskine *Inst. Law Scot.* (1773) III. ix. § 21 Where the husband predeceases, neither widow nor children can claim a right in any part of the heirship moveables.

Hence **Predecea·sed** *ppl. a.*, previously or formerly deceased; **Predecea·ser,** one who dies before another.

1599 Shaks. *Hen. V*, v. i. 76 Will you mocke at an ancient Tradition began vppon an honourable respect, and worne as a memorable Trophee of predeceased valor? 1880 Muirhead *Gaius* Digest 506 The prætors admitted the survivor of husband or wife to *bonorum possessio ab intestato* of the predeceaser, next after cognates. *Ibid.* 520 He or she might take..the usufruct..of a third part of the predeceaser's estate.

† **Predece·ss,** *v. Obs. nonce-wd.* [Back-formation from Predecessor.] *trans.* To precede, be the predecessor of.

1747 H. Walpole *Lett.* (1846) II. 192 Lord John Sackville predecessed me here.

Predecession (prīdĭse·ʃən). *rare.* [n. of action f. stem of Predecess-or; cf. med.L. *prædēcessiōn-em* (Du Cange).] The action or condition of preceding in any position; the being a predecessor.

1647 Ward *Simp. Cobler* 51 Progenitors have had them for four and twenty predecessions. 1855 Ht. Martineau *Autobiog.* (1877) III. 255 How much Judaism owes to Egyptian predecession.

† **Predece·ssive,** *a. Obs. rare*⁻¹. [f. as prec. + -ive.] That has gone before; preceding.

1599 Massinger, etc. *Old Law* I. i, Our noble and wise prince has hit the law That all our predecessive students Have missed, unto their shame.

Predecessor (prīdĭse·səɹ, pred-). Also 6 præ-; 5–6 predy-, predi-; 4 -ur, 5 -ar, 5–7 -our, -oure, 7 -er. [ME. *predecessour* = F. *prédécesseur* (13th c. in Hatz.-Darm.), ad. late L. *prædecessor* (Rutil. *c* 420), f. *præ*, Pre- A. + *dēcessor* one who goes away, departs, or dies, agent-n. from *dēcēdĕre* to go away, depart. Often used as the equivalent of L. *præcessor, antecessor.*]

1. One who has held (and ceased to hold) any office or position before the present holder; one who has preceded in the position.

[1292 Britton I. i. § 6 Si la fraunchise ne soit graunté par nous ou par nos predecessours.] *c* 1375 *Sc. Leg. Saints* x. (*Mathou*) 326 Of þi predecessare. *Ibid.* xxxi. (*Eugenia*) 416 Þe emperoure Oto, þat wes predecessoure Of þe gud emperoure henry. 1494 Fabyan *Chron.* VII. 464 The newe pope..whiche also lyke to his predecessour was a Frensheman. 1560 Daus tr. *Sleidane's Comm.* 307 b, My predecessours, Byshoppes of Rome. 1607 Topsell *Four-f. Beasts* (1658) 163 The Elephant..with his teeth digged up the ground and shewed her the naked body of her predecessor, intimating thereby..how unworthily she had marryed with a man, murtherer of his former wife. 1768 Gray in *Corr. w. Nicholls* (1843) 83 Next day Hinchliffe made his speech, and said not one word (though it is usual) of his predecessor. 1861 Craik *Hist. Eng. Lit.* I. 83 Eadmer's immediate predecessor in the see of St. Andrews was Turgot.

b. A thing to which another has succeeded.

1742 Young *Nt. Th.* II. 319 To-day is Yesterday return'd;.. Let it not share its predecessor's fate. 1853 Kane *Grinnell Exp.* xxix. (1856) 248 This is the first clear day..Compared with the gloomy haziness of its predecessors, it was cheering. 1883 *Pall Mall G.* 2 June Suppl., This Supplement..will be republished together with its predecessor.

2. An ancestor; a forefather.

c 1400 *Three Kings Cologne* 56 Þe kyngis citee þe wich her predecessours and þe Chaldeys of olde tyme had byseged and destruyed. 1432–50 tr. *Higden* (Rolls) II. 199 Somme women haue childer like to theyme, somme like to the fader, and somme like to their predecessores afore tyme. 1553 Eden *Treat. Newe India* (Arb.) 4 We may perceue such magnanimitie to haue ben in our predicessours. 1599 Shaks. *Hen. V*, I. ii. 248 Your Highnesse..Did claime some certaine Dukedomes, in the right Of your great Predecessor, King Edward the Third. 1656 Cowley *Verses Sev. Occas.*, *To Roy. Soc.* v, All long Errors of the Way, In which our wandring Predecessors went. 1848 R. I. Wilberforce *Doctr. Incarnation* xii. (1852) 323 Considering the vast number of ancestors which each individual had in the twenty-seventh generation, there can scarcely have been a Jewish parent in the time of David,..who was not, according to the flesh, a predecessor of our Lord.

† **3.** One who takes precedence. *Obs. rare.*

a 1400–50 *Alexander* 1723 Predicessour of princes & pere to þe sonn.

† **4.** One who goes before as a leader or guide.

1412–20 Lydg. *Chron. Troy* IV. xxxiii. (MS. Digby 230) lf. 154/1 Þat þou shalt firste be my predecessour And goo aforn depe doun in helle. *c* 1450 tr. *De Imitatione* III. lxi. 143 He [Jesus] shal be our helpe, þat is our leder & oure predecessour. 1656 tr. *Comenius' Gate Lat. Unl.* § 955 If they [Christians] knew their own priviledges, and composed themselves according to the pattern of their Predecessor.

5. *attrib.* and *Comb.*

1680 E. F. *Life Edw. II* 21 He exactly follows his Predecessor-precedent to the Life. 1683 J. Wilson in *Cloud of Witnesses* (1810) 216 That which their great doctor had yielded and their predecessor council had approven. 1723 Dr. Wharton *True Briton* No. 57 II. 498 This French Author celebrates his Predecessor Countrymen. 1858 Carlyle *Fredk. Gt.* III. v. (1872) I. 167 'The old castle of the Schellenbergs' (extinct predecessor Line).

Hence **Predece·ssoress,** † **Predece·ssrix,** a female predecessor; **Predece·ssorship,** the office of a predecessor.

1591 Percivall *Sp. Dict.*, *Decession*, a predecessorship, *decessio*. 1640 R. Baillie *Canterb. Self-convict.* 119 After the example of his glorious Father and renowned predecesrix Elizabeth. 1822 *Blackw. Mag.* XII. 657 They will find no obstruction from the melodious pages of their predecessoresses.

Predeclare (prīdĭklē·ɹ), *v. rare.* [f. Pre- A. 1 + Declare; cf. obs. F. *prédéclarer* (16th c.).] *trans.* To declare or announce beforehand.

1633 Massinger *Guardian* I. i, I do not carry An almanack in my bones, to pre-declare What weather we shall have. *a* 1711 Ken *Hymns Evang.* Poet. Wks. 1721 I. 77 For God Incarnate shalt [thou] the Way prepare, His wonderful Salvation pre-declare. 1855 Milman *Lat. Chr.* XIV. x. (1864) IX. 355 It is believed by few that the Priest..has the power of irrevocably predeclaring the doom of his fellow men.

Predecree (prīdĭkrī·), *sb. rare.* [Pre- A. 2.] A decree pronounced beforehand.

1831 Lytton *Godolphin* xxvii, Of all supernatural belief, that of being compelled by a predecree,..seems the most fraught at once with abasement and with horror. 1832 — *Eugene A.* III. vi, The invisible and giant hand..at whose pre-decree we hold the dark boons of life and death.

Predecree, v. rare. Also 7 pre-. [f. PRE- A. 1.] trans. To decree beforehand; to foreordain.

Pre-dedicate, -dedication: see PRE- A. 1, 2.

Predefine (prīdǐfəi·n), v. [f. PRE- A. 1 + DEFINE v.; cf. late L. praedefinīre.] trans. To define, limit, appoint, or settle previously; to predetermine.

Hence **Pre·defined** ppl. a., **Pre·defining** vbl. sb.

Predefinition. [f. PRE- A. 1.] A predetermination (in quot. 1847 = PREDESIGNATE 2 b). Hence **Predefinite** (prī-), predetermination.

Predeliberate (prī-), v. rare. [f. PRE- A. 1 + DELIBERATE v.; cf. obs. F. prédélibérer (16th c. in Godef.).] trans. To deliberate beforehand, to premeditate. Hence **Predeliberated** ppl. a., previously deliberated.

Pre·deliberation, previous deliberation.

Predelineate (prī-), v. rare. To delineate beforehand. So **Predelineation**, previous delineation.

Predella (prědě·la). [a. It. predella (predě·lla) a stool, footstool, kneeling-stool; prob. f. OHG. pret a board + -ella, dim. suffix.]

1. The step or platform upon which an altar is placed, an altar-step, foot-pace; also, a painting or sculpture upon the vertical face of this.

2. A raised shelf at the back of an altar; also (more usually) a piece of painting or sculpture on the front of such a shelf, forming an appendage to the altar-piece above it : = GRADINO.

Predesign (prīdǐzəi·n), v. rare. [f. PRE- A. 1 + DESIGN v.] trans. To design, appoint, purpose, or contrive beforehand : see DESIGN v. 7, 8, 10.

Pre·designate (-mět), v. rare. [f. PRE- A. 1.]

1. trans. To designate or specify beforehand.

2. Logic. To designate by prefixing a sign of quantity.

Predesignate (prīdě·sǐgnāt), ppl. a. [ad. L. praedēsignāt-us.] a. Designated or specified beforehand. b. Logic. Having a sign of quantity prefixed.

Predesignation (prīdēzǐgnēi·ʃən). [n. of action from pres. : see -ATION.]

1. The action of predesigning, or of predesignating; previous designation, appointment, or specification.

2. Logic. The designation by prefixing a sign of quantity to the predicate.

Predesignatory (prīdē·sǐgnətəri, -dēz-), a. [f. PREDESIGNATE v. + -ORY 2.] Having the function of predesignating; in quot. = Prefixed as a sign of quantity to a proposition (cf. prec. 2).

Predestinarian (prīdestinēə·riăn), sb. and a.
A. sb. One who believes or maintains the theological doctrine of predestination, esp. in an extreme form; a fatalist.
B. adj. Of, pertaining to, concerning, or relating to predestination; holding or maintaining the doctrine of predestination.

Hence **Predestinarianism**, the doctrine of predestinarians.

†Pre·destinate, a. Obs. rare. [f. PRE-DESTINE v. + -ATE¹, or ad. late L. praedestinātus.]

Predestinate (prīdě·stinǐt), ppl. a. and sb. [ad. L. praedestinātus, pa. pple. : see next.]

1. Theol. Foreordained by the eternal purpose or decree of God; b. to whatever destiny.

2. b. to any specified fate or lot in this life or after death; also transf.: Foreordained by divine decree. Const. to, or inf. with to.

Predestinate (prīdě·stinēit), v. [f. PRE- + L. destināre; or ad. L. praedestināre, f. PRE- + destināre to make fast, establish, determine, appoint.]

1. Theol. To foreordain by a divine decree or purpose.

Predestinately, adv. [f. PREDESTINATE ppl. a. + -LY².] In a 'predestinate' manner; by predestination.

Predestination (prīˌdestinēi·ʃən). [ad. L. praedestinātiōn-em.]

Predestinative (prīdě·stinātiv), a. rare.

Predestinator (prīdě·stinēitəʳ). [agent-n. in L. form f. PREDESTINATE v.: or + -OR 2.]

Predestine (prīdě·stin), v. [a. F. prédestiner (12th c. in Hatz.-Darm.), or ad. L. praedestināre : see PREDESTINATE v.]

Predial (prī·diăl), a. (sb.) Also 7 – praedial. [ad. med.L. praediālis, f. L. praedium estate, manor : see -AL.] So F. prédial (16th c.).

Predicable (pre·dikăb'l), a. and sb. [a. F. prédicable adj. and sb. (1581 in Hatz.-Darm.), or ad. L. praedicābile; in med.L. that may be affirmed, predicable, neut. praedicābile, pl. -bilia, as sb.]
A. adj. That may be predicated or affirmed; capable of being asserted.
B. sb. In Aristotelian Logic : One of the classes or kinds of predicates.

Predicament (prīdi·kăment). [a. F. prédicament, or ad. late L. praedicāmentum.]

Predicamental (prīˌdikămental), a. Also 7 pre-. [f. prec. + -AL.] Of or pertaining to a predicament, or the predicaments.

Hence **Predicamentally** adv.

Predicant (pre·dikănt), a. and sb. Also 6-7 pre-. [ad. L. praedicans, -āntem, pres. pple. of praedicāre to cry in public, proclaim, in late L. preach.]

Predicate (pre·dikēit), v. Also 7 pres. pple. **predicating**. [f. L. praedicāt-, ppl. stem of praedicāre to cry in public, proclaim, declare, in late L. preach.]

Predication (predikēi·ʃən). Also 6-7 pre-. [ME. a. OF. predicacion (12th c. in Hatz.-Darm.), mod.F. prédication (13th c.) :— L. praedicātiōn-em.]

(Dictionary columns — headwords include:) **Predicate**, **Predicative**, **Predicator**, **Predicatory**, **Predicable**, **Predicability**, **Predicant**, **Predicted**, **Prediction**, **Predicatory**, **Predicament**, **Predicature**, **Predicant** (Predikant), **Predict**, **Predictable**, **Predictive**, **Predictor**, **Prediction**, **Predictory**, **Predilation**, **Prediluvial**, **Prediluvian**, **Prediluvian**, **Predirect**, **Prediscover**, **Predispose**, **Predisposed**, **Predisposition**, **Predistinguish**, **Predivination**, **Predominance**, **Predominant**, **Predominantly**.

(Dictionary columns — headwords include:) **Predominate**, **Predominance**, **Predominating**, **Predominatingly**, **Predomination**, **Predominator**, **Predomine**, **Predominion**, **Predominy**, **Predominium**, **Predominize**, **Predoom**, **Predoominable**, **Predoominate**, **Predoominating**, **Predoominatingly**, **Predoominator**, **Predorsal**, **Predy**, **Pre-election**, **Pre-elect**, **Pre-electing**, **Pre-election**, **Pre-elemental**, **Pre-elementation**, **Preem**, **Pre-dy**, **Preen**, **Freem**, **Pre-eminence**, **Pre-eminent**, **Pre-eminently**, **Pre-emption**, **Pre-emptive**, **Pre-emptor**, **Preen**.

PREEN.

b. *fig.* As type of a thing of small value.

[Dense dictionary entries for **Preen** sb., **Preen** v.1, **Preen** v.2 — column text illegible at this resolution.]

Pre-engage, v.

trans. To bind in advance by a pledge or promise; to put under obligation beforehand.

[Entries for **Pre-engaged**, **Pre-engagement**, **Pre-establish**, **Pre-establishment**, **Pre-estimate**, **Pre-eternity**, **Preue**, **Pre-examine**, **Pre-examination**, **Pre-excel**, **Pre-excellence**, **Pre-excellent**, **Pre-exist**, **Pre-existence**, **Pre-existent** — illegible.]

PRE-EXISTENCIST.

[Entries for **Pre-existiary**, **Pre-existimation**, **Pre-existing**, **Pre-exposition**, **Preface** — illegible.]

PREFECT.

[Entries for **Preface** v., **Prefaced**, **Prefacer**, **Prefacial**, **Prefacing**, **Pre-famous**, **Pre-fashion**, **Prefation**, **Prefator**, **Prefatorial**, **Prefatorily**, **Prefatory**, **Prefect** — illegible.]

PREFECT (cont.)

[Entries for **Prefectoral**, **Prefectorial**, **Prefectorian**, **Prefectship**, **Prefectual**, **Prefectural**, **Prefectorate**, **Prefecture**, **Prefectureship**, **Prefer** — illegible.]

PREFER.

[Entries for **Prefer** v., **Preferability**, **Preferable**, **Preferableness**, **Preferably**, **Preference**, **Preferent**, **Preferential** — illegible.]

Preferentialism. [f. PREFERENTIAL + -ISM.] The system of giving preference in the fixing of a tariff; see PREFERENCE, PREFERENTIAL b.

Preferentialist, an advocate of preference in tariff relations.

Preferentially, adv. [f. PREFERENTIAL a. + -LY².] In a preferential manner, by preference.

Preferment. [f. PREFER + -MENT.]

Preferred (prĭfōᵊrd), ppl. a. [f. PREFER + -ED¹.]

Preferrer (prĭfōᵊrᵊr).

Preferring (prĭfōᵊriŋ), vbl. sb. [f. PREFER + -ING¹.]

Prefertilization.

Prefestinate, v. Obs. rare⁻¹.

† Preferrable, -ible, a. Obs. [f. PREFER-ABLE.]

Prefiguration. [ad. late L. praefigūrātiōn-em.]

Prefigurative, a.

Prefiguratively, adv.

Prefigure (prĭfī·gᵊr), v. [ad. L. praefigūrāre.]

Prefigured, ppl. a.

Prefiguring, ppl. adj.

Prefigurement. [f. prec. + -MENT.]

† Prefine, prefyne, sb. Law. Obs.

Prefine, v. [ad. L. praefīnīre (Cic.)]

† Prefinite, ppl. a. [ad. L. praefīnīt-us.]

Prefinition. [ad. L. praefīnītiōn-em.]

Prefix (prīfiks), sb. [ad. mod.L. praefixum.]

Prefix (prĭfi·ks), v. [ad. L. praefīg-ĕre.]

† Prefixed, ppl. a.

Prefixion (prĭfi·kʃᵊn). [ad. L. praefixiōn-em.]

Preform (prĭfō·ᵊm), v. [a. OF. preformer, ad. L. praefōrmāre.]

Prefixure. [f. PREFIX sb. + -URE.]

Prefixal (prĭfi·ksᵊl), a.

Prefixation.

Prefoliation. Bot. [f. PRE- 1. and FOLIATION.]

† Prefoliation, n. of action. Obs.

Prefool, Preforeceps = PRE- 1. and praefoemina(e). [as prec. + -ED¹.]

Preform, v. [ad. L. praefōrmant-em.]

Preformant.

† Prefract, a. Obs. [ad. L. praefrāctus.]

Preformation. [f. PRE- 1. + FORMATION.]

Preformationism. So **Preformist** = PREFORMATIONIST.

Preformationist, the doctrine or theory of preformation (sec 2.)

Preformative (prĭfō·ᵊmᵊtiv), a. (sb.)

Preformism. Biol. [f. PREFORM v. + -ISM.]

Prefrontal (prĭfrᵊntᵊl), a. (sb.)

Prefrontals = PRE- 1. and FRONTALS.

Pre-genial (prĭdʒī·nial), a.

Preglacial (prĭglē·ʃial), a.

Pregnable (pre·gnᵊbᵊl), a.

Pregnance, n. of action. Obs.

Pregnancy (pre·gnᵊnsi). [f. PREGNANT a.² + -ANCY.]

Pregnant (pre·gnᵊnt), a.¹ [a. OF. preignant.]

Pregnant, a.² [ad. L. praegnant-em.]

Pregnantly, adv.¹ [f. PREGNANT a.¹ + -LY².]

Pregnantly, adv.² [f. PREGNANT a.² + -LY².]

Pregnate, v. [f. L. praegnāt-, ppl. stem of praegnāre.]

Pregnation. [f. as PREGNATE + -ION.] = PREGNANCY.

† Pregna·tress. *Obs. rare⁻¹.* [f. as fem. of L. *pregnātor* (not found) + -ESS¹.] A (feminine) agent or power that generates or brings to birth.

Pregna·vate, obs. form of PREGRAVATE.

Pre·grand, *pregra·nd, a. Obs. rare⁻¹.* [ad. L. *prægrand-is* very large: see PRE- A. 6 and GRAND 2.] Extraordinarily large.

† Pre·gravate, *v. Obs. rare.* Also *præ-* [f. præ, PRE- A. 5 + *gravāre* to weigh down, f. *gravis* heavy.] *trans.* To weigh down, overweight.

Pre·gravate, *v. Obs. rare.* Also *præ-* [f. præ, PRE- A. 5 + *gravāre* to weigh down, f. *gravis* heavy.]

† Pregrava·tion. *Obs. rare.* [n. of action f. prec.]

Pre·gravitate, *v.* To gravitate more (than something else).

† Progre·dience. *Obs. rare⁻¹.* [ad. L. type *prægrediēntia*, f. *prægredi* to go before or in front.] A going before or in front.

† Progre·ss. *Obs.* [ad. L. *prægressus*, n. of action f. *prægredi*: see prec.] Going before, antecedence, precedence.

Pregu·st, *v. Obs. rare⁻¹.* [ad. L. *præzustāre*.] *trans.* To taste before.

Pre·gustant. *Obs.*

† Pregusta·tion. *Obs.* [n. of action f. L. *prægustāre* (Godef.).] A tasting before, a foretaste.

Pregusta·tor. *Obs.*

† Pregu·station. *Obs.*

‡ Prehallux, *præ-* (prīhæ·lʌks), *sb. Anat.* and *Zool.* [mod.L., f. præ, PRE- B. 3 + HALLUX.] A first or additional digit on the inner side of the tarsus of certain Mammalia, Reptilia, and Batrachia, and supposed to represent an additional digit.

Prehallu·ces, pl. of PREHALLUX.

Prehaminea·ceæ, *-ent,* obs. ff. PRE-EMINENCE.

Pre·hend, *v. Obs. rare.* [ad. L. *prehendĕre* to grasp, seize, catch, for earlier *prehendĕre* (Thurn). f. præ, PRE- + *handĕre*, cognate with Gr. *χανδ-άνειν* to hold. Sometimes perh. aphetic f. APPREHEND.] *trans.* To seize, catch, apprehend.

Prehe·nsible, *a. rare.* [f. L. *prehens-,* ppl. stem of *prehendĕre* (see PREHEND) + -IBLE. So F. *préhensible.*] Capable of being grasped.

Prehe·nsile, (prīhe·nsil), *a. Chiefly Zool.* [f. L. *prehens-* (buffon), f. as prec. + -ILE. -ILE.] Capable of prehension; having the capacity of gra-ping or laying hold of anything.

Prehe·nsion. *Obs. rare.* [ad. L. *prehensiōn-em* seizing, apprehending, n. of action f. *prehendĕre* (see PREHEND). So F. *préhension* (1400 in Godef.).] 1. The action of taking hold (physically); grasp, seizing. Chiefly *Zool.*

Prehe·nsive, (prīhe·nsiv), *a. rare.* [f. L. *prehens-,* ppl. stem of *prehendĕre* (see PREHEND) + -IVE.] Capable of seizing or laying hold; PREHENSILE. Hence **Prehe·nsiveness.**

Prehe·nsor. *rare.* [as prec. + -OR 2.] One who that which lays hold of anything.

Prehe·nsory, *a. rare.*

† Prehensu·rient, *a. Obs.* [see -URIENT.]

Prehe·nsorium. *Zool.* [mod.L., f. *prehensor*, see -ORIUM.] An apparatus or arrangement of parts adapted for prehension; *spec.* applied to a formation of the legs in spiders and insects.

Prehe·nsory, (prīhe·nsəri), *a. rare.* See *prec.* + -ORY 2.

Pre-ima·gine, (prīimæ·dʒin), *v.* [f. PRE- A. 1 + IMAGINE; cf. med.L. *præimāginārī* (1132 in Du Cange).] *trans.* To imagine beforehand; in quot. a 1651, to preconceive, presuppose.

So **Pre-ima·gination.** Also **† Pre-ima·ginate.**

† Pre-ina·nimate, *v. Obs. rare.* [PRE- A. 1.] *trans.* To 'inanimate', vivify, or inspire beforehand.

Pre-inca·rnate, *a.* [PRE- B. 1 + INCARNATE 2.] Existing previous to the Incarnation.

Pre-inca·rnate, *v.* [f. PRE- B. 1 + INCARNATE.]

Prehisto·ric, (prīhistɒ·rik), *a.* [f. PRE- B. 1 + HISTORIC 2. So F. *préhistorique*.] Of, belonging to, or existing in the period antecedent to history, or to the first historical accounts of a people.

So **Prehisto·rian,** a prehistoric; hence **Prehisto·rically** *adv.*

Prehisto·ric, (prīhistɒ·rik), *a.* [f. PREHISTORIC + -IC.]

Prehisto·ry. [f. PREHISTORIC + -Y.]

Prehni·te, (prē·nəit, prē·nit). *Min.* [ad. G. *prehnit* (Werner 1789), f. the name of Colonel von Prehn, who brought it from the Cape of Good Hope.]

† Prei·ndicate. *Obs.*

Preincarna·tion.

Pre-indi·cate, *v.*

Pre-indesignate, (prīindesi·gnāt, -der-), *a.*

Pre-insti·nct, *rare.* [PRE- A. 2.] A previous or pre-existing instinct.

Pre-instru·ct, *v.* [PRE- A. 1.] *trans.* To instruct beforehand. So **Pre-instru·ction,** instruction in advance.

Prei·nte, obs. form of PRINT.

Pre-inte·nd, (prīinte·nd), *v.*

Pre-inte·rpret, (prīinte·rpret), *v.* [PRE- A. 1.] *trans.* To interpret beforehand. So **Pre-inter-preta·tion,** interpretation in advance.

Pre-i·ntimate, (prīi·ntimeit), *v.* [PRE- A. 1.] *trans.* To intimate beforehand; to suggest beforehand.

Pre-into·ne, (prīintō·n), *v. Eccl.* [PRE- A. 1.] *trans.* To intone the introductory part of a melody in a low voice for the officiant, who then intones it aloud.

Pretre, obs. f. PRAYER. **Preis(e,** obs. ff. PRAISE, PRICE. **Preive,** obs. f. PROVE.

Prejacent (prīdʒē·isĕnt), *a. (sb.)* [ad. L. *præjacent-em*, pr. pple. of *præjacēre* to lie in front.]

† Pre·judicacy. *Obs. rare⁻¹.* Preconceived opinion, prepossession, prejudice.

† Prejudi·cial, *a.¹ Obs.* [app. f. L. *præjudicĭum* (see PREJUDICE sb.) + -AL.] Preconceived.

Prejudica·te, *ppl. a.* [ad. L. *præjudicāt-us,* pa. pple. of *præjudicāre*: see next.]

Prejudicate, *v.* [f. L. *præjudicāt-,* ppl. stem of *præjudicāre*, f. præ, PRE- A. 1 + *jūdicāre* to judge.] 1. *trans.* To judge beforehand; to prejudge.

Prejudi·cated, *ppl. a.*, prejudiced, prejudged.

Prejudica·tely. 1275 **Prejudi·cial.**

Prejudica·tely, *adv.*

† Prejudica·ting *vbl. sb.* and *ppl. a.*, prejudging, prejudicating.

† Prejudica·tion. *Obs.*

Prejudi·cative, *a.*

Prejudica·tor.

Prejudica·tory, *a. Obs. rare⁻¹.*

Prejudica·tion. *Obs.*

† Prejudica·tive, *a. Obs.*

Prejudica·tion. *Obs.*

Prejudi·ciator, *rare⁻¹.*

† Prejudi·catory, *a. Obs. rare⁻¹.*

Pre·judice, (pre·dʒudis), *sb.* Also 4-6 -yse, 6 (prejudysce), 5-7 prejudyce, 6 -ice, 6-7 pre-. [a. F. *préjudice* (13th c. in Littré), ad. L. *præjūdicĭum* a preceding judgement or decision, a precedent; damage, prejudice, f. præ, PRE- A. 1 + *jūdicĭum* judgement, sentence.]

† Preke. *Obs.* Also 7 preak. [Of unknown origin.] A polyp, an octopus.

Pre·late, (pre·lĕt), *sb.* Also 3-6 prelat. [a. OF. *prelat* (11-12th c.), ad. eccl. L. *prælāt-us,* sb. use of pa. pple. in med.L. as sb., a civil or ecclesiastical dignitary.] 1. An ecclesiastical dignitary of exalted rank and authority.

Prelacy, obs. f. PRELATE. **Pre·late,** *v.* **Prela·tic,** *a.* **Prela·tical,** *a.*

Prelatehood. [f. PRELATE + -HOOD.] The state of a prelate; the estate of prelates.

+ Prelatery (pre'lǝtǝri). Obs. [f. PRELATE sb. after nicety, poverty, etc.] The essential quality or essence of a prelate.

Pre'lately, a. rare. [f. PRELATE sb. + -LY.] Prelatical.

Prela'teship. The office of a prelate; the tenure of this office; also, with poss. pron., as a title (a'ter lordship).

Prelate'ss. A female prelate; an abbess or prioress.

Prelates (pre'lāts). [f. PRELATE sb. + -ESS.]

Prelatial (prǐlǣʹʃǎl), a. [f. PRELATE + -AL.] Of, pertaining to, or proper to prelacy or a prelate.

Prelatic (prǐlǣʹtǐk), a. [f. PRELATE sb. + -IC.] 1. That is a prelate; of, pertaining to, of the nature or character of, or like a prelate; prelately.

Prela'tical, a. (sb.) [as prec. + -AL.]

Prela'tically, adv.

Prela'ticalness.

Prelatie'alness.

Prela'tion (prǐlēʹʃǎn). Now rare or Obs.

Prela'tise, -ize, v.

Prela'tism. [See -ISM.] Prelacy, lordly episcopacy; adherence to this. (A hostile term.)

Pre'latist (pre'lātist). [f. PRELATE sb. + -IST.]

Prela'tize (pre'lǎtǎiz), v.

Pre'latry (pre'lǎtri). [f. as prec. + -RY.] Prelacy.

Prela'tress, a female lecturer. rare.

Prela'ture (pre'lǎtiǔr). [ad. med.L. prælātūra.]

Prelatry. Obs. = PRELACY 2.

Prelaty (pre'lǎti). [f. as prec. + -Y.]

Prelect, pre- (prǐle'kt), v. [L. prælect-.] 1. I. Utterance, pronunciation. Obs.

II. 2. The action of preferring or condition of being preferred; preferment, exaltation, promotion; pre-eminence, superiority, primacy; preference.

Prele'ct, pre- (prǐle'kt), v. 1. I. 1. trans. To choose in preference to others, lecture upon.

Prele'ction, pre- (prǐle'kʃǎn), sb. [ad. L. prælection-em.] 1. A public lecture or discourse.

+ Prela'tiah, a. Obs. rare⁻¹. Prelatical.

Prelism, a. Obs. rare⁻¹.

Prelate'ss.

+ Pre'late, sb. 1. The action of placing before.

Pre'lection, n., trans. to make the subject of prelection.

Prele'ctor, pre- (prǐle'ktǝr). [a. L. prælector.]

Prele'gal, a. Obs. rare.

Prele'ctress, a female lecturer. rare.

Prele'gate (pre'lǐgēt), v.

+ Prela'te, n. Obs. rare.

+ Prelimit (prǐlǐ'mǐt), v. 1. To limit or set bounds to beforehand.

Prelibation. Obs. [ad. L. prælibātion-em a tasting beforehand, an offering of the first-fruits.]

1. A tasting beforehand by anticipation; a foretaste. Chiefly fig.

2. The office or superiority of a prelate.

Prelimita'tion. [f. PRE- A 2 + LIMITATION.] The action of prelimiting; an instance of this.

Prelingual (prǐlǐ'ŋgwǎl), a. [f. PRE- B 1 + LINGUAL.] Antecedent to the development or acquirement of language.

Prelinpinpin, in powder of prelinpinpin: a quack medicine.

Preliography, prœli-. [f. L. prœli- battle + -(O)GRAPHY.] A description of battles.

Prelocutor. Sc. Obs. Also 7 preloquutour. [as med.L. prælocutor (L. L. prælogui to speak beforehand or before another), sometimes erron. used in med.L. prælogui.]

Preliminarily, adv. [f. next + -LY 2.] In a preliminary manner; as an introduction.

Preliminary (prǐlǐ'mǐnǎri), a. and sb. (adv.)

Prelibatory (prǐlǐ'bǝtǝri), a. and sb. Obs.

A. adj. 1. Preliminary; preparatory.

B. sb. 1. A subordinate step, measure, statement, etc., that precedes another to which it is introductory or preparatory.

Preludious (prǐlūʹdǐǎs), a. rare. [f. next + -OUS.]

Prelude (pre'liūd, prǐliūd), sb. Also 6 preludie, 6-7 prelude. [a. F. prélude (Rabelais, 1532), ad. late or med.L. prælūdium, f. præludere to prelude.]

1. Preliminary play, before the real performance.

2. A preliminary performance, action, event, or course of action, introductory to and more important than, or introductory, preface.

Prelude (prǐliūʹd), v. Also 7 præ-. [ad. L. prælūdere, or ad. F. préluder.]

Prelusion (prǐliūʹʒǎn), sb. [ad. L. prælūsion-em.]

Prelusive (prǐliūʹsǐv), a. [f. L. prælūs-.]

Prelusory (prǐliūʹsǝri), a. [f. late or med.L. prælūsorius.]

Prelusorily, adv.

Preludiously.

Russell Frozen Pirate II. viii. 146

Prematurate (prǐmæ'tiǔrēt), a.

Premature, a. [L. præmatūrus.]

Prematurely, adv.

Prematureness.

Prematurity (prē-, præmǎtiūʹrǐti). [ad. F. prématurité (16th c. in Littré).]

+ Prema'x, Obs. rare.

Premaxilla (prēmæksǐ'lǎ). Zool. [mod.L., f. PRE-B + MAXILLA, after next.]

Premaxillary, a.

Prematura'tion, Obs. rare.

Prematurate, v. Obs. rare.

Pre'max, sb.

Premea'sure, v.

+ Preme'dial, a.

Premedi'ament, Obs. rare.

Premeditate (prǐme'dǐtēt), v. [ad. L. præmeditāt-, ppl. stem of præmeditāri.]

Premeditately, adv.

Premeditation (prǐmedǐtēʹʃǎn). [ad. F. préméditation, or ad. L. præmeditation-em.]

Premeditative, a.

Premeditator.

Premeditative (prǐme'dǐtǝtǐv), a. rare.

Premeditator (prǐme'dǐtētǝr).

Pre-mention, v.

Premise (pre'mǐs, prǐmǎiz), sb. [ad. med.L. præmissa.]

Premiss.

Premit, v.

Premise (prǐmǎiz), v.

Premollition.

Premonish, v.

Premonition.

Premonitor.

Premonitory.

Premonstrant.

Premonstratensian.

Premontane, a.

Premorse, a.

Premotion.

Premise (pre'mǐs), sb.

Premial (prēʹmǐǎl), a. rare. [ad. L. præmiāl-is.]

Premiant, a.

Premiate, v.

Premiation.

Premious (prēʹmǐǎs), a. Obs. rare⁻¹. [ad. L. præmiōs-us.]

Premeditation. Premediter.

Premie (prǐmī). Also -ya. [a. obs. F. premie.]

Premiership (prǐmǐǝʃǐp, prēʹmǐǝr-). [f. PREMIER + -SHIP.] 1. The office of a premier or prime minister.

2. The state of being first in position or rank, as in a competition.

Premier (prē-, prǐmǐǝr). [a. F. premier, f. L. prīmārius.]

Premil'lenarian, a. and sb.

Premillennial (prǐmǐle'nǐǎl), a. [f. PRE- B 1 + MILLENNIAL.]

Premillennialism.

Premillennialist.

Premillennially, adv.

Premillennian, a.

Premiate.

Premium (prīʹmǐǎm). [ad. L. præmium.]

Premonish.

Premire, obs. form of PREMUNIRE.

Prem'iour. [a. AF. premiour.]

Premium.

Premisal (prī́mǎizǎl). *?Obs.* [f. PREMISE *v.* + -AL.] The action of premising; the making of a prefatory or introductory statement; stating (of something) as a premiss.

Premise, premiss (pre′mis), *sb.* [a. F. *premisse*, later *prémisse* (14th c.), also obs. and less usual *premisse* (a foregoing), a setting before' Cotgr.), ad. med.L. *præmissa* (*propositio*, *sententia*), in Logic, a proposition set in front, a premiss, fem. of proposition *præmiss-us*, pa. pple. of L. *præmittĕre* to send before: see PREMISE *v.*]

Premise (prī́maiz), *v.* [f. PREMISE *sb.*, or ad. L. *præmittĕre*, f. *præ-* + *mittĕre* to send: see *set* before, f. *præ*, PRE- A 1 + *mittĕre* to send.]

Premiss (pre′mis), *sb.* = PREMISE *sb.*

Premium (prī́miŏm), *sb.* Pl. **-iums**, formerly also **-ia**. [L. *præmium* booty, profit, advantage, reward, f. *præ*, PRE- A 1 + *eməre* to buy, orig. to take.]

Premolar (prī́mōu′lǎr), *a.* and *sb.* [PRE- B 1 + MOLAR. Cf. F. *pré-molaire*.]

Premonish (prī́mɔ′niʃ), *v.* Now *rare*. [f. *præmonĕre* to forewarn.]

Premonition (prēmŏni′ʃən), *sb.* Now *rare*. [ad. obs. F. *premonition*, ad. L. *præmonition-em.*]

Premonitive (prī́mɔ′nitiv), *a.* *rare*. [f. *præmonit-*, ppl. stem of *præmonēre.*]

Premonitor (prī́mɔ′nitər). [a. late L. *præmonitor* forewarner: see PREMONISH.]

Premonitory (prī́mɔ′nitəri), *a.* and *sb.* [ad. late L. *præmonitori-us.*]

Premonstrant (prī́mɔ′nstrǎnt), *sb.* and *a.* [ad. mod.L. *præmonstrant-em.*] = PREMONSTRATENSIAN.

Premonstratensis, *sb.* = PREMONSTRATENSIAN.

Premonstrate, *ppl. a.* *Obs. rare*. [ad. L. *præmonstrat-us*, pa. pple. of *præmonstrāre.*] Foreshown.

Premonstrate, *v.* *Obs.* [f. ppl. stem of L. *præmonstrāre* to show beforehand, f. *præ*, PRE- A 1 + *monstrāre* to show.]

Premonstration, *sb.* *Obs.* [ad. L. *præmonstration-em.*]

Premonstratensian, *sb.* and *a.* [med.L. *Præmonstrātensis* (see next) + -AN.] A member of the Roman Catholic order of regular canons founded by St. Norbert at Prémontré, near Laon, Île de France, in 1119.

Premonstration (prēmɔnstrē′ʃən). [ad. late L. *præmonstration-em*, n. of action f. *præmonstrāre*: see PREMONSTRATE *v.*] The action of premonstrating or showing beforehand; a showing forth, making known, indication, or manifestation beforehand.

Premonstra-tor *rare*. [a. L. *præmonstrator* agent-n. f. *præmonstrāre*: see PREMONSTRATE *v.*] One who or that which shows forth beforehand.

Premonstrate (prī́mɔ′nstreit), *v.* *Obs.*

Pre-mortem, *a.* [a. L. *præ mortem* before death: opposed to *post-mortem*.]

Premortise, *v. trans.*

Premote, *v.* *Obs. rare.* = PROMOTE *v.*

Premotion (prī́mōu′ʃən). [ad. med.L. *præmotion-em*, n. of action f. late L. *præmovēre* to move (anything) beforehand: see PREMOVE.]

Premove, *v.* *Obs.* [ad. L. *præmovēre*, f. *præ*, PRE- A 1 + *movēre* to MOVE.]

Premunire (prēmiuni′ri). *Obs.* = PRÆMUNIRE.

Premultiply, *v. Math.* [PRE- B 1 d + MULTIPLY *v.*] *trans.* To multiply by (as a PREFACTOR, *q. v.*).

Premunition (prēmiuni′ʃən). *Obs. rare.* [ad. L. *præmunition-em.*]

Premunitory (prī́miu′nitəri), *a.* [f. L. *præmunīre* to fortify in front + -ORY.]

Pren, obs. form of PRINCE.

Prend, *sb.* *Obs.* [?for *?reprend*, from F. *re-prendre.*] A repaired crack.

Prend, *v.* *Obs. rare.* [ad. F. *prend-re*.] *trans.* To take.

Prender (pre′ndǎr). *Law.* [sb. use of F. *prendre*, inf., to take.] The power or right of taking without its being offered.

Prene, obs. form of PREEN.

Prenegard. *Obs.* The F. phrase *prenez garde*, take care.

Pre-nephritic: see PRE- B 1. **Prengte, Prenk**: *see* PRANK, PRINK.

Prenoble, *v.* *Obs.* [PRE- A 4 + NOBLE *a.*] Pre-eminently noble. So † Pre-noble *a.* *Obs.*, *trans.* to ennoble pre-eminently.

Prenomen: *see* PRÆNOMEN.

Prenominal (prī́nɔ′minǎl), *a.* [f. L. *prænōmin-*, stem of PRÆNOMEN + -AL: cf. NOMINAL.]

Prenominate (prī́nɔ′mineit), *v.* *Obs.* [f. late L. *prænominat-*, ppl. stem of *prænomināre.*]

Prenotion (prī́nōu′ʃən), *sb.* Now *rare*. [ad. L. *prænotion-em* a previous notion, preconception, innate idea (Cic.), transl. Gr. πρόληψις of the Epicureans: see PRE- A 2 and NOTION.]

Prenotary (pre′nŏtəri). *Obs.* Forms: 5 prenotory, 6 -arie, prenygatory [etc.]

Prenote (prī́nōu′t), *v.* [ad. L. *prænotāre* to mark before, in late L. to predict: see PRE- A 1 and NOTE *v.*]

Prenotice (prī́nōu′tis), *sb.* [PRE- A 2.] Previous notice or intimation.

Prenotification (prī́nŏtifikē′ʃən), *sb.* Previous notification.

Prenotion (prī́nōu′ʃən), *sb.* [ad. late L. *prænotion-em.*]

Prenticehead. *Obs.* [f. PRENTICE *sb.* + -HEAD.]

Prentice (pre′ntis), *sb.* Now *arch.* and *dial.* [Aphetic f. APPRENTICE *sb.*]

Prenticehood. [f. as prec. + -HOOD.]

Prenticeship. Now *arch.* [f. as prec. + -SHIP.]

Prenunciation, *sb.* *Obs.* [ad. L. *prænuntiation-em.*]

Prenunciate, **-nuntiate**: *see* prec.] *Obs.*

Pre-objective, *a.* *rare*. [PRE- B 1 d.]

Pre-oblige, *v.* *Obs. rare.*

Pre-observe, v. trans. To observe beforehand.

Pre-observation. see PRE- B. 1 d.

Pre-observational a. see PRE- B. 1 d.

Preoccupancy (pri̯ǫ·kiúpănsi), sb. [f. PRE- A. 3 + OCCUPANCY.]

Preoccupant (pri̯ǫ·kiúpănt), a. and sb. [f. PRE- A. 3 + OCCUPANT.]

Preoccupate, v. Obs. [f. ppl. stem of L. præoccupāre to PREOCCUPY: see OCCUPATE v.]

Pre-occupate, a. rare⁻⁰. [ad. L. præoccupātus.]

Preoccupation (pri̯ǫ·kiúpēi·ʃən), sb. [ad. L. præoccupātiōn-em, n. of action from præoccupāre.]

Preoccupied, ppl. a. [f. next + -ED¹.]

Preoccupy (pri̯ǫ·kiúpəi), v. [f. PRE- A. 1 + OCCUPY.]

Preocular (pri̯ǫ·kiúlǎɹ), a. (sb.) Also præ-.

Pre-oesophageal, a. Obs. rare.

Pre-ominate, v. Obs. rare.

Preomnostomy, -omosternal. see PRE- A. 4.

Pre-operate, v. rare.

Pre-operation. rare.

Pre-operculum. Also -ule. Anglicized form of PRE-OPERCULUM.

Pre-opercular, præ-.

Pre-operculum, præ- (pri̯ǫ·pɜ·ɹkiúlǝm), sb.

Pre-option (pri̯ǫ·pʃǝn).

Pre-oral, præ- (pri̯ǫ·rǎl), a. [f. PRE- B. 3 + ORAL, f. L. ōs, ōr- mouth.]

Pre-ordain (pri̯ǫdēi·n), v. [f. PRE- A. 1 + ORDAIN v.]

Pre-ordinance, [f. PRE- B. 1 + ORDINANCE.]

Pre-ordination (Hilary c 350), F. préordination.

Pre-orbital (pri̯ǫ·ɹbitǎl), a. (sb.) Anat. and Zool.

Preordinate, ppl. a. Obs.

Pre-ordinate, v. Obs.

Pre-order, v. [f. PRE- A. 1.]

Pre-organic, a.

Pre-ornate, v. Obs. rare.

Prep. Short for PREPARATION (sense 1 c).

Prepaid: see PREPAY.

Prepalaeolithic (præ·pǝli·ǫl·pǝk), a. Anthropol.

Preparable (pre·pǎrǎb'l), a. rare. [f. PREPARE + -ABLE.]

Preparate, ppl. a. Obs. [ad. L. præparātus.]

Preparation (pre·pǎrēi·ʃǝn), sb. [a. F. préparation (13th–14th c. in Hatz.-Darm.), ad. L. præparātiōn-em, n. of action f. præparāre to PREPARE.]

Preparative (pri̯pæ·rǎtiv), a. and sb. [ME. preparatif, a. F. préparatif, -ive adj., -ive sb., ad. med.L. præparātīvus (in libertus Magnus (a 1255) and Aquinas): see PREPARE and -ATIVE.]

Preparatively (pri̯pæ·rǎtivli), adv. [f. next + -LY².]

Preparator (pre·pǎrēi·tǝɹ), rare. [a. late L. præparātor, agent-n. f. præparāre to PREPARE.]

Preparatorily (pri̯pæ·rǎtǝrili), adv. [f. next + -LY².]

Preparatory (pri̯pæ·rǎtǝri), a. and sb. [ad. med.L. præparātōrius (Digest), f. præparātor a preparer.]

Prepare (pri̯pɛǝ·ɹ), v. [a. F. préparer (14th c. in Hatz.-Darm.), ad. L. præparāre, f. præ- PRE- + parāre to make ready.]

Preparedness (pri̯pɛǝ·rednes, pri̯pɛǝ·rednes), [f. prec. + -NESS.]

Preparement, Obs. rare. [f. PREPARE v. + -MENT.]

Preparer (pri̯pɛǝ·rǝɹ). [f. as prec. + -ER¹.]

Prepare, v.

Preparing, ppl. a. [f. as prec. + -ING².]

Prepay (pri̯pēi·), v. [f. PRE- A. 1 + PAY v.]

Prepaid, ppl. a.

Prepayment (pri̯pēi·mǝnt), [f. PREPAY + -MENT.]

Prepense (pri̯pe·ns), a., adv. [Substituted for earlier prepensed, PREPENSED, OF. purpensé, pourpensé.]

Pre·per·ception. [PRE- A. 2.] Previous perception.

Preper·ceptive a., characterized by preperception.

Prepeteneal rare. see PRE- B. 3.

Pre·petition. [PRE- A. 2.] Petition beforehand, previous petition.

Prepi·gmental, pituitary see [PRE- B. 1.]

Pre·pious see PRE- A. 6. **Pre-placental** see [PRE- B. 1.]

Prepla·cental, -plot see [PRE- B. 1.]

Prepo·llence. Now rare or Obs. [f. as prec.: see PREPOLLENT.] The quality or fact of being prepollent.

Prepo·llency. Now rare or Obs. [f. as prec.: see -ENCY.] The quality or fact of being prepollent; greater prevalence.

Prepo·llent a. Now rare. [ad. L. præpollent-em, pr. pple. of præpollēre.] Having superior power, weight, or influence; predominating, prevailing.

Pre·polex, pre-. Anat. and Zool. [mod. L. f. pre, PRE- 3 + POLLEX.] A rudimentary structure, sometimes osseous, similar to the prehallux, found in certain animals on the radial border of the hand or fore-foot, and supposed to represent an additional digit.

Prepo·nd, v. Short for next or preponderate.

Prepo·ndance, adv. In the Institutions in, vii, no He..preponderch the gyrer before all thynges gyuen.

Prepo·nderance. [ad. L. type, etc.]

Prepo·nderancy. [f. as prec.: see -ANCY.] The quality or fact of being preponderant; an instance of this.

1. Superiority of physical weight.

2. Superiority in number or amount.

3. Superiority of power, influence, or importance.

Prepo·nderant a. [ad. L. præponderant-em, pr. pple. of præponderāre.] a. Surpassing in weight; outweighing, heavier. b. Surpassing in influence, power, or importance; predominant.

Hence **Prepo·nderantly** adv.

Prepo·nderate, v. [f. L. præponderāt-, ppl. stem of præponderāre.]

I. Intransitive senses.

1. To weigh more ; to be heavier; to incline the balance; to turn the scale.

b. fig. To have the greater moral or intellectual weight.

2. To descend or incline downwards, as on a scale or end of a balance, on account of greater weight; to weigh or be weighed down; to show a preponderance. Also fig.

II. Transitive senses.

3. To weigh more than, exceed in weight; to turn the scale when weighed against (something else); to outweigh. Obs.

b. fig. To outweigh in importance, value, or influence. Obs.

Prepo·nderating ppl. a. [PREPONDERATE v.] That preponderates, is superior in weight, influence, power, amount, number, etc.

Hence **Prepo·nderatingly** adv., in a preponderating or surpassing degree; predominantly.

Prepondera·tion. Now rare or Obs. [n. of action l. L. præponderation-em.]

1. The action or fact of preponderating or exceeding in weight; preponderance.

2. To gravitate or incline more strongly. rare.

Prepo·nderous, a. [f. PREPONDER, etc.: see prec.] Preponderant, outweighing.

Prepo·nderous a., PREPONDERATE, etc.] Exceeding in weight, amount, or number; having the preponderance.

Preposi·tion (prepæ·ziŋ), sb. [ad. L. præposition-em a putting before, a preposition, n. of action from præpōnere to put before: see PREPONE, -SITION.]

Preposi·tional, a. [f. prec. + -AL.] pertaining to, or proper to a preposition.

Preposi·tionally, adv. [f. prec. + -LY².] In a prepositional manner; with the force or meaning of a preposition.

Prepo·sitive (prepǫ·zĭtĭv), a. (sb.) [ad. late L. præpositīvus (Diomedes) that is set before (in gramm.), f. ppl. stem of præpōnere to put before: see -IVE. cf. F. prépositif (14th c. in Hatz.-Darm.).]

Proper to be placed before or prefixed.

Preposi·ture. The office of a præpositus or provost of a collegiate church or priory.

Prepossess, v. [f. PRE- A. 1 + POSSESS v.]

1. trans. To take or get possession of beforehand, or before another; to have prior possession of. Now rare.

b. refl. with of or with? To possess oneself of beforehand; to take for oneself or make one's own beforehand; also in pass. to be prepossessed. Obs.

2. To possess (a person) beforehand or cause (him) to be preoccupied or pre-engaged with or by a feeling, notion, etc.; to imbue, inspire, or affect strongly beforehand. Chiefly in pass.

3. To cause (a person) to have a feeling or opinion beforehand against or in favour of a person or thing; to bias, prejudice ; now chiefly, To impress favourably beforehand. Chiefly in pass.

Prepossessing, ppl. a. [f. prec. + -ING².] That prepossesses.

Prepossession. [n. of action f. PREPOSSESS v.: see PRE- A. 2 and POSSESSION.]

1. The having or taking of possession beforehand; prior possession or occupancy. Now rare.

2. The condition of being mentally prepossessed; a preconceived opinion which tends to bias the mind; inclination or favourable antecedent opinion; prejudice, predisposition, liking.

Prepossessor. Obs. or rare. [PRE- A. 2 + POSSESSOR.] A previous possessor.

Prepost, Obs. rare. [ad. L. præpost-us, contr. f. præpositus, sb. use of pa. pple. of præpōnere to place before.] = PREPOSITUS; provost.

Prepo·stor, **Pre·postor.** The name given in some English public schools to those senior boys who are entrusted with much of the discipline of the school, esp. out of the class-room; now usually PREPOSTOR, q.v. Also ag. and in fig. context.

Prepostor, variant of PRÆPOSTOR.

Prepo·sterate, v. Obs. rare⁻¹. [f. ppl. stem of L. præposterāre PREPOSTEROUS.] To reverse, thwart, [f. præpostor-us PREPOSTEROUS (Cotgr.).]

To make (preposterous); to reverse, invert; to overturn; to pervert.

Prepo·sterize, v. [f. PRE- + POSTERIZE.]

Prepo·sterous, a. [ad. L. præposter-us, reversed, perverted, absurd (f. præ before + poster-us coming after, following) + -OUS. Cf. obs. F. prépostère (Cotgr.).]

1. Having or placing last that which should be first : inverted in position or order. Now rare.

2. Contrary to the order of nature, or to reason or common sense ; monstrous ; irrational, perverse, foolish, nonsensical ; in later use, utterly absurd.

Prepo·sterously, adv. [f. prec. + -LY².] In a preposterous order or manner.

1. In an inverted or reversed order or position ; with the latter part before the former ; hind-side before. Now rare.

2. Contrary to the order of nature, to reason or common sense ; irrationally, absurdly.

Prepo·sterousness. [f. as prec. + -NESS.] The quality of being preposterous; perversity ; unreasonableness; absurdity.

Prepo·tence (prepǫ·tĕns), a. [ad. F. prépotence, ad. L. præpotentia.]

1. Superior power or influence ; predominance, prevalence.

2. Biol. The quality or state of being prepotent.

Prepotency (prepǫ·tĕnsĭ), [ad. L. præpotentia.] = PREPOTENCE and -ENCY.]

1. The quality of being prepotent; superior power or influence ; predominance, prevalence.

2. Biol. The greater power of transmitting hereditary features or qualities; having a stronger fertilizing influence.

Prepo·tent (prepǫ·tĕnt), a. [ad. L. præpotent-em, pr. pple. of præpos+e to be more or very powerful, to have the superiority.]

1. Having greater power, force, influence, or authority ; pre-eminent.

2. Biol. Having power of transmitting to offspring one's own hereditary characters in preponderating degree.

Prepu·beral, **-pubertal,** a. [PRE- B. 1.]

Prepu·bic, pre- a. [PRE- B. 1.] Pertaining to the prepubis, Situated in front of the pubis.

Prepu·bis, pre- a. [PRE- B. 1.] The pre-acetabular portion of the pubis, in Ornithopoda and Dinosauria.

Prepuce (prīpiūs). Anat. [a. F. prépuce (13th c. in Godef.), ad. L. præpūtium, of unknown origin.]

Prepubes, pre- Also -ez. [PRE- A. 1. + -puberal.]

Prepu·tial (prepiū·ʃăl), a. [f. L. præpūti-um prepuce + -AL.] Of or pertaining to the prepuce.

Pre·pyramidal, a. Anat. [PRE- B. 1.]

Prepyriform, pre- a. Anat. [PRE- B. 1.]

Prepyriform, a. [PRE- B. 1.]

Pre-Raphael (prīrăf·ăĕl), a. (sb.) [f. PRE- A. 1 + Raphael, the name of the painter (1483-1520).]

Hence **Pre-Raphaelite** adj. = pre-Raphaelitism.

Pre-Raphaelism, *prera¹b-, prø-*. [f. as prec. + -ism.] The artistic principles of the Pre-Raphaelite Brotherhood; by way of distinction, to the set of the painters who preceded Raphael; see quot. 1882 s.v. Pre-Raphaelitism.

Pre-Raphaelist *stic* a = next, B.

Pre-Raphaelite, *preraphaelite, prø-* (*prī'rǣfəᵊləit, -æᵊl-*). Also *a.* Also *-Raffael-*. [f. Pre- + the proper name *Raphael* (It. *Raffaello, Raffaele*) + -ite 1.]

A. sb. 1. An artist who aims at producing work in the spirit which generally imbued art before the time of Raphael (or, more especially, before his later work and that of his successors); *spec.* one of the group of English artists, including Holman-Hunt, Millais, and D. G. Rossetti, who *c*1848 called themselves the 'Pre-Raphaelite Brotherhood' (P. R. B.).

2. One of the painters who preceded Raphael.

B. adj. (or attrib. use of sb.)

1. Of, belonging to, or characteristic of the Pre-Raphaelites, or their principles and style.

Pre-Raphaelitic, *preraph-, prø-* (-¹t¹k), *a.* In these pre-Raphaelite productions.

Pre-Raphaelitism, *preraph-, prø-* (-oᵊtī¹), *a.* rare. [f. as prec. + -ism.] Resembling the work of the Pre-Raphaelites.

Preremote, -renal, etc.: see Pre- B. 1, 3, etc.

Prerept, *v.* Obs. rare. [f. L. *præcept-, ppl.* stem of *præripere* to snatch away in front of another.]

Prereption. Obs. rare. In 7 *præ-*. [f. action from L. *præripĕre, prærept-*.]

Prerogative (*prĭro̅'gătĭv*), *sb.* (and *a.*) [Pre- A. 1.]

Prerequire (-kwoi·r), *v.* Also 7 *præ-* [Pre- A. 1.]

Prerequired *ppl. a.*, previously required.

Prerequisite (-kwizit), *a.* and *sb.* [Pre- A. 2 + Requisite *a.* and *sb.*]

Prerequisition. Obs. rare. [Pre- A. 1.] Requisition beforehand, previous requirement.

Pre-resolve, *v.* Now rare. Also 7 *præ-*. [Pre- A. 1.] *a. ppl. aptle*. Previously resolved; *b. intr.* To resolve beforehand.

Prerogative (-tᵊv), *a.* rare. [f. prec.]

Prerogatively, *adv.* rare. [f. Prerogative *a.* + -ly².]

Prerogative (*continued*)

Prerogative writ. A writ issued on extraordinary occasions in the exercise of the royal prerogative: see quots.

Prerogatived (*prĭro̅'gătĭvd*), *ppl. a.* [f. as prec. + -ed.] Enlowed with or possessed of a prerogative.

Prerogative-monger, motion, party.

Prerupt, *ppl. a.* Obs. rare. [ad. L. *præruptus* broken or torn off.]

Prerupted *ppl. a.* rare.

Presa (*prē'za*). *Mus.* [It., = a taking, from *presa, pp. ppte. fem.*] (See quot. 1898.)

Presage (*pre'sᵊdʒ, prĭ-*; formerly *prĭsē'dʒ*), *sb.* [a. F. *présage, ad. L. præsāgium* a foreboding.]

1. Something that portents, foreshows, or gives warning of that which is about to happen; an indication of a future event; an omen, sign, portent.

2. Of, pertaining to, or arising from prerogative or special privilege; held, enjoyed, or exercised by exclusive prerogative or privilege; privileged.

4. Short for Prerogative court: see 6.

5. *attrib.* and *Comb.*, as *prerogative-monger, motion, party;* prerogative case, a cause within the jurisdiction of the prerogative court; prerogative copy, a book of which the copyright is a prerogative of the crown; prerogative lawyer, a lawyer retained in behalf of the royal prerogative; prerogative man, an advocate or supporter of prerogative; prerogative office = prerogative court: see 6.

6. Having precedence or priority; having the right to lead, leading; *spec.* in *prerogative-, etc.*

Presageful, *a.* Obs. rare. [f. Presage *sb.*]

Presagient, *a.* Obs. rare. Also *præ-*. [ad. L. *præsāgiens*, pres. pple. of *præsāgīre* to presage: see Presage *v.*]

Presaging, *vbl. sb.* [-ing¹.]

Presaging, *ppl. a.* [-ing¹.]

Presagingly, *adv.* In a presaging manner.

Presagious, *a.* Obs. [f. L. *præsāgium* Presage + -ous.]

Presagition. Obs. rare. [f. L. *præsāgītiōn-em*.]

Presagement. [f. Presage *v.* + -ment.]

Presbyope (*pre'sbiøoʊp*), *prez-*). *rare⁻⁰*. [f. Gr. πρεσβυ- old + ωψ, ωπ- eye.] A person affected with presbyopia.

Presbyopia (*pres-, prezbiøo̅'pia*). Rarely in anglicized form **presbyopy**.

Presbyopic (*pres-, prezbio̅'pik*), *a.*

Presbyopy (*prĭzbī'øpi*), *vbl. sb.* [-ing¹.]

Presbyte (*pre's-, prez-*). Obs. 6 presbiter. [a. late L. *presbyter* (Tertullian), ad. Gr. πρεσβύτερος, in Y. T. the Cleargie: see either Presbyters or Deacons.]

Presbyter (*pre's-, prez-bĭtəɹ*). Also 6 presbiter. [a. late L. *presbyter* (Tertullian), ad. Gr. πρεσβύτερος.]

1. Of or pertaining to a presbyter or priest; consisting of presbyters.

Presbyteral (*prezbī'tĕral*), *a.* [ad. med.L. *presbyterālis* (755 in Du Cange): see Presbyter + -al¹.]

Presbyterate (*prezbī'tĕrat*), *sb.* [ad. Short for *presbyterate*: see next.] Constituted of presbyters or by a presbytery.

Presbyterate (-ᵊt), *v.* Also 9 -trate. [f. prec.] *trans.* To constitute or organize according to the Presbyterian system.

Presbyterial, *a.* and *sb.* [ad. med.L. *presbyterialis* (Ordo Rom. in Du Cange, etc.): see Presbyter + -al.]

Presbyterian (*pres-, prezbitēʳ'rĭən*), *a.* and *sb.* [f. late L. or eccl. L. *presbyterium* in 13th c. an almoner, Froissart).]

A. adj. 1. Pertaining to, or characterized by, government by presbyters or elders; applied to a form or system of church polity (see below).

Presbyterianism (*pres-, prezbitēʳ'rĭanĭz'm*). [f. prec. + -ism.]

Presbyterianize (*-aiz*), *v.* [f. Presbyterian + -ize.]

2. A body of presbyters; the order of presbyters.

3. Of or pertaining to presbyters or priests, or the priestly order.

B. *sb.* One who maintains the Presbyterian system of church government ; a member or adherent of a Presbyterian church.

Presbyterianize, *v.* [f. as prec. + -IZE.] *a. trans.* To make Presbyterian ; to organize according to the Presbyterian system.

Presbyterianly, *adv.* [f. as prec. + -LY 2.] In a Presbyterian manner or direction.

Presbyterianism, *rare.* [f. PRESBYTER + -ISM.] *a.* = PRESBYTERIANISM.

‖ Presbyterium, *sb.* *Eccl.* [Christian L. (Cyprian, 4250), ad. Gr. πρεσβυτέριον, -τερϊον (N.T.).] A council of elders, Jewish or Christian ; in eccl. Gr. the office of a presbyter, also the meeting-place of presbyters or elders.]

Presbytery (pre's, pre'zbĭtəri). Plu. 5 *-teries.* [See PRESBYTER.] The office of presbyter ; = PRESBYTERATE 1.

1. A part of a church, esp. of a cathedral or other large church, reserved for the clergy.

2. The office of a presbyter ; eldership or priesthood ; = PRESBYTERATE 1.

3. A body of presbyters or elders (in the early church ; also in a general sense, usually with allusion to 4.

4. In the Presbyterian system : A body or assembly of presbyters or elders, consisting of all the ministers, and one ruling elder (or sometimes two) from each parish or congregation within a particular local area, constituting the ecclesiastical court next above the kirk-session and below the synod (*see* PRESBYTERIAN *a.* 1).

‖ Prescapular (prī-skæ·piŭliə), *a.* [f. PRE- A.4 + L. *scapula* shoulder-blade.] That part of the scapula or shoulder-blade above (or in quadrupeds, anterior to) the spine or median axis. Hence **Pres·capu·lar,** *a.* placed to the spine or long axis of the shoulder-blade ; *sb.* the *prescapularis* or *supraspinatus* muscle.

Pre-scene, -scholastic: *see* PRE- A. 2, B 1 d.

Prescience (prī·ʃiĕns). [a. F. *prescience* (13th c.), ad. late L. *præscientia* (Tertull.) foreknowledge.] Knowledge of events before they happen ; foreknowledge.

Prescient (prī·ʃiĕnt), *a.* Also 2 **pre-**. [a. F. *prescient*, ad. L. *præscient-em,* pr. pple. of *præscire* to know before, f. *præ,* PRÆ- A.1 + *scīre* to know.] Having foreknowledge or foresight ; foreseeing.

Presciently (prī·ʃiĕntli), *adv.* In a prescient manner ; with prescience.

Prescind (prĭsi·nd), *v.* [ad. L. *præscind-ĕre* to cut off before.] **1.** *trans.* To write first or beforehand ; to predict in writing ; to describe beforehand. *Obs.*

‡ 2. Appointed or fixed by prescription. *Obs.*

Prescribe (prĭskrəi·b), *v.* [ad. L. *præscrīb-ĕre* to write before, f. *præ,* PRÆ- A.1 + *scrīb-ĕre* to write.]

I. *trans.* To write or lay down beforehand as a guide or rule of action ; to direct, enjoin, order, or appoint authoritatively.

II. *intr.* To make a claim by prescription ; to assert a prescriptive right or claim (*to* or *for* something ; *also with* *in, against,* *clause*).

PRESCRIBED. 1299 PRESCRIPTION. PRESCRIPTION. 1300 PRESENCE.

Prescribed (prĭskrəi·bd), *ppl. a.* [f. prec. + -ED 1.] Laid down, appointed or fixed beforehand ; ordained, appointed, set, fixed, defined.

Prescriber (prĭskrəi·bəi). [f. as prec. + -ER 1.] One who prescribes.

Prescript (prī·skript), *a.* and *sb.* [ad. L. *præscript-us,* pa. pple. of *præscrīb-ĕre* to PRESCRIBE.]

A. *adj.* That which is prescribed or appointed ; written or explicit direction or injunction.

B. *sb.* That which is prescribed or laid down ; an ordinance, law, command, precept, rule, direction, injunction.

Prescriptible (prĭskri·ptib'l), *a.* *rare.* [f. L. *præscript-* (see prec.) + -IBLE ; or F. *prescriptible.*] That may be prescribed ; derived from or founded on prescription.

Prescription (prĭskri·pʃən). [a. F. *prescription* (13th c. in Hatz.-Darm.), ad. L. *præscription-em* a writing before or in front, a title, introduction ; a preface, precept, rule ; in law, an inhibition or limitation (ppl. stem *præscript-*: *see* PRESCRIBE).]

1. The action of prescribing or appointing beforehand ; that which is prescribed or appointed ; written or explicit direction or injunction.

2. *Law.* The action or fact of prescribing ; the acquisition of a right, title, etc., by virtue of long uninterrupted use.

Prescriptive (prĭskri·ptiv), *a.* [ad. late L. *præscriptiv-us* relating to a legal exception or demurrer : *see* PRESCRIPT *sb.* and -IVE.]

1. That prescribes or directs ; giving definite, precise directions or instructions.

2. Of or pertaining to prescription ; acquired, sanctioned, or established by prescription or long-continued usage or custom.

Prescriptively (prĭskri·ptivli), *adv.* by prescription ; by recognized custom.

Presence (pre·zĕns). Also 4-6 **pre·s-**, **-one,** 5 **-ence,** 6 **-ense,** **presense,** 7 **presens.** [a. F. *presence* (11th c. in Littré) :—L. *præsentia,* f. *præsent-,* pr. pple. of *præesse* to be before : *see* PRESENT.]

1. The fact or condition of being present ; the state of being before, in front of, or in the same place with a person or thing ; being there ; attendance, company, society, association.

2. The place in front of or around a person ; the immediate vicinity of a great personage ; the presence-chamber.

3. *Presence of mind*: readiness and composure of mind in a sudden or difficult situation.

4. The bearing, carriage, air, or demeanour of a person ; mien, aspect.

Presence-chamber.

† **Pre·sency.** *Obs. rare.*

Presensation (prisen·ʃən).

Presension (prisen·ʃən).

Present (pre·zant), *a.* (*adv.*)

Present (pre·zant), *sb.*

Present (prize·nt), *v.*

Presentable (prize·ntǎb'l), *a.*

Presental (prīze·ntăl), *a.* Obs. as prec.+ -AL 1, after *Accidental,* etc.] = PRESENTAL 8.

†Presenta·neous, *a.* Obs. [f. L. *praesentāneus* operating quickly (Plin.), f. *praesent-* PRESENT *a.* + suffix *-āne-us* + -OUS.] Acting immediately or speedily; = PRESENT *a.* 9 b.

†Pre·sentary, *a.* Obs. Also 7 pre-. [ad. L. *praesentāri-us* that is at hand, ready, quick. f. *praesent-em*: see PRESENT *a.* + -ARY 1.] = PRESENT *a.* 6, 8.

Presentation (prezentēi·ʃən). [ME. a. OF. *presentation* (12th c. in Littré, mod.F. *présentation*), or ad. late L. *praesentātiōn-em,* n. of action f. *praesentāre* to PRESENT.] The action of presenting.

I. 1. The action of presenting or introducing a person: see PRESENT *v.* 1. a. The formal bringing or presenting of a person before God, as a religious act: see PRESENT *v.* 1 b.

Presentative (prīze·ntătiv), *a.* [In senses 1, 2 ad. med.L. type *praesentātīv-us*: see PRESENT *v.* and -ATIVE. In sense 3 directly f. PRESENT *v.*; cf. REPRESENTATIVE.]

Presentee (prezentī·). [a. AF. *presentee* = F. *présenté,* pa. pple. of *presenter* to PRESENT: see -EE 1.]

Presenter (prīze·ntəɪ). [f. PRESENT *v.* + -ER 1. See also PRESENTOR.] One who presents, in various senses of the verb.

Presential (prīze·nʃəl), *a.* nonce-wd., a be liever in the Real Presence: see PRESENCE 2, REAL *a.* 8.

Presentiality (prīzenʃiæ·lĭti). The condition or character of being presential.

Presentially (prīze·nʃăli), *adv.* [f. med.L. *praesentiāl-* + -LY 2.] Cf. med.L. *praesentiāliter.* In a presential manner; in the way of actual presence; as being present.

Presentialness. Now *rare* or Obs. [f. as prec. + -NESS.] The quality of being present; presentiality.

Presentiate, *v.* [irreg. f. PRESENT *a.* + -ATE 3.] *trans.* To make or render present in place or time; to cause to be perceived or realized as present.

Presentific (prīzentĭ·fik), *a.* Obs. rare. [f. L. type *praesenti-* PRESENT *a.* + *-fic(us):* see -FIC.] Making or rendering present.

Presentifically, *adv.* Obs. [f. prec. + -AL + -LY 2.]

Presenti·fy, *v.* Obs. rare. [f. L. type *praesenti-*: see -FY.] Of or pertaining to presence; having or implying actual presence with a person or in a place; present.

Presentive (prīze·ntiv), *a.* [irreg. f. PRESENT *a.* + -IVE; used for distinction from the etymologically incorrect *Presentative.*]

Presentiveness. [f. prec. + -NESS.]

Presentient (prīse·nʃiənt), *a.* [ad. L. *praesentient-em,* pr. pple. of *praesentīre* to PRESENT *v.*]

Presentiment (prīze·ntiment, prīse·n-). Also 8 presentiment. [See PRE- A. 2 and SENTIMENT.]

Presently (pre·zentli), *adv.* [f. PRESENT *a.* + -LY 2.]

Presenting (prīze·ntiŋ), *vbl. sb.* [f. PRESENT *v.* + -ING 1.] The vbl. sb. of the verb PRESENT, in its various senses. Also *attrib.*

Pre·senting, *ppl. a.* [-ING 2.] That presents, in various senses of the verb; that presents or shows itself.

Presentist (pre·zentist). [f. PRESENT *a.* + -IST.] An advocate of the present; in quot., One who believes that the prophecies of Scripture, esp. of the Apocalypse, are at present in course of fulfilment: opp. to PRETERIST and FUTURIST.

Presentment (prīze·ntment). Also 5 presentement (Cotgr.): see PRE- A. 2 and SENTIMENT.

Presentness (pre·zentnes). [f. PRESENT *a.* + -NESS.] The quality or condition of being present in place, time, or thought.

Presentor (prīze·ntəɪ). [Early mod.E. *presentour,* a. AF. *presentour* = F. *présenteur,* agent-n. f. *presenter* to PRESENT: see -OR.]

Presentoir. Obs. [In mod.French form.]

Preservative (prīzə·ɪvătiv), *a.* and *sb.* [a. F. *préservatif,* -*ive* (14th c. in Oresme).]

Preservation (prezəɪvēi·ʃən). [a. F. *préservation* (14th c. in Godef.), or ad. med.L. *praeservātiōn-em:* see PRESERVE *v.*]

Preserve (prīzə·ɪv), *v.* [a. OF. *preserver.*]

Preservatize ... against error from a pound. 1890 Allbutt's Syst. Med. VIII. 2b. (absolute use of adj.)

1. a. A medicine that preserves health, protecting from or preventing disease; a safeguard against poison or infection; a prophylactic.

Preservative, a. and sb. ...

Preservative-our, Obs. rare ...

Preserve, v. [a. F. *préserver* ...]
1. trans. To keep safe from harm or injury ...
2. trans. To keep safe from perishing ...
4. To keep (game) undisturbed for personal use in hunting, shooting, or fishing ...

Preserved (prězě·rvd), ppl. a. [f. prec. + -ED¹.]

Preserver (prězě·rvə̆r). [f. PRESERVE v. + -ER¹.]
1. A person who preserves.

Preserving (prězě·rviŋ), vbl. sb. ...
Preserving, ppl. a. ...

Preswme, obs. form of PRESUME.
Pre-shadow: see PRE- A. 2.

Preside (prězəi·d), v. Also / pre-, Sc. preceid, -ceid. [a. F. *présider* (13th c. in Littré), ad. L. *præsidēre* ...]
1. intr. To occupy the chair or seat of authority in any assembly, or at the ordinary meetings of a society or company; to act as chairman or president.

Presidence (prězi·dĕns, prě·-). [a. F. *présidence* (14th c. in Hatz.-Darm.), ad. med. L. *præsidentia*: see PRESIDENT.]

Presidency (prě·zidĕnsi, prě-). [= med. L. *præsidentia* (1165 in Bonaventura), L. *præsidens*, -ent-: see PRESIDENT and -ENCY.]

President (prě·zidĕnt, prě·-), sb. Also 4-5 presedent, 5-6 presydent ...
1. The office or function of president; presidentship, chairmanship; superintendence, direction; also, the term during which a president holds office.

Presidential, a. and sb. [f. PRESIDENT + -IAL.]

Presidentially, adv. ...

Presidentship. [See -SHIP.] The office or function of a president; the period over which this extends.

Presidency ...

Presidiary (prĕsi·diări), a. and sb. [ad. L. *præsidiārius* ...]

Presidio (prĕsi·dio, prĕsĭ·dio). [Sp., a garrison ...]

Presignification (prĕsi·gnifikēi·ʃən). Now rare. [ad. L. *præsignificātiōn-em* ...]

Presignify (prĕsi·gnifəi), v. [ad. L. *præsignificāre* ...]

Presolve (prĕsǫ·lv), v. [PRE- A. 1 + SOLVE v.]

Pre-solution. [PRE- A. 1 + SOLUTION.] A preliminary or prior solution (of a difficulty).

Presome, **Presomption**, obs. ff. PRESUME, PRESUMPTION.
Presonar, obs. form of PRISONER.
Presound, -ound, obs. ff. PROFOUND sb.²

Presphenoid (-sfīˈnoid). *Anat.* [f. PRE- A. 4 + SPHENOID.] The anterior part of the sphenoid bone of the skull, which forms a separate bone in (human) infancy. Hence **Presphenoidal** (prī:-sfinoi·dăl) *a.*, of or pertaining to the presphenoid.

1854 OWEN *Skel. & Teeth* in *Orr's Circ. Sc.* I. *Org. Nat.* 193 The basisphenoid and presphenoid form a single bone, and the chief keel of the cranial superstructure. *Ibid.* 251 The superior turbinals extend .. below into the presphenoidal sinus. 1855 HOLDEN *Hum. Osteol.* (1878) 85 The front part of the body, termed 'presphenoid', has two centres of its own. 1872 MIVART *Elem. Anat.* 83 The anterior part of the body, or pre-sphenoidal part. 1881 — *Cat* 60 The occipital, two parietals, two frontals, two temporals, the sphenoid, the presphenoid, the ethmoid—which ten bones compose the cranium, or skull proper.

Prespinal, -splenomegalic: see PRE- B. 3, 1.

Press (pres), *sb.*[1] Forms: α. 3–7 **presse**, (4 **presce**), 4– **press**. β. 3–6 **pres** (*dative* 3–4 **prese, prece**), 4–6 **prees, prese, prece**, 5 **preesse**, *Sc.* **preys**, 5–6 **preas, preese**, *Sc.* **preis**, 5–7 **preace, preasse**, 6 *Sc.* **preise, preiss**, ? **prais**, 6–7 **prease**. [Two distinct forms: α. ME. *presse*, a. F. *presse* (11th c. in Littré) = Pr. *pressa*, It. *pressa*, verbal sb. from stem of F. *presser* = It. *pressare*, L. *pressāre*, freq. of *premĕre*, *press-um* to press; or ? Romanic fem. sb. from *press-us, -a, -um*, pa. pple. of *premĕre*; β. ME. *prēs, prees*, in 16–17th c. *prese, preas(e, preace*, found as a parallel form only in early senses. The relation of this to the Fr. and the α-forms presents difficulty. Cf. the two corresponding forms of the verb, *press* and *prese, prease*, and see Note below. (The spelling *pres* generally means *prēs*, but may be sometimes = *press*. *Press* in Barbour is doubtful, and may have been = *prēs*.)]

I. In reference to crowding, pressure of persons, circumstances, affairs, etc.

1. The condition of being crowded or thronged; a crowd, a throng, a multitude. *arch.*

α. a 1225 *Ancr. R.* 168 Me is loð presse. a 1400 *R. Brunne's Chron. Wace* (Rolls) 11255 (Petyt MS.) Grete presse was at the procession. c 1400 *R. Gloucester's Chron.* (Rolls) App. XX. 190 Þe king forþ com & out of þe presce [*v.r.* pres] mid strengþe him nom. c 1400 *Destr. Troy* 2157 The pepull was depertid & the presse voidet. 1500–20 DUNBAR *Poems* lxxvii. 50 Great was the press of peopill dwelt about. 1557 N. T. (Genev.) *Matt.* viii. 1 Great presse of people folowed him. 1581 W. STAFFORD *Exam. Compl.* iii. (1876) 76 As in a presse going in at a straight, the formost is driuen by him that is nexte hym. 1601 SHAKS. *Jul. C.* I. ii. 15 Who is it in the presse, that calles on me? a 1657 SIR J. BALFOUR *Ann. Scotl.* (1824–5) II. 170 The presse so augmented, that the Ducke was forced to returne with speed to his lodgeing. 1741–3 WESLEY *Extract of Jrnl.* (1749) 45 It was some time before I could possibly get out of the press. 1866 WHITTIER *Our Master* xiv, We touch him in life's throng and press, And we are whole again. 1891 C. E. NORTON *Dante's Purgatory* x. 64 Round about him there seemed a press and throng of knights.

β. c 1290 *S. Eng. Leg.* I. 101/30 [She] cam ant touchede þe lappe of ore louerdes cloþes ene Ase he eode In grete prece. c 1330 R. BRUNNE *Chron. Wace* (Rolls) 11242 So þey ches, ffor to departe þer mykel pres. 13.. *E. E. Allit. P.* B. 880 Þay..distresed hym wonder strayt, with strenkþe in þe prece. c 1386 CHAUCER *Wife's Prol.* 522 Greet prees at Market maketh deere ware. c 1390 — *Truth* 1 Flee fro þe prees. c 1440 *Promp. Parv.* 412/2 Prees, or thronge, *pressura*. 1480 CAXTON *Chron. Eng.* cxcviii. 177 Anon doth hym oute of prece [*ed.* 1520 prees]. 1500–20 DUNBAR *Poems* xv. 33 Convenient tyme, lasar, and space, But haist or preiss of grit menȝie. 1526 TINDALE *Mark* v. 27 She cam into the preace [*Great, Rhem.* preasse, *Genev.*, 1611 prease] behynde hym and tewched hys garment. 1558 PHAER *Æneid* III. G ij b, The preas with crooked paws [the Harpies] are out. 1590 SPENSER *F. Q.* I. iii. 3 Far from all peoples preace. 1601 B. JONSON *Poetaster* v. ii, Those whom custome rapteth in her preasse. 1613 SHAKS. *Hen. VIII*, IV. i. 77 Great belly'd women,..would shake the prease And make 'em reele before 'em. 1700 DRYDEN *Iliad* I. 338 When didst thou thrust amid the mingled preace [*rime* peace]?

b. A throng or crush in battle; the thick of the fight; an affray or mêlée.

† Phr. *proud in pres*, said of a knight: see PROUD *a.*

α. 1375 BARBOUR *Bruce* II. 430 Thai prikyt then out off the press [*rime* wes]. c 1489 CAXTON *Sonnes of Aymon* i. 44 Grete was the presse and the bataylle fyers. c 1500 *Lancelot* 867 And in the press so manfully them seruith, His suerd atwo the helmys al to-kerwith. 1610 DONNE *Pseudo-martyr* 264 They..are seldom drawen to any presse or close fight. c 1764 GRAY *Triumphs Owen* 24 There the thundering strokes begin, There the press, and there the din. 1849 MACAULAY *Hist. Eng.* vii. II. 168 He..fought, sword in hand, in the thickest press.

β. c 1330 R. BRUNNE *Chron. Wace* (Rolls) 720 At which bataille þe Troiens lees, & fledde fro þat mykel prees. c 1350 *Will. Palerne* 3848 Bliue with his burnes he braide in-to prese. c 1400 *Destr. Troy* 1201 Mony peryshhet in þe plase er þe prese [*mispr.* prise] endit. c 1489 CAXTON *Blanchardyn* li. 194 He brake & departed the grete preesses, so that his enmyes made waye byfore his swerde. a 1500 *Sir Beues* 3087 (Pynson) Beuys thoroughe the preas dyd ryde. 1513 DOUGLAS *Æneis* x. xiv. *heading*, Hym to ravenge his lyfe lost in the pres [*ed.* 1553 preis]. 1523 LD. BERNERS *Froiss.* I. cvii. 129 They..russhed into yᵉ thyckest of the preace. 1550 LYNDESAY *Sqr. Meldrum* 1135 Than Makferland that maid the prais, From time he saw the Squyeris face, Upon his kneis he did him yeild. 1596 SPENSER *F. Q.* IV. iv. 34 Into the thickest of that knightly preasse He thrust.

† **c.** *In press*: in a crowd, crowded together, in the thick of the fight. *Obs.*

β. 1509 HAWES *Past. Pleas.* xliv. (Percy Soc.) 213, I marveyle muche of the presumption Of the dame Fame so puttyng in ure Thy great prayse, saiyng it shall endure For to be infinite evermore in prease [*rime* cease]. 15.. *Adam Bel* 143 in Hazl. *E. P. P.* II. 144 Among them all he ran, Where the people were most in prece, He smot downe many a man. 1581 MULCASTER *Positions* xvi. (1887) 74 Here will desire throng in prease, though it praise not in parting. 1587 FLEMING *Contn. Holinshed* III. 1986/2 The Scots..ran sharplie forward.., and without anie mercie, slue the most part of them that abode furthest in prease.

2. The action or fact of pressing together in a crowd; a crowding or thronging together.

α. 1595 SHAKS. *John* v. vii. 19 With many legions of strange fantasies, Which, in their throng and presse to that last hold, Confound themselues. 1617 MORYSON *Itin.* I. 134 There was such a presse to kisse his feet. c 1823 BYRON *Juan* XIII. xviii, Give gently way, when there's too great a press. 1833 HT. MARTINEAU *Tale of Tyne* iv, The press of vessels near the port is very awful. 1849 MACAULAY *Hist. Eng.* iii. I. 369 The great press was to get near the chair where John Dryden sate.

β. c 1290 *S. Eng. Leg.* I. 15/494 Þat folk him siwede with gret pres. c 1375 *Sc. Leg. Saints* ii. (*Paulus*) 87 For to here hym wes sik prese, Þat fawt of rowme gret þar wes. c 1489 CAXTON *Sonnes of Aymon* xxiv. 504 By the grete prees & stampyng of their horses. 1560 DAUS tr. *Sleidane's Comm.* 24 b, Where was suche prease of the people, that harnessed men had muche a do to kepe them backe. a 1643 W. CARTWRIGHT *Lady Errant* II. iv, Our loves what are they But howerly Sacrifices, only wanting The prease and tumult of Solemnity?

† **3.** The condition of being hard pressed; a position of difficulty, trouble, or danger; a critical situation; straits, distress, tribulation. *Obs.* or *arch.*

α. 1375 BARBOUR *Bruce* III. 129 The King wes then in full gret press. c 1440 *York Myst.* xlviii. 289 In harde presse whan I was stedde, Of my paynes ȝe hadde pitee. 1627–77 FELTHAM *Resolves* I. lxxv. 115 Such Cordials, as frolick the heart, in the press of adversity.

β. a 1300 *Cursor M.* 5608 Born in þat sith was moyses Þat þe folke was in þat pres [*Trin.* prees]. c 1330 R. BRUNNE *Chron.* (1810) 311 In alle þis grete pres praied þe kyng of France, Þe Scottis suld haf pes þorgh Edward sufferance. 1523 LD. BERNERS *Froiss.* I. ccclvii. 577 They wolde not medell, nor be in no busynesse nor prease. 1573 J. DAVIDSON *Commend. Vprichtnes* 153 Bot cheifly anis he was put to ane preace, Quhen that the Quene of tressoun did accuse him. 1601 J. MELVILL *Diary* (Wodrow Soc.) 496 But pruff thy preass can nocht be understude.

4. Pressure of affairs; urgency, haste, hurry.

α. 1641 *Vind. Smectymnuus* xi. 111 Poore men cannot have their Presse wayted on, as your greatnesse may. 1836 *Going to Service* vi. 69 Roused to the press of an occasion, as if she acquired double power of diligence. 1883 *Fortn. Rev.* May 734 The eager press of our modern life. 1888 LIGHTHALL *Yng. Seigneur* 52 What..is your press about going to England?

β. a 1400–50 *Alexander* 3382 For no prayer ne preese [*v.r.* pres] ne plesaunce on erth..rynne shuld he neuer. c 1400 *Destr. Troy* 11910 Þan the grekes..With proses and pres puld vp þere ancres. 1533 BELLENDEN *Livy* II. xxii. (S.T.S.) I. 222 The fray and noyis..causit þe Veanis to rusche with maist preiss to harnes. a 1547 SURREY *Æneid* II. 430 Amid the flame and armes ran I in preasse.

† **5.** Phr. *To put oneself in press*: (?) to exert oneself, use one's endeavour, set oneself, undertake. (Cf. PRESS *v.* 17.) *Obs.*

α. 1540 HYRDE tr. *Vives' Instr. Chr. Wom.* (1541) 135 b, Lest she be to homely, to put her self in presse, in company of her seruauntes, namely if she be yonge.

β. 1387–8 T. USK *Test. Love* Prol., That I..wil putten me in prees to speke of loue. c 1420 LYDG. *Assembly of Gods* 1755 When the Son of Man put hym in prese, Wylfully to suffre dethe for mankynde. a 1529 SKELTON *Bowge of Courte* 44 But than I thoughte I wolde not dwell behynde; Amonge all other I put myselfe in prece. 1542 RECORDE *Gr. Artes* Pref. a iij, Yet am I bolde to put my selfe in preasse with suche abilitie as God hathe lente me.. to helpe my countrey men. 1551 BIBLE (Matthew) *Ps.* xxii. 21 *note*, The common people of the Iewes, who cruelly & furiously put them selues in prease agaynst Christe, cryinge, crucifie him, crucifie him. 1560 DAUS tr. *Sleidane's Comm.* 208 We see hym put hymselfe in prease, to occupie a place in thys most noble consistorye.

† **b.** *To put in preace*: ? to exercise, put in practice. (Perh. a Spenserian misuse.) *Obs. rare.*

β. 1579 SPENSER *Sheph. Cal.* Oct. 69 The vaunting Poets found nought worth a pease, To put in preace emong the learned troupe.

II. In reference to the physical act or process. (Rarely in β-form.)

6. The act of pressing (something); pressure.

1513 DOUGLAS *Æneis* III. i. 73 But eftir that the thrid syon of treis,..I schupe to haue wprevin with mair preise [*rime* peice]. 1899 E. J. CHAPMAN *Drama Two Lives, Dream's End.* 95 The proud lips meet with icy press. 1903 D. McDONALD *Garden Comp.* Ser. II. 82 Give it [the bulb] a gentle press sufficient to more than half bury it.

7. A mark made by pressing; a crease; *fig.* an impression.

1601 SIR W. CORNWALLIS *Ess.* II. xl. (1631) 175 Meditation goeth with so faint a presse in my braine, that it is soon wiped out. a 1688 VILLIERS (Dk. Buckhm.) *Restoration* (1775) 95 May their false lights undo 'em, and discover presses, holes, strains and oldness in their stuffs.

8. The action of pressing (forward).

1893 *Daily News* 14 Apr. 2/2 The press forward of the horse against the stress of the blast. 1895 *Ibid.* 16 May 6/3 Russia is beginning to feel uncomfortable from the press forward of Chinese in her Asiatic States.

9. *Naut.* *Press of sail, canvas* (formerly *press sail, prest sail, pressing sail*): 'as much sail as the state of the wind, etc., will permit a ship to carry' (Smyth *Sailor's Word-bk.*). Cf. CROWD *sb.*[3] 3 b.

The earlier variants *press sail*, etc., leave the origin obscure.

1592 NASHE *Four Lett. Confut.* Wks. (Grosart) II. 240 I my self,..make my stile carry a presse saile. a 1642 SIR W. MONSON *Naval Tracts* III. (1704) 331/2 Keeping the Sea..with a contrary Wind, foul Weather, and a press Sail. 1693 *Lond. Gaz.* No. 2888/2 All Night we run along the shore with a press Sail. 1710 J. HARRIS *Lex. Techn.* II. s. v. *Prest Sail*, A Ship at Sea is said to carry a Prest Sail, when she carries all that She can possibly Croud. 1772 *Phil. Trans.* LXIV. 129 We .. carried a pressing sail, with hopes of reaching Torbay before dark. 1794 NELSON in Nicolas *Disp.* (1845) I. 372 The gale.. obliged me to carry a press of sail to clear the shore towards Cape Corse. 1806 A. DUNCAN *Nelson* 61 He bore away with a press of sail for Malta. 1836 MARRYAT *Midsh. Easy* xxvi, Foaming in her course, and straining under the press of sail. 1884 H. COLLINGWOOD *Under Meteor Flag* 92, I carried on under a heavy press of sail.

III. An instrument or machine by which pressure is communicated. (Only in form *press*.)

10. An instrument used to compress a substance into smaller compass, denser consistency, a flatter shape, or a required form: usually distinguished by prefixing a qualifying word, expressing purpose, as *baling, coining, copying, packing, rolling, sewing, stamping press*, the name of the thing pressed, as *bonnet, cheese, clothes, cotton, hay, napkin press*, or the power or mechanical contrivance employed, as *cam, hydraulic, screw, toggle press*; etc.

1362 LANGL. *P. Pl.* A. v. 127 Þenne I drouȝ me a-mong þis drapers,..Among þis Riche Rayes lernde I a Lessun,.. Putte hem in a pressour [*v.r.* presse (so in B.); C. VII. 21 pressours] and pinnede hem þer-Inne. c 1440 *Promp. Parv.* 412/2 Presse, or pyle of clothe, *panniplicium, pressorium*. 1483 *Cath. Angl.* 290/2 A Presse for clathe, *lucunar, panniplicium, vestiplicium*. 1513 *Act 5 Hen. VIII*, c. 4 § 1 Divers Strangers..dry calander Worsteds with Gums, Oils, and Presses. 1532 MORE *Confut. Barnes* VIII. Wks. 797/1 Stretched out as it wer in the presse or tenter hokes of a strong fullar. 1570 LEVINS *Manip.* 84/31 A Presse for backs, *prælium*. 1674 in J. Simon *Irish Coins* (1749) 133 To import such a quantitie of copper blocks or chipps as may possible with two presses, to be coyned by the spring ensueing. 1727–41 CHAMBERS *Cycl.* s. v., *Rolling Press*, is a machine used for the taking off prints from copper-plates. 1776 WITHERING *Brit. Plants* (1796) I. 31 Directions for drying..Specimens of Plants..First prepare a press, which a workman will make. 1787 M. CUTLER in *Life*, etc. (1888) I. 269 Another great curiosity was a rolling press, for taking the copies of letters or any other writing. 1824 J. JOHNSON *Typogr.* II. xv. 553 Hydraulic Presses..are now deemed a valuable acquisition to the printing profession. 1846 J. BAXTER *Libr. Pract. Agric.* (ed. 4) II. 77 The wood is fit for..screws for presses, spokes for wheels, chairs, &c. 1858 SIMMONDS *Dict. Trade, Copying-press, Copying Machine*, a press for taking duplicate or manifold impressions on damped paper from manuscripts by a lever. 1873 E. SPON *Workshop Rec.* Ser. I. 394/1 The necessary tools for small [bookbinding] work are: .. a sewing press; a cutting press [etc.]. *fig.* c 1374 CHAUCER *Troylus* I. 559 And so kan leye oure Iolyte on presse. And bryng oure lusty folk to holynesse.

b. The apparatus for inflicting the torture of *peine forte et dure*: see PRESS *v.*[1] 1 b.

a 1734 NORTH *Lives* (1826) I. 287 He would not plead to the country..till the press was ready; and then he pleaded, and was, at last, hanged. 1839 W. H. AINSWORTH *J. Sheppard* III. xv, The ponderous machine, which resembled a trough, slowly descended upon the prisoner's breast. Marvel, then, took two iron weights, each of a hundred pounds, and placed them in the press.

11. An apparatus for expressing or extracting the juice, or the like, out of anything: usually designated by prefixing the name of the substance extracted, as *wine, oil, cider, sugar press*, etc.

a 1380 *Minor Poems fr. Vernon MS.* lii. 131 Til grapes to þe presse beo set, Þer renneþ no red wyn in raþe. 1382 WYCLIF *Isa.* lxiii. 3 The presse I trad alone. 1398 TREVISA *Barth. De P. R.* XVII. cxii. (Bodl. MS.), Þe faster oile reneþ oute of þe presse..þe better it is acounted. 1483 *Cath. Angl.* 291/1 A Presse for wyne, *bachinal, calcatorium* [etc.]. 1530 PALSGR. 258/1 Presse for lycour, *pressouer*. 1553 EDEN *Treat. Newe Ind.* (Arb.) 40, 28. suger presses, to presse ye sugre whiche groweth plentifully in certaine canes or redes of the same countrey. 1616 SURFL. & MARKH. *Country Farme* 430 Put them in a haire cloth or hempen bagge, for to presse in a presse that hath his planke hollow and bending doweneward. 1707 MORTIMER *Husb.* (1721) II. 328 After your Apples are ground they should be..committed to the Press. 1825 J. NICHOLSON *Operat. Mechanic* 291 Presses used for expressing liquors are of various kinds.

† **b.** *Press of Herophilus* [Gr. ληνός (Herophilus, in Galen), L. *torcular Herophili*]: the enlarged reservoir at the union of the four sinuses of the dura mater, opposite the tuberosity of the occipital bone. *Obs.*

1578 BANISTER *Hist. Man* v. 78 The quadruplication of Dura mater..is called a presse, & lyeth betwene the brayne and Cerebellum. 1594 T. B. *La Primaud. Fr. Acad.* II. 150 [A vessel] which both the Greeke & Latine physicions call by a name that signifieth a presse, because the blood is pressed into it for the nourishing of the braine.

12. In the Jacquard loom, The mechanism which disengages the needles or wires which are not to act from the lifting-bar.

1875 URE *Dict. Arts* (ed. 7) III. 3 The name *press* is given to the assemblage of all the pieces which compose the moveable frame BB.

13. A machine for leaving the impression of type upon paper, vellum, or other smooth surface; a machine for printing, a printing-press. Often qualified, as *Stanhope, Albion, Michle press*, etc.

[1507 in Blades *Caxton* Plate vii. (from Ascensius Bk.), Prelum Ascensianum.] 1535 [see d.] 1536 J. RASTELL *Will*, My house in St. Martyns, with my presse, notes and lettres comprised in the same. 1565 COOPER *Thesaurus*, *Prelum*, a presse that eyther Printers or any other occupation vseth. 1574 *Will of Johane Wolfe*, All the presses, letters, furniture, etc., belonging to the arte of pryntyng. 1588 *Marprel. Epist.* (Arb.) 22 Waldegraues printing presse and Letters were takken away. 1594 R. ASHLEY tr. *Loys le Roy* 22 Then the gouernour of the Presse taketh these last chasies or fourmes, and laieth them on the marble of his Presse. 1598 STOW *Surv.* 394 Therin [the Ambry,] Islip, Abbet of Westminster, first practized and erected the first Presse of booke Printing that euer was in England, about..1471. 1683 MOXON *Mech. Exerc., Printing* ii. ¶ 1 His Presses have a solid and firm Foundation. 1827 HALLAM *Const. Hist.* (1876) III. xiii. 3 The privilege of keeping presses was limited to the members of the stationers' company. 1853 *N. & Q.* 1st Ser. VIII. 10/1 Charles Earl Stanhope, whose versatility of talent succeeded in abolishing the old wooden printing-press, with its double pulls, and substituting .. the beautiful iron one, called after him the 'Stanhope Press'. 1873 H. SPENCER *Stud. Sociol.* (1882) 126 The last achievement in automatic printing—the Walter-Press. 1896 HOWELLS *Impressions & Exp.* 11 A second-hand Adams press of the earliest pattern and patent.

b. Used as an inclusive name for the place of business of which the printing-press is the centre, in which all the stages and processes of printing are carried on; a printing-house or printing-office. Often used in the names of such printing establishments, e.g. the Clarendon Press, Oxford, the Pitt Press, Cambridge, the Aldine Press, Leadenhall Press, Chiswick Press, etc. Hence, contextually, for the *personnel* of such an establishment, the compositors or printers, printer's readers, etc.

1579 GOSSON *Sch. Abuse* To Rdr. (Arb.) 18 Because you are learned amende the faultes freendly, which escape the Presse. 1589 *Pasquil's Ret.* A iij b, That worke shall come out of the Presse like a bryde from her chamber. 1590 NASHE *Pasquil's Apol.* I. B j, When he carried his coppie to the Presse. 1641 J. JACKSON *True Evang. T.* III. 200 While these Sermons were betweene the Pulpit, and the Presse. 1647 CLARENDON *Hist. Reb.* IV. § 104 The Presses swell'd with the most virulent Invectives against them. a 1656 BP. HALL *Rem. Wks.* (1660) 82 We should not have such libellous presses. 1670 G. H. *Hist. Cardinals* I. III. 87 There is a Press..for all Foreign Languages. 1797 *Monthly Mag.* III. 46 An elegant and splendid edition of 'Archimedes', from the Clarendon Press. 1841 MACAULAY *Ess., L. Hunt* (1887) 594 The Athenian Comedies..have been reprinted at the Pitt Press and the Clarendon Press under the direction of Syndics and delegates. 1849 — *Hist. Eng.* vii. II. 263 The Dutch arms..were scarcely so formidable to James as the Dutch presses. 1900 H. HART (*title*) Notes on A Century of Typography at the University Press, Oxford, 1693–1794.

c. The printing-press in operation, the work or function of the press; the art or practice of printing.

1579 FULKE *Confut. Sanders* 661 His report is more to bee credited then the Printers presse. 1641 *More's Rich. III*, Ded., Having for many yeares escaped the presse. 1656 EARL MONM. tr. *Boccalini's Advts. fr. Parnass.* I. XXXV. (1674) 42 Of all Modern inventions..the precedency ought to be given to the Press..; and that now the Press had.. for ever secured the past and present labours of the Vertuosi. 1663 R. L'ESTRANGE (*title*) Considerations and Proposals in Order to the Regulation of the Press. 1791–1823 D'ISRAELI *Cur. Lit., Licensers Press*, Under..William III..the press had obtained its perfect freedom. c 1880 TENNYSON *Despair* xvi, These are the new dark ages, you see, of the popular press.

d. In phrases belonging to 13, b, or c, as *at, in, † under (the) press*, in the process of printing, being printed; *off the press*, finally printed, issued; † *out of press*, = prec., also out of print (*obs.*).

1665 BOYLE *Occas. Refl.* Introd. Pref. (1848) 11 Papers.. discovered to have been lost when some of the rest were to be *at the Press. 1823 J. BADCOCK *Dom. Amusem.* p. viii, After the volume has been at press upwards of a year. 1535 JOYE *Apol. Tindale* (Arb.) 21 One bothe to wryte yt and to correcke it *in the presse. 1545 LELAND *New-Year's Gift* (1549) C iv, Part of the exemplaries,..hath bene empryntede in Germany, and now be in the presses chefely of Frobenius. 1642 CHAS. I in Clarendon *Hist. Reb.* v. § 399 A Declaration now in the Press. 1670–1 T. PIERCE in *Lett. H. More* (1694) 43, I have a Book in the Press. 1764 BURKE *Let. to J. Dodsley* 9 Feb. (in *Westm. Gaz.* 12 Jan. (1898) 2/1) I suppose that by this our work is in the press. 1900 *Advertisement*, In the press, and shortly will be published, a new work by [etc.]. 1823 J. BADCOCK *Dom. Amusem.* p. iv, The first intelligence..of the sheets being in hand, was the announcement that they were also '*off the press'. 1622 PEACHAM *Compl. Gent.* xiii. (1634) 128 His peeces have been long since worne *out of press. 1674 NEWTON in Rigaud *Corr. Sci. Men* (1841) II. 367 Hearing that Mr. Kersey's book is out of press, I desire you would send in the fourth part. 1612 SIR R. NAUNTON in *Buccleuch MSS.* (Hist. MSS. Comm.) I. 113 The great work of his Chrysostome then *under press. 1721 *Lond. Gaz.* No. 5961/2 A Memorial of the Grocers..said to be under the Press.

e. In many other phrases, in which *press* passes from the literal sense 13 into that of c, as *to bring, put, commit, send, submit to the press; to carry, see through the press; to come to, pass, undergo the press; to correct the press*, i.e. the printing, or the errors in composing the type.

1582 T. WATSON *Centurie of Loue* Ep. Ded., The world.. called vpon mee, to put it to the presse. 1597 MORLEY *Introd. Mus.* 75 If I had seene it before it came to the presse, it should not have passed so. 1605 *Gunpowder Plot* in *Harl. Misc.* (Malh.) III. 5 Being about to commit them to the press. 1631 MASSINGER *Emperor East* Ded., Such trifles of mine as have passed the press. 1646 EARL MONM. tr. *Biondi's Civil Warres* II. To Rdr., I know not whether they may ever undergoe the Presse. 1649 W. DUGDALE in *Lett. Lit. Men* (Camden) 175 Soe may be correct the presse, which will be an especiall matter. 1691 WOOD *Ath. Oxon.* II. 696 A stop was made for some years of bringing the second [vol.] to the Press. a 1764 LLOYD *Author's Apol.* Poet. Wks. 1774 I. 2 But when it comes to press and print You'll find, I fear but little in't. 1800 *Med. Jrnl.* III. 274 It will be submitted to the Press in the course of the ensuing mouth. 1848 HALLIWELL *Ingelend's Disobed. Child* (Percy Soc.) Pref., It was formerly a very common practice to correct and alter the press whilst the impression was being taken. 1867 E. QUINCY *Life J. Quincy* 477 My father took an active interest in this publication, and corrected the press himself. 1869 SIR J. T. COLERIDGE *Mem. Keble* (ed. 2) 265 A translation..is now being carried through the press. *Mod.* In his absence, I am to see the book through the press.

f. *Freedom* or *liberty of the press*: free use of the printing-press; the right to print and publish anything without submitting it to previous official censorship; see LIBERTY 2 b, and quots. So in *free press, unfettered press*, etc.

[1644 (*title*) Areopagitica; a Speech of Mr. John Milton for the Liberty of Vnlicenc'd Printing To the Parlament of England.] 1680 R. L'ESTRANGE (*title*) A Seasonable Memorial,..upon the Liberties of the Presse and Pulpit. 1681 W. DENTON *Jus Cæsaris* ad fin., An Apology for the Liberty of the Press. 1769 BLACKSTONE *Comm.* IV. xi. 151 The liberty of the press is indeed essential to the nature of a free state; but this consists in laying no previous restraints upon publications, and not in freedom from censure for criminal matter when published. 1771 SMOLLETT *Humph. Cl.* 15 July, He said, he should always consider the liberty of the press as a national evil, while it enabled the vilest reptile to soil the lustre of the most shining merit. 1789 *Constit. U. S.* Amendm. i, Congress shall make no law.. abridging the freedom of the press. 1827 HALLAM *Const. Hist.* (1876) III. xv. 167 The liberty of the press consists, in a strict sense, merely in an exemption from the superintendence of a licenser. 1903 in *Westm. Gaz.* 11 Aug. 8/2 It has been pointed out over and over again,..that the licence of the Press is not the liberty of the Press.

g. (Also *periodical* or *public press, daily press*, etc.) The newspapers, journals, and periodical literature generally; the newspapers and journals of a country, district, party, etc., as the French Press, the London Press, the Conservative Press, the religious press, the secular press, etc. Hence, sometimes the title of a newspaper, as *The Press, The Scottish Press, The Aberdeen Free Press*, etc.

This use of the word appears to have originated in phrases such as *the liberty of the press, a servile* or *shackled press, to write for the press*, etc., in which 'press' originally had sense c above, but was gradually taken to mean the products of the printing-press. Quotations before 1820 are mostly transitional, leading gradually up to this sense.

1797 *The Press* (Dublin) No. 1. 1 By some fatality of late, the Press of the harassed country has been either negligent or apostate; it has been a centinel a-sleep on its post...It is now proposed to establish a newspaper, to be solely and unalterably devoted to the people of Ireland and their interests, under the appellation of *The Press*. 1798 *Anti-Jacobin* No. 36. 281 For this purpose, the Press was engaged, and almost monopolized in all its branches: Reviews, Registers, Monthly Magazines, and Morning and Evening Prints sprung forth in abundance 1807 *Edin. Rev.* X. 115 Unlimited abuse of private characters is another characteristic of the American press. 1827 COBBETT in *Weekly Polit. Reg.* 11 Jan. 53 Silencing the press would not enable them to pay the interest of the debt. 1820 *Lond. Mag.* I. 569 The Manager has thought it his duty to suspend the Free List during the representation, the public press excepted. *Ibid* 575 The gentlemen-critics of the daily press. 1823 *Edin. Rev.* XXXVIII. 349 (*Article*) The Periodical Press. *Ibid.*, If he had not had the fear of the periodical press before his eyes. *Ibid.* 359 The staple literature of the Periodical Press may be divided into Newspapers, Magazines, and Reviews. *Ibid.* 360 This paper [the *Morning Post*] we have been long used to think the best..that issued from the daily press. 1828 *Lancet* 19 Jan. 595/1 Sir Astley Cooper, in a silly speech at a public dinner, talked of the 'reptile press'. 1840 *Penny Cycl.* XVI. 194/1 The two principal persons..at this time concerned in the newspaper press. *Ibid.* 195/1 Capital to the amount of £500,000 at least is invested in the daily press of London, of which two-thirds..may be represented by the morning papers. 1843 RUSKIN *Arrows of Chace* (1880) I. 3, I seldom, therefore, read..the ordinary animadversions of the press. 1862 TROLLOPE *Orley F.* xiii, There was also a reporter for the press. 1885 SIR C. P. BUTT in *Law Times Rep.* LIII. 61/2 After so much discussion..in the public press on this question. *Mod.* The book has been favourably noticed by the press.

IV. 14. A large (usually shelved) cupboard, esp. one placed in a recess in the wall, for holding clothes, books, etc.; in Scotland, also for provisions, victuals, plates, dishes, and other table requisites. Cf. CLOTHES-PRESS 1. Also *attrib.*

c 1386 CHAUCER *Miller's T.* 26 His presse ycovered with a faldyng reed. 1398 TREVISA *Barth. De P. R.* XVIII. cv. (1495) gg iv/1 Whanne the cloth is to longe in presse & thicke ayre. a 1533 LD. BERNERS *Huon* cxi. 384 There were presses..in the whiche presses were gownes and robes of fyne golde, and ryche mantelles furryd with sabyls. 1552 in *Bury Wills* (Camden) 142, I gyve her my newe cubbord with the presse in yᵉ and too great books the Bybyll and the New Testament, with the Booke of the Kings Statuts. 1566 *Eng. Ch. Furniture* (1866) 67 One sepulcre—sold to Johnne orson and he haith made a presse therof to laie clothes therein. 1598 SHAKS. *Merry W.* III. iii. 226 In the house, & in the chambers, and in the coffers, and in the presses. 1600 J. PORY tr. *Leo's Africa* III. 125 Each chamber hath a presse curiously painted and varnished belonging thereunto. 1686 *Inv.* in *Essex Rev.* (1906) XV. 172 Two chayers, one presse cubbord. 1709 HUGHES *Tatler* No. 113 ¶ 9 A Press for Books [with four shelves]. 1753 SMOLLETT *Ct. Fathom* (1784) 35/2 He should..conceal himself in a large press or wardrobe, that stood in one corner of the apartment. 1790 BURNS *Tam o' Shanter* 125 Coffins stood round like open presses, That shaw'd the dead in their last dresses. 1802 FINDLATER *Agric. Peebles* iii. 41 The ambry, or shelved wooden press, in which the cow's milk, and other ..provision are locked up. 1859 JEPHSON *Brittany* xiii. 221 In a press with glass doors, she showed me some beautiful reliquaries. 1888 BARRIE *Auld Licht Idylls* ii. 50 A 'press' or cupboard containing a fair assortment of cooking utensils. 1892 *Pall Mall G.* 16 Jan. 7/3 The Sliding Book-Press at the British Museum. *Ibid.*, The principle of a sliding or hanging press is entirely peculiar to the British Museum, and hardly could have originated elsewhere than in a building possessing..floors and ceilings entirely grated.

V. *attrib.* and *Comb.*

15. General combinations: **a.** attributive, (*a*) of a press (senses 10, 11), as *press-bar, -beam, -block, -board, -frame, -plunger, -shop*, etc.; (*b*) of or pertaining to the printing-press, to printing, or to journalism, as *press-censorship, -correspondent, -folk* (cf. PRESSMAN), *-girthing, -mohawk, -organ, -people, -reader, -worker*. **b.** [from the vb. stem.] Used to press, pressing, as *press-barrel, -box, -harrow*. **c.** objective genitive, as *press-builder, -building, -haunter, -maker, -mauler*. **d.** instrumental, as *press-made, -noticed, -ridden* adjs.

1839 URE *Dict. Arts* 158 (*Bookbinding*) The *pressbar, or beam, has two holes upon its under surface, for securing it to two pegs standing on the top of the chest. 1794 *Rigging & Seamanship* 55 *Press-barrels are old tar-barrels filled with clay, and laid on the sledge or drag to add weight when the rope is closing. 1803 *Naval Chron.* X. 477 The [old] tar barrels..are applied to the purpose of serving as a weight in laying..rope, and are called press barrels. 1825 J. NICHOLSON *Operat. Mechanic* 448 (*Oil-mill*), 16, the first *press-box, (also hollowed out of the block,) in which the grain is squeezed, after it has come for the first time from below the mill-stones. 17, the second press-box, at the other end of the block, for squeezing the grain after it has passed a second time under the pestles. 1890 W. J. GORDON *Foundry* 194 Associated with Smith, he [Richard Hoe's father] had turned his attention to *press building in general. 1896 T. L. DE VINNE *Moxon's Mech. Exerc. Printing* 410 Press-building was not a distinct trade in 1683. 1887 *Pall Mall G.* 9 Aug. 5/1 An aggressive and oppressive *press-censorship. 1900 *Macm. Mag.* May 36 One of our *press-correspondents at the present day. 1729 SWIFT *Wks.* (1841) II. 98 Mist..happened to reprint this paper in London, for which his *press-folk were prosecuted. 1825 J. NICHOLSON *Operat. Mechanic* 448, Fig. 460 is the elevation of the pestle and *press-frame, their furniture, the mortars, and the press-pestles. 1840 J. BUEL *Farmer's Comp.* 146 For pulverizing stiff clays, Concklin's *press harrow is an admirable instrument. 1597 G. HARVEY *Trimming Nashe* Wks. (Grosart) III. 67 To all ballet-makers, pamphleters, *presse haunters, boon pot poets, and such like. 1886 *Pall Mall G.* 4 Sept. 14/1 The original introducer of *press-made pens. 1900 *Daily News* 11 May 3/.. The .. theory that this is a capitalist- and Press-made war. 1705 J. DUNTON *Life & Err.* 244 He has been an indefatigable *Press-mauler, for above these Twenty years. 1849 THACKERAY *Box of Novels* Wks. 1900 XIII. 399 The nation ..looks upon the *press-Mohawks..as it did upon the gallant young noblemen who used a few years since to break the heads of policemen. 1906 in *Westm. Gaz.* 24 Sept. 4/2 One of the best *Press-noticed books he had ever published. 1895 *Daily Tel.* 27 Aug. 4/7 The pernicious example..was followed by more than one Parisian *press-organ. 1880 C. G. W. LOCK *Workshop Receipts* Ser. III. 361/1 The die is easily reached by lifting the chamber *c*, which is done by attaching the same to the *press-plunger and elevating the latter. 1849 LONGF. *Kavanagh* xiii. (1857) 228 This country is not priest-ridden, but *press-ridden. 1798 *Times* 28 June 1/3 At the back of the said dwelling-house are also a *press shop and other conveniences for carrying on the Business of a Merchant.

16. Special combs. **a.** from senses 10, 11: **press-cake**, = MILL-*cake* (*a*); **press-copy** *sb.*, a copy of writing made by transfer in a copying-press; hence **press-copy** *v.*; **press-drill**, (*a*) = LAND-*presser*; (*b*) see quot. 1884; † **press-fat**, a vat used for collecting the produce in an oil- or wine-press; **press-forged** *a.*, forged by pressure; **press-house**, the house or building containing a press; a place where pressing is done; **press-iron**, = PRESSING IRON; **press-key**, a thumb-screw used to tighten and hold the cords of a sewing-press, in bookbinding; **press-pack** *v.*, *trans.* to pack or compress (something) into small compass by means of a press (Webster 1864); **press-pin**, the lever of a screw press: **press-plate**, (*a*) in Bramah's press = FOLLOWER *sb.* 5; (*b*) a plate of metal placed between the press-boards of a standing press; **press-pole**, a pole used in pleaching: see quot.; **press-printing**, printing by a press; a method of printing porcelain: see quot.; **press-ware**: see quot.

1839 URE *Dict. Arts* 629 It comes out in large thin solid cakes, or strata, distinguished by the term *press-cakes. 1858 GREENER *Gunnery* 43 Two pieces of lignum vitæ are placed on the broken press-cakes in each sieve. 1792 GOUV. MORRIS *Let. to Lady Sutherland* 22 Aug., I will fold up in this a *press copy of my last, because the original may have been drowned. 1834 *Penny Cycl.* II. 224/2 In such soils an artificial pan may be formed by the land-presser or *press-drill. 1884 KNIGHT *Dict. Mech.* Suppl., *Press Drill*, a drilling machine largely used in gun and sewing machine work. 1611 BIBLE *Haggai* ii. 16 When one came to the *presse-fatte [1885 *R.V.* winefat] for to draw out fiftie vessels out of the presse, there were but twentie. 18..

Daily News 14 Nov. 6/5 His gun, Captain Jaques explained, would be made of a few hollow, *press-forged, cold-drawn, taper cylinders of alloyed steel. 1744 *N. Jersey Archives* XII. 211 To Be Sold... A new Fulling-Mill, *Press-House and Dye-House. 1878 J. INGLIS *Sport & W.* iv. 34 The huge lever is strained and pulled at by the press-house coolies. 1900 *Westm. Gaz.* 25 Oct. 7/2 Allowing the populace to enter the press-house of the vineyard. 1892 ZANGWILL *Children of Ghetto* I. 45 He taught them how to handle a *press-iron. 1839 URE *Dict. Arts* 1031 Upon the top of the ram, the *press-plate or table.. rests, which is commonly called the follower, because it follows the ram closely in its descent. 1868 *Report U. S. Commissioner Agric.* (1869) 257 Two men use the *press-pole,..the other uses the pleaching-hook. The pole is thrust through behind each stout vertical sapling, when both men pull gently and equally. Thus bent back a little, the third man cuts it two-thirds through, cutting obliquely downward with the pleaching-hook. 1875 URE *Dict. Arts* (ed. 7) III. 620 There are two distinct methods of printing in use for china and earthenware; one is transferred on the bisque, and is the method by which the ordinary printed ware is produced,..called '*press-printing'. 1612 STURTEVANT *Metallica* 38 *Press-ware or Mould-ware is any thing that can bee made, wrought, or formed of clay and earth,.. by Presse and Mould, or by pressing and moulding.

b. (connected with printing and journalism): **press agent**, a man employed in connexion with a theatre or the like to attend to the advertising, and the reporting of the performances; **press-blanket**, a piece of flannel or felt used on a printing-press to equalize the impression of the type; **press-box**, a shelter for newspaper reporters in the open air, as at a cricket or football match; **press-boy**, a boy employed as messenger in a printing-office; in the United States, a machine-boy; **press cutting**, a paragraph, article, or notice, cut from a newspaper; also *attrib.* as *press-cutting agency*; **press-gallery**, a gallery or part of the house at any public meeting, set apart for reporters; esp. that in the House of Commons or other legislative chamber; **press-law**, a law as to the licensing of printing, esp. of the newspaper press; **press-proof, -revise**, the last proof examined before printed matter goes to press; **press-stone**, the bed of a printing-press; **press-tradition**, handing down in print.

1905 *Westm. Gaz.* 12 Dec. 9/2 A series of scrimmages on that side of the field remote from the *press-box. 1890 *Cent. Dict.*, *Machine-boy*, in the United States known as feeder or *press-boy. 1888 *Pall Mall G.* 4 May 11/1 A Visit to a *Press-cutting Agency... For some time an agency has been at work for supplying newspaper references—at so much per hundred cuttings or a yearly subscription. 1899 *Westm. Gaz.* 5 May 2/3 Mr. Chamberlain has recently made a feeling protest against government by Press-cutting agency. 1901 *Cycl. Tour. Club Gaz.* Oct. 389 The press cuttings that lie before us. 1884 YATES *Recoll.* II. vii. 286, I..was in the *press-gallery of the Chamber..on the 14th May. 1897 [see GALLERY *sb.* 3 d]. 1897 MRS. E. L. VOYNICH *Gadfly* ix, A new *press-law was expected. 1683 MOXON *Mech. Exerc., Printing* xi. ¶ 17 The *Press-Stone should be Marble, though sometimes Master Printers make shift with Purbeck. 1675 J. SMITH *Chr. Relig. Appeal* I. 16 Conveyed down to us in the same way of pen or *press-tradition that other writings are.

[*Note.* The origin of the β forms *prēs, prees, preas, prese, prease, preace*, is not clear. So far as concerns the lengthened vowel, they go with the similar forms of the verb *prēse-n, preese, prease*, beside the ordinary *press-en*, PRESS *v.*[1] These agree with *cease, lease, decease* from OF. or ME. *cesse, lesse*, ME. *decesse*, also with *beast, feast*, in which original short *e* before *ss, st* is lengthened. (See Note to PRESS *v.*[1]) The special difficulty in the sb. is that ME. *prēs* had no final *e* (the 15–16th c. *-e* being only graphical), so that it cannot be identified with OF. and ME. *presse*. Could it be an Eng. derivative from the long-vowel stem of the vb. *prēs-e(n*? As a formation, it appears to be distinct from *presse, press*, and might have been treated as a separate word *prease* or *preace*; but being obsolete, and its senses (so far as they went) coinciding with those of *press*, it has for convenience been treated as a parallel form of this word.]

Press (pres), *sb.*[2] Now *rare.* [An alteration of or substitution for PREST *sb.*[1] 5, as in PRESS *v.*[2], and PRESS-MONEY.]

1. The impressing of men for service in the navy or (less frequently) the army; compulsory enlistment; = IMPRESS *sb.*[2], IMPRESSMENT[2]. Now *Hist.*

[1592 KYD *Sol. & Pers.* I. v. 27 A common presse of base, superfluous Turkes May soon be leuied. (But this may be PRESS *sb.*[1], crowd.)]

1599 MINSHEU *Sp. Dict.*, *Léva*, a presse or taking vp men for the war. 1601 R. JOHNSON *Kingd. & Commw.* (1603) 99 He giueth his captaines commissions to take vp souldiers through the whole Realme, (not by presse, as with us) but by striking vp the drumm. 1615 *Trade's Incr.* in *Harl. Misc.* (Malh.) III. 304 The general press that was made of men from all the coasts to man the ships. 1667 *Lond. Gaz.* No. 154/2 The Press for Seamen is great, and several Captains are imployed to raise men both in Denmark and Lubec. 1676 I. MATHER *K. Philip's War* (1862) 139 At Boston there is a Press in order to sending forth another Army to pursue the enemy. a 1715 BURNET *Own Time* (1766) II. 9 It looked liker a press than a levy. 1761–2 HUME *Hist. Eng.* (1806) III. xlix. 779 An English army of twelve thousand foot and two hundred horse was levied by a general press throughout the kingdom. 1771 *Junius Lett.* lix. (1797) II. 196 With regard to the press for seamen.. bounties..have a limit. 1793 NELSON in Nicolas *Disp.* (1845) I. 299, I have only got a few men.., and without a press I have no idea our Fleet can be manned. 1803 *Naval Chron.* IX. 328 There was a very hot press last night throughout Plymouth. 1894 C. N. ROBINSON *Brit. Fleet* 413 The 'Press' does..derive its name..from the 'prest' or 'imprest' money paid to the man on entry as an earnest of his wages on enlisting in the King's service.

† **b.** A warrant or commission giving authority to impress recruits. *Obs.* exc. *Hist.*

1596 SHAKS. 1 *Hen. IV*, IV. ii. 13, I haue mis-vs'd the Kings Presse damnably. I haue got, in exchange of a hundred and fiftie Souldiers, three hundred and odde Pounds. 1667 DRYDEN *Wild Gallant* Epil. 22 They shrink like seamen when a press comes out.

† **c.** = PRESS-MONEY. *Obs.*

1626 *Faithful Friends* I. ii, *Marc.* Hold thee, here's gold; furnish thyself with speed:..These shall along with us too. Receive your press. *Calve.* Oh, good captain, I have a wife, indeed, sir. *Marc.* If she be a striker, I will press her too.

2. *transf.* and *fig.* Impressment into service of any kind; a requisition.

1667 *Decay Chr. Piety* viii. ¶ 44, 233 'Tis this Fear [of singularity] that engages many in it; and though it hath too many voluntiers, yet sure 'tis this press that helps to make up its numbers. 1670 EACHARD *Cont. Clergy* 119 If men of knowledge, prudence, and wealth, have a phansie against a living of twenty or thirty pounds a year, there is no way to get them into such an undertaking, but by sending out a spiritual press. 1855 W. SARGENT *Braddock's Exped.* 166 To be reminded that such things as a Press of private means for the benefit of the State still existed. 1894 *Daily News* 25 July 5/6 The Central Government [of China] has placed an emergency press upon the fleet of the China Merchants Company to be taken when necessary for transport of troops.

3. *attrib.* and *Comb.*, as *press-boat, -ketch, -smack, -vessel* (a vessel employed in pressing seamen). See also PRESS-GANG, PRESS-MONEY, etc.

1688 LUTTRELL *Brief Rel.* (1857) I. 457 The next day the presse boats went down the river to presse seamen. 1696 *Lond. Gaz.* No. 3164/1 On Board any of His Majesty's Ships of War, or Hire-Ships, or on any Press-Vessels, or Tenders. 1702 *Flying Post* Apr. 4/7 Some Press-Ketches in that [Dublin] Harbour have pressed 400 Seamen within a few Days, and..a great many are voluntarily come in. 1745 *Proj. Manning Navy* 6 Those who are daily dragg'd into the Press-Smacks.

† **Press**, *a.* *Obs.* [ad. L. *press-us*, of style, compressed, concise, also close, exact, accurate, precise; in origin pa. pple. of *premĕre* to press.] Concise, compendious; close, precise, exact, minute: chiefly of language.

c 1611 CHAPMAN *Iliad* XIV. Comm. 199 Homers maner of writing..is so presse, and puts on with so strong a current, that it farre ouer-runnes the most laborious pursuer. 1615 CROOKE *Body of Man* 432 There is a double acception of the word *Caput* among Physitions, one strickt & presse, another large and ample. 1661 RUST *Origen & Opin.* in *Phnix* (1721) I. 33 They observe not those terms and conditions, being drawn away from a press and careful attendance to them. 1675 R. BURTHOGGE *Causa Dei* 329 Of which persuasion [that the World should have End by Fire]..were all the Stoicks; Seneca is press and full, *At illo tempore, solutis Legibus, fine modo fertur* [etc.].

Press (pres), *v.*[1] Forms: α. 4–5 **press-en, -yn**, 4–7 **presse**, 6– **press** (5 **pres**). *Pa. t.* and *pple.* **pressed**; also 4– **prest** (4 **yprast**). β. 4–7 **prese**, 4–5 **prece** (4–7 **praise**), 5–6 **preace**, 5–7 *Sc.* **preis, -ss**, 5–7 (*dial.* 8–9) **prease**, 6–7 **preasse**, 9 *dial.* **preese, -ze**. [Two forms: α. ME. *press-en*, a. OF. *press-er* (13th c. in Littré) = It. *pressare*:— L. *pressāre*, freq. of *premĕre, press-um* to press. β. ME. *prēse(n, prēce(n*, with lengthened vowel: cf. *prēs, prees, prese*, parallel form of PRESS *sb.*[1], and see Note below. The β form prevails in branch III, where it appears to be the earlier; it is rare in I and II.]

I. Literal and directly connected senses. Primarily *trans.*

1. *trans.* To act upon (a body) with a continuous force directed towards or against it (the body by or through which the force is exerted being in contact with that acted upon); to exert a steady force against (something in contact), e.g. by weight (downwards), or by other physical agency or voluntary effort (in any direction); to subject to pressure.

[13.. *E. E. Allit. P.* B. 1249 Prestes & prelates þay presed to deþe.] c 1385 CHAUCER *L. G. W.* 1787 (*Lucrece*) And as she wok hire bed she felte presse. c 1440 *Promp. Parv.* 412/2 Pressyn, *premo, comprimo, presso*. c 1445 LYDG. *Nightingale* 152 Like hem that pressen vpwards of entent In the pressour. 1592 SHAKS. *Rom. & Jul.* III. ii. 60 Thou and Romeo presse one heauie beere. 1656 tr. *Hobbes' Elem. Philos.* (1839) 211 Of two moved bodies one presses the other, when with its endeavour it makes either all or part of the other body to go out of its place. 1820 SHELLEY *Sensit. Pl.* II. 21 Her step seemed to pity the grass it prest. 1839 G. BIRD *Nat. Philos.* 89 The layer of fluid would be submitted to unequal pressure, being in a pressed by the long column, and in A pressed only by the shorter column. *Ibid.* 341 The plane glass against which it is pressed. 1893 W. S. GILBERT *Utopia* 1, You only need a button press.

b. *To press* (*to death*): to execute the punishment of *peine forte et dure* upon (a person arraigned for felony who stood mute and would not plead): see PEINE. *Obs.* exc. *Hist.*

1554 *Dial. on Laws Eng.* II. xli. 133 He shalbe pressed to death [see PEINE]. 1604 G. DUGDALE *Disc. Pract. Eliz. Caldwell* B ij, According to the Law, he was adiudged to be prest, receiuing his iudgement on the Saturday, to be executed on Munday following. *Ibid.*, [He] was prest. 1675 3 *Inhumane Murthers* 6 The same day he was pressed, being very willing to dye. 1770 *Chron.* in *Ann. Reg.* 129/2 Cooowry at first refused to plead, but being taken down and shewn the apparatus for pressing him to death, if he refused, he relented. 1900 *Daily News* 31 Dec. 6 There can be no doubt that it was in 1736 that the barbarous practice of 'pressing to death' was last resorted to.

c. As a sign of affection or courtesy (with a person, the hand, etc. as object).

1700 DRYDEN *Iliad* VI. 173 She..press'd Th' illustrious infant to her fragrant breast. 1780 COWPER *Doves* 26 'Tis then I feel myself a wife, And press thy wedded side. 1810 SCOTT *Lady of L.* II. xxxvii, The Minstrel's hand he kindly pressed. 1832 TENNYSON *Miller's Daughter* 160 She..rose, and..press'd you heart to heart.

d. *intr.* To exert pressure; to bear with weight or force *on, upon, against*.

1815 J. SMITH *Panorama Sc. & Art* I. 76 The column sustained by the bottom of such a vessel..is therefore no more than what would press upon the bottom of a vessel Y. *Ibid.* 232 To make the surfaces intended to be in contact, press against each other simultaneously and uniformly in every part. 1837 W. IRVING *Capt. Bonneville* III. 240 The heavy buffalo..are easily overtaken by the Blackfeet; whose fleet steps press lightly on the surface. 1878 HUXLEY *Physiogr.* 88 Since air possesses weight, it necessarily presses upon any object exposed to its influence.

2. *trans.* To cause to move in some direction or into some position by pressure; to push, drive, thrust. (With various advbs. and preps.)

c 1410 *Master of Game* (MS. Digby 182) xxiv, If..þe foote and þe knees haue..ypressede þe grasse a doune. a 1425 *Cursor M.* 11829 (Trin.) Þe dropesy so to gider him prest. c 1440 *Promp. Parv.* 412/1 Precyn in, *ingero*. *Ibid.* 412/2 Presse downe, *deprimo, reprimo*. 1526 TINDALE *Luke* vi. 38 Good measure, pressed doune, shaken to gedder, and runnynge ouer. 1697 DAMPIER *Voy.* I. xviii. 495 The Wind being on our broad side, prest her down very much. 1824 R. STUART *Hist. Steam Engine* 196 The steam presses the pistons or valves forward in that direction. 1832 R. & J. LANDER *Exped. Niger* I. xi. 84 The weight of his..ornaments almost pressed him to the ground. 1842 TENNYSON *Locksley Hall* 90 Baby fingers, waxen touches, press me from the mother's breast. 1899 *Allbutt's Syst. Med.* VII. 250 The blood pressed up the vena cava can be aspirated into the right heart.

b. *fig.* (usually with *down*).

a 1340 HAMPOLE *Psalter, Cant.* 497 Noght pressid down in þe luf of þis warld. 1382 WYCLIF *Bible* Pref. Ep. i. 61 Pictagorax..more wilnyng other mennus thingis shamfastli to lernen, than his owne vnshamfastli to prece forth [*sua impudenter ingerere*]. 1576 FLEMING *Panopl. Epist.* 82 We felt the burthen of necessitie pressing downe our shoulders. 1668 R. STEELE *Husbandman's Calling* vii. (1672) 188 The husbandman..hath weights to press him down, and therefore hath need of wings to lift him up.

3. To extract by pressure; to express; to squeeze (juice, etc.) *out of* or *from* something.

1388 WYCLIF *Gen.* xl. 11 Therfor Y took the grapis, and presside [c 1430–40 *MSS. I. & S.* presside hem] out in to the cuppe which Y helde. c 1420 *Liber Cocorum* (1862) 49 Sethe hom in water .. Þen take hom up; presse a non þe water of hom. 1526 *Pilgr. Perf.* (W. de W. 1531) 246 b, This..shall presse out teares of our eyes. 1697 DRYDEN *Virg. Georg.* I. 412 To gather Laurel-berries, and the Spoil Of bloody Myrtles, and to press your Oyl. 1744 BERKELEY *Siris* § 212 Wine is pressed from the grape. 1830 M. DONOVAN *Dom. Econ.* I. 13 It is very probable, that it was much the same word as is used..in Gen. ix. 21, viz. יין from יָנָה to press out.

4. To subject to pressure so as to reduce to a particular shape, consistence, smoothness, thinness, or bulk, or so as to extract juice, etc. from; to compress, squeeze.

c 1430–40 [see prec., quot. 1388]. 1549 *Act 3 & 4 Edw. VI*, c. 2 § 8 That no person shall..put to sale here within the Realme..any cloth being pressed to be..worne here within the Realme of England. 1555 EDEN *Decades* 3 They neuer eate *Iucca* excepte it be first sliced & pressed. 1562 J. HEYWOOD *Prov. & Epigr.* (1867) 137 He hath turnd his typpet and prest it so close, That for a turnd typpet it hath a fayre glose. 1659 LEAK *Waterwks.* 1 The Aire may be prest, but not the Water. 1715 DESAGULIERS *Fires Impr.* 45 You have always more dense Air in the Room, it being more press'd. 1764 HARMER *Observ.* x. iv. 155 Into these they put the curds, and binding them up close, press them. 1796 MRS. GLASSE *Cookery* xxi. 339 Press them as long as there is any milk in the almonds. 1844 G. DODD *Textile Manuf.* iii. 106 'Pressing' it [cloth] between hot iron plates and smooth millboard.

† **5.** To print: = IMPRESS *v.*[1] 4. *Obs.* or *arch.*

1579 FULKE *Confut. Sanders* 691 Howe proue you that this picture was pressed when that leafe came to Correction? 1637 LAUD *Relat. Confer.* Ep. Ded. (1639) A iij b, The Discourse upon this Conference stayed so long, before it could endure to be pressed. 1857 T. H. WARREN *By Severn Sea* 32 He who pressed, He who bound.

II. Figurative senses, denoting actions compared to physical pressure. Usually *trans.*

6. *trans.* (*fig.* of 1.) Of an enemy, an attacking force, etc.: To bear heavily on, to assail with much force; to reduce to straits; to beset, harass. Now chiefly in *hard pressed*.

1375 BARBOUR *Bruce* x. 316 [He] presyt the folk that thar-in ves, Swa that nocht ane the ȝet durst pas. c 1400 *Destr. Troy* 8606 Polidamas, the pert, was presset so fast, Þat he was wonen in wer, & away led. 1560 DAUS tr. *Sleidane's Comm.* 353 The horsemen pressed him before, and the fotemen gaue the onset at his back. 1607 TOPSELL *Four-f. Beasts* (1658) 101 All of them being pressed with Dogs or other wilde Beasts, will fly unto a man for succour. 1686 tr. *Chardin's Coronat. Solyman* 94 The Generalissimo ceas'd not to press the Armenians. 1693 *Mem. Cnt. Teckely* II. 153 The Place was pressed with vigour enough till the 11th of September. 1769 ROBERTSON *Chas. V*, IV. Wks. 1813 V. 405 The castle of Milan was pressed more closely than ever. 1893 FORBES-MITCHELL *Remin. Gt. Mutiny* 23 Although hard pressed at first, the force eventually gained a..victory.

† **b.** Of a tyrant, adverse circumstances, etc.: To oppress; to crush, reduce to distress or misery; to load or burden with impositions or restrictions; to distress, afflict. *Obs.*

c 1400 *Destr. Troy* 5093 Non proffer, apon payne, to prese hym no more. c 1425 WYNTOUN *Cron.* I. 1663 (Cotton MS.) Na man sulde swa hardy be Hym to presse, to tak or sla. 1553 T. WILSON *Rhet.* (1580) 202 Chrisogonus here that moste can doe, will presse vs with his power. 1585 T. WASHINGTON tr. *Nicholay's Voy.* III. xiii. 95 Yet are they pressed wyth a more grieuous tribute. 1609 BIBLE (Douay) *Hist. Table* II. 1079 The children of Israel were pressed with servitude in Ægypt. 1633 P. FLETCHER *Purple Isl.* III. xix, So when a tyrant raves, his subjects pressing, His gaining is their losse. 1720 OZELL *Vertot's Rom. Rep.* II. x. 153 The People, press'd by Hunger, called loudly for Bread. 1793 SMEATON *Edystone L.* § 102, I should not be able to..get out when there pressed with danger.

c. To affect with a feeling (physical or mental) of pressure, constraint, or distress; to weigh down, burden, oppress (the feelings, mind, spirits, etc.).

1604 SHAKS. *Oth.* III. iv. 177, I haue this while with leaden thoughts beene prest. 1656 RIDGLEY *Pract. Physic* 259 When he ascends a steep place, he is pressed with an unusual difficulty of breathing. 1695 PRIOR *Ode Queen's Death* vi, If prest by Grief our Monarch stoops. 1738 WESLEY *Ps.* LXXXVIII. i, These horrid Clouds that press my frighted Soul.

† **d.** Of a difficulty or the like: = BESET *v.* 3 b.

1654 JER. TAYLOR *Real Pres.* 35 On the other side no inconvenience can presse our interpretation of 'spiritual eating Christ by faith'. 1662 STILLINGFL. *Orig. Sacr.* III. i. § 8 The Atheist in denying a Deity, must assert something else instead of it, which is pressed with the same, if not greater difficulties, and proved by far less reason.

e. To put to straits, as by want of time, space, means, etc.: in passive, usually with *for*. (Cf. 8 b.)

1678 HICKES in Ellis *Orig. Lett.* Ser. II. IV. 47, I..am very sensible how much you press yourself to keep correspondence with me. 1813 MACAULAY in *Life & Lett.* (1880) I. 42 Being pressed for room, I will conclude. 1817 COBBETT *Wks.* XXXII. 354 In writing the last Number I was pressed for time. 1845 DISRAELI *Sybil* III. iii, I am pressed for business, but I will wait and watch over him till the crisis is passed. 1861 CRAIK *Hist. Eng. Lit.* I. 89 He had felt continually pressed by the necessity of economising his paper or parchment. 1866 G. A. LAWRENCE *Sans Merci* xiv, You can have money sooner, if you are much pressed for it.

7. *intr.* To produce a strong mental or moral impression *upon*; in mod. use usually (*fig.* from 1 d), to bear heavily, weigh *upon* (the mind, etc.).

1561 T. NORTON tr. *Calvin's Inst.* I. 5 Least they shoulde in al thinges seme to despise him, whoes maiestie still presseth vpon them. 1802 MAR. EDGEWORTH *Moral T.* (1816) I. xvii. 144 The reflection that he had wasted his time..pressed upon his mind. 1838–9 FR. A. KEMBLE *Resid. in Georgia* (1863) 131 People in the South, pressed upon by northern opinion.

8. *trans.* To urge on, impel or try to impel to action; to constrain, compel, force.

[The frequency of *prese* forms in 8, 9, 9 b, perh. indicates some association with the intr. senses in III.]

α. 1390 GOWER *Conf.* I. 217 Sodeinly the jugge he nom.. and hath him pressed, That he the sothe him hath confessed. 1590 SHAKS. *Mids. N.* III. ii. 184 Why should hee stay whom Loue doth presse to go? What loue could presse Lysander from my side? 1611 BIBLE *Acts* xviii. 5 Paul was pressed in spirit, and testified to the Iewes, that Iesus was Christ. 1758 J. S. *Le Dran's Observ. Surg.* (1771) 164 The Patient being pressed to go backwards, went behind the Tent. 1861 MAY *Const. Hist.* (1863) I. i. 62 They [the Commons] could withhold the supplies, and press the king with representations against his ministers.

β. 1565 *Reg. Privy Council Scot.* I. 372 Thair Majesteis heirtofoir hes na wayis preissit ony personis in the fre use of thair conscience. 1580 *Ibid.* III. 281 They have nevir persuadit nor preissit his Majestie to this hour. 1586 J. CARMICHAEL *Let.* in *Wodrow Soc. Misc.* (1844) 444 Turncotes..if they were preasit, they wald be readie to cap, and cope, and surpleis. 1623 PR. CHARLES *Let.* (in *Athenæum* 24 Feb. (1872) 241/2) Ye euer promised that the King [my] father should be no farder preaced in matters of religion. a 1627 MIDDLETON *Mayor of Quinborough* I. (1661) 8 Great Constantine our Noble Father,..therefore prais'd me into this profession.

b. Said of danger, business, etc., or of time. Now only *absol.* or *intr.* To compel haste or dispatch; to be urgent; to be pressing; to demand immediate action. (Cf. 6 e.) So mod.F. *le temps presse*; *le péril presse*.

c 1440 *York Myst.* xl. 192 Here may we notte melle of more at þis tyde, For prossesse of plaies þat precis in plight. 1683 TEMPLE *Mem.* Wks. 1731 I. 396 The Prince wou'd have had me stay, but..I pretended some Letters press'd me, and so went away. 1748 *Col. Rec. Pennsylv.* V. 44 Let it be done with Dispatch, for the time presses. 1823 SCOTT *Peveril* xxviii, Do you think I will read all these?..I mean, is there any thing which presses? *Mod.* Time presses: I must go.

c. To impel to rapid movement; to urge on, hasten, drive quickly. *rare.*

1611 BIBLE *Esther* viii. 14 So the posts..went out, being hastened, and pressed on by the kings commandement. 1856 KANE *Arct. Expl.* II. xx. 198, I..pressed my dogs for the hut.

d. With the movement as obj.: To urge, hasten, execute quickly.

1742 COLLINS *Oriental Ecl.* IV. 9 Fast as they prest their flight. 1821 SCOTT *Kenilw.* xiii, Tressilian and his attendants pressed their route with all dispatch.

9. To urge by words or arguments; to try hard to persuade; to importune, beg, beseech, entreat (a person *to do* something or *for* something).

α. 1593 BILSON *Govt. Christ's Ch.* 273 They be Ieromes owne words that I presse you with. 1596 SHAKS. *Merch. V.* IV. i. 425 You presse mee farre, and therefore I will yeeld. 1617 MORYSON *Itin.* I. 23 Neither they nor any other would take the least reward of mee, though I pressed them to receiue it. 1698 FRYER *Acc. E. India & P.* Pref., More than Four hundred Queries..to which I was pressed for Answers. 1748 *Anson's Voy.* III. x. 409 He was much pressed to go into a neighbouring apartment. 1800 DE QUINCEY in 'H. A. Page' *Life* (1877) I. iii. 53 To avoid being pressed..to stay another day. 1875 JOWETT *Plato* (ed. 2) I. 15, I will share the enquiry with you, but I will not press you if you would rather not.

β. 1623 PR. CHARLES *Let.* (in *Athenæum* 24 Feb. (1872) 241/2) Which the Pope so earnestlie preases to be added.

b. *intr.* or *absol.* To use urgent entreaty; to ask or seek importunately. Const. *for* or *inf.*; formerly also *on, upon* (a person).

β. 1401 *Pol. Poems* (Rolls) II. 33 Freer, what charity is this, to prease upon a rich man, and to intice him to be buried among you from his parish church? 1529 MORE *Dyaloge* III. Wks. 214/1 He was in his examinacion sore preaced vpon to tell for what intent he made such a sermon ready. a 1699 LADY A. HALKETT *Autobiog.* (1875) 43 As much as was fitt to prese for the reason.

α. a 1533 LD. BERNERS *Huon* clvi. 599 Kynge Arthur hath sore pressed on me to haue my dignyte & realme. 1648 in *Hamilton Papers* (Camden) 220 My Lord Newcastle hes prest mouch for his dispach, and a comision for the North. 1709–10 ADDISON *Tatler* No. 121 ¶ 1 There was a Gentlewoman below who..pressed very much to see me. 1766 GOLDSM. *Vic. W.* viii, And spread his vegetable store And gaily pressed, and smiled. 1833 HT. MARTINEAU *Manch. Strike* ix, Don't press for an answer yet. 1895 LAKE in *Law Times* XCIX. 468/1, I applied for this on the 9th May, and pressed for it day by day.

10. *trans.* To urge, insist on the doing of (something); to solicit, request (a thing) earnestly. Const. *on, upon* (a person).

1625 BURGES *Pers. Tithes* 16 The Apostles peremptory command more then once pressed in the Gospel. 1673 *Essex Papers* (Camden) I. 93 The discontented part of yᵉ Citty press, that yᵉ Election last mentiond may be confirm'd. 1710 PRIDEAUX *Orig. Tithes* iii. 143 *note*, St. Ambrose very earnestly presseth the payment of Tithes. a 1716 BLACKALL *Wks.* (1723) I. 294, I suppose, it was not press'd upon such, by the Apostles, as a Duty. a 1770 JORTIN *Serm.* (1771) I. iv. 65 Such a person might earnestly press the observance of a duty which himself had so well fulfilled. 1834 *Tracts for Times* No. 40. 2 This material part of piety..had not been sufficiently pressed on my people. 1899 *Allbutt's Syst. Med.* VII. 591 Nothing now remained but to press the use of anti-pneumococcic serum.

11. To urge, insist on the belief, admission, or mental acceptance of (something); to impress (a thing) upon the mind, emphasize, inculcate earnestly; to present earnestly, plead with insistence (a claim, etc.). Const. *on, upon* (a person, his attention, etc.).

1625 BURGES *Pers. Tithes* 35 It must be pressed..vpon the Magistrate, that he is bound in Conscience to pull down all Churches, once superstitiously prostituted to Popish Idolatry. 1692 BENTLEY *Boyle Lect.* ix. 303 The Apostle presseth this advice in the text. 1781 COWPER *Conversation* 104 Remember, if you mean to please, To press your point with modesty and ease. 1836 J. GILBERT *Chr. Atonem.* vi. (1852) 174 Thus are we brought again to the conclusion already pressed upon attention. 1875 JOWETT *Plato* (ed. 2) I. 379 Crito is but pressing upon him the opinions of the many. 1878 STUBBS *Const. Hist.* III. xviii. § 664. 129 Letters ..in which he..presses on the potentates of east and west the great opportunity for ecclesiastical union.

12. To urge, thrust (something to be taken or accepted) *upon* a person.

1797 MRS. RADCLIFFE *Italian* i, He pressed the offer so repeatedly and respectfully that at length she accepted it. 1815 W. H. IRELAND *Scribbleomania* 285 *note*, He..refused the first ecclesiastic dignities, which were unsolicitedly pressed upon him. 1879 M. PATTISON *Milton* v. 63 The garden-house in Aldersgate-street had before been found too small for the pupils who were being now pressed upon Milton.

13. To push forward (arguments, views, considerations, positions, etc.).

1665 SIR T. HERBERT *Trav.* (1677) 355 Nor am I willing to press these conjectures any further. 1766 FORDYCE *Serm. Yng. Wom.* (1767) I. i. 17, I press not any farther an argument so exceedingly plain. 1856 FROUDE *Hist. Eng.* I. ii. 130 Charles had no desire to press matters to extremities. 1874 STUBBS *Const. Hist.* I. x. 320 Stephen pressed his advantage.

III. Senses connected with the notion of a crowd or throng, or of pushing one's way as in a throng: cf. PRESS *sb.*[1] 1. Primarily *intr.* Here the β forms are usually the earlier, and predominate till c 1600.

As L. *premĕre* and *pressāre* and OF. *presser* were only transitive, the intransitive use appears to have been developed in Eng., and perh. in connexion with the notion of pressing or crowding upon each other.

14. *intr.* To come closely to or about a person or place; esp. of a number of persons: to come up or gather in a crowd; to crowd, throng. Also *fig.*

β. 13.. *Gaw. & Gr. Knt.* 830 Mony proud mon þer presed, þat prynce to honour. 13.. *Cursor M.* 2796 (Gött.) Þe mare þat loth [= Lot] þaim [þus] bisoght, Þe mare þai presid [*Trin.* pressed] and sesid noght. c 1440 *Bone Flor.* 1082 They presyd abowte syr Sampson all. 1526 TINDALE *Luke* vi. 19 All the people preased to touche hym. 1559 *Mirr. Mag., Worcester* xvii, I could not passe, so sore they on me preast. 1569 STOCKER tr. *Diod. Sic.* I. xxxii. 38 Commanding them to preace and talke with the Captaynes. 1593 SHAKS. 3 *Hen. VI*, III. i. 19 No humble suters prease to speake for right. 1610 HOLLAND *Camden's Brit.* (16..) 175 By reason of the multitude preasing up to him.

α. c 1400 *Song Roland* 635 Ingler, and arnold, of th.. peres, I say, Pressen to the prince in þer palle wed.. c 1400 *Destr. Troy* 8227 Then the grekes..Oppressit ho.. with pyne, pressit full hard. 1642 H. MORE *Song Soul* (..) I. II. lvii, The crosse lines of a Rhomboides That from the.. meeting to all angles presse. 1648 in *Hamilton Pape..* (Camden) 210 The enemy presseth harde upon us. 17.. GIBBON *Decl. & F.* xii. (1869) I. 341 The nations of German.. who perpetually pressed on the frontiers of the empire. 18.. HT. MARTINEAU *Manch. Strike* ix, The most thinking m.. in the crowd pressed towards the waggon. 1876 C. .. DAVIES *Unorth. Lond.* 106 Consisting..of 'thoughts th.. had been pressing in upon his own soul'. 1881 HEN.. *Cornet of Horse* xxvi, All the sailors pressed up, eager .. know how the pursuit had been shaken off.

b. *trans.* To crowd upon, throng. *Obs.* or *arc..*

1549–62 STERNHOLD & H. *Ps.* cxlii. 7 When thou art goo.. to me, the just shall presse me round about. 1582 N. .. (Rhem.) *Luke* viii. 45 Maister, the multitudes throng a.. presse thee [*Vulg.* te comprimunt et affligunt; WYCLIF 13.. thringen and turmentyn thee, 1388 thristen and disesen the.. TINDALE, etc. thruste the and vexe the; *Geneva*, thrust th.. and treade on thee; 1611 throng thee and prease the.. *Revised*, press thee and crush thee]. c 1586 C'TE.. PEMBROKE *Ps.* LVI. iv, They presse me neere, my sou.. in snare to take.

c. *Naut.* *To press sail* = to crowd sail: s.. CROWD *v.*[1] 9, and cf. *press of sail*, PRESS *sb.*[1] 9.

1860 *Merc. Marine Mag.* VII. 98 Press on sail, to see.. you can come in.

15. *intr.* To push or strain forward, as throug.. a crowd or against obstacles or hindrances; to pu.. one's way, advance with force or eagerness; .. hasten onward, urge one's way.

β. c 1330 R. BRUNNE *Chron.* (1810) 112 After þis f.. praised Steuen with alle his here, Þe castellis he seised, .. he hat neuer ere. c 1330 — *Chron. Wace* (Rolls) 13.. Among þe moste euere he presed, His harde strokes noug.. ne sesed. c 1385 CHAUCER *L. G. W.* 642 (*Cleopatra*) In w.. the polax presith he & sche. c 1400 *Destr. Troy* 5138 .. þai past fro þat pales, preset vnto horse. 1526 TINDA.. *Phil.* iii. 14, I forget that which is behynde me..and pre.. vnto the marke apoynted. a 1599 SPENSER *F. Q.* VII. vi. .. The Giantesse..boldly preacing-on raught forth her ha.. 1603 FLORIO *Montaigne* II. x. (1632) 226 Sometimes th.. prease out thicke and threefold. 1621 BRATHWAIT *N..* *Embassie*, etc. (1877) 257 Two iollie shepheards, that .. hither prese.

α. c 1400 *Destr. Troy* 2156 And þus pertid þe persons .. presset to þere ynnes. c 1407 LYDG. *Reson & Sens.* 5.. Ay the more I gan to presse The more my Ioy[e] g.. tencresse. 14.. in *Tundale's Vis.* (1843) 158 Efthyr th.. full fast I prest. 1500–20 DUNBAR *Poems* xxxiii. 49 V.. no mess pressit this prelat, For sound of sacring bell n.. skellat. 1560 DAUS tr. *Sleidane's Comm.* 136 So made w.. for their fellowes without, which immediately pressed .. with a strong power. 1660 BOYLE *New Exp. Phys. Me..* xvii. 110 Air would..press in at some little Avenue or oth.. 1738 WESLEY *Ps.* LXXXIX. iv, With Reverence and religi.. Dread His Servants to his House should press. 1810 SCO.. *Lady of L.* III. xiv, Pressing forward like the wind. 18.. BRYANT *Iliad* I. v. 138 Trojans, great in mastery of stee.. Press on!

† **b.** *refl.* in same sense. *Sc. Obs. rare.*

c 1425 WYNTOUN *Cron.* II. 1310 Qwha wiþe in walde pre.. hym out, þan hym behuffit to mak entre. *Ibid.* VII. 2.. (Cotton MS.) Wiþe al þe kynge of Inglandis mycht .. pressit hym [*Wemyss MS.* He schupe him] to þe cite ric..

16. *intr.* To push one's way, thrust oneself, a.. vance into a person's presence, or into a place, bold.. presumptuously, or insistently; to approach vent.. ously, to venture; to push oneself forward, obtru.. oneself, intrude. *arch.*

β. 1377 LANGL. *P. Pl.* B. XIV. 212 Þere þe pore pres.. bifor þe riche with a pakke at his rugge. c 1394 *P. .. Crede* 749 So of þat beggers brol a bychop schal worþ.. Among þe peres of þe lond prese to sitten. c 1460 *Urba.. tatis* 25 in *Babees Bk.* 13 Amonge þe genteles gode & hen.. Prece þou not vp to hyȝ for no þyng. 1535 COVERDA.. *Prov.* xxv. 6 Prease not in to yᵉ place of greate m.. — *Ecclus.* xiii. 10 Prease not thou vnto him, that thou .. not shott out. 1587 TURBERV. *Trag. T.* (1837) 14 The peevis.. puttocke may not preace in place where Eagles are. 1.. J. CARPENTER *Solomon's Solace* viii. 32 Forbidden to pre.. forth to do the priests office. 1615 CHAPMAN *Odyss.* IV. 6.. Men's knowledges have proper limits set, And should n.. prease into the mind of God.

α. 1393 LANGL. *P. Pl.* C. XVII. 55 There þe poure pres.. by-fore with a pak at hus rygge. 1599 SANDYS *Euro.. Spec.* (1632) 76, I will not here presume to presse in with .. determination upon this great difference and question. 1.. DEKKER & WEBSTER *Hist. Sir T. Wyatt* D.'s Wks. 1.. III. 88 Pardon me Madam, that so boldly I presse in.. your Chamber. 1714 SWIFT *Imit. Horace* II. vi. 89 Y.. ne'er consider whom you shove, But rudely press before.. duke. 1885 G. MACDONALD *Diary Old Soul* 16 May, .. would go near thee—but I cannot press Into thy presen.. —it helps not to presume.

† **b.** *refl.* To presume, take upon oneself. *ra..*

1500–20 DUNBAR *Poems* XXXV. 14 Me thocht Deme Forto.. ..said on this maneir..preiss the nocht to stryfe aganis .. quheill. 1535 STEWART *Cron. Scot.* (Rolls) I. 4 And pr.. the nocht my purpois till impung.

† **17.** *intr.* To strive, try hard, endeavour, attem.. *to do* something (usually with eagerness or haste.. to aim at, strive or endeavour after somethin.. Also in weaker sense: To essay, undertake, ta.. in hand. *Obs.* (So F. *presser* in Froissart (Godef..

β. c 1374 CHAUCER *Troylus* I. 446 To seen her goo.. look be gan to prese [*rimes* encrese, cece]. c 1380 WYC.. *Wks.* (1880) 166 Ȝonge children presen faste to be p.. c 1475 *Rauf Coilȝear* 615 To cum to this Palice he pre.. to preif. 1513 DOUGLAS *Æneis* x. xi. 193 Athir way

Supplement, p. 3873; Corrigenda, p. 4092; Spurious words, p. 4093; Books quoted, p. 4094

Press, v.[2] Pa.t. and ppple. pressed; also 6–8 prest. [Altered from or substituted for PREST, by association with PRESS v.[1]; see PRESS-MONEY.]

Pressible, (pre-sib'l), a.[1] rare. [f. PRESS v.[1] + -IBLE.] ... That may be pressed: in various senses of the verb.

Pressable, a.[1] rare. [f. PRESS v.[1] + -ABLE.] Liable to be pressed or taken by a press-gang.

Press-bed. Obs. exc. dial. A bed constructed to fold up, when not in use, into a press.

Pressed, ppl. a.[1] [f. PRESS v.[1] + -ED.]

Presser (pre·sǝɹ). Also 6 -or. [Partly f. PRESS v.[1] + -ER[1]; partly from PRESSOUR, with change of suffix.] One who presses. Applied to workmen in various trades.

Pressing, vbl. sb.[1] [f. PRESS v.[1] + -ING[1].]

Pressingly, adv. [f. PRESSING ppl. a. + -LY[2].]

Pression (pre·ʃǝn). Now rare. [a. F. pression (= Ital. pressione, Sp. presion), ad. L. pression-em.] The action of pressing; pressure.

Pressive (pre·siv), a. Now rare. [f. L. press- (see PRESS v.[1]) + -IVE.]

Pressor (pre·sǝɹ). Ornith. [ad. f. L. pressor, agent-n. from press-, ppl. stem of premĕre to PRESS.]

Pressirostral, a. [f. PRESSIROSTRES + -AL.]

Pressirostres, sb. pl. Ornith. [mod.L.]

Pressman (pre·smæn). [f. PRESS sb.[1] + MAN sb.[1]] 1. A man engaged in a wine-press. 2. A man who operates or manages a printing-press.

Pressmark. [PRESS sb.[1] + MARK.] In libraries, a mark or number written or stamped in or on each book.

Press-master. [f. PRESS sb.[2] + MASTER sb.] One who was authorized to impress recruits.

Press-money, = prest-money. Now only Obs. Also 6 prease-, 7 preassed-. [Orig. prest-money, f. PREST sb.[2] + MONEY.]

Pressness. [f. PRESS a. + -NESS.]

Prest, sb.[2] [a. OF. prest.] 1. Money advanced, a loan; esp. to the sovereign in an emergency. 2. Money paid in advance for work undertaken, or expenses to be incurred.

Press-paper. [ad. F. presse-papier.]

Press-room. [f. PRESS sb.[1] + ROOM sb.] 1. The room in a printing-office in which the presses stand, and where the printing is done.

Press-room. [f. PRESS sb.[2] + ROOM.] 2. Obs.

Press-sail = press of sail. Obs.

Pressurage. Sc. form of PRESSURE.

Pressual, a. Obs. rare. [f. PRESSURE.]

Pressure (pre·ʃʊɹ), sb. [a. obs. F. pressure (12th c. in Godef.), ad. L. pressūra, f. press-, ppl. stem of premĕre to PRESS.]

Pressure-work. [f. PRESS sb.[1] + WORK sb.]

Prest, v. Obs. rare. [f. PREST sb.[2] or OF. prester.]

PREST.

Prest, *a.* and *adv. Obs.* Also 3–6 preste, 5 prest, (prast), 6 preast, 7 Sc. priest, (7 *erron.* pressed). [a. OF. *prest* (11th c. in Littré), in mod.F. *prêt* = Pr., Cat. *prest*, It., Sp., Pg. *presto* —late or pop. L. *præst-us* ready (7 cent. in Salic Law), earlier L. *præstō* (*præstō*) adv., near at hand, in readiness, at one's service; supposed to be contr. from **præsitō, † pro* before, in front + *sit-* of *sitās*, abl. of *situs* situation.]

A. *adj.* **1.** Ready for action or use; at hand; prepared, or in proper order.

2. Often in association with *ready, readily*.

†Prest[2], *sb.* Obs. rare. Also 7–8 press[e. [Of uncertain origin.] A sheet of parchment or the like.

†Prest[3], *v.* Obs. [f. PREST *sb.*[1].] *trans.* To engage or hire the services of (a person) or the use of (a ship, etc.) by giving part-payment in advance.

†Prest[4], *v.* Obs. rare[1]. [f. PREST *sb.*[2].] *trans.* To press.

†Prest[5], *ppl. a.* = PRESSED *ppl. a.*[1].

†Prest[6], *v.* Obs. [a. OF. *prester* (11th c. in Godef. Compl.), mod.F. *prêter* to furnish, place at one's disposal, lend, pay in advance (= It. *prestare*, ...

Prestable, *a. Sc.* Now rare. Also 7 -ible. [a. obs. F. *prestable* (mod.F. *prêtable*) leviable, that may be lent (Cotgr.), also, ready to afford or give (16th c. in Godef.), f. *prester*: see PREST *v.*[1] and -ABLE.] Capable of being paid or advanced; payable; capable of being performed or discharged.

Prestance. *rare*[1]. [f. as next + -ANCE. Cf. F. *prestance* (pregât fm), ad. It. *prestanza* (med. L.)...] Surpassing excellence; pre-eminence.

†Prestancy, *Obs. rare*[1]. [ad. L. *præstantia*, f. *præstant-em* PRESTANT: see next and -ANCY.] Priority, superiority, pre-eminence.

Prestant, *a. Mus.* [See quot.] The open diapason of an organ, sometimes of 16 feet, sometimes of 8 feet in length.

PRESTER JOHN.

†Præstantious, *pre-, a. Obs. rare*[1]. [f. L. *præstantia* excellence, PRESTANCY + -OUS.] Characterized by excellence; excellent.

Prestate (pre'stēt), *n. Rom. Law.* [pl. stem of L. *præstāre* to stand before, to stand good for, vouch for, answer for: see PREST *sb.*[1] and -ATE[3].] *trans.* To undertake, take upon oneself; become responsible for; to furnish, manifest.

Prestation (prestā'ʃən). [a. F. *prestation*...] The action of lending, rendering, etc., ad. L. *præstātiōn-em*, n. of action f. *præstāre*: see PREST *v.*[1], PRESTATE.] The action of paying, of rendering service, what is due by law or custom...

†Preter. Obs. [a. L. *prætēr*, adv. or prep.] A ruler likened to Prester John; one who is supreme (in a particular sphere).

1. A serpent, the fire of which was fabled to cause death by swelling.

2. A burning or scorching whirlwind.

Prestern, presternum. [f. PRE-+ STERNUM.]

1. *Entom.* = PROSTERNUM.

2. *Comp. Anat.* The front part of the sternum.

Pre-sternal, *a.*, or pertaining to the pre-sternum, in *præ-sternal* region, etc.

Presthood, obs. form of PRIESTHOOD.

Prestidigital, *a. Obs. rare*[1]. [f. after next and *digital*.] Light-fingered; practising sleight of hand.

PRESTISSIMO.

The practice of juggling, sorcery, or magic; deception or illusion by such practice; conjuring.

Prestidigitator (prestidi'giteitər). Also in F. form prestidigitateur (prestidigitæ:tœ:r). [a. F. *prestidigitateur* (prestidigitatœr)... 1831), f. *preste* nimble (ad. It. *presto*, L. *præstus*: see PRESTO) + L. *digit-us* a finger + *-ateur*, L. *-ātor* agent-suffix...] One who practises sleight of hand or legerdemain; a juggler, a conjurer; hence *fig.*

Prestidigitatory, *a.* Of, belonging to, or of the nature of prestidigitation or legerdemain.

Prestige (pre'stidʒ, pre:sti:ʒ). [a. F. *prestige* (16th c. in Littré) an illusion, esp. in pl. *deceits*, impostures, delusions, jugling or consenting tricks (Cotgr.), in mod.F. illusion, magic, glamour, ad. L. *præstigium* a delusion, illusion, usually in pl. *præstigia* juggler's tricks, for **præ-strigium* (*præstringere* to blind fast [*præstringere oculos* to blindfold, hence, to dazzle the eyes]: see PRESTRICT + -ION.]

†1. An illusion; a conjuring trick; a deception. Usually *pl. Obs.*

2. Influence, reputation or standing derived from former achievements...

Prestigiate, *v. Obs. rare*[1]. [f. L. *præstigi-um* (see PRESTIGE) + -ATE[3].]

Prestigiation, *Obs. rare*[1]. The practising of juggling or legerdemain; the exhibition of deceptive or delusive feats.

Prestigious, *a.* [f. as prec. + -OUS.] Practising legerdemain, juggling, or magic; deceptive, illusory.

PRESTLY.

†Prestly, *adv. Obs.* Also 4–5 pristly, prystly, 6 preastly. [f. PREST *a.* + -LY[2].]

1. Readily, quickly, promptly, immediately.

Prestmoney, earlier form of PRESS-MONEY.

Prestness. [f. PREST *a.* + -NESS.] Readiness, preparedness.

†Presto (pre'stō), *a.*[1], *adv.*[1], *sb.*[1] *Music*. [It. *presto* quick, quickly (*tempo presto* quick time); L. *præst-us*, f. earlier *prest* adv., at hand, ready, in red L. prompt, quick: see PREST *a.*]

A. *adj.* or *adv.* A direction indicating rapid performance: in quick time: fast.

Presto, *a.*[2], *adv.*[2], *sb.*[2] [a. It. *presto* adj. and adv., quick, quickly = the same word as prec., but the inc uses are unconnected in Eng.]

A. *adv.* (*interj.*) Quickly, immediately, at once.

Prestolate, *v. Obs. rare*[1]. [f. L. *præstolāt-*, ppl. stem of *præstolāri* to wait for, wait for: see -ATE[3].] *trans.* To wait.

Prestool, obs. form of PRIESTHOOD.

Prestoler (Rabelais), *n.* [F. *prestoler*...

Prestrict, *v. Obs. rare*[1]. [f. L. *præstrict-*, ppl. stem of *præstringere*: see below.] *trans.* To bind, tie fast.

†Prestriction, *Obs. rare*[1]. [ad. late L. *præstrictiōn-em* binding fast, n. of action f. *præstringere*: see next.] The binding or tying up of the divers; blindfolding, binding.

Prestringe, *v. Obs. rare.* [ad. L. *præstring-ere* to bind fast, to touch upon, mention, f. *præ*, PRE + L. *stringere* to draw tight, to touch.] *trans.* To touch upon, mention, refer to.

Prest-sail = press of sail: see PRESS *sb.*[1] 9.

Pre-study = PRE- A. 1. Prestwoode, obs. form of PRIESTHOOD. Presubmittant, Presubliminal: see PRE- A. 3, B. 3.

Presul (prē'səl). *rare.* [a. L. *præsul* a dancer in public, the leader of the *Salii* (dancing priests), hence in late L. a præsident, a prelate, bishop, f. *præsilīre*, *præsul-um*, to dance before others, f. *præ* before, in front + *salīre* to leap, dance.] A prelate, a bishop. Hence **Pre'sulate**, the tenure of office of a 'presul'.

†Prosultor. *Obs. rare*[1]. In 7 præsu-. [Late L. *præsultor* one who dances before others, agent-n. f. *præsilīre*: see prec.] One who leads the dance.

†Prou:mury, *a. Obs. nonce-wd.* [f. after DE-SULTORY: see PRE- A. and prec.] Characterized by leaping forward, presumptuous.

Presumable (prī:z:ə'mäb'l), *a.* [f. PRESUME *v.* + -ABLE; so F. *présumable* (16th c. in Godef.).] 1. Capable of being presumed or taken for granted; probable, likely.

Presumably, *adv.* [f. prec. + -LY[2].]

†Presumant, *a. Obs. rare*[1]. [ad. F. *présu-mant*, pres. pple. of *présumer* to PRESUME.] Presuming, presumptuous.

PRESUME.

Presume (prīzū'm), *v.* Also 4 -sewme, -seume, 6 preswme, 6 presume, 7 presumme. [a. F. *présumer* (12–13th c. in Hatz.-Darm.), ad. L. *præsūmere* to take before, anticipate, in late L. to take for granted, assume, suppose, dare, f. *præ*, PRE- A. 1 + *sūmere* to take.]

†1. *trans.* To take possession of without right: to usurp, seize. *Obs. rare.*

2. To take upon oneself, undertake without adequate authority or permission; to venture upon.

a. with simple object.

b. with *inf.*: To be so presumptuous as; to take the liberty; to venture, dare (*to do* something).

3. To assume oneself, presume without proof; take for granted, presuppose.

†4. *intr.* To presume, to take upon oneself; to form expectation of, look for. *Now rare Obs.*

5. *trans.* To presuppose, to assume as reasonably certain.

6. *intr.* To press forward presumptuously; to advance or make one's way over-confidently into an unwarranted position or place; to aspire presumptuously; to presume to, *fig. Now rare or Obs.*

7. *intr.* with *on*, *upon* (*of*): to rely upon, count upon, take for granted; to form expectation of, look for. *Now rare Obs.*

Presumedly (prīzū'medli), *adv.* [f. prec. + -LY[2].] As is or may be presumed; supposedly.

Presumer (prīzū'mər). [f. prec. + -ER[1].] One who presumes.

PRESUMED.

Presumed (prīzū'md), *ppl. a.* [f. prec. + -ED[1].] Assumed before or without proof; taken for granted; anticipated, expected.

Presumedly (prīzū'medli), *adv.* [f. prec. + -LY[2].] As is or may be presumed; supposedly.

Presuming, *vbl. sb.* [f. PRESUME *v.* + -ING[1].] The action of the verb PRESUME; presumption.

Presuming, *ppl. a.* [f. PRESUME *v.* + -ING[2].] That presumes; presumptuous, arrogant, forward.

PRESUMPTUOSITY.

4. A ground or reason for presuming or believing; presumptive evidence.

Presumption (prīzʌm'pʃən). Forms: 3 presum-cioun, 4 -sumptiun, 4- presumption; also 4 -cioun, -cioun, -suncioun. [a. F. *présomption* (11–12th c. in Hatz.-Darm.), *presumpcïun* (12–13th c. in Hatz.-Darm.), ad. late L. *præsūmptiōn-em* (5th c.), f. *præsūmpt-*, ppl. stem of *præsūmere* to PRESUME.]

1. Seizure and occupation without right; usurpation; presumptuous assumption (of an office): cf. PRESUME *v.* 1, 2.

2. The taking upon oneself of more than is warranted by one's position, right, or (formerly) ability; forward or over-confident opinion or conduct; arrogance, pride, effrontery, assurance.

3. Ground or reason for presuming or believing; warranting inferences.

4. *Law.* Presumption of fact: the inference of a fact not certainly known, from known facts.

Presumptive (prīzʌm'ptiv), *a.* (*sb.*) [a. F. *présomptif, -ive* (13th c. in Godef.) presumptuous, (15th c.) of the nature of presumption, ad. late L. *præsūmptīv-us*...]

Presumptively, *adv.* [f. prec. + -LY[2].]

Presumptuosity, *Obs. rare*[1]. [f. as next + -ITY.] Usurpation.

Presumptuous (prĭzŏmptiŭas), a. Also 4 -somptious, 5 -sumptuous, -uous, 5–6 -tuous, -tuous.e, 6. OF. *presuntuex* (14th c. in Hatz.-Darm.), *presumptueux*, mod.F. *présomptueux*, ad. L. *praesumptiōsus*, late variant of the regular *praesumptiōsus* PRESUMPTION, perh. influenced by *sumptuōsus*, f. *sumptus* (see SUMPTUOUS).

...

Presumptuously, adv. [f. prec. + -LY 2.]

...

Presumptuousness, n. [f. as prec. + -NESS.]

...

Presuppose (prĭsŭpō
uz), v. ...

Presupposing, ...

Presupposal (prĭsŏpō
uzal), ...

Presupposition ...

Hence **Presuppositionless** a., without presuppositions.

Presupponible a. ...

Presydent, obs. f. PRESIDENT, PRESIDENT.

Presyne, ...

Presylvian, ...

Presystole (prĭsĭstŏli), ...

Pretax, v. ...

Pretaxable, ...

Pretaxation ...

Pre-temporal (prī-), a. ...

Pretemporary, a. ...

Pretemporal ...

†Pretence, pretense, v. Obs. [Back-formation from *pretence* n.: see PRETENCE n.; or f. late L. *pretens-*, ppl. stem of *praetendĕre*: see PRETENSE v.]

Pretenced, pretensed (-enst), ppl. a.

Pretenceful, a. ...

Pretenceless, a. ...

Pretend (prĭtend), v. Also 7 pre-. [ad. L. *praetendĕre* to stretch or hold before, put forward, allege, pretend, f. *prae*, PRE- + *tendĕre* to stretch, extend, TEND. So F. *prétendre* (14th c. in Littré).]

Pretendable, a. rare. [f. PRETEND v. + -ABLE.]

Pretendant, -ent (pretendŏnt, -ent), sb. and a. [a. F. *prétendant* (16th c. in Littré), pr. pple. of *prétendre* to PRETEND: see as sb.).]

Pretended, ppl. a. [f. PRETEND v. + -ED 1.]

Pretendedly, adv. [f. prec. + -LY 2.]

Pretender (prĭtendŏr). [f. PRETEND v. + -ER 1.]

Pretendership, ...

Pretending, ppl. a. [f. PRETEND v. + -ING 2.]

Pretendingly, ...

†Pretendence. Obs. rare. [f. PRETEND v. + -ENCE.]

Pretendment, ...

Pretendant, variant of PRETENDANT.

Pretension (prĭtenĭŏn). Also 7 -pretention. [ad. med.L. *pretentiō* (c1150 in Thomas Aquin. Summ. Theol., etc.), or ad. F. *prétention* (in 16th c. rarely *pretension*, Godef.).]

Pretensional, ...

Pretensioned, ...

Pretensious, obs. variant of PRETENTIOUS a.

Pretensive (prĭtensiv), a. Also 7 -ive. [f. late L. *praetens-*, ppl. stem of *praetendĕre* PRETEND + -IVE.]

Pretensively, adv.

Pretensory, a. Obs. rare⁻¹.

Pretent, v. Obs. rare. [ad. L. praetentāre.]

Pretentative, a. Obs. rare⁻¹.

Pretention, sb. form of PRETENSION.

Pretentious, a.

Pretentiously, adv.

Pretentiousness.

Preterit.

Preter, præter-, prefix.

Preter-Christian, a.

Preterdiplomatic, a.

Preterdivine, a.

Preterhuman, a.

Preterimperfect, a. (sb.) Gram.

Preterist.

Preterit, -ite (preʹtĕrit), a. and sb.

Preterite-present, a. (sb.) Gram.

Preterition (prētĕriʹʃən).

Preteritness.

Preterlapsed, ppl. a. rare.

Preterlegal, a. rare.

Preterminable, a. Obs. rare⁻¹.

Pretermission (prētĕrmiʹʃən).

Pretermit (prētĕrmiʹt), v.

Preterito-presential, a. Gram.

Preteritive (prĕteʹritiv), a.

Pretermitted, ppl. a.

Preternatural, a.

Preternaturalism.

Preternaturalist.

Preternaturality.

Preternaturally, adv.

Preternaturalness.

Preterperfect (prētĕrpɜːfekt), a.

Preterpluperfect, a.

Preterperfection.

Pretertiary, a.

Pretextatian.

Pretextatized.

Preternaturals.

Pretext, v. Obs.

Pretervection.

Pretextuous, a. Obs. rare⁻¹.

Pretext (prēteʹkst), v.

Pretextless, a.

Pretextate, a. Obs.

Pretor, -orian, etc.: see PRÆTOR, etc.

Pretorture, v.

Pretexture.

Pretextine, a. Obs.

Pretone, sb.

Pretonic, a. Phonology.

Pretoxtature.

Prettify (priʹtifai), v. colloq.

Prettily (priʹtili), adv.

Prettiness (priʹtinĕs).

Pretty (priʹti), a.

Prettyish, a.

Prettyism.

Pretty, adv. Forms: see prec. [The adj. in adverbial use.]

Prettify, v.

Prettyism.

Prettyity.

Pretty-pretty, a. and adv.

Prettyish, a.

Pretzel, bretzel.

Preu, prew, a. Obs.

Preux, prevor, a.

Preve, Preeve.

Preux (prø), a. [mod.F. preux valiant.]

Prevail, sb. Obs. rare.

Prevail (priveil), v.

Prevailable, a.

Prevailing, ppl. a.

Prevailingly, adv.

Prevailment.

Prevalence (prevalens).

Prevalescence.

Prevalency.

Prevalent (prevalent), a.

Prevalently, adv.

Prevaricable.

Prevaricant.

Prevaricate, v.

Prevaricating.

Prevarication (priværikeiʃən).

Prevaricative, a.

Prevaricator.

Prevaricatory, a.

Preveance.

Prevenance.

Prevene, v.

Prevenience.

Prevenient (priveenient), a.

Preveniently adv., antecedently, previously.

† Prevenire, pron. See PRÆMUNIRE.

† Prevent, ppl. a. Obs. [ad. L. prævent-us, pa. pple. of prævenire to PREVENT.] Prevented, in various senses; chiefly as pple.: see the verb.

Prevent (prĭve·nt), v. [f. L. prævent-, ppl. stem of prævenire: see PREVENE and cf. prec.]

I. † 1. trans. To act before, in anticipation of, in preparation for (a future event, or a point of time, esp. the time fixed for the act); to act as if the event or time had already come. Obs.

2. trans. To act before or more quickly than (another person or agent); to anticipate in action. Now rare and arch.

† 3. intr. or absol. To come, appear, or act before the time or in anticipation. Obs.

4. trans. To be beforehand with (a person or agent); to anticipate in action. Now rare and arch.

5. To foreanull, balk, or baffle by previous or precautionary measures. Obs. or merged in 7.

6. To cut off beforehand, debar, preclude (a person or other agent) from, deprive of a purpose, expectation, etc. Now rare or merged in 7.

† 7. To forestall, to meet in front; to meet with hostility or opposition, to confront. Obs.

† 8. To come in front of, to meet in front; to meet with welcome or succour; to meet with hostility or opposition, to confront. Obs.

† 9. To keep (something) from befalling oneself; to escape, evade, or avoid by timely action. Obs.

† 10. To frustrate, defeat, bring to nought, render void or nugatory (an expectation, plan, etc.). Obs.

† 11. intr. or absol. To use preventive measures. Usually with constr. Obs.

III. † 12. causative. To hasten, bring about or put before the time or prematurely; to anticipate.

Preventable (prĭve·ntăb'l), a. Also 8 erron. -ible. [f. PREVENT v. + -ABLE.] That may be prevented, capable of prevention.

Hence **Pre·ventableness**.

Preventative (prĭve·ntătiv), a. and sb. Also 8 erron. -itive. [f. PREVENT v. + -ATIVE. See also PREVENTIVE.]

A. adj. = PREVENTIVE 2, 3. In 7.

B. sb. = PREVENTIVE.

Preventer (prĭve·ntəɹ). [f. PREVENT v. + -ER.] One who prevents.

Preventing, ppl. a. [See -ING.] That prevents, in various senses of the vb.

Hence **Pre·ventingly** adv.

Preventional, a. rare. [f. PREVENTION + -AL.] = PREVENTIVE. Hence **Preventionalist**.

Preventive (prĭve·ntiv), a. and sb. [f. L. type *præventiv-us, f. prævent-, ppl. stem of prævenire: see PREVENE and PREVENT; cf. inventive. So mod.F. préventif.]

A. adj. † 1. That comes or goes before something else; preventient, anticipatory. Obs.

2. That anticipates in order to ward against; precautionary; that keeps from coming or taking place; that acts as a hindrance or obstacle.

B. sb. 1. That which prevents or hinders.

2. Med. Having the quality of preventing or keeping off disease; prophylactic.

Preventively, adv. [f. prec. + -LY².] In a preventive manner; in way of prevention.

Preventorium, sb. [mod.L. præventorium.] foresight.

Preview (prĭvi·ū), v. rare. [f. PRE- A. 1 + VIEW v.] trans. To view or preview beforehand; to foresee.

Preview (prĭvi·ū), sb. rare. [f. PRE- A. 1 + VIEW sb.] A previous view, inspection, or survey.

Previge, obs. Sc. form of PRIVILEGE.

Previous (prĭ·vias), a. (adv.) Also 7 pre·vious. [f. L. prævi-us going before, leading the way (f. præ, PRE- A. 1 + via way) + -OUS.]

1. Going before or in front; leading the way. (fig. in quot.) Obs.

2. Coming or going before (in time or order); foregoing, preceding, prior, antecedent.

3. With to: Coming before, preceding, antecedent to. Now rare; cf. B.

b. With to: Coming before, preceding, antecedent to. Now rare; cf. B.

c. Qualifying (and usually hyphened to) a ppl. or compound adj.; antecedently.

Previous question, in parliamentary procedure: the question whether a vote shall be taken on the main question or issue, moved before the main question comes up.

d. Previous Examination (Cambridge University): the first examination for the B.A. degree; colloquially called Little-go.

B. adv. = PREVIOUSLY; usually previous to = before, prior to.

Previously (prĭ·viasli), adv. [f. prec. + -LY².]

1. At a previous or preceding time; before, beforehand, antecedently.

Previousness (prĭ·viasnes). [f. as prec. + -NESS.] The quality or fact of being previous.

Previse (prĭvai·z), v. [f. L. prævis-, ppl. stem of prævidere.]

† 1. trans. To provide, supply, furnish. Const. of a thing. Obs. rare.

2. To foresee; to forecast. rare.

Prevision (prĭvi·ʒən), sb. Also 7-9 pre·vision-en, 9 -vision. [a. F. prévision (14th c. in Littré), ad. L. type prævision-em, n. of action f. prævidere PREVIDE.]

The action or faculty of foreseeing; knowledge of or insight into the future; foresight, foreknowledge.

b. With a and pl. An instance of this; a prophetic or anticipatory vision or perception.

Hence **Prevision** v. trans., (a) to endow with prevision; (b) to foresee.

Previsor (prĭvai·zəɹ). [f. prec.] One who foresees.

Prevost, obs. form of PROVOST.

Prevoyance (prĭvoi·ans). rare. [a. F. prévoyance.] Foresight. So **Prevoyant** a. [a. F. prévoyant.]

Prey (prē), sb. Forms: 3 preie, 3-6 praie, 3-7 preye, 4 preeye, 4 praeie, 4-7 praye, 5-6 prei, 6 praie, 7 preie; also 4-6 pray, 5-7 praie. [a. OF. preie, preje (11th c.), mod.F. proie:—L. præda booty, prey, also a beast of prey.]

1. Goods taken in war or by pillage or violence; booty, spoil, plunder. Formerly often with pl. † to prey, † to prey as a verb. arch.

2. An animal hunted or killed, esp. (now only) by carnivorous animals for food; quarry. Also fig.

3. The fact of being preyed upon, or the condition of being a victim.

PRICKLE.

¶1. A thing to prick with; a goad. *Obs.*

Prickle (prik'l), *sb.*[2] [Derivation obscure.] A wicker basket, esp. for fruit or flowers.

Pricklenose (prik'l-nouz). A derisive name for a tailor.

Prickling, *sb.* [f. PRICK *v.* + -LING[1].]

Prickle, *v.* [Partly f. PRICKLE *sb.*[1]]

1. *trans.* (or *absol.*) To prick, as with a goad or other sharp instrument; hence, to goad, instigate.

Prickle-back. Also 8-9 *bag.* [f. PRICKLE *sb.*[1] + BACK *sb.*] Name of the three-spined stickleback.

Prickled (prik'ld), *a. Obs.*

Prickle-pear. *Obs.* [f. PRICKLE *sb.*[1] + PEAR *sb.*] = PRICKLY-PEAR.

Prickless, *a.* Having no pricks; without a sting; thornless.

PRICKLY HEAT.

Prickliness. [f. PRICKLY + -NESS.] The quality of being prickly.

Prickling, *ppl. a.* [f. PRICK *v.* + -LING[1].]

1. Having, armed with, or full of prickles; aculeate.

2. Having a sensation as of many pricking points; smarting, as if full of tender prickings.

3. *Special collocations:* prickly ash; prickly broom, the whin or furze; prickly comfrey; prickly fern; prickly pole; prickly poppy.

Prickly heat, a common name for *Lichen tropicus*, an inflammatory disorder of the sweat glands.

PRICKLY PEAR.

Prickly pear, the name given to various species of the cactaceous genus *Opuntia*, prickly plants with pear-shaped fleshy edible fruit; also the fruit itself. Formerly also *Prick-pear, Prickle-pear, Pricked pear.*

Prick-madam. *Herb.* 7 *Obs.* Also 7 prick-my-dame.

Prick-mark. [f. PRICK *sb.* 10 + MARK *sb.*]

Prick-me-dainty, *sb.* and *a. Now Sc.* or *arch.* Also prickmedainty, prickmydainty.

A. *sb.* 'One who dresses in a finical manner, or is ridiculously exact in dress or carriage' (Jam.).

B. *adj.* Affectedly nice in dress or manners.

Prick-post. [f. PRICK *sb.* + POST *sb.*]

Pricknickety, -nikity, *a. Sc.* arbitrary var. of PERSNICKETY.

Prick-seam. Also *Prick-seem.* = PRICK-SEAM.

Prickwood. [See PRICK 14.]

Pricky (prik'i), *a.*

PRIDE.

Pride (praid), *sb.*[1] Forms: see A. below.

1. *orig. pricked song:* Music sung from written or 'pricked' as, distinguished from that sung from memory or by ear.

2. *trans.* A written descant or accompanying melody to a 'plain-song' or simple theme.

Prick-song (prik'sŋŋ). *Mus. Obs. exc. Hist.*

PRIDE.

II. 6. Magnificence, splendour; pomp, ostentation, display.

1. A high or overweening opinion of one's own qualities, attainments, or estate, which gives rise to a feeling and attitude of superiority over and contempt for others; inordinate self-esteem.

2. The exhibition of this quality in attitude, bearing, conduct, or treatment to others; arrogance; haughtiness.

3. A consciousness or feeling of what is befitting or due to oneself or one's position, which prevents a person from doing what he considers to be beneath him or unworthy of him; esp. as a good quality; legitimate, 'honest', or 'proper pride'; self-respect; also as a mistake or misapplied feeling, 'false pride'.

4. A feeling of elation, pleasure, or high satisfaction derived from some action or possession, etc.

5. That of which any person or body of persons is proud; that which causes a feeling of pride in those to whom it belongs; hence, the flower, the best, of a class, country, etc.

Pride, (praid), *v.* Forms: 3 *south.* prude (ii); 4 Acc. 1416 prede (-); 5 prydde, 6 *Sc.* prydy. 8-9 prided.

1. *refl.* To ornament or adorn magnificently or proudly. *Obs.*

2. *refl.* To make proud, fill with pride; to display (oneself) proudly. Chiefly in *pass.*, to be made or become proud.

Prided, *ppl. a.*, filled with pride.

Prideful (praid'fūl), *a. Chiefly Sc.* [f. PRIDE + -FUL.] Full of pride; proud, arrogant.

Prideless, *a.* [f. PRIDE *sb.*[1] + -LESS.] Devoid of pride (either in good or bad sense); having, feeling, or manifesting no pride.

Pridian (prid'iăn), *a. rare.* [ad. L. *prīdiān-us.*] Of or belonging to the day before, of a former day.

Pride-gavel. *Sc. local.* [app. f. PRIDE *sb.*[1] + GAVEL *sb.*]

Prideling (praid'liŋ), *nonce-wd.* [f. PRIDE *sb.*[1] + -LING.] A 'child' of pride.

PRIDED.

Prydy, (praid'i), *v. Obs. exc. dial. Sc.* prydy, 9 *dial.* preedy.

Prie, obs. form of PRY *v.*

Pride-dieu (pridy). [F., lit. 'pray God']. A desk made to support a book or books, and having a foot-piece on which to kneel; a praying-desk, kneeling-desk.

Prier (prai'er), *sb.* Also 6 *pryer*. [f. PRY *v.* + -ER[1].] One who pries.

Pries, obs. form of PRICE *sb.*

Priest (prist), *sb.* Forms: 1-4 préost, 2-5 prost, 3-4 preost, 3-6 prest(e), preest(e), 4-6 preist, 4-7 priest.

1. An official minister of religious worship.

2. In hierarchical Christian churches: a clergyman in the second of the three holy orders, above a deacon and below a bishop, having authority to administer the sacraments and pronounce absolution.

3. In general sense: A clergyman, a member of the clerical profession, a minister of religion.

Priest.

4. A sacrificing priest, a minister of the altar.

5. An official minister of a pagan or non-Christian religion; originally implying sacrificial functions, but in later use often applied to the functionaries of any religious system, whether sacrificial or not.

6. *fig.* One whose office is likened to that of a priest, *as a priest of nature, of science,* etc.

b. *attrib.* and *Comb.*

Priesthood. Forms: see PRIEST + -HEAD.

Priestal. [f. PRIEST *sb.* + -AL.] Pertaining to or having the character of a priest or priests; sacerdotal.

Priestcraft (prī′stkrȧft). **1.** The craft of a priest; the exercise of priestly functions.

2. Priestly craft, or policy; the arts used by ambitious and worldly priests to impose upon the multitude to further their own interests.

Priestdom (prī′stdăm). [f. PRIEST *sb.* + -DOM.] **†a.** The office of a priest, priesthood.

†Priesterly, *a.* *Obs. rare⁻¹.* [app. ad. G. *priesterlich*, f. *priester* PRIEST + *-lich*, -LY.] Priestly.

†Priestery. *Obs. rare⁻¹.* [f. PRIEST *sb.* + -ERY.] Priests collectively; a body or company of priests. (*contemptuous.*)

Priestess (prī′stĕs). [f. PRIEST *sb.* + -ESS.] **1.** A female priest; a woman who holds the position and performs the functions of a priest, or (loosely) of a minister of religion.

Priesthood (prī′sthŭd). **1.** The office of a priest, priesthood.

Priestless, *a.* [f. PRIEST *sb.* + -LESS.] Without a priest; having, or not attended by, a priest.

Priestlike (prī′stlaik), *a.* [f. PRIEST *sb.* + -LIKE.] Like, or resembling, a priest; priestly.

Priestliness (prī′stlinĕs). Priestly quality or character.

Priestling (prī′stliŋ). [f. PRIEST *sb.* + -LING¹.] A little, young, petty, or insignificant priest. (*Usually contemptuous.*)

Priestly (prī′stli), *a.* (*adv.*) [f. PRIEST *sb.* + -LY¹.]

Priestship. *Obs. rare.* [f. PRIEST *sb.* + -SHIP.]

Priest-ridden (prī′st‚ridˌn), *ppl. a.* [f. PRIEST *sb.* + RIDDEN.]

Priestship, *etc.*

Priestly.

Prig, *sb.*¹ Also 5–6 **prigg**, **prygge** (7 *prydy*). [App. another form of SPRIG *sb.* (null). Cf. PRAG *sb.*] **†1.** A prig, *brial* usually collective.

Prig, *sb.*² [Origin unascertained. Cf. PIG *sb.*] A small pan of brass or tin; a small kettle.

Prig, *sb.*³ **6.** A precisian in speech or manners; one who cultivates or affects a propriety of culture, learning, or morals, which offends or bores others.

†Prig, *v.*¹ *Obs. or dial.* [Origin obscure.] **1.** *intr.* To haggle about terms, to try to drive a hard bargain.

Prig, *sb.*⁴ **1.** *trans.* To steal. [*Thieves' Cant.*]

Prig, *v.*³ [In sense 1 goes with PRIG *sb.*³ 2, both being orig. Rogues' Cant.]

Prigging, *vbl. sb.*¹ *slang.* [f. PRIG *v.*¹] **1.** *intr.* To chaffer, to higgle or haggle about the price of anything.

†Priggish, *a.*

†Prigman, *prito*, *obs. pa. t.* of PRITCH *v.*

Prim, *sb.*¹ Now local. [app. f. PRIM, short for PRIMROSE.] A name of the privet.

Prim, *sb.*² [Origin doubtful: perh. a generalized use of the proper name *Prill*, short for *Priscilla*, which according to Elworthy is very common in West Somerset.]

†Prill, *sb.*¹ *Obs. rare.* [Origin obscure: perh. var. of BRILL *sb.*¹]

Prim, *a.* [Origin obscure.] Precise, formal, affectedly nice or demure.

Prime (praim), *a.* (*sb.*) [ad. F. *prime* adj. now only in certain phrases]...

Prime, *sb.*

Primecocks, obs. form of PRINCOX.

Primeful, *a. Obs. nonce-wd.* [f. PRIME *sb.* + -FUL.] Characterized by being in the prime.

Primegilt, *Sc. Obs.* In 6-7 prymegylt, -gilt, 8 primegilt.

Primely (praimli), *adv.* [f. PRIME *a.* + -LY.]

Prime Minister [PRIME *a.*; MINISTER *sb.* 3.]

Prime-minister, *v.*, *nonce-wd.*, *intr.*

Primeness (praimnes). [f. PRIME *a.* + -NESS.]

Primer (praimə, primə), *sb.* [...]

Primer (prai'mər), *sb.* [...]

Primero (prime·ro), *sb.* [Italian *primiera*]

Great Primer type.

b. Long Primer, a size between Small Pica and Bourgeois, of 89 ems to a foot. *Two-line long primer* = PARAGON (type).

Long Primer type.

Primerole (prime·roul), *sb. Obs.* [ME. *primerole*]

Primetide, prime-tide. *Obs.* [f. PRIME *a.* or *sb.* + TIDE.]

Prime-sign, pri'msign, *v. Obs.* [f. *prim-sign*]

Prime-temps. *Obs.*

Prime-time. *Obs.* [f. PRIME *a.* + TIME, prob.]

Primeur (prinœr). [Fr., the quality or condition of being quite new.]

Primeval, primæval (praimī·văl), *a.* (*sb.*) [f. L. *primæv-us*]

Primeval, primaeval (praimī·văl), *adv.*

Primevity, primævity. *Obs. rare.* [f. prec.]

Primeval-ous. *Obs.*

Primigenial (primidʒī·nial), *a.* [ad. L. *primigeni-us*]

Primigenious (primidʒī·nias), *a. rare.* [ad. L. *primigeni-us*]

Primigenous (praimi·dʒinəs), *a. rare.* [ad. L. *primigen-us*]

Primigenious, -ious.

Primary, obs. anal. dial. form of PRÆMUNIRE.

Primine (prəi'məin). *Bot.* [f. *prim*- + -INE [1].] The first of the two coats or integuments of an ovule; i.e. &. (originally), the outer one; but subsequently &. applied to the inner, as being formed first.

Priming (prəi'miŋ), *vbl. sb.*[1] [f. PRIME v.[1] + -ING[1].]

1. The action of PRIME v.[1]

2. *concr.* The gunpowder which was placed in the pan of a fire-arm and to which the match or spark was applied; also, the train of powder connecting a fuse with a charge in blasting, etc.

3. The preparing (of a surface) for painting, by coating it with a body colour. Also *transf.*

4. *concr.* &. The substance or mixture used by painters for the preparatory coat. &. A coat or layer of the substance. Also *fig.*

Primipara (prəi'mipăra). *Med.* [mod.L., f. *primus* first + *parĕre* to bring forth.] A female that brings forth for the first time.

Primiparous (prəi'mipărəs), *a.* bearing a child (or young) for the first time.

Primitiæ (prəi'mitii). *L. pl.* [L.] First-fruits.

Primitial (prəi'miʃăl), *a.* Now rare. Also † *errron.* -stiall.

Primitive (pri'mitiv), *a.* and *sb.* Forms: *a.* 5 *primitif*, prymytyf, 6 *primityve*, (*premative* -.[etc.] *b.* 5 *primitive*, 6-yve), 6 *primatiue*, -yve, prymatyfe, -ive, 5- *primitive*. [ME. *primitif*, a. F. *primitif* (14th c. in Hatz.-Darm.), ad. L. *primitiv-us* first or earliest of its kind, f. *primit-* first, f. *primere* to PRIMITE.]

Primly (prim'li), *adv.* [f. PRIM *a.* + -LY[2].] In a prim or precise manner, with primness.

Primmer, obs. spelling of PRIMER *sb.*[1]

Primness (prim'nes). [f. PRIM *a.* + -NESS.] The quality of being prim; formal or affected preciseness.

Primogenial, -genian, -genious, -geneous *a.*, erroneous forms of PRIMIGENIAL, -GENIAN, -GENIOUS *a.*, q.v. in imitation of *primogenit*, *-geniture*, etc., in which the first element is *L. primō*.

Primogenit, *a.* and *sb.* rare. [f. L. *primōgenit-us* properly two words, *prīmō genitus*, first born, f. *prīmō* adv., first + *genit-us*, pa. pple. of *gignĕre* to bring forth.]

Primogenital (prəi'moʤe'nităl), *a.* [ad. late L. *primōgenitāl-is* (Tertull.), f. *prīmōgenit-us*.]

Primogenitary (prəi'moʤe'nitări), *a.* [f. *primōgenit-us* (see above) + -ARY[1].]

Primogenitive (prəi'moʤe'nitiv), *a.* and *sb.* [f. *primōgenit-us* + -IVE.]

Primogenitor (prəi'moʤe'nitər). [a. med.L. *primōgenitor*, f. *prīmō* adv., first + *genitor* father, begetter.] First parent, earliest ancestor; *loosely*, forefather, progenitor.

Primogeniture (prəi'moʤe'nitjər). Now *rare.* [f. *prīmō* + -GENITURE.]

Primordial (prəi'mordiăl), *a.* (*sb.*). Also *a.* 5 *erron.* pre-. [ad. late L. *prīmōrdiāl-is* that is first of all, original, f. *prīmōrdium* (see 2).]

Primordiality (prəi'mordiæ'liti), *adv.* [f. prec. + -LY[2].]

Primordian (prəi'mordiăn). *Obs.* [a. F. *prune de Damas* 'plum of Damascus'; in L. *prunum Damascenum*.] A kind of early plum.

Primordiate, *a. Obs. rare.* [f. L. *prīmordi-us* (see next) + -ATE[2].] = PRIMORDIAL *a.*

Primordium (prəi'mordiəm). Pl. **-ia.** [L. *primordium* sb., orig. neut. of *primordius* adj., original, f. *prīmus* first + *ordīrī* to begin.]

Primp (primp), *v. dial.* [Related to PRIM *v.*]

Primrose (pri'mro¨z), *sb.* (*a.*). Forms: 5 prymerose, prime rose, 5-6 prymerose, prymrose, 5-7 primerose, 6 pryme rose, prim-rose, prime-rose, primerose, (primrose). [Late ME. *prime rose*, a. OF. *primerose*, med.L. *prima rosa* lit. 'first rose'.]

Primrose, *v.* [f. prec.] *trans.* To make prim; to dress (up) or deck neatly or showily; to dispose or arrange primly.

Primy, *a. poet.* [f. PRIME *sb.*[1] + -Y[1].]

Primit. *Obs.* [Derivation unknown.]

Primrose-peerless. [See the two words.]

Primrose.

Primroser (primē-əzə). [f. PRIMROSE sb. + -ER.]

Primrosy (primrōzi), a. [f. PRIMROSE sb. + -Y.]

Primose.

Primrosed (primrōzd), a. [f. PRIMROSE sb.]

Primrosy.

Primrose.

Primula (prī-miŭla). Bot. [L. med. L. primula, fem. of primus adj. of primus first.]

Primum frigidum (prai-mŏm frid·dĭdŏm). Obs.

Primum mobile (prai-mŏm mǫ-bili). [med. L.]

Primy (prai-mi), a. rare. [f. PRIME sb. 4 + -Y.]

Prin, sb. Obs. rare⁻¹. [Origin unknown.]

Primness.

Primo (prī-mo), adv. rare. [It.]

Primus. [L. primus first: see PRIME a.]

Prince. [a. F. prince (= Pr. princep, princes, It. principe, Sp. principe, Pg. principe), ad. L. princip-em, princeps first, chief, principal.]

Prince.

Prince's-feather.

Prince's-metal. [From Prince Rupert of the Rhine, who invented it.]

Prince-elector. (= Ger. Kurfürst.)

Princehead. Obs.

Princehood. Obs.

Princeite (prin·sʌit). Name of a small resin.

Princekin (prin·skin). [f. PRINCE sb. + -KIN.]

Princeless, a. rare. [f. PRINCE sb. + -LESS.]

Princelet (prin·slet). [f. PRINCE sb. + -LET.]

Princelike, a. (and adv.). [f. PRINCE sb. + -LIKE.]

Princeliness (prin·slines). [f. PRINCELY + -NESS.]

Princeling (prin·sliŋ). [f. PRINCE sb. + -LING.]

Princely (prin·sli), a. [f. PRINCE sb. + -LY.]

Princely, adv. Now rare. [f. as prec. + -LY.]

Princess (prin·ses, prinse·s), sb. Also 5 princes, 5-7 princes, pryncess. [ME. princesse, a. F. princesse.]

Princecraft. rare. [f. PRINCE sb. + CRAFT.]

Princedom (pri·ndəm). [f. as prec. + -DOM.]

Princehood.

Princeship (prin·sship). [f. PRINCE sb. + -SHIP.]

Prince Regent (PRINCE 10 a, and REGENT.)

Prince royal. Also prince-royal.

Princess dowager.

Princess. **Princesse.** **Prince-worthy.** **Prince-wood.** **Prinely.** **Principal.**

Princesse-ship. **Princedom.** **Princely.** **Princeship.** **Prinely.**

Princess. **Prince-wood.**

Principality. **Principate.** **Principance.** **Principality.**

Principal. **Principally.** **Principality.** **Principance.** **Principle.** **Principial… ** **Principiant.**

Principiality. **Principle.**

determines the nature of something; essential characteristic or character; essence.

1662 Gerbier *Princ.* 1 The three chief Principles of Magnificent Building, viz. Solidity, Conveniency, and Ornament. 1706 Phillips s.v., The Epicurean Principles, are Magnitude, Figure, and Weight. 1817 Jas. Mill *Brit. India* II. v. iii. 388 This was the principle and essence of his plan. 1862 Maurice *Mor. & Met. Philos.* IV. v. § 35. 163 [This] indeed must involve the very principle and meaning of the subject with which he is occupied.

7. A general law or rule adopted or professed as a guide to action; a settled ground or basis of conduct or practice; a fundamental motive or reason of action, esp. one consciously recognized and followed. (Often partly coinciding with sense 5.)

c 1532 Du Wes *Introd. Fr.* in *Palsgr.* 895 To teche and instruct by the principles and reules made by divers well expertz auctours. 1590 Greene *Never too late* (1600) 61 You keepe the prouerbe for a principle, to bed with the Bee and vp with the Lark. 1656 Evelyn *Diary* 8 July, Some Quakers..; a new phanatic sect, of dangerous principles, who shew no respect to any man, magistrate or other. 1762–71 H. Walpole *Vertue's Anecd. Paint.* (1786) III. 68 He painted the great staircase, and as ill, as if he had spoiled it out of principle. 1763 Johnson 1 July in *Boswell*, This shews that he has good principles. 1785 Reid *Intell. Powers* vi. vi, There are also first principles in morals. 1844 Disraeli *Coningsby* viii. iii, Before I support Conservative principles, ..I merely wish to be informed what those principles aim to conserve. 1853 J. H. Newman *Hist. Sk.* (1873) II. i. iv. 183 The barbarian lives without principle and without aim.

b. Used *absol.* for *good, right,* or *moral principle*: An inward or personal law of right action; personal devotion to right; rectitude, uprightness, honourable character. (Also in *pl.*)

1653 Cromwell *Speech* 4 July in *Carlyle*, If I were to choose any servant..I would choose a godly man that hath principles..Because I know where to *have* a man that hath principles. 1697 Collier *Immor. Stage* (1698) 287 The management of the Stage..strikes at the Root of Principle, draws off the Inclinations from Virtue, and spoils good Education. 1704 J. Harris *Lex. Techn.* I. s.v., We say, a Person is a *Man of Principles*, when he always acts according to the Eternal Rules of Morality, Virtue and Religion. 1722 De Foe *Moll Flanders* (Bohn) 45 Thus my pride, not my principle..kept me honest. 1874 Bancroft *Footpr. Time* i. 87 He had brilliant powers, but little principle. 1894 F. Watson *Genesis a true Hist.* v. 103 The religion of the prophets..the religion of principle rather than of law, and of morality rather than of ritual. *Mod.* A man of high principle.

c. Phr. *On principle* (usually in sense b): as a matter of (moral) principle; on the ground of fixed rule or obligation; from a settled (conscientious) motive.

[Cf. quot. 1762–71 in 7.] 1824 Landor *Imag. Conv.* xxxii. II. 267 Principles do not much influence the unprincipled, nor mainly the principled. We talk on principle, but we act on interest. 1835 J. H. Newman *Par. Serm.* (1837) I. i. 10 Outward acts, done on principle create inward habits. 1871 Lowell *Pope* Prose Wks. 1890 IV. 26 There was a time when I could not read Pope, but disliked him on principle. 1894 *Westm. Gaz.* 3 May 5/3 He was acting as counsel for an insurance company, and they told him that they were defending on principle.

8. A general fact or law of nature by virtue of which a machine or instrument operates; a natural law which furnishes the basis of the construction, or is exemplified in the working, of an artificial contrivance; hence, the general mode of construction or operation of a machine, etc. (Cf. 5 b.)

1802 Paley *Nat. Theol.* iii. § 2 (1819) 24 Constructed upon strict optical principles; the self-same principles upon which we ourselves construct optical instruments. 1829 *Nat. Philos.* I. ii. 8 (Usef. Knowl. Soc.) The principle of the Archimedian Screw is occasionally adopted in the wheel-form. 1838 W. Bell *Dict. Law Scot.* s.v. *Patents*, The subject of a patent must be something vendible. A mere principle or method would not be sufficient; but if the patent were actually for a process or thing produced, it would not be a valid objection that the specification described it as a method. *a* 1842 in Meeson & Welsby *Reports* VIII. 806 *note*, In this specification the plaintiff did not claim a patent for a mere principle, but for a mode of applying a well-known principle, viz. the heating of air, by means of a mechanical apparatus, to fires and furnaces. 1858 Lardner *Handbk. Nat. Phil.* 255 This thermometer is sometimes varied in its form and arrangement, but the principle remains the same.

b. A general fact which forms the basis of any artificial device (e.g. of a system of measurement).

1821 J. Q. Adams in C. Davies *Metr. Syst.* iii. (1871) 121 The real original connection between the cubic foot and the English bushel was not formed by avoirdupois weights and water, but by the easterling pound of twelve and fifteen ounces and Gascoign wine. It was the principle of the quadrantal and congius of the Romans, applied to the foot and the nummulary pound of the Greeks. *Ibid.* 179 Thus the gallon of wheat and the gallon of wine, though of different dimensions, balance each other as weights..This observation applies, however only to the original principle of the English system.

†9. A motive force or appliance, as in a machine.

1631 Milton *Univ. Carrier* ii. 10 And like an Engin mov'd with wheel and waight, His principles being ceast, he ended strait. 1830 *Chron.* in *Ann. Reg.* 84/1 Much attention was excited in the neighbourhood of Portland-place, by the appearance of a steam-carriage, which made its way through a crowded passage, without any perceptible impulse..; one gentleman directed the moving principle, and another appeared to sit unconcerned behind.

III. Rudiment, element.

†10. a. *pl.* The earliest or elementary parts of a subject of study; elements, rudiments. *Obs.* or merged in 5.

1534 Elyot *Doctr. Princes* 7 These be the principles and chiefe introduction to the right..gouernance of a publike weale. 1638 Junius *Paint. Ancients* 10 The first principles ..of these Arts of imitation. 1706 Phillips s.v., Principles are the first Grounds and Rules..otherwise call'd Elements and Rudiments; as the Principles of Geometry, Algebra, Astronomy, &c.

†b. *concr.* A rudiment of a natural structure; a germ, embryo, bud. *Obs.*

1721 Bradley *Philos. Acc. Wks. Nat.* 109 All the Trunk of a Tree..is fill'd with Principles or little Embrio's of Branches. 1732 Berkeley *Alciphr.* iii. § 1 Sometimes by Principle we mean a small particular seed, the growth or gradual unfolding of which doth produce an Organized Body, animal or vegetable.

†11. A component part, ingredient, constituent, element. *Obs.* (exc. as in c).

Proximate *principle*, Ultimate *principle*: see these words.

1615 Crooke *Body of Man* 33 There are two materiall principles, the Crassament or substance of the seede..and Bloud. 1644 *Bury Wills* (Camden) 187 My body I committ to the earth whereof it was framed, knowing it must returne to its first principles. 1655 Fuller *Hist. Camb.* (1840) 101 Within few years hither came a confluence of buyers, sellers, and lookers-on, which are the three principles of a fair. 1732 Berkeley *Alciphr.* ii. § 1 Sometimes by Principles we mean the parts of which a whole is composed, and into which it may be resolved. Thus the Elements are said to be principles of compound bodies. And thus words, syllables, and letters are the principles of Speech.

†b. *Old Chem.* Chiefly in *pl.*: The five supposed simple substances or elements of which all bodies were believed to be composed; classed into three *active* (or Hypostatical) *principles*, by which the sensible properties of the body were supposed to be determined, called respectively *spirit* (or *mercury*), *oil* (or *sulphur*), and *salt*; and two *passive principles*, called *water* (or *phlegm*), and *earth* (or *caput mortuum*). *Obs.*

1650 T. Vaughan *Anthroposophia* 22, I speak not of Kitchin-stuffe, those three Pot-Principles Water, Oyle and Earth, or as some Colliers call them Mercury Sulphur and Salt. 1658 Sir T. Browne *Hydriot.* iii. 44 When the heavy Principle of Salt is fired out, and the Earth almost only remaineth [in burnt bones]. 1661–1706 Hypostatical Principles [see Hypostatical 2]. 1727–41 Chambers *Cycl.* s.v. 1799 G. Smith *Laboratory* I. 334 In this manner are extracted from roses the three principles, spirit, oil, and salt.

c. In later chemical use: One of the constituents of a substance as obtained by chemical analysis; usually restricted to a constituent which gives rise to some characteristic quality, or to which some special action or effect is due, as in *active, bitter, colouring, neutral principle.*

Of these, *bitter principle*, is almost the only one commonly used; for the rest *constituent* or *matter* is preferred.

1732 Arbuthnot *Rules of Diet* in *Aliments*, etc. (1736) 265 By which Principles they [spices] are heating, and act strongly. 1769 E. Bancroft *Guiana* 299 It is but seldom that either Animal or Vegetable Poisons derive their deleterious properties from either of these principles. 1799 [see Narcotic *a.* 1]. 1813 Sir H. Davy *Agric. Chem.* iii. (1814) 94 The narcotic principle is found abundantly in opium. *Ibid.*, The bitter principle is very extensively diffused in the vegetable kingdom. *Ibid.* 123 When any vegetable principle is acted on by a strong red heat, its elements become newly arranged. 1831 T. P. Jones *Convers. Chem.* xxviii. 282 Those distinct compounds which exist ready formed in a plant, are called its *proximate*, or *immediate principles*..sugar, starch, and gum are proximate principles, and these we obtain by proximate analysis. 1842 Parnell *Chem. Anal.* (1845) 284 To coagulate various animal principles which may be present. 1874 Garrod & Baxter *Mat. Med.* (1880) 98 The increase of the colouring matter and other principles of the bile in the evacuations from the bowels. 1875 H. C. Wood *Therap.* (1879) 26 The active principle of the vegetable astringents is tannic acid,..it is almost their sole therapeutic principle. 1879 *Chemical Society, Instr. to Abstractors* P 16 Basic substances should invariably be indicated by names ending in *-ine*, as aniline..the termination *-in* being restricted to certain neutral compounds, viz. glycerides, glucosides, bitter principles, and proteids, such as palmitin, amygdalin, albumin.

†Principle, *v. Obs.* [f. prec. sb.]

1. *trans.* To ground (any one) in the principles or elements of a subject; to impress with principles of action; to instruct, teach, train, indoctrinate; to influence by instruction. (See also Principled 1 a.)

1608 D. T[uvil] *Ess. Pol. & Mor.* 124 b, Simplicitie hath principled her selfe with stronger Axiomes then heeretofore. 1651 *Fuller's Abel Rediv., Regius* (1867) I. 152 Urhanus Regius was born..of honest parents, who principled him in the rudiments of learning. *a* 1661 Fuller *Worthies, Durham* (1662) i. 300 Pious and orthodox Professors to have Principled and Elemented the Members therein with Learning and Religion. 1690 Locke *Hum. Und.* i. iii. § 22 Such, who are careful (as they call it) to principle Children well. 1760 Sterne *Serm.* vi. (1773) 73 He had been so principled and instructed as to observe a scrupulous nicety..in the lesser matters of his religion.

b. To act upon or influence (one) as a principle; to dispose to some course of action.

1712 M. Henry *Serm. Death R. Stretton* Wks. 1853 II. 302/2 O that grace might..principle you with a concern for their spiritual lives. *a* 1716 South *Serm.* (1744) XI. 305 It is not the mere interest of his own salvation, but of God's honour, that principles and moves him in the whole course of his actions.

2. To be the principle, source, or basis of; to give rise to, originate.

1650 T. Vaughan *Anima Magica* 2 They would ground Nature on Reasons fram'd and principl'd by their own Conceptions. 1668 Owen *Nat. & Power Indwell. Sin* xv. 259 All neglect of private duties is principled by a weariness of God. 1675 R. Burthogge *Causa Dei* 242 Not conceiving how any lower Being should be able to inspire and principle it [world].

Hence **Pri·ncipling** *vbl. sb.*

1649 in *Perfect Diurnall* 26 Mar., Public Schools for the better education and principling of youth in virtue and justice. 1692 Locke *Educ.* § 70 If the foundation of it be not laid in the Education and Principling of the Youth, all other Endeavours will be in vain.

Principled (pri·nsip'ld), *ppl. a.* Now *rare* (exc. in comb.). [f. prec. + -ed [1], but in later use as if f. Principle *sb.* + -ed [2].]

1. Imbued with or established in principles; trained or instructed in certain principles of action; holding or habitually actuated by particular principles; that is so or such on principle. Often in parasynthetic combs., as *high-*, *honest-*, *right-principled.* a. In predicate, or following its noun.

1642 Milton *Apol. Smect.* Wks. 1851 III. 277 He shall be to me so as I finde him principl'd. 1657 Titus *Killing no Murder* 12 What are the people in Generall but Knaues, Fooles, and Cowards; principled for Ease, vice, and Slavery? 1700 T. Brown *Amusem. Ser. & Com.* 126 Poets are better Principled than to hoard up Trash. 1712 Berkeley *Passive Obedience* To Rdr., Take care they go into the world well principled. 1799 Washington *Lett.* Writ. 1893 XIV. 196, I am principled against this kind of traffic in the human species. 1886 Ruskin *Præterita* I. 423 She was firm, and fiery, and high principled.

b. In attributive relation, preceding its noun.

1655 *Nicholas Papers* (Camden) II. 279, I think him..a very honest, right principled man in the mayne. *a* 1744 Pope (J.), He seems a settled and principled philosopher, thanking fortune for the tranquillity he has by her aversion. 1774 tr. *Helvetius' Child of Nature* II. 224 A Knave, Fanny, is a principled impostor, who, guided by self-interest,..acts in defiance to the Law. 1846 Urwick *J. Howe* 29 Though a principled Nonconformist, he was on intimate terms with Tillotson.

2. Having good or right principles; actuated by moral considerations; devoted to rectitude; upright, honourable. (The opposite of *unprincipled*.)

1697 C. Leslie *Snake in Grass* (ed. 2) 224 Now let any honest-Hearted People judge, whether these be found Principled Men, that can Turn, Conform, and Transform to every Change according to the Times. 1785 G. A. Bellamy *Apology*, etc. IV. 63 He was the most principled man I ever was acquainted with. 1856 Bagehot *Biog. Stud.* 36 To expect..a principled statesman from such a position, would be expecting German from a Parisian or plainness from a diplomatist.

3. Founded on or involving a principle; instilled into or settled in the mind as a principle.

1784 J. Barry in *Lect. Paint.* (1848) I. 73 A loose mechanical abridgment..of the other more entire, principled, and more perfect art. 1824 Southey *Bk. of Ch.* (1841) 526 A steady and principled resistance. 1865 Bushnell *Vicar. Sacr.* ii. iii. 127 That the love is a principled love, grounded in immovable convictions of right.

Princke, obs. form of Prink.

†Pri·ncock, -cox. *Obs.* exc. *dial.* Forms: α. 6 pryn-, 6–7 (9) princox; also 6 -coxe, -cockes, -cocks, -kox, -kockes (7 primecocks). β. 6–7 princock, (prime-cocke, primcock), 9 (*dial.*) princy-cock. [Etymol. and original form obscure; the form *-cocks*, *-cox* appears earlier than *-cock*. See Note below.]

A pert, forward, saucy boy or youth; a conceited young fellow; a coxcomb. *humorous* or *contemptuous.*

α. 1540 Palsgr. *Acolastus* R ij b, *Aco.* Wylt thou gold .i. any pieces of golde? *Lais.* This chayne my lyttell prycke .i. I wolde fayne haue this chayne (of golde) my pretye pryncockes, or my ballocke stones. *a* 1553 ?Ingelend *Nice Wanton* (1560) A iv b, What ye pryncockes, begin ye to raue? 1568 *Hist. Jacob & Esau* v. x. in Hazl. *Dodsley* II. 260 It is your dainty darling, your prinkox, your golpol. 1592 Nashe *P. Penilesse* (ed. 2) 23 A Caualier of the first feather, a princockes that was but a Page the other day in the Court. 1592 Shaks. *Rom. & Jul.* i. v. 88. 1602 *2nd Pt. Return fr. Parnass.* iii. ii. 1197 Your proud uniuersity princox thinkes he is a man of such merit the world cannot sufficiently endow him with preferment. 1606 Warner *Alb. Eng.* xvi. cv. (1612) 410 And dares the Primecocks interrupt me in my loue, quoth she? 1636 Heywood *Loves Mistr.* ii. i. Wks. 1874 V. 113 Who doe you thinke maintaines this princox in his *Pontificalibus*? 1821 Scott *Kenilw.* vii, Well-a-day—God save us from all such misproud princoxes! 1825 Brockett *N. C. Gloss.*, *Princox*, a pert or forward fellow.

β. 1562 Phaer *Æneid* ix. D d ij, Euryalus,..Fyne princock fresh of face furst vttring youth by buds vnshorne. 1570 Levins *Manip.* 159/1 A Princocke, *precox, lascivus.* 1589 *Mar Martine* A iij, Siker, thous bot a pruid princock thus reking of thy swinke. 1598 Florio, *Pinchino*, a pillicock, a primcock, a prick, a prettie lad, a gull, a noddie. 1611 *Ibid.*, *Pinchino*, a prime-cocke, a pillicocke, a darlin, a beloued lad. 1617 Minsheu *Ductor.* A Princocke, a ripe headed yong boy. 1674 Ray *N. C. Words* 37 A *Princock*, a pert, forward Fellow. 1719 *Gloss. Angl. Nova*, *Princock*, a forward Youth, a brisk Spark. 1828 *Craven Gloss.* (ed. 2), *Princy-cock*, a term used here in addressing a young person. 1869 *Lonsdale Gloss.*, *Princy-cock*, a dandified, conceited young fellow.

b. *attrib.* or as *adj.*; esp. in *princock-boy.*

1595 *Locrine* ii. iv. Naught reck I of thy threats, thou princox boy. 1598 Florio, *Herba da buoi*..vsed for a princock boy [1611 a prime-cock-boy], a fresh man, a milke

sop, a nouice, or fresh water souldier. 1611 Coryat *Crudities* 414 Proud princocke scholars that are puffed vp with the opinion of their learning. 1621 Br. Mountagu *Diatribæ* 367 Such vpstart princox Youths as you. 1634 Canne *Necess. Separ.* (1849) 25 They shall be called asses, geese, fouls, dolts, princock boys, beardless boys,..new come out of the shell, &c. *a* 1668 Davenant *Play-house to let* v. i, Proud Princock-Cæsar hardly seems to mind him.

[*Note.* One suggestion is that the first element is *prime*, but though *primecock* is used by Florio, this looks rather like an etymological manipulation; other early writers held it for an alteration of L. *præcox* 'early, precocious'. Apparently the word was originally of slang or low use, perh. somewhat obscene or equivocal; cf. quot. 1540, and the synonyms in Florio.]

Princod, a pincushion: see Preen *sb.* 4.

†Pri·ncum. *Obs. colloq.* [? Mock-latin f. Prink *v.*[2]] Nicety of dress, behaviour, etc.

1690 D'Urfey *Collin's Walk thro. Lond.* i. 41 An aukward fear..That my behaviour may not yoke With the nice Princums of that Folk.

Princum-prancum: see Prinkum-prankum.

†Prine. *Obs. rare.* [ad. late L. *prin-us* (Vulg.), a. Gr. πρῖν-ος holm oak, ilex. Cf. OF. *prin* (Godef.).] Also *prine tree*: The holm or evergreen oak; ilex.

a 1400 *Pistill of Susan* 342 (Vern. MS.) Þat roþly cherl.. seide bifore þe prophet: þei pleied bi a prine [*MS. Phil.* pryne; *MSS. Ing., Cott.* pyne; Vulg. (Dan. xiii. 58) *sub prino*]. 1609 Bible (Douay) *Susanna* i. 58 Tel me, under what tree thou tookest them speaking one to an other. Who said: Under a prine tree [1611 a holme tree].

Prine, obs. form of Preen, pin, brooch.

†Pri·ngle, *sb. Obs. dial.* Also prindle. [Origin unascertained: perh. from the surname *Pringle.*] A silver coin: see quots.

1683 G. Meriton *Yorks. Dial.* 183 Here's good Tobacco, Wife, it cost a Pringle [*v.r.* prindle]. [1697 (ed. 3) *Gloss.*, *Pringle*, a little silver Scotch Coin about the bigness of a penny, with two xx. on it.]

Pringle, *v.* [Alteration of Prinkle *v.* (app. influenced by *tingle*).] *intr.* To have a prickly and tingling sensation.

1889 Doyle *Micah Clarke* xxi, You must be still pringling from the first [hand-grip]. *Ibid.* xxxii, My eyes ached and my lips pringled with the smack of the powder. 1894 — *Round Red Lamp* xii. 230 There was something in this sudden, uncontrollable shriek of horror which chilled his blood and pringled in his skin.

†Prink, *v.*[1] *Obs.* exc. *dial.* Pa. t. in 4 (?5) preynte, preynkte, prengte, prent, prentede, prynkid; 9 *dial.* prenk'd, prinked. [app. connected with OE. *princ* (or *prince*) a blink, a wink, a twinkle of the eye (Defensor *Lib. Scint.* ix. (1889) 43).]

1. *intr.* To wink, to give a wink.

1377 Langl. *P. Pl.* B. xiii. 112 Þann conscience curteisliche a contenaunce he made, And preynte [*v.rr.* prentede, prynkid; 1393 C. xvi. 121 preynte, prengte] vpon Pacience to preie me to be stille. *Ibid.* xviii. 21 'Is Piers in þis place?' quod I, and he preynte [*v.rr.* twynclid, prent; 1393 C. xxi. 19 preynkte] on me. *c* 1380 *Sir Ferumb.* 1238, & þan sche preynte with hure eȝe oppon hur chamberere þar sche stod. ?*a* 1800 in W. Walker *Bards Bon-Accord* (1887) 634 The dear, the lovely blinkin' o't [an eye]..plagues me wi' the prinkin' o't. 1873 *St. Paul's Mag.* Mar. 259 Professedly prudish..they..nod, osculate, prink, quiz.

2. *trans. To prink the eye*: to wink.

c 1380 *Sir Ferumb.* 4507 With þat Richard preynte ys eȝe, Oppon ys feleschip þat was him neȝe. *a* 1900 in *Eng. Dial. Dict.* s.v., He never prinked his eyes for the night. 'Evvent prenk'd an eye far tha neight.

¶ The following are perh. incorrect uses, which may have arisen from confusing this with Prink *v.*[2] 2 b.

1776 Anstey *Election Ball* i. 241 How she simpers and prinks while the glass is before her. 1841 C. H. Hartshorne *Salopia Antiq.* Gloss. 536 *Prink*, to look at, gaze upon, as a girl does at herself in a glass.

Prink (priŋk), *v.*[2] Also 6 princke. [Known from *c* 1570; evidently related to Prank *v.*[4], in similar senses (occurring 1546): see Note below.]

†1. *trans.* with *up*: (?) To set up, exalt; to display ostentatiously, show off. *Obs.*

1573 Twyne *Æneid* xi. Hh iv b, Fortune whom she did disgrace Oft times agayne doth rayse and prinkes him up in prouder place. 1581 J. Bell *Haddon's Answ. Osor.* 407 He so chaufeth and moyleth in sturryng the coales in princkyng upp the glory of this whothouse.

†b. *intr.* (?) To make ostentatious display; also *to prink it. Obs.*

1573 *New Custom* i. i. in Hazl. *Dodsley* III. 6 See how these new-fangled prattling elves Prink up so pertly of late in every place. 1576 Gascoigne *Philomene* xxi. To get more grace by crummes of cost And princke it out hir parte. 1600 J. Lane *Tom Tel-troth* 254 Some princk and pranck it.

2. *trans.* To make spruce or smart; to deck or dress *up* with many petty adornments; esp. *refl.* to deck oneself out, dress oneself *up. colloq.*

1576 Gascoigne *Steele Gl.* Ep. Ded., Now I stand prinking me in the glasse. 1579–80 North *Plutarch* (1595) 1010 When he [Demetrius] was to make any preparation for warre, he had not then..his helmet perfumed, nor came not out of the Ladies closets, picked and princt to go to battell. 1600 Breton *Pasquill's Mad-Cappe* (1626) B j, Who hath not seene a logger headed Asse..Prinking himselfe before a Looking-glasse? 1705 tr. *Bosman's Guinea* 142 The Women prink up themselves in a particular manner. 1775 in F. Moore *Songs & Ball. Amer. Rev.* (1856) 100 All prinked up in full bag-wig. 1784 Cowper *Task* vi. 303 To gather king-cups in the yellow mead, And prink their hair with daisies. 1808 Southey *Chron. Cid* 246 Since midnight they had done nothing but prink and prank themselves. 1828 *Craven Gloss.* (ed. 2), *Prenk, Prink, Pronk*, to decorate, to dress in a showy, affected manner. 1871 B. Taylor *Faust* (1875) II. i. ii. 8 Adorned and prinked with wondrous art, Yet so grotesque that all men start.

transf. 1876 Blackie *Songs Relig. & Life* 95 Nor, where flowers prink the mead with diverse hue. 1877 — *Wise Men* 63 My Ctesibias, who not with gold And silver only prinks his princely hall. 1899 Crockett *Kit Kennedy* i, The flowers which have slept,..prink themselves again, and give forth a good smell.

b. *intr.* (for *refl.*) To dress or deck oneself up, make oneself look smart. *colloq.*

1709 D'Urfey *Pills* (1719) I. 177, I hate a Fop that at his Glass Stands prinking half the Day. 1753 Miss Collier *Art Torment.* i. ii. 59 She was every day longer prinking in the glass than you was. 1858 O. W. Holmes *Aut. Breakf.-t.* ii. (1865) 15 Ironing out crumpled paragraphs, starching limp ones, and crimping and plaiting a little; it is as natural as prinking at the looking-glass. 1898 *Daily News* 8 Aug. 5/4 The young man, after an appropriate time spent in his room, prinking, appears in all the glory of starch and perfumery.

3. *trans.* Of a bird: To trim (the feathers); to preen. Also b. *intr.*

1575 Gascoigne *Weeds, Farew. Mischief* vi, But marke his plumes, The whiche to princke he dayes and nights consumes. 1820 Scott *Monast.* xxiv, Meantime he went on with his dalliance with his feathered favourite,..'Ay, prune thy feathers, and prink thyself gay—much thou wilt make of it now'. 1878 B. Taylor *Deukalion* i. i. 21 Yonder bird Prinks with deliberate bill his ruffled plumes.

b. 1877 Lanier *Mocking Bird* 11 This bird..perched, prinked, and to his art again.

4. *intr.* To be pert or forward. *dial.*

1828 *Craven Gloss.* (ed. 2), *Prenk, Prink, Pronk*, to be forward or pert. *Ibid.*, *Prenkin*, pert, forward. 1863 Mrs. Toogood *Yorks. Dial.*, She's a prenkin, forward, lass.

Hence **Prinked** (priŋkt) *ppl. a.*, **Pri·nking** *vbl. sb.*; also **Prink** *sb.*, the act of prinking or making spruce; **Pri·nker**, one who dresses up with minute care. (All *colloq.*)

1579–80 North *Plutarch* (1676) 579 To apparel himself so sumptuously, and to be more fine and prinked then became a private man. 1699 Farquhar *Constant Couple* v. ii, I knew, sir, what your powdering, your prinking, Your dancing, and your frisking, would come to. *a* 1700 B. E. *Dict. Cant. Crew*, *Prinkt up*, set up on the Cupboards-head in their Best Cloaths, or in State. Stiff-starched. 1783 tr. *Rollin's Belles Lettres* (ed. 10) I. ii. 49 He compares this florid prinked eloquence to young people curled out and powdered. 1864 Webster, *Prinker*, one who prinks; one who dresses with much care. 1883 Howells *Register* ii. That just gives me time to do the necessary prinking. 1895 *Westm. Gaz.* 6 Aug. 3/1 Most..of the present Bench..have had a full-dress 'prink' in front of the large looking-glass ..before venturing to make their first appearance in court.

[*Note.* The late appearance of Prank *v.*[1] and Prink *v.*[2] makes it difficult to refer them to an ablaut stem *prink*, *prank*, *prunk*, or to suppose *prink* to represent an earlier *preŋk*, an umlaut deriv. of *prank.* It seems more likely that *prink* was formed from *prank*, with the thinner vowel sound, to express a more slight or petty action, or perhaps in the reduplicated formation *prink-prank*, *prink* and *prank*, as in *clink-clank*, *crinkle-crankle*, *jingle-jangle*, etc. It may have also been associated with or influenced by Prick *v.* 20: cf. Prinkle. There is no decisive evidence.]

Prink, *v.*[3] *dial.* [app. related to Prank *v.*[3]] ?To walk jauntily or affectedly. Hence **Pri·nking** *vbl. sb.*

1697 C. Leslie *Snake in Grass* (ed. 2) 41 Thou, and thy Godfather Fox can know a Saint from a Devil, without speaking, but not without a little Mincing and Prinking. 1803 Mary Charlton *Wife & Mistress* II. 28 'Oh', says she, mincing and prinking, 'I find, Mrs. Maunder, that you have been so unlucky as to affront Boden'. 1880 *W. Cornwall Gloss.*, *Prink*, to walk jauntily.

Prinkle (pri·ŋk'l), *v. Sc.* [Origin obscure; in sense 1, perh. a modification of Prickle *v.*; in sense 2, perh. dim. or frequent. of Prink *v.*[1] See Pringle *v.*]

1. *intr.* To have a thrilling sensation, such as the feeling of 'pins and needles'; to tingle, prickle. Hence **Pri·nkling** *vbl. sb.*

1721 Kelly *Sc. Prov.* 396 I'll gar your Daup [*note* Backside] dirle [prinkle, smart]. 1807 Hogg *Song*, '*Sing on, sing on*' i, My blude ran prinklin' through my veins, My hair begoud to steer, O. 1818 — *Brownie of B.* I. xii. 270 Are ye an angel o' light..that ye gar my heart prinkle sae wi' a joy that it never thought again to taste? 1819 W. Tennant *Papistry Storm'd* 175 The dulefu' dart, That sent a prinklin' to his heart Mair fierce than burr or nettle.

2. *intr.* To twinkle, scintillate, sparkle.

1724 Ramsay *Vision* xvii, Starrie gleims..prinkled, and twinkled. 1851 Mayne Reid *Rifle Rangers* xi, His rays, prinkling over the waves, caused them to dance and sparkle with a metallic brightness. *Ibid.* xii, The humming-birds.. prinkled over the parterre like straying sunbeams.

†Pri·nkum-pra·nkum. *Obs.* Also princum-prancum. [In sense 1, reduplication of *prankum*, Prancome, related to Prank *sb.*[1]; in sense 3 related to Prank *a.* and *v.*[4]: cf. also Du. *pronckeprincken*, *pronckepinken* to glitter in a fine dress (Oudemans).]

1. A prank, freak, frolic, trick.

1596 Nashe *Saffron Walden* Wks. (Grosart) III. 191, I wil not present into the Arches, or Commissaries Court, what prinkum prankums Gentlemen (his nere neighbors) haue whispred to me of his Sister.

2. = Cushion-dance.

a 1635 Randolph *Muses' Looking-Gl.* v. i, No wanton jig, I hope: no dance is lawful But prinkum-prankum! *a* 1668 Davenant *Playhouse to Let* v. i, Call in the Fidlers..Yet let 'em play us but princum and prancum, And we'll pay at last, or els we'll thank 'um. 1698 *Dancing Master* 7 Then he lays down the Cushion before a Woman, on which she kneels and he kisses her, singing, 'Welcom, Joan Sanderson, welcom, welcom'. Then she rises, takes up the Cushion, and both dance, singing, 'Prinkum-prank'um is a fine Dance, and shall we go dance it once again..., and shall we go dance it once again?'

3. Fine attire, fine clothes and adornments: cf. Princum. See also quot. 1725.

1715 tr. *C'tess D'Aunoy's Wks.* 408 Yonder she hides her self, because she was not dress'd up in her Princum Prancums. 1725 *New Cant. Dict.*, *Mistress Princum-Prancum*, such a stiff, over-nice, precise Madam.

Pri·nky, *a.* [f. Prink *v.*[2]; cf. Pranky.] Prinked up, decked out; spruce-looking; precise.

1834 *New Monthly Mag.* XLII. 442 Nothing can be more at variance than the aristocratic-looking houses half buried in gloom..in May Fair, and those prinky green and white dwellings, where city folks enjoy themselves. 1895 *Chicago Advance* 18 Apr. 1025/3 The idea may suggest itself that prinky, medieval, despised China has been making a resistance which amounts to something.

Print (print), *sb.* Forms: 4 prient(e, pryente, preynte, 4–5 preent(e, 4–6 prente, printe, prynte, 4–7 preinte, 5 preynt, (prend), 4–6 (7– *Sc.*) prent, 5– print. [ME. (= obs. Du. *printe* (Kilian), Du., Da. *prent*, MLG., LG. *prente* print, impression), a. OF. *priente* (1317 in Godef.), *preinte* impression of a seal, etc., f. *prient, preint*, pa. pple. of *preind-re*, *priemb-re* to press, stamp:— L. *prem-ĕre* Press *v.*[1]]

A. Illustration of Forms.

a 1300 *Cursor M.* 557 (Cott.) Als prient [*Gött.* preinte, *F.* prent] of seel in wax es thrist. 13.. *Sir Beues* (A.) 1244 To schewe þe prente of me sele! *a* 1340 Hampole *Psalter* iv. 7 Þe prynt we bere of þi light. 1340 *Ayenb.* 81 His ryȝte pryente, þet is þe ymage of his sseppere. *c* 1380 Wyclif *Serm.* Sel. Wks. I. 92 Sum..fordiden soone Cristis prente. 1390 Gower *Conf.* I. 60 My lady therupon Hath such a priente of love grave. 1393 Langl. *P. Pl.* C. xviii. 73 A badde peny with a good preynte [*v.rr.* preente, prente]. *a* 1400–50 *Alexander* 3162 To Porrus vnder my print. *c* 1400 *Three Kings Cologne* 101 Þe same preent is made, boþe in gold and in copyr. *c* 1440 *Promp. Parv.* 412/1 Preente (*K.* prend, *S.* preynt), *effigies, impressio.* 1512 *Act* 4 *Hen. VIII*, c. 19 § 14 Pennys..havynge the prente of the Coigne of this realme. 1555 Eden *Decades* 219 The printe of his feete. 1583 *Reg. Privy Council Scot.* III. 583 Libellis baith in write and prent. *a* 1660 *Contemp. Hist. Irel.* (Ir. Archæol. Soc.) I. 203 They issued a declaration in preinte. 1785 Burns *To J. Smith* vii, To try my fate in guid black prent.

B. Signification.

I. General non-typographical senses.

* *An impression or impress.*

1. The impress made in a plastic material by a stamp, seal, die, or the like; a distinctive stamped or printed mark or design, as on a coin.

a 1300 [see A.]. *c* 1315 Shoreham *Poems* i. 1205 Caracter, þet is prente ycliped, Nys non of eliinge. 1382 Wyclif 1 *Macc.* xv. 6 Y suffre the for to make smytyng [*gloss* or printe; 1388 prynte] of thin own money in thi regyoun. *c* 1450 *Godstow Reg.* 295 He strengthed hit with the prynte of his seale. 1463–4 *Rolls of Parlt.* V. 501/2 Sealed with a double prynt of Leede at the ende therof. 1523 *Act* 14 & 15 *Hen. VIII*, c. 12 All suche farthinges..shall haue vppon the one side thereof the printe of the port collice. 1548–9 (Mar.) *Bk. Com. Prayer*, *Communion* Rubric, That the breade ..for the Communion bee made..without all maner of printe, and somethyng more larger and thicker than it was. 1599 Davies *Immort. Soul* x. ii, As the Wax retains the Print in it. 1660 F. Brooke tr. *Le Blanc's Trav.* 69 That famous Idol made of the tooth of a Monkey..The King of Pegu ..sent yearely Ambassadours thither, to take the print of it upon Amber.

†b. A symbolic mark, a character; a badge.

1382 Wyclif 1 *Sam.* Prol., Samarytans also the fyue bokis of Moyses wryten in as feele lettris, oonli in figuris and printis dyuersynge. 1387 Trevisa *Higden* (Rolls) III. 11 [Solomon] fond vp figures and prentis to be grave in precious stones. 1399 Langl. *Rich. Redeles* ii. 108 Þat comounes of contre..Sholde knowe be hir quentise þat þe kyng loued hem Ffor her priuy prynte passinge anoþer. 1546 Langley *Pol. Verg. De Invent.* i. vi. 13 b, Afore that time [of Esdras] the Hebrues and Samarites vsed all one carecters and print of their letters.

c. See quot. (A doubtful sense.)

1840 Parker *Gloss. Archit.* (ed. 3) 169 *Print, Prynt*, a plaister cast of an ornament, or an ornament formed of plaister from a mould. The term is used in the record of St. Stephen's chapel. [Founded upon instances of *prynts*, *preynts*, in accounts cited in J. T. Smith *Antiq. of Westminster* (1807) pp. 203, 217, 219–21, of uncertain meaning but prob. belonging to sense 1. Hence, with modifications, in recent Dicts.]

2. *fig.* a. An image or character stamped upon the mind or soul, *esp.* the Divine likeness (in allusion to Gen. i. 27); a mental impression. Now *rare.*

c 1315 Shoreham *Poems* i. 450 For wanne me takeþ þis sacrement, His soule prente takeþ. 1413 *Pilgr. Sowle* (Caxton) i. xiii. (1859) 10 Deformynge in hym self the prent and the figure, that god hath set in hym. 1583 Babington *Commandm.* vii. (1622) 58 Which needeth no proofe besides ..that print which in his conscience euerie one carrieth about. 1642 R. Carpenter *Experience* ii. viii. 196 To lay him low, and make him supple to take the print of Humility. 1855 Tennyson *Maud* i. i. 8 Sooner or later I too may passively take the print Of the golden age.

b. An image or likeness of anything.

1388 Wyclif *Ezek.* xxviii. 12 Thou a preente of licnesse, ful of wisdom, perfit in fairnesse, were in delicis of paradijs of God. *c* 1470 Henryson *Mor. Fab.* vii. (*Lion & Mouse*) xix, It bair the prent of my persoun. 1513 More *Rich. III*

Wks. 61/1 This is quod he, yᵉ fathers owne figure, this is his own countenance, yᵉ very prent of his visage.

†c. Form, appearance. *Sc. Obs. rare.*

c 1450 Holland *Howlat* 854 The pure Howlatis appele completly was planyt,..He besocht..That thai wald pray Natur his prent to renewe. 1535 Stewart *Cron. Scot.* (Rolls) III. 415 Hir plesand prent, hir perfit portrature, Exceidit far all vther creatuir.

3. *gen.* Any indentation in a surface, preserving the form left by the pressure of some body, as the print of a foot in the ground; also, by extension, a mark, spot, or stain produced on any surface by another substance.

c 1400 Maundev. (Roxb.) xi. 47 Ȝet may men see in þe roche þe prynte of oure Lorde hend. 1474 Caxton *Chesse* 116 The prynte of the hors shoo and nayles abode euer in his vysage. 1546 Phaer *Bk. Childr.* (1553) Q viij, The swellyng or puffyng vp..pressed wyth the finger, there remaineth a print. 1601 Holland *Pliny* II. 141 A faire medicine to cure..the black prints remaining after strokes. 1712 Arbuthnot *John Bull* iii. i, He would pinch the children..so hard that he left the print of his forefingers and thumb in black and blue. 1853 Kane *Grinnell Exp.* xxix. (1856) 239 Returning..we saw the recent prints of a bear and two cubs. 1867 Murchison *Siluria* ii. (ed. 4) 29 Smaller ripples..together with apparent rain-prints [in stratified rocks]. 1900 *Westm. Gaz.* 25 Sept. 5/1 Informed that the Finger-print Office had stated that the finger-prints ..were identical with those of a convicted person.

†b. A vestige, trace, indication. *Obs.*

a 1548 Hall *Chron.*, *Edw. IV* 223 b, That no print or shadowe should remain of the adverse faccion, in his realme. 1615 G. Sandys *Trav.* 228 The inhabitants..yet retaine some print of the Punicke language. *a* 1668 Lassels *Voy. Italy* (1670) II. 160 Hard by it appeare some prints of the Temple of Venus and Cupid. *a* 1715 Burnet *Own Time* (1766) I. 247 Scarce any prints of what he had been remained.

** *An instrument for impressing.*

4. An instrument or apparatus which produces a mark or figure by pressing; a stamp or die; a mould. Also *fig.*

c 1470 Henry *Wallace* v. 606 The prent off luff him punȝeit at the last So asprely. 1586 in *Wills & Inv. N. C.* (Surtees) II. 139, v printes for gingbreade 12ᵈ. 1594 *Ibid.* 245, vj printes for printinge jens-breade, 3/4ᵈ. 1660 Stanley *Hist. Philos.* ix. (1701) 419/2 Matter is the print, mother, nurse, and productrix of the third essence. 1789 O'Brien *Calico Printing* E viij, Some treacle and lamp-black may be mixed and diffused with a pad..over the face of the print [i.e. the 'block' used in block-printing of calicoes]. 1847–78 Halliwell, *Print*, a mould for coin, &c.

b. *Cutlery.* (See quot.)

1839 Ure *Dict. Arts* 379 In order to make the bolster of a given size, and to give it..shape and neatness, it is introduced into a die, and a swage placed upon it; the swage has a few smart blows given it by the striker. This die and swage are, by the workman, called prints.

c. *Founding.* A support for the core of a casting.

1864 Webster s.v., *Core print*, a projection on a pattern, forming a mortise in the mold made from it, to receive a portion of the core that does not appear in the casting, for the purpose of holding the core in place. 1884 *Spon's Mechanic's Own Bk.* (1893) 37 Prints are extensions of the cores, which project through the casting and into the sides of the mould, to be held by the sand or flask.

*** *A thing impressed.*

5. A pat of butter, moulded to a shape.

1768 Sterne *Sent. Journ.* (1778) II. 128 He had brought the little print of butter upon a currant leaf. 1777 in J. Hancock *His Bk.* (1898) 216 Mrs. Smith sent up..a print of Butter. 1877 *Cornh. Mag.* Feb. 175 Saucers of cream and prints of butter were to be found upon the dresser.

6. A printed cotton fabric; a piece of printed cotton cloth. Often *attrib.*

1837 Marryat *Dog-fiend* xl, Shrouding herself..in her cotton print cloak. 1852 Hawthorne *Blithedale Rom.* iii. I. 31 She was dressed as simply as possible, in an American print. 1858 Lytton *What will he do* i. xiv, In a coloured print, of a pattern familiar to his observant eye in the windows of many a shop. 1883 Stevenson *Silverado Sq.* 133 He chose the print stuff for his wife's dresses. 1891 T. Hardy *Tess* xvii, Mrs. Crick..wore a hot stuff gown in warm weather because the dairymaids wore prints. 1893 J. Ashby Sterry *Naughty Girl* vi, Their print frocks..were gone. 1899 *Prospect. Calico Printers' Assoc.*, Certain markets are closed to English prints owing to hostile tariffs.

II. Typographical uses.

7. The state of being printed, printed form: in phrases. a. *In print.* (*a*) In a printed state, in printed form. Cf. also sense 14. So *Into* (†*unto*) *print.*

1482 J. Paston in *P. Lett.* III. 300 A Boke in preente off the Pleye off the Chess. *c* 1493 in *Christ Church Canterbury Lett.* (Camden) 59, I can nat thynke yt lykely that ther shall come ony moo of them yn prentys, as be that I her off them that selle such bokys. 1529 More *Dyaloge* iii. Wks. 245/2 The worke..by theyr authorities so put vnto prent, as all the copies should come whole vnto the bysshoppes hande. 1533 *Test. Ebor.* (Surtees) VI. 38 A antiphoner in prynt. 1563 Winȝet *Four Scoir Thre Quest.* To Rdr., Wks. 1888 I. 60 To put furth our mynd in prent at hame. 1606 *Choice, Chance*, etc. (1881) 45 My Mistris was saluted by a spruse companion that lookt like a letter in print. [Cf. sense 14.] 1617 Moryson *Itin.* ii. 71 A certaine dangerous seditious Pamphlet was of late put forth into print. 1712 Steele *Spect.* No. 509 ⁋1 My present Correspondent, I believe, was never in Print before. 1816 Byron *Eng. Bards & Sc. Rev.* 51 'Tis pleasant, sure, to see one's name in print; A book's a book, although there's nothing in't. *a* 1839 Praed *Poems* (1864) II. 6 Rush like a hero into print.

(*b*) Of a book or edition: On sale at the publisher's, not yet sold out.

1880 (*title*) The American Catalogue...Author and Title Entries of Books in Print and for Sale...July 1, 1876.

b. *Out of print* (of a book or edition): no longer to be bought at the publisher's, sold out.

1674 Boyle *Excell. Theol.* i. v. 194 Divers excellent little Tracts, which..are already out of print. 1865 *Prospectus of E. E. T. S.* 6 Half the Publications for 1866..are out of print, but will be gradually reprinted.

8. *concr.* Language embodied in a printed form; printed lettering; typography; esp. with reference to size, form, or style, as *small print, clear print.*

1623 Massinger *Dk. Milan* i. i, And if you meet An officer preaching of sobriety, Unless he read it in Geneva print Lay him by the heels. 1657 T. Atkin in Fuller *Worthies* (1662) ii. 309 Forty years since he could not read the biggest Print without Spectacles, and now there is no Print so small,..but he can read it without them. 1773 Johnson *Let. to Boswell* 5 July in *Life*, I can now write without trouble, and can read large prints. 1856 Emerson *Eng. Traits, Voy. Eng.* Wks. (Bohn) II. 12 The sea-fire shines in her wake... Near the equator, you can read small print by it.

b. *fig.* (Cf. also 1623 in a.)

1623 Wither in *C. Butler's Fem. Mon.* Ad Author. 28 An Abstract of that Wisdome, Power, and Loue, Which is imprinted on the Heav'ns aboue In larger volumes, for their eies to see That in such little prints behold not thee. 1637 Suckling *Aglaura* i. i, Well, Ile away first, for the print's too big If we be seene together. 1844 Dickens *Mart. Chuz.* xxvi, All the wickedness of the world is Print to him.

†9. A printing-press (with its accessories). Hence, the work of the press, the process of printing. *Obs.* Cf. Press *sb.*[1] 13.

1507 Jas. IV in *Dict. Nat. Biog.* (1887) X. 187/1 To furnis and bring home ane prent, with all stuff belangand tharto, and expert men to use the samyne for imprenting..of the bukis of our lawis. 1538 Coverdale *Prol. N. T.* Wks. (Parker Soc.) II. 36 The turning of a letter is a fault soon committed in the print. 1549 Coverdale, etc. *Erasm. Par. Eph.* Prol., Neither translated ready to the Prynte nor yet appointed certaynle to be translated. 1691 Wood *Ath. Oxon.* I. 134 Mʳ. Doctor Stevens..espyed certain false allegations in his Masters book, whilst it was under the print in London.

10. An impression of a work printed at one time; an edition.

1535 Joye *Apol. Tindale* (Arb.) 20 When these two pryntes (there were of them bothe aboute v thousand bokis printed) were al soulde..the dewch men prynted it agen..in a small volume lyke their firste prynt. 1623 T. James in *Ussher's Lett.* (1686) 304 To compare old Prints with the new. 1634 *Raynold's Byrth Mankynde* Pref. 1 In the other prints, there lacked matter necessary to the opening and declaration of the Figures. 1887 *Daily News* 11 July 3/2 Notwithstanding an immense 'print', the papers rapidly reached a premium of, in some cases, 300 per cent.

11. A printed publication; *esp.* a printed sheet, news sheet, newspaper; *the prints* = the press. Now chiefly *U. S.*

1570 Dee *Math. Pref.* A ij, Will they prouoke him, by worde and Print. 1651 Cleveland *King's Disguise* 44 A Psalm of mercy in a miscreant print. 1654 *Nicholas Papers* (Camden) II. 108 The English letters came not till last evning and soe late as I could not see the prints, but heare they conteyne little. 1696 H. Sampson in *Thoresby's Corr.* (ed. Hunter) I. 246 Manuscripts, if lost, can never be made good, as prints may. 1727 Swift *Imit. Horace* ii. vi. 115 Inform us, will the emp'ror treat? Or, do the prints and papers lye? 1777 J. Adams in *Fam. Lett.* (1876) 234 The particulars you will have..in the public prints. 1779 Sheridan *Critic* i. ii, I believe, Mr. Puff, I have often admired your talents in the daily prints. 1871 Morley *Crit. Misc.* Ser. i. *Condorcet* (1878) 52 The freedom of the press, the multitude of the public prints, were all so many insurmountable barriers against a French Cromwell. 1892 *Nation* (N. Y.) 22 Dec. 470/3 Of course, the Government prints take in each case the opposite view.

b. A printed copy (of a bill in parliament).

1828 in Picton *L'pool Munic. Rec.* (1886) II. 329 That the intended Bill..be read.., and Prints of the Bill circulated. 1831 *Ibid.* 331 Laid before the Council a Print of the Bill.

12. A picture or design printed from a block or plate; an impression from an engraved or otherwise prepared plate. Hence *in print*, quot. 1662.

In a general sense, including impressions from a raised surface as in wood-engravings, and from sunken lines as in copperplate and steel engravings; also from a flat surface as in lithographs; but sometimes excluding lithographs and etchings, and otherwise variously restricted.

1662 Evelyn *Chalcogr.* iii. 38 With eight more Prints [i.e. woodcuts by Dürer] of this subject. *Ibid.* iv. 45 After Raphaels death, did Julio Romano publish some of his own designes in print. *Ibid.* 48 Diogenes..a very rare print [i.e. a chiaro-scuro]. *Ibid.* v. 129 Copies are in Prints much more easily detected, then in paintings. *Ibid.* 141 An Universal, and choice Collection of prints and cuts. 1703 Maundrell *Journ. Jerus.* (1732) 7 Were fastned to the Wall two or three old Prints. 1710 J. Harris *Lex. Techn.* II. s.v., Prints or Cutts, as we sometimes call them. *a* 1745 Jon. Richardson *Ess. Prints* Wks. (1792) 262 He hath etched several valuable prints. 1755–73 Johnson s.v., It is usual to say wooden prints and copper plates. 1762–71 H. Walpole *Vertue's Anecd. Paint.* (1786) II. 206 There is a print of him, painted by John Lyvyus, and engraved by Vosterman. 1774 Goldsm. *Nat. Hist.* (1776) II. 307 In such a case..there is no other substitute but a good print of the animal to give an idea of its figure. 1815 J. Smith *Panorama Sc. & Art* II. 732 This combination of the two modes of colouring prints has a good effect. 1801 Craig *Lect. Drawing* vii. 384 The earliest specimen that we have of it is in a print, by Albert Durer. 1898 Pennell *Lithography* 54 From 1817 onwards the great lithographic houses issued their prints by 'hundreds and thousands'. 1901 *Blackw. Mag.* Nov. 663/1 Garish coloured prints and execrable oleographs.

13. *Photogr.* A picture produced from a negative: see Print *v.* 14.

1853 R. Hunt *Man. Photogr.* 22 Attempts are being made, at this time, to fix the images produced by the Daguerreotype—perfect prints, it is true, but which are as light as the vapour from which they are produced. 1855 Hardwich *Man. Photogr. Chem.* 293 Some advise that on removal from the colouring Bath the print should be soaked in new Hypo for ten minutes. 1879 *Cassell's Techn. Educ.* III. 207 A good print may be obtained by a person who is unskilled in making a negative. 1893 *Photogr. Ann.* 50 Rough paper for prints in silver is now on the market, and certainly gives most pleasing results.

III. Transferred uses, of uncertain origin.

By Nares and others derived from the typographical sense, 'from the exact regularity and truth of the art of printing, which was at first deemed almost miraculous'. But printing was not new in 1576 and in various respects this explanation seems doubtful, though Shakspere plays on the two senses of 'in print' in *Two Gent.* ii. i. 175, *A. Y. L.* v. iv. 94, and the phrase may sometimes have been so taken: cf. quot. 1881, and 1606 in sense 7. The use in reference to the ruff, 14 b, may yet prove to be the earlier, though not evidenced in the quots.

14. In phrase *in print*: In a precise and perfect way or manner; in exact order, with exactness or preciseness; to a nicety. Now *dial.*

1576 Fleming *Panopl. Epist.* 357 Considering that what soeuer is vttered in such mennes hearing, must bee done in printe, as wee say in oure common Prouerbe. 1580 Lyly *Euphues* (Arb.) 407 Concerning the body, as there is no Gentlewoman so curious to haue him in print, so is there no one so careles to haue him a wretch, onlye his right shape to shew him a man. 1583 Greene *Mamillia* ii. Wks. (Rtldg.) 316/1 Dames now-a-days..Pac'd in print, brave lofty looks, not us'd with the vestals. 1588 Shaks. *L. L. L.* iii. i. 173, I will doe it sir in print. 1591 — *Two Gent. Verona* ii. i. 175 All this I speak in print, for in print I found it. 1621 Burton *Anat. Mel.* iii. ii. iv. i. (1676) 328/1 A young lover ..must..speak in Print, walk in Print, eat and drink in Print, and that which is all in all, he must be mad in Print. 1658 Gurnall *Chr. in Arm.* verse 14. xi. § 1 (1669) 97/2 If his heart be on his Garden, O how neatly it is kept! it shall lie, as we say, in print. 1692 Locke *Educ.* § 22 Not design'de to lie always in my young Master's Bed at home, and to have his Maid lay all Things in print, and tuck him in warm. *a* 1700 B. E. *Dict. Cant. Crew* s.v., *To set in Print*, with Mouth skrew'd up and Neck Stretcht out. 1854 Miss Baker *Northants. Gloss.* s.v., She's always in print, and so is her house. 1881 *Leicestersh. Gloss.* s.v., 'The house is as neat as print'..'Shay kips all 'er plazes in print', is high praise for a servant who keeps her own part of the house neat and clean.

†b. With a sb.: *A man, fool* (etc.), *in print*, a perfect or thorough man, fool, etc. *Obs.*

1604 Dekker *Honest Whore* i. Wks. 1873 II. 10, I am sure my husband is a man in print, for all things else, save only in this. 1611 Cotgr. s.v. *Bosse*, *Sot en bosse et platte peinture*, a foole in print, asse in graine, compleat coxcombe, absolute hoydon. 1633 Massinger *Guardian* ii. i, Is he not, madam A monsieur in print? What a garb was there!

†c. Applied, *a* 1600 to *c* 1630, to the exact crimping, goffering, or set of the plaits or pleats of the ruffs then worn. Nearly always in the phrases *to set the ruff in print*, or *the ruff stands in print.* See also Print *a.* 1, Printed 1 b. Said also of *clothes. Obs.*

Quot. 1628 appears to mean a ruff of the size or pattern worn by Puritans: cf. 1614 in Printed 1 b. There may also be a reference to the small print of Geneva Bibles: cf. 1623 in sense 8.

1598 E. Gilpin *Skial.* (1878) 58 Neat as a Merchants ruffe, that's set in print. 1602 Middleton *Blurt, Master Constable* iii. iii. 105 Your ruff must stand in print; and for that purpose, get poking-sticks. 1615 *Band, Ruffe, & C.* (Halliw.) 5 The presse Ruffe Cuffe and Band (what reason's in't) And yet desire they still should stand in print. 1616 J. Lane *Contn. Sqr.'s T.* xi. 363 Yet these mote sett their ruffes and clothes in print, Yea, keepe them so: elles dames will looke a squint. 1625 B. Jonson *Staple of N.* i. i, Put on my girdle, rascal: fits my ruff well? *Lin.* In print. 1628 Earle *Microcosm.*, *Shee Precise Hypocr.* (Arb.) 63 Shee is a Nonconformist in a close Stomacher and Ruffle of Geneua Print, and her puritie consists much in her Linen. *a* 1642 Suckling *To Ld. Lepington* Poems (1648) 18 It is so rare..to see Ought that belongs to young Nobility In print (but their own clothes) that we must praise.

d. Said of the beard or hair. So also *out of print*, out of proper order, in disorder. *Obs.* or *dial.*

1605 Chapman *All Fools* v. i. H iv b, Tis such a picked fellow, not a haire About his whole Bulke, but it stands in print. 1649 Gaule *Holy Madn.* 91 His (a proper squire's) Beuer cocks, Feather waggs, Locks bouer, and Beard stands in print. 1851 *N. & Q.* 1st Ser. IV. 12/1 An old Somersetshire servant..used to say..'Take care, Sir, you'll put your hair out of print'.

IV. 15. *attrib.* and *Comb.*, in sense 1, as *print-mark*; in sense 6, as *print-broker*; in sense 7, as *print-blurred* adj.; in sense 12, as *print-collector*, *-pedlar*; **print-cutter**, (*a*) a person occupied in cutting prints; (*b*) a knife for cutting photographic prints; **print hand**, handwriting imitating or resembling print: so **print letters**; **print-holder**, (*a*) a small frame for holding a photograph or engraving; (*b*) a device for holding a photographic print flat or in a desired position (*Cent. Dict.*); **print-room**, a room in a museum or the like, containing a collection of prints; **print-state**, state or condition of an engraving, resulting from the number of impressions that have been previously printed; **print-trimmer** = *print-cutter* (*b*); **print-washer**, an apparatus for washing photographic prints after fixing. See also Print-seller, -shop.

1905 *Academy* 30 Dec. 1362/1 They have done duty so often, that they are now like battered wood-blocks, and only *print-blurred. 1851 Mayhew *Lond. Labour* I. 374/1 The '*print-brokers', who sell 'gown-pieces' to the hawkers or street-traders. 1880 Warren *Book-plates* xii. 126 A *print-collector, an ex-librist, and a herald. 1851 in *Illustr. Lond. News* 5 Aug. (1854) 119/3 (Occupations of People) *Print colourer, *print cutter, print mounter. 1773 Goldsm. *Stoops to Conq.* iv. Wks. (Globe) 668/2, I can read your *print hand very well. 1826 Miss Mitford *Village* Ser. ii. 250 (*My Godfather*) The letter in print-hand, proper to the damsel of six years old. 1837 Dickens *Pickw.* lii, It ain't my father's writin', 'cept this here signatur in *print letters. 1701 *Lond. Gaz.* No. 3694/4 A bright-bay Gelding near 16 hands,..a *Print-Mark pretty high on the near Buttock. 1804 *Europ. Mag.* XLV. 360/1 An open saloon, where are petty book-stalls and *print-pedlars. 1902 *Blackw. Mag.* Nov. 616/2 Had '*print-states' been numbered consecutively by the old publishers, we should now have graduated prices. 1890 *Photogr. Ann.* II. 57 If a circular *print-trimmer is used, the print, if albumen, can be cut while damp. 1889 E. J. Wall *Dict. Photogr.* 261 [Advt.] 'Optimus' rocking *print-washer. 1892 *Photogr. Ann.* 480 Combined Tank and Print Washer..will accommodate any plate rack up to half-plate size.

Print, *a.* Now only *dial.* Also *Sc.* prent. [In sense 1 perh. pa. pple. of Print *v.*; cf. quot. 1513 in sense 2 b, also MDu. *geprent*; but possibly sometimes attrib. or adj. use of Print *sb.*]

1. Printed.

1475 *Bk. Noblesse* (Roxb.) 84 Late us..bring forthe..the golde and silver of coyne and print money that every of us senatours and statis haven. 1542 in *Archæologia* (1887) L. i. 46 Item a prynte masse boke. 1816 Scott *Antiq.* xxvi, She can speak like a prent buke. 1864 Mrs. Lloyd *Ladies Polc.* 103, I can't spake like print books—never could. 1865 J. Young *Pictures* 64 (E. D. D.) Thou com'st wi' some prent scrap in han'.

b. Of a ruff: cf. Print *sb.* 14 c, Printed 1 b. *New print*, ?newly printed, pressed, or goffered.

1600 Rowlands *Lett. Humours Blood* (Hunter. Cl.) 52 [They] are foorth comming sir, and safe enough Sayes goodman Broker, in his new print ruffe.

2. *dial.* Clear, bright (of moonlight, etc.).

1736 Pegge *Kenticisms* s.v. (E. D. S.), The moon shines print. 1787 Grose *Provinc. Gloss.* s.v., Print star, or moon-light. 1875 *Sussex Gloss.*, *Print-moonlight*,..very clear moonlight. 1887 *Kent Gloss.* s.v., The night is print;..The moonlight is very print.

Print (print), *v.* Forms: 4 prente, 4–5 (6– *Sc.*) prent, 4–6 prynt(e, 5 preent(e, 5–6 printe, 6– print. *Pa. pple.* printed: *Sc.* 6 prent, 6– prentit. [ME. *prente-n*, *printe*, known from *c* 1350, app. f. the earlier *prente*, *printe*, Print *sb.*, like OF. *emprienter*, *empreinter*, f. *empriente*, *empreinte*, Imprint *sb.* The vb. corresponds to MDu., Du. *prenten*, WFris. *printjen*; MLG., LG. *prenten* (whence Da. *prente*, Sw. *prenta*), also app. f. the corresp. sb., MDu. *prente*, *printe*, Du. *prent*, MLG. *prente*, a. OF. *priente*, *preinte.* Cf. also obs. F. *printer* to coin or stamp money (1544, Liège, in Godef.).]

I. General senses.

1. *trans.* To impress or stamp (a surface) with a seal, die, or the like; to mark with any figure or pattern, impressed or coloured; to brand. Said also of footsteps upon soft or yielding ground.

1340–70 *Alex. & Dind.* 256 Whan we sihen þi sonde wiþ þi sel prented, We kenden þi couaitise. *c* 1400 Maundev. (Roxb.) xxv. 117 Þis monee es prynted on bathe þe sydes. *c* 1466 Sir J. Paston in *P. Lett.* II. 294 The other ij. pottys be prentyd with that merchauntys marke. 1637 G. Daniel *Genius this Isle* 26 The Naiades..the willing Sand shall print. 1697 Dryden *Virg. Georg.* iii. 308 He..treads so light, he scarcely prints the Plains. 1708 *Lond. Gaz.* No. 4421/8 Stoln.., a black Mare.., printed in the near Hip. 1750 Gray *Elegy* 116 + 4 Little footsteps lightly print the ground. 1820 W. Irving *Sketch Bk.* I. 194 A spot that has been printed by the footsteps of departed beauty. 1879 *Cassell's Techn. Educ.* IV. 246/2 The butter is then salted..and then moulded and printed.

†b. *fig.* To stamp, brand, stain. *Obs.*

c 1380 Wyclif *Wks.* (1880) 473 Crist..forfendide hem to prynte þer soulis to myche wiþ erþly godis. *c* 1440 *York Myst.* xxxvi. 111 Sette þat he saide.., As he þat was prente full of pride, 'Jewes kyng am I', comely to knawe, Full playne. 1598 E. Gilpin *Skial.* (1878) 21 It is Cornelius that braue gallant youth, Who is new printed to this fangled age.

†c. To coin (money). *Obs.*

1393 Langl. *P. Pl.* C. xviii. 80 God coueiteþ nat þe coygne þat crist hym-self prentede. 1432–50 tr. *Higden* (Rolls) VIII. 265 He caused halpenys and ferthynges to be printed and made rownde. 1533 Bellenden *Livy* iv. xxiii. (S.T.S.) II. 135 Becaus na siluer was as ȝit prentit in rome, thay cunȝeit grete sovmes of brasin money. 1567 *Sc. Acts Jas. VI* (1814) III. 29/1 That our Souerane Lord..may cause prent, and cunȝe gold and siluer of sic fynes as vtheris cuntreis dois.

2. To impress or stamp (a form, figure, mark, etc.) in or on a yielding substance; also, by extension, to set or trace (a mark, figure, etc.) on any surface, by carving, writing, or otherwise.

c 1400 Maundev. (1839) v. 62 And in that roche Is prented the forme of his body. 1494 in *Somerset Med. Wills* (1901) 318 A basyn and lavor of siluer, myne armes printed thereon. 1494 Fabyan *Chron.* 3 Lyke the Prentyse that hewyth the rowgth stone, And bryngeth it to square,..That the mayster after may..prynte therin his fygures and his story. 1536 Bellenden *Cron. Scot.* (1821) I. 195 On the ta side of this money was prentit ane croce, and his face on the tothir. 1611 Bible *Lev.* xix. 28 Ye shall not make any cuttings in your flesh for the dead, nor print any markes vpon you. 1658 A. Fox *Würtz' Surg.* ii. xxv. 158 The plaisters.. growing hard there, would print a hole into the flesh. 1789 E. Darwin *Bot. Gard.* II. 90 Thrice round the grave Circaea prints her tread. 1812 J. Wilson *Isle of Palms* iii. 834 The child prints many a playful kiss Upon their hands. 1890 'R. Boldrewood' *Col. Reformer* (1891) 156 If you'd only had those patterns printed out slowly and indelibly.., you'd have known it was no joke [to be tattooed].

b. *fig.* To impress (an image, thought, saying, etc.) upon the heart, mind, or memory; to fix in the mind.

c 1374 Chaucer *Troylus* ii. 851 (900) Euery word þat sche of hire herde Sche gan to prentin in h[i]re herte faste. *c* 1420 ?Lydg. *Assembly of Gods* 1784 Remembre hit well and prynte hit in thy mynde. 1513 Douglas *Æneis* iv. i. 8 Deip in hir breist so wes his figur prent. 1563 *Homilies* ii. *Matrimony* (1859) 505 This sentence is very meet for women to print in their remembrance. 1678 Cudworth *Intell. Syst.* 681 Contrived by a Perfect Understanding Being or Mind..which hath every where Printed the Signatures of its own Wisdom upon the Matter. *a* 1704 T. Brown *Imit. 1st Sat. Persius* Wks. 1730 I. 53 Then will grey hairs on all thou say'st print awe. 1850 Tennyson *In Mem.* lxxix, And hill and wood and field did print The same sweet forms in either mind.

3. To press (anything hard) into or upon a yielding substance, so as to leave an indentation or imprint. Also with *in*.

1382 Wyclif *Jer.* xxxii. 44 Prented in shal be the sel. 1530 Palsgr. 666/2 Let me printe your seale in a pece of waxe, me thynketh it is antique. *a* 1541 H. S. in *Wyatt's Penit. Ps.* Prelim. Sonn. 15 In princes' hearts God's scourge y-printed deep, Ought them awake out of their sinful sleep. 1599 Shaks. *Hen. V*, Prol. 27 Horses..Printing their prowd Hoofes i' th' receiuing Earth. 1697 Dryden *Virg. Georg.* i. 101 If the Soil be barren, only scar The Surface, and but lightly print the Share. 1884 Tennyson *Becket* ii. ii, Only the golden Leopard printed in it Such hold-fast claws.

†b. *fig.* To fix in or on (something). *Obs. rare.*

1398 Trevisa *Barth. De P. R.* viii. xiv. (Tollem. MS.), Þe sonne entrynge in to þat parti of þe signe prenteþ in his bemis more scharpely [orig. *acrior radios imprimit*] þan he dooþ in þe ende. 1513 Douglas *Æneis* vii. v. 132 His sycht vnmovyt to the erd dyd he prent.

c. *Founding.* To make an impression of in a mould with a core-print or with a pattern.

1895 in *Funk's Standard Dict.*

†4. To commit (anything) to writing; to express in written words; to inscribe. *Obs.*

c 1400 *Destr. Troy* 11772 This poynt is not prynted in proces þat are now. *c* 1430 *Hymns Virg.* 114 The hiȝest lessoun þat man may lere..Yf þou haue grace to holde & heere, Is playnli printid in þoulis booke. *c* 1440 *York Myst.* xxvi. 76 Loo! sir, þis is a periurye To prente vndir penne. 1588 Shaks. *Tit. A.* iv. i. 75 Heauen guide thy pen to print thy sorrowes plaine.

†5. To form in a mould; to cast, shape. *Obs. rare.*

1530 Palsgr. 157 A moulde, to moulde or print a thyng in. 1558 Warde tr. *Alexis' Secr.* (1568) 110 b, Things that remain in the fire without melting, wherein men print very well all maner of metall. *Ibid.* 114 b, Untill that turninge downwarde the mouldes, they come out. And if in case they be not wel printed,..you may put them in agayne.

II. Senses relating to typography.

6. To make or produce (a book, picture, etc.) by the application to paper, vellum, or any similar substance, in a press or machine, of inked types, blocks, or plates, bearing characters or designs. (In printing for the blind, embossed characters, without ink, are produced.)

In this sense *enprynte, emprynte*, is found earlier, and was app. at first more in use: see Imprint *v.*

[1474 Caxton *Chesse* Pref., By cause thys sayd book is ful of holsom wysedom..I haue purposed to enprynte it.] 1511 *Pilton Churchw. Acc.* (Som. Rec. Soc.) 62 Item for a new processionary printed..xvjᵈ. 1533 *Gau's Richt Vay* 109 (Colophon) Prentit in Malmw Be me Ihone Hochstraten the xvi day of October Anno md xxxiii. 1560 Daus tr. *Sleidane's Comm.* 160 Englishe Bibles were printed at Paris. 1603 Jas. I in Ellis *Orig. Lett.* Ser. i. III. 78, I sende you herewith my booke latelie prentid: studdie and profite in it. 1633 Prynne *Histriomastix* To Rdr., They are now new-printed in farre better paper than most Octavo or Quarto Bibles. 1639 Gentilis *Servita's Inquis.* (1676) 882 Things of importance ought equally to be handled, as well in those that are Printed, as in those that are to Print. 1660 F. Brooke tr. *Le Blanc's Trav.* 22 He procured me the Mappe of Babylon, or Bagdet, printed upon a Cotton. 1711 Abp. King in *Swift's Lett.* (1767) III. 239 The Spectators are likewise printing in a larger and a smaller volume. 1718 Hearne *Collect.* (O. H. S.) III. 426 'Tis about half printed off. 1720 *Lond. Gaz.* No. 5850/3 His Majesty's Picture, printed in natural Colours. 1775 Johnson in Boswell *Life* 10 Oct., Maps were printing in one of the rooms. 1839 Ure *Dict. Arts* 217 The copper-plate printing of calico is almost exactly the same as that used for printing engravings on paper from flat plates. 1887 *Chicago Advance* 19 May 306/1 She..prints it herself with the cyclostyle. 1906 L. Giles *Musings Chinese Mystic* 31 The philosopher's works, in Kuo Hsiang's standard edition, were printed for the first time in the year 1005 A.D.

7. Said of an author or editor, not of the actual printer: a. To cause (a manuscript, book, etc.) to be printed; to give to the press.

1530 Palsgr. 666/1 Whan wyll you printe your booke, *quant voules vous faire imprimer vostre liure!* 1669 Sturmy *Mariner's Mag.* vii. Aaaa ij b, Being desired by some Friends..to Print it,..I have so done. 1678 Bunyan *Pilgr.* i. Author's Apol., Some said, John, print it; others said, Not so;..At last I thought, Since you are thus divided, I print it will; and so the case decided. 1789 Burns *Capt. Grose's Peregrin.* i, A chield's amang you taking notes, And, faith, he'll prent it. 1897 J. W. Clark *Barnwell* Introd. 9 My first idea was to print the Latin text alone.

b. To express or publish in print (ideas, etc.).

1638 Baker tr. *Balzac's Lett.* (vol. II) 23 They thinke it not enough to do me wrongs unlesse they print them too. 1672 Villiers (Dk. Buckhm.) *Rehearsal* v. (Arb.) 133 I'l be reveng'd on them too: I will both Lampoon and print 'em too, I gad. 1751 Labelye *Westm. Br.* 107 My Intention, in Printing and distributing this Plan..is..to ease the Minds of many Persons. 1874 Blackie *Self-Cult.* 17 Young men of course may..have opinions on many subjects, but there is no reason why they should print them.

†c. To designate in a printed statement, describe in print as. *Obs. rare.*

1611 Beaum. & Fl. *King & no King* iii. ii, My safest way were to print myself a coward. *c* 1646 Milton *New Forcers Consc.* 11 Men whose Life, Learning, Faith and pure intent Would have been held in high esteem with Paul, Must now be nam'd and printed Hereticks.

8. *intr.* or *absol.* a. Of a person (in senses 6, 7): To exercise the vocation of a printer; to employ the press in printing. †*Print upon*, to print an edition of a book immediately after that published by (the author or editor), in order to appropriate some of the profits (*obs.*).

1699 Bentley *Phal.* Pref. 5 Before they ventur'd to Print, which is a Sword in the Hand of a Child. 1716 Hearne *Collect.* (O. H. S.) V. 324 There may be danger they may print upon you, unless you print more Copies. 1733 Pope *Hor. Sat.* ii. i. 100 In durance, exile, Bedlam or the Mint,— Like Lee or Budgel, I will rhyme and print. 1771 Luckombe *Hist. Print.* 25 [Caxton] printed likewise for..Henry VIIth. 1802 Syd. Smith *Wks.* (1859) I. 13/2 Every man who prints, imagines he gives to the world something which they had not before, either in matter or style.

b. Of type, a block, a plate: To yield an impression on paper, etc. c. Of a manuscript or of literary matter: To run *up* or amount in type (to so much). *rare.*

1886 Tupper *My Life as Author* 282, I wish there was space here to say more about all this; but the great book before me would print up into several volumes. 1904 *19th Cent.* Apr. 672 Here scarcely a line has been added: but the plate 'prints', and the plate began by *not* printing.

9. *trans.* To mark (paper, etc.) with printed characters or designs.

1727–41 Chambers *Cycl.* s.v. *Printing*, The wetting of the paper ought to be done two or three days before printing it.

10. To take an impression from (a forme of type, a plate, block, etc.); to use in printing.

1727–41 Chambers *Cycl.* s.v. *Printing*, Engraving several plates of Sandro Boticello's design, and printing them off this new way. 1839 *Encycl. Brit.* (ed. 7) XVIII. 573/1 These machines, however, are better adapted to printing stereotype plates, to which a curved form could be given. 1875 Knight *Dict. Mech.* 1335/2 The stone is then etched, washed out, and printed.

11. To write in imitation of typography; to form (letters) in the style of printed letters; also *absol.*

1837 Dickens *Pickw.* xxxvii, ⁋ Mr. Weller..here's a letter for you'..'It can't be from the gov'ner', said Sam, looking at the direction..'He always prints, I know, 'cos he learnt writin' from the large bills in the bookin' offices'. *Mod.* A little boy, who cannot write yet, has *printed* me a letter.

III. Technical senses analogous to II.

12. *trans.* To stamp or mark (a textile fabric, as cotton or oilcloth), by hand or machinery, with a pattern or decorative design in one or more colours. Also *absol.*

1588 Hickock tr. *Frederick's Voy.* 7 b, Goods and marchandize that come out of the kingdom of Cambaia, as cloth of Bumbast white, painted, printed, great quantitie of Indico [etc.]. 1600 in Nichols *Progr. Q. Eliz.* (1823) III. 505 One coveringe for a Frenche gowne of lawne, embrodered all over with fountaines, snaikes,..and other devises, upon silver chamblet prented. 1700 *Act* 11 & 12 *Will. III*, c. 10 All Calicoes, painted, dyed, printed or stamped there [in E. Indies] shall not be worn or otherwise used within the Kingdom of England. 1712 *Act* 10 *Anne* c. 19 There shall be..Paid for and upon..all Callicoes to be so Printed, Stained, Painted or Dyed..the Sum of Three Pence for every yard in length. 1758 Franklin *Lett.* Wks. 1887 III. 7 There are also fifty-six yards of cotton, printed curiously from copper plates. 1839 Ure *Dict. Arts* 214 The manufacturer..can print at whatever hour he may receive an order... Under the patronage of parliament, it was easy..to buy printed calicoes.

b. *Print on* (in *Calico-printing*): to apply (the colouring matter of the design) upon the surface by printing.

1839 Ure *Dict. Arts* 215 Four different methods are in use for imprinting figures upon calicoes..the fourth is by a system of copper cylinders..by which two, three, four, or even five colours may be printed on in rapid succession. *Ibid.* 222 Some mordants..liquefy in the course of a few days; and being apt to run in the printing-on make blotted work. *Ibid.* 241 Print on the resist to preserve the white.

13. *Pottery.* To transfer to the unglazed surface a decorative design in colour from paper, or in oil from a gelatine sheet or bat, the colour in the latter case being dusted on afterwards. With the pottery, or the design, as obj.

1839 Ure *Dict. Arts* 1017 The old plan of passing the biscuit into the muffle after it had been printed... The [glue] cake..is..transferred to the surface of the glazed ware which it is intended to print. *Ibid.* 1029 M. Saint Amans ..says the English surpass all other nations in manufacturing a peculiar stoneware..as also in printing blue figures upon it.

14. *Photogr.* To produce (a positive picture) by the transmission of light through a negative placed immediately upon the sensitized surface, or, in an enlarging camera, before it. Also with *off*, *out.*

1851 Hunt *Photogr.* 80 The Printing Process...It is..a negative picture,..a matrix which is capable of yielding a vast number of beautiful impressions. I have had as

Supplement, p. 3873; Corrigenda, p. 4092; Spurious words, p. 4093; Books quoted, p. 4094

Printable, *a.* ... Capable of being printed ...

Printed, *ppl. a.* [f. PRINT *v.* + -ED¹.] ...

Printer ... **1.** A person who prints, in any sense of the word; one engaged in impressing or stamping marks or designs upon a surface, as a calico-printer ...

Printery ... A printing-office.

Printing, *vbl. sb.* [f. PRINT *v.* + -ING¹.] The action of the verb PRINT, in various senses; an instance of this.

Printing-house.

Printing-ink.

Printing-office.

Printing-press.

Priodont ...

Priol, obs. form of PAIR-ROYAL.

Prion ...

Priodontes ...

Prior ...

Prioress ...

Prioress ... A nunnery or convent presided over by a prioress.

Priorhede, *Obs. rare⁻¹.*

Priori, *a.* and *adv.*

Priorie, obs. form of PRIORY.

Priority ...

Priorly, *adv.*

Priorship ...

Priory ...

Prisage, *sb.¹*

Priscian ...

Priscianist ...

Prise, *v.*

Prise, *sb.³* and *v.¹*

Prism ...

Prismal, *a.*

Prismated, *a.*

Prismatic, *a.* [ad. Gr. πρισματ-, πρίσμα: see PRISM and -IC.] **1.** Of or pertaining to, or produced by a prism; prismatic.

[This page of the Oxford English Dictionary is printed in extremely dense, small type across six columns. The principal head-words in order of appearance are transcribed below.]

Prismatic, a. Now rare.

Prismatical, a. Now rare.

Prismatically, adv.

Prisma-tico-, combining form of PRISMATIC.

Prismatoid.

Prismatoid-al, a.

Prismatoidal, a.

Prismatical, a.

Prismed (priz'md), a.

Prismoid (priz'moid), sb.

Prismoid-al, a.

Prismy (priz'mi), a.

Prison (priz'n), sb.

Prison (priz'n), v.

Prisonable.

Prisoned (priz'nd), ppl. a.

Prisoner (priz'nər), sb.

Prisoner's base.

Prison-bar. pl.

Prison-door.

Prison-fellow. Obs.

Prison-gate.

Prison-house.

Prisoning, vbl. sb.

Prisoning, ppl. a.

Prisonment. Now rare.

Prisonous.

Prisonry.

Prisonerment.

Pristinary. Obs. rare.

Pristinate, a. (sb.) Obs.

Pristine (pri'stin), a.

Prithee (pri'ðə), int. phr.

Pritch (pritʃ), sb.

Pritchel (pri'tʃl), sb. dial.

Pritch-aule. Obs. rare.

Prittle-prattle (pri'tl, prae'tl), sb.

Prittle-prattle, v. Obs.

Prius (prai'ɒs). [L.]

Priusable, bad form of prevable, PROVABLE.

Privacy (prai'vəsi, pri'vəsi).

Privado (privā'do). Obs.

Privat-docent, dozent (prīvā't dōtsent').

Private (prai'vət), a. and sb.

2306 Supplement, p. 3873; Corrigenda, p. 4092; Spurious words, p. 4093; Books quoted, p. 4094

Privisant, a. Obs. rare. Also 5 pryui-sant. [Form and meaning obscure: perh. erron.]

Privit, obs. form of PRIVET.

Privitate, Sc. Obs. rare. [app. ad. L. type *privitātem*: see next.]

Privity (privi). Now chiefly *techn.* (in Law, etc.). Forms: 3-5 privete, -vite (also 4-6 pre-; 3-5 pryv-, -va-; 4-6 pre-), 7 privitie, 6- privity. [ME. privete, -ite, a. OF. privete, priviteit (a 1200 in Godef.) privacy, a secret, etc., ad. L. type *privitās*, abstr. n. f. prīv-us private, peculiar: see -ITY.]

† **1 A.** A thing that is kept hidden or secret. A divine or heavenly mystery; a secret of nature. *The book of priuyty (privities)*, the Apocalypse. Obs.

† **b.** A secret matter, design, purpose, or plan; a secret. Obs.

† **2.** The condition of being private; privacy, seclusion, retirement; concealment, secrecy; chiefly in phr. *in privity*, in privacy, in private. Obs.

† **3.** Private or secret fellowship; intimacy, familiarity. Obs.

4. Private or secret knowledge of; participation in the knowledge of something private or secret. Obs.

5. The fact of being privy to something; participation in the knowledge of something private or secret, usually implying concurrence or consent; private knowledge or cognizance.

6. *Law.* Any relation between two parties recognized by law, e.g. that of blood, covenant, tenure, lease, service, etc.; mutual interest in any transaction or thing.

Privy (privi), a., sb. (adv.) and v. techn. (in Law, etc.). Forms: 3- pri-, 4-6 pry-; 3-6 (7-) ve (4 Sc. -wy) 4 -vel, -vie, 4-5 -vee, -vay (5 Sc. -way), 4-6 -vie, -veye (5 -ve(e), 5-7 -vie; 6-7 privi). [ME. prive, privi, etc., a. F. privé (12th c. in Littré), private, tame; as sb. privy place.]

A. adj.

† **1 A.** That is of one's own private circle or companionship; intimate, familiar; = PRIVATE a. 1.

2. Of or pertaining exclusively to a particular person or persons; one's own; = PRIVATE a. 5; of an attendant, etc., personal. Obs. exc. in PRIVY CHAMBER, COUNSEL, COUNSELLOR, SEAL.

3. Of language: idiomatic. Obs. rare.

4. Acting or done in secret or by stealth; secret, clandestine, furtive, surreptitious, sly. (Often opposed to *apert*, *pert*: arch.)

5. Withdrawn from public sight, knowledge, or use; kept secret or concealed; hidden; secluded. arch.

6. Of material things.

II. Of things.

III. In specific collocations with sb.

8. *Privy evil* (Falconry), a disease of the hawk; see quot. *Privy tithe*, the 'small' or vicarial tithe. *Privy verdict*, a verdict given to the judge out of court.

B. sb.

9. Privy purse. **a.** The allowance from the public revenue for the private expenses of the monarch. **b.** Short for *Keeper of the Privy Purse*, an officer of the royal household charged with the payment of the private expenses of the sovereign.

10. Privy signet: see SIGNET.

11. *Absol.* or elliptical uses of the adj. Cf. OF. *privé*, *private*, in various subst. uses.]

C. adv. = PRIVILY adv.; privately, secretly, in secret.

Privy (privie), obs. var. PRIVET.

Privy chamber. Now Hist. [PRIVY a. 2.]

Privy council, councillor. [ME. from 17th c. occasionally, and in 19th c. often spelt councillor plar.]

Privy counsellor, counciller. [ME. from 17th c. occasionally, and in 19th c. often spelt councillor plar.]

Privy-counsellorship, -councillorship. [See -SHIP.]

Privy seal. Forms: see PRIVY and SEAL. [PRIVY a. 2 1 b. private or secret seal.]

1. The seal affixed to documents that afterwards to pass the Great Seal; also to documents of less importance which do not require the Great Seal. In Scotland, A seal which authenticates a royal grant of personal or assignable rights.

b. The office in which documents were prepared and the privy seal affixed to them. Obs.

Prizable, priseable (prai·zăb'l), a.[1] Now chiefly dial. Also 7 priseable. [f. PRIZE v. 1 -ABLE.] Capable of being, or worthy to be, prized; valuable.

Prizable, -eable, var. PRISABLE a.

Prizal, Obs. rare. [f. PRIZE v. 1 or sb. 1 -AL.] Estimate of worth; appraisement; valuation.

† Prizal, sb. form of PRICE sb.1 Obs.

Prize (praiz), sb.1 For earlier forms (price, prise, prize, etc.) see PRICE sb.1 [A differentiated variant of ME. *pris*, *prise*, now PRICE sb. The latter was formerly, and in some dialects is still, *prize*, *prise* (prait), and its plural in 16-18th c. was very commonly *prises*, *prices*. The corresp. verb is also *prise*, PRIZE v. 1 Cf. also the forms of PRICE sb.2, v.]

2. A sum of money or a thing of value, offered for competition by chance or hazard, as by trying who shall throw the highest or other specified number at dice, or draw a particular ticket from among a large number to which no advantage attaches, as in a lottery.

3. fig. Anything striven for or worth striving for; a thing of value won by or inspiring effort.

4. attrib. and Comb. **a.** attrib. (a) That gains a prize, awarded in a competition or exhibition; also fig. such as would or might gain a prize; supremely excellent of its kind, first-class. (b) That is offered or gained as a prize. (Often hyphened.)

Prize (praiz), sb.2, β.-4-7 prise, 5-7 price, 6-7 pryse, 6- prize. [ME. prise, a. F. prise taking, capture, orig. fem. pa. pple. of prendre to take. Hence prize-money, prize-master, etc.]

1. The act of taking; capture, seizure. Obs.

2. That which is taken or seized.

3. attrib. and Comb., as prize brandy, cause, goods, property, ship; prize agent, an agent authorized for the sale of prizes taken in maritime war; prize court, which adjudicates concerning prizes; prize crew, a crew of seamen placed on board a prize ship to bring her into port; prize-master, an officer appointed to command a prize ship; prize-office (see quot. 1706). See also PRIZE-MONEY.

Supplement, p. 3873; Corrigenda, p. 4092; Spurious words, p. 4093; Books quoted, p. 4094

c 1590 GREENE Fr. Bacon xiii. 41 Thou'rt worthy of the title of a squire, That durst, for proof, of thy affection And for thy mistress' favour, prize thy blood. 1590 C'TESS PEMBROKE Antonie 264 But terror here and horror, naught is seene: And present death prizing our life each hower [orig. Et la presente mort nous marchande à tous coups].

3. To value or esteem highly, to think much of. (The current sense.)

α. 1375 BARBOUR Bruce I. 239 And suld think fredome mar to pryss Than all the gold in warld that Is. c 1470 Gol. & Gaw. 1207, I aught as prynce him to prise for his prouese. c 1615 SIR W. MURE Sonn. ix, In bewty, (loue's sueit object), ravischt sight Doth some peculiar perfectioun pryse [rime lyes]. 1665 BOYLE Occas. Refl. VI. iii, That we..prise many [customs] of our own onely because we never consider'd them. β. c 1586 C'TESS PEMBROKE Ps. CXXXIX. x, My God, how I these studies prize, That doe thy hidden workings show! 1618 E. ELTON Exp. Rom. vii. (1622) 136 A blessing that cannot be sufficiently prized. 1681 FLAVEL Meth. Grace xxxv. 583 When we would express the value of a thing, we say, we prize it as our eyes. 1725 POPE Iliad I. 237, I..prize at equal rate Thy short-liv'd friendship, and thy groundless hate. a 1720 SEWEL Hist. Quakers (1795) I. 53 Prize your time now, while you have it. 1891 Speaker 11 July 36/2 The Swiss seem more and more to prize..the Referendum and the Initiative.

γ. 1375–1643 [see PRICE v. 5].

†**b.** With negative: Not to value at all, to think nothing of, care nothing for. Obs.

c 1600 SHAKS. Sonn. cxliii, Not prizing her poore infants discontent. 1611 — Wint. T. IV. iv. 386 Had [I] force and knowledge More then was euer mans, I would not prize them Without her Loue.

II. †**4.** To commend or extol the worth, excellence, or merit of; = PRAISE v. 3. Obs. northern.

α. 1375 BARBOUR Bruce x. 776 Of this deid,..The Erll wes prisit gretumly. 1456 SIR G. HAYE Law Arms (S. T. S.) 11 Ilke man did sum thing, that was mekle to lowe and to pris. 1500–20 DUNBAR Poems xliii. 45 Sic ladyis wyiss, Thay ar to pryis. 1567 Satir. Poems Reform. v. 16 Gif him all thankis..And pryse his name with all 3our micht.

Prize, prise, v.² Forms: α. 6 pryse, 6–7 prise; β. 7– prize. [f. PRIZE sb.³] trans. To seize, take, capture; to seize as forfeited, to confiscate. Obs. exc. as in b.

α. 1535 COVERDALE Dan. iii. 29 All people..which speake eny blasphemy agaynst the God of Sydrac, Misac and Abdenago, shal dye, and their houses shalbe prysed. 1581 LAMBARDE Eiren. II. iv. (1588) 177 If any bee afterward found offending,..their armour and weapon shall be prised, ..to the use of the Queenes Maiestie. c 1611 CHAPMAN Iliad XI. 385 To kill the five Hippasides And prise their arms. β. 1602 WARNER Alb. Eng. x. lv. (1612) 245 The Queene of Scots from Ours almost her Crowne and life had prizde.

b. spec. To make a prize or seizure of; to seize (a ship or her cargo) as a prize of war.

α. 1568 C. WATSON Polyb. 60 b, The Romans being both more in number and valianter men, prised her [the Rhodians' ship] without labour and toke the Rhodian. 1600 HAKLUYT Voy. (1810) III. 236 The one [ship]..being prised near Silley by a ship of which I am part owner. 1622 MALYNES Anc. Law-Merch. 145 If it happen a Ship to be prised for debt or otherwise to bee forfeited, yet the Mariners hire is to be payed. β. 1886 American XII. 67 It was explained that the David J. Adams was prized for concealing her name and her sailing-port.

Prize, prise (prəiz), v.³ [f. PRIZE sb.⁴] **1.** trans. To raise or move by force of leverage; to force up; esp. to force open in this way.

1686 PLOT Staffordsh. 344 They easily prize up bushes, furses, or broom by the very roots. 1688 R. HOLME Armoury III. xx. (Roxb.) 246/1 The Forked end is strucken deep in the ground each side the root and so drawn or prised vp. 1808 JAMIESON, To prize up, to force open, to press up a lock or door. 1818 SCOTT Hrt. Midl. vi, The door was..assailed with sledge-hammers, iron crows [etc.].. with which they prized, heaved and battered for some time with little effect. 1822 — Pirate vii, There stands yonder a chest, from which the lid has been just prized off. 1840 DICKENS Barn. Rudge lxiv, Many men..were seen..striving to prize it [the jail door] down with crowbars. 1897 Pall Mall Mag. June 254 The lock was broken, and the lid bore signs of having been prised. fig. 1824 PRIOR Burke (1854) 232 Thus this famous measure..became the lever by which to prize its authors out of office.

2. To compress (cured tobacco) in a hogshead or box. Southern U. S.

1867 SMYTH Sailor's Word-bk., Prizing,..also, the act of pressing or squeezing an article into its package, so that its size may be reduced in stowage. 1889 BRUCE Plant. Negro 183 To the moment that the leaf is prized in the hogshead.

Hence **Prizing, prising** vbl. sb.; also attrib.

1867 [see 2]. 1890 Daily News 14 July 2/8 This pad prevented the splintering of wood, although the prising power would be the same. 1891 ATKINSON Last of Giant-Killers 166 More hammering and more prising with the gavelocks and crowbars.

Priseable: see PRIZABLE.

Prized (prəizd), ppl. a. [f. PRIZE v.¹ + -ED¹.] **1.** Greatly valued; highly esteemed.

1538 in Lett. Suppress. Monasteries (Camden) 209 The prysed memoryes and perpetuall renowned factes of the famouse princes of Israel. 1856 KANE Arct. Expl. II. xvii. 180 Two of our most prized comrades. 1873 EMERSON Let. 3 May in Westm. Gaz. 7 Aug. (1906) 3/3, I am glad you have seen my prized friend, your Uncle George.

†**2.** = PRICED. In quot. 1642, High-priced, expensive. Obs. or dial.

1642 HARCOURT in Macm. Mag. XLV. 289/2 Some prittee small laces, but not prized ones; for I will spare your pursse as much as may be. 1682 FLAVEL Fear 44 'Tis a low priz'd commodity in my eyes. 1710 HEARNE Collect. 19 Mar. (O.H.S.) II. 362 The priz'd Catalogue wch I have seen. (Priced is still so pronounced by some.)

Prize-fight (prəi·zfəit). [app. a late back-formation from next.] A public contest between prize-fighters; a boxing-match for money.

1824 W. N. BLANE Excursion 508 There had just been a 'prize fight' well attended by noblemen and gentlemen. 1857 HUGHES Tom Brown II. v, The stories he had heard of men being killed in prize-fights rose up horribly before him. 1898 Daily News 18 Nov. 4/5 Sir John Bridge said this contest was not, in his opinion, a sparring match, but a prize-fight. He held that fighting for money was a prize-fight, and that was illegal.

Prize-fighter (prəi·zfəitəɹ). [orig. f. PRIZE sb.² + FIGHTER, from the phr. 'to fight a prize' or 'prizes'; in later use associated with PRIZE sb.¹]

†**a.** orig. One who 'fought a prize' (see PRIZE sb.²); one who engaged in a public fighting-match or contest. Obs. **b.** In mod. use, A professional pugilist or boxer, who fights publicly for a prize or stake; 'one that fights publicly for a reward' (J.).

1703 LUTTRELL Brief Rel. (1857) V. 316 Yesterday, one Cook, a prize fighter, was condemned at the Old Baily for killing a constable last May fair was twelve month. 1725 St. Mary le Bow, Durham, Par. Reg., Jane, daughter of Thomas Barrett, Prize fighter, bap. 28 April. 1727 POPE, etc. Art Sinking 122 It is proposed..that Mr. Figg with his prize-fighters, and Violante with the rope-dancers, be admitted in partnership. 1753 SMOLLETT Ct. Fathom (1784) 117/2 The sword..he brandished over the chevalier's head, with the dexterity of an old prize-fighter. 1796 MORSE Amer. Geog. II. 104 The encouragement given to prize-fighters and boxers. 1828 SCOTT F. M. Perth xiv. 1861 Sat. Rev. 7 Dec. 587 He..had the wit and luck to bring over that bulky prizefighter [Heenan] to make a sensation in England.

fig. 1829 CARLYLE Misc. (1857) II. 17 Not that we would say Voltaire was a mere prize-fighter.

So **Pri·ze-fighting** sb. and a.

1720 SWIFT T. Tub, Hist. Martin § 2 Hence the origine of that genteel custom of Prize-fighting. a 1763 BYROM Verses Figg & Sutton i, Long was the great Figg, by the prize Fighting Swains, Sole Monarch acknowledg'd of Mary-bone Plains. 1796 MORSE Amer. Geog. II. 108 The barbarous diversions of boxing and prize-fighting. 1878 N. Amer. Rev. CXXVII. 289 Countries that have not been civilized by prize-fighting. 1890 Review of Rev. II. 510/2 Prize-fighting in the ordinary sense of the term—i.e., a fight for money with fists, fought out to the bitter end—is absolutely illegal.

Prizeless (prəi·zlés), a. [f. PRIZE sb.¹ + -LESS.] Without a prize; not having gained a prize.

1897 Westm. Gaz. 11 Feb. 3/2 The kind old lady who went about consoling the prizeless dogs at Cruft's. 1899 Ibid. 3 Aug. 2/3 On the return of Harry and Robert home from school; Robert laden with prizes, Harry prizeless.

Prizeless, obs. form of PRICELESS.

Prize-list: see PRIZE sb.¹ 4 b, sb.³ 3.

Prizeman (prəi·zmæ̆n). [f. PRIZE sb.¹ + MAN sb.¹] A man who wins a prize (esp. for excelling in learning or art).

1800 Cambr. Univ. Cal. Title-p., A list of the..Medallists and Prize-men. Ibid. 15 Members' Prizemen. Ibid. 22 Seatonian Prizemen. 1834 Edin. Rev. LIX. 133 The mere prize-man is often dismissed in a few lines. 1856 LEVER Martins of Cro' M. xiv, He's more than that..he is the great prize man of the year in Trinity. 1896 Current Hist. (Buffalo) VI. 463 In his third year he [Lord Kelvin] came out as second wrangler and Smith's prizeman.

†**Pri·zement**. Obs. Also 6 prisement, 7 pricement. [f. PRIZE v.¹ + -MENT.] The act of 'prizing' or valuing; valuation, appraisement.

1566 Richmond Wills (Surtees) 189 All theis to remayne at the house thare withoute prisement so longe as any of the Phillipson name shall dwell at the said house. 1631 WEEVER Anc. Fun. Mon. 274 According to the pricement at the suppression. a 1700 in Keble Life Bp. Wilson vi. (1863) 203 When sufficient men are sworn to prize children's goods..the executors..must take all things according to the prizement.

Pri·ze-mo·ney. [f. PRIZE sb.³] Money realized by the sale of a prize (esp. one taken in maritime war), and distributed among the captors.

1757 J. LIND Lett. Navy i. 23 All ships are equally entitled to their share of prize-money. 1800 J. WEBBE in Gurw. Wellington's Desp. (1837) I. 128 Likely to obtain neither fame nor prize money. 1887 BESANT The World went xxiv, The prize-money..amounted to a very pretty sum.

Prizer¹ (prəi·zəɹ). Now rare. Forms: 5 pryzer, 5–6 prysar(e, 6 prisar, pryser, -or, 6–7 priser, 7 prisor, prizor, 7– prizer. [f. PRIZE v.¹ + -ER¹.] One who prizes.

†**1.** One who estimates the value, or determines the price, of something; an appraiser. Obs.

1427 in Trans. Stirling Nat. Hist. & Archæol. Soc. (1902) 57 The pain of the Pryzer, if he be negligent & punish not. c 1440 Promp. Parv. 413/2 Prysare, or settar at price, yn a merket, or oþer placys. 1505 Berwick Reg. in Hist. MSS. Comm., Var. Collect. I. 7 No bowcher..shall breke nor cut out any flysh to sell exsept the said prysers ber present. 1549 Records of Elgin (New Spald. Cl.) I. 97 Alexander Wynchester [and five others] electit prisers of flesche. 1552 in Picton L'pool Munic. Rec. (1883) I. 59 Assessors and Prysors. a 1625 SIR H. FINCH Law (1636) 472 The prisors to take them of the price if they prise too high. 1654 H. L'ESTRANGE Chas. I (1655) 194 Charges of driving to be set by a priser of the forrage.

2. †**a.** One who values or esteems something at a specified (high, low, etc.) rate. Obs. **b.** One who values or esteems something highly.

c 1611 CHAPMAN Iliad XVI. 762 Too much prizer of thyself. 1657 Mrs. Hobson's Brass in Chancel of Clewer Ch., A despiser of yᵉ world and a high Prizer of yᵉ Lord Christ.

1691 NORRIS Pract. Disc. 33 But now, are the Children of Light such Prizers of Time?

Pri·zer². arch. Also 6 priser. [f. PRIZE sb.² + -ER¹.] One who engages in a 'prize' or contest; a prize-fighter.

1599 B. JONSON Cynthia's Rev. IV. v, I haue a plot vpon these prizers. 1600 SHAKS. A. Y. L. II. iii. 8 Why would you be so fond to ouercome The bonnie priser of the humorous Duke? 1679 MRS. BEHN Feign'd Curtizan v, And fought like prizers, not as angry rivals. 1823 SCOTT Quentin D. xxxv, You shall be fought for in real mêlée. Only..the successful prizer shall be a gentleman. 1845 BROWNING Luria I. 52 The brace of prizers fairly matched Poleaxe with poleaxe.

Prize-ring (prəi·z₁riŋ). [f. after PRIZE-FIGHT: see RING sb.¹ 13.] A ring or enclosed space (now a square area enclosed by poles and ropes) for prize-fighting; hence transf. the practice of prize-fighting (cf. the turf = horse-racing); also attrib. belonging to prize-fighting, characteristic of prize-fighters.

1840 BLAINE Encycl. Rur. Sports § 4000 Two of the members of 'the ancient prize-ring' in actual combat. 1848 THACKERAY Van. Fair lxiv, Captain Rook with his horse-jockey jokes and prize-ring slang. 1861 J. CRAWFURD in Trans. Ethnol. Soc. I. 367 One of this race had nearly carried off the championship of England in the prize-ring. 1884 Times (weekly ed.) 17 Oct. 2/2 Better..not to introduce into political controversy the language of the prize-ring.

Prizing (prəi·ziŋ), vbl. sb.¹ Forms: see PRIZE v.¹ [f. PRIZE v.¹ + -ING¹.] The action of PRIZE v.¹; † determination of price or value, appraising; valuing, estimation (obs.); high estimation.

c 1440 Promp. Parv. 414/1 Prysynge, licitatio. 1499 Exch. Rolls Scotl. XI. 436 The prising of the said landis. 1552 HULOET, Prisynge or settynge pryce, licitatio. 1678–9 LUTTRELL Brief Rel. (1857) I. 6 The latter end of this month came out his majesties proclamation for prizeing of wines. [The proclamation has 'to set the Prices of all kinds of Wines'.] 1907 Daily Chron. 9 Oct. 6/4 It was a fit prize for a feat that stood above all prizing.

Prizing, vbl. sb², 3: see PRIZE v.², 3.

‖**Pro** (prōᵘ). The L. preposition prō before (of place), in front of, for, on behalf of, instead of, in return for, on account of, etc. [Cognate with Gr. πρό forward, before, in front of, earlier than, Skr. prá before; more remotely related to OTeut. for, fora, Eng. for, fore.]

A. as prep. in various Latin phrases, more or less used in Eng. (See also PRO AND CON.)

1. pro a·ris et fo·cis, for altars and hearths; for the sake of, or on behalf of, religion and home.

1621 BURTON Anat. Mel. III. iv. I. iii. (1676) 398/1 When I see two superstitious Orders contend pro aris & focis, with such have and hold, de lana caprina. 1741 HUME Ess. iv. 48, I wou'd only perswade Men not to contend, as if they were fighting pro aris & focis. 1859 LOWELL Biglow P. 12 They serve cheerfully in the great army which fights even unto death pro aris et focis.

2. pro bo·no pu·blico, for the public good.

a 1726 GILBERT Cases in Law & Equity (1760) 113 It is pro bono publico, in which they are included.

3. pro confe·sso, for or as confessed or admitted: chiefly in Law.

1631 in Crt. & Times Chas. I (1848) II. 141 As if they had taken it pro confesso that he is living. 1776 Claim of Roy Rada Churn 17/1 in Trial J. Fowke, etc., The Court.. had informed them, if they did not [support their case by affidavit], the negative of the question put would be taken pro confesso.

4. pro fo·rma (-ă), for form's sake; as a matter of form; in the way of formality. Also attrib.

1573–80 G. HARVEY Letter-bk. (Camden) 77 To give the choyce of a thousand thankes for every gewegawe; and sumtymes tooe for very meere Nifilles as it were only pro forma tantum. 1623 J. CHAMBERLAIN in Crt. & Times Jas. I (1848) II. 425 Which is thought to be done rather pro formâ than ex animo. 1788 Gentl. Mag. LVIII. 73/1 The cession of the Crimea by the Porte was contrary to the Alcoran, and was therefore admitted merely pro forma. 1882 BITHELL Counting-ho. Dict. (1893) s.v., When a document is drawn up or a process gone through after a prescribed model, and with the special object of complying with some legal requirement it is said to be done pro formâ.

5. pro hac vice, for this turn or occasion (only).

1653 in Rashdall & Rait New College (1901) 178 Wee therefore shall pro hac vice nominate the 13 Seniors and Officers for the carrynge on the government of the said Colledge. 1715 S. SEWALL Diary 29 Mar., Made Mr. Little Clark pro hac vice, Mr. Cooke being sick of the Gout. 1873 Oxford Univ. Gazette 18 Nov. 312 The following gentlemen have been nominated by the Vice-Chancellor and Proctors to examine pro hac vice this Term.

6. pro indivi·so (Law), 'as undivided': applied to a right shared by two or more persons without division: see quot.

1607 COWELL Interpr., Pro Indiuiso, is a possession, and occupation of lands, or tenements belonging vnto two or more persons, whereof none knoweth his seuerall portion, as Coparceners before partition.

7. pro ra·ta (-ă) [= 'for the rate': RATE sb.¹ 2], in proportion to the value or extent (of his interest), proportionally. Also attrib. or as adj., proportional.

[1354 Rolls of Parlt. II. 260/1 Les Eschetours sont chargez ..a respoundre des parcelles des ditz rentes et fermes Pro rata temporis.] 1575 Reg. Privy Council Scot. II. 468 To mak payment of thair part of the said taxatioun pro rata. 1642 tr. Perkins' Prof. Bk. v. § 310 (1657) 118 His wife shall not have dower of that which the other copercener had pro rata. 1877 L. W. M. LOCKHART Mine is Thine xv. (1879)

134 I'll take my pro ratâ allotment. 1901 Daily Tel. 9 Mar. 9/7 The Preference issue will be offered pro rata to shareholders at 115.

8. pro re na·ta (-ă), 'for the affair born, i.e. arisen'; for some contingency arising unexpectedly or without being provided for; for an occasion as it arises. Also attrib.

1578 in Spottiswood Hist. Ch. Scot. VI. (1677) 295 It is in the power of the Eldership to send out qualified persons to visit pro re nata. 1765 BLACKSTONE Comm. I. ii. 174 It was formerly left to the crown to summon, pro re nata, the most flourishing towns to send representatives to parliament. 1885 A. P. PETER in Law Times 10 Jan. 185/1 Such orders are only granted pro re natâ, and must be renewed on each fresh occasion arising. Mod. At a pro re nata meeting of the Town Council, it was resolved, etc.

†**b.** So **pro-re-nascent** a. (obs. nonce-wd.), arising unexpectedly.

1647 WARD Simp. Cobler 50 In pro-re-nascent occurrences, which cannot be foreseen.

9. pro ta·nto, 'for so much', so far, to such an extent. Also attrib.

1780 BENTHAM Princ. Legisl. ii. § 4 Any one who reprobates any the least particle of pleasure as such..is pro tanto a partizan of the principle of asceticism. 1882 Macm. Mag. XLVI. 437 Anything which reduces the amount of payments to be made out of the country pro tanto reduces the loss. 1885 Law Times LXXVIII. 387/1 The land tax was redeemed and pro tanto personal estate converted into real estate.

10. pro te·mpore, for the time, temporarily; attrib. or as adj. temporary. (Abbrev. pro tem.)

1468 Paston Lett. II. 325 The tythandes did goode pro tempore. 1625–6 J. CHAMBERLAIN in Crt. & Times Chas. I (1848) I. 73 The Lord Chamberlain is like to be Lord Steward this parliament, pro tempore. 1748 J. LIND Lett. Navy ii. (1757) 70 Another might be appointed pro tempore to command his ship. 1759 E. W. MONTAGU, jr. Anc. Republics 353 The pro tempore Dictator soon came to be perpetual. 1828 Reg. Deb. Congr. IV. 787 President Pro Tempore..The Senate proceeded to the election of a President pro tem. 1846 H. GREVILLE Diary (1883) 159 Called to-day upon Craven..who is pro tem. private secretary to Normanby.

B. Pro- sb. **1.** An argument for or in favour of something, as opposed to one against it. (Now usually in PRO AND CON, q. v.) **b.** A person who sides or votes in favour of some proposal.

c 1400 Beryn 2577 That I may the bet perseyve al inconvenience, Dout, pro, contra, and ambiguite, Thurh yeur declaracioune. 1509 HAWES Past. Pleas. vi. (Percy Soc.) 26 Provyng the pro well from the contrary. 1784 GEO. III in G. Rose's Diaries (1860) I. 61 Mr. Pultney..should have stood amongst the Pros. 1790 M. CUTLER in Life, etc. (1888) I. 462 The pros are afraid to bring it forward until the return of several members on their side of the question.

2. Tally of pro: see TALLY sb.

Pro, pro., a familiar abbreviation of various wds., as proproctor and other combs. of PRO- pref.¹ 4, also professional.

1848 J. H. NEWMAN Loss & Gain iii. 17 When he came to Oxford..he reverenced even the velvet of the Pro. 1861 H. KINGSLEY Ravenshoe xiv, He had past the Pro's at Magdalen turnpike, and they never thought of stopping him...Both the Proctors were down at Coldharbour turnpike. a 1884 M. PATTISON Mem. (1885) 229, I had acted as proproctor to Green, the other pro being Kay. 1885 J. K. JEROME On the Stage 86 The poor players helped each other as well as they could, but provincial Pros. are—or, at least, were—not a wealthy class. 1887 Scott. Leader 19 Dec. 4/1 A match..between six professional golfers and six amateurs resulted in favour of the 'pros.' by three holes. 1890 Daily News 18 Sept. 5/3 'Master or Pro.'..the burning question of whether school cricket should be under the dominion of the schoolmaster or the professional cricketer. 1903 19th Cent. Sept. 464 Taverns frequented by 'pros', as music-hall artistes are popularly called.

Pro-, prefix.¹ The Latin adv. and prep. (see above), used in combination with verbs and their derivatives, and sometimes with other words not of verbal derivation.

(Unlike the Gr. προ-, the L. was originally and usually prō-; but in some compounds it was occasionally and in others usually or always shortened to prŏ-.)

A large number of Latin words so formed were retained in popular use in French (as in the other Romanic langs.); many others were taken into French in earlier or later times as learned words, and were thence taken into English. In later times words of this kind have been adopted or adapted in English directly from Latin, or have been formed immediately from Latin elements.

In OF. the prefix had often the popular form por-, pur-, pour- (see PUR-); but this, in many words, was subseq. changed back to the Latin form in pro-.

I. As an etymological element. The following are the principal uses in Latin and English. (All words of this class appear as Main words.)

1. a. Forward, to or towards the front, from a position in the rear, forth, out, into a public position; as prōclāmāre to call out, PROCLAIM, prōdūcĕre to lead forth, PRODUCE, prōfundĕre to pour forth (PROFUSE), prōjicĕre to throw forth, PROJECT, prōminēre to jut out (PROMINENT), prōnuntiāre to speak out, PRONOUNCE, prōpōnĕre to put forth, PROPONE, PROPOSE, prōtrūdĕre to thrust forth, PROTRUDE. **b.** To the front of, down before (the face of), forward and down: as prōcidĕre to fall forward or down (PROCIDENCE), prōclīvis sloping downward, PROCLIVE, prōculcāre to trample down, PROCULCATE, prōcumbĕre to fall down forwards (PROCUMBENT), prōflīgāre to dash down (PROFLIGATE), prōlābī, prōlaps- to slip down forwards (PROLAPSE), prōsternĕre, prōstrāt- to strew or lay flat before one, to PROSTRATE.

c. Forth from its place, away; as prōdĕre to give away, betray (PRODITION), prōdigāre to drive away, dissipate (PRODIGAL), prōfugĕre to flee away (PROFUGATE). **d.** Forward, onward, in a course or in time; as prōcēdĕre to PROCEED, prōcessus PROCESS, prōcrastināre to defer till the morrow, PROCRASTINATE, prōgredī to step forward, PROGRESS, prōmināre to drive onward (PROMENADE), prōmovēre, prōmōt- to move onward, PROMOVE, PROMOTE, prōpellĕre to drive forward, PROPEL. **e.** Out, with outward extension; as prōductilis able to be drawn out, PRODUCTILE, prōlixus PROLIX, prōpāgāre to plant out, PROPAGATE, prōtrahĕre, prōtract- to drag out, PROTRACT. **f.** Before in place, in front of; as prohibēre to hold in front, hold back, PROHIBIT, prōscrībĕre to write in front, PROSCRIBE, prōtegĕre to cover in front, PROTECT. **g.** Before in time, in anticipation of, in provision for; as prōdigium PRODIGY, prōloquī to speak before (PROLOCUTION), prōvidēre to foresee, PROVIDE. **h.** For, in preparation for, on behalf of; as prōcinctus girt for, PROCINCT, prōcūrāre to take care for, PROCURE, prōsperus wished for, PROSPEROUS, prōficĕre to do service to, PROFIT. **i.** With worn-down or obscure force; as prōcērus tall, PROCEROUS, prŏfānus PROFANE, prŏfundus deep, PROFOUND, prōlēs offspring (PROLETAIRE), prōmerēre to deserve, PROMERIT, prōmiscuus mixed, PROMISCUOUS, prōverbium PROVERB, prōvincia PROVINCE.

2. Frequently prefixed in Latin to names of relationship, answering to Eng. 'great' or 'grand', F. grand and petit; as avus grandfather, pro-avus great-grandfather, amita aunt, father's sister, pro-amita great-aunt, grandfather's sister, gener son-in-law, prōgener grandson-in-law, granddaughter's husband. So pronepos great-grandson, great-nephew, PRONEPHEW, PRONEPOT, proneptis great-grand-daughter, great-niece, PRONIECE, PRONEPT.

3. Pro- for PRÆ-, PRE-. In late and mediæval Lat. pro- was sometimes substituted for præ-, prē-, partly through confusion of sense, partly perhaps under the influence of words from Greek, such as prologus, prophēta, proscænium. Examples of this are frequent in ME., where, however, as in med.L. MSS., it is often difficult to say whether pro- was intended, or was merely a scribal or copyist's error, due to confusion of the written e and o. Examples will be found among the cross-references.

II. As a living prefix.

4. In Latin prō- in the sense 'for', 'instead of', 'in place of', was prefixed to a sb., app. originally in prepositional construction, as prō consule (one acting) for a consul, afterwards combined with the sb., as prōconsul = deputy-consul; so prōdictātor, prōflāmen, prōgubernātor, prōlēgātus, prōmagister, prōpræfectus, prōprætor; also in a few names of things, as prōnōmen PRONOUN, prōtūtēla deputy-guardianship.

English has examples of pro- prefixed **a.** to names of persons (officials or functionaries), 'acting as deputy', as pro·-Grand Ma·ster, pro-gua·rdian, pro-legate, pro-provincial, pro-provost, pro-regent, pro-seneschal, pro-tetrarch, pro-treasurer, pro-tribune, pro-warden, etc.; also PROCONSUL, PROPROCTOR, PRORECTOR, etc. **b.** to names of things, as pro-rea·lity (something serving the purpose of a reality), pro·-ski·n, pro·-ve·rb [after pronoun], etc.; also PRO-CATHEDRAL, PRO-LEG, etc. **c.** to an adj., as pro·-e·thical, serving as a substitute for what is ethical; pro·-su·bstantive (see quot.): hence pro-substantively adv.

1892 H. SPENCER Princ. Ethics I. II. ii. § 123. 337 We must class them as forming a body of thought and feeling which may be called *pro-ethical; and which, with the mass of mankind, stands in place of the ethical properly so called. 1902 R. R. MARETT in Personal Idealism 250 Religion..as often as it happens to take the side of salutary practice.. is probably [a] more effectual 'pro-ethical sanction' [than law]. 1898 Daily Chron. 21 Nov. 5/1 Having served with pre-eminent distinction the office of Deputy Grand Master, he was in 1891 elected *Pro-Grand Master, a distinction which can only be understood when it is recalled that the Prince of Wales himself is Grand Master. 1868 Digby's Voy. Medit. Pref. 17 Digby's *pro-guardian was a man of considerable celebrity. 1656 BLOUNT Glossogr., A *Prolegate,..a Deputy Legat, or one that stands for a Legat. 1902 Westm. Gaz. 25 Jan. 4/2 In the name of the Trinity, Thomas, *Pro-Provincial of Canterbury, Joseph, Provincial of York, Laurence, Provincial of Caerleon, deplore the evil state of the Established Church. 1858 in Stat. Univ. Oxford (1863) 158 *Pro-Provost. 1877 E. R. CONDER Bas. Faith iv. 185 This kind of idealised symbol or concept serves as a *pro-reality, which we can reason about as though it were real. 1798 HELEN M. WILLIAMS Tour Switzerland I. 238 (Jod.) Don Amatori Solani *proregent, professor extraordinary, and enjoying numerous other titles. 1657 W. RAND tr. Gassendi's Life Peiresc II. 84 Cadafalcius *Pro-senescal of Digne. 1886 H. SPENCER in 19th Cent. May 763 There is produced a new skin, or rather a *pro-skin. 1794 E. BANCROFT Res. Perm. Colours I. 176 Such compositions ..assume the form of substantive colours, without being such in reality;..I beg leave..to call them *pro-substantive topical colours. Ibid. 390 Of the Uses of Quercitron Bark, in producing Topical Yellow and other Colours, 'pro-substantively, upon Cotton and Linen. 1647 TRAPP Comm. Luke viii. 3 His vicar-general, or *protetrarch. 1645 WOOD Life Jan. (O.H.S.) I. 115 For the space of three yeares he was a *protribune [mispr. protobune] of horse under Charles Lewis elector Palatine. In 1641 he was sent into Ireland..

where he served in the quality of a tribune for two yeares. 1907 J. M. GRAINGER Studies K. Jas. Bible 19 Do is sometimes used as a *pro-verb, to avoid repetition of an antecedent verb. 1861 NEALE Notes Dalmatia, etc. 169 *Pro-Vicar of the Bishop in the southern part of his diocese. 1857 in Stat. Univ. Oxford (1863) 83 *Pro-Warden.

5. In sense 'for, in favour of, on the side of'.

This use is entirely modern, and has no precedent or analogy in Latin. It appears to have arisen from the use of pro in PRO B. 1 b, or in PRO AND CON. To a certain extent, combinations with pro- take the place of those with PHILO-, as philo-Turk, philo-publican. They appear to have begun c 1825, but to have been comparatively rare up to 1896, since which date they have swarmed in the journalistic press, usually in antithesis to formations in anti- expressed or understood. Pro-Boer and anti-British were terms of opprobrium during the South African War, 1899–1902.

a. Prefixed to a sb., sb. phr., or adj., forming adjs. with sense 'favouring or siding with (what is indicated by the second element)'; as pro-alien, -American, -annexation, -Asiatic, -Boer, -British, -Catholic, -Chinese, -clerical, -educational, -English, -foreign, -French, -Irish, -Japanese, -moral, -negro, -opium, -papist, -patronage, -popery, -rebel, -Russian, -slavery, -tariff reform, -transubstantiation, -Turk, -Turkish, -war, etc. Where the form of the second element permits, as in pro-Boer, pro-Catholic, pro-negro, pro-papist, pro-Turk, these are also used as sbs. = 'one who is on the side of, or favours . . ., a partisan or adherent of . . .'. **b.** In comb. with a sb. (or verb-stem) + -ER or -ITE, forming a nonce-sb. = 'one who favours or sides with . . .'; as pro-Boarder (one in favour of a School Board), -breecher (a partisan of breeches), -flogger (one who favours flogging), -slaver (a pro-slavery man); pro-liquorite (one in favour of the unrestricted sale of alcoholic drinks). **c.** In comb. with a sb. or adj. (or directly from those in a.) + -ISM, forming abstract sbs. = 'the principle or character of being in favour of . . .', as pro-alcoholism, -Boerism, -capitalism, -clericalism, -Russianism, -Semitism, -slaveryism. Many of these are of opprobrious or hostile use.

1898 Westm. Gaz. 27 Apr. 6/3 Owing to the *pro-American tone of the English Press. 1899 FITZPATRICK Transvaal 21 In demolition of Sir T. Shepstone's *pro-annexation arguments. 1902 Daily Chron. 7 May 4/7 The *pro-Boarders were out-voted. 1899 Westm. Gaz. 23 May 1/3 Liberals need not trouble to be more *pro-Boer than the Boers themselves. 1901 J. CHAMBERLAIN Sp. Ho. Comm. 18 Feb., We have had six pro-Boers speaking in this debate..and not one Liberal Imperialist. 1900 Dundee Advertiser 23 Aug. 4 Lord Rosslyn brings the novel charge of *pro-Boerism against us. 1901 Daily News 28 June 3/4 This trumpet blare of Triumphant Democracy..almost unnerves us into *pro-capitalism. 1831 SOUTHEY in Q. Rev. XLIV. 284 The Roman Catholics and the *pro-Catholics, and their infidel allies, had incessantly employed the periodical press in aid of their cause. 1839 Morn. Herald 22 Oct., The opinions of the *pro-educational and anti-slavery parties throughout the country. 1898 M. DAVITT in Westm. Gaz. 14 July 2/1 The *pro-English minority in the United States..are attempting a very hazardous enterprise for the future peace of the Republic. 1903 Daily Chron. 30 June 3/7 The *pro-floggers in the United States are constantly appealing to the condition of Delaware in proof of the efficacy of flogging. 1897 Westm. Gaz. 8 Apr. 2/2 If Russia can arrange a *pro-Greek settlement, do not let us denounce her. 1904 Daily Chron. 2 Dec. 4/3 Some of the pro-Greeks [those in favour of retaining Greek in the Previous Examination] at Cambridge would be ready to vote for an anti-Greek motion on the Oxford lines. 1897 Daily News 22 Feb. 9/3 The *pro-Hellenic manifestations in the streets..have..produced an unfavourable impression among business men. 1901 Daily Chron. 28 Oct. 4/3 Mr. Chamberlain..described Sir Henry Campbell-Bannerman as the leader of the pro-Boer and Little Englander and *pro-Irish party. 1896 Daily News 7 Mar. 5/7 Kim-Hong-Tsu, the Premier [of Corea], and seven other *pro-Japanese Ministers were beheaded and their corpses dragged through the streets. 1896 M. DAVITT in Westm. Gaz. 15 Dec. 4/2 If the Irish Land Commission were not a practically packed *pro-landlord tribunal. 1895 Voice (N. Y.) 19 Sept. 3/4 It has even been admitted by *proliquorites that the voters of New Jersey would under the Initiative and Referendum adopt county, municipal, and township local option. 1895 Pop. Sci. Monthly Sept. 649 It may be well to call the..tendencies favorable to virtue, *pro-moral. 1892 Pall Mall G. 20 Apr. 6/1 Mr. Malins headed the *pro-negro party when the secession..took place. 1839 Conservative Jrnl. 26 Jan., The interests of.. a *pro-papist popularity-hunting viceroy. 1841 J. ROBERTSON in Charteris Life v. (1863) 125 The anti-patronage men and the *pro-patronage Non-intrusionists split among themselves. 1828 SYD. SMITH in Lady Holland Mem. (1855) I. 217 A deputation of *pro-Popery papers waited on me today to print, but I declined. 1829 WHEWELL in Life (1881) 127 He is supported by the pro-popery Ministry. 1897 Daily News 25 Jan. 5/7 The *pro-Rhodes feeling in Capetown..is strong to unreason. 1890 Columbus (Ohio) Dispatch 29 Aug., The so-called United Brethren known as liberals or *pro-secretists. 1856 in L. W. SPRING Kansas (1885) 48, I tell you I'm *pro-slave. 1858 N. York Tribune 29 Dec. 6/4 The *Pro-Slavers all went home without any action. 1843 WHITTIER What is Slavery? Prose Wks. 1889 III. 106 In the midst of grossest *pro-slavery action, they are full of anti-slavery sentiment. 1856 G. D. BREWERTON War in Kansas 124 'The hour and the man' of Free-State-ism, or *Pro-Slavery-ism, for we can scarce say which, is yet to come. 1839 J. ROGERS Antipopopr. VI. ii. 222 One sense tells that a *pro-transubstantiation passage is in the Bible. 1896 Daily News 3 Apr. 4/7 The curious anomaly

that some of our strongest anti-Turk politicians on the Armenian question should at the same time be in favour of a *pro-Turk policy in Egypt. 1899 Ibid. 6 Mar. 8/5 The *pro-vaccinist statisticians.

Pro- (pro), pref.², repr. the Gr. preposition πρό, meaning 'before' (of time, position, preference, priority, etc.), forming in Greek many compounds —verbs, substantives, and adjectives. Of the sbs. and their derivatives more than 60 were adopted in late Latin as technical terms of rhetoric, philosophy, natural history, art, and Jewish or Christian religion (e.g. problēma, proboscis, prodromus, prolēpsis, prologus, prophēta (prophētia, prophēticus, prophētizāre), propolis, proscænium, prostylus, protasis). With the revival of learning many more Greek terms were latinized. Many of these latinized forms of both periods have been adopted or adapted in the modern languages generally, and have subsequently served as models for the formation of new combinations from Greek (less commonly from Latin) elements, in the nomenclature of modern science and philosophy. The older and more important of the English words so derived appear in their alphabetical order as Main words. Those in which pro- is more obviously a prefix to a word itself used in English, or which are merely technical terms, follow here.

1. In sense 'Before in time': forming (a) sbs., chiefly scientific terms denominating the earlier, or (supposed) primitive type of an animal, plant, organ, or structure (with derived adjs.); (b) adjs. meaning 'previous to or preceding that which is expressed by the second element'.

Pro-agonic (-ăgǫ·nik) a., Path., preceding a paroxysm. **Pro-a·mnion,** the primitive amnion in the embryonic stage of some animals; hence **Pro-amnio·tic** a., pertaining to the pro-amnion. ‖**Pro-amphibia** (-æmfi·biă) sb.pl., Zool., the (hypothetical) primitive or ancestral amphibious animals. **Pro-angiosperm** (-æ·ndʒiospə̄m), Bot., a primitive or ancestral angiosperm, from which the existing angiosperms are supposed to have been developed; hence **Pro-angiospe·rmic** a. **Pro-bapti·smal** a., preceding or preparatory to baptism. **Prochorion** (-kō·riǫn), Embryol., the vitelline membrane or integument of the ovum, which develops into the chorion. **Pro-di·alogue** (nonce-wd.), an introductory dialogue. **Prodissoconch** (-di·sokǫŋk), Zool. [Gr. δισσό-s double + CONCH], a name suggested for the early shell of the oyster. **Pro-ethnic** (-e·þnik) a., Philol. [see ETHNIC], anterior to the division of the primitive Aryans into separate nations or peoples, or of any people or race into separate tribes. **Progametange** (-gæ·mitændʒ), **-gameta·ngium,** Biol., 'an immature or resting gametangium' (Cent. Dict.). **Proganoid** (-gæ·noid), Ichthyol., a. of or belonging to the primitive (fossil) ganoid fishes; sb. a primitive ganoid. **Proganosaur** (-gæ·nosǭɹ), Palæont. [Gr. γάνος brightness + σαῦρος lizard], sb. a member of the order Proganosauria of extinct reptiles; adj. belonging to this order. **Progy·mnosperm,** Bot., a primitive or ancestral gymnosperm, from which the existing gymnosperms are supposed to have been developed; hence **Progymnospe·rmic** a. **Proko·smial** a., nonce-wd. [Gr. κόσμος world: see COSMOS], existing before the cosmos or universe. **Proma·mmal,** Zool., one of the (hypothetical) Promammalia or primitive mammals; so **Promamma·lian** a. **Prome·ristem,** Bot., primary meristem, protomeristem. **Pronymph** (prōᵘ·nimf), Entom. [see NYMPH 3], a stage in the development of some dipterous insects, intervening between the larval and pupal stages (cf. propupa below); hence **Prony·mphal** a. ‖**Pro-œstrum** (-ī·strǫm, -e·s-), Zool., the period immediately preceding that of the œstrum or sexual excitement in animals; so **Pro-œ·strous** a., preceding the œstrum; belonging to the pro-œstrum. **Prope·ptone** (see quot. 1895). ‖**Properistoma** (-pĕri·stǫmă), **Properistome** (-pe·ristōᵘm), Embryol. [cf. PERISTOME], the lip of the primitive mouth of a gastrula; hence **Properi·stomal** a. ‖**Prophy·llon,** Bot. (pl. -phylla), [Gr. φύλλον leaf]: see quot. ‖**Propupa** (-piū·pă), Entom., a stage in the development of some insects, as the cochineal-insect, intervening between the larval and pupal stages (cf. pronymph above). **Prorenal** (-rī·năl) a., Embryol. [see RENAL], belonging to the primitive kidney or segmental body. ‖**Proscolex** (-skōᵘ·leks), Zool., pl. proscolices (-skōᵘ·lisīz) [Gr. σκώληξ worm], the first embryonic stage of a cestode or tape-worm, from which the scolex is developed by budding; hence **Pro-scolecine** (-skōᵘ·lĭsəin) a., pertaining to a proscolex. ‖**Prospora·ngium,** Bot. (pl. -ia) = prozoosporange. **Protrypsin** (-tri·psin), Phys. Chem., a substance formed in the pancreas, and afterwards converted into trypsin; also called trypsinogen. **Prozoosporange** (-zōᵘ·o₁sporæ·ndʒ), Bot., a stage in the development of certain fungi, which produces a thin-walled process into which the protoplasm passes and divides into zoospores.

1876 tr. Wagner's Gen. Pathol. 621 The termination is doubtful, and transition into the *pro-agonic stage not rare. 1890 BILLINGS Med. Dict., *Pro-amnion, term applied by van Beneden and Julin to an area around the head of the very young embryo in which there is no mesoderm, the ectoderm and endoderm being in direct contact, and which is soon obliterated by the ingrowth of mesoderm. 1889 Q. Jrnl. Microsc. Sc. Dec. 290 Long after the true amnion has been quite completed the head gradually emerges from this *pro-amniotic pit. 1901 Nature 14 Mar. 462/2 Connected through a series of hypothetical *Proamphibia or Protetrapoda with equally hypothetical Selachian-like animals. 1886 Ibid. 25 Feb. 389/1 The ancestral '*pro-angiosperms' are supposed to have borne leaves such as are found diminished or masked in so many of their existing descendants. Ibid 389/2 Such was the nature of plants in their '*pro-angiospermic' stage. 1840 G. S. FABER Christ's Disc. Capernaum viii. 230 note, Cyril has devoted to his painful '*probaptismal instruction no fewer than eighteen Lectures. 1879 tr. Haeckel's Evol. Man II. xix. 157 This *prochorion very soon disappears, and is replaced by the permanent outer egg-membrane, the chorion. 1884 Athenæum 12 July 41/1 In the *pro-dialogue to the 'Isle of Gulls' one of the characters says, 'I cannot see it out.' 1888 JACKSON in Proc. Boston Soc. Nat. Hist. XXIII. 543 In the oyster..this shell is not single but double-valved, and ..as it precedes the dissoconch or true shell, I suggest the name *prodissoconch, or early double shell. 1864 MAX MÜLLER Sc. Lang. Ser. II. viii. (1868) 383 Deriving both from a common Aryan or *pro-ethnic source. 1887 R. S. CONWAY Verner's Law in Italy § 5 Medial s between vowels.. became voiced (z) in pro-ethnic Italic. 1889 NICHOLSON & LYDEKKER Palæont. II. xlix. 959 *Proganoid Series. Ibid. 965 The last group of the Proganoids. 1900 OSBORN in Amer. Naturalist Oct. 797 More probable than that the avian phylum should have originated quite independently from a quadrupedal *proganosaur. 1886 Nature 25 Feb. 389/2 In the remote past..the cambium layer may have existed in an irregular or fugitive manner in the 'pro-angiospermic', as it did in the '*pro-gymnospermic' stem. 1855 BAILEY Mystic (ed. 2) 36 Where the *pro-kosmial forms of thought abide. 1889 Proc. Zool. Soc. 262 If not the '*Promammal' of Haeckel, it may perhaps have been a near relative of some such transitional form. 1876 tr. Haeckel's Hist. Creat. xxi. II. 235 The unknown, extinct Primary Mammals, or *Pronammalia..probably possessed a very highly developed jaw. 1898 tr. Strasburger's Bot. I. 90 The tissues. are distinguished as primary and secondary, according as they are derived from the *promeristem or secondary meristem. 1895 D. SHARP in Camb. Nat. Hist. V. 164 The process of forming the various organs goes on in the *pronymph, till the 'nymph' has completed its development. Ibid., The *pronymphal state may be looked upon as being to a great extent a return of the animal to the condition of an egg. 1900 W. HEAPE in Q. Jrnl. Microsc. Sc. Nov. 6 '*Pro-œstrum or the *Pro-œstrous Period..I have adopted to describe the first phases of generative activity in the female mammal at the beginning of a sexual season. 1901 Brit. Med. Jrnl. No. 2097. 593 There is the 'pro-œstrum' ('the coming in season')..characterised by..a pro-œstrous discharge..most usually of mucus. 1895 Syd. Soc. Lex., *Propeptone, also termed Hemialbumose, one of the intermediate products formed during the conversion of albumins into peptones in gastric digestion. 1897 Allbutt's Syst. Med. III. 292 The action of the gastric juice upon the albuminous constituents of the food is indicated by the presence of syntonin, propeptone and peptone. 1879 tr. Haeckel's Evol. Man I. viii. 220 At the thickened edges of the gastrula, the primitive mouth-edge (*properistoma), the endoderm, and the exoderm pass into each other. 1898 tr. Strasburger's Bot. 462 The leaves borne on the stalks of the flowers are designated Bracteoles or *Prophylla. 1895 Syd. Soc. Lex., *Propupa, that stage in insect development immediately preceding the pupa. 1898 PACKARD Text-bk. Entomol. III. 627 It passes into what Riley terms the pro-pupa, in which the wing-pads are present. 1888 HUXLEY & MARTIN Elem. Biol. 169 The *pro-renal (segmental) duct; a conspicuous thick-walled tube seen, on either side, lying within the somatic mesoblast. 1895 Syd. Soc. Lex., *Proscolecine, belonging to a Proscolex. 1870 ROLLESTON Anim. Life 250 Embryo or *proscolex of an ordinary Taenia, armed..with six spines. 1888 ROLLESTON & JACKSON Anim. Life 233 That the proscolex may develope in an alimentary canal is proved by P. J. Van Beneden's discovery of proscolices with scolices in all stages of growth in the intestine of the Lump-fish. 1887 tr. De Bary's Fungi 163 When it [Polyphagus Euglenæ] has reached a certain size,..it shows itself in many specimens to be a sporangium, or, if the term is preferred, a *prosporangium. Ibid. Explan. Terms 498 Prosporangium, in Chytridieæ: vesicular cell the protoplasm of which passes into an outgrowth of itself, the sporangium, and becomes divided into swarm-spores. 1900 Lancet 27 Oct. 1187/1 The pancreatic zymogen, trypsinogen or *protrypsin.

2. Of local position: forming sbs. and adjs., chiefly anatomical and zoological terms (often correlated with words in META- and MESO-); (a) in adjectival relation to the second element, denoting either 'an anterior or front (thing of the kind)', or 'an anterior or front part (of the thing)'; (b) in prepositional relation to the second element = 'lying before or in front of (the thing)'.

Pro-a·tlas, Zool. [ATLAS sb.¹ 2] (see quots.). ‖**Procerebrum** (-se·rĭbrǫm), Anat., the front part of the cerebrum or brain; the fore-brain, prosencephalon; hence **Procerebral** a. **Procnemial** (-knī·miăl) a., Anat. [Gr. κνήμη leg, tibia], situated in front of the tibia. ‖**Pro-epimeron** (-epimī·rǫn), Entom., the epimeron of the prothorax of an insect, the second sclerite of either propleuron; hence **Pro-epime·ral** a. ‖**Pro-episte·rnum,** Entom., the episternum of the prothorax, the anterior sclerite of either propleuron; hence **Pro-episte·rnal** a. ‖**Pro-o·steon,** Ornith. [Gr. ὀστέον bone], an ossification in each anterior lateral process of the sternum in certain birds. ‖**Propara·pteron,** Entom., the parapteron of the prothorax; hence **Propara·pteral** a. ‖**Prople·xus** (also anglicized **Pro·plex**), Anat., (a) Wilder's term for the choroid plexus of either of the lateral ventricles of the brain; (b) 'the analogue in the Vertebrata generally of the brachial plexus in man' (Syd. Soc. Lex.). ‖**Pro-postscute·llum,** ‖**Pro-præscu·tum,** Entom., the postscutellum and præscutum (respectively) of the prothorax of an insect; hence **Pro-postscute·llar, Pro-præscu·tal** adjs. ‖**Propygidium** (-pəidʒi·diǫm), Entom., the segment immediately in front of the pygidium in certain beetles. ‖**Proscapula** (-skæ·piŭlă), Ichth., the outer bone of the scapular arch, usually passing forwards and articulating with its fellow of the opposite side, and supporting the cartilage or bone which bears the pectoral fin; hence **Prosca·pular** a. ‖**Proscutellum** (-skiute·lǫm), ‖**Proscutum** (-skiū·tǫm), Entom., the scutellum and scutum (respectively) of the prothorax; hence **Proscute·llar, Proscu·tal** adjs. ‖**Prosygapo·physis** = PREZYGAPOPHYSIS.

1886 GÜNTHER in Encycl. Brit. XX. 447/2 The first two vertebræ are differentiated as axis and atlas, and in front of the latter there may be [in Reptiles] a rudiment of another vertebra, which has been distinguished as the *proatlas. 1889 NICHOLSON & LYDEKKER Palæont. II. xlv. 897 It has been suggested that certain bony splints overlying the arch of the atlas in Crocodiles represent a vertebra intercalated between the latter and the cranium, for which the name proatlas has been proposed. It is, however, by no means proved that these splints do not belong to the atlas vertebra. 1895 Syd. Soc. Lex., *Procerebral, belonging to the Procerebrum. 1890 BILLINGS Med. Dict., *Procerebrum, Prosencephalon. 1854 OWEN Skel. & Teeth (1855) 64 The proximal end of the tibia..: two ridges are extended from its upper and anterior surface: the strongest of these is the '*procnemial' ridge. 1895 Syd. Soc. Lex., *Proëpimeral, *Proëpimeron, *Proëpisternal, *Proëpisternum. 1868 W. K. PARKER Shoulder-Girdle Vertebr. (Ray Soc.) 144 In the genus Rhea ..there is, on each side, an osseous centre in front of the first rib: it ossifies the costal process, and, projecting forwards as a wing in front of the sternal ribs, may be called the '*pro-osteon'. 1896 NEWTON Dict. Birds 910 Thus in Rhea, Gallinæ, Turnix, Lestris and the Passeres, each anterior lateral process has its pro-osteon,..but in many other forms..these processes possess no special centre of ossification. 1882 WILDER & GAGE Anat. Techn. 485 *Proplexus. 1899 D. SHARP in Camb. Nat. Hist. VI. 187 A similar plate anterior to the pygidium is called *propygidium. 1833 F. WALKER in Entomol. Mag. I. 21 The semihyaline spots on the *proscutellum are much larger in this species. 1872 MIVART Elem. Anat. 46 But in some Chameleons, a prominence is developed from each *prozygapophysis, which may be a metapophysis.

Proa (prōᵘ·ă), ‖**prahu** (prā·u). Forms: 6–7 parao, paroe, 7 paro, 7–8 paroo; 7–9 prau, praw, (7 prawe); 7–9 prow, (7 provoe, proe); 9 praoe, 8– proa, (9 proah); 9 prahu. [ad. Malay ڤراو p(ĕ)rā(h)ū a boat, a rowing or sailing vessel; in Pg. parao, Du. prauw, F. prao, pro. The forms prow and proa are assimilated to the Eng. PROW (sb.²) and its Pg. equivalent proa.]

A Malay boat propelled by sails or by oars; spec. a sailing boat of a particular type used in the Malay Archipelago.

It is about thirty feet long, has both stem and stern sharp, adapting it to sail equally well in either direction; one side is curved as in other vessels, the other is flat and straight and acts as a lee-board: to steady the boat a small canoe or the like is rigged parallel to it in the manner of an outrigger see OUTRIGGER 2).

1582 N. LICHEFIELD tr. Castanheda's Conq. E. Ind. I. xxv. 62 b, The next day..there came in two little Paraos, to the number of twelue men. 1599 HAKLUYT Voy. II. I. 258 We left our boats or Paroes. 1606 MIDDLETON Voy. C iij b, An howre after..came a prawe or a canow from Bantam. 1623 St. Papers, Col. 188 Others violently kept their men from entering Limco's prau. 1625 PURCHAS Pilgrims I. III. x. § 1. 239 The King sent a small Prow. 1653 H. COGAN tr. Pinto's Trav. ii. 35 She imbarqued herself in sixteen.. fishermens Paroos. 1698 FRYER Acc. E. India & P. 20 They are Owners of several small Provoes..and Canooses. 1700 S. L. tr. Fryke's Voy. E. Ind. 30 They were carried off in little Praw's, or small Boats, on Board the Men of War. 1726 SHELVOCKE Voy. round World 437 We saw several flying prows, but none came near us. 1745 P. THOMAS Jrnl. Anson's Voy. 130 The Pinnace..brought with her an Indian Paroo, which you may see very well described by Capt. Cooke. 1785 FRANKLIN Lett. Wks. 1840 VI. 477 We have no sailing boats equal to the flying proas of the South Seas. 1831 TRELAWNEY Adv. Younger Son I. 220 They are called by Europeans, owing to the wonderful rapidity with which they sail, flying prows. 1850 W. STANTON in Merc. Marine Mag. (1860) VII. 107 Prahus frequently anchor here. 1883 R. A. PROCTOR in Contemp. Rev. Oct. 571 At Bima every proa and boat was forced from its anchorage and flung on the coast.

attrib. and Comb. 1699 DAMPIER Voy. II. I. 111 The Dutch ..do often buy Proe-bottoms for a small matter of the Malagans..and convert them into Sloops. 1904 World Mag. Apr. 21/1 Six lusty proa-men paddled her along.

†**Proach, proche,** v. Obs. [= AF. proscher (Britton).] Aphetic form of APPROACH v.

[1292 BRITTON III. xxiv. § 2 Sauvement gardez qe nul ne les prosche jekes autaunt qe il eynt respoundu.] 1426 LYDG. De Guil. Pilgr. 18761 3eue thow be hardy and bolde For to proche to hir presence. c 1470 HENRY Wallace V. 987 The day was downe, and prochand wes the nycht. 1563 SACKVILLE Mirr. Mag., Induct. i, The wrathful winter prochinge on a pace. 1600 FAIRFAX Tasso VI. xxxix, To make their forces greater, proaching nire.

†**Proadju·tor.** Obs. rare⁻⁰. [f. PRO-¹ + L. adjūtor helper, aider.] (See quot.)

1623 COCKERAM II, A chiefe Author, proadiutor.

‖**Proæ·resis, -ai·resis.** [a. Gr. προαίρεσις a choosing one thing before another, f. προαιρεῖσθαι to choose before.] A deliberate choice, a resolution.

1644 MILTON Educ. Wks. 1851 IV. 387 That act of reason which in Ethics is called Proairesis.

Pro-agonic: see PRO-² 1.

Proague, Proak, obs. ff. PROG sb.², PROKE.

Proal (prōᵘ·ăl), a. Physiol. [f. Gr. πρό before + -AL.] Having a forward direction or motion: said of the lower jaw in mastication.

1888 COPE in Amer. Nat. Jan. 7 note, The propalinal mastication is to be distinguished into the proal, from behind forwards,..and the palinal, from before backwards.

†**Pro·alizer.** Obs. rare⁻¹. [f. *proalize (ad. Gr. προαλίζ-ειν to collect before) + -ER¹.] An empiric, a herb doctor.

1577 B. GOOGE Heresbach's Husb. IV. (1586) 191 Cardus Benedictus, or blessed Thistle, which the Empirickes, or common Proalisers, doe commend for sundrie..Vertues.

Pro-amnion to -amphibia: see PRO-² 1.

Pro-anaphoral (prōᵘ₁ănæ·fŏrăl), a. [f. PRO-² + Gr. ἀναφορά offering + -AL.] Applied to that part of the Eucharistic service (esp. in the Greek rite) which precedes the anaphora or more solemn part (the consecration, great oblation, communion).

1850 NEALE East. Ch. I. III. i. § 8. 319 In every Liturgical family there is one Liturgy, (or at most two,) which supplies the former or proanaphoral portion to all the others. 1866 BLUNT Annot. Bk. C. P. 148. 1878 C. E. HAMMOND Ant. Liturgies p. xxxi, Another division of the service is into the Anaphora and the Pro-anaphoral part.

Pro and con. Forms: 5–7 pro et contra, pro and contra, 7 pro et con, 6– pro and con. [Abbreviation of L. pro et contra for and against. The and instead of et probably originated as an English reading of the character &.]

A. adv. phr. For and against; in favour and in opposition; on both sides. So pro or con.

1426 LYDG. De Guil. Pilgr. 5663, I tauhtë folkys to argue Pro & contra, yong & olde. 1480 CAXTON Chron. Eng. ccliii, Wherof aroose a grete Altercacion..pro and contra. 1572 R. H. tr. Lavaterus' Ghostes To Rdr. (1596) A ij, The matter throughly handled Pro and Con. 1577 DEE Gen. & Rare Mem. 10 Much..may be here sayd, Pro, et Contra. 1636 JACKSON Creed VIII. iii. § 6, I will not determine pro or con, that [etc.]. 1710 ADDISON Tatler No. 224 ¶ 3 The whole Argument pro and con in the Case of the Morning-Gowns. 1813 BYRON Let. to Murray 25 Jan., The rest.. has never yet affected any human production 'pro or con'. 1863 READE Hard Cash xxxvii, I have no objection to collect the evidence pro and con.

b. attrib. or as adj.

1715 M. DAVIES Athen. Brit. I. Pref. 25 Several Pro and Con-Pamphlets.

B. sb. phr. (now always, in pl., pros and cons.) Reasons for and against; reasonings, arguments, statements, or votes on both sides of a question. (In quot. 1809, favourable and adverse fortunes.)

[c 1400, 1509: see PRO B. 1.] 1589 R. HARVEY Pl. Perc. 20 Such a quoile about pro and con, such vrging of Ergoes. 1591 Troub. Raigne K. John i. 405 Why stand I to expostulate the crime With pro & contra? 1640 BROME Antip. III. iv, The pro's and contras in the windings, workings, And carriage of the cause. 1704 SWIFT T. Tub i. § 24 A Quill worn to the Pith in the Service of the State, in Pro's and Con's upon Popish Plots. 1713 Humble Plead. for Gd. Old Way 259 Seeing the pros and cons did run equal so that the determination depended on the moderator's casting vote. 1809 MALKIN Gil Blas VII. vi. ¶ 14 A..true narrative of all my pros and cons, my ins and outs, since that.. separation of ours. 1880 HUXLEY in Life (1900) II. ii. 21, I felt justified in setting all the pros and cons of the case.

C. as vb. To weigh the arguments for and against; to debate both sides of a question.

1694 CONGREVE Double-Dealer Ded., When a man in soliloquy reasons with himself, and pro's and con's, and weighs all his designs, we ought not to imagine that this man either talks to us or to himself. 1762 STERNE Tr. Shandy VI. xvi, My father's resolution of putting me into breeches..had..been pro'd and con'd, and judicially talked over betwixt him and my mother about a month before. 1818 KEATS Lett. Wks. 1889 III. 138 The topic was the Duke of Wellington—very amusingly pro-and-con'd. 1835 SOUTHEY Doctor cv. III. 324 He was no shilli-shallier, nor ever wasted a precious minute in pro-and-conning.

Proane, Proaness, obs. ff. PRONE a., PRONENESS. **Pro-angiosperm, -atlas**: see PRO-² 1, 2.

Pro aris et focis: see PRO 1.

Prose, obs. form of PROSE.

Proat (prōᵘt), v. dial. Also prote. [Origin obscure: cf. POTE v. and PROD v.] To poke. Hence **Proter** dial., a poker.

1654 FULLER Comm. Ruth (1868) 141 Like sullen chickens ..proating under an old wood-pile. a 1825 FORBY Voc. E. Anglia, Proter, a poker. 1888 Sheffield Gloss., Prote, to poke.

†**Proau·ctor.** Obs. rare⁻⁰. [a. L. proauctor remote ancestor, founder: see PRO-¹ 2.]

1623 COCKERAM, Proauctor, the chiefe author.

‖**Proaulion** (proǫ·liǫn). Archæol. [a. Gr. προαύλιον a vestibule, f. πρό, PRO-² + αὐλή a court, with dim. ending -ιον.] A portico or colonnade outside a church or temple, opening into the narthex.

1842 BRANDE Dict. Sci. etc., Proaulion, in Architecture, the same as vestibule. 1850 NEALE East. Ch. I. II. ii. § 48. 215 The Proaulion, or porch, is..sometimes a lean-to against the west end of the narthex. 1869 TOZER Highl. Turkey I. 78 The proaulion, or porch, a corridor supported on the outside by light pillars. Ibid., Passing onwards from the Proaulion, we enter the narthex.

Prob, dial. variant of PROBE v.

Probabiliorism (prǫbăbi·lioriz'm). [f. as next + -ISM.] The doctrine of the probabiliorists; according to which, in opposition to probabilism, it is claimed that that side on which the evidence preponderates is more probably right and therefore ought to be followed.

1845 GLADSTONE Glean. (1879) VII. 152 Probabilism is by no means the universal or compulsory doctrine of the Roman theologians...It is confronted by a system called Probabiliorism: which teaches that, when in doubt among several alternatives of conduct, we are bound to choose that which has the greatest likelihood of being right. 1882–3 Schaff's Encycl. Relig. Knowl. III. 1931 Probabiliorism.. demands that the more probable opinion shall always be chosen. 1885 Catholic Dict. s.v. Moral Theology.

Probabiliorist (prǫbăbi·liŏrist). [= F. probabilioriste, mod.L. probabiliōrista, f. L. probābilior more probable, compar. of probābilis: see -IST.] One who holds the doctrine of probabiliorism.

1727–41 CHAMBERS Cycl. s.v. Probabilists, Those who oppose this doctrine [of the Probabilists], and assert, that we are obliged, on pain of sinning, always to take the more probable side, are called probabiliorists. The Jansenists, and particularly the Port-royalists, are probabiliorists. 1768 J. BARETTI Acc. Mann. & Cust. Italy II. 49 The vain disputes between the..Probabilists and the Probabiliorists, have long divided our friars into nearly equal parties. 1885 Catholic Dict. 602/2 The Probabiliorists put no restraint on liberty, where a man was convinced on solid grounds that the balance of evidence was decidedly in favour of his liberty.

Probabilism (prǫ·băbiliz'm). [= F. probabilisme, f. as next: see -ISM.]

1. R. C. Casuistry. The doctrine, orig. propounded by Molina, a Spanish Dominican, in the 16th century, that in matters of conscience on which there is some disagreement among authorities, it is lawful to follow any course in support of which the authority of a recognized doctor of the Church can be cited.

1842 in BRANDE Dict. Sci., etc. 1844 W. G. WARD Ideal Chr. Ch. (ed. 2) 326 The very interesting controversies of the last and previous centuries on probabilism. 1845 [see PROBABILIORISM]. 1872 JERVIS Gallican Ch. II. v. 164 The doctrine of Probabilism..popularly identified with the Jesuits, did not strictly speaking, originate with this body. 1886 SIDGWICK Hist. Ethics iii. 151.

2. Philos. The theory that there is no absolutely certain knowledge, but that there may be grounds of belief sufficient for practical life.

1902 BALDWIN Dict. Philos. II. 344 The term probabilism is also used to describe the theory which mediates between a sceptical view regarding knowledge, and the needs of practical life.

Probabilist (prǫ·băbilist). Also 7 probablist. [= F. probabiliste (17th c.), ad. mod.L. probabilist-a, f. L. probābil-is PROBABLE: see -IST.]

1. One who holds the casuistic doctrine of probabilism.

1657 J. SERGEANT Schism Dispach't 93 Then indeed I shall not refuse to..rank them [men who call us Papists] in Dr. H's Predicament of Probablists. 1727–41 CHAMBERS Cycl., Probabilists, a sect, or division, among the Romanists, ..holding, that a man is not always obliged to take the more probable side, but may take the less probable, if it be but barely probable. 1882–3 Schaff's Encycl. Relig. Knowl. III. 1931 In 1665 Alexander VII felt compelled to disavow a number of the propositions of the Probabilists.

2. Philos. One who holds the philosophical theory of probabilism.

1847 WEBSTER, Probabilist. 1. A term applied to those who maintain that certainty is impossible, and that probability alone is to govern our faith and actions.

Hence **Probabili·stic** a. [see -ISTIC], pertaining to probabilists or probabilism.

1864 Chambers's Encycl. VI. 131/1 In that [R. C.] church his [Liguori's] moral theology..a modification of the so-called 'probabilistic system' of the age immediately before his own, is largely used in the direction of conscience.

Probability (prǫbăbi·lĭti). [ad. F. probabilité (14th c. in Littré), ad. L. probābilitātem, f. probābil-is PROBABLE: see -ITY.]

1. The quality or fact of being probable; the appearance of truth, or likelihood of being realized, which any statement or event bears in the light of present evidence; likelihood.

1551 T. WILSON Logike (1580) 30 b, In..gatheryng of conjectures that are doubtfull, when probabilitie onely and no assured knowledge, boulteth out the truthe of a matter. 1623 J. MEADE in Ellis Orig. Lett. Ser. I. III. 150 Other reports there are, but without any probability of truth, and therefore I will not mention them. 1736 BUTLER Anal. Introd. 3 Probability is the very Guide of Life. 1823 J. GILLIES tr. Aristotle's Rhet. II. xxiii. 348 Truth and probability are the causes of assent. 1881 FROUDE Short Stud. (1883) IV. II. iii. 197 The soundest arguments..went no farther than to establish a probability.

b. In, † by probability: probably; considering what is probable. (Now always with all.)

a 1602 W. PERKINS Cases Consc. (1619) 140 In probabilitie they could not bee either many or great. 1615 W. LAWSON Country Housew. Gard. (1626) 23 The compasse and roomth that each tree by probabilitie will take and fill. 1617 MORYSON Itin. II. 62 The Lord Deputies going into the field,..in all probability could not be for some two moneths after. 1697 LUTTRELL Brief Rel. (1857) IV. 202 Otherwise in probability they had fallen into the hands of the French. 1880 HAUGHTON Phys. Geog. ii. 50 These cliffs corresponding in all probability to ancient lines of faults.

2. An instance of the fact or condition described in 1; a probable event, circumstance, belief, etc.; something which, judged by present evidence, is likely to be true, to exist, or to happen.

1576 FLEMING Panopl. Epist. 375 Hee beginneth..with the infancie of Alexander which ministred manifest and manifold probabilities of things which came afterwards to passe. 1680 T. GRANGER Div. Logike 80 Many probabilities concurring preuaile much. 1769 Junius Lett. xvi. (1820) 71 Arguments..have been drawn from inferences and probabilities. 1856 FROUDE Hist. Eng. I. ii. 152 Wolsey's return to power was discussed openly as a probability. 1866 GEO. ELIOT F. Holt xl, You must not strain probabilities in that way.

b. pl. Probabilities of the weather; weather forecasts. U. S.

Old Probabilities, a humorous name for the chief signal-officer of the U. S. Signal Service Bureau.

1875 O. W. HOLMES Old Vol. Life, Crime & Automatism (1891) 327 No priest or soothsayer that ever lived could hold his own against Old Probabilities. 1886 Pop. Sci. Monthly Aug. 546 The official publications embrace the 'probabilities' and the so-called 'weather-maps'.

3. Math. As a measurable quantity: The amount of antecedent likelihood of a particular event as measured by the relative frequency of occurrence of events of the same kind in the whole course of experience; estimated by the ratio of the number of successful cases to the whole number of possible cases.

1718 DE MOIVRE (title) The Doctrine of Chances: or, a Method of Calculating the Probability of Events in Play. 1788 REES Chambers' Cycl., Probability of an event, in the Doctrine of Chances, is greater or less according to the number of chances by which it may happen, compared with the whole number of chances by which it may either happen or fail. 1838 DE MORGAN Ess. Probab. Pref., At the end of the seventeenth century, the theory of probabilities was contained in a few isolated problems, which had been solved by Pascal, Huyghens, James Bernoulli, and others. 1884 tr. Lotze's Logic II. ix. 369 For each draw the probability of a white ball being drawn would = 7/30, so that the probability of two whites being drawn in succession would = 7/30 · 7/30 = 49/900. 1892 H. GOODWIN in Contemp. Rev. Jan. 60 To speak of a certain possible event as having a probability of three to one..is to use language in a strictly defined sense.

Probabilize (prǫ·băbiləiz), v. [f. L. probābil-is PROBABLE + -IZE.] trans. To render probable or likely.

1802–12 BENTHAM Ration. Judic. Evid. (1827) III. 13 By means of it the fact is probabilized: rendered, in a greater or less degree, probable. a 1832 — Deontol. iv. (1834) II. 210 The considerations which tend to probabilize success. 1846 S. R. MAITLAND Ess. Reform. Eng. (1849) 314 That he may take his turn at probableizing [the story], and pass it on.

Probable (prǫ·băb'l), a. (sb.) [a. F. probable (14th c. in Littré), or ad. L. probābil-is that may be proved, probable, credible, f. probāre to try, test, approve, make good: f. prob-us good: see -ABLE.]

1. Capable of being proved; demonstrable, provable. Now rare.

1485 Surtees Misc. (1888) 43 Which..duly examined by hym..and no thing probable object ayenst the same, the.. Maire..decreed and finally determyned [etc.]. a 1548 HALL Chron., Hen. VII 33 It is probable by an inuincible reason and an argument infallible. 1659 MILTON Civ. Power Wks. 1851 V. 312 No man in religion is properly a heretic,..but he who maintains traditions or opinions not probable by scripture. 1678 SIR G. MACKENZIE Crim. Laws Scot. II. xiii. § 2 (1699) 209 Executions by a Barrons Officer are valid, though not given in Writ, and that the same are probable by Witnesses. 1865 GROTE Plato I. xix. 536 Neither proved nor probable.

†**2.** Such as to approve or commend itself to the mind; worthy of acceptance or belief; rarely in bad sense, plausible, specious, colourable. (Now merged in the modern sense 3.)

1387 TREVISA Higden (Rolls) I. 339 It is more probable and more skilful [= reasonable], þat þis lond was from þe bygynnynge alwey wiþoute suche wormes. 1467–8 Rolls of Parlt. V. 622/2 As it appereth by probabill persuacions of Philosofers. 1538 STARKEY England I. iv. 119, I can not wel tel what I schal say, your resonys are so probabyl. 1593 SHAKS. 2 Hen. VI, III. ii. 178 It cannot be but he was murdred heere, The least of all these signes were probable. 1639 S. DU VERGER tr. Camus' Admir. Events 129 One of his most probable excuses was to frame some journeyes out of towne. a 1715 BURNET Own Time (1823) I. II. 401 His schemes were probable. 1780 JEFFERSON Corr. Wks. 1859 I. 280 He assigns the most probable reasons for that opinion. 1872 JERVIS

Gallican Cæ. II. v. 165 It was proclaimed that an opinion was probable, and might therefore be safely followed in practice, which had the sanction of any single theologian of established reputation.

† b. Of a person : Worthy of approval, reliable.
1597 Nashe *Theatre of God's Judgem.* ... *1611* There is not one example here mentioned, but it hath a credible or probable Author for the avoucher of it. *1682* G. Touman *Knox's Descr. 223* If this be but the single opinion of a probable Doctor, we may have the same asserted by an infallible one.

3. Having an appearance of truth ; that may in view of present evidence be reasonably expected to happen, or to prove true ; likely.

† Probableness.

† Probate, ... Obs.

Probation (prŏbēɪ·ʃən), sb. ...

Probational (prŏbēɪ·ʃənəl), a. and sb. ...

Probationary (prŏbē·ʃənəri), a. ...

Probationer (prŏbē·ʃənər). ...

Probative (prŏ·bătiv), a. ...

Probator (prŏbē·tər). ...

Probatory ...

Probe (prŏub), sb. ...

Probe, v. ...

Probing (prŏu·biŋ), vbl. sb. ...

Probity (prŏ·bĭti, prō·bĭti). ...

Problem (prŏ·blɛm), sb. ...

Problematic (prŏblɛmæ·tik), a. ...

Problematical (prŏblɛmæ·tikăl), a. ...

Problematically, adv. ...

Problematist ...

Problemize ...

Problemist ...

Probe ...

Proboscidate ...

Proboscide ...

Proboscidea ...

Proboscidean, -ian ...

Proboscideous, a. ...

Proboscides ...

Proboscidiferous ...

Proboscidiform. Having the form or shape of a proboscis ; proboscis-like.

Probosciformed, *a.* [f. L. Pro- + Proboscis + -Formed.] Proboscis-shaped.

Proboscis-monkey.

Proboscidian.

Proboscis (prŏbŏ'sis). *Pl.* **proboscides** (-idi̇z), **proboscises** (-siz).

1. An elephant's trunk; also applied to the long flexible snout of some other mammals, as the tapir and proboscis-monkey.

Proboscis-worm.

Procaccio.

Procacious.

Procacity.

Procation.

Procacious.

Procaiacion.

Procambium, *Bot.*

Procarp, *Bot.*

Procatalepsis, *Rhet.*

Procatarctic.

Procedendo, *Law.*

Procedure (prosī'diūr). Also **7 procedoor, -or, 8–9 procedure.** [a. F. *procédure* (1507 in Godef. Compl.), f. *procéder* to Proceed: see prec.]

1. The fact or manner of proceeding with any action, or in any circumstance or situation; a system of proceeding; proceeding, in reference to its mode or method; conduct, behaviour.

Proceed (prosī'd), *v.* Forms: 4–8 procede, 6–7 -ceede, 6 -cedde (e,-sede, proceed), 6– proceed.

1. *intr.* To go, move, or travel forward; to make one's way onward; *esp.* to move onward after interruption or stoppage, or after reaching a certain point; to continue one's movement or travel.

Proceeder. 1407 PROCELLARIAN. PROCERITIC. PROCERITY. 1408 PROCESS.

Proceeder.

Proceeding, *ppl. a.*

Proceeding, *vbl. sb.*

1. The action of going onward; advance, onward movement or course.

Procellarian (prosĕlē·riăn), *a.* and *sb. Ornith.*

Procellarious.

Procello.

Procellous, *a. Obs.*

Procephalic, *a. Zool.*

Procerebrum.

Proceres.

Proceritic.

Procerity (prosē·rĭtī). Now *rare.* [ad. obs. F. *procérité* (15th c. in Godef.) or ad. L. *procēritāt-em* height, tallness.]

1. Tallness, loftiness, height; length.

Procerous.

Process (prŏ·ses, prō·ses), *sb.* Forms: 4 proces, 4–5 -cesse, 6–7 -cesse, -ces, -cess, -ces, 6– process. [ME. *proces*, a. F. *procès* (13th c. in Godef.), ad. L. *prōcess-us* advance, progress, process, lapse of time, f. *prōcēd-ere* to Proceed.]

1. The fact of going on or being carried on, as an action, or a series of actions or events; progress, course.

PROCOELIA. 1413 PROCREATING. PROCREATION. 1414 PROCTOR.

‖ **Procoelia** (prosī·liă), *Anat.* Pl. -**ia.** [mod. L. (Wilder), f. Gr. πρό, πρό- + κοιλία a hollow: cf. Coeliac.] A prosencephalic ventricle; either of the lateral ventricles of the brain.

‖ **Procoelia** (prosī·liă), *a. Comp. Anat.* [f. Pro- + ex. + κοιλο- hollow + -ous: see prec.] Concave or cupped in front: applied to vertebræ; distinguished from *opisthocoelous* and *amphicoelous*.

‖ **Proconsul** (prŏkǭ·nsŏl). [L. *proconsul*, from the earlier phrase *pro consule* 'one acting for the consul': see Pro- 1 and Consul.]

Procrastinate (prŏkræ·stǐnēt), *v.* [f. L. *procrastināt-*, ppl. stem of *procrastināre*: see next. So f. *procrastinē*, pres. pple. of *procrastin-*.]

Procrastination (prŏkræstǐnē·ʃən). [ad. L. *procrastinātiōn-em*: see prec.]

Procrastinator (prŏkræ·stǐnētǝɹ). [agent-n. f. L. form from Procrastinate v.: see -or 2.]

Procreant (prō·krǐănt), *a.* (*sb.*) [ad. L. *procreant-em*, pr. pple. of *procreāre*: see next.]

Procreate (prō·krǐēt), *v.* Now *rare.* [f. L. *procreāt-*, ppl. stem of *procreāre*: see next.]

Procreation (prōkrǐē·ʃən). [ME. a. OF. *procreacion* (14th c. in Littré), mod.F. *procréation*, ad. L. *procreātiōn-em*, n. of action f. *procreāre*: see above.]

Procreative (prō·krǐētiv), *a.* [f. L. type *procreātīv-us*: see -IVE.]

Procreator (prō·krǐētǝɹ). *rare.* [a. L. *procreātor*, agent-n. f. *procreāre*: see -or.]

Procrustean (prŏkrʌ·stĭăn), *a.* [f. next + -AN.]

‖ **Procrustes** (prŏkrʌ·stīz). [L., a. Gr. Προκρούστης, the stretcher-out, f. προκρούειν.]

Procryptic (prŏkri·ptik), *a. Zool.* [f. Pro- 2 + Cryptic.]

Procto- (prǫ·ktŏ), before a vowel **proct-**, combining form of Gr. πρωκτός anus, used to form modern scientific terms, chiefly medical and surgical, rarely zoological.

Proctor (prǫ·ktǝɹ), *sb.* [A syncopated form of *procurator*, Procurator, through *procutor*, *proketour*, *proctour*, etc. Cf. Praxy = Procuracy; also the ME. weakening of Procure v. to *prater.*]

Proctor (prǫ·ktǝɹ), *v.* [f. prec. sb.]

Proctoral (prǫ·ktǝrăl), *a.* [f. Proctor sb. + -AL.] Of or pertaining to a proctor.

Procurable (prǒkiū·răb'l), *a.* [f. Procure v. + -ABLE.]

Procuracy (prǒ·kiurăsǐ), *sb.* [f. Procur-e + -ACY.]

Procurance (prǒkiū·răns). *rare.* [f. Procure v. + -ANCE.]

Procuration (prǒkiurē·ʃən). [ME. *procuraciun*, a. OF. *procuracion* (12th c. in Littre), ad. L. *procūrātiōn-em*, n. of action f. *procūrāre*: see -ATION.]

Procurator (prǒ·kiurētǝɹ). [a. OF. *procuratour* (13th c. in Hatzf.-Darm., mod.F.-*eur*), ad. L. *procūrātor*, agent-n. f. *procūrāre*: see Procure.]

PROCURATOR.

3. In the medieval universities, one of two or more representative officers, of whom one was elected by each of the 'nations' into which the students and Regent Masters were divided, having financial, electoral, and disciplinary functions.

†b. The procurer of a loan: cf. PROCURATION 4 b. *Obs. rare.*

Procuratory (prɒˈkiūrătəri), *a.* and *sb.* [ad. late L. *prōcūrātōri-us* belonging to an agent or manager: cf. PROCURATOR and -ORY 2; hence L. *prōcūrātōrium sb.*, whence B.]

Procurer (prɒˈkiūrə(r)). [f., agent-n. from *procure vb.*] ...

6. To prevail upon, induce, persuade, get (a person) to do something. *Obs. or arch.*

PROCURESS. 1419 **PRODIGAL.** **PRODIGAL** 1420 **PRODIGY.**

Procuress.

Prodigal (ˈprɒdɪgəl), *a.* and *sb.* [ad. OF. *prodigal* (13th c. in Godef.), ad. L. *prōdigāl-is*, f. *prōdig-us*: see PRODIGE and -AL.]

Prodigy (ˈprɒdɪdʒɪ). [ad. L. *prōdigium*, f. *prōdigere*.]

PRODITED. — PRODUCE. — PRODUCE. — PRODUCING.

PRODUCT. — PRODUCTIVE. — PRODUCTIVELY. — PROFANATE.

†**Profana·tic**, a. nonce-wd. [app. f. PROFANE, with word-play on FANATIC.] Infatuated with profanity.

Profanation (prɒfanēi·ʃən). Also 6-8 prophanation.

Profanatory (prɒfæ·natəri), a. [f. as PROFANATE + -ORY.] That tends to profane; profaning.

Profane (prɒfēi·n), a. Also 4-8 prophane.

Profane (prɒfēi·n), v. Also 4-8 prophane.

†**Profa·ned**, ppl. a. Also 6-8 prophaned.

Profanely (prɒfēi·nli), adv. Also 6-8 prophanely.

†**Profa·neness**. rare. Obs.

Profaner (prɒfēi·nəɹ). Also 6-8 prophaner.

Profa·nish, a. rare. Obs.

Profanation, prophe-. Obs. rare⁻¹.

Profanity (prɒfæ·niti). Also late L. profanitas.

Profa· noness. rare. Obs. rare⁻¹.

†**Profa·ssise**, v. Obs. rare⁻¹.

†**Profa·neling**, prophe-. Obs. rare⁻¹.

Prof, Profe, Profs, Prove. Abbreviations.

Profe·ction (prɒfe·kʃən). Astrol. Obs. rare.

Profe·ctional, a. Obs.

Profe·cting, vbl. sb.

Profe·ctive, a. rare. Obs.

†**Profe·ctual**, a. Obs.

†**Profe·r.** Obs. Forms of PROFFER.

†**Profe·ss**, sb. Obs. Also 3-4 professe (prouesse).

†**Profe·ss**, a. Obs.

Profess (prɒfe·s), v. [f. L. profess-, ppl. stem of profitērī to profess.]

Profe·ssable, a. rare.

Profe·ssant. rare. Obs.

Profe·ssed (prɒfe·st), ppl. a. Also 5-8 profest.

Profe·ssedly (prɒfe·sedli), adv.

Profe·ssing, vbl. sb.

Profe·ssing, ppl. a. [as prec. + -ING².]

Profession (prɒfe·ʃən). [ME. a. F. profession (12th c. in Hatz.-Darm.), ad. L. professiōn-em a public declaration; a business or profession that one publicly avows, n. of action f. profitērī to PROFESS.]

Professional (prɒfe·ʃənăl), a. (sb.) [f. prec. + -AL.]

†**Professionalism.** [f. prec. + -ISM.]

Professionalist. [f. as prec. + -IST.]

Professionality. [f. as prec. + -ITY.]

Professionalize, v.

Professionally, adv.

Professionate, a. Obs. rare⁻¹.

Professionless, a. [f. prec. + -LESS.]

†**Professionary**, a. Obs.

†**Professor** (prɒfe·səɹ), sb. [a. F. professeur or ad. L. professōr-em.]

Professo·rate. [f. as PROFESSOR + -ATE.]

Professorial (prɒfesō·riăl), a.

Professo·rially, adv.

Professoriate (prɒfesō·riĕt). [f. as prec. + -ATE.]

Professo·rious, a.

Professorship.

Professorship (profe·ǝship). [f. PROFESSOR + -SHIP.]

Professoress (profe·sǝres). [f. PROFESSOR + -ESS.] A female professor.

Professorial (profesō·riăl), a. [f. L. professōri-us belonging to a public teacher (see PROFESSOR) + -AL.]

Professorially (profesō·riăli), adv.

Professoriate (profesō·riět). [as prec. + -ATE.] A body of professors; the professorial staff of a university.

Proffer (prǫ·fǝɹ), v.

Proffer (prǫ·fǝɹ), sb.

Proffered (prǫ·fǝɹd), ppl. a.

Profferer (prǫ·fǝrǝɹ). One who proffers; one who makes an offer.

Proffering (prǫ·fǝriŋ), vbl. sb.

Proficience (profi·ʃens). Obs.

Proficiency (profi·ʃensi).

Proficient (profi·ʃent), a. and sb.

Proficiently (profi·ʃentli), adv.

Proficuous (profi·kiŭǝs), a. Obs. rare⁻¹.

Profile (prōu·fil, -faɪl), sb.

Profile (prōu·fil, -faɪl), v.

Profiling-machine.

Profit (prǫ·fit), sb.

Profit (prǫ·fit), v.

Profitable (prǫ·fitǎb'l), a.

Profitableness (prǫ·fitǎb'lnes).

Profitably (prǫ·fitǎbli), adv.

Profiter (prǫ·fitǝɹ).

Profiterole (profi·tǝroul).

Profitful, *a. (and sb.)* Obs. [f. PROFIT + -FUL.] Profitable.

Profiting, *vbl. sb.* [f. PROFIT v. + -ING.] The action of the verb PROFIT: † improving; benefiting, etc.

Profitless, *a.* [f. PROFIT sb.] Void of profit; unprofitable, useless.

Profitly, *adv.* Obs. rare⁻¹. [f. PROFIT sb. + -LY.] Profitably.

Profity. Obs. In 5 profitee, 6 profittyo. [? PROFIT sb. + -Y (if the examples are not erroneous)] Profit.

Profligacy (prɔˈfligăsi). [f. PROFLIGATE a.] The quality, state, or condition of being profligate.

Profligate (prɔˈfligĕt), *a. and sb.* [ad. L. *prōflīgāt-us* overthrown, ruined; wretched, vile, dissolute, abandoned, pa. pple. of *prōflīgā-re* to dash to the ground, cast down, overthrow, overwhelm, ruin, dispatch, f. *prō-*, PRO- 1 + *-flīg-āre* for *flīg-ĕre* to strike down, dash.]

Profligately, *adv.* [f. as prec. + -LY ².]

Profligateness. Now rare. [f. as prec. + -NESS.] The quality or character of being profligate.

Profligation (prɔfliˈgeiʃən). Now rare. [ad. L. *prōflīgātiōn-em*, n. of action f. *prōflīgā-re*: see PROFLIGATE.]

Profluence (prɔˈfluəns). Now rare. [ad. L. *prōfluentia* a flowing forth, f. *prōfluent-em*: see next.]

Profluency (prɔˈfluənsi). Obs. rare⁻¹. [f. as prec.]

Profluent (prɔˈfluənt), *a.* [ad. L. *prōfluent-em*, pr. pple. of *prōfluĕre* to flow forth, f. *prō-*, PRO- 1 + *fluĕre* to flow.] Flowing forth or onward; current, stream, flow.

Profluous, *a.* Obs. rare⁻¹. [f. as prec.]

Profluvious, *a.* Obs. rare⁻¹. [Of the nature of, or causing, a profluvium or flux.]

Profluvium (prɔˈfluviəm). Pl. -ia. [L., f. *prōfluvi-us* adj. flowing, f. *prōfluĕre*: see PROFLUENT.] A flowing forth; a copious flow or discharge, a flux.

Profulgent, *a.* Obs. rare⁻¹. [f. L. *prō-*, PRO- 1 + *fulgent-em*: see FULGENT.] Shining forth.

Profound (prɔˈfaund), *a.* [ME. *profounde, -ound*, a. OF. *profund, -ont* (mod.F. *profond*), ad. L. *profund-us* deep, f. *prō-*, PRO- 1 + *fund-us* bottom.]

1. Deep (as a physical or material quality).

2. Having great or considerable downward (or inward) measurement; of great depth.

3. Situated or extending far beneath the surface; deep-seated; deep-reaching.

4. Of a person: Characterized by intellectual depth; that penetrates or has penetrated deeply into a subject of knowledge, study, or thought; having great insight into or knowledge of something; very learned.

5. Of feelings, etc.: Deep-seated, heartfelt, intense.

Profound, *sb.* [f. the adj.] The depth of the sea or other deep water; the deep sea, 'the deep'. *poetical.*

Profound, *v.* Obs. rare. [f. the adj.]

Profoundly, *adv.* [f. PROFOUND a. + -LY ².] In a profound manner or degree; deeply.

1. To or at a great depth or distance from the surface.

2. With intellectual depth; with great insight or penetration into a subject.

Profoundness. [f. as prec. + -NESS.] The quality of being profound; PROFUNDITY.

Profund, -e, obs. forms of PROFOUND.

Profunda (prɔˈfʌndə). *Anat.* [L. fem. of *profundus* deep, PROFOUND: cf. *arteria.*] A distinguishing name of various deep-seated arteries and veins, in the neck, arm, leg, and other parts.

Profundipalmar (prɔfʌndiˈpælmə), *a. Anat.* [f. *profunda* deep + *palmaris*.] Deep-seated in the palm of the hand.

Profundiplantar (-ˈplæntə), *a. Anat.* [as prec. + *plantar*.] Deep-seated in the sole of the foot.

Profunditude. Obs. [irreg. f.] = PROFUNDITY.

Profundity (prɔˈfʌnditi). [ad. L. *profunditas*, f. *profundus*: see PROFOUND.] The quality of being profound; depth.

1. Depth, in a physical sense.

2. Depth of intellect, insight, knowledge, etc.

3. Intensity, thoroughness, extremeness of degree.

Profuse (prɔˈfjuːs), *a.* [ad. L. *profūs-us* poured forth, spread out, lavish, immoderate, profuse, prop. pa. pple. of *prō-fundĕre* to pour forth.]

1. Of persons or agents: Expending, bestowing, or producing abundantly; lavish, liberal to excess; extravagant, wasteful, prodigal.

2. Of things: Produced, existing, or supplied in great abundance.

Profusely, *adv.* [f. as prec. + -LY ².] In a profuse manner; in profusion or abundance; lavishly, wastefully.

Profuseness. [f. as prec. + -NESS.] The quality or state of being profuse; lavishness.

Profusion (prɔˈfjuːʒən). [a. F. *profusion* (16th c.), or ad. L. *profūsiōn-em*, n. of action f. *profundĕre* to pour forth.]

1. The action of pouring forth; outpouring, effusion (of a liquid); spilling, shedding. Now rare.

Prog (prɔg), *v.¹* *dial.* Also 7 progue, 7-8 progg.

1. Food, victuals; provender; esp. *colloq.*, provisions for a journey or excursion; *slang*, food.

Prog, *sb.¹* *dial.* Also 7 progge, 7-8 progg, progue. [perh. f. PROG v.¹]

Prog, *v.²* *dial.* Also 9 progue.

Prog, *v.³* Also 7 progg.

Progenerate (prɔˈdʒenəreit), *v.* Obs. exc. *dial.* Also 6 prog-, progue. [Origin and sense-history obscure.]

Progenital, *a.* rare. [f. L. *prōgenit-*: see PROGENITOR + -AL. Cf. GENITAL.]

Progenitive (prɔˈdʒenitiv), *a.* [f. L. *prōgenit-*: see PROGENITOR + -IVE.] Having the quality of producing offspring or progeny.

Progenitor (prɔˈdʒenitə). [ME. *progenitour*, a. AF. *progenitour*, OF. *progeniteur*, ad. L. *prōgenitor*, agent-n. f. *prōgignĕre* to beget.]

Progenitorship. [f. PROGENITOR + -SHIP.]

Progenitress (prɔˈdʒenitrɪs). [f. PROGENITOR + -ESS.] A female progenitor; an ancestress.

Progenitrix (prɔˈdʒenitrɪks). [a. late L. *progenitrix*, fem. of *progenitor*.] = prec.

Progeniture (prɔˈdʒenitjʊə). [ad. med.L. *progenitura*.]

Progeny (prɔˈdʒeni). [ME. *progenie*, a. OF. *progenie*, ad. L. *prōgeniēs* descent, family, offspring, f. *prōgignĕre* to beget.]

1. The offspring of a father or mother, or of both; issue, children collectively; more widely, descendants.

2. Offspring, progeny.

d. More vaguely, expressing relation or character: cf. CHILD 2b, 13.

Progermination. *rare*. [f. L. *progerminā-re* to germinate.] Springing forth; birth, propagation.

Progger. Now *dial*. [f. PROG v.1 + -ER.] One who progs, begs, or solicits; a beggar.

Progging (prg·giŋ), *vbl. sb.* [f. PROG v.1 + -ING.] Soliciting, begging. Foraging.

Progging-iron, *butcher's* instrument.

Proggins: see PROG sb.2

Proglottis (prglo·tis), *a.* [irreg. f. PROGLOTTIS + -IC.] Of or pertaining to a proglottis.

Proglottid (prglo·tid), *Zool.* [f. Gr. προγλωττίς.] = next; or its F. form.

Proglottis (prglo·tis), *Zool*. Pl. **-ides** (-ĭdīz.)

‖Prognosis (prgnǭ·sis). Pl. **-oses** (-ǫsīz.) [a. Gr. πρόγνωσις a recognizing beforehand, foreknowledge, in medicine a prognosis, f. προγινώσκειν to know beforehand: see PRO-2 and GNOSIS. In F. *prognose*.]

Prognostic (prgno·stik), *sb.* [ad. L. *prognōstica*, *-cum*, sb. use of neut. sing. of *prognōsticus* PROGNOSTIC *a.*]

Prognostic (prgno·stik), *a.* [f. L. *prognōsticus*, *-ca*, *-cum*, or f. Gr. προγνωστικός, f. προγινώσκειν: see PROGNOSTIC *sb.*]

Prognosticable (prgno·stikăb'l), *a.* [f. L. *prognōstic*-āre to PROGNOSTICATE + -ABLE.]

Prognosticate (prgno·stikē̆t), *v.* [f. L. *prognōsticāt-*, ppl. stem of *prognōsticāre*: see PROGNOSTIC *sb.*]

‖Programma (progrægm·ə). *Obs.* Pl. **programmata** (-ə·tə.)

Programmatic (prō̆grəmæ·tik), *a.* + *-ism.* [f. Gr. πρόγραμμα, -γραμματ-, PROGRAM + -IC.]

Programme, program (prō̆u·grăm), *sb.* Forms: **a.** 7– **program**, (7-grame). **β.** 9– **programme.** [a. F. *programme*.]

Progredient (progrī·di̯ent), *a.* (sb.) *rare*. *Obs.*

Progress (prō̆u·gres, prǫ·-), *sb.* [a. L. *prōgressus*.]

Progress (progre·s), *v.* [f. prec.]

Progression (progre·ʃən). [a. F. *progression* (1495 in Hatz.-Darm.), ad. L. *prōgressiōn-em* a going forward, advancement, progression, n. of action f. *prōgredī*: see PROGRESS *sb.*]

Progressional (progre·ʃənăl), *a.* [f. prec. + -AL.]

Progressionist (progre·ʃənist). [See -IST.] An advocate of or believer in progress; a progressist, a progressive.

Progressist (prō̆u·gresist), *sb.*

Progressist. [ad. F. *progressiste* sb. *progressista* : see PROGRESS sb. and -IST.] One who favours or advocates progress, esp. in political or social matters; a reformer, a progressive.

Progressive (progre·siv), a. [ad. F. *progressif*, -*ive* (14th c. in Hatz.-Darm.), f. L. *progress*- : see PROGRESS sb. and -IVE.]

1. Characterized by stepping, walking, or otherwise moving onward, as in the locomotion of men and animals generally; executed, as a movement, step by step; moving on or forward.

2. Passing on from one member or item of a series to the next; proceeding step by step; successive.

3. *generally.* Moving forward or advancing (in space); of the nature of onward motion.

Progressively, adv. [f. prec. + -LY.]

Progressiveness. The quality or character of being progressive.

Progressivism. [f. PROGRESSIVE + -ISM.] The principles of a progressive or progressist; advocacy of, or devotion to, progress.

Progressivist = PROGRESSIVE sb.

Progressivity (progresi·viti), rare. [as prec. + -ITY.] = PROGRESSIVENESS.

Progressor (progre·sɔɹ), rare. [a. late L. *progressor*, agent-n. f. *progredi* : see PROGREDIENT.] One who progresses or makes progress; in quot. a 1626, one who makes a state progress or tour.

Pro-guardian: see PRO-1.

Progynæum (prodʒinī·um), Bot. [f. Gr. πρό before + γύναιον.] (See quot. 1886.)

Progynosperm: see PRO-1.

Pro hac vice: see PRO-1.

Prohelm, henry, etc.: see PROEM, etc.

Prohessian (prohe·siăn), Math. [f. PRO-1 + HESSIAN sb.] (See quots.)

Prohibit (prohi·bit), v. Also pa. -hibet. [f. L. *prohibit-*, ppl. stem of *prohibēre* to hold back, prevent, forbid, f. *pro* in front + *habēre* to hold.]

1. *trans.* To forbid (an action or thing) by or to a command or statute; to interdict.

2. To debar, preclude, hinder, or declare (an action or thing) by physical means.

Prohibited, ppl. a. [f. prec. + -ED1.] Forbidden; interdicted, debarred.

Prohibiter (prohi·bitəɹ). One who prohibits or forbids; = PROHIBITOR.

Prohibition (prohibi·ʃən). [a. F. *prohibition* (1327 in Godef.), ad. L. *prohibition-em*, n. of action f. *prohibēre* to PROHIBIT.]

1. The action of forbidding by or by authority; an edict, decree, or order forbidding or debarring; a negative command.

2. *spec.* The forbidding by law of the manufacture and sale of intoxicating liquors, as for consumption.

Prohibitionary, a. [f. prec. + -ARY1.] Relating to prohibition.

Prohibitionism (prohibi·ʃəniz'm). [f. as prec. + -ISM.] One who advocates or favours prohibition, *spec.* of the manufacture and sale of intoxicating liquors.

Prohibitionist. [f. as prec. + -IST.] One who advocates or favours prohibition.

Prohibitive, a. [f. prec. + -IVE (in Hatz.-Darm.); see PROHIBIT ppl. a. and -IVE.]

1. Having the quality of prohibiting; that forbids or restrains from some course of action; prohibitory.

Prohibitor (prohi·bitəɹ). [a. L. *prohibitor*, agent-n. from *prohibēre*: see PROHIBIT.]

Prohibitory (prohi·bitəri), a. [ad. L. *prohibitōri-us*, f. *prohibitor*: see prec. and -ORY.]

Project (prɒ·dʒekt), sb. [ad. L. *projectum*, something thrown forth or out, neut. sing. of *projectus*, pa. pple. of *projicĕre*: see next.]

1. A plan, draft, scheme, or table of something arranged; a design or pattern according to which something is made.

Project (prɒdʒe·kt), v. [f. L. *project-*, ppl. stem of *projicĕre* to throw forth, f. *pro* forth + *jacĕre* to throw.]

I. Of mental operations.

1. *trans.* To plan, contrive, devise, or design.

II. Of physical operations.

Projectile (prodʒe·ktil), a. and sb. Also **projectil**. [ad. mod.L. *projectil-is*, f. L. *project-*, ppl. stem of *projicĕre*: see PROJECT v.]

Projectist. One who forms projects; a schemer or contriver.

Projecting, ppl. a. [f. as prec. + -ING2.] That projects.

Projection (prodʒe·kʃən), sb. [ad. L. *projection-em*, n. of action f. *projicĕre*: see PROJECT v.]

1. The action of throwing or shooting forth.

Projector (prodʒe·ktəɹ). [agent-n. f. PROJECT v.: see -OR.] One who projects or plans; a schemer.

Projectivity (prɒdʒekti·vĭti). rare. [f. prec. + -ITY.] Projective quality; power or capacity of geometrical projection.

Projectment. Obs. [f. PROJECT v. + -MENT. Cf. F. projectement (16th c.).] The formation of a project; a project formed, a scheme, plan, design.

Projector (prɒdʒe·ktɐ). [a. L. *projectōr*, agent-n. f. *projicĕre* to PROJECT: see -OR. In F. *projecteur*.]
1. One who forms a project, who plans or designs some enterprise or undertaking; a founder.

Projet (prɒʒe). [a. F.: see PROJECT sb.]
1. The project or draught of a proposed treaty, etc.

Projicient. Obs. rare. [ad. L. *projicient-em*, pres. ppl. of *projic-ĕre* to PROJECT.] One or that which throws a thing forward or forth.

Proke, obs. form of PROG, PROKE v.

Proker. Obs. [? f. PROKE v.] A poker.

Prokofiev.

Proking, vbl. sb. Now only dial.

Prokomial. see PRO-² 1.

Prokyrnont, obs. form of PROCUREMENT.

Prolabial. a. [f. L. *labial*.] Of or pertaining to the prolabium.

Prolabium. Anat. [mod.L. *prolābium*, f. L. *pro*, Pro-1 + LABIUM.] The prominent or outer part of a lip.

Prolapse, sb. Obs. nonce-wd. [ad. L. *prolapsus*, pa. pple. of *prolābī* to PROLAPSE.]

Prolapse, v. Obs. [ad. L. *prolaps-*, ppl. stem of *prolābī*.]

Prolapsion. Obs. [ad. L. *prolapsiōn-em*.]

Prolapsus (prolæ·psɒs). Path. [late L. *prolapsus*.]

Prolate, v. Obs. [ad. L. *prolāt-*: see PROLATE a.]

Prolate (prɒ·lĕt), a. [ad. L. *prolāt-us*.]

Prolation (prɒlēiʃən). Obs. [ad. L. *prolātiōn-em*.]

Prolative (prɒlēi·tiv). a. [ad. late L. *prolātīv-us*.]

Prole, obs. form of PROWL v.

Proleg (prɒu·leg). Entom. [f. PRO-¹ 4 b + LEG.]

Prolegomenon (prɒlĕgɒ·menɒn). Pl. **-mena** (-ă). [a. Gr. *προλεγόμενον*, neut. of pres. pple. pass. of *προλέγειν* to say beforehand, f. *προ*, Pro-² + *λέγειν* to say.]

Prolegomenal.

Prolegomenary.

Prolepsis (prɒle·psis). [a. Gr. *πρόληψις*.]

Proleptic (prɒle·ptik), a. (sb.) [ad. Gr. *προληπτικός*.]
1. Of, pertaining to, or characterized by prolepsis or anticipation; anticipative, anticipatory; spec. in Med. predictive, prognostic.
2. Path. Recurring at a periodical disease, of the paroxysm recurs each time at an earlier hour.

Proleptical, a. Obs. rare⁻¹. [f. prec. + -AL.]

Proleptically, adv. [f. prec. + -LY².] In a proleptic manner; by prolepsis.

Prole (prɒul). [Lat. *prōlēs* offspring.] Progeny, offspring; in phrase *sine prole* (abbrev. *s.p.*), without offspring or issue.

Proletaire (prɒlĕtɛə·ɹ). [a. Fr. *prolétaire*.]

Proletarian (prɒlĕtɛə·riăn), a. and sb. [f. L. *prōlētāri-us* a PROLETAIRE + -AN.]

Proletarianism. [f. prec. + -ISM.]

Proletariat, -ate (prɒlĕtɛə·riăt, -ĕt). [a. F. *prolétariat*.]

Proletary (prɒu·lĕtări), a. and sb. [ad. L. *prōlētāri-us*.]

Proletical, a. Obs. rare⁻¹.

Prolicide (prɒu·lisəid). [f. L. *prōli-*, *prōlēs* offspring + -CIDE.]

Prolicient.

Prolific (prɒli·fik), a. [ad. med.L. *prōlific-us*.]

Proliferate (prɒli·fĕrĕit), v. [f. as next + -ATE³.]

Proliferation (prɒlifĕrēi·ʃən). [ad. med.L.]

Proliferous (prɒli·fĕrɒs), a. [f. L. *prōli-*, *prōlēs* offspring + -ferous.]

Prolification (prɒlifikēi·ʃən). [ad. med.L. *prōlificātiōn-em*.]

Prolificacy (prɒli·fikăsi). [f. PROLIFIC + -ACY.]

Prolificate (prɒli·fikĕit), v. [f. as prec. + -ATE³.]

Prolificity (prɒlifi·siti). [f. PROLIFIC + -ITY.]

Prolificly (prɒli·fikli), adv. [f. PROLIFIC + -LY².]

Prolificness. [f. PROLIFIC + -NESS.]

Prolify (prɒu·lifəi), v. Obs. rare. [ad. med.L. *prōlificāre*.]

PROLIGEROUS.

Proligerous (proli·dʒěras), *a*. [f. L. type (or mod.L.) *proliger* (f. *prōl-es* offspring + *-ger* bearing) + -OUS : cf. F. *proligère*.]

Bearing offspring ; generative ; germinative. *Proligerous disk or layer* (Embryol.), a layer formed by the aggregation of cells on the outside of an ovum supposed to be germinative.

Prolix (prǒ·liks, prŏliks·), *a*. [a. F. *prolixe* (14th c. in Littré) or ad. L. *prōlix-us* extended, long, prolix, etc. app. etymologically, that has flowed forth', f. *prō-*, Pro-[1] + *lix-us*, pa. pple. of *liquēre* to flow, to be liquid.]

1. Of long duration, lengthy, protracted. † a. In general. *Obs*.

2. Of a person : Given to or characterized by tedious lengthiness in discourse or writing ; long-winded.

Prolixly, *adv*. [f. PROLIX *a*. + -LY[2]] In a prolix manner.

Prolixness (see PROLIX *a*.). [as prec. + -NESS.] = PROLIXITY.

Proll, -e, **Proller**, obs. ff. PROWL *v*., PROWLER.

Prolocute, *v*. *Obs. rare*[-1]. [f. L. *prōlocūt-*, ppl. stem of *prōloquī* to speak out.]

Prolocution (proʊlok[y]u·ʃən). [ad. L. *prōlocūtiōn-em*, n. of action from *prōloquī* to speak forth, declare, here identified with *prōloquī* to speak forth.]

† Prolocutory, *a*. *Obs. rare*[-1]. [f. prec. : see -ORY.]

Prolocutress (see PROLOCUTOR). = next.

† Prolocutrix (proʊlok[y]u·triks), *Obs*. [a. L. *prōlocūtrīx*, fem. of *prōlocūtor*.] A female prolocutor ; a spokeswoman.

Prologist (prɒ·lŏdʒist), *rare*. [f. next + -IST.] The writer or speaker of a prologue.

PROLOGIST.

Prologize (prɒ·lŏdʒaiz, prǒl-), *v*. See also PROLOGUIZE. [f. Gr. προλογίζειν to speak the prologue : see PROLOGUE *sb*., and -IZE.]

Prologizer. [f. prec. + -ER[1].] The speaker of a prologue.

Prologue (prɒ·lɒg, prǒ·lǒg), *sb*. [a. F. *prologue*, ad. L. *prologus*, a. Gr. πρόλογος.]

1. The preface or introduction to a discourse or performance ; a preliminary discourse, proem, preface, preamble.

2. One who speaks or recites the prologue to a play on the stage.

Prologue, *v*. [f. prec. *sb*.: cf. obs. F. *prologuer*.]

1. *trans*. To introduce or furnish with a prologue.

2. *fig*. To introduce, preface.

PROLONGE.

† 3. To spend (time) in introductory remarks. *Obs*.

Prologuer (prɒ·lŏgər, prǒ·l-). Also 6 pro-loger. = PROLOGIST.

Prologuize (prɒ·lŏgwaiz, prǒ·l-), *v*. = PROLOGIZE.

Prolong (proʊlǒ·ng), *v*. [ad. late ME. *prolonge*, a. OF. *prolonger* (13th c. in Littré), variant of F. *prolonger* (Hatzfeld), f. Late L. *prōlongāre*, f. *prō-*, Pro-[1] + *longus* long.]

1. *trans*. To lengthen out in time ; to extend in duration ; to cause to continue or last longer ; continue.

2. To extend (time or a period) so as to cause delay ; to protract, 'waste'. *Obs*.

Prolongable (proʊlǒ·ŋgəb'l), *a*. [f. prec. + -ABLE.] Capable of being prolonged or lengthened.

Prolongate (proʊ·lǒŋgeit), *v*. [f. ppl. stem of the L. *prōlongāre* to PROLONG : see -ATE[3].] *trans*. To prolong, lengthen.

Prolongation (proʊlǒŋgei·ʃən). [a. F. *prolongation* (14th c. in Littré), ad. late L. type *prōlongātiōn-em*, n. of action f. *prōlongāre* : see PROLONG.]

1. Lengthening or extension in time ; extension of the duration of anything.

2. To extend (time or a period) so as to cause delay ; to protract.

3. The lengthening or prolonging of a syllable, etc.

Prolonge (proʊlǒ·nʒ), *Milit*. [F. *prolonge*.] A rope composed of three pieces joined by two open rings, and having...

PROLONGED.

...a book at one end, and a toggle at the other, forming part of the equipment of a gun-carriage, and used for various purposes, esp. for moving a gun when unlimbered.

Prolonged (proʊlǒ·ŋd), *ppl. a*. [f. PROLONG *v*. + -ED[1].] Lengthened, extended (in space or time).

Prolonger. [f. PROLONG *v*. + -ER[1].] One who or that which prolongs ; see the verb.

Prolonging (proʊlǒ·ŋiŋ), *vbl. sb*. [f. as prec. + -ING[1].] The action of the verb PROLONG ; *spec*.

Prolusion (proʊl[y]u·ʒən). [ad. L. *prōlūsiōn-em*, a prelude, preliminary exercise, n. of action f. *prōlūdere* to play or practise beforehand.]

1. A display introductory to a game, performance, or entertainment ; a prelude, preliminary essay or attempt.

† Proloyne, *v*. *Obs*. Also 5 -oigne. [a. OF. *proloignier*, *pro-longer* or *por-*, *portloigner* : see PURLOIN.] It is here intermediate between the popular OF. *porloigner*, and the learned or latinized *prolonger* ; so it has thus been coinciding with both, and is therefore placed separately.]

1. *trans*. To entice away, kidnap (a person) ; to make away with, to steal : = PURLOIN *v*. 2.

2. To put far away ; to remove : = PURLOIN *v*. 1, PROLONG *v*. 7.

3. To put off, postpone : = PROLONG *v*. 8.

Prolusion (proʊl[y]u·ʒən). [ad. L. *prōlūsiōn-em* : as prec.]

PROMERIT.

Promenade (prǒměnā·d, -ā·), *sb*. Forms : 6 *promenade*, (*purmenade*), 7 *pourmenade*, 7- *promenade*. [a. F. *promenade* (1557 in Hatz.-Darm.), f. *promener* to lead forth, take for a walk, refl., *se promener* to take a walk, altered from OF. *pormener* (11th c. in Cotgr., 1611) *pourmenade* a walk, *pourmener* 'to walke (trans.), to stirre vp and downe'—late L. *prōmināre* (Appel.) to drive onward (a beast), f. *prō* forward, forth + *mināre* to threaten, in rustic and late L. *mināre* to drive (beasts), f. *mināre*, f. *mināri* to conduct, lead. See also -ADE, -ADO.]

1. A walk (taken usually at a leisurely pace) for exercise or amusement, or (esp.) to and fro for display, or in a formal manner as part of a social ceremony. Also applied to exercise taken in this way, in a carriage, on horseback, or in a boat.

2. A place for walking or promenading ; a walk, *esp*. a paved public walk for social resort.

Promenade, *v*. [f. prec. *sb*.: cf. F. *promener*.] Also 6 *Sc*. promi-neida (in vb. *a*. promineding).

1. *intr*. To make a promenade ; to walk about or take exercise on horseback, or in a carriage, etc. ; esp. for amusement or display ; to parade.

2. *trans*. To make a promenade through, to walk about (a place) in a leisurely or stately way.

3. In causal sense—*v. promener*) : To lead (a person, etc.) about a place, esp. in the way of display.

Promenader (prǒměnā·dər). [f. prec. + -ER[1].] One who promenades.

Promerit (promĕ·rit), *v*. Now *rare*. [ad. L. *prōmeritus*, pa. pple. of *prōmerēre*, *-ērī*, f. *prō-*, Pro-[1] + *merēre*, *-ērī* to merit, deserve.]

1. *trans*. To merit, gain, win, gain over, procure.

2. To merit, deserve ; to win or procure by merit.

PROMERIT.

...times, when they came to make petition for the Imperial crowne, were wont by some worthy office to promerit the favour of the Church before.

Prominence (prǒ·minĕns), *sb*. [a. obs. F. *prominence* (16th c. in Hatz.-Darm.), ad. L. *prōminentia* a jutting out, projection : see PRO-MINENT and -ENCE.]

1. The fact or condition of being prominent.

2. That which is prominent ; a projection, protuberance.

3. *Solar*, a projecting cloud of incandescent hydrogen, etc., above the chromosphere of the sun, best seen during an eclipse.

Prominent (prǒ·minĕnt), *a*. [ad. L. *prōminent-em*, pr. pple. of *prōminēre* to jut out, project, be prominent, f. *prō-*, Pro-[1] + *minēre* to project.]

1. Jutting or standing out above or beyond the adjacent surface ; projecting, protuberant.

2. *fig*. Standing out so as to strike the eye ; conspicuous.

Prominently (prǒ·minĕntli), *adv*. [f. prec. + -LY[2].] In a prominent manner or degree.

PROMISCUOUS.

Prominence : see PROMISCUOUS.

Prominism : see PROMISCUOUS.

Promiscuous (promiskiu·əs), *a*. [f. L. *prōmiscu-us* mixed, indiscriminate, in Gram. epicene (f. *prō-* + *miscēre* to mix) + -OUS.]

1. Consisting of members or elements of different kinds grouped together without order ...

of mixed and disorderly composition or character; also, with *pl. sb.*, of various kinds mixed together.

1603 KNOLLES *Hist. Turks* 283 About them..the promiscuous common people, doubling and redoubling the praises of the King, and Huniades. 1621 BURTON *Anat. Mel.* Democr. to Rdr. 20 Hee told him that hee saw a vast multitude and a promiscuous. 1667 MILTON *P. L.* I. 380 While the promiscuous croud stood yet aloof. 1692 BENTLEY *Boyle Lect.* ii. 41 The Apostle who was to speak to such a promiscuous Assembly. 1752 HUME *Ess. & Treat.* (1777) I. 222 The characters of nations are very promiscuous in the temperate climates. 1830 LYELL *Princ. Geol.* (1875) I. I. iii. 46 He conceived the strata to have settled down from this promiscuous mass. 1875 HELPS *Soc. Press.* xx. 291 What Milverton contemptuously would call our miscellaneous and promiscuous essays.

b. Rarely of a single thing.

1663 BUTLER *Hud.* I. i. 99 It had an odd promiscuous Tone, As if h' had talk'd three Parts in one. 1711 POPE *Temp. Fame* 22 Sudden I heard a wild promiscuous sound.

2. That is without discrimination or method; done or applied without respect for kind, order, number, etc.; confusedly mingled, indiscriminate.

1605 BACON *Adv. Learn.* II. vii. § 3 Axioms which are promiscuous and indifferent to several sciences. 1650 HOBBES *De Corp. Pol.* 179 To forbid the promiscuous Use of Women. 1678 R. L'ESTRANGE *Seneca's Mor.* (1776) 334 The common and promiscuous lot both of good men and bad. 1751 JOHNSON *Rambler* No. 144 ¶ 9 Secrets are not to be made cheap by promiscuous publication. 1772 — 31 Mar. in *Boswell*, Promiscuous hospitality is not the way to gain real influence. 1816 SCOTT *Old Mort.* ii, The profane custom of promiscuous dancing—that is, of men and women dancing together in the same party. 1853 J. H. NEWMAN *Hist. Sk.* (1873) II. I. i. 28 At Metz he [Attila] involved in one promiscuous massacre priests and children.

b. Of an agent or agency: Making no distinctions; undiscriminating.

1633 E. PORTER in *Donne's Poems* 405 Why should death, with a promiscuous hand, At one rude stroke impoverish a land? 1688 R. HOLME *Armoury* II. 310/1 Promiscuous Birds..feed on Flesh, Insects, Fruit, or Grain, as the Raven. a 1763 SHENSTONE *Ess.* vi. (1765) 21 A well-discriminated landscape was..to be preferred to a distant and promiscuous azure. 1900 A. LANG *Hist. Scot.* I. i. 5 People..still polyandrous or promiscuous in the relation of the sexes.

3. Of common gender; epicene. *rare.*

a 1637 B. JONSON *Eng. Gram.* I. x, The promiscuous, or epicene, which understands both kinds. 1878 VILLARI *Life & Times Machiavelli* (1898) I. III. vii. 130 There were three sexes, male, female and promiscuous.

†**4.** That forms part of a promiscuous or mingled company; hence (*slang*), a term of depreciation or contempt. *Obs.*

1753 SMOLLETT *Ct. Fathom* (1813) I. 162 One may see with half an eye that he is no better than a promiscuous fellow. 1785 CRABBE *Newspaper* 233 This, like the public inn, provides a treat, Where each promiscuous guest sits down to eat. 1889 GRETTON *Memory's Harkb.* 58 'Go back to bed, you promiscuous old bird!' 'Promiscuous' was just then a term in slang use.

5. Casual, carelessly irregular. *vulgar* or *colloq.*

1837 DICKENS *Pickw.* xxxiv, I walked in..just to say good mornin', and went, in a permiscuous manner, up-stairs, and into the back room. 1883 L. OLIPHANT *Altiora Peto* I. 5 On the beach, where he will, in the most promiscuous and accidental manner, certainly go for a stroll.

6. quasi-*adv.* = PROMISCUOUSLY.

1671 MILTON *P. R.* III. 118 Glory he receives Promiscuous from all Nations, Jew, or Greek. 1695 ADDISON *King* 110 And Planks, and Arms, and Men promiscuous flow'd. 1747 FRANCIS tr. *Horace, Sat.* II. ii. 99 Roast, and boil'd, when you promiscuous eat, When fowl and shell-fish in confusion meet. 1813 SHELLEY *Q. Mab* II. 153 Old age and infancy Promiscuous perished.

b. = PROMISCUOUSLY 2. *vulgar.*

1885 G. ALLEN *Babylon* xiv, Colin only kissed her now and again quite promiscuous like. 1901 A. FORBES *Odd Fish* 92 You get a barrel o' the reds, and send it aboard just permiscuous like.

Promiscuously (promi·skiuˌəsli), *adv.* [f. prec. + -LY [2].]

1. In a promiscuous manner; without distinction, discrimination, or order; indiscriminately; at random, in confusion.

1610 HOLLAND *Camden's Brit.* (1637) 100 These [coins] passed promiscuously as mony from one to another. 1641 WILKINS *Math. Magick* I. xvii. (1648) 124 Both which names are sometimes used promiscuously. 1693 *Lond. Gaz.* No. 2888/2 The body of their Fleet lay promiscuously to Leeward of one another. 1777 ROBERTSON *Hist. Amer.* (1778) II. v. 119 Horsemen and infantry plunged in promiscuously. 1840 MACAULAY *Ess., Clive* (1887) 542 The dead bodies, a hundred and twenty-three in number, were flung into it promiscuously and covered up.

†**b.** *colloq.* Without 'standing upon the order of one's going'; unceremoniously; promptly. *Obs.*

1609 ROWLANDS *Knaue of Clubbes* 37, I bad him vanish most Promiscuously, And not Contaminate my company.

2. *colloq.* Casually, incidentally.

1812 *Sporting Mag.* XL. 153 Witness promiscuously found the bottle..amongst some rubbishing things, quite empty. 1843 MRS. ROMER *Rhone, Darro*, etc. II. 300 'Let us go to Africa!' exclaimed a friend of mine quite promiscuously (as the Cockneys have it). 1871 L. STEPHEN *Playgr. Eur.* 16 The stone was dropped promiscuously by a flying dragon, and picked up by a passing peasant.

Promi·scuousness. *rare.* [f. as prec. + -NESS.] The quality or state of being promiscuous; promiscuity.

1727 BAILEY vol. II, *Promiscuousness*, mixedness. 1775 in ASH. 1818 in TODD; and in mod. Dicts.

Promise (prǫ·mis), *sb.* Forms: 5–6 promis, -ys, -isse, -ysse, 6 -yse, 7 -iss, 5– promise. β. 5 promess, 5–6 -es, -esse, 6–7 *Sc.* -eis. [ad. L. *prōmiss-um* a promise, sb. use of neut. pa. pple. of *prōmitt-ĕre*: see PROMIT *v.* The β forms represent F. *promesse* (13th c.):—med.L. *prōmissa* a promise.]

1. A declaration or assurance made to another person with respect to the future, stating that one will do, or refrain from, some specified act, or that one will give or bestow some specified thing. (Usually in good sense, implying something to the advantage or pleasure of the person concerned.)

Breach of promise: see BREACH *sb.* 3 b.

c 1400 MAUNDEV. (1839) v. 40 No straungere cometh before him, but that he maketh him sum promys and graunt, of that the sowdan asketh. c 1430 LYDG. *Min. Poems* (Percy Soc.) 39 This man for trust of femynyne promysse, Wolde telle out alle. a 1548 HALL *Chron., Edw. IV* 225 Geuyng them faire wordes, and makyng large promises. ? a 1550 *Knt. of Curtesy* 280 His promysse he wil not breke. 1605 SHAKS. *Macb.* V. viii. 21 These Iugling Fiends..That keepe the word of promise to our eare, And breake it to our hope. 1613 PURCHAS *Pilgrimage* (1614) 631 Which Boferes after with like perfidiousnes, and breach of promise, requited on three thousand Marochians. 1768 BLACKSTONE *Comm.* III. ix. 158 A promise is in the nature of a verbal covenant. 1785 PALEY *Mor. Philos.* III. I. v, Promises are not binding, where the performance is unlawful. 1838 W. BELL *Dict. Law Scot.*, *Promise and Offer*...An offerer is not bound until his offer is accepted. A promiser is bound as soon as the promise reaches the party to whom it is made. 1845 STEPHEN *Comm. Laws Eng.* (1874) II. 55 There is in strictness a distinction between a promise and a contract; for the latter involves the idea of mutuality which the former does not. 1877 FROUDE *Short Stud.* (1883) IV. I. v. 52 Becket had broken his promise to submit to the Constitutions.

β. c 1412 HOCCLEVE *De Reg. Princ.* 1772 Whanne I þe mette, & sy þin heuynesse, Of comfort, sone, made I þe promesse. c 1470 HENRY *Wallace* VI. 866 A promes maid to meit Wallace but let. *Ibid.* XI. 947 The tym was past by Off the promess the quhilk at he was bund. 1489 CAXTON *Faytes of A.* IV. iv. 238 Hys promesse and affyaunce made. 1530 PALSGR. 258/2 Promesse, *promesse*.

2. In religious use: One of the Divine assurances of future good or blessing, recorded in the Scriptures as made to particular persons on various occasions, or conceived as given to mankind through Christ; *spec.* that made to Abraham with respect to his posterity (Gen. xii. 2, etc.).

1502 ATKYNSON tr. *De Imitatione* III. xviii. 211 The promes of god. 1526 TINDALE *Heb.* vi. 12 Them, which thorow fayth and pacience inheret the promyses. 1567 *Gude & Godlie B.* (S.T.S.) 3 The threitning of God maid to them that brekis his commandementis, and his promeis made to them that keipis them. 1659 T. ALLEN (*title*) A Chain of Scripture Chronology..in VII periods, viz., From the Creation to the Flood, the Flood to the Promise, the Promise to the Law, the Law to the Temple, the Temple to the Captivity.., the Captivity to the Return, the Return to the Death of Christ. 1707 WATTS *Hymn*, '*Begin, my tongue*' ii, Sing the sweet promise of his grace, And the performing God. 1819 SCOTT *Ivanhoe* xxxii, 'So help me the promise', ..said Isaac,..'as no such sounds ever crossed my lips!'

b. *Land of promise* (tr. τὴν γῆν τῆς ἐπαγγελίας, Heb. xi. 9): = PROMISED *land*. Also *fig.*

1535 COVERDALE *Heb.* xi. 9 By faith was he a straunger in the londe of promes [WYCL. the loond of biheest]. 1662 STILLINGFL. *Orig. Sacr.* II. v. § 8 Not..meerly a Covenant for the Land of Promise. 1851 DIXON *W. Penn* xv. (1872) 131 To all these exiled sects America was the land of promise. 1865 J. H. INGRAHAM *Pillar of Fire* (1872) 570 Their land of heaven is our land of promise also.

c. *Bow of promise*, the rainbow (in allusion to Gen. ix. 12–17).

1827 SARAH E. MILES *Hymn*, '*Thou who didst stoop below*' iii, To see a Father's love Beam, like a bow of promise, through the cloud. 1850 S. DOBELL *Roman* viii, Thoughts that shining through To-morrow's tears shall set in our worst cloud The bow of promise.

3. *transf.* The thing promised; *contextually* (with *claim*) = the fulfilment of a promise.

1526 TINDALE *1 John* ii. 25 This is the promes that he hath promysed vs, even eternall lyfe. 1594 SHAKS. *Rich. III*, III. i. 197 He clayme that promise at your Graces hand. 1646 H. LAWRENCE *Comm. Angells* 168 They hope to attaine the promise of God, that is, the thing promised. 1864 TENNYSON *En. Ard.* 455 He stood once more before her face, Claiming her promise.

4. *fig.* That which affords a strong or reasonable ground of expectation of something to come, esp. of future good; a pledge, earnest, forerunner, pre-indication (*of* something); something that leads one confidently to expect (good) results.

To give (*afford*, etc.) *promise*: to afford expectation *of* something, esp. good. *Of great* (*high*, etc.) *promise*: such as leads one to expect future excellence; very promising.

c 1532 DU WES *Introd. Fr.* in *Palsgr.* 922 A gyrle..full of swete promyse. 1599 SHAKS. *Much Ado* I. i. 14 A yong Florentine,..He hath borne himselfe beyond the promise of his age. 1697 DRYDEN *Virg. Past.* IV. 23 Fragrant Herbs (the promises of Spring). 1700 — *Cymon & Iph.* 329 Like a fiery meteor sunk the sun, The promise of a storm. 1748 GRAY *Alliance Educ. & Govt.* 21 The vernal Promise of the Year. 1828 MACAULAY *Ess., Hallam* (1887) 55 A historical novel of high merit, and of still higher promise. 1832 HT. MARTINEAU *Hill & Vall.* i. 16 Remarking on the fine promise of fruit. *Mod.* This scholarship is given for promise, rather than for attainment.

†**b.** A mental feeling of assurance. *Obs.*

a 1625 FLETCHER *Noble Gent.* IV. iv, I have a constant promise she's my own.

5. *Comb.*, as *promise-breach*, *-breaker*, *-maker*, *-monger*; *promise-bound*(*en*, *-crammed* adjs.; *promise-breaking*, *-fulfilling*, *-keeping*, *-making*, *-performing* sbs. and adjs.

a 1548 HALL *Chron., Hen. VI* 133 b, He, whiche is a promise breaker, escapeth not alwaie free. 1592 NASHE *P. Penilesse* Wks. (Grosart) II. 10, I am quite vndone through promise-breach. 1602 SHAKS. *Ham.* III. ii. 99, I eate the Ayre promise-cramm'd, you cannot feed Capons so. 1603 — *Meas. for M.* I. ii. 77 He was euer precise in promise keeping. a 1639 W. WHATELEY *Prototypes* II. xxvi. (1640) 48 A thankfull receiving of Gods promises..proveth faith to the promise-maker. 1771 WESLEY *Wks.* (1872) VI. 85 It is hard to speak of..these promise-mongers, as they deserve. 1772 FLETCHER *Logica Genev.* 160 A merciful, gracious promise-keeping God. 1813 SCOTT *Trierm.* II. xx, As promise-bound, I bid the trump for tourney sound. 1849 MACAULAY *Hist. Eng.* vi. II. 11 If..he had also turned dissembler and promise-breaker. 1864 TENNYSON *En. Ard.* 835 Awed and promise-bounden she forbore.

Promise (prǫ·mis), *v.* Forms: see prec. [Appears early in 15th c.; f. prec. sb.]

1. *trans.* To make promise of; to give verbal assurance of; to undertake or engage, by word or writing addressed to another person, to do or refrain from (some specified act), or to give or bestow (some specified thing): usually to the benefit or advantage of the person concerned. Often with dative (with or without *to*) of the person to whom the promise is made. **a.** with simple direct object, expressing the thing or act promised.

c 1420 ? LYDG. *Assembly of Gods* 227 Oon thyng suerly I will yow promyse. ? a 1500 *Chester Pl.* xiii. 6 Vnto whom I was promised, before the world began, to pay ther ransome and to become man. 1508 FISHER *7 Penit. Ps.* xxxii. Wks. (1876) 23 He promyseth dampnacion to them that refuseth penaunce; to them that dooth it, forgyvnes. 1548–9 (Mar.) *Bk. Com. Prayer, Catechism*, They did promise and vowe three thinges in my name. 1611 SHAKS. *Wint. T.* IV. iv. 237, I was promis'd them against the Feast. 1736 BUTLER *Anal.* I. iii. Wks. 1874 I. 69 The wonderful power and prosperity promised to the Jewish nation in the Scripture. 1802 MAR. EDGEWORTH *Moral T.* (1816) I. xii. 97 She would not promise what..she could not perform. 1872 FREEMAN *Gen. Sketch* xvi. § 5. 335 All the princes promised free constitutions to their people.

b. with obj. clause, expressing the act.

c 1420 ? LYDG. *Assembly of Gods* 482 Ye me promysyd That my myght of noon shuld haue be dyspysyd. 1470–85 MALORY *Arthur* x. lix. 515, I promyse yow that I shalle be with yow by that day, yf I be vnslayne or vnmaymed. 1548–9 (Mar.) *Bk. Com. Prayer, Catechism*, Your Godfathers and Godmothers dyd promyse for you that ye should kepe Goddes commaundementes. 1690 DRYDEN *Don Sebastian* Pref., I dare boldly promise for this Play, that in the Roughness of the Numbers..you will see somewhat more masterly..than in..any of my former Tragedies. 1726 SWIFT *Gulliver* II. viii, I made him promise he would come to see me at my house. 1864 TENNYSON *Aylmer's Field* 417 Him..she promised that no force, Persuasion, no, nor death could alter her.

c. with inf., expressing the act.

1467 *Mann. & Househ. Exp.* (Roxb.) 558 [The parker] hathe promessed me to make it as wel as he kane fore me. a 1548 HALL *Chron., Edw. IV* 228 The Constable had promised to the kyng and the duke, to render vp to them the towne of sainct Quintynes. 1603 SHAKS. *Meas. for M.* I. ii. 75 He promis'd to meete me two howres since. 1737 POPE *Hor. Epist.* II. i. 178 When..we..promise our best Friends to rhyme no more. 1848 THACKERAY *Van. Fair* xli, The Baronet promised to take charge of the lad at school.

2. *absol.* or *intr.* To make a promise; to engage to do or give something. In quot. 1869, to undertake responsibility, stand sponsor *for* another.

1447 BOKENHAM *Seyntys* (Roxb.) 26 Now haf I acomplysyd Brefly, lych as I yow promysyd In the prologe. a 1533 LD. BERNERS *Huon* lxxxiv. 266 Desyre hym to render to you your londes as he promysyd. 1651 HOBBES *Leviath.* II. xx. 102 He that promiseth, hath no right in the thing promised. 1716 *Wodrow Corr.* (1843) II. 145, I cannot promise upon this so very soon, we having much public business. 1777 BURNS '*I dream'd I lay*' ii, Fickle fortune ..promis'd fair, and perform'd but ill. 1842 TENNYSON *Dora* 44 Dora promised, being meek. 1869 — *Pelleas & Ettarre* 15 There were those who knew him near the King And promised for him: and Arthur made him knight.

3. *spec.* (*trans.*) To engage to give (e.g. a daughter) in marriage to another; to betroth. *To be promised*, to be engaged or betrothed. *arch.*

a 1548 HALL *Chron., Hen. VII* 60 The lady Mary..was promysed to kyng Charles. a 1553 UDALL *Royster D.* III. ii. (Arb.) 42 Haue you he will (he sayth) and haue you he must. *C. Custance.* I am promised duryng my lyfe, that is iust. 1596 SHAKS. *Tam. Shr.* I. ii. 262 Her father..will not promise her to any man, Vntill the elder sister first be wed. 1738 SWIFT *Pol. Conversat.* i. 35 If she ben't marry'd, at least she's lustily promis'd.

†**b.** *pass.* To be engaged; to have an engagement. *Obs.*

1601 SHAKS. *Jul. C.* I. ii. 293 *Cassi.* Will you suppe with me to Night, Caska? *Cask.* No, I am promis'd forth.

4. *To promise oneself* (something): to entertain the (pleasing) expectation of. Const. as in 1 a, b, c.

1617 MORYSON *Itin.* I. 42 Nothing were more pleasant..then Sea-voyages, if a man might promise himselfe a good wind, and a reasonable gale. 1639 N. N. tr. *Du Bosq's Compl. Woman* I. 21 There are some who promise to themselves, never to discover their secrets. 1746 *Col. Rec. Pennsylv.* V. 45, I promise myself that you will proceed to some less exceptionable Method. 1832 HT. MARTINEAU *Each & All* iv. 53 She ran out, promising herself that she would be back in ten minutes. 1869 'MARK TWAIN' *Innoc. Abr.* xii, We ..promised ourselves that we would call around some time .., and finish the game.

5. *colloq.* With *obj. cl.* or *parenthetically*, and with *dat.* of person: To convey assurance of some fact, to assert confidently or emphatically, to declare; almost always in phrase *I promise you* = I assure you, I tell you plainly.

a. with reference to the future, as a strong assertion of one's intention. (Nearly coinciding with 1 b, but often implying a threat of something disadvantageous or unpleasant.)

c 1440 *Generydes* 1603 Thu shalt dye to morow.., And what that euer be..That wolle for the entrete.., He shall not spede I yow promysse. 1538 STARKEY *England* I. i. 25, I promys you I schal neuer pretermyt occasyon..of helpyng my cuntrey. 1777 DIBDIN *Quaker* I. i, You wont get a lamb out of our fold, I promise you. 1825 THIRLWALL tr. *Tieck's Pictures* 80 Well, I promise you, you shall find I do not come again.

b. in assurance of a statement as to the present. (Cf. EXPECT *v.* 6.) Now *arch.* or *dial.*

1469 J. PASTON in *P. Lett.* II. 349 He losythe sore hys tyme her, I promyse yow. 1535 in *Lett. Suppress. Monasteries* (Camden) 74 The comyssioners, I promyse you, have been very necligent. 1599 SHAKS. *Much Ado* IV. ii. 47, I do not like thy looke I promise thee. 1655 tr. *Com. Hist. Francion* XII. 37 The Nights, I promise you, are very cold. 1705 ADDISON *Italy* (1733) 212 For, I promise, I long for it. 1749 FIELDING *Tom Jones* XVIII. i, I promise thee it is what I have desired. 1841 F. E. PAGET *Tales of Village* (1852) 466, I promise you I'm preciously tired already. 1862 THACKERAY *Round. Papers, Peal of Bells*, Magnificent dandies, I promise you, some of us were.

6. *fig.* To afford ground of expectation of; to cause or lead one to expect (something good or bad); to give pre-indication of. Const. as in 1 a or c.

1594 ? GREENE *Selimus* 1102 My life forepassed in Pleasure's court Promises weak resistance in the fight. 1617 MORYSON *Itin.* I. 3 The houses promise more beauty outwardly then they haue inwardly. 1665 SIR T. HERBERT *Trav.* (1677) 125 Berry is a Village which promises much at a distance, but when there, deludes the expectation. 1722 DE FOE *Col. Jack* (1840) 4 He..promised to be stout when grown up. 1832 HT. MARTINEAU *Life in Wilds* v. 56 A plan..which promised fair to supply the butcher with employment. 1855 TENNYSON *Maud* I. I. xvii, I play'd with the girl when a child; she promised then to be fair. 1878 H. H. GIBBS *Ombre* 25 If his own hand be such as not to promise him at least two or even three tricks. 1891 *Law Times* XC. 459/2 An atmosphere of public discussion which promises future storms.

b. *absol.* or *intr.* To encourage expectation, to give tokens: usually with adv., as *fair*, *well*.

1601 SHAKS. *All's Well* II. i. 146 Oft expectation fails, and most oft there Where most it promises. 1686 tr. *Chardin's Coronat. Solyman* 88 The Harvest..promis'd no better then the last year. 1687 A. LOVELL tr. *Thevenot's Trav.* I. 14 The weather promising fair. 1768 J. BYRON *Narr. Patagonia* (1778) 133 He promised the fairest for holding out, being a very strong young man. 1847 MARRYAT *Childr. N. Forest* iv, Humphrey, the second, promised well. 1887 GISSING *Thyrza* I. ii. 29 It promises for another fine day to-morrow.

Promised (prǫ·mist), *ppl. a.* [f. prec. + -ED [1].] Undertaken to be done or given; of which promise is made. *Promised land*: the land of Canaan, as promised to Abraham and his posterity (Gen. xii. 7, xiii. 15, etc.); hence allusively applied to heaven, or to any place of expected felicity.

1538 ELYOT, *Sponsus*..promysed. 1545 *Ibid.*, *Desponsus*, et *desponsa*, affianced or promised in mariage. 1667 MILTON *P. L.* III. 531 Over the Promis'd Land to God so dear. 1697 DRYDEN *Virg. Georg.* III. 133 The fiery Courser..Shifts Place, and paws, and hopes the promis'd Fight. 1862 BP. C. WORDSWORTH *Hymn*, '*O day of rest and gladness*' iii, From thee, like Pisgah's mountain, We view our Promised Land. 1881 LADY HERBERT *Edith* 140 Edith was Lord St. Aubyn's promised bride.

Promisee (prǫmisī·). Also **promissee.** [f. as prec. + -EE.] The person to whom a promise is made: esp. in legal use, correlative to PROMISOR.

1733 SWIFT *Advice to Freemen Dublin* Wks. 1745 VIII. 239 The persons..possessed of the sole executive power.., and hundreds of expectants, hopers, and promissees. 1785 PALEY *Mor. Philos.* III. I. v. 107 The promise is to be performed in that sense in which the promiser apprehended at the time that the promisee received it. 1846 GROTE *Greece* I. xx. II. 110 The tie which binds a man to any special promisee towards whom he has taken the engagement of an oath. 1875 POSTE *Gaius* I. Introd. (ed. 2) 11 The intention of the promissor must accord with that of the promissee. *Ibid.* II. Comm. 203 The payee, promisee, or creditor, is.. defined by the class term 'bearer' or 'holder'.

Promiseful (prǫ·misfŭl), *a. rare.* [f. PROMISE *sb.* + -FUL.] **a.** Full of or accompanied by promises. **b.** Full of promise or pre-indication of good; promising.

1598 SYLVESTER *Du Bartas* II. ii. II. *Babylon* 96 Som he wins with promisefull intreats,..and som with rougher threats. 1883 *Chicago Advance* 25 Jan., From the Rocky Mountain Districts, never more promiseful, comes the unchanged cry. 1908 *Daily Chron.* 9 June 3/2 Our rivers are promiseful enough of sport.

Promiseless (prǫ·mislės), *a. rare.* [f. as prec. + -LESS.] Devoid of promise.

1882 J. A. HEWITT *Summer Songs* 3 The promiseless calm of the present Was dull with the dusk of night.

Promiser (prǫ·misəɹ). [f. PROMISE *v.* + -ER [1]. (See also PROMISOR, PROMISSOR.)] One who or that which promises; the maker or giver of a promise.

1530 TINDALE *Answ. More* IV. xi. Wks. (1573) 336/2 Faith ..shall receaue according to the truth of the promiser. 1632 MASSINGER *City Madam* III. ii, I must be A doer, not a promiser. 1771 MRS. GRIFFITH *Hist. Lady Barton* II.

122 That sweet promiser Hope. 1775 JOHNSON *Tax. no Tyr.* 22 An idle promiser of kingdoms in the clouds. 1864 *Realm* 6 Apr. 2 We may always distrust the universal promiser.

Promising (prǫ·misiŋ), *vbl. sb.* [f. as prec. + -ING [1].] The action of the verb PROMISE; the making of a promise or promises.

1513 DOUGLAS *Æneis* VIII. x. 38 Lo, my reward heyr, and my promising Fulfillit justly. 1530 PALSGR. 258/2 Promysing, trouthe plyghtynge, *fianceilles*. 1607 SHAKS. *Timon* V. i. 23 Promising, is the verie Ayre o' th' Time;..Performance, is euer the duller for his acte.

Pro·mising, *ppl. a.* [f. as prec. + -ING [2].] That promises.

1. *lit.* That makes a promise or promises; that engages to do or give something. *rare.*

1720 SWIFT *Fates Clergymen* Wks. 1755 II. II. 30 He was hardly drawn to attend upon some promising lord. 1838 E. BROWN *Serm.* xi. 252 Will the promising God ever permit the name of Christ to be forgotten?

2. *fig.* Affording expectation of good; showing signs of future excellence or success; likely to turn out well; full of promise; hopeful. (The prevailing sense.)

1601 SHAKS. *All's Well* III. iii. 3 We..lay our best loue and credence Vpon thy promising fortune. 1654–66 EARL ORRERY *Parthen.* (1676) 544 My Prince's condition was so promising. 1709 STANHOPE *Paraphr.* IV. 512 That so promising and plentiful a crop might not be lost. 1770 HARRIS in *Priv. Lett. Ld. Malmesbury* (1870) I. 194 He is a very promising man; and will I think do honour to his name and his country. 1860 TYNDALL *Glac.* I. v. 37 The weather was not quite clear, but it was promising. 1878 BOSW. SMITH *Carthage* 90 This was not a promising beginning.

Pro·misingly, *adv.* [f. prec. + -LY [2].] In a promising manner; so as to cause expectation of good.

a 1691 BOYLE *Hist. Air* (1692) 49, I speak the less promisingly of what I am to say in the remaining part of this paper. 1748 RICHARDSON *Clarissa* (1811) V. xxvii. 272 Clarissa must be the name, if promisingly lovely. 1861 W. BRINTON in *Peaks, Passes & Glac.* Ser. II. I. 423 The weather cleared, and left the summits of the surrounding mountains promisingly covered with snow.

So **Pro·misingness**, promising quality.

1665 BOYLE *Occas. Refl.* IV. *Transition* (1848) 289 Notwithstanding the Serenity and Promisingness of the Morning. 1727 in BAILEY vol. II.

Promisor (prǫ·misǭɹ). *Law.* [f. PROMISE *v.* + -OR: cf. PROMISER, PROMISSOR.] The person who makes a promise: correlative to PROMISEE.

1846 in WORCESTER citing CHITTY. 1875 POSTE *Gaius* II. Comm. (ed. 2) 171 The obligation of the promisor. *Ibid.* III. § 100 A stipulation to convey on the day before the death of the promisee or promisor is invalid.

†**Promi·ss,** *a. Obs. rare.* In 7 -isse. [ad. L. *prōmiss-us* hanging down, prop. pa. pple. of *prōmitt-ĕre*: see PROMIT *v.*] Hanging down; long and pendent.

1637 HEYWOOD *Dial.* iv. Wks. 1874 VI. 190, I know him by his promisse beard. 1657 TOMLINSON *Renou's Disp.* 375 Promisse and not broad leafs.

†**Pro·missary.** *Obs. rare.* [f. L. *prōmiss-*, ppl. stem of *prōmittĕre* (see PROMIT *v.*) + -ARY [1].]

1. (?) = PROCURATOR.

c 1485 *Digby Myst.* (1882) III. 237, I am pylat pr[o]mmyssary and presedent.

2. = PROMISEE.

1655 T. WHITE *Grounds Obed. & Govt.* 36 He who maketh a promise to another, so it be a perfect one,..puts himselfe and his promissary into a rank of agency and patiency.

Promisse, obs. form of PROMISE, PROMISS.

Promissee, variant of PROMISEE.

†**Promi·ssion.** *Obs.* [a. F. *promission* (12th c. in Hatz.-Darm.), ad. L. *prōmissiōn-em* a promising, n. of action from *prōmitt-ĕre*: see PROMIT *v.*] = PROMISE *sb.* (esp. in sense 2): orig. and chiefly, as in 2 b, in phrase *land of promission*.

c 1250 *Gen. & Ex.* 4131 [Moses] Saȝ ðe lond of promission. a 1300 *Cursor M.* 6924 Þis Ieus, fild wit vn-resun, In-to þe land o promission Thoru moyses ne come þai noght. c 1400 MAUNDEV. Prol. (1839) 1 Holy Lond..men callen..the lond of Promyssioun. 1480 CAXTON *Chron. Eng.* I. (1520) 6 b/2 Eleazar and Iosue deuyded the lande of promyssyon to ye chyldren of Israell. 1588 PARKE tr. *Mendoza's Hist. China* 316 So great store of prouision yt it seemeth to be ye land of promission.

c 1440 CAPGRAVE *St. Kath.* III. 1429 At this eyte dayes ende, as was promyssion, Cometh oure lady wyth lyght doun from euene. c 1440 *Gesta Rom.* xxxiv. 134 (Harl. MS.) This is a grete promission that thowe makest to me. 1529 FRITH *Pistle to Chr. Rdr.* Wks. (1829) 469 We..are the children of promission as Isaac was. 1560 DAUS tr. *Sleidane's Comm.* 217 b, Chyldren..which are also partakers of the godly promission.

Promissive (promi·siv), *a.* Now *rare.* [ad. late L. *prōmissīv-us* promising, applied to the future tense: see PROMISE and -IVE.] Conveying, implying, or having the character of a promise; promissory.

a 1635 NAUNTON *Fragm. Reg.* (Arb.) 24 She amazed them with a kind of promissive disputation. 1650 HOBBES *De Corp. Pol.* 186 All Declarations..concerning Future Actions and Omissions, are either Promissive, as 'I will do, or not do'; or Provisive, As for example, 'If this be done or not done, this will follow'; or Imperative, as 'Do this, or do it not'. 1677 GALE *Crt. Gentiles* II. IV. 356 God's Wil reveled in his Word is either promissive or preceptive. a 1703 BURKITT *On N. T.* Matt. xi. 12 Which words are both restrictive and promissive. 1824 L. MURRAY *Eng. Gram.* (ed. 5) I. vi. 119 Instead..of making a separate mood for every auxiliary verb, and introducing moods Interrogative, Optative, Promissive, Hortative, Precative, &c. we have exhibited such only as are obviously distinct. 1850 *Proc. Philol. Soc.* IV. 186 Shall (2, 3) and will (1) [are called] promissive.

Promissor (promi·sǫɹ). [a. L. *prōmissor* a promiser, agent-n. f. *prōmitt-ĕre*: see PROMIT *v.*]

†**1.** *Astrol.* = PROMITTOR. *Obs.*

1621 BURTON *Anat. Mel.* I. ii. I. iv, If ♄ by his revolution, or transitus, shall offend any of those radicall promissors in the geniture. *Ibid.* III. iii. I. ii. (1651) 596 By direction of the significators to their several promissors. 1696 PHILLIPS (ed. 5), *Promitters* or *Promissors*, a Term in the Genethliack part of Astrology, so called because they promise in the Radix something to be accomplished, when the Time of direction is fulfilled.

2. *Rom. Law*, etc. One who makes a promise: = PROMISOR.

1644 [H. PARKER] *Jus Pop.* 12 This wide gaping promissor. 1859 SANDARS *Instit. Justinian* III. xv. (ed. 2) 423 If the promissor attempted to defeat the condition by preventing its being fulfilled, he was treated as if he had promised *pure*, and the thing could be demanded from him at once. 1875 POSTE tr. *Gaius* I. Introd. (ed. 2) 11 The intention of the promissor must accord with that of the promissee. *Ibid.* III. Comm. 362 A unilateral convention is one where there is a single promissor and a single acceptor.

Pro·missorily, *adv. rare.* [f. next + -LY [2].] In a promissory manner; in the way of a promise.

1646 SIR T. BROWNE *Pseud. Ep.* V. xiv. (1650) 217 Nor was he [Jephthah] obliged by oath unto a strict observation of that which promissorily was unlawfull.

Promissory (prǫ·misəri), *a.* [ad. med.L. *prōmissōri-us* (Bonaventura a 1274), f. L. *prōmissor*: see above and -ORY [2].]

1. Conveying, containing, or implying a promise; of, pertaining to, or of the nature of a promise.

1649 JER. TAYLOR *Gt. Exemp.* II. Disc. ix. 115 [It] require[s] the sanction of promissory oaths. 1696 LORIMER *Goodwin's Disc.* vii. 71 A form of words which..was..promissory of Eternal Life upon a possible condition. 1782 MISS BURNEY *Cecilia* VIII. viii, Her imagination,—that source of promissory enjoyment. 1851 HT. MARTINEAU *Hist. Eng.* 1800–15 II. I. (1878) 259 Popham's Circular to the British merchants, promissory of a rich trade. 1890 BRIDGETT *Blunders & Forgeries* iv. 107 The binding power of a promissory oath.

b. *Promissory note*: a signed document containing a written promise to pay a stated sum to a particular person (or to the bearer), either at a specified date, or on demand.

1710 *Lond. Gaz.* No. 4699/4 A Bill to make Promissory Notes more effectual. 1711 SWIFT *Jrnl. to Stella* 10 May, To lend Stella twenty pounds, and to take her note promissory to pay it in half a year. 1766 BLACKSTONE *Comm.* II. xxx. 446 If a man..gives a promissory note, he shall not be allowed to aver the want of a consideration in order to evade the payment. 1833 HT. MARTINEAU *Berkeley the Banker* I. iv. 81 A bank note is a promissory note for a definite sum; and it must be stamped.

2. *fig.* Conveying a 'promise' or indication of something to come, esp. of good; full of promise, promising, prognosticatory.

1839–48 BAILEY *Festus* xxiii. (ed. 4) 294 A promissory Being unfulfilled. 1891 *Harper's Mag.* Jan. 205/1 The tender glow of evening,..so promissory of the splendid days to come. *Ibid.* Apr. 728/1 She nodded her head with a look promissory of horrors.

†**Pro·mit,** *sb. Sc. Obs.* [f. next.] = PROMISE *sb.* 1, 2.

1501 DOUGLAS *Pal. Hon.* III. lxxvi, In thair promittis thay stude euer firme and plane. 1567 *Gude & Godlie B.* (S.T.S.) 113 My beleue is in thy word, And all thy promittis maist and leist.

†**Promi·t,** *v. Obs.* Forms: 5–6 promit, -itt(e, -yt(te (5 *pa. t.* promit, -ytt). β. 5 promette. [ad. L. *prōmitt-ĕre* to let go or send forth, to put forth; to promise, give hope of; to foretell; f. *prō*, PRO- [1] + *mitt-ĕre* to let go, send. The β form a. F. *promett-re* (10th c. in Godef.) to promise.]

1. = PROMISE *v.* 1, 2.

1425 *Rolls of Parlt.* IV. 297/2 Promyttyng and behotyng ..to do, kepe, observe and fulfille..al yat shall be decreed. 1432–50 tr. *Higden* (Rolls) VI. 93 Promittynge if he myȝhte escape þat pestilence, þat he wolde dye in goynge pilgremages. 1456 SIR G. HAYE *Law Arms* (S.T.S.) 141 He has payit thame all that he promyttit thame. 1527 in Fiddes *Wolsey* II. (1726) 141 Promytting..that from heyceforth I shall never retorn agen to the said heresies. a 1584 MONTGOMERIE *Cherrie & Slae* 1131 Promitting, unwitting, Ȝour hechts ȝou neuir huiked.

β. c 1422 HOCCLEVE *Jereslaus's Wife* 802 If your pardon Yee me promette. 1432–50 tr. *Higden* (Rolls) V. 435 Y promette feithefully to be rulede by hym. c 1489 CAXTON *Blanchardyn* xxiii. 78 'Syre', sayd the pucell, 'I promette you that youre hoste shalbe al to gydre contented of you'.

b. = PROMISE *v.* 5 a.

1484 CAXTON *Fables of Æsop* V. xvi, I promytte and warne the that yf thow come nyghe me I shalle slee the with this grete clubbe.

¶**2.** Erroneous for PERMIT: perh. scribal error.

c 1500 *Joseph Arim.* (E.E.T.S.) 32 He..commaunded hym he sholde promytte and suffre the seruauntes of almyghty god to passe out of pryson. 1523 [COVERDALE] *Old God & New* (1534) E j, They were promitted and suffred to retreate. 1565 *Reg. Privy Council Scot.* I. 330 The Quenis Majestie promittis thame to tak of her awin woddis as may serve to the bigging of neidfull houssis for the labouraris.

¶ The alleged sense 'To disclose, to publish, to confess' is a figment founded on a misquotation: see below.

a 1548 HALL *Chron., Hen. VII* 33 b, Pardone of all offences and crymes committed, and promocions and rewardes for obeynge to the kynges request. [Misquoted in *Cassell's Encycl. Dict.* 'of all offences and crimes promitted': whence in *Cent. Dict.*, and (def.) in *Funk's Stand. Dict.*]

Promittor (promi·tǫɹ). *Astrol.* Also 7 -er. [f. prec. + -OR. Cf. PROMISSOR.] A planet which 'promises' or prognosticates that some event will take place on its arriving at some particular aspect with another planet, star, or point of the heaven (the *significator*); also applied to such an aspect.

1647 LILLY *Chr. Astrol.* clxvii. 719 Consider the Profections of Significators and Promittors. 1671 SALMON *Syn. Med.* I. xxxiv. 71 The Quality of the Disease shall be discerned from the Promittor or afflicting Planet. 1696 Promitters [see PROMISSOR 1]. 1819 J. WILSON *Dict. Astrol.* s. v., ♄ and ♂ are anaretic promittors, and promise to destroy the life of the native when the hyleg is directed to them. ♃ and ♀ are promittors of good when directions to them are fulfilled.

‖**Promnesia** (prǫmnī·siă). *Psychic Science.* [mod.L., f. Gr. πρό, PRO- [2] + -μνησία memory.] (See quot.)

1903 MYERS *Human Personality* I. p. xx, *Promnesia*, the paradoxical sensation of recollecting a scene which is only now occurring for the first time; the sense of the *déjà vu*. *Ibid.* II. 264 That sensation of already remembering what is happening or is just about to happen, to which some authors have applied the too wide term paramnesia, but for which *promnesia* seems a more exact and distinctive name.

†**Pro·mont.** *Obs. rare.* [Shortened from PROMONTORY, as if f. PRO- [1] + L. *mont-em* MOUNT *sb.* [1]] = PROMONTORY.

1612 DRAYTON *Poly-olb.* i. 151 A Promont jutting out into the dropping south. a 1627 MIDDLETON *Changeling* I. i, Our citadels Are plac'd conspicuous to outward view On promonts' tops. 1631 CHETTLE *Trag. Hoffmann* B j b, Ile to yon promonts top, and their suruey, What shipwrackt passengers the belgique sea Casts from her fomy entrailes.

†**Pro·montore.** *Obs. rare.* [f. L. *prōmontōrium* PROMONTORY: cf. F. *promontoire* (15–16 c. in Hatz.-Darm.).] = prec.

1623 LITHGOW *Trav.* I. 22 Capo Bianco in Calabria.. being the furthest promontore of Italy. *Ibid.* X. 448 Without it is quadrangled, and within round; hauing two degrees of incircling promontores, supported by Marble pillars, and Allabaster arches. 1657 THORNLEY tr. *Longus' Daphnis & Chloe* 82 Coming to a Promontore which ran into the Sea.

Promontorial (prǫmǫntō·riăl), *a. rare.* [f. L. *prōmontōri-um* PROMONTORY + -AL.] Of, pertaining to, or resembling a promontory.

1875 ALEX. SMITH *New Hist. Aberdeen.* I. i. 1 From its semicircular shape it may be called promontorial.

Promontoried (prǫ·mǫntərid), *a.* [f. PROMONTORY + -ED [2].] Formed into or furnished with a promontory or projection.

1649 G. DANIEL *Trinarch., Hen. V* cccxxviii, The floating Bodies, promontoried, Reaks An Exhalation. 1844 FABER *Sir Lancelot* (1857) 51 The green hill-tops and promontoried steeps. 1891 *Cornh. Mag.* June 649 They see the promontoried backs and small heads and long necks of some of those ungainly beasts [camels].

b. as *pa. pple.* Pierced as by a promontory.

1877 BLACKMORE *Erema* II. xxxi. 141 In bays and waves of rolling grass, promontoried, here and there, by jutting copse or massive tree.

†**Promonto·rious,** *a. Obs. rare.* [f. as prec. + -OUS.] Of the nature of a promontory; lofty and prominent. (In quots. *fig.*)

1615 T. ADAMS *Eng. Sickness* Serm. ii. Wks. 1861 I. 422 The Papists brag of their numerous multitude, and promontorious celsitude. 1618 — *Happiness Ch.* ibid. II. 497 The ambitious man's mountain is his honour, and who dares find fault with so promontorious a celsitude?

‖**Promontorium** (prǫmǫntō·riŭm). [med.L.: see next.] **a.** = next, 1. **b.** = next, 2.

1652–62 HEYLIN *Cosmogr.* Introd. (1674) 19/1 Promontorium, is a high Mountain which shooteth it self into the Sea, the utmost end of which is called a Foreland, or Cape. 1831 [see next, 2]. 1871 *Daily News* 23 Jan., This long bluff.. its promontorium throws forward, as it were, two sheltering wings for batteries stationed in the narrow waist behind.

Promontory (prǫ·mǫntəri). Also 7 -ary, promontory. [ad. med.L. *prōmontōri-um*, alteration (after *mont-em* MOUNT *sb.* [1]) of L. *prōmunturi-um* a mountain ridge, a headland, promontory; referred by some to *prōminēre* to jut forward.]

1. A point of high land which juts out into the sea or other expanse of water beyond the line of coast; a headland.

1548 UDALL, etc. *Erasm. Par. Acts* xiii. 46 Barnabas and Saul went to Seleucia, whiche is a great promontorye, or peake on the weste parte of Antioche. 1553 EDEN *Treat. Newe Ind.* (Arb.) 8 Euen vnto the promontorie or landes ende of the people, called *Cimbri*. 1559 W. CUNNINGHAM *Cosmogr. Glasse* 80 The parallele.., goth by the promontory of good hope. 1659 GALE *Crt. Gentiles* I. I. viii. 44 Corsica ..called by the Grecians..the Horny Iland; because of its many Promontories, and angles. 1725 POPE *Odyss.* X. 221 From yonder Promontory's brow, I view'd the coast. 1876 GREEN *Stray Stud.* 60 Monaco stands on a promontory of rock which falls in bold cliffs into the sea.

b. *transf.* and *fig.*

1603 OWEN *Pembrokeshire* (1892) 196 The begynning of his Raigne is the Period or farthest Promontorye of the certaine antiquities of this Realme. 1832 W. IRVING *Alhambra* I. xxi. 307 They doubled the promontory of the mountains, and arrived in sight of the famous Puente del Pinos. a 1854 H. REED *Lect. Brit. Poets* (1857) II. xv. 205 Standing on the promontory of the present, to feel the air rising from the shadowy waters of the past. 1860 TYNDALL *Glac.* I. ix. 63 The avalanche..was hidden from us by a rocky promontory.

2. *Anat.* Applied to certain prominences or protuberances of the body.

Promontory of the sacrum, an angular prominence formed by the junction of the last lumbar vertebra with the sacrum. *Promontory of the tympanum*, a protuberance of the inner ear caused by the projection of the cochlea.

1831 R. KNOX *Cloquet's Anat.* 111 The sacrum is articulated to the fifth lumbar vertebra...Its junction with the spinal column forms a projecting angle named the Promontory (*promontorium*). *Ibid.* 567 The Promontory (*Promontorium*)..is another pretty broad tubercular eminence, of a variable form, which limits the fenestra ovalis below. 1881 MIVART *Cat* 298 Another opening, called the fenestra rotunda, lies below and behind the promontory.

3. *attrib.* (or *adj.*) Resembling a promontory, projecting, outstanding.

1579 FENTON *Guicciard.* VII. (1599) 284 On the top of the mountaine called the Promontorie hill. c 1590 GREENE *Fr. Bacon* iv. 6 Welcome..To Englands shore, whose promontory cleeues, Shewes Albion is another little world. 1693 DRYDEN *Juvenal* vi. 153 A Promontory Wen, with griesly Grace, Stood high, upon the Handle of his Face. 1726 POPE *Odyss.* XIX. 281 His bending head O'er which a promontory shoulder spread. 1809 CAMPBELL *Gertr. Wyom.* III. xxv, Each bold and promontory mound.

Promorph (prōu·mǫɹf). *Biol.* [a. Ger. *promorph* (Haeckel), f. Gr. πρό, PRO- [2] + μορφή form.] A primitive or fundamental form.

1889 *Nature* 28 Feb. 409/2 An addition of three pages on 'the fundamental form (promorph)'.

Promorphology (prōuːmǫɹfǫ·lŏdʒi). *Biol.* [ad. Ger. *promorphologie* (Haeckel): see PRO- [2] and MORPHOLOGY.] The morphology of fundamental forms; the branch of morphology that treats of organic forms from a mathematical standpoint; stereometric morphology. So **Promorpholo·gical** *a.*, of or pertaining to promorphology; whence **Promorpholo·gically** *adv.*; **Promorpho·logist**, one who is versed in promorphology.

1878 BELL *Gegenbaur's Comp. Anat.* 2 General Anatomy has to do with the fundamental forms of animal organisms (Promorphology). 1883 P. GEDDES in *Encycl. Brit.* XVI. 843/2 *note*, As promorphology develops the crystallography of organic form, so mineralogy..becomes parallel to morphology. *Ibid.* 844/2 The classification into bilateral and radiate forms which usually does duty for more precise promorphological conceptions. *Ibid.* 845/1 These homoplastic or homomorphic forms, as Haeckel has shown, come as fairly within the province of the promorphologist. 1890 *Cent. Dict.*, Promorphologically. 1895 *Syd. Soc. Lex.*, *Promorphology*, morphology, as relating to a few fundamental types.

Promotable (promōu·tăb'l), *a.* [f. next + -ABLE.] That may be or is to be promoted; deserving of promotion.

1726 M. DAVIES *Athen. Brit.* III. 31 Scarce sufferable, much less promotable or remunerable *Alibi*. 1887 MORLEY *Sp.* in *Scott. Leader* 31 Mar., Resident Magistrates are removable, and, if I may coin a word, 'promotable' by the Executive Government.

Promote (promōu·t), *v.* [f. L. *prōmōt-*, ppl. stem of *prōmovēre* to move forward, advance: see PRO- [1] and MOVE *v.* So obs. F. *promoter* to instigate (14th c. in Godef.).]

I. 1. *trans.* To advance (a person) *to* a position of honour, dignity, or emolument; *esp.* to raise to a higher grade or office; to prefer.

1387 TREVISA *Higden* (Rolls) VII. 145 Þe emperour i-smyten aȝen promoted hym sone into a bisshop [L. *promovit in episcopum*]. 1401 *Pol. Poems* (Rolls) II. 94 Preestes, wich to fatte benefices wolde be promotid. 1535 COVERDALE *Ps.* xxxvi[i]. 34 He shal so promote the, that thou shalt haue the londe by enheritaunce. 1685 STILLINGFL. *Orig. Brit.* iv. 167 Leontius his way was, to promote onely those in the Church, he was beforehand sure of. 1874 GREEN *Short Hist.* iii. § 5. 140 Boniface..was promoted to..the Archbishopric of Canterbury.

b. *Chess.* To raise (a pawn) to the rank of a piece. (Cf. to QUEEN.)

1803 [see PROMOTION 1 b]. 1900 *Westm. Gaz.* 12 May 3/3 Compelled to promote a Pawn to a piece. 1904 H. J. R. MURRAY in *Brit. Chess Mag.* Dec. 466 [In Malay chess] a pawn may be promoted to the rank of any superior piece, but promotion takes place, not when the Pawn reaches the eighth line, but only after a further diagonal move.

2. To further the growth, development, progress, or establishment of (anything); to help forward (a process or result); to further, advance, encourage. (Formerly also with *on*.)

1515 BARCLAY *Egloges* IV. (1570) C vj/1 Such rascolde drames promoted by Thais,..Or by suche other newe forged Muses nine. 1526 *Pilgr. Perf.* (W. de W. 1531) 12 b, This gyfte expelleth all vyce, and promoteth all vertue. 1577 HANMER *Anc. Eccl. Hist.* (1619) 236 The Emperour..went about to promote christian religion. 1644 DIGBY *Nat. Soul* iv. § 5. 390 All the causes and helpes that promote on its impotent desires. 1698–9 (Mar. 8) *Minute Bk. S. P. C. K.*, The Journal of the Hon[ble] Society for Promoting Christian Knowledge. 1703 J. TIPPER in *Lett. Lit. Men* (Camden) 305 You will promote the Sale of it as much as possibly you can. —1765 A. DICKSON *Treat. Agric.* (ed. 2) 79 Vegetation is promoted..by communicating to the earth the food of plants, and enlarging their pasture. 1849 MACAULAY *Hist. Eng.* ii. I. 191 It could in no way promote the national interest. 1874 GREEN *Short Hist.* ii. § 1. 60 Commerce and trade were promoted by the justice and policy of the Kings.

b. To support actively the passing of (a law or measure); now *spec.* to take the necessary steps for obtaining the passing of (a local or private act of parliament).

1721 *Col. Rec. Pennsylv.* III. 138 The parties concerned in promoting this Bill. 1863 H. COX *Instit.* 170 Many bills promoted as private bills, largely affect public as well as private interests.

II. †3. To put forth or forward into notice or attention; to publish, promulgate; to assert, advance (a claim). *Obs.*

1480 CAXTON *Chron. Eng.* ccxxv. 230 The kynges nedes were put forth and promoted as touchyng the kyngdom of Fraunce. 1555 in Strype *Eccl. Mem.* (1721) III. App. xlvi. 139 The false surmised articles promoted by Hugh Raulins, priest. 1563 BONNER in Strype *Ann. Ref.* (1709) I. xxxiv. 342 That the oath shall be promoted in open place, where there shall be a convenient assembly of people to witness the same. 1662 STANLEY *Hist. Chaldaick Philos.* (1701) 18/1 An Intellectual incorruptible pattern, the Print of whose Form He promoted through the World. 1683 MOXON *Mech. Exerc., Printing* i, Gutenberg..promoted His claim to the first Invention of this Art.

†**4.** To incite, prompt, move (*to* something). *Obs. rare.*

1450–1530 *Myrr. our Ladye* 27 The aungels of god..to helpe vs in time of prayer, & to promote our prayers towarde god. 1646 H. LAWRENCE *Comm. Angells* 80 The Angell keepers ..promote to all good, oppose all evill.

5. To cause to move forward in space or extent; to extend. *Obs.* exc. *dial.*

1652 NEEDHAM tr. *Selden's Mare Cl.* 274 None of them ever attempted to promote their Empire beyond the bounds thereof. 1660 BOYLE *New Exp. Phys. Mech.* i. (1682) 16 Other eminent Astronomers would promote the Confines of the Atmosphere to exceed six or seven times that number of Miles. 1683 MOXON *Mech. Exerc., Printing* i, William Caxton (..who first brought it to Oxford) promoted it to London also. a 1705 RAY *Creation* I. (1714) 201 Francis Pirara promotes the life of the Brazilians beyond the term we have set it. 1872 *Spectator* 7 Sept. 1137 'Sure it's I will promote her for your honour', where the word 'promote' was used..in its strict meaning of 'cause to move forward'.

III. †6. To inform against (a person); to lay an information of (a delinquency, etc.); also *intr.* or *absol.* to act as informer. Cf. PROMOTER 3. *Obs.*

14.. *Chester Pl.* (Shaks. Soc.) II. 82 Taverners, tapsters of this cittie, Shalbe promoted heare by me, For breakinge statutes of this cuntrey. 1550 LATIMER *Last Serm. bef. Edw. VI* Serm. (1562) 130 [129] There lacke men to promote the kinges officers when they do amisse, and to promote al offenders. 1566 DRANT *Horace, Sat.* IV. C j b, I am not one that doth promote, why art thou frayde of me? 1596–1623 [see PROMOTING *ppl. a.* 1].

7. *Eccl. Law.* To set in motion (the office of the ordinary or judge) in a criminal suit in an ecclesiastical court; to institute (a suit *ex officio promoto*) by permission of the ordinary.

1681 CONSET *Pract. Spir. Courts* I. ii. § 1 (1700) 5 Its Official [*sc.* of the Court of Arches] is the proper and competent Judge to take cognizance of all Ecclesiastical Causes whatsoever not only at the Instance of Parties, but also of his meer Office, or when 'tis promoted. *Ibid.* I. ii. § 3 (1700) 7 It is left to the election of the Plaintiff to elect in which Court he will institute or promote his Cause. 1789 SIR W. SCOTT in Haggard *Rep. Consist. Court* (1822) I. 14 This is a case of Office promoted [= *ex officio promoto*] against Thomas Calcott, for..erecting tombs in the church-yard.. without leave of the Ordinary. 1837 LUSHINGTON in Curteis *Rep. Eccl. Cas.* (1840) 601 Mr. Williams [Vicar of Hendon], who promotes the office of the judge, has brought a charge against a parishioner of chiding and brawling. 1849 DICKENS *Dav. Copp.* xxix, The office of the judge promoted by Tipkins against Bullock for his soul's correction. 1889 (May 11) ABP. BENSON in *Read v. Bp. of Lincoln* (Roscoe) 36 The archbishop's office was promoted against him [Bp. Wood of Lichfield, 1681]. *Ibid.* 37 The suit [*Lucy v. Bp. St. Davids*] was promoted ex officio before the archbishop. 1895 SIR R. PHILLIMORE *Eccl. Law* (ed. 2) 837 In every ecclesiastical court there are two modes of procedure—the civil and the criminal. In criminal proceedings the office of the judge is promoted, [i.e.] inasmuch as all spiritual jurisdiction is in the hands of the bishop or ordinary, his office or function is set in motion. *Ibid.* 956 The Criminal Suit is open to every one whom the ordinary allows to promote his office, and the Civil Suit to every one showing an interest.

†**Promo·te,** *ppl. a. Obs.* [ad. L. *prōmōt-us*, pa. pple. of *prōmovēre* (see prec.); or abbreviated from *promoted*.] Promoted.

c 1530 *Crt. of Love* 1261 For where a lover thinketh him promote, Envy will grucch, repyning at his wele.

†**Promo·tement.** *Obs. rare*[−1]. [f. PROMOTE *v.* + -MENT.] = PROMOTION 2.

1670 EVELYN *Sylva* xxii. (ed. 2) 105 Some commend the strewing a few Oats at the bottom of the fosses or pits..for a great promotement of their taking.

Promoter (promōu·təɹ). Forms: α. 5–6 promotour, -oure, 6 *Sc.* -ar, 6–9 -or, 5– -er. β. 6–8 promooter, 7 -mouter. [AF. and early mod.E. *promotour* = F. *promoteur* (1336 in Hatz.-Darm.) one who promotes, an official procurator in an ecclesiastical court, † a business agent, ad. med.L. *prōmōtor*, agent-n. f. *prōmovēre* to PROMOVE. But from 16th c. commonly spelt with *-er*, as if f. PROMOTE *v.* + -ER [1]. The β forms occur only in sense 3.]

I. 1. One who or that which promotes, advances, or furthers any movement or project; a furtherer, an encourager.

1450–1530 *Myrr. our Ladye* 237 A comforter to them that are desolate, a promoter to the rightful, an helper to the synful. 1494 FABYAN *Chron.* VII. 445 Of whiche oppynyon ..a great furtherer or promoter. 1553 BECON *Reliq. Rome* (1563) 85 The firste promoters..to haue Images in churches. a 1568 ASCHAM *Scholem.* (Arb.) 82 In tyme they be Promoters of both openlie. 1660 BOYLE *New Exp. Phys. Mech.* xx, That great and learned promoter of experimental philosophy, Dr. Wilkins. 1737 BRACKEN *Farriery Impr.* (1756) I. 78 A powerful Diuretic, or Promoter of Urine. 1781 D. WILLIAMS tr. *Voltaire's Dram. Wks.* II. 135 Money is the best promoter of matrimony. 1840 *Penny Cycl.* XVII. 277/1 In 1837 the bills for making four distinct lines of railway to Brighton had been referred to one committee. An unprecedented contest arose between the promoters of the competing lines. 1847 HELPS *Friends in C.* I. 106 There are two great classes of promoters of social happiness. 1878 LECKY *Eng. in 18th C.* II. v. 35 [The] leading promoter [of the University] was the Chancellor, Bishop Elphinstone.

b. *Legisl.* One who takes steps for, or actively supports, the passing of a law; now *spec.* one of those who take the necessary steps for obtaining the passing of a local or private act of parliament.

1741 MIDDLETON *Cicero* I. vi. 441 Cicero himself was the promoter of it, and procured a decree to his satisfaction. *Ibid.* 551 Cælius was the promotor of this law. [Cf. 1840 in 1.] 1863 H. COX *Instit.* I. iv. 20 With respect to these [local acts] various preliminaries..are..required to be observed by the promoters of the several bills. *Ibid.* I. ix. 172 The promoters of each bill are required to prove compliance with the standing orders of both Houses.

c. *Finance.* One who promotes, or takes the requisite steps for, the formation of a joint-stock company; one who is a party to the preparation or issue of the prospectus; a company-promoter. In consequence of the amount of swindling too often resorted to, the term has in popular use acquired an opprobrious sense: cf. PROMOTERISM.

1876 *World* V. No. 106. 5 A promoter, *quoad* promoter, is not necessarily a bad man. 1884 W. C. SMITH *Kildrostan* 80 He..cursed Himself, his friend, and all the ravenous crew Of jobbers and promoters. 1889 *Times* 18 Mar. 9/3 The promoter of a company is accountable for what he omits to do, as well as for what he does. 1890 *Act* 53 & 54 *Vict.* c. 64 § 3 A promoter in this section means a promoter who was a party to the preparation of the prospectus. 1894 *Westm. Gaz.* 15 Nov. 8/1 *Official Receiver.* Is he a company promoter? *Witness.* Oh, no; he is far too respectable for that.

2. One who promotes or advances another in dignity or position.

14.. [see PROMOVER]. 1670 G. H. *Hist. Cardinals* III. 301 They are disinterested, and no passionate promotors of their Kindred. 1868 FREEMAN *N. Conq.* II. vii. 80 Harold ..appears as a special promoter of German churchmen.

II. †3. One whose business was to prosecute or denounce offenders against the law; originally an officer appointed by the crown; later, one who prosecuted in his own name and that of the sovereign, and received a part of the fines as his fee; a professional accuser, an informer. *Obs.*

α. 1485 *Rolls of Parlt.* VI. 347/1 The Office of oure Promotoure, by us graunted unto hym by oure Lettres Patents. 1509 BARCLAY *Shyp of Folys* (1570) 140 b, Sergeaunt, Atturney, Promoter, Judge or Scribe, Will not feele thy matter without a priuie bribe. 1566 *Roy. Proclam.* 10 Nov., Such as be infourmers vpon penall lawes and Statutes, commonly called promoters. 1603 HOLLAND *Plutarch's Mor.* 421 Aristogiton the sycophant or false promotor, being condemned to death for troubling men with wrongfull imputations. 1603 [see RELATOR 2]. 1607 COWELL *Interpr.*, *Promoters*..be those, which in popular and penall actions doe deferre the names, or complaine of offenders, hauing part of the profit for their reward...They belong especially to the Exchequer and kings bench. a 1661 FULLER *Worthies*, *Northampton* (1662) 287 [Henry VII] made Empson Promoter General, to press the Penal-Statutes all over the land.

β. 1573 TUSSER *Husb.* (1878) 147 His eies be promooters, some trespas to spie. 1598 GRENEWEY *Tacitus' Ann.* IV. vii. (1622) 99 The promooters [L. *delatores*], a race of men found out for a common ouerthrow and destruction. 1607 R. C[AREW] tr. *Estienne's World of Wonders* 158 Prowling promouters. 1653 MILTON *Hirelings* Wks. 1851 V. 358 Tyndarus and Rebuffus, two canonical Promooters. 1670 BLOUNT *Law Dict.*, Promooters.

†**b.** An officer appointed to prosecute students before the Rector for debts or offences, in some of the Scottish universities. Now only *Hist.* repr. med.L. *promotor*.

[1482 *Munim. Univ. Glasguensis* (Maitl. Club) II. 9 De electione Promotoris Universitatis et eius officio.] 1854 *Ibid.* II. Table p. iv, A Promotor or General Sindic to be elected annually for the recovery of University debts, and the detection of contraventions of the Statutes. The Promotor to bring offenders before the Lord Rector... The Promotor's oath.

c. *Eccl. Law.* The prosecutor of a suit in an ecclesiastical court.

1754 HUME *Hist. Eng.* I. viii. 172 Laics should not be accused in spiritual courts, except by legal and reputable promoters and witnesses. 1821 LAMB *Elia* Ser. I. *Oxford in Vacation*, Amid an incongruous assembly of attorneys, attorneys' clerks, apparitors, promoters, vermin of the law, among whom he sits 'in calm and sinless peace'. 1876 LD. PENZANCE in *Willis v. Bp. of Oxf.* in *Law Rep.*, *Prob. Div.* II. 198 The promoter in this proceeding of 'duplex querela' complains in his libel that having been duly presented..the bishop has refused to institute him. *Ibid.*, That the result of the examination satisfied him (the defendant) that the promoter was *non idoneus et minus sufficiens in literatura*. 1889 E. S. ROSCOE *Bp. of Lincoln's Case* 1 The promoters in the suit were E. Read, W. Brown, T. F. Wilson, and J. Marshall. The respondent was the Lord Bishop of Lincoln. 1895 SIR R. PHILLIMORE *Eccl. Law* (ed. 2) 992 The promoter of the office of the judge is bound not only to give in articles, but also a correct copy to the defendant.

III. 4. A descriptive appellation in the Scottish universities (or some of them) of the official who presented students for degrees. *Obs.* exc. *Hist.*

Properly in Latin form *promotor*, but sometimes represented historically by the Eng. form.

1894 W. L. LOW *D. Thomson* iv. 93 It was his turn to act as Promotor or 'Father' of the new graduates. 1898 A. C. FRASER *T. Reid* iv. 46 In the last year of each course, as 'promoter', he presented his undergraduates to receive the Master's degree [at King's Coll., Aberdeen].

Hence **Promo·terism**, the reprobated practice or conduct of promoters of joint-stock companies.

1882 (*title*) Last Words of Thomas Carlyle on Trades-Unions: Promoterism and the Signs of the Times. 1882 *Edin. Courant* 27 Oct. 6/7 Word-painting of the diabolical promoterism of the day.

Promoting (promōu·tiŋ), *vbl. sb.* [f. PROMOTE *v.* + -ING [1].] The action of the verb PROMOTE.

1. Advancement, furtherance, helping forward; the 'getting up' of joint-stock financial companies.

1485 *Rolls of Parlt.* VI. 276/1 The..preferring of..Justice and promoteinge and rewardeinge Vertue. 1529 RASTELL *Pastyme, Hist. Pap.* (1811) 54 [He was accursed] for promotynge of benefices by symony. 1648 MILTON *Observ. Art. Peace* Wks. 1851 IV. 560 To give the first promoting.. to his own tyrannical designs in England. 1771 LUCKOMBE *Hist. Print.* 41 For the promoting of their pious designs. 1890 *Pall Mall G.* 3 July 2/2 Company-promoting has become a business.

†**2.** The action of a PROMOTER (sense 3); accusing, denouncing. *Obs.*

1581 SAVILE *Tacitus' Hist.* II. x. (1591) 58 Annius Faustus ..condemned of promoting.

Promo·ting, *ppl. a.* [f. as prec. + -ING [2].] That promotes, in various senses.

†**1.** That lays an information; that is a promoter or informer. *Obs.*

1596 HARINGTON *Apol. Ajax* Aa vj b, Least some hungrie promoting fellowes should beg it as a concealement. 1604 DRAYTON *Owl* 547 Steps in this false spy, this promoting wretch, Closely betrays him that he gives to each. 1623 SANDERSON *Serm.* (1657) 121 Informing, and promoting, and pettifogging make-bates.

2. That furthers, assists, or fosters. Chiefly in comb., as *company-promoting*, *health-promoting*.

1871 'M. LEGRAND' *Cambr. Freshm.* 250 Hunting the Drag..is so innocent, so health-promoting, and in every way so praiseworthy an amusement. 1904 *Westm. Gaz.* 1 Feb. 2/2 Colossal company-promoting swindlers.

Promotion (promōu·ʃən). Also 5–6 -cio(u)n, -cyon. [a. F. *promotion* (14th c. in Hatz.-Darm.), ad. L. *prōmōtiōn-em*, n. of action f. *prōmovēre*: see PROMOVE.]

1. Advancement in position; preferment.

On promotion, on the way to promotion, on trial; *to be on one's promotion*, to conduct oneself with a view to promotion (also *colloq.* to marriage).

1429 *Rolls of Parlt.* IV. 344/2 Ne for promotion or fortheryng of any persone to Office. 1523 LD. BERNERS *Froiss.* I. cccxxvii. 511 With his promocyon of popalyte the romayns were apeased. 1540 *Test. Ebor.* (Surtees) VI. 119, I give to Dorithe and Anne my doughters xl *li*, to be equallye devyded betwixte them towarde ther mariadge or other promocion. 1613 SHAKS. *Hen. VIII*, V. ii. 23 The high promotion of his Grace of Canterbury, Who holds his State at dore 'mongst Purseuants, Pages, and Foot-boyes. 1693 LUTTRELL *Brief Rel.* (1857) III. 81 Disgusted that he was not in the late promotion made a marshall of France. 1751 EARL ORRERY *Remarks Swift* (1752) 23 In point of power and revenue, such a deanery might be esteemed no inconsiderable promotion. 1785 CRABBE *Newspaper* 312 Promotion's ladder, who goes up or down. 1857 BUCKLE *Civiliz.* I. x. 602 In that period promotion depended solely on merit.

1836 *Lett. fr. Madras* i. (1843) 4 Several Irish girls apparently on their promotion. 1848 THACKERAY *Van. Fair* xxxix, The little kitchen-maid on her promotion. *Ibid.* xliv, 'I remember when you liked 'em, though'..'That was when I was on my promotion, Goosey', she said. 1888 W. E. HENLEY *Bk. Verses* 4 A square, squat room (a cellar on promotion). 1902 MISS E. P. THOMPSON in *Gentl. Mag.* Dec. 583 When the canonised saints have been worked out, he has recourse to those, as it were, 'on their promotion'.

b. *Chess.* The elevation of a pawn to the rank of a higher piece.

1803 P. PRATT *Studies of Chess* (1804) I. 30 Of promoting a pawn to be a queen, rook, &c. When a pawn has penetrated to the farthest rank on the adverse side of the board, he is rewarded with promotion to the *highest vacant* dignity. 1900 *Westm. Gaz.* 12 May 3/3 If a player..is forced..to the promotion which involves the loss of the game. *Ibid.* 22 Dec. 3/3 A trio of promotion problems..representing three different types of promotion side by side.

2. The action of helping forward; the fact or state of being helped forward; furtherance, advancement, encouragement.

1483 *Caxton's Chron. Eng.* V. N viij b, To the quyete state of the chyrche and to the promocion of the fayth. 1584 *Reg. Privy Council Scot.* III. 702 To the promotioun and furtherance of the gospell. 1664 POWER *Exp. Philos.* III. 183 An Authentick discouragement to the promotion of the Arts and Sciences. 1725 T. THOMAS in *Portland Papers* VI. (Hist. MSS. Comm.) 100 There is a navigable river.. which is a great promotion of the trade of the town. 1845 S. AUSTIN *Ranke's Hist. Ref.* III. 60 Institutions for the promotion of learning. 1862 SIR B. BRODIE *Psychol. Inq.* II. vii. 233 The great agent in the promotion of civilization is the advancement of knowledge.

b. The getting up of a joint-stock company.

1886 *Law Times* LXXX. 310/1 The plaintiff..was interested in the promotion of the Georgia Gold Mines Company Limited. 1898 *Westm. Gaz.* 8 June 7/1 He had not personally reaped the benefit of some of his promotions.

†**3.** The laying of an information against any one. *Obs.*

a 1536 TINDALE *Exp. Matt.* v–vii. 71 Couetousnes & promocion and such like,..are that ryghte hand and right eye that must be cut of & plucked out that the whole man peryshe not. [But this quot. perh. belongs to sense 1.]

†**4.** ? Motion or stirring of the mind. *Obs.*

1526 *Pilgr. Perf.* (W. de W. 1531) 136 Passyons of ire, enuy, sclaunderous wordes or other promocyons. 1656 STANLEY *Hist. Philos.* IV. (1701) 134/1 They held..That nothing judgeth but by interior promotion, and the judgment of true and false consists of inward touch.

†**5.** Advance, getting on, progress made. Cf. PROMOVE *v.* 5. *Obs.*

1649 JER. TAYLOR *Gt. Exemp.* I. Sect. 7. 108 Whether it were truly or in appearance, in habit or in exercise of act it is certain the promotions of the holy Childe [Luke ii. 52] were great, admirable, and as full of wonder as of sanctity.

6. *attrib.* (in sense 2 b) *promotion allowance*, *expense*, *money*; (in 1) *promotion examination*.

1882 *Pall Mall G.* 13 July 6/1 The General Hydraulic Power Company... No promotion money is to be paid. 1898 *Engineering Mag.* XVI. 32 *note*, The Edinburgh arbitrator took the actual cost of promotion as the test of the promotion allowance. 1899 *Westm. Gaz.* 4 Dec. 10/1 To look into the promotion expenses. 1903 *Daily Chron.* 17 Oct. 3/7 The..promotion examinations are at hand.

Promotive (promōu·tiv), *a.* (*sb.*) [f. as PROMOTE *v.* + -IVE, after MOTIVE *a.* Cf. Anglo-L. *prōmōtīvus* (1337 in Du Cange).] Having the quality of promoting; tending to the promotion (*of* a thing).

1644 J. GOODWIN *Innoc. Triumph.* (1645) 76 They will use [it] rather in a destructive, then promotive way thereunto. 1680 *Relig. Dutch* v. 46 Promotive to the advancement of Christian Religion. 1711 SHAFTESB. *Charac.* III. Misc. II. iii. 98 Corroborative of Religion, and promotive of true Faith. 1824 MISS MITFORD *Village* Ser. I. 277 The air is so promotive of growth. 1882 FAIRBAIRN in *Contemp. Rev.* XLII. 860 Agencies powerfully promotive of human progress.

B. *sb. nonce-use.* That which promotes or furthers something.

1793 W. TAYLOR in *Monthly Rev.* XII. 286 To evolve its real promotives.

Hence **Promo·tiveness**, the quality of being promotive; tendency to promote or further.

a 1866 J. GROTE *Exam. Utilit. Philos.* (1870) 251 He has defined utilitarianism as the philosophy which values one thing simply in regard of actions, viz. their promotiveness of happiness. 1874 P. SMYTH *Our Inher.* xi. 224 To set forth..their promotiveness to the fulness of thought as well as the material comforts of..man.

†**Promo·tor.** *Obs. rare*[−1]. [a. med.L.: see PROMOTER.] A procurator, prolocutor, or proctor.

1706 tr. *Dupin's Eccl. Hist.* 16th C. II. III. i. 2 Hercules Sevecollus, Promotor of the Council.

†**Promotorial** (prōumotō·riăl), *a. Obs.* [f. med.L. *prōmōtor* (see prec.) + -IAL; cf. obs. F. *promotoriel* (1589 in Godef.), = med.L. **prōmōtōrius*.] Of or pertaining to a procurator; *promotorial letters*, letters of attorney.

1631–3 J. DURIE in *Presbyt. Rev.* (1887) 301 [The King] had promised to give mee Promotoriall letters to further this end. *Ibid.* 303 How..to goe to the King of Sweden for his Promotoriall Letters towards ye Lutheran princes.

Promotress (promōu·trės). [f. PROMOTER + -ESS [1].] A female promoter. So [in L. form] **Promo·trix**, in same sense.

1622 H. SYDENHAM *Serm. Sol. Occ.* II. (1637) 107 A promotresse and bawd to error. 1678 ANTH. WALKER *Funeral C'tess Warwick* 48 The greatest Mistress, and Promotress ..of a new Science—The Art of obliging. 1892 *Cornh. Mag.* July 14 The promotress of mothers' meetings. 1650 J. LLOYD *Prim. Episc.* 17 A zealous promotrix of the Schism of the Donatists.

†**Promo·val.** *Sc. Obs. rare.* [f. PROMOVE *v.* + -AL.] Promotion, furtherance, advancement.

1683 RENWICK *Serm.*, etc. (1776) 570 For promoval and defence of Reformation. 1687 in Shields *Faithful Contendings* (1780) 300 For the promoval and defence of these testimonies. a 1693 *Urquhart's Rabelais* III. xxix. 240 Steadable for the promoval of the good of that Youth.

†**Promo·ve,** *v. Obs.* [ad. L. *prōmovēre* to move forward, promote: see PRO- [1] and MOVE *v.* Cf. OF. *por-*, *promovoir*, mod. *promouvoir*, perh. the immediate source.]

1. *trans.* = PROMOTE *v.* 1.

c 1425 *Found. St. Bartholomew's* (E.E.T.S.) 34 The sone of Stevyne..the whiche promoyd Theobalde..in-to the Archebisshope of Cawntirbery. 1513 DOUGLAS *Æneis* VII. Pref., Lat euery nobyll Prynce..luf vertew and iustice, beat vyce, punys euyll men, and promowe gud men. a 1578 LINDESAY (Pitscottie) *Chron. Scot.* (S.T.S.) I. 62 [He] laborit daylie to promove his freindis to honour and dignatie. 1671 J. BRYDALL *Law Eng. Nobility & Gentry* (1675) 2 Nobility being then a Quality or Dignity, whereby a Man is..promoved out of, and above the Estate of the vulgar.

2. = PROMOTE *v.* 2.

c 1400 *Apol. Loll.* 51 Prelats promouing, or secular lordis procuring þat þat clerk lord in þat maner, þei synnen deadly. 1566 *Act. Gen. Assembly Ch. Scot. to Eng. Ch.* 19 To promove the Kingdom of Jesus Christ. a 1641 SUCKLING *Loving & Beloved* Poems (1646) 5 It is impossible, nor can Integrity our ends promove. 1677 GALE *Crt. Gentiles* II. III. 19 Making use of the Christian Religion only as a blind or politic medium to promove their gain. 1702 C. MATHER *Magn. Chr.* IV. iv. (1852) 77 The 'sons of the prophets', whose establishment 'in the present truth', I am..under an obligation to promove.

3. To move mentally, provoke, instigate, incite.

c 1477 CAXTON *Jason* 10 To this promouid him enuye and disloyal detraccion. 1637 GILLESPIE *Eng. Pop. Cerem.*

Promovent, *pa. pple.* (sb.) [ad. L. *promovent-em*, pr. pple. of *prōmovēre*: see next.]

Promove, *v.* Obs. [ad. L. *prōmovēre* to move forward, advance, promote.]

Promoving, *vbl. sb.* Obs.

Prompt, *sb.* [In branch I. ad. L. *promptus* readiness, f. *promere*; in III. f. Prompt *v.*; in II. f. Prompt *a.*]

Prompt, *a.* (*adv.*) [a. F. *prompt* (13th in Godef. *Compl.*), or ad. L. *promptus* drawn forth, brought to light, manifest; at hand, ready, quick, prepared, disposed, inclined.]

Prompt, *v.* [f. Prompt *a.*, or Prompt *sb.* III.]

Promptitude, *sb.* [a. F. *promptitude*, in Cotgrave (1611) *promptitude*: see Prompt *a.* and -TUDE.]

Promptive, *a.* rare. [f. L. *prompt-* (see Prompt *a.*) + -IVE.]

Promptly, *adv.* [f. Prompt *a.* + -LY.]

Promptness. [f. Prompt *a.* + -NESS.]

Prompt-book, *sb.*

Prompter. Also 5-6 *ar(e*, -owre. [f. Prompt *v.* + -ER.]

Prompting, *vbl. sb.* [f. Prompt *v.* + -ING.]

Promptitude.

Promptuary, *sb.* (*a.*) [ad. L. *promptuārium* a store-room, repository; cf. F. *promptuaire* a store-room.]

Promptuous, *a.* rare. [f. Prompter + -ESS.] A female prompter.

Promulgate, *ppl. a.* Obs. [ad. L. *prōmulgāt-us*, pa. pple. of *prōmulgāre*: see Promulge.]

Promulgate, *v.* [f. L. *prōmulgāt-*, ppl. stem of *prōmulgāre* to expose to public view, publish: see Promulge.]

Promulgation. [ad. L. *prōmulgātiōn-em*, n. of action f. *prōmulgāre*: see Promulgate.]

Promulgator. [ad. L. *prōmulgātor*, agent-n.]

Promulge, *v.* [ad. L. *prōmulgāre*.]

Promulger. [f. prec. + -ER.]

Promuscis (prōmˈʌsis), *sb.* [L. *prōmuscis*, -idem (see next) + -ATE.]

Promuscis.

Promycelium (prōmaiˈsiliʊm). *Bot.* Rarely in Eng. form **Promycele.** [mod. L. f. Pro- + MYCELIUM.]

Promygale.

Pronaos (prōnēˈɒs), *sb.* [L., a. Gr. πρόναος.] Now chiefly an *official archaism.*

Pronate, *ppl. a.* rare. [ad. late L. *prōnāt-us*, pa. pple. of *prōnāre*: see next.] Bent into a prone position; bent forward and downward.

Pronate, *v.* [f. late L. *prōnāt-*, ppl. stem of *prōnāre* to bend forward, f. *prōn-us* Prone *a.*] *trans.* To render prone.

Pronation (prōnēˈʃən). *Physiol.* [a. F. *pronation* (16th c. in Hatz.-Darm.), also *pronatio*, ad. med.L. *prōnātiō-em*, n. of action f. *prōnāre*: see prec.] The action of pronating.

Pronator (prōnēˈtər), *sb.* [a. mod.L. *pronator* agent-n., f. *prōnāre*: see Pronate *v.*] A muscle that effects or assists in pronation.

Prone, *sb.* Now rare. Also 7 *proan.* [a. F. *prône* (12th c. in Hatz.-Darm.), also *prosne*, ad. med.L. *prōtana.*]

Prone, *a.* [ad. L. *prōn-us* inclined forward, bending downward.]

Pronely, *adv.* [f. Prone *a.* + -LY.]

Proneness. [f. Prone *a.* + -NESS.]

Pronephew, *sb.* Obs. [ad. L. *pronepōs* great-grandson; but cf. F. *proneveu*, -veux.]

Pronephric, *a.* [f. next + -IC.]

Pronephros, nephros (prōneˈfrɒs, -nefrɒs), *sb.* [mod.L.: f. Pro- + Gr. νεφρός kidney.] *Anat.*

Pronephew.

Prong (prɒŋ), *sb.* [Known only from c 1440: app. = MLG. *prange*, *pronge* a pinching, pinch, also Du. *prange*, *prang* a pinching, confinement.]

Prong, *v.* [f. Prong *sb.*] *trans.* To prick, stab, or pierce with a prong.

Prongbuck (prɒŋbʌk). [f. Prong *sb.* + Buck.]

Prongbud.

Prongos, the female of the pronghorn.

Pronged (prɒŋd), *a.* [f. Prong *sb.* + -ED[2].] Furnished with or having prongs.

Pronghorn (prɒŋhɔːn), *sb.* [f. Prong *sb.* + Horn.]

Prong-horned, *a.*

Pronity. Obs. rare. [f. *prōn-us* Prone + -ITY.] Inclination, propensity.

Pronominal (prōnɒˈminăl), *a.* (*sb.*) [ad. L. *prōnōmināl-is* belonging to a pronoun (Priscian), f. *prōnōmen* Pronoun.]

Pronominally, *adv.* [f. prec. + -LY.]

Pronomination (prǫnǫmineɪ·ʃən). [In sense 1 Pro- 1 + Nomination, imitating Gr. ἀντωνομασία. Antonomasia; in sense 2 f. L. *prōnōmen* Pronoun = -ation.]

† 1. = Antonomasia. *Obs.*

2. Indication or reference by means of a pronoun.

‖ Prononce (prǫnǫ·ns), *a.* [Fr. pa. pple. of *prononcer* to Pronounce.] Pronounced, emphasized; strongly marked or defined; conspicuous, noteworthy.

Pronotary, etc.: see Prognostic, etc.

Pronotum ... The dorsal part of the prothorax of an insect; the anterior division of the notum, as distinct from the *mesonotum* and *metanotum*.

Pronoun (prǫu·naun). [f. Pro- 1 + Noun, after F. Pronom, L. *prōnōmen*.] One of the Parts of Speech : a word used instead of a noun substantive, to designate an object without naming it ...

Pronounce (prǫnau·ns), *v.* [ME. *pronuncen*, *pronunce*, a. OF. *pronuncier* (1277 in Godef. Compl.), for earlier *purnuncier* (mod.F. *prononcer*)—late L. *prōnuntiāre* for clg. *prōnūntiāre* to proclaim, announce, rehearse, narrate, pronounce, f. *prō-* + *nuntiāre* to announce: cf. Announce, Enounce.]

I. 1. *trans.* To utter, declare, or deliver (a sentence or statement) formally or solemnly ...

2. *trans.* To give utterance to; to utter, speak, articulate (a word or words); to make, or produce (a vocal sound) (*obs.*). Also *absol.*

3. To declare aloud, proclaim, announce, make known ; to tell, narrate, report. *Obs.* or merged in 1.

4. To affirm, assert authoritatively or definitely; to declare as one's opinion or judgement, or as a known fact. **a.** with simple compl. or inf.

b. *intr.* To make a statement or assertion, esp. now always, an authoritative or definite one; to pass judgement, give one's opinion or decision. Now usually const. *on* or *upon*; also *for* (in favour of) or against.

Pronounceable (prǫnau·nsəb'l), *a.* [f. prec. + -able.] Capable of being pronounced.

Hence **Pronounceabi·lity**.

Pronounced (prǫnau·nst), *ppl. a.* [See -ED 1.]
1. Spoken, uttered, articulated.
2. *fig.* Firmly of Prayer ... marked; pronounced.

Pronouncedly (prǫnau·nsedli), *adv.* [f. prec. + -LY 2.] In a pronounced manner or degree; markedly, decidedly, distinctly.

Pronouncement (prǫnau·nsmənt). [f. Pronounce v. + -MENT: cf. OF. *prononcement* (13th c.).]
1. The action or act of pronouncing ; a formal statement ; an authoritatively made ; an opinion or decision given ; a declaration, assertion.
2. The act or condition of being pronounced.

Pronouncer (prǫnau·nsəɹ). [f. Pronounce v. + -ER 1.] One who pronounces.

Pronouncing (prǫnau·nsiŋ), *vbl. sb.* [f. as prec. + -ING 1.] The action of the verb Pronounce.
1. Utterance, articulation, pronunciation.
2. With reference to the mode of pronunciation of a letter, syllable, word, or language. Also *attrib.*
3. The giving of an authoritative opinion or decision, judgement, announcement.

Pronouncing, *ppl. a.* [-ING 2.] That pronounces ; expressing a pronouncement.

Pronta·to (prǫntaɪ·to), *adv.* [It.] *Mus.*

Pronuba (prǫu·niubă). *Rom. Antiq.* [L. *prōnuba* a woman who attended a bride, f. *prō-* (found in *prōnubus*) to arrange a marriage, f. Pro- 1 + stem of *nūb-ĕre* to marry.] A woman presiding over or assisting in the ceremonies and offices of marriage.

Pronunciamento (prǫnʌnsiəme·nto), *lit.* a pronouncement, espr. a proclamation, manifesto; often applied to one issued by insurrectionists, esp. in Spanish-speaking countries.

Pronuncial. [f. L. *prōnuntiāl-is* f. *prōnuntium*: see Pronunciation.] Of or pertaining to pronunciation.

Pronunciate (prǫnʌ·nsiit), *ppl. a. Obs. rare.* [ad. L. *prōnuntiāt-us*, pa. pple. of *prōnuntiāre* to Pronounce.]

Pronunciate (prǫnʌ·nsieit), *v. Obs. rare.* [f. ppl. stem of L. *prōnuntiāre* to Pronounce.] *trans.* To pronounce, declare.

Pronunciation (prǫnʌnsiːeɪ·ʃən). Also 6–8 -noun, 7 -non-. [f. OF. *pronuntia-tion*, ad. L. *prōnuntiātiōn-em*, n. of action f. *prōnuntiāre* to Pronounce.]
1. The pronouncing or uttering of a word; the mode in which a word is pronounced.
2. Oratorical utterance; delivery; spec. elegant or eloquent delivery. *Obs.*
+ 3. The action of pronouncing authoritatively or ordaining; promulgation; a pronouncement. *Obs.*
4. Illustration of Forms.

‖ Pronunciato, *f.* [see Pronounced.]

Pronunce, var. of Pronounce.

Pronze, etc.: see Prone, Pronominate, etc.

PROOF.

Proof (prūf), *sb.* Forms: *a.* preve, preve, prief, *etc.* see below. [ME. *preove*, *proeve*, *preve*, from OF. *pruève*, *preuve* (11th c. in Littré), earlier *prueve*, *prove* (12th c. in Littré) are assimilated to the vowel of F. *prouver*, Eng. Prove.]

I. That which makes good or proves a statement; evidence sufficient (or contributing) to establish a fact or produce belief in the certainty of something.
† 1. To make proof : to put to the test, to try.
2. The action or an act of testing or making trial of anything, or the condition of being tried; test, trial, experiment ; examination, probation ; essay.
3. The action of testing or making trial of anything, or the condition of being tried ; test, trial, examination, probation ; essay.
4. *a.* First or trial print taken from a plate ; also used as equivalent to Print (*sb.* 13). *Obs.*
b. *Photog.* A first or trial print taken from a plate; also used as equivalent to Print (*sb.* 13).
5. *Mech.* The proof were the blog's whale that he has in his gate armours make him hardy ...
6. The testing of cannon and fire-arms by firing a heavy charge, or by hydraulic pressure.
7. *a.* A surgeon's probe. *Obs. rare.*
b. A test-tube. (*b*) An apparatus for testing the strength of gunpowder.
8. The standard of strength of distilled alcoholic liquors (or of vinegar) ; now, the strength of a mixture of alcohol and water having a specific gravity of 0·9183, and containing 0·495 of its weight, or 0·5727 of its volume, of absolute alcohol.
9. *Typog.* A trial or preliminary impression taken from composed type, in which typographical errors may be corrected, and alterations and additions made.
10. Armour of tried or proved quality.
11. The standard of strength of distilled alcoholic liquors ...
12. *Typog.* A trial or preliminary impression ...
13. *Engraving.* Originally, An impression taken by the engraver from an engraved plate, stone, or block, to examine its state during the progress of his work ...
14. A coin or medal struck as a test of the die (*obs.*); also, one of a limited number of early impressions of coins struck as specimens.
15. *Sir A. Barton in Surtees Misc.* (1888) 77 Then he put on the armere of proof.
16. *Typog.* A definite number of ems placed in the composing-stick as a pattern of the length of the line. *Obs.*
17. *Bookbinding.* The rough uncut edges of the shorter or narrower leaves of a book, left in trimming to show that it has not been cut down.
18. *attrib.* and *Comb.* **a.** General Combs., in senses 1–4, as *proof-needle, -object, -paper, -passage, -plate, -reading, -sheet, -stone*; proof-*reading*, etc. as *proof-armed, -proof*, etc.; objective, as *proof-reader*; instrumental, as *proof-corrected*; locative, as *proof-house, -master, -mortar* (Mortar *sb.*), *-sleigh* ... **b.** Special Combs.: *proof-arm* n., connect-rod ; *proof-charge*; *proof-house*, *-master*; *proof-leaf* = Proof-sheet; *proof-mark*; *proof-plane*; *proof-spirit*; *proof-staff*.

† Proful, *a. Obs. rare.* [f. Proof *sb.* + -ful.]

Proof-spirit. ...

Proof-sheet ...

Proofy (prū·fi), a., dial. ...

Pro-ostracum ...

Pro-otic (prō·ǫtik, -ōtik), a. and sb. ...

Prop (prǫp), sb.[1] ...

b. In Coal-mining ...

Prop, sb.[2] Also 6 proppe. ...

Pro-pepsin ...

Pro-os-aeon ...

Prop (prǫp), sb.[3] [= MDu. proppe, Du. prop ...

Prop, sb.[4] U.S. ...

Prop, sb.[5] Short for PROPOSITION.

Prop (prǫp), v.[1] Also 6 proppe. ...

b. ...

2. ...

Prop, v.[2] Also 6 proppe. [Known from 13th c.; app. directly f. PROP sb.[2] ...

Propædeutic (proupīdiū·tik), a. and sb. ...

B. adj. ...

Propædeutical a. = PROPÆDEUTIC a. ...

Propagable (prǫ·pagab'l) a. ...

Propagand (prǫpagæ·nd). ...

Propaganda (prǫpagæ·nda). [a. It. (Sp., Fg.) propaganda = propagandē, from propaganda fide 'congregation for propagating the faith': see sense 1.] ...

Propagandism (prǫpagæ·ndiz'm). ...

Propagandist (prǫpagæ·ndist), sb. (a.) ...

Propagandistic a. ...

Propagandize (prǫpagæ·ndiz), v. ...

Propagate (prǫ·pageit), v. ...

Propagation (prǫpagēi·ʃən). ...

Propagational, a. rare. ...

Propagative (prǫ·pageitiv), a. ...

Propagator (prǫ·pageitǫɹ). ...

Propagatory, a. ...

Propagatress, a. ...

Propage, v. obs. rare. ...

Propagule (prǫ·pagiūl). ...

Propagulum, -la. rare. ...

Propale, v. ...

Propalinal, a. ...

Propane (prǫu·pein). Chem. ...

Propaparental ...

Proparasceve (prǫupærasī·v), rare. ...

Proparent ...

Pro-parergal ...

Propargyl (prǫupā·ɹdʒil). Chem. ...

Proparoxytone (prǫupærǫ·ksitoun) a. and sb. ...

Propassion ...

Propata ...

Propathy, obs. rare. ...

Propatagium ...

propepsi, pl. propedes = PRO-LEG. ...

Propel (prǫpe·l), v. ...

Propellent (prǫpe·lənt), a. and sb. ...

Propeller (prǫpe·lǫɹ). ...

Propelling, vbl. sb. and ppl. a. ...

Propend, v. Obs. ...

Propendency. Obs. rare. ...

Propense (prǫpe·ns), a. ...

Propensed, ppl. a. Obs. ...

Propensely (prǫpe·nsli), adv. Now rare. ...

+2. Premeditatedly, intentionally: = **Prepense**-ly. (See **Prepense** *a. 2.*) *Obs.*

Propenseness (prope·nsnes). Now *rare.* [f. as prec. + -ness.] The quality of being propense.

1. Proneness, inclination, propensity; favourable disposition; liability.

Propension (prope·nʃən). Now *rare.* [= F. *propension* (1595 in Godef. *Compl.*), ad. L. *prōpensiōn-em* inclination, propensity, n. of action f. *prōpendēre*: see **Propend**.]

1. The action, fact, or quality of 'propending' or inclining to something; inclination, 'leaning', propensity. = **Propensity** 1.

b. favourable inclination: = **Propensity** 1 b.

c. Liability, tendency: = **Propensity** 1 c.

+2. Tendency to move in some direction or to take some position; inclination, as of the scale of a balance. (Cf. **Propensity** 2.) *Obs.*

Hence +Propensioner *Obs.*, one who or that which has or causes a propension to something.

+Propensitude, *a.* [See prec. + -tude.] **Propensity.** *Obs.—¹*

Propensity (prope·nsĭti). [f. L. *prōpens*-, ppl. stem of *prōpendēre* (see **Propend**) + -ITY.]

1. The quality or character of being 'propense' or inclined to something; inclination, disposition, tendency, bent. Const. *to, towards* (rarely *for, of*) with *sb.*, or *to* with *inf.*; a disposition or inclination to some action, course of action, habit, etc.; bent of mind or nature.

b. A disposition to favour, benefit, or associate oneself with some person, party, etc.; favourable inclination, good will.

†Propensive, *a.* [f. as prec. + -ive.] Mental inclination, liking. Is **Propensity**. Mental inclination, liking. *b.* psychical inclination, leaning.

Propensity (prope·nsĭti). [f. as prec. + -ITY.] so ll. prˑpensitā (Veitch.)

1. The quality or character of being 'propense' or inclined to something; inclination, disposition, tendency, bent. Const. *to, towards* (rarely *for, of*) with *sb.*, or *to* with *inf.*

[Dense multi-column dictionary text continues across the columns for the entries **Propenseness, Propension, Propensity, Propensive, Propense, Propenyl, Propenoic, Propone, Proper, Properdine, Properistoma, Properisispome, Properly, Properate, Properation, Properchant, Properhede, Property, Prophesier** *et al. The detailed etymological and citation content is not legibly reproducible at this resolution.]*

Properness. Now *rare.* [f. as prec. + -ness.] The quality of being proper.

1. The fact of belonging specially to something; special quality or character; peculiarity.

2. Excellence, goodness; esp. of appearance; goodliness, handsomeness, elegance, comeliness.

3. Fitness, suitableness; becomingness, propriety, that which is 'proper'.

†Propertary, Propertary. [f. **Property** *sb.* + -ARY.] cf. **Proprietary** (to which **propertary** was in early use conformed): the forms of **Property**.] = **Proprietary** *a.* 1, *b.* A.

Propertied (prope·rtid), *ppl. a.* [f. **Property** *sb.* + -ED².]
1. Having a specified property; quality, faculty, or disposition.

Property (prope·rti). Forms: see below. [ME. *proprete*, a. OF. *proprete, -eit, propriete.*]

1. The condition of being owned by or belonging to some person or persons (cf. **Proper** *a.* 1); hence, the fact of owning a thing; the holding of something as one's own; the right (esp. the exclusive right) to the possession, use, or disposal of anything (usually of a tangible material thing); ownership, proprietorship. = **Proprietary** 1.

Prophesier. [f. **Prophesy** *v.* + -ER¹.] One who prophesies; a prophet, seer.

1. The action, function, or faculty of a prophet; divinely inspired utterance or discourse; *spec.* in Christian theology, utterance flowing from the revelation and impulse of the Holy Spirit.

†Prophecy-monger. [f. prec. + **Monger**.] One who deals in, repeats, or occupies himself with prophecies.

Prophesiable, *a.* In ? -cyable. [f. **Prophesy** *v.* + -able.] Capable of being prophesied.

Prophesie, obs. form of **Prophecy, Prophesy.**

Prophesier (prˑfîˈsāˌə). Also 5-7 -cier, 8 -syer. [f. next + -ER¹.] One who or that which prophesies; *esp.* one who preaches; *a.* a prophet; a prognosticator.

Prophesy (prɔ·fĕsəi), v. Forms: 4-5 profecy, 5 -ecie; 5-6 prophecie, -esien, 5-6 -ecie, 5-7 -esie, -ecy, 5- prophesy. [ME. a. OF. prophecier (14 c.) :- late L. *prophetare, -ciare, -cier, f. prophecie, -ecie Prophecy. The modern differentiation of prophesy and prophecy sb. was not established till after 1700, and has no etymological basis, prophesy being at first a mere spelling variant in both sb. and vb. For the pronunciation of the final vowel, cf. verbs in -fy, also multiply.]

Prophesying (prɔ·fĕsəi·iŋ), vbl. sb. [f. prec. + -ING[1].] The action of the verb PROPHESY; speaking by divine inspiration; foretelling the future; expounding divine mysteries or preaching unto edification, as practised in apostolic times.

Prophet (prɔ·fĕt), sb. Forms: 4-5 profete, 3 -fiete, 4-5 -fet, 4-5 -fett, 5 -fett, 4-5 prophete, 4- prophete (6-prophit, 6 G.-phelite). [ME. prophete, fete, a. F. prophète (11th c. in Littré), ad. L. prophēta (prophētēs), ad. Gr. προφήτης an interpreter, proclaimer, spokesman, expounder, one who speaks for another, a prophet; f. πρό forth, before, for + φητης speaker, f. φά- to speak.]

Prophethood (prɔ·fĕthud). [f. PROPHET sb. + -HOOD.] The position or office of a prophet.

Prophetic (prŏfe·tik), a. (sb.) [a. F. prophétique (15th c. in Hatz.-Darm.), or ad. late L. prophēticus, a. Gr. προφητικός :- see PROPHET sb. and -IC.]

Prophetically (prŏfe·tikăli), adv. [f. prec. + -LY[2].]

Propheticism (-fe·tisi·zm). [f. as prec. + -ISM.]

Propheticly (prŏfe·tikli), adv. Obs. rare. [f. as prec. + -LY[2].]

Prophetism (prɔ·fĕtizm). [f. PROPHET sb. + -ISM.]

Prophetize (prɔ·fĕtəiz), v. [a. F. prophétiser, or ad. med.L.]

Prophetizing, vbl. sb.

Prophetless, a. Without a prophet or inspired teacher.

†Prophetly, a. Obs. rare. [f. as prec. + -LY[1].] Prophet-like, befitting a prophet.

Prophetocracy. [f. PROPHET + -CRACY.] Government by a prophet.

Prophet-ship. [f. as prec. + -SHIP.] The office or function of a prophet.

Prophet's-flower, prophet-flower.

Prophetship (prɔ·fĕtʃip). [f. PROPHET sb. + -SHIP.] The office or function of a prophet.

Prophoric (prŏfɔ·rik), a. rare. [ad. Gr. προφορικός, f. προφορά utterance, f. προφέρειν to bring forth.] Characterized by utterance, enunciation, or emission.

Prophragm (prɔ·frăm). [prophragma.]

Prophylactic (prŏfilæ·ktik), a. and sb. [ad. Gr. προφυλακτικός, f. προφυλάσσειν to keep guard before : see PRO- and PHYLACTIC. So F. prophylactique (16th c. in Hatz.-Darm.).]

Prophylaxis (prŏfilæ·ksis). [mod.L., f. Gr. προ- + φύλαξις a watching, guarding, after PROPHYLACTIC.] Med. The preventive treatment of disease.

Propine (prŏpəi·n), v. Obs. exc. Sc. and dial. [ad. L. propīnāre to drink to one's health, pledge; to give to drink, administer, furnish, ad. Gr. προπίνειν.]

Propination (prŏpinē·ʃən). [ad. L. propīnātiōn-em a drinking to one's health, n. of action f. propīnāre to PROPINE.]

Propinquate (prŏpi·ŋkwēt), v. Obs. rare. [f. L. propinquāt-, ppl. stem of propinquāre to approach, draw near.]

Propinque (prŏpiŋ·k), a. rare. [ad. L. propinqu-us near, neighbouring, derivative of prope near; cf. longinque-us distant, from longe far.] Near in space, neighbouring, at hand.

Propinquitous, a. rare-.

Propinquity (prŏpi·ŋkwĭti). [ME. propinquite, a. OF. propinquité (14th c. in Godef.), ad. L. propinquitāt-em nearness, proximity, relationship, f. propinqu-us: see PROPINQUE and -ITY.]

†Propinquous, a. rare-1. [f. L. propinqu-us near + -OUS.] Near, neighbouring, proximate.

Propio-, propion-, Chem., a formative derived from PROPIONIC, entering into the names of compounds related to propionic acid. The chief are:

Propionic (prŏpiŏ·nik), a. Chem. [ad. F. propionique, f. propion + -IC.]

Propionate (prɔ·piŏnēt). [f. as prec. + -ATE.]

Propitiable (prŏpi·ʃiăb'l), a. [ad. L. propitiābilis, f. propitiāre: see PROPITIATE and -ABLE.]

Propitiate (prŏpi·ʃiēt), v. [f. L. propitiāt-, ppl. stem of propitiāre to render propitious or favourably inclined; to appease, conciliate.]

Propitiation (prŏpiʃiē·ʃən). [a. F. propitiation (12th c. in Littré) or ad. late L. propitiātiōn-em, n. of action from propitiāre to PROPITIATE.]

Propitiator (prŏpi·ʃiētǝɹ). [a. late L. propitiātor, agent-n. from propitiāre to PROPITIATE.]

Propitiatorily (prŏpi·ʃiătǝrili), adv. [f. next + -LY[2].] In a propitiatory manner; by way of propitiation.

Propitiatory (prŏpi·ʃiătǝri), a. and sb. [ad. late L. propitiātōri-us (a 200 in Vulg.), f. propitiāt-: see PROPITIATE and -ORY.]

Propitious (prepɪˈʃəs), a. Forms: 5 propycyous, 5-7 -piti(o)us, 6- propitious. [Late ME. a. OF. *propicius*, -*eux* (a 1140 in Godef.), f. L. *propitius*: see PROPICE: see -OUS.]

1. Disposed to be favourable; well-disposed, favourably inclined; gracious.

Proplex, -exus: see PRO- 2 2.

† **Proplexity.** *Obs.* [For *perplexity*, by confusion with *pro-*.] Perplexity.

Propolis (ˈprɒpəlɪs). [L. (Plin.), a. Gr. πρόπολις.] The substance with which bees stop up the holes in their hives.

Proponation. Improperly **proponium.**

Proport, -port. *Obs.* *rare*⁻¹. [Short for *proportion.*] = PROPORTION *sb.* 4.

Proport, v. *Sc. Obs.* [a. OF. *proporter* (1118 in Godef.), variant of *porporter* to PURPORT.]

Proportion (prəˈpɔːʃən), *sb.* [ME. *proporcioun*, a. F. *proportion* (13th c. in Littré), ad. L. *proportion-em* proportion, comparative relation, analogy, symmetry, agreement, harmony.]

Proportionability. 1479 **PROPORTIONATE.** **PROPORTIONATE.** 1480 **PROPOSE.**

Propose (prəˈpəʊz), v. [a. F. *proposer* (12th c. in Littré), f. *pro-*, PRO- 1 + *poser* to POSE, substituted for L. *propōn-ĕre* (cf. F. COMPOSE, etc.)]

Proposable (prəˈpəʊzəbl), a. [PROPOSE v. + -ABLE.] Capable of being or fit to be proposed.

Proposal (prəˈpəʊzəl). [f. PROPOSE v. + -AL.]

Proposer. [f. PROPOSE v. + -ER 1.]

Proposition (prǫpǫzi·ʃǫn). [ME. *proposicioun*, a F. *proposition*, ad. L. *propositiōn-em* a setting forth, purpose, theme, statement...]

Proposer (prǫpōu·zǝɹ). [f. PROPOSE v. + -ER¹.]

Proposing (prǫpōu·ziŋ), vbl. sb. [f. as prec. + -ING¹.]

Propositional (prǫpǫzi·ʃǫnǎl), a. [f. prec. + -AL.]

Propositionize, v. rare.

Pro-positantical, a.

Propound (prǫpau·nd), v. [A later form of PROPONE, through the intermediate *propoune*, *propowne*: cf. COMPOUND, EXPOUND.]

Propound (prǫpau·nd), sb.

Propounder (prǫpau·ndǝɹ). [f. prec. + -ER².]

Propoundment. rare.

Propoundness. rare.

Pro-priling, sb.

Propping, vbl. sb. [f. PROP v. + -ING¹.]

Pro-pronounced.

Propraetor (prǫprī·tǝɹ), sb. Also PRO-PRAETOR.

Propraetorial, a. [f. prec. after PRAE-TORIAL.]

So Propraetorian a., in same sense.

Propre, obs. form of PROPER a. and v.

Proprefect, praefect (prōu·prī·fekt). [f. PRO-¹ + PREFECT.]

Proprefecture. [f. as prec. from PREFECTURE.]

Proprete, -tie, etc. obs. forms of PROPERTY.

†Propriatary, Obs. rare⁻¹. [f. L. *propriāt-*, ppl. stem of *propriāre* to make one's own, f. *proprius* PROPER.]

†Propriate, a.

†Propriate, v.

†Propriation. Obs. rare⁻¹.

Propriety (prǫprǝi·ti). [ad. L. *propriētāt-em* property.]

Propriethead. rare⁻¹.

Proprietor (prǫprǝi·ǝtǝɹ). [irreg. f. *propriet*(or or *propriet*(y) + -AGE.]

Proprietarian (prǫprǝi·ǝtēǝ·riǎn), sb. (a.)

Proprietarious, a. Obs. rare⁻¹.

Proprietary (prǫprǝi·ǝtǎri), sb. late L. *proprietāri-us* (Paulus) proprietary, in med L. also sb. a proprietor...

†Proprietor. Obs. rare⁻¹.

Proprietor (prǫprǝi·ǝtǝɹ). [ad. med.L. *proprietor*, agent-n. f. *proprietāre*.]

Proprietorial (prǫprǝi·ǝtō·riǎl), a. [f. prec. + -AL; cf. *dictatorial*, *senatorial*, etc.]

Proprietorship (prǫprǝi·ǝtǝɹʃip).

†Proprietory, sb. and a. [erron. var. f. PRO-PRIETARY, going with the anomalous PROPRIETOR.]

Proprietress (prǫprǝi·ǝtres). [f. PROPRIETOR + -ESS.]

Proprietrix. [L. fem. of PROPRIETOR.]

Pro-proctor (prōu·prǫ·ktǝɹ). [f. PRO-¹ + PROCTOR.]

† Propugnation. Obs. [ad. L. prŏpugnātiōn-em, n. of action f. prŏpugnāre: see PROPUGN.] Defence, protection, vindication.

Propugnator. [ad. L. prŏpugnātor.] A defender, champion.

† Propugn, v. [ad. L. prŏpugnāre.] One who champions; a defender, champion.

† Propugnatory, a. rare. [f. L. prŏpugnāt- ...] ...

† Propulsation. Obs. [ad. L. prŏpulsātiōn-em, n. of action f. prŏpulsāre: see PROPULSE.] So obs. **Propulsation** (Cotgr.)

Propulse, v. [ad. L. prŏpulsāre, frequent. of prŏpellĕre to PROPEL.] Defence, or repelling.

Propulsion. [ad. L. prŏpulsiōn-em.] The action of driving forth or away; impulse.

Propulsive, a. [f. L. type *prŏpulsīv-us, f. prŏpuls-: see PROPULSE.] Impelling, propelling.

Propulsory, a. rare. [f. as PROPULSIVE.] Propulsive quality; propulsion.

Propulsive, v. rare. [f. L. prŏpuls-.] Propulsive quality; propulsion.

Propylite (prō̆·pĭləit), a. (sb.). [f. Gr. πρόπυλον a gate: see PROPYLON.] The action of driving or pushing forward or onward.

Propylitic. Having the quality of propelling, or the tendency to propel, that drives or urges forward or onward.

Propylon (prō̆·pĭlǫn). Pl. -pylons or in Gr. form -pyla (-pĭla.) ...

Prow (prou). [a. F. proue, ad. L. prōra.] 1. The prow of a ship: see PRORE.

Prorate, v. Chiefly U.S. [f. pro rata.]

Prorite, v. Obs. rare.

Prorogate, v. [ad. L. prorogāt-.]

Prorogation (prŏrogē·ʃən). [a. F. prorogation.]

Prorogue (prōrōu·g), v. [a. F. proroger.]

Prosaism (prō̆·zēĭz'm). [ad. F. prosaïsme.]

Prosaic (prozē·ĭk), a. [ad. med.L. prosaicus.]

Prosaical, a. [f. prec. + -AL.]

Prosaically, adv. [f. prec. + -LY.]

Prosaicalness.

Prosaicism (prozē·ĭsiz'm). [f. PROSAIC a. -ISM.]

Prosaicness.

Prosand (prō̆·sǎnd), adv. Obs. rare.

Prosapia, Obs. rare.

Prosar Obs. ...

Prosateur.

Prose (prōuz), sb. (a.). [a. F. prose, ad. L. prōsa.]

Prosaist (prō̆·zēist). [f. as prec. + -IST.]

Proscholium, Obs. rare. [med.L. proscholium, f. Gr. πρό, PRO- + schola.]

Proscind, v. Obs. rare. [ad. L. prōscindĕre.]

Proscribe (prŏskrǒi·b), v. [ad. L. prōscrībĕre.]

Proscript, sb. and a. rare. [ad. L. prōscript-us.]

Proscription (prŏskri·pʃən). [ad. L. prōscrīptiōn-em.]

Proscriptive (prŏskri·ptiv), a. [f. L. prōscript-.]

Proscriptively, adv. [f. prec. + -LY.]

Proscriptiveness.

Prose (prōuz), sb. (a.). [a. F. prose, ad. L. prōsa.] A piece of prose, as opp. to a poem; a composition in prose; a prose exercise.

[Oxford English Dictionary — this page comprises closely-set dictionary columns. Principal entries reading across the columns:]

Prose (continued): 6. Comb., as prose-inditing sb. and adj., prose-like adj.; † prose-master, a master of prose, one who excels in prose composition; prose-poem, a prose work having the style or character of a poem; so prose-poes, prose-poetry; † prose-printer, a printer of prose (in quot.); † prose author); prose-writer, one who writes or composes prose, an author who writes in prose; so prose-writing.

Prose (prōz), v. †1. trans. To turn into or write in prose; to translate or turn into prose.

Prosect (prosĕ·kt), v. rare. [Formed (after next) on L. prōsect-, ppl. stem of prōsecāre to cut away or off, cut up, f. PRO-1 + secāre to cut.] To dissect (a dead body, or part of one) in preparation for anatomical demonstration.

Prosection (prosĕ·kʃən), dissection for purposes of anatomical demonstration; the function of a prosector.

Prosector (prosĕ·ktər). [a. late L. prōsector.]

Prosecutable (prɒ·sĕkiūtăbl), a. [f. PROSECUTE v. + -ABLE.] That may be prosecuted; liable to prosecution.

Prosecute (prɒ·sĕkiūt), v. Also 6 prose-qwuit, -quit, 6-7 -quite; 7 pa. pple. (L.) prosecute. [f. L. prōsecūt-, ppl. stem of prōsequī to follow.] 1. trans. To follow up, pursue; to persevere in, follow out, go on with (some action, undertaking, or purpose) with a view to completing or attaining it.

Prosecution (prɒsĕkiū·ʃən). Also 6 prosecucion. [a. F. prosecution (1549 in Godef.).] The action of prosecuting.

Prosecutive, a. Obs. rare. Also 7 -quu-tive. [f. prosecute.] Proceeding still in the prosecution of rythmous speech.

Prosecutor (prɒ·sĕkiūtər). [a. med.L. prōsecūtor, agent-n. f. prōsequī to PROSECUTE.] 1. One who follows up or carries out any action, project, or business.

Prosecutrix (prɒ·sĕkiūtriks). Pl. -trices. [L. n. med., prōsecūtrix, fem. agent-n. f. as prec.+-TRIX.] A female prosecutrix.

Proselenic (prosĕlī·nik), a. Obs. rare. [f. Gr. σελήνη moon + -IC.] Existing before the moon.

Proselyte (prɒ·sĕlait), sb. Also 4-7 proselite, -lyt, -lite. [a. F. proselyte (13th c. in Littré).]

Proselytical, a. Obs. rare. Of or pertaining to proselytes or proselytism.

Proselytism (prɒ·sĕlaitiz'm). [a. F. proselytisme (1721 in Hatz.-Darm.).] 1. The act of becoming or being a proselyte; the state or condition of a proselyte.

Proselytist (prɒ·sĕlaitist). [f. as prec.+-IST.] One who proselytizes; a proselytizer.

Proselytize (prɒ·sĕlaitaiz), v. [f. as prec.+-IZE.] 1. intr. To make proselytes.

Proselytizer (prɒ·sĕlaitaizər). 1. One who proselytizes; one who makes or endeavours to make proselytes.

Proseman (prōz·măn). [f. PROSE sb. + MAN sb.] A man who writes prose, a prose author.

Proseminary (prosĕ·minări). [f. PRO-2 1 + SEMINARY sb. So L. proseminarium.] A preparatory seminary or school.

Proser (prōz·ər). 1. A writer of prose; = PROSAIST 1.

Prosify, v. rare. [f. PROSE sb.+-FY.] 1. trans. To turn into prose; to make prosaic.

Prosily (prō·zili), adv. 1. Chiefly humorous. Also prosely. [f. late L. prōsa or PROSE sb.+-LY1.] 1. In a prosy or dull manner; tediously.

Prosiness (prō·zinĕs). [f. PROSY + -NESS.] The quality of being prosy; dullness and tediousness of writing or speech.

Prosing (prō·ziŋ), vbl. sb. [f. PROSE v. + -ING1.] 1. Prose-writing, prose composition.

Prosenchyma (prosĕ·ŋkimă). [mod.f. Gr. πρός to + ἔγχυμα, f. ἐγχεῖν to pour in.] Bot. Tissue consisting of elongated cells closely placed with their ends interpenetrating.

Prosilient (prosi·liĕnt), a. rare. [ad. L. prōsilient-, pres. pple. of prōsilīre to leap forth.] Leaping forth; fig. outstanding, prominent.

Prosimian (prosi·miăn), a. and sb. Zool. [mod.f. prōsimiae, generic name (Brisson 1756), f. PRO-2 1 + simia ape.] a. adj. Belonging to the Prosimiæ.

Prosiphonal (prosi·fonăl), a. Zool. [f. PRO-2 + SIPHON + -AL.] Of a chambered shell: Having the siphonal funnel directed forward, as in the Prosiphonata, a primary group of chambered cephalopods now extinct.

Prosiphonate (prosi·fonet), a. Zool. [f. as prec.+-ATE2.] Having the siphon directed forwards, as in the Prosiphonata.

Prosish (prō·ziʃ), a. Of the nature of prose, prosaic.

Prosit (prō·sit), int. [L., 'may it be useful'.] A toast: Good luck! good health!

Prosocele (prō·sosīl), Anat. [mod.L., f. Gr. πρόσω forward + κοίλη cavity.]

Proso- before a vowel pros-, combining form of Gr. πρόσω forward.

Prosobranch (prō·sobraŋk), a. and sb. Zool.

Prosocoele (prō·sosīl), Anat. Also prosocele.

Prosodemic, a. [f. Gr. δῆμος people.]

Prosodetic, a. Zool.

Prosodial (prosō·diăl), a. [f. PROSODY + -AL.] Of or pertaining to prosody; prosodic.

Prosodiacal (prosodai·ăkăl), a. [f. as prec.]

Prosodian (prosō·diăn). [f. as prec.] A prosodist.

Prosodical (prosō·dikăl), a. [f. PROSODIC + -AL.] Of or pertaining to prosody.

Prosodist (prɒ·sodist). [f. PROSODY + -IST.] One skilled or learned in prosody.

Prosody (prɒ·sodi). [ad. L. prosōdia, a. Gr. προσῳδία.] The science of versification.

Prosoma (prosō·mă). Zool. Also in anglicized form prosome. [mod.L., f. Gr. πρό before + σῶμα body.]

Prosonomasia (prosonomē·siă). Rhet. [mod.L., a. Gr. προσονομασία.] An incorrect opening or channel in a sponge.

‖ **Prosopalgia** (prɒsopæ·ldʒiă). *Path.* [mod.L., f. Gr. πρόσωπ-ον a face (f. πρός to + ὤψ, ὠπ- eye, face) + ἄλγος pain. Cf. F. *prosopalgie.*] Facial neuralgia; face-ache.

1831 SOUTH *Otto's Pathol. Anat.* 454 It is not surprising that..prosopalgia, ischias nervosa, &c. should be considered as arising from inflammation of the medullary part and sheaths of the nerves. 1862 *New Syd. Soc. Year-bk. Med. & Surg.* 150 Case of Prosopalgia from a cranial tumour. 1876 tr. *von Ziemssen's Cycl. Med.* XI. 200 Prosopalgia is one of the forms of neuralgia..most frequently met with.

Hence **Prosopalgic** (-æ·ldʒik) *a.*, pertaining to or affected with prosopalgia.

1890 in *Cent. Dict.* 1895 in *Syd. Soc. Lex.*

Prosopial (prɒsōᵘ·piăl), *a. Ornith.* [f. PROSOPI-UM + -AL.] Belonging to the prosopium.

1895 MIVART in *Proc. Zool. Soc.* 369 On either side a large aperture, the two forming the posterior prosopial nares.

‖ **Prosopis** (prɒsōᵘ·pis). [In sense 1, late L. *prosōpis*, a. Gr. προσωπίς (an unidentified plant), applied as generic name (Linnæus 1767); in sense 2, mod.L. generic name (Fabricius 1804).]

1. *Bot.* A tropical and subtropical genus of leguminous trees and shrubs, of the suborder *Mimoseæ*, often prickly or thorny, bearing spicate green or yellow flowers, and usually fleshy pods. *Prosopis juliflora* is the mesquit or honey-locust.

1851 MAYNE REID *Scalp Hunt.* xxxii, Peering cautiously through the leaves of the prosopis.

2. *Zool.* A genus of solitary bees of the family *Andrenidæ*.

1887 JEFFERIES *Field & Hedgerow* (1889) 205, I think there were four species of wild bee at these early flowers, including the great bombus and the small prosopis with orange-yellow band. 1901 LD. AVEBURY in *Daily Chron.* 25 May 3/1 On the evolution of the hive bee from the less highly organised Prosopis—which has a short, simple tongue, no brushes or baskets on the legs, and leads a solitary life.

Prosopite (prɒsōᵘ·pait). *Min.* [ad. G. *prosopit* (Th. Scheerer 1853), f. Gr. πρόσωπον face, mask: see -ITE[1].] A hydrous fluoride of aluminium and calcium, occurring in colourless, white, or greyish crystals.

1854 DANA *Min.* 502 Prosopite..occurs at the tin mines of Altenberg. 1899 *Amer. Jrnl. Sc.* Ser. IV. VII. 53 If the assumptions made in the foregoing are justified, the Utah mineral is prosopite.

‖ **Prosopium** (prɒsōᵘ·piŏm). *Ornith.* Pl. **-ia.** [mod.L. (Mivart 1895), ad. Gr. προσωπεῖον a mask, f. πρόσωπον face.] Term for the whole of the bones and ossifications in front of the cranio-facial articulation in parrots.

1895 MIVART in *Proc. Zool. Soc.* 365 The Bony Beak or Prosopium. [*Note*] By this term I intend to denote the whole ossified mass in front of the cranio-facial articulation and the articulations of the zygomata and palatines. It includes the premaxilla, the maxillæ, maxillo-palatine processes, the nasals, and the ethmoidal and turbinal ossifications of the beak. *Ibid.* 369 The greater extension ventrad of the apex of the prosopium.

Proso-poetical (prōᵘzopo,e·tikăl), *a. rare.* [f. *proso-*, assumed comb. form of L. *prōsa* PROSE (see -O) + POETICAL.] Properly 'of the nature of prose poetry'; but in quots. app. taken in the sense 'of the nature of metrical prose or prosaic verse'.

1858 C. A. COLE *Mem. Hen. V*, p. xliii, The present Metrical, or rather Proso-poetical, History. 1895 *Month* June 230 Thomas of Elmham—in his..proso-poetical History of Henry V.

† **Prosopo·graphy.** *Obs.* [f. Gr. πρόσωπον face, person: see -GRAPHY. Cf. F. *prosopographie.*] A description of the person or personal appearance.

1577 tr. *Bullinger's Decades* (1592) 613 Prosopographie is a picturing or representing of bodily lineaments. 1577–87 HOLINSHED *Chron.* (1807) II. 110 Thus farre of the acts and deeds of Stephan: now..touching the prosopographie or description of his person. 1654 Z. COKE *Logick* 212. 1813 *Monthly Mag.* XXXVI. 330 An historic character, says a German professor, should consist of two parts, the *prosopography*, or description of the person, and the *ethopea*, or description of the mind and manners.

Prosopolepsy (prɒsōᵘpo,le·psi, -lī·psi). ? *Obs.* [ad. Gr. προσωποληψία (a Hebraism of the N.T.) acceptance of the face or person, f. προσωπολήπτης an acceptor of the face or person, f. πρόσωπον face + λαμβάνειν to take, accept.] Acceptance or 'acception' of the face or person of any one (see ACCEPTION 2, PERSON 13); respect of persons, undue favour shown to a particular person; partiality.

1646 BUCK *Rich. III* Ded., The Historiographer, veritable; free from all Prosopolepsyes, or partiall respects. 1678 CUDWORTH *Intell. Syst.* I. iv. § 36. 567 The Assumption of it was neither Fortuitous nor Partial, or with Prosopolepsie (the Acception of Persons) but bestowed upon it justly for the Merit of its Vertues. 1849 E. B. EASTWICK *Dry Leaves* 116 The English rule is a model of justice. There is no prosopolepsy in it; no respect of persons. All men are equal, and have equal rights.

Hence † **Prosopole·psian** *Obs.*, one given to 'prosopolepsy'; a 'respecter of persons'.

1647 J. HEYDON *Discov. Fairfax* 11 God's no Prosopolepsian, he respects the poore as well as the rich.

Prosopologist (prɒsopɒ·lŏdʒist). *nonce-wd.* [f. Gr. πρόσωπον face + -LOGIST.] One who studies or treats of the face. So **Prosopo·logy** (*rare*⁻⁰), the scientific study of the face, physiognomy.

1820 *Blackw. Mag.* VI. 651 As this author limits his observations to the face, we propose to term him, and all such, prosopologists, discoursers on the face. 1858 MAYNE *Expos. Lex.*, *Prosopologia*, term for a dissertation on the countenance: prosopology.

† **Proso·popey.** *Obs.* Also -eie, -eye. [ad. L. *prosōpopœia*: see next, and cf. F. *prosopopée* (16th c. in Littré).] = next.

1577 tr. *Bullinger's Decades* (1592) 613 Prosopopeie is wher those are brought in to speake that do not speake. 1605 *Answ. Supposed Discov. Rom. Doctr.*, etc. 2 He warreth..against poetically or childishlie feigned Prosopopeis, and Chimeres of his owne creation. *a* 1641 BP. MOUNTAGU *Acts & Mon.* (1642) 89 The Prophet himselfe..speaks by Prosopopey concerning them. *a* 1693 *Urquhart's Rabelais* III. Prol., Who with their very countenance..express their consent to the Prosopopeie.

‖ **Prosopopœia** (prɒsōᵘpopī·ă). Also 6 -oiia, 6–9 -eia, (*erron.* 6–8 -cea, 7 -oia). [L. (Quintil.), a. Gr. προσωποποιία personification, representation in human form or with human attributes, f. πρόσωπον face, person + ποιεῖν to make.]

1. A rhetorical figure by which an imaginary or absent person is represented as speaking or acting; the introduction of a pretended speaker.

1561 DAUS tr. *Bullinger on Apoc.* (1573) 91 We vnderstand these things to be spoken by a figure called Prosopopeia: that is, by the fayning of a person. 1581 SIDNEY *Apol. Poetrie* (Arb.) 24 His notable Prosopopeias, when he maketh you as it were, see God comming in his Maiestie. 1609 R. BARNARD *Faithf. Sheph.* 67 Prosopopeia; the feigning of a person: when wee bring in dead men speaking, or our selues doe take their person vpon vs, or giue voice vnto senselesse things. 1787 GREGORY tr. *Lowth's Lect.* (1816) I. xiii. 280 Prosopopœia, or Personification. Of this figure there are two kinds: one, when action and character are attributed to fictitious, irrational, or even inanimate objects; the other, when a probable but fictitious speech is assigned to a real character. 1877 MORLEY *Crit. Misc.* Ser. II. 153 This is his one public literary Equivocation..it was resorted to..to give additional weight by means of a harmless prosopopoeia to an argument for the noblest of principles.

2. A rhetorical figure by which an inanimate or abstract thing is represented as a person, or with personal characteristics: = PERSONIFICATION 1. (Formerly included in prec. sense: see quots. 1609, 1787 there.)

1578 TIMME *Calvine on Gen.* 142 Clemency and gentleness..is attributed thereto, by a figure called Prosopopoiia. 1649 ROBERTS *Clavis Bibl.* 276 The universall triumph and gladnesse as it were of all creatures (in an elegant Prosopopeia) is intimated. 1732 BERKELEY *Alciphr.* v. § 22 Sentiments, and vices, which by a marvellous prosopopœia he converts into so many ladies. 1884 A. LAMBERT in *19th Cent.* June 947 Prosopopœia has no place even in popular science.

b. *transf.* Applied to a person or thing in which some quality or abstraction is as it were embodied; an impersonation, embodiment (*of* something).

1826 DISRAELI *Viv. Grey* I. x, Don't start..and look the very Prosopopeia of Political Economy! 1867 MACFARREN *Harmony* iv. (1876) 152 Everywhere at once..the prosopopœia of ubiquity.

Hence **Prosopopœ·ial, Prosopopœ·ic, -ical** *adjs.*, pertaining to, of the nature of, or involving prosopopœia.

1577 tr. *Bullinger's Decades* (1592) 622 To this place now doo belong the *Prosopopeiall speeches of God. 1652 URQUHART *Jewel* Wks. (1834) 292, I could have used..apostrophal and prosopopœial diversions. 1883 COTTERILL *Does Science Aid Faith?* (1886) 57 A poetic and *prosopopœic representation of the attribute of Divine wisdom. 1576 FLEMING *Panopl. Epist.* 192 He hath a *Prosopopoical speach to his countrie.

Prosopulmonate (prɒsopʊ·lmŏnĕt), *a. Zool.* [f. Gr. πρόσω forward + PULMONATE.] Pulmonate in front: applied to those pulmonate or air-breathing gastropod molluscs which have the pulmonary sac in front (opp. to *opisthopulmonate* (see OPISTHO-); cf. PROSOBRANCHIATE).

1877 HUXLEY *Anat. Inv. Anim.* viii. 514 The animal is thus more or less prosopulmonate.

Prosopyle (prɒ·sopoil). *Zool.* [f. Gr. πρόσω forward + πύλη a gate.] A small aperture by which an endodermal chamber in a sponge communicates with the exterior. Hence **Prosopylar** (prɒsɒ·pilăɹ) *a.*, pertaining to, having, or constituting a prosopyle.

1887 SOLLAS in *Encycl. Brit.* XXII. 413/2 (*Sponges*) To avoid ambiguity we shall for the future distinguish [this] kind of opening as a prosopyle. 1888 — in *Challenger Rep.* XXV. p. xiv, The recesses, known as flagellated chambers, communicate with the cavity of the sac (*paragaster*) each by a single wide mouth (*apopyle*), and with the exterior by a small pore (*prosopyle*). 1890 *Cent. Dict.*, *Prosopylar.*

Prospect (prɒ·spekt), *sb.* [ad. L. *prōspect-us* a look out, view, f. *prōspic-ĕre* to look forward, f. *prō*, PRO-[1] + *specĕre* to look. Cf. F. *prospect* (16th c. in Littré).]

I. 1. The action or fact of looking forth or out, or of seeing to a distance; the condition (of a building, or station of any kind) of facing or being so situated as to have its front in a specified direction; outlook, aspect, exposure. *Obs.* passing into 2.

1432–50 tr. *Higden* (Rolls) I. 147 The water of Cilicia, which hathe prospecte ageyne the yle of Cipresse [L. *sinum qui prospicit contra insulam Cyprum*]. *Ibid.* II. 11 Briteyne is..sette as vn to the prospecte of Speyne [*ad prospectum Hispaniæ sita est*]. 1560 BIBLE (Genev.) *Ezek.* xl. 44 Without the inner gate were the chambers of the singers in the inwarde courte..and their prospect was towarde the South. 1601 HOLLAND *Pliny* I. 119 [Armenia] confineth vpon the Medians, and hath a prospect to the Caspian sea. 1691 RAY *Creation* II. (1692) 4 This [erect] Figure is most convenient for Prospect, and looking about one. 1845 STOCQUELER *Handbk. Brit. India* (1854) 265 The atmosphere tolerably clear,..and the prospect, for the most part, clear and open: this is the autumn, if autumn there be at Dorjeling.

† **b.** A place which affords an open and extensive view; a look-out. *Obs.*

c 1586 C'TESS PEMBROKE *Ps.* CII. xi, From the prospect of thy heav'nly hall Thy eye of earth survey did take. 1611 CORYAT *Crudities* 164 People may from that place as from a most delectable prospect contemplate and view the parts of the City round about them. 1667 MILTON *P. L.* III. 77 Him God beholding from his prospect high,..Thus..spake. 1885 BIBLE (R. V.) *1 Kings* vii. 4 And there were prospects [1611 windowes] in three rows, and light was over against light in three ranks.

2. An extensive or commanding sight or view; the view of the landscape afforded by any position.

1538 ELYOT, *Prospectus*..a syght farre of, a prospecte. 1594 NORDEN *Spec. Brit. Pars* (Camden) 23 A..howse of pleasure vpon the topp of a mount..: it is seene farr of, and hath most large and pleasant perspecte [*sic*]. 1613 PURCHAS *Pilgrimage* (1614) 436 The streets are strait, yeelding prospect from one gate to another. 1634 SIR T. HERBERT *Trav.* 216 [St. Helena] giues a large prospect into the Ocean. 1657–83 EVELYN *Hist. Relig.* (1850) I. 28 Take we next a prospect of the earth's surface, and behold from the lofty mountains how the humble valleys are clothed with verdure. 1778 M. CUTLER in *Life*, etc. (1888) I. 68, I had a fine prospect of the whole army as it moved off. 1818 MISS MITFORD in L'Estrange *Life* (1870) II. ii. 23 There is but one place in all Berkshire which has a really fine commanding prospect. 1853 PHILLIPS *Rivers Yorksh.* iv. 128 A most striking prospect over sea and land. 1860 TYNDALL *Glac.* I. vii. 49 The prospect was exceedingly fine.

b. *In (within)* or *into prospect*: in or into a position making it possible to see or to be seen; within the range or scope of vision; in or into sight or view; within view. Also *fig. arch.*

1555 EDEN *Decades* 13 Within the prospecte of the begynnynge of Cuba, he founde a commodious hauen. 1599 SHAKS. *Much Ado* IV. i. 231 Euery louely Organ of her life, Shall come..Into the eye and prospect of his soule. 1605 [see 8]. 1664 BUTLER *Hud.* II. iii. 486 The Knight..Was now in prospect of the Mansion. 1685 BAXTER *Paraphr. N. T.* Matt. iv. 8 By all Kingdoms is meant, many that were within prospect. 1738 GRAY *Tasso* 5 Nor yet in prospect rose the distant shore. 1800–24 CAMPBELL *Dream* iv, Yon phantom's aspect..would appal thee worse, Held in clearly measured prospect.

3. That which is looked at or seen from any place or point of view; a spectacle, a scene; the visible scene or landscape.

a 1633 AUSTIN *Medit.* (1635) 278 What a prospect is a well-furnish'd Table? 1662 J. DAVIES tr. *Mandelslo's Trav.* 58 The windows of all the houses..were beset with Lamps, before which were placed Vessels of Glass fill'd with waters of several colours, which made a very delightful prospect. 1693 *Humours Town* 3, I had rather look up to see the welcome prospect of your House. 1711 SWIFT *Jrnl. to Stella* 25 Aug., He is ravished with Kent, which was his first prospect when he landed. 1727–46 THOMSON *Summer* 1438 Heavens! what a goodly prospect spreads around, Of hills, and dales, and woods, and lawns, and spires. 1763 JOHNSON in *Boswell* 6 July, But, Sir, let me tell you, the noblest prospect which a Scotchman ever sees, is the high road that leads him to England. 1798 WORDSW. *Peter Bell* I. xvi, On a fair prospect some have looked. 1859 DICKENS *Lett., to Mrs. Watson* 31 May, A snug room looking over a Kentish prospect.

‖ **b.** A vista; a long, wide, straight street; an avenue of houses. (Russian, esp. used of the great avenues of St. Petersburg; e.g. *Nevsky Prospekt.*)

† **4.** The appearance presented by anything; aspect. *Obs. rare.*

1604 SHAKS. *Oth.* III. iii. 398 It were a tedious difficulty, I thinke, To bring them to that Prospect. 1709 MRS. E. SINGER *Love & Friendship* 36 in *Prior's Poems*, On the Plain when she no more appears, The Plain a dark and gloomy Prospect wears. 1715 LEONI *Palladio's Archit.* (1742) II. 8 By Prospect is understood the first show or appearance that a Temple makes to such as approach it... Those which have their Porticos only in front, may be said to have the Prospect *Prostylos*.

† **5.** A pictorial representation of a scene or the like; a view, a picture, a sketch. *Obs.*

1649 EVELYN *Diary* 20 June, I went to Putney and other places on the Thames to take prospects in crayon to carry with me into France, where I thought to have them engrav'd. 1695 E. BERNARD *Voy. fr. Aleppo to Tadmor* in *Misc. Cur.* (1708) III. 119 We have since procured a Curious Prospect of these Noble Ruins, taken on the Place. 1708 J. CHAMBERLAYNE *St. Gt. Brit.* II. III. x. (1737) 435 The Prospects of it [the Bass], as represented in Slezer's Theatrum Scotiæ, will sufficiently shew the Difficulty of Access to it. 1762–71 H. WALPOLE *Vertue's Anecd. Paint.* (1786) II. 180 His works are mentioned in the royal catalogue, particularly prospects of his majesty's houses in Scotland.

II. † **6.** A mental view or survey; a look, inspection, examination; also, an account or description. *Obs.*

1625 BACON *Ess., Truth* (Arb.) 501 'To see the Errours..in the vale below': So alwaies, that this prospect, be with Pitty. *a* 1648 LD. HERBERT *Hen. VIII* (1683) 10 Our King being thus setled in his Throne, took several prospects upon all his neighbouring Princes. 1677 *Govt. Venice* 266 Let us now take a Prospect of their Governours, I mean, consider the Manners and Maxims of their Nobility. *a* 1718 PENN *Tracts* Wks. 1726 I. 248, I take a Serious Prospect of the Spiritual Nature and Tendency of the Second Covenant. 1764 GOLDSM. (*title*) The Traveller; or, a Prospect of Society.

7. A scene presented to the mental vision, esp. of something future or expected; a mental vista.

1641 DENHAM *Sophy* v. i, Man to himselfe Is a large prospect. 1672 GREW *Anat. Plants, Idea Philos. Hist.* § 63 How far soever we go, yet the surmounting of one difficulty is wont still to give us the prospect of another. 1736 BUTLER *Anal.* I. Concl., Wks. 1874 I. 144 All expectation of immortality..opens an unbounded prospect to our hopes and our fears. 1785 T. BALGUY *Disc.* 26 True knowledge will perpetually mortify us with the prospect of our own weakness and ignorance. 1879 *Cassell's Techn. Educ.* IV. 95/1 The torch which illuminated the path of the youth, and opened new prospects to his eager views.

8. A mental looking forward; consideration or knowledge of, or regard to something future.

1605 SHAKS. *Macb.* I. iii. 74 To be King Stands not within the prospect of beleefe. 1662 EVELYN *Chalcogr.* 102 Not..without Prospect had to the benefit of such as will be glad of instruction. *a* 1703 BURKITT *On N. T.* John xix. 22 The providence of God hath a prospect beyond the understanding of all creatures. 1779–81 JOHNSON *L. P., Dryden* Wks. II. 400 His prospect of the advancement which it [navigation] shall receive from the Royal Society. 1862 STANLEY *Jew. Ch.* (1877) I. viii. 157 It was a Pisgah, not of prospect, but of retrospect.

b. *esp.* Expectation, or reason to look for something to come; that which one has to look forward to. Often *pl.*

1665 MANLEY *Grotius' Low C. Warres* 281 For the future, nothing remained, but a prospect of Tyranny and slavery. 1667 MARVELL *Corr.* Wks. (Grosart) II. 223 If anything be particularly in your prospects,..you will do well to give us timely advice. *c* 1775 JOHNSON *Lett., to Mrs. Thrale* (1788) I. 259 Our gay prospects have..ended in melancholy retrospects. 1849 MACAULAY *Hist. Eng.* v. I. 535 The prospect which lay before Monmouth was not a bright one. 1860 TYNDALL *Glac.* I. xxiii. 165 Seeing no prospect of fine weather, I descended to Saas. 1881 FROUDE *Short Stud.* (1883) IV. II. iii. 196 He was careless about his personal prospects.

c. *In prospect*: within the range of expectation; expected, or to be expected: now chiefly of something personally advantageous.

1779 BURKE *Corr.* (1844) II. 286 Every thing in prospect appears to me so very gloomy. 1833 HT. MARTINEAU *Manch. Strike* iv. 55 Allen longed to..forget all that had been done, and all that was in prospect. *Mod.* He has nothing in prospect at present.

III. † **9.** Short for *prospect-glass*: see 11. *Obs.*

1639 R. BAILLIE *Lett., to W. Spang* 28 Sept., The King himself beholding us through a prospect, conjectured us to be about 16 or 18,000 men. 1685 BURNET *Lett.* iii. (1686) 169, I looked at this Statue..through a little prospect that I carried with me. 1743 HUME *Ess., Rise Arts & Sc.* (1817) I. 106 A man may as reasonably pretend to cure himself of love, by viewing his mistress through the artificial medium of a microscope or prospect.

IV. 10. *Mining.* **a.** A spot giving prospects of the presence of a mineral deposit.

1839 MARRYAT *Diary Amer.* Ser. I. II. 129 Finders, who would search all over the country for what they called a good prospect, that is, every appearance on the surface of a good vein of metal. 1882 *Rep. to Ho. Repr. Prec. Met. U. S.* 180 There are also a number of prospects being opened up in the vicinity. 1895 in *Daily News* 11 July 5/4 This demand [in California] is more for developed properties than for mere 'prospects' which may or may not become mines.

b. An examination or test of the mineral richness of a locality or of the material from which the ore, etc. is extracted.

1855 *Melbourne Argus* 10 Jan. 4/6 The result of a few prospects that have been made at a spot..has been very satisfactory.

c. A sample of ore or 'dirt' for testing; also, the resulting yield of ore.

1879 ATCHERLEY *Boërland* 115 The thrill of pleasure..with which the digger contemplates his first good 'prospect' in the pan. There they are—some bright and yellow, others inky black, little rounded nuggets of every shape. 1890 'R. BOLDREWOOD' *Miner's Right* (1899) 33/1 When the first 'prospect', the first pan of alluvial gold-drift, was sent up to be tested, we stopped work and joined the anxious crowd, who pressed around. 1891 *Melbourne Age* 2 Sept. 5/3 The average prospect will not exceed from 2 to 6 oz. per dish.

V. 11. *attrib.* and *Comb.*, as (from 1 b) *prospect ground, tower*; (from 10) *prospect hole, operation, pan, shaft, work*; **prospect-glass**, a 'prospective glass', telescope, field-glass.

1617 *Fight at Sea* A iij, Who in a *prospect glasse perceiued them to bee the Turkes Men of Warre. 1871 CARLYLE in *Mrs. Carlyle's Lett.* (1883) I. 257 Susan..had from her windows, with a prospect-glass, singled me out on the..deck of the steamer. 1848 BUCKLEY *Iliad* 406 They rushed by the *prospect-ground and the wind-waving fig-tree. 1877 RAYMOND *Statist. Mines & Mining* 303 Most of these are as yet mere *prospect-holes, and can boast of but little rich ore. 1880 SUTHERLAND *Tales of Goldfields* 12 He stood up with the dripping *prospect-pan in his hand. 1877 RAYMOND *Statist. Mines & Mining* 56 As determined by the *prospect-shafts, the channel falls toward his end on a steep grade. 1900 *Daily News* 25 Sept. 5/1 The Lord of the Manor determined to restore it to its original purpose of a *prospect-tower. 1882 *Rep. to Ho. Repr. Prec. Met. U. S.* 290 *Prospect work is all that has thus far been done.

† **Pro·spect**, *ppl. a. Obs. rare*⁻¹. [ad. L. *prōspect-us*, pa. pple. of *prōspic-ĕre*: see prec.] Open to view, clearly visible.

a 1619 FLETCHER, etc. *Q. Corinth* III. i, I wear a Christall casement 'fore my heart...Let it be prospect unto all the world.

Prospect (see below), *v.* [In branch I, ad. L. *prōspect-āre*, frequent. of *prōspic-ĕre*: see above; in branch II, a new formation from PROSPECT *sb.* IV.]

I. (pro,spe·kt).

† **1.** *intr.* To look forth or out; to front or face; to afford a prospect in some direction. *Obs.*

1555 EDEN *Decades* 79 It prospecteth towarde that parte of Aphrike. 1598 SYLVESTER *Du Bartas* II. i. IV. *Handie-Crafts* 206 Sixteen fair Trees.. Whose equall front in quadran form prospected As if of purpose Nature them erected. 1613 PURCHAS *Pilgrimage* (1614) 437 Their houses are low..and prospect into the streets.

† **2.** *trans.* Of a person: To look out upon or towards; to look at, view, see at a distance. Of a building or the like: To front, face; to lie or be situated towards; to command a view of. *Obs.*

1555 EDEN *Decades* 140 The highest towre of his palaice, from whense they myght prospecte the mayne sea. 1578 BANISTER *Hist. Man* I. 20 Openyng the window of light, on the clearer side, prospecting the Sunne. 1579 FENTON *Guicciard.* (1618) 223 He cast a mine on that side which prospects Pizifalcona. 1677 [see PROSPECTING *vbl. sb.* 1]. 1698 FRYER *Acc. E. India & P.* 150 The College of the Carmelites is on an high Mount, prospecting the whole City.

† **3.** *trans.* To foresee, look for, expect; to anticipate. *Obs. rare.*

1652 GAULE *Magastrom.* 152 How many accidents fall out fatally, that can have no second cause ordinatly assigned to them, much less prospected in them. 1671 FLAVEL *Fount. Life* xviii. Wks. 1731 II. 52/1 The infinite Wisdom, prospecting all this, ordered that Christ should first be deeply humbled.

II. *Mining*, etc. (prɒ·spekt). Originally *U.S.*

4. *intr.* To explore a region *for* gold or other minerals.

1848 [see PROSPECTING *ppl. a.* 2]. 1850 B. TAYLOR *Eldorado* ix. (1862) 88 Dr. Gillette came down..with a companion, to 'prospect' for gold among the ravines in the neighborhood. 1872 BESANT & RICE *Ready Money Mortiboy* iii, 'Went prospecting to Mexico'—'What's prospecting, Dick?' 'Looking for silver'. 1885 MRS. C. PRAED *Head Station* (new ed.) 64 I've sent my mate to prospect for a new claim. 1898 MORRIS *Austral Eng.*, *Prospect v.*, to search for gold. In the word, and in all its derivatives, the accent is thrown back on to the first syllable.

b. *fig.* To search about, look out *for* something.

1867 E. NASON in *N. Eng. Hist. & Gen. Reg.* XXI. 5 Mr. Webster..finding himself almost pennyless,..came to Boston, 'prospecting' for employment. 1870 LOWELL *Study Wind.* I. 7, I hope she was prospecting with a view to settlement in our garden. 1872 R. B. MARCY *Border Rem.* 145 A professional mesmerist..'prospecting' for subjects to exercise his powers upon after a lecture. 1884 *N. Eng. Hist. & Gen. Reg.* XXXVIII. 340, I have prospected in the records, from the middle of the sixteenth to the middle of the seventeenth centuries.

5. *trans.* **a.** To explore or examine (a region) for gold or other minerals. **b.** To work (a mine or lode) experimentally so as to test its richness.

1858 *N. York Tribune* 20 Sept. 7/2 [He] left Cherry Creek, near Pike's Peak, on the 27th of July, having satisfactorily 'prospected' a rich gold region. 1865 VISCT. MILTON & CHEADLE *N. W. Passage* xii. (1901) 222 The three miners..discovering that they were close to the Athabasca, had turned back to prospect the sources of the McLeod. 1877 RAYMOND *Statist. Mines & Mining* 162 A shaft is being sunk to prospect the ground.

c. *fig.* To survey as to prospects.

1864 D. A. WELLS *Our Burden & Strength* 10 Let us now cautiously prospect the resources of the future. 1867 F. FRANCIS *Angling* vii. (1880) 264 Prospect the place, look for an open space. 1892 *Daily News* 12 Apr. 5/5 In prospecting the new year, he saw grounds for caution, but none for alarm.

6. *intr.* Of a mine, reef, or ore: To give (good or bad) indications of future returns; to 'promise' (well or ill). Also, to turn out, prove (rich or poor) on actual trial.

1868 F. WHYMPER *Trav. Alaska* xxv. 282 If a speculation promises well, they may answer, 'It prospects well'. 1877 RAYMOND *Statist. Mines & Mining* 60 The dirt on the bed-rock is very rich, having prospected from $5 to $10 to the pan. 1897 *Daily News* 3 Nov. 9/5 This stone is very rich in places, and some of it prospects fully 20 ounces to the ton.

Prospecting, *vbl. sb.* [f. prec. + -ING[1].] The action of the verb PROSPECT.

† **I. 1.** (pro,spe·ktiŋ) Viewing, seeing. *Obs.*

1677 GILPIN *Demonol.* (1867) 416 The expression..intimates that the way which Satan took was different from common prospecting or beholding.

II. *Mining* (prɒ·spektiŋ).

2. Surveying as to prospects; exploring or examining for minerals; the experimental working of a mine or reef.

1857 J. D. BORTHWICK 3 *Years California* vi. 124 We abandoned it [our claim], and went 'prospecting'. 1872 RAYMOND *Statist. Mines & Mining* 283 Little real mining has been carried on, while much prospecting has taken place. 1887 R. MURRAY *Geol. & Phys. Geog. Victoria* 157 Tracts..which,..in spite of careful prospecting, failed to yield gold.

b. *attrib.* Used, made, or done in prospecting, as *prospecting drill, mill, shaft, work*; **prospecting claim**, the first claim, marked out by the discoverer of the deposit.

1877 RAYMOND *Statist. Mines & Mining* 37 Prospecting-drills will be used..to make a thorough exam nation of the best-appearing veins on the whole estate. 1880 *Daily Tel.* 3 Dec., Hundreds of men..began to sink what are called 'prospecting shafts', and a vast amount of low grade mineral was brought to bank. 1890 'R. BOLDREWOOD' *Miner's Right* v, This..would be but half the size of the premier or prospecting claim. *fig.* 1891 *Athenæum* 23 May 662/2 Nothing could well look less promising..than the first appearances which..greeted Dr. Atkinson on his prospecting visit to Danby.

Prospecting, *ppl. a.* [f. as prec. + -ING[2].]

† **1.** That looks forward or foresees; provident.

1681 FLAVEL *Meth. Grace* Ep. to Rdr. 14 Man being a prudent and prospecting creature, hath the advantage of all other creatures in his foreseeing faculty.

2. *Mining* (prɒ·spektiŋ). That prospects or searches for indications of gold, etc.

1848 *N. York Lit. World* 3 June (Bartlett), Two or three men with a bucket, a rope, a pick-axe, and a portable windlass...This..is a prospecting party. 1882 H. LANSDELL *Through Siberia* I. 213 There must be a prospecting party made up.

Prospection (pro,spe·kʃən). Now *rare*. [n. of action f. L. *prōspic-ĕre*: see PROSPECT *sb.*]

1. The action of looking forward; anticipation; consideration of or regard to the future; foresight.

1668 H. MORE *Div. Dial.* I. ix. (1713) 18 A Principle that has a Prospection for the best, that rules all. 1668 HOWE *Bless. Righteous* (1825) 185 This is great wisdom in prospection; in taking care of the future. 1802 PALEY *Nat. Theol.* xviii. (1819) 282 That the prospection, which must be somewhere, is not in the animal, but in the Creator. 1832 CARLYLE in *Misc. Ess.* (1872) III. 238 Such retrospections and prospections bring to mind an absurd rumour.

b. A seeing or beholding, a view.

1897 in *Chicago Advance* 29 July 135/2 The higher sense gives prospection of a spiritual King and a spiritual Canaan.

2. The action of prospecting for gold or the like: see PROSPECT *v.* II.

1908 *Westm. Gaz.* 31 Mar. 11/3 The directors authorised ..the prospection of the swampy land..with a view to ascertaining the possibility of working this.

Prospective (pro,spe·ktiv), *a.* and *sb.* [As adj. ad. obs. F. *prospectif, -ive*, or med.L. *prōspectīv-us* belonging to or affording a prospect, f. L. *prōspect-*, ppl. stem of *prōspic-ĕre*: see PROSPECT *sb.* and -IVE. As sb. a. obs. F. *prospective* (1553 in Godef.) a view, prospect; but in senses 1 and 2 short for *prospective glass*. Sometimes corresponding to the earlier PERSPECTIVE, q. v.]

A. *adj.* **1.** Characterized by looking forward into the future; also, † having foresight or care for the future; provident (*obs.*).

c 1590 GREENE *Fr. Bacon* xiii. 12 By prospective skill I find this day shall fall out ominous. 1658 A. FOX tr. *Würtz' Surg.* II. xiv. 100 Be moderate, prospective, and cautious in stitching, and not too hasty. 1690 CHILD *Disc. Trade* Pref. (1694) C vj b, The French King and King of Sweden are..circumspect, industrious and prospective too in this Affair. 1850 L. HUNT *Autobiog.* II. ix. 7 He was a retrospective rather than a prospective man.

† **2.** Used or suitable for looking forward or viewing at a distance (*lit.* and *fig.*). *Prospective stone*: cf. PROSPECTIVE GLASS 1. *Obs.*

1603 H. CROSSE *Vertues Commw.* (1878) 128 That olde Witch Lamea, who as the Poets frame, had broade prospectiue eyes to pull out and in at pleasure. *a* 1635 NAUNTON *Fragm. Reg.* (Arb.) 60 It seemes nature..to pleasure him the more, borrowed of Argus, so to give unto him a prospective sight. 1652 ASHMOLE *Theat. Chem. Brit.* Prol. 8 By the Magicall or Prospective Stone it is possible to discover any Person in what part of the World soever.

† **3.** Fitted to afford a fine prospect or extensive view. Hence *fig.* Elevated, high, lofty. *Obs.*

1588 GREENE *Metamorphosis* Wks. (Grosart) IX. 88 Desirous to heare what the meaning of this monument seated so prospectiue to Neptune, should be. 1632 LITHGOW *Trav.* IV. 139 Being situate on moderate prospectiue heights. *Ibid.* IX. 416 A pleasant and prospectiue Countrey. *a* 1814 *Apostate* III. iii. in *New Brit. Theatre* III. 328 It ..cannot be, that one so great, So lofty and prospective in his virtue, Should fall to such perdition. *a* 1817 T. DWIGHT *Trav. New Eng.*, etc. (1821) II. 106 Above this plain, after ascending a moderate acclivity, lies another; both of them handsome grounds, and the latter finely prospective.

4. That looks or has regard to the future; operative with regard to the future.

1800 *Proc. E. Ind. Ho.* in *Asiat. Ann. Reg.* 112/1 The usages and customs of this country have authorised a certain species of oaths, which he would denominate prospective oaths, as they generally are so. 1802 PALEY *Nat. Theol.* xiv. § 2 (ed. 2) 275 It is not very easy to conceive a more evidently prospective contrivance, than that which, in all viviparous animals, is found in the milk of the female parent. 1828 MACAULAY *Ess., Hallam* (1887) 58 A prospective law, however severe,..would have been mercy itself compared with this odious act. 1868 M. PATTISON *Academ. Org.* v. 188 The fellowship should convey a prospective obligation to the prosecution of the studies intended to be promoted by the endowment. 1884 SIR J. PEARSON in *Law Rep.* 27 Chanc. Div. 354 The language of the 26th section is entirely prospective and not retrospective.

5. That looks forward or is looked forward to; that is in prospect; expected, hoped for; future.

1829 SOUTHEY *Sir T. More* (1831) I. 372 No measure which indicates prospective policy was taken. 1853 C. BRONTE *Villette* xii, All the pupils above fourteen knew of some prospective bridegroom. 1863 FAWCETT *Pol. Econ.* II. iii. 150 Not only a large prospective but even a large immediate profit would be returned. 1884 *Truth* 13 Mar. 376/2 A silly lordling and prospective peer.

B. *sb.* Formerly (prɒ·spektiv).

† **1.** A magic mirror: = PROSPECTIVE GLASS 1. Also *fig. Obs.*

[*a* 1430 *Chaucer's Sqr.'s T.* 226: see PERSPECTIVE *sb.* 2.]

1595 DANIEL *Delia* xxii, This heart made now the prospectiue of care. 1596 FITZ-GEFFRAY *Sir F. Drake* (1881) 76 Highe throne, wherein all vertues made their seate, True prospective of immortalitie. 1604 DANIEL *Vis. 12 Goddesses* Ded., And withal delivers her a Prospective, wherein she might behold the Figures of their Deities, and thereby describe them. 1625 BACON *Ess., Seeming Wise* (Arb.) 215 It is a Ridiculous Thing..to see what shifts these Formalists haue, and what Prospectiues, to make Superficies to seeme Body, that hath Depth and Bulke. 1626 — *Sylva* § 98 Such Superficiall Speculations they have; Like Prospectives, that shew things inward, when they are but Paintings.

† **2.** A field-glass, spy-glass, or telescope; *pl.* spectacles; = PROSPECTIVE GLASS 2. Also *fig. Obs.*

1630 J. TAYLOR (Water P.) *Fennor's Defence* Wks. II. 149/2, I haue look't ouer with my best Prospectiues, And view'd the tenor of thy base Inuectiues. *a* 1635 CORBET *Poems* 91 Lastly of fingers, glasses we contrive, And every fist is made a prospective. 1657 W. MORICE *Coena quasi Κοινὴ* ii. 35 Turning the wrong end of the Prospective, to make things at hand seem to be farr off. 1674 *Depos. Cast. York* (Surtees) 233 To follow his calling..of pollishing glasses for prospectives and specktacles and mycroscopes. 1727 A. HAMILTON *New Acc. E. Ind.* I. i. 14 Those on board the Ship, saw, by their Prospectives, what was acted Ashore.

3. The action of looking out (*lit.* or *fig.*); cf. PROSPECT *sb.* 1. † *At prospective*: on the look-out (*obs.*). *In prospective*: in view (*lit.* or *fig.*); in prospect or anticipation. Now *rare*.

1599 B. JONSON *Cynthia's Rev.* II. Wks. (Rtldg.) 79/1 A quarter past eleven, and ne'er a nymph in prospective. 1616 J. LANE *Cont. Sqr.'s T.* XI. 19 But lo, as Canac stoode at prospective, Her glasse discried from farr a troopes arive. 1746–7 HERVEY *Medit.* (1818) 217 Now the day is gone, how short it appears! When my fond eye beheld it in prospective, it seemed a very considerable space. 1866 MRS. H. WOOD *St. Martin's Eve* ix, Four thousand a year now, and six in prospective!

† **4.** A scene, a view: = PROSPECT *sb.* 3. *Obs.*

1599 PORTER *Angry Wom. Abingd.* in Hazl. *Dodsley* VII. 269 As prospectives, the nearer that they be, Yield better judgment to the judging eye. *a* 1639 WOTTON *Life Dk. Buckhm.* in *Reliq.* (1651) 93 The whole Scene of affairs was changed from Spain to France; there now lay the prospective. 1745 P. THOMAS *Jrnl. Anson's Voy.* 188 When the Canal runs in a strait Line, as they usually do, it makes a Prospective at once stately and agreeable.

† **5.** A pictorial view; *fig.* a description: cf. PROSPECT *sb.* 5, 6. *Obs. rare.*

1658 T. HIGGONS tr. *Busenello* (title), A Prospective of the Naval Triumph of the Venetians over the Turk. 1660 (*title*) A Landskip: or a Brief Prospective of English Episcopacy, Drawn by three skilfull hands in Parliament: Anno 1641.

† **6.** A place for viewing, a look-out: = PROSPECT *sb.* 1 b. *Obs. rare*⁻¹.

1616 R. C. *Times' Whistle*, etc. 145 Be ther placd A prospective vpon the top o' th' mast, Wherein 'tis fitt that carefull diligence Keep evermore his watchfull residence.

† **b.** A point of view. *Obs.*

1603 DANIEL *Def. Rhyme* H iv, Men, standing according to the prospectiue of their owne humour, seeme to see the selfe same things to appeare otherwise to them, than either they doe to other, or are indeede in themselues.

† **7.** The art of drawing in perspective: = PERSPECTIVE *sb.* 3; also, a perspective view. *Obs.*

1601 B. JONSON *Poetaster* III. i, I studie architecture too.. I'd haue a house iust of that prospectiue. 1620–55 I. JONES *Stone-Heng* (1725) 42 The whole Work in Prospective, as when entire. *Ibid.*, The Ruin yet remaining drawn in Prospective. 1662 GERBIER *Princ.* (1665) 5 An Exact Architect must have the Art of Drawing, and Prospective. 1684 *Contempl. St. Man* I. ii. (1699) 22 Those who work in Prospective, will so paint a Room, that the Light entring only through some little Hole, you shall perceive beautiful and perfect Figures and Shapes.

b. *Her.* (See quot.) Also *Comb.* **prospective-wise**, in perspective.

c 1828 BERRY *Encycl. Herald.* I. Gloss., *Perspective*, or *Prospective*, is used, in blazon, to express divisional lines forming a kind of pavement with diminishing squares in perspective, as *paly barry*, or *barry bendy, in perspective*, or *prospective wise*.

† **Prospe·ctive glass.** *Obs.*

1. A magic glass or crystal, in which it was supposed that distant or future events could be seen. Also called *glass prospective*. Also *fig.*

a 1584 *Tom Thumbe* 298 in Hazl. *E. P. P.* II. 190 This cunning doctor tooke A fine prospective glasse, with which he did in secret looke Into his sickened body downe. *c* 1590 GREENE *Fr. Bacon* v. 110 In a glasse prospectiue I will shew Whats done this day in merry Fresingfield. 1609 ROWLEY *Search for Money* (Percy Soc.) 26 If every conjurer had such a prospective glasse of his owne, they would never deale so much with the Divell as they doe. 1628 MILTON *Vacation Exerc.* 71 A Sybil old..That..in Times long and dark Prospective Glass Fore-saw what future dayes should bring to pass.

2. A spy-glass, field-glass, telescope. Also *pl.* spectacles, binocular glasses. Cf. PERSPECTIVE *a.* 2.

1626 CAPT. SMITH *Accid. Yng. Seamen* 33 The Gunners scale is made in brasse at Tower Hill, with prospectiue glasses. 1672 *Phil. Trans.* VII. 5063 He likewise shew'd his Highness a little Prospective Glass, made according to Mr. Newtons new Invention. 1696 tr. *Du Mont's Voy. Levant* xiii. 168 He frequently observ'd what was done in the City from his Seraglio, by the help of some excellent Prospective-Glasses. 1738 NEAL *Hist. Purit.* IV. 22 Discovering by prospective glasses that they were coming down to attack him.

fig. 1634 WITHER *Emblemes, Medit. on Pict.*, A glimpes farre off, through Faith's prospective glasse. 1641 MILTON *Animadv.* Wks. 1851 III. 191 These free-spoken, and plaine harted men that are the eyes of their Country, and the prospective glasses of their Prince. 1678 DONNE *Olimpia* 150 And with the Prospective Glasses of their Ambition daily surveyed all Italy.

Prospe·ctively, *adv.* [f. PROSPECTIVE + -LY[2].] In a prospective manner.

1. With outlook upon or consideration of the future, with foresight; also, in anticipation or expectation of something to come.

1828 *Blackw. Mag.* XXIII. 418 Prospectively maintaining the same harmony between the existing powers of the tree, and the exigencies of its new situation. 1868 M. PATTISON *Academ. Org.* iv. 103 An annual outlay..is applied—prospectively as scholarship, or retrospectively as fellowship.

2. With bearing upon or application to the future.

1863 H. COX *Instit.* I Rules which..prospectively declare the rights and obligations which the State will enforce. 1885 *Law Times Rep.* LII. 168/2 The Judicature Act 1875.. cannot..apply prospectively to the Bankruptcy Act of 1883.

† **3.** = PERSPECTIVELY *adv.* 3 (for which in quot. it may be an error; but cf. PROSPECTIVE *sb.* 7).

1557 RECORDE *Whetst.* H j, These nombers can not be expressed aptly in flatte, but prospectiuely, as Dice maie be made in protracture.

Prospe·ctiveness. [f. as prec. + -NESS.] The quality or character of being prospective.

1817 COLERIDGE *Biog. Lit.* xviii. (1882) 172 There is a want of that prospectiveness of mind, that surview, which enables a man to foresee the whole of what he is to convey. 1824 T. E. HOOK *Sayings & Doings* III. 343 The symptomatic prospectiveness of the disease.

Prospectless (prɒ·spektlės), *a.* [See -LESS.]

1. Having no prospect or outlook.

1656 S. H. *Gold. Law* 103 Wert thou hous'd in some dark or Prospectless ground room. 1770 H. WALPOLE *Let. to G. Montagu* 11 June, A palace as dismal and prospectless as if it stood 'on Stanmore's wintry wild'!

2. Without prospects for the future.

1878 FLOR. MONTGOMERY *Seaforth* III. i, Your boys..were born as penniless and as prospectless as mine. 1889 MRS. OLIPHANT *Poor Gentleman* II. ii. 27 A penniless, prospectless young man.

Prospector (prɒspe·ktəɹ, prɒ·spektəɹ). Also -er. [a. late L. *prōspector* one who looks out, foresees, or provides, agent-n. f. *prōspic-ĕre*: see PROSPECT *sb.*] One who prospects; in quots., one who explores a region for gold or the like: see PROSPECT *v.* 4, 5.

1857 J. D. BORTHWICK 3 *Years California* vi. 124 A 'prospecter' goes out with pick and shovel, and a wash-pan; and..digs down till he reaches the dirt in which it may be expected that the gold will be found. 1862 *Times* 8 Apr., Mr. Disraeli may be a good prospecter, and he may make the best of his 'claim', but the result is nil. 1884 *Ibid.* 18 Apr. 8 All the trains..bring in new settlers and prospectors.

Prospectus (prɒ,spe·ktɒs). Pl. **prospectuses** (rarely in L. form **prospectūs**). [a. L. *prōspectus* (-ūs) a view, PROSPECT *sb.* So F. *prospectus* (1723 in Hatz.-Darm.).] A description or account of the chief features of a forthcoming work or proposed enterprise, circulated for the purpose of obtaining support or subscriptions.

1777 *Life Goldsmith* G.'s Wks. 1786 I. Pref. 31 A design for executing an universal dictionary of arts and sciences, the *prospectus* of which he actually printed and distributed among his acquaintance. 1791 BOSWELL *Johnson* an. 1747, His 'Dictionary of the English Language', was announced to the world by the publication of its Plan or Prospectus. 1845 R. W. HAMILTON *Pop. Educ.* iv (ed. 2) 62 The extent of injurious influence upon the public mind of certain *prospectūs* of education. 1855 MACAULAY *Hist. Eng.* xix. IV. 322 To put forth a lying prospectus announcing a new stock. 1890 SIR R. ROMER in *Law Times Rep.* LXIII. 685/2 The plaintiff applied for shares in this company on the faith of the prospectus. *Mod.* He has obtained the prospectuses of several schools.

attrib. 1895 *Pall Mall Gaz.* 3 July 3/1 A rich specimen,.. though not for prospectus purposes. 1900 *Westm. Gaz.* 19 Apr. 9/1 The results..are distinctly disappointing when compared with the prospectus estimates.

† **Prosper,** *a. Obs. rare.* [ME. *prospere*, a. F. *prospère* (14th c. in Littré) or ad. L. *prosper, prosper-us* favourable, fortunate, prosperous: of uncertain origin. The form *prospre* is a. OF. *prospre* (12th c. in Littré).] Prosperous, successful.

c 1374 CHAUCER *Boeth.* I. pr. iv. 8 (Camb. MS.) Thilke man.. þat maade alwey assawtes ayeins the prospere [*v. r.* prospre] fortunes of poore feeble fookkes. 1513 DOUGLAS *Æneis* VIII. v. 59 We pray the vissie, that thou may cum heyr Wyth prosper presens and full happy fute. *Ibid.* XI. xiv. 88 The pepill Tuscane..Seand the exempill and prosper chans that tyd Of thar stowt duke.

Prosper (prɒ·spəɹ), *v.* [a. F. *prospére-r* (14th c. in Littré), ad. L. *prosperā-re* to cause (a thing) to succeed, to render fortunate, also absol., in late L. also to propitiate (God), in pass. to prosper, f. *prosper* adj.: see prec.]

1. *intr.* Of a person, community, etc.: To be prosperous, fortunate, or successful; to flourish, thrive, succeed, do well.

c 1460 FORTESCUE *Abs. & Lim. Mon.* xvi. (*heading*), How the Romaynes prospered whiles that hade a grete counsell. 1526 *Pilgr. Perf.* (W. de W. 1531) 16 b, They wente hole togyder, and prospered ryght well in theyr iourney. 1651 HOBBES *Leviath.* III. xxxiii. 202 Why wicked men have often prospered in this world. 1786 *Scotch Paraphr.* VII. iii Who, that tries th' unequal strife Shall prosper in the end? 1864 TENNYSON *En. Ard.* 48 Enoch..so prosper'd that at last A luckier or a bolder fisherman..did not breathe. 1884 RUSKIN *Pleas. Eng.* 75 No false knight or lying priest ever prospered, I believe, in any age.

b. *intr.* Of things: To flourish; to turn out well.

c 1529 in *Archæologia* (1882) XLVII. 51 We will the said religion to prospere according unto the foundacion of the house. 1535 COVERDALE *Ps.* i. 3 What soeuer he doth, it shal prospere. *a* 1720 SEWEL *Hist. Quakers* (1795) II. VII. 11 If such doings as this ever prosper. 1870 MORRIS *Earthly Par.* (1890) 358 Well did all things prosper in his hand.

c. *intr.* Of plants: To thrive, to flourish.

1553 EDEN *Treat. Newe Ind.* (Arb.) 41 There were also vynes..planted in this Ilande, where they prosper so wel, that [etc.]. 1682 SIR T. BROWNE *Chr. Mor.* III. § 4 Where such Plants grow and prosper.

2. *trans.* To cause to flourish; to promote the prosperity or success of; to be propitious to.

1530 PALSGR. 668/1, I beseche Jhesu prospere you in all your busynesses. 1593 NASHE *Christ's T.* 61 b, God.. cherrisht and prosperd them with all the blessings hee could. 1642 *Declar. Lords & Com., Ordinance* 13 Apr. 3 For prospering the common cause. 1784 COWPER *Task* VI. 1024 Whose frown can disappoint the proudest strain, Whose approbation prosper—even mine. 1855 KINGSLEY *Westw. Ho!* xxiii, If Heaven prospered them, they might seize a Spanish ship.

Hence **Pro·spering** *vbl. sb.* and *ppl. a.*

c 1557 ABP. PARKER *Ps.* xx, This prayth for kinges Good prosperinges, Theyr realmes to have defence. 1604 EARL STIRLING *Parænesis to Pr. Henry* lxxvii, Every State by long experience findes, That greatest blessings prosp'ring Peace imparts. 1854 E. G. HOLLAND *Mem. J. Badger* xviii. 349 The pastor of a prospering church.

† **Pro·sperable,** *a. Obs. rare.* [f. prec. + -ABLE.] **a.** Prosperous, likely to prosper. **b.** Able or inclined to give prosperity; propitious.

c 1422 HOCCLEVE *Learn to Die* 112 Horrible is thy presence and ful greevable To him þat yong is strong and prosperable. 1611 SPEED *Hist. Gt. Brit.* IX. xxiii. § 46 Vnlesse God be prosperable to his purpose.

† **Pro·sperance.** *Obs. rare*⁻¹. [f. L. *prosperāre* to PROSPER: see -ANCE.] = PROSPERITY.

1502 ARNOLDE *Chron.* (1811) 162 God the yeuar of all goodnes graunte the prosperaunce and happy encreses.

† **Pro·sperately,** *adv. Obs. rare*⁻⁰. [f. *prosperate*, ad. late L. *prosperāt-us* prospered + -LY[2].]

1573–80 BARET *Alv.* P 786 Prosperately, fortunately, with good lucke, *secundis auibus.*

Prosperation (prɒspərē·ʃən). *rare.* Now only *dial.* [ad. late or med.L. *prosperātiōn-em*, n. of action f. *prosper-āre* to PROSPER. Cf. obs. F. *prosperation* (1512 in Godef.).] Prosperity.

c 1470 HARDING *Chron.* LXXXVII. xii. (MS. Arch. Seld. B. 10) Þe Churche [might haue be] preserued in greate prosperacioun. 1828 *Craven Gloss.* (ed. 2), *Prosperation*, success, good luck. 1856 HINCHLIFFE *Hist. Barthomley* 145 One old song..was always sung at these meetings [Annual Churchwardens' Dinner],..which I insert below..'Come, brave boys, prosperation Be to the Church and Nation!' 1883 BURNE *Shropsh. Folk-Lore* 471 [At Much Wenlock] each of the new burgesses was required to stand up in turn and empty the cup to the toast of 'Prosperation To the Corporation'.

Pro·spered (-əɹd), *ppl. a.* [f. PROSPER *v.* + -ED[1].] Caused to prosper, blest with prosperity.

1651 CROMWELL *Let. to Speaker* 4 Sept. in *Carlyle*, That the fear of the Lord, even for His mercies, may keep an Authority and a People so prospered, and blessed,..humble and faithful. 1661 BOYLE *Style of Script.* (1675) 230 Wherein her Prospered Sedulousness gave her an Understanding much above her Age and Sex.

Prosperer (prɒ·spərəɹ). *rare.* [f. as prec. + -ER[1].] **a.** One who is prosperous or flourishing. **b.** One who causes prosperity.

1633 D. R[OGERS] *Treat. Sacram.* I. 161 A man that is no prosperer in grace. 1643 TRAPP *Comm. Gen.* xlix. 10 Others render *Shiloh*..The Peace-maker, The Prosperer.

Prosperity (prɒspe·riti). [ME. a. F. *prospérité* (*prosperitet* a 1140 in Littré), ad. L. *prosperitās, -tātem* good fortune, success, prosperity, f. *prosper, prosper-us*: see PROSPER *a.* and -ITY.] The condition of being prosperous, successful, or thriving; good fortune, success, well-being.

a 1225 *Ancr. R.* 194 Uor þe uttre uondunge is mislicunge in aduersite, & in prosperite þet limpeð to sunne. 1382 WYCLIF *1 Macc.* ii. 47 The werk hadde prosperite in her hondis. 1406 HOCCLEVE *La male regle* 34 Prosperitee is blynd, & see ne may. 1500–20 DUNBAR *Poems* lxxx. 11 God give the guid prosperitie, Fair fortoun and felicitie. 1607 SHAKS. *Cor.* II. i. 188 You haue, I know, petition'd all the Gods for my prosperitie. 1638 BAKER tr. *Balzac's Lett.* (vol. II.) 68 A Moderatour in prosperitie; and a guide in adversitie. 1795 BURKE *Corr.* (1844) IV. 284 Prosperity is not apt to receive good lessons, nor always to give them. 1862 RUSKIN *Unto this Last* iv. 143 The prosperity of any nation is in exact proportion to the quantity of labour which it spends in obtaining and employing means of life. 1874 GREEN *Short Hist.* vii. § 2. 357 The cause which prosperity had ruined revived in the dark hour of persecution.

b. *pl.* Instances of prosperity, prosperous circumstances.

1340 *Ayenb.* 24 Þe guodes of hap byeþ heȝnesses, richesses, delices, and prosperites. 1598 GRENEWEY *Tacitus, Ann.* VI. v. (1622) 128 The vitious and bad triumph with so great prosperities. 1632 SIR T. HAWKINS tr. *Mathieu's Unhappy Prosperitie* 231 Shewing all prosperities of the world were but trifles, and counterfet gems, compared with eternall felicitie. 1856 MRS. BROWNING *Aur. Leigh* II. 467 What then, indeed, If mortals are not greater by the head Than any of their prosperities?

c. *attrib.* and *Comb.*

1647 TRAPP *Comm. Mark* iv. 17 These are prosperity-proselytes, holy-day servants,..neuter passive Christians. 1889 *Standard* 16 Apr., The Budget which Mr. Goschen introduced..might have been a 'Prosperity' Budget, had the requirements of the country been normal. 1901 *Lady's Realm* X. 655/2 Households, who shall watch the prosperity-bringing fire with mingled joy and awe.

Prosperous (prɒ·spərəs), *a.* [a. obs. F. *prospereus* (15th c. in Godef.) = It. *prosperoso*: see PROSPER *a.* and -OUS.]

1. Having continued success or good fortune; consistently successful; flourishing, thriving.

1472–3 *Rolls of Parlt.* VI. 30/2 The first yere of your moost prospereux reigne. 1531 TINDALE *Exp. 1 John* (1537) 58 Oure brethren were in prosperouser state then we. 1591 SHAKS. *1 Hen. VI*, I. i. 32 The Battailes of the Lord of Hosts he fought: The Churches Prayers made him so prosperous. 1638 JUNIUS *Paint. Ancients* 88 In this same plaine and prosperous way of emulation. 1771 *Junius Lett.* l. (1820) 260 In the most prosperous state of his fortune he was always the very man he is at present. 1878 JEVONS *Prim. Pol. Econ.* 7 Political Economy inquires into the causes which make one nation more rich and prosperous than another.

2. Promoting or conducing to success; bringing prosperity; favourable, auspicious, propitious.

1445 in *Anglia* XXVIII. 273 While goodis be had in habundaunce & prosperous chauncis be falle. *c* 1460 J. METHAM *Wks.* (E.E.T.S.) 153 Yt ys prosp[er]us that day to pase the see with marchaundyse, and to wedde a wyfe. 1555 EDEN *Decades* 247 We sayled euer with prosperous wynde. 1599 NASHE *Lenten Stuffe* (1871) 58 To try what kind of flesh-meat was most nutritive and prosperous with a man's body. 1772–84 *Cook's Voy.* (1790) V. 1697 We..had a prosperous gale, and plenty of provisions. 1871 R. ELLIS *Catullus* lxiv. 237 A prosperous hour shall bring to thee happy returning.

3. *Comb.*, as *prosperous-looking* adj.

1899 CROCKETT *Kit Kennedy* 31 'But, Lilias, you are well dressed, and prosperous-looking', said the man.

Prosperously (prɒ·spərəsli), *adv.* [f. prec. + -LY[2].] In a prosperous manner.

1. Successfully, with continued good fortune.

1503–4 *Act* 19 *Hen. VII*, c. 38 § 2 Your moste noble & royall Estate longe prosperously to endure. 1617 MORYSON *Itin.* I. 251 Vpon Friday the eleuenth of October, we sayled prosperously. *a* 1714 SHARP *Wks.* V. iv. 297 We are willing to trust God with any other concern, so long as that concern goes on prosperously. 1849 MACAULAY *Hist. Eng.* vi. II. 71 For a time the intrigue went on prosperously and secretly.

2. Favourably, propitiously. *rare.*

1596 DRAYTON *Leg.* iv. 39 Be now abundant prosp'rously to aide The Pen prepar'd.

Prosperousness (prɒ·spərəsnės). [f. as prec. + -NESS.] The quality or condition of being prosperous; prosperity, success.

1648 BOYLE *Seraph. Love* i. (1700) 3, I seldom use endeavours, whose prosperousness is more welcome to me, than those that aspire to serve Lindamor. 1812 G. CHALMERS *Dom. Econ. Gt. Brit.* 459 Yet, was that prosperousness accompanied, by unfavourable exchanges, and several bankruptcies.

Prosphygmic (prɒ,sfi·gmik), *a. Phys.* [f. PRO-[2] + Gr. σφυγμ-ός the pulse + -IC: cf. SPHYGMIC.] Preceding the beat of the pulse.

1898 *Allbutt's Syst. Med.* V. 469 This is the period of 'getting up pressure', the 'prosphygmic interval' as Allbutt terms it. *Ibid.* 930 This apparent origin of the murmur is suggested by the great protraction of the 'prosphygmic' interval.

‖ **Prosphysis** (prɒ·sfisis). Pl. **-es** (-īz). *Path.* [mod.L., a. Gr. πρόσφυσις a growing on or to something, an attachment, adhesion, f. πρός to + φύσις growth, cf. προσφύεσθαι to grow to or upon.] An adhesion; morbid adhesion of parts.

1693 tr. *Blancard's Phys. Dict.* (ed. 2), *Prosphysis*, a Coalition, or growing together, as when two Fingers are connected to each other. 1704 J. HARRIS *Lex. Techn.* I. 1727–41 CHAMBERS *Cycl.* s.v. *Adhesion*, Anatomists sometimes observe prosphyses, or Adhesions of the lungs to the sides of the thorax, the pleura, and diaphragm. 1842 DUNGLISON *Med. Lex.*, *Prosphysis*, adhesion... In a more limited sense, this word means morbid adhesion of the eyelids, either between themselves, or with the globe of the eye.

† **Pro,spi·cient,** *a. Obs. rare.* [ad. L. *prōspicient-em*, pr. pple. of *prōspic-ĕre* to look forward.] Having foresight; provident. So † **Prospi·cience** *Obs.*, † **Prospi·ciency** *Obs.*, the action or quality of looking forward; foresight.

1654 R. CODRINGTON tr. *Iustine* xliii. 503 But fortune prospicient to the Original of Rome, did provide a Woolf to give suck to the children. 1656 BLOUNT *Glossogr.*, *Prospicience*, providence, fore-sight. [So 1775 in ASH; 1828 in WEBSTER; and in recent Dicts.] 1817 T. L. PEACOCK *Melincourt* vii, Well-grounded prospiciencies of hopelessness and helplessness. *Ibid.* xvi, The second [reason] is most refined, abstract, prospicient, and canonical.

† **Pro,spi·cuous,** *a. Obs. rare.* [f. L. *prōspicu-us* that may be seen afar, conspicuous (f. *prōspic-ĕre*: see prec.) + -OUS.] Conspicuous; also, app., distinguished, 'fair to behold'.

1605 A. WARREN *Poore Mans Passions* E iij, Dutifull Loyalty would humbly greete My Person, passing the prospicuous streete. 1632 LITHGOW *Trav.* x. 499 The incircling Coast a nest of Corporations; and Meandring Forth from tip-toed Snadoun, the prospicuous mirrour for matchlesse Maiesty. 1656 BLOUNT *Glossogr.*, *Prospicuous*, goodly or fair to see or behold, or which may be seen afar off. 1688 R. HOLME *Armoury* III. 393/1 An Eagles head ..is an adornment only added to the handle to make it more prospicuous.

Prosporangium: see PRO-[2] 1. **Pross**, obs. Sc. and mod. dial. f. PROSE. **Prosse**, obs. erron. f. PROWESS; var. of PRUCE *Obs.* **Prosses(se**, obs. ff. PROCESS. **Prossession**, obs. f. PROCESSION.

† **Prossyllogism.** *Logic. Obs. rare.* [f. Gr. πρός in addition (added) to + SYLLOGISM. Cf. PROSYLLOGISM.] A syllogism added after either premiss of the principal syllogism, and furnishing the proof of that premiss.

1620 T. GRANGER *Div. Logike* 281 A Prossyllogisme is a reason, or proofe set after the principall Syllogisme, or some part thereof... Here both the proposition, and assumption are prooued by their Prossyllogismes.

Prostaphæresis, etc., obs. erron. ff. PROSTH-.

† **Prostasy.** *Obs. rare*⁻¹. In 7 proes-. [ad. L. *prostasia* office of a president, a. Gr. προστασία a standing before or in front, f. προστάτης one who stands in front.] Precedence, pre-eminence.

1661 H. D. *Disc. Liturgies* 41 [We] shall willingly allow him proestasie in that Art and Practise.

Prostate (prɒ·stēⁱt), *sb.* (*a.*) *Anat.* [ad. med.L. *prostat-a* the prostate, ad. Gr. προστάτ-ης one who stands before, agent-n. from προϊστάναι to set before: cf. στατός placed, standing. (So F. *prostate.*)] A large gland, or each of a number of small glands, accessory to the male generative organs, surrounding the neck of the bladder and the commencement of the urethra, in man and other Mammalia.

(In first quot. app. confounded with the seminal vesicles.)

1646 SIR T. BROWNE *Pseud. Ep.* 189 An Horse or Bull may generate after castration, that is, from the stock.. of seminall matter, already prepared and stored up in the Prostates or glandules of generation. *c* 1720 W. GIBSON *Farrier's Guide* I. ii. (1738) 17 There are several glandular bodies situated..immediately before the seed bladders [in the horse], and are therefore called Prostates. 1804 ABERNETHY *Surg. Obs.* 234 The chief cases..are those of enlarged prostates. 1847–9 *Todd's Cycl. Anat.* IV. 146/1 In shape the prostate resembles a Spanish chesnut. 1888 ROLLESTON & JACKSON *Anim. Life* 31 It is in accordance with general usage to speak of both of [the two other] sets of glands [in the male rabbit] as 'prostates', the smaller as the 'anterior' and the larger as the 'posterior prostates'.

b. *attrib.* or *adj.*, esp. in *prostate gland*.

(In first quot. applied to the gland of Bartholin in the female, the homologue of the Cowperian gland.)

1754–64 SMELLIE *Midwif.* I. 94 On each side of the *Meatus urinarius* are two small..openings the tubes of which.. come from the prostate gland. 1840 G. V. ELLIS *Anat.* 582 The prostate gland..is situated at the front of the pelvis, and near the symphysis pubis.

Hence **Prostata·lgia**, pain in the prostate (Dunglison, 1842); **Prostatectomy** (prɒstăte·ktŏmi) [Gr. ἐκτομή cutting out], excision of the prostate, or of part of it; ‖ **Prostatitis** (-əi·tis) [-ITIS], inflammation of the prostate; hence **Prostatitic** (-i·tik) *a.*; **Prosta·tolith** [-LITH], a calculus formed in the prostate; **Prostato·meter** [-METER], 'an instrument for measuring the prostate' (*Syd. Soc. Lex.*); ‖ **Pro·statorrhœ·a** (-rī·ă) [Gr. ῥοία flux], a discharge, esp. of mucus, from the prostate; **Prostatotomy** (-ɒ·tŏmi) [Gr. τομή cutting], incision of the prostate; **Pro·stato-ve·sical** *a.* [L. *vesica* bladder], belonging to the prostate and bladder.

1890 BILLINGS *Nat. Med. Dict.*, *Prostatectomy. 1904 *Brit. Med. Jrnl.* 17 Dec. 1641 Prostates removed by perineal prostatectomy. 1890 *Cent. Dict.*, *Prostatitic. 1895 *Syd. Soc. Lex.*, *Prostatitic*, belonging to, or affected with, prostatitis. 1844 DUNGLISON *Med. Lex.*, *Prostatitis. 1860 SIR H. THOMPSON *Dis. of Prostate* (1868) 53 The morbid anatomy of acute prostatitis. 1895 *Syd. Soc. Lex.*, *Prostatolith..*Prostatometer. 1858 MAYNE *Expos. Lex.*, *Prostatorrhœa. 1899 CAGNEY *Jaksch's Clin. Diagn.* ix. (ed. 4) 425 Their presence in large numbers..indicates prostatorrhœa. 1890 BILLINGS *Nat. Med. Dict.*, *Prostatotomy. 1878 T. BRYANT *Pract. Surg.* (1879) II. 85 The dumb-bell calculus is usually *prostato-vesical or encysted.

Prostatic (prɒstæ·tik), *a.* [f. as PROSTATE + -IC: cf. F. *prostatique* and Gr. προστατικός.] Pertaining to, produced by, or connected with the prostate. *Prostatic body, gland*, the prostate.

1836–9 *Todd's Cycl. Anat.* II. 459/1 Very little is known as to the uses of the prostatic body. 1846 G. E. DAY tr. *Simon's Anim. Chem.* II. 359 The prostatic fluid..mixes with the semen..at the moment of emission. 1870 ROLLESTON *Anim. Life* Introd. 54 [Birds have no] accessory glands ..appended to the generative canals..as..the Cowperian, the prostatic glands, and the vesiculae seminales.

Prostemmate (prɒste·mĕt). *Zool.* [f. PRO-[2] 2 + Gr. στέμμα, -ματ- a wreath: see STEMMA.] An organ of unknown function situated in front of the eyes in some apterous insects of the lowest type of the order *Collembola*. Hence **Prostemma·tic** *a.*, pertaining to or of the nature of a prostemmate.

1895 *Cambr. Nat. Hist.* V. 193 Some of the Collembola possess a very curious structure called the prostemmatic or ante-ocular organ... The prostemmate is placed slightly in front of the group of ocelli.

† **Proste·rn**, *v. Obs.* [a. F. *prosterner* (15th c. in Littré), ad. L. *prōsternĕre* to strew in front, throw down, prostrate, f. *prō*, PRO-[1] 1 b + *sternĕre* to lay flat.] *trans.* To cast down, lay flat, prostrate. (Chiefly *refl.* or *pass.*) Hence † **Proste·rning** *vbl. sb.* = PROSTERNATION.

c 1489 CAXTON *Blanchardyn* xxv. 93 His doughter Beatryse ..prosterned or casted her self doune byfore her faders feet, on her knees humbly. 1588 A. KING tr. *Canisius' Catech.* 79 We maist humblie and laulie prosterne our selfs. 1612 J. GORDON *Εἰρηνοκοινωνία* E iij, In..prayers there is a threefold kinde of gesture..: the first is a falling downe or prosterning of the body: the second is..a bowing downe of the head to the ground. The third is kneeling.

Prosternal (pro,stɔ̄·ɹnăl), *a. Entom.* [f. PRO-STERNUM + -AL.] Of or pertaining to the prosternum of an insect.

1868 *Rep. U. S. Commissioner Agric.* (1869) 93 They [*Elateridæ*] extend the prothorax so as to bring the prosternal spine..to the anterior part of the mesosternal cavity.

† **Pro·sternate,** *v. Obs.* [f. ppl. stem of med.L. *prōstern-āre*, collateral form of L. *prōstern-ĕre*: see PROSTERN.] *trans.* = PROSTERN *v.*

1593 NASHE *Christ's T.* (1613) 78 Wholy haue I bequeathed my penne and my spirit, to the prosternating and ensorrowing the frontiers of sinne. 1651 BIGGS *New Disp.* § 85 Trip up and prosternat our strength. 1653 E. CHISENHALE *Cath. Hist.* 394 Prosternating her lofty Spires,..to the ground.

† **Prosterna·tion.** *Obs.* [a. F. *prosternation* (1599 in Hatz.-Darm.), n. of action from F. *prosterner* or L. *prōstern-āre*: see prec.] The action of prostrating or condition of being prostrated; prostration. Also *fig.*

1622 DONNE *Serm.* (ed. Alford) V. 93, I shall rise..from the prostration, from the prosternation of Death. 1650 CHARLETON *Paradoxes* 17 Before the Patient hath suffered too great a prosternation of spirits. *a* 1652 J. SMITH *Sel. Disc.* II. i. (1821) 33 Prosternations, uncouth gestures, and strange rites of worship. 1768 [W. DONALDSON] *Life Sir B. Sapskull* I. xii. 127 To the humiliating attitude of prosternation. 1819 H. BUSK *Banquet* II. 30 You call the oaks to witness the deceit, In prosternation at their aged feet.

‖ **Prosternum** (pro,stɔ̄·ɹnŏm). *Entom.* [mod.L., f. PRO-[2] 2 + STERNUM.] The sternal, ventral, or under segment of the prothorax of an insect.

1826 KIRBY & SP. *Entomol.* III. xxxv. 544 The *sternum* or breast-bone of insects consists mostly of three distinct pieces..the first of these pieces, the *sternum* of the *antepectus* or *prosternum*. 1833 E. DOUBLEDAY in *Entomol. Mag.* I. 474 The prosternum..occupies the lower part of the prothorax. 1895 *Cambr. Nat. Hist.* V. 102.

‖ **Prosthaphæresis** (prɒsþăfī·ɹĭsis). *Astr.* Pl. **-eses** (-ĭsīz). Also 7–8 *erron.* prosta-; 8–9 -eresis. [mod.L., a. Gr. προσθαφαίρεσις previous subtraction, f. πρόσθε(ν before + ἀφαίρεσις: see APHÆRESIS.] The correction necessary to find the 'true', i.e. actual apparent, place of a planet, etc. from the mean place; the equation of the centre. (In quot. 1677 in more general sense.)

1633 H. GELLIBRAND in T. James *Voy.* R ij, The Prosthaphæresis of the ☉ orbe. 1669 STURMY *Mariner's Mag.* II. 102 To Rectifie the Tables of the Sun's Declination..by Prostaphæreses. 1677 R. CARY *Chronol.* I. I. I. vii. 19 The Months alternatively of 29, and 30 Days, except where necessity did require a Prosthaphæresis, either a Subduction, or else an Adjection of one or more Days. 1810 VINCE *Astron.* x. 96 The difference of these two angles is called the equation of the planet's center, or prosthapheresis. 1882 MORTON *Astronomers* 51 Tables of the prosthapheresis and nychthemeron are given.

Hence **Prosthaphære·tical** *a.*, of, pertaining to, or involving prosthaphæresis. *rare* or *Obs.*

1635 GELLIBRAND *Var. Magn. Needle* 5 Its..necessary for the Seaman who sailes by his Compasse, continually to search the variation, that so by the Prosthaphæreticall application thereof, the true point of the compasse..may be rectified. 1690 LEYBOURN *Curs. Math.* 813 Called the Prosthaphæretical Time, because it is wont sometimes to be added to, sometimes..taken from the Time of the middle Syzygy.

‖ **Prostheca** (prɒsþī·kă). *Entom.* [mod.L., ad. Gr. προσθήκη an addition, appendage, f. προστιθέναι to put to, add. Cf. F. *prosthèque.*] A process on the mandibles in certain coleopterous insects. Hence **Prosthe·cal** *a.*, pertaining to the prostheca.

1826 KIRBY & SP. *Entomol.* III. xxxiii. 356 *Prostheca*..a subcartilaginous process attached to the inner side, near the base, of the *Mandibulæ* of some *Staphylinidæ*. 1879 J. WOOD-MASON in *Trans. Entomol. Soc. Lond.* 152, I refer to the prostheca of Kirby and Spence, and to the structures homologous with it in beetles other than Staphylinidæ.

Prosthenic (prɒspe·nik), *a.* (*sb.*) [f. Gr. πρό (PRO-[2] 2) + σθένος strength + -IC.] Having preponderance of strength in the anterior limbs or part of the body. *sb. pl. Ent.* Insects so characterized.

1863 DANA [see *Metasthenic* in META- 3].

‖ **Prosthesis** (prɒ·spĭsis). [L., a. Gr. πρόσθεσις addition, f. προστιθέναι to put to, add. Cf. F. *prosthèse.*]

1. *Gram.* The addition of a letter or syllable at the beginning of a word.

(The qualification 'at the beginning' may have arisen from associating προς- with προ-.)

1553 T. WILSON *Rhet.* (1580) 180 *Prosthesis.* Of Addition. As thus: He did all to beratle hym. Wherin appeareth that a sillable is added to this woorde (rattle). 1657 J. SMITH *Myst. Rhet.* 170 *Prosthesis*..A figure (contrary to *Aphæresis*) whereby a letter or syllable is added to the beginning of a word. 1876 DOUSE *Grimm's Law* 208 'Prosthesis' belongs to a..class of terms..denoting arbitrary processes, whose intrusion into the realm of language should be viewed with..suspicion.

2. *Surg.* That part of surgery which consists in supplying deficiencies, as by artificial limbs or teeth, or by other means.

1706 PHILLIPS (ed. Kersey) s.v., In Surgery *Prosthesis* is taken for that which fills up what is wanting, as is to be seen in fistulous and hollow Ulcers, filled up with Flesh by that Art: Also the making of artificial Legs and Arms, when the natural ones are lost. 1902 *Encycl. Brit.* XXVII. 417/2 Dental Prosthesis.

Prosthetic (prosthe'tik), a. [ad. mod.L. *prosthetic-us*, ad. Gr. προσθετικός or the nature of addition, giving additional power, f. προσθετος added, vbl. adj. of προστιθεναι: see prec. and -IC. Cf. F. *prosthétique*.]

Prosthesis (pro'sthesis). *Surg.* [mod.L.]

Prosthetically, adv.

† Prostibule. Obs. rare⁻⁰.

† Prostibulous, a. Obs. rare.

Prosting.

† Prostitrice. rare⁻¹.

Prostitute (pro'stitiut), ppl. a. and sb. [ad. L. *prostitut-us* (see *prostitute* v.).]

Prostitute (pro'stitiut), v.

Prostitution (prostitiū'ʃən). [ad. late L. *prostitution-em*.]

Prostitutor (pro'stitiutər).

† Prostomium. [mod.L.]

Prostrate (pro'streit), ppl. a. and sb. [ad. L. *prostrat-us*: see PROSTERN.]

Prostrate (pro'streit), v.

Prostration (prostreī'ʃən).

Prostrative, a. rare.

† Prosubstantive, a.

† Prosult. Obs. rare⁻¹.

Prosy (prō'zi), a. [f. PROSE sb. + -Y.]

Prosylite, obs. form of PROSELYTE.

Prosyllogism (prosi'lədʒiz'm). *Logic.* [ad. med.L. *prosyllogism-us* (Boeth.), ad. Gr. προσυλλογισμός: see PRO- and SYLLOGISM.]

Prot-, the form of PROTO- used before a vowel.

Protactinic, a. rare. [ad. Gr. πρωτακτις.]

Protagon (prō'tagɔn) (Liebreich).

Protagonist (protæ'gɔnist), sb. [ad. Gr. πρωταγωνιστης.]

Protamin.

Protandrous (protæ'ndrəs), a. *Bot.*

Pro tanto: see PRO 9.

Protase.

Protasis (pro'tasis), sb.

Protatic (protæ'tik), a.

Protean (prō'tiən, protī'ən), a.

Protect (prote'kt), v. [f. ppl. stem of L. *protegere*: see prec. Cf. rare obs. F. *protecter*.]

† Protect, ppl. a. Obs.

Protecting, ppl. a.

Protection (prote'kʃən). [ad. L. *protection-em*.]

Protectional, a.

Protectionary, a.

Protectionism (prote'kʃəniz'm), sb.

Protectionist (prote'kʃənist), sb. [f. prec. + -IST.]

Protectant (prote'ktənt).

Protecte, var. PROTECT.

Protectible.

Protective (prote'ktiv), a. [f. L. *protect-* + -IVE.]

Protectively, adv.

Protector (prote'ktər), sb. [a. AF. *protectour*, agent-n. f. L. *protector*: see PROTECT.]

Protectorate (prote⋅kتور̊t), sb. [f. PROTECTOR sb. + -ATE¹: cf. doctorate.]

Protectorship.

Protectress, var. PROTECTRESS.

† **Protectorial**, a. [f. late L. *prōtectori-us* PROTECTORY + -AL.]

Protectorian, a. and sb. [f. as prec. + -AN.]

Protectorless, a. [f. PROTECTOR + -LESS.]

Protectory, a. and sb. [f. as prec. + -LY.]

Protecture. Obs. rare⁻¹.

Protectrix (prote⋅triks). [med.L., fem. of *protector* PROTECTOR.]

Protectrice.

Protend (prote⋅nd), v. Now rare. [ME. ad. L. *protendĕre* to stretch forth, extend: f. PRO- + *tendĕre* to stretch; cf. obs. F. *protendre* (1404 in Godef.) to extend, a variant of *pourtendre*: see PORTEND.]

Protension (prote⋅nʃən). rare. [ad. late L. *prōtension-em*, n. of action f. PROTEND.]

Protensity (prote⋅nsiti), sb. [f. next + -ITY.]

Protensive (prote⋅nsiv), a. rare. [f. L. *prōtens-* ppl. stem of *protendĕre* to PROTEND + -IVE.]

Proteolysis (prout̄iˌɒ⋅lisis). *Phys. Chem.* [mod.L., f. PROTEO-, assumed combining form of PROTEIN + Gr. λύσιϲ a loosening, solution.]

Proteolytic (prout̄iˌˌɒli⋅tik), a. [f. prec. + -IC.]

Proteose (prout̄iˌ·ous). *Chem.*

Proterandrous (prŏtĕræ⋅ndrŏs), a. [f. PROTERO- + -ANDROUS: cf. PROTANDROUS.]

Proterandry.

Protero-gynous (proterɒ⋅dʒinəs), a. [f. PROTERO- + -GYNOUS.]

Proterogyny.

Protervious, a. Obs. rare⁻¹.

Protervity.

Protest (prout̄est), sb. [a. F. *protest*, now *protêt*, f. *protester*: see next.]

Protest (prŏte⋅st), v. [a. F. *protester* (14th c. in Littré), ad. L. *prōtestārī* (also in Gael.) to declare formally in public, testify, protest, f. PRO- + *testārī* to be or serve as a witness, f. *testis* witness.]

Protestancy (prŏ⋅testənsi), sb. [f. next + -CY.]

Protestant (prŏ⋅testănt), sb. and a. [a. Ger. *Protestant*, or F. *protestant*, ad. L. *prōtestant-, -ans,* pr. pple. of *prōtestārī* to PROTEST.]

Supplement, p. 3873; Corrigenda, p. 4092; Spurious words, p. 4093; Books quoted, p. 4094.

2335

Church of England, in distinction from 'Dissenters', 'Chapel-goers', and the like.

1823 A. Knox in *K. & Jebb's Corr.* (1834) II. 122 What perverse influence the nick-name of protestant has had on our church. 1905 A. Cooper-Marsdin *Church or Sect* i. 7, I refuse to call myself a Protestant except..when I wish to declare..that I am not a Papist.

II. *General.* Often stressed (prote·stănt).

3. One who protests. a. One who makes protestation or declaration; *esp.* one who protests devotion [Fr. *protestant*]; a suitor. *rare.*

1648 Herrick *Hesper., To Anthea, who may command,* etc. i, Bid me to live, and I will live Thy Protestant to be. 1904 *Daily Chron.* 5 May 3/3 That is how we find among her 'protestants' Mr. Denis O'Hara, whose love-chase is the theme of this, as of the earlier story.

b. One who protests against error (partly etymological, partly *fig.* from 1 or 2).

1836–7 Sir W. Hamilton *Metaph.* (1877) I. v. 91 We must be protestants, not infidels in philosophy. 1903 G. F. Browne *St. Aldhelm* 297 Abbat Failbe was the first Protestant in these islands, for Adamnan says that he 'protested'...A Protestant is one who asserts his own belief in a definite and positive form.

c. One who makes a protest *against* any decision, proceeding, practice, custom, or the like; a protester. (Often with allusion to senses 1 and 2.)

1853 Maurice *Proph. & Kings* xix. 328 The protestant against sensual and divided worship. 1862 — *Mor. & Met. Philos.* IV. ix. § 108. 629 To hope that he would be the effectual protestant against all North West passages. 1885 *Century Mag.* June 328/1 No great moral value can be attached to a protest against evil-doing at which the protestant has connived. 1896 Bp. Gore *Rom. Cath. Claims* (1904) App. i. 206 When John the Baptist appeared, he appeared as a protestant against the actual development which the inspired religion had received. 1906 *Daily Chron.* 4 May 3/4 Lawrence Rivers, protestant against compulsory games, champion of the right to do with schoolboy leisure as schoolboy pleases.

B. *adj.* 1. Of, pertaining to, or of the nature of Protestants or Protestantism. (In the earliest quots., = *protesting*, and, in reference to the Continent, = *Lutheran*.)

1539 Cromwell in *St. Papers Hen. VIII*, I. 605 The States Protestantes have geven their petition more then 4 dayes passed, but as yet thEmperours Commissioners have geven no answer therto. 1548 Coverdale *Actes Disput.* 195 These be the Prynces and estates protestantys & all which do stond to the confessyon geuen at Augspurg called the germanys confession. 1584 *Leycesters Commw.* (1641) 97 Complaining on all hands of our protestants Bishops and Clergy. 1607 Topsell *Four-f. Beasts* Ep. Ded., D. Gesner..was a Protestant Physician. 1644 Evelyn *Diary* 6 Mar., To heare & see the manner of the French Protestant Churches service. 1648 *Eikon Bas.* xxvii. 277 That scarce any one [of them]..either was, or is a true Lover,..or Practiser of the Protestant Religion, established in England. 1654 (Dec. 7) *Resolution in Jrnls. Ho. Comm.* VII. 397/2 The True Reformed Protestant, Christian Religion, as it is contained in the Holy Scriptures, ..shall be asserted and maintained, as the publick Profession of these Nations. 1679 Evelyn *Diary* 28 Nov., This Duke [Monmouth], whom for distinction they call'd the Protestant Duke.., the people made their idol. c 1687 Burnet *Orig. Mem.* i. (1902) 153 She does the protestant interest more service than all her ill-affects can do it a prejudice. 1688 Kennett in *Magd. Coll. & Jas. II* (O. H. S.) 258 There was a Protestant, or rather Providential, wind. 1688 *Act 1 Will. & Mary* c. 6 (Coronation oath), Will you to the utmost of your Power maintain the Laws of God, the true Profession of the Gospel and the Protestant Reformed Religion established by Law? 1689 Sancroft in Gutch *Coll. Cur.* I. 447 The Bishops and Clergy of England are unmoveably fixt to the Protestant religion; and absolutely irreconcileable both to Popery and arbitrary power. 1700 Pepys *Let.* 12 Apr., All the King of France does against his Protestant subjects. 1827 Barrington *Personal Sk.* 243 The term 'Protestant ascendancy' was coined by Mr. John Gifford..and became an epithet very fatal to the peace of Ireland. 1828 *Act 9 Geo. IV*, c. 17. § 2 (*Declaration*) The Protestant Church as it is by Law established in England. 1854 [see Catholic B. 3]. 1899 Bp. Stubbs *Visitation Charges* (1904) 343 *The Protestant Religion* is, I think, the historical and reasonable expression for collective application. 1903 F. W. Maitland in *Camb. Mod. Hist.* II. xvi. 594 That Protestant principle which refers us to the primitive Church.

b. **Protestant Dissenter**: see Dissenter 2 c. **Protestant Episcopal**, official style of the church in U. S. descended from and in communion with the Church of England.

1672 Dk. Buckhm. *Sp.* in *Proc. Ho. Lords* (1742) I. 165 That you would give me leave to bring in a Bill of Indulgence to all Protestant Dissenters. 1688, 1689, 1826, 1839 [see Dissenter 2 c]. 1780 in W. S. Perry *Hist. Amer. Episcopal Ch.* (1885) II. 21 On motion of the Secretary it was proposed that the Church known in the province as Protestant be called 'the Protestant-Episcopal Church', and it was so adopted.

2. Also (prote·stănt). Protesting; making a protest.

1844 Ld. Houghton *Mem. Many Scenes, Tintern Abbey* 182 We of this latter, still protestant age, With priestly ministrations of the sun,..Maintain this consecration. 1890 G. S. Hall in *Amer. Jrnl. Psychol.* Jan. 61 A private protestant tribunal, where personal moral convictions preside. 1899 *Echo* 1 Nov. 1/4 Artlessly protestant against the vicious vanities of smart society.

Hence **Pro·testantdom**, the Protestant communities collectively; **Pro·testantlike** *a.*, like or after the manner of a Protestant; **Pro·testantly** *adv.*, in a Protestant manner; consistently with Protestantism.

1579 Fulke *Refut. Rastel* 739 An argument of authority negatiue, is naught and protestantlike. 1659 Milton *Civ. Power* Wks. 1851 V. 312 To protestants..nothing more protestantly can be permitted then a free and lawful debate. 1676 *Doctrine of Devils* 21 If there have not been..even in Protestantdom some too, that..give heed to such doctrines. 1896 D. L. Leonard in *Papers Ohio Ch. Hist. Soc.* VII. 98 Probably by most of Christendom, if not also by most of 'Protestantdom', we are as yet unheard of.

† **Protesta·ntical**, *a. Obs.* [f. prec. + -ical.] Of, pertaining to, or of the nature of a Protestant; inclined to or of the nature of Protestantism; = Protestant *a.* 1. (Sometimes with hostile or opprobrious implication.)

1592 Bacon *Observ. Libel* Wks. 1879 I. 382/2 A third kind of gospellers called Brownists..affirm that the protestantical church of England is not gathered in the name of Christ, but of Antichrist. 1612 T. James *Corrupt. Scripture* iv. 97 They had euery where almost omitted Photius words, being very Protestanticall in this Translation.

Pro·testantish, *a. rare.* [f. as prec. + -ish[1].] = prec. Hence **Pro·testa·ntishly** *adv.*

1680 R. L'Estrange *Answ. Litter of Libels* 8 Something ..which might give the Protestantish Authour occasion of that flourish. 1685 H. More *Refl. Baxter* 24 As if he insinuated himself Popishly and Protestantishly affected in one Breath. 18.. in Flügel *Eng.-Germ. Dict.* (1891), Louis Philip has been very Protestantish in his predilections.

Protestantism (prǫ·tĕstăntiz'm). [f. as prec. + -ism. Cf. F. *protestantisme.*]

1. The religion of Protestants, as opposed to Roman Catholicism; the condition of being Protestant; adherence to Protestant principles.

1649 Milton *Eikon.* xv. 142 In the setling of Protestantism, thir [Papists'] aid was both unseemly and suspicious. 1726 Jos. Trapp *Popery* III. 205 There were Schisms..long before Popery, and consequently much longer before Protestantism..was in Being. 1775 Burke *Sp. Conc. Amer.* Wks. III. 53 But the religion most prevalent in our northern colonies is a refinement on the principle of resistance: it is the dissidence of dissent, and the protestantism of the protestant religion. 1790 — *Fr. Rev.* 30 It was still a line of hereditary descent..though an hereditary descent qualified with protestantism. 1849 Macaulay *Hist. Eng.* vi. II. 54 When the Jesuits came to the rescue of the papacy ..Protestantism..was stopped in its progress, and rapidly beaten back from the foot of the Alps to the shores of the Baltic. 1895 Bp. Gore *Creed of Christian* x. (ed. 7) 60 She [Ch. of Eng.], more than any other branch of the Church Catholic, holds together Church authority, Bible authority, and individual conscience. The Church of Rome makes much of one; Protestantism makes much of the other two.

2. Protestants, or the Protestant churches, collectively.

1662–3 South *Serm.* (1727) V. 60 The only thing that makes Protestantism considerable in Christendom, is the Church of England. a 1677 J. Harrington *Grounds Monarchy* II. § 108 The slow assistances sent to his Daughter, in whose safety and protection Protestantism was at that time so much concern'd. 1902 *Daily Chron.* 28 July 7/3 Protestantism, meaning by that all the non-Roman Catholic persuasions, has held its own, but the Roman Catholics are still steadily dwindling.

3. The condition of protesting; an attitude of protest or objection. *rare.*

1854 H. Spencer in *Westm. Rev.* Apr. 388 There, needs, then, a protestantism in social usages. 1855 Thackeray *Newcomes* I. 366 How his protestantism against her doctrines should exhibit itself on the turf.

Protestantize (prǫ·tĕstăntəiz), *v.* [f. as prec. + -ize.] a. *trans.* To render Protestant; to convert to or permeate with the principles of Protestantism. b. *intr.* To follow Protestant practices. Hence **Pro·testantized** *ppl. a.*, **Pro·testantizing** *vbl. sb.* and *ppl. a.*; also **Pro·testantizer**, one who protestantizes.

1834 *Fraser's Mag.* X. 720 The grants which they still retain for the express purpose of Protestantising Ireland. 1851 J. H. Newman *Cath. in Eng.* 339 Are Protestantizing priests and monks the only evidence of the kind which they could get? 1882 Bp. R. T. Davidson, etc. *Abp. Tait* II. xxiv. 199 He would further 'Protestantise' the Church of England. 1895 *Daily News* 24 May 5/6 He belonged to a Protestantised Jewish family, eminent in the financial world. 1906 W. Walker *Calvin* vii. 203 Another considerable element valued the Protestantising of Geneva more for its political than for its religious results. 1908 *Dublin Rev.* Apr. 308 He was a Protestantizer who formed a party of Calvinists in his Church.

Protestation (prǫtĕstēⁱ·ʃən). [a. F. *protestation* (13th c. in Littré), ad. late L. *prōtestātio* (in Itala, 2 Macc. vii. 6), n. of action f. *prōtest-ārī* to Protest.] The action of protesting; that which is protested.

1. A solemn affirmation of a fact, opinion, or resolution; a formal public assertion or asseveration. *To make protestation*, to protest in a solemn or formal manner.

1340 Hampole *Pr. Consc.* 9593, I make here a protestacion, Þat I wil stand til þe correccion Of ilka rightwyse lered man. c 1386 Chaucer *Miller's Prol.* 29 First I make a protestacioun, That I am dronke I knowe it by my soun. 1526 *Pilgr. Perf.* (W. de W. 1531) 98 With a meke protestacyon deny it, & clere your selfe. 1559 *Declar. Doctrine* in Strype *Ann. Ref.* (1709) I. viii. 116 Although in our last protestation made before the honourable auditory at Westminster, we sufficiently set forth in few words the sum of our faith. 1591 Shaks. *Two Gent.* iv. iv. 133, I know they are stuft with protestations, And full of new-found oathes, which he will breake As easily as I doe teare his paper. 1663 Cowley *Verses & Ess., Cromwell* (1669) 64 If there had been any faith in mens vows and protestations. 1733 Neal *Hist. Purit.* II. 437 They entered into a solemn Protestation to stand by each other with their lives and fortunes. 1838 Dickens *Nich. Nick.* xxviii, Many protestations of friendship, and expressions anticipative of the pleasure which must inevitably flow from so happy an acquaintance. 1895 *Westm. Gaz.* 4 Oct. 10/1 The great 'Church of the Protestation', which is being erected at Spires as a memorial of the origin of the name 'Protestant' at the famous Reichstag in that city in 1529.

† b. *By, with, under* (*a*) *protestation*, with the assertion of the reservation or stipulation, under the condition (*that*). Cf. Protest *v.* 5. *Obs.*

1425 *Rolls of Parlt.* IV. 267/2 Yat he myghte speke under protestation, to yat ende. 1480 *Coventry Leet Bk.* 444 With a protestacion that the seid Priour & Couent may be at their liberte at all tymes to refourme & adde more. *Ibid.* 454 The answeres..made..to þe bill of Compleynt made be þe priour of Couentre, be protestacion þat his answer at all tymes hereafter may be altered, added þerto, amended or otherwyse reformed at eny tyme requisite. 1576 *Reg. Privy Council Scot.* II. 577 Under protestatioun that thay na wayis grant the narrative..to be of veritie.

2. *Law.* † a. In pleading, an affirmation or denial, introduced in form of a protest, of some allegation the truth of which the pleader cannot directly affirm or deny without duplicating his plea, and which he cannot pass over lest he should be held to have tacitly waived or admitted it (see quot. 1628). *Obs.*

By protestation, by way of or in the form of a protestation.

1471–3 in *Calr. Proc. Chanc. Q. Eliz.* (1830) II. Pref. 55 Thomas seith, by protestacion, that the mater contened in the seid bill is insufficient to put hym to answer therto. 1551 in Leadam *Sel. Cas. Crt. Requests* (Selden) 57 And he beyng thereof so seysed dyed of such estate thereof by protestacion seysed. 1579 *Expos. Termes Law* 162 b/2 *Protestation* is a sauinge to the partie (that so pleadeth by protestation) to bee concluded by any matter alledged or obiected against him, vpon which he cannot ioin issu. 1628 Coke *On Litt.* 124 b, Protestation..is an exclusion of a conclusion that a party to an action may by pleading incurre, or it is a safegard to the party which keepeth him from being concluded by the plea he is to make, if the issue be found for him. 1797 Tomlins *Law Dict.* s.v., The use of a Protestation in pleading seems to be this, *viz.* When one party alleges or pleads several matters, and the other party can only offer, or take issue on one of them, he protests against the others.

b. *Sc. Law.* (See quot. 1838.)

1571 *Reg. Privy Council Scot.* II. 92 Thay will proceid and minister justice alsweill be geving of protestationis and decretis. 1633 *Acts of Sederunt* 12 Dec. (1790) 46 Act anent Expences in Protestations. 1739 *Ibid.* 7 July 325. 1838 W. Bell *Dict. Law Scot.* s.v., Where a pursuer, advocator or suspender, after having raised an action, fails to insist in it, his opponent, by means of protestation, may compel him either to proceed or to suffer the action to fall... [This] is done by delivering to one of the Outer-house clerks, a note for insertion in the minute-book of the Court of Session...This note..is called a protestation.

3. A solemn or formal declaration of dissent or objection; = Protest *sb.* 4.

1641 J. Jackson *True Evang. T.* III. 194 After a thousand Complaints, Dissertations, Protestations against their Errors. 1661 Wood *Life* 1 Apr. (O. H. S.) I. 391 Mr. Brent desir'd them..to read a paper..containing a protestation in the name of all the fellowes, under a public notarie's hand, against the admission of Sir Thomas Clayton to the wardenship of Merton coll. 1793 *Acc. Proc. Camb. agst. W. Frend* 194, I Robert Tyrwhitt, a non-regent master of arts, do, within ten days, make this open and legal protestation against the said grace. 1803 Jefferson *Writ.* (1830) IV. 7 Spain had entered into a protestation against our ratification of the treaty. 1849 Stovel *Introd. Canne's Necess.* p. xxxiii, Its burning fetters have provoked..protestation, resistance, dissent, in various forms, civil and sacred.

b. = Protest *sb.* 4 b.

1624 (May 26) in Rogers *Protests of Lords* (1875) I. 2 Therefore the Lords, spiritual and temporal, in the higher House of Parliament, now assembled, do hereby declare and pronounce, and cause this protestation to be entered on record, in the rolls of this Parliament. 1641 (Sept. 9) *Ibid.* 6 [The first formal protest with Reasons in the Journals of the House] We whose names are underwritten did dissent, and having, before the putting of the question, demanded our right of protestation, did accordingly make our protestation: That [etc.]. 1700 (April 4) *Ibid.* 139 We cannot but enter this our protestation against a second reading of this Bill. 1722 *Jrnls. Ho. Lords* XXII. 73/1 The restraining the Assertions, used in Protestations, to the Apprehension or Opinion of the Lords protesting.

4. *attrib.*, as *protestation meeting, money* (2 b).

1589 *Pappe w. Hatchet* (1844) 36, I drew neere the sillie soule whom I found quiuering in two sheetes of protestation paper [alluding to the Marprelate tract 'The Protestation']. 1661 *Acts of Sederunt* 4 July (1790) 78 The supplication of Richard Wairde, lately clerk of the bills, under the usurpers, mentioning him to have in his hands severall sums of money, consigned as protestation-money. 1908 *Nation* (N. Y.) 6 June 342/2 Protestation meetings have been held.

Protestator (prǫ·tĕstēⁱtəɹ). *rare*⁻⁰. [a. mod.L. *prōtestātor*, agent-n. from *prōtestārī* to Protest.] One who protests; a protester.

1847 in Webster.

Protestatory (prote·stătəri), *a. rare.* [f. L. *prōtestāt-*, ppl. stem of *prōtestārī* to Protest + -ory[2]. So F. *protestatoire.*] Pertaining to or of the nature of a protest.

a 1624 Bp. M. Smith *Serm.* (1632) 27 The answere is partly indignatory..partly protestatory. 1887 *Standard* 23 Dec. 3/2 These concessions were not favourably received by the

National Party, who went so far as to threaten further protestatory elections.

Prote·sted, *ppl. a.* [f. Protest *v.* + -ed[1].]

1. Solemnly or † publicly asserted.

1605 Marston *Dutch Courtezan* IV. i, And don all the offices of protested gallantrie for your sake. c 1620 Fletcher & Mass. *Lit. Fr. Lawyer* I. i, Thou wouldst not willingly Live a protested coward, or be call'd one?

† 2. That has made or joined in a protest or protestation. *Obs. rare*⁻¹.

1641 Milton *Animadv.* iv. Wks. 1851 III. 219 In this age.. God hath renewed our protestation against all those yet remaining dregs of superstition. Let us all goe, every true protested Brittaine throughout the 3 Kingdoms, and render thanks to God the Father of light.

3. That is protested against, objected to, or done or given under protest. *Protested bill*: see Protest *v.* 2.

1849 Thackeray *Friendship* Wks. 1900 VI. 626, I will disown you, and cut you off with a protested shilling. 1864 O. W. Holmes *Banker's Secret* Poet. Wks. (1895) 310 The moral market had the usual chills Of Virtue suffering from protested bills.

Protester (prote·stəɹ). [f. as prec. + -er[1].]

1. One who makes a protestation or solemn affirmation.

1601 Shaks. *Jul. C.* I. ii. 74 Were I a common Laugher, or did vse To stale with ordinary Oathes my loue To euery new Protester.

2. One who makes a protest or remonstrance.

1651 C. Cartwright *Cert. Relig.* I. 103 To annex their Religion as a codicill to an appeal of a company of Protesters against a decree at Spira. 1794 Burke *Rep. Lords' Jrnls.* Wks. 1842 II. 601 The reasons against the article, alleged in the protest, were by no means solely bottomed in the practice of the courts below, as if the main reliance of the protesters was upon that usage. 1822 L. Hunt in *Examiner* 25 May 322/2 The Grenvilles and other protesters against improper expenses. 1885 *Manch. Exam.* 14 May 6/1 The motion was carried by 54 to 4, the protesters being [etc.].

b. *Sc. Hist. pl.* Those Presbyterians who in 1650 protested against the union with the Royalists; also applied to those who on various later occasions formally protested against acts or decisions of the church courts.

1660 Douglas in Wodrow *Hist. Suff. Ch. Scot.* (1721) I. Introd. 12 That it may be they were mistaken for some of their Brethren the Protesters, to whom..the King's Return is Matter of Terror. 1722 *Wodrow Corr.* (1843) II. 630 His pieces he wrote in the debate with the Protesters contain.. many things as to the History of this Church. 1816 Scott *Old Mort.* v, They had parted..at the time when the kingdom of Scotland was divided into Resolutioners and Protesters. 1855 *Summary Principles U. P. Ch.* 2 In May 1733 the Assembly refused to hear fully the reasons which the protesters had to urge. 1882–3 *Schaff's Encycl. Relig. Knowl.* I. 409/2 His father..belonged to the extreme Covenanting party of Protesters.

3. One who protests a bill or other commercial document.

1849 De Quincey *Eng. Mail Coach* Wks. 1862 IV. 295 If it is by bills at ninety days after date that you are made unhappy—if noters and protesters are the sort of wretches whose..shadows darken the house of life.

Prote·sting, *vbl. sb.* [f. Protest *v.* + -ing[1].] The action of the verb Protest. a. Protestation, solemn declaration; remonstrance. b. The formal declaration of the non-payment of a bill when duly presented.

1599 ? Shaks. *Pass. Pilgr.* vii, Yet in the mids of all her pure protestings, Her faith, her othes, her teares, and all were ieastings. 1702 Rowe *Tamerl.* I. i. 344 'Twas well my Heart was cautious of believing Thy Vows, and thy Protesting. 1722 *Jrnls. Ho. Lords* XXII. 74/1 The Liberty of Protesting, with Reasons, being an unquestionable Right and essential Privilege of the whole Peerage. 1809 R. Langford *Introd. Trade* 20 The..act..authorises the protesting of inland bills for non-acceptance.

Prote·sting, *ppl. a.* [f. as prec. + -ing[2].] That protests: in various senses of the verb.

1681 Wood *Life* 6 June (O. H. S.) II. 542 The outrage committed on the old lady Lovelace..they pluck'd her out of her coach, and called her 'old protesting bitch'. 1703 Rowe *Ulyss.* v. i. 1967 A protesting, faithless, villain Friend.

Prote·stingly, *adv.* [f. prec. + -ly[2].] In a protesting manner; by way of protest.

1888 R. Dowling *Miracle Gold* I. vii. 125 She looked at him protestingly. 1894 *Temple Bar Mag.* CII. 328 The maid..stood protestingly in the background.

Protestor (prote·stəɹ). [Early mod.E. *protestour*, ad. obs. F. *protesteur*, f. *protester*: see Protest *v.* and -or.]

† 1. = Protester 1. *Obs.*

1550 Bale *Image Both Ch.* I. v. 64 The present protestours of the veritie, here liuing in the world. 1691 Wood *Ath. Oxon.* II. 493 He was..a protestor for a Community of wealth, as well as of women.

2. = Protester 2.

1706 Hearne *Collect.* 5 Feb. (O. H. S.) I. 178 Dr. Cawley was the more taken notice of upon Acc^t of his Being one of the Protestors. 1780 *Hist. Eur.* in *Ann. Reg.* 121/2 He contended, that the protestors..possessed property equal, if not superior, to the petitioners. 1885 *Manch. Exam.* 13 Feb. 5/1 It is asserted by the protestors that three names should have been so forwarded.

b. = Protester 2 b. Also *attrib.*

1693 *Apol. Clergy Scot.* 78 They pretend..that the generality of the Godly did adhere to the Protestors, that the Publick Resolutioners had made defection. a 1715 Burnet *Own Time* I. (1724) I. 55 A great division followed in the Kirk: Those who adhered to these resolutions were called the Publick Resolutioners: But against these some of those bodies protested, and they, together with those who adhered to them, were called the Protestors. 1834 H. Miller *Scenes & Leg.* viii. (1857) 110 Urquhart of Cromarty ..had lately 'counterfeited the Protestor'. 1900 *U. P. Mag.* May 209/2 When the foundations of the Protestor Synod were laid [1737–8], he was one of seven.

Protetrarch: see Pro-[1] 1.

‖ **Proteus** (prōᵘ·tius, prōᵘ·tiŭs). [L. *Prōteus*, a. Gr. Πρωτεύς proper name.]

1. *Gr.* and *Rom. Mythol.* A sea-god, the son of Oceanus and Tethys, fabled to assume various shapes.

c 1400 *Rom. Rose* 6319 Protheus, that coude him chaunge In every shap, hoomly and straunge. 1620 T. Granger *Div. Logike* 137 More mutable then Proteus. 1639 S. Du Verger tr. *Camus' Admir. Events* a j b, Falsehood is ..capable of more different formes, than the..Proteus of Poets. 1806 Wordsw. *Sonn., The world is too much with us* 13 So might I..Have sight of Proteus rising from the sea; Or hear old Triton blow his wreathed horn.

2. Hence allusively, One who, or that which, assumes various forms, aspects, or characters; a changing, varying, or inconstant person or thing.

1585 J. Hart *Æsop's Fables* 111 A Protheus..vnstedfast in word and ded. 1589 Cooper *Admon.* 28 Such a subtile Protheus hee is, that he can turn himself into all maner of shapes. 1685 *Gracian's Courtier's Orac.* 76 He is a wise Proteus that is holy with the holy,..serious with the serious, and jovial with the merry. 1703 Maundrell *Journ. Jerus.* 4 Mar. (1810) 17 Being such Proteus's in religion, that no body was ever able to discover what shape or standard their consciences are really of. 1823 R. Hall *Wks.* (1841) V. 62 Mental phenomena form a Proteus which is constantly changing its aspect.

3. *Zool.* and *Biol.* a. A name for the protozoon now called Amœba. (Now disused as a generic name.) Also *proteus animalcule*, † *p. insect.*

1802 Bingley *Anim. Biog.* (1813) III. 492 Some..if viewed in a microscope, will be found to contain, among several other animalcules, the Proteus. 1806 Priscilla Wakefield *Dom. Recreat.* vi. 85, I shall find plenty of the Proteus insect in it. 1888 Rolleston & Jackson *Anim. Life* 256 *Amœba Proteus* or *A. princeps*, the Proteus animalcule..is to be found in the upper layers of soft ooze at the bottom of still clear lakes, ponds, and ditches.

b. A genus of tailed amphibians with persistent gills, having four short slender legs and a long eel-like body, found in subterranean caves in Austria.

1825 Kirby *Hab. & Inst. Anim.* II. xxii. 419 The Proteus is about a foot in length..the body is cylindrical. 1854 Owen *Skel. & Teeth* in *Orr's Circ. Sc.* I. *Org. Nat.* 188 In the proteus the last segment of the fore-limb divides into three rays. 1860 Gosse *Rom. Nat. Hist.* 76 The proteus, a strange sort of salamander found in the lakes of immense caverns in Illyria.

c. The name given to a group of bacteria, some of which are saprophytes and some pathogenic.

1896 *Allbutt's Syst. Med.* I. 529 The list of putrefactive organisms includes various forms of proteus (vulgaris, mirabilis, Zenkeri), for which formerly the name bacterium termo had to do duty. 1897 *Ibid.* III. 748 Dr. Booker states that a group which he calls the 'proteus' group of bacteria was represented in fifteen out of nineteen cases.

4. a. *attrib.* Changeable like Proteus, protean. *Proteus animalcule, insect* = sense 3 a. b. *Comb.* as *Proteus-like* adj. and adv.

1687 Dryden *Hind & P.* III. 818 O Proteus Conscience, never to be tied! 1718 *Entertainer* No. 34. 233 Who it is, that Proteus like has so often shifted his Meaning. 1733 Cheyne *Eng. Malady* II. viii. § 4 (1734) 196 In such a Proteus-like Distemper. 1834 *Tait's Mag.* I. 599/1 The fantastic tricks of this Proteus principle, became most amusing. 1839 Carlyle *Chartism* iv. (1858) 22 English commerce with its..immeasurable Proteus Steam-demon, makes..all life a bewilderment.

Hence [irreg.] † **Proteu·sian** *a. Obs.* = Protean.

1689 T. Plunket *Char. Gd. Commander* 51 Proteusian pranks, unthought of mysteries.

Protevangel (prōᵘtˌivæ·ndʒĕl). Also irreg. **pro·to-eva·ngel** (see Proto-). [ad. next: cf. Evangel[1]. So F. *protévangile.*] = next, 2.

1875 *Expositor* 413 It is entirely absent even from his interpretation of the Protevangel of Gen. iii. 1878 F. Ferguson *Pop. Life Christ* x. 105 The meaning of Eden's protevangel. 1882–3 *Schaff's Encycl. Relig. Knowl.* I. 503 The grace under which the patriarchal protevangel manifested itself.

‖ **Protevangelium** (prōᵘtˌevændʒe·liŭm). Also (after Gr.) -ion. [mod.L., f. Gr. πρῶτ-ος first, primitive (see Proto- 1) + L. *evangelium*: see Evangely.] A primitive or original gospel.

1. Name of an apocryphal gospel, attributed to St. James the Less.

1715 Proto-Evangelion [see Pseudepigraphal]. 1851 Longf. *Gold. Leg.* III. *Nativity* Introitus 11 The Nativity of our Lord, As written in the old record Of the Protevangelion.

2. Applied to the promise concerning the seed of the woman implied in the curse upon the serpent (Gen. iii. 15), regarded as the earliest utterance of the gospel. (In quot. 1892 in extended sense.)

1874 H. R. Reynolds *John Bapt.* ii. 113 Going right back to the protevangelium uttered in paradise. 1892 Westcott *Gospel of Life* 186 The whole narrative of the Creation and the Fall, and not one isolated verse, contains, when rightly apprehended, the real Protevangelium, the primitive Gospel of the world.

So **Protˌeva·ngelist**, a first or original evangelist or bringer of good tidings.

1864 Carlyle *Fredk. Gt.* XVI. viii. IV. 371 *note*, The true protevangelist of the thing.

Protext (prōᵘ·tekst). *rare.* [f. Pro-[1] 3 or Pro-[2] + Text *sb.*; cf. *context.*] The preceding context of a passage.

1641 J. Jackson *True Evang. T.* II. 141 The..alliance that the text hath with the protext, or verse immediately foregoing. 1886 *N. & Q.* 7th Ser. II. 279/1 See Baring-Gould's 'Curious Myths of the Middle Ages', p. 600 (ed. London, 1881), and the protext.

‖ **Prothalamion** (prōᵘþălēⁱ·miǫn). Also (in mod. Dicts.) -ium. [Invented by Spenser, after *epithalamion*, Epithalamium: see Pro-[2].] 'A preliminary nuptial song' (Stanf.).

1597 Spenser (*title*) Prothalamion, or a Spousall Verse. 1612 Drayton *Poly-olb.* xv. Argt. 8 At Oxford all the Muses meet her And with a Prothalamion greet her. 1627 — *Miseries Q. Margaret* Poems (1748) 141 Poets write prothalamions in their praise Until men's ears were cloy'd with the report. [1896 *Spectator* 31 Oct. 594/1 'Prothalamion'. Spenser must have invented this word, as it does not exist in either Greek or Latin, to express the idea of a song of greeting to happy lovers before the actual wedding-day had arrived.]

Prothallial (proþæ·liăl), *a. Bot.* [f. next + -al.] Pertaining to or of the nature of a prothallium. So **Protha·llic**, **Protha·lline** *adjs.*

1876 J. H. Balfour in *Encycl. Brit.* IV. 160/1 In Ferns the alternation consists of two dissimilar generations,—a sexual or prothallial generation, and an asexual generation. 1882 J. M. Crombie *ibid.* XIV. 555/1 Their fecundating influence is rather exercised on the prothalline elements of the growing thallus. 1890 *Cent. Dict.*, *Prothallic.*

‖ **Prothallium** (proþæ·liŭm). *Bot.* Pl. **prothallia.** [mod.L., f. Pro-[2] 1 + Gr. θαλλίον, dim. of θαλλός: see Prothallus, Thallus.] In vascular cryptogams (ferns, horsetails, club-mosses, etc.), A minute cellular structure or thallus, produced by the germination of the spore, and bearing the sexual organs (antheridia and archegonia); forming the first of the two alternate generations, much simpler than, and as it were introductory to, the fully-developed (asexual) plant. (Sometimes including also the similar Protonema of mosses.)

1858 Carpenter *Veg. Phys.* § 402 This Marchantia-like expansion has received the name of *prothallium*, and it is on this little membranous body, that the archegonia and pistillidia make their appearance. 1872 Oliver *Elem. Bot.* II. 286 From the germinating spore [of Ferns] arises a small, green, leafy expansion, called a prothallium, which gives off delicate root-fibres from its under surface. 1875 Bennett & Dyer *Sachs' Bot.* 335 In the Ferns and Equisetaceæ the prothallium resembles the thallus of the lowest Hepaticæ.

Prothalloid (proþæ·loid), *a.* [f. next + -oid.] Resembling, or having the form of, a prothallus.

1890 in *Cent. Dict.* 1897 *Naturalist* 178 The brown radicles are a prothalloid growth.

‖ **Prothallus** (proþæ·lŏs). *Bot.* Pl. **prothalli** (-əi). [mod.L., f. Pro-[2] + Gr. θαλλός shoot: see Thallus.] = Prothallium.

1854 J. H. Balfour in *Encycl. Brit.* V. 144/1 *Equisetaceæ.* ..The spore when sprouting, produces a pro-embryo or pro-thallus, which at first appears as a green-lobed leaf supported on a stalk. 1857 Berkeley *Cryptog. Bot.* § 32. 45 The spores germinate and produce a more or less foliaceous mass, which after impregnation bears fruit containing bodies like the original spores, or a plant capable of bearing such spores, in which case it is called a prothallus. 1908 *Athenæum* 16 May 608/1 The fern-plant..is typically a land-plant...But one phase of its life-cycle, the small green prothallus or fore-plant, is essentially an aquatic phase.

Prothelminth, -ic, -thelmis: see Proto- 2 b.

‖ **Prothesis** (prǫ·þĭsis). [a. Gr. πρόθεσις a placing before or in public, as in the phrase of ἄρτοι τῆς προθέσεως the showbread (LXX and N.T.), f. Pro-[2] 2 + θέσις placing: cf. προτιθέναι to place before, set out (food, etc.).]

1. *Eccl.* The placing of the elements, etc., in readiness for use in the eucharistic office; hence, the table upon which these are placed, a credence-table, or the part of a church where this stands.

In the Greek Church, the preparation and preliminary oblation of the elements, performed by the priest and deacon (more fully *office of prothesis*); hence, the table upon which this is done (*table* or *altar of prothesis*), or the place where this table stands (*chapel of prothesis*).

1672 Cave *Prim. Chr.* I. vi. (1673) 140 The Prothesis, or place where things were prepared in order to the Sacrament. 1711 Hickes *Two Treat. Chr. Priesth.* (1847) I. 322 The use of a Prothesis, or another table from whence he may fetch them [bread and wine]. 1883 Beresf. Hope *Worship & Ord.* 92 We have the Altar with its attendant table of Prothesis.

2. (See quots.)

1812–29 Coleridge in *Lit. Rem.* (1838) III. 93, I would thus class the pentad of operative Christianity:—

	Prothesis, Christ, the Word.	
Thesis, the Scriptures.	*Mesothesis*, the Holy Spirit.	*Antithesis*, the Church.
	Synthesis, the Preacher.	

1830 *Ibid.* IV. 423 *note*, As a synthesis is a unity that results from the union of two things, so a prothesis is a primary unity that gives itself forth into two things.

3. *Gram.* The addition of a letter or syllable at the beginning of a word: commonly, but less etymologically, called Prosthesis.

1870 March *Ags. Gram.* § 48. 31 Real prothesis is pretty common in Greek.

¶ 4. *Surg.* Erron. used for Prosthesis 2.

1842 Dunglison *Med. Lex.*, *Prothesis* [ed. 1857 adds *Prosthesis*], that part of surgery, whose object is to add to

the human body some artificial part, in place of one that may be wanting.

Prothetic (proþe·tik), *a.* [ad. Gr. προθετικ-ός having a purpose in view, also of or for prefixing, prepositional, f. προτιθέναι to place before.]

1. *Gram.* Prefixed at the beginning of a word; also, less etymologically called Prosthetic.

1833 S. Kenrick in *Philol. Museum* II. 348 That the ω in the longer form is merely prothetic and no part of the root. 1888 *Athenæum* 24 Nov. 704/2 In II. 156 Prof. Sterrett has again misunderstood this prothetic iota; read ἰσφαγέντι. 1900 H. Harrison in *N. & Q.* 9th Ser. VI. 514/2 Wrayton...Its prothetic w is due to false analogy.

2. That is posited before; antecedent. *rare*⁻¹.

1839–52 Bailey *Festus* xix. (ed. 5) 301 In hope to know the great unknowable, The all prothetic universal I.

¶ 3. *Surg.* Erron. used for Prosthetic 2.

1899 *Nature* 23 Nov. 77/1 The introduction of a section upon prothetic appliances.

Prothe·tical, *a.* [f. as prec. + -al.] ? Having the quality of putting forth into view, or exhibiting.

1837 *Fraser's Mag.* XVI. 91 A poet is necessarily a synthetical, if, indeed, he be not rather a higher, a prothetical agent. *Ibid.* 258 The language of Scripture..the style not being so much symbolical or typical as *prothetical*, if we may coin the word; the natural things which we too generally understand as figures of speech..being used not only as direct exponents of the spiritual,..but as one and the same with them.

Prothe·tically, *adv.* [f. prec. + -ly[2].]

1. (Cf. prec.)

1838 *Fraser's Mag.* XVII. 167 The genuine poet works synthetically, or even in higher guise, prothetically, and never analytically.

2. *Gram.* By prothesis or prefixion.

1885 *Trans. Amer. Philol. Assoc.* XVI. App. 33 Letters added prothetically.

Prothistorian: see Proto- 1. **Prothocall, -coll, -gall, -goll**, obs. ff. Protocol.

† **Prothodaw.** *Obs. humorous nonce-wd.* [f. *protho-*, Proto- + Daw *sb.* 2 a.] A prime simpleton, a noodle of the first rank.

a 1548 Hall *Chron., Hen. V* 73 That an Arche foole cannot forge a lye for his pleasure, but a prothodawe wyll faine a glose to mainteine his folish fantasie.

Prothonotary, etc., var. Protonotary, etc.

Prothoplasmator, -pla(u)st(e: see Proto-.

Prothoracic (prōᵘþoræ·sik), *a. Entom.* [f. mod.L. *prothōrax, -thōrăcem* (see next) + -ic: cf. Pro-[2] 2, and *thoracic.*] Of or pertaining to the front of the thorax; pertaining to or situated on the prothorax.

1826 Kirby & Sp. *Entomol.* III. xxxiv. 412 The lower margin of the prothoracic cavity has a notch. 1836–9 *Todd's Cycl. Anat.* II. 883 In the Coleoptera..the pro-thoracic.. segments are largely developed. 1887 *Athenæum* 16 Apr. 518/1 The existence of prothoracic glands in certain species.

‖ **Prothorax** (proþōᵘ·ræks). *Entom.* [mod.L.: see Pro-[2] 2 and Thorax.] The first of the three thoracic somites, or divisions of the thorax of an insect, which bears the first pair of legs. Its upper surface consists of the *pronotum* or central ridge, and the two *propleura*, one on each side.

[1824 Audouin in *Ann. des Sc. Nat.* I. 119 Nous nommerons *Prothorax* le premier segment... Le prothorax, le mésothorax, et le métathorax réunis, constituent le Thorax.] 1826 Kirby & Sp. *Entomol.* III. xxxv. 531, I adopt likewise the terms..*prothorax, mesothorax, metathorax*, to signify the three segments into which the thorax of Linné, or the upper side of the trunk, is resolvable. 1877 Huxley *Anat. Inv. Anim.* vii. 437 The longicorn Beetles produce a sound by the friction of the tergum of the prothorax upon a process of that of the mesothorax.

Prothyalosomal: see Proto- 2 b.

Prothyl, -yle, variants of Protyle.

‖ **Prothyrum** (prǫ·þirŏm). [L. (generally in pl. *prothyra*), ad. Gr. πρόθυρον a front-door, a porch, f. πρό, Pro-[2] + θύρα a door.] The porch or vestibule of an ancient Greek or Roman house.

1706 Phillips, *Prothyrum*, a Porch at the outer Door of an House, a Fence of Pales or Rails, to keep off Horses or Carts from the Door. 1834 *Gentl. Mag.* CIV. I. 53 The Roman Villa after Vitruvius...The principal features noticed are the Prothyrum, vestibule, or lobby.

Prothysteron, Protichnite: see Proto- 2 b.

‖ **Protime·sis.** *Obs.* [mod.L., a. Gr. προτίμησις, n. of action f. προτιμᾶν to honour before or above.] Estimation of one thing above another; preference.

a 1638 Mede *Wks.* (1672) 285, 'I will have mercy and not sacrifice'; it is no Antithesis, but a Protimesis, that 'I had rather have mercy than sacrifice'.

Protiodide (protəi·ǒdəid). *Chem.* Also **proto-iodide.** [*prot-*, Proto- 3.] A combination of iodine with another element or radical, containing the smallest proportion of iodine: opposed to Per-iodide. Formerly also called † **Protio·duret.** Now usually otherwise expressed, as *protiodide of iron* = ferrous iodide, $Fe I_2$; *protiodide* or *protioauret of mercury* = mercuric iodide, $Hg I_2$.

1836 J. M. Gully *Magendie's Formul.* (ed. 2) 120 Preparation of the Proto-Ioduret of Mercury. 1836–41 Brande *Chem.* (ed. 5) 677 Iodide of Calcium..may also be obtained by digesting hydrate of lime with protiodide of iron. 1854 Scoffern in *Orr's Circ. Sc.*, *Chem.* 499 The protoiodide [of mercury]..is a beautiful red compound.

‖ **Protista** (proti·stă), *sb. pl. Biol.* [mod.L. (= Ger. *Protisten*, Haeckel 1868), a. Gr. πρώτιστα, neut. pl. of πρώτιστ-ος the very first, superl. of πρῶτος first.] A third kingdom of organized beings, proposed by Haeckel to include those of the simplest structure, not definitely distinguished as either animals or plants (thus comprising the Protozoa and Protophyta, with those forms indeterminately assigned to either group); corresponding to the *Primalia* of Wilson and Cassin (see Primal 5).

1878 Bell *Gegenbaur's Comp. Anat.* 75 The plan of uniting all the lower organisms which cannot be regarded as Animals or Plants into the Kingdom of the Protista. 1908 M. Hartog in *Contemp. Rev.* Apr. 486 The physiology of the Protista (organisms which have the character of isolated cells).

Hence **Protist** (prōᵘ·tist), an organism of the group *Protista*, a protozoon or protophyte; also *attrib.* = *protistan*; **Proti·stan** *a.*, of or belonging to the *Protista*; *sb.* = *protist*; **Proti·stic** *a.*, of the *Protista*.

1869 Huxley *Crit. & Addr.* xii. (1873) 314 Some of the *Monera* acquired tendencies towards the Protistic, others towards the Vegetal, and others towards the Animal modes of life. 1877 F. Bateman *Darwinism* 33 The second group of the Protistic Kingdom—the Amœboida or Protoplasta. 1889 Geddes & Thomson *Evol. Sex* x. 129 In [Volvox], which is best regarded as a multicellular protist. *Ibid.* xi. 152 Loose protist colonies like Volvox or Ampullina. 1897 *Nat. Science* Oct. 234 The modes of reproduction among Protists are many and various. 1908 M. Hartog in *Contemp. Rev.* Apr. 489 The Protistic parent that loses its individuality in its offspring when it divides.

Proto- (prōᵘ·to), before a vowel or *h* properly **prot-** (prōᵘt), or with *h* (prōᵘþ), repr. Gr. πρωτο-, combining form of πρῶτος first, which became πρωτ- before a simple, and πρωθ- before an aspirated vowel.

In compounds already used in Greek, and many of later formation, the Greek practice (represented by the forms *proto-, prot-, proth-*) is retained, but in modern formations, esp. in group 2 below, the tendency is to leave *proto-* unchanged: e. g. *proto-apostate, proto-hippus.*

Words in *proto-* requiring for any reason individual treatment will be found as main words; those not so treated follow here, in three groups, showing the use of *proto-*, (1) in general language; (2) in terms of zoology and biology; (3) in chemical terminology.

1. In various words of rare occurrence or nonce-words, often self-explaining: *proto-* (which, when prefixed to a word already in English, is usually hyphened) denoting (*a*) 'First in time, earliest, original, primitive', as in † *prot-*, *proto-historian*, *proto-apostate, -bishop, -chemistry, -chronicler, -god, -heresiarch, -ideal, -metaphrast, -parent, -pattern, -protestant, -sinner, -tyrant*; (*b*) 'First in rank or importance, chief, principal', as in † *proto-abbaty* (= abbacy), *-architect, -chemist, -devil, -groomship, -justiciaryship, -magnate, -rebel, -traitor*; also the following: **Proto-dea·con** (-diacon) [Gr. πρωτοδιάκονος], a chief deacon (in the Greek Church). † **Proto-fo·rester** (protho-) [med.L. *protoforestarius*], chief forester. **Proto-go·spel** = Protevangelium. **Pro·tograph** [see -graph], a first or original writing. **Proto-histo·ric** *a.*, belonging or relating to primitive history, or the beginnings of historical records. **Proto-Ma·rk**, an assumed original writing which formed the basis of the existing Gospel of Mark; so **Proto-Ma·tthew.** † **Proto-na·tural** *a. Obs.*, primarily natural, belonging to the original nature of a thing. † **Proto-nota·tor**, a first or principal recorder of a court. **Proto-patria·rchal** *a.*, belonging to a chief patriarch. † **Pro·to-plot** *Obs.*, an original plot or scheme. **Proto-pre·sbyter** = Protopope. † **Proto-pri·mitive** *a.*, earliest among the primitive, most primitive. † **Proto-scri·niary** (*erron.* scrinerary), a chief keeper of records, etc. **Proto-typo·grapher**, the earliest or chief printer. **Protove·stiary** [med.L. *prōtovestiārius*], the chief keeper of a (royal) wardrobe. **Protozeu·gma** (see quot.). Also Protocanonical, Protomartyr, Protopope, Prototype, etc.

1647 M. Hudson *Div. Right Govt.* I. viii. 63 All Histories and Chronicles..since Moses the *Prothistorian of the world. a 1661 Fuller *Worthies, Somerset.* (1662) III. 21 Glassenbury being the *Proto-Abbaty then and many years after. 1827 Hallam *Const. Hist.* xv. II. 475 *note*, Sir James Montgomery, the false and fickle *proto-apostate of whiggism. 1859 Hobhouse *Italy* I. 93 Sansovino was *proto-architect to the empire of St. Mark. 1641 Heylin *Hist. Episc.* II. (1657) 18 James the *Proto-Bishop, the first that ever had a fixt Episcopall Sea, was ordained Bishop of Hierusalem, by Peter, James and John the sonnes of Zebedee. 1907 *Edin. Rev.* Jan. 34 Anastasius..sent the *proto-chemist, Johannes Isthmius, to end his fraudulent career in the Fortress of Petra. 1650 T. Vaughan (*title*) Anthroposophia Theomagica: Or a Discourse of the Nature of Man and his state after death; Grounded on his Creator's *Proto-Chimistry. *Ibid.* 9 He that knows how to imitate the Proto-Chymistrie of the Spirit by Separation of the Principles wherein the Life is Imprisoned. 1604 Parsons *3rd Pt. Three Convers. Eng., Relat. Trial* 61 Though he be the Protestants *Protochronicler. 1698 J. Crull *Muscovy* 314 He hath also a *Proto-Deacon. 1896 *Westm. Gaz.* 27 May 6/2 Two archpriests, accompanied by proto-diacons, come forward. 1694 Motteux *Rabelais* v. xiii, Oh you Devils,.. *Proto-Devils, Panto-Devils, you would wed a Monk, would you? [1617 Minsheu *Ductor*, *Protoforestarius*, was he whom the auncient Kings of this Realme made cheefe of Winsour Forest.] 1631 Weever *Anc. Fun. Mon.* 644 This Hugh was high Justice, Gardian, or Prothoforester of England. 1900 *Nature* 8 Mar. 437/2 So strangely complex a pantheon was set up that the *protogod was almost whelmed by the sanctifications of himself. 1841 Myers *Cath. Th.* III. § 46. 176 If it be admitted that an authentic *protograph of the Bible, with incontestably Divine signature..does not exist. 1822 *New Monthly Mag.* V. 342 The *protogroomship of the horse. 1844 W. Kay in *Fleury's Eccl. Hist.* III. 188 *note*, The words..may simply refer to the fact of Simon's being the *proto-heresiarch. 1880 *Trans. Royal Hist. Soc.* VIII. 191 The great school of *protohistoric mythology. 1901 *Pilot* 26 Jan. 102/2 Our knowledge of prehistoric and protohistoric times..increases daily. 1716 M. Davies *Athen. Brit.* III. *Diss. Physick* 40 The same *Proto-Ideal Purpose of drawing out the Primogenial Physick of the Grecians to its first aboriginal Offspring. 1611 Speed *Hist. Gt. Brit.* IX. ix. § 31. 588 The Earle of Kent, whom..the King remooued from the *Proto-Iustitiariship (or high office of his Chiefe Iustice). 1822 *New Monthly Mag.* V. 342 Creating him a *protomagnate of Persia. 1883 Schaff *Hist. Ch.* II. XII. lxxix. 600 He used the Hebrew Matthew ..or a lost *proto-Mark. 1865 De Morgan in *Athenæum* 13 May 653/3 Billingsley, the English *protometaphrast of Euclid. a 1653 Binning *Serm.* (1845) 68 This is the *proto-natural obligation. 1720 Strype *Stow's Surv.* II. v. xxviii. 387/1 The Maior's Clerk, together with the Common Clerk of the City, and the Sheriff's Clerks sat before them, to note..all the Matters objected...And one was *Protonotator, from whose Note all the rest took each his Copy of Writing. 1603 J. Davies *Microcosm.* (Grosart) 23/1 Since our *Proto-parents' lowest fall, Our wisdome's highest pitch (God wot) is low. c 1820 Coleridge in *Lit. Rem.* (1838) III. 218 Aye! here is the *ovum*,..the proto-parent of the whole race of controversies. 1658 Bramhall *Schism Guarded* IV. i. x, His *Protopatriarchal power was acknowledged. 1657 J. Watts *Vind. Ch. Eng.* 86 We are to..eye Christ beyond them, especially, as the *Proto-Patterne. 1584 *Leycesters Commonw.* (1641) 91 Their Architipe or *Proto-plot which they follow (I meane the conspiracy of Northumberland and Suffolke in King Edwards dayes). 1882–3 *Schaff's Encycl. Relig. Knowl.* III. 1942 There is a *proto-presbyter or proto-pope at each cathedral ..in the Græco-Russian Church. 1694 J. Smith *Doctr. Lord's Day* 70 Sunday was accounted by the *Protoprimitive Fathers the Seventh day in the order of Creation. 1604 Parsons *3rd Pt. Three Convers. Eng.* 355 One of the first *Protoprotestants of England. 1714 Lockhart *Mem. Affairs Scot.* 9 His son..thence acquired the title of *proto-rebell. 1907 A. Lang *Hist. Scot.* IV. iv. 80 Queensberry, now regarded by Cavaliers as 'the proto-rebel', was Privy Seal. 1670 G. H. *Hist. Cardinals* I. III. 85 He had under him twelve Scrineraries, and one *Proto-Scrinerary. 1702 *Burlesque L'Estrange's Quevedo* 279 Lucifer, the *Proto-Sinner of Heaven. 1570–6 Lambarde *Peramb. Kent* (1826) 284 Thomas that *Prototraitour and rebell to his Prince. 1656 Blount *Glossogr.*, *Prototypographer.., the cheif Printer. 1880 Blades in *Athenæum* 18 Dec. 814/3 He left Bruges to return to his native country and become its proto-typographer. 1657 W. Rand tr. *Gassendi's Life Peiresc* Ep. Ded. 4 Nimrod the mighty Hunter, and *Proto-Tyrant of the world. 1774 Warton *Hist. Eng. Poetry* (1840) I. iii. 132 *Protovestiary or wardrobe keeper of the palace of Antiochus at Constantinople (c 1070). 1657 J. Smith *Myst. Rhet.* 180 *Protozeugma,..when the Verb or Adjective is expressed in the beginning of the clause or sentence; and omitted after.

2. In numerous modern scientific and technical terms (sbs. and adjs.). The second element is properly of Greek origin, less frequently of Latin.

a. Prefixed to adjs. from names of countries or races, forming adjs. denominating primitive or original tribes, languages, writings, works of art or manufacture, styles of architecture, etc.: as *proto-Arabic, -Babylonian, -Caucasic, -Celtic, -Corinthian, -Doric, -Egyptian, -Elamite, -Greek, -Ionic, -Phœnician, -Semitic.* Also with nouns denoting natives or inhabitants, as *proto-Mede.*

1889 Sayce in *Contemp. Rev.* Dec. 905 An alphabet and language which have been termed *Protoarabic. 1889 I. Taylor *Orig. Aryans* iii. 182 The higher culture of the Semites, which again was derived from the *proto-Babylonian people. 1899 R. Munro *Prehist. Scot.* III. 246 The horned weapons are products of the *proto-Celtic stratum which lies chronologically between the earlier megalithic chambers and the later Gaulish tumuli. 1894 E. Robinson in *Nation* (N.Y.) 31 May 405/2 Of the early styles,..and, most of all, the so-called '*proto-Corinthian'. 1907 *Athenæum* 6 July 20/2 In one of the primitive graves laid bare..in the Forum was found a small vase of the proto-Corinthian class. 1876 Birch *Rede Lect. Egypt* 21 The architect invents the *protodoric column. 1901 A. J. Evans in *Oxf. Univ. Gaz.* 12 Feb. 339/1 A survival of this *Proto-Egyptian class in the Libyan regions. 1901 *Pilot* 26 Jan. 103/1 Hitherto..called 'Mycenæan' or *proto-Greek art. 1890 *Cent. Dict.* s. v., [Figure] *Proto-Ionic Capital, discovered in the Troad. 1889 I. Taylor *Orig. Aryans* iii. 184 Non-Aryan tribes, such as the *proto-Medes,..the Etruscans, and the Picts. 1893 F. Adams *New Egypt* 38 An expedition of acquisition, a truly *Proto-Phœnician trait!

b. In terms, chiefly of Zoology or Biology: usually designating an (actual or hypothetical) original or primitive form, type, organism, structure, etc. ‖ **Prota·mnion**, a hypothetical primitive amniotic animal, the supposed common

ancestor of mammals, birds, and reptiles. ‖ **Protamœ·ba**, a genus of Protozoa having lobate pseudopodia like the amœba (cf. Protogenes); hence **Protamœ·ban**, *a.* belonging to or having the characters of this genus; *sb.* a member of this genus; **Protamœ·boid** *a.*, resembling a protamœba. **Prota·mphirhine**, the ancestral type of the amphirhine or double-nostrilled vertebrates. ‖ **Prota·stacus** [Gr. ἀστακός lobster, crayfish], the ancestral type of the *Astacidæ* or crayfishes; hence **Prota·stacine** (-səin) *a.* **Protaxo·nial** *a.*, in *Morphology*, having the parts arranged about a single primary or main axis; of or pertaining to *Protaxonia.* **Prote·mbryo**: see quot.; hence **Protembryo·nic** *a.* ‖ **Protence·phalon**, the first of the three primary cerebral vesicles of the embryo. **Prothe·lminth** [Gr. ἕλμινς, ἑλμινθ- worm], a protozoön of the order *Prothelmintha*, comprising most of the *Infusoria*, regarded as representing an ancestral type of worms; hence **Prothelmi·nthic** *a.*; so ‖ **Prothe·lmis**, a hypothetical ancestral type of worms. **Prothyalosomal** (proþəiˌălosōᵘ·măl) *a.*, pertaining to the *prothyalosoma* [Gr. ὕαλος glass + σῶμα body], 'Van Beneden's name (1883) for the envelope of the nucleolus of an ovum' (*Syd. Soc. Lex.*). ‖ **Prothysteron** (proþi·stĕrǫn) *Rhet.* [Gr. πρωθύστερον] = Hysteron proteron. **Protichnite** (-i·knəit), *Palæont.* [see Ichnite], one of the fossil tracks found in the Potsdam sandstone of Canada, supposed to be those of a trilobite or allied animal. **Pro·toblast** [see -blast], (*a*) a cell of a primitive or simple form, consisting of a mass of protoplasm with no investing membrane or cell-wall; (*b*) 'the nucleus of the ovum' (*Syd. Soc. Lex.*). **Protobla·stic** *a.* = Holoblastic. **Protobla·stoderm**, the primitive blastoderm or investing layer of the fertilized ovum. **Proto-ca·rinate**, *a.* belonging to those primitive birds having a carinate or keeled breast-bone; *sb.* one of such birds. **Protoce·rcal** *a.*, *Ichth.*, having a tail-fin of the primitive form, continuous with the dorsal and ventral fins. **Pro·tocere** (-sīᵊɹ) [Gr. κέρας horn], the rudiment of the antler of a deer, the process developed in the first year. ‖ **Protoce·rebrum**, the anterior cerebral vesicle of the embryo, which develops into the cerebrum; hence **Protoce·rebral** *a.* **Protocœlo·mate**, an animal belonging to the *Protocœlomata*, a proposed division of *Metazoa* characterized by a primitive enteric cavity with simple cœlomic sacs, as most sponges; hence **Protocœloma·tic** *a.* **Pro·toconch** (-kǫŋk) [see Conch], the embryonic shell in certain cephalopods; hence **Protoco·nchal** *a.* **Protodi·pnoan**, a hypothetical primitive dipnoan. **Pro·todome** *Cryst.*, a primary Dome. **Protodyna·stic** *a.*, *Anc. Hist.*, belonging to the first or earliest (Egyptian) dynasties. **Protofo·rami·nifer** (pl. -foramini·fera), a primitive foraminifer. ‖ **Protoga·ster** [Gr. γαστήρ stomach]: see quot. **Protoga·stric** *a.* [as prec.], (*a*) a term designating two lobes, one on each side, towards the front of the gastro-hepatic area of the carapace in brachyurous Crustaceans; (*b*) pertaining to the protogaster. **Protole·mur**, a term including various extinct insectivorous mammals as the supposed ancestral types of the lemurs. ‖ **Protoma·la** [L. *māla* jaw], each member of the first pair of jaws or mandibles in the Myriapoda; hence **Protoma·lal**, **Protoma·lar** *adjs.* **Protome·ristem** *Bot.*, the meristem or generating tissue of the youngest parts of plants; primary meristem (Russow (in Ger.) 1872). **Proto·merite** [Gr. μέρος part], the first or anterior segment of a polycystid gregarine, as distinguished from the larger posterior segment (*deuteromerite* or *deutomerite*); hence **Protomeri·tic** *a.* **Protome·sal** *a.*, *Entom.* [Gr. μέσος middle], applied to a series of cells in the wings of hymenopterous insects; now called the second, third, and fourth submarginal or cubital cells. **Pro·tomorph** [Gr. μορφή form], a primitive or original form; so **Protomo·rphic** *a.*, having the primitive or simplest form or structure. **Protomy·xoid** *a.*, resembling *Protomyxa* [Gr. μύξα slime], a genus of myxopodous Protozoa. ‖ **Protone·phron** [Gr. νεφρός kidney], the primitive kidney in the embryo of vertebrates, consisting of the *pronephron, mesonephron*, and *metanephron*; hence **Protone·phric** *a.* **Protonu·cleate** *a.*, having a primitive nucleus; belonging to the *Protonucleata*, a hypothetical group of Protozoa regarded as the ancestors of all other animals. **Proto-o·rganism**, a primitive or unicellular organism, animal or vegetable; a protozoön or protophyte. **Proto-o·rnithoid** *a.* [Gr. ὄρνις, ὀρνιθ- bird], of the most ancient or primitive birdlike type. **Protophlo·em** *Bot.*, the tissue from which the phloem is developed; the primitive phloem of a fibro-vascular bundle (Russow (in Ger.) 1872). **Protopo·dial** *a.*, pertaining to a *protopodium*. **Proto·podite** [see Podite], in Crustacea, the first or basal joint of a limb, which articulates with its somite; hence **Protopodi·tic** *a.* ‖ **Protopo·dium** [see Podium 2 b], a primitive or typical foot in Molluscs. **Pro·toprism** *Cryst.*, a primary prism. **Protopy·ramid** *Cryst.*, a primary pyramid. **Protosei·smograph** [see Seismograph], an instrument for recording the beginning or first trace of an earthquake shock. **Protosi·phon**, the primitive or rudimentary siphon or siphuncle in the protoconch of certain cephalopods; also ‖ **Protosipho·nula.** **Protoso·mite**, each of the rudimentary somites or segments of the embryo in arthropods and annelids; hence **Protosomi·tic** *a.* **Pro·tospasm** *Path.*, a local spasm preceding a general convulsion. **Protospe·rmatoblast** [see Sperm and -blast], term for certain cells from which spermatozoa are formed: see quot. **Protospo·ngian** *a.*, designating a primitive stage in the development of a sponge. **Pro·tospore** *Bot.*, a primary spore or spore-like body in certain fungi, corresponding to the prothallium in higher cryptogams. **Proto·stoma** [Gr. στόμα mouth]: see quot. for *protogaster.* **Protosystema·tic** *a.*, *Cryst.*, belonging to a primary system. **Proto·tergite** *Entom.* [L. *tergum* back], the first dorsal segment of the abdomen of an insect. **Proto·toxin**: see quot.; so **Prototo·xoid** = *protoxoid*: see Toxin and Toxoid. **Protove·rtebra**, (*a*) *Comp. Anat.* in Carus's nomenclature (1828) applied to the ribs reckoned as the first set of vertebræ; (*b*) *Embryol.* each of the segments, formerly considered as primitive (temporary) vertebræ, in the early embryo of a vertebrate; hence **Protove·rtebral** *a.*, pertaining to or of the nature of a protovertebra. **Protove·rtebrate** *a.*, (*a*) furnished with protovertebræ; (*b*) belonging to the *Protovertebrata*, the hypothetical ancestral forms of vertebrate animals. ‖ **Proto·vum**, an ovum in its first or primitive stage, e.g. before impregnation, or (in the case of a meroblastic ovum) before the formation of the food-yolk (cf. Metovum). **Protoxylem** (-zəi·lem) *Bot.*, the tissue from which the xylem is developed; the primitive xylem of a fibro-vascular bundle. **Proto·zonite** *Entom.* [Gr. ζώνη girdle], each of the primitive or rudimentary segments of the body of an insect in the embryonic stage. **Protu·reter**, the primitive ureter, the excretory duct of the *protonephron.* See also Protohippus, Protophyte, Protozoa, etc.

1879 tr. *Haeckel's Evol. Man* xviii. II. 134 This unknown common parent-form is the Primitive Amnion Animal (*Protamnion*). In external appearance the Protamnion was most probably an intermediate form between the Salamanders and the Lizards. 1877 Huxley *Anat. Inv. Anim.* ii. 79 It is open to doubt..whether either *Protamœba, Protogenes*, or *Myxodictyum* is anything but one stage of a cycle of forms. 1883 J. E. Ady in *Knowledge* 15 June 355/2 The thousands of other *protamœboid creatures. 1869 Huxley *Crit. & Addr.* xii. (1873) 317 From this *'Protamphirhine' were developed, in divergent lines, the true Sharks, Rays, and Chimæræ; the Ganoids, and the Dipneusta. 1880 — *Crayfish* vi. 344 The common *protastacine form is to be sought in the Trias. 1878 — in *Proc. Zool. Soc.* 787 A Crustacean..which we may call provisionally *Protastacus.* 1887 *Proc. Boston Soc. Nat. Hist.* 397 The stages of holoblastic ova may be..classified as follows..(1) The ovum or Monoplast..; (2) the first stage of segmentation..; (3) the second stage of segmentation... We have proposed to classify these stages under the name of *Protembryo. 1887 T. J. Parker in *Proc. Zool. Soc.* 37 The..unpaired portion of the *protencephalon (embryonic fore-brain). 1879 tr. *Haeckel's Evol. Man* xvii. II. 76 The common parent-form of the whole Worm tribe (the *Prothelmis*). 1873 Dawson *Earth & Man* iii. 45 Some of the most ancient sandstones have their surfaces covered with rows of punctured impressions (*Protichnites, first foot-prints). 1880 *Libr. Univ. Knowl.* (U.S.) VII. 772 The sandstone beds which contain the protichnites. 1872 Packard *Embryol. Stud. Hexapodous Insects* (Peabody Acad. Sci. I. Mem. III.) 6 The primitive blastodermic skin..or as it might be termed, *protoblastoderm. 1901 *Ibis* Apr. 343 That in Rhea we have represented the *proto-carinate wing-type of to-day. 1892 J. A. Thomson *Outl. Zool.* xx. 403 The end of the notochord in the tail is quite straight (protocercal and diphycercal). 1885 Wilder in *N. York Med. Jrnl.* 28 Mar. 354 *Protocerebrum, a monomial..significant equivalent for..cerebral rudiment. 1884 Hyatt in *Proc. Boston Soc. Nat. Hist.* 113 Anatomically, the Sponges may be called Metazoa protocœlomata...We can readily transform a *protocœlomate into a trochocœlomate by destroying the horizontal parts of the partitions. 1883 *Ibid.* XXIII. 542 The *protoconch of Owen, in Cephalopods, is the early shell which precedes the conch, or true shell. Professors Hyatt and Brooks consider the protoconch in cephalous molluscs as..probably derived from the periconch of Scaphopods. 1878 Gurney *Crystallogr.* 52 The former [dome] is distinguished as the *protodome. 1902 *Daily Chron.* 6 Oct. 3/1 The period of the first three dynasties ..requires a designation of its own,..the word '*protodynastic' appears to be suitable. 1875 Dawson *Dawn of Life* viii. 215 Eozoon [etc.], our *proto-foraminifera. 1879 tr. *Haeckel's Evol. Man* viii. I. 193, I shall call the central cavity of the Gastrula-body the primitive intestine (*protogaster*), and its opening the primitive mouth (*protostoma*). 1877 Huxley *Anat. Inv. Anim.* vi. 313 The latter is..subdivided into two epigastric lobes, two *protogastric lobes, a median mesogastric lobe, two metagastric lobes and two urogastric lobes. 1887 Heilprin *Distrib. Anim.* III. ii. 343 By Trouessart they [certain mammals of tertiary age] are all ranged with the Insectivora as the group of the *protolemurs. 1883 Packard in *Proc. Amer. Philos. Soc.* June 198 [In *Myriapoda*] the *protomala consists of two portions, the *cardo* and *stipes*, while the hexapodous mandible is invariably composed of but one piece,..which corresponds to the stipes of the myriapodous protomala. *Ibid.* 203 The *protomalal and deutomalal arthromeres. 1881 *Nature* XXIII. 288/1 Dr. Jakob Eriksson describes in a lengthened paper the *protomeristem of the roots of Dicotyledons. 1882 Vines *Sachs' Bot.* 550 The young anther consists at first of a small-celled proto-meristem in which a fibro-vascular bundle becomes differentiated lying in the axis of the connective. 1888 Rolleston & Jackson *Anim. Life* 858 [In] the *Polycystidea* [the body] is divided by two septa into three segments...The first segment is the epimerite; it is the part from which the other two segments bud out...The second segment is the *protomerite, the third and by far the largest, the deuteromerite. 1826 Kirby & Sp. *Entomol.* III. xxxv. 632 The medial areolets of the Intermediate Area..form three distinct series; these may be called the *protomesal, deuteromesal, and tritomesal, reckoning from the postcostal areolets. 1876 J. J. G. Wilkinson *Hum. Sc. & Div. Rev.* 58 The growth of evils from their first wicked thoughts or germs, from their true *protomorphs, tiny and unperceived, to monstrous destructions. 1859 *Todd's Cycl. Anat.* V. 476/1 The integumentary *protomorphic line. 1867 H. Spencer *Princ. Biol.* § 290 II. 289 A protomorphic layer, which differentiates in opposite directions. 1883 P. Geddes in *Encycl. Brit.* XVI. 846/2 The writer has attempted to explain the forms of free and united cells as specializations of a (*protomyxoid) cycle in which variations of functional activity are accompanied by the assumption of corresponding forms. 1879 tr. *Haeckel's Evol. Man* xxv. II. 412 In all low Skulled Animals (*Craniota*), without amnion..the primitive kidneys (*protonephra*), though much modified,..act permanently as urine-secreting glands. 1861 *N. Syd. Soc. Year-bk. Med.* 113 Genesis of the *Proto-organisms found in Calcined Air, and in Putrescible Substances that have been heated to 150°. 1895 *Syd. Soc. Lex.*, *Protoörganism*, one of the simplest of organised beings, capable of being referred either to the animal or vegetable kingdom. 1883 W. Sikes in *Harper's Mag.* Feb. 332/2 Slab ..extending the..area of *proto-ornithoid forms of life from longitude 72° to 4°. 1884 Bower & Scott *De Bary's Phaner.* 390 The first primitive elements of the phloem, Russow's *protophloem. 1898 tr. *Strasburger's Bot.* I. i. 105 In fully-developed vascular bundles the protoxylem and protophloem cease to perform their functions. 1870 Rolleston *Anim. Life* 94 (Common Crayfish) The appendages of the..post-abdominal segments consist of a biarticulate '*protopodite' [etc.]. 1877 Huxley *Anat. Inv. Anim.* vi. 273 Two pairs of appendages, composed each of a protopodite, terminated by an endopodite and exopodite. 1880 Gill in *Smithsonian Rep.* 361 The valve of the siphon [in Cephalopods] is a true foot or *protopodium, and the two lateral folds are pteropodia. 1895 Story-Maskelyne *Crystallogr.* 283 The hexagonal deutero-prism..is identical in features with the *proto-prism...The horizontal sections of the proto- and deutero-prisms are regular hexagons. *Ibid.* 291 The trigonal *proto-pyramid may be regarded..as being a limiting case of the ditrigonal proto-pyramid. 1881 *Friends' Intelligencer* XXXVIII. 556 The *protoseismograph and the microseismograph,..with which Professor Palmieri.. may detect the first faintest quiver which hints the coming earthquake. 1893 Hyatt in *Proc. Boston Soc. Nat. Hist.* 103 An aperture through which the *protosiphonula communicated with the protoconch. 1877 Huxley *Anat. Inv. Anim.* v. 213 Generally, the development of the *protosomites, as these segments might be called, does not occur until some time after the embryo has been hatched. *Ibid.* vi. 250 As with Annelids, the segmentation of the body results from the subdivision of the mesoblast by transverse constrictions into protosomites. 1890 *Cent. Dict.*, *Jacksonian epilepsy* .., epilepsy in which the spasms are local...Such spasms are also called *monospasms*, or, when they are followed by general convulsions, **protospasms*. 1899 *Allbutt's Syst. Med.* VII. 289 With this monospasm or proto-spasm there is often a tendency to generalisation. 1889 *Q. Jrnl. Microsc. Sc.* Dec. 251 *note*, The spermatozoa of the Decapods studied by him [Sabatier] arise in large cells, the '*protospermatoblasts'. 1884 Hyatt in *Proc. Boston Soc. Nat. Hist.* 86 We have not been able to separate the *Protospongian stage of Haeckel from the ascula. 1878 Gurney *Crystallogr.* 72 These are sometimes called the *protosystematic planes. 1895 Story-Maskelyne *Crystallogr.* 110. 1904 *Brit. Med. Jrnl.* 10 Sept. 567 We have three different toxins with different toxicity and different avidities to the antitoxin, viz. the *prototoxin, the deuterotoxin, and the tritotoxin. *Ibid.* 568 The prototoxin with the greatest avidity for the antitoxin and with the greatest toxicity..but..being comparatively labile it changes after some time into *prototoxoid. 1877 Huxley *Anat. Inv. Anim.* v. 225 The mesoblast becomes divided into a series of quadrate masses, like the *protovertebræ of a vertebrate embryo. 1881 Mivart *Cat* 325 On each side of the medullary groove and notochord a series of quadrate thickenings appear, termed protovertebræ. 1890 Billings *Nat. Med. Dict.*, *Protovertebra*, primitive segment of the mesoderm; myotome. When the name was given the myotomes were supposed to be the rudiments of the vertebræ. **Protovertebral column* or *plate*, a thick column of cells lying along the medullary groove, from which by segmentation the protovertebræ are formed. 1879 tr. *Haeckel's Evol. Man* I. 223 The **protovum* is thus transformed into the *metovum* (after-egg) which is many times larger..but..is only a single..cell. 1889 tr. *Strasburger's Bot.* viii. 86 We have found..in the wood portion (the xylem) of the fibro-vasal bundle, the primary wood, the *Protoxylem, composed of primary wood-parenchyma and of vessels. 1898 *Ibid.* I. i. 105 The protoxylem occupies the innermost, the protophloem the outermost side of a procambium strand. 1872 Packard *Embryol. Stud. Diplax* etc. (Peabody Acad. Sci.

PATUS 2). Hence **Protra·cheate,** *a.* belonging to the *Protracheata*; *sb.* an animal of this class.

1878 BELL *Gegenbaur's Comp. Anat.* 255 In the Protracheata the nervous system remains in a lower condition. 1879 *Athenæum* 19 July 83/1 One of his hypothetical animals, a protracheate, may be said to have been actually discovered ..in the primitive air-breathing Arthropod Peripatus.

Protract (pro₁træ·kt), *sb.* [ad. L. *prōtractus* a prolonging, protraction, f. *prōtract-*, ppl. stem of *prōtrah-ĕre*: see next.]

†1. Prolongation or extension (of time); hence, delay, procrastination. *Obs.*

1536 *St. Papers Hen. VIII*, II. 298 The doing therof will aske a protracte of tyme. *a* 1640 SIR J. OGLE in *Sir F. Vere's Comm.* (1657) 143 By protract of time, and casualties of war, he found his numbers wasted. 1646 *Unhappy Game at Scotch & Eng.* 4 The difference would only be in the protract of time, not in the nature of the thing.

†2. A delineation, drawing. Cf. PORTRAIT. *Obs. rare.*

1585 T. WASHINGTON tr. *Nicholay's Voy.* II. xix. 53 b, I made the draughtes and protractes heere represented vnto you [orig. *ie fey les pourtraicts icy representez*].

3. [f. the vb.] A 'protracted meeting': see PROTRACTED 1, quot. 1860. *U.S. colloq.*

1908 *Mission Field* Jan. 343 There is always a great religious awakening at the annual revival or 'protract'... When the 'protract' is over their emotions are calmed and every man returns to his own 'vine and fig tree'.

Protract (protræ·kt), *v.* Also 7 -traicte. [f. L. *prōtract-*, ppl. stem of *prōtrah-ĕre* to draw forth, to prolong, extend, defer, f. *prō*, PRO-¹ 1 + *trah-ĕre* to draw. With sense 6 cf. PORTRAY, the direct repr. of *prōtrahĕre* through OF. *portraire.*]

I. †1. *trans.* To extend or prolong (time) so as to cause delay; to waste (time). *Obs.*

a 1548 HALL *Chron., Edw. IV* 240 b, All these faire wordes wer onely delaies to protracte tyme. *a* 1660 *Contemp. Hist. Irel.* (Ir. Archæol. Soc.) II. 84 His father would protraicte time the best he could. 1769 ROBERTSON *Chas. V*, II. Wks. 1813 V. 296 This they did merely to protract time.

2. To lengthen out (an action); to cause to continue or last longer; to extend in duration; to prolong. (The chief current sense.)

1563 [see PROTRACTING *vbl. sb.* 1]. 1591 SHAKS. *1 Hen. VI*, I. ii. 120 Else ne're could he so long protract his speech. 1614 SYLVESTER *Bethulia's Rescue* II. 439 But, with thy Dayes thy Dolours to protrack, Thou shalt from hence unto Bethulia pack. 1700 DRYDEN *Sigism. & Guiscardo* 334 But I..Protracting life have liv'd a day too long. 1838 THIRLWALL *Greece* V. xxxix. 101 Their stay was protracted for some weeks. 1855 MOTLEY *Dutch Rep.* v. iii. (1866) 699 The dance upon the sward was protracted to a late hour.

†3. To put off, defer, postpone (an action).

(The date of the first quotation is very doubtful.)

[1477 NORTON *Ord. Alch.* Introd. in Ashm. (1652) 3 Sin protracts the gifts of Heaven.] 1553 *Act 7 Edw. VI*, c. 1 § 16 If any Auditor..willingly protract or delay the taking of the same Accompt. *a* 1648 LD. HERBERT *Hen. VIII* (1683) 369 If the Interview..must needs follow (which yet he wished were protracted). 1776 GIBBON *Decl. & F.* v. (1869) I. 97 He attempted, however, to prevent, or at least to protract, his ruin. 1808 ELEANOR SLEATH *Bristol Heiress* IV. 219 Lord L——s' marriage, which had been protracted ..was celebrated in Grosvenor-square.

†b. To put off, defer (a person). *Obs. rare.*

1737 WHISTON *Josephus, Antiq.* XI. iv. § 4 Desire..to delay and protract the Jews in their zeal.

†4. *intr.* To make delay, to delay. *Obs.*

1611 BIBLE *Neh.* ix. 30 Yet many yeres diddest thou forbeare [*marg.* protract ouer] them. 1677 *Govt. Venice* 293 They had not lost the Battle of Vaila, had they..protracted but ten days.

II. 5. *trans.* To extend in space or position.

a 1658 J. DURHAM *Exp. Rev.* vi. (1680) 31 Concerning Christs Body on earth, or ubiquitie of his humanitie, or bodily presence with his churches, or for protracting of his Body. 1749 SMOLLETT *Regicide* v. vii. To save his country, and protract his blaze Of glory, farther still! *a* 1850 WORDSW. (Ogilvie), Many a ramble, far And wide protracted, through the tamer ground Of these our unimaginative days.

†b. To extend or amplify the signification of anything; to 'stretch'. *Obs. rare.*

1698 FRYER *Acc. E. India & P.* 363 If any thing happen to oppose common Sense, they protract the meaning [of the prophecy] Mysteriously or Anagogically.

III. 6. To draw, represent by a drawing [so med.L. *prōtrahĕre*]; *spec.* to draw to scale; to delineate by means of a scale and protractor (lines, angles, a figure); to plot out.

1563 SHUTE *Archit.* B ij b, An Architecte must .. haue experte knowladg in drawing and protracting the thinge, which he hath conceyued. 1607 [see PROTRACTION 5]. 1669 STURMY *Mariner's Mag.* v. 6 After you have taken the Angles..You must Protract or lay down the Figure. 1766 *Compl. Farmer* s.v. *Surveying*, How to measure a close, or parcel of land, and to protract it, and give up the content. 1881 E. HULL in *Nature* 22 Dec. 177/2 If we protract to a true scale the outlines of certain tracts of the British Isles.

Protracted (protræ·ktėd), *ppl. a.* [f. prec. + -ED¹.]

1. Lengthened, extended, prolonged; **a.** in time.

1746–7 HERVEY *Medit.* (1767) I. 62 (*Tombs*) The divine Redeemer expired in tedious and protracted Torments. 1855 HALIBURTON *Nat. & Hum. Nat.* I. I. 2 It's a gentleman that calculates to hold a protracted meeten here to night. 1860 BARTLETT *Dict. Amer.*, *Protracted Meeting*, a name given in New England to a religious meeting, protracted or continued for several days. 1864 BRYCE *Holy Rom. Emp.* xix. (1875) 354 The miseries of a protracted war.

b. in space.

1784 COWPER *Task* I. 257 Their shaded walks And long protracted bowers.

2. Drawn out; = PROLATE *a.* 1.

1816 tr. *Lacroix's Diff. & Int. Calculus* 662 The protracted or contracted cycloid.

†3. Delayed, tardy. *Obs.*

1838 tr. *Strauss' Early Life Lutheran Clergym.* ii. 12 A cart appeared with the protracted produce of the fields.

4. Drawn to scale; plotted out; see prec. 6.

1696 *Col. Rec. Pennsylv.* I. 498 The Courses and protracted figure thereof. 1808 PIKE *Sources Mississ.* II. App. 51 Lieutenant Wilkinson has copied and carries with him a very elegant protracted sketch of the route.

Hence **Protra·ctedly** *adv.*, in a protracted or long-continued way; **Protra·ctedness,** long continuance or extent.

1847 WEBSTER, *Protractedly.* 1862 F. HALL *Hindu Philos. Syst.* 29 Pursuing it with due heed, continuously, and protractedly. 1893 F. ADAMS *New Egypt* 122 When.. he told me that he himself..had received an order..I whistled protractedly, and decided offhand on going up to Cairo. 1888 TALMAGE *Serm.* in *N. Y. Witness* 29 Feb., In regard to what is the protractedness and immensity of influence of one good woman in the church and world.

Protracter, obs. variant of PROTRACTOR.

(The only form in BAILEY (originally), and in JOHNSON; also a variant in later Dicts.)

Protra·ctible, *a.* [f. as PROTRACT *v.* + -IBLE.] Capable of being protracted or lengthened out.

1830 *Westm. Rev.* Oct. 434 In the infinitely protractible part with which, under his plan,..jury trial is preceded.

Protractile (protræ·ktil, -əil), *a. Zool.* [f. as prec. + -ILE: cf. *contractile.*] Capable of being lengthened out or extended.

1828 STARK *Elem. Nat. Hist.* I. 135 Echidna...Toothless, but the palate aculeated;..tongue protractile. 1861 HULME tr. *Moquin-Tandon* II. v. 268 A special organ..sometimes internal and protractile. 1878 BELL *Gegenbaur's Comp. Anat.* 298 A narrow coiled continuation of this leads to the protractile ovipositor.

Hence **Protracti·lity,** the quality or fact of being protractile.

1849–52 *Todd's Cycl. Anat.* IV. 1146/2 The Chameleon presents us with the most complete protractility of the organ [the tongue].

Protracting (protræ·ktiŋ), *vbl. sb.* [f. PROTRACT *v.* + -ING¹.] The action of PROTRACT *v.*

1. Lengthening out, prolonging, extending (of time, or of action in time); † dilatory action (*obs.*).

a 1548 HALL *Chron., Hen. VI* 89 b, The duke of Bedford.. not content with their whisperynges and protractyng of tyme. 1563 GOLDING *Cæsar* I. (1565) 31 b, The Galles were now weary with long protracting of the war. 1601 FULBECKE *1st Pt. Parall.* (1602) 75 The tedious and odious protracting of suits. 1622 CALLIS *Stat. Sewers* (1647) 114 If any danger be likely to ensue by the protracting of time.

†b. The putting off or postponement of an action; deferring. *Obs.*

1581 SAVILE *Tacitus, Hist.* III. xx. (1591) 125 More oftentimes profiteth and helpeth hee by protracting, then venturing rashly. 1608 *Mem.* in *Buccleuch MSS.* (Hist. MSS. Comm.) 76 The protracting of a plantation until the Ward come to years.

2. Extending in space. *rare.*

a 1658 [see PROTRACT *v.* 5].

3. Drawing or plotting out to scale; delineation.

1669 STAYNRED *Fortification* Title-p., The Scale, for speedy Protracting of any Fort. 1766 *Compl. Farmer* s.v. *Surveying*, These squares and long squares need no protracting; for you need only to multiply the chains and links of the length, by the chains and links of the breadth.

4. *attrib.* and *Comb.*, denoting instruments used in protracting (sense 3), as *protracting-bevel, -needle, -pin*; **protracting quadrant,** a protractor.

1669 STURMY *Mariner's Mag.* IV. xi. 178 To know the Rhomb between any two Places..by a Protracting Quadrant. 1701 MOXON *Math. Instr.* 16 *Protracting Pin*, a taper piece of brass with a Point of Silver, to draw black Lines on Mathematical Paper, and a small Head..which holds a fine Needle to prick off any Degree and part from the Protractor. 1766 *Compl. Farmer* s.v. *Surveying*, Having drawn lines with the point of the compasses, or a protracting-needle, the intersections represent the angles. 1875 KNIGHT *Dict. Mech.*, *Protracting-bevel*, a plotting-instrument having a protracting sector and a prolongation of one radius, which forms a rule.

Protracting (protræ·ktiŋ), *ppl. a.* [f. as prec. + -ING².] That protracts, delays, or defers; delaying, time-consuming.

1600 R. CHURCH *Fumée's Hist. Hungary* 29 He might rather molest them by a protracting fight. 1822 'B. CORNWALL' *Dram. Scenes, Jul. the Apostate* i, Never! A dull, protracting, melancholy word That in an alien language, talks despair.

Protraction (protræ·kʃən). [a. F. *protraction* (1499 in Godef.), or ad. late L. *prōtractiōn-em*, n. of action from *prōtrah-ĕre*: see PROTRACT *v.*] The action of protracting.

I. 1. The lengthening out or extension of time or of the duration of anything; drawing out, prolongation; † delay, postponement (*obs.*).

1535 *Act 27 Hen. VIII*, c. 4 § 1 Without longe tarienge and protraction of time. 1608 D. T[UVIL] *Ess. Pol. & Mor.* 112 By reason of his protractions and delayes. 1610 HEALEY *Vives' Comm. St. Aug. Citie of God* (1620) 10 That Fabius that ..by his cunning protraction blunted the fury of Hannibal. *a* 1677 HALE *Prim. Orig. Man.* 92 As to the fabulous protractions of the age of the World by the Egyptians or others, they are uncertain idle Traditions. 1734 tr. *Rollin's Anc. Hist.* IV. VIII. xiii. 83 Such are his usual protraction, delays, distrusts and fearful precaution. 1868 E. EDWARDS *Ralegh* I. xxi. 473 The long protraction of the suit must have been occasioned by difficulties.

2. Drawing forth or out.

1681 tr. *Willis' Rem. Med. Wks.* Vocab., *Protraction*, a drawing forth at length. 1895 *Syd. Soc. Lex.*, *Protraction*, extraction; as of a foreign body from a wound.

3. A stretching out or extension; the action of a protractor (muscle).

1890 in *Cent. Dict.* 1899 *Allbutt's Syst. Med.* VII. 285 In this area one may distinguish, more or less completely, protraction and retraction of the upper arm.

4. The lengthening of a vowel, syllable, or word; = PROLONGATION 3.

a 1849 POE *Fancy & Imag.* Wks. 1865 III. 381 He also too frequently draws out the word Heaven into two syllables—a protraction which it never will support.

II. 5. The drawing to scale or laying down of the figure of any surface, esp. of a piece of land.

1607 NORDEN *Surv. Dial.* III. 128 The difference is onely in the protraction: for where the one protracteth the worke, by the degrees, found by the fall of the wandring Index: so the other protracteth from the degree, whereupon the needle falleth. 1669 J. FLAMSTEAD in *Phil. Trans.* IV. 1109 The protraction of the Star's way in this appearance will be facile. 1774 M. MACKENZIE *Maritime Surv.* 66 Protract carefully, with a large Protractor, the several Angles written in the Field-book; and also calculate trigonometrically the most material Distances: judge of the Accuracy of the Protraction by its Agreement with the Calculation. 1823 SCORESBY *Jrnl. Whale Fish.* 268 The distances by protraction, and the estimated distances of five or six headlands,..generally coincided to within 1½ miles. 1866 LIVINGSTONE *Last Jrnls.* (1873) I. x. 270 By protraction Rua Point was distant 33 miles.

b. That which is protracted; a chart or plan drawn or laid down to scale; a survey.

1669 STURMY *Mariner's Mag.* II. viii. 73 Any Chart or Protraction whatsoever. 1810 G. CHALMERS *Caledonia* II. 62 Employing five years in drawing their protractions of the country..on a vast scale of 3000 feet to an inch.

†**Protra·ctive,** *a. Obs.* [f. L. *prōtract-* (see PROTRACT *v.*) + -IVE.] Characterized by or tending to protraction; lengthening out, delaying.

1606 SHAKS. *Tr. & Cr.* I. iii. 20 Our workes,..nought else But the protractiue trials of great Ioue. 1687 DRYDEN *Hind & P.* III. 1103 He saw, but suffer'd their Protractive Arts. 1796 *Mod. Gulliver's Trav.* 149 By this protractive work, fresh mischief grows. 1819 H. BUSK *Vestriad* IV. 675 Protractive alleys the trim grove deform.

Protractor (protræ·ktəɹ). Also 7–8 -er. [a. med.L. *prōtractor*, agent-n. f. *prōtrah-ĕre* to PROTRACT.] One who or that which protracts.

1. One who lengthens out or prolongs time or any action; † one who puts off, delays, or postpones action (*obs.*).

1611 COTGR., *Delayeur*, a delayer, deferrer, protractor, prolonger, lingerer, wiredrawer... *Prolongeur*, a prolonger, protracter, a wyre-drawer, delayer. 1661 BLOUNT *Glossogr.* (ed. 2), *Protractor* (Lat.), a prolonger or drawer out. 1697 BURGHOPE *Disc. Relig. Assemb.* 144 The protractors and delayers of due preparation. 1727 BAILEY (vol. II.), *Protracter*, one who protracts. 1737 BOLINGBROKE *Stud. & Use Hist.* viii. (1777) 277, I know not what part the protractors of the war..intended to take. 1755 JOHNSON, *Protracter*, one who draws out any thing to tedious length.

2. An instrument, generally having the form of a graduated semicircle, used in setting off and measuring angles.

1658 PHILLIPS, *Protractor*, a certain Mathematical instrument made of brasse, consisting of the Scale and Semicircle, used in the surveying of Land. 1669 PEPYS *Diary* 4 Feb., This parallelogram is not, as Mr. Sheres would, the other day, have persuaded me, the same as a Protractor. 1712 J. JAMES tr. *Le Blond's Gardening* 92 Measure the Angle marked upon the Plan with the Protractor. 1727 BAILEY and 1755 JOHNSON, *Protracter*. 1889 *Anthony's Photogr. Bull.* II. 421 The application of an ordinary horn protractor will at once show the angle included in every instance.

3. A surgical instrument: see quots.

1727–41 CHAMBERS *Cycl.*, *Protractor*, an instrument used in surgery, to draw out any foreign or disagreeable bodies from a wound or ulcer; in like manner as the forceps. 1731 BAILEY, *Protracter*. 1736 *Ibid.* (folio), *Protracter*, *Protractor*. 1895 *Syd. Soc. Lex.*, *Protractor*, an instrument for extracting foreign bodies from wounds.

4. *Anat.* A muscle which serves to protract or extend a limb or member. Also *protractor muscle*.

1861 HULME tr. *Moquin-Tandon* II. v. ii. 276 Four muscles, two of which are protractors, and two retractors. 1870 ROLLESTON *Anim. Life* Introd. 96 One pair of protractor muscles may be present. 1871 HUXLEY *Anat. Vertebr. Anim.* 49 The *psoas minor*..is a protractor of the pelvis.

5. (See quot.)

1875 KNIGHT *Dict. Mech.*, *Protractor*,..an adjustable tailor's pattern, expansible to agree in its proportions with the particular measurements and capable of being secured in the obtained adjustment.

†**Protra·cture.** *Obs.* Also *erron.* 6–7 -our, -or. [f. as PROTRACT *v.* + -URE: cf. *portraiture.*]

1. Representation by a figure; drawing.

1551 RECORDE *Pathw. Knowl.* I. Defin., Without perspectiue knowledge, it is not easy to iudge truly the formes of them in flatte protracture. 1557 — *Whetst.* G iv, I will..set forth a brief explication of their names, with the protracture of the figures. 1613 M. RIDLEY *Magn. Bodies* 51 Having the formes and protractors of creeping things.. drawne in past-boord. 1634 W. WOOD *New Eng. Prosp.* II. xx. (1865) 107 They make curious baskets with intermixed colours and protractures of antique Imagerie.

2. Figure, shape, form, outline.

1551 RECORDE *Pathw. Knowl.* II. lv, Circles are regulare formes, that is to say, such formes as haue in their protracture a iuste and certaine proportion. 1581 DERRICKE *View Irel.* II. E iij b, His skirtes be verie shorte..And Irishe trouses more to put their straunge protractours out. 1607 TOPSELL *Four-f. Beasts* (1658) 411 It is her fashion and protracture to lie thus when she [the hamster] is angry.

Protraiote, obs. form of PROTRACT *v.*

Protreptic (protre·ptik), *a.* and *sb.* [as adj. ad. Gr. προτρεπτικ-ός fitted to urge on, hortative, instructive, f. πρό, PRO-² + τρέπ-ειν to turn, direct the course of; as sb. ad. late L. *protrepticon* (-*um*) = Gr. προτρεπτικόν, neuter of the adj.]

A. *adj.* Directive, instructive, didactic.

1658 PHILLIPS, *Protreptick*, doctrinal, or giving instructions. 1850 MAURICE *Mor. & Met. Philos.* (1854) I. 47 The discipline of the habit or character he [Clement] would call protreptic.

B. *sb.* A book, writing, or speech intended to exhort or instruct; an exhortation, instruction.

1656 BLOUNT *Glossogr.*, *Protreptick*, a book of instruction, a doctrinal. 1678 CUDWORTH *Intell. Syst.* 125 To rank Anaximander amongst the Divine Philosophers, as he [Clement] doth in his Protreptick to the Greeks. *Ibid.* 371 That this Pythagorick Prayer was directed to the Supreme Numen and King of Gods, Jamblichus thus declares in his Protrepticks. 1899 A. B. COOK in *Classical Rev.* Nov. 418/1 In the mind of Ischomachus' wife the bear-dance.. bulked larger than the protreptics of her husband.

So **Protre·ptical** *a.*, of protreptic nature.

1667–8 BP. WARD *Serm. Infidelity* (1670) 3 The means used ..are partly Didactical, and partly Protreptical. 1895 R. G. MOULTON *Proverbs* p. x, Early proverbs are philosophical, not protreptical.

Protriæne (prōᵘtrai,īn). *Zool.* [f. PRO-² + TRIÆNE.] In sponges, a triæne whose three prongs or cladi project forwards from the shaft.

1887 SOLLAS in *Encycl. Brit.* XXII. 417/1 (*Sponges*) The arms make different angles with the shaft: when recurved a grapnel or *anatriæne* is produced, when projecting forwards a *protriæne*, and when extended at right angles an *orthotriæne*.

Protribune: see PRO-¹ 4.

†**Protri·te,** *a. Obs.* [ad. L. *prōtrīt-us* worn away, in late L. trite, vulgar, pa. pple. of *prōter-ĕre* to tread under foot: see PRO-¹ and TRITE *a.*] Worn out, trite, threadbare, hackneyed.

1604 T. WRIGHT *Passions* I. iii. 12 The fourth [Passion] most protrite and manifeste unto the world, is their Inconstancie. *Ibid.* v. 214 What else meane those protrite words of the Psalme. 1659 GAUDEN *Tears Ch.* II. xv. 195 They are but old and rotten errours, protrite and putid opinions of the ancient Gnosticks.

Protrudable (protrū·dăb'l), *a.* [f. next + -ABLE.] Capable of being protruded, protrusible.

1881 DARWIN *Veg. Mould* (1882) 17 This part corresponds.. with the protrudable trunk or proboscis of other annelids.

Protrude (protrū·d), *v.* [ad. L. *prōtrūd-ĕre* to thrust or push forward or forth, f. *prō*, PRO-¹ 1 a + *trūd-ĕre* to thrust.]

†1. *trans.* To thrust forward (some detached body): to push or drive onward. *Obs.*

1620 VENNER *Via Recta* vii. 112 They protrude and driue downe the meates from the stomacke, before they be digested. *a* 1704 LOCKE (J.), When the stomach has performed its office upon the food, it protrudes it into the guts. 1769 E. BANCROFT *Guiana* 284 The arrow is by a single blast of air from the lungs, protruded through the cavity of the reed. 1822–34 *Good's Study Med.* (ed. 4) IV. 121 A series of spasmodic contractions..gradually increase in strength..and protrude the child into the world. *fig.* 1654 H. L'ESTRANGE *Chas. I* (1655) 169 Nothing is more familiar than for several Factions..to protrude and drive on one and the same design.

†b. *intr.* To shoot out. *Obs.*

1626 BACON *Sylva* § 328 If the spirits be not merely detained, but protrude a little, and that motion be confused and inordinate, there followeth putrefaction.

2. *trans.* To push or thrust into any position; to thrust forth or stick out (an organ or part) into a projecting position; to cause to project; to extend.

1646 SIR T. BROWNE *Pseud. Ep.* III. xx. 156 If beholding a candle we protrude either upward or downeward the pupill of one eye, the object will appeare double. 1664 POWER *Exp. Philos.* I. 36 Those black filaments or optick nerves, which are sheathed in her [the snail's] horns which she can retract or protrude. 1730–46 THOMSON *Autumn* 1311 When young Spring protrudes the bursting gems. 1828 G. W. BRIDGES *Ann. Jamaica* II. xv. 236 The linen jacket which he wore was protruded by a broken rib. 1841–71 T. R. JONES *Anim. Kingd.* (ed. 4) 131 From each tube a polyp is protruded, of a brilliant grass-green colour.

†b. *transf.* To bring to the surface, as a rash.

a 1776 R. JAMES *Diss. Fevers* (1778) 17 Let the physician but remove the fever, and..no miliary eruptions will be protruded.

c. *fig.* To obtrude, put forth obtrusively.

1840 THACKERAY *Pict. Rhapsody* Wks. 1900 XIII. 321 Critics, who..protrude their nonsense upon the town. 1841 CATLIN *N. Amer. Ind.* II. lviii. 255, I would protrude my opinion to the world.

3. *intr.* To stick out; to project or jut out beyond the surrounding parts.

a 1626 BACON (Webster 1828–32), The parts protrude beyond the skin. 1771 [see PROTRUDING below]. 1802 *Med. Jrnl.* VIII. 219 If the other hand should protrude, it may be encountered by a similar expedient. 1860 TYNDALL *Glac.* I. xxii. 155 The rocks which protrude from the snow at the base of the last spur of the mountain. 1868 FARRAR *Seekers* I. vi. (1875) 75 A common soldier had spied a pair of feet protruding from under the curtains.

Hence **Protru·ded, Protru·ding** *ppl. adjs.*

1771 LUCKOMBE *Hist. Print.* 241 The *P* is kerned, that its propensity may cover the back of the protruding angle of *A*. 1810 SOUTHEY *Kehama* II. xi, The protruded brow. 1841–71 T. R. JONES *Anim. Kingd.* (ed. 4) 7 The protruded filaments are able to coalesce. 1904 W. M. RAMSAY *Lett. to Seven Ch.* xxvii. 394 A coiled serpent with raised head and protruding tongue.

Protrudent (protrū·dĕnt), *a.* [ad. L. *prōtrūdent-em*, pres. pple. of *prōtrūd-ĕre* to PROTRUDE.] Protruding, projecting, protuberant, prominent.

1891 LD. HOUGHTON *Bookworm* in *Stray Verses* 9 Earnest underlip protrudent. 1893 *Scribner's Mag.* Aug. 180/2 The lofty, protrudent corner made by the dropping of the high-road into the curious transverse valley.

Protrusible (protrū·sib'l), *a.* [f. L. *prōtrūs-*, ppl. stem of *prōtrūd-ĕre*: see prec. and -IBLE.] Capable of being protruded or thrust out.

1836–9 *Todd's Cycl. Anat.* II. 400/1 A sharp horny dart.. readily protrusible through the aperture. 1870 ROLLESTON *Anim. Life* Introd. 58 The tongue may be..protrusible, as in other Reptiles.

Protrusile (protrū·sil, -əil), *a.* [f. as prec. + -ILE, after L. type **prōtrūsilis*.] Adapted to be extended or thrust out, as a limb, tentacle, etc.

1847 in WEBSTER citing GARDNER. 1849 JOHNSTON in *Proc. Berw. Nat. Club* II. No. 7. 366 Mandibles large and protrusile. 1867 J. HOGG *Microsc.* II. iii. 574 The mouth is furnished with a protrusile proboscis.

Protrusion (protrū·ʒən). [a. F. *protrusion*, ad. L. type **prōtrūsiōn-em*, n. of action f. *prōtrūd-ĕre* to PROTRUDE.]

1. The action of protruding (in various senses of the vb.); the fact or condition of being protruded.

†a. Thrusting forward or onward. *Obs.*

1646 SIR T. BROWNE *Pseud. Ep.* VII. xviii. 381 He was.. not to bee removed by the force or protrusion of three men. 1660 BOYLE *New Exp. Phys. Mech.* i. 21 You will finde the Sucker forcibly carryed up to the top of the Cylinder, by the protrusion of the external Air. 1787 BRADLEY *Fam. Dict.* s.v. *Cantharides*, Such Motions as are necessary for the Protrusion forwards or Ejectment of the Water.

b. The action of thrusting or pushing out an attached part; the condition of being protruded.

1646 SIR T. BROWNE *Pseud. Ep.* III. xvii. 148 That the distinctive parts of sexes are onely different in position, that is inversion or protrusion. 1783 POTT *Chirurg. Wks.* II. 13 The falling down or protrusion of some part. 1833 LYELL *Princ. Geol.* III. 340 The notion of deluges accompanying the protrusion of mountain-chains. 1880 C. & F. DARWIN *Movem. Pl.* 62 Shortly before the protrusion of the leaves.

c. The fact of projecting or jutting out.

1853 KANE *Grinnell Exp.* viii. (1856) 56 The protrusion of these abutting faces into the waters of the sound.

2. *concr.* That which protrudes or juts out; a protruded part, a protuberance, a prominence.

1704 SWIFT *T. Tub* xi. Wks. 1760 I. 123 [They] looked upon all extraordinary dilatations of that member as protrusions of zeal, or spiritual excrescencies. 1805 *Med. Jrnl.* XIV. 19 Between this ridge and the protrusion abovementioned. 1862 S. LUCAS *Secularia* 96 The fantastic gables, pinnacles, and protrusions, which intercepted the light. 1884 BOWER & SCOTT *De Bary's Phaner.* 66 They ..are covered by a protrusion of the epidermis.

Protrusive (protrū·siv), *a.* [f. L. *prōtrūs-*, ppl. stem of *prōtrūd-ĕre* to PROTRUDE + -IVE.]

1. Having the power or tendency to thrust forward or onward; propulsive.

1676 H. MORE *Remarks* 172 Though it add nothing to the elasticity of the Air, seeing it has a pressure and protrusive force in it. 1728 J. CHAMBERLAYNE *Relig. Philos.* (1730) I. iv. § 13 The Protrusive Motion of the Bowels. 1822–34 *Good's Study Med.* (ed. 4) IV. 144 The protrusive force of the surrounding muscles.

2. Characterized by thrusting oneself forward; obtrusive.

1840 CARLYLE *Heroes* iii. (1858) 267 A true English heart breathes, calm and strong, through the whole business; not boisterous, protrusive. 1893 *Chicago Advance* 16 Nov., His protrusive, unrestrained, ill-regulated idiosyncracies.

3. Protruding, projecting, protuberant.

1858 CARLYLE *Fredk. Gt.* III. iv. (1872) I. 156 The 'Austrian lip'—protrusive underjaw, with heavy lip disinclined to shut. 1876 GEO. ELIOT *Dan. Der.* vii, The chin protrusive, and the cervical vertebræ a trifle more curved.

Hence **Protru·sively** *adv.*, **Protru·siveness.**

1831 CARLYLE *Sart. Res.* I. x, To him thou, with sniffing charity, wilt protrusively proffer thy hand-lamp. 1890 *Cent. Dict.*, Protrusiveness.

Protrypsin: see PRO-² 1.

Prottore, -our, obs. ff. *prouder*, comp. of PROUD.

Protuberance (protiū·bĕrăns). [f. PROTUBERANT: see -ANCE. So F. *protubérance* (1738 in Hatz.-Darm.).]

1. The fact or condition of being protuberant; bulging out or projecting in a rounded form.

1681 tr. *Willis' Rem. Med. Wks.* Vocab., *Protuberance*, a bunching forth above the rest. 1756–82 J. WARTON *Ess. Pope* (ed. 4) I. vii. 361 The firmness and protuberance of the Muscles in each limb. 1836 *Random Recoll. Ho. Lords* xiv. 342 His eyes have a sunken appearance, owing to the protuberance of his eye-brows. 1874 *Imperial Gazetteer* s.v. *Australia*, The whole figure..very well proportioned, but frequently marred by the protuberance of the abdomen.

2. That which is protuberant; a rounded prominence, projection, or swelling; a knob, a bump.

1646 SIR T. BROWNE *Pseud. Ep.* III. xix. 154 A cartilagineous substance without any spondyles, processes, or protuberance whatsoever. 1658 — *Gard. Cyrus* iii. 47 The Rhomboidal protuberances in Pineapples maintaining this Quincuncial order unto each other. 1794 S. WILLIAMS *Vermont* 82 Under the throat there is a fleshy protuberance. 1859 W. S. COLEMAN *Woodlands* (1866) 106 On the leaf of the Poplar..large reddish-coloured protuberances.

b. *Solar protuberance* = solar PROMINENCE (2 b).

1874 tr. *Lommel's Light* 167 The so-called protuberances afforded an instant and crucial test of the truth of Kirchhoff's hypothesis. 1907 *Daily News* 25 Dec. 4 Janssen was in the Malay Peninsula making his observations of the solar 'protuberances', otherwise masses of blazing hydrogen.

Protu·berancy. [f. as prec. + -ANCY.]

1. Protuberant condition; bulging out; = prec. 1.

1654 GAYTON *Pleas. Notes* IV. xxii. 276 When..a protuberancy of the lip should be the certeine signe of the true heir to the Crowne. 1692 RAY *Disc.* I. iii. (1693) 34 The protuberancy of the dry Land above the common Superficies of the Ocean. 1718 J. CHAMBERLAYNE *Relig. Philos.* (1730) II. xx. § 23 The Earth..is not perfectly globular, but has a greater Protuberancy under the Equator. 1822–34 *Good's Study Med.* (ed. 4) III. 185 The other [cause of squinting arises] from an oblique position and greater protuberancy of the cornea.

†2. A rounded projection; = prec. 2. *Obs.*

1653 H. MORE *Antid. Ath.* II. x. (1712) 72 Why has he four Knees,..as also a Protuberancy under his Breast to lean on? 1760 MILLES in *Phil. Trans.* LI. 537 Small protuberancies sometimes appear, like the knots of trees.

Protuberant (protiū·bĕrănt), *a.* [ad. late L. *prōtūberant-em*, pres. pple. of *prōtūber-āre* to swell or bulge out, f. L. *prō*, PRO-¹ + *tūber* a hump, swelling. So F. *protubérant* (16th c. in Littré).]

1. Bulging or swelling out beyond the surrounding surface; prominent.

1646 SIR T. BROWNE *Pseud. Ep.* III. iv. 113 These..follicles are found in both sexes, though somewhat more protuberant in the male. 1661 GLANVILL *Scepsis Sci.* xxvi. (1665) 162 One mans eyes are more protuberant, and swelling out. 1747 HERVEY *Medit.* II. 122 Mountains vastly uneven and protuberant. 1807 G. CHALMERS *Caledonia* I. II. vi. 292 Eocha III..is remembered for his protuberant nose. 1869 PHILLIPS *Vesuv.* iv. 130 The protuberant northern base of the dome of Vesuvius.

b. *fig.* That forces itself upon notice, prominent.

1822 GALT *Provost* xxxiii, The effect of this, however, was less protuberant in our town than in many others. 1895 R. BURTON in *Forum* (N.Y.) Apr. 251 A foil to the protuberant ugliness of the theory.

†2. Moulded or done in the round; figured in relief, or rising above the surface. *Obs.*

1676 TOWERSON *Decalogue* 109 God..forbade all images whatsoever, particularly all protuberant ones. 1696 BP. PATRICK *Comm. Exod.* xx. 4 The former was a protuberant Image, or a Statue made of Wood, Stone, &c. *Ibid.* xxviii. (1697) 538 Abarbinel saith the Letters were protuberant as they are upon Coins, or upon Wax.

Hence **Protu·berantly** *adv.*, in a protuberant, bulging, or prominent manner.

1836 LANDOR *Peric. & Asp.* cliii. Wks. 1846 II. 417/1 They serve as graven images, protuberantly eminent and gorgeously uncouth.

Protuberantial (protiūbĕræ·nʃăl), *a.* [f. L. type **prōtūberanti-a* PROTUBERANCE + -AL. So F. *protubérantiel.*] Of the nature of, or belonging to (the solar) protuberances.

1880 *Nature* XXI. 436/2 The mixture of protuberantial vapours in the sun. 1882 *Ibid.* XXVII. 111/1 The spectrum is that of protuberantial gases and of matter still unknown.

Protuberate (protiū·bĕreit), *v. rare.* [f. late L. *prōtūberāt-*, ppl. stem of *prōtūberāre*: see PROTUBERANT.] *intr.* To bulge out; to form a rounded prominence.

1578 BANISTER *Hist. Man* I. 26 The inner region..hath cauities..which on the outer side agayne do protuberate and giue forth. 1650 BULWER *Anthropomet.* 11 Hippocrates..writes, That the head sometimes doth more remarkably protuberate at the eares, then either forward or backward. 1721 BRADLEY *Philos. Acc. Wks. Nat.* 126 We see the..Fore-legs half out, and the other just beginning to protuberate through the skin. 1822–34 *Good's Study Med.* (ed. 4) II. 483 Mesenteric enlargement..felt in the form of knots protuberating in the abdomen.

b. *trans.* To cause to bulge out or project. *rare.*

1884 A. A. WATTS *Life A. Watts* I. 302 The manly breast protuberated by waistcoats fashioned like a doublet.

Hence **Protu·berated** *ppl. a.*, swollen or bulged out; **Protu·berating** *vbl. sb.*, a swelling; **Protu·berating** *ppl. a.*, bulging out.

1683 A. SNAPE *Anat. Horse* v. xii. (1686) 221 The fourth Bone..is smooth, not being hollow nor *protuberated as the rest are. 1755 NEDHAM in *Phil. Trans.* XLIX. 230 The circumference of which was full, and protuberated. 1667 *Phil. Trans.* II. 564 Suffering grievous *Protuberatings of the bones in his Arms. 1615 CROOKE *Body of Man* 973 These Rack-bones haue in the middle *protuberating, round and embowed bodies. 1776 WITHERING *Brit. Plants* (1796) I. 285 In others, the nectary is blunt, scarcely protuberating.

†**Protubera·tion.** *Obs.* [n. of action f. late L. *prōtūberāre* to PROTUBERATE.] A swollen or bulged part, a protuberance.

1615 CROOKE *Body of Man* 903 The sixt Nerue..neare the inner protuberation of the arme distributeth many surcles into the skinne of the cubit. 1670 H. STUBBE *Plus Ultra* 125 A..Souldier..having grievous protuberations of the bones in his armes. *c* 1720 W. GIBSON *Farrier's Guide* I. vi. (1738) 97 The foremost of which receives the Protuberation of the Stifle bone.

†**Protu·bered,** *ppl. a. Obs. rare*⁻¹. [f. late L. *prōtūber-āre* (see PROTUBERANT) + -ED¹.] Swollen or bulged out.

1578 BANISTER *Hist. Man* I. 21 The cauities wherin the protubered heads of the ribbes are setled.

†**Protu·berous,** *a. Obs. rare*⁻¹. [f. stem *protuber-* of PROTUBERANT, etc. + -OUS, after *tuberous.*] = PROTUBERANT. So **Protubero·sity,** = PROTUBERANCE; a rounded bulge or boss. *rare.*

1666 J. SMITH *Old Age* (1676) 183 The one being protuberous, rough, crusty, and hard; the other, round, smooth, spongy, and soft. 1859 R. F. BURTON *Centr. Afr.* in *Jrnl. Geog. Soc.* XXIX. 314 The forehead converges to a central protuberosity, where phrenclogists locate eventuality.

Protu·rb, *v. humorous nonce-wd.* [ad. L. *prōturb-āre* to drive forth in confusion, f. *prō*, PRO-¹ 1 a + *turbāre* to confuse: cf. *perturb*, *disturb.*] *trans.* To drive forth or chase out.

1845 STANLEY in *Life* I. x. 342 Some undergraduates..saw Ward rush out from the Theatre—'proturbed', as they imagined by the Bedell.

Protureter: see PROTO- 2 b.

Pro-tutor (prōᵘ,tiū·təɹ). *Sc. Law.* [f. PRO-¹ + TUTOR *sb.* Cf. med.L. *prōtūtor*, F. *protuteur* (1762 in *Dict. Acad.*).] One who acts as 'tutor' or guardian to one in the state of pupillarity, though not legally appointed as such. So **Protu·tory,** the charge of a pro-tutor.

1665 *Acts of Sederunt* 10 June (1790) 93 Whatsoever person or persons shall..intromett with the means and estate of any minor, and shall act in his affairs as pro-tutors, haveing no right of tutory or curatory established in their persons, they shall be lyable. 1681 [see PRO-CURATOR]. *a* 1722 FOUNTAINHALL *Decis.* (1759) I. 10 Kilrie had meddled with the charter-chest..which the Lords did not find sufficient to make him protutor. 1773 ERSKINE *Inst. Law Scot.* I. vii. § 28 Pro-tutors..may be sued by the minor in an action for accounting, even during the pro-tutory, though proper tutors or curators are not bound to account till their office determine. 1838 in W. BELL *Dict. Law Scot.*

‖**Protyle** (prōᵘ·təil). Also prothyle, -yl. [irreg. f. Gr. πρωτ(ο-, PROT(O- first, primary, primitive + ὕλη 'timber, material', in philosophical lang. 'matter'; see HYLE, and cf. πρώτη ὕλη first matter or substance (Aristotle *Metaph.*).

If a combination of the two words had been made in Greek, it would have been *πρωθύλη, in Latin form *prōthylē*. Moreover, in Eng., ὕλη as second element usually becomes *-yl*, as in *methyl*, *ethyl*, *carbonyl*, etc.; thus the regular form would be *prothyl*.]

A name proposed for the hypothetical original undifferentiated matter, of which the chemical substances provisionally regarded as elements may be composed.

1886 W. CROOKES *Address* in *Rep. Brit. Assoc.* 568 Let us picture the very beginnings of time...Before even the sun himself had consolidated from the original protyle. [*Note*] We require a word analogous to protoplasm to express the idea of the original primal matter existing before the evolution of the chemical elements. The word I have ventured to use for the purpose is compounded of πρό (earlier than) and ὕλη (the stuff of which things are made). 1891 [F. C. S. SCHILLER] *Riddles of Sphinx* 189 Prothyle, the undifferentiated basis of chemical evolution. 1903 *Daily Chron.* 24 Apr. 5/1 That hypothetical substance—the 'prothyl'—of which the entire material universe, suns, planets, comets, and nebulæ, is made. 1905 *Academy* 4 Feb. 108/1 At present theory seems to suggest that this ether, originally 'invented' to account for the phenomena of light, and called the 'luminiferous ether', is really the *prima materia* of the ancients, the *Urstoff* of the Germans, the *protyle* of Sir William Crookes.

‖**Protypon** (prōᵘ·tipǫn). *Anc. Arch.* Pl. -a. [a. Gr. πρότυπον, f. as next.] (See quots.)

1601 HOLLAND *Pliny* II. 552 To set up Gargils or Antiques at the top of a Gavill end, as a finiall to the crest tiles, which in the beginning he called *Protypa.* [*margin*] Moulds or patterns. 1857 BIRCH *Anc. Pottery* (1858) I. 167 These early reliefs, called *protypa*, or bas reliefs, and *ectypa*, or high-reliefs, were also used for decorating houses and halls.

‖**Protypus** (prōᵘ·tipǫs). *Obs.* Also in anglicized form **pro·type.** [f. Gr. πρό, PRO-² + τύπος TYPE.] (See quot. 1656.)

1656 BLOUNT *Glossogr.*, *Protype*.., that is made for an example or copy: an image or form whereof moulds are made, in which things of mettal or earth are cast. 1662 EVELYN *Chalcogr.* (1769) 16 The *protypus* was of wax for efformation.

Prou, obs. f. PROW *sb.*¹ and ²; var. PROW *v. Obs.*

Proud (praud), *a.* (*sb.*, *adv.*) Forms: see below. [Late OE. *prút*, *prûd* = ON. *prúð-r* brave, gallant, magnificent, stately (whence Icel. *prúður*, MSw. *prudh*, MDa. *prud*); both prob. a. OF. *prūd*, *prōd*, nom. *prūz*, *prōz* (= **prūt-s*, **prōt-s*) valiant, doughty, gallant (11th c. in Godef.), in mod.F. *preux* = Prov. *proz*, *pro*, Cat. *prou*, It. *prode* valiant, Rhæto-Rom. *prus* pious;—late L. **prōd-is* profitable, advantageous, useful (*prōde* neut. in Itala *a* 200); app. either the source of, or taken from, the first element of L. *prōd-esse* to be of value, be good. See also PREUX, PROW *a.*, and cf. PRIDE.]

A. Illustration of Forms.

α. 1–5 prūt, 5 prute, 3–5 prout, -e, 5–6 prowte. *Compar.* 4 prottore, -our, 5 prutter, -yr.

a 1050 *Liber Scintill.* xlvi. (1889) 152 Pryte heage utawyrpð & wiþerwyrdnyss prute (*sublimes*) genyþerude. *a* 1225 *Ancr. R.* 276 Eaðe meiht to beon prut! *c* 1290 *S. Eng. Leg.* I. 225/197 Oure maister was so prout, Lucefer, for his fairhede, þat he ful sone out. 1297 R. GLOUC. (Rolls) 9539 King stefne was þe boldore & þe prottore [*v.r.* prottour] uor þis cas. *c* 1440 *Eng. Conq. Irel.* 57 Ne for no good chaunce, he was not the Pruttyr [*v.r.* prutter]. *Ibid.* 145 Spare the meke, and wreke Ham on the Prowte. *c* 1440 *Gesta Rom.* lxv. 280 (Harl. MS.) And when he was this i-lyved, he wex prout. 1553 *Respublica* (Brandl) v. vii. 17 Zo thieke prowte howrecop.

β. 1–4 prúd, 4–6 prude, (4–5 prode), 4–6 proude, 4–7 prowd(e, 4– proud. *Compar.* 3 pruder, prudder, 5 prodder. *Superl.* 3 prudest, 4 pruddest, proddest, 5 pruddist.

c 1000 in Napier *O.E. Gloss.* 226/233 *Arrogantes*, modig: *vel* prud. *c* 1175 *Lamb. Hom.* 57 Prud ne wreiere ne beo þu noht. *a* 1225 *Ancr. R.* 296 He is þinge prudest, and him is scheome loðest. *c* 1330 R. BRUNNE *Chron.* (1810) 289 Þe proude kyng Pharaon, þat chaced Israel. *c* 1350 *Will. Palerne* 2942 Þe proddest of hem alle. 13.. *E. E. Allit. P.* B. 1300 Þe pruddest of þe province. *Ibid.* 1772 Þe prowde prynce of Perce. 13.. *Cursor M.* 2415 (Cott.) Fra þaa prude folk had hir sen. *Ibid.* 27571 Oft bitides þat man es Bicummen prode for halines. *a* 1400–50 *Alexander* 4375 Þe playne purperyn see full of prode fischis. *c* 1400 *Destr. Troy* 2743 The pruddist of payone, prise men of honde. *a* 1450 *Myrc* 1129 Hast þou..þe prodder be mad, For any ofyce þat þow hast had? 1535 COVERDALE *Job* xxxv. 12 Because of the wickednesse off proude tyrauntes.

B. Signification.

Senses 6 and 7 come nearest to the OF. and ON. The unfavourable sense, so early in Eng., may be due to the aspect in which a Norman *prud barun* or *prode chevalier* presented himself to the English peasant or townsman. (Cf. the two senses of L. *superbus*.)

I. 1. Having or cherishing a high or lofty opinion of oneself; valuing oneself highly on account of one's position, rank, attainments, possessions, etc.; Usually in a bad sense: Disposed to take an attitude of superiority to and contempt for others; arrogant, haughty, overweening, supercilious.

a 1050 *Liber Scintill.* xvii. (1889) 85 Sawl prutes byð forlaeten. *c* 1175 *Lamb. Hom.* 5 Ne beo þu þereuore prud ne wilde. *Ibid.* 43 Prud heo was swiðe and modi. *c* 1290 *Beket* 980 in *S. Eng. Leg.* I. 134 [He] is prouȝt and conteckor. 1362 LANGL. *P. Pl.* A. III. 172 Ne to depraue þi persone with a proud herte. 1484 CAXTON *Fables of Æsop* IV. xx, None ought to be prowd ageynst his lord, but ought to humble hym self toward hym. 1526 *Pilgr. Perf.* (W. de W. 1531) 18 Some be as proude as Nabugodonosor. 1560 DAUS tr. *Sleidane's Comm.* 119 They are as bragge and as proude as pecockes. 1613 SIR E. HOBY *Counter-snarle* 54 Hee was a proud insolent Delegate. 1711 SWIFT *Jrnl. to Stella* 20 Nov., Lord Strafford is as proud as Hell. 1782 MISS BURNEY *Cecilia* IX. vi, They say he's as proud as Lucifer. 1784 COWPER *Task* VI. 96 Knowledge is proud that he has learned so much; Wisdom is humble that he knows no more. 1820 BYRON *Mar. Fal.* II. i. 210 The vile are only vain; the great are proud. 1841 W. SPALDING *Italy & It. Isl.* II. 16 Claims not less arrogant than those of the proudest popes in the middle ages. 1859 TENNYSON *Geraint & Enid* 347 Turn, Fortune, turn thy wheel and lower the proud.

b. Const. *of* (the thing, quality, action, etc. which constitutes the ground of pride). See also 2.

1422 tr. *Secreta Secret., Priv. Priv.* 154 Haue knowynge of thy-Selfe, and be not Prute of so hey vyrchipp. *c* 1510 MORE *Picus* Wks. 17/2 If thou haste receiued it: why arte thou prowde therof, as thoughe thou haddst not receiued it. 1593 SHAKS. *2 Hen. VI*, IV. x. 77 Iden farewell, and be proud of thy victory. 1616 R. C. *Times' Whistle* III. 959 Most of our women are extreamly proud Of their faire lookes. 1707 NORRIS *Treat. Humility* vii. 317 If a man were to be proud of anything, it should be what the angels were proud of,.. their intellectual endowments. 1809–10 COLERIDGE *Friend* (1865) 140, I should be more inclined to be ashamed than proud of myself if they had. 1859 GEO. ELIOT *A. Bede* ii, An ornament of which she was much prouder than of her red cheeks.

c. Preceded by a sb. in comb. = proud of...

1682, etc. [see PURSE-PROUD]. 1863 W. C. BALDWIN *Afr. Hunting* viii. 354, I could make four or five spans of.. good and well-matched oxen..and I am now becoming a little ox-proud. 1904 *Globe* 27 Oct. 4/4 No one can prevent the woman who is jewel-proud..from bedecking herself with gems on every possible and a few impossible occasions.

2. Highly sensible of, or elated by, some honour done to one; feeling oneself greatly honoured by some act, fact, or relation; taking pride or having high satisfaction in something; in early use (as still in *dial.*) sometimes merely = gratified, pleased, glad. Often const. *of*, or with *inf.*

c 1250 *Gen. & Ex.* 1414 Wið gold, and siluer, and wið srud, Ðis sonde made ðe mayden prud. 1377 LANGL. *P. Pl.* B. XIII. 59 Pacience was proude of þat propre seruice, And made hym muirth with his mete. *c* 1400 *Destr. Troy* 262 Pelleus of the proffer was proude at his hert. 1593 SHAKS. *Rich. II*, III. iii. 191 Faire Cousin, you debase your Princely Knee, To make the base Earth proud with kissing it. 1677 DRYDEN *Apol. Heroic Poetry* Ess. (Ker) I. 182 The author of the *Plain Dealer*, whom I am proud to call my friend. 1781 COWPER *Charity* 308 A divine ambition, and a zeal, The boldest patriot might be proud to feel. 1784 BURNS '*There was a lad*' iv, He'll be a credit to us a', We'll a' be proud o' Robin. 1902 LD. KITCHENER in *Westm. Gaz.* 30 July 5/1 This..will, I am sure, be well understood by the Army I have been so proud to command.

3. Having a becoming sense of what is due to or worthy of oneself or one's position; unwilling to stoop to what is beneath one; characterized by lofty self-respect; feeling or showing a proper pride.

1738 POPE *Epil. Sat.* II. 205 *F.* You're strangely proud. *P.* So proud, I am no Slave: So impudent, I own myself no Knave. 1761 GRAY *Sketch* 1 Too poor for a bribe and too proud to importune. 1828 CARLYLE *Misc., Burns* (1857) I. 233 Many a poet has been poorer than Burns; but no one was ever prouder. 1833 TENNYSON *Lady Clara Vere de Vere* ii, Your pride is yet no mate for mine, Too proud to care from whence I came.

4. *transf.* Of actions, etc.: Proceeding from or indicating pride; arrogant, haughty, presumptuous; arising from lofty self-respect.

1390 GOWER *Conf.* II. 379 Ther was..many a proud word spoke also. 1535 COVERDALE *Prov.* vi. 17 There be sixe thinges, which the Lorde hateth...A proude loke, a dyssemblynge tonge [etc.]. 1701 *Stanley's Hist. Philos.*, *Biog.* 9 This Philosophy [the Stoick] has..charmed a World of People by its Proud and Ostentatious Principles. 1790 COWPER *Mother's Picture* 110 Higher far my proud pretensions rise—The son of parents pass'd into the skies. 1853 tr. *F. Bremer's Homes New World* II. xxvii. 311 The Indians, like the Greenlanders, look down upon the white race with proud contempt.

5. That is a ground or cause of pride; of which one is or may be proud (now usually in good sense); affording high satisfaction or gratification.

a 1340 HAMPOLE *Psalter* xix. 8 Þai ere on heghe, and has þaire delite in proude honours and vayn. *a* 1577 GASCOIGNE *Herbs, Weeds*, etc. Wks. (1587) 304 Not one of these rebuketh avarice And yet procureth prowd pluralities. *c* 1600 SHAKS. *Sonn.* xxv, Let those..Of publike honour and proud titles bost. 1746–7 HERVEY *Medit.* (1767) I. 57 (*Tombs*) Where is Honour, with her proud Trophies of Renown? 1831 LAMB *Elia* Ser. II. *Ellistoniana*, One proud day to me he took his roast mutton with us in the Temple. 1840 DICKENS *Barn. Rudge* xlviii, 'It is a proud sight', said the secretary. 1868 FREEMAN *Norm. Conq.* II. vii. 44 The proud inheritance of their stainless loyalty.

II. 6. As a poetic or rhetorical epithet. **a.** Of persons, their name, etc.: Of exalted station, of high degree, of lofty dignity; lordly.

a 1250 *Prov. Ælfred* 5 in *O. E. Misc.* 102 Eorles prute, knyhtes egleche. *c* 1374 CHAUCER *Anel. & Arc.* 147 A nobere ladye proude and nuwe. *c* 1425 WYNTOUN *Cron.* IV. viii. 1148 Donald-Erchsone-Heggebouð King wes xiiii. winter provd. 1599 SHAKS. *Much Ado* III. i. 50 Nature neuer fram'd a womans heart, Of prowder stuffe then that of Beatrice. 1742 GRAY *Spring* ii, How low, how little are the Proud. 1805 SCOTT *Last Minstr.* VI. i, High though his titles, proud his name, Boundless his wealth as wish can claim. 1854 CHR. G. ROSSETTI *Poems* (1904) 180/1 In the grave will be no space For the purple of the proud.

b. Of things: Stately, majestic, magnificent, grand, 'gallant', splendid. (Referring to aspect.)

c 1290 *S. Eng. Leg.* I. 301/41 A noble churche huy founden þare, with walles faire and proute. *a* 1300 *Cursor M.* 3249 Ring and broche war selli prude. *c* 1400 *Destr. Troy* 435 With pelur and pall & mony proude rynges. 1530 PALSGR. 321/2 Prowde or stately, *fier*. 1602 MARSTON *Antonio's Rev.* III. ii, Tis not yet prowde day: The neat gay mist[r]es of the light's not vp. 1678 WOOD *Life* 28 June (O. H. S.) II. 410 The ruins..do shew that it hath been a verie statelie and proud fabrick. 1794 MRS. RADCLIFFE *Myst. Udolpho* xv, And through the waters view on high The proud ships sail, and gay clouds move. 1840 THIRLWALL *Greece* VII. lv. 91 Ecbatana..one of the proudest cities of the ancient world.

†c. *transf.* Highly pleasing (to other senses), 'grand'. *Obs. rare.*

c 1375 *Sc. Leg. Saints* vii. (*Jacobus minor*) 705 Persawand prowd sawoure þare Of sottyne [sodden] flesche.

7. Characterized by great vigour, force, or vitality, such as indicates or suggests pride: in various applications. †**a.** Of warriors (or their acts): Valiant, brave; mighty; esp. in phr. *proud in pres* (*prece*), valiant in conflict (see PRESS *sb.*¹ 1 b).

c 1330 *Sir Tristr.* 57 To Marke þe king þai went Wiþ kniȝtes proude in pres. *c* 1400 *Destr. Troy* 2132 To purvey a pepull pruddest of werre. *Ibid.* 6719 Presset hym with payne, & with proude strokes. *c* 1420 *Avow. Arth.* xlvii, Thenne he wente to the dece, Be-fore the pruddust in prece. 1523 LD. BERNERS *Froiss.* I. ccl. 371 The ii squiers within were right hardy and prowde. 1591 CONINGSBY *Jrnl. Siege Rouen* in *Camden Misc.* I. 58 Thus have you the most prowd sally that any capten here can tell of to their memorie. 1697 DRYDEN *Virg. Georg.* IV. 27 The youthful Prince, with proud allarm, Calls out the vent'rous Colony to swarm.

b. Of animals: Spirited, high-mettled; marked by vigorous and fearless activity; moving with force and dignity. (Chiefly *poet.*)

c 1407 LYDG. *Reson & Sens.* 3714 Bestys that be proude: As boors, lippardys, and lyouns. 1588 SHAKS. *Tit. A.* II. ii. 21, I haue dogges my Lord, Will rouze the proudest Panther in the Chase. 1667 MILTON *P. L.* IV. 858 The Fiend repli'd not,.. But like a proud Steed reind, went hautie on, Champing his iron curb. 1780 COWPER *Table-Talk* 523 Give me the line that ploughs its stately course Like a proud swan, conquering the stream by force.

c. Of the sea or a stream: Swelling, swollen, high, strong, in flood.

1535 COVERDALE *Job* xxxviii. 11 Here shalt thou laye downe thy proude and hye wawes. 1590 SHAKS. *Mids. N.* II. i. 91 Which falling in the Land, Hath euerie petty Riuer made so proud, That they haue ouer-borne their Continents. 1611 BIBLE *Ps.* cxxiv. 5 Then the proud waters had gone ouer our soule. 1828 BUCHAN *Ballads N. Scot.* I. 247 The wind was loud, the stream was proud, And wi' the stream gaed Willie. 1894 *Field* 1 Dec. 838/1 In the big rivers of upper Sweden and Norway, the grayling lives in the turmoil and 'proud' water.

d. Of organic structures: Overgrown, exuberant, too luxuriant; swelling or swollen, tumid. (*a*) Said of the sap: Swelling; rising or circulating vigorously; also, said locally of plants, or parts of them, as buds, shoots, grain. (See also WINTER-*proud.*) (*b*) Applied to overgrown flesh in a healing wound: see also PROUD FLESH.

[1586 A. DAY *Eng. Secretary* II. (1625) 78 *Metaphora*..as if we should say..corne by the stately length and weighty eare it carrieth, to be proud.] 1593 SHAKS. *Rich. II*, III. iv. 59 As we..wound the Barke, the skin of our Fruit-trees, Least being ouer-proud with Sap and Blood, With too much riches it confound it selfe. 1607 TOPSELL *Four-f. Beasts* (1658) 279 Used by Physitians for taking down of proud swelling wounds. 1648 MARKHAM *Housew. Gard.* III. x. (1668) 79 Now sap in flowers is strong and proud. 1664 EVELYN *Sylva* 32 About the beginning of March (when the buds begin to be proud and turgid). 1764 *Museum Rust.* III. xxxiv. 152 Ten acres of wheat, which, after Christmas, seemed proud. 1825 BROCKETT *N. C. Gloss.*, *Proud*, luxuriant. 'Corn's varra proud.' 1844 STEPHENS *Bk. Farm* II. 515 If the winter has been open and mild, the autumn-wheat plant will have grown luxuriantly,..so..that it may have become *proud*, that is, in a precocious state of forwardness for the season.

8. Sensually excited; 'swelling', lascivious. ? *Obs.*

1590 SPENSER *F. Q.* I. x. 26 In ashes and sackcloth he did array His daintie corse, proud humors to abate. 1593 SHAKS. *Lucr.* 712 The flesh being proud, Desire doth fight with grace. 1641 HINDE *J. Bruen* vii. 27 Who having made their flesh proud by pampering, do now..cast off all feare of God.

b. *spec.* Of certain female animals, as bitches, mares, elephants: In a state of sexual excitement; 'in heat'. ? *Obs.*

1575 TURBERV. *Venerie* vii. 17 A fayre Bitch..the whiche you may make to goe proude in this wyse. 1590 COKAINE *Treat. Hunting* B iij b, A Brach is..nine daies full proude. 1615 tr. *De Monfart's Surv. E. Indies* 17 To take them [wild elephants]..they make vse of a female, when shee goeth proud, in her heate [etc.]. 1727 BRADLEY *Fam. Dict.* I. Ee j b/2 Make Broth thereof and of this give her some twice or thrice, and she will infallibly grow proud. 1781 P. BECKFORD *Hunting* (1802) 62 Watch over the bitches with a cautious eye, and separate such as are going to be proud, before it be too late.

9. *dial.* or *local.* 'Large; projecting in any direction; of a roof: high-pitched'; also 'said of a fulcrum when it is placed too near the lever end' (*E. D. D.*); and in other transferred uses: see quots.

1825 JAMIESON, *Proud*, applied to a projection in a haystack, during the act of rearing it, whence it needs dressing in a particular quarter. 1857 P. COLQUHOUN *Comp. 'Oarsman's Guide'* 13 It has been the custom to fill oars very square, to make them row proud; but there are few men capable of enduring proud oars for any length of time..not rowing the stroke out is attributable to these proud fillings. 1866 *S. W. Linc. Gloss.* s.v., 'The nails [in a horseshoe] stand out too proud'; 'The board's a bit too proud, it wants spoke-shaving off.' *Mod.*, 'You are too proud': said of or to a person who, trying to raise something with a crowbar or other lever, places the point too far under the object to be lifted (= too far beyond the fulcrum).

10. *Phrases.* **a.** *Proud tailor*: a local name for the goldfinch, from its showy plumage.

1770 D. BARRINGTON in *Archæologia* (1775) III. 33 A goldfinch still continues to be called a proud tailor in some parts of England. 1829 *Glover's Hist. Derby* I. 151 *Fringilla Carduelis*, Goldfinch, Thistle-Finch, Proud Tailor. 1876–82 *Yarrell's Brit. Birds* (ed. 4) II. 118 *note*, In some of the Midland counties it is termed 'Proud Tailor'.

b. *To do* (a person) *proud* (colloq.): to make proud, confer an honour upon, gratify highly.

1819 *Metropolis* I. 220 'You do me proud', said the general. 1837 THACKERAY *Ravenswing* i, Madam, you do me proud. 1884 *Milnor* (Dakota) *Teller* 22 Aug., The people of Milnor have done themselves proud in building a school house. 1899 *Daily News* 1 June 6/4 The sun did himself proud...For once the tents were not actually crammed throughout the afternoon.

†c. *To make it proud*: to behave proudly or haughtily. *Obs.* (See MAKE *v.*¹ 68 h.)

c 1460 *Towneley Myst.* xxx. 263 She can make it full prowde with iapes and with gynnes. 14.. *Tundale's Vis.* 486 Þis hogy best..His sette to swolo covetous men þat in erþe makyd hit prowd and towȝe.

†**C.** as *sb. Obs.*

1. A proud person; one of high degree.

c 1400 *Destr. Troy* 13696 Pirrus with that proude presit to þe temple, Weddit þat worthi, & as wif held. 1535 STEWART *Cron. Scot.* (Rolls) II. 24 Wes neuir proud of sic auctoritie Moir wirschip wan. *a* 1586 in Pinkerton *Anc. Scot. Poems* (1786) 190 He luifit that proude in paramouris.

2. Pride. *rare.* (*Prude* (*ü*) was also early southern ME. spelling of *pryde*, PRIDE.)

c 1440 *Gesta Rom.* i. 4 (Harl. MS.) Alle þat is in þe wordle oþer it is fals coueitise of flesch, or fals coueitise of yen, or prowde of lif.

D. as *adv.* Proudly, in a proud manner (in various senses).

13.. *Cursor M.* 28515 Lucheri has don me scrud Me-self and bere my bodi prud. *c* 1425 *Cast. Persev.* 1793 in *Macro Plays* 130 Heyl, prinse, proude prekyd in palle! 1534 MORE *Treat. Passion* Wks. 1272/2 Men maye call hym a foole that beareth hymselfe prowde, because he ietteth about in a borowed gown. 1857 [see 9 above].

E. *Comb.* **a.** parasynthetic, as *proud-blooded*, *-crested*, *-minded*, *-paced*, *-pillared*, *-quivered*, *-spirited*, *-stomached*: see also PROUD-HEARTED.

b. adverbial, as *proud-blind* (blinded by pride), *-exulting*, *-glancing*, † *-pied* (proudly or splendidly variegated), † *-pight*, *-prancing*.

1589 *Broughton's Let.* ix. 31 Put on your spectacles you purblind and *proud-blind Pharisee. 1759 MASON *Caractacus* Poems (1774) 261 *Proud-crested soldier! 1798 *Poetry* in *New Ann. Reg.* 168 To leave him, *proud-exulting in his pains. 1596 SHAKS. *Tam. Shr.* II. i. 132, I am as peremptorie as she *proud minded. 1616 *Marlowe's Faust.* Wks. (Rtldg.) 120/2 On a *proud-pac'd steed, as swift as thought. *c* 1600 SHAKS. *Sonn.* xcviii, When *proud pide Aprill (drest in all his trim) Hath put a spirit of youth in euery thing. *c* 1400 *Laud Troy Bk.* 11191 Many a *proude pight pynacle Stode a-boute that tabernacle. 1902 L. F. BRUSE in *Academy* 28 Sept. 258/1 *Proud-prancing Æschylean words. 1838 DICKENS *Nich. Nick.* xiii, *Proud-stomached teachers.

†**Proud,** *v. Obs.* [OE. *prūtian*, ME. *prouden*, f. *prút* PROUD *a.*]

1. *intr.* To be proud; to behave proudly.

a 1000 *Aldhelm Gloss.* 1161 in Napier *O.E. Glosses* 32/1 *Fastu*, i. *elatione*, prutunge. *c* 1000 *Corp. Chr. Coll. Cambr. MS.* 191, 29 Þæt hi wyllon modiȝȝan oððe prutian. *Ibid.* 168 Hwanon hi modiȝian magon oððe prutian. *c* 1325 *Deo Gratias* 18 in *E. E. P.* (1862) 129 A noþur Mon proudeþ as doþ a poo. 1382 WYCLIF *Job* xv. 20 Alle his daȝis the vnpitous man proudeth. *a* 1618 SYLVESTER *Henry Gt.* 117 There prowdeth Pow'r, here Prowesse brighter shines.

b. To be lively or wanton. (Cf. PROUD *a.* 8.)

c 1330 *Arth. & Merl.* 264 Mirie time is Auerille..Ȝong man wexeþ jolif, & þan proudeþ man & wiif.

2. *trans.* To make proud; to puff up with pride.

c 1425 *St. Mary of Oignies* II. ii. in *Anglia* VIII. 153/12 Nor she was depressed wiþ reproues ne prouded wiþ hir preisynges. 1606 WARNER *Alb. Eng.* XVI. cii. 403 Yee whom Nature hath or Fortune prowded. 1606 SYLVESTER *Du Bartas* II. iv. II. *Trophies* 1333 As Sin breeds Sin, and Husband marr's the Wife, Sister prouds Sister, Brother hardens Brother, And one Companion doth corrupt another.

Hence †**Prou·ded** *ppl. a.*, made proud, overswollen; †**Prou·der,** ? one who behaves proudly.

1602 WARNER *Alb. Eng.* IX. lii. 236 The prouded Flesh from sins excesse to waine. 1565 W. ALLEN *Def. Cath. Doctr. Purgatory* II. viii. 191 Goddes Churche..hathe by the spirite of God beaten downe your prouders, the Arrians: the Macedonians: the Anabaptistes. 1577 FULKE *Confut. Purg.* 298 [quoting prec.] Our prowders the Arians.

Proudens, obs. form of PRUDENCE.

†**Prou·dfall.** *Obs. rare*⁻¹. [f. PROUD *a.* + (?) FALL *sb.*¹] ? The front hair, the forelock.

c 1400 *Destr. Troy.* 3025 The shede þurghe the shyre here shone as þe lilly, Streght as a strike, straght þurgh the myddes, Depertid the proudfall pertly in two, Atiret in tressis trusset full faire.

Proud flesh. [See PROUD *a.* 7 d (*b*).] Overgrown flesh arising from excessive granulation upon, or around the edges of, a healing wound.

c 1400 *Lanfranc's Cirurg.* 78 An hori elde wounde þat haþ summe greete crustis, or ellis..sum gret proud fleisch to hiȝe [Lat. *carnem superfluam grossam*]. 1597 A. M. tr. *Guillemeau's Fr. Chirurg.* 50 b/2 Aboue the ordinary fluxions, therin engendreth proude fleshe. 1685 BOYLE *Enq. Notion Nat.* vii. 323 In wounds, proud-flesh, and perhaps funguses, are as well produced and entertained by the aliment brought to the wounded part, as the true and genuine flesh. 1779 *Gentl. Mag.* XLIX. 80 If fungus, commonly called proud-flesh, should appear, a dressing of dry lint will mostly soon repress it. 1880 M. MACKENZIE *Dis. Throat & Nose* I. 526 The formation of 'proud flesh' on the edges of the wound.

Hence **Prou·d-flesh** *v. trans.*, to cause a growth of proud flesh upon (in quot. *fig.*).

1876 S. LANIER in *Life & Lett. B. Taylor* (1884) II. xxviii. 693 The additional forcing of such a tendency..becomes positively hurtful through proudfleshing the artistic conscience.

Proudful (prau·dfŭl), *a.* Now *dial.* [f. PROUD *a.* + -FUL: cf. PRIDEFUL.] Full of pride; abounding in pride; proud. (In quot. 1900 as *adv.*)

1340 *Ayenb.* 217 Prouduol cloþinge ne wynþ naȝt of god. *a* 1578 LINDESAY (Pitscottie) *Chron. Scot.* (S.T.S.) I. 81 [They] began to delet [= delate] his proudfull ambitioun and disdaining of the peipill. 1881 W. C. SMITH in *Mod. Sc. Poets* III. 243 She leaves his proudfu' mither Draggin through the dowie heather. 1900 'ZACK' (GWEN. KEATS) *Tales Dunstable Weir* (1901) 135 (Devon dial.) He moved that free and yet that proudful I couldn't but call to mother to mark him.

Prou·d-hea·rted, *a.* Having a proud heart or spirit; proud, haughty.

?*a* 1366 CHAUCER *Rom. Rose* 1491 Proude-herted Narcisus. 14.. in *Harrow. Hell* Introd. 25 The horss hath xxv propertes,..iiii off a lyon..prowd-herted, brod-brestid, iiii good legis, and a stowte stern. 1456 SIR G. HAYE *Law Arms* (S.T.S.) 116 Oft dois hautane proud-hartit men to wyn los in armes, mare for pride na prow. 1593 SHAKS. *3 Hen. VI*, v. i. 98 And so, prowd-hearted Warwicke, I defie thee. *a* 1803 *Young Benjie* iv. in Child *Ballads* IV. (1886) 282/1 And he was stout, and proud-hearted, And thought o't bitterlie. 1861 TROLLOPE *Framley P.* I. xi. 236 It is hardly possible that the proud-hearted should love those who despise them; and Lucy Robarts was very proud-hearted.

So **Prou·d-heart** *sb.*, a name for a proud-hearted person; *a.*, proud-hearted.

1362 LANGL. *P. Pl.* A. v. 45 Pernel proud-herte [C. VII. 3 proute-herte] platte hire to grounde,..And beo-hiȝte to him þat vs alle maade, Heo wolde [etc.]. 1819 KEATS *Lamia* II. 285 Leaving thee forlorn..For all thine impious proud-heart sophistries. 1887 MORRIS *Odyss.* II. 324 Those young and proud-heart lords.

Proudish (prau·diʃ), *a.* [f. PROUD *a.* + -ISH¹.] Somewhat proud, rather proud.

1658 COKAINE *Trappolin* IV. i, I do remember my self well enough, yet Eo, Meo, and Areo, have made me something proudish. 1688 PENTON *Guard. Instruct.* (1897) 44 Especially when they are a little proudish. 1827 DISRAELI *Viv. Grey* VI. i, Had some little with a proudish air.

†**Prou·dling.** *Obs. rare.* [f. as prec. + -LING¹.] A proud person; a 'son' or 'daughter of pride'.

a 1618 SYLVESTER *Henry Gt.* 152 Milde to the Meek, to Proudlings sterne and strict. 1628 SIR W. MURE *Doomesday* 196 There, the Ambitious...Of base contempt is made the pryse; The Proudling pestred downe.

†**Prou·dly,** *a. Obs. rare*⁻¹. [f. as prec. + -LY¹.] Of proud manner; proud-looking.

c 1400 *Laud Troy Bk.* 2136 Duk Nestor was ful of wratthe and ire Toward Antenor, that proudely sire.

Proudly (prau·dli), *adv.* Forms: see PROUD *a.* and -LY². [Late OE. *prūtlīce*: see -LY²; ME. *prudeliche*.] In a proud manner; with pride.

1. With excessive self-esteem; with an attitude or air of superiority; haughtily, arrogantly.

a 1050 *Liber Scintill.* lviii. (1889) 178 Prutlice [*superbe*] witan. *a* 1225 *Leg. Kath.* 577 Þa onswerede þe an swiðe prudeliche, þus, to þe prude prince. *c* 1380 *Sir Ferumb.* 534 Fyrumbras ansuerde him agayn prouteliche & sayde:..'Ich hem wolde wel conquere wiþ my swerd trenchaunt'. 14.. *Tourn. Tottenham* 30 in Hazl. *E. P. P.* III. 84 How prudly among vs thy dogter he craues. 1560 DAUS tr. *Sleidane's Comm.* 192 b, He aunswered contemptuously & proudlye. 1621 MOLLE *Camerar. Liv. Libr.* III. x. 178 [She] thinketh the proudlier of herselfe. 1671 MILTON *Samson* 55 Proudly secure, yet liable to fall By weakest suttleties. 1788 COWPER *Negro's Compl.* 56 Prove that you have human feelings, Ere you proudly question ours! 1831 FOSTER in *Life & Corr.* (1846) II. 197 A long and proudly imperious reign of corruption.

b. With lofty satisfaction or self-respect; with a high sense of honour done to one, or of what is worthy of one; with elation or exultation.

1753 A. MURPHY *Gray's Inn Jrnl.* No. 23 Rather than drag a feverish Life under an huge Load of Misery, he proudly resolves to put an End to his Sufferings. 1855 MACAULAY *Hist. Eng.* xiii. III. 290 A rule which, as far back as the days of the Plantagenets, had been proudly declared by the most illustrious sages of Westminster Hall to be a distinguishing feature of the English jurisprudence. 1871 FREEMAN *Norm. Conq.* IV. xvii. 79 A conquest which is proudly contrasted with the petty exploits of the first Cæsar in the same island.

2. With an aspect or manner suggesting pride; grandly, magnificently, splendidly; † gallantly, valiantly (quot. *c* 1420); with spirited and dignified movement; with vigour or force, exuberantly.

c 1050 *Byrhtferth's Handboc* in *Anglia* (1885) VIII. 311 Eac hig prutlice gymað þæs miotacismus gefleard. *c* 1300 *Vices & Virt.* 107 Ne he ne scal to prudeliche bien isc(r)edd. 13.. *K. Alis.* 3413 (Bodl. MS.) Many stede there proudely lep. *c* 1400 *Destr. Troy* 371 A chamber full choise..þat proudly was painted with pure gold ouer. *c* 1420 *Brut* 370 Proutly & manly he quitte hym on his aduersarye. *a* 1547 SURREY *Æneid* II. (1557) C ij, The pillers eke proudly beset with gold, And with the spoiles of other nations. 1597 SHAKS. *2 Hen. IV*, v. ii. 130 The Tide of Blood in me, Hath prowdly flow'd in Vanity, till now. 1670 CAPT. J. SMITH *Eng. Improv. Reviv'd* 73 The best season is when the Sap is ready to stir, not when it is proudly stirring. 1671 MILTON *P. R.* IV. 34 An Imperial City..With Towers and Temples proudly elevate On seven small hills. 1899 F. T. BULLEN *Way Navy* 40 We swept proudly up to the anchorage off Buncrana.

Proudness (prau·dnės). Now *rare.* [f. PROUD *a.* + -NESS.] The quality of being proud; pride.

1. Lofty self-esteem, arrogance, haughtiness.

1500–20 DUNBAR *Poems* ix. 116, I synnit..In he exaltit arrogance and folye, Prowdnes, derisioun, scorne and vilipentioun. 1552 LATIMER *Serm. Gospels* iv. 173 He fell..in suche a hatred and proudenes agaynst God. 1588 A. KING tr. *Canisius' Catech.* Kj, Thair proudnes is intolerable. 1860 PUSEY *Min. Proph.* 465 Isaiah accumulates words, to express the haughtiness of Moab..as if we were to say 'pride, prideful, proudness, pridefulness'. 1902 E. H. COOPER *20th Century Child* xii. (1905) 231 They [crabs] should be kept in a bucket for a week, said a small child firmly, 'to calm down their proudness'.

2. Proud show, splendour, magnificence.

1606 WARNER *Alb. Eng.* XVI. ci. 401 Nature wrongd by Arte, of Prowdnes more than need.

Proues, -ese, -esse, obs. ff. PROWESS.

Prouey(e, obs. f. PURVEY. **Prouffer, -ffre,** obs. ff. PROFFER. **Prounȝe,** obs. Sc. form of PRUNE *v.*

Proustite (prū·stait). *Min.* [a. F. *proustite* (1832), after J. L. Proust, a French chemist, the discoverer: see -ITE¹.] Native sulpharsenide of silver, occurring in crystals or granular masses of a cochineal-red colour; also called *ruby silver* or *light-red silver ore*.

1835 C. U. SHEPARD *Min.* II. II. 120 Proustite. Aphotistic Melacone-Blende. 1872 *Catal. Min. W. Nevill* 20 Proustite in large crystals. 1893 CHAPMAN *Blowpipe Pract.* 15 Proustite..is recognized by its deep or bright red colour.

Prout(e, Prouwis, obs. ff. PROUD, PROWESS.

Provable, proveable (prū·văb'l), *a.* Also 4–5 prevable, (5 -bulle), 6 proov(e)able. [a. OF. *pro(u)vable* (*c* 1225 in Godef.) that can be proved, worthy of approbation, ad. L. *probābil-is* PROBABLE. The form *prevable* is f. *preve* (see PROVE); *proveable* (usual from 17th to early 19th c.) affects direct formation from PROVE *v.*]

1. Capable of being proved; of which the truth or validity can be established; demonstrable.

c 1400 *Rom. Rose* 5414 And if thee thinke it is doutable It is thurgh argument provable [*orig.* c'est bien par argument prouvable]. *c* 1400 *Apol. Loll.* 7 It is not aȝen þe feiþ, or prouable aȝen þe trowþ. 1561 T. NORTON *Calvin's Inst.* I. xv. (1634) 79 They seem to say somewhat by reason proveable, yet..there is no stedfast certainty in their reasons. 1651 BAXTER *Inf. Bapt.* 272 He makes it fully proveable from Scripture. 1729 BUTLER *Serm., Hum. Nat.* i. *note*, [This] is a mere question of fact..not proveable immediately by reason. 1873 M. ARNOLD *Lit. & Dogma* (1876) 280 This being proveable from Scripture. 1889 *Spectator* 23 Nov., The steady prosecution of every provable case of sanitary neglect.

†2. Such as approves itself to the mind; worthy of acceptance or belief; plausible; = PROBABLE 2

Supplement, p. 3873; Corrigenda, p. 4092; Spurious words, p. 4093; Books quoted, p. 4094

Provably, proveably (prǒ'văbli), adv. [f. prec. + -LY⁴. Cf. AF. provablement.] In a provable manner: f. a. so as to approve itself to the mind, with likelihood (obs.); b. in a way proved; demonstrably.

†Proval, Obs. rare⁻¹. The act of proving or testing.

Provand (prǒ'vănd). Also 4-5 provande. [= MLG. and early mod.Du. provande.] Food, provisions, provender; esp. the food and fodder provided for an army.

Provant (prǒ'vănt). [app. a. MLG. provant, later form of provande PROVAND; sometimes confounded with PROVENT sb. Formerly provant.] 1. Provand, provender; an allowance of food.

†Frovant-master, Obs. [f. PROVANT sb.] The officer in charge of the provisioning; the commissary.

Prove (prūv), v. Forms: a. prove, etc. β. preove, preve, etc. ... To make trial of, try, test.

Proved (prūvd), ppl. a. Forms: see PROVE v. 1. Tried, tested; hence, That has stood a trial or test; approved, trustworthy, tried.

Proveable, -ably: see PROVABLE, -ABLY.

†Provect, a. Obs. [ad. L. provect-us.] Advanced (in years); mature, adult. b. sb. Something grown or become old.

Proveditor (provē'ditor). [ad. Ital. provveditore, n. of action f. provveder-e: see above.] 1. Advance, proficiency; advancement.

Provectant. Math. [f. L. provect- (see prec.)] +

Provedore (provēdō'r). Also 6 provador, vedor, 7 vidor,a(-)r, 7 -vidore, 8 -vidoro. [ad. Pg. provedor, Venetian dial. providore, the agent-n. from the vb. repr. L. providēre to PROVIDE.]

Provence, **Provençal**: see next.

Provence (prŏvã'ns, prǒ'vĕns). [a. F. Provence:—L. prōvincia PROVINCE.]

Provend (prǒ'vĕnd), sb. Obs. Also 4-6 provende. [a. F. provende (12th c. in Littré) f. prebend.]

Provender (prǒ'vĕndər), v. [f. prec.] 1. trans. To provide with a prebend. 2. To provide (horses, etc.) with provender; to feed.

Provender (prǒ'vĕndər), sb. Also 4-7 provendre, 5 -dour, -dere, -dyr, 6 provandor, prawnder. [a. OF. provendre (13th c. in Godef.), a phonetic variant of provende PROVEND.]

†Provenient, a. Obs. rare. [ad. L. provenient-em, pr. pple. of provenīre.]

Provent, Obs. erron. form of PREVENT.

Provene (provī'n), v. Obs. rare. [ad. L. provenīre to come forth, arise, succeed.]

Provene, obs. form of PROVINE.

Provenance (prǒ'vĕnăns). [a. F. provenance, f. provenant, pr. pple. of provenīr.] The fact of coming from some particular source or quarter; origin, derivation.

Provençal (prǒvă'nsăl, F. provãsal). Also 6-7 provincial. [a. F. provençal.]

Provencial¹, obs. form of PROVINCIAL.

Provencial², a. Of or relating to Provence or its inhabitants. (See next.)

Provenience (provī'nĭĕns). [f. L. provenient-em, pr. pple. of provenīre to come forth.]

Provent, sb. Obs. [a. L. provent-us, f. provenīre.]

Provenue, -venew. [a. F. provenu.]

Prover (prū'vər). Also 4 -ere, 5 -ar, -owr. [f. PROVE v. + -ER¹.]

Proverb (prǒ'vərb), sb. Also 4-7 proverbe. [a. F. proverbe (13th c.):—L. prōverbium.] 1. A short pithy saying in common and recognized use; a concise sentence, often metaphorical or alliterative in form.

Proverb (prǒ'vərb), v. [f. prec.] 1. trans. To utter in the form of a proverb.

Proverbial (provə'rbĭăl), a. Also 4-7 proverbiall. [ad. late L. prōverbiālis, f. prōverbium.] 1. Resembling, characteristic of, or of the nature of a proverb. 2. Such as is expressed in a proverb or proverbs.

Proverbialist. One who originates, uses, or records proverbial sayings.

Proverbiality. The quality of being proverbial. Addiction to the use of proverbs.

Proverbialize, v. 1. *intr.* To make or utter proverbs. Hence **Proverbializing** *vbl. sb.* 2. *trans.* To make or convert into a proverb; to use proverbially; to speak of in a proverb, *rare.*

Proverbially, adv. 1. In a proverbial manner; by way of, by means of, or as a proverb; according to the proverb.

Proverbic, a. rare. Of, pertaining to, or of the nature of proverbs.

Proverbio-logy. The scientific study of proverbs.

†Proverbise, v. To style or call proverbially.

Proverbity. Obs. rare⁻¹. [Ultimately from L. prōverb-ia advanced, pa. pple. of prōverbīre.]

†Proverbize. See PROVERBISE.

Provexity. Obs. rare⁻¹.

†Proviable, a. Obs. rare⁻¹.

Proviance. Sc. Obs. rare.

Proviant (prǫ'viǎnt). Also 7 provant, 9 proviand. [a. G. proviant, Du. proviand, in It. provianda, apparently an altered form of provenda.]

Pro-vicar: see PRO-14.

Pro-vice-chancellor. One of the deputies appointed by the vice-chancellor of a university on his election; an assistant or deputy vice-chancellor.

Providable (prǫvai'dǎb'l), a. rare. [f. PROVIDE v. + -ABLE.] Capable of being provided.

Provide (prǫvai'd), v. Also 5–6 provyde, Sc. -wyde, -wide, 6 -vyd. [ad. L. prōvid-ēre to see before, foresee, look after, attend to, be cautious, f. prō- PRO-1 + vidēre to see. Cf. PURVEY, a doublet of this through OF., in earlier Eng. use. *Provide* was app. distinct from PURVEY at the L. end in certain senses, and its use may have been promoted by the fact that *providence* was already in use for *purveyance.*]

I. †1. *trans.* To foresee. *Obs.*

2. *intr.* To exercise foresight in taking due measures in view of a possible event; to make provision or adequate preparation. *Const. for, against.*

3. *intr.* To equip or fit out (a person, etc.) with what is necessary for a certain purpose; to furnish or supply with something implied. In quot. 1628, to provide or furnish with a lodging.

Provident (prǫ'vidĕnt), a. [ad. L. prōvidēnt-, prōvidēns, pr. pple. of prōvidēre to PROVIDE. Cf. PRUDENT.]

1. Foreseeing; that has foresight of and makes provision for the future, or for some future event; exercising or characterized by foresight. *Providential* = *providential* (FRIENTCH 4, 8.)

2. Economical; frugal, thrifty, saving.

Providential (prǫvidē'nʃăl), a. [ad. L. prōvidentia PROVIDENCE + -AL. So F. providentiel (18-cth c. in Hatz.-Darm.)]

1. Of the nature of or characterized by providence; exercised by, proceeding from, or due to divine providence.

2. Of, pertaining to, or ordained by divine providence; *providential right*, the 'divine right' of kings. (Obs.)

3. *transf.* A person who acts or appears in the character of Providence. *colloq.*

Providence (prǫ'vidĕns), sb. [a. F. providence (13th c. in Hatz.-Darm.), ad. L. prōvidentia foresight.]

Providentialist. One who believes in providence.

Providentially, adv. [f. PROVIDENTIAL + -LY 2.] 1. With foresight and providing care; prudently. *Obs.* 2. By the ordination of divine providence.

Providentialness. The quality of being providential.

Providently, adv. [f. PROVIDENT + -LY 2.] In a provident manner. 1. With thought and providing care; prudently.

Provider (prǫvai'dəj). Also 6 -or. [f. PROVIDE v. + -ER 1.] One who provides or supplies; a purveyor.

Providing, vbl. sb. [f. PROVIDE v. + -ING 1.] The action or the verb PROVIDE; furnishing, supplying; provision; (preparation (obs.).

Providore (prǫ'vidōəj), Also 6 -or. [f. Sp. proveedor, Pg. provedor.]

Providore: see PROVED-.

Province (prǫ'vins). Also 4 (Sc.) prowince, 5 prouynce. [a. F. province (13th c. in Godef. Compl.), ad. L. prōvincia an official duty, a charge.]

I. 1. *prōvincia* as official duty or charge. Of uncertain derivation: that which offers itself at first sight, from *prō-*, PRO-1 + *vincere* to conquer (although it may in later times have affected the application of the word) does not explain the earliest known use in Latin.

II. 1. *Eccl.* The district within the jurisdiction of an archbishop or a metropolitan.

2. *Rom. Antiq.* A territory outside Italy, under Roman dominion, and administered by a governor sent from Rome.

Provincial (prǫvi'nʃăl), a. and sb. [a. F. provincial (13th c. in Hatz.-Darm.), or ad. L. prōvinciāl-is, f. prōvincia: see prec. and -AL.]

A. *adj.* Of or belonging to a province or provinces.

Provincialism (prǫvi'nʃălizm). [f. PROVINCIAL + -ISM.]

1. *Politics.* Attachment to one's own province.

Provincialize (provinʃǝlǝiz), v.

Provinciality (provinʃiˈæliti).

Provincialism (proˈvinʃǝlˌiz'm).

Provincialist (proˈvinʃǝlist).

Provinciate, v.

Provine (prǝˈvəin), v.

Proving (prūˈviŋ), ppl. a.

Proving (prūˈviŋ), vbl. sb.

Provirus.

Provision (proˈviʒǝn), sb.

Provision (proˈviʒǝn), v.

Provisional (proˈviʒǝnal), a. (sb.)

Provisionality (prǝvɪʒǝˈnæliti).

Provisionally (proˈviʒǝnali), adv.

Provisionary (proˈviʒǝnǝri), a.

Provisioned (proˈviʒǝnd), ppl. a.

Provisioner (proˈviʒǝnǝr).

Provisioness, a female provisioner.

Provisionless, a.

Provisionment.

Proviso (proˈvəizou).

Provisor (proˈvəizǝr).

Provisorily (provəiˈzɒrili), adv.

Provisory (proˈvəizǝri), a.

Provocation (prɒvǝˈkeiʃǝn).

Provocative (proˈvɒkǝtiv), a. and sb.

Provocatively, adv.

Provocativeness.

Provocatory (proˈvɒkǝtǝri), a.

Provocatress (proˈvɒkǝtres).

Provocatrix.

Provokable (proˈvoukǝb'l), a.

Provoke (proˈvouk), v.

Provokement. Obs.

Provoker (proˈvoukǝr).

Provoking (proˈvoukiŋ), ppl. a.

Provokingly (proˈvoukiŋli), adv.

Provost (proˈvost).

PROVOST.

As to the etymological and phonetic relations of the OE. and Teutonic forms, see Note below.

One set or placed over others ; a superintendent, president, head, chief ; used generally as an equivalent of the uses of PRÆPOSITUS in ancient and med.Latin, and of the descended terms in French and other languages ; *esp.* as the proper title of certain ecclesiastical and secular officers in England and Scotland, as a rendering of French *prevost, provost,* formerly used to designate various officials ; see Cotgr. s. v. *Prevost,* and cf. PREVOST.

I. In ecclesiastical and scholastic use.

1. The head or president of a chapter, or of a community of religious persons ; in conventual bodies properly the official next in rank to the abbot. — Pl. *prioresses*

2. The specific title of the heads of certain educational colleges.

II. A secular officer, etc.

†3. One appointed to preside over or super-

intend something ; usually the representative of the supreme power in a district or sphere of action ; formerly used as a translation of various Latin titles, as *præpositus, prætor, proconsul, procurator,* etc. ; also in the sense of *viceroy,* prime minister, and the like.

†b. *transf.* Applied to the archangel Michael as leader of the heavenly host. *Obs.*

4. An officer charged with the apprehension, custody, and punishment of offenders.

5. The chief magistrate of a town. *b.* In obsolete or historical uses, *esp.* (*b*) in reference to French, Flemish, or other foreign cities, in which also it sometimes passes into sense 6.

†6. The chief magistrate of a town. *b.* In obsolete or historical uses, *esp.* (*b*) in reference to French, Flemish, or other foreign cities, in which also it sometimes passes into sense 6.

6. An officer charged with the apprehension, custody, and punishment of offenders.

7. A Provost or Captayne of men of warre.

8. An assistant fencing-master.

9. *attrib.* and *Comb.* : provost-cell, a cell for confining military prisoners ; †provost-place, in phr. *to sit provost-place,* to preside ; †provost-seal, the official seal of a provost of a borough ; provost-sergeant, a sergeant of the military police : cf. sense 7.

c. The chief police official of some of the colonies in the West Indies, etc.

Provost, *v. rare.* Also *provo* (cf. PROVO). [f. prec. *sb.* sense 7.] *trans.* To hand over to the provost-marshal to be dealt with summarily and (formerly) to receive corporal punishment. Hence **Pro**vosting *vbl. sb.*

Provostal (provō'stăl), *a. rare.* [f. Provost *sb.* + -AL, after obs. F. *provostal* (Cotgr. 1611), mod.F. *prévôtal.*] Of or pertaining to a provost.

Provost-marshal. Also 6 propheast, 6, 9 -martial. [f. PROVOST *sb.* + 5, 7 + MARSHAL *sb.*] commonly held to be an irregular representation of OF. *prevost des mareschaus* (de France), 'provost of the marshals (of France),' 15th c. in Littré : see Note below.

Provosty (prə'vŏsti). Now *Hist.* [PROVOST *sb.* + -RY : cf. F. *Prévôterie,* local name (in Godef.), variant of OF. *prevosterie* the tribunal of a *prévôt.*]

1. The office or jurisdiction of a provost.

†2. The benefice of a collegiate provost : see PROVOST 1 ; the revenue derived from such a benefice ; rarely, the office of provost of an educational college ; = PROVOSTSHIP 1.

†Provostship (prə'vŏstšĭp). Now *Hist.* [PROVOST *sb.* + -SHIP.]

1. The office or dignity of a provost.

2. The residence of a provost. *nonce-use.*

Provostship (prō'vŏstšĭp). *nonce-use.*

Provro̅wve, obs. form of PROVE.

Prow (prau), *sb.[1]* Now chiefly *literary.* Forms : 6 proo, 7 proe, prow ; 6–8 prowe, 7 prou, -e, 7–8 prow. [a. F. *proue* (16th c. Rabelais), earlier *prou̅e* prow. For details, and the pronunciation, see Note below.]

1. The fore-part of a boat or ship ; the part immediately about the stem.

†b. Sometimes applied specially to the fore-part-deck holding the bow-guns, and hence to a discharge of shot from these. *Obs.*

2. *transf.* A ship. *poet.* (Cf. KEEL *sb.[1]* 2.)

PROW.

PROW. 1531 PROWLER. PROWLERY. 1532 PROXY.

Encounter matt. 1809 BYRON *Juan* ii. clxiv, At last her father's prows put out to sea.

4. *attrib.* and *Comb.,* as *prow gun, ornament, side* ; *prow-shaped a.,* of the shape of a ship's prow, i. e. projecting in a point in front.

†Prow (prau), *sb.[2]* *Obs.* [a. OF. *prou, preu, prod* (mod.F. *preux*) : — late pop.L. *prōde*, *prōdis* advantage, orig. neut. adj.]

Prow (prau), *a.* Now *arch.* [ME. *prou, prow, prowe,* a. OF. *prou, preu, prud, proud, prud.*]

†Prow (prau), *v. Obs. rare.* In 4 prowe, prou. [f. prec. adj.]

Prow, Malay boat : see PROA.

Prowd (e, obs. f. PRUDENCE.

†Prower. *Obs.* [a. F. *proveur,* -*our,* agent-n. f. *prover* to purvey.] 'Purveyor, provider of necessaries' (Skeat, *Notes to P. Pl.*).

Prowess (prou'es). Now chiefly *literary.* Forms : 3–5 prouesse, 3–7 prowesse, prowes, 4–5 prouese, 5 prowes, -*is,* -ys, prouelis, 5–7 proesse, 6 proues, prowes, prowesse, 5–7 prowesse, proves. [ME. *prouesse, prowesse,* a. OF. *proesse, prooesse, prouesse* (mod.F. *prouesse*).]

1. Valour, bravery, gallantry, martial daring ; manly courage, active fortitude.

†2. Moral goodness or excellence ; virtue. *Obs.*

†Prowessed (prau'est), *a. Obs. rare.* [f. prec. + -ED 2.]

Prowessful, *a. rare.* [f. prec. sb. + -FUL.] Full of prowess ; valorous, valiant.

†Prowful, *a. Obs. rare.* [f. PROW *sb.[2]* + -FUL.] Profitable, advantageous.

Prowl (praul), *sb.* Forms : 6–7 proller, 7–8 proler, 8– prowler. [f. next.]

Prowl (praul), *v.* Forms : 4 prolle, 5 pralle, 6–8 proll, prole, 7 prowle ; 8– prowl. [Origin obscure.]

1. *intr.* Originally, To go or move about, esp. in search of or looking for something ; hence, to go, rove, roam, or wander about, in search of what can be found, esp. of plunder or prey, or with predatory intent.

†Prowler. *Obs. rare[-1].* [f. as prec. + -ERY.] The action or practice of a prowler ; a mode of plunder or dishonest gain ; a swindle.

Prowling, *vbl. sb.* Forms : see PROWL *v.* The action of the verb PROWL in various senses.

Prowling, *ppl. a.* Forms : see PROWL *v.*

Prowly, obs. form of PROUDLY, PROLE.

Prowoky, obs. form of PROVOKE.

Prowort, -*out,* variants of PROWER *Obs.*

Prowse, Prowto, obs. f. PROWESS, PROUD.

†Prox (prŏks), *v. Obs. rare.* [f. PROX *sb.[2]* or *a.*] *trans.* To plunder, pilfer.

Proxenus (prŏk'sēnŭs). Also in Gr. form proxenos. Pl. proxeni (-ī). [mod.L., a. Gr. πρόξενος, f. πρό, Gr. + *b* guest, stranger.]

†Proximad, *adv. Anat.* [f. L.

next + -*ad* : see DISTRAD.] In the direction of its point of attachment : opp. to DISTAD.

Proximal (prŏk'sĭmăl), *a. Obs.* [ad. L. *proxim-us* nearest, superl. adj.] *proxŏ̄*

1. Next in position, adjacent : = PROXIMATE *a.* 1.

†b. Lying very near or close to something : = PROXIMATE *a.* 2.

2. *Anat.* Situated toward's the centre of the body, or the point of origin or attachment of a limb, bone, or other structure : opp. to DISTAL.

Proximate (prŏk'sĭmāt), *a.* [ad. L. *proximāt-us,* pa. pple. of *proximāre* to draw near, approach, f. *proxim-us* nearest.]

1. Closely neighbouring immediately adjacent, next, nearest (in space, serial order, quality, etc.) ; *esp.* next in a series.

Proximateness. [f. as prec. + -NESS.] The fact of being proximate ; nearness in position.

Proxime (prŏk'sĭm), *a. Obs.* [ad. L. *proxim-us* nearest, superl. adj.] 1. Next in position, adjacent ; near.

Proximity (prŏksĭ'mĭti). [a. F. *proximité,* ad. L. *proximitāt-em,* f. *proximus* nearest.]

†Proximo (prŏk'sĭmō). [L. *proximo* (sc. *mense*) in the next (month).]

Proxy (prŏk'sĭ), *sb.* Forms : 5 prokesy, prokecy, 6 proxesy, 5 procsy, 6–7 proxie, 6– proxy. [Apparently contracted from PROCURACY or PROCURATION ; cf. Proctor.]

PROXY.

ment instead of another; the action of a substitute or deputy : — Procuract 1, Procuration 2.

†2. A document empowering a person to represent and act for another ; a letter of attorney : — Procurate 2, Procuration 2 b. *Obs. exc. as b.*

b. *spec.* A writing authorizing a person to vote instead of another, at an election, a meeting of shareholders, etc., or as formerly in the House of Lords ; hence, a vote so given. (Cf. also 4.)

3. A person appointed or authorized to act instead of another; an attorney, substitute, representative, agent. (Cf. Proctor 3, Procuration 2.)

4. *U. S. local* (Rhode Isl. and Conn.). orig. A written vote for the legislative assembly sent by a deputy ; hence, loosely applied to the voting-papers or votes generally.

II. †5. *Eccl.* Provision or entertainment for a visiting bishop or his representatives; an annual payment by incumbents to the ordinary, in commutation of this : — Procuract 3, Procuration 3. *Obs.*

Proxy, *v.*, to act or vote by proxy.

Proxyhood, **Proxyship**, the office or function of a proxy or substitute.

Proyne, obs. form of Prune *v.*² and Prune.

Prose, obs. form of Prey.

Pruce, *Obs.*

†Pruce. *Obs.* Forms : 4 pruys, 4-5 prus, 4-6 pruce, 5-7 pruse, (5 prewce, prewe 6, 8 pruss, pruske). [M.E. *Prus*, a. AF. *Prus*, *Pruce*, OF. *Pruce* ...] Prussia.

Prude, obs. form of Proud.

Prudence (prū´dens). Also 6 *Sc.* prowdence, *proudens.* [a. F. *prudence* (13th c. in Littré) ...]

Prudent (prū´dent), *a.* [a. F. *prudent* (c 1300 in Godef. *Compl.*) ...]

PRUDENTIAL.

1. Of persons (rarely of inferior animals): Sagacious in adapting means to ends; careful to follow the most politic and profitable course; having or exercising sound judgement in practical affairs; circumspect, discreet, worldly-wise.

†2. Wise, discerning, sapient. *Obs.* (exc. as included in 1.)

3. Of conduct, action, etc.: Characterized by, exhibiting, or proceeding from prudence; politic, judicious. *The prudent* : that which is prudent.

Hence Prudence *a.*, of the nature of, or characteristic of, a prude; **Prudely** *adv.*, in the manner of a prude.

Prudent, *a.* [a. F. *prudent* ...]

Prudential (prūden´ʃal), *a.* (adv.), *sb.* [f. L. *prudentia* PRUDENCE ...]

A. *adj.* **1.** Of, belonging to, or of the nature of prudence ; involving prudence ; characterized or prescribed by forethought and careful deliberation.

2. Of persons: Exercising prudence ; (in New England) Appointed to conduct the affairs of a town, society, etc. ; cf. B. 1 a.

†4. Alleged term for a 'company' of vicars. *Obs.*

†Pru´dency. *Obs.* [ad. L. *prūdentia.*] = Prudence.

B. *sb.* **1.** Matters that fall within the scope or province of prudence ; *esp.* (in *U. S.*) matters of local government and administration for which there is no need to go to the law courts.

2. *pl.* **Prudentials**, prudential considerations.

†Prudhomme. Also as Fr. **prud'homme** (prüdŏm). [a. F. *prud'homme* ...]

Prudish (prū´diʃ), *a.* [f. Prude + -ish¹.]

1. Having the character of a prude ; maintaining or affecting extreme propriety of behaviour.

2. *fig.* Of things : Extremely prim, formal, or rigid.

Prudishly (prū´diʃli), *adv.* In a prudish manner ; with prudery.

Prudishness (prū´diʃnes). [f. as prec. + -ness.] = Prudishness.

Prudishness (prū´diʃnes). [f. as prec. + -ness.]

Prudish´ness. [f. Prudish + -ness.]

Prudist. *Obs. rare.* [f. Prude + -ist.]

Prudity (prū´diti), *rare.* [f. Prude + -ity.] = Prudery.

†Prue. *Obs.*

Pruessa, var. Prowess.

Pruff, obs. var. of Proof, Prove.

Prunella. See Prunello.

PRUNE.

Prune (prūn), *sb.* Forms : see below. [a. F. *prune* (13th c. in Littré)—*med.*L. *pruna*, fem. sing. from *prūnum*, neut. pl. cf. L. *prūnum* a plum, a. Gr. προῦνον, later form of προῖμον a plum.]

A. *Illustration of Forms.*

B. *Signification.*

†1. The fruit of the plum-tree ; a plum ; also, the tree, *Prunus domestica.* (exc. as in c. and 2.)

2. The dried fruit of several varieties of the common plum-tree, prepared by drying; hence, the fruit itself, as an article of food.

3. *transf.* The dark reddish purple colour of the juice of prunes; also called *prune-purple.* Also *attrib.*

4. *Phrase.* **Prunes and prism** : see quot. 1855.

Prune (prūn), *v.*¹ *Obsolescent.* [ME. *prune*, *proine*, of uncertain origin, but in its phonetics apparently French ...]

1. To cut or lop superfluous branches or twigs from (a vine, tree, or shrub), in order to promote fruitfulness, induce regular growth, etc. ; to trim.

5. *refl.* To preen oneself, pride oneself. *Obs.*

†Prunel. *Obs.* Also 6 -elle, 6-8 -ell. [a. F. *prunel*, variant of *brunelle* Brunel.]

PRUNELET.

Prunelet (prū´nelet), *sb.* [? ad. F. *prunellette*.] A little green prune.

Prunella (prūne´lă). *Obs.* [Of uncertain history ...]

2. *Pharmacy.* Chiefly in comb. **prunella salt**, **prunella salt**, in *mod.*L. *sal prunella* : 'prunella stone' ...

Prunella (prūne´lă). *Bot.* [mod.L. alteration of *Brunella*, generic name in Tournefort and Linnæus ...]

Prunella (prūne´lă). Also 7, 9 prunella, 8 -ello, 9 -elloe. [Altered from ? or from F. *prunella* 'any kind of little plums or Prune' (Florio), dim. of F. *prune* a Prune ...]

Prunello (prūne´lō). Also 7, 9 prunella, 8 -ello, 9 -elloe.

Prunel-lus, Prunel´lum. *Obs. rare.*

Pruner (prū´nǝr). [f. Prune *v.*¹ + -er¹.] One who prunes trees or vines.

Prunery (prū´nǝri), *rare.* [f. Prune *v.*² + -ery.] The place where prunes are grown.

Pruniferous (prūni´ferǝs), *a.* *rare.* [f. L. *prūni-ferus*.] Bearing plums or stone-fruits.

Pruniform (prū´nifǫrm), *a.* [f. L. *prūni-* + -form.] Having the form of a prune.

Pruning (prū´niŋ), *vbl. sb.* [f. Prune *v.*¹ + -ing¹.] The action of Prune *v.*¹

PRUNUS

Prunus (prū´nǝs). *Bot.* [L. *prūnus* plum-tree, a. Gr. προῦνος, προῖμος plum ...] A genus of trees and shrubs, nat. ord. *Rosaceæ*, containing the common sloe, bullace, plums, apricot, myrobalan, and many other species of sub-species, bearing drupaceous fruits.

Prurience (prū̇′riĕns). [as PRURIENT: see -ENCY.]

1. The physical fact or sensation of itching.

2. *fig.* Mental itching or craving.

3. = PRURIENCY 2.

Pruriency (prū̇′riĕnsi). 1. The quality of itching, itchingness. *rare.*

2. *fig.* Having an itching desire or curiosity, or an uneasy or morbid craving. *rare.*

3. Liking for or tendency towards impure or lascivious thought; an instance of this.

Prurient (prū̇′riĕnt), *a.* [ad. L. *prūrient-*, *-entem*, pres. pple. of *prūrīre* to itch, long, be wanton. Cf. obs. F. *prurient* (1598 in Godef.).]

1. That itches physically, itching. *rare.*

2. *fig.* Having an itching desire or curiosity, or an uneasy or morbid craving. *rare.*

3. Given to the indulgence of lewd ideas; impure-minded; characterized by lasciviousness of mind.

4. *Bot.* Applied to plants which cause an itching or slightly stinging sensation. *rare.*

5. *Comb.*, as *prurient-minded* adj.

Pruriently, *adv.* [f. prec. + -LY.] In a prurient manner.

Pruriginous (prūrij′inǝs), *a.* (Also 8 -genous, 9 -ginous.) [ad. F. *prurigineux* (1495 in Godef. *Compl.*), ad. late L. *prūrīginōs-us* adj., f. *prūrīgō*: see next.] 1. Affected by or liable to prurigo or itching; pertaining to or of the nature of prurigo.

Prurigo (prūrai′gou). [a. L. *prūrīgō* itching, irritation.] *Path.* A chronic disease of the skin.

Pruriousness, *rare.* [f. *prūriōse* adv.: see -NESS.] = PRURIENCE 3.

Prurit-, comb. form of PRURITUS.

Pruritant, *a.* and *sb.* *Obs. nonce-wd.* Satirical perversion of *puritan*, in allusion to L. *prūrītus* itching.

Pruritation, *a.* and *sb.* *Obs. rare*. [n. of action from *prūrītāre*, freq. of *prūrīre* to itch.] A continual or recurring itching; *fig.* a restless desire, a craving.

Pruritic (prūrit′ik), *a.* [f. next + -IC.] Pertaining to or of the nature of pruritus.

Pruritus (prūrai′tǝs). [L. *prūritus* (-us-item), f. *prūrīre* to itch.] *Path.* Itching of the skin without visible eruption.

†Prurity. *Obs. rare*. [f. stem of L. *prūrīre* (see above) + -ITY.] = PRURIENCY 1.

Prus. *obs. form of* PRUCE.

†Prusiano (prūsiä′ne). [Sp., = Prussian.] A finch or bunting (*Passerina versicolor*) of Mexico and Texas, so called from its blue colour. *1890 in Cent. Dict.*

Prusite. *Obs. rare.* [var. of PRUCE.] Pruce or spruce beer.

Prussian (prǝ′ʃǝn), *a.* and *sb.* [f. mod.L. *Prussian-us* adj., f. *Prussia*: see Note below. So F. *prussien.*]

A. *adj.* 1. Of or pertaining to Prussia or its inhabitants; also, designating things actually or reputedly coming from Prussia.

Prussian blue: a deep blue pigment of great body and covering power, consisting essentially of hydrated ferric ferrocyanide.

Prussian brown, Prussian green, pigments derived from or allied to Prussian blue.

†3. Hence, *Chem.* Prussian acid = PRUSSIC acid.

Prussian alkali: potassium ferrocyanide.

B. *sb.* A native or inhabitant of Prussia; the ethnic territory, the duchy, or the kingdom.

Prussianism. [f. PRUSSIAN *a.* + -ISM.] The national spirit or political system of Prussia.

Prussianize (prǝ′ʃǝnaiz), *v.* [f. PRUSSIAN *a.* + -IZE.] *trans.* To render Prussian or like Prussian in organization or character. Hence **Prussianization**, the action or process of Prussianizing; **Prussianizing** *vbl. sb.* and *ppl. a.*

Prussiate (prǝ′sieit), *sb.* *Chem.* [a. F. *prussiate* (Morveau, *etc. Nomencl. Chim.* 1787).] *Chem.* A salt of prussic acid.

†Prussin. *Chem.* *Obs.* Also *-ine.* An early name for CYANOGEN, CN (a polymer of it), as a derivative of Prussian blue.

Prussite. *Obs. rare.* = PRUSSIATE.

So † *Prutenical a.*, in same sense.

Pry (prai), *sb.*[1] [f. PRY *v.*[1]]
1. An act or the action of prying; a peeping or inquisitive glance.

2. An inquisitive person. Cf. *Paul Pry.*

†Pry, *sb.*[2] [Deviation unknown.] A name given locally to various rigid glaucous grasses and species of *Carex*, esp. *C. paradoxa.*

†Pry, *sb.*[3] [Deviation unknown.] Also ?-pie. The lime-tree or linden.

Pry (prai), *v.*[1] Now *dial.* Also ? pry. [Deviation unknown.] 1. *intr.* To look closely or curiously; to peep or peer, to look narrowly; to peer inquisitively or impertinently; to spy.

2. *trans.* To look for, look through, or look at closely; to observe narrowly.

Pry (prai), *v.*[2] [f. PRY *sb.*[1]] To raise or move by force of leverage; to force up.

Prying, *ppl. a.* [f. PRY *v.*[1] + -ING[2].] That pries; inquisitly or impertinently curious; inquisitive; diligently inquiring.

Prying, *vbl. sb.* [f. PRY *v.*[1] + -ING[1].] The action of PRY *v.*[1]; narrow peering or examination; inquisitive search.

Pryingly, *adv.* [f. prec. + -LY[2].] In a prying manner; narrowly, closely, inquisitively.

Pry-pole. *Obs.* [f. PRY *v.*[2] + POLE *sb.*[1]] A pole used as a 'pry' or lever.

Pryse, pryce. *Hunting, arch.* Also *prise*, **pryce.** [ME. a. OF. *pris, prise*, *priz.*]

Prye, *obs. form of* PRY.

Pryse, *prise*, obs. ff. PRICE, PRIZE, PRIZE.

†Prytaneum (pritai′ĭŏm). *Gr. Antiq.* Also 9 *-eium*, *-eion*. [L. *prytaneum*, a. Gr. *πρυτανεῖον*: see next.] The public hall of a Greek state or city, in which the sacred fire was kept burning.

†Prytanis (pri′tanis). *Gr. Antiq.* Pl. *-nes* (-nīz). Also 7 in Anglicized form *prytan*, *-ane*. [L. *prytanis*, a. Gr. *πρύτανις* a prince, ruler, chief, at Athens a president.]

Prytany (pri′tani). *Gr. Antiq.* Also *prut-.* [ad. Gr. *πρυτανεία*, f. *πρύτανις* PRYTANIS.] 1. The presidency of the Athenian senate; the office or dignity of a prytanis. Also *transf.*

2. Each of the ten divisions of the Athenian Council of Five Hundred during its presidency; also the period of time during which each such division presided.

Psalloid. *rare.* [ad. Gr. ψάλις + -OID.] *Anat.* [ad. mod.L. *psalloides*, irreg. f. Gr. *ψαλίς* + *-οειδής*] A structure resembling a stringed instrument; applied to a part of the *fornix* of the brain (*corpus psalloides*), from the lines in it suggesting the strings of a musical instrument, whence also called *lyra* (see LYRA 4).

Psalm (sām), *sb.* Forms: see below. [ad. L. *psalm-us*, a. Gr. *ψαλμός* a twitching (of the strings of a harp), a song sung to the harp, f. *ψάλλειν* to twitch, twang, play (with the fingers), sing to a harp (in LXX and N.T.). The OE. *(p)salm* was app. a. L. directly.]

1. A sacred song or hymn; esp. one of those included in the 'Book of Psalms'; also, a version or paraphrase of any of these.

2. *spec.* Any one of the sacred songs or hymns of the ancient Hebrews which together form the 'Book of Psalms' (see b); a version or paraphrase of any of these, esp. as sung (or read) in public or private worship. The prevailing use throughout.

b. *The Psalms, the Book of Psalms.* Name of one of the books of the Old Testament, forming the hymn-book of the Jewish church, and used also in Christian worship from the earliest times; the Psalter. Often called the *Psalms of David*, in accordance with the belief that the greater part of them were composed by David king of Israel.

Psalm-book, *sb.* A book of psalms; *spec.* a metrical version of them for public worship.

Psalmist (sā′mist, sǝ-). [ad. late L. *psalmista*, a. Gr. *ψαλμιστής* f. *ψάλλειν*: see PSALM *sb.*] The writer or author of a psalm or psalms; almost always with def. art. as a title for David considered as the author of the Psalms, or as a designation of the author of any one of them.

†Psalmister. *Obs.* Also *psalmister, -itere*; *(poet.)* -ster. [ad. OF. *(psalmistre)*, = PSALMIST.]

Psalmistry. *Obs. rare*. [f. PSALMIST + -RY.]

Psalmodial (sælmou′dial), *a.* [f. PSALMODY + -AL.] Of, pertaining to, or having the character of psalmody.

Psalmodic (sælmɔ′dik), *a.* [= F. *psalmodique*, ad. Gr. *ψαλμῳδικός*.] Of or pertaining to psalmody; having the style or character of psalmody.

Psalmodical (sælmɔ′dikăl), *a.* = prec.

Psalmodist (sæ′lmǝdist). [f. PSALMODY + -IST.] One who practises or is skilled in psalmody; a singer of psalms.

Psalmodize (sæ′lmǝdaiz), *v.* [f. PSALMODY + -IZE.] *intr.* To practise or use psalmody; to sing psalms.

Psalmody (sæ′lmǝdi, sā′-). [ad. late L. *psalmodia*, a. Gr. *ψαλμῳδία* singing to a harp, f. *ψαλμός* PSALM + *ῳδή* song, ode.]

1. The action, practice, or art of singing psalms (or sacred vocal music in general), including hymns and anthems, esp. in public worship.

Psalmograph, *Psalmographer*, *Psalmographist.* One who writes psalms; the composer of a psalm or psalms.

Psalmographer. The author of a psalm or psalms.

Psalmography. The writing or composition of psalms.

Psalmy (sā′mi), *a.* *nonce-wd.* [f. PSALM *sb.* + -Y[1].] Of or disposed for a psalm.

Psalter (sǝ′ltǝr, sā′-). Forms: see below. [In OE. *saltere*, a. OHG. *psalteri, psalte-* (= mod. Ger. *psalter*), ad. late L. *psaltērium*: see PSALTERY.] 1. The Psalms of David collectively.

PSALTER.

Psalter (ps—).

I. 1. The Book of Psalms, as one of the books of the Old Testament.

b. a translation or particular version (prose or metrical) of the Book of Psalms: e.g. a Latin, English, Chinese Psalter; the Prayer-book Psalter, the Scotch Metrical Psalter.

b. Applied to a kind of wind instrument.

Psaltery (-t'əri).

Psalterian (psælt-, -pilt'ri-an).

† **b.** Psalter. Applied to a kind of wind instrument.

PSALTRESS.

Psaltress.

Psaltry, obs. form of PSALTERY.

PSAMMITE

Psammite (psæm-mait, sæ-mait). Min. rare.

Psammo-, combining form.

Psammoma (psæmōmă). Path.

Psammophis

Psamite

Psamm-

PSEUDO-

Pseudo- (psi—, sīdō).

Pseudaxis

Pseudo-, combining form. 2. Special combinations.

Pseudo-, combining form.

Psithurism (psi·pûri·m), *rare*. [irreg. for *psithyrism*, ad. Gr. ψιθυρισμός or ψιθυρισμ-ός, f. ψιθυρίζειν to whisper.] Whispering; a whispering noise, as of leaves moved by the wind.

Psittac-, repr. Gr. ψιττακ-, L. *psittac-*us parrot, in various words.

Psittaceous (psitā·shəs), *a*. [f. L. *psittac-*us parrot + -eous.] Like or akin to the *Psittacidæ* or parrots.

Psittacine (psi·tăsin), *a*. [f. L. *psittac-*us + -ine.]

Psittacosis (psitəkō·sis), *Path.* [f. Gr. ψιττακός parrot + -osis.] An infective disease communicated to man from parrots.

Psoadic (psŏæ·dik), *a*. *Anat*. [f. next + -ic.] Of or pertaining to the psoas muscle.

Psoas (psō·ăs). *Anat.* [Properly pl. of *psoa*, a. Gr. ψόα, ψύα, pl. ψόαι, ψύαι, the muscles of the loins.]

Psora (psō·ră). *Path.* [a. Gr. ψώρα itch, mange, = L. *scabies*.] A contagious skin disease; the itch.

Psoriasis (psŏrai·ăsis), *Path.* [mod.L., a. Gr. ψωρίασις, f. ψωριᾶν to have the itch, f. ψώρα itch.] A disease of the skin.

Psorosperm (psō·rŏspəm), *a*. as prec. + Gr. σπέρμα seed.] An individual or a group of Sporozoa.

Psychagogic (psəkăgŏ·dʒik), *a*. [ad. Gr. ψυχαγωγικός attractive to the mind, persuasive, f. ψυχαγωγ-ός winning of the mind, persuasion, f. ψυχαγωγεῖν: see next. In mod.F. *psychagogique*.] Influencing or leading the mind or soul; persuasive, attractive.

Psychagogue (-æg·g). [ad. Gr. ψυχαγωγός, f. ψυχή + ἄγειν to lead; leader of departed souls, said of Hermes. So mod.F. *psychagogue*.]

Psyche (psī·kī), *a*. [a. Gr. ψυχή (in L. *psychē*) breath, life, soul.] The animating principle, the soul.

Psychiater (psəkiai·təɹ), [mod.f. Gr. ψυχή + ἰατρ-ός healer, physician.] One who treats mental disease: an alienist.

Psychiatric (-æ·trik), *a*. (*sb*.) as prec.

Psychiatrics (rarely -atric, -atrik). The theory or practice of psychiatry.

Psychiatrist (psəkai·ătrist), [f. next + -ist.] A student or professor of psychiatry.

Psychiatry (psəkai·ătri). [f. Gr. ψυχή PSYCHE + -λατρεια healing, medical treatment (f. ἰατρός healer).]

Psychic (psai·kik, saik-), *a*. and *sb*. [ad. Gr. ψυχικός of the soul or life: in mod.F. *psychique*.]

Psychofugal [after CENTRIPETAL], tending away from the brain.

Psychogony (-gŏni), also in mod.L. form **psychogonia** (-gōʊ·niă), [f. Gr. ψυχή + -γονία generation.]

Psychogram (sɑi·kŏgræm), 'A spirit-writing'; a writing or message supposed to come from a spirit, or to be produced by psychical agency.

Psychogony [as prec. + -GRAPH.]

Psychographer [as -GRAPHER.]

Psychographic (psɑikŏgræ·fik), *a*. [f. next + -ic.]

Psychography (psɑikŏ·grăfi). [f. Gr. ψυχή, PSYCHO- + -γραφία, -GRAPHY.]

Psychologer (psɑi·kŏlŏdʒəɹ), [f. PSYCHOLOG-Y + -ER.] = PSYCHOLOGIST.

Psychologian (-olō·dʒiăn). = PSYCHOLOGIST.

Psychologic (psɑikŏlŏ·dʒik), *a*. (*sb*.) [ad. L. *psychologicus*: see PSYCHOLOGY + -IC.]

Psychological (psɑikŏlŏ·dʒikăl), *a*. 1. Of, pertaining to, or of the nature of psychology; dealing with or relating to psychology.

Psychologically (-ăli), *adv.* 1. In a psychological manner; in relation to psychology.

Psychologism (psɑi·kŏlŏdʒiz'm). Idealism as opposed to sensationalism.

Psychologist (psɑi·kŏlŏdʒist). One who makes a study of, or is skilled in, psychology; a student or teacher of the science of mental phenomena.

Psychology (psɑikŏ·lŏdʒi). [ad. mod.L. *psychologia* (f. Gr. ψυχή soul + -λογία -LOGY), in F. and Ger. *psychologie*. See note below.] The science of the nature, functions, and phenomena of the human soul or mind.

Psychometer (-ŏ·mïtəɹ). 1. One who has the psychometric faculty, or practises psychometry (sense 1). 2. An instrument for measuring the duration of mental states or processes.

Psychometric (-mĕ·trik), *a*. Of, pertaining to, or of the nature of psychometry (in either sense).

Psychometry (-ŏ·mïtri). 1. The measurement of the duration and intensity of mental states or processes.

Psychopannychy (psɑikŏpæ·nikĭ, f. Gr. ψυχή soul + παννυχία all-night vigil). Obs.

Psychopath. ... One affected with psychopathy; a mentally deranged person.

Psychopathic, *a.* (and *sb.*) 1. a. Of, pertaining to, or of the nature of mental disease. b. Subject to or affected with mental disease, mentally deranged.

Psychopathist. One who studies or treats psychopathy or mental disease; an alienist.

Psycho-pathology. The pathology of the mind; the science of mental disease.

Psychopathy ... Path. [f. Gr. ...] Mental disease or disorder; 'mental disorder considered apart from cerebral disease' (Billings).

Psycho-physical, *a.* [f. as prec. + *-AL*: cf. *physical*.] Of or pertaining to psycho-physics; having to do with psychology and physics, or the connexion of the psychical and the physical.

Psycho-physicist. One versed in psycho-physics.

Psycho-physiology. The department of physiology which deals with mental phenomena; physiological or experimental psychology.

Psychoplasm ... Psychopomp ... Psychostatics ... Psychotherapeutic ... Psychotherapy ...

Psychro-. ... combining form of Gr. ... cold.

Psychrometer ... Meteor. An instrument for measuring the relative humidity of the air.

Psychrophobia ... Dread of or sensitiveness to cold.

Ptarmigan. Forms: a 6 termagan, tarmigan, 7 termigant, termagant, tormichan, 8 tormiean, tarmichan, tarmachan, 8– ptarmigan, (9 ptarnacan, -gan). [In Lowland Sc. ...] A bird of the grouse family (*Lagopus mutus*) ...

Pt. Words beginning with this combination of consonants are all (with the exception of the fancifully mis-spelt *ptarmigan*) from Greek, in the combination is frequent.

Pterion ... Anat. [mod.L., f. Gr. ...] In craniology: the region of the wing of the sphenoid ...

Pteris 1555 **Pterygo-** **Pterygode.** 1556 **Ptolemaic**

Pteris ... Bot. [mod.L. (Linné), f. Gr. ...] A genus of ferns with feathery leaves.

Pterodactyl ... Palæont. Also **-yle**. An extinct flying reptile of the Mesozoic period.

Pteroma ... Pteron ... Pteropod ... Pterygo- ... Pterygode ...

Ptolemaic, *a.* [f. *Ptolemy* + *-AIC*.] Of or pertaining to Ptolemy, a celebrated astronomer who lived at Alexandria in the second century A.D.

Column 1 — PTOLEMAICAL

the earth, which was supposed to be stationary: it was, with modifications, the accepted theory till the time of Copernicus and Kepler.

2. Of or pertaining to the Ptolemies, the Macedonian Greek rulers of ancient Egypt from the death of Alexander the Great to Cleopatra.

Ptomaine (tōˈmǝin, tōˈmaˌiːn). *Chem.* [ad. F. *ptomaïne*, blunderingly formed by Professor Selmi of Bologna, f. Gr. πτῶμα fallen body, corpse: see -INE².] A class of substances, some of them poisonous, produced in animal and vegetable matter during decomposition.

Ptosis (tōˈsis). *Path.* [a. Gr. πτῶσις falling, fall.]

Ptyalin (ˈtaɪəlɪn). *Physiol. Chem.* [f. Gr. πτύαλον saliva + -IN¹.]

Puberty (piuˈbǝˌti). [ME. *puberte* (1474 in Hatz.-Darm.), ad. L. *pūbertās*, *-tāt-* the age of maturity, the signs of puberty, f. *pūber* or *pūbēs*: see PUBER.]

1. The state or condition of having become functionally capable of procreating offspring.

Pubescent (piuˈbesǝnt), *a.* (*sb.*). [a. F. *pubescent* (1516 in Hatz.-Darm.), ad. L. *pūbescent-*, *-ens*, pres. pple. of *pūbēscĕre* to become downy or hairy, to attain puberty, to ripen.]

Pubic (piuˈbik), *a.* [f. PUBES + -IC.] Of, pertaining to, or connected with the pubes or pubis.

Public (pʌblik), *a.* and *sb.* [a. F. *public*, *-ique* (14th c.), ad. L. *pūblicus*, altered from *poplicus*, *populicus* (f. *populus* people), by the infl. of *pūbēs* adult population.]

A. *adj.*

1. Of or pertaining to the people as a whole; that belongs to, affects, or concerns the community or nation.

B. *sb.*

1. Of or pertaining to the people as a whole.

Lower half

Publicate, *v. rare⁻¹.* [f. ppl. stem of L. *pūblicāre*.] = PUBLISH.

Publican (pʌbˈlikǝn). Forms: 3–4 *puplican*, 4 *poplican*, *publican*, 4 *pupplicane*, 5 *publican*, *publycane*, 6 *publicane*; also 5 *publicain* (14th c. in Hatz.-Darm.), ad. L. *pūblicānus* a farmer-general of the revenues, later a tax-gatherer.

Publication (pʌblikeɪˈʃǝn). [ME. *publicacioun* (14th c. in Hatz.-Darm.), a. OF. *publicacion*, or ad. L. *pūblicātiōn-em*, n. of action f. *pūblicāre* to PUBLISH.] The action of publishing, or the condition of being published.

Public house. See PUBLIC *a.* 3 c.

Public school. A school under various meanings.

Publican, *sb.²* *Eccl. Hist.* Forms: 5 *Puplican*, *puplican*, *-quan*, 7 *Publican*. [ME. *Pop(e)lican-*, *Publican*, altered from med. *Pop(e)lican-* (v.–v.) PUBLICAN, in allusion to, or by confusion with, L. *pūblicānus* PUBLICAN.]

Publicanism (pʌbˈlikǝnɪz'm). The fact or profession of being a publican.

Publication (as above).

Publicist (pʌbˈlisist). [a. F. *publiciste* (1762 in Dict. Acad.), f. L. *pūblic(us)* + -IST.]

Publicity (pʌbˈlisiti). [a. F. *publicité* (18th c. in Hatz.-Darm.), ad. med.L. *pūblicitāt-em*.] The quality or condition of being public; the condition or fact of being open to public observation or knowledge.

Publicly (pʌbˈlikli), *adv.* [f. PUBLIC *a.* + -LY².] In a public manner; in the presence or with the knowledge of people generally; with publicity; openly; without concealment.

Public school. (as above)

Public-spirited, *a.* Characterized by public spirit (PUBLIC *a.* 8 b.); animated or prompted by zeal for the public good; directed to the common good.

Hence **Public-spiritedly** *adv.*, with public spirit; **Public-spiritedness**.

Publish (pɒˈblɪʃ), *v.* Forms: see below. [ME. *publise*, *-ish*, *-lisch*, etc., ad. *Publiss-*, lengthened stem of OF. *publier*, *publier*, (later) *publier*, ad. L. *pūblicāre* to make public, confiscate, (L. *pūblic-us* Public.]

1. *trans.* To make publicly or generally known; to declare or report openly or publicly; to tell or noise abroad; to proclaim, promulgate, disseminate (a creed or system).

b. To make generally accessible or available for acceptance or use; to place before or offer to the public. *Obs.* exc. as said of doing this by the medium of a book, journal, or the like.

c. *spec. in Law.* *To publish one's will:* see quot. 1845. *To publish a libel:* to communicate a libel to one or more persons.

2. *spec.* To issue or cause to be issued for sale to the public (copies of a book, writing, engraving, piece of music, or the like); said of an author, editor, or *spec.* of a professional publisher.

b. *Comm.* One whose business is the issuing of books, newspapers, music, engravings, or the like, as the agent of the author or owner; one who undertakes the printing and distribution of copies of such works, and their distribution to the booksellers and other dealers, or to the public.

Puck (pʌk), *sb.¹* *Obs.* exc. *dial.* [OE. *pūca*.] **1.** A malicious or evil spirit or demon of popular superstition.

Puck, *sb.²* *dial.* [Origin uncertain.] A fat unripe or half-formed nut or the like.

Pucker (pʌkər), *v.* [prob. a frequentative or diminutive of Poke.] **1.** *intr.* To contract or gather into wrinkles, small folds, cockles, or bulges; to become drawn together into irregular wrinkles or corrugations.

2. *trans.* To draw together or contract into wrinkles, bulges, or fullnesses.

Pucker, *sb.* **1.** A ridge, wrinkle, or corrugation of the skin or other substance; a number of small wrinkles running across and into one another.

2. *fig.* A state of agitation or excitement; a flutter, a fuss. *colloq.*

Pudding (pudɪŋ), *sb.* Forms: 3–4 poding, 4–6 podyng, (4–6 -ynge), puddyng; 5–6 pudding, 6 puddyng, 6– pudding. [ME. *poding*, of uncertain origin.]

Pudding-bag. A bag in which a pudding is boiled.

†Pudding-grass. Obs. Pennyroyal.

Pudding-pie. A name for various forms of pastry; esp. a dough pudding containing meat, baked in a dish; a tart made with pie-crust and custard; see quot. 1829.

†Pudding-prick. Obs. A slender wooden skewer (see PRICK sb. 14) with which the ends of a gut containing a pudding were fastened. Often in similative phrase: see quots. 1561, 1611.

Pudding-stone. A composite rock consisting of a mass of rounded pebbles cemented together by a siliceous matrix; conglomerate.

†Pudding-time. Obs. The time when puddings or puddings are to be had; hence fig., a time when one is in luck; a favourable or lucky time.

Pudding-wife.

Puddle (pɒˈdl), sb. Forms: 4-5 podel, 4-6 podil, 4-8 pudel, 6-7 poddel, 5-7 pudeil, (6 -elle, -il, 6-7 -ell), 6 poddell, poddle, 6 Sc. pwdyll, 6-7 pudle; 6- puddle. [ME. podel, puddel, app. dim. from OE. pudd, furrow, *pudda, *pudel, etc.]

Puddle (pɒˈdl), v. Forms: see prec. [f. PUDDLE sb.]

Puddler (pɒˈdlər). [f. PUDDLE v. + -ER¹.] One who puddles; spec. a workman employed in puddling iron.

Puddle (pɒˈdl), ppl. a. [f. prec. + -ED¹.]

Puddling, ppl. a. [as prec. + -ING².]

Puddling, vbl. sb. [as prec. + -ING¹.]

Puddy (pɒˈdi), a. [f. PUDDLE sb. + -Y¹.]

Pudency (piūˈdensɪ). [ad. L. pudentia.]

Pudenda. pl. of PUDENDUM.

Pudendal (piūˈdendəl), a. [f. PUDENDUM + -AL.]

Pudendous (piūˈdendəs), a.

Pudendum (piūˈdendəm). Usually in pl. pudenda.

†Puder, Puderer, obs. ff. PEWTER, PEWTERER.

Pudge (pʌdʒ), dial. and colloq. Also Sc. podge (pɒdʒ).

Pudgy (pʌˈdʒi), a. [f. PUDGE² + -Y¹.]

Pudibund (piūˈdibʌnd), a. rare. [ad. L. pudibund-us easily ashamed, bashful, modest, also shameful, f. pudēre to make or be ashamed; cf. -BUND.]

Pudic (piūˈdik), a. [ad. F. pudique (15th c.), ad. L. pudīc-us modest, chaste.]

Pudicity (piūˈdisɪti). [ad. F. pudicité (14th c.), ad. L. pudicitās.]

Pudor (piūˈdɔr). [L. pudor shame, modesty.]

†Pudu (pʊˈdū). [Native Chilian name.]

Pudibundity.

Pueblo (pweˈblo). [Sp., = people, population, town, village.]

Puerile (piūˈərɪl, -aɪl), a. [ad. F. puérile (15th c.), ad. L. puerīlis.]

Puerilism (piūˈərɪlɪz'm).

Puerility (piūərɪˈliti). [ad. F. puerilité (15th c.), ad. L. puerīlitātem.]

Puerper (piūˈərpər). [L. puerpera, f. puer boy, child + parere to bear.]

Puerperal (piūˈərpərəl), a. [f. L. puerper-us bearing a child + -AL.]

Puerperium (piūˈərpɪərɪəm).

Puet, Puefellow, obs. ff. PEWIT, FEW-FELLOW.

Puff (pʌf), sb.¹ Forms: 3, 6 puf, 6 puff, 7- puff. [f. PUFF v.]

Pug (pʌg), *sb.*[1] Now only *dial.* [Origin obscure: more than one word.]

Pug (pʌg), *v.*[1] [Origin obscure.] ...

Puggy (pʌgi), *a.*[2] *dial.* [f. *pug* *vb.* *dial.*] Moist, clammy.

Pugil (dᵛ̇ldᵹil), *sb.* [ad. L. *pugill-us* a handful, f. root *pug-* as in *pugn-us* fist.]

Pugilism (pi̇ʊdᵹiliz'm), *sb.* The art or practice of fighting with fists; boxing. Also *fig.*

Pugilist (pi̇ʊdᵹilist), *sb.* One who practises the art of boxing; a boxer, a fighter; *fig.* a vigorous controversialist.

Pugilistic (pi̇ʊdᵹilistik), *a.* ...

Pug nose, **pug-nose** (pʌgnō·z). [f. Pug *sb.*]

Pug-mill. [app. f. Pug *v.*[1] + Mill *sb.*[1]] ...

Pug-piles, *sb. pl.* ...

Pugnacious (pʌgnēⁱ·ʃəs), *a.* [f. L. *pugnāci-*, *pugnax* ...] Disposed to fight; given to fighting; quarrelsome; contentious.

Pugnacity (pʌgnæ·siti), *sb.* [ad. L. *pugnācitās*.] The condition or character of being pugnacious.

Pugnant, *sb.* ...

†Pugnant, *a.*[1] ... Conflicting, hostile, opposed, repugnant.

Puggree, puggaree (pʌ·gri, pʌ·gəri). Also ... A light turban or head-covering worn by Indian natives.

Pugil... etc.

Puissant (pi̇u·isənt, piwi·sənt, piwɪsæ·nt), *a.* ...

Puissance ...

Puissantly (see *prec.*), *adv. arch.* ...

Puke, *v.*[1] ... To vomit.

Pukish, *a.*[1] ...

Pul, *sb.* ...

Pulchritude (pʌ·lkritiūd). ... Beauty.

Pule, *v.* ... To cry in a thin or weak voice; to whine.

Pulicose, pulicous (pi̇u·likōs, -kəs), *a.* [ad. L. *pūlicōsus*, f. *pūlic-, pūlex* flea.] Abounding in fleas; fleasy.

Puling, *ppl. a.* ...

Pulick Mountain. ...

Pulk (pʌlk). Now *local.* ...

Pull (pul), *sb.* [OE. *pull*, found beside *pll*, Poll *sb.*[1] ...] The act, action, or faculty of pulling.

Pull (pul), *v.* [f. Pull *sb.*] ...

Pull (pul), *v.* Forms: 1 pullian, 4–5 pullen, -yn, 4–7 pulle, 4–5 poyll, poylle, poull, 5c. and *n. dial.* 5–8 pow, 8 *pow*, 9090, poogh). [OE. *pullian* (with compound *a-pullian*), rare, and of uncertain etymology.

I. *trans.* To pluck or take away (anything) by force from where it grows or is set or attached; – PLUCK B. 1.

II. To exert upon (anything) a force that tends to snatch, or drag or draw it away; or tug at.

III. In technical senses, with specific objects expressed or understood.

IV. Phrases.

V. With adverbs.

Pullable (pu'lăb'l), *a.* [f. PULL *v.* + -ABLE.] Capable of being pulled.

Pullace, variant of PULLACE.

Pullan, variant of PILAU.

Pullastrine (pulæ'strin), *a. Ornith.* [Zool.]

Pull-back. 1. The action or an act of pulling back.

Pull-devil, a bundle of fish-hooks fastened back to back.

Pull-door.

Pulle, obs. form of PULL, POLE.

Pulled (puld), *ppl. a.* [f. PULL *v.* + -ED 1.]

Pullen (pu'len). *Obs. exc. dial.* Forms.

Puller (pu'lər). [f. PULL *v.* + -ER 1.] One who or that which pulls, in various senses of PULL *v.*

Puller-on: a provocative of thirst.

Pullery, *Obs.* Forms: 5 pulare, 6 pullory, -rye, -rie, 9 poultry. [app. a f. Poultry.]

Pullet (pu'let). Forms: 4 polet, pulet, 5 polette, -yt, 6 poullet, poullette, 6 pullette. [a. F. *poulet* young fowl, dim. of *poule*

1. Poultry; barn-door or domestic fowls; the flesh of these as food. Also *attrib.*, as *pullen-market.*

Column headers (top half)

PULLETIER. 1581 PULLING. PULLING. 1582 PULMO-.

Pulletier. Cf. also F. *pouletie* fem. young hen. The early instances, being pl., do not show whether the sing. was *pullet* or *pullete*.

1. A young (domestic) fowl, between the ages of chicken and mature fowl; but formerly often most more loosely; *spec.* and *techn.* a young hen from the time she begins to lay till her first moult, after which she is a full-grown hen or fowl.

2. Name of a bivalve mollusc, *Tapes pullastra*, more fully *Pullet Carpet-shell*.

3. attrib. and Comb., as *pullet-broth*, *sperm*.

Pullet, error in Phillips, etc. for PALLET *sb.*[2].

† Pulletier. *Ren. Antiq. Obs.* rare. [a. OF. *pouletier* poultry-keeper, poultry-dealer, f. *poulet* chicken.] The keeper of the sacred chickens observed for purposes of augury.

Pulletin, obs. form of POULTRY.

Pulley (pŭ·lĭ), *sb.*[1] Forms: see below. [ME. *poleye*, *poley*, etc.]

a. 4-5 *poley*, *poyle*, *pl.* *polies*, *poylleyes*; *polye*, *pole*, 5-6 *pulley*, *pollye*, 6 *polly*.

b. ...

Pulley (pŭ·lĭ), *sb.*[2] [Alteration of POLEYN, a. F. *pouleine*] ...

Pulley, v. [f. PULLEY *sb.*[1]] *trans.* To raise or hoist with or as with a pulley. Also *fig.*

Pulli-, combining form of L. *pullus* chick, chicken.

Pulligraph. ...

Pullicate (pŏ·lĭkeĭt), *sb.* Also 8-9 pulicate, *q dial.* pulacate. ...

Pulling, *vbl. sb.* [See -ING [1].] That pulls.

Pull-over. 1. (*phr.* to *pull over* = the PULL *sb.*] ...

Pull-up. [f. vbl. *phr.* to *pull up*: see PULL v. 31 c.] ...

Pulley-haul (pu·lĭ-hŏ·l), *v.* and *sb. colloq.* Also *attrib.* ...

Pulma-, combining form of L. *pulmo*, *pulmon-em* lung.

Bottom half

PULMONAD. 1583 PULP. PULP. 1584 PULPIT.

Pulmonad. ...

Pulmonary (pŭ·lmŏnări), *a.* (*sb.*) [ad. L. *pulmōnāri-us*, f. *pulmo*, *pulmōn-em* lung: see -ARY [1].] CF. F. *pulmonaire.*

Pulmonaria (pŏlmŏnē··riă), *Bot.* [mod.L.] ...

Pulmonate (pŭ·lmŏneĭt), *a.* and *sb.* [ad. mod.L. *pulmonāt-us*, f. L. *pulmo*, *-ōn-em* lung: see -ATE [2].]

Pulmonectomy. ...

Pulmonic (pŏlmŏ·nĭk), *a.* (*sb.*) [a. F. *pulmonique* (16th c.), f. L. *pulmo*, *-ōn-em* lung.]

† Pulmonarian. ...

Pulmonial. ...

Pulmoniferous (pŏlmŏnĭ·ferəs), *a.* Zool. ...

Pulmonifer. ...

Pulp (pŏlp), *sb.* [ad. L. *pulpa* the fleshy portion of the animal body, also the pulp of fruit, the pith of wood; cf. F. *poulpe* (R. Estienne 1539), *polpe*, *pulpe* (Cotgr. 1611).] A soft, moist, homogeneous or formless substance or mass: in various applications.

Pulp (pŏlp), *v.* [f. PULP *sb.*] *trans.* To reduce to pulp or to a pulpy mass.

Pulpamen (pŏlpē·men), *sb.* [L.] ...

Pulpatoon (pŏlpătū·n), *Obs.* [Cf. Sp. *pulpeton*, augm. of *pulpeta*, 'a slice of stuffed meat'. A dish made of rabbits, fowls, etc., in a crust of forced meat.]

Pulped (pŏlpt), *ppl. a.* ...

Pulpefaction. ...

Pulpify. ...

Pulpiness (pŏ·lpĭnes), *sb.* ...

Pulpit (pŭ·lpĭt), *sb.* [ad. L. *pulpitum* a scaffold, stage, platform for public representations, speeches, or platform for public representations.]

1. In reference to ancient times: A scaffold, stage, or platform for public representations, speeches, etc.

2. A raised structure consisting of an enclosed platform, usually supplied with a desk, seat, and book, in a church or chapel from which the preacher in a church or chapel delivers the sermon, and in which some denominations the officiating minister conducts the service. Hence, to *occupy the pulpit*.

3. *transf.* The occupants of the pulpit; the preachers, Christian ministers or the Christian ministry as occupied with preaching.

4. *attrib.* and *Comb.*

nent living Ministers. 18.. (*title*) The Christian World Pulpit. 18.. (*title*) The Metropolitan Tabernacle Pulpit.

4. Applied to other places elevated so as to give the occupant a conspicuous position, or enable him to direct or address others.

† **a.** An elevated royal pew or seat in a church.

?1370 *Robt. Cicyle* 59 (Vernon MS.) Ye kyng to churche com ful riht..And in his þouht a sleep him tok In his pulput as seiþ þe bok. 1485 *Rutland Papers* (Camden) 22 The King and the Quene..shall retourne to their seages roiall and of estate, in the said pulpitt, wherin when thei are sett, the rulars of the quere shal begynne this postcommon, *Intellige* [etc.].

b. † The poop of a ship, from which directions were given (*obs.*); the harpooner's standing-place on a whaler.

1513 Douglas *Æneis* viii. iii. 46 Eneas tho..Maid ansuer from the pulpit of the schip [L. *puppi ab alta*]. 1888 Goode *Amer. Fishes* 250 All vessels regularly engaged in this fishery are supplied with a special apparatus, called a 'rest' or 'pulpit', for the support of the harpooner as he stands on the bowsprit.

c. An auctioneer's desk or platform. Now *local.*

1738 Fielding *Hist. Reg.* ii. Wks. 1784 III. 329 Why are you not at the auction? Mr. Hen has been in the pulpit this half-hour. 1777 Sheridan *Sch. Scand.* iv. i, Come, get to your pulpit, Mr. Auctioneer. 1798 *Hull Advertiser* 9 June 2/2 The Exchange and W. Bell's pulpit are at the service of every broker and auctioneer. 1889 *N. W. Linc. Gloss.* (ed. 2).

5. *attrib.* and *Comb.* **a.** Of or belonging to a pulpit, as *pulpit bible, cushion, door, stair*, etc.

1631 Weever *Anc. Fun. Mon.* 49 A beaten-out pulpit cushion. 1641 *Rutland MSS.* (1905) IV. 531 Payd for the pulpet velvet and the velvet of the carving, *xli.* xvjs. 1848 G. Struthers *Hist. Relief Ch.* v. in *United Presb. Fathers* 278 Mr. Boston heard the pulpit door open. 1900 Crockett *Fitting of Peats* i. in *Love Idylls* (1901) 5 The top of the shut pulpit Bible.

b. Of, pertaining to, or characteristic of the pulpit as the place of preaching, as *pulpit eloquence, key, oratory, service, style, thunder*, etc.

1609 *Ev. Woman in Hum.* i. i. in Bullen *O. Pl.* IV, Another in a rayling pulppet key Drawes through her nose the accent of her voice. 1649 Milton *Eikon.* Pref., Wks. 1851 III. 334 The Prelats and thir fellow-teachers..whose Pulpit-stuffe..hath bin the Doctrin and perpetuall infusion of Servility and wretchedness to all thir hearers. *c* 1686 South *Serm., Prov. xxii.* 6 (1727) V. i. 31 Filled with Wind and Noise, empty Notions and Pulpit-tattle. 1751 J. Brown *Shaftesb. Charac.* 33 In France, the applauded pulpit eloquence is of the enthusiastic..species. 1895 J. J. Raven *Hist. Suffolk* 204 With caricature as well as pulpit-thunder he carried the war into the enemy's quarters.

c. Referring to the occupant of a pulpit (often uncomplimentary), as *pulpit drone, drum, mountebank, orator; pulpit-thumper*, etc.

1546 J. Heywood *Prov.* ii. vii. (1566) I ij, Though this appeere a proper pulpet peece, Yet whan the fox preacheth, then beware your geese. 1649 G. Daniel *Trinarch., Her. V*, lxx, And Pulpit Drums awake the Iland round; All Boanerges. 1650 Milton *Tenure Kings* (ed. 2) 47 That men may yet more fully know the difference between Protestant divines and these pulpit firebrands. 1673 [R. Leigh] *Transp. Reh.* 11 Your weapons of offence..you might have reserv'd for some of your pulpit-officers. 1682 T. Flatman *Heraclitus Ridens* No. 72 (1713) II. 191 How do they make one of these Pulpit-thumpers? 1705 Hickeringill *Priest-cr.* iv. (1721) 226 The Pulpit-prater (that has his Religion in his Tongue and Eyes, I mean, his Sermon-Notes). 1772 Nugent tr. *Hist. Fr. Gerund* I. 564 Henceforth those Pulpit-Drones..let not a braggart of a Frenchman praise. 1824 Southey *Bk. of Ch.* xiii. (1841) 230 Though he [Bp. Pecock] censured these pulpit-bawlers, as he called them. 1828 Webster, *Pulpit-orator*, an eloquent preacher.

d. Special Combs.: **pulpit-cloth**, an ornamented cover of the reading-desk of a pulpit; **pulpit-cross**, a cross set up in a burying-ground or in a place where there was no church, from the steps or raised base of which sermons were often preached; a preaching-cross; † **pulpit-friar**, a preaching friar; **pulpit-glass**, a sand-glass placed on a pulpit to indicate the time to the preacher; † **pulpit-man**, a preacher; † **pulpit-prayer**, a prayer said in the pulpit (as distinguished from those read in the service).

1552 in *Inv. Ch. Surrey* (1869) 44 One *pulpit clothe. 1711 Addison *Spect.* No. 112 ¶ 2 He has likewise given a handsome Pulpit-Cloth,..at his own Expence. 1598 Stow *Surv.* (1603) 333 About the middest of this [Pauls] Churchyeard is a *Pulpit Crosse of timber, mounted vpon steppes of stone,..in which are sermons preached..euery Sundaye in the forenoone. 1555 Eden *Decades* 165 Iohn Cacedus the *pulpitte fryer of the order of saynt Frances. 1907 *Daily Chron.* 4 Nov. 4/7 Probably the most modern *pulpit-glass in existence is that which adorns the pulpit of the Chapel Royal, Savoy. It is timed for eighteen minutes only, and was placed in the chapel in 1867. [Cf. quots. 1591, 1852, s. v. Hour-glass.] 1582 Allen *Martyrd. Father Campion* (1908) 8 Many Protestantes..ever afterward contemned their vulgar *pulpit men in comparison of him. 1681 Evelyn *Diary* 5 Nov., Dr. Hooper..is one of yᵉ first rank of pulpit men in the nation. 1684 Baxter *Twelve Argts.* § 20. 35 They have all that you have (*Pulpit Prayer and Sermon, and sometimes a Chapter). 1697 Burghope *Disc. Relig. Assemb.* 92 Every pulpit-prayer made by a man's private spirit is valued much above the Common Prayer.

Hence (mainly *nonce-words*) † **Pu·lpitable, Pu·lpital, Pu·lpitary, Pulpi·tic, Pulpi·tical** *adjs.*, connected with, appropriate to, or characteristic of the pulpit as the place of preaching; hence **Pulpi·tically** *adv.*, in a pulpitical manner; **Pu·lpitful**, enough to fill a pulpit; **Pu·lpitish** *a.*, resembling a pulpit performance or preaching; **Pu·lpitism**, a characteristic of language or style of preachers and sermons; **Pu·lpitless** *a.*, lacking a pulpit or a place as preacher; **Pu·lpitly** *adv.*, with regard to the pulpit or preaching; **Pulpito·latry**, 'worship' of the pulpit or of preaching.

1772 Nugent tr. *Hist. Fr. Gerund* II. 84 This the exordium of my *pulpitable functions. *Ibid.* 511 The famous *pulpital performances of..Friar Gerund. 1846 Poe *Colton* Wks. 1864 III. 27 He converses fluently,..but grandiloquently, and with a tone half tragical, half pulpital. *c* 1784 J. Brown *Hist. Brit. Ch.* (1820) I. 120 The *pulpitary contention between Popish and Protestant preachers was great. 1845 *Ecclesiologist* IV. 117 A slight poetical licence, a mere *pulpitic exaggeration. 1775 Ash, Suppl., *Pulpitical. 1883 Clark Russell *Strange Voy.* I. xvi. 229 Not a little impressed by the pulpitical twang and rattle of his north-country notes. 1751 Chesterf. *Lett.* (1792) III. ccxlv. 123 To proceed then regularly and *pulpitically; I will first shew you, my beloved [etc.]. 1680 V. Alsop *Mischief of Imposit.* xiii. 99 Whether he gave..any encouragement..to vomit up a whole *Pulpitful of Gall. 1847 Webster, *Pulpitish. 1881 *Ch. Rev.* No. 589. 177 The common-places and *pulpitisms which have gone so far to make volumes of sermons odious. 1889 *Chicago Advance* 7 Feb., Some of them are *pulpitless, and some..want a change of pulpit. 1872 H. W. Beecher *Lect. Preaching* I. 24 As it is dangerous personally, so it is dangerous *pulpitly. 1853 *Ecclesiologist* XIV. 409 The *pulpitolatry of another arrangement is almost incredible.

Pu·lpit, *v.* [f. Pulpit *sb.*] **a.** *trans.* To provide with a pulpit, or place in the pulpit. **b.** *intr.* To officiate in the pulpit, to preach. Hence **Pu·lpited** *ppl. a.*, **Pu·lpiting** *vbl. sb.*

1529 More *Dyaloge* I. Wks. 151/1 Yet would thei long to be pulpeted. *c* 1540 *Old Ways* (1892) 39 Affter he had doone with his pulpitynge. 1653 Milton *Hirelings* (1659) 84 It is not necessarie..that Men should sit all thir life long at the feet of a pulpited Divine. 1729 Byrom *Jrnl. & Lit. Rem.* 19 Feb. (Chetham Soc.) I. ii. 330 He said..that he was in priest's orders, but..that he had done with pulpiting. 1865 E. Burritt *Walk Land's End* vi. 209 Mat and seat the rotunda..; pulpit at the central column of the great buildings such men as her preaching rolls may supply. 1867 O. W. Holmes *Guard. Angel* xiii, The young girl sat under his tremendous pulpitings. 1904 *Edin. Rev.* July 147 Orderly, vulgarised, 'materialised, pulpited, prosperous England.

Pulpitarian (pulpitēə·riăn), *sb.* (*a.*) [f. Pulpit *sb.* + *-arian*, as in *trinitarian*, etc.] A preacher, a pulpiteer; also, one who regards the pulpit or preaching as the chief feature of worship.

1654 Whitlock *Zootomia* 139 You may take away the Pewes, where all are Pulpitarians. *a* 1670 Hacket *Abp. Williams* I. (1692) 90 Directions, that had netled the aggrieved Pulpitarians. 1860 *Medical Times* 15 Sept. 266/1 Some of the most 'popular' of..modern pulpitarians.

B. *adj.* Savouring of the pulpit; sermonical.

1887 *Daily News* 15 Oct. 3/6 Some fastidious critics may consider Dr. Bayne's style somewhat pulpitarian.

Pulpiteer (pulpitiə·ɹ), *sb.* [f. Pulpit *sb.* + -eer.] A preacher by profession; usually with contemptuous implication.

1642 Howell *Twelve Treat., True Inform.* (1661) 16 By the incitement of those fiery pulpiteers. 1679 *Answ. to Appeal fr. Country to City* 15 Against his Over-hot Churchmen we'l set the Mechanique Pulpiteers and Tub preachers. 1738 Neal *Hist. Purit.* IV. 464 The mouths of the High Church pulpiteers were encouraged to open as loud as possible. 1860 Tennyson *Sea Dreams* 20 A heated pulpiteer, Not preaching simple Christ to simple men. 1861 Tulloch *Eng. Purit.* i. 27 Travers..seemed by far the more clever and successful pulpiteer.

Hence **Pulpitee·r** *v. intr.*, to preach; chiefly in **Pulpitee·ring** *vbl. sb.* and *ppl. a.*

1812 *Religionism* 11 If your men a pulpiteering go. 1877 T. Sinclair *Mount* (1878) 48 A commonplace everyday pulpiteering king. 1883 *Spectator* 23 June 811 A thoughtful Scotchman who has no weakness for pulpiteering.

Pu·lpiter. [f. Pulpit *sb.* or *v.* + -er[1].] A preacher, a Pulpiteer.

1600 Shaks. *A. Y. L.* iii. ii. 163 O most gentle pulpiter [Spedding's emendation; Folios Iupiter], what tedious homilie of Loue haue you wearied your parishioners withall. 1681 Hickeringill *Vind. Naked Truth* ii. 4 As some Pulpiters have also had. 1894 *Speaker* 2 June 613/1 The sanitary drain-maker does more for morals than the pulpiter.

Pu·lpitize, *v. nonce-wd.* [f. Pulpit *sb.* + -ize.] **a.** *intr.* To pulpiteer, to preach. **b.** *trans.* To discuss or deal with in the pulpit. Hence **Pu·lpitizing** *vbl. sb.*

1651 Biggs *New Disp.* § 240 Cryed up even to pulpitising. 1798 Coleridge *Lett., to T. Poole* (1895) 18 Parson Warren did certainly *pulpitise* much better. 1875 *Contemp. Rev.* XXV. 798 The whole subject of how to encounter these enigmas..must be popularised and pulpitised.

Pu·lpitry. [f. Pulpit *sb.* + -ry.] The work or service of the pulpit; preaching; the conventional talk of the pulpit; sermonizing.

1606 Warner *Alb. Eng.* xv. xc. (1612) 389 For Fare And greater Ease than Studie them or Pulpetrie can spare. 1641 Milton *Reform.* ii. ¶ 1 To teach thus were meer pulpitry to them. 1861 K. H. Digby *Chapel St. John* (1863) 55 But perhaps you do not like pulpitry.

Pulpless (pʊ·lplės), *a.* [-less.] Lacking pulp.

1778 Lightfoot *Flora Scot.* I. 268 Barren Strawberry..the fruit is dry and pulpless. 1875 *Dental Cosmos* XVII. 521 Ridiculous demands, such as for devitalization of pulps in pulpless teeth.

Pulpose (pʊ·lpōs), *a.* *rare*[−0]. [ad. L. *pulpōsus* fleshy, f. *pulpa* Pulp.] = Pulpous.

1858 Mayne *Expos. Lex.*, *Pulposus*..of the consistence of pulp; having or full of pulp; pulpy: pulpose.

So † **Pulpo·sity**, pulpousness. *Obs. rare*[−0].

1721 Bailey, *Pulposity*, fulness of Pulp, Substance, etc.

Pulpous (pʊ·lpəs), *a.* [ad. L. *pulpōs-us* (see prec.): cf. F. *poulpeux* (1539 R. Estienne in Hatz.-Darm.).] Of the nature of or consisting of pulp; resembling pulp; pulpy.

1601 Holland *Pliny* I. 561 The leaues verily that this graine Rice doth beare, be pulpous and fleshy. 1660 Ingelo *Bentiv. & Ur.* ii. (1682) 119 A small mass of pulpous substance for the Brain. 1725 *Bradley's Fam. Dict.* s. v. *Pear Tree*, This flower is succeeded by a pulpous fruit. 1796 De Serra in *Phil. Trans.* LXXXVI. 503 A soft and pulpous matter, like that which is found in unripe antheræ. 1876 Ruskin *Fors Clav.* lxix. 397 The special type of youthful blackguard..more or less blackly pulpous and swollen.

Hence **Pu·lpousness**, *rare*, pulpy consistency.

1727 in Bailey vol. II.; whence 1755 in Johnson; and in mod. Dicts.

Pulpy (pʊ·lpi), *a.* [f. Pulp *sb.* + -y.] Of the nature of, consisting of, or resembling pulp; soft, fleshy, succulent; also *fig.* flabby.

1591 Sylvester *Du Bartas* i. iii. 860 Long'st thou for Butter? bite the poulpy part [of coco] And never better came to any Mart. 1694 J. Ray in *Lett. Lit. Men* (Camden) 200 The hard-bill'd [birds] touch not pulpy fruits. 1799 Kirwan *Geol. Ess.* 330 Moist, pulpy, incoherent, argillaceous masses. 1800 tr. *Lagrange's Chem.* II. 417 The pulpy matter of the brain. 1843 Carlyle *Past & Pr.* ii. xvii, Some score or two of years ago all these were little red-coloured pulpy infants. 1863 Geo. Eliot *Romola* xxxix, His mind was perhaps a little pulpy from that too exclusive diet. 1905 J. H. McCarthy *Dryad* 263 To make its way through ground as muddy and pulpy as a swamp.

‖ **Pulque** (pu·lke). [Sp. Amer. *pulque*, of uncertain origin.

According to F. X. Clavigero *Istoria antica del Mexico* 1780–81 (Eng. trans. 1787 I. 435), neither Sp. nor Mexican, but from Araucanian *pulcu*, the generic name for the intoxicating beverages used by the Indians. See J. Platt in N. & Q. 9th s. IX. 226 (1902), where other suggestions are also mentioned.]

A fermented drink made in Mexico and some parts of Central America from the sap of the agave or maguey (*Agave americana*).

1693 *Lond. Gaz.* No. 2848/1 The Viceroy Commanded, That the Indian Natives should not..consume any Mays in the making of a Drink common among them, called *Pulche*. 1796 Morse *Amer. Geog.* I. 729 Pulque is the usual wine or beer of the Mexicans, made of the fermented juice of the Maguei. 1843 Prescott *Mexico* i. v. (1850) I. 133 The older guests continued at table, sipping *pulque*, and gossiping about other times. 1900 *Speaker* 8 Sept. 619/2 The peon with money only bought pulque or gambled.

b. *attrib.* and *Comb.*: **pulque-brandy**, a strong intoxicating spirit distilled from pulque.

1888 Mrs. M. E. Blake & Mrs. Sullivan *Mexico* 12 A corner cantine has its handful of quiet pulque-drinkers.

Pulsant (pʊ·lsănt), *a.* *rare.* [ad. L. *pulsānt-em*, pr. pple. of *pulsāre*: see next.] Pulsating.

1891 H. Tuckley *Under the Queen* 254 An atmosphere which is pulsant still with the mighty issues over which noble women have wept, and great men have bled, for a thousand years.

Pulsate (pʊ·lseᵗt), *v.* [f. L. *pulsāt-*, ppl. stem of *pulsāre* to push, strike, beat, freq. of *pellĕre, puls-* to drive, strike, beat.]

1. *intr.* To expand and contract rhythmically, as the heart or an artery; to exhibit a pulse; to beat, throb. (Chiefly in scientific use.)

1794 E. Darwin *Zoon.* I. x. 49 The heart of a viper or frog will continue to pulsate long after it is taken from the body. 1813 Sir H. Davy *Agric. Chem.* (1814) 215 From the moment the heart begins to pulsate till it ceases to beat, the aeration of the blood is constant. 1899 *Allbutt's Syst. Med.* VII. 239 It has been asserted that the brain cannot pulsate in the closed cranium.

b. *fig.* or in figurative allusion, of life, feeling, etc.

1847 Emerson *Poems, Saadi* vii, Leaves twinkle, flowers like persons be, And life pulsates in rock or tree. 1858 O. W. Holmes *Aut. Breakf.-t.* iv, What strains and strophes of unwritten verse pulsate through my soul when I open a certain closet in the ancient house where I was born! 1883 *Schaff's Encycl. Relig. Knowl.* 2318 The Punic blood of his descent is visibly pulsating in his style.

2. *intr. gen.* To strike upon something with a rhythmical succession of strokes; to move with a regular alternating motion; to exhibit such a movement; to beat, vibrate, quiver, thrill.

1861 *Times* 22 Oct., The air pulsates with the flash of arms in the sunlight. 1867 Lewes *Hist. Philos.* (ed. 3) I. p. cii, The sensation excited..by that undulation pulsating on our tympanum. 1881 G. Forbes in *Nature* 18 Aug. 361/1 Dr. Bjerknes reproduces this experiment by causing two drums to pulsate in concord, the one above the other. 1884 H. Spencer in *19th Cent.* Jan. 10 The spectroscope proves..that molecules on the Earth pulsate in harmony with molecules in the stars.

3. *trans.* To agitate with a Pulsator (sense 2).

1891 *Blackw. Mag.* Sept. 322 The stuff to be pulsated.

Hence **Pu·lsating** *vbl. sb.* (also *attrib.* in sense 3, as *pulsating-pan*); **Pu·lsating** *ppl. a.*, that pulsates, exhibiting a pulsation or pulse.

1807–26 S. Cooper *First Lines Surg.* 247 An aneurism is generally a pulsating tumour, arising from a dilated, ruptured, or wounded artery, and filled with blood. 1880 Günther *Fishes* 312 Heart replaced by pulsating sinuses.

1891 *Blackw. Mag.* Sept. 322 We throw marked diamonds into the pulsating-pan, and we never fail to recover them.

Pulsatile (pʊ·lsătil, -əil), *a.* Also 6 -yle, 7 -il. [f. L. type **pulsātilis*, f. *pulsāre, pulsāt-*: see prec. and -ile.]

1. *Anat.* and *Physiol.* Having the capacity or property of pulsating or throbbing, as the heart, an artery, a tumour, etc.; exhibiting pulsation.

† *Pulsatile vein*, old name for an artery, *spec.* the aorta.

1541 R. Copland *Guydon's Quest. Chirurg.* H j b, The braunche of the vayne pulsatyle that commeth fro the left syde. 1684 tr. *Bonet's Merc. Compit.* i. 11 You could no sooner press this Pulsatile Tumour with your Fingers, but [etc.]. 1858 H. Spencer *Ess.* I. 332 Every heart is at first a mere pulsatile sac. 1872 Mivart *Elem. Anat.* x. (1873) 432 Such pulsatile structures are called lymphatic hearts.

b. Of, or characterized by, pulsation; pulsatory.

1684 J. P. tr. *Fambresarius' Art Physic* i. 64 Under the Pulsatil Actions are comprehended the Motions of the heart. 1728 Nicholls in *Phil. Trans.* XXXV. 444 Such a Tumor will rather have a pulsatile Dilatation, than a Pulsation, for its true Diagnostick. 1897 *Allbutt's Syst. Med.* IV. 647 Instances..of the common tendency towards 'pulsatile or rhythmic activity' manifested by all living matter.

2. Of a musical instrument: Played by striking or percussion; percussive: see Percussion 2 c.

1769 *Mus. Dict.* 194 (T.) The rattle, among the ancients, is a musical instrument of the pulsatile kind. 1864 Engel *Mus. Anc. Nat.* 102 The Assyrians employed in their musical performances stringed, wind, and pulsatile instruments in combination. 1887 *Athenæum* 5 Nov. 612/3 The 'pulsatile instruments covered with skin' begin with the hymnal Mridanga, said to be invented by Brahma himself, and its modern form, the Bānya and Tabla.

Hence **Pulsatility** (-i·lĭti), the quality of being pulsatile (sense 1).

1835–6 *Todd's Cycl. Anat.* I. 243/1 The distinguishing characteristic of the third form of nævus is its pulsatility. *Ibid.* 460/2 A pulsatility scarcely inferior to that of an aneurism.

‖ **Pulsatilla** (pʊlsăti·lă). *Bot., Pharm.* Also anglicized 6 **pulsatill**, 7 **-il**. [med.L., dim. of *pulsāta* beaten, driven about; according to Linnæus *Philos. Botan.* 166 'from the beating of the flower by the wind': cf. the name Anemone.

Cf. also Pena & Lobel *Stirpium Adversaria Nova* (1570) 114 Pulsatilla, an Sylvestris Anemone. Huius comosi et tremuli seminum pappi quia huc atque illuc vel levissimo quoque flatu pultarentur, Pulsatillam barbari vocitarunt, Anemonemque.]

The Pasque-flower, a species of Anemone (*A. Pulsatilla*); in Tournefort, *c* 1700, a generic name; now in *Bot.* the name of a subgenus including this (then called *P. vulgaris*) and other species; also, in pharmacy, the extract or tincture of this plant.

[1578 Lyte *Dodoens* iii. lxxii. 420 Passe flower is called in Latine *Pulsatilla*.] 1597 Gerarde *Herbal* ii. lxxiii. 309 In English Pasque flower..and after the Latin name Pulsatill. [1706 Phillips, *Pulsatilla*, a Plant call'd Pasque-Flower, the distilled Water of which is excellent for cleansing and curing Wounds.] 1876 tr. *von Ziemssen's Cycl. Med.* VI. 727 Bednar [has recommended] for some cases [of whooping-cough] the extract of pulsatilla. 1890 *Daily News* 7 Jan. 6/2 Take at the same time three drops of tincture of pulsatilla every half hour until relief is obtained. 1890 Billings *Nat. Med. Dict.*, *Pulsatilla*, the herb of *Anemone Pulsatilla* and *A. pratensis*, and of *A. patens*, var. *Nuttalliana*, collected soon after flowering..; diaphoretic and emmenagogue.

Pulsation (pʊlsēⁱ·ʃən). [ad. L. *pulsātiōn-em*, n. of action f. *pulsāre*: see Pulsate.]

I. The action, or an act, of pulsating or pulsing.

1. The movement of the pulse in a living animal body; rhythmic dilatation and contraction, as of the heart, an artery, etc.; beating, throbbing.

1541 R. Copland *Galyen's Terap.* 2 F ij b, Yf there be all redy vehement pulsacyon, in such wyse that there is no more hope of the curacyon of the sayd partyes. 1615 Crooke *Body of Man* 859 This motion of the Arteries is called *pulsus* or pulsation..which is absolued by dilatation and contraction. 1664 Power *Exp. Philos.* i. 9 In a greater Louse you might see this pulsation of her heart through her back also. 1804 Abernethy *Surg. Obs.* 229 The pulsation of the artery was not felt. 1876 Bristowe *The. & Pract. Med.* (1878) 501 Dilatation and pulsation of the larger veins.

b. with *pl.* A beat, throb (of the heart, an artery, etc.); = Pulse *sb.*[1] 1 c.

c 1645 Howell *Lett.* i. i. xxxvii, The Physitians hold, that in evry well dispos'd body, ther be above 4000 Pulsations evry hour. 1747 H. Brooke *Fables, Female Seducers* Poems (1810) 413/2 Her frame with new pulsations thrill'd. 1834 J. Forbes *Laennec's Dis. Chest* (ed. 4) 659 The affection is distinguished by the pulsations of the heart appearing more audible in the back..than in the region of the heart itself.

c. *fig.* Cf. Pulse *sb.*[1] 2.

1765 Sterne *Tr. Shandy* VIII. xvi, It could neither give fire by pulsation, nor receive it by sympathy. 1848 H. Rogers *Ess.* (1874) I. vi. 327 The pleasure..of beholding the pulsations, so to speak, of intellectual life. 1885 *Manch. Exam.* 15 Apr. 3/1 A little book..warm with the pulsation of individual thought.

2. *gen.* Rhythmical beating, vibration, or undulation: cf. Pulse *sb.*[1] 4.

1658 J. Rowland *Moufet's Theat. Ins.* 1104 They [worms] move from place to place with a certain drawing and pulsation. 1850 Tennyson *In Mem.* xii, As a dove..Some dolorous message knit below The wild pulsation of her wings. 1870 Emerson *Soc. & Solit., Art* Wks. (Bohn) III. 17 The pulsation of a stretched string or wire gives the ear the pleasure of sweet sound.

b. with *pl.* A beat, a vibration, an undulation; = Pulse *sb.*[1] 4 b.

1831 Brewster *Nat. Magic* ix. (1833) 243 A low continuous murmuring sound beneath his feet, which gradually changed into pulsations as it became louder. 1840 R. H. Dana *Bef. Mast* xviii. 52 No sound heard but the pulsations of the great Pacific! 1866 Dk. Argyll *Reign Law* iii. (1867) 137 The pulsations of the wing in most birds are so rapid that they cannot be counted. 1878 Huxley *Physiogr.* xi. 171 In the open sea, the wave or pulsation is propagated, but the mass of the water..remains stationary.

II. 3. The action of striking, knocking, or beating; with *pl.* A stroke, knock, blow; in quot. 1891 one made by a pulsator (see Pulsator 2).

1656 Blount *Glossogr.*, *Pulsation*, a beating, striking, knocking or thumping. 1768 Blackstone *Comm.* III. viii. 120 The Cornelian law *de injuriis* prohibited pulsation as well as verberation; distinguishing verberation, which was accompanied with pain, from pulsation, which was attended with none. 1891 *Blackw. Mag.* Sept. 322 A large flap of wood bestows a smart box on the ear,..on the surface of no. 2 pan. I estimated the number of these pulsations at 110 per minute.

Hence **Pulsa·tional** *a.* (*rare*), of, pertaining to, or characterized by pulsation.

1882 *Contemp. Rev.* Oct. 636 The striations seen athwart the tail..would be explained..as due to the observed pulsational manner in which the envelopes are raised.

Pulsative (pʊ·lsătiv), *a.* Now *rare.* [f. ppl. stem of L. *pulsāre*: see Pulsate and -ative.]

1. = Pulsatile 1, Pulsatory. Now *rare.*

1398 Trevisa *Barth. De P. R.* v. lxi. (Bodl. MS.), Þis veyne hatte pulsatif and is nedefulle to bringe quantite of blood and spurtes to þe lunges. *c* 1400 *Lanfranc's Cirurg.* 112 It is riȝtful þat an arterie schulde arise vpward from byneþe, for þe blood þat is in him is sutil, & his meuynge is pulsatif. 1563 T. Gale *Antidot.* i. vi. 4 Great inflamations..doe induce payne, and pulsatiue dolour. 1668 Culpepper & Cole *Barthol. Anat.* Man. iv. xii. 348 A pulsative pain of the teeth. 1842 *Blackw. Mag.* LII. 786 Others..have laid bare to us the very pulsative heart of America.

† **2.** = Pulsatile 2. *Obs.*

1695 J. Edwards *Perfect. Script.* iv. 176 All other Musical Instruments..whether Pulsative or Pneumatick.

Hence **Pu·lsatively** *adv.* (in quot., with a blow or ? a series of blows).

1881 Blackmore *Christowell* xv, Handling him by the head, against the wall, pulsatively, [he] stirs up the muffled drum of his outer ear.

Pulsator (pʊlsēⁱ·təɹ, pʊ·lsătəɹ). [agent-n. in L. form from *pulsāre*: see Pulsate and -or.]

1. One who or that which knocks or strikes: see quots.; in quot. 1753 the Death-watch. *rare.*

1656 Blount *Glossogr.*, *Pulsator*, one that knocks or strikes. 1730–6 Bailey (folio), *Pulsa'tor*, the plaintiff or actor. 1753 Chambers *Cycl. Supp.*, *Pulsator*, a name given by some writers to that species of beetle, commonly known among us by the name of the death-watch. 1755 Johnson, *Pulsa'tor*, a striker, a beater. 1836 E. Howard *R. Reefer* xx, The pulsator, with pointed toe.., would make a progress in a direct line.

2. A machine, working on the principle of the jigger, for separating diamonds from the earth in which they are found.

1890 *Pall Mall G.* 13 Feb. 2/1 The residue of divers stones of divers sorts and sizes is then jogged about with more water in the 'pulsator'..The machine is a huge framework of graduated sieves and runlets. 1901 *Ibid.* 1 July 8/2 The finer material is graded by the screens of the trommel, and passes direct to the four compartments of a pulsator or jigger of the type used at Kimberley.

3. = Pulsometer 2.

1884 Knight *Dict. Mech.* Suppl., *Pulsator*, a name for the *Pulsometer*.

Pulsatory (pʊ·lsătəri), *a.* [f. Pulsate: see -ory[2].] Having the quality of pulsating; characterized by or of the nature of pulsation; acting or moving in intermittent pulses.

1613 Wotton *Let. to Sir E. Bacon* 27 May, in *Reliq.* (1672) 418 These external evils do not so much trouble us, as an inward pungent and pulsatory ach within the skull. 1747 Langrish *Muscular Motion* iii. § 129 in *Phil. Trans.* XLIV, Let us now..examine whether the nervous Æther is transmitted from the Brain to the Heart, in a pulsatory Manner, at equal Distances of Time. 1822–34 *Good's Study Med.* (ed. 4) I. 535 A pulsatory motion is always felt by the fingers when applied to a leaden water-pipe. 1878 G. B. Prescott *Sp. Telephone* 206 A merely intermittent or pulsatory current.

b. = Pulsatile 1.

1802 *Med. Jrnl.* VIII. 4 A pulsatory swelling at the fore part of the elbow joint. 1868 Duncan tr. *Figuier's Insect World* Introd. 12 Malpighi and Swamerdam..discovered in different insects a pulsatory organ occupying the median line of the back, which appeared to them to be a heart.

Pulsche, obs. form of Polish *v.*

Pulse (pʊls), *sb.*[1] Forms: α. 4–5 **pous, pows**, 4–6 **pouce**, 5 **pouse, powce**; β. 4–6 **puls**, 6 **poulce, poulse, pulce**, 5– **pulse**. [ME. *pous, pouce*, a. OF. *pous* (*c* 1175 in Godef. *Compl.*), *pousse*:—L. *puls-us* (*vēnārum*) the beating of the veins, f. *puls-*, ppl. stem of *pellĕre* to drive, beat; altered in mod.F. to *pouls*, and in late ME. to *pulse* after L.]

1. The 'beating', throbbing, or rhythmically recurrent dilatation of the arteries as the blood is propelled along them by the contractions of the heart in the living body; esp. as felt in arteries near the surface of the body, e.g. in the wrists and temples; usually in reference to its rate and character as indicating the person's state of health: often in phr. *to feel* († *taste*) *one's pulse.* (A pulse also occurs exceptionally in the veins.)

Formerly sometimes construed erron. as a plural.

α. *c* 1330 R. Brunne *Chron. Wace* 9011 He tasted his pous, saw his vryn, He selde he knew his medycyn. 1340 Hampole *Pr. Consc.* 822 His pouce es stille, with-outen styringes. *c* 1380 Wyclif *Serm.* Sel. Wks. I. 151 A fisician lerneþ diligentli his signes, in veyne, in pows. *c* 1412 Hoccleve *Jonathas* 604 He sy hire vryne & eeke felte hir pous. 1470–85 Malory *Arthur* xvii. xv. 712 They..felte his pouse to wyte whether there were ony lyf in hym. 1530 Palsgr. 257/1 Pouce of the arme, *pouce*.

β. 1398 Trevisa *Barth. De P. R.* v. i. (Tollem. MS.), Þe arteries takeþ þe spirite of þe herte, and bereþ forþe to make þe puls. 1483 *Cath. Angl.* 293/2 A Pulse, *pulsus*. 1530 Palsgr. 158 The poulce of a mannes arme. *Ibid.* 259/1 Pulce of mannes arme, *pous*. 1578 Banister *Hist. Man* vii. 95 Phisitions..take counsell at the pulse. 1590 Shaks. *Com. Err.* iv. iv. 55 Giue me your hand, and let mee feele your pulse. 1773 T. Percival *Ess.* II. 65 In twenty minutes my pulse rose to 88. In half an hour they sunk to 82. 1876 Foster *Phys.* i. iv. (1879) 155 The average rate of the human pulse or heart-beat is 72 a minute.

b. *Venous pulse*: see quot.

1897 *Syd. Soc. Lex.*, P[ulse], *venous*, a term applied..1. To a pulse carried on from the arteries through the capillaries into the veins, *e.g.* in a secreting salivary gland. 2. To the backward propagation of a pulsation, *e.g.* in tricuspid regurgitation, when pulsation is seen in the great veins and the liver. 3. To variations of pressure in the great veins due to the movements of respiration.

c. Each successive beat or throb of the arteries, or of the heart. Usually in *pl.*

c 1430 *Pilgr. Lyf Manhode* ii. xlvii. (1869) 94, I tastede his pouces, but..i fond nouht, in sinewe ne in condyt ne in veyne. 1566 Painter *Pal. Pleas.* I. 92 To take hede to the mutacion of his poulces. 1664 Power *Exp. Philos.* i. 41 At every pulse of the Auricle you might see the blood passe through this Channel into the heart [of the lamprey]. 1710 J. Clarke *Rohault's Nat. Phil.* (1729) I. 193 If we will be at the Trouble to count how many Pulses of the Artery there are in the first twenty Vibrations. 1887 Bowen *Æneid* ii. 726, I, whose pulses stirred not at javelins showered in the fray.

d. As a vague or incidental measure of time.

1626 Bacon *Sylva* § 32 For the space of ten pulses. *Ibid.* § 366 A Spoonfull of Spirit of Wine, a little heated, was taken, and it burnt as long as came to 116. Pulses.

† **e.** *concr.* The place where the pulse occurs or is felt; esp. in the wrist; also an artery or 'pulsating vein'. *Obs.*

c 1374 Chaucer *Troylus* iii. 1065 (1114) Þer-with his pous and pawmes of his hondes Þei gan to frote. 1398 Trevisa *Barth. De P. R.* xvi. lxxxvii. (Tollem. MS.) The saphire keleþ moche in hete of brennynge feueres yf he is honged nyȝe þe pulses and þe veynes of þe herte [L. *juxta venas cordis pulsatiles*]. 1541 R. Copland *Guydon's Quest. Chirurg.* Q iv b, Wastyng of a brawne, and chyefly of a poulce, so that when it is pynched it abydeth vpryght. 1614 W. B. *Philosopher's Banquet* (ed. 2) 16 The Artiries..are also called Pulses. 1623 Cockeram, *Pulse*, a beating veine.

† **f.** Excessive or violent throbbing, palpitation.

1607 Topsell *Four-f. Beasts* (1658) 4 [It] strengthneth the heart, emboldneth it, and driveth away the pulse and pusillanimity thereof.

2. In various figurative or allusive uses, denoting life, vitality, energy, feeling, sentiment, tendency, drift, indication, etc.; with *pl.*, a throb or thrill of life, emotion, etc.

c 1540 [see b]. 1595 Shaks. *John* iv. ii. 92 Thinke you I beare the Sheeres of destiny? Haue I commandement on the pulse of life? 1619 Visct. Doncaster in *Eng. & Germ.* (Camden) 201 Setting downe my observations upon the pulse of the affayres which I am neerer to feele. 1745 H. Walpole *Lett.* (1846) II. 91 All this will raise the pulse of the stocks. 1804 Wordsw. '*She was a phantom*' iii, And now I see with eye serene The very pulse of the machine. 1865 R. S. Hawker *Prose Wks.* (1893) 43 Had this instrument [a barometer], the pulse of the storm, been preserved, the crew would have received warning of the..hurricane.

b. Phr. *To feel* († *try*) *the pulse* († *pulses*) *of* (fig.): to try to discover the sentiments, intentions, drift, etc. of; to 'sound'.

c 1540 tr. *Pol. Verg. Eng. Hist.* (Camden) I. 288 Godwinus, having no small confidence, after hee hadd once felte his pulses and perceaued his diet. 1639 S. Du Verger tr. *Camus' Admir. Events* a iv, I have runne over some pieces of them, only as to feele their pulse, and informe my selfe of their language and Country. 1707 Freind *Peterborow's Cond. Sp.* 263 With whom my Lord had occasion to talk and to feel his Pulse. 1869 Swinburne *Ess. & Stud.* 5 He only who has felt the pulse of an age can tell us how fast or slow its heart really beat towards evil or towards good.

† **3.** A stroke, blow, impact; an attack, assault. (Cf. *impulse, repulse*, and Pulse *v.* 3 b.) *Obs.*

1587 Fleming *Contn. Holinshed* III. 1024/1 The commons..ran all into the towne: and there ioine themselues togither to abide the pulse. 1677 Gale *Crt. Gentiles* II. iv. 309 Every bodie that is moved by an externe pulse is inanimate. *a* 1687 Petty *Treat. Naval Philos.* i. ii, The quick and effectual pulse of the water upon the Rudder.

4. The rhythmical recurrence of strokes, vibrations, or undulations; beating, vibration.

1657 W. Morice *Coena quasi Κοινὴ* xv. 218 Like the pulse of the flowing Sea. 1660 Boyle *New Experim. Phys.-Mech.* xxvii. 208 So weak a pulse as that of the ballance of a Watch. 1665 Hooke *Microgr.* xvi. 100 That there is such a fluid body..which is the *medium*, or Instrument, by which the pulse of Light is convey'd. 1850 Tennyson *In Mem.* lxxxvii, The measured pulse of racing oars Among the willows. 1876 Blackie *Songs Relig. & Life* 157 Pulse of waters blithely beating, Wave advancing, wave retreating.

b. Each of a rhythmical succession of strokes or undulations; a single vibration or wave; a beat.

1673 Newton in Rigaud *Corr. Sci. Men* (1841) II. 350 To suppose that there are but two figures, sizes, and degrees of velocity or force, of the ethereal corpuscles or pulses. 1704 — *Optics* (1721) 326 The Vibrations or Pulses of this Medium..must be swifter than Light. 1756 Burke *Subl. & B.* iv. xi, When the ear receives any simple sound, it is struck by a single pulse of the air, which makes the ear-drum and the other membranous parts vibrate. 1827 Keble *Chr. Y.*, *Evening* i, The last faint pulse of quivering light.

c. *Pros.* and *Mus.* A beat or stress in the rhythm of a verse or piece of music.

1885 J. Lecky in *Philol. Soc. Proc.* p. v, Varieties of metre were caused (*a*) by altering the division and coalescence of pulses, as in passing from dactyl to anapest..(*b*) by altering the number of pulses into which the stress-group was divided (substitution of triplets in binary metre, and of duplets in ternary).

5. *attrib.* and *Comb.* (almost all in sense 1 or 2). **a.** attrib., as *pulse-beat, -beating, -place, -rate, -stroke, -throb, -tick.* **b.** objective, etc., as *pulse-counter, -feeling* sb., adj., *pulse-like, -moving, -quickening, -stirring* adjs. **c.** Special Combs.: **pulse-breath** *Path.* (see quots.); **pulse-curve** = *pulse-tracing*; **pulse-glass**, a glass tube with a bulb at each end, or at one end only, containing spirits of wine and rarified air, which when grasped by the hand exhibits a momentary ebullition, which is repeated at each beat of the pulse; † **pulse-pad** *Obs. nonce-wd.* [Pad *sb.*[2] 3], humorous appellation for a medical man; **pulse-tracing**, the curve traced by a sphygmograph, indicating the character of a pulse-wave; † **pulse-vein** *Obs.*, a 'vein' or blood-vessel in which there is a pulse, an artery; † **pulse-watch** *Obs.*, Floyer's name for a sand-glass used for estimating the rate and character of the pulse; **pulse-wave**: see quot. 1897.

1841 Emerson *Addr., Method Nat.* Wks. (Bohn) II. 222 We do not take up a new book, or meet a new man, without a *pulse-beat of expectation. 1862 C. R. Hall in *Trans. Med.-Chirurg. Soc.* XLV. 167 By the term '*pulse-breath', I wish to signify..an audible pulsation communicated to the breath as it issues from the mouth by each beat of the heart. 1881 *Syd. Soc. Lex.*, *Breath, pulse*, a term applied to a pulsatile movement of the expired air in cases of phthisis, where there is a large cavity either close to the heart and the aorta, or separated from them only by indurated structures. 1809 Malkin *Gil Blas* ii. iv. ¶ 3 The little *pulse-counter set himself about reviewing the patient's situation. 1890 Billings *Nat. Med. Dict.*, *P[ulse] curve. 1899 *Allbutt's Syst. Med.* VII. 239 *note*, The pulse curve is usually anacrotic. 1829 *Nat. Philos.* I. ix. 56 (Usef. Knowl. Soc.) The instrument called a *pulse-glass is a glass tube with a bulb at each end of the form represented. 1575 Banister *Chyrurg.* i. (1585) 6 The paine [of an absces] is *pulslike beating mixt with pricking and some itching. 1706 Baynard in Sir J. Floyer *Hot & Cold Bath.* ii. 272 These *Pulse-pads, these Bedside Banditti. 1644 G. Plattes in *Hartlib's Legacy* (1655) 262 They say, that divers who were esteemed dead have been annointed with old Oyl in the five principal *pulse-places, and revived. 1879 *St. George's Hosp. Rep.* IX. 799 The temperature had fallen to 99°; the *pulse-rate was 110. 1832 Motherwell *Poems* (1847) 86 Feel every *pulse-stroke thrill of good. 1855 Browning *Old Pict. in Florence* vi, One whom each fainter *pulse-tick pains. 1896 *Allbutt's Syst. Med.* I. 314 This change is only maintained during the bath; after it the *pulse-tracing returns to its former standard. 1658 A. Fox *Würtz' Surg.* v. 353, I called for help, intreating them to cut the *pulse vein on my left temple. 1706 Hearne *Collect.* 17 Dec., Sir Joh. Floyer [is printing] an Invention of a *Pulse-Watch wᶜʰ being nicely set and adjusted to a Man's Constitution tels him when his Blood & that is out of order. 1707 Floyer *Physic. Pulse-Watch* Pref., I caused a Pulse-Watch to be made which run 60 Seconds, and I placed it in a Box to be more easily carried, and by this I now feel Pulses. 1753 [see Pulsiloge]. 1851 Carpenter *Man. Phys.* (ed. 2) 348 When the tonicity of the arteries is less than it should be, their walls yield too much to the *pulse-wave. 1897 *Syd. Soc. Lex.*, P[ulse]-waves, the component elements of the apparently simple movement of the pulsating artery, as detected by the sphygmograph. These are chiefly the summit wave, in which the line of ascent ends; the tidal or first secondary wave, due to the distension of the arteries; and the dicrotic or great secondary wave, produced probably by the aortic recoil.

Pulse (pʊls), *sb.*[2] Forms: (3 **pols-**, 4 **pols', puls'**), 5–7 **puls**, 6 **poulse, poults**, *dial.* **pousse**, 7 **powse, pulce**, 8–9 *dial.* **pouse**, 6– **pulse**. [a. OF. *pols, pouls, pous* (Godef.), in mod.Norm. dial. *pouls*, in other dialects *poul, pou*:—L. *puls* pottage made of meal, pulse, etc. See also Pults.]

1. The edible seeds of leguminous plants cultivated for food, as peas, beans, lentils, etc. **a.** *collective singular*: sometimes const. as *pl.*

1297 [see Pulse-corn]. 1355–6 *Abingdon Acc.* (Camden) 6 De j quarterio pols' vendito. 1388–9 *Ibid.* 53 Et de xij d. de puls' vendito. 1548 Udall, etc. *Erasm. Par. Matt.* xiii. 77 Whiche of it selfe is lest among al pulse. 1591 Sylvester *Du Bartas* i. ii. 644 In Cods the Poulse, the Corn within the Ear. 1616 Surfl. & Markh. *Country Farme* 570 Pulse (as we call them) that is..such graine as is inclosed in coddes or huskes. 1694 Westmacott *Script. Herb.* 92 Field Beans and Powse do feed horses. 1780 Cowper *Progr. Err.* 215 Daniel ate pulse by choice—example rare! *a* 1822 *Old Rime* in *Gentl. Mag.* XCII. i. 15/1 Thee eat thy pouse, and I will drink my beer. 1826 Southey in *Q. Rev.* XXXIII. 406 A soup composed merely of a few pulse. 1865 Sir T. Seaton *Cadet to Colonel* ix. 165 To search for and secure all grain, flour, pulse, and food of every description.

b. with *a* and *pl.* A kind or sort of such seeds.

1555 W. Watreman *Fardle Facions* i. v. 52 The priest may not loke vpon a beane, for that it is iudged an vncleane puls. 1604 E. G[rimstone] *D'Acosta's Hist. Indies* vii. iv. 505 They sowed their land for bread and pulses, which they vsed. 1681 tr. *Belon's Myst. Physick* 47 All sorts of Milk-meats, Sauces, Pulces, Fruits. 1707 Mortimer *Husb.* (1721) I. 141 There are several other Pulses or Seeds mentioned in many Authors. 1758 R. Brown *Compl. Farmer* ii. (1760) 86 The least of all pulses is the lentil.

2. a. *collective sing.* (sometimes const. as *pl.*) Plants yielding pulse; esculent leguminous plants.

1388–9 *Abingdon Acc.* (Camden) 53 Et de xij d. de stramine puls' vendito. 1542 Udall *Erasm. Apoph.* 304 Deriued of the moste vsed Poultz called cicer. 1555 Eden *Decades* 260 All kyndes of pulse, as beanes, peason, tares, and suche other. 1697 Dryden *Virg. Georg.* i. 110 Where Vetches, Pulse, and Tares have stood, And Stalks of Lupines grew. 1760–72 tr. *Juan & Ulloa's Voy.* (ed. 3) I. 123 Here are no pulse or pot-herbs of any kind. 1807 Crabbe *Parish Reg.* i. 141 High climb his pulse in many an even row. 1870 Yeats *Nat. Hist. Comm.* 48 Pulse grows everywhere.

b. *individual sing.* (with *pl.*) An esculent leguminous plant, or a species of such.

c 1440 *Pallad. on Husb.* vii. 55 For fodder now is tyme, and euery puls.

3. *attrib.* and *Comb.*, as *pulse crop*, † *-shell* (*shale*), *-stick* (cf. *pea-stick*), *tribe*; also Pulse-corn.

a 1661 Holyday *Juvenal, Sat.* xiv, A pulse-shale more I value, than the whole town's praise. 1785 Martyn *Rousseau's Bot.* iii. (1794) 39 The leguminous or pulse tribe. 1830 *Kyle Farm Rep.* 35 in *Libr. Usef. Knowl., Husb.* III, A luxuriant pulse crop of itself fertilizes the soil. 1869 Blackmore *Lorna D.* vii, A hook and a bit of worm on it,..or a blow-fly, hung from a hazel pulse-stick.

Pulse (pʊls), *v.* Also 6 **pulce**. [ad. L. *pulsāre* to push, drive, strike, beat, freq. of *pellĕre* to drive, strike, beat. In sense 1 prob. in part from F. *pousser*, formerly *polser, poulser* (15th c. in Littré); in other senses more directly connected in use with Pulse *sb.*[1], and *pulsate, pulsation*, etc.]

† **1.** *trans.* To drive, impel; to drive *forth*, expel. *Obs.* (exc. as in 4).

1549 *Compl. Scot.* xv. 125 Necessite pulsis and constrenȝes me to cry on god. *Ibid.* xvi. 139 ȝour ignorance, inconstance, ande inciuilite, pulcis ȝou to perpetrat intollerabil exactions. 1573 Twyne *Æneid* x. (1584) Q v, Pulst forth through spite from princely throne [L. *Pulsus ob invidiam solio*]. 1586 *Reg. Privy Council Scot.* IV. 111 The Douglassis wes pulsit up to this be thame quha advanceit thame-selfis to be farrest in his Hienes secreitis. 1666 J. Smith *Old Age* (1752) 203 The heart..doth..cast it [the blood] forth, and pulse it to all, even the extremest parts.

2. *intr.* To beat, throb, as the heart, etc.: = Pulsate 1 (but now only in literary use).

1559, 1664 [see Pulsing *ppl. a.*]. 1668 Culpepper & Cole *Barthol. Anat.* i. xxxvii. 82 For the Umbilical Arteries of a live Child being bound, as yet cleaving to the Mother..they pulse between the Ligature and the Child. 1691 Ray *Creation* i. (1692) 35 The Heart, when separated wholly from the Body in some Animals, continues still to pulse for a considerable time. 1864 Dutton Cook *Trials of Tredgolds* II. 118 The heart pulsed very, very feebly; his eyes were closed again. 1895 F. E. Trollope *F. Trollope* I. i. 6 The warm blood pulsed beneath high-waisted gowns.

b. *fig.* or in figurative allusion, in reference to life, energy, influences, feelings, etc.: = Pulsate 1 b: cf. Pulse *sb.*[1] 2.

1818 Keats *Endym.* i. 105 The mass Of nature's lives and wonders puls'd tenfold. 1874 Green *Short Hist.* v. § 1. 216 The throb of hope and glory which pulsed at its outset..died into inaction or despair. 1888 *Times* 26 June 9/5 The outward and sensible expression of the never-resting flow of thought, action, and feeling which pulses through it [London].

3. *intr. gen.* To perform or exhibit a rhythmic movement; to beat, vibrate, undulate: = Pulsate 2.

1851 Carlyle *Sterling* ii. i. (1872) 88 Playing and pulsing like sunshine or soft lightning. 1873 J. Geikie *Gt. Ice Age* iv. 41 The heat of the sun..pulses through the great piles of ice that cumber the higher elevations of Alpine countries. 1883 *Harper's Mag.* June 117/1 The thermal water..pulsed out of the cleft of the rock. 1904 M. Hewlett *Queen's Quair* ii. vii. 285 You could hear the regular galloping of a horse, pulsing in the dark like some muffled pendulum.

¶ **b.** To make recurrent sallies or attacks.

1851 Carlyle *Sterling* i. iv. (1872) 30 His studies were..pulsing out with impetuous irregularity now on this tract, now on that. 1865 — *Fredk. Gt.* xx. v. (1872) IX. 89 Such charging and recharging, pulsing and repulsing, has there been. *Ibid.* vii. 146 Broglio, on the other hand, keeps violently pulsing out, round Ferdinand's flanks.

4. *trans.* To drive or send out in or by pulses or rhythmic beats.

1819 Keats *Isabella* vi, The ruddy tide Stifled his voice, and pulsed resolve away. 1861 Lowell *Washers of Shroud* ii, Pale fireflies pulsed within the meadow-mist Their halos, wavering thistledowns of light. 1876 Mrs. Whitney *Sights & Ins.* II. iii. 371 Life is not dead, but living?..coming down and out, always;..pulsed into us, not set outside of us to grasp and define.

† **Pu·lse-corn.** *Obs. rare.* Also 3 **polscorn.** [f. Pulse *sb.*[2] + Corn *sb.*[1]] = Pulse *sb.*[2] 1 a, 2 a.

1297 in Rogers *Agric. & Prices* (1866) II. 174/2 (Cheddington) Polscorn. 1558 Warde tr. *Alexis' Secr.* 24 b, All sortes of pulse corne, as Pease, Beanes, Tares, and Fitches.

Pulseful (pʊ·lsfŭl), *a.* *rare.* [f. Pulse *sb.*[1] + -ful.] Full of pulses, pulsations, or throbbing.

a 1861 D. Gray *Poet. Wks.* (1874) 193 The partridge cowers beside thy loamy flow In pulseful tremor.

Pulseless (pʊ·lslės), *a.* [f. as prec. + -less.]

1. Having or exhibiting no pulse or pulsation, as a body in which the heart has ceased to beat.

1748 Richardson *Clarissa* (1810) VIII. xxiii. 100 While warm, though pulseless, we pressed each her hand with our lips. 1822 Shelley *Hellas* 142 His cold pale limbs and pulseless arteries. 1875 Bedford *Sailor's Pocket Bk.* viii. (ed. 2) 302 In shock the injured person lies pale, faint,..almost pulseless.

2. *fig.* and *gen.* Devoid of life, energy, or movement; void of feeling, unfeeling, pitiless (quot. 1856); motionless; lifeless.

1856 Aytoun *Bothwell* ii. ix, There he stood, the pulseless man, The calculating lord. 1861 E. S. Kennedy in *Peaks, Passes*, etc., Ser. ii. I. 170 So often as she came, so often there floated on the pulseless air the gentle moan 'Mort Aratsch'. 1873 W. S. Mayo *Never Again* xxxii, Better than Joys of pale and pulseless Life, The agony of Strife.

Hence **Pu·lselessness.**

1853 Dunglison *Med. Lex.*, *Pulselessness*, asphyxia. 1889 *Sat. Rev.* 20 July 85/2 [He] points out the difference between the meanings of the terms asphyxia and apnoea, the former standing for pulselessness and the latter for breathlessness.

‖ **Pulsellum** (pʊlse·lŏm). *Zool.* Pl. **-a.** [mod. L., f. *puls-*, ppl. stem of *pellĕre* to drive, after Flagellum.] A modified form of flagellum found in spermatozoa and certain infusorians, serving to propel the body through a liquid medium.

1880 Kent *Infusoria* I. 429 Among the free-swimming monoflagellate Infusoria as at present known, where the locomotive appendage without exception fulfils during natation the rôle of a tractellum, its recognition by such title in contradistinction to a propelling organ or pulsellum is uncalled for. 1885 E. R. Lankester in *Encycl. Brit.* XIX. 859/1 The flagellum of the Flagellata is totally distinct from the pulsellum of the Bacteria.

Pulshe, obs. form of Polish *v.*

† **Pulsidge.** *Obs.* Humorous blunder for Pulse.

1597 Shaks. *2 Hen. IV*, ii. iv. 25 You are in an excellent good temperalitie: your Pulsidge beates as extraordinarily, as heart would desire.

Pulsi·fic, *a.* Now *rare.* [f. L. *puls-us* Pulse *sb.*[1] + -fic.] Producing or causing the pulse or pulsation of the arteries; also, characterized by pulsation, pulsatory, throbbing.

1634 T. Johnson tr. *Parey's Chirurg.* viii. xix. 314 Cruell symptomes doe follow, as pulsifique paine, a feaver, restlessnesse. *Ibid.* xx. vii. 772 The oppression of the vitall and pulsifick faculty by a cloud of grosse vapours. 1678 Cudworth *Intell. Syst.* i. iii. § 17. 161 A pulsifick corporeal quality in the substance of the heart itself, is very unphilosophical and absurd. 1710 T. Fuller *Pharm. Extemp.* 425 The pulsific Motion of the Blood continually thrusting on. 1853 Dunglison *Med. Lex.*, *Pulsific*, that which causes or excites pulsation. 1897 in *Syd. Soc. Lex.*

† **Pu·lsiloge.** *Obs.* [ad. mod.L. *pulsilogium*, f. *puls-us* Pulse *sb.*[1], after *horologium*, Horologe.] (See quots.)

[1753 Chambers *Cycl. Supp.*, *Pulsilogium*, a name given by authors to a pulse-watch, or instrument to measure the celerity of the pulse.] 1812 *Edin. Rev.* XX. 185 Sanctorio..applied the pendulum to determine the quickness of the pulse, forming what he called a *pulsiloge*, in which the string suspending a ball was gradually shortened, till its vibrations corresponded with the beats.

Pulsimeter (pʊlsi·mĭtəɹ). [f. L. *pulsus* Pulse *sb.*[1] + -meter. Cf. Pulsometer.] An instrument for measuring the rate or force of the pulse. Also *attrib.*, as *pulsimeter watch.*

1842 in Dunglison *Med. Lex.* 1894 *Brit. Med. Jrnl.* 26 May 1132/1 The advantages claimed for the 'Pulsimeter' watch are economy of time, accuracy of record, and the possibility of taking the pulse in the dark without any inconvenience to the patient.

Pu·lsing, *vbl. sb.* [f. Pulse *v.* + -ing[1].] The action of the vb. Pulse: rhythmical beating, throbbing, or flowing.

1839 Bailey *Festus* xix. (1852) 281 Ceaseless as the pulsings of the blood. 1843 Carlyle *Past & Pr.* iii. xv, The pulsings of his own soul, if he have any soul, alone audible. 1894 Crockett *Raiders* 133, I could hear..the pulsing of the sea.

Pu·lsing, *ppl. a.* [f. as prec. + -ing[2].] That beats, throbs, or flows with rhythmic cadence.

1559 Morwyng *Evonym.* 359 This oyll anoynted vpon the pulsing veynes, where they appeare moste. 1664 Power *Exp. Philos.* i. 4 If you divide the Bee..near the necke, you shall..see the heart beat most lively, which is a white pulsing vesicle. 1879 *Cassell's Techn. Educ.* IV. 250/2 The pulsing torrent rushes through the arteries.

Pulsion (pʊ·lʃən). Now *rare.* [ad. L. *pulsio, -ōn-em*, n. of action from *pell-ĕre, puls-* to drive, push.] The action of driving or pushing. In first quot., the beating of the pulse.

1634 T. Johnson tr. *Parey's Chirurg.* v. iii. (1678) 107 There may ensue..a deadly interception of the pulsion of the brain. 1656 tr. *Hobbes' Elem. Philos.* (1839) 214 One motion is pulsion or driving, another traction or drawing. Pulsion, when the movent makes the moved body go before it; and traction, when it makes it follow. 1731 S. Hales *Stat. Ess.* I. 111 If this great quantity [of sap] were carried up by pulsion or trusion. 1836–48 B. D. Walsh *Aristoph., Clouds* i. iv, Pulsion, and prension.

attrib. 1897 *Allbutt's Syst. Med.* III. 363 Acquired malformations [of the œsophagus]—Pressure pouches..pharyngeal pouches, pharyngoceles, pulsion diverticula.

Pulsive (pʊ·lsiv), *a.* Now *rare.* [f. L. *puls-*, ppl. stem of *pell-ĕre* to drive, impel + -ive.]

1. Having the quality of driving or impelling; constraining, compelling; impulsive; propulsive.

1602 Marston *Antonio's Rev.* iv. iii, What I here speake is forced from my lips By the pulsive straine of conscience. *a* 1687 Petty *Treat. Naval Philos.* i. i. § 85 The Tractive and Pulsive forces upon swimming Bodies. 188. R. G. H[ill] *Voices in Solitude* 83 The whirl of the wheels went on at length With the pulsive strain of their started strength.

† **2.** Beating or throbbing as the heart, etc. *Obs.*

1611 J. Taylor (Water P.) *Coriat's Commend.* Wks. ii. 91/1 Such a straine That shall euen cracke my pulsiue pia mater In warbling thy renowne by land and water. 1630 — *Descr. Eng. Poetry* ibid. 248/2 In end my pulsiue braine no Art affoords, To mint or stamp, or forge new coyned words.

Pulsometer (pʊlsǫ·mĭtəɹ). [irreg. f. L. *pulsus* Pulse *sb.*[1] + -meter, after *barometer*, etc.]

1. = Pulsimeter.

1858 Mayne *Expos. Lex.*, *Pulsometrum*, term for an instrument for measuring or calculating the variations of the pulse: a pulsometer.

2. A name for a kind of steam-condensing vacuum-pump, with two chambers so arranged that the steam is condensed in, and the water admitted to each alternately: so called from the pulsatory action of the steam. Also *pulsometer pump.* (Not being a *measuring* instrument, it is preferably called *pulsator.*)

1875 Knight *Dict. Mech.*, *Pulsometer*,..a form of vacuum pump. 1881 *Mechanical World* 24 Dec. Advt., The Pulsometer Engineering Company Limited. 1891 *Daily News* 2 Sept. 3/1 The water is heated by means of a horizontal tubular boiler, a six-horse power engine, a centrifugal pump, and two pulsometer pumps. 1900 F. T. Bullen *Idylls of Sea* 265 My heart worked like a pulsometer.

† **Pu·lsor.** *Obs.* *rare*[−1]. [agent-n. from L. *pellĕre, puls-* to drive, impel: see -or 2.] One who or that which drives or impels.

1666 J. Smith *Old Age* (1676) 242 The great artery..is to us the most apparent Pulsor; we can feel the blood to be forced along its Cavity.

Pulsshe, obs. form of Polish *v.*

Pult, parallel form of Pilt *v.* and *sb.* *Obs.*

Pultaceous (pʊltēⁱ·ʃəs), *a.* [f. L. *puls, pultem* pap, pottage + -aceous.]

1. Of the nature or consistency of pap or of a poultice; soft, semi-fluid, pulpy.

1668 *Phil. Trans.* III. 751 He first denyeth, that the Testes are glandulous or pultaceous. 1738 Stuart *ibid.* XL. 327 A soft white pultaceous Matter. 1835–6 *Todd's Cycl. Anat.* I. 71/1 In infancy the brain is extremely soft, almost pultaceous. 1896 *Allbutt's Syst. Med.* I. 403 Pultaceous or even solid food may be remarkably well borne.

2. Of the nature or class of pulse.

1762 tr. *Busching's Syst. Geog.* III. 667 Barley, peas and other pultaceous grain.

Pultar, -er, etc., **Pulterer, Pult(e)rie**, obs. forms of Poulter, etc.

Pultas, obs. or dial. form of Poultice.

† **Pu·lter.** *Obs.* *rare*[−1].

In quot. prob. an error for *pultre*, Poultry, fowls. (The whole passage is composed in the language of falconry, and some of the allusions are obscure.)

1399 Langl. *Rich. Redeles* ii. 165 But þe blernyed boynard þat his bagg stall, Where purraileis pulter was pynnyd ffull ofte, Made þe ffawcon to ffloter and fflussh ffor anger, That þe boy hadd be bounde þat þe bagge kepte.

Pultes, -ess, -ice, obs. or dial. ff. Poultice.

† **Pulti·fical**, *a.* *Obs.* *rare*[−0]. [f. L. *puls, pultem* pottage + -fic + -al.]

1656 Blount *Glossogr.*, *Pultifical*,..wherewith Pottage, Pap, or such like meat is made.

Pultis(e, -oss, Pultre, Pultron(e, -oon, -owne, obs. ff. Poultice, Poultry, Poltroon.

† **Pults.** *Obs.* *rare.* [app. ad. med.L. *pultes* any victuals prepared by boiling (Du Cange), pl. of L. *puls, pultem* pap, pottage (see Pulse *sb.*[2]): cf. It. *pulta, polta* 'grewell, battre, or pap' (Florio).] Soft boiled food, pap, pottage.

c 1550 Lloyd *Treas. Health* S ij, Geue vnto the pacient..two pennye weightes of bay beris made to pouder wyth a soft Egge or pults, without doubt the pacyent shalbe made hole.

‖ **Pultun** (pʊ·ltʊn). *E. Ind.* Also **pultan, -on, -oon.** [Hindī *paltan*, ad. Tamil and Telugu *paṭālan*, ad. Eng. *battalion* (the Eng. word having been first adopted in Southern India).] A regiment of infantry in India.

1800 Wellington in *Gurw. Desp.* (1834) I. 21*, I..shall probably destroy some campoos and pultans, which have been indiscreetly pushed across the Kistna. 1883 *Q. Rev.* Apr. 294 *Campos* and *pultuns* (battalions) under European adventurers. 1895 Mrs. B. M. Croker *Village Tales* (1896) 60, I know lots of Sahibs in a pultoon (i.e. regiment) at Bareilly.

‖ **Pulu** (pū·lū). [Hawaiian.] A fine yellowish silky vegetable wool obtained from the base of the leaf-stalks of the Hawaiian tree-ferns, *Cibotium menziesii, C. chamissoi*, and *C. glaucum.*

1858 Simmonds *Dict. Trade*, *Pu-lu*, a species of brown thistle-down imported from the Sandwich islands, to mix with silk in the manufacture of hats. 1864 in Webster. 1888 Hillebrand *Flora Hawai Is.* 546 The base of the leaf stalks is densely covered with a soft and glossy yellowish wool, which is used for stuffing mattresses and pillows, and under the name of pulu forms a regular article of export to California.

† **Puluere**, obs. f. Pilliver, pillow-case, pillow.

c 1350 *Will. Palerne* 681 He wende ful witerly sche were in is armes; ac peter! it nas but is puluere.

† **Pu·lver**, *sb.* *Obs.* [ad. L. *pulver-em* (nom. *pulvis*) powder, dust.] Powder, dust.

1502 Atkynson tr. *De Imitatione* iii. ix. 204 Good lorde, I speke to the of my presumpcion, natwithstandinge that I am but puluer & asshes. 1535 Stewart *Cron. Scot.* (Rolls) II. 423 In puluer small gart birne thame euerie one. 1599 A. M. tr. *Gabelhouer's Bk. Physicke* 28/1 Mixe these prænominated pulvers..addinge heerunto the Suger.

b. Pulver Wednesday = Ash-Wednesday.

c 1454 Agnes Paston in *P. Lett.* I. 270 Wretyn at Norwyche on Pulver Wedenesday.

† **Pu·lver**, *v.* *Obs.* [ad. L. *pulver-āre*, f. *pulver-*: see prec.] *trans.* To reduce to powder, to pulverize. Hence † **Pu·lvered** *ppl. a.*, † **Pu·lvering** *vbl. sb.*, sprinkling of ashes; *pulvering day*, Ash Wednesday.

1621 G. Sandys *Ovid's Met.* vii. (1626) 129 As pulvered flints [*ed.* 1632 lime of flints] infurnest under ground By sprinkled water fire conceive. 1754 T. Gardner *Hist. Dunwich* 193 On pulvering Days, when Disposition of the said Lands was made, but not confirmed till St. Nicholas's Day. 1778 [implied in Pulverer].

Pulverable (pʊ·lvĕrăb'l), *a.* [f. as prec. vb. + -able.] Capable of being crushed or ground down to powder; pulverizable.

1657 *Physical Dict.*, *Pulverable*, hard things (as oyster-shells) brought to pouder. 1680 Boyle *Produc. Chem. Princ.* iv. 167 Some liquid substances afforded by wounded plants, that..turned into consistent and pulverable bodies. 1789 Nicholson in *Phil. Trans.* LXXIX. 274 If a little mercury be added to melted zinc, it renders it easily pulverable. 1869 J. E. Halliday in *Student* II. 228 Trap-rock,..very soft and pulverable.

Pulveraceous (pʊlvĕrēⁱ·ʃəs), *a.* *Bot.* and *Zool.* [f. L. *pulver-em* powder, dust + -aceous.] Covered or sprinkled with powder; pulverulent.

1864 Gray in Webster.

† **Pulverain.** *Obs.* [Corruption of Fr. *pulvérin* (*c* 1600 in Littré), = It. *polverino*, f. *polvere*:—L. *pulverem* powder.] A powder-horn, esp. one for priming-powder. 1890 in *Cent. Dict.*

† **Pu·lveral**, *a.* *Obs.* *rare.* [f. L. *pulver-em* Pulver *sb.* + -al.] In the state of powder.

1657 Tomlinson *Renou's Disp.* 178 Solid..or pulverall, which must be snuffed up.

† **Pu·lverate**, *v.* *Obs.* [f. L. *pulverāt-*, ppl. stem of *pulverāre* to powder: cf. Pulver *v.*] *trans.* To reduce to powder, to pulverize.

1615 G. Sandys *Trav.* 65 They litter them in their owne dung, first dried in the Sunne and puluerated. 1657 Tomlinson *Renou's Disp.* 60 Some cannot be so exactly pulverated by beating.

Pulveration (pʊlvĕrēⁱ·ʃən). [ad. L. *pulverātiōn-em*, n. of action f. *pulverāre*: see prec.] Reduction to powder or dust; pulverization.

1623 Cockeram, *Pulueration*, a beating into powder. 1733 Tull *Horse-Hoeing Husb.* v. 43 No further..than the Hoe-Plow could turn it up, and help it in its Pulveration. 1866 C. W. Hoskyns *Occas. Ess.* 103 The deep and perfect pulveration of the soil.

‖ **Pulveratores** (pʊlvĕrătō·rīz), *sb. pl.* *Ornith.* [mod.L., pl. of *pulverātor*, agent-n. from L. *pulverāre* to powder; in F. *pulvérateurs* (Buffon 1771).] Birds which habitually roll themselves in the dust, as the *Rasores.*

† **Pulveratricious** (pʊlvĕrătri·ʃəs), *a.* *Obs.* [f. mod.L. *pulverātrix, -trīc-em* (see next) + -ious.] Of, belonging to, or characteristic of birds that roll themselves in the dust.

1661 Lovell *Hist. Anim. & Min.* Introd., Birds, which..are pulveratricious and wild; as the Peacock, japonian, and turky. 1678 Ray *Willughby's Ornith.* iii. ii. 371 The colour of the feathers..comes near to that of pulveratricious birds. 1688 R. Holme *Armoury* ii. 313/1 Pulveratricious [is] an earthly kind of colour, mouse-colour. *Ibid.*, *Pulveratriceous*, covered with a dusty colour.

‖ **Pulveratrix** (pʊlvĕrēⁱ·triks). *Ornith.* *rare.* Pl. **-atri·ces.** [mod.L., fem. of *pulverātor*, agent-n. from *pulverāre* to powder (sc. *avis* bird); in F. *pulvératrice* (Littré).] A bird which cleanses itself by wallowing in dust.

Cf. Aristotle's κονιστικοί, *Hist. An.* 9. 49 B. 10.

1770 G. White *Selborne* 8 Oct., Ray remarks that birds of the *Gallinæ* order, as cocks and hens, partridges and pheasants, are *pulveratrices*, such as dust themselves..Common house-sparrows are great *pulveratrices*, being frequently seen grovelling and wallowing in dusty roads.

† **Pulvereous**, *a.* *Obs.* *rare*[−0]. [f. L. *pulvereus* dusty (f. *pulver-em* powder, dust) + -ous.]

1656 Blount, *Pulvereous*, dusty, of dust, full of dust.

† **Pu·lverer.** *Obs.* *rare.* [f. Pulver *v.* + -er[1].] A pulverizer, an instrument for pulverizing the soil.

1778 [W. Marshall] *Minutes Agric.*, *Digest* 54 *note*, If used as a Pulverer and Compressor of fallows, this acting Bar ought to be set deeper.

Pulverescence (pʊlvĕre·sĕns). *Bot.* [f. as next + *-escence*: see -ence.] Incipient powderiness; tendency to become powdery.

1828 R. K. Greville *Sc. Cryptog. Flora* VI. 338 Hoary, with a white pulverescence. 1858 Mayne *Expos. Lex.*, *Pulverescentia*..of a vegetable surface when covered with a kind of *farina*..as in the *Chenopodium purpureum*: pulverescence. 1897 in *Syd. Soc. Lex.*

Pulverescent (pʊlvĕre·sĕnt), *a.* [f. L. *pulver-em* dust + -escent.] Tending to fall into powder; becoming powdery.

1805 Mushet in *Phil. Trans.* XCV. 168 It was..found to be very fine ore of iron in a pulverescent state.

Pulverilentous, obs. f. Pulverulentous.

Pulverine (pʊ·lvĕrin). Also **-in.** [Cf. It. *polverina* dust, fine powder.] Ashes of barilla.

1836 in Smart. 1858 Simmonds *Dict. Trade*, *Pulverine*, barilla ashes.

Pulverizable (pʊ·lvĕrəizăb'l), *a.* [f. Pulverize *v.* + -able. So F. *pulvérisable* (Littré).] Capable of being pulverized or reduced to powder.

1660 tr. *Paracelsus' Archidoxis* ii. 60 Boil them until they are pulverisable. 1794 G. Adams *Nat. & Exp. Philos.* I. xi. 462 An earthy pulverizable matter. *c* 1865 J. Wylde in *Circ. Sc.* I. 18/2 Tin becomes pulverisable..at high temperatures.

† **Pu·lverizate**, *ppl. a.* *Obs.* [ad. *pulverizāt-us*, pa. pple. of late L. *pulverizāre* to Pulverize.] Pulverized, reduced to powder.

1471 Ripley *Comp. Alch.* xi. vi. in Ashm. (1652) 182 Lyke as Saffron when yt ys pulveryzate.

† **Pu·lverizate**, *v.* *Obs.* [f. ppl. stem of late L. *pulverizāre*: see prec.] *trans.* = Pulverize.

1597 A. M. tr. *Guillemeau's Fr. Chirurg.* 49 b/1 That all these Poulders be verye diminutlye pulverisated. 1599 — tr. *Gabelhouer's Bk. Physicke* 1/2 Pulverisate it verye smalle. 1604–13 R. Cawdrey *Table Alph.*, *Pulverizated*, beaten or broken into dust, or powder.

Pulverization (pʊlvĕrəizēⁱ·ʃən). [n. of action f. late L. *pulverizāre* to pulverize: cf. F. *pulvérisation* (Oudin 1642).]

1. The action of pulverizing; reduction to the state of powder or dust.

[1657 *Physical Dict.*, *Pulverication*, bringing to pouder.] 1658 Phillips, *Pulverization*, a breaking to dust, a reducing into powder. 1763 Mills *Pract. Husb.* II. 197 Brought to that state of pulverization, in which alone plants can thrive well. 1846 J. Baxter *Libr. Pract. Agric.* II. 64 Rains, alternate frosts, and thaws, greatly assist its pulverization.

b. *techn.* The separation (of a liquid) into minute particles, as spray.

1861 *N. Syd. Soc. Year-Bk. Med.* 207 Method of rendering Medicated Liquids Respirable by Pulverisation. 1863 *Ibid.* 421 Pulverization of liquids for Therapeutic Purposes.

c. *fig.* Crushing morally, reducing to nullity, utter demolition (of arguments, statements, etc.).

1873 Morley *Rousseau* II. i. 42 This criticism..marks a beginning of true democracy, as distinguished from the mere pulverisation of aristocracy. 1884 *Chr. World* 13 Mar. 192/5 The complete pulverisation of their case by the Minister whom they approached. 1897 *Windsor Mag.* Jan. 282/2 That the *Saturday Review* devote to your pulverisation two pages and a 'par'.

2. *concr.* A pulverized product or material.

1896 in *Columbus* (Ohio) *Dispatch* 18 Mar. 11/3 The pulverizations gradually find a place on the lowest levels of the ocean.

Pulverizator (pʊ·lvĕrəizēⁱtəɹ). [Agent-noun from late L. *pulverizāre* to pulverize: so mod.F. *pulvérisateur* (Littré).] An instrument for reducing to powder; also, an apparatus for scattering powder or ejecting liquid in the form of spray.

1890 *Kew Bulletin* 191 It is mixed as a powder..and blown with 'pulverizators' on to the vine leaves. 1894 *Dublin Rev.* Oct. 433 There have been many patents taken out in Russia for injectors or pulverisators.

Pulverize (pʊ·lvĕrəiz), *v.* [ad. late L. *pulverizāre*, or F. *pulvériser* (Paré 16th c.), † *polveriser* (14th c. in Hatz.-Darm.), f. L. *pulverem*: see Pulver *sb.*]

1. *trans.* To reduce to powder or dust; to comminute, to triturate. Also *refl.*

1585 T. Washington tr. *Nicholay's Voy.* ii. xxii. 60 b, A drugge..which being puluerised and tempered in water, they rubbe vppon..the bodye. 1605 Sylvester *Du Bartas* ii. iii. iii. *Law* 1142 The zealous Prophet with just fury mov'd..pulveriz'd their Idol. *c* 1790 Imison *Sch. Art* ii. 69 Let it dry, and then pulverize it. 1868 Rogers *Pol. Econ.* xii. (1876) 154 Cultivable land must be pulverised and watered. 1869 J. Martineau *Ess.* II. 235 The solid ground of life was pulverizing itself away.

b. *techn.* To divide (a liquid) into minute particles or spray.

1807 J. Barlow *Columb.* vi. 230 Stroke after stroke with doubling force he plied, Foil'd the boar Fiend and pulverized the tide.

2. *fig.* To demolish or destroy, to break down utterly; to 'smash'.

1631 Massinger *Believe as you List* i. ii, You shall..Feel really that we have iron hammers To pulverize rebellion. 1684 Baxter *Twelve Argts.* Post. M ij, Between both which Truth and Peace is broken, and the Church pulverized. 1813 *Examiner* 17 May 313/1 Which, like a clap of thunder, has pulverized..chimerical hopes. 1864 J. H. Newman *Apol.* iii. (1865) 117 The theory of the *Via Media* was absolutely pulverized. 1895 Col. Maurice in *United Service Mag.* July 428 The four battalions..were..pulverised and driven helter-skelter partly among the defendants.

b. To dissipate in minute portions. *rare.*

1834 Sir W. Hamilton *Discuss.* (1852) 373 The responsibility was so pulverized among a passing multitude of nameless individuals.

3. *intr.* To crumble or fall to dust; to become disintegrated. Also *fig.*

1801 *Farmer's Mag.* Apr. 147 If they are ploughed in November or December, the rains, snow, and frost, make them pulverize easily. 1860 Emerson *Cond. Life, Worship* Wks. (Bohn) II. 394 The stern old faiths have all pulverized. 1866 Lawrence tr. *Cotta's Rocks Class.* (1878) 267 Sometimes these varieties [of limestone] pulverise to a crystalline sand.

4. *intr.* Of a bird: To roll in the dust; to take a dust-bath. *rare.* 1890 in *Cent. Dict.*

Hence **Pu·lverized** *ppl. a.*; **Pu·lverizing** *vbl. sb.* and *ppl. a.*

a 1693 *Urquhart's Rabelais* iii. xxxiv. 288 That..pul-

Supplement, p. 3873; Corrigenda, p. 4092; Spurious words, p. 4093; Books quoted, p. 4094

Pulverizer ... One who or that which pulverizes; an instrument or machine that reduces to powder; also *techn.* one that reduces a liquid to spray.

Pulverous (pɒ·lverəs), *a.* [f. L. *pulver-* dust + -OUS.] Powdery; dusty.

Pulverulence ... [as next, as if from a L. *pulverulentia*: see -ENCE.] Dustiness, powder.

Pulverulent (pɒlve·riŭlent), *a.* [f. L. *pulverulent-us* dusty, f. *pulver-em* dust, powder: see -LENT. So mod.F. *pulvérulent* (1801 in Littré).]

Pulvil, Pulville: see PULVIL, PULVILLO.

Pulvillar ... [f. L. *pulvill-us* little cushion + -AR.] Of or pertaining to a pulvillus; cushion-like, pad-like.

Pulville, Pulvillio: see PULVIL, PULVILLO.

Pulvillus (pɒlvi·ləs), *sb.* [L., contr. from *pulviscul-us, dim.* of *pulvinus* cushion.]

Pulvinar (pɒlvəi·nɑɹ), *sb.* [L.]

Pulvinaria (pɒlvinɛˈriə), *sb.* [mod.L.]

Pulvinate (pɒ·lvineit), *a.* [ad. L. *pulvinat-us* made into or like a cushion, f. *pulvin-us* cushion: see -ATE.]

Pulvinic (pɒlvi·nik), *a.* *Chem.*

Pulvinule (pɒ·lvinɪul), *sb.* *Bot.* [ad. L. *pulvinul-us* little cushion, pillow, bank.]

Pulvinus (pɒlvəi·nəs), *sb. Bot.* [L.]

Pulviplume ... *Ornith. sb.* [ad. *pulviplūma*, f. L. *pulvi-s* dust + *plūma* plume, feather.]

Pulviscle ... *sb.* *Chem.* dim. of *pulvis* dust.]

Pulwar (pɒ·lwɑɹ). *E. Ind.* Also *pulwaul*, *pulwah*. [Hind.]

Puly (piū·li), *a.* [? f. PULE v. + -Y.] Given to puling; puling, sickly.

Puly-haul *v.* [? redupl. f. HAUL v.]

Pulyah (v.), obs. form of PULL v.

Pulza-oil (pɒ·lza·ɔil). A fixed oil obtained from the seeds of the Physic-nut.

Puma (piū·mã). [a. Sp. *puma* (pū·mă), a. Peruv. *puma*.] A large American feline quadruped, *Felis concolor*, also called COUGAR.

Pumelo: see POMELO, SHADDOCK.

Pumelose, -yse, obs. ff. PUMICE, Pumel, -elle, obs. ff. *pulvis-us* cushion, pillow, bank. (Also used in L. form.)

Pumex (piū·meks), *sb.* [L. *pūmex.*] = PUMICE sb.

Pumicate *v.* rare⁻º. [f. L. *pūmicāt-*, ppl. stem of *pūmicāre*, f. *pūmex.*] *trans.* To smooth with pumice. So † **Pumica·tion.**

Pumice (pɒ·mis), *sb.* Forms: see below.

Pumiced (pɒ·mist), *ppl. a.*

Pumiceous (piūmi·ʃəs), *a.*

Pumicer (pɒ·mise), *sb.* rare.

Pumicose (piū·mikōs), *a.* rare.

Pumiculum ... *Obs. rare⁻¹.*

Pumil, Pumila, obs. ff. POMMEL.

Pumilio, pumilo, *Obs.* rare. Also *pumilion*, *pumilon*.

Pumice-stone (pɒ·mis·stōn), *sb.*

Pumilous ... *Obs. rare.*

Pummel, Pummell, obs. ff. POMMEL sb. and v.

Pummel, *sb.*, a parallel form of POMMEL sb.

Pummel (pɒ·m'l), v. Also = POMMEL, pommle, pomele, pumel.

Pummage, Pummice, obs. ff. POMAGE, PUMICE.

Pummy, Pummyse: see POMMEY, PUMICE.

Pump (pɒmp), *sb.1* Also 5-7 pompe, pumpe (5-6 pomp, 6 poumpe): see also PLUMP.

Pump (pɒmp), *sb.2* Also 6-8 pompe, poump, 6-7 pomp.

Pump (pɒmp), *v.* Also 6 pompe, poump, pompen, 7 pompe, etc.

Pumpage (pɒ·mpedʒ). [f. PUMP sb.1 + -AGE.] The work done at pumping, the quantity pumped.

Pump-ball, obs. synonym of PUMPET, PUMPING-BALL.

PUMP-BRAKE. 1593 **PUMPKIN.** **PUMPKIN-HEAD.** 1594 **PUNAISE.**

Pump-brake. The handle of a (ship's) pump, esp. one having a transverse bar for several persons to work at it; = BRAKE *sb.*[6] 1 b.

Pumpe, obs. form of POMP, POMP.

Pumped (pɒmpt), *ppl. a.* [f. PUMP *sb.*[2] + -ED[2].]
1. Obtained by pumping. *Pumped-up* (*fig.*), raised by an effort likened to pumping; artificially worked up; laboured: cf. PUMP v. 8.

2. *Pumped-out* (also *pumpod*), exhausted or out of breath with exertion; winded: cf. PUMP v. 12.

Pumpeo: *nonce-wd.* [f. PUMP v. + -EE[1] 2.]

Pumpelmousse, variant of POMPELMOOSE *Obs.*

Pumper (pɒmpə(r)). [f. PUMP v. + -ER[1].]
1. One who or that which pumps or works a pump.

Pumping, *vbl. sb.* [f. PUMP v. + -ING[1].] The action of the verb PUMP in various senses.

Pumping, *ppl. a.* [as prec. + -ING[2].] That pumps; in *quot.* 1812, issuing as from a pump.

Pumping-ball, *sb.* [History obscure.]

Pumpion. Also 7–9 pompkin, 8–9 pumpkin, 7. pompion. [An altered form of *pumpion* (see POMPION).]

Pumpkin (pɒmˈkin). Also 7–9 pompkin, 8–9 pumpkin, 7. pumpkin. [An altered form of *pumpion* (see POMPION), With the terminal conformed to the *-kin* of many sbs.]

Pump-handle, *sb.* The handle by which a pump, esp. the ordinary hand- or horse-pump, is worked; also *transf.* (see quot. 1794.)

1. The large fruit of a cucurbitaceous plant (*Cucurbita Pepo*), egg-shaped or nearly globular with flattened ends; widely cultivated for the fleshy edible layer next to the rind, which is used in cookery, esp. for pies, and as a food for cattle; *in U.S.* applied *spec.* to particular varieties in distinction from the squash.

b. *U.S. slang.* A person or matter of importance; esp. in phrase *some pumpkins* (or *punkins*).

c. An over-sensitive person.

2. *fig.* Applied contemptuously to the body or person; hence 'a stupid, self-important person'.

3. *attrib.* and *Comb.*, as *pumpkin-field*, *-patch*, *-pie*, *-plant*, etc.

Pumpkin-head. *U.S. colloq.* a. A head having the hair cut short like that of a pumpkin.

Pumpkinification. Also *pumpkinsation*.

Pumpkin-seed. a. The flattish oval seed of the pumpkin.

Pum.pless. [See -LESS.] Without a pump.

Pum.pman. Also pumpsman. A man who works a pump; *spec.* one who attends to the pump in a coal or other mine.

Pump-rod. A rod (ROD *sb.* 9 z) connecting the plunger of a pump with the motive power; in mines a heavy iron or wooden beam or system of beams.

Pump-room. A room or building where a pump is worked; *spec.* a place at a spa where the medicinal water is dispensed for drinking, etc.

Pump-tree. A length of tree-trunk used as the body or stock of a hand-pump, or a water-pipe; the stock, barrel, or cylinder of a pump.

Pump-water. Water obtained from the surface of the soil by means of a pump, as distinguished from *rain-water*, *spring-water*, etc.

Pump-well. A casing or compartment in a ship in which the pumps work; the 'well' of a ship. b. A well having a pump combined with it; a receptacle in which water is collected to be removed by pumping.

Pun, *sb.* [Related to PUN v.[2].]
1. A layer or bed of clay to prevent leakage. *local.*

2. A punner, a pounder, a rammer. *local.*

Pun, *v.*[1] [Goes with PUN *sb.*]
1. *trans.* To pound. [Now rare.]

2. *spec.* (in technical use.) To consolidate by pounding or ramming down (as earth or rubble, in setting poles, etc., or making a roadway); = POUND v.[1] 6.

Pun, *v.*[2] [Also 7–8 punn.] Appears first, with its cognate PUN *sb.*[1], soon after 1660. Of unascertained origin; see Note below.]

Puna (ˈpuːnə). [Peruvian, in mixed *a*. 1. A high bleak plateau in the Peruvian Andes.

Punaise (pyˈneːz). *Obs. exc. as Fr.* Forms:—a. 6- punaise (-piəna·z); 7–9 punese, punaise, 8. 6–8 punie, 7 punay. *b. 6–9 punie*.

PUNATOO. 1595 **PUNCH.** **PUNCH.** 1596 **PUNCH-BOWL.**

Punatoo. (pmˈtuː). [Cingalese.] The preserved pulp of the fruit of the palmyra palm, used as food.

Punay, variant of PUNEE *Obs.*

Punce, obs. var. POUNCE *sb.*[1] 4.

Punce, dial. var. POUNCE *sb.*[3] and v.; obs. f. PUNCH *sb.*[1] 7 and v.

Punch (pɒntʃ), *sb.*[1] Also 5–6 punche, 6. punsche. [A collateral form of POUNCE *sb.*[1], used in certain senses, chiefly related to uses of PUNCH v.[1], or shortened from PUNCHEON[1], with which it is synonymous in nearly every sense.]
1. A dagger; = PUNCHEON[1] 1. *Obs. rare.*

2. An instrument or tool for pricking, piercing, perforating, or making a hole in anything.

Punch (pɒntʃ), *sb.*[2] [Cf. PUNCH v.[1].] An act of punching; a straight or thrusting blow, in mod. usage generally one delivered with the fist; also (*obs. or dial.*) a kick; = POUNCE *sb.*[3] 7.

Punch (pɒntʃ), *sb.*[3] Also 7 punche, puntch. [Origin uncertain.]

Punch, *sb.*[4] A short, thick, punchy person; a Norfolk breed of draught horses; cf. PUNCHY *a.*

Punch (pɒntʃ), *sb.*[5] [Short for PUNCHINELLO.]

Punch (pɒntʃ), *sb.*[6] [? f. PUNCH *sb.*[2].]

Punch (pɒntʃ), *v.*[1] colloq. *rare*—[1]. [f. PUNCH *sb.*[2].]

Puncha, var. PUNCHAYET.

Punchable, *a.* [f. PUNCH v.[1] + -ABLE.] Capable of being punched; † *spec.* of coin.

Punch-bowl. [f. PUNCH *sb.*[3] + BOWL *sb.*[2].]
1. A bowl in which the ingredients of punch are mixed, and from which it is served out; also *transf.*

'Punch's' wife (see later). Also *attrib.* in *Punch and Judy show*, etc.; see also 3.

Punch, *sb.*[4] 2. *Now chiefly dial.*

Punched (pvnʃt), *ppl. a.*

Puncheon (pvnʃən).

Puncher (pvnʃəɹ).

Punchinello (pvnʃinelo).

Punchiness.

Punching (pvnʃiŋ), *vbl. sb.*

Punchy (pvnʃi), *a.*

Punct.

Puncta, pl. of **Punctum**.

Punctate (pvŋktət), *a.*

Punctatim.

Punctation.

Punctiform (pvŋktifɔɹm), *a.*

Punctilio (pvŋktilio).

Punctilious (pvŋktiliəs), *a.*

Punctiliousness.

Punct, *v.*

Punction.

Punctist.

Punctive, *a.*

Punctual (pvŋktiuəl), *a.*

Punctualist.

Punctuality (pvŋktiuæliti).

Punctually, *adv.*

Punctualness.

Punctuate (pvŋktiueit), *v.*

Punctuation (pvŋktiueiʃən).

PUNCTUATIONIST. **PUNDIGRION.** **PUNDIT.** **PUNGLED.**

Punctuationist. 5. *Nat. Hist.* — PUNCTATION 2.

Punctuative (pʌ'ŋktiu̯eitiv), *a.* [f. as PUNCTUATE v. + -IVE: see -ATIVE.] Of, pertaining to, or serving for punctuation (sense 3).

Punctuator (pʌ'ŋktiu̯eitər), agent-n. f. *punctuate* to PUNCTUATE v. One who punctuates.

Punctulate (pʌ'ŋktiu̯let), *a. Nat. Hist.* [ad. *punctulatus*, f. as next.] Marked or studded with punctules; minutely punctate.

Punctulated (-eited), *ppl. a.* [as prec. + -ED.] Consisting of small points or dots; dotted. *Obs.*

Punctule (pʌ'ŋktiu̯l), *Nat. Hist.* [ad. mod.L. *punctulum*, pl. -a, [ad. L. *punctul-um*, dim. of *punctum* point.] A small *Nat. Hist.*, etc., a small punctum.

Punctulation (pʌŋktiu̯le'ʃən), *Nat. Hist.* [f. mod.L. *punctul-um* as after prec. *ppl. a.* + -ATION.] The condition of being punctulate; minute punctation; also *concr.*, a number or mass of punctules.

Puncture (pʌ'ŋktiu̯r), *sb.* [ad. L. *punctūra*, f. *punct-, punct-, ppl. stem of *pungĕre* to prick: see -URE.]

1. An act, or the action, of pricking; a prick, perforation with a sharp-pointed instrument or object; its recent use *spec.* an accidental perforation of a pneumatic tire, as of a bicycle.

Puncture, *v.* [f. prec. sb.]

1. *trans.* To subject to pressure; to pierce with a sharp point; to prick; to perforate: esp. in *Surgery.* Also said of the instrument.

Puncture, *sb.* [See PUNCHER.]

Pundigrion. *Obs.* rare. [app. related, either as earlier form or derivative, to PUN [q.v.] q.v.]

Pundit (pʌ'ndit). Also ? *pandet,* 4-5 *poundhag,* 9 *pandeh, pandit.* [Hind. *panḍit* — Skr. *paṇḍita* learned, skilled; as sb., a learned man.]

1. In India, a learned Hindū...

Pundit ... b. *transf.* A learned expert or teacher.

Pundle. *var.* of POINDLAR Sc. *Obs.*

Pung (pʌŋ), *sb.* *U.S.* [Shortened from *tom-pung...*]

Punge, *var.* of PUNGE, *sb.* *Obs.*

PUNGY. **PUNICIN.** **PUNISHER.** **PUNISHING.** **PUNKLING.**

Pungy (pʌ'ŋgi). *U.S. local.* [Origin obscure: cf. PUNG sb.²] In Massachusetts, 'A small boat like a sharpey'; in Chesapeake Bay, a kind of fast-sailing schooner used in the oyster-trade.

Puniard. obs. form of PONIARD.

Punic (piū'nik), *a.* and *sb.* Also 5 -yk, 6 -ik, 7 -ike, -icke, -quo, -ioque, 7-8 -ick. [ad. L. *Pūnic-us* Carthaginian: f. *Pūnus, Pœnus* a Carthaginian: also purple. Cf. F. *punique* (15th c. in Littré).]

1. Belonging to Carthage; Carthaginian.

Punicin (piū'nisin). *Chem.* [See -IN.]

1. [f. L. *Pūnic-a* pomegranate.] (See quots.)

2. [f. L. *pūnicus* purple.] The colouring matter obtained from the purple whelk (PURPLE sb. 3); the purple of the ancients.

Punily (piū'nili), *adv.* [f. PUNY a. + -LY.] In a puny manner; weakly.

Puniness (piū'nines). Also § *punyness.* [f. PUNY a. + -NESS.] The state or quality of being puny; littleness and feebleness.

Punish (pʌ'niʃ), *v.* Forms: see below. [a. F. *puniss-,* extended stem (in *puniss-, punissant,* etc.: see -ISH²) of *F. punir* — *punire* to punish, in earlier L. *pœnīre, f. pœna* Gr. *ποινή* fine, penalty, requital, punishment, PAIN sb.]

1. *trans.* To cause to suffer for an offence; to subject to judicial chastisement as retribution or requital, or as a caution against further transgression; to inflict a penalty on.

Punisher (pʌ'niʃər). Forms: see PUNISH. [f. PUNISH v. + -ER¹.] One who punishes.

Punishing (pʌ'niʃiŋ), *vbl. sb.* [f. PUNISH v. + -ING¹.] The action of the vb. PUNISH; an instance of this; punishment.

Punishing, *ppl. a.* [f. as prec. + -ING².]

Punishment (pʌ'niʃmənt). Forms: see PUNISH. [a. AF. *punisement* (in Britton) = OF. *punissement,* f. *punir* to PUNISH: see -MENT.]

1. The action of punishing or the fact of being punished; the infliction of a penalty in retribution for an offence.

Punishworthy, *a.* rare. [f. PUNISH v. + -WORTHY.] Deserving of punishment.

Punition (piūni'ʃən). Now rare. Forms: [-icion, [-ition,] *punicion,* 5 -ycion. [a. F. *punition...*]

Punitive (piū'nitiv), *a.* [ad. med.L. *pūnitīv-us* (Bonaventura c 1250), f. *pūnit-,* ppl. stem of L. *pūnire* to PUNISH.]

Punitory (piū'nitəri), *a.* [ad. late L. *pūnitōrius, f. pūnit-,* ppl. stem of *pūnire* to PUNISH.]

Punk (pʌŋk), *sb.*¹ rare arch. Forms: 6-7 *punck,* 6 *puncke, punke, punque, pung,* 7-9 *punk.* [Origin obscure.]

Punka(h (pʌ'ŋkɑ), *sb.* [E. Indies. Forms: 7 *punkaw, punkah, panha, punker, panka,* 9 *punkah, punka, punka.*]

Punkling. *Obs.* rare⁻¹. [as prec. + -LING².] A little or young punk.

Punky, *sb.* local. Also punkie.

Punky (pŏŋki), *a.* Chiefly *U.S.* [f. PUNK *sb.*]

Punler, variant of POINDLAE *Sc. Obs.*

Punnable, *a.* [f. PUN *v.*1] Capable of being; punned upon; susceptible of puns.

Punnage (pŏnedʒ). Now rare. [f. PUN *sb.*]

Punner1 (pŏrnə). Now rare. [f. PUN *v.*1 -ER1.]

Punner2 (pŏrnə). [f. PUN *v.*2] a variant of POUNDER *sb.*2]

Punnet (pŏ'net). local. Also punnit. [Of obscure origin.]

Punning (pŏ'niŋ). *vbl. sb.*1 [f. PUN *v.*1]

Punning (pŏ'niŋ). *ppl. a.* [f. PUN *v.*1]

Punster (pŏ'nstə). [f. PUN *sb.* + -STER.]

Punt (pŏnt), *sb.*1 [OE. *punt* (in 10–11th c. glossaries), ad. L. *pontō* in sense of Gallic transport (Caes. *B.C.* III. 29).]

Punt, *sb.*2 [f. PUNT *v.*2]

Punt, *sb.*3 [Goes with PUNT *v.*3] An act of punting.

Punt, *sb.*4 Glass-making. [ad. F. *pontil*.]

Punta1. *Obs.* Also *pl.* **puntes** (in *anglicised*) **Pointall**.

Punt, *sb.*5 [f. PUNT *v.*1] The hollow at the bottom of a wine-bottle. = KICK *sb.*2 1.

Punt, *sb.*6 [ad. F. *pointe*] a point.

Punt (pŏnt), *v.*1 [ad. F. *ponter*, in same sense (in *Dict. Acad.* 1718); according to Hatz.-Darm., of unknown origin.]

Punt, *v.*2 [ad. F. *pointer*] To play at card-games, as basset, faro, and baccarat: To lay a stake against the bank.

Punted (pŏ'nted), *ppl. a.*1 [f. PUNT *sb.*1 and *v.*1 + -ED.]

Punted, *ppl. a.*2 [f. PUNT *v.*3] Obtained by punting.

Puntee, variant of PUNTY 1.

Puntel, variant of PONTIL [ad. Sp. *puntel*]

punt-fisher, one who fishes from a punt; **punt-fishing**; **punt-gun**, a gun used for shooting water-fowl from a punt; **punt-gunner**, **punt-gunning**; punt-pole, the long pole used in propelling a punt; **punt-shooting**, **-shooting** = *punt-pole*; punt-well, a well in a fishing-punt in which to deposit fish.

Punter1 (pŏ'ntə). [f. PUNT *v.*2 + -ER1.]

Punter2. [f. PUNT *v.*1 + -ER1.] In earlier use, one who goes fishing or shooting in a punt; often a *punt-gunner*. Now: one who punts or manages a punt.

Puntist (pŏ'ntist). [f. PUNT *v.*3 + -IST.]

Puntsman (pŏ'ntsmǎn). [f. PUNT *sb.*1 + MAN1 = PUNTSMAN. PUNTSMAN.]

Punto1 (pŏ'ntō). Also 6–8 (in senses 1–3) **punto**. [a. It. or Sp. *punto*— L. PUNCTUM.]

Punto2. *Cards.* Also **ponto** (pŏ'ntō).

Puntman, variant of PUNTSMAN.

Punty (pŏ'nti). Glass-making. Forms: also as PUNT, PUNTO, PONTEL, PONTIL.

Pun-up (pŏ'nŏp). *vbl. sb.* [f. PUN *v.*1]

Puny (piū'ni), *a.* and *sb.* [a. OF. *puisné*, *puisnié* later *puîné*, f. *puis*— L. *postea* afterwards + *né*— L. *nātus* born.]

Punyish, variant of PUNISH.

Punyship, variant of PUNISHER.

Pup (pŏp), *sb.* Also 8 **pupp**. [Shortened form of PUPPY *sb.* Cf. PUP *v.*]

Pupa (piū'pǎ), *sb.* [L. *pupa* girl, doll.]

Pupal (piū'pǎl), *a.* [f. PUPA + -AL.] Of or pertaining to a pupa.

Puparial (piupēə'riǎl), *a.* [f. next + -AL.] Of or pertaining to a puparium.

Puparium (piupēə'riɵm). [mod.L., f. PUPA + -ARIUM, after *barbarium*, *ovarium*, etc.]

Pupate (piū'pēt), *v.* [f. PUPA + -ATE3.] *intr.* To become a pupa or chrysalis.

Pupa-case. [f. prec. + CASE *sb.*2] The horny case or sheath of a pupa or chrysalis.

Pupation (piupē'ʃǎn). The formation of the pupa.

Pup-barn, *Obs. rare*—1. [app. f. MLG. *puppe*, *pupp*, MDu., MFris. *poppe*, Du., Fris. *pop* doll (ad. L. *pupa*) + BARN1.]

Pupe, *Obs. rare.* [a. F. *pupe*.] = PUPA 1.

Pupelo (piū'pilō). *U.S. local.* A name in New England for cider-brandy.

Pupiform (piū'pifǎrm), *a.* [ad. mod.L. *pupiformis*, f. PUPA: see -FORM.]

Pupa (piū'pǎ). *Conch.* [mod.L. *pupa*. See PUPA *sb.*] A genus of pulmonate molluscs.

Pupigerous (piupi'dʒerǎs), *a.* [f. PUPA: see -GEROUS + -OUS.]

Pupil (piū'pil), *sb.*1 and *a.* [ad. OF. *pupille* (14th c. in Godef.), or ad. L. *pūpillus* (14th c. in Godef.), ad. L. *pūpillus*, dim. of *pūpus* boy, child; *pūpilla*, dim. of *pūpa* girl.]

Pupil (piū'pil), *sb.*2 [ad. F. *pupille* (15th c.), ad. L. *pūpilla* the pupil of the eye, the same word as *pūpilla* female child: see prec.]

Pupilage, pupillage (piū'piledʒ). [f. PUPIL *sb.*1 + -AGE.]

Pupilar, pupillar (piū'pilǎ), *a.*1 [ad. L. *pūpillāris*.]

Pupilary, pupillary (piū'pilǎri), *a.*2 [f. PUPIL *sb.*2]

Pupilate, variant of PUPILLATE.

Pupiled, pupilled (piū'pild), *a.* [f. PUPIL *sb.*1]

Pupillarity (piupilǎ'riti). *Sc. Law.*

Pupillate, pupillize (piū'pilǎt), *v.* [f. L. *pūpilla*.]

Pupillometer (piupilŏ'mitǎ). [f. L. *pūpilla* pupil + -METER.]

Pupil-monger. *Obs.* [f. PUPIL *sb.*1 + MONGER.]

Pupil teacher. A boy or girl preparing to be a teacher, who spends part of the period of preliminary education in compulsory attendance under the supervision of the head teacher, and concurrently receives general education either from the head teacher or from a tutor.

Column 1 (PUPIL-TEACHERDOM)

their general education. (Introduced as 'Central Classes' about 1874 ; much developed 1888–98.)

1869 *Daily News* 13 Jan. 5/1 A Committee to inquire into the working of the pupil-teacher system in England and Wales. 1900 *Westm. Gaz.* 14 Apr. 2/2 It should be noted that the London School Board have just had harnessed the cost of their pupil-teacher training-centres. 1900 *Daily Chron.* 29 Nov. 6/6 A compulsory system of pupil-teacher candidates. 1903 *Westm. Gaz.* 21 July 2/1 There are, at this moment, some 30,000 pupil-teachers, of the ages 16 to 18, attending institution called pupil-teacher centres. 1903 *Morn. Adv. Pupil-Teacher* 506 3 So Obviously it would not be possible to drop the Pupil Teacher system as a source for the supply of adult teachers.

¶ 'Pupil teacher' in Milton : see PUPIL *sb.*[1] 3.

Hence **Pupil-tea·cherdom**, the body or institution of pupil-teachers ; **Pupil-tea·chership**, the post or office of a pupil-teacher ; **Pupil-tea·chery**, the work or position of a pupil-teacher.

1903 *Westm. Gaz.* 26 June 3/1 How can one complain about the teachers...now that we've opened "pupil-teacherdom to all alike ? 1878 T. Hardy *Return* (1890) 192 If I could not get a "pupil-teachership in London school... I could stay with you and be governess to Georgina and Myrtle. 1890 W. T. Green *How are Heroes ? Zool.* I. 321 Self (George Eliot), too, has been variously described : as 'Apotheosis of 'Pupil-Teachery'.

‖ **Pupipara** (pi͡u·pi·pär͡a), *sb. pl. Entom.* [mod. L. neuter *pl.* of *pūpiparus* bringing forth pupæ (*f. parĕre* to bring forth).] A division of *Diptera* in which the young are born in, or ready to pass into, the pupal state. Also called *Nymphiparæ*.

1835 LIBRARY *Orig. 6 Nat. Ins.* iii. 41 The case of the so-called Pupipara not constituting a true exception. 1858 BELL *Gegenbaur's Comp. Anat.* 759 The complete fusion of the ventral chord into one somewhat long knot, in the case of Pupipara.

Hence **Pupiparous** (pi͡u·pi·pär͡as) *a.*, of or pertaining to the *Pupipara* ; producing or bringing forth young already advanced to the pupal state.

1826 KIRBY & Sp. *Entomol.* III. xxix. 63 Pupiparous, continuing in the matrix of the mother during the larva state, and coming forth in that of pupa. 1835, 1845 [see NYMPHIPAROUS]. 1891 W. CLARK *Van der Hoeven's Zool.* I. 321 Pupiparous insects lack the blood of mammals and birds.

‖ **Pupivora** (pi͡u·pi·v͡or͡a), *sb. pl. Entom.* [mod. L. neuter *pl.* of *pūpivor-us* devouring pupæ.] A division of hymenopterous insects containing those, such as the Ichneumon-flies, which deposit their eggs in the larvæ of other insects, chiefly *Lepidoptera*. Hence **Pupivora** [as in 1.], a member of the *Pupivora* ; **Pupivorous** (pi͡u·pi·vĕr͡as) *a.*, of or pertaining to the *Pupivora* ; devouring the pupæ of other insects ; parasitic on pupæ.

The name *Pupivora* was introduced by Latreille 1806-9, as that of his second family of Hymenoptera. They correspond nearly to the *Entomophaga* of Westwood. 1898 SHARP, Pupivorous.

[*...continues...*]

Column 2 (PUPPETRY 1609)

...and do them muche reuerence.

Puppet-clack (-clæk [Cf. CLACK *sb.*[5].] — PUPPET-VALVE.

1741 DESAGULIERS *Exper. Philos.* II. 472 If the Steam is stronger than you want, it may lift up the Valve, and go out at the Puppet-clack alias the *Puppet Clack*.

Puppet-head, variant of POPPET-HEAD.

Puppetish, *a. rare.* Also 6 popetish. [f. PUPPET *sb.* + -ISH.] Pertaining to or of the nature of a puppet. (Cf. PUPPET *sb.* b.)

1599 BALE *Image Both Ch.* II. H iv, Holye wakyne hypocrysye, for processyon and sensinge wyth other Popetish gaudis.

Puppetly, *a. Obs. rare.* Also 6 popetish, pupitily. [f. as prec. + -LY.]

1599 BALE (see -LY).

Column 3 (PUPPET-SHOW 1610)

hobby, toy (e.g. *il en fait sa poupée*), whence app. in Eng. 'a dog used as a plaything', a toy dog ; a sense unknown to French. The doll and nonce-senses of F. *poupée* are usually represented in Eng. by PUPPET *sb.*[1] 1, 2.

+ 3. 'Get-up' or dress as a puppet (sense 1 or 2) ; one with a New doth the body ; to trick out with... *Obs.*

4. Something compared to a puppet or set of puppets. *pl.* False or pretended divinities. *Obs.*

Puppet-show (-ʃ͡oʊ). Also 7 poppet-, 6–7 puppet. A show, display, or exhibition of puppets ; *esp.* a dramatic performance of, or puppets ; a puppet-play.

Hence **Puppet-shower**, **Puppet-show·man**, a man who exhibits or manages a puppet-show.

Puppet-valve. Also poppet-valve. [f. PUPPET *sb.* + VALVE.] A disk valve which is opened by being bodily lifted from its seat, not by turning upon a hinge.

Column 4 (PUR right)

[*Column of entries for PUR, PUPPY-DOG, PUPPYDOM, etc.*]

Lower Column 1 (PUR 1611)

+ **Pur**, v. *Obs.* [Origin uncertain.] A name given to the Knave or Jack in the game of post and pair (see POST *sb.*[4]). Also *attrib.* pur-chop, pur-dog, *f* a card which would take the Knave.

1592 LYLY *Midas* v. ii, Mine armes are all armorie, gules, vert, pur, purre, pur-post, purre, &c. 1608 D. JONSON *Masque Christmas, Enter...* Post and Pair, with a pair-royal of aces in his hat, his garments all done over with Pairs and Purs. *Ibid.*, Post and Pair wants his pur-chop, and his pur dogs.

Pur, obs. f. POOR, PORE, PURE, PURRE.

Pur-, prefix. The usual AF. form of OF. *por-, pur-*, mod.F. *pour-* = L. *prō-, prō-*, prep. and pref. (see PRO- *pref.*[1]), which in the native forms of these two words fell together with the prefix came into early ME. through OF. still retained in numerous words as purchase, purfle, purlieu, purloin, purport, purpose, purpresture, pursue, purvey, and their derivatives, as well as in the earlier forms of words in which it has been since altered to the L. form, as promenade, etc.

Purail, -aile, -rall, var. of PORAIL *Obs.*, poor people.

+ **Purale, puralee**. *Old Law.* Forms : 3–4 purale, pouralee, 4 pouraleye, puralie, puraille, 5 puralee, 6–7 pur-, 6 puraleigh 7 puralie. [AF. *puralee* (a latinized *puralea*) = OF. *porallee* a going through, f. OF. *por-, pur-* forth, forth there interchanging with *por-* (-L. *per-*) in OF. *paraler* to go through. Taken into AF. and ME. equivalent of L. *perambulatio*, PERAMBULATION, whence also PURALLEE.] A perambulation made to determine the boundaries of a county, manor, parish, or district.

Lower Column 2 (PURBLINDLY 1611)

...tam de Wychewode, elargando bundas predictas : et...quod predictus hamelettus (Haneberghe) est infra las puralees ejusdem forestæ.

Puranic (pi͡urænik), *a.* (*sb.*) Also panranic, -ik (pourā́nik), pooranic. [f. prec. + -IC. *Puranic* follows the Skt. *pauraṇika.*] Of or pertaining to the Puranas.

1809 COLEBROOKE *Trans. in Asiat. Res.* IX. 275 The Indians, who have legendary story of their saints also seem to be engrafted on the Puranic tales of the orthodox sect. 1889 Max Müller *Rig Veda* I. 244 In the epic and puranic literature this has grown into a definite sect.

Puraventure, erron. var. of PERADVENTURE.

Purbeck (pɜ͡ərbek). Named of a peninsula on the Dorsetshire coast ; in full, Isle of Purbeck ; used *attrib.* to designate the stone quarried there, or things made of this, and the geological formation there typically developed.

Purblind (pɜ͡ərblai͡nd), *a.* Forms : 3–4 pur-blind, -blynd, 4 purblinde, 7 pore-, pure-, 4–6 purblynd, poreblinde, etc. ; 3–6 pur-blind, 6–7 pur-blinde, 7 pore-blinde. [ME. *pur blind*, poure blynd, in which *pur* (*pure*) was intensive = 'quite blind' : see PURE *adv.* 3 and PUR- 1.]

+ 1. Quite or totally blind. *Obs. rare.*

2. Of impaired or defective vision, in various senses : **a.** Blind of one eye (*obs.*). **b.** Short-sighted, near-sighted ; *c.* (Sometimes app.) dim-sighted, dim-sighted from age. **d.** Partially blind ; almost blind ; dim-sighted, generally, or without particularization.

Lower Column 3 (PURBLINDNESS 1612)

Purblindness. [f. PURBLIND *a.* + -NESS.] The quality of being purblind (*lit.* and *fig.*).

1598 HOLLAND, Purblindnes, *Luscus.* 1611 B. JONSON *Epicene* II. i, My short-sightednesse is growne to a meere blindnesse of their eies with the powder of white Marjoram.

Purcha·sable (pɜ͡ər·tʃəsæ͡bl), *a.* Also 7 purchasable. [f. PURCHASE *v.* + -ABLE.] That may be purchased. + **a.** That may be obtained in any way ; acquirable ; procurable (*obs.*). **b.** Capable of being or liable to be bought for money.

Lower Column 4 (PURCHASE 1612)

meeting with any property. 1694 LUTTRELL *Brief Rel.* I. Dec. (1857) III. 486 All their profits are laid up... St. Madison, finding... themselves that the... II. **The process of making one's profit or gaining one's sustenance in any way ; *esp.* of doing this in an irregular way, as by begging, or by shifts of any kind ; shifting for oneself.**

the Facility of gaining the same with smaller Force. 1726 SHELVOCKE *Voy. round World* 241 When we came to make purchases to raise her again,..[we] found she did not hang so heavy. 1793 SMEATON *Edystone L.* 198 The compound purchase, called the Runner and Tackle. 1820 SCORESBY *Acc. Arctic Reg.* II. 455 We had no other means of performing this singular evolution than by attaching purchases to the ice from the ship. 1899 F. T. BULLEN *Log Sea-waif* 47 A derrick was rigged over the main-hatch with a double chain purchase attached.

15. *fig.* A 'hold', 'fulcrum', or position of advantage for accomplishing something; a means by which one's power or influence is increased.

1790 BURKE *Fr. Rev.* 232 A politician, to do great things, looks for a power, what our workmen call a purchase; and if he finds that power, in politics as in mechanics, he cannot be at a loss to apply it. 1809 KNOX & JEBB *Corr.* I. 547 This may give us a purchase, by which we may gain over people, from irreligion, to religion. 1853 MIALL *Bases Belief* II. xvii. (1861) 97 They diminish the amount of evil to be contended with, and they provide a firmer purchase for the power which contends with it. 1868 LIDDON *Serm. Spec. Occas.* vii. (1897) 150 The will has a subtle but strong purchase over the understanding in matters of belief.

IV. 16. *attrib.* and *Comb.*: in sense 6, as *purchase-book, -deed, -making, -price, -sum*; in sense 6 b, as *purchase officer, system*; in sense 13, as *purchase-block* (BLOCK *sb.* 5), *-fall* (FALL *sb.*[1] 26), *gear, power, -tackle*; also **purchase-land**, land acquired by purchase. See also PURCHASE-MONEY.

1838 *Civil Eng. & Arch. Jrnl.* I. 148/2 With the assistance of double and single *purchase-blocks. c 1860 H. STUART *Seaman's Catech.* 36 Purchase or shoulder blocks are used for masting, dismasting, or heaving down, or heaving off vessels on shore, or anything where immense strain is required. 1753 CHAMBERS *Cycl. Supp.*, **Purchase-book*, ..the name given to a book..containing an account of all the purchases made. 1907 *Expositor* Dec. 498 The description of *purchase-deeds in the time of Jeremiah is suggestive of Babylonian usage. 1898 C. BRIGHT *Submar. Telegraphs* iv. 150 Not only can the cable be cut in shallow water near the coast by any small steamer with *purchase gear that will raise an anchor, but [etc.]. 1485 in *Somerset Medieval Wills* (1901) 254, I bequethe to Henry, my sonne, all my *purchesse londes that I haue purchessed oute of the manor of Comtone. 1891 *Daily News* 5 Mar. 3/5 That they should re-open the whole question of purchase and the terms granted to *purchase officers. 1884 *Sword & Trowel* Feb. 49 Jesus paid the *purchase-price. 1898 *Westm. Gaz.* 30 Sept. 7/2 To issue 370,000 fully paid shares to the old company as purchase price for the undertaking. 1793 SMEATON *Edystone L.* § 122 *note*, The term *Purchase-Tackle has of late years been applied to this kind of block.

Purchase (pɜ̄·ɹtʃės, -ās), *v.* Forms: α. 3 porchas(s)i, -chasy, 3-4 -chacy, -i, -e(n, 3-6 -chase. β. 4 pourchase, 4-6 -chace, -chasse, 5 -chasshe, -chaas. γ. 3 purchaci, -chasy, 3-5 -chacen, 4-5 -chasen, 4 -chasce, -chayse, -chaise, -chece, 4-6 -chas, -chass(e, -chess, 4-7 -ches, 4-8 -chace, 5 -chese, 4- purchase; (5 percheas). [ME. a. AF. *purchacer*, = OF. *por-*, *pur-*, *pourchacier*, *-chassier*, *-chasser* (11th c. in Hatz.-Darm.) to seek for, seek to obtain, procure, or bring about, f. *por, pur, pour*:—L. *prō* for + *chacier, chassier, chasser*:—pop. L. *captiāre* to catch, hunt, CHASE; cf. It. *procacciare* to endeavour to get, to procure. (The ONF. dialect forms *porcachier*, and *por-*, *purcacier*, *pourkacier*, *pourkachier*, do not appear to be represented in Eng.)]

I. †1. *trans.* To try to procure or bring about; to contrive or devise (esp. something evil) *to* or *for* a person. *Obs.*

1297 R. GLOUC. (Rolls) 9685 Þat hii ne ssolde purchasy non uvel þe king ne non of his. 1340 *Ayenb.* 8 He..þet deþ oþer por'haceþ ssame oþer harm to oþren. 1422 in E. Déprez *Études de diplomat. angl.* (1908) 37 Yat the saide Johan Moreau ..ne purchase ne do no noyowe thyng..to owre seide rewme. 1481 CAXTON *Godeffroy* 76 Wel they apperceyued certaynly that themperour pourchassed for them alle the euyl that he myght. 1483 — *Cato* g j b, Whan they seken and purchasen the losse and the dethe of yonge chyldren. 1549 *Compl. Scot.* viii. 74 3e, vndir the cullour of frendschip, purchessis my final exterminatione.

†b. With subordinate clause or infinitive. *Obs.*

1390 GOWER *Conf.* III. 162 Wherof thou thenkest to deserve Thi princes thonk, and to pourchace How thou myht stonden in his grace. 1426 LYDG. *De Guil. Pilgr.* 4731 Wher thow..dist purchace Thy temptacioun to enchace. 1483 CAXTON *Gold. Leg.* 408b/1, I shalle soo pourchaas to sette suche a clothe in thy lommes. 1523 LD. BERNERS *Froiss.* I. cxl. 168 Duke Johan of Brabant, purchased greatly that yᵉ erle of Flaunders shulde haue his doughter in maryage. 1549 *Compl. Scot.* viii. 73 My mortal enemeis purchessis to rais my liberte.

†2. To exert oneself for the attainment of some object; to endeavour; to strive. *Obs.* **a.** *refl.*

[= OF. *se porchacier* 's'efforcer, s'activer' (11th c.).]

[1292 BRITTON v. xii. § 3 Le tenaunt se purchace de amesurer la dowarie [*transl.* let the tenant proceed for admeasurement of the dower].] c 1330 R. BRUNNE *Chron. Wace* (Rolls) 7314 Þey..byddem go purchace þem best, To seke oþer lond & lede. c 1450 LOVELICH *Grail* li. 331 Pharans purchased him that ilke day..that he hadde geten hym An Asse.

b. *intr.*

1481 CAXTON *Godeffroy* 191, I wote not how many poure pylgryms that wente pourchasshyng yf they myght fynde ony vytaylles in the countre. 1523 LD. BERNERS *Froiss.* I. cxlvii. 177 The Cardynall..purchased somoche that a truse was taken bytwene yᵉ kynges of Englande and of Fraunce. a 1533 — *Huon* lxxxii. 253 He purchaseth for

your deth. 1607 SHAKS. *Timon* III. ii. 52 That I should Purchase..for a little part, and vndo a great deale of Honour. 1674 EARL ESSEX *Let.* 17 Mar. (1770) 204 Mr. justice Jones purchased hard for it [to be made chief Justice].

†3. *trans.* To bring about, cause, effect, produce; to obtain, procure, manage. Const. *to* or *for* a person, or with dative. *Obs.*

c 1330 *Arth. & Merl.* 216 Nil Ich me nothing auentour, To purchas a fole gret honour. 1375 BARBOUR *Bruce* VII. 496 And went..to hunt & play, Forto purchase thame venysoun. 1390 GOWER *Conf.* Prol. 129 The werre wol no pes purchace. c 1489 CAXTON *Sonnes of Aymon* ix. 232 None ought not to complayne my deth, sith that I have purchaced it myself. a 1533 LD. BERNERS *Huon* lxvii. 231 Ye haue founde here an yll brother, syn he hath purchased for you so moche yll. 1641 J. JACKSON *True Evang. T.* III. 176 As a Priest, he did earne, and purchase peace. 1678 SIR G. MACKENZIE *Crim. Laws Scot.* II. *Acts Convict.* (1699) 285 Accused, and pursued be vertue of Crimes purchast be him.

†b. *intr.* To arrange, make provision, provide. Const. *for*. *Obs.*

c 1386 CHAUCER *Man of Law's T.* 775 Ffor wynd and weder almyghty god purchace And brynge hire hoom. c 1430 LYDG. *Min. Poems* (Percy Soc.) 176 In every ffelaship so for thysilf purchace. 1483 CAXTON *G. de la Tour* lxxxiii, Lyke the lyonesse..of all her faons she loueth best hym that best can purchace for hym self. 1523 LD. BERNERS *Froiss.* I. lxxii. 93, I trust I shall purchase for suche a capitayne, that ye shal be all reconforted.

II. †4. *trans.* To procure for oneself, acquire, obtain, get possession of; to gain. *Obs.*

[a 1135 *Leges Wilhelm. Conq.* (MS. c 1230) I. xiv, Li apelur jurra sur lui..que pur haur nel fait ne pur auter chose, se pur sun dreit nun purchacer.] c 1290 *S. Eng. Leg.* I. 87/32 Þat huy [Ursula] þe purchace clene maidenes: with þe to habbe in þi boure. 1297 R. GLOUC. (Rolls) 360 Corineus..wende alond to honti..Vor to porchassi hom mete. c 1330 R. BRUNNE *Chron. Wace* (Rolls) 14463 He purchased hym, þorow robberye, Men ynowe, & fair nauye. c 1386 CHAUCER *Pars. T.* ¶ 992 He hopeth for to lyue longe and for to purchacen muche richesse for his delit. c 1460 *Oseney Reg.* 38 All thynges þe which the church of Saynte Marye..lawfully hath i-purchased [L. *adepta est*]. 1549 *Compl. Scot.* xii. 100 It sal be ane lang tyme or the romans can purches sa grit ane armye contrar 3ou. 1600 SURFLET *Countrie Farme* I. iv. 11 The water..purchaseth from the lead an euill qualitie. 1630 *R. Johnson's Kingd. & Commw.* 314 If..two or three united Cantons purchase any bootie by their peculiar Armes. 1703 M. MARTIN *Western Isles* 287 With these rude hooks, and a few sorry fishing lines, they purchas'd fish for their maintenance.

b. To obtain from a constituted authority (a mandatory or permissive instrument, as a brief, a licence, etc.); *spec.* in *Law*, *To purchase a writ*, to sue out, to obtain and issue a writ; hence, to commence an action. *Obs.* exc. *Hist.*

[1292 BRITTON II. xvii. § 4 Si le bref fust purchacé avaunt la disseisine.] a 1300 *Cursor M.* 19606 And þar-on purchest he þar breue For to seke..Cristen men. c 1425 *Eng. Conq. Irel.* 6 Whan Macmorgh hade the kynges lettres thus y-purchasede. 1553 BECON *Reliques of Rome* (1563) 238 b, All thoe yᵗ purchasen letters of any Lordes court. 1849 MACAULAY *Hist. Eng.* ii. I. 153 He could not alienate one acre without purchasing a licence. 1876 DIGBY *Real Prop.* v. § 2. 222 *note*, 'Purchasing' a writ was the usual expression for commencing an action by suing out a writ, for which the usual fees must be paid, notwithstanding the provision of Magna Carta (c. 40), 'Nulli vendemus..justitiam'.

†c. To gain, get to, reach (a port). *Obs. rare*[−1].

?1587 R. TOMSON *Voy. W. Ind.* in Hakluyt *Voy.* (1589) 582 One of the shippes of our company..went that night with the land: thinking in the morning to purchase the port of S. John de Vllua.

5. *spec. Law.* To acquire (property, esp. land) otherwise than by inheritance or descent; sometimes, to get by conquest in war. *Obs.* or *arch.*

[1278 *Rolls of Parlt.* I. 10/2 Pur ceo qe la terre est de ancient demene le Roy u nul neste put purchaser par la commune ley.] 1303 [implied in PURCHASER 2]. c 1330 [see PURCHASED *ppl. a.* 1]. 1375 BARBOUR *Bruce* I. 433 Ga purches land quhar euir he may, For tharoff haffys he nane perfay. 1398 TREVISA *Barth. de P. R.* VI. xiv. (Bodl. MS.), Þe fadir..purchaseth lond and heritage for his children alwey [L. *acquirere..non desistit*]. c 1425 *Eng. Conq. Irel.* 30 Al hys thoght & all hys wylle, was nyghte & day, wyth all hys myght to wend in-to Irland..to do hym yn adventur, lond to purchace yn vnked land. 1435 *Rolls of Parlt.* IV. 487/1 The Manoirs, Londes,..and Possessions, purchaced or amortised. 1503-4 *Act 19 Hen. VII*, c. 15 § 4 Yf eny bondeman purches eny londes..in fee symple. 1606 SHAKS. *Ant. & Cl.* I. iv. 14 His faults in him..Hereditarie, Rather then purchaste. 1682 [see PURCHASED].

†b. *intr.* To acquire possessions; to become rich. *Obs.*

1340 HAMPOLE *Pr. Consc.* 1332 Swilk men purchaces and gaders fast, And fares als þis lyfe suld ay last. c 1386 CHAUCER *Prol.* 608 He [the Reve] koude bettre than his lord purchace; ffnl riche he was astored pryuely. 1390 GOWER *Conf.* II. 194 Riht so is Coveitise afaited To loke where he mai pourchace. 1623 WEBSTER *Devil's Law-case* IV. i, Were all of his mind, to entertain no suits But such they thought were honest, sure our lawyers Would not purchase half so fast. 1623-33 FLETCHER & SHIRLEY *Night-Walker* I. i, Why should that Scrivener..Purchase perpetually, and I a rascal?

6. *trans.* To acquire by the payment of money or its equivalent; to buy. (Now the chief sense.)

1377 LANGL. *P. Pl.* B. XVII. 252 And purchace al þe pardoun of Pampiloun & Rome. 1393 *Ibid.* C. IV. 32 And porchace 30w prouendres while 3oure pans lasteþ. 14.. *Voc.* in Wr.-Wülcker 602/18 *Peronizo*, to purchase. 1611 BIBLE *Gen.* xxv. 10 The field which Abraham purchased of the sonnes of Heth. 1611 COTGR., *Acheter*, to buy, to purchase. a 1727 NEWTON *Chronol. Amended* v. (1728) 339

He that received money of the People for purchasing things for the Sacrifices. 1765 BLACKSTONE *Comm.* I. iv. 214 To buy wool for her majesty's use, to purchase oyl for her lamps. 1837 DICKENS *Pickw.* ii, 'We must purchase our tickets,' said Mr. Tupman.

b. *fig.* To obtain, acquire, or gain (something immaterial) at the cost or as the result of something figured as the price paid; *esp.* to acquire by toil, suffering, danger, or the like; to earn, win; to bring upon oneself, incur (mischief).

c 1400 tr. *Secreta Secret., Gov. Lordsh.* 51 He þat gyues his good to hem þat hauys no myster, he purchases no louynge þerof. c 1450 LOVELICH *Grail* xliii. 476 For be that deth be hym Ouercam, And purchaced lif to Every Cristen Man. 1456 *Paston Lett.* I. 405, I..do purchasse malgre to remembre of evidenses lakkyng by negligence. 1521-2 *Wolsey* in Furnivall *Ballads fr. MSS.* I. 335 Þat þou may purches hevyn to mede. 1548-77 VICARY *Anat.* Ep. Ded. (1888) 6 [They] purchased eternal prayse by their study and cunning in Phisicke and Surgery. 1680 OTWAY *Orphan* I. i, The Honours he has gain'd are justly his; He purchas'd them in War. 1709 STEELE & SWIFT *Tatler* No. 68 ¶ 4 He that commends himself, never purchases our Applause; nor he who bewails himself, our Pity. 1741 tr. *D'Argen's Chinese Lett.* xx. 141 At length they all perish'd, and made the Japonese purchase their Death by the Loss of 3000 of their Soldiers. 1778 MISS BURNEY *Evelina* (1791) II. xxx. 180 Dearly, indeed, do I purchase experience! 1871 FREEMAN *Norm. Conq.* IV. xviii. 183 The victory was purchased by the death of Rhiwallon.

III. 7. *Naut.* To haul in, draw in (a rope or cable); *spec.* to haul up (the anchor) by means of the capstan; hence, to haul up, hoist, or raise (anything) by the aid of a mechanical power, as by the wheel-and-axle, pulley, or lever. Cf. PURCHASE *sb.* III.

From quot. a 1625 this appears to have arisen as a nautical use of sense 4, with the notion of 'gaining', applied at first to hauling in a rope with the two hands so as to 'gain' one portion after another, and to have been extended to hauling with the capstan, and so at length to the advantage gained by any mechanical power.

1567 *Admiralty Crt. Act* XII., 29 May, [Commission is awarded]..to recover, purchase, wey and bring to lande one sonken or wrecked shipp. a 1625 *Nomencl. Navalis* (Harl. MS. 2301) lf. 60 b, To Purchase Wee Call the gaining or Coming in of a Roape by our haling of it in with our handes, or heauing of it in at yᵉ Capstaine or otherwise Purchasing; as the Capstaine doth purchase apace that is it drawes in the Cabell apace, or the Tackles doe purchase, and the Contrarie where wee cannot purchase with the Roape, Tackle, or the like Neate. 1627 CAPT. SMITH *Seaman's Gram.* I. xvi. (1692) 80. 1704 J. HARRIS *Lex. Techn.* I. 1711 W. SUTHERLAND *Shipbuild. Assist.* 141 Pendants of the Main and Foremast ought to be as big as the Shrowds, since they purchace a great Weight of Boats and Anchors. 1726 SHELVOCKE *Voy. round World* 180 In purchasing the anchor, the cable parted, and I lost it. 1768 J. BYRON *Narr. Patagonia* (ed. 2) 28 We were usually obliged to purchase such things as were within reach by means of large hooks fastened to poles. 1793 SMEATON *Edystone L.* § 143 In this situation a strong hawser..being passed under one of the arms of the anchor,..the whole suspension was in that manner purchased. *Ibid.*, *note*, A piece of strong timber overlaying the bows of a vessel, containing sheaves, or a roller for purchasing the anchor. 1835 MARRYAT *Jac. Faithf.* ii, Purchase the anchor I could not; I therefore slipped the cable. 1836 — *Midsh. Easy* xxiv, After one or two attempts, he lowered down the steps and contrived to bump her [an old lady] on the first, from the first he purchased her on the second, and from the second he at last seated her at the door of the carriage.

Purchased (pɜ̄·ɹtʃest), *ppl. a.* [f. prec. + -ED[1].]

†1. Obtained by effort, entreaty, or the like; acquired, procured, gotten; of land, Acquired otherwise than by inheritance. Also *fig.* *Obs.*

c 1330 R. BRUNNE *Chron.* (1810) 87 Heritage þat lyues & leues to þe eldest sonne, Purchased þing men gyues, woman weddyng to mone, Or tille a man is strange for his seruise oftsone. 1483 *Cath. Angl.* 294/1 Purchest (A. Purchessyde), *adeptus.* 1568 BIBLE (Bishop's) *Eph.* i. 14 Unto the redemption of the purchased possession. 1596 SHAKS. *Merch. V.* IV. i. 90 You haue among you many a purchast slaue. 1682 WARBURTON *Hist. Guernsey* (1822) 90 Purchased estates, acquêt or conquêt...Strictly, acquet is such as is purchased before marriage.

†b. Incurred by one's act or conduct. *Obs.*

1611 BEAUM. & FL. *Knt. Burn. Pestle* IV. iii, He is dead, Grief of your purchas'd anger broke his heart.

2. Bought with money or other equivalent.

1823 BYRON *Juan* XIII. lxxvi, An English autumn, though it hath no vines..Hath yet a purchased choice of choicest wines. 1825 T. HOOK *Sayings* Ser. II. *Sutherl.* (Colburn) 44 Purchased roses decked her furrowed cheeks.

Pu·rchase-mo:ney. The sum for which anything is or may be purchased. Also *fig.*

a 1763 SHENSTONE *Wks.* (1764) II. 293, I would part with the purchase-money, for which I have less regard. 1818 COBBETT *Pol. Reg.* XXXIII. 57 The purchase money of farms is estimated upon the amount of rent. 1832 HARR. MARTINEAU *Life in Wilds* ix, Labour is still the purchase-money of everything here. 1890 'R. BOLDREWOOD' *Col. Reformer* (1891) 259 He..retained the proceeds..with which to pay off his purchase-money.

Purchaser (pɜ̄·ɹtʃėsəɹ). Forms: 4 purchasour, 5 -oure, -owre, purchesour, 6 -asser, 6-8 -asor, 6- purchaser. [ME., a. AF. *purchasour*, = OF. *porchaceor*, later *pur-*, *pourchaseur*, agent-n. from *porchacier*, *pourchasser* to PURCHASE.]

†1. One who acquires or aims at acquiring possessions; one who 'feathers his nest'. *Obs.*

In quot. c 1386, many explain *purchasour* as 'conveyancer'.

which is possible; but cf. quot. 1591 and PURCHASE *v.* 5 b, quot. 1623-33.

1303 R. BRUNNE *Handl. Synne* 1105, Y se men þat purchasours are, Þat coueyte catel with sorwe & kare. c 1386 CHAUCER *Prol.* 318 A Sergeant of the Lawe..Of fees and robes hadde he many oon, So greet a purchasour was nowher noon; Al was fee symple to hym in effect; His purchasyng myghte nat been infect. c 1440 *Partonope* 6427, I haue lyued as a sowdyor A poure man but no purchasoure. 1591 GREENE *Disc. Coosnage* (1592) 11 Think you some lawyers coulde be such purchasers, if al their pleas were short, and their proceedinges iustice and conscience?

†b. One who procures or brings something about. *Obs. rare*[−1].

1653 WHITFIELD *Treat. Sinf. Men* vi. 25 Is he not the Author and purchasor of peace?

†c. *Mining.* See quot. 1747; cf. CAVER. *Obs.*

?1556 in Pettus *Fodinæ Reg.* (1670) 95 That no Purchasors shall let or stop any Miners from any Wash-trough at any time. 1747 HOOSON *Miner's Dict.* s.v. *Mineral time*, Purcassers [are] Poor People that daily go to the Mines, with their Hammers, Bags, or Penny-wiskets, searching in the Deads that are daily drawn and tem'd on the Hillocks, for any Bits of Ore that they can find therein. *Ibid.*, Also Purchasers are all to go away from the Works when that time is expired.

2. *Law.* One who acquires land or property in any way other than by inheritance.

1303 R. BRUNNE *Handl. Synne* 9453 Also with purchasours ry3t so hyt fareþ, Alle þat þey bygge, here eyrēs bareþ. c 1540 in J. R. Boyle *Hedon* (1875) App. 71 Yf anye suche inherytor or purchessor absent them selfes [etc.]. 1642 tr. *Perkins' Prof. Bk.* viii. § 539. 235 If husband and wife be joynt purchasers unto them and unto the heires of the husband of lands. 1766 BLACKSTONE *Comm.* II. xiv. 220 The first purchasor..is he who first acquired the estate to his family, whether the same was transferred to him by sale, or by gift, or by any other method, except only that of descent. *Ibid.* xv. 241 If I give land freely to another, he is in the eye of the law a purchasor. 1833 *Act 3 & 4 Will. IV*, c. 106 § 1 (Act for Amendment of Law of Inheritance), The Words 'the Purchaser' shall mean the Person who last acquired the Land otherwise than by Descent, or than by any Escheat, Partition, or Inclosure.

3. One who purchases for money; a buyer.

1625 MASSINGER *New Way* II. i, I must have all men sellers, and I the only purchaser. 1712 ADDISON *Spect.* No. 511 ¶ 4 The Purchaser..pays down her Price very chearfully. 1849 MACAULAY *Hist. Eng.* iii. I. 371 He was instantly discerned to be a fit purchaser of every thing that nobody else would buy. 1900 E. L. BANKS *Newsp. Girl* 129 Plenty of things are not for sale until a purchaser comes.

Purchasing (pɜ̄·ɹtʃėsiŋ), *vbl. sb.* [-ING[1].] The action of the verb PURCHASE in various senses. In quot. 1747, the gathering of ore from the waste heap: cf. PURCHASER 1 c.

13.. *K. Alis.* 5197 In water and londe [is] his purchaceyng. Boþe hij eteth flesshe and fysshe. 1375 BARBOUR *Bruce* II. 579 And swa thar purchesyng maid thai. 1386 [see PURCHASER 1]. 1494 FABYAN *Chron.* VI. clxx. 164 As they weente in purchasynge of prayes. 1595 in Willis & Clark *Cambridge* (1886) II. 733 Monye..for the purchasing of some competent landes. 1656 EARL MONM. tr. *Boccalini's Advts. fr. Parnass.* II. xxxvi. (1674) 188 The purchasing of Eternity to her name. 1747 HOOSON *Miner's Dict.* S j, Sauntle [is] the first pee or bit of Ore that the Cavers find in a morning by Purchasing. 1800 in Picton *L'pool Munic. Rec.* (1886) II. 193 A fund..for the purchasing Potatoes.

b. *attrib.*, as *purchasing power, value.*

1675 EARL ESSEX *Lett.* (1770) 221, I am not in a purchasing condition. 1861 *Sat. Rev.* XIII. 640/1 If we could suddenly double the whole quantity of sovereigns and their equivalents in England, the purchasing value of each coin would ..be reduced to exactly one half of its former amount. 1863 FAWCETT *Pol. Econ.* II. iv. (1876) 137 The cost of living is augmented, and wages possess less purchasing power.

Purcholis, -ious, obs. forms of PORTCULLIS.

Pur-chop: see PUR[2].

†Purcinct, *sb. Obs.* Also 4 pursaunt, poursent, 4-5 purseynt, 5 -cynct. [a. AF. *purceynt*(*e* = OF. *porceinte*, sb.fem., *porceint*, sb. masc., from *porceindre*:—L. *prōcingĕre*, *prōcinctus*: see next and PROCINCT.] = PRECINCT *sb.*, PROCINCT *sb.*[1]; compass.

[1292 BRITTON VI. v. § 3 Hors de la purceynte del Counté ne est nul tenu a receyvere somounse. 1304 *Year Bk.* 32 *Edw. I*, Trin. Term (Rolls) 261 Dens la purceynt de meisme le bois.] 13.. *E. E. Allit. P.* A. 1034 Vch pane of þat place [the new Jerusalem, *Rev.* xxi. 12] had þre 3atez, So twelue in poursent I con asspye. [Some read *poursent*, and explain as 'pursuit, sequence, order'.] 13.. *Ibid.* B. 1385 Þe place, þat plyed þe pursaunt wyth-inne, Was longe & ful large. 1382 WYCLIF 2 *Kings* xi. 8 3if eny man comme with in the purseynt of the temple, be he slayn. 1437 *Rolls of Parlt.* IV. 503/1 The suburbes and the Purseynt of ye same citee. 1495 *Act 11 Hen. VII*, c. 39 § 1 Viewe of franciplegge within the purcynct of the seid Manoir.

†Purcinct, purseynt, *ppl. a. Obs.* [a. OF. *porceint, -saint* (:—L. *prōcinctus*), pa. pple. of *porceindre*:—L. *prōcingĕre*: see PROCINCT.] Girt about, enclosed; = PRECINCT *ppl. a.*

1303 R. BRUNNE *Handl. Synne* 8914 Ne quest take of endytement Yn holy cherche, oþer 3erde purseynt.

Purcoloys, -culleis, obs. ff. PORTCULLIS.

Purcy, Purcyfant, obs. ff. PURSY, PURSUIVANT.

‖Purdah (pɜ̄·ɹdā). *E. Indies.* Also **purda, pardah, parda** (*erron.* **purdow, purder**). [a. Urdū and Pers. پرده *pardah* veil, curtain.]

1. A curtain; *esp.* one serving to screen women from the sight of men or strangers.

1800 *Misc. Tracts* in *Asiat. Ann. Reg.* 64/1 A purdow, or skreen, of a yellow kind of gauze, being dropt before the door. 1809 LD. VALENTIA *Trav.* I. 100 He led me to a small couch close to the purdah, and seated me on his right hand ..between his mother and himself, though she was invisible. 1844 KINGLAKE *Eöthen* i, They passed through no door, but only by the yielding folds of a purder. a 1858 D. WILSON in *Life* (1860) II. xv. 126 Purdahs or curtains of all colours hung from the crenated arches.

b. As typical of the seclusion of Indian women of rank; hence *fig.* the system of such seclusion.

1865 *Daily Tel.* 25 Nov. 8/6 As an Occidental, she will not like that tame bird's life inside the lattice cage and the pardah which Oriental wives must bear. 1893 W. S. BURRELL & EDITH E. CUTHELL *Indian Mem.* 23 The veil of the purdah hangs less heavily over Mahommedan than over Bengali women. 1905 *19th Cent.* Mar. 486 The purdah has been hardly any drawback to the women born with any talent for ruling.

2. A striped cotton cloth, or other material, of which curtains are made.

1858 SIMMONDS *Dict. Trade*, *Purdah*, an Indian cotton cloth, with white and blue stripes, used for curtains, etc.

3. *attrib.* and *Comb.*, chiefly in reference to sense 1 b, as *purdah lady, walla* [see WALLAH], *woman*; *purdah party, system*; *purdah-like* adj.

1847 MRS. SHERWOOD in *Life* xxi. (1854) 356 Amina was.. particularly dark for a purdah walla, or one, according to the Eastern custom, who is supposed always to sit behind a purdah, or curtain. 1894 S. S. THORBURN *Asiat. Neighbours* iv. 68 Of all his [Peter the Great's] social reforms, the greatest was the abolition of the purdah system for Russian ladies. 1902 *19th Cent.* Nov. 818 Purdah women are a comparatively small proportion of their sex.

Hence **Purdahed** (pɜ̄·ɹdād) *a.*, screened or secluded by a purdah; curtained; 'cloistered'.

1832 MRS. MEER ALI *Observ. Mussulmans India* I. xiv. 380 The hour is passed in lively dialogues with the several purdahed dames.

Pur-dog: see PUR[2].

Purdo·nian. Also -ion, -ium. [f. *Purdon*, name of the introducer.] Trade-name of a form of coal-scuttle.

1851 W. S. BURTON *Trade Catal., Lond. Internat. Exh.*, Purdonion. 1856 H. LOVERIDGE *Trade Catal.*, Purdonian. 1870 *Auction Catalogue* 29 Apr., A cocoanut mat, cinder sifter, japanned purdonium and scoop. 1901 *Ibid.*, An iron curb fender and oak coal purdonium with scoop and liner.

Purdy (pɜ̄·ɹdi), *a. rare.* Now *dial.* Surly, ill-humoured.

1668 SHADWELL *Sullen Lover* v, 'Slife, one shan't speak to you one of these days, you are grown so purdy. 1672 — *Miser* IV, Why you saucy fellow you, what's to do with you? Ha, are you so purdy? a 1825 FORBY *Voc. E. Anglia*, *Purdy*, surly; ill-humoured; self-important.

Pure (piūəɹ), *a.* (*sb., adv.*) Forms: 3-5 pur, 4- pure. (Also 4 pu3r, por(e, 4 (6 *Sc.*) puyr(e, puir(e, 5 poure, 5-6 pewr(e, puer, 6 pour.) [a. OF. *pur*, fem. *pure* (12th c. in Littré), = Pr. *pur*, Sp., It. *puro*:—L. *pūru-s* clean, clear, unmixed, pure, chaste, etc.]

I. In physical sense.

1. a. Not mixed with anything else; free from admixture or adulteration; unmixed, unalloyed; often qualifying names of colours. **b.** *esp.* Not mixed with, or not having in or upon it, anything that defiles, corrupts, or impairs; unsullied, untainted, clean. **c.** Visibly or optically clear, spotless, stainless; in quots. 1481, 1652, clear, transparent. Rarely const. *from.*

(There is a wide range of sense here, but lines of division cannot well be drawn among the quotations, many of which unite more than one shade of meaning.)

1297 R. GLOUC. (Rolls) 184 So clene is al so þat lond & mannes blod so pur [*v. rr.* puir, pure]. *Ibid.* 3178 O cler leom wiþoute mo þer stod fram him wel pur. c 1300 *St. Brandan* 313 Caliz and cruetz, pur cler crestal. 13.. *E. E. Allit. P.* A. 227 So was hit clene & cler & pure, Þat precios perle þer hit was py3t. 1362 LANGL. *P. Pl.* A. IV. 82 A present al of pure Red gold. 1398 TREVISA *Barth. De P. R.* XIII. ii. (Bodl. MS.), To make pitte water clene and pure. 1481 CAXTON *Myrr.* III. vi. 140 The mone is not so pure that the sonne may shyne..thurgh her as thurgh an other sterre. 1590 SPENSER *F. Q.* II. vii. 15 At the well-head the purest streames arise. 1638 JUNIUS *Paint. Ancients* 42 To have his minde..like unto a pure, bright looking-glasse. 1652 GAULE *Magastrom.* 7 One reads them with the pure glass of Gods word: the other by his own false and fallacious perspicils. 1750 GRAY *Elegy* 53 Full many a gem of purest ray serene, The dark unfathom'd caves of ocean bear. 1784 COWPER *Task* II. 508 To filter off a crystal draught Pure from the lees. 1797 *Encycl. Brit.* (ed. 3) XVI. 33/1 There can be but one proper species of red;..all other shades being adulterations of that pure colour, with yellow, brown, &c. 1800 tr. *Lagrange's Chem.* II. 308 If alcohol be re-distilled, and reduced to two-thirds, you will obtain it very pure. This is what is called Rectified Alcohol. 1804 J. GRAHAME *Sabbath* 42 The morning air pure from the city's smoke. 1839 URE *Dict. Arts* 414 A mixture of prussian blue and cochineal pink..in preference to a pure blue. 1853 W. GREGORY *Inorg. Chem.* (ed. 3) 74 In consequence of the great solvent power of water, it is never found pure in nature. 1860 TYNDALL *Glac.* I. xxv. 187 The snow was of the purest white.

†d. Intact, unbroken, perfect, entire. *Obs. rare.*

1607 TOPSELL *Four-f. Beasts* 716 Twenty of these hornes pure, and so many broken.

e. Of a musical sound or voice: Free from roughness, harshness, or discordant quality; smooth, clear: *spec.* in *Mus.* and *Acoustics*, said of tones that are perfectly in tune, i.e. whose vibration-ratios are mathematically exact, so as to give no beats: esp. as opp. to *tempered*.

1872 F. JACOX *Aspects Authorship* iii. 44 The pure and most tuneful voice of Miss Clara Novello. 1873 HALE *In His Name* vi. 49 The voice was a perfectly clear and pure tenor. 1889 J. LECKY in Grove *Dict. Mus.* IV. 70/2 If..all the consonant intervals are made perfectly smooth and pure, so as to give no beats, the tuning is then called Just Intonation.

II. In non-physical or general sense.

2. Without foreign or extraneous admixture; free from anything not properly pertaining to it; simple, homogeneous, unmixed, unalloyed.

Pure naturals: see NATURAL *sb.* 5.

1377 LANGL. *P. Pl.* B. XIII. 166 Þere nys neyther..Pope, ne patriarch þat puyre reson ne schal make þe meyster of alle þo men. 1487 in *Surrey Archæol. Soc. Collect.* III. 163, I Elizabeth Uvedale..in my pure widowhood make and ordain my will. 1614 PURCHAS *Pilgrimage* I. ix. (ed. 2) 47 In the time of Elisa or Dido, the Phœnicean or Punike, which she carried into Africa, was pure Hebrew, as were also their letters. 1642 *Answ. Observ. agst. King* 23 'Tis Adams pure naturalls, impure nature that makes a Subject covet to be a King. 1724 A. COLLINS *Gr. Chr. Relig.* 81 The Sadducees profess'd to follow the pure text of Scripture, or to interpret it according to the literal sense. 1864 BOWEN *Logic* vi. (1870) 148, I know at once, or by Immediate Inference,—that is, by an act of Pure Thought. 1882 MINCHIN *Unipl. Kinemat.* 130 The strain at a point is said to be pure strain if the principal axes (axes of the strain ellipse) are not rotated by the strain.

b. In reference to descent or lineage: Of unmixed descent, pure-blooded.

c 1475 *Rauf Coilȝear* 20 In point thay war to parische, thay proudest men and pure. 1568 GRAFTON *Chron.* II. 286 To people the towne with pure Englishe men. 1827 ROBERTS *Voy. Centr. Amer.* 137 He was an Indian of pure blood. 1853 J. H. NEWMAN *Hist. Sk.* (1873) II. I. i. 24, I consider Attila to have been a pure Hun. 1866 G. MACDONALD *Ann. Q. Neighb.* xxvii, That horse..is very nearly a pure Arab.

c. *Law.* Having no condition annexed; absolute, unconditional. *Pure alms*: cf. ALMOIGN 2.

[Cf. cl. L. *pūrus*, unconditional, absolute; med.L. *pūra* (*et perpetua*) *eleēmosyna* (a 1100), AF. *pure* (*et perpetuele*) *almoigne*; also F. *pur et simple* (Montesquieu 1747).]

1536-7 *Award. conc. St. Bartholomew's Hosp., Oxford* 3 Feb., The which said Hospital, King Edward the third.. gave and granted unto the predecessors of the said Provost and Scholars [of Oriel]..in free pure and perpetual alms. 1713 *Act 13 Anne*, c. 6 § 8 To have and to hold the said Canonship or Prebend to the said Colwell Brickenden..and his Successors..in pure and perpetual Alms. 1818 COLEBROOKE *Obligations* 151 [If] one be conditional or deferred for a term, while the other is a pure and simple engagement. 1880 MUIRHEAD *Gaius* II. § 244 Sabinus and Cassius think that a conditional legacy to him is valid, but not a pure one.

d. Of a subject of study or practice: Restricted to that which essentially belongs to it; not including its relations with kindred or connected subjects. (Often denoting the simply theoretical part of a subject, apart from its practical applications, as in *pure mathematics*; opp. to APPLIED 2, MIXED 7.) Also said of a student or practitioner who confines himself to one particular subject or branch of a subject.

1641 WILKINS *Math. Magick* I. ii. (1648) 12 Mathematicks ..is usually divided into pure and mixed; and though the pure doe handle only abstract quantity..that which is mixed doth consider the quantity of some particular determinate subject. 1750 JOHNSON *Rambler* No. 14 ¶ 5 The difference between pure science, which has to do only with ideas, and the application of its laws to the use of life. 1858 MAYNE *Expos. Lex.* s. v., In England..the profession is ostensibly divided into three distinct branches, viz. *pure* physicians, or those who profess to act only in medical cases; *pure* surgeons, or those who practise surgery alone; and surgeon-apothecaries, or general practitioners. 1883 *Encycl. Brit.* XV. 752/2 Pure Mechanism, or Applied Kinematics: being the theory of machines considered simply as modifying motion. 1903 R. B. CARTER *Doctors & Work* i. 4 A small number of operating, or so-called 'pure' surgeons. *Mod.* He is a pure physicist; he does not know chemistry.

e. *Logic.* Of a proposition or syllogism: opp. to MODAL *a.* 4.

1697 tr. *Burgersdicius his Logic* I. xxviii. 112 A Pure Enunciation is that in which it is not express'd how the Parts cohere...Modal, in which it is. *Ibid.* II. xiv. 60 A Pure [Syllogism] is that which consists of Propositions pure. ..Modal either of one or both Modal. 1725 WATTS *Logic* II. ii. § 4 When a proposition merely expresses that the predicate is connected with the subject, it is called a *pure proposition*; as, every true christian is an honest man: But when it includes also the way and manner wherein the predicate is connected with the subject, it is called a *modal proposition*; as, when I say, it is necessary that a true christian should be an honest man. 1827, 1870 [see MODAL *a.* 4].

f. *Gram.* (*a*) In Greek (καθαρός), of a vowel: Preceded by another vowel. Of the stem of a word: Ending in a vowel. Of a consonant (as *s*): Not accompanied by another consonant. (*b*) In Arabic, etc., of a syllable: Ending in a vowel, open.

1650 E. REEVE *Introd. Gr. Tongue* 24 Nounes ending in δα, θα, ρα, or pure α, do make the Genitive in ας. *Ibid.*, Adjectives in ις, having or not pure [e.g. εὐνατρις, εὐνάτριδος]. 1776 J. RICHARDSON *Arab. Gram.* v. 14 [Syllables] are divided into *pure* and *mixed*; the pure consisting only of one consonant and one vowel,..the mixed of two consonants joined by a vowel. 1818 BLOMFIELD tr. *Matthiæ's Gr. Gram.* I. 218 Verbs pure, whose final syllable ω is preceded by a diphthong. 1870 E. ABBOTT tr. *Curtius' Gr. Gram.* I. vi. 57 In the formation of the acc. sing. of Masc. and Fem., the

true vowel-nature of the stem declares itself, πόλι-ν, πολύ-ν; and the voc. sing...contains the pure vowel stem.

3. Taken by itself, with nothing added; ... and nothing else; nothing but ..., nothing besides ..., no more than ...; mere, simple.

Often in phr. *pure and simple*, following the sb. (cf. 2 c).

1297 R. GLOUC. (Rolls) 794 He isei þat he moste attenende Vor pur meseise vorfare. c 1375 *Sc. Leg. Saints* ii. (*Paulus*) 1026 For pure pytte & loy þai gret. c 1400 MAUNDEV. (Roxb.) xxxii. 144 Many..diez for pure elde withouten sekenes. 1494 FABYAN *Chron.* v. cvii. 81 The .ii. sonnes of Mordred were constrayned of pure force to seche stronge holdes for theyr refuge. 1593 SHAKS. 2 *Hen. VI*, II. i. 157 Alas Sir, we did it for pure need. 1639 FULLER *Holy War* IV. xix, Knowing no more how to sway a sceptre then a pure clown to manage a sword. 1724 A. COLLINS *Gr. Chr. Relig.* 79 This distinction is the pure invention of those who make the objection. 1861 M. PATTISON *Ess.* (1889) I. 38 His delay in setting out was due to pure procrastination and dilatoriness. 1875 JOWETT *Plato* (ed. 2) I. 29 That of which we are speaking is knowledge pure and simple.

b. In emphatic or intensive sense: Nothing short of ..., absolute, sheer, thorough, utter, perfect, complete.

1297 R. GLOUC. (Rolls) 1917 He was..pur mesel þo & he bicom in is baptizinge hol of al is wo. c 1400 *Destr. Troy* 1817 Pelleus..sourdit into soure greme, And Priam reprouyt as a pure fole. 1472-3 *Rolls of Parlt.* VI. 36/1 Contynuyng alwey in his pure malice and envy. 1611 CHAPMAN *May-Day* v. Plays (1889) 303/1 His master hath such a pure belief in his wife, that he's apt to believe any good of her. 1794 GODWIN *Cal. Williams* 182, I believed that misery more pure than that which I now endured had never fallen to the lot of a human being. 1870 RUSKIN *Let.* in *Athenæum* 30 Sept. (1905) 428/3 Dickens was a pure modernist—a leader of the steam-whistle party *par excellence*. 1908 BUCHAN *Watcher by Threshold* 145 A lot of pure nonsense.

†c. That is the thing itself, not something else; true, real, genuine; very. *Obs.*

1297 R. GLOUC. (Rolls) 2308 He..sede he was purost eyr to be icrouned to kinge. *Ibid.* 6603 In a toun in barcssire.. out of þe erþe pur blod sprong ywis. 13.. *E. E. Allit. P.* B. 704 Wel ny3e pure paradys mo3t preue no better. c 1386 CHAUCER *Knt.'s T.* 421 The pure fettres of his shynes grete Weren of his bittre salte teeres wete. c 1400 *Laud Troy Bk.* 6636 He..persed his Armure,..That it come to his flessche pure. 1534 MORE *Comf. agst. Trib.* I. Wks. 1162/2 Til the pure panges of death pulled their heart fro their play.

III. Free from corruption or defilement.

4. Free from admixture of anything debasing or deteriorating; unadulterated, uncorrupted, uncontaminated; conforming accurately to a standard of quality or style; faultless, correct.

13.. *K. Alis.* 84 Thus he asaied the regiouns, That him cam for to assaile:—In puyr maner of bataile. 1390 GOWER *Conf.* II. 214 Mi ladi..is the pure hed and welle And Mirour and ensample of goode. 1526 TINDALE *Jas.* I. 27 Pure devocion and undefiled. 1540 PALSGR. *Acolastus* Ep. to King A iij b, In suche places of your realme as the pureste englyshe is spoken. 1617 MORYSON *Itin.* I. 182 At Geneua many French Gentlemen and Students comming thither..did speake pure French. 1768 GIBBON *Decl. & F.* I. (1838) V. 21 The purest disciples of Zoroaster escaped from the contagion of idolatry. 1849 MACAULAY *Hist. Eng.* ii. I. 165 They had been oppressed, and oppression had kept them a pure body. 1882 PEBODY *Eng. Journalism* xvi. 124 His taste, if severe, was pure.

5. Free from moral defilement or corruption; of unblemished character or nature; unstained or untainted with evil; guiltless, innocent; guileless, sincere. Rarely const. †*of* (obs.), *from* (arch.). Often absol., *the pure* (*sc.* persons).

a 1340 HAMPOLE *Psalter* xiii. 4 He..þat is pure in werkis and clen in thoghtis. 1481 CAXTON *Myrr.* I. xiv. 48 To saue his sowle whiche God hath lent to hym pure and clene to thende that he shold rendre it such agayn. 1526 TINDALE *Matt.* v. 8 Blessed are the pure in herte. *Ibid.*, *Acts* xx. 26, I am pure from the bloud of all men. *Ibid.*, *Titus* i. 15 Unto the pure are all thynges pure. 1667 MILTON *P. L.* VIII. 506 Nature her self, though pure of sinful thought. 1719 WATTS *Hymns* I. lxxxvi, How should the sons of Adam's race Be pure before their God? 1790 PALEY *Horæ Paul.* Concl., His morality is everywhere calm, pure, and rational. 1849 MACAULAY *Hist. Eng.* vii. II. 171 A friendship as warm and pure as any that ancient or modern history records. 1851 TENNYSON *To Queen* vii, Her court was pure; her life serene. 1855 MACAULAY *Hist. Eng.* xiii. III. 265 He protested.. that his hands were pure from the blood of the persecuted Covenanters.

†b. Applied mockingly to Puritans; also to Quakers. *Obs.*

1598 MARSTON *Sco. Villanie* I. i, Lucia, new set thy ruffe; tut, thou art pure, Canst thou not lispe 'good brother', looke demure? 1602 B. JONSON *Poetaster* IV. i, To helpe 'hem to some pure landresses, out of the citie. 1785 G. A. BELLAMY *Apology* II. 45 My mother, from being one of the pure ones, had changed her religion to that of a methodist.

6. Sexually undefiled; chaste.

c 1430 LYDG. *Min. Poems* (Percy Soc.) 8 Alle clad in white, in tokyn of clennes, Lyke pure virgines. 1588 A. KING tr. *Canisius' Catech.* in *Cath. Tractates* (S.T.S.) 209 That blissit Marie remaines still puir virgine. 1591 SHAKS. 1 *Hen. VI*, v. iv. 83 And yet forsooth she is a Virgin pure. 1671 MILTON *P. R.* I. 134. 1771 tr. *Horstius' Parad. Soul* App. 21 Hail you, the Sea's bright Star, Who God's pure Mother are. 1904 *Hymns A. & M.* No. 55 A maiden pure and undefiled Is by the Spirit great with child.

7. Free from ceremonial defilement; fit for sacred service or use; 'clean'.

1611 BIBLE *Ezra* vi. 20 The Priestes and the Leuites were purified together, all of them were pure, and killed the Passeouer. 1613 PURCHAS *Pilgrimage* II. xvi. (1614) 159 His [a Jew's] wife hath prepared his dinner, pure meats purely dressed.

IV. 8. *slang* or *colloq.* (?orig. *ironical*). A general term of appreciation: Fine, excellent, capital, jolly, nice, splendid. Now *rare* or *Obs.*

1675 WYCHERLEY *Country Wife* III. i, I was quiet enough till my husband told me what pure lives the London ladies live abroad with their dancing, meeting and junketing. 1695 CONGREVE *Love for L.* v. ii, O I have pure news, I can tell you, pure news. a 1720 VANBRUGH *Journ. to London* I. ii, A slice of it [goose pie] before supper to-night would have been pure. 1734 MRS. DELANY in *Life & Corr.* (1861) I. 508 Well, is it not pure that we shall meet in a fortnight? 1747 GARRICK *Miss in her Teens* II, The door's double locked, and I have the key in my pocket. *Biddy.* That's pure. 1884 HENLEY & STEVENSON *Deacon Brodie* I. iii. Sc. 3 (1892) 35 O, such manners are pure, pure, pure!

b. In conjunction with another adj.: *Pure and ...* = nice and ..., fine and ...; excellently, satisfactorily; thoroughly (= C. 1: cf. 2 above). Now *dial.* (See AND *conj.* 4.)

1742 FIELDING *Jos. Andrews* II. xiv, They [*sc.* hogs] were all pure and fat. 1788 CHARLOTTE SMITH *Emmeline* (1816) IV. 271 You would have been pure and happy to drive about in a one-horse chaise. 1769 ROMAINE *Let.* 27 Oct. (1795) xxvii. 122, I saw Lady H— —, who was pure and well. 1865 *Let. to Editor*, In answer to the question 'How do you do?' in Cornwall..they say 'Pure and well, thank you'.

c. *dial.* Quite well, in good health: = PURELY 4 b.

1854 *N. & Q.* 1st Ser. IX. 527/1 The word pure is commonly used in Gloucestershire to express being in good health... 'I hope, Zur, the ladies be all pure.' 1900 *Eng. Dial. Dict.*

B. *sb.* (or *absol.*)

1. That which is pure; purity. *poet.*

a 1625 LODGE *Misc. Pieces* ii. Wks. 1883 IV, Her eies shrowd pitie, pietie, and pure. 1667 MILTON *P. L.* VIII. 627 Union of Pure with Pure. 1873 BROWNING *Red Cott. Nt.-cap* II. 735 How heaven's own pure may seem To blush. 1874 TENNYSON *Vivien* 35 The mask of pure Worn by this court. 1898 G. MEREDITH *Odes Fr. Hist.* 6 Earth's warrior Best To win Heaven's Pure.

†2. 'Pured' fur: see PURED 2, PUREE[1]. *Obs.*

1512 *Acc. Ld. High Treas. Scot.* IV. 213 For lyning of the said Tanne weluus goune within with puyr.

†3. A kept mistress. *Obs. slang.*

1688 SHADWELL *Sqr. Alsatia* II. i, Where's..the Blowing, that is to be my Natural, my Convenient, my Pure. a 1700 B. E. *Dict. Cant. Crew*, *Pure*, a Mistress. 1725 in *New Cant. Dict.*

4. A 'pure' physician or surgeon; see the adj., sense 3 d. *Med. colloq.*

1827 *Lancet* 15 Dec. 434/2 Do the Pures profess a kind of surgery in the abstract? 1843 SIR J. PAGET *Let.* 19 Dec. in *Mem.* vi. (1901) 148 The election of the pures in London was not I am told general. [*Note*, The 'pures' were the surgeons in consulting practice.]

†5. [Cf. PURE *v.* 1 b.] *Tanning.* Dogs' dung or other substance used as an alkaline lye for steeping hides. Also in *comb.* as *pure-collector, -finder, -finding*. (Also spelt *pewer, puer*.)

1851 MAYHEW *Lond. Labour* II. 142 Dogs'-dung is called 'Pure', from its cleansing and purifying properties. *Ibid.*, The name of 'Pure-finders'..has been applied to the men engaged in collecting dogs'-dung from the..streets. *Ibid.*, There are about 30 tanyards..and these all have their regular Pure collectors. 1858 SIMMONDS *Dict. Trade*, *Puer*, a tanner's name for dogs' dung. *Ibid.*, *Pure, Pewer*.

C. *adv.*

1. Absolutely, entirely, thoroughly, quite.

In early use from sense 3 b of the adj.; in 18th c. *slang* or *colloq.*, from sense 8 b; now *dial.* or *Obs.*

1297 R. GLOUC. (Rolls) 1542 He bicom sone þer after pur gidy & wod. 1340 HAMPOLE *Pr. Consc.* 2499 He says 'our ille dedys er pur ille wroght, Bot our gud dedis pur gud er noght'. c 1394 *P. Pl. Crede* 170 Þe pris of a plou3-lond.. To apparaile þat pyler were pure lytel. c 1491 CAXTON *Chast. Goddes Chyld.* 89 It is pure easy..to folow god and serue hym in tyme of tranquylite. 1560 DAUS tr. *Sleidane's Comm.* 37 This yere [1522] departed Reucline, a pure aged man [*ætate gravis*]. 1710 SWIFT *Jrnl. to Stella* 23 Sept., Ballygall will be a pure good place for air. 1750 *Let.* 29 May in *Mrs. Delany's Life & Corr.* (1861) II. 548 Your amiable and worthy sister is pure well. 1810 *Splendid Follies* I. 78 The course will be pure swampy in some parts.

2. Purely, in various senses; simply, merely; rightly; chastely. *poet. rare.*

c 1460 G. ASHBY *Dicta Philos.* 590 A kynge shude be right besy and studious To gouerne his Roiaulme & his people pure. 1601 SHAKS. *Twel. N.* V. i. 86 For his sake, Did I expose my selfe (pure for his loue) Into the danger. 1602 — *Ham.* III. iv. 158 O throw away the worser part of it, And liue the purer with the other halfe.

3. Qualifying an adj. of colour (chiefly *white*): Purely, with no admixture of any other colour.

(Not always clearly distinguishable from *pure* adj.: cf. a pure white rose: a rose which colour is a pure white.)

1297 R. GLOUC. (Rolls) 182 So clene & vair & pur 3wit among oþere men hii beþ. 1530 PALSGR. 259/2 Pure white sylke, *soye bissine*. 1611 SHAKS. *Wint. T.* III. iii. 22. a 1618 SYLVESTER *Spectacles* xxxiv, The Lily (first) pure-whitest Flow'r of any. 1853 W. GREGORY *Inorg. Chem.* (ed. 3) 256 Gold is distinguished by its pure yellow colour.

D. *Comb.*: **a.** parasynthetic, as *pure-blooded, -bosomed, -coloured, -eyed, -mannered, -minded, -sighted*, etc. **b.** adverbial and complemental, as *pure-bred, -driven, -living, -washed.*

1886 C. SCOTT *Sheep-Farming* 157 Breeding *pure-blooded rams for sale. 1868 *Rep. U.S. Commissioner Agric.* (1869) 10 Specimens of *pure-bred domestic fowls. 1634 MILTON *Comus* 213 O welcom *pure-ey'd Faith, white-handed Hope, ..And thou unblemish't form of Chastity. 1896 ARR. BENSON in *Nat. Church* Feb. 51/2 Pray we for a temperate, a *pure-living people. 1819 SHELLEY *Peter Bell* VI. xxxiv, The most sublime, religious, *Pure-minded poet. 1596

SPENSER *Hymn Heavenly Love* 276 All earthes glorie.. [will] Seeme durt and drosse in thy *pure-sighted eye. 1801 BLOOMFIELD *Rural T.* 86 On the *pure-wash'd sand.

Pure, *v.* [a. OF. *purer*:—L. *pūrāre* to purify (with religious rites), f. *pūrus* PURE.]

†1. *trans.* To make pure; to cleanse, purify, refine (*lit.* and *fig.*). *Obs.* exc. as in b.

c 1340 HAMPOLE *Prose Tr.* 16 Þat saule þat es purede in þe fyre of lufe of Godd. 13.. *E. E. Allit. P.* B. 1116 Þou may..pure þe with penaunce tyl þou a perle worþe. c 1400 MAUNDEV. (Roxb.) xxxiii. 149 Þe whilk pissemyres kepez bisily and pures þe gold and disseuerez þe fyne gold fra þe vnfyne. c 1460 G. ASHBY *Dicta Philos.* 90 Ye must pure youre selfe fyrst withoute blame. 1581 T. HOWELL *Devises* (1879) 217 As fyre by heate the Golde doth fine and pure. 1608 MIDDLETON *Fam. Love* III. iii, If you be unclean..you may pure yourself. 1635 HEYWOOD *Hierarch.* v. 242 The Light, pur'd and refin'd.

b. *Tanning.* To cleanse (hides) by steeping them in a bate or alkaline lye. (Cf. PURE *sb.* 5.)

1883 *Workshop Receipts* Ser. II. 366/2 They [calf-skins] are then unhaired and fleshed in the usual manner, pured with a bate of dog's dung. 1907 *Camb. Mod. Hist. Prospectus* 100 Bating or puring as it is called, is a process by which all but a very small amount of the natural grease is removed from the skin.

†2. (?) *intr.* To become pure. *rare.*

c 1315 SHOREHAM *Poems* I. 67 And aldey he to senne falleþ, Her ne moje nau3t pury Of serewnessche.

Pure, obs. form of PORE *v.*, POOR.

Pureanis, i.e. *pure anis*: see PUIRANIS.

Pure-blind(e, obs. forms of PURBLIND.

†Pured, *ppl. a.* (*sb.*) *Obs.* Also 5 purid, -yd. [f. PURE *v.* + -ED[1].]

1. Purified, cleansed; refined.

13.. *Gaw. & Gr. Knt.* 633 Gawan was for gode knawen, & as golde pured. c 1400 MAUNDEV. (1839) xx. 217 Bordured alle abouté with pured Gold. c 1430 LYDG. *Min. Poems* (Percy Soc.) 173 Wedyde the cokkelle frome the puryd corne. 1509 HAWES *Past. Pleas.* xvii. K j b, Mercury..About the ayre castinge his pured lyght. 1513 *Bradshaw's St. Werburge, Balade to Auctour* (E.E.T.S.) 200 This delicious werke Thus surely sette by pured science.

2. Of fur: Trimmed or cut down so as to show one colour only. (Cf. PURE *a.* 1 a.)

Pured gris or *grey*, the grey fur of the back of the squirrel in winter, without any of the white of the belly. *Pured calabre, miniver*, the white belly part of these furs, with the dark or grey sides trimmed off. (Cf. also b, and PUREE.)

Beside pured miniver (*minutus varius puratus, menever puree*), the 14-16th c. records have also *m. v. dimidio puratus*, half-pured miniver, in which a narrow strip of the grey colour was left at the edges. (John Hodgkin.)

13.. *Gaw. & Gr. Knt.* 154 With pelure pured apert þe pane ful clene. *Ibid.* 1738 In a mery mantyle..furred ful fyne with feller, wel pured. [1363 *Rolls of Parlt.* II. 279 Et q'ils ne usent..Cloche, Mantel, ne Goune, fururez de menevoir purez.] c 1420 *Chron. Vilod.* cccxxxi, Þe mantyl þᵗ was furuyd wᵗ puryd gray. c 1450 *Brut* 434 Thanne was don on the Bisshop an abbite..of fyne Scarlet furrid with purid werke. 1463-4 *Rolls of Parlt.* V. 505 Their wyfes, may use and were the forseid Furres of Mattrones, Funes, Letyce, pured Grey, or pured Menyver. 1503 *Acc. Ld. High Treas. Scot.* II. 221 Payit to Pyeris Mainiryng, Maister of the Quenis wardrob, for vj tymir of pured calabar to the samyn, ilk tymir xxxiiijs. 1505 *Ibid.* III. 43 For xvj bakkis of pured gray; ilk pece xvjd.

b. *ellipt.* as *sb.* 'Pured' miniver: cf. next.

c 1435 *Chron. London* (1905) 95 Ther was putte vpon the bisshop a cardynall habyte off Skarlette furred with puredd. c 1450 *Ibid.* 131 A fferrys coope of ffyne scarlett flurred with puryd. c 1450 LOVELICH *Merlin* 4460 In the kynges tyme ..that aftyr the schal regnen in pured & palle.

‖Puree[1], purray. *Obs.* Also 4 purree, 5 purry. [a. AF. *purée*, for F. *puré*, pa. pple. of F. *purer*: see PURE *v.*] = PURED 2 b, i.e. pured or pure white miniver, the belly fur of the grey squirrel in winter, used in the furring of garments.

(In the London Letter Bks. in AF. form *puree*; in 15th c. Sc. as *puray, purray*.)

1351 *Lett. Bk. F. Lond.* lf. 208 Furree de Pellure come de meneueyr, Gris, Purree, Destranlyng, Popell' Desquirels, Bys des Conyns des leures. 1365 *Lett. Bk. G. Lond.* lf. 162 b, Item q' nul del mister enremettre ventres de calabre en furours de puree [in Lett. Bk. H. lf. 39 *in fururis puratis*] ne de menever ne de Bissh [tr. in Riley *Mem. Lond.* (1868) 329 No one of the trade shall mingle bellies of calabre with furs of puree, or of minever, or of bisshes]. 1429 *Sc. Acts Jas. I* (1814) II. 18 Þat na man sal weir clathis of silk na furringis of mertrikis, funȝeis, puray, na grece, na nane oþir riche furring bot allanirly knychtis [etc.]. 1455 *Sc. Acts Jas. II* ibid. 43 The vþir lordis of parliament to haif ane mantill of rede rycht sa oppinnit befor and lynyt with silk or furryt with cristy gray, grece, or purray, togiddir with ane hude of the sammyn clath, and furryt as saide is.

‖Purée[2] (pürē). Rarely in anglicized form **pu·ry.** [F. *purée* (*puree de pois* pea-soup, 1314 in Hatz.-Darm.), of uncertain and disputed origin.

Hatz.-Darm. take *purée* as the ppl. sb. from the OF. vb. *purer*, in sense 'to squeeze, press out'. Others would identify it with OF. *porée* (see PORRAY), from which it cannot always be separated in sense; cf. med.L. *purea, pureya*, as well as *porea* (1231 in Du Cange), in sense 'pea-soup'. See Scheler, Littré, Brachet.]

A kind of broth or soup made of vegetables, meat, or fish, boiled to a pulp and passed through a sieve. Also *fig.*

1824 BYRON *Juan* XV. lxxi, Alas! I must leave undescribed the gibier, The salmi, the consommé, the *purée* [*rime* way]. 18.. — *Let. to Bowles* Wks. (1846) 603/2 *note*, This stanza contains the *purée* of the whole philosophy of Epi-

curus. 1887 G. R. SIMS *Mary Jane's Mem.* 84 Mutton cutlets fried in cod liver oil with pury. 1896 *Allbutt's Syst. Med.* I. 392 Pounded fish may be cautiously given, pounded mutton or beef in purée. 1897 *Ibid.* II. 521 A purée of potato.

Purel(l, Sc. var. PORAIL *Obs.*, poor people.

Purely (piū·ɹli), *adv.* [f. PURE *a.* + -LY[2].] In a pure manner or degree: in various senses.

1. Without (physical) admixture, esp. of anything that stains or impairs; cleanly, clearly, spotlessly.

1509 HAWES *Past. Pleas.* XX. (Percy Soc.) 97 The fayre carbuncle, so ful of clerenes, That in thee truely dyd moost purely shyne. c 1600 DRAYTON *Elegy to Lady I. S.* 65 The Sunnes rayes..Bent on some obiect, which is purely white. 1824 MISS MITFORD *Village* Ser. I. (1863) 120 The purely grey rouleau..showed its mixture of black and white. 1864 TENNYSON *Aylmer's Field* 458 The soft river-breeze..on him breathed Far purelier in his rushings to and fro.

†b. So as to make pure or clean; so as to cleanse. *Obs.*

1576 BAKER *Jewell of Health* 232 b, Washe dilygentlye and purelie the bodie. 1611 BIBLE *Isa.* I. 25, I will..purely purge away thy drosse. 1669 WORLIDGE *Syst. Agric.* 27 It may be purely separated from its Husk by a Mill. 1683 MOXON *Mech. Exerc., Printing* xi. ¶ 13 These Ribs must be purely Smooth-fil'd and Pollish'd.

2. Without mixture of anything different (in non-physical or general sense); simply, merely; exclusively, solely; ... and nothing else: often implying 'entirely' (cf. b, and ENTIRELY 3).

c 1350 *Will. Palerne* 4219 We alle..neuer-more for no man mowe be deliuered..but purli þourh 3our help. c 1380 WYCLIF *Wks.* (1880) 47 Þat þei putte not glosis vnto þe reule..but..sympliche and pureliche to seie & to write þe reule. c 1450 tr. *De Imitatione* II. v. 45 Lete no þyng be gret or hye or acceptable to þe, but purely god. 1552 HULOET, Purely, *liquido, mere, pure, puriter, Syncere.* 1662 J. DAVIES tr. *Mandelslo's Trav.* 5 Whether they had been..set there in the air purely for show. 1710 BERKELEY *Princ. Hum. Knowl.* § 122 Reasonings and controversies purely verbal. 1883 GILMOUR *Mongols* xxxi. 362 The Government duty they have to perform seems to be purely formal. 1890 *Academy* 8 Nov. 415/2 There were..no children of origin purely Egyptian.

†b. Of degree or extent: Absolutely, thoroughly, perfectly, completely, fully, utterly, entirely. *Obs.*

1297 R. GLOUC. (Rolls) 1512 Þe king louede is wif anon so purliche & so vaste þat al is herte onliche on hire on he caste. 1377 LANGL. *P. Pl.* B. XIII. 260 Ne [may] masse make pees amonges cristene peple, Tyl pruyde be pureliche fordo. c 1400-50 *Alexander* 167 And þe province of Persee purely distruye. 1585 J. HILTON *Recant.* in Fuller *Ch. Hist.* (1655) x. vi. § 27 The said Errours..I utterly abjure, forsake, and purely renounce. a 1656 HALES *Gold. Rem.* III. *Serm.*, etc. (1673) 44 A Gentleman..purely ignorant, yet greatly desirous to seem learned.

†c. Really, actually, truly, genuinely. *Obs.*

1297 R. GLOUC. (Rolls) 3323 Icholle make þi sulue..Abbe al þe fourme of þe erl as þou were purliche he. 1393 LANGL. *P. Pl.* C. XVI. 226 He haþ the power þat seynt peter hadde, He haþ pureliche þe pot with þe same salue.

d. *Law.* Without conditions, unconditionally.

1427 *Rolls of Parlt.* IV. 327/1 Yᵉ open declaration..subscribed pureli and simply. a 1661 FULLER *Worthies* (1662) I. 183 This his gift was a gift indeed, purely bestowed on the colledge, as loded with no detrimentall Conditions. 1880 MUIRHEAD *Gaius* III. § 113 If I have stipulated purely, he may stipulate conditionally.

3. Without mixture of anything deteriorating or debasing; without blemish, corruption, baseness, or uncleanness; faultlessly; properly, rightly, correctly; guilelessly, innocently, chastely.

1526 *Pilgr. Perf.* (W. de W. 1531) 158 To behaue you purely, &..to apply yourselfe to labour in the seruyce of god. 1537 (*title*) The Byble, whych is all the holy Scripture: In whych are contayned the Olde and Newe Testament truelye and purely translated into Englishe by Thomas Matthewe. 1606 SHAKS. *Tr. & Cr.* IV. v. 169 Faith and troth, Strain'd purely from all hollow bias drawing. 1674 T. FLATMAN *To Mr. Faithorn* 6 One line speaks purelier Thee, than my best strain. 1823 BYRON *Juan* XIV. xcii, Or Germany, where people *purely* kiss.

b. So as to be ceremonially clean.

1613 [see PURE *a.* 7].

4. *slang* or *colloq.* Finely, excellently, capitally; nicely, satisfactorily, very well. Now *rare* or *Obs.*

1695 CONGREVE *Love for L.* II. ii, You can keep your countenance purely, you'd make an admirable player. 1712-13 SWIFT *Jrnl. to Stella* 1 Jan., Am I not purely handled between a couple of puppies? 1756 A. MURPHY *Apprentice* II. ii, That will do purely. a 1845 HOOD *Last Man* xxi, To see me so purely drest.

b. *dial.* Quite well, in good health. (Used predicatively like an adj.; cf. *well, ill, poorly.*)

1809 MAR. EDGEWORTH *Absentee* xvi. (*Tales* 1825 X. 321), If the ladies' prayers are of any avail, you ought to be purely. 1828 *Craven Gloss.* (ed. 2) s.v., 'How's thy mam?' 'Purely, thank ye.' 1857 HUGHES *Tom Brown* I. ii, Well I never! you do look purely. 1859 THACKERAY *Virgin.* xxxiv, 'I hope the dear ladies are well, sir?' 'The ladies are purely.'

Pureness (piū·ɹnės). [f. PURE *a.* + -NESS.] The quality of being pure; purity.

1. Freedom from admixture; simplicity, homogeneity.

c 1485 *Digby Myst.* (1882) III. 322 Þis soft metell led, nat of so gret puernesse. a 1618 RALEIGH (J.), An essence..of absolute pureness and simplicity. 1675 R. VAUGHAN *Coinage* 14 A proof of the pureness of the metal. 1695 LD. PRESTON *Boeth.* v. 240 His knowledg..remaineth in the Pureness & Simplicity of its Presence.

2. Freedom from defilement or blemish; cleanness; faultlessness, correctness.

1528 PAYNELL *Salerne's Regim.* O ij b, Many fynnes and skales betoken the purenes of the fysshes substance. a 1568 ASCHAM *Scholem.* II. (Arb.) 144 In all this good proprietie of wordes, and purenesse of phrases which be in Terence. a 1698 TEMPLE *Ess. A. & M. Learn.* Wks. 1760 I. 157 Great Pureness of Air, and Equality of Climate.

3. Freedom from moral blemish; innocence; sincerity; chastity.

1398 TREVISA *Barth. De P. R.* XIV. xxxv. (1495) 480 Mount Synay hyghte the mount of purenesse and of clennesse, for none myght come to the mount but those that were clene in bodi and in soule. 1526 TINDALE 2 *Cor.* I. 12 With godly purenes. 1591 SPENSER *Daphn.* xxx, She in purenesse heauen it self did pas. 1624 QUARLES *Sion's Sonn.* xv. 7 Virgin purenes. 1708 H. DODWELL *Nat. Mort. Hum. Souls* 149 To manage all Disputes..with..Pureness from Humane Passions. 1840 CLOUGH *Dipsychus* I. ii. 41 And thou, clear heaven, Look pureness back into me.

4. Ceremonial cleanness.

[Cf. quot. 1398 in 3.] 1607 *Schol. Disc. agst. Antichr.* I. ii. 78 Holy purenes from all communion with vncleane Gentiles. 1643 MILTON *Divorce* II. vi. Wks. 1851 IV. 77 Inflicting death..for the mark of a circumstantiall purenes omitted.

Purete, -ty, obs. forms of PURITY.

Purfle (pɜ̄·ɹf'l), *sb.* Forms: 4 porfyl, -fil, purf(i)el, 4-5 purfil(e, -fyle, 4-6 -fyl, 5-6 -fell, -full, 6 -ful, -fyll, -fele, -phell, 6- purfle. Also (in sense 2) 6 purflue; (in sense 3) 7 porfil(e, -phile, 7-8 pourfil. See also PROFILE. [a. OF. *porfil* (c 1215 in Godef.), later *pourfil* (1316, and 1611 in Cotgr. in sense 2), a border or edge; = Pr. *perfil*, Sp. *perfilo*, med.L. *perfilum*, It. *profilo*, PROFILE; prob. verbal sb. from *profilare, perfilāre*, etc.: see PURFLE *v.*]

1. A border; *esp.* a wrought or decorated border; the embroidered border or edge of a garment.

In ordinary use app. obs. after 1610; revived as an archaism in 19th c. (But cf. quot. c 1758 in PURFLE *v.* 1.)

13.. *E. E. Allit. P.* A. 216 Of precios perle in porfyl pyȝte. 1362 LANGL. *P. Pl.* A. IV. 102 Til..perneles porfyl [*v. rr.* purfil, purfyl] be put in heore whucche. c 1430 LYDG. *Min. Poems* (Percy Soc.) 37 A lewde wretche to were a skarlet gowne, Withe a blac lamb furre without purfile of sable. c 1440 *Promp. Parv.* 416/2 Purfyle of a clothe, *limbus*. a 1450 *Knt. de la Tour* (1906) 30 This astate that ye use of gret purfiles and slitte cotes. 1530 PALSGR. 259/2 Purfyll or hemme of a gowne, *bort*. a 1548 HALL *Chron., Hen. VIII* 2 b, The Trapper of his Horse, Damaske gold, with a depe purfell of Armyns. 1609 HOLLAND *Amm. Marcell.* XIV. vi. 10 Inner garments..beset with long jagges and purfles. 1610 — *Camden's Brit.* II. *Irel.* 148 They cast ouer these their mantells or shagge Rugges..with a deep fringed purfle. 1731 BAILEY, *Purfle*, a Sort of antient Trimming for Womens Gowns, made of Tinsel, Thread, &c., called also Bobbin-Work. 1813 HOGG *Queen's Wake* 292 Furnaced pillars..upright ranged in horrid array, With purfle of green o'er the darksome gray. 1821 JOANNA BAILLIE *Met. Leg., Lady G. Baillie* Concl., Betty's skill Leaves her in purfle, furbelow, or frill, No whit behind. 1894 *Athenæum* 5 May 571/2 The portrait of the gracious court lady in her ruff and purfles.

b. = PURFLING 1 c (as of a violin).

1706 PHILLIPS (ed. Kersey), *Purfle*..Also a kind of Ornamentation about the Edges of Musical Instruments, particularly of Viols, Violins, &c. 1905 HAWEIS *Old Violins* 125 He runs his purfle into his monogram with attendant flourishes.

†2. *Her.* A bordering line. *Obs.*

1562 LEIGH *Armorie* (1597) 90 b, This pale was giuen after it had a chiefe; because they were both of one colour, there goeth no purfle betweene. 1572 BOSSEWELL *Armorie* II. 27 That terme is so frequented, because two colors, or any mettal or colour, be gradately inferred one into the other, that no partition but onely the Purflue maie be seene betwene them.

†3. The contour or outline of anything; a representation of the outline; = PROFILE *sb.* 1, 3. *Obs.*

In this sense app. a new adoption from Fr., and there from It. Soon superseded by *profile*.

1601 HOLLAND *Pliny* XXXV. x. II. 535 Hee woon the prise and praise from them all in making up the pourfils and extremities of his lineaments. 1610 GUILLIM *Heraldry* II. iii. 42 The naked and bare proportion of the outward lineaments thereof, or the outward Tract, Purfle, or shadow of a thing. *Ibid.*, The Portraicting out of any thing vmbrated, is nothing else but a sleight and single draught or Purfle, traced out with a Pensill. 1669 A. BROWNE *Ars Pict.* 83 Draw the lines of porphile (i.e. the outmost stroak) of a Face with lake and white.

†b. *In purfle*, as seen from one side; = *in profile* (PROFILE *sb.* 2). *Obs.*

1605 B. JONSON *Masque Blackness*, The backs of some were seen; some in purfle, or side; others in face. 1686 AGLIONBY *Painting Illustr.* 132 Cimabue his Picture is yet to be seen,..made in Porfil. *Ibid.* 268 All the left Side was seen in Porfile. 1706 PHILLIPS, *Pourfil*, (a Term in Painting) as A Face drawn in Pourfil, i.e. side-way; a Side-face.

Purfle (pɜ̄·ɹf'l), *v.* Forms: 4-5 purfile, -fyle, 5 -fill, 5-6 -fell, -fyll, 5-7 -fel, 6 -fyl, -fulle, -phle, 6- purfle. Also 7 (sense 5) pourfil(l, pourfle. [a. OF. *porfiler* (1371 in Godef.), later *porphyler, pourfiler* to border, adorn the border of, adorn, = Pr., Sp. *perfilar*, It. *profilare*, med.L. *perfilāre* (Du Cange), f. L. *prō* or *per* + *filum* thread: see PROFILE *v.*]

1. *trans.* To border; to decorate with a wrought or ornamental border; *esp.* to adorn (a robe) with a border of thread work or embroidery; to trim with gold or silver lace, pearls, fur, etc. *arch.*

c 1325 in *Rel. Ant.* II. 19 Hir wede, Purfiled with pellour doun to the teon. c 1386 CHAUCER *Prol.* 193, I seigh his sleues ypurfiled at the hond With grys. c 1460 *Wisdom* Stage Dir., in *Macro Plays* 36 A mayde, in a wyght clothe of golde..purfyled with menyver. 1470-85 MALORY *Arthur* I. xxvii. 74 Kyng Ryons had purfyled a mantel with kynges berdes. c 1500 *Melusine* xxxv. 240 Robes of cloth of gold, & fourred with Ermynes, & purfylled all with precyous stones. 1502 *Privy Purse Exp. Eliz. of York* (1830) 83 Item for blake crewle to purfulle therosys vjd. a 1548 HALL *Chron., Hen. VIII* 214 The knightes of the bath in uiolet gounes with hoddes purfeled with Miniuer lyke doctors. 1611 COTGR., *Pourfiler d'or*, to purfle, tinsell, or overcast with gold thread, etc. a 1625 FLETCHER *Woman's Prize* III. ii, Line the gown through with plush perfumed, and purfle All the sleeves down with pearl! c 1758 W. THOMSON *Hymn to May* ix, A silken camus,..Purfled by Nature's hand! 1803 W. TAYLOR in *Ann. Rev.* I. 332 Like a garment embroidered in chenille, and purfled with beads, and spangles, and foil. 1840 H. AINSWORTH *Tower of Lond.* (1864) 4 The Bishop of Ely, who, in his character of lord high chancellor, wore a robe of scarlet, open before, and purfled with minever.

fig. 1607 *Lingua* IV. ii. in Hazl. *Dodsley* IX. 417 This [*Tragedus*] gorgeous-broider'd with rich sentences, That [*Comedus*] fair and purfled round with merriments.

†b. To work (a design) in embroidery. *Obs.*

1601 HOLLAND *Pliny* XIII. xi. I. 392 To weave and purfle letters in their cloths, after the manner of embroiderie.

c. *intr.* or *absol.* To do purfling; 'to hem a border', *Cent. Dict.*

†2. *trans.* To give to (leaves, flowers, etc.) a border or edge of a particular kind; to ornament with such a border: in *pa. pple.*, denoting the outline, contour, or distinctive colouring of the edge.

1562 BULLEYN *Bulwark, Bk. Simples* 49 b, Leaues.. purfled aboute with iagges, or small teeth like a sawe. 1578 LYTE *Dodoens* II. lii. 212 The great Tulipa, or rather Tulipa ..of colour very diuers..and purfled about the edges or brimmes with yellowe, white, or red. 1640 PARKINSON *Theat. Bot.* IV. v. 428 Flower..consisting of five small pure white leaves, pointed at the ends, and sometimes a little purfled about the brims, and with a wash of purple.

3. In technical applications. **†a.** *Her.*, etc. To border or edge with a line of a different colour or tincture. (See also PURFLED *ppl. a.*[1] 2.) *Obs.*

1634 PEACHAM *Gentl. Exerc.* I. xxvi. 91 A faire blew deepned with lake, and purfled with liquid gold.

b. *Arch.*, etc. To ornament (the edge or ridge of any structure) *with* crockets, etc.; cf. PURFLED 3.

1844 ROCK *Ch. of Fathers* II. vi. 108 All the edges [of the mitre] were purfled with a border of exquisitely-wrought crockets in silver gilt. 1852 *Ibid.* III. i. 390 To this chest [shrine] the goldsmith..gave an architectural form: it had ..its tall crest purfled with knobs of sparkling jewels to run along the ridge of its steeply-pitched roof.

c. To adorn (the back or belly of a violin or other instrument) with a border of inlaid work: see PURFLER, PURFLING 1 c.

4. In vague or extended sense: To adorn, ornament, beautify.

c 1470 HENRYSON *Mor. Fab.* VIII., *Preach. Swallow* ix, Flouris..Quhilk..Phebus with his goldin bemis gent Hes purfellit and payntit plesandly. 1592 GREENE *Upst. Courtier* D ij, A nose, Autem nose, purphled pretiouslie with pearle and stone like a counterfait worke. 1615 CROOKE *Body of Man* 94 The close Meshes whereof, are purfled with curled veines. 1871 R. ELLIS *Catullus* i. 2 Who shall take thee, the new, the dainty volume, Purfled glossily, fresh with ashy pumice [*arida modo pumice expolitum*]?

†5. *trans.* To draw in profile, to outline; to draw. Also *absol.* or *intr.* *Obs.*

1601 HOLLAND *Pliny* XXXV. x. (1634) II. 539 Apelles..had no sooner pourfiled a little about the visage, but the king presently tooke knowledge thereby of the partie that had played this pranke by him. *Ibid.* xii. 551 [She] used ordinarily to marke upon the wall the shaddow of her lovers face by candle light and to pourfil the same afterwards deeper, that so shee might enjoy his visage yet in his absence.

Purfled (pɜ̄·ɹf'ld), *ppl. a.*[1] [f. prec. + -ED[1].]

1. Bordered; *esp.* having a decorative or ornamental border; bordered with embroidery, gold lace, fur, etc.; fringed; in vaguer use, embroidered, decorated. Also *fig.*

c 1470 *Compl. Christ* 284 in *Pol. Rel. & L. Poems* (1866) 178 What shalle than prophyte þi gowne purfylled? 1520 *Treat. Galaunt* 141 So many purfled garmentes furred with non sequitur With so many penyles purses hath no man sawe. 1600 HOLLAND *Livy* VII. i. 250 All of the Patritij, sitting like Consuls, with their purfled and pourpled long robes in yvorie chaires of estate. 1634 MILTON *Comus* 995 Flowers of more mingled hew Then her purfl'd scarf can shew. a 1717 PARNELL *Misc.* (1807) 30 The purfled border deck'd the floor with gold. 1870 ROSSETTI *Poems, Jenny* 117 But must your roses die, and those Their purfled buds that should unclose?

b. *transf.* Of a person: Decorated with purfling.

1362 LANGL. *P. Pl.* A. II. 9 Þenne was I war of a wommon wonderliche cloþed, Purfylet with pelure þe riccheset vppon eorþe. a 1450 *Knt. de la Tour* (1906) 30 Thus she shall be beter purfiled and furred thanne other ladies and gentill women. 1901 *Westm. Gaz.* 23 Oct. 2/1 The Austrian knights with mace and battle-axe, the plumed and purfled *Landvogts* from Bern.

†c. *transf.* Applied as a border. *Obs.*

1652 COLLIER in *Benlowes' Theoph.* Pref. Verses, But brighter Theophil behold, Whose Vest is wrought with purfled Gold.

†2. *Her.* Said of a charge having a bordering line, or a border or edging of another tincture: see also quot. 1868, and cf. PURFLEWE. *Obs.*

1562 LEIGH *Armorie* (1597) 91 The Fesse was first, & then the Cantone was giuen in rewarde. Being of one colour,

Purfler (pɜːˈflə). [f. PURFLE v. + -ER.] One who purfles; spec. one who inlays the ornamental borders in violins.

Purflew, a. Her. Obs. Also 6-7 purfue, 7-8 purflieu.

Purfling (pɜːˈflɪŋ), vbl. sb. [f. PURFLE v. + -ING.]

Purfly, a. T. and S. rare. [= PURFLED ppl. a.]

Purgable, a. [f. PURGE v. + -ABLE.] Capable of being purged.

Purgament. [ad. L. purgament-um, f. purgare to cleanse, PURGE: see -MENT.]

Purgation (pɜːˈɡeɪʃən). [a. OF. purgacion (13th c. in Hatz.-Darm.), ad. L. purgātiōn-em, n. of action from purgāre to PURGE.]

Purgative (pɜːˈɡətɪv), a. and sb. [a. F. purgatif, -ive (14th c. in Hatz.-Darm.), ad. late L. purgātīv-us.]

Purgatorial (pɜːɡəˈtɔːrɪəl), a. [f. late L. purgātōri-us or med.L. purgātōri-um (see PURGATORY) + -AL.]

Purgatorian (pɜːɡəˈtɔːrɪən), a. and sb.

Purgatorious, a. Obs. rare.

Purgatory (pɜːˈɡətərɪ), sb. Forms: 4-7 purgatorie, 4-5 -tori, 5-6 -torye, 4-7 purgatory; also -purgatorie, 4-6 -tory, 5-6 -torye, 4-6 purgatore, 4-6 -torie, 5-6 -tory. [a. OF. purgatore.]

Purgatory (pɜːˈɡətərɪ), a. [ad. post-cl. L. purgātōri-us, f. purgāt-, ppl. stem of purgāre to PURGE: see -ORY.]

Purge (pɜːdʒ), sb. [f. PURGE v.]

Purge, v. Obs. rare. [app. for *porge, ad. L. porrigere, contr. form of porrigere to reach out, extend, put forth, f. por- = prō forth + regere to lead straight.]

Purgeable, a. [f. PURGE v. + -ABLE.]

Purged (pɜːdʒd), ppl. a. [f. PURGE v. + -ED.]

Purger (pɜːˈdʒə). [f. PURGE v. + -ER.]

Purgery (pɜːˈdʒərɪ). [a. F. purgerie (1838 in Littré).]

Purging (pɜːˈdʒɪŋ), vbl. sb. [f. PURGE v. + -ING.]

Purgy, a. Obs. rare. [app. for *pursy, ad. L. -: see -Y.]

Purle, obs. form of PEARL, PURL.

Purification (pjʊərɪfɪˈkeɪʃən). [a. F. purification (13th c. in Hatz.-Darm.), or ad. L. pūrificātiōn-em (Pliny), n. of action from pūrificāre to PURIFY.]

Purificative (pjʊəˈrɪfɪkeɪtɪv), a. rare. [a. F. purificatif, -ive purificatory (15th c.), f. pūrificat-.]

Purificator (pjʊəˈrɪfɪkeɪtə). [Agent-n. in L. form, f. L. pūrificāre to purify: see -OR.]

Purificatory (pjʊəˈrɪfɪkeɪtərɪ), a. and sb. [f. L. pūrificāt-, ppl. stem of pūrificāre to PURIFY.]

Purified (pjʊəˈrɪfaɪd), ppl. a. [f. PURIFY + -ED.]

Purifier (pjʊəˈrɪfaɪə). [f. as prec. + -ER.]

Puriform (pjʊəˈrɪfɔːm), a. Path. [f. L. pūs, pūr- matter + -FORM.] Having the form or character of pus; resembling pus.

Purify (pjʊəˈrɪfaɪ), v. [a. F. purifier (12th c. in Hatz.-Darm.), ad. L. pūrificāre, f. pūr-us pure + -ficāre, -fy.]

Purim (pjʊəˈrɪm, ˈpjʊərɪm). [Heb. pūrīm, pl. of pūr, a foreign word (perh. Assyrian or Persian) explained in Esther iii. 7, ix. 26 as Heb. pūr lot.]

Purine (pjʊəˈriːn). Phys. Chem. Also un-systematically purin.

Puriri (puˈriːriː). [Native Maori name.]

PURISM. 1621 **PURITANISM.** **PURITANIZE.** 1622 **PURL.**

Purism (piū″riz'm). [ad. F. *purisme*, f. *pur* PURE: see -ISM.] Scrupulous or exaggerated observance of, or insistence upon, purity or correctness, esp. in language or style.

Purist (piū″rist). [f. as prec., f. *pur* PURE; or (sense 2) *purus* PURE + -IST.]
1. One who aims at, affects, or insists on scrupulous or excessive purity, esp. in language or style; a stickler for purity or correctness.
2. One who maintained that the New Testament was written in pure Greek.

Hence **Puri′stic, Puri′stical** *adjs.*, characteristic of a purist; characterized by purism.

Puritan (piū″ritan). *sb.* (and *a.*) [f. *pūritas* PURITY + -AN. Perh. formed in French or mod.Latin: cf. F. *puritain* (Ronsard 1564), mod.L. *pūritāni* (Du Cange).]

A. *sb.*
1. *Hist.* A member of the party of English Protestants who regarded the reformation of the church under Elizabeth as incomplete, and called for its further 'purification' from what they considered to be unscriptural and corrupt forms and ceremonies retained from the unreformed church; subsequently, often applied to any who separated from the established church on points of ritual, polity, or doctrine, held by them to be at variance with 'pure' New Testament principles.

2. Applied, chiefly in reproach or ridicule, to one who is, affects to be, or is accounted extremely strict, precise, or scrupulous in religion or morals.

3. *transf.* A member of any religious sect or party that advocates or aspires to special purity of doctrine or practice.

4. *attrib.* In sense 'of any (non-religious) party or school who practises or advocates strict or extreme adherence to its principles.'

B. *adj. a.* Of, pertaining to, or characteristic of the Puritans; strict and scrupulous in religious observances. **b.** That is a Puritan.

Puritanism (piū″ritaniz'm). [f. PURITAN + -ISM.]
1. The Puritan system; the doctrines and principles of the Puritans; Puritan opinion or practice.

Puritanize (piū″ritanəiz), *v.* [as prec. + -IZE.]
1. *intr.* (with *it*.) To act the puritan; to practise, conform to, or affect puritanism.
2. *trans.* To make puritan, imbue with puritanism.

Hence **Puritaniza′tion**; **Puritani′zing** *ppl. adjs.*

Puritiane, *v.* To act the puritan; to practise, conform to, or affect puritanism.

Puritanly, *adv.* After the manner of a puritan.

Purity (piū″riti). Forms: 3-6 *purete*, 4-5 *purte*, 4-6 *puryte*, 5 *purite*, 6-7 *puritie*, 6 *puritye*. [ME. *purete* (rare), a. OF. *purete* (13th c. in Hatz.-Darm.); but usually, from the beginning of 13th c. in the later F. form *pureté*, mod.F. *pureté*, ad. L. *pūritāt-em*.]
1. In physical sense: The state of being unmixed; freedom from admixture of any foreign substance or matter; absence of any other ingredient; esp. freedom from matter that contaminates, defiles, corrupts, or debases; physical cleanness.
2. In non-physical or general sense: The state of being unmixed; freedom from any foreign or extraneous element; esp. from such as corrupt or debase; unalloyed or unadulterated condition; faultlessness, correctness.
3. Moral or spiritual cleanness; freedom from moral corruption, from ceremonial or sexual uncleanness; innocence, chastity; ceremonial cleanness.
4. Of persons, their faculties, actions, attributes, etc.: Freedom from moral corruption, from ceremonial or sexual uncleanness, etc.; innocence, chastity.
5. *quasi-concr.* Pure substance or part.
6. *quasi-concr.* An embodiment of purity; a stainless being. *nonce-use.*

Purkinjean, *a. Anat.* and *Phys.* Also erron. *-gian*. [f. *Purkinje*, name of a Bohemian physiologist (1787-1869) + *-AN*.] Pertaining to or named after Purkinje: applied to various anatomical structures, etc., as the *Purkinjean capsules* in the cement of a tooth (see quot. 1854); *Purkinjean vesicle*, the nucleus of the ovum, discovered by Purkinje in 1825, also called *germinal vesicle*.

Purl (pɜrl). *sb.*[1] Forms: 6 *pyrle*, 6-9 *purle*, 7 *purl* (in senses 2, 5, also *peark*), see PEARL th.[1] Also *perl*, *pirl*. [Of obscure origin.]
I. **1.** Thread or cord made of twisted gold or silver wire, used for bordering and embroidering. *Pearl* *perl*: see quot. 1882. *Silk purl*: see quot. 1899.
II. † **3.** 'The pleat or fold of a ruff or band' (Fairholt), as worn about 1600; a frill.
III. 5. Knitting. (Often *pearl*.) An inversion of the stitches, producing a ribbed appearance of the surface. (See PEARL sb.[1] 4.)

Purl (pɜrl), *sb.*[2] [Origin unascertained (?related to prec.).] A formerly liquor made by infusing wormwood or other bitter herbs in ale or beer. Also later, a mixture of hot beer with gin (also called *dog's nose*), sometimes also with ginger and sugar; in repute as a morning draught.

Purl (pɜrl), *sb.*[3] *Obs. exc. Hist.* Also 7 *perle*. [Origin unascertained.] A rill.

Purl (pɜrl), *v.*[1] [Goes with PURL *sb.*[1] 5.] *trans.* To embroider with gold or silver thread; to edge or border with a purl or twist; to fringe, or frill.

Purl, *v.*[2] Also 6 *pyrl(e*, *pirl(e*. [? *pirle*, freq. of PURL *v.*[4], of which *pirl* may be a variant.]
1. *intr.* To revolve or whirl round rapidly, as a wheel; to spin round, as a peg-top, a whirligig, etc.
2. *intr.* To wheel round suddenly, as when falling; to be overturned.
3. *trans.* and *intr.* To turn upside down, overturn, upset, capsize; to turn heels over head, turn a somersault.
4. *Purl, v.[4]* *Obs.* Variant of PROWL *v.*

Purl, var. PIRL *v.*, to twist, spin.

Purlieu, lieu'd, *v.* (in 4 *purlieu, -loy, -loie*, ff. PURLIEU.) To enclose within a purlieu.

Purler (pɜrlər). *colloq.* [f. PURL *v.*[2] + -ER[1].] A throw or blow that hurls any one head-foremost; a knock-down blow; cf. PURL *sb.*[4]

Purl. 1623 **PURLIEU.** **PURLIEU-MAN.** 1624 **PURPENSE.**

Purlicue, purl. Also spelt *purlicue*. *Sc.* Now *rare*. Also *purlieu, -ieue, -loyroe*, *perlocue, -leque, -likew*, *pirlicue, -lieeue, -liquey*, *purleyoue*. See Note below.
1. 'A dash or flourish at the end of a word in writing'; a school-term, Aberd.' (Jamieson 1808.)
2. 'The peroration, or conclusion of a discourse; also used to denote the discourse itself, Strathmore, Roxb.' (Jam. 1825.)
3. See quot. 1825. (The practice is now obsolete.)

Purlin, -ine (pɜrlin). Also 6-9 *purline, -lyne, -loyn, -loyne, -lyng, -ling*; 7-9 *purline, 8 -lin*; (parting, *perling* :) 5 *perloyn*, 6 *-loyne, -lin, 9 *purlin*. [History uncertain; the forms suggest a Fr. origin; but no suitable source is forthcoming.] A horizontal beam, usually one of two or more, which run along the length of a roof, resting upon the principal rafters, and supporting the common rafters or boards of the roof.

Purling, *vbl. sb.*[1] [f. PURL *v.*[2] + -ING[1].] The action of PURL *v.*[2]; chiefly referring to the sound.

Purling, *vbl. sb.*[2] [f. PURL *v.*[1] + -ING[1].] The action of PURL *v.*[1]: making away with; pilfering, filching.

Purloin (pɜrloin'), *v.* Forms: 5-6 *perloyn(e*, 5-7 *purloyn(e*, (5 *perlogne*, 6-7 *purloin*). [a. AF. *purloigner, purloin-*, in senses *laire*, put far off, estrange; also *purluigner, parlonger, f. pur-*, *pour-* = L. *pro-* + *loign, loin* far, distant, ad. L. *longē* far off.]
1. *trans.* To put away, remove to a distance; to make away, do away with, remove.
2. To steal.

Hence **Purloi′ned** *ppl. a.*; **Purloi′ning** *vbl. sb.* and *ppl. a.*

Purloiner (pɜrloin'ər). [f. PURLOIN *v.* + -ER[1].] One who purloins; a petty thief, a pilferer.

Purlieu (pɜrliū). Forms: 5-6 *purlewe, -lue, -lewe, -lieu, -lu*, 6-7 *purley, -lie*, etc. [app. a. AF. *puralé, puralee*, etc.] A district on the fringe or border of a forest; originally, one that, after having been (wrongly, as was thought) included within the bounds of the forest, was disafforested by a new perambulation, but still remained in some respects, especially as to the hunting or killing of game, subject to provisions of the Forest Laws.

Purlieu-man, † purley-man (pɜrliū-, pərlē man). Also 6 *purle-*, *purlieu-man*. [f. prec. + MAN *sb.*] The owner of freehold land within the purlieu of a forest.

Purpense, variant of PURPRENSE.

Purple, *-ly*, *-lyn(e*, *-lyon*, obs. ff. PURPLE.

Purpart, **Purprend**, **Purpor**, var. forms of PURPRENSE.

Purpose-, combining form from L. *purpos-*, *-posit-*.

Purpose (pɜrpos), *sb.* Forms: 4 *purpos*, 4-5 *purpoos*, 5 *purpose*, *-pos*, etc. [a. AF. *purpos* (= OF. *porpos*, *propos*), f. *purposer*: see PURPOSE *v.*]

Purport, *sb.* Law. *Obs. or arch.* [- med.L. *proport*, *purport* (in Fleta), *purpresa* (1366) *partie* hæreditatis, pro divisio hæreditatis (Du Cange).] Law or custom: see PART *sb.*

Purparty, **Purpart**. Law. *Obs.* Forms: 4 *purpartie*, 4-5 *pourpartie*, -*pairtie*, 5-6, 8 *purparty*. [a. AF. *purpartie* (Britton 1292)] A part, portion, or share of property or an inheritance.

Purpense, v. Obs. ... To think, purpose.

Purple, a. and sb. ...

Purple-fish. ...

Purplely, adv. ...

Purpose, sb. ...

Purpose, v. ...

Purposeful, a. ...

Purposefulness. ...

PURPOSELESS | 1629 | **PURPUR.** | **PURPUR.** | 1630 | **PURPURIZE.**

Purposeless. Purpose-like. Purposely. Purposer. Purposing. Purposive. Purposiveness. Purpure. Purpuration. Purpure (sb.). Purpurescent. Purpurate. Purpurean. Purpureal. Purpuriparous. Purpurine. Purpuroid. Purpurous. Purr. Purre. Purree. Purrel. Purfle. Purrock. Purring. Purse.

Purse-bearer.

The bearer or carrier of a purse; one who has charge of the money of another or of a company; a treasurer, bursar.

Purse-pride. Pride of purse or wealth; the self-esteem or arrogance of the wealthy.

Purse-proud, a. Proud of wealth; puffed up on account of one's wealth.

Purse-cutter. A thief who cuts purses and abstracts their contents; a cutpurse.

Pursed, *ppl. a.* 1. Drawn into close folds or wrinkles; drawn together, puckered. Usually *with up.*

Purseful, *a. nonce-wd.* That has a full purse, opulent, wealthy.

Purselin, -lan, obs. ff. PORCELAIN, PURSLANE.

Purseless, *a.* Having no purse; without a purse.

Purse-master. Chiefly *Sc. pl.* A purse-bearer, treasurer, bursar.

Purser (pɜ·ɹsəɹ). Also 5 pursour, porser, pursor, -our, 4-9 pursar, 5-7 purcer.

Purseless ...

Purse-net. A bag-shaped net, the mouth of which can be drawn together with cords; used especially for catching rabbits, also as a ballast-net.

Purse-seine. A net, or one of the two sliding rings, closing a silk or leather purse.

Purse-ring. A ring, or one of the two sliding rings, closing a silk or leather purse.

Purse-seine. A net so shaped or seine which may be pursed or drawn into the shape of a bag, used for catching small fish.

Purse-string. Usually *in pl.* The two purse or purse is closed; hence in various *fig.* phrases, as *to hold the purse-strings,* to control the expenditure of money; *to tighten or loosen the purse-strings,* to be sparing, or generous, in spending money.

Purset, obs. form of POSSET.

Purse-taker. A highwayman or robber who deprived persons of their purses.

Pursewort. An old name for the weed Shepherd's purse.

Pursy, Pursivant, and *sb.* Obs.

Purslane. A low succulent herb, *Portulaca oleracea,* widely distributed throughout tropical and warmer temperate regions, used in salads, and sometimes as a pot-herb, or for pickling.

Purslet (pɜ·ɹslet). Also 6 purslett. A small or tiny purse or bag.

Purslive, obs. form of PURSIVE.

Pursual (pɜɹsiū·al). Forms: 1-4 pursue.

Pursuance (pɜɹsiū·ăns). Also 7 pour-, 7-8 pursuence.

Pursuant (pɜɹsiū·ănt), *sb.* and *a.* Also 4 poursuant.

Pursue (pɜɹsiū·, -syū·), *v.* Forms: see below.

I. Intransitive uses.

1. To follow with hostility or enmity; to seek to injure (a person); to persecute; to harass, worry, torment.

II. To go in chase or pursuit.

Pursuer (pɜɹsiū·əɹ). Forms: 4 pursuere, -suere, 5 suour, 5-6 persewar, 4-7 pera-souar, 4- pursuer.

Pursuing, Pursuingly: see PURSUE *v.*

Pursuit (pɜɹsiū·t). Forms: 4 purseut, 4-5 -suet, 4-6 -suyt(e, 4-7 -suite, 5-6 -sewt, 5-7 -suite, 6 -suyte, 6 -suyt, 7 -suit. &c.

Pursuivant (pɜ·ɹswivănt), *sb.* Forms: 4-5 pursefulant, 5 persu-, 4-5 -suyvaunt, 5 -ewyvant, 6-pursyvant, -yvaunt, 6 -eou-, -eew-, 6-7 -uivant; also 6-7 pursevant, -ewyvant, -owyvant, 6 -eowant, -sant, -aphant, -aivant, -oyfant, 5-6 persevaund. [ME. a. OF. pour-, poursuivant, F. poursuivant, ...]

Pursuivant, v. Obs.

Pursy, a. Obs.

Pursy, sb.

Purtenance, sb.

Purvey, sb.

Purvey, v.

Purveyable, a.

Purveyal, rare⁻¹.

Purveyor, sb.

Purwannah, parwannah. East Ind.

Purwinkle, -wynkle, obs. ff. PERIWINKLE².

Pus, sb.

Push, sb.¹

Push, v.

PUSH.

2. intr. To thrust with a pointed weapon, stick, or the like (const. *at*); to tilt, fence; to use a spear, short sword, poniard, etc.

3. intr. To thrust with the horns; chiefly biblical. Also *trans.* – PUTT.

5. trans. To thrust out, stick out (an organ or part).

6. intr. To exert pressure upon something in the way described in 1.

7. intr. To make one's way with force or persistence (as against difficulty or opposition). With various adverbs and preps.

8. intr. To put forth vigorous effort or endeavour; to press, be urgent in request or solicitation; to aim at with endeavour to attain; to try or work strenuously for, press for; to seek actively, labour after. Now *rare*.

PUSH-.

Push, *sb.* [f. PUSH *v.*, or PUSH *sb.*[1]], in combination.

Pu·shful, *a.* [f. PUSH *v.* + -FUL.]

Pu·shing, *vbl. sb.* [f. PUSH *v.* + -ING[1].]

Pu·shing, *ppl. a.* [f. PUSH *v.* + -ING[2].]

PUSHER

Pusher (*pu·ʃəɹ*).
1. One who or that which pushes (*lit.* and *fig.*).

Hence **Pu·shingly** *adv.*, **Pu·shingness**.

Push-pin (*pu·ʃpin*). [f. PUSH + PIN *sb.*[1]]

PUSS.

Puss (*pus*), *sb.*[1]

Pu·sillani·mity.

Pusley, **Pusoun**, obs. ff. PURSLANE, POISON.

Puss, *int.*

PUSS-CAT.

Puss-cat, form of PUSSY-CAT.

Pussa·te, sb. form of PUSSAT.

Pu·ss-clover. *U.S.* The hare's-foot clover, *Trifolium arvense*.

Pu·ssel, **pusele**, obs. forms of PUCELLE.

Pussley (*pu·sli*). Also *pusley*. A corruption of PURSLANE, common in *U.S.*

Pussy (*pu·si*), *sb.*

Pussy-cat. [In quot. 1527 a Du. *puist*.]

Pussy-willow. A popular name in *U.S.* for the American glaucous willow, *Salix discolor*.

Pust, obs. f. PUS.

Pu·ss-moth. [f. Puss + MOTH: see quot. 1826.]

Pustulant (*pu·stiŭlănt*), *a.* and *sb.*

Pustulate (*pu·stiŭlĕt*), *a.* [ad. late L. *pustulātus*.]

Pustulate (*pu·stiŭlĕt*), *v.*

PUSTULOUS.

Pustulation (*pʌstiŭlē·ʃən*). [ad. late L. *pustulātiōn-em*.]

Pustule (*pʌ·stiŭl*).

Pustulous (*pʌ·stiŭləs*), *a.*

Pustulate (*pu·stiŭlĕt*), *a.* and *sb.*

PUT

Put (*put*), *sb.*[1]

Put (*put*), *v.*

Pu·t-off, *sb.*

Put, *sb.*[2]

Put (*put*), *sb.*[3]

Put, *v.*[2]

Where the notion of motion in space is subordinated to that of relation.

11. To place (a thing or person) *in* or *into* the hands or power of, *in* or *under* the care of a person; formerly also *in*, *to* (a person's etc.).

12. To place, set, or cause to be in some place or position, in a general or figurative sense, or when the name of a thing or place stands for its purpose, as *to put a person to bed, to school, in ward, in prison, to put a thing to sale, on the market, on the stage*, etc.

13. To place with or *to*, in a way of addition. Const. *to* (*unto*), *in*.

14. To place, insert, or enter (a name or an item) in a list, account, or table.

15. To place (a thing or person) in a scale of estimation or a classification; to allot a place to in thought, opinion, or statement; also, to regard or suppose (a thing) to be (so-and-so) (also).

23. To impose (something) *on*, *upon* (*to, uponto*) a person, etc.

25. To place, bring, *into*, or reduce a person or thing to some state or condition; as...

27. To posit, suppose, assume. With obj. cl.

28. To force or drive (a person, etc.) to the performance of some action, e.g. of making a choice, playing a certain card, etc.

IV. In combination or construction of the transitive verb with prepositions.

31. Put on. — intr. To strive, proceed against, take measures against; to attack; to prosecute. [*fr.* from i.d.] *Sc.* With indirect appositions.

34. Put off. — trans. To delay, defer.

35. Put abroad. *trans.* To spread abroad, unfurl, display. *Obs.*

36. Put aside. See simple senses and ABIDE.

37. Put asunder. *trans.* To separate.

38. Put away. See simple senses and AWAY.

41. Put down and **Down** adv. *To put one's foot down :* see Foot sb. 28.

42. Put forth.

43.

44. Put in.

45. Put off.

46.

47. Put out.

48.

49.

50. Put over.

e. *Naut. intr.* To put in to shore; to turn in, take shelter.

1797 F. Baily *Jrnl. Tour N. Amer.* (1856) 195 We pushed off..and after going about twenty miles, were obliged to put-to on account of the wind. 1807 P. Gass *Jrnl.* 163 We put to at a branch of fresh water, under high cliffs.

f. *pass.* To be reduced to straits: = *to be put to it*: see 28 c (*b*).

1803 *Pic Nic* No. 6 (1806) I. 221 He is,..like myself, hard put to at times for a little money. 1886 T. Hardy *Mayor Casterbr.* iv, We must needs be put-to for want of a wholesome crust. 1889 M. Gray *Reproach Annesley* II. ii, Terble hard putt to they be to beat out the time.

52. Put together. **a.** See simple senses and Together.

c 1440 *Promp. Parv.* 417/2 Put to-geder, but not onyd, *contiguus.* 1690 Locke *Hum. Und.* I. ii. 9 Upon the first Occasion that shall make him put together those Ideas in his Mind and observe whether they agree or disagree.

b. *trans.* To combine, unite (parts) into a whole; to join, e.g. in marriage.

c 1440 [see a]. 1530 Palsgr. 671/2 Sythe they be ones put togyther by the lawes of holy churche, I wyll never put them asonder. 1651 H. More *Second Lash* in *Enthus. Tri.*, etc. (1656) 218 It is you that have put things together so ill-favouredly. 1687 Abp. Wake *Prep. for Death* 10 That those few directions I have here put together, may be as truly useful to you. 1793 Smeaton *Edystone L.* § 271 Every thing was ready in the yard for putting together.

† c. *refl.* To join, combine, unite. *Obs. rare.*

1556 *Aurelio & Isab.* (1608) P v, The Quene and the ladies put them againe together for to geve Affranio a very bitter sopper.

d. To form (a whole) by combination of parts; to construct, compile, compose, compound.

1530 Palsgr. 676/1 He can spell, but he can nat put to gyther. 1638 Junius *Paint. Ancients* 18 Our mind putteth the whole figure out of those visible parts together. 1825 *New Monthly Mag.* XV. 212/2 This figure can be taken to pieces and put together with the greatest ease. 1862 *Temple Bar Mag.* VI. 401, I put together some account of a series of incidents. 1889 Fr. A. Kemble *Far Away & Long Ago* xii, His figure was ill put together.

e. To combine mentally; to add or reckon together, to sum; often in *pa. pple.*, taken or considered together, in a body, collectively.

To put this and that together: to consider two facts or circumstances together and draw a conclusion from them. So *to put two and two together*: see Two.

1622 Mabbe tr. *Aleman's Guzman d'Alf.* II. 195 All this put together..was nothing, being compared with her retirednesse of life. 1707 J. Stevens tr. *Quevedo's Com. Wks.* (1709) 351 Put that and that together. 1748 Richardson *Clarissa* vii. (1810) 70 All these things put together, excited their curiosity. 1861 *Temple Bar Mag.* I. 468 He knew more than all the old school put together. 1865 Dickens *Mut. Fr.* III. xv, He puts this and that together.

f. *Cricket.* To make up, 'compile', as a 'score'.

1890 *Field* 31 May 784/3 Webbe and O'Brien..put together thirty-nine runs for the third wicket. *Ibid.* 21 June 919/2 The largest score they have ever put together in a first-class engagement.

53. Put up.

***a.** *trans.* To put into a higher position; to raise; to lift: see simple senses and Up *adv.*, also the sbs. Back, Hair, Shutter, etc.

a 1300 *Cursor M.* 5833 (Cott.) Þe water o þe flum þou ta And put it vp apon þe Land. *a* 1400 *Sir Beues* 3040 Beues wiste wel and sede, Put vp a pensell, lest Saber vs drede. *a* 1500 *MS. Ashm.* 344 lf. 19 (Chess) And must he nedis put vp his pon & mated in c. 1503 Dunbar *Thistle & Rose* 54 The purpour sone..Throw goldin skyis putting vp his heid. 1605 Shaks. *Macb.* IV. ii. 78 Why then (alas) Do I put vp that womanly defence? 1662 J. Davies tr. *Olearius' Voy. Ambass.* 75 Married Women put up their hair within their Caps or Coifs. 1861 Hughes *Tom Brown at Oxf.* ix, There were others sneering..and that puts a fellow's back up. 1889 M. Gray *Reproach Annesley* v. i, Shopkeepers had hastily put up their shutters. 1897 Flor. Montgomery *Tony* (1898) 17 You will put up the windows in the tunnels, won't you?

spec. (*b*) To fix up for public view, to post up. Hence, of a cricketer: To score (so many runs); orig. to have them put up on the scoring board.

1833 *Act* 3 & 4 *Will. IV*, c. 46 § 113 Such rules..shall..be put up, either in print or in writing, on such place..as the ..council shall think proper. 1860 *Baily's Mag.* I. 428 Grundy put up 11 and 16. 1890 *Globe* 7 June 1/4 He put up notices requesting visitors to leave the plants alone.

(*c*) To set up or mount (a person, esp. a jockey) on horseback; to employ as a jockey.

1888 *Times* 26 June 4/5 Would they put up a jockey they believed to be dishonest? 1893 *Illustr. Sporting & Dram. News* 15 Apr. 183/1 Some trainers believe in putting up stable boys instead of jockeys.

(*d*) To put or bring (a play, etc.) on the stage for performance. Cf. *put on*, 46 a.

1890 F. Barrett *Between Life & Death* II. xxvi. 148 A new spectacle was..put up for rehearsal after Christmas. 1891 *New Rev.* Dec. 506 A manager..may 'put up' the 'Midsummer Night's Dream'.

b. *Hunting.* To cause (game) to rise from cover; to rouse, start.

?*c* 1475 *Hunt. Hare* 112, Y wylle ryde and putt her vp. 1575 Turberv. *Falconrie* 131 Let him which hath the Hearoner (that is the make Hawke) put up the Hearon. 1629 H. Burton *Truth's Triumph* 308 A spaniell..puts vp many a foule. 1711 Addison *Spect.* No. 131 ¶ 2 In Town, ..I..put up such a Variety of odd Creatures, that they foil the Scent. 1805 Southey *Lett.* (1856) I. 345 Camp is in good health, and put up a hare. 1890 *Longm. Mag.* June 222 We put up a couple of tigers.

(*b*) *intr.* for *refl.* To rise: (in *Angling*) of a fish.

1600 Surflet *Countrie Farme* II. liv, When as the sappe putteth vp and commeth to the barke. 1890 *Field* 31 May 790/1 The trout that put up here and there were after a tiny speck of midge-like character.

c. *trans.* To cause to spring up or grow; of a beast, to develop or 'cut' (a tooth).

1626 Bacon *Sylva* § 549 It is reported, that hartshorn shaven, or in small pieces, mixed with dung and watered, putteth up mushrooms. 1854 *Jrnl. R. Agric. Soc.* XV. II. 321 These teeth are put up when the calf is six months old.

d. *Cricket.* To hit (a ball) so that it rises high.

1845 W. Denison *Cricketer's Compan.* p. ix, Had the chances from the ball being put up been taken advantage of. 1890 *Field* 31 May 790/2 Holden next put a ball up to long-on.

e. To 'raise' (a shout). *rare.*

1892 *Quiver* Mar. 359/1 They put up a great shout of admiration.

f. To raise in amount.

1890 *Harper's Mag.* Oct. 758/1 His governor..had quite lately put his allowance up a hundred pounds. 1892 *Sat. Rev.* 26 Nov. 617/2 Making preparations to put up the price still higher.

g. *colloq.* To show, exhibit (a game, play). *To put up an appearance* (*north. dial.* and *Sc.*), to make one's appearance.

1832 Ht. Martineau *Tales Pol. Econ.* II. IV, *Demerara* i. 10 A few of the sluggards who had not put up their appearance at the proper hour. 1892 *Field* 30 Jan. 133/3 Pettitt put up a good game..but it was not severe enough for the English champion. 1897 *Outing* (U.S.) XXX. 431/1 Able to put up a game at golf that the youngster will find hard to beat.

****h.** † (*a*) To send or hand up to a superior for consideration; to present (a petition, etc.). *Obs.*

1360 Langl. *P. Pl.* A. IV. 34 Þene Pees com to parlement and put vp a Bille, Hou þat Wrong a3eyn his wille his wyf hedde I-take. 1439 *Rolls of Parlt.* V. 9/1 In a Petition putte up to the Kyng. 1530 Palsgr. 676/1, I wyll put up a complaynt agaynst the. 1589 *Pasquil's Ret.* C iij b, The reuerend Elders of Martinisme had neuer put vppe any Billes of endightment against her the last Parliament.

(*b*) To offer (prayer or worship) to God or a divine being 'on high'; to present a petition to any exalted personage.

1641 [see Putting *vbl. sb.*[1] 9]. 1709 Strype *Ann. Ref.* I. xlvi. 502 Our church..put up prayers to God in the behalf of it. 1757 Hume *Ess., Nat. Hist. Relig.* § 4 (1788) II. 377 The Lacedemonians..always during war, put up their petitions very early in the morning, in order to be beforehand with their enemies. 1848 Thackeray *Van. Fair* lix, The coarse tyrant..to whom she had been forced to put up petitions for time, when the rent was overdue. 1889 F. C. Philips *Ainslie's Courtsh.* xiii, Prayers for fine weather were put up. 1889 Doyle *Micah Clarke* xxv, At dinner I heard him put up thanks for what he was to receive.

† i. To bring (a person) up before a magistrate; to bring into court on some charge; to accuse formally. *Obs.*

c 1440 *Alphabet of Tales* 121 On a tyme he was ferd to be putt vp at þe sene [*in synodo accusari*]. 1526 Tindale *Matt.* x. 19 When they put you vp, take no thought howe or what ye shall speake. 1541 in Foxe *A. & M.* (1563) II. 1194/2 All these were put up for railing against the Sacramentes and Ceremonies.

j. To propose for election or adoption.

1573 G. Harvey *Letter-bk.* (Camden) 2 Sinc mi grace amongst the rest was put up in the hous. *Ibid.* 3. 1682 *Enq. Elect. Sheriffs* 31 [They] both put up and Voted for Sir Humphrey Nicolson, and Mr. Box. 1692 R. L'Estrange *Fables* cxvi, The Beasts Met in Councel to Chuse a King. There were Several Put up. *a* 1859 Macaulay in *Encycl. Brit.* (1885) XIX. 137/1 Soon after this debate Pitt's name was put up by Fox at Brookes's.

(*b*) *intr.* for *refl.* To offer oneself for election; to stand as a candidate.

1705 Hearne *Collect.* 20 Dec., He..modestly declin'd it. The like did also Dr. Hudson, who was desir'd by divers to put up. 1870 Doyle *Firm Girdlestone* xviii, He put up at Murphytown in the Conservative interest.

(*c*) *fig.* To 'set up' *for*, offer (to do something).

1892 *Quiver* Sept. 872/2, I am not master enough of the occult sciences to put up for defending Dan's character as a charmer.

(*d*) *trans.* (with mixture of lit. sense): To bring forward (a person) to stand up and speak.

1889 Doyle *Micah Clarke* xxxv, What use to put a witness up, when he was shouted down..and threatened by the Chief Justice? 1890 *Blackw. Mag.* CXLVIII. 597/1 He was the only speaker the Conservatives could put up..to answer or criticise Mr. Gladstone.

k. To send or hand in (a communication) to be published in a church in the course of the service; esp. in reference to banns; also, to publish (banns).

1685 S. Sewall *Diary* 26 Mar., I put up a note to pray for the Indians. 1830 *Examiner* 306/2, I then went and put up the banns. 1842 Marryat *Perc. Keene* xxxii, We are to be put up in church next Sunday, and it takes three Sundays. 1892 *Cornh. Mag.* July 46 Their banns had been put up in the East End parish.

l. To offer for sale by auction, or for competition.

1706 *Lond. Gaz.* No. 4287/3 The Buyer to pay down 2 Guineas each Lot, or to be put up again. 1856 *Leisure Hour* V. 279/2 The lot was put up again, to be knocked down for six and threepence. 1892 *Chamb. Jrnl.* 3 Dec. 773/2 Oughtn't the post..to have been put up for public competition? 1899 Goldw. Smith *United Kingd.* I. 108 He [Richard I] put everything up to sale.

m. † (*a*) *intr.* ? To advance *to*, approach; or ? to make up *to*, address oneself *to* a person (*obs.*). (*b*) *trans.* To submit (a question, etc.) *to* a person: cf. 22, 22 b. *rare.*

?1728 Swift *Discovery* 17 Wks. 1755 IV. I. 298 With this he put up to my lord, The courtiers kept their distance due. 1906 *Harper's Mag.* June 68/1 When he finally put it up to me what I would do,—'It would depend', I answered, 'on what it was the woman has done'.

*** **n.** To place in a receptacle for safe keeping; to stow away; to put into a bag, pocket, box, or the like; to lay aside out of use, put by (somewhat *arch.*); to lay up in store, lay by for future use (now *rare* or *obs.*); to pack up, do up, make up into a parcel, or place in small vessels or receptacles so as to be kept ready for use.

To put up one's pipes: see Pipe *sb.*[1] 1 e. (Cf. *put away*, 38 e; *put by*, 40 g.)

c 1368 Chaucer *Compl. Pite* 54, I haue put my compleynt vp agayne, ffor to my foos my bille I dar not shewe. 1382 Wyclif *Luke* xii. 19 Soule, thou hast many goodis kept [*v. r.* put vp] in to ful manye 3eeris. 1588 Shaks. *L. L. L.* IV. i. 109 Thou hast mistaken his letter..Here, sweete, put up this. 1637 Gataker *Serm., On* 1 *Tim.* vi. 6, I. 134 They might not pocket or put up ought to carry away with them. 1651 French *Distill.* v. 125 Put it up in bottles. 1825 *New Monthly Mag.* XV. 406/1 It will keep sweet a very long time put up in good flour barrels. 1883 Mrs. F. Mann *Parish Hilby* iv, If you aren't for any more whist,..we may as well put up the cards. 1889 F. Barrett *Under Str. Mask* II. xiv. 76, I took the money..and put it up in the pocket-book. 1892 *Field* 21 May 778/1 The housekeeper..had put us up plenty of edibles and drinkables.

(*b*) To put into the sheath, to sheathe (a sword); also *absol.* to sheathe one's sword (cf. Draw *v.* 33 b). Also *fig. arch.*

c 1470 *Golagros & Gaw.* 1123 Thai..Put up thair brandis sa braid, burly and bair. 1526 Tindale *John* xviii. 11 Put vppe thy swearde into the sheath [Gk. βάλε, Vulg. *mitte*]. 1592 Shaks. *Rom. & Jul.* I. i. 72, I do but keepe the peace, put vp thy Sword. 1602 Middleton *Blurt Master Constable* v. ii, *Font.* I'm arm'd: let him come in...*Imp.* Goe, goe, put vp. 1608 Dod & Cleaver *Expos. Prov.* 164 To be wary how we carry our tongues, that they be safely put up from doing of hurt, and never unsheathed. 1775 Sheridan *Rivals* v. iii, Put up, Jack, put up..—how came you in a duel? 1826 Scott *Woodst.* xxv, None shall fight duellos here...Put up, both of you.

(*c*) To shut up, enclose (a beast for fattening, a meadow for hay).

1607 Topsell *Four-f. Beasts* (1658) 517 They put up a Hog to fatting. 1799 Washington *Writ.* (1893) XIV. 225 Before the period arrives for putting them up as porkers. 1854 *Jrnl. R. Agric. Soc.* XV. II. 401 The stall beasts are ..put up in sheds in October. 1892 J. C. Blomfield *Hist. Heyford* 2 'Ings', or meadows put up for hay.

(*d*) To settle (any one) to rest or repose; to settle (a patient) in bed.

1800 *Med. Jrnl.* III. 36, I just applied simple dressing,.. putting him up in blankets, with no hope of his recovery. 1860–6 Flor. Nightingale *Nursing* 39 Everything you do in a patient's room, after he is 'put up' for the night, increases tenfold the risk of his having a bad night.

(*e*) To deposit, stake (a sum of money); to pay up. Also *absol.* *U.S.* and *Colonial.*

1884 *Boston* (Mass.) *Jrnl.* 16 Aug., A wealthy Bostonian yesterday wagered $2000, and put-up the money, that Mr. Blaine's majority in New York State would exceed 40,000. 1891 C. Roberts *Adrift Amer.* 126, I will pick you up if you choose to put up a couple of dollars.

o. (*a*) To lodge and entertain (man or beast).

1766 Goldsm. *Vic. W.* xxii, The hired horse that we rode was to be put up that night at the inn. 1828 *Blackw. Mag.* XXIII. 375 Mr. Hunt..was 'put up' in the ground-floor of his Lordship's house. 1867 Trollope *Chron. Barset* xx, Mr. Robarts went to the inn, put up his horse, and then ..sauntered back up the street. 1890 'R. Boldrewood' *Col. Reformer* (1891) 129 Can you put us up for the night?

(*b*) *intr.* for *refl.* or *pass.* To take up one's lodging, to 'stop' (at an inn, etc.).

1727 *Philip Quarll* (1816) 32 We put up at the first cottage. 1753 *Scots Mag.* Oct. 483/1 The inns where their waggons put up. 1840 Dickens *Barn. Rudge* xxxv, Let's either go on to London, sir, or put up at once. 1884 D. C. Murray in *Graphic* Xmas No. 5/3 Would it not be better..to put up here for the night?

p. *fig.* † (*a*) *trans.* To 'pocket', submit to, endure, suffer quietly, patiently, or tamely (an affront or injury); 'to pass unrevenged' (J.) *Obs.* (now displaced by *put up with*: see (*b*)).

1573 G. Harvey *Letter-bk.* (Camden) 48 All this I put up quietly. 1600 W. Watson *Decacordon* (1602) 91 Abuses.. which, with honour, he can neuer put vp at their hands. 1604 Shaks. *Oth.* IV. ii. 181. 1628 Earle *Microcosm.* lv. (Arb.) 79 He can put vp any iniury sooner then this. 1752 Fielding *Amelia* IX. iii, He who would put up an arrest, would put up a slap in the face. 1832 *Philol. Museum* I. 477 The ridicule which the minister..might put up from his jocose friend.

(*b*) *To put up with*: to submit to (an injury), 'to suffer without resentment' (J., 1765): = (*a*); in wider sense, To bear, endure, tolerate, do with (anything inconvenient or disagreeable); 'to take without dissatisfaction' (T., 1818).

1755 P. Supple in *Connoisseur* No. 100. 605 All these indignities I very patiently put up with. 1761 Colman *Genius* No. 9 in *Prose on Sev. Occas.* (1787) I. 90 This loss ..would have been the least, and most easily to be put up with. 1839 De Quincey *Casuistry Rom. Meals* Wks. 1854 III. 280 Whether Pope ever put up with four o'clock dinners again, I have vainly sought to fathom. 1887 Jessopp *Arcady* viii. 235 [An] organ grinder..hunted out of London streets, where they will not put up with him.

**** **q.** *trans.* *To put* (a person) *up to* (colloq.): (*a*) To make conversant with or aware of; to inform of, instruct in (something, originally some artifice or expedient).

1812 J. H. Vaux *Flash Dict.* s. v., To suggest to another, the means of committing a depredation,..is termed, putting him up to it. 1824 *Hist. Gaming*, etc. 18 Those who had been 'put up' to the secrets, or made acquainted with the manner of doing the flats. 1828 *Examiner* 589/1, I want you to put the people at the inn up to my not coming. 1891 *Cornh. Mag.* Oct. 357 He put me up to one or two things worth knowing.

(*b*) To stir up, instigate, incite, induce, persuade (*to* some action, etc., or *to do* something).

1824 in G. T. Curtis *D. Webster* (1870) I. 266 'You find it hard work enough this morning, I think', said Mr. Webster. 'Yes, Sir', said the boatman, 'it puts a man up to all he knows, I assure you'. 1849 E. FitzGerald *Lett.* (1889) I. 193 You must not believe however that it is only chance which puts me up to this exertion. 1889 M. Gray *Reproach Annesley* IV. i, Always putting them up to mischief. 1892 *Gd. Words* Sept. 584/1 He put me up to try to get into Harris's secrets.

***** **r.** To erect, set up (a building or other structure); to construct, build.

1818 in Willis & Clark *Cambridge* (1886) I. 573 The making a Bridge and putting up the Gates at the end of that walk. 1857–8 Sears *Athan.* xii. 102 A building which ..God put up carpenter-fashion. 1873 H. Spencer *Stud. Sociol.* xi. 287 Here are lighthouses we have put up to prevent shipwrecks. 1879 Trollope *Thackeray* i. 58 A bust to his memory was put up in Westminster Abbey.

s. To make up or compose by union of individuals or parts; *spec.* in *Angling*, to make up or construct (an artificial fly).

1892 *Harper's Mag.* May 870/1 Prussia, together with the remaining states, puts up sixteen army corps. 1892 *Field* 17 Sept. 454/1 When putting up a new fly, the wings, hackle, and body are painted over with the paraffin. *Ibid.* 10 Dec. 901/2 Our guest put up a cast of midges.

t. *fig.* To concoct or plan in combination with others; to prearrange, preconcert (a robbery, or any iniquitous or underhand piece of work). Orig. and chiefly *Thieves' slang*: see also Put-up *ppl. a.* 1.

1810–38 [see Put-up *ppl. a.* 1]. 1856 *Leisure Hour* V. 542/2 Her account..affords a good example of the style of 'putting up' a house robbery. 1892 *Illustr. Sporting & Dram. News* 13 Aug. 790/1 Barclay put up a job to ruin old Overton.

VI. 54. In numerous idiomatic, proverbial, and other phrases, as *to put to the* Blush, *to the* Push; *to put in one's* Pocket, *in* Requisition, *into* (*out of*) *one's* Head, *into one's* Mouth, *out of* Countenance, *out of* Court, *out of* Joint, *out of the* Way; *to put the* Change *upon*, *a* (*good*, etc.) Face *upon*, *one's* Foot *in it*, *too fine a point upon it* (Point *sb.*[1] B. 1 d), *one's* Shoulder *to*, Spurs *to*; *to put a* Bone *in any one's hood*, *the* Cart *before the horse*, *the finger in the* Eye, *one's best* Foot *foremost*, *one's* Nose *out of joint*, *one's hand to the* Plough, *pen to* Paper, *a* Spoke *in one's wheel*, etc., etc., for which see the sbs.

Put, putt (pɒt), *v.*[2] Pa. t. and pa. pple. **putted** (pɒ·tĕd). [The same word as prec., used in particular senses differentiated by pronunciation and by the use of the regular weak conjugation.

This is not merely the Sc. pronunciation of Put *v.*[1], which in Sc. is conjugated *pit, pat, putten* or *pitten*; while this is *putt, puttit, puttit*, and in current use felt as a distinct verb. But the regular weak conjugation formerly occurred in Eng. with senses belonging to Put *v.*[1]]

† 1. *intr.* To push, shove, butt; = Put *v.*[1] 1 d. *To put on*: to push gently, nudge. *Sc. Obs.*

1513 Douglas *Æneis* IX. x. 91 The beste..Can allreddy wyth hornis fuyn and put. 1583 *Leg. Bp. St. Androis* 477 How everie wyfe on vther puttis, Bidding the bischop pay for his guttis. 1630 Rutherford *Lett.* (1862) I. vii. 54 It were time for us, by prayer, to put upon our master-pilot Jesus, and to cry, 'Master, save us: we perish'. 1637–50 Row *Hist. Kirk* (Wodrow Soc.) 436 He sent one who, putting on me, awakened me. 1768 Ross *Helenore* 38 (Jam.), I putted o' you for to set you free.

2. *trans.* To throw or hurl (a stone or weight) from the shoulder, as an athletic exercise; = Put *v.*[1] 2. *Sc.*

[*c* 1300–: see Put *v.*[1] 2.] 1724 Ramsay *Gentle Sheph.* II. iv, When thou ran, or wrestled, or putted the stane. 1816 Scott *Antiq.* xxix, Auld Edie, that kens the rules of a' country games better than ony man that ever drave a bowl, or threw an axle-tree, or putted a stane. 1816 — *Old Mort.* iv, Would the bumpkins but wrestle, or pitch the bar, or putt the stone.

b. *intr.* = Put *v.*[1] 2 b.

[*c* 1300–1535: see Put *v.*[1] 2 b.] ?*a* 1800 *Rose the Red & White Lilly* xviii. in Scott *Minstr. Scot. Bord.*, O it fell anes, upon a time, They putted at the stane. 1820 [see Putter *sb.*[2] 1]. *Mod. Sc.* Let's try who can putt farthest!

3. *Golf.* To strike the ball gently and carefully (with the Putter), so as to make it roll along the surface of the Putting-*green*, with the object of getting it into the hole. Usually *intr.*; also *trans.* with the ball as obj. *orig. Sc.*

1743 [implied in Putter *sb.*[2] 2 a]. 1833 G. F. Carnegie *Golfiana* in R. Clark *Golf* (1875) 150 Well he plays the spoon and iron, but He fails a little when he comes to putt. 1857 *Golfer's Man.* in *Chambers's Inform. for People* 696/1 Some golfers put almost exclusively with a metal club, an iron or cleek. 1892 *English Illustr. Mag.* X. 59 It seems a little matter..to drive your ball up in one and 'put' into the hole in two more. 1894 *Times* 16 June 16/1 He..approached with his iron with great effect, and putted in most deadly style.

Put (put), *ppl. a.* Also 7 *Sc.* **putt.** [pa. pple. of Put *v.*[1]] Placed, set, appointed, etc.: see Put *v.*[1] Usually with an adverb, as **put-aside** (in quot. *absol.*); **put-away** (Put *v.* 38 e); **put-down** (41: in quot., degraded, 41 c); **put-off** (45: in quots., † cast away, abject (*obs.*); deferred, postponed, 45 c); **put-out** (47: in quots., 47 f (*d*), m (*c*)). See also Put-on, Put-up *ppl. adjs.*

1868 Yates *Rock Ahead* I. viii, The *put-aside and rejected of Gilbert Lloyd. 1891 Kipling *Light that Failed* (1900) 261 It was this *put-away treasure that he was trying to find. 1860 Gen. P. Thompson *Audi Alt. Part.* III. cxliii. 126 It ought to be asked in parliament, if parliament was not a *put-down thing and a plaything of the minister. 1636 B. Jonson *Discov., Princeps*, I am a wretch and *put of man, if I doe not reverence and honour him. 1871 Mrs. H. Wood *Dene Hollow* xxxix, A put-off wedding sometimes brings ill-luck. 1899 F. V. Kirby *Sport E. C. Afr.* xi. 118 Grunting in a *put-out sort of way. 1907 *Westm. Gaz.* 24 Oct. 10/3 The put-out work of some West End tailors.

Put, obs. f. Pit *sb.*[1], Pith; var. Putt *sb.*[1]

Put- (put), the stem of Put *v.*[1] in combination with adverbs, forming sbs. derived from adverbial combinations of the verb (see Put *v.*[1] V.): as **put-back,** an act of putting back, or something that puts back; a set-back; **put-by,** an act of putting by or setting aside; **† put-forth,** an act of putting forth, or ? one who puts forth; in quot. an imposture, pretence, or ? an impostor, pretender; **put-out,** an act of putting out (in quot., of putting a player 'out' at baseball); **put-up,** a place to 'put up' in, a lodging, 'quarters'. Also rarely with a preposition, as **put-upon,** an act of 'putting upon' any one, or fact of being 'put upon' (see Put *v.*[1] 23 f); an imposition. See also Put-off *sb.*

a 1697 J. Aubrey *Lives, Hobbes* (1898) I. 333 For ten yeares together his thoughts were..chiefly intent on his 'De Cive', and..his 'Leviathan', which was a great *putt-back to his mathematicall improvement. 1549 Latimer *Serm. Ploughers* (Arb.) 36 There be so manie put offes, so many *put byes, so many respectes, and considerations of worldly wisedome. 1549 [see Put-off 1]. 1628 Feltham *Resolves* Ser. II. lvi. (1647) 175 The cast of the eye, and the put-by of the turning hand. 1581 Mulcaster *Positions* xxxix. 205 Learning empouerished in purses, though replenished in *putfurthes by such interceptours. 1896 Knowles & Morton *Baseball* 83 Every base that was run was ticked off..and every '*put-out' and every 'assist' was shown on the painted plan. 1892 *Longm. Mag.* Oct. 564 We must get a *put-up at Queen's Gate. 1889 J. K. Jerome *Three Men in Boat* iv, The presence of your husband's cheeses in her house she would..regard as a '*put upon'.

† Putage. *Obs.* [a. OF. *putage* (Godef.), f. *pute* harlot, Pute + -age.] Fornication on the part of a woman; whoredom. (Cf. Putery.)

1480 Caxton *Ovid's Met.* XII. iii, Yt pleseth me better that men saye that Helayne is a good wyf than she had doon putage. 1670 Blount *Law Dict.*, *Putage*, fornicatio ex parte fœminæ. 1706 in Phillips (ed. Kersey).

† Putai·le, -ay·le. *Obs.* [In form = OF. *putaille* (Godef.) a body of harlots, a harlotry; but the sense appears to be that of Pedaile, q. v.] Rabble; (?) foot-soldiers.

13.. *Coer de L.* 1286 They slowe knyghtes and gret putayle Off Sarezynys that mys-belevyd. *Ibid.* 4291 Folk of armes ..fyffty thousent With other smal putayle, That ther com into the batayle. *c* 1450 *Merlin* xiii. 192 The saisnes.. were well x ml. of horse-men, with-oute the putaile that ronne vp and down and robbed the peple.

† Putain. *Obs.* Also 4 **-aine,** (**-eyn**), 4–5 **-ayn,** 6 **-ane,** 7 **pewtene.** [a. OF. *putain*:—late popular L. **puttānem*, acc. of *putta*:—L. *pūtida* stinking, disgusting. (See Schwan *Gram. Altfr.* ed. 2, § 341, 352.)] A whore, a prostitute, a strumpet.

Fitz-a-putain (Anglo-Fr.) = whoreson: see Fitz.

a 1300, etc. [see Fitz]. *c* 1380 Wyclif *Serm.* Sel. Wks. II. 27 Puplicans and puteyns trowiden to him. 1560 Rolland *Seven Sag.* Prol. iii, Ane prydfull pure Putane, At quhais wordis men wald tak small disdane. 1603 *Philotus* lxxxiii, Fals pewtene, hes scho playit that sport, Hes scho me handlit in this sort?

‖ **Putamen** (piutēɪ·mĕn). [L. *putāmen* that which falls off in pruning or trimming, husk, shell, f. *putāre* to prune.]

1. *Bot.* The endocarp of a fruit when hard and woody, as the 'stone' of a plum, etc.; rarely applied to the shell of a nut.

1830 Lindley *Nat. Syst. Bot.* 84 Fruit a drupe, with the putamen sometimes separating spontaneously from the sarcocarp. 1885 Goodale *Physiol. Bot.* (1892) 176 A fragment of the hard shell of a nut or of the putamen of a drupe.

2. *Anat.* The outer zone or segment of the extraventricular portion of the grey matter of the brain (*nucleus lenticularis*).

1890 in Billings *Nat. Med. Dict.* 1899 *Allbutt's Syst. Med.* VII. 334 [Certain lesions] in the lenticular nucleus in its outer segment or putamen.

3. The tough membrane or skin which lines the inside of the shell of an egg.

1890 in *Cent. Dict.* 1897 in *Syd. Soc. Lex.*

Putaminous (piutæ·minəs), *a. rare.* [f. L. *putāmen* (*-min-*) + -ous.] Of the nature of or pertaining to a shell, husk, or putamen.

1597 A. M. tr. *Guillemeau's Fr. Chirurg.* 26 b/2 Some putaminous substance chaunced to be theron [the teeth] hardened. 1660 Hickeringill *Jamaica* (1661) 28 The outward crust, or putaminous husk, being broken, appears full of little kernells, or nuts. Also in mod. Dicts.

† Putanie. *Obs.* [Cf. It. *puttana*.] = Putain (for which the instances may be misprints).

1566 *Pasquine in Traunce* 28 Some are called Celestines,.. other Carmilitanes, and some Putanies also. *Ibid.*, *note*, Putanies be those Nunes that we call the greene Friers on strawbery banke.

† Pu·tanism. *Obs. rare*—°. [f. Putain + -ism: cf. F. *putanisme*, It. *puttanismo*.] (See quot.)

1696 Phillips, *Putanism*, the Trade and Living of a Whore. 1721 in Bailey, and in later Dicts.

† Puta·tion. *Obs.* [ad. L. *putātiōn-em*, n. of action from *putāre* to cleanse, prune, reckon, consider, think.]

1. The pruning or trimming of trees.

c 1440 *Pallad. on Husb.* XII. 50 Putacioun autumnal celebrate Is now in vyne & tre ther nys no coold. 1623 Cockeram, *Putation*, a lopping of trees.

2. The action of considering or reckoning; supposition, estimation.

1658 Phillips, *Putation*,..a thinking, reputing, or esteeming. 1670 Baxter *Life Faith* III. viii. 322 It is not possible ..by any putation, estimation, or misjudging whatsoever.

Hence **† Puta·tionary** *a.*, based on hypothesis or theory, suppositional; **† Puta·tioner,** a theorizer.

1657 G. Starkey *Helmont's Vind.* 86 An insufferable task for an old Putationer. 1658 — *Pyrotechny* III. ii, A lazie person, or a conceited Putationer. 1669 W. Simpson *Hydrol. Chym.* 207 In a putationary and consequently deceitful philosophy.

† Putati·tious, *a.* *Obs.* [f. L. *putāt-us*, thought, supposed, pa. pple. of *putāre* to think: see prec. and -itious [1].] Of a supposed, reputed, or imaginary sort.

1660 tr. *Paracelsus' Archidoxis* II. 50 An inhibition might be imposed on such putatitious, imaginary Physicians. 1671 J. Webster *Metallogr.* xxix. 380 The putatitious transmutation of Iron doth otherwise not happen. 1674 R. Godfrey *Inj. & Ab. Physic* 145, I found neither Truth nor Knowledge in my Putatitious Doctrine.

Hence **† Putati·tiously** *adv.*, supposedly, reputedly, in reckoning merely.

1660 H. More *Myst. Godl.* VIII. iv. 375 Even as Christ was righteous, who was not putatitiously and imaginarily righteous, but really so indeed.

Putative (piū·tătiv), *a.* [a. F. *putatif* (14–15th c. in Hatz.-Darm.), or ad. late L. *putātīv-us* (Tertullian *c* 200), f. *putāt-us*: see prec. and -ive.] That is such by supposition or by repute; commonly thought or deemed; reputed, supposed.

Putative marriage, in *Canon law*, a marriage which though legally invalid was contracted in good faith by at least one of the parties.

1432–50 tr. *Higden* (Rolls) III. 331 Philippus,..fader putatiue of the noble conqueroure Alexander. 1530 *Test. Ebor.* (Surtees) VI. 92 John Beilbie, my sone putative. *a* 1548 Hall *Chron., Edw. IV* 196 Of al hys other putatyue (I dare not say fayned) frendes..he had bene clerely abandoned. 1577 tr. *Bullinger's Decades* (1592) 688 Neither is the Scripture it selfe ashamed, to call Marie..not the putatiue or supposed, but the true and naturall mother. 1681 Flavel *Meth. Grace* vi. 130 Let their blasphemous mouths call it in derision putative righteousness, (*i.e.*) a mere fancied or conceited righteousness; yet we know assuredly Christ's righteousness is imputed to us, and that in the way of faith. 1765 Blackstone *Comm.* I. xvi. 458 If such putative father, or lewd mother, run away from the parish, the overseers..may seize their rents, goods, and chattels, in order to bring up the said bastard child. 1858 Sears *Athan.* II. xi. 240 He [Christ] imparts not a putative, but a subjective, righteousness to the believer.

1811 (Febr.) Ld. Meadowbank in *Brymner v. Riddell* (Ct. of Session), Here there was a putative marriage, acknowledged by all the friends of both parties, and by the general admission..of the legality of that marriage. 1825 Rt. Bell (*title*) Report of a case of legitimacy under a putative marriage [Brymner v. Riddell] tried..1811. 1876 P. Fraser *Husb. & Wife Law Scotl.* (ed. 2) I. 152 The children born of such a putative marriage are, by the law of Scotland legitimate, though the marriage be null.

Hence **Pu·tatively** *adv.*, in a putative way or manner; supposedly, reputedly.

1716 M. Davies *Athen. Brit.* II. 220 He subjoin'd also that Christ did not really suffer, but only Putatively in people's Fancies. 1851 P. Colquhoun *Rom. Civ. Law* II. § 1078 Putatively married persons have the same privilege. 1903 McNeill *Egregious English* 109 Mr. Davidson is a Scot, and Mr. Yeats, putatively at any rate, an Irishman.

† Pu·tatory, *a.* *Obs. rare*—°. [ad. late L. *putātōrius*, f. *putāre* to prune.] (See quot.)

1656 Blount *Glossogr.*, *Putatory*, of or belonging to cutting, dressing or pruining of Trees.

† Put-bone. ? The knuckle-bone or astragalus.

1664 E. Browne in *Sir T. Browne's Wks.* (1836) I. 45 Mr. Osborne sent my father a calf, whereof I observed the knee joynt, and the neat articulation of the put bone, which was here very perfect. I dissected another bull's heart. *Ibid.* 48 In a putbone the unfortunate casts are outward, the fortunate inward.

Put-card: see Put *sb.*[3]

† Put-case. *Obs.* [f. the phrase *put case*: Put *v.*[1] 22.]

1. The act of putting a case; a supposition or hypothesis.

1565 Jewel *Def. Apol.* IV. ix. § 3 What a foolishe putcase, and what a fond whatif is that, to saie, What if a Pirate inuade the Arke of Noe? 1577 tr. *Bullinger's Decades* (1592) 282 They with their innumerable perchances and put-cases do make the treatise of restitution so tedious.

2. A person skilled in putting cases; one who states or argues hypothetical cases.

a 1734 North *Lives, Ld. Guildford* I. 20 He used to say that no man could be a good lawyer that was not a put-case.

Putchamin, early form of Persimmon.

Putcher (pɒ·tʃəɹ). *local.* [The same as *putchen, -con, -in*, recorded in the Eng. Dial. Dict. from Shropsh., Worcester, Warwick, Gloucestersh., in sense 'eel-basket, wicker eel-trap'. Origin unknown. Cf. Putt *sb.*[2]] A conical basket or wicker trap for catching salmon (see quot. 1885).

1873 *Act* 36 & 37 *Vic.* c. 71 § 21 (1) Licenses for fishing weirs, fishing mill dams, putts, putchers, fixed nets, and other fixed instruments or devices. 1883 *Fisheries Exhib. Catal.* 51 Models of Salmon Nets..Weirs with fish-passes.. Putchers, [etc.]. 1884 *Daily News* 1 Sept. 6/7 In the [Severn] estuary large hauls were made with the nets and putchers in July and August. 1885 *Daily Tel.* 18 Aug., Putchers.. are funnel-shaped baskets of wicker-work set at right angles to the shore, into which the salmon press themselves in trying to press through, and are unable to return.

‖ **Putchuk, putchock** (pɒ·tʃɒk). Also 7 **pochok,** 8–9 **putchick,** 9 **patchuk.** [Dukhnī or Southern Hindustānī پچک *pachak*; origin doubtful: widely prevalent as a trade name.] The root of the plant *Aplotaxis auriculata* (*Aucklandia Costus* of Falconer), a native of Kashmīr, exported to China and other Eastern countries, and used as a medicine and for making the Chinese joss-sticks.

(*Native*) *green putchuk*, a name for the root of the Chinese *Aristolochia recurvilabra*, used in medicine.

[1588 T. Hickock tr. *C. Frederick's Voy.* 5 Aboundaunce of Opioum, Assa Fetida, Puchio, with many other sorts of drugs.] 1617 R. Cocks *Diary* (Hakl. Soc.) I. 294, 5 hampers pochok. 1704 in C. Lockyer *Trade Ind.* (1711) 77 Putchuck or Costus dulcis. 1727 A. Hamilton *New Acc. E. Ind.* I. xi. 126 Nothing of it is usefull but the Root, called Putchock, or Radix dulcis. 1802 Capt. Elmore *Brit. Mariners Direct.* 129 Putchick, shark fins, olibanum. 1845 Stocqueler *Handbk. Brit. India* (1854) 34 Bombay..supplies..grain, oils, putchock, seeds, tobacco, and soap, from the northern coast. 1858 Simmonds *Dict. Trade Prod.*, Putchuk.

† Pute, *sb. rare*—[1]. [a. F. *pute* = Pr., Sp. *puta*, It. *putta*, late pop. L. *pūtta*:—L. *pūtida* stinking: cf. Putain.] A whore, strumpet, prostitute.

c 1380 Wyclif *Serm.* Sel. Wks. I. 293 Þei ben foule putis.

Pute (piūt), *a.* Now *rare* or *arch.* [ad. L. *putus* clean, pure, used in the phrase *purus* (*ac*) *putus* = *purissimus*.] In phrases *pure pute, pure and pute*, pure, clean, mere.

c 1619 Bp. Hall *Via Media* § 5 Arminius..acknowledges faith to be the pure pute gift of God. 1657 Sanderson *Serm.* Pref. § 24 A pure pute Christian. *a* 1734 North *Exam.* II. iv. § 49 (1740) 256 Dangerfield had the Honour to be a single Discoverer of a pure and pute Sham-plot, Name and Thing. 1906 R. Kipling *Puck of Pook's Hill, Hal o' Draft* 240 Only you and I chance to be pure pute asses.

Pute, obs. form of Pit *sb.*[1]

Puteal (piū·tĭăl), *sb. Rom. Antiq.* [a. L. *puteal*, (*-āle*), orig. neuter of *puteālis*: see next.] The stone curb surrounding the mouth of a well.

[1832 Gell *Pompeiana* II. xiii. 27 A marble mouth or *puteale*.] 1850 Leitch tr. *C. O. Müller's Anc. Art* (ed. 2) § 379 *note*, The Capitoline puteal has adopted a younger figure of Hermes. 1862 E. Falkener *Ephesus* I. iv. 63 Vestiges of a circular building, the small size of which renders it probable that it formed a puteal.

† Pu·teal, *a.* *Obs. rare.* [ad. L. *puteālis*, f. *puteus* pit, well.] Of or pertaining to a well or pit.

1656 Blount *Glossogr.*, *Puteal*, of or belonging to a pit or well. 1657 Tomlinson *Renou's Disp.* 219 The best water, therefore, is fontane, fluvial, and puteal water.

Puteanic (piūtĭˌæ·nik), *a.* *Chem.* [f. L. *puteān-us* pertaining to a well (f. *puteus* well) + -ic.] In *puteanic acid*: see quot.

[1834 Haenle in *Kastner's Archiv*, Nurnberg, XXVI. 399 Ich bezeichne sie daher..mit dem Namen Brunnensäure (*Acidum puteanum*).] 1838 T. Thomson *Chem. Org. Bodies* 156 Puteanic acid..discovered, in 1835, by M. Haenlé, apothecary at Lahr, in the ochre which deposits abundantly in the wells of that neighbourhood...It is a resinous-looking body, transparent when in thin crusts, having a strong lustre, and a brown colour. It has no smell.

Puten, error for Petun, q. v., quot. 1600–14.

Puter, obs. form of Pewter.

† Pu·tery. *Obs.* Also 4 **putrie,** 4–5 **-erie,** 5 **putrye, -ree, -erye.** [a. OF. *put(e)rie* whoredom, f. *pute*: see Pute *sb.*: -ery [1].] Unchastity (properly in a woman); harlotry, prostitution.

c 1380 Wyclif *Wks.* (1880) 10 Þes pharisees geten hem moo holderis vp for here putrie þan for here trewe prechyng. *c* 1386 Chaucer *Pars. T.* ¶ 812 What seye we eek of Putours þat lyuen by the horrible synne of putrie, and constreyne wommen to yelden to hem a certeyn rente of hire bodily puterie? *c* 1440 *York Myst.* xxiv. 30 We haue hir tane with putry playne. 1483 Caxton *G. de la Tour* lj, In puterye and in synne mortalle or dedely he [the deuylle] hath grete power.

Putfalle, obs. form of Pitfall.

† Put-gallary, putt-, var. of Pot-gallery, *Obs.*

1658 *Lease* in *N. & Q.* 10th Ser. (1908) IX. 212/2, 4 Putt Gallaries, or shedds, built over the mill stream upon the wharfe thereof, in Paris Garden.

† Put-gally. *Obs.* Also 6 **putt-.** [ad. Du. and Fl. *put-galg* a bascule to raise water from a well, in Hexham *put-galge* 'a swipe to drawe up water out of a well', in Kilian *put-galghe*, 'tollenon, pertica putealis'; f. *put* well, pit + *galge*, gallows, post of a draw-well.] A bascule or lever fixed on a high fulcrum and having a counterpoise on the handle, by means of which water is lifted from a well or pit; a swipe or sweep.

1584–5 *Indenture* 27 *Eliz.* in *N. & Q.* 8th Ser. (1894) V. 346/2 With free egresse and regresse thorowe the same waye, and with free accesse, egresse and regresse to the Putt gally, findinge wherewith to drawe and carrye the same water aweye, And together also withe like accesse egresse and regresse to the litle well there. 1611 Cotgr., *Bascule*, a swipe, scoope, or put-gally to draw vp water withall.

† Puther[1], obs. form of Pewter.

1562 in J. R. Boyle *Hedon* (1875) App. 206 A litle brasse pott, two puther dublers, two dishes of puther.

Puther[2], obs. and dial. form of Pother.

Putid (piū·tid), *a.* Now *rare.* [ad. L. *pūtid-us* stinking, foul, f. *pūtē-re* to stink: see -id [1].]

† 1. Stinking, rotten, putrid. *Obs.*

1659 Gauden *Slight Healers* (1660) 21 Some putid or corrupt humors in the body.

2. *fig.* Foul, base; morally or intellectually 'rotten' or worthless. (Often merely a term of contempt or execration.)

1580 Fulke *Dang. Rock* xviii. Wks. (Parker Soc.) II. 391 O putid and absurd slanders! 1635–56 Cowley *Davideis* I. Notes, Wks. (1669) 28 Made up..by the putid officiousness of some Grammarians. 1681 Baxter *Answ. Dodwell* iv. 28 A chain of forgeries or putid falshoods. *a* 1734 North *Exam.* III. vii. § 70 (1740) 556 He hath..framed so putid a Libel upon his Lordship. 1818 J. C. Hobhouse *Hist. Illustr.* (ed. 2) 216 To reject this narration as a putid fable.

Hence **Puti·dity** [ad. med.L. *pūtiditās*, *c* 1150 in Thomas *Thesaur.*], **Pu·tidness,** the quality of being putid, rottenness; **Pu·tidly** *adv.*

1659 Gauden *Tears Ch.* II. xvi. 199 High-tasted sawces.. applied to tainted meats, to make their putidness less perceptible. 1864 Webster, Putidity, Putidness. 1897 *Sat. Rev.* 7 May 552/2 What we most feebly and putidly nowadays call a lady-doctor.

Putlog, putlock (pɒ·tlɒg, -lɒk), *sb.* [The form *putlock* appears to have been the earlier; derivation obscure; ? from *put*, pa. pple. of Put *v.*[1]]

One of the short horizontal timbers of a scaffolding, on which the scaffold-boards rest; one end is inserted at right angles in a hole left in the wall for that purpose (*putlog-hole*), the other being supported by the ledger.

α. 1645 *Docum. St. Paul's* (Camden) 143, Putlocks for scaffolding 3763. 1688 R. Holme *Armoury* III. 262/1 Putlocks, pieces of Spar put into the Sides of the Wall to lay Boards on for the Bricklayer to stand and work up high Walls. 1727–41 Chambers *Cycl.*, *Putlogs*, or *Putlocks*, in building. 1823 P. Nicholson *Pract. Build.* 591 Putlogs or Putlocks; in scaffolding, the transverse pieces, at right angles to the wall. 1866 *Standard* 12 June 7/2 The putlock..came away, and a bricklayer..was precipitated from a considerable height to the ground.

β. 1703 Moxon *Mech. Exerc.* 251 *Putlogs*..pieces of Timber, or short Poles, about 7 Foot long. 1862 E. Falkener *Ephesus* iv. 85 The walls are for the most part disfigured by small square holes (like those left by putlogs). 1901 *J. Black's Carp. & Build., Scaffold.* 89 Scaffold poles, putlogs, and boards are rented..most largely to builders.

b. *Comb.* **Putlog-, putlock-hole,** one of a series of small square holes left in the brickwork or stonework of a wall to receive the ends of the putlogs.

1757 Smeaton in *Phil. Trans.* L. 202 Putlock-holes for the scaffolding. 1878 McVittie *Christ Ch. Cathedral* 61 Small holes were found running through the wall at different heights, resembling putlock holes.

Hence **Pu·tlog** *v. trans.*, to insert in the manner of a putlog.

1908 *N. & Q.* 10th Ser. VII. 483/1 A beam putlogged into the north and south walls.

Put-off (put,ǫ·f), *sb.* Pl. **put-offs.** [f. the verbal phrase *put off* (Put *v.* 45).] An act of putting off, in various senses.

1. An act of dismissing a question, argument, etc., or the person propounding it, by evasion or the like; a pretext for not doing something, or for deferring it till later (cf. 2); an evasion, a shift.

1549 Latimer *3rd Serm. bef. Edw. VI* (Arb.) 79 Nowe they haue theyr shyftes, and theyr putofs sainge, we maye not go before a lawe, we maye breake no order. 1549 E. Becke *Bible* (Matthew's) Prol., Then should neyther Goddes cause nor poore mans matters haue so many putoffes, so many put byes & delayes. *a* 1704 T. Brown *Dial. Dead, Friendship* Wks. 1711 IV. 59 He..repay'd my past Services with..base Put-offs. 1823 Bentham *Not Paul* 42 Promises, put-offs, evasions—and, after all, no performance. 1886 Stevenson *Kidnapped* xxii, I think I would have asked farther, but Alan gave me the put-off. 'I am rather wearied', he said.

2. An act of deferring or postponing something; postponement, delay, procrastination; a putting a person off to a later time.

1623 R. Carpenter *Conscionable Christian* 28 Instantly, as the occasion is giuen, without put-offs to aftertimes, or any tedious protraction. ?1625 Jas. I in *Waller's Poems* (1711) p. ix, No Put-offs, my Lord, answer me presently. 1759 Franklin *Ess.* Wks. 1840 III. 425 What the governor's set-off could not effect, was to be reattempted by this put-off. 1827 Moore *Mem.* (1854) V. 157 Expecting..to receive a put-off from Lady Holland for the evening.

3. *lit.* A putting off or setting down a person from a vehicle or a vessel, esp. a boat. *rare.*

1825 Hone *Every-day Bk.* I. 603 This delay..is occasioned by 'laying to' for 'put offs' of single persons and parties, in Thames wherries.

Put-off, *ppl. a.*: see Put *ppl. a.*

Put-on (put,ǫn; stress var.), *ppl. a.* [pa. pple. of *to put on*: see Put *v.* 46.]

1. Placed upon the person, as clothing.

1894 Miss Broughton *Beginner* xii, The Russian net or her accurately put-on veil.

b. *transf.* of the person: Clothed, dressed (with qualifying adv., as *well* or *ill*). *Sc.* and *north. dial.*

1815 Scott *Guy M.* l, I'm no just that weel put on. 1887 Mabel Wethersal *Two North-Country Maids* xxiii, It changes lassies when they look so trim, and well put on. 1896 Barrie *Marg. Ogilvy* ix. (1897) 167 The first thing I want to know about her is whether she was good-looking, and the second how she was put on.

2. *fig.* Assumed, affected, feigned, pretended.

1621 Fletcher *Wildgoose Chase* III. i, With such a reverend put-on Reservation Which could not miss. 1775 Mme. D'Arblay *Early Diary* 28 Feb., He assumed no manner of superiority; nor yet..affected a certain put-on equality. 1884 Church *Bacon* iii. 58 The put on and worldly life.

† Pu·tor. *Obs. rare.* [a. L. *pūtor* stench, f. *pūtēre* to stink.] (See quot.)

1656 Blount *Glossogr.*, *Putor*, a stink or ill savor.

† Putour. *Obs.* [app. AF. *putour*, collateral form of OF. *putier* Putyer.] A whoremonger; a pimp; a fornicator.

c 1386 [see Putery]. 1393 Langl. *P. Pl.* C. VII. 172 Lady, to þy leue sone lowte for me nouthe, That he haue pyte on me putour [*v. r.* putrour] of hus pure grace and mercy.

Put-out, *sb.* and *ppl. a.*: see Put-, Put *ppl. a.*

† Pu·t-pin. *Obs.* [f. Put *v.*[1] + Pin.] = Push-pin.

1592 Nashe *Foure Lett. Confut.* (1593) 52, I will play at put-pinne with thee for all that thou art woorth. 1658 J. Harrington *Prerog. Pop. Govt.* I. ix. (1700) 260 His Put-pin is pretty: The Emperor puts Power into the hands of the Electors; and the King of Poland puts Power into the hands of the Gentlemen. 1665 Glanvill *Scepsis Sci.* xxiii. 178 He..will not leave the Throne to play with Beggars at Put-pin, or be fond of Tops and Cherry-stones.

Putred, obs. erron. form of Putrid.

† Pu·trede. *Obs. rare.* Also **-ride.** [ad. L. *putrēdo*: see below.] Rotting, putridity.

c 1400 *Lanfranc's Cirurg.* 86 If þat þe membre be drie.. & þei han greet putride [MS. B. putrede] & rotschipe.

† Putre·dinal, *a.* *Obs.* Also 7 **putri-.** [a. F. *putrédinal* (16th c. in Godef.), f. late L. *putrēdo, -inem*: see Putredo and -al.] Proceeding from or characterized by putrefaction.

1574 J. Jones *Nat. Beginning Grow. Things* 18 It is the naturall heate, become putredinall or rotten. 1666 G. Harvey *Morb. Angl.* xv. 178 Lice..engendred out of their clammy sweat, by a putredinal heat that attends them.

† Putre·dinous, *a.* *Obs.* [ad. F. *putrédineux* (Cotgr. 1611), f. as prec.: see -ous.] = prec.; also *fig.* filthy, abominable.

1641 Burges *Serm. bef. Ho. Com.* 5 Nov. 60 All putredinous vermine of bold Schismaticks and frantick Sectaries glory in her ashes. 1708 *Brit. Apollo* No. 35. 3/2 From Putredinous Humours this ill doth proceed. 1711 G. Cary *Phys. Phylactick* 209 Most Putredinous Sectaries.

‖ **Putredo** (piutrī·do). *Obs.* [Late L. *putrēdo* rottenness, putridity, f. *putrēre* to rot: cf. *torpēdo* f. *torpēre*.] Putrefaction; *spec.* in *Path.*, hospital gangrene (*Syd. Soc. Lex.*).

1704 F. Fuller *Med. Gymn.* (1718) 161 Accounting for things by Occult Qualities, Putredo's and the like.

Putrefacient (piūtrĭfēɪ·ʃĕnt), *a.* (*sb.*) [ad. L. *putrefacient-em*, pres. pple. of *putrefacĕre* to make rotten: see next.] = Putrefactive.

1883 *American* VI. 173 One of which is..a putrefacient poison. 188. *Alienist & Neurol.* IX. 363 Putrefacient action on the blood and tissues after the lapse of some hours.

B. *sb.* A putrefactive agent or substance.

1890 in *Cent. Dict.*

† Putrefa·ct, *v.* *Obs.* Also 7 **putri-.** [f. L. *putrefact-*, ppl. stem of *putrefacĕre* to make rotten, f. *putrēre* to be rotten (f. *puter, putr-* rotten) + *facĕre* to make.] *trans.* To make rotten, to putrefy.

1597 A. M. tr. *Guillemeau's Fr. Chirurg.* 33 b/2 To prevente the same [bone] to be..putrefacted and corrupted.

Hence **† Putrefa·cted** *ppl. a.*, putrefied; **† Putrefa·ctible** *a.*, capable of putrefaction; putrescible.

1602 Marston *Antonio's Rev.* IV. iv, Vermine bred of putrifacted slime. 1634 Peacham *Gentl. Exerc.* I. xviii. 60 Grosse and putrefacted vapours, that issue from the eyes. 1651 Biggs *New Disp.* § 287 As often as any putrefactible or cadaverizable thing is ingested in the stomack.

Putrefaction (piūtrĭfæ·kʃən). Forms: 5–9 (*erron.*) **putri-,** 6 **putry-,** 5– **putre-;** 5 **-faccio(u)n, -faccyon, -factioun,** 6– **-faction.** [a. OF. *putrefaction* (14th c. in Littré), or ad. L. *putrefactiōn-em*, n. of action f. *putrefacĕre*: see prec.]

1. The action or process of putrefying; the decomposition of animal and vegetable substances, with its attendant unwholesome loathsomeness of smell and appearance; rotting, corruption.

In quot. 1432–50, applied to a corrupting pestilence.

1432–50 tr. *Higden* (Rolls) V. 339 A grete dragon, thro the pestilente putrefaccion of whom moche peple diede in the cite. 1533 Elyot *Cast. Helthe* III. xv. (1541) 72 b, It shal be necessary for them..to be circumspecte in eatyng meate yt shortly will receiue putrifaction. 1661 J. Childrey *Brit. Baconica* 55 Heat and moisture are the greater disposers to putrifaction. 1789 W. Buchan *Dom. Med.* (1790) 63 Animal substances have a constant tendency to putrefaction. 1833 Marryat *P. Simple* xxx, The body is never allowed to remain many hours unburied in the tropical climates, where putrefaction is so rapid. 1875 Huxley & Martin *Elem. Biol.* (1883) 26 All the forms of putrefaction which are undergone by animal and vegetable matters are fermentations set up by Bacteria of different kinds.

b. Decomposition of tissues or fluids in a living body, as in ulceration, suppuration, or gangrene.

c 1400 *Lanfranc's Cirurg.* 51 Þe which quytture schulde corrupte þilke lyme [= limb] & brynge him to putrifaccioun [*v. r.* putrefactioun]. 1460–70 *Bk. Quintessence* 21 Alle philosophoris seyn þat þe feuere contynuele is gendrid of putrifaccioun of blood and of corrupcioun of humouris in it. 1579 Langham *Gard. Health* (1633) 403 Mirrhe preserueth from putrifaction, both the intrals and all outward sores, wounds, and vlcers. 1605 Bacon *Adv. Learn.* I. vi. § 9 That putrefaction is more contagious before maturitie than after. 1756 Gray *Let. to Wharton* 25 Mar., I maintain that one sick rich patient has more of pestilence and putrefaction about him than a whole ward of sick poor. 1806 *Med. Jrnl.* XV. 492 It is attended with great debility, and there is frequently a great tendency to putrefaction and mortification.

† 2. In reference to inorganic matter, esp. in *Alchemy*: The disintegration or decomposition of a substance by chemical or other action; also, the oxidation or corrosion of metals, etc. *Obs.*

1471 Ripley *Comp. Alch.* v. iii. in Ashm. *Theat. Chem. Brit.* (1652) 148 And Putrefaccyon may thus defyned be After Philosophers sayings it ys of Bodyes the fleyng, And in our compound a dyuysyon of thyngs thre. 1610 B. Jonson *Alch.* II. v, Name the vexations, and the martyrizations of Mettalls...Sir, Putrefaction, Solution, Ablution, Sublimation [etc.]. 1626 Bacon *Sylva* § 291 Metals give Orient and Fine colours in Dissolutions..likewise in their Putrefactions or Rusts. 1671 J. Webster *Metallogr.* viii. 128 A certain metallick body..that is of an easie solution and putrefaction.

3. *concr.* Decomposed or putrid matter.

1605 Bacon *Adv. Learn.* I. vi. § 11 The mosse vppon the wall, which is but a rudiment betweene putrefaction, and an hearbe. 1634 Sir T. Herbert *Trav.* 39 In the midst is a hole, discending to the bottome, which receiues that putrefaction and vncleannesse, issuing from the melting bodies, which are laid there naked..exposed to the sunnes fiery rage. 1692 Bentley *Boyle Lect.* iv. 134 They would readily [deposit their eggs] in all Putrefaction, even in a mucilage of bruised spiders.

4. *fig.* Moral corruption and decay.

a 1631 Donne *Select.* (1840) 164 We bring elements of our own; earth of covetousness, water of unsteadfastness, air of putrefaction, and fire of licentiousness. 1750 Johnson *Rambler* No. 47 ¶ 14 Sorrow..is the putrefaction of stagnant life, and is remedied by exercise and motion. 1871 Tyndall *Fragm. Sci.* (1879) II. ix. 148 Rome, and the other cities of the Empire, had fallen into moral putrefaction. 1907 *Edin. Rev.* Jan. 22, It is thanks to heretics that orthodoxy has been kept from putrefaction.

Hence **† Putrefa·ctious** (putri-) *a. Obs.*, of the nature of, or full of putrefaction; putrefying, putrid.

1609 W. M. *Man in Moone* D iij, Your complexion..shall be of a saffron colour; your cheekes, thinne; your nosethrils putrifactious;..your breath, noysome. 1616 R. C. *Times' Whistle* v. 2178 Drunkennesse, whose putrefactious slime Darkens the splendour of our common wealth.

Putrefactive (piūtrĭfæ·ktiv), *a.* (*sb.*) Also 6–7 **putri-.** [a. F. *putréfactif, -ive* (14th c. in Littré), f. L. *putrefact-*: see Putrefact and -ive.]

1. Causing or inducing putrefaction; putrefying.

1545 Elyot *Dict.* H h vj b/1, *Septicus*,..putrifactife, or corrosife. 1601 Holland *Pliny* XXVIII. ix. II. 321 Their blood is corrosiue by nature, and putrifactiue. 1610 Markham *Masterp.* II. clvi. 460 The medicines are either corrosiue, putrifactiue, or caustick. 1744 Berkeley *Siris* § 69 Where the obstruction is attended with a putrefactive alkali. 1830 M. Donovan *Dom. Econ.* I. 99 The existence of some putrefactive ferment. 1899 *Allbutt's Syst. Med.* VI. 165 Putrid softening is due to the invasion of putrefactive bacteria.

2. Of, pertaining to, produced or characterized by putrefaction; indicative of putrefaction. *Putrefactive fermentation*, putrefaction scientifically viewed as a species of fermentation.

1646 Sir T. Brown *Pseud. Ep.* II. vi. 95 Making putrifactive generations correspondent unto seminal productions ..when the Ore corrupteth into Bees, or the Horses into hornets. 1676 Wiseman *Chirurg. Treat.* (J.), If the bone be corrupted, the putrefactive smell will discover it. 1758 Reid tr. *Macquer's Chem.* I. 111 The third generates an alkaline salt;..this last sort takes the name of the Putrid or Putrefactive Fermentation. 1815 Kirby & Sp. *Entomol.* iv. (1818) I. 87 The authors..had mistaken for lice some other species of insects, which are not unfrequently found in putrefactive sores. 1838 *Penny Cycl.* X. 237/2 Fermentation is of three kinds: the vinous, producing alcohol; the acetous, yielding vinegar; and the putrefactive, of which the products are very variable and usually fetid.

† 3. Undergoing or subject to putrefaction; putrefying; corruptible. *Obs.*

1610 Markham *Masterp.* II. clxxiii. 487 It cleanseth al putrifactiue humors. 1661 Feltham *Resolves* II. xvii. Wks. (1677) 194 If momentary and putrefactive man can undiscerned and unburthen'd bear so much about him.

† B. *sb.* A substance which causes putrefaction; a putrefactive agent. *Obs.*

1610 Markham *Masterp.* II. clvi. 461 The corrosiues are weaker then the putrifactiues, and the putrifactiues are weaker then the caustickes.

Hence **Putrefa·ctiveness,** the quality of being putrefactive. 1864 in Webster.

† Putrefa·ctory, *a.* *Obs. rare.* Also **putri-.** [f. as prec. + -ory [2].] = Putrefactive *a.*

1650 Bulwer *Anthropomet.* 251 Their way is, to cut a man in pieces, and then put him into a Putrifactory Vessel.

Putrefiable (piū·trĭfəiˌăb'l), *a.* [f. Putrefy + -able.] Capable of being putrefied; putrescible.

1883 W. T. Belfield *Relat. Micro-Org. to Disease* 60 For absorption of putrefiable materials. 1884 *19th Cent.* Feb. 325 Some epidemic agent..which converts putrefiable impurities into a specific poison.

Putrefied (piū·trĭfəid), *ppl. a.* [f. Putrefy + -ed [1].] Rendered putrid; rotten.

1526 *Pilgr. Perf.* (W. de W. 1531) 202 b, Many other beestes and wormes be gendred of the erth onely, or other putrefyed matter. *a* 1640 J. Ball *Answ. to Canne* II. (1642) 55 As rotten and putrified stuffe to be cast out. 1724 R. Welton *Chr. Faith & Pract.* 359 Their hearts are filthy and corrupt like those putrefied carcasses. 1765 A. Dickson *Treat. Agric.* (ed. 2) 370 The dung..is still to be considered as vegetables in a putrefied state.

Putrefier (piū·trĭfəiˌəɹ). [f. Putrefy + -er [1].] A putrefying agent. Also *fig.*

1651 Biggs *New Disp.* § 118 Putrefyers of the blood. 1883 *Workshop Receipts* Ser. II. 196/2 A series of experiments upon putrefiers and antiseptics. 1895 *Voice* (N. Y.) 9 May 5/4 Who are the putrefiers of society to-day?

Putrefy (piū·trĭfəi), *v.* Also 5–6 **putry-,** 6–9 **putrify.** [a. F. *putréfi-er*, ad. L. *putrefacĕre* (see Putrefact), with the ending *-fy*, as if from a L. **putrificāre* (whence the spelling *putrify*): see Putrification and -fy.]

1. *trans.* To render putrid; to cause to rot or decay with a fetid smell. Now *rare.*

1432–50 tr. *Higden* (Rolls) V. 117 This Galerius..hade the partes interialle of his breste and exterialle putrefiede [*putrefacto pectore*] and corrupte so soore..that [etc.]. 1528 Roy *Rede me* Epist. (Arb.) 25 For one rotten apple lytell and lytell putrifieth an whole heape. 1591 Shaks. 1 *Hen. VI*, IV. vii. 90 They would but stinke, and putrifie the ayre. 1659 Pearson *Creed* iv. (1662) 242 The bodies were often left upon the Crosse till the sun and rain had putrified and consumed them. 1784 Cowper *Task* II. 184 God..bids a plague Kindle a fiery boil upon the skin, And putrefy the breath of blooming health. 1863 *Intell. Observ.* IV. 103 (tr. *Pasteur's Researches*) Let us putrefy lactate of lime sheltered from air.

† b. *Alchemy* and *Old Chem.* To decompose chemically; to subject to any decomposing or destructive process, e. g. to oxidize. *Obs.*

1471 Ripley *Comp. Alch.* v. li. in Ashm. *Theat. Chem. Brit.* (1652) 160, I have the tought How thou the Bodys must Putrefy. 1651 French *Distill.* i. 14 Things are sooner putrefied in cloudy weather then in faire. *Ibid.* v. 118 Putrefie them together in Balneo the space of three dayes.

† c. *fig.* To corrupt morally or socially; to destroy the purity or soundness of; to render corrupt. *Obs.*

1538 Bale *Thre Lawes* 1927 We charge you no more thys lawe to putryfye. 1593 G. Harvey *Pierce's Super.* in G. G. Smith *Eliz. Crit. Ess.* (1904) II. 260 Out vpon ranke and lothsome ribaldry that putrifieth where it should purify. 1685 Baxter *Paraphr. N. T.* Matt. v. 13 The World is putrified with the corruption of all sin.

2. *intr.* To become putrid; to decay with an offensive smell; to decompose, rot, 'go bad'.

1412–20 Lydg. *Chron. Troy* III. xxviii, Aboue the grounde if the body lye That by all reason it must putryfye. 1539 Elyot *Cast. Helthe* 37 Suche is the nature of hony, that it suffreth not the bodies to putrifie. 1692 Bentley *Boyle Lect.* iv. 134 He suffer'd those things to putrefy in Hermetically sealed glasses. 1774 Goldsm. *Nat. Hist.* (1776) I. 314 In the cold arctic regions, animal substances, during their winter, are never known to putrefy. 1838 Thomson *Chem. Org. Bodies* 1010 Albumen and fibrin putrefy very quickly.

b. Of the tissues or fluids in a living body: To become putrid or gangrenous; to fester, suppurate.

c 1500 [see Putrefying *vbl. sb.*]. 1540–54 Croke *Ps.* (Percy Soc.) 11 Myne old sores do breake out agayn, And are corrupte and putrefie. 1660 R. Coke *Power & Subj.* 170 No Physitian can rightly cure any disease or wound until the venemous matter which putrifies inwardly be drawn out. 1871 Tyndall *Fragm. Sci.* (1879) I. v. 176 The blood would putrefy and become fetid.

c. *fig.* To become corrupt or decay, morally, socially, or in any non-physical sense.

1526 Tindale 1 *Pet.* i. 4 An inheritaunce immortall and vndefiled, and that putrifieth not. 1597 Hooker *Eccl. Pol.* v. lxxvi. § 4 The name of vnrighteous persons shall putrifie. 1675 Traherne *Chr. Ethics* 29 Raising up some persons thereby to be like salt among corrupted men, least all should putrifie and perish. 1720 T. Boston *Hum. Nat. Fourfold St.* (1797) 114 We putrified in Adam as our root.

Putrefying (piū·trĭfəiˌiŋ), *vbl. sb.* [-ing [1].] The action of the verb Putrefy; putrefaction.

1471 Ripley *Comp. Alch.* III. xvi. in Ashm. *Theat. Chem. Brit.* (1652) 143 And hete of Askys and balnys for putrefying. *c* 1500 *Melusine* xxiii. 157 The venym that was within the wounde caused grete putrefyeng & rotyng of his fleshe.

Pu·trefying, *ppl. a.* [-ing [2].] That putrefies.

a. *intr.* Undergoing putrefaction; rotting. Also *fig.*

1611 Bible *Isa.* i. 6 Wounds, and bruises, and putrifying sores. 1746–7 Hervey *Medit.* (1818) 157 Alas! a mass of putrefying clay. 1839 Darwin *Voy. Beagle* xi. 231 The ground is concealed by a mass of slowly putrefying vegetable matter. 1896 *Allbutt's Syst. Med.* II. 789 These 'putrefactive' bacteria are..present..in putrefying liquids.

b. *trans.* = Putrefactive *a.* 1. *rare.*

1758 J. S. *Le Dran's Observ. Surg.* (1771) 298 From a continual Use of putrefying Medicines.

† Pu·trer. *Obs. rare.* [f. *putrie*, Putery + -er [1].] A whoremonger; a fornicator.

c 1303 [see Putour]. ?14.. in Arnolde *Chron.* (1811) 90 Ye shall enquyre yf there bee putrer comon hasurdur contrary mayntener of quarels..or other comon mysdoers be dwellyng wythin the warde.

Putrescence (piutre·sĕns). [f. L. *putrescent-em* Putrescent: see -ence. Cf. F. *putrescence* (18th c. in Littré).] The action or process of rotting or becoming putrid; incipient or advancing rottenness.

1646 Sir T. Browne *Pseud. Ep.* IV. x. 202 They prevent.. putrescence of humors. 1783 Johnson *Let. to Mrs. Thrale* 22 Sept., You would not have me for fear of pain perish in putrescence. 1800 *Phil. Trans.* XC. 165 As soon as a great degree of putrescence has taken place, the luminous property of the fishes is destroyed. 1802 *Trans. Soc. Arts* XX. 213 Having always a putrescence *per se*, or tendency to putrify. 1861 Wynter *Soc. Bees* 197 (*Preserved Meats*) How did this putrescence arise?

b. *concr.* Putrescent or rotting matter.

1843 Carlyle *Past & Pr.* III. x, Nameless masses of putrescence, useful only for turnip-manure. 1898 *Westm. Gaz.* 29 Aug. 2/3 The sanitary inspector described one of the lots as 'perished, diseased, and rotten'...Is the only penalty..the carting away of the putrescence and the burying of it at the bottom of the sea?

c. *fig.*; esp. Moral rottenness or corruption.

1840 Carlyle *Heroes, Luther*, The European World was asking him: Am I to sink ever lower into falsehood, stagnant putrescence, loathsome accursed death? 1865 Ruskin *Arrows of Chace* (1880) II. 141 A putrescence through the constitution of the people is indicated by this galled place.

Putrescency (piutre·sĕnsi). [f. as prec. + -ency.] The state or condition of being putrescent.

1756 C. Lucas *Ess. Waters* III. 151 This..corrects the putrescency, blunts the acidity. 1794 Sullivan *View Nat.* I. 148 When these bodies are only at the commencement of putrescency. 1837 M. Donovan *Dom. Econ.* II. 33 Putrescency is no blemish, in the opinion of many nations...The inhabitants of Terra del Fuego find the putrid flesh of the whale and seal quite agreeable.

Putrescent (piutre·sĕnt), *a.* [ad. L. *putrēscent-em*, pr. pple. of *putrēsc-ĕre* to grow rotten, inceptive of *putrēre* to be rotten. Cf. F. *putrescent* (16th c. in Godef.).]

1. Becoming putrid; in process of putrefaction.

1732 Arbuthnot *Rules of Diet* in *Aliments* 257 The State of a putrescent Alkali. 1818–20 E. Thomson *Cullen's Nosol. Method.* (ed. 3) 240 Scorbutus. In cold countries occurring after living on putrescent, salted animal food. 1834 *Brit. Husb.* I. 225 Putrescent manures..all animal and vegetable substances which can be reduced through decomposition, fermentation, and putrefaction, into such a state as will render them fit to assist the melioration of the land. 1881 Tyndall *Floating Matter Air* 67 Bacteria were numerous in the exposed tubes, and soon afterwards all three of them became thickly muddy and putrescent.

2. Of, pertaining to, or accompanying putrescence.

1775 Sir E. Barry *Obs. Wines Ancients* 10 Stronger Wines are more apt to degenerate..into a vapid, ropy, and at length a putrescent state. 1849–52 *Todd's Cycl. Anat.* IV. 862/1 We find game, in a putrescent state, eaten as a luxury. *fig.* 1876 Blackie *Songs Relig. & Life* 40 He saw God's features, in the dim putrescent light Of his own sick imaginings.

Putrescible (piutre·sĭb'l), *a.* [f. L. *putrēsc-ĕre* to grow rotten + -ible. Cf. F. *putrescible* (14th c. in Godef.), and Putrible.] Liable to rot or become putrid; subject to putrefaction.

1797 Pearson in *Phil. Trans.* LXXXVIII. 28 It does not appear to be putrescible, nor form a viscid solution with water. 1815 Millard *Time's Telesc.* (1825) 87 The white cabbage is the most putrescible. 1878 Tyndall in *19th Century* Mar. 505 The substances after having been superheated remain putrescible, though they do not putrefy.

Hence **Putrescibi·lity** [cf. F. *putrescibilité* (Littré)], the quality of being putrescible.

1800 Hatchett in *Phil. Trans.* XC. 393, I..suspect, that strong..muscular fibre..is not of easy putrescibility. 1881 Tyndall *Floating Matter Air* 101 The putrescibility of pheasant..was exceeded by that of snipe, partridge, and plover.

Putrescine (piutre·səin). *Physiol. Chem.* Also erron. **-in.** [f. as prec. + -ine [5].] One of the ptomaines or cadaveric alkaloids: see quots.

1887 A. M. Brown *Anim. Alkaloids* 36 Putrescine $C^4H^{12}N^2$.—Like the preceding ptomaines is obtained from the flesh of the mammifera and herring brines. It is a limpid, slightly oily liquid, the odour of which resembles that of sperm. 1896 *Allbutt's Syst. Med.* I. 588 Brieger ..has isolated and named a number of these ptomaines, such as putrescine, cadaverine, neurine, &c. 1897 *Ibid.* II. 788 Some [alkaloids] such as cadaverine, putrescine, and choline are but slightly poisonous. 1899 Cagney *Jaksch's Clin. Diagn.* v. (ed. 4) 188 These observers..established the identity of Brieger's putrescin with tetramethylendiamine.

† Pu·trible, *a.* *Obs. rare.* [ad. late L. *putribilis* corruptible, f. *putrēre* to rot: see -ible.] Liable to become putrid; = Putrescible.

1620 Venner *Via Recta* vi. 97 Olives..breed a putrible and vnwholsome nourishment. *Ibid.* vii. 122 They..fill the body with crude and putrible humours.

Putrid (piū·trid), *a.* (In 6–7 *erron.* **putred.**) [a. L. *putrid-us* rotten, f. *putrēre* to rot, f. *puter* rotten. Cf. F. *putride* (14th c. in Godef.).]

1. Of organic bodies or substances: In a state of decomposition; rotten.

1598 Marston *Sco. Villanie* I. Proem. (1599) 171 Quake guzzell dogs, that liue on putred slime, Skud from the lashes of my yerking rime. 1692 Bentley *Boyle Lect.* iv. 131 [He] made innumerable trials with the putrid Flesh of all sorts of Beasts and Fowls. 1730 tr. *Leonardus' Mirr.*

Supplement, p. 3873; Corrigenda, p. 4092; Spurious words, p. 4093; Books quoted, p. 4094

PYRAMICAL

Pyramical, *a.* *Obs.* [irreg. f. L. *pyramis*, a. Gr. πυραμίς + -ICAL.] = PYRAMIDAL.

Pyramid (pɪ'ramid), *sb.* Forms: see below.

A. Illustration of Forms.

α. 4–7 *pi*ʹramis, 6–8 *py*ʹramis; *pl.* 6–7 *pira*ʹmides, *pyra*ʹmides; (7 *pyra*ʹmidis, *pyra*ʹmidis, 8 *pira*ʹmidies); *sing.* (3 syll.) 6–7 *pyra*ʹmides (4 *mute*), *pyra*ʹmidis.

β. 6–7 *pyramid*, *piramide*, 7 *piramid*, 7 *pyramidis*; *pl.* 7 *pyramides*, *pi*ʹramids, 7–9 *pyra*ʹmides.

B. Signification.

1. A monumental structure built of stone or the like, with a polygonal (usually square) base, and sloping sides meeting at an apex; *orig.* and *esp.* one of the ancient structures of this kind in Egypt.

2. The form of a pyramid; in *Geom.* a solid figure bounded by plane surfaces, of which one (the base) is a polygon of any number of sides, and the other surfaces triangles having as bases the sides of the polygon, and meeting at a point (the vertex) outside the plane of the polygon.

3. *Arch.* Any structure of pyramidal form, as a spire, pinnacle, obelisk, etc. Also applied to a gable.

4. Any material thing or object of pyramidal form; a number of things arranged or heaped up in this form, a pyramidal pile.

5. *fig.* or *allusively* (from prec. senses).

6. *Cryst.* A set of faces belonging to a single crystallographic form and, if symmetrically developed, meeting in a point.

7. *Anat.* Applied to various parts or structures of more or less pyramidal form.

PYRAMIDAIRE

Pyramidaire [after *millionaire*], a person to whom a pyramid is erected is a monument.

Pyramidal (pɪ'ramidal), *a.* (*sb.*) [ad. med. L. *pyramidal-is* (1507 in Hatz.-Darm.).]

1. Of or pertaining to a pyramid; sloping, as of the sides of a pyramid; *rare.*

2. Of the nature or shape of a pyramid; resembling a pyramid.

PYRAMOIDAL

Pyramidine, *v.* [f. PYRAMID *sb.* + -INE.] *intr.* To form in a pyramidal or pyramidising manner.

Pyramido- combining form from Gr. πυραμίς.

Pyramis, earliest form of PYRAMID, *q.v.*

PYRAUSTA

PYRETO-

PYRETOID

PYRITOUS

pyritous smell is generally perceptible. 1794 SULLIVAN *View Nat.* II. 112 All pit coal is more or less pyritous. 1839 URE *Dict. Arts* 337 Pyritous Copper; Kupferkies; a metallic looking substance, of a bronze-yellow colour. 1852 TH. ROSS *Humboldt's Trav.* I. vi. 235 Ravines, of which the pyritous strata have borne for ages the imposing names of 'Minas de oro!' 1881 BODDY *Hist. Salt* iv. 34 Those sulphates so prevalent in the..pyritous beds of the Lias.

† **Py·rity,** *a. Obs.* [f. PYRITE + -Y.] Containing pyrite or pyrites.

1757 tr. *Henckel's Pyritol.* 175 Small or poor ores, which are commonly quartzy, mock-leady, and pyrity. *Ibid.* 302 Neither pyrity nor vitriolic.

Pyrk e, obs. forms of PERK *sb.*[1] and *v.*[1]

Pyrl(e, obs. forms of PIRL, PURL *sb.*[1] and *v.*[1]

Pyro (pəi·ro). *Photogr.* Abbreviation of PYROGALLIC *acid* or PYROGALLOL, extensively used as a developing agent. Often *attrib.* and in *Comb.*, as in *pyro-developer*, *-solution*, etc.

1879 *Cassell's Techn. Educ.* III. 294 The proper developing agent for collodio-bromide plates is..known as the alkaline pyro-developer. 1885 C. G. W. LOCK *Workshop Receipts* Ser. IV. 376/2 Take enough of the pyro solution in your developing tray to well cover the plate. 1892 *Photogr. Ann.* II. 44 Pyro and other photo chemicals are violent poisons. 1893 *Brit. Jrnl. Photogr.* XL. 747 Pyro is used in conjunction with sodium sulphate. 1905 *Westm. Gaz.* 5 Aug. 14/2 One of the chief merits of the pyro-developed negative.

b. *Comb.*, indicating a mixture of pyrogallic acid with another substance, as a developer: e.g. *pyro-ammonia*, *-lime*, *-metol*, *-potash*, *-soda*; **pyro-carbonate**, pyrogallic acid with carbonate of soda.

1885 C. G. W. LOCK *Workshop Receipts* Ser. IV. 357/1 The pyro-lime developer becomes violet and brown in use. 1890 *Anthony's Photogr. Bull.* III. 108 Now a word about developers. I have tried them all...Ferrous oxalate pyro-soda, pyro-potash, hydroquinone, etc. *Ibid.* 312, I have developed a good many dozens of exposures, and with pyro-ammonia or pyro-carbonate I have not yet got an unevenly developed film. 1907 *Westm. Gaz.* 2 Mar. 18/2 A green-brown or brown-black colour, such as is given by a pyro-metol developer or pyro-soda not too heavily dosed with sulphite.

Pyro- (pəi·ro, piro), before a vowel or *h* sometimes **pyr-** (but more freq. *pyro-*), repr. Gr. πυρο-, combining form of πῦρ fire, forming the first element in many terms belonging to various arts and sciences. (The second element is properly of Greek, but sometimes of Latin or English origin.)

1. In various terms, chiefly scientific or technical, in the sense Of, relating to, done with, caused or produced by fire.

Pyrocla·stic *a. Geol.* [Gr. κλαστός broken: cf. CLASTIC], consisting of fragments broken through the action of volcanic fire, or comminuted in the process of eruption. **Py·rocone,** a cone of flame, as in the blow-pipe flame. **Py·ro-engra·ver,** an artist who practises PYROGRAVURE or poker-work. **Pyrognomic** (-gnǫ·mik, -gnōᵘ·mik) *a.* [Gr. γνώμη means of knowing, mark, token]: see quot. **Pyrognostic** (-gnǫ·stik) *a. Min.* [Gr. γνωστικός pertaining to knowledge: after *diagnostic*, *prognostic*, etc.], applied to, or relating to, those characters of a mineral that are ascertained by means of the flame of a blow-pipe or of a Bunsen burner; so **Pyrogno·stics** *sb. pl.*, pyrognostic characters, or the branch of mineralogy that deals with them. † **Py·romachy,** *Obs. nonce-wd.* [cf. Gr. πυρομαχεῖν to contend with fire], fighting with fire. **Pyromagne·tic** *a.*, applied to a dynamo invented by Edison, the working of which depends on the diminution of the magnetization of iron with increase of temperature. **Pyroma·nia,** insanity characterized by an impulse to set things on fire, incendiary mania; so **Pyroma·niac** *sb.*, one affected with pyromania; *adj.*, pertaining to or affected with pyromania; also **Pyromani·acal** *a.* **Py·rometamo·rphism** *Geol.*, metamorphism resulting from the action of heat; so **Py·rometamo·rphic** *a.*, of, pertaining to, or characterized by pyrometamorphism. **Pyromo·rphous** *a. Min.* [Gr. μορφή form], having the property of crystallizing after fusion by heat (cf. *pyromorphite* in 2). **Pyrona·phtha,** an illuminant made from the waste products of the distillation of Baku petroleum. † **Pyronomics** (-nǫ·miks), † **Pyro·nomy** (-ǫ·nŏmi) [? after *economics*, *economy*], the phenomena and laws of the action of fire or heat. **Pyrophanous** (pəirǫ·fănəs) *a. Min.* [Gr. -φανης appearing; cf. *diaphanous*], having the property of becoming transparent or translucent when heated (cf. *pyrophane* in 2). ‖ **Pyropho·bia** *Path.* [see -PHOBIA], 'morbid dread of fire' (Billings *Nat. Med. Dict.* 1890). **Py·rophone** (-fōᵘn) [Gr. φωνή voice, sound], a musical instrument devised by Kastner, having a series of glass tubes each containing two hydrogen flames burning close together, which by pressing down a key are caused to separate, and then produce a sound. **Pyropu·ncture** *Surg.*, 'puncturing with red-hot needles' (Billings); a puncture so made. **Py·roscope** [see -SCOPE], an instrument invented by Leslie, *c* 1825, for measuring the intensity of radiant heat, consisting of a differential thermometer having one bulb covered with silver. **Pyrosi·lver,** a trade name for electro-plated goods in which the silver is 'burnt in', i.e. fixed more firmly by means of heat. **Pyrosophy** (-ǫ·sŏfi) [Gr. σοφία wisdom], 'the knowledge of the nature and properties of fire or heat' (Mayne *Expos. Lex.*). **Py·rostat** [Gr. στατός standing: cf. *heliostat*, *thermostat*], 'an automatic draft-regulator for chimneys, smoke-pipes, and smoke-stacks' (*Cent. Dict.*). **Pyroste·reotype,** a printing plate in relief cast from an intaglio burnt in a wooden block by means of a blade, or of steel plugs, heated by a gas-flame; used esp. for printing music; also, short for *pyrostereotype process* (Knight *Dict. Mech.* 1875–84). † **Pyrotheo·logy,** the part of natural theology which is founded on the laws and phenomena of fire. **Pyrothonide** (-ǫ·þonəid) [Gr. ὀθόνη linen, sail-cloth], an empyreumatic oil, formerly used in medicine, obtained by burning linen, hemp, or cotton in a closed vessel.

1888 RUTLEY *Rock-Forming Min.* 124 Breccias and tuffs, whether of *pyroclastic origin or not. 1897 GEIKIE *Anc. Volcanoes Gt. Brit.* I. 14 All kinds of pyroclastic detritus discharged from volcanic vents. 1880 W. A. ROSS in *Nature* XXI. 275/1 The blue *pyrocone produced by the blowpipe from an ordinary gas-burner. 1897 *Daily News* 27 Mar. 6/7 Henri Guénard, the eminent draughtsman, painter, aquafortist, *pyro-engraver, and engraver in colours. 1882 OGILVIE (Annandale), **Pyrognomic*, applied to certain minerals which, when heated to a certain degree, exhibit a glow of incandescence, probably arising from a new disposition of their molecules. 1849 DANA *Geol.* iii. (1850) 207 *note*, *Pyrognostic Characters.—In an open tube gives off a small quantity of water. 1851 RICHARDSON *Geol.* v. 76 Bromel, a French mineralogist,..being the first who classified mineral substances according to their pyrognostic qualities. 1593 G. HARVEY *Pierces Super.* Wks. (Grosart) II. 66, I looke for Agrippas dreadfull *Pyromachy: for Cardans multiplied matter, that shall delude the force of the Canon. 1887 *Times* 9 Sept. 14/5 The *pyro-magnetic dynamo will allow of the waste heat being utilized for other purposes. 1842 DUNGLISON *Med. Dict.*, **Pyromania*. 1847 tr. *von Feuchtersleben's Med. Psychol.* (Syd. Soc.) 293 An irresistible impulse to incendiarism (pyromania). 1867 MAUDSLEY *Physiol. Mind* 273 Instances of..homicidal monomania, kleptomania, pyromania, and suicidal monomania. 1887 *Amer. Jrnl. Psychol.* I. 191 *Pyromaniacs rarely incriminate themselves. 1897 *Westm. Gaz.* 2 Apr. 7/2 A dangerous pyromaniac has been discovered in Brooklyn..[who] has set over twenty tenements on fire.. simply for the pleasure of seeing them burn. 1879 RUTLEY *Stud. Rocks* xii. 208 Commonly called metamorphic action, but which might more properly be designated *pyro-metamorphic action. *Ibid.*, *Pyro-metamorphism, by which rocks originally stratified..come to be subsequently acted on by heat, and so transformed into what are commonly called the metamorphic rocks. 1847 WEBSTER, **Pyromorphous*, in mineralogy, having the property of crystallization by fire. 1834 *Tait's Mag.* I. 39 *Pyronomics, hydrostatics, phrenology,..and other crabbed sciences. 1601 GILL *Treat. Trinitie* Wks. (1635) 220 They which understand the rules of *Pyronomie, know what I say. 1858 MAYNE *Expos. Lex.*, *Pyronomia*, term for the doctrine of the nature and use of fire: pyronomy. 1836 SMART, **Pyrophanous*, rendered transparent by heat. 1882 *Nature* XXVI. 304/1 This phenomenon, which Kastner called the interference of flames, was the..starting-point of Kastner's *Pyrophone or Flame-Organ, which he patented in 1873. 1828 WEBSTER, **Pyroscope*. 1832 *Nat. Philos.* II. *Therm. & Pyrom.* iv. 44 (U. K. S.) When one ball of the differential thermometer is smoothly covered with thick silver leaf, or inclosed in a polished sphere of silver, and the other ball is naked, it forms the pyroscope. 1883 *Fisheries Exhib. Catal.* 78 Neal's Patent *Pyro-Silver Cutlery. 1832 L. HUNT *Sir R. Esher* (1850) 244, I would willingly elude the experiment, and take the wings of the ancient *pyrosophy. 1846 J. C. BROWN tr. *Arbousset's Narr.* xxi. (1852) 309 Who can tell all the ingredients which may enter into the product of a pyrosophy so new? 1755 tr. *Pontoppidan's Nat. Hist.* Pref. 7 That circumstantial examination..which hath been undertaken and executed by Fabricius, in his *pyro- and hydro-theology. 1857 DUNGLISON *Med. Lex.*, **Pyrothonide*.

2. In names of minerals and rocks, usually indicating some property exhibited or alteration produced by the action of fire or heat; sometimes denoting a fiery red or yellow colour.

Pyrallolite (-æ·lǒləit) [Gr. ἄλλος other; Nordenskiöld 1820, in Ger.: see -LITE], an altered form of pyroxene, usually of a whitish or green colour, which changes colour when heated. † **Pyra·ntimonite,** obs. synonym of KERMESITE. **Pyrargillite** (-ā·ɪdʒiləit) [Gr. ἄργιλλος clay; Nordenskiöld 1833, in Ger.], an alteration product of iolite, which has a clayey smell when heated. **Pyrargyrite** (-ā·ɪdʒirəit) [Gr. ἄργυρον silver; Glöcker 1831, in Ger.], a dark red silver ore, a native sulphide of silver and antimony. † **Pyrau·xite,** obs. synonym of *pyrophyllite*. **Pyroaurite** (-ǭ·rəit) [L. *aurum* gold; Igelström 1865, in Sw.], hydrate of magnesium and iron, which has a golden-yellow colour when heated. **Py·rochlore** (-klōᵊɪ) [Gr. χλωρός greenish-yellow; Wöhler 1826, in Ger.], a niobo-titanate of calcium, cerium, and other bases, occurring in octahedral crystals of a brown colour, becoming greenish-yellow when strongly heated. **Pyrochroite** (-krōᵘ·əit) [Gr. χροιά colour; Igelström 1864, in Ger.], a pearly-white foliated hydrate of manganese, which becomes coloured when heated. † **Pyrochro·tite,** obs. synonym of *pyrostilpnite*. **Pyro·clasite** [Gr. κλάσις fracture], **Pyrogua·nite** [GUANO], names given to hard guano. **Pyro·melane** [Gr. μέλας black; C. U. Shepard 1856, 'because it turns black when heated', Chester *Names Min.*], a reddish mineral (prob. titanite), found in the gold sands of N. Carolina. **Pyrome·line** [Gr. μήλινος yellow; Kobell 1852, in Ger.], hydrous sulphate of nickel, pale yellow or greenish white. **Pyro·meride** [Gr. μέρ-ος part], a granitoid rock containing felspathic spherules thickly disseminated (Watts *Dict. Chem.*). **Pyromo·rphite** [Gr. μορφή form; Hausmann 1813, in Ger.], chlorophosphate of lead, occurring in green, yellow, or brown crystals; so called because the globule produced by melting assumes a crystalline form on cooling. † **Py·rophane** (-fēⁱn) [Gr. -φανης appearing], a variety of opal which absorbs melted wax, and consequently becomes translucent when heated (cf. HYDROPHANE); also sometimes = FIRE-*opal*. **Pyro·phanite** [Gr. φανός bright; A. Hamberg 1890], titanate of manganese found in brilliant red crystals and scales. **Pyrophyllite** (-fi·ləit) [Gr. φύλλον leaf; R. Hermann 1829, in Ger.], a hydrous silicate of aluminium, occurring in foliated masses which exfoliate when heated. **Pyrophysalite** (-fi·săləit) [Gr. φυσαλλίς bubble; Berzelius 1806, in Sw.], a coarse, nearly opaque variety of topaz, which swells up when heated. **Pyropi·ssite** [Gr. πίσσα pitch; Kenngott 1853, in Ger.], a greyish-brown earthy friable substance, consisting of a mixture of hydrocarbons, which when heated melts into a mass resembling pitch. **Pyrore·tin** [Gr. ῥητίνη resin; Reuss 1854], a resin occurring in masses in brown coal, in the vicinity of basaltic dykes, in Bohemia; hence **Pyrore·tinite,** 'the part of pyroretin which dissolves in hot alcohol and deposits in cooling' (Chester *Names Min.*). **Pyro·rthite** [ORTHITE; Berzelius 1818] an impure mineral resembling orthite, but containing carbonaceous matter, and hence burning when strongly heated. **Py·roschist** (-ʃist), a highly bituminous schist or shale, which burns or yields inflammable gas when heated. **Pyrosclerite** (-skliᵊ·rəit) [Gr. σκληρός hard; Kobell 1834, in Ger.], a green mineral allied to the chlorites, forming seams in serpentine: so called 'because a fragment becomes very hard when heated before the blow-pipe' (Chester *Names Min.*). **Pyrosiderite**: see PYRRHOSIDERITE. **Pyrosmalite** (-ǫ·zmăləit) [orig. (in Ger.) *pirodmalit* (Hausmann 1808), f. Gr. ὀδμαλέος stinking; altered by Karsten 1808, after Gr. ὀσμή smell], a chloro-silicate of iron and manganese, occurring in dark green or brown crystals, which when heated give off an odour of chlorine. † **Pyrosti·bite,** obs. synonym of KERMESITE. **Pyrosti·lpnite** [Gr. στιλπνός shining; Dana 1868], a sulphantimonide of silver, occurring in minute bright red crystals; also called *fire-blende*. † **Pyrote·chnite,** obs. synonym of THENARDITE.

1822 CLEAVELAND *Min.* (ed. 2) I. 426 **Pyrallolite*, this new mineral occurs both massive, and in crystals...This mineral..has received its name..in allusion to its changes of color from white to dark, and from dark to white, before the blowpipe. 1837 DANA *Min.* 256 Pyrallolite. Tersilicate of Magnesia. 1866–8 WATTS *Dict. Chem.* IV. 753 *Pyrallolite*, name of a series of decomposition-products of augite and occasionally of hornblende, consisting mainly of magnesian hydrosilicates. They blacken when heated, then burn white if in contact with the air. 1834 *Amer. Jrnl. Sc.* July 387 **Pyrargillite*. 1841 *Penny Cycl.* XIX. 153/1 *Pyrargillite* occurs in four-sided prisms, with bevelled edges and massive. 1849 NICOL *Min.* 500 Dark *pyrargyrite or antimonial silver-blende. 1866–8 WATTS *Dict. Chem.* IV. 753 Pyrargyrite. Dark-red silver ore. Ruby silver.. occurring in rhombohedral crystals. 1868 DANA *Min.* (ed. 5) 179 *Pyroaurite...Perfectly soluble in muriatic acid. 1830 *Amer. Jrnl. Sc.* XVIII. 392 *Pyrochlore from Norway in zircon syenite. 1866 LAWRENCE tr. *Cotta's Rocks Class.* (1878) 39 Pyrochlore occurs as an accessory in granite and syenite. 1868 DANA *Min.* (ed. 5) 177 *Pyrochroite...Occurs in veins, 1 to 2 lines broad. 1856 C. U. SHEPARD in *Amer. Jrnl. Sci. & Arts* Ser. II. XXII. 97 The altered guano is composed..of two mineral species, which I have called *pyroclasite and glaubapatite. *Ibid.* 96 *Pyro-guanite minerals. The three following species occur at Mong's Island. *Ibid.* 96 *Pyromelane. Found in crystalline grains of the size of kernels of Indian corn. 1866–8 WATTS *Dict. Chem.* IV. 762 **Pyromeline*. 1865 LAWRENCE tr. *Cotta's Rocks Class.* 218 *Pyromeride..in addition to the usual quartz crystals, contains balls of felsite. 1814 ALLAN *Min. Nomencl.* 29 Brown and green lead ore..*pyromorphit. 1842 BRANDE *Dict. Sci.*, etc., *Pyromorphite*, native phosphate of lead. 1794 KIRWAN *Min.* (ed. 2) I. 291 It is said that some *pyrophanes are found in Armenia which are transparent while exposed to the sun, and opake at night. 1830 *Edin. Philos. Jrnl.* VIII. 183 The name *pyrophyllite is given to it on account of its exfoliation on exposure to heat. 1862 DANA *Man. Geol.* § 67. 62 Pyrophyllite, a mineral resembling talc in appearance and soapy feel. 1808 *Nicholson's Jrnl.* XIX. 33 Mineralogical Description..of a Stone, called *Pyrophysalite. 1866 BRANDE & COX *Dict. Sci.*, etc., s.v. *Mineralogy* 531/2 *Pyropissite. 1868 DANA *Min.* (ed. 5) 344 **Pyroretinite*, part of *Pyroretin of Reuss. 1881 *Jrnl. Chem. Soc.* XL. 359 Four resins belonging to the retinite group, viz., Pyroretin, Reussinite, Leucopetrite, and Euosinite. 1828 WEBSTER s.v., *Pyrorthite is in black plates, thin and almost parallel. 1866 LAWRENCE tr. *Cotta's Rocks Class.* (1878) 330 *Pyroschist is..very bituminous and ..dark-brown or black-coloured argillaceous shale. 1862 DANA *Man. Geol.* § 8. 82 They [nickel and chrome] occur also in the *pyrosclerite and Williamsite of Chester Co. Pa. 1896 CHESTER *Dict. Names Min.*, *Pyrosclerite*,..a micaceous mineral, one of the uncertain alteration products classed with vermiculite. 1816 R. JAMESON *Syst. Min.* (ed. 2) III. 311 *Pyrosmalite or native Muriate of Iron. 1852 SHEPARD *Min.* (ed. 3) 160 Pyrosmalite..heated in a tube yields water. 1868 DANA *Min.* (ed. 5) 93 *Pyrostilpnite...Fireblende... Lustre pearly-adamantine. Color hyacinth-red.

3. In Chemistry, *pyro-* is prefixed to the name of a substance or to an adjective forming part thereof, in order to name a new substance formed by destructive distillation or other application of heat.

Names thus formed appeared first in the *Méthode de Nomenclature Chimique* of De Morveau, Lavoisier, etc. 1787. Many of the substances originally so called have subsequently received other names.

a. Prefixed to the adj. denominating an acid († sometimes an ether or spirit), to form the name of a new acid, etc. The substances properly so denominated were themselves mostly acids, but sometimes anhydrides or other derivatives. † **Pyroace·tic** *acid* = PYROLIGNEOUS *acid*; † **pyro-acetic** *ether* or *spirit*, early name of ACETONE. **Pyroaliza·ric** *acid*, $C_8H_4O_3$ = PHTHALIC *anhydride*. **Pyro-arse·nic** *acid*, $H_4As_2O_7$, an acid produced by the action of heat on arsenic acid expelling H_2O. **Pyrocamphre·tic** *acid*, $C_{10}H_{14}O_4$. **Pyrocatechu·ic** *acid* = *pyrocatechin*: see b. † **Pyroci·tric** = CITRACONIC. † **Pyrocome·nic** = PYROMECONIC. † **Pyrofe·llic** = *pyrolithofellic*. † **Pyroglu·cic** *acid* = *pyrodextrin*: see b. † **Pyroguaia·cic** *acid* = GUAIACOL. † **Pyroki·nic** *acid* = QUINIDE. † **Pyrole·ic** = SEBACIC. † **Pyroli·thic** = *pyro-uric*, CYANURIC. **Pyrolithofe·llic** *acid*, $C_{20}H_{34}O_3$: see quot. **Pyrolivi·lic** *acid* [OLIVIL], $C_{20}H_{26}O_5$. † **Pyroma·lic** = MALEIC. **Pyroma·ric** *acid*: see quot. 1866–8. **Pyromelli·tic** *acid*, $C_{10}H_6O_8$. **Pyrope·ctic** *acid*: see quot. **Pyrophospha·mic** *acid*, $P_2NH_5O_6$. **Pyrophospho·ric** *acid*, $H_4P_2O_7$, a tetrabasic acid, produced as a glass-like solid, by the action of heat on phosphoric acid. **Pyroracemic** *acid* = PYRUVIC *acid*. † **Pyroso·rbic** = *pyromalic*, MALEIC. **Pyrosulphu·ric** *acid*, $H_2S_2O_7$ = $(HSO_3)_2+O$: see quots. **Pyrotere·bic** *acid*, $C_6H_{10}O_2$; also called *hexenoic acid*. **Pyro-u·ric** = CYANURIC. Also in the names of salts of these acids, as **Pyroarsenate, -citrate, -phosphamate, -sulphate,** etc. See also PYROGALLIC, PYROMECONIC, PYROMUCIC, PYROTARTARIC, PYRUVIC.

1815 HENRY *Elem. Chem.* (ed. 7) II. 281 The peculiar fluid, which Derosne has termed 'pyro-acetic ether, but to which Mr. Chenevix is of opinion, the less definite name of pyro-acetic spirit will be better adapted. 1859 FOWNES *Man. Chem.* (ed. 7) 396 Acetone: pyroacetic spirit.. A peculiar inflammable volatile liquid, designated by the above names. 1868 *Nat. Encycl.* I. 115 A..volatile inflammable fluid called pyro-acetic spirit. 1876 *Mat. Med.* (ed. 6) 296 *Pyroarsenate of soda, isomorphous with the pyrophosphate of that base. 1882 *Encycl. Brit.* XIV. 91/2 The methylated gallic ether or *pyrocatechuic acid. 1838 T. THOMSON *Chem. Org. Bodies* 62 Dumas subjected the pyr-citric acid in *pyrocitrate of lead to an ultimate analysis by means of oxide of copper. 1810–26 HENRY *Elem. Chem.* II. 216 **Pyro-citric Acid*. M. Lassaigne has given this name to an acid, produced by the destructive distillation of citric acid. 1838 T. THOMSON *Chem. Org. Bodies* 338 Of pyrocitric and pyrotartaric ethers. 1863–8 WATTS *Dict. Chem.* I. 992 Citraconic acid (Pyrocitric acid), $C_5H_6O_4$. (Lassaigne, 1822.) 1873 WATTS *Fownes' Chem.* 739 *Pyrocomenic acid is a weak acid. 1873 RALFE *Phys. Chem.* 59 Submitted to dry distillation, lithofellic acid loses 1 atom of water and is converted into *pyrofellic acid. 1843 *Chem. Gaz.* 1 Dec. 725 *Pyroguaiacic Acid obtained by the Distillation of Guaiacum Resin. 1858 MAYNE *Expos. Lex.*, **Pyrokinate*,..a combination of pyrokinic acid with a salifiable base. 1832 *Encycl. Brit.* VI. 430/1 *Pyrokinic acid is formed when kinic acid is distilled in a retort. 1836 SMART, **Pyrolithic*, an epithet applied to an acid obtained from uric acid. 1897 *Syd. Soc. Lex.*, *Pyrolithic acid*, the same as Pyro-uric acid. 1866–8 WATTS *Dict. Chem.* IV. 760 **Pyrolithofellic acid*,..an acid oil produced by the dry distillation of lithofellic acid, the chief constituent of some kinds of oriental bezoar. 1847 WEBSTER, **Pyromalate* [citing URE]. 1810–26 HENRY *Elem. Chem.* II. 225 When malic acid is heated out of the contact of air, it sublimes, and the sublimed crystals possess characters differing from those of the original acid. When thus altered, it has been called **pyromalic acid*. 1865–8 WATTS *Dict. Chem.* III. 784 Maleic Acid. (Pyromalic acid, Pyrosorbic acid.) 1857 MILLER *Elem. Chem.* III. 501 *Pyromaric acid. 1866–8 WATTS *Dict. Chem.* IV. 760 Pyromaric acid..obtained by subjecting pimaric acid to dry distillation. 1882 *Jrnl. Chem. Soc.* XLII. 850 Crystals of ammonium *pyromellate. *Ibid.* 851 *Pyromellic acid. 1851 *Chem. Gaz.* 15 Sept. 341 A new acid, to which he [Erdmann] has given the name of *pyromellitic acid. 1866–8 WATTS *Dict. Chem.* IV. 769 When pectin..is heated to 200°, water and carbonic anhydride are evolved, and *pyropectic acid remains in the form of a black substance, insoluble in water, but soluble in alkaline liquids...Frémy deduces the formula $C_{14}H_{..}O_9$. 1864 *Jrnl. Chem. Soc.* XVII. 237 It seems preferable to adopt the names given by Laurent... These are *pyrophosphamic and pyrophosphodiamic acids. 1866–8 WATTS *Dict. Chem.* IV. 766 Laurent (1850) suggested that these acids were amic acids derived from pyrophosphoric acid, the first being *pyrophosphamic acid*, $P_2NH_5O_6$, and the second *pyrophosphodiamic acid*, $P_2N_2H_6O_5$, and these formulæ have been confirmed by the more recent analyses. *Ibid.*, *Pyrophosphamate of Ammonium is obtained as a gummy mass. 1836–41 BRANDE *Chem.* (ed. 5) 492 Phosphoric acid, after it has been exposed for some time to heat, yields, when saturated with bases, salts possessed of certain peculiarities, which have hence been termed *pyrophosphates. 1869 ROSCOE *Elem. Chem.* 159 If common sodium phosphate be heated to redness, water is driven off, sodium pyrophosphate remains. 1832 *Encycl. Brit.* VI. 380/1 Mr. Clarke..called the newly modified acid *pyrophosphoric acid. 1850 DAUBENY *Atom. The.* x. 334. 1866–8 WATTS *Dict. Chem.* IV. 539 Pyrophosphoric acid is converted into metaphosphoric acid when heated to redness, and into orthophosphoric acid when boiled with water. *Ibid.* 537 Intermediate between ortho- and meta-phosphates there are at least three distinct classes of salts, the most important of which are *pyrophosphates* or *paraphosphates*. 1837 R. D. THOMSON in *Brit. Ann.* 339 *Pyroracemic acid. 1866–8 WATTS *Dict. Chem.* IV. 770 Pyroracemic acid is a liquid having a faint yellowish colour, smelling like acetic acid. 1894 MUIR & MORLEY *Watts' Dict. Chem.* IV. 363 Pyroracemic or Pyruvic acid, $C_3H_4O_3$ = $CH_3.CO.CO_2H$. 1865–8 *Pyrosorbic: see *Pyromalic*. 1872 *Jrnl. Chem. Soc.* XXV. 669 Proofs that sulphuric and *pyrosulphuric acids are really distinct compounds. 1875 WATTS *Dict. Chem.* VII. 1140 Disulphuric, Pyrosulphuric, or Anhydrosulphuric Acid; Nordhausen Sulphuric Acid. 1894 MUIR & MORLEY *Watts' Dict. Chem.* IV. 582 Potassium pyrosulphate, $K_2S_2O_7$, is formed by heating K_2SO_4 with half its weight of H_2SO_4 till acid ceases to come off at an incipient red heat. 1866–8 WATTS *Dict. Chem.* IV. 776 **Pyroterebic Acid*..belonging to the acrylic series..is a liquid boiling at 210°, and smelling of butyric acid. *Ibid.*, **Pyroterebrate of silver*, $C_6H_9AgO_2$, crystallises with difficulty, and blackens on exposure to light. 1810–26 HENRY *Elem. Chem.* II. 413 The liquid, when filtered and evaporated, yielded small white needles which were pure *pyro-uric acid. 1836–41 BRANDE *Chem.* (ed. 5) 564 Cyanuric Acid...Scheele first described this acid under the name of *pyrouric acid*.

b. Prefixed to a sb. (Now often superseded by other names.)

† **Pyrobe·nzoline** = LOPHINE, $C_{21}H_{16}N_2$. **Pyrocatechin** (pəiro₁kæ·tĭtʃin), also called *catechol*, *pyro-catechuic acid*, and *oxyphenic acid*, $C_6H_6O_2$, produced by the dry distillation of catechu, kino, and other substances, forming broad white strongly shining laminæ, and rhombic or small rectangular prisms. **Py·rocoll** [Gr. κόλλα glue]: see quot. **Pyrode·xtrin,** a product of the action of a high temperature upon starch. **Pyrogly·cerin,** diglycerin = $C_3H_5(OH)_2.O.C_3H_5(OH)_2$. **Pyrogly·cide,** diglycide, $C_3H_5(OH).O_2.C_3H_5(OH)$. **Pyroguai·acin,** a crystalline substance, $C_{14}H_{18}O_3$, produced by the dry distillation of gum guaiacum. † **Pyroqui·nol** = HYDROQUINONE. † **Pyroste·arin**: see quot. See also PYROXANTHIN, -XANTHOGEN, and PYROXYLIN.

1857 MILLER *Elem. Chem.* III. 263 *Pyrobenzoline (lophine). *Ibid.* 349 Catechin..yields a crystallizable substance termed *pyrocatechin, or oxyphenic acid. 1878 KINGZETT *Anim. Chem.* 236 Pyrocatechin was discovered in human urine by Müller and Ebstein. 1897 *Allbutt's Syst. Med.* IV. 555 Mühlmann has put forward the view that the symptoms of Addison's disease are due to chronic poisoning with pyrocatechin. 1881 *Jrnl. Chem. Soc.* XL. 295 The authors propose to call it *pyrocoll, because of its mode of formation from gelatin. 1894 MUIR & MORLEY *Watts' Dict. Chem.* IV. 359 Pyrocoll, $C_{10}H_6N_2O_2$, a product of the distillation of gelatin when free from fat but containing albumen, casein or gluten. 1858 *Chem. Gaz.* 1 May 178 *Pyrodextrine..is precipitated by baryta. 1866–8 WATTS *Dict. Chem.* IV. 758 Pyrodextrin is a solid, brown, friable mass, shining and tough when moist. Inodorous and tasteless...[It] dissolves readily in water, forming a brown adhesive gum. 1861 *Chem. News* III. 111/2 *Pyroglycerine oxidises phosphorus, potassium, and copper. 1854–72 WATTS *Dict. Chem.* II. 894 The hypothetical body glycide, $C_3H_6O_2$..is the alcohol of the glycidic ethers, and is related to glycerin in the same manner as *pyroglycide to pyroglycerin. 1866–8 *Ibid.* IV. 771 **Pyrostearin*, the name applied by Berzelius to the less fusible portion of the distillate obtained by distilling empyreumatic oils with water.

c. Also in the derivative names of certain hydrocarbon compounds and groups: **Py·razine** [Azo- + -INE], a ring-group; **Py·razole** [Azo- + L. *oleum* oil], a compound; **Py·rone** [-ONE], a ring-group; the analytical formulæ of which respectively are

$$N\left\langle{CH:CH \atop CH:CH}\right\rangle N,\quad \left\langle{CH:N \atop CH:CH}\right\rangle NH,\quad CO\left\langle{CH:CH \atop CH:CH}\right\rangle O.$$

Hence *Pyrazoleblue*, a dye substance ($C_{20}H_{14}N_4O_3$).

1805 MUIR & MORLEY *Watts' Dict. Chem.* III. 349.

Pyro-acetic to **-arsenic**: see PYRO- 3 a.

Pyro-acid (pəi·ro₁æ·sid). *Chem.* Also 9 † **pyracid.** An acid formed from another acid by dry or destructive distillation: see PYRO- 3.

1835–6 *Todd's Cycl. Anat.* I. 47/1 The other animal acids ..are artificially produced...Such as the..animal pyroacids. 1838 T. THOMSON *Chem. Org. Bodies* 11 Sometimes the saturating power of a vegetable acid is not altered by converting it into a pyroacid. 1866–8 [see PYROGEN b].

Pyro-aurite, etc.: see PYRO- 2.

† **Pyroba·llogy.** *Obs.* [Altered from PYROBOLOGY, after Gr. βάλλειν, to throw.] The study of the art of casting fire, i.e. of artillery.

1738 [see PYROBOLOGY, quot. 1728]. 1759 STERNE *Tr. Shandy* II. iii, He was enabled, by the help of Gobesius's military architecture and pyroballogy, translated from the Flemish, to form his discourse with passable perspicuity.

Pyro-benzoline: see PYRO- 3 b.

† **Pyrobo·lic,** *a. Obs. rare*⁻¹. [f. PYRO- + Gr. βολή a throw + -IC.] (See quot.)

(Perh. due to a misunderstanding of *parabolic*.)

1628 R. HOLME *Armoury* III. xiv. (Roxb.) 12/1 A pyrobolick Mirrour is such a Glass that casts forth fire in a moment of tyme by the suns heat.

† **Pyrobo·lical,** *a. Obs.* [f. as prec. + -AL.] Relating to the art of casting fire, i.e. ? to artillery, or ? to fireworks. So † **Pyro·bolist** [F. *pyroboliste*, Ger. *pyroballist*], one who makes or manages artillery or fireworks; † **Pyrobo·logy** [F. *pyrobologie*, 18th c.], † **Pyro·boly,** the art of making or managing fireworks, pyrotechny.

1728 CHAMBERS *Cycl.* s.v. *Pyrotechny*, Some call Pyrotechny by the name Artillery;. Others chuse to call it Pyrobology [*ed.* 1738 *adds* or rather pyroballogy], *q.d.* the Art of Missile Fires. 1729 SHELVOCKE *Artillery* III. 165 To fire several Pyrobolical Machines, which are used upon Rejoicing Occasions. *Ibid.* 169 Nothing..that may be of Use to the diligent and expert Pyrobolist. 1732 *Hist. Litteraria* III. 110 He called together the most expert of the Fire-workers and Pyrobolists. *Ibid.* IV. 114 If the Chinese have been so ancient in the Mystery of Pyroboly and Pyrotechnics.

Pyro-camphretic, etc.: see PYRO- 1, 2, 3 a, b.

Pyro-carbonate: see PYRO b.

Pyro-che·mical, *a. rare.* [f. med. or early mod.L. *pyrochymia*, *-icus*, in F. *pyrochimie*, *-chimique*: see PYRO- 1 and CHEMICAL.] Pertaining to the chemical action of fire. Hence **Pyro-che·mically** *adv.*, by the chemical action of fire.

1839 G. ROBERTS *Dict. Geol.*, Pyro-chemically formed.. through the instrumentality of fire, as crystals of prismatic felspar on the walls of a furnace in which copper slate and ore have been melted.

Pyrodin (pəi·rōᵘdin). *Med.* [f. Gr. πυρώδης like fire + -IN[1].] A crystalline substance consisting essentially of acetyl-phenyl-hydrazine, $C_6H_5N_2H_2(C_2H_3O)$, used as an antipyretic.

1890 BILLINGS *Nat. Med. Dict.*, *Pyrodine*. 1897 *Syd. Soc. Lex.*, *Pyrodin*. 1899 CAGNEY *Jaksch's Clin. Diagn.* (ed. 4) 352 Observed in cases of poisoning by naphthol, carbolic acid, pyrodin, and chinin.

Py·ro-ele·ctric, *a. Min.* [PYRO- 1.] Applied to certain crystals which on being heated become electrically polar, i.e. exhibit positive and negative electricity at opposite ends (the effects being reversed while cooling). Hence **Py·ro-electri·city,** the property of being pyro-electric.

1834 in *Encycl. Brit.* VIII. 595/1 Pyro-electricity. 1853 *Pharm. Jrnl.* XIII. 112 The crystals..are..pyroelectric. 1864–72 WATTS *Dict. Chem.* II. 411 In Crystals:—Pyro-electricity. 1871 B. STEWART *Heat* § 167 Haüy was the first to remark that those crystals are pyroelectric which are deficient in symmetry. 1895 [see PYRITOID]. 1899 O. LODGE *Mod. Views Electr.* § 63 (heading) Pyro-electricity.

Pyro-engraver, -fellic: see PYRO- 1, 3 a.

Pyroet, Pyrog, obs. ff. PIROUETTE, PIROGUE.

1707 *Curios in Husb. & Gard.* 206 The Savages..transport Plants in their Pyrogs.

Pyrogallic (pəi·rogæ·lik), *a. Chem.* [f. PYRO- 3 + GALLIC *a.*[2]] Produced from gallic acid by the action of heat: in *pyrogallic acid*, an acid substance, $C_6H_6O_3$ (strictly a trihydric phenol, $C_6H_3(OH)_3$, hence systematically named *pyrogallol*), which crystallizes in long flat colourless prisms, soluble in water; much used as a reducing agent in photography (see PYRO) and otherwise. Hence *pyrogallic developer*, etc.

1836 BRANDE *Man. Chem.* (ed. 4) 933 Pyrogallic acid has been analyzed by Berzelius under the name of gallic acid. 1838 T. THOMSON *Chem. Org. Bodies* 86 Braconnot.. showed that when gallic acid is sublimed, it is converted into a substance possessing quite different properties... He therefore gave it the name of pyrogallic acid. 1856 E. A. HADOW in *Orr's Circ. Sci., Pract. Chem.* 194 After the pyrogallic solution has apparently done its utmost. 1861 *Photogr. News Alm.* in *Circ. Sc.* (c 1865) I. 160/1 There are two methods of development; with pyrogallic acid and with gallic acid. 1869 ROSCOE *Elem. Chem.* 417 On heating, gallic acid splits up into carbon dioxide and pyro-gallic acid or trihydroxyl benzol. 1878 ABNEY *Photogr.* (1881) 103 A pyrogallic-acid developer.

Hence **Pyroga·llate,** a salt of pyrogallic acid; **Pyroga·llein,** a product of the action of air on an ammoniacal solution of pyrogallic acid; † **Pyroga·llin** (*rare*), **Pyroga·llol,** synonyms of pyrogallic acid.

1836 BRANDE *Man. Chem.* (ed. 4) 933 Ammonia, soda, and potassa, form soluble *pyrogallates. 1878 ABNEY *Photogr.* (1881) 98 The alkaline pyrogallates have..an affinity for the halogens. 1866–8 WATTS *Dict. Chem.* IV. 758 *Pyrogallein, an uncrystallisable product. 1876 HARLEY *Mat. Med.* (ed. 6) 422 Heated to 410°, gallic acid is..converted into *pyro-gallin and carbonic anhydride. 1876 *Encycl. Brit.* V. 564/2 Trihydric phenols comprising..pyrogallic acid (or *pyrogallol). 1899 *Allbutt's Syst. Med.* VIII. 580 The remedies..found most useful are tar, chrysarobin, and pyrogallol.

Pyrogen (pəi·rŏdʒen). *rare.* [f. PYRO- + -GEN; lit. 'fire-producer', or 'fire-produced'.] A term proposed in various senses. † **a.** A name for electricity considered as a material substance; the 'electric fluid'. † **b.** (See quot. 1866–8.) **c.** A substance which, when introduced into the blood, produces fever; a pyrogenetic agent.

a. 1858 MAYNE *Expos. Lex.*, *Pyrogen*, a term proposed for electricity considered as a material substance possessing weight. 1854 in WEBSTER.

b. 1866–8 WATTS *Dict. Chem.* IV. 759 *Pyrogen*, a name applied by Dumas to pyro-acids and other products of the action of heat on organic bodies.

c. 1895 *Allbutt's Syst. Med.* I. 157 In 1875 I prepared a substance, which I ventured to call pyrogen, from putrid extract of flesh.

Pyrogeneous, erron. form of PYROGENOUS.

‖ **Pyroge·nesis.** [f. PYRO- 1 + GENESIS.] The generation of fire or heat.

1858 in MAYNE *Expos. Lex.* 1890 in *Cent. Dict.*

Pyrogenetic (pəi·ro₁dʒĭne·tik), *a.* [f. PYRO- 1 + -GENETIC.] **a.** Having the property of producing heat, esp. in the body; thermogenetic. **b.** Having the property of producing fever.

1858 MAYNE *Expos. Lex.*, Pyrogenetic. 1875 tr. *von Ziemssen's Cycl. Med.* I. 255 What the chemical natures of these pyrogenetic processes may be, we have never learnt. 1885 *Buck's Ref. Handbk. Med. Sc.* II. 226 Not the least curious phenomenon of the pyrogenetic mechanism is the influence that increases the resistance to cold. 1896 *Allbutt's Syst. Med.* I. 155 Artificial fever produced by the introduction of pyrogenetic substances.

Pyrogenic (-dʒe·nik), *a.* [f. as PYROGEN + -IC.]

† **1.** *Geol.* = PYROGENOUS 1 a. *Obs. rare.*

1853 TH. ROSS *Humboldt's Trav.* III. xxxii. 370 The ancient pyrogenic rocks which I found near Parapara.

† **2.** *Chem.* Name for a supposed peculiar acid, now identified with formic acid. *Obs.*

1864–72 WATTS *Dict. Chem.* II. 684 Tünnermann (Pogg. Ann. xv. 307) thought that he had discovered two peculiar acids, to which he gave the names of *pyrogenic* and *amylenic acids*.

3. *Phys.* and *Path.* = PYROGENETIC b.

1877 ROBERTS *Handbk. Med.* (ed. 3) I. 80 Dr. Burdon-Sanderson found..that by injecting certain fluids—which he terms 'pyrogenic'—..fever could be excited. 1896 *Allbutt's Syst. Med.* I. 157 The pyrogenic substance was perhaps a body analogous to the unformed ferments.

Pyrogenous (-ǫ·dʒĭnəs), *a.* Erron. -geneous. [f. as PYROGEN + -OUS.]

1. Produced by fire or heat. **a.** *Geol.* Of rocks: = IGNEOUS *a.* 2. **b.** *Chem.* Applied to a substance produced by the combustion of another substance.

1839 G. ROBERTS *Dict. Geol.*, *Pyrogenous*,..produced by the agency of fire. 1845 J. PHILLIPS *Geol.* in *Encycl. Metrop.* VI. 763/1 The phenomena of pyrogenous rocks. 1858 MAYNE *Expos. Lex.*, *Pyrogenus*,..pyrogeneous. Applied by Berzelius to empyreumatic oils and resins, i.e. those produced by distillation of organic substances.

2. Producing fire, heat, or fever: = PYROGENETIC.

1890 *Cent. Dict.* s.v., Pyrogenous action in the blood. 1897 *Syd. Soc. Lex.*, *Pyrogenous*...2. *Med.* Fever-producing, pyrogenetic.

Pyroglucic to **-gnostics**: see PYRO- 1, 3 a, b.

Pyro·graphy. [f. PYRO- 1 + -GRAPHY.]

† **1.** A description of fire-arms. *Obs.*

1684 tr. *Agrippa's Van. Arts* xxii. 67 The several varieties of Guns and Fire-vomiting Engines, of which lately my self have written a..Treatise, Entituled *Pyrographie*.

2. a. A method of wood-carving by means of heated metallic plates or cylinders in relief, by which the design is burned into the substance of the wood (Knight *Dict. Mech.* 1875).

b. The art of making drawings or designs on wood, bone, etc. by means of a heated metallic point: = POKER-WORK.

1891 MRS. MAUDE *Pyrography* iii. 43 Bone and Ivory form very delicate grounds for Pyrography in small work. 1895 MRS. STEVENS in *Proc. 14th Convent. Teach. Deaf* 366 The 'Legend of Sleepy Hollow', done in pyrography on the wood-work of a fire-place.

So **Py·rograph** *v. intr.*, to practise pyrography or poker-work; **Pyro·grapher, Pyro·graphist,** one who practises or is skilled in pyrography; **Pyrogra·phic** *a.*, pertaining to, done by, or using pyrography; **Pyrogravure** (pəi·ro₁grăviūᵊɪ) = PYROGRAPHY 2 b, poker-work.

1891 MRS. MAUDE *Pyrography* iv. 56 The general tones of the animal to be *Pyrographed. *Ibid.* v. 80 Pyrographed frames for sepia drawings. 1811 JOS. SMITH in *Fowler Corr.* (1906) 204 To send you the *Pyrographic Picture you ordered of me. 1895 MRS. STEVENS in *Proc. 14th Convent. Teach. Deaf* 366 Some very fine specimens of pyrographic work. 1891 MRS. MAUDE *Pyrography* ii. 28 A very clever lady *Pyrographist. 1888 *Sci. Amer.* 9 June 353 *Pyrogravure is a new method of engraving in black, reddish brown, bister, etc., by the use of a red hot metallic point. 1901 *N. Amer. Rev. Adv.* Feb. 2 This panel and the rest of the wood-work are in pyrogravure.

Pyroguaiacic to **-kinic**: see PYRO- 2, 3 a, b.

Pyrogue, obs. form of PIROGUE.

Pyroheliometer: = PYRHELIOMETER.

‖ **Pyrola** (pi·rŏlă). *Bot.* Also 7 **pirola**; and in anglicized form. 6 **pyrole,** 7 **pyrol.** [med. or mod.L. dim. of *pyrus*, med.L. for *pirus* pear-tree; in F. *pirole*. So called from the resemblance of the leaves to those of the pear-tree.] A genus of plants, type of the N.O. *Pyrolaceæ*, often viewed as a sub-order of the *Ericaceæ*, consisting of smooth herbs, with running underground stems, evergreen usually entire and rounded leaves, and simple racemes of flowers; several of the species are known as *wintergreen*.

Formerly including some allied plants now removed to other genera, as *Moneses grandiflora* (*Pyrola uniflora*) and *Chimaphila* (*Pyrola*) *umbellata*.

1578 LYTE *Dodoens* I. xcii. 134 Pyrola groweth in shadowy places, and moyst wooddes. *Ibid.* 135 Greene Pyrole is also good to be layde vpon woundes, vlcers, & burnings. 1651 DAVENANT *Gondibert* II. vii. iii, New wounds..such..As balm nor juice of pyrol never heals. 1672 JOSSELYN *New Eng. Rarities* 67 Pirola, or Winter Green, that kind which grows with us in England is common in New-England, but there is another plant which I judge to be a kind of Pirola, and proper to this Country. 1834 MARY HOWITT *Sk. Nat. Hist., The Garden* xii, I found within another wood The rare Pyrola blowing.

Hence **Pyrolaceous** (-ēⁱ·ʃəs) *a.*, belonging to the *Pyrolaceæ* (Mayne *Expos. Lex.*, 1858).

Pyrolatry (pəirǫ·lătri). [f. PYRO- + Gr. λατρεία service, worship: cf. IDOLATRY.] The worship of fire, fire-worship.

1669 GALE *Crt. Gentiles* I. II. ix. 144 Their Pyrolatrie, or fire-worship, which they learnt from the Chaldeans. 1839 MOORE *Hist. Irel.* I. ii. 26 The Pyrolatry, or Fire-worship, of the early Irish. 1891 MAX MÜLLER *Phys. Relig.* 241 Anything like pyrolatry or worship of fire, as a mere element, is foreign to the character of the Greeks.

Hence **Pyro·later** (-or), [cf. IDOLATER], a fire-worshipper.

1801 SOUTHEY *Thalaba* VIII. *note*, The fires..having too near an analogy to the religion of the pyrolators.

Pyroleter (pəirǫ·lĭtəɪ). [f. Gr. πῦρ fire + ὀλετήρ destroyer.] An apparatus for extinguishing fire, consisting of a double pump by which solutions of hydrochloric acid and sodium bicarbonate are mixed in a cylinder, and the carbonic acid generated by the reaction is projected upon the fire.

1878 *Ure's Dict.* IV. 712 The pyroleter is a small double pump worked by hand, which sucks up from tubes on either side muriatic acid and a solution of carbonate of soda.

Pyroligneous (pəi·ro₁li·gniəs), *a.* [a. F. *pyro-ligneux* (De Morveau and Lavoisier, 1787), f. PYRO- + L. *lignum* wood.] Produced by the action of fire or heat upon wood. *Pyroligneous acid*: a crude acetic acid (wood vinegar) obtained by the destructive distillation of wood. So *pyroligneous alcohol*, *ether*, *spirit*, methyl alcohol.

[1787 DE MORVEAU, LAVOISIER, etc. *Nomencl.* 150 Noms nouveaux: *Acide pyro-ligneux*. Esprit acide empyreumatique du bois.] *c* 1790 tr. *De Morveau's*, etc., *Table Chem. Nom.* (*Encycl. Brit.* (ed. 3) IV. 598) 21 Pyro-ligneous acid. Spirit of wood. 1810–26 HENRY *Elem. Chem.* I. 336 Liquid products of value are collected, an impure vinegar called pyroligneous acid. 1822 P. TAYLOR in *Philos. Mag.* 31 Oct. 316 This spirit, which, from its greater resemblance to æther than to any other substance, I have called pyroligneous æther. 1861 *Photogr. News* 3 May 211/2 Pyroligneous Spirit, known also as pyroxylic spirit, wood alcohol, and wood naphtha. 1873 E. SPON *Workshop Receipts* Ser. I. 64/1 Some turpentine being drawn from green trees abound[s] with a pyroligneous acid. 1876 HARLEY *Mat. Med.* (ed. 6) 336 Pyroligneous æther or wood naphtha,—a fluid quite distinct from mineral naphtha, which is a simple hydrocarbon.

So † **Pyroli·gnic,** † **Pyroli·gnous** *adjs.* in same sense; **Pyroli·gnate,** † **Pyroli·gnite** [so in Fr.; see -ITE[1] 4 b], a salt of pyroligneous acid, an impure or crude acetate.

1823 J. BADCOCK *Dom. Amusem.* 22 Acetate of Lime. Sometimes termed *Pyrolignate of Lime. *a* 1799 J. BLACK *Lect. Elem. Chem.* (1803) II. 374 An acid now called *pyro-lignic (pyro-xylic). 1805 NISBET *Dict. Chem.*, *Table Nomencl.* i. 359 *Pyrolignic radical*, basis of acid distilled from birch and other woods. [1787 DE MORVEAU, LAVOISIER, etc. *Nomencl.* 208 *Pyro-lignite de chaux, etc.] *c* 1790 tr. *De Morveau's*, etc., *Tabl. Chem. Nom.* (*Encycl. Brit.* (ed. 3) IV. 598) 21 Pyro-lignite of lime, Pyrolignite of zinc, etc. 1839 URE *Dict. Arts* 223 The pyrolignite of iron called iron liquor in this country, is the only mordant used in calico-printing for black, violet, puce, and brown colours. 1790 KERR tr. *Lavoisier's Elem. Chem.* 260 The Combinations of *Pyro-lignous Acid with the Salifiable Bases. 1823 J. BADCOCK *Dom. Amusem.* 21 Pyrolignous acid, about twice the strength of vinegar..possesses a dull, acidulous, offensive smack.

Pyroline, *Chem.*, var. of PYRROLINE.

Pyrolithic to **Pyrolivilic**: see PYRO- 3 a.

Pyrology (pəirǫ·lŏdʒi). *rare.* [ad. mod.L. *pyrologia*: see PYRO- 1 and -LOGY.] The science or study of fire or heat; now *spec.* that branch of chemistry which deals with the application of fire to chemical analysis, etc.

[1669 R. WITTIE (*title*) Pyrologia Mimica; or an Answer to Hydrologia Chymica of W. Simpson...In Defence of Scarborough-Spaw. 1692 D. BOTTONI (*title*) Pyrologia Topographica, id est, de Igni dissertatio, juxta loca cum eorum descriptionibus.] 1731 *Hist. Litteraria* III. 348 The Discoveries made by the modern Philosophers in Pneumaticks, Hydrology, Pyrology, &c. 1797 W. OKELY (*title*) Pyrology; or the Connection between Natural and Moral Philosophy. 1875 W. A. ROSS (*title*) Pyrology or Fire Chemistry.

Hence **Pyrolo·gical** *a.*, pertaining to or involving pyrology; **Pyro·logist,** one versed in pyrology.

a 1799 BLACK is cited by Webster (1828) for *Pyrologist*. 1881 W. A. ROSS in *Knowledge* No. 7. 137 The young 'pyrologist', or blowpipe chemist. 1881 *Eng. Mechanic* 27 May 284/1 Even with his pyrological methods, he would have difficulty in determining the carbonic acid in a pinch of soot. 1883 *Ibid.* 20 July (*title*) Easy Lessons in Blowpipe Analysis and Pyrological Mineralogy.

Pyrolusite (pəiro₁lŭ·səit). *Min.* [ad. Ger. *pyrolusit* (Haidinger 1827), f. Gr. πυρο- (PYRO-) + λοῦσις washing + -ITE[1]: from its use, when heated, for discharging colour from glass.] Native dioxide of manganese, MnO_2, a common ore of black or dark-grey colour and metallic lustre.

1828 *Edin. Jrnl. Sc.* IX. 304 An account of pyrolusite or prismatic manganese ore. 1839 DE LA BECHE *Rep. Geol. Cornwall*, etc. xv. 610 Pyrolusite, or grey and black ore, containing from 70 to 99 per cent. of peroxide of manganese. 1868 DANA *Min.* (ed. 5) 166 Pyrolusite parts with its oxygen at a red heat, and is extensively employed for discharging the brown and green tints of glass. Hence..whimsically entitled by the French *le savon des verriers*.

Pyromachy to **-malic**: see PYRO- 1, 3 a.

Pyromancy (pəi·romænsi, pi·ro-). Now *rare.* Forms: 4 **piromance, -aunce,** (**perimancie**), 5–6 **piromancy,** (5 **-cye,** 6 **-cie**), 5– **pyromancy,** (5 **-cye,** 6–7 **-cie,** 7 **-ty**). [a. OF. *piromance*, *pyromancie* (14th c. in Godef. *Compl.*), ad. late L. *pyromantia*, a. Gr. πυρομαντεία: see PYRO- and -MANCY.] Divination by fire, or by signs derived from fire.

1362 LANGL. *P. Pl.* A. XI. 158 Nigromancye and perimancie. 1390 GOWER *Conf.* III. 45 The craft..That Geomancie cleped is,..And of the flod his Ydromance, And of the fyr the Piromance. *c* 1400 [see HYDROMANCY]. 1496 *Dives & Paup.* (W. de W.) I. xxxvi. 77/1 Pyromancye. that is wytchecrafte done in the fyre. *c* 1590 GREENE *Fr. Bacon* ii. 15 Thou art read in Magicks mystery, In Piromancy, to diuine by flames. 1630 J. TAYLOR (Water P.) *Water Cormorant* Wks. III. 12/2 By Fire he hath the skill of Pyromanty. 1855 SMEDLEY *Occult Sc.* 292 Pyromancy, by which conjectures were made from the motions of the sacrificial flame.

So **Py·romancer,** one who divines by fire; **Pyroma·ntic** *a.*, pertaining to or practising pyromancy; † *sb.* = *pyromancer*.

c 1400 *Apol. Loll.* 96 Þus are callid..piromauncers þat wirkun bi þe fire. *c* 1590 GREENE *Fr. Bacon* ix. 72 The Pyromanticke Genij. 1608 DAY *Law Trickes* IV. ii, Skill in pyromantique rules. 1638 SIR T. HERBERT *Trav.* (ed. 2) 215 Many Witches, Sorcerers, Inchanters, Hydro and Pyromantiques, and other Diaboliques.

Pyromania to **-maric**: see PYRO- 1, 3 a.

Pyromeco·nic, *a. Chem.* [f. PYRO- 3 + MECONIC.] In *pyromeconic acid*, a crystalline bitter acid, $C_5H_4O_3$, occurring in large transparent tables; it is obtained by the dry distillation of meconic or of comenic acid. Hence **Pyrome·conate,** a salt of this acid.

1836 BRANDE *Man. Chem.* (ed. 4) 1023 Pyromeconic Acid. This acid is among the products of the destructive distillation of the meconic acid; it is a crystalline sublimate, which fuses at a temperature of about 250°. *Ibid.* The neutral pyromeconate of lead. 1838 T. THOMSON *Chem. Org. Bodies* 82 Pyromeconic acid..was first examined by Robiquet in 1832. 1866–8 WATTS *Dict. Chem.* IV. 761 With bromine water it yields bromopyromeconic acid ($C_5H_3BrO_3$)... Chloride of iodine converts it into iodopyromeconic acid ($C_5H_3IO_3$).

† **Py·romel.** *Obs.* [f. PYRO- + L. *-mel* honey.] An old name for treacle.

1897 in *Syd. Soc. Lex.*

Pyromelane to **-metamorphism**: see PYRO-.

Pyrometer (pəirǫ·mĭtəɪ). [f. PYRO- + -METER.] † **a.** *orig.* An instrument for measuring the expansion of solid bodies under the influence of heat. *Obs.* **b.** Any instrument for measuring high temperatures, usually those higher than can be measured by the mercurial thermometer.

Such instruments have been made on a variety of principles, depending on the expansion, contraction, or fusion of solids, the radiation, conduction, etc. of heat, the production of electrical or chemical action, etc.

1749 *Gentl. Mag.* XIX. 361/2 The Draught of an accurate Pyrometer or Instrument to measure the Extension or Contraction, of Metal, or other Rods,..invented by Mr. Withurst of Derby. 1793 W. & S. JONES *Catal. Optical, etc. Instr.* 8 Pyrometers, shewing the expansion of metals. 1796 KIRWAN *Elem. Min.* (ed. 2) I. Pref. 10, I..examined..their fusibility in various degrees of heat by the help of Mr Wedgewood's pyrometer. 1812 SIR H. DAVY *Chem. Philos.* 73 Clay contracts considerably in dimensions by a very intense heat, and on the measure of its contractions the pyrometer of Wedgwood is founded. 1906 *Westm. Gaz.* 16 July 4/2 Special furnaces which are controlled by the assistance of electrical pyrometers. 1907 *Athenæum* 18 May 609/3 A modification of Prof. Féry's radiation pyrometer, which in principle consists of receiving in a concave mirror the total radiation of a hot plate.

Hence **Pyrome·tric, Pyrome·trical** *adjs.*, pertaining to a pyrometer or to pyrometry; of the nature of, or measurable by, a pyrometer; formerly said of effects due to the expansive power of great heat; **Pyrome·trically** *adv.*, in the manner of, or by means of, a pyrometer; **Pyro·metry,** the measurement of very high temperatures.

1800 tr. *Lagrange's Chem.* I. 20 This pyrometer [Wedgewood's] consists of two parts, one of which, called the Gage, serves to measure the degrees of diminution or contraction: the other consists of small cylinders of clay, called *Pyrometric Pieces. 1837 HERSCHEL in Babbage *Bridgew. Treat.* App. I. 237 The elevation of strata by pyrometric expansion of the subjacent columns of rock. 1839 URE *Dict. Arts* 1016 Pyrometric balls of red clay, coated with a very fusible lead enamel, are employed in the English potteries to ascertain the temperature of the glaze kilns. 1791 *Phil. Trans.* LXXXI. 107 The substances employed..must have been influenced in their length by *pyrometrical and hygrometrical effects. 1834–6 BARLOW in *Encycl. Metrop.* (1845) VIII. 460/2 *Pyrometrical beads*, technically called *trials*, ..are made in the form of small hoops, of Egyptian black clay. 1865 MISS METEYARD *Wedgwood* II. 160 Thos. and John Wedgwood..about 1740 introduced what they termed pyrometrical beads..formed of prepared clay. 1778 *Phil. Trans.* LXVIII. 419 (heading) An Essay on *Pyrometry and Areometry. *Ibid.* 421 The occasion which led me to Pyrometry. 1830 HERSCHEL *Stud. Nat. Phil.* 319 The dilatation of bodies by heat forms the subject of..pyrometry. 1897 ROSE in *Mining Jrnl.* 30 Jan. 143/3 Pyrometry and the testing..of alloys continue to receive much attention.

Pyromorphite, -morphous: see PYRO- 2, 1.

Pyromucic (pəi·ro₁miū·sik), *a. Chem.* [f. PYRO- 3 + MUCIC: cf. F. *pyromucique* substituted for *pyromuqueux* (De Morveau and Lavoisier 1787).] In *pyromucic acid*, an acid, $C_5H_4O_3$, metameric with pyromeconic acid, produced by the dry distillation of mucic acid, and occurring in white glistening scales or needles. So *pyromucic alcohol*, *chloride*, *ether*, etc.

1794 G. PEARSON tr. *De Morveau*, etc. *Table Chem. Nom.* 22 Radical Pyro mucic. 1819 J. G. CHILDREN *Chem. Anal.* 281 Pyromucic acid has been lately discovered by M. Houton Labillardière. 1836–41 BRANDE *Chem.* (ed. 5) 1072 When mucic acid is subjected to destructive distillation it yields..pyromucic acid.

Hence **Pyromu·camide,** an amide of pyromucic acid, $C_5H_5NO_2$; *Dipyromucamide*, $C_5H_6N_2O$; **Pyromu·cate,** a salt of pyromucic acid; **Pyromu·cyl,** the radical $C_5H_3O_2$ of pyromucic acid; also † **Pyromucous** *a.* = *pyromucic*, † **Pyromucite** = *pyromucate*.

1790 KERR tr. *Lavoisier's Elem. Chem.* 263 Table of the Combinations of Pyro-mucous Acid with the Salifiable Bases. *Ibid.* 260 Pyro-mucite of lime. 1819 J. G. CHILDREN *Chem. Anal.* 284 Pyromucate of barya is composed of acid 57.7 barya 42.2. 1847 *Chem. Gaz.* V. 85 Pyromucamide differs essentially from this body. 1856–8 WATTS *Dict. Chem.* IV. 763 The pyromucates of the alkali-metals are..difficult to crystallise. *Ibid.* 765 Dipyromucamide forms white, shining laminæ, easily soluble in alcohol and ether, less soluble in water. 1881 *Jrnl. Chem. Soc.* XL. 715 Ethylamine pyromucate when distilled with phosphorus pentachloride yields pyromucyl chloride.

Pyronaphtha to **Pyronomy**: see PYRO- 1.

Pyrone: see PYRO- 3 c.

Pyrope (pəi·rōᵘp). Forms: 4 **pirope,** 7 **pirop,** 7–9 **pyrop,** 9 **pyrope**; also in Lat. form 6 **piro·pus,** 7–9 **pyro·pus,** (*pl.* -i). [a. OF. *pirope* (13th c. in Godef.), ad. L. *pyrōpus* gold-bronze, also a kind of gem, a. Gr. πυρωπός gold-bronze, lit. 'fiery-eyed', f. πῦρ, πυρ- fire + ὤψ eye, face.]

† **1.** In early use applied vaguely to a red or fiery gem, as ruby or carbuncle. *Obs.*

13.. *K. Alis.* 5682 Jacynkte, Piropes, Crisolites. 1553 EDEN *Treat. Newe Ind.* (Arb.) 14 *Piropi* (whiche are a kind of Rubies or Carbuncles). 1602 CAMPION *Eng. Poesie* vii. in G. G. Smith *Eliz. Crit. Ess.* (1904) II. 345 The glossy Pirop faines to blaze, But toucht cold appeares, and an earthy stone. 1625 LISLE *Du Bartas, Noe* 154 Two pyrops are her eyes Or flaming carbuncles. 1795 SOUTHEY *Joan of Arc* II. 84 Rubies and amethysts..With the gay topaz,..and the emerald's hue, And bright pyropus.

2. *Min.* Applied by Werner, 1803 (*Pyrop*), to the Bohemian garnet or fire-garnet, a deep-red gem.

1804 *Edin. Rev.* III. 301 The pyrop, which has lately exfoliated from the class of garnets, has no difference but superior beauty. 1805–17 R. JAMESON *Char. Min.* (ed. 3) 91 Precious garnet, pyrope and iron-sand. 1840 BROWNING *Sordello* VI. 411 Cool citrine-crystals, fierce pyropus-stone. 1868 DANA *Min.* (ed. 5) 267 The original pyrope is the kind containing chrome. 1888 RUTLEY *Rock-Forming Min.* 112 Pyrope, or magnesia-alumina garnet.

Pyropectic to **Pyrophone**: see PYRO-.

Pyrophore (pəi·rŏfōᵊɪ). *rare.* [a. F. *pyrophore* (1762 in *Dict. Acad.*), ad. mod.L. *pyrophorus*.] **1.** = PYROPHORUS 1; also applied to a substance which takes fire on contact with water.

1884 KNIGHT *Dict. Mech.* Supp., *Pyrophore*..a body which has the faculty of inflaming by contact with air or water.

‖ **2.** [prop. Fr.] A fire-fly of the genus *Pyrophorus*: see PYROPHORUS 2.

1885 *B'ham Weekly Post* 26 Dec. 1/4 These insects had been brought from Mexico, where they are to be found in the forests. Their scientific name is the pyrophore.

Pyrophoric (-fǫ·rik), *a.* [f. next + -IC.] Of, pertaining to, or of the nature of a pyrophorus; having the property of taking fire on exposure to air. Also **Pyrophorous** (-ǫ·fŏrəs), *a.*

1828 WEBSTER, *Pyrophorous*, pertaining to or resembling pyrophorus. 1836 BRANDE *Man. Chem.* (ed. 4) 1119 A residue..which burns like tinder when heated, and at a high temperature is pyrophoric. 1866–8 WATTS *Dict. Chem.* IV. 766 The pyrophoric character is exhibited by all the more easily oxidable metals. 1876 HARLEY *Mat. Med.* (ed. 6) 247 At a higher temperature this is completely decomposed, leaving a pyrophoric mixture of lead and carbon.

‖ **Pyrophorus** (pəirǫ·fŏrŏs). Pl. **-i** (-əi). [mod. L., ad. Gr. πυροφόρος fire-bearing.]

1. *Chem.* Any substance capable (esp. in a finely divided state) of taking fire spontaneously on exposure to air. In early use applied *spec.* to *Homberg's pyrophorus*, a substance made by heating alum with lamp-black, starch, sugar, or flour.

1778 M. CUTLER in *Life*, etc. (1888) II. 204 That these acids may produce such appearances is probable from the easy experiment of Pyrophorus. 1798 *Monthly Mag.* Jan. 20/1 There is a particular composition, known to chemists by the name of pyrophorus, because it possesses the property of being liable to spontaneous inflammation in the open air. It was composed by Homberg. 1842 PARNELL *Chem. Anal.* (1845) 345 The metallic cobalt thus obtained acts as a pyrophorus when it comes in contact with the air. *c* 1860 FARADAY *Forces Nat.* iv. 109 *note*, Lead Pyrophorous..is a tartrate of lead which has been heated in a glass tube to dull redness as long as vapours are emitted.

2. *Entom.* A genus of beetles (named by Illiger, 1809) of the family *Elateridæ* (see ELATER[1] 2), found in tropical and subtropical America, containing the most brilliantly luminous 'fire-flies'.

Pyrophosphamic, -phoric: see PYRO- 3 a.

Pyro-photograph (pəi·ro₁fōᵘ·tŏgraf). [f. PYRO- 1 + PHOTOGRAPH.] A photographic picture burnt in on glass or porcelain. Hence **Pyro-photogra·phic** *a.*, of, pertaining to, or of the nature of a pyro-photograph, or of pyro-photography. **Pyro-photo·graphy,** a process in which heat is used to fix a photographic picture.

1869 *Photogr. Jrnl.* 15 Oct. 136 Pyro-photography, or fire-proof photography, is the production of transparent glass photographs by means of fusible pigments, the latter being attached to a film rendered sensitive to the action of light. *Ibid.*, The pigments of the pyro-photographic pictures. *Ibid.* 137 It is this almost incredibly delicate graduation of hygroscopic power, imparted to the film by exposure..to light, that is utilized for the production of pyro-photographs. 1875 H. VOGEL *Chem. Light* xiv. 213 We shall see..that there are other means of producing such pyro-photographs. *Ibid.* xv. 257 Section ix.—Pyro-Photography with Salts of Chromium.

Pyrophyllite to **Pyrosilver**: see PYRO-.

Pyropus, L. form of PYROPE; var. PEROPUS *Obs.*

‖ **Pyrosis** (pəirōᵘ·sis). *Path.* [mod.L., a. Gr. πύρωσις setting on fire, burning, f. πυροῦν to set on fire.] An affection characterized by a burning sensation in the stomach and œsophagus, with eructation of watery fluid; water-brash.

1789 CULLEN *Mat. Med.* II. 248 The pyrosis, frequent in this country under the name of the Water-brash. 1843 R. J. GRAVES *Syst. Clin. Med.* Introd. Lect. 32 The preparation of bismuth used in pyrosis. 1847 E. J. SEYMOUR *Severe Dis.* I. 9 The next morbid condition of the stomach is what is called pyrosis or water-brash.

Pyrosmalite: see PYRO- 2.

Pyrosome (pəi·rosōᵘm). *Zool.* [ad. mod.L. *Pyrosōma* (also in Eng. use), f. Gr. πῦρ fire (PYRO-) + σῶμα body.] An animal of the genus *Pyrosōma*, consisting of highly phosphorescent compound ascidians, the individuals being united into a free-swimming colony in the form of a hollow cylinder closed at one end.

1812 tr. *Peron's Voy. S. Lands* in *Pinkerton's Voy.* XI. 760 What..of those Pyrosomes shaped like an enormous finger of a glove..which cover the sea with their innumerable hosts? 1834 *Lancet* 20 Sept. 1013/2 Compound tunicata, as the pyrosoma and the botryllus. 1856 WOODWARD *Mollusca* III. 344 The Pyrosomes are often gregarious in vast numbers. 1883 C. F. HOLDER in *Harper's Mag.* Jan. 187/2 The most glorious fire bodies of the sea, the salpa and pyrosoma, the latter a pelagic aggregation of individuals, forming a hollow cylinder, closed at one end, from five inches to five feet in length.

Pyrosophy to **Pyrosulphuric**: see PYRO-.

Pyrotartaric (pəi·ro₁tartæ·rik), *a. Chem.* [f. PYRO- 3 a + TARTARIC: cf. F. *pyrotartarique*, substituted for *pyrotartareux* (De Morveau and Lavoisier 1787).] In *pyrotartaric acid*, $C_5H_8O_4$, a colourless crystalline substance, obtained by the dry distillation of tartaric acid. So *pyrotartaric anhydride*, $C_5H_6O_3$; *pyrotartaric ether*, etc.

1794 G. PEARSON tr. *De Morveau*, etc. *Table Chem. Nom.* 15 Basis of Pyro-tartaric Acid. 1815 HENRY *Elem. Chem.* (ed. 7) II. 208 From the experiments of Fourcroy and Vauquelin, it appears that the pyrotartaric acid is a peculiar species. 1819 J. G. CHILDREN *Chem. Anal.* 280 Pyrotartaric acid..is solid, extremely acid to the taste, and reddens vegetable blues strongly. 1866 ODLING *Anim. Chem.* 36 Diatomic Fatty Acid Series: $C_5H_8O_4$ Pyrotartric.

Hence **Pyrota·rtranil,** $C_{11}H_{11}NO_2$, formed by heating aniline with the acid; **Pyrotartrani·lic** *acid*, $C_{11}H_{13}NO_3$ (hence **Pyrotartra·nilate,** a salt of this); **Pyrota·rtrate,** a salt of pyrotartaric acid; **Pyrota·rtrimide,** the imide of this acid; and other derivatives. Also † **Pyro-ta·rtarous, -tarta·reous** *a.* = *pyrotartaric*; † **Pyrota·rtarite, -ta·rtrite** = *pyrotartrate*.

1790 KERR tr. *Lavoisier's Elem. Chem.* 261 The name of Pyro tartarous acid is given to a dilute empyreumatic acid obtained from purified acidulous tartarite of potash by distillation in a naked fire. *c* 1790 tr. *De Morveau's*, etc. *Table Chem. Nom.* (*Encycl. Brit.* (ed. 3) IV. 598) Pyro-tartareous acid. *Ibid.*, Pyro-tartarite of lime. 1805 NISBET *Dict. Chem.*, *Table Nomencl.* i, Pyrotartareous, Pyrotartrites. 1817 T. THOMSON *Chem.* (ed. 5) II. 150 The French chemists distinguished them by the names of *tartarous* and *pyrotartarous* acids; which were afterwards changed into those of *tartaric* and *pyrotartaric* acids. 1836 BRANDE *Man. Chem.* (ed. 4) 960 The pyrotartrates of ammonia, potassa,..and lime, are very soluble. 1856 *Jrnl. Chem. Soc.* VIII. 172 Pyrotartanil. *Ibid.* 173 Pyrotartanilic acid is a very stable though rather weak acid. *Ibid.*, Pyrotartanilate of ammonia. 1866–8 WATTS *Dict. Chem.* IV. 775 Pyrotartranil..is easily soluble in..aqueous alkalis, by which when heated it is converted into pyrotartranilic acid. *Ibid.*, Pyrotartrimide forms small needles or hexagonal plates belonging to the trimetric system.

Pyrote, obs. form of PIRATE.

Pyrote·chnian. *rare*⁻⁰. [f. PYROTECHNY + -AN] = PYROTECHNIST.

1731 BAILEY vol. II, *Pyrotechnian*, *Pyrotechnician*, a maker of fire works, one skill'd in Pyrotechny.

Pyrotechnic (pəi·ro₁te·knik), *a.* and *sb.* [f. Gr. πυρο-, PYRO- + τεχνικ-ός, f. τέχνη art; or f. PYROTECHNY + -IC.]

A. *adj.* Pertaining to pyrotechny.

† **1.** Of or pertaining to the use of fire in chemistry, metallurgy, or gunnery. *Obs.*

1704 J. HARRIS *Lex. Techn.* I, *Pyrotechnick-Art*, is the Art of Chymistry, so called..because Fire is the chief Instrument the Chymist makes use of in the separating.. the purer Substances of mixt Bodies. 1731 BAILEY vol. II, *Pyrotechnick*, *Pyrotechnical*, of or pertaining to Pyrotechny [1736 (folio) *adds* or the art of gunnery].

2. Of or pertaining to fireworks, or the art of making or managing them; of the nature of a firework.

1825 C. M. WESTMACOTT *Eng. Spy* I. 64 The pyrotechnic artiste. 1837 SIR F. PALGRAVE *Merch. & Friar* Ded. (1844) 11 The pyrotechnic cases in which the powder is to be contained. 1869 H. AINSWORTH *Hilary St. Ives* II. xviii, The glories of extinct Vauxhall pale the modern pyrotechnic displays. 1873 *Board of Trade Notice* in Bedford *Sailor's Pocket Bk.* iii. (1875) 68 The Pyrotechnic Light, commonly known as a Blue Light, every 15 minutes.

b. *fig.* Resembling or suggesting fireworks; esp. said of a brilliant or sensational display of wit, rhetoric, etc.

1849 MISS MULOCK *Ogilvies* xxiv, Sending forth his bon-mots in a perfect shower of scintillations, so that his conversation became quite a pyrotechnic display. 1897 'IAN MACLAREN' (J. Watson) *Bonnie Brier Bush, Dr. Old School* iv. 133 This was considered to be rather a pyrotechnic display of Elspeth's superior memory than a serious statement.

B. *sb.* **1.** = PYROTECHNIST. *rare.*

1817 *Blackw. Mag.* I. 470 Like the fiery wheel of some skilful Pyrotechnic.

2. *pl.* **Pyrotechnics. a.** = PYROTECHNY 1, 3.

1729 SHELVOCKE *Artillery* III. 169 The whole Excellence.. of Pyrotechnics doth not consist in the Construction of Rockets. 1834 DE QUINCEY *Autob. Sk.* Wks. 1853 I. 41 All subjects..from the Thirty-nine Articles..down to pyrotechnics, legerdemain..thaumaturgy and necromancy.

b. A display of fireworks; also *transf.* of lightning; in quot. 1840, the juggler's trick of pretending to eat fire.

1840 BARHAM *Ingol. Leg.* Ser. I. *Leech Folkest.*, He was eating fire!..the attention of the multitude was absorbed by the pyrotechnics of Mr. Merryman. 1850 B. TAYLOR *Eldorado* i. (1862) 10 Broad scarlet flashes of lightning, surpassing any celestial pyrotechnics I ever witnessed. 1861 N. A. WOODS *Pr. Wales in Canada* 108 The long deferred fireworks for the people came off at last. The pyrotechnics were very fine. 1884 ROE *Nat. Ser. Story* ix, A great black cloud..was the background for the electric pyrotechnics.

c. *fig.* Brilliant displays. (Cf. A. 2 b.)

1901 *Spectator* 17 Aug. 220/1 Orchestral pyrotechnics can be infinitely more exciting. 1905 *Daily Chron.* 16 Aug. 3/1 An Edinburgh graduate, in the period illuminated there by the kindling pyrotechnics of Professor Blackie.

Pyrote·chnical, *a.* [f. as prec. + -AL.]

† **1.** = PYROTECHNIC A. 1. *Obs.*

1610 HEALEY *St. Aug. Citie of God* 169 The warlike artes were Minerva's charge, the pyrotecknicall, or such as worke in fire,..Vulcans. 1753 *Chambers' Cycl. Supp.*, *Ball*, in the military and pyrotechnical arts, is a composition..of the combustible kinds, serving to burn and destroy, give light, smoak, stench, or the like. 1800 T. GREEN *Diary L. Lit.* (1810) 233 Count Rumford, with all his pyrotechnical devices.

2. = PYROTECHNIC A. 2.

1755 JOHNSON, *Pyrotechnical*, engaged or skilful in fireworks. 1765 R. JONES *Fireworks* vi. 254 A variety of pyrotechnical representations. 1801 STRUTT *Sports & Past.* IV. iii. 334 Some of the actors concerned in the pyrotechnical shows. 1862 M. HOPKINS *Hawaii* 99 The pyrotechnical display created..the greatest astonishment.

b. *fig.* = PYROTECHNIC A. 2 b.

1825 *Eng. Life* I. 194 All the warmth of her nature was exhausted by her manner: there was a sort of pyrotechnical blaze, without any real heat. 1898 *Chicago Advance* 17 Feb. 211/2 The hysterical and pyrotechnical fashion of the French.

Hence **Pyrote·chnically** *adv.*, in a pyrotechnical manner; by means of fireworks; *fig.* like fireworks.

1867 E. DOWDEN *Contemp. Rev.* VI. 51 He can mention 1789 without exploding pyrotechnically. 1883 *Daily News* 11 Sept. 3/1 Gala nights with Chinese lanterns and 'the mouse ran up the clock' done pyrotechnically.

† **Pyrotechni·cian.** *Obs. rare.* [f. PYROTECHNIC + -IAN, after *mechanician*, *physician*, etc.] One skilled in pyrotechny; a maker of gunpowder, etc., or of fireworks (= next).

1729 SHELVOCKE *Artillery* III. 169 To consult able Pyrotechnicians. 1731 [see PYROTECHNIAN].

Pyrotechnist (paɪ·rǒte·knist). [f. next + -IST: cf. botanist, etc.] One employed or skilled in pyrotechny; a maker or displayer of fireworks.

Pyrotechny (paɪ·rǒtekni). [a. F. pyrotechnie (1556 in Hatz.-Darm.) or mod.L. pyrotechnia (also formerly in English use), f. Gr. πῦρο- PYRO- + -τέχνη art.] The art of employing fire; with various connotations.

†1. (Military pyrotechny.) The manufacture and use of gunpowder, bombs, fire-arms, etc. Obs.

2. Pyrotechnics; the art of making fireworks, or of managing fires.

3. The making and managing of fireworks for scenic display, for military use, or as signals, etc.

Pyrotechnical, a. [f. as prec. + -AL.]

Pyroterebic to **Pyrotlionide**: see PYRO-.

Pyro-uric acid: see PYRO- 3 a.

Pyroxanthin (paɪrǒksæ·nþin). Chem. [f. PYRO- 3 b + Gr. ξανθ-ός yellow + -IN¹.] A yellow crystalline substance.

Pyroxene (paɪ·rǒksiːn). Min. [f. Gr. πῦρο- fire + ξένος stranger.] A mineral.

Pyroxenic (paɪrǒkse·nik), a.

Pyroxylic (paɪrǒksi·lik), a.

Pyroxylin (paɪrǒ·ksilin). Chem.

Pyrrhic (pi·rik), sb.² and a. Prosody.

Pyrrhic, sb.¹ A metrical foot in ancient Greek.

Pyrrhichian (pǐri·kiǎn), a.

Pyrrhicist (pi·risist).

Pyrrhonism (pi·rǒniz'm). Also 8 pyrro-. [as prec. + -ISM.]

Pyrrhonist (pi·rǒnist). Also 7 pyrro-.

Pyrrhonize (pi·rǒnaiz), v.

Pyrrhotine (pi·rǒtin). Min.

Pyrrhotite (pi·rǒtait). Min.

Pyrrhocorax (pirǒ·kǒræks). [Named 1825.]

Pyrrhol (pi·rǒl). Chem.

Pyrrholite (pi·rǒlait). Min.

Pyrrhonic (pǐrǒ·nik), a.

Pythagoric (piθægǒ·rik, pai-), a. [ad. L. Pythagoricus, a. Gr. Πυθαγορικός.] = PYTHAGOREAN.

Pythagorical, a. [f. as prec. + -AL.]

Pythagorically, adv.

Pythagorean (paiθægori·ǎn), a. and sb.

Pythagorian, a. and sb.

Pythagorism (pai·θægǒriz'm).

Pythagorist, a disciple of Pythagoras.

Pythagorize, v.

Pythia (pi·þiǎ). Gr. Antiq. The priestess of the Pythian Apollo at Delphi.

Pythiad (pi·þiæd), pai-.

Pythian (pi·þiǎn), pai-. a. [as prec.]

Pythic (pi·þik), a. [ad. L. Pythicus.]

Pythogenic (paiþo·dʒenik), a. [f. Gr. πύθω to rot + -γεν-.]

Python¹ (pəi·þǒn, pai·-). Also 7 pithon(e. [a. L. Pȳthōn, a. Gr. Πύθων, name of the serpent fabled to have been slain near Delphi by Apollo.]

Python² (pai·þǒn, pi·þǒn). Zool.

Pythoness (pai·þǒnes). Forms: 4-6 phitones, phiton(e, 4-6 phitonesse, 7 phytonisse. [a. OF. phitonisse.]

A woman supposed, or professing, to have a familiar spirit; also a witch.

Pythonic (paiþǒ·nik), a. [ad. L. pythonicus.] Of or pertaining to, or resembling, a python.

Pythonism (pai·þǒniz'm).

Pythonissa. Now rare.

Pythonist (pai·þǒnist).

Pythonoid (pai·þǒnoid), a.

Pyx (piks), sb. Also 5-7 pixe, pyxe, (5-6 pixt, 6 pyxt). [ad. L. pyxis.]

Pyx (piks), v. [f. prec. sb.]

Pyxidium (piksi·diǒm). Bot. Pl. pyxidia.

Pyxis (pi·ksis). Pl. pyxides. [L. pyxis: see PYX.]

Q.

Q (kiū), the seventeenth letter of the modern and the sixteenth of the ancient Roman alphabet, was in the latter an adoption of the Greek *Q* (*ḳoppa*) of some of the early Greek alphabets. The Phoenician letter from which this was derived had the forms *Q*, *φ*, *Ϙ*, and was used as the sign for the deeper or more guttural of the two *k*-sounds which exist in the Semitic tongues (Hebrew ק, Arabic ق). Though this sound had no real equivalent in Greek, it is found in early inscriptions, e.g. as the initial of *Ḳόρινθος* Corinth, but was not accepted as a letter of the Athenian alphabet, being retained only as a numerical symbol = 90. In Latin, however, *Q* was regularly employed, in combination with V, in representing the double sound (kw) which arose partly from the labialized velar guttural, as in *quis*, *quattuor*, and partly from a palatal *k* followed by the labial semi-vowel, as in *quae*. In the Romanic tongues this Latin combination was either retained with its original value, or in certain cases (esp. in Fr.) was modified to a simple *k*-sound. In the former case the spelling with *qu*- has commonly been retained, even where the sound has at a later period been reduced to (k).

The Latin *qu*- might naturally have been adopted in OE. orthography to represent the Common Teutonic initial combination *kw*- (for which Wulfila employed the special sign ϙ); but though *qu*- is found in the earliest glosses, which, as in the Kentish glosses, the ordinary OE. symbol for the sound was *cw*- (in early use also *cu*-). After the Conquest *qu*- was again introduced, though at first sparingly employed; *quatterne* appears in the Laud MS. of the OE. Chron., an. 1137, the *Lambeth Hom.* have *quic*, *quiken* (but *cwen*), and Ormin has *qwarrterrne cwen*, though regularly using *cw*- except in *quafferan*. In the 13th c. the usage varies in different MSS., and sometimes even in the same text. The earlier version of Laȝamon has regularly the later *cw*-; the *Leg. St. Kath.* and *Jul.* have *-w-*, but *qu*- in *quod*; and the *Ancren Riwle* usually *cu*-, even in French words, but also *qu*-, esp. in French words. In *Gen. & Exod.* there is no *cu*-, only *qu*- or *qua*- being used. By the end of the 13th c. *cw*- was entirely discontinued, and *qu*- (or its variants *qw*-, *gw*-) was the established spelling for all cases of the sound (kw), whether of English, French, or Latin origin. The author of the *Ayenbite*, however, also writes *kw*-, and this, as well as *kv*-, is occasional. Scottish scribes preferred *quh*- (*qwh*-, *quh*-), which is also, though more rarely, used in northern English MSS.; this orthography survived till the 17th c., and is defended by H. Hume (*Orthogr. Brit. Tongue* 18) as a more correct method of representing than *wh*-. On the other hand *wh*- was freely written by northern scribes in the 14-15th c. in place of *qu*-, as *whilk*, *whenne*, *white* = *quick*, *quene*, *quite*; and alliteration of original *qu*- with *wh*- is not infrequent in some poems, as the *Wars of Alexander*, *Destr. Troy*, and *Morte Arthur*. The pron. implied by this is still current in the northern and north-midland counties (not in Scotland): see esp. the words QUAINT, QUEME, QUEY, QUICK.

2. Of English words or phrases. **a.** Q = Queen; Q. q. = query, question; q. (in a ship's log) = squalls; †q. = *quasi*, QUOD, *St. Clu.* ℔; Q.B. = Queen's Bench; Q.C. = Queen's Counsel (hence q. = Quartermaster); Q.M. = Quartermaster; Q.M.G. = Quartermaster-General; Q.T., q.t. = quiet, *slang*. **c.** † qd. = *quod*, QUOTH; Qn., q. = quarter, quire; qt. = quart, quantity; qu. = query.

3. In plural words or phrases. **a.** = Queens (*Book of St. Albans*); Q's = question-marks. † b. **b.** an *exclam.* of surprise.

† **Qua**, *obs.* form of CUE *sb.*[2]; see also QU.

‖ **Ghat, Qheche, Qhom, qhwom, Qhython-tyci,** obs. ff. WHAT, WHENCH, WHOM, WHENINTHE.

† **Qu, Q,** var. of CUE *sb.*[1], half-a-farthing. *Obs.* **1.** Rules for knowing the numbers which the Old Pt. [1624] I. 64 (T2 Halfpenny) Rather pray there be no fall of money for then wilt thou go for a q. **1507** *II. Return fr. Parnass.* I. i. 134 Aboue saltpre and three qus of brede. **1589** *Jewels* (1608) 27 Some ... divide the Farthing into a Quu, the Q into a Quee.

† **Qua** (kwā), *adv.* Also qua, quē. [L., the abl. sing. fem. of *qui* who.] So far as; in the capacity of. *Obs.*

II. Abbreviations.

1. Of Latin words or phrases. † **a.** Q in medieval notation = 500; q. qu. = QUASI, as if; q. = *quadrans* farthing. *Obs.* **b.** † q. d. = *quasi dictum* 'as if said'; (= *quasi dicat* 'as if one should say', etc.; † q. e. = *quod est* 'which is'; v. v. = *quod vide* 'which see'. † **c.** From the language of medical prescriptions: q. l. = *quantum libet*, q. pl. = *quantum placet* 'as much as one pleases'; q. s. = QUANTUM SUFFICIT; q. v. = *quantum vis* 'as much as you wish'. **d.** Formulæ placed at the end of mathematical problems, etc.: Q.E.D., Q.E.F., Q.E.I., = *quod erat demonstrandum*, *faciendum*, *inveniendum*, 'which was to be demonstrated, done, found'.

Quab, *sb.*[2] *Obs. exc. dial.* (quob). Also 7 quabbe. [= Da. *kwabbe* a boggy place; cf. MLG. *quabbel* slime, and see QUAG.] A marshy spot, a bog. Cf. QUABMIRE.

Quab, *v. Obs. exc. dial.* (quob). [var. of QUAP *v.*; cf. Ga. *quabbeln* in same sense.] *intr.* To beat, throb, quiver. Hence **Quabbing** *ppl. a.*

Qua-bird (kwā-bǭd), *U.S. Also* 8 quaw-. [*qua*, imitative of its note + BIRD.] The Night Heron of North America, *Nycticorax naevius* or *Gardeni*.

† **Qua-bling**, *Obs. rare*[—1]. [? + -LING.] A goby or gudgeon.

† **Quabmire**. *Obs. rare*[—1]. [Q QUAB *sb.*[2] + -bire, but found earlier.] A quagmire.

Quacha, obs. form of QUAGGA.

† **Qua-cham**. *Obs. rare*[—1].

1a. Obs. form of CUE *sb.*[1]; see also QU.

Quack (kwæk), *sb.*[1] Also 7 quake. [Abbrev. of QUACKSALVER.]

1. An ignorant pretender to medical or surgical skill; one who boasts to have a knowledge of wonderful remedies; an empiric or impostor in medicine. = CHARLATAN 2.

2. *trans.* One who professes a knowledge or skill concerning subjects of which he is ignorant. = CHARLATAN 2.

3. *attrib.* and *Comb.*, as quack-advertisement, -bill, -bookseller, -doctor, -medicine, etc.; also quack-adoring, -ridden adjs.

Quack (kwæk), *sb.*[2] [Imitative: cf. Du. *kwak*, q. *quack*, Sw. *quack* (of ducks or frogs), Icel. *kvak* twittering of birds. See also QUAKE *int.*] The harsh cry characteristic of a duck; a sound resembling, or imitating this. **b.** *humorously.* A duck.

Quack (kwæk), *v.*[1] Also 7 quake, 6 quacke, 6 quacke. [Imitative.] **1.** *intr.* To cry as a duck; to make the sound of a duck. **2.** *trans.* To make a harsh sound like the note of a duck; to make a noisy outcry. Hence **Quacking** *vbl. sb.*

Quack (kwæk), *v.*[2] [f. QUACK *sb.*[1]] To play the quack; to practise as a quack.

Quackery (kwæ-kəri), *nonce-wd.* [f. QUACK[2] + -ERY.] The characteristic practice of a quack; charlatanry.

Quackish (kwæ-kiʃ), *a.* [f. QUACK *sb.*[1] + -ISH.] Of the nature of a quack or quackery.

Quackle (kwæ-k'l), *v.* *Obs. exc. dial.* [Imitative: cf. QUACK *sb.*[2]] *intr.* To choke.

Quack-quacking *vbl. sb.*

Quacksalver (kwæ-kˌsælvə). Also 6-7 quack(e)-, 7 quaksaluer. [a. early mod. Du. (16th c.) *quacksalver*, f. *quack*-salve + -er.] 1. One who quacks, or talks pretentiously; a charlatan.

Quacksalving, *sb.* The practice of a quacksalver.

Quadern, *a square*: see QUADRAIN *sb.*[1]

Quadle, obs. variant of CODDLE *v.*, to boil.

Quadra (kwǫ·drä), *sb.* [L. *quadra*, used by Vitruvius in sense 1.]

1. a. The plinth or socle of a podium. **b.** A fillet, that above or below the scotia in the Ionic base.

Quadrable (kwǫ·dräb'l), *a. Math.* Also 8 -ible. [ad. L. type *quadrābilis*, f. *quadrāre* to square.] Capable of being represented by an equivalent square, or of being expressed in a finite number of algebraic terms.

Quadragenarian (kwǫ·drædʒi·ne·riăn), *a.* and *sb.* [f. L. *quadrāgenārius*, f. *quadrāgēni* distrib. of *quadrāgintā* forty) + -AN.] **a.** *adj.* Forty years old. **b.** *sb.* A person forty years of age.

Quadragesima (kwǫ·drădʒe·sima), *sb.* [med. L. *quadrāgēsima* (sc. *dies*) fortieth, fem. of *quadrāgēsimus* fortieth.]

1. The first Sunday in Lent.

Quadragesimal (kwǫ·drădʒe·simăl), *a.* and *sb.* [ad. med. L. *quadrāgēsimālis*.]

† **Quadragesimal-lia**, *rare.* [neut. pl. of late *quadrāgēsimālis*.]

Quadragesimals, *sb. pl.*

Quadrain, *a square*: see QUADRAIN *sb.*[1]

Quadrans, *Obs.* variant of QUATRAIN.

Quadral (kwǫ·dräl), *a.* and *sb.* [f. QUADR(I)- + -AL.]

Quadrangle (kwǫ·dræŋg'l), *sb.* [a. F. *quadrangle*, ad. late L. *quadrangulum*, neut. of *quadrangulus* (see next), f. *quadr-* QUADRI- + *angulus* angle.]

1. A quadrilateral figure; a square.

Quadroon.

1. a. One who is the offspring of a white and a mulatto; one who has a quarter of negro blood. b. *rarely.* One who is a fourth in descent from a negro, one of the parents in each generation being white.

b. transf. Applied to the offspring resulting from similar admixture of blood in the case of horses, or from crossing in the case of animals or plants.

Quadroxalate (kwǫdrǫˈksælăˈt). *Chem.* [f. QUADR(I-) + OXALATE.] A compound containing four equivalents of oxalic acid; esp. *quadroxalate of potash.*

Quadroxide. *Chem.* [f. QUADR- + -OXIDE.]

Quadru- (kwǫˈdrǫ), a variant of QUADRI-; restricted to a few formations in which the second element begins with *p*, as *quadruped*, *quadruplex*, and their derivatives.

Quadrumana (kwǫˈdrɤmænă), *n. pl.*

Quadrumanous (kwǫˈdrɤmǟnɤs), *a.* Also **quadrumanal** (-mǟn-). [f. + -ous.] Belonging to the order of QUADRUMANA; four-handed.

Quadruped (kwǫˈdrɤpĕd). [ad. L. *quadrupēd-*, *quadrupēs* four-footed.]

A. *adj.* Four-footed. Also *transf.* of things.

Quadrupedal (kwǫˈdrɤpĕdăl), *a.* Of or being a quadruped; the fact of being a quadruped.

Quadruple (kwǫˈdrɤp'l, kwǫdrūˈp'l), *a.* and *sb.* [a. F. *quadruple*, ad. L. *quadruplum*, *quadruplus*.]

A. *adj.* 1. *Electric Telegraphy.* Applied to a system by which four messages can be sent over one wire at the same time.

2. *Engineering.* Applied to an engine in which the expansion of the steam is used four times in cylinders of increasing diameter.

Quadruplicate (kwǫdrūˈplikǟt), *a.* and *sb.*

Quadruply (kwǫˈdrɤpli), *adv.* [f. QUADRUPLE + -LY.] Four times; in a fourfold degree or manner.

Quaere, Quære (kwīˈri). *Obs. rare⁻¹.* [Onomatopoeic.]

Quaff (kwǫf, af), *v.* [QUAFF v.] An act of quaffing, or the liquor quaffed; a deep draught.

Quag (kwæg), *sb.* Also 6, 8 quagge, 7 quagge. [Related to QUAG v.; cf. QUAB, QUAW, also to QUAGMIRE.] A marshy or boggy spot, a place covered with a layer of turf which shakes or yields when walked on.

Quaggy (kwæˈgi), *a.* [f. QUAG sb. or v.]

Quagmire (kwæˈgmaiǝ̯r). [app. f. QUAG sb. + MIRE.] 1. A piece of wet, boggy, soft ground that shakes or yields under the feet; a bog, a marsh.

Quaich, quaigh (kwěx). *Sc.* Forms: 4-7 8 quaich, 4-6 quayle, 4-7 quaile, 5 qwayle, 7 quaigh. [a. Gael. *cuach* cup, ad. L. *caucus* (Gr. καῦκα) cup.]

Quail (kweⁱl), *sb.* Forms: 4-7 quaille, 4-6 quayle, 4-7 quaile, 7 quaile, 5 qwayle, 5 qwaile, 7 quail. [a. OF. *quaille* (F. *caille*) = Prov. *calha*, It. *quaglia*, Cp. *codix*, med.L. *quaccula* (Du. *kwakkel*) and OHG. *quatala*, of imitative origin.] 1. A migratory bird allied to the partridge (family *Perdicidæ*).

Quail, *v.¹* [Of obscure origin.] 1. intr. Of persons, plants, etc.: To fail, break down, come to nothing. *Obs.*

Quail, v.[2] Obs. exc. dial. Forms: 5–6 quayle, 7 qualle. [a. OF. *quailler*, F. *cailler* = It. *quagliare*, Pg. *coalhar*, Sp. *cuajar*:—L. *coāgulāre* to COAGULATE.]

1. *intr.* To curdle, coagulate.

Quailer v.[1] Obs. A place where quails are kept, esp. to be fattened for food.

Quailing (kwē·liŋ), *vbl. sb.*[1] [f. QUAIL v.[1] + -ING[1].] The action of giving way, failing, losing heart, etc.

Quail-pipe. [f. QUAIL sb. + PIPE.] A pipe or whistle on which the note of the quail (usually the female) can be imitated, in order to lure the birds into a net; a quail-call. Also used allusively, of fg.

Quaint (kwēnt), a. Also 4–7 queint, etc. Forms: a. 3–4 cointe, (3 kointe 4 coint(e, coynte, koynt(e) quoynte, (3 owointe, 4 quointe, quoynt), 4–6 coynte, (4 quainte, 4 quoynte), quinte, 5 qwainte, 4–6 quaint. β. 4–8 queint, 6 quent, qwent; 4–5 quaynt, 5 qwaynt, qwaint), quainte, 5 qwaintte, 4–6 quaint, 6 weynte, qwhaynte, whaynt(e; 4–5 weynt, 8–9 whaint, whent, 9 wheant.

Quaintance. Obs. = 1 quaynt-, 4–6 quentance, (5 qw-), 6 quaynta(u)nce; 5–7 quentaunce, 5 quyntans. [cf. QUAINT v.]

Quaintise. Obs. rare. [a. OF. *queintise*, *cointise*, *cuintise* (F. *cointise*), f. *cuint*, *quaint* QUAINT a.]

Quaintance. Obs. Also 4 coynt, 4–6 quaynt. [See ACQUAINT v., and OF. *cointier*.]

Quair(e, obs. form of QUIRE sb., WHERE adv.

Quaiver, pl. of quaif, obs. var. COIF.

Quake (kwēk), sb. Forms: *Inf.* 1 cwacian, (cwacc-, cnoac-) quaca(n; 2 kwak-, 3 owak-, 4 quaken(e, 4 quake, 5 qwakyn, 4–6 qvaks, 5 qvake, 5–north. whake, 5–6. St. quaik, 9 St. quaik, 5 *north.* quoke.

Quake (kwēk), v. Also 6 quayk.

Quakerism (kwē·kǝriz'm), [f. QUAKER + -ISM.] The principles or practice of the Quakers, or Society of Friends.

Quakerly, a. [f. QUAKER + -LY[1].] Like a Quaker; befitting a Quaker.

Quaking (kwē·kiŋ), *vbl. sb.* [f. QUAKE v.[1] + -ING[1].]

Quaking-grass. [f. prec.] A popular name of the grasses *Briza*, esp. *B. media*.

Quakily, (kwē·kili), *adv.* [f. next + -LY[2].]

Quaky (kwē·ki), a. [f. QUAKE v. + -Y[1].]

Qual, obs. form of WHALE a.

Quale (kwē·li), sb. Obs. or arch. [a. L. *quale*, neut. sing. of *qualis* of what kind.]

Quaking (kwē·kiŋ), *ppl. a.* [f. as prec. + -ING[1].]

Qualifiable, a. rarⁱ. [f. QUALIFY v. + -ABLE.]

Qualification (kwǫlifikē·∫ǝn). [ad. med.L. *qualificātiōn-*, n. of action from *qualificāre*: see QUALIFY v. and -ATION.]

Qualificative (kwǫ·lifikētiv), a. [ad. med.L. type *qualificātīv-us*: see prec. and -IVE.]

Qualificator (kwǫ·lifikētǝr). [a. med.L. agent-n. from *qualificāre* to QUALIFY.]

Qualificatory (kwǫ·lifikǝtǝri), a.

Qualified (kwǫ·lifǝid), *ppl. a.* [f. QUALIFY v. + -ED[1].]

Qualifier (kwǫ·lifǝiǝr). [f. QUALIFY + -ER[1].]

Qualify (kwǫ·lifǝi), v. Also 6 qualifie, 6–7 qualifie. [ad. F. *qualifier* (15th c.), or ad. med.L. *qualificāre*, f. L. *quālis* of what kind + facere to make.]

Quantum sufficit (kwǫ̆ntəm sŭ·fit).

Quantiplicity (kwǫntiplí·sĭti).

Quantity (kwǫ·rĕl).

Quarrel (kwǫ·rĕl).

Quarrelled.

Quarreller.

Quarrelling.

Quarrelous.

Quarrelsome (kwǫ·rĕlsəm).

Quarrelsomely adv.

Quarrelsomeness.

Quarry (kwǫ·ri).

Quarring.

Quarromes.

Quarrian.

Quarry (kwǫ·ri). sb.[1] Forms: 5 quar[e]y, quarry, 6 quarie, quarrie (7 -ay, quarie), 6 -quarry; (9 dial. whary) ... [a. med.L. quarreia (1266 in Du Cange), var. of L. quareria, etc. See QUARRER, q.v. See also QUAR sb.[2], QUARREL sb.[3]]

1. An open-air excavation from which stone for building or other purposes is obtained by cutting, blasting, or the like; a place where the rock has been, or is being, cut away in order to be utilized.

Quarry, sb.[2] [f. QUARRY sb.[1]] A square candle.

Quarry, sb.[3] Forms: see QUARRE. ... [f. quarré (now quarry) a square piece, in use of quarry QUARRY a.]

Quarry, a.[1] Obs. Also 4-5 quarre, (4 -oy, quare,) (quarie), 6 quarye; 7 quarrie.

Quarry, sb.[4] Obs. rare. In 6-7 quar(r)ie. 1. Clotted, coagulated.

Quarry (kwǫ·ri). v.[1] [f. QUARRY sb.[2]]

1. trans. a. To teach (a hawk) to seize its quarry.

Quarry (kwǫ·ri). v.[2] [f. QUARRY sb.[1]]

To obtain or extract by laborious methods.

Quarryman (kwǫ·ri,man). One employed in quarrying; one who works in a quarry.

Quart (kwǫrt). sb.[1] [a. F. quarte fem. of OF. quart:—L. quarta, fem. of quartus fourth.]

1. A position in fencing (see quart.). — QUART sb.[2]

Quart (kwǫrt). sb.[2] Forms: 5 qwh-, qwrte, 5 qwerte, 5 quarte, -tt, whart, wharte, 6-7 quart. [app. a. ON. *kvert, neut. of *kverr:—L. quartus fourth.]

1. The fourth part of a gallon, or two pints.

Quart (kǭrt). sb.[3] Forms: 5 qwh-, qwrte, 5-7 quarte, (6 -tt, whart), 4- quart. [a. quarte fem. (13th c. in sense 1) and quart masc. (= It. quarto, quarto, Sp. cuarta, quarto,) repr. L. quarta, -tum, fem. and neut. of quartus fourth.]

Quart (kwǫrt). v.[1] [f. quarter (Molière). f. quart sb.[3]] a. intr. To use the position 'quart' in fencing.

Quartan (kwǫ·rtăn). a. and sb. Also 4-7 quartaine, 4-7 -ain(e), 5-6 -ayn(e); 4-6 quartanye(n), (4-etc.), 5- quartane. [ad. F. quartaine, -ain.] ... a. adj. 1. Path. Of a fever or ague.

Quartation (kwǫ·rtē·ʃǫn). [f. L. quart-us fourth + -ATION.] The operation of combining silver with gold so that the latter metal forms one quarter of the whole.

Quarter (kwǫ·rtǝ(r)), sb. Also 4 quartere, 4-7 quarter, (5 quartre, -ir, 5-6 -our, -ur, 6-7 quartter, 6 cart-), 4- quarter. [a. AF., OF. quarter, -ier (= Pr. quartier):—late L. quartarius a fourth part (of a measure), f. quartus fourth. see QUART sb.[3]]

I. Of four equal or corresponding parts into which anything is or may be divided.

1. Of things generally.

2. a. The fourth part of a pound.

b. The fourth part of a hundredweight = 28 lbs.

c. The fourth part of a cwt. of wool, etc.

3. a. The fourth part of a year, esp. as divided by the recognised Quarter-days.

4. One of the four parts into which a road is divided by the horse-track and the wheel-rails.

II. The fourth part of some usual measure or standard.

III. Senses denoting locality, and transferred use.

12. The region lying about or under one of the four principal points of the compass or divisions of the horizon.

13. Region, district, place, locality.

IV. Technical uses, in most of which the original sense is much obscured.

19. Carpentry. A piece of wood, four inches wide by two or four inches thick.

20. a. Farriery. One side of a horse's hoof.

21. A bed or plot in a garden.

22. Naut. a. The upper part of a ship's side between the after part of the main chains and the stern.

24. One of the four parts into which a road is divided by the horse-track and the wheel-rails.

27. General combs. (sense 1), as quarter-beam, -bb, -face, -flood, -hogshead, -inch, -lock, -mile, pay, -pint, -ream, -ton, etc., quarter-faced adj., quarter-yearly adv.

*quarter carrier of that honour which His enemy comes in. *a* 1634 RANDOLPH *Amyntas* v. 6 They do caper Like *quarter Fairies at the least. 1610 HEALEY *St. Aug. Citie of God* IV. xi. (1620) 160 A *quarter ruler with his brethren and sisters. *c* 1640 J. SMYTH *Lives Berkeleys* (1883) I. 116 The lawes..as some have written, were as *quarter-tirants.

†**28.** (Sense 8 a) = 'quarter's', 'quarterly', as *quarter-allowance, -almoner, -feast, -fee, -salary, -sermon, -service, -supper.* Also QUARTER-DAY, -SESSIONS, -WAITER.

1727 BOYER *Dict. Fr.-Angl., Quartier*,..*Quarter-allowance. 1599 SANDYS *Europæ Spec.* 9 With an eye perhaps that themselves would be his *quarter Almoners. 1609 B. JONSON *Silent Woman* II. ii, It is his *quarter-feast, sir. 1615 J. STEPHENS *Satyr. Ess.* 11 Clearkes and other knaves ..Will take a pention or a *quarter-fee. 1583 STUBBES *Anat. Abus.* II. (1882) 77 Preaching their *quarter sermons themselues. *a* 1555 LATIMER *Serm. & Rem.* (1845) 243 Any services in your churches, either trental, *quarter-service, or other. 1592 in *Acts Priv. Counc.* N. S. XXII. 564 Irysche customes as..*Quartersupers called Quidraighe.

29. *Naut.* (sense 22 a) as *quarter-badge, -bitt, -boat, -check, -davits, -fast, -netting, -port, -rail, -railing, -stanchions* (cf. quots.). See also *quarter-board, -cloth, -ladder, -timbers* in 30, and QUARTER-GALLERY, -LINE, -PIECE, -WIND.

1807 ROBINSON *Archæol. Græca* IV. xiv. 390 To the ἀκροστόλια in the prow answered the ἄφλαστα, *quarter-badges, in the stern. 1867 SMYTH *Sailor's Word-bk., Quarter-badge*, artificial galleries; a carved ornament near the stern of those vessels which have no quarter-galleries. 1805 Sir E. BERRY 13 Oct. in Nicolas *Disp.* (1846) VII. 118 *note*, I ordered the weather *quarter-boat to be cut away. 1840 R. H. DANA *Bef. Mast* vi. 13 The watch on deck were lowering away the quarter-boat. 1833 MARRYAT *P. Simple* (1863) 41 Request that he will cast off the *quarter check. 1898 J. CONRAD *Nigger of Narcissus* 246 Let go your quarter-checks!..The ropes splashed heavily, falling in the water. 1867 SMYTH *Sailor's Word-bk.*, *Quarter-davits*, pieces of iron or timber with sheaves or blocks at their outer ends, projecting from a vessel's quarters, to hoist boats up to. 1846 A. YOUNG *Naut. Dict.* 117 *Fast*, a rope or chain by which a vessel is secured to a wharf or quay. They are called bow, head, *quarter, and stern fasts. 1769 FALCONER *Dict. Marine* (1780), *Quarter-Netting*, a sort of net-work, extended along the rails on the upper part of a ship's quarter. 1867 SMYTH *Sailor's Word-bk.*, *Quarter-Nettings*, the place alloted on the quarters for the stowage of hammocks. *Ibid.*, *Quarter-ports*, those made in the after side-timbers and especially in round-stern vessels. 1769 FALCONER *Dict. Marine* (1780), *Quarter-rails*, are narrow-moulded planks, generally of fir, reaching from the top of the stern to the gangway. *c* 1850 *Rudim. Navig.* (Weale) 139 *Quarter-rails*, rails fixed into stanchions from the stern to the gangway, and serving as a fence. 1809 W. IRVING *Knickerb.* (1861) 200 Anthony..was leaning over the *quarter-railing of the galley. 1860 LONGF. *Wayside Inn, Saga K. Olaf* xx, He sat concealed,..behind the quarter-railing. 1846 A. YOUNG *Naut. Dict.* 243 **Quarter-stanchions*, strong stanchions in the quarters of a square-sterned vessel, one of which forms the outmost boundary of the stern on either side: it connects the main rail with the taffrail; [etc.].

30. Special combs., as **quarter-ail** = QUARTER-ILL; †**quarter-ale**, an 'ale' or festival held by the people of a certain quarter (? or quarterly); **quarter-angled** *a.*, at a quarter of a right angle; also *Her.* = QUADRATE *a.* 5; **quarter-aspect**, quartile-aspect (Worcester 1860, citing Brande); **quarter-back**, in American football, a player stationed between the forwards and half-backs; (see also quot. 1895); †**quarter-basin**, *Sc.* (?); **quarter-bell**, a bell in a clock which sounds the quarters; **quarter-bend**, a section of pipe bent into a quarter-circle (Knight *Dict. Mech.* Suppl. 1884); **quarter-bill**, *Naut.* (see quot.); **quarter-binding**, a style of bookbinding with narrow leather back and no leather corners; **quarter-blanket**, a small blanket for a horse's back (Knight); **quarter-block**, *Naut.* a block fitted under the quarter of a yard; †**quarter-blow** (cf. QUARTER 26 a, and *quarter-stroke*); **quarter-board**, †some kind of board used in carpentry; also *Naut.* in *pl.* (see quot. 1846); †**quarter-book**, ? a book containing quarterly accounts; **quarter-boot**, a leather boot used to protect the heels of a horse's fore-feet from being injured by the hind feet (Knight); **quarter-bound** *a.*, in Bookbinding (see *quarter-binding*); **quarter-boy**, a quarter-jack in the form of a boy; **quarter-bred**, of animals: having one fourth good blood (Ogilvie, 1882); †**quarter-bullet** (see quot.); **quarter-butt**, in Billiards, a cue smaller than the HALF-BUTT; **quarter-cask**, (*a*) a quarter-hogshead; (*b*) a quarter-butt; †**quarter-cast**, *a.* of a horse (see quot.); **quarter-clock**, a clock that strikes the quarters; **quarter-cloth**, (*a*) *Naut.* (see quot.); (*b*) = *quarter-blanket*; **quarter-coal**, a periodical allowance of coal made to miners (Gresley *Gloss. Coal-mining* 1883); **quarter-column**, *Mil.* (see quots.); †**quarter-cord**, *Mining* (see quot. 1747); **quarter-course**, *U.S.*, a quarter-mile racing-course; **quarter-crack**, a crack on the inner quarter of a horse's fore-hoof (*Syd. Soc. Lex.* 1897); †**quarter-curtsey**, a slight curtsey; **quarter-cut**, plank cut to a quarter of an inch in thickness; **quarter-distance**, *Mil.* a distance intermediate between half and close distance; **quarter-fishes** [FISH *sb.*²], *Naut.* 'stout pieces of wood hooped on to a mast to strengthen it' (*Cent. Dict.*); †**quarter-foot** = *quarter-hoof*; †**quarter-four**, (?); **quarter-galley**, *Naut.* 'a Barbary cruiser' (Smyth); **quarter-grain**, the grain of wood in the plane of the medullary fibres and radially from the centre, shown when a log is quartered; †**quarter-ground** (Isle of Man) = QUARTERLAND; †**quarter-head**, a brad or flat-nail with a bill or projection at the head; †**quarter-heel** = QUARTER 20 c; **quarter-hollow**, a concave moulding, having an arc which is approximately a quadrant; also *attrib.*, or *adj.*, as in *quarter-hollow tool* (*Cent. Dict.* 1891); †**quarter-hoof**, ? a hoof with one of the quarters cut (cf. *quarter-cast*); **quarter-hoop**, a hoop on the quarter of a cask; also *attrib.*; **quarter-hung** *a.*, of a gun: having trunnions with their axis below the line of bore (Knight); **quarter-iron**, a boom-iron on the quarter of a yard; **quarter-ladder**, *Naut.* (see quots.); **quarter-left**, *Mil.* one quarter of a right-angle towards the left; **quarter-light**, a side-window in the body of a close carriage, as distinct from the door-light; **quarter-miler**, one who is good at running a quarter-mile race; †**quarter-moon**, (*a*) a crescent moon; (*b*) = QUADRATURE 4 b; †**quarter-night**, the time when a quarter of the night has passed; **quarter-note**, *Mus.* a crotchet; also *attrib.* as *quarter-note rest*; **quarter-pace**, a resting-place or landing on a stair, containing a quadrant or 'quarter-turn'; **quarter-partition**, a partition whose framework is made of quarters; **quarter-pierced** *a.*, *Her.* (see quots.); **quarter-plate**, a photographic plate measuring $3\frac{1}{4} \times 4\frac{1}{4}$ inches; also, a photograph taken on a plate of this size; also *attrib.*; **quarter-ply** *a.* (?); **quarter-point**, *Naut.* = QUARTER 10 b; **quarter-pointed** *a.*, *Her.* (see quot.); **quarter-pole**, a pole marking the quarter-mile on a race-course; **quarter-quibble**, ? a poor or weak quibble; **quarter-race**, *U.S.*, a quarter-mile race; **quarter-rack**, a rack which regulates the striking of the quarters in a clock; †**quarter-ranger**, ? the ranger or keeper of a certain quarter; **quarter-repeater**, a repeater-watch which strikes the quarters; **quarter-rest**, *Mus.* a rest equal in time to a quarter-note, a crotchet-rest (*Cent. Dict.*); **quarter-right**, *Mil.* one quarter of a right angle towards the right; †**quarter-road**, an ordinary road with quarters separated by horse-track and ruts; **quarter-round**, a convex moulding having an outline of a quarter-circle, an ovolo or echinus; also *attrib.*, or *adj.*, as *quarter-round tool*; †**quarter-sack**, a sack capable of holding a quarter of grain; **quarter-sawed** *a.*, of wood: quartered; **quarter-screw**, one of the four screws in a compensation balance by which the watch is regulated; **quarter-seal**, a seal pertaining to the Chancery of Scotland, having the shape and impression of a fourth part of the Great Seal; **quarter-section** (U. S. and Canada), a quarter of a square mile of land, 160 acres; **quarter-sights**, sights engraved on the base-ring of a cannon in quarter degrees (Smyth); **quarter-slings**, *Naut.* (see quot.); **quarter-snail** (see quot.); **quarter-space** = *quarter-pace* (Nicholson, 1823); †**quarter-spells**, some game; **quarter-square**, the fourth part of the square of a number; **quarter-stroke**, †(*a*) = *quarter-blow*; (*b*) the stroke with which a clock marks the quarters; **quarter-stuff**, (*a*) = *quarter-timber* b; (*b*) = *quarter-cut* (Knight); **quarter-tackle**, *Naut.* (see quot.); †**quarter-tale**, reckoning (grain) by quarters; **quarter-timber**, †(*a*) quartered timber; (*b*) timber in the form of quarters (sense 19); (*c*) *Naut.* in *pl.* (see quot. 1846); **quarter-tone**, *Mus.* one half of a semitone; **quarter-track** = *quarter-course*; **quarter-turn**, (*a*) a rifle in which the shot makes a quarter of a revolution in the length of the barrel; (*b*) a bend of a quarter of a circle; also *attrib.*; **quarter-twist** = prec. a; **quarter-vine**, an American vine (*Bignonia capreolata*), the stem of which readily divides into quarters (*Cent. Dict.*); †**quarter-voided** *a.*, *Her.* = *quarter-pierced*; **quarter-watch**, *Naut.* a ship's watch composed of one-fourth of the crew; **quarter-wheeling**, turning through a quarter of a circle; †**quarter-wood** = *quarter-timber*.

1797 J. BILLINGSLEY *View Agric., Somerset* 249 A disorder provincially called the *quarter-ail, which is a mortification beginning at the hock. 1574 *Provise in Lease* in Worsley *Hist. Isle Wight* 210 If the Quarter shall need..to make a *Quarter-Ale, or Church-Ale. 1775 ADAIR *Amer. Ind.* 269 Rushed off with impetuous violence, on a *quarter-angled course. 1895 *Westm. Gaz.* 8 Nov. 2/1 Your '*quarter-backs', as half-backs were then called, waited for the ball to roll out. 1899 W. CAMP in Badminton *Football* xxii. 286 Seven rushers or forwards,..a quarter-back, who stands just behind this line; two half-backs [etc.]. 179. BURNS *Lass Ecclefechan* i, A mickle *quarter basin. 1872 ELLACOMBE *Bells of Ch.* in *Ch. Bells Devon* viii. 393 The four *quarter bells were cast. 1769 FALCONER *Dict. Marine* (1780), *Quarter-Bill*, a roll, or list, containing the different stations, to which all the officers and crew of the ship are quartered, in the time of battle, and the names of all the persons appointed to those stations. 1794 *Rigging & Seamanship* I. 157 *Thick-and-thin*, or *Quarter block*, is a double block..used to lead down the topsail-sheets and clue-lines. *c* 1860 H. STUART *Seaman's Catech.* 38 Topsail sheets when made of chain are rove through gins instead of quarter blocks. 1555 W. WATREMAN *Fardle Facions* II. x. 221 Thei [Tartares] fighte all with a *quarter blow, and neither right downe, ne foyning. 1589 GREENE *Menaphon* (Arb.) 85 Breaking a few quarter blowes with such countrey glances as they coulde. 1638 HEYWOOD *Wise Wom.* IV. Wks. 1874 V. 330, I had my wards, and foynes, and quarter-blowes. 1452 in Willis and Clark *Cambridge* (1886) I. 282 The selyng boord..shalbe *quartere borde an inche thyk. 1497 *Naval Acc. Hen. VII* (1896) 296 Sawyng of certeyn tymbre into plankes [&] quarterbordes. 1548 *Privy Council Acts* (1890) II. 174 Quarter boord, iijml. 1846 A. YOUNG *Naut. Dict.* 242 *Quarter-Boards* or *Top-gallant Quarter-Boards*, a thin bulwark boarding, forming an additional height to the bulwarks at the after part of a vessel. They also get the name of *Topgallant bulwarks*. 1679–88 *Secr. Serv. Money Chas. & Jas.* (Camden) 146 His allowance..for returning the *quarter books to Sr Edmund Turner. 1826 SOUTHEY *Vind. Eccl. Angl.* 260 The machinery ..by which his own *quarter-boys in Fleet-street perform their office. 1900 *Academy* 28 Apr. 365/1 The grotesque 'quarter-boys'—corpulent cherubs on either side of the clock—beat the quarters on the dial. 1627 CAPT. SMITH *Seaman's Gram.* xiv. 69 *Quarter Bullets is..any bullet quartered in foure or eight parts. 1873 BENNETT & CAVENDISH *Billiards* 27 The cue-butt or *quarter-butt is larger in diameter than the cue, about 5 feet long, and leathered at the bottom. 1711–2 *Advt.* in *Spectator* (1891) 904, 22 Hogsheads and 3 *quarter Casks of new Bene-Carlos Barcelona Wine..at..5*l.* per Hogshead and 25*s.* per Quarter Cask. 1727 BAILEY vol. II, *Quarter-cast* (with Horsemen), a Horse is said to cast his Quarter, where for any Disorder in the Coffin, there is a Necessity to cut one of the Quarters of the Hoof. 1626 DONNE *Serm.* lxxiii. 748 There was never heard *Quarter-clock to strike. 1884 F. J. BRITTEN *Watch & Clockm.* 217 [A] Quarter Clock..[is] a clock that strikes or chimes at the quarter hours. 1769 FALCONER *Dict. Marine* (1780), *Quarter-cloths*, long pieces of painted canvas, extended on the outside of the quarter-netting from the upper part of the gallery to the gangway. 1894 *Field* 9 June 828/3 The names of his two horses embroidered on the quarter cloths. 1879 *Cassell's Techn. Educ.* IV. 218/2 The *quarter-column is the formation..most employed when large bodies of troops are working together. 1884 *St. James's Gaz.* 21 Aug. 5/2 A battalion of eight companies in quarter-column, that is, in column of companies one behind the other. 1747 HOOSON *Miner's Dict.* Q iij b, *Quartercord* [is] a Measure used in laying out of Flats, 'tis a superficial Measure, and one fourth part of a Mear; it is a Square, each side being seven Yards and one Quarter long. 1851 TAPPING *Gloss. Mining Terms* (E. D. S.), s.v., So long as a mine is wrought..everything upon the quarter cord belongs to the miner. 1885 *Century Mag.* XXX. 397/2 '*Quarter-courses' usually consisted of two parallel paths, and were run by two horses at a time. 1753 SMOLLETT *Ct. Fathom* (1784) 147/1 A *quarter curtsey, or slight inclination of the head. 1895 *Westm. Gaz.* 30 Mar. 3/1 The skin of..all kinds of racing eights, is known as '*quarter cut'. 1796 *Instr. & Reg. Cavalry* (1813) 164 The rear..[divisions] quicken their march, and close up to *quarter distance. 1842 ALISON *Hist. Europe* (1849–50) XIV. xciv. § 7. 7 They were drawn up in two lines, but the enemy chiefly in quarter-distance columns. 1711 *Lond. Gaz.* No. 4888/4 A *quarter Foot the near Foot behind. 1776 G. SEMPLE *Building in Water* 66 A nine Foot Pantile-lath or a *Quarter-four. 1745 P. THOMAS *Voy. S. Seas* 58 We found here in the Road.. two *Quarter Galleys. 1867 [see HALF-GALLEY]. 1703 T. N. *City & C. Purchaser* 187 The *Quarter-grain..is that Grain which is seen to run in straight Lines towards the Pitch. 1825 J. NICHOLSON *Operat. Mechanic* 612 Clear them [laths] into thicknesses by the quarter grain. 1593 *Statutes Isle Man* (1821) 76 To pay for every *Quarter Ground in respect of their..Custom Turves. 1703 T. N. *City & C. Purchaser* 35 *Quarter-heads, or Bill-brads for soft Wood-floors. 1727 A. HAMILTON *New Acc. E. Ind.* I. vii. 67 Their Shoes..very low and stiff at the *Quarter-heels. 1713 *Lond. Gaz.* No. 5148/12 A *Quarter-hoof on one of his hind Feet. 1885 *Census Instruct.*, *Quarter Hoop Maker, Bender, Shaver. *c* 1860 H. STUART *Seaman's Catech.* 75 On each quarter is a *quarter-iron that opens with a hinge to allow the topmast studding sail booms to be raised or lowered. 1769 FALCONER *Dict. Marine* (1789), *Quarter-Ladders*, two ladders of rope, depending from the right and left side of a ship's stern. 1867 SMYTH *Sailor's Word-bk.*, *Quarter-Ladder*, from the quarter-deck to the poop. 1832 *Regul. Instr. Cavalry* II. 93 The..command will be given, Squadrons..*Quarter or Half Left. 1881 *Daily News* 15 Sept. 3/2 The engine..struck the side of the three last carriages..smashed a number of the '*quarter lights'. 1890 W. J. GORDON *Foundry* 157 The thick glass in the quarter-lights, the thinner plate in the door-lights, are not bought for nothing. 1899 *Daily News* 19 July 6/5 The *quarter-miler was only just leading. 1601 HOLLAND *Pliny* I. 121 With horned points like to a *quarter moone. 1665–6 *Phil. Trans.* I. 55 The Course of irregular Tides about the Quartermoons. *c* 1386 CHAUCER *Miller's T.* 330 A Monday next, at *quarter-night, Shall fall a reyn. 1763 J. BROWN *Poetry & Mus.* v. 63 *Quarter-Notes..an Interval which no human Ear can precisely distinguish. 1773 BARRINGTON *Singing of Birds* in *Phil. Trans.* LXIII. 263 Such a minute interval..when a quarter-note for example might be required. 1825 J. NICHOLSON *Operat. Mechanic* 594 Where the height of a story is considerable, resting places are necessary, which go under the name of *quarter-paces, and half-paces, according as the passenger..has to describe a quadrant or semi-circle. 1858 *Skyring's Builders' Prices* (ed. 48) 11 The Plates and Braces in *Quarter Partitions must be added. 1842–59 GWILT *Archit.* (ed. 4) § 2024 The scantlings of the timbers of a quarter partition should vary according to the extent of bearing. 1678 PHILLIPS (ed. 4), *Quarter Pierced*, in Heraldry is when there is a hole of a square form made in the middle of a Cross. 1893 CUSSANS *Her.* (ed. 4) 63 The Cross..If..that part where the limbs are conjoined be removed, it is termed Quarterly-pierced. A Cross with a square aperture in its centre, smaller than the last example, is Quarter-pierced. 1890 *Anthony's Photogr. Bull.* III. 273 A 'half-plate' or a '*quarter-plate' lens. *Ibid.*, A beginner buying his first quarter-plate outfit. 1856 OLMSTED *Slave States* 3 Three yards of ragged and faded *quarter-ply carpeting. 1727–41 CHAMBERS *Cycl.* s.v. *Point*, Half of that, or 2° 48′ $\frac{3}{4}$, [is] a *quarter point. 1769 FALCONER *Dict. Marine* (1789), The quarter-points of the Compass..are distinguished..by the word *by*. 1840 MARRYAT *Olla Podr.* III. 26 How was it possible that a man could navigate a ship with only one quarter point of the compass in his head? 1825–9 W. BERRY *Encycl. Her.*, *Quarter-pointed*,..extending from dexter chief towards the base, and terminated in the fesse point. It..is just one-fourth part of a partition per saltier. 1894 *Outing* (U.S.) XXIV. 142/2 Held his place until the *quarter-pole was reached. 1663 DRYDEN *Wild Gallant* I. i. Wks. 1882 II. 35 A bare clinch will serve the turn; a carwichet, a *quarter-quibble, or a pun. 1729 T. COOKE *Tales*, etc. 96 Quarter-quibbles made his Heart right glad. 1792 *Descr. Kentucky* 12 His time is employed in *quarter-races, cock-fights. 1885 *Century Mag.* XXX. 397/2 In North Carolina..quarter-races were much esteemed. 1884 F. J. BRITTEN *Watch & Clockm.* 219 The *quarter rack ..falls against the bent arm of the hour rack hook. *a* 1613 OVERBURY *Characters, Sargeant* Wks. (1856) 163 The gallowes are his purlues, in which the hangman and hee are the *Quarter-rangers. 1884 F. J. BRITTEN *Watch & Clockm.* 224 In a *quarter repeater the last hour is struck, and afterwards the number of quarters that have elapsed since. 1832 *Regul. Instr. Cavalry* II. 72 The Troops..wheel *quarter right. *Ibid.* 90 The previous command is given, Squadrons quarter or half-right. 1767 A. YOUNG *Lett. to People* 282 A broad-wheel waggon will go in any *quarter-road. 1706 PHILLIPS (ed. Kersey), *Echinus*..is termed..Ovolo by the Italians; but the English Workmen commonly call it the *Quarter-round. 1753 HOGARTH *Anal. Beauty* xii. 171 Let us observe the 'ovolo', or quarter-round, in a cornice. 1851 TURNER *Dom. Archit.* II. vi. 272 The arches and purlins are well moulded, with the quarter round and fillet. 15.. *Merie Tales of Skelton* S.'s Wks. 1843 I. p. lxx, The miller hauying a great *quarter sacke. *a* 1661 FULLER *Worthies, Cambridge* I. (1662) 156 Quarter-sacks were here first used, men commonly carrying..eight bushels of Barly. 1884 F. J. BRITTEN *Watch & Clockm.* 25 Drawing out the *quarter screws of the balance nearest the fast position..and setting in the ones nearest to slow position. 1706 *Act 6 Anne* c. 11 Art. xxiv, The privy seal..*quarter seal and seals of Courts now used in Scotland. 1879 LD. BEACONSFIELD *Sp.* 18 Sept. 2/3 Every man of fair character who comes to Canada, has a right..to obtain what is called a *quarter-section of land. 1882 *Contemp. Rev.* Aug. 233 Each township, section, and quarter-section..marked off by mounds and posts. 1876 VOYLE & STEVENSON *Milit. Dict.* 385/2 In smooth-bore guns, *quarter-sights are cut on the upper quarter of the base ring, and numbered up to 3°. 1867 SMYTH *Sailor's Word-bk.*, *Quarter-Slings*, are supports attached to a yard or other spar at one or both sides of (but not in) its centre. 1884 F. J. BRITTEN *Watch & Clockm.* 219 [The] *Quarter Snail..[is] the snail used in the quarter part of clocks and repeating watches. 1448 in Bacon *Ann. Ipswich* 105 John Lackford accused for cheating at Games called Whistilds, Prelleds, and *Quarter spells. 1841 *Penny Cycl.* XIX. 199/2 A table which gives the squares of the halves of numbers will, by the addition of the squares of the halves or *quarter-squares, give the product. 1550 AYLMER *Harborowe* H, They must know their *quarter strookes, and the waye how to defende their head. 1589 *Marprel. Epit.* D ij, Such a precher..as this, would quickly with his quarter strokes, ouerturne al religion. 1780 COWPER *Table Talk* 531 The clock-work tintinnabulum of rhyme,.. such mere quarter-strokes are not for me. 1712 J. JAMES tr. *Le Blond's Gardening* 71 They make use..of *Quarter-Stuff for large Plinths and Facias. 1799 *Naval Chron.* II. 389 Timber..blocks, quarterstuff, candles. 1815 *Falconer's Mar. Dict.* (ed. Burney), *Quarter-tackle*, a strong tackle fixed occasionally upon the quarter of the main- or fore-yard, to hoist boats and heavy packages into and out of the ship. 1641 BEST *Farm. Bks.* (Surtees) 132 For burying of Corne by *Quarter-tayle..to have 6*d.* a quarter for barley, 4*d.* a quarter for oates. 1601 HOLLAND *Pliny* I. 488 The *quarter timber, or that which runneth with foure grains, is simply the best. 1846 A. YOUNG *Naut. Dict.* 243 *Quarter-timbers*, the framing timbers in a vessel's quarter. 1776 BURNEY *Hist. Mus.* (1789) I. ii. 23 A Diesis or *Quarter-tone. 1811 BUSBY *Dict. Mus.* s.v., The Quarter-tone is of two kinds, viz. the major-enharmonic..and the enharmonic minor. 1866 ENGEL *Nat. Mus.* ii. 45 The seven intervals of the Hindu Scale..are subdivided into twenty-two *srooti*, corresponding to quarter-tones. 1888 J. C. HARRIS *Free Joe*, etc. 10 There was a *quarter-track,..if he chose..horse-racing. 1810 *Sporting Mag.* XXXVI. 272 A *quarter turn, which is the kind of rifle the line uses. 1661 MORGAN *Sph. Gentry* II. iii. 29 Or..a Crosse *quarter-voided azure. 1708–11 *Milit. & Sea Dict.* (ed. 4) II, *Quarter-Watch* is when a Quarter of the Ship's Company watches, which is us'd in Harbour, when there is no Danger. 1769 FALCONER *Dict. Marine* (1789), *Faire la petite Bordée*, to set the quarter-watch. 1887 G. B. GOODE *Fisheries U. S.* V. ii. 229 On the whaling ground.. they stand 'quarter-watches'. 1727–41 CHAMBERS *Cycl.*, *Quarter-wheeling*..in the military art, is a motion whereby the front of a body of men is turned round to where the flank was. 1611 in *Cheshire Gloss.* 275 *Quarter wood att the wiche howses.

Quarter (kwǭ·ɹtəɹ), *v.* Also 4–6 quartre. [f. QUARTER *sb.* AF. *quarteré* is found *c* 1350.]

1. *trans.* To cut into quarters; to divide into four equal or equivalent parts. Also with *out* (cf. 2 b). **a.** things in general.

c 1430 *Two Cookery-bks.* 18 Take a Capoun..quarter hym. *c* 1500 in *Prymer* (E. E. T. S.) 171 Take a penyworthe of hyt, and quarter hyt in fowre. *c* 1590 MARLOWE *Faust.* vii, The streets..Quarter the town in four Equivalents. 1646 SIR T. BROWNE *Pseud. Ep.* 284 As for the divisions of the yeare, and the quartering out this remarkable standard of time (etc.). 1735 POPE *Donne Sat.* IV. 136 He knows.. Whose place is quarter'd out, three parts in four. 1796 MRS. GLASSE *Cookery* xiv. 260 Pare and quarter your apples and take out the cores. 1860 READE *Cloister & H.* lvi, So [to] halve their land instead of quartering it.

b. the body of a person, *esp.* of a traitor or criminal. (Cf. quots. for HANG *v.* 3, DRAW *v.* 4.)

1387 TREVISA *Higden* (Rolls) VIII. 291 His body was i-quartred and i-sent into dyvers places of Engelonde. 1440 J. SHIRLEY *Dethe K. James* 23 The said hongman smot of thare hedes, and there quartard hem. 1508 KENNEDIE *Flyting w. Dunbar* 416 Hang Dunbar, Quarter and draw. 1601 SHAKS. *Jul. C.* III. i. 268 Infants quartered with the hands of Warre. 1723 DE FOE *Col. Jack* (1840) 292 Being discovered, betrayed,..hanged, quartered, &c. 1849 MACAULAY *Hist. Eng.* v. I. 614 A few..were set apart for the hideous office of quartering the captives.

transf. and *fig.* 1595 SHAKS. *John* II. i. 506 Hang'd in the frowning wrinkle of her brow!—And quarter'd in her heart. 1632 LITHGOW *Trav.* I. 2 The very Gospell it selfe,.. is quartered, mangled, and reiected. 1824–8 LANDOR *Imag. Conv.* Wks. 1846 I. 259 At present the one hangs property, the other quarters it.

c. *Mech.* To fix cranks on (a shaft), to make wrist-pin holes in (a driving-wheel), a quarter of a circle apart (Knight *Dict. Mech.* 1875).

2. To divide into parts fewer or more than four. Also with *out*.

14.. *Sir Beues* (M.) 4239 Dede bodyes quarterrid in thre. 1552 HULOET, Quarter or trymme a garden, *deformare aream*. 1596 SPENSER *F. Q.* VI. ii. 44 Clad all in gilden armes, with azure band Quartred athwart. 1599 T. M[OUFET] *Silkwormes* 55 Send Witte the knife to quarter out their meate as need requires. 1627 CAPT. SMITH *Seaman's Gram.* xiv. 69 Quarter Bullets is..any bullet quartered in foure or eight parts. 1634 MILTON *Comus* 29 This Ile..He quarters to his blu-hair'd deities. *a* 1800 *K. Malcolm & Sir Colvin* in Child *Ballads* II. 62/2 Here is a sword..Will quarter you in three.

†**b.** *To quarter out*: To mark out, outline. *Obs.*

1600 SURFLET *Countrie Farme* III. xxvii. 484 The iuice [of the fig] doth constraine the skin to fall into wreathes and to quarter out a thousand shapes. 1616 SURFL. & MARKH. *Country Farme* 158 You shall quarter out a bed for Leekes.

3. *Her.* **a.** To place or bear (charges or coats of arms) quarterly upon a shield; to add (another's coat) to one's hereditary arms; to place in alternate quarters *with*.

14.. *Tournam. Tottenham* 153 in Hazl. *E. P. P.* III. 89 The chefe was of a ploo mell,..Quartered with the mone lizt. 1572 GASCOIGNE *Deuise of Maske* Wks. (Roxb.) I. 85 Confessing that he..bare the selfe same armes that I dyd quarter in my Scute. 1605 CAMDEN *Rem., Rythmes* 25 King Edward the third when he first quartered the Armes of France with England. 1628 COKE *On Litt.* Pref., This faire descended Family de Littleton,..quartereth many faire Coates. 1762–71 H. WALPOLE *Vertue's Anecd. Paint.* (1786) I. 152 [Henry's] sacrificing the gallant earl of Surrey for quartering the arms of England, as he undoubtedly had a right to quarter them. 1854 HAWTHORNE *Eng. Note-bks.* (1883) I. 493 The royal banner of England, quartering the lion, the leopard, and the harp. 1880 DIXON *Windsor* III. ix. 89 Norfolk..had quartered his wife's arms.

absol. 1727–41 CHAMBERS *Cycl.* s.v. *Quartering*, The King of Great Britain quarters with Great Britain, France, Ireland, Brunswick, &c. 1893 CUSSANS *Heraldry* (ed. 4) 171 Neither would their issue—being unable to quarter—be permitted to bear their maternal coat.

b. To divide (a shield) into quarters, or into any number of divisions formed by vertical and horizontal lines.

1590 SPENSER *F. Q.* II. i. 18 In his silver shield He bore a bloodie Crosse that quartred all the field. 1727–41 CHAMBERS *Cycl.*, *Counter-quartered*..denotes the escutcheon, after being quartered, to have each quarter divided again into two. 1868 BROWNING *Ring & Bk.* VI. 237 Our arms are those of Fiesole itself, The shield quartered with white and red.

4. To put (soldiers or others) into quarters; to station, place or lodge in a particular place. Also *pass.* = to have one's abode, lodging, etc.

1594 SHAKS. *Rich. III*, v. iii. 34 Where is Lord Stanley quarter'd, do you know? 1665 MANLEY *Grotius' Low C. Warres* 221 The Duke of Parma all this Winter, quarter'd his men in the village of Brabant. 1723 DE FOE *Col. Jack* (1840) 233 After this campaign I was quartered at Cremona. 1795 WELLINGTON in Gurw. *Desp.* (1837) I. 2 The 33rd Regiment was landed and quartered at Poole. 1822 W. IRVING *Braceb. Hall* I. 4, I am again quartered in the panelled chamber. 1882 B. D. W. RAMSAY *Recoll. Mil. Serv.* I. i. 5 He was then quartered in Edinburgh as a lieutenant.

b. With *on, upon*: To impose (soldiers) upon (a householder, town, etc.), to be lodged and fed.

1683 *Apol. Prot. France* ii. 29 He quartered his Men upon those of the Protestant Religion. 1815 J. W. CROKER in *C. Papers* 14 July (1884), Blucher has quartered a guard of Prussians on him. 1874 GREEN *Short Hist.* viii. § 3. 485 Soldiers were quartered on recalcitrant boroughs.

transf. and *fig.* 1663 BUTLER *Hud.* I. ii. 274 He'd suck his Claws And quarter himself upon his Paws. 1714 *Spect.* No. 595 ¶ 6 You have Quartered all the foul Language upon me, that could be raked out of the Air of Billingsgate. 1812 L. HUNT in *Examiner* 24 Aug. 531/1 Those upon whom the Attorney-General is pleased to quarter his attentions. 1874 GREEN *Short Hist.* iii. § 5. 139 Italian clergy were quartered on the best livings of the Church.

5. *intr.* To take up (one's) quarters; to stay, reside, lodge. (Freq. in 17th c.)

1581 SAVILE *Tacitus, Hist.* II. lxvi. (1591) 91 That they and the cohorts of Batauians should quarter together. 1624 CAPT. SMITH *Virginia* III. ii. 49 That night they quarterd in the woods. 1670 R. MONTAGU in *Buccleuch MSS.* (Hist. MSS. Comm.) I. 482 The whole army..will quarter there for some time. 1723 DE FOE *Col. Jack* (1840) 240 The man in whose house I quartered was exceedingly civil to me. 1781 HAMILTON *Wks.* (1886) VIII. 44, I quarter, at present, by a..warm invitation, with General Lincoln. 1863 COWDEN CLARKE *Shaks. Char.* x. 262 An atmosphere of manner belonging to those who have quartered in various countries.

transf. 1668 CULPEPPER & COLE *Barthol. Anat.* Manual I. v. 312 A remarkable Vein about the Heart..quartering on the one side, without another on the other side.

b. With *on* or *upon*. (Cf. 4 b.) ? *Obs.*

1650 FULLER *Pisgah* II. v. 122 The Canaanites quartered ..hard on the men of Asher. 1681 *Lond. Gaz.* No. 1583/4 A body of men should be sent to quarter upon the Country.

6. To give quarters to; to furnish with quarters or lodgings. ? *Obs.*

1681 W. ROBERTSON *Phraseol. Gen.* (1693) 1040 To quarter, *hospitio accipere*. 1682 BUNYAN *Holy War* (Cassell) 177 They had called his soldiers into the town [and] coveted who should quarter the most of them.

absol. 1667 *Ormonde MSS.* in *10th Rep. Hist. MSS. Comm.* App. v. 56 [Certain] inhabitants of the said towne, refuse to quarter or pay the allowances for quartering.

7. *Naut.* To assign (men) to a particular quarter on board ship; to place or station for action.

1695 T. SMITH *Voy. Constantinople* in *Misc. Cur.* (1708) III. 6 The Captain quartered his Men, and the Decks were cleared. 1748 *Anson's Voy.* III. viii. 378 He had not hands enough remaining to quarter a sufficient number to each great gun. 1769 FALCONER *Dict. Marine* (1780) G g ij, The marines are generally quartered on the poop and forecastle. 1809 J. DALE in *Naval Chron.* XXIV. 78 The Europeans..had been quartered to the upper deck guns.

8. *Naut.* **a.** *intr.* To sail with the wind on the quarter, *i.e.* between beam and stern.

1627 CAPT. SMITH *Seaman's Gram.* vii. 31 When you goe before the wind, or quartering. 1628 DIGBY *Voy. Medit.* (1868) 83 Quartering with one tacke abord till you gett your chace vpon your beame. 1725 DE SAUMAREZ in *Phil. Trans.* XXXIII. 424 Sometimes sailing right before the Wind, then quartering.

b. *intr.* Of wind: To blow on a ship's quarter.

1720 DE FOE *Capt. Singleton* xi. (1840) 192 She came down upon us with the wind quartering.

c. Of a sea: To strike (a ship) on the quarter.

1890 CLARK RUSSELL *Ocean Trag.* I. v. 94 The sea had quartered her and swept..along her lustrous bends.

9. *Build.* To construct (a wall or partition) with quarters of wood.

1703 T. N. *City & C. Purchaser* 278 The Walls being quarter'd and Lathed between the Timber. 1848 *Jrnl. R. Agric. Soc.* IX. II. 570 The former [circle] above the brickwork being quartered and plastered.

10. To range or traverse (ground, etc.) in every direction. Said esp. of dogs in search of game.

1700 J. COLLIER *2nd Def. Short View* 118 He has rang'd over a great deal of Ground, and Quarter'd the Fields of Greece and Italy. 1760–72 H. BROOKE *Fool of Qual.* (1809) IV. 139 They crossed and quartered the country at pleasure. 1766 PENNANT *Brit. Zool.* (1768) II. 235 Who pass over the fields and quarter the ground as a setting dog. 1788 WOLCOTT (P. Pindar) *Sir J. Banks & Emp. of Morocco* Wks. 1812 II. 94 Just like a Pointer quartering well his ground. 1873 TRISTRAM *Moab* viii. 143 To traverse and quarter these ruins is a good day's work. 1888 *Antipod. Notes* 6 Two boats are ..quartering the sea, as a..pointer quarters a turnip-field.

b. *intr.* To range to and fro; to shift from point to point.

1857 HUGHES *Tom Brown* II. v, They quarter over the ground again and again, Tom always on the defensive. 1873 G. C. DAVIES *Mount. & Mere* x. 76 The hounds quartered to and fro.

c. *intr.* To drive from side to side of the road.

In quot. 1834 app. a misinterpretation of sense 11.

1834 DE QUINCEY *Autob. Sk.* Wks. 1862 XIV. 296 The postillion..was employed..eternally, in *quartering*, *i.e.*, in crossing from side to side, according to the casualties of the ground. 1886 ELWORTHY *W. Somerset Word-bk.*, *Quarter* to drive uphill in such a way that the horse crosses the road backwards and forwards so as to diminish the gradient.

d. *intr.* To move in a slanting direction.

1894 *Outing* (U.S.) XXIV. 387/1 The bird quartered past the Judge who had only cut a bunch of feathers from it. 1895 *Ibid.* XXVI. 401/1 We..changed our direction so as to 'quarter' by them.

11. *intr.* To drive a cart or carriage so that the right and left wheels are on (two of) the quarters of a road, with a rut between. Also, of a horse: To walk with the feet thus placed; hence, to walk in front of the wheel.

This is also the sense of F. *cartayer*, Walloon *quateler* (Littré), which are etymologically related to the Engl. word.

1800 TUKE *Agric.* 300 Two-horse carts should be drawn by the horses abreast..by which means they would be enabled to quarter or stride the ruts. 1806–7 J. BERESFORD *Miseries Hum. Life* (1826) II. xxvii, A rugged narrow lane in which the ruts refuse to fit your wheels and yet there is no room to quarter. 1847 *Jrnl. R. Agric. Soc.* VIII. II. 277 The carting off the cabbages..is done with a quarter-cart, as it is termed in Suffolk, having the shafts so placed that the horse walks before the right hand wheel; in other words, it 'quarters'. 1859 MRS. GASKELL *Round the Sofa* 20 We had to quarter, as Randal called it, nearly all the way along the deep-rutted miry lanes. 1879– In dialect glossaries (Shropsh., Chesh., etc.).

b. *intr.* To drive to the side in order to allow another vehicle to pass. (Cf. QUART *v.*²)

1849 DE QUINCEY *Eng. Mail Coach* Wks. 1862 IV. 334 Every creature that met us would rely upon us for quartering. 1866 GEO. ELIOT *F. Holt* 1 Elderly gentlemen in pony-chaises, quartering nervously to make way [etc.].

c. To set (the shafts of a cart) so that the horse walks in front of one of the wheels.

1847 *Jrnl. R. Agric. Soc.* VIII. II. 268 The shafts are quartered, so that the horses (usually two) walk in the furrow followed by one wheel.

12. *intr.* Of the moon: To begin a fresh quarter. Also with *in*.

1789 G. KEATE *Pelew Isl.* 227 They would have had weather until the moon quartered. 1833 MARRYAT *P. Simple* (1863) 157 The new moon's quartered in with foul weather.

Quarterage (kwǭ·ɹtərėdʒ). Also 4 qwarter-, 5 quater-, 6 quartrage, -errage, quarterege, 6–8 quartridge, (6 -redge), 7–8 -eridge, (7 -eridg, 8 -erridge). [f. QUARTER *sb.* + -AGE; perh. a. OF. *quarterage* (Godef.).]

1. A contribution, subscription, tax, or other charge paid by a person every quarter; a quarterly payment made by one.

1389 in *Eng. Gilds* (1870) 3 Which wardeins schul gadere þe qwarterage of bretheren & sustren. 1452 in Gross *Gild Merch.* II. 69 All maner fynnys, amercyments & quarteragys. 1529 in *Vicary's Anat.* (1888) App. xiv. 251 So Alweys that the sayde quarterage be lawfullye demaunded. 1602 DEKKER *Satirom.* Wks. 1873 I. 262 You shall not brag that your Vizeroyes or Tributorie kings have done homage to you, or paide quarterage. 1708 *Brit. Apollo* No. 42. 1 Most of our subscribers having paid their Quarterridges [etc.]. 1795 BURKE *Tracts Popery Laws* Wks. 1842 II. 434 They trade and work in their own native towns as aliens, paying, as such, quarterage, and other charges and impositions. 1887 *Times* 20 Jan. 4/3 The plaintiff had not paid his quarterages.

2. A sum paid to, or received by, a person every quarter; a quarter's wages, allowance, pension, etc.

1423 *Leet Bk.* in Sharp *Cov. Myst.* (1825) 207 Thei shall have ij men of every ward, every quarter, to help them to gather þer Quarterage. *c* 1515 *Cocke Lorell's B.* 4 Than came a pardoner with his boke, His quarterage of euery man he toke. 1590 TARLTON *News Purgat.* (1844) 82 He, being then bare of pence, because his quarterage was not come in. 1666 PEPYS *Diary* 8 Jan., My uncle Thomas with me to receive his quarterage. 1727 SWIFT *Richmond Lodge & Marble Hill*, An idle Rogue, who spends his Quartridge In tippling at the Dog and Partridge. 1830 D'ISRAELI *Chas. I*, III. xvii. 370 A half-starved Clerk, eked out his lean quarterage, by these merry perquisites. 1892 *Cornh. Mag.* July 27 He must wait till his new quarterage came before he could pay.

3. Quarters, place of abode; quartering of troops, or the expense of this. *rare.*

1577 HOLINSHED *Chron., Scot.* I. 485 The Scots that lay in Kelso, and other places keeping their quarterage on the bordures. 1647 in Picton *L'pool Munic. Rec.* (1883) I. 143 Agreed that a Ley..be imposed upon the Towne for payeing of the Quarterage of the horse. *Ibid.*, These burdens of quarterage. 1841 *Tait's Mag.* VIII. 562 Common sense is driven out of her native quarterage in the brain. 1873 O'CURRY *Lect. Ancient Irish* I. xvi. 336 Any noble residence at which they [great stewards] intended to claim the free quarterage due to their official dignity.

4. *attrib.*, as *quarterage-bill, -book, -day, -fee.*

1533 in Sharp *Cov. Myst.* (1825) 214 Paid to the mynstrell at quarterage day..viijd. 1692 *Lond. Gaz.* No. 2799/4 A large Folio Book..called the Carmens Quarteridg-Book. 1771–2 *Ess. fr. Batchelor* (1773) II. 192 The Quarterage-bill, like all others, must pass through both houses of parliament. 1894 *Times* 19 Oct. 6/2 The 'quarterage' fees of 4*s.* per annum per member.

Quarter-cart: see QUARTER *v.* 11 (quot. 1847).

Quarter-cleft, *a.* and *sb.* Chiefly *dial.* Also 7 -cliff, 9 -clift. [See CLEFT *sb.* and *ppl. a.*]

A. *adj.* (See quots.) *rare*—°.

1850 OGILVIE, *Quarter-cleft Rod*, a rod cleft at one end, the cleft extending to one-fourth of its length. 1882 *Ibid.*, *Quarter-cleft*, said of timber cut from the centre to the circumference.

B. *sb.* **1.** Wood cleft in four; quartered wood; also, one of the pieces produced by cleaving in four.

1641 BEST *Farm. Bks.* (Surtees) 15 Wee gette the biggest of [the willows] riven with iron wedges into quarter-cliffe. *Ibid.*, Shorte forke-shaftes, made of seasoned ashe, and quarter cliffe. 1887 *Scott. Leader* 21 Sept. 6 A large stick known in Tipperary as a 'quarter-clift'.

2. A slightly-crazed or 'half-cracked' person.

1831 *Fraser's Mag.* IV. 327 A mere nincompoop, or quarter-cliff or what else you will that implies feebleness of intellect. 1896 *Chambers' Jrnl.* V. 139 (*Ulster Proverbs*, etc.) An eccentric person..is said..to 'want a square of being round'. The next degree of aberration constitutes a 'quarter clift'. 1880 *Antrim & Down Gloss.*, *Quarter cleft*, a crazy person.

Quarter-co(u)sen, -cozin, corrupt varr. of CATER-COUSIN.

1656 in BLOUNT *Glossogr.* 1681 in W. ROBERTSON *Phraseol. General* (1693) 1040.

Quarter-day. [QUARTER *sb.* 8 a.] One of the four days fixed by custom as marking off the quarters of the year, on which tenancy of houses usually begins and ends, and the payment of rent and other quarterly charges falls due.

In England and Ireland the quarter-days are Lady Day (March 25), Midsummer Day (June 24), Michaelmas (Sept. 29), and Christmas (Dec. 25). The name is also sometimes applied to the Scottish terms of Candlemas (Feb. 2), Whitsunday (May 15), Lammas (Aug. 1), and Martinmas (Nov. 11).

1480 in *Eng. Gilds* 315 Ther shall be iiij quarter dayys that every Brother..shall assemble at our comen hall. 1586 HARYNGTON in *Leisure H.* (1884) 630/2 All which somnes shal be duly paide each quarter-day. 1596 *Edw. III*, III. ii, What, is it quarter-day, that you remove, And carry bag and baggage too? 1660 FULLER *Mixt Contempl.* (1841) 197 A gentleman had two tenants, whereof one..repaired to his landlord on the quarter-day. 1767 BLACKSTONE *Comm.* II. 124 Rent..for the occupation of the land since the last quarter day. 1805 SOUTHEY *Ball. & Metr. T.* Poet. Wks. VI. 80, I was idle, and quarter-day came on, And I had not the rent in store. 1840 DICKENS *Barn. Rudge* xiii, The twenty-fifth of March,..one of those unpleasant epochs termed quarter-days. *fig.* 1641 BROME *Joviall Crew* II. Wks. 1873 III. 382 If ever any just or charitable Steward was commended, sure thou shalt be at the last Quarter-day. 1851 THACKERAY *Eng. Hum.* ii. (1876) 174 [They] had..a happy quarter-day coming round for them.

Qua·rter-deck. *Naut.* †**a.** Originally, a smaller deck situated above the HALF-DECK (q. v.), covering about a quarter of the vessel. *Obs.* **b.** In later use: That part of the upper or spar-deck which extends between the stern and after-mast, and is used as a promenade by the superior officers or cabin-passengers.

1627 CAPT. SMITH *Seaman's Gram.* ii. 6 The halfe Decke is from the maine mast to the stearage, and the quarter Decke from that to the Masters Cabin called the round house, wch is the vtmost of all. 1667 DENHAM *Direct. Paint.* I. 55 Each Captain from his Quarter-deck commands. 1748 *Anson's Voy.* I. iii. 29 Many of the principal Officers were on the quarter-deck, indulging in the freshness of the night air. 1840 R. H. DANA *Bef. Mast* xxiii. 67 The chief mate walking the quarter-deck, and keeping a general supervision. 1884 PAE *Eustace* 67 I'd have you to remember that you are not on the quarter-deck just now.

fig. 1853 LYTTON *My Novel* I. x, Too old a sailor to think that the State..should admit Jack upon quarterdeck.

attrib. 1712 E. COOKE *Voy. S. Sea* 167 Each Ship is to answer the other with a Quarter-Deck Gun. 1797 NELSON in A. Duncan *Life* (1806) 42 A Spanish officer looked over the quarter-deck rail. 1828 P. CUNNINGHAM *N. S. Wales* (ed. 3) II. 299 When surgeon of a brig of war, my quarter-deck promenade was confined to eight paces. 1840 R. H. DANA *Bef. Mast* ix. 29 The quarter-deck dignity and eloquence of the captain.

Hence **Qua·rter-decker, -deckish** (see quots.).

1867 SMYTH *Sailor's Word-bk.*, *Quarter-Deckers*, those officers more remarkable for etiquette than for a knowledge of seamanship. *Ibid.*, *Quarter-Deckish*, punctilious, severe. 1889 A. CONAN DOYLE *Micah Clarke* 244 It's your blue-coated, gold-braided..quarter-deckers that talk of canes.

Quartere, obs. form of QUARTER *sb.*

Quartered (kwǭ·ɹtəɹd), *ppl. a.* [f. QUARTER *v.*]

1. Cut into quarters; divided in four; *spec.* of quarter-cleft timber, which being afterwards cut into planks shows the grain to advantage.

1502 *Priv. Purse Exp. Eliz. of York* (1830) 74 For twoo quartred bourdes with vysys. 1601 YARINGTON *Two Lament. Trag.* IV. iii. in Bullen *O. Pl.* IV, Bull always strips all quartered traitors quite. 1626 CAPT. SMITH *Accid. Yng. Sea-men* 32 Musquet shot, Colyuer shot, quartred shot. 1719 LONDON & WISE *Compl. Gard.* 187 The most convenient..is a Lattice of quarter'd Wood, or Heart of Oak. 1805 WORDSWORTH *Prelude* II. 83 Through three divisions of the quartered year. 1854 P. B. ST. JOHN *Amy Moss* 21 These palisades were formed of quartered oak.

b. *Her.* Of a shield or arms: Divided or arranged quarterly. Of a cross: Quarterly-pierced.

1486 *Bk. St. Albans, Her.* D ij b, Certan armys ther be quarterit and irrasit as here apperis, the Wich..ar called quarterit armys irrasit. 1864 BOUTELL *Her. Hist. & Pop.* xvi. 235 He assumed the quartered arms on his accession to the ducal dignity. 1893 CUSSANS *Heraldry* (ed. 4) 166 The earliest known example of a quartered shield occurs on the monument of Eleanor..wife of Edward the First.

†**c.** Of a building: Cruciform. *Obs. rare*—¹.

1591 PERCIVALL *Sp. Dict.*, *Cruzero en edeficio*, a kinde of quartered building, *Structura quadriuiatis*.

2. *Mil.* Lodged in or belonging to quarters.

1611 SHAKS. *Cymb.* IV. iv. 18 When they heare their Roman horses neigh, Behold their quarter'd Fires. 1824 WIFFEN *Tasso* I. vi, To breme winter's wing The quartered hosts give place.

3. Belonging to a quarter or part of the horizon.

1671 MILTON *P. R.* IV. 202 And on the earth Nations besides from all the quarter'd winds.

4. Having quarters of a specified character.

The sense in first quot. is not clear: the F. orig. has *quarrés* 'square'.

[1481 CAXTON *Godefrey* 286 His armes grete and wel quartred.] 1641 BEST *Farm. Bks.* (Surtees) 3 The lambes that forbeare grasse the longest prove..the straightest, and best quartered. 1891 *Cent. Dict.* s.v., A short-quartered horse. *Ibid.*, Low-quartered shoes.

5. *Carpentry.* Made of quarters.

1842–59 GWILT *Archit.* (ed. 4) § 2024 The framework of timber used for dividing the internal parts of a house into rooms is called a partition or quartered partition.

Quarterer (kwǭ·ɹtərəɹ). [f. QUARTER *v.* + -ER ¹.] One who quarters, in various senses of the verb; *esp.* one who takes up quarters, a lodger.

1648 C. WALKER *Hist. Independ.* I. 66 If these quarterers offer violence..they are protected. 1681 W. ROBERTSON *Phraseol. Gen.* (1693) 1040 A quarterer or hang-man. *a* 1800 *Dk. Athole's Nurse* ix. in Child *Ballads* IV. 131 Had you a quarterer here last night,..We are come to clear his lawing. 1881 GREGOR *Folk-lore* 37 Now and again there was a quarterer [a class of beggar] in the family.

†**Qua·rteret.** *Obs. rare.* [f. QUARTER *sb.* 14 or 13 + -ET.] A small quarter or allotted space.

1598 BARRET *Theor. Warres* V. iv, The 3000 launciers are deuided and allodged into 6 quarterets. *Ibid.* Gloss. 252 *Quarteret*, is the diminutiue of quarter.

Quarter-evil. 1. = QUARTER-ILL.

a 1722 LISLE *Observ. Husb.* (1757) 290 The joint-murrain in calves..by others is called the quarter-evil. 1800 TUKE *Agric.* 312 A complaint very prevalent amongst calves, when a year old, is called the..quarter evil..The calves are first seized in one quarter, and are lame. 1841 DICK *Man. Vet. Science* (1862) 148 In two or three hours the animal is dead, from the Quarter-evil. 1898 *Allbutt's Syst. Med.* I. 548 Rabbits, which are relatively refractory to quarter-evil.

2. [QUARTER *sb.* 23.] An inflammation of part of the udder (*Syd. Soc. Lex.* 1897).

Quarterfoil, †**-foyle**, erron. ff. QUATREFOIL.

Quarter-gallery. *Naut.* [QUARTER *sb.* 22.]

1. A kind of balcony with windows, projecting from the quarter of a large vessel; cf. GALLERY 2 d.

1769 in FALCONER *Dict. Marine* (1789) D ij. 1796 NELSON 10 Mar. in Nicolas *Disp.* (1846) VII. xxxvii, The very heavy gales..carried away the starboard quarter-gallery. 1830 SCOTT *Demonol.* x. 363 He saw that the captain had thrown himself into the sea from the quarter-gallery. 1836 MARRYAT *Midsh. Easy* xiii, Pulled them out of the quarter gallery. 1867 [see *Quarter-badge*, in QUARTER *sb.* 29].

attrib. 1797 NELSON Feb. in Nicolas *Disp.* (1845) II. 342 A soldier..having broke the upper quarter-gallery window.

2. A small projection on the quarter of a ship, containing lavatory accommodation (*Cent. Dict.*).

Quarter-guard. *Mil.* [QUARTER *sb.* 14 c.] A small guard mounted in front of each battalion in a camp, at about eighty paces distant.

1741 S. SPEED in *Buccleuch MSS.* (Hist. MSS. Comm.) I. 399 Col. Cockran's and Brigadier Lowther's Regiments.. were not able to give more than nine men for their quarter-guard. 1758 WATSON *Milit. Dict.* (ed. 5) s.v. *Guard*, Quarter Guards are more for preserving the Peace and Tranquillity within the Regiment..than for a Security against the Enemy. 1844 *Regul. & Ord. Army* 32 On these occasions, the Tents of the Quarter Guards are to be struck. 1892 R. KIPLING *Ball., East & West* 89 When they drew to the Quarter-Guard, full twenty swords flew clear.

Quarter-gunner. *Naut.* An officer subordinate to the gunner, whom he assists in all departments of his work (cf. quots. 1769, 1846).

1627 CAPT. SMITH *Seaman's Gram.* viii. 35 The Master Gunner hath charge of the ordnance..the rest of the Gunners, or quarter Gunners to receive their charge from him. 1702 *Royal Declar.* 1 June in *Lond. Gaz.* No. 3815/2 The Trumpeter, Quarter Gunners, Carpenters Crew [etc.]. 1769 FALCONER *Dict. Marine* (1780) s. v., The number of quarter-gunners in any ship is always in proportion to the number of her artillery, one quarter-gunner being allowed to every four cannon. 1804 *Med. Jrnl.* XII. 476 One of his Majesty's frigates, on board of which her husband served in the quality of a quarter-gunner. 1846 A. YOUNG *Naut. Dict.* 242 *Quarter-Gunner*, in a ship of war, an able seaman, generally one of the gunner's crew, appointed to act as his assistant under the gunner's mates.

Quarter-ill. An inflammatory disease of cattle and sheep (*symptomatic anthrax*), causing putrefaction in one or more of the quarters. Called also *quarter-evil, black quarter*, etc.

1797 BAILEY & CULLEY *View Agric. Northumb.* 130 The loss of lambs is sometimes very considerable..from..the 'quarter-ill'. 1834 YOUATT *Cattle* 362 The first symptoms are those of quarter ill. 1855 STEPHENS *Book Farm* (ed. 2) II. 185 Another effect of the same febrile affection in calves in autumn is the quarter ill or evil. 1881 GREGOR *Folk-lore* 186 When the quarter-ill made its appearance [etc.].

Quartering (kwǭ·ɹtəriŋ), *vbl. sb.* [f. QUARTER *v.* + -ING ¹.] The action of the verb.

1. Division into four equal parts; also, division in general.

1610 W. FOLKINGHAM *Art of Survey* I. ix. 23 The quartering of the sweard of Ant-hils, casting their ballas't, and playning their Plots for pasture. 1694 *Phil. Trans.* XVIII. 70 The halving, trisecting, quartering, &c. is performed by extracting the Square Root,..&c. of the Terms. 1727–41 [see QUARTERIZATION]. 1895 *Pall Mall Gaz.* 18 Jan. 10/3 Even in 'quartering'—the term for breaking up the great nodules of flint—it is not muscle, but eye, that tells.

2. *Her.* The dividing of a shield into quarters; the marshalling or bringing in of various coats upon one shield, to denote the alliances of one family with the heiresses of others.

1592 WYRLEY *Armorie* 4 An other thing that is amisse..is the quartering of many marks in one shield, coate, or banner. 1595 *Blanchardyn* ii. (1890) 15 Then questioned he with his Master, of the blazonry of armes, and ye quartering of these coates. 1605 CAMDEN *Rem.* (1636) 225 Quartering of Coates, beganne, first..in Spaine in the Armes of Castile and Leon. 1727–41 CHAMBERS *Cycl.* s.v., Quartering, in heraldry, the act of dividing a coat into four or more quarters..by parting, couping, &c. *Ibid.*, Colombiere reckons twelve sorts of quarterings. 1893 CUSSANS *Her.* (ed. 3) 166 Quartering..was not generally adopted until the end of the Fourteenth Century. The manner in which various coats are brought in, and marshalled by Quartering [etc.].

b. *pl.* The various coats marshalled upon a shield; rarely *sing.*, one of these coats.

1719 ASHMOLE *Berkshire* II. 214 A Surcoat..of the Quarterings impaled with Fetiplace. 1763 C. JOHNSTON *Reverie* II. 55, I have nine quarterings more than he. 1826 DISRAELI *Viv. Grey* VI. iv, He did nothing but.. think of the quarterings of his immaculate shield. 1879 GEO. ELIOT *Theo. Such* ii. 41 Some of them..belong to families with many quarterings.

transf. 1833 MARRYAT *P. Simple* (1863) 229 The pride of colour is very great in the West Indies, and they have as many quarterings as a German prince in his coat of arms.

3. The assigning of quarters to a person; the action of taking up quarters; † a place in which one is or may be quartered.

1605 BP. MOUNTAGU *App. Cæsar* xviii. 235 Heaven..is not ..so narrowed..that there cannot bee divers Designations, Regions, Habitations, Mansions, or Quarterings there. 1767 H. WALPOLE *Lett.* (1846) II. 177 A motion for inquiring into useless places and quarterings.

b. *spec.* The billeting of soldiers; the fact of having soldiers quartered upon one; the provision of quarters for soldiers.

1646 SIR E. NICHOLAS in *N. Papers* (Camden) 68 Your Honours frends at Winterborne are well, but much oppressed with quarterings. 1667 *Ormonde MSS.* in *10th Rep. Hist. MSS. Comm.* App. v. 58 Your petitioner was heretofore charged with the quartering of two private souldiers. 1705 *Lond. Gaz.* No. 4098/2 The Inhabitants..much impoverished by the Quartering of Soldiers. 1867 SMILES *Huguenots Eng.* xii. (1880) 225 In anticipation of the quartering of the dragoons on the family, his wife had gone into concealment.

4. *Build.* **a.** The placing or using of quarters in construction. **b.** Work formed of quarters. **c.** Wood in the form, or of the size, of quarters.

1703 T. N. *City & C. Purchaser* 232 Quartering..signifies the putting in of Quarters. Sometimes 'tis us'd to signifie the Quarters themselves. 1825 J. NICHOLSON *Operat. Mechanic* 580 The braces should be rated..at a superior price to that of the quarterings. 1854 *Jrnl. R. Agric. Soc.* XV. 255 Farms..built of quartering and weather boarding.

5. Driving on the quarters of a road.

1815 SCOTT *Paul's Lett.* (1839) 207 The French postilions ..contrived, by dint of quartering and tugging, to drag us safe through. 1825 C. M. WESTMACOTT *Eng. Spy* I. 313 No ruts or quarterings now.

6. The moon's passage from one quarter to another; also = QUARTER 8 b.

1854 L. TOMLINSON tr. *Arago's Astron.* 67 Changes of weather are not more frequent at the moon's quarterings than at any other period. 1880 L. WALLACE *Ben-Hur* 234 Before the new moon..passes into its next quartering.

7. *attrib.* and *Comb.*, as *quartering-block, -knife*; **quartering-belt**, a belt connecting pulleys which have their axles at right angles to each other (Knight *Dict. Mech.* 1875); **quartering-hammer**, a steel-hammer with which the rough masses of flint are shaped for flaking (*ibid.*); **quartering-machine**, a machine for boring the wrist-pin holes in driving-wheels a quarter of a circle apart (*ibid.*); †**quartering-money**, money paid in lieu of giving quarters to soldiers.

1688 in Wodrow *Hist. Ch. Scot.* (1721) I. 283 Exacting Cess or Quartering-money for more Soldiers than were actually present. 1818 COBBETT *Pol. Reg.* XXXIII. 425 Why do they..resort to gags, dungeons, halters, axes, and quartering-knives? 1855 MACAULAY *Hist. Eng.* xii. III. 218 Those who were doomed to the gallows and the quartering block.

Quartering (kwǭ·ɹtəriŋ), *ppl. a.* [f. QUARTER *v.* + -ING ².] That quarters, in senses of the vb.

1591 SHAKS. *1 Hen. VI*, IV. ii. 11 You tempt the fury of my three attendants, Leane Famine, quartering Steele, and climbing Fire. 1692 *Capt. Smith's Seaman's Gram.* I. xvi. 76 *The Ship goes Lasking, Quartering, Veering, or Large*; are terms of the same signification, viz. that she neither goes by a Wind nor before the Wind, but betwixt both. 1708–11 *Milit. & Sea Dict.* (ed. 4) II, *Quartering*, is when a Gun lies so, and may be so travers'd, that it will shoot on the same Line, or Point of the Compass as the Quarter bears. 1765 *Museum Rusticum* IV. 341 The track was just of a proper breadth for post-chaises and all quartering carriages to run in. 1769 FALCONER *Dict. Marine* (1789), *Vent Largue*, a large, or quartering wind. 1860 MAURY *Phys. Geog. Sea* (Low) xx. § 815 Through the former [ocean] the wind is aft; through the latter quartering. 1893 *Times* 13 June 12/1 Sheets trimmed for a quartering breeze.

†**Quarteriza·tion.** *Obs. rare*—°. (See quot.)

1727–41 CHAMBERS *Cycl.*, *Quarterization*, *Quartering*, part of the punishment of a traitor, by dividing his body into four quarters.

Quarter-jack.

1. [JACK *sb.*¹ 6.] A jack of the clock which strikes the quarters.

1604 MIDDLETON *Father Hubburd's T.* Wks. (Bullen) VIII. 54 The quarter-jacks in Paul's, that are up with their elbows four times an hour. 1771 [see JACK *sb.*¹ 6]. 1874 T. HARDY *Far fr. Mad. Crowd* I. xvi. 190 A little canopy with a quarter-jack and small bell beneath it.

2. [JACK *sb.*⁷] A jack-boot cut down.

1809 A. *Sir Frantic the Reformer* 75 His first born Long with these boots did's shanks adorn, Until..He made them into quarter-jacks.

Qua·rterland. A certain division of land in the Isle of Man, originally the fourth part of a *treen* or *balla*; also the class of lands included in such divisions.

Called 'Quarter of Land' in 1593 (*Statutes* 76); see also *quarter-ground* s.v. QUARTER *sb.* 30.

1645 *Statutes Isle Man* (1821) 107 Lands and Tenements in the said Island called Farme Lands or Quarter Lands. 1798 J. FELTHAM *Tour Isl. Mann* iv. 46 Divisions of land prevail here, termed Quarterlands. It is uncertain how they obtained the name. 1845 TRAIN *Isle Man* I. 31 For each four quarterlands he made a chapel. 1865 *Notes & Queries* Ser. 3 VIII. 310/2 Treens..usually contain from three to four quarterlands. *Ibid.*, Quarterlands, which are estates of inheritance, vary in size, and contain from 120 to 140 acres. 1890 A. W. MOORE *Surnames Isle Man* 211 The lowlands about the church are still intack, not quarterland. 1900 — *Hist. Isle Man* II. vii. 873.

Quarter-line. *Naut.*

1. The position of ships in a column when each successive vessel has its bows abaft the beam of the one in front, and a little to one side.

1875 BEDFORD *Sailor's Pocket Bk.* I. (ed. 2) 22 A Column is said to be in Quarter Line when the ships are ranged in one line abaft each others' beam, but not right astern.

2. a. A line from a vessel's quarter.

1888 R. C. LESLIE *Sea-painter's Log* vii. 146 The quarter-line is cast overboard.

b. An additional line fastened to the underside of a seine to assist in drawing it in (*Cent. Dict.*).

Quarterly (kwǭ·ɹtəɹli), *a.* and *sb.* Also 6 -lie. [f. QUARTER *sb.* + -LY ¹.] **A.** *adj.*

1. That takes place, is done, etc., every quarter of a year; relating to, or covering, a quarter of a year. † *Quarterly waiter* = QUARTER-WAITER.

1563 in *Maitl. Club Misc.* (1833) 32 Takand ilk quarter 22*s* 6*d*. As the capitane of the said Gardis quarterlie acquittances proporttis. 1688 MIEGE s. v., The quarterly Seasons of Devotion, called the Ember-weeks. 1727 BOYER *Fr.-Angl. Dict.* s. v. *Quartier*, *Officier de Quartier*, a quarterly Waiter. 1750 WESLEY *Wks.* (1872) II. 205 We had a Quarterly Meeting. 1802 MISS EDGEWORTH *Moral T.* (1816) I. xix. 158 Quarterly and half-yearly payments. 1862 SALA *Ship-chandler* 37 Mine is a quarterly hiring, and my quarter is out to-morrow. 1885 *Law Times* LXXIX. 191/1 The necessity of having a quarterly gaol delivery.

transf. 1694 W. HOLDER *On Time* i. 22 The Moon..makes also four Quarterly Seasons within her little Year.

2. Pertaining or relating to a quarter (in other senses). † *Quarterly book*: (see quot. 1776). *Quarterly wind*, a wind on the quarter.

1769 FALCONER *Dict. Marine* (1789), *Vent de quartier*, a quarterly, or quartering wind. 1776 JOHNSON *Let. to Wetherell* 12 Mar. in *Boswell* II. 14 We must..superadd what is called the quarterly-book, or for every hundred books so charged we must deliver an hundred and four. 1889 *Standard* 16 Mar. 3/8 The wind..was..quarterly.

B. *sb.* A quarterly review, magazine, etc.

1855 in OGILVIE *Suppl.* 1871 BESANT & RICE *Ready-money Mort.* iv, He had written papers for what were vaguely called the Quarterlies. 1882 MISS BRADDON *Mt. Royal* III. i. 10 'Oh, there are the new Quarterlies', seeing a package on the table.

Quarterly (kwǭ·ɹtəɹli), *adv.* (*a.*, *sb.*) [-LY ².]

1. Every quarter of a year; once in a quarter.

1458 in Sharp *Cov. Myst.* (1825) 208 To go with þe wayts to gader their wages quarterly. 1509 *Act 21 Hen. VIII* c. 13 § 28 Chaplains..daily or quarterly attending. 1581 MULCASTER *Positions* xli. (1887) 234 That there were no admission into schooles, but foure times in the yeare quarterly. *a* 1633 AUSTIN *Medit.* (1635) 234 They be Times that Quarterly bring us in Revenew for our temporall profit. 1712 ADDISON *Spect.* No. 295 ¶ 1 She should have 400*l.* a Year for Pin-money, which I obliged my self to pay Quarterly. 1878 JEVONS *Prim. Pol. Econ.* 53 Managers, officers, secretaries, and others, are paid quarterly, or sometimes half-yearly.

2. *Her.* In the four divisions of a shield formed by a vertical and a horizontal line drawn through the fess point; usu. with reference to two tinctures, charges, or coats of arms, placed in the diagonally opposite quarters.

c 1450 HOLLAND *Howlat* 391 He bare quarterly..the armes of the Dowglass. 1525 LD. BERNERS *Froiss.* II. clxviii. 191 He bare syluer and sables quarterly. 1592 WYRLEY *Armorie* 91 Sir Neal Loring, who fairly Arms put on Quarterly white and red. 1684 *Lond. Gaz.* No. 1952/4 The Arms of the said Count, being in an Eschutcheon Four Coats quarterly. 1765 H. WALPOLE *Otranto* iii. (1798) 51 A banner with the arms of Vicenza and Otranto quarterly. 1824 SCOTT *St. Ronan's* xviii, A white lion for Mowbray, to be borne quarterly, with three stunted or scrog-bushes for Scrogie. 1893 CUSSANS *Her.* (ed. 3) 163 Their daughter..is entitled to bear both her Father's and her Mother's Arms quarterly.

b. With ref. to the division of the shield into quarters, or to blazoning it by quarters. *Quarterly-quartered*, having one or more quarters divided in four; so *quarterly-quartering*.

1610 GUILLIM *Heraldry* v. i. (1611) 238 If they be charged, then I hold it best blazoned quarterly. 1705 HEARNE *Collect.* 21 Dec. (O. H. S.) I. 136 His Arms, quarterly parted per Cross. 1709 STRYPE *Ann. Ref.* Introd. i. 8 This [shield] impaled quarterly, 1. The arms of Scotland. 2. The arms of England. The third as the second. The fourth as the first. 1864 BOUTELL *Her. Hist. & Pop.* iii. (ed. 3) 16 The Grand Quarters of which the first and the fourth..are Quarterly-quartered. *Ibid.* xiv. 142 The Marshalling now proceeds by Quarterly Quartering.

c. *ellipt.* as *adj.* = divided quarterly, or (by extension) into any number of parts by lines at right angles to each other, as *quarterly of eight*; also as *sb.* = a shield divided or charged quarterly.

1869 W. S. ELLIS *Antiq. Her.* x. 228 Aubrey de Vere.. transmitted his..coat of Quarterly to his descendants.

d. *Quarterly-pierced*: (see quots.).

1780 EDMONDSON *Body Her.*, *Gloss.* II, Quarterly Pierced, is used to express a square hole in a saltire, a cross milkrine, &c. through which aperture the field is seen. 1893 CUSSANS *Her.* (ed. 3) 63 If..that part where the limbs [of the cross] are conjoined be removed, it is termed Quarterly-pierced.

†**3. a.** Into four parts. **b.** At four equidistant points on a circle. **c.** Through each quarter of a town. *Obs. rare.*

a. 1576 GASCOIGNE *Philomene* (Arb.) 107 They tore in peces quarterly The corps. **b.** 1605 CAMDEN *Rem.* (1637) 167 A Wing with these foure Letters, F. E. L. D. quarterly about it. **c.** *a* 1690 SPALDING *Troub.* (1828) I. 199 The baillies went quarterly about, to cause ilk inhabitant subscrive.

Quarterman.

†**1.** ? One of the quarter-guard. *Obs. rare*—¹.

1599 in *Harington's Nugæ Antiquæ* (ed. Park 1804) I. 274 The deathes of our captaines were revenged by our quartermen and scoutsmen, who..slewe 7 of the rebells, whiche awaited to force the quarter.

2. A foreman-shipwright.

1793 SMEATON *Edystone L.* § 62 That species of foreman shipwright, called a Quarter-man in Plymouth dock. 1803 R. PERING in *Naval Chron.* XV. 135 The quartermen..give an account of the work performed to the job office. *Ibid.* 137 Quartermen of shipwrights and caulkers..have apprentices. 1862 SMILES *Engineers* II. 30 [He] was then a foreman of shipwrights, called a quarterman, in Plymouth Dock.

Quartermaster (kwǭ·ɹtəɹmɑːstəɹ). [In sense 1 app. from QUARTER *sb.*¹ 16; sense 2 (from QUARTER *sb.* 13) is app. the original meaning of F. *quartier-maître*, Du. *kwartier-meester*, G. *quartier-meister*, etc., and may have been adopted from one or other of these languages.]

1. *Naut.* A petty officer who attends to the steering of the ship, the binnacle, signals, stowing of the hold, etc.

1442 *Rolls Parlt.* V. 60/1 The Maisters of the Shippes, Quarter Maisters, Shipmen and Soudeours. 1509 BARCLAY *Shyp of Folys* (1570) 77 iij, Purser and Captayne, Quarter master, Lodesman. 1549 *Compl. Scot.* vi. 41 Euery quartar master til his auen quartar. 1626 CAPT. SMITH *Accid. Yng. Seamen* 5 The *quarter Maisters* hath the charge of the hold for stowage, rommageing, and trimming the shippe; and of their squadrons for their watch. 1643 *Declar. Commons, Reb. Irel.* 50 He is one of the Quarter-masters of the Dunkirke Frigot. 1708 *Royal Proclam.* 20 May in *Lond. Gaz.* No. 4440/1 The Midshipmen,..Quarter-Master, Quarter-Masters Mates,..and Serjeants of Marines. 1836 MARRYAT *Midsh. Easy* xxvi, Up with the helm, quarter-master.

b. *transf.* Steering-gear.

1882 *Standard* 26 Dec. 2/1 She will have a brigantine rig, ..and [be] steered by a steam 'quartermaster'. 1899 F. T. BULLEN *Way Navy* 37 Like everything else in this giant vessel, the steam quartermaster is on an immense scale.

2. *Mil.* An officer, ranking as lieutenant, attached to each regiment, with the duties of providing quarters for the soldiers, laying out the camp, and looking after the rations, ammunition and other supplies of the regiment.

1600 DYMMOK *Ireland* (1843) 33 The small losse we susteyned..was multiplied upon the rebell by our quarter and skoutmasters. *a* 1653 GOUGE *Comm. Heb.* vi. 18 A quartermaster, who goeth before hand to prepare quarters for souldiers. 1721 DE FOE *Mem. Cavalier* (1840) 97 The king ..made him a quarter-master to a troop of Cuirassiers. 1803 WELLINGTON *Let. to Col. Stevenson* 16 Sept. in Gurw. *Desp.* (1837) II. 308, I rather believe that your Quarter Masters have 1000 bullocks for each regiment. 1893 FORBES-MITCHELL *Remin. Gt. Mutiny* 150 Our quartermaster divided among us a lot of shirts and underclothing.

b. Quartermaster-general, a staff-officer who is chief of the department exercising control over all matters relating to the quartering, encamping, marching and equipment of troops.

1701 *Lond. Gaz.* No. 3732/1 The said Quartermaster-General and Adjutant-General Baron Riedt were sent out to view the Ground. 1813 WELLINGTON *Let. to Sir G. Collier* 19 Aug. in Gurw. *Desp.* (1838) XI. 15, I enclose a letter to the Quarter Master General directing that the Infantry now in the horse ships at Bilbao may be removed. 1876 BANCROFT *Hist. U. S.* V. xliv. 35 Mifflin, who in August had been appointed quartermaster-general.

c. Quartermaster-sergeant, a non-commissioned officer, ranking as a staff-sergeant, who assists the quartermaster in his duties.

1869 E. A. PARKES *Pract. Hygiene* (ed. 3) 300 The Serjeant-major and Quarter-master-serjeant are entitled to two rooms and a kitchen.

†**3.** One who shares authority with another to the extent of a fourth. *Obs.*

Prob. *transf.* from sense 2, with pun on *quarter* = one fourth; cf. QUARTER *sb.* 27 d.

1550 LATIMER *Last Serm. bef. Edw. VI* 111 They do it, because they will be quarter maister with their husbandes: Quarter maister? nay halfe maisters: yea some of them will be whole maisters. 1607 COLLINS *Def. Bp. Ely* I. i. 7 Discerne you no better betweene Popes and Councels, which are the Church in effect? or shall these play quarter-masters with the Pope? 1685 R. BURTON *Eng. Emp. Amer.* ii. 28 The English Nation..might have made themselves Quarter-Masters, at least with the Spaniards.

†**4.** A gild-official, having charge of the gildsmen in a quarter of the town. *Obs.*

1646 in G. Tate *Alnwick* II. xvii. 338 It is agreed that none of the wood shall be sould but with the consent of the four quartermaisters. [1868–9 G. TATE *Alnwick* II. xvii. 338 Wood and bark were therefore bought for the whole company, by officers called quartermasters, who allotted to each tanner a proportional share of every purchase.]

Hence **Qua·rtermaster** *v.*, to perform the duties of a quartermaster (hence *quartermastering* vbl. sb.); **Quartermasteriveness**, the qualities of a quartermaster (*nonce-wd.*); **Quartermastership**, the office of quartermaster (so also *Quartermaster-generalship*).

1745 *Observ. Conc. Navy* 44 Sales of Ensignships, Adjutancies, Quarter-Master-ships, &c. 1824 MCCULLOCH *Scotland* I. 370 His organ of quarter-masteriveness must have been woefully in arrear. 1880 *Times* 8 Jan. 8/6 Questions of massing, manœuvring, or quartermastering. 1890 *Daily News* 3 Nov., The quartermastership..of the district around Metz. 1876 BANCROFT *Hist. U. S.* VI. Index 553 [Greene] resigns [the] quartermaster-generalship abruptly.

†**Quartern**, *sb.*¹ *Obs.* Forms: 1 cweartern, -en, cwart-, cwiartern, 1–2 cwart-, quartern, 3 cwarrt-, quarterne, cwart-, quarterne. [Of obscure origin, poss. an alteration of OE. *carcern*, *carcern*, ad. L. *carcer*.] A prison.

c 995 *Rushw. Gosp.* Matt. xxv. 39 Hwonne we þe segun untrymne ððe in quartern? *c* 1000 ÆLFRIC *Exod.* xl. 3 Þa dyde hiz man on cweartern..and þus cweartternes hirde betæhte hiz Iosepe. *c* 1154 *O. E. Chron.* an. 1137 Hi dyden heom in quarterne. *c* 1200 ORMIN 6168 Himm þatt i cwarrterne lip Forrbundenn. *Ibid.* 18187 Inntill quarrterne worrpenn. *c* 1205 [see QUALE¹ b]. *a* 1225 *Leg. Kath.* 670 Al þe cwarterne þet his come leitede a leie.

Quartern (kwǭ·ɹtəɹn), *sb.*² Forms: 3–7 quartron, (4 -run, -roun, -eroun, quaterone, 6 -eren), 5–7 quarteron, (5 -eron, -rone), 6–7 quarterne, (7 soterne), 7–9 *Ir.* cartron, 9 quar-

Quarteron, -oon, variants of QUADROON.

Quarter-piece.

Quarter-sessions.

Quarterstaff. 1. A stout pole, from six to eight feet long and tipped with iron, formerly used as a weapon by the English peasantry.

2. Righting or earnest with the quarterstaff.

Quarter-tense, corrupt f. QUATER-TEMPS (q.v.).

† Quarterth, a. Obs. [QUARTER sb. + -TH.] Fourth (part).

Quarter-waiter. In To Rd., His receipts amounted not to the half nor quarterth part of a common Apothecaries Bill.

Quarter-winder. Belonging to the lower class of Gentlemen-Ushers, who remained in waiting for a quarter of a year.

Quarter-wind. a. A wind blowing on a vessel's quarter. b. A wind from one of the cardinal points.

† Quartessence. Obs. rare⁻¹. [f. L. quarta + ESSENCE.] An essence one degree less pure than a quintessence.

Quarter, quartette (kwǫ̆·tet). Also 9 -tett. [f. F. quartette, ad. It. quartetto: see -ETT.]

† Quartetto. (kwartĕ·to.) ? Obs. [It. a. It. quartetto, a quartet of.]

Quarto (kwōrtō). Also written 4to, 4°. [L. (in) quarto, (in the fourth (of a sheet), abl. sing. of quartus fourth.]

1. The size of paper obtained by folding a whole sheet twice, so as to form four leaves, in which a half the height is not markedly in excess of the breadth. Orig. and chiefly in pl., in quarto.

2. A book composed of paper of this size; a quarto-volume.

Quarto-deciman (kwōrto·desimăn), sb. (a. quarto-boil (see quot. 1869), ...

Quartodecimal, a. = prec.

Quartodecimanism, the views or practice of the Quartodecimans.

Quartzodecimarian = prec.

Quart-major : see QUART sb. 2.

Quart-pot, a vessel for containing the measure of a quart.

Quartz (kwǫrts). Min. [a. G. quarz (first in MHG.) of uncertain origin: hence also Du. kwarts, F. quartz, It. quarzo.]

A widely diffused mineral, massive or crystallizing in hexagonal prisms; in a pure form consisting of silica or silicon dioxide (SiO_2), but varying greatly in colour, lustre, etc., according to the different impurities it contains.

Quartze, obs. f. of QUARTER sb.

Quartzi-, in comb. f. QUARTZ.

Quartzite (kwǫ·rtsəit). Min. Also 7 -site. A compact, granular rock, consisting essentially of quartz.

Quartzoid (kwǫrtsoid). A crystal having the form of a double six-sided pyramid.

Quartzose (kwǫrtsōs), a. [f. as prec. + -OSE.] Mainly or entirely composed of quartz; of the nature of quartz.

Quartzous (kwǫrtsŏs), a. Quartzose.

Quartzy (kwǫ·rtsi), a. [f. as prec. + -Y¹.] Of the nature of quartz; resembling quartz.

Quarvel, ?error for quarred: see QUAR sb.²

Quary, Quas, Quash variants.

Quash (kwǫʃ), v. Forms: 4-5 quasse, (5 qwas-), 4 quasch, 5 qv-, quaunch, quaysh, quaysch-, 6-quash. [In branch I, ad. OF. quasser = assail, f. L. (see below). In branch II, ad. L. quassāre, casse, quassi, frequentative of quatere, casser to break, smash, etc.]

I. 1. trans. To annul, to make null or void (a law, decision, election, etc.); to throw out or reject (a writ, indictment, etc.); to put an end to, stop completely (legal proceedings).

II. 2. trans. To crush, dash in pieces.

QUASHEE. 35 QUATENUS. QUATER-CENTENARY. 36 QUATRE.

Quashee (kwǫ·ʃi), quashie (kwǫ·ʃi). [Ashantee or Fantee Kwasi, a name commonly given to a child born on Sunday.] A negro personal name, adopted as a general name for any negro.

Quashey, rare⁻¹. [See quot. and cf. QUASH sb.¹]

Quasi (kwā·səi), adv. and pref. [L. quasi as, as it were, almost.]

Quasi-, combining form.

Quasquicentennial.

Quass, Quassia.

Quassation.

Quassia (kwǫ·ʃia). Also ff. QUASSIA.

Quassin, Quassine.

Quat.

Quatch.

Quaternary (kwatǫ·rnări, a. and sb. [ad. L. quaternārius, f. quaternī four together; fours.]

Quaternion (kwatǫ·niǫn). [ad. late L. quaterniō, -ōn-em, f. quaternī four together: cf. obs. F. quaternion (Godef.).]

Quaternity (kwatǫ·rniti). [ad. late L. quaternitās, f. quaternī.]

Quatorzain (kat·ǫrzein). Also 6 quatorzaine. [a. F. quatorzain.]

Quatorze (katǫ·rz). [F. quatorze fourteen.]

Quatre (kā·tǝr). Also quater. [F. quatre four.]

Supplement, p. 3873; Corrigenda, p. 4092; Spurious words, p. 4093; Books quoted, p. 4094.

2387

QUEBRACHO. 39 QUEEN. QUEEN. 40 QUEEN.

Queen (kwīn), n. [Forms and history as above.]

1. To be a queen; to act or rule as queen; to have pre-eminence like a queen.

2. To rule over a people.

3. To rule over as a queen.

Chess. To advance (a pawn) to the opponent's end of the board, where it acquires the power of, and is replaced by, a queen or such other piece as the player may choose.

Queen Anne. The Queen of Great Britain and Ireland who reigned from 1702 to 1714.

Queening (kwī·niŋ). A variety of apple.

Queen-mother. [See QUEEN *sb.* 2 c.]

1. The country ruled over by a queen.

Queen'ite. [f. QUEEN *sb.* + -ITE.]

Queen'ite. [f. QUEEN *sb.* + -ITE.]

Queening. [See QUEENING.]

Queenless (kwī·nlės), *a.* [-LESS.]

Queenlike (kwī·nlaik), *a.* [-LIKE.] Like a queen.

Queenliness (kwī·nlinės). The condition or quality of being queenly.

Queenly (kwī·nlĭ), *a.* [f. QUEEN *sb.* + -LY1.]

Queen-mother (kwī·nmŏðə).

QUEER (kwīə), *a.* [Of obscure origin.]

1. Strange, odd, peculiar, eccentric.

2. Bad; worthless.

3. Out of sorts; giddy, faint, ill.

Queer, *a.*[2] Thieves' cant. Forms: 6 quyer, queer, etc.

Queer (kwīə), *v. slang.* [f. QUEER *a.*[1] or *a.*[2]]

1. To quiz or ridicule; to puzzle.

Queening (kwī·niŋ).

Queer (kwīə), *v.* Forms: 6 queir, quey, que(e)re, 7 quere.

Queering, *vbl. sb.*

Queerish (kwī·rĭʃ), *a.* Also 9 quear-.

Queerity.

Queerly (kwīə·lĭ), *adv.* [f. QUEER *a.*[1] + -LY[2].]

Queerness (kwīə·nės).

Quelling (kwe·liŋ), *vbl. sb.* [f. QUELL.]

Quelling (kwe·liŋ), *ppl. a.*

†Que'llio. [ad. Sp. *cuello* neck, collar.] A Spanish ruff. Also *attrib.*

†Quelm, *v.* [OE. *cwelman*, *cwilman* = OS. *quelmian* = OHG. *quelman* (MHG. *quelmen*).]

Quelme, *obs. var. of* WHELM.

Quelp, *obs. f.* WHELP. **Quelque-chose:** see KICKSHAW.

†Queme, *sb.* Obs. Also 2-3 weme, 3 wheme.

Queme (kwīm), *a. etc. north. dial.* Forms: α. 3 weme, 5 queme, 4-5 quem, 5 qweme, 7-8 Sc. quim, 7-8 weem, 9 weam.

Queme (kwīm), *v.* Obs. exc. *arch.*

QUENCH (kwenʃ), *v.* Forms: 3 *Orm.* cwennkenn, 3-5 quenche, 3-6 quenchen, 4- quench.

I. *trans.* **1.** To put out, extinguish (fire, flame, or light, *lit.* or *fig.*). **b.** Also *with out.* Now *rhet.*

II. **7.** *intr.* (for *reflexive*). **†8.** Of fire, a burning thing, etc.: To be extinguished; to go out, to cease to burn.

Quenchable (kwe·nʃăb'l), *a.* [f. prec. + -ABLE.]

Quenched (kwenʃt) *ppl. a.*, extinguished.

†Quenchless, *a.*

Quench-coal. [f. QUENCH + COAL.]

Quencher (kwe·nʃə).

Quenching (kwe·nʃiŋ), *vbl. sb.* [f. QUENCH *v.* + -ING[1].]

QUERCITRON

Quercetin (kwǝ·rsĭtin), *sb.* Chem.

Quercine (kwǝ·rsein), *a.* [ad. L. *quercinus*.]

Quercite (kwǝ·rsəit), *sb.* Chem.

Quercitannic, *a.* Chem.

Quercitrin (kwǝ·rsĭtrin). Chem.

Quercitron (kwǝ·rsĭtrən), *sb.* Chem. [Abbreviated f. *quercicitron.*]

QUERCIVOROUS. (top of column)

Queror'trie a., derived from *quercitrin*, as in *quercitric acid* (Watts *Dict. Chem.* 1868). Quercitrin, the yellow crystalline colouring matter of quercitron bark.

Quer'cin-us. [f. L. *quercus* oak + *-ous* *browning*.] Feeding on oak-leaves.

Quercle, obs. form of QUIRE.

+Quercaline, a. *Obs. rare—*. [ad. mod.L. *quercalin-us*, f. *quercus* oak.] —QUERCINE *a*.

Querdling: see CODLING²

+Quere, v. *Obs.* Also 4 *squire*. [a. OF. *quer-re* (in conj. *quier-*, *quer-*) f. L. *quærere*: see INQUIRE.] To ask, inquire.

Querier (kwi·ri·ər). [f. QUERY *v.* + -ER¹.] One who queries; also *slang*, a chimney-sweep who asks for work.

+Querimon, *Obs. rare—*. [ad. late L. *querimon-ia*], also 7 *quere-* and *-ous*. [f. as QUERIMONY + -OUS.] Full of, addicted to, complaining.

+Querimonious, *a.* [f. L. *querimonia* complaint + -OUS.] Complaining.

Querimony (kwi·riməni). [ad. L. *querimonia*, f. *queri* to complain: cf. F. *querimonie* (16th c.).] Complaint, complaining.

+Querist (kwiə·rist). [f. L. *quær-* to ask + -IST; cf. QUERENT, QUERY.] One who asks or inquires; a questioner, interrogator.

Querister, variant of CHORISTER.

Querk, **Querken**, variants of QUIRK.

Querl, variant of CURL *sb.* and *v.*

Quern (kwə̄ɹn). Forms: 1 *cweorn*, *cwyrn*, *cwyrn*, 3-7 *quern*, etc. [OE. *cweorn*, *cwyrn*, *cwyrne* fem.]

+Queror, obs. form of CONQUEROR.

Querpo, obs. form of CUERPO. *Obs.*

Querstfull, *a.* —FUL.

+Quesal. variant of QUETZAL.

Quest (kwest), *sb.¹* Also 7 *quer*-. [ad. L. *quærent-em*, prps. pple. of *quærere* to seek + -ER¹.]

QUEST. (bottom of page)

+Quest, *sb.²* *Obs.* [Related to QUETHE *v.*, as *bequest* (q.v.) to *bequeath*.] A bequest.

Quest (kwest), *v.* [f. OF. *quester* (*quêter*), f. *queste* QUEST *sb.¹*]

+Quest-house. *Obs.* The house at which the inquests in a ward or parish were commonly held.

Questing (kwe·stiŋ), *vbl. sb.* [f. QUEST *v.* + -ING¹.] The action of the vb. in various senses.

Questing (kwe·stiŋ), *ppl. a.* [f. as prec. + -ING².] That quests, in senses of the vb.

Question (kwe·stʃən), *sb.* Also 4 *questiun*, 4-6 *-oun*, *questyon*, 4-7 *-ioun*, *-ion*, etc. [a. AF. *questiun*, OF. *question* (11th c.), ad. L. *quæstion-em*, n. of action from *quærere* to seek: cf. QUEST, QUERY.]

Question (kwe·stʃən), *v.* [ad. F. *questionner* (13th c.), f. *question* QUESTION *sb.*]

Questionability. = QUESTIONABLENESS.

Questionable (kwe·stʃənəb'l), *a.* [f. QUESTION *v.* + -ABLE.]

Questionableness. [f. prec. + -NESS.] The state of being questionable; doubtfulness, etc.

Questionably, *adv.* [f. as prec. + -LY².] In a questionable manner.

+Questional, *a.* [f. QUESTION *sb.* + -AL.] Relating to questions.

Questionary, *sb.* [ad. med.L. *quæstionāri-us* = QUESTIONER.]

Questionary (kwe·stʃənəri), *a.* [ad. med.L. *quæstionāri-us*: see QUESTION *sb.* and -ARY¹.] Having the form of a question; consisting of questions; conducted by means of questioning.

Supplement, p. 3873; Corrigenda, p. 4092; Spurious words, p. 4093; Books quoted, p. 4094

Questionless (kwe·styŏnlės), a. and adv.

A. adj. Not admitting of question; unquestionable, indubitable.

B. adv. Without question, beyond all question; unquestionably; undoubtedly.

Hence **Que·stionlessly** adv. a. = QUESTIONLESS

B. Without asking questions.

Questman. [f. QUEST + MAN.]

1. A member of a 'quest'; one appointed to make official inquiry into any matter; *spec.* † **a.** a parish or ward official elected annually (see quot. 1706). *Obs.*

†**b.** An inquisitor. *Obs.*

2. = QUESTION 1. *Obs.*

†**Questmonger.** *Obs.* Also 6 -**manger, 7 -moonger.** [f. QUEST sb. + MONGER.] One who made a business of conducting inquests.

Questor (kwe·stŏr). Also 4-6 questour. [ad. L. quæstor, agent-n. f. quærĕre to ask, seek (cf. QUESTION).] hence also **L. quaestour, f. questour.**]

1. *R. C. Ch.* An official appointed by the Pope or by a bishop to grant indulgences on the gift of alms to the Church; a pardoner.

2. *Rom. Antiq.* (see QUÆSTOR).

Quetch, quitch, v. *Obs. exc. dial.* Forms: 1 cweccan, (cw-), 7 quech(e), 6 quetch, 4-6 qu(i)tch, quyche.

†**1.** *trans.* To shake; to brandish; to drive, chase.

†**b.** *intr. (and early ME.)*

2. *intr.* To shake; tremble. *Obs.*

†**3.** *intr.* To stir or move from one place to another; to go, run, hasten. *Obs.*

4. *intr.* Of persons (or animals): **a.** To move the body or any part of it; to stir; in later use *esp.* to writhe, twitch (with pain), not usually in negative clauses. *Obs. exc. dial.*

b. To assign by will; to bequeath.

†**7.** To bestow, deliver. *rare⁻¹.*

Quethe, var. QUED(E, bad. Quethen, -un, var. WHETHEN, whence. Quethen, -ur, obs. ff. WHETHER. Queton, obs. f. WHETSTONE.

Quetzal (ket·sal). Also quezal, quesal. Zo. [Sp. *quetzal,* shortened from Aztec *quetzalli* a tail-feather of the bird called *quetzaltotl* (f. the comb. form of *quetzalli* + *tototl* bird).] An exquisitely coloured bird (*Pharomacrus mocinno*) of Central America, belonging to the Trogon family; the cock is remarkable for its long tail-coverts, of a resplendent golden-green colour.

Queue (kiū). *sb.* [F. prec. sb.]

1. To put up (the hair) in a queue.

2. *intr.* To move (in, in a line of people.

Queued (kiūd), a. *Her.* Also 7 queved. *double-queued.*

2. *Her.* Furnished with a tail; in comb.

3. *Her.* Also 7 queve. [f. prec. sb. + -ING¹.]

Queying, obs. form of QUEYNING.

Quey (kwē). *Sc.* and *north. dial.* Forms: 4-5 qwy, 5-7 quye, 6 quy, 6-7 quey; 5 quoy, 8 quyhe.

Quibble (kwi·b'l), *sb.* [dim. of QUIB.]

†**1.** A play upon words, a pun. *Obs.*

†**b.** An instance of punning style.

2. A quirk; an evasion; a quibbling argument.

Quibble (kwi·b'l), *v.* [f. prec. sb.]

1. *intr.* To play upon words, to pun.

2. *intr.* To argue in a purely verbal way; to evade the real point by a quibble.

b. To quibble *away:* to trifle or deal unfairly *with,* by quibbling. *rare.*

Quibbler (kwi·blər). One who quibbles, in senses of the vb.

Quibbling (kwi·bliŋ), *vbl. sb.* [-ING¹.] The action of the verb QUIBBLE. Also *with a* and *pl.*

Quibbling (kwi·bliŋ), *ppl. a.* [-ING².] That quibbles; characterized by quibbles.

Hence **Qui·bblingly** adv.

Quibi (kwi·bī). *Obs. rare⁻¹.* [? A fanciful extension of QUIB.]

†**Quible.** *Obs. rare⁻¹.* Also 6-byble. [Of obscure origin.] A pun or quibble.

Quibble, -ler, obs. ff. QUIBBLE, -LER.

Quiblet (kwi·blet). *Obs. exc. U.S.* [f. QUIB or QUIBBLE + -ET².] = QUIBBLE sb. 2.

Quice. obs. form of QUEIST.

Quich, -e, obs. ff. QUICK. **a.** see also QUETCH v.

+Quico. *Obs. rare⁻¹.* [Of obscure origin.] Only in *quice-tree* = gorse, whin.

Quice, Quich, variants of QUEIST, QUETCH.

Quick (kwik), *a.,* *sb.¹,* and *adv.* Forms: *a.* 1 cwic(u), (cw-), 2-4 quic, (-u, cwike), -i 3 cwike, 3 cwike, 4 cuic, 4 quike, 4-5 quyke, 5 quyk, 3-6 quic, 6 quicke, quik(e, 6-7 quick; *β.* 3-5 quic(k)e, quyk(k)e (5 qu-), 5 quike, quyk, 5 quikke, quyk(k)e, 5 quyke, quikke; *γ.* 3-6 quyk, quick, 6-7 quicke, quike, 6-7 quyck, -e; *δ.* 3 north. 5 qwyk(k, quek, 4-7 quik(e, quyk(k.

A. *adj.*

I. Living, endowed with life, in contrast to what is naturally inanimate.

b. Of persons (or animals): **a.** living; not dead or inanimate. *Now dial. or arch.*

c. Of the flesh or parts of the body. *Obs.*

†**d.** Of fire: Burning, alight. *Obs.*

†**e.** Of water or other liquids: Running, flowing.

†**f.** Of plants or their parts: Living, growing; green, fresh, flourishing.

†**g.** Of quicksilver: Mobile, shifting, readily yielding to pressure. Now *rare.* Cf. QUICKSAND.

h. Composed of living plants, esp. hawthorn, as *quick fence, -hedge,* etc. Cf. *quickhaw(?),* mound.

2. Of persons and animals: **a.** With child, said of a female in the stage of pregnancy at which the motion of the fœtus is felt. *Now rare or Hist.*

b. As complement to subject of *intr.*

†**11. †a.** Of coals: Live, burning. *Obs.*

b. Of flame or flames: Burning strongly or briskly. Also of an oven: Exposed to a brisk fire. *Obs.*

†**12.** Of water, springs, etc.: Lively, full of vigour or acting vigorously; *spec.* sparkling. *Obs.*

†**13.** Of places or times: Full of activity or business; busy. Cf. brisk. *Obs.*

Aztec Emperor was reserved for imperial wear.

Queue-rock (also 6 quick, 7 quoy-, quynch, 9 queych roch, etc.) = QUEY.

Hence **Quey·rock** (also 6 quick, 7 quoy-, quynch, etc.)

Qui, obs. form of QUEY, WHY.

†**Quib,** sb. *Obs.* 5-6 -be, 7 -bbe. [App. ad. (orig. in *pl.*), L. *quibus,* dat. or abl. *pl.* of *qui* 'who, which', a word of frequent occurrence in legal documents and hence associated with 'quirks and quillets' of law.

b. a. 'The tail-piece of a violin or other instrument.' **b.** 'The tail of a note' (Stainer & Barrett *Dict. Mus. Terms* 1876).

15. Of wine and other liquors: Brisk, effervescent. *Obs.*

16. Of persons: Prompt, expeditious, active; acting with energy or despatch.

17. Of feelings: Lively, vivid, keen, strongly felt.

18. Of a taste or smell: Sharp, pungent, brisk. Also of things in respect of taste or smell. *(rare.)*

19. Of light: Sharp, piercing, vivid.

20. Of the eye, ear, etc.: Keen or rapid in its function; capable of ready or swift perception.

21. Mentally active or vigorous; of ready apprehension or wit; prompt to learn, think, invent, etc.

22. Of speech or writing: Lively, caustic. *Obs.*

23. Moving, or able to move, with speed. *b.* Of time: Lasting a short time. *c.* Of fire: Burning fiercely. Also *advb.*

III. Having in a high degree the vigour of energy characteristic of life; and hence distinguished by, or capable of, prompt or rapid action or movement.

24. Of movement or ascension: Rapid, swift.

27. Of a curve, turn, etc. : Sharp.

28. With constructions: **a.** with *to* and *infin.*

b. with *in.*

c. with *of.*

IV. 29. Combs. (chiefly parasynthetic adjs., as *quick-answered*, *-born*, *-chapt*, *-eared*, *-handed*, *-hearted*, *-nosed*, *-paced*, *-scented*, (*-sensedness*), *-sited*, *-spirited*, (*-sprighted*), *-tempered*, *-thoughted*, *-voiced*, *-winged*). Also **QUICK-EYED**, **-SIGHTED**, **-WITTED**.

I. a. *pl.* (Without article or *-s*.) Living persons. (Chiefly in echoes of Acts x. 42 or the Apostles' Creed, in phr. *quick and dead*.)

b. *Elliptical or absolute uses passing into sb.*

2. a. *The quick*: The tender or sensitive flesh in any part of the body, as that under the nails or beneath callous parts; also, the tender part of a sore or wound. Usu. in phr. *to the quick*. †Also *without article*.

b. *fig.* with ref. to persons, chiefly in phrases denoting acute mental pain or irritation, as *touched*, *galled*, *stung*, etc. *to the quick*.

c. *transf.* of things (esp. immaterial things): The central, vital, or most important part.

d. With *a* and *pl.*: A tender, sensitive, or vital part.

3. *Comb.* with present participles, as *quick-acting*, *-burning*, *-coming*, *-conceiving*, *decaying*, *-designing*, *-devouring*, *-fading* (see quot. f.), *-firing*, *-flowing*, *-glancing*, *-growing*, *-guiding*, *-labouring*, *-moving*, *-piercing*, *-relishing*, *-returning*, *-rolling*, *-running*, *-scenting*, *-seeing*, *-shifting*, *-sighting*, *-spouting*, *-stepping*, *-thriving* (chiefly *adj.*).

b. *fig.* with ref. to persons, chiefly in phrases denoting acute mental pain or irritation.

c. *transf.* of things.

4. *Comb.* with pples., as *quick-compounded*, *-drawn*, *-gone*, *-raised*, *-wrought* adjs.

D. Special combs. or phrases.

quick anatomy: an epithet of an actor or other performer who quickly changes costume or appearance.

†quick-firer, a quick-firing gun.

†quick-hatch, **quick-loader**, a device to enable a gun to be loaded quickly.

quick-match (see sense B.).

quick-mire (see D.).

quick saver, *Naut.*

quick-scab (in horses).

quick-set [G. *quick-wasser*].

quick-stick(e), quickly.

quick-water [G. *quick-wasser*].

Quick-grass: see QUITCH.

quick-in-the-hand (= *Noli-me-tangere*), a plant.

Quick-chaws, obs. variant of **Kickshaw**.

Quick (kwik), *sb.*

Quickbeam. *Obs. exc. dial.* The mountain-ash, or rowan-tree.

Quicken (kwi'k'n), *sb.* The mountain-ash.

Quicken (kwi'k'n), *v.*

I. Transitive senses.

1. To give or restore life to; to make alive; to vivify or revive; to animate.

b. *fig.*

Quick-chaws, obs. variant of KICKSHAW.

2. To give, add, or restore vigour to (a person or thing); to stimulate, stir up, rouse, excite, inspire.

3. To make faster, to accelerate.

b. a feeling, faculty, action, course of things, etc.

II. Intransitive senses.

4. To come to life.

5. To hasten, accelerate, grow speed.

6. To receive life, to become living.

Quickening, *vbl. sb.*

Quick-grass: see QUICK.

Quickener (kwi'k'nər), *sb.*

Quickened, *ppl. a.*

Quickening, *ppl. a.*

Quickening-grass.

Quicken-tree (see QUICKEN *sb.*)

Quick-eyed, *a.* Having a quick eye.

Quickhatch (kwi'khætʃ). Also *4-5* **quiquehatch**, *9* **quickhatch**. An adaptation of the Cree (Indian) name, given by Richardson as *okeecoohagew* or *-gew*, by Watkins (1865) as *kwekwaahoo*; from other Algonkian dialects come the forms CARCAJOU and KINKAJOU. The wolverine.

Quick-in-the-hand (= *Noli-me-tangere*).

Quickly (kwi'kli), *adv.* Forms: 1 **cwic-**, **cwyc-**, **cucian**, 3 **quikie**, 5 **quykke (?)**, 1 **quiken**, and presumably from QUICK *a.*, but the exact nature of the ending is not clear.

Quickly (kwi'kli), *adv.* Forms: 1 **cwiclice**, **cwyclice**, 3 **quikliche**, 5 **qwykliche**(?), etc. Cf. QUICK *a.*

1. In a living or lively manner; with animation or vigour; also, with strong feeling, sensitively. *Obs.*

b. With speed or rapidity; with rapid motion.

2. Rapidly, with haste or speed.

a. Describing the rate of progress in a motion, action, or process, without consideration of the time at which it begins and ends.

b. Denoting that a thing is little or no interval between a given point in time and the doing of an act or happening of an event.

c. Denoting that there is little or no interval between a given point in time and the doing of an act or happening of an event.

Quick march, *Mil.*

1. A march in QUICK TIME. Also *transf.*

2. Used as a command to soldiers to march in quick time (see quots. 1802 and 1833).

Quick-match. A quick-burning match used for firing cannon, igniting fire-works, shells, etc., consisting of cotton-wick soaked in a composition of gum, spirits, water, and gunpowder.

Quickness (kwi'knes), *sb.*

1. Life, vitality, vital principle. *Now rare.*

2. Without article: Loose yielding sand.

3. Animation, liveliness, briskness, vigour, freshness, etc. *Obs.*

4. Physical: esp. of the eyes or sight.

Quicken (kwi'k'n), *v.*

Quickening (kwi'k'niŋ), *vbl. sb.*

Quicken-tree.

Quick time, *Mil.*

Quick-witted, *a.*

b. Menial; of the mind, etc.

Quickness continued.

Quicksand (kwi'ksænd). ME. [f. QUICK *a.* 10.]

1. A bed of extremely loose wet sand, easily yielding to pressure and thus readily swallowing up any heavy object resting on it.

b. *fig.*

Quickset (kwi'kset), *sb.* Also **5-6** **quyk-sette**, etc.

1. Live slips or cuttings of plants, set in the ground to grow, esp. those of whitethorn or other shrub of which hedges are made.

2. A quickset hedge or hedges.

Quickset, *v. Obs.* [f. QUICKSET *sb.*]

Quickset, *ppl. a.*

Quicksilver (kwi'ksilvər), *sb.* [OE. *cwicseolfor*—OHG. *quecsilbar*, *-silabar* (mod. *Quecksilber*), etc.]

1. The metal mercury, so called from its liquid state and ready motion.

2. *fig.* and *attrib.*

Quicksilver, *v.* [f. prec. *sb.*]

Quickset: see QUICKSET.

Quick-sighted, *a.* Having quick sight.

N. Carpenter *Geog. Del.* ii. v. (1635) 71 Quick-siluer.. will gather it selfe to a round body. 1669 Worlidge *Syst. Agric.* (1681) 309 This Column of Quick-silver in the Tube, is supported by the weight of the Air Ambient. 1782 Cowper *Progr. Err.* 21 Like quicksilver, the rhetoric they display Shines as it runs, but grasped at slips away. 1825 J. Neal *Pro. Jonathan* I. 326 A profusion of little rain-drops; like spattered quicksilver. 1870 Yeats *Nat. Hist. Comm.* 360 Quicksilver is met with pure in minute globules, but for the purposes of commerce it is obtained from one of its ores,—cinnabar, a red sulphide of mercury.

2. Used allusively. **a.** with reference to the quick motion of which the metal is capable.

1562 J. Heywood *Prov. & Epigr.* (1867) 165 She is quycke syluer. 1622 Bacon *Hen. VII* 192 Perkin (who was made of Quick-silver, which is hard to hold or imprison) began to stirre. 1820 Scott *Abbot* xix, Thou hast quicksilver in the veins of thee to a certainty. 1889 *Boy's Own Paper* 17 Aug. 730/3, I..had come off the journey with my veins full of quicksilver.

b. with ref. to its use in mirrors (see the vb.).

1851 Robertson *Serm.* Ser. ii. xii. (1864) 166 The dull quicksilver of their own selfishness behind the glass.

3. *attrib.* and *Comb.* **a.** attributive, in senses 'consisting of, containing, pertaining to, etc. quicksilver', as *quicksilver bath, battery, earth, field, globe, mine, ore, plaster, ship, tank, valve, water*, etc.

1552 Huloet, Quyckesyluer earth, *antrax.* a 1631 Donne *Poems, Apparition*, In a cold Quicksilver bath. 1685 *Lond. Gaz.* No. 1996/1 The Quick-Silver Ships may be expected this month at Cadiz. 1751 Mrs. Delany *Autobiog.* (1861) III. 53 Quick-silver-water is the most effectual remedy for worms. 1756–7 tr. *Keysler's Trav.* (1760) IV. 152 Cinnabar or quicksilver ore. 1839 Marryat *Phant. Ship* iii. (1874) 25 In the centre of the ceiling hung a quicksilver globe, a common ornament in those days. 1877 Raymond *Statist. Mines & Mining* 19 A very important quicksilver-field is about to be opened in the far north. *Ibid.* 260 A..clever arrangement of quicksilver-tanks.

b. attrib. in sense 'resembling quicksilver (in quickness of movement)', as *quicksilver mind, rebel, rogue, temper.*

1655 Gurnall *Chr. in Arm.* V. § 4 (1669) 94/1 Labour therefore in hearing the Word to fix thy quick-silver mind. 1676 W. Hubbard *Happiness of People* 29 These are *Inquieta ingenia* of Quick-silver tempers. 1796 Earl Balcarres in Bryan Edwards *Proc. Maroon Negroes* (1796) 35 Until such time as these quick-silver rebels are under lock and key. 1863 Cowden Clarke *Shaks. Char.* xiv. 360 That prince of quicksilver rogues—Master Autolycus.

c. objective, and obj. genitive, as *quicksilver-feeder, -fixation, -producing* adj., *-reduction*, etc.

1834 Macaulay *Ess., Pitt* (1887) 306 The periwig company, and the Spanish-jack-ass-company, and the quicksilver-fixation-company. 1877 Raymond *Statist. Mines & Mining* 19 Coming south from Trinity, the next quicksilver-producing locality..is in the Coast Range. 1882 *Rep. Ho. Repr. Prec. Met. U.S.* 507 A quicksilver feeder has been devised for feeding mercury to gold mills.

Hence **Qui·cksi·lverish** *a.*, somewhat quicksilvery (hence **Qui·cksi·lverishness**); **Qui·cksi·lvery** *a.*, of the nature of, resembling, quicksilver.

1611 Cotgr., *Vif-Argentin*, quicke-siluerie. 1829 *Anniversary, Honeycomb & Bitter Gourd* 118 The flighty and quicksilvery youth of the parish. 1852 Mrs. Craik *Agatha's Husband* II. i. 17 She had..a certain quicksilverishness of manner, jumping here there everywhere like mercury on a plate. 1891 T. Hardy *Tess* (1900) 70/2 The quicksilvery glaze on the rivers and pools.

Quicksilver (kwi·ksi:lvəɹ), *v.* [f. prec. sb.] To treat, imbue, or mix with quicksilver; *esp.* to coat (the back of glass) with an amalgam of tin in order to give a reflecting power.

1704 Newton *Optics* (1721) 94 Metal..reflects not so much Light as Glass quick-silver'd over does. 1799 G. Smith *Laboratory* I. 178 How to Quicksilver the inside of Glass Globes, so as to make them look like Looking-glass. 1831 Brewster *Optics* i. 4 The glass is always quicksilvered on the back, to make it reflect more light.

Hence **Qui·cksi·lvered** *ppl. a.* (in early quots. *fig.*). **Qui·cksi·lvering** *vbl. sb.*, the action or process of coating, etc., with quicksilver; also *concr.* a coating of quicksilver or amalgam.

1599 E. Sandys *Europæ Spec.* (1632) 80 Those nimble and quicksilverd braines which itch after change. c 1645 Howell *Lett.* (1650) I. iv. 21 The Leaden-heeld pace of the one, and the Quick-silver'd motions of the other. 1753 Parsons in *Phil. Trans.* XLVIII. 380, I took a quicksilver'd glass. 1825 J. Nicholson *Operat. Mechanic* 728 The quicksilvered tin-foil adheres..firmly to the glass.

Quick step, qui·ckstep.

1. *Mil.* The step used in marching in quick time. Also quasi-*adv.*, at a quick step.

1802–1876 [see Quick time]. 1875 W. McIlwraith *Guide Wigtownshire* 51 We now move, quick-step, over the pasture-fields.

transf. 1877 Talmage 50 *Serm.* 26 Nearly all the verses of the Bible have a quick-step.

2. *Mus.* A march in military quick time.

1811 Busby *Dict. Mus.*, *Quick-step*, a species of march generally written in two crotchets in a bar. 1885 *Harper's Mag.* Feb. 384/1 The drum..beats a..quickstep. 1897 H. Porter *Campaigning with Grant* in *Century Mag.* Apr. 826 Bands were playing stirring quicksteps.

Quick-stick(s: see Quick *a.* D.

Quick time. *Mil.* A rate of marching which in the British army now consists of 128 paces of 33 inches each (= 118 yards) in a minute, or four miles an hour. Formerly the rate per minute was 108, then 116, and latterly 120 paces of 30 inches each (cf. quots. and Double-quick).

1802 James *Milit. Dict.*, *Quick Step*, or *Quick Time*, is 108 steps of 30 inches each, or 270 feet in a minute, and is the step used in all filings of divisions. *Quickest Step*, or *Quickest Time* is 120 steps of 30 inches each, or 300 feet in a minute. 1833 *Regul. Instr. Cavalry* I. 18 *The Quick Step.* The cadence of the slow pace having become..habitual to the recruits, they are..to be taught to march in 'quick time', which is 108 steps in a minute, each of 30 inches. 1876 Voyle & Stevenson *Milit. Dict.*, *Quick-time*, a pace soldiers ordinarily march at, viz. 3·3 miles an hour. *Ibid.* s.v. *Step, Quick step*, a military step of 30 inches, with a cadence..of 116 per minute, in the British army. It constitutes what is technically called *quick time* in marching.

b. quasi-*adv.* In quick time.

1816 Scott *Old Mort.* x, Come, come, Mrs. Janet—march, troop—quick time.

†**Quick tree.** *Obs. rare*$^{-1}$. = Quicken *sb.*1

1548 Turner *Names Herbes* (E. D. S.) 54 Myrica, otherwyse named tamarix..The Poticaries of London vse nowe for thys quik tree.

Quick-witted, *a.* (Stress variable.) [f. *quick wit* + -ed2.] Having a quick or ready wit; mentally acute, sharp, clever.

1530 Tindal *Pent., Lev.* Prol. (1884) 297 Allegoryes make a man qwick witted. 1596 Shaks. *Tam. Shr.* v. ii. 38 How likes Gremio these quicke-witted folkes? 1693 Dryden *Juvenal* iii. (1697) 50 Quick-Witted, Brazen-fac'd, with fluent Tongues. 1702 Mead *Mech. Acc. Poisons* Wks. (1775) 50 Impatient, ready to action, quickwitted. 1824 Miss Mitford *Village* Ser. i. (1863) 133 There is always great freshness and originality in an uneducated and quick-witted person. 1870 Lowell *Among my Bks.* Ser. i. (1873) 189 The cultivated and quick-witted men in whose familiar society he lived.

Hence **Quickwi·ttedness.**

1863 Cowden Clarke *Shaks. Char.* x. 257 He has French quick-wittedness, French good temper. 1883 P. Schaff *Hist. Church* Per. i. II. lxxxiii. 712 The curiosity and quick-wittedness of the Samaritan Magdalene.

Qui·ckwood. [f. Quick *a.* 3.] = Quick *sb.* 3, Quickset. (Chiefly *attrib.*)

1473–4 *Durham Acc. Rolls* (Surtees) 645 Pro..plantacione de le Whikwod. 1696 Aubrey *Misc.* (1721) 104 A Pond..adjoyning to a Quick-wood-hedge. 1769 *Adome Inclos. Act* 10 All the new quick-wood fences. 1800 Tuke *Agric.* 91 White thorn (provincially quickwood) constitutes the most common fence throughout the Riding. 1892 J. D. Hood *Waterspouts Yorksh. Wolds* 25 Rooting up a strong quickwood fence.

Qui·ck-work. *Naut.* (See quots.)

1711 W. Sutherland *Shipbuild. Assist.* 162 Quick-work; that part of a Ship's Sides both within and without Board, above the Channel-wales and Decks. 1730 Capt. W. Wrigglesworth *MS. Log-bk. of the 'Lyell'* 21 Sept., This morning begun to Caulk the Quick Work on the Quarter deck. 1776 Falconer *Dict. Marine* (ed. 2), *Quick-Work*,..a general name given to all that part of a ship which is under the surface of the water when she is laden. 1780 *Ibid.* (ed. 3), *Viberd*, the quick-work, or that part of a ship's side..comprehended between the drift-rails and the waist-rail. c 1850 *Rudim. Navig.* (Weale) 139 *Quickwork*. A denomination given to the strakes which shut in between the spirketing and clamps. 1867 Smyth *Sailor's Word-bk.*, *Quick-Work*, is also applied to that part of the inner upper-works of a ship above the covering board. Also, the short planks worked inside between the ports...In general parlance quick-work is synonymous with spirketting.

†**Quicqui·dlibet.** *Obs. rare*$^{-1}$. [L., f. *quicquid* whatever + *libet* it pleases.] Whatever one pleases, anything whatsoever.

1647 Ward *Simp. Cobler* 22 A multimonstrous maufrey of heteroclytes and quicquidlibets.

‖**Quid** (kwid), *sb.*1 [L. *quid* what, anything, something, neut. sing. of *quis* who, any one, etc.]

1. That which a thing is. Cf. Quiddity 1.

1606 Marston *Parasitaster* i. ii, My age Hath seene the beings and the quide [*sic*] of things. 1611 L. Barry *Ram Alley* in Dodsley (1874) X. 363 A widow that has known the quid of things. 1675 [Br. Croft] *Naked Truth* 25 The quid, the quale, the quantum, and such-like quack-salving forms. 1727–41 Chambers *Cycl.* s.v., Hence we have two kinds of *quids*, nominal..and real. 1875 Jowett *Plato* (ed. 2) I. 270 When I do not know the 'quid' of anything how can I know the 'quale'?

†**2.** = Quiddit, Quiddity 2. *Obs. rare*$^{-1}$.

1576 Gascoigne *Steele Gl.* (Arb.) 77 That Logike leape not ouer euery stile..With curious quids to maintaine argument.

3. *U.S.* (abbrev. of *tertium quid.*) A name given to a section of the Republican party in 1805–11.

1805 Jefferson *Writ.* (1830) IV. 45 Those called the third party, or Quids. 1882 H. Adams *J. Randolph* (1884) 182 He belonged to the third party, the quiddists or quids, being that tertium quid..which had no name, but was really an anti-Madison movement.

Quid, *sb.*2 *slang.* [Of obscure origin.]

1. A sovereign; †a guinea.

(Pl. usually without *-s*, as *two quid, a few quid*, etc.).

1688 Shadwell *Sqr. Alsatia* iii. i, Let me equip thee with a Quid. 1791–3 in *Spirit Pub. Jrnls.* (1799) I. 244 The man..rarely has more than from thirty to fifty quids a year. 1796 *Mod. Gulliver* 163 The twenty last are worth full forty quid. 1834 H. Ainsworth *Rookwood* III. iii. xiii. 166 One quid, two coach wheels. 1883 Besant *All in Garden Fair* ii. x, It isn't two quid a week that will keep a young gentleman of your powers.

†**2.** *pl.* (with *-s*.) Money, cash. *Obs. rare.*

a 1700 B. E. *Dict. Cant. Crew.*

Quid (kwid), *sb.*3 [var. of Cud *sb.* q.v.] A piece of something (usu. of tobacco), suitable to be held in the mouth and chewed.

1727 in Bailey vol. II. 1731 *Gentl. Mag.* I. 349 Spitting about the church..As if he'd got a quid in's mouth. 1789 G. Keate *Pelew Isl.* 27 Beetle-nut and Chinam, of which they had always a quid in their mouths. 1833 Marryat *P. Simple* (1863) 89 The first lieutenant..perceived that he had a quid of tobacco in his cheek. 1883 Stevenson *Silverado Sq.* (1886) 68 His mind was..revolving the problem of existence like a quid of gum.

fig. 1805 W. Hunter in *Naval Chron.* XIII. 35, I chewed my Quid of bitterness.

†**Quid,** *v.*1 *Obs.* Forms: 1 **cwyddian,** 2–3 **cwidden, quidd(i)en.** [OE. *cwiddian*, f. **cwidi*- Quide (q.v.).] *trans.* and *intr.* To say, speak.

c 1000 Ælfric *Hom.* II. 388 Crist hi befran hu men cwyddodon be him. c 1200 Ormin 3048 Þatt illke word wass cwiddedd ær. c 1205 Lay. 9825 Bi-þenc þu a þine quides þe þu sulf quiddest. c 1275 *Woman Samaria* 55 in *O. E. Misc.* 85 Nv quiddeþ men, þat cumen is Messyas.

Quid, *v.*2 [f. Quid *sb.*3]

1. *intr.* To chew tobacco; to chew the cud.

1775 in Ash. 1778 *Gentl. Mag.* July 311/1 The cow chews her cud, and the man, when he chews tobacco, calls it quidding. 1893 *Surrey Gloss.*, *Quidding*, chewing the cud. 'The heifer's getting better, she's quidding all right'.

2. *trans.* Of horses: To let (food) drop from the mouth when half chewed.

1831 Youatt *Horse* (1847) 258 The Horse quids his hay, and gulps his water. 1888 W. Williams *Princ. Vet. Med.* (ed. 5) 376 Soreness of the throat is indicated by 'quidding of the food'.

Hence **Qui·dder,** a horse which 'quids' (*Cassell's Encycl. Dict.* 1886).

‖**Quidam** (kwəi·dăm). *rare.* [L., f. *qui* who: cf. Quædam.] Somebody; a certain person.

1579 E. K. *Ded. Spenser's Sheph. Cal.* Post-scr., So many vnworthy Quidams, which catch at the garlond which to you alone is dewe. 1624 Bedell *Lett.* xi. 143 Who were these quidams that laid hands on Scory? a 1641 Bp. Mountagu *Acts & Mon.* (1642) 48 Some *Individuum vagum*, a certaine *Quidam* in the Clouds.

Hence **Quida·mity,** an allusion to 'somebody'.

1892 *Athenæum* 9 July 65/1 A retort lay ready to his hand more effective than any indulgence in *quidam*-ities.

†**Qui·ddany,** *sb.* *Obs.* Also 7 **quiddanet, -onie, quidenie,** 7–8 **quiddeny, -ony,** 8 **quidony.** [ad. obs. F. *codignat, condoignac*, etc. (mod.F. *cotignac*, It. *cotognato*) = med.L. *codōniātum*, var. of *cydōniātum*, f. L. *cydōnia*: see Quince, and cf. Codiniac, Cotiniate, Quinidiniac.] A thick fruit-syrup or jelly; orig. and properly, one made from quinces.

1616 Bullokar *Eng. Expos.*, *Quidianet*, a sweete mixture thicker than a sirupe, and not so thicke nor stiffe as marmalet. 1638 tr. *Bacon's Life & Death* (1651) 42 That which they call Quiddeny of Quinces. a 1655 Sir T. Mayerne *Archimag. Anglo-Gall.* No. 150 (1658) 101 Boyle the Syrrup, untill it be as thicke as for quiddonie. 1695 Westmacott *Script. Herb.* 203 Sloes in the form of a Quiddeny, or Marmalade. 1712 tr. *Pomet's Hist. Drugs* I. 133 It is us'd in Rob or Quiddony, made with Damask-Rose-Water. 1736 Bailey *Househ. Dict.* 494 Quiddany of Quinces.

Hence †**Qui·ddany** *v. trans.*, to make into a quiddany. (In quot. *fig.*)

1647 Ward *Simp. Cobler* 18 He will..Quidanye Christ with Sugar and Rats-bane.

Qui·ddative, *a. rare.* [For *quidditative*; cf. *qualitive, quantitive.*] = Quidditative.

1642 J. Jackson *Bk. Conscience* 18 Find out the very quiddative nature and being of Conscience. 1727–41 Chambers *Cycl.* s.v. *Quiddity*, What is essential to a thing is said to be quiddative—as quiddative knowledge. 1898 *Dublin Rev.* Oct. 299 The quiddative unity of things.

Quiddenie, -eny, varr. Quiddany.

Qui·dder, (? *a.* and) *adv.* *Sc. rare.* [Cf. Norw. dial. *kvidra* to dart about.] Only in phr. *quick and quidder*, quickly, forthwith.

In first quot. perh. as adj. = 'alive and lively'.

1633 *Fife Witch-Trial* in *Statist. Acc. Scotl.* XVIII. 658 He gave her, soul and body, quick and quidder full to the devil. 1866 Edmondston *Gloss. Shetl. & Orkn.*, *Quick-and-Quidder*, swiftly, quickly.

Quiddist: see Quid *sb.*1 3, quot. 1882.

Quiddit (kwi·dit). Now *arch.* = Quiddity 2.

1592 Greene *Upst. Courtier* in *Harl. Misc.* (Malh.) II. 232 These lawiers haue..such quibs & quiddits. a 1613 Overbury *A Wife*, etc. (1638) 188 He makes his Will in forme of a Law-case, full of quiddits. 1635 Heywood *Hierarch.* iv. 202 He..Stretches each Quiddit of the Law to finde Him culpable. 1838 Hor. Smith *Tor Hill* II. 221 Rhyming couplets, quirks, quiddits and riddles. 1855 Browning *Old Pict. Florence* xx, The first of the new..Beats the last of the old; 'tis no idle quiddit.

†**Qui·dditative,** *a.* *Obs.* [f. Quiddit-y + -ative. See also Quiddative.]

1. Pertaining to the quiddity or essence of a thing.

1650 Charleton *Paradoxes* 9 The quidditative and peculiarly expresse causes of all those admirable effects of the Loadstone. 1656 [? J. Sergeant] tr. *T. White's Peripat. Inst.* 220 The quidditative notion of an Element.

2. Full of equivocations, quirky.

1611 Cotgr., *Quidditatif*, quidditatiue, doubtfull, obscure, full of quirkes, fraught with quiddities. 1637 Gillespie *Eng. Pop. Cerem.* i. ix. 31 A weak and easily penetrable hedge of some quidditative Cautions.

Hence †**Qui·dditatively** *adv.*

c 1600 *Timon* iv. iii. (1842) 66 The moone may bee taken..either specificatiuely, or quidditatiuely, or superficially, or catapodially.

Quiddity (kwi·diti). [ad. schol. L. *quidditas*: see Quid *sb.*1 and -ity; so F. *quiddité* (14th c.).]

1. The real nature or essence of a thing; that which makes a thing what it is.

1569 J. Sanford tr. *Agrippa's Van. Artes* 21 The true demonstration..is that whiche is made (as the Logitioners

speake) by Quiddites, and by the proper difference of thinges. 1628 T. Spencer *Logick* 75 Dissent is in the qualitie not the quidditie, or being of the subject. 1670 Maynwaring *Vita Sana* x. 106 These notions being too..remote from the quiddity, essence and spring of the Disease. 1710 Berkeley *Princ. Hum. Knowl.* § 81 The positive abstract idea of quiddity, entity, or existence. 1828 De Quincey *Rhetoric* Wks. 1862 X. 76 The quiddity, or characteristic difference, of poetry as distinguished from prose. 1897 S. S. Sprigge *Life of T. Wakley* xiii. 125 The quiddity of each attitude was the desire to curtail the privileges of the hospital surgeons.

b. Something intangible. *rare*$^{-1}$.

1774 Burke *Sp. Amer. Tax.* Wks. 1842 I. 158 Fighting for a phantom; a quiddity; a thing that wants, not only a substance, but even a name.

2. A subtlety or captious nicety in argument; a quirk, quibble. (Alluding to scholastic arguments on the 'quiddity' of things.)

1539 Taverner *Gard. Wysed.* i. 18 b, [He] must nat playe with hys sophemes and quyddities. 1579 Fulke *Heskins' Parl.* 475 Hee saith hee will not vse the quiddities of the schooles, but plaine examples. 1678 R. Barclay *Apol. Quakers* § 12. 371 To find out and invent subtile Distinctions and Quiddities. 1731 *Plain Reas. for Presbyt. Dissent* 138 The most honest cause is often run down with the torrent and speat of law-quirks and quiddities. 1807 W. Irving *Salmag.* (1824) 33, I humbly solicit..A quiddity, quirk, or remonstrance to send. 1877 C. Geikie *Christ* xxv. (1879) 281 Their..quiddities and quillets, and casuistical cases.

Comb. 1863 De Morgan *Pref.* in *From Matter to Spirit* 40, I went back to the old quiddity-mongers.

b. Subtlety (of wit); ability or tendency to employ quiddities.

1600 W. Watson *Decacordon* (1602) 140 How shall euer those come in heauen, that haue neither qualitie of body to get it..nor quidditie of wit to keepe it? 1881 W. S. Gilbert *Patience*, To stuff his conversation full of quibble and of quiddity. 1884 R. Buchannan in *Pall Mall G.* 16 Apr., With the intellectual strength and bodily height of an Anak, he possessed the quiddity and animal spirits of Tom Thumb.

Quiddle (kwi·d'l), *sb. dial.* and *U.S.* [f. Quiddle *v.*] A fastidious person.

1856 Emerson *Eng. Traits* vi. 108 The Englishman is very petulant and precise about his accommodation..a quiddle about his toast and his chop [etc.].

Quiddle (kwi·d'l), *v.* Now chiefly *dial.* and *U.S.* [Of obscure origin: cf. *twiddle, fiddle*.]

1. *intr.* **a.** To discourse in a trifling way.

1567 Edwards *Damon & Pithias* in Hazl. *Dodsley* IV. 81 Set out your bussing base, and we will quiddle upon it. 1587 Fleming *Contn. Holinshed* III. 1275/2 Which name of the Marishes, Marshes, or Moores, if it like them to expound it, as I doubt not but manie will quiddle therevpon. 1863–70 [see Quiddling].

b. To trifle, waste time (*with*).

1832 in Webster. a 1877 in J. Cook *Orthodoxy* iv. (1882) 81 Don't quiddle with the goody little notes to Gibbon by Milman and others.

†**2.** *trans.* To trifle or play with. *Obs.*

a 1652 Brome *City Wit* iii. i. Wks. 1873 I. 311 *Cras.* How does she feel your hand? *Lin.* O, she does so quiddle it, shake it, and gripe it!

Hence **Qui·ddling** *vbl. sb.* and *ppl. a.* Also **Qui·ddler,** a trifler.

1832 in Webster. 1860 Emerson *Cond. Life* iv. (1861) 92 Neither will we be driven into a quiddling abstemiousness. 'Tis a superstition to insist on a special diet. 1863 W. Phillips *Speeches* vii. 181 Lawyers, bound by quiddling technicalities. 1870 H. Stevens *Bibl. Histor.* Introd. 14 He indulged in..bibliographical quiddling about the mechanical and manufacturing points of the books.

Quiddonie, -y, variants of Quiddany.

†**Quide.** *Obs.* Forms: 1 **cwyde,** 1–2 **cwide,** 3 **quede, queðe,** 3–4 **quide,** 4 **qwede.** [OE. *cwide* (*cwyde*) = OS. *quidi*, OHG. *quidi, chwiti*, etc., ON. *kviðr* verdict:—OTeut. **kwidi-z*, f. the root **kweþ-* to say, Quethe.]

1. A saying, speech, statement.

c 888 K. Ælfred *Boeth.* iii. § 4 Is þis nu se cwide þe þu me ʒeo sædest? c 1080 *O. E. Chron.* (Parker MS.) an. 1070 Se ar'b..mid strangan cwydan þæt ylce ʒefæstnode. c 1205 Lay. 9141 Hit wes ʒare iqueðen, þa quides beoð nu soðe. a 1250 *Owl & Night.* 685 Alvered seide of olde quide [etc.].

b. A promise. *rare*$^{-1}$.

c 1250 *Gen. & Exod.* 1463 He bad god..ðat he sulde fillen ðat quede, ðe he abraham quilum dede.

2. A will, legacy, bequest.

950 in Thorpe *Diplom.* 500/1 Ðis is Byrhtrices & Ælfswyðe his wifes nihsta cwide. Þe hi cwædon..on heora maʒa gewitnesse. a 1050 *Liber Scintill.* xliv. (1889) 146 On cwyde þinum læf þearfum. c 1205 Lay. 14857 Ich forʒiue ælchere widewe hire lauerdes quide. 13.. *K. Alis.* 8020 To have theo kyngis qwede, Muche bataile was heom myde.

Quidenie, variant of Quiddany.

Quider, obs. form of Whither.

†**Quidi·fical,** *a.* *Obs. rare*$^{-1}$. [f. Quid *sb.*1 + -(i)fic + -al.] Quibbling, captious.

1542 Udall *Erasm. Apoph.* 124 Diogenes mockyng suche quidificall trifles saied [etc.].

Quidighe, var. Cuddy1. (See Quidrathe.)

†**Quidlit,** obs. var. of (or misprint for) Quiddit or Quillet. (In quot. *attrib.*)

1598 Gilpin *Skial.*, *Satyr* ii. 43 Then whats a wench but a quirke, quidlit case, Which makes a Painters pallat of her face?

Quidnunc (kwi·dnʌŋk). [f. L. *quid* what + *nunc* now.] One who is constantly asking: 'What now?' 'What's the news?'; hence, an inquisitive person; a gossip; a newsmonger.

1709 Steele *Tatler* No. 10 ¶ 2 The Insignificancy of my Manners..makes the Laughers called me a Quid Nunc. 1782 Cowper *Wks.* (1837) XV. 126 Acknowledge, now..that I should make no small figure among the quidnuncs of Olney. 1832 W. Irving *Alhambra* II. 95 He was a sort of scandalous chronicle for the quid-nuncs of Granada. 1874 L. Stephen *Hours in Library* (1892) I. x. 352 Some wretched intrigue which had puzzled two generations of quidnuncs.

attrib. 1880 *19th Cent.* VII. 191 Not for the mere gratification of quidnunc curiosity.

Hence **Quid-nunc-ism, Quidnunckery,** curiosity, love of news or gossip. *nonce-wds.*

1804 in *Spirit Pub. Jrnls.* VIII. 93 His attachment to quidnunckery is as constant as ever. 1847 J. Cairns *Let.* in *Life* xi. (1895) 281 The ne plus ultra of disappointed religious quid-nunc-ism.

Quidony, variant of Quiddany.

‖**Quid pro quo** (kwid prōᵘ kwōᵘ), *sb.* [L. *quid* something, *pro* for, *quo* (abl. of *quid*) something.]

1. One thing in place of another; *orig.* and *esp.* one medicinal substance used for another, either intentionally, fraudulently, or by mistake.

1565 Calfhill *Answ. Martiall* 32 b, A leude Apoticarie, that vnderstandeth not his bil, but giueth *Quid pro Quo*. 1601 Holland *Pliny* II. A vj b, *Succedan*, that drug which may be used for default of another. The Apothecaries call such *Quid pro quo*. 1654 R. Whitlock *Zootomia* 60 The Apothecaries themselves, both take, and receive (from Herbe-women) *Quid pro Quo*, one thing for another, many, many Times. 1738 Steward in *Phil. Trans.* XL. 449 A Mistake..and a putting of *quid pro quo* (as 'tis commonly express'd). 1804 *Edinb. Rev.* III. 416 Referring the proximate cause of this disease to a deficiency of azote is only substituting *quid pro quo*.

b. The action or fact of using or putting one thing for another; the result of this; a mistake or blunder consisting in such a substitution.

1679 Everard *Discourses* 35 A Capital *quid pro quo* of Estate of the most part of the Potentates of Europe. 1687 Miege *Grt. Fr. Dict.*, *Quid-pro-quo* or mistake, *un Qui pro quo*. 1727–41 Chambers *Cycl.* s.v. *Quid*. A northern physician, in a printed thesis on *quid pro quo's*, owns ingenuously, that they are very frequent. 1824 Lady Morgan *Salvator Rosa* I. v. 263 He..produces the most ludicrous *quid pro quo's* by misapplied erudition, witty absurdities, and naïve questions. 1843 Thackeray *Misc. Essays* (1885) 44 A laughable *quid pro quo*..occurred to him in a conversation.

†**c.** One who assumes a false character. *Obs.*

1689 Hickeringill *Modest Inquiries* ii. 10 Have we not still..some (*Quid pro quo's*, amongst us) Papists in Masquerade?

2. One thing (or action) in return or exchange for another; tit for tat.

1591 Shaks. *1 Hen. VI*, v. iii. 109, I cry you mercy, 'tis but *Quid* for *Quo*. 1608 Middleton *Mad World* ii. iv. 44 Let him trap me in gold, and I'll lap him in lead; *quid pro quo*. 1705 Hickeringill *Priest-cr.* iv. (1721) 206 Every Church is the Old-Exchange, Spiritual Things in exchange for Carnal Things; Heaven for Earth; *Quid pro Quo*. 1727 Boyer *Dict. Royal* II. s.v. *Quid*. To give one *Quid-pro-quo* (or tit for tat). 1820 Combe *Dr. Syntax* ii. xxix. (186.) 167, I shall be able..to bestow What you will find a *quid pro quo*. 1871 M. Collins *Mrq. & Merch.* II. ix. 276 The tradesman gets his *quid pro quo*.

attrib. 1861 T. A. Trollope *La Beata* II. xvii. 187 A system of conduct based on the theory of a quid-pro-quo purchase.

†**Quidrathe.** *Obs. rare.* Also **-raighe.** [Ir. *cuid* part, portion + *ráithe* quarter of a year.] A quarterly tax, payment, or entertainment.

1570 in *11th Rep. Dep. Kpr. Irel.* 235 An Irish custom of £10 sterling called quidrathe. 1592 in *Acts Privy Council* N.S. XXII. 564 Unlawfull taxacions of Iryshe customes as Quony, Quoshirs, Nightsupers called Quidighe, Quartersupers called Quidraighe, Hueryе for their horses or anie other like taxes.

Quie, obs. form of Quey.

†**Quiell,** obs. var. Keel *sb.*1 (after F. *quille* or Pg. *quilha*).

1582 N. Lichefild tr. *Castanheda's Conq. E. Ind.* 336 They have no quiell, but are flat-bottomed.

†**Quiennal.** *Obs. rare.* In 4 **qui-, quyenal.** [For *quinquennal*, on anal. of Bi-, Triennal, q.v.] A dispensation or indulgence for five years.

c 1380 Wyclif *Sel. Wks.* III. 398 Freris..mony times bringen veyne pardouns, quienals, and oþer veyne privilegies. — *Wks.* (1880) 66 To paie..for pardons, quyenals, priuylegies, for assoilyngis of wowes, & many feyned iapis.

Quier, obs. form of Queer *a.*2

Quier(e, obs. forms of Choir, Quire *sb.*1

Quierie, obs. variant of *querry* Equerry.

Quiesce (kwəi‚e·s), *v.* [ad. L. *quiēscĕre* to be quiet, f. *quiēs* Quiet *sb.*]

1. *intr.* To become quiescent; to subside *into*.

1833 *Wild Sports of West* I. 27 Did tired nature quiesce for a moment, I was..roused with a tornado of..sounds. 1888 Howells *Annie Kilburn* xxx. 330 The village, after a season of acute conjecture, quiesced into..sufferance of the anomaly.

2. *intr.* Of a letter: To become silent; said of the feeble consonants in Hebrew when their sound is absorbed in that of a preceding vowel.

1828 Stuart *Elem. Heb. Lang.* (1831) 25 A moveable consonant is one which is sounded, and does not quiesce or coalesce. 1853 J. R. Wolf *Practical Heb. Gr.* 8 The letters אהוי are said to quiesce in the vowels after which they are placed.

Quiescence (kwəi‚e·sĕns). [ad. late L. *quiēscentia*: see Quiescent and -ence.] The state of being quiescent; quietness; an instance of this.

a 1631 Donne *Lett.* lxxx. Wks. (ed. Alford) VI. 397 Bless them with a satisfaction and Quiescence. 1664 Power *Exp. Philos.* Pref. 11 That there is no such thing in the World as an absolute quiescence. 1751 Johnson *Rambler* No. 137 ¶ 2 To sleep in the gloomy quiescence of astonishment. 1812 Woodhouse *Astron.* xxiii. 239 The anomalous retrogradations and quiescences of the planets. 1830 Lyell *Princ. of Geol.* (1875) II. ii. xxx. 177 The local quiescence or dormant condition of the subterranean igneous causes. 1879 Proctor *Pleas. Ways Sc.* ii. 29 The usual condition of the air..is one of motion, not of quiescence.

b. *spec.* in Hebrew grammar: see Quiesce *v.* 2.

1828 Stuart *Elem. Heb. Lang.* (1831) 54 Quiescence sometimes happens when the *Evi* would (by analogy) have a vowel. 1853 J. R. Wolf *Practical Heb. Gram.* 112 This quiescence consists in such letters losing their consonantal power when preceded by certain vowels.

Quiescency (kwəi‚e·sĕnsi). [See prec. and -ency.] = Quiescence.

1649 Bulwer *Pathomyot.* ii. i. 82 To find a quiescency in many Muscles working. 1664 Power *Exp. Philos.* i. 70 When the Animal Spirits are in Quiescency. 1824 Landor *Imag. Conv., Southey & Porson* Wks. 1853 I. 79/2 Much of this quiescency induces debility. 1882–3 Schaff *Encycl. Relig. Knowl.* I. 465 His Godhead..was in a state of quiescency during his humiliation.

Quiescent (kwəi‚e·sĕnt), *a.* and *sb.* [a. ppl. stem of L. *quiēscĕre* to Quiesce. So mod.F. *quiescent.*] **A.** *adj.*

1. Motionless, inactive, at rest.

1646 Sir T. Browne *Pseud. Ep.* 190 The active or moving side..the weaker or more quiescent part. 1710 Berkeley *Princ. Hum. Knowl.* § 114 A man in a ship may be said to be quiescent with relation to the sides of the vessel. 1753 Chambers *Cycl.* Suppl. *App.* s.v. *Force*, The pressure of the quiescent body against the obstacle that hinders it to move. 1812 Woodhouse *Astron.* i. 3 The pole, which is the place of a quiescent star. 1874 Lubbock *Orig. & Met. Ins.* iv. 63 The quiescent and death-like condition of the pupa.

†**b.** *Quiescent reason*, the fallacy of sorites.

1656 Stanley *Hist. Philos.* viii. (1.) xxxii, Sorites..is called also ἡσυχάζων λόγος, the quiescent reason, because the way to withstand it, is by stopping, and withholding the assent.

2. Of a letter: Not sounded, silent; *spec.* in Hebrew grammar (see Quiesce *v.* 2). *Quiescent verb*: (see quot. 1853).

1609 C. Butler *Fem. Mon.* (1634) p. iv, The E silent or quiescent, which yieldeth no sound. 1711 J. Greenwood *Eng. Gram.* 301 Other Letters..are quiescent or silent. 1807 G. Chalmers *Caledonia* I. i. iv. 160 The Irish Raths have the same origin, the [th] being quiescent. 1807 Hurwitz *Elem. Heb. Lang.* 101 According to the system of reading by points, the letters אהוי are in many instances quiescent. 1853 J. R. Wolf *Practical Heb. Gram.* 111 Quiescent verbs are those in which one of the feeble letters אהוי occurs as a radical letter.

b. Of a person: Silent, not speaking. *rare.*

1791 Boswell *Johnson* an. 1784. 17 May, Johnson was very quiescent to-day.

B. *sb.* **1.** A quiescent letter.

1727 in Bailey, vol. II. 1807 Hurwitz *Elem. Heb. Lang.* 134 Whenever a letter is written and not pronounced, it is called by Hebrew Grammarians..an invisible quiescent, or a mute. 1831 Lee *Hebr. Gram.* (1832) 36 The..letters, considered either as consonants or quiescents, will occasionally be changed for one another. 1882–3 F. Brown in Schaff *Encycl. Relig. Knowl.* I. 583/1 The weaker Shemitic gutturals and the quiescents.

2. A quiescent verb (see 2 above).

1831 Lee *Hebr. Gram.* (1832) 222 We do not think it necessary here to divide these verbs into Defectives and Quiescents as has usually been done.

Quie·scently, *adv.* [f. prec. + -ly2.] In a quiescent manner; at rest; in repose.

1805 Foster *Ess.* ii. iii. 146 Quiescently regarding the conclusions. 1887 *Twin Soul* I. xiii. 131 They float quiescently upon the fleecy clouds.

†**Quie·sceous,** *a.* *Obs. rare*$^{-1}$. [irreg. f. Quiesce *v.* + -ous.] Belonging to quiescence.

1688 R. Holme *Armoury* ii. 388/2 The Sense of Ease and Rest..it shall be termed The Quiesceous sense.

Quiese, obs. form of Queest, wood-pigeon.

Quiet (kwəi·ĕt), *sb.* Also 4–6 **quyet(e, quiete,** 7 **quiett.** [ad. L. *quiēt-*, stem of *quiēs* rest, repose, quiet. An AF. *quiete* may have existed beside *quieté* Quiety.]

1. Absence of disturbance or tumult; peaceful condition of affairs in social or political life.

13.. *Cursor M.* 29341 (Cott. Galba), [Cursed] er þai þat..robbes or reues on ani side, Whare pese and quiet suld bityde. c 1375 *Sc. Leg. Saints* iii. (*Andrew*) 519 Þe quyet of our lord Ihesu, luk in vnreste ʒe turne nocht now. 1470–85 Malory *Arthur* xx. xvii, In this realme wyll be now no quyete but euer stryf and debate. 1542–3 *Act* 34 & 35 *Hen. VIII*, c. 27 § 119 Lawes and ordinaunces for the..good quiet of his saide dominion of Wales. 1651 Hobbes *Leviath.* iv. xlvi. 380 To whom the care of the Publique quiet is committed. 1763 Burke *Corr.* (1844) I. 43 Why is not the nation's quiet secured, and its independance asserted? 1874 Bancroft *Footpr. Time* i. 104 A long period of almost absolute quiet followed the establishment of the empire.

personified. 1590 Spenser *F. Q.* i. i. 41 Carelesse Quiet lyes, Wrapt in eternall silence farre from enimyes. 1632 Milton *Penseroso* 45 Join with thee calm Peace, and Quiet, Spare Fast, that oft with gods doth diet. 1754 Gray *Pleasure* 53 Humble quiet builds her cell.

b. Absence of noise or (rapid) motion; calmness, stillness.

a 1400 *Stockh. Medical MS.* ii. 382 in *Anglia* XVIII. 316 Ageyn cowrs of watyr wyll he flete, ʒif þe water renne in good quiete. 1602 Marston *Antonio's Rev.* i. i. Wks. 1856 I. 73 No breath disturbs the quiet of the ayre. 1816

Shelley *Alastor* 393 A smooth spot Of glassy quiet mid those battling tides Is left. 1867 Smiles *Huguenots Eng.* iii. (1880) 51 It was only the quiet that preceded the outbreak of another storm.

2. Freedom from external disturbance, molestation, interruption, or noise; †freedom from work or occupation; rest, repose.

1340 Hampole *Pr. Consc.* 9128 Whare alle ryghtwyse men salle won at ees, In ioyfulle quyete, and rest, and pese. c 1430 Lydg. *Min. Poems* (Percy Soc.) 249 Lat me nat reste nor have no quyete, Occupye my soule with spiritual travayl. 1494 Fabyan *Chron.* vii. ccxxx. 256 This foresayd countesse..with her sonne..was in quyete of theyr countrey and castell. 1592 Greene *Conny catching* iii. 12 She seeing him laid in bed..commits him to his quiet. 1638 R. Baker tr. *Balzac's Lett.* (vol. II) 26, I have too much care of my own quiet, to goe about to trouble his. 1749 Fielding *Tom Jones* viii. xi, An arrant vixen of a wife soured his domestic quiet. 1865 Hook *Lives Abps.* III. 301 It often happens that a man, turbulent in his youth, will make great sacrifices to procure peace and quiet in his old age.

pl. 1650 Weldon *Crt. Jas. I*, 185 More beneficiall to the Subjects in respect of their quiets.

b. Freedom from mental agitation or excitement; calm or peace of mind.

a 1628 Preston *New Covt.* (1634) 421 As wondrous quiet and peaceablenesse, and calmnesse in the heart. 1688 Lady R. Russell *Lett.* I. lxxi. 156 Such letters as yours, Sir, do not disturb my quiet. 1726 Swift *Corr.* Wks. 1841 II. 586 An accident that must be so fatal to my quiet. 1840 Lady C. Bury *Hist. of Flirt* vi, A matter that concerns my quiet.

3. The condition of remaining quiet, of refraining from disturbance, hurry, exertion, etc.

1559 *Mirr. Mag., Henry VI*, vii, My mynde to quyet bent, had not bene tossed so. c 1586 C'tess Pembroke *Ps.* cxxxi, None more [than me] for quiet might compare Ev'n with the babe. 1604 E. G[rimstone] *D'Acosta's Hist. Indies* v. v. 343 That God was a great Lord, who with great quiet and leasure performeth his workes. 1750 Johnson *Rambler* No. 74 ¶ 12 Knowledge and genius are often enemies to quiet, by suggesting ideas of excellence. 1889 Pater *G. de Latour* (1896) 41 How becomingly..that self-respecting quiet sat upon their high-bred figures.

4. Freq. in phrases *at*, †*in*, and †*out of quiet*, with vbs. of being, remaining, maintaining, etc.

1377 Langl. *P. Pl.* B. i. 121 God..garte the heuene to stekye and stonden in quiete. c 1450 tr. *De Imitatione* ii. vi. 46 An evel conscience is euer dredful and oute of quiete. 1533 Frith *Another Bk. agst. Rastell* Prol. (1573) 61 They could neuer be at quiet..untill they had dronken his bloud. 1577 *Test. XII Patriarchs* (1604) 101 Bear your losses willingly, and be not out of quiet for it. 1699 Burnet *39 Art.* i. (1700) 21 Every part of it is at quiet till it is put in motion. 1771 Jefferson *Writ.* (ed. Ford) II. 129 Matters..are too much in quiet to send you news from hence. 1830 Scott *Demonol.* viii. 266 The country remained at quiet. 1886 Stevenson *Dr. Jekyll* 54 Mr. Utterson began..to grow more at quiet with himself.

†**b.** With adjs., esp. *at* (*a*) *good* (or *better*) *quiet*.

c 1470 Henry *Wallace* viii. 587 The ost he maid in gud quyet to be. 1603 Knolles *Hist. Turks* (1638) 62 The other Christian Princes also being at no better quiet. 1652 Cotterell *Cassandra* iv. (1676) 68 He began to be at a little better quiet. 1663 Pepys *Diary* 30 June, My differences with my uncle Thomas at a good quiett, blessed be God!

Quiet (kwəi·ĕt), *a.* Forms: 4–7 **quyet,** (4–6 **-te,** 6 **-tt**), 5 **quiete,** 6 **quyat, quyit, queat,** 8 *Sc.* **quait,** 6– **quiet.** [a. OF. *quiete* or ad. L. *quiētus*, pa. pple. to *quiēscĕre* to come to rest, f. root of *quiēs* rest, Quiet *sb.* The popular Fr. form *coi* is represented by Coy *a.*]

I. 1. Of persons (or animals): Making no stir, commotion, or noise; causing no trouble or disturbance; remaining at rest; not moving or acting.

1382 Wyclif *1 Thess.* iv. 11 We preyen ʒou..that ʒe be quyet, and do ʒoure nede. 1560 Daus tr. *Sleidane's Comm.* 277 b, Obteyne of the Clergie, that they wyll be quiet, tyll suche tyme as the other States may declare [etc.]. 1586 Warner *Alb. Eng.* i. vi. (1612) 24 Lycus..did cast his haughtie armes abroad, as who would say, be queat. 1715 Ramsay *Christ's Kirk Gr.* ii. vi, Let gae my hands, I say, be quait. 1738 Swift *Polite Conv.* Wks. 1883 IX. 403, I wish you would be quiet, you have more tricks than a dancing bear. 1837 Mrs. Sherwood *Henry Milner* iii. iii. 44 The young men began to call to them crying, 'Whisht, whisht, what ails the curs?—quiet there, Viper'. 1843 Miall in *Nonconf.* III. 635 Rebecca's rights once obtained we will be as quiet as mice.

b. (Also of nature or disposition.) Habitually or naturally peaceful or averse to making stir, noise, etc. Of an animal: Gentle.

1432–50 tr. *Higden* (Rolls) II. 167 The peple of the sowthe is meke and quiete. 1535 Coverdale *1 Chron.* xxii[i]. 9 The sonne which shal be borne vnto the, shal be a quyete man. 1609 Bible (Douay) *Mic.* iv. *comm.*, Quiet patient people..suffering persecution with alacritie of minde. 1669 Clarendon *Ess.* Tracts (1727) 148 Quiet and easy natures are like fair weather. a 1720 Sewel *Hist. Quakers* (1795) I. Pref. 18 They always were quiet and never made any resistance. 1811 *Sporting Mag.* XXXVIII. 212 The defendant did not put the question..whether it were a quiet horse? 1840 Dickens *Barn. Rudge* vi, Barnaby is not in his quietest humour to-night. 1863 *Q. Rev.* July 262 It is a great relief to quiet people when the Easter ceremonies are wound up.

†**c.** *Sc.* in specific senses: Acting or living quietly; remaining hid or secret; fast asleep. *Obs.*

1533 Gau *Richt Vay* 17 Thay that ar quiet and fals flatterers. 1536 Bellenden *Cron. Scot.* x. vii, Traistyng..sum quiet personis liand ay in wait to inuaid hym. 1632 Lithgow *Trav.* x. 444, I could not beleeue, that the Patrone of so great a Monarchy, could be so quiet; yea, as quiet as a Countrey Baron is with vs. 1651 Weldon *Crt. Jas. I*, 107 Loveston replies, He is quiet (which in the Scottish dialect is fast asleep).

2. Of things: Not active; not moving or stirring; also, making no noise; still.

Quiet disease, latent hip-joint disease in children (*Syd. Soc. Lex.* 1897). †*Quiet letter*, a quiescent letter.

1599 Shaks. *Hen. V*, iii. ii. 36 For Pistoll, hee hath a killing Tongue, and a quiet Sword. 1658 P. Goodwin *Myst. Dreams* in Spurgeon *Treas. Dav.* Ps. cxxvii. 2 The Hebrew word..being with *aleph*, a quiet or resting letter. 1798 Wordsw. *Tintern Abbey* 47 An eye made quiet by the power Of harmony. 1816 Scott *Antiq.* iii, The dust was very ancient, peaceful, quiet dust about an hour ago. a 1889 Eliza Cook *Poems* (Rtldg.) 51, I prize the soul That slumbers in a quiet eye. 1898 J. Hutchinson in *Arch. Surg.* IX. 330 Doubts might have been felt as to whether the induration was really malignant. It was quite quiet.

b. Free from excess; not going to extremes; moderate, gentle; *esp.* of colour, dress, style, etc.: Not obtrusive, glaring or showy.

1560 Daus tr. *Sleidane's Comm.* 261 b, That for the appeasing of religion, they would use lawfull and quiet remedies. 1634 Sir T. Herbert *Trav.* 5 Now you shall have a quiet breath and gale, and suddenly an unexpected violent gust. 1685 Dryden *Horace, Odes* iii. xxix. 54 The tide of bus'ness..Is sometimes high, and sometimes low, A quiet ebb, or a tempestuous flow. 1768 Sterne *Sent. Journ.* (1778) I. 63 (*Remise Door*), I made them a quiet bow, and wished them a good passage to Dover. 1838 Lytton *Alice* 21 A woman of quiet and pleasing exterior. 1856 Ruskin *Mod. Paint.* III. iv. App. 346 The beautiful quiet English of Helps. 1885 R. L. & F. Stevenson *Dynamiter* 185 He was conscious of a certain regular and quiet sound. 1889 *Catholic News* 15 June 8/6 There was a quiet trade in pigs.

c. Avoiding or escaping notice; private, secret, underhand. (In older use only *Sc.*)

a 1578 Lindesay (Pitscottie) *Chron. Scot.* (S. T. S.) I. 87 He..send quyit messagis to his freindis. a 1600 Montgomerie *Misc. Poems* xviii. 65 Thair companie [it] wes not quyet, Bot or they wist they wer beuryde. 1609 Skene *Reg. Maj.* 52 (*Acts Robt. III*, c. 2) The kings lieges, are trubled in their lands, be volunter and quyet recognitions, made be the overlords. 1899 *Westm. Gaz.* 29 Dec. 8/2 'Quiet cases' meaning the insurance of lives without the knowledge of the persons so insured.

II. 3. Free from disturbance, molestation, or annoyance; not interfered or meddled with; left in peace. **a.** of a state, condition, procedure, etc.

1382 Wyclif *1 Tim.* ii. 2 That we lede quyet and pesyble lyf. c 1450 *St. Cuthbert* (Surtees) 3720 In quiete prayers he contenued. c 1532 Du Wes *Introd. Fr.* in Palsgr. 921 A quyete slepe is right necessary and delycious. 1560 Daus tr. *Sleidane's Comm.* 94 b, If they maye have their Religion quiet untill the counsell, they are also contented to become contributaries. 1601 R. Johnson *Kingd. & Commw.* (1603) 96 They sent..to Cæsar, to intreat a quiet passage through the Romana province. 1642 Fuller *Holy & Prof. St.* (1648) 18 Though prayer purchaseth blessings, giving praise doth keep quiet possession of them. 1766 Blackstone *Comm.* II. 304 The grantor may covenant..for the grantee's quiet enjoyment.

†**b.** of a person, people, or country. Also const. *from*. *Obs.*

1558 Goodman *How to Obey* 175 Hauing your Realme free from strangers, and quiete from all enimies. 1599 Shaks. *Much Ado* ii. i. 266 While she is heere, a man may liue as quiet in hell, as in a sanctuary. 1611 Bible *Job* iii. 26, I was not in safetie, neither had I rest, neither was I quiet. 1655 Fuller *Ch. Hist.* ii. iii. § 26 That the abbot should be quiet from the bishop's right. 1671 Milton *P. R.* iii. 360 Long to enjoy it quiet and secure.

†**c.** Quit, clear. *Obs. rare*$^{-1}$.

1473–4 in Swayne *Sarum Church-w. Acc.* (1896) 16, iiijs. vijd. the which ben forgeven them..and so they ben quyete.

4. Characterized by the absence of all strife, bustle, stir, or commotion; also, free from noise or uproar, silent, still.

1514 Barclay *Cyt. & Uplondyshm.* (Percy Soc.) 11 Than..Wedlocke was quyet & pleasaunt without stryfe. 1596 Shaks. *1 Hen. IV*, v. i. 25, I could be well content To entertaine the Lag-end of my life With quiet houres. 1611 Bible *Wisd.* xviii. 14 While all things were in quiet silence. 1655 Fuller *Ch. Hist.* iii. xii. § 27 He chose a quiet county before a cumbersome kingdom. 1791 Mrs. Radcliffe *Rom. Forest* x, In the second chamber all was quiet and in order. 1831–3 E. Burton *Eccl. Hist.* i. (1845) 9 If the state of things might be described as at all quiet. 1856 Kane *Arctic Explor.* II. xxiv. 204 We gave two quiet hours to the memory of our dead brother. 1872 Ruskin *Eagle's N.* § 179 My hope..that the streams of the Isis and Cherwell will be kept pure and quiet.

b. Remote from scenes of activity; retired.

1500–20 Dunbar *Poems* (S. T. S.) xliii. 33 In quyet place,..They can, percaice, Purchess some grace. a 1578 Lindesay (Pitscottie) *Chron. Scot.* (S. T. S.) I. 187 They..past to the wall heid at ane quyit place quhair the watches might haue no sight of them. 1738 Gray *Propertius* iii. 105 Then to my quiet Urn awhile draw near. 1861 H. Kingsley *Ravenshoe* xxxvii, As soon as he and Lady Ascot were seated on a quiet sofa.

c. Partaken of, or enjoyed, in quiet.

1837 Dickens *Pickw.* xxvi, To have a quiet cup of tea. 1892 Anstey *Voces Pop.* Ser. ii. 85 A cup of coffee, and a quiet cigar.

5. Of the mind, conscience, etc.: Not troubled or distressed; free from agitation or excitement. So also of persons in respect of the mind, etc.

1535 Coverdale *Prov.* xv. 15 A quyete herte is as a contynuall feast. 1552 *Bk. Com. Prayer* Commun., With a quiet conscience. 1558 Goodman *How to Obey* 230 That you cannot be quiete in conscience. 1593 Shaks. *Rich. II*, i. iii. 96 Truth hath a quiet breast. 1631 Gouge *God's Arrows* i. § 5. 8 The bond of a Creditor, so lies on the debter, that he is not quiet till it be discharged.

†**6.** Sheltered from the wind. *Obs. rare.*

1596 Dalrymple tr. *Leslie's Hist. Scot.* I. 30 In the scoug of the craig and castell is a verie quyet hauining place. 1697 Dryden *Virg. Georg.* iv. 10 For thy Bees a quiet Station find, And lodge 'em under Covert of the Wind.

III. †**7.** Used as *adv.* = Quietly. *Obs. rare*$^{-1}$.

1573 Tusser *Husb.* (1878) 63 More profit is quieter found (where pastures in several bee).

8. Quasi-*sb.*, in phr. *On the quiet*, privately, in secret. (Abbrev. *q. t.*: see Q II. 2.) *slang* or *colloq.*

1873 *Slang Dict.* s.v., 'On the quiet', clandestinely, so as to avoid observation, 'under the rose'. 1881 *Punch* 8 Jan. 4/1 I'd just like to have a bit of chinwag with you on the quiet about the..troubles of a Cabby. 1889 H. O'Reilly *50 Yrs. on Trail* 7 Having on the quiet found out a passenger steamboat.

9. *Comb.*, as *quiet-eyed, -mannered, -minded, -spoken, -tempered*; *quiet-going, -living, -looking, -moving, -seeming* adjs.

1780 S. J. Pratt *Emma Corbett* (ed. 4) I. 107, I can..impress the quiet-seeming sentiment. 1825 J. Neal *Jonathan* II. 124 An old, stately, quiet-looking negro. 1848 Dickens *Dombey* iii, She was a quiet-tempered lady. *Ibid.* iv, He was a slow, quiet-spoken..old fellow. 1886 H. F. Lester *Under two Fig Trees* 59 The exciting incidents which now and then ruffle the life of even the most quiet-going family. 1888 Bryce *Amer. Commw.* II. ii. xlii. 119 A larger sum than a quiet-living man can need.

Quiet (kwəi·ĕt), *v.* Also 6 **quyet.** [ad. med.L. *quiētāre*, f. L. *quiētus* Quiet *a.*]

†**1.** *trans.* To quit, acquit (oneself or another). c 1440 *Generydes* 2861 Eche of hem iij so wele quiete them ther. 1472–3 *Rolls Parlt.* VI. 50/1 That your said suppliaunt..be discharged, relesed and quieted, of almaner..fynes, paynes [etc.].

2. To make quiet (in various senses); to reduce to quietness:

a. a person or people, a material thing, etc.

1550 Crowley *Way to Wealth* 269 Quiet thy selfe therfore, and striue not againste the streame. 1599 Shaks. *Hen. V*, v. i. 54 Quiet thy Cudgell, thou dost see I eate. 1609 Holland *Amm. Marcell.* 109 Those savage nations whom he had quieted. 1665 Manley *Grotius' Low-C. Warres* 570 A very difficult piece of Work..to quiet all the right side of the Rhine. 1786 Mad. D'Arblay *Diary* 8 Nov., I did what was possible to quiet her, but to no purpose. 1855 Macaulay *Hist. Eng.* xii. III. 211 In trying to quiet one set of malecontents, he had created another. 1866 G. Macdonald *Ann. Q. Neighb.* vi. (1878) 73 She knew she had no chance of quieting the girl.

b. a feeling or emotion, *esp.* of fear.

1526 *Pilgr. Perf.* (W. de W. 1531) 2 b, His naturall inclinacyon and appetyte can neuer be sacyate, contented and quieted. 1552 *Bk. Com. Prayer* Commun., If there be any of you which..cannot quiet his own conscience. 1748 *Anson's Voy.* ii. xi. 253 This quieted our apprehensions for some days. 1855 Macaulay *Hist. Eng.* xi. III. 32 The event quieted the fears of one party. 1888 Bryce *Amer. Commw.* III. lxxxviii. 190 In order to quiet these suspicions the comptroller played a very bold game.

c. a disturbance, dissension, etc.

1560 Daus tr. *Sleidane's Comm.* 174 The byshop wyl sende thether..to quiet the controversy. 1601 J. Wheeler *Treat. Comm.* 33 Till the said King Edward had quieted the troubles with his subiects at home. 1674 *Essex Papers* (Camden) I. 193 Some companys of yᵉ Guard being comanded together to quiet yᵉ Tumult. 1792 Burke *Let. to R. Burke* Corr. IV. 4 Measures which may quiet the unhappy divisions of the country. 1846 Trench *Mirac.* iv. (1862) 147 Quieting with a word the tempest in their bosoms. 1875 Jowett *Plato* (ed. 2) V. 360 The motion..quiets the restless palpitation of the heart.

3. To settle or establish in quiet. Chiefly *Law.*

c 1586 C'tess Pembroke *Ps.* lxxxii. iii, You should unto the weake extend Your hand, to loose and quiet his estate. 1654 G. Goddard *Introd. Burton's Diary* (1828) I. 190 A Bill for quieting the possession of the government. 1668 *Ormonde MSS.* in *10th Rep. Hist. MSS. Comm.* App. V. 69 Your petitioner..made surrender of his estate unto the Crowne so soone as he was quieted in the possession thereof. 1884 Sir J. Bacon in *Law Rep.* 27 Chanc. Div. 47 The Plaintiffs are entitled..to be quieted in the possession they have had for so many years.

4. *intr.* To become quiet. Also *to quiet down.*

1791 Paine *Rights of Man* (ed. 4) 27 The mind can hardly..conceive the possibility of its quieting so soon. 1851 Mayne Reid *Scalp Hunt.* xxxii. 247, I have never seen buffaloes 'quieting' down before. 1865 Mrs. Whitney *Gayworthys* II. 237 By and by she quieted, and, from pure exhaustion, fell asleep.

Hence **Qui·eted** *ppl. a.*

1894 E. F. Benson *Dodo* 185 The darkened house, the quieted movements.

†**Quietance.** *Obs.* [ad. med.L. *quiētāncia*, f. *quiētāre* to Quiet: see -ance] = Quittance 2.

1451 *Rolls Parlt.* V. 224/1 Libertees, Fraunchises and Quietaunces conteyned in the same. 1571 *Act* 13 *Eliz.* c. 29 All manner of Liberties, Franchises, Immunities, Quietances and Privileges.

Quietant (kwəi·ĕtănt). [f. Quiet *v.* + -ant1.] Anything that makes quiet or soothes.

1875 H. C. Wood *Therap.* (1879) 340 As a nocturnal quietant and hypnotic, it would appear to offer very great advantages.

†**Quieta·tion.** *Obs.* Also 6 **quietacion, -cyon, quyat-, quyetacyon, -cion.** [ad. med.L. *quiētātiōn-em*, n. of action f. *quiētāre* to Quiet. Cf. obs. F. *quietacion* (Godef.).] The action of quieting; the state of being quieted or quiet.

1502 W. Atkynson tr. *De Imitatione* iii. xl. 229 If thou seke here rest, how shalt thou come to euerlastyng rest & quietacion in heuen? 1526–9 Ld. Dudley in Ellis *Orig. Lett.* Ser. iii. II. 84 For the quyatacion of the Kyngs subgetts.

1640 J. Stoughton *Def. & Distrib. Divinity* iii. 90 Such a fruition of all good..as brings with it a perfect quietation of the natural appetite. a 1711 Ken *Anodynes* Poet. Wks. 1721 III. 427 From God I ease or succour find, And Quietation to my Mind.

Quiete, variant of Quiety *Obs.*

Quieten (kwəi·ĕt'n), *v.* [f. Quiet *a.* + -en5.]

1. *trans.* To make quiet.

1828 in *Craven Gloss.* 1844 *N. Brit. Rev.* I. 182 To 'quieten' the children..is not English. 1853 Mrs. Gaskell *Ruth* III. x. 280, I will stay,..partly to quieten the fears of this poor, faithful fellow. 1888 *Chamb. Jrnl.* 7 Apr. 223 The incident did not quieten the audience.

2. *intr.* To become quiet. Commonly with *down*.

1890 C. Dixon *Stray Feathers* v. 67 They soon quieten down. 1897 *Westm. Gaz.* 21 Aug. 5/1 Towards the close the market quietened.

Hence **Qui·etener,** = next. (Cf. Quietant.)

1882 *Fraser's Mag.* XXV. 35 The poisonous method of giving soothing or narcotic quieteners to children.

Quieter (kwəi·ĕtəɹ). [f. Quiet *v.* + -er1.] One who or that which makes quiet.

a 1541 Wyatt in *Tottel's Misc.* (Arb.) 45 The bodyes ease, and troubler of my heart: Quieter of minde. 1547–64 Bauldwin *Mor. Philos.* (Palfr.) 140 It is also a satisher or ioyfull quieter of the minde. 1832 Southey *Lett.* (1856) IV. 261 Half an hour of some goodly grave old book..as a quieter for the night.

†**Qui·etful,** *a.* *Obs. rare*$^{-1}$. [f. Quiet *sb.* + -ful.] Full of quiet; calm.

c 1440 Hylton *Scala Perf.* (W. de W. 1494) iii. xv, A quyetful langynge with a trusty desyrynge to heuenly Joye.

Quietie, variant of Quiety *Obs.*

Qui·eting, *vbl. sb.* [f. Quiet *v.* + -ing1.] The action of the vb.

a 1548 Hall *Chron., Hen. VIII*, 179 He..for quietyng of his conscience called together the best lerned of the realme. a 1652 J. Smith *Sel. Disc.* x. 511 A pacifying and quieting of all those riots and tumults. 1783 Mad. D'Arblay *Diary* 18 Jan., I felt so fagged..that I really wanted quieting and refitting. 1861 Goldw. Smith *Irish Hist.* 105 To withhold the capital 'grace' concerning the quieting of titles to land.

Qui·eting, *ppl. a.* [-ing2.] That quiets.

1659 A. Hay *Diary* (S. H. S.) 80 There is a quieting rest under Christ's wings. 1759 H. Walpole *Lett. to Mann* 9 Feb. (1846) III. 432 The Parliament has taken a quieting-draught. 1839 I. Taylor *Anc. Chr.* I. 22 The quieting recollection that they themselves are members of a series. 1846 Trench *Mirac.* xxxii. (1862) 450 The Lord spoke these quieting words to his disciples.

Quietism (kwəi·ĕtiz'm). [ad. It. *quietismo* (whence also F. *quiétisme*, mod.L. *quietismus*, etc.): see Quiet *a.* and -ism.]

1. A form of religious mysticism (originated prior to 1675 by Molinos, a Spanish priest), consisting in passive devotional contemplation, with extinction of the will and withdrawal from all things of the senses; hence, any form of mysticism in which such principles are enjoined.

The *Guida spirituale* in which Molinos expounded his views was published at Rome in 1675, and condemned by the Inquisition in 1685.

1687 in Burnet *Lett.* (1688) Suppl. 46, I will here digress a little from the business of Quietism. 1698 tr. *Fenelon's Maxims of Saints* Introd., There are but a few people that have not heard of Molinos, and his Doctrine of Quietism. 1773 Wesley *Wks.* (1872) XIII. 25 Her [Madame Guion's] writings will lead any one who is fond of them, into unscriptural Quietism. 1838 Sir J. Stephen *Eccl. Biog.* (1850) II. 70 Quietism, indigenous in the East, is an exotic in this cold and busy land of ours. 1873 C. M. Davies *Unorth. Lond.* 200 To avoid the Charybdis of carnalism, there is no need to seek the Scylla of Quietism.

2. A state of calmness and passivity of mind or body; repose, quietness, tranquillity.

1772 *Town & Country Mag.* 86 This discovery deprived him of all his quietism. 1795 Jefferson *Writ.* (1859) IV. 122 That quietism into which people naturally fall after first sensations are over. 1836 *Fraser's Mag.* XIII. 526 They could..disturb his quietism by acrimonious attacks.

Quietist (kwəi·ĕtist). [ad. It. *quietista* (F. *quiétiste*): cf. prec. and -ist.]

1. One who believes in or practises Quietism, or any form of mysticism resembling it.

1685 Burnet *Letter from Rome* (1689) 205 A state of inward quietness, from which the name of Quietists was given to all his followers. 1687 *Lond. Gaz.* No. 2269/3 They write from Rome that the Pope had assisted a third time at a Congregation held concerning the Quietists. 1732 Berkeley *Alciphr.* iii. § 14 The disinterested Stoics (therein not unlike our modern Quietists). 1840 Thirlwall *Greece* VII. liii. 14 He conceived a like admiration for the Indian quietists. 1893 C. G. Leland *Memoirs* I. 23 Reading works by Mystics, Quietists, and the like.

2. One whose attitude towards political or social movements is analogous to Quietism in religion.

1798 Charlotte Smith *Yng. Philos.* IV. 393, I will not talk to you about politics because you are among the moderates and quietists. 1834 Southey *Doctor* cii. (1862) 232 He was not like him a political quietist from indifference. 1871 R. H. Hutton *Ess.* II. 442 He was, in political and social conviction, a democratic quietist; one might almost say a fatalist.

3. *attrib.* or as *adj.*

1856 R. A. Vaughan *Mystics* (1860) II. xi. ii. 224 The Quietist doctrine of unconsciousness. 1860 O. W. Holmes *Elsie V.* xxviii. (1891) 413 Hymns..of the Methodist and Quietist character. 1873 Morley *Rousseau* II. x. 29 Rousseau raised feeling, now passionate, now quietist.

Quietistic (kwəiĕti·stik), *a.* [f. prec.: see -istic.] Belonging to, or characteristic of, quietists.

1850 H. Bushnell *God in Christ* 321 They make a study of the mystic and quietistic writers. 1876 *Macm. Mag.* XXXIV. 194 He displays..the most tender love and quietistic resignation.

Quietive (kwəi·ĕtiv). [f. Quiet *v.* + -ive.] That which tends to produce quiet; a sedative.

1894 Bruce *Paul's Concept. Chr.* xx. 365 It is his quietive amid disgusts.

Qui·etize, *v. rare*$^{-1}$. [f. Quiet *a.* + -ize.] *trans.* To make quiet.

1791 Mad. D'Arblay *Diary* (1842–6) V. vi. 271 Solitude, and patience, and religion, have now quietized both father and daughter into tolerable contentment.

Qui·etless, *a. rare*$^{-1}$. [f. Quiet *sb.* + -less.] Devoid of quiet.

1839 Bailey *Festus* (1852) 376 The moon..comes haunting the cold earth..quietless.

Quietlike, *a.* and *adv.* *Sc.* [See -like 2 b.] Apparently quiet; quietly.

c 1470 Henry *Wallace* v. 577 All his four men bar thaim quietlik. *Mod. Sc.* Your horse is a quietlike beast.

Quietly (kwəi·ĕtli), *adv.* Forms: 5–6 **quyetly, -lie, 6 quietlie, -ely,** 6– **quietly,** (9 *dial.* **whietly**). [f. Quiet *a.* + -ly2.] In a quiet manner; without molestation, peacefully; without excitement, tumult, or noise; without moving or stirring, etc.

1494 Fabyan *Chron.* i. iv. 11 He was stablysshed in his Realme quyetly. 1535 Coverdale *1 Sam.* xxiv. 4 Dauid stode vp and cut of the typpe of Sauls garment quyetly. 1568 Grafton *Chron.* II. 378 They entred into the Citie, and there abode quietly. 1611 Tourneur *Ath. Trag.* i. ii. Wks. 1878 I. 35 That he may sleepe the quietlier. 1729 Butler *Serm. Hum. Nat.* ii. Wks. 1874 II. 20 Let every one then quietly follow his nature. 1793 Smeaton *Edystone L.* § 227 A weight of lead..which, in all such trials as had hitherto been made thereof, had lain quietly. 1878 Huxley *Physiogr.* xvii. 281 When the river..quietly deposited mud and sand.

Quietness (kwəi·ĕtnĕs). Forms: 5–7 **quietnes(se, 6 quyetnes(se,** 7 **quiett-, quyettnes,** 6– **quietness.** [f. as prec. + -ness.] The condition of being quiet or undisturbed; absence of noise, motion, or excitement; calmness, tranquillity.

c 1450 tr. *De Imitatione* i. ix. 10 Þou shalt neure finde quietnes but in meke subieccion under a prelate. 1526 *Pilgr. Perf.* (W. de W. 1531) 142 It is lesse labour and more quietnes. a 1578 Lindesay (Pitscottie) *Chron. Scot.* (S.T.S.) I. 185 Althocht the conspiratouris thocht to have this matter..in quyetnes, yet..the king of France gat wit of the samin. 1682 Norris *Hierocles* 71 The knowing man..will learn quietness and sedateness. 1730 Earl of Oxford in *Swift's Lett.* (1768) IV. 25 Enjoying the fruit of his victory, peace and quietness. 1807 Wordsw. *White Doe* i. 294 Happy in the shy recess Of Barden's lowly quietness. 1874 Gladstone in *Contemp. Rev.* Oct. 664 A word spoken in quietness..can rarely fail to be in season.

†**b.** With *a* (not followed by *that*). *Obs.*

a 1548 Hall *Chron., Hen. V* 75 b, To set all thynges in a quietnes. 1549 Latimer *2nd Serm. bef. Edw. VI* (Arb.) 73 That she wold let the great man haue a quietnes in hyr Lande. 1596 Shaks. *Merch. V.* iv. i. 12, I..am arm'd To suffer, with a quietnesse of spirit [etc.].

†**Qui·etous,** *a.* *Obs. rare.* [f. Quiet *sb.* + -ous.] Quiet, peaceful. Hence †**Qui·etously** *adv.*

1550 Bale *Image Both Ch.* 84 b, Quietously to rest for a season. *Ibid.* 93 b, Bringing men to a quietous holde and sure stay in the Lord.

Qui·etsome, *a.* *Obs.* exc. *dial.* [f. Quiet *a.* + -some.] Quiet.

1595 Spenser *Epithal.* 326 Let the night be calme and quietsome. 1876 *Whitby Gloss.*, *Quietsome*, retired; silent.

Quietude (kwəi·ĕtiūd). [a. F. *quiétude* (c 1500) or ad. late L. *quiētūdo*, f. *quiēt-us* Quiet *a.*] = Quietness; rest, calm, tranquillity.

1597 A. M. tr. *Guillemeau's Fr. Chirurg.* 46 b/2 That parte requireth nothinge els then quietude. 1675 Otway *Alcibiades* iii. i, How sweet a Quietude's in Fetters found. 1755 J. Shebbeare *Lydia* (1769) II. 3 Love,..urged his bosom too vehemently, to suffer a moment's quietude or delay. 1832 Lytton *Eugene A.* i. v. 28 Philosophy has become another name for mental quietude. 1877 'H. A. Page' *De Quincey* II. xvi. 29 The quietude of the Meadows..made them his favourite resorts.

‖**Quietus** (kwəi‚ī·tŭs). [Short for next.]

1. A discharge or acquittance given on payment of sums due, or clearing of accounts; a receipt.

1540 *Act* 32 *Hen. VIII* (Pardon), Such issues fines or amerciaments..and haue his or their Quietus for the same. 1623 Webster *Duch. Malfi* iii. ii, You had the tricke in Audit time to be sicke, Till I had sign'd your Quietus. 1688 Evelyn *Diary* 15 Mar., I gave in my account about the Sick and Wounded, in order to have my quietus. 1780 Burke *Sp. Econ. Reform* Wks. 1826 III. 297 A final acquittance, (or a *quietus*, as they term it) is scarcely ever to be obtained [from the exchequer]. 1887 *48th Dep. Keeper's Rep.* 628 The several Books..being preserved, and..the satisfaction or *quietus* being therein entered.

†**2.** A discharge from office or duty. *Obs.*

c 1670 Wood *Life* an. 1650–1, 16 Jan. (O. H. S.) I. 166 Had A. W. continued postmaster a little longer, he had, without doubt, received his quietus. 1687 Luttrell *Brief Rel.* (1857) I. 401 Sir Francis Withens, a judge of the Kings bench, hath his quietus. a 1711 Ken *Hymnotheo* Poet. Wks. 1721 III. 155 The Guardian to relieve, Who his Quietus shall in Heav'n receive. 1788 Walpole *Letters* (1902) 104 A Veteran Author ought to take out his quietus as much as the Superannuated of any other Profession.

3. Discharge or release from life; death, or that which brings death.

1602 Shaks. *Ham.* iii. i. 75 When he himselfe might his quietus make With a bare bodkin. 1768–74 Tucker *Lt. Nat.* (1834) II. 639 Some obtain their quietus without any signs of pain at all. 1775 Sheridan *Rivals* v. iii, If an unlucky bullet should carry a quietus with it. a 1839 Praed *Poems* (1864) II. 65 Sought his quietus in a duel. 1872 Baker *Nile Tribut.* v. 65 This shot, far from producing a quietus, gave rise to a series of convulsive struggles.

b. Final settlement or extinction.

1806–7 Beresford *Miseries Hum. Life* (ed. 5) I. 233 We have now, I think, given a quietus to the parlour. 1885 Clodd *Myths & Dr.* i. iv. 73 This law gave the quietus to theories of common origin.

4. (By assoc. with *quiet*.) Something which quiets or represses.

1824 Miss Ferrier *Inher.* xxxii, This disaster..had the effect of a quietus upon Miss P. for some time. 1855 Thackeray *Newcomes* II. 304 The nurse ran to give its accustomed quietus to the little screaming infant.

Hence †**Quietus** *v. trans.*, to discharge. *Obs.*

1688 in Ellis *Corr.* II. 22 The other Powell and Holloway, who are quietus'd.

‖**Quietus est.** *Obs.* [(med.)L. = 'he is quit'.] = Quietus.

1427–8 *Rolls Parlt.* V. 409/2 That thei haue not theire Quietus est out of the Eschequier. 1530 Latimer *Rem.* (Parker Soc.) 309 To have..your quietus est sealed with the blood of our Saviour Christ. 1594 Carew *Huarte's Exam. Wits* (1616) 217 That Steward..salued vp all his reckonings, and got his quietus est. 1681 Luttrell *Brief Rel.* (1857) I. 74 On Monday the 11th of Aprill the lord cheif justice Scroggs received his quietus est. 1706 Phillips (ed. Kersey), *Quietus est*..a Phrase us'd by the Clerk of the Pipe and Auditors in the Exchequer, in their Acquittances and Discharges given to Accountants: A *Quietus est* granted to the Sheriff likewise discharges him of all Accounts due to the Queen.

†**Qui·ety.** *Sc. Obs. rare.* In 6 **quiete, -tie,** 7 **quyetie.** [a. OF. *quieté, quité* (Godef.):—L. type **quiētāt-em*, f. *quiēt-us* Quiet *a.*] Quietness.

c 1470 Henryson *Mor. Fab.* ii. (*Town & C. Mouse*) xxxi, Blissit be sober feist in quiete [*ed.* 1621 quyetie]. 1528 Lyndesay *Dreme* 283 Secreit synnis done in quietie.

Quife, Quig, Quight, obs. ff. Coif, Whig, Quite.

‖**Qui-hy** (kwəi‚həi). Also **-hi.** [Urdū (Hindi) كوئي هي *koī hai* 'is (*hai*) any one (*koī*) there?' a call used in India to summon a servant.] An Anglo-Indian, esp. one belonging to the Bengal Presidency.

1816 'Quiz' (*title*), The Grand Master, or Adventures of Qui Hi in Hindostan. 1822 *Blackwood's Mag.* Aug. 133 So if you are neither a qu, hy [sic] nor a politician [etc.]. 1834 Medwin *Angler in Wales* I. 7 An apparition..not unusual at that refuge for Indians, a 'qui hi'. 1864 Trevelyan *Compet. Wallah* (1866) 170 Old Quihyes, with clogged livers and shattered nerves.

attrib. 1840 E. E. Napier *Scenes & Sports For. Lands* II. iv. 91, I sent to my Qui Hi friend an Arab pony.

Quik(e, quikk(e, etc., obs. ff. Quick *a.* and *v.*

Quil, obs. form of While, Which.

†**Quilate.** *Obs.* Also 6 **quillat(e.** [a. Sp. or Pg. *quilate*: cf. Killat.] = Carat, q.v.

1577 Frampton *Joyfull Newes* ii. 55 They shall put the water lower, in Quillats. 1622 Mabbe tr. *Aleman's Guzman d'Alf.* i. 27 Shee would rather die..then..faile one quilate in the touch and finenesse of her punctualitie. 1622 *Ibid.* ii. 320 Hee teacheth vs the quilates and aloy of that gold.

Quilc, obs. f. Which. **Quile,** var. Coil *sb.*5 haycock, While. **Quiler,** var. Quoiler.

†**Quilicom.** *Obs. rare*$^{-1}$. [Of obscure formation.] App., an idle fancy, conceit, or quibble.

1644 Quarles *Barnabas & B.* (1651) 43 It is enough for me to know, that God is a good man..and for all other Quilicoms, they shall never trouble my braines.

Quilis, -ist, obs. forms of Whiles, Whilst.

Quilk, obs. form of Which.

Quill (kwil), *sb.*1 Forms: 4–7 **quil,** 5 **quyl, qwil, qvylle,** 6 **quyll,** 6– **quill.** [Of obscure etym.: cf. LG. *quiele*, G. *kiel*, dial. *keil* (MHG. *kil*), quill (of a feather).]

†**1.** A hollow stem or stalk, as that of a reed; a smooth piece of stem between two joints. *Obs.*

1412–20 Lydg. *Chron. Troy* i. vi, They take a quil..or a large can, And in the ende this stone they set. c 1440 *Promp. Parv.* 421/1 Qvylle, stalke, *calamus*. 1688 R. Holme *Armoury* ii. 84/2 Of a Tree..the Quill, is the Cane, or space between two such joints.

b. A piece of reed or other hollow stem on which yarn is wound; hence, a bobbin, spool, or pirn of any material.

14.. *Voc.* in Wr.-Wülcker 613/1 *Spola*, a Quyl, or a Spole. 1547 Salesbury *Welsh Dict.*, *Prikied edafedd*, a quyll of yorne. 1610 Guillim *Heraldry* iv. vii. (1611) 204 Hee beareth Argent three Weauer's Shuttles Sable tipped and furnished with Quils of Yarne. 1635 *Roxb. Ball.* (1890) VII. 142 If I should a Weaver have,..Either wind silk, or fill his quills, 'tis either I can fit. 1771 Mrs. Delany *Lett.* Ser. ii. I. 382 Neither by force or art can I get the present quill off the spindle. 1831 G. R. Porter *Silk Manuf.* 221 The quantity of silk wound upon each of these quills is necessarily but small. 1886 Elworthy *W. Som. Word-bk.*, *Quill*, to wind the yarn from the hank or skein on to a bobbin, called a quill, for the weaver's shuttle.

c. A musical pipe, made of a hollow stem.

1567 Turberv. *Epit.*, etc. 56 Assist mee with your skilfull Quilles and listen when I call. 1633 P. Fletcher *Purple Isl.* xi. ii, Who now shall teach to change my oaten quill For trumpet 'larms. 1720 Philips *Pastorals* iv. 28 Yet Colinet..My fingers guided on the tuneful Quill. 1749 Collins *Superstit. Highlands* ii, There, must thou wake

perforce thy Doric quill. **1598** BROWNING *Poets Croisic* xlviii, Joining the Delphic quill and Getic trump.

d. A piece of cinnamon or cinnamon bark curled up in the form of a tube. Also, the extent to which such bark curls up in drying.

+2. A small pipe or tube; *esp.* a small water-pipe. *Obs.*

c. The hollow steel mandrel of a seal-engraver's lathe, into which the engraving tools are fitted.

3. The tube or barrel of a feather, the part by which it is attached to the skin. Sometimes extended to include the shaft, or used loosely in the sense of 'feather' (*esp.* one of the strong wing- or tail-feathers) and *poet.* for 'wing'.

b. The feather of a large bird (usually a goose) formed into a pen by pointing and slitting the lower end of the barrel.

4. One of the hollow sharp spines forming part of the covering of a porcupine.

5. The hollow cylindrical plaits or folds of a ruff (Nares); *a.* quilled ruff. *Obs.*

6. quill-plaster (see 5.) Obs.

7. (In full quill-stroke.) A particular stroke in the game of billiards.

Quillai (kila'i). Also *quillay*. [Chilian (Araucanian) *quillai, quillay, quillan*.] The soap-bark tree of Chili (*Quillaja saponaria*): see next. Also *attrib.*, as *quilla-bark, -tree*.

Quillaia (kwilā'yǎ). *var.* of QUILLAJA. [mod.L., prec.] **a.** A genus of S. American rosaceous trees, the bark of which possesses soap-like properties. **b.** The quillai-tree (see prec.); or its bark (also *quillaia-bark*).

Quillate, variants of QUILATE, carat.

Quill-driver. [f. QUILL sb.1 + DRIVER.] One who works with a quill or pen; a clerk or author. (Chiefly with contemptuous force.)

Hence **Quill-driving** vbl. sb.1

Quilled (kwild), *a.* and *ppl. a.* [f. QUILL sb.1 and *v.* + -ED.]

1. Having the form of a quill or quills.

a. of cinchona bark: see QUILL sb.1 1 d.

b. of cloth: see QUILL sb. 5 V. 1. Also (of persons) *quilled up*: wearing a quilled ruff.

2. Furnished with quills, as a porcupine.

Quillet1 (kwi'let). *sb.*2 Also 7 *quirp*, 7-9 *quillit.* [? Abbrev. of QUILLITY; cf. *quip, quirp*.] A verbal nicety or subtle distinction; a quirk, quibble.

b. *transf.* A thick covering (= or soft bed).

+2. A hamlet. *Obs.*

Quillet2 (kwi'let). *sb.*3 Also 7 quillit. [Of doubtful origin.] A small plot or narrow strip of land. Now only *local* or *dial.*

Quillity. *Obs. rare.* [f. QUIL + -ITY.] A quibble, a subtlety.

Quilling (kwi'liŋ), *vbl. sb.* [f. QUILL *v.* + -ING.] **1.** The action of the vb. QUILL; *esp.* filling a quill with thread or yarn.

2. A ribbon, strip of lace or other material gathered into small cylindrical folds resembling a row of quills.

+Quilmeasure. *Obs. rare.* Also 7 quillety.

Quillon (kī'yon). [Fr. (1611 in Cotgr.), app. f. *quille* ninepin: see QUILL sb.1] One or other of the two arms forming the cross-guard of a sword.

Quilly (kwi'li), *a. rare.* [f. QUILL sb.1 + -Y.] Resembling a quill; pertaining to quills.

Quilt (kwilt), *sb.* Forms: *a.* 3 cowlte, *pl.* quoltes, 4 quylte, quylt, 4–6 quylte, quylt, 4–7 quilte, quylt, 6–8 quilt, 5– quilt. [a. OF. *cuilte, coilte, coute, cute*, etc.:—L. *culcita*.]

1. A bed-covering of woven material, consisting of two layers of cloth with a layer of wool, feathers, etc. between them.

b. *transf.* A thick covering (= or soft bed.)

2. To fasten together (two pieces or thicknesses of material) by stitches or lines of sewing.

Hence **+Quiltedly** *adv. Obs. rare*—1.

Quilter (kwi'ltə). [f. QUILT *v.* + -ER1.] A person who quilts; an apparatus for quilting.

Quilting (kwi'ltiŋ), *vbl. sb.* [f. QUILT *v.* + -ING1.]

1. The action of making, sewing together, etc.

2. Quilted material; quilted work. **b.** Material for making a quilt. A kind of cloth with a diagonal pattern resembling the appearance of an ordinary quilt.

3. *dial.* and *U.S.* A quilting-party.

4. *attrib.* as *quilting-needle, -seam*; *quilting bee, -feast, -frolic, -party* (*U.S.*), a gathering of girls held for the purpose of making a quilt, and serving as an occasion for enjoyment; *quilting-cotton*, raw cotton prepared for stuffing quilts; *quilting frame*, a frame on which a counterpane is stretched during the process of quilting.

Quiltster. *Obs.* A flooring.

Quim (kwim). *sb.* Also 7 quiminy. [Of obscure origin; cf. QUEEN 10 a, and SQUEX.] A variety of peaches (F. *spercularis*).

Quin1 (kwin). *Obs.* [Of obscure orig.; cf. QUEEN 10 a, etc.] A variety of cockle. *Obs.*

Quin2 (kwin). *Sc. vb.* cont. Cox sb.1 3. *Obs.*

Quina (kwi'nǎ). [Sp.] = QUININE. Also china-china.

Quinamine (kwinæ'min). *Chem.* Also quinammina, Quinamidine, artificial isomeric alkaloids obtained from quinamine.

Quinary (kwai'nǎri), *a.* [ad. L. *quinarius*.] **1.** Pertaining to, consisting of, or arranged in fives; consisting of five (things or parts).

2. Proceeding by fives; on the principle of, or relating to the number five.

Quinate (kwi'nāt). *a. Bot.* [f. L. *quini*] Composed of five leaflets; quinquefoliolate.

Quince (kwins). *sb.* Forms: 3-6 quynce, 4-6 quynse, coyns, 4-7 quynce, quynse, 5-6 quence, 6-7 quynse, 5– quince. A well-known fruit of a golden colour resembling an apple, with an austere flavour.

Quincentenary (kwinsente'nǎri), *sb.* and *a.* A five-hundredth anniversary, or its celebration.

Quinch (kwintʃ). *v. Obs.* [var. of QUINCH *v.*] *intr.* To move, stir, make a slight noise; to start, flinch.

Quincunx (kwi'nkŋks). [L. *quincunx* (*quinque-+uncia*), five-twelfths, f. *quinque* five + *uncia* a twelfth.]

1. *Astrol.* An aspect of planets in which they are at a distance of 5 signs or 150 degrees from each other.

2. An arrangement or disposition of five objects so placed that four occupy the corners, and the fifth the centre, of a square or rectangle.

Quincuncial (kwinkŋ'nʃǎl), *a.* [L. *quincunciālis*.] **1.** Pertaining to, characterised by, the quincunx.

2. *Bot.* Of aestivation: Having five leaves so placed.

Quindecagon (kwinde'kǎgon). *Geom.* A plane figure having fifteen angles.

Quindecemvir (kwindē'semvə). *Rom. Antiq.* [L.] A member of a body, commission, etc., of fifteen men.

Quindecima (kwinde'simǎ). *Mus.* [It.] The fifteenth; an interval of two octaves.

Quinia (kwi'niǎ). *Chem.* [ad. mod.L. *quinium*.] = QUININE.

+Quinible. *a.* and *sb. Obs. rare.* Also 5 quynyble. [Irreg. f. L. *quini* five, on anal. of *treble, quatreble*.] *Mus.* A high part sung above the treble.

Quina (kwi'nǎ). *Chem.* = QUININE.

Quinina (kwinai'nǎ). *Chem.* = QUININE.

| QUININE. | 65 | QUINQUAGESIMA. | QUINQUAGESIMAL. | 66 | QUINQUIFID. |

Quinine (kwinī·n, -in, U.S. kwaī·nain). Also **quinin**. [f. QUINA + -INE [2].] An important alkaloid ($C_{20}H_{24}N_2O_2$) found in the bark of various species of cinchona and remigia, used largely in medicine as a febrifuge, tonic, and antiperiodic, chiefly in the form of the salt, sulphate of quinine, which is popularly termed quinine.

Quinidine (kwini·din). *Chem.* Also **-ina**.

Quininism (kwī·ninizm). *Path.* [f. QUININE + -ISM.]

Quini·narin. *Chem.* [f. QUININE + (AL)IZARIN.]

Quinine (kwinā·iz), v. *Chem.* 3rd Suppl. 1736.

Quink. *Sc.* [? Imitative of the cry.]

Quinnat (kwi·nat). [?f. N. Amer. Indian: Clatsop *tʃkwínnat*,*tʃkwínnax*, Chinook *ikwánin* (Gibbs *Chinook Vocab.* 1863).] The king-salmon; the Californian, Columbian, or Chinook salmon (*Oncorhynchus chouicha* or *quinnat*) of the N. Pacific coast.

Quinnet (kwi·net), *dial.* Also 9 quinet, &c.

Quinoa (kī·noa, kwinō·a). [Sp.]

Quinoidine (kwinoi·din). *Chem.* Also **-ina**.

Quinol (kwī·nǫl). *Chem.* Also **-ol.**

Quinoline (kwi·nǫlin). *Chem.* Also **-olein** (-).

Quinologist (kwinǫ·lǫdʒist). [f. QUINA + -OLOGY + -IST.]

Quinology (kwinǫ·lǫdʒi). [f. QUINA + -OLOGY.]

Quinone (kwi·nōn, kwinō·n). *Chem.*

Quino·va-mic, a. *Chem.*

Quinova·tannic, a. *Chem.*

Quinoo·vic, a. *Chem.*

Quinovin (kwinō·vin), *Chem.* Also **quinovia**.

Quinovic (kwī·noa, kwinō·vik), *kinovic.* a. *Chem.*

Quino·vate, kinovate [-ATE I c.], a salt of quinovic acid (Mayne *Expos. Lex.* 1855).

Quinovin, kino·vin [-IN [3]], an amorphous bitter compound found in (false and other) cinchona-barks.

Quinoyl (kwi·nǫil). *Chem.* Also **kinoyle,** quinoil. *b.* (See quot. 1843.)

†Quinquae-dron. *Math.* *Obs.* rare⁻¹. [f. L. *quinque* + QUADRATE.] A thirty-second power.

Quinquagenarian (kwinkwǫdʒínǟ·rijǎn), sb. and a. [f. as next + -AN.]

Quinquagenary (kwinkwǒ·dʒinǟri), a. [f. L. *quinquāgēnārius*, distrib. f. *quinquāgēni* fifty : cf. F. *quinquagénaire*.]

Quinquangular (kwinkwæ·ŋgiūlā), a. [f. med. L. *quinquangul-us,* f. L. *quinque* + *angul-us* ANGLE, corner : pentagonal.]

Quinquartic·ular, a. [ad. med. L. *quinquarticulār-is,* f. *quinque* + *articulus* ARTICLE.]

Quinquatria (kwinkwē·tria), sb. pl. *or* **quinquatrus,** rare. [L. *quinquātrūs* pl.]

Quinque- employed in combs. in L. from *quinque* five.

†Quinque·lian, a. *Obs.* rare⁻¹. [f. L. QUINQUE- + -LIAN.]

Quinque-angle, -angled, -angular adjs., **quinquangular,** †conjugate, -conjugate, -articulate, -capsular, -costate, -dentate, †-dentated, -digitate(d), -farious, -fid, -fistular(y), †-lateral, -lobate, -lobed, etc.

Quinquefid see QUINQUIFID.

Quinquefolious (kwinkwifō·liǎs), a. [ad. L. *quinquefoli-us* (Pliny) five-leaved, f. *quinque* + *folium* leaf.]

Quinquennial (kwinkwe·nial), a. [as next + -AL.]

†Quinquennium (kwinkwe·niǒm). Pl. **-ennia.** [L., *quinquennium* + *-annus* year.] A period of five years : *spec.* in Canon Law 1480.

Quinquepartite (kwinkwe·pā'tǎit), a. [ad. L. *quinquepartīt-us,* f. *quinque* + *partīt-us* divided.]

Quinqueparted (kwinkwe·pātǎd), a.

Quinqueque·partition, n. rare.

Quinquereme (kwi·nkwirīm), a. and sb. [ad. L. *quinquerēm-is,* f. *quinque* + *rēmus* oar.]

Quinquevalence (kwinkwe·valěns). [-ENCE.]

Quinquevalent (kwinkwe·valěnt), a. [f. L. *quinque* + *valent-em*.]

Quinquivalve (kwi·nkwivalv), a. *Bot.* Also 8-9 *quinque-*. [f. *quinque-* + VALVE.]

Quinquivirate (kwinkwi·virět), n. rare. [ad. L. *quinquevirātus*.]

| QUINQUINA. | 67 | QUINTAN. | QUINTANT. | 68 | QUINTUPLE. |

Quinquina (kwinkwī·na). *Med.* Also 7 **kinkina, 8 kinquina.** *See also* QUINA, QUINA. Sp. spelling of Peruvian (Quichuan) *kina-kina* or *kina-kina,* redupl. of *kina* bark, Quina.

†Quinquivalent (kwinkwi·valěnt), a. *Chem.*

Quinquivirate see QUINQUEVIRATE.

†Quinquiplicate, v. *Obs.* rare⁻¹. [f. ppl. stem of L. *quinquiplicāre* : cf. DUPLICATE v.]

Quinquity, error⁻¹. [f. L.]

Quinse (kwins), sb.¹ Also 6 **quinse, kinse.** [Origin obscure. The form *cuinse,* cited by Halliwell from the *Bk. of Hunting* 1586, may be a misprint : the *Bk. St. Albans* gives 'A Floouer Mynsed' as the proper term.]

†Quinse, v. *Obs.* rare. Also 6 **quinse, kinse.**

†Quinsell. *Obs.* Also 6 **-sell.** [ad. F. *quinzain.*]

Quinsy (kwi·nzi). *Forms:* 4-7 **qwinsy,** **quinesy,** 5 qweynose. β. 5 **quynacy,** **quenesy,** 6 quynance, &c. [Aphetic f. ME. *quinaci,* *quinci,* a. OF. *quinancie, squinancie*.]

Quinta (kī·nta). [Sp. and Pg., orig. denoting a house and farm let at a rent of one-fifth (*quinta parte*) of the produce of the latter.] A country-house or villa in Spain or Portugal.

Quintagena·rian, erron. f. QUINQUAGENARIAN.

Quintain (kwi·ntǎin). *Obs.* exc. *Hist.* *Forms:* 4-6 **quintain,** 5-7 **quintin,** β. 6-8 **quintin,** -tine, etc. [a. OF. *quintaine* (13th c.).] 1. An object set up to be tilted at.

Quinta (kwi·nta), sb., a., and v. *Med.* [a. F. *quintaine*.]

Quintain (kwi·ntǎn). See QUINTAIN.

Quinquina, obs. form of QUININE.

Quint (kwint), sb.¹ Also 6 **quinte.** [a. F. *quint* sb. (sense 1), or *quinte* f. (senses 2 and 3) :—L. *quint-us,* -a, -um, ordinal to *quinque* five.]

1. A tax of one-fifth.

2. *Mus.* a. An interval of a fifth.

Quintal (kwi·ntǎl). *Forms:* 4-7 **quintal,** 5-7 quyntall, etc. [a. F. *quintal* (13th c.).]

Quintan (kwi·ntǎn), a. and sb. [ad. L. *quintāna* (sc. *febris*), fem. of *quintānus* i. *quintus* fifth.]

Quintan (kwi·ntǎn), v. Also 7 **quintayne.**

†Quintant. *Obs.* rare⁻¹. [f. L. *quint-us* fifth, after QUADRANT sb.] The fifth part of a circle.

†Quintary. *Obs.* rare⁻¹. [f. *quint-us* fifth : cf. QUINARY.] A multiple of five.

Quinte (kēnt). [F. : see QUINT sb.²] 1. The third or parry of the eight taught in fencing-schools. Also *attrib.*

Quintennial, var. of QUINQUENNIAL.

Quintenary, var. of QUINQUENARY.

Quinternion (kwintŏ·niǒn). [ad. L. *quinque* + *ternion*.]

Quinteron, -oon, variants of QUINTROON.

Quintessence (kwinte·sěns), sb. Also 5 **-essense, -isence, quintessaunce,** 7 -escence. [a. F. *quintessence,* †quinte essence (14th c.), or ad. med.L. *quinta essentia* (cf. L. *quinta essentia*).]

Quintessence (kwinte·sěns), v. Now rare.

†Quintessenciate (1611 in Cotgr.). rare.

†Quinti·lle. *Obs.* rare⁻¹. [ad. sp. *quintillo* f. *quinto* fifth : cf. QUADRILLE.]

Quintessential (kwintise·nʃǎl), a. [f. QUINTESSENCE sb. + -IAL : cf. *essential* and F. *quintessentiel*.]

Quintessentiality (kwintise·nʃiæ·liti), rare.

Quintessentialize (kwintise·nʃǎlǎiz), v. [f. prec. + -IZE.]

Quintet, quintett (kwinte·t). *Mus.* Also **-tte, -tto.** [ad. F. *quintette* (also ad. It. *quintetto*).]

Quintic (kwi·ntik), a. and sb. *Math.* [f. L. *quint-us* fifth + -IC.]

Quintile (kwi·ntǎil), a. and sb. *Astrol.* [ad. L. *quintīl-is* fifth : see quartile.]

Quintin, variant of QUINTAIN.

Quintole (kwi·ntōl). *Mus.* [Obscurely f.]

Quintroon (kwintrū·n). rare. Also **quinteroon, quinteron, quintroon.**

Quintuple (kwi·ntiūpl, kwintiū·pl), a., sb., and v. [a. F. *quintuple* (16th c.), or ad. late L. *quintuplus*.]

A. *adj.* Fivefold : multiplied by five.

B. *sb.* A quantity or sum five times as much as a great.

Quintuple (kwi·ntiūpl). v. To multiply by five ; to make five times as much or as great.

Quintuplet (kwi'ntiuplet). [f. QUINTUPLE a.] A set of five things, &c. (see QUINTUPLE.)

Quintuplicate, v. and a.

Quintuplication.

Quintuply, adv.

Quintus (kwin'tɒs).

Qui'nyie. Sc. Obs. Also 6 quinze, -yie, 7.

Quinzaine (kwinzeːn, F. kɛ̃zɛn). rare.

Quinzieme (F. kɛ̃zjɛm). Forms: 5 quyn-(s)ieme, -syeme, -zyme, 6 quinsime, -sī(s)me, -zyme, 5-6 quinsime, 6-sien, -siesme, 7-siesme, 8 -sieme, 9 -sieme. [a. F. quinziesme, -ieme.] A tax or duty of a fifteenth.

Quindene.

Quinze (kwinz, F. kɛ̃z). [a. F. quinze—L. quindecim fifteen.] A card-game.

Quip, sb.

Quip, v.

Quipo, obs. form of QUIPU.

Quipping.

Quipu (kiːpuː, kwiːpuː). Also quipo, quippu, &c.

Quire, sb.[1]

Quire (kwaiəɹ), sb.[2]

Quire, obs. f. QUARRY and QUEER.

Quire, v.

†Quirister, obs. f. CHORISTER.

Quiritary (kwiˈritari).

Quiritation.

Quirk (kwɜːk), sb.

Quirk, v.

Quirked (kwɜːkt), ppl. a.

Quirkish.

Quirky (kwɜː·ki), a.

Quirl, variant of QUERL.

Quirquincho.

Quirt (kwɜːt), sb. U.S.

†Quirt, v.[1] Obs. rare.

Quirt (kwɜːt), v.[2] U.S.

Quirtam, adv.

Quisby (kwizbi), sb. slang.

Quisby, a.

Quisby (kwizbi), a. slang.

Quischen, -on, etc., obs. forms of CUSHION.

Quisco(kos obs. form of CUISSE.

†Quish, obs. form of CUISSE.

Quishan, -en, etc., obs. forms of CUSHION.

Quisle, obs. form of WHISTLE.

†Quiscu'lian, a.

Quisquiliary.

Quisquilious (kwiskwiˈliɒs), a.

Quit (kwit), sb.[1]

Quit (kwit), a.

Quit (kwit), v.

Quitch, sb.[1]

Quitch, sb.[2]

Quitch, sb.[3], obs. variant of COACH.

†Quitchinroo, obs. form of COCHINEAL.

Quitclaim (kwitkleːm), sb.

Quitclaim, v.

2. To renounce, resign, give up (a possession, claim, right, pursuit, etc.).

Quite (kwəit), *adv.* Forms: 4–6 quyte, 5 quhyt, 5–6 quyt, 6 quyght, 6–7 quight, 4–quite. [f. *quit* a.]

1. Completely, wholly, altogether, entirely; to the fullest extent or degree.

1. With verbs, esp. in the pa. pple., denoting the thorough completion of the action. †Formerly also in phr. *quite and clean*: see CLEAR *adv.* 6.

b. With *quit* taken as vb.

†**Quitclaimance.** *Obs. rare⁻¹.* In 4 quiteclamance. [a. AF. *quiteclamaunce,-aunce* (Britton, etc.).]

†**Quitelaimance.** *Obs. rare⁻¹.* In 4 quiteclamance, etc.

Quits (kwits), *a.* and *v.* Forms: 4–5 quyte, 5 *sc.* quhyt, 5–6 quyt, 6 quyght, 4–quite. [f. *quit* a.]

d. With superlatives.

e. With substantives preceded by *a*, or in *pl.*

Quit-claim (kwit·klēm), *sb.* [f. QUIT *v.* + CLAIM.]

Quittance (kwi·tăns), *sb.* Forms: 3 cwitt-aunce, 4 quitance, 5 quyt-, quyte-, quyet-, 5–6 quittaunce (also 5 -awnce, 5–6 -aunce, -auns), 7 quitt-, 6– quittance. [a. OF. *quitance, quittance*, etc.]

Quitter (kwi·tər), *sb.²* [f. QUIT *v.* +-ER¹.]

†**1.** One who frees, discharges, etc. *Obs.*

Quitter, obs. f. *quitter*, twitter.

Quit-rent, *a. rare.* [f. QUITTER *sb.²*] Affected with quitter-bone.

Quitting (kwi·tiŋ), *vbl. sb.* [f. QUIT *v.* +-ING¹.]

Quittor, variant of KITTISOL.

Quittor, quittor (kwi·tər), *sb.¹* Now rare. Forms: 3–4 quiture, 4 quyt-, 5 quet-, (5 -ur), 6–7 quitture, (7-ur); 5 quewter, quest-, quitoure, 5 quytoure, whitour, whytoure, 7 quittour; 3 quater, (5 qur-), 5–9 whyver, 5–6 -ver. & 6; 6 quwvyr, quawier, 6–7 quaver, etc. [OE. *cwifer*]

Quittor, obs. f. *quitter,* twitter.

†**Quirical** (kwai·rikəl), *a. Obs. rare⁻¹.* [f. QUIRE *sb.*]

Quiver (kwi·vər), *sb.¹* Forms: 1 *cwifer,* 3 *cwiuer, couer,* 4 *quy-,* 5–6 *quyuer,* (6 *que-*), 5–7 *quiuer,* 6 *quiver.* [OE. *cwifer.*]

Quiver (kwi·vər), *a. Obs. exc. dial.* Forms: 1 *cwifer,* 3 *cwiuer, couer, quer,* 4 *quyuer,* (6 *que-*), 5–7 *quiuer,* 6 *quiver.*

Quiver (kwi·vər), *v.¹* *trans.* To put into or as into a quiver. Chiefly in *pa. pple.*; cf. QUIVERED 2.

Quiver (kwi·vər), *v.²* *intr.* To tremble, shake, vibrate, esp. with a slight but rapid agitation.

Quiver-full. [f. QUIVER *sb.¹* +-FUL.] As much as a quiver can hold.

Quivered (kwi·vərd), *ppl. a.* Chiefly *poet.* [f. QUIVER *sb.¹* + -ED¹.]

Quivering (kwi·vəriŋ), *vbl. sb.* [f. QUIVER *v.²* + -ING¹.] The action of the vb.

Quivering (kwi·vəriŋ), *ppl. a.* [-ING².]

Quiveringly (kwi·vəriŋli), *adv.* [f. prec. + -LY².]

†**Quiverly,** *adv. Obs.* [f. QUIVER *a.* + -LY².] Actively, quickly, smartly.

Quixote (kwi·ksōt), *sb.* Also 7 -ot, 8 -iot, 9 -ote. [The name of the hero of Cervantes' romance *Don Quixote*.]

Quixotic (kwiksɔ·tik), *a.* [f. QUIXOTE + -IC.]

Quixotism (kwi·ksōtiz'm). [f. QUIXOTE + -ISM.]

Quiz (kwiz), *sb.¹* dial. and U.S. [Prob. transferred use of prec., by association with *question* or *inquisitive.*]

Quiz (kwiz), *sb.²* Also 8 *quis.* [Of obscure origin.]

Quizzable, *a.* [f. QUIZ *v.* + -ABLE.]

Quixotry (kwi·ksōtri). Also 8 *-ery.* [f. QUIXOTE + -RY.]

Quiz (kwiz), *v.¹* [f. QUIZ *sb.²*]

Quiz (kwiz), *v.²* [Cf. QUIZ *sb.¹*]

Quizzer (kwi·zər). [f. QUIZ *v.* + -ER¹.]

Quizzical (kwi·zikəl), *a.* [f. QUIZ *sb.²* + -ICAL.]

Quizzicality (kwizikæ·liti). [f. prec. + -ITY.]

Quizzically (kwi·zikəli), *adv.* [f. QUIZZICAL + -LY².]

Quizzification. [f. QUIZZIFY + -FICATION.]

Quizzify (kwi·zifəi), *v. rare⁻¹.* [f. QUIZ + -FY.]

Quizziness, *rare⁻¹.* [f. QUIZZY + -NESS.]

Quizzing (kwi·ziŋ), *ppl. a.* [f. QUIZ *v.* + -ING².]

Quizzing, *vbl. sb.* [f. QUIZ *v.* + -ING¹.]

Quizzing-glass. [f. QUIZZING *vbl. sb.*]

Quizzing-glass. *rare.*

Quizzism (kwi·ziz'm), *rare.* [f. QUIZ *sb.²* + -ISM.]

Quizzity, *rare⁻¹.* [f. QUIZ *sb.²* + -ITY.] Oddity.

Quizzy (kwi·zi), *a.* [f. QUIZ *sb.²* + -Y¹.]

Quo. *dial.* variant of QUOTH.

†**Quoad** (kwō·æd), *adv.* [L., 'as far as,' as much as.]

Quirable, *a. rare.* [f. QUIRE *v.²* + -ABLE.]

Quod (kwɒd), *sb.* slang. Also var. *quad.* A prison.

Quod (kwɒd), *v.* [f. QUOD *sb.*] *trans.* To put in prison.

Quod, Quod-a, obs. var. QUOTH, QUOTHA.

Quodam, obs. var. QUONDAM.

Quoddlibetarian. [L.]

Quodling, obs. form of CODLING.

Quods, var. CODS. [Cf. *Od's death,* etc.]

Quodlibet (kwɒ·dlibet). Also 6 *quot-.* [a. med.L. *quodlibet* a subtle or captious question in scholastic disputation, f. L. *quod* what + *libet* it pleases.]

Quodlibetic (kwɒdlibe·tik), *a.* [f. prec. + -IC.]

Quodlibetical (kwɒdlibe·tikəl), *a.* [f. next + -AL.]

Quodlibetically, *adv.* [f. prec. + -LY².]

Quoin (kwɔin), *sb.* [var. of COIN *sb.*]

1. Any question in philosophy or theology proposed as an exercise in argument or disputation.

Quoit (kwɔit), *sb.* Forms: 6 *coyte,* 6–8 *quoyte,* 7 *quoite,* 7– *quoit.*

Quoin. The key-stone, or any one of the wedge-shaped stones (voussoirs) of an arch. *rare.*

Quoin (koin), *v.* [See prec. and COIN *v.*]

Quoining, *vbl. sb.*

Quoit (koit, kwoit), *sb.* Forms: 4–7 coyte, quayt–, quoyte, quaite, quoit–.

Quoiting, *vbl. sb.*

Quoiter.

Quojo.

Qnoll (kwōl). [Aboriginal name. *(Dasyurus macrurus)* of Australia.]

†**Qnominus, quo minus.** [L.]

‖**Quomodo** (kwǒ·mŏdǒ), quo modo.

†**Quomodocunque,** *adv.*

Quondam (kwǫ·ndæm), *adv., sb.,* and *a.*

Quoniam (kwǒ·niæm), *sb.*

Quook, obs. *pa. t.* of QUAKE.

Quop (kwǫp), *v.* Obs. exc. *dial.*

Quor, Quore, obs. variants of WHERE, CORE.

Quorister, obs. form of CHORISTER.

‖**Quorum** (kwō·rǫm). [L.]

‖**Quotable** (kwō·tǎb'l), *a.* [QUOTE *v.* + -ABLE.]

Quotableness, Quotableness.

‖**Quotal,** *a.* [L. *quot* + -a (-ary).]

Quote (kwōut), *sb.* Obs. rare. Also 5 quoote, 6 cote, 7 coat.

Quotation (kwotēi·ʃǎn).

Quote (kwōut), *v.* [QUOTE *v.*]

Quoter.

Quoth (kwōþ), *v.*

Quotennial, *a. rare⁻¹.* [L. *quotennis.*]

Quoter (kwōu·tǎr). One who quotes.

†**Quoth-dial,** *a.* Obs. rare⁻¹.

Quoth (kwōþ), *v. (pa. t.)* Said.

†**Quotha** (kwōu·þǎ), *interj.*

Quotidian (kwotī·diǎn), *a.* and *sb.*

Quotient (kwōu·ʃent). Forms: 5 quotient, 5–6 quotiente, 6 (7 quocient).

Quotiety, *sb.* Obs. rare⁻¹.

Quotity (kwō·titi), *rare.* [a. F. *quotité.*]

Quotum, *sb.*

Quotity, *sb.*

Quotidiary, *adv. rare.*

Quotidianary, *a.* Obs. rare⁻¹.

Quotidianly, *adv. rare.* [+ -LY².] Daily.

Quo warranto. A King's Bench writ formerly in use.

Qu-, freq. ME. (esp. northern) var. of QU- (and WH-).

Quowka, Sc. var. of QUAKE *v.*

Quoy, Sc. variant of QUEY, heifer.

Quoy-duck, obs. form of COY-DUCK.

Quoyl, obs. form of COIL.

Quoyn, Quoyne, Quoyntaunce, obs. ff. QUOIN, etc.

Quoyqueth, Quoyt, obs. ff. QUOIT.

Quoyn, obs. form of COIN *sb.*

Quuok, obs. *pa. t.* QUAKE *v.*

Quuqu, obs. *pa. t.* QUAKE *v.*

Quy-, a common ME. variant of QUI-.

Quy, obs. form of QUEY.

Qv-, occasional ME. var. of QU- and WH-.

Qv-, abbrev. of QUERY.

R.

R (ɑ̄ɹ), the eighteenth letter of the modern and seventeenth of the ancient Roman alphabet, is derived through early Greek Ρ, P from the Phoenician 𐤓, representing the twentieth letter of the early Semitic alphabet. In general the character denotes an open voiced consonant in the formation of which the point of the tongue approaches the palate a little way behind the teeth; in many languages this is accompanied by a vibration of the tongue, in which case the *r* is said to be 'trilled'. This trill is almost or altogether absent in the *r* of modern standard English, which moreover retains its consonantal value only when it precedes a vowel; in other positions it has been vocalized to an ə-sound, in this Dictionary denoted by (ɹ), and even this is entirely lost after certain vowels. The earlier history of these sounds is somewhat obscure, as scholars differ in their views as to the formation of *r* in OE. times. In Scotland *r* is still strongly trilled in all positions, and other varieties of the sound are characteristic of certain districts, as the burred *r* of Northumberland and the reverted *r* of the south-west. By southern speakers *r* is frequently introduced in hiatus, esp. in the phrase *the idea(r) of*; in vulgar speech it is heard even in such forms as *draw(r)ing*.

In all periods of English, *r* has exercised a marked effect upon a preceding vowel. In OE., *e* and *a* before *r* + consonant became *eo*, *ea*, as in *steorfan* starve, *deorc* dark, *heorte* heart, *eorþe* earth; *hearm* harm, *wearp* warp. In late ME. and early mod.E. *er* usually became *ar*, *ear*, as in (*sterve*) starve, (*derk*) dark; (*herte*) heart, (*erthe*) earth, the date and extent of the change varying in different dialects. In a few cases (as *clerk*, *sergeant*, *Derby*) the spelling with *er* has been retained, while *ar* (ɑ̄ɹ) is pronounced. In mod.E. (prob. from about 1650) *e* (or *ea*) and *i* before *r* in close syllables have fallen together in one obscure vowel (ɜ̄), as in *berth*, *birth* (bɜ̄ɹþ), *dearth* (dɜ̄ɹþ), *dirt* (dɜ̄ɹt), often not distinguished from (ɒ̄), as in *bur* (bɒ̄ɹ), *burn* (bɒ̄ɹn). The vowel-lengthening exemplified in these words is common to all cases in which *r* is not followed by a vowel, as *far* (fɑ̄ɹ), *farm* (fɑ̄ɹm), *for* (fǭɹ), *horse* (hǭɹs). The effect of *r* is also seen in the use of open vowels instead of the normal close ones, as in *care* (kēᵊɹ), *here* (hīᵊɹ), *moor* (mūᵊɹ), *floor* (flōᵊɹ). In a few words the vowel has been affected by a preceding *r*, as in *break* (brēⁱk), *great* (grēⁱt), *broad* (brǭd).

OE. *r* usually represents Germanic *r*, but in some cases takes the place of Germ. *z* (Goth. *z* or *s*), as in *éare* ear (Goth. *ausô*), *mára* more (Goth. *maiza*), *hord* hoard (Goth. *huzd*); hence the variation in verbal forms, as *léosan*, *loren*; *céosan*, *coren*. It was rarely dropped (as in *specan* to speak, for usual *sprecan*); but metathesis was frequent, and many of the forms resulting from this have been retained in the later language, as *beornan* to burn, *berstan* to burst, *hors* horse, *fryhtu* fright, North. *þirda* third. In some Scottish texts of the 15–16th c. there is a similar tendency to transpose *r* (as *trage* targe, *rehress* rehearse, *scruge* scourge), and it is sometimes neglected in rimes (as *large : age*).

Among the native words beginning with *r* in modern Eng. are a certain number which in OE. have initial *hr-*, as *hring* ring, *hræfn* raven, *hréod* reed. This *h* was usually written down to the close of the OE. period, but had probably been dropped in speech at a somewhat earlier date; in the northern Gospels it is often erroneously prefixed, as in *hræst* rest, *hreafere* reaver, *hrioppa* reap. On the other hand, *w* before *r* was retained so late (being still pronounced in some Scottish dialects) that confusion between *wr-* and *r-* is comparatively rare, chiefly occurring with the words *rack*, *wrack*, and *rap*, *wrap*.

I. 1. Illustrations of the literary use of the letter or its name.

c 1000 ÆLFRIC *Gram.* iii. (Z.) 6 *Semivocales* syndon seofan: ..*r*, *s*, *x*. ? 1460 in *Archæologia* (1842) XXIX. 331 There was an V and thre arres to-gydre. c 1460 *Pol. Rel. & L. Poems* 2, iij ares for iij Richardes þat bene of noble fames. 1530 PALSGR. 34, R in the frenche tonge shalbe sounded as he is in latyn without any exception. 1599 H. BUTTES *Dyets drie Dinner* M viij b, Oysters.. in those Moneths that have the letter R. in their names. 1636 B. JONSON *Eng. Gram.* (1640) 47, R is the Dogs Letter and hurreth in the sound. 1727–41 CHAMBERS *Cycl.* s.v., The Hebrews allow the *r* the privilege of a guttural; that is, they never double it. a 1854 CAROLINE B. SOUTHEY *Poet. Wks.* (1867) 21, R's whose lower limbs Beyond the upper bulged unseemly out. 1888 *Cornh. Mag.* Oct. 365 The letter R is not yet menaced with extinction in Washington.

b. *The 'r' months*: Those months in the name of which an *r* occurs (September to April), during which oysters are in season (cf. quot. 1599 above). So also *r-less month*.

1764 CHESTERF. *Lett.* cccxlvi, Here is no domestic news of changes and chances in the political world, which, like oysters, are only in season in the R months, when the Parliament sits. 1856 LOWELL *Lett.* (1894) I. iv. 301, I don't believe even the oysters found out what r-less month it was. 1888 *Pall Mall G.* 21 Sept. 7/2 The 'r' months have, however, opened at Brussels in the usual way; the Zeeland and Ostend oysters..made their welcome appearance.

2. Used to denote serial order, as 'R Battery', 'MS. R', etc., or as a symbol of some thing or person, a point in a diagram, etc.

II. Abbreviations.

1. Of Latin words or phrases. **a.** † R (in mediæval notation) = 80. R. = *rex* king, *regina* queen. In medical prescriptions: R, ℞ = *recipe* take. **b.** R.I.P. = *requiescat in pace*, 'may he (or she) rest in peace'; or *requiescant in pace*, 'may they rest in peace'.

2. Of English words and phrases: **a.** R. = Rabbi, radius, Railway, Reaumur, † rest, right, River, † rogue, Royal, *Naut.* run (see quots. 1706 and 1867), rupee; also various proper names, as Richard, Robert, etc.; r (*Naut.* in log-book) = rain; *r* = radius vector. R.A. = Rear Admiral, Royal Academy or Academician, (*Astron.*) right ascension; R.C. = Roman Catholic; R.H. = Royal Highness; R.M. = Resident Magistrate; R.N. = Royal Navy; R.S. = Royal Society; R.V. = Revised Version (of the Bible); R.W. = Right Worthy or Worshipful. Also ℟ = response (to a versicle.)

c 1330 R. BRUNNE *Chron.* (1810) 156 To mak certeyn partie, R. a quitance toke. 1588 J. MELLIS *Briefe Instr.* Dvj, Set the same down..on this Creditor side..with an R before it, signifying rest. 1625 MASSINGER *New Way* IV. ii, My hand hissing..with the letter R printed upon it. 1654 SIR E. NICHOLAS in *N. Papers* (Camden) II. 48 Beseech her R.H. that nothing that comes from me may in any kinde be taken notice. 1662 STILLINGFL. *Orig. Sacr.* II. iv. § 3 R. Solomon makes this hill to be Kirjath-jearim. 1676 GLANVILL *Ess. Philos. & Relig.* title-p., Joseph Glanvill.. Fellow of the R.S. 1706 *Lond. Gaz.* No. 4216/3 All such Seamen.., that are made Run, for not repairing to their Duty, shall have their R's taken off. 1813 *Examiner* 17 May 316/1 Far above the mediocrity of most of our R.A.'s. 1819 *Pantologia* X. F j b, Then the radius vector *r* is expressed by either of the following formulæ. 1867 SMYTH *Sailor's Word-bk.*, R. in the muster-book means run, and is placed against those who have deserted, or missed three musters. 1881 *Athenæum* 5 Nov. 603/2 The year of his R.A.-ship. 1896 *Expositor* Aug. 126 Here the R.V... has rightly translated.

b. *The three R's*: Reading, (W)riting, (A)rithmetic. See also quots. 1879, 1892.

The phrase is said to have originated with Sir W. Curtis (1752–1829) who proposed it as a toast.

1828 *Mirror* V. 75/1 The three R's—Reading, Writing, and Rithmetic. 1864 *Reader* 30 Jan. 134 Middle-class schools, in which education is pushed beyond the three 'R's'. 1879 *Athenæum* 5 Apr. 431/1 Romanism, Ritualism, and Rationalism, the three 'r's' of theological controversy. 1892 *Academy* 31 Dec. 602/3 Rhetoric, reflexion, and repetition—those three R.s of the inexperienced bookmaker.

3. R.S.V.P., abbrev. of the French phrase *répondez s'il vous plaît*, 'reply, if you please': commonly placed in one of the corners of invitation-cards. Also *attrib.*

a 1845 BARHAM *Ingol. Leg.* III. *House Warming* 289 Quadrilles in the afternoon, R.S.V.P. 1883 ANNIE THOMAS *Mod. Housew.* 92 Attend strictly to the R.S.V.P. corner of your 'at home' cards.

† Ra. *Sc. Obs.* Also 6 **rae, raye.** [= ON. *rá* (Da. and Sw. *rå*), Du. *ra* (Kilian *rae*, *rha*, *rah*), MLG. *rå*, MHG. *rahe* (G. *rahe*, *raa*):—Comm. Teut. **rahâ* pole, stake. In Sc. prob. adopted from ON., or Du.] A sail-yard.

1494 *Accts. Ld. High Treasurer Scot.* (1877) I. 253 Ane gret mast, ane ra. *Ibid.*, Thir rais and the takling. 1513 DOUGLAS *Æneis* v. xiv. 8 Thai .. Set in a fang, and threw the ra abak. 1566 KNOX *Hist. Ref.* (1846) I. 109 Our Schotish schippis war stayed, the sayles tackin from thare rayes. 1589 *Munim. Irvine* (1890) I. 76 To fens and arreist the same schipis..and take the saillis fra the rais.

Ra, obs. f. RAW; obs. north. f. ROE. **Raack**, obs. f. RACK *sb.*⁷ **Raad**, var. RAD *a.*² *Obs.* **Raaf**, obs. f. RAFF *sb.*³ **Raak**, obs. f. RAKE *sb.*¹

Raas(e, obs. forms of RACE *sb.*¹, RASE *v.*¹

Rab¹ (ræb). [ad. F. *rabot* in same sense; cf. RABBIT *sb.*³] A wooden beater, formed like a crutch, used for mixing the ingredients of mortar.

a 1825 FORBY *Voc. E. Anglia.* 1860 WORCESTER cites LEONARD. 1875 KNIGHT *Dict. Mech.* 1850/1.

Rab². *dial.* = RAD *sb.*² (q.v.).

1830 LOUDON *Cottage Arch.* § 840 Cob is used for filling in the framework, which is previously lathed with stout slit oak... This sort of work is called rab and dab.

† Ra·band. *Sc. Obs.* Also rai-. [f. RA + BAND: cf. Da. and Sw. *råband*, Du. *raband* (Kilian *raeband*), G. *rah-*, *raaband*, and ON. *rábenda* to bend a sail.] A roband or robbin.

1513 DOUGLAS *Æneis* III. iv. 110 Do lows the rabandis, and lat doun the sail. 1549 *Compl. Scot.* vi. 40 Cut the raibandis, and lat the mane sail and top sail fal.

Rabanet, variant of RABINET.

Rabarber, obs. form of RHUBARB.

† Rabat¹. *Obs. rare*⁻⁰. Also 5 **rabet.** [a. F. *rabot* = Pg. *rabôte*.] A carpenter's plane.

c 1440 *Promp. Parv.* 421/2 *Rabet*, yryne tool of carpentrye, *runcina*. 1530 PALSGR. 260/1 Rabat an yrone for a carpentar, *rabot*. 1572 HULOET, *Rabat*, a playne that carpenters vse, *runcina*.

† Rabat². *Sc. Obs. rare.* Also 6 **rabbat.** [a. F. *rabat* a turned-down collar.] = REBATO.

(Recent Dicts. give *rabat* in senses of the mod. F. word.)

1578 *Inv. R. Wardr.* (1815) 231 Huidis quaiffis collaris rabattis. *Ibid.* 234 Ane rabbat of hollane claith.

Rabat, obs. form of RABBET *sb.*

† Rabate, *sb. Obs. rare.* Also **rabbate.** [a. OF. *rabat*, *rabbat* sb. to *rabattre*: see next, and cf. REBATE *sb.*] Diminution; lessening, drawing in.

1589 PUTTENHAM *Eng. Poesie* II. xi[i]. (Arb.) 109 In his altitude he wil require diuers rabates to hold so many sizes of meetres. *Ibid.* III. xi. 173 Your figures of rabbate be as many (as the 'figures of addition'.)

† Rabate, *v. Obs.* Also 6 **rabbate.** [a. F. *rabattre* to beat down, etc.; the more usual form in Eng. is *rebate*.] = REBATE *v.* in various senses.

1489 *Sc. Acts Jas. IV* (1814) 222 And samekle..to be defalkit and Rabatit in þe price of þe said siluer. 1530 PALSGR. 677/2, I rabate a porcyon out of a great somme. 1585 A. POULET *Letter-bk.* (1874) 69 Rabating so many of my number.. cannot be any way chargeable. 1632 GUILLIM *Heraldry* III. xx. (ed. 3) 228 She [a Hawk] is sayd to Rabate, when by the motion of the bearers hand she recouerth the fist.

Hence † **Rabated** *ppl. a.*; † **Rabating** *vbl. sb.*

1589 PUTTENHAM *Eng. Poesie* III. xi. (Arb.) 173 Sometimes by adding sometimes by rabbating of a sillable or letter. *Ibid.* xxv. 310 The full and emptie euen, extant, rabbated, hollow, or..other figure and passion of quantitie.

Rabate, obs. form of RABBET *sb.* and *v.*

Rabatine. *rare*⁻¹. [app. f. F. *rabat* RABAT² + -INE.] A low collar.

1821 SCOTT *Kenilw.* xxiii, Reform..that precise ruff of thine for an open rabatine of lace and cut work.

Rabato, variant of REBATO *Obs.*

† Rabattued, *a. Obs. rare*⁻¹. [f. F. *rabattu* (pa. pple. of *rabattre* RABATE) + -ED.] Blunted.

1562 J. SHUTE tr. *Cambini's Turk. Wars* 1 b, Scanderbeg .. delighted .. with his companiones to use the launce, and the rabattued sworde.

Rabbat, Rabbate, varr. RABAT², RABATE. *Obs.*

Rabbatte, obs. form of RABBIT *sb.*¹

Rabbenet, obs. form of RABINET.

Rabbet (ræ·bėt), *sb.* Forms: 5 **rabit**, 5–8 **rabet**, 6 **rabat(e, -att, -ett, rabbott-**, 8–9 **rabbit**, 7– **rabbet.** See also REBATE. [a. OF. *rabat*, *rabbat* the act of beating down, a check, abatement in price, recess in a wall, etc., sb. from *rabattre* to beat back or down: see REBATE *v.*]

I. 1. a. A channel, groove, or slot (usually of rectangular section) cut along the edge or face of a piece (or surface) of wood, stone, etc., and intended to receive the edge or end of another piece or pieces, or a tongue specially wrought on these to fit the groove. **b.** A rectangular recess made along a projecting angle or arris.

Both forms are extensively used in Carpentry in joining or framing wood, the two pieces being commonly either in the same plane or at right angles to each other. In a *double rabbet* (b) the shoulder on one piece fits into the rabbet of the other. In Masonry, a rabbet (b) is often made to receive the edge of a door, window, etc.; in picture-frames the rabbet receives the edges of the glass.

1404 [see *rabbet-stock* in 3]. c 1425 WYNTOUN *Cron.* III. ii. 332 Thare he made than rak & rak Quhyll conyhe and rabet bath he brak. c 1440 *Promp. Parv.* 421/2 Rabet, in a werke of carpentrye, *runctura*, *incastratura*. 1538 LELAND *Itin.* I. 55 By pulling one or all wold cum downe, briste high in rabettes, and serve for Deskes. 1593–4 in Swayne *Sarum Church-w. Acc.* (1896) 299 Yotting in of the hookes and hewinge of the Rabbottes. 1663 GERBIER *Counsel* 68 Oaken Windows with a double Rabet. 1711 W. SUTHERLAND *Shipbuild. Assist.* 46 Cut the Rabbit of the Keel, Stem and Stern-post the exact Bigness of your Plank. 1793 SMEATON *Edystone L.* § 51 The windows, shutters and doors .. falling into a rabbet, when shut, their outside formed a part of the general surface. 1830 HEDDERWICK *Marine Arch.* 257 The rabbet is cut out in form of a V, having its breadth equal to the thickness of the garboard-plank. 1870 H. MEADE *New Zealand* 324 The parts are joined by scarfing with a bevelled rabbet at the juncture.

2. † **a.** A tongue to fit into a groove. *Obs.* **b.** One of the sides of a rabbet made in an arris; a shoulder, a ledge.

1678 MOXON *Mech. Exerc.* I. 103 Upon this Rabbet rides a Block with a Groove in its under side .. made fit to receive the Rabbet on the Planck. 1728 DESAGULIERS in *Phil. Trans.* XXXV. 606 A square Hole .. to receive a Piece .. shutting close with a Rabbet or Shoulder. 1826 KIRBY & SP. *Entomol.* I. IV. 544 So as to form a cavity all round of a proper width to closely receive the rabbet. 1867 J. HOGG *Microsc.* I. iii. 188 The dotted ring shows the rabbet on which the centre-piece rests.

3. *attrib.*, as *rabbet-iron*, *-joint*, *measure*, *-plane*, *-saw*, † *-stock*; **rabbet-head** (see quot.).

1830 LOUDON *Cottage Arch.* § 282 The *rabbet-head of a window is a Scotch term for what in England is called the reveal of a window. 1552 HULOET s.v. *Rabat*, *Runcina* is the *rabet iron. 1832 WEBSTER, *Rabbeted*, united by a *rabbet joint. 1838 J. BRITTON *Dict. Archit.* 387 The junction thus effected being called a rabbet-joint. 1886 *Pall Mall G.* 26 July 4/2 A frame whose '*rabbet' measure is 96 by 72 inches. 1678 MOXON *Mech. Exerc.* I. 67 The *Rabbet-plain ..is to cut part of the upper edge of a Board..square down into the Board. 1881 YOUNG *Every man his own Mechanic* 92 The rabbet or rebate plane. 1875 KNIGHT *Dict. Mech.* 1850/1 *Rabbet-saw. 1404 *Durham Acc. Rolls* (Surtees) I. 396, j *rabitstoke cum ij screws. 1572, 1688 [see CLAVESTOCK].

II. † **4.** *Fencing.* The act of beating down an opponent's weapon. *Obs. rare*⁻¹.

c 1450 *Fencing with two handed Sword* in *Rel. Ant.* I. 309 Thy stoppis, thy foynys .. Thy spryngys, thy quarters, thy rabetis also.

5. An elastic beam fixed so as to give a rebound to a large fixed hammer; a spring-pole.

1825 J. NICHOLSON *Operat. Mechanic* 335 The hammer in its ascent strikes against this beam, called the rabbit, which by its elasticity reacts upon the hammer [etc.]. 1831 J. HOLLAND *Manuf. Metal* I. 241 An elastic rabbet or spring pole to give a rebound to the hammer. 1852 MORFIT *Tanning & Currying* (1853) 231 Two vertical pieces, supporting horizontally a rabbit, or wooden spring.

Rabbet (ræ·bėt), *v.* Forms: 4, 8 **rabit**, 5 **rabat**, **-yt**, 5–9 **rabet**, (7 **-ett**), 6 **rabate**, **rabbat**, **-ott**, **-itt**, 8 **rabbit**, 7– **rabbet.** [app. f. RABBET *sb.*, but found earlier than this in the vbl. sb. *rabityng* (Wyclif), the second vowel of which makes direct adoption of F. *rabattre* unlikely.]

1. *trans.* To join or fix by means of a rabbet or rabbets. Also with *in*.

1565 COOPER *Thesaurus*, *Trabes compactiles*,.. Joygned or rabbated one within the other. 1620 BEST *Farm. Bks.* (Surtees) 153 Hee is..to sawe the rayles and postes, and sett them in a groundsell, and rabbitt them in to the rayle above. 1693 EVELYN *De La Quint. Compl. Gard.* II. *Orange-Trees* ii. 5 A double Cloison made of Boards well Rabetted. 1829 *Nat. Philos.* I. *Heat* x. 60 (U. K. S.) It should have a wooden cover, rabbeted in.

2. To form a rabbet in; to provide with a rabbet; to cut *away* or *down* as in making a rabbet.

1572 HULOET, To rabate or make suche chaumfreyes in any thing. 1667 PRIMATT *City & C. Build.* 63 Suppose that a Window hath four lights, and double rabbetted for Ornament. 1679 MOXON *Mech. Exerc.* I. 148 The Window Frame hath every one of its Lights rabbetted on its outside about half an Inch into the Frame. 1711 W. SUTHERLAND *Shipbuild. Assist.* 25 When that is trim'd, scarf'd, and rabbited, mind to set it very streight. 1794 W. FELTON *Carriages* (1801) I. 12 The middle rails are..rabbetted on the top for the boarding or pannels. 1877 COUES & ALLEN *N. Amer. Rod.* 229 The general face is rabbeted down externally. *Ibid.* 532 The outer portion is rabbeted away.

3. *intr.* To join *on* or lap *over* by means of a rabbet.

c 1850 *Rudim. Navig.* (Weale) 101 The upper piece rabbeting on the lower piece. *Ibid.* 119 It rabbets over the ends of the deals.

Rabbet, obs. form of RABBIT *sb.*¹

Rabbeted (ræ·bėtėd), *ppl. a.* [f. RABBET *v.*] In which a rabbet is cut.

1797 *Monthly Mag.* III. 145 The door shuts without noise, by means of a spring affixed in the rabitted jamb. c 1850 *Rudim. Navig.* (Weale) 101 Built with rabbeted or ciphered plank. 1869 SIR E. REED *Shipbuild.* ii. 19 The..steam-ship 'Persia'..has also a solid rabbeted keel.

Rabbeting (ræ·bėtiŋ), *vbl. sb.* [f. RABBET *v.* + -ING¹.] The process of grooving boards, etc. by cutting rabbets, or of fitting rabbeted boards together; also the groove or rabbeted portion of such boards.

1382 WYCLIF *Exod.* xxxvi. 22 Two rabitynges weren bi eche tables, that the tone to that other myȝt be ioyned. c 1440 *Promp. Parv.* 421/2 Rabetynge to-gedyr of ij. bordys, *supra in* knyttynge, or ioynynge. 1463 *Mann. & Househ. Exp.* (Roxb.) 193 Settyng in of hedys of pypys and barells, and rabating of xl. ber pypys. 1530 PALSGR. 260/1 Rabettyng of bordes, *rabetture*. 1658 PHILLIPS, *Rabbetings*, a term in Navigation, the letting in of the planks to the keel. 1678 MOXON *Mech. Exerc.* I. 67 When two Boards are thus lapped on the edges over one another, this lapping over is called Rabbetting. 1769 FALCONER *Dict. Marine* (1776), *Assembler*, to unite the several pieces of a ship, as by rabbeting, scarfing, scoring, tenanting, &c. 1869 SIR E. REED *Shipbuild.* iii. 48 The rabbeting has now been almost universally dispensed with.

Rabbett(e, obs. forms of RABBET, RABBIT.

Rabbi (ræ·bəi, ræ·bi), *sb.* Forms: 4–5 **rabi**, 4–6 **raby**, 5 **rabe**, 7 **rabbie**, 8 **rabby**, 6– **rabbi.** [a. (orig. through L. *rabbi*, Gr. ῥαββί) Heb. רבי *rabbī* 'my master', f. רב *rabh* master, with pronominal suffix. Cf. OF. *rabi*, *rabbi* (mod.F. *rabbin*).]

1. A title of respect (in use since the first century B.C.) given by the Jews to doctors of the law.

a. As a form of address. (In English use only in translations or echoes of N.T. passages.)

c 1000 *Ags. Gosp.* John i. 38 Hi cwædon to him 'rabbi', þæt is ȝecweden & ȝereht lareow, 'hwar eardast þu?' a 1300 *Cursor M.* 15766 Iudas .. lepe him to, 'Aue rabi', coth he. 1377 LANGL. *P. Pl.* B. XVIII. 50 'Aue, rabby!' quod that ribaude, and threw redes at hym. c 1386 CHAUCER *Sompn. T.* 479 God liketh nat that Raby men vs calle. c 1450 HOLLAND *Howlat* 94 Befor the Pape .. on kneis he fell; said 'Aue Raby'. 1526 TINDALE *Matt.* xxiii. 8 Ye shall not suffre youre selves to be called Rabi. a 1550 *Image Hypocr.* I. 172 in *Skelton's Wks.* (1843) II. 416/1 Wher they may haue metinge With lordes and with ladyes, To be called Rabyes. 1611 BIBLE *John* i. 38 They said vnto him, Rabbi, (which is to say being interpreted, Master) where dwellest thou?

b. Prefixed to personal names.

1340 HAMPOLE *Pr. Consc.* 7685 Raby Moyses says alle þis. 1387 TREVISA *Higden* (Rolls) III. 365 Avicenna preyseþ hym wel..and Raby Moyses. 1541 R. COPLAND *Guydon's Quest. Chirurg.* Y iij b, Rabymoyses..approued water dystylled of a leane gotes mylke. 1587 GOLDING *De Mornay* xxix. 470 The same man whom .. the Chronicle of the Iewes calleth Rabbi Iohanan. 1677 HALE *Prim. Orig. Mank.* III. vii. 285 The Blew and Red Men of Rabbi Elcha, that came out of the Mountains of Armenia. 1727–41 CHAMBERS *Cycl.* s.v., Rabbi Juda is said to have composed the Mischna...in the IId century. 1838 *Penny Cycl.* XII. 92/2 The Jerusalem Talmud appears to have been compiled..by Rabbi Jochonan.

2. A Jewish doctor of the law. In mod. Jewish use properly applied only to one who is authorized by ordination to deal with questions of law and ritual, and to perform certain functions.

When used in pl. as the designation of a class (*the rabbis*), the reference is usually to those Jewish teachers or writers who have more commonly been called *rabbins*.

1484 CAXTON *Fables of Alfonce* i, A Rabe of Lucanye sayd to his sone in this maner. 1599 SANDYS *Europæ Spec.* (1632) 226 Each Synagogue hath his Rabbi, to expound their Law. 1641 MILTON *Animadv.* ii. Wks. (1851) 207 The gowned Rabbies..were of opinion that hee was a friend of Beelzebub. 1688 R. HOLME *Armoury* III. 221/1 The Jews..are Married in the open Aire, either in the Streets or Gardens, by their Rabbies. 1788 GIBBON *Decl. & F.* l. (ed. Milman) V. 22 The dreams and traditions of the Jewish rabbis. 1838 LYTTON *Leila* IV. v, I have been summoned into the presence of their chief rabbi. 1838 *Penny Cycl.* XII. 92/2 The Rabbis of Tiberias and Babylon wrote numerous commentaries upon it [the Mishna]. 1897 *Allbutt's Syst. Med.* II. 391 The early and almost universal seizures of medical officers, of the clergy and rabbis.

† **b.** *transf.* One whose learning, authority, or office is comparable to that of a Jewish rabbi. (Freq. contemptuous.) *Obs.*

1553 BALE *Gardiner's 'De vera Obed.'* To Rdr. A vij b, Yf these ruffling rabbies in theyr Sermons & aduised Orationes said and wrote the truthe. 1629 L. OWEN *Spec. Jesuit.* 1 These great Rabbies that call themselues Iesuites. 1647 N. BACON *Disc. Govt. Eng.* I. ii. (1739) 3 The deep obligement of the People unto these their Rabbies [the Druids]. 1691 WOOD *Ath. Oxon.* II. 175 This book.. pusled the Presbyterian Rabbies for a time.

3. *Comb.*, as *Rabbi-like* adj.

1611 COTGR., *Rabinique*, Rabbie-like, of the Rabbies.

Hence † **Ra·bbi** *v. trans.*, to call 'Rabbi'. *Obs.*

1583 STUBBES *Anat. Abus.* I. K iv, He who hath moni enough shalbe rabbied and maistered at euery word.

Rabbin (ræ·bin). Also 6 **rabbyn**, 6–7 **-ine**, 7 **-yne**; 6 **rabyne**, 6–7 **-ine**, 7–8 **-in.** [a. F. *rabbin* or ad. med.L. *rabbīnus*: cf. It. *rabbino*, Pg., Sp. *rabino*.

The source of the *n* in these forms is obscure: it may have originated in pl. forms (*rabbins*, *rabbini*) on the supposition that the pl. of the Heb. word was **rabbin* (cf. *assassin*, *bedouin*, etc.).]

= RABBI 2 (but mainly used in *pl.* to designate the chief Jewish authorities on matters of law and doctrine, the most important of whom flourished between the second and thirteenth centuries of the Christian era).

1579 E. K. in *Spenser's Sheph. Cal.* Gen. Argt., According to the opinion of the best Rabbins..God made the worlde in that Moneth. 1612 BREREWOOD *Lang. & Relig.* 239 The Talmud and Targum..and the books of the latter rabbines. 1676 GLANVILL *Ess. Philos. & Relig.* v. 22 'Tis said in the Talmud, If two Rabbins differ [etc.]. 1741 WATTS *Improv. Mind* I. iv. § 1 For a lawyer to learn Hebrew and read the Rabbins. 1832 W. IRVING *Alhambra* II. 23 Instructed..in the language of birds, by a Jewish Rabbin. 1852 THACKERAY *Esmond* I. xi, All the parsons, cardinals, ministers, muftis, and rabbins in the world.

† **b.** = RABBI 2 b. *Obs.*

1531 ELYOT *Gov.* III. xxv, Some of those Rabines..which in comparison of the sayde noble doctours be..unnethe lettered. 1531 TINDALE *Exp. 1 John* 5 We remayne all blynde generally, as well our great Rabynes..as the lay people. 1606 in *Crt. & Times Jas. I* (1848) I. 65 Their masters and rabbins, the Jesuits. 1632 LITHGOW *Trav.* I. 35 She is both the Spouse, and the mother of God, saith a Rabbin of theirs.

c. Used as *pl.* (see etym. note).

1826 SIR W. DRUMMOND *Orig.* iii. 105 Many of the Rabbin have understood by Baal Berith the Lord of the Covenant. 1860 MOTLEY *Netherl.* (1868) I. v. 146 A match for the doctors, bishops or rabbin of Europe.

Rabbinate (ræ·binět). [f. prec. + -ATE: cf. F. *rabbinat*.] **a.** The office or dignity of a rabbi. **b.** The period during which some one is a rabbi. **c.** *coll.* Rabbis as a body or class.

1702 C. MATHER *Magn. Chr.* IV. ii. § 8. 146 He .. seemed inclinable to the Jewish Rule about the Rabbinate. 1881 *Encycl. Brit.* XIII. 681 Gradually the Talmud .. was abandoned almost entirely to candidates for the rabbinate. 1890 *Jewish Intelligence* Mar. 35 During the Rabbinate of Dr. Adler. 1892 ZANGWILL *Childr. Ghetto* I. 27 The Rabbinate was invited to address the philanthropists.

Rabbindom (ræ·bindəm). [f. as prec. + -DOM.] The rule and government of rabbis; the sphere of rabbinical authority.

1889 BRUCE *Kingd. God* xi. 266 The state of matters which prevailed in Rabbindom. 1890 E. JOHNSON *Rise Christendom* 32 The twelfth century is the great age of early Rabbindom.

Rabbinet, obs. form of RABINET.

Rabbinic (răbi·nik), *a.* and *sb.* [f. RABBIN + -IC, prob. after med. or mod.L. *rabbinic-us*. Cf. F. *rabbinique* (1611), It. *rabbinico*, Pg., Sp. *rabinico*.] **A.** *adj.* = RABBINICAL.

1612 SELDEN *Illustr. Drayton's Poly-olb.* v. 168 The Rabbinic conceit upon the Creation. 1678 CUDWORTH *Intell. Syst.* I. iv. § 30. 469 Those Rabbinick Writers commonly interpret certain places of the Scripture to this sence. a 1711 KEN *Hymnarium* Poet. Wks. 1721 II. 146 To extract from Mud rabbinick Gold. 1879 FARRAR *St. Paul* I. 136 Illiterate men, untrained in the schools of..rabbinic wisdom.

B. *sb.* Rabbinical Hebrew.

1832 in WEBSTER. 1878 *Academy* 606/3 A good means of, and help in, practising Rabbinic.

Rabbinical (răbi·nikăl), *a.* [f. as prec. + -AL.]

1. Of things: Pertaining to, or characteristic of, the rabbins, their learning, writings, etc.

1622 BOYS *Wks.* 4 It is a Rabinicall conceit, that the last Psalme hath thirteene Halleluiahs [etc.]. 1713 ADDISON *Guard.* No. 138 ⁋ 7 A Rabbinical story which has in it the oriental way of thinking. 1779–81 JOHNSON *L. P., Cowley* (1790) I. 37 In the following verses we have a Rabbinical opinion concerning Manna. 1856 STANLEY *Sinai & Pal.* I. i. 34 The grotesqueness and absurdity of the Rabbinical interpretations.

b. *spec.* of the later form of the Hebrew language or character used by the rabbins.

1727–41 CHAMBERS *Cycl.* s. v. *Hebrew*, Modern, or Rabbinical Hebrew character, is a good neat character, formed of the square Hebrew by rounding it. *Ibid.*, The rabbinical Hebrew must be allowed a very copious language. 1817 COLERIDGE *Biog. Lit.* 55 Of the Hebrew..the remainder seemed to be in the Rabbinical dialect.

2. Of persons: Belonging to the class of rabbis or rabbins; resembling a rabbi; occupied with or skilled in rabbinical literature.

1642 MILTON *Apol. Smect.* i. Wks. (1851) 282 The Masoreths and Rabbinicall Scholiasts. 1711 ADDISON *Spect.* No. 221 ⁋ 10 We had a Rabbinical Divine in England. 1826 SYDNEY SMITH *Serm. Charity* Wks. 1859 II. 248/1 A very short..apologue, taken from the Rabbinical writers. 1838–9 HALLAM *Hist. Lit.* II. II. viii. § 45. 349 Hugh Broughton was a deeply learned and rabbinical scholar.

Hence **Rabbi·nically** *adv.*, in a rabbinical manner.

1684 N. S. *Crit. Enq. Edit. Bible* App. 286 Vossius..who so greedily catches at dreams more than Rabbinically. a 1751 BOLINGBROKE *Fragm.* lxi. Wks. 1754 V. 456 If he [the apostle] understood it as Locke did, he reasoned very rabinically. 1833 *New Monthly Mag.* XXXVII. 149 Responding most rabbinically to the serjeant on this knotty matter.

† Ra·bbinish, *a. Obs. rare*⁻¹. = RABBINICAL.

1652 GAULE *Magastrom.* 123 Errors of paganish, rabbinish, and other magicians and astrologers.

Rabbinism (ræ·biniz'm). [f. RABBIN + -ISM: cf. F. *rabbinisme*, Pg., Sp. *rabinismo*.]

1. The teaching or doctrines of the rabbins.

1652 GAULE *Magastrom.* 43 The key of doctorall and magisteriall rabbinismes and cabalismes. 1833 *Blackw. Mag.* XXXIII. 628 Rabbinism has continued full of trivial observances. 1887 *Spectator* 1 Oct. 1307 The history of mediæval rabbinism.

2. A rabbinical expression; a peculiarity of the language of the rabbins. 1832 in WEBSTER.

Rabbinist (ræ·binist). [f. as prec. + -IST: cf. F. *rabbiniste*, It. *rabbinista*, Pg., Sp. *rabinista*.] An adherent or follower of the rabbins; *esp.* among the Jews, one who accepts the teaching of the Talmud and the rabbins, in contrast to the Karaites, who reject tradition.

1599 *Broughton's Lett.* x. 35 You .. shew you are a great Rabbinist. 1609 BP. HALL *Pharis. & Chr.* (1627) 408 At deadly fevd with the other Iewes, which they now call Rabbinists. 1727–41 CHAMBERS *Cycl.* s. v. *Caraite*, If a Caraite would become a rabbinist, he should never be received by the other Jews. 1863 J. G. MURPHY *Comm. Gen.* i. 4 According to the Pharisees and Rabbinists. 1882 FARRAR *Early Chr.* II. 66 *note*, The Rabbinists also felt this.

Hence **Rabbini·stic, Rabbini·stical** *adjs.*

1599 *Broughton's Lett.* vii. 24 Glorying of your reading Rabbinisticall. 1676 *Doctrine of Devils* 174 What-ever besotted Rabbins, and Rabbinistical men prate..I care not. 1888 B. PICK in *Librar. Mag.* Mar. 247 The last Doctors of the Law in the chain of Rabbinistic succession.

Rabbinite (ræ·binəit). [f. as prec. + -ITE¹.] = RABBINIST. 1832 in WEBSTER.

Hence **Rabbini·tic** *a.*

1884 SCHAFF *Encycl. Relig. Knowl.* III. 2095/2 The Pharisaic-rabbinitic system of tradition.

Rabbinize (ræ·binəiz), *v. rare.* [f. as prec. + -IZE: cf. F. *rabbiniser*.]

1. *intr.* To adopt or conform to rabbinism. ? *Obs.*

a 1641, 1652 [see *Rabbinizing* ppl. a.].

2. *trans.* To imbue with rabbinism.

1835 J. HARRIS *Gt. Teacher* (1837) 54 The whole of their law had become rabbinized and overlaid with traditions.

Hence **Ra·bbinized, Ra·bbinizing** *ppl. adjs.*

a 1641 BP. MOUNTAGU *Acts & Mon.* (1642) 110 A man thoroughly enspired with a Rabbinising spirit. 1652 GAULE *Magastrom.* 44 The rabbinizing and Christianizing magicians and astrologers. 1894 BRUCE *Paul's Concept. Chr.* xx. 377 The bane to be dreaded is a rabbinised church.

Ra·bbinship. *rare.* [f. as prec. + -SHIP.] Rabbinate; the personality of a rabbi.

1599 *Broughton's Lett.* ix. 29 How knoweth your Rabbinship that he is no Grecian? 1852 [see RABBISHIP].

Rabbious, variant of RABIOUS.

† Ra·bbish, *a. Obs.* Forms: 4 **rabbisshe**, 5 **rabbishe**, **-isch**, **-yshe**, **rabyssh**, **-sch.** [? f. OF. *rabi*, *rabbi* rabid, raging + -ISH, or directly from the OF. fem. *rabice*, *rabiche*, the ending being associated with *-ish*.] Unruly, turbulent; inconsiderate, rash; rough or precipitate in action.

1387 TREVISA *Higden* (Rolls) VIII. 85 Þan þe rabbisshe peple..up wiþ staves, battes, and stoones. 1398 — *Barth. De P. R.* II. xix. (1495) 45 By rabbyssh foole hardynesse he takyth moore vpon hym than he maye doo. 1494 FABYAN *Chron.* VII. 357 Many of the rabbishe and wylde commoners, were in full purpose to haue defended the cytie.

Hence † **Ra·bbishly** *adv.*; † **Ra·bbishness.** *Obs.*

1387 TREVISA *Higden* (Rolls) VIII. 147 A manere kyndeliche rabbischnesse of wit. c 1400 *Harl. Contin.* ibid. VII. 523 Me wondreth gretlich that ȝe demeth ȝoure bischop so rabbischlich. c 1475 *Partenay* 4690 He..A chambre perceiued, in went rabbishly. 1494 FABYAN *Chron.* v. cxxxvi. 123 The kynge handelyd the body of Seynt Denys so rabbysshely, yᵗ he brake one of his armes.

Rabbiship (ræ·bəi-, ræ·bi₍ʃip). [f. RABBI + -SHIP.] The office of rabbi.

1649 PENN *No Cross* Wks. 1782 II. 21 He came .. to overthrow their rabbyship. 1702 C. MATHER *Magn. Chr.* IV. ii. § 8. 146 The Jewish Rule, about the Rabbinate, Love the Work, but Hate the Rabbiship [ed. 1852 rabbinship]. 1886 *Daily News* 23 Dec. 5/7 His two sons quarrelled for the Rabbi-ship.

Rabbit (ræ·bit), *sb.*¹ Forms: 5–6 **rab(b)ette**, 5–7 **rabet**, 6–8 **rabbet**, (6 **-atte**), 7 **rabytt**, 8 **-it**, 8– **rabbit.** [app. of Northern French origin: cf. Walloon *robett* (Remacle). The primitive seems to occur in Flem. *robbe* (Kilian, De Bo; the latter also gives *ribbe*, *rubbe*), dim. *robbeke(n*; the ultimate etym. is unknown. If F. *rabouillère* (the burrow made by the female rabbit to kindle in) is connected, the ME. *rabet* may be more primitive in form than the Walloon and Flem. words.]

1. A common burrowing rodent of the hare-family (*Leporidæ*), esp. the common European species, *Lepus Cuniculus*, which is naturally of a brownish-grey colour, but in domestication also white, black, or pied. † Orig. applied only to the young animal, the full-grown one being called a CONY.

1398 TREVISA *Barth. De P. R.* XVIII. lxvii. 277 Conynges ..bringeþ forþe many rabettes & multiplieþ ful swiþe. c 1440 *Anc. Cookery* in *Househ. Ord.* (1790) 457 Then take conynges parboyled, or elles rabets, for that are better for a lorde. 1502 *Privy Purse Exp. Eliz. York* (1830) 13 A present of Rabettes and quayles. 1576 TURBERV. *Bk. Venerie* lxiii. 178 The Conie beareth her Rabettes xxx dayes, and then kindeleth. 1607 TOPSELL *Four-f. Beasts* (1658) 89 If two males be put to one female, they fight fiercely; but they will not hurt the rabbets. 1653 WALTON *Angler* viii. 171 Take the flesh of a Rabet or Cat cut smal. 1768 PENNANT *Brit. Zool.* I. 91 Rabbets will breed seven times a year. 1846 J. BAXTER *Libr. Pract. Agric.* (ed. 4) I. 334 The rabbit lives to the age of eight or nine years. 1885 E. CLARK in *Nature* XXXI. 264/1 Large tracts are still honeycombed by the ubiquitous biscacha, a gigantic rabbit.

2. *transf.* **a.** Applied contemptuously to a person. **b.** A shadow resembling the form of a rabbit, cast by the hands upon a wall. **c.** (See quot. 1878.) **d.** (See quot. 1882.) See also WELSH RABBIT.

1597 SHAKS. 2 *Hen. IV*, II. ii. 91 Away, you horson upright Rabbet, away. 1849 *Plymouth Her.* 21 Apr., Shadows .. strong enough for children to make *rabbits* with their fingers upon a wall. 1878 BESANT & RICE *By Celia's Arbour* xxx, Even if you did happen to have a 'rabbit', that is one of the coats lined with white fur. 1882 *Standard* 4 Sept. 6/2 Though somewhat of a 'rabbit', as a horse that runs 'in and out' is sometimes called.

3. *attrib.* and *Comb.* **a.** Simple attributive, as *rabbit-burrow*, *-cleve*, † *-hay*, *-hole*, *-house*, *-hutch*, *-paw*, *-pie*, *-run*, *-skin*, *-stock*, *-warren*.

1752 SIR J. HILL *Hist. Anim.* 423 Deserted *rabbet-burrows, or any other hollows of a like kind. 1883 E. PENNELL-ELMHIRST *Cream Leicestersh.* 420 A gallant fox getting to ground in a rabbit-burrow. 1869 BLACKMORE *Lorna D.* xiii, I went all along on the ridge of the *rabbit-cleve. 1725 BRADLEY *Fam. Dict.* s.v. *Woodcock*, Your Net must be like your *Rabbet-Hays. 1705 BERKELEY *Cave Dunmore* in Fraser *Life* (1871) 507 The earth turned up at the entrance of a *rabbit-hole. 1885 LADY BRASSEY *The Trades* 264 We were assured..that there were no rabbit-holes in the fields. 1839 W. CHAMBERS *Tour Belgium* 77/1 A little garden..containing a *rabbit hutch. 1851 in *Life A. Fonblanque* (1874) 499 A principal ingredient in this *rabbit-pie. 1876 T. HARDY *Ethelberta* xxxiii, Every detail of barrow, path, and *rabbit-run. 1829 RICHARDSON *Zool. Brit. Amer.* I. 218 The winter skins of this animal [the American Hare] are imported by the Hudson's Bay Company under the name of *rabbit-skins. 1848 DICKENS *Dombey* vi, He hung the rabbit-skin over his left arm. 1861 R. F. BURTON *City of Saints* 590 They were dressed in the usual rabbit-skin cape. 1805 DICKSON *Pract. Agric.* II. 1204 *Rabbit-stock demands, on the whole, but little regard. 1775 ASH, **Rabbit-warren*. 1800 MAR. EDGEWORTH *The Will* i, There is that rabbit-warren near Clover Hill. 1890 E. REEVES *Homeward Bound* 295 It is almost as thickly populated as a rabbit warren.

b. Objective and obj. genitive, as *rabbit-breeder*, *-breeding*, *-catcher*, *-chase*, *-chasing* (sb. and adj.), *-coursing*, *-destroyer*, *-fancier*, *-keeper*, *-management*, *-rearer*, *-shooting*, *-trapper*.

1885 *Census Instruct.*, *Rabbit Breeder, Catcher, Destroyer. 1848 MAUNDER *Treas. Nat. Hist.* 560/1 Otherwise .. will *Rabbit-breeding turn out a losing speculation. 1897 *Outing* (U. S.) XXIX. 436/1 A genuine *rabbit-chase. *Ibid.*, The season of *rabbit-chasing begins .. in October. 1895 *Ibid.* XXVI. 426/2 The *rabbit-chasing pups. 1891 *Pall Mall G.* 23 Dec. 6/3 Fond of what they call *rabbit-coursing. 1848 MAUNDER *Treas. Nat. Hist.* 560/1 The ingenuity of *rabbit-fanciers has been shown in the production of various breeds. 1848 *Chambers's Inform. People* I. 628/2 Experienced *rabbit-keepers conceive too frequent breeding to be injurious. 1805 DICKSON *Pract. Agric.* II. 1203 The hazard and uncertainty of *rabbit-management. 1848 *Chambers's Inform. People* I. 629/1 The duty of the *rabbit-rearer. 1819 *Pantologia* X. s.v., An occasional reduction..is found necessary .. in which case *rabbit-shooting is a pleasant diversion. 1888 G. M. FENN *Dick o' the Fens* 326 'Ay', said the *rabbit-trapper.

c. Similative and parasynthetic, as *rabbit-mouth*, *-shoulders*; *rabbit-backed*, *-eared*, *-like* adjs.; *rabbit-wise* adv.

1778 FOOTE *Trip Calais* III. Wks. 1799 II. 370 Red-faced, *rabbet-back'd. 1885 W. J. E. CRANE *Bookbinding for Amateurs* 71 The book will be *rabbit-backed'. 1835–40 HALIBURTON *Clockm.* (1862) 183 That little..*rabbit-eared runt of a pig. 1836–9 TODD *Cycl. Anat.* II. 52/2 The light *rabbit-like hyrax. 1849 *Sk. Nat. Hist.*, *Mammalia* IV. 6 Body short, thick, and rabbit-like. 1833 DISRAELI 29 June in *Corr. w. Sister* (1886) 21 Handsome..but with one great fault, a *rabbit mouth. 1784 J. BARRY in *Lett. Paint.* ii. (1848) 94 The excesses and deficiencies in the human form,.. *rabbit shoulders, pot belly. 1846 MRS. GORE *Eng. Char.* (1852) 139 A starveling cat roasted *rabbit-wise.

4. Special combs.: **rabbit-bandicoot**, a small Australian marsupial of the genus *Peragale*; **rabbit-berry**, the buffalo-berry of N. America; **rabbit-brush**, **-bush**, a common shrub (*Bigelovia graveolens*) of western N. America, giving shelter to jack-rabbits; **rabbit-fish**, the name of several fishes having points of resemblance to a rabbit, as (*a*) the British fishes *Chimæra monstrosa* and the striped rock-gurnard, (*b*) an American fish of the genus *Lagocephalus* with teeth resembling a rabbit's incisors; **rabbit-foot (clover)** = HARE'S-FOOT 1; **rabbit-moth**, a N. American bombycid moth, *Lagoa opercularis*; **rabbit-mouth sucker**, a N. American fish (see quot.); **rabbit-rat** = HAPALOTE; **rabbit-root**, the wild sarsaparilla, *Aralia nudicaulis*; **rabbit-spout** *dial.*, a rabbit-burrow; **rabbit-squirrel**, a S. American chinchilla, esp. *Lagidium Cuvieri*; † **rabbit-starter**, a young rabbit; **rabbit-weed**, a N. American plant.

1832 BISCHOFF *Van Diemen's Land* II. 28 (Morris) There are two kinds, the rat and the *rabbit bandicoot. 1896 SPENCER *Thro' Larapurta Land* 34 The white tips of the tails of the rabbit-bandicoot. 1807 P. GASS *Jrnl.* 30 Small red berries, the Indian name for which in English means *rabbit berries. 1861 R. F. BURTON *City of Saints* 591 An expanse of white sage and large *rabbit-bush. 1848 MAUNDER *Treas. Nat. Hist.* 560/1 **Rabbit-fish*, a local name for the Northern Chimæra, or King of the Herrings. 1880 DAY *Fishes Gt. Brit.* I. 57 Streaked gurnard,..rock gurnard, rabbit fish. 1883 SIMMONDS *Dict. Usef. Animals*, *Rabbit-fish*, a name for *Tetrodon lævigatus*..an American fish. 1884 MILLER *Bot. Dict.*, *Trifolium arvense*, Hare's foot Clover or Trefoil, *Rabbit-foot, of N. America. 1882 JORDAN & GILBERT *Syn. Fishes N. America* 144 *Quassilabia lacera*, Hare-lip Sucker..*Rabbit-mouth Sucker. a 1833 RICHARDSON in Hooker *Flor. Bor. Amer.* I. 274 The Crees use the root of this plant..under the name of..(*Rabbit-root). 1886 *Field* 27 Feb. 266/3 Here they..run him into a *rabbit-spout in the gorse. 1651 WELDON *Crt. Jas. I* 125 Little children did run up and downe the King's Lodgings, like little *Rabbit-starters about their boroughs. 1750 G. HUGHES *Nat. Hist. Barbados* VI. 172 The Thistle, or *Rabbit-weed. 1884 E. INGERSOLL in *Harper's Mag.* Sept. 502/2 Sorry bunch-grass and sad rabbit-weed.

† Ra·bbit, *sb.*² *Obs.* Also **rabit.** [Of obscure origin.] A wooden drinking-vessel.

1685 MERITON *Praise Yorksh. Ale* 1 Stronge Beer in Rabits and cheating penny Cans. a 1700 B. E. *Dict. Cant. Crew*, *Rabbits*, Wooden Kanns to Drink out of, once used on the Roads, now almost laid by.

Ra·bbit, *sb.*³ [a. F. *rabot*.] = RAB¹ (q.v.).

1890– in OGILVIE and later Dicts.

Rabbit (ræ·bit), *v.*¹ [f. RABBIT *sb.*¹]

1. *intr.* To hunt for or catch rabbits. Chiefly in *pres. pple.*

1832 *Meanderings of Mem.* I. 20 Beer never bound him rabbiting again. 1861 HUGHES *Tom Brown at Oxf.* xxx, She liked .. coming to look at them fishing or rabbiting. 1873 G. W. KITCHIN *Hist. France* I. III. viii. 341 This man caught three Flemish students rabbiting in his warren.

2. *intr.* To crowd *together* like rabbits.

1892 *Sunday Mag.* Sept. 602 The common people..rabbit together in miserable warrens.

Rabbit (ræ·bit), *v.*² *Vulgar.* [Prob. a fanciful alteration of *rat* in *od rat* (OD¹), *drat*.] A meaningless word used as an imprecation = DRAT, etc. Also *drabbit*, *od(d) rabbit* (see OD¹ 1 b).

1742 FIELDING *J. Andrews* III. viii, 'Rabbit the fellow' cries he. 1768 GOLDSM. *Good-n. Man* III, Rabbit me, but little Flanigan will look well in anything. 1787 GROSE *Provinc. Gloss.*, *D'rabbit it*, a vulgar exclamation or abbreviation of God rabbit it, a foolish evasion of an oath. N. 1831 ROBY *Trad. Lancash.* Ser. II. (1879) II. 196 Rabbit thee, Will, but the luggage will break thy back. 1880 MRS. PARR *Adam & Eve* xxix. 397 Drabbit the maid! 1889 DOYLE *Micah Clarke* 302 Rabbit me! but you are to be envied.

Rabbit, variant of RABBET *sb.* and *v.*

Rabbiter (ræ·bitəɹ). [f. RABBIT *v.*¹ + -ER¹.] One who hunts rabbits; a rabbit-catcher. Also of a dog (quot. 1883).

1872 BLACKMORE *Maid of Sk.*, The five young rabbiters. 1883 C. READE in *Harper's Mag.* June 97/1 He's the best rabbiter you ha' got. 1887 *Blackw. Mag.* Dec. 826 These rabbiters insisted on being shifted out to more rabbity country.

Rabbiting (ræ·bitiŋ), *vbl. sb.* [f. as prec. + -ING¹.] Hunting, shooting, or catching rabbits.

1841 J. T. HEWLETT *Parish Clerk* I. 90 A day's rabbiting or rat-catching. 1875 W. S. HAYWARD *Love agst. World* 27 The day's 'rabbitings' on the heath with Giles' ferrets and Giles' terriers.

b. *Comb.* in sense 'useful for rabbiting'.

1884 *Western Morning News* 5 Sept. 2/5 White Rabbiting Spaniels. 1889 *Dogs* ii. 12 A capital rabbiting dog.

Rabbitish (ræ·bitiʃ), *a. rare.* [f. RABBIT *sb.*¹ + -ISH.] Characteristic of a rabbit.

1834 BECKFORD *Italy* II. 14 My nose having lost all relish for rabbitish odours. 1852 in *Life A. Fonblanque* (1874) 498 That is just the most rabbitish thing you could do.

Rabbitry (ræ·bitri). [f. RABBIT *sb.*¹ + -RY.] A place in which rabbits are kept; a collection of rabbits.

1838 LOUDON *Suburban Gardener* 712 The Rabbitry.—.. The warren may either be close to the rabbit-house, or at any convenient distance. 1854 WOOD *Anim. Life* (ed. 2) 273 A curious circumstance occurred in my rabbitry. 1886 *Poultry*, etc. 17 Sept. 463 Rye flour may be used to an advantage in the rabbitry.

† Rabbit-sucker. *Obs.* [Properly an appositive comb., but in some of the transf. uses *rabbit* may have been taken as objective.]

1. A sucking rabbit, a very young rabbit.

c 1460 J. RUSSELL *Bk. Nurture* 457 Rabettes sowkers, þe furþer parte from þe hyndur, ye devide. *Ibid.* 697 Rabettes sowkere. 1591 LYLY *Endym.* Wks. 1858 II. 70, I preferre an olde cony before a rabbet sucker, and an ancient henne before a young chicken peeper. 1605 *Tryall Chev.* v. ii. in Bullen *Old Pl.* 1884 III. 350 If Dicke Bowyer be not writ a bountifull benefactor in hell..I am a rabbit sucker. 1630 J. TAYLOR (Water P.) *Gt. Eater of Kent* 6 This same noble Nicke..hath made an end of an hogge all at once, as if it had bin a rabbet-sucker.

2. *transf.* (See quots.)

1608 DEKKER *Lanth. & Candlelight* E, The commodities that are taken vp are cald Pursenets..They that take up are the Rabbet-suckers. 1663 COWLEY *Cutter of Colman St.* IV. vi, I'm .. mistaken if thou beest not cheated of it all .. by such Rabbet-suckers as these. a 1700 B. E. *Dict. Cant. Crew*, *Rabbet-suckers*, young Unthrifts taking up Goods upon Tick at excessive rates. 1725 *New Cant. Dict.*, *Rabbet-sucker*,.. also a Name given to Pawn-brokers and Tally-men.

Rabbity (ræ·biti), *a.* [f. as prec. + -Y¹.] Abounding in rabbits; somewhat like a rabbit.

1887 [see RABBITER]. 1892 *Field* 10 Dec. 883/2 Any gamey or rabbity district. 1897 W. C. HAZLITT 4 *Generations* II. 207 The legs are the only edible part..and..are of a rabbity flavour.

Rabble (ræ·b'l), *sb.*¹ (and *a.*). Forms: 4 **rabel**, **-ul**, 6 **rabell**, **-il(l**, **-yll**, **rabbell**, 6–7 **rable**, 6– **rabble.** [Possibly connected with RABBLE *v.*¹, the root-notion being that of hurry and confusion; but the respective dates of sb. and vb. make the relationship somewhat uncertain. In early examples the idea of a string or series seems to be prominent.]

A. † **1.** A pack, string, swarm (of animals). *Obs.*

13.. *Gaw. & Gr. Knt.* 1703 [The dogs] runnen forth in a rabel. *Ibid.* 1899 Renaud com..& alle þe rabel..ryȝt at his helez. 1513 DOUGLAS *Æneis* XI. ix. 29 The rawk vocit swannis in a rabyll. a 1529 SKELTON *P. Sparowe* 1313 He brought out a rable Of coursers and rounses. 1591 SYLVESTER *Du Bartas* I. v. 909 Flies, Butterflies, Gnats, Bees, and all the rabbles Of other Insects.

2. A tumultuous crowd or array of people, a disorderly assemblage, a mob.

1513 DOUGLAS *Æneis* XIII. iv. 63 In lang rabill the wemen ..fled. a 1529 SKELTON *E. Rummyng* 382 Now in cometh another rabell. Fyrst one with a ladell [etc.]. a 1568 ASCHAM *Scholem.* I. (Arb.) 69, I sawe..cum out of London ..a great rable of meane and light persons. 1667 PEPYS *Diary* (1879) IV. 349 At last the rabble broke up and so I away. 1713 BERKELEY *Guard.* No. 39 ⁋ 5 They seemed rather a confused rabble than a regular army. 1756 C. LUCAS *Ess. Waters* III. 332, I narrowly escaped the insolence...of an inraged rabble. 1840 THIRLWALL *Greece* VII. 249 He was accompanied..by a mixed rabble of strangers and disfranchised citizens. 1858 FROUDE *Hist. Eng.* III. xiv. 194 He went unwillingly, with followers little better than a rabble.

b. Applied contemptuously to a class or body of persons, imagined as collected in a mob.

1529 MORE *Dyaloge* III. Wks. (1557) 228/1 That we should not haue such a rabell [of priests]. 1560 DAUS tr. *Sleidane's Comm.* 249 b, Monkes and Freers and all that relygious rabbell. 1652–62 HEYLIN *Cosmogr.* I. (1682) 183 That rabble of 39 Kings...mentioned by Hector Boetius. 1671 J. WEBSTER *Metallogr.* ii. 29 The numerous, and almost innumerable rabble of the School-men. 1741 WARBURTON *Div. Legat.* II. iv, Jupiter, Mercury, Bacchus, Venus, Mars, and the whole rabble of licentious deities. 1790 BURKE *Pres. St. Aff.* Wks. 1826 VII. 100 To class himself with that rabble of murderers. 1847 TENNYSON *Princ.* VI. 290 To mob me up with all The soft and milky rabble of womankind.

c. *The rabble*, the common, low, or disorderly part of the populace († or of a company); the mob.

1553 BALE *Vocacyon* in *Harl. Misc.* (Malh.) I. 357 Than was all the rable of the shippe..called to the reckeninge. 1581 J. BELL *Haddon's Answ. Osor.* 215 b, The meane and inferiour subjectes, even the rascall rable and multitude. 1625 N. R. *Camden's Hist. Eliz.* I. 101 A few of the rabble of the people raising a tumult. 1676 MARVELL *Mr. Smirke* Wks. 1875 IV. 80 None but the noisy rabble love to hear anything scurrilous or railing. 1711 ADDISON *Spect.* No. 18 ⁋ 6 It is not the Taste of the Rabble, but of Persons of the greatest Politeness. 1813 SHELLEY *Q. Mab* VII. 166 His name unheard, Save by the rabble of his native town. 1873 SYMONDS *Grk. Poets* Ser. I. iii. 86 Theognis complains that the rabble rule the state with monstrous laws.

transf. 1691 T. H[ALE] *Acc. New Invent.* p. xlvi, As to the Rabble of Readers..Water would have served their turns as well.

d. Without article: Persons of the lowest class.

1726 DE FOE *Hist. Devil* II. v. (1840) 235 The devil makes use of scoundrels and rabble, beggars and vagabonds. 1736 T. SHERIDAN in *Swift's Lett.* (1768) IV. 67 You live in Dublin among a parcel of rabble. 1856 MRS. STOWE *Dred* II. xxxii. 321 There is always an abundance of excitable rabble to be got for a drink of whiskey.

† **e.** = RABBLEMENT 1 d. *Obs. rare*⁻¹.

1720 BOLINGBROKE 1 Jan. in *Swift's Lett.* (1766) II. 23 The hurry and rabble of an impertinent town.

3. A disorderly collection, a confused medley (of things). **a.** Of material things. *rare.*

1524 BARCLAY *Cyt. & Uplondyshm.* (Percy Soc.) p. xxxiii, The boorde or table, With dishes charged twentie in a rable. 1585 R. SMITH *Let.* in Foxe *A. & M.* (1583) 1690/2 Builde they neuer so strongly: yet downe shall theyr rabble fall. 1581 J. BELL *Haddon's Answ. Osor.* 40 A wonderfull rabble of wormeeaten pictures. 1803 W. TAYLOR in *Ann. Rev.* I. 431 A rabble of books of all ages, sizes [etc.].

b. Of immaterial things. (In later use only with direct reference to sense 2.)

1549 COVERDALE, etc. *Erasm. Par. Rom.* 14 All oure desyres of transitorye pleasures, whose whole rable maye well be called the body of synne. 1562 JEWEL *Apol. Ch. Eng.* v. ix. (Parker Soc.) 89 Pardons, crosses, censings, and an endless rabble of ceremonies. 1633 HART *Diet of Diseased* Introd. 26 A rabble of remedies, which may so easily be abused. 1768–74 TUCKER *Lt. Nat.* (1834) II. 401 Reason..overpowered by the rabble of appetites, passions, and opinions. 1847 H. ROGERS *Ess.* I. v. 259 A seditious rabble of doubts. 1861 EMERSON *Soc. & Solit.*, *Old Age* Wks. (Bohn) III. 134 We live in youth amidst the rabble of passions.

† **4.** A long string or series *of* words, etc., having little meaning or value. *Obs.*

c 1388 *Wyclif's Sel. Wks.* III. 466 Nouþer God ne alle his seintus willen heren men for no rabul of wordis, ne curiouse florischynge in ryme. 1545 BRINKLOW *Lament.* (1874) 88 A rable of vncommaunded tradicions. 1589 PUTTENHAM *Eng. Poesie* III. xxiii. (Arb.) 271 Such a rable of scholastical precepts which be tedious. 1641 EARL MONM. tr. *Biondi's Civil Warres* v. 170 Hee told them a long rabble of reasons, why hee had sate downe in that place. 1656 — tr. *Boccalini's Advts. fr. Parnass.* I. vi. (1674) 10 So horribly tedious did that rabble of discourse appear.

b. A rigmarole. (Cf. RABBLE *v.*¹) Now *dial.*

1592 CHETTLE *Kind-harts Dr.* (1841) 20 When I had read this rabble, wherein I founde little reason, I laide it by. c 1660 FORBES *Defence* 63 (Jam.) Such doting dreames..fitter to bee an addition to rables .. then to be reputed profound pointes of Christian wisedome. 1649 J. H. *Motion to Parl. Adv. Learn.* 28 This would amount to a long rabble, and degenerate into some Satyre or Pasquill. 1876 *Mid-Yorksh. Gloss.* s.v., He made sike a rabble on it, I couldn't understand a word he said.

c. Hurried or confused talk or reading.

Perh. directly from RABBLE *v.*¹, but cf. 2 e above.

1868 BROWNING *Ring & Bk.* IV. 34 To hear the rabble and brabble, you'd call the case Fused and confused past human finding out.

5. *Comb.*, as *rabble-driver*; *rabble-charming*, *-chosen*, *-courting*, *-rousing* adjs.

1686 SOUTH *Serm.* (1693) 455 With this powerfull, senseless Engine the Rabble-driver shall be able to carry all before him. a 1716 *Ibid.* (1717) VI. 56 The Rabble-charming words, which carry so much Wild-fire wrapt up in them. 1802 SYD. SMITH *Wks.* (1859) I. 10/2 Vulgar violence and the eternal repetition of rabble-rousing words. 1839 *Times* 10 Apr., Wounded the pride of this rabble-courting despot. 1853 T. N. TALFOURD *Castilian* II. iii, A council rabble-chosen.

B. *attrib.* passing into *adj.*

1. Of persons: Forming a rabble; of or belonging to the rabble.

1549 LATIMER *3rd Serm. bef. Edw. VI* (Arb.) 93 You my rable people that are wronged in the world, aske of my father in your distresses. 1656 EARL MONM. tr. *Boccalini's Advts. fr. Parnass.* I. lxxix. (1674) 107 To procure them that number of followers of the rabble sort of people. a 1683 OLDHAM *Wks.* (1685) 9 Let rabble Souls..Stoop their vile Necks. 1778 *Heroic Ep. to Unfort. Monarch* 7 Silent, and watchful of the rabble-band. 1832 *Lincoln Herald* 23 Dec. 4/5 This old war-cry of the Newark blues, or rather the rabble part of them. 1885 LOWE *Bismarck* I. 548 His only resource left was .. to concentrate his rabble army around..Sedan.

2. Of things, actions, etc.: Characteristic of, appropriate to, the rabble.

1603 FLORIO *Montaigne* II. xii. (1632) 317 In the rabble case-canvasing of our plea-courts. 1692 DRYDEN *Cleomenes* Pref., To gratifie the barbarous Party of my Audience, I gave them a short Rabble-Scene. a 1734 NORTH *Exam.* (1740) 306 How could any one of English Education..swallow such a low Rabble Suggestion. 1780 JOHNSON *Let. to Mrs. Thrale* 10 June, To burn the jails .. was a good rabble trick. 1848 ANNA JAMESON in Mrs. Macpherson *Mem.* (1878) 248 There are some disturbances here...mere rabble-work.

3. *Rabble-fish*, the worthless or less valuable fish of a catch. (Cornwall.)

1862 COUCH *Fishes* I. 85 Other fishes..are collectively known by the name of rabble-fish, as being rejected from the market. 1880–4 DAY *Fishes Gt. Brit.* II. 335 Things are altered now, much of this rabble-fish going to Billingsgate and other large inland markets.

Rabble (ræ·b'l), *sb.*² Also 7 **rabil.** [a. F. *râble*, earlier *roable*, *rouable*:—med.L. *rotabulum*, L. *rutābulum* fire-shovel, f. *ruĕre* to rake up.]

† **1.** A kind of shovel used by charcoal-burners to remove the covering from the burned pile. *Obs.*

1664 EVELYN *Sylva* xxx. 100 Two or three days it will only require for cooling, which..they assist, by taking now off the outward covering with a Rabil or Rubber.

2. 'A kind of rake' (Halliwell).

3. An iron bar sharply bent at the end, used for stirring and skimming molten metal in puddling; also, a steam-pipe used for the same purpose.

1864 *Q. Jrnl. Sc.* I. 493 A stirring tool called a rabble by which the workman stirs the melted iron. 1868 JOYNSON *Metals* 67 The steam tube, or 'rabble', being bent on the end, so as to inject the steam on the liquid metal. 1877 RAYMOND *Statist. Mines & Mining* 383 The slag is now drawn with a rabble into molds prepared for it.

Rabble (ræ·b'l), *v.*¹ *Obs.* exc. *dial.* Forms: 5–6 **rable**, 8 *Sc.* **raible**, 9 **rabble.** [= Du. *rabbelen* to speak indistinctly, (L)G. *rabbeln* to talk hurriedly and thoughtlessly; also, to struggle, wriggle, Sw. *rabbla upp* to rattle over.]

1. a. *trans.* To utter (words or speech) in a rapid confused manner. Also with *forth*, *off*, *out*, *over*. **b.** *intr.* To speak or read in this fashion; to gabble. (Cf. RABBLE *sb.*¹ 4.)

14.. *Prov. Solomon* in *MS. Cantab. Ff.* ii. 38 lf. 24 (Halliw.) Let thy tunge..rable not wordes recheles owt of reson. c 1410 LOVE *Bonavent. Mirr.* xviii. 44 (Sherard MS.) In the seyinge of the pater noster they..rablen it forth with oute deuocioun. 1450–1530 *Myrr. our Ladye* 53 [Do] not rable them out togyther as though ye wolde say them all at ones. 1583 FOXE *A. & M.* 1663/2 Thus father Traues you may see my rashnes to rable out the scriptures without purpose, ryme, or reason. 1647 J. CARTER *Plain Expos.* 60 The Lords prayer is rabled ouer without..vnderstanding or reuerence. 1785 BURNS *Holy Fair* xvii, Wee Miller..Orthodoxy raibles. 1859– In various northern glossaries.

2. *intr.* To work in a hurried slovenly manner. *dial.* **b.** *trans.* To rattle *up*.

1862 MRS. H. WOOD *Channings* I. 5 'It looks as though it had been rabbled up for the purpose', cried Hurst in his schoolboy phraseology. 1869 *Lonsdale Gloss.*, *Rabble*,..in sewing, to take too long stitches, and without due care to finish the work neatly. 1880 *Jamieson's Dict.*, *Rabble*,..to do any kind of work in a careless and hurried manner.

Rabble (ræ·b'l), *v.*² Also 8 **rable.** [f. RABBLE *sb.*¹ 2.]

1. *trans.* To attack or assail (a person or his property) as, along with, or by means of, a rabble; to mob. *To rabble out of*, to drive from (a place) in this way.

The word was especially used to describe the attacks made upon the Episcopalian clergy in Scotland by bands of Presbyterians in the last few days of 1688 and early months of 1689, and is frequently employed by historical writers in reference to this.

1644 HOWELL *Twelve Treat.* (1661) 132 The same kind of riotous Rascals which rabbled the K. out of Town. 1690 *Acc. Pres. Persec. Ch. Scot.* 26 Some who were then very active in rabbling the Clergy. 1694 GIBSON in *Lett. Lit. Men* (Camden) 227 He fail'd not to cast in his mite when the Episcopal Clergie were rabbl'd. c 1714 *Culloden Papers* (1815) 336 The magistrates thought fitt to stirre up a mob and rable them. 1818 SCOTT *Hrt. Midl.* vii, The aughty-nine, when I was rabbled by the collegeaners. 1860 A. L. WINDSOR *Ethica* iv. 190 He was continually receiving missives threatening to rabble his house.

2. *intr.* To become a rabble.

1813 SIR R. WILSON *Priv. Diary* II. 448 We rabbled, while he [the enemy] never loosened his solidity.

Hence **Ra·bbled** *ppl. a.*

1855 MACAULAY *Hist. Eng.* xviii. IV. 186 William .. thought that the rabbled curates had been hardly treated.

Rabble (ræ·b'l), *v.*³ [f. RABBLE *sb.*²] *trans.* To stir, skim, or rake with a rabble.

1877 RAYMOND *Statist. Mines & Mining* 392 Just before tapping it is rabbled for five minutes. 1894 BOWKER in *Harper's Mag.* Jan. 420 The molten metal is thoroughly stirred, or 'rabbled' to make it uniform.

Rabblement (ræ·b'lmĕnt). Also 6 **rabel-**, 6–7 **rablement.** [f. RABBLE *sb.*¹ + -MENT.]

1. = RABBLE 2. Now *dial.*

1548 UDALL, etc. *Erasm. Par. Mark* i. 10 Thither flocked a great rablement of souldiers. 1586 J. HOOKER *Girald. Hist. Irel.* in *Holinshed* II. 96/1 Two or three field peeces ..scattered Thomas and his rablement. 1665 J. WEBB *Stone-Heng* (1725) 127 We are not then to wonder, that .. such a promiscuous Rabblement were in great Confusion. 1833 LAMB *Elia* II. *Productions Mod. Art*, A rabblement at the heels of Rosinante. 1837 *New Monthly Mag.* LI. 118 A rude and noisy rabblement whom he could not command. 1877– In various dial. glossaries (Northumb., Lanc., Som.).

† **b.** = RABBLE 2 b. *Obs.*

1549 CHALONER *Erasm. on Folly* M iii, Dunsmen, and.. Albertistes, together with the whole rablement of Sophisters. 1605 CAMDEN *Rem.* (1637) 199 Church-robbers, Traitours, and other of the same rabblement. 1674 BR. BROWNRIG *Serm.* I. xxi. 284 Usurers, Brokers, and the like rabblement of City-thieves.

transf. 1599 NASHE *Lenten Stuffe* 25 All the foure footed rablement of herbagers and grasse champers.

c. = RABBLE 2 c. Now *rare.*

1601 SHAKS. *Jul. C.* I. ii. 245 As hee refus'd it, the rabblement howted. 1612 *Trav. Four Englishm.* 95 Messengers ..sent to raise vp all the whole rabblement thereabout vpon us. 1748 THOMSON *Cast. Indol.* II. xlv, The hubbub of the rabblement. 1813 LD. THURLOW *Poems* 23 The rudest rabblement With their ill darts upon her bosom glanc'd. 1841 H. SMITH *Moneyed Man* I. i. 12 Some of the passing rabblement ordered him to desist.

d. Confusion, disturbance, or tumult like that of a rabble; riotous conduct. *rare.*

1590 SPENSER *F. Q.* I. xii. 9 The raskall many..Heaped together in rude rablement. 1731 *Gentl. Mag.* I. 115 Rabblement, Brabblement, or Squabblement. 1888 STEVENSON *Black Arrow* 177 This impulse of rablement was not restrained without a certain clamour of voices.

† **2.** = RABBLE 3 b. *Obs.*

c 1550 *Will of Deuyls* (Collier) 8 The rablement of..feined and domme ceremonies. 1607 *Scholast. Disc. agst. Antichr.* I. ii. 66 The rabblement of Roman rites which Augustine ..brought in. 1650 G. COLLIER *Vindic. Sabbath* (1656) 44 The rabblement of Romish holi-daies.

† **3.** = RABBLE 4. *Obs.*

1545 JOYE *Exp. Dan.* ix, An hole rabblement of significations and signes of an abominable desolation. 1581 MARBECK *Bk. of Notes* 843 Prayer consisteth not in a rabblement of words. 1612 tr. *Benvenuto's Passenger* I. i. § 19. 73 An whole rablement of flim flam tales. 1714 GAY *Sheph. Week* Proem, A rout and rabblement of critical gallimawfry.

b. = RABBLE 4 b. Now only *dial.*

1567 RECORDE *Judic. Ur.* I, I wyll..overpasse the greate rablement, only taking one generall sentence. 1694 GATAKER *Disc. Apol.* 85 In both his Rabblements fraught with Ribaldrie. 1665 J. WEBB *Stone-Heng* (1725) 34 To reckon up the rest of the Rab'lement is needless. 1855 ROBINSON *Whitby Gloss.*, *Rabblement*, a long random discourse.

Rabbler [f. RABBLE v.[2] + -ER.] One who rabbles; one of a rabble.

Rabble sb.[1] [f. RABBLE v.[2]]

Rabble sb.[2]

Rabbling, vbl. sb.[1] [f. RABBLE v.[2] + -ING.]

Rabbling, vbl. sb.[2] [f. RABBLE v.]

Ra·bbling, a. Disorderly, rowdy.

Rabi, obs. form of RABBET.

†Ra·biate, a. Obs. rare—. [a. med.L. *rabidus*.] Rabid.

†Ra·biator, Sc. rare. [Perh. a later form of RUBIATOR.] A violent, noisy, greedy person.

†Ra·bical, a. Obs. rare—. [f. L. *rabi·es* + -IC + -AL.] Pertaining to rabies.

Rabid (ræ·bid), a. [f. L. *rabidus*, f. *rabĕre* to rave, rage, be mad.]

Rabi·tic, a. [Irreg. f. RABIES.]
Rabid.

†Rabone, var. RABONE sb.[1] and v.

Raboot, obs. Sc. form of REBUT v.

†Ra·bulane, Obs. rare—. [?Obscure formation: cf. RABULE n.1.]

†Ra·bulous, a. Obs. rare—. [f. L. *rabula* a brawling or wrangling advocate.] Scurrilous.

Rabut, obs. Sc. var. REBUT sb. and v.

Raby, obs. f. RABBI, RABBY.

Rabies (ræ·bii̯z). [a. L. *rabies*, f. *rabĕre* to rave.] Canine madness; hydrophobia.

†Rabin. Obs. Forms: rabin, -yn. An ancestor, progenitor.

Raboon, obs. form of RABBIT.

Racamode, a. Obs. Also § racom-, racomode.

†Ra·bin, a. Obs. Also 6 racom-, racomode.

RACE (re̯is), sb.[1] Forms: 3–4 ras, 4–5 raas, 4–6 rase, Sc. rais, 4–7 race, rais, raise, 6 Sc. raice.

Race (re̯is), sb.[2] [Origin unknown.]

†Race, sb.[3] Obs. rare. [? var. of RASE (RAZE) sb.[1], in sense[?].]

Race, sb.[4] Obs. rare.

Race-course, sb. [f. RACE sb.[1] + COURSE.]

Race (re̯is), sb.[5] Also 6–7 race, 7 race.

Race (re̯is), v.[1] [f. RACE sb.[1]]

Race (re̯is), v.[2] [var. of RASE (RAZE) v.[1], in sense[?].]

Racemate (ræ·sĕme̯it). Chem. [f. RACEMIC + -ATE.]

Raceme (ræ·siːm). Bot. [ad. L. *racemus* a cluster of grapes, etc.]

b. To charge an excessive rent for (land). ?*Obs.* 1581 RICH *Farew.* (1846) 11 Landes be so racked at such a rate. 1628 WITHER *Brit. Rememb.* VII. 751 Yet stand their Farmes already rackt so high, That they have begger'd halfe their Tenantry. 1641 BROME *Joviall Crew* Wks. 1873 III. 356 What Acre of your thousands have you rack'd? 1766 *Museum Rusticum* VI. 145 Open fields may be as high racked as inclosures.

c. To oppress (a person) by extortions or exactions, *esp.* of excessive rent; to bear hard upon (one's purse, etc.).
1584 T. LUPTON *Dreame Devil & Dives*, Wo woorth the time that ever we rackt our tenants. 1594 *1st Part Contention* (1843) 34 Because I would not racke the needie Commons. 1600 HEYWOOD *1st Pt. Edw. IV*, Wks. 1874 I. 69 Oh, good Sir Humfrey, do not rack my purse. 1624 CAPT. SMITH *Virginia* VI. 210 Here are no hard Landlords to racke vs with high rents. *a* 1674 CLARENDON *Hist. Reb.* X. § 122 The declared Delinquents [were] racked to as high compositions. 1791 NEWTE *Tour Eng. & Scot.* 124 The same increase of luxury which would induce the landlord to rack his tenant [etc.]. 1862 J. A. ST. JOHN *Four Conq. Eng.* II. 303 Racking the people with impost, and collecting treasure from all parts. 1883 S. C. HALL *Retrospect* II. 315 Implying that tenants were to be racked to the utmost. *absol.* 1774 CUMBERLAND in *Westm. Mag.* II. 600 In vain the steward racks, the tenants rave. 1823 BYRON *Juan* IX. xv, Let *this* one toil for bread—*that* rack for rent.

†d. To extort (money, etc.). *Obs.*
1591 SPENSER *M. Hubberd* 1306 Each place..fild with treasure rackt with robberies. 1622 FLETCHER *Sea-Voy.* I. i, Here lies all..The money I ha' rack'd by usury. *a* 1680 BUTLER *Rem.* (1759) I. 310 When there is no more to be racked out of the People upon any other Pretence. *absol.* 1603 H. CROSSE *Vertues Commw.* (1878) 58 It is neither right, nor honest, to racke, extort, and purloyne from other.

e. To exhaust (tenants, land, etc.) by exactions or excessive use. Also with *out*.
1778 *Family In-compact* 6 Her Lands and Tenants almost rack'd. 1850 *Jrnl. R. Agric. Soc.* XI. II. 717 Soon after it was enclosed it was racked out by over-cropping. 1856 FROUDE *Hist. Eng.* (1858) II. x. 410 It was thought, too, that they had racked their estates. *Ibid.* III. xv. 283 Using..their last opportunity of racking out their properties.

†5. *To rack a horse's wind*: to open his lungs. *Obs. rare.*
1607 MARKHAM *Caval.* III. (1617) 45 The first chase will (as the Northerne man saies) racke your Horses winde, and so prepare him to his labor. 1614 — *Cheap Husb.* I. i. 8 Trauaile moderately in the morning, till his winde be rack'd, and his limbes warmed.

Rack (ræk), *v.*[4] [Of obscure origin: cf. RACK *sb.*[6] The F. *racquassure*, by which Palsgr. renders 'racking', appears to be otherwise unknown.] *intr.* Of animals, *esp.* horses: To move with the gait called a rack.
1530 [see RACKING *vbl. sb.*[4]]. 1589 PEELE *Eclogue to Earl Essex* xii, His rain-deer racking with proud and stately pace. *c* 1626 *Dick of Devon* I. iii. in Bullen *Old Pl.* (1883) II. 23 Ile..trott up hill with you and racke downewards. 1671 *Lond. Gaz.* No. 627/4 Bay Gelding..trots and racks. 1829 *Sporting Mag.* XXIII. 266 There can be little doubt of his having racked a mile in even less than I stated. 1843 MARRYAT *M. Violet* xx. 157 No one ever saw him trotting or galloping; he only racks.
fig. *a* 1661 FULLER *Worthies, Northampton.* (1662) 292 He was thorough-paced in all Spiritual Popery..but in secular Popery..he did not so much as rack.

Rack (ræk), *v.*[5] [ad. Prov. (Gascon) *arracar* in same sense, f. *raca* the stems and husks of grapes, thick dregs: cf. obs. F. *vin raqué* 'small or course wine, squeezed from the *marc* or dregs of the grapes' (Cotgr.).]

1. *trans.* To draw off (wine, cider, etc.) from the lees. Also with *off*.
c 1460 J. RUSSELL *Bk. Nurture* 115 The reboyle to Rakke to þe lies of þe rose, þat shalle be his amendynge. 1519 [see RACKED *ppl. a.*[4]]. 1633 *Naworth Househ. Bks.* (Surtees) 330 To the cooper for rackinge 2 hogsheades of sack. 1694 FALLE *Jersey* ii. 71 [To] ferment, rack and bottle our Cidar. 1741 *Compl. Fam.-Piece* I. v. 275 Rack off your Wine into another Vessel. 1846 J. BAXTER *Libr. Pract. Agric.* (ed. 4) II. 416 Whenever the wine becomes dry, rack off the clear into a clean and sulphured cask. 1880 *Act* 43 & 44 *Vict.* c. 24 § 64 The proprietor of spirits..may..vat, blend, or rack them in the warehouse. *absol.* 1830 M. DONOVAN *Dom. Econ.* I. 303 It will be necessary to rack off from one cask to another. *transf.* 1683 A. SNAPE *Anat. Horse* I. xxviii. (1686) 64 Serving as a Pipe to rack the Urine as it were out of the Bladder of the Young.

b. *fig.* in various senses.
1653 GAUDEN *Hierasp.* 74 Rack him off further, and refine him from the lees of sensual and inordinate lusts. 1696 BROOKHOUSE *Temple Open.* 17 Christ Racks off his Truth from Vessel to Vessel. 1809 MALKIN *Gil Blas* v. i. ¶ 73 Every morning I wrote down in my pocket-book such anecdotes as I meant to rack off in the course of the day. 1861 SALA in *Temple Bar Mag.* II. 302 His speech was of the finest jackeen just racked through a cask of Cork whisky.

†2. To empty (a cask) by racking. *Obs. rare.*
1626 BACON *Sylva* § 306 Rack the one Vessell from the Lees. 1703 *Art & Myst. Vintners* 65 Rack your Cask very clean, and let it remain full of water all night.

Rack (ræk), *v.*[6] *Naut.* [Of obscure origin: perh. a use of *v.*[2] or *v.*[3]] (See quots.)
1769 FALCONER *Dict. Marine* (1776), *Racking*, the fastening two opposite parts of a tackle together, so as that any weighty body suspended thereby shall not fall down, although the rope..should be loosened by accident. 1841 DANA *Seaman's Man.* 119 *Rack*, to seize two ropes together, with cross-turns. 1882 NARES *Seamanship* (ed. 6) 131.

Rack, obs. var. RAKE *sb.*[4], *v.*[1] and *v.*[3]; obs. north. and Sc. f. RECK; pa. t. of REKE *v.* *Obs.*

†**Racka**, obs. form of ARECA.
1625 PURCHAS *Pilgrims* III. 304 Their lading..was principally dryed Coco Nuts..and Racka Nuts.

Rackan (ræ·k'n), **reckon** (re·k'n). *Obs.* exc. *north. dial.* Forms: 1 racente, racete, 4 rakente, 5 rakende, racand, 6 raken, racon, 9 rackan; 4 recawnt, 5–6 rekand, 5 rekande, rekanth, -enth, 6 reckand, -en, recon, 7 reckan, 9 reckon. [OE. *racente* wk. f. = ON. *rekendi* (usually in pl. *rekendr* as if from sing. **rekandi*), OHG. *rahchinza* (Graff): cf. RAKENTEIE. In ME. and later use only north. dial., and chiefly in forms *rek-*, *reckan(d*, which app. represent the Scand. rather than the OE. word (but forms with *rak-*, *rack-*, prevail in the comb. *rackan-crook*).]

†1. A chain, fetter. *Obs.*
c 888 K. ÆLFRED *Boeth.* xvi. § 2 Þæt he wearð ʒebunden mid hira racentum. 971 *Blickl. Hom.* 43 Hie hine hæfdon ʒebreatodne mid fyrenum racentum. *a* 1050 *Liber Scintill.* (1889) 59 ʒebeorscipas swylce racetan..forfleo lusta. 13.. *E. E. Allit. P.* C. 188 Þer ragnel in his rakentes hym rere of his dremes. *a* 1400–50 *Alexander* 5128, I send ʒow..twa hundred & ten..of rekanthes of rede gold. 14.. *Sir Beues* (MS. N.) 1636 Þe jailers liggen bothe dede & Beues liþ bounde in rakende.

2. A chain or other apparatus by which cooking vessels are suspended over a fire; now usually a vertical bar pierced with holes, into one of which the pot-hook is inserted.
1400 *Test. Ebor.* (Surtees) I. 268 Unum recawnt de catenis ferreis. 1445 *Ibid.* II. 194, j. rekand de ferro. 1485 *Ibid.* III. 300, j pare of coberdis, ij potte-hyngyls, j racand. 1534 in Peacock *Eng. Ch. Furniture* (1866) 186 Thre racons wt a peire of galows of yron. 1566 *Richmond. Wills & Inv.* (Surtees) 184, j paire of tongs, j iron scummer and one recken. 1582 BEST *Farm. Bks.* (Surtees) 172 One recon,..one fier shole, one paire of tanges. 1674–91 RAY *N. C. Words* 58 Reckans, Hooks to hang Pots or Kettles on over the Fire. 1876 *Mid-Yorksh. Gloss.* s.v., A pot-hook..sliding through a hole in the bottom piece of the reckon.

Rackan-crook. *north. dial.* Forms: 5–6 raken-, 6 rakon-, racon-, rackyn-, rayckin-, rakin(ge)-, 6, 9 rackin-, 7–9 racken-, 9 rackan-, rack-an'-; 7 rekin-, 7–9 reckin-, 9 reckon-. [f. prec. + CROOK. *Rackan-hook* is used in the same sense in mod. dial.] A rackan serving as a pot-hook, or a pot-hook used with a rackan.
1469–70 *Durham Acc. Rolls* (Surtees) 280 In repar..unius rakencroke, iiijd. 1564 *Wills & Inv. N. C.* (Surtees 1835) 223 Gibcrokes, rakincroke, and racks,..two Rayckincrokes and iiij spetes. 1648 *Lancash. Tracts Civil War* (Chetham Soc.) 254 The very racken crocks and pot hooks. 1684 MERITON *Yorksh. Dialogue* 39 Hing the Pan ore'th fire ith Rekin-Creauk. 1781 J. H. *Gloss. N. E. Words* (E. D. S.), *Rannle-balk*, a piece of wood in a chimney, from which is hung the pot-crook, or racken-crook. 1869– In dialect glossaries (Lonsdale, Rochdale, Sheff., Northumb.).

Rackarock (ræ·kärǫk). [f. RACK *v.*[3] + A *a.*[2] + ROCK *sb.*] An explosive consisting of potassium chlorate and nitrobenzol. Also *attrib.*
1885 *Daily News* 12 Oct., A six-pound cartridge of rackarock. 1891 *Times* 8 Oct. 5/4, 200 lb. of rackarock powder..were set off. 1891 THORPE *Dict. Appl. Chem.* I. 84/2 The rackarock cartridges were not fired electrically.

Rackat, obs. form of RACKET.

Ra·ck-bar.
1. *Mech.* [f. RACK *sb.*[2] 6.] A bar fitted with a rack or racks.
a 1824 A. SCOTT in *Trans. Highl. Soc.* (1824) VI. 31 The teeth of these two spur-wheels are to work..into the teeth of the rack-bars. 1879 *Cassell's Techn. Educ.* IV. 395/1 A strong semicircle of cast iron, with which the telescope is connected by a rack-bar.
2. *Naut.* [f. RACK *v.*[3]] (See quot.)
1867 SMYTH *Sailor's Word-bk.*, *Rack-bar*, a billet of wood used for twisting the bight of a swifter round, in order to bind a raft firmly together.

Rack-bolt, variant of RAG-BOLT.
1793 SMEATON *Edystone L.* § 58 Of trenails, screws, and rack-bolts 2500 each.

†**Ra·ck-bone.** *Obs.* [RACK *sb.*[4]] A vertebra.
1615 CROOKE *Body of Man* 775 The transuerse processes of the racke-bones of the necke. *Ibid.* 800 The last spondels or rackbones of the chest. 1656 W. D. tr. *Comenius' Gate Lat. Unl.* (1659) 259 The chine or back bone..is made up of four and thirty rack-bones. *c* 1720 W. GIBSON *Farrier's Guide* I. v. (1738) 67 The Rack-bones that are between the sixth Vertebrae of the Chest, and the middle of the Os sacrum.

Rackcoone, obs. form of RACOON.

Ra·ck-deal. [f. RACK *sb.*[2]] Deal set up in a rack or framework and dried by exposure to the air.
1807 C. VANCOUVER *Agric. Devon* (1813) 96 The floor above is made of rack deal, or any soft wood plank. 1835 WHITE in *Parl. Rep. Timber Duties* 206 By being cut out with the sap running to them, they would be both sappy and slabby; those are what we call rack deals. 1887 *Dict. Archit.* s.v. *Rack*, The name of the framework in which deals or boards are placed on end for air-drying...Hence the term 'rack deals'.

Racked (rækt), *ppl. a.*[1] [f. RACK *v.*[1] + -ED[1].] Driven along, as clouds by the wind.
1858 KINGSLEY *Poems* 150 Winds, upon whose racked eddies, far aloft, My thoughts in exultation held their way.

Racked (rækt), *ppl. a.*[2] [f. RACK *sb.*[2] or *v.*[2] + -ED.] Fitted with a rack or racks.
1890 *Anthony's Photogr. Bull.* III. 128 A metal racked frame to fit inside a plain wooden box.

Racked (rækt), *ppl. a.*[3] [f. RACK *v.*[3] + -ED[1].]
1. That is racked, in various senses of the vb.; stretched, strained, tortured by stretching, etc.
1571 GOLDING *Calvin on Ps.* iv. 1 Wheras some translate thys woord (for ever)..I do reject as a racked translation. 1583 STUBBES *Anat. Abus.* II. i. (1882) 24 They will be sure to make price of their racked cloth, double and triple more than it cost them. 1611 CHAPMAN *Widowes T.* Wks. 1873 III. 59 Much more worth than the rackt value. 1632 LITHGOW *Trav.* x. 484 The maintayning of my Lame and Racked body. 1867 TROLLOPE *Chron. Barset* I. i. 11 He endeavoured to tell the truth, as far as his poor racked imperfect memory would allow him. 1894 HALL CAINE *Manxman* v. xix. 341 The torn heart and racked brain could bear no more.
2. Of rent: Raised to excess. Cf. RACK-RENT.
1583 STUBBES *Anat. Abus.* II. i. (1882) 29 He might haue it freely for this racked rent. 1668 R. L'ESTRANGE *Vis. Quev.* (1708) 164 Impositions, hard Services, and Rackt Rents. 1725 RAMSAY *Gentle Sheph.* II. i, Never did he stent Us in our thriving with a racket rent. 1799 J. ROBERTSON *Agric. Perth* 404 Racked rents..disable the tenant to improve.
b. Of men, their living, etc.: Oppressed by or subjected to extortion or excessive rent.
1628 WITHER *Brit. Rememb.* II. 1713 That Crew of Spendthrifts..Were now, among their racked Tenants faine To seeke for shelter. 1643 PRYNNE *Sov. Power Parl.* II. 30 Weekely or monethly assessements and contributions..exceeding many mens racked incomes. 1781 COWPER *Expost.* 304 Thy racked inhabitants repine, complain.
3. **Racked-out**, (*a*) completely exhausted; (*b*) passed through with suffering.
1870 SIR S. NORTHCOTE in *Life* (1890) II. xii. 30 The old racked-out tobacco and corn lands. 1900 W. A. ELLIS *Life Wagner* 332 The harvest of the last outlived, or rather racked-out Summer.

Racked (rækt), *ppl. a.*[4] [f. RACK *v.*[5] + -ED[1].] Drawn off or emptied by racking.
1519 HORMAN *Vulg.* 294 b, Whither so euer I go: I haue with me racked wyne. 1563 T. GALE *Antidot.* II. 83 In the latter drinke we haue vsed to put in racked Renishe Wyne. 1626 BACON *Sylva* § 306 Powre the Lees of the Racked Vessell into the vnracked Vessell. 1764 *Mass. Gazette* No. 3149/4 Good rack'd and refin'd Cyder.

Rackee, obs. f. RAKI. **Racken**, north. and Sc. var. RECKON. **Racken-**, var. RACKAN-CROOK.

Racker[1] (ræ·kəɹ). [f. RACK *v.*[3] + -ER[1].]
1. One who racks, in senses of the vb.
1565 COOPER *Thesaurus*, *Contortor legum*, a racker of lawes. 1607 DEKKER *Knt.'s Conjur.* (1842) 72 Landlords dare not quarter themselves here, because they are rackers of rents. *a* 1656 HALES *Gold. Rem.* (1688) 15 These Rackers of Scripture are by St. Peter stiled Unstable. 1725 RAMSAY *Gentle Sheph.* II. i, Rackers aft tine their rent. 1820 SOUTHEY in *Q. Rev.* XXIII. 568 The constant employment of rackers and executioners.
†2. (See quot.) *Obs. rare*[—1].
1688 R. HOLME *Armoury* III. 70/1 The Farmer, or Racker, or Dairy-Man..hold Lands..from the Lords thereof upon Rack or half-Rack, that is upon the yearly value or half value, having no certain term of holding [etc.].

Racker[2] (ræ·kəɹ). [f. RACK *v.*[4] + -ER[1].] A racking horse.
1829 *Sporting Mag.* XXIII. 266 The racker comes to us from our North Western territory. 1856 THOREAU *Lett.* (1865) 146 The swiftest equine trotter or racker.

Racker[3] (ræ·kəɹ). [f. RACK *v.*[5] + -ER[1].]
1. One who racks wine or other liquor.
1611 COTGR., *Frelateur*, a racker of wine. 1865 *Pall Mall G.* 1 Apr. 8 Harris was what is called a racker.
2. An apparatus for racking.
1846 TIZARD *Brewing* (ed. 2) xx. 551 The Floating Racker. [Description follows.]

†**Ra·cket**, *sb.*[1] *Obs. rare.* Also 4–5 raket. [Etym. obscure.] Some game played with dice.
c 1374 CHAUCER *Troylus* IV. 432 (460) Canstow pleyen raket, to and fro, Netle in, dokke out, now this, now that, Pandare? 1387–8 T. USK *Test. Love* I. ii. (Skeat) 166, I haue not plaid raket, Nettle in, Docke out. 1430–40 LYDG. *Bochas* v. xxix. (1554) 140 Kyng Phrahartes, in token he was unstable, Sent him three dees, forged square of golde, To play racket as a chylde chaungeable.

Racket (ræ·kėt), *sb.*[2] Forms: 6 rackat, -it, *Sc.* rakkett, rakcat, 6–7 rackette, 8 -ett, 5– racket; 6–9 raquet, 7 -ett, 9 racquet. See also RAQUETTE. [a. F. *raquette* (16th c.) = Sp., Pg. *raqueta*, It. *racchetta*, *lacchetta*, of uncertain origin (see Littré and Devic): hence also Du. *raket* (in Kilian *racket*), G. *rakete*, *-ette*.]
1. A bat used in the games of rackets, tennis, etc., consisting of a network of cord or catgut stretched across a somewhat elliptical frame formed of a bent strip of wood, to the base of which a handle is attached.
1500–20 DUNBAR *Poems* xiv. 66 Sa mony rakkettis, sa mony ketche-pillaris. 1540 [see b]. 1574 NEWTON *Health Mag.* 6 Striking and receaving the balle with a raquet. 1624 CAPT. SMITH *Virginia* II. 27 The Beaver..His taile somewhat like the forme of a Racket. 1690 LOCKE *Hum. Und.* xxi. § 9 A Tennis-Ball, whether in motion by the stroke of a Racket, or lying still at rest. 1763 C. JOHNSTON *Reverie* II. 206 He was seated at table with a parcel of shuttle-cocks before him, and mending a racket. 1805 SCOTT *Last Minstr.* II. xxxi, Like tennis-ball by raquet tossed. 1808 PIKE *Sources Mississ.* (1810) 100 [In Lacrosse] one catches the ball in his racket, and..endeavors to carry it to the goal. 1828 D'ISRAELI *Chas. I*, I. ii. 22 In the tennis-court he toiled with the racquet. 1890 C. G. HEATHCOTE *Lawn Tennis* 208 The main object of modern lawn tennis is to meet the ball with a full racket.

fig. 1589 GREENE *Menaphon* (Arb.) 51 Finding opportunitie to giue her both bal and racket. 1610 HEALEY *St. Aug. Citie of God* (1620) 616 Friuolous pamphlets, the very rackets wherewith Greece bandieth ignorant heads about. 1705 HICKERINGILL *Priest-cr.* II. iii. 38 Antichrist is the common Tennis-Ball that every malicious Racket bandies and tosses against each other. 1809 MALKIN *Gil Blas* VIII. ix. ¶ 9 You have a racket for every ball; nothing comes amiss to you.

b. A game of ball played by two persons, who strike the ball alternately with their rackets and endeavour to keep it rebounding from a wall. Now always *pl.* Also *fig.*
1529 LYNDESAY *Compl.* 175 Sum gart him raiffell at the rakcat: Sum harld hym to the hurly hakcat. 1540 HEYWOOD *Four P. P.* 882 All the soules were playnge at racket. None other rackettes they hadde in honde [etc.]. 1610 GUILLIM *Heraldry* IV. xii. 221 Such [games] are..Racket, Balloone. 1748 RICHARDSON *Clarissa* (1811) III. xxxii. 191 All his address and conversation is one continual game at raquet. 1822 HAZLITT *Table-t.* II. vii. 161 Rackets..is, like any other athletic game, very much a thing of skill and practice. 1890 E. O. P. BOUVERIE *Rackets* 359 The game of rackets is now exclusively played in a court enclosed in four walls.

†2. A military engine (see quot.). *Obs. rare*[—1].
1535 COVERDALE 1 *Macc.* vi. 51 He made all maner ordinaunce: handbowes, fyrie dartes, rackettes to cast stones.

3. A snow-shoe made after the fashion of a racket (sense 1), as used in Northern America.
1613 PURCHAS *Pilgrimage* VIII. iv. 753 Their Dogges..haue rackets tied vnder their feet, the better to runne on the snow. 1677 W. HUBBARD *Narrative* II. 130 Unless they carried Rackets under their Feet, wherewith to walk upon the Top of the Snow. 1758 *Michmakis & Maricheets* 55 Much more capable with their legs only, than we with our rackets. 1790 BEWICK *Hist. Quadrup.* (1792) 111 The sportsman pursues in his broad rackets or snow-shoes. 1875 TEMPLE & SHELDON *Hist. Northfield, Mass.* 84 Travel was next to impossible, except upon rackets.
b. A broad wooden shoe for man or horse to enable them to walk over marshy ground.
1864 in WEBSTER.

4. *Ornith.* A bird's tail-feather shaped like a racket, a spatule. (*Cassell's Encycl. Dict.* 1887.)

5. *attrib.* and *Comb.*, as (sense 1) *racket-frame*, *-maker*, *-seller*; *racket-like* adj.; (sense 1 b) *racket-ball*, *-bat*, *-court*, *-ground*, *-match*, *-player*; (sense 3) *racket-string*; **racket-press** (see quot.).
1651 OGILBY *Æsop* (1665) 164 Like *Racket-Bals with Argos's I sport And the whole Ocean is my Tennis-Court. 1837 THACKERAY *Ravenswing* vi, Who hit [him] across the shoulders with a *racket-bat. 1604 MIDDLETON *Father Hubbard's T.* Wks. (Bullen) VIII. 103, I am no day from the line of the *racket-court. 1860 *All Year Round* No. 66. 366 It is thoroughly inconvenient and defective as a racket-court. 1837 DICKENS *Pickw.* xli, This area..was the *racket-ground. 1893 NEWTON *Dict. Birds* 168 The outermost pair [of feathers] are enlarged at the end in a *racquet-like form. 1611 COTGR., *Raquetier*, a *Racket-maker. 1838 JAS. GRANT *Sk. Lond.* 57 Employed to supply the *racket-players with balls. 1890 C. G. HEATHCOTE *Lawn Tennis* 204 Among those [implements] which..are useful, may be mentioned the *racket press to keep the racket from warping. 1808 PIKE *Sources Mississ.* (1810) 75 The pressure of my *racket strings brought the blood through my socks and mockinsons.

Racket (ræ·kėt), *sb.*[3] Also 8–9 racquet. [Prob. onomatopœic. Gael. *racaid*, sometimes cited as the source, is no doubt from Eng.]
1. Disturbance, loud noise, uproar, din; usually such as is produced by noisy or disorderly conduct on the part of one or more persons.
In quot. 1597 with pun on *sb.*[2]
1565 ABP. PARKER *Corr.* (Parker Soc.) 234, I send you a letter sent to me of the racket stirred up by Withers. 1597 SHAKS. 2 *Hen. IV*, II. ii. 23 But that the Tennis-Court-keeper knowes better then I, for it is a low ebbe of Linnen with thee, when thou kept'st not Racket there. *a* 1641 BP. MOUNTAGU *Acts & Mon.* (1642) 323 Antonius..hearing what racket the Parthians kept in Syria. 1712 STEELE *Spect.* No. 336 ¶ 3 After all this Racket and Clutter [etc.]. 1792 *Elvina* II. 98 We wanted quiet, not racket. 1877 BLACK *Green Past.* xlii. (1878) 336 A quiet country life—no racket except the roosters in the morning.
b. With *a* and *pl.* An instance of this.
1622 MABBE tr. *Aleman's Guzman d'Alf.* II. 261 Then will shee keepe a racket, and cry out. 1683 *Pol. Ballads* (1860) I. 243 And made such a riot..That never before such a racket was known. 1741 RICHARDSON *Pamela* (1824) I. 53 Your daughter has made a strange racket in my family. 1777 MAD. D'ARBLAY *Early Diary* 7 Apr., The drums and trumpets again made a racket. 1824 SCOTT *St. Ronan's* i, Such dashers occasioned many a racket in Meg's house. *fig.* 1855 J. H. NEWMAN *Callista* (1890) 87 There is such a racket and whirl of religions on all sides of me.
c. A noisy expression of opinion or feeling; clamour, outcry; excitement or fuss (*about* something, or *with* a person).
1652 CULPEPPER *Eng. Physic.* 182 What a noise Authours have made of Roses, what a 'Racket' they have kept up. 1755 J. SHEBBEARE *Lydia* (1769) II. 270 She was astonished..at the racket which was made about a son of such a creature. 1789 CHARLOTTE SMITH *Ethelinde* (1814) I. 11 Though her father has always made such a racket with her.
2. The noise and whirl of society; excessive social excitement or dissipation.
1784 R. BAGE *Barham Downs* I. 118 Charm'd with dress and trumpery, with racket and dissipation. 1822 SCOTT 4 Sept. in *Fam. Lett.* (1894) II. xviii. 149, I did not wish for you in the midst of all this racquet of mirth and war. 1850 THACKERAY *Lett., to Mrs. Brookfield*, With all this racket and gaiety, do you understand that a gentleman feels very lonely? 1886 *Spectator* 6 Feb. 175/1 Dr. Johnson..did not live in the racket of Society.
b. A large or noisy social gathering.
1745 ELIZA HEYWOOD *Female Spect.* No. 12 (1748) II. 269 She told me, that when the number of company for play exceeded ten tables, it was called a racquet. 1750 JOHNSON *Rambler* No. 97 ¶ 4 To idle amusements, and to negligence of domestic business, to wicked rackets. 1876 T. HARDY *Ethelberta* (1890) 402 She'll have her routs and her rackets as well as the high-born ones.
3. *slang.* A trick, dodge, scheme, game, line of business or action.
1812 J. H. VAUX *Flash Dict.*, *Racket*, some particular kinds of fraud and robbery are so termed. 1851 MAYHEW *Lond. Labour* I. 224/1, I did wear a shovel hat when the Bishop of London was our racket. 1884 *Bread-winners* 183 That's just our racket. 1891 KIPLING & BALESTIER *Naulahka* vi, What's your lay? What's your racket?
4. An exciting or trying situation or experience; an ordeal. *To stand the racket*, (*a*) to hold out against strain or wear and tear; (*b*) to face the consequences of an action.
1823 'J. BEE' *Dict. Turf*, '*Racket*—to stand the', when one of a set stands forward to bear all the blame. 1827 T. WILSON *Pitman's Pay* II. 63 Sic tussels nobbit pluck could settle, For nowse less could the racket stand. 1837 WHITTOCK *Bk. Trades* (1842) 404 (*Shoemaker*) Upon this..preparation depends his work standing the racket of adverse seasons. 1878 BESANT & RICE *Celia's Arb.* xxxii. (1889) 237, I escaped and came out of the whole racket unwounded.
5. *Sc.* A hard blow; a severe slap.
1710 RUDDIMAN *Douglas Æneis, Gloss.* s.v. *Rak*, More frequently..we use Racket, as he gave him a racket on the lug, i.e. a box on the ear. 1810 *Cock's Simple Strains* 135 (Jam.) The wabster lad bang'd to his feet, An' gae 'im a waefu racket.

†**Ra·cket**, *v.*[1] *Obs.* Also 7 rackat. [f. RACKET *sb.*[2]]
1. *trans.* To strike with, or as with, a racket; to toss or bandy about. Chiefly *fig.*
1603 FLORIO *Montaigne* III. ix. (1613) 540 The Gods perdie doe reckon and racket us men as their tennis balles. 1609 B. JONSON *Case is Altered* IV. iv, Then think, then speak,..And racket round about this body's court These two sweet words, 'tis safe. 1631 R. H. *Arraignm. Whole Creature* xiv. § 2. 244 They are moveable as Shittlecockes, or Tennis Balls, now racketed here, now there. 1795 G. SCROPE *Epit. on himself* (St. Michael's, Coventry), Here lyes an Old Toss'd Tennis ball Was Racketted from Spring to Fall.
b. *To racket away*: To lose (money) in playing with a racket.
1612 WEBSTER *White Devil* II. i, I shall not shortly Racket away five hundred crowns at tennis But it shall rest upon record!
2. *To racket it*: To carry a racket. *rare*[—1].
1605 CHAPMAN, etc. *Eastw. Hoe* I. i, There's thy fellowe Prentise, as good a Gentleman borne as thou art..But does he pumpe it or Racket it?

Racket (ræ·kėt), *v.*[2] [f. RACKET *sb.*[3]]
1. *intr.* To live a gay life, to take part in social excitement. Also with *about*.
1760 GRAY *Lett., to Dr. Clarke*, Poems (1775) 282 Company and cards at home, parties by land and water abroad, and..racketing about from morning to night. 1792 *Elvina* II. 132 Sir Edward will not allow Elvina to racket any more for some time. 1833 MACAULAY in *Life & Lett.* (1880) I. 346, I have been racketing lately, having dined twice with Rogers and once with Grant.
2. *intr.* To make a noise or racket; to move about in a noisy way.
1827 CAPT. HARDMAN *Waterloo* 16 A ball from their infantry went through my jacket. Took the skin off my side, and made me racket. 1851 S. JUDD *Margaret* xvii. 151 The wind blazed and racketed through the narrow space between the house and the hill. 1897 R. KIPLING *Captains Courageous* iv. 86 The pots and pans..jarred and racketed to each plunge.
b. To get *up* with noise and confusion.
1847 ALB. SMITH *Chr. Tadpole* lii. (1879) 445 They're..obliged to racket up too early in the morning to catch the train, to take anything.
3. *trans.* To keep lively, to disturb, destroy (also with *away*), etc. by racketing. *rare.*
1753 RICHARDSON *Grandison* (1781) VI. xxvii. 166 Dearly do we love racketing; and, another whisper, some of us to be racketed. 1777 LADY S. LENNOX in *Life & Lett.* (1901) I. 261 The racketting their health so entirely away. 1827 HONE *Every-day Bk.* II. 820 A racketty life had racketted his frame. 1866 H. WARD BEECHER in *Hom. Rev.* May 421 We hear the whole land racketed with the disturbance produced by labor and capital.

Racketer[1] (ræ·kėtəɹ). *rare.* Also 6 rakketter. [f. RACKET *sb.*[2] + -ER[1].]
1. One who plays with a racket.
1581 MULCASTER *Positions* xxvii. (1887) 105 The rakketters in tennyse play..must shew them selues nymble. 1860 *All Year Round* No. 66. 366 These listless racketers rarely, if ever, hit the ball twice before it dropped.
2. One who wears, or walks on, rackets or snow-shoes (*Funk's Stand. Dict.* 1893).

Ra·cketer[2]. *rare.* [f. RACKET *sb.*[3] or *v.*[2] + -ER[1].] A gay or noisy person.
1661 *Sir A. Haslerig's Last Will* 3 The discontented Party..may find our impregnant City a ready Foster-Mother to nurse these distempers in her ranting Racketers. 1754 RICHARDSON *Grandison* (1781) I. xvi. 109 At a private concert last night..and again to be at a play this night: I shall be a racketer, I doubt.

Racketing (ræ·kėtiŋ), *vbl. sb.* [f. RACKET *v.*[2] + -ING[1].] The action of the vb., esp. in sense 1; an instance of this.
1753 [see RACKET *v.*[2] 3]. 1795 SCOTT 23 Aug. in *Lockhart*, I wish they may come down soon, as we shall have fine racketting. 1822 — 25 June in *Fam. Lett.* (1894) II. xviii. 139 Late hours and raqueting. 1843 MIALL in *Nonconf.* III. 745 No racketing of engines to turn his domain into a modern Babel. 1886 BARING-GOULD *Mehalah* 183 There'll be junketings and racketings.

Racketing (ræ·kėtiŋ), *ppl. a.* [f. as prec. + -ING[2].] That rackets, in senses of the vb.; characterized by racket or racketing.
1763 ELIZ. CARTER in *Mem.* (1808) I. 362 We live a very racketting life at the Hague. 1821 JEFFREY in Cockburn *Life* II. lxxxvi, We have had a racketing feverish life since we came here. 1847 W. IRVING in *Life & Lett.* (1864) IV. 25 One of the most racketing cities in the world. 1895 BESANT *Westminster* iii. 88 A place filled with noisy, racketing, even uproarious life.

Racketry (ræ·kėtri). [f. RACKET *sb.*[3] + -RY.] Systematic or continuous noise or disturbance.
1884 in Bryce *Amer. Commw.* II. 639 The non-voters..constitute the muscle and sinew of the campaign racketry—a word made indispensable by political conventions. *Ibid.* 640 All this racketry has been going on..for seven minutes.

Ra·cket-tail. [f. RACKET *sb.*[2]] A (bird's) tail shaped like a tennis-racket; hence used as a name for various species of humming-birds and motmots having tails of this form.
1851 JARDINE *Contrib. Ornith.* 111 The beautiful species S[*pathura*] *Underwoodii*, with its white boots and racket tail. 1861 GOULD *Humming Birds* III. Pl. 162 *Spathura Underwoodi*, white-booted Racket-tail. *Ibid.* 164 *S. Peruana*, Peruvian Racket-tail. 1893 NEWTON *Dict. Birds* 446 The lateral feathers may..suddenly enlarge into a terminal spatulation as in the forms known as 'Racquet-tails'.
So **Ra·cket-tailed** *a.*, having a racket-tail.
1812 SHAW *Gen. Zool.* VIII. I. 317 The Racket-tailed Humming Bird is a rare species, and is a native of South America. 1833 JARDINE *Humming-Birds* II. 110 Rough-legged Racket-tailed Humming-Bird. 1894 *Naturalist on Prowl* 178 The ever-changing..notes of the Racket-tailed Drongo.

Rackette, obs. form of RACKET *sb.*[2]

Racket-wheel, variant of RATCHET-WHEEL.
1794 W. FELTON *Carriages* (1801) I. 78 The brace is fixed to a spindle..and is there confined by a small racket-wheel and ketch. 1837 *Penny Cycl.* IX. 150/1 There is also a racket-wheel to prevent its unwinding.

Rackety (ræ·kėti), *a.* Also -tty. [f. RACKET *sb.*[3] + -Y.]
1. Addicted to making a racket; noisy, gay, fond of excitement.
1773 BERRIDGE *Chr. World Unmasked* (1812) 27 Some players are rude and rackettty. 1857 KINGSLEY *Two Years Ago* I. vii. 192 This strange metamorphosis in the rackety little Irishman. 1885 *Manch. Exam.* 9 Apr. 5/3 The rackety winds of March and April.
2. Characterized by noise, excitement, dissipation, or disturbance.
1827 [see RACKET *v.*[2] 3]. 1840 HOOD *Up the Rhine* 61 Foreign travelling is very racketty work. 1865 CARLYLE *Fredk. Gt.* x. ii. (1872) III. 221 He..studies and learns amazingly in such a rackety existence.
¶ 3. = RICKETY.
1824 W. IRVING *T. Trav.* I. 55 An old rackety inn, that looked ready to fall to pieces.

Ra·ckful. [f. RACK *sb.*[2]] The fill of a rack.
1898 C. G. ROBERTSON *Voces Academ.* 190 A rackful of sticks and pipes.

Rackin-crook, variant of RACKAN-CROOK.

Ra·cking, *vbl. sb.*[1] [f. RACK *v.*[1] + -ING[1].] The action of driving before the wind. *rare*[—1].
1631 *Celestina* Prol. A vj b, Those rackings to and fro of the clouds.

Ra·cking, *vbl. sb.*[2] [f. RACK *v.*[2]] a. Fitting with, placing in, etc., a rack or racks. b. The washing of ore on a rack (Knight 1875).
1888 *Daily News* 18 July 2/6 Restitution of 'pennies' if the girls do their own racking.

Racking (ræ·kiŋ), *vbl. sb.*[3] [f. RACK *v.*[3]]
1. The action of stretching, extending, straining, etc.; pulling tight or making fast by rack-lashings. Also with *down*.
1463–4 *Rolls Parlt.* V. 501/1 Brode Cloth..after almanere rakkyng, streynyng or teyntyng therof. 1565 JEWEL *Repl. Harding* (1611) 364 It cannot be drawen, nor by racking can be stretched to any other sense. 1577 HOLINSHED *Chron.* II. 1751/2 Thys grieuous racking and extending of this worde Procurement. 1764 CHURCHILL *Gotham* 12 The daily, nightly racking of the brains, To range the thoughts. 1853 SIR H. DOUGLAS *Milit. Bridges* 170 The oars and poles were used as ribands for racking. 1876 VOYLE & STEVENSON *Milit. Dict.*, *Racking-down*, an operation performed with the aid of rack-lashing in laying a gun or mortar platform.
b. Torturing by means of the rack.
1494 FABYAN *Chron.* VII. 490 Dyuerse tourmentes, as rakkynge, heddynge, and hangynge. 1560 DAUS tr. *Sleidane's Comm.* 284 All racking and torture, that exceadeth a meane, is uncerten and perillous. *a* 1653 GOUGE *Comm. Hebr.* xi. 36 If racking, if scourging..be reall persecutions, then were theirs reall. 1732 NEAL *Hist. Purit.* I. 429 He had condemned racking for grievous offenders, as contrary to Law. 1868 BROWNING *Ring & Bk.* v. 13 Noblemen were exempt, the vulgar thought, From racking.
c. Raising (of rents) to an excess. Also with *up*.
1581 W. STAFFORD *Exam. Compl.* iii. (1876) 82 This rackynge and hoyssing vp of Rentes. 1627 HAKEWILL *Apol.* (1630) 522 By unconscionable racking of rents and wresting from them excessive fines. 1690 CHILD *Disc. Trade* (1694) 50 The racking up of rents in the years 1651 and 1652.
2. The undergoing or causing of strain, distortion, or dislocation.
1739 LABELYE *Short Acc. Piers Westm. Bridge* 18 The Frames could move..without any Danger of racking or straining. 1793 SMEATON *Edystone L.* § 306 Nothing to oppose the racking of the frame. 1868 *Rep. Munitions War* 267 The 'Bellerophon' could pass the forts at New York within 200 yards without suffering except by racking. 1869 SIR E. REED *Shipbuilding* ii. 23 This plan..has the important advantage of opposing the racking of the floor plates longitudinally.
attrib. 1865 A. L. HOLLEY *Ordnance & Armor* 212 The 'racking' system, by means of heavy projectiles at low velocities.
3. Intense pain.
1896 *Allbutt's Syst. of Med.* I. 680 Violent aching of the head..with racking in the bones.

Ra·cking, *vbl. sb.*[4] [f. RACK *v.*[4]] Of a horse: The action or fact of moving with a rack.
1530 PALSGR. 260/2 Rackyng of a horse in his pace, *racquassure*. 1607 MARKHAM *Caval.* IV. 5 Taking his time-keeping from trotting, and his motion of legges from ambling, and so compound this which is called a Traine, or Racking. 1725 BRADLEY *Fam. Dict.* s.v. *Rules for buying Horses*, Racking..'tis the same Motion as Ambling, only it is a sweeter Time. 1828 J. PALMER *Jrnl. Travels* 51 Racking is a favourite ambling pace.

Racking (ræ·kiŋ), *vbl. sb.*[5] [f. RACK *v.*[5]] Drawing off wine, etc. from the lees.
c 1475 *Liber Niger* in *Househ. Ord.* (1790) 74 The rackinge, coynynge, rebatinge, and other salvations of wynes. 1626 BACON *Sylva* § 305 It is in common Practise, to draw Wine, or Beere, from the Lees, (which we call Racking). 1703 *Art & Myst. Vintners* 23 The usual times for Racking, are Midsummer and Alhallontide. 1783 B. J. BROMWICH *Exper. Bee-keeper* 59 If it does not become fine after the first racking, the operation should be repeated. 1846 J. BAXTER *Libr. Pract. Agric.* (ed. 4) I. 169 The manufacture of cider may be divided into twelve heads:..8. The racking.
b. *attrib.*, as *racking-back*, *-can*, *-cellar*, *-cock*, *-engine*, *-faucet*, *-hose*, *-pump*, *-shed*, *-tap*, *-vessel*.
1846 TIZARD *Brewing* (ed. 2) xx. 547 A more perfect racking-engine than such as are in ordinary use. *Ibid.*, The racking tap. 1890 *Pall Mall G.* 4 Aug. 3/1 The cask..is further cleaned with steam..before being allowed to roll off into the 'racking shed', where it is filled with porter. 1892 H. E. WRIGHT *Handy Bk. Brewers* 37 'Settling backs' or 'racking backs'. *Ibid.* 42 The fermenting or racking vessels. *Ibid.* 503 Racking hose..and racking cocks.

Ra·cking, *vbl. sb.*[6] [f. RACK *v.*[6]] A piece of spun yarn or other material used for racking ropes.
1711 W. SUTHERLAND *Shipbuild. Assist.* 143 Racking and Seizing for the Parrel. *c* 1860 H. STUART *Seaman's Catech.* 34 It will greatly assist the spunyarn racking. 1882 NARES *Seamanship* (ed. 6) 116 Cast off the racking.

†**Ra·cking**, *vbl. sb.*[7] [f. *rack* WRACK *v.* Cf. RACK *sb.*[5]] Wrecking, destruction.
1689 *Pol. Ballads* (1860) II. 8 The Queen and Prince banisht for what none dares own, Unless for the racking and ruin o' the state.

Ra·cking, *ppl. a.*[1] [f. RACK *v.*[1] + -ING[2].]
1. Of clouds: Driving before the wind.
1590 MARLOWE *2nd Pt. Tamburl.* IV. iv, Draw my chariot swifter than the racking clouds. 1697 DRYDEN *Æneid* IV. 361 Drives the racking clouds along the liquid Space. 1808 SCOTT *Marm.* III. xxii, Of middle air the demons proud, Who ride upon the racking cloud.
2. Of winds: Driving, carrying along.
1667 MILTON *P. L.* II. 182 The sport and prey Of racking whirlwinds. 1840 CARLYLE *Heroes* iii. (1858) 255 The racking winds..whirl them away again.

Racking (ræ·kiŋ), *ppl. a.*[2] [f. RACK *v.*[3]]
1. Extortionate; exacting.
1580 SIDNEY *Arcadia* I. (1598) 2 The court of affection, held by that racking steward, Remembrance. 1636 FEATLY *Clavis Myst.* vii. 90 Hee layeth the blame on..racking Landlords. 1649 BP. HALL *Cases Consc.* (1650) 12 Let those..learn to make no lesse conscience of a racking bargain. 1817 SCOTT *Search after Happiness* xvi, Cursed war and racking tax Have left us scarcely raiment to our backs.
†b. Let at rack-rents. *Obs. rare*[—1].
a 1619 BEAUM. & FL. *Wit without M.* I. i, Your racking Pastures, that have eaten up as many singing Shepherds, and their issues, as Andeluzia breeds.
2. Torturing; causing intense pain, physical or mental.
1667 MILTON *P. L.* XI. 481 Maladies Of gastly Spasm, or racking torture. 1693 CONGREVE in *Dryden's Juvenal* xi. (1697) 296 The most racking Thought, which can intrude. 1752 HUME *Ess. & Treat.* (1777) II. 106 A man lying under the racking pains of the Gout. 1806–7 J. BERESFORD *Miseries Hum. Life* (1826) VI. xxii, Getting up for a journey with a racking headache. 1873 G. C. DAVIES *Mount. & Mere* viii. 57, I had been kept awake by a most racking tooth-ache.
3. Straining, dislocating; breaking under strain.
1868 *Rep. Munitions War* 262 To neutralize the vibration, when struck a racking blow on one side. 1874 THEARLE *Naval Archit.* 118 Great racking strains are set up, tending to alter the relative positions of the beams to each other and to the ship's side. 1895 R. KIPLING in *Pall Mall G.* 25 Oct. 3/2 Spirits, goblins, and witch-people were moving about on the racking ice.
Hence **Ra·ckingly** *adv.*, in a racking or exhausting manner.
1857 *Chamb. Jrnl.* VIII. 33 They will certainly become..monotonous by virtue of being so rackingly relevant.

Ra·cking, *ppl. a.*[3] [f. RACK *v.*[4]]
1. Of a horse: Moving with a rack.
1562 *Richmond. Wills* (Surtees) 166 One old rackynge nagg. 1585 *Wills & Inv. N. C.* (Surtees 1860) 108 My rackinge blacke nagge. 1817 PAULDING *Letters fr. South* (1835) I. 86, I bought a new horse,—one of your capital racking ponies, as they are yclept.
fig. *a* 1661 FULLER *Worthies, Staffordsh.* (1662) 41 He himself became a racking but no thorough-paced Protestant.
2. *Racking pace* = RACK *sb.*[6]
1611 COTGR., *Amble*,..an ambling, or racking pace. 1676 *Lond. Gaz.* 1138/4 Two Cart-Geldings,..a little racking-pace. 1721 DUDLEY in *Phil. Trans.* XXXI. 167 A Moose..shoves along side-ways, throwing out the Feet, much like a Horse in a racking pace. 1819 REES *Cycl.* XXIX. s.v. *Rack*, The racking pace is much the same as the amble.

Ra·cking, *ppl. a.*[4] *Naut.* [f. RACK *v.*[6]] That fastens ropes together.
1867 SMYTH *Sailor's Word-bk.* s.v. *Nippering*, Fastening nippers by taking turns crosswise between the parts..These are called racking turns. 1882 NARES *Seamanship* (ed. 6) 34 It is..secured with a racking seizing. 1886 J. M. CAULFEILD *Seamanship Notes* 3 Secure..reef-pendant to boom with a racking or rolling hitch.

†**Rack jack.** *Obs. rare*[—1]. A racket.
1582 STANYHURST *Æneis* I. (Arb.) 22 Dare ye..Too raise such raks iaks on seas, and danger vnorderd?

Ra·ck-lashing. *Mil.* [f. RACK *v.*[3]] A lashing consisting of a piece of stout rope fastened to a short tapering stick, by means of which it may be twisted tight.
1834–47 J. S. MACAULAY *Field Fortif.* (1851) 74 A piece of smaller scantling is laid on the top of the plank..to which it is secured with rack-lashings. 1859 F. A. GRIFFITHS *Artil. Man.* (1862) 257.

Rackle (ræ·k'l), *a.* *Obs.* exc. *Sc.* and *north. dial.* Forms: 4–5 rakel, -il, 4–6 -yl, (5 -yll), racle, 6 ra(c)kle, *Sc.* rakill, 7 rackel, 8 raucle, 9 rackle, rau(c)kle. [Of obscure origin.] Hasty, rash, impetuous, headstrong; rough or coarse in action; also *Sc.* possessed of rude strength, vigorous at an advanced age. a. of persons:
a 1300 in Horstm. *Altengl. Leg.* (1875) 37 To rakele þo þei were, ʒware fore þo huy fullen þere. 13.. *E. E. Allit. P.* C. 526 He þat is to rakel to renden his cloþez, Mot efte sitte with more vnsounde to sewe hem togeder. *c* 1430 LYDG. *Min. Poems* (Percy Soc.) 30 To wyving be thou nat racle. 1433 — *St. Edmund* II. 512 The kyng, nat rakel, but of hih prudence. 1570 LEVINS *Manip.* 129/8 Rakyl, *insolens*. *c* 1670 *Poor Man's Cup* in G. Hickes *Spirit of Popery* (1680) 10 Samson was a Rackel and Rough-handed Saint, ready to Pelt the Philistines on all occasions. 1785 BURNS *Jolly Beggars* 4th Recit., Then niest outspak a raucle carlin. 1826 T. WILSON *Pitman's Pay* I. lxvi, Te guide a rackle ram-stam wife. 1876 WAUGH *Hermit Cobbler* (Lancash. dial.) 29 Is there ony news o' that rackle (reckless) brother o' thine?
b. of things, actions, feelings, etc.
c 1374 CHAUCER *Troylus* III. 380 (429) Eche rakil dede, and eche unbridelid chere. *c* 1386 — *Manciple's T.* 185 A thousand folk hath rakel Ire Fully fordoon. *Ibid.* 235 Wostow wherof a rakel tonge serueth. 1406 HOCCLEVE *La Male Regle* 83 His rakil wit only to him souffysith. *c* 1550 R. BIESTON *Bayte Fortune* Aij, Thy tounge is racle, thy wit is rechles. 1786 BURNS *Earnest Cry & Prayer* xxii, Auld Scotland has a raucle tongue.
Comb. 1715 *Wodrow Corr.* (1843) II. 39, I suspect this will be a very rackle-handed committee.
? Hence †**Rackle** *v. intr.*, to act rashly or roughly. *Obs. rare*[—1].
c 1374 CHAUCER *Troylus* III. 1593 (1642), I nil not rakle as for to greven here.

Rackleness (ræ·k'lnės). *Obs.* exc. *dial.* [f. RACKLE *a.* + -NESS.] †a. Rashness, hastiness. *Obs.* b. *Sc.* (See quot. 1825).
c 1386 CHAUCER *Manciple's T.* 179 O euery man be war of rakelnesse Ne trowe no thyng withouten strong witnesse. 1549 COVERDALE, etc. *Erasm. Par. James* 29 True godlynes can in no wise agree with racklenes of tongue. 1825 JAMIESON Suppl., (*Rackleness*), *Raucleness*, vigour and freshness in an advanced period of life.

Ra·ckless, *a.* *rare*[—1]. [f. RACK *sb.*[3] + -LESS.] Produced without a rack.
1867 G. GILFILLAN *Night* ix. 310 Rackless torture.

Rackless, obs. (north. and Sc.) f. RECKLESS.

†**Ra·ckly**, *adv.* *Sc. Obs. rare*[—1]. In 6 raklie. [? f. RACKLE *a.* + -LY[2].] Rapidly, impetuously.
c 1470 HENRYSON *Mor. Fab.* XI. (*Wolf & Sheep*) xix, Went never hound mair haistelie fra the hand, Quhen he wes rynnand maist raklie at the ra.

Rackoon(e, obs. forms of RACOON.

Ra·ck-pin.
1. [f. RACK *v.*[3]] = RACK-STICK.
1859 J. BROWN *Rab & F.* (1862) 33, I had to brain him wi' a rack-pin.
2. [f. RACK *sb.*[2]] One of the pins supporting the rack-boards in an organ.
1881 W. E. DICKSON *Pract. Organ-building* 91 The rack-board..may be placed on its rack-pins, and the feet dropped into their places.

Rack-punch. [f. RACK *sb.*[7] + PUNCH.] Punch made with arrack.
1713 STEELE *Guard.* No. 143 ¶ 3 Rack-punch, quickned with brandy and gun-powder. 1752 FIELDING *Amelia* Wks. 1775 X. 155 The governor..trumpeted forth the praises of his rack-punch. 1848 THACKERAY *Van. Fair* vi, He insisted upon having a bowl of rack punch; everybody had rack punch at Vauxhall.

Ra·ck-rent, *sb.* [f. RACK *v.*[3] 4 + RENT. *Rack-rented* is found in 1591.] A very high, excessive, or extortionate rent; a rent equal (or nearly equal) to the full value of the land.
1607 J. NORDEN *Surv. Dial.* v. 80 An obseruing and painefull husband..thriueth as well vpon his farme of rack rent, as many..Freeholders. 1715 *Act Reg. Papists* in *Lond. Gaz.* (1716) No. 5455/3 Any Farmer or Tenant at Rack-Rent. 1745 *Season. Adv. Protest.* 18 They steal from their Neighbours, to enable them to pay the Land-Jobber his Rack-Rent. 1828 JAS. MILL *Brit. India* I. II. v. 184 *note*, One third to the cultivator, and two thirds to the proprietor, would be accounted a rackrent in England. 1879 H. GEORGE *Progr. & Pov.* II. ii. (1881) 111 They lived on the potato, because rack-rents stripped every thing else from them.
attrib. 1778 [W. MARSHALL] *Minutes Agric.* 4 Dec. 1775 *Obs.*, The rack-rent Gentlemen of landed property. 1834 *Tait's Mag.* I. 17/1 Every year growing worse than the last in this rack-rent country.
transf. and *fig.* 1608 MIDDLETON *Fam. Love* I. ii, *Nil muliere levius*. Tut, man, every one knows their worth When they are at a rack rent. 1768 *Woman of Honor* II. 178 Subjecting to the rack-rent of avarice and insolence that country of theirs.

Ra·ck-rent, *v.* [f. prec.]
1. *trans.* To subject (a person) to the payment of rack-rent.
1748 RICHARDSON *Clarissa* (1811) I. xiii. 83 It was a maxim with his family..never to rack-rent old tenants or their descendants. 1879 H. GEORGE *Progr. & Pov.* 105 Who rack-rent the cultivators most mercilessly.
absol. 1856 LEVER *Martins of Cro' M.* 138 He hunted, and drank, and feasted and rack-rented.
2. To let (a farm, etc.) at a rack-rent.
1882 in OGILVIE.
Hence **Rackre·ntable** *a.*, capable of being rack-rented; **Ra·ck-rented** *ppl. a.* (in quot. 1591 app. f. the sb.); **Ra·ck-renting** *vbl. sb.* and *ppl. a.*
1591 SYLVESTER *Du Bartas* I. iii. 1154 The needy, hard-rack-rented Hinde. 1856 LEVER *Martins of Cro' M.* 398 Is it rack-renting..would make them popular? 1875 MAINE *Hist. Inst.* vi. 175 They were the first 'tenants at will'..and..were always theoretically rackrentable. 1893 PEEL *Spen Valley* 120 The appeal of the poor rack-rented tenantry. 1897 *Westm. Gaz.* 9 Sept. 7/1 Even the most rack-renting of landlords will find..the impossibility of extortion.

Ra·ck-rental. *rare*[—1]. The value (of land) at rack-rent.
1812 SOUTHEY in *Q. Rev.* VIII. 328 The rack-rental of England in that year [1803] was about forty millions.

Ra·ck-renter.
1. One who pays rack-rent.
1680 *Spirit of Popery* 45 If they were Rack-renters. 1733 TULL *Horse-hoeing Husb.* Pref. 6 'Tis a publick Calamity, that the Lands of a Country must be all or mostly in the Hands of Rack-Renters, whose Interest it is..that they never may be improv'd. 1807 VANCOUVER *Agric. Devon* (1813) 224 These meadows the rack renters are bound to dress after every third crop of hay. 1826 COBBETT *Rur. Rides* (1885) II. 236 The farmers were real yeomen, and not miserable rack-renters.
2. One who exacts rack-rent.
1880 *Times* 23 Oct. 6/5 Not..one [landlord] in 500 [will] be found to merit the name of 'rack-renter'.

†**Rack-sauch.** *Sc. Obs. rare*[—1]. [f. RACK *v.*[3] + SAUCH, sallow, willow.] A gallows-bird.
1508 DUNBAR *Flyting* 245 Filling of tauch, rak sauch, cry crauch, thow art our sett.

Ra·ck-staff. ? *Obs.* (See quots.)
1611 COTGR., *Frayoire*, the racke-staffe, or nog of a mill; the little peece of wood which rubbing against the hopper makes the corne fall from it. 1688 R. HOLME *Armoury* III. 340/2 The parts of a Wind-Mill..The Rack-staff, that shakes the Shough. 1847–78 HALLIWELL, *Rack-staff*, a kind of pole or staff used for adjusting the mill-stones.

Ra·ck-stick. [f. RACK *v.*[3]] A stick used for tightening a rope placed round anything.
1859 F. A. GRIFFITHS *Artil. Man.* (1862) 258 Rack-sticks, and lashings. *Ibid.* 259 The..officer carries the rack sticks.

Rackt, obs. form of *raked*, RAKE *v.*[1]

†**Rack vintage.** *Obs.* (See quot. 1617.)
1540 *Act 32 Hen. VIII*, c. 14 For the freight of euery tun wyne at the racke vintage, xvi s. 1617 MINSHEU *Ductor*, *Racke vintage*, An. 32. H. 8. cap. 14, is a second vintage or voyage for wines by our Merchants into Fraunce, &c. [Hence in Blount and later Dicts.]

Rack-wind: see RACK *sb.*[1] 3.

Rackyn-croke, obs. form of RACKAN-CROOK.

Racle, obs. f. RACKLE *a.* **Racoille**, var. RECUEIL *v.* **Racolta**, var. RACCOLTA. **Racommode**, var. RACCOMMODE. **Racon**, obs. f. RACKAN.

‖**Raconteur** (rakontör). [F., f. *raconter* to relate: see RECOUNT *v.*[1]] One skilled in relating anecdotes or stories.
1829 DISRAELI *Yng. Duke* I. xii. (1831) 97 Stamped the illustrious narrator as the most consummate *raconteur*. 1855–6 THACKERAY *Four Georges* (1861) 183 Scott..the very best *raconteur* of his time. 1885 *Manch. Exam.* 13 Apr. 5/7 He was a good *raconteur*. No one knew more good stories or could tell them so well.
So **Raconteuse** (-töz), a female raconteur.
1863 OUIDA *Held in Bondage* (1870) 46 'There's not one of you men now-a-days like Selwyn', began the old *raconteuse* again. 1892 *Daily News* 2 Aug. 5/1 Let us admit that she is a good raconteuse, for the sake of grammar.

Racoon, raccoon (rǎkū·n, rækū·n), *sb.* Forms: 7 (see etym. note; also) racoone, -oune, -owne, 7–8 rackoon, (7 rack-, rockoone), 7– raccoon, 8– racoon. See also COON and RATTOON. [Powhatan (Virginia) dialect of Algonquian. The following quots. show more precise reproductions of the native word:
1608 CAPT. SMITH *True Relat.* Wks. (Arb.) 19 Couered with a great Couering of Rahaugcums. *Ibid.* 23 Presents of Deare, bread, Raugroughcums. *c* 1610 W. STRACHEY *Virginia* (1849) I. x. 122 There is a beast they call arocoune, much like a badger. *Ibid.* 183 *Dict. Ind. Lang.*, *Arathkone*, a beast like a fox. 1624 CAPT. SMITH *Virginia* II. 27 There is a beast they call Aroughcun, much like a badger. *Ibid.* III. ii. 48 A great robe, made of Rarowcun skinnes.]
An American nocturnal carnivore of the genus *Procyon*. The common N. American species is *P. lotor*, a grayish-brown furry animal with bushy tail and sharp snout.
1619 MIDDLETON *Love & Antiq.* 19 Minck, Stote, Miniuer, Racoone, Moashye, Wolueriue. 1632 T. MORTON *New Eng. Canaan* v. (1838) 54 The Racowne is a beast as bigg..as a Foxe, with a Bushtayle. 1672 JOSSELYN *New Eng. Rarities* 17 The Raccoon liveth in hollow trees. 1712 E. COOKE *Voy. S. Sea* 326 Of wild Creatures, there are Raccoons, Hares, Rabbits, &c. 1774 GOLDSM. *Nat. Hist.* (1776) IV. 333 The racoon, which some authors have called the Jamaica rat, is about the size of a small badger. 1809 W. IRVING *Knickerb.* (1861) 204 They were gallant bush-whackers and hunters of racoons by moonlight. 1856 BRYANT *Winter Piece* 52 The lighter track Of fox, and the racoon's broad path, were there. 1895 *Outing* (U. S.) XXVI. 434/2 The American racoon..is practically a bear.
b. *attrib.* and *Comb.*, as *racoon-hunt*, *-hunting*, *-skin*; **racoon-berry** *U.S.*, the May-apple or mandrake (Miller, 1884); **racoon-bridge** (see quot. 1791); **racoon-oyster** *U.S.* (see quots. 1883–4).
1624 [see etym. note]. 1670 D. DENTON *Descr. New York* (1845) 2 Bevers, Otter, Raccoon skins, with other Furrs. 1791 W. BARTRAM *Carolina* 445 No other bridge than a sapling felled across it, which is called a raccoon bridge. 1809 A. HENRY *Trav.* 131 Racoon-hunting was my..daily employ. 1864 C. GEIKIE *Life in Woods* xix. (1874) 317, I remember one racoon hunt. 1883 SIMMONDS *Useful Animals*, *Raccoon Oysters*, a variety of American oysters from Appalichicola Bay, Florida. 1884 GOODE *Nat. Hist. Usef. Aquatic Anim.* 752 From..overcrowding the shells of the individual Oysters become very narrow and greatly elongated; the peculiar forms which result are known to oystermen as 'Raccoon Oysters' or 'Cats-tongues'.
Hence **Racoo·n** *v. intr.*, to walk about at night, like a racoon. *nonce-wd.*
1855 MRS. GASKELL *North & S.* xiii, She heard him pacing about (racooning, as she and Edith used to call it)..long after she began to listen as she lay in bed.

Racord, obs. Sc. form of RECORD.

Racovian (rǎkōu·viǎn), *a.* and *sb.* [f. *Rakow*, a town in Poland + -IAN.] a. *adj.* Of or pertaining to Rakow, or to the Unitarians (Socinians) who made it their chief centre in the 17th century. b. *sb.* An adherent of the doctrines taught at Rakow.
1652 (*title*) The Racovian Catechisme. 1768–74 TUCKER *Lt. Nat.* (1834) II. 474 Should another Edwards do me the honour to make another Mr. Locke of me by calling out, Racovian! 1837 HALLAM *Hist. Lit.* III. ii. § 39 The Racovian institution was broken up and dispersed in 1638. *a* 1861 CUNNINGHAM *Hist. Theol.* (1864) II. xxiii. 177 The Racovian Catechism fills very nearly two hundred pages.

Racquet, -ette, varr. RACKET *sb.*, RAQUETTE.

Ract, obs. Sc. form of RACK *sb.*[1]

Racunnis, etc., obs. Sc. forms of RECOGNIZE.

Racy (rēⁱ·si), *a.* Also 7 racie, rasy, 8 razie. [f. RACE *sb.*[2] 10 + -Y[1].]
1. Of wine or other liquors, vegetable juices, fruits, etc.: Having a characteristically excellent taste, flavour, or quality. So of taste, flavour, etc.
1654 GAYTON *Pleas. Notes* III. vi. 102 The generous oyle of Sack, nitty, roapy, and rasy. 1676 WORLIDGE *Cyder* (1691) 210 If ground early then is the cider more racy. 1756–7 tr. *Keysler's Trav.* (1760) IV. 244 The racy flavour and strong body of this wine. *a* 1774 GOLDSM. *Surv. Exp. Philos.* (1776) II. 243 The juices which are nourished in the vegetable world by the solar heat, are light, pungent, and racy. 1800 MOORE *Anacreon* i. 12 His lip exhaled..The fragrance of the racy tide. 1849 SIR J. STEPHEN *Eccl. Biog.* II. 228 The grapes they yield are ponderous and racy, like the clusters of Eshcoll.
fig. *c* 1650 DENHAM *Progr. Learn.* 68 Might make old Homer's skull the Muses' hive; And from his brain that Helicon distil Whose racy liquor did his offspring fill. 1832 DE QUINCEY *Rhetoric* Wks. 1862 X. 50 English divinity ceased to be the racy vineyard that it had been in ages of ferment and struggle.
†b. Of plants: Full of sap, succulent. *Obs.*
1675 EVELYN *Terra* (1729) 25 Some Plants, the most racy, and charg'd with Juice..thrive well amongst Rocks.
2. a. Of persons: Having a distinctive quality or vigour of character or intellect; lively, spirited, full of 'go'. So of actions, qualities, etc.
1668 DRYDEN *Even. Love* II. i, A colony of Spaniards, or spiritual Italians, planted among us, would make us much more racy. 1849 C. BRONTË *Shirley* ix, Yorkshire has such families here and there..peculiar, racy, vigorous; of good blood and strong brain. 1852 MISS MITFORD *Recoll.* II. 147 My friend the rector, raciest of men, is an Oxford divine of the old school. 1854 BLACKMORE *Clara Vaughan* lxi, That genial racy smile, which very few could resist.
b. Of animals or their parts: Showing high breeding or good blood.
1841 'WILDRAKE' *Cracks of the Day* 190 The *racy* Mango won him the St. Leger. 1885 *Century Mag.* XXXI. 118 The Gordon setter..should have..a narrow deep chest with racy front. 1889 *Pall Mall G.* 21 Aug. 2/1 His [a horse's] head having a racy, determined look.
†c. Of a sense: Noble, superior. *Obs. rare*[—1].
1675 R. BURTHOGGE *Causa Dei* 400 There are things Good, and things Evil to this High and Racy Sense, as well as to Inferiour Ones.
3. Of speech, writing, etc.: Having a characteristic sprightliness, liveliness, or piquancy.
a 1667 COWLEY *Answ. Verses fr. Jersey*, Brisk racy Verses, in which we The Soil from whence they came, tast, smell, and see. *c* 1817 GIFFORD *Let.* in Smiles *Mem. J. Murray* (1891) II. xxi. 47 His style is racy and vivid. 1841 D'ISRAELI *Amen. Lit.* (1867) 291 The conversations of Sir Thomas More were racy. 1895 J. HOLLINGSHEAD *My Lifetime* I. xxiv. 232 A rich imagination, and the power of racy narrative.

4. Of pleasure, enjoyment, etc.: Peculiarly agreeable or rich.
1690 SHADWELL *Am. Bigot* II, 'Tis difficulty makes the pleasure high and racy. 1847 LYTTON *Lucretia* (1853) 166 There was a racy, wholesome gusto in his enjoyment of novelty. 1862 BURTON *Bk. Hunter* (1863) 163 The active racy enjoyments of life—those enjoyments in which there is also exertion and achievement.
5. Of the air: Pure, exhilarating.
1838 LYTTON *Alice* VIII. vii, Theresa's merry laugh sounded clear and musical in the racy air.
6. Phr. *Racy of the soil*, characteristic of a certain country or people (chiefly used with ref. to Ireland).
1870 *Daily News* 16 Feb., It is racy of the soil; and would not admit of transplantation to England or Scotland. 1889 *Spectator* 26 Oct., This popular [Irish] superstition..is so racy of the soil, that it is really deserving of a much wider publicity.

Racyn, obs. form of RAISIN.

Racyonal, obs. form of RATIONAL.

Rad (ræd), *sb.*[1] Abbrev. of RADICAL *sb.* 5.
1831 *Lincoln Herald* 7 Jan., The tricolor rads of this Borough. 1851 COL. HAWKER *Diary* (1893) II. 344 Hooted at by the scum and rads at this dirty end of the town. 1882 BESANT *All Sorts* (1884) 139 He is the reddest of red-hot Rads and the most advanced of Republicans.

Rad, *sb.*[2] [Abbrev. of RADDLE *sb.*[1]] In phr. *rad and dab*: see RADDLE *sb.*[1] 2.
1887 in *Dict. Archit.* VII.

Rad (ræd), *a.*[1] and *adv.* *Obs.* exc. *dial.* Forms: 1 hrad, hræd, 1–3 ræd, 3–6 rade, 5–6 radde, 3–6 (9 *dial.*) rad. [OE. *hrad*, *hræd* = OHG. *hrad*, *hrat*, ON. *hrað-r* (MSw. *radh*).]
A. *adj.* Quick, hasty, speedy; active, prompt, ready; eager, elated.
a 700 *Epinal Gloss.* 741 *Percitus*, hraed [*Erfurt* hrad]. *c* 888 K. ÆLFRED *Boeth.* iv, Þu þe on hrædum færelde þone heofon ymbhweorfest. *c* 897 — *Gregory's Past.* xxxviii. 280 Sie æʒhwelc mon swiðe hræd & swiðe ʒeornfull to ʒehieranne. *c* 1000 *Ags. Gosp.* Matt. xxvi. 41 Se gast is hræd [*Hatton MS.* ræd], þæt flæsc ys untrum. *c* 1205 LAY. 12318 Þer fore wes þe king glad & þiderward wes swiðe ræd. *c* 1250 *Gen. & Ex.* 2730 Ðu art of dede and o word to rad. *a* 1310 in Wright *Lyric P.* 45 Wymmen..beoth to rad upon huere red, To love [etc.]. *c* 1400 *Destr. Troy* 917 The freike..raght to his Ryng in a rad haste. *c* 1425 *Seven Sag.* (P.) 1290 The tormentours wer ful rade To do tha[t] the Emperour bade. *c* 1470 HENRY *Wallace* VII. 526 Cast we doun all, we mycht be demyt our rad. 1570 LEVINS *Manip.* 7/41 Radde, *agilis*, *promptus*. 1876 *Whitby Gloss.* s.v., 'Either too rad or too sad', as a variable person, over-elated or, otherwise, depressed. 1887 *S. Chesh. Gloss.*, *Rad*, quick, ready.
†B. *adv.* Quickly, readily, soon. *Obs.*
c 1250 *Gen. & Ex.* 998 Al ðat euere ðe louerd bad dede abraham redi and rad. 13.. *Gaw. & Gr. Knt.* 862 Ryche robes ful rad renkkez hem broʒten. *c* 1400 *Destr. Troy* 9233 He made hym redy full rad, ron to the toun. 1486 *Bk. St. Albans* F j b, Then ar thay glad In hope thay shall hym haue & renne so rad. *c* 1525 *Priests of Peblis* 1190 Thow thocht I was not wort ane prene, And that I am, ful rade on the will be sene.

Rad (ræd), *a.*[2] *Obs.* exc. *Sc.* Also 3 raad, 3–5 radd, rade, 4–6 radde, 6 raed; 4, 8 rede; 4–8 red, 5 redd, 6 redde. [a. ON. *hræddr* (Sw. *rädd*, Da. *ræd*) frightened, afraid, pa. pple. of *hræða* to frighten.] Frightened, afraid, alarmed. Const. *of*, *for*, and infin.
c 1200 ORMIN 2170 Ʒho drefedd wass & radd off Godess engell. 13.. *Cursor M.* 5097 Bes noght rad bot mas godd chere. *Ibid.* 23024 Þai for him sal be sa redd. *a* 1340 HAMPOLE *Psalter* lxv. 8 All erthly lufers was rad for pyne. 1375 BARBOUR *Bruce* XII. 431 Thai war rad till byd fichting. *a* 1400–50 *Alexander* 2510 Þan am I redd all oure rewme be reft vs for euire. *c* 1450 *St. Cuthbert* (Surtees) 4627 For few perills were þai radd. 1513 DOUGLAS *Æneis* II. ii. 18 Semyng ful red, Behalding Troiane rowtis on athir hand. *c* 1600 MONTGOMERIE *Cherrie & Slae* 1392, I am red His hastyness bred us mishap. *a* 1708 *Outlaw Murray* xxvi. in Child *Ballads* V. 192/1, I am right rad of treasonrie. 1791 LEARMONT *Poems* 284, I'm rede I tine the way.

Rad, obs. f. RAID *sb.*, obs. pa. t. READ, REDE, RIDE.

†**Radcolle.** *Obs.*[—0] A radish. (Cf. REDCOLL.)
1483 *Cath. Angl.* 298/1 Radcolle, *raphanus*.

Radd(e, variants of RAD *a.*[1] and *a.*[2]

Radde, obs. f. RAID; obs. pa. t. READ, REDE.

Raddish, obs. form of RADISH.

Raddle (ræ·d'l), *sb.*[1] *Obs.* exc. *dial.* Also 6 radel(l, -yll, 8 roddle, 9 ruddle. [a. AF. *reidele* (Wright *Vocab.* 168), OF. *reddalle*, *ridelle*, *rudelle* (14th c. in Du Cange) a stout stick or pole, the rail of a cart (so mod.F. *ridelle*), of obscure origin.]
1. †a. The rail of a cart. *Obs. rare*[—0].
1530 PALSGR. 260/2 Radyll of a carte, *costee*.
b. *north. dial.* and *U.S.* A wooden bar with upright pegs, used to keep the threads of the warp in place while it is being wound upon the beam.
1848 in WORCESTER. 1883 *Almondbury Gloss.*
2. A slender rod, wattle, or lath, fastened to or twisted between upright stakes or posts to form a fence, partition, or wall (in the latter case usually plastered over with clay, whence the phr. *raddle and daub* or *dab*, applied to walls or houses made in this way).
1577 HARRISON *England* II. x[ii.] in *Holinshed* 84 b, The houses of the Brytons were slitely set vppe with a few postes and many radles, the like whereof almost is to be seene in the fenny countries vnto this day. 1686 PLOT *Staffordsh.* 233 Small stakes driven into the ground..and interwoven with broom and other raddles. 1736 PEGGE *Kenticisms* (E.D.S.), *Raddis-chimney*, a chimney made of studs, lathes, or raddles, and covered with lome or lime. 1868 *Sussex Gloss.* in Hurst *Horsham* (1889), *Ruddles*, long supple sticks of greenwood interwoven between upright sticks to make a hedge. 1869– In dial. glossaries (Lanc., Chesh., Som.).
attrib. 1736 PEGGE *Kenticisms* (E.D.S.), *Raddle-hedge*. 1778 [W. MARSHALL] *Minutes Agric., Observ.* 167 A live roddle Hedge..is, perhaps, the Ultimate of Farm hedge-making. 1785 HUTTON *Bran New Wark* (E.D.S.) 372 The girl unsneck'd the raddle heck. 1786–1805 H. TOOKE *Purley* (1829) II. 258 A raddle hedge, is a hedge of pleached or plashed or twisted or wreathed twigs or boughs.
3. A piece of wattled work; a hurdle, door, hedge, etc. made with intertwined raddles.
1886 *Cheshire Gloss.* s.v., Long sticks were wound together between the timber, forming a sort of basket-work or raddle. 1892 J. LUCAS tr. *Kalm's England* 398 In only a few places were there any 'Raddles', or wooden hurdles.

Raddle (ræ·d'l), *sb.*[2] Also 6 radel, raddell, 7–8 radle. [var. RUDDLE, q.v.: cf. also REDDLE.]
1. Red ochre, RUDDLE.
1523 [see *raddle-mark* below]. 1577 B. GOOGE *Heresbach's Husb.* (1586) 16 b, Stone, marble, sande, gravell, raddell, chalke, &c. 1631 J. BURGES *Answ. Rejoined, Lawfuln. Kneeling* 21 The raddle doth signifie more then the brand alone. 1699 T. BROWN in R. L'Estrange *Colloq. Erasm.* (1711) 402 To revive the decay'd Red and White in their cheeks with raddle and chalk. 1757 DYER *Fleece* I. 321 See that thy scrip have store of..marking pitch and raddle. 1805 DICKSON *Pract. Agric.* (1807) I. 360 *note*, Raddle..has lately been used with advantage on some lands. 1853 LANDOR *Last Fruits, Let. Wiseman* vi. 194 He would whistle the sheep into the ancient fold, marking them with his raddle.
transf. 1603 OWEN *Pembrokeshire* (1891) 83 'Nod glas' which in Englishe is blewe radle or blewe markinge stone.
b. A coarse red layer. *nonce-use.*
1860 THACKERAY *Round. Papers* xxxii, To hide..a yellow cheek behind a raddle of rouge.
2. *attrib.* and *Comb.*, as *raddle-ground*, *-mark*; *raddle-red* adj.
1523 FITZHERB. *Husb.* § 52 Se that they [the sheep] be well marked, both eare-marke, pitche-marke, and radelmarke. 1577 B. GOOGE *Heresbach's Husb.* (1586) 18 A raddell and a stonie grounde is discerned by the eye. 1897 *Contemp. Rev.* June 765 The then new and raddle-red penny postage stamps.

Ra·ddle, *sb.*[3], variant of RABBLE *sb.*[2]
1875 in KNIGHT *Dict. Mech.*

Raddle (ræ·d'l), *v.*[1] Also 6 rathel. [f. RADDLE *sb.*[1]] *trans.* To weave or twist together (like raddles), to intertwine, interlace.
1671 *St. Foine Improved* 18 To wrap or wreath or raddle the spiks or teeth of the Harrow. 1719 DE FOE *Crusoe* II. v, They came at last to build up their Huts..very handsomely; raddling or working it up like Basket-work all the way round. 1747 HOOSON *Miner's Dict.* I j b, They are made of Boards or of Sticks radled together. 1824 in *Craven Dialect.* 1867 SMYTH *Sailor's Word-bk.*, *To raddle*, to interlace; as in making boat's gripes and flat gaskets. 1869– In dial. glossaries (Yks., Lanc., Som.).
Hence **Ra·ddled** *ppl. a.*[1]
1562 WITHALS *Dict.* 41 b/1 A hartheled wall, or ratheled..*paries craticius*. 1876 *Whitby Gloss.*, *Raddled*, wrought or painted in a zigzag pattern.

Raddle (ræ·d'l), *v.*[2] [f. RADDLE *sb.*[2]] *trans.* To paint or mark with raddle; to colour coarsely with red or rouge.
1631 J. BURGES *Answ. Rejoined, Lawfuln. Kneeling* 21 Hee that beside a pitch-brande, doth raddle the heads of his fat sheepe, doth more then marke them. 1848 THACKERAY *Lett.* 1 Nov., A chief raddled over with war-paint. 1879 SALA *Paris herself again* (1880) I. viii. 120 They do not even go so far as to raddle themselves. Rouge is apparently too dear.
Hence **Ra·ddled** *ppl. a.*[2]
1681 CHETHAM *Angler's Vade-m.* iv. § 7 (1700) 35 Perhaps within an Hour again the bright ones will be taken, and the radled Worms refused. 1854 THACKERAY *Newcomes* xx, Those whitened and raddled old women.

Raddle (ræ·d'l), *v.*[3] *north. dial.* [Perh. f. RADDLE *sb.*[1] (as if = to beat with a raddle).] *trans.* To beat, thrash.
1688 SHADWELL *Sqr. Alsatia* II. i, I'st raddle the bones o' thee. 1818 SCOTT *Rob Roy* vii, I'se raddle Dick the miller's bones for him. 1855 *Bon Gaultier Ballads* 171 Raddle him well, till he roar again.

†**Ra·ddled**, *a.* *Obs. rare*[—1]. [Of obscure origin.] Fuddled.
1694 MOTTEUX *Rabelais* v. xxxix, A..sottish Fellow, continually raddled, and as drunk as a Wheelbarrow.

Ra·ddleman. [f. RADDLE *sb.*[2]] A digger of, or dealer in, raddle. †Applied allusively to Rutlandshire, and to a disease in wheat. *Obs.*
1622 DRAYTON *Poly-olb.* xxiii. 268 Little Rutlandshire is tearmed Raddleman. *a* 1661 FULLER *Worthies, Rutland* (1662) 347 Rutland *Raddleman*..*Rad* here is the same with *red* (onely more broadly pronounced)..*Raddleman* then is a *Reddleman*. 1798 *Ann. Agric.* XXVI. 177 *Raddleman*, ear-cockle, the disease in wheat due to *Vibrio tritici*. *Sal.* 1881 in *Leicestersh. Gloss.*

Ra·ddling. *dial.* Also 7, 9 radling. [f. RADDLE *sb.*[1] + -ING[1].]
1. A raddle, rod, twig, etc.
1616 *Salford Portmote Rec.* (1902) 121 Any sprinkelings radlings or any other woode. 1626 *Manchester Court Leet Rec.* (1886) III. 114 John Wright..got Radlings in the grounds of Elizabeth Mosley. 1736 PEGGE *Kenticisms* (E.D.S.), *Raddles*..in some countries called *raddlings*. *a* 1796 — *Derbicisms*, *Radlings*, long slender poles for

Supplement, p. 3873; Corrigenda, p. 4092; Spurious words, p. 4093; Books quoted, p. 4094

[This is a densely-set dictionary page from the Oxford English Dictionary. The principal headwords and entries across the four upper columns include:]

Radicose, *a. Bot. rare*

Radicular (rædīk·iŭlăɹ), *a.*

Radiculariā

Radicule (ræ·dikiŭl), *Bot.*

Radie, obs. Sc. form of READY.

Radience, variant of RADIANCE, RADIANT.

Radiescent (rēdiĕ·sĕnt), *a.*

Radiisium

Radio- (rē·diŏ), comb. form of RADIUS.

Radio-active, *a.*

Radio-conductor

Radiodynamic

Radiogoniometer

Radiograph (rē·diŏgrăf), *sb.*

Radiographer

Radiographic

Radiographically

Radiography

Radiolaria

Radiolarian

Radiole

Radiolite

Radiometer (rēdiǫ·mĕtăɹ)

Radiomicrometer

Radiophone (rē·diŏfŏun), *sb.*

Radiophonic

Radiophony

Radioscopy

Radious, *a. Bot. rare*

Radish (ræ·dĭʃ)

Radius (rē·diŭs). *Pl.* radii

Radix (rē·diks). *Pl.* 7-9 radixes (rē·diksiz), 7- radices. [a. L. *radix* (stem *radic*-) a root.]

Radman (ræ·dmăn), *Eng. Hist.*

Radness, Sc. and north. Obs.

Radnesse

Radon, obs. Sc. f. REDDEN.

Radour, var. RADDER, Radres, obs. Sc. f. RETHER.

Radula (ræ·diŭlă)

Radulate

Raduliferous, *adjs.*

Raduliform, *a.*

Radure, var. RADDOUR? Radyll, -y(e)she, obs. ff. RIDDLE 1.

Rae, var. RA, ROE.

Rafe, obs. Sc. Rae(s)che: see REACH.

Raff (ræf), *sb.1* Also 4-5 (9) raf, 6-7 raffe.

Raff, *sb.2* Also raffe, raffle. [Of obscure origin: cf. obs. F. *rafer* to catch, or snatch.]

Raffe (ræf), *U.S.* Also raffee, raffle.

Raffery, *rare*

Raffia (ræ·fiă), *variant of* RAFFIA.

Raffiosos

Raffish

Raffle (ræ·f'l), *sb.1*

Raffle, *sb.2*

Raffle, *v.1*

Raffle, *v.2*

Raffling

Raffly

Rafle (ræ·f'l), *v.1*

Rafia, variant of RAFFIA.

Rafiol, obs. var. ravioli.

Raffinose

Rafer, *Obs. rare*

Raffler (ræ·flăɹ)

Rafsed

Raft (ráft), *sb.1* Also 5-6 rafte, 5-6 rafte.

Raft, *sb.2*

Raft, *v.*

Rafter (ráftăɹ), *sb.1*

RAGGED.

4. *Her.* = RAGULY.

Ragged Robin. One of the popular names of a wild-flower, *Lychnis Flos-cuculi.* Also *attrib.*

Ragged staff. [RAGGED *a.*1]

Ragged school. A free school for the education of the poorest class.

Hence **Raggedish**, somewhat ragged. **Raggedy** (*a.* Raggety *a.*), ragged appearance.

Ragged (ræg'd), *a.*2 (or *pple.*) *dial.* [Of obscure origin; connexion with prec. is not clear.] Covered with fruit; thickly laden.

Ragged (ræg'd), *ppl. a.* [f. RAG *v.*] Subjected to the process of ragging (*vbl. sb.*3).

Raggedemuffin, obs. form of RAGAMUFFIN.

Raggedly (ræ'gedli), *adv.* In a ragged manner.

Raggedness (ræ'gednes). [f. RAGGED *a.*1 + -NESS.] The fact or condition of being ragged.

Ragger [RAG *v.*1 + -ER 1.] One who sorts needles by means of a rag.

Raggery (ræ'geri). *rare.* [RAG *sb.*1 + -ERY.]

Ragghe, obs. f. RAG *sb.*2 **Raggi,** var. RAGI.

Ragging, *vbl. sb.*1 [RAG *v.*1 + -ING 1.]

Ragging, *vbl. sb.*2 [f. RAG *v.*2]

Raggle (ræ'g'l), *sb.*1 *Sc. Obs.* — Straggling order.

Raggle, *sb.*2 *U.S.* [f. RAGGLE *sb.*1 + -LE.] A rag, a strip (of fur, etc.).

Raggle (ræ'g'l), *v.* [f. RAGGLE *sb.*1] To cut a raggle in (stone). **b.** = HOUSE *v.* 4. Hence **Raggling** *vbl. sb.*

RAGLAN.

Raggle, var. of RAGGLE *sb.*1

Ragman. The document by which the Scottish nobles in 1291 acknowledged Edward I as their overlord.

Ragman's roll. *Hist.* [f. prec. + ROLL *sb.*]

Raglan (ræ'glan). [f. the name of Lord Raglan, British commander in the Crimean war.] An overcoat without shoulder seams, the sleeve going right up to the neck. Also *attrib.*

RAGLER.

Ragler. = RAGMAN.

Ragly, obs. form of RALLY *v.*

Ragman. [ad. (sense 1) raggeman, rageman, -mon, 6 Sc. ragment. [f. RAG *sb.*1 + MAN.]

Ragman 2. Forms: 3-5 rageman, 4-mon, -ment; 4, 6 Sc. ragment.

Ragman 3. = RAGMAN *a.* b.

RAG-TAG.

Ragout (ragū'), *sb.* Forms: 7 ragoust; 8-ragoo, 8 ragouz, 8-9 ragou. [f. F. *ragoût.*]

Ragstone (ræ'gstoun). [f. RAG *sb.*2 + STONE *sb.*]

Rag-tag (ræ'gtæg), *sb.* (and *a.*) [f. RAG *sb.*1 + TAG.]

Rag-time. *U.S.* Music in which there is frequent syncopation, as in many negro melodies.

RAGULED.

Ragule, variant of RAGULY.

Raguled, *a.* *Her.* Also 6 raguelеd. [f. as next, with various termination.] = RAGULY.

Raguly (ræ'giuli), *a.* *Her.* Also 6 raguelе. [Of obscure formation: perh. based on *rag*, *ragged*, or *ragge.*] Of a cross or other bearing: Having short oblique projections resembling the stumps of branches cut off close to the stem.

Ragusye, obs. form of ARGOSY.

† **Rag-water.** *Obs. Cant.* [Cf. prec.] Some sort of strong-waters.

Ragwort 1. [RAG *sb.*1]

Rag-wheel. 1. A wheel having projections which catch into the links of a chain passing over it, as in a chain-pump; a sprocket-wheel.

Ragwork. [f. RAG *sb.*2] Masonry composed of flattish pieces of ragstone, having an undressed surface.

Ragworm. [f. RAG *sb.*2] A sand-worm.

Ragwort 1. [Prob.f. RAG *sb.*1, in reference to the ragged form of the leaves.]

RAIK.

Ragwort 1. The popular name of several species of the genus *Senecio*, esp. the Common Ragwort, *Senecio Jacobæa.*

Rahdar (rä'där), Anglo-Ind. Also 6 rahdari. A road-keeper, toll-gatherer.

Rahdaree, variant of REHATOUR. *Sc.*

† **Rahatour,** variant of REHATOUR. *Sc.*

Rai (räi), *Zool.* Also *raja* (pl. *R. raia* (pl.

Raia, -aw, obs. ff. RAJA(H). **Raiah,** obs. f. RAJAH. **Raian,** var. RAYAN.

Raid (re·d), *sb.* Forms: 5-6 rade, 5 raide, 5-9, 9 reid. [In form a var. of ROAD, revived by Scott and subsequently adopted in general use, with extension of meaning.]

Raid, *v.* [f. RAID *sb.*] **1.** *intr.* To go upon, or take part in a raid.

Raider (re·dɐr). [f. RAID *v.* + -ER 1.] Onc who raids; a plundering invader, a marauder.

Raik (re·k), *sb.* *Sc. Obs.* [f. RAIK *v.* Cf. ON. *reik.*]

Raik (re·k), *v.* Now *dial.* Forms: 3-5 raike, 4-5 rayk(e, 5 raike, 6 reike, 6-7 reik; also 6-7 raik, 7 rake. [ME. *raiken*, ad. ON. *reika* to wander.]

RAIK.

Raik, *v.* Forms: 3-5 raike, 4-6 rayk(e.

† **Rail,** *sb.*1 *Obs.* [OE. *hrægl*, *rægl*.]

Rail (re·l), *sb.*2 Forms: 4-6 raille, 4-7 raile, 5 reyle, 5-7 raill(e, 5- rail. [ME. *raile*, a. OF. *reille* (12th c. in Godef.), *raille*, :—L. *regula* straight stick, bar, rod, etc.]

Rail (re·l), *sb.*3 [a. F. *râle* (16th c. in Palsgr., *rasle*), f. OF. *raale.*]

RAIL.

Rail, *sb.*4 Obs. A gown or dress. [See RAIL *sb.*1]

Rail (re·l), *v.*1 [f. RAIL *sb.*2] 1. *trans.* To furnish with a rail or rails.

Rail, *v.*2 [a. F. *railler* (16th c. in Littré), to jest, banter.] 1. *intr.* To utter abusive language.

Hence **Railing,** conveyance by rail, or the charges for this.

Rail (rēˀl), sb.¹ An act of railing or reviling.

Rail (rēˀl), sb.⁴ A bird. Also **rayle**.

Rail, v.¹ *intr.* To utter abusive language.

Rail, v.⁴ To provide (vines, etc.) with rails; to train on rails.

Railage (rēˀlˑēdʒ), sb. Conveyance by rail; the charge for this.

Railer, sb.¹ One who rails; a reviler.

Railery, obs. form of RAILLERY.

Raillery (rēˀlˑəri), sb. Good-humoured ridicule, banter.

Railless (rēˀlˑles), a. Devoid of rails; having no railway.

Railler, sb. One who practises raillery.

Railly, v. Obs. Also rayly, raillie.

Railroad (rēˀlˑrōd), sb. A road laid with rails; a railway.

Railroad, v. To convey by railroad.

Railroading, vbl. sb.

Railway (rēˀlˑwē), sb. A way or road laid with rails.

Raim, v. Obs. To ransom, redeem; to recover (a heritage).

Raiment (rēˀmənt), sb. Clothing, clothes, dress, apparel.

Rain (rēˀn), sb.¹ The condensed vapour of the atmosphere, falling in drops.

Rain, v. To fall as or like rain.

Rainbow (rēˀnˑbō), sb. A bow or arch exhibiting the prismatic colours, formed in the sky opposite to the sun by the reflection, double refraction, and dispersion of the sun's rays in falling drops of rain.

Rainer. [f. RAIN v. + -ER 1.] One who rains.

† Raines. Obs. Forms: a. 4-6 reynes, 5 raynes, raygnes, 5-6 raynes, 6 rein(e)s, Sc. renes, 6-7 raine, 6 rayne. β. 5 rayne. [f. Rayens, obs. f. Rennes: see def.] The place-name occurs in the form Reynes 1480 in the Play (surname etc.) also 1489 in Paston Lett. (1895) III. 358.

Rainbow (continued)

Rainbowy, a. [f. RAINBOW sb. + -Y.] Of the nature of a rainbow.

† Rainbreed, a. mance-toad. Producing rain.

Raindeer, obs. form of REINDEER.

Rain-drop, rain-drop. [OE. regndropa OHG. regentropfo (G. -tropfen), MSw. reghndropi (Sw. regndroppe : see RAIN sb.) and DROP sb.]

Rain-fowl. 7 Obs. L. = RAINBIRD 1.

Rain-water. [OE. regn-, rēnwæter = Du. regenwater, MHG. regenwater (G. -wasser), ON. regnvatn (Sw. -vatten) : see RAIN sb. and WATER.] Water that falls from the clouds as rain.

Rain-water.

Raint, v.

Rainy, a. [OE. regnig, rēnig : see RAIN sb. and -Y 1.] Characterized by rain.

RAISE.

Raid, obs. form of RAYED.

Raip, north. and Sc. var. ROPE.

Raird, var. REIRD. Rain, obs. Sc. f. RARE, ROAR.

Raisable, a. [f. RAISE v. + -ABLE.] Capable of being raised.

Raise, sb. 1 [f. RAISE v.]

† Raise, sb. 2 north dial. [a. ON. hreysi, hreysar, a heap of stones, a cairn.]

Raise, sb. 3 Obs. (See REISE.)

Raise, sb. 4 north dial.

Raise, v. [ME. reisen, reȝen.]

Rakeism. A. *adj.* 1. Of persons : Of the nature of, or resembling a rakehell, or rakehells.

B. 2. *sb.* = RAKE-HELL 1.

Rakeism. *rare* —1.

Rake-kennel. *Obs. rare* —1. A scavenger.

Ra'kel. *Obs. exc. dial.* Abbrev. of RAKE-HELL.

Rakeless. *rare.*

Rakeless. *sb.*

†Rakely. *a.* *Obs.* —1.

Ra·ke-mould. *Obs. rare* —1.

Rakentee. *Obs.* Forms: ... 1 raoenteah ... 3 raketee.

Raker (rēi·kəɹ). Also 4 *rakyr.*

1. One who rakes.

2. *spec.* A scavenger, street-cleaner.

Raking (rēi·kiŋ), *vbl. sb.*

1. The action of the vb., in various senses.

2. *concr.* That which is collected with a rake.

4. An implement for raking : *spec.* a. A tool used by charcoal-burners.

Billiards. (See quot. 1788.)

Rakery. Now *rare.*

Raking (rēi·kiŋ), *ppl. a.*

Rakeshame. (*rēi·kʃeim.*)

Raking (rēi·kiŋ), *ppl. a.*

†Rakes. *Obs. rare* —1.

Ra·ke-shamed *a.*, disreputable, disgraceful. *Obs.*

Rake-soil : see RAKE *sb.*3 5 b.

Raket, obs. form of RACKET *sb.*1

Rakete, -tein, etc., var. RAKENTEIE. *Obs.*

Ra·ke-vein *Obs.* —1. A leading vein of ore (cf. quot. and RAKE).

Raki (rāki·, rɑ·ki). Forms : 7 racokoe, 8 rakia, 8-9 rakie, 9 racah, 7- raki.

Rakily (rēi·kili), *adv.*

Raki·sh (rēi·kiʃ), *a.*2 [See notes below.]

1. *Naut.* Of a ship : Having an appearance indicative of smartness and fast sailing, freq. with suggestion of suspicion or piratical character.

2. Of a hawk's wings : Smart-looking.

3. In a rakish manner; jauntily.

Rakishly (rēi·kiʃli), *adv.*

Rakishness (rēi·kiʃnes).

So Ra·kishness, the quality of being rakish.

Rakk·ʃo, obs. ff. RACK, RECK.

Rakle, obs. f. RACKLE *a.*

Rakn·o, obs. f. RECKON *v.*

†Ra·kyl. *Obs. rare* —1.

Rakyl (*rēi·kil*), *sb.*

†Rāle (rāl). *Path.* [F. *râle*, *rasle* (Cotgr. 1611).]

Rale (rēil), *ppl. a.*

†Raling (*rēi·liŋ*), *vbl. sb.* *Obs. rare* —1.

Rakish (rēi·kiʃ), *a.*1

Ra·ling. *vbl. sb.* *Obs. rare* —1.

Ralliance [f. RALLY *v.*1 + cf. *dalliance*.] The act of rallying.

Ralliaria, -ry, variants of RALLERY.

Ralli-car, -cart. [See def.] A form of light two-wheeled driving-trap.

†Ra·llier. One who rallies.

Rallier. [f. RALLY *v.*2 + -ER 1.] One who banters.

Ra'lly (rē·li), *v.*1 [f. RALLY *v.*1]

I. A rapid reunion for concentrated effort, *esp.* of an army after repulse or disorganization.

Rallye (*rēi·li, ra·li*), *sb.* *Ornith.* [F. mod.L. *rall-*... etc.]

Ra·lly (rē·li), *v.*1

1. *trans.* To reunite, rouse, stimulate (a person or animal).

II. *intr.*

Rallo, -lly, obs. forms of RALLY.

III. To attack vigorously.

IV. *Sporting.* To bant.

Rally. santry, or good-humoured ridicule ; to make fun of.

Ra'lly (rē·li), *v.*2 All in chorus called out *mais.*

Rallying (rē·liiŋ), *vbl. sb.*1 The action of RALLY *v.*1

Rally'ing, *vbl. sb.*2

Rallying, *ppl. a.*1 [f. RALLY *v.*1 + -ING 1.]

Rallying, *ppl. a.*2

Rallyman. That rallies, banters, etc.

Rallymentt : see RALLIMENT.

Ralstonite (rǫ·lstonəit). *Min.* [Named (1871) after J. G. Ralston its discoverer : see -ITE.]

Ram (ram), *sb.*1 Forms : 1-2 ramm, 4-7 ramme, 5-6 rame, rambe, 1- ram. [OE. *ram*(*m*), *romm* = M(L)Du., M(L)G., OHG. and MHG. *ram* (*ramm-*) : see RAM *v.*2]

1. A male sheep ; in domestication, one kept for breeding purposes, a tup.

Ram, *sb.*2 *rare.* Ore. *Black ram*, bog-iron.

Ram (ram), *sb.*3 *Naut.* Length 'over all' of a boat.

Ram (ram), *sb.*4

Ram (ram), *v.*1

1. To beat down the earth with a heavy implement, so as to make it hard and firm.

Ram (ram), *v.*2

Ram (ram), *v.*3

Ramadan (ramadān·). Forms : 1 ramadan, 1-7 ramadan, 7-9 ramadhan, 8 -dam, ramzan, 8-9 rhamazan, 6 ramassan etc. [a. Arab. رمضان *ramaḍān*.]

Ramage (ra·mēdʒ), *sb.*1 Also 7 *ramago*. [a. OF. *ramage*.]

†Rama·geness. *Obs.*

Ramage, *a.* Also 6-7 (9) *ramage.*

†Ramage, *v.* *Obs.* —1.

Ramagious, -gous, -geus, 6-gious, a. Forms.

†Ramass. *Obs. rare* —1.

Ramassh, obs. forms of RAMMEL.

Ramakin, variant of RAMEKIN.

Ramal (rēi·mal), *a.* [f. L. *rām-us* branch.]

Ramass (ramæ·s), *v.* *arch.*

Ramass, *sb.*1 *Obs. rare* —1.

Ramass, *sb.*2 Forms : 6 ramash,

This page consists of densely printed Oxford English Dictionary columns. The main headwords visible include entries such as: rammass, Ramble, Ramble-berry, Rambler, Rambling, Ramblingly, Rambooze, Rambustious, Rambutan, Rame, Rameous, Ramekin, Ramie, Ramed, Ramellose, Rament, Ramentaceous, Ramicorn, Ramiculose, Ramiferous, Ramification, Ramified, Ramiflorous, Ramiform, Ramify, Ramist, Rammilie, Ramiparous, Ramiram, Ramming, Rammish, Rammel, Rammed, Rammer, Rammy, Ramoon, Ramoose, Ramose, Ramp, and related forms.

RAMPISH. 135 RAMULUS. RAMUS. 136 RANCOROUS.

RANCOROUSLY. 137 RANDOM. RANDOM. 138 RANE.

Rancour, **-re**, obs. ff. RENCOUNTER *sb.*

Rancour (ræŋkəɹ), *sb.* Forms: 4–6 rankor, -our, (5 -ours, -owre, -ure), 6 ranckor, 6–7 rauker; 4 rancours, 5–6 rancoure, 3– rancour, 4– rancour. [a. OF. *rancor*, *-our*, *-ier*, *raunkour*, in the Vulgate.] bitter grudge.

1. Inveterate and bitter ill-feeling, grudge, or animosity; malignant hatred or spitefulness.

†2. Rancid smell; rancidity; rankness. *Obs. rare.*

3. A strip of leather placed under the quarters of a boot or shoe, to make this heel before the lifts of the heel are attached.

Rancour, *v.* Now rare or *Obs.* [f. prec.]

Rand (rænd), *sb.* Also 7 (in sense 3 a) rann. [OE. *rand*, *rond* (margin, etc.) = MDu. *rant*.]

†Rand, *v.* Obs. *rare*⁻. [ad. F. *rand*.] to melt (tallow).

†Randall, obs. var. RANDOM.

Randan (rænda·n), *sb.¹* [var. of *random* RAN-DOM, with assimilation of the vowels.]

Randan (rænda·n), *sb.²* A boat rowed by three persons: *see latest quot.*)

Randan, *sb.³* form of RANDOM.

Randle (ræ·nd'l), *sb.* dial. Also -dann. [?]

Random (ræ·ndəm), *sb.*, *adv.*, and *a.* Forms: 4 raundoun, 4–6 randon, -oun, (6 rawn-), 6–7 randome, 7– random. [a. F. *randon*.]

Random, *adv.* and *a.*

I. **†1.** Impetuosity, great speed, force, or violence (in riding, running, striking, etc.): chiefly in phr. *with (or in) great random.*

2. The direction (of a rake vein, etc.).

†3. *Hawking.* (See quot. 1486.)

Rane, obs. form of RANGE.

Ranedeer, obs. form of REINDEER.

†Ranee (rā·nī), *sb.* Also 7 ranny, 8 r(h)anny, 9 ranee, rani, rani, 7 (Hind) rāni = Skr. *rājñī* fem. of *rājā* in ELIJAH.] A Hindu queen.

Rane, obs. form of RANGE; obs. pa. t. RUN.

Ranegate, obs. form of RENEGATE.

†Ranforce, *v.* *Obs.* Also 6 -forse. [ad. F. *renforcer* RENFORCE.]

Rang, *Sc.* Now *rare* or *Obs.* dial. [Of obscure origin.]

Rang-, in Comb.

†Rangale. *Obs.* Chiefly *Sc.* Forms: 4 ren-galle, 4–5 rangale, -aill, 6 -all, rangall, 7 [ad. OF. *ringaille* (Vtace, etc.).]

Rangant, *v.* [f. *sc. rangant*, pr. pple. of *ranger* to RANGE.] = FIMBRIATE (*q.v.*).

†Rangat¹. *Sc. Obs.* [Of obscure origin.] Disorder, disturbance, noise.

†Rangat². *Sc. Obs.* [cf. prec.]

Range (rēⁱndʒ), *sb.¹* Forms: 4 renge, 5 rawnge, 5 rang, 6 raunge, 6– range. [a. OF. *range* row, rank.]

I. 1. A row, line, file or rank of persons (†*spec.* of hunters or fighting men) or animals. Now *rare*.

Range (rēⁱndʒ), *sb.²* Forms: 4–5 Sc. raung, 6 (*dial.*) rawnge, 5 r. range, (*dial.*) r. raunge, 6 ranges, 6– range. [a. F. *range.*]

I. 1. To place, set, or station (persons, rarely animals) in a row, line, or rank; to draw up, arrange (an army, etc.) in ranks.

II. intr. 7. To move hither and thither or comparatively large area; to rove, roam, wander, stray. *Const.* with various advbs. and preps. (*see* quot.).

Range (re-ndʒ), *sb.* ...

Ranged (re-ndʒd), *ppl. a.* ...

†Ranged, *ppl. a.* Obs. [f. RANGE *sb.*] Sifted; made of sifted flour.

Ranger (re-ndʒər), *sb.* ...

Rangership (re-ndʒərʃip). [f. RANGER] ...

Ranging (re-ndʒiŋ), *vbl. sb.* [f. RANGE *v.*]

Ranging, *ppl. a.* [f. RANGE *v.* + -ING.] That ranges, in senses of the vb.

Ranging-lath, a lath employed to guide the tool in cutting glass; **ranging-line, -pole, -rod, -stick**, a line, pole, etc. used in surveying or measuring, for setting out straight lines; **ranging-rim**.

Rangle, v. Obs. [Of obscure origin.]

†Rangy, *a.* Obs. rare. [f. RANGE *sb.* + -Y.]

Rangy (rei-ndʒi), *a.* Chiefly *U.S.* [f. RANGE *sb.*]

Rangerine (re-ndʒərəin), *a. Zool.* [f. RANGER *(gier)* reindeer + -INE.] Resembling the reindeer.

Rani, var. RANEE.

Raniform (rei-niform), *a.* [f. *rani-* comb. form of L. *rāna* frog + -FORM.] Frog-shaped.

Ranina (ranai-na), *sb.* Zool. ...

Ranine (rei-noin), *a.* [ad. mod.L. *rānīnus, f. rāna* frog: see -INE.]

Ranny, obs. form of RANGE *sb.*[1]

Rani-gerine, *a.* [f. med.L. *rangifer (f. rangifére)* reindeer + -INE.]

Ranivorous (rani-vorəs), *a.* [f. *rani-* (see *raniform*) + -VOROUS.] Frog-eating.

Rank (ræŋk), *a.1* Also 6 G. *ranke*, 6-7 *ranck*, 6-8 *rank*. [OE. *ranc*, *rang*, rare, usually supposed to be OHG. *kranc*, *kring* RING.]

Rank (ræŋk), *sb.2* Also 6-7 *ranke, ranck*, (7 *ranckes*). [a. OF. *ranc* (mod.F. *rang*); see RANGE *sb.*]

Rank (ræŋk), *v.* Also 6-7 *ranke, ranck*, (7 *rancke*). [f. RANK *sb.2*]

Ranked (ræŋkt), *ppl. a.1* [f. RANK *sb.2* + -ED.]

Ranked, *ppl. a.2* [f. RANK *a.1*] Rancid.

Ranken, v. Obs. rare. Also 7 *rancken*.

Ranker (ræŋkər), *sb.* [f. RANK *sb.* or *v.*]

Rankful, *a.* rare. [f. RANK *a.1* + -FUL.] Rank.

Rankle (ræŋk'l), *v.* Forms: 4-5, 7 (9) *rancle, rankil, -kyll, 6-7 wrankle, 7 -el; 4 rancle; rancre, var. dial. RANKER; 7 wrankle, 6-9 wrankle.* [a. OF. *rancler, draoncler* (Godef.)]

Rankling (ræŋkliŋ), *vbl. sb.* [f. RANKLE *v.* + -ING.] The action of the vb.

Rankly (ræŋkli), *adv.* [f. RANK *a.* + -LY.]

Rankness (ræŋknes). [OE. *rancnes*: see RANK *a.1* and -NESS.]

Ranksman. rare. [f. RANK sb.¹] a. (See quot. 1880.) b. One drawn up with others in a rank.

Rankum. Obs. rare⁻¹. b. A noisy chorus.

Rankyll, obs. form of RANKLE v.

Rann (ran). [Ir.] A verse, a strain.

Ranna, Ranndon, Rannoo, Rannegald, obs. ff. RANK a., RANDOM, RANEE, RANNIGAL.

Rannel-tree. Sc. and north. dial. Also 9 rannell-, rantle, rangel-, 8–9 Sc. rantle-tree.

Ran'nigal. Sc. and north. dial. Also 9 rannegald, 9 rannygill. [Alteration of renegade.]

Ranny (ræ'ni). Obs. exc. dial. Also 9 -ey.

Ranny, Sc. var. RANDY c., also 8 RANEE.

Ran-pick, -pike[d]: see RAMPICK, -PIKE[D].

Ranque, obs. form of RANK sb.

Ransack (ræ'nsæk), sb. [f. the vb. Cf. ON. rannsak.] The act of ransacking.

Ransack (ræ'nsæk), v. Forms: 3–7 ransake (3-en, 5-yn; 4 ron-, 5 raun-; also 5 ranske, 7-runtle, 6 ransik, -sake, 8 -sac), 6- ransack. [a. ON. rannsaka (Sw. ransaka, Da. ransage), f. rann house (= Goth. razn, OE. ærn) + -saka, ablaut-var. of sakja to seek; cf. sake to blame, accuse, harm. Guernsey dial. ran-sagüer, ransacked are from Eng.]

Ransacker (ræ'nsækər). [f. prec. + -ER¹.] One who ransacks; a pillager.

Ransacking (ræ'nsækiŋ), vbl. sb. [f. as prec. + -ING¹.] The action of the verb RANSACK.

Ransackle, v. Obs. exc. north. dial. [f. RANSACK v. + -LE.] trans. To ransack.

Ransail, Ransalman: see RANCEL, -MAN.

Ransom (ræ'nsəm), sb. Forms: 4–7 raun-sum (4 -coun, -oun-e, -oum, -coum), 4–6 ransoun, 4–7 raunsom, 5 -somme, 6-7 ransum, 5 ransome, 6–7 ransome.

1. The action of procuring the release of a prisoner or captive by paying a certain sum, or of obtaining one's own freedom in this way; the fact or possibility of being set free on this condition; the paying of money to this end.

†b. To search, explore, penetrate. Also intr. Obs.

2. The sum or price paid or demanded for the release of a prisoner or the restoration of captured property.

b. To redeem, deliver, in religious sense.

Ransomable (ræ'nsəməb'l). [f. prec. + -ABLE.] Capable of being ransomed.

Ransomed (ræ'nsəmd), ppl. a. [f. as prec. + -ED¹.] Freed by means of a ransom, delivered, redeemed.

Ransomer (ræ'nsəmər). [f. as prec. + -ER¹.] 1. One who ransoms; a redeemer. 2. Obs. One of the representatives of the Order of our Lady for the redemption of captives, founded by St. Peter Nolasco in 1223.

Ransoming (ræ'nsəmiŋ), vbl. sb. [f. as prec. + -ING¹.] The action of the vb. RANSOM.

Ransomless (ræ'nsəmlĕs), a. [f. as prec. + -LESS.] Without ransom.

Rant (rænt), v. [a. obs. Du. ranten, randten to rave, rage.] 1. intr. (†or with it). To talk or declaim in an extravagant high-flown manner; to use bombastic language.

Rant (rænt), sb. [f. prec. vb.] 1. A high-flown, extravagant, or bombastic manner; a piece of turgid declamation; a tirade.

Ran-tan (ræ'ntæn), sb. and v. [Echoic: cf. RAN-DAN.]

Rant-tan (ræntæ'n), adv. [Echoic.]

Ranter (ræ'ntər), sb. [f. RANT v. + -ER¹.] 1. One who rants, declaims noisily or bombastically, esp. in preaching.

Ranter. 1649 CROMWELL Let. 14 Nov. (Carlyle), There went also with this party, Sir Thomas Armstrong, Colonel Trevor, and most of their great ranters.

Ranterish (ræ'ntəriʃ), a. [f. RANTER + -ISH¹.] 2. b. Of or pertaining to the Ranters.

Ranterism (ræ'ntəriz'm). [f. RANTER + -ISM.] The practices or doctrines of Ranters.

Ranting (ræ'ntiŋ), vbl. sb. [-ING¹.] The action of the vb. RANT in various senses.

Ranting, ppl. a. [-ING².] That rants, in senses of the verb.

Rantipole (ræ'ntipōl), sb. (and a.) Now rare. 1. A romp; a wild, ill-behaved or reckless person; a scold, termagant.

Rantism, Obs. rare. [f. RANT v. + -ISM.] The practice of baptism by sprinkling.

Rantism. 1672 H. MORE Brief Reply 251 The Rantism.

Rantize, v. Obs. rare. [ad. Gr. βαντίζειν to sprinkle.] trans. To baptize by sprinkling; to sprinkle. (Used with reference to baptism by sprinkling instead of immersion.)

Rantle, dial. var. ROWAN-TREE. Rantle-tree.

Rantling, vbl. sb. Obs. rare⁻¹. Squeaking.

Rantoone, v. Obs. A form of tricking formerly in use (see quot. 1869).

Rantree, -try, dial. variants of ROWAN-TREE.

Ran'tum-scan'tum, int., sb., and a. Also 8 -skantum. A riming comb., perh. suggested by RANT v.

Ranty, a. Sc. and north. dial. Also 8 rantie, rantee. [f. RANT v. + -Y.] 1. Wild, unruly; riotous. b. Lively, jolly, merry. 2. Blazing, roaring.

Rantypole, variant of RANTIPOLE.

Ranty-tanty, north. dial. and Sc. A weed. [Cf. RANTY-TANTY.]

Rannule, (ranule), sb. Path. [a. rānula a little frog; the swelling of the tongue in cattle.] A cystic tumour under the tongue, caused by the obstruction of the salivary ducts or glands.

Ranunculaceous (rănʌ'ŋkjuleĭʃəs), a. [f. RANUNCULUS + -ACEOUS.] Belonging to the Natural Order Ranunculaceæ, of which Ranunculus is the typical genus.

Ranunculus (rănʌ'ŋkjuləs), sb. Pl. -culuses, (7-8 -us's, 8 -uses) and -culi. [L. ranunculus little frog, tadpole; also a medicinal plant, perh. crowfoot (Pliny): dim. of rāna frog.] A genus of plants (also called CROWFOOT) widely diffused in temperate regions; the common species with yellow flowers are popularly known by the name of BUTTERCUPS.

Rap (ræp), sb.¹ Forms: 4–6 rappe, (8 wrap), 4-6 rap. [Related to RAP sb.²; cf. also frap vb. and G. rappen to beat, drub, is of obscure history.] 1. A blow or stroke, esp. one inflicted on a person. Orig. applied to severe blows with weapons, with a stick or the like, not causing serious hurt.

Rap (ræp), sb.² [Of obscure origin; there is no evidence of connexion with G. rappe, the name of a small coin.] 1. A counterfeit coin, worth about half a farthing, which passed current for a halfpenny in Ireland in the 18th c., owing to the scarcity of genuine money. Now only Hist.

Rap (ræp), sb.³ [Of obscure origin.] A skein containing 120 yards of yarn.

Rap (ræp), sb.⁴ [Of obscure origin.] A skein.

Rap (ræp), sb.⁵ Also 4-6 rappe, (7 wrap). [Related to RAP sb.¹; cf. also frap vb. and G. rappen to beat, drub, is of obscure history.] Sw. rapp to beat, drub, is of obscure history.

Rap (ræp), v.¹ Also 4-6 rappe. [Of obscure origin.] 1. trans. To strike, smite; esp. to rap at or on. Also absol.

Rap, v.² [Of obscure origin.] To exchange, barter.

Rap, used imitatively; see RAP sb.¹ and v.¹

Rapacious (răpeĭ'ʃəs), a. [f. L. rapāci-, rapax grasping (f. rapĕre to seize) + -OUS.] 1. Giving to grasping or taking for oneself; inordinately greedy; grasping, extortionate.

Rapaciously (răpeĭ'ʃʌsli), adv. [f. prec. + -LY².] In a rapacious manner; greedily.

Rapaciousness (răpeĭ'ʃʌsnĕs). [f. prec. + -NESS.] The quality of being rapacious; rapacity.

Rapacity (răpæ'siti). [ad. L. rapācitāt-em, f. rapāci-, rapax: see RAPACIOUS and -ITY.] The quality or fact of being rapacious; the exercise of rapacious tendencies.

Raparee, obs. var. RAPPAREE.

Rape (reĭp), sb.¹ [a. AF. rap, raap, rape (Britton, etc. in Anglo-L. rapa), back-formation from RAPE v.¹] 1. The act of carrying anything away by force; violent seizure (of goods), robbery. Obs. exc. dial.

Rape (reĭp), sb.² [a. AF. rape, rap: cf. med.L. rapum, rapa, a division, portion.] One of the six administrative divisions of the county of Sussex.

Rape (reĭp), sb.³ [? ad. L. rāpa, rāpum turnip.] The common turnip, Brassica Rapa; also, the plant Brassica Napus.

Rape (reĭp), sb.⁴ [ad. L. rāpa, rāpum.] The refuse of grapes after the wine has been pressed out, used in making vinegar.

Rape (reĭp), sb.⁵ [a. AF. raper, rape, med.L. rapum, rapa.] 1. The act of seizing and carrying off by force; abduction. 2. The act of violating a woman; ravishment.

Rape (reĭp), v.¹ [a. AF. raper, OF. raper: cf. med.L. rapare.] 1. trans. To seize and carry off by force; to snatch. 2. To ravish, violate (a woman).

RAPE

Rape, sb.[1] The act of carrying away a person, esp. a woman, by force.

1. Sometimes (as in quot. 1450) involving also sense 2.

2. Violation or ravishing of a woman.

3. With *a* and *pl.* An instance of this.

4. *concr.* One (esp. a woman) who is raped.

Rape, sb.[2] *Obs. exc. dial.* [a. F. *râpe*, *raspe* Kluge *sb.*] A rape, rough file.

Rape, sb.[3] *n. and pl.* Also 5 *rappe*. [Of unknown origin; first found in Domesday Book, but possibly of OE. origin.]

Rape, sb.[4] *n.* Also 7 *rap*, 4 *rope*. [Of unknown origin.]

Rape, sb.[5] [ad. L. *râpum* nent., *râpa* fem., a turnip. In sense 2 perh. partly from F. *râpe* turnip, *rave*; cf. L. (now obs. or dial.) *rape*, *rabe*(*n*, *râbe*(*n* turnip.]

1. (With *a* or in *pl.*) a. A turnip (? or radish).
 b. A plant of rape (2 b). *Obs.*

2. As a plant-name. †a. The common turnip. *Obs.* b. The plant *Brassica napus*, usually grown as food for sheep. c. The plant *Brassica campestris oleifera*, largely cultivated on the continent for its seed, from which oil is made; coleseed.

Rape, sb.[6] [ad. L. *râpum*.]

3. *Wild rape*, Charlock or Field-Mustard.

raspa (1201 in Du Cange). In II properly *rapé*, a. F. *râpé* (:—OF. *raspeit*, :—L. *râpe*.) [f. *râpe*.]

I. 1. The stalk of grape-clusters, or refuse of grapes from which the wine has been expressed, used in making vinegar.

II. †4. (More fully *Rape wine*, F. *vin râpé*.) Wine made either from the rape (sense 1 above) by addition of water, or from fresh grapes and light wine placed together in a cask. *Obs.*

†5. The grapes used in making vinegar. *Obs.*

Rape, obs. form of REAP sb. (sheaf.)

†Rape, a. and adv. *Obs. rare.* [Back-formation from RAPELY adv.] A. adj. Quick, hasty.
B. adv. Hastily.

†Rape, v.[1] *Obs.* Also *inf.* 3-4 rapen, 5 rapyn.
[a. ON. *hrapa* (MSw. rapa) to hasten.]

Rape, v.[2] *Obs.* [Prob. ad. L. *rapĕre* to seize, take by force: cf. AF. *raper* (1400 in Godef.), L. *râpere*.

Rape-cake, sb. *Comm.* ad. Cl. Dn. *raapaand* *oleifera*, used chiefly for the production of oil.

Raper, obs. form of RAPIER, ROPER.

Raperee, obs. form of RAPPAREE.

Raripseed. The seed of the Rape (esp. *Brassica campestris oleifera*), used chiefly for the production of oil.

2. To carry off (a person, esp. a woman) by force. *Obs.*

3. To ravish, commit rape on.

Raped, *ppl. a.*[1]

Rape, sb.[7] *Obs.* Also 4 *rappe*, *rapp*, 5 *rapey*(e. [f. *râpé*, pa. pple. of *râper* to scrape, grate: cf. RAPPEE.] A dish in medieval cookery, composed of many ingredients grated, stamped, or pounded, and highly seasoned.

Rape-cake. A flat cake made of rapeseed pressed into this form after the oil has been extracted from it.

Rapea, variant of RAPÉ, RAPPEE.

†Rapeful, *a.* [f. RAPE sb.[1] + -FUL.] Given to, or characterized by, rape or violence.

†Rapely, adv. *Obs.* Also 3 -liche, 4 -liche, -lyche.

Rapen, variant of RAPE *v.*

Rapent, obs. Sc. form of REPENT *v.*

Rape-oil. A thick brownish-yellow oil expressed from rapeseed, used chiefly for lubricating and in the manufacture of soap and india-rubber.

Raper, obs. form of RAPIER, ROPER.

Raperee, obs. form of RAPPAREE.

Rapeseed. The seed of the Rape (esp. *Brassica campestris oleifera*), used chiefly for the production of oil.

Raphael, sb. Also *raf-*. [the name of Raphael (It. *Raffaello*), one of the great artists (1483–1520) of the Italian Renascence, + -ESQUE.] After the style of Raphael.

Raphaelism (ræ'fēel·ism). *Bot.* Also *raf-*. [f. RAPHAEL + -ISM.]

Raphania (ræfī'niă). *Path.* [mod.L. f. *raphanus* radish + -IA.] A name given by Linnæus to a form of ERGOTISM, on the supposition that it was due to the use of grain containing seeds of species of *Raphanus*.

Raphany, variant of RAPÉ, RAPPEE.

†Rapeful, *a.* [f. RAPE sb.[1] + -FUL.]

Raphide (ræ'fəid). *Bot.* Also 8 raph, 8-9 raphes, pl. *rhaphe*. [mod.L. a. Gr. *ῥαφίς*, seam, suture (f. the skull, a wound, etc.).]

Raphael, variant of RAFFLE.

Raphis (rā'fis). *Bot.* Also rha-. Pl. raphides.

Raphorte, variant of RAPPORT *Obs.*

Rapic, variant *a. Chem.* [f. RAPE sb.[5] + -IC.]

Rapid (ræ'pid), *a.* and *sb.* [ad. L. *rapidus*, f. *rapĕre* to seize, carry off: see RAPE *v.*]

A. adj. 1. Moving, or capable of moving, with great speed; swift, very quick.

2. Characterized by speed: a. of motion.
 b. of speech: Extremely quick.

3. Quick in action, thought, etc.

4. *Phys.* Of rapidity, rapid succession.

B. sb. 1. (in *pl.*) A part of a river where the bed descends more rapidly.

Rapidity (răpi'dĭtĭ), *sb.* [ad. L. *rapiditas*: see RAPID and -ITY. Cf. F. *rapidité* (1611 in Cotgr.).] The quality of being rapid; celerity; velocity; swiftness of motion or action.

Rapidly (ræ'pidlĭ), adv. In a rapid manner, with rapidity; swiftly, quickly. Sometimes hyphened to *pal. adj.*)

Rapidness. Now rare. [-NESS.] = RAPIDITY.

Rapier (rē'pĭəɹ), *sb.* Also 6 *rapyer*, 6-7 *rapire*, 7-8, 9 *-per*, *-yer*, *-yre*.

Rapine (ræ'pĭn, -in), *sb.* [a. F. *rapine* (14th c. in Godef.).]

Rapinous, a. *Obs.* [f. RAPINE *sb.* + -OUS, or ad. OF. *rapineux* (14th c. in Godef.).]

Rapist (rē'pĭst), *sb.* [f. RAPE *sb.*[1] + -IST.] One guilty of rape.

Raploch (ræ'plȯx), *sb.* and *a. Sc.* Also 6 *rapeloch*, *raiploch*, *rapploch*, *-lack*, *raplach*, *-loch*. [Of obscure origin.]

Rappee (ræpī'), *sb.* [ad. F. (*tabac*) *râpé*, pa. pple. of *râper* to RASP (see def.).]

Rapper (ræ'pəɹ). Forms: 4 *rappar*, *-er*. 1. One who raps or knocks; a spirit-rapper.

Rapparee (ræpărī'). Forms: *a.* 7 *rappery*, *pl.* -*ies*, *rap(p)ories*. *β.* 7-8 *rappare*, 8 *rapperee*, 7- *rapparee*. [a. Ir. *rapaire* 'a short pike, a rapparee' (O'Reilly); cf. *repaire* 'a robber, a trencherous violent person', ibid.; the *β.* forms app. originated in the *pl.*, after the southern Irish *pl.* *rapairidhe*.]

Rapper, -ier, etc. So. forms of RAPIER.

Rappee, variant of RAPLY adv. *Obs.*

Rapping, -y, etc. forms of RAPPAREE.

Rapping (ræ'pĭŋ), *vbl. sb.*[1] [f. RAP *v.*[1]]
1. The action of striking or knocking sharply.
2. *concr.* That which is rapped out.

Rapper (ræ'pəɹ), *sb.* [f. RAP *v.*[1] + -ER.]

Rappist (ræ'pĭst), *sb.* *U.S.* [See def.] A member of an American religious sect named from its leader, George Rapp.

Rapport (răpōɹ't, F. rapōr), *sb.* Also 7 *rapoort* (*rappoort*), *raport*, *rapore*. [a. F. *rapport*, f. *rapporter*.]

Rapporteur (rapɔrtœr). *Obs. rare.*

Rapprochement (raprɔ̃ʃmɑ̃). [F. f. *rapprocher* (f. re- + approcher APPROACH) + -MENT.] A coming or bringing together, an establishment of harmonious relations.

Rapscallion (ræpskæ'lyən), *sb.* [Later form of RASCALLION.] A rascal, rogue, vagabond, scamp.

Rapt (ræpt), *ppl. a.* [See prec.]
1. Carried away, transported, carried off.
2. Transported, enraptured, etc.

†Rapt, *sb.* [f. RAPT *pa. pple.*: cf. RAPE.]

†Rapt, v. *Obs.*
1. *trans.* To carry away by force.
2. To transport, enrapture, entrance.

[This is a densely printed Oxford English Dictionary page containing entries for **Rap, tap** *through* **Rase***. The body text is set in extremely fine multi-column dictionary type, including the following headwords:]*

Rap, tap, v. — **Ra·p-ta·p**, v. — **Raptatory** — **Ra·pter** — **Ra·ptery** — **Rapting**, ppl. a. — **Raptor** — **Raptly**, adv. — **Raptness** — **Raptorial** — **Raptril** — **Rapture** — **Rapture**, v. — **Raptured**, ppl. a. — **Ra·ptureless** — **Rapturing** — **Rapturist** — **Raptu·rize** — **Rapturous** — **Rapy** — **Rape** — **Rapyer** — **Raquet** — **Raquette** — **Rare** (dense) — **Rarefaction** — **Rarefy**

Rarely — **Rareness** — **Rarety** — **Rarify** — **Rary-show** — **Rasamala** — **Rasant** — **Rare-ripe** — **Raritude** — **Rarity** — **Rascal** — **Rascaldom** — **Rascality** — **Rascally** — **Rascalism** — **Rascalry** — **Rascasse** — **Rasch** — **Rase**

RASE. 157	RASH.	153	RASP.

RASE.

Wyclif *Prof. Epist.* iv.yh Whanne he scrapide or rasile awey any maner writyng. 1486 *Bk. St. Albans*, D ij b. The colouris be raset out as oon colaure in rasyng ware take awey from an olde rage.

c. *transf.* and *fig.* (chiefly from b.)

1. To erase, obliterate (writing), orig. by scraping with a knife. (Freq. in 16-17th c., now *rare* or *Obs.*)

1390 **Gower** *Conf.* II. 21 Lich to the bok in which is raset The lettre, and mai nothing be rad. 1508 **Fisher** *7 Penit. Ps.* li. Wks. (1876) 101 So lytke maner as letters be done awaye whan they be rased.

Rased (raˈzd), *ppl. a.* [f. **RASE** *v.*[1] + -ED[1].] Cut, scraped, altered by erasure, demolished, etc.

† **Ra·sen.** *Obs.* Forms: 1 ræsan, 4, 7 rasen, 6-7 rayson, etc.

† **Raser[1]**. *Obs.* Also 6 rasier(e. [a. OF. (now dial.) *rasier*, -ere (13th c. in Godef.): see also **RASURE**[2].] A dry measure containing about

† **Raser[2]**. *rare.* [f. **RASE** *v.*[1]] One who rases.

Rash, *sb.*[1] Also 4-6 rasche, 5 rashe, 6 rash, (9 rashe). [Prob. onomatopœic (cf. *clash*, *crash*, *dash*, etc.)

1. *intr.* To dash or rush violently.

Rash, *v.*[1] Chiefly *Sc.* Now *rare* or *Obs.*

Rash·ful, *a. rare.* [f. **RASH** *a.* + -FUL.]

Rashing, *vbl. sb.* [f. **RASH** *v.*[1] + -ING[1].]

Rash·ling. *Obs.*

† **Rashly**, *adv. rare.* [f. **RASH** *a.* + -LY[2].]

Rashly (raˈʃli), *adv.* [f. **RASH** *a.* + -LY[2].]

1. Quickly, rapidly, hastily. *Obs. exc. dial.*

2. In a rash or inconsiderate manner.

Rashness (raˈʃnes), [f. **RASH** *a.* + -NESS.] The quality of being rash; inconsiderate haste or boldness; an instance of this, a rash act.

Rasier, variants of **RASER**[1], *Obs.*

Rasing (reɪˈzɪŋ), *vbl. sb.*[1] [f. **RASE** *v.*[1] + -ING[1].]

Rasion (reɪˈʒən). Now *rare* or *Obs.* [ad. L. *rāsiōn-em* (Cælius), or *a* action 1 *rādere* to scrape.

RASP.

Rasp (rasp), *v.*[1] Also 6 rape, 6-7 raspe [Related to **RASPE** *v.*[1] and? *perh.* a back-formation from it. Now chiefly *dial.* and *Sc.*]

1. *tr.* To scrape or rub with a rasp or other rough instrument.

Raspberry (raˈspberi), Also 7-8 raspis-berry.

Rasped (raspt), *ppl. a.* [f. **RASP** *v.*[1] + -ED[1].]

Rasping (raˈspɪŋ), *vbl. sb.*[1] [f. **RASP** *v.*[1] + -ING[1].]

Rasping (raˈspɪŋ), *ppl. a.*[1] [f. **RASP** *v.*[1] + -ING[2].] That rasps, in senses of the vb.

Raspy (raˈspi), *a.*[1] Of a rasping nature; harsh, grating.

† **Raspis**[1]. *Obs.* [Echoic of *brushing* sound.]

† **Raspis**[2]. *Obs.* Forms: a. 6 raspyse, -ass, 6 raspise, -iso, -yoo, 7 raspas, -asse, 8 -isse. B. 6 respise, 6-iae, 7 respass.

† **Ra·spis**[2]. *Obs.* Forms: a. 6 raspyse, -ass...

† **Raster.** *Obs. rare.* [? f. **RASE** *v.*[1] + -STER.]

Rastle, variant of **WRESTLE** *v.*

Rastle, obs. form of **RAITHOOT**.

Rastel. *Obs. rare.* [a. OF. *rastel* (*ratel*, mod.F. *râteau*) rake, f. L. *rastellum*, dim. of *rastrum* rake.]

RAT.

Rat (rat), *sb.*[1] Forms: 1 ræt, 4-6 ratte, 6 ratt, 5- rat.

1. a. Any of numerous rodents of the genus *Mus*, esp. *M. decumanus*, the common grey, brown, or Norway rat, and *M. rattus*, the black or old English rat.

b. *transf.* Applied to anim[a]l of other species.

2. *slang* (orig. *U.S.*) Used ironically in *pl.* to express incredulity 'humbug', 'nonsense'.

RATELIKE.

Ra·telike, adv. *Obs. rare⁻¹.* — RATEABLY.

Ratell, obs. form of RATTLE (q.v.).

Ra·tely, adv. *Obs. rare⁻¹.* [f. RATE sb.¹ + -LY ?] — RATEABLY.

Rater¹.

Ra·tement. *Obs. rare.* [f. RATE v.¹ + -MENT.] Rating, valuation.

Rater¹. [f. RATE v.² + -ER¹.] One who rates or scolds.

Rater² (rēi·tǝɹ). [f. RATE v.¹ + -ER¹.] One who reproves or scolds.

Rat-goose. *Ornith.* [Given by Willughby, app. as a local name.] A kind of wild-goose, supposed to be the brent-goose.

Rath, sb. [Ir. *rath*, earlier pron. (rǟ).] *Irish Antiq.* An enclosure (usually of a circular form) made by a strong earthen wall, and serving as a fort and place of residence for the chief or a tribe; a hill-fort. (Often incorrectly ascribed to the Danes.)

Rath, a.¹ See RATHE.

Rathe, sb. obs. form of RAITH.

Rathe, a. In 3 rap(e, rath. [a. ON. *rað* → OE. *hræð* RATH sb.]

Rathe (rēið), adv., adj. *Obs.* [OE. *hræðe, hraðe.*]

Rathe, v. *Obs. exc. dial.* Also 5 rath.

Rathe, v.² *Obs.* Also *raith, rappenn.*

Rath-ripe, **rathe-ripe.**

RATING.

Rathe-ripe, rath-ripe.

Ra·thely, adv. *Obs.*

Rathe·rish, adv. *colloq.*

Rathest, a., adv. *Obs. exc. dial.*

RATIO.

Ra·ting, *vbl. sb.¹*

Ratio (rēi·ʃio, rēi·ʃo). [L. *ratiō*, -*ōn*-, f. *rat-*, ppl. stem of *rērī* to think.]

Ratio·cinate, v.

Ratiocina·tion.

Ratiocinative.

Ration (ræ·ʃǝn, rēi·ʃǝn).

RATIONAL.

Ra·tionable, a.

Ra·tional, a. and sb.

Ra·tionable, a. *Obs.*

Rattle-bag.

Rattle-brain.

So Rattle-brained, a., characterized by foolish noisy levity of character or conduct.

Rattled snake = RATTLESNAKE.

Rattle-gold. Sc. Obs.

Rattle-head. Obs.

Rattle-mouse.

So Rattle-headed a. = RATTLE-BRAINED.

Rattle-pate. — RATTLE-HEAD.

So Rattle-pated = RATTLE-HEADED.

Rattler (ræt·ləɹ).

Rattlesome, adj.

Rattlesnake (ræt·lsnēik).

Rattling (ræt·liŋ), ppl. a.

Rattle.

Rattly (ræt·li), a.

Ratton (ræt·n). Now Sc. and north. dial.

Rattoner, Obs. rare.

Ratton, obs. variant of RATTAN.

Rat-trap.

Raucle, a. Sc. and north. dial.

Rauk, a. Sc. and north. dial.

Raucidity (rǭsi·diti), Obs. rare.

Raucity (rǭ·siti).

Raucous (rǭ·kəs), a.

Raucousness.

Raught, pa. pple. and pa. t. of REACH.

Raughty, var. RAFTY a.

Raunge, obs. form of RANGE v.

Raught, obs. or archaic pa. t. and pa. pple. of REACH.

Raute. Min.

Raujpoot, variant of RAJPOOT.

Rauk, a. Sc. Obs. Also 6 rawk.

Raukie = var. RAWKY.

Raukle, Sc. variant of RACKLE a.

Raunce rare.

Raun, variant of RAWN.

Random, -don'e, -doun, obs. ff. RANDOM.

Rauning, a. [var. RAWNING; but in Cornwall glossaries explained as 'raveling, ravenous', as if r. rauin, 'to devour greedily'.]

Raunge, obs. f. RANGE v.

Rauns = RANSOM, -try: see ROWAN-TREE.

Raupo (rau·po, rau·pē). Also 7 a. rapou (Maori.) [A New Zealand bulrush (Typha Augustifolia) used for building houses, thatching roofs, etc. Also attrib.]

Rauque (rǭk), a. rare. [a. F. rauque, ad. L. raucus.]

Raut, dial. var. ROWT v.

Rauven, variant of RAVEN.

Rauvage (ræ·vedʒ), n. [var. RAVAGE.]

Ravage (ræ·vedʒ), sb.

Ravage (ræ·vedʒ), v.

Ravagement, Obs. rare. [a. F. ravagement.]

Ravager (ræ·vedʒəɹ).

Ravaging, vbl. sb.

Ravaging, ppl. a.

Rava-lling, var. RAVELLING.

Ravan, var. RAVIN sb.

Rave (rēiv), v.

Rave, sb.

Rave, sb.

Rave, v.

Ravel (ræ·v'l), v.

Ravel, sb.

Ravel, sb.

Ravel, variant of RABBLE v.

Raveled, -elled, ppl. a.

Ravelin (ræ·vlin). Also 6-7 ravelline, -lin, ravellin, (8 ravlin); 6 ravelline, -yne, 7-8 raveline; 6-7 ravelin.

Raveling, variant of RAVELLING.

Ravel-bread, obs. forms of RAVELIN.

Ravelly, a.

Ravelling (ræ·vliŋ), vbl. sb. [f. RAVEL v.]

Ravelled (ræ·v'ld), ppl. a.

Ravelment (ræˈv'lmĕnt). [f. RAVEL v.¹ + -MENT.] Entanglement, confusion. Also with *a*.

Raven (ræˈv'n). *sb.*¹ Forms: α. 1 hræfn, (h)remn, remn; 3 rauen, 4 rauen, ravin, -yn, (5 rawyn, -ine, ravyne), 4-5 rauen; 3-7 rauen, 4-ravven. β. 1 (h)refn, 3 refn, reafen, 3-5 reven, 4-5 revyn, (4 revon, 5 revon), 6 Sc. revin, 7 rem, 1-3 rem. [Comm. Teut.: OE. *hræfn* = OHG. (*h*)raban (MHG. *rabe*, ON. *hrafn* (MSw. *hrafn*).]

1. A widely-distributed corvine bird (*Corvus Corax*) of Europe and Asia, of large size...

2. The figure of a raven on the flag of the Danish vikings; also, the flag itself or the warlike power typified by this.

3. *Astron.* The southern constellation *Corvus*.

Raven, *sb.*² Forms: 6 rau, rayvne, 6-7 rau, -rauen, 7 rauin, -yn, 7-9 ravin. [ad. F. *ravine* (†rabine, raveine, 12th c.):—L. *rapīna* RAPINE. The orig. sense of the word is lost in Fr., see RAVIN².]

1. Robbery, rapine. *Obs.*

2. Ravenous or voracious eating.

Ravener (ræˈvĕnəɹ). [f. RAVEN v. + -ER¹.] One who ravens; a robber, plunderer.

Raveness (ræˈvĕnĕs). [f. RAVEN *sb.*¹ + -ESS.] A she-raven.

Ravening (ræˈv'nĭŋ), *vbl. sb.* [f. RAVEN v.] **1.** The action of the vb. in various senses.

†2. Madness, rabies. Also with *pl.*: A fit of madness. *Obs.*

Ravening, *ppl. a.* [f. RAVEN v.]

Ravenous (ræˈvĕnəs), *a.* [a. OF. *ravineus, -ous*, etc. (see Godef.):—pop. L. OF. *ravinens, -os, -ous*, etc.]

Ravin (ræˈvĭn), *sb.*¹ [See RAVEN *sb.*²]

Ravine (raˈvain), *sb.* A deep narrow hollow or gorge, a mountain cleft, properly one worn by a torrent.

Raving (ræˈvĭŋ), *vbl. sb.* [f. RAVE v. + -ING¹.]

Raving, *ppl. a.* [f. RAVE v. + -ING².]

†Raving, *a.* *Obs. rare.* Also 6 *attrib.*

Ravingly (ræˈvĭŋli), *adv.* [f. RAVING *ppl. a.* + -LY².] In a raving manner.

Ravinous, obs. form of RAVENOUS.

†Ravioli. *Obs. rare.*

‖Ravish (ræˈvĭʃ), *v.* Forms: 4-5 ravys-, ravisch, -ish, 4-6 raviss(e, -ysch, -ysh, (6-yssh), 4-7 ravish. [a. OF. *raviss-*, lengthened stem of *ravir* to seize, take away violently.]

1. *trans.* To seize and carry off (a person); to take by violence, to tear or drag away (*rare* in place or person).

†2. *In pass.* To be carried away from a belief, state, etc. *Obs.*

3. To carry away, transport (a person); to carry away with rapture; to fill with ecstasy of delight; to entrance. Also *const. from*.

4. To seize and take away as plunder or spoil; to seize upon (a thing) by force or violence; to make a prey of.

Ravishable, *a.* [f. RAVISH v. + -ABLE.]

Ravished (ræˈvĭʃt), *ppl. a.* [f. prec. + -ED².]

Ravishedly, *adv.* [f. RAVISHED + -LY¹.]

Ravishedness. *Obs. rare.* [f. RAVISH v.]

Ravisher (ræˈvĭʃəɹ). [a. OF. *ravisseur*, etc.]

Ravishing (ræˈvĭʃĭŋ), *vbl. sb.* [-ING¹.]

Ravishing, *ppl. a.* [-ING².] That ravishes; carrying away, rapturous.

Ravishingly, *adv.*

Ravishment (ræˈvĭʃmĕnt). [a. F. *ravissement*.]

‖Ravissant (raviˈsɑ̃), *a.* [F.]

Ravish-, obs. variant of REVEST v.

Ravle, dial. form of RAVEL v.

Ravyn, obs. forms of RAVEN *sb.*¹, RAVIN¹.

Ravyner, obs. forms of RAVENER.

Raw (rǭ), *a.* [sb.] Forms: α. 1 hreaw, hrew, (hréow), 3 raʒe, 4 rawe, 4-6 rawe, 8 north. 3 raw, 8 Sc. raw. [Comm. Teut.: OE. *hréaw* = Fris. *râ, ré,* OS. *hrâo* (hro-, LG. *raw,* rå), MDu. (Du.) *rauw,* OHG. *hrô, rô* (MHG. *rô,* G. *roh*), ON. *hrá-r* (Sw. *rå,* Da. *raa*):—OTeut. *hrawo-,* pre-Teut. *krawo-* related to Olr. *crú,* Lat. *cruor,* Skr. *kravĩ,* raw flesh.]

1. Uncooked, not prepared for use as food by the action of fire or heat.

RAW
Raw-bone, a. and -d.
+ Raw-bone, a. — Raw-boned.
Raw-boned, a.
Rawchter, obs. Sc. form of RAFTER.
+ Rawed, a.
+ Rawen, -eyne, obs. variants of ROWEN.
Rawenge, Rawonge, obs. Sc. ff. REVENGE, RAVEN.
+ Raw-flesh, obs. rare⁻¹. = RAW-FLESH.
Rawght, etc. pa. t. REACH v.¹
Raw-head.
Rawhide, see RAW a. 2 c.
Rawin, Rawing, dial. variant of rowing ROWEN.
Rawish (roi·ʃ), a.
Rawk, vapour, fog : see ROKE.
Rawk, variant of RAUK a., hoarse. Obs.

+ Rawky, a.¹ Obs. rare⁻¹.
Raw-ly, a.² rare.
Rawll, obs. f. ROLL.
Rawlins.
Rawly, adv.
+ Raw-neck, obs. rare⁻¹. = RAW-HEAD.
Rawness (rō·nes).
Rax, sb.¹ Sc.
Raxle, Obs.
Ray (rē¹), sb.¹
Rax, v. Sc. and north. dial.
Rax, sb.² Sc. and north. dial.

RAY
Ray (rē¹), sb.²
Ray, sb.³ Obs.
Ray, sb.⁴
Ray (rē¹), sb.⁵
Ray, v.¹
Ray (rē¹), v.²
Ray, v.³
Ray, v.⁴
Rayah (rā·ja). Also raiah, raya.
Rayat (rā·ı). Also rayet, raʹyat.

RAYNE
Rayah
Rayle.
Rayling.
Raylay.
Rayle, obs. f. RAIL.
+ Rayed, ppl. a.²
Rayed (rēid), ppl. a.¹
Rayful, a.
+ Ray-grass.
Rayle, Rail, Rayl.
Rayless (rēʹles), a.
Rayment.
Rayn, Rayne, obs. ff. RAIN, REIGN, REIN.
Rayne.

| RAYNOLL. | 185 | RAZOR. | RAZOR. | 186 | RE-. |

† **Raynoll.** Obs. Also 5 ? **raynole.** [Form and origin uncertain: cf. *raynolles* in Cotgr.] pl. Small cakes or balls made of pork with a large number of other ingredients.

Rayn'ye, obs. form of RAINY a.

Rayoun, variant of RAION sb.

Rayon (rēˈˌn, *f.* raion). [a. F. *rayon* (1539), f. *rai* (mod.) RAY sb.[1]]

1. A ray of light. *rare.*

2. = RADIUS a.

Rayonnance. *rare* [...]

† **Rayona** (rēˈyonǎ), a. [f. prec., or app. pple. of *rayonne* RAION.]

Rayme, obs. form of RAIN sb.

Rayneceocie, obs. variant of RAJPOOT.

† **Raze**, sb.[1] ...

† **Raze**, sb.[2] Obs. *rare*—[1]. (See quot.)

† **Raze**, sb.[3] Obs.

Raze (rēz), sb.[4] ...

Raze, obs. form of RACE sb.[5], RAISE v.[1]

Razee (rǎzīˈ), sb. [f. F. *rasé*, pa. pple. of *raser* to RAZE v.[1]] *Naut.*

Razee (rǎzīˈ), v. [f. prec.] *trans.*

Razen, obs. form of RAISIN.

...

Razor (rēˈzǎɹ). Forms: ... [a. OF. *rasor*, *rasour*, etc.]

1. A sharp-edged instrument, specially used for shaving the beard or hair.

Razor, a keen edge, *fig.* a narrow foothold, a critical situation (cf. *razor's edge* in 1 b): razorgrass, a West Indian sedge (*Scleria flagellum* or *scindens*) with sharp-edged leaves...

† **Razorable**, a. *rare*—[1]. [f. RAZOR sb.] Capable of, or fit for, being shaved.

Razor-back. sb. and a. [f. RAZOR sb.]

So **Razor-backed** a.

Razor-bill. [f. RAZOR sb. + BILL sb.[2]]

1. A name given to various birds.

Razor-fish. [f. RAZOR sb.]

Razor-grinder. 1. One who grinds or sharpens razors.

Razor-shell. [f. RAZOR sb.]

Razure, variant of RASURE.

Rasty, obs. form of RACY.

† **Razzia** (rǎˈzǐǎ). [a. F. *razzia*, ad. Algerian Arab. *ɣāzīah*, var. Arab. *ghazwah*, *ghazāh* war, battle, military expedition, raid against infidels, f. *gharw* to make war.]

Re-, prefix, of Latin origin, with the general sense of 'back' or 'again', occurring in a large number of words directly or indirectly adopted from Latin, or of later Romanic origin...

Re-abridge, v. [RE- 5 a.] *trans.* To abridge again.

Reabsorb, v. [RE- 5 a. Cf. F. *réabsorber* (Littré).] *trans.* To absorb anew or again; to take in again by absorption.

Hence **Reabsorbed** ppl. a., **Reabsorbing** vbl. sb.

Reabsorption. [RE- 5 a. Cf. F. *réabsorption* (Littré).] The action of reabsorbing, or fact of being reabsorbed; *spec.* in *Path.*

Reaccess. [RE- 5 a.]

1. Return, renewed access.

† 2. Re-accession (to the throne). Obs. *rare*—[1].

So **Reaccession**

Reaccommodate, v. [RE- 5 a.] Cf. F. *réaccommoder* (Littré). *trans.* To accommodate, adjust, or fit afresh or again.

So **Reaccommodation.**

Reaccompany, v. [RE- 5 a.] *trans.* To accompany again; † to escort back.

Reaccomplishment. A second accomplishment or fulfilling.

Reaccount, v. [RE- 5 a.] *trans.* To count again or over.

Reaccumulate, v. [RE- 5 a.] *trans.* To accumulate again.

Re-accrue, v. [RE- 5 a.] † *trans.* To gather again.

Reach (rītʃ), sb.[1] Forms: 6 reche, reache, 6-7 reatch, 7 reach, 6- reach. See also RETCH sb.[1]

1. An act of reaching.

I. An act or the act of reaching out with the arm (*esp.* to take hold of something); a stretching out the hand. Also *transf.* and *fig.*

II. Power of, or capacity for, reaching.

5. The extent to which a person can stretch out the arm or hand, *esp.* so as to touch or grasp something.

the Reach of the most wealthy private Gentleman. 1781 Cowper Conv. 586 Who .. plucks the fruit placed more within his reach. 1871 Rossetti Dante at Verona lxxxii, How the Prince Sunned himself out of Dante's reach.

c. transf. of things, in various applications.

c1586 C'tess Pembroke Ps. xlvi. v, Our rock on Jacob's God we found, Above the reach of harmes. 1596 Shaks. Merch. V. iv. i. 10 No lawful meanes can carrie me Out of his enuies reach. a1656 Bp. Hall Rem. Wks. (1660) 106 The Almighty is above all the reach of these unquiet perturbations. a1687 Petty Pol. Arith. (1690) 103 All of these ten Millions of People are obedient to their Sovereign, and within the reach of his power. 1827 Hood Hero & Leander ci, Just past the reach Of foamy billows he lies cast. 1875 Encycl. Brit. I. 337/1 To plough deeply .. places them [weeds] out of the reach of frost.

d. Power of reaching far.

1825 J. Wilson Noct. Ambr. Wks. 1855 I. 40 Although he has weight length and reach .. yet has he lost every battle.

6. Capacity or power to perform or achieve some action, attain to some state or condition, etc. (Chiefly with preps., as in 5 b.) a. of persons.

1576 Fleming Panopl. Epist. 18 Whom to annoy is beyond my reache and abilitie. 1592 Babington Comf. Notes Gen. I. § 9 The mouing of others .. to consider what wanteth to a multitude in this land, and to relieue them according to their reaches. 1711 Hearne Collect. (O. H. S.) III. 176 His Learning was above yᵉ common Reach. 1784 Cowper Task iii. 40 The fault is obstinate, and cure beyond our reach. 1820 W. Irving Sketch Bk. I. 28 A picture of active yet simple virtues, which are within every man's reach. 1880 L. Stephen Pope vii. 163 Anything like sustained reasoning was beyond his reach.

b. of things.

1611 Tourneur Ath. Trag. ii. iv, Any circumstance That stood within the reach of the designe Of persons. 1690 Locke Hum. Und. ii. xxi. § 21 In respect of Actions, within the reach of such a Power in him. 1711 W. King tr. Naudé's Refined Politics iii. 91 A very great design with a long reach, and contrived with much judgment. 1800-24 Campbell Margaret & Dora ii, Dora's eyes of heavenly blue Pass all painting's reach. 1865 M. Arnold Ess. Crit. ii. (1875) 58 The highest reach of science is, one may say, an inventive power.

† c. Of the voice: Range, compass. Obs.

1597 Morley Introd. Music 7 That compasse was the reach of most voyces. 1674 Evelyn Diary (1827) II. 392 Mrs. Knight .. who sang incomparably, and doubtlesse has the greatest reach of any Englishwoman. a1680 Butler Rem. (1759) II. 429 All he does is forced, like one that sings above the Reach of his Voice.

7. Capacity or power of comprehension; extent of knowledge or of the ability to acquire it; range of mind or thought.

1586 A. Day Eng. Secretary i. (1625) iv, The ignorant .. hereof, whose reach hath not been so ample as others. 1601 Holland Pliny I. 168 His high reach and deep wit, whereby he apprehended the knowledge of all things vnder the cope of heauen. 1667 Milton P. L. x. 793 Let this appease The doubt, since humane reach no further knows. 1671 — Samson 1380 How thou wilt here come off surmounts my reach. 1709 Pope Ess. Crit. 47 Be sure your self and your own reach to know, How far your genius, taste, and learning go. 1750 Johnson Rambler No. 79 ¶ 3 Has a long reach in detecting the projects of his acquaintance.

b. In prep. phrases, as above, beyond, out of (one's) reach. (Cf. 5 b.)

1542 Udall Erasm. Apoph. i. § 23 This saiyng .. whiche is fathered on Socrates .., What is aboue our reach, we haue naught to doe withall. 1572 H. Middelmore in Ellis Orig. Lett. Ser. ii. III. 5, I sayd they were matters owt of my reache, and farre from myne acquayntawnce. 1613 Purchas Pilgrimage i. xii. (1614) 60 Many things they [Planets] foretold to Alexander .. beyond the reach of men. 1671 Milton Samson 62 Which herein Happ'ly had ends above my reach to know. 1711 Addison Spect. No. 58 ¶ 1 If my Readers meet with any Paper that in some Parts of it may be a little out of their Reach. 1842 Macaulay Fredk. Gt. Ess. (1877) 663 Nothing beyond the reach of any man of good parts.

c. In phr. of (a) great (deep, etc.) reach. (Very common c1585–1710; in later use only without article.)

1586 J. Hooker Hist. Irel. in Holinshed II. 143/1 In matters of policie he was verie prudent, and of a great reach. 1603 Knolles Hist. Turks (1621) 1128 A man of greater reach and courage. 1641 Milton Reform. ii (1851) 54 Men more audacious, and precipitant, than of solid and deep reach. 1686 tr. Chardin's Coronat. Solyman 103 They that had a deeper reach, were not so positive in their judgments. 1720 Steele Tatler No. 246 ¶ 8 Plumbeus acknowledges Levis a Man of a great Reach. 1763 J. Brown Poetry & Mus. v. 54 If one .. delivered his Stories in Verse, another of inferior Reach and Invention would naturally give them .. in plain Prose. 1875 Stedman Victorian Poets 151 To claim that they have been overrated, and are not men of high reach.

8. Of the mind or mental powers: Range of efficiency in speculation, acquisition of knowledge, penetration, etc.

c1580 Sidney Ps. xxxvi. iv, Pleasures past the reach of mind. 1597 Hooker Eccl. Pol. v. lxiii. § 1 The mysteries of our religion are above the reach of our understanding. 1662 Stillingfl. Orig. Sacr. ii. vi. § 2 The events .. must be such as do exceed the reach of any created intellect. 1725 Watts Logic (1736) 271 Matters of Fact .. which lye beyond the Reach of our own personal Notice. 1744 Berkeley Siris § 337 The most refined human intellect, exerted to its utmost reach.

b. With a. (Approximating to sense 12 c.)

1657 J. Sergeant Schism Dispach't 261 Hath not this Dr. of Divinity a strange reach of reason? 1707 Curios. in Husb. & Gard. 5 Those who have a sufficient Reach of Understanding to comprehend the .. ordinary Course of Nature. 1773 Life N. Frowde 21 Perhaps no Child of my Years had ever more Cunning, or a readier Reach of Thought. 1875 Jowett Plato (ed. 2) III. 186 The 'Utopia' of Sir Thomas More .. shows a reach of thought far beyond his contemporaries.

9. Range; scope; extent of application, effect, influence, etc.

1546 J. Heywood Prov. (1867) 2 Their sentences include so large a reache. 1570 Dee Math. Pref. 37 These wordes .. the reach of their meaning, is farther, then you woulde lightly imagine. 1600 Heywood 2nd Pt. Edw. IV, Wks. 1874 I. 99 My simple wit Can never found a judgment of such reach. 1858 Buckle Civiliz. (1869) II. vii. 378 When we compare the shortness of his life with the reach and depth of his views. 1875 Whitney Life Lang. vi. 100 A process of wide reach and abundant results in English.

10. Range (of carrying or traversing). a. of a gun, or shot.

1571-91 Digges Pantom. (1591) 179 The first parte of the violent course of Gunners, commonly termed the peeces pointe blanke reache. 1662 J. Davies tr. Mandelslo's Trav. 28 They could not go by, without coming within reach of our Muskets. 1698 T. Froger Voy. 21 In order to level the shot within reach of the Place. 1748 Anson's Voy. ii. v. 171 Captain Saunders alarmed them unexpectedly with a broadside, when they flattered themselves they were got out of his reach. 1805 in 19th Cent. (1899) Nov. 725 We were now without any opponent within reach of our guns.

b. of the eye or sight.

1623 Milton Ps. cxxxvi. 94 Above the reach of mortall ey. 1667 — P. L. xi. 380 The Hemisphere of Earth .. Stretcht out to amplest reach of prospect lay. 1709 Addison Tatler No. 119 ¶ 2 Those Heavenly Bodies which lie out of Reach of Humane Eyes. 1875 Manning Mission H. Ghost xiii. 353 The capacity and the reach of the eye are developed by practice, and by experience.

c. of the voice.

1797 Mrs. Radcliffe Italian xii, The travellers .. were soon beyond the reach of the voices.

11. Power or possibility of getting to (or as far as) some place, person, or object; distance or limit from which some point may be reached. Only in prep. phrases, as in 5 b.

1784 Cowper Task vi. 263 That has .. within his reach A scene so friendly to his favourite task. 1806-7 J. Beresford Miseries Hum. Life (1826) ii. i, No knife in your pocket nor house within reach. 1833 Ht. Martineau Briery Creek ii. 23 Mrs. Temple had never been very happy while within reach of markets and shops. 1859 Dickens T. Two Cities i. v, All the people within reach had suspended their business.

III. That which reaches or stretches.

12. A continuous stretch, course, or extent: a. of some material thing or space.

1609 Bible (Douay) Ezek. xvii. 3 A great eagle with great winges, with a long reach of members. 1638 Junius Paint. Ancients 68 Darksome night .. dimming the spacious reach of heaven. 1674 N. Fairfax Bulk & Selv. Contents, The outmost reach of Body must needs be bounded. 1803 Naval Chron. IX. 440 Exposed to the whole reach of the Western Ocean. 1866 Blackmore Cradock Nowell x, The glades and reaches of gentle park and meadow.

b. of time.

1814 L. Hunt Feast of Poets 49 His look with the reach of past ages was wise. 1869 Phillips Vesuv. xii. 323 Some mountains are now constantly active, and have been so in all the reach of history.

c. of immaterial things. (Cf. 8 b.)

1838-9 Hallam Hist. Lit. II. iii. ii. § 66. 452 A prodigious reach of learning distinguishes the theologians of these fifty years. 1869 Goulburn Purs. Holiness iv. 31 A reach of love, and wisdom, and power to which it is impossible to set bounds.

d. The space over which something extends or is distributed.

1850 H. Miller Footpr. Creat. i. (1874) 9 The marine and fresh-water animals having each their own reaches.

13. spec. a. That portion of a river, channel, or lake which lies between two bends; as much as can be seen in one view. Also the portion of a canal between two locks, having a uniform level.

1536 in R. G. Marsden Sel. Pl. Crt. Adm. (1894) I. 58 The same catche beyng under sayle in the reche over agaynste Lymehowse callyd Limehowse Reche. 1562 Phaer Æneid viii. X iv, They pluckyng swift their Ores, that .. tyre their lims, And reatches long they win. 1609 Holland Amm. Marcell. 33 Rasing as it goes the high bankes with their curving reaches. 1724 De Foe Mem. Cavalier (1840) 95 The king .. examined every reach and turning of the river. 1792 A. Young Trav. France 99 The river presents one reach, crossed by the bridge, and then dividing into two fine channels. 1880 Haughton Phys. Geog. v. 242 Occasionally threading some narrow channel, to enter again some magnificent reach.

† b. A bay. Obs.

1526 Tindale Acts xxvii. 39 They spied a certayne reache [Gr. κόλπος] with a banke. 1601 Holland Pliny v. xxix. I. 108 All the coast thereof is very full of creekes and reaches. 1650 Fuller Pisgah v. vii. 156 The opposite shoar, on the same side of the Sea, but .. over a reach, or bay. 1736 Ainsworth Eng.-Lat. Dict., A reach at sea, duorum promontoriorum intervallum.

c. A headland or promontory. Obs. exc. U. S. (local).

1562 Phaer Æneid i. A iij, On either side the reaches hie .. And vnder them the still sea lyeth. 1626 Capt. Smith Accid. Yng. Seamen 17 A headland, a furland, a reatch, a land marke. 1687 E. F. Life Edw. II. in Select. fr. Harl. Misc. (1793) 45 Twice had they gained St. Vincent's rock, but, from that reach, were hurried back, with sudden gusts and tempests. 1897 in Cent. Dict.

14. A bearing-shaft or coupling-pole.

1868 Routledge's Ev. Boy's Ann. 478 The Reach, or bearing-shaft [of a bicycle] is the most important portion. 1875 Knight Dict. Mech. 1887/1 A reach for a certain description of city wagon is shown in Fig. 4190.

15. = Rache sb.²

1897 M. H. Hayes Points of Horse xx. (ed. 2) 222 If it runs down the nose in the form of a line of no great width, it is known as a 'reach' or 'stripe'.

† **Reach**, sb.² Obs. rare. [f. Reach v.²] An act of clearing the throat, or of retching.

1575 Laneham Let. (1871) 41 [He] cleered his vois with a hem and a reach, and spat oout withal. 1736 Ainsworth Eng.-Lat. Dict., A reach, or reaching to vomit, vomendi nisus.

Reach (rītʃ), v.¹ Forms: α. Infin. 1 ræ̂can, 3 ræchen, 2, 4 rechen, (5 -yn); 4–5 reche, (5 ric(c)he, 6 rech), 4–5 reiche, (5 reyche, 6 Sc. reich), 6 reache, (7 reatch), 6– reach. Pa. t. (a) 1 ræ̂hte, 3 rehte, 4 reiȝte, reighte; 1, 3 râhte, 4 raȝte, 4–5 raghte; 4 rauhte, rauȝte, -tte, 5 rawȝte, 4–6 raughte, (6 roughte); (and pa. pple.) 4 raht, 4–5 raȝt, 4–6 raght, (4–5 ragh, 5 Sc. racht); 4–5 rauht, (4 rahut, 5 rauth, rauȝt, (4 rauȝht, 5 rawȝt), 5–9 raught, (5 rawght, rought, 6 erron. wrought), Sc. raucht, (6 rawcht); also pa. pple. 4 i-rawt. (b) 4–6 reched, (4 recched, 5 rechid, reychid), 6–7 reach'd, 7 reachd, reacht, 6– reached. β. 4, Sc. 5–6 reke, (4 reque, 5 Sc. rek), 5–6 (9) Sc. reik, (6 reyk), 8 Sc. reek, ryke, (9 rike). Pa. t. 4 reked, 6 Sc. reikit. [OE. ræ̂can (also geræ̂can) = OFris. reka, rets(i)a, resza, MDu. (Du.) reiken, MLG. reiken, reken, OHG. (G.) reichen:—OTeut. *raikjan of uncertain relationship.

The various parts of the verb exhibit considerable variety of form at different periods. In ME. the normal vowel ē of the infin. and pres. is sometimes replaced by ā, ī, or ī. The latter is unusual; the other two (see Ratch v.¹ and Retch v.¹) have probably been developed by back-formation from the pa. t. raught, on the analogies of catch, caught and stretch, straught. Mod. dial. forms differing from the standard reach are reit(t)ch, rey(t)ch (Yks.), raich, reigh.k (Lanc.), rache, rayck (Devon), etc., in addition to the northern forms with final -k (as in streek beside stretch), which are recorded from c1400 and survive as reek, ryke (Sc.), reak, raik (Yks.), reik, reyk (Lanc.), etc.

The normal West Saxon form of the pa. t. was rǽhte, giving ME. rehte, reihte (rare). From the typically northern OE. ráhte came the usual ME. raughte, which continued in general use down to c1600, and was frequently employed for half a century later, but is now only archaic, or dialectal in the forms raucht (Sc.), rought (Lanc., Chesh., Staff.) and raught (West Midl.). The new preterite form reached (cf. northern reekit) appears about 1400, but is comparatively rare before 1600. For other modern dial. variants of the pa. t. and pa. pple. (mostly due to analogy) see the Eng. Dial. Dict.

In addition to ræ̂can, OE. had also the form geræ̂can, the use of which is naturally prominent in those senses in which stress is laid on the full completion of the action (see sense 4). In some senses (as 4 b, 4 c, and 5) the verb occurs chiefly or exclusively in the preterite form raught, which in later use was perhaps not clearly associated with reach in its other applications.]

I. Transitive senses.

1. To stretch out, extend, hold out or forth (one's hand, arm, etc.).

c897 K. Ælfred Gregory's Past. C. xxxvi. 246 Ic ræhte mine hond to eow. a900 Cynewulf Christ 1620 In þæt hate fyr .. þær hy leomu ræcað .. to bærnenne. c1000 Ælfric Gen. xxxviii. 28 Se oðer ræhte forð his hand. a1300 Cursor M. 19791 To saint petere sco raght hir hand. c1400 tr. Secreta Secret., Gov. Lordsh. 83 Drynke he a syrupe of roses .. and after, reche out his armes a lityll. 1481 Caxton Reynard (Arb.) 54 He raught out his right foot and dubbed me in the necke. 1565 Jewel Def. Apol. (1611) 375 Iulius Cæsar raught out his foot for Pompeius Pœnus to kisse. 1662 J. Davies tr. Olearius' Voy. Ambass. 19 Some of us would have reach'd their arms over the Table, to take the Goblet. 1755 Ramsay To Jas. Clerk 48 [He] will at naithing stap or stand, That reeks him out a helping hand. 1850 Tennyson In Mem. lxxx, Unused example from the grave [shall] Reach out dead hands to comfort me.

b. Of a tree: To extend (its branches).

1613 Shaks. Hen. VIII, v. v. 54 He shall flourish, And like a Mountaine Cedar, reach his branches, To all the Plaines about him. 1667 Milton P. L. v. 213 Where any row Of Fruit-trees .. reachd too far Thir pamperd boughes.

c. To thrust (a weapon) forth or up by stretching out the arm.

1596 Spenser F. Q. iv. iii. 33 At that instant reaching forth his sweard .. He smote him. 1829 W. Tennant Papistry Storm'd (1827) 93 He raucht his halbert up, and brack An image that stood starin' out.

† d. To launch, direct, aim. Obs.—¹.

1591 Spenser M. Hubberd 840 He would his impudent lewde speache Against Gods holie Ministers oft reach.

2. To hold out (a thing) and give (it) to a person; to hand to one. Also const. with dat., and occas. with simple object.

α. a1000 Boeth. Metr. xxix. 62 Hærfest to honda herbeendum ripa [bleda] receð. c1000 Ags. Gosp. John xiii. 26 He ys se ðe ic ræce [Hatton MS. ræche] bedyppedne hlaf. a1300 Cursor M. 3649 (Cott.) Quen it [mete] es dight þou it him reche [Fairf. salle þou hit reiche]. c1369 Chaucer Dethe Blaunche 47, I .. bade one reche me a booke. 1432-50 tr. Higden (Rolls) VII. 35 His stappemoder rechid to hym a pece that he myghte drynke. 1535 Coverdale Ruth iii. 15 Reach me the cloke yᵗ thou hast on the, & holde it forth. 1581 in Confer. ii. (1584) M iij, The Greke testament being reached vnto him, he refused to reade it. 1613 Shaks. Hen. VIII, iv. ii. 4 Reach a Chaire, So now (me thinkes) I feele a little ease. 1655 Fuller Ch. Hist. i. i. § 5 It pleased God with a strong hand and stretched-out Arme, to reach the Gospel unto them. 1760-72 H. Brooke Fool of Qual. (1809) II. 59 Taking out your picture .., I reached it to her. 1827 Blackw. Mag. Sept. 339/2, I reached him the letter.

absol. a1300 Cursor M. 790 (Cott.) Quen sco þis frutte biheild, Sco .. tok and ette and raght adam.

β. 1513 Douglas Æneis v. vii. 42 Reik to the man the price promist. 1567 Satir. Poems Reform. iii. 230 With that he rais and reikit me this bill. 1862 Hislop Prov. Scot. 129 [She] cried 'Reik me this, reik me that'.

b. With advbs., as back, down, forth, out, round, up. † Also to reach up, to surrender.

a1400-50 Alexander 758 Obire recouyre me þi rewme, or reche vp þe girdill. Ibid. 817 Þis renke & his rounsy þai reche vp a croune. 1508 Dunbar Tua Mariit Wemen 148 Thai .. raucht the cop round about full off riche wynis. 1548 Udall, etc. Erasm. Par. Luke xxiv. 198 [He] brake it, and then raught it forth to theim. 1631 Weever Anc. Funeral Mon. 517, I caused some of the Nailes to be reached vp to me. 1642 Rogers Naaman 172 Beg of the Lord to reach you out the Lord Jesus. 1760-72 H. Brooke Fool of Qual. (1809) III. 5 The burdened trees reached forth fruits of irresistible temptation. 1865 Kingsley Herew. iv, The beaker I reach back More rich than I took it.

† c. With immaterial object: To give, yield, render; to grant, bestow, communicate, etc. Obs.

c961 Æthelwold Rule St. Benet (Schröer 1885) 139 Þara anra, þe for neode him þenunge æt þæs mynstres ingange ræcan scylon. a1300 Cursor M. 5308, I sal þe to þe kinge beteche, And siþen þe mi blissing reche. 13.. E. E. Allit. P. B. 1369 Vche duk .. Schulde com to his court .. to reche hym reuerens. c1470 Henryson Mor. Fab. iv. (Fox's Confess.) xvi, Heir I reik the [= thee] full remissioun. 1659 Hammond On Ps. cxv. 1 Unworthy of the least of all thy goodness, abundantly reached out unto us. a1718 Rowe (J.), Through such hands The knowledge of the gods is reach'd to man.

3. a. To deal or strike (a blow); † to give (a wound). Const. to, at, or dat. Now rare.

1375 Barbour Bruce ii. 420 To philip sic rout he raucht, .. He gert him galay disyly. c1400 Sowdone Bab. 1347 He raught a stroke to Ferumbras. c1470 Golagros & Gaw. 630 Schir Rannald raught to the renk ane rout wes vnryde. a1553 Udall Royster D. iv. iv. (Arb.) 66, I with my distaffe will reache hym one rappe. 1577-87 Holinshed Chron. II. 57/2 Gegathus raught Haco such a wound, that the vpper part of his liuer appeared bare. 1666 Sancroft Lex Ignea 24 God hath reacht us now an Universal Stroke. 1760-72 H. Brooke Fool of Qual. (1809) II. 19 A sudden punch which he reached at the nose of his lordship. 1847 Chalmers Romans xxx. II. 82 Faith .. reaches that exterminating blow whereby the body of sin is destroyed.

† b. To give (a kiss). Obs. rare—¹.

13.. Gaw. & Gr. Knt. 2351 Þou kyssedes my clere wyf, þe cossez me raȝtez.

4. To succeed in touching or grasping with the outstretched hand (or with something held in it), or by any similar exertion.

971 Blickl. Hom. 207 Se hrof .. wæs þæt man mid his handa nealice geræcean mihte. a1000 Satan 169 Eala .. þæt ic mid handum ne mæg heofon geræcan. a1300 Cursor M. 24464 Me-thoght moght i .. wit mi hand him ans reche .. I suld ha ben all hale. 1377 Langl. P. Pl. B. xi. 353 Who tauȝte hem on trees to tymbre so heighe, There noither buirn ne beste may her briddes rechen. 1530 Palsgr. 680/2, I reche a thyng with my hande .. I can nat reache it, myne arme is to shorte. 1591 Shaks. Two Gent. iii. i. 156 Wilt thou reach stars, because they shine on thee? a1704 Locke (J.), Having let down his sounding-line, he reaches no bottom. 1747 Gray Cat 22 She stretch'd in vain to reach the prize. 1858 Kingsley Poems 113 If I could but reach that hand.

† b. To obtain by seizure or otherwise; to procure, gain, acquire, get possession of. Obs.

a900 O. E. Chron. an. 885 Þa metton hie xvi scipu wicenga & wiþ þa ȝefuhton, & þa scipo allę ȝeræhton, & þa men ofslogon. a1000 Ibid. an. 918 Hie ne meahton nanne mete geræcan. 11.. Ibid. (MS. C.) an. 1066 Hi ne micte þa brigge oferstiȝan, ne siȝe ȝerechen. a1250 Owl & Night. 106 Tho hit bi-com that he haȝte, And of his eyre briddes y-raȝte. a1300 Cursor M. 1912 Þe beist[es] thoght selcutli god þat þai hade raght þair kindle fode. c1394 P. Pl. Crede 733 After .. his rychesse is rauȝt he schal ben redy serued. a1542 Wyatt Poet. Wks. (1861) 67 With hapless hand no man hath raught Such hap as I. 1603 Drayton Bar. Wars ii. xlv, Then had yee raught Fames richest Diadem. 1612 — Poly-olb. ix. 290 All his diuelish wit, By which he raught the Wreath.

† c. To seize in the hand; to take or lay hold of; to carry off. Obs.

c1330 R. Brunne Chron. (1810) 229 A trestille Edward rauht, þat heuy was of pais. c1375 Sc. Leg. Saints xxi. (Clement) 453 He .. hyre in armys racht & hyre embrasit. a1400-50 Alexander 5284 Scho .. raȝt him by þe riȝt hand & raikis to a chambre. c1470 Harding Chron. cv. vi, Great people yᵗ daye the death hath raught. a1547 Surrey Æneid ii. 272 Then raught they hym .. twise winding him about. 1591 R. Wilmot Tancred & Gismunda iii. iii, She raught the cane, And with her owne sweet hand she gaue it me. 1606 Shaks. Ant. & Cl. iv. ix. 30 The hand of death hath raught him. a1626 Middleton Mayor of Queenborough iv. ii. 155, I was surprised by villains, and so raught.

absol. 1667 Milton P. L. xi. 94 Least .. his now bolder hand Reach also of the Tree of Life, and eat.

transf. 1587 Mirr. Mag., Porrex vii, Can I complayne of this reuenge she raught? 1642 Fuller Holy & Prof. St. iv. xix. 338 Princes are not to reach, but to trample on recreations.

† d. To receive, catch, suffer. Obs.

c1400 Song Roland 756 Of the hethyn hound no harm he reches. c1410 Sir Cleges 193 As he knelyd on hys knee, .. He rawght a bowe on hys hede. c1450 Mirour Saluacioun 2554 Of the Jewes cruwelle mykel persecucioune he raght.

† e. To fetch, heave (a sigh). Obs. rare—¹.

1580 Stanyhurst Æneis i. (Arb.) 33 Groane sighs deepe reaching with tears his lyers ful he blubbred.

5. Const. with preps. and advbs. a. To take or snatch from a person or thing; to take away, hence, out, up. Now only arch.

a1400-50 Alexander 799* Þou must rewle all my realm qwen I am raght hyne. 14.. Sir Beues (MS. M) 837 Thes knyghtes, that Beues raught fro Bradmond. 1481 Caxton Reynard (Arb.) 21 Tybert .. raught out his ryght colyon. 1563 Mirr. Mag. ii. Rich. III, xx, [The king] of kyngdome I bereft, His life also from him I raught away. 1587 Turberv. Trag. T., First History, He raught a truncheon from a pine by chaunce. 1593 Nashe Christ's T. (1613) 179 Many in their prime and best yeares are raught hence. 1634 Jackson Creed viii. xix. § 12 Those bodies, which being alive shall be raught up into the air. 1718 Ramsay Christ's Kirk Gr. iii. xviii, They frae a barn a kabar raught. 1863 W. Lancaster Praeterita 51 Old confusions, which .. Raught from my helm the garland of its praise.

b. To draw or bring towards oneself (esp. to take down) from a certain place or position; to lift up, take († or pull) down, etc.

c1450 Merlin 697 The damesell .. raught hym vp be the honde. 1483 Caxton Gold. Leg. 61 b/1 He .. ran and raught doun the Calf that they had made. 1545 Ascham Toxoph. i. (Arb.) 66 Ill fortune me that daye befell, Whan first my bowe fro the pynne I roughte. 1647 Crashaw Steps to Temple 67 Men of martyrdom, that could reach down With strong arms their triumphant crown. 1649 R. Hodges Plain. Direct. 17 He raught it from the shelf, when I wrought it with him. 1746 Collins Ode to Fear 33 [The Bard] reach'd from Virtue's hand the patriot's steel. 1830 Marryat King's Own xxiii, [He] reached down his hat. 1868 Holme Lee B. Godfrey viii. 43 She reached from the .. shelf her .. cup of ink.

† c. To take in, to, or unto, oneself. Obs.

1588 Kyd Househ. Phil. Wks. (1901) 253 First wold I that the parched earth did riue and raught me in. 1591 Spenser M. Hubberd 441 That same [rod] hath Iesus Christ now to him raught. 1660 Bloome Archit. C b, Calimachus .. reached unto himselfe the Basket.

6. To succeed in touching with a weapon or with the hand in delivering a blow († hence, to strike or smite).

Beowulf 556 Ic aglæcan orde geræhte. 13.. Guy Warw. (A.) 1477 Gii þat on wiþ his swerd rauȝt. c1350 Will. Palerne 1193 What rink so he rauȝt he ros neuer after. c1400 Sowdone Bab. 2923 Richard raught him with a barr of bras. c1489 Caxton Sonnes of Aymon ii. 63 He .. rought hym wyth soo grete a myghte, that sterke deed he ouerthrew hym. 1609 Heywood Brit. Troy xii. cvi, The inuincible Dardanian with one stroke, Raught Aiax Beauer and unplumed his hed. 1809 Roland Fencing 126 If you can conveniently reach your adversary upon the longe.

b. To succeed in affecting or influencing by some means; to impress, convince, win over, etc.

1667 Milton P. L. iv. 801 Assaying by his Devilish art to reach The Organs of her Fancie. a1713 Ellwood Autobiog. (1714) 45 Being sensible that I was thoroughly reach'd; and the Work of God rightly begun in me. 1851 Dixon W. Penn x. (1872) 83 Men's opinions must be reached by reason, not by force. 1887 Times (weekly ed.) 14 Oct. 15/3 They [the merchants] know how Chinese are to be reached.

7. a. Of things (or of persons in respect of some part of the body): To come into contact with, to touch; to extend so far as to touch.

a1225 Juliana 56 Hu hit grond in hwet so hit rahte. a1300 Cursor M. 24390 It raght mi hert al thoru þe rote. c1384 Chaucer H. Fame iii. 284 With hir feet she therthe reighte, And with hir heed she touched hevene. 1393 Langl. P. Pl. C. xx. 144 Þe paume haþ power to .. receuen þat þe fyngres rechen. 1667 Milton P. L. ii. 1029 A Bridge of wondrous length .. reaching th' utmost Orbe Of this frail World. Ibid. iv. 988 His stature reacht the Skie. 1704 Pope Windsor F. 193 Now his shadow reach'd her as she run, His shadow lengthen'd by the setting sun.

b. Of immaterial things, in various applications derived from 7 a and 8, esp. to succeed in affecting or influencing.

c1400 Song Roland 190 To help the, þat no harm þe reche. c1489 Caxton Sonnes of Aymon x. 267 The stroke slided a syde & kyt a sondre all That it rought. 1613 Shaks. Hen. VIII, ii. ii. 89 Who can be angry now? What Enuy reach you? a1625 Beaum. & Fl. Bonduca iv. iii, There is no mercy in mankind can reach me. 1675 H. More in R. Ward Life (1710) 347 Nor does that [conclusion] reach the present Controversie. 1712 Addison Spect. No. 287 ¶ 3 Liberty should reach every Individual of a People. 1761 Gray Odin 48 Pain can reach the Sons of Heav'n! 1786 Burns Twa Dogs 213 There's sic parade, sic pomp, an' art, The joy can scarcely reach the heart. 1844 Ld. Brougham Brit. Const. xvii. (1861) 259 Libels .. which the ordinary process of the law reached, and would have been quite sufficient to punish.

8. To come to, arrive at (a place, object, or point in space), to get up to or as far as.

c1330 R. Brunne Chron. Wace (Rolls) 1320 Two dayes þey sailled .. lond ne hauene reche þey ne myght. 13.. E. E. Allit. P. B. 10 Reken with reverence þay rechen his auter. 1563 B. Googe Eglogs, etc. (Arb.) 109 Now was the Son got vp aloft, and raught the mydle Lyne. 1609 Holland Amm. Marcell. xxv. vi. 273 Sooner than a man would have thought [they] raught the banke on the further side. 1684 R. Waller Nat. Exper. 110 The point not onely again reacht the Line, but passed beyond it. 1709 Steele Tatler No. 107 ¶ 2 You may easily reach Harwich in a Day. 1808 Scott Marm. i. xi, The steps of stone, By which you reach the donjon gate. 1860 Tyndall Glac. i. xiv. 96 Brought him to rest before he had reached the bottom.

b. With personal object, in various applications.

1706 E. Ward Wooden World Diss. (1708) 22 Those strong unexpected Turnadoes .. sometimes reach him as far as Brasil and Jamaica. 1894 Hall Caine Manxman iii. xv. 177 Pete's letter had reached him.

c. Of sounds: To come to (the ear, a person or place).

1649 G. Daniel Trinarch., Hen. IV, lxxx, Fame had before the escape of Richard told .. wᵗʰ raught her open Ears. 1671 Milton Samson 177, I hear the sound of words; thir sense the air Dissolves unjointed e're it reach my ear. 1727 Gay Fables i. xxxi. 11 My name, perhaps, hath reach'd your ear. 1784 Cowper Task ii. 5 Where rumour of oppression and deceit .. Might never reach me more! 1828 Scott F. M. Perth xix, The alarm reached the royal residence. 1874 Micklethwaite Mod. Par. Churches 10 Every syllable should reach the ears of the auditors.

d. Of the eye, a gun, etc.: To carry to (a point).

1667 Milton P. L. xii. 556 Eternitie, whose end no eye can reach. 1669 Sturmy Mariner's Mag. v. xii. 72 What degree the Gun must be Mounted to, to reach the Mark. 1732 Pope Ess. Man i. 240 What no eye can see, No glass can reach.

9. To arrive at, to attain or come to (a point in time, a condition, quality, etc.): a. of persons.

1590 Spenser F. Q. i. vi. 29 Till ryper yeares he raught. 1604 Shaks. Oth. i. ii. 24 As proud a Fortune As this that I haue reach'd. 1647-8 Cotterell Davila's Hist. Fr. (1678) 2, I hope I shall be able to reach the proper order. 1709 Pope Ess. Criticism 145 Nameless graces which no methods teach, And which a master-hand alone can reach. 1727 Gay Fables i. xxxix. 35 He reach'd the height of power and place. 1789 Trifler No. 35. 448 Our poets .. frequently reach the climax of absurdity. 1801 Strutt Sports & Past. ii. i. 60, I believe few, if any, of the modern archers in long shooting, reach four hundred yards. 1874 Green Short Hist. v. § 3. 228 Wyclif .. had already reached middle age.

b. of things.

1667 Milton P. L. iii. 197 Thy desire .. leads to no excess That reaches blame. 1691 Locke Lower. Interest Wks. 1727 II. 7 But supposing the Law reach'd the Intention of the Promoters of it. 1724 A. Collins Gr. Chr. Rel. 215 The means .. will not reach that end. 1784 Cowper Task i. 696 In the eye Of public note, they reach their perfect size. Ibid. iv. 662 His faculties .. there only reach their proper use. 1888 Burgon Lives 12 Gd. Men x. II. 262 This little work reached a second edition.

10. a. To succeed in understanding or comprehending. ? Obs.

1605 B. Jonson Volpone iv. i, Sir P. I reach you not. Lady P. Right, sir, your policy May bear it through thus. a1627 Middleton Wom. beware Wom. v. i, But how her fawning partner fell I reach not. 1662 Dryden Wild Gallant iv. i, I do not reach your meaning, Sir. a1715 Burnet Hist. Ref. iii. Pref. 3 The Meaning of this dark Expression I do not reach. a1822 Shelley Tasso 16 The words are twisted in some double sense That I reach not.

b. To succeed in acquiring or obtaining.

1638 Junius Paint. Ancients 303 Zenodorus .. could not reach the art of tempering the metalls as it was used by the ancients. c1709 Prior Charity 4 Had I all knowledge .. That thought can reach, or science can define. 1782 Cowper Charity 304 Knowledge such as .. only sympathy like thine could reach. 1842 J. Aiton Domest. Econ. (1857) 318 Paying a small sum yearly, .. according as I could conveniently reach it.

11. To stretch; to draw or pull out † or in; † to extend (one's power). Obs. exc. dial. (Cf. Ratch v.¹ 3, Retch v.¹)

971 Blickl. Hom. 191 Min heafod sceal beon on eorþan gecyrred, & mine fet to heofenum geræhte. c1275 Serving Christ 5 in O. E. Misc. 90 Crist .. on rode was rauht. 1297 R. Glouc. (Rolls) 4820 Ȝoure fon ssolle hor poer among ow wide reche. a1375 Lay Folks Mass Bk. App. iv. 348 He rauhte þe Rolle .. Wiþ his teth. ? a1400 Morte Arth. 2549 Than they raughte in the reyne and a-gayne rydes. c1420 Pallad. on Husb. iv. 682 An huge breste, No litel wombe, and wel out raught the side. 1607 Topsell Four-f. Beasts (1658) 167 Whilest the members are reached and stretched with many strains and convulsions. 1648-60 Hexham Dutch Dict., Het leder Recken, to Stretch or Reach out leather. 1823 Moor Suffolk Words s.v. Reech, A pair of small shoes require to be reached.

II. Intransitive senses.

12. To make a stretch with the arm or hand; to extend the arm, hold out the hand. Also of the arm or hand: To stretch out.

Beowulf (Z.) 748 Ræhte ongean feond mid folme. a1225 Ancr. R. 338 Hwon God beot þe, recheð forð mid boðe honden. c1305 St. Andrew 95 in E. E. P. (1862) 101 Here armes whan hi vpward reiȝte bicome as stif as treo. c1400 N. Love Bonavent. Mirr. xxxix. (B. N. C.) 92 The disciples seten .. so þat þey alle myȝte reche into þe myddes and ete of one disshe. 1538 Starkey England i. ii. 48 The ye to se, .. the fote to go, the hand to hold and rech. 1667 Milton P. L. ix. 779 What hinders then To reach, and feed at once both Bodie and Mind? 1785 Burns Jolly Beggars 5th Air, Let me ryke up to dight that tear.

b. Const. to or unto (a person or thing), usually with implication of catching († or striking) at. Now only dial. (also absol., to help oneself at table).

a1000 Satan 437 Efe .. ræhte þa mid handum to heofoncyninge. 13.. Sir Beues (A.) 2445 Þe lionesse seyȝe þat sight And rauȝt to B[eues], with out faile. c1400 Destr. Troy 10882 Ho raght to hym radly, reft hym his sheld. 1586 J. Hooker Hist. Irel. in Holinshed II. 7/1 But these two .. raught to their weapons. 1671 H. M. tr. Erasm. Colloq. 192 Reach to the Pompions, there's an end of the Lettices. 1674 Brevint Saul at Endor 232 This Paiment, however reacht to, is, they say, presented to God by the Pope. 1847 Halliwell, Reach-to, to reach out one's hand, so as to help oneself. 1890 Austin Clark For Love of Lass iii, Now do as the missus bids you, and reach to. Your father's son 'll be always welcome at my table.

c. Const. after, for (a thing).

c1386 Chaucer Prol. 136 Whan she dronken hadde hir draughte, ful semely after hir mete she raughte. 1571 Campion Hist. Irel. ii. ix. (1633) 118 A Gentleman .. raught in the morning for some paper. 1591 Spenser M. Hubberd 1336 Rouring up himselfe, for his rough hide He gan to reach. 1737 [S. Berington] G. de Lucca's Mem. (1738) 33

I was .. reaching for my Sword to defend myself to the last Gasp.

d. To grasp or clutch at. (lit. and fig.)

1562 J. Heywood Prov. & Epigr. (1867) 106 Master Sexten .. Gredily raught at a goblet of wyne. 1593 Shaks. 2 Hen. VI, i. ii. 11 Put forth thy hand, reach at the glorious Gold. 1655 Fuller Ch. Hist. ix. Ded., The Third reached not at all at Honor. 1732 Neal Hist. Purit. (1822) I. 66 Stretching the laws to reach at those whom they could not fairly come at an other way. 1818 Keats Endym. iii. 372 Wherefore reach At things which, but for thee, .. Had been my dreary death?

e. fig. of mental striving.

1646 P. Bulkeley Gospel Covt. ii. 131 The soule is of an intelligent nature, reaching after the knowledge of high and hidden things. 1845-6 Trench Huls. Lect. Ser. ii. vii. 261 Some of old had been reaching out after this. 1870 J. H. Newman Gram. Assent i. v. 109 His mind reaches forward with a strong presentiment to the thought of a Moral Governor.

13. To make a stretch of a certain length; to succeed in stretching one's arm, etc., so far.

a1300 Cursor M. 1840 Na creatur in liue .. moght to grund or reche or riue. Ibid. 11673 Þe frut hu sulde man reche vnto. 13.. Sir Beues (A) 1623 [Beues] knette þe rop þar while Ase hiȝ ase a miȝte reche. c1408 Lydg. Compl. Bl. Knt. xvi, With myn hede unto the welle I raughte. c1450 Merlin 344 He lifte vp his swerde .. and he slytte the shelde as fer as that he raught. 1484 Caxton Fables of Æsop ii. xiii, He cowde not reche to the mete with his mouthe. 1535 Coverdale Eccl. vii. 23 She wente .. so depe that I might not reach vnto her. 1581 J. Bell Haddon's Answ. Osor. 471 By reaching beyond his reach, he reacheth nothing at all. 1590 Shaks. Mids. N. iii. ii. 289, I am not yet so low, But that my nailes can reach vnto thine eyes. 1667 Milton P. L. vi. 140 With solitarie hand Reaching beyond all limit. absol. 1667 Milton P. L. ix. 593 All other Beasts .. envying stood, but could not reach.

b. transf. and fig. in various applications.

a1300 Cursor M. 27332 Als ferre als he may reche, þe forme o scrift til him he teche. 1570-6 Lambarde Peramb. Kent (1826) 257 As farre as I can reache by coniecture. 1591 Shaks. Two Gent. i. ii. 87 Lu. Melodious were it, would you sing it. Ju. And why not you? Lu. I cannot reach so high. 1611 Bible Lev. v. 7 marg., His hand cannot reach to the sufficiencie of a lambe. 1633 Bp. Hall Hard Texts, N. T. 51 This woman hath herein reached beyond your conceit. 1653 H. More Antid. Ath. ii. vii. § 5, I might now reach out to Exotick Plants.

14. To stretch out (continuously), to extend; to project a certain distance (above, beyond, etc.).

α. a1000 Riddles lxvii. 7 (Gr.) Ic eom mare þonne þes middangeard .. wide ræce ofer engla eard. a1000 Cædmon's Gen. 990 Ræhton wide ȝeond werþeoda wrohtes telȝan. a1300 Cursor M. 2232 Do we wel and make a toure, .. þat may reche heghur þan heuen. Ibid. 8080 (Gött.) Lang and side þair leues wern And recched al a-boute þair ern. ? a1366 Chaucer Rom. Rose 1022 Hir tresses yelowe .. Unto hir helys down they raughten. c1400 Maundev. (Roxb.) iii. 9 Þe schadowe rechez vnto Lempny. 1526 Pilgr. Perf. (W. de W. 1531) 77 b, Saynt Austyn asketh a questyon: How hye recheth the hous of perfeccyon. 1623 Gouge Serm. Extent God's Provid. § 15 A partition .. which reached up to the floore of the garret. 1687 A. Lovell tr. Thevenot's Trav. i. 21 The Portico .. reaches along the whole front of the Church. 1751 Labelye Westm. Br. 28 These Frames reached about 2 Feet above the common High-water Mark. 1822 Latham Gen. Hist. Birds II. 63 The wings reach very little beyond the base. 1875 Bryce Holy Rom. Emp. v. (ed. 5) 72 These vast domains, reaching from the Ebro to the Carpathian mountains.

β. c1375 Sc. Leg. Saints xviii. (Egipciane) 1320 Þe sone cane fare bemys strek, þat fra þe hewine til erd can rek. 1462 Extr. Burgh Rec. Peebles (1872) 144 The sayde .. akeris of land .. on the northt half of the gat rekand to the Wenlaw. 1513 Douglas Æneis iii. ix. 12 His berd Rekand doun the lenth neir of a ȝerd. 1824 Mactaggart Gallovid. Encycl. 191 He sought for through-ban's that wad rike.

b. Of immaterial things, in various applications.

a1000 Sal. & Sat. 293 Yldo .. ræceþ wide langre linan. 1340 Hampole Pr. Consc. 6311 Þe mercy of God .. reches over alle, bathe fer and nere. 1443 Pol. Poems (Rolls) II. 211 Hir contemplacioun rauht up to the hevene. 1535 Coverdale Dan. iv. 22 Thy greatnesse increaseth, and reacheth vnto the heauen. a1656 Hales Gold. Rem. (1688) 1 How far his intent and meaning reacht. 1718 Freethinker No. 2. 10 His Jurisdiction reaches even to the Councils of Princes. 1769 Junius Lett. i. 9 It reaches beyond the interest of individuals. 1871 Freeman Norm. Conq. (1876) IV. xviii. 131 The exclusion of Englishmen reached even to men of Norman descent born in England.

c. Of a period of time, or with reference to duration of time.

1340 Hampole Pr. Consc. 554 Þe tother part .. reches fra þe begynnyng Of mans lyfe un-til þe endyng. 1535 Coverdale Lev. xxvi. 5 The wyne haruest shal reache vnto the sowynge tyme. 1622 Callis Stat. Sewers (1647) 110 These things .. do reach from the beginning of the Lease to the top of the Inheritance. 1711 Addison Spect. No. 159 ¶ 4 That Portion of Eternity which is called Time, .. reaching from the Beginning of the World to its Consummation.

d. To suffice, be adequate or sufficient to (also with infin.). Chiefly of money. ? Obs.

1377 Langl. P. Pl. B. xiv. 230 His rentes ne wol nauȝte reche, no riche metes to bugge. 1456 Sir G. Haye Law Arms (S. T. S.) 168 He aw till allow thai gudis as payment of his costis .. in alsferr as thai mycht reke. 1642 Rogers Naaman 159 Abilities will not reach to suffer for God, though they seeme to act for him. a1657 Bradford Plymouth Plant. (1856) 215 Every one was to pay .. what yᵉ profite of yᵉ trade would not reach too. 1733 Tull Horse-Hoeing Husb. xi. (Dubl.) 142 As much of the middle sort of Wheat as his Money would reach to purchase.

e. To amount to.

1596 Shaks. 1 Hen. IV, iv. i. 129 Hotsp. What may the Kings whole Battaile reach vnto? Ver. To thirty thousand. 1887 Stubbs Mediev. & Mod. Hist. 360 Another sum of the same amount, reaching .. to £120,000.

15. † a. To move, proceed, go, spread. Obs.

Some examples would also admit of being taken in sense 16, the history of which is somewhat obscure, in the absence of quotations for the 15th and 16th centuries.

a1000 Riddles xvi. 27 (Gr.) Siþþan ic þurh hylles hrof geræce. c1205 Lay. 16265 Bruttes weoren bælde & rehten ouer walde. c1330 R. Brunne Chron. Wace (Rolls) 5003 Tydynges ronne, þat ouer al reches; .. þat Romayns were aryue on land. c1374 Chaucer Troylus ii. 447 Up he stert & on his way he raught. a1400-50 Alexander 3852 Þus raȝt he fra þis reuir be many ruȝe waies.

† b. To go on, or proceed to (a place or point); to run into; to penetrate to. Obs.

a1300 Cursor M. 15788 (Cott.) Ilk dint þat þai him gaf it reked to þe ban. c1400 Beryn 168 To othir placis of holynes þey rauȝte. a1400-50 Alexander 5510 [Alexander] Raȝt on to þe reede See & rerid þare his tentis. c1425 Wyntoun Cron. i. x. 554 Fra north on sowth the streme it strekys In tyll the Rede Se quhille it rekys.

c. Naut. To sail on a reach; (see also quot. 1867).

1832 Marryat N. Forster v, The sloop wearing round, reached in for the land. 1867 Smyth Sailor's Word-bk., Reaching, sometimes used for standing off and on .. A vessel also reaches ahead of her adversary. 1884 Hunt's Yachting Mag. Apr. 150 A rattling breeze .. got up .. and she reached along like a schooner.

16. To attain or succeed in coming to a place, point, person, etc.; † to come up (to).

1632 J. Hayward tr. Biondi's Eromena 21 Posting on with such diligence that by darke night hee reached to Caleri. 1651 Cromwell Let. 4 Aug. in Carlyle, To give the enemy some check, until we shall be able to reach up to him. 1719 De Foe Crusoe i. xviii. (1840) 318 They could not reach back to the boat before it was dark. 1749 Fielding Tom Jones iii. vii, The public voice .. seldom reaches to a brother or a husband, tho' it rings in the ears of all the neighbourhood. 1802 H. Martin Helen of Glenross III. 19 When we had reached to this stage of our proposed journey.

b. With other constructions. Also with specification of distance covered in attaining to a point.

1591 R. Wilmot Tancred & Gismunda i. ii, He neuer sought, with vast huge mounting towers To reach aloft, and ouer-view our raigne. 1622 Drayton Poly-olb. xxii. 1222 Hastings that before raught hither with his rear, And with King Edward join'd. 1627 Sir R. Granville in Ld. Lansdowne's Wks. (1732) II. 336 We had not raught a musket-shot out of the Town. 1760-72 H. Brooke Fool of Qual. (1809) IV. 138 At length, reaching near the door. 1799 E. Du Bois Piece Family Biog. III. 55 Continually receding until they have both reached as far as they can go.

c. Of the eye, a gun, etc.: To carry.

1632 Holland Cyrupædia 166 They gave backe from thence foot by foot .. so farre as a dart shot raught from the wall. 1698 Fryer Acc. E. India & P. 40 The Power of the English, who command as far as their Guns reach. 1885 G. Allen Babylon i, As far as the eye could reach in either direction.

17. To attain to an achievement, condition, etc. Now rare or Obs.

a1300 Cursor M. 20026 A thusand year moght i noght reke .. Til tend part of hir louing. 1303 R. Brunne Handl. Synne 1930 Alle þe penaunce þat þou mayst do Ne may nat reche here godenes to. c1330 — Chron. (1810) 195 In armes is þer none þat to þie renoun reches. 1594 Shaks. Rich. III, i. i. 159 Another secret close intent, By marrying her, which I must reach vnto. 1603 Owen Pembrokeshire vii. (1891) 55 Great aboundance of Wheat, barlie and other graine, not rechinge in finenes to Castlemartyn. 1633 Bp. Hall Hard Texts O. T. 373 By no humane meanes which thou canst reach unto.

b. Const. with infin. Now rare.

a1300 Cursor M. 11385 Elles moght not kinges thre Haf raght to ride sa ferr ewai. 1387 Trevisa Higden (Rolls) II. 217 And he may not reche for to greue oþere, þan he bycomeþ angry and cruel to hym self. 1871 Farrar Witn. Hist. iv. 142 They could only reach to lay their garlands of admiration at his feet.

† c. To attain to (knowledge of). Obs.

1582 N. T. (Rhem.) Mark vi. 3 note, His countrie-folks .. not reaching to his godhead and divine generation did take offence or scandal of him. 1594 Hooker Eccl. Pol. iii. viii. § 6 Festus .. heard him, but could not reach unto that whereof he spake. 1653 H. More Antid. Ath. ii. v. § 5 To conclude there is no such thing as Reason and Demonstration because a natural Fool cannot reach unto it.

18. To undergo stretching. rare. Now only dial.

1362 Langl. P. Pl. A. iv. 148 Bi him that rauhte on the roode. c1440 Promp. Parv. 425/1 Rechyn, as lethyr, dilato, extendo. 1570 Levins Manip. 88/32 To Reche, distendi. 1823 Moor Suffolk Words, s.v. Reech, If your hat be too small it will 'reech i' the wearing'.

† 19. To start up. Obs.—¹

a1450 Le Morte Arth. 3191 Hys chambyrlayns wakyd hym ther wᵗ all, And woodely oute of hys slepe he raught.

Reach (rītʃ), v.² Now only dial. (cf. Retch v.²). Also 5 areche, 6–7 reche. [OE. hræ̂can, = ON. hrækja to spit, f. OE. hráca, ON. hráki spittle, expectorated matter.

The apparent absence of the word in literature from the OE. period to the 15th c. is remarkable, but there can be no doubt of its continuity.]

† 1. a. intr. To spit; also, to make an effort to clear the throat, to hawk. Obs.

c897 K. Ælfred Gregory's Past. C. v. 43 Ȝif he ðonne ðæt wif wille forsacan, ðonne hræcð hio him on ðæt neb foran. c1000 Sax. Leechd. I. 148 Wið ȝeposu & wið þæt man hefelice hræce, ȝenim ðas wyrte [etc.]. [c1460 J. Russell Bk. Nurture 290 Areche, ne spitt to ferre, ner be ye slow of herynge.] 1545 Raynold Byrth Mankynde 58 Crieng or reching so loude as she can, so to stere her selfe. 1565 Cooper Thesaurus, Screo, to reache in spittyng.

† b. trans. To spit or bring up (blood or phlegm). Obs.

c1000 Sax. Leechd. I. 142 Ȝyf hwa blod swiþe hræce, genime ðysse ylcan wyrte [etc.]. c1550 Lloyd Treas. Health (1585) L ij, Gume of a Peache tre geuen to hym that rechit or spitteth bloud, helpeth greatly. 1601 Holland Pliny II. 59 For them that raught vp bloud at the mouth, he prescribeth to take Mints in a broth. 1606 — Sueton. 189 Hee never durst once spit and reach up fleame.

2. intr. To make efforts to vomit; to retch.

In 18th c. freq. to reach to vomit (cf. Reaching vbl. sb.²). 1575 Gascoigne Hearbes Wks. 165, I poore soule which close in caban laye, And there had reacht til gaule was wel neare burst. 1636 Brathwait Rom. Emp. 47 As hee was reaching or striving to vomit. 1748 Richardson Clarissa (1811) IV. xliii. 285, I shall reach confoundedly, and bring up some clotted blood. a1776 R. James Diss. Fevers (1778) 51 She .. reached to vomit very much.

Reachable (rī·tʃăb'l), a. [f. Reach v.¹]

† 1. Able to reach to. Obs. rare—¹.

1633 T. Adams Exp. 2 Peter ii. 10 A tower reachable to heaven!

2. That may be reached.

1824 L. M. Hawkins Mem. II. 5 note, My father .. had strong oak shutters put on the outside of all the reachable windows in our house. 1873 W. S. Mayo Never Again xvii. 229 If through the sense of smell Her heart were reachable.

Reache, variant of Recche v. Obs.

Reached, ppl. a. rare—¹. [? f. Reach v.¹ 11.] ? Stretched, strained.

1650 Weekes Truth's Confl. ii. 45 It doth arise from their own reached and unworthy carriages towards God.

Reachelesse, obs. form of Reckless.

Reacher (rī·tʃəɹ). [f. Reach v.¹ + -er ¹.]

1. One who or that which reaches.

1594 Greene & Lodge Looking Gl. G.'s Wks. (Rtldg.) 120/1 Hold in your rapier; for though I have not a long reacher, I have a short hitter. 1598 Florio, Recatore, a bringer, a reacher. 1667 Wood Life (O. H. S.) II. 111 [Prynne] spoke to Jennings the reacher of the records that he should let him have any record. 1819 Byron Juan ii. clxv, The highest reachers Of eloquence in piety and prose. 1899 Daily News 9 Oct. 6/2 Shamrock .. has proved herself to be a good runner, a fine reacher.

† b. A certain type of beggar. Obs.—¹

1607 Dekker Jests to make you Merry 35 There is a new company arising, .. and these call themselues Reachers, they walke together Male and Female [etc.].

† 2. An exaggerated statement, 'stretcher'. Obs.

1613 Purchas Pilgrimage ii. x. (1614) 157 Adrian had a Vineyard eighteen miles square, which hee hedged with those slaine carkasses, as high as a man can reach (a reacher I thinke). a1661 Fuller Worthies, Monmouth. iv. (1662) 51. I can hardly believe that Reacher, which another writeth of him, that with the palms of his hands he could touch his knees, though he stood upright.

Reaching (rī·tʃiŋ), vbl. sb.¹ [f. as prec.]

1. The action of Reach v.¹, in its various senses. Also with out, up.

c950 Lindisf. Gosp. John Intr. 7/3 Mið ræcing [L. porrectione]. Ibid. 8/11 Mið racing honda [L. extensione manuum]. c1440 Promp. Parv. 425/2 Rechynge, or stretchynge, extensio. 1591 Percivall Sp. Dict., Alcance, ouertaking, obteining, pursuing, reaching. 1662 Betty Verney 19 Apr. in Mem. Verney Fam. (1899) IV. 21 The reaching up of my armes. 1760 Law Spir. Prayer i. 55 A natural .. reaching after that eternal light. 1875 Whitney Life Lang. viii. 138 The reaching-out of the bodily organs. 1884 Sat. Rev. 14 June 783/2 According to all accepted tenets, mere running and reaching [in yacht-racing] is poor work.

b. With a and pl. An instance of this.

1785 Burke Sp. Nabob Arcot Wks. 1842 I. 333 All the reachings and graspings of a vivacious mind. 1846 Ruskin Mod. Paint. (1883) ii. i. i, Reachings forward unto the things that are before. 1871 Spencer Princ. Psych. II. § 300. 82 All reasoning .. is a reaching of the unknown through the known.

† 2. A reach or stretch of country. Obs.—¹

1727 in M. A. Richardson Hist. Table-bk. Leg. Div. (1843) I. 401 There are many hills and reachings for many miles.

3. Comb. reaching-post (see quot.).

1815 Burney Falconer's Mar. Dict., Reaching-Post, in rope-making, a post .. fixed in the ground at the lower-end of a rope-walk. It is used in stretching the yarn by means of a tackle.

Rea·ching, vbl. sb.² Now dial. [f. Reach v.²] The action of retching † or (in OE.) spitting. Also pl. (freq. in 18th c.).

c1000 Sax. Leechd. II. 174 Þis sint tacn adlies magan; ærest ȝelome spætunga oððe hræcunga. 1601 Holland Pliny xxiv. iv, The said barke .. is greatly commended for the reaching and spitting of blood. 1655 Culpepper Riverius i. vi. 24 Coughing, Yawning, Reaching, and Hiccoughs. 1719 De Foe Crusoe (1858) 481 First hungry, then sick again, with reachings to vomit. 1777 G. Forster Voy. round World II. 238 They groaned most pitifully, had violent reachings.

Reaching (rī·tʃiŋ), ppl. a. [f. Reach v.¹ + -ing ².] That reaches, in senses of the vb.

1. Of the hand, etc.: Stretching out to or after something; able to reach far.

1593 Shaks. 2 Hen. VI, iv. vii. 86 Great men haue reaching hands. 1681 T. Flatman Heraclitus Ridens No. 31 (1713) I. 200 A sad Experiment I have made Of the long reaching Arm of Kings. 1817 Keats Sleep & Poetry 362 Fauns and satyrs taking aim At swelling apples with a frisky leap And reaching fingers.

b. Characterized by reaching forward (with the legs. Cf. Reach sb. 5).

1866 Blackmore Cradock Nowell xxv, She broke from the long stride of her trot into a reaching canter.

2. Having great (mental) reach; far- or deep-reaching. (Freq. in 17th c. Now rare.)

a. of thoughts, views, plans, etc.

c1400 tr. Secreta Secret., Gov. Lordsh. 106 It ys nedfull .. [to] chese a sotell man, þat hauyn most stalworth tokenyng, and most rechand argument. c1592 Marlowe Jew of Malta i. ii. 219 A reaching thought will search his deepest wits. 1674 Boyle Excell. Theol. ii. v. 207 To have so reaching and attentive a prospect of all things. a1718 Penn Maxims Wks. 1726 I. 840 St. James gives a short Draught of the Matter, but very full and reaching. 1836 Browning Life of Strafford (1891) 140 The views of the lord deputy, somewhat more reaching than their own, startled them.

b. of the mind, etc.; rarely of persons.

1582 Stanyhurst Æneis Ep. Ded. (Arb.) 3 Such reaching wyts, as bend theyre endewours too thee vnfolding thereof. 1594 Willobie Avisa 2 Then Pallas gaue a reaching head, With deepe conceites, and passing wit. 1664 Power Exp. Philos. iii. 161 The reaching soul of the renowned Descartes. 1845 Bp. Wilberforce Let. 27 May in A. R. Ashwell Life (1879) I. vii. 269 A very clever reaching mother.

3. Stretching; capable of stretching. rare—¹.

1651 N. Bacon Disc. Govt. Eng. ii. viii. (1739) 46 They saw that in such cases of Treason the King's honour was made of reaching Leather.

† 4. ? Attractive, 'fetching'. Obs.—¹

1607 Beaumont Woman Hater v. i, My Book-strings are sutable, and of a reaching colour.

Hence **Rea·chingly** adv.

1664 H. More Exp. 7 Epist. iii. 31 Very reachingly and comprehensively Prophetical.

Reachless (rī·tʃlės), a. [f. Reach v.¹ + -less.] That cannot be reached.

1628 Sir W. Mure Doomesday 318 What glorious lights Must beautifie those reachlesse hights. 1825 Hone Every-day Bk. I. 951 The hot little dog looking wistfully into the reachless warm water. 1863 Ld. Lytton Ring Amasis I. 121 Aloof upon her reachless rock, sat cold the Loreley.

Hence **Rea·chlessness**. rare—¹.

1861 Lytton & Fane Tannhäuser 26 As one should love a star .. who knows The distance of it, and the reachlessness.

Reachless, obs. variant of Reckless.

Reach-me-down, a. and sb. [Reach v.¹ 5 b.]

A. adj. Of clothes: Exposed for sale in a finished state, ready for wearing, ready-made; also, cast-off, second-hand.

1862 Thackeray Philip xxiv, The most splendid reach-me-down dressing gowns. 1887 Pall Mall G. 22 Jan. 4/1 The reach-me-down finery of the East-end exquisite.

B. sb. A ready-made or second-hand garment. Chiefly pl.

1877 Besant & Rice Harp & Cr. xv. 148 Two new pairs of second-hand machine-made reach-me-downs. 1884 World 3 Dec. 13/1 The wide-awakes, billycocks, ulsters, and reach-me-downs.

attrib. 1869 Routledge's Ev. Boy's Ann. 674 We preferred going to a reach-me-down store, as Prawle styled it.

Reachy (rī·tʃi), a. rare. [f. Reach sb.¹ + -y.] That has a long reach.

1888 Poultry 27 July 377 Game Cocks (four)—First (Plattin) a beautiful Black Red, very reachy, capital style.

Reack, obs. variant of Rick.

Reacknow·ledge, v. [Re- 5 a. In early use suggested by L. recognoscĕre or F. reconnoître.]

† 1. trans. To recognize, confess, acknowledge.

1550 J. Coke Eng. & Fr. Heralds § 225 (1877) 123 You, syr herald of Fraunce, .. for ever herafter, shall reacknowledge your dutie, gevynge place to the heralde of Englande. 1555 Harpsfield in Bonner's Homilies 10 He teacheth vs in oure prayers, to reacknowledge oure selues synners.

† 2. To reconnoitre, explore. Obs. rare—¹.

1622 F. Markham Bk. War v. ix. 196 To find out and reacknowledge the natures, dispositions and inclinations of all the Enemies Commanders.

3. To acknowledge again or anew.

1640 Habington Edw. IV 70 King Henry set at libertie went .. to Pauls Church, the Clergy, Nobility, and Commonalty reacknowledging all obedience to him. 1657 J. Sergeant Schism Dispach't 614 If then .. they have broke in peeces his Church, and renounced the only-certain grounds of his law, they must .. restore both to their former integrity by reacknowledging them. 1735 Pope Lett. (1735) I. 232 This puts me in mind of reacknowledging your continu'd Endeavours to enrich me.

Hence **Reacknow·ledgement, -ledging.**

1598 Florio, Resipiscentia, .. a reacknowledging. 1611 Ibid., Riconoscenza, reacknowledgement.

Reacquai·nt, v. [Re- 5 a.] trans. To make acquainted again; to bring back into acquaintance.

1647 H. More Song of Soul iii. i. xii, Tract of time at least all memory Will quite debarre, that reacquainten mought My self with mine own self.

So **Reacquai·ntance**, renewed knowledge.

1668 H. More Div. Dial. iii. ii. (1713) 183 Your reacquaintance of those many and most noble Truths that Philotheus recovered into your Mind.

Reacquire, v. [Re- 5 a. Cf. F. réacquérir (15th c. in Littré).] trans. To acquire anew.

a1691 Boyle Hist. Air (1692) 225, I perceived one of them .. that had almost quite lost its colour, to have reacquired a very fair blew. a1711 Ken Hymnotheo Poet. Wks. 1721 III. 361 Their penitential Tears .. Had strove lost Heav'n and Love to re-acquire. 1805 W. Taylor in Ann. Rev. III. 291 The established interests .. would, after the first novelty of an independant choice, shortly reacquire their natural ascendancy. 1884 Sir J. Pearson in Law Times Rep. L. 712/2 By losing an English domicil, he re-acquired a Scotch domicil, his domicil of origin.

Hence **Reacqui·red** ppl. a.

1839 James Louis XIV, II. 299 To ensure durability to the reacquired power of the queen. 1880 C. & F. Darwin Movem. Pl. 524 This regeneration of the tips and reacquired sensitiveness.

So † **Reacqui·st** v. Obs. rare—¹.

1635 J. Hayward tr. Biondi's Banish'd Virg. 166, I will endeavour to re-acquist you the kingdome or dye in the attempt.

† **Reacqui·te**, v. [Re- 5 a.] trans. To requite.

1534 Cromwell in Merriman Life & Lett. (1902) I. 395, I shall accompt my self bounden to reaquite your gentilnes with semblable pleasures. a1548 Hall Chron., Rich. III (1809) 405 His bountyfulnes and liberalitie whiche they would God wyllynge shortly reacquyte. 1594 T. Bedingfield tr. Machiavelli's Florentine Hist. (1595) 166 So might he also hope in time to come, to be reacquited.

React (ri,æ·kt), v.¹ [See Re- 2 a and Act v. Cf. F. réagir (18th c.), late L. reagĕre (5th cent.).]

1. intr. To act in return, or in turn, upon some agent or influence. Also without const.

Sometimes used loosely when previous action is merely implied or possible.

1644 Digby Nat. Bodies xvi. 141 If fire doth heate water, the water reacteth againe .. vpon the fire and cooleth it. 1724 Swift Answer Misc. (1735) V. 21 Because, the Soul her Power contracts, And on the Brother Limb re-acts. 1772 Wesley Wks. (1872) V. 233 God does not continue to act upon the Soul, unless the Soul re-acts upon God. 1831 Macaulay Sp. in Ho. Comm. 5 July, Government and society are cause and effect—they re-act on each other. 1880 McCarthy Own Times IV. l. 61 Applause reacts upon the orator.

b. spec. in Chem. of the action of reagents.

1797 Encycl. Brit. (ed. 3) IV. 415/1 The nitrous acid soon .. reacts on the other metals, and dissolves them. 1845 G. E. Day tr. Simon's Anim. Chem. I. 359 Chyle of different qualities may react with varying energy on the lymphatic glands.

2. intr. To act, or display some form of energy, in response to a stimulus; to undergo a change under some influence. Const. to (in recent use).

1656 tr. Hobbes' Elem. Philos. (1839) 393 Though all sense .. be made by reaction, nevertheless it is not necessary that every thing that reacteth should have sense. 1856 Kane Arct. Expl. II. v. 67 The less severe cases .. are beginning to feel the influence of their new diet; but Wilson and Brooks do not react. 1882 Vines tr. Sachs' Bot. 895 The tendency to expand is increased by darkness .. : light has the contrary effect, and the one half always reacts more powerfully than the other. 1891 F. Darwin in Nature 409 Plants may gain .. various aptitudes for reacting to light and gravitation.

3. intr. To act in opposition to some force. Const. against.

1861 M. Arnold Pop. Educ. France p. xx, I know that some individuals react against the strongest impediments. 1871 Daily News 31 Jan., He .. did all that lay in him to react against the cry, à Berlin.

4. intr. To move or tend in a reverse direction; to return towards a previous condition.

1875 Tennyson Queen Mary iv. iii. 246 Heaven help that this re-action not re-act Yet fiercelier under Queen Elizabeth. 1893 Westm. Gaz. 29 Nov. 2/1 His father was a strong Wesleyan, and the son, as was natural, reacted towards the Church of England. 1896 Daily News 5 Nov. 7/4 Silver reacted 2¼, but rallied 1⅞ on dealings.

† 5. trans. a. To exercise in turn. b. To drive back, to reflect. Obs.

1646 Sir T. Browne Pseud. Ep. 386 The spirits of many .. meeting no assimilables wherein to react their natures, must certainely anticipate such naturall desolations. 1678 Cudworth Intell. Syst. i. v. 731 Every thing that suffered and reacted motion, especially polite bodies, as looking-glasses.

Hence **Rea·cting** vbl. sb. and ppl. a.

1611 Florio, Reattióne, a reacting, or reaction. 1685 J. Chamberlayne Coffee, Tea, & Choc. 60 The acting and re-acting which they have one upon another. 1833 Chalmers Const. Man (1835) I. iv. 173 The actings and reactings that take place between man and man. 1871 Morley Voltaire (1886) 5 A kind of reacting sympathy. 1896 Allbutt's Syst. Med. I. 245 Some modification in the reacting tissue.

Re-act (rī,æ·kt), v.² [f. Re- 5 a + Act v.] trans. To act, do, or perform a second time.

a1656 Bp. Hall Invisible World iii. v, Encouraging a man, by the prosperous event of his sin, to re-act it. a1711 Ken Preparatives Poet. Wks. 1721 IV. 18, But .. I fear my treacherous Will Wou'd live re-acting the like Ill. 1755 Smollett Quix. iv. xv, The gay shepherdesses and gallant swains, who sought to renew and react the pastoral Arcadia. 1833 I. Taylor Fanat. vi. 144 They .. wait only the leave or bidding of circumstances to re-act their part.

Reaction (ri,æ·kʃən). [f. Re- + Action; cf. React v.¹ and F. réaction (a 1610).

Florio (1611) uses 'reaction' to render It. reattione (mod. reazione): see Reacting vbl. sb.]

1. Repulsion or resistance exerted by a body in opposition to the impact or pressure of another body.

1644 Digby Nat. Bodies xvi. 139 Of reaction .. in locall motion, that each agent must suffer in acting and acte in suffering. 1748 Hartley Observ. Man i. i. 47 It must be compressed in return, by the Re-action of the Skull. 1800 Vince Hydrost. i. (1806) 11 The reaction of the sides of the vessel against the fluid. 1881 Encycl. Brit. XII. 524/2 The reaction of the jets caused the rotation of the machine.

fig. 1643 Sir T. Browne Relig. Med. i. § 5 It is the method of Charity to suffer without reaction. a1660 Hammond Serm. xxi. Wks. 1684 IV. 687 In such a Soul as this, there is a perpetual re-action, an impatience of the presence of any thing which may trash, incumber or oppress it.

2. The influence which a thing, acted upon or affected by another, exercises in return upon the agent, or in turn upon something else.

1772 Wesley Wks. (1872) V. 232 A continual action of God upon the Soul, and a re-action of the Soul upon God. 1792 A. Young Trav. France 434 The effects of high or low prices on agriculture, and the re-action of culture on price. 1863 Tyndall Heat i. 2 Action and reaction have thus gone on from prehistoric ages to the present time. 1876 L. Stephen Eng. Th. 18th C. I. i. 12 Mr. Darwin's observa- tions upon the breeds of pigeons have had a reaction on th[e] structure of European Society.

b. Chem. The action of one chemical agent o[n] another, or the result of such action.

1836 J. M. Gully Magendie's Formul. (ed. 2) 9 The grea[t] care that is requisite to prevent the re-action of this acid [is] an objection to its use. 1862 Miller Elem. Chem. (ed. [..]) III. 67 Owing to the feebler affinities of these elements, th[e] reactions take place with less vehemence. Ibid. 435 Th[e] vegetable bases when in solution have generally a decided alkaline reaction upon test papers.

3. Phys. and Path. a. The supervention of a[n] opposite physical condition, as the return of hea[t] after cold, or of vitality after shock.

1805 W. Saunders Min. Waters 498 If an intire immersio[n] in cold water be employed, and the body be in a fit state [to] produce reaction, a full .. perspiration will follow. 18[..] Abdy Water Cure (1843) 165 The first impulse to the r[e]action of the heart has been found to have been given b[y] these means. 1875 H. C. Wood Therap. (1879) 652 Th[e] cold bath, when not followed by a healthy reaction, is an[y]thing but a tonic.

b. The response made by the system or a[n] organ to an external stimulus.

Reaction of degeneration, 'a gradual diminution and fina[l] loss of faradic excitability of both nerves and muscles, co[n]sequent on degeneration and atrophy of both' (Syd. Soc. Lex.). A variety of this is called Reaction of exhaustion. 1896 Allbutt's Syst. Med. I. 359 This condition is know[n] as the reaction of degeneration, and is found in seriou[s] injury or disease in the motor nuclei of the anterior cornu. 1899 Ibid. VII. 347 The reaction to light was lost in bot[h] eyes.

4. A movement towards the reversal of an exist[-]ing tendency or state of things, esp. in politics; return, or desire to return, to a previous conditio[n] of affairs; a revulsion of feeling.

In 1816 referred to as a French use of the word (Edinb. Re[v.] XXVII. 480).

1801 Hel. M. Williams Fr. Rep. I. xii. 122 If I hav[e] delayed sending you the sketch of the re-action at Naple[s] [etc.]. 1816 Scott Old Mort. xliv. note, That perpetuatin[g] of factious quarrels, which is called in modern times Re[-] action. 1836 Hor. Smith Tin Trump. (1876) 161 Like ever[y] other excess, fanaticism provokes a reaction. 1875 Jowet[t] Plato (ed. 2) IV. 256 In the ancient as well as the moder[n] world there were reactions from theory to experience.

5. attrib. and Comb., as (sense 3) reaction perio[d], stage, time; reaction engine or machine, [a] small apparatus in which the motive power i[s] derived from the reaction exerted by escapin[g] steam; reaction process, a method of treatin[g] galena, depending on the chemical reaction whic[h] follows upon roasting and fusing (Raymond 1881); reaction wheel, a water-wheel impelled by th[e] reaction of escaping water.

1868 Model Steam Eng. (1895) 82 *Reaction or resistanc[e] engines, described at pages 7 and 8. 1863 Ganot Physic[s] § 380 In *reaction machines steam acts by a reactive forc[e] like water in the hydraulic tourniquet. 1897 Syd. Soc. Le[x.] s.v., *Reaction-period, the period of reaction or return [of] vitality after a shock. 1899 Allbutt's Syst. Med. VI. 619 I[n] the *reaction-stage of many cases of local asphyxia, there [is] distinct evidence of heat. 1893 Outing (U.S.) XXII. 152/[..] It appears .. that the *reaction time varies with the loudnes[s] of the report. 1881 Encycl. Brit. XII. 524/2 The old *re[-] action wheel consisted of a vertical pipe balanced on [a] vertical axis, and supplied with water.

Hence **Rea·ctional** a., characterized by reaction; **Rea·ctionally** adv.

1856 J. Grote in Cambr. Ess. 87 Under certain circum[-] stances the mind may be likely to move reactionally. 189[..] Hughes Medit. Fever v. 207 This artificial reduction o[f] temperature is followed by a slight reactional rise.

Reactionary (ri,æ·kʃənări), a. and sb. [f. Reaction + -ary ¹. Cf. F. réactionnaire (19th c.).]

A. adj. 1. Of, pertaining to, or characterized by, reaction.

1847 Grote Greece ii. xxxvi. IV. 497 The intensity of th[e] subsequent displeasure would be aggravated by this re[-] actionary sentiment. 1879 McCarthy Own Times II. xvii[i.] 40 The results of the year that followed were decidedl[y] reactionary.

2. Inclined or favourable to reaction.

1858 Froude Hist. Eng. III. 161 The reactionary member[s] of the council had suggested a call of parliament. 187[..] Jowett Plato (ed. 2) III. 174 The fixed ideas of a reactionar[y] statesman.

B. sb. One who favours or inclines to reaction.

1858 Froude Hist. Eng. IV. 485 The reactionaries .. watched for some change of fortune.

Rea·ctionist, sb. and a. [f. as prec. + -ist.] A marked or professed reactionary.

1862 Merivale Rom. Emp. lii. (1865) VI. 266 As usua[l] with reactionists in social life, .. they mistook the cause o[f] the disease. 1883 Jrnl. Educ. XVIII. 137 Nobody excep[t] the chronic reactionist and constitutional grumbler want[s] to keep back the colored people.

b. attrib. or as adj.

1858 Froude Hist. Eng. xiii. III. 177 To the clergy and the reactionist lords he would not yield a step. 1866 Pal[l] Mall G. 21 Feb. 4/2 The Liberals .. did not expect that the reactionist tendencies of the Government would be expressed so strongly.

Rea·ctive (ri,æ·ktiv), a. and sb. [f. React v.¹ + -ive. Cf. F. réactif (18th c.), It. reattivo.]

A. adj. † 1. Repercussive, echoing. Obs.—¹

1712 Blackmore Creation 357 Ye fish, assume a voice, with praises fill The hollow rock, and loud reactive hill.

2. Acting or operative in return.

Supplement, p. 3873; Corrigenda, p. 4092; Spurious words, p. 4093; Books quoted, p. 4094

REACTIVELY.

body that acts, is at the same instant both active and re-active.

Reactivity. [f. REACTIVE + -ITY, after *activity*.] The state or power of being reactive.

Re-actuate, v. [Re- 5 b.] *trans.* To make actual again; to restore to activity.

Reacuntar, obs. Sc. f. RECOUNTER.

Read (rīd), *sb.[1]* Obs. *exc. dial. or techn.* Also 4 (g *dial.*) rede, 5 g *Sc.* reid, 8–9 reed. [OE. *reada*, of obscure origin.] The stomach of an animal; in later use only *spec.* the fourth stomach of a ruminant.

Read (rīd), *sb.[2]* [f. READ v.] An act of perusal; a spell of reading; also *Sc.*, a run of a book, etc., for the purpose of reading it.

Read (rīd), v. Pa. t. and pa. pple. *read*. Forms: *pres.* ī rédan, (-on, rǽdan, *north.* réda, 3 rǣden(2), raden, 2–4 rede(n, 3 redyn ; *pres.*) 2–4 rade, 3–6 reda, 5–6 reade, 3–6 reid, reid, 6 (8 *Sc.*) read ; (3) 6–7 reade, 6–read.

Read (rīd), v. Pa. t. and pa. pple. *read*. To read out. transf. and fig. in various applications.

Read, obs. f. RED a., var. RIDE v., obs. f. REED.

Readable (rī′dăb′l), a. [f. READ v.] Capable of being read, legible.

Readdress, v. [RE- 5 a.] *trans.* To address oneself again.

Read.pt, v. [RE- 5 a.] To re-adapt.

Read.pt, v. [RE- 5 a.] To re-adapt.

Readeption. So **Readaptation**; **Read.pt.ive** a ; **Read.pt.iveness.**

Reade or **Reede,** sb. Obs. [See RE- 5 a and ADEPT a., ADEPTIO(N), a. C., etc.] Obs.

Readept, v. Obs.

Reader (rī′dər), sb. Forms: 1 rǣdere, 4–6 redar(e, 4–6 reder(e, 6 Sc. reidar, ridar, reider), 5–present [f. READ v. + -ER.]

Readerless, a. Having no reader.

Readership, sb. [f. READER + -SHIP.]

Readily, adv. Forms: 4–6 redely, 4 redili, 5–6 (7) redely), 4 redili; also (5) readily.

READILY.

READINESS.

1. Promptly, in respect of the voluntariness of the action; hence, with alacrity or willingness; willingly, cheerfully.

2. Promptly, in respect of the time of action; quickly, without delay; also, without difficulty, with ease or facility.

3. Promptly, in respect of the facility or ease of action; easily.

Readiness (re′dinĕs), sb. [f. READY a. + -NESS.]

1. The quality, state or condition of being ready.

2. Promptness in voluntary action ; prompt compliance, willingness, etc.

3. A state of preparation : †a. Without reference to time.

b. In reference to a particular time or occasion.

4. The condition or fact of being ready or fully prepared. *rare.*

Reading, vbl. sb. [f. READ v. + -ING.]

READING.

READING.

Reading (rīˈdiŋ), ppl. a. [f. READ v. + -ING².]

Reading boy, a boy who reads copy aloud to the corrector of the press.

Readmit (rĭˈdmit), v.

Readjourn (rĭˈdʒərn), v.

Readjust, v.

Readjustment, n.

Readminister, v.

Readmission, n.

Readmittance, n.

Readopt, v.

Readoption, n.

Readorn, v.

Readvance, v.

Readvertency, n.

Readvertise, v.

Ready (rĕˈdi), a.

Ready, v.

Ready-made, ppl. phr.

Ready-money, a.

Ready-reckoner, n.

Ready-witted, a.

Reaffirm, v.

Reaffirmation, n.

Reafforest, v.

Reafforestation, n.

Reaggravate, v.

Reaggravation, n.

Reaggregate, v.

Reaggregation, n.

Real (rīˈal), n.

Real (rīˈal), a. and n.

Realgar

REAL

Realgar (rĭ'algär). Also 8 **realgal**. [... from Arab. ...] The native or artificial disulphide of Arsenic (1 b.), also called red (sulphide of realgar) of arsenic and red orpiment, used as a pigment and in pyrotechnics.

Reali, variant of REALLY adv. Obs.

Realie, obs. Sc. form of REALLY adv.

Real¹gnment [RE-5 a.] A new alignment.

Realism (rī'alĭz'm). [f. REAL a.² + -ISM; perh. after F. réalisme or G. realismus.]

1. Philos. n. The scholastic doctrine of the objective or absolute existence of universals, of which Thomas Aquinas was the chief exponent. (Opposed to NOMINALISM and CONCEPTUALISM.) Also in later use: The attribution of objective existence to a subjective conception.

2. Belief in the real existence of matter as the object of perception (natural realism); also, the view that the physical world has independent existence, and is not ultimately reducible to universal mind or spirit. (Opposed to IDEALISM 1.)

3. Inclination or attachment to what is real; tendency to regard things as they really are; any view or system contrasted with IDEALISM 2.

Realist (rī'alĭst), sb. (and a.) [f. REAL a.² + -IST; cf. F. réaliste.]

1. One who occupies himself with things rather than words. Obs. rare.

2. Philos. An adherent or advocate of Realism (as opposed either to NOMINALIST or to IDEALIST).

Realistic (rīalĭ'stĭk), a. [f. prec. + -IC.]

1. Characterized by artistic or literary realism; representing things as they really are.

Reality (rĭæ'lĭtĭ). [ad. F. réalité, or med.L. realitat-, realitas.]

1. The quality of being real or having an actual existence.

Realizable (rī'alăizăb'l), a. [f. REALIZE v. + -ABLE.] 1. REALIZE sb.²

1. The quality of being real or having a real existence.

REALIZABLENESS

Realizableness, Realizability adv.; also **Realizability** (in recent Dicts.).

Realization (rīalăizē'shən). [f. REALIZE v. + -ATION.] The action or result of realizing.

1. The action of making real or investing with reality; the process of becoming or being made real; conversion into real fact.

Realize (rī'alăiz), v. [f. REAL a.² + -IZE; cf. F. réaliser.]

1. trans. To make real, to give reality to (something merely imagined, planned, etc.); to convert into real existence or fact; to show the reality or truth of (a statement).

Realizing (rī'alăizĭŋ), ppl. a. [f. prec. + -ING.] The action of REALIZE v.²

Really (rī'alĭ), adv.² Also ε -riallich, 6 Sc. realie. [f. REAL a.² + -LY².]

1. In a real manner; in reality; in point of, or as a matter of, fact; actually.

REALM

Realm (relm). Forms: ? realsy (? re-aly', 6 re-allme), 7 realy; ε -realme, 4 reaume, 4-5 reume, regme(e, 4-6 reaume, 4-5 realme, 4-6 reme, 4-5 reame, realme, Sc. reime, 6 reaum, 4-6 reaulme, reaume, realme. [a. OF. reialme, reiaume, realme, etc.]

1. A kingdom. Now chiefly Hist., and in such phrases as "Statutes of the Realm."

Realme, obs. (erron.) form of REAM sb.³

Realty (rī'altĭ). Also 5 realte, 7 -tie. [f. REAL a.¹ + -TY.]

1. Royalty; royal state, dignity, or power.

REAM

Ream, sb.¹ Forms: 1 hréam, 2-3 ream, 3-5 rem, reme, 6-7 reme. [OE. hréam.] Cry, outcry, shouting.

Ream, sb.³ Also 3 realm, rem, ream, reem, rem. [OE. Ardam, of obscure origin.]

Ream, v.¹ trans. 1 hréam, 2-3 ream, 3 reme, reme, 6 rime. [OE. hréaman, to cry out.]

Realness (rī'lnes). [f. REAL a.² + -NESS.] The fact or quality of being real; reality, truth.

Ream, obs. variant of REALME.

Ream, sb.[1] Obs. exc. dial. Forms: 3 remien, 4 reme, 6–7 reme, 9 dial. ra·y·me, r(h)eom. [ME. *rēmien*, of obscure origin. Cf. REAM v.[3]]

Ream, v.[1] [f. REAM sb.[1]]

Ream, v.[2] techn. Also reem. [Of somewhat doubtful origin: perh. a survival in special sense of RE-, v.prefix to make room, open up.

Ream, v.[3] Also reem, rem-. [Of obscure origin; found only in 1 ayamon, usually along with *ream* REAM v.[1]]

Re-amass, v. rare. [RE- 5 a.] trans. To bring or heap together again.

Re-amend, v. [RE- 5 a.] trans. To amend again.

Reamer (rī'mar). [f. REAM v.[2] + -ER[1].]

Rea·ming, vbl. sb.[1] [f. REAM v.[1] + -ING[1].]

Rea·ming, vbl. sb.[2] [f. REAM v.[2]]

Reaming, variant of REEMING vbl. sb.

Rea·ming, ppl. a.[1] rare. [f. REAM v.[3]]

Rea·ming, ppl. a.[2] Chiefly Sc. [f. REAM v.[1]]

Reanimation (rī,ænimē'ʃən). [f. prec.]

Rea·nimate, v. [f. RE- 5 a + ANIMATE a.]

Rea·nimate, v. [f. RE- 5 a + ANIMATE v.]

Reanimation (rī,ænimē'ʃən). [f. prec.]

Rean (rēn). Obs. exc. dial. Forms: 6 reian, 7 reane, 7, 9 reaon, 9 reen, 9 rean, etc.

Re-anchor, v. [RE- 5 a.] trans. and intr. To anchor again.

Reane, obs. form of RANE sb. and REN.

Reanimate, a. rare. [Cf. next and ANIMATE a.]

Reannex (rī,ænə'ks). [f. RE- 5 a + ANNEX v.]

Reannexation (rī,ænəksē'ʃən). [Cf. prec. and ANNEXATION.]

Reanoint, v. [RE- 5 a.] trans. To anoint again.

Reanswer, sb. [f. RE- + ANSWER sb.]

Reanswer, v. [RE- 5 a. + ANSWER v.]

Reanson, obs. form of RANSOM v.

Reap (rīp). v.[1] Forms: see below. [OE. *rīpan* or *ripan* (North. *riopa* etc.), *rypan*, *ropan*]

Reap (rīp), sb.[1] Forms: 1 reopa, 4–5 repe, 4–5 rope ... [OE. *rēapa*, *rīpa*, *rēpe*, *rip*.]

Reap (rīp), sb.[2] [OE. *rīp* related to *ripan* REAP v.[1]]

Reap (rīp), v.[2] Now only dial. [Var. of RIP v.]

Re-apparel, v. [RE- 5 a.] trans. To apparel again. Hence Re-appa·relling vbl. sb.

Rea·pable, a. rare. [f. REAP v.[1] + -ABLE.]

Reape, obs. var. RIPE v.[1]; obs. var. ROPE sb.

Reaper (rī'par). Forms: 1 ripere, 4 reaper, (5 repere, 6 reper). [f. REAP v.[1]]

Reapparel, v. [RE- 5 a.]

Reappeal, v. Also 5 -appel. [f. RE- + APPEAL v.]

Reapparel, variant of REAPPAREL v. Obs.

Reappear, v. [RE- 5 a.] intr. To appear again.

Reappearance. [f. prec. + -ANCE.] The act of appearing again; a second or fresh appearance.

Reapplication. [RE- 5 a.; cf. next.] A fresh application.

Reapply, v. [RE- 5 a.] To apply again.

Reappoint, v. [RE- 5 a.] trans. To appoint again. Hence Reappoi·nted ppl. a.

Reappoint, sb. Obs. rare. [var. RAPPORT or REPORT sb., + A- pref. 11.] A report.

Reapportion, v. Obs. [var. REPONE v., as if f. RE- + APPOSE v.] intr. and trans. To repose.

Reappraise, v. Obs. [f. RE- + APPRAISE v.]

Reappropriate, v. [RE- 5 a.] trans.

Reap-silver. Obs. rare. [f. REAP v.[1] + SILVER.]

Reap-time. Obs.[1] [var. as prec. + TIME.] Harvest-time.

Reappear, sb. Obs. rare. [var. RAPPORT or REPORT sb., + A- pref. 11.]

Reap-hook. [f. REAP v.[1]] A reaping-hook.

Reaping (rī'piŋ), vbl. sb. [f. REAP v.[1]]

†Reap-man. Obs. Forms: 1 hrip(p)emonn, 2 ripman, 4 repeman, 5–6 repmon. A reaper.

Reaquite, variant of REACQUITE v. Obs.

Rear (rīar). sb.[1] Obs. exc. dial.

Rear (rīar). sb.[2] Also 7 reer, reere. [OE. *hrēa(m)*; cf. RARE a.[1]]

Rear (rīar), a.[1] Now dial. Also 7 reer, reare. [OE.]

Rear (rīar), a.[2] Forms: 1 hrer, 4–7 (9 dial.) rere, 6 reare, 6–7 (9 dial.) rear, 7–9 reare, 6, 8 reer. [OE.]

Rear (rīar). sb.[3] Forms: 1 rēran, 3 reren, 4–6 rere, 7 reyr, (6–7 dial.) reare, 6–7 rear. [OE.]

Rear (rīar), v.[1] [OE. *rǣran*]

Rear (rīar), v.[2] [f. prec. sb.]

REAR-ADMIRAL. [f. REAR-.]
1. A flag-officer in the navy, the next in rank below a vice-admiral. (See ADMIRAL.)

Rear-arch. *Arch.* Also **rere-**. [f. REAR- + ARCH.] The inner arch of a window or door-opening, when differing in size or form from the external arch. (Cf. REAR-VAULT.) Also *attrib.*

Rear-banquet, see REBE-BANQUET.

Reard, variant of REDD, noise.

Rardors, obs. variant of REREDEMAIN *Obs.*

Reared (rī·ɘd), *ppl. a.* [f. REAR *v.*[1] + -ED[2].]
1. Raised, elevated, exalted.

Rear (rīəɹ), *v.*[2] *Obs. exc. dial.* Also 5-9 **rere**. [Of obscure origin.] *trans.* To cut up or carve (a goose, etc.)

Rear (rīəɹ), *v.*[1] [OE. rǽran = ON. reisa.]

† Rear, *v.*[3] *Naut.* Of obscure origin and meaning.

† Rear, *v.*[4] = ARREAR *adv.*

† Rear-foast. *Obs.* [f. REAR- + FEAST.] The latter meal, supper.

† Rear-freight. *Obs.* [Alteration of REFRAIT, after REAR- and FREIGHT.] Refrain, burden.

Rear-guard (rī·ɹgaːd), *Mil.* Forms: 5-8 **reregard**, 5 **rere-**, 6 Sc. **rearegard** ; 6 Sc. **reir-**, 7 **rere-**, 7 **roreguard**, etc. [a. OF. rereguarde, rereguard (13th c.) rearguard.] 1. That division of an army which marches in the rear.

Variously written **roarguard**, **rearguard**, and **rear-guard**.

Rearing (rī·riŋ), *vbl. sb.* [f. REAR *v.*[1]] The action of the vb. in various senses.

Re-arrange, *v.* [f. RE- + ARRANGE *v.*] To arrange anew.

Re-arrangement. [f. prec.] Fresh or different arrangement.

So **Re-arra·ngeable** *v.* ; **Re-arra·ngement**.

Re-array, *v.* [RE- *5 a.*] To array again.

Re-arrest, *v.* [RE- *5 a.*] To arrest again.

So **Re-arre·st** *sb.*

Rear-rib = REAR-VAULT (1844).

Re-arve, *v.* [RE- *5 a.*] To carve again.

So **Re-arva·l**.

Rear-shaft, see REAR-VAULT (1844).

Rear-support, variant of REBE-SUPPER *Obs.*

Rear-vassal. *Hist.* Also **rere-**. [f. REAR- + VASSAL, after f. *arrière-vassal*.]

Rear-vault. *Arch.* Also **rere-**. [f. REAR-, after f. *arrière-vousteure*.] The vaulted space connecting an arched window- or door-head with the arch in the inner face of the wall.

Rearward (rī·ɹwəd), *adv.* [f. REAR- + -WARD.] 1. Situated in the rear.

Rearward (rī·ɹwəd), *sb.*[2] [f. as prec.] Towards the rear ; backward.

Reascend, *v.* [RE- + ASCEND.] To ascend again.

Reascent. [f. prec.] 1. The act of reascending.

So **Reasce·ndant**, *ent-a.*; **Reasce·ndancy, -ency**.

Reascensi·on.

Rease, obs. f. RAISE *v.*[1], var. REBE *Obs.*, obs. Sc.

Roasod, variant of RESEED *a.*, raised.

† Reasonable, *sb.* ASSEMBLANCE[2.] Resemblance.

Reasm, Resm, obs. forms of RAISIN.

Reasiness see READY *a.*

Re-a·sk, *v.* [RE- *5 a.*] To ask again.

Reason (rī·z'n), *sb.* Forms: 2 resun, 3-4 -oun, (5 reisoun), 3-5 reyson, 4-5 reison ; 4-6 reson, (5 rayson), 4-7 rayson, (5 reasoun, -un) ; 4-6 resoun, 5 resun, 6 Sc. rason. β. 3 reosun, (4-5 ressoun, ressun), 4-7 reson, (6 Sc. resson) ; 7- reason. [a. OF. reisun, resun, raison, raison etc.]

Reason (rī·z'n), *v.* Forms: 4-6 **rosoun**, 4-7 **reson**, etc. [a. OF. raisoner (raisonner).]

12. In verbal phrases denoting the conformity of something to the dictates of reason: †**a.** *Reason will* or *would*. *Obs.*

a 1300 *Cursor M.* 11663 'Ioseph', sco said, 'fain wald i rest'.. 'Gladli', said he, 'þat wil resun'. 1377 LANGL. *P. Pl.* B. x. 112 Whi shulde we [etc.]?..resoun wolde it neuere. 1423 *Rolls of Parlt.* IV. 257/2 Hit semeth resoun wolde he shuld have the disavaille therof, and not the Marchant. 1433 *Ibid.* 424/2 To be as reson will, Chief þereof. 1526 TINDALE *Acts* xviii. 14 Yf it were a matter of wronge,.. reason wolde that I shuld beare you. [So COVERDALE & 1611.] 1597 SHAKS. 2 *Hen. IV*, IV. i. 157 Our Cause [is] the best; Then Reason will, our hearts should be as good.

b. *It stands* († *with* or) *to reason*.

1528 PAYNEL *Salerne's Regim.* B iij, Consyderynge then that mans eies be colde of nature: hit standeth with reason they shulde be washed with colde water and not with hotte. 1612 SHELTON *Quix.* I. i. I. 6 For it stood greatly with reason, seeing his Lord and Master changed his estate and vocation, that he should alter likewise his denomination. 1632 HOLLAND *Cyrupædia* 149 It standeth to good reason, that they who repose mutuall trust one in another, will joyntly sticke to it. 1698 C. BOYLE, etc. *Ep. Phalaris Exam.* 137 It stands to reason, that he thought the Expression common enough; or else he would not have us'd it. 1873 BLACK *Pr. Thule* xxiv, Of course it stands to reason that the rich never have justice done them in plays and stories: for the people who write are poor.

13. In prepositional phrases (chiefly *Obs.*), denoting agreement with, or opposition to, what reason directs or indicates:

†**a.** *By reason* (= OF. *par raison*). Also rarely *by good* (or *right*) *reason*, *by no reason*. *Obs.*

a 1300 *Cursor M.* 14742 Mi hus agh be, [be] right resun Hus o praier and of orisoun. 13.. *K. Alis.* 3937 The kyng ..n'olde him sle, bote by resoun. *c* 1400 MAUNDEV. (1839) x. 120 Seynt Petre the Apostle, and thei that camen aftre him, han ordeynd to make here Confessioun to man; and be gode Resoun: for [etc.]. *a* 1425 *Cursor M.* 10535 (Trin.) Shal no mon bi no resoun Aȝeyn hir haue no wicke chesoun. *a* 1450 *Knt. de la Tour* (1868) 53 Thei that seethe the good and takithe the evelle, by reson they shulle repent hem. 1523 LD. BERNERS *Froiss.* I. xviii. 26 He delyuered them sufficient by reason, to pay all their small charges. 1563 *Mirr. Mag., Collingbourne* 145 b, The gylty alwayes are suspicious, And dread the ruyne that must sewe by reason.

b. *In reason.* Also *in all* or *any reason*; † *upon reason*.

a 1400-50 *Alexander* 1670 Aske it at Alexander quat þou will apon reson, And I sall grant. 1597 SHAKS. 2 *Hen. IV*, II. ii. 53 Keeping such vild company as thou art, hath in reason taken from me, all ostentation of sorrow. 1598 — *Merry W.* I. i. 229 In any reason. 1603 — *Meas. for M.* III. i. 250 In all reason. 1650 T. B[AYLEY] *Worcester's Apoph.* 97 The Law could not in reason take notice of any such thing. 1678 BUNYAN *Pilgr.* I. (1862) 68 Had he had a thousand souls, they had in reason been cast away. 1712 BUDGELL *Spect.* No. 277 ¶ 12, I am willing to do anything in reason for the Service of my Country-women. 1823 KEBLE *Serm.* iii. (1848) 65 To..consider fairly, what effect, in all reason, their believing it ought to have on themselves. 1898 G. B. SHAW *Plays* I. (*Unpleasant*) 186 If you want a cheque for yourself..you can name any figure you like—in reason.

†**c.** *Of reason.* Also with *all*, *good*. *Obs.*

1413 *Pilgr. Sowle* (Caxton 1483) IV. xxx. 78 They shall.. brynge hit in to good couenable fourme as to suche a lord bilongeth of reson. 1449 in *Wars Eng. in France* (Rolls) I. 493 Purveaunce shalbe made for you in such wise as of reasone ye shal holde you wel contente. 1523 FITZHERB. *Husb.* § 12 In some places they sowe bothe pees and beanes vnderforowe: and those of reson must be sowen betyme. 1533 BELLENDEN tr. *Livy* v. ii, May it nocht be said to him of gude resoun: 'Thow has ȝerelie wagis, suffir þareof ȝerelie laubouris?' 1664 H. MORE *Antid. Idolatry* ix. 103 The Council of Trent .. must of all reason be conceived to mean these very Circumstances.

†**d.** *Out of reason.* *Obs.*

c 1400 *Destr. Troy* 2222 We may boldly vs byld with bostis out of Reason. 1480 CAXTON *Chron. Eng.* ccxix. 209 Mortimer disgised him with wonder riche clothes out of al maner reson. 1576 FLEMING *Panopl. Epist.* 385 You sell the same..to your Brother too deere and out of reason.

†**e.** *Through* (*good* or *right*) *reason.* *Obs.*

13.. *Sir Beues* (MS. A.) 48 Man, whan he falleþ in to elde, Feble a wexeþ..þourȝ riȝt resoun. *c* 1325 *Chron. Eng.* 842 in Ritson *Metr. Rom.* II. 305 Ant so thourh god resoun He yeld hem heore tresoun. *c* 1330 R. BRUNNE *Chron. Wace* (Rolls) 3628 After Belyn, Gurgoint his sone Hadde þe heritage þorow resone.

†**f.** *With* (or *to*) *reason.* Also with *no*. *Obs.*

c 1290 *S. Eng. Leg.* I. 44/359 Seint Ieme ne miȝhte habbe þe soule..with no resun ne riȝhte. *a* 1300 *Cursor M.* 14705 Þe werckes þat i werc in his nam, Quat man þan mai wit resun blam. *c* 1330 *Amis & Amil.* 874 Then seyd thai al with resoun, Sir Amis schuld ben in prisoun. 14.. *Sir Beues* (MS. M.) 179 Syr Guy answered hym with reason And sayd: 'Alas, for here is treason!' *c* 1489 CAXTON *Sonnes of Aymon* vii. 159 As ye knowe, I wolde be reformed with rayson to the sayenge of his barons. 1556 HOBY tr. *Castiglione's Courtyer* Epist. A iij b, Because you may see him confirme with reason the Courtly facions. 1615 T. ADAMS *White Devill* 37 These ride in the open streetes, whiles the other lurke in close woods—and to reason, for [etc.].

†**g.** *Without* (*right*) *reason.* *Obs.*

a 1300 *Cursor M.* 16296 Qui smites þou me wit-vten right resun. *c* 1330 R. BRUNNE *Chron.* (1810) 150 Men mad tille him grete mone, it was without reson. 1390 GOWER *Conf.* III. 42 Delicacie in loves cas Withoute reson is and was. 1484 CAXTON *Life of Æsop* 2 b, He.. went in without rayson and hath eten al the fygges. 1568 GRAFTON *Chron.* II. 629 This multitude..spoyled, robbed and rifled, without reason or measure.

14. A matter, act, proceeding, etc., agreeable to reason; in phrases *it is reason* or *reason is* (also with *good*, *great*), *it is no* (or *not*) *reason*, *to think* (*it*) *reason*, etc. Freq. *c* 1400–1650; now *rare*.

So OF. *il est raison*, *c'est* (*bien*) *raison*, *c'est raison et droit*, etc.

c 1320 *Cast. Love* 1096 'Þat is skile', quaþ Jhesu, 'and good reson'. 1340 HAMPOLE *Pr. Consc.* 6891 Þarfor it es reson and ryght, Þat þai ay se þat grysely syght. 1423 *Rolls of Parlt.* IV. 257 Hit is no reson that the Maister take his worship of another mannes harme. 1454 *Ibid.* V. 248/1 In suche wyse as it can be thought reason unto our Tresorer. 1523 LD. BERNERS *Froiss.* I. 348 It is reason that it shulde so be. *a* 1533 — *Gold. Bk. M. Aurel.* D d vi, Reason is, that I succour thy povertee with moneie. 1577 B. GOOGE *Heresbach's Husb.* I. (1586) 25 b, It is good reason to sowe timely in wette groundes. 1625 BACON *Ess., Marriage* (Arb.) 264 It were great Reason, that those that haue Children, should haue greatest care of future times. 1676 HOBBES *Iliad* I. 129, I thought it reason th' Argives should collect. 1686 tr. *Chardin's Coronat. Solyman* 100 It was not reason to punish the innocent with the Guilty. 1809 MALKIN *Gil Blas* VI. ii. ¶ 2 It is but reason that you should distrust our purity. 1818 T. L. PEACOCK *Nightmare Abbey* iv, 'Do you know, sir, that Marionetta has no fortune?' 'It is the more reason, sir, that her husband should have one'. 1864 MANNING *Let. to Pusey* 28 It is, however, but reason that I should rejoice.

†**b.** In parenthetic phrases, *as reason is* (or *was*), *as* (*it*) *is reason*, etc. *Obs.*

c 1386 CHAUCER *Prol.* 847 Telle he moste his tale as was reson, By foreward and by Composicion. 1535 COVERDALE *Baruch* ii. 6 We with oure fathers (as reason is) are brought to open shame. 1596 DANETT tr. *Comines* (1614) 198 To which his commandement I obeyed as reason was. 1604 E. G[RIMSTONE] *D'Acosta's Hist. Indies* I. xxii. 74 If we shall give that respect to the authoritie of Plato (as it is reason), we must [etc.]. 1671 MILTON *Samson* 1641 What your commands impos'd I have perform'd, as reason was, obeying.

†**c.** *And reason*, placed after a statement. *Obs.*

1563 MAN *Musculus' Commonpl.* 279 They do sufficiently confesse.. that the sacrament is not the very grace itselfe, and reason. *c* 1592 MARLOWE *Jew of Malta* IV. i, *Barabas.* I'd cut thy throat, if I did. *Ithamore.* And reason too. 1671 MILTON *P. R.* III. 122 To whom our Saviour fervently reply'd. 'And reason; since his word all things produc'd'.

†**d.** Similarly *and good reason*, *and* (rarely *as*) *reason good*. *Obs.* (Cf. 8 a.)

1593 SHAKS. 2 *Hen. VI*, IV. ii. 171 Wee'l haue the Lord Sayes head... *Cade.* And good reason. 1657 W. RAND tr. *Gassendi's Life Peiresc* I. 75 He wrote most frequently (and good reason) to his Father and Uncle. 1714 MRS. MANLEY *Adv. Rivella* 60 Lord Crafty, as Reason good, immediately assumed the Management of his Lady's Affairs. 1757 MRS. GRIFFITH *Lett. Henry & Frances* (1767) I. 115 True love.. never attacks us but once, and reason good, because it lasts us for life.

†15. That treatment which may with reason be expected by, or required from, a person; justice; satisfaction; chiefly in phr. *to do* (*one*) *reason* (tr. F. *faire raison*). *Obs.*

c 1400 MAUNDEV. (Roxb.) xxxi. 141 Þai do resoun and trewth till ilke man, als wele to pouer as to riche. *c* 1420 *Anturs of Arth.* xxviii, Welecome, worthely wyghte! Thou sall hafe resone and ryghte. *c* 1477 CAXTON *Jason* 72 b, To holde them in pees reson and justice. *a* 1533 LD. BERNERS *Huon* x. 30, I shal do hym reason yf it be founde that I haue done any wronge. 1588 SHAKS. *Tit. A.* I. ii. 278, I.. [am] resolu'd withall To doe my selfe this reason, and this right. 1638 R. BAILLIE *Lett. & Jrnls.* (1841) I. 94 If they gett reason, it is thought they are both undone. *Ibid.* 132 The Thesaurer...required that his Grace would see justice done upon him...The Commissioner promised him reason. 1651 tr. *De-las-Coveras' Don Fenise* 301 The more I endeavoured by faire meanes to oblige him to doe me reason, the more I excited him to derision.

b. With reference to drinking. *Obs.* exc. *arch.*

1594 PLAT *Jewell-ho.* III. 62 Quaffing companions.. wil require reason at their hands as they terme it. 1663 DRYDEN *Wild Gallant* I. i, First I'll drink to you, Sir; upon my faith I'll do you reason, Sir. 1698 FRYER *Acc. E. India & P.* 279 After.. every one's Health has reason done it, they take off the Table-Cloth. 1819 SCOTT *Ivanhoe* xlii, I pray you.. to do me reason in a cup of wine. 1826 — *Woodst.* xix, Nor was his follower slow in doing reason to the royal pledge.

†**c.** Satisfaction by a duel. *Obs.*[−1]

1619 in *Crt. & Times Jas. I* (1849) II. 120 Sir Edward Villiers told him himself was the man. 'I hope', said the other, 'you will do me reason'. Thereupon a challenge was made and accepted.

†16. A reasonable quantity, amount, or degree. Also *spec.* the measure by which a miller took his toll. *Obs.*

1426 LYDG. *De Guil. Pilgr.* 10614 As touchyng off the melle, Thow myghtest ther..be-holden A mesure Wych (by folkys oppynyoun,) Bereth the name off 'Resoun'. *c* 1430 *Pilgr. Lyf Manhode* II. xv. (1869) 80 At the mille peraventure ye haue seen a mesure that is cleped resoun. *Ibid.* III. xvii. 144 Millewardes also that filleth here resoun, with oute cleping of resoun. 1591 SPENSER *M. Hubberd* 887 In case his paines were recompenst with reason. 1598 GRENEWEY *Tacitus, Ann.* VI. vi. (1622) 130 Agrippina not contented with reason, and greedy of rule. 1599 SHAKS. *Much Ado* V. iv. 74 *Bene.* Do not you loue me? *Beat.* Why no, no more than reason. 1675 EARL ESSEX [A. CAPEL] *Lett.* (1770) 15. I have not yet heard precisely what terms mr. Thinne stands upon, but in case he will take reason.. it would be a great convenience to me to be provided of a dwelling in town.

†**b.** Moderation. *Obs.*[−1]

1615 LATHAM *Falconry* (1633) 93 When she hath cast them againe, giue her her breakefast of good meat, with reason in the quantity.

†17. *To have reason* (tr. F. *avoir raison*): to be right (esp. in making a statement). *Obs.* (Cf. 8 b.)

1557 NORTH *Gueuara's Diall Pr.* I. x. (1568) 13 b, This if they had demaunded of the true God, they should haue had reason. 1594 CAREW *Huarte's Exam. Wits* 8 Aristotle excepteth naturall Philosophie, saying, a yoong man is not of fit disposition for this kind of doctrine, wherein it semeth he hath reason. 1624 BEDELL *Lett.* vi. 95 The King himselfe said aloud, that both sides had reason. 1667 DRYDEN & DK. NEWCASTLE *Sir M. Mar-all* III. i, *Sir Mart.* You have reason, sir. *Mood.* There he is again too; the town phrase. 1704 SWIFT *Mech. Operat. Spir.* Misc. (1711) 285 The Objectors have Reason, and their Assertions may be allowed. 1771 *Junius Lett.* xliii. (1804) II. 181 Louis XIV had reason when he said 'the Pyrenees are removed'.

18. The fact or quality of being agreeable to the reason; such a († procedure or) view of things as the reason can approve of.

c 1470 *Golagros & Gaw.* 331 Ressaue him reuerendly, as resoun in lyis. 1599 SHAKS. *Hen. V*, V. ii. 358 Wee haue consented to all tearmes of reason. 1601 — *Jul. C.* III. ii. 113 Me thinkes there is much reason in his sayings. 1653 WALTON *Angler* ii. 47 This is reason put into Verse, and worthy the consideration of a wise man. 1667 MILTON *P. L.* IX. 738 His perswasive words, impregn'd With Reason, to her seeming, and with Truth. 1732 BERKELEY *Alciphr.* II. § 4 There is reason in what you say. 1819 SHELLEY *Cenci* II. ii. 17 Nay, there is reason in your plea; 'twere hard. 1880 T. HARDY *Wessex Tales, Fellow-Townsmen* iii. (1896) 124 There was reason in Mrs. Downe's fear—that he owned.

b. In phrases *to hear*, *listen to*, or *speak reason*.

1535 STEWART *Cron. Scot.* I. 596 For na counsall that tyme wald he heir ressoun. 1545 ELYOT s.v. *Ius*, *Ius dicis*, thou speakest reason. 1599 SHAKS. *Much Ado* I. iii. 5 You should heare reason. *Ibid.* V. i. 41 There thou speak'st reason. 1664 J. WILSON *A. Comnenius* V. iii, Troth he speaks reason. 1719 DE FOE *Crusoe* II. iii, The rogues were now more capable to hear reason than to act reason. 1765 GOLDSM. *Good-n. Man* I, When I'm determined I always listen to reason, because it can then do no harm. 1832 HT. MARTINEAU *Hill & Valley* vi. 101 The people were now in a condition to hear reason. 1880 T. HARDY *Wessex Tales, Fellow-Townsmen* iii. (1896) 124 Her impression is that your wife will listen to reason.

IV. †19. The exercise of reason; the act of reasoning or argumentation. *Obs.*

c 1330 *King of Tars* 276 The doughter dude overcome hem bothe Beo riht reson and evene. *c* 1440 *York Myst.* xxxvii. 255, I schall þe proue be right resoune. 1542 RECORDE *Gr. Artes* (1575) 8 Reason is the expressing of a iust matter with witty persuasions, furnished with lerned knowledge. 1565 JEWEL *Repl. Harding* (1611) 361 Wee may not argue by reason in this sort [etc.]. 1620 T. GRANGER *Div. Logike* 8 That part of euery proposition that goeth afore in reason, howsoeuer the words be placed, is the Theme there handled. 1647 H. MORE *Poems* Interpr. Gen. 433, I understand by Reason, the deduction of one thing from another.

†20. Consideration, regard, respect. *Obs.*

c 1385 CHAUCER *L. G. W.* 728 *Thisbe*, And certeyn as by reson of hir age Ther myght haue ben bitwixe hem mariage. 1398 TREVISA *Barth. De P. R.* XVIII. liii. (Bodl. MS.), Amptes .. take grete charge of heyr comyn profite and haue þerof reson and mynde. 1533 BELLENDEN tr. *Livy* III. xxiv, More respect suld haue bene had to ressoun of þe senatouris þan to ony ressoun of þare vassalege or meritis.

†21. Way, manner, method; *spec.* the method of a science. *Obs.*

c 1380 WYCLIF *Serm.* Sel. Wks. I. 15 ȝif men avysiden hem on þis resoun, noone shulde juge bi mannis lawe. 1530 PALSGR. 889 And by lyke reason forme they *tintouin*, *charivaris*, and suche lyke. 1551 RECORDE *Pathw. Knowl.* Argts., The fourth booke teacheth the right order of measuringe all platte formes, and bodies also, by reson Geometricall. 1643 in Clarendon *Hist. Reb.* VI. § 353 We cannot believe the intermixture of the present ecclesiastical government with the civil state to be other than a very good reason.

†**b.** Possibility of action or occurrence. Const. *but*. *Obs. rare.*

1591 SHAKS. *Two Gent.* II. iv. 212 When I looke on her perfections, There is no reason, but I shall be blinde. *c* 1592 MARLOWE *Jew of Malta* V. ii, Since things are in thy power, I see no reason but of Malta's Wrack. 1596 SHAKS. *Tam. Shr.* II. i. 409, I see no reason but suppos'd Lucentio Must get a father.

†22. *Math.* = RATIO 2. *Obs.*

c 1374 CHAUCER *Boeth.* II. pr. vii. 44 (Camb. MS.) Al the enuyronynge of the erthe abowte ne halt but the resoun of a prikke at regard of the gretnesse of heuene. *c* 1400 tr. *Secreta Secret., Gov. Lordsh.* 86 If it be yn tokenynge fleumetyke, a lityll [medicine] after þe qualyte & resoun of þe tokenynge. 1570 BILLINGSLEY *Euclid* XI. def. i. 312 There are..three reasons or meanes of measuring, which are called commonly dimensions. 1587 GOLDING *De Mornay* xiv. 212 There is the same reason in the proportion of eight vnto six that is of fower vnto three. 1614 T. BEDWELL *Nat. Geom. Numbers* I. 8 Like-plaines haue a doubled reason of their correspondent sides. 1678 COCKER *Arithm.* vi. 60 A third [number], which shall have such reason to the one, as the other hath to unite. 1713 BERKELEY *Hylas & Phil.* iii. Wks. 1871 I. 337 The moments or quantities of motion in bodies are in a direct compounded reason of the velocities and quantities of Matter contained in them.

V. 23. *attrib.* and *Comb.* (chiefly objective and obj. gen.), as *reason-plating* (after *armour-plating*), *-poisoning*, *-renderer*, *-scanner*, *-worship*; *reason-derived*, *-proof* adjs.; **reason-ring**, a ring bearing a 'reason' or motto.

1874 W. WALLACE *Hegel's Logic* § 36. 61 A *reason-derived knowledge of God is the highest problem of philosophy. 1870 *Spectator* 24 Dec. 1536/1 If his heavy artillery could not penetrate the thick *reason-plating of the statesmen, it was passion-proof. 1888 F. M. CRAWFORD *With the Immortals* I. 69 Doctor Saul Ascher, who died an abstract death from *reason-poisoning. 1849 *Westm. Rev.* Oct. 442 A man who on this topic.. is pretty nearly *reason proof. 1589 PUTTENHAM *Eng. Poesie* III. xix. (Arb.) 236 This assignation of cause the Greekes called Etiologia...We also call him the *reason-rendrer. 1877 W. JONES *Finger-ring* 426 Among the motto or '*reason' rings, as they were termed, is an example.. found in 1823, at Thetford. 1591 SYLVESTER *Du Bartas* I. iii. 970 *Reason-scanners have resolved all, That heavie things, hang'd in the Aire must fall. 1893 G. A. DENISON in *Ch. Times* 24 Mar. 315 *Reason-worship, the parent of all heresies.

Reason (rīˑz'n), *sb.*[2] Forms: 6 resun, 7 resen, 8 reson, *dial.* resen, 7– reason. [var. RASEN, q.v.] = RAISING-PIECE. Also *attrib.* with *piece*.

a 1548 [see RAISING-PIECE]. 1611 COTGR., *Architrave*,...the reason peece, or master beame (in buildings of timber). 1674–91 [see RASEN]. 1703 T. N. *City & C. Purchaser* 183 Betwixt them and the Sell, or Reson. 1736 PEGGE *Kenticisms* (E. D. S.), *Resen*, the raising; 'tis much the same as the wall-plate. 1875 KNIGHT *Dict. Mech.* 1899/1 *Reason-piece*, a timber which lies under the beams on the brick or timber in the side of a house.

Reason (rīˑz'n), *v.* Forms: 4 resun, 5 resoune, 5–7 reson, 6 rai-, rayson, reason, *Sc.* resson, 5– reason. [ad. OF. *raisoner* (F. *raisonner*):—late L. *ratiōnāre* to discourse, f. *ratiōn-em*: see REASON *sb.*[1] In sense 1 perh. aphet. for AREASON.]

†1. *trans.* To question (a person); to call (one) to account. = AREASON *v.* *Obs. rare.*

13.. *Cursor M.* 8676 (Gött.), I knew wel..Of þis tresun scho had me don. I hir resuned þan al-sua son. *c* 1430 *Syr Gener.* (Roxb.) 2829 Generides thoo he [Anazaree] gan reason Whi the Sowdon did him in prison. *a* 1578 LINDESAY (Pitscottie) *Chron. Scot.* (S.T.S.) I. 33 Quhen he had pansit in this maner wp and doun and ressonit himself for his slouthfulnes.

†2. *intr.* To hold argument, discussion, discourse or talk *with* another. *Obs.*

The precise sense depends greatly on the context.

1483 CAXTON *G. de la Tour* L vj, Yf one begynne to resoune and talke with yow of suche mater, lete hym alone. *c* 1489 — *Sonnes of Aymon* i. 32 Thenne he resoned wyth his prynces and barons. 1530 PALSGR. 680/1 By that tyme that I have reasonned a lytell with hym I shall soone fele his mynde. 1568 GRAFTON *Chron.* II. 127 He sent for the Maior and Shirifes of London, with whome he reasoned greuously for the escape of one called John Gate. 1596 SHAKS. *Merch. V.* II. viii. 27, I reason'd with a Frenchman yesterday, who told me [etc.]. 1611 BIBLE 1 *Sam.* xii. 7 Now therefore stand still, that I may reason with you before the Lord. 1671 MILTON *P. R.* IV. 233 How wilt thou reason with them, how refute Thir Idolisms, Traditions, Paradoxes?

†**b.** (Without const.) To argue, discourse, converse, talk. *Obs.*

1526 *Pilgr. Perf.* (W. de W. 1531) 99 Glotony commeth in full subtylly, & reasoneth full craftely, sayenge [etc.]. 1551 ROBINSON tr. *More's Utop.* II. (1895) 271 That no man shalbe blamed for reasonynge in the mayntenaunce of his owne religion. 1594 SHAKS. *Rich. III*, IV. iv. 537 Away towards Salsbury, while we reason here, A Royall battell might be wonne and lost. 1611 BIBLE *Matt.* xvi. 7 And they reasoned among themselues, saying, It is because we haue taken no bread.

†**c.** Const. *about*, *against*, *of*, *on* (a matter). *Obs.*

1551 ROBINSON tr. *More's Utop.* II. (1895) 270 He, as sone as he was baptised, began..to reason of Christes religion. 1588 SHAKS. *L. L. L.* I. i. 95 How well hee's read, to reason against reading. 1599 — *Hen. V*, III. vii. 38 My Horse.. 'tis a subiect for a Soueraigne to reason on. 1667 MILTON *P. L.* II. 558 Others apart sat on a Hill retir'd,..and reason'd high Of Providence, Foreknowledge, Will, and Fate.

d. To employ reasoning or argument *with* a person, in order to influence his conduct or opinions.

1847 MARRYAT *Childr. N. Forest* iv, All he could do was ..to reason with him. 1875 JOWETT *Plato* (ed. 2) V. 72 Mankind must be reasoned with before they are punished.

3. *intr.* To think in a connected, sensible, or logical manner; to employ the faculty of reason in forming conclusions (in general, or in a particular instance).

In early use not clearly distinguished from 2 b.

1593 SHAKS. *Rich. II*, I. iii. 277 [Q. 1] Teach thy necessity to reason thus,—There is no vertue like necessity. 1620 T. GRANGER *Div. Logike* 2 God doth not reason, or discourse. 1651 HOBBES *Leviath.* II. xxix. 168 Kings deny themselves some such necessary Power..: wherein they reason not well. 1667 MILTON *P. L.* IX. 765 Hee hath eat'n and lives, And knows, and speaks, and reasons, and discernes, Irrational till then. 1713 ADDISON *Cato* V. i, It must be so—Plato, thou reason'st well. 1782 COWPER *Doves* i, Reasoning at every step he treads, Man yet mistakes his way. 1810 CRABBE *Borough* xix, Temptation came; I reason'd, and I fell. 1846 RUSKIN *Mod. Paint.* II. III. i. xiv. § 5 Though we cannot, while we feel deeply, reason shrewdly.

b. Const. *from* (premises or data); *about*, *of*, *upon* (a subject).

1651 HOBBES *Leviath.* III. xlii. 280 By Reasoning from the already received Scripture. 1695 BLACKMORE *Pr. Arth.* I. 398 He reason'd deep of Heav'ns mysterious Ends. 1785 PALEY *Mor. Philos.* I. vii, To reason about his duty. 1812 SIR H. DAVY *Chem. Philos.* 3 If the phenomena are reasoned upon,.. the enquirer is guided by analogy. 1822 SHELLEY *Faust* II. 341 Oh! He is far above us all in his conceit: Whilst we enjoy, he reasons of enjoyment. 1844 H. H. WILSON *Brit. India* II. xi. II. 489 Reasoning from experience of the past abuses.. they anticipated a like result from the present.

4. With object-clause:

a. To question, discuss *what*, *why*, etc.

1529 BRIGHTWELL [Frith] *Ep. to Christian Rdr.* 111 b, If thou woldist reason why God doth thus. 1594 SHAKS. *Rich. III*, I. iv. 94, I will not reason what is meant heereby, Because I will be guiltlesse from the meaning. 1596 — 1 *Hen. IV*, II. iii. 107, I must not haue you henceforth, question me, Whether I go: nor reason where-about. 1855 TENNYSON *Lt. Brigade* 14 Their's not to reason why. 1864–8 BROWNING *J. Lee's Wife* IV. i, I will be quiet and talk with you, And reason why you are wrong.

b. To argue, conclude, infer *that*, etc.

1587 R. THORNE in Hakluyt *Voy.* (1589) 257, I reason, that as some sicknesses are hereditarious,..so this inclination or desire of this discouerie I inherited of my father. 1727 POPE & GAY *What passed in London* Swift's Wks. 1751 VI. 262 She reasoning, that it would be time enough..after the Comet had made its appearance.

c. To say by way of argument. *nonce-use.*

1840 DICKENS *Barn. Rudge* I, 'What have I done', reasoned poor Joe.

5. *trans.* **a.** To discuss or argue (a matter). Now *rare.*

1526 *Pilgr. Perf.* (W. de W. 1531) 187 b, They wyll reason yᵉ mysteryes of our fayth, whiche be aboue reason. 1560 DAUS tr. *Sleidane's Comm.* 175 b, Ther should be chosen two divines to reason the matter. 1605 BURGES *Pers. Tithes* 26 Thence a tender conscience may iustly thus reason the case. 1660 *Trial Regic.* 116 [He] was pleased to do me, and several other Gentlemen..the favour to reason the Law with us. 1808 MAR. EDGEWORTH *Moral T.* (1816) I. 205, I am in no humour to reason that point.

b. To explain, support, infer, deal with, by (or as by) reasoning. *nonce-uses.*

1605 SHAKS. *Lear* I. ii. 114 Though the wisedome of Nature can reason it thus, and thus, yet Nature finds it selfe scourg'd by the sequent effects. 1607 — *Cor.* V. iii. 176 This Boy, that cannot tell what he would haue, Doe's reason our Petition with more strength, Than thou hast to deny't. 1732 POPE *Ess. Man* I. 18 Say first, of God above, or Man below, What can we reason, but from what we know? 1821 SHELLEY *Prometh. Unb.* III. iv. 22 It saw much, Yet idly reasoned what it saw.

6. **a.** To bring (a person) *into*, *out of* (a state of mind, etc.) by reasoning.

1599 SHAKS. *Hen. V*, V. ii. 165 These fellowes of infinit tongue, that can ryme themselues into Ladyes fauours, they doe alwayes reason themselues out againe. 1653 H. MORE *Conject. Cabbal.* 233 Men commonly reason themselves into an allowance of sin, by pretending humane infirmities or natural frailties. 1749 FIELDING *Tom Jones* XV. ii, You know us better than to talk of reasoning a woman out of her inclinations. 1785 PALEY *Mor. Philos.* I. vii, A man, who has to reason about his duty, when the temptation to transgress it is upon him, is almost sure to reason himself into an error. 1893 FORBES-MITCHELL *Remin. Gt. Mutiny* 289 David tried to reason him out of his fears.

b. To put *down* by reasoning.

1686 GOAD *Celest. Bodies* II. i. 155 This.. is the grand popular objection, which Cries, not reasons us down. 1713 ADDISON *Cato* I. i, Love is not to be reason'd down, or lost In high ambition.

7. To think *out*, to arrange the thought of, in a logical manner.

1736 BUTLER *Anal.* I. vi. Wks. 1874 I. 124 There is no hint or intimation in history, that this system was first reasoned out. 1851 THACKERAY *Eng. Hum., Swift* (1858) 34 They are reasoned logically enough. 1874 CARPENTER *Ment. Phys.* I. ix. (1879) 414 By thus reasoning-out the probable consequences of an action, motives.. may lose more or less of their force.

8. To provide with reason; to accompany with a reason. *nonce-uses.*

1562 J. HEYWOOD *Prov. & Epigr.* (1867) 161 Which.. Sheweth thy nose better sesond than thy hed resond. 1796 BURKE *Reg. Peace* i. Wks. 1826 VIII. 129 This offer so reasoned plainly implies, that [etc.].

Reason, obs. form of RAISIN.

Reaˑsonabiˑlity. *rare.* [f. as next + -ITY.] Reasonableness.

1897 *Advance* (Chicago) 22 July 105/1 The reasonability of man, and the reasonability of the contention of God with his sinful creature.

Reasonable (rīˑz'nǎb'l), *a.*, *adv.*, and *sb.* Forms: 4 raison-, reison-, 4–5 resoun-, (5 resun-), 4–7 reson-, 5–6 reason-, 6 reson-, 5– reasonable (also 4–6 -abil, -abyll, etc.; 5 resenable, 6 reasnable). [a. OF. *raison*(*n*)*able*, *reson*(*n*)*able*, etc. (mod. F. *raisonnable*), f. *raison*, *reson*, etc. REASON, after L. *ratiōnābilis* RATIONABLE. The 15th c. form *resenable* may represent the earlier *resnable* RENABLE, q.v.]

A. *adj.* **I.** Endowed with reason. = RATIONAL *a.* 1. Now *rare.* **a.** of persons or living things, esp. *reasonable creature* († or *beast*).

c 1374 CHAUCER *Boeth.* V. pr. iv. 128 (Camb. MS.) Man is a resonable two foted beest. *Ibid.* pr. vi. 133 The commune Iugement of alle creaturis resonablis .. is this þat god is eterne. 1456 SIR G. HAYE *Law Arms* (S. T. S.) 64 Or lang tyme be gane, thare sall men that ar callit resonable do mare bestly dedis. 1502 *Ord. Crysten Men* (W. de W. 1506) Prol. 2 Every creature resonable unto whome god hathe gyuen mynde and understandynge. 1588 KYD *Househ. Phil.* Wks. (1901) 251 Man, a reasonable creature whose dignity doth come so neere the Angels. 1650 JER. TAYLOR *Holy Living & Dying* (1870) 7 Let your employment be such as may become a reasonable person. 1725 WATTS *Logic* III. ii. § 5 If every Creature be reasonable, every Brute is reasonable. 1791 BURKE *App. Whigs* Wks. 1826 VI. 218 For man is by nature reasonable.

b. of the soul or intellectual powers.

1390 GOWER *Conf.* III. 378 Thilke intelligence In mannys soule resonable Hath schape to be perdurable. *c* 1425 *Found. St. Bartholomew's* (E.E.T.S.) 45 In his slepe he was raueshid from his resonable wyttys. 1538 STARKEY *England* I. ii. 40 Some sayd that man was no thyng els but hys resonabul soule. 1595 SHAKS. *John* III. iv. 54 My reasonable part produces reason How I may be deliuer'd of these woes. 1648 *Shorter Catech.* § 22 Christ..became man by taking to Himself a true body and reasonable soul. 1736 CHANDLER *Hist. Persec.* Introd. 2 Every Man is bound..to make the best use he can of his reasonable powers. 1838–9 HALLAM *Hist. Lit.* II. II. iii. § 6. 102 The reasonable soul of mankind is not numerically one.

c. *fig.* 1610 SHAKS. *Temp.* V. i. 81 Their vnderstanding Begins to swell, and the approching tide Will shortly fill the reasonable shore.

2. Having sound judgement; sensible, sane. = RATIONAL *a.* 1 b. Also, not asking for too much.

13.. *E. E. Allit. P.* B. 724 Fyfty fyn frendez..þat..restful were & resounable & redy þe to serue. *c* 1386 CHAUCER *Wife's Prol.* 441 Sith a man is moore resonable Than womman is, ye moste been suffrable. 1573 G. HARVEY *Letter-bk.* (Camden) 10 He is able to satisfi ani reasnable natural philosopher in that point. 1638 JUNIUS *Paint. Ancients* 39 Reasonable and judicious Readers will not dislike the same digression. 1669 STURMY *Mariner's Mag.* II. 46 To give any reasonable Man an answer to any useful Question in the Art of Gunnery. 1751 SMOLLETT *Per. Pic.* xxxix, Those polite, candid, reasonable watermen demanded a Louis d'or for that service. 1769 *Junius Lett.* I. 10 We are governed by counsels from which a reasonable man can expect no remedy but poison. 1808 GOUV. MORRIS in Sparks *Life & Writ.* (1832) III. 369 If mankind were reasonable they would want no government. 1883 ANNA K. GREEN (Mrs. Rohlfs) *Hand & Ring* iii, 'Ferris is a reasonable man', said the coroner.

b. Requiring the use of reason. *nonce-use.*

1611 SHAKS. *Wint. T.* IV. iv. 409 Is not your Father growne incapable Of reasonable affayres?

†3. Able to discourse or discuss matters; ready of tongue or speech. Also const. *of*. *Obs.*

c 1369 CHAUCER *Dethe Blaunche* 534 Loo how goodely spake thys knyghte..I..fonde him so tretable Ryght wonder skylful and resonable. 1387 TREVISA *Higden* (Rolls) VIII. 25 He was.. resonabel of speche, and wel i-lettred. *c* 1400 *Rom. Rose* 2214 Wherfore be.. Goodly of word, and resonable Bothe to lesse and eek to mar.

†**b.** Of language: Marked by reasoning. *Obs.*

1387 TREVISA *Higden* (Rolls) I. 11 After so noble spekers þat sownede at þe beste; and of hem faire facounde and resonable speche, folowed and streynede all her lyf tyme. 1390 GOWER *Conf.* III. 136 Rethorique the science Appropred to the reverence Of wordes that ben resonable.

4. Agreeable to reason; not irrational, absurd or ridiculous.

a 1300 *Cursor M.* 26767 Stedfast and stabil Sal scrift be, þat es resonabil, And noght als neus þat er tan. *c* 1340 HAMPOLE *Prose Tr.* 24 Charite.. lith both ine loue of God and of thyne evyne cristene, and þere fore it is resounable that he that hath cherite vse both. 1390 GOWER *Conf.* III. 210 Pite...Makth that the god is merciable, If ther be cause resonable. 1411 *Rolls of Parlt.* III. 650/2 Atte such resonable tyme as it likyth the forsaid Lord.. to assigne. 1494 FABYAN *Chron.* VI. clxxxv. 184 This pylgryme.. layde for hym many resonable excuses, as well for his age as otherwyse. 1573 G. HARVEY *Letter-bk.* (Camden) 1 Uppon a reasnable vew of the matter. 1594 SHAKS. *Rich. III*, I. ii. 136 It is a quarrell iust and reasonable, To be reueng'd on him that kill'd my Husband. 1655 STANLEY *Hist. Philos.* III. (1701) 78/1 That God, not chance, made the World and all Creatures, is demonstrable from the reasonable disposition of their parts. 1725 DE FOE *Voy. round World* (1840) 154 Something which it was much more reasonable to worship. 1796 BP. WATSON *Apol. Bible* 232 So far from this genealogy being a solemn truth, it is not even a reasonable lie. 1858 GREENER *Gunnery* 359 The reasonable assumption would be that this bullet would range a greater distance if projected at the same velocity. 1877 E. R. CONDER *Bas. Faith* i. 3 The conviction would be reasonable, for it would be based upon universal experience.

†**b.** That may reasonably be used. *Obs.*[−1]

1465–6 *Act 5 Edw. IV* in Bolton *Stat. Irel.* (1621) 37 The Bowes [to be] of Ewe, Wych-hassell, Ashe, Awburne, or any other reasonable tree.

5. Not going beyond the limit assigned by reason; not extravagant or excessive; moderate.

a. of requests, desires, wishes, expectations, etc.

a 1366 CHAUCER *Rom. Rose* 1499 This prayer was but resonable, Therefor god held it ferme and stable. *c* 1399 *Pol. Poems* (Rolls) II. 5 Axe of thi God, so schalt thou nought be werned Of no request, which is resonable. 1561 WINȜET *Cert. Tractates* Wks. (S. T. S.) I. 4 Our resonable desyris being knawin. 1581 J. HAMILTON in *Cath. Tract.* (S. T. S.) 76 This demand appeiret ressonabill to sum, that thay could not reiect the same. 1832 HT. MARTINEAU *Life in Wilds* iv. 55 The reasonable wishes of the whole people. 1882 A. W. WARD *Dickens* iv. 91 He never had a reasonable want which he could not and did not satisfy.

b. of amount, size, number, etc., or of things in respect of these properties.

13.. *E. E. Allit. P.* A. 523 What resonabele hyre be naȝt be runne, I yow pay in dede and þoȝte. *c* 1380 WYCLIF *Sel. Wks.* III. 200 Men and wymmen schulden lyven in.. resonable abstynence of mete. 1477 *Rolls of Parlt.* VI. 178/2 Suche resonable costs and expenses, as shall happen to be done. 1504 *Bury Wills* (Camden) 98, I wyll that J. P. shall by my house..for xl li...to be payd in resonablyll yeerys as he can agre wᵗ myn executo'ˢ. 1573 TUSSER *Husb.* (1878) 20 Rent corne to be paid, for a reasnable rent. 1632 LITHGOW *Trav.* vi. 256 Nothing will sinke into it, of any reasonable weight. 1653 WALTON *Angler* ii. 41, I long to be doing; no reasonable hedge or ditch shall hold me. 1755 COLMAN & THORNTON *Connoisseur* No. 68 ¶ 9 The old lady had the hardiness to squint at the sum total, and declared 'it was pretty reasonable, considering'. 1849 MACAULAY *Hist. Eng.* II. 206 Doing a great service on reasonable terms to the Church of which he was a member. 1895 *Bookman* Oct. 25/2 A straightforward, readable narrative in a very reasonable compass.

c. Moderate in price; inexpensive.

1667 COLLINS in Rigaud *Corr. Sci. Men* (1841) II. 471 Mr. Stephens...will undertake it when paper is more reasonable. 1805 W. IRVING in *Life & Lett.* (1864) I. 148 This part of Paris is tranquil and reasonable. 1885 *Field* 3 Oct. 502/2 Feeding materials...are unusually reasonable just now.

†**d.** *Law.* *Reasonable aid*: (see quot.). *Obs.*

1607 COWELL *Interpr.*, *Reasonable ayde*, is a duty that the Lord of the Fee claimeth holding by Knights service or in soccage to marie his daughter, or to make his sonne Knight.

6. Of such an amount, size, number, etc., as is judged to be appropriate or suitable to the circumstances or purpose.

1436 *E. E. Wills* (1882) 104 Beyng yn Resonable helth of body. 1523 FITZHERB. *Husb.* § 62 If the beaste be fatte, and any reasonable meate vpon hym. 1560 DAUS tr. *Sleidane's Comm.* 251 We trust surely, that moste men..wil be content for reasonable [L. *tolerabilis*] wages rather to followe oure campe, than theirs. 1614 LATHAM *Falconry* (1633) 116 Put it into a pipkin or posnet with some reasonable store of faire water. 1755 FRANKLIN *Autobiog.* Wks. 1887 I. 252 All.. forage..is to be taken for the use of the army and a reasonable price paid for the same. 1784 COWPER *Task* II. 623 A man o' the town dines late, but soon enough, With reasonable forecast and dispatch, To ensure a side-box station at half-price. 1849 MACAULAY *Hist. Eng.* V. I. 656 They were determined to prosecute.. unless a reasonable sum were forthcoming, and .. by a reasonable sum was meant seven thousand pounds.

†**b.** Of a fair, average, or considerable amount, size, etc. *Obs.* (Freq. *c* 1590–1650.)

1588 PARKE tr. *Mendoza's Hist. China* 317 There are many prouinces.. that euery one of them is as bigge as a reasonable kingdome. *Ibid.* 337 They saw two reasonable riuers, vppon whose bankes there were many vines. 1597 MORLEY *Introd. Mus.* 63, I haue a Brother..a reasonable musition for singing. 1612 WOODALL *Surg. Mate* Wks. (1653) 9 My self have had reasonable experience in piercing wounds. 1653 GREAVES *Seraglio* 154 A Customer, who receiveth custom of the buyers and sellers of slaves, which amounteth to a reasonable sum in a year, for the toll is very great. 1725 SWIFT *Gulliver* I. vi, A barrel of their liquor a reasonable draught.

†7. Proportionate. Also const. *to*. *Obs. rare.*

c 1460 FORTESCUE *Abs. & Lim. Mon.* x. (1885) 132 Also moche salte as by thair coniecture ys ressnable to the nombre off þe men, women, and childeren. 1546 *Reg. Privy Council Scot.* I. 51 The said Dame Marioun to haue ane ressonable terce of Eglintoun. 1766 BLACKSTONE *Comm.* II. 492 The shares of the wife and children was called their reasonable parts, and the writ *de rationabili parte bonorum* was given to recover it.

8. *Comb.*, as *reasonable-bladed*, *-minded*, adjs.

1764 *Museum Rust.* III. 373 You cannot possibly hurt the gut,.. which no reasonable-bladed pen-knife can touch. 1895 *Outing* (U.S.) XXVII. 226/2 Enough for any reasonable minded person.

B. *adv.* Reasonably. **a.** With adjs. and advbs.

1470–85 MALORY *Arthur* x. lxxvi, I helde hym resonable hote though ye had not holpen me. 1523 LD. BERNERS *Froiss.* I. ccclvi. 574 The first day the wynde was reasonable good for them. 1583 STOCKER *Civ. Warres Lowe C.* I. 16 b, The minister.. made a reasonable long exhortation. 1603 KNOLLES *Hist. Turks* (1638) 185 The common people began to like reasonable well of the Turks. 1698 FRYER *Acc. E. India & P.* 66 There is also a reasonable handsome Buzzar. 1835–40 HALIBURTON *Clockm.* (1862) 180 Reasonable well, I give you thanks, sir, said he.

b. With verbs. *rare*[−1].

c 1550 *Disc. Common Weal Eng.* (1893) 326 Thincke youe that..he did not speake..reasonable.

C. *absol.* as *sb.* †**a.** A reasonable being. *Obs.*

c 1400 *Rom. Rose* 6760 In al this caas and in semblables If that ther ben mo resonables He may begge as I telle you here. 1620 T. GRANGER *Div. Logike* I. xxvi. 57 A mixt action in reasonables is voluntarie, because there is some consent of will, or self-motion. 1633 BP. HALL *Occas. Medit.* § 24 That woeful hostility, which is exercised betwixt us reasonables.

b. A reasonable person. *rare*[−1].

a 1814 *Savoyard* I. i. in *New Brit. Theatre* IV. 360 What, fool, are you one of the reasonables too?

Reasonableness (rīˑz'nǎb'lnės). [f. prec.]

†1. The quality of being reasonable or rational; rationality. *Obs.*

c 1511 *1st Eng. Bk. Amer.* (Arb.) Introd. 27 These folke lyuen lyke bestes without any resonablenes. 1620 T. GRANGER *Div. Logike* II. vi. 231 *Reasonablenesse is in man vniuersally. *a* 1677 HALE *Prim. Orig. Man.* I. i. 16 Porphiry ..and some others have been bold to make reasonableness not the specifical difference of the Humane Nature.

b. The fact or quality of being amenable to reason, or of acting or thinking in a sensible manner.

1533 UDALL *Floures* 168 b, Lette your goodnes or resonablenes be som refuge or succour vnto my folyshnes. 1576 FOXE *A. & M.* (ed. 3) II. 1884/1, I haue heard you talke this houre and a halfe, and can heare no reasonablenes in hym. 1736 BUTLER *Anal.* I. v. 134 A settled moderation and reasonableness of temper. 1850 KINGSLEY *Alt. Locke* Pref. (1879) 105 The self-restraint, the reasonableness, the chivalrous honour of the men. 1873 M. ARNOLD *Lit. & Dogma* 379 For the right inculcation of the method and secret of Jesus, we need the *epieikeia*, the sweet reasonableness, of Jesus.

2. Of actions, opinions, words, etc.: The fact of being based on, or agreeable to, reason.

1568 Q. ELIZ. in H. Campbell *Love-lett. Mary Q. Scots* (1824) App. 10 They shall..judge thereby the reasonableness of the things propounded. 1581 SIDNEY *Apol. Poetrie* (Arb.) 23 May I not presume a little further, to shew the reasonablenes of this worde *Vates*? 1641 SMECTYMNUUS *Vind. Answ.* II. 44 The reasonablenesse or unreasonablenesse of this we determine not. 1712 *Spectator* No. 524 ¶ 2 A serious Reflection on the Reasonableness of Virtue, and great Folly of Vice. 1751 SMOLLETT *Per. Pic.* xli, He saw the reasonableness of her fear. 1825 MᶜCULLOCH *Pol. Econ.* II. ii. 74 All have been impressed with the reasonableness of the maxim which teaches that those who sow ought to be permitted to reap. 1860 TYNDALL *Glac.* I. viii. 60 To acknowledge the reasonableness of my remarks.

b. Moderateness, cheapness. *rare.*

1742 FIELDING *J. Andrews* II. xiii, They had no objection to the reasonableness of the bill, but many to the probability of paying it. 1813 *Guide Watering Places* 289 The reasonableness of this place, joined to the beauty of its situation, draws to it a considerable number..during the season.

Reasonably (rīˑz'nǎbli), *adv.* [f. as prec.]

1. According to reason, with good reason, justly, properly.

1377 LANGL. *P. Pl.* B. XIV. 100 Ricchesse riȝtfulliche ywonne and resonablelich yspended. 1456 SIR G. HAYE *Law Arms* (S. T. S.) 66 He gave to man wit and resoun, knaulage and discrecioun to governe him resonably. *a* 1533 LD. BERNERS *Huon* cxlix. 563 He wolde gyue hym as moche golde & syluer as he coud resonably demaunde. 1585 T. WASHINGTON tr. *Nicholay's Voy.* III. iii. 74 Reasonably to consider aswel the time past, present, and too come. 1651 HOBBES *Leviath.* II. xxvi. 150 One may very reasonably distinguish Laws in that manner. 1718 *Freethinker* No. 87 ¶ 9 He can reasonably blame only Himself. 1830 MISS MITFORD in L'Estrange *Life* (1870) II. xiii. 302 The French Revolution is most happily over; never was anything French so reasonably conducted. 1879 LUBBOCK *Addr. Pol. & Educ.* iii. 49 The results which we might reasonably expect from a more enlightened system of education.

2. At a reasonable rate; † to a reasonable extent.

? *a* 1400 *Morte Arth.* 1508 Raunsone me resonabillye, as I may over reche, Aftyre my renttez in Rome may redyly forthire. 1422 tr. *Secreta Secret., Priv. Priv.* 191, xijᵉ causes enduceth a man to louse his wif reissonnabli and tempora[l]li. 1600 SURFLET *Countrie Farme* II. ii. 351 When you see that all the water is consumed.. boile them altogither reasonablie.

3. Sufficiently, suitably, fairly.

c 1502 *Joseph Arim.* (E.E.T.S.) 47 Verely she was heled, and lefte her styltes thore, And on her fete wente home resonably well. 1589 PUTTENHAM *Eng. Poesie* III. xxiii. (Arb.) 278 The Earle..could reasonably well speake French. 1638 JUNIUS *Paint. Ancients* 15 The helpe of a reasonably good wit. 1665 MANLEY *Grotius' Low C. Warres* 720 A town.. reasonably well fortified, having therein a strong garrison. 1791 MRS. RADCLIFFE *Rom. Forest* ii, Their distress was reasonably great. 1861 DICKENS *Gt. Expect.* v, There was a reasonably good path now.

†**b.** With vbs.: Fairly or pretty well. *Obs.*

1586 A. DAY *Eng. Secretary* I. (1625) 76 It is reported.. that you are growne prettely skilled in Instruments whereon you play reasonably. 1613 PURCHAS *Pilgrimage* VI. ii. (1614) 566 To which also the computation of Herodotus dothe agree reasonably in the time.

†4. Normally, naturally. *Obs.*[−1]

1615 CROOKE *Body of Man* 335 The Infant borne the seuenth month is reasonably borne and liueth.

†**Reaˑsonal**, *sb.* and *a.* *Obs. rare.* [f. REASON *sb.*[1] + -AL, after RATIONAL *sb.* and *a.*] **a.** *sb.* = RATIONAL *sb.*[2] 2. **b.** *adj.* = RATIONAL *a.* 2.

1577 *Test. 12 Patriarchs* (1706) 46 Put on the stool of priesthood, the crown of righteousness, the reasonal of understanding. 1594 CAREW *Huarte's Exam. Wits* (1616) 286 [They] make their children defective, as well in the powers reasonall, as in the naturall.

†**Reasonate**, *v.* *Obs.*[−1] (? error for *resonate*, to resound, shout.)

1631 R. H. *Arraignm. Whole Creature* xii. § 4. 127 He cryes out of a suddaine.. like that passionate Orator, that reasonates; Oh tempora! Oh mores!

†**Reaˑsoned**, *a.* *Obs.*[−1] [f. REASON *sb.*[1]] Provided with reason or reasoning power.

1521 FISHER *Serm. agst. Luther* Wks. (1876) 345 These heretykes all be it they .. were fell wytted men and depely resoned .. yet were they disceyued.

Reasoned (rīˑz'nd), *ppl. a.* [f. REASON *v.* + -ED[1].] Characterized by or based on reasoning, carefully studied. Also with *out*.

1684 T. BURNET *Th. Earth* I. II. x. 297, I do generally distinguish of two sorts of opinions in all men, Inclination-opinions, and Reason'd-opinions. 1815 J. C. HOBHOUSE *Substance Lett.* (1816) I. 304 The official letter of Lord Clancarty..which is a sort of renewed and reasoned declaration. 1862 H. SPENCER *First Princ.* II. vi. § 61 (1875) 192 All reasoned-out conclusions whatever must rest on some postulate. 1874 L. STEPHEN *Hours in Library* (1892) II. vi. 200 He prefers nature to law, instinct to reasoned action.

Hence **Reaˑsonedly** *adv.*

1836 A. WALKER *Beauty in Woman* 281 The Greeks, either intuitively or reasonedly, distinguished the three species of beauty as to the Figure.

Reasoner (rīˑz'nəɹ). [f. as prec. + -ER[1].]

1. One who reasons.

1548 ELYOT, *Ratiocinator*,.. a disputer, a reasoner. 1551 T. WILSON *Logike* X vj, Vpon such matters as are necessary ..for the godlye reasoner to teache. 1639 ROUSE *Heav. Univ.* Advt. (1702) 3 By too many of the great Reasoners of the age. 1741 WARBURTON *Div. Legat.* II. 642 Our Reasoner has here mistaken the very question. 1769 *Junius Lett.* xix. 82 A correspondent.. censures him for a bad reasoner. 1864 BOWEN *Logic* ix. 271 The ambiguities of language which..originally led the reasoner astray.

†2. A keeper of accounts. *Obs.*[−1]

1509 *Plumpton Corr.* (Camden) 205 John Wythers, his Surveyor & generall Reasonner.

†**Reaˑsonfully**, *adv.* *Obs.*[−1] [f. REASON *sb.*[1] + -FUL + -LY[2].] Reasonably.

1387–8 T. USK *Test. Love* III. i. (Skeat) l. 136 Reasonfulli maye he sey, yᵗ mercy bothe right and lawe passeth.

Reasoning (rīˑz'niŋ), *vbl. sb.* [f. REASON *v.* + -ING[1].] The action of the vb. REASON, *esp.* the process by which one judgement is deduced from another or others which are given.

c 1374 CHAUCER *Troylus* IV. 1046 (1018), I may wel maken ..My resoninge of goddes purveyaunce. — *Boeth.* V. pr. v. 131 (Camb. MS.) Yif þat wit and ymaginacion stryuen ayein resonynge. 1494 FABYAN *Chron.* IV. lxix. 47 For resonyng and profe of this was after assygned vii. score Iewes. 1538 STARKEY *England* I. iv. 137 Hyt ys a commyn faute in resonyng, to lay a faute ther as non ys. 1587 GOLDING *De Mornay* i, There is no reasoning against those which denie the Principles. 1643 MILTON *Divorce* Introd. (1851) 4 Who.. make it their chief designe to envie and cry-down the industry of free reasoning. 1725 DE FOE *Voy. round World* (1840) 313 A little reasoning with them brought some of the men to their senses. 1781 COWPER *Table-t.* 53 Such reasoning falls like an inverted cone, Wanting its proper base to stand upon. 1866 GEO. ELIOT *F. Holt* (1868) 29 The Rector was helped to this chain of reasoning by Harold's remarks.

b. With *a* and *pl.* An instance of this.

1552 EDW. VI *Jrnl.*, etc. (Roxb.) 457 The reasonings be in my deske. 1611 BIBLE *Luke* ix. 46 There arose a reasoning among them, which of them should be greatest. 1651 HOBBES *Govt. & Soc.* ix. § 1. 135 Socrates is a man, and therefore a living creature, is a right reasoning, and that most evident. *a* 1720 SEWEL *Hist. Quakers* (1795) I. ii. 101 Several people accompanied him, and he had great reasonings with them. 1812 L. HUNT in *Examiner* 14 Dec. 785/2 He would not enter into a reasoning on the subject. 1880 L. STEPHEN *Pope* vii. 163 The reasonings in the Essay are confused, contradictory, and often childish.

c. *attrib.*, as *reasoning faculty*, *ground*, *power*, *thread*.

1728 POPE *Dunc.* I. 179 Or quite unravel all the reas'ning thread. 1775 HARRIS *Philos. Arrangem.* Wks. (1841) 325 Of all the animals we see around us, man alone possesses the reasoning faculty. 1781 COWPER *Conversat.* 431 The reasoning power vouchsafed of course inferred The power to clothe that reason with his word. 1875 E. WHITE *Life in Christ* I. i. 14 Such contradictory arguments as these, the reasoning-grounds.. of two opposing schools.

Reasoning (rīˑz'niŋ), *ppl. a.* [f. as prec. + -ING[2].] That reasons, in senses of the vb.

1665 GLANVILL *Def. Van. Dogm.* 80 Thus was the reasoning World despoil'd of that Freedom which is the priviledge of Humane Nature. 1737 POPE *Hor. Epist.* I. i. 185 That reas'ning, high, immortal Thing, Just less than Jove. 1781 COWPER *Hope* 143 Then praise is heard instead of reasoning pride. 1821–2 SHELLEY *Chas. I*, II. 158 All that makes the age of reasoning man More memorable than a beast's. 1870 J. H. NEWMAN *Gram. Assent* I. iv. 91 After all, man is not a reasoning animal.

Hence **Reaˑsoningly** *adv.*

1886 H. JAMES *Bostonians* III. III. xxxvi. 111 'That's not the way', Verena went on, reasoningly.

†**Reaˑsonist.** *Obs. rare.* [f. REASON *sb.*[1] or *v.* + -IST.] A professed reasoner.

1610 HEALEY *St. Aug. Citie of God* (1620) 843 But what say our great Reasonists unto those ordinary things which are so common? *a* 1740 WATERLAND *Chr. Vind. agst. Infid.* Wks. 1823 VIII. 67 Such persons are now commonly called reasonists and rationalists, to distinguish them from true reasoners and rational inquirers.

Reasonless (rīˑz'nlės), *a.* (and *adv.*). [f. REASON *sb.*[1] + -LESS.]

1. Not endowed with reason. = IRRATIONAL *a.* 1.

1398 TREVISA *Barth. De P. R.* XVIII. lii. (Bodl. MS.) 273/1 [The ant is] a litel beste wiþoute prince and resonles. *c* 1412 HOCCLEVE *De Reg. Princ.* 3659 If he tho weies take wolde That beestes resonles vsen and holde. 1581 PETTIE *Guazzo's Civ. Conv.* II. (1586) 80 b, Nature .. giuing a very long life to many reasonlesse creatures. 1604 T. WRIGHT *Passions* V. § 4. 201 Beasts, though reasonlesse, yet in loue follow this generall instinct and inclination of reason. 1633 W. STRUTHER *True Happines* 14 Three instances prove the same: The first is from reasonlesse creatures. 1877 BLACKIE *Wise Men* 250 So great a gap Betwixt the reasonless and the reasoning life A favouring God hath set.

b. Of natural forces or their results: Acting or produced without the aid of reason.

1867 H. MACMILLAN *Bible Teach.* ii. (1870) 36 The forces of nature..are not reasonless, merciless forces. 1895 *Q. Rev.* Apr. 492 A purely reasonless concourse of atoms.

2. Devoid of ordinary reason; senseless.

1421 HOCCLEVE *Complaint* 222 Yet homly reason know I nevertheles; not hope I founden be so resonles as men demen. 1592 GREENE *Groatsw. Wit* (1617) 24 Reasonlesse Roberts, that hauing but a Brokers place, asked a Lenders reward. 1628 WITHER *Brit. Rememb.* III. 626 Now, most thou need'st it, be not reasonlesse. 1671 F. PHILLIPS *Reg. Necess.* Ep. Ded. 1 These unhappy times have brought forth a sort of reasonless men, whose humors and phancies.. makes them unwilling to submit to Laws. 1868 BROWNING *Ring & Bk.* IV. 11 This rabble's-brabble of dolts and fools Who make up reasonless unreasoning Rome.

3. Not grounded upon reason or reasons; not supported by any reason.

1553 GRIMALDE *Cicero's Bk. Offices* III. (1558) 124 That is reasonlesse that some say [etc.]. 1591 SHAKS. 1 *Hen. VI*, V. iv. 137 This proffer is absurd, and reasonlesse. 1658 T. WALL *Charact. Enemies Ch.* 23 Casting a fraudulent shew of reason upon those things which are indeed reasonless. 1794 ANNA SEWARD *Lett.* (1811) IV. 34 The shallow, reasonless oratory, which is so perpetually shifting its ground. 1874 T. N. HARPER *Peace through Truth* Ser. II. I. p. xx, The feelings of the great body of the people, even though reasonless, ought to be respected.

†**b.** of a reason. (Common *c* 1600–50.) *Obs.*

a 1603 T. CARTWRIGHT *Confut. Rhem. N. T.* (1618) Pref. 26 To affirme that a substantiall reason.. should be iudged reasonlesse. 1634 CANNE *Necess. of Separ.* (1849) 210 It is likely he saw that there was no help for him there, and therefore only makes use of this reasonless reason. 1670 G. H. *Hist. Cardinals* I. I. 20 The good Father..made me a long discourse,.. alleging reasonless reasons.

†4. *adv.* Without reason. *Obs. rare*[−1].

1632 BROME *Crt. Beggar* IV. iii, Since reasonlesse you layd those wrongs upon me.

Hence **Reaˑsonlessly** *adv.*, **Reaˑsonlessness.**

1889 *Harper's Mag.* Apr. 721/2 Reasonlessly, silently, all her anger against him vanished. 1891 MAX MÜLLER *Pres. Addr. Brit. Assoc.* in *Nature* 3 Sept., He saw.. that there is no possible transition from reasonlessness to reason.

Reasoune, obs. form of REASON *sb.*[1]

Re-aspiˑre, *v.* [RE- 5 a.] To aspire again.

1621 S. WARD *Life of Faith* 2 It would pittie one to see how lamely and blindly hee re-aspires thereunto. 1646 E. F[ISHER] *Mod. Divinity* (ed. 2) 222 The soule is thereby made to re-aspire towards..that chief good, even God.

Reassaiˑl, *v.* [RE- 5 a.] To assail again.

1579 FENTON *Guicciard.* II. (1599) 67 The king complayned ..that he did not eftsoones reassayle with a new supply [of vessels] the rocke of Yschia. 1665 GLANVILL *Def. Van. Dogm.* 75 And possibly could with an humor brisk enough have reassailed the spirit of proud and unreasonable presumption. 1851 C. L. SMITH tr. *Tasso* III. xxxi, Then showed her front and re-assailed the foe.

Reassauˑlt, *sb.* [RE- 5 a.] A renewed or repeated assault.

1611 FLORIO, *Riassalto*, a re-assault. 1631 R. BYFIELD *Doctr. Sabb.* 3 Never so subtle or serpentine in malice to a re-assault. *a* 1711 KEN *Urania* Poet. Wks. 1721 IV. 471 The Chaste..By Watching, Prayr, Fasts, Alms, Lust's Fury quell, and all its reassaults repell.

Reassauˑlt, *v.* [RE- 5 a.] *trans.* To assault or attack again.

1654 H. L'ESTRANGE *Chas. I* (1655) 24 One Turner a Doctor of Physick, reassaults it in these six Queries. 1674 T. FLATMAN *Agst. Thoughts* Poems 102 Then they throng again, And reassault me with a trebled pain. *a* 1711 KEN *Hymnotheo* Poet. Wks. 1721 III. 220 Soon as this lower World becomes our own, We with success may reassault the Throne. 1851 C. L. SMITH tr. *Tasso* III. xxiii, She covered her fair head..And re-assaulted him.

Reassay, *v.* [RE- 5 a.] **a.** *intr.* To make a fresh attempt. **b.** *trans.* To test the purity of (metals) again. Hence **Reassaˑying** *vbl. sb.*

1598 FLORIO, *Rattentare*, to reattempt, to reassaie. 1665 BRATHWAIT *Comment Two Tales* 140 In this sort she reassaies to course him before she leave him. 1677 *Touchstone* in Rigland *Assay Gold & Silver W.* 71 Four grains out of every twelve ounces that is marked, is..to be detained and kept for a reassaying. 1898 *Daily News* 2 May 6/7 They require hall-marked silver to be re-assayed.

†**Reassecure**, *v.* *Obs. rare*[−1]. [RE- 5 a.] *trans.* To make secure again.

1654 EARL MONM. tr. *Bentivoglio's Warrs Flanders* 384 Thinking that it was sufficient for them to reassecure their Neutralities which had been violated.

Reasseˑmblage. [RE- 5 a.] A collecting, meeting, or gathering together again.

1744 HARRIS *Three Treat.* I. notes (1765) 264 New Beings arise from the Re-assemblage of the scattered Parts. 1792 *Ann. Reg., Chron.* 49 A reassemblage of the mob was apprehended. 1815 SOUTHEY in *Q. Rev.* XIII. 482 It will not now be doubted that Buonaparte had this reassemblage in view. 1890 WEISSMANN in *Nature* 6 Feb. 319 The giving off, circulation, and reassemblage of gemmules.

Reassemble (rīǎseˑmb'l), *v.* [RE- 5 a. Cf. F. *rassembler*, † *reassembler* (14th c.).]

1. *trans.* To bring together again, to collect anew.

1494 FABYAN *Chron.* VII. ccxlvi. 289 Kynge Phylyp reassembled his Knyghtes, and sped hym towarde the countrey of Poytoys. *c* 1520 BARCLAY *Jugurth* xxxi. 43b, Whan Metellus (as sayd is) had reasembled them againe: he began in fewe wordes to pray and exhort them. 1667 MILTON *P. L.* I. 186 Reassembling our afflicted Powers, Consult how we may henceforth most offend Our Enemy. 1751 JOHNSON *Rambler* No. 157 ¶ 12, I was reassembling my scattered sentiments. 1762–71 H. WALPOLE *Vertue's Anecd. Paint.* (1786) V. 267 King Charles's collection, which his royal highness wished as far as possible to re-assemble. 1863 COWDEN CLARKE *Shaks. Char.* vii. 173 Her old father pathetically endeavours to reassemble his wandering ideas.

refl. 1818 SCOTT *Rob Roy* viii, Morris, whose scattered wits had hardly yet reassembled themselves.

2. *intr.* To meet, come together, again.

1611 COTGR., *Recouvenir*, to reassemble, reunite. *c* 1645 HOWELL *Lett.* I. II. xix. (1890) I. 133 At the dissolution of the last Assembly at Lodun, where he solemnly gave his word, to permit them to re-assemble when they would six months after. 1677 COLES *Eng.-Lat. Dict.*, To Reassemble, *rursum convenire*. 1821 SHELLEY *Hellas* 1003 If Greece must be A wreck, yet shall its fragments re-assemble. 1882 J. HAWTHORNE *Fort. Fool* I. xviii, They would reassemble in London once more.

Hence **Reasseˑmbling** *vbl. sb.*

1611 COTGR., *Ralliement*, a rallying, reassembling, reuniting. 1817 *Parl. Deb.* 247 Mr. Hunt's parliament at Spa-fields was prorogued, and at the re-assembling received a royal message. 1863 H. COX *Instit.* I. vi. 32 This rule.. applies as well to the original meeting of a Parliament as to its reassembling after prorogation.

Reasseˑmbly. [RE- 5 a. Cf. obs. F. *réassemblée* (1606–9 in Godef.)] = REASSEMBLAGE.

1611 FLORIO, *Radunanza*, a re-assemblie. 1632 H. SEILE *Augustus* xlviii. 157 The Soldiers..he dispersed..all about Italy, in 32. Colonies:.. for their more speedy reassembly, if need should require. 1779–81 JOHNSON *L. P.*, *Young* Wks. IV. 278 The re-assembly of the atoms that compose the human body. 1896 *Daily Chron.* 25 Aug. 3/5.

Reassert (rīǎsɜˑɹt), *v.* [RE- 5 a.]

1. *trans.* To assert (a statement, claim, etc.) again.

a 1665 J. GOODWIN *Filled w. the Spirit* (1867) 162 We might re-assert our former argument for the divinity of the Holy Ghost. 1726 POPE *Odyss.* XVII. 147 With equal fury, and with equal fame, Shall great Ulysses re-assert his claim. 1771 *Junius Lett.* lvi. 293 You replied with abuse, and re-asserted your charge. 1835 LYTTON *Rienzi* V. v, I re-asserted each right, and proved it. 1879 FROUDE *Cæsar* xxii. 368 They had an opportunity of reasserting their independence.

refl. 1840 MILL *Diss. & Disc.* (1875) I. 417 The natural tendency.. reasserted itself. 1854 KINGSLEY *Alexandria* Pref. 10 These laws will..reassert themselves.

†2. To reassign (a person) *to* a condition. *Obs.*[−1]

1675 SOUTH *Serm.* (1823) I. 297 Gross ingratitude in the person.. made free, forfeits his freedom, and re-asserts him to his former conditions of slavery.

3. To claim (a thing) again. *rare.*

1725 POPE *Odyss.* I. 52 To warn the wretch, that young Orestes grown To manly years shou'd re-assert the throne. 1853 KANE *Grinnell Exp.* xxv. (1856) 202 Both of these documents reassert the name of Albert Land for the large tract of high lands.

Hence **Reasseˑrting** *vbl. sb.*

1697 C. LESLIE *Snake in Grass* (ed. 2) 233 A fair occasion ..towards the Re-asserting of the Good Old Cause.

Reasseˑrtion. [RE- 5 a.] A repeated assertion, a reaffirmation.

1848 R. I. WILBERFORCE *Doctr. Incarnation* xii. (1852) 327 The glowing words in which Scripture describes the privileges of Christians, are regarded.. as a re-assertion of the claims of nature. 1880 E. WHITE *Cert. Relig.* 106 A resolute reassertion by scholars of the Baconian laws of scientific interpretation.

So **Reasseˑrtor**, one who asserts again.

1859 SMILES *Self-Help* iii. (1860) 48 A recent reassertor of the power of perseverance.

Re-asseˑss, *v.* [RE- 5 a.] *trans.* To assess anew.

1803 W. TAYLOR in *Ann. Rev.* I. 427 Whatever taxes are laid on the rent of land, must be re-assessed by the grower of corn on the produce. 1813 — in *Monthly Mag.* XXXVI. 7 This.. will be re-assessed with a profit on the poor. 1884 *Law Times Rep.* L. 142/1 The rateable value of certain property having been re-assessed at a much higher sum.

So **Re-asseˑssment.**

1777 BURROW *Rep.* IV. 2291 Personal Estate is not generally rated to the Poor, throughout the Kingdom; and very seldom to the Land Tax, unless upon a Re-assessment. 1886 *Pall Mall G.* 10 Aug. 8/2 There had been lately in London a quinquennial reassessment.

†**Reassiege**, *v.* *Obs. rare*[−1]. [RE- 5 a.] *trans.* To lay siege to anew.

1577 HOLINSHED *Hist. Scot.* 412/1 Which occasioned the castell of Edenborough to be reasseeged and inuironed both by sea and land.

Reassiˑgn, *v.* [RE- 5 a.] To assign anew.

1611 COTGR., *Reconsigner*, to reconsigne, reassigne, reappoint. 1721 in BAILEY [hence in later Dicts]. 1893 *Voice* (N. Y.) 8 June, Generally on the occasion of a new sovereign all lands were reassigned.

So **Reassignaˑtion** (Bailey 1721); **Reassiˑgnment** (Worcester 1850).

Reassiˑmilate, *v.* [RE- 5 a.] To assimilate anew. So **Reassimilaˑtion.**

1828 in WEBSTER. 1876 DOUSE *Grimm's L.* 111 A partial, but now arrested reassimilation.

Reassoˑciate, *v.* *rare.* [RE- 5 a.] *refl.* and *intr.* To come together again.

1494 FABYAN *Chron.* VII. 552 Some euyll dysposyd .. reassociat them, and sayde and cryed that [etc.]. 1809 A. HENRY *Trav.* 124 The Indian families.. separate in the winter season,.. and re-associate in the spring and summer.

Reassoˑrt, *v.* [RE- 5 a.] *trans.* To assort again. So **Reassoˑrtment.**

1779 FORREST *Voy. N. Guinea* 294 He took care to provide .. reassortments of stock, which he safely deposited in his warehouse. 1870 ORTON *Andes & Amazons* II. xxxii. (1876) 438 Wool is generally taken to that city.. to be re-assorted and repacked. 1872 W. S. SYMONDS *Rec. Rocks* vi. 193 The whole mass has evidently been reassorted by water.

†**Reassort**, obs. variant of RESORT *v.*

1535 in *Lett. Suppress. Monasteries* (Camden) 85 There was here suche frequence of women commyng and reassorting to this monastery.

Reassoune, obs. Sc. form of REASON *sb.*[1]

Reassume (rīǎsiūˑm), *v.* [f. RE- 5 a + ASSUME *v.* Cf. Sp. *reasumir*, Pg. *reassumir*, It. *riassumere*. See also RESUME *v.*, with which this word formerly coincided in many of its senses.]

1. *trans.* To take, or take up, again (a material thing laid down or handed to another).

1494 FABYAN *Chron.* VII. 319 Pandulph toke yᵉ Crowne of the Kynge,..yᵉ Kynge reassumyd the Crowne of Pandulph. 1628 FELTHAM *Resolves* II. xxi. 70 Beware him, as an Enemie, apt to re-assume his Armes. 1679 *New Advice* in *Roxb. Ball.* (1883) IV. 548 Painter, once more thy Pencil reassume. *a* 1766 MRS. F. SHERIDAN *Sidney Bidulph* V. 44, I shall break off here, and shall re-assume my pen in the evening. 1848 C. C. CLIFFORD tr. *Aristophanes, Frogs* 18 No nonsense, Xanthias; reassume your pack.

b. To revoke, take back (a grant, gift, etc.).

1609 DANIEL *Civ. Wars* III. lxxxix, His successour .. did reuocate And re-assume his liberalities. 1675 H. NEVILE *Machiavelli's Prince* vii. Wks. 209 Lest the next Pope should.. reassume all that Alexander had given him. 1726 POPE *Odyss.* XVI. 476 She waves her golden wand, and reassumes From ev'ry feature every grace that blooms. 1792 CHARLOTTE SMITH *Desmond* I. 129 What then should prevent a nation from re-assuming grants? 1816 SCOTT *Antiq.* xviii, His lands.. lay waste till they were reassumed by the emperor as a lapsed fief.

†**c.** To rescind, recall (a vote). *Obs.*

1685 S. SEWALL *Diary* 22 Oct., Deputies reassume their vote as to the treasurer, and consent with the magistrates. 1716 B. CHURCH *Hist. Philip's War* (1867) II. 128 The Lieut. Governour.. told them except they did Re-assume that Vote..they should sit there till the next Spring.

2. **a.** To take back (a person) into close relationship with oneself.

1610 DONNE *Pseudo-martyr* 13 The seuerity which the Church vsed towards them,..and her bitternesse and auerseness, from re-assuming them, euen after long penances, into her bosome. 1647 N. BACON *Disc. Govt. Eng.* I. xlvi. (1739) 76 He reseized and reassumed the English, in partnership with the Norman in their ancient right of Government. 1667 MILTON *P. L.* X. 225 Into his blissful bosom reassum'd In glory as of old.

b. To take back (a thing) as a constituent part.

1691 RAY *Disc.* II. ii. (1732) 74 Carried off by the rivers and reassumed by the sea. 1741 MONRO *Anat.* (ed. 3) 22 The Marrow .. is reassumed into the Mass of Blood. 1883 *Cath. Dict.* (1897) 744/1 St. Thomas says.. that all the particles of blood which Christ shed in his Passion were reassumed by him in His resurrection.

3. To take again upon oneself:

a. a shape or form, a garb or something worn.

1624 HEYWOOD *Gunaik.* I. 31 By the bankes of Nilus reassumed her humane shape. 1660 F. BROOKE tr. *Le Blanc's Trav.* 221 The.. Steward of houshold.. caused him to reassume his apparell. 1719 J. T. PHILIPPS tr. *Thirty-four Confer.* 283 At the great Day of Accompts the Souls shall re-assume their former Bodies. 1771 MRS. GRIFFITH *Hist. Lady Barton* II. 271, I could again be weak enough.. to reassume those rosy fetters. 1855 LONGF. *Hiaw.* XII. 301 Then the birds, again transfigured, Reassumed the shape of mortals. 1873 B. STEWART *Conserv. Force* § 157 The heat thus spent reassumes the form of molecular motion.

b. a charge, office, exercise of power, etc.

1632 SIR T. HAWKINS tr. *Mathieu's Unhappy Prosp.* I. 24 Hee should re-assume the charge [which] had beene taken from him. 1670 MILTON *Hist. Eng.* I. Wks. (1851) 25 Elidure now in his own behalf re-assumes the Government. 1726 AYLIFFE *Parergon* 162 After Henry the VIIIth had re-assum'd the Supremacy. 1774 tr. *Helvetius' Child Nat.* II. 245 At last, reason reassumed her empire. 1821 SHELLEY *Prometh. Unb.* III. i. 58 The tyranny of heaven none may retain, Or reassume, or hold. 1885 M. ARNOLD in *Pall Mall G.* 3 Nov. 3/2 To reassume an office at sixty-two is not the same thing as to assume it at thirty-two.

c. a character, attribute, quality, feeling, etc.

1632 MASSINGER *Maid of Hon.* V. ii, I conjure you To re-assume your order [of knighthood]. 1655 tr. *Com. Hist. Francion* XII. 23 Little and little he began to reassume his Spirits. 1671 MRS. BEHN *Forc'd Marriage* I. iii, Go, reassume your beauty; dry your eyes. 1712 STEELE *Spect.* No. 432 ¶ 4 These little Republicks reassume their National Hatred to each other. 1785 G. A. BELLAMY *Apol.* IV. 37 Upon rejoining the company, he reassumed his good humour and politeness. 1810 SOUTHEY *Kehama* XXIV. iv, Then did the Man-God re-assume His unity. 1899 *Allbutt's Syst. Med.* VIII. 482 The quality of reassuming turgescence or excitement.

d. a right, title, name, etc.

1660 T. M. *Hist. Independ.* IV. 101 The Lords (who had now reassumed their Native right by taking their places in the higher House). 1761 GRAY *Odin* 92 Night Has reassum'd her ancient right. 1813 EUSTACE *Class. Tour* (1821) IV. 328 Whether Italy be destined to re-assume her honors. 1830 LYTTON *P. Clifford* xxxiii, He had re-assumed his hereditary name. 1847 MRS. A. KERR tr. *Ranke's Hist. Servia* vi. 114 They re-assumed the title of Dahi.

e. *refl.* To return to one's natural character.

1682 N. O. *Boileau's Lutrin* I. 149 Then Reassume your self, forbear to Doat. 1811 *Henry & Isabella* I. 168 She instantly combated what she considered an ungenerous suspicion, and reassumed herself.

f. *absol.* To take office again. *Obs. rare.*

1716 B. CHURCH *Hist. Philip's War* (1867) II. 3 Soon after this was the Revolution, and the other Government Re-assumed.

4. To take, resume (one's place) again.

1640 in Rushw. *Hist. Coll.* III. (1692) I. 43 Mr. Solicitor.. reassumed the Chair again. 1670 DRYDEN *Conq. Granada* I. ii, But now my Reason re-assumes its Throne. *a* 1711 KEN *Hymnotheo* Poet. Wks. 1721 III. 84 The scatter'd Atoms of each humane Mold.. Shall.. re-assume in Men their pristine site. 1789 CHARLOTTE SMITH *Ethelinde* (1814) IV. 131 Again reassuming his place at the breakfast-table. 1821 SHELLEY *Ess. & Lett.* (1852) II. 255 We could easily reassume our station with the spring at Pugnano or the baths. 1841 CLOUGH *Poems* (1862) 8 The day may come I yet may re-assume My place.

5. To recommence, take up again, resume:

†**a.** speech, discourse, thought, a subject, etc.

Very common in the 17th and 18th centuries.

1608 WILLET *Hexapla Exod.* 818 After the Iewes had made answere..the Lord presently reassumeth that speech. 1660 INGELO *Bentiv. & Ur.* II. (1682) 102 They might afterwards re-assume their delightful conversation. 1682 VERNON *Life Heylin* 183 He again re-assumes the Argument and confutes all that Bellarmin and others produce for it. 1715–6 *Town Talk* No. 4 Mr. Arthur reassumed the discourse. 1755 B. MARTIN *Mag. Arts & Sc.* I. 11 We will re-assume the Subject of the Ptolomaic System.

b. a practice, action, occupation, etc.

Common in the 17th and 18th centuries.

1624 BP. MOUNTAGU *Gagg* 244 A thing prohibited in the councell of Laodicea, but re-assumed, and long time frequented in the Church. *a* 1641 — *Acts & Mon.* (1642) 144 They re-assumed the work upon warrant of Cyrus his former Edict. 1702 ECHARD *Eccl. Hist.* (1710) 492 Those kind of Spectacles were already over, and not to be reassumed the same day. 1756 TOLDERVY *Hist. 2 Orphans* III. 12 Our company reassumed their march; and..arrived in good time. 1791 CHARLOTTE SMITH *Celestina* (ed. 2) I. 220 To quiet the perturbation of her mind by re-assuming her usual occupations. 1824 in *Spirit Pub. Jrnls.* (1825) 508 Mary Stuart having brought some superb diamonds into France, the ladies of the Court re-assumed the wear of them.

†**c.** With *inf.* *Obs. rare.*

1646 FULLER *Wounded Consc.* (1841) 313, I re-assume to personate a wounded conscience.

†**d.** *intr.* To resume, continue speaking, after a pause. *Obs.*

1719 J. T. PHILIPPS tr. *Thirty-four Confer.* 32 Then they re-assumed and said. 1768 STERNE *Sent. Journ.* II. 110 *Case of Conscience*, I own it is necessary, re-assumed the master of the hotel, that [etc.]. 1796 CHARLOTTE SMITH *Marchmont* I. 60 'Ah, my dear love!' reassumed this admirable woman, after a short pause.

†6. To repeat. *Obs. rare.*

1631 R. BYFIELD *Doctr. Sabb.* 17, I re-assume that your

Re-beck, *Obs.* trans. To beckon back, to recall, reclaim.

Re-become, v. [RE- 5 a.] intr. (with cmpl.) To become again.

Re-beget, v. trans. To beget again or a second time. Hence **Re-begetting** vbl. sb.

Re-begin, v. To begin again or anew. Hence **Re-beginning** vbl. sb.

Re-beguile, v. trans. To beguile again.

Re-behold, v. trans. To behold, or look upon, again.

Rebel (re'bĕl), a. and sb. A. adj.

B. sb.
b. of animals. Obs. rare.
c. Law. One who resists or disobeys a legal command or summons. Now only spec. in Sc. Law.

Rebel (rĕbe'l), v. intr. To rise in opposition or armed resistance against the rightful or established ruler or government of one's country.
b. To resist, oppose, or be disobedient to, some one having authority or rule.
c. transf. and fig.

Rebel·lant, a. Obs. rare. Rebelling.

Rebeller (rĕbe'lər). Now rare. One who rebels; a rebel.

†Rebel, sb. Obs. [L. REBEL (perh. on analogy of prec.) or ad. med.L. rebellium.]

Rebellion (rĕbe'lyən). Forms: 4-5 rebellyoun, 4-6 -ioun; 5 rebelyon, belyone, 5-6 rebell'yon, 4-6 -rebellion. [a. F. rebellion (14th c.), ad. L. rebellion-em a renewal of war, revolt, rebellio, f. rebell-is REBEL a.]
1. Organized armed resistance to the ruler or government of one's country; insurrection, revolt.
b. With a and pl. An instance of this.
2. To resist, oppose, or be disobedient to, some one having authority or rule.
b. transf. of the hand, head, a weapon, etc.
3. Of things: Opposition or resistance to manipulation or treatment; refractory. Of diseases, sores, etc.

Rebelliously (rĕbe'lyəsli), adv.

Rebelliousness (rĕbe'lyəsnes). The state of being rebellious.

Rebeldom (re'bĕldəm). [f. REBEL sb. + -DOM.]

Rebellow (rĕbe'lō), v. intr. To re-echo, return in a loud echo.

Rebind (rĕbəi'nd), v. trans. To bind again, in senses of the vb.; esp. to give a new binding to (a book). Hence **Re-binding** vbl. sb.

Rebirth (rĭbə̄·þ). [RE- 5 a.] A second birth (physical or spiritual); also fig. of things.

Rebite, v. [RE- 5 a.] trans. To bite again.

Reblossom (rĭblo'səm), v. intr. To blossom again.

Reboant (re'bŏant), a. Chiefly poet.

Reboation (rĭbŏē'ʃən), n.

†Rebody, v. trans.

Reboil, v. To ferment a second time.

Reboil (rĭboi'l), v.

Rebolt, v.

Rebore, v.

Reborn (rĭbō·rn), pa. pple. and ppl. a.

Reborrow (rĭbo'rō), v.

Rebottle, v.

Rebound (rĭbau'nd), v.
1. intr. To spring back from force of impact.

Rebound (rĭbau'nd), sb.
3. The act of bounding back after striking; resilience, recoil.

Rebounding (rĭbau'ndiŋ), ppl. a. [-ING²]

Rebounding, vbl. sb. [-ING²]

Rebrace, v.

Rebreathe, v.

Rebribe, v.

Rebring, v. trans. To bring back.

Rebuck, obs. form of REBUKE v.

Rebuckle, v. trans. To buckle again.

Rebucous, see REBUKOUS.

Rebud, v. [RE- 5 a.] intr. To bud again.

Rebuff (rĭbʌ'f), sb.

Rebuff (rĭbʌ'f), v. trans.

Rebuild (rĭbi'ld), v. trans. To build again; to reconstruct. Hence **Rebuilding** vbl. sb., an operation of rebuilding.

Recaptor (rīkæ·ptǝɹ). 1. One who retakes by capture; *esp.* one who makes a recapture at sea.

Recapture (rīkæ·ptiǔɹ), *sb.* [f. RE- + CAPTURE.]

1. The fact of taking, or being taken, a second time; recovery or retaking by capture.

2. That which is captured again.

Recapture (rīkæ·ptiǔɹ), *v.* [RE- 5 a.] *trans.*

To capture again.

Recaption (rīkæ·pʃǝn), *sb.* [f. RE- + CAPTION.]

Recarbon (rīkaˑɹbǝn), *v.*

Recarry (rīkæ·ri), *v.* 1. *trans.* To carry, bear, or convey, back or again.

Recash (rīkæ·ʃ), *v.* [RE- 5 a.] *trans.* To convert into flesh again.

Recarriage (rīkæ·rǐdʒ). Also 6 recariage. [f. RE- + CARRIAGE: cf. next.]

Recatch (rīkæ·tʃ), *v.* [RE- 5 a.] To catch again.

Recatholize, *v.* Obs. rare⁻¹. [RE- 5 a.]

Recaudo, obs. form of RECADO.

Recauleacence (rīkǭlesens), *sb.* *Bot.*

Recaulk (rīkǭˑk), *v.* [RE- 5 a.] *trans.* To caulk again.

Recche, reche, *v.* Obs.

Recche (RECK)

Recede (rĭsīˑd), *v.* [f. RE- + CEDE *v.*]

Recedence (rĭsīˑdens), *sb.*

Recedent (rĭsīˑdent), *a.* Med.

Receding (rĭsīˑdiŋ), *ppl. a.*

Recedure (rĭsīˑdiŭɹ). Arch.

Receipt (rĭsīˑt), *sb.* Forms: 4-6 receyt, 4-6 resseyt, 4-7 receite, 5-6 receyte, 7-8 receit, (5-6 a-), 4 resseit, 4-5 resait, 6 rasait, rossayt(-ayt, 5-6 resayte, 5-7 receit, (5-6 a-), 4 resaite, 6 resait, 5-6 resavte, 5 receipt, etc. [ME. receite, receit, a. AF. (ONF.) receite, receyte = OF. recete, recoite.]

Receipt (rĭsīˑt), *v.* [f. prec.]

Receiptless, *a.* [RECEIPT *sb.* + -LESS.]

Receiptor, *sb.* [RECEIPT *sb.* + -OR.]

Receivable, *a.* [a. AF. *receivable* (1304), var. OF. *recevable*, in later use f. RECEIVE *v.* + -ABLE.]

Receivability, **Receivableness**.

Receival (rĭsīˑvăl). Now rare. [f. RECEIVE *v.* + -AL.]

Receive (rĭsīˑv), *v.* Forms: 4-6 receyve, 4-6 receive, (5-6 a-), 4 resseyve, resceyve, 5-6 resave, resaive, 5-6 receyue, 4-5 resayve, 5 ressave, etc.

Receiver (rĭsīˑvǝɹ), *sb.* [a. AF. *receivour*, var. OF. *receveor*, OF. *-ur* = *recevre* to take).]

Receivership (rĭsīˑvǝɹʃip).

RECEIVE.

7. To take into (one's mind); to apprehend mentally; to understand; to learn.

II. 8. To admit (a person) into some relation with oneself, esp. to familiar or social intercourse; to treat in a familiar or friendly manner.

b. To admit to one's presence. *rare.*

10. To meet, welcome or greet (a person) in a specified manner.

b. To admit to membership of a society or class or to partnership in work; to take in *among* other persons or things. *Const. with.*

12. To take or accept (a person) in some capacity.

13. To take, accept, regard, hear, etc. (anything offered or presented, or to which attention is given) in a specified manner or with a specified expression of feeling.

14. To take, accept, regard, hear, etc. (anything offered or presented, or to which attention is given) in a specified manner or with a specified expression of feeling.

b. To take for, regard as, etc. (Cf. 13.)

15. To accept an authority, rule, or practice; to admit the truth or validity of; to make use of.

16. To contain, comprise, hold.

c. To give assent to, to pass (a law). *Obs.*

III. 17. To have (anything) given or handed to oneself; to get from another or others. Also *receiving* = being received.

b. To get a letter, etc.; brought to oneself or delivered into one's hands.

17. a. To get (a person) into one's custody, control, vicinity, society, etc. *Now rare or Obs.*

b. To get, come into, possession of (a town, country, etc.). *rare.*

RECEIVER.

5. As the name of certain parts of apparatus or machinery, intended to receive and contain something.

b. The receptacle for mercury in a barometer.

Receiver-generalship.

Receiving *(rǐsī·vĭŋ), vbl. sb.* [ING 1.]

b. An apparatus which receives and reproduces sounds transmitted from another part of an electric circuit; that part of a telephone which is applied to the ear.

Receiver-general, n. A chief receiver, esp. of public revenue.

Re-cement, v. [RE- 5 a.] To join together again with, or as with, cement; to unite firmly or closely.

Re-celebrate, v. [RE- 5 a.] trans. To celebrate or commemorate again.

Recency *(rǐsěn·sĭ).* [ad. RECENT: see -ENCY.]

Recent *(rǐ·sĕnt), a.* [ad. L. recent-, recens, or a. F. récent (16th c.).]

1. Lately done or made; that has lately happened or taken place, etc.

b. Fresh; not affected by decay, decomposition, or loss of moisture.

2. Lately formed, created, originated, or begun; new-born.

Re-centre, v. [RE- 5 a.] trans. To centre again. Hence Re-centring *ppl. a.*

Rerceipt, *obs. f.* RECEIPT.

Recently, *adv.* [f. RECENT a. + -LY.] At a recent date; not long before or ago; lately, newly.

Recentness, *obs. f.* RECENTNESS.

Recentity *(rǐsěn·tĭti).* [f. RECENT + -ITY.]

Recency.

Re-circuit, v.

RECEPTIBLE.

Recept *(rǐ·sĕpt), sb.* [ad. L. recept-um.]

Receptacle *(rǐsě·ptăk'l).* [a. F. réceptacle, ad. L. receptāculum, f. recept-: see RECEIVE.]

1. That which receives and holds a thing; something into which another thing may be put; a container, vessel, place, or space; a repository.

2. *Bot.*

Receptaculous, *a. Bot.*

Receptacular *(rěseptæ·kiŭlar), a. Bot.*

Receptary *(rǐ·sĕptări), sb. and a.*

Reception *(rǐsě·pʃən).* [ad. med.L. receptiōn-, L. receptiōn-em, n. of action f. recipĕre to RECEIVE.]

Receptive *(rǐsě·ptĭv), a.*

Receptibility *(rǐsepti·bĭlĭti).* [f. next: see -BILITY.]

Receptible *(rǐsě·ptĭb'l), a.* Now rare. [ad. late L. receptibilis: see -IBLE and -BLE.]

1. That may be received; receivable.

Reception (rĭsĕpʃən). Also 5 recepcion. [a. F. *réception* (13–13th c.), or ad. L. *receptiōn-em*, n. of action f. *recipere* to RECEIVE.]

1. The action or fact of receiving or getting.

2. a. *Astrol.* The fact of each of two planets being received into the other's house, exaltation, or other dignity.

b. The action of receiving (esp. persons), or fact of being received, into a place, company, state, etc.

c. The action of receiving or being received, in a formal or ceremonious manner.

d. An occasion of ceremonious receiving; an assemblage of persons for this purpose.

2. The action of receiving, or taking in, physically or spatially. Also *transf.*

b. The action of receiving mentally.

3. The action of accepting or admitting; acceptance, admittance, approbation.

b. Const. *of*.

4. a. The condition or state of being received, or accepted without evidence of its truth.

5. The action of receiving, or fact of being received, in a certain manner; kind or manner of reception. (Usually with qualifying adj.)

Receptible (rĭsĕptĭb'l). Also 9 -icious. [ad. L. *receptĭbilis* or -icius : see RECEIPT and -IBLE.] Capable of being received.

Receptive (rĭsĕptĭv), a. [ad. med.L. *receptīvus* : see RECEIPT and -IVE, and cf. obs. F. *receptif*.]

1. Having the quality of or capacity for, receiving; able to receive; pertaining to, or of the nature of, reception.

b. Const. *of*.

2. *spec.* (in senses of 1).

b. Capable of receiving or taking in other substances.

Receptively *adv.*

Receptiveness (rĭsĕptĭvnĕs). [f. prec. + -NESS.] Receptivity. (Common in recent use.)

Receptivity (rĭsĕptĭvĭti). [= prec. + -ITY.]

1. The quality of being receptive; ability or readiness to receive or take in. (Common in 19th c., esp. with ref. to the mind.)

Receptment. [-F. *receptement* RESENTMENT.] The act or practice of harbouring criminals.

Receptor (rĭsĕptɔɹ). [ad. late L. *receptor*, agent-n. f. *recipere* to RECEIVE.]

1. One who receives, or gives reception to.

2. A telephonic receiver.

Receptory, *sb.* Obs. [ad. late L. *receptōrium* : see RECEIPT and -ORY, and cf. obs. F. *receptoire* (16th c.).] A receptacle.

Receptual, a. *Psychol.* Pertaining to receptive; receptive.

Recess (rĭsĕs), *sb.* [ad. L. *recess-us*, f. *recedere* to RECEDE.]

1. The act of receding or going back or away, from a certain point. (Used chiefly of the motion of things, and *esp.* of water, the sea, or the heavenly bodies.)

b. *transf.* A dislike or departure of a thing.

2. *transf.* or *fig.* (from senses 1 and 6).

3. The act of retiring, withdrawing, or departing (from or to a place); withdrawal, departure.

b. A departure *from* some state or standard.

Recess (rĭsĕs), *v.* [f. RECESS *sb.*]

1. *trans.* To place in a recess or in retirement; to set back or away.

b. *spec.* To set (part of a wall or other structure) in a recess. Also *refl.*

Recessive, a. [f. L. *recess-*, ppl. stem of *recedere* to RECEDE + -IVE.] Tending to recede.

b. *Phonetics* (of accent).

Recessively *adv.*, in a receding manner.

Recess, var. of RECEASE *sb.* Obs.

Rech, obs. f. REACH *sb.* and v.¹, RICH v.

Rechabite (rĕkabəit). [ad. biblical L. *Rechabīta*, rend it pl. to rendit: Heb. בֵּית־רֵכָב *Rēkhābīm*.]

1. One of a Jewish family descended from Jonadab, son of Rechab, which refused to drink wine or live in houses. Hence (*a*) one who abstains from intoxicating liquors; *now spec.* a member of the Independent Order of Rechabites, a benefit society founded in 1835; (*b*) a dweller in tents.

Hence **Rechabitism**, the practice of abstaining from intoxicating liquors; the principles or practice of the friendly society of Rechabites.

Rechace, obs. var. of RECHASE.

a. f. the act of buying back or redeeming.

Rechafe, v. [RE- 5 a + CHAFE *v.*] A repeated chafing.

Rechange, *v.* Obs. Cf. RECHAUFFE *v.*) *trans.*

Rechange, *sb.* Also 9 *Sc.* rechenge(a, 5–6 rechaunge, 6 rechaynge. [f. RE- 5 a + CHANGE *sb.*]

1. The re-exchange on a bill. Obs.

Rechant, v. [a. F. *rechanter*.]

Recharge (rĭtʃɑɹdʒ), *sb.* Also 9 recharge. [f. next.]

1. A fresh charge or load.

Recharge (rĭtʃɑɹdʒ), *v.* Now *rare.* [f. RE- + CHARGE *sb.*, prob. after F. *recharger* (1433–).]

1. A fresh charge or load.

Recharter, v. To charter again; to give a new charter to. Hence **Rechartering** *vbl. sb.*

Rechase, v. Obs. Also 5 rechace, 5–6 rechace. [a. F. *rechasser* (13th c.; OF. also *rechacer*), f. *re-* + *chasser* : see CHASE *v.*]

1. *trans.* To chase again or in turn. Obs.

2. *Hunting.* To chase (a deer) back into the forest. Obs.

Rechauffe (reʃofe), *sb.* [F., *pa. pple.* of *rechauffer*.] A warmed-up dish.

Re-chaw, v. [RE- 5 a.] To chaw again.

Rechew, v. [RE- 5 a.] To chew again.

Recheat (rĭtʃiːt), *sb.* [Of obscure origin: cf. RECHASE *v.*] *Hunting.*

Recheate, obs. form of REACH, RETCH.

Rechelesnes, -ness, var. RECKLESSNESS.

Recidivation. Obs. Also 5 resydyua-cion, 5–6 -iuation, 6 -evatyon; 7 resid-recyndcation (-ation, etc.). [a. F. *recidivation* :— late L. *recidivation-em*.] Relapse into sin, error, crime, etc.; backsliding, apostasy. (Very common in 17th c.)

Recidive (rĭsɪdɪv), *a.* and *sb.* Obs. rare. [ad. F. *récidive*.]

Recidivist (rĭsɪdɪvɪst). [a. F. *récidiviste*.] One who relapses into crime.

Recidivity. rare. [as prec. + -ITY.] Tendency to relapse. Obs.

Recidivous, a. Obs. rare. [f. L. *recidīvus* + -OUS.] Liable to fall back or relapse.

Recincture, v. *rare.*

Recinct, *sb.* Obs. rare. [ad. L. *re-cinct-*, ppl. stem of *recingere*.] A girdle.

Recipe (rĕsɪpɪ), *sb.* [L. *recipe*, take (used sing. imper. of *recipere* to RECEIVE), used by physicians (abbreviated R, Rc) to head prescriptions, and hence spelt out and similar uses.]

A. *v. imper.* = 'Take'. Obs.

B. *sb.*

1. A formula for a medical preparation; a prescription, or the remedy prepared in accordance with this.

2. A statement of the ingredients and procedure necessary for the making or compounding of some preparation, esp. of a dish in cookery; a receipt.

Supplement, p. 3873; Corrigenda, p. 4092; Spurious words, p. 4093; Books quoted, p. 4094

Recipiangle (rĭsi·piæŋg'l), *sb.* [a. F. *réciproque*, f. stem of L. *recipĕre* : see ȢRECEIVE and ANGLE.] An instrument formerly used (chiefly in France) for measuring of angles, esp. in fortification. (See first quot.)

Recipience (rĭsi·piĕns). *rare.* [f. as next : see -ENCE.] The act or process of receiving.

Recipiency (rĭsi·piĕnsi). [f. RECIPIENT : see -ENCY.] Receptivity; reception.

Recipiend (rĭsi·piĕnd). *rare.* [f. L. *recipiend-*, gerundial stem of *recipĕre* to RECEIVE + -AND, perh. after F. *récipiendaire*.]

Recipiendary (rĭsipiē·ndări). *rare.* [f. L. *recipiend-* : see RECIPIEND.]

Recipient (rĭsi·piĕnt), *a.* and *sb.* [ad. L. *recipient-em*, pres. pple. of *recipĕre* to RECEIVE : cf. F. *récipient* (16th c.).]
A. *adj.* That receives ; is capable of receiving ; receptive.
B. *sb.* 1. One who or that which receives, in senses of the vb.
2. *Chem.* A receiver ; a (glass) vessel for receiving or holding a liquid. ? *Obs.*

Reciprocable (rĭsi·prŏkăb'l), *a.* *rare.* [f. L. *reciprocā-re* (see RECIPROCATE) + -BLE.] Capable of reciprocating.

Reciprocal (rĭsi·prŏkăl), *a.* and *sb.* [f. L. *reciproc-us* RECIPROQUE + -AL.]
A. *adj.*

†1. Having, or partaking of, an alternate backward and forward motion. (Said *esp.* of tides.) *Obs.*
2. Of the nature of, pertaining to, a return made for something given ; felt, shown, etc., in return ; correspondent.
†b. Of actions : Alternate, alternating. *Obs.*
2. *Math.* in *reciprocal curves, figures, polars, quantities, triangles,* etc. (Cf. quots.)
3. *Gram.* Of pronouns and verbs, or their signification : **a.** Reflexive.
b. Expressing mutual action or relationship.
c. Convertible, synonymous, equivalent in meaning or force. *Obs.*
4. *Math.* Inversely.
5. Conversely.
B. *sb.* **1.** One who is sent back. *Obs. rare*[-1].
2. A thing corresponding to another ; a counterpart, etc.
3. *Math.* **a.** A function or expression so related to another that their product is unity ; the inverse.

Reciprocality (rĭsiprŏkæ·lĭti). [f. prec. + -ITY. Cf. RECIPROCALTY.] Reciprocity.

Reciprocalize, *v.* [f. L. *reciproc-us* : see RECIPROCAL and -IZE.]

Reciprocally (rĭsi·prŏkăli), *adv.* [-LY[2].]

Reciprocalty. *Obs. rare.*

Reciprocant. *Math.* [ad. L. *reciprocant-em,* pres. pple. of *reciprocāre* to RECIPROCATE.] A differential invariant.

Reciprocate (rĭsi·prŏkē·t), *v.* [f. L. *reciprocāt-, ppl.* stem of *reciprocāre,* f. *reciproc-us* RECIPROQUE.]
1. *intr.* To pass, return ; to have a backward direction. *Obs.*
2. *trans.* To give and receive in return or mutually ; to interchange ; † to have in common.
3. *intr.* To make an interchange ; † to have a mutual relation. *Obs.*

Reciprocation (rĭsiprŏkē·ʃən). [ad. L. *reciprocātiōn-em,* n. of action f. *reciprocāre* : see RECIPROCATE. Cf. F. *réciprocation* (16th c.).]
†1. A Reflexive action ; a reflexive mode of expression. *Obs.* (Cf. RECIPROCAL *a.* 3.)

Reciprocative (rĭsi·prŏkē·tiv), *a.* [f. RECIPROCATE + -IVE.]

Reciprocator (rĭsi·prŏkē·təɹ). [Agent-n. in L. type, f. RECIPROCATE *v.*] One who, or that which, reciprocates.

Reciprocatory (rĭsi·prŏkĕtəri), *a.* [f. as RECIPROCATE *v.* + -ORY[1].]

Reciprocitarian. [f. next, after *Trinitarian* etc.] One who advocates reciprocity in trade.

Reciprocity (resiprŏ·siti). [ad. F. *réciprocité* (1729), or L. type *reciprocitāt-em,* f. *reciproc-us* RECIPROQUE.]
1. The state or condition of being reciprocal ; a state or relationship in which there is mutual action, influence, giving and taking, correspondence, etc., between two parties or things.

Recital (rĭsai·tăl). Forms: 6 recytall, 6-7 recital(l, (6 reasyt-, recyt-), 6- recital. [f. RECITE *v.* + -AL[5].]
1. A rehearsal, account, or description of some thing, fact, or incident ; also (esp. in early use), an enumeration or detailed account of a number of things, facts, etc. ; a relation of the particulars of an event, transaction, etc.

Recitation (resitē·ʃən). [ad. L. *recitātiōn-em,* n. of action f. *recitāre* to RECITE *v.* : cf. F. *récitation* (14-15th c.).]
1. The action of reciting or repeating aloud ; the repetition of something (or of a passage, etc.) from memory.

Recitationist. [f. prec. + -IST.] One who recites.

Recitative (resitări·v), *a.[1]* and *sb.* *Mus.* [ad. It. *recitativo* RECITATIVO ; cf. F. *récitatif sb.*]

Recitative (resităti·v), *a.[2]* [f. RECITE *v.* + -ATIVE.] Of the nature of, in the style of, recitative (see B).

Recitatively (resitē·tivli), *adv.* [-LY[2].] By way of citation.

Recitativo (retʃitătī·vo). [It., f. ppl. stem of *recitare* to RECITE + -ivo : see RECITATIVE *sb.*]

Recitator (re·sitētəɹ). *rare.* [ad. L. *recitātor,* agent-n.]

Recite (rĭsəi·t), *v.* Forms : 5-7 recyte, 6 resyte, -syght, -zyt, 6-7 rasight ; 5-6 recite, (6 -cite, 3c -ceat), 5- recite. [a. OF. *reciter* (14th c.), or ad. L. *recitāre* to read out, recite aloud, repeat, f. *re-* RE- + *citāre* to cite, CITE.]
1. *trans.* To repeat or utter aloud (something previously composed, heard, or learned by heart) ; now esp. to repeat to an audience (a piece of verse or other composition) from memory in an appropriate manner.

Recited (rĭsəi·tĕd), *ppl. a.* [f. RECITE *v.* + -ED[1].] Repeated, mentioned, etc.

Reciter (rĭsəi·təɹ). [f. RECITE *v.* + -ER[1].] One who recites.

Recital. (See under RECITE.)

Recitement. *rare.* [f. RECITE *v.* + -MENT.]

Recitation. (See earlier.)

Reciting (rĭsəi·tiŋ), *vbl. sb.* [-ING[1].] The action of the vb. RECITE.

Recivilization. [RE- 5 a.] The action of recivilizing again.

Recivilize (rīsi·viləiz), *v.* [RE- 5 a.] To civilize again.

RECK.

Reck (rek), sb.[1] Obs. exc. dial. Forms: 6 recke, reake, Sc. rak, rack. [f. RECK v.]

1. Care, heed, consideration, regard.

2. In phr. What reck? What matters it?

3. Sc. Reckoning.

Reck, sb.[2] dial. variant of RACK sb.[2] 5 d.

Reck, variant of RICK, WREAK sb.

Reck (rek), v. Forms: a. inf. α. 1 rēcan, recc(e)an, 2–5 recchen, (recthen), (and Pres.). 3 recche, rychche, 4–5 reche(n), 2–5 reche(n), reiche, royche. β. 3–6 rekke(n), 4–7 recke, 4–6 rek, 6–reck, (4 wreoke), 4–6 roke, 6–7 (wreake); north. and Sc. 4–6 rek, 5–8 reck. γ. Sc. rak. δ. 5 Pa. t. 4–5 rōhte, 3–5 roȝt(e, 4–6 roght(e, 4 rout, 3–5 route, rough, rowth, Sc. rought; 4–6 raught, 5–6 wreaked, Sc. rakit.

245

RECKLESS.

Reckless (rek'les), a. Also 6 reckles, etc. Forms: a. 1 recceléas, recéléas, 3 reccheles, recheles, etc.

1. Of persons: Careless, heedless. a. Careless in respect of (one's conduct, reputation, or charge) or caution.

b. Rash, foolhardy.

2. Of actions, conduct, things, etc.: Characterized or distinguished by († negligent carelessness or) heedless rashness.

Recklessly (rek'lesli), adv. Forms: see RECKLESS a. [f. RECKLESS a. + -LY[2].]

246

RECKON.

1. In a reckless manner; † a. Carelessly, negligently.

Recklessness (rek'lesnes). [f. RECKLESS a. + -NESS.] The quality of being reckless.

Reckon (rek'n), v. Forms: a. 1 reconian, reken, (2–3 reknen); 3–4 rekne, (4 reken, recken), 6–9 reckon.

247

RECKON.

Reckoner (rek'nar). Also 3 rikenare, 5 rekenar. 1. One who reckons, in senses of the vb.

Reckon-crook, var. RACKAN (-CROOK).

Reckoning (rek'niŋ), vbl. sb. Forms: see RECKON v.

248

RECKONING.

RECLAIM.

Reclaim (rikle'm), v. Forms: see CLAIM v.

1. trans. † 1. Falconry. To call back (a hawk).

2. To reclaim; to bring back (a person or animal) from a wrong course of action, etc., to a right course.

Supplement, p. 3873; Corrigenda, p. 4092; Spurious words, p. 4093; Books quoted, p. 4094

Recognizance.

Recognizant, a. [f. Recognize-: cf. Cognizant.] That recognizes, affords recognition or acknowledgement; perceptive.

Recognize, v.¹

Recognize (re·kgnəiz), v.¹

Recognition (rekəgni·ʃən), sb.

Recognize, v.² Law.

Recognized, ppl. a. [f. Recognize v.¹ + -ed¹.]

Recognizee (rekəgnəizī·), [in Law.]

Recognizer (re·kgnəizəɹ), [f. Recognize v.¹ + -er¹.] One who recognizes; a reviser.

Recognizing, vbl. sb. [f. as prec. + -ing¹.] The action of the vb. Recognize¹.

Recoil, v.

Recoilment. 255 RECOLLECTABLE. RECOLLECTED. 255

Recoilment. Now rare or Obs. Also 7 recoil-, recoyle-.

Recoin, v.

Recoinage (rīkoi·nedʒ). [f. Re- 5 a + Coinage.]

Recoil (rīkoi·l), v.

Recollectable, a.

Recollect, v.

Recollected, ppl. a.

Recollectedly, adv.

Recollectedness.

Recollection (rekəle·kʃən).

Recollective, a.

Recollet (re·kəlet).

Recolonize, v.

Recolonization.

Recolour, v.

Recomb, v.

Recombine, v.

Recommence, v.

Recomfort, v. Obs. exc. arch.

2442 Supplement, p. 3873; Corrigenda, p. 4092; Spurious words, p. 4093; Books quoted, p. 4094

†Recomfortable. *Obs.*

Recomfort. *Obs.*

†Recomforture, *vbl. sb. Obs.* [f. prec. + -ING.] Encouragement, consolation.

†Recomfortless, *a. Obs.*

†Recom̄forture, *Obs.*

Recommand. *Obs.*

Recommence, *v.* [Re- 5 a.]

Recommence-ment.

†Recommencen.

Recommend, *v.* [ad. L. recommendāre (13th c.)]

1. To commend or commit (oneself or one's soul or spirit) *to* God, his keeping, etc.

2. With consignment.

3. To inform (a person). *Obs. rare⁻¹.*

4. To commend, praise.

5. To mention or introduce (a thing) with approbation.

6. To make (a person or thing) acceptable.

Recommendable, *a.*

Recommendably, *adv.*

Recommendation.

Recommendatory, *a.*

Recommendee. *rare.*

Recommender.

†Recommend- *mise. Obs. rare.*

†Recommit, *v.¹ Obs.*

Recommit, *v.²*

†Recommit-ment.

Recommitment.

Recommittal. [Re- 5 a.]

Recommixture. *Obs.⁻¹* [Re- 5 a.]

Recomfortable. *Obs.*

Recommunicate, *v.* [Re- 5 a.]

Recompact, *pa. pple.*

Recompact.

Recompanse.

Recompany, *v.*

Recompass, *v.*

Recompel, *v.*

Recompensable, *a.*

Recompensation.

Recompense, *v.*

Recompense, *sb.*

Recompenser. *rare.*

Re-compenser. *rare.*

Recompensing, *vbl. sb.*

Recompensive, *a. rare⁻¹.*

Recompile, *v.*

Recompilement.

Recompilation.

Recomplain, *v.*

Recomplete, *v.* See **Recompletion.**

Recomplicate, *v.*

Recom포sition.

Recompose, *v.* [Re- 5 a.]

Recomposition.

Recomposer. *rare⁻¹.*

Recompound, *v.* [Re- 5 a.]

Recompoundable.

Recomprehend.

Recomputation.

Recompt.

Reconcentrate.

Recon, *v.*

Reconceive, *v.*

Reconcentration.

Reconcilable, *a.*

Reconcilableness.

Reconcilably, *adv.*

Reconcile, *v.* [ad. L. reconciliāre.]

1. To bring (a person) into friendly relations to or with (oneself or another) after an estrangement.

2. To restore to harmony.

3. To restore to communion.

4. To make (one thing) consistent with another.

Reconcilement.

Reconcer.

Reconciliation.

Reconciliatory, *a.*

Reconciling, *vbl. sb.*

Reconcile.

Reconcilement.

Reconciler.

Recondite.

Reconditely.

Reconquer.

Reconquering.

Recontract.

Supplement, p. 3873; Corrigenda, p. 4092; Spurious words, p. 4093; Books quoted, p. 4094

1597 Beard *Theatre God's Judgem.* (1612) 415 [He] sent him..a dispensation to put away his wife..and to recontract Anne of Bretaigne, the widow of Charles the eight lately deceased. 1622 J. Reynolds *God's Revenge* II. ix. 160 My soule hath made my peace with God, and my heart desires to recontract it both with thyselfe and her. 1647 N. Bacon *Disc. Govt. Eng.* I. Sum. Concl. (1739) 201 For the sense of State once contracted into a Privy Council, is soon recontracted into a Cabinet-Council, and last of all into a Favourite or two.

So **Recontra·ction.**

1861 Bumstead *Ven. Dis.* (1879) 297 Continuous dilatation is likely to be attended with untoward symptoms and is always followed by a strong tendency to recontraction.

Recontr-: see Reconter v.

†**Reco·ntre.** *Sc. Obs. rare*⁻¹. [var. of Recounter *sb.* Cf. Rencontre.] An encounter.

1570 Buchanan *Chamæleon* Wks. (S.T.S.) 50 [The Queen had] to wryte to hir lieutenentis to mak ye regent be put sauf in Scotland, and so he wes without any recontre.

Reconvale·sce, *v.* [Re- 5 a. Cf. late L. *reconvalēre* (Du Cange).] *intr.* To become convalescent again. So **Reconvale·scence** [cf. med.L. *reconvalescentia* (1341)]; **Reconvale·scent** *a.*

1767 *Douglas Trial* 57 The proof brought of Lady Jane's reconvalescence. 1790 Beatson *Nav. & Mil. Mem.* II. 261 They once more got to sea, where the troops were joined by their reconvalesced men from the isle of Wight. 1824 Scott *St. Ronan's* xvi, His reconvalescence was attended with..debility, it seemed both of mind and body. 1871 *Standard* 14 Jan., The glowing patriotism of the reconvalescent soldiers has perhaps not abated.

†**Reconvalidation.** *Obs. rare*⁻¹. [Re- 5 a.] A renewed confirmation.

1525 Bp. J. Clerk *Let. to Wolsey* (MS. Cott. Vit. B. vii. lf. 126), The Venetians, who hathe made stykyng hetherto to agre withe the Emperor..for the reconvalidation off the ligge by them brokyn.

Reconve·ne, *v.* [Re- 5 a. Cf. med.L. *reconvenīre* (13th c.), F. *reconvenir* (1347 in Godef.).] *trans.* and *intr.* To convene again.

1647 Clarendon *Hist. Reb.* IV. § 24 There was a worse accident than all these which fell out..about the time of the two Houses reconvening. 1676 Hale *Contempl.* I. 101 He is..then sent into the high Priest's Hall; then re-convened before the Council.

†**Reconvent,** *v. Obs.* [Re- 5 a.] *trans.* To reassemble. Hence **Reconventing** *vbl. sb.*

1589 Warner *Alb. Eng.* V. 571 He reconuenting armes therefore,..Died to his countrie's friends a friend. 1611 Florio, *Reconuentione*, a reconuenting.

Reconvention (rīkǫnve·nʃən). [a. F. *reconvention* (13th c. in Littré). Cf. med.L. *reconventio* (14th c.). See Re- and Convention.]

†1. An agreement made in return. *Obs.*

c1449 Pecock *Repr.* III. xviii. 397 As bi boond and withoute eny reconvencioun or couenant of bond expressid or priueli understonde forto ȝeue aȝen.

2. *Law.* A counter-charge; a counter-action brought against the plaintiff by the defendant in a suit. †Also *transf.* in general use.

1538 *Extr. Aberd. Burgh Rec.* (1844) 158 My lord prowest..humely menis, schawis, and, be the way of reconuentioune, compleniis [etc.]. 1629 Mabbe tr. *Fonseca's Dev. Contempl.* 423 Hee vnderstood by sinne in that place, the sinne of adulterie, for otherwise..the reconuention had not beene so strong and forcible. 1633 Ames *Agst. Cerem.* II. 303 In vie of those grounds, laid by the Repl. against humane significant Ceremonies, out of the second Commandement, the Rej. by way of Reconvention faineth two grounds to the contrary. 1726 Ayliffe *Parergon* 83 An Appeal in a cause of Convention does not impeach and hinder the Execution of a Sentence in a Cause of Re-convention. 1760–5 Burn *Eccl. Law* (1797) II. 137 But in these cases of re-convention, the parties must proceed together in the contesting of suit. 1838 W. Bell *Dict. Law Scot.* 823 Where an action is brought in Scotland by a foreigner,..his adversary in the suit is entitled, by reconvention, to sue the foreigner on a counter-claim. 1884 *Law Rep.* 9 App. Cases 582 A claim in reconvention is in substance nothing else than a cross action brought by the defendant against the plaintiff.

†3. The reassembling (of Parliament, etc.). *Obs.*

1641 Sir E. Dering in Rushw. *Hist. Coll.* III. (1692) I. 393 My humble motion therefore is this, I beseech you to declare, That upon this our Reconvention, your Order of the 8th. of September is out of date. 1664 Evelyn *Diary* 24 Nov., The heads of the speech he made at the re-convention of the Parliament, which now began to meet.

Reconve·rge, *v. rare.* [Re- 5 a.] *intr.* To converge again.

1847 De Quincey *Secret Societies* Wks. 1857 VII. 289 Armies of brave men,..by the clapping of hands, in a moment have reconverged in battle array.

Reconversion (rīkǫnvɜ·ɹʃən). [Re- 5 a.] Conversion back to a previous state. a. Of persons, *spec.* in religious sense.

1599 Sandys *Europæ Spec.* (1632) 181 The Popes refusall to reblesse the King upon his sodaine reconversion. a1628 F. Grevil *Sidney* (1652) 237 Those cob-webs of re-conversion in Queen Maryes dayes, I had no intent to meddle with. 1655 Fuller *Ch. Hist.* III. Ded., He could recount his Reconversion, after his foul Offences of Adulterie and Murder. 1778 Johnson in *Boswell* 30 Mar., How often are the primary motives of our greatest actions as small as Sibbald's, for his re-conversion. 1817 Coleridge *Biog. Lit.* (Bohn) 97, I cannot doubt, that the difference of my metaphysical notions from those of Unitarians in general contributed to my final re-conversion to the whole truth in Christ. 1867 Freeman *Norm. Conq.* (1876) I. App. 680 The Danish Chroniclers assert a repentance and reconversion.

b. Of things.

1783 Priestley in *Phil. Trans.* LXXIII. 426 The reconversion of air into water, by decomposing it in conjunction with inflammable air. 1830 Lyell *Princ. Geol.* I. 83 The reconversion of the sedimentary into the crystalline by subterranean fire. 1881 Armstrong in *Nature* XXIV. 449/1 Internal as well as external work may be reconverted into heat, but until the reconversion takes place, the heat which did the work does not exist as heat.

Reco·nvert, *sb.* [Re- 5 a.] One converted a second time.

1843 Gladstone *Glean.* (1879) V. 34 She has made (we refer to the latter part of the sixteenth century) converts and reconverts by thousands—nay, even by millions.

Reconvert (rīkǫnvɜ·ɹt), *v.* [Re- 5 a. Cf. med.L. *reconvertĕre* (Du Cange), F. *reconvertir* (1591 in Godef.), It. *reconvertire* (Florio).]

1. *trans.* To convert back to a previous state: a. persons, *spec.* in religious sense.

1611 Cotgr., *Reconvertir*, to reconuert. 1649 *Alcoran* 278 We..sent him to preach to more then an hundred thousand persons, that we reconverted. 1670 Milton *Hist. Eng.* IV. Wks. (1847) 520/2 About this time the East Saxons, who..had..renounc'd the Faith, were by the means of Oswi thus reconverted. 1737 Wesley *Wks.* (1872) I. 50, I myself having known many Papists..reconverted. 1849 Macaulay *Hist. Eng.* x. II. 647 In December ambition had converted him into a rebel. In January disappointment reconverted him into a royalist. 1882 Saintsbury *Short Hist. Fr. Lit.* III. vii, He soon distinguished himself by reconverting a considerable number of persons to the Roman form of faith.

b. things.

1662 Petty *Taxes* 17 Money; which being paid to the King, is again reconverted into corn. 1762 Mills *System Pract. Husb.* I. 160 There will be no danger of it's re-converting the soil into a bog. 1783 Priestley in *Phil. Trans.* LXXIII. 427 The result was such as to afford a strong presumption that the air was re-converted into water. 1862 Ansted *Channel Isl.* IV. xx. (ed. 2) 474 The islanders in Jersey replaced much of their arable land by orchards. These have since..been re-converted.

2. *Logic.* To transpose again the subject and predicate of (a proposition). Cf. Convert v. 4 b.

1864 Bowen *Logic* vi. 161 It is evident that, by reconverting the Converse, we ought to regain the Convertend. *Ibid.*, This is reconverted simply into 'Some men are mortals'.

3. *Law.* To change back again into something of equivalent value. Cf. Convert v. 15.

1884 Sir E. E. Kay in *Law Times Rep.* L. 56/2 It does not decide that if the court or a trustee sell more than is necessary there is any equity to reconvert the surplus for the benefit of the heir-at-law.

Hence **Reconve·rted** *ppl. a.*; **Reconve·rtible** *a.*, capable of being reconverted.

1738 Wesley *Ps.* LXXX. xxiii, King of a re-converted Land. 1886 *American* XII. 251 That these waves are reconvertible into heat.

Reconvey (rīkǫnvē·), *v.* [Re- 5 a.]

1. *trans.* To convey († or escort) back to a previous place or position; to convey in a reverse direction. Now *rare.*

1506 in *Mem. Hen. VII* (Rolls) 286 After the King had showed him his chamber and would he should take no further pains the King would have somewhat reconveyed him. 1636 *Destr. Troy* 10 Then, that we should our Sacriledge restore And reconveigh their gods from Argos shore, Chalcas perswades. 1707 *Curios. in Husb. & Gard.* 77 There are Vehicles in Plants, to reconvey towards the Roots, the Juices that were mounted up into the Stem. 1766 *Phil. Trans.* LVII. 125 The nerves may..become incapable of conveying the commands of the will, and yet remain sufficiently capable of re-conveying sensible perceptions. 1846 McCulloch *Acc. Brit. Empire* (1854) I. 25 The water that thus overspread the country would be reconveyed to the sea at ebb tide.

2. *Law.* To make over again or restore to a former owner.

1665 Brathwait *Comment Two Tales* 64 She repents her of her Gift. Gladly would she have him re-convey it to her. 1682 Dryden *Satyr* 78 He buys the Purchase, with design t'improve; And like some prudent Kinsman reconvey What the wild Heir hath vainly thrown away. 1734 *Act* 7 *Geo. II*, c. 16 § 2 For redisponing or reconveying the said Lands and Estate in any Manner of Way. 1818 Cruise *Digest* (ed. 2) II. 91 If the mortgagor pays the money borrowed on a certain day, the mortgagee will reconvey the lands. 1881 *Act* 44 & 45 *Vict.* c. 41 (Conveyancing Act), Then B. and C...will at the request and cost of A...reconvey the premises to A.

absol. 1858 Ld. St. Leonards *Handy Bk. Prop. Law* xiv. 94 If a mortgagee will not re-convey upon payment of the principal and interest, and costs, and the right to redeem is still open, the mortgagor may..compel a redemption.

Reconvey·ance. [Re- 5 a.] The act of reconveying; *spec.* in *Law*, restoration to a previous owner.

1767 S. Paterson *Another Trav.* I. 84 The conveyance was almost as astonishing as the re-conveyance. 1768 Blackstone *Comm.* III. xxvii. 439 As by setting aside fraudulent deeds, decreeing re-conveyances, or directing an absolute conveyance merely to stand as a security. 1804 Eugenia de Acton *Tale without Title* I. 154 Soon after its reconveyance to its owners, Lady Laura was again very ill. 1858 Ld. St. Leonards *Handy Bk. Prop. Law* xiv. 89 His prior disposition will..still remain good, nor will a re-conveyance to him upon paying off the money affect the validity of the will.

Reconvi·ct, *v.* [Re- 5 a.] *trans.* To convict again. Hence **Reconvi·cted** *ppl. a.*

1884 *Contemp. Rev.* July 73 *note*, An old offender was re-convicted for a violent assault upon a woman. 1891 H. Matthews in *Law Times* XCII. 96/2 The earning of marks..will extend to reconvicted licence-holders serving the remanets of former sentences.

So **Reconvi·ction.**

1892 *Daily News* 2 Dec. 6/6 Were it the rule..that a longer sentence was to be expected at each reconviction, crime would at once largely diminish.

Reconvo·ke, *v.* [Re- 5 a. Cf. F. *reconvoquer* (Cotgr.).] *trans.* To convoke again.

1837 Carlyle *Fr. Rev.* I. vii. viii, To reconvoke his Assembly Members by sound of drum. 1872 *Echo* 23 Aug. 5 The French Cardinals have requested his Holiness to reconvoke the Council to some French city.

Recool-, obs. Sc. var. *recule* Recoil v.

†**Recoo·per.** *Obs. rare.* [app. irreg. f. L. *recuper-āre* to Recuperate.] Recovery.

1652–60 in Gilbert *Contemp. Hist. Irel.* (1879) I. i. 1 All men desirous of honor, must trie theire fortune, in the recooper therof, but none escaped. *Ibid.* III. i. 49 Either the destruction of a whole nation or the recooper of a kingdome.

†**Recope.** *Obs.*⁻¹ [app. a. OF. *recope* (not recorded in this sense), f. *recoper* (-*couper*) to sound (a bell).] A hunting-note on the horn.

c1400 *Master of Game* (MS. Digby 182) xxxiii, And after þe iiij mote euen forthwith þei shulde blowe ij recopes, as þus: trut, trut, trororororowte.

†**Recopilation.** *Obs. rare.* [ad. Sp. *recopilacion*, f. *re-* Re- + *copilacion*, n. of action f. *copilar*:—L. *compilāre* to Compile.] = Recompilation.

1622 Mabbe tr. *Aleman's Guzman d'Alf.* I. iii. 197 Besides these Ordinances, they had many other...So that it might be said of them, that they were another new Recopilation, or gathering together of those of Castile. 1656 in Blount *Glossogr.* (citing Selden).

Re-co·pper, *v.* [Re- 5 c.] *trans.* To sheathe (a vessel) again with copper.

1857 *Merc. Marine Mag.* (1858) V. 12 The ship has to be hove down and re-coppered. 1897 *Mission. Herald* (Boston) June 219 These repairs, including the recoppering of the vessel.

Reco·py, *v.* [Re- 5 a.] *trans.* To copy again.

1710 Shaftesb. *Adv. to Author* III. ii. 146, I have a very fair Hand offer'd, which may save me the trouble of re-copying. a1779 Tweddell *Rem.* xxxix. (1798) 200 If I have time to recopy, also, my remarks upon the Crimea,..I will send one copy home. 1895 *Forum* (N.Y.) Nov. 354 Paul Verlaine recopied here his Saturnian poems on the paper of the administration.

Record (re·kǫɹd), *sb.* Also 4–6 **recorde**, 5 *Sc.* **racord.** [a. OF. *record* (*recort*, *recor-s*, etc.), f. *recorder* to Record. Cf. Sp. *recuerdo*, It. *ricordo*. The original stressing (reco·rd) is found in verse as late as the 19th c.]

I. 1. *Law.* The fact or attribute of being, or of having been, committed to writing as authentic evidence of a matter having legal importance, *spec.* as evidence of the proceedings or verdict of a court of justice; evidence which is thus preserved, and may be appealed to in case of dispute. Chiefly in phrases †*of* (common in 15–16th c.), †*in*, *by*, *on* or *upon record.*

a1300 *Cursor M.* 9711 Ne dom agh haf right na record, Ar we ben all at an a-cord. 1423 *Rolls of Parlt.* IV. 201/2 Pair namys also, to be entred of record, what and how thei determyne. 1455 *Paston Lett.* I. 364 As it apperith pleynlye by accompt made of the sayd office of Constabulrye, remaynyng in the Kyngs Cheker at Westminster of record. 1523 Fitzherb. *Surv.* 20 Whan a mater..is past by verdyt ..and entred in the kynges recordes there it resteth of recorde, and also yf a dede or a patent be inrolled there it remeyneth of recorde in lyke maner. 1596 Bacon *Max. & Uses Com. Law* (1630) 50 These Estates are created by word, by writing, or by record. *Ibid.* 81 So that he for-see that he pay Debts vpon Record, first debts to the King, then vpon Iudgements. 1603 Shaks. *Meas. for M.* II. ii. 40 To fine the faults, whose fine stands in record, And let goe by the Actor. a1677 Hale *Prim. Orig. Man.* II. x. 235 Which was accordingly done, and remains of Record in the Exchequer. 1700 Tyrrell *Hist. Eng.* II. 837 These Letters..remain upon Record in the Tower on the Clause Roll of this Year. 1766 Blackstone *Comm.* II. 119 All estates-tail are rendered liable to be charged for payment of debts due to the king by record of special contract. 1818 Cruise *Digest* (ed. 2) V. 55 The manor..was let at a greater rent, or appeared upon record to be of a greater value.

fig. 1709 Hearne *Collect.* 12 Jan. (O. H. S.) II. 163 An Ass upon Record cried up for a man of..learning.

b. In phr. *Matter* (*thing*, *debt*, etc.) *of record.* Also *debt by record.*

1433 *Rolls of Parlt.* IV. 424/1 Thay to abide enacted as þinges of recorde. 1472–3 *Ibid.* VI. 52/2 Any relesse, arbetrament, or any other plee, not matier of Recorde. 1596 Bacon *Max. & Uses Com. Law* (1630) 62 This Fine is called a Feofment of Record, because that it includeth all that the Feofment doth. 1642 tr. *Perkins' Prof. Bk.* x. § 655. 283 If it were by Matter of Record it should be good without attornment. 1766 Blackstone *Comm.* II. xxx. 464 A debt of record is a sum of money, which appears to be due by the evidence of a court of record. 1827 Hallam *Const. Hist.* (1876) I. i. 15 It then became a matter of record, and could not be impeached. 1842 Stephen *Comm. Laws Eng.* II. II. v. 187 Another species of debt by record is that upon adjudgment; which is, where any sum is adjudged to be due from one party to the other, in an action in a court of record.

c. *Court of record*: a court whose proceedings are formally enrolled and valid as evidence of fact, being also a court of the sovereign, and having authority to fine or imprison. So †*Judge of record.*

[1419 *Liber Albus* in Riley *Munim. Gildh.* (Rolls) I. III. I. 217 Si issint soit qe mesme le defendaunt veigne en court ce recorde, etc.] 1451 *Rolls of Parlt.* V. 219/1 Your Offices in youre Courtes of Record. 1581 Lambarde *Eiren.* I. xiii. (1602) 59 It maketh not a little..for the credit of the Iustices [of the Peace]..., that they are numbred amongst the Iudges of Record. 1607 Cowell *Interpr.* s.v., Queene Elizabeth ..made the Consistory Court of the University of Cambridge a Court of Record. 1641, 1765 [see Court *sb.*¹ 11]. 1768 Blackstone *Comm.* III. iii. 25 That the very erection of a new jurisdiction with power of fine and imprisonment makes it instantly a court of record. 1844 Stephen *Comm. Laws Eng.* III. v. vi. 442 The Commissioners [of Sewers] are a court of record and may fine and imprison for contempts. 1865 F. M. Nichols *Britton* I. 136 *note*, It was decided in later times, that the county court, though sitting by virtue of the King's writ.., had not the powers of a court of record. 1888 [see Court *sb.*¹ 11].

†d. *To have record*: to be entitled to have one's judicial acts and decisions enrolled. *Obs.*

1581 Lambarde *Eiren.* I. xiii. (1602) 60 Bracton..writing of a speciall case, where the Sherife in his Countie hath Record. [1865 F. M. Nichols *Britton* I. 136 *note*, The sheriff..is treated by our Author as the King's Justiciary, and as having the power of record incident to that office.]

2. The fact or condition of being preserved as knowledge, *esp.* by being put into writing; knowledge or information preserved or handed down in this way. Freq. in phrases (†*of*,) *on* or *upon record.*

c1386 Chaucer *Sompn. T.* 409 Syn Ennok was or Elise Han freres been, that fynde I of record. 1390 Gower *Conf.* III. 166 For this I finde ek of record, Which the Cronique hath auctorized. 1470–85 Malory *Arthur* I. ii, By all record he was dede or euer kynge Vther came. 1570–6 Lambarde *Peramb. Kent* (1826) 177, I finde on Recorde that the Priory at Bylsington was first advaunced by John Maunsell. 1588 J. Mellis *Briefe Instr.* F vij b, Yee must haue a seuerall booke of record, wherein you shall record the copy of letters of charge. 1606 Shaks. *Tr. & Cr.* I. iii. 14 Euery action that hath gone before, Whereof we haue Record. 1628 Wither *Brit. Rememb.* 7 The gloriout things, That stand upon record of mortall Kings. a1720 Sewel *Hist. Quakers* (1722) I. Let. to King, Remarkable Cases, which I thought worthy to be kept upon Record, and not buried in Oblivion. 1815 Shelley *Alastor* 25 In charnels and on coffins, where black death Keeps record of the trophies won from thee. 1884 *Times* 2 Dec. 10 Having beaten the highest break on record.

†3. Attestation or testimony of a fact; witness, evidence, proof. In early use chiefly in phrases *by record of*, *to take record* (*at*). *Obs.*

13.. *E. E. Allit. P.* A. 830 Lombe was taken þere, By trw recorde of ayþer prophete. 1377 Langl. *P. Pl.* B. xv. 85 ȝe..louten to þis lordes..Aȝeine ȝowre reule and Religion, I take record at Ihesus. 1417 in *E. E. Wills* (1882) 39 Syf þer be eny man or woman þat wil say þat I howght hem eny goud, and swere vppon a boke by record of goud men, y wyl þat dey be payd. 1465 *Paston Lett.* II. 223 The qwych peticion I made diverse tyme to fore moche recorde. 1533 More *Debell. Salem* Wks. 1011/1 Where one is openly and notably suspected of heresye, and sufficient recorde and witnesse agaynste hym. 1547 Hancock in Strype *Eccl. Mem.* (1721) II. I. ix. 115, I awnswered that he spake those words betwyxt him and me, but yf I had record of them he would not speak them. 1646 H. Lawrence *Comm. Angells* 90 Of which I could give you account enough upon as good record as story can give us of any thing.

†b. *To bear record*: to bear witness. *Obs.*

Tr. AF. *porter record* (Britton): cf. Bear v. 2 c.

13.. *Coer de L.* 4591 With Kyng Richardes armes pourtrayed In sygne to bere record That Kyng Richard was her ovyr-lord. 1390 Gower *Conf.* I. 70 Forto bere hierof record He sende ous hider bothe tuo. 1413 *Pilgr. Sowle* (Caxton) I. xii. (1859) 9 Of this wyl I bere hym good record, that he has clerely kepte hys byleue in to this last ende. 1526 Tindale *John* i. 34 And I sawe yt, and have borne recorde, that thys ys the sonne off God. 1542–5 Brinklow *Lament.* (1874) 107 All that reade their workes maye beare recorde with them agaynst your lyes. 1611 Bible [in a number of passages, after earlier versions].

†c. *To take* or *call to record*: to call to witness. *Obs.* (Cf. Call v. 20 c.)

1390 Gower *Conf.* I. 7 That I take to record..The comun vois, which mai noght lie. 1494 Fabyan *Chron.* I. xiv. 14 Gonorilla..callynge her goddes to recorde, sayd, she loued hym more than her owne soule. 1526 Tindale *Acts* xx. 26, I take you to recorde this same daye that I am pure from the bloud of all men. 1535 Coverdale *Deut.* xxx. 19, I take [1611 call] heauen and earth this daye to recorde ouer you. 1591 Sylvester *Du Bartas* I. vi. 344, I call to record that same Roman Thrall Who..Fled through the desart.

†d. A witness. *Obs.* (In later use only in Biblical language.)

1526 Tindale *Acts* v. 32 We are his recordes as concernynge these thynges. 1568 *Wills & Inv. N. C.* (Surtees 1835) 291 Recordes hereof thomas Barker..and Thomas Slogen wt others. 1593 Shaks. *Rich. II*, I. i. 30 Heauen be the record to my speech. 1768 Sterne *Sent. Journ.* I. 33 (*In the Desobligeant*) God is my record,..that I do not speak it vauntingly.

II. 4. *Law.* An authentic or official report of the proceedings in any cause coming before a court of record, together with the judgement given thereon, entered upon the rolls of court and affording indisputable evidence of the matter in question.

The reference in Cowell (quot. 1607) is to Sir R. Brooke *La Graunde Abridgement* (1573) II. 192.

1455 *Rolls of Parlt.* V. 341/1 Fynes, obligacions, reconysaunces, and othir recordes upon the same. 1472 *Ibid.* VI. 63/1 And therupon Juggement ayenst him yeven: as in the Record therof, wherof the Copie hereto is annexed, more playnly it is conteyned. 1568 Grafton *Chron.* II. 836 All attaynders..were adnichilated, and the recorde of the same adiudged to be defaced. 1597 Skene *De Verb. Sign.* s.v. *Recordum*, Ilk lauchfull court..hes thair awin recordes in all sik actiones as are..decided before them. 1607 Cowell *Interpr.* s.v., That caveat of Brooke..that an act committed to writing in any of the King's Courts during the terme wherein it is written is alterable & no record; but that terme once ended and the said Act duly enrolled, it is a record. 1628 Coke *On Litt.* 260 The Rolles being the Records or memorialls of the Judges of the Courts of Record ..admit no auerment, plea, or proofe to the contrarie. And if such a Record be alleaged, and it be pleaded, That there is no such Record, it shall be tried only by it selfe. 1765 Blackstone *Comm.* I. Introd. 69 The judgment itself, and all the proceedings previous thereto, are carefully registered and preserved, under the name of records, in public repositories set apart for that particular purpose. 1825 *Act* 6 *Geo. IV*, c. 86 § 11 All the said Judgments and Verdicts shall be deemed to be and shall become Records of the said Sheriff to all Intents and Purposes whatsoever. 1838 W. Bell *Dict. Law Scot.* 1025 It is then transferred to the record and read aloud to the jury, who are asked, 'Is this your verdict?'

b. A copy of the material points, pleadings, and issue between defendant and plaintiff on a matter of law, constituting the case to be decided by the court; hence, a case so constituted or presented.

1627 Powell *Attornies Almanacke* Title-p., Such as shall have occasion to remoue any Person, Cause, or Record from any inferiour Court to any the higher Courts at Westminster. 1768 Blackstone *Comm.* III. 317 The record is a history of the most material proceedings in the cause, entered on a parchment roll,..in which must be stated the original writ and summons, all the pleadings [etc.]. 1817 W. Selwyn *Law Nisi Prius* (ed. 4) II. 1087 A person having a bare authority, and not being a party to the record, is not prevented from being a witness. 1824 J. Marshall *Const. Opin.* (1839) 329 In cases where a state is a party on the record the question of jurisdiction is decided by inspection. 1827 Hallam *Const. Hist.* (1876) III. xiii. 19 No record was ever removed thither [to the Star chamber] upon assignment of errors in an inferior court. 1885 *Encycl. Brit.* XIX. 219/1 Since the Judicature Acts (1873) there has been no record properly so called, in civil cases, though it has not been expressly abolished.

c. Phr. *To travel out of the record* (see quot. 1770). Also *transf.*, to go off the subject. So *to keep to the record.*

1770 Chatham *Sp.* 11 Dec. in *Junius Lett.* (1772) I. Pref. 18 *note*, The court..are so far confined to the record, that they cannot take notice of any thing that does not appear on the face of it; in the legal phrase, they cannot travel out of the record. 1772 *Junius Lett.* I. Pref. 18 If I stated the merits of my letter to the King, I should imitate Lord Mansfield, and travel out of the record. 1840 W. L. Garrison in *Life* II. 430 [He] will speak to a point that is pertinent, and not travel out of the record. 1861 Dickens *Gt. Expect.* xviii, Never mind what you longed for. Keep to the record.

d. *Sc. Law.* A minute, subscribed by the counsel on both sides and by the judge (in the Court of Session by the Lord Ordinary), by which the parties to a suit mutually agree to hold certain pleadings as a full and final statement of the facts and pleas on which their case rests.

The record when finally adjusted and authenticated by the Lord Ordinary or the inferior judge is said to be *closed*. For details of the practice, which dates from the Act of 1825, see Bell's *Dict. Law Scot.* s.v.

1825–6 *Act* 6 *Geo. IV*, c. 120 § 10 The Record so made up and authenticated shall be held as foreclosing the parties from the statement of any new averments in point of fact. 1850 *Act* 13 & 14 *Vict.* c. 36 § 2 Where Defences are lodged, and unless the Record shall be closed upon the Summons and Defences, the Record shall be made by Revisal.

5. An account of some fact or event preserved in writing or other permanent form; a document, monument, etc., on which such an account is inscribed; also, *transf.* any thing or person serving to indicate or give evidence of, or preserve the memory of, a fact or event; a memorial. Freq. in *pl.*, a collection of such accounts, documents, etc. Also, in recent use, a tracing or series of marks, made by a recording instrument.

1611 Bible *Ezra* vi. 2 There was found..a rolle, and therein was a record thus written. 1655 H. Vaughan *Silex Scint.*, *Agreement*, I wrote it down. But one that saw And envyed that Record [etc.]. 1790 Cowper *In Mem. Thornton* 48 Thy bounties all were Christian, and I make This record of thee for the Gospel's sake. 1822 Shelley tr. *Calderon* II. 163 In my wisdom are the orbs of Heaven Written as in a record. 1841 *Penny Cycl.* XIX. 332/2 The journal stamp on a letter is a record that it has passed through the post-office. 1876 *Nature* XV. 101/2 Thus a permanent record is made of every signal that is sent. 1881 I. Taylor *Alphabet* I. 16 The very earliest record which we possess of any actual event is the scene depicted on a fragment of an antler [etc.].

transf. 1594 Shaks. *Rich. III*, IV. iv. 28 [Thou] breefe abstract and record of tedious dayes. c1600 — *Sonn.* lv, The living record of your memory. 1790 Cowper *Receipt Mother's Pict.* 54 The record fair That memory keeps, of all thy kindness there. 1797 Wordsw. *Old Cumbld. Beggar* 89 The villagers in him Behold a record. 1842 Tennyson *Gardener's Dau.* 173 Shaping faithful record of the glance That graced the giving.

pl. 1581 Savile *Tacitus, Hist.* IV. xl. (1591) 199 To communicate a copie to the Senate of the Princes recordes and papers. 1615 Bedwell *Arab. Trudg.* Talby, This I translated for the office of the Records in the Towre well neare thirtie yeares since. 1697 Dryden *Virg. Past.* IX. 63 Why, Daphnis, dost thou search in old Records, To know the Seasons when the Stars arise? 1751 Johnson *Rambler* No. 143 ¶ 8 That no records were so durable as poems. 1781 Cowper *Conversat.* 615 Who..Could fetch from records of an earlier age,..His rich materials. 1819 Shelley *Cenci* IV. i. 58 My parchments and all records of my wealth. 1841 *Penny Cycl.* XIX. 336/2 The Victoria Tower..has been named as a likely repository for the public records. 1875 Helps *Soc. Press.* III. 50 No historical records remain of this great transaction.

transf. a1610 Parsons *Leicester's Ghost* (1641) 28 Can this injurious World so quickly blot A name so great out of records of fame. 1662 Bp. Hopkins *Funeral Serm.* (1685) 13 The records of the grave. 1759 Mason *Caractacus* Wks. 1811 II. 97 That black hour, (May Memory ever raze it from her records). 1843 Mill *Logic* I. i. § 5 Either in the records of our own experience or in the discourse of others.

b. An account or reckoning of past time. *rare.*

1611 Bible *Transl. Pref.* ¶ 3 For conseruing the record of time in true supputation. 1711 Pope *Temp. Fame* 112 Who measured earth..And traced the long records of lunar years.

c. The leading facts in the life or career of a person, *esp.* of a public man; the sum of what one has done or achieved.

App. of American origin, but now in common Eng. use.

1856 H. Greeley *Sp.*, *on Lincoln* 20 Mar. 133 A candidate must have a slim record in these times. 1879 Tourgee *Fool's Err.* xi. 49 Contending so hotly over each other's records during and before the war. 1888 *Century Mag.* May 3 My literary record—so far as I had made a record.

d. A performance or occurrence remarkable among, or going beyond, others of the same kind; *spec.* the best recorded achievement in any competitive sport. Freq. in phr. *to beat* or *break the record*: to surpass all previous performances.

1883 W. Wilson *Swim. Instructor* 137 The following records are given. 1884 *Longm. Mag.* Feb. 483 This performance, which beat all previous records was considered a very fine one.

III. †6. Reputation, repute, account. *Obs.*

c1386 Chaucer *Sompn. T.* 341 Dronkenesse is eek a foul record Of any man and namely in a lord. 1390 Gower *Conf.* II. 230 Protheus of his record Which was an Astronomien. *Ibid.* III. 326 Sche was a womman of record And al is lieved that sche seith. c1470 Henry *Wallace* IX. 1133 Off him he maid bot lycht record.

†7. Memory, remembrance, recollection. *Obs.*

13.. *Minor Poems fr. Vernon MS.* xlix. 61 Long record of þat malice. c1400 tr. *Secreta Secret.*, *Gov. Lordsh.* 116 It fallys þat þou chese of wyse men & of Skreueyns..of sotyll record. 1577–87 Breton *Flourish upon Fancy* (1879) 55/1 When that in minde I feede upon the freshe recorde of thee. 1601 Shaks. *Twel. N.* V. i. 253 O that record is liuely in my soule.

†8. *Sc.* Reply; tale, statement. *Obs.*

c1470 Henry *Wallace* VII. 1260 Schir Jhon Menteth..Till Wallace come, and maid a playne record. *Ibid.* X. 1145 To that langage Cumyn maid na record. c1475 *Rauf Coilȝear* 729 The king fell in carping, and tauld his Intent To mony gracious Grome he maid his record.

†9. Accord, reconcilement. *Obs. rare*⁻¹.

c1400 *Rule St. Benet* 63/654 For our enmes sal we pray, Til a recorde be redy ay.

†10. A musical note. *Obs. rare*⁻¹.

1582 T. Watson *Centurie of Love* xi, O Goulden bird..Whose sweete records and more then earthly voice..did then my griefe asswage.

†11. = Recorder². *Obs. rare.*

†c1475 *Sqr. lowe Degre* 1075 With sytolphe and with sautry songe With fydle, recorde, and dowcemere. 1589 Puttenham *Eng. Poesie* II. i. (Arb.) 79 Melodious instruments, as Lutes, Harpes, Regals, Records, and such like.

†12. = Recorder¹. *Obs. rare.*

a1550 *Vox populi* 702 in Hazl. *E. P. P.* III. 292 The laweare and the landelorde, The greate reave and the recorde, The recorde I mean is he That hath office or els ffee.

IV. 13. *attrib.* and *Comb.* a. objective and objective genitive, as *record bearer*, *bearing*, *-breaking*, *keeper*, *-maker*, *-making.*

1549 Coverdale, etc. *Erasm. Par. 2 Thess.* i. 9 b, You, which trusted in Christ at our *recorde bearing. — *Erasm. Par. 2 John* 54 Thys is the true doctrine, whiche you haue receaued of true *recorde bearours from the begynnyng. 1581 Marbeck *Bk. of Notes* 216 Those faithfull christen men, that heard and sawe Christ, and were his record bearers. 1886 *Pall Mall G.* 10 July 6/1 This Henley Regatta has been a *record-breaking one. 1715 Willis *Notitia Parl.* I. Pref. 3 Deputy *Record Keeper of the Tower. 1884 *Longm. Mag.* Feb. 480 Some severe strictures on the '*record-makers' [in cycling]. *Ibid.*, Whilst I am writing in familiar style of 'records' and '*record-making'.

b. *attrib.* in senses 4 and 5, as *record-bottle*, *commission*, *committee*, *-cross*, *-office*, *-room*, *-stone.*

1853 Kane *Grinnell Exp.* xxv. (1856) 203 Planting a flagstaff, with a *record-bottle below it. 1811 *First Ann. Rep. Rec. Ireland* App., The Statutes..which have been published under the English *Record Commission. 1841 *Penny Cycl.* XIX. 336/1 The Record Commission was renewed six several times between the years 1800 and 1831. 1802 *Ann. Rep. Comm. Public Rec.* § 2 The *Record Committee of the House of Commons. 1836 Miss Pardoe *River & Desert* II. 17 The hand..which had planted the *record-cross, and the tributary wreath. 1800 *First Rep. Public Rec.* 18 Upon Inquiry into the *Record Offices of the Sheriffs [etc.]. 1855 Singleton *Virgil* I. 141 Nor people's record-offices beheld. 1800 *First Rep. Public Rec.* App. Pl. i, *Record Room for Principal Clerks of Session. 1812 *Sporting Mag.* XXXIX. 172 Convicted by the magistrates at the record-room, Northampton. 1836 J. H. Newman in *Lyra Apost.* (1849) 53 So, let the cliffs and seas of this fair place Be named man's tomb and splendid *record-stone.

c. *attrib.* in sense 5 d, passing into *adj.*

1893 Lydekker *Horns & Hoofs* 135 The 'record' dimensions are..a length of 13½ in., with a girth..of 6¼ in. 1895 *Times* 2 Jan. 13/1 Record prices have been made.

Record (rīkǭ·ɹd), *v.* Also 5 *Sc.* **racord**, 6 **reccord.** [ad. OF. *recorder* (in most senses of the Eng. word) = Sp. *recordar*, It. *ricordare*:—L. *recordāre* (classical *recordārī*), f. *re-* Re- + *cord-*, *cor* heart: cf. *accord*, *discord*, etc.]

I. †1. *trans.* a. To get by heart, to commit to memory, to go over in one's mind. b. To repeat or say over as a lesson, to recite. *Obs.*

a1225 *Ancr. R.* 256, & makie so þeo þet bereð þet word recorden hit ofte biuoren hire, er heo go ut. c1330 R. Brunne *Chron.* (1810) 172 Better him wer..Þe seruise of his song recorded & lered. c1374 Chaucer *Troylus* III. 2 (51) Lay al this mene while Troilus Recordyng his lesson in this manere. c1477 Caxton *Jason* 37 If ye will recorde the lessons and epistles of loue by the space of ten yere. 1542 Udall *Erasm. Apoph.* 250 b, Anon the crowe recorded also the other woordes whiche she had so often heard. 1579 Spenser *Sheph. Kal.* Apr. 30 If hys ditties bene so trimly dight, I pray thee, Hobbinoll, recorde some one. a1656 Hales *Gold. Rem.* I. (1673) 142 The Gardiner whilst he prunes his Vines and Arbours, may record some one of David's sonnets.

†c. To take to heart, give heed to. *Obs.*⁻¹

1390 Gower *Conf.* II. 250 He tolde him many a dredful sawe Bot Jason wolde it noght recorde.

2. To practise (a song, tune, etc.). In later use only of birds (cf. 3); †freq. (c1580–1620) = to sing or warble (a tune, etc.).

1413 *Pilgr. Sowle* (Caxton 1483) v. viii. 99 When they hadde these instrumentes they recorded songes besyly tylle that they were..parfyte ynowe in al maner musike. 1580 Lyly *Euphues* (Arb.) 278 Where vnder a sweete Arbour of Eglentine, the byrdes recording theyr sweete notes [etc.]. 1601 Dolman *La Primaud. Fr. Acad.* (1618) III. 760 The young little nightingales harken to the old, and do record by themselues apart, the songs which they heard. a1654 Selden *Table-t.* (Arb.) 95 You see a Bird by often whistling to learn a tune, and a Month after record it to her self. 1834 E. Jesse *Glean. Nat. Hist.* Ser. II. 84 This tune..I could distinctly hear it inwardly whistle, or, in the language of bird-fanciers, record it.

†b. To sing of or about (something); to render in song. *Obs.*

1576 Gascoigne *Philomene* (Arb.) 110 Then Phylomene records the rewth Which craueth iust remorse. 1597 Lyly *Wom. in Moon* III. i. 79 Let vs go walke the woods, Where warbling birds recorde our happines. 1592 Shaks. *Two Gent.* V. iv. 6 Here can I..to the Nightingales complaining Notes Tune my distresses, and record my woes.

3. *intr.* Of birds (rarely of persons): To practise or sing a tune in an undertone; to go over it quietly or silently. Now only *techn.*

c1510 Barclay *Mirr. Gd. Manners* (1570) E vj, Therfore first recorde thou, as birde within a cage,..thy tunes tempring longe, And then..forth with thy pleasaunt songe. 1530 Palsgr. 681/2 This byrde recordeth all redy, she wyll synge within a whyle. a1592 H. Smith *Serm.* (1637) 429 Like a bird that is taught to record, when he had sung it he sang it again. 1619 Fletcher *M. Thomas* III. iii, Ye may record a little, or ye may whistle, As time shall minister; but, for main singing, Pray ye satisfy yourselves. 1727–41 Chambers *Cycl.* s.v., The cock thrush is distinguished from the hen in recording, the first being more loud and frequent in it than the second. 1773 Barrington in *Phil. Trans.* LXIII. 250, I have known instances of birds beginning to record when they were not a month old. 1871 Darwin *Desc. Man* I. ii. 55 The young males [birds] continue practising, or, as the bird-catchers say, recording, for ten or eleven months.

†b. To sing or warble. *Obs.*

1590 Lodge *Rosalind* (Hunter. Cl.) 37 Partlie to heare the melodie of the sweete birdes which recorded. 1592 Kyd *Sp. Trag.* II. iv. 28 Harke, Madame, how the birds record by night. 1613–6 W. Browne *Brit. Past.* II. iv, While the nymph did earnestly contest Whether the birds or she recorded best.

II. †4. *trans.* To call to mind, to recall, recollect, remember. *Obs.*

1303 R. Brunne *Handl. Synne* 4191 Treytur! recorde what þou hast herde Seyde and sunge yn al þe werlde. 1340 *Ayenb.* 142 Huanne he recordeþ þet lif of iesu crist and his holy passioun. c1400 *Rule St. Benet* 11 Þat ye be noght for-getil,..And tat ye recorde wel þe cumantemens of god. 1480 Caxton *Chron. Eng.* lxxxv, Do we so..that men mowe recorde the worthynesse of knyght hode. 1530 Palsgr. 681/2 When I recorde the gentyll wordes he hath had unto me, it maketh my herte full sorye for hym. 1599 T. M[oufet] *Silkwormes* 65 For they recording what they were of late Dare not yet mount aboue their former state. a1656 Hales *Gold. Rem.* I. (1673) 4 Do you already know your duty? it serves to commemorate, and to make you record it. 1789 Cowper *Annus Mem.* 34 An era..Which joyful I will oft record, And thankful, at my frugal board.

absol. c1440 *Jacob's Well* 181, I haue seyd my synne in herte recordynge. c1460 *Launfal* 831 The Kyng recorded tho, And bad hym bryng hys lef yn syght.

†5. To meditate, ponder (something) *with* oneself. *Obs.*

c1374 Chaucer *Boeth.* I. pr. i. 2 (Camb. MS.) While þat I stille recordede thise thinges with myself. 1583 Stocker *Civ. Warres Lowe C.* II. 46 Certaine dayes of deliberation are giuen to the prisoner to record with himselfe, who or what his enemies be. 1586 A. Day *Eng. Secretary* I. (1625) 86 We shall record with our selues, in what league, amity or duty, we haue before-time stood charged.

†6. *intr.* a. To have mind or recollection *of* a person or thing. *Obs.*

1382 Wyclif *Gen.* viii. 1 The Lord forsothe recordide of Noe. — *Isa.* lxiii. 11 He recordide of the dayes of the world. 1509 Hawes *Past. Pleas.* I. (Percy Soc.) 9 Recorde of Saturne, the first kyng of Crete. 1567 *Triall Treas.* (1850) 28 Recorde of Dionisius, a king of much fame.

†b. To think or meditate *on* a thing or person. Also with *in.* *Obs.*

c1374 Chaucer *Troylus* III. 1130 (1179) Evermore on this night ye recorde, And beth wel ware ye do no more amys. c1430 Lydg. *Min. Poems* (Percy Soc.) 125 Recorde on Fraunce and Parys the fayre citee. 1430–40 — *Bochas* VIII. i. (1558) 3 Recorde on Cyrus, and many other mo. 1531 Tindale *Expos. Matt.* vi. 34 (c1550) 82 b, To kepe the couenaunt of the Lorde thy God, and to recorde therin daye and night. 1560 Becon *New Catech.* Wks. I. 488 Let not the boke of this lawe departe out of thy mouth, but recorde therein daye and nyght. a1604 R. Hall *Life Bp. Fisher* xxii. (ed. Baily, 1655) 206 Himselfe praying all the way, and recording upon the words which he before had read.

†7. a. To remind (one) of (a thing). *Obs. rare*⁻¹.

c1386 Chaucer *Prol.* 829 Ye woot youre foreward and I it yow recorde.

†b. *refl.* To remember. Also const. *of.* *Obs.*

1413 *Pilgr. Sowle* (Caxton 1483) I. xv. 9 Ful wel I me record, of this mater ne touchyd I no word. 1422 tr. *Secreta Secret., Priv. Priv.* 150 A man sholde hym recorde of thynges that afore hath bene.

III. †8. *trans.* To relate in words; to tell or narrate orally. Also *intr.* in *to hear record*, to hear tell (*of* a person). *Obs.* (in later use only as *transf.* from 9).

13.. *Cursor M.* 19122 (Gött.) Bi his fadir sitt he sall, Till he record haf vs all, þat he spac feirst wid prophecis. 1340 *Ayenb.* 59 Þet is þe zenne of þan þet zuo bliþeliche recordeþ hare dedes and hare prowesses. 1390 Gower *Conf.* I. 36 In this wise, as I recorde, The man is cause of alle wo. a1450 *Knt. de la Tour* (1868) 52 Beting hem self [and] recordyng her synne tofore the pepille. 1500–20 Dunbar *Poems* lix. 13 Quhois crewall sclander seruis deid, And in my name all leis recordis. 1550 Lyndesay *Sqr. Meldrum* 1520 Thair dwelt in Fyfe ane aged Lord That of this Squyer hard record. 1738 Wesley *Hymn*, '*To Thee, O Father of Mankind*' ii, Who in th' Assembly of the Just Will still record thy Praise.

†b. Const. *to* or *unto* (a person). *Obs.*

1375 Barbour *Bruce* I. 72 Thai all concordyt, That all thar spek suld be recordyt Till Schyr Eduuard. 1390 Gower *Conf.* III. 49 Somwhat of his aventures, To thee, mi Sone, I wol recorde. c1470 Henry *Wallace* X. 542 The Bruce than in his mynd remordyt Thai wordis suth that Wallace had him recordyt. c1500 *Melusine* 102 The erle..demanded of Raymondin where he had be so long, and he recorded to hym alle his auenture.

†c. To declare as one's verdict. *Obs.*

1377 Langl. *P. Pl.* B. xviii. 197, I, Riȝtwisnesse, recorde thus with treuth, That her peyne be perpetuel. 1393 *Ibid.* C. IV. 474 After the dede that ys ydo, the dome shal recorde, Mercy other no mercy. a1400 *Pistill of Susan* 60 Riȝtwys Jugement recordet þei none.

9. To relate in writing; to narrate or mention in a written account; to put or set down in writing; to put on record. Also, in recent use, of telegraphic and other instruments: To set down (a message, etc.) in some permanent form.

In later use the sense of setting down in a written or permanent form becomes the prominent one; early examples are more closely connected with sense 8.

13.. *E. E. Allit. P.* B. 25 Me mynez on one amonge oþer, as Maþew recordez. c1375 *Sc. Leg. Saints* xxxi. (*Eugenia*) 239 It nedis nocht to recorde here þe dole. c1430 Lydg. *Min. Poems* (Percy Soc.) 47 Clerkys recorde, by gret auctoryte, Hornes wer yove to bestys for dyffence. 1554–9 in *Songs & Ball.* (1860) 2 Yet God made hyme promys, as Scrypture dothe reccord. 1579 E. K. *Gloss. Spenser's Sheph. Cal.* May 54 Which story is first recorded of Plutarch, in his booke of the ceasing of oracles. 1601 Dolman *La Primaud. Fr. Acad.* (1618) III. 828 Plinie recordeth many other wonders concerning these beasts. 1662 Stillingfl. *Orig. Sacr.* II. iii. § 1 After he hath recorded those faults, he seeks not to extenuate them. 1696 Whiston *Th. Earth* III. (1722) 253 Their Numbers were exactly taken, and are as exactly Recorded. 1771 *Junius Lett.* I. 259 The services you have done the nation..have been faithfully recorded. 1820 W. Irving *Sketch Bk.* II. 265 The last words of his that are recorded, are worthy the greatness of his soul. 1860 Tyndall *Glac.* II. xxi. 343, I have recorded certain winter measurements made on the Mer de Glace. 1873 F. Jenkin *Electr. & Magn.* xxii. § 5 Sometimes the Morse signals are indicated to the ear or eye without being recorded. 1895 [see Recorder¹ 4].

fig. 1601 Daniel *To C'tess Cumbld.* xvi, This note (Madam) of your Worthinesse Remaines recorded in so many Hearts. 1647 H. More *Song of Soul* I. I. i, What so under eye Doth fall, or is record in memorie. 1726 Pope *Odyss.* XVII. 580 Just and unjust recording in their mind. 1782 Cowper *Truth* 161 In faithful memory she records the crimes, Or real or fictitious, of the times.

absol. c1425 Wyntoun *Cron.* II. Prol. 30 Wiþe Orosius we wil discorde In til our dat qwhen we racorde Befor or fra þe byrtht of God.

refl. 1818 Scott *Ivanhoe* ix, By this name the stranger had recorded himself in the books of the tourney.

b. To have (a gift, etc.) properly recorded; to give (a verdict or vote).

1596 Shaks. *Merch. V.* IV. i. 388 That he doe record a gift Heere in the Court of all he dies possest Vnto his sonne [etc.]. a1856 Cushing *Law & Pract. Legisl. Assemblies U.S.* VI. iii. 708 If they do not apply until afterwards, they can only be permitted to record their votes by leave of the house. 1884 *Manch. Exam.* 10 May 5/4 There is only one verdict which those who disapprove of it can record.

†10. To bear witness to (a fact, etc.); to attest, confirm. Also *absol.*, to testify. *Obs.*

1377 Langland *P. Pl.* B. IV. 157 Alle riȝtful recorded þat resoun treuthe tolde. 1387 Trevisa *Higden* (Rolls) VIII. 348 Þese were i-sent to the popes court for to have þese covenauntes recorded by þe popes billes. c1440 *Promp. Parv.* 426/1 Recordyn, or bere wytnesse, *testificor.* 1476 in *Surtees Misc.* (1888) 35 Thys wyll we recorde and bere wittenesse be thys lettre of record sealed with our seales. 1514 Barclay *Cyt. & Uplondyshm.* (Percy Soc.) p. xlvi, That can Amintas record and testify. 1570 Levins *Manip.* 171/21 To Recorde, *contestari.* 1607 Shaks. *Timon* IV. iii. 4 Let me be recorded by the righteous Gods, I am as poore as you.

absol. 1393 Langl. *P. Pl.* C. v. 29 To take red at Reson, that recorde sholde By-fore the kyng and Conscience. c1460 *Towneley Myst.* xii. 327 It was a mery gle, sich hard I neuer none, I recorde.

†b. To call to witness. *Obs. rare*⁻¹.

1586 Marlowe *1st Pt. Tamburl.* V. ii, For all blot of foul inchastity, I record Heaven, her heavenly self is clear.

†IV. 11. To pertain or belong *to* (one). *Obs.*⁻¹

c1500 *Lancelot* 606 Hyme lakid nocht that to a lord recordith.

Re-cord (rīkǭ·ɹd), *v.* [f. Re- 5 a + Cord v.¹] *trans.* To cord again, in senses of that vb.

1797 *Term Rep.* VII. 182 All that they had done was to measure the wood and re-cord a very small part of it. 1869 *1st Rep. Dep. Kpr. Irel.* 14 The document sought is usually found in a few minutes, and the piece re-corded and returned to its place.

Recordable (rīkǭ·ɹdăb'l), *a.* [f. Record v. + -able.] Capable of being recorded, admitting of record.

1483 Caxton *Gold. Leg.* 258/2 Thou that arte called to the lyf perdurable..to refection not recordable. 1815 Jane Austen *Emma* xxxviii, Of very important, very recordable events. 1858 Carlyle *Fredk. Gt.* IX. xi. II. 541 Prince Lichtenstein..does nothing else recordable in Berlin.

Reco·rdal. *rare*⁻¹. [-al.] = Record *sb.*

1859 T. S. Henderson *Mem. E. Henderson* i. 13 Boyish escapades which are not worth recordal.

†**Reco·rdance.** *Obs. rare.* [a. OF. *recordance* (13th c.) = It. *ricordanza*: or f. Record v. and -ance.] Remembrance.

1490 Caxton *Eneydos* xvi. 61 Hauynge noo mynde ne recordaunce for to goo conquere the cytees. *Ibid.* xxv. 90 For often commeth in mynde, to theym of good recordaunce [etc.]. 1592 Wyrley *Armorie* 145 Recordaunce make with griefe and dolefulnes. 1630 J. Taylor (Water P.) *Verbum Sempiternum* Wks. III. 131/2 This Booke againe, againe, Recordance brings.

So †**Reco·rdancy.** *Obs. rare*⁻¹.

1654 Cokaine *Dianea* IV. 364, I know the Recordancie of thy vertues have no need of Commiserations.

Reco·rdant, *a. rare*⁻¹. [f. as prec. + -ant.] Containing a record, reminiscent.

1813 in *Parr's Wks.* (1828) VIII. 656 Monument or memorial recordant of the virtues..of man.

Recordar, obs. Sc. form of Recorder².

Reco·rdate, *v. rare*⁻¹. [f. ppl. stem of L. *recordārī* to Record.] *trans.* To remember, recollect.

1830–2 Carleton *Traits* (1843) I. 131 When Rose recovered, she seemed as if trying to recordate what had happened.

Recordation (rekǫɹdē·ʃən). [a. OF. *recordation* (14–16th c.), or ad. L. *recordātiōn-em* (hence also Sp. *recordacion*, It. *ricordazione*), n. of action f. *recordārī* to Record.]

†1. The faculty of remembering or recollecting.

1398 Trevisa *Barth. De P. R.* v. iii. (Bodl. MS.), In the hyndermeste [cell of the brain is] recordacioun and mynde. 1594 T. B. *La Primaud. Fr. Acad.* II. 163 For this cause some Philosophers attribute vnto man beside memorie both recordation and remembrance. 1666 J. Smith *Old Age* (ed. 2) 46 Another receptacle for the intelligible species, which they call Reminiscency or Recordation.

†2. Remembrance or recollection *of* something.

c1450 tr. *De Imitatione* III. xxiv. 94 Of þe recordacion of þe manyfolde benefetes of god. 1475 *Bk. Noblesse* (Roxb.) 3 The recordacion of actis and dedis in armes of so many famous..Kingis. a1540 Barnes *Wks.* (1573) 351/2 They doe..pray vnto them in remembraunce and recordation of the first fruits. 1579 Fenton *Guicciard.* (1618) 147 Ioyning to that new offence a recordation of old iniuries done against him. 1609 [Bp. W. Barlow] *Answ. Nameless Cath.* 159 It strooke a..recordation of their former disloyaltie into our first parents. 1657 W. Morice *Coena quasi Κοινὴ* Diat. v. 244 The recordation thereof, and external acknowledgment of Christ to be the Redeemer [etc.].

attrib. 1748 Richardson *Clarissa* (1811) III. x. 71 Let me call myself back to my recordation-subject. Thou needest not remind me of my Rosebud.

†3. An act of commemorating or making mention; a commemorative account. *Obs.*

1598 Yong *Diana* Pref., Discurring most of those townes and places in it with a pleasant recordation of my pen. 1609 [Bp. W. Barlow] *Answ. Nameless Cath.* 69 A short, but pithy and worthy recordation of Her Clement gouernment. 1670 Walton *Life Donne* 63 Methinks they be persons that seem to challenge a recordation in this place.

4. The action or process of recording or committing to writing.

1802–12 Bentham *Ration. Judic. Evid.* (1827) I. 279 Notation: or say recordation, registration, scription, note taking. 1831 *Examiner* 723/2 An accurate recordation or representation of the transactions of an individual. 1877 Burroughs *Taxation* 326 It is difficult to perceive upon what principle recordation is necessary.

attrib. 1802–12 Bentham *Ration. Judic. Evid.* (1827) II. 94 Every cause is recordation-worthy, unless in so far as some special reason can be shewn to the contrary.

Recordative (rīkǭ·ɹdātiv), *a.* [a. obs. F. *recordatif* (16th c.) or ad. late L. *recordātīv-us* (once): see Recordate v. and -ive.] Commemorative.

1551 Gardiner in Foxe *A. & M.* (1563) 795/1 A sacrifice recordative of that only sacrifice of the crosse. 1607 *Schol. Disc. agst. Antichr.* I. i. 32 There be Papists that tollerate Images only for their signification and as they are recordatiue. 1811–31 Bentham *Ess. Lang.* Wks. 1843 VIII. 297 Recordative of the matter of thought. 1898 *Month* June 646 In the few sentences recordative of his teaching.

Hence **Reco·rdatively** *adv.*

1633 Ames *Agst. Cerem.* II. 291 If we admitte of significant Images, as religious Ceremonies, I would fain know how we in England can condemne, those that worship..them commemoratively or recordatively.

†**Recordator.** *Obs.*⁻¹ [a. med.L. *recordātor*, f. *recordārī* to Record.] = Recorder¹.

1691 Wood *Ath. Oxon.* I. 246 Dav. Middleton of Gwenock, Recordator of North-Wales.

Recorded (rīkǭ·ɹdėd), *ppl. a.* [f. Record v. + -ed¹.] †a. Tuned or musically rendered. *Obs.*

b. Put on record, preserved in writing.

1568 T. Howell *Arb. Amitie* (1879) 83 With loyes the Nightingal gan rayse, hir right recorded song. 1603 Shaks. *Meas. for M.* II. iv. 61, I (now the voyce of the recorded Law) Pronounce a sentence. 1606 — *Mach.* v. v. 21 To the last Syllable of Recorded time. 1871 Freeman *Hist. Ess.* Ser. I. i. 27 An age of recorded history for one nation, is an age before recorded history for another. 1877 *Nature* XVI. 446/2 The recorded ascents to the height of 21,000 feet are extremely few.

Hence **Reco·rdedly** *adv.*

1893 *Temple Bar* Apr. 511 Mrs. Charles Kemble, an actress, recordedly, and a character.

Recorder¹ (rīkǭ·ɹdəɹ). Also 4–5 **recordour.** [Orig. a. AF. *recordour*, OF. *recordeour*, *-eur* (14th c.); in later use partly f. Record v. + -er¹.]

1. A certain magistrate or judge having criminal and civil jurisdiction in a city or borough.

The Recorder was originally a person with legal knowledge appointed by the mayor and aldermen to 'record' or keep in mind the proceedings of their courts and the customs of the city, his oral statement of these being taken as the highest evidence of fact. (See Riley *Munimenta Gildhallæ* I. 42–3.) The recorder of London, to whom most of the early evidence refers, is still appointed by the court of aldermen; in other cities and boroughs the appointment is made by the crown, the duties of the office being regulated by the Municipal Corporations Act of 5 and 6 William IV and subsequent enactments. The court of Quarter-Sessions is held by the recorder on dates fixed by himself.

[c1325 in Riley *Munim. Gildh.* (Rolls) II. I. 151 Solonc le record des Recordours de la Gilhale. 1347 *Rolls of Parlt.* II. 186/1 Au Mair & au Recordour & as Aldermannes de mesme la Citee. 1419 *Liber Albus* in Riley *Munim. Gildh.* (Rolls) I. III. I. 182 Et si les parties pleident a jugement, le jugement serra done par bouche de loure Recordoure. *Ibid.* I. 308 Sacramentum Recordatoris. Vous jurrez, qe vous serrez foialx et loialx..a la citee de Loundres, en loffice du Recordour.]

1426 in *Surtees Misc.* (1888) 8 [At York] Richard Russell, Thomas Bracebryg, aldermen, Gui Rouclyff, recordour. 1463–4 *Rolls of Parlt.* V. 504/2 Aldermen or Recorders of the same Cite [London]. a1548 Hall *Chron.*, *Hen. VIII* 142 b, Whatsoeuer was saied by the Recorder, in his excuse, was taken as..a dissimulacion or a mocke. 1594 Shaks. *Rich. III*, III. vii. 30 His answer was, the people were not vsed To be spoke to, but by the Recorder. 1607 Cowell *Interpr.* 1630 *Galway Arch.* in *10th Rep. Hist. MSS. Comm.* App. V. 476 The Recorder of this towne..shall have per annum tenn poundes sterling. 1642 Calthrop *Liberties London* 23 That the Recorder shall or may *ore-tenus*,..record and certifie the Customs being traversed. And his certificate shall be as strong in the Law as the verdict of 22 men. 1709 Steele *Tatler* No. 39 ¶ 4 [He] has, by Advice of the Recorder of Oxford, brought this Action. 1765 Blackstone *Comm.* I. 76 The customs of London differ from all others in point of trial: for, if the existence of the custom be brought in question, it shall not be tried by a jury, but by certificate from the lord mayor and aldermen by the mouth of their recorder. 1850 Ht. Martineau *Hist. Peace* V. iii. II. 244 Boroughs having a Recorder have separate Courts of Quarter-Sessions of the peace. 1886 *Encycl. Brit.* XX. 160/1 The recorders of Dublin and Cork are judges of the civil bill courts in those cities.

transf. 1593 Donne *To C'tess Huntingdon* xvii, I but your Recorder am in this..A ministerial notary.

†b. The chief justice of an East Indian settlement. *Obs.*

1800 *Asiatic Ann. Reg.*, *St. Papers* 5/2 So much of the charter..for erecting the Courts of Recorder at Madras and Bombay, as relates to the appointment of Recorder.

†2. A witness. *Obs.*

c1440 *Promp. Parv.* 426/1 Recordowre, wytnesse berer, *testis.* 1522 *Knaresborough Wills* (Surtees) I. 14 Also I wyll John Wylkes..and Richard Roundell to be recorders with other moo. 1556 *Richmond Wills* (Surtees) 87 Recorders hereof, Lawranse Robinson..withe other mo. 1607 Cowell *Interpr.* s.v., I find not that wee in our Courts (especially in the Kings Courts) stand much upon the number of recorders or witnesses for the strength of the testimonie which the record maketh.

3. One who records or sets down in writing.

Recorder of the Great Roll, a former officer of the Scottish Court of Exchequer, also called *Clerk of the Pipe.*

1537 Bible (Matthew) *1 Kings* iv. 3 Josaphath the sonne of Ahilud the recorder. 1640 Bp. Hall *Episc.* II. xix. 198 Faithfull recorders of all occurrences that befell the Church. 1771 Luckombe *Hist. Print.* 10 He had got Corsellis into his hands, as the recorder imports, so many years before. 1830 D'Israeli *Chas. I*, III. xvii. 370 The faithful recorder of our once country-customs. 1834 *Act* 4 & 5 *Will. IV*, c. 16 (*title*) An Act to abolish the Office of Recorder of the Great Roll or Clerk of the Pipe in the Exchequer in Scotland. 1871 Blackie *Four Phases* i. 3 A faithful..recorder of what he heard and saw.

4. A recording apparatus; *esp.* a device in a telegraphic instrument for recording the signals received. (See also *siphon recorder.*)

1873 F. Jenkin *Electr. & Magn.* xxiii. § 6 Keeping..the glass tube end of the recorder within a very narrow strip of paper. 1876 *Nature* XV. 102/1 The Recorder consists of a powerful electro-magnet [etc.]. 1895 *Daily News* 29 Jan. 6/5 The Thompson and Marsden Patent Recorder..is a machine to be attached to the indicator posts of steam vessels for recording..every order as it is given by the master from the bridge to the engineer below.

Reco·rder². *Obs.* exc. *Hist.* Forms: 5–6 **recordre**, 5 *Sc.* **-our**, 6 *Sc.* **-ar**, (5 **recourder**), 5– **recorder.** [app. f. Record v. (senses 2 and 3) + -er¹.] A wind instrument of the flute or flageolet kind (see quot. 1626).

1430–40 Lydg. *Bochas* II. xv. (1554) 54 b, Pan..Of recorders fond fyrst the melodies. c1450 Holland *Howlat* 759 The rote, and the recordour,..The trumpe, and the talburn. 1542 Udall *Erasm. Apoph.* 5 b, Yf a manne would fayn bee reputed a good player on the recordres. 1598 Yong *Diana* 475 One of them plaied on a Lute; another on a Harpe; another made a maruellous sweet countertenour vpon a Recorder. 1626 Bacon *Sylva* § 221 The Figure of Recorders, and Flutes, and Pipes are straight; But the Recorder hath a less Bore and a greater; Above, and below. 1683 Tryon *Way to Health* 655 Flutes or Recorders are a brave noble Instrument, being skilfully handled. 1719 D'Urfey *Pills* (1872) IV. 94 All maids that make trial of a Lute or a Viol,..If you like not this Order, come try my Recorder. 1773 Barrington in *Phil. Trans.* LXIII. 250 A musical instrument, formerly used in England, called a recorder. 1791 Cowper *Iliad* x. 14 Pipes, and recorders, and the hum of war.

†b. One of the pipes of an organ. Also *transf.*

1613 *Organ Specif. Worcester Cathedral*, The particulars of the great organ..1 recorder of mettal, a stopt pipe. 1650 Bulwer *Anthropomet.* 92 In the curious Machin of speech, the Nose is added as a Recorder, to advance the melodious eccho of the sound.

†c. *transf.* One who plays a recorder. *Obs.*⁻¹

1630 J. Taylor (Water P.) *Gt. Eater Kent* 5 Such are poets, trumpetters, cornets, recorders, pipers, bag-pipers.

Recordership (rīkǭ·ɹdəɹʃip). [f. Recorder¹ + -ship.] The office, or term of office, of a recorder.

1553 *Shrewsbury MSS.* in *15th Rep. Hist. MSS. Comm.* App. X. 13 It ys supposed to be incident to his office of recordarshipp. 1678 Lady Chaworth in *12th Rep. Hist. MSS. Comm.* App. V. 45 To confirme your Lordship's election to the Recordership of Grantham. 1689 J. Bent *Bloody Assizes* 13 To whose influence..he attributed his dismission from the Recordership. 1835 *Fraser's Mag.* XII. 64 The fees of registration and recordership. 1884 *Law Times* LXXVII. 248/1 County Court judges could retain their recorderships after their appointment.

Recording (rīkǭ·ɹdiŋ), *vbl. sb.* [-ing¹.] The action of the vb. Record in various senses.

†1. Remembrance, recollection; meditation. *Obs.*

1340 *Ayenb.* 55 Þe blisse þet hi habbeþ ine þe recordinge. 1382 Wyclif *2 Tim.* i. 5 Takinge recordinge [*gloss* or mynde] of that feith, that is in thee. 1483 Caxton *G. de la Tour* N iv b, They whiche kepe them self fro recordynge of ony wordes. 1519 Horman *Vulg.* 277 Huntyng is a playn recordyng of warre. 1559 *Homilies* I. *Exhort. Holy Script.* B j, Continual readyng and recordyng of Gods worde.

2. The practising or singing of birds.

1530 Palsgr. 261/1 Recordyng of byrdes, *patois.* 1611 Cotgr., *Resonnance*,..a recording, as of birds. 1681 W. Robertson *Phraseol. Gen.* (1693) 1053 The recording of birds, *modulatio avium alterna.* 1773 Barrington in *Phil. Trans.* LXIII. 250 The next stage in the notes of a bird is termed, by the bird-catchers, recording. 1852 Miss Pratt *Nat. Songst.* 49 This practising is by bird fanciers called recording.

3. The action of setting down or putting on record. Also *attrib.*

1662 Stillingfl. *Orig. Sacr.* IV. i. § 1 So certain a recording of them, as may be least liable to any suspicion of imposture or deceit. 1684 I. Mather (*title*) An Essay for the recording of Illustrious Providences. 1838 W. Bell *Dict. Law Scot.* 827 This recording is necessary, in order that the deed may have the benefit of the statute. 1898 *Daily News* 15 Aug. 7/1 Recording fees are regulated solely by the miners themselves.

Recording (rīkǭ·ɹdiŋ), *ppl. a.* [-ing².] That records, now *esp.* in phr. *recording angel.*

1761 Sterne *Tr. Shandy* V. viii, The recording angel, as he wrote it down, dropp'd a tear upon the word. 1781 Cowper *Conversat.* 551 Marble and recording brass decay. 1781 — *Table-t.* 21 When recording History displays Feats of renown. 1841 Lane *Arab. Nts.* I. 30 Every believer is attended by two guardian and recording angels. 1870 Burton *Hist. Scot.* lxv. (1873) VI. 2 Had the Romans been a recording people like the Normans [etc.]. 1873 F. Jenkin *Electr. & Magn.* xxii. § 7 The electro-magnet of the recording instrument.

Re·cordless, *a.* [f. Record *sb.* + -less.] Having no record or records; unrecorded.

1892 A. E. Lee *Hist. Columb.* (Ohio) I. 62 The line which separates the extinct and recordless races from the races known to history.

Recordour, -dre, obs. ff. Recorder².

Re-cork (rīkǭ·ɹk), *v.* [Re- 5 a.] *trans.* To cork again; to provide with new corks.

1843 *Penny Cycl.* XXVII. 464/1 Such also are most liable to the aggressions of insects, and must frequently be recorked. 1884 *Graphic* 23 Aug. 207/2, I ordered the..bottles to be refilled, recorked, and served a second time.

†**Recorporification.** *Obs.*⁻¹ [Re- 5 a.] A making or becoming corporeal again.

1666 Boyle *Orig. Formes & Qual.* 216 This Factitious Vitriol may not be barely a new Production, but partly a Recorporification.

So †**Recorporify** *v.*; **Recorporize** *v.*

1694 Salmon *Bate's Dispens.* (1713) 490/2 The recorporified Spirits have a greater Sphere of Activity..than the Substances purely natural. 1781 *Westm. Mag.* IX. 74 Spirits re-corporised render the water colder than the salts do, out of which they were drawn.

†**Recotising,** *vbl. sb. Her. Obs.*⁻¹ [Re- 5 a.] A second cotising.

1586 Ferne *Blaz. Gentrie* II. 69 The Fret is as it were a recotizing of the feeld: but in Armes bended or cotized, the cullors conteined be equally deuided with the feeld.

Recou·ch, *v. rare*⁻¹. [Re- 5 a.] *intr.* To couch again, to retire again to rest.

a1639 Wotton *Poems*, civ *Psalm* vii, Then savage Beasts creep from the silent Wood,..Who when at Morn they All recouch again, [etc.].

Recouer(e, -ir, obs. ff. Recover *sb.* and *v.*

Recouncile, obs. form of Reconcile v.

†**Recou·nsel,** *v. Obs.* Forms: α. 4 **reconseyle**, 4 (6 *Sc.*) **-sale**, 5 **-saille**; 4 **reconcele**, **-seyll**, 4–5 **-sail**, 6 *Sc.* **-saill**, **-sale**; 4–5 (6 *Sc.*) **recounsel**, 5 **-selle**, 6 *Sc.* **-sell**, **-cel(l.** β. 4 **recounseil**, 5 **-seille**, 5–6 **-seyll**, 4–5 **-sail**, 6 *Sc.* **-saill**, **-sale**; 4–5 (6 *Sc.*) **recounsel**, 5 **-selle**, 6 *Sc.* **-sell**, **-cel(l.** [a. OF. *reconseiller*, ad. L. *reconciliāre* after *conseiller* to Counsel. The forms in Eng. follow those of the simple vb.]

1. *trans.* = Reconcile v. 1 and 2.

13.. *Propr. Sanct.* (Vernon MS.) in *Archiv neu. Spr.* LXXXI. 308/55 Crist forsoþe was in heuene þe goode workes Reconseylinge To him-self. 1382 Wyclif *Matt.* v. 24 Go first for to be recounseilid to thi brother. c1450 *Mirour Saluacioun* 2370 And with his blode vs to godde his fadere to reconsaille. 1482 Caxton *Trevisa's Higden* II. xxiii. 98 b, Jason recounseylled and toke ayene his wyfe media. 1533 Gau *Richt Vay* (S. T. S.) 42 We war inimis with god bot now we ar reconsalit be the deid of his sone.

2. *Sc.* = Reconcile v. 4.

1501 Douglas *Pal. Hon.* Prol. 94 O Nature Quene, and O ȝe lustie May,..Recounsell me out of this greit affray. 1533 Bellenden *Livy* I. xi. (S. T. S.) I. 63 He kest him to recounsell him agane to the favoure of his pepill. 1563 Winȝet *Wks.* (S. T. S.) II. 4 He apperis weil to hef bene reconcelit vnto his fauour.

3. = Reconcile v. 5 and 5 b. Also, to bring back, or admit again, to allegiance.

1375 Barbour *Bruce* IX. 740 Thou has a quhill renyit thi fay; Bot thou reconsalit now mon be. 1496 *Dives & Paup.* (W. de W.) VII. xviii. 305/2 Yf ony curate..recounseyll hym that wyll not amende hym..he doth symonye. 1572 *Sc. Acts Jas. VI* (1814) III. 72/1 Quhill thay haue recounsallit tham selfis to the trew Kirk submittand þame selfis to the Discipline thairof. a1578 Lindesay (Pitscottie) *Chron. Scot.* (S.T.S.) II. 76 Mr. George [Wishart] ansuerit..he wald..be recounsellit in ony thing his conscience movet him.

4. = Reconcile v. 6.

c1450 *St. Cuthbert* (Surtees) 7147 Þe new kirke was recounsaile Solemply, and reparailde. 1496 *Dives & Paup.* (W. de W.) I. lxiv. 108/2 Yf it [pollution] myght be preued, ther sholde noo preeste synge ne saye noo masse therin, ne bodye be buryed tyll it [the churchyard] were recounseylled ayen by the bysshop. 1533 Bellenden *Livy* V. xxiii, Þat þe templis of þe goddis (quhilkis war pollutit & violet be Inemyis) suld be recounseld, renewit, & purifyit.

5. To recover, regain. *rare*⁻¹.

c1400 Maundev. (Roxb.) Pref. 2, I trowe wele þat within a lytill tyme oure riȝt heritage..schuld be recounsailed and putte in to þe handes of þe right heyers of Ihesu Criste.

Hence †**Recou·nseller**; **Recou·nselling** *vbl. sb.*

a1340 Hampole *Psalter* xliv. 3 Þe warld resayued grace of recouncelynge. 1388 Wyclif *Deut.* v. 5 Y was recounselere and mediatour bitwixe God and ȝou in that tyme. — *Isa.* lx. 10 In my recounselyng Y had merci on thee. 1483 *Cath. Angl.* 301/2 A Recounsillynge, *reconsiliacio.*

Recounsile, -syle, obs. ff. Reconcile v.

†**Recou·nt,** *sb.*¹ *Obs.* [f. Recount v.¹, in early use perh. after OF. *raconte* (Godef.).] Account, narrative, narration.

c1489 Caxton *Blanchardyn* liii. 204 And for the recounte of their adventure, they chased Subyon [etc.]. 1582 T. Watson *Centurie of Love* lx, No Night with sleepe shall close mine eyes at all, Before I make recount of such a debt. a1635 Naunton *Fragm. Reg.* (Arb.) 34 In recount of whom I proceed with Sir Philip Sidney.

Recount (rīkau·nt), *sb.*² [Re- 5 a; cf. Recount v.²] A new count; a second or subsequent enumeration (*esp.* of votes in an election).

1884 *Pall Mall G.* 22 Nov. 7/2 In reply to the Conservative application for a re-count. 1890 *Times* 21 Oct. 5/4 The Government Census Bureau has refused to make a recount of the population of New York.

Recount (rīkau·nt), *v.*¹ Also β. 5–6 **recompte**, 6 **-coumpte.** [a. ONF. and AF. *reconter*, *recunter* (12th c.) f. *re-* Re- + *conter* to Count. Cf. also F. *raconter*.]

1. *trans.* To relate or narrate; to tell in detail; to give a full or detailed account of (some fact, event, etc.). Also const. *to* (a person).

α. 1456 Sir G. Haye *Law Arms* (S. T. S.) 7 As is recountit be Sanct Gregore the haly doctour. 1483 Caxton *G. de la Tour* K iij b, Gladde to here telle and recounte the goodness of them. a1533 Ld. Berners *Huon* lxxxiii. 262, I am ashamyd to recounte it. 1599 Nashe *Lenten Stuffe* 41 To recount *ab ouo*..howe the Herring first came to be a fish. 1617 Moryson *Itin.* I. 186 He ceased not to bewaile my misery, and to recount my Tragedy. 1653 H. Cogan tr. *Pinto's Trav.* ix. 28 He recounted unto me, that he had in all but six thousand men. 1782 Miss Burney *Cecilia* IX. v, Mrs. Hill wept for joy in recounting how well she succeeded. 1809 Malkin *Gil Blas* VII. ii. ¶ 2, I recounted..all that had passed..without garbling the facts in any particular. 1858 Doran *Crt. Fools* 269 The two..fell to recounting to each other many a good story.

β. c1477 Caxton *Jason* 45 b, I shal recompte to yow my lyf and all myn astate. 1568 Grafton *Chron.* II. 803 With ye which aunswere John Greene returned, recompting the same to king Richarde. 1575 Turberv. *Venerie* i. 3, I have thought good to recompte this historie.

b. (With plural object.) To relate in order; to enumerate by particulars.

α. 1483 Caxton *Gold. Leg.* 428 b/1 Who that coude recounte alle the myracles doon by hym. a1533 Ld. Berners *Huon* xxi. 60 Yf I sholde recounte all the aduentures,..it sholde be to longe a processe to show it. 1584 R. Scot *Discov. Witchcr.* x. ii. (1886) 143 Macrobius recounteth five differences of images. 1667 Milton *P. L.* VII. 112 To recount Almightie works What words or tongue of Seraph can suffice? 1745 Fielding *True Patriot* Wks. 1775 IX. 304 To enumerate all those vices which I have already declined recounting. 1816 J. Scott *Vis. Paris* (ed. 5) 267 These are advantages and gratifications which it makes one almost feverish to recount. 1870 M. D. Conway *Earthw. Pilgr.* viii. 113 Rites and prayers, recounting to God the items of his magnificence.

β. 1561 Daus tr. *Bullinger on Apoc.* Pref. (1573) 3 He

Recount (rī·kau·nt), *v.*³

Recountable, *a.* rare.

Recountal (rīkau·ntal).

Recounter, *sb.*¹ rare.

Recounter, *sb.*² Obs.

Recountermand. Obs.⁻¹

Recountless, *a.* Obs.⁻¹

Recounting, *vbl. sb.*

Recoup (rīkū·p), *v.*

Recoup, *sb.* Law.

Recouper.

Recouple (rīkŏ·p'l), *v.*

Recourage. Obs.⁻¹

Recourse (rīkōᵒ·rs), *sb.*

Recourse, *v.* Obs.

Recourseful, *a.* Obs.⁻¹

Recourt, *v.*

Recover (rīkŏ·vəɹ), *sb.*

Recover (rīkŏ·vəɹ), *v.*

Recoverable (rīkŏ·vərăb'l), *a.*

Recoverableness.

Recoverance. Obs.

Recover, *v.*² Also re-cover.

Supplement, p. 3873; Corrigenda, p. 4092; Spurious words, p. 4093; Books quoted, p. 4094

Supplement, p. 3873; Corrigenda, p. 4092; Spurious words, p. 4093; Books quoted, p. 4094

Rectorate (re̱ktŏrĕt). [ad. L. RECTOR + -ATE¹; cf. med.L. *rectōrātus* (1382 in Du Cange).] The office or position of a rector; the period during which the office is held.

Rectoress (re̱ktŏres). [f. RECTOR + -ESS.]
1. A female ruler or governor. *Obs.*
2. The wife of the rector of a parish.

Rectorial (rektōʳri·ăl), *a.* Of or pertaining to a university rector; connected with the office or election of a rector.

Rectorship (re̱ktŏʳship). [f. RECTOR + -SHIP.]
1. The office of ruler or governor; government, rule.

Rectory (re̱ktŏri). [ad. med.L. *rectōria* (1294 in Du Cange), or ad. med.L. *rectōria* (1263 ibid.): see RECTOR and -Y³.]

Rectrix (re̱ktriks). *Pl.* **rectrices** (rektrəi·sīz). [L., fem. of RECTOR ruler.]
1. A female ruler or governor. *Obs.*

Rectual, obs. form of RECTAL.

Rectum (re̱ktŏm). *Anat.* and *Med.* [a. L. *rectum* (sc. *intestinum*), neut. of *rectus* straight.]

Recubation. *Obs. rare.* [L. *recubātiōn-em*, n. of action f. *recubāre* to recline.]

Recueil (rĕkœ·y). *Pl.* Forms: 5 recuel, recuyle, recueyll, 5–6 recule, 6 recuell, -cuoil, -cewle, 6 recoil, 6–7 (9) recueil. [a. F. *recueil* (14th c.).]
1. A literary compilation or collection.

Recumbency (rĕkŏ·mbensi). [f. as next: see -ENCY.]

Recumbentibus. *Obs.* Also 7 -bend-. [A humorous use of L. *recumbentibus*, abl. pl. of *recumbens*: see RECUMBENT.] A knock-down blow.

Recumbent (rĕkŏ·mbent), *a.* [ad. L. *recumbent-em*, pr. pple. of *recumbĕre*.]

Recuperate (rĭkiū·pĕreⁱt), *v.* [f. L. *recuperāt-*, ppl. stem of *recuperāre* to recover, f. RE- + *capere* to take, seize.]

Recuperation (rĭkiūpĕreⁱ·ʃən). [ad. L. *recuperātiōn-em*, n. of action f. *recuperāre*: see prec. Cf. F. *récupération* (16th c.).]

Recuperative (rĭkiū·pĕrătiv), *a.* [ad. L. *recuperātīvus*: see RECUPERATE and -IVE.]

Recuperator (rĭkiū·pĕreⁱtəʳ). [a. L. *recuperātor*.]

Recuperatory (rĭkiū·pĕrătŏri), *a.* [ad. L. *recuperātōrius*: see RECUPERATE and -ORY.]

Recur (rĭkəʳ·), *v.* [ad. L. *recurrĕre* to run back, f. RE- + *currĕre* to run.]

Recure, *sb.* *Obs.* Forms: 5 recūr, -cuer, -cure, -keur, 5–7 recure. [f. next, or aphetic of RECOVER *sb.*]

Recure, *v.* *Obs.* Also 5 *Sc.* recuir. [ad. L. *recūrāre*, or aphetic of RECOVER *v.*]

Recured, *ppl. a.* *Obs.* [f. prec.]

Recureful, *a.* *Obs.* [f. RECURE *sb.* + -FUL.]

Recureless, *a.* *Obs.* That cannot be cured; incurable.

Recurement. *Obs. rare.* [f. RECURE *v.* + -MENT.]

Recurer. *Obs.* [f. RECURE *v.* + -ER¹.] One who helps or aids.

Recurred (rĭkəʳ·d), *ppl. a.* [ad. L. *recurv-us*: cf. RECUR *v.*]

Recurrence (rĭkŏ·rĕns). [f. as next: see -ENCE.]
1. Return (of a thing, state, event, etc.); renewed, frequent, or periodical occurrence.

Recurrent (rĭkŏ·rĕnt), *a.* and *sb.* [ad. L. *recurrent-em*, pr. pple. of *recurrĕre*: see RECUR *v.*]

Recurring (rĭkəʳ·riŋ), *ppl. a.* [-ING².]

Re-current (rīkŏ·rĕnt), *a.* [RE- + CURRENT *a.*]

Recurrency. *Obs. rare.* [f. RECURRENT: see -ENCY.]

Recursant, *a.* *Obs. rare.* [ad. L. *recursant-em*.]

Recurvant (rĭkəʳ·vănt), *a.* *Her.* [ad. L. *recurvant-em*, pr. pple. of *recurvāre*.] Bowed, embowed, recurved.

Recurvate (rĭkəʳ·veⁱt), *a.* [ad. L. *recurvāt-us*, pa. pple. of *recurvāre*.] Bent back again.

Recurvation (rīkəʳveⁱ·ʃən). [ad. L. *recurvātiōn-em*.]

Recurve (rĭkəʳ·v), *v.* [ad. L. *recurvāre*, f. RE- + *curvāre*: see CURVE *v.*]
1. *trans.* To bend (a thing) back or backwards.

2. intr. (Chiefly of a wind or current): To turn back in a curve upon its previous direction.

Recurved (rĭkœ̄·rvd), *ppl. a.* [f. prec. + -ED.] Bent back; having a backward curve. In 19th c., esp. in scientific use.

† Recu·rvity, *Obs. rare.* [See RECURVE *a.* and -ITY.] The fact of being recurved.

Recurve, used in *Bot.* as comb. form of L. *recurvus*, as **recu·rvo-patent**, bent back and spreading; **recu·rvo-ternate**, bent back and divided into three parts.

Recurvous (rĭkœ̄·rvŏs), *a. rare.* [f. L. *recurvus* + -OUS.] Recurved, bent back.

Recus, obs. Sc. form of EXCUSE.

Recusance (re·kiuzăns, rĭkiu·zăns), [f. as next: see -ANCE.] = next.

Recusancy (re·kiuzănsi, rĭkiu·zănsi). [ad. L. type *recūsantia*: see RECUSANT and -ANCY.] The action or practice characteristic of a recusant.

1. *Hist.* Refusal, especially on the part of Roman Catholics, to attend the services of the Church of England; from c1570 to 1791 this was punishable by a fine, and involved many disabilities.

Recusant (re·kiuzănt, rĭkiu·zănt), *sb.* and *a.* [ad. L. *recūsant-em*, pres. pple. of *recūsāre* to REFUSE. Cf. F. *récusant* (Littré).]

A. 1. *Hist.* One, especially a Roman Catholic (*Popish recusant*), who refused to attend the services of the Church of England.

† Recu·sative, *a. Obs. rare⁻¹.* [See late L. *recūsātīvus* peritinory: see RECUSE and -IVE.] That tends to refuse or prohibit.

Recu·sator, *n.* and *a. Sc. Law. Obs. rare.* [ad. med.L. *recūsator*, agent-n. f. *recūsāre*: see prec. and -OR.]

† Recu·satory, *a. Obs. rare.* [ad. L. type *recūsātōri-*: see next and -ORY.] Of or belonging to recusing; containing a recusation.

Recuse (rĭkiū·z), *v. Now rare.* Also 5 *Sc.* **recous**. [ad. F. *récuser* (13th c. in Littré), ad. L. *recūsāre* to refuse, make an objection, f. re- RE- + *causa* CAUSE.]

Red (red), *sb.* and *a.* Forms: 1 **réad**, 2–3 **read**, 3 **reed**, 3–6 **rede**, 4–6 **redd(e**, (*comp.* 4 **reddere**, 5 **ur**)... 4–8 **red**, (6 **rid**, 7– **red**. [Common to all OFris. *rād*, OS. (M.Du., MLG.) *rēd* (Du., LG. *rood*), OHG., MHG. *rōt* (mod.G. *rot*), ON. *rauðr* (Sw., Da. *rød*), Goth. *rauþs*=OTeut. *raudo-z* :–pre-Teut. *roudho-*, from the *e*-grade of the ablaut series *reudh-, roudh-, rudh-*.]

A. adj. I.

1. Having, or characterized by, the colour which appears at the lower or least refracted end of the visible spectrum, and is familiar in nature as that of blood, fire, various flowers (as the poppy and rose) and ripe fruits (whence the frequent epithets *red as blood, fire, a rose, cherry*, etc.).

2. Of red, flame, lightning, etc. (*lit.* and *fig.*), and of objects lit up by these.

3. As a conventional (chiefly *poet.*) epithet of gold. Now only *arch.*

4. Of the sky or sun, esp. at dawn or sunset; hence of dawn, the end, etc.

5. Golden, made of gold. Now only *thieves' slang.* † *Red ones, gold coins.*

6. As an epithet of the cent (formerly made of copper), usually in negative expressions.

7. Of the cheeks (or complexion) and lips (as a natural healthy colour); hence also of persons.

8. Of the colour (of blood); Dyed with red.

9. As an epithet of the sea; Dyed with red.

10. Stained or covered with blood. Used *absol.*, *quasi-sb.*

B. With pres. pples.

II. In various special applications.

12. In combinations, forming attributive compounds, as *red-brick* (floor), *red-leather* (trunk), etc.

13. As first element in names of colours, forming compound adjs. or sbs., as *red-brown, -fallow, -gold, -orange, etc.*

14. Forming parasynthetic adjectives, as *red-cheeked, -coated, -eyed, -handed, -headed, -jellied, -nosed, etc.*

15. In general use. (See also RED-BEARDED, -CHEEKED, -COATED, -EYED, -HANDED, -HEADED, -JELLIED, -NOSED, etc.)

15 a. With *n. pples.*, as *red-clad, -dabbled, -dyed, -lined, -litten, -painted, -plowed, -written.*

b. In the distinctive names of species or varieties of birds, fishes, moths, etc. (See also RED-BACKED, -BELLIED, -BILLED, -BREASTED, etc.)

c. With *prns.*, in complemental use, as *red-branching, -burning, -flowering, -gleaming, -kissing, -ripening, -streaming, -swelling.* Also objective, as *red-molding.*

III. In special applications.

16. As a distinctive epithet of things in which the colour forms a natural or obvious mark of kind or class.

c. In names of plants. See also RED-COLE, -ROOT, etc.

17. Used more or less descriptively and distinctively with generic or generic names of animals, birds, fishes, plants, and minerals.

Supplement, p. 3873; Corrigenda, p. 4092; Spurious words, p. 4093; Books quoted, p. 4094

REDDING. 297 REDE. REDE. 298 REDE.

Redding, *sb.*
2. A kind of apple; the ruddock. *rare*.

†**Redding**, *vbl. sb.* var. READING *sb. Obs.*

Redding (reˑdiŋ), *vbl. sb.* [f. RED *v.* + -ING¹.] The action of making red.
1. The action of separating combatants, or of arranging, tidying, clearing up, etc.
2. *Comb.* a redding-blow or -stroke, a blow received by a person trying to separate combatants.
n. redding-comb, an ordinary hair-comb.

Reddish (reˑdiʃ), *a.* Also 4 redissche. [f. RED *a.* + -ISH¹.]
1. Somewhat red, red-tinted.
2. In names of animals and plants.
2. *Comb.* a. Qualifying adjs. and sbs. of colour.
b. Parasynthetic, as reddish-bellied, -coloured, -haired, -headed, and similative, as reddish-looking.
Hence **Reˑddishness**.

Reddish, obs. form of RADISH.

Reddi·tion, *Obs.* [a. F. reddition or ad. L. redditiōn-em, n. of action f. reddĕre to give back, to RENDER.]
1. Restoration of something taken or received.
2. The application of a comparison, or the clause containing the application.
3. Rendering, translation.

†**Reˑdditive**, *a.* and *sb. Obs.* [ad. L. redditīvus: see prec. and -IVE.]
A. *adj.* That answers to something already said; correspondent, correlative.
B. *sb. Gram.* A word which answers to one already used; a correlative.

Reddle (reˑd'l), *sb.* var. RUDDLE: cf. also RADDLE¹. Red ochre, ruddle.
Hence **Reˑddle** *v. trans.*, to paint or wash over with reddle.

Reˑddleman. [f. prec.] = RADDLEMAN.

Reddon, obs. pl. pa. t. READ *v.*

†**Reˑddour**, *Obs.* Forms: 4-5 reddure, -our, 4-7 reddour, -or, 5 redour. [a. ONF. reddur, redor, ridur, etc. (mod.F. raideur, roideur), f. reddir, redir (mod.F. raidir, roidir).] Severity, strictness, rigour; also, harshness, harsh treatment.

Reddour, variant of RADDOUR¹. *Obs.*

Reˑdding, var. of REDDER¹ *v.*

Reˑddman. *Sc.* [f. RED *sb.¹ +* -s- = MAN.] *Mining.* A man employed in clearing away rubbish from the workings of a mine.

Reddur·e, variants of REDDOUR³. *Sc. Obs.*

Reddure, variant of REDDOUR². *Sc. Obs.*

Reˑddy (reˑdi), *a.* Now *rare.* Also 4-6 redy. [f. rede RED *sb.* + -Y¹.] †a. Red, ruddy. *Obs.* (With names of colours.) Reddish.

Rede (rīd), *sb.¹* Now arch. or poet. and dial. Forms: 1-3 red, 3 reod, reed, (read), 3-5 red, (3-7 Sc.), reede, reide, (4-6 Sc.), 3-7 reed, (5-7 Sc.), 4-7 reid, 5 redd, 5 rede. [Common Teut.: OE. réd masc. = OFris. réd, OS. ráð (MDu., rát, rāde, Du. raad), OHG. rât (G. rath, rat), ON. ráð (Sw. råd, Da. raad)—OTeut. *rǣdo-z (? and *rǣdo-m), f. the stem of the vb. *rǣdan to READ or REDE.]
1. A counsel or advice given by one person to another.
2. Counsel or advice in general.
3. Counsel, decision, or resolve taken by one or more persons; a plan, design, or scheme devised or adopted.
4. A scheme, plan, or method for attaining some end; a principle or course of action, mode of procedure.
5. The faculty of deliberation, or the exercise of this; judgement, prudence, reason. *Obs.*
6. The act of taking counsel together, or of assembling for this purpose; a council. *Obs.*
7. Tale, narrative, story; a saying, proverb.
8. Speech. *Obs. rare⁻¹.*

Reˑddyish, obs. form of REDDISH.

Rede, *sb.² Obs. rare⁻¹.* The clew made among the reeds when fishing.

Rede (rīd), *v.* Now *arch.* or *poet.* and *dial.* Forms: 1 rǣdan, 2 -n, 2 readan, 3 raden, 4 redyn; (and *Sc.*), 1-2 réden, 3-6 (*Sc.*) read, (3-9 *v.*), -6 reed, (5, 7 *v.*), 4-5, 8 reed, 5 redyn; 8 *Sc.*) rede, 4, 6-8, 9 redde, 3 radde, 5-6 redde, 4-6 reade, 6 reade. *Pa. tense.* 1 redde, 4 red, 1 rædde, 5 read, 2-3 radde. [Common Teut.: OE. rǣdan str. vb.]
I. †1. *trans.* To have or exercise control over.
2. *trans.* To advise or counsel (a person).
II. †4. *intr.* To take counsel together or with another, to deliberate. Also of one person: To take counsel (or others. *Obs.*)
III. 6. *trans.* To advise or counsel (a person).

Rede, *sb. Obs. rare.* Also 5 reede. [Of obscure origin.] A small trench or furrow.

Rede (rīd), *v.¹ Obs.* To READ.

red, To dele faire landes: þam bi-tuixt, c1275 R. BRUNNE.

Redeˑ·dicate, *v.* Also as *pa. pple.* [RE- 5a.]
To dedicate anew.
Hence **Redeˑdicaˑtion**.

Redeem (rĭdīˑm), *v.* Forms: 5 radme, redeym, 5-6 redeme, (5 redem), 6-7 redeeme, 6-7 redeem, 7- redeem. [ad. F. rédimer or ad. L. redimĕre to buy back, f. red-, RE- + emĕre to buy.]
1. *trans.* To buy back (a thing held or claimed by another).
2. To free or release (a person) by payment; to make payment for (a thing held or claimed by another).
3. To ransom, liberate, free (a person) from bondage, captivity, or punishment; to save (one's life) by paying a ransom.
4. To rescue, save, deliver. Also *with out.*
5. To regain, recover (an immaterial thing).
6. To free from a charge or claim.
7. To make amends for; to compensate (an error, fault, etc.).
8. To pay off or clear (a debt, obligation, etc.).
9. Of persons: To make amends or atonement for, to compensate for.
10. Of qualities, actions, etc.: To make up for, compensate for, counterbalance.

Redeemˑable, *a.* Also 6 redimable. Capable of being redeemed.
Hence **Redeeˑmableness**, **Redeeˑmably** *adv.*

Redeeˑmer (rĭdīˑməᵊ). Also 6 redeemer, redemer, redimar. [f. REDEEM *v.* + -ER¹.]
1. One who redeems, in religious sense: God or Christ regarded as saving man from sin or its effects.
2. One who redeems (in other senses).

Redeeˑming, *ppl. a.* [-ING².] That redeems, in various senses.
So **Redeeˑming** *vbl. sb.*

Redeˑemless, *a. rare.* [f. as prec. + -LESS.] Incapable of being redeemed; irrecoverable; admitting of no redemption.

Redeˑfy, *v.* [RE- 5a.] To defy again.

Redeiˑfy, *v.* [RE-.] To deify again.

Redeˑify, obs. form of RE-EDIFY.

Redeˑine (rĭdaiˑn), *v.* [RE- 5a.] To define again.
So **Redefiˑnition**.

Redeˑinal, *a. Obs.* Forms: 2 REDE *sb.¹*; also redefull, f. REDE *sb.¹ +* -FUL.] Wise, prudent, full of counsel.

Redeliˑver (rīˑdĭlĭˑvəᵊ), *v.* [RE-.]
1. *trans.* To liberate, free, restore (a person).
2. To hand over, give up, restore again.

Redelivery (rīdīˈvəri). [Re–.] The action of giving back again, restitution; restoration; also, the action of setting free again, liberation.

Redeliver, v. trans. To demolish again.

Redemolish, v. [Re– 5 a. Cf. F. *redémolir* (Cotgr.).] trans. To demolish again.

Redemp-, in *Redempt*, *Redemptible*, etc.

† Redemp, v. [ad. L. *redimĕre*.] trans. To redeem.

† Redemp', ppl. a., pple. and ppl. a. Obs. rare.

† Redemp'tion (rĭdemˈʃən). Obs. rare.

Redemptible, a. [ad. L. type *redemptibilis*: see REDEMPT and -IBLE.] Redeemable.

Redemp'tine. [f. REDEMPT-OR + -INE.]

Redemption (rĭdemˈʃən). Also 4–6 -cio(u)n, -cyo(u)n, etc., 5–6 redemcion, 6–7 redemtion. [f. *redemption* (13th c. in Littré), or ad. L. *redemption-em*, n. of action f. *redimĕre* to REDEEM.]
1. Deliverance from sin and its consequences by the atonement of Jesus Christ.

Redemptional, a. [f. prec. + -AL.] Of or pertaining to redemption; redemptive.

Redemptioner. [f. REDEMPTION + -ER.]

Redemptionist. [f. as prec. + -IST.]

Redemptive (rĭdemˈptiv), a. [ad. L. type *redemptivus*: see REDEMPT and -IVE.] Tending to redeem, redeeming.

Redempt'ory, a.

Redemption (rĭdemˈʃən). Now rare. Also -sun, 5–0 -our, 6 Sc. -oun. [ad. F. *rédempteur*, OF. *redemptor*, Godef.), or L. *redemptor*.]

Redemptorist (rĭdemˈptŏrist). [ad. F. *rédemptoriste*: see prec. and -IST.]

Redemptory, a. [ad. L. type *redemptorius*: see REDEMPT and -ORY.]

Redemptress. [f. REDEMPTOR + -ESS.]

Redemptrice, Obs. form of REDEMPTRESS.

Rede-nigrate, v. [Re– 5 a.] To blacken or darken again.

† Redent'ed, ppl. a. Obs. rare⁻¹. [f. *redent* + -ED².] Formed like the teeth of a saw; dented, indented.

Redepo'sit, v. [Re– 5 a.] A depositing again.

Redep'osit, v. [Re– 5.] To deposit again.

Rede'velop, v. [Re– 5.] To develop again.

Redevelopment. [Re– 5.]

Redevote, v. [Re– 5.] To devote anew.

Redewable, variant of REDEVABLE a. Obs.

† Re-devise, v. Obs. rare⁻¹. [Re–.]

Red-eye.

Redescend (rīdĭseˈnd), v. [Re–.] To descend again.

Redescribe (rīdĭskraiˈb), v. [Re– 5 a. Cf. F. *redécrire*.] To describe again.

Red fish, red-fish.

— dense columned content —

Red-footed, a. Having red feet. Chiefly in *red-footed falcon*, the orange-legged hobby (*Falco vespertinus*).

Red-foo'ted, a. Having red feet.

Red-handed, a.

Red-head.

Red-headed, a.

Red-heart, red-heat.

Red-heeled.

Red herring.
1. A herring cured in this way.

Red horse, red-horse. U.S.

Redintegrate (redinˈtĕgrĕt), a. [ad. L. *redintegrāt-us*, pa. pple. of *redintegrāre*: see REDINTEGRATE v.] Restored to a perfect state.

Redintegrate (redinˈtĕgrĕt), v. [f. ppl. stem of L. *redintegrāre* to make whole again, restore, renew, f. RED- + *integrāre* to INTEGRATE.]
1. trans. To restore to a state of wholeness, completeness or unity; to renew, re-establish, in a united or perfect state.

Redly, **Redmain**, **Redness**, **Redolent**, etc.

b. Const. *to* (a person) *into* (a state). *rare.*

+2. To re-establish (a person) *in* a place. Also *refl.*, *Obs. rare.*

b. To re-establish (a person) *in* (+*into*) a position, condition, etc.

b. To become reunited again.

Hence **Redintegrated** *ppl. a.*

Redintegration. [ad. L. *redintegrātiōn-em.*]

1. Restoration, renewal.

+b. *Chem.* The restoration of any body or matter to its former state.

2. *spec.* as *Chem.*

Redintegrator. *rare⁻¹.* [f. as prec. + -IVE.] Tending to redintegrate.

Redintegrator. *rare⁻¹.* That which redintegrates.

Redip, *v.* [RE- 5 a.] To dip again ; *spec.* to rebaptize. Hence **Redipped** *ppl. a.*

Rediract, *v.* [RE- 5 a.] *U.S. Law.*

Rediscern, *v.* [RE- 5 a.] *trans.* To discern anew or in a new direction.

b. *intr.*

Rediscount, *v.* [RE- 5 a.] *trans.* To discount again.

Rediscover, *v.* [RE- 5 a.] *trans.* To discover again.

Rediscovery. [RE- 5 a.] The act of rediscovering ; a renewed discovery.

Redisburse, *v.* [RE- 5 a.] *trans.* To pay back again. So **Redisbursement.**

Redischarge, *v.* [RE- 5 a.] *trans.* To discharge or disburden again.

Redispatch, *v.* [RE- 5 a.] *trans.* To dispatch again.

Redisperse, *v.* [RE- 5 a.] *trans.* To disperse again.

Redispose, *v.* [RE- 5 a.] *trans.* To dispose again. Also with *of.*

Redistill, *v.* [RE- 5 a.] *trans.* To distil again.

Redistillation. [RE- 5 a.] The action of redistilling ; renewed distillation.

Redistribute, *v.* [RE- 5 a.] *trans.* To distribute anew.

Redistribution. [RE- 5 a.] A fresh distribution, esp. of Parliamentary seats.

Redistributive, *a.* [RE- 5 a.] Of or belonging to redistribution of seats.

So **Redistributory** *a.*

Redistrict, *v.* *U.S.* [RE- 5 a., prob. after RE- 5 f.] *trans.* To divide or apportion anew into districts.

Redition. [ad. L. *reditiōn-em.*] The action of going or coming back ; return.

Redive, *v.* [RE- 5 a.] *intr.* To dive again.

Redivivus, *a.* [L.] Living red again.

Redivorce, *v.* [RE- 5 a.] *trans.* To restore to life. So **Redivived** *ppl. a.*

Red land. [RED sb. + LAND.]

Red lead, red-lead. [See LEAD sb. 2.] An oxide of lead, largely used as a pigment.

Red-legged, *a.* Having red legs.

Red letter.

1. (Chiefly *pl.*) A letter made with red ink, or with some red pigment, esp. as used in ecclesiastical calendars to indicate saints' days and church festivals.

2. *attrib.*, as *red-letter almanac, mark, name* ; *red-letter day* a saint's day or other festival indicated in the calendar by red letters.

Redling. variant of REDLING.

+Redling, *sb.* *rare⁻¹.* — REDSHANK 2.

+Redly, *v.* *rare.* [app. f. RED a. + -LY.] *trans.* & *intr.* To make red.

Redly, *adv.*¹ [f. RED a. + -LY ².] In a red manner, with a red appearance or colour.

+Redly, *adv.*² [var. of RADLY, RIDDLE.]

+Redlys. *Obs.* [repr. OE. *rēdlīce.*]

Red-making *sb.* Also **red-man.**

+1. *Alchemy.* Red sulphide of mercury.

2. [See RED d. 5 c.] A (or *the*) North American Indian ; a redskin.

Redly, *v.* Also red-do.

Redmond, *sb.* *rare⁻¹.*

Red-mouth *sb.* [RED sb. + MOUTH.]

Rednass, *-ness.* *Sc.* var. of REDNESS.

Red-necked, *a.* Having a red neck ; used *spec.* in names of birds, etc.

Redness (re'dnes). [f. RED a. + -NESS.] The state or quality of being red ; red colour.

Red-nose.

1. *a. attrib.* Red-nosed, as a red nose, *type.*

b. *sb.*

Red-nosed, *a.* Having a red nose. Also *transf.* in names of birds, etc.

Redo, *v.* [RE- 5 a.] Also **redo.**

1. To do over again or afresh.

2. To recreate (a room).

+Redoing, *ppl. a.* [f. L. *redol-ēre* (see prec.) + -ING ².] Redolent.

Red ochre. A variety of OCHRE, commonly red in colour.

Redolence. [a. OF. *redolence* (Godef.), f. *redolent-* : see next.] Sweet smell, fragrance, perfume.

Redolency. [f. next + -ENCY.]

Redolent (re'dŏlent), *a.* [a. OF. *redolent*, *redolant-em*, pr. pple. of *redolēre*, f. *red-* + *olēre* to emit a smell. Cf. ODENT a.]

1. Having or diffusing a pleasant odour ; sweet-smelling, fragrant, odorous. Now *rare.*

b. *fig.*

2. Smelling, stench. *Obs. rare⁻¹.*

3. *transf.* and *fig.* (Const. *of, with.*) Strongly suggestive or reminiscent of, or impregnated with, some quality, etc.

Redolently, *adv.* In a redolent manner.

+Redonate, *v.* *rare.* [RE- 5 a. + DONATE.] To give back.

+Redonation. *Obs. rare⁻¹.* [See prec. and -ATION.] The action of giving back.

Redonda, *sb.*

Redonde, obs. form of REDOUND.

Redondilla (redŏndi'lja). [Sp., dim. f. *redonda*, fem. of *redondo* round.] In Spanish poetry, a stanza of riming verse.

Re-doom, *v.* [RE- 5 a.] To doom again.

Redor, variant of REDOVER.

Redorne, Redos, variants of REREDOS.

Redoub(e, redoubble, vars. of REDOUBLE.

Redouble (rĭdɒ'b'l), *v.* Also 6–7 *redub*(*b*)*le.*

1. *trans.* To double (a thing) ; to make twice as great.

2. *intr.* To be doubled ; to become twice as great or as much. Also to become doubly strong in some respect.

+3. To repeat. *Obs.*

Redoubled, *ppl. a.* [f. prec. + -ED ¹.]

Redoublement (6th *redoublement*).

Redoubling, *ppl. a.* [f. as prec. + -ING ².] Doubling, repeating ; re-echoing, resounding.

Redoubt (rĭdɒut), *sb.* [a. F. *redoute*, ad. med.L. *reducta*, *redotta*, etc.]

1. *Fortif.* An outwork or fieldwork, usually of a square or polygonal shape, and with little or no means of flanking defence.

b.

2. *Fortif.*

3. A public amusement-hall in Germany used for gambling and entertainments ; also *transf.* an assembly held there, esp. a masked ball.

+Redoubt, *v.¹* *Obs.* [a. OF. *redouter*, *redoubter*, f. *red-* + *douter* to DOUBT.]

1. *trans.* To fear, dread ; to stand in awe or apprehension of (a person, etc.).

Redoubtable, *a.* [a. OF. *redoutable*, *-doubtable*, f. *redouter* : see REDOUBT *v.¹*]

1. To be feared or dreaded ; formidable.

REDOUBTABLENESS

Redoubtable (rĭdout'ăb'l), *ppl. a.*

Redoubtably, *adv.*

Redound, *v.*

Redound, *sb.*

Redowa (rĕd'owă), *sb.*

Redpoll, -pole.

Redpoll, -polled.

Redpepper.

Redsear, Redshank.

Redraw, *v.*

Redrawer; Redrawing

Redress (rĭdres'), *v.*

Redress (rĭdres'), *sb.*

Redressable

Redresser

Redressing (rĭdres'ing), *vbl. sb.*

Redressive, *a.*

Redressless, *a.*

Redressment

Redressor, Redresser

Re-drill, *v.*

Redrive, *v.*

Redross, *obs.*

Red-rot

Red-rumped, *a.*

Redruthite (rĕd'ruthəit), *sb.*

Red-sanders.

Red-sear, *v.*

Red-shank's, redshank.

Red-shank's-end

Redship.

Redshire, -share, *a.*

Red-short, *a.*

Red-shortness

Red-shouldered, *a.*

Red-spider.

Red-spotted, *a.*

Redstart (rĕd'stārt), *sb.*

Red-streak. ... **Red-tape, red tag.** ... **Red-tapish** ... **Red-tapism.** ... **Red-tapist.** ... **Red-throated.** ... **Red-top.** ... **Reduce** ... **Redubble** ... **Rednoe** ...

Reduce, v. ...

Reduceable ... **Reducement** ... **Reducend** ... **Reducent** ... **Reducer** ... **Reducibility** ... **Reducible** ...

Reducibleness. … Every thought…unmistakable…to his glorious attributes, reducible to this first kind of evil thoughts.

Reducing, *ppl. a.* [f. as prec. + -ING 2.] That reduces, in senses of the vb.

Reduct, *sb. Obs.* [f. L. reduct-us, pa. pple. of reducere.]

Reduct, *v. Obs.* [f. ppl. stem of L. reducere.]

Reducibility. [ad. F. réductibilité, or f. as prec. + -IBLE, -ITY.] Reducibility (Ogilvie 1882).

Reduction. (rĭdɒ̈k·ʃən). Also 5–6 reduccion, -cyon. [a. F. réduction, or ad. L. reductiōn-em.]

Reductive (rĭdɒ̈k·tiv), *a.* and *sb.* Now rare.

Reduct, *sb.* …

Redundance (rĭdɒ̈ndăns). [See prec. and next.] The state or quality of being redundant; superabundance, superfluity.

Redundancy. The state or quality of being redundant.

Reduction-compasses, *pl.* …

Reductionist, … who favours reduction (in the number of licensed houses).

Redundantly, *adv.* In a redundant manner.

Redundate. *Obs.* [f. L. redundāt-, ppl. stem of redundāre to REDOUND.] Overflow.

Redundate, *v. Obs. rare*–[f. as prec.]

Reduplicate (rĭdiū·plĭkĕt), *a.* and *sb.* [ad. late L. reduplicāt-us: see REDUPLICATE *v.*]

Reduplicate (rĭdiū·plĭkeit), *v.* [f. late L. reduplicāt-, ppl. stem of reduplicāre.]

Reduplicating, *ppl. a.* [f. as prec. + -ING 2.]

Reduplication (rĭdiūplĭkei·ʃən). [ad. late L. reduplicātiōn-em: see REDUPLICATE *v.* and -ATION, and cf. F. réduplication (1520).]

Reduplicative (rĭdiū·plĭkātiv), *a.* and *sb.* [ad. late L. reduplicātiv-us: see REDUPLICATE *v.* + -IVE.]

Reduplicatively, *adv.* (Cf. A. 1 above.)

Reduplicatory, *a. rare*–[f. as REDUPLICATE *v.* + -ORY.] Repetitional.

Redux (rī·dɒks), *a. Path.* [L., f. *redūcĕre* to bring back, REDUCE.] Of crepitation or other physical signs: Indicating the return of an organ to a healthy state.

Ree, *sb.¹* A stream, channel, river.

Red weed, red-weed. An American plant or plants.

Red wheat. A variety of the common wheat, of a reddish colour.

Red ware¹. A coarse kind of unglazed pottery.

Red ware². A kind of seaweed, *Laminaria digitata*; common tangle.

Redwing, red-wing. A common variety of thrush (*Turdus iliacus*).

Red ware³. *Sc.* [See WARE *sb.*] A kind of seaweed.

Red-vented: see RED *a.* 14 *b.*

Redwood, -wud, *a. Sc.* [RED *a.* + WOOD *a.*] Mad, furious, distracted.

Red-wood. Wood of a red colour, obtained from various different trees, chiefly of tropical regions.

Red-winged, *a.* Having red wings.

Reduvid (re·diūvĭd), *a.* and *sb.* Belonging to or of the family *Reduviidae*, the typical genus of which is *Reduvius.*

Redwater. A disease in cattle and sheep.

Ree (rī), *sb.*[2] [Variant of REEVE *sb.*[2] It is not clear which is the more original form.] The female of the ruff.

Ree, obs. form of READ, REE *sb.*

Ree (rī), *sb.*[4] [Of obscure origin: the form *reeve* also occurs locally.]
1. A walled enclosure for sheep, cattle, or swine.
2. A yard where coal is stored for sale.

Ree (rī), *a.* & *sb.*[5] [Of unknown origin.] Excited, esp. with drink; elevated; crazy, delirious.

Ree (rī), *sb.*[6] & *v.* [Of obscure origin: the various forms indicate a ME. *rēʒe(n*), but their relationship to the synonymous REEVE *sb.*[2] and *rew* or *rue* (Devonshire) is not clear.]
1. *trans.* To clean or sift (winnowed grain, peas, etc.).

Ree, obs. f. REEN, RHINE.
¶ **Reebok** (rē′bŏk). Also 8-book, 9 rheebok, rhebuck.

Re-echo, *v.* [f. RE- + ECHO *v.*]
1. *intr.* To echo (again), resound.

Reechy (rī′tʃi), *a.* Obs. exc. *dial.* Also 6 rechy, 6 reekie. [f. *reech* REEK *sb.*[1] & *v.*[1]] Smoky; squalid, dirty; rancid.

Reed (rīd), *sb.*[1] Forms: 1 hréod, (hréad, 2-5 reod, (3 rode, reode), 3-6 rede, (4 ride, rieþe), 4-5 red, (4 reud, reheed), 4-7 reede, 6- reed.

Reedbird.
1. A bird which frequents reeds, *rare*[−1].
2. *spec. n. A.* A North American singing-bird, *Dolichonyx oryzivorus*; the bobolink or ricebunting. Also *attrib.*

Reed-bunting. [REED *sb.*[1]] The reedsparrow (*Emberiza schœniclus*).

Reed, obs. f. READ, RED, REDE, REDE *sb.*[1] & *v.*
Reeded (rī′dĕd), *ppl. a.* [f. REED *sb.*[1]]
1. Overgrown with reeds.

Reeder (rī′dar). Also 5 reede, 6 reider. [f. REED *sb.*[1] + -ER[1].]
1. One who thatches with reeds; a thatcher.

Reed-grass.
1. A name given to various reed-like grasses.

Re-edify (rī-e′difai), *v.* [f. RE- a.[1]]
1. *trans.* To rebuild (a house, or other building, a wall, city, street, etc.).

Reedify, *rare*, var. of RE-EDIFY.

Re-edit, *v.* To edit again.

Re-educate, *v.* [RE- 5 a.] *trans.* To educate again.

Re-edition, *v.* A second edition; a re-editing.

Reed-mace. [REED *sb.*[1]] *n. A.* An aquatic plant, *Typha latifolia*, common on the margins of ponds and lakes, having long eminferous leaves and tall stems, the latter terminated by dense cylindrical spikes of small brownish flowers. Also called *cat's-tail* or *cat's-tail*, and *bulrush.*

Reed-pipe. [REED *sb.*[1]]
1. An obs. reed-pen. Obs. *rare*[−1].

Reed-sparrow.
1. A common British bird, *Emberiza schœniclus*, frequenting reedy places. Also called *Reed-bunting*, n. The sedge-warbler.

Reedling (rī′dliŋ).

Reedy (rī′di), *a.* Also 4 reeddy, 6 redy. [REED *sb.*[1] + -Y[1].]
1. Abounding with, full of, reeds; characterized by the presence of reeds.

Reef, *sb.*[1] Forms: 6 riffe, 6-8 reef, reefe, reif, (6-9 rif), rife. [ME. *riff*, *rif*; cf. ON. *rif*, Sw. *ref*, Da. *rev*.]
1. A narrow ridge or chain of rocks, shingle, or sand, lying at or near the surface of the water.

Reef, *sb.*[2] Forms: 6 riffe, 6-8 riff, 8- reef. [− Du. *rif* (in Kilian also *rift*), MLG. *rif*, *ref*, Sw. *ref*, Now *rev*, Da. *ref.*]
1. A horizontal portion of a sail.

Reef

Reefer [f. REEF sb.]

Re-efformation. Obs. rare

Reefing

Reefy

Reeing, rying

Reefs, var. RIFF, midriff.

Reefed

Reek [OE. réc]

Reeks, variant of REAKS sb.

Reek-staffold, ?stavail: see RICK sb.

Reeky

Reel [OE. hréol]

Reel

Reel

Reelable

Reel-bird.

Re-elect

Re-election. [RE- 5 a.]

Reeled

Reeler (rī·ləɹ). [f. REEL v.² + -ER¹.]

1. One who reels or winds yarn, cord, etc., upon a reel; also, one who employs such workers.

1598 FLORIO, *Innaspatore*, a reeler or winder of yarne. 1611 COTGR. s.v. *Garde*, *Faire la garde*, to make fast; (a phrase vsed by reelers, or winders of yarne). 1776–7 [see REELED *ppl. a.*]. 1825 J. NICHOLSON *Operat. Mechanic* 395 The slubs which may have been left in the silk by the negligence of the foreign reeler. 1844 G. DODD *Textile Manuf.* vi. 175 When the winder or reeler has purchased the cocoons [etc.]. 1891 *Textile Industries* 12 Dec. 61/1 However careless the reeler may be, the reel is stopped instantly.

b. (See quot.)

1893 L. KELLNER *Soldiers at Sea* 50 Told off as Reelers, to haul in the reel, which tests the ship's rate of progress.

c. The grasshopper-warbler, *Locustella nævia*.

1871–4 NEWTON *Yarrell's Brit. Birds* I. 385 In the more marshy parts of England .. this bird has long been known as the 'Reeler'—from the resemblance of its song to the noise of the reel used.. by the hand-spinners of wool.

d. *Cant* (after *peeler*). A policeman.

1879 *Macm. Mag.* Oct. 502/1 A reeler came to the cell and cross-kiddled (questioned) me.

† 2. An instrument for reeling. *Obs. rare*⁻¹.

1598 FLORIO, *Indenenatoio*, a reeler or reeling sticke. 1629 MASSINGER *Picture* v. i, *Ubaldo*. I have not spittle enough to wet my fingers When I draw my flax from my distaff. *Ricardo*. Nor I, strength To raise my hand to the top of my reeler.

Re-e·levate, *v.* [RE- 5 a.] To elevate again.

a 1834 COLERIDGE cited by WORCESTER (1846). 1873 J. GEIKIE *Gt. Ice Age* xxii. 290 Then, finally, the land was re-elevated to its present level. 1895 *Minutes 9th Nat. Counc. Congreg. Ch.* (U.S.) 242 To re-elevate the standard of scholarship which has been so unfortunately.. lowered.

So **Re-eleva·tion.** (Chiefly *Geol.*)

1817 J. SCOTT *Paris Revis.* (ed. 4) 395 Resting its re-elevation on the foundation of popular choice. 1868 LYELL *Princ. Geol.* II. xxxi. (ed. 10) II. 187 It seems impossible to explain the position of this buried hut, without imagining, first a subsidence..then a re-elevation. 1876 PAGE *Adv. Text-bk. Geol.* xiv. 258 The frequent subsidences and re-elevations.

Reel foot. *Sc.* [? f. REEL *sb.*¹] A club-foot. So **Reel-footed** *a.*

1867 H. SCOTT *Fasti Eccl. Scotic.* II. 586 A reel foot marred his personal appearance. 1887 SERVICE *Dr. Duguid* i. xxiii. 155 James being reel-fitted. 1908 *Brit. Med. Jrnl.* 19 July 209 A child .. is 'reel-footed' if there is a club-foot.

Re-eligibi·lity. [f. next + -ITY.] Eligibility for re-election to the same office.

1787 HAMILTON *Federalist* No. 72 With a positive duration [of the presidency]..I connect the circumstance of re-eligibility. 1788 JEFFERSON *Let.* 7 Feb., There is another strong feature in the new constitution, which I..strongly dislike. That is, the perpetual re-eligibility of the President. 1888 BRYCE *Amer. Commw.* II. xli. II. 103 The governor..is elected directly, not..by a college of electors...Some States limit his re-eligibility.

Re-e·ligible, *a.* [RE- 5 a.] Capable of being re-elected to the same office.

1802 *Ann. Reg.* 644 The president is to exercise his functions for ten years, and to be indefinitely reeligible. 1843 *Penny Cycl.* XXVI. 26/2 The person so appointed to vacate is not re-eligible for the ensuing year. 1884 *Law Times* 8 Mar. 3 The Examiners above-named are re-eligible.

Reeling (rī·liŋ), *vbl. sb.*¹ [f. REEL *v.*¹ + -ING¹.] The action of staggering, etc.

1375 BARBOUR *Bruce* XIII. 265 The king Robert be thair relyng Saw thai war neir discomfyting. 1495 *Trevisa's Barth. De P. R.* (W. de W.) v. xx. 126 The passyons of the teeth ben dyuers..brekynge, and brusynge.., relynge and wag[ging] and fallynge. a 1500 *Peebles to Play* ii, For reiling thair micht na man rest, For garray and for glew. a 1591 H. SMITH *Six Serm.* (1594) 89 As if he should say, neither the winds blowing..nor the ships reeling..should..waken him from his sleepe. 1607–12 BACON *Ess., Counsel* (Arb.) 312 They will..be full of inconstancye,..like the reeling of a drunken Man. 1664 H. MORE *Myst. Iniq.* 329 Singing and dancing and drinking and reeling were usual concomitants of all the Pagan Holy-days. 1736 E. ERSKINE *Serm.* Wks. 1871 II. 406 The Avenger of thy blood will take care of thee in public reelings. 1781 COWPER *Conversat.* 862 Though such continual zigzags in a book, Such drunken reelings, have an awkward look. 1899 *Allbutt's Syst. Med.* VII. 69 [A gait] in which there is unsteadiness, titubation, and reeling like a drunken man.

Comb. 1610 SHAKS. *Temp.* v. i. 279 Trinculo is reeling ripe: where should they Finde this grand Liquor that hath gilded 'em? 1706 E. WARD *Wooden World Diss.* (1708) 100 When he's reeling drunk ashore, he takes it for granted to be a Storm abroad.

Reeling (rī·liŋ), *vbl. sb.*² [f. REEL *v.*² + -ING¹.]

1. The action of winding on a reel.

1589 RIDER *Bibl. Schol.*, A Reeling, *alabratio*. 1603 DEKKER *Grissil* v. i, Janiculo, leave your fish-catching, and you your reeling. 1853 *Public Gen. Acts* 179 Abuses ..in the Reeling of the Yarns. 1727–41 CHAMBERS *Cycl.* s.v. *Reel*, The reel used..in the reeling or winding of silks. 1789 *Trans. Soc. Arts* VII. 143 It was..afterwards reeled off from those bobbins, and in the reeling passed through warm water. 1803 W. TAYLOR in *Ann. Rev.* I. 432 The purchases [of silk] are made about the end of August when the reelings terminate. 1884 MCLAREN *Spinning* (ed. 2) 235 The processes of twisting, reeling, and scouring.

b. *attrib.* and *Comb.*, as *reeling apparatus, arrangement, establishment, machine, stick*.

1598 FLORIO, *Indenenatoio*, a reeler or reeling sticke. 1835 URE *Philos. Manuf.* 265 The reeling apparatus used in France. 1853 — *Dict. Arts* (ed. 4) II. 616 The cocoons are prepared at the reeling establishment into raw silk. *Ibid.*, The reeling machines in the Tyrol. 1887 *Encycl. Brit.* XXII. 61/2 A sectional view of the reeling apparatus and arrangements..is shown in fig. 12.

2. The production of a humming sound.

1747 R. MAXWELL *Bee-Master* (1750) 35 This reeling is occasioned, by a great many of the Bees flying, and making a confused Motion and Noise in the..Hive. 1899 *Longm. Mag.* Dec. 152 It was more sustained than the longest reeling of the grasshopper warbler that I have heard.

Reeling (rī·liŋ), *ppl. a.* [f. REEL *v.*¹ + -ING².]

1. That reels, in senses of the vb.

1577 HOLINSHED *Chron.* I. 69/1 Honorius, perceiuing the reeling state of the empire, determined foorthwith to recouer it. 1602 MARSTON *Ant. & Mel.* I. Wks. 1856 I. 17 With that he totterd from the reeling decke, And downe he sunke. 1649 JER. TAYLOR *Gt. Exemp.* III. Ad § 16. 177 With troubled spirits and a reeling faith. 1697 DRYDEN *Virg. Past.* v. 46 Daphnis did Rites to Bacchus first ordain; And holy Revels for his reeling Train. 1768 ROSS *Helenore* I. 55 The man..in his fury, an' in his reeling eyn, Thinks that the ane he wanted she had been. 1781 COWPER *Expost.* 306 War lays a burden on the reeling state. 1849 LONGF. *Building the Ship* 242 The stress and the strain Of the wind and the reeling main.

2. Characterized by reeling; causing to reel.

1614 MARKHAM *Cheap Husb.* IV. x. (1668) 99 If your Goats be troubled with the Staggers or Reeling Evil. 1875 MANNING *Mission H. Ghost* ii. 54 That sort of gross reeling intoxication by which men..shame themselves in the streets. 1895 *Westm. Gaz.* 27 Feb. 1/1 The Liberal Party suffered a reeling blow yesterday.

Hence **Ree·lingly** *adv.*

1621 LADY M. WROTH *Urania* 481 Suddenly, and reelingly he ran with his last fury vpon him. 1657 J. SERGEANT *Schism Dispach't* 62 Is this a sober discourse, which falls reelingly to the ground of it self, when none pushes it?

† **Reel-pot.** *Obs. rare*⁻¹. [f. REEL *v.*¹] One who makes the (drinking) pot go round.

1604 T. M. *Black Bk.* in *Middleton's Wks.* (Bullen) VIII. 28 There I heard how many perjurds [were] in France, and how many reel-pots in Germany.

‖ **Reem** (rīm). [a. Heb. ראם *rᵉēm* (also רים *rēym* in Job xxxix. 9–10), rendered in the Vulgate by *rhinoceros* and *unicornis*, and by Wyclif and later Eng. versions, *unicorn*.] The Hebrew name of an animal mentioned in the Old Testament, now identified with the wild ox.

1719 YOUNG *Par. Job* Wks. 1757 I. 215 Will the tall Reem, which knows no Lord but Me, Low at the crib, and ask an alms of thee? [1845 KITTO *Cycl. Bibl. Lit.* s.v., From the fact that the reêm is classed in scripture with bulls or bullocks..it has been concluded that he was of the bovine species, and probably the buffalo or wild ox. 1886 W. HOUGHTON in *Academy* 24 Apr. 292 The identification of the Hebrew *reēm* with the wild ox (*Bos primigenius*) is one of the most certain of all Bible animal names.]

Reem, obs. f. REALM, REAM; var. REME *v.*, to cry, shout; obs. f. RIME, hoarfrost.

Re-embark (rī,embā·ɹk), *v.* Also 7–8 reim-. [RE- 5 a. Cf. F. *rembarquer* (1549), It. *rimbarcare* (Florio), Sp. *reembarcar*.]

1. *trans.* To put (a person or thing) on board ship again. Also † const. *into*.

1611 COTGR., *Rembarquer*, to reimbarke, to put into a ship againe. 1654 H. L'ESTRANGE *Chas. I* (1655) 18 The Admirall re-imbarques all and..plies for the Southward Cape. 1687 LOVELL tr. *Thevenot's Trav.* II. 171 Goods..which..he was necessitated to reimbark. 1702 *Lond. Gaz.* No. 3850/3 They were reimbarking the Troops on board the Ships. 1758 *Ann. Reg.* I. 101/1 They were..hoisted into the ship, and..re-imbarked into the boats. 1836 MACGILLIVRAY tr. *Humboldt's Trav.* xviii. 230 The boat having been got up, they re-embarked their instruments and provisions.

refl. 1622 CAPT. SMITH *Wks.* I. 257 Reimbarking myselfe in a Bark of 60 Tuns.

fig. 1647 WARD *Simp. Cobler* (1843) 80 It may re-imbarque themselves and you all into a deadly relapse of scorne and calamity.

2. *intr.* To go on board ship again. Also const. *in*.

1585 T. WASHINGTON tr. *Nicholay's Voy.* II. v. 35 We had made our accompt to reimbarke and depart. 1747 CARTE *Hist. Eng.* I. 288 The Danes still re-imbarking when they found opposition in any place, and landing in some other. 1777 ROBERTSON *Hist. Amer.* II. v. 23 He ..issued orders that the army should be in readiness next day to reimbark for Cuba. 1856 KANE *Arct. Expl.* II. xxviii. 279, I called my officers together..and prepared to re-embark. 1878 GLADSTONE *Prim. Homer* xi. 131 After re-embarking, he exasperates the monster with his pungent addresses.

fig. a 1711 KEN *Edmund* Poet. Wks. 1721 II. 159 His Soul, which while he slept at Anchor lay, Began to reimbark. 1812 *Examiner* 24 Aug. 542/2 In such a cause his very selfishness is a security for his not re-embarking.

transf. 1751 SMOLLETT *Per. Pic.* ci, He re-embarked in his hackney-coach.

Hence **Re-emba·rking** *vbl. sb.*

1611 FLORIO, *Rimbarcamento*, a re-imbarking. 1790 BEATSON *Nav. & Mil. Mem.* I. 321 Brigadiers Graham and O'Farrel..agreed to the reimbarking of the troops.

Re-embarka·tion. Also 8 reim-. [RE- 5 a.] The action of re-embarking.

1726 *Lond. Gaz.* No. 5470/2 They knew nothing of the Reimbarkation. 1757 SMOLLETT *Hist. Eng.* xviii. § 5 After the re-embarkation of the troops. 1790 BEATSON *Nav. & Mil. Mem.* I. 323 They unanimously declared themselves for the reimbarkation. 1847 GROTE *Greece* II. xxxvi. IV. 471 They repulsed the Athenians from the sea-shore and secured a safe re-embarkation.

So **Re-emba·rkment.** [Cf. F. *rembarquement*.]

1758 *Ann. Reg.* I. 66/1 The smaller [squadron]..was designed..to favour the landing and reimbarkment.

Re-emba·ttle, *v.* In 7 reim-. [RE- 5 a.] *trans.* To draw up again in battle array.

1667 MILTON *P. L.* VI. 794 They..at the sight Took envie, and aspiring to his highth, Stood reimbattell'd fierce.

Re-embe·llish, *v.* Also 7 re-im-. [RE- 5 a.] *trans.* To embellish anew. Hence **Re-embe·llishing** *vbl. sb.*

1611 FLORIO, *Rimbellire*, to re-imbellish. *Ibid.*, *Rabbellimento*, a rebeautifying, a re-embellishing. 1655 tr. *Com. Hist. Francion* II. 43 Ceruse and Vermillion were not capable to re-imbellish my face.

Re-embo·dy, *v.* Also 7, 9 reim-. [RE- 5 a.] To embody again. a. *trans.*

1802 JAMES *Milit. Dict.* s.v., The militia is disbanded, and partially reimbodied for 28 days in every year during peace. 1862 MERIVALE *Rom. Emp.* lvii. (1865) VII. 121 It became necessary to re-embody the prætorian and the urban guards. 1873 in B. Stewart *Conserv. Force* vii. 173, I propose..now to reëmbody my views in a more popular form.

† b. *intr.* for *refl.* (See EMBODY 5 b.) *Obs.*

a 1691 BOYLE (J.), Quicksilver broken into little globes, the parts brought to touch immediately reimbody.

Re-embo·som, *v.* Also 7 reim-. [RE- 5 a.] *trans.* To embosom again.

1641 HEYLIN *Hist. Episc.* II. (1657) 369 Some..had been Reconciled and reimbosomed with the Church. 1656 — *Surv. France* 56 [Henry IV. of France] once more re-embosom'd himself into the Roman Synagogue. 1878 BROWNING *La Saisiaz* 129 Treasure oft was disembosomed...Disembosomed, re-embosomed.

Re-embra·ce, *v.* Also 7 re-im-, reim-. [RE- 5 a. Cf. F. *rembrasser*, † *rembracier*.] *trans.* and *intr.* To embrace again, in *lit.* and *fig.* senses.

1611 FLORIO, *Rimbracciare*, to imbrace againe, to re-imbrace. 1633 PRYNNE *1st Pt. Histrio-m.* 57 Why should you re-embrace..the things, which you haue thus abiured? 1655 tr. *Com. Hist. Francion* IX. 4 His Daughter and her Sweetheart coming to re-imbrace each other. a 1711 KEN *Preparatives* Poet. Wks. 1721 IV. 48 When their Souls they re-embrace. 1742 YOUNG *Nt. Th.* v. 1044 He takes his Leave, To re-embrace in Extasies, at Eve. 1855 BROWNING *In a Year* i, Bitterly we re-embrace, Single still. 1858 CARLYLE *Fredk. Gt.* VIII. iii. (1872) III. 13 His Majesty, who wept like a paternal bear, on reëmbracing Wilhelmina.

So **Re-embra·ce** *sb.*, a renewed embrace; **Re-embra·cement.**

1611 FLORIO, *Rabbracciamenti*, re-imbracements. 1868 BROWNING *Ring & Bk.* XI. 2316 If, fighting quietly, the jaws enjoy One re-embrace in mid back-bone.

Re-embroi·l, *v.* [RE- 5 a.] To embroil again.

1718 BLACKMORE *Alfred* x. (1723) 363 Lest this audacious Tribe..Disturb the Throne and re-embroil the State.

Re-emburse, -ment, obs. ff. REIMBURSE, -MENT.

Reeme, obs. f. REALM, REAM *sb.*³, RIME.

Re-emerge, *v.* [RE- 5 a.] To emerge again.

1775 CHANDLER *Trav. Asia M.* (1825) I. 94 It will gradually re-emerge, and become dry and green as before. 1837 CARLYLE *Fr. Rev.* III. II. iii, A question emerges,..is put off, submerged; but always reemerges bigger than before. 1879 M. ARNOLD *Mixed Ess., Falkland* 227 But is it meant, ..that after all, political liberty re-emerged in England..?

So **Re-eme·rgence; Re-eme·rgent** *a.*; **Re-eme·rsion.**

1801 COLERIDGE *Lett.* (1895) 365 Flashes of lightning, that seemed almost to alternate with the flash-like re-emersions of the waning moon. 1837 CARLYLE *Fr. Rev.* III. II. iii, By its frequent reemergence and by its rapid enlargement of bulk,..this question [etc.]. 1865 GEIKIE *Scen. & Geol. Scotl.* ix. 248 Since its first re-emergence it has doubtless been often sunk and raised anew. 1895 *Forum* (N. Y.) Apr. 254 Cases of fallen and still fitfully re-emergent nobility.

Reeming (rī·miŋ), *vbl. sb.* Also reaming. [See REAM *v.*³] (See quot. 1846.) Also *Comb.*, as *reeming-beetle, -iron*.

1750 BLANCKLEY *Nav. Expos.* 130 *Reeming Irons*, are used by the Caulkers for opening the Seams of the Planks of Ships on the Stocks before caulked. 1846 A. YOUNG *Naut. Dict.*, *Reeming*, in shipbuilding, opening the seams of the planks with iron wedges, called reeming-irons, in order that the oakum used in caulking may be more readily admitted. 1867 SMYTH *Sailor's Word-bk.* 566 *Reeming-Beetle*, a caulker's largest mallet. 1875 KNIGHT *Dict. Mech.* 1905/2 The tool is a reeming-iron struck by a reeming-beetle.

Re-emi·ssion. [RE- 5 a: cf. next.] A second or subsequent emission; a re-issue.

1740 W. DOUGLASS *Disc. Curr. Brit. Plant. Amer.* 10 In the following Years no more new Emissions, but some Re-emissions of the remainder. 1801 YOUNG in *Phil. Trans.* XCII. 46 Its remaining many months as if in a latent state, and its subsequent re-emission by the action of heat.

Re-emi·t, *v.* [RE- 5 a.] *trans.* To emit again; esp. *U. S.*, to reissue (bills, bank-notes, etc.). Hence **Re-emi·tting** *vbl. sb.* (in quot. *attrib.*).

1740 W. DOUGLASS *Disc. Curr. Brit. Plant. Amer.* 10 The Province..have since A. 1702 emitted and re-emitted Bills of public Credit. *Ibid.* 17 The three Upper Counties.. emitted 30,000 *l.* which have generally been continued out by re-emitting Acts from Time to Time. 1759 FRANKLIN *Ess.* Wks. 1840 III. 203 The trustees of the loan office might reëmit the same sums. 1884 *American* VIII. 311 The notes are not held, when redeemed, but re-emitted.

Re-employ·, *v.* [RE- 5 a.] *trans.* To employ again; to take back into employment. So **Re-employ·ment.**

1611 COTGR., *Remployer*, to reimploy. 1883 STEVENSON *Silverado Sq.* 147 Begging me to re-employ him again. 1893 *Columbus* (Ohio) *Disp.* 7 Aug., It is to be hoped that relief will come, in the way of re-employment, before cold weather sets in.

Reen (rīn). Also reene, rheen. A variant (and more phonetic) spelling of the south-western RHINE, a ditch.

1829 J. L. KNAPP *Jrnl. Nat.* 142 A pale blue shrew..has been seen about the margin of our reenes, and the deep marsh ditches. 1864 G. F. BERKELEY *Life & Recoll.* I. 241

The wide deep reens or ditches that intersect these marshy meadows. 1867 *Macm. Mag.* June 164 It is intersected.. by several large dykes, called in the language of the country 'rhines' or 'rheens'.

Reen, var. REAN; obs. f. REIN(DEER).

Re-ena·ble, *v.* Also 6–7 re-in-. [RE- 5 a.]

† 1. *trans.* To rehabilitate, restore. *Obs.*

1586 T. B. *La Primaud. Fr. Acad.* I. (1594) 600 The reinabling of such as before were not capable of offices or dignities. 1611 SPEED *Hist. Gt. Brit.* IX. xiv. § 7. 612 They were also forbidden..to reenable the late King against the authoritie of this Parliament. 1629 DONNE *Serm.* V. 440 When God hath thus created a new heart, that is, Re-enabled me by his Ordinance.

2. To make able again.

1633 T. ADAMS *Exp. 2 Peter* iii. 18 Thus are we re-enabled to pay him the debt of glory. 1834 *Good's Study Med.* (ed. 4) II. 616 To require..many months before the patient was re-enabled to take his station in society.

So † **Re-ena·blement.** *Obs.*

1648 W. MOUNTAGUE *Devout Ess.* I. Ep. Ded. A 4 b, The propitiating of Almighty God, towards Your reinablement to afford them all..succors.

Re-ena·ct, *v.* [RE- 5 a.]

1. *trans.* To enact (a law, etc.) again. Hence **Re-ena·cting** *vbl. sb.*

a 1676 HALE *Prim. Orig. Man.* IV. viii. (1677) 369 That Precept .. was no other than the re-enacting of that old Commandment. 1705 ARBUTHNOT *Coins*, etc. (1727) 259 The Construction of Ships was forbidden to Senators, by a law made by Claudius, Tribune of the people,..and re-enacted by the Julian Law of Concussions. 1832 BABBAGE *Econ. Manuf.* xxxiii. (1835) 363 *note*, In 1825 an attempt to re-enact some of the most objectionable was made. 1865 H. PHILLIPS *Amer. Paper Curr.* II. 38 All the regulations of the prior resolution..were herein re-enacted.

2. To act or perform again; to reproduce.

1854 J. S. C. ABBOTT *Napoleon* (1855) I. v. 89 Napoleon had no desire to see the Reign of Terror re-enacted in the cities of Italy. 1856 'STONEHENGE' *Brit. Rural Sports* 464/1 My yachting friends need never expect to see her with her present rig re-enacting the America.

So **Re-ena·ction, Re-ena·ctment.**

1803 *Hist. Europe* in *Ann. Reg.* (1804) 14/2 Lord Limerick positively asserted that the re-enactment of those bills was absolutely necessary for the tranquillity of the country. 1855 H. CLARKE *Dict.*, Reenaction. 1860 FORSTER *Gr. Remonstr.* 2 The Petition..was but the affirmation and re-enactment of the precedents of the three foregoing centuries.

Re-ena·mour, *v.* [RE- 5 a.] *trans.* To inflame again with love. In *pass.*

a 1711 KEN *Anodynes* Poet. Wks. 1721 III. 417 Love saw me cool, I by his Rod Shall re-enamour'd be of God.

Re-enchai·n, *v.* Also 7–8 re-in-. [RE- 5 a.] *trans.* To enchain again.

1611 COTGR., *Renchainer*, to reinchaine, to chain, or bind in chaines, againe. 1718 *Free-thinker* No. 90 ¶ 7 He becomes an easy Captive to the first Person, who shall endeavour to re-inchain him. 1837 R. WILSON *Pleas. Piety* IV. 93 Ham's haughty King collects his armed hosts To re-enchain the ransomed of the Lord.

† **Re-encha·rge,** *v. Obs. rare*⁻¹. [RE- 5 a.] ? To charge again.

1600 HOLLAND *Livy* VIII. xxxix. 310 The Dictator .. cried unto the Colonels .. to reencharge and renew the medley againe with him.

† **Re-encloi·ster,** *v. Obs.* In 7 re-in-. [RE- 5 a.] *trans.* To shut up again in a cloister.

1632 LITHGOW *Trav.* VI. 286 Bidding farewell to the Church of St. Saluatore, and being re-incloystred againe.

Re-encou·nter, *sb.* Also 6–7 rein-, re-in-. [f. RE- + ENCOUNTER *sb.*; cf. RENCONTRE *sb.*, RENCOUNTER *sb.*] † a. A meeting, encounter, *esp.* a hostile one. *Obs.* b. A renewed meeting.

1525 LD. BERNERS *Froiss.* II. xxix. 34/1 Without any busynesse or reencounter we came to the captall. 1577–87 HOLINSHED *Chron.* I. 85/2 The Saxons had the victorie in that reincounter. 1603 HOLLAND *Plutarch's Mor.* 443 So many pleasant speeches and lively reencounters. 1611 FLORIO, *Rancontro*, a reencounter, a meeting againe. 1666 S. PARKER *Free & Impart. Censure* (1667) 32 After many reiterated controversial Re-incounters with Aurelius. 1737 L. CLARKE *Hist. Bible* (1740) I. I. 68 This Re-encounter had not a little ruffled Jacob's mild disposition. 1794 GODWIN *Cal. Williams* 77 Mr. Falkland's servants, hearing the bustle of the re-encounter [etc.].

Re-encou·nter, *v.* Also 6–7 re-in-. [f. RE- + ENCOUNTER *v.*; cf. RENCONTRE *v.*, RENCOUNTER *v.*] † a. To encounter, *esp.* in a hostile manner. *Obs.* b. To encounter or meet again.

1523 LD. BERNERS *Froiss.* I. ccxiv. 267 They..robbed all that countrey, for there was none that reencountred them. 1577–87 HOLINSHED *Chron.* I. 164/2 Bicause the Danes .. were reencountred..so often as they did encounter [etc.]. 1600 *Gowrie Conspir.* C 2, His owne seruants..hauing put his maiestie in saftie, re-encountred the sayd Earle and his seruantes. 1611 FLORIO, *Rancontrare*, to reincounter or meete againe. c 1630 RISDON *Surv. Devon* § 65 (1810) 63 Both armies met again, and re-encountered. 1639 FULLER *Holy War* II. x. (1840) 63 The Pagans, little suspecting to be reencountered, gave themselves over to mirth and jollity.

† **Re-encou·ntry.** *Obs.*⁻¹ = RE-ENCOUNTER *sb.*

1568 GRAFTON *Chron.* II. 266 For I thinke verely that your aduersarie king Phillip will meete with you to fight, and ye shall find many streight passages and reencountries.

Re-encou·rage, *v.* In 6–7 rein-. [RE- 5 a.] *trans.* To encourage again.

1598 FLORIO, *Rinfrancare*, to reincourage. 1670 MILTON *Hist. Eng.* IV. 138 The Abbot Austin.., reincourag'd by the exhortations of Gregory.., came safe to the Ile of Tanet.

So **Re-encou·ragement.**

a 1766 J. BROWNE *Willie & Old Wernock* 329 But O, (my Wernock) how am I to thee Obligen, for thy keene re-encouragements.

Re-endear, *v.* In 6–7 re-in-. [RE- 5 a.] *trans.* To endear again. So **Re-endea·rment.**

1606 BP. HALL *Contempl., O. T.* XX. xii, As a man..puts himself into some deserving action, whereby he may hope to re-indeare him selfe. 1654 H. L'ESTRANGE *Chas. I* (1655) 212 Resolued he was no opportunity should escape him which might promove his re-endeerment with them.

Re-endow, *v.* Also 8 re-in-. [RE- 5 a.] *trans.* To endow again.

1607 HIERON *Wks.* I. 390 How much is vented away by such meanes, by which..many an impouerished and spoiled church [might be] re-endowed. 1761 *London & Environs* IV. 102 The hospitals .. being built, and re-indowed at the public expence. 1869 *Spectator* 24 July 861/1 Concessions which re-endow the Free Church with an extra half-million.

So **Re-endow·ment.** Also *attrib.*

1869 *Spectator* 24 July 861/1 Re-endowment even with half a million is re-endowment. 1884 *Manch. Weekly Times* 11 Oct. 4/6 A re-endowment of the Protestant denomination. 1897 *Daily News* 10 Mar. 9/4 In aid of the Re-endowment Fund of Guy's Hospital.

Reene, var. REAN, REEN; obs. f. REIN.

Re-e·nergize, *v.* [RE- 5 a.] *trans.* To energize anew, impart fresh energy to.

1803 ANNA SEWARD *Lett.* (1811) VI. 108 You, my friend, have..affectionate interests, which combine to reenergize your mind. 1887 *Chicago Advance* 5 May 274 The true way to re-energize the languishing institution.

Re-enfeo·ff, *v.* Also 7 rein-, re-in-. [RE- 5 a; cf. REFEOFF *v.*] *trans.* To enfeoff anew; to enfeoff in return (the original feoffor).

1540 in *Eng. Gilds* (1870) 256 Who, soe being seised, shall re-enfeoffe the said seaven who shall survive. 1628 COKE *On Litt.* 208 b, If the Condition be, That the Feoffee shall re-infeoffe the Feoffor [etc.]. 1642 tr. *Perkins' Prof. Bk.* iii. § 241. 107 If my Feoffee in Fee of one Acre of Land, doe reinfeoff mee of the same acre [etc.]. 1765 *Act 5 Geo. III*, c. 26 *Preamble*, With power also to the surviving trustees.. to re-enfeoff other trustees to the same uses. 1865 NICHOLS *Britton* II. 209 *note*, It was not uncommon for a layman to enfeoff a church on condition of being reenfeoffed to hold of the church.

So **Re-enfeo·ffment.**

1661 J. STEPHENS *Procurations* 55 So warranty is extinguished by Re-infeoffment or Descent of Land to the same person that had the Warranty. 1870 *Eng. Gilds* 256 *marg.*, When only seven feoffees remain living, a re-enfeoffment, to fourteen, shall be made.

Re-enflame, variant of REINFLAME.

Re-enfo·rce, *sb.* = REINFORCE *sb.*

1886 *American* XII. 141 The gun is a small one,.. composed of two concentric cylinders, the inside one being of steel, the outside or reënforce of cast iron.

Re-enfo·rce, *v.* [f. RE- + ENFORCE *v.*; cf. REINFORCE and RENFORCE. Now rare in English, but common in American use.]

1. *trans.* To strengthen, give fresh or additional strength to.

c 1586 C'TESS PEMBROKE *Ps.* LXXXVI. v, Thou, Jehova, .. With strength my weaknesse re-enforce. 1605 K. LONG tr. *Barclay's Argenis* v. x. 364 He was with these and the like speeches re-enforcing his anger. a 1630 S. PAGE *Broken Heart* (1637) 177 To magnifie him, and to reenforce his Petition, he calleth him *Deum salutis*. a 1711 KEN *Hymnarium* Poet. Wks. 1721 II. 49 Thou to thyself dost Glory raise, By re-enforcing our Decays. 1883 *Harper's Mag.* Nov. 886/2 The sonority of this re-ervoir is expected materially to re-enforce the volume of tone. 1888 STEVENSON *Gentlemen in Fiction*, The opinions.., though .. re-enforced with excellent images, are not peculiar..to Hamlet.

b. *refl.* To strengthen or encourage (oneself) afresh. *rare.*

1589 in Hakluyt *Voy.* (1812) V. 588 Who after one battle were never able to reenforce themselves against him. 1599 B. JONSON *Cynthia's Rev.* III. iii, And then, if she shall coily recoil, and signify your repulse, you are to reenforce yourself with [etc.].

2. *Mil.* To strengthen with additional forces († or supplies); to support by fresh numbers.

1596 DANETT tr. *Comines* (1614) 24 Then vsed we to re-enforce them with new supplies. 1613 PURCHAS *Pilgrimage* IV. ii. 295 The Magi .. himselfe re-enforcing his power, and bidding battell..was taken aliue. 1693 *Mem. Cnt. Teckely* IV. 62 They thought only upon reposing themselves, and re-enforcing their Army by detachments out of the neighbouring Garrisons.

transf. 1885 J. L. ALLEN in *Harper's Mag.* Apr. 709/2 With my house re-enforced by a housekeeper,.. there would be nothing more to desire. 1896 *Paterson Mag.* VI. 305/1 The pioneers have been re-enforced.

† b. To collect again; to reassemble. *Obs.*

1594 KYD *Cornelia* Argt., His purpose was to have re-enforc'd a newe Armie. 1599 SHAKS. *Hen. V*, IV. vi. 36 The French haue re-enforc'd their scatter'd men.

3. To strengthen (any part of an object) by additional support.

1883 *Harper's Mag.* Nov. 887/1 The re-entrant angles.. are re-enforced..with..pilasters. 1897 *Outing* (U.S.) XXX. 278/2 It goes to the brazing furnace, where the joints are re-enforced and solidified.

† 4. *intr.* To renew one's efforts: to insist. *Obs.*

1624 BP. MOUNTAGU *Gagg* 3 Though he fall off to-day, hee will re-enforce to-morrow, though he faile to-day, he will assay to-morrow. 1642 JER. TAYLOR *Episc.* (1647) 325 This account we have from S. Cyprian, and he reenforces againe upon the same charge in his Epistle.

Hence **Re-enfo·rceable** *a.*, capable of being re-enforced (*Funk's Stand. Dict.* 1895); **Re-enfo·rcer,** one who re-enforces; **Re-enfo·rcing** *vbl. sb.*

1611 FLORIO, *Rafforzamento*, a re-enforcing. 1884 *Century Mag.* Mar. 929/1 Writers who are more properly feeders and reënforcers of life itself.

Re-enfo·rcement. [f. as prec. + -MENT: cf. REINFORCEMENT and RENFORCEMENT.] The act of re-enforcing, or the state of being re-enforced; that which re-enforces; a fresh supply.

1602 R. JOHNSON *Kingd. & Commw.* (1603) 139 Populous, because of reenforcements after checks or ouerthrows. 1651 BP. MOUNTAGU *Diatribæ* 41 Without a generall re-enforcement from authority. 1681 GLANVILL *Sadducismus* II. 126 Having resolved upon this Reenforcement, I writ again to my Honoured Friend. 1775 P. SCHUYLER in Sparks *Corr. Amer. Rev.* (1853) I. 78 That a reënforcement may be speedily sent into Canada. 1853 KANE *Grinnell Exp.* xlv. (1856) 411 We devoured eagerly the seal, of which, by good fortune, we had several re-enforcements. 1882 *Rep. to Ho. Repr. Prec. Met. U. S.* 472 The natural head of water needs the re-enforcement of pumping apparatus to enable it to reach the highest point of the mine.

Re-enfra·nchise, *v.* Also 7 re-in-. [RE- 5 a.] *trans.* To enfranchise († set free) again. So **Re-enfra·nchisement.**

1611 FLORIO, *Raffrancare*, to re-enfranchise or set at libertie. 1660 INGELO *Bentiv. & Ur.* II. (1682) 147 A price paid down for the re-infranchising of inslav'd Men. 1888 G. W. CABLE in *Libr. Mag.* (U.S.) May 16 The slow doling out of re-enfranchisement to the best intelligence of Southern white society.

Re-enga·ge, *v.* Also 7 rein-, re-in-. [RE- 5 a. Cf. F. *rengager* (16th c.).] To engage again. Hence **Re-enga·ging** *vbl. sb.* a. *trans.*

1611 COTGR., *Rengager*, to reingage. 1825 J. NICHOLSON *Operat. Mechanic* 20 The disengaging and reengaging of the moving parts. 1828 SOUTHEY *On a Picture*, etc. xiv, If then the power to thee were given In that cold form its life to re-engage. 1870 *Act 33 & 34 Vict.* c. 67 § 8 Any soldier who being in army service has commenced the twelfth year from his first enlistment .. may..be reengaged.

b. *intr.*

1678 BUTLER *Hud.* III. iii. 182 It put him in so fierce a Rage He once resolv'd to re-ingage. 1864 CARLYLE *Fredk. Gt.* XVII. i. (1872) VII. 3 Brühl has ever since rather held back; would not reëngage at all. 1876 VOYLE & STEVENSON *Milit. Dict.* 335/1 Soldiers who have declined to re-engage abroad, and have been sent home at the public expense, will not be permitted to re-engage in this country.

So **Re-enga·gement.**

1731 BAILEY Vol. II. (ed. 2), *Re-ingagement*, an engaging again. 1828 *Lights & Shades* II. 286 He stayed to see Madame Vestris commence her re-engagement. 1870 *Act 33 & 34 Vict.* c. 67 § 8 Re-engagement of soldiers.

Re-enge·nder, *v.* In 6–8 rein-, re-in-. [RE- 5 a. Cf. F. *rengendrer* (13th c.).] To engender again. Hence **Re-enge·ndering** *ppl. a.*

1545 RAYNOLD *Byrth Mankynde* 3 Yᵉ thynne or superficial skyn, skale it, or fall it of, neuer so often, yet in the place of it is reingendryd nue. 1611 COTGR., *Rengendrer*, to reingender. 1641 MILTON *Animadv.* iv. Wks. 1851 III. 219 As if a man should taxe the renovating and re-ingendring Spirit of God with innovation. 1751 tr. *Rousseau's Discourse* 35 What star may be inhabited, what insects reingender themselves in an extraordinary manner..?

So **Re-enge·nderer.**

1611 COTGR., *Rengendreur*, a reingendrer.

Re-engine, *v.* [f. RE- 5 a + ENGINE *v.* 4.] *trans.* To furnish (a ship) with new engines.

1888 *Daily News* 9 Nov. 3/7 The Admiralty have decided to re-engine those ships [etc.]. 1889 *Standard* 9 Mar., Certain ships required to be re-engined.

† **Re-engo·rge,** *v. Obs.* Also 7 rein-. [RE-.] *refl.* Of water: To pour back *into*, *in* a place.

1610 HOLLAND *Camden's Brit.* I. 208 When the sea re-engorgeth it selfe backe againe into the sea. 1632 LITHGOW *Trav.* x. 466 My head hanging downeward, and the water reingorging it selfe in my throat with a strugling force.

Re-engraft: see REINGRAFT.

Re-engra·ve, *v.* [RE- 5 a.] *trans.* To engrave again. Hence **Re-engra·ved** *ppl. a.*

a 1711 KEN *Hymnarium* Poet. Wks. 1721 II. 99 They joy to see God's Image re-engrav'd. 1776 DA COSTA *Elem. Conchol.* ii. 35 He had them re-engraved; and therefore many shells appear twice in his work. 1806 W. TAYLOR in *Monthly Mag.* XXII. 133 Doppelmayer had a fac-simile of this chart re-engraved. 1889 *Pall Mall G.* 1 Feb. 2/1 The re-engraved plates are nine in number.

Re-enjoi·n, *v.* Also 7 rein-. [RE- 5 a.] *trans.* To enjoin again.

1611 COTGR., *Rejoindre*, to reinioyne, reordaine vnto, reimpose vpon. 1748 RICHARDSON *Clarissa* (1811) V. 36, I besought Miss Lloyd to re-enjoin secrecy to every one. 1892 *Current Hist.* (U.S.) Aug. 134 Re-enjoining the duty of loyalty to the Republican Government in France.

Re-enjoy·, *v.* Also 7 rein-. [RE- 5 a.] *trans.* To enjoy again.

1605 EARL STIRLING *Alexandr. Trag.* I. Chor., Those that th'earth chargde .. Theyr ashie lodgings leaue, To re-enioy the light. a 1648 LD. HERBERT *Hen. VIII* (1683) 159 That Charles, Duke of Bourbon should re-injoy his former estate. 1670 COTTON *Espernon* II. v. 241 To the end they might re-enjoy the licence of War. a 1711 KEN *Hymns Evang.* Poet. Wks. 1721 I. 53 'Tis Heav'n to me to re-enjoy my Dear. 1751 ELIZA HEYWOOD *Betsy Thoughtless* II. 221, I am preparing to return to my country-seat, where I hope to re-enjoy..tranquility.

So **Re-enjoy·ment.**

1611 COTGR., *Rejouissance*, a reinioyment, repossession, reinioying. 1631 QUARLES *Div. Poems, Samson* Medit. xx, Whose sweet enjoyment..leaves a thirst Of reenjoyment, greater than the first. 1668 FRANCO *Truth Springing* 46 The re-injoyment of those infinite Delights the Soul lost. 1815 MRS. PILKINGTON *Celebrity* III. 148 The result was, a re-enjoyment of illicit pleasures.

Re-enki·ndle, *v.* Also 7 re-in-. [RE- 5 a.] *trans.* and *intr.* To kindle again, *lit.* and *fig.*

1650 JER. TAYLOR *Holy Living* I. § 2 ¶ 4. 20 Renew and re-inkindle your purpose by short ejaculations. 1651 — *Serm. for Year* I. xii. 136 They went out, never to be re-enkindled. a 1711 KEN *Anodynes* Poet. Wks. 1721 III. 394 Love re-enkindled in my frozen Soul. 1753 [see RADIAL *a.* 1]. 1879 L. SHEPHERD tr. *Guéranger's Liturg. Year* I. 195 The piety of her children was re-enkindled.

Re-enla·rge, *v.* Also 7 rein-. [RE- 5 a.] *trans.* To enlarge, set at large, again.

1611 FLORIO, *Ringrandire*, ..to re-enlarge. 1632 QUARLES *Div. Poems, Samson* vi, When time,..By his benignant power, had reinlarg'd Their captive senses. 1823 BENTHAM *Not Paul* 376 Peter imprisoned, enlarged, recommitted, examined, and reenlarged.

Re-enli·ghten, *v.* [RE- 5 a.] *trans.* To enlighten again.

1691 E. TAYLOR tr. *Behmen's Divine Essence* xviii. 275 Re-enlightening the Soul.

Re-enli·st, *v.* Also rein-. [RE- 5 a.] *intr.* and *trans.* To enlist again.

1828–32 in WEBSTER. 1837 *Penny Cycl.* IX. 443/1 At the end of his time of service a seaman may re-enlist for a like period. 1850 R. G. CUMMING *Hunter's Life S. Afr.* (1902) 109/1 He declared himself..penitent,..and, expressing a wish again to join the service, I re-enlisted him. 1869 *Pall Mall G.* 7 Jan. 1/2 Many men..take the bounty with no other intention than that of deserting in order to re-enlist.

So **Re-enli·stment.**

1847 in WEBSTER. 1866 *Pall Mall G.* 3 Jan., This drawback would be greatly lessened if we could secure re-enlistments in greater numbers.

Re-enli·ven, *v.* [RE- 5 a.] *trans.* To inspire with new life or vigour.

a 1660 HAMMOND *Wks.* (1684) IV. 660 To clear up as much as we can, and re-inliven this light within us. 1681 *Whole Duty Nations* 31 When the times..of Re-inlivening all things shall come. a 1711 KEN *Psyche* Poet. Wks. 1721 IV. 293 May Love, they cry'd, Lord, re-enliven'd be. 1809–10 COLERIDGE *Friend* (1865) 145 Does not war create or re-enliven numerous branches of industry as well as peace?

Re-enro·l(l, *v.* [RE- 5 a.] *trans.* To enrol again. So **Re-enro·lment.**

1889 *Voice* (N.Y.) 8 Aug., The third and final day of the Republican re-enrollment. 1893 *Daily News* 27 Dec. 5/5 Dr. Jameson..is re-enrolling many of the men to form a permanent police force.

Re-enshri·ne, *v.* [RE- 5 a.] *trans.* To enshrine again.

a 1711 KEN *Preparatives* Poet. Wks. 1721 IV. 48 God-man his Angels will enjoyn, Saints hallow'd Dust to re-enshrine. 1815 J. C. HOBHOUSE *Substance Lett.* (1816) I. 104 Relics.. to be re-adjusted and re-enshrined by a second St. Louis.

Re-ensla·ve, *v.* Also 7 rein-, re-in-. [RE- 5 a.] *trans.* To enslave again. Hence **Re-ensla·ving** *vbl. sb.*

1657 HAWKE *Killing is M.* 12 The Army presaging what dangerous..consequences might ensue to the reinslaving of the people. 1691 BEVERLEY *Mem. Kingd. Christ* 3 It would be wholly impossible to Re-inslave these Nations. 1807 HAZLITT *Pol. Ess.* (1819) 406 If this increase would be an evil..the re-enslaving the country would be a good. 1856 OLMSTED *Slave States* 95 A man who had been free, but.. was reënslaved.

So **Re-ensla·vement.**

1862 in *Cent. Dict.* 1883 *Contemp. Rev.* Nov. 686 The whites would undoubtedly disfranchise the blacks if they could.. but none assuredly would ever again consent to their re-enslavement.

Re-ensphe·re, *v.* Also 7 re-insphear. [RE- 5 a.] *trans.* To ensphere again.

1684 T. HOCKIN *God's Decrees* 152 He could not re-ensphere himself into the same happy condition he did lose. *Ibid.* 277 The faln angels could not be re-insphear'd into their primitive blessed condition.

Re-ensta·mp, *v.* Also 8 rein-. [RE- 5 a.] *trans.* To enstamp or imprint again.

a 1703 BURKITT *On N. T., Romans* viii. 39 Will he leave them after his image is engraven, and reinstamped upon them? c 1750 J. NELSON *Jrnl.* (1836) 191 He doth actually destroy the works of the devil, and re-enstamp the image of God in their souls. 1776 JOS. NEILL 23 *Serm.* 257.

† **Re-e·nter,** *sb. Obs.* [RE- 5 a.] = RE-ENTRY.

1574 tr. *Littleton's Tenures* 74 Yelding to the lessoure.. a certeine rent, and for defaut of paiment a reenter. 1639 *Records of Dedham* (Mass.) (1892) III. 58 In case yᵗ payment be not yearly made..it shall be lawfull for ye said Town to make a Reenter vpon ye premises.

Re-enter (rī,e·ntəɹ), *v.* [RE- 5 a + ENTER *v.* Cf. F. *rentrer* (12th c.).]

1. *intr.* To enter again. Const. † *in*, *into*, *upon*.

1483 CAXTON *Gold. Leg.* 129/1, I shal reentre nakyd agayn in to therthe. 1494 FABYAN *Chron.* VI. clxxxix. 191 He warred vpon the Danys that then were reentrede into Northumberlande. 1515 BARCLAY *Egloges* I. (1570) A iij 2 When the good is gone..Seldome the better re-entreth in the place. 1551 ROBINSON tr. *More's Utop.* II. (1895) 283 The other, at theyre retourne home, agayn reentre euery one into his own place. 1618 ROWLANDS *Sacred Mem.* 35. I doe command and charge that forth thou come, And neuer to reenter any more. 1651 HOBBES *Leviath.* II. xxix. 174 There is no possibility for the Soveraignty to re-enter. 1726 POPE *Odyss.* XXI. 246 Re-enter then, not all at once. 1825 J. NICHOLSON *Operat. Mechanic* 499 An air was then performed by bells; after which the two figures reentered. 1861 tr. *Montalembert's Monks of West* I. 354 He descended..to re-enter into a rustic solitude. 1870 *Act 33 & 34 Vict.* c. 67 § 5 When any such soldier is directed to re-enter upon army service.

b. *Law.* To enter again upon possession of lands or tenements.

1461 *Rolls of Parlt.* V. 485/1 In the same halfendele to reentre, and it in their first state to hold. 1485 *Ibid.* VI. 321/2 The forsaid Blaunch and her said Feoffes to reenter into the said Ten[emen]ts. 1503–4 *Act 19 Hen. VII*, c. 29 *Schedule*, It shalbe lefull to the seide Abbas..to reentre into the seid grounde. 1607 COWELL *Interpr.* s.v. *Reentry*, If I doe condition with the Leasee, that for nonpayment of the rent at the day it shalbe lawful for me to reenter. 1622 CALLIS *Stat. Sewers* (1647) 45 If A. or his heirs pay to B. Ten pounds within a certain day, that they might re-enter. 1818 CRUISE *Digest* (ed. 2) I. 396 The feoffee will re-enter, or bring an action to recontinue the possession. 1849 MACAULAY *Hist. Eng.* ii. I. 179 The royalist nobility and gentry reentered on their confiscated estates.

c. In stage-directions. (Cf. ENTER *v.* 1 b.)

1693 CONGREVE *Old Batchelour* v. i, Enter Sharper... Reenter Sharper.

2. *trans.* To enter (a place, etc.) again.

1442 T. BECKINGTON *Corr.* (Rolls) II. 246 The Lord Usak ..re-entred the said cite by the same ladder. 1494 FABYAN *Chron.* VI. cxcviii. 205 In whiche season he made great prouysion to reenter the lande of Englande. 1570 FOXE *A. & M.* (ed. 2) 255/2 He was content that Thurstinus should reenter hys realme. 1667 MILTON *P. L.* II. 397 Those bright confines, whence..we may chance Re-enter Heav'n. a 1711 KEN *Hymnotheo* Poet. Wks. 1721 III. 220 Once more we to re-enter Bliss will try. 1778 MISS BURNEY *Evelina* (1791) II. xxxi. 195, I re-entered the drawing-room. 1830 LYTTON *P. Clifford* xxv, Mauleverer slowly re-entered his carriage. 1898 *Allbutt's Syst. Med.* V. 111 The air re-enters the minute bronchi and air-vesicles.

† b. To enter again into possession of (a thing); to regain (possession). *Obs. rare.*

1590 SOUTHWELL *M. Magd. Funeral Teares* (1823) 115 Hee should after death re-enter possession of that inheritance which Adam lost. 1706 PHILLIPS (ed. Kersey), *To Re-enter*, to enter upon, or take Possession of again.

† 3. *Sc.* To lodge (a person) again *in* a place.

1566 *Reg. Privy Council Scot.* I. 454, I am content..that my saidis freindis tak and reentir and put me within the castellis. 1574 *Ibid.* II. 379, I sall re-enter agane the said Roger in presoun quhen I sall be requirit.

4. To enter again in a book or register.

1839 *Act 2 & 3 Vict.* c. 11 § 4 The Senior Master shall forthwith re-enter the same [judgment] in like Manner as the same was originally entered. 1885 *Law Times* LXXIX. 25/1 Another [notice] must be given before the plaintiff can re-enter the cause for trial.

5. *techn.* a. In hand calico-printing: To apply (the secondary colours), to ground in.

1839 [see the *vbl. sb.* below].

b. In engraving: To cut (imperfect or worn lines) deeper in the plate.

1854 FAIRHOLT *Dict. Terms Art* s.v., [The] line is re-entred with a sharp graver, and cut to the proper depth.

Hence **Re-e·ntering** *vbl. sb.*

1638 JUNIUS *Paint. Ancients* 309 The very..reentring into the presence of things will instantly suggest unto us..how to order and place every figure. 1839 URE *Dict. Arts* 216 The grounding in or re-entering (*rentrage*) of the other colours is the next process.

Re-e·ntering, *ppl. a.* [f. prec. + -ING².]

1. *Re-entering angle*, an angle pointing inward.

1696 PHILLIPS (ed. 5) s.v. *Angle*, Re-entring Angle, is that which re-enters into the body of the place. 1723 CHAMBERS tr. *Le Clerc's Treat. Archit.* I. 95 The Inner or Re-entering Angles. 1805–17 R. JAMESON *Char. Min.* (ed. 3) 175 Salient, and never re-entering angles. 1877 HUXLEY & MARTIN *Elem. Biol.* 43 The branches spring from the re-entering angle between the stem and the leaf.

b. So *re-entering bend, line, order, place, wall.*

1830 E. S. N. CAMPBELL *Mil. Dict.* 182 The object of the Re-entering Places of Arms is to flank the branches of the covered way. 1841 *Penny Cycl.* XIX. 346/1 To break the lines of parapet near the gorges, so as to form re-entering bends. 1873 TRISTRAM *Moab* v. 74 Each of the flanking or re-entering walls extending in an obtuse angle from it. 1876 VOYLE & STEVENSON *Milit. Dict.* 335/1 Re-entering order of battle. 1885 W. C. COUPLAND *Spir. Goethe's Faust* vi. 208 The industrialism of the present is only a point in a re-entering historic line.

2. Returning into a place.

1850 GROTE *Greece* II. lxvi. (1862) VI. 9 The re-entering exiles from Peiræus, and the Horsemen..blended again together into one harmonious .. democracy.

Re-entertai·n, *v.* [RE- 5 a.] To entertain again; to readmit. So **Re-entertai·nment.**

1611 SPEED *Hist. Gt. Brit.* IX. xi. § 4. 555 Peirs of Gaueston..whose reentertainement the dying King had so seriously forbidden. a 1680 CHARNOCK *Attrib. God* (1834) I. 191 Till the true sense of God be reentertained in the soil where it ought to grow.

Re-enthra·ll, *v.* Also 7 rein-. [RE- 5 a.] *trans.* To enthrall again.

1622 DONNE *Serm.* CXIX. V. 107 Neither is this..to re-enthrall you to a necessity of communicating all your sins. 1632 LITHGOW *Trav.* VI. 241 Ierusalem was reinthralled and seazed vpon by Saladine. 1644 HEYLIN *Stumbling-block* Tracts (1681) 651 That..we should not re-inthral our selves to the lusts of men.

Re-enthro·ne, *v.* [RE- 5 a; cf. REINTHRONE.] *trans.* To enthrone again.

1654 tr. *Scudery's Curia Pol.* 117, I am at last..ready to invest and re-enthrone John King of Hungary. a 1711 KEN *Hymns Festiv.* Poet. Wks. 1721 I. 368 When Jesus re-enthron'd on high, His Spirit sent. — *Preparatives* ibid. IV. 72 My Mind, which now I re-enthrone.

So **Re-enthro·nement** (Webster 1847); † **Re-enthro·nize** *v.* = REINTHRONIZE.

1620–55 I. JONES *Stone-Heng* 43 Vortigern was re-enthroniz'd.

Re-enti·ce, *v.* In 6 rein-. [RE- 5 a.] *trans.* To entice again.

1580 WARNER *Alb. Eng.* v. xxvi, And reintise the Club-God Dys, And all his diuells to daunt.

Re-entoi·l, *v.* [RE- 5 a.] To entoil again.

1606 SYLVESTER *Du Bartas* II. iv. II. *Trophies* 777 What frantick fury art thou mov'd with-all..(By powr-full Charms) to re-entoyl my Cares?

Re-e·ntrance. [RE- 5 a.] A renewed or repeated entrance.

1594 HOOKER *Eccl. Pol.* IV. ix. § 2 Their whole religion in time will have reentrance. 1597 *Ibid.* v. xxii. § 4 The first step of their re-entrance into Life. 1661 GLANVILL *Van. Dogm.* 32 That the pores of the brain..are more easily opened to the spirits which demand re-entrance. 1775 ROMANS *Florida* App. 62 It being too dark to attempt a re-entrance of the reef, I was forced to heave the vessel too. 1883 H. DRUMMOND *Nat. Law in Spir. W.* (ed. 2) 168 The successful re-entrance of importunate desires.

Re-e·ntrant, *a.* (and *sb.*). [f. RE- + ENTRANT. Cf. F. *rentrant*.] = RE-ENTERING *ppl. a.* 1 and 1 b.

1781 J. T. DILLON *Trav. Spain* 462 He could find nothing which seemed to confirm the opinion relating to the salient and reentrant angles. 1825 J. NICHOLSON *Operat. Mechanic* 588 When the faces form a re-entrant angle, common dove-tailing is preferable. 1876 TAIT *Rec. Adv. Phys. Sc.* v. (ed. 2) 108 Any re-entrant line whatever may be supposed to be traced. 1883 *Harper's Mag.* Nov. 887/1 The re-entrant angles of the splay.

b. *sb.* A re-entrant angle in a fortification.

1900 'LINESMAN' *Words by Eyewitness* iii. (1902) 41 A.. crackle of musketry from the occupants of the re-entrant.

Re-entry (rī,e·ntri). [RE- 5 a. Cf. F. *rentrée*.]

1. *Law.* The act of re-entering upon possession of lands, tenements, etc., previously granted or let to another.

1461 *Rolls of Parlt.* V. 485/1 With lyke clause of reentre reserved. 1473 *Ibid.* VI. 70/1 Though he wold entre into the seid maners,..yet anon theruppon reentre is made ayen uppon hym. 1540 *Act 32 Hen. VIII*, c. 17 The leassor .. to haue no action reentre or other remedy for nonpayment of the same. 1581 in W. H. Turner *Select. Rec. Oxford* (1880) 414 Wᵗ a clause of re-entrie for none payment of the rente.., and also a re-entrye for not doinge reparacions. 1611 BARRY *Ram Alley* H, Although thou boughtst the beyre, Yet hath the slaue made a re-entry. 1644 QUARLES *Sheph. Orac.* xi, They plead for want of dressing Our Garden's forfeited, and they are pressing Hard for reentry. 1766 in Burrow *Rep.* (1776) IV. 1936 No Re-entry shall in such Case be given, unless the Demand be precisely and strictly followed. 1818 CRUISE *Digest* (ed. 2) IV. 113 No right of entry or re-entry can be assigned. 1876 DIGBY *Real Prop.* x. § 1. 381 A lease usually contains a proviso for re-entry by the lessor in the event of the breach of any of the covenants entered into by the lessee.

† b. Resumption *of*, return *to*, a right or station.

1471 *Arriv. Edw. IV* (Camden) 39 The reentrie and perfecte recover of the iuste title and right of owr sayd soverayngne Lord Kynge Edward the Fowrthe, to his realme and crowne of England. 1586 T. B. *La Primaud. Fr. Acad.* I. (1589) 374 Convicted for conspiring the reentrie of Tarquinius race unto the Kingdome of Rome.

2. The act of re-entering or coming back into a place, etc.; a second or new entry.

1494 FABYAN *Chron.* VII. 636 To haue his counceyll for maters concernyng theyr charge as reentre into this lande & other. 1601 DANIEL *Civ. Wars* VII. xxxi, Every Port And Shore close-shut debarres their reentry. 1603 HOLLAND *Plutarch's Mor.* 922 Those of Phila had made a reentrie into the citie, and chased out the tyrants. a 1653 GOUGE *Comm. Hebr.* iii. (1655) 8 To return to sinne..is to make way for the Devils re-entry. a 1680 CHARNOCK *Attrib. God* (1834) II. 127 Will [he] lose the glory..by suffering his foiled adversary to make a re-entry? 1821 SCHOOLCRAFT *Trav.* 98 We..effected the crossing and re-entry of the lake. 1884 'CAVENDISH' *Whist* (ed. 14) 5 A player cutting into one table, whilst belonging to another, loses his right of re-entry into that latter.

b. *Card of re-entry*, in whist, a card which by winning a trick gives the lead to a player at an advanced stage of the hand.

1884 'CAVENDISH' *Whist* (ed. 14) 127 Plain suits should be led like trumps..if all the trumps are out, and the leader or his partner has certain cards of re-entry in other suits.

† 3. *Sc.* The act of putting (a person) back *in* a place. *Obs. rare*⁻¹.

1566 *Reg. Privy Council Scot.* I. 454 For re-entre of the said Erle .. in ward.

4. The act of setting down or recording again; the fact of being so set down; the entry thus made.

1839 *Act 2 & 3 Vict.* c. 11 § 4 Such officer shall be entitled for any such Re-entry to the Sum of One Shilling. 1885 *Law Times Rep.* LII. 574/2 The re-entry was erroneous, and ought to be struck out. 1887 *48th Rep. Dep. Kpr. Records* 628 A memorandum .. of the judgment, &c., was to be left for the purpose of re-entry in the book.

Re-enu·nciate, *v.* [RE- 5 a.] *trans.* To enunciate again. So **Re-enunciation.**

1881 [see RE- 5 a]. 1888 *Chicago Advance* 20 Dec. 832 The New Testament does not re-enunciate and re-enact the old law. 1895 A. J. BALFOUR in *Daily News* 9 Sept. 5/1 A mere re-enunciation of my belief.

† **Re-enve·rse,** *v. Obs.* [ad. F. *renverser* to RENVERSE.] *trans.* To reverse.

1603 FLORIO *Montaigne* II. xii. (1632) 322 Plato saith, that ..the Starres, and the Sunne do some times re-enverse the motion we perceive in them. 1610 DONNE *Pseudo-martyr* x. 274 Bridgewater, which cals himselfe Aquipontanus, ouerturning and re-enuersing his name with his conscience.

Reepe, obs form of REAP.

Reeper, reaper (rī·pəɹ). *Anglo-Indian.* [ad. Mahratti *rip* (Yule).] (See quots.)

1734 in J. H. Wheeler *Madras in Olden Time* (1862) III. 148 Paid the Banksall Merchants for the house poles, country reapers, &c. necessary for house building. 1858 SIMMONDS *Dict. Trade*, *Reepers*, laths, or longitudinal sections of the palmyra palm, used for building purposes in the East; the trunk of the tree is split into 8 for reepers, and these are dressed with an adze. 1886 YULE & BURNELL *Anglo-Ind. Gloss.*, *Reaper*. The small laths, laid across the rafters of a sloping roof to bear the tiles, are so called in Anglo-Indian house-building.

Re-epi·tomize, *v.* [RE- 5 a.] *trans.* To present again in smaller compass.

1655 FULLER *Wounded Consc., Antheologia* (1867) 377 A small scantling of some three acres, which..re-epitomized the delicacies of all the rest.

Re-equi·p, *v.* [RE- 5 a.] *trans.* To equip again. So **Re-equi·pment.**

1804 LARWOOD *No Gun Boats* 12 Re-equipping Line-of-Battle Ships. *Ibid.* 17 The process of re-equipment being thus obvious. 1823 SOUTHEY *Penins. War* I. 743 The government had already begun to take measures for re-equipping them. 1889 *Voice* (N.Y.) 24 Oct., To get education and re-equipment for Christian Work.

Ree-raw (rī·rǭ), *a.* (and *sb.*). [Anglo-Irish, prob. of echoic origin.] Rough, riotous, noisy.

1842 S. LOVER *Handy Andy* xxxvii, The joining of many voices in a 'ree-raw' chorus indicated that a carouse was going forward within. 1863 LE FANU *House by Churchyard* (ed. 2) II. 44 There was something cynical in his ree-raw independence. 1864 ANSTER tr. *Faustus* pt. II. I. (1887) 48 A wild, ree-raw, self-willed tumultuous throng.

b. *sb.* A drinking-bout; a noisy romp.

1854 DICKENS in *Househ. Wds.* VIII. 75/2 For the one word drunk,..I find..on the ran-tan, on the re-raw, groggy. 1867 KENNEDY *Banks Boro* xxxi, Wouldn't the little boys .. have a fine ree-raw at prison bars at play time!

† **Reere.** *Obs. rare.* Also 4 rere. [Of obscure origin, perh. related to ROAR *v.*, but cf. also REAR *sb.*¹] Noise, shouting; a shout.

c 1330 R. BRUNNE *Chron. Wace* (Rolls) 10207 Alle þe ernes ..Schul crie & ȝelle, & make rere. 1567 GOLDING *Ovid's Met.* XIII. (1593) 320 These words were spoke with such a reere as verie well became An angrie Giant. 1571 — *Calvin on Ps.* xvii. 1 Hypocrites make stout bragges, and lift up their voyce with lowd reere, in token of affiance.

Re-ere·ct, *v.* [RE- 5 a.] *trans.* To erect again, *lit.* and *fig.* Hence **Re-ere·cting** *vbl. sb.*

1598 DRAYTON *Heroic. Ep.* (1605) 89 Bring marble mines to re-erect those walls. 1631 HEYLIN *St. George* 220 Temples demolished..in the time of Diocletian: and reerected by.. Maximinianus. 1679 PRANCE *Addit. Narr. Pop. Plot* 30 This re-erecting of Abbies by Q. Mary. a 1711 KEN *Preparatives* Poet. Wks. 1721 IV. 14 Conscience, thy Throne I'll re-erect. 1835 in Willis & Clark *Cambridge* (1886) I. 333 To re-erect or restore on some other site, the Old Gateway. 1882–3 SCHAFF *Encycl. Relig. Knowl.* III. 2172 He re-erected the Court of High Commission in 1664.

So **Re-ere·ction.**

1655 FULLER *Ch. Hist.* VI. vi. 359 She was legally empowred for the re-erection of these Convents. 1861 SMILES *Engineers* II. 28 He also had regard to durability as an important point in its re-erection.

Reermouse, variant of REARMOUSE.

Reer-supper, variant of RERE-SUPPER *Obs.*

Rees, variant of REIS (Pg. money), RESE.

Re-esca·pe, *v.* [RE- 5 a.] To escape again.

1727 BROOME *Poems* 120 Lest hid in Shades, Thro' the dusk Air he re-escape to Troy. 1902 *Daily Chron.* 15 Aug. 3/6 After sundry depredations he was recaptured, only to re-escape.

† **Reescate,** *v. Obs. rare*⁻¹. [ad. It. *riscattare*, Sp. *rescatar*:—pop.L. **re-ex-captāre*.] *trans.* To redeem, ransom.

c 1645 HOWELL *Lett.* v. xxxii. (1650) I. 168 The great honour you have acquir'd by your gallant comportment in Algier in reescating so many English slaves.

Reese, reeze (rīz), *v.*¹ *Obs.* exc. *dial.* [? Back-formation from REESED.] *intr.* To become rancid.

1784 TWAMLEY *Dairying* 712 Butter..will reeze or get of a tallowy nature; fat Bacon will reeze so far as the fat melts. 1886 *Rochd. Gloss.*, *Reese*, to grow rancid, as bacon.

† **Reese, reeze,** *v.*² *Obs.* [Of obscure origin: cf. REEST *v.*²] *trans.* To burn, scorch, smoke.

1618 T. ADAMS *Heaven made sure* Wks. (1629) 902 For a while they bee reezed in Purgatory. 1633 — *Exp. 2 Peter* ii. 4 His priests..were reesed or smoked with the incense offered to the idol. 1698 M. LISTER *Journ. Paris* (1699) 147 It is little less than Quicklime, and burns and reeses all it touches.

Reese, var. RESE *sb.* and *v.*; dial. var. ROOSE *v.*

Reesed, reezed (rīzd), *ppl. a.* Also 5 resside, 6 re(e)s'd, 7 reised; 8 reased, 9 reazed. [Later form of REST *a.*; cf. REASTY.] Rancid.

1496 *Bk. St. Albans* C vij, Upon that powdre do a litill larde that is resside. 1598 BP. HALL *Sat.* IV. ii. 36 Once a weeke, perhaps, for nouelty, Reez'd bacon soords shall feast his familie. 1598 MARSTON *Sco. Villanie* I. iii. 183 What Academick starued Satyrist Would gnaw rez'd Bacon? 1607 MARKHAM *Caval.* VII. (1617) 56 Their insides are..in colour yellow like reesed bacon. 1641 *Curates Conference* in *Harl. Misc.* (Malh.) IV. 376 He .. looks like a piece of reesed bacon, ever since the plot failed. 1727 BRADLEY *Fam. Dict.* s.v. *Garget*, Put in a little reased bacon and boil them altogether. 1883 *Almondbury Gloss.*, *Reezed* or *Reazed*, a term applied to rancid bacon.

Reeshle: see REESLE.

Reesk (rīsk). *Sc.* Forms: 5 reysk, 6 resk, 9 reisk, reisque, reesk. [a. Gael. *riasg* 'a moor, fen, or marsh; coarse mountain-grass'.]

1. A piece of moorish or mossy ground producing coarse worthless grass or rushes; unproductive soil or land of this description.

1466 *Reg. Arbroath* (Bann. Club) II. 152 The marchis of Gwtheryn..passand eist the Greyn Reysk to Laithan Den. 1540 in *5th Rep. Hist. MSS. Comm.* 609/1 The..merchis.. begynnand in the west in the myddis of the resk betuix the ..landis. 1804 TARRAS *Poems* Gloss. 156 *Reesk*, ground full of rough-rooted weeds, something like rushes. 1813 G. ROBERTSON *Agric. Kincardinesh.* 317 The greater part of the original soil..is either a moss..or it is, what in this and in the adjacent county of Aberdeen, is provincially called Reisque, or Reisk.

2. Coarse grass growing on moorish ground.

1794 *Statist. Acc. Scotl.* XII. 576 Large tracks of ground producing a coarse kind of grass, called by the country people reesk. 1812 D. SOUTER *Agric. Banffsh.* App. 59 If a field be cold and canker'd, or overgrown with reesk, year old fauch will agree best.

Hence **Ree·sky** *a.*, producing reesk.

1804 TARRAS *Poems* 7 Aft we've seen them fain, Dink owre the bent to the reiskie den.

Reesle (rī·s'l), **reeshle** (rī·ʃ'l), *sb. Sc.* Also reestle. [Of onomatopœic origin.] A loud clatter; a rattling blow.

a 1774 FERGUSSON *Tron Kirk Bell* Poems (1845) 44 I'd bring ye a reesle down. a 1810 TANNAHILL *Come hame* Poems (1846) 145 I'll lend you a reestle wi' this, owre your back. 1880 JAS. E. WATT *Poet. Sketches* 52 A reeshle like thunder was heard at the door.

Ree·sle, ree·shle, *v. Sc.* Also reessil, reishle, etc. [Cf. prec.]

1. *intr.* To make a loud clattering noise.

1819 TENNANT *Papistry Storm'd* (1827) 44 Doors reessil'd up, and made a blatter. 1826 D. ANDERSON *Poems* 92 Gar'd ..their shin-banes reeshle i' their hose. 1895 CROCKETT *Men of Moss-hags* 31 That blind and unkindly wind reestling and soughing about the house.

2. *trans.* To beat with rattling blows.

1853 WATSON *Poems* 91 (E. D. D.), Whan Scotlan' had reissl't the rascals [etc.]. 1887 SERVICE *Life Dr. Duguid* v. 31 He reishled the main author o' thae tricks weel.

Reeso(u)n, obs. forms of REASON *sb.*¹

Re-espou·se, *v.* [RE- 5 a.] To espouse again.

a 1618 SYLVESTER *Elegie to Marg. Wyts* 80 Metkerk had her Mother re-espous'd. 1652 BENLOWES *Theoph.* XIII. lxxvi, The Corps but fails to be refin'd And re-espous'd unto the Glorifi'd high Minde.

Hence **Re-espou·sal.**

1817 G. S. FABER *Eight Dissert.* (1845) I. 357 *note*, The repudiation, long desolation, and ultimate reëspousal, of the Levitical Church, are described at large in Isaiah liv. 1–14. 1827 — *Sacr. Cal. Prophecy* (1844) III. 299 The set time of the Reëspousal of Judah.

Reest (rīst), *sb. Obs.* exc. *dial.* Forms: 1 réost, 7, 9 reest, 9 reist, riest, reost, reece; 6–7 (9) rest. Also *wreest* WREST. [OE. *réost*, of obscure origin: cf. G. *rist* ploughshare (Grimm), Sw. *rist* (MSw. *rist-iern*) coulter.

G. *rist* may be for *riest*, repr. an OHG. **riost*: cf. OHG. *riostra, riostar, riester, rister*, etc. (mod.G. dial. *riester, rister*) ploughshare, plough-handle, the stem of which agrees with the OE. form. It is doubtful, however, whether Sw. *rist* can be separated from ON. *ristill* ploughshare (mod. Norw. *ristel* coulter, also Gael. *ristealt* a kind of plough used in the Hebrides), which may rather be a derivative of *rista*, to cut, than an adaptation of the OHG. word. The Du. or Flem. equivalent of the latter is given by Kilian as *ryster, reyster*, with the meaning 'plough-staff'.]

† a. The share-beam of a plough. *Obs.* b. A mould-board. c. A piece of wood or iron fixed beneath the mould-board.

c 725 *Corpus Gloss.* 656 *Dentalia*, sules reost. a 1000 *Gloss.* in Wr.-Wülcker 219/2 *Dentale, i. est aratri pars prima in qua vomer inducitur quasi dens*, sule-reost, *uel* proc. ? 14.. *MS. Lansdowne* 560 fol. 47 b, *Restis*, a rest of a plow. 1523 FITZHERB. *Husb.* § 3 The rest is a lyttell pece of woode, pynned fast vpon the nether ende of the stylt, and to the sharebeame in the ferther ende. 1616 SURFL. & MARKH. *Country Farme* v. vi. 532 The spindles, the rest,..the plowfoot, the culture, and the share. 1688 R. HOLME *Armoury* III. 333/1 The Reest, is the Boards on the side of the Plow that turns over the Furrow. 1886 *Chesh. Gloss.*, *Reest*, the mould-board of a plough. 1887 *Kentish Gloss.*, *Chef*, the part of a plough on which the share is placed, and to which the *reece* is fixed.

attrib. 1894 *Northumbld. Gloss.*, *Reest-, reest-cleet*,..a thin piece of iron fastened under the lower edge of the mowdy-boord (mould-board) of a plough.

Reest (rīst), *v.*¹ *Obs.* exc. *dial.* Also 7 reast, 7, 9 reist. [Of obscure origin: cf. REST *a.* and REESED.] *intr.* Of bacon, etc.: To become rancid. Hence **Ree·sted** *a.*, rancid.

c 1440 *Promp. Parv.* 431/1 Reestyn', as flesche, *ranceo*. 1530 PALSGR. 688/2, I reest, I waxe of yll taste, as bacon dothe. 1616 SURFL. & MARKH. *Country Farme* I. xxiv. 107 The scalding of Hogges keepeth the flesh whitest,..neither is the Bacon so apt to reast as the other. 1634 W. WOOD *New Eng. Prosp.* (1865) 39 This kind of fish..is so fat, that it can scarce be saved against winter without reisting. 1869 *Lonsdale Gloss.*, *Reested*, rancid, spoiled, as bacon from being badly kept. 1894 *Northumbld. Gloss.*, *Reest*, to become rancid. Reested or reesty bacon—rancid bacon.

Reest (rīst), *v.*² *Sc.* and *north. dial.* Also 6, 9 reist. [Of obscure origin: cf. REESE *v.*² and Da. *riste* to grill or broil, f. ON. *rist* gridiron.]

1. *trans.* To dry or cure (herring, bacon, etc.) by means of heat or smoke.

1508 DUNBAR *Flyting* 187 Thow purehippit, vgly averill,.. Reistit and crynit as hangit man on hill. a 1590 MONTGOMERIE *Sonn.* xxv, Rau rid herring reistit in the reik. 1692 *Sc. Presbyt. Eloq.* (1738) 138 Take them up by the Heels, reest them in the Chimney of Hell, and dry them like Bervy Haddocks. 1816 SCOTT *Bl. Dwarf* ix, Let us cut up bushes and briers,..set fire to them, and smoke that auld devil's dam as if she were to be reested for bacon. 1832–53 W. CROSS in *Whistle-Binkie* Ser. III. 16 But ne'er say a herring is dry until it be reestit and reekit.

2. *intr.* To become smoke-dried.

1725 RAMSAY *Gentle Sheph.* II. i, A large ham hangs reesting in the neuk. 1820 SCOTT *Guy M.* xxvi. *note*, The salmon is usually dried by hanging it up, after being split and rubbed with salt, in the smoke of the turf fire.., where it is said to reist, that preparation being so termed.

Reest (rīst), *v.*³ *Sc.* and *north. dial.* Also reist. [Prob. a var. of REST *v.*, or identical with *reest*, aphetic form of Sc. *arreest*, to ARREST. The precise relationship to RESTIVE *a.* is not clear.] *intr.* Of horses: To stop suddenly and refuse to proceed. Hence **Ree·sting** *vbl. sb.* and *ppl. a.*

1786 BURNS *To Auld Mare* xiv, In cart or car thou never reestet. 1816 SCOTT *Antiq.* xv, Our powny reists a bit, and it's dooms sweer to the road. *Ibid.* xxiv, The butcher's reisting powny. 1826 J. WILSON *Noct. Ambr.* Wks. 1855 I. 250 Like horses that never reest. 1895 CROCKETT *Men of Moss-hags* xxvi. 197 Reesting and terror among horses are mostly but over-sharpness in hearing.

fig. 1890 SERVICE *Notandums* xix. 124, I was like to reist and to sten at the doctor's orders.

Reest, obs. form of REST.

Re-establish (rī,estæ·bliʃ), *v.* [RE- 5 a. See also RESTABLISH.] *trans.* To establish again.

1. To establish (a person or thing) again *in* a former place, position, or state; to restore to a previous place or position. Also const. *among*.

1483 CAXTON *Gold. Leg.* (1493) 268 b/1 Thus was the precious tree of the crosse reestablysshid in his place. 1586 WILKES in Motley *Netherl.* x. (1860) II. 99, I had not much to do.. to re-establish in her Majesty..a singular good opinion of you. 1606 G. W[OODCOCKE] *Hist. Ivstine* XVI. 67 He could now deliuer them..and re-establish them in their former peace. a 1648 LD. HERBERT *Hen. VIII* (1683) 87 He purpos'd to re-establish Henry d'Albret in the Kingdom of Navarre. 1728 ELIZA HEYWOOD tr. *Mme. de Gomez's Belle A.* (1732) II. 215 A Nation on whose Throne his Ancestors had sat for a long Series of Ages, would not fail to protect and re-establish him. 1838 LYTTON *Alice* I. ix, He has been kind to me, and re-established me among my flock. 1858 FROUDE *Hist. Eng.* IV. 311 He expected that..he could re-establish the English party in a decisive superiority.

b. To fix or set up again. *rare.*

1669 J. ROSE *Eng. Vineyard* (1675) 35 Re-establish your props, and with your foot tread the earth close to the roots. 1827 STEUART *Planter's G.* (1828) 24 The same writer.. mentions, that it was a common practice to reestablish large Trees..that had been blown down. 1847 GROTE *Greece* II. xxxiv. (1862) III. 233 The bridge was re-established.

2. To set up again in a status or condition similar to the former one; to restore.

1559 *Fabyan's Chron.* II. 571 In the foresaied parliament also was the booke of seruice..reestablished. 1579 FENTON *Guicciard.* II. 77 The better to reestablish their gouernment, they had in their parliament..instituted a kind of pollicie. 1631 WEEVER *Anc. Funeral Mon.* 137 One hundred and sixe Abbeyes of this Order were built and reestablished. 1676 TOWERSON *Decalogue* 161 The great design of the gospel was to re-establish natural worship. 1705 ARBUTHNOT *Coins*, etc. (1727) 257 Theodosia..was..afterward re-established and possessed by the Genoese, under the name of Cafa. 1769 GOLDSM. *Hist. Rome* (1786) I. 62 Some young men .. undertook to re-establish monarchy. 1863 BRIGHT *Sp., Amer.* 26 Mar. (1876) 127 He had a fair chance of re-establishing his business. 1866 CRUMP *Banking* ix. 193 America was..re-establishing a metallic currency.

3. To restore (one's health or strength) to the usual state; to set (ill-health) right again. Usually in *pass.* († also with person as subj.).

1697 [see the *vbl. sb.* below]. 1709 STEELE *Tatler* No. 7 ¶ 18 His Health being so well re-established by the Baths. 1735–6 BERKELEY *Let. to Johnson* 12 Mar. in Fraser *Life* vii. 245 My ill-health, which is now pretty well re-established. 1766 J. WILKES *Let.* 3 May, I thank my dearest daughter for her obliging solicitude about my health. I am now quite re-established. c 1850 *Arab. Nts.* (Rtldg.) 268 The jeweller ..felt his strength re-established. a 1859 MACAULAY *Hist. Eng.* XXV. V. 288 With health so far re-established that he was able to take exercise on horseback.

b. To restore to a proper condition.

1812 G. CHALMERS *Dom. Econ. Gt. Brit.* 144 To see her.. reestablish her financial affairs, in so short a period, after the conclusion of war. 1822 DE QUINCEY *Confess.* 61 About fifteen shillings I had employed in re-establishing..my dress.

4. To reassure. *rare*⁻¹.

1722 DE FOE *Plague* (1754) 212 These things re-establish'd the Minds of the People very much.

Hence **Re-esta·blishable** *a.*; **Re-esta·blisher; Re-esta·blishing** *vbl. sb.*

1599 SANDYS *Europæ Spec.* (1632) 161 The soveraigne restorers of vertue, and re-establishers of an happy world. 1611 COTGR., *Restablissable*, reestablishable. 1611 SPEED *Hist. Gt. Brit.* VI. xlvi. § 9. 260/2 He addressed himselfe with his Armie to the reestablishing of the Ilands subiection. 1697 DRYDEN *Virgil, Life* ✱2 b, The wholesomness of the Air..contributed..to the re-establishing of his Health.

Re-esta·blishment. [f. as prec. + -MENT.] The act of re-establishing; the fact or condition of being re-established; restoration to a previous position or state.

1586 T. B. *La Primaud. Fr. Acad.* I. (1594) 302 Their creation after the image of God,..and..their reestablishment into the same image. 1651 HOBBES *Leviath.* III. xliii. 331 The re-establishment of the Kingdome of God in Christ. a 1679 W. OWTRAM *Serm.* (1682) 43 The reestablishment of the nation upon its antient laws. 1751 SMOLLETT *Per. Pic.* lxxxi, I repaired to Bath for the re-establishment of my health. 1788 GIBBON *Decl. & F.* lxx. VI. 575 All persons should assemble..to provide for the re-establishment of the good estate. 1817 SHELLEY *Rev. Islam* Pref., The re-establishment of successive tyrannies in France. 1884 BLACK *Jud. Shaks.* v, The re-establishment of the Catholic faith.

† b. Restoration to health. *Obs.*

Re-estate, v. Obs. (Very common in 17th c.)

Reested, ppl. a. Dried by heat or smoke.

Reesty, a. Sc. [f. REEST v.³ + -Y.] Inclined to reest or stop; given to reesting.

Reesty, Reesy, varr. REASTY, REASE, rancid.

Reest, dial. variant of RIGHT, ROOT.

Reestel, obs. form of RIVEL sb.

Re-eva·porate, v. [RE- 5 a.] To evaporate again. So **Re-evapora·tion**.

Reeve (riv), sb.¹ Now chiefly Hist. Forms: 1 ᵹeréfa, ᵹeréfa, réfa, 2 trefe, 3 ref-, 5-7 refe, 6 reeffe, Sc. reif; 7-8 (9) rive, 6-7 reave, 4-6 -reeve. [OE. ᵹeréfa, earlier ᵹiréfa, of uncertain orig.]

Reeve (riv), sb.² [Of obscure orig.: the form REE sb.² is found earlier, but is less frequent.] The female of the RUFF (Tringa pugnax).

Reeve (riv), sb.³ [Of obscure origin.] A long narrow strip. ? Obs.

Reeve-ship. Forms: 1 ᵹeréfscipe, 3 refeschipe, 7 reeveship. [f. ᵹeréfa REEVE sb.¹] The office of a reeve.

Reeve (riv), v.¹ Now only dial. [Of obscure origin.] (also in comb. reeving-sieve).

Reeve (riv), v.² Chiefly Naut. [Of obscure origin.]

Reever, rare-¹. [Of obscure origin.] A wooden instrument for collecting the crushed apples from the cider-mill.

Re-exalt, v. [RE- 5 a.] To exalt again. So **Re-exalta·tion**.

Re-exa·mination. [RE- 5 a.] A second or further examination.

Re-exa·mine, v. [RE- 5 a.] trans. To examine again.

Re-exca·vate, v. [RE- 5 a.] To excavate again. So **Re-excava·tion**.

Re-excha·nge, sb. [RE- and EXCHANGE sb.]

Re-excha·nge, v. trans. To exchange again.

Re-exci·te, v. [RE- 5 a.] trans. To excite again. Hence **Re-exci·ted** ppl. a.

Re-exci·tation. The partial re-excitation of some faded current of parental instinct.

Re-execute, v. [RE- 5 a.] trans. To execute again. So **Re-execu·tion**.

Re-exe·rcise, v. [RE- 5 a.] trans. To exercise again.

Re-exert, v. [RE- 5 a.] trans. To exert again. So **Re-exe·rtion**.

Re-exhale, v. [RE- 5 a.] trans. To exhale again.

Re-exhaust, v. [RE- 5 a.] trans. To exhaust again. Hence **Re-exhau·sted** ppl. a.

Re-exhi·bit, v. [RE- 5 a.] To exhibit again. So **Re-exhi·bition**.

Re-exist, v. intr. To exist again. So **Re-exi·stence**; **Re-exi·stent** a.

Re-exi·stence. **Re-exi·stent** a.

Reesed, rancid: see REESED.

Reese, variant of REESE, REOSE v.

Ref., abbr. of REFERENCE, etc.

† **Refa·bric**, v. Obs.-¹ To reconstruct.

Re·face, v. [RE- 5 a.] To renew the face or surface (on a building, stone, etc.).

Refa·ction. variant of RIFACIMENTO.

‡ **Refa·ction**. variant of RIFACIMENTO.

Re·fashion, v. [RE- 5 a.] To fashion again. Hence **Re·fashioned** ppl. a.; **Re·fashioning** vbl. sb.

Re·fasten, v. [RE- 5 a.] trans. To fasten again. Hence **Re·fastening** vbl. sb.

Re-father, v. nonce-wd. [RE- 5 a.] trans. To make (one) again a father.

Refa·vour, v. Obs.-¹ To favour again.

Refe, obs. f. REAVE v., REEF sb.², REEVE sb.¹

Refe·ct, ppl. a. and sb. Obs. [ad. L. refectus, pa. pple.] Refreshed, restored.

Refe·ct, v. rare. [f. L. refect-.] To refresh, restore, renew; etc.

Refe·ction. [a. F. refection, ad. L. refectiōn-em, n. of action f. reficĕre.]

Refe·ctive, a. rare. [f. L. refect-.] Refreshing, restoring, nourishing.

Refe·ctory. Obs. Also refecioun, etc. [ad. med.L. refectiōnem.]

Refe·ctory. [ad. late L. refectōrium.] A room in a monastery or convent, in which meals are taken.

Refectorer, -orar. Obs. [Anglo-Fr.] One who has charge of the refectory.

Refecto·rian. rare. [See next and -AN.]

Refe·l, v. arch. and Obs. [ad. L. refellĕre.] trans. To refute, confute, disprove (an argument, etc.).

Refe·ller. One who refels or refutes.

Refe·nce, v. [RE- 5 a.] To fence again.

Refer, v. [a. F. référer, ad. L. referre to carry back, refer.]

Referable ...

Referee ...

Reference (reˈfĕrĕns), sb. [f. prec.]

Referendal ...

Referendary ...

Referendum ...

Referent ...

Referential ...

Re-ferism ...

Referment ...

Refine (rĭˈfaɪn), v.

Refined (rĭˈfaɪnd), ppl. a.

Refinedly (rĭˈfaɪnɛdlɪ), adv.

Refinedness ...

Refinement ...

Refiner ...

Refinery ...

Refining ...

Refit ...

Refitment. *vbl. sb.* The act of refitting; a refit.

Refitting, *vbl. sb.* The action of the vb. in various senses.

Refix, *v.* To fix again; to establish anew.

Refixion.

Reflaç, revelaik. *Obs.*

Reflate, from CONFLATE *v.*

Reflect, *v.*

I. *Transitive senses.*
1. To turn or direct in a certain course, to divert; to turn away or aside, to deflect.
2. To bend, give or cast back.

II. *Intransitive senses.*

Reflection, reflexion. Also Re-, reflection.

Reflectional.

Reflective, *a.* and *sb.*

Reflectively, *adv.*

Reflectiveness.

Reflectly, *adv.*

Reflecto-meter.

Reflector.

Reflex, *a.* and *sb.*

Reflexed, *ppl. a.*

of it in reflex discoveries. 1736 Butler *Anal.* Diss. ii. 311 It does not appear, that Brutes have the least reflex Sense of Actions as distinguished from Events. 1850 M'Cosh *Div. Govt.* III. i. (1874) 331 When the reflex moral faculty, or the conscience, surveys virtuous action, it proclaims it good.

4. Coming by way of return or reflection.

1822 Hazlitt *Table-t.* Ser. II. xviii. (1869) 376 It is the immediate pursuit, not the remote or reflex consequence that gives wings to the passion. 1833 Chalmers *Const. Man* (1834) I. ii. 100 The secondary or reflex gratification which there is in the consciousness of benevolence. 1866 Dk. Argyll *Reign Law* i. (ed. 4) 12 That knowledge has a reflex influence on our knowledge of ourselves.

5. *Phys.* **a.** *Reflex action*, involuntary action of a muscle, gland, or other organ, caused by the excitation of a sensory nerve being transmitted to a nerve-centre, and thence 'reflected' along an efferent nerve to the organ in question.

1833 *Proc. Royal Soc.* III. 210 He [Dr. M. Hall] distinguishes muscular actions into three kinds:..thirdly, those resulting from the reflex action above described [see Reflect v. 4]. 1840 *Penny Cycl.* XVI. 153/1 In decapitated animals (in which the reflex actions are more remarkable than under any other circumstances). 1851 Carpenter *Man. Phys.* (ed. 2) 518 From the best judgment we can form of the actions of the Star-fish,..we may fairly regard the greater number of them as simply reflex. 1872 Darwin *Emotions* i. 35 Coughing and sneezing are familiar instances of reflex actions.

b. Of the nature of, characterized by, or connected with, such action.

1833 M. Hall in *Proc. Royal Soc.* III. 210 On the Reflex Function of the Medulla Oblongata and Spinalis. 1840 *Penny Cycl.* XVI. 151/2 When the spinal chord remains, its passage may be indicated by the phenomena of reflex motion. 1878 Foster *Phys.* II. i. § 2. 208 The ganglion in fact acted as a reflex centre. 1899 *Allbutt's Syst. Med.* VII. 618 The natural and imperious reflex cough being diminished..by the depth of coma.

6. *Gram.* Reflexive.

1873 Earle *Philol. Eng. Tongue* (ed. 2) § 469 The accusative pronoun of all the persons performed for a long period the double office of a direct and a reflex pronoun.

Reflex (rĭfle·ks), *v.* [f. L. *reflex-*, ppl. stem of *reflectĕre* to Reflect.]

1. *trans.* To bend, fold back, recurve; = Reflect *v.* 2. Chiefly *Her.* and *Bot.*, and only in pa. pple. (cf. Reflexed *ppl. a.* 4).

1572 Bossewell *Armorie* II. 48 The fielde is verte, twoo Apes..combattante, with tayles reflexed. 1610 Guillim *Heraldry* VI. vii. (1611) 280 A chaine..passing betweene his fore legs and reflexed ouer his backe. 1655 Fuller *Wounded Consc., Ornithologie* (1867) 244 This Eagle had its bill..reflexed back again into his mouth. 1760 J. Lee *Introd. Bot.* II. xvii. (1765) 107 The Stigma bipartite and acute, with the lower Lacinia reflexed. 1771 *Antiq. Sarisb.* 182 A monster lying at his feet, with his head reflext on his tail. 1861 Mrs. Lankester *Wild Fl.* 125 The petals are reflexed, and turn over. 1868 Cussans *Her.* 209 *note*, Their tails passing between their legs, and reflexed over their backs. 1875 Darwin *Insectiv. Pl.* iv. 71 With the outer tentacles slightly reflexed.

†**2.** To reflect (light, vision, etc.). *Obs.*

c1380 [see Reflexed *ppl. a.* 1]. a1586 *Satir. Poems Reform.* xxxvii. 22 Ay moir brycht and burning is þe beymis Off Phebus face, þat fastast ar reflexit. 1594 R. Ashley tr. *Loys le Roy* 4 The Sun beames reflexed doe heate. 1658 tr. *Porta's Nat. Magic* VIII. 230 The Cockatrice..giveth venimous wounds with the beams of his eyes: which being reflexed upon himself,..kill the Author of them.

†**b.** To throw, cast (beams) *on* a place. *Obs.*

1586 Marlowe *1st Pt. Tamburl.* III. i, For neither rain can fall upon the earth, Nor sun reflex his virtuous beams thereon. 1591 Shaks. *1 Hen. VI*, v. iv. 87 May neuer glorious Sunne reflex his beames Vpon the Countrey where you make abode.

†**3.** To reflect, mirror, image (an object). *Obs.*

1633 Drumm. of Hawth. *Entertainm. Charles* Wks. (1856) 228 When Iber's streams reflex'd thy glorious face! 1657 W. Rand tr. *Gassendi's Life Peiresc* II. 96 Contemplate the Image being reflexed by the Retina and restored.

†**4.** *intr.* Of heat: To strike *upon* a thing, and be reflected. *Obs.*[—1]

1632 Lithgow *Trav.* VI. 292 What with..the great heate reflexing vpon the sand, and from the sand to our faces, we were miserably turmoiled.

†**5.** To reflect, meditate, etc., *on* a subject. *Obs.*

1631 R. H. *Arraignm. Whole Creature* iv. 22 To drive this naile further to the very head: reflexing more fully on the Prodigals huskes.

†**Reflexcye.** *Obs. rare*[—1]. [app. f. Reflex *sb.* or *a.* + -cy, but perhaps a misprint.] Reflection.

1589 *Almond for Parrat* 16 The very reflexcye of my fury, shall make thee driue thy father to the gallows, for begetting thee.

Reflexed (rĭfle·kst), *ppl. a.* [f. Reflex *v.*]

1. Of light, etc.: Reflected, thrown back; due to, or caused by, reflection.

c1380 Wyclif *Sel. Wks.* II. 299 Þe þridde si3t is reflexid when it comeþ bi dyvers meenes, and þei ben on divers kyndis, as þe moone is seen a3ens ni3t. 1595 J. King *Queens Day Serm.* in *Jonas* (1618) 690 Our loue to other..comming as broken and reflexed beames from our loue to God. 1615 Jackson *Creed* IV. III. viii. § 5 Any reflexed splendour from the favourable aspect of earthly majesty. 1662 Bargrave *Pope Alex. VII* (1867) 134 This glass..will render the reflexed species of the outward object full and large.

†**2.** Directed backwards. Cf. Reflex *a.* 3. *Obs.*

1656 in Clarendon *Hist. Reb.* XV. § 113 When we take a reflexed [1704 reflex] view of our past actions. 1659 *Gentl. Calling* (1696) 102 Cheating has usually a reflexed efficacy, and deceives none more than those that use it. a1676 Hale *Prim. Orig. Man.* I. i. (1677) 20 By considering the reflexed acts of our Understanding, whereby we know many acts of our own minds and Soul.

†**3.** = Reflex *a.* 4. *Obs. rare*[—1].

1667 *Decay Chr. Piety* v. ¶ 11 This secondary and reflext apologie for Christs law.

4. Turned, bent, or folded back. Cf. Reflex *v.* 1.

1733 Miller *Gard. Dict.* (ed. 2) s.v. *Cassia*, Barbadoes Cassia, with a reflex'd Cup, and pointed leaves. 1818 Kirby & Sp. *Entomol.* xxi. (ed. 2) II. 238 The reflexed head simulating a tail curled over its back. 1854 Hooker *Himal. Jrnls.* II. xx. 77 Inflated reflexed bracts, that conceal the flowers. 1882 *Garden* 7 Oct. 312/2 A very handsome and full reflexed flower.

Comb. 1777 Lightfoot *Flora Scot.* II. 755 Reflex'd-leav'd Hypnum.

b. (See quot.)

1836 Rafinesque *Amer. Nations* I. ii. 66 The Resupinate or Reflexed Group [of American languages]: where the roots or nouns substantive are reversed, following the adjectives or epithets, which are prefixed.

Reflexibi·lity. [f. next + -ity. Cf. F. *réflexibilité* (14th c., Oresme; but in mod. use adopted from English).] Capability of being reflected.

1673 Newton in Rigaud *Corr. Sci. Men* (1841) II. 351 Whence it is that the same rays exhibit the same colours, when separated by any other means; as by their different reflexibility. 1728 Pemberton *Newton's Philos.* 370 The sun's light differs in reflexibility, those rays being most reflexible, which are most refrangible. 1797 Brougham in *Phil. Trans.* LXXXVII. 375 It is evident, that neither reflexibility nor refrangibility will account for either sort of rings. 1808 Herschel *ibid.* XCIX. 267 In consequence of the different reflexibility of the differently coloured rays.

Reflexible (rĭfle·ksĭb'l), *a.* [f. Reflex *v.* Hence F. *réflexible.*] Capable of being reflected.

1706 W. Jones *Syn. Palmar. Matheseos* 301 The Light of the Sun consists of Rays that are differently Reflexible and Refrangible. 1794 J. Hutton *Philos. Light*, etc. 29 Such an opinion, as that heat is a thing eradiated and reflexible. 1822 Imison *Sc. & Art* I. 229 The waves of sound being thus reflexible, nearly in the same manner as the rays of light.

So **Refle·xile** *a. nonce-wd.*

1797 Brougham in *Phil. Trans.* LXXXVII. 384 The rays which are most flexible..are most refrangible, reflexile, and flexile.

†**Refle·xing,** *ppl. a. Obs. rare.* [f. Reflex *v.* + -ing [2].] That reflects, in senses of the vb.

1606 J. Raynolds *Dolarney's Prim.* (1880) 62 The hot reflexing rayes Of bright Apollo. 1632 Lithgow *Trav.* x. 488 This reflexing heart..Can by experience conster well, your Churches Sire and Dame.

Reflexion, -al, -ist: see Reflection.

†**Reflexious,** *a. Obs. rare*[—1]. [f. Reflex *sb.* + -ious.] Of the nature of a reflection.

1680 J. Aubrey in *Lett. Eminent Persons* (1813) II. 255 But shee needed neither borrowed shades, nor reflexious lights, to set her off.

†**Reflexity.** *Obs.* [f. as Reflex *a.* + -ity.]

1. Shining, reflection. *rare*[—1].

c1485 *Digby Myst.* (1882) III. 441 Heyl, oryent, as þe sonne In his reflexite!

2. Reflexibility. *nonce-use.*

1797 Brougham in *Phil. Trans.* LXXXVII. 361, I now tried to measure the different degrees of reflexity, &c. of the different rays.

Reflexive (rĭfle·ksiv), *a.* and *sb.* [ad. L. type *reflexivus: see Reflex *v.* and -ive. Cf. F. *réflexif, -ive* (Cotgr. 1611), Sp. *reflexivo*, It. *riflessivo*, and see also Reflective.] **A.** *adj.*

1. a. Capable of turning or bending back. *rare.*

1588 J. Read tr. *Arcæus' Compend. Meth.* 60 b, Who would not feare the force, the pearcing and power reflexiue of Quicksiluer. 1884 A. Daniell *Princ. Physics* xiv. 413 The reflexive power of flame is nearly the same as that of tracing-paper.

†**b.** Capable of reflecting light. *Obs. rare.*

1676 Boyle in *Phil. Trans.* XI. 787, I found the Confining surface very strongly reflexive.

†**c.** Reflected (as light). *Obs. rare*[—1].

1676 Hale *Contempl.* II. 201 Though the Glory of thy Essence, cannot receive any increase by this reflection, yet thou art pleased everlastingly to perpetuate this thy reflexive Glory.

†**2.** Of mental operations: Turned or directed back upon the mind itself. *Obs.*

1640 Bp. Reynolds *Passions* xxviii. 295 In those two Offices of Reason, the Transient and Reflexive act, that whereby we looke Outward on others; or Inward on our selves. 1656 Jeanes *Mixt. Schol. Div.* 42 Then the mind in it's reflexive workings can proceed *in infinitum*. a1708 Beveridge *Priv. Th.* I. (1730) 1 Being not capable of a reflexive act, they know it not.

†**b.** Capable of, inclined to, or characterized by, reflection or serious thought; reflective. *Obs.*

1653 H. More *Antid. Ath.* II. v. (1712) 53 Man, in whom there is a principle of more fine and reflexive Reason. 1655–87 — *App. Antid.* (1712) 193 This must be in a knowing, passive, and reflexive Subject. 1684 T. Burnet *Th. Earth* I. 287 To the attentive and reflexive, to those that are unprejudic'd. 1752 *School of Man* (1753) 37 Their sensitive soul bears such marks of a reflexive intelligence.

†**3.** Reciprocal, correspondent. *Obs.*

c1642 *Contra-Replicant's Complaint* 18 There is likewise a neare consanguinity, and reflexive benevolence of aspects between Lawes and Princes. 1681 Flavel *Right. Man's Ref.* 178 Nor..are our thoughts as Gods in respect of reflexive comprehension.

†**4.** Reflecting on a person. *Obs. rare*[—1].

a1716 South *Serm.* (1744) X. 174, I would fain know what man..there is that does not resent an ugly reflexive word.

5. *Gram.* Of pronouns, verbs, and their signification: Characterized by, or denoting, a reflex action on the subject of the clause or sentence.

1837 G. Phillips *Syriac Gram.* 114 The ordinary method of expressing a reciprocal or reflexive sense. 1861 Max Müller *Sc. Lang.* viii. 299 The mere addition of certain letters, which give to every verb a negative, or causative, or reflexive, or reciprocal meaning. 1867 J. Hadley *Ess.* xi. 205 A shortened form of the reflexive pronoun.

6. Of a reflex character.

1871 Farrar *Witn. Hist.* iv. 138 He reduced religion to a reflexive ceremony of empty proprieties. 1888 J. T. Gulick in *Linn. Soc. Jrnl.* XX. 200/2 Reflexive Selection is the exclusive generation of those better fitted to the relations in which the members of the same species stand to each other.

B. *sb.* †**1.** An object reflecting light. *Obs.*[—1]

1686 Goad *Celest. Bodies* I. ix. 27 That there may be found as much variety in them as in other Reflexives, i.e. Plain, Convex or Concave Glasses.

2. A reflexive verb or pronoun.

1866 *Trans. Phil. Soc.* 88 We are still capable of forming a double set of reflexives. 1867 J. Hadley *Ess.* xi. 209 The reflexive which serves to express the passive is a causal reflexive.

Refle·xively, *adv.* [f. prec. + -ly [2].] In a reflexive or reflecting manner, by way of reflection (in various senses).

1674 *Govt. Tongue* 223 Not only directly..but reflexively also, in respect of what may rebound to our selves. 1678 Cudworth *Intell. Syst.* I. v. 636 Reflexively examining himself whether he have a phantasm, or sensible idea, belonging to every word, or no. a1716 South *Twelve Serm.* (1717) VI. 105 Ay, but he spoke slightly and reflexively of such a Lady. 1858 Caswall *Poems* 192 Thyself by nurture, meditation, grace, Reflexively reveal'd. 1867 C. J. Smith *Syn. & Antonyms, Abeyance*, The term has been transferred reflexively from the person waiting to the thing waited for.

Refle·xiveness. [f. as prec. + -ness.] The state or quality of being reflexive.

1667 H. More *Div. Dial.* I. II. 234 There not being that Reflexiveness..in Brutes in their suffering as in rational Creatures. 1881 Westcott & Hort *Grk. N. T.* II. App. 144 The reflexiveness is so direct that a refusal to admit the rough breathing introduces language completely at variance with all Greek usage.

So **Reflexi·vity.**

1653 H. More *Antid. Ath.* III. xvi. 137 Ready from every part to be reflected if the clouds had any such reflexivity in them. 1891 Mrs. H. Ward tr. *Amiel's Jrnl.* 32 Less reflexivity and more plasticity..would raise the style of Vinet.

Refle·xly, *adv.* [f. Reflex *a.* + -ly [2].] In a reflex manner. (Common in recent use.)

1839 Hallam *Hist. Lit.* IV. iii. § 20 No body can act reflexly on itself. 1875 H. C. Wood *Therap.* (1879) 255 Contraction of the pupil before dilatation..is probably caused reflexly by irritant action of the atropia.

Reflexo·genous, *a. Path.* [f. Reflex *a.*: see -o.] Producing reflex action. So **Reflexoge·nic** *a.* (*Cent. Dict.* 1891.)

1899 *Allbutt's Syst. Med.* VI. 521 Certain bone surfaces are similarly very dependably 'reflexogenous'.

†**Refle·xure.** *Obs. rare*[—1]. [See Reflex *v.* and Flexure.] A bend or fold.

1578 Banister *Hist. Man* VIII. 100 The thinne Membran ..made in reflexures, should nourish the substaunce of the brayne.

†**Refli·rt,** *v. Obs. rare*[—1]. In 7 reflurt. [Re-.] *trans.* To toss back again.

1652 *News fr. Low-Countr.* 11 If carping Momes shall flurt in Podex's face A Flout,..Podex, with a full Breath, reflurts it back.

†**Refloa·t,** *sb. Obs. rare.* [ad. obs. F. *reflot*: see Re- 2 a and Float *sb.* 2.] A flowing back; reflux, ebb (of the tide).

1594 [see Float *sb.* 2]. 1626 Bacon *Sylva* § 907 The Maine Float and Refloat of the Sea..which is..Part of the Diurnal Motion.

So †**Refloa·t** *v.*[1] *intr.*, to flow back, ebb. *Obs.*[—0]

1632 Sherwood, To reflote, *refloter.*

Refloat (rĭflōu·t), *v.*[2] [Re- 5 a.] *trans.* To float, set afloat, again. Hence **Refloa·ting** *vbl. sb.*; also **Refloata·tion.**

1871 *Daily News* 14 Jan., The necessary operations for the refloating of the French war vessel. 1883 *Manch. Exam.* 24 Oct. 7/1 The company undertook to refloat, at their own expense, any vessel that went ashore in the canal. 1892 *Pall Mall G.* 22 Nov. 2/1 The refloating of all the colonial loans..By such a refloatation there would be a saving of about one per cent.

Refloenge, obs. form of Reflowing *vbl. sb.*

Refloo, obs. form of Reflow *v.*

†**Reflo·re,** *v. Sc. Obs. rare*[—1]. In 6 refloir. [f. Re- 5 a + -*flore*, as in *deflore* Deflower.] *trans.* To cause to flourish again; = Reflower *v.* 1.

1560 Rolland *Crt. Venus* I. 295 With superabundant Mirth, melodie, thow dois my hart refloir.

Reflore·scence. [Re- 5 a; or f. L. *reflōrēscĕre* to flower again + -ence.] A blossoming again, a second florescence.

1721 in Bailey. a1792 Horne *Disc.* xvi. Wks. 1809 IV. 302 By the reflorescence of that mortal part which he drew from the stem of Jesse. 1880 Swinburne *Stud. Shaks.* 17 A famous..example of this reflorescence.

So **Reflore·scent** *a.*

1897 *Dublin Rev.* Oct. 398 The classic forms so exuberantly reflorescent in the sixteenth century.

Reflourish (rĭflʊ·rĭʃ), *v.* [f. Re- 5 a + Flourish *v.*, orig. after L. *reflōrēscĕre.*] *intr.* To flourish anew. Chiefly *fig.* (Common in 17th c.)

a1340 Hampole *Psalter* xxvii. 10 And my fleysse reflorist

[L. *refloruit*]. 1544 Leland *N. Y. Gift* in *Itin.* (1768) I. p. xxiii, The old Glory of your renowmid Britaine [shall be seen] to reflorisch thorough the Worlde. 1558 Phaer *Æneid* Gen. Sum. a ij b, A land where their Kyngdome should reflorishe. 1615 G. Sandys *Trav.* 83 Cypresse: a tree destinated to the dead; in that once being cut it neuer reflourisheth. 1675 Plume *Life Hacket* in *Cent. Serm.* p. i, Afterwards, when Christian religion reflourished, the Christian Church resumed these studies again. 1776 R. Chandler *Trav. Greece* (1825) II. 135 He saw the city reflourishing under the auspices of the emperor Hadrian. 1853 G. Johnston *Nat. Hist. E. Bord.* I. 229 The love of flowers..reflourishes..in the autumn of our age.

†**b.** Const. with *inf.* (after the Vulgate). *Obs.*

1582 N. T. (Rhem.) *Phil.* iv. 10, I rejoyced in our Lord excedingly, that once at the length you have reflorished to care for me [L. *refloruistis pro me sentire*]. 1613 Day *Dyall* x. (1614) 266 Little have they Reflourished to care for them, to use a phrase of theirs.

Hence **Reflou·rishing** *vbl. sb.* and *ppl. a.*

1621 H. Farley *St. Paul's* title-p., All such as beare good will to the reflourishing estate of the said Chvrch. 1627 Hakewill *Apol.* (1630) 230 Their resurrection, and refloureshing againe. 1657 W. Rand tr. *Gassendi's Life Peiresc* II. 238 The reflourishing Glory of that most excellent and Beneficent King Renatus. 1728 Earbery tr. *Burnet's St. Dead* II. 108 The Wicked are no Objects of Hope nor of Reflourishing. 1775 S. J. Pratt *Liberal Opin.* xciv. (1783) III. 191 The reflourishing fortunes of the benevolent Blewitt.

So **Reflou·rishment.** *rare*[—1].

1611 Speed *Hist. Gt. Brit.* IX. ix. § 95. 535/2 The Welsh seeing these round proceedings in England, the peace and reflorishment whereof they feared, labored for reconciliation.

Reflow, *sb.* [Re- 2 a.] A reflux, refluence, ebb of the tide.

1610 Holland *Camden's Brit.* I. 37 By the reflow or ebbe of the Ocean. 1793 Smeaton *Edystone L.* § 197 This matter..would in time block up the Humber, was it not for the powerful re-flow of that river's tide. 1832 De la Beche *Geol. Man.* (ed. 2) 131 A quick flow or reflow of the water. 1860 Maury *Phys. Geog. Sea* § 136 (Low) 47 The grand equatorial flow and reflow which is performed by the waters of all the great oceans.

Reflow, *v.*[1] Now *rare.* [Re- 2 a, orig. after L. *reflŭere.*] *intr.* To flow back; *esp.* of the tide, to ebb. Freq. in phr. *flow and reflow.*

1387 [see Reflowing *vbl. sb.*]. 1432–50 tr. *Higden* (Rolls) I. 57 The see Pontike reflowethe not as other sees. *Ibid.* 425 A lytelle welle in the costes of Ruthlande,..whiche dothe not floo and refloo in the maner of a see. 1535 Stewart *Cron. Scot.* I. 373 Syne as the flude begouth for till reflow [etc.]. 1555 Eden *Decades* 119 They see the seas by increase and decrease to flowe and reflowe. 1589 Fleming *Virg. Georg.* IV. 71 At creekes reflowing past the which the water cannot go. 1776 Burrow *Rep.* IV. 2163 It is said that the king has a right, as high as the sea flows and reflows. 1810 Crabbe *Borough* i. 216 The billows..strike with furious force, And then re-flowing, take their grating course. 1852 *Humber Conserv. Act* 2038 So far as the tide flows or reflows.

b. *fig.* and in fig. context.

1609 J. Davies *Holy Roode* Ded., Those [pleasures] will runne to Helles impure, While these to Eden faire reflow againe. 1677 Gale *Crt. Gentiles* IV. 15 As al Creatures flow and reflow to God, as the Ocean or plenitude of al Being. 1721 R. Keith tr. *T. à Kempis, Solil. Soul* xii. 197 My Affection floweth and refloweth here and there and every where. 1818 Byron *Ch. Har.* IV. xcii, An universal deluge, which..ebbs but to reflow!

Reflow, *v.*[2] *rare.* [Re- 5 a.] To flow again.

1817 Byron *Mazeppa* xiv, Life reassumed its lingering hold,.. My blood reflow'd, though thick and chill. a1832 Crabbe *Woman* i, She..bids the spring of hope re-flow That languish'd in the fainting heart.

Reflow·er, *v.* [Re- 5 a.]

†**1.** *trans.* To cause to flower or flourish again.

1598 Sylvester *Du Bartas* II. ii. I. *Ark* 66 As the Sommer sweet-distilling drops..Re-greens the Greens, and doth the Flowrs re-flowr [F. *refleurir*]. 1606 *Ibid.* IV. II. *Magnificence* 805 Her sight re-flowres th' Arabian Wilderness. a1649 Drumm. of Hawth. *Poems* Wks. (1711) 39 To make peace prosper, justice to reflow'r.

2. *intr.* To flower again (Ogilvie *Suppl.* 1855).

Reflow·ing, *vbl. sb.* [f. Reflow *v.*[1] + -ing [1].] The action of the vb.; refluence.

1387 Trevisa *Higden* (Rolls) III. 369 The floenge..of the see þer as at oon tyme and refloenge to gedre. 1555 Eden *Decades* 58 Whiche rowghnes or reflowinge, the Spanyardes caule Resacca. 1613–16 W. Browne *Brit. Past.* I. v, Our teares should make the flood, not her reflowing. 1654 Earl Monm. tr. *Bentivoglio's Warrs Flanders* 224 The flowing and reflowing of the Tide will oppose them. 1813 J. C. Hobhouse *Journey* (ed. 2) 454 The change which..took place in the flowing and reflowing of the stream.

So **Reflow·ing** *ppl. a.*

1609 Holland *Amm. Marcell.* 196 With a returne of the current and reflowing waves it dasheth upon the temple of Apollo Sminthius. 1896 *Daily News* 29 Feb. 5/5 Coming up..on the crest of the re-flowing tide.

Refluction, variant of Refluxion *Obs.*

Refluctua·tion. *rare*[—0]. [Re- 2 a.] A flowing back (Webster 1828–32).

†**Reflue,** *v. Obs. rare.* [ad. L. *reflŭere*: see Refluent and Reflow *v.*[1]] *intr.* To flow back.

1545 Raynold *Byrth Mankynde* 30 This skynny flappes close the passage and defende, that nothynge canne rebound, ne reflue backe agayne. *Ibid.* 44 Sum part therof reflueth, and is reuerted to the womans brestes, ther to becum mylke.

Refluence (re·fluĕns). [See Refluent and -ence.] A flowing back; a reflux.

c1592 Marlowe *Jew of Malta* III. iv, The wastfull sea, Whose billowes..Shall ouerflow it with their refluence. 1615 Crooke *Body of Man* 167 To hinder the refluence or returne of the..vnprofitable humors. 1621 Lodge *Summary of Du Bartas* 106 In the sea, betwixt Norway, and Scotland, there is clerely obserued a flow and refluence. 1817 Shelley *Rev. Islam* XII. ix, Like the refluence of a mighty wave Sucked into the loud sea. 1861 Mrs. Browning *Psyche & Pan* 4 The gentle river..cast up Psyche, with a refluence brave, Upon the flowery bank.

transf. and *fig.* a1592 Greene *Jas. IV*, IV. iii, One hornpipe further, a refluence back, and two doubles forward. 1842 Alison *Hist. Europe* lxxiv. § 78 The refluence of its legions over the Rhine and the Pyrenees..prostrated the financial affairs of the Empire.

So †**Re·fluency.** *Obs. rare.*

1615 Crooke *Body of Man* 400 By..what affluencies and refluencies this perpetuity is accomplished. 1648 W. Mountague *Devout Ess.* I. vi. § 2. 58 How all things sublunary move..in an interchangeable flowing and refluencie.

Refluent (re·flŭĕnt), *a.* [ad. L. *refluent-em*, pres. pple. of *reflŭere* to flow back, f. *re-* Re- 2 a + *flŭere* to flow.]

1. Flowing back, reflowing:

a. of the sea, waves, rivers, etc.

1712 Blackmore *Creation* III. 139 Do not the Rivers..to the Hills convey the Refluent Wave..? 1725 Pope *Odyss.* v. 549 Then backward sweep The refluent tides, and plunge him in the deep. 1791 Cowper *Iliad* XII. 30 All those [rivers] with refluent course Apollo drove Nine days against the rampart. 1812 Brackenridge *Views Louisiana* (1814) 37 In lower Louisiana, there are a great number of lakes from the refluent waters of the Mississippi. 1873 T. W. Higginson *Oldport Days* ii. 36 All night the phosphorescent water..washes with long, refluent waves along their sides.

transf. 1842 Alison *Hist. Europe* lxxxiv. § 1 The once triumphant Peninsular hosts, refluent through the passes of the Pyrenees. 1856 R. A. Vaughan *Mystics* (1860) II. 78 To give him a hold against any refluent doubt that might threaten to sweep him back.

b. of blood, the spirits, life, etc.

1699 Garth *Dispens.* 91, I show'd of old, how vital Currents glide, And the Meanders of their refluent Tide. 1714 *Spring* in Steele *Poet. Misc.* 109 When to his Heart the refluent Spirits came. 1789 E. Darwin *Bot. Gard.* II. (1791) 77 Slow-ebbing life with refluent crimson breaks O'er their wan lips. 1816 Southey *Lay of Laureate* lxix, I felt the refluent blood forsake my face. 1872 Geo. Eliot *Middlem.* xxxii, Too languid to sting, he had the more venom refluent in his blood.

c. *Phys.* of blood or other fluids.

1704 Ray *Creation* II. (ed. 4) 319 To discharge the refluent Blood into the next adjacent Trunk. 1822–34 *Good's Study Med.* (ed. 4) IV. 347 The ammoniacal salt of the refluent urine. 1898 *Allbutt's Syst. Med.* V. 924 The heading back will..fill the ventricle still more with refluent aortic blood.

2. Characterized by refluence, *esp.* tidal.

1741 Monro *Anat. Nerves* (ed. 3) 21 This..Reflux it was ..., which gave Rise to another Division of the Nerves into arterious or effluent, and venous or refluent. 1798 *Anti-Jacobin* No. 28 Wherever man is found, or refluent oceans roll. 1864 Tennyson *Boädicea* 28 A phantom colony smoulder'd on the refluent estuary.

†**3.** Directed backwards. *Obs. rare*[—1].

1741 Shenstone *Judgm. Hercules* 424 If o'er their lives a refluent glance they cast, Their's is the present who can praise the past.

†**Re·fluous,** *a. Obs. rare.* [f. L. *reflu-us* refluent + -ous.] Refluent; recurring.

1628 Sir W. Mure *Spirit. Hymn* 274 That Day shall rest Heauen's rolling spheares, Earth's refluous tumults. 1650 Fuller *Pisgah* II. 62 Seeing the stream of Jordan..was not supplied with any reciprocall or refluous tide out of the Dead Sea.

Reflurt: see Reflirt *v. Obs.*

Reflux (rī·flɒks). [f. Re- 2 a + Flux: cf. F. *reflux* (16th c.), Sp. *reflujo* (-*fluxo*), It. *riflusso.*]

1. A flowing back, return, refluence: **a.** of the sea (esp. in phr. *flux and reflux*), rivers, water, air, etc.

c1430 Lydg. *Min. Poems* (Percy Soc.) 194 Man hath of erthe slowthe and hevynesse, Flux and reflux by watir made unstable. 1601 Holland *Pliny* I. 43 Hereunto addeth Aristotle..that no liuing creature dieth but in the reflux and ebbe of the sea. 1686 Plot *Staffordsh.* 56 Which in some measure may cause the flux and reflux of the green Sea. 1719 De Foe *Crusoe* I. xv, The great draught and reflux of the..river. 1761 *Ann. Reg.* I. 95 Fluxes and refluxes of the sea..continued till six o'clock next morning. 1804 C. B. Brown tr. *Volney's View Soil U.S.* 67, I cannot determine how far eastward the Delaware then extended the reflux of its waters. 1830 Lyell *Princ. Geol.* I. 117 The heat and cold which surround the globe are in a state of constant and universal flux and reflux. 1869 E. A. Parkes *Pract. Hygiene* (ed. 3) 110 Ill-contrived sewers permitting a large reflux of air into the houses.

b. in *transf.* and *fig.* uses.

1632 J. Hayward tr. *Biondi's Eromena* 129 The refluxes of so unjust a fortune in a Princesse of so great merit. 1670 R. Coke *Disc. Trade* 69 After all this flux and re-flux of vexation and charge to the certain undoing of one or both parties. 1711 Shaftesb. *Charac.* (1737) I. 271 The alterations which happen in manners, and the flux and reflux of politeness, wit, and art. 1800 Colquhoun *Comm. Thames* Introd. 25 The flux and reflux of Commercial Property..on the Thames. 1849 Macaulay *Hist. Eng.* vii. II. 189 A violent and rapid reflux of public feeling.

c. *Phys.* of the blood.

1653 Harvey *Anat. Exerc.* I. xiii. (1673) 81 [The blood] comes..into the ear of the heart in so great abundance, with so great flux, and reflux [etc.]. 1707 Floyer *Physic. Pulse-watch* 15 The Circulation of our Blood, whose reflux to the Heart is promoted by..Respiration. 1834 J. Forbes *Laennec's Dis. Chest* (ed. 4) 511 The reflux of blood into the jugular veins from coughing or a prolonged expiration. 1899 *Allbutt's Syst. Med.* VI. 40 The intra-ventricular pressure becomes lowered from reflux through the valve.

2. *attrib.* and *Comb.*, as *reflux current, theory, tide*; **reflux catheter**, a double-channel catheter, in which the liquid passes by one duct and returns by the other (Knight *Dict. Mech.* Suppl. 1884); **reflux trap**, a trap in a drain or sewer to prevent a back current of foul air.

1852 Wiggins *Embanking* 51 This is to sustain any current that may take place at the reflux tide. 1892 *Daily News* 30 Dec. 3/4 As far as practical, the up current of air (when existing) is prevented by reflux traps. 1898 *Allbutt's Syst. Med.* V. 975 The current impelled by the right ventricle.. is met by the reflux current from the left ventricle. 1899 *Ibid.* VI. 234 The reflux theory seems at present the more probable for most cases.

†**Reflu·xion.** *Obs.* Also refluction. [ad. med.L. *refluxiōn-em*, n. of action f. *reflŭere*: see Refluent.] = Reflux.

1597 A. M. tr. *Guillemeau's Fr. Chirurg.* 4 b/1 The refluxione of badd humors vnto the wounded parte. 1635 Swan *Spec. M.* vi. § 2 (1643) 202 The next..question propounded, was concerning the fluxion and refluxion of the sea. 1654 Gayton *Pleas. Notes* IV. xvii. 279 Are they more daring at the ebullition of the blood, or at the circular refluxion?

Refly·, *v.* [Re-.] *intr.* To fly back or again.

1611 Florio, *Riuolare*, to flie againe, to refly. a1711 Ken *Hymns Evang.* Poet. Wks. 1721 I. 142 Thus spake the Seraph, and to Bliss reflew. — *Hymns Festiv.* ibid. 351 Gabriel..to Heav'n reflown, Attended at the Throne. 1866 Crichton *Nat. Ramble Orcades* 63 Many individuals were flying and reflying from and to the spot.

Refo·cillate, *v.* Now *rare.* [ad. late L. *refocillāre* to warm into life again, revive: see Re- 5 a and Focillate.] *trans.* To revive, refresh, reanimate, comfort (a person, the spirits, senses, etc.).

1611 Coryat *Crudities* 93 The first view thereof did euen refocillate my spirits and tickle my senses with inward joy. 1680 Aubrey *Lives* (1898) II. *Prynne* 174 About every 3 houres his man was to bring him a roll and a pott of ale to refocillate his wasted Spirits. 1694 Motteux *Rabelais* v. (1737) 230 In Arbors, some themselves refocillate. 1760 Sterne *Tr. Shandy* III. xxxviii, The nose was comforted, nourish'd, plump'd up, refresh'd, refocillated, and set a growing for ever.

Hence †**Refo·cillating** *ppl. a. Obs.*

1697 R. Peirce *Bath Mem.* II. ii. 279 These Disorders.. were greatly increased..so that she was not fit for any, but refocillating Means (to palliate the most urging Symptomes).

Refocilla·tion. Now *rare.* [ad. med. or mod. L. *refocillātiōn-em*, n. of action f. *refocillāre*: see prec. + -ation.] The action of the verb; refreshment, reanimation, reinvigoration.

1576 Foxe *A. & M.* (ed. 3) 1615/1 What paynes..would not hee willyngly haue suffered, to haue had some refocillation and tyme of refreshyng? 1620 Donne *Serm.* xliii. 414 He..kindly performed all offices of ease and refocillation to these way-faring strangers. 1656 E. Reyner *Rules Govt. Tongue* 225 For recreation of the minde, and refocillation of the spirits. 1824 Coleridge *Lett.* (1895) II. 621, I need for myself solace and refocillation of animal spirits. 1872 Jacox *Asp. Authorsh.* 3 Refocillation is a favourite resource —whatever the word may be—with authors not a few.

†**b.** A means of refreshment. *Obs. rare*[—1].

1608 Middleton *Mad World* III. ii, Some precious cordial, some costly refocillation.

Refo·cus, *v.* [Re- 5 a.] To focus again.

c1865 J. Wylde in *Circ. Sc.* I. 149/2 Having..refocussed the lenses, the brass cap..should be put on. 1895 *N. Amer. Rev.* Feb. 173 A pulpit..capable of re-focusing religion.

Refo·ld, *v.* [Re- 5 a.] *trans.* To fold again. Hence **Refo·lding** *vbl. sb.*

1594 Daniel *Cleopatra* Wks. (1717) 293 And having ended, with a Sigh refolds Thy Letter up. 1611 Florio, *Ridupplicare*, to redouble or refold. *Ibid.*, *Ripiego*, a refolding vp againe. 1852 Surtees *Sponge's Sp. Tour* (1893) 327 Having mastered its contents, the captain refolded and replaced it where he found it. 1892 Zaehnsdorf *Bind. Books* (1892) 7 Refolding would in such a case be most detrimental. 1899 *Allbutt's Syst. Med.* VIII. 344 She will refold and rearrange all clothing and bedding in the store-room.

Refo·nt. *rare.* [ad. F. *refonte*: see Font *sb.*[2] and cf. Refount.] A recast, recasting.

1833 *New Monthly Mag.* XXXVII. 47 The impending refont of the political structure of Germany. 1833 S. Austin *Charact. Goethe* iii. 220 The fragment of the *Achilleis*, or his refont of *Reinecke Fuchs.*

Refoorme, obs. form of Reform *v.*

Refoo·t, *v.* [Re- 5 a.] *trans.* To put a new foot in (a boot or stocking).

1851 Mayhew *Lond. Labour* II. 6/2 Stocking-legs for the supply of 'jobbing worsted', and for re-footing. *Ibid.* 34/1 The back and the remainder of the front having been used for refooting boots. 1880 *Plain Hints Needlework* 116 It is in this last meaning probably that this word [*sc.* stilt] is used in Lincolnshire to describe the re-footing a stocking.

†**Reforce,** *v. Obs.* [ad. OF. *reforcier, reforcer*, f. *re-* Re- + *forcer*: see Force *v.*]

1. *trans.* To reinforce, strengthen, make stronger.

c1489 Caxton *Blanchardyn* 113 He byganne to reforce his callynge, cryinge wyth a hyghe voyce. c1500 *Melusine* 175 Thus bygan ayen the batayll to be reforced. 1546 *Reg. Privy Council Scot.* I. 54 He sall send men of experience for reforsing of strenthis and biggein of the samyn.

2. *intr.* To become stronger, be reinforced.

c1489 Caxton *Blanchardyn* 110 Nothyng coude playse nor brynge hym tyll his hertys ease, But euer more reforced and redoubled his sorowe. c1500 *Melusine* 290 There reforced the batayll.

Refo·rest, *v.* [Re- 5 a.] *trans.* To cover again with forest; to reafforest. Also *absol.*

1881 *Q. Rev.* July 56 Large tracts of land are being re-forested. 1882 *Nature* XXV. 527 Attention is called to the necessity of re-foresting.

So **Reforesta·tion**; **Reforestiza·tion** (Ogilvie 1882); **Refo·restize** *v.* (Webster 1897).

1887 Molony *Forestry W. Afr.* 90 How different would it have been had there been some system of conservancy or re-forestation.

Refo·rfeit, *v.* [Re- 5 a.] To forfeit again.

1667 *Decay Chr. Piety* v. ¶ 12 Those who by a new set of impossible commands should..reforfeit themselves again.

Refo·rge, *v.* [Re- 5 a. In early use prob. ad. OF. *reforgier* (15th c.; mod.F. *reforger*).]

1. *trans.* To forge (metal or articles of metal) over again.

1426 Lydg. *De Guil. Pilgr.* 16048 Take ageyn ther olde Armure..Wych they ha broke, and lost in veyn; Lat hem reforge hem newe ageyn. 1813 *Metrical Remarks* 42 To reforge the fetters they had broke. 1846 Holtzapffel *Turning* II. 536 Continually re-forging the blade, to the manifest deterioration of the steel.

2. To refabricate, fashion afresh.

1542 Udall *Erasm. Apoph.* 144 b, Thou doest disguyse and reforge thyn owneself into a woman. 1614 Sylvester *Bethulia's Rescue* IV. 242 There, did no drunken Groom.. against Heav'n blasphemous Oathes re-forge. 1899 *Daily News* 20 Apr. 3/2 Whether they should retain this Act..or whether they should throw it aside and leave the necessity of re-forging it at some future time.

Hence **Refo·rger,** one who forges anew. *rare.*

1548 Udall *Erasm. Par. Luke* xxiv. 187 Christe beeyng a newe reforger of the olde lawe.

Reform (rĭfǭ·ɹm), *sb.* [f. next, or ad. F. *réforme* (1640) = Sp. *reforma*, It. *riforma.*]

1. The amendment, or altering for the better, of some faulty state of things, *esp.* of a corrupt or oppressive political institution or practice; the removal of some abuse or wrong.

1663 Butler *Hud.* I. ii. 538 No Sow-gelder..but cry'd Reform! 1706 Phillips (ed. Kersey), *Reform*, Reforming, Reformation. 1730–6 Bailey (folio), *Reform*,..a reestablishment or revival of a former neglected discipline; also a correction of reigning abuses. 1786 Han. More *Florio* Dramas, etc. (1827) 181 He said when any change was brewing, Reform was a fine name for ruin. 1820 Shelley *Œd. Tyr.* I. 113 Bœotia, choose reform or civil war! 1844 H. H. Wilson *Brit. India* II. 118 His unwilling consent.. rendered him still more than ever hostile to all projects of reform. 1874 Micklethwaite *Mod. Par. Churches* 80 Reform was needed, and not total abolition.

b. A particular instance of such amendment; a change for the better.

1781 Cowper *Conversat.* 804 Great changes..have occurred, And blest reforms, that I have never heard. 1795 Burke *Regic. Peace* iv. Wks. IX. 58 This new constitution of theirs, which had been announced as a great reform. 1855 Macaulay *Hist. Eng.* xii. III. 209 To reduce those endowments..would have been a reform worthy of a good prince and of a good parliament. 1883 *Law Times* 20 Oct. 408/1 The public and the Profession were alike urgent in calling for sweeping reforms.

2. Amendment of conduct; reformation of persons or character.

1784 Cowper *Task* II. 321 What vice has it subdued? whose heart reclaimed By rigour, or whom laughed into reform? *Ibid.* v. 618 Remorse begets reform. 1843 *Penny Cycl.* XXV. 155/2 Institutions auxiliary to those for Punishment (Houses of Reform).

3. Improvement or rectifying of something faulty or inexact.

1856 Emerson *Eng. Traits, Wealth*, Roger Bacon explained precession of the equinoxes, [and] the consequent necessity of the reform of the calendar.

4. a. A religious order created by the reduction of another to stricter observances. *rare.*

Copied by Chambers from the *Dict. de Trévoux* (1721).

1727–41 Chambers *Cycl.* s.v., In this sense the order of St. Bernard is said to be only a reform of that of St. Benedict. 1869 *Chambers' Encycl.* s.v. *Recollet*, A reform of the Cistercian order of nuns in Spain was called by the same name.

†**b.** A reformed person. *Obs. rare.*

1756 Amory *Buncle* (1770) I. 118, I became a thorough reform from that hour.

†**5.** *Mil.* A discharge or dismissal. *Obs. rare*[—1].

1698 Luttrell *Brief Rel.* (1857) IV. 416 Another reform of 25 men more will be made out of each troop of guards, which will reduce them to 150 each troop.

6. *attrib.*, as *Reform League, Parliament, party, school*; **Reform Act** or **Bill**, an act or bill to amend the system of parliamentary representation, especially those brought in and passed in 1831–2.

1831 (*title*) A Chart exhibiting a list of the Names of the Majority and Minority, on the Second Reading of the English Reform Bill. 1832 F. N. Rogers (*title*) Parliamentary Reform Act, 2 Will. 4. c. 45. With notes. 1851 Borrow *Lavengro* c, I think of the two, the liberal or reform party were the most inveterate. 1859 Bartlett *Dict. Amer.* 359 *Reform School.* 1862 C. Knight *Pop. Hist. Eng.* VIII. xvii. 310 The dreaded Reform Parliament was to assemble at the end of January, 1833. 1865 Bright *Sp., Reform* 27 Aug. (1876) 377, I am not afraid of the principles of the Reform League.

Reform (rĭfǭ·ɹm), *v.*[1] Also 4 refoorme, reffourme, 4–7 refourme. [ad. OF. *reformer* (12th c.; mod.F. *réformer*), or L. *reformāre*, f. *re-* Re- + *formāre* to form; hence also Sp. *reformar*, It. *riformare.*

For early examples of the purely literal sense 'to form again', see *v.*[2]]

†**1.** *trans.* To renew, restore, re-establish (peace).

c1340 Hampole *Prose Tr.* 3 This name Ihesu..wastys discorde, reformes pese. 1387 Trevisa *Higden* (Rolls) VII. 103 Pees was reformed in þis manere [L. *pax reformata est*]. 1483 Caxton *Gold. Leg.* 182/1 In theyr solempnytees pees was reformed bytwene the lombardes and the emperour of Rome. 1556 *Chron. Gr. Friars* (Camden) 16 That pesse shulde be reformyd be-twene Yngland and France.

†**2.** To convert, bring back, or restore (a thing or person) *to* the original form or state, or to a previous condition. *Obs.*

c1340 Hampole *Prose Tr.* 14 Whene þe myghtes of þe saule er refourmede by grace to þe dignyte and þe state of þe firste condicione. c1375 *Sc. Leg. Saints* v. (*Johan*) 136 Sancte Iohne..tuk vpe þe pecis small, and..be his prayere þar fut-hate reformyt þam to þe fyrste state. 1390 Gower *Conf.* I. 144 His mannes forme a3ein he tok, And was reformed to the regne In which that he was wont to regne. c1430 Lydg. *Min. Poems* (Percy Soc.) 206 Suche as be pensyff make hem glad and murye, Distrauhte in thouhte refourme hem to resoun. c1485 *Digby Myst.* (1882) v. 120 What reformyth the sovle to his first light? *Ibid.* 127 Baptem..reformyth the soule..to the glorious lykenesse of god eternall. 1579 Tomson *Calvin's Serm. Tim.* 815/2 It is true nowe that God is reuealed to vs when he reformeth vs to his image.

†**b.** Without const. To restore (a person) to a normal state of mind, or to consciousness. *Obs.*

1382 Wyclif *1 Sam.* xvi. 23 Dauid took an harp, and smoot with hys hoond, and Saul was refourmyd [L. *refocillabatur*], and li3ter he hadde. — *Judith* xiii. 30 [xiv. 7] After forsothe that, the spirit taken a3een, he is reformed [L. *recreatus*], he fel doun to hir feet, and honourede hir.

†**3.** To restore (a building) after destruction, decay, or damage; to rebuild, repair. *Obs.*

c1375 *Sc. Leg. Saints* xxii. (*Laurence*) 582 Lumbardis had brynt it in were..Þane gat he men of craft to wyrk & to reforme þis haly kyrk. 1480 Caxton *Chron. Eng.* III. (1520) 23 b/2 He refourmed the temple of God better and encreased the cytee of Iherusalem. a1578 Lindesay (Pitscottie) *Chron. Scot.* (S.T.S.) I. 57 The castell..was reformit againe new better nor it was befoir. 1606 Warner *Alb. Eng.* XIV. lxxxvii, Reforming first their thrise-reard wall. 1667 Milton *P. L.* IX. 101 Seat worthier of Gods, as built With second thoughts, reforming what was old!

4. To convert into another and better form; to amend or improve by some change of form, arrangement, or composition; to free from previous faults or imperfections. †Also const. *unto, into.* Now *rare.*

13.. *Gaw. & Gr. Knt.* 378 Þen carppez to syr Gawan þe kny3t in þe grene, 'Refourme we oure for-wardes, er we fyrre passe'. 1382 Wyclif *Phil.* iii. 21 Oure Lord Jhesu Crist, the which schal refoorme the body of oure mekenesse. c1450 Holland *Howlat* 77 His halynace Throw prayer may purchace To reforme my foule face. 1495 *Act 11 Hen. VII*, c. 24 § 1 Panells..shall herafter be reformed by addicions and taking oute of names of persones by discrecion of the same Justices. 1565 Jewel *Repl. Harding* (1611) 315 The Water of Baptisme by the working of the holy Ghost, is reformed vnto a Diuine power. 1589 Greene *Menaphon* (Arb.) 79 Those eyes, faire eyes, too faire to be describde, Were those that earst the Chaos did reforme. 1615 W. Lawson *Orch. & Gard.* xi. (1623) 34 Neither let any man euer so much as thinke,..it is vnprobable..to reforme any tree. 1634 W. Tirwhyt tr. *Balzac's Lett.* (vol. I) 208 He would needes reforme all the fortifications of those strong places we passed by; he trode on no earth at which he carped not. 1687 Dryden *Hind & P.* III. 1030 'Tis prudence to reform her into ease. 1727–41 Chambers *Cycl.* s.v. *Calendar*, Romulus's calendar was reformed by Numa, who added two more months. 1769 Sir W. Jones *Palace Fortune* Poems (1777) 23 Describ'd the seasons, and reform'd the year. 1796 H. Hunter tr. *St.-Pierre's Stud. Nat.* (1799) II. 26 Persons who have been disfigured..have it in their power to reform their looks. 1853 J. H. Newman *Hist. Sk.* (1873) II. I. ii. 95 He patronised learning and poetry, and he reformed the calendar.

absol. 1340 *Ayenb.* 81 Þis uayrhede..reformeþ and agrayþeþ and him yelt his ry3te pryente.

†**b.** To correct, emend (a book, writing, chart, etc.); to recast, improve by revision and alteration. *Obs.*

1498 in *Archæol. Jrnl.* XLIII. 169 Pd..for mendyng and reformyng an Article of our ordinances viijd. 1528 in *Vicary's Anat.* (1888) App. xiv. 249 To peruse, oversee, examyne, Refourme, & correcte suche Bookes and ordynaunces. 1563 North *Gueuara's Dial. Pr.* (ed. 2) title-p., Now newly revised and corrected,..refourmed of faultes escaped in the first edition. 1621 Burton *Anat. Mel.* II. ii. III. 320, I would ..Correct those errors in Navigation, reforme Cosmographicall Chartes, and rectifie longitudes. 1631 Weever *Anc. Funeral Mon.* 489 Geffery Chaucer, whose life is written at large, by Thomas Speght, (who by old copies, reformed his workes). 1705 Hearne *Collect.* 8 Sept. (O.H.S.) I. 42 The original Author of the *Private Devotions*, wch Dr. Hicks..reform'd. c1779 R. Cumberland in *Lett. Lit. Men* (Camden) 412, I have reformed the passages you pointed out, and..written a Prologue.

c. *Law.* To revise and amend a judgement (*obs.*); to allow an instrument to be corrected or construed according to the original intention, when an error has been committed in it.

c1670 Hobbes *Dial. Com. Laws* (1681) 63 Erroneous Judgments are only to be reform'd by the High Court of Parliament. 1755 Magens *Insurances* I. 440 His Majesty is disposed..to have the Judgement reformed, in case the Pleas of the adverse Party, so suing, should be found valid. 1824 Simons & Stuart *Rep. Cases Chanc.* I. 210 *marg.*, A Court of Equity will reform an Instrument which, by the mistake of the Drawer, admits of a construction inconsistent with the true Agreement of the Parties, although the Party seeking to reform it himself drew the Instrument.

5. To make a change for the better in (an arrangement, state of things, practice or proceeding, institution, etc.); to amend or improve by removal of faults or abuses.

1432 *Rolls of Parlt.* IV. 405/1 To have ye saide first Statute of newe refourmed. 1494 Fabyan *Chron.* II. I, Callynge a counsayl he refourmed many thynges for the weale of hys realme. 1560 Daus tr. *Sleidane's Comm.* 180 b, Howe the state of the weale publike, as well ciuile, as ecclesiasticall maye or ought to be reformed [L. *emendari*]. 1594 Hooker *Eccl. Pol.* IV. viii. § 4 There hath arisen a sect in England, which..seeketh to reform even the French reformation. 1651 Hobbes *Leviath.* II. xxx. 177 To doe no more than reforme the Common-wealth. 1727 Gay *Fables* I. xiv, A Monkey to reform the times, Resolv'd to visit foreign climes. 1788 Gibbon *Decl. & F.* xlix. V. 155 After a long series of scandal, the apostolic see was reformed and exalted by the austerity and zeal of Gregory VII. 1845 S. Austin *Ranke's Hist. Ref.* I. 121 He was bound by the concessions he made in 1489 to reform the administration of justice. 1867 Smiles *Huguenots Eng.* i. (1880) 2 There were many eminent churchmen who sought to reform it [the Church] from within.

absol. 1480 *Bury Wills* (Camden) 63 And the seid priour of the same monasterie to refourme and to make a direccion therof. 1643 Denham *Cooper's H.* 116 May no such storm Fall on our Times, where ruine must reform. 1849 Macaulay *Hist. Eng.* i. (1890) I. 49 A body of members anxious to preserve, and a body eager to reform.

†**b.** *ironically.* To alter *to* a worse state. *Obs.*

1649 C. Walker *Relat. & Observ.* II. 35 For, in the interim, they garrisoned Black Fryars and S. Pauls, reforming it, from the Church of God, to a den of thieves, &c.

c. To take away, remove entirely, by (or by way of) reformation.

1660 South *Serm. Matt.* xiii. 52 In those Days, when the Revenues of the Church were not wholly reformed from it. 1694 Atterbury *Serm. 1 Peter* iv. 8 (1726) I. 78 Our Adversaries..who cry'd us down, as Men that were Reforming away Good Works. 1897 Labouchere in *Daily News* 17 Mar. 3/7 His idea of reform was to reform the Armenians off the face of the globe.

6. To put a stop or end to (an abuse, disorder, malpractice, etc.) by enforcing or introducing a better procedure or conduct; †to amend (a fault committed).

1390 Gower *Conf.* III. 136 Wherof full many a gret debat Reformed is to good astat. 1399 Langl. *Rich. Redeles* Prol. 21 If reson ne had reffourmed the mysseheff and the mysserule. c1430 *Stans Puer ad Mensam* 89 (Lamb. MS.), A rodde reformeþ al her neclygence. 1530 Palsgr. 682/2 If I have done any thynge amysse, I wyll reforme it. 1545 Brinklow *Compl.* 6 Such abuses as are to be reformed in the realme. 1596 Spenser *F. Q.* v. ii. 28 Sir Artegall undid the evill fashion, And wicked customes of that Bridge refourmed. 1619 Sir R. Naunton in *Fortescue Papers* (Camden) 96 The best remedies they can for reforming what they find faultie. 1687 T. Brown *Saints in Uproar* Wks. 1730 I. 83, I am resolved..to reform these disorders. 1715 De Foe *Fam. Instruct.* I. iii. (1841) I. 63 We are resolved to reform several practices..in their behaviour. 1802 Mar. Edgeworth *Moral T.* i, He could reform every abuse.

†**b.** (Chiefly *Sc.*) To repair, redress (a wrong, loss, damage, etc.), to make up, make good. *Obs.*

1456 Sir G. Haye *Law Arms* (S.T.S.) 185 To reforme all harmes and scathis that suld be done throu his men. 1461 *Paston Lett.* II. 15 Seyng they have had gret wrong, besechyng my Lorde that it myght be reformed. 1535 Stewart *Cron. Scot.* I. 459 Beseikand him..to reforme the greit dampnage and cryme Tha had sustenit. 1549 *Compl. Scot.* ix. 77 Ther eftir thai reformit the distructione of the tempil. 1609 Skene *Reg. Maj., Forme of Proces* 126 b, Vntill ..he be summoned,..and his expenses payed and reformed to him.

c. To correct, put right (an error or mistake).

1542–3 *Act 34 & 35 Hen. VIII*, c. 27 § 113 Al errours in plees personall shalbe reformed by billes, to be sued before the saied presidente. 1571 Digges *Pantom.* III. xi. R iv b, But if ye finde any discrepance or variaunce betweene them, ye shall by the ayde of some skilfull Artificer refourme it in the lesser. 1784 Cowper *Tiroc.* 445 Young heads are giddy, ..And make mistakes for manhood to reform.

†**d.** To remove (a fault or blemish) by some treatment. *Obs. rare.*

1589 Puttenham *Eng. Poesie* III. xxiv. (Arb.) 293 Euery man may..reforme by arte, the faultes and imperfections that nature hath wrought in them. 1675 Hobbes *Odyssey* (1677) 250 Then we bare your body to the fleet, And there the blemishes thereof reform With water fair and warm.

7. To bring, lead, or force (a person) to abandon a wrong or evil course of life, conduct, etc., and adopt a right one; to bring about a thorough amendment in (a person, his conduct, etc.).

1413 *Pilgr. Sowle* (Caxton) II. lii. (1859) 54 Sathan..myght not be refourmyd by cause of his vnchangeabylyte. 1494 Fabyan *Chron.* v. lxxxiii. 61, ii. holy Byshoppes..came into Brytaygne to refourme the Kynge, and al other that erryd from the waye of trouth. 1535 Coverdale *Prov.* v. 23 Because he wolde not be refourmed, he shal dye. 1575–85 Abp. Sandys *Serm.* 60 Those wilful cubbes, which neither by teaching nor by example will be reformed must feele the smart of the rod. 1631 Gouge *God's Arrows* I. § 46. 81 What usurer, what deceiver is reformed by this Plague? 1680 Burnet *Rochester* (1692) 61 A man is never thoroughly reformed till a new principle governs his thoughts. 1715 De Foe *Fam. Instruct.* I. iv. (1841) I. 84 Will you call my father's desire to reform your life, a putting hard upon you? 1796 H. Hunter tr. *St.-Pierre's Stud. Nat.* (1799) III. 540 As we must not go to ruin the men whom we wish to reform. 1819 Shelley *Cenci* I. i. 74 You gave out that you have half reformed me. 1846 J. Baxter *Libr. Pract. Agric.* (ed. 4) I. p. xxxi, Far be it from us to discourage any effort made to reform juvenile offenders. 1871 Ruskin *Fors Clav.* ix. 6, I have not the slightest intention..of setting myself to mend or reform people.

b. Const. *from*, †*of*, †*to*, †*unto*.

1422 tr. *Secreta Secret., Priv. Priv.* 204 He rebukid the forsayden breenys and bourkeyns..and ham to Pees reformed. c1450 Holland *Howlat* 875 To reforme the Howlat, of faltis full fell. 1477 Earl Rivers (Caxton) *Dictes* 16 To reforme the euyl disposed vnto goodnesse.

1697 Potter *Antiq. Greece* III. xi. (1715) 99 The Grecians were much reform'd from the Inhumanity..of their own Ancestors. 1714 Swift *Pres. St. Aff.* Wks. 1755 II. I. 214 The house of Hanover..is the nearest branch of our regal line reformed from popery. 1858 Carlyle *Fredk. Gt.* x. i. (1872) III. 204 Lieutenant Buddenbrock..is now reformed from those practices.

†**c.** To reprove, punish, chastise (a person) for some fault. *Obs.*

1484 Caxton *Fables of Æsop* II. Pref., By cause they were not customed to be refourmed ne chastysed, whan ony of them was corrected and punysshed, they were gretely troubled. 1535 Coverdale *Jonah* (heading), Ionas is angrie, and complayneth of God which refourmeth him. 1577 Harrison *England* II. iv. (1877) I. 103 At these meetings also..roges, and runnagates, are often reformed for their excesses. 1596 Spenser *F. Q.* v. i. 21 He..The lady to alight did eft require, Whilest he reformed that uncivill fo.

d. *refl.* (also with *heart, life*, etc. as obj.) To improve one's own conduct, character, etc.

1512 *Act 4 Hen. VIII*, c. 19 *Preamble*, The seid Frensche Kyng..the Decree of the enterdiccion dispysyng will not therby reforme himselfe. 1535 Coverdale *2 Esdras* xiv. 34 Yf so be that ye wil subdue youre owne vnderstandinge, and refourme youre hert [etc.]. 1597 Shaks. *2 Hen. IV*, v. v. 72 And as we heare you do reforme your selues, We will according to your strength, and qualities, Giue you aduancement. 1727 De Foe *Syst. Magic* I. i. (1840) 14 How justly might they bid him hold his tongue, and go and reform his life, before he pretended to instruct them.

transf. 1552 Latimer *Serm. & Rem.* (Parker Soc.) 182 The wind and waters obeyed him, and reformed themselves according to his word.

†**8.** To instruct, inform (a person). *Obs. rare.*

1535 Coverdale *Isa.* xl. 12 Who hath refourmed [1611 directed] the mynde of the Lorde? Or who is of his councel to teach him? 1560 Becon *New Catech.* II. Wks. 1564 I. 312 The Prophete Esaye also sayeth, who hath refourmed the Spiryte of the Lorde?

†**9. a.** *Hawking.* (See quot.) *Obs. rare*[—1].

1486 *Bk. St. Albans* A vj b, Sum tyme yowre hawke countenansis as she piked hir, and yet she proynith not, and then ye most say she Reformith hir federis and not piketh hir federis.

†**b.** To cut down or back to a desired length; to trim, prune. *Obs.*

1574 R. Scot *Hop Gard.* (1578) 17 You must pyle them vp immediately after they are cut, sharped, reformed in length and smoothed. 1615 W. Lawson *Country Housew. Gard.* (1626) 35 Snub his top..with a sharpe knife, and take him cleane away, and so you may vse any Cyon you would reforme. 1667 Milton *P. L.* IV. 625 We must be ris'n And at our pleasant labour, to reform Yon flourie Arbors. 1697 Dryden *Virg. Georg.* II. 605 Shall we doubt..To sow, to set, and to reform their growth?

†**c.** To bring into a better state, to improve.

1607 Norden *Surv. Dial.* v. 237 This peece of ground.. hath had much labour and great cost bestowed on it, and the ground little or nothing the more reformed.

†**10.** *Mil.* [After F. *réformer.*] To form into a new regiment or company; to break up, partially or completely, for this purpose; hence also, to disband, dismiss from the service. *Obs.*

1604 E. Grimstone *Hist. Siege Ostend* 183 He hath casziered and dismissed aboue 600 men, as well Commanders and Sargeants, as commissaries and Treasurers,..hee hath also reformed the common soldiers. 1629 Wadsworth *Pilgr.* vii. 71 His regiment being reformed into one company, was giuen to Captaine Rhisby. 1664 Pepys *Diary* 31 Oct., If you must reform two of them, be sure let him command the troop that is left. 1706 Phillips (ed. Kersey) s.v., In Military Affairs, to Reform, is to reduce a Body of Men, either disbanding the Whole, and putting the Officers and Soldiers into other Bodies, or only breaking a Part, and retaining the rest. 1768 Sterne *Sent. Journ.* II. 51 (*Le Patissier*) At the conclusion of the last peace, his regiment being reformed,..he found himself..without a livre.

11. *intr.* (for *refl.*) To abandon wrong-doing or error; to free oneself from misconduct or fault.

1582 N. Lichefield tr. *Castanheda's Conq. E. Ind.* I. xxi. 54 The Catuall did reforme, and make himselfe friendes with him. 1643 Sir T. Browne *Relig. Med.* I. § 3 We have reformed from them, not against them. 1680 H. More *Apocal. Apoc.* 356 How necessary it is to reform from the Roman impurities. 1736 Butler *Anal.* I. iii. 47 Those who have gone on for some time in the ways of Vice, and have afterwards reformed. 1769 *Junius Lett.* xiv. 61 It is possible the young man may, in time, grow wiser and reform. 1865 Pusey *Truth Eng. Ch.* 80 If..the Church of England reformed by herself [etc.]. 1857 Freeman *Norm. Conq.* (1876) I. App. 637 He reformed and rose to the rank of Ealdorman.

Re-form, reform (rīfǭ·ɹm), *v.*[2] Also 4 refourme, 5 *Sc.* refurm. [Orig. identical with prec., but in later use a new formation from Re- 5 a and Form *v.* Cf. F. *reformer.*] *trans.* and *intr.* To form a second time, form over again.

trans. a1340 Hampole *Psalter* iv. 7 Þe light of his grace þat refourmes in vs his ymage. 1390 Gower *Conf.* I. 273 And riht so in the same forme In fleissh and blod he schal reforme..the qwike and dede. c1425 Wyntoun *Cron.* II. vi. 484 Til wyttyr þaim for hir pete How mankynde mycht refurmyt be. 1594 Kyd *Cornelia* II. 360 The formes of things doe neuer die, Because the matter that remaines Reformes another thing thereby. 1656 Stanley *Hist. Philos.* v. (1701) 181/1 When the Soul by cogitation reforming these things, which are conceived in Opinion by Memory and Sense [etc.]. 1695 Woodward *Nat. Hist. Earth* II. (1723) 105 Its prime Errand was to Re-form and New-mold the Earth. 1798 Landor *Gebir* IV. 128 She had words to speak, She form'd them and reform'd them. 1821 Byron *Juan* III. lix, Our little selves re-form'd in finer clay. 1875 *Ure's Dict. Arts* (ed. 7) II. 924 The formation goes on continuously, so that..a fresh deposit..is re-formed in about twenty years.

intr. 1899 Cagney tr. *Jaksch's Clin. Diagn.* v. (ed. 4) 158 This precipitate re-formed on the further addition of the dye.

b. *Mil.* (See Form *v.* 8.)

trans. 1802 James *Milit. Dict.* s.v., When a line of several battalions hath passed another..it may be reformed in the following manner. 1835 Lytton *Rienzi* II. iii, Order was again restored, and the line reformed. 1859 F. A. Griffiths *Artil. Man.* (1862) 13 Unfix Swords. Re-form Company.

intr. 1847 *Infantry Man.* (1854) 97 No advanced guard.., after carrying a post, should..be permitted to advance without reforming. 1854 J. S. C. Abbott *Napoleon* (1855) II. xx. 311 At that well known..voice, the flying troops immediately re-formed.

Reformable (rĭfǭ·ɹmăb'l), *a.* [f. Reform *v.*[1] + -able: cf. F. *réformable* (16th c. in Godef. *Compl.*).] Capable of being reformed; admitting or susceptible of reformation.

1483 in *Eng. Gilds* (1870) 337 Provided allway..that hit be reformabyll and corrigabill by the Mayre. 1533 Cranmer *Let. to Hen. VIII* in *Misc. Writ.* (Parker Soc.) II. 271, I find them as conformable and reformable as any number with whom I have communed. 1563 Abp. Parker in Ellis *Orig. Lett.* Ser. II. II. 271 Other disorders reformable by ecclesiasticall lawes. 1647 Hammond *Power of Keys* iv. 76 To make the Christian offender by that meanes ashamed and reformable. 1711 G. Hickes *Two Treat. Chr. Priesth.* (1847) I. 163 The reformable mal-administration of church censures. 1832 *Fraser's Mag.* VI. 486 The boy was criminal, but in my judgment reformable.

Hence †**Refo·rmableness.** *rare*[—1].

a1591 R. Greenham *Wks.* (1599) 32 Little children, whether in teachablenes to good, or reformablenes from sinne.

†**Reformade.** *Obs.* [ad. next: see -ade 3.] = Reformado 1.

c1645 T. Tully *Siege of Carlisle* (1840) 8 With him came some white coats, and about 200 of reformades. 1661 *Sir A. Haslerig's Last Will & Test.* 3 Our baffled Reformades, and desperate Decoys of our late disbanded Army. 1696 tr. *Du Mont's Voy. Levant* xiv. 176 A sort of Officers that never go to War, almost like our Reformades. 1733 Neal *Hist. Purit.* II. 525 David Hyde, one of the Reformades, first drew his sword in Palace yard.

attrib. c1645 T. Tully *Siege of Carlisle* (1840) 26 The partye, consisting of 42, all reformade officers. 1685 Crowne *Sir C. Nice* I. 8 They..march in Publick with their Baggage, ..and a whole train of Reformade sinners.

b. *To ride reformades*, to serve as volunteers.

1682 Bunyan *Holy War* 104 There were also some from the Court that rode Reformades, for the love that they had to the King Shaddai.

So †**Reformader.** *Obs.* (In quot. *attrib.*)

c1642 in *Glover's Hist. Derby* (1829) I. App. 71 Two hundred and forty of the Lord Brooke's reformader troupe, which behaved themselves all very gallantly.

Reformado (refǭɹmā·do). [a. Sp. *reformado* (= Pg. *reformado*, It. *riformato*, F. *réformé*): ad. L. *reformātus*, pa. pple. of *reformāre* to Reform.]

1. *Mil.* **a.** An officer left without a command (owing to the 'reforming' or disbanding of his company) but retaining his rank and seniority, and receiving full or half pay; a 'reformed' officer.

b. A volunteer serving in the army (or navy) without a commission, but with the rank of an officer. Now only *Hist.*

1598 B. Jonson *Ev. Man in Hum.* III. v, Into the likenesse of some of these Reformado's had he moulded himselfe so perfectly. 1640 in Rushw. *Hist. Coll.* III. (1692) I. 68 That the Earl of Crauford's Troop, and those other Officers in the Army that go under the name of Reformadoes, are an unnecessary Charge. 1647 Sprigge *Anglia Rediv.* III. ii. (1854) 143 The castle was manned with 700 men, divers of them reformadoes. 1660 Pepys *Diary* 1 Oct., Mr. Mansell, a poor Reformado of the Charleses, came to see me. 1724 De Foe *Mem. Cavalier* (1840) 85 There was about thirty officers, who, having no soldiers,..served as reformadoes with the regiment. 1755 Carte *Hist. Eng.* IV. 311 Moving his majesty that the loyal Scotch officers, formed into a company of reformadoes,..might be cashiered. 1814 Scott *Wav.* xliv, Jinker..had been reduced, with several others, by the advice of the Baron of Bradwardine, to the situation of what he called reformed officers, or reformadoes. 1891 Gardiner *Hist. Civil War* III. liii. 177 The Reformadoes were at last to be actually ejected from London.

transf. 1643 Trapp *Comm. Gen.* xiv. 16 Kings cared not for soldiers (no more did the King of Sodome for Abraham, and his Reformadoes). a1679 T. Goodwin *Christ the Mediator* v. xviii. Wks. 1863 V. 331 The devil again put out of trade, and made a reformado.

2. One who is (or has) reformed in some respect; also, one who favours reform; a reformer.

a1632 Weever (T.), This was one of Celestin the pope's caveats for his new reformadoes. 1642 *View Print. Book int. Observat.* 22, I promise him upon that to turn Reformado. 1654 Whitlock *Zootomia* 502 Now see the Rocks our false Reformado splits on. a1734 North *Exam.* II. iv. § 146 (1740) 310, I promise hereafter to be a Reformado, or no Writer at all. 1787 *Gentl. Mag.* LVII. II. 1053/1 Never surely did any Turkish or Algerine reformado slash his subject of conversion with a spirit so zealous. 1823 Byron *Juan* x. xiii, Even shuffling Southey..Would scarcely join again the 'reformadoes', Whom he forsook to fill the laureate's sty. 1857 *Blackw. Mag.* LXXXI. 394 Have I not set fast brothers by the ears..And sometimes roused the reformado's zeal?

3. a. *attrib.*, as *reformado officer, saint, Scot, sect, soldier*, etc.

1644 *Ordinance* 26 Mar. in Husband *Coll. Pub. Ord. Ho. Parlt.* (1646) 446 The condition of Reformadoe Officers. 1664 Butler *Hud.* II. ii. 116, I grant You are a Reformado Saint. *Ibid.* 648 She..o'er her shoulder Chastiz'd the Reformado Soldier. a1680 — *Rem.* (1759) II. 128 Three Reformado Sects joined in one..will not serve to maintain one Pedant. 1724 De Foe *Mem. Cavalier* (1840) 85 My reformado Scots having observed that the town port [etc.].

b. Used after a sb., as *captain, gentleman, knight reformado.*

1609 B. Jonson *Sil. Wom.* v. ii, His Knights reformados are wound vp as high, and insolent, as euer they were. 1617 Moryson *Itin.* II. 166 Wee tooke thirteene prisoners, among whom was a Captaine Reformado (as they terme them, for honour of antiquitie). 1691 *Proc. agst. French* in *Select. fr. Harl. Misc.* (1793) 475 Himself leading his own guard of gentlemen reformadoes.

†**Refo·rmalist.** *Obs. rare*[—1]. [irreg. f. Reform *sb.*, perh. an error for Reformatist: cf. next.] A reformer.

1611 Speed *Hist. Gt. Brit.* IX. xv. § 44. 636/2 By instigation of the discontented reformalists.

†**Refo·rmalizing,** *ppl. a. Obs. rare*[—1]. [Perh. an error for *reformatizing*: cf. prec.] Seeking or pretending to reform.

1614 W. Loe *Serm. Bliss of Br. Beauty* 25 (T.), Christ's doctrine [is] pure, correcting all the impure glosses of the reformalizing Pharisees.

Reformation (refǭɹmē^ɪ·ʃən). Also 6 refourmation. [ad. L. *reformātiōn-em*, n. of action f. *reformāre* to Reform: cf. F. *réformation* (13th c. in Godef. *Compl.*).]

†**1.** Restoration (of peace). Cf. Reform *v.*[1] 1.

c1440 *Gesta Rom.* I. xlvii. 196 (Harl. MS.), Wher so euer he knewe þat eny discorde or vnrest was Regnynge, he labovrid to make Reformacion of pes. 1568 Grafton *Chron.* II. 156 The Legate..laboured so to the king, that a reformation of peace was spoken of.

2. Improvement in form or quality; alteration to a better form; correction or removal of defects or errors; †reparation, rebuilding.

c1425 Wyntoun *Cron.* II. i. 108 Off Babilon bathe towire and town Scho made gude reformacion. 1468 *Paston Lett.* II. 314 Maister John Smyth, that..was none holsom counceller yn the reformacion of the last testament. 1528 in *Vicary's Anat.* (1888) App. xiv. 249 [To] examine, Refourme, & correcte..alle suche of the saide Actes and Ordynaunce As vppon the examinacion and Reformacion of theym they shalle thynke to be good and Resonable. c1543 in Parker *Dom. Archit.* (1859) III. 79 To make..a new halle..and reformacon honourable for the quenes loggyng. *Ibid.*, With reformation of your conduyts there. 1594 Blundevil *Exerc.* III. I. xvi. (1636) 311 Unlesse the Kalenders be reformed..(for the Roman reformation is not so exactly true as it might be). 1600 Rowlands *Lett. Humours Blood* xii. 18 Fine Phillip comes vnto the Barbers shopp, Wheer's nittie lockes must suffer reformation. 1663 Gerbier *Counsel* d 3, All such as the very aspects of number of Brick-buildings, since the reformation of a Gotis relick building, hath manifested to have been the main cause. 1776 Adam Smith *W. N.* I. v. I. 49 Even before the late reformation of the gold coin of Great Britain. 1829 Simons & Stuart *Rep. Cases Chanc.* I. 218 Whether a Court of Equity will refuse to reform an Instrument..because it happened to be drawn by the Party seeking that reformation. 1855 Brewster *Newton* II. xxiii. 311 When the public attention was called to the reformation of the Kalendar.

†**b.** Improvement in health. *Obs. rare*[—1].

1772 Johnson *Let. to Mrs. Thrale* 19 Oct., This is to be my home long enough to receive a letter, which will, I hope, tell me that you are busy in reformation.

3. Improvement of (or in) an existing state of things, institution, practice, etc.; a radical change for the better effected in political, religious, or social affairs.

c1460 Fortescue *Abs. & Lim. Mon.* xv. (1885) 148 How also þe lawes mey be amendet in suche thynges as thay neden reformacion in. a1548 Hall *Chron., Hen. VIII* 60, I will do for a reformacion of this matter as much as a priest may do. 1588 Burghley in Ellis *Orig. Lett.* Ser. I. III. 28 Yf I fynde not a due and spedye reformation of all disorders among you. 1662 J. Davies tr. *Olearius' Voy. Ambass.* 3 In consequence of the Reformation of Religion, both lost the Authority they had in this City. 1713 Berkeley *Guardian* No. 62 ¶ 10 The reformation of the Church and that of learning began together. 1782 Cowper *Flatting Mill* 14 Alas for the poet! who dares undertake To urge reformation of national ill. 1833 Alison *Hist. Europe* ii. II. 65 If they [bands] are slowly and cautiously unbent, it is Reformation; if suddenly removed,..it is Revolution. 1856 Froude *Hist. Eng.* (1858) I. ii. 99 Wolsey talked of reformation, but delayed its coming.

b. *spec.* (with capital). The great religious movement of the 16th century, having for its object the reform of the doctrines and practices of the Church of Rome, and ending in the establishment of the various Reformed or Protestant Churches of central and north-western Europe.

1563 Winjet *Wks.* (S.T.S.) I. 67 We ar sa tribulit be 3ow.. for nocht assenting generalie to 3our prætendit reformatioun. 1588 Fregeville *Reformed Politicke* 44 To the end to ship the Clergy in the League, they wer perswaded, that within six moneths the Reformation should be vtterly extinguished. 1657 Trapp *Comm. Ps.* cl. 4 That grave and simple Psalmodie ..so much used of old, and by this blessed Reformation restored to the Church). 1685 Evelyn *Diary* 22 Dec., The first Popish Nuncio that had ben in England since the Reformation. a1715 Burnet *Own Time* I. 10 Some few.. did lean so grosly to Popery, that the heat and violence of the Reformation became the main subject of their sermons. 1772 T. Warton *Sir T. Pope* 133 The liberal Pontiff did not consider..that he was undermining the papal interest, and bringing on the Reformation. a1862 Buckle *Misc. Wks.* (1872) I. 85 The English Reformation..during the early period of its progress,..did not produce a single man of genius.

†**c.** A reformed order (of friars). *Obs. rare*[—1].

1706 tr. *Dupin's Eccl. Hist. 16th C.* II. IV. xi. 449 These [friars] also being divided yet farther into different Reformations, Leo X. commanded them all to be reduced under the single Title of Reformed.

Refraination. *Obs.*

Refrainment (rifrē'nment). *rare.* [f. as prec. + -MENT.] Restraining, abstinence.

Refraint, obs. form of REFRAIN v.

Refraining (rifrē'niŋ), *vbl. sb.* [f. REFRAIN v. + -ING¹.] The action or fact of restraining, abstaining, etc.

Refrakate, obs. variant of REFRACT v.

Refrain, *irreg. var.* of REFRAINATION or REFRENATION. *Obs.* Chiefly *Astral.*

† Refranation. *Obs.* [ad. L. type *Refrænātio*.]

Refrangibility. [f. next + -ITY.] The property of being refrangible; the degree to which this property is present.

Refrangible (rifræ'ndʒib'l). [ad. L. type REFRACT v.] Capable of being refracted; admitting of, susceptible to, refraction.

Refrenation. *Obs.* [ad. L. *refrēnātiōn-em,* n. of action f. *refrēnāre*.] 1. The action of refraining or restraining.

Re-freney. *Obs.* forms of REFRAIN v.

Re-frenzy, v. *Obs.* To throw again into a frenzy.

Refresh (rifre·ʃ), v. Now *collog.* [f. next:]

Refresher (rifre·ʃəɹ). [f. as prec. + -ER¹.]

Refreshful (rifre·ʃful), *a.* [f. REFRESH v. + -FUL.] Full of refreshment; refreshing.

Refreshfully (rifre·ʃfuli), *adv.* [f. prec. + -LY².] In a refreshful manner.

Refreshing (rifre·ʃiŋ), *vbl. sb.* [f. REFRESH v. + -ING¹.]

Refreshing, *ppl. a.* [f. as prec. + -ING².]

Refreshingly, *adv.* [f. prec. + -LY².]

Refreshment (rifre·ʃment). [a.OF. *refreschement,* *refreschissement.*]

Refret, retret, var. REFREID v. *Obs.*

Refrettime.

Refrey, obs. var. of REFRAIN v.

Refreyde, obs. f. REFREID v. *Obs.*

Refricate, v. *Obs.* [f. ppl. stem of L. *fricāre* to rub.]

† Refrication. *Obs.* [as prec. L. types of FRICATION.]

Refriction. [RE-5 a.] Renewed friction.

Refrigerant (rifri'dʒĕrănt), *a.* and *sb.* [a. F. *réfrigérant* (16th c.), or ad. L. *refrigerant-em,* ppl. pple. of *refrigerāre*.]

Refrigerate (rifri'dʒĕreit), v. [f. L. *refrig-er-āt-,* ppl. stem of *refrigerāre* to REFRESH + -ATE³.]

Refrigerated, *ppl. a.* Now *rare.* [ad. L. *refrigerātus,* pa. pple. of *refrigerāre.*]

Refrigerating, *ppl. a.* [f. as prec. + -ING².] That refrigerates; producing, pertaining to, connected with, natural or artificial refrigeration.

Refrigeration (rifri'dʒĕrei·ʃən). Also 5 refrygeracion, 6 -cyoun. [ad. L. *refrigerātiōn-em,* n. of action f. *refrigerāre* to REFRIGERATE. Cf. F. *réfrigération* (16th c. in Littré).]

Refrigerative (rifri'dʒĕrătiv), *a.* and *sb.* [a. F. *réfrigératif,* -ive (15th c.), ad. L. *refrigerāt-* (see REFRIGERATE), + -IVE.]

Refrigerator (rifri'dʒĕreitəɹ). [f. as REFRIGERATE + -OR.]

Refrigeratory (rifri'dʒĕrătəɹi), *a.* and *sb.* [ad. med.L. *refrigerātōri-us,* a.OF. *refrigeratoire* (Godef.).]

Refrigery (rifri'dʒĕri). [ad. late L. *refrigeri-um* (see prec.), a.OF. *refrigerie* (Godef.).]

Hence Refrigeravtiveness.

Refuge (riū·dʒ), *sb.* [a. F. *refuge* (12th c.), ad. L. *refugi-um,* f. *refugere* to flee back, f. *re-* RE- + *fugere* to flee.]

Refuge (riū·dʒ), v. Now rare. [f. the sb., or ad. F. refugier, refuger (15th c.), usually refl. se refugier, to take refuge.]

1. trans. To afford a refuge, asylum, or retreat to (a person); to shelter, protect. Also occas. in pass., to be refuged, to have taken refuge.

†b. refl. To take refuge; to flee for refuge to a place. Obs.

2. intr. To take refuge; to seek shelter or protection. Also fig.

Refugee (refiudʒī·). [ad. F. refugié, pa. pple. of refugier: see REFUGE v.]

1. One who, owing to religious persecution or political troubles, seeks refuge in a foreign country; orig. applied to the French Huguenots who came to England after the revocation of the Edict of Nantes in 1685.

†b. transf. or fig.

2. attrib. and Comb., as refugee camp, etc.

Refulgence (rifɐ·ldʒens). [ad. L. refulgentia: see next.] The quality of being refulgent; splendour, brightness, radiance.

Refulgency (rifɐ·ldʒensi). ? Obs. [See prec. and -ENCY.] = REFULGENCE.

Refulgent (rifɐ·ldʒent), a. [ad. L. refulgent-em, pres. pple. of re- RE- + fulgēre to shine.] Shining with, or reflecting, a brilliant light; radiant, resplendent, gleaming.

Hence Refu·lgently adv.

Refulge (rifɐ·ldʒ), v. [ad. L. refulgēre.] intr. To shine brightly. Obs. rare.

Refund (rifɐ·nd), v.[1] [ad. OF. refunder, refonder.]

1. trans. To pour back, pour in or out again (lit. and fig.). Obs. rare.

Refund (rifɐ·nd), v.[2] [ad. F. refonder (refunder): pay back, repay, restore.]

Hence Refu·nded ppl. a.; Refu·nding vbl. sb.

Refu·nder. One who refunds.

Refundment (rifɐ·ndment). [f. REFUND v.[2] + -MENT.] The act of refunding.

Refurbish (rifɐ·bɪʃ), v. [RE- 5 a.] trans. To furbish anew; to repolish, do up again.

Hence Refu·rbished ppl. a.; Refu·rbishment.

Refu·rnish, v. [RE- 5 a.] Also 4 refous, 4-5 (7) refuss, 5 refurnysh, 6 refnrnish, Sc. refour.

Refuse (refiū·s), sb. and a. Also 4 refous, 4-5 refus, 5-7 refuse, 6 refuse, Sc. refous, 6-7 reffuse, (6 refuge), 4- refuse. [a. OF. refus, -refuse.]

Refusable (rifiū·zəb'l), a. [f. REFUSE v. + -ABLE, or ad. OF. refusable.]

Refuse (rifiū·z), v. Forms: 4 refuse, refuss, 5-7 refuse, 6 refuce, refuze, (refusse, refuys), 4- refuse.

1. trans. To decline to take or accept (something offered or proffered).

Refusal (rifiū·zal). Also 5 refusaile, 5-7 refusall, -fusel, (7 Sc. refussall). [f. REFUSE v. + -AL.]

Refuser (rifiū·zəɹ). One who refuses.

Re-fuse (rīfiū·z), v. [RE- 5 a.] To fuse or melt again.

Hence Re-fu·sed ppl. a.; Re-fu·sing vbl. sb.

Refu·table, a. [f. L. refutāre: see REFUTE.] Capable of being refuted.

Hence Refu·tably adv.; Refu·tability.

Refutal (rifiū·tal). rare. [f. REFUTE v. + -AL.] = REFUTATION.

Refutation (refiutēi·ʃən). [ad. L. refutātiōn-em, n. of action f. refutāre to REFUTE. Cf. F. réfutation.] The action of refuting or disproving a statement, charge, etc.; confutation.

Refute (rifiū·t), v. [ad. L. refutāre, or a. F. réfuter.]

Hence Refu·ted ppl. a.; Refu·ting vbl. sb.

Refu·ter. One who refutes.

Regain (rigēi·n), v. [ad. F. regagner.]

1. trans. To gain or win back again; to recover possession of (something). Also absol.

2. To win back, recover, for another.

Hence **Regai′ned** *ppl. a.*, **Regai′ning** *vbl. sb.* and *ppl. a.* Also **Regai′nable** *a.*, **Regai′ner**.

Regai′nment. [f. prec. + -MENT.] The action of regaining.

Regal (rī′găl), *a.* and *sb.*[1] Also **regall**, **(6 -ale)**, **(7 -gall)**. [a. F. *regal*, *-ale*, or *regalis*, f. *reg-*, *rex* king: see -AL.]

A. *adj.* **1.** Of or belonging to a king; royal.

2. Resembling or befitting a king: royal, splendid, magnificent, stately, etc.

3. Befitting, or resembling, a king; kingly; hence, splendid, magnificent, stately, etc.

Regal (rī′găl), *sb.*[2] Also **6 regalle**, **reyrgal**, **regol**, **7 rigoll**, **-ole**, **7 rigalle**, **6-9 regall**, **(6 -alle)**. [a. F. *régale* (16th c., in Rabelais *régale*), ... cf. It. *regale* (Florio).]

1. Chiefly *pl.* A small portable organ formerly in use, having one, or sometimes two, sets of reed-pipes played with keys by the right hand, while a small bellows was worked by the left hand. Now chiefly *Hist.* (common *c* 1550–1625).

2. *pl.* ... A pair of regals.

3. *fig.* or *in fig. context.*

Regal, *sb.*[3] *Obs.* rare⁻¹.

Regal, *v.*[1] *Obs.*

Regal, *v.*[2] *Obs.*

Regale (rĭgē′l), *sb.*[1] Also **7 regall**, **regalle**. [ad. med.L. *regāle*, neut. sing. of *regālis* REGAL *a.* See also REGALIA[1].]

1. ... The right, on the part of the kings of France, of enjoying the revenues of vacant bishoprics and abbacies, and of presenting to benefices dependent on these.

2. A royal right or privilege. *Obs.*

Regale (rĭgē′l), *sb.*[2] Also **6 regalle**, **reygal**, **7-rigoll**, **-ole**, **7 rigalle**, **6-9 regall**, **(6 -alle)**. [a. F. *régale* (16th c., in Rabelais *régale*); ... cf. It. *regale* (Florio).]

Regale (rĭgē′l), *v.* [ad. F. *régaler* (Cotgr.).] **1.** *regulary*, *bp.* and *fig. regular*: see REGALO.

2. To entertain or treat (a person, etc.) in a choice manner. Also *ironical* (quot. 1856).

3. To gratify, please, delight, by a gift, deference, etc. rare.

Regalement (rĭgē′lmĕnt). Also **6-7 regalment**. [a. F. *régalement* (16th c.): cf. -MENT.] **1.** The act of regaling; refreshment, entertainment.

2. A complimentary present. *Obs.* rare.

Regaler. [f. REGALE *v.* + -ER[1].] One who or that which regales (Ogilvie, 1882).

Regalia[1] (rĭgē′liă). Also **7-8 regalia's**. [L., *pl.* of *regāle* REGALE *sb.*[1]] **1.** Rights appertaining to a king; royal powers or privileges.

2. The emblems or insignia of royalty; the crown, sceptre, and other distinctive ornaments of a king or queen which are used at coronations.

3. *pl.* The decorations or insignia of an order.

Regalia[2] (rĭgā′liă). *Obs. rare⁻¹.* [a. Sp. *regalía* royal privilege (see REGALO).] A Cuban or other large cigar of superior quality.

Regalian (rĭgē′liăn), *a.* [ad. F. *régalien* (1690): see REGAL *a.* and -IAN.] Pertaining to a sovereign, regal.

Regalism (rī′găliz'm). [f. REGAL *a.* + -ISM.] The doctrine or practice of the supremacy of the sovereign in ecclesiastical matters.

Regalist (rī′gălist). [a. F. *régaliste* (16th c.): see prec. and -IST.] A supporter of regalism.

Regality (rĭgæ′litĭ). Also **5-6 -tie**, **6-yte**, **-ytye**, **-tee**, **6-7 -tie**, **5-6 -ryalite**, **(5-... AF. and OF.) *regalité* (Langtoft, etc.), ... **1.** Royalty, sovereignty, kingship, sovereign rule or jurisdiction.

2. A country or district subject to royal authority, a kingdom; a monarchical state.

3. *Sc.* Territorial jurisdiction of a royal nature granted by the king. Now only *Hist.*

Regality[2], *Obs. rare⁻¹.* [irreg. f. REGALE *v.*] Regalement, entertainment.

Regalize, *v.* [f. REGAL *a.* + -IZE.] *trans.* To make regal or royal.

Regally (rī′gălĭ), *adv.* [f. REGAL *a.* + -LY[2].]

Regalo (rĭgā′lo). Now rare. Also **7-8 regallo**, **regalo**. [ad. It. (also Sp. and Pg.) *regalo* a present, gift, etc., the *sb.* related to *regulare* to REGALE; the etym. of the stem is obscure (see ...]

Diez and Körting). The erroneous form *regalio* is common in the second half of the 17th century: *regalia* is less usual.] A present, esp. of choice food or drink; a choice or elegant repast or entertainment, etc. (see REGALE *sb.*[2]).

Regalty. *Obs.* Forms: **4-5 regalté**, **4-6 regalte**, **(4-, 4-tee)**, **6 regaltie**, **(7-5yte)**, **7-8 6-regaltie**, **(5 -tye, 6 -ye)**, **6 rigalie**. [a. AF. *regalty*, *regalté* = It. ... **1.** Royalty, royal prerogative, kingship; kingdom. (Very common *c* 1350–1550.)

Regard (rĭgārd), *sb.* Also **4-7 regarde**, **(5 -aird)**. [a. OF. *regard* (12th c.), now regarded as masc., f. *regarder*: see REGARD *v.*]

1. A look, glance, or gaze. Also **†2.** Aspect, appearance (*obs.*); look (of person).

3. The fact of taking care of, or paying attention to (something said or done). *Obs.*

4. Reference to a person or thing. Chiefly in phr. *to have (a) regard to.*

5. Observant attention or heed bestowed upon or given (a matter); consideration of a question or problem. Also *pl.* (cf. sense 2).

6. In prepositional phrases.

7. Esteem, affection, kindly feeling.

8. A looking or attention in order to direct one's actions or conduct. *Obs.*

9. Care in doing something; close attention to some principle or method.

10. A thing or circumstance looked to, or taken into account, in determining action or conduct; a consideration.

Regard (rĭgārd), *v.* Also **6 regarde**, **6-7 regard**. [a. F. *regarder*, *-greater*, OF. *regarder*: see REGARD *sb.*] **1.** To look at, gaze upon, observe.

Regardable. ... [f. REGARD v. + -ABLE], or s. f. Regardable (14th c.] Worthy of being regarded, noticeable. (Common in 17th c.)

Regardage. Obs. rare⁻¹. [f. REGARD + -AGE.] An allowance for providing fresh guards for robes.

Regardancy. Obs. rare. [See next and -ANCY.] The fact of being regardant.

Regardant, (rĭgā'dănt), a. and sb. Also 6 (9) -aunt, -ard. [a. F. regardant, pres. pple. of regarder to REGARD.]

A. adj. I. Law (now only Hist.) Attached to a manor; only in villein regardant (†also const. to).

b. Her. Looking backward.

Regardful, (rĭgā'ʼdfŭl), a. [f. REGARD sb.] 1. Heedful, attentive, observant.

b. To pay attention (to), take heed.

Regardfully, adv. [f. prec. + -LY.] Attentively, respectfully.

Regarding, vbl. sb. [f. REGARD v.]

b. = REGARD sb.

Regardless, (rĭgā'ʼdlĕs), a. [f. REGARD sb.]

b. Without const. (Chiefly in attrib. use)

Regardlessly, adv. [as prec. + -NESS.]

Regardlessness. [as prec. + -NESS.] Heedlessness, carelessness.

Regardship. Obs. rare⁻¹. [f. REGARD sb. + -SHIP.]

Regatta, (rĭgæ'ta, -gā'-). Also 7 regato, 7-8 regatta, 8 regata. [It. (Venetian) regatta or regata 'a strife or contention or struggling for the maistrie' (Florio) : hence also F. régate.]

Regel, variant of RIGOL Obs.

Regelate, (rĭ'dʒĕleit), v. [f. RE- 5 a + L. gelāre to freeze (cf. CONGEAL).]

Regelation, (rĭdʒĕleiʼʃən). [f. prec. and GELATION.] The action of freezing together again.

Regence. Obs. rare. [a. F. régence = REGENCY.]

Regency, (rĭ'dʒĕnsi). [ad. med.L. regentia (1418 in Du Cange), or f. REGENT : see -ENCY.]

1. a. Rule; government. Obs.

b. spec. The position or office of ruler; exercise of rule or authority; government, dominion, control.

Regenerable. Obs. rare⁻¹. [f. REGENERATE v. + -ABLE.]

Regeneracy. rare⁻¹. [f. REGENERATE a. + -CY.] The state of being regenerate.

Regenerant. rare⁻¹. [See next and -ANT.]

Regenerate, (rĭdʒĕ'nĕreit), ppl. a. and sb. [ad. L. regenerātus.]

Regenerate, (rĭdʒĕ'nĕreit), v. [f. L. regenerāt-, ppl. stem of regenerāre : see RE- and GENERATE v., and cf. F. régénérer (13th c.).]

Regeneration, (rĭdʒĕnĕreiʼʃən). Also 4-6 -acion, etc. [ad. L. regenerātiōn-em, n. of action f. regenerāre : see -ATION. Cf. F. régénération (13th c.).]

Regenerative, (rĭdʒĕ'nĕreitiv), a. (and sb.). [ad. F. régénératif, -ive (14th c.), or med.L. regenerātīv-us : see REGENERATE v. and -IVE.]

Regenerator, (rĭdʒĕ'nĕreitə(r)). [f. REGENERATE v. + -OR.]

Regeneratory, a. rare. [as REGENERATIVE: see -ORY.]

Regeneratress. rare⁻¹. [-ESS: cf. next.] A female regenerator.

Regeneratrix. rare⁻¹. [See REGENERATOR and GENERATRIX.] A female regenerator.

Re-genesis. [RE- 5 a.] The state, fact, or process, of producing or being reproduced.

Regent, (rĭ'dʒĕnt), sb. [subst. use of next.]

1. a. That which rules, governs, or has supremacy; a ruling power or principle. Now rare.

b. Regent (congregation or) house; the upper of the two houses into which the Senate of Cambridge University was formerly divided.

Regentess. rare⁻¹. [f. REGENT sb. + -ESS.] A female regent.

Regentship. [f. REGENT sb. + -SHIP.]

Regerminate, (rĭ-), v. [RE- 5 a.] To germinate again.

Regerminating, vbl. sb.

Regerminative, a.

Regest, sb. Obs. [ad. OF. regeste (11th c.; mod.F. régeste) or L. regesta register.]

Regest, v. Obs. [ad. L. regest-, pa. ppl. stem of regerĕre.]

Regestary, obs. form of REGISTRY.

Register, v. ... To register. ... To cast up, reckon, retort.

† **Regestry**, obs. form of REGISTER.

† **Regestion**. Obs. rare. ... Retort, reply.

† **Regestry**, obs. form of REGISTER. [See RUGEST v. and REGISTER.]

Regest (rīˈdʒest), sb. ... (Of obscure origin and meaning.)

Regian. Obs. ... An upholder of regal authority; a royalist.

Regible, a. Obs. rare⁻⁰. ... Governable.

† **Regible**, a. Obs. rare⁻¹.

Regicidal (redʒiˈsaidăl), a. ... Pertaining to, characterized by, inclined to, regicide.

Regicidation. nonce-wd. = REGICIDE 2.

Regicide ¹ (reˈdʒisaid). [f. L. rēgi-, stem of rex king + -CIDE 1: cf. F. régicide (16th c.).] ... One who kills a king, esp. his own king; one who commits the crime of regicide.

Regicide ² (reˈdʒisaid). [f. prec. + -CIDE 2.] The killing or murder of a king.

Regicidism. [f. prec. + -ISM.] The practice or principle of regicide.

Regie, **regime** (reˈʒiːm, reˈʒim). [F., ad. L. regimen.] = REGIMEN 2.

Regift, **regifical** ...

Regild, v. ... trans. To gild again.

Regimen (reˈdʒimen). [ad. L. regimen.] ...

Régime, **regime** (reˈʒiːm). [F., ad. L. régimen REGIMEN 2.] = REGIMEN 2.

Regiment (reˈdʒimənt), sb. Also 5–6 regement. [ad. late L. regimentum, f. L. regĕre to rule: see -MENT, and cf. F. régiment (1314).]
1. Rule or government over a person, people, or country; esp. royal or magisterial authority.
† 6. A rule, regulation, ordinance. Obs.
† b. Naut. (See quots.) Obs.

Regiment (reˈdʒiment), v. [f. prec.]
1. trans. To form into a regiment or regiments.
b. To form (persons, now esp. workers) into a definitely organized body or group.

Regiminal (redʒiˈminăl), a. Med. [f. REGIMEN + -AL.] Of or pertaining to, of the nature of, regimen.

Regina (rīˈdʒainə). [L.: fem. of rex king.] ... A queen.

Régine. Obs. ... Queen.

Reginal (rīˈdʒainăl), a. [ad. med.L. rēginālis, f. rēgina queen.] ... Of or pertaining to a queen; queenly, queenlike.

Regio- ...

Region (rīˈdʒən). [ad. AF. regiun, OF. region (mod. Godef.).] a. Of or pertaining to a queen; queenlike.

Region.
1. A realm or kingdom. Obs.
2. A large tract of land; a country; a more or less defined portion of the earth's surface, etc.
3. A separate part or division of the world or universe, as the air, heaven, etc.

Regional (rīˈdʒənăl), a. [ad. late L. regiōnāl-is: see prec. and -AL, and cf. mod.F. régional.]
1. Of or pertaining to, connected with, a particular region.
2. Pertaining to a special part of the body.

Regionalism (rīˈdʒənăliz'm). [f. prec. + -ISM.] Tendency to, or practice of, regional systems or methods; localism on a regional basis.

Regionalist (rīˈdʒənălist). [f. as prec.] ...

Regionality (rīˌdʒənˈæliti).

Regionally (rīˈdʒənăli), adv.

Regionary (rīˈdʒənări), a. and sb. [ad. late L. regiōnārius: see REGION and -ARY 1.]
A. adj. Of or pertaining to a region.
B. sb.

Regioned (rīˈdʒənd), ppl. a. [f. REGION + -ED 2.] Divided into regions; placed in a region.

Regionic, -al ... Regional.

Regioun, obs. form of REGION.

Register (reˈdʒistə), sb.¹ Forms: 4–6 regestre, registre, 5 registere, 6 registre, 6–7 (9) registre, 7– register; 4–6 registry, etc.
1. A book or volume in which regular entry is made of particulars or details of any kind which are considered of sufficient importance to be exactly and formally recorded; a written record or collection of entries thus formed; a list, catalogue.

Register, sb.² [prob. from Thermometer to be its own Register.]

Register (reˈdʒistə), v. [ad. med. L. registrāre, f. registrum.]
1. trans. To enter or cause to be entered formally in a register.

† b. *Sc. Lord Register* = Lord Clerk Register (see ch. 1 § b). *Obs.*

5. *intr.* To manipulate the registers of an organ.

Hence **Registerable** = Registrable.

Register book = Register sb. 1 c or d.

† Registrary, obs. rare. [f. med.L. *registeri-um*, cf. Registre sb.] *v.* + ery.]

† Registral, a. *Obs.* Chiefly *Sc.* [f. ppl. stem of med.L. *registrare*: see prec.] *trans.* To register (in *lit.* and *fig.* sense).

Registrant (re·dʒistrănt). [ad. L. *registrant-em*, pr. pple. of *registrāre*: see Registrate.]

Registrar (re·dʒistrā·r). [f. Register v. + -AR²; cf. the earlier Registrer and Registrary.]

Registrarship (re·dʒistrā·rʃip). [f. prec. + -ship.]

Register-office. An office at which a register of any kind is kept, or where registration is made.

Registering (re·dʒistəriŋ), *vbl. sb.* [f. Register v. + -ing¹.] The action of recording, or entering in a book, etc.

Registership (re·dʒistərʃip). The office of registrar.

Registration (redʒistrē·ʃən). [ad. med.L. *registration-em*, n. of action f. *registrāre* to Register: see Registrate.]

Registry (re·dʒistri). [f. Register v. + -ery.]

† Registure. *Obs.* rare⁻¹. [f. Register + -ure.] = Registrature.

Regnal (re·gnăl), a. [ad. med.L. *regnālis*, f. *regn-um* kingdom, Reign sb.]

Regnancy (re·gnănsi). [f. next + -cy.]

Regnant (re·gnănt), *ppl. a.* [ad. L. *regnant-em*, pres. pple. of *regnāre* to Reign. Cf. F. *régnant*.]

Rego (rī·goʊ). *Obs.* rare⁻¹. [? f. med.L. *regula.*]

Regrade (rīgrē·d), v. [Re- 5 a.] *trans.* To regrade.

Regrate (rīgrē·t), v.¹ *Obs.* [ad. OF. *regrater* (12th c.).]

Regratery (rīgrē·təri). [f. Regrate v.¹ + -ery.]

Regrede (rīgrī·d), v. *Obs.* rare. [ad. L. *regredī* to go back.]

Regredience. *Obs.* rare. [f. L. *regredient-em.*]

Regress (rī·gres), sb. [ad. L. *regress-us*, f. *regred-ī*, *regress-* to go back.]

Regma (re·gma). *Bot.* [mod.L.]

Regmacarp. *Bot.*

Regn, obs. form of Reign.

Regnacioune, -acyon, var. Renegation *Obs.*

Regressive (rĭgre·siv), *a.* [f. REGRESS *v.*]

1. Retrogressive; returning, passing back.

2. Proceeding from effect to cause, or from particular to universal.

Regression (rĭgre·ʃǝn). [ad. L. *regressiōn-em*, n. of action f. *regredī*: see REGRESS *v.*]

1. Return to a subject.

2. Recurrence or repetition (of a word or statement).

3. The action of returning to or towards a place or point of departure.

Regressive (rĭgre·siv), *a.*

Regret (rĭgre·t), *sb.* [f. the vb.]

Regret (rĭgre·t), *v.* [a. F. *regretter*, OF. also *regreter* and *regrater*: see REGRATE *v.*[2]]

1. To remember, think of (something lost), with distress or longing; to feel (+ or express) sorrow for the loss of (a person or thing).

2. To grieve at, feel mental distress on account of (some event, fact, action, etc.).

Regretful (rĭgre·tfŭl), *a.* [f. REGRET *sb.* + -FUL.] Full of regret; feeling or expressing regret.

Regretfully, *adv.*

Regretfulness.

Regrettable (rĭgre·tǎb'l), *a.* [a. F. *regrettable*, f. *regretter*: see REGRET *v.* and -ABLE.] Deserving of, calling for, regret.

Regrettably, *adv.*

Regreet (rĭgrī·t), *v.* [RE- 5 a.]

Regreet, *sb.*

Regrind (rīgrəi·nd), *v.* [RE- 5 a.] *trans.* To grind again.

Regrow (rīgrōu·), *v.* [RE- 5 a.] *intr.* To grow again.

Regulable.

REGULAR.

Regular (re·gi̯ŭlǎɹ), *a.* and *sb.* [ad. L. *rēgulāris*, f. *rēgula* RULE.]

Regularity (regi̯ŭlæ·rĭti). [f. prec. + -ITY.]

Regularize (re·gi̯ŭlǎɹǝiz), *v.* [f. REGULAR + -IZE.]

Regularly (re·gi̯ŭlǎɹli), *adv.* [f. REGULAR + -LY[2].]

REGULATE.

Regulate (re·gi̯ŭleit), *v.* [f. late L. *rēgulāt-*, ppl. stem of *rēgulāre* (5th c.), f. *rēgula* RULE.]

Regulation (regi̯ŭlē·ʃǝn). [f. REGULATE *v.* + -ION.]

Regulative (re·gi̯ŭlǎtiv), *a.* [f. REGULATE *v.* + -IVE.]

Regulator (re·gi̯ŭleitǎɹ). [agent-n. f. L. *rēgulāre* to REGULATE: cf. F. *régulateur*, lt. *regolatore*.]

Regulatory (re·gi̯ŭleitǎɹi), *a.* [f. REGULATE *v.* + -ORY[2].]

Regulatress, *rare*[-1]. [See REGULATOR and -ESS[1].] A female regulator.

Reguline (re·gi̯ŭlǎin, -līn), *a.* *Chem.* [f. REGULUS + -INE[1].] Of or pertaining to, of the nature of, regulus.

Regulize, *v. rare*[-1]. [f. REGULUS + -IZE.]

‖Regulus (re·gi̯ŭlǒs). Pl. **reguli** (re·gi̯ŭlǎi). [L.]

Regurgitate, v. [ad. med.L. regurgitāre, f. re- RE- + late L. gurgitāre (16th cent.).] ...

Regurgitation ...

Reh, re3, rei, v. Obs.

Rehiche adv. ; **Re-hahip**. Obs.

Rehn'bile, v. Sc. Obs. rare ... var. of REABLE

Rehabilitate ...

Rehabili'tation ...

Rehabli'tion. Obs. rare.

Rehle, v. ...

Rehn'low, v. ...

Rehaye, ...

Rehammer, v. [RE- 5 a.] To hammer again.

Behandle, v. [RE- 5 a.] To handle ...

Rehaunt ...

Reheta, ...

Rehearse, ...

Rehea'ten, v. Obs.

Rehe'tour. Obs. rare.

Reheat, v. [RE- 5 a.] trans. To heat again.

Reheater. ...

Reheating, vbl. sb.

Rehelm, v. [RE- 5 a.]

Rehedte, variant of REHETE v.2 Obs.

Rehete, ...

Rehelm, v. ...

Rehire, v. [RE- 5 a.]

Rehire, v.

Rehoi'st, v.

Rehonour, v.

Rehou'se, v.

Rehearse, ...

Rehumanize, v.

Rehu'mble, v. rare.

Rehumilia'tion. rare. [RE- 5 a.]

Rehypo'thecate, v. ...

Reid, ...

Re-identifica'tion. [RE- 5 a.] The action of identifying again.

Reif, ...

Reil, ...

Reign, sb. ...

Reign, v. ...

2. A thing rejected as something. *Obs. rare*

†Reject, pa. pple. and *ppl. a. Obs.* [ad. L. *reject-us*, pa. pple. of *rejicĕre* to REJECT.]
= REJECTED.

Reject (rĭdʒe̅kt), *v.* Also 6-8. *rejekk-*. [f. L. *reject-*, ppl. stem of *reicĕre* (*rejicĕre*) to throw back, f. re- RE- + *jacĕre* to throw. Cf. also F. *rejeter* vb. of *rejeter*, mod.F. *rejeter*: see JET v.2]

1. *trans.* To refuse to recognize, (to allow,) acquiesce in, submit to, or adopt (a rule, command, practice, etc.); to refuse credit to (a statement).

2. To refuse to have or take for some purpose; to set aside or throw away as useless or worthless.

3. To cast back or throw.

4. To expel from the mouth or stomach.

5. *Math.* To drop.

6. To refuse (something offered); to decline to receive or accept.

7. To refuse to grant, entertain, or agree to.

8. *Ent.* [Not admitted between other parts.]

†b. *absol.* or *intr.* To be disobedient. *rare*

c. To deny (one who makes a request). *Obs.*

†b. To cast (a fault, etc.) back upon a person. Also *const. in*.

Rejectable, *a. Obs. rare.* That may be, or ought to be, rejected.

†Rejectamenta (rĭdʒektame̅ntă), *sb. pl.* [mod.L., pl. of *rejectamentum*: see REJECT v. and -MENT.]

Rejectaneous, *a. Obs.* [ad. L. *rejectāneus* (coined by Cicero to render the Stoic ἀπο-προηγμένα), f. *rejectus*: see REJECT; cf. *extraneous*, *spontaneous*, etc.]

†Rejecta'neous, *a. Obs.* [ad. L. *rejectāneus*]

Rejecter (rĭdʒe̅ktər). One who rejects.

†8.a. To refer (a matter or person) to another for decision. Also *const. into* a place. *Obs.*

†b. To cast (a fault, etc.) back *upon* a person.

†Rejectible, *a. Obs.* = REJECTABLE.

Rejecting, *ppl. a.* [f. pres. pple. of REJECT v. + -ING2.] In a rejecting manner.

Rejection (rĭdʒe̅kʃən). [a. F. *rejection* (16th c.), or ad. L. *rejectiōn-em*, n. of action f. *rejicĕre* to REJECT.] The action of rejecting or the state of being rejected.

Rejective, *a.* [f. as REJECT v. + -IVE.] That rejects, or tends to cast off (Webster 1828-32.)

Rejectment (rĭdʒe̅ktmĕnt). [f. as prec. + -MENT. Cf. REJECTAMENT.]

†Rejectment. *Obs. rare.* [ad. mod.L. *rejectamentum*: see mod.L.]

†Rejectamenta.

Rejector (rĭdʒe̅ktər). One who rejects.

† Rejerk'r, *v. Obs.* [RE-5 a.] *trans.* To jerk back.

†Rejoice, *v.* Obs. [f. next. A. next.]

3. *Phys.* Excremental matter.

REJOICE

Rejoice (rĭdʒoi̅s), *v.* Forms: 4-6 *reioyse*, (5 *reyowse*), *reyyoyse*, *reyjoyse*, *5-6 reioys), reioyce-*, 6-7 *rejoyce*, (6 *-joyse*, *-joies*, 4-6 rejoice, (5 -see, 6 Sc. reioie); 5-7 *rejoyce*, (7-8 rejoye), 5 *rejoice*, 8 *reioische*, *-ashe*, 4-5 rejoyschie, 4-9 rejoice. [a. OF. *rejoir-*, *rejoiss-*, lengthened stem of *rejoir* (later *réjouir*, mod.F. *réjouir*), f. re- RE- + *joir* to JOY v.]

Rejoicer (rĭdʒoi̅sər). One who rejoices.

Rejoicing, *vbl. sb.* [-ING2.]

†Rejoin, *sb. Obs.* [f. next.]

REJOIN

Rejoin (rĭdʒoi̅n), *v.1* Also 5-7 *rejoyne*, 6 *reioynne*, 7 *rejoigne*. [a. F. *rejoindre* (12th c.), f. re- RE- + *joindre* to JOIN.]

Rejoin (rĭdʒoi̅n), *v.2* Also 5-7 *rejoyn*, (6-7 *rejoyne*). [ad. F. *rejoin-* (see prec.), or f. RE- 5 a. + JOIN v.]

1. *trans.* To join again, reunite (persons or things, or one to or with another).

Rejoindure.

Rejoinder (rĭdʒoi̅ndər), *sb.* Also 5-6 *reioynder*, 6 *reioyndre*, 7 *rijoinder*. [a. AF. *rejoinder*, *rejoindre*, inf. used *subst.*]

Rejoindure, *v. Obs.* [prob. ad. F. *rejoindre* (see prec. and JOINDER), with ending assimilated to -URE.]

†Rejoint, *v.1* Obs. rare–1. [Of obscure origin: cf. REJOULT v.] *trans.*

Rejoint (rĭdʒoi̅nt), *v.2* [f. as REJOIN *v.2*] *trans.* To joint together again.

Rejoin so, *v. Obs.* [f. REJOIN v. + -so.]

Rejolt, *sb.* Obs. rare.

Rejolt, *v.* [f. RE- + JOLT v.]

Rejoneed, *v. Obs.* To cure or recur to the mind after the manner of a bump or thump.

Rejourn, *v.* Also 6 *reiourne*. [prob. ad. F. *rejourner* (see prec. and JOURN), with ending assimilated to -URN.]

Rejoyn, see prec. forms of REJOIN v.

Rejoyce, obs. forms of REJOICE v.

Rejource, *v. Obs.* [RE- + JOUNCE v.]

REKE

Reke, *sb.* Obs. [Related to next: cf. ON. *reka*.]

Reke, *v.1* Obs. Forms: *4 rak(e*, *7 rake.* Pa. t. and *pa. pple.* 4 *rake*.

Reke, *v.2* Obs.

Reke, obs. form of RECK, REACH, REEK vbs.

Rejuvenescence (rĭdʒu̅vĭne̅sens). Also 7, 9 *-escence*. [f. as prec. + -ENCE.] A renewal of youth, physical, mental, or spiritual. Also fig.

Rejuvenescent, *a.* [f. as prec. + -ENT.]

Rejuvenescency, *sb.* Now rare.

† Rejuvenescent, *a.* [f. as prec. + -ENT.]

2. *trans.* and *refl.* To make joyful or happy; to cause to rejoice. Also *absol.*

Rejuvenate (rĭdʒu̅vĕnēt), *v.* [f. L. *juvenis* young, after F. *rajeunir*: cf. REJUVENESCE.]

Rejuvenise, *v.* [f. as prec. + -ISE.]

Rejuvenize, *v.* [f. as prec. + -IZE.]

Rejuvenation.

Rekels, obs. form of RECKON v.

Rekendle.

Rekenyng, obs. ff. RECKONING *vbl. sb.*

Rekindle, *v.* [RE- 5 a.]

1. *trans.* To kindle again, set fire to afresh.

2. *intr.* To take fire again.

3. *refl.* To make glow again.

Rela'be, *v. Obs. rare.* [RE- 5 a.] *trans.* and *intr.* To lade again.

Rela'tion.

RELAPSE

Relapse (rĭla̅ps), *sb.* Also 6 relaps. [ad. L. *relapse*, f. *relapsus* pa. pple. of *relābi*. Cf. RELAPSE v.]

Relapse (rĭla̅ps), *v.* Also 6-7 *relaps*. [ad. L. *relaps-*, ppl. stem of *relābi* to slip or slide back, f. re- RE- + *lābi* to slide, slip, fall.]

1. A falling back into error, heresy, or wrong-doing; backsliding.

Relapsarian.

Relapsation.

Relapse.

Relapse (rĭlæps'), *ppl. a.* War *rare*.

Relapse (rĭlæps'), *ppl.* stem of *relabi* to slip back: see Relapsed.

1. *intr.* To fall back into wrong-doing or error; to backslide; *spec.* to fall again into heresy after recantation. Const. *into, to*; also without const.

b. *intr.* To fall back into an illness after partial recovery or from a convalescent state. *Obs.*

2. To fall back or sink again into (*to*) any state, practice, etc.

3. To cause to fall back. *Obs.*

Relapsed (rĭlæps't), *ppl. a.* [*prec. + -ED¹.*] Fallen back into a previous condition.

Relapse (rĭlæps'), *sb.* [f. prec. + -ER¹.] One who relapses.

Relapsing (rĭlæps'iŋ), *vbl. sb.* [f. as prec. + -ING¹.] The action of the vb. Relapse.

Related.

Relasping, *ppl. a.* [-ING².] That relapses.

Relate (rĭlē't), *v.* [ad. L. *relāt-*, *ppl.* stem of *referre*, taken substantively: see Relate D.]

1. *trans.* I. In pass. **a.** To be borne or carried in *between* things. *Obs.*

2. To recount, narrate, tell; *spec.* Hearsay to begin in farm a relaxh and contemptuous neglect of or bane and despicle an Enemy.

Relate (rĭlē't), *v.* [f. Relate *v.* + -ABLE.] **a.** That may be narrated. **b.** That may be brought into relation with something else.

Relate (rĭlē't), *a.* *Obs. rare⁻¹.* [ad. L. *relātus.*] Related.

Relatio (rĭlē'ʃɪo), *sb. Law.* The recantation of a relate quality is of this kind, whose conjunction is the relation itself.

Related (rĭlē'tĕd), *ppl. a.* (*and sb.*) [f. prec. + -ED¹.]

1. Narrated, recited; † referred to. *rare.*

2. *a.* Brought into relation *to*, or associating *with*; something else. Also *absol.* without const.

b. Having mutual relation or connexion.

c. *Of persons:* Connected by blood or marriage (*to* another, or each other).

b. To connect, to establish a relation.

2. *One who relates:* a narrator, historian.

Relation (rĭlē'ʃən), *sb.* Also 4-7 **relacion**, (5-cioun, 6-cyon). [a. F. Relation, or ad. L. *relātiōn-em*: see Relate *v.* and -ion.]

1. The action of relating in words; narration, recital, account; report. In early use *esp.* in phr.

2. *a.* Connexion, reference, respect; relationship; (*or one's*) narrative, account, statement.

b. *Law.* (see quot. and Information 5 b.)

Related (rĭlē'tĕd), *ppl. a.* [f. prec. + -ED¹.]

Relational (rĭlē'ʃənăl), *a.* [f. prec. + -AL.]

Relationship (rĭlē'ʃənʃɪp), *sb.* [as prec. + -SHIP.] The state of being related; a condition or character imported by relation.

Relatist.

6. The position which one person holds with respect to another on account of some social or other connexion between them; the particular mode in which persons are mutually connected by circumstances.

7. The aggregate of the connexions, or modes of connexion, by which one person is brought into touch with another or with society in general.

Relatedness, the state or condition of being related.

Relatival (relătəi'văl), *a.* Chiefly *Gram.* [f. Relative + -AL.] Of or pertaining to a relative or relation.

Relative (re'lătiv), *a.* and *sb.* [ad. F. *relatif*, *-ive* (13th c.), or L. *relatīv-us*: see Relate *v.* and -IVE.] **A.** *adj.*

I. *Gram.* Relating or referring to an antecedent term; *esp. relative pronoun.*

Relator.

†4. A relationship. *Obs. rare.*

Relativism (re'lătiviz'm), *sb.* The doctrine of relativism.

Relativist (re'lătivist), *sb.* One who holds the doctrine of relativism.

Relativity (relătivi'tĭ), *sb.* [as prec. + -ITY.] The fact or condition of being relative, relativeness.

Relator (rĭlē'tər), *sb.* Also 7 -our. [a. L. *relātor*, agent-noun.]

1. A relater, narrator. (Common 1600-1750.)

Relatrix.

Relax (rĭlæks'), *v.* [ad. L. *relaxāre*, f. re- Re- + *laxāre* to loosen, f. *laxus* loose, Lax *a.*]

1. *trans.* **a.** To slacken.

b. To make less strict, severe, or rigid.

c. To diminish the force or tension of.

2. To make less strict, severe, or rigid.

Relaxant (rĭlæk'sănt), *a.* and *sb. Med.* [ad. L. *relaxant-em.*] **A.** *adj.* Causing, or distinguished by, relaxation.

Relaxation.

Relaxate (rĭlæks'ēt), *v. Obs. rare.* [f. L. *relaxāt-*, ppl. stem of *relaxāre.*]

Relaxation (rilăksē'ʃən). [ad. L. *relaxātiōn-em*, or ad. F. *relaxation* (1314).]

1. Partial (†or complete) remission of some penalty, burden, duty, etc.; also, the document granting such remission.

2. The action of unbending the mind from severe application; recreation or ordinary occupations.

RELAXATIVE

3. Path. A loosening or slackening of the fibres, nerves, joints, etc., of the body; diminution of firmness or tension.

1646 BACON *Sylva* § 730 Bathing or Anointing give a Relaxation or Emollition. 1661 LOVELL *Hist. Anim.* 20 A relaxation of the nerves and ligaments.

4. Extension of meaning: a release or freedom from strictness or severity.

a 1646 W. SLATER *Exp. 4th ch. Rom.* (1650) 216, I ... can but wonder, How the severest of Judges ... Popish Seminaries hath gotten relaxation.

5. Abatement of intensity, vigour, or energy.

1695 WOODWARD *Nat. Hist. Earth* II. ii. (1723) 142 Relaxation of the Heat.

Relaxative, *a.* and *sb.* [f. RELAX *v.*, after LAXATIVE. Cf. RELAXANT.]

A. *adj.* Tending to relax; of the nature of relaxation. *rare.*

1611 FLORIO, *Rilassativo,* laxative or relaxative in operation.

B. *sb.* A means of relaxing; *esp.* a relaxing medicine. *Obs.*

1692 B. JONSON *Magn. Lady* iii. iv. It is a pureness, a kind of soppage ... that are troubled with ... and therefore you must use relaxatives.

So Relaxatory *a. rare.*

1581 J. BELL *Haddon's Answ. Osor.* 202 They would graunt plenarie remission of sinnes; and would make out their Bulles relaxatory.

Relaxed (rĭlæ·kst), *ppl. a.* [f. RELAX *v.*]

1. Freed from restraint or restrictions; not strict or precise, † esp. in observing a religious rule.

1646 G. DANIEL *Eclog. v.* 74 The Florentine proceeds to duller fodes; But Stronger flew from all relaxed Soules.

2. Slackened, mitigated, or modified in respect of strictness.

1671 WOODHEAD *St. Teresa* II. xxx. 187 A Monastery of our Lady of Carmel of the *Relaxed* order.

3. Path. A loosening of some part of the body: Deprived of firmness or of normal firmness; rendered soft or feeble.

1646 SIR T. BROWNE *Pseud. Ep.* 117 This part in Deere ... sometimes becomes so relaxed and pendulous.

Relaxer. *rare.* [f. RELAX *v.* + -ER¹.]
One who, or that which, relaxes or loosens.

1816 SHELLEY *Rosal.* ♦ Helen 1170 His mien Sunk with the sound relaxedly.

Relaxing, *ppl. a.* [f. as prec. + -ING¹.] Causing or producing relaxation; enervating.

1779 FLORIO, *Rilassante,* a relaxing. 1869 LOWES in *Phil.*

RELEASE

Relay (rĭlē·), *sb.*¹ [ad. F. *relay* (13th c.), of obscure origin.]

† **1. Hunt.** Of a hunter: One of the fresh hounds ① upon the track of the deer. Also *absol. Obs.*

1410 *Master of Game* (MS. Digby 182) Prol., He shold but be deere passe and go to be fees ... and relay his hounds upon be fees. *Ibid.,* If it so be, bat he hunter hav habe relayes of houndes.

2. To chase by relays : to provide with, or place by, fresh relays.

3. *intr.* To get a fresh relay.

Re-lay (rĭ-lē·), *v.* Also *relay.* [RE- 5 a.] *trans.* To lay again, in various senses. Also *absol.*

Relayer. *rare.* [ad. F. *relayeur.*]

RELEASE

Release (rĭlī·s), *sb.*¹ Forms: 3-6 relea, 4-6 relees, -lese, -lees, (4 -leoce, -leesse, 5 relece, -leoyt); 4-5 releyshe, -leeshe, (4 -leasshe), 5 relesche, relheshe; 5- release, (6 -leace, -lease). [ad. OF. *reles, relais* (13th c.), *relaisse* (var. *relascher*):—L. *relaxāre* to RELAX.]

I. 1. Abatement, alleviation, or remove (labour, pain, etc.). *Obs.*

2. An intermission of, or release from, suffering, trouble, etc.

3. Relaxation, relief. *Obs.*

4. Remission or pardon of an offence, penalty, debt, etc.

5. Deliverance or liberation from trouble, pain, sorrow or the like.

II. In certain technical senses.

6. The action of setting free, or the fact of being set free, from restraint or confinement ; permission to go free ; also, a document giving formal discharge from captivity.

7. The action or right of freeing, or act of being freed.

8. The act of letting go something or held in a certain position.

RELEASEE

Releasee (rĭlīsī·). *Law.* [f. RELEASE *v.* + -EE¹.] One to whom an estate is released.

RELEASEMENT

Releasement (rĭlī·smĕnt). [RELEASE *v.*]

1. The act of releasing, or the fact of being released, from prison, obligation, debt, trouble, etc. (Very common. *c* 1650–1800.)

1611 UDALL, tr. *Erasm. Par. Acts* viii. 32 No answere made he before him his releasement.

2. Relaxation, remission, or removal of a thing.

Releaser (rĭlī·sər). [f. RELEASE *v.*¹ + -ER¹.]
One who, or that which, releases or sets free.

Releasor (rĭlī·sɔɹ). *Law.* [f. RELEASE *v.*¹ + -OR.]
One who makes an estate or claim in favour of another. (See RELEASEE *v.* 3 and 4 b.)

Releave, *obs.* form of RELIEF *sb.*¹

Releasing, *vbl. sb.* [f. RELEASE *v.*¹ + -ING¹.]
The action of the vb. in various senses.

Relect, *obs.* form of RELEGATE *v.*

Relection. [f. L. *relect-,* ppl. stem of *relegere* to read again ; cf. LECTION, PRELECTION.]

Relegate (re·lĭge't), *v.* Also 7 *relig-.* [f. ppl. stem of L. *relēgāre,* f. RE- RE- + *lēgāre* to send.]

1. To remove (oneself) to a distance *from* something.

2. To consign to some unimportant or obscure place; to consign to a place or position, *esp.* one of inferiority.

3. To banish ; to send *into* exile ; to banish *to* a particular place. (Cf. RELEGATION 1.) Also *refl.,* to remove (oneself) to a distance *from* somewhere.

Relegation (relĭgē·ʃən). [ad. L. *relēgātiōn-,* n. of action f. *relēgāre* to RELEGATE.]

1. The action of banishing ; the state of temporary exile or banishment. In *Roman Antiq.* banishment of a person, or to a specified distance from Rome, for a limited time and without loss of civil rights. Also *attrib.*

RELENT

Relent (rĭle·nt), *v.* [app. f. RE- + LENT a. (in sense of L. *lentus*) pliant, flexible.]

1. *intr.* To melt under the influence of heat; to assume a liquid form; to dissolve into water. *Obs.*

2. *intr.* To soften ; to become less hard or rigid ; to grow soft or tender.

3. *intr.* To soften (one's mind, etc.) ; to cause (a person) to relent.

4. *intr.* To relax in severity ; to slacken.

† b. To relent, to repent (of) ; to regret. *Obs.*

† c. To pity. *Obs. rare.*

Hence † Relented *ppl. a.*

† Relentful, *a. Obs. rare.*

Relenting, *ppl. a.* [f. as prec. + -ING².]
That relents, in various senses of the vb.

Hence Relentingly *adv.*

Relentless, *a.* [f. RELENT *v.* + -LESS.] Incapable of relenting ; pitiless.

Relentlessly, *adv.* [f. prec. + -LY².]
In a relentless manner.

Relentlessness. [f. as prec. + -NESS.]
The quality of being relentless.

Relentment (rĭle·ntmĕnt). *Now rare.* [f. RELENT *v.* + -MENT.] The act of relenting; softening of disposition. Also *concr.*

† Relenture. *Obs. rare.* [f. RELENT *v.* + -URE.]

RELEVATOR

Relesche, *obs.* form of RELEASE *sb.*¹ and *v.*¹

Relessee, *Law.* var. RELEASEE.
Relessor, *Law.* var. RELEASOR.

Relet (rīle·t), *v. rare.* [RE- 5 a.] *trans.* To let again.

Re-letting, *vbl. sb.*

Relevance (re·lĭvăns). Also *Sc.* **reliv-.** [f. RELEVANT : see -ANCE.] Relevancy.

Relevancy (re·lĭvănsi). Also 6 *Sc.* **reliv-.** [f. RELEVANT : see -ANCY.]

1. Bearing upon, connected with, pertinent to, the matter in hand : pertinence or applicability.

2. *Sc. Law.* Legally pertinent or sufficient.

Relevant (re·lĭvănt), *a.* Also *Sc.* **relivant.** [ad. med.L. *relevant-em* (1481 in Du Cange), pres. pple. of L. *relevāre* to raise up, etc. (see RELIEVE *v.*) : cf. F. *relevant* (17th c. in Littré).]

1. Bearing upon, connected with, pertinent to, the matter in hand : Bearing upon or sufficiently connected with the matter in hand.

2. *Sc. Law.* Legally pertinent or sufficient ; ... that justifies a legal action or answer.

Relevate (re·lĭveʹt), *v.* [f. ppl. stem of L. *relevāre* to raise up, etc.]

1. *trans.* To raise the spirits of (a person) ; to restore to cheerfulness.

2. To raise, elevate. Hence **Relevated** *ppl. a.*

Relevation (relĭvē·ʃən), *n.* [ad. L. *relevātiōn-em,* n. of action f. *relevāre.*]

So Relevator, one who raises.

† Relevavith. *Obs. rare.* [ad. L. *relevavit* 'he has relieved', 3rd sing. perf. indic. of *relevāre*: see RELIEVE *v.* 8.] Also *Ag.*

Releve(n, obs. forms of RELIEVE *v.*

† Relev'y. *sb.[2] Obs. rare—[1].* [ad. It. *rilievi,* pl. of *rilieve* RELIEF.] Relief.

Relevy, *v. Sc. obs. rare—[1].* [irreg. ad. L. *relevāre* or F. *relever*: see RELIEVE *v.*] *trans.* To raise or set up again.

Relewe, obs. Sc. form of RELIEVE *v.*

Relewy, Releyit, obs. Sc. pa. pple. of RELIEVE *v.*

Reliability. (rĭlaĭəbⁱlⁱti). [f. next + -ITY.]

The quality of being reliable, reliableness.

Reliable, (rĭlaĭəb'l), *a.* [f. RELY *v.[1]* + -ABLE.]

That may be relied upon; in which reliance or confidence may be put; trustworthy, safe, sure.

Reliableness (rĭlaĭəb'lnɛs). [f. prec. + -NESS.]

The quality or state of being reliable.

Reliably (rĭlaĭəbli), *adv.* [f. as prec. + -LY.]

In a reliable manner.

Reliance (rĭlaĭəns). [f. RELY *v.[1]* + -ANCE.]

1. The († or an) act of relying; the condition or character of being reliant; dependence, confidence.

b. Without const.

Reliant (rĭlaĭənt), *a.* [f. as prec. + -ANT.]

Having reliance or confidence; confident, trustful.
(Cf. SELF-RELIANT.) Also const. *on.*

Relic (rɛlik). Forms: 3-7 reliks, 4-6 lyke, relik, 4-7 relike, 4-5 relyke, (5 realyke), 6-8 relick, 8- relic. [f. OF. *relique,* ad. L. *reliquiæ* pl. remains.] See RELIQUE.

1. In religious use, *esp.* in the Roman Catholic and Greek Churches: Some object, such as a part of the body or clothing, an article of personal use, or the like, which remains as a memorial of a departed saint, martyr, or other holy person, and as such is carefully preserved and held in esteem or veneration.

† b. Applied to the sacred objects of the ancient Jewish and pagan religions.

† c. A precious or valuable thing. *Obs. rare.*

2. Something kept as a remembrance or souvenir of a person, thing, or place; a memento.

3. The remains of a meal or of food; remnants, scraps, leavings. Now *rare.*

4. A surviving trace of some practice, fact, idea, quality, etc. In early use chiefly *pl.*

5. The widow of a man.

6. An object invested with interest by reason of its antiquity or associations with the past.

† 8. *pl.* Remains, remnants, residue. Also *sing.*

Relicary. *rare.* [ad. Sp. *relicario*: see RELIQUARY.] A shrine for relics.

Re-lick, *v.* [RE- 5 a.] *trans.* To lick again.

† Relickly, *adv. Obs. rare—[1].* [f. RELIC + -LY.] As a relic; carefully.

Relict (rɛlikt), *sb.* [ad. L. *relict-us, -a, -um,* pa. pple. of *relinquĕre* to leave behind, RELINQUISH; in sense 2 more immediately ad. med.L. *relicta* sb. or OF. *relicte* (14th c.).]

1. RELIQUE, *q.v.* and sb. 2. Now *rare* or *Obs.*

2. The widow of a man.

Relicary. See RELICARY.

Relief [1] (rĭlīf). Forms: 4-6 relef, (5-6 leffe), relefe, 5-7 releefe, -leif, (5 relyf, relyef), 5-7 releife, 6 releeffe, -refe, relyeffe, -leeve, (6 Sc. -lieve), 7 relyve; 4-6 releve, -love, (6 Sc. -lieve), reliefe; 6 OF. *relief,* vbl. sb. from *relever* to RELIEVE.]

I. A payment, varying in value and kind according to rank and tenure, made to the overlord by the heir of a feudal tenant on coming into possession of the vacant estate.

b. *pl.* That which is left behind or rejected; leavings; refuse. *Obs. rare.*

2. Relict. *v. Obs.* [as prec.; f. DERELICT.]

1. Allowed to remain untouched or undisturbed.

2. Left by death, surviving.

3. *Law:* Left by the recess of the sea.

b. Abandoned, deserted.

Relict, *sb.* [f. L. *relict-us,* etc.]

II. The remains of food left after a meal; leavings, scraps.

2. The remains of something broken off, etc.

Relief (rĭlīf). Forms: 3-5 relef, (5 -leffe), 4-7 relif, -lyf, (4 pl. -lyves), releff, 5 reliffe, -leve, (pl. -leves, -lyve), 6-6 relief, (6-love); 6 relief, rilief (plied); *relic, reliery,* 'that remnant .. of meat left at a meal', also 'rubbidge, or the ruines of over-thrown houses' (Cotgr.); cf. *Prov. relieu, Sp. relieve, It. rilievo,* whence, with its corresponding to RELIEVE *v.,* and literally meaning 'that which is lifted or removed'.

1. **a.** That which is left or given up by one.

b. The remains of a thing; remainder; residuum.

† c. The surviving portion of a person. *Obs.*

II. A payment, etc.

Relieve, *v.* [RE- 5 a.]

II. †6. To lift or raise up again. *Obs.*

7. intr. To rise again. Also in *pass.*, to have risen from childbed. *Obs.*

III. †9. To bring (a matter) into prominence; to make clear or evident. *Obs.*

†**10.** To raise up, make higher. *Obs. rare.*

Reliever (rĭliˑvə̆z). Also 6-*or.* [f. RELIEVE *v.*]

Relieving (rĭliˑviŋ), *vbl. sb.* [f. as prec. + -ING¹]

†Relievement. *Obs.* Also 5-6 releve-, 7 releaue-. [a. OF. *releve-, relievement*, f. *relever* to RELIEVE.] The act of relieving; relief.

Relievo (rĭliˑvo). Also 7 releuo, 8 releivo, 8-9 rilievo. [ad. It. *rilievo* (*rilyeˑvo*): see RE-LIEF¹, and cf. ALTO-, BASSO-, MEZZO-RELIEVO.]

Relighting (rĭlaiˑtiŋ), *vbl. sb.* [f. as prec. + -ING¹.] The action of the vb. RELIGHT, in various senses.

Relight, *v.* [RE- 5 a.]

Religate, *v. rare.* [L. *religāt-*, ppl. stem of *religāre* to bind up or back : see RE- and LIGATE *v.*] *trans.* a. *Surg.* To bind up (a vein). *Obs.* b. To bind together or unite (people). *c.* To constrain. Also *absol.* Hence **Religaˑtion** (*rel-*), *vbl. sb.*

Religation, *rare.* [ad. L. *religātiōn-em*, n. of action f. *religāre* : see last and -ATION.] The action of tying or binding up (lit. and fig.)

Religieuse (religyȩ̄z). † Also as *pl.* [F. *religieuse* fem. of next.] A woman (bound by religious vows, or devoted to a religious life) : a nun.

† Religieux (religyȩ̄). Now *rare* or *Obs.* [F.] A member of a religious order.

Religio-, combining form of RELIGION or RELIGIOUS, as in *religio-educational, -magical, -military, -philosophical, -scientific,* etc.

Religion (rĭliˑdʒən). Forms: 3-4 religiun(e, 4-5 -ioun, 5-6 -yon(e, 5-6 -ion, 7 religioun ; 3-6 religyon, 4 -un, -ioun, 5-6 -ion ; 4 relligioun, (11th c.), 6 *religeon,* or 5-6 *religion,* etc. [a. AF. *religiun* (11th c.), OF. *religion, religiun, -ion,* F. *religion.*]

Religional, *a.* [f. prec. + -AL.]

Religionary, sb. and a. [F. *religionnaire.*]

Religioner (rĭliˑdʒənəz). [f. as prec. + -ER¹.]

Religionism (rĭliˑdʒəniz'm). [f. as prec. + -ISM.]

Religionist (rĭliˑdʒənist). [f. as prec. + -IST.]

Religionize (rĭliˑdʒənəiz), *v.* [f. as prec. + -IZE.]

Religioˑse, *a. Obs. rare.* [ad. L. *religiōsus.*]

Religioˑsity. [ad. late L. *religiōsitās:* see RELIGIOUS and -ITY.]

Religious (rĭliˑdʒəs), *a.* and *sb.* Forms: 3-5 religius, 4 religyus, -ous, -eous, -eus, 4-5 -ios, -ieus, -ious, 4-6 -yous, 5 -iouse, 4-6 -you(u)s, 5 -youse, 6 -youse, 7 -eous. [a. AF. *religius, -ious,* OF. *religius, -ious* (F. *religieux*), ad. L. *religiōsus,* f. *religiōn-em* : see RELIGION and -OUS.]

Religiously (rĭliˑdʒəsli), *adv.* [f. RELIGIOUS + -LY².]

Religiousness (rĭliˑdʒəsnes). [f. as prec. + -NESS.]

Religiˑous-ite, -ity, *varr.* RELIGIOSITY.

Relik(e, -lyke, obs. forms of RELIC.

Reliˑmb, *v.* [RE- 5 a.] *trans.* To provide with new limbs.

Reˑligation, *Obs.* In 4-5 -de, 5 -ion, -ite, 6 -ity. [f. RELIGIOUS + -(I)TY : cf. RE-LIGIOSITY and cf. F. *religiosité.*]

Religue, obs. form of RELIC.

Reline (rī-), *v.* [RE- 5 a.]

Reˑling, *v. Obs. rare.* [RE- 5 a.]

Reˑlinquish (rĭliˑŋkwiʃ). Also 5-6 relinquye, -lyngqushe, -lenquysh, etc. [ad. OF. *relinquiss-,* lengthened stem of *relinquir* (11th c. in Godef.), L. *relinquĕre,* f. RE- + *linquĕre* to leave.]

Relinquishment (rĭliˑŋkwiʃment). [f. prec. + -MENT.]

Relique (relik). Now *rare* or *Obs.* [F. *relique.*]

Reliquary (reˑlikwări), *sb.* [F. *reliquaire* (14th c. in Godef.) = Sp. *relicario,* It. *reliquario, reliquiario,* ad. med.L. *reliquiārium,* f. L. *reliquiæ* : see RELIQUIÆ and -ARY¹.] A small box, casket, shrine, or other receptacle, in which a relic or relics are kept.

Reliquary, *a. rare.* [f. as prec. + -ARY².]

Relique, obs. form of RELIC.

Reliquiæ (rĭlikˑwiī), *sb. pl.* [L., f. *relinquĕre* to leave : see RELIC.] **1.** Remains of any kind; esp. in Geol. remains of early animals or plants. **2.** *Eccl.* Relics.

Religioˑus, obs. form of RELIGIOUS.

Relk, obs. variant of RELIC.

Reliˑquid, *a. Obs. rare.* [RE- + L. *liquidus.*] Remaining, left.

Reliquiˑ, variant of RELIC.

RELIQUIAL.

Reliquial, a. *nonce-wd.*

Reli·quian, a. *Obs.—¹* [f. L. *reliquia* relics.]

Re·liquies, *pl. Obs. rare.* [ad. L. *reliquiæ.*]

Reliquism, *nonce-wd.* The veneration of relics.

Relish (re·liʃ), *sb.¹* [Later form of RELES, with shifting of stress (cf. *rellesse* s.v. RELISHED) and assimilation of the ending to -ISH ².]

1. A taste or flavour; the distinctive taste of anything.

b. *fig.* or in fig. context.

c. *transf.* A trace or tinge of some quality; a suggestion; a sample or specimen; a small quantity.

2. An individual taste or liking.

3. An appetizing or pleasing flavour; a savoury or piquant taste.

b. *fig.*

4. Enjoyment of the taste or flavour of something; the pleasure of tasting or enjoying something agreeable; liking, zest.

Relish, *sb.²* [cf. *relish* v.]

Re·lish, *sb.² Mus. Obs.*

Relish, *sb.³* [ad. OF. *relais.*]

Relish (re·liʃ), *v.¹* [f. RELISH *sb.¹*]

1. *trans.* To give a relish to (a thing); to make pleasant to the taste.

b. To have a taste, tinge, or trace (of some quality or thing); to partake of.

2. To taste in a particular way; to have a specified relish.

3. *trans.* To appreciate, understand.

4. To enjoy, take pleasure or delight in.

5. *intr.* To have a (or the) taste of something; to savour or smack of, have a touch or trace of.

6. *fig.* To be agreeable or pleasant; to find acceptance or favour (with one).

7. *trans.* (in a period of time) over again.

RELISH.

Relish, *v.²* [cf. RELISH *sb.²*]

Re·lishable, *a.* Capable of being relished; enjoyable.

Re·lished, *ppl. a.* Having a (specified) relish.

Relisher, *rare.* [f. as prec. + -ER ¹.]

Re·lishing, *ppl. a.* [f. as prec. + -ING ¹.]

Re·lishment, *rare.* [f. RELISH + -MENT.]

† Re·lisom, *a. Obs. rare—¹.*

Reli·shy, *a. rare.* [f. RELISH + -Y.]

Re·listen, *v.* [RE- 5 a.]

Relive (riˈliv), *v.¹* [RE- 5 a + LIVE *v.*]

Relive (riˈliv), *v.²* [RE- 5 a + LIVE *v.*]

Re·livener, *v. Obs. rare.* [f. OF. *reviver.*]

† Reli·ver, *v.¹ Obs. rare.*

† Re·liver, *v.² Obs.*

RELUCTANCE.

† Belong, *v. Obs. rare.* [ad. F. *ralonger.*]

Relook, *v.* [RE- 5 a.]

Relove, *v.* [RE- 5 + LOVE *v.*]

Reload, *v.¹* [RE- 5 a.]

Relo·cate, *v.* [RE- 5 a.]

Relo·cation, *sb.* [ad. L. *relocation-em.*]

Relu·cent, *a. rare.* [ad. L. *relucent-em.*]

Relu·cence, **-ency**, *rare.* [f. prec.]

Relo·ok, *v.*

Reluct (riˈlʌkt), *v.* [ad. L. *reluctārī*.]

Relu·ctance, *-ancy.*

RELUCTANCY.

1. The act of struggling against something; resistance, opposition.

2. The property, in a magnetic circuit, of opposing to a certain extent the passage of the magnetic lines of force. (Cf. RESISTANCE.)

3. Unwillingness, disinclination. Freq. in phr. *with* (*or without*) *reluctance.* († Also *rarely pl.*)

4. Characterized by unwillingness, disinclination, or distaste.

† 3. A struggle or qualm of conscience. *Obs.*

† 4. Regret, sorrow. (Cf. RELUCTANCY 4.) *Obs.*

Reluctant (riˈlʌktănt), *a.* [ad. L. *reluctant-*, pres. pple. of *reluctārī* to struggle against, f. re- RE- + *luctārī* to struggle : cf. LUCTATION.] Hence also F. *réluctant* (rare), It. *rilattante.*]

1. Struggling; writhing.

2. Offering resistance or opposition to something. *rare.*

3. Making resistance or opposition; unwilling, disinclined.

Relu·ctantly, *adv.* [f. prec. + -LY ².] In a reluctant manner; unwillingly.

Reluctate (riˈlʌkteit), *v. Obs.* [f. ppl. stem of L. *reluctārī*: see RELUCTANT.]

1. *intr.* To offer resistance or to strive or struggle against something; to show reluctance.

b. To feel reluctance or do something. *rare—¹.*

2. *trans.* To strive against, refuse, reject. *rare—¹.*

† Reluctation, *sb.*

Reluctation (rel'ʌkteiʃən), *sb.* [ad. late L. *reluctātiōn-em* (Quicherat); see pres. and -ATION.]

1. Struggle, resistance, opposition, of or in the case of things or persons.

2. Reluctance, unwillingness.

RELUSANT.

Relume (riˈljuːm), *v.* [ad. late L. *relūmināre* (cf. RE-LUMINE) + LUME.]

Relu·mine (riˈljuːmin), *v.* [f. RE- 5 + LUMINE.]

1. *trans.* To light again; rekindle (a light, flame, fire, *lit. or fig.*); to cause to burn afresh.

2. To make clear or bright again.

3. To rally (a person).

† Relu·mination, *sb.* [ad. late L. *relūminātiōn-em* : see next and -ATION.] Fresh illumination.

† Reluyse, *v. Obs. rare—¹.*

RELUYSE.

† Reluyse, *v. Obs. rare.*

Rely (riˈlai), *v.¹* [ad. OF. *relier* to bind together, etc., f. re- (RE- 1) + *lier*, L. *ligāre* to bind.]

1. *trans.* To gather (soldiers, followers, etc.) together; to assemble, to rally. *Obs.*

2. To put trust or confidence in a person or thing. *Somewhat rare.*

Rely (riˈlai), *v.²* [ad. OF. *relier.*]

Relyings, *vbl. sb.*

Re·lyke, obs. form of RELIC.

Relyn, obs. inf. of RAIL *v.⁴*

Re·make, *v.* [RE- 5 a.] *trans.* To make again or over again.

Re·mail, *v.* [RE- 5 a.]

REMAIN.

1. The act of remaining; residence, abode.

† b. *with pl.* A remainder. *Obs.*

2. That which is left; remainder, remnant; a remaining part or fragment.

3. A remaining or surviving part or fragment of something. *Now rare.*

† 4. A remainder of stores or forces; also, a list or inventory of military stores taken at the appointed time. *Obs.*

† 5. A literary relic. *Obs. rare.*

6. *pl.* A dead body, a corpse; remains.

Remain (riˈmein), *v.* [ad. OF. *remain-*, tonic stem of *remaindre, remanoir*, :—L. *remanēre* to stay behind, f. re- RE- + *manēre* to stay, remain.]

Remain

Remainder

Remand

Remanent

Remanence

Remark

Remarkable

Remarry

1638 FORD *Lady's Trial* v. ii, This gentleman, Benatzi, Disguised as you see, I have re-married. 1859 SALA *Tw. round Clock* (1861) 170 She..had married a very foolish rich old banker, and at his death, remarried a more foolish and very poor duke.

Hence **Rema·rried** *ppl. a.*

1848 *Blackw. Mag.* Apr. 447 *note*, In the middle ages re-married queens lost their title.

Rema·ss, *v.* [RE- 5 a.] *trans.* To mass together again.

1839–48 BAILEY *Festus* x. 105 The hour..When all shall be remassed in one great creed, All being shall be rebegotten.

Remass, variant of RAMASS *v.*[1] *Obs.*

Rema·st, *v.* [RE- 5 a.] *trans.* To fit with a new mast or masts.

1781 *Westm. Mag.* IX. 265 While the Bedford was re-masting. 1804 LARWOOD *No Gun Boats* 18 The prefects of the ports will re-ship their rudders, re-mast the Flotilla.

Rema·sticate, *v.* [RE- 5 a.] *trans.* To masticate again. Hence **Rema·sticated** *ppl. a.*

1828–32 in WEBSTER. 1840 tr. *Cuvier's Anim. Kingd.* 135 The aliment thus remasticated descends directly into the third stomach. 1843 OWEN *Lect. Compar. Anat.* ix. (1846) I. 105 When it is presented to them in its remasticated state.

So **Remastica·tion**.

1828–32 in WEBSTER. 1837 YOUATT *Sheep* 423 After it has been returned for remastication,..and reduced to a pultaceous mass. 1859 *Todd's Cycl. Anat.* V. 538/1 The softened bolus..is destined to receive a thorough..remastication.

Rema·tch, *v.* [RE- 5 a.] To match again.

1856 MASSON *Ess., Theor. Poetry* 421 Who walks amid Nature's appearances, divorcing them, rematching them, interweaving them. 1871 DARWIN *Desc. Man* II. xiv. (1890) 408 [He] has repeatedly shot..one of a pair of jays,..and has never failed..to find the survivor re-matched.

† **Remauldit**, *a. Obs. rare*⁻¹. [ad. OF. *remauldit*, pa. pple. of *remau(l)dire*: cf. MALEDICT *a.*] Accursed.

1471 CAXTON *Recuyell* (ed. Sommer) 498 O deyanyra ryghte remauldyt vnhappy and moste cursid serpente.

Remaynand(e, variants of REMAINANT *Obs.*

† **Remay·ne**, *v. Obs. rare.* [ad. OF. *remainer, -me(i)ner*, etc., f. *re-* RE + *mener* to lead: cf. mod.F. *ramener*.] *trans.* To lead or bring back.

1481 CAXTON *Myrr.* I. xii. 37 Musyque accordeth alle thinges that dyscorde..& remayne[th] them to concordaunce. *Ibid.* 38.

Remaynent, variant of REMAINANT *Obs.*

† **Remba·r**, *v. Obs. rare.* [ad. F. *rembarrer*: see RAMBARRE.] *trans.* To shut out, repel.

1588 A. KING tr. *Canisius' Catech.* 53 b, Quha according to thair authoritie suld and may rembar the wolues, defend the sheip. 1600 O. E. [M. SUTCLIFFE] *Repl. Libel* II. Pref. 1 Sufficient hath bin saide..to rembarre the malice of N. D. his encounters.

Rembarbe, erron. f. *reubarbe* RHUBARB.

Remberge, variant of RAMBARGE.

1867 SMYTH *Sailor's Word-bk.* 568.

‖ **Remblai** (rañbl*ɛ*). Also in pl. form **remblais**. [F., f. *remblayer* to embank, f. *re-* RE- + *emblayer* to heap up: see DÉBLAI.]

1. *Fortif.* The earth used to form a rampart, mound, or embankment.

1794 *Amer. State Papers, Mil. Aff.* (1832) I. 99 (Stanf.), The demolition of the old fort very much advanced, and very little remblais made. 1802 JAMES *Milit. Dict.*, *Remblai* (Fr.), earth collected together for the purpose of making a bank, way, &c. 1828 J. M. SPEARMAN *Brit. Gunner* (ed. 2) 215 The earth obtained from the ditch forms the remblai, or elevation. 1876 VOYLE & STEVENSON *Milit. Dict.* 337/1 In general, the number of cubic feet contained in the *remblai* has been furnished by the *deblai*, so as to balance each other.

2. *Mining.* Material used to fill up the excavations made in a thick seam of coal.

1867 W. W. SMYTH *Coal & Coal-mining* 138 The remblais or stowage is found to be so closely packed as to form a very good roof for driving under.

Re·mble, *v. dial.* [Of obscure origin.] *trans.* To move, stir. Hence **Re·mbling** *vbl. sb.*

1579 W. WILKINSON *Confut. Familye of Loue* 56 They must take heede that in the rembling thereof they crush not all their bones in sunder. 1674 RAY *N. C. Words* 38 To *Remble*: Lincoln, to move or remove. 1864 TENNYSON *North. Farmer* I. viii, I stubb'd 'um oop wi' the lot, an' raaved an' rembled 'um out. *Ibid.* xv, A weänt niver give it..to Robins—a niver rembles the stoäns.

† **Remblere**. *Obs. rare*⁻¹. A puzzle, riddle.

1599 NASHE *Lenten Stuffe* 39 Whiles I am shuffling and cutting with these long coated Turkes, would any antiquarie would explicate vnto mee this remblere, or quidditie..?

Rembnand, obs. form of REMNANT *sb.*

Rembrandtesque (rembrɑnte·sk), *a.* [f. the name of *Rembrandt*, the great Dutch painter and etcher (1608–1669), + -ESQUE.] Resembling the manner or style of Rembrandt.

1879 *Encycl. Brit.* IX. 324/1 Life-size figures full of animation in the faces, 'radiant with Rembrandtesque colour.' 1888 LIGHTHALL *Yng. Seigneur* 121 The windmill was one of those rembrandtesque relics [etc.].

Re·mbrandtish, *a.* [f. as prec. + -ISH.] Somewhat after the style of Rembrandt.

c 1860 STANNARD *Examples Art* 211 Desirous of rescuing ..some Rembrandtish etching. 1880 E. FITZGERALD *Lett.* (1889) I. 459 With some Rembrandtish Light and Shade.

So **Re·mbrandtism**, the style of Rembrandt.

1849 RUSKIN *Sev. Lamps* iii. § 13. 77 Rembrandtism is a noble manner in architecture, though a false one in painting.

† **Rembu·rsement**. *Obs.*⁻¹ [a. F. *remboursement*: see REIMBURSEMENT.] = REIMBURSEMENT.

1586 BURGHLEY in *Leicester's Corr.* (Camden) 358 The states would not agree to make the remboursement of these thinges, if your lordships warrant had not past for the same.

† **Reme**, *sb.*[1] *Obs. rare.* [ad. L. *rēmus* (It., Sp. *remo*).] An oar.

a 1300 *K. Horn* 1623 (Harl. MS.), Þe see bigan to flowen ant hy faste to rowen, hue aryueden vnder reme in a wel feyr streme. 1511 *Guylforde's Pilgr.* (Camden) 13 Armour was first ther [in Candia] deuysed and founde,..so was yᵉ makyng of remys, and rowynge in bootes.

† **Reme**, *sb.*[2] *Obs. rare*⁻¹. [? var. of RIM *sb.*[1]; see also RYME.] Surface.

a 1300 *Cursor M.* 4779 He sagh a-pon þe watur reme [*v.r.* reime] Caf flettand dunward [with] þe strem.

† **Reme**, *v.*[1] *Obs.* Also 7 **reem**. [OE. *hrēman, hrȳman* (for **hrīeman*), f. *hrēam* REAM *sb.*[1] Both *hrēman* and *hrȳman* are normal forms in OE.: the former is distinct from the rarer *hrēman* to boast, = OS. *hrōmian*, OHG. *(h)ruomian* etc. (G. *rühmen*).]

1. *intr.* To cry, call out, shout; also, to cry out in grief or pain, to scream, yell; to lament, weep.

c 897 K. ÆLFRED *Gregory's Past. C.* lv. 429 Se cliopað [L. *cum voce*], se ðe dearninga syngað; ac se hremð [L. *cum clamore*], se ðe openlice..syngað. c 950 *Lindisf. Gosp.* John xi. 31 Hia..gaas to ðæm byrgenne þætte hreme ðer. c 1000 ÆLFRIC *Exod.* xxii. 23 ȝif ȝe him deriað, hiȝ hrymað to me, and ic gehire hira hream. c 1200 *Trin. Coll. Hom.* 89 Þo þe after him comen remden lude stefne. c 1275 *Sinners Beware* 167 in *O. E. Misc.* 77 Remen heo schule and grede Deope in helle grunde. 13.. *Sir Beues* (MS. A) 1592 Þe gailers þat him scholde ȝeme, Whan hii herde him þus reme [etc.]. 13.. *E. E. Allit. P.* A. 858 ȝe remen for rauþe wyth-outen reste. c 1400 *Laud Troy Bk.* 2902 Whan that thei herd wymmen so remed, Thei hadde meruayle what it myght be. ? a 1500 *Chester Pl.* (Shaks. Soc.) I. 229 This frecke begines to reme and yole. 1674 RAY *N. C. Words* 38 To *Reem*, to Cry: Lancashire.

2. *trans.* a. To utter (a shout). b. To call out (something). *rare.*

c 1220 *Bestiary* 664 Ðanne remen he alle a rem, so hornes blast oðer belles drem. a 1225 *Ancr. R.* 242 ȝif me remde lude fur! fur! þet te chirche bernde!

† **Reme**, *v.*[2] *Obs. rare.* [var. (in SE. dialects) of ME. *ryme*:—OE. *rȳman*: see RIME *v.*, and cf. REAM *v.*[3]]

1. *trans.* a. To leave, depart from (a land). b. To clear (a place) *of* persons.

a 1300 *K. Horn* 1364 (Camb. MS.), Þu makedest me fleme, And þi lond to reme. c 1330 *Arth. & Merl.* 4398 (Kölbing), .viii. þousand þo hadde Lot, Þat wele him holpe..þe waies & þe paþes ȝeme, & of þe Sarrains hem reme.

2. *intr.* To clear a way; to make way (for one).

13.. *K. Alis.* 3347 He is the furste with sweord that remith, Thou art the furste with hors that flemeth. c 1400 *St. Alexius* (Trin. MS.) 505 Remeþ me [*Laud MS.* ȝiueþ me roum], for godis lone, And leteþ me go to my sone.

Reme, obs. form of REALM, REAM *sb.*[2], RIM.

† **Re·meable**, *a. Obs. rare*⁻¹. [ad. L. *remeābilis*, f. *remeāre* to return.] Capable of returning.

1610 BP. ANDREWES 96 *Serm., Holy Ghost* iii. (1629) 626 So is the Spirit best fitted, made remeable, and best exhibited to us.

Remeable: see REMEVABLE.

† **Remeal, -mel**, variants of RAMEAL *sb. Obs.*

1622 R. HAWKINS *Voy. S. Sea* (1847) 96 In Brazill..they eate this meale mingled with remels of sugar, or malasses. 1662 *Stat. Irel.* (1765) II. 412 Melasses or remeals the hundred weight.

Remeant (rī·miănt), *a. rare.* [ad. L. *remeant-em*, pres. pple. of L. *remeāre*, f. *re-* RE- + *meāre* to pass: cf. *permeate*.] Returning.

1848 KINGSLEY *Saint's Trag.* II. ix, Most exalted Prince, Whose peerless Knighthood, like the remeant sun, After too long a night, regilds our clay.

Remea·sure (rī-), *v.* [RE- 5 a.] *trans.* To measure again, in various senses of the vb.

1590 SPENSER *F. Q.* III. vii. 18 Her wearie Palfrey..she freshly dight, His late miswandred wayes now to remeasure right. 1600 W. WATSON *Decacordon* (1602) 9 With like measure to his brother giuen, it should be remeasured to him againe. 1651 BAXTER *Inf. Bapt.* 238 Their Faith and Integrity in re-measuring (or reforming) the Temple of God. a 1711 KEN *Anodynes* Poet. Wks. 1721 III. 396 Assur'd of Supplemental Years, By your re-measuring the Spheres. 1785 G. A. BELLAMY *Apology* II. 204 This obliged me to re-measure back the road I had just come. 1814 SCOTT *Wav.* xv, Measuring and re-measuring, with..tremendous strides, the length of the terrace. 1874 BEDFORD *Sailor's Pocket Bk.* v. 119 The line should be..re-measured in the boat.

So **Remea·surement**.

1895 *Daily News* 10 Sept. 3/1 The re-measurement will increase Defender's time allowance by two seconds.

† **Re·med**, *v. Obs.*⁻¹ [See REMEDE, REMEDY *v.*, and cf. REMEDLESS *a.*] *trans.* To remedy.

1590 FENNE *Frutes*, etc. Gg ij b, And how to remed wrong with right the man had no respect.

Remede, remeid (rĭmī·d), *sb.* Now *arch.* Forms: 5 **remed, remmede, remyde**, 5–6 **ramed(e**, 6 **-meid**), 5– **remeid**, (6 **-meide, -maid**), 6–8 **-mead**, 6–9 **-meed**, 4– **remede**. [a. OF. *remede, remide* (12th c.; mod.F. *remède*), ad. L. *remedium* REMEDY. After the 15th c. only a Sc. form.] Remedy, redress.

Remeid of Law (Sc.), the obtaining of justice by appeal from an inferior to a superior court (see Jamieson, s.v.).

c 1374 CHAUCER *Troylus* IV. 889 He desyreth..With yow to been al night, for to devyse Remede in this. c 1375 *Sc. Leg. Saints* ii. (*Paul*) 38 Quham it bittis, it mon be ded, þar agane is no remed. 1423 JAS. I *Kingis Q.* cxxxviii, Lat me se Gif thy remede be pertynent to me. 1466 *Plumpton Corr.* (Camden) 17 Therfore provide by your wisdome such remmede in his behalfe, as you semes best. 1549 *Compl. Scot.* Prol. 13 Ane desolat prince, distitute of remeide, ande disparit of consolatione. 1585 JAS. I *Ess. Poesie* (Arb.) 42 Ane greif to them, who mereits it indeid: Yet for all thir appearis there some remeid. 1649 BP. GUTHRIE *Mem.* (1702) 7 They resolv'd upon Application to his Majesty for remeed. 1711 RAMSAY *On Maggy Johnstoun* xiii, We must..when we're auld return to dust, Without remead. 1785 BURNS *Prayer to Sc. Repr.* xviii, Strive, wi' a' your wit and lear, To get remead. 1828 *Blackw. Mag.* XXIV. 915 The matter was..past all earthly remede. 1868 G. MACDONALD *R. Falconer* I. 306 He made one remorseful dart after the string,..but it was gone beyond remeid.

† b. *Coining.* = REMEDY *sb.* 4. *Obs.*

1565 *Act. Dom. Conc.* 22 Dec. in Keith *Hist. Ch. Scot.* (1734) App. 118 That thair be cunzeit ane Penny of Silvir.. of Weicht ane Unce Troce-weicht, with twa Granes of Remeid. 1591 *Reg. Privy Council Scot.* IV. 620 All the saidis assayis keipit the just fynnes..and past nocht beneth the granis of remeid prescrivit in the same Actis.

Remede, remeid (rĭmī·d), *v. Sc. Obs.* exc. *arch.* Forms: 5 **remed**, 6–7 **remeid**, (6 **-maid**), 7–8 **remeed**, 8 **remead**, 5, 9 **remede**. [ad. OF. *remedier*: see REMEDY *v.*] *trans.* To remedy, cure, redress, amend. Also *absol.*

13.. in Wyntoun *Cron.* VII. 3625 Succoure Scotland and remede, That stad is in perplexyte. c 1375 *Sc. Leg. Saints* vii. (*James less*) 94 Mannis sonne fra þe ded Is rysine al synnys to remed. *Ibid.* xxxi. (*Eugenia*) 284 Scho..prayt hyme parcheryte to remed hyr Infyrmyte. 1500–20 DUNBAR *Poems* xxii. 56 May nane remeid my melady Sa weill as ȝe. *Ibid.* lxxiii. 5 Remeid in tyme, and rew nocht all to lait. 1579 *Reg. Privy Council Scot.* III. 155 Without his Hienes petifullie considder thair caise and remeid the same. 1596 DALRYMPLE tr. *Leslie's Hist. Scot.* I. 24 It is gude..to kure and to remeid diuers dolouris of the skin. 1640 R. BAILLIE *Canterb. Self-convict.* 103 To remeed their wicked follies, the English expressely ordained their communion Table to stand in the body of the church. 1711 *Countrey-Man's Let. to Curat* 22 They desire him..to remeed the Enormities among the Corrupt Conformists. 1752 E. ERSKINE *Serm.* Wks. 1871 III. 480 What would remead these evils? [1847 EMERSON *Poems, Monadnoc*, Thou dost succour and remede The shortness of our days.]

Reme·deless, *a.* and *adv.* In 9 **remead-, remeid-**. [f. REMEDE *sb.*] Remediless(ly).

a 1849 J. C. MANGAN *Poems* (1859) 457 That dusk realm where all is ended, Save remeadless dole. 1850 BLACKIE *Æschylus* I. 231 Spit not your rancour On this fair land remeidless.

† **Reme·der**. *Sc. Obs. rare*⁻¹. In 6 **remeidar**. [f. REMEDE *v.* + -ER[1].] One who remedies.

1535 STEWART *Cron. Scot.* II. 487, I pray to God, remeidar of all thing, Gif I mycht se in my tyme sic ane king.

Remediable (rĭmī·diăb'l), *a.* Also 5 **-medy-**, 6 **-mede-**. [a. F. *remédiable* (15th c.), or ad. L. *remediābilis* curative, curable, f. *remediāre* to REMEDY: see -ABLE.]

† 1. Capable of remedying; remedial. *Obs.*

c 1491 *Chast. Goddes Chyld.* 46 Suche medycynes may be spedefull and remedyable. 1596 DALRYMPLE tr. *Leslie's Hist. Scot.* x. 397 Layng medicine remedeable to her warking woundis.

2. Capable of being remedied or redressed.

1570 LEVINS *Manip.* 4/9 Remediable, *recuperabilis*. 1600 E. BLOUNT tr. *Conestaggio* 311 Labouring to remedie that which he thought remediable. 1641 H. AINSWORTH *Orth. Found. Relig.* 37 Mans misery is remediable through the mercy of God. 1707 SLOANE *Jamaica* I. p. lxxxii, They.. were, when remediable, chiefly cured by the infusion of goose-dung. 1758 JOHNSON *Idler* No. 3 ⁋ 7 This want..may seem easily remediable by some substitute or other. 1828 SOUTHEY in *Q. Rev.* XXXVII. 540 It is an evil..which will be found remediable, if the proper and obvious remedies are ..applied. 1875 JOWETT *Plato* (ed. 2) V. 135 Where injustice, like disease, is remediable, there the remedy must be applied in word or deed.

Hence **Reme·diableness** (Bailey, 1727, vol. II); **Reme·diably** *adv.* (Webster, 1847).

Remedial (rĭmī·diăl), *a.* [ad. L. *remediālis*, f. *remedium* REMEDY: see -AL.] Affording a remedy, tending to relieve or redress.

1651 N. BACON *Disc. Govt. Eng.* II. xviii. (1739) 96 These Laws were but penal, and not remedial for the parties wronged. 1707 CHAMBERLAYNE *Pres. St. Eng.* II. xiv. 189 This Court proceeds..ordinarily..granting out Writs Mandatory and Remedial. 1765 BLACKSTONE *Comm.* I. 55 The remedial part of a law is so necessary a consequence of the former two [etc.]. 1770 BURKE *Pres. Discont.* Wks. 1842 I. 135/1 Every good political institution must have a preventive operation as well as a remedial. 1850 McCOSH *Div. Govt.* IV. ii. (1874) 473 The Gospel professes to be remedial, and remedial of an evil affecting the laws of God. 1862 GOULBURN *Pers. Relig.* III. ix. (1873) 236 That suffering is a medicine, remedial though bitter.

Hence **Reme·dially** *adv.*

1796 BURKE *Regic. Peace* i. (1892) 83 It is, preventively, the assertor of its own rights, or remedially, their avenger. 1840 ARNOLD in Stanley *Life* (1844) II. ix. 175 Before anything is ventured remedially. 1875 E. WHITE *Life in Christ* V. xxxi. (1878) 534 It is God acting, no longer according to the course of law,..but remedially above law.

† **Reme·diate**, *a. Obs.*⁻¹ [? f. L. *remediāt-*, ppl. stem of *remediāre* to REMEDY.] Remedial.

(Perh. an error for *remedial* or *remediant*.)

1605 SHAKS. *Lear* IV. iv. 17 (Qq.), All you vnpublisht vertues of the earth Spring with my teares, be aydant, and remediat [1st Fol. -ate] In the good mans distress.

Re-mediate, *v.* [RE- 5 a.] To mediate again.

a 1652 BROME *Mad Couple* III. i, I will re-mediate for you to the Widow.

Remediation (rĭmīdiˌēⁱ·ʃən). *rare.* [n. of action f. L. *remediāre* to REMEDY.] The action of remedying.

1818 BENTHAM *Ch. Eng.* Pref. 54 On this subject, and on this state of things, remediation..requires that something should be said. 1826 — in *Westm. Rev.* VI. 499 Towards remediation, a disposition has of late been expressed by those on whom it depends.

Remediless (re·mĭdilės, rĭme·dilės), *a.* (and *adv.*) Forms: 5–7 **remedyless**, (8 **remedie-**), 6 **remeadi-**, 6 (*Sc.*) 7 **remidi-**, 7 **remeedi-**, 6– **remediless**. [f. REMEDY *sb.* + -LESS: cf. REMEDELESS and REMEDLESS. The orig. stressing was *reme·diless*, with the *e* long.]

1. Of persons, etc.: Destitute of remedy; having no prospect of aid or rescue. Now *rare* or *Obs.*

14.. *MS. Cantab. Ff.* I. 6, lf. 131 (Halliw.), Thus welle y wote y am remedylesse, For me no thyng may comforte nor amend. 1532 MORE *Confut. Tindale* Wks. 602/1 He shall for lacke of such preuencion and help, fall into such raylyng and blasphemy, and then is he remedilesse. 1556 J. HEYWOOD *Spider & F.* ii. 158 Being cleare remediles from cure Of all my paines. c 1592 MARLOWE *Jew of Malta* v. ii, I'll rear up Malta, now remediless. 1621 DONNE *Serm.* xv. 149 When the last enemie shall watch my remedilesse body and my disconsolate soule. 1757 W. THOMPSON *R. N. Advoc.* 21 Poor remediless, aggrieved and tortured Men. 1786 BURKE *Charges agst. W. Hastings* Wks. 1813 XII. 243 He demanded these in such a manner that being 'remediless' I was obliged to comply with what he required.

b. Destitute of legal remedy.

1590 SWINBURNE *Testaments* 169 It seemeth..vniust also, that they, especially the creditors, should be remedilesse all that while. 1616 in Cary *Rep. Chancery* (1650) 122 Whither the Chancery may relieve B...or else leave him utterly remedilesse and undone. 1667 *Ormonde MSS.* in *10th Rep. Hist. MSS. Comm.* App. V. 59 Your petitioner is herein altogether remedylesse. 1670 in *Phenix* (1721) I. 393 Such Judgments on Jurors leaue them remediless of relief. 1700 *Col. Rec. Pennsylv.* I. 577 Finding yᵉ petitioner to be left remediless by yᵉ Courts.

† c. In quasi-*adv.* use: Without or beyond all remedy. *Obs.* (common in 16th c.)

c 1485 *Digby Myst.* (1882) IV. 1124 It is bot in vayn Thus remedilesse to mak compleyn. 1531 TINDALE *Exp. 1 John* (1537) 18 The same synneth agaynste the holye gooste remedylesse. 1542 UDALL *Erasm. Apoph.* 82 Sir, ye must remedylesse be obediente to me, and rewled by me. 1567 *Gude & Godlie B.* (S. T. S.) 147 We ar exilit remedilles. 1601 HOLLAND *Pliny* I. 46 Whosoever drinketh, is sure to die of it, remedilesse, and yet without paine. 1674 HICKMAN *Quinquart. Hist.* (ed. 2) 86 They maintain not, that any is left remediless in a state of damnation.

2. Of trouble, disease, etc.: Not admitting of remedy; incapable of being remedied, cured, or redressed. (Very common in 16–17th c.)

1513 BRADSHAW *St. Werburge* I. 3160 Alas, remedylesse is our lamentacyon. 1548 CRANMER *Catech.* 115 b, He is able to delyuer us out of al troubles.., although they seme to mans reason remediles. 1581 MULCASTER *Positions* xxxiii. (1887) 119 In all these measure is a mery meane, and immoderatenes a remeadilesse harme. 1640 R. BAILLIE *Canterb. Self-convict.* Pref. 11 It were better by much, before the remeedilesse stroke be given, to be well advised. 1671 FLAVEL *Fount. Life* x. 29 This renders their misery the more remediless. 1715 M. DAVIES *Athen. Brit.* I. 66 Those more inward Resentments..seem almost remediless and irreconcileable. 1775 MASON *Mem. Gray* in *G.'s Poems* 136 Such persons as die of that most remediless..of all distempers, a Consumption. 1791 COWPER *Iliad* XVII. 189 So, at once Shall remediless ruin fall on Troy. a 1822 SHELLEY *Prose Wks.* (1888) I. 404 There is no terror in the countenance, only grief—deep, remediless grief. 1875 E. WHITE *Life in Christ* III. xix. (1878) 254 The law is and will be, that remediless suffering shall follow sin.

† 3. Of vices, etc.: Incurable, incorrigible. *Obs.*

1604 T. WRIGHT *Passions* IV. ii. § 6. 138, I must say this vice in them to be remedilesse, because it hath bene in euery age..and neuer amended. 1625 JACKSON *Creed* v. xliv. § 1 It is the remediless remainder of our first parents' pride. 1675 BAXTER *Cath. Theol.* II. v. 83 We hold also that his vicious necessity of disposition is curable, and not remediless and desperate. 1690 E. GEE *Jesuit's Mem.* 99 Sharp execution of Justice upon the obstinate and remediless.

† 4. *adv.* Remedilessly. *Obs. rare*⁻¹.

a 1614 D. DYKE *Myst. Self-deceiving* (ed. 8) 50 It makes him twice, yea, remediless miserable.

Remedilessly (see prec.), *adv.* Now *rare.* [f. prec. + -LY[2].] Without or beyond remedy. (Common in 17th c.)

1556 *Olde Antichrist* 74 b, We must remidilesly confesse them to be voide of all charitie. 1596 DRAYTON *Legends* iii. 409 Like one whose House remedilesly burning [etc.]. 1609 BP. HALL *Disswas. Poperie* Wks. (1627) 642 A cruell religion, that sends poore infants remedilesly vnto the eternall paines of hell. 1612 DRAYTON *Poly-olb.* xiv. 30 Remedilesly drown'd in sorrow day and night. 1669 CLARENDON *Ess.* Tracts (1727) 126 The government of it is actually and remedilessly altered. 1747 *Col. Rec. Pennsylv.* V. 111 Thus remedilessly exposed to any Attempts the Enemy shou'd be pleased to make. 1808 W. TAYLOR in *Monthly Mag.* XXVI. 111 Yet to these clerks of the magistrates..all the objects of national commiseration are thus remedilessly to be consigned. 1868 MIALL *Congregationalism Yorks.* 66 My place was remedilessly lost.

Remedilessness. Now *rare* or *Obs.* [f. as prec. + -NESS.] The state or condition of being remediless; incurableness.

1601 DENT *Pathw. Heaven* 364 Concerning the torments of hell, I do note three things..the extremity, perpetuity, and remidilesnesse thereof. 1684 HOWE *Redeemer's Tears* Wks. (1846) 88 They show the remedilessness of thy case. a 1758 EDWARDS *Hist. Redemption* II. i. (1793) 200 The remedilessness of their disease might by long experience be seen.

† **Reme·diously**, *adv. Obs. rare*⁻¹. [f. as REMEDY *sb.* + -OUS + -LY[2].] Remedially.

1659 *Bibliotheca Regia* Pref. 9 His last sleep took from him most remediously all the arts of government.

† **Re·medist**. *Obs. rare*⁻¹. [f. REMEDY *sb.* + -IST.] One who seeks out medical remedies.

1716 M. DAVIES *Athen. Brit.* III. *Diss. Physick* 12 Such were call'd..Magists.., Prophylactists, Remedists [etc.].

Reme·ditate, *v.* [RE- 5 a.] *trans.* To meditate (on) again.

1855 LYNCH *Rivulet* IX. vii, Let me remeditate the truth, That Christ did for and with us bleed.

So **Remedita·tion**. † Const. *of.*

1642 W. PRICE *Serm.* 28 In a kind of remeditation of what obscenities he hath beene a spectator. 1676 *Life Father Sarpi* in *Brent's Counc. Trent* 26 [He] gave himself to a remeditation of what he had formerly observed.

† **Re·medless**, *a. Obs. rare.* [Cf. REMED *v.* and REMEDELESS.] Remediless.

1590 FENNE *Frutes*, etc. Ffiij b, In vaine it is to vexe thy self where cause is remedles. *Ibid.* Gg iij, 'Tis past with us and remedles, wherefore no longer mourne.

Remedy (re·mĭdi), *sb.* Also 6 **remeady**. [a. AF. *remedie, remedy* (= OF. *remede* REMEDE *sb.*), ad. L. *remedium*, f. *re-* RE- + *med-* stem of *medērī* to heal: cf. *medical, medicine*.]

1. A cure for a disease or other disorder of body or mind; any medicine or treatment which alleviates pain and promotes restoration to health. † Also without article.

a 1225 *Ancr. R.* 120 Lo her aȝeines wreððe monie kunnes remedies, & frouren a muche vloc, & misliche boten. a 1340 HAMPOLE *Psalter* xv. 3 He þat felis him seke he sekis remedy. c 1386 CHAUCER *Prol.* 475 Of remedies of loue she knew perchaunce. 1398 TREVISA *Barth. De P. R.* VII. lix. (Bodl. MS.), Aȝenste venemouse postemes..men schal ordeyne a remedy warlich and sone. c 1440 *Gesta Rom.* i. 2 (Harl. MS.), I pray þe tell me if þer be ony remedye ayenst my deth. 1484 CAXTON *Fables of Poge* x, [He] mynistyred alwey his pylles to euery man that came to hym for ony remedy. 1560 DAUS tr. *Sleidane's Comm.* 91 For verely tyme itselfe wyl at laste bring remedy also unto moste daungerous diseases. 1577 B. GOOGE *Heresbach's Husb.* II. (1586) 68 b, Nature hath appointed remedies in a readinesse for all diseases. 1651 WITTIE tr. *Primrose's Pop. Err.* I. 42 For remedies doe cure without a physician, but not a physician without remedies. 1697 DRYDEN *Virg. Georg.* III. 701 This Remedy the Scythian Shepherds found. 1702 J. PURCELL *Cholick* (1714) 181 The only Remedy is to lay the Bone open. 1830 SCOTT *Demonol.* v. (1831) 140 The Scottish law did not acquit those who accomplished..remarkable cures by mysterious remedies. 1875 H. C. WOOD *Therap.* (1879) 688 Whenever it is desired to give a powerful remedy in increasing doses until its physiological effect is produced, it should always be given by itself.

b. *transf.* or *fig.* in various uses.

a 1300 *Cursor M.* 27816 Again þis sin [sloth] remedi es [*v.r.* best medcyn is]—Haf gastli ioi and hope o blis. 1340 HAMPOLE *Pr. Consc.* 3394 Ilk man here lyghtly may Swilk remedys thurgh grace wyn, Þat may fordo al veniel syn. 1387 TREVISA *Higden* (Rolls) IV. 11 Alisaundre was i-poysoned..and axede a tool to slee hymself in remedie of sorwe [L. *in remedium doloris*]. 1485 CAXTON *Chas. Gt.* 244 For yᵉ remedye of theyr soules themperour gaf..for almesse xij C vnces of syluer. 1576 FLEMING *Panopl. Epist.* 25 Your wisedome and knowledge are remedies available, to cut off the course of suche an infecting canckar. 1607–12 BACON *Ess., Counsel* (Arb.) 318 For which inconveniences the doctrine of Italy..hath introduced Cabanett Councelles, a remedy worse than the disease. 1693 DRYDEN *Juvenal* xvi. (1697) 386 Withdraw thy Action, and depart in Peace; The Remedy is worse than the Disease. 1718 PRIOR *Solomon* II. 352 Our griefs how swift! our remedies how slow! 1781 COWPER *Truth* 273 God replies, 'The remedy you want I freely give: The book shall teach you'. 1819 SHELLEY *Cyclops* 88 Can you show me some clear water spring, The remedy of our thirst? a 1862 BUCKLE *Civiliz.* (1873) II. viii. 582 The only remedy for superstition is knowledge.

† c. *By remedy of*, by the help or means of. *Obs.*

1398 TREVISA *Barth. De P. R.* XVII. lxi. (Bodl. MS.), A fige tre is made to bere wele frute bi remedie of a tre þat is icleped Caprificus. 1579 LYLY *Euphues* (Arb.) 108 If women be not peruerse they shall reap profite by remedye of pleasure.

2. A means of counteracting or removing an outward evil of any kind; reparation, redress, relief.

a 1225 *Ancr. R.* 180 We schulen nu speken of þe uttre vondunge, & techen þe þet habbeð hire, hu heo muwen, .. ivinden remedie, þet is elne, aȝeines hire. a 1340 HAMPOLE *Psalter* cxix. 3 Þe rightwis man sekis remedy of god, how þere ill lippis may be amendid. 1413 *Pilgr. Sowle* IV. xiii. (Caxton 1483) 63 Now seye me what the semeth in this mater that we may ordeyne a remedy for this grete meschyef. 1483 CAXTON *G. de la Tour* C ij, Sith it pleseth yow that I shall dye withoute remedye and withoute mercye. a 1500 *Sir Beues* 57/66² (Pynson), Certys, nowe wol he by hyr lye, But if ye fynde some remedy. 1560 DAUS tr. *Sleidane's Comm.* 388 He fleeth to the last remeady which untill that time he had purposelye reserved. 1585 T. WASHINGTON tr. *Nicholay's Voy.* IV. xxxv. 158 Iupiter was honored amongst them for a remedy of stormes and tempests. 1634 SIR T. HERBERT *Trav.* 35 The Nobles, when they saw no remedie, ..submitted to Curroon. 1687 A. LOVELL tr. *Thevenot's Trav.* II. 186 The human remedies which Sea-men use against Spouts, is to furle all the Sails, and to fire some Guns with shot against the Pipe of the Spout. 1747 *Col. Rec. Pennsylv.* V. 93 Such a Defect in the Government as stands in need of the most speedy Remedy. 1774 BURKE *Corr.* (1844) I. 473 Popular remedies must be quick and sharp, or they are very ineffectual. 1837 GORING & PRITCHARD *Microgr.* 168 In this respect..we have a remedy against those optical deceptions. 1851 CARLYLE *Sterling* I. i, It by no means appeared what help or remedy any friend of Sterling's..could attempt in the interim.

b. *There is no remedy* (= way out of it, help for it, alternative) *but*, etc.

c 1386 CHAUCER *Knt.'s T.* 1216 Ther nas noon oother remedie ne reed, But taketh his leue, and homward he him spedde. 1523 LD. BERNERS *Froiss.* I. 72 Ther is no remedy but to fight, & to abyde fortune. 1568 GRAFTON *Chron.* II. 293 There was no remedy but he must fight with him. 1642 ROGERS *Naaman* 20 There had beene no remedy, but he must have dyed upon his owne sword. 1719 DE FOE *Crusoe* (Globe) 267 We had no Remedy, but to wait and see what the Issue of Things might present.

† c. *No remedy*, unavoidably. *Obs.*

1538 BALE *Thre Lawes* 1700 Yet must it geue place to Gods worde, no remedye. 1550 CROWLEY *Epigr.* 242 The vengeaunce of God muste fall, no remedye, Vpon these wicked men. 1598 SHAKS. *Merry W.* II. ii. 127 You must send her your Page, no remedie. 1617 BP. ANDREWES 96 *Serm., Holy Ghost* x. (1629) 706 In default of this (no remedie) the common hammer must come.

† d. *What remedy?* what help for it? *Obs.*

1500–20 DUNBAR *Poems* xv. 43 The lord sumtyme rewaird will it; Gife he dois not, quhat remedy? 1598 SHAKS. *Merry W.* v. v. 250 Well, what remedy?..what cannot be eschew'd, must be embrac'd. 1608 ARMIN *Nest Ninn.* (1842) 21 Now you must be hanged says the king...What remedie? sayes hee. 1628 EARLE *Microcosm.* (Arb.) 35 He sayes it must not bee so, [y]it is strait pacified, and cryes what remedie.

3. Legal redress.

1450 *Paston Lett.* I. 174, I pray you requyre hym on my Lord ys behalf to compleyn to Justice..[for a] remedie. 1583 STUBBES *Anat. Abus.* II. (1882) 10 To go to lawe, and spende all that euer he hath, and yet come by no remedie neither.. 1651 HOBBES *Leviath.* II. xxii. 118 Left to the remedie, which the Law of the place alloweth them. 1766 BLACKSTONE *Comm.* II. 199 Even this right of property will fail, or at least it will be without a remedy, unless I pursue it within the space of sixty years. 1819 J. MARSHALL *Const. Opin.* (1839) 154 Without impairing the obligation of a contract, the remedy may certainly be modified. 1891 *19th Cent.* Dec. 857 Where injury to character takes the form of aspersion, the primary remedy is in a court of law.

4. *Coining.* The small margin within which coins as minted are allowed to vary from the standard fineness and weight. (Cf. REMEDE *sb.* b.) Also called *tolerance*.

1423 *Rolls of Parlt.* IV. 257/1 As touching ye remedie of vid of the pound of Troie, the Kyng will be avised. 1675 R. VAUGHAN *Coinage* 24 The remedies do make so small a difference that it is not considerable. 1805 EARL OF LIVERPOOL *Treat. Coins Realm* 102 They authorised a large remedy to be taken..and did not require the Officers of the Mint to make their coins as perfect as possible, but authorised or suffered them to coin just within the remedy. 1867 *Chamb. Jrnl.* 16 Feb. 106/2 For silver coin, the 'remedy' or margin of error is fixed at one pennyweight per pound Troy. 1875 KNIGHT *Dict. Mech.* 1916/1 The remedy on United States silver coin is 1½ grains to the piece.

5. At various schools (as still at St. Paul's and Winchester): A time specially granted for recreation; a half-holiday.

1518 COLET *Statute* in Gardiner *Regist. St. Paul's School* (1884) 381, I will also they shall haue noo remedies—yff the maister graunteth eny remedies he shall forfett xls.. Except the kyng or a arche bisshopp or a bisshopp..desyre it. 1580 in Boys *Hist. Sandwich* (1792) 228, I ordeine, that the master..shall not give remedie or leave to plaie aboue once in a week. 1593 *Rites & Mon. Ch. Durh.* (Surtees) 75 To recreat themselves when they had remedy of there master. 1656 in Gardiner *Regist. St. Paul's School* (1884) 382 *note*, [At Newport..it was provided that] each Thursday afternoon..shall be a remedy or time of recreation. 1866 MANSFIELD *School-Life at Winchester* (1870) 49 Remedies were not a matter of right, but were always applied for..on Tuesday or Thursday. 1893 *Ch. Times* 22 Dec. 1331/2 His lordship afterwards (the *Pauline* reports)..exercised his privilege of desiring a 'remedy' (or half-holiday) on Wednesday.

Remedy (re·mĭdi), *v.* Also 6 **remydy**. [a. OF. *remedier* (cf. REMEDE *v.*), or ad. L. *remediāre*, f. *remedium* REMEDY *sb.*]

1. *trans.* † a. To grant (one) legal remedy; to right (one) in respect of a wrong suffered. *Obs.*

1414 *Rolls of Parlt.* IV. 57/1 Byfore hene [= any] of the persones that weren..Commissioners upon myn enditement, ..I myghte not have been remedied. *Ibid.* To have been remedied of the wronges that we have had. 1454 in Ellis *Orig. Lett.* Ser. II. I. 120 That they shuld be remedyed, and he remedyed them not. 1549 LATIMER *3rd Serm. bef. Edw. VI* (Arb.) 92 There is one [Judge]..wyll remedye you, if you come after a ryghte sorte vnto him. a 1662 HEYLIN *Laud* I. (1671) 113 Of which Indignity he complained to the Duke,..and was remedied in it.

b. To bring remedy to (a person, diseased part, etc.); to heal, cure, make whole again. Now *rare.*

1470–85 MALORY *Arthur* XIII. viii. 622 It shal so heuye me at their departynge that..there shal no manere of Ioye remedye me. 1502 *Ord. Crysten Men* (W. de W. 1506) I. iv. E j b, The synner..is fro yᵉ moost gretest payne remedyed. 1541 R. COPLAND *Galyen's Terap.* H h iij b, When the party yᵉ should be holpen & remydyed is hyd in the dypenes of the body. 1590 SPENSER *F. Q.* III. v. 32 Into the woods..shee went, To seeke for hearbes that mote him remedy. 1607 TOPSELL *Four-f. Beasts* (1658) 271 If one Horse do die of it, all his fellows that bear him company will follow after, if they be not remedied in time. 1795 SOUTHEY *Joan of Arc* I. 57 Some pious sisterhood, Who..may likeliest remedy The stricken mind.

2. To cure (a disease, etc.); to put right, reform (a state of things); to rectify, make good.

1412–20 LYDG. *Chron. Troy* I. v. (1555), There is a lawe ysette..that may not be ylette Nor remedyed. *Ibid.* vi, All her ill was holpe and remedyed. 1469 *Paston Lett.* II. 375 With Goddys grace it schall be remedyed well inow. 1509 HAWES *Past. Pleas.* XVIII. (Percy Soc.) 81, I thanke you for your love,..But I your cause can nothing remedy. 1567 MAPLET *Gr. Forest* 37 It being wrought and tempered ..remedieth all kinde of swelling. 1596 DRAYTON *Legends* iii. 389 They tooke up Armes to remedie their wrong. 1651 N. BACON *Disc. Govt. Eng.* II. ii. (1739) 14 The House of Lords shall remedy all offences contrary to the Law of Magna Charta. 1654 BRAMHALL *Just Vind.* ii. (1661) 7 A sharp fit of a feuerish distemper, which a little time..will infallibly remedy. 1754 SHERLOCK *Disc.* I. i. 49 They cannot remedy the Corruption that has spread thro' the Race of Mankind. 1768 GOLDSM. *Good-n. Man* III. i, That shall be remedied without delay. 1814 SOUTHEY *Roderick* XXI. 417 Repentance taketh sin away, Death remedies the rest. 1853 BRIGHT *Sp., India* 3 June (1876) 8 A great deal has been done to remedy the deficiency. 1858 J. H. NEWMAN *Hist. Sk.* (1873) III. v. i. 436 Evils which threaten to continue we try to remedy.

† 3. *absol.* To provide a remedy. Const. *for, of.*

c 1440 LYDG. *Hors, Shepe & G.* 387 For ache of bonys & also for brosoure It remedieth & dooth men ese ful blyve. c 1477 CAXTON *Jason* 42 Ye be seke of the maladye of loue wherof no man may remedye but youre lady.

Hence **Re·medying** *vbl. sb.*

1570 FOXE *A. & M.* (ed. 2) 1221/1 For the remediying and redressyng of those foresayd iniuries. 1597 A. M. tr. *Guillemeau's Fr. Chirurg.* 30 b/2 To the remedyinge and curinge of the which, we ought to tye the Arterye. 1641 WILKINS *Math. Magick* I. iii. (1648) 18 For the remedying of such abuses the Ancients did appoint divers officers.

Remee·t (rī-), *v.* [RE- 5 a.] To meet again.

1644 QUARLES *Sheph. Orac.* iii, The time will come, wherein We shall remeet, and never part agin. a 1657 R. LOVEDAY *Lett.* (1663) 11 When I re-met with them they had been so lost to my memory, that [etc.]. 1859 F. MILLS in *Athenæum* 9 July 49 Ere the shining valves remeet.

Hence **Remee·ting** *vbl. sb.*

1648 HERRICK *Hesper., Parting Verse*, 'Tis to be doubted whether I next yeer, Or no, shall give ye a re-meeting here. 1684 *Lond. Gaz.* No. 1994/3 At the remeeting of the said States..these Points will be farther spoken of.

Remeeving, -mefe, obs. varr. REMOVING, REMOVE. **Remeid**: see REMEDE *sb.* and *v.* **Remel**, see REMEAL and RIMMEL. **Remelant**, var. REMENANT *Obs.*

Reme·lt (rī-), *v.* [RE- 5 a.] To melt again.

a. *trans.* 1626 BACON *Sylva* § 771 The Crude Materialls of Glasse, mingled with Glasse, already made and Re-moulten. 1775 R. CHANDLER *Trav. Greece* (1825) II. 180 They re-melted the old dross and scum, and found ore. 1833 LYELL *Princ. Geol.* III. 185 If the lavas could be remelted. 1897 *Allbutt's Syst. Med.* II. 938 Those who remelt the pig brass, and are called 'founders'.

b. *intr.* 1793 SMEATON *Edystone L.* § 274 It was perceived to re-melt and unite with the fresh metal. 1865 MASSON *Rec. Brit. Philos.* 78 Into what Empyrean will it remelt when the separating film bursts?

Hence **Reme·lted** *ppl. a.*, **Reme·lting** *vbl. sb.*

1796 PEARSON in *Phil. Trans.* LXXXVI. 431 Perhaps metals in general are rendered purer..by remelting. 1839 URE *Dict. Arts* 1127 The roasting of the mattes and their treatment by four successive re-meltings. 1861 FAIRBAIRN *Iron* 142 Molten crude iron, or..remelted pig or refined iron.

Remember (rĭme·mbəɹ), *v.* Forms: 4–6 **remembre**, (5 **-menbre**), 5–6 **remembyr**, (5 **-bur**, 6 **-bar**, *Sc.* **-bir**), 6– **remember**, (6 *Sc.* **ra-**). [ad. OF. *remembrer* (11th c.), = Prov. and Sp. *remembrar*, It. *rimembrar*:—late L. *rememorārī*, f. *re-* RE- + *memor* mindful: see REMEMORATE *v.*]

I. 1. *trans.* To retain in, or recall to, the memory; to bear in mind, recollect (a thing, person, fact, event, saying, etc.).

c 1330 R. BRUNNE *Chron.* (1810) 327 Edward may remembre þe trauaile & þe pyn. 1382 WYCLIF *Tobit* ii. 6 Remembrende that woord, that the Lorde seide by Amos. c 1420 LYDG. *Assembly of Gods* 154 Remembre your name was wont to be egall. 1484 CAXTON *Fables of Æsop* I. xviii, Euer I shal remembre the grace whiche thou hast done to me. 1560 DAUS tr. *Sleidane's Comm.* 80 b, They should remembre themselves to be earth and asshes. 1609 HOLLAND *Amm. Marcell.* 217 A thing that no man could remember done since Dioclesian and Aristobulus time. 1678 BUNYAN *Pilgr.* I. (1900) 35 Let this mans misery be remembred by thee. 1750 JOHNSON *Rambler* No. 26 ⁋ 2, I was..left by my father, whom I cannot remember, to the care of an uncle. 1833 TENNYSON *Dream Fair Wom.* xx, The times when I remember to have been Joyful. 1875 JOWETT *Plato* (ed. 2) IV. 130 We must remember the place held by Parmenides in the history of Greek philosophy.

fig. 1732 POPE *Hor. Sat.* II. ii. 73 The stomach..Remembers oft the School-boy's simple fare. 1833 TENNYSON *Two Voices* 423 My frozen heart began to beat, Remembering its ancient heat.

b. With *inf.* To bear in mind, not to forget, *to* do something.

c 1430 LYDG. *Min. Poems* (Percy Soc.) 12 Remembryng the highe lord to queme. 1461 *Paston Lett.* II. 27 Remembre to take a wryht to chese crowneres in Norffolk. 1535 LYNDESAY *Satyre* 3054 My Lords,..Remember to reforme the consistorie. 1610 SHAKS. *Temp.* III. ii. 99 Remember First to possesse his Bookes. 1733–4 BERKELEY in Fraser *Life* vi. 218 You will also remember to take bonds for the money. 1781 COWPER *Convers.* 103 But still remember..To press your point with modesty and ease.

† c. Const. *with* oneself. *Obs. rare.*

1563 B. GOOGE *Eglogs*, etc. (Arb.) 86 As ofte as I remembre with my self, The Fancies fonde [etc.]. 1613 DAY *Festivals* viii. (1615) 240 That you remember with your selves, who it is that hath made you Fathers of Children.

† d. *Remember your courtesy*, be covered. *Obs.* (The precise origin of the phrase is not clear; compare *leave your courtesy* in *Mids. N.* IV. i. 21, and the following passage: c 1560 WEVER *Lusty Juventus* C ij, Well sayd maister doctor...I pray you be remembred, and couer your head.)

1588 SHAKS. *L. L. L.* v. i. 103, I doe beseech thee remember thy curtesie. I beseech thee apparell thy head. [Cf. *Haml.* v. ii. 108.] 1598 B. JONSON *Ev. Man in Hum.* I. i, Pray you remember your court'sy..Nay, pray you be covered.

2. To think of, recall the memory of (a person) with some kind of feeling or intention.

1382 WYCLIF *Isa.* lxii. 6 ȝee that remembren the Lorde, ne beth stille. 1490 CAXTON *Eneydos* xix. 69 So shall I remembre elysse as longe as lyffe shall abyde wythin me. 1535 COVERDALE *Eccl.* xii. 1 Remembre thy maker in thy youth, or euer the dayes of aduersite come. 1560 DAUS tr. *Sleidane's Comm.* 314 We must also remember the dead. 1671 MILTON *P. R.* III. 434 Yet he at length..Remembring Abraham by some wond'rous call May bring them back. 1791 BURNS *Lament for Glencairn* x, I'll remember thee, Glencairn, And a' that thou hast done for me! 1841 LANE *Arab. Nts.* I. 111, I will do thee an act of kindness for which I shall be remembered.

b. To bear (a person) in mind as entitled to a gift, recompence, or fee, or in making one's will; hence, to fee, reward, 'tip'.

1470 *Paston Lett.* II. 407 Also my brother Edmonde is not yet remembryd. He hathe not to lyff with, thynk on hym. 1563 BP. SANDYS in Ellis *Orig. Lett.* Ser. I. II. 195 This Contrie..bringith nothing forth fitt to remember youe withall. 1599 *Aberdeen Regr.* (1848) II. 188 The..counsall..lykvayes ordanis Mr. Peter Blakburne, minister, to be rememberit for the interteneing of the said Mr. George. 1605 SHAKS. *Mach.* II. iii. 23 Anon, anon, I pray you remember the Porter. 1802 MAR. EDGEWORTH *Moral T.* (1816) I. xi. 93 He assured the hostler, that he would remember him the next day. 1871 *Punch* 16 Sept. 113/1 Mr. Keane Hunter is manœuvring to be remembered in Alderman W.'s will.

† 3. To record, mention, make mention of (a thing, person, etc.). *Obs.* (common c 1430–1660).

c 1430 LYDG. *Min. Poems* (Percy Soc.) 73 Remembryd by scriptures we fynde and rede, Holsum and holy it is to thynke and pray. 1483 CAXTON *Gold. Leg.* 261/1 Her deth and..her assumpcion wherof the Scripture remembryth no thynge. 1577–87 HOLINSHED *Chron.* III. 963/2 About the same time that the armie before remembred, was set forward into Scotland. 1620–55 I. JONES *Stone-Heng* (1725) 4 History hath not remembred the Ruins of any ancient Buildings digged up in Anglesey. 1652 NEEDHAM tr. *Selden's Mare Cl.* 62 The Carians possessed the Sea. Their Sea-Dominion is remembred by Diodorus Siculus. 1749 FIELDING *Tom Jones* III. iv, That phenomenon in the face of the former which we have above remembered.

† b. To commemorate. *Obs.*

1430–40 LYDG. *Bochas* I. xiv. (1554) 30 This knightly man ..Set up pillers for a memoriall Which remembred his conquests. 1535 COVERDALE *Numb.* v. 15 It is..an offeringe of remembraunce, that remembreth synne. 1610 SHAKS. *Temp.* I. ii. 405 The Ditty do's remember my drown'd father. 1658 *Whole Duty Man* iii. § 17 His mercies, especially those remembred in the Sacrament, his giving Christ to die for us.

† c. To mention by way of reminder. *Obs. rare.*

1621 ELSING *Debates Ho. Lords* (Camden) 36 L. Ch. Justice moved whether to proceed against Michell...and remembred the message to the Lower House to sytt as a House this afternoone.

d. To (have mind of and) mention (a person, his condition, etc.) in prayer.

1602 SHAKS. *Ham.* III. i. 90 Nimph, in thy Orisons Be all my sins remembred. 1613 — *Hen. VIII*, v. i. 73 In thy Prayres remember Th' estate of my poore Queene. 1836 SIMEON in Carus *Life* (1847) xxxiii. 794, I intreat the favour of you to remember at the throne of grace one, who [etc.].

4. *absol.* or *intr.* To have or bear in mind; to recall to the mind; also, to exercise or possess the faculty of memory.

1390 GOWER *Conf.* III. 122 Which yifth men cause to remembre, If any Sor be left behinde. 14.. *Tundale's Vis.*, etc. (1843) 101 In verrey sothe, as I remembur can. 1548 ELYOT, s.v. *Memoria*, Sens any manne coulde remembre. 1588 SHAKS. *L. L. L.* I. i. 258 That shallow vassall..which as I remember, hight Costard. a 1631 DONNE *Poems* (1650) 22 So, in forgetting thou remembrest right. 1690 LOCKE *Hum. Und.* I. iv. § 20 To remember is to perceive any thing with memory, or with a consciousness, that it was known or perceived before. 1752 GRAY *Lett., to Walpole* (1900) I. 219 As I remember, there were certain low chairs, that looked like ebony. 1822 COLERIDGE *Lit. Rem.* (1836) I. 336 Beasts and babies remember, that is, recognize: man alone recollects. 1819 SHELLEY *Prometh. Unb.* I. 561 Past ages crowd on thee, but each one remembers.

b. To have mind, memory, or recollection *of* something. Now *rare* (in later quots. *Sc.*).

c 1386 CHAUCER *Pars. T.* ⁋ 85 At euery tyme þat I remembre of þe day of doom, I quake. c 1440 *Partonope* 3502 Remembring of the Joy he had before. 1523 LD. BERNERS *Froiss.* I. cccxxvii. 339 Sir Johan Chandos remembred of a knyfe that he had in his bosome. 1613 SHAKS. *Hen. VIII*, I. ii. 190, I remember of such a time, being my sworn seruant, The Duke retein'd him his. 1642 MILTON *Apol. Smect.* Wks. 1851 III. 285 And yet he can remember of none but Lysimachus Nicanor, and that he mislikt and censur'd. 1760–72 H. BROOKE *Fool of Qual.* (1809) II. 54 Among.. female fashions..I remember but of one [etc.]. 1808 SCOTT *Mem.* in *Lockhart* i. (1842) 6/1, I remember of detesting the name of Cumberland. 1851 H. STEPHENS *Bk. Farm* (ed. 2) I. 594/1, I remember of another case in which there was no appearance of a lamb.

† c. Const. *on* or *upon*. *Obs.*

c 1386 CHAUCER *Nun's Pr. T.* 213 Remembring on his dremes that he mette. 1430–40 LYDG. *Bochas* IX. xiv. (1558) 26 He gan remembre anone..Vpon a verse written in yᵉ Sautere. 15.. *Impeachm. Wolsey* in Furniv. *Ballads fr. MSS.* I. 352 Remembyr on Thomas of Canterbury. 1588 A. KING tr. *Canisius' Catech.* 9 b, Remember on me, o lord.

† d. To make mention *of* a thing. *Obs. rare*⁻¹.

1531 ELYOT *Gov.* II. xiii, Plinie remembreth of a dogge whiche..assaulted the murdrer of his maister.

5. *refl.* To bethink or recollect, † to think or reflect upon (oneself). Now *rare.*

c 1386 CHAUCER *Pars. T.* ⁋ 135. I wol remembre me alle the yeres of my lyf, in bitternesse of myn herte. c 1440 *Generydes* 583, I may not ease my hert..That doth me harme whanne I remembre me. 1484 CAXTON *Chivalry* 10 And thenne he remembryd hym a lytyl and after sayd [etc.]. a 1548 HALL *Chron., Hen. VIII* 194 The Cardinal somewhat remembred hym selfe and sayd, wel my lord I am content to obey. 1592 SHAKS. *Rom. & Jul.* I. iii. 9 Nurse come backe againe, I haue remembred me, thou'se heare our counsell. 1605 — *Lear* IV. vi. 233 Thou old, vnhappy Traitor, Breefely thy selfe remember. 1891 *Illustr. Lond. News* Christmas No. 21/1, 'I long for home'. But she remembered herself. 'That's only a momentary feeling'.

† b. Const. *of* or *on*; = 4 b, 4 c. *Obs.*

13.. *E. E. Allit. P.* C. 326 Þenne I remembred me ryȝt of my rych lorde. c 1386 CHAUCER *Melib.* ⁋ 33 Remembreth yow upon the pacient Job. c 1450 LONELICH *Merlin* 581 (Kölbing), Sche hire remembrid of fadyr and modyr bothe. 1545 *St. Papers Hen. VIII*, I. II. 806, I cannot remember me of any others [fit to be captains]. 1622 MABBE tr. *Aleman's Guzman d'Alf.* II. 308, I remembred my selfe of my Hostesse. 1651 tr. *De-las-Coveras' Don Fenise* 94 Remembering himselfe of the recitall which Rufine had made him. 1760–72 H. BROOKE *Fool of Qual.* (1809) III. 88, I remembered me of my gallant messmates.

c. With obj. clause. (Cf. sense 1.) Now *arch.*

c 1374 CHAUCER *Troylus* I. 384 Remembring him, that love to wyde y-blowe Yelt bittre fruyt. 1428 *Lett. Marg. Anjou & Bp. Beckington* (Camden) 43 Treuly, I can not remembre me, that ever I wrote to yow. 1470–85 MALORY *Arthur* VIII. ii. 275 The kyng merueilled why she dyd soo, and remembryd hym how her sone was sodenly slayne with poyson. 1589 *Hay any Work* 48 O now I remember me, he has also a charge to prouide for. a 1648 LD. HERBERT *Hen. VIII* (1683) 39 Remembring himself, that it was time to visit his Army..he takes leave of the Ladies. 1700 CONGREVE *Way of World* II. ix, Now, I remember me, I'm married. 1817 BYRON *Manfred* III. iv. 8, I do remember me, that in my youth..I stood within the Coliseum's wall.

6. a. *impers.* (*It*) *remembers me* [after OF. (*il*) *me remembre*], I remember. Now *arch.*

c 1374 CHAUCER *Compl. Mars* 150 What his compleynt was, remembreth me. c 1386 — *Wife's T.* 469 Whan that it remembreth me Up-on my yowthe. 1484 CAXTON *Fables of Æsop* I. iv, I am certayne & me remembreth wel that the dogge lend to her a loof of brede. 1814 CARY *Dante, Par.* XX. 137 It doth remember me, that I beheld The pair of blessed luminaries move. 1831 SCOTT *Cast. Dang.* i, It may remember you that I undertook..to temporize a little with the Scots.

† b. Of a thing: To recur to (one). *Obs.*⁻¹

1608 *Yorksh. Trag.* I. ix, When the dread thought of death remembers you.

c. *To be remembered*, to remember; also const. *of.* Now *obs.* exc. *dial.* (common c 1450–1600).

c 1440 *Generydes* 619 Ther is a land I am remembryd wele, Men call it Perse. 1470–85 MALORY *Arthur* IX. xxi. 370 Soo whan the quene loked vpon sir Tristram she was not remembryd of hym. 1509 BARCLAY *Shyp of Folys* (1570) 46, I am remembred that I haue often sene Great wordly riches ende in pouertie. c 1590 MARLOWE *Faust.* x, Are you remembered how you crossed me in my conference with the Emperor? 1605 *1st Pt. Jeronimo* III. ii. 53 Are you remembred, Don, of a daring message, And a proud attempt? 1828 *Craven Gloss.* s.v., An ye be remembered, i. e. if you remember.

II. 7. To remind (a person); esp. to put (one) in mind *of* a thing or person. † Also const. *upon, with.* Now *arch.* or *dial.*

c 1386 CHAUCER *Frankl. T.* 515 This was as thise bookes me remembre The colde frosty seson of Decembre. c 1449 PECOCK *Repr.* I. iv. 22 Thouȝ he wolde reherce tho pointis ..of the lawe forto remembre the iugis and the peple ther upon. 1451 *Paston Lett.* I. 190 Item, to remembre T. Denyes of the tale that Fyncheham told. 1530 PALSGR. 683/1, I shal remembre him of it whan he gothe to bedde. 1604 T. WRIGHT *Passions* VI. 320 These...I thought good briefly to set downe..to remember the Reader, that hereafter he may benefit himselfe of them. 1641 R. MARRIOT *Serm.* 25 The third was a Golden letter, which remembred him with the joyes of Heaven. 1745 *Fortunate Orphan* 68 Emanuel.. remember'd Azem of his Promises. 1808 *Edin. Rev.* Jan. 285 He takes care to remember us of Dr. Johnson's saying. a 1850 ROSSETTI *Dante & Circ.* I. (1874) 98 She remembered me many times of my own most noble lady.

b. With inf. or obj. clause. Now *dial.* (Very common in 17th c., esp. with *that*.)

c 1449 PECOCK *Repr.* I. iv. 21 If a bischop..wolde remembre hem, exorte hem, and stire hem..forto kepe certeyn moral vertues. 1474 *Rolls of Parlt.* VI. 113/1 Remembryng us that it appered unto us [etc.]. 1540–1 ELYOT *Image Gov.* (1556) 48 b, Fyrste he wolde remembre hym for what cause he hath called hym. 1596 NASHE *Saffron Walden* 11 Let me remember thee to do this one kindnes more for me. 1638 CHILLINGW. *Relig. Prot.* I. iii. § 77. 177, I am to remember you, that many Attributes in Scripture, are not notes of performance but of duty. 1670 BAXTER *Cure Ch. Div.* Pref. 1, I write it to remember the Teachers of the Churches, what principles they have to preach. 1703 J. SAVAGE *Lett. Antients* xxvii. 88 Remembring him that Liberality to Friends is the best way of hoarding Treasure. 1748 RICHARDSON *Clarissa* (1811) II. 239 The edge of the opened door, which he ran against, remembered him to turn his welcome back upon me. 1877– in dial. glossaries (Lancs., Chesh., Lincs., Warw., Shropsh.).

† 8. To recall (a thing or person) *to* a person. Also with double object, obj. clause, and without const. *Obs.*

1382 WYCLIF *John* xiv. 26 He schal..schewe, or remembre, to ȝou alle thingis. c 1440 CAPGRAVE *Life St. Kath.* III. 1379 Loke on ȝour ryng! It wyll remembyr ȝow ȝour gloryous weddyng. a 1470 TIPTOFT *Tulle on Frendsh.* (Caxton 1481) A ij, Syth my master Seuola remembrid unto me how Lelius hath resouned with him. 1531 ELYOT *Gov.* I. iv, Remembryng to hym the daunger of his iuell example. 1617 WITHER *Fidelia* in *Juvenilia* (1633) 456 Every severall object that I see Doth severally (methinkes) remember thee. 1649 MILTON *Eikon.* Pref., By onely remembring them the truth of what they themselves know to be heer miss-affirmed. 1672 *Mede's Wks.* p. xl, I remembred to him, how often I heard him wonder [etc.].

† b. To mention (one's affection, respect, etc.) by way of message *to* another. *Obs.*

1586 A. DAY *Eng. Secretary* II. (1625) 63 Sir, my humble dutie remembred unto you and my good Mistresse, you may please to understand [etc.]. 1625 USSHER in *Lett. Lit. Men* (Camden) 132, I pray remember my hearty affeccion unto my Lord of Landaff. 1672 MARVELL *Corr.* Wks. (Grosart) II. 408 Pray remember my respects to your Partner.

c. To mention (a person) *to* another as sending a friendly greeting. Also without const.

1560 GRESHAM in Burgon *Life* I. 302 To whom it may please you, I maye be remembered. 1613 SHAKS. *Hen. VIII*, IV. ii. 160 Remember me In all humilitie vnto his Highnesse. a 1674 CLARENDON *Surv. Leviath.* (1676) 6 To remember me kindly to Mr. Hobbes. 1713 STEELE *Guardian* No. 171 ⁋ 3 Remember me to the lion. 1780 *Phil. Trans.* LXX. 452 He begs to be remembered to you with best compliments. 1804 in *G. Rose's Diaries* (1860) II. 86 Mrs. Tomline desires to be most kindly remembered. 1872 BLACK *Adv. Phaeton* xxvi. 353 Katty Tatham desires to be remembered with you.

Re-me·mber, *v. nonce-wd.* [RE- 5 b.] *trans.* a. To put together again. b. To supply with a new member.

1871 SPENCER *Princ. Psychol.* II. VII. vii. 377 Mind..is a thing we can form no notion of without *re-membering*, re-*collecting* some of our mental acts. 1894 BLACKMORE *Perlycross* 389 A British tar..a true heart of oak, re-membered also in the same fine material.

Reme·mberabi·lity. [f. next + -ITY.] The fact of being rememberable.

1839 J. ROGERS *Antipopopr.* x. § 2. 255 The easy rememberability of the Bible system.

Rememberable (rĭme·mbərăb'l), *a.* Also **remembr-**. [f. REMEMBER *v.* + -ABLE: cf. obs. F. *remembrable*.] Capable or worthy of being remembered. (Common in 19th c.)

1611 COTGR., *Memorable*, memorable, remembrable, worthie of memorie. 1803 HAZLITT *Pol. Ess.* (1819) 399 When all is done, nothing rememberable has been said. a 1842 ARNOLD *Serm. Chr. Life* (1845) 296 A change..of any rememberable kind. 1881 SHAIRP *Asp. Poetry* v. 143 More rememberable than any blank verse since Milton's.

Hence **Reme·mberably** *adv.*

1800 SOUTHEY *Lett.* (1856) I. 133 The moral features of the people [are] more accurately and rememberably painted. 1809 *Ibid.* II. 157 Say what you have to say as perspicuously..and as rememberably as possible.

Rememberance, obs. form of REMEMBRANCE.

Remembered (rĭme·mbəɹd), *ppl. a.* [-ED[1].]

† 1. Already mentioned. *Obs. rare.*

c 1425 *Found. St. Bartholomew's* (E. E. T. S.) 31 Whan the remembrid priour was ȝit a-lyue. 1589 PUTTENHAM *Eng. Poesie* (Arb.) 115 Besides all the remembred points of Metricall proportion, ye haue yet two other sorts.

2. Recalled to or kept in memory. Also in combs., as *sad-, well-remembered*.

1638 JUNIUS *Paint. Ancients* 17 That the Artificer after a well-remembred knowledge, should invent something of his owne. 1745 *Matrimony pro & con* 3 O! to recall the sad-remember'd Day. 1754 RICHARDSON *Grandison* (1811) I. xxxiii. 253 As dear to me..as her brother from his remembered bravery. 1805 WORDSW. *Prelude* I. 161 No little band of yet remembered names. 1863 GEO. ELIOT *Romola* ix, Far in the backward vista of his remembered life.

Rememberer (rĭme·mbərəɹ). [-ER[1].] One who, or that which, remembers († or reminds).

c 1449 PECOCK *Repr.* II. vi. 171 Bi this rememoraunce the rememberer..schal be the more stirid. a 1542 WYATT in *Tottel's Misc.* (Arb.) 45 Forgetter of payn, remembrer of my wo. 1579 G. HARVEY *Letter-bk.* (Camden) 61 Lett this ilfavorid letter suffize for a..remembrer in that behaulfe. 1614 RALEIGH *Hist. World* III. (1634) 89 Artaxerxes called Mnemon, that is to say the Mindful or the Rememberer. 1754 RICHARDSON *Grandison* (1781) IV. vii. 62 What a rememberer, if I may make a word, is the heart! 1809 SYD. SMITH *Wks.* (1859) I. 174/1 The maker of verses and the rememberer of words. 1876 F. HARRISON *Choice Bks.* (1886) 376 The recollections are very often the inventions of the rememberer.

Reme·mbering, *vbl. sb.* [-ING[1].] The action of the vb. REMEMBER; an instance of this. † *In remembering*, in remembrance or memory.

c 1375 *Sc. Leg. Saints* xl. (*Ninian*) 532 Of þat merwale in remembryng. c 1449 PECOCK *Repr.* v. xii. 547 Into the remembring of persones not being religiose. 1521 J. T. *Prol. Bradshaw's St. Werburge* 40 Who on this wolde haue remembrynge..wolde dispise all thynges..mundayne. 1585 T. WASHINGTON tr. *Nicholay's Voy.* Ep. Ded., Doth it not deserue diligent marking and remembring? 1673 *True Worship of God* 51 A Remembring and Renewing of our Baptismal Vow. 1740 J. CLARKE *Educ. Youth* (ed. 3) 88 The Matter is well worth the remembring. 1846 MASKELL *Mon. Rit.* I. p. clxxxv, Wearying the reader with continued rememberings of much, which we might have wished away.

Reme·mbering, *ppl. a.* [-ING[2].] That remembers († or reminds); † mindful *of* a thing.

c 1449 PECOCK *Repr.* v. xii. 546 Wherfore it is resonable,.. that her outward habit be mad to hem into such..a remembring signe. c 1586 C'TESS PEMBROKE *Ps.* CXIX. G. i, Grave deeply in remembring mind My trust, thy promise true. 1625 BACON *Ess., Great Place* (Arb.) 293 Be not too sensible, or too remembring, of thy Place, in Conuersation. a 1676 HALE *Prim. Orig. Man.* (1677) 21 Touching the knowledge of Brutes, touching their remembring Faculty. 1790 PENNANT *London* (1813) 498 Death..shaking his remembering hour-glass. 1822 GALT *Provost* xxix, During the remembering prayer, Mr. Pittle put up a few words for criminals under sentence of death. 1886 SWINBURNE *Death Sir H. Taylor* in *Athenæum* 10 Apr. 488/1 Clothed round with reverence of remembering hearts.

Remembir, obs. Sc. form of REMEMBER.

Remembrance (rĭme·mbrăns), *sb.* Also 4–6 **-aunce**, 5 **-a(u)nse, -ans**, 6 **-auns**, 4–8 **remember-**. [a. F. *remembrance* (11th c.; AF. *-aunce*): see REMEMBER and -ANCE, and cf. It. *rimembranza*.]

1. (Without article.) Memory or recollection in relation to a particular object, fact, etc. In early use esp. in phrases *to have in r.*, *to call to r.* (see CALL *v.* 20 b).

13.. *Coer de L.* 6926 Whoso hadde sene hys cuntenaunse, Wolde euer had hym in remembraunse. 1390 GOWER *Conf.* I. 5 He schal drawe into remembrance The fortune of this worldes chance. c 1450 *Merlin* 49 The moste remembraunce that I shall haue, shall be vpon yow, and on yowre nedes. 1530 PALSGR. 351 Here is to be called to remembraunce what I sayd afore of *quel*. 1535 COVERDALE 2 *Macc.* xii. 42 They..besought God, that the fawte..might be put out of remembraunce. 1611 BIBLE *Transl. Pref.* ⁋ 7 He hath for euer bound the Church vnto him, in a debt of speciall remembrance. 1667 MILTON *P. L.* III. 704 Worthiest to be all Had in remembrance alwayes with delight. 1725 POPE *Odyss.* XIII. 501 This ever grateful in remembrance bear. 1826 J. G. STRUTT *Sylva Brit.* (1830) 5 Secured to remembrance by the pencil. 1871 R. ELLIS tr. *Catullus* lxiv. 231 Look that..deep-laid in steady remembrance These our words grow greenly.

b. Const. *of*, † inf., or † clause. Formerly freq. in phrases *to have r. of*, *to put* (one) *in r. of*.

c 1385 CHAUCER *Knt.'s T.* 188 This maked Emelye han remembrance To do honour to May. — *Monk's T.* 728 Of honestee yit hadde he remembrance. 1465 *Paston Lett.* III. 482 This might..put him in remembrance what time he hath lost. 1555 EDEN *Decades* 43 You put me so often in remembrance of your departure. 1586 A. DAY *Eng. Secretary* II. (1625) 38 His presence I am resolved shall no more disquiet me, by hearing or remembrance of him. 1623 BINGHAM *Xenophon* 101 Yet it is honest..that remembrance be had rather of that which is good, than of the bad. 1678 CUDWORTH *Intell. Syst.* I. v. 693 Though all Learning be not the Remembrance of what the Soul once before actually understood in a Pre-existent State. 1784 COWPER *Task* VI. 252 What he views of beautiful or grand..Prompts with remembrance of a present God. 1816 J. WILSON *City of Plague* II. ii. 231 Remembrance rises faint and dim Of sorrows suffer'd long ago.

2. That operation of the mind which is involved in recalling a thing or fact; recollection. Freq. personified, or in fig. context.

c 1374 CHAUCER *Anel. & Arc.* 211 So thirlethe with the poynt of Rememberaunce þe swerde of sorowe..Myn hert bare of blisse. 1500–20 DUNBAR *Poems* lxxii. 105 Than rudelie come Remembrance Ay rugging me, withoutin rest. 1595 SHAKS. *John* v. vi. 12 Vnkinde remembrance: thou, & endles night, Haue done me shame. 1671 MILTON *Samson* 952 Not for thy life, lest fierce remembrance wake My sudden rage. 1690 LOCKE *Hum. Und.* II. xix. § 1 The same Idea, when it again recurs without the Operation of the like Object on the external Sensory, is Remembrance. 1785 REID *Intell. Powers* I. i. 16 When the word perception is used properly..it is never applied to things past. And thus it is distinguished from remembrance.

† b. Faculty or power of remembering or recalling to mind. *Obs.* (Cf. next.)

c 1420 LYDG. *Assembly of Gods* 998 To whom Vertew sent embassatours three, Reson, Discresion, & Good Remembraunse. 1509 FISHER *Funeral Serm. C'tess Richmond* Wks. (1876) 291 She was good in remembraunce & of holdyng memorye. 1538 *Bury Wills* (Camden) 133, I, Barbara Mason, ..beyng..in hooll mynd and good remembrauns, make this my present testament. 1577 NORTHBROOKE *Dicing* (1843) 143 The witte thereby is made more sharpe, and the remembrance quickened. 1610 SHAKS. *Temp.* II. i. 232 This Lord of weake remembrance. 1631 WIDDOWES *Nat. Philos.* 52 The wittie excell in remembrance, the dull in memorie.

3. With possess. pron. (One's) memory or recollection; also, in later use, (one's) power of remembering (cf. prec.).

c 1374 CHAUCER *Troylus* III. 919 (968) Can I not seyn..If sorow it put out of her remembraunce. c 1410 HOCCLEVE *Mother of God* 45 Fecche that lady in thy remembrance. 1490 CAXTON *Eneydos* xxii. 80 Come to her remembraunce the grete iustyces..vnto her tolde. a 1533 LD. BERNERS *Huon* I. 167 Call to your remembraunce how that..Adam & Eue was dyffendyd fro yᵉ etinge of fruyte. 1604 E. G[RIMSTONE] *D'Acosta's Hist. Indies* IV. xxv. 401 They must confesse themselves of all the sinnes they have committed, to their remembrance. 1660 *Trial Regic.* 44 To the best of my remembrance, he sate there four days together. 1754 RICHARDSON *Grandison* (1781) IV. x. 87 The obliging wife would banish from his remembrance the petulant mistress. 1819 SHELLEY *Cyclops* 145 Pour: that the draught may fillip my remembrance. 1864 SKEAT *Uhland's Poems* 170 But now is my remembrance weak with eld.

b. The point at which one's memory of events begins, or the period over which it extends.

1565 COOPER *Thesaurus*, *Memoria patrum*, in the time and remembrance of our fathers. 1601 SHAKS. *All's Well* IV. iii. 126 Fro the time of his remembrance to this very instant disaster. 1667 MILTON *P. L.* VIII. 203 Thee I have heard relating what was don Ere my remembrance. 1771 SMOLLETT *Humph. Cl.* 2 June, Let. ii, I know but one other method.., which..has been practised successfully more than once in my remembrance.

4. The memory († or thought) which one has *of* a thing or person.

c 1386 CHAUCER *Pars. T.* ⁋ 157 The fourth point, that oughte make a man have contrition, is the sorweful remembrance of the good dedes that he hath lefte to don here in erthe. 1490 CAXTON *Eneydos* xxii. 78 Anguishe & calamyte, ..wherof yᵉ remembraunce greued hym ryght sorowfully. 1551 ROBINSON tr. *More's Utop.* II. (1895) 302 The remembraunce of theire poore indigent and begerlye olde age kylleth them up. 1590 SHAKS. *Mids. N.* IV. i. 164 My loue To Hermia..Seems to me now as the remembrance of an idle gaude. 1655 GURNALL *Chr. in Arm.* verse 11. I. iii. (1669) 27/1 These add to his sin, and the remembrance of his sin will adde to his torment. 1725 POPE *Odyss.* XIII. 224 Yet had his mind thro' tedious absence lost The dear remembrance of his native coast. 1792 WORDSW. *Descrip. Sketches* 519 Why does their sad remembrance haunt the mind? 1849 MACAULAY *Hist. Eng.* vii. II. 229 Between him and the court was interposed the remembrance of one terrible event.

b. With *a* and *pl.* A recollection, reminiscence.

1601 SHAKS. *All's Well* I. iii. 140 By our remembrances of daies forgon. 1610 — *Temp.* v. i. 138 How sharpe the point of this remembrance is. [1706–7 FARQUHAR *Beaux' Strat.* IV. ii, But cussen Mackshane, vil you not put a remembrance upon me?] 1788 GIBBON *Decl. & F.* xlix. V. 158 A faint remembrance of their ancestors still tormented the Romans. 1809 CAMPBELL *Gertr. Wyom.* I. i, Although the wild-flower on thy ruined wall..a sad remembrance bring. 1819 SHELLEY *Peter Bell 3rd* v. x, These obscure remembrances Stirred such harmony in Peter.

c. The surviving memory of a person.

1579 W. WILKINSON *Confut. Familye of Loue, Brief Descr.*, Kyng Edward the vi., a Prince of blessed remembrance. 1611 BIBLE *Exod.* xvii. 14, I will vtterly put out the remembrance of Amalek from vnder heauen. 1698 TATE & BRADY *Ps.* cxii. 6 The sweet Remembrance [1696 Memorial] of the Just Shall flourish when he sleeps in Dust. 1812 SOUTHEY *Omniana* I. 110 He might have secured for himself a lasting and respectful remembrance.

d. *pl.* Greetings expressive of remembrance.

1789 COWPER *Let. to Newton* 1 Dec., With our joint affectionate remembrances to yourself and Mrs. Newton. 1804 in *G. Rose's Diaries* (1860) II. 87 Kindest remembrances to all our good friends. c 1850 *Arab. Nts.* (Rtldg.) 528 He bid me also be sure and give his kindest remembrances to you.

5. † a. *In (into, rarely for) remembrance*, as a memorial or record; *to put in remembrance*, to put on record. *Obs.*

1390 GOWER *Conf.* III. 183 Into remembrance He dede upon him such vengance. *Ibid.* 294 Thei for evere in remembrance Made a figure in resemblance Of him. 1426 LYDG. in *Pol. Poems* (Rolls) II. 132 To put his title in remembraunce, Whiche that he hath to Inglond and to Fraunce. 1490 CAXTON *Eneydos* vi. 24 Of which were fourmed lettres for to write..in remembraunce perpetual be thinges that [etc.]. 1511 *Guylforde's Pilgr.* (Camden) 27 By token of a fayre stone layde for remembraunce. 1535 COVERDALE *Zech.* xiii. 2, I will destroye the names of Idols out off the londe: so that they shal nomore be put in remembraunce.

b. *In* († *the*) *remembrance of*, in memory of.

c 1400 MAUNDEV. (Roxb.) xxxiv. 153 Þeroff he drinkez..in remembraunce of his fader. 1483 CAXTON *Cato* F vij, It is sayd that there is as yet in the same place a pytte in mynde and remembraunce of the sayd myracle. ? a 1500 *Wycket* (1828) 6 Do ye this in the remembrance of me. 1581 PETTIE tr. *Guazzo's Civ. Conv.* II. (1586) 105 That the..life of the people of Arpines, should be spared in the remembraunce of Tullie. 1613 PURCHAS *Pilgrimage* I. xiii. 63 The day in remembrance thereof [was] yeerely solemnized with fasting the Euen. 1697 DRYDEN *Æneid* VI. 680 In remembrance of so brave a Deed, A Tomb, and Fun'ral Honours I decreed.

† 6. Mention, notice. *Obs.*

1375 BARBOUR *Bruce* III. 558 Quhen that he herd mak remembrance Off the perellys that passyt war. 1390 GOWER *Conf.* I. 156 As the bok makth remembrance, Alphonse was his propre name. c 1440 *Generydes* 2177 Till he was putte [from] his enheritaunce, Wherof be fore was made remembraunce. 1531 ELYOT *Gov.* I. xviii, I can finde no notable remembrance that it was used of auncient tyme. 1607 TOPSELL *Four-f. Beasts* (1658) 497 He saith he found the remembrance of it in the Grecian books. 1631 WEEVER *Anc. Funeral Mon.* 650 This towne..requireth some large remembrance from mee.

† b. A commemorative discourse or mention; a memorial inscription. *Obs.*

1509 FISHER *Funeral Serm. C'tess Richmond* Wks. (1876) 289 Here after foloweth a mornynge remembraunce had at the moneth mynde of the noble prynces Margarete. 1598 BARNFEILD *Poems* (Arb.) 119 A Remembrance of some English Poets. 1599 SHAKS. *Hen. V*, I. ii. 229 Lay these bones in an vnworthy Vrne, Tomblesse, with no remembrance ouer them.

† 7. The act of reminding or putting in mind. *Book of remembrance*, a memorandum-book, a record. *Ring of remembrance* (see quot. 1659). *Obs.*

1461 *Paston Lett.* II. 64 It is not for no lak of remembrans, for I sent to hym thryis or fowyr tymys ther for. 1465 *Ibid.* 202 He sent me word that Wyllyam Worceter had a boke of remembraunce of recaytys. 1535 COVERDALE *Num.* v. 15 It is..an offeringe of remembraunce, that remembreth synne. 1565 COOPER *Thesaurus*, *Memorialis liber*, a booke of remembrance. 1597 HOOKER *Eccl. Pol.* v. lxv. § 4 It serueth, namely, for a signe of rememberance to put vs in minde of our dutie. 1611 BIBLE *Mal.* iii. 16 The Lord hearkened and heard it, & a booke of remembrance was written before him. 1659 HOWELL *Vocab.* xxxiv, A ring of remembrance, viz. two or three interchain'd [cf. COTGR., *Souvenance*,..a Ring with many hoopes, whereof a man lets one hang downe when he would be put in mind of a thing].

attrib. a 1626 W. SCLATER *Comm. Mal.* (1650) 186 He hath also, then, his remembrance-book, his register, for the ungodly.

† b. *Bill of remembrance*, a royal letter of authority. *Obs.*

1481 in *Muniment. Magd. Coll. Oxf.* (1882) 15 Dayly to atende tyll I myte haue T. S. at leysere and than breke yᵉ matere and schew to hym yᵉ byll of remembranse. 1580 HOLLYBAND *Treas. Fr. Tong*, *Vn placet*, a bill of remembraunce to an Officer from the prince, a bill of processe. 1582 N. LICHEFIELD tr. *Castanheda's Conq. E. Ind.* 69 He gave him other possessions and rents and a bill of remembraunce to make him Lorde.

† c. *Clerk of the Remembrance*, = REMEMBRANCER 1 a. *Obs.*

The Act cited by Cowell is one establishing *un Clerc de la remembrancie*.

1607 Cowell *Interpr.* s.v. *Remembrancer*, These [Remembrancers of the Exchequer] anno 37 Ed. 3. Cap. 4. be called clerks of the Remembrance. [Hence in later Dicts.]

†8. A note or entry serving as a record or reminder; a memorandum. *Obs.*

1430–1 *Rolls of Parlt.* IV. 376/1 Make oute a remembrance under her seall..resityng ye issue yat is joyned. 1465 *Paston Lett.* II. 202 As for such bokys as he hath hyre at hom he wol doo loke yf any remembraunce canne be founde therof. 1586 A. Day *Eng. Secretary* II. (1625) 63, I haue laden for your account..according to your remembrance sent vnto me for the same,..seuen Buts of Sack. 1601 Holland *Pliny* II. 172 Set down vnder the hand of the sayd prince, in a priuat note-book of remembrances. a1676 Hale (J.), Those proceedings and remembrances are in the Tower, beginning with the twentieth year of Edward I.

†b. A reminder given by one person to another; a remark of this nature. *Obs.*

1597 Shaks. *2 Hen. IV*, v. ii. 115, I do commit into your hand, Th'vnstained Sword..With this Remembrance; That you vse the same [etc.]. 1612 Woodall *Surg. Mate* Wks. (1653) 1 Brief remembrances touching the particular instruments for the Surgeons Chest. 1638 Chillingw. *Relig. Prot.* I. v. § 29. 264 But let the understanding Reader, take with him three or four short remembrances.

c. A reminder given by some thing or fact; a thing or fact serving to remind one of something. Now *rare.*

1617 Moryson *Itin.* I. 107 The Orange trees..are greene in winter, giuing at that dead time a pleasant remembrance of Sommer. 1663 Gerbier *Counsel* 21 To knock their head against that of the doore, for a remembrance, that they were not to passe the threshold. 1739 Wesley *Wks.* (1872) I. 174, I was not suffered to conclude my subject; a good remembrance that I should, if possible, declare, at every time, the whole counsel of God. 1789 [see Remark sb.[1] 3 c]. 1806–7 J. Beresford *Miseries Hum. Life* (1826) I. Introd., What..[are] dressing and undressing but stinging remembrances of the privileged nakedness of the savage?

9. An article serving to remind one person of another; a keepsake, souvenir; a token.

1425 *E. E. Wills* (1882) 63. I wil þat Iohn Ondeley haf a coueryd pece of siluer..for a remembraunce of me. 1463 *Bury Wills* (Camden) 34, iij of my beste gownys..for a remembraunce to thinke vpon me. c1532 Du Wes *Introd. Fr.* in Palsgr. 1023 Do nat you bryng me some remembraunce or token from them? 1611 Tourneur *Ath. Trag.* II. i, Here's the sad remembrance of his life, Which, for his sake, I will for euer weare. 1724 in *Swift's Lett.* (1768) IV. 13, I desire your acceptance of a ring, a small remembrance of my father.

b. A memorial or record of some fact, person, etc. Now *rare.*

c1470 Henry *Wallace* XI. 1458 Go nobill buk,..Now byd thi tym, and be a remembrance. a1533 Ld. Berners *Gold. Bk. M. Aurel.* (1546) G, His wordes and counsels remayne for a remembraunce. 1590 Spenser *F. Q.* I. i. 2 On his brest a bloodie Crosse he bore, The deare remembrance of his dying Lord. 1607 Topsell *Four-f. Beasts* (1658) 192 That figure which is engraven at Rome in a Marble pillar, being a remembrance of some Triumph. 1822 B. Cornwall *Dram. Scenes, Rape Proserpine*, And is this fountain left alone For a sad remembrance.

†c. A heraldic device. *Obs. rare*[−1].

1470–85 Malory *Arthur* IX. xxx. 384 Tristram..commaunded..his seruaunt to ordeyne hym a blak sheld with none other remembraunce therin.

Reme·mbrance, *v. rare.* [f. the sb.: cf. Remembrancing *vbl. sb.*] *trans.* To remind.

1593 Nashe *Christ's T.* Wks. (Grosart) IV. 261 Let vs looke for the sworde next to remembrance and warne vs. 1656 G. Collier *Answ.* 15 *Quest.* Ded., The best return I am able to make you, is, remembrancing you of your duty.

Remembrancer (rĭme·mbrănsəɹ). [a. AF. *remembrancer*: see Remembrance *sb.* and -er[1].]

1. †a. A local official of some kind. *Obs. rare*[−1].

1430–1 *Rolls of Parlt.* IV. 386/1 Robt. Holme Esquyer, Remembrauncer of Guyen..suyng for the good of the Corone of oure Soverayn liege Lorde the Kyng, and for the parties of the Duche of Guyen.

b. The name of certain officials of the Court of Exchequer.

(a) The *King's* (or *Queen's*) *Remembrancer*, an officer responsible for the collection of debts due to the sovereign; now an officer of the Supreme Court. (b) The *Lord Treasurer's Remembrancer*. Now only *Hist.* (abolished by Act 3 & 4 Will. IV, c. 99 § 41). (c) The *Remembrancer of the First Fruits*, responsible for the collection of all compositions for first fruits and tenths. Now only *Hist.* (abolished by Act 1 & 2 Vict. c. 20 § 1).

[1354 *Rolls of Parlt.* II. 271/2 Que come en l'Escheqer soient diverses offices & places, Gardein de la Pipe, & de la Somons, Remembrancers.] 1455 *Ibid.* V. 342/2 Remembrauncer of the Kynges Eschequier. 1464 *Ibid.* 520/1 The Office of oure Remembrancer in oure Eschequer. 1566 *Act 8 Eliz.* c. 16 § 2 Her or their Graces Officers of Remembrauncer and the Treasourers Remembrancer. 1607 Cowell *Interpr.* s.v., Remembrancers of the Exchequer (*Rememoratores*) be three officers, or clerks, one called the Kings Remembrancer...The third is called the Remembrancer of the first fruites. 1652 *Act 14 Chas. II*, c. 21 § 3 That the several Remembrancers of the said Court..make true and perfect Copies of..such other Seizure and Inquisicion. 1724 Swift *Drapier's Lett.* Wks. 1755 V. II. 68 The lord Palmerstown is first remembrancer, worth near 2000*l.* per annum. 1797 *22nd Rep. Sel. Committee on Finance* 4 Upon entering into the Details of the Constitution of this Court, the Officers who first present themselves are the Remembrancers. 1838 *Act 1 & 2 Vict.* c. 20 § 11 Henry Warre Esquire, the present Remembrancer of First Fruits and Tenths. 1887 Pollock *Land Laws* 8 *note*, These rents are now received by the Queen's Remembrancer a few days before the beginning of Michaelmas term.

†c. *Queen's Remembrancer*, an officer having the administration of the Queen Consort's affairs. *Obs.*

[? 1644 *Cal. St. Papers Chas. I, Dom.* (1890) 212 There has always been an officer called the Remembrancer to the Queens of this nation.] 1647 Haward *Crown Rev.* 5 Clerke in the Office of the Queenes Remembrancer.

d. An official of the Corporation of the City of London, whose chief duty now is to represent that body before Parliamentary Committees and at Council and Treasury Boards.

'From the records of the City of London, in the Town Clerk's Office, it appears that the office of Remembrancer was instituted in 1570–1' (*Archaeologia*, 1855, XXXVI. 106).

1710 J. Chamberlayne *St. Gt. Brit.* II. III. 631 Mr. John Johnson, Remembrancer [of the City of London]. 1770 in *Examiner* (1812) 4 May 286/1 Lord Denbigh came up to the City Remembrancer. 1802–12 Bentham *Ration. Judic. Evid.* (1827) II. 590 *note*, In the official establishment of the city of London there still exists one officer, the remembrancer [etc.]. 1837 *Municip. Corporations* (Eng. & Wal.) *2nd Rep., London* 45 The Remembrancer is elected by the Common Council. 1882 *Times* 1 Mar. 9/6 Mr. Robarts..was elected City Remembrancer in 1878, at a salary of 1,500*l.* per annum.

2. One who reminds another; in former use, *esp.* one engaged or appointed for that purpose. (Common in 16–17th c.)

1523 Skelton *Garl. Laurel* 864 To be your remembrauncer, madame, I am bounde. 1571 Golding *Calvin on Ps.* xxxix. 13 God knoweth welynough without a remembrancer, that men have but a short journey to walk upon earth. 1645 Durye *Israel's Call* 28 You have put me in this place, to be your remembrancer in the name of the Lord. 1687 R. L'Estrange *Answ. Diss.* 22, I think it would not do Amiss, if the Dissenter should Counter-Advise his Remembrancer upon Two or Three of these Last Points. 1771 Smollett *Humph. Cl.* 28 Apr., Let. ii, If I had not been an ass, I should not have needed a remembrancer. 1835 Browning *Paracelsus* II. 42 What does this Remembrancer set down concerning life? 1865 *Examiner* 18 Mar. 161 It is his chosen office to be Remembrancer of all wrongs.

3. *fig.* of things; also, a thing serving to remind one; a reminder; a memento, souvenir.

1589 G. Harvey *Pierces Supererog.* Wks. (Grosart) II. 138 Consideration is a good Counsellour: & Reading, no badd Remembrancer. 1594 Kyd *Cornelia* III. i. 13 Sweet teares of loue, remembrancers to tyme. 1607 Donne in *Four C. Eng. Lett.* (1880) 62 No searching vehemencies..made you need so shadowy an example or remembrancer. 1666 J. Davies *Hist. Caribby Isles* 297 Their stomacks are their Clocks and Remembrancers. 1778 [W. Marshall] *Minutes Agric., Digest* 144 This Diary is the basis of the other accounts, and serves as an almost-infallible Remembrancer. 1809 Malkin *Gil Blas* x. ii. ¶ 10, I fell dangerously ill there; and that timely remembrancer was the cause of bringing back your son to you. 1867 Howells *Ital. Journ.* 252 A bit of the sacred wood for a remembrancer.

b. A reminder *of* something.

c1610 Sir J. Melvil *Mem.* (1735) 286, I had indited a long Letter..as a Remembrancer of his former Promises. 1682 Wheler *Journ. Greece* III. 263 There are some Remains of noble Structures, Remembrancers of their prosperous State. 1766 Goldsm. *Vic. W.* iii, Premature consolation is but the remembrancer of sorrow. 1829 Southey *Sir T. More* (1831) II. 253 You have in them speaking remembrancers of mortality. 1851 Hawthorne *Ho. Sev. Gables* v, The..freckles, friendly remembrancers of the April sun and breeze.

c. Used as the title of a book or pamphlet.

1585 Higins (*title*) The Nomenclator, or Remembrancer of Adrianus Iunius..., conteining proper names and apt termes for all thinges. 1628 Wither (*title*) Britain's Remembrancer, containing a Narration of the Plague lately past. 1670 Barksdale (*title*) A Remembrancer of Excellent Men. 1749 H. Walpole *Lett.* (1846) II. 288 There was a Remembrancer on that subject ready for the press. 1788 (*title*) Egerton's Theatrical Remembrancer, a list of all dramatic performances. 1867 (*title*) The Churchman's Daily Remembrancer, Meditations from Standard Divines.

†d. A register or record. *Obs.*

1671 N. Philipot (*title*) Reasons..for a Registry or Remembrancer of all Deeds and Incumbrances of Real Estates.

e. A memorandum-book.

1842 Thackeray *Fitz-Boodle Papers, Dorothea*, Taking from her waist a little mother-of-pearl remembrancer, she notes them down.

†3. One who sends remembrances to another.

1700 Pepys *Let.* 8 Feb., Captain Hatton, who was my guest to-day and your kind remembrancer.

4. One who seeks to remember.

1798 Edgeworth *Pract. Educ.* (1811) II. 245 Here are things mentioned which will assist the young remembrancer.

Hence **Reme·mbrancership**, the office of remembrancer.

1882 *Times* 1 Mar. 9/6 The Court of Common Council looked upon the Remembrancership as a post given for the term of a year only.

Reme·mbrancing, *vbl. sb.* [See Remembrance *sb.* and *v.*] The act of remembering or reminding; a reminder.

c1449 Pecock *Repr.* II. viii. 188 That men visite and haunte for the seide eende of solempne remembrauncing tho placis and tho ymagis, which it is sure God to chese. 1627 W. Sclater *Exp. 2 Thess.* (1629) 290 Minding, Remembrancing, putting in minde of dutie. 1800 Coleridge *Piccolom.* I. ii. 134 This is no more than a remembrancing That you are now in camp. 1825 Lamb *Elia* Ser. II. *Barbara S——*, [These little books] were precious to her for their affecting remembrancings.

†**Reme·mbrative**, *a.* and *sb. Obs.* [f. Remember *v.* + -ative; cf. Rememorative.]

A. *adj.* Mindful; keeping in, or bringing to, mind.

14.. *Pol. Rel. & L. Poems* (1866) 38 Riche is it nat,.. Saue an hert [that] is reme[m]bratyf to you in eueri stounde. c1449 Pecock *Repr.* v. xii. 546 No more conuenient, redier, and ofter seen .. remembratijf signe .. couthe be founde. 1662 J. Chandler *Van Helmont's Oriat.* 269 Where that remembrative memory is not a distinct act.

B. *sb.* A memorial, reminder.

?c1470 G. Ashby *Active Policy* 11 Ye had lafte to vs.. sum remembratife Of a personne lerned & Inuentif.

Remembre, -bur, -byr, obs. ff. Remember.

†**Reme·morable**, *a. Obs. rare*[−1]. [Cf. Rememorate *v.*] Memorable.

a1641 Bp. Mountagu *Acts & Mon.* (1642) 316 Many excellent and rememorable acts.

†**Reme·morance**. *Obs.* [a. OF. *rememorance* (13th c.): see next and -ance, and cf. It. *rimemoranza* (Florio).] Remembrance.

c1449 Pecock *Repr.* II. vi. 171 Bi this rememoraunce the remembrer, if he wole, schal be the more stired to araie and dispose him thidirward. c1470 Harding *Chron.* LXIII. v, Nowe menne it call, by all rememoraunce, Constantyne noble. 1549 *Compl. Scot.* i. 21 Is nocht that nobil toune extinct furtht of rememorance?

†**Reme·morant**, *a. Obs. rare*[−1]. [ad. L. *rememorant-em*, or a. F. *remémorant*: see next and -ant.] Mindful.

1549 *Compl. Scot.* xx. 175 Than thir tua armes past to githir in gude accord, nocht rememorant of there deidly ald fede that vas betuix them.

†**Reme·morate**, *v. Obs.* [ad. ppl. stem of late L. *rememorārī* (Tert., Vulg.), -*āre*: see Remember, and cf. F. *remémorer* (16th c.), It. *rimemorare*.] a. *trans.* To remind, put in mind (of). Also *absol.* b. *intr.* To remember. Hence †**Reme·morating** *vbl. sb.*

1460–70 in C. Innes *Sk. Early Sc. Hist.* App. (1861) 506 Pleis it your lordchypis to be rememmorat the vrangous occupatioun of our landis. 1606 Bryskett *Civ. Life* 121 Whether our learning be but a rememorating of things which we knew formerly, or else a learning a new. *Ibid.* 128 We shall euer find the like difficulties, whether we rememorate or learne anew. a1670 Hacket *Cent. Serm.* (1675) 691 Ascension-day..rememorates every year that He is gone up into heaven. 1685 *Gracian's Courtiers Orac.* 68 To inform, is far better than to put in mind. Sometimes we are to rememorate, sometimes advise.

Rememora·tion. Now *rare.* [ad. late L. *rememorātiōn-em* (Vulg.): see prec. and -ation, and cf. F. *remémoration* (14th c.).] The action of remembering (†or reminding); an instance of this, †a recalling to mind.

c1449 Pecock *Repr.* II. viii. 182 The rememoracioun or the remembraunce of thilk thing..must needis be the febler. 1597 J. King *On Jonas* (1618) 431 The same word of the Lord againe repeated in my text tieth mee to a rememoration of the same particulars. 1624 Bp. Mountagu *Gagg* 318 The Protestants..use them for helps of piety, in rememoration, and more effectuall representing of the Prototype. 1654 Jer. Taylor *Real Pres.* 129 A representing of his body crucified, a rememoration of his crucifixion. 1893 Saltus *Madam Sapphira* 172 In unconscious rememoration of the famous retort.

†**Reme·morative**, *a.* and *sb. Obs.* [f. as Rememorate *v.* + -ive, perh. after a med.L. *rememorātīvus: cf. F. *remémoratif* (1527).]

A. *adj.* Serving to remind. Also const. *of*.

c1449 Pecock *Repr.* II. ii. 136 The setting vp of ymagis in chirchis and the vsing of hem as rememoratijf or mynding signes. 1625 Bp. Mountagu *App. Cæsar* 287 Only [a] representative, rememorative, and spirituall Sacrifice. a1641 — *Acts & Mon.* (1642) 90 Ἱστορικόν, Rememorative of actions done.

B. *sb.* A reminder.

1624 Bp. Mountagu *Gagg* 315 This Serpent..was a Rememorative of salvation extended by the Sonne of God. 1676 *Life Father Sarpi* in *Brent's Counc. Trent* 39 With little Notes of his own.., but so short,..that one may easily perceive that..he wrote to himself alone for rememoratives.

†**Reme·morize**, *v. Obs. rare*[−1]. [Cf. Rememorate *v.*] *trans.* To recall to mind.

1634 Sir T. Herbert *Trav.* 110 Melek Bahaman perceives the losse of his liberty when past recovery, rememorizes his sonnes advice [etc.].

Re-me·morize (rī-), *v.* [Re- 5 a.] *trans.* To commit again to memory.

1869 A. J. Ellis *E. E. Pronunc.* II. vi. § 3. 618 Even those who employed it would have to re-memorize every word in the language.

†**Reme·mory**, *sb. Obs. rare*[−1]. [Cf. Rememorance.] Remembrance.

c1470 Harding *Chron.* XIV. ii, He made theim wryten, for long rememory, To rule the Isle by theim perpetually.

†**Re·menant**. *Obs.* Forms: α. 4–6 remenant(e, -aunt(e, (4 -ont, 5 -ent), 4–5 -and, 5 remunaunde, remynaunte. β. 4–6 remanant, 5–6 -aunt(e, 5 *north.* and *Sc.* -and, -aunde, (5 *Sc.* ra-). γ. 5 remelant, -aunt, -awnt, remulant. [a. OF. *remenant*, *remanant* (AF. -*aunt*), pres. pple. of *remenoir*, *remanoir* to Remain. See also Remainant and Remnant.]

1. The rest or remainder of a number of persons or (rarely) things; the others. Also *pl.*

α. 13.. *K. Alis.* 5707 The remenaunt than fleigh on hast, Bisiden into a riche cite. c1385 Chaucer *L. G. W.* Prol. 304 Fyrst sat the god of loue & thanne this queene..And sithyn al the remenant by & by. c1400 Maundev. (Roxb.) xi. 42 Þe remenant he putte in presoun. 1470–85 Malory *Arthur* I. iii. 39 Kyng Vthers men .. slewe many peple & putt the remenaunt to flight. 1546 *Supplic. Poore Commons* (E. E. T. S.) 63 Not withstandynge that the remenaunt of the sturdy beggers..do daylye..stere vs thereunto. *pl.* c1330 R. Brunne *Chron. Wace* (Rolls) 3338 Belyn & Brenne..wente..To..take truage of þe remenauntz [*v.r.* heue trewage at Remanans].

β. c1330 *Arth. & Merl.* 6210 (Kölbing), A þousand & mo þai slowen, Þe remanant of hors drowen. 1375 Barbour *Bruce* VII. 337 Till thar host the remanand fled. c1400 Maundev. (Roxb.) vii. 27 Twa of þam er wonder hie and wyde also, and þe remanand er no3t so hie. c1470 Henry *Wallace* III. 185 The ramanand apon thaim folowit fast. 1534 More *Treat. Passion* Wks. 1310/2 He myghte thereby haue giuen occasyon of enuye..to Iudas, or peraduenture grefe to the remanant. 1573 J. Tyrie in *Cath. Tract.* (S. T. S.) 17 Ye and the remanant of your propheites ar alluterlie separat from the trew kirk.

2. The rest or remainder of a thing or aggregate of things; that which, or all that, is left over.

α. c1315 Shoreham I. 1060 Beter hys þat hy a lyte do her..And foluelle þat remenaunt Ine purgatoryes tense. ?a1366 Chaucer *Rom. Rose* 1024 Hir nose, hir mouth, and eye and cheke Wel wrought, and alle the remenaunt eke. c1400 Maundev. (1839) xxi. 230 In alle the remenant of the World, ne myghte a man fynde a more reverent man. 1430 *E. E. Wills* (1882) 87 All the Remenent of my gode & Catell y bequeth to my wif. 1473 in Arnolde *Chron.* (1811) 245 The whiche I reserue to the performyng of the remenaunt off my legates conteyned in this mi testament. 1536 *Act 28 Hen. VIII*, c. 11 § 11 Suche rent and seruyces, as for the remenaunt of the sayde yere, shall vppon euery suche lease be due. 1560 Daus tr. *Sleidane's Comm.* 54 Claude, Duke of Guise..had gathered up the remenaunt of the Frenche armye dispersed at the battle of Pavie.

β. c1375 *Sc. Leg. Saints* xvi. (*Magdalene*) 79 Þe remanand dystribut scho to pure mene. 1423 Jas. I *Kingis Q.* clxxi, Spend wele, therefore, the remanant of the day. 1477 Earl Rivers (Caxton) *Dictes* 68 A wyseman ought..to kepe wele the remanaunt of his good. 1566 in Peacock *Eng. Ch. Furniture* (1866) 88 The Remanaunt to the poore.

γ. c1440 *York Myst.* xxvii. 23 The remelaunt parted schall be. 1462 *Paston Lett.* II. 98, ij c. and l. mark to bene payed at this Estern and the remulant at Mihelmasse. And of the remulant the Kyng shuld be answered.

b. = Remainder I. *rare*[−1].

1544 tr. *Littleton's Tenures* 51 Yf the lorde wil graunt the homage of his lande by his dede to another, sauynge to hym the remenaunt of the seruyces.

3. A remaining thing or part; a remnant.

c1330 R. Brunne *Chron.* (1810) 16 The tothere remenant [F. *le remanaunt*] of the north son salle thei nomen. 1406 *E. E. Wills* (1882) 13 All the remenauntys of my godys, y wyll they be preysyd & parttyd in thre. *Ibid.* 37 Also ij remenauntz of the Lynne bed. 1433 *Rolls of Parlt.* IV. 452/1 The same Clothe to be sold for a remenaunt..and nat for a Clothe.

4. *A remenant*, for the future, henceforward.

c1330 R. Brunne *Chron.* (1810) 115 3e wite wele a-remenant [F. *desore*] & forsoth 3e kenne, Þat Inglis & Normant be now ons men.

Remenbre, obs. form of Remember.

Reme·nd (rī-), *v.* [Re- 5 a.] To mend again.

1592 Wyrley *Armorie, Ld. Chandos* 73 What harme they should His countrie do, that he remend it would.

†**Reme·ne**, *v. Obs.* [perh. a. OF. *remener* to bring back; but the senses are app. not OF., and may be based upon those of Mean *v.*[1]]

1. *trans.* To make mention of; to commemorate; to recall to mind.

13.. *Gaw. & Gr. Knt.* 2483 Mony a-venture .. þat I ne tyȝt, at þis tyme, in tale to remene. c1400 tr. *Secreta Secret., Gov. Lordsh.* 56 He shal turne hym to þe poeple to prayse hem..and remene [*pr.* remeue] & recomend her gode maneres. c1440 *Macro Plays* (E. E. T. S.) 67/960 Put yt, Lorde, in-to my thowte! Thi olde mercy, let me remene.

2. To compare; to apply by way of comparison or illustration. Const. *to*.

1377 *Pol. Poems* (Rolls) I. 216 This good ship I may remene To the chivalrye of this londe. 1387 Trevisa *Higden* (Rolls) II. 371 Þat by þe tale þat is i-feyned þe sooþ by tokenynge may be remened [*printed* remeued: L. *referatur*] to þat þat is sobeliche i-doo in deede. 1390 Gower *Conf.* I. 51 To thi matiere Of love I schal hem so remene, That thou schalt knowe what thei mene. [Cf. II. 348.] c1440 *York Myst.* xii. 50 Þe dewe to þe gode halygaste May be remened [*printed* remeued] in mannes mynde.

3. To interpret, expound, explain. Also *absol.*

1382 Wyclif *Neh.* viii. 9 Esdras..and the Leuitus, remenyng [1388 expownynge; L. *interpretantes*] to al the puple. *Ibid.* 13 That he remene to them the woordis of the lawe. c1440 Capgrave *Life St. Kath.* IV. 2271 This same figure oure clerkis thus remene.

Hence †**Reme·ning** *vbl. sb.*; also †**Reme·nour**, interpreter, translator. *Obs.*

1382 Wyclif *Ezra* Prol., Leuende the sens of scripture he folewide the errour of eche remenour. — *Prov.* Prol., The remenyng .. of the thre volumes of Salomon. *Ibid.*, The translacioun of the seuenty remenoures. — *Ecclus.* xlvii. 18 In prouerbis, and comparisouns, and in remenyngus.

Remenent, -ont, varr. Remenant *Obs.*

Rement, obs. form of Raiment.

†**Rementimuta·tion**. *nonce-wd.* A second or fresh change of mind.

1650 B. *Discolliminium* 45. I and my Friends shall be allowed the full benefit of all the variations, interpretations,..mentimutations, rementimutations,..that I and my Mare can devise or possibly imagine.

†**Reme·rce**, *v. Obs. rare*[−1]. [app. f. Re- + -*merce* as in Commerce *v.*] *trans.* To ransom.

1559 Baldwin *Mirr. Mag., Earl Northumbld.* G v, And that we might this matter set on fyre From Owens iayle, our cosin we remerst.

†**Reme·rciment**. *Obs. rare.* [a. F. *remerciment*, f. *remercier*: see Remercy *v.*] *pl.* Thanks.

1654 Flecknoe *Ten Years Trav.* iv. 8 To whom I answered (after my most humble remerciments for so high a favour) That as I yet wanted nothing [etc.]. 1777 C'tess Ossory in Jesse *Selwyn & Contemp.* (1844) III. 189 Begging you to accept our kindest remercimen[t]s for your good company.

†**Reme·rcy**, *sb. Obs. rare.* [Cf. next and Mercy.] Thanks. Also *pl.*

1542 Udall *Erasm. Apoph.* 163 b, Persones by hym conquered and subdued, who did..not rendre thankes ne saie remercies for that they had been leat..to escape. 1600 B. Jonson *Cynthia's Rev.* v. ii. Wks. (Rtldg.) 95/2 Remercie, madame, and these honourable censors. 1606 *Sir G. Goosecappe* III. i, Remercy, my more then English pages.

†**Reme·rcy**, *v. Obs.* [ad. F. *remercier* (15th c.), f. *re-* Re- + *merci* thanks, Mercy.] To thank.

c1477 Caxton *Jason* 28 b, Thenne Jason remercyed and thanked the noble Quene Myrro. 1484 — *Fables of Alfonce* xii, I remercye and thanke yow gretely. 1568 in Maskell *Mon. Rit.* (1846) III. 264 Wyth al my hert I remercye and thanke thee. 1590 Spenser *F. Q.* II. xi. 16 She him remercied as the Patrone of her life. 1592 Wyrley *Armorie* 115 With thanks rewards remercied was our paine.

Reme·rge (rī-), *v.* [Re- 5 a.] To merge again.

1850 Tennyson *In Mem.* xlvii, That each, who seems a separate whole,..should fall Remerging in the general Soul. 1901 *Spectator* 17 Aug. 221/2 A remoter realm, out of which we emerged, and into which we again remerge.

Remetamo·rphose, *v.* Also 7 -ise. [Re- 5 a.] *trans.* To change back again.

1598 J. Dickenson *Greene in Conc.* (1878) 138 When Vlisses mates turn'd from men to beastes..they would in no sort be remetamorphosed. 1636 Heywood *Loves Mistress* I. i. Wks. 1874 V. 92 If men be growne thus savage, oh you powers, Remetamorphise mee into an asse.

Reme·te, *v. rare*[−1]. [Re-] *trans.* To mete out in return.

1647 Trapp *Comm., Matt.* vii. 2 God delights to give men their own,..to re-mete them their own measure.

Remeue, obs. variant of Remove *v.*

†**Reme·vable**, *a. Obs.* [f. *remeve*, var. Remove *v.* + -able.] Capable of being moved; liable to remove, or to be taken away.

1422 tr. *Secreta Secret., Priv. Priv.* 215 Thoures [= towers] of trees reme[v]able thou shalte I-have ouer al, and Knyghtes there-in wel armyd. c1430 Lydg. *Min. Poems* (Percy Soc.) 193 The world so wyd, the air so remevable,.. The fyr so hoot and sotil of nature. 1461 *Rolls of Parlt.* V. 493/2 Afore tyme they were datyf and remevabill.

Remeve, obs. variant of Remove *v.*

†**Reme·vement**. *Obs. rare.* [f. *remeve*, var. Remove *v.* + -ment.] Removal, transference.

1437 *Rolls of Parlt.* IV. 510/1 Withoute eny remevement to be hadde of him into the seid prison. 1439 *Ibid.* V. 29/2 The..delyverance and remevement of the said Recordes.

Remewe, obs. variant of Remove *v.*; variant of Remue *v. Obs.*

‖**Remex** (rī·meks). Pl. **remiges** (re·midʒīz). [L. *rēmex*, f. *rēmus* oar.]

†1. A rower. *Obs. rare*[−1].

1674 Petty *Disc. Dupl. Proportion* 57 If one Remex or Skuller move [a boat of]..3 inches draught 12000 feet forward in 3600 seconds: then 4 like Rowers [etc.].

2. *Ornith.* One of the principal feathers of a bird's wing, by which it is sustained and carried forward in flight; a wing-quill. Chiefly *pl.*

1767 G. White *Selborne* xii, Peculiar crimson tags..at the ends of five of the short remiges. 1797 *Encycl. Brit.* (ed. 3) XIII. 505/2 The primary and secondary wing-feathers are called *remiges*. 1874 Coues *Birds N. W.* 269 The wings.. have but six remiges, in addition to the ten primaries. 1887 *Athenæum* 16 Apr. 517/3 The absence..of the fifth cubital remex, its coverts only being developed.

Remeynant, variant of Remainant *Obs.*

Remiform (re·mifǫɹm), *a. rare*[−0]. [f. L. *rēmus* oar.] Shaped like an oar.

1860 Worcester (citing Smart, but app. by mistake for *reniform*): hence in later Dicts.

†**Re·migable**, *a. Obs. rare*[−1]. [f. L. *rēmigāre*: see next and -able.] That one may row over.

1685 Cotton tr. *Montaigne* xxx. (1869) 167 Where steril remigable marshes, now Feed neighb'ring cities, and admit the plough.

Re·migate, *v. rare.* [f. ppl. stem of L. *rēmigāre*, f. *rēmex* Remex.] *intr.* To row.

1623 Cockeram, *Remigate*, to row, or row backe. 1873 Leland *Egypt. Sketch Bk.* 260 The rascally darkeys..declined 'tracking' (which is pulling), or remigating (which is rowing).

Remiga·tion. *rare.* [ad. L. *rēmigātiōn-em*: see prec. and -ation.] The action of rowing.

Erroneously defined by Cockeram and Blount, through association of the initial letters with the prefix *re-*.

1623 Cockeram, *Remigation*, a rowing backe. 1656 Blount *Glossogr.*, *Remigation*, a rowing or sailing back again. 1842 *Blackw. Mag.* LII. 726 A man, versed in Latin and Greek, is not, therefore, acquainted with the mechanic laws of remigation or of shipbuilding.

Remi·gial, *a. rare.* [f. L. *rēmigi-um* rowing, or (in mod. use) f. *remig-es* (see Remex) + -(i)al.] Serving to propel; now *Ornith.*, of or pertaining to the remiges of a bird's wing.

1592 R. D. *Hypnerotomachia* 21 His hands tooke fast hould upon the remigiall bones of the Eagles pinions. 1879 Newton in *Encycl. Brit.* X. 712/1 In this the remigial streamers do not lose their barbs.

†**Remigrable**. *Obs. rare*[−1]. [See next and -able.] Capable of changing back again.

1669 W. Simpson *Hydrol. Chym.* 255 They themselves are yet remigrable into a more simple element.

Remigrate (re·migreˈt, rīmai·greˈt), *v.* [orig. (with stress *re·migrate*) f. ppl. stem of L. *remigrāre*; in later use f. Re- 5 a + Migrate *v.*]

†1. *intr.* To change back again. *Obs.*

1601 Chester *Love's Mart.*, etc. (1878) 177 Ought into nought can neuer remigrate. 1651 Biggs *New Disp.* ¶ 288 Whatsoever that is truly vital hath once degenerated .. never remigrates again from the winter of its privation. 1680 Boyle *Scept. Chem.* II. 126 The rest, which is incomparably the greater part of the Liquor, will remigrate into Phlegm.

2. To migrate again or back.

1623 Cockeram, *Remigrate*, to returne vnto his first dwelling. 1790 Bewick *Hist. Quadrup.* 104 In autumn, the Deer, with the fawns bred during the summer, remigrate northward. 1802 Montagu *Ornith. Dict.* (1831) 523 The Turtle[dove]..re-migrates the beginning of September. 1893 F. Adams *New Egypt* 40 It is not till..a sultan re-migrated from Tunis to the East, that Egypt once more found herself the seat of empire.

Remigra·tion. [See prec. and Migration.] The action of remigrating; return.

1608 Willet *Hexapla Exod.* 35 The Pythagoreans and Platonists..dreame of the remigration and returne of the soule to the bodie. a1676 Hale *Prim. Orig. Man.* II. x. (1677) 233 There was a Return of the Jews under Cyrus, which continued in Partial Remigrations for some time after. 1759 B. Martin *Nat. Hist. Eng.* I. 170 *note*, The Time of their Remigration is soon after Harvest. 1859 Darwin *Orig. Spec.* xii. (1878) 331 The first migration when the cold came on, and the re-migration on the returning warmth.

Remile, variant of Rimel *Obs.*

Re-mi·mic, *v.* [Re- 5 a.] To mimic again.

1856 De Quincey *Confess.* 98 The scene in the poem, that had been originally mimicked by the poet from the sky, was here re-mimicked and rehearsed to the life.

Remind (rĭmai·nd), *v.* Also 7 re-mind. [f. Re- 5 a + Mind *v.*]

1. *trans.* To recall (a thing) to one's own mind; to remember, recollect. Now *rare* or *Obs.*

1645 Wither *Vox Pacif.* 189 Let him re-minde, what Attributes were given. 1675 R. Burthogge *Causa Dei* 194 Whosoever seriously Reminds the Circumstance of Time wherein the Apostle wrote .. will easily agree that [etc.]. 1706 Watts *Horæ Lyr.* II. *Victory of Poles over Osman*, This the fierce Saracen wore, (for, when a boy, I was their captive, and remind their dress). 1788 Shirrefs *Poems* (1790) 167 Ye'll now remind the happy show'r o' rain. 1826 Anderson *Poems* 36 (E. D. D.), Their merry homefair I remind. 1859 Bartlett *Dict. Amer.*, *To Remind*, for remember; as 'the company will please remind'. A New York vulgarism.

†b. To bring to mind, to recall to another's mind. *Obs. rare.*

1647 N. Bacon *Disc. Govt. Eng.* I. lvii. (1739) 104 The issue whereof may remind, that too much countersecurity from the King to the people, is like so many Covenants in Marriage. 1669 Earl Orrery *Black Prince* III, O! do not wound me by reminding Things Which rather Trouble than Repentance brings.

2. To put (one) in mind *of* something. (Also *ellipt.* with omission of personal obj.)

1660 Jer. Taylor *Duct. Dubit.* I. i. rule 1 § 16 It hath no other force upon the Conscience but that it re-minds us of a special obligation to thankfulness. 1675 R. Burthogge *Causa Dei* 91 This Re-minds me of the second thing which I propounded to be evinced. 1697 J. Sergeant *Solid Philos.* Cij, By re-minding them often of such Important Truths. 1751 Eliza Heywood *Betsy Thoughtless* II. 39, I must intreat you will give me leave to remind you of the consequences. 1791 Mrs. Radcliffe *Rom. Forest* ix, You do well to remind me of this. 1847 Marryat *Childr. N. Forest* xi, They would always have reminded me of such a melancholy accident. 1884 F. M. Crawford *Rom. Singer* I. 19 It reminds me of him and his ways.
ellipt. 1887 *Pall Mall G.* 11 Jan. 14/1 Many of the names remind of celebrated episodes. 1887 E. Johnson *Antiqua Mater* 260 Little but the mere name Christus to remind of the current beliefs of Judaism.

b. Const. with *inf.* or obj. clause.

1662 H. More *Philos. Writ.* Pref. Gen. (1712) 5 That the High Priest .. might be re-minded not to do..any thing contrary to the laws thereof. 1670 H. Stubbe *Reply Def. Roy. Soc.* (1671) 14, I must remind this Adversary that the person I designed to accompany..was a Carmelite. 1675 Earl Essex *Lett.* (1770) 206, I must also again remind you to advise Mr. Harbord to go more plainly to work. 1741–2 Gray *Agrippina* Wks. 1884 I. 107, I might remind my mistress that her nod Can rouse eight hardy legions. 1820 Shelley *Œd. Tyr.* II. i. 78 Allow me to remind you, grass is green. 1867 Dickens *Lett.* (1880) II. 287 The time of year reminds me how the months have gone. 1875 Jowett *Plato* (ed. 2) IV. 408 We may be reminded that in nature there is a centripetal as well as a centrifugal force.

Hence **Remi·ndal**, the act of reminding.

1883–8 Bp. Walsham How *Comm. N. T.* (S. P. C. K.) Matt. xxii. 3 The remindal and summons to the feast were made by John the Baptist.

Reminder (rĭmai·ndəɹ). [f. prec. + -er[1].] Something which reminds, or is intended to remind, one; mention made for the purpose of reminding.

1653 H. More *Antid. Ath.* I. v. § 2 There is an active and actuall Knowledge in a man, of which these outward Objects are rather the re-minders then the first Begetters or Implanters. 1831 Arnold in Stanley *Life* (1844) I. vi. 270, I know it is good to have these sobering reminders. 1838 Dickens *Lett.* (1880) I. 11 Your .. reminder of the subject of a pleasant conversation. 1880 Meredith *Tragic Com.* (1881) 211 Time passed, whole days: the tender reminder had no effect on him!

b. *Path.* in *pl.* Secondary syphilitic symptoms.

1897 *Allbutt's Syst. Med.* II. 260 They escape the class of phenomena grouped as 'reminders' (the intermediate stage) and are to all appearance cured. 1897 J. Hutchinson in *Arch. Surg.* VIII. 230 In 1880 a mild attack of syphilis occurred, not, however, followed by reminders.

Remi·ndful, *a.* [f. as prec. + -ful.]

1. Mindful, retaining the memory, *of*.

1810 Southey *Kehama* XI. i, Reminful of revengeful thoughts. a1845 Hood *Bianca's Dream* xxxii, Meanwhile, reminful of the convent bars, Bianca did not watch these signs in vain. 1891 Meredith *One of our Conq.* III. x. 209 He was in some amazement at himself, reminful of the different nature of our restraining power [etc.].

2. Reminiscent, reviving the memory, *of*.

1864 R. A. Arnold *Cotton Fam.* 85 The dropping patter so reminful of their blameless inactivity. 1867 E. Yates *Forlorn Hope* xiv, A thousand little reminiscences..each touchingly reminful of something pleasant.

Remi·nding, *ppl. a.* [-ing[2].] That reminds. Hence **Remi·ndingly** *adv.*

1887 A. Austin *Pr. Lucifer* IV. ii, The stroke of the reminding hour when I Should from your voice be willing to depart. 1890 'Annie Thomas' *On the Children* III. i. 8 'You've forgotten',..Florence said remindingly.

†**Remi·ndless**, *a. Obs.*[−1] [-less.] Forgetful.

1657 W. Morice *Coena quasi Κοινὴ* x. 119 Those remindless persons, whom we sometimes see to go about to seek that which they carry in their hands.

†**Re·ming**, *vbl. sb. Obs.* [f. Reme *v.*[1] + -ing[1].] Calling, crying, lamenting, etc.

c1200 *Trin. Coll. Hom.* 197 Þat hie ne muge heren here remenge, ne here gal. c1220 *Bestiary* 666 For here mikle reming rennande cumeð a gungling. a1400 *Pol. Rel. & L. Poems* (1903) 252 Fletus, *Anglice* Reminge. c1400 *Destr. Troy* 8511 He hade no ruthe of hor remyng, ne þe rank teris. ?a1500 *Chester Pl.* (E. E. T. S.) 448 To..putt them into great Torment, wher Reeminge, Grinninge were fervent.

Remi·ngle, *v.* [Re- 5 a.] To mingle again.

1853 C. Bronte *Villette* xxv, That slight rod of Moses could, at one waft, release and re-mingle a sea spell-parted. 1866 Felton *Anc. & Mod. Gr.* I. I. v. 76 A backward movement commenced by sea, and remingled..Greeks with those from whom they had been severed.

Reminisce (reminis), *v.* [Back-formation from next: still somewhat colloquial or jocular.]

1. *trans.* and *intr.* To recollect, remember.

1829 [J. R. Best] *Pers. & Lit. Mem.* 304 Some of my readers may reminisce—the word shall never enter my vocabulary—a political squib, let off towards the conclusion of the American war. 1896 A. Lang in *Longm. Mag.* June 219 She could not have remembered much of Keats...How do people remember anything? How do they reminisce?

2. To indulge in reminiscences.

1882 *Pall Mall G.* 8 Sept. 4 There is probably no reason why old Bohemians as well as other people should not 'reminisce'. 1892 M'Crie *Public Worship Presbyt. Scot.* i. 48 Before his wife's death, so he reminisced, he always went to church.

Reminiscence (reminisĕns). Also 6 -cens, 7 -cience. [a. F. *réminiscence* (14th c.), or ad. late L. *reminiscentia* (Tert.), f. *reminisci* to remember, f. *re-* Re- + **men-* (see Mind).]

1. The act, process, or fact, of remembering or recollecting; sometimes *spec.* the act of recovering knowledge by mental effort (cf. *recollection*).

1589 Puttenham *Eng. Poesie* III. xxv. (Arb.) 312 By long and studious obseruation rather a repetition or reminiscens naturall. 1639 N. N. tr. *Du Bosq's Compl. Woman* II. 84 There are those who teach on Plato's grounds, that Inclination comes from a certain Reminiscence. 1655 Stanley *Hist. Philos.* III. (1701) 78/1 Thus is all her Learning only reminiscence, a recovery of her first knowledge. 1692 South *Serm.* (1697) I. 361 The other part of memory, called Reminiscence: which is the Retreiving of a thing, at present forgot, or but confusely remembred. 1744 Berkeley *Siris* § 315 The Peripatetics themselves distinguish between reminiscence and mere memory. 1791 Cowper *Four Ages* 23 Knows he his origin? can he ascend By reminiscence to his earliest date? 1867 Lewes *Hist. Philos.* (ed. 3) I. 291 The ingenious doctrine of the soul's reminiscence of a former apprehension of truth. 1879 Calderwood *Mind & Br.* 266 Embryology presents us with a modification of Plato's doctrine of reminiscence.

2. (Chiefly *pl.*) a. A recollection or remembrance, as a mental fact.

1813 Shelley *Q. Mab* VII. 52 Vague dreams have rolled, And varied reminiscences have waked. 1836 J. Gilbert *Chr. Atonem.* i. (1852) 5 The passive indolence which .. easily mistakes its mere reminiscences for the result of inquiry. 1887 Lowell *Democr.* 94 Memory which at my time of life is gradually becoming one of her own reminiscences.

b. A recollection or remembrance of some past fact or experience related to others; freq. (in *pl.*), the collective memories or experiences of a person put into literary form.

1811 L. M. Hawkins *C'tess & Gertr.* I. 96 Till his feelings were ascertained...his friends were not wanting in these reminiscences. 1843 Prescott *Mexico* (1850) I. 248 As he listened to these reminiscences of the sailors. 1868 Farrar *Seekers* Introd. 3 Contemporary reminiscences of that day of desperate disaster.

3. An expression, feature, fact, etc., which recalls something else.

1860 Pusey *Min. Proph.* 153 Other reminiscences of the words of Amos are only a part of the harmony of Scripture. 1873 Mivart *Elem. Anat.* vi. 229 There is a singular and striking reminiscence of vertebræ in the three arches of the bony skull. 1876 Humphreys *Coin-coll. Man.* xxvi. 396 [The Saturnalia] of which the vivid reminiscence still exists in the modern Carnival.

Hence **Remini·scence** *v.*, to 'reminisce'; **Remini·scenceful** *a.*; **Remini·scencer**.

1888 Frith *Autobiog.* III. iii. 30 The..reminiscencer who is fond of talking of matters that can be of no interest to anyone but himself. 1889 *Edin. Rev.* Jan. 64 The reflective reminiscenceful character common to all the writings of the Apocrypha. 1890 Sara J. Duncan *Social Depart.* 327 Orthodocia was delightful when she reminiscenced.

†**Remini·scency**. *Obs.* [See prec. and -ency.] The faculty of reminiscence.

1655–87 H. More *App. Antid.* (1712) 205 If you'll say that Memory is in the Brain, but Reminiscency in the Conarion [etc.]. 1666 S. Parker *Free & Impart. Censure* (1667) 38 In his Phædo, he fairly argues for the Souls Immortality from its presupposed Reminiscency. 1732 *Hist. Litteraria* IV. 206 The Rules of Reminiscency require, that [etc.].

Remini·scent, *sb.* [f. as next.] A relater or writer of reminiscences.

1822 C. Butler *Reminisc.* (ed. 3) I. 4 No one ever discovered a passion for literature at an earlier hour in his life than the Reminiscent. 1837 *Blackw. Mag.* XLII. 76 This reminiscent is not a good converser. 1869 Bagehot *Lit. Stud.* (1879) II. 331 It is the excellence of a reminiscent to have a few good stories.

Reminiscent (reminisĕnt), *a.* [f. L. *reminiscent-em*, pres. pple. of *reminisci*: see Reminiscence.]

1. Pertaining to, characterized by, reminiscence.

1765 *Universal Mag.* XXXVII. 356/2 Men, in their sentient, imaginative, and reminiscent part,..are..subject to diseases. 1837 Southey *Doctor* cxxix. (1848) 327 The Biographer, or Historian,..or rather the reminiscent relator of circumstances. 1855 Bagehot *Lit. Stud.* (1879) I. 1 The evident fiction of reminiscent age—striving and failing to remember. 1890 'R. Boldrewood' *Miner's Right* (1899) 146/2 The most careful reminiscent accuracy.

b. Having reminiscence *of* something.

1830 *Fraser's Mag.* I. 151 A more perfect state of being—a state of which it is reminiscent and anticipant. 1836–7 Sir W. Hamilton *Metaph.* xxxiv. (1859) II. 278 Some other state of existence, of which we have been previously conscious and are now reminiscent.

2. Of the nature of reminiscence or reminiscences.

1863 *Cornh. Mag.* VII. 391 Some of the charms of youth reminiscent in the grey dignity of acknowledged age. 1883 J. Burroughs in *Century Mag.* Nov. 103/2 There is..a pensive, reminiscent feeling in the air itself. 1892 *Independent* 25 Nov. 220/2 The talk on the way was reminiscent.

3. Evoking a reminiscence *of* a person or thing.

1880 *Academy* 13 Nov. 352 He is strangely reminiscent of Millais. 1891 *Speaker* 2 May 527/2 The verse..is.. reminiscent of the style of Rowe.

Hence **Remini·scently** *adv.*

1891 Cotes *2 Girls on a Barge* 23 'The Cadet', quoth Girton, reminiscently, 'did that rather well.'

Reminisce·ntial, *a.* [f. Reminiscence: cf. *essential*.] Of the nature of, pertaining to, reminiscence; of a reminiscent character.

1646 Sir T. Browne *Pseud. Ep.* Pref. A iij, Would Truth dispense, we could be content, with Plato,..that Intellectuall acquisition were but Reminiscentiall evocation. 1682 — *Chr. Mor.* III. § 10 Trust not too much unto suggestions from reminiscential Amulets, or artificial Memorandums. 1853 Lowell *Moosehead Jrnl.* Pr. Wks. 1890 I. 1 At the sound of the name, no reminiscential atoms..stirred and marshalled in my brain. 1869 Mrs. H. Wood *Roland Yorke* III. 70 Just as Roland Yorke had seen them in his reminiscential visions. 1891 W. C. Hudson *Man with a Thumb* i. 7 As the old man indulged his reminiscential vein.

Hence **Reminisce·ntially** *adv.* (In recent Dicts.)

†**Remini·scion**. *Obs. rare.* [irreg. f. L. *reminiscī* + -ion.] Reminiscence.

1607 Chapman *Bussy d'Ambois* Plays 1873 II. 85 This strange vision..stir[s] my thoughts With reminiscion of the Spirits promise. 1688 R. Holme *Armoury* II. 415/2 Reminiscion is the remembring a thing out of mind.

Remini·scitory, *a. rare*[−1]. [f. as prec. + -itory.] Of the nature of reminiscence.

1827 Lytton *Pelham* lxxiii, I still bore a reminiscitory spite against Mr. Job Jonson.

Remi·nt (rī-), *v.* [Re- 5 a.] To mint again.

1823 De Quincey *Lett. to Yng. Man* Wks. 1860 XIV. 84 In other cases, when there happen to exist double expressions for the same notion, he called in and reminted them as it were. 1896 Sir R. P. Edgcumbe *Pop. Fallacies Bimetallism* 121 When the western nations of Europe agree again to remint silver upon a fixed ratio.

Remiped (re·miped), *sb.* and *a.* *Zool.* [ad. F. *rémipède*, f. L. *rēmus* oar + *ped-*, *pēs* foot.] a. *sb.* One of an order of coleopterous insects having tarsi adapted for swimming (Brande *Dict. Sci.* 1842); also, a crustacean of the genus *Remipes* (Webster 1847). b. *adj.* Having feet that are oar-shaped, or used as oars (Webster 1864).

So **Re·mipede** *sb.*

1826 Kirby & Sp. *Entomol.* xxix. III. 170, I have some suspicion that..the remipedes, *Notonecta*, *Sigara*, &c. may find their prototypes among the *Crustacea*.

†**Remi·se**, *sb.*[1] *Obs.* Also 5 **remysse**, 7 **remyse**. [a. F. (in early use prob. AF.) *remise*, vbl. sb. f. *remettre* to remit: cf. late L. *remissa* remission (of sins).]

1. *Law.* A transfer of property.

1473 *Rolls of Parlt.* VI. 75/1 Any Graunte or Grauntes, Ratifications, Confirmations, Remysse or Releases to hym ..made. 1485 *Ibid.* 342/2 Annexions, Remises, Releases or Pardones, to theym..made or had. 1766 Blackstone *Comm.* II. App. iv. § 3. p. xv, This recognition, remise, quit-claim, warranty, fine, and agreement.

2. A remission or cessation of sickness. *rare*[−1].

1603 Florio *Montaigne* III. xiii. 653, I have notwithstanding some remyses or intermissions yet.

3. ?Return, recompense.

a1578 Lindesay (Pitscottie) *Chron. Scot.* (S. T. S.) I. 136 We come now..to thai [= thy] maiestie to gett support, promiss and richt remise [*v.r.* riche revenues] thairfoir.

4. The act of remitting money; a remittance.

1667 Temple *Let.* Wks. 1731 II. 39 They have remitted by this Ordinary to his Excellency a hundred and thirty thousand Crowns, which is the third Remise of about that Sum. 1682 Scarlett *Exchanges* 16 Its necessary that the Remise be confirmed by the following Post. 1689 *Myst. Iniq.* 38 In order whereunto great Remises of Mony were already ordered him from the French Court.

‖**Remise** (rəmīz), *sb.*[2] [F.; see prec.]

1. A house or shelter for a carriage; a coach-house.

1698 W. King tr. *Sorbière's Journ. Lond.* 4 Divers of the Citizens Houses, have Port-cochezs to drive in a Coach, or a Cart either, and Consequently have Courts within, and mostly Remises to set them up. 1768 Sterne *Sent. Journ.* I. 62 The Remise Door. *Ibid.* 73 (*The Remise*), Mons. Dessein came up with the key of the Remise in his hand, and forthwith let us into his magazine of chaises. 1841 Lady Blessington *Idler in France* II. 135 In former days sledges were considered as indispensable in the winter *remise* of a grand seigneur in France.

b. (Ellipt. for *voiture de remise*.) A carriage hired from a livery-stable, of a better class than the ordinary hackney-carriage.

1698 M. Lister *Journ. Paris* (1699) 142 Many of the *Fiacres* or Hackneys, and all the *Remises*, have one large Glass before. 1753 A. Murphy *Gray's Inn Jrnl.* No. 45 Without the Expence of a Remise, you may visit Boileau. 1818 Lady Morgan *Autobiog.* (1859) 200 We got into our *remise*—that special French carriage which never breaks down, drawn by horses that never tire.

2. *Fencing.* A second thrust made after the first has missed and while still upon the lunge; the act of making a thrust of this kind.

1823 Roland *Art Fencing* 86 The Remise is made upon your adversary's quitting your blade to make a feint as a return too soon after having parried your attack. 1861 Chapman *Review Art Fencing* I. 20 The remise is provoked by opportunities afforded in the adversary's play, and in that respect differs essentially from the Reprise, a redoubling of the Attack.

3. In some card-games, as quadrille and reversis: a. (See quot. 1830.) b. A stake in the pool.

1830 'Eidrah Trebor' *Hoyle made familiar* 36 Remise is when they who stand the game do not make more tricks than they who defend the pool, and then they lose by remise. *Ibid.* 40 Should..there be three remises, or stakes, in the pools, then it is at the option of any player to take a card or not. 1850 *Hand-bk. Games* (Bohn) 309 One of the players making the reversis..would then prevent your having the remises out of the pool.

†**Remise**, *a. Obs.*[−1] [a. F. *remis(e*, pa. pple. of *remettre*: see next.] Delayed, postponed.

c1510 Barclay *Mirr. Gd. Manners* (1570) B v, In sentence remise is lesser iniury, Then in headling sentence pronounced hastely.

Remise (rĭmai·z), *v.*[1] Also 5–6 remyse. [f. F. *remis(e*, pa. pple. of *remettre*:—L. *remittĕre* to Remit. Cf. Remiss *v.*]

†1. *trans.* To put back again *in* or *into* a place, state, etc.; to replace; to convert again *into*; to send back *to* a place. *Obs.* (freq. in Caxton).

1481 Caxton *Godfrey* Prol. 1 Tadresse and remyse theym in theyr auncyent Fraunchyses and lyberte. 1485 — *Chas. Gt.* 181 Floripes remysed the relyques in the coffret. c1500 *Melusine* xxvi. 207, I remyse hym in your possession. 1512 *Helyas* in Thoms *Prose Rom.* (1828) III. 76 They saw the king and the quene remised and set in good love and unite of hert togither. *Ibid.* 82 To five of them he remised the chaynes about theyr neckes. 1598 Sylvester *Du Bartas* I. ii. 164 Yet think not that this Too-too-much remises Our thoughts to noughts; it but the Form disguises. 1623 Bingham *Xenophon* 1 His Mother made intercession for him, set him at libertie, and remised him to his gouernment.

†b. To bring *together* again; to lead back again. *Obs. rare.*

c1500 *Melusine* 134 The king..remysed hys folke togidre, and made to withdraw them al the lytil pas. *Ibid.* 137 He full wel remysed hys folke into the tounne.

2. *Law.* To give up, surrender, make over to another, release (any right, property, etc.).

1487 *Rolls of Parlt.* VI. 390 Ye remysed and relessed..all the residue of the said Fee Ferme. 1491 *Act 7 Hen. VII*, c. 18 Your seid suppliant..them remised and quite claymed ..unto the seid late pretended Kyng. 1612 in *O'Flaherty's West Connaught* (1846) 258 Wee..have remised, released, and .. quitt claimed .. all that our right.., interest, [etc.]. 1655 Fuller *Waltham Abb.* 10 Peter Duke of Savoy remised and quit-claimed from him and his Heirs..the right and claim he had. 1766 Blackstone *Comm.* II. xx. 324 The words generally used therein are 'remised, released, and for ever quit-claimed'. 1841 *Penny Cycl.* XIX. 375/2 The operative words of release are remise, release, renounce, and for ever quit claim.

†3. To remit or send (a letter or reply). *Obs.*

1633 T. Stafford *Pac. Hib.* I. viii. 62 Remising therefore onely this Answer, that he despised their Forces. *Ibid.* II. vi. 164 All which may appeare by a Letter remised from the said Iames unto him.

Remi·se, *v.*[2] *Fencing.* [f. Remise *sb.*[2] 2.] *intr.* To make a remise.

1889 *Fencing* (Badminton Libr.) 96 It is wrong to remise on a riposte made by a disengagement in the low line.

†**Remi·ss**, *sb. Obs.*[−1] [Cf. Remise *sb.*[1]] Relaxation. (But perh. an error for *remissnes*.)

1589 Puttenham *Eng. Poesie* I. xix. 32 Such manner of men as by negligence of Magistrates and remisses of lawes euery countrie breedeth great store of.

Remiss (rĭmi·s), *a.* Forms: 5–6 **remys**, **-ysse**, (6 **-yshe**), 5–7 **remisse**, (6 **-is**, **-isshe**, 7 **-ish**), 6– **remiss**. [ad. L. *remiss-us*, pa. pple. of *remittĕre* to Remit.]

†1. a. Dissolved, liquid. *Obs. rare.*

c1420 *Pallad. on Husb.* I. 1126 White wax, hard picche, remysse [L. *remissum*] ammonyake—This iij commyxt therefore is good to take. Or thus: ammoniak remysse and figis.

†b. *Med.* Weakened in consistency or colour; dilute. *Obs.*

?a1412 Lydg. *Two Merch.* 323 His vryne was remys, attenuat, By resoun gendryd of frigidite. 1547 Boorde *Brev. Health* lxxiii. 25 b, An uryne that is pale of colour..yf it be remyshe, then there is great coldnes in the body. 1625 Hart *Anat. Ur.* II. iv. 69 The vrine became of a remisse and light colour, such as it was wont to be.

†c. Of sounds: Weak, soft, low. *Obs.*

1530 Palsgr. Introd. 16 They gyve..unto theyr consonantes but a sleight and remisshe sounde. 1650 Bulwer *Anthropomet.* 203 Instruments which have a more acute or treble sound when the strings are stretched, and a lower and more remiss when they are loosened. 1653 R. Sanders *Physiogn.* 246 The voice acute and smooth, or remiss, with a little trembling.

†d. Of taste: Faint, slight. *Obs. rare*[−1].

1655 Culpepper, etc. *Riverius* v. iii. 126 The Taste..is lessened when it scarce perceiveth remiss savors and strong savors but a little.

2. Of persons: Slack in the discharge of a task or duty; careless, negligent.

c1450 tr. *De Imitatione* I. xxiii. 20 Þou shalt gretly sorwe þat þou hast be so remysse [L. *remissus*] & so negligent. 1472–5 *Rolls of Parlt.* VI. 155/2 If any Custumer or Comptrollour of any Porte, be necligent or remisse in noon pakkyng of the same Clothes. c1510 Barclay *Mirr. Gd. Manners* (1570) D ij, If thou be in office..Be not more remis, do not thy duetie lesse. 1567–8 *Reg. Privy Council Scot.* I. 610 Certifeing the personis..that beis fund remysse or negligent in the premissis. 1602 Warner *Alb. Eng.* XII. lxxi. 296 As well as too remisse in choyce, we may be too precise. 1660 Young *Table of Statutes* 44 Officers remisse to collect rates. 1696 Bentley *Boyle Lect.* ix. (1724) 346 Who can tell, if..they might not in long tract of time have grown remiss in the duties..of Religion? 1776 C. Lee in Sparks *Corr. Amer. Rev.* (1853) I. 158 Though I confess I am naturally remiss, I have not neglected my duty in this point. 1838 Thirlwall *Greece* IV. 55 The satrap..had become as remiss as before in making the stipulated payments. 1893 *Academy* 10 June 497/1 He was a very remiss correspondent.

b. Of conduct, actions, etc.: Characterized by carelessness, negligence, or inattention.

1502 Atkynson tr. *De Imitatione* I. xxiii. 173 Than shalte thou repent full sore of thy remysse and neclygent lyfe. 1509 Barclay *Shyp of Folys* 206 b, Idylnes By wayes remys and dranynge neglygence Of all other synne is rote. 1656 Earl Monm. tr. *Boccalini's Advts. fr. Parnass.* I. xxxviii. (1674) 50, I, in the beginning of my Principality seemed to be of a remiss spirit, and totally incapable of the great affairs of State. 1675 Traherne *Chr. Ethics* 169 To exert almighty power in a remiss and lazy manner, is infinitely base and dishonourable. 1712 Addison *Spect.* No. 471 ¶ 6 Hope..keeps the Mind awake in her most Remiss and Indolent Hours. 1817 Jas. Mill *Brit. India* II. v. viii. 663 [He] was appointed, under the..expectation that he would supply what had been remiss in the conduct of his predecessor. 1886 *Illustr. Lond. News* 20 Feb. 194/2 It was remiss in Aunt Louisa not to have offered to be her chaperon.

†c. Idle; free from labour. *Obs. rare*[−1].

1566 Adlington *Apuleius* 45 With great lamentation was ordained a remisse time for that day.

3. Characterized by a lack of strictness or proper restraint; lax, loose. ?*Obs.*

c1450 tr. *De Imitatione* I. xxv. 37 He þat euermore sekiþ þo þinges þat are most laxe and most remisse, shal euer be in anguissh. 1540–1 Elyot *Image Gov.* Pref., By the lasciuiouse and remisse educacion of Varius Heliogabalus, he grewe to be a person moste monstruouse in liuyng. 1583 Stubbes *Anat. Abus.* I. (1879) 76 This ouer great leuitie and remisse libertie in the education of youthe. 1624 in Rushw. *Hist. Coll.* (1659) I. 160 So dangerous it is for Princes by a remiss comportment, to give growth to the least Error. 1651–3 Jer. Taylor *Serm. for Year* (1678) 224 A seldom restraint, —a remiss discipline. 1751 Johnson *Rambler* No. 157 ¶ 3 Many among my fellow-students took the opportunity of a more remiss discipline to gratify their passions.

†b. Not strict or severe in punishing; lenient.

1568 Grafton *Chron.* II. 927 They were gentle and remisse to a great number, and specially to such as offended by cohercion and feare. 1613 *Edict agst. Priv. Combats* title-p., Straitly charging all officers and other His Majestie's subjects to use no conniuencie, or remisse proceedings toward such offenders. 1651 N. Bacon *Disc. Govt. Eng.* II. xxii. (1739) 102 Coming in by the people's favour, he was obliged to be rather remiss than rigorous.

4. Free from vehemence or violence; also, defective or lacking in force or energy.

1550 T. Nycolls *Thucidides* 14 The one is more vehemente for to moue mens hartes, the other more remys and gentle. 1586 B. Young *Guazzo's Civ. Conv.* IV. 189 Euen so after meate,..our will prone to wickednesse, is become more remisse and temperate. 1644 Bulwer *Chiron.* 32 The Hand restrained and kept in is an argument of modesty..sutable to a milde and remisse declamation. 1695 Woodward *Nat. Hist. Earth* IV. (1723) 210 Its Motion becomes more languid and remiss. 1707 Floyer *Physic. Pulse-Watch* 364 A remiss Pulse, is when it is small and slow. 1752 Hume *Ess. & Treat.* (1777) I. 179 The passion must neither be too violent nor too remiss. 1837 Sir W. Hamilton *Metaph.* xlv. (1870) II. 493 Pain or dissatisfaction experienced, when the energy elicited is either inordinately vehement or too remiss.

†b. Not intense or strong; moderate, mild. *Obs.* (common in 17th c., esp. of heat and cold).

1573 P. More *Almanack* E vj, But all euills shall seeme more remisse and tolerable than they were the laste yere. 1610 Holland *Camden's Brit.* I. 2 The cold with us is much more remisse than in some parts of France and Italie. 1654 H. L'Estrange *Chas. I* (1655) 123 The King fell sick of the Small-Pocks, but the malignity was very remisse, and gentle. 1686 Goad *Celest. Bodies* I. ix. 28 Her Warmth is so remiss and slack, that she seemeth to befriend a Cold Influence.

†c. Moderate, low, slight (degree). *Obs.*

1620 T. Granger *Div. Logike* 104 Note that these middles haue contrariety in them in the remisse, or remote degree. 1657 Austen *Fruit Trees* II. 18 Distinct and severall works of Nature, in moderate and remisse degrees, are all promoted at the same time. 1670 W. Simpson *Hydrol. Ess.* 104 Retaining the same..properties in a remiss degree.

†5. Diminished in tension; slack, loose, relaxed.

1623 Jas. I in Rushw. *Hist. Coll.* (1659) I. 115 Not alwayes to use his spurs and keep strait the rein, but sometimes to use the spurs and suffer the reins more remiss. 1644 Bulwer *Chiron.* 37 The turned up Hand, the Thumbe bent in, and the other Fingers remisse. 1667 Milton *P. L.* VI. 418 What availes Valour or strength,..quelld with pain Which all subdues, and makes remiss the hands Of Mightiest.

Remiss (rĭmi·s), *v. rare.* [f. L. *remiss-*, ppl. stem of *remittĕre* to Remit; cf. Remise *v.*[1]] *trans.*

†1. *trans.* To remit; to resolve or dissolve; to mitigate; to let go, pass over. *Obs.*

c1500 *Melusine* 335 Al that ye shal doo with good wyll I remysse it to your penaunce. 1541 R. Copland *Galyen's Terap.* H hij b, It behoueth asmoche to intende & augment the vertue of the said medycament, as it shulde be remyssed & dymynysshed in yᵉ depth of the body. 1573 P. More *Almanack* F j b, Oftentymes the drought shall be remyssed and tempered with shoures. 1605 Daniel *Philotas* IV. ii, Words, if they proceed of leuity Are to be skornd,..or of injury To be remiss'd or vnacknowledged. 1656 S. H. *Gold. Law* 103 Once, yea twice have I spoken, but for future wil be wiser, and so compress and remiss it.

†2. To assign, adjudge. *Obs. rare*[−1].

1525 Ld. Berners *Froiss.* II. ccix. [ccv.] 643 The herytage was remyssed and iudged into the handes and possessyon of the Erle of Brayne.

†3. To send back (an answer). *Obs. rare*[−1].

1633 Stafford *Pac. Hib.* I. xix. 113 Answere was remissed by the President, that the State was well perswaded of his loyaltie.

4. *Law.* = Remise *v.*[1] 2.

1809 R. Langford *Introd. Trade* 108, I, A. B... having remissed, released, and for ever quit claim to C. D... of all ..debts, dues, duties.

Hence †**Remi·ssable** *a.*, remissible. *Obs.*[−1]

a1550 *Image Hypocr.* in *Skelton's Wks.* (1843) II. 425/1 It is..synne..Ageynst the Holy Gost, That is not remissable.

†**Remi·ssal**. *Obs. rare.* Forms: 5 **remyssaylle**, (-**moss**-), 6 **-aile**, **remissaile**, 7 **remissal**. [a. AF. **remissaille*: see prec. and -al.] *pl.* That which is left over; remains; *esp.* the remains of a meal.

1387–8 T. Usk *Test. Love* Prol. (Skeat) l. 108 The almoigner, that hath drawe up in the cloth al the remissailes, as trenchours, and the relief, to bere to the almesse. c1430 *Stans Puer* 48 Laade nat thy trenchour withe many remyssailes. c1444 Lydg. in *Pol. Poems* (Rolls) II. 220 The poore man stant hungry at the gate, Of remossaylles he wold be partable. a1618 Raleigh *Rem.* (1644) 114 Death hath..left you now to be Lees, and remissalls of your wearyish and dying dayes.

Remi·ssful, *a. rare.* [f. Remiss *v.* or *a.*]

†1. Full of remission; merciful. *Obs. rare*[−1].

1603 Drayton *Bar. Wars* I. xi, As though the heauens, in their remissfull doome, Tooke those best lou'd, from worser daies to come.

2. Full of remissness; careless, negligent.

1836 *Tait's Mag.* III. 569 Taking up a vial of physic from the table, he tapped his remissful patient on the shoulder. 1892 *Field* 3 Dec. 880/1 The outlay for road repair under such remissful management.

Remissibi·lity. [See next and -ity.] The state or condition of being remissible.

1698 Norris *Pract. Disc.* IV. 146 Those places of Scripture ..must and ought to be understood not of Actual Remission ..but of a Remissibility or State of Pardon. 1729 Stackhouse *Body Divin.* IV. i. § 2 (1776) II. 423 That which is previous to repentance consists in a bare remissibility of sin. 1780 Bentham *Princ. Legisl.* xvii. § 25 The eleventh and last of all the properties that seem to be requisite in a lot of punishment is that of remissibility.

Remissible (rĭmi·sib'l), *a.* [a. F. *rémissible* (15th c.), or ad. L. *remissibilis*; see Remiss *v.* and -ible.] Capable or admitting of remission; that may be remitted.

1577 Fulke *Answ. True Christian* 90 Thou wouldest vouche safe to pardon, and to make it remissible. a1594 R. Greenham *Wks.* (1599) 70 If you turne to the Lord.. your sin is remissible. 1627–77 Feltham *Resolves* II. ix. 177 Some sins..they allow..to be such as deserue Punishment, although..remissible. a1703 Burkitt *On N. T.* Heb. ix. 22 Though man had repented,..yet his sins could not have been remitted, had not this blood made it remissible. 1875 Poste *Gaius* III. (ed. 2) 452 An obligation remissible by the private individual whose primary rights are violated.

Hence **Remi·ssibleness**, remissibility.

a1658 O. Sedgwick (*title*), The Anatomy of secret Sins, [etc.],..Together with the remissibleness of all sin.

Remission (rĭmi·ʃən). Also 4 **remis(s)iun**, 4–6 **remissioun**, **-yssio(u)n**, 5–6 **-issyon**, **-ys(s)yon**, etc. [a. OF. *remission*, ad. L. *remissiōn-em*, n. of action f. *remittĕre* to Remit. The order in which the senses appear in English differs widely from their natural development: cf. the note to Remit *v.*]

1. Forgiveness or pardon *of* sins (cf. 2) or other offences.

a1225 *Ancr. R.* 346 In remission, & in uorȝiuenesse of alle þine sunnen. a1300 *Cursor M.* 20048 Þai sal haue..crist aun beniscun, And o þair sin remisiun. c1380 Wyclif *Sel. Wks.* II. 11 And Joon cam..preching þe baptism of penaunce in remission of synnes. 1447 Bokenham *Seyntys* (Roxb.) 7 Of myn old and newe transgressyoun That I may haue a plener remyssyoun. 1483 Caxton *Cato* 5 Of the sacryfyse that thauncyentes made to god for to haue remyssion of theyr synnes. 1560 Daus tr. *Sleidane's Comm.* 4 If he repent of his owne accorde, and desyre remission of his offence. 1651 Hobbes *Leviath.* III. xxxviii. 245 In .. Scripture, Remission of Sinne, and Salvation from Death and Misery, is the same thing. 1788 Gibbon *Decl. & F.* xlix. V. 123 The gift which he had conferred on the Roman pontiff for the remission of his sins. 1846 Browning *Lett.* (1899) II. 212 As naughty children punished by mistake are promised a remission of next offence. 1884 *Catholic Dict.* (1885) 5/1 Absolution from Sin is a remission of sin which the priest.. makes in the Sacrament of Penance.

2. (Without *of*.) Forgiveness or pardon granted for sins or offences against divine law; the cancelling of, or deliverance from, the guilt and penalties of sin; †also, power of obtaining such pardon.

c1325 *Chron. Eng.* 634 in Ritson *Metr. Rom.* II. 296 The spere That Charlemayne was wonet to bere To-fore the holy legioun, That is of gret remissioun. 1362 Langl. *P. Pl.* A. xi. 277 A robbere hadde remission raþere þanne þei alle. c1430 Lydg. *Min. Poems* (Percy Soc.) 239 O blissed Jhesu! do remissioun To alle that axe mercy on ther kne! 1500–20 Dunbar *Poems* viii. 28 Pray now for him .. Unto the Lord ..To gif him mercie and remissioun. 1579 Lyly *Euphues* (Arb.) 174 Remember..how he sweat water and bloud for thy remission. 1614 Raleigh *Hist. World* II. (1634) 250 Ingratitude and rebellion after his so many benefits, so many remissions, so many miracles wrought. 1685 Baxter *Paraphr. N. T.* Acts ii. 39 The Messiah with his Grace of Remission, and the Spirit, is promised. 1715 De Foe *Fam. Instruct.* (1841) I. 25 He gives repentance and remission.

b. Pardon for a political, legal, or other offence. Now only *Hist.*

1429 *Pol. Poems* (Rolls) II. 145 Be rightful juge,.. Thy right ay sugre with remyssioun. 1535 Lyndesay *Satyre* 4093 But doubt, ȝe salbe hangit, But mercie or remissioun. 1568 Grafton *Chron.* II. 863 Sir Thomas Broughton..was at hande..vtterly dispairing of pardon and remission. 1591 Shaks. *Two Gent.* I. ii. 65 My pennance is, to call Lucetta backe And aske remission, for my folly past. 1613 Purchas *Pilgrimage* VIII. xii. 671 If any were found dishonest, they were put to death without remission. 1687 A. Lovell tr. *Thevenot's Trav.* I. 95 Whosoever are taken stealing of Mastick, are without remission sent to the Galleys. 1864 Kirk *Chas. Bold* I. viii. 376 They entreated, therefore, that letters of remission might be granted to them for this fault.

†c. *Sc.* With *a* and *pl.* A formal pardon; a document conveying this. *Obs.*

1456 Sir G. Haye *Law Arms* (S. T. S.) 52 That all maner of man, that had bene before tyme banist out of Rome, suld cum agayne, and thai suld..have remissiounes. 1535 Lyndesay *Satyre* 1132, I dreid, without ȝe get ane remissioun,..The spirituall stait sall put ȝow to perditioun. 1546 *Reg. Privy Council Scot.* I. 34 The remissioun grantit to the Capitane of Dumbertane, and all his complices..sall presentlie be past throw the signet. 1609 Skene *Reg. Maj.* 158 Gif he quha is accused, alledges ane remission, he sall produce the samine in judgement.

†d. An inclination towards pardon. *Obs. rare*[−1].

1603 Shaks. *Meas. for M.* v. i. 503, I finde an apt remission in my selfe; And yet heere's one..I cannot pardon.

†3. a. Release from a debt or payment. *Obs.*

1362 Langl. *P. Pl.* A. vii. 83 To ha Reles and Remission on þat Rental I be-leeue. 1382 Wyclif *Deut.* xv. 1 To whom is owed eny thing,..he shal not mowe aȝen aske it, for ȝeer of remyssioun of the Lord it is. 1607 Shaks. *Cor.* v. ii. 90 Though I owe My Reuenge properly, my remission lies In Volcean brests. 1608 Willet *Hexapla Exod.* 838 They.. only went vp..in the seuenth yeare of remission twice.

†b. Release, liberation, deliverance, from captivity, etc.; respite. *Obs.*

1432–50 tr. *Higden* (Rolls) II. 291 From whiche victory of Abraham, somme men say the yere of Iubile to haue taken originalle, for that remission of captif men. 1582 N. T. (Rhem.) *Luke* iv. 19 To preach to the captiues remission, ..to dimisse the bruised unto remission. 1635 Pagitt *Christianogr.* I. iii. (1636) 162 For remission of soules the Patriarch graunts no Indulgences. 1761 Goldsm. *Misc. Wks.* (1837) I. 471 Some remission from the war gave them leisure to form schemes of future prosperity.

†c. Release from work or exertion. *Obs. rare.*

1382 Wyclif *1 Macc.* x. 34 Alle solempne days..be alle dais of ynmunite..and of remission, to alle Jewis that ben in my rewme. — *2 Cor.* viii. 13 Forsoth not that it be remyssioun, or slouthe, to othere,..to ȝou tribulacioun.

4. The action of remitting or giving up partially or wholly: a. of a debt, tax, etc.

1382 Wyclif *Prol. Bible* iii. 6 Also in the vij. ȝeer shal be remissioun of dette to citeseynes and kynnesmen. a1719 Addison (J.), Not only an expedition, but the remission of a duty or tax, were transmitted to posterity after this manner. 1841 Elphinstone *Hist. Ind.* II. 491 His remissions [of taxes], as far as they were carried into effect, were productive of great inequality. 1884 *Law Rep.* 9 App. Cases 624 He does not ask for any remission of any portion of his obligation.

b. of a penalty or punishment. Also *attrib.*

1736 Butler *Anal.* I. iii. Wks. 1874 I. 58 Circumstances of aggravated guilt prevent a remission of the penalties. 1741 Betterton *Eng. Stage* II. 51 Queen Mary..immediately granted..a Remission of her Father's Execution for that of Transportation. 1797 Mrs. Radcliffe *Italian* xxvi, The consequence of this confession was a remission of punishment. 1861 Pearson *Early & Mid. Ages Eng.* 177 This was an illegal remission of an important part of the penalty. 1884 *Catholic Dict.* 442/1 The indulgence..was no mere remission of canonical penance. 1893 *Daily News* 9 Mar. 6/7 He [a convict] was punished by the forfeiture of remission marks.

†c. *Law* = Remise *sb.*[1] 1. *Obs. rare*[−1].

c1450 *Godstow Reg.* (E. E. T. S.) 100 He remytted to them and quyte-claymed...And for þis knowlechyng, remission, fyne, and accorde [etc.].

†5. Relaxation; lessening of tension; slackening of energy or application. *Obs.*

1579 Lyly *Euphues* (Arb.) 112 As too much bending breaketh the bowe, so too much remission spoyleth the minde. 1580 *Ibid.* 383 As the Musitians tune their strings, who..either by intention or remission, frame them to a pleasant consent. 1614 Raleigh *Hist. World* v. iii. § 18. 474 Such accompt of

Remon'stratory, a. [f. as prec. + -ORY².] Expostulatory.

Remon'strator (remó'nstrətə). [f. REMONSTRATE v. + -OR.] One who remonstrates; a remonstrant.

Remonstration (remónstrē'ʃən). [ad. med.L. remonstrātiōn-em, n. of action f. remonstrāre.]

Remon'strative, a. [f. REMONSTRATE v. + -IVE.] Of or characterized by remonstrance; expostulatory.

Remord, v. Obs. [ad. L. remordēre to bite again.]

Remora (re'mŏra). [a. L. remora delay.]

Remorse (rimǒ'rs), sb. [a. OF. remors.]

Remorseful, a. [f. prec. + -FUL.]

Remorseless, a. [f. prec. + -LESS.]

Remorselessly, adv.

Remorselessness.

Remote (rimōu't), a. [ad. L. remōt-us, pa. pple. of removēre to REMOVE.]

Remotely, adv. [f. REMOTE a. + -LY².]

Remoteness. [-NESS.]

Remotion (rimōu'ʃən). Now rare. Also 5 remosion, 6-9 -cion, -oyone, etc. [a. obs. F. remotion (13-16th c.), or ad. L. remōtiōn-em, n. of action f. removēre to REMOVE.]

Remount, v. [OF. remonter, f. RE- + monter to MOUNT.]

Remount, sb. [f. prec., or ad. OF. remont.]

Removability. [f. next: see -ITY.]

Removable (rimūv'əbl). a. [f. REMOVE v. + -ABLE.]

Removal (rimū'văl). [f. REMOVE v. + -AL.]

Remove (rimū'v), v. [a. OF. remov-er, -oir, remuev-, remeuv-.]

1581 SAVILE *Tacitus, Hist.* I. lxii. (1591) 35 When al was in order ready to march, they cal to sound the remoue. 1622 F. MARKHAM *Bk. War* v. iii. 171 All things being assured, he may then cause the Drumme-maior to beat a remoue.

†c. A period of absence from a place. *Obs.*—1

1603 SHAKS. *Meas. for M.* I. i. 44 In our remoue, be thou at full, our selfe.

6. The space or interval by which one person or thing is remote from another, in time, place, condition, etc.; distance.

1628 FELTHAM *Resolves* II. [I.] xiv. 41 The soules Perspective glasse: whereby, in her long remoue, shee discerneth God. 1686 GOAD *Celest. Bodies* II. xii. 329 A Sign that ♄ is more frigid than ♃, by reason of his greater remove. 1771 WESLEY *Wks.* (1872) V. 385 A giddy, careless temper is at the farthest remove from the whole religion of Jesus Christ. 1845 R. W. HAMILTON *Pop. Educ.* iv. (ed. 2) 66 He would see that scale recede from him to as distant a remove as that where it now stands. 1876 MEREDITH *Beauch. Career* xxxii, As mountains gather vastness to the eye at a certain remove.

b. A step or stage in gradation of any kind; especially in phr. *but one* (or *a*) *remove from*.

1633 G. HERBERT *Temple, Jordan* ii, Must all be vail'd, while he that reads, divines, Catching the sense at two removes? 1668 R. STEELE *Husbandman's Calling* ix. 225 How can I glorifie my Maker, that am but one remove from a piece of..sinful earth? 1741 RICHARDSON *Pamela* (1824) I. 123 It might be well enough if you were..but a remove or two from the dirt you seem so fond of. 1850 M^cCOSH *Div. Govt.* (1852) 193 Events are explained by other events separated from them by a thousand removes. 1864 BRYCE *Holy Rom. Emp.* viii. (1875) 126 Yet nascent feudality was but one remove from anarchy.

c. A degree in descent or consanguinity.

1766 GOLDSM. *Vic. W.* i, Our cousins, too, even to the fortieth remove, all remembered their affinity, without any help from the heralds' office. 1789 HUNTER in *Phil. Trans.* LXXIX. 161 These puppies are the second remove from the Wolf and Dog. 1852 DICKENS *Bleak Ho.* i, I am not prepared to inform the Court in what exact remove he is a cousin.

7. *attrib.*, as *remove-ticket*.

1805 NELSON 26 Apr. in Nicolas *Disp.* (1846) VI. 416, I directed Captain Schomberg to make out the proper Remove-Tickets for the wages due to the said men.

Remove (rĭmū·v), *v.* Forms: α. 4–5 **remeeve**, 4–6 **remeue, -meve**, (5 **-mevyn, -mewe, -mefe, -meff**). β. 4–7 **remoue**, (5 **-mouyn**), 6–7 **remooue**, 7 **-moove**, 5– **remove**; 4 **remo(u(n, remuve** (8 *Sc.*), 4–5 **remow(e**, 5 *Sc.* **ra-**), 5 **remown(e**; also *north.* and *Sc.* 5 **remofe, -muf(f**, 5–6 **-mufe**, 6 **-moif**, 5–6 **ramuff, -muif**. [a. OF. *remeuv-*, *remouv-* and *remov-*, the stressed and unstressed stems of *remouvoir*:—L. *removēre*, f. *re-* RE- + *movēre* to MOVE. On the variation of form see MOVE *v.*]

I. *trans.* 1. To move or shift from or out of the place occupied; to lift or push aside; to lift up and take away; to take off.

The precise connotation varies to some extent with the nature of the object and the intention of the moving.

a 1300–1400 *Cursor M.* 17288 + 99 (Cott.), Who sal vus helpe to remou þat heuy stone? *c* 1400 MAUNDEV. (Roxb.) xxxiii. 150 Þe tendre erthe was removed fra his place and þare become a valay. *c* 1460 *Towneley Myst.* xxvi. 369 Which shall of us systers thre remefe the stone? 1530 PALSGR. 685/1 Remeve this thynges out of the waye. 1535 COVERDALE *Job* vi. 17 When they be set on fyre, they shalbe remoued out of their place. 1611 BIBLE *Transl. Pref.* ¶ 5 Translation it is..that remooueth the couer of the well, that wee may come by the water. 1669 STURMY *Mariner's Mag.* II. vi. 65 On the other Edge make a Line of Equal Parts, with an Ear in like manner to remove at pleasure. 1683 MOXON *Mech. Exerc., Printing* xxiv. ¶ 19 A Spring in the Tympan removes the Paper in this interval of Time. 1775 S. J. PRATT *Liberal Opin.* lxxxi. (1783) III. 101 Having, as the tea-equipage was removing, some intention to take his leave. 1837 DICKENS *Pickw.* ii, 'What's that?' he inquired, as the waiter removed one of the covers. 1843 YOUATT *Horse* (1848) 313 The shoe having been removed, the smith proceeds to rasp the edges of the crust.

b. To take away, withdraw, from a place, person, etc.; †to raise, abandon (a siege). Also *refl.* to betake oneself away.

c 1425 WYNTOUN *Cron.* III. v. 769 He..hym ramowit þan in hy, And agane hayme in Medy. 1530 PALSGR. 685/1 Remeve you from thence, my frende. *Ibid.*, I remeve my selfe out of the place I am in. 1560 DAUS tr. *Sleidane's Comm.* 90 So were the warders removed from the gates the same day. 1585 T. WASHINGTON tr. *Nicholay's Voy.* I. xv. 16 They resolued to remoue their siege, and to imbarke themselues with their ordinance. 1648 MILTON *Ps.* lxxxviii. 69 Lover and friend thou hast remov'd And sever'd from me far. 1667 — *P. L.* VIII. 119 God to remove his wayes from human sense, Plac'd Heav'n from Earth so farr. 1697 DRYDEN *Virg. Georg.* I. 201 Jove..Remov'd from Humane reach the chearful Fire. 1729 LAW *Serious C.* xv. 273 We can..remove ourselves from objects that inflame our passions. 1819 SCOTT *Ivanhoe* i, [The swine] made..no haste to remove themselves from the luxurious banquet of beech-mast and acorns. 1850 M^cCOSH *Div. Govt.* IV. i. (1874) 464 The Epicureans removed their Gods far above the care and supervision of human affairs.

c. To take or convey away from a place; †to keep apart, separate. Also *removed*, taken away by death.

1459 *Test. Ebor.* (Surtees) II. 227 Y^t thei..delyuere vn to George Chaworth..alle his stuffe that he hath at Alfreton, ..he to remeve them at his awne wille. 1596 SHAKS. *1 Hen. IV*, II. ii. 11 That Rascall hath remoued my Horse, and tied him I know not where. 1610 — *Temp.* II. i. 110 She too, Who is so farre from Italy remoued, I ne're againe shall see her. 1633 P. FLETCHER *Purple Isl.* IV. xi, A border citie these two coasts removing. 1748 *Anson's Voy.* II. vi. 195 Mr. Brett had hitherto gone on in collecting and removing the treasure without interruption. 1816 SOUTHEY *Ess.* (1832) I. 191 The latter was early removed from a world which his Talents..were..fitted to adorn. 1850 TENNYSON *In Mem.* Prol. 37 Forgive my grief for one removed, Thy creature, whom I found so fair.

d. To put (a person) out of the way; to assassinate, murder.

1653 A. WILSON *Jas. I* 65 The Prince..being removed, the Earl of Salisbury (another obstacle) dying six moneths after the Prince [etc.]. 1655–6 T. ROSS in *Cal. St. Papers, Dom.* (1882) 196, I cannot divine how, except by removing Cromwell, to which one of them had specially devoted himself. 1889 *Times* (weekly ed.) 31 May 6/2 An elaborate article to-day, declares that Dr. Cronin was 'removed' by the Clan-na-Gael after trial and conviction.

e. In *pass.* Of dishes: To be replaced or followed *by*, after removal.

1840 LADY C. BURY *Hist. of Flirt* iv, There was fish and soup, removed by boiled chickens and bacon. 1852 THACKERAY *Shabby Genteel Story* iii, Boiled haddock, removed by hashed mutton.

2. To move, shift, transfer or convey from one place to another; to change the place or situation of (†also with *place* as obj.); †to lead (a force) to another place.

13.. *Guy Warw.* (A.) ccxcvi, Lete him be stille, Neuer more remoun him y nille, No do him hennes lede. 1388 WYCLIF *2 Sam.* xx. 12 He remouyde Amasa fro the weie in to the feeld. *c* 1400 *Destr. Troy* 3113 Ho..beckonet hym boldly ..his place to Remeve. *c* 1420 *Pallad. on Husb.* II. 177 Letuce is to be sette in Ianyueer.., the plantes to remeue In Feueryeer. 1494 FABYAN *Chron.* VI. clxxi. 166 Than he remeuyd his people, and in sondry places faughte with the Danys. 1523 FITZHERB. *Husb.* § 129 If thou wylte remoue & set trees gete as many rotes with them as thou can. *a* 1548 HALL *Chron., Edw. IV* 215 He politiquely..determined in great haste to remove his whole army. 1560 DAUS tr. *Sleidane's Comm.* 301 You ought not to haue removed or chaunged the place without the consent of the Emperour. 1613 PURCHAS *Pilgrimage* III. ii. (1614) 234 Their tents, which with themselues, their flockes, and substance, they remoued vp and downe from place to place. 1703 MOXON *Mech. Exerc.* 343 Then removing the string the space of 15 degrees in the Quadrant. 1765 *Museum Rust.* IV. 170 This row being thus planted, the line was removed two feet forwards. 1815 J. SMITH *Panorama Sc. & Art* II. 178 Remove the needle from the situation P to the situation R. 1839 KEIGHTLEY *Hist. Eng.* II. 25 Elizabeth was now removed to Canterbury. 1876 HOLLAND *Sev. Oaks* xi. 151 [He] is about to remove his residence from among us.

refl. *c* 1375 *Lay Folks Mass. Bk.* (MS. B) 301 Þo prest wil after in þat place Remow [*v.r.* remo] him a litel space.

absol. 1615 W. LAWSON *Country Housew. Gard.* (1626) 17 The onely best way..to haue sure and lasting Sets, is neuer to remoue: for euery remoue is an hinderance.

†b. *Law.* To transfer (a cause or person) for trial from one court of law to another. Also *refl.*

1507 *Cal. Anc. Rec. Dublin* (1889) I. 394 Writes of privelage to remowe ple othir ples owte of the cowrt of the citte. 1607 COWELL *Interpr.* s.v. *Habeas Corpus*, is a writ the which a man..may haue out of the Kings bench, thereby to remooue himselfe thither..and to answer the cause there. 1627 T. POWELL (*title*) The Attornies Almanacke, provided ..for..all such as shall have occasion to remove any person, cause or record, from an inferior Court to any the higher Courts at Westminster. 1744 [see REMOVER[2] 2].

†c. *Chess.* To move (a piece). Also *absol.* *Obs.*

1562 ROWBOTHUM *Playe of Cheasts* B ij, Oftentymes the game is lost by remouinge the Rookes Paune or Knyghtes Paune one roume. *a* 1585 MONTGOMERIE *Cherrie & Slae* 215, I gat sik chek, Quhilk I micht nocht remuif nor nek, Bot eyther staill or mait.

3. To send or put (a person) away; to compel (one) to go from, or quit, a place.

c 1380 WYCLIF *Serm.* Sel. Wks. I. 401 3if..þou have a wickide servaunt.., putte him out of his office and remeeve him fer awey. *c* 1425 WYNTOUN *Cron.* II. xvi. 1416 Of neid þaim behuffit To be banyst and ramowyt Fra þar gud, þar kyn, þar kytht. 1432–50 tr. *Higden* (Rolls) VIII. 329 A knyȝhte..promysede to brynge an hoste of Scottes to remove hym from that sege. 1567 *Gude & Godlie B.* (S. T. S.) 86 From thy face thow sall thame swyith remufe. 1581 *Reg. Privy Council Scot.* III. 396 Thay on nawyse suld..molest, rais or remove any of the auld tennentis. *c* 1600 SHAKS. *Sonn.* xxv, Then happy I that loue and am beloued Where I may not remoue nor be remoued. 1667 MILTON *P. L.* XI. 96 To remove him I decree, And send him from the Garden. *a* 1768 ERSKINE *Inst. Law Scot.* II. vi. § 49 (1773) 273 Warning must be used in order to remove a tenant in a common lease. 1838 W. BELL *Dict. Law Scot.* 848 The tenant is..entitled to continue his possession.., until legally removed by the landlord.

b. To put (one) away from, or out of, a position or office; to depose, dismiss.

1388 WYCLIF *1 Kings* xv. 13 He remouyde Maacha,..that sche schulde not be princesse in the solempne thingis. 1433 *Rolls of Parlt.* IV. 477/2 That the seid Sergeauntz be remeved at the ende of every Yere. 1502 ARNOLDE *Chron.* (1811) 36 The Aldermen of the forsayd cite that eueri yere they ben remeued..and that they so remeued be not chosen ayen the next yere. 1520 *Caxton's Chron. Eng.* III. 20 b/2 The Trybunes were remeved every yere. 1553 in Hakluyt *Voy.* (1886) III. 18 And the person so remoued not to be.. accepted..from the time of his remoue, any more for an officer. 1775 BURKE *Sp. Conc. Amer.* 87 That the said Chief Justice and other Judges..shall hold his and their office..and shall not be removed therefrom but when [etc.]. 1874 STUBBS *Const. Hist.* xii. (1896) I. 511 *note*, None of the sheriffs now removed were employed again.

†c. To raise (a siege). *Obs.* (See RAISE *v.* 28.)

1387 TREVISA *Higden* (Rolls) VIII. 329 William de Reeth ..behiȝt þe kyng þat he wolde..bryng þe oost of Scottes..to remeve þe seege..of Berwyk. 1480 CAXTON *Chron. Eng.* ccxxxv. 257 This same yere the king with a grete host entred the see to remeue the sege of rochel. 1586 MARLOWE *1st Pt. Tamburl.* IV. iii, Let us..hasten to remove Damascus' siege. 1640 YORKE *Union Hon.* 245 He was sent..to remove the siege of the City of Rochel in France.

†d. To clear off, dispose of. *Obs. rare.*

1609 HOLLAND *Amm. Marcell.* 131 In the high tops whereof were balists fitly placed, which removed the defendants that kept lower. 1652 NEEDHAM tr. *Selden's Mare Cl.* 168 Having thus refuted, or upon good ground removed som Opinions of antient Lawyers.

4. To take away (*from* a person), to relieve or free one from, some feeling, quality, condition, etc., esp. one of a bad or detrimental kind; †to do away with, put an end to (a practice).

c 1374 CHAUCER *Troylus* I. 691 And for-thy wolde I fayn remeve Thy wrong conceyte. *c* 1400 tr. *Secreta Secret., Gov. Lordsh.* 108 Gouerne hem wel, and..remowe fro hem all þaire wronges. *c* 1449 PECOCK *Repr.* II. ix. 196 Wherbi is excludid and wilned of Crist to be removed, that eny man schulde worschipe God bi eny outward ymagis. *Ibid.*, Crist in the same chapiter..removed pilgrimagis. 1567 *Gude & Godlie B.* (S. T. S.) 74 Lord..Remufe fra me all frawardness. 1596 SHAKS. *Tam. Shr.* I. ii. 72 She moues me not, or not remoues at least Affections edge in me. 1610 — *Temp.* II. ii. 79 If hee haue neuer drunke wine afore, it will goe neere to remoue his Fit. 1667 MILTON *P. L.* XII. 290 When they see Law can discover sin, but not remove. 1770 *Junius Lett.* xxxix. (1788) 217 In the repeal of those acts..the parliament have done everything but remove the offence. 1809 *Med. Jrnl.* XXI. 260 That general debility..which time and attention will in all probability very speedily remove. 1874 GREEN *Short Hist.* vii. § 6. 405 The death of Norfolk and Northumberland removed the dread of civil war.

†b. To put away (a feeling, thought, etc.) *from* oneself; to set aside. *Obs.*

1388 WYCLIF *Eccl.* xi. 10 Do thou awei ire fro thin herte, and remoue thou malice fro thy fleisch. *c* 1440 *Alph. Tales* 106 It is impossible to remove ill thoghts fro þe with other mens prayers. 1535 COVERDALE *Eccl.* xii. 1 Put away displeasure out of thy hert, & remoue euell from thy body. [1611 (xi. 10) Therefore remoue sorrow from thy heart, and put away euill from thy flesh.] 1703 EARL ORRERY *As you Find it* III. i, You had best remove this Scruple quickly.

†5. To change, transform, *into* something. *Obs.*—1

c 1430 *Pilgr. Lyf Manhode* I. xli. (1869) 25 And therfore I haue wrethe in myn herte whan ye remeeuen [F. *mues*] it in to quik flesh.

†6. To go away from, to quit (a place or position). *Obs. rare.*

c 1440 *Generydes* 3223 Too all his ost he gave a speciall charge,..They shuld remeve that place ij myle large. *c* 1450 *St. Cuthbert* (Surtees) 7514 Ane [bishop] þe whilk by symony þe se gat; with in sex moneths remoued he þat.

†7. To move or stir (a part of the body). *Obs.*

1483 CAXTON *Gold. Leg.* 262 b/2 Whan the tyraunte sawe that he remeuyd yet his lyppes..[he] smote hym wyth hys knyf to the herte. 1523 LD. BERNERS *Froiss.* I. ccclxix. 606 The church that day was so full of noblenesse, that a man might nat a remoued his fete. 1585 T. WASHINGTON tr. *Nicholay's Voy.* II. xxi. 58 b, Pulling and remouing your ioyntes as before is said.

†8. To move or persuade (one) *out of* or *from* a purpose or resolve. Also without const. *Obs.*

1483 CAXTON *Gold. Leg.* 184/2 He wold haue comen unto our presence but that hys conscyence hath remeuyd hym. 1523 LD. BERNERS *Froiss.* I. ccxxxi. 314 They coude nat remoue him out of that purpose. *a* 1548 HALL *Chron., Edw. IV* 24 b, All the tounes round about, were permanent and stiffe on the parte of kyng Henry, and could not be remoued. 1647 MAY *Hist. Parl.* I. viii. 94 But the King was hard to be removed from his resolution. 1654 tr. *Martini's Conq. China* 167 Nor would he ever be removed from this unhumane sentence.

†b. To move, affect (the heart). *Obs. rare*—1.

?1600 LYLY *Love's Metam.* IV. ii, Men, whose loues are built on truth, and whose hearts are remoued by curtesie.

II. *intr.* 9. To go away or depart from a place; to move off to somewhere else.

α. 13.. *K. Alis.* 7238 He with-seith alle homage..And bad you remeve out of his lond. *a* 1400–50 *Alexander* 1975 Remefe agayn to þi realm or þou sall it rewe. *c* 1450 *Merlin* 61 They seide 'Sir, we haue no talents to remeve fro hens'. 1495 *Trevisa's Barth. De P. R.* VIII. xviii. xij/2 The mone makyth a man vnstable chaungeable & remeuynge abowte fro place to place.

β. *c* 1375 *Sc. Leg. Saints* xviii. (*Mary Egypt*) 1090 Þu sal na mycht haf to remofe [from the abbey]. *c* 1400 *Rowland & O.* 730 The Oste remowede & forthe thay ȝede,..To þaire Iournaye þay hye. *c* 1470 HENRY *Wallace* XI. 315 Wallace off France a gudly leiff can tak. The kyng..Gret langour tuk quhen Wallace can ramuff. 1568 GRAFTON *Chron.* II. 378 From thence they remoued to Saint Albons, and came thether on Christmas Euen. 1585 T. WASHINGTON tr. *Nicholay's Voy.* I. xv. 16 [He] remooued..to assiege the castle of Tripoli. 1680 J. COLE *Of Death* 51 Hee would rather chuse to stay here, and live in the same [earthly pleasures], then remove to enjoy the heavenly. 1661 GLANVILL *Van. Dogm.* 198 He said, he'd remove into another room. 1706 E. WARD *Wooden World Diss.* (1708) 28 He..begs a Certificate, when he removes from the Ship. 1796 *Hist. Ned Evans* II. 104 From which few ever remove but to torture.

b. *spec.* To change the place of one's (temporary or permanent) residence; also of a tenant, to quit a house or holding.

1399 LANGL. *Rich. Redeles* III. 301 A new þing þat noyeth nedy men and oþer, Whanne realles remeveth and ridith þoru tounes. 1478 *Paston Lett.* III. 229 My Lord of Suffolk is remevyd in to Suffolk..and my lady purposed to remeff after on thys day. 1530 PALSGR. 685/1, I remeve, as an armye or the trayne of a prince or gret man removeth from one place to an other. 1555 *Sc. Acts Mary* (1814) II. 494/1 The warning of all tennentis and vtheris to flit and remoue fra landis mylnis fischingis and possessiouns quhatsumeuer. 1633 FORD *Broken H.* II. i, This house, methinks, stands somewhat too much inward; we'll remove Nearer the court. 1697 DRYDEN *Virg. Georg.* I. 57 Proserpine.. importun'd by Ceres to remove, Prefers the Fields below to those above. 1722 DE FOE *Plague* (1754) 6 This Frenchman..was one who, having liv'd in Long-Acre..had removed for fear of the Distemper. 1756 *Act of Sederunt* 14 Dec., Where the tenant hath not obliged himself to remove without warning. 1838 W. BELL *Dict. Law Scot.* 848 In order to authorise judicial removing, the tenant..must be warned by the landlord to remove. 1855 BREWSTER *Newton* II. xxi. 252 Newton received this letter when he was removing from Jermyn Street to Chelsea.

†c. To shift one's place or position. *Obs.*

1340 HAMPOLE *Pr. Consc.* 7365 In helle salle be þan swa gret thrang, Þat nane may remow for other ne gang. *c* 1475 *Rauf Coilȝear* 861 The lenth of ane rude braid he gart him remufe. *a* 1533 LD. BERNERS *Huon* lv. 186 He remoued no more for the stroke then it had ben a strong walle. 1562 ROWBOTHUM *Playe of Cheasts* A v b, Their office is not to remoue but in necessitie, and chiefelye for the succoure of theyr kynge. 1595 SAVIOLO *Practise* H ij b, Remoue with your right foot a little back toward his left side. 1656 BEALE *Chess* 8 The King removeth but one house at a time.

10. Of things: To change place; to move off or away; to depart, disappear, etc.

1423 JAS. I *Kingis Q.* clxxxviii, In perfyte Ioy, that neuir may remufe. 1481 CAXTON *Myrr.* I. vi. 29 There cheualrye contynued long, And frothens after it remeuid in to Fraunce. 1535 COVERDALE *Isa.* liv. 10 The mountaynes shall remoue, & the hilles shal fall downe. *c* 1586 C'TESS PEMBROKE *Ps.* LII. ix, My trust on his true love Truly attending Shall never thence remove. 1662 STILLINGFL. *Orig. Sacræ* III. ii. § 17 Those particles will necessarily remove into that empty space. 1704 POPE *Autumn* 29 Ye trees that fade when autumn-heats remove. *a* 1792 BURNS *Posie* vii, I'll swear.. That to my latest draught o' life the band shall ne'er remove. 1839–48 BAILEY *Festus* xviii. 174 And sigh That truth from that Heaven should ever remove. 1896 A. E. HOUSMAN *Shropshire Lad* xxxvi, But ere the circle homeward hies Far, far must it remove.

†b. To change *into* something. *Obs. rare*—1.

1674 PLAYFORD *Skill Mus.* III. 5 That which is an eighth shall remove into a fifth.

†11. To move, stir; to be in motion. *Obs.*

a 1400–50 *Alexander* 2943 Sir Dary..Rerys hym vpp & remevys in hys sete riche. *a* 1450 *Knt. de la Tour* (1868) 37 She might not stere nor remeue more thanne a stone. 1509 HAWES *Past. Pleas.* xxiv. (Percy Soc.) 108 These are the v. wyttes remeuing inwardly. *c* 1555 HARPSFIELD *Divorce Hen. VIII* (Camden) 251 The head thus being above, the body beneath in water, wagging and removing to and fro. 1601 HAKLUYT tr. *Galvano's Discov.* 46 There is further a kinde of herbe there growing, which followeth the sunne, and remooveth after it.

Removed (rĭmū·vd), *ppl. a.* [f. prec. + -ED[1].]

1. Distant in relationship by a certain degree of descent or consanguinity.

Properly denoting a degree in descent, as *first cousin once removed* = a cousin's child; but in later use freq. employed in vague designations of distant relationship, as *cousin seven times removed*.

a 1548 HALL *Chron., Hen. V* 53 Barbara doughter to therle of ziliec cosyn germain removed to kyng Henry. 1594 PARSONS *Confer. Success.* II. iv. 75 Edmond was but nephew remoued, that is to say, daughters sonnes sonne to the said king Richards other uncle. 1611 SHAKS. *Wint. T.* IV. iv. 802 Those that are Iermaine to him (though remou'd fiftie times) shall all come vnder the Hang-man. 1687 MIÈGE *Gt. Fr. Dict.* II. s.v. *Cousin*, A Cousin once removed, *Cousin issu de germain*. 1738 SWIFT *Pol. Conversat.* 62 He's my Cousin-German, quite remov'd. 1748 SMOLLETT *Roderick Random* xviii, My grandfather's brother's daughter..rabbit it! I have forgot the degree; but this I know that he and I are cousins seven times removed. 1841 LYTTON *Money* I. vii, Cousin to the deceased, seven times removed. 1852 DICKENS *Bleak Ho.* i, He is a cousin, several times removed.

transf. 1600 SHAKS. *A. Y. L.* V. iv. 71 Vpon a lye, seuen times removed.

2. †a. Remote; retired, secluded. *Obs.*

1600 SHAKS. *A. Y. L.* III. ii. 360 Your accent is something finer, then you could purchase in so removed a dwelling. 1609 DOWLAND *Ornithop. Microl.* 54 Imperfection is made not only by the neere part of the Notes, but also by the remoued part. 1632 MILTON *Penseroso* 78 Or if the Ayr will not permit, Som still removed place will fit.

†b. Separated by time or space. *Obs. rare.*

1601 SHAKS. *Twel. N.* V. i. 92 His false cunning..grew a twentie yeeres remoued thing While one could winke. 1628 FELTHAM *Resolves* II. [I.] xxxiii. 105 They haue the aduantage of being beleeued, before a remoued friend.

†c. Segregated or set apart. *Obs. rare*—1.

1611 BIBLE *Ezek.* xxxvi. 17 Their way was before me as the vncleannesse of a remooued woman.

d. Lifted or taken away.

1645 [see HARDLY *adv.* 10]. 1683 MOXON *Mech. Exerc., Printing* xxii. ¶ 8 He removes the other Transpos'd Page into the place of the first remov'd Page. 1688 R. HOLME *Acad.* I. iii. 22/1 If the under Chief had been the colour of the Field, then it had been termed a Chief removed, or fallen out of its place. *a* 1716 SOUTH *Serm.* (1823) V. 281 Nobody..languishes with the remembrance of a removed sickness. 1748 RICHARDSON *Clarissa* (1768) I. 93 He took the removed chair, and drew it..near mine.

3. In predicative use: Remote, separated, or distant *from* something, in *lit.* and *fig.* senses.

1617 MORYSON *Itin.* I. 214 He was like neuer to be redeemed, being farre remoued from Christians, who onely trade vpon the Coasts. 1690 LOCKE *Hum. Und.* I. iii. § 1 They are farther removed from a title to be innate. 1756 C. LUCAS *Ess. Waters* I. 172 [He] is not, in knowledge or rationality, three degrees removed from the brute. 1864 BRYCE *Holy Rom. Emp.* vi. (1875) 77 A corrupt tongue, equally removed from Latin and from modern French.

Hence **Remo·vedness**.

1604 SHAKS. *Wint. T.* IV. ii. 41, I haue eyes vnder my seruice, which looke vpon his remouednesse. 1845 *Blackw. Mag.* LVII. 147 It has a middle removedness or estrangement from the ordinary speech of men. 1892 *Temple Bar* Jan. 59 The impressions this garden gave were of removedness, of light and shadow, of grass and roses.

†**Remo·veless**, *a.* *Obs. rare*—1. [f. REMOVE *sb.* or *v.* + -LESS.] Incapable of being removed.

c 1592 MARLOWE *Massacre Paris* II. iv, As now you are, so shall you still persist, Removeless from the favours of your King.

Remo·vement. [f. REMOVE *v.* + -MENT.]

†1. The act of removing from place to place.

1630 *R. Johnson's Kingd. & Commw.* 495 In their travels and removement they are governed by their Stars, and observing the North pole, they settle according to its motion.

2. The act of taking, or the fact of being taken, away; removal.

1845–6 TRENCH *Huls. Lect.* Ser. II. v. 223 All the alleviations and removements of pain and disease. 1862 DARWIN *Fertil. Orchids* i. 48 The derangement in the complex mechanism had hindered the removement of the pollinia.

†**Remo·vent**, *a.* *Obs. rare*—1. [ad. L. *removent-em*, pres. pple. of *removēre* to REMOVE.] Producing removal.

1625 *Debates Ho. Commons* (Camden) 86 To shew..the remedyes both removent and promovent.

Remover[1] (rĭmū·vəɹ). [f. REMOVE *v.* + -ER[1].]

1. One who, or that which, removes or takes away; *spec.* in modern use, a furniture-remover.

1594 SOUTHWELL *M. Magd. Funeral Teares* 56 b, Where the thing remooued was remoouer of it selfe. 1607 HIERON *Wks.* I. 367 If the desirer of our saluation, and the remoouer of all hinderances to it, do yet leaue sinne behind. 1624 T. SCOTT *Vox Regis* 23 Which Court was the onely..discouerer and remoouer of all such mightie enormities. 1860 GOSSE *Rom. Nat. Hist.* 108 We must see them..engaged as the scavengers of the forest-wilds of the tropics; the removers of fallen trees. 1861 HUGHES *Tom Brown at Oxf.* III. 264 Grey had discovered a benevolent remover of furniture.

†b. *fig.* A poison. *Obs. rare*—1.

1625–6 SHIRLEY *Maid's Revenge* III. ii, *Shar.* A rat! give him his bane..*Ans.* Pray let me see a remover at twelve hours; I would be loth to kill the poor thing presently.

2. One who changes his place; a restless or stirring person. *rare.*

c 1600 SHAKS. *Sonn.* cxvi, Loue is not loue Which alters when it alteration findes, Or bends with the remouer to remoue. 1607–12 BACON *Ess., Fortune* (Arb.) 378 An hastye Fortune maketh an Enterpriser, and Remover (The French hath it better *Entreprenant*, or *Remuant*).

†b. A hive from which the bees are made to remove. *Obs. nonce-use.*

1609 C. BUTLER *Fem. Mon.* (1634) 153 Having first placed these two stalls, the Remover (that is driven) and the Receiver, as near as may be to one another.

†**Remo·ver**[2]. *Obs. rare.* [f. as prec. + -ER[4].]

1. The act of moving; movement. *rare*—1.

1663 H. COGAN tr. *Pinto's Trav.* xxv. 95 At the first sight of him, he would have turned back out of the remover of conscience, and true repentance.

2. *Law.* (See quot. and REMOVE *v.* 2 b.)

1744 JACOB *Law Dict.*, *Remover* is where a Suit or Cause is removed out of one Court into another.

Removing (rĭmū·viŋ), *vbl. sb.* [-ING[1].]

1. The action of removing from a place; removal to another place or residence; †also, change, alteration.

1340 HAMPOLE *Pr. Consc.* 6365 Þe son sal þan in þe este stande, With-outen removyng, ay shynande. *c* 1430 *Pilgr. Lyf Manhode* I. xlii. (1869) 25 Many oothere remeeuinges [F. *remuemens*] of which were to longe to holde parlement. 1535 COVERDALE *Ezek.* iii. 12, I herde the noyse of a greate rushinge and remouynge off the most blissed glory off the Lorde out off his place. 1555 EDEN *Decades* 35 In contynual remoouinge as the nature of warre requyreth. 1620 T. GRANGER *Div. Logike* 108 Vegetation, and locomotion are powers of growing, augmentation, mooving, remoouing. 1719 DE FOE *Crusoe* I. (Globe) 268 We waited a great while, though very impatient for their removing. 1750 MRS. DELANY *Life & Corr.* (1861) II. 566, I have not heard from my brother a great while; I suppose his removing has hurried him.

attrib. *a* 1601 LAMBARDE *Dict. Angl. Top.* (1730) 48 Batarsey, the removinge House of the Byshoppes of Yorke. 1684 E. CHAMBERLAYNE *Pres. St. Eng.* I. (ed. 15) 177 There is the Removing Wardrobe, which always attends upon the Person of the King.

2. The action of removing, shifting, taking or putting away; also, an instance of this.

1425 LYDG. *De Guil. Pilgr.* 6372 With-outen any remowyng Off the Eyen in myn hed Into myn Eryn. 1535 COVERDALE *Heb.* xii. 27 No doute that same..signifieth the remouynge awaye of those thinges. 1563 HYLL *Art Garden.* (1593) 127 The better also they wil prosper, if after euery remoouing..the blades bee cut. 1642 DRUMM. OF HAWTH. *Skiamachia* Wks. (1711) 193 Such particulars, as..will much conduce to the removing of all these mistakes. 1712 J. JAMES tr. *Le Blond's Gardening* 116 The Transporting and Removing of Earth is a vast and excessive Charge. 1818 in Willis & Clark *Cambridge* (1886) I. 573 The removing of the present walk with the two trees. 1882 E. C. ROBERTSON in *Proc. Berw. Nat. Club* IX. 507 The removing of the earth brought to view an immense collection of skeletons.

3. *Sc. Law.* The removal of a tenant by, or at the instance of, the landlord; †also, a notice requiring a tenant to remove.

1555 *Sc. Acts Mary* (1814) II. 494/1 Na forther laying furth of stressis and removing vpone wednisday to be vsit in tyme to cum. 1588 *Reg. Privy Council Scot.* IV. 270 The executioun of ane precept of removing. *Ibid.*, He putt the copy of the removing..in the said Johnis bosome. 1683 *Acts Sederunt* (1790) 156 Act appoynting Advocations and Suspensions of Decreets of removeing. *a* 1768 ERSKINE *Inst. Sc. Law* II. vi. § 51 (1773) 274 A landlord's title to prosecute a removing..cannot be questioned by a tenant who derives his possession from him. 1838 W. BELL *Dict. Law Scot.* 848 In order to authorise judicial removing, the tenant..must be warned by the landlord to remove.

So **Remo·ving** *ppl. a.*

1643 [ANGIER] *Lanc. Vall. Achor* 22 Desire to see this Forreiner..led some of note and worth into a teadious and removing captivitie. 1870 *Daily News* 5 Sept. 6 Sometimes upon a pile of mattresses or bedding..were to be seen the removing householder himself and his wife and family.

Remow, obs. form of REMOVE *v.*

†**Remp**, *v.* *Obs. rare.* [Of obscure origin.] *intr.* To act hastily; to hasten.

c 897 K. ÆLFRED *Gregory's Past. C.* xx. 148 Oft mon bið swiðe rempende, & ræsð swiðe dollice on ælc weorc & hrædlice. *c* 1330 R. BRUNNE *Chron. Wace* (Rolls) 3492 Þe Bretons sawe þer syde ȝede lowe, Þey rempede þem to reste a þrowe.

†**Rempa·re**, *v.* *Obs. rare.* Also **renpayre.** [ad. F. *remparer*: see RAMPIRE *v.*] *trans.* To strengthen, fortify. Also *absol.*

1525 LD. BERNERS *Froiss.* II. cxiii. 336 Than he newe renpayred the towne, and furnished it with newe men of warre. 1549 EDW. VI *Jrnl.* (Roxb.) 236 The gates of the hous to be rempared; peple to be raysed. 1581 MULCASTER *Positions* xxxvii. 148 Our state then must reiect the multitude, and rempare with the cunning.

‖**Rempli** (ranpli), *a.* *Her.* Also 8 **remply.** [F., pa. pple. of *remplir* to fill up.] (See quots.)

1725 COATS *Dict. Her.*, *Remply*, that is, fill'd up, denoting that all the Chief is fill'd up with a square Piece of another Colour, leaving only a Bordure of the proper Colour of the Chief about the said Piece. 1780 EDMONDSON *Compl. Body Heraldry* II. Gloss. s.v., When a chief is filled with any other metal, or colour, leaving only a border round the chief of the first, it is then called a *Chief Rempli*.

†**Remuable**, *a.* *Obs. rare.* [a. OF. *remuable* (14th c.): see REMUE *v.* and -ABLE.]

1. That may remove (= depart) or be removed; changeable, unstable.

c 1374 CHAUCER *Troylus* IV. 1633 (1682) And this may length of yeres nought fordo, Ne remuable fortune deface. 1390 GOWER *Conf.* III. 256 For where honour is remuable, It oghte wel to ben avised. *c* 1430 LYDG. *Min. Poems* (Percy Soc.) 122 In this world here is none abidyng place, But that it is by processe remuable.

2. Capable of movement.

c 1374 CHAUCER *Boeth.* V. pr. v. 131 (Camb. MS.) The ymaginacion comth to Remuable [L. *mobilibus*] beestis, þat semyn to han talent to fleen or to desiren any thing.

†**Remuant**, *a.* *Obs. rare.* Also 7 **-ent.** [a. F. *remuant*, pres. pple. of *remuer* to REMUE.] Inclined to remove; restless, changeable.

1625 W. B. *True School War* 12 Those Busibodies, or as the French haue it better, those Remuant spirits, that.. haue rather defaced than built. 1654 *Nicholas Papers* (Camden) II. 92, I protest I am so pationatly troubled for the remuant humour of our frend that I know not what to say. 1659 O. WALKER *Oratory* 66 Fixing his fancy (remuent, and volatile) upon one object.

†**Remue·**, *sb.* *Obs. rare*—1. [a. OF. *remue* (Godef.).] Movement forward, advance, progress.

1433 LYDG. *St. Edmund* III. 1217 [They] stood stylle as ston, sore in themsylff amasyd..Fro ther werk myhte no remews make.

†**Remue·**, *v.* *Obs.* Forms: 3–4 **remuwe**, 3–5 **remue**, (4 **-u, -uye**), **remwe**; 3–7 **remew**, 4–5 **remewe**, (4 **-eue**). [a. OF. *remuer* (11th c.), f. *re-* RE- + *muer*:—L. *mūtāre* to change: cf. It. *rimutare*, med.L. *remūtāre* (Du Cange). It is sometimes not clear whether the forms *remeue* and *remewe* belong here, or to *remeve*, obs. variant of REMOVE *v.*]

1. *trans.* To remove, shift, or transfer, to another place; to move from a place.

1297 R. GLOUC. (Rolls) 5522 Remwe in to anoþer stude þi pauilon. *c* 1325 *Chron. Eng.* 744 in Ritson *Metr. Rom.* II. 301 Afterward..That he hade leyen..Sixti wynter under molde, An abbot him remue wolde. *c* 1386 CHAUCER *Sqr.'s T.* 172 The hors of bras þat may nat be remewed It stant as it were to the ground yglewed. *c* 1420 *Pallad. on Husb.* II. 280 Sette ek noon almaundes but grete and newe; And hem is best in Feueryeer remewe. 1600 FAIRFAX *Tasso* XIII. lxx, That faith wherewith he could remew The stedfast hils.

refl. *c* 1380 *Sir Ferumb.* 77 He stynte & þoȝte noȝt remuye hem [= him] þere til he ha foȝt is fille. 1430–40 LYDG. *Bochas* IX. v. (1558) 23 b/1 And secretly he gan him selfe remue, To be bathed in a preuy stue.

b. To remove to a distance; to put, take, or keep away *from*.

13.. *E. E. Allit. P.* B. 1673 Þou, remued fro monnes sunnes, on mor most abide. *c* 1400 tr. *Secreta Secret., Gov. Lordsh.* 93 All þare-by is vnderstandant, and neghys negh, þat þat ys remued of farre. *c* 1420 *Pallad. on Husb.* I. 777 Yet is the chalk or cley lond forto eschewe, And from the rede also thy garth remewe.

2. To remove (a person) from a position or office; to put away, dismiss.

1297 R. GLOUC. (Rolls) 11455 Þis tueie erles acorded were þere þat iremewed [*v.r.* yremuwed] al clene þe frenssemen were. *c* 1330 R. BRUNNE *Chron.* (1810) 312 To þe we pleyn vs here, Him for to remue þorgh comon assent. 1390 GOWER *Conf.* I. 318 Witt and resoun conseilen..that I scholde will remue And put him out of retenue. 1412–20 LYDG. *Chron. Troy* II. xii. (1555) G v b, She can make a man for his welfare,..Whan be least weneth, for to be remewed.

b. To raise (a siege). *rare*—1.

c 1330 R. BRUNNE *Chron.* (1810) 100 Þerfor þe duke him dight, as man of grete value, Roberd Bellyse with myght, þe sege þei wend remue.

3. To remove entirely; to take or clear away.

1297 R. GLOUC. (Rolls) 11613 Bruggen hii breke oueral, hii ne bileuede ssip non..þat hii ne remuede echon. *c* 1350 *St. Peter* 197 in Horstm. *Altengl. Leg.* (1881) 51 He bad þam stir oway þe stone And remu al þe erth oway. 1390 GOWER *Conf.* III. 21 In no wise The drunkeschipe of love aweie I mai remue be no weie. 1426 LYDG. *De Guil. Pilgr.* 4446, I remewe, in especial, Clene with-outen & with-Inne, The fylthe of euery maner synne.

4. To transfer, translate; to change, alter.

c 1330 R. BRUNNE *Chron. Wace* (Rolls) 164 Geffrey..fro Breton speche he did remue & made it alle in Latyn. 1340 *Ayenb.* 104 Wyþoute him to chongi, wyþoute him remue ine none manere. *c* 1403 LYDG. *Temple Glas* 1182 Vices eschew,..And for no tales thin hert not remue.

5. *intr.* To move off or away, to depart, to go.

1340–70 *Alex. & Dind.* 137 (*heading*) How alixandre remewid to a flod þat is called phison. *c* 1400 MAUNDEV. (1839) v. 38 And whan hem lyst, they remewen to other Cytees. *c* 1430 *Hymns Virgin* (1867) 20 Þouȝ we wolden from þee remewe, In ech place þou art present. 1482 WARKW. *Chron.* (Camden) 2 Kynge Edwardes hooste..remewed from the sege, and were affrayed.

6. To stir, to alter one's position, to move.

a 1350 *St. Stephen* 519 in Horstm. *Altengl. Leg.* (1881) 34 Þe body remude..And left to saint Steuen half þe graue. 1390 GOWER *Conf.* II. 316 As if a goshauk hadde sesed A brid, which dorste noght for fere Remue. *c* 1430 *Syr Gener.* (Roxb.) 5359 He hath forbede..That noon of hem shul remew, Him to help or reskew.

Hence †**Remu·ing** *vbl. sb.*, removal. *Obs. rare.*

13.. *K. Alis.* 7821 Theo lewed folk prayed theo kyng, Of him to make remuwyng. 1497 *Naval Acc. Hen. VII* (1896) 229 Payed..to c men..attendyng about the remewyng of the Regent.

Remuent, variant of REMUANT *Obs.*

Remuf(e, -muff, obs. Sc. forms of REMOVE *v.*

Remu·gient, *a.* *rare*—1. [f. pres. pple. of L. *remūgīre*, f. *re-* RE- + *mūgīre* to bellow.] Resounding, rebellowing.

1660 H. MORE *Myst. Godl.* III. iii. 63 Trembling and tottering Earth-quakes accompanied with remugient Echoes and ghastly murmurs from below.

Remulant, variant of REMENANT *Obs.*

†**Remuled**, *a.* *Obs.*—1 [ad. OF. *remulé*, found only in the passage here translated.] Mutilated.

1481 CAXTON *Godfrey* li. 93 Atyns was a Greke..the moost fals, vntrewe man that euer was. And so he wel semed, ffor he had his nosethrellys remuled and tourned.

Remunaunde, variant of REMENANT *Obs.*

Remu·nerable, *a.* *rare.* [See next and -ABLE.] That may be rewarded; deserving of reward.

1593 NASHE *Christ's T.* (1613) 134 Shall he not (of all other) doe him the most remunerablest seruice? 1641 J. JACKSON *True Evang. T.* II. 159 The righteousnesse of the cause..is as necessary to remunerable suffering, as fuell to make a fire. 1716 M. DAVIES *Athen. Brit.* III. 31 [A neutrality] which how plausible soever to the Commonalty of sure Cards or Self-Interests, is yet scarce sufferable, much less promotable or remunerable *Alibi*.

Hence **Remunerabi·lity.** *rare*—1.

1659 PEARSON *Creed* (1816) I. 570 If there were no other consideration, but..of the liberty and remunerability of human actions.

Remunerate (rĭmiū·nĕreʹt), *v.* [f. L. *remūnerāt-*, ppl. stem of *remūnerārī* (later *-āre*), to reward, f. *re-* RE- + *mūnus* a gift; cf. F. *rémunérer*.]

1. *trans.* To repay, requite, make some return for (services, etc.).

1523 CROMWELL in Merriman *Life & Lett.* (1902) I. 313 Entending to remembre and also remunerate the olde acquayntaunces. 1594 J. DICKENSON *Arisbas* (1878) 37, I will remunerate your kindnesse with most ample recompence. 1607 DEKKER *Sir T. Wyat* Wks. 1873 III. 90 She no doubt, with royall fauour will remunerate The least of your desertes. 1612 T. TAYLOR *Comm. Titus* ii. 13 That was to teach righteousnesse, but this to remunerate it.

2. To reward (a person); to pay (one) for services rendered or work done.

1588 SHAKS. *Tit. A.* I. i. 398 Is she not then beholding to the man..? Yes, and will Nobly him remunerate. 1606 WARNER *Alb. Eng.* XIV. lxxxii. 343 Should Succession fault in not remunerating thee With such a Monument. *a* 1661 FULLER *Worthies* (1840) II. 534 The king remunerated them both, the former with an addition of honour, the latter with an accession of estate. 1849 THACKERAY *Pendennis* xiv, The great Hubbard had acted legitimate drama for twenty nights, and failed to remunerate anybody but himself. 1855 MACAULAY *Hist. Eng.* xx. IV. 526 Dryden..received thirteen hundred pounds for his translation of all the works of Virgil, and was thought to have been splendidly remunerated.

refl. 1838 DICKENS *Nick. Nick.* ii, To remunerate themselves for which trouble.., they only charged three guineas each man.

b. Of things: To recompense or repay (one).

1849 COBDEN *Speeches* 34 The principle that our exclusive trade with the colonies remunerates us for the expense of colonial establishments. 1867 H. MACMILLAN *Bible Teach.* ix. (1870) 188 There are few plants that remunerate so largely the labours of the husbandman.

†3. To give as compensation. *Obs. rare*—1.

1595 *Locrine* II. iii, For your houses burnt We will remunerate you store of gold.

Hence **Remu·nerated** *ppl. a.*; **Remu·nerating** *vbl. sb.* and *ppl. a.*; also **Remu·neratee·**, one who receives remuneration.

1611 COTGR., *Remuneration*, a remuneration, remunerating. 1816–30 BENTHAM *Offic. Apt. Maximized, Extr. Const. Code* (1830) 14 The benefit of it diffuses itself among any, who..are in any way connected with the remuneratee. 1825 *Ibid.*, *Observ. Peel's Sp.* (1830) 32 The very field for which it is proposed to engage their remunerated services. 1843 MARRYAT *M. Violet* xliv, Objects that bring no remunerating value. 1846 J. BAXTER *Libr. Pract. Agric.* (ed. 4) I. 272 The farmer..would get a more remunerating crop from his land than he would obtain under a system of thinner sowing.

Remuneration (rĭmiūnĕrēʹ·ʃən). [a. F. *rémunération*, or ad. L. *remūnerātiōn-em*, n. of action f. *remūnerārī*: see prec.] Reward, recompense, repayment; payment, pay.

1477 EARL RIVERS (Caxton) *Dictes* 6 He shal gyue remuneracion to the goode for theyr goodnesse. *c* 1500 *Melusine* 39 For the salary & remuneraciour of alle the seruyse that euer ye dide vnto his fader. 1590 SWINBURNE *Testaments* 147 So it bee doon in regard of good will, and affection, and not in hope of gaine or remuneration. 1606 SHAKS. *Tr. & Cr.* III. iii. 170 O let not vertue seeke Remuneration for the thing it was. *a* 1653 GOUGE *Comm. Heb.* iii. 5 To be faithfull in the trust that is reposed in one ..deserveth much commendation, and procures also remuneration. 1726 AYLIFFE *Parergon* 188 When such Grant or Donation is liberally and freely bestow'd without any Prospect of an evil Remuneration. 1832 HT. MARTINEAU *Ireland* ii. 26 The remuneration of the Catholic clergy in Ireland being principally derived from marriage fees. 1853 J. H. NEWMAN *Hist. Sk.* (1873) II. I. ii. 83 The indignant author would accept no remuneration at all.

Remunerative (rĭmiū·nĕrătiv), *a.* [f. as REMUNERATE *v.* + -IVE: cf. mod.F. *rémunératif*.]

†1. Inclined to remunerate. *Obs. rare*—1.

1626 *Disc. Pr. Henry* in *Select. Harl. Misc.* (1793) 262 That remunerative he was of services, and considerative of those that deserved and needed.

2. That remunerates or rewards.

a 1677 MANTON *Exp. Lord's Pr.* Matt. vi. 11 Wks. 1870 I. 154 Not from his strict remunerative justice, but out of his grace. 1678 CUDWORTH *Intell. Syst.* I. v. 690 Men..become fit objects for remunerative justice to display itself upon. 1833 I. TAYLOR *Fanat.* ii. 40 Our acquiescence in retributive proceedings as well penal as remunerative.

3. That brings remuneration; profitable.

1859 SMILES *Self-Help* viii. 209 He advanced by degrees to more remunerative branches of employment. 1865 H. PHILLIPS *Amer. Paper Curr.* II. 72 The scheme did not prove remunerative nor a source of revenue. 1880 C. R. MARKHAM *Peruv. Bark* 334 Although chinchona cultivation is a remunerative public work..the experiment is still in its infancy.

Hence **Remu·neratively, Remu·nerativeness.**

1652 GAULE *Magastrom.* 27 But remuneratively let your starres and planets not onely signe, but cause good fortune or reward. 1877 *Fraser's Mag.* XV. 39 Their time is more remuneratively occupied. 1895 *Manch. Guard.* 14 Oct. 5/5 Of the remunerativeness of the enterprise there can be no doubt, apart from the net gain to the cultivators.

Remu·nerator. *rare.* [a. late L. *remūnerātor*, or f. REMUNERATE *v.* + -OR. Cf. F. *rémunérateur* (16th c.).] One who remunerates; a rewarder, recompenser.

1688 BOYLE *Final Causes Nat. Things* ii. 84 The children of God will by their most bountiful remunerator be thought fit to inhabit the New world. 1828 LANDOR *Imag. Conv., Rousseau & Malesherbes*, You have no right, sir, to be the patron and remunerator of inhospitality.

Remu·neratory, *a.* [f. as REMUNERATE *v.* + -ORY: cf. F. *rémunératoire* (16th c.).] Serving to remunerate; affording remuneration.

1586 A. DAY *Eng. Secretary* I. (1625) 22 Remuneratorie, being a gratefull relation of courtesies, benefits or good turnes receiued. 1617 MORYSON *Itin.* III. 219 The gift of vtensile goods..is of so little force, as with death it is not confirmed, except it be remuneratory. 1751 JOHNSON *Rambler* No. 145 ¶ 4 Remuneratory honours are proportioned at once to the usefulness and difficulty of performances. 1765 BLACKSTONE *Comm.* I. 56 Human legislators have for the most part chosen to make the sanction of their laws rather vindicatory than remuneratory. 1844 M. HENNELL *Soc. Syst.* 118 Legislation..will be remuneratory, and distribute the honour and glory due to pre-eminent virtue.

Remurmur (rĭmɜ·ɹmɜɹ), *v.* Chiefly *poet.* [ad. L. *remurmurāre*: see RE- and MURMUR *v.*]

1. *intr.* To give back or give forth a murmuring sound; to resound with murmurs.

1697 DRYDEN *Virg. Georg.* IV. 667 The Realms of Mars remurmured all around. 1718 MOTTEUX *Quix.* (1733) II. 276 A pleasant Rivulet..remurmurs over the whitest Pebbles. 1747 T. GIBBONS *Elegy Col. Gardiner* v, Heav'n high Crystal Domes remurmur with the Sound. 1870 BRYANT *Iliad* II. XXI. 279 The banks around Remurmured shrilly.

b. To answer with murmurs *to* a sound.

1697 DRYDEN *Æneid* XI. 695 A jarring Sound..Like that of Swans remurm'ring to the Floods. 1703 POPE *Thebais* 166 Eurota's banks remurmur'd to the noise. 1762–9 FALCONER *Shipwr.* I. 34 Yonder cave, Whose vaults remurmur to the roaring wave.

c. Of sounds: To echo in murmurs.

1717 POPE *Iliad* X. 563 A low groan remurmur'd through the shore. 1790 A. WILSON in *Poems & Lit. Prose* (1876) II. 17 Crying and sighing Remurmured through the glen.

2. *trans.* To repeat in murmurs.

1704 POPE *Winter* 64 The trembling trees..Her fate remurmur to the silver flood. 1789 J. WHITE *Earl Strongbow* I. 202 The woods, the valleys, the mountains around..daily remurmur the effusions of my misery.

Hence **Remu·rmuring** *ppl. a.*

1740 SOMERVILLE *Hobbinol* II. 464 While thy remurm'ring Streams Danc'd by, well pleas'd. 1757 DYER *Fleece* I. 608 Deep remurmuring cords Of th'ancient harp.

†**Remurmura·tion.** *Obs. rare.* [ad. late L. *remurmurātiōn-em*: see prec. and -ATION.] The action of murmuring or protesting.

1612 W. SCLATER *Key* (1629) 214 So see we many practising vsurie, without any remurmuration of conscience, through errour of iudgement. 1623 R. CARPENTER *Conscionable Christian* 38 To him..there is no condemnation, or remurmuration of conscience for sinne.

Remuta·tion. *rare*—1. [RE- 5 a.] The action of changing back again.

a 1843 SOUTHEY *Doctor* ccxvii. (1848) 584 The mutation or rarefaction of water into air takes place by day, the remutation or condensation of air into water by night.

Remynaunte, variant of REMENANT *Obs.*

Remyssale, variant of REMISSAL *Obs.*

Remyt, obs. form of REMIT *sb.*

†**Ren**, *sb.* *Obs. rare.* [f. *renne*, obs. f. RUN *v.*; cf. Du. *ren*, G. *renn*, ON. *renna*.] A run, course.

c 1250 *Gen. & Ex.* 1 Man og to luuen ðat rimes ren, ðe wisseð wel ðe logede men [etc.]. *c* 1386 CHAUCER *Reeve's T.* 159 The wyf cam lepynge Inward with a ren. *c* 1440 *Promp. Parv.* 429/1 Ren, or rennynge, *cursus*.

†**Ren**, *v.* *Obs.*—1 [?for *rene*:—OE. *rēnian*, *regnian* to set in order.] *trans.* To clear a way for.

a 1340 HAMPOLE *Psalter* lxxxiv. 14 Rightwisnes of penaunce for oure syn sal ga bifor him in vs, that is, it sall ren his cumynge in til vs.

Ren, obs. form of RAIN *sb.*[1], REIN *sb.*[1], RUN *v.*

Renable (re·năb'l), *a.* *Obs.* exc. *dial.* Also 5 **renabol, -abulle, -abyll, resnabyl**, 7 **rennible**, 9 *dial.* **-able, runnable.** [a. OF. *renable*, *resnable* (AF. also *rednable*), *reis-*, *raisnable*, etc., :—L. *ratiōnābil-em* reasonable, RATIONABLE. The sense of 'eloquent' appears to be characteristic of AF. In later use prob. assoc. with *renne* RUN *v.*]

1. Of persons: Ready of speech, eloquent: speaking or reading fluently or distinctly; †esp. in phr. *renable of tongue*. (Cf. REASONABLE *a.* 3.)

c 1290 *Beket* 1336 in *S. Eng. Leg.* I. 144 Non of heom þar nas, Þat he preisede muche þis heiȝe man for he so renable was. 1297 R. GLOUC. (Rolls) 8572 Renable was he noȝt of tonge, ac of speche hastif. 1377 LANGL. *P. Pl.* B. Prol. 158 A raton of renon most renable of tonge. 1387 TREVISA *Higden* (Rolls) VIII. 25 He was..resonabel [*v.r.* renable, renabel] of speche [L. *eloquens*], and wel i-lettred. *c* 1400 *Ywaine & Gaw.* 200 Of tong sho was trew and renable, And of hir semblant soft and stabile. *c* 1460 *Towneley Myst.* xxi. 110 Men calle hym a prophete, a lord fulle renabyll. 1781 J. HUTTON *Tour to Caves* (ed. 2) Gloss., *Renable*, loquacious, and never at a stop or inconsistent in telling a story. 1868 SEDGWICK *Mem. Cowgill Chapel* 72 (E. D. D.), Some lassie who was bright and renable was asked to read for the amusement of the party.

b. Of speech, etc.: Ready, fluent, plain.

1387 TREVISA *Higden* (Rolls) I. 11 Noble spekers, þat.. faire facounde and resonable [*v.r.* renable] speche folowed and streynede all her lyf tyme. *c* 1400 tr. *Secreta Secret., Gov. Lordsh.* 103 Þe ffyfte [virtue], þat he be curtays..and ..of renable speche. *a* 1450 MYRC 1008 Hast þou also prowde I-be..for þow hast a renabulle tonge? 1643 BP. HALL *Devout Soul* ii. (1646) 5 Not [he] that hath the most rennible tongue (for prayer is not so much a matter of the lips, as of the heart). 1674 N. FAIRFAX *Bulk & Selv.* 33 We choose the renablest words belonging to the former, wherewith to set forth the latter. 1895 *E. Anglian Gloss.*, *Rennable*, plain, easy to be understood.

†2. Reasonable, moderate. *Obs. rare*—1.

1340 *Ayenb.* 95 Þyse þri þinges byeþ nyeduolle to alle þe þinges þet in þe erþe wexeþ. Guod molde, wocnesse norissynde, and renable hete.

Re·nably, *adv.* *Obs.* exc. *dial.* Also 4 **renab(le)liche**, 9 *dial.* **runnably.** [f. prec. + -LY[2].]

1. Fluently, readily.

13.. *Sir Beues* (A.) 2074 Forþ þer com on redi reke, Þat renabliche kouþe frensch speke. *c* 1386 CHAUCER *Friar's T.* 211 Som tyme we..speke as renably and faire and wel As to the Phitonissa dide Samuel. 1895 *E. Anglian Gloss.*, *Runnably*, currently; smoothly; without hesitation. Often *Renably* in Suffolk.

†2. To a reasonable extent; moderately. *Obs.*—1

c 1315 SHOREHAM III. 19 Þou schel haue..mete and cloþes renableliche, And lyf ine herte blisce.

Renagado, obs. form of RENEGADO.

Renaissance (rĭnēʹ·săns, F. rənɛsɑ̃s). [F., f. *renaître* to be born again, after *naissance* birth: cf. RENASCENCE.]

1. The great revival of art and letters, under the influence of classical models, which began in Italy in the 14th century and continued during the 15th and 16th; also, the period during which this movement was in progress.

1845 FORD *Handbk. Spain* II. 745 At the bright period of the *Renaissance*, when fine art was a necessity and pervaded every relation of life. 1854 LOWELL *Keats* Prose Wks. 1896 I. 244 In him we have an example of the renaissance going on almost under our own eyes. 1873 PATER *Renaissance* 2 The word Renaissance indeed is now generally used to denote..a whole complex movement of which that revival of classical antiquity was but one element or symptom.

b. *ellipt.* The style of art or architecture developed in, and characteristic of, this period.

1840 T. A. TROLLOPE *Summer in Brittany* II. 234 That heaviest and least graceful of all possible styles, the 'renaissance' as the French choose to term it. 1851 RUSKIN *Stones Ven.* I. i. 23 This rationalistic art is the art commonly called Renaissance, marked by a return to pagan systems. 1859 JEPHSON & REEVE *Brittany* 268 The cathedral front is a huge mass of barbarous Renaissance.

c. *attrib.* with *architecture*, *building*, etc.

1851 RUSKIN *Stones Ven.* I. App. xi. 370 A choice little piece of description this, of the Renaissance painters. 1857 — *Pol. Econ. Art* ii. 103 Verona possesses..the loveliest Renaissance architecture of Italy. 1860 G. A. SPOTTISWOODE in *Vac. Tour* 98 We..contented ourselves with what we saw of its heavy-looking renaissance buildings. 1880 CAULFIELD & SAWARD *Dict. Needlework*, *Renaissance Braid Work*.—This is also known as Renaissance Lace.

2. Any revival, or period of marked improvement and new life, in art, literature, etc.

1872 MORLEY *Voltaire* 4 Voltairism may stand for the name of the Renaissance of the eighteenth century. 1882 *Athenæum* 23 Dec. 857/2 The most satisfactory among the signs of a theatrical renaissance.

Renai·ssant, *a.* *rare.* [a. F. *renaissant*, pres. pple. of *renaître*: cf. RENASCENT.] = prec. 1 c.

1864 MISS COBBE *Italics* 14 The great artistic ages, classic and Renaissant. 1886 *Ch. Times* 17 Sept. 686 Gothic is most appropriate for ecclesiastical buildings and Renaissant for gin-shops, theatres and restaurants.

Renal (rī·năl), *a.* and *sb.* [a. F. *rénal*, or ad. late L. *rēnālis*, f. *rēn* kidney: see REINS.]

A. *adj.* Of or pertaining to the reins or kidneys.

1656 BLOUNT *Glossogr.* s.v. *Vein*, *Renal veins*, the kidney veins. 1704 J. HARRIS *Lex. Techn.* I, *Renal Artery*, is said by some, to come out of the Aorta, and to enter into the Kidneys. *c* 1720 W. GIBSON *Farrier's Dispens.* i. (1734) 27 By its extraordinary detersive qualities, it scours and cleanses the renal passages. 1788 BAILLIE in *Phil. Trans.* LXXVIII. 357 The renal capsules had undergone no change. 1840 E. WILSON *Anat. Vade M.* (1842) 309 The Renal arteries are two large trunks given off from the sides of the aorta. 1872 HUXLEY *Physiol.* v. 105 The renal excretion has naturally an acid reaction.

B. *sb.* A renal artery.

1899 *Allbutt's Syst. Med.* VI. 274 In ten [cases] the upper extremity lay between the inferior mesenteric and the renals.

†**Re·naldry.** *Obs. rare*—1. [f. *Renald*, obs. var. REYNARD + -RY: cf. obs. F. *renarderie*.] Guile, cunning, craft.

1612 tr. *Passenger of Benvenuto* I. iv. 269 She vsed all malitious Renaldrie [It. *volpina malitia*] to the end I might stay there this night.

Rename (rī-), *v.* [RE- 5 a.] *trans.* To name again; *esp.* to give another or new name to.

a 1660 HAMMOND *Serm.* (1850) 423 By that odious re-naming of sin. 1665 J. WEBB *Stone-Heng* (1725) 62 It is scarcely worth re-naming, much less answering to. 1675 SHERBURNE *Sphere Manilius* 66 [Philippi] afterwards renamed from Philip..its Reedifier. 1869 TOZER *Highl. Turkey* II. 354 The features of the district were renamed. 1897 *Atlantic Monthly* LXXIX. 36 Then must we have a new vocabulary and re-name the professions.

Re·nardine, *a.* *rare*—1. [f. *Renard* var. REYNARD.] Pertaining to Reynard the Fox. So †**Re·nardism** = REGNARDISM (Blount 1661).

1886 *Athenæum* 7 Aug. 165/2 There has been much learning expended..on the question of why the lion was king in the Renardine tales.

Renascence (rĭnæ·sĕns). Also 9 **re-** (rī-). [See RENASCENT and -ENCE.]

1. The process or fact of being born anew; rebirth, renewal, revival.

1727 EARBERY tr. *Burnet's St. Dead* 187 The Souls have a kind of Renascence, or παλιγγενεσία, a new Life, a new World, and all things new. 1827 COLERIDGE in *Lit. Rem.* (1839) IV. 393 The perpetuity and continued re-nascence and spiritual life of Christ.

2. = RENAISSANCE 1.

1869 M. ARNOLD *Cult. & An.* 159 The great movement which goes by the name of the Renascence. [*Note*] I have ventured to give to the foreign word *Renaissance* an English form. 1874 GREEN *Short Hist.* vii. 390 Here, as elsewhere, the Renascence found vernacular literature all but dead.

transf. 1872 MORLEY *Voltaire* 5 The four-score volumes which he wrote, are the monument..of a new renascence.

†**Rena·scency.** *Obs.* [See next and -ENCY.] = RENASCENCE 1.

1654 EVELYN tr. *Freart's Archit.* Ep. Ded. a 4 This [science] of Architecture..ows her renascency amongst Us to Your Majesties encouragements. *Ibid.* II. i. 91 A renascency from his own Ashes like the Phœnix. 1682 SIR T. BROWNE *Chr. Mor.* III. § 25 Job would not only curse the day of his Nativity, but also of his Renascency.

Renascent (rĭnæ·sĕnt), *a.* and *sb.* [ad. L. *renascent-em*, pres. pple. of *renascī*, f. *re-* RE- + *nascī* to be born.] A. *adj.* That is being born again, reviving, springing up afresh.

1727 BAILEY (vol. II), *Renascent*, springing up, or being born again. 1747 *Gentl. Mag.* XVII. 212/2 Care must also be taken to prevent any external impression on the renascent bark. 1773 J. ROSS *Fratricide* VI. 552 (MS.) To console her cares, And give renascent vigour to her frame! 1812 SOUTHEY *Omniana* II. 95 These are the first rudiments of the renascent plant. 1849 THACKERAY *Pendennis* lvi, Pen's renascent desire to see his little conquest again. 1883 SYMONDS *Shaks. Predec.* ii. (1900) 22 The genius of youthfulness, renascent,..was dominant in that age.

B. *sb.* One who takes part in a renaissance.

1898 *Amer. Jrnl. Philol.* Apr. 115 This we owe to the Greek renascents and to their maintenance of the best standards—the three stars of Attic tragedy.

Rena·scible, *a.* *rare*—0. [f. L. *renasc-ī* (see prec.) + -IBLE.] Capable of being born or produced again (Johnson 1755). Hence **Renascibi·lity** (Bailey 1721); **Rena·scibleness** (Bailey, vol. II, 1727).

†**Renash**, *v.* *Obs. rare*—1. [Of obscure origin.] *intr.* ?To toss the head.

c 1475 in *Archæologia* (1814) XVII. 293 A rayne of lethir hungry tied fro the hors hede unto the girthis beeneth betwene the ferthir bouse of the hors for renasshyng.

Renat(e, obs. forms of RENNET *sb.*[2]

†**Rena·te**, *ppl. a.* *Obs. rare.* [ad. L. *renāt-us*, pa. pple. of *renascī*.] Reborn, reincarnate.

1570 LEVINS *Manip.* 30/43 Renate, *renatus*. *c* 1614 FLETCHER, etc. *Wit at Sev. Weap.* I. ii, And to confirm yourself in me renate, I hope you'll find my wits legitimate! 1660 STANLEY *Hist. Philos.* IX. (1701) 428/2 So one man often renate, is named Æthalides, Euphorbus, Hermotimus, Pyrrhus, and lastly Pythagoras.

†**Rena·te**, *v.* *Obs. rare.* [f. L. *renāt-*, ppl. stem of *renascī*: see RENASCENT.] a. *pass.* To be born again. b. *intr.* To form again.

c 1546 JOYE in Gardiner *Declar. Joye* (1546) 91 b, Thus we electe, called & renated of the Spirit, know ye father in Christ. *a* 1548 HALL *Chron., Hen. VII* 32 A pernicious fable and ficcion..to feyne a dead man to be renated and newely borne agayne. 1578 BANISTER *Hist. Man* VIII. 104 The watrie humor being effused may renate or grow agayne.

Rena·vigate, *v.* *rare*—0. [RE- 5 a.] To navigate again. So **Renaviga·tion** (Phillips 1658).

1611 COTGR., *Renaviger*, to renauigate, sayle backe, or sayle ouer againe. 1623 in COCKERAM. 1721– in BAILEY and later Dicts. 1828–32 WEBSTER s.v., To renavigate the Pacific Ocean.

†**Renay**, *sb.* *Obs.* Also **reney, renye.** [ad. OF. *reneié*, pa. pple. of *reneier*: see next.] A renegade, apostate.

13.. *Coer de L.* 4070 Quod the renay: 'Mercy I crye!' 1340 *Ayenb.* 19 He ys wel renay, þet þet land þet he halt of his lhorde deþ in-to þe hond of his uyende. *Ibid.*, Ine þri maneres is man ycleped reney and uals cristen. ?*a* 1400 *Morte Arth.* 2795 The renye relys abowte and rusches to þe erthe, Roris fulle ruydlye, bot rade he no more.

†**Renay·, reny·**, *v.* *Obs.* Forms: α. 4 **renai(e, -aye**, 4–6 **renay**, (5 **renn-, reyn-**); 4 **reneie**, 4–6 **reney(e**, 5 **reneyhe.** β. 4–6 **reny(e**, 6 **renie.** [a. OF. *reneier*, *renier* (*renoier*, etc.):— pop. L. *renegāre*: see RENEGUE, and cf. DENY *v.*]

1. *trans.* To renounce, abjure (one's faith, God, lord, etc.).

α. *a* 1300 *Cursor M.* 8995 Leuedis he luued,..Þat did him drightin to renai. *a* 1330 *Otuel* 524 Me ne stant nouȝt of þe swich awe, Þat þou sschalt make me reneie mi lawe. 1377 LANGL. *P. Pl.* B. XI. 121 Though a Crystene man coueyted his Crystenedome to reneye [etc.]. *c* 1400 MAUNDEV. (Roxb.) xi. 42 Þe emperour Iulyan Apostata, whilk reynayd and forsuke Cristen fayth. *c* 1440 CAPGRAVE *Life St. Kath.* IV. 976 We haue heere a mayde whiche with obstinacye Reneyeth [*v.r.* reneybithe] oure lawes. *c* 1475 *Partenay* 2173 Me moste here-After our lord to renay, And in sarisine lau beleue. 1534 MORE *Comf. agst. Trib.* III. Wks. 1212/1 Hee ..geueth..parte to suche as willinglye will reney their faith. [1900 RALEIGH *Milton* 219 He renayed his ancestry.]

absol. 1340 *Ayenb.* 19 Alþaȝ he by be his ziggingе cristen, he renayþ be dede. *c* 1380 WYCLIF *Sel. Wks.* III. 371 Lest I..be drawen to renaye, and sey, Who is Lord?

β. 1375 BARBOUR *Bruce* IX. 739 Thow has a quhill renyit thi fay. *c* 1400 *Sowdone Bab.* 2254, I shalle..make the to renye thy laye. 1483 CAXTON *Gold. Leg.* 20/2 It is redde in this-toryes, whan he renyed and forsoke our Lord [etc.]. 1511 *Guylforde's Pilgr.* (Camden) 44 He shall be compelled incontynentlye to renye his fayth and crystendome. 1579 J. STUBBES *Gaping Gulf* C iv, The king of Nauarre..had felt the poynt thereof if he had not to hys honour..renied hys God. 1602 WARNER *Alb. Eng.* XI. lxix. 285 For that thow should'st reny thy Faith, and her therby possesse, The Soldan did capitulat.

refl. 1549 CHALONER *Erasm. on Folly* M ij b, They dishort vs from sinne, but I renie myselfe, if euer they coulde cunningly diffine, what that should be, we call sinne.

b. To recant (an opinion). Also *absol.*

a 1529 SKELTON *Replyc.* 87 Fayne were ye to reny, And mercy for to cry, Or be brende by and by. *c* 1533 *Song* in Strype *Eccl. Mem.* (1721) I. App. xliv. 121 Which opynions wer good for thee to renay.

2. a. To deny, disown (an utterance). *rare*—1.

c 1440 *Partonope* 1835 That I haue sayde In no wyse for me shall be renayed [*printed* remayed].

b. To deny the truth of (a statement).

1510–20 *Compl. too late maryed* (1862) 16 For to saye that therin is servage In maryage, but I it reny, For therin is but humayne company. 1512 *Helyas* in Thoms *Prose Rom.* (1828) III. 66 She blusshed all red,..but not withstandinge she wende well assuredly to have renied al the case.

3. a. To refuse, decline (a gift). *rare.*

13.. *Gaw. & Gr. Knt.* 1821 Ho raȝt hym a riche rynk [= ring]..Bot þe renk hit renayed, &..sayde, 'I wil no giftez for gode'.

b. To refuse *to* do something. *rare*—1.

c 1489 SKELTON *Death Earl Northumbld.* 78 The commons renyed ther taxes to pay Of them demaunded and asked by the kynge; With one voice importune they plainly sayd nay.

†**Renay·ed, reni·ed**, *ppl. a.* *Obs.* [f. prec. + -ED[1], after OF. *reneié*: see RENAY *sb.*] Apostate, renegade.

a 1300 *Cursor M.* 23111 Wreches mistruand, Þat renaid ar traiturs and fals. 13.. *St. Erkenwolde* 11 in Horstm. *Altengl. Leg.* (1881) 266 Þene wos this reame renaid mony ronke ȝeres. *c* 1380 *Sir Ferumb.* 4673 If Fyrumbras may beo taan, þat lik false reneyed man. *a* 1400 *Pistill of Susan* 198 Þo Ros vp with rancour þe Renkes reneyed. 1585 T. WASHINGTON tr. *Nicholay's Voy.* I. xi. 13 b, This Caddi was a renyed Christian. 1590 SIR J. SMYTHE *Disc. conc. Weapons* 41 b, The Ianissaries..being Christian mens children renied.

†**Renay·ing**, *vbl. sb.* *Obs.* [f. RENAY *v.* + -ING[1].] The action of renouncing or abjuring.

a 1300 *Cursor M.* 29406 If he in renaijng lijs, efter þat he es monest thris. *c* 1386 CHAUCER *Pars. T.* ¶ 719 Reneying of god and hate of his neighebors. *c* 1440 *Jacob's Well* 131 On..is renaying; whan a man forsakyth god, & becomyth a iewe or a sarazene. 1529 MORE *Dyaloge* II. Wks. 179/1 It was a plaine renaying of Christes faith to doo anye obseruaunce therto.

†**Renay·rie, renoy·rie.** *Obs. rare.* [a. OF. *reneierie*, *renoierie*: see RENAY *v.*] Apostacy.

1340 *Ayenb.* 17 He him to-delþ in þri little boȝes..þe þridde [is] renoyrye. *Ibid.* 19 Þe þridde ontreuþe þet comþ of prede ys renayrie.

Rence, Sc. variant of RAINES *Obs.*

Rence, rench, obs. or dial. forms of RINSE *v.*

Rench, obs. form of WRENCH *v.*

†**Re·ncian.** *Obs. rare.* [a. OF. *rentien* (Godef.), of obscure origin.] Some kind of cloth.

a 1272 *Luue Ron* 106 in *O. E. Misc.* 96 Ne byt he wiþ þe lond ne leode, Vouh ne gray ne rencyan. *c* 1275 *Serving Christ* 70 in *O. E. Misc.* 92 Ne geyneþ vs..þe robes of russet ne of rencyan.

Rencky: see RENKY *a.*

Rencontre (renkǫ·ntəɹ, F. rɑ̃kõtr'), *sb.* Also 8 **-countre**, 9 **-conter.** [a. F. *rencontre* (13th c.), vbl. sb. f. *rencontrer*: see next and cf. RENCOUNTER *sb.*]

The form is given by Blount (1656, etc., copying Cotgrave), but later Dictionaries down to the Webster of 1864 recognize only *rencounter*.]

1. = RENCOUNTER *sb.* 3.

1619 in *Eng. & Germ.* (Camden) 95 The nice termes his Ma^{ty} standeth in with the French King..makes it necessary to acquaint you with a rencontre I had at Antwerp. 1705 VANBRUGH *Country House* I. iv, *Baron.* We have not seen one another since we were schoolfellows before. *Marquis.* The happiest rencontre! 1788 MME. D'ARBLAY *Diary* 2 Aug., One of the letters..was written just after I had communicated to her my singular rencontre with this lady. 1845 STOCQUELER *Handbk. Brit. India* (1854) 82 The accidental rencontre of a vessel homeward bound awakens family recollections. 1884 'H. COLLINGWOOD' *Under Meteor Flag* 117 The rencontre was disagreeable, and, to shorten it as much as possible, Isabel..turned back.

b. *Her.* (See quots.)

The existence of the use in Eng. is doubtful; quot. 1727–38 is ultimately derived from the *Dict. Universel* of Furetière (1690).

1725 COATS *Dict. Her.*, *Rencontre*, or *an Rencontre*, is a French Phrase signifying, that the Face of a Beast stands right forward, as if it came to meet the Person before it. 1727–38 CHAMBERS *Cycl.*, *Rencontre* or *rencontre*, in heraldry is applied to animals when they show the head in front, with both eyes, etc. *Ibid.*, He bears sable, in rencountre, a golden fleece.

2. = RENCOUNTER *sb.* 1.

1688 in Ellis *Orig. Lett.* Ser. II. IV. 154 Then had happened a rencontre betwixt a party of his Majesty's Army and that of the Prince of Orange. 1803 MRQ. WELLESLEY in Gurw. *Wellington's Desp.* (1838) II. 609 *note*, I have not yet discovered whether the battle was occasioned..by an accidental rencontre of the armies before the truce had commenced. 1824 SILLIMAN *Tour fr. Hartford to Quebec* (ed. 2) 157 *note*, Lord Howe..was killed near Ticonderoga..in a rencontre the day preceding the..assault.

b. = RENCOUNTER *sb.* 1 b.

1754 RICHARDSON *Grandison* (1781) III. xxviii. 293, I referred to my known resolution of long standing, to avoid a meditated rencontre with any man. 1772 *Chron.* in *Ann. Reg.* 125/2 A rencontre has just happened..between the Marquis de Fleury..and an officer..They fought with pistols. 1826 SCOTT *Woodst.* xxvii, Perhaps there mingled with his resolution a secret belief that such a rencontre would not prove fatal. 1848 THACKERAY *Van. Fair* lv, The secret of the *rencontre* between him and Colonel Crawley was buried in the profoundest oblivion.

c. = RENCOUNTER *sb.* 1 c.

1666–7 PEPYS *Diary* 18 Feb., He was mighty witty, and she also making sport with him very inoffensively, that a more pleasant rencontre I never heard. 1874 C. GEIKIE *Life in Woods* xxi, I was very much amused at a rencontre between the 'captain'..and one of the passengers, who.. had come on board without having money to pay his fare.

3. = RENCOUNTER *sb.* 2. ?*Obs.*

1677 GALE *Crt. Gentiles* IV. II. ix. I. 476 The affaires of war: wherein oft the most inconsiderable rencontres or occurrences produce the greatest changements. 1770 in Jesse *Selwyn & Contemp.* (1844) III. 3 By the..despair and misery which the poor waggoner testified on this unlucky *rencontre*, I guessed we had done some great mischief.

†**Renco·ntre**, *v.* *Obs. rare.* Also 7 **-ter.** [ad. F. *rencontrer*: see RENCOUNTER *v.*] *trans.* a. To encounter, to meet with. b. To oppose, reverse.

1654 *Nicholas Papers* (Camden) II. 67, I was stoped be the manie disorders and deficulties that I rencontred at my first comming. 1680 HICKERINGILL *Ceremony-Monger* v. Wks. 1716 II. 427 To Rancounter and Ruffle the whole course of Nature, and make Heaven a Pair of Stairs to Hell.

Rencounter (renkau·ntəɹ), *sb.* Also 6 **rencounter, -countre**, 7 **rancounter, -tre.** [ad. F. *rencontre*: see prec. and cf. RE-ENCOUNTER *sb.*]

1. An encounter or engagement between two opposing forces; a battle, skirmish, conflict.

1523 LD. BERNERS *Froiss.* I. lxxxiv. 106 At the first rencounter many were ouerthrowen. 1562 J. SHUTE tr. *Cambini's Turk. Wars* 56 Amorathe and Aladino..in the rencountre that they had with Selim [etc.]. 1588 ALLEN *Admon.* 59 Recounte all the..rencounters of a very fewe Catholikes against the heretikes and rebelles in Flanders. 1632 LITHGOW *Trav.* IX. 419 Tartars are not..so manly as the Polonians, who counter-blow them at rancounters. 1682 LUTTRELL *Brief Rel.* (1857) I. 169 There lately happened a rancounter between some forces of the French.. and some Spaniards. 1709 STEELE *Tatler* No. 28 ¶ 8 There are mentioned several Rencounters between..Detachments of the Swedish and Russian Armies. 1781 JEFFERSON *Corr.* Wks. 1859 I. 288 Three little rencounters have happened with the enemy. 1865 CARLYLE *Fredk. Gt.* XXI. iv. (1872) X. 36 The Russian Armies had only to show themselves to beat the Turks in every rencounter.

b. A hostile meeting or encounter between two adversaries; a duel; †sometimes *spec.* (after French usage) distinguished from a regular duel by being unpremeditated. Also without article.

Supplement, p. 3873; Corrigenda, p. 4092; Spurious words, p. 4093; Books quoted, p. 4094

Rencounter (renkəu'ntəɹ), v. Now rare. Also *-cunter*. [ad. F. *rencontrer*: cf. prec. and RENCOUNTER sb.]

1. *trans.* To meet or encounter (an army, person, etc.) in hostile fashion; to engage (one) in fight.

†b. *intr.* To encounter each other in battle.

2. *trans.* To meet or fall in with (a person, etc.).

†b. *intr.* To meet together, or fall in together.

Rend, sb. [f. the verb: cf. RENT sb.]

1. A rent, split, division. *Obs. rare.*

Rend (rend), v. [OE. *rendan*. Forms: 1 *rendan* (*hrendan*), 3–4 *renden*, 4–5 *rende*, (4 *reende*, 5 *-yn*, *reynd*), 6– rend. *Pa. t.* and *pa. ppl.* 1 *rendde*(*d*)e, 3–6 *rente*, 4– rent.]

1. *trans.* To tear, to pull violently or by main force, *off*, *out of*, or *from* a thing or place; to tear *off* or *away*.

Render (rendəɹ), sb.[1] [f. RENDER v.]

One who rends or tears.

Render (rendəɹ), sb.[2] Also 4 rendre, 8 -dare. [a. F. *rendre* to render.]

Render (rendəɹ), v. [a. F. *rendre*, = Pr., Sp., Pg. *render*, It. *rendere*.]

Renderable (rendəɹab'l), a. rare. [f. prec. + -ABLE.] Capable of being rendered.

Rendered (rendəɹd), ppl. a. [f. RENDER v.] Molten, or curled.

Renderer (rendəɹəɹ). [f. RENDER v. + -ER.] One who renders, in senses of the vb.

Rendering (rendəɹiŋ), vbl. sb. [-ING.]

1. The action of rendering, surrendering, yielding, giving, etc.; also, that which is rendered.

Render-set, v., and sb. [RENDER v. + SET.]

Rendezvous (rendezvous, -davous, -vous), sb. Forms: α. 7 rendezvous, ... β. 7 randevoo, -vous, -vowse, ... γ. 7–8 rendevous, -devouze ...

1. *Mil.* A place appointed for the assembling of troops or armed forces.

Rendible, a.[1] [f. REND v. + -IBLE.] That may be rent (Worcester 1864).

Rendible, a.[2] rare. [f. RENDER v. + -IBLE.]

Rendition (rendɪʃən). [a. obs. F. *rendition* (Sp. *rendición*), f. *rendre* to RENDER.]

1. The surrender of a place, garrison, possession, etc. (common in 17th c.)

Renounce

Renouncer (rĭnau·nsǝɹ). [f. RENOUNCE v. + -ER.] One who renounces.

Renunciation.

Renouncing (rĭnau·nsiŋ), vbl. sb. [f. as prec.] The action of the vb., in various senses; renunciation. Also, an instance of this.

Renovation

Renovate

Renovant

Renounce, obs. form of RENOUNCE v.

Renouncement (rĭnau·nsmĕnt). [a. F. renoncement (13th c.).] = RENUNCIATION.

Renounceable, a. rare⁻¹. [f. prec. + -ABLE.] That may be renounced.

Reno·vable

Renovate (re·nǝvǝt), v. [f. L. renovāt-, ppl. stem of renovāre, f. re- RE- + novāre to make new, f. novus new.]

Renovation

Renovator (re·nǝveɪtǝɹ). [a. L. renovātor, agent-n. f. renovāre to RENOVATE; cf. F. rénovateur.] One who renovates.

Renove, v. Obs. [ad. OF. renover, renouver.] trans. To renew.

Renovel, v. Obs. Also 4-5 renouel. [ad. OF. renoveler, renouveler, f. L. re- RE- + novellus NOVEL.] trans. To renew.

Reno·vation

Reno·vesical, a. Path. [f. reno- combining form of L. rēn kidney.] Connected with the kidneys and bladder.

Renovize

Renovate

Renown (rĭnau·n), sb. Forms: 4-7 re-noun(e, 5-6 re-, 5-7 renowne (-oun, -ownne), 5-6 renoune, 8-9 renown. [a. AF. renoun, renon, OF. renom, renum.]

Renowne, obs. form of RENOUNCE v.

Renowned (rĭnau·nd), ppl. a. Also 5-7 renowned. [f. as RENOWN v. + -ED¹; cf. RE-NOWNE.] Celebrated; famous; covered with renown.

Renowner (rĭnau·nǝɹ). [f. as prec. + -ER.] One who celebrates or makes famous.

Renowning, vbl. sb.

Renownful, a. rare. [-FUL.]

Renownless, a. rare. [-LESS.] Devoid of renown; unrenowned.

Renoyre, variant of RENAYRE Obs.

Renpayre, variant of REMPAIR v. Obs.

Rens, obs. Sc. form of RHENISH a.

Rensch, Rense, obs. forms of RINSE v.

Rensselaerite (rensĕlē·ǝrǝit, rĕnslē·ǝrǝit). Min. [Named in 1837 after Gov. Stephen Van Rensselaer.] A variety of talc.

Rent, sb.¹ Forms: 1-7 rent, 3-7 rente (5-6 rente, rent, etc.). [OE. rent, ad. OF. rent(e.]

Rent, sb.² [f. RENT v.²] A rent or item of revenue or income.

Rent (rent), sb.³ [f. RENT v.¹] 1. The result of rending or tearing apart; a separation of parts produced by tearing or violence.

Rent (rent), sb.⁴ [var. of RAND sb.¹; cf. RENT v.²] 1. The rail of rending or tearing; a laceration.

Rent (rent), v.¹ [a. OF. renter, f. rente; see RENT sb.¹] 1. trans. To provide with revenues; to endow.

Rent (rent), v.² [f. RENT sb.¹] 1. intr. To pay rent for; to hold, occupy on, say, by payment of rent.

Rent (rent), v.³ Also ppl. rent. [a. var. of REND v.] trans. To tear, pull asunder or in pieces.

Rentable (re·ntǝb'l), a. [f. RENT v.² + -ABLE.] 1. Liable to pay rent. b. That may be rented, or let out at a rent.

Rentage (re·ntǝdʒ). [f. RENT sb.¹ + -AGE.] Rent, rental, or rent-charge.

Rental (re·ntal), sb. Also 4-5 rentall, 6 rentall, -ayll. ad. AF. rental (Godef.), or ad. Anglo-Lat. rentāle (Du Cange).] 1. A list or register of the rents due by tenants.

Rental-charger, Law. One who rents or holds land at a rental.

Rentaller (re·ntalǝɹ). Sc. Also 6 -alar, 6-7 -aller. [f. prec. sb. or vb. + -ER¹.] 1. One who holds property at a rental.

Rent-charge, Law. A rent forming a charge upon lands, etc., granted or reserved by deed to one who is not the owner, with a clause of distress in case of arrears.

Rentage. See RENTAGE.

Renten, v. Obs.

Renter (re·ntǝɹ). [a. F. renteur.]

Rentage

Rented (re·ntĕd), ppl. a. [f. RENT v.² + -ED¹.] 1. Possessed of, or endowed with, property yielding a revenue or income.

Repay'ing *ppl. a.*; also **Repay'al**, repayment; **Repay'er**, one who repays.

Repay'ment (rī·pēˈmént). *sb.*

Repayable, **-ayl**, **-yl**, varr. REPAEL *v. Obs.*

Repe, obs. form of REAP.

Repeal (rĭpīˈl), *v.¹*

Repeal (rĭpīˈl), *v.²*, variant of REPEL *v.*

Repeal (rĭpīˈl), *sb.*

Repealable (rĭpīˈlăbʼl), *a.*

Repealer (rĭpīˈləɹ).

Repeat (rĭpīˈt), *v.*

Repea·se, *Obs.* Also **repayse**.

Repeat (rĭpīˈt), *sb.*

Repeal·ment. *Obs.*

Repeatedly, *adv.*

Repeater (rĭpīˈtəɹ).

Repea·ting, *vbl. sb.*

Repea·ting, *ppl. a.*

Repe·coating, *ppl. a.*

Repedation. *Obs.*

Repeal (rĭpēˈl), *v.*

Repell (rĭpēˈl), *v.*

Repe·llance, **-ency.**

Repellant (rĭpeˈlănt), *a.* and *sb.*

Repe·llence, **-ency.**

Repe·llancy (rĭpeˈlănsi).

Repellent (rĭpeˈlént), *a.* and *sb.*

Repe·ller.

Repe·lling, *vbl. sb.*

Repe·lling, *ppl. a.*

Repe·nce.

Repend, *v.*

Repe·nedant, obs. form of REPENTANT.

Repensation. *Obs. rare⁻¹.*

Repent (rĭpeˈnt), *a.*

Repent (rĭpeˈnt), *v.*

REPENTABLE

Repentable, *a.* [f. prec. + -ABLE] Capable of being repented of; † repentant.

† Repentaille. *Obs.* [F., f. *repentir* to REPENT: see -AILLE.] Repentance.

Repentance (rǐpe·ntăns). Also 4–6 -aunce, (5 -aunse), 4 -anee, (5 -ans, -once), 6 -vonce. [a. F. *repentance* (12th c.): see REPENT *v.* and -ANCE, and cf. *Olsp. repentencia* (13th c.).]

1. The act of repenting or the state of being penitent; sorrow, or contrition for past action or conduct; an instance of this.

REPENT

† Repent, *a.* *Obs. rare⁻¹.* [f. REPENT *v.*, or f. L. *repent-* ppl. stem.] Repentant.

Repentance, *obs. f.* REPENTANCE.

REPERCUSSION

Repercussion (rī·pɔːkʌ·ʃən). Also 6 -par-. [a. F. *repercussion* (14th c.), or ad. L. *repercussiōn-em*, n. of action f. *repercutere*: see REPERCUSS and -ION.]

1. The action of a thing in forcing or driving back an impinging or advancing body; also, the power of doing this. Now *rare*.

REPERTORIUM

Repertorium (repətɔ·riʌm). [L., f. *repert-*, ppl. stem of *reperīre* to find: cf. next.] A catalogue, list. **b.** A storehouse, repository.

REPERTORY

Repertory (repˈərtɔri). Also 6 *erron.* report-. [See prec. and -ORY.]

1. An index, list, catalogue or calendar.

REPERUSAL

Reperusal (rī-). *rare.* [RE- 5 a: cf. next.] A second perusal.

REPERUSE

Reperuse (rī-), *v.* [RE- 5 a.] *trans.* To peruse again or repeatedly.

REPINE

Repine (rǐ-əi·n), *v.* Also 6–7 repyne. [app. f. RE- + PINE *v.*, but the formation is unusual.]

1. *intr.* To be not contented discontent or dissatisfaction; to fret, murmur, or complain.

REPLACE

Replace (rī-), *v.* [f. RE- 5 a + PLACE *v.*; perh. after F. *remplacer* (1549) in later use.]

1. *trans.* To restore to a previous place or position; to put back again (in 1° *refl.*) a place.

REPLATE

Replate, *v.* [RE- 5 a.] *trans.* To plaster over.

Replate (rī-), v. [RE- 5 a.] trans. To plate afresh; to renew the plating on.

Replay (rī-), v. [RE- 5 a.] trans. To play (a match, etc.) again. Hence **Replay** sb. a replayed match.

Reple, obs. form of RIPPLE sb.

Repleder, var. f. RE- + †LEAD v.; cf. OF. *replaider* (13th c.), f. re-pledge (16th c. in Littré).

Replegiare, v. Obs. Law. [med.L.: see REPLEVIN.] = REPLEVIN v.

Replenish, sb. rare. [f. the vb.] A fresh supply (of money); a refill.

Replenish (rī'plĕnish), v. Forms: 4-5 replenye, 5-7 -esch, 6-7 -isshe, -ische; 4-6 -plenissh, -iash, 6 -nishe, 4-7 replenissh, -nash, 5-6 replenisch, -pleynsch, 6 ?replynysah. See also REPLENISSH and REPLEVISH v.

Replenisher. [f. as prec.] One who replenishes or refills.

Replenishing, vbl. sb.

Replenishingly, adv.

Replenishment (rī'plĕnishment).

Replete (rī'plīt), a. Now rare.

Replete (rī'plīt), v. Obs.

Repletion (rī'plīshǎn). Forms: 4-5 replecioun, 5-6 replecion, -tion, 5-6 replecioun, 6 replexion; 5- repletion.

Replevin (rī'plĕvin), sb. Law. [prec.]

Replevin, v.

Repleviable, a. Law. Also 5-7 repleviable.

Replevisable, a. Law. Also 6-7 -is(e)a-ble.

Replevish v. Obs. Also 6-7 -ish.

Replevisor.

Replevy (rī'plĕvi), v. Now rare.

Replial. Obs.

Replicant. Obs. rare.

Replicate (re'plikit), a. (sb.) [ad. L. replicāt-, pa. pple. of replicāre = REPLY v.]

Replicate (re'plikeit), v. [f. L. replicāt-, pa. pple. of replicāre.]

Replication (replikei'shǎn). Also 4-5 replicacioun, 5-6 -cion.

Replicatory, a. rare.

Replier (rī'plaiǎr). One who replies.

Reply (rī'plai), v. Forms: 4-5 replie, 4-6 replye, 5- reply.

Replire, variant of REPLEVIE v. Obs.

Replight, v. [RE- 5 a.] To plight afresh.

Replique. Obs. rare.

Reply (rī'plai), sb. Also 6 replie, 7 replye.

Reply (rĭplăi·), sb. Also 4 *replye*, 4-7 *replye*, 5-6 *replie*. [ad. OF. *replier* to fold again, turn back, reply (mod.F *replier* to fold again, turn, coil) :—L. *replicāre*: see REPLICATION.]

¶ Repoint, v. *Obs. rare*—¹. [a. obs. F.*repoin-, repoign-*, stem of *repoindre*:—L. *repungĕre* to prick against: see POINGANT.]

Report (rĭp·ȯ·rt). sb. Also 5-6 *raport, reaport*. [a. OF. *report* or *raport* (mod.F. *rapport*), vbl. sb. f. *reporter, rapporter*: see REPORT v.]

Report (rĭp·ȯ·rt), v. [a. F. *reporter* :—L. *reportāre*: see REPORT sb.]

Reportable (rĭpō·rtăb'l), a. [f. prec. + -ABLE.] Capable or worthy of being reported.

Reportage (rĕpŏrtē·dȝ). [a. F. *reportage*.]

Reportative, a. *rare*—¹. [as prec. + -ATIVE.]

Reported, -edly: see REPORT v.

Reporting, vbl. sb. [-ING¹.]

Reportingly, adv. *Obs. rare*. [f. REPORTING + -LY².]

Reportorial (rĕpŏrtō·riăl), a. [irreg. f. RE-PORT v. or REPORTER: see -ORIAL.]

Repository (rĭpŏ·zitŏri), a. *Obs. rare*—¹. [ad. late L. *repositōri-us*.]

Repost, obs. form of REPOSE.

Reposture, sb. *rare*. [f. REPOST v. + -URE.]

Repour, v. *Obs.* [RE- 5 a.]

Repousse (rẹpū·sē), a. and sb. [a. F. *repoussé*, pa. pple. of *repousser* to push back.]

Repp, variant of REP sb.²

Repp'l, obs. form of REPEAL.

Repped, a. [f. REP sb.² + -ED².]

Reprehend (reprĭhe·nd), v. Also 4 *reprehende*. [ad. L. *reprehendĕre* to hold back, check, blame.]

Repose (rĭpō·z), sb.¹ [ad. L. *depose, dispose, suppose*, etc.: cf. RE-POSE and POSE.]

Repose (rĭpō·z), sb.² [a. F. *repos* (OF. *repous*), f. *reposer*: see next.]

Repose (rĭpō·z), v.¹ [ad. L. *repōn-ĕre* to put back into the same place, *Obs.*]

Repose (rĭpō·z), v.² [a. F. *reposer* (11th c.) :—late L. *repausāre*: see RE-POSE and POSE.]

Representation. ... 3. The exhibition of character and action upon the stage; the (or a) performance of a play. ...

b. Acting, simulation, pretence. *rare*⁻¹.

4. The action of placing a fact, etc., before another or others by means of discourse; a statement or account, *esp.* one intended to convey a particular view or impression of a matter in order to influence opinion or action. ...

b. Insurance. A special statement of facts relating to the risk involved, made by the insuring party to the insurer or underwriter before the subscription of the policy. ...

5. A formal and serious statement of facts, reasons, or arguments, made with a view to effecting some change, preventing some action, etc.; hence, a remonstrance, protest, expostulation. ...

Re-presenta·tion (rī-). [RE- 5 a.] A renewed presentation or presenting. ...

Representa·tional (reprizenā·ʃǝnal). [f. REPRESENTATION + -AL.] Pertaining to, or of the nature of, representation; also, holding the doctrine of representationism. ...

Representa·tionism. ... The doctrine that the immediate object of the mind in perception is only a representation of the real object in the external world. ...

Representa·tionist. ... An adherent of the doctrine of representationism.

Representative (reprizéntǎtiv), *a.* and *sb.* ...

A. *adj.* **I.** Serving to represent, figure, portray, or symbolize. Also const. *of* (the thing figured, etc.). ...

2. One who (or that which) represents a number of persons in some special capacity; *spec.* one who represents a section of the community as member of a legislative body; a member of Parliament (of U.S.) of the House of Representatives. ...

Representatively, *adv.* [-LY¹.] In a representative manner; in respect of representation.

Representative·ness. The character of being representative. ...

Represe·ntator (reprentā·tǎ). [a. late L. ... Tertull.), agent-n. f. *repraesentāre* to REPRESENT.] †1. A representative or representer. *Obs. rare.* ...

Represe·nt (reprizént·). [as prec. + -ER¹.] Cf. also REPRESENTOR. ...

Represe·nting, *ppl. a.* [-ING².] That represents. ...

Represe·ntment. [-MENT : cf. prec. and -ORY.] Representative. ...

Re-prese·ntment (rī-). [RE- 5 a : cf. PRESENTMENT.] Renewed presentment. ...

Repress (rī-, -prés·), *sb.* [f. REPRESS *v.*, or ad. REPREME and REPRIME.]

Repress (riprés·), *v.*¹ [ad. L. *repress-*, ppl. stem of *reprimĕre*, f. *re-* RE- + *premĕre* to PRESS.]

1. *trans.* To check, restrain, put down or keep under (something bad or objectionable). ...

b. To put down, quell (a rebellion, riot, etc.). ...

2. To check (a person) in action. ...

Re-press (rī-), *v.*² [RE- 5 a.] To press again. ...

Repre·ssal. *Obs. rare*⁻¹. [-AL.] Repression.

Repre·sser, *agent-n.* f. REPRESS + -ER¹. One who, or that which represses.

Repre·ssible, *a.* ... That may be repressed.

Repre·ssion (riprécén). [ad. L. type *repressiōn-*.] The action of repressing ... Also const. *of*.

Repre·ssive (riprés·iv), *a.* [f. REPRESS *v.* + -IVE : cf. F. *répressif*, -*ive*, and med. L. *repressīvus*.] Having the nature of, or tending to, repression. ...

Hence **Repre·ssively,** *adv.*, **Repre·ssiveness.**

Repre·ssor. ... One who, or that which represses.

Reprevable, Repreve, obs. ff. REPRIEVABLE, REPRIEVE.

Repri·eval (riprī·val). Also 6-7 repriual. [f. REPRIEVE *v.* + -AL.] The action of reprieving; reprieve.

Repri·eve (riprī·v), *v.* ... [First in *pa. pple. reprevd*, app. ad. AF. *repris*, *pa. pple. of reprendre:* see REPRIEVE *sb.*] ... 1. *trans.* To take back, send back to prison; to detain on remand. *Obs.* ...

2. To respite, or temporary escape from trouble, calamity, etc. ...

Repri·eve, obs. form of REPROOF, REPROVE.

Repri·mand (reprimænd), *sb.* [ad. F. *réprimande*, earlier *reprimende* (= Sp. *reprimenda*, It. *riprimenda*), ... f. L. *reprimendus*, gerundive of *reprimĕre* to REPRESS.] A severe reproof; rebuke. ...

Repri·mand (reprimǎnd), *v.* Also 7 -mand. [ad. F. *réprimander* (1642), f. the *sb.*] ...

Repri·nt (rī-), *v.* [RE- 5 a.]

1. *trans.* To rebuke, reprove or censure (a person) sharply or severely. ...

Repri·nt (rī-), *sb.* [f. the vb.]

1. A reproduction in print of any matter already printed; a new impression of a work previously printed, without alteration of the matter. ...

2. Printed matter used as copy to be set up again. ...

REPRINTED.

Reprinter (-). [f. prec. + -ER¹.] One who reprints, or who publishes a reprint.

Reprintal (rīprīntǎl), n. Forms: 5 reprisail, 5-7 -ale, 6-7 -aill, -6 -aill), 7 repressal; 7-reprisal; -also 7-8 reprisall, 6-8 -aall, 7-reall. [a.OF. re-prisaille (found in AF. in 1352): see REPRISE v. and -AL. The mod.F. représailla (recorded in 19th c.) is ad. It. ripresaglia (f. ripreso), or med.L. repressalia (see Du Cange), whence also Sp. represalia, -aria.]

I. 1. (Without article or plural.) The act or practice of seizing the property (or persons) of subjects of another nation, in retaliation for loss or injury suffered from these or their countrymen. Now only Hist.

2. Letters (or Commission) of reprisal, official warrant authorizing an aggrieved subject to exact forcible reparation from the subjects of another state: see MARQUE 1 and 2. † Also ellipt. in sense sense (quot. 1472).

3. An act of retaliation for some injury or attack; spec. in warfare, the infliction of similar or severe injury or punishment on the enemy, e.g. by the execution of prisoners taken from them.

4. Without article (see 3).

II. † 5. = REPRISE sb. 2. Obs. rare⁻¹.

6. (Chiefly pl.) A return or compensation: a sum or amount paid or received as compensation.

REPRISE.

† 7. = REPRISE sb. 4. Obs. rare⁻¹

8. Arch. (See REPRISE sb. 6, quot. 1888.)
Hence **† Repri·sal** v. intr., to make reprisal.

Repri·sary, a. [See next and -ARY.] Authorizing reprisals.

Reprise (rīprəiz′), sb. [a. F. reprise (pres. priso, 7-8 reprise. [a. F. reprise (13th c., f. re-pris, pa.pple. of reprendre to take back, resume, etc. (see next); cf. Sp. and Pg. represa, It. ripresa.]

1. In phr. to make reprisals (cf. 4 b).

2. A deduction, charge, or payment (such as a rent-charge or annuity) falling to be made yearly out of a manor or estate. Chiefly pl. in phrase above, besides, beyond, or † over, reprises.

† 3. a. The taking of a thing as a prize. Obs.

4. a. Something taken back or recovered; a thing retaken; spec. (Mus.) a repetition, a recapitulation; reception. † Obs.

5. Recompense, requital; reception. † Obs.

† b. Respite; the act of taking something by way of retaliation. Obs.

† c. The act of recapturing a vessel taken by the enemy; also, the vessel so taken. Obs. rare⁻¹

4. A resumption or renewal of an action; a separate occasion of doing something. Chiefly in phr. at or in.. reprises. Also † by reprises, alternately. Somewhat rare.

5. To compensate (a person). Cf. REPRISE sb. 3 a.

6. Arch. (see later quots.)

7. Music. † A. A refrain. Obs.⁻¹ b. A cadence.

† Reprise, v. [ad. F. reprise.] † 1. trans. To begin again, start afresh. rare⁻¹

2. To take back again.

3. To withdraw from trouble or punishment; to reprieve. rare.

b. To recoup (oneself). rare⁻¹

Reproach (rīprō·tʃ), sb. Also 5-7 reproche, 6-7 reproch. [a. F. reproche, pres. repróche (12th c.), f. reprochier (mod. reprocher) to reproach: see next.]

1. A source or cause of disgrace or shame: a person, etc.; a fact, matter, feature or quality bringing disgrace or discredit upon one.

b. A thing, animal, or person forming a source of disgrace or discredit.

2. Shame, disgrace, opprobrium, or blame, incurred by or falling upon a person or thing. † In reproach, blamed, censured.

b. in. To heap scorn or contempt upon; reproaching.

3. To withdraw from trouble or punishment; to reprieve.

b. To take or hold back out of a sum.

REPROACHABLE. 487 REPROBATE.

REPROBATE. 488 REPRODUCE.

Re·probacy. [f. REPROBATE a.: see -ACY.]
The state or condition of being reprobate.

† Re·probance. Obs. rare⁻¹

† Reprobarian, sb. and a. Obs. rare. [f. RE-PROBATE sb. or v.] sb. One who professes the doctrine of reprobation. b. adj. Relating to reprobation.

Reprobate (re·prǒbet), sb. [ad. L. repro-bāt-us: see next.]

1. One rejected by God; one who has fallen away from grace or religion; one lost in sin.

2. An abandoned or unprincipled person; one whose character is utterly bad; a scamp.

Reprobate (re·prǒbet), a. Also 5-7 as pa. pple. 5 L. reproba·t-, 6 pa. pple. of reprobāre; to reprove.]

1. trans. To disapprove of, censure, condemn.

Re·probative, a. rare⁻¹ [ad. L. type reprobāre, agent-n. f. reprobāre.]

Re·probatory, a. [as prec. + -ING².]

† Reprobatress. Obs.

Reproduce (rīprǒdiū·s), v. [f. RE- 5 a + PRO-DUCE v., after F. reproduire.]

1. trans. To bring again into material existence; to create or form anew; spec. in Biol. to form (a lost limb or organ) afresh; to generate (new individuals).

Hence **Re·probatively** adv. rare⁻¹

Reproductory, *a. rare⁻¹.* [Cf. prec. and -ORY.] 'Pertaining to or used in reproduction' (Webster 1847).

Reprofa'ne, *v.* [RE- 5 a.] To profane anew.

Reprofe'ss, *v.* [RE- 5 a.] *trans.* To profess again.

Reproffer, *v. Obs. rare⁻¹.* [RE- 5 a.] *intr.* Of a sling : to turn back into the water again.

Repro'ject, *v.* [RE- 5 a.] To plan again.

Repromise, *v. Obs.* [ad. L. *reprōmittĕre*, f. re- RE- + prōmittĕre to promise.] *intr.* To promise in return. Hence **Repromised** *ppl. a.*

Repro'mise, *v. Obs.* Also 4 -mysioun, -miscioun, 4-5 -mysseioun, 6 mysson. [a. OF. *repromission,* or ad. L. *repromission-em,* f. *repromittĕre* see nxt.] A counter-promise, a promise made in return. *Land of repromission,* the promised land.

Repromulgate (*rī-*), *v.* [RE- 5 a.] *trans.* To promulgate again. Hence **Repromulga'tion.**

Reproof (rĭprū'f). Forms : 4 reproef, 4-5 reprof, 4-6 reprofe, 5-7 reproofe, (6-proufe), 5-reprof; 4-6 reproue, (4-pruue), 5-reprove, 5-prove; 4-5 reproffe, 5-8 reproofe. [a. OF. *reprove* (AF. also *repreove*), vbl. sb. f. *reprover* to REPROVE.]

Re-proof (*rī-*). [RE- 5 a.] A fresh proof.

Repro'val (rĭprū'văl), *sb.* [f. REPROVE *v.* + -AL.] The act of reproving; reproof.

Repro've (rĭprū'v), *v.* Forms : 4-7 re-proue, (4-pruue), 5-7 reprove.

Repro'ver (rĭprū'vər). [f. REPROVE *v.* + -ER.] One who reproves.

Repro'ving, *vbl. sb.* [f. as prec. + -ING¹.] The action of the verb in various senses; reproof.

Repro'ving, *ppl. a.* [-ING².] That reproves.

Repro'vingly, *adv.* [f. prec. + -LY².] In a reproving manner.

Reprovi'sion (*rī-*), *v.* [RE- 5 a.] *trans.* To supply with a fresh stock of provisions.

Repro've, *var. repra've Obs.*, to reproach.

Reprune (*rī-*), *v.* [RE- 5 a.] To prune again.

Reprw', *obs. form of* REPROVE.

Repry, *obs. variant of* REPRIEVE.

Repryla'ble, *obs. form of* REPROVABLE.

Reps (reps), *variant of* REP².

Re-pu'ster, *Obs. rare⁻¹.*

Reptant (re'ptant), *a.* [ad. L. *reptant-,* -ans, pr. pple. of *reptāre* to creep.] Creeping, crawling, repent.

Reptation (reptēi'ʃən), *Obs.* [ad. L. *reptātiōn-em,* f. *reptāre.*] The action of creeping or crawling.

Reptatory, *a. rare⁻¹.* [f. L. *reptāt-,* stem of L. *reptāre* to creep (see -ORY.)] 'Having the character of reptation' (Webster 1864, citing Dana).

Reptile (re'ptil, -tăil), *sb.* [ad. late L. *reptile* (Boëthius) : cf. next and -ILE.]

Reptile (re'ptil, -tăil), *a.*

Reptilian (reptī'li̯ăn), *a.* and *sb.*

Republic (rĭpŭ'blik), *sb.*

Republican (rĭpŭ'blikăn), *a.* and *sb.*

Republicanism (rĭpŭ'blikănizm). [f. prec. + -ISM : cf. F. *républicanisme.*]

Republicanize (rĭpŭ'blikănăiz), *v.* [f. REPUBLICAN + -IZE.]

Republication (rī-), *sb.* [RE- 5 a.]

Republish (rīpŭ'bliʃ), *v.* [RE- 5 a.]

Republisher (rīpŭ'bliʃər).

Republishment.

Repudiable (rĭpiū'di̯ăb'l), *a.* [ad. L. *repudiābilis.*] That may be repudiated.

Repudiate (rĭpiū'di̯ēit), *v.*

REPUDIATE.

2. In general use: Rejected, set aside.

Repudiate (rĭpiū·dĭeit), *v.* [f. L. *repudiāt-*, ppl. stem of *repudiāre* to divorce, reject, etc., f. *repudium* REPUDY *sb.*]

1. *trans.* **a.** Of a husband: To put away or cast off (his wife); to divorce, dismiss.

2. To cast off, disown (a person or thing).

3. To reject (an authority or its claims).

4. To refuse to accept a thing (as a duty, obligation, etc.); to decline.

5. To refuse to acknowledge or discharge (a debt or other obligation).

6. To reject (opinions, conduct, etc.) with condemnation or abhorrence.

Hence **Repu·diating** *vbl. sb.* and *ppl. a.*

Repudiation (rĭpiūdĭei·ʃən). *v.* [ad. L. *repudiātion-em*, n. of action f. *repudiāre*: see prec. and -ATION, and cf. F. *répudiation* (15th c.).] The action of repudiating or fact of being repudiated.

1. Divorce (of a wife).

2. Rejection, refusal, disowning.

Hence **Repu·diationist**, *U.S.*, one who advocates the repudiation of a public debt.

Repudiative (rĭpiū·dĭeitĭv), *a.* [-IVE.] Characterized by repudiation or rejection of something.

Repudiator (rĭpiū·dĭeitɔɹ). *n.* [a. L. *repudiator*, agent-n. f. *repudiāre* to REPUDIATE.] One who repudiates; *esp.* one who advocates the repudiation of a public debt.

Repudiatory, *a. rare.* [f. REPUDIATE *v.* + -ORY.] Characterized by repudiation (of debts).

Repu·dious, *a. rare.* [ad. L. *repudiōsus* (Plautus): see next and -OUS.] = REPUDIATE A. 3. [So quot. 1656.]

Repu·dy, *sb.* Obs. rare. [ad. L. *repudium*.] Divorce; repudiation.

Repu·dy, *v.* Obs. rare. [ad. L. *repudiāre.*] **1.** To cast off, reject. **2.** = REPUDIATE *v.*

Repugn (rĭpiū·n), *v.* Also 4-7 repugne, 6 -pougne, 4-6 repugne, 5-6 repugnge (re-). [a. F. *repugner*, ad. L. *repugnāre* to fight (ob-f. *impugn*.]

1. To contradict or contravene (something).

2. To fight or contend against, to resist or repel (a person).

b. To fight, strive, or contend *against* a person or thing. Now *rare*.

c. To oppose, offer resistance to; to resist or refuse.

3. To object or offer resistance to a thing, proceeding, etc. *Obs.*

4. *intr.* To be contrary or contradictory, be inconsistent or incompatible, *with* a thing.

b. To fight, strive, or contend *against* a person or thing.

c. To be contrary (to); to be opposed or repugnant (to).

d. To offer or make resistance; to resist (Obs.)

5. *trans.* To repel with disgust or aversion. *Obs.*

6. To oppose, resist, or contend against (some-thing); to repel or reject; to refuse, etc.

Hence **Repu·gning** *vbl. sb.* and *ppl. a.*

REPUGNABLE.

b. *trans.* To affect (one) with repugnance or aversion. Also *absol.*, to cause repugnance.

2. Opposition or resistance of mind or feeling.

In later use = REPUGNANCE 3.

†Repu·gnable, *a.* [f. prec. + -ABLE.] Capable of being repugned or refuted.

1879-80 NORTH *Plutarch, Marcellus* (1612) 315.

Repugnance (rĭpʊ·gnăns). Also 5-6 repugn-[a.F. *répugnance*, ad. L. *repugnantia*: see REPUGN *v.* and -ANCE.]

1. Contradiction, inconsistency; contrariety op-position or disagreement of ideas or statements. Also *with a* and *pl.*

b. *concr.* An instance of this.

2. Opposition or resistance to action; tendency to oppose.

3. Opposition or resistance to action; tendency to oppose. *Obs.*

†4. Opposition or contrariety between or of things. *Obs.*

5. Antipathy, aversion, strong dislike. Now somewhat *rare* (common *to*). *Obs.*

b. Without consent, *esp.* of two or more things in this relation to each other.

2. Making or offering resistance (to a person or thing); opposing, resisting, hostile, antagonistic, refractory.

Repugnancy (rĭpʊ·gnănsi). Also -ANCE *rare.* Now *rare* (common *-ANCE* 1560-1800).

1. Contradiction, inconsistency, etc. = REPUG-NANCE 1. Now *rare* (common *-ance* 1560-1800).

†2. Contrariety, opposition. *Obs. rare.*

†3. Antipathy, aversion. *Obs.*

Repugnant (rĭpʊ·gnănt), *a.* and *sb.* [a. F. *répugnant* (1372) or ad. L. *repugnant-em*, pres. pple. of *repugnāre* to REPUGN.]

A. *adj.* **1.** Contrary or contradictory to, inconsistent or incompatible *with*, at divergent *from*, standing *against*, something else.

2. Contrary or opposed; hostile, antagonistic.

†b. Resisting, offering resistance.

B. *sb.* That which is repugnant or contrary.

Repugnantly, *adv.* [f. prec. + -LY.] In a contrary, contradictory, or inconsistent manner.

†Repu·gnate, *v. Obs. rare.* [f. L. *repugnāt-*, ppl. stem of *repugnāre*.] *intr.* To be repugnant.

Repugnatorial, *a.* Serving as a defence; applied to certain glands or pores in Diplopoda, from which a malodorous fluid can be emitted.

†Repu·gnatory, *a. Obs. rare.* [ad. med.L. *repugnātōrius.*] Defensive.

Repu·gner, *rare.* [f. REPUGN *v.* + -ER.] One who repugns.

Repugning, *vbl. sb.* [-ING.] Opposition, resistance.

Repugning (rĭpiū·niŋ), *ppl. a.* [-ING.] That repugns; resisting, or opposed to something, *Obs.*

Repu·iter (rĭpiū·tɔɹ), *v. Obs. rare.* [RE-.] To pull back again.

Repull, *v.* [Re- 7 a.] To pull back again.

Repu·llulate, *v. Obs. rare.* [f. L. *repullulāt-*, ppl. stem of *repullulāre* (Pliny): see PULLULATE.]

1. *intr.* To bud or sprout again. Also *fig.*

Hence **Repu·llulating** *ppl. a.*

Repullulation (rĭpʊliūlei·ʃən). [f. prec. Cf. F. *répullulation.*] **1.** The repullulating or budding again of plants. *Obs.*

2. *Path.* Of diseases: To start afresh; to recur.

REPULLULATIVE. — 495 — REPULVERATION. — REPUMICATE. — 496 — REPUTATION.

Repu·llulative, *a.* [f. REPULLULATE *v.* + -IVE.] Having the faculty of sprouting again.

Repu·llulescent, *a.* [as prec., f. L. *repullulēscere.*] Reviving, springing up afresh.

Repu·lpit (rĭ-), *v.* [RE- 5 a.] *trans.* To re-store to the pulpit.

Repulse (rĭpʊ·ls), *sb.* [a. L. *repulsus* or *repulsa*, f. *repell-*, ppl. stem of *repellere* to REPEL. Cf. obs. F. *repulse*, *repolse* (Godef.).]

1. The act of repelling an assailant or hostile force; the fact of being driven back in an engagement or assault.

b. An act or mode of repelling an injury, etc.

2. Refusal of a request, suit, etc.; denial, rejection, rebuff.

3. The act of forcing or driving back; the fact of being forced back. Now *rare.*

4. To affect with repulsion. *rare*-1.

Hence **Repu·lseless** *a.* That cannot be repulsed (Webster 1847).

Repulse (rĭpʊ·ls), *v.* [f. L. *repuls-*, ppl. stem of *repellere* to REPEL; cf. also obs. F. *repulser* (mod. *repousser*), ad. L. *repulsāre.*]

1. *trans.* To drive or force back (an assailant); to repel by force of arms.

2. To drive or force back, to repel by force the onset of (something).

b. To force or drive back (a person); to repulse.

Repulsion (rĭpʊ·lʃən). Also 5-6 repulcion, -em, -ion, 6-7 -tion. [ad. late L. *repulsion-em*, n. of action f. *repellere*: see REPULSE *sb.* and -ION (cf. F. *repulsion* (1450 in Godef.).]

†1. Repudiation, divorce. *Obs. rare.*

1421-2 *Lydg. Chron. Troy* v. xxxvi. (1555), He .. The Kinges daughter hath vtterly forsake And in ashame did a libell make And forge a note of repulsion. **1430** *Ld. Hyghre* (Rolls) VI. 381 The quene .. takynge a libelle of repudy, of repulsion, entende a monastery.

2. The action of forcing or driving back or away. Now *rare.*

3. *Physics.* The action of that, or the property of, by which they fly from one another. (Opposed to ATTRACTIVE.)

b. Feeling of aversion, dislike, or disgust.

Repulsiveness (rĭpʊ·lsĭvnes). The state or quality of being repulsive or disagreeable.

Repulsory (rĭ-), *a.* [ad. L. *repulsōrius*, f. *repuls-*: see prec.] = REPULSIVE *a.*

Repurge, *v.* [RE- 5 a.] *trans.* To make purge again.

Repumicate, *v. Obs. rare.* [ad. L. *re-pumicāre* (ob. text.), f. *pumex* PUMICE.] [See quots.] To scour.

Repumiceance, *Obs.* — PURVEYANCE

Repu·mp (rĭ-), *v.* [RE- 5 a.] *trans.* To pump again. — *intr.* To pump again or in return. So **Repu·mpment.**

Repu·nish (rĭ-), *v.* [RE-.] To punish again or in return. Also *Repu·nishment.*

Repurchase (rĭ-), *sb.* [RE- 5 a.] Renewal of a purchase, buying back. (Common in recent use.)

Repurchase (rĭ-), *v.* [RE- 5 a.] *trans.* To purchase again, to buy back.

Repure (rĭpiū·ɹ), *v.* [RE-.] To purify again.

Repurify (rĭ-), *v.* [RE-.] To purify again. Hence **Repu·rifying** *vbl. sb.*

Repurple (rĭ-), *v.* [RE- 5 a.] *trans.* To make purple again.

Repursue (rĭ-), *v.* [RE- 5 a.] *trans.* To pursue again. So **Repu·rsuit** [RE- 5 a.] Renewed pursuit.

Repurveyance, *Obs.* = PURVEYANCE

Reput·h (rĭ-), [RE-.] *intr.* To push in return.

Repute (rĭpiū·t), *v.* [a. F. *réputer*, ad. L. *reputāre* to reckon, count, f. *re-* + *putāre* to reckon, think.]

1. To consider or account to be something; to deem, esteem, judge.

2. To hold in repute, to esteem.

Reputability (rĭpiūtăbi·lĭti). [See next and -ITY.] The quality or state of being reputable.

Reputable (rĭpiū·tăb'l), *a.* [f. REPUTE *v.* + -ABLE. Cf. obs. F. *réputable* (Godef.).]

1. Held in or worthy of repute or credit.

2. Having a good reputation; of good repute; estimable, honourable, respectable.

Hence **Reputableness**, *'being of good Repute'* (Bailey vol. II. 1727).

Reputably (rĭpiū·tăbli), *adv.* [f. REPUTABLE + -LY.] In a reputable or respectable manner.

Reputate (rĭ-), *ppl. a.* and *v. Obs. rare.* [f. L. *reputāt-*, ppl. stem of *reputāre*.] To repute.

Reputation (rĭpiūtei·ʃən). Also 4-6 repu-tacioun, -cion, -cyon, -cyoun, 6 -cioun, 4-6 reputacioun, 6 -cyon, etc. [ad. L. *reputātiōn-em*, n. of action f. *reputāre*: see prec. and -ATION (cf. F. *réputation* (14th c.).]

1. The common or general estimate of a person with respect to character or other qualities; the relative estimation or esteem in which a person or thing is held. In phrases.

2. The common or general estimate of a thing with respect to its character or other qualities.

3. The honour or credit of a particular person in general; good name, good report, or fame in general.

b. Specific repute or credit for some quality or attainment.

4. The condition, quality, or being highly regarded or esteemed; credit, note, or distinction; also, respectability, good report.

Reputative (rĭpiū·tătĭv), a. [ad. L. type *reputātīv-us* see REPUTE v. and -IVE.] Considered or regarded as such; putative.

Reputatively, adv. [f. prec. + -LY 2.] By repute or reckoning, reputedly; putatively.

Repute (rĭpiū·t), sb. [f. the vb.]

1. Opinion, estimate. Obs. rare.

†b. The reputation of (having or being) something. Obs.

2. Relative estimation; rank or position. Obs.

3. Reputation, distinction, honour, credit.

4. The reputation of a particular person.

b. in phr. by repute.

Repute (rĭpiū·t), v. Also 5 repotate, 6 reputate. [ad. F. reputer (1294 in Godef.), or L. reputāre, f. re- RE- + putāre to reckon, think, etc.]

1. trans. To consider, think, esteem, reckon (a person or thing) to be, or as being, something. a. with simple complement.

†b. The reputation of having or being something. Obs.

†2. To account oneself to have something. Obs.

3. To regard, reckon, account as something.

4. To have or hold (one) in repute or esteem; to think (well, etc.) of; to value. Also, to hold in worth or something. Obs.

Reputed (rĭpiū·tĕd), ppl. a. [f. REPUTE v.]

†1. Held in repute. Obs. rare.

†2. Supposed, accounted, reckoned (to be some-

Requiem (re·kwĭĕm, rī·kwĭĕm), sb. [L. requiem, acc. of requies 'rest', the first word of the Introit in the Mass for the Dead, 'Requiem æternam dona eis, Domine', etc.]

1. R.C. Ch. A special mass said or sung for the repose of the souls of the dead. Also Mass of Requiem (common in early use).

2. A musical setting of a mass for the dead.

†3. Rest, repose, quiet. Obs.

Requiescence (rekwĭe·sĕns), sb. [L. requiescĕre to rest, repose: see QUIESCENCE.] A state of quiescence, rest, repose.

†**Requisable**, a. Obs. rare. [ad. L. requirĕre.] Capable of being required.

Require (rĭkwəi·ə(r)), v. [ad. L. requīrĕre, f. re- RE- + quærĕre to ask, seek.]

Repugnance (rĭpŏ·gnăns), sb. [a. F. repugnance, or ad. L. repugnantia.]

Resconse, obs. form of RESPONSE.

†2. Asking for rescission, obs. rare⁻¹.

Resconse, v. Obs. rare. Also **-sconce**, **-sconse**.

Recounter, -tre: see RECOUNTER sb. and v.

Rescouth, obs. form of RESCUE v.

Rescounter, sb. Obs. Also **6 -conter**, **-counter**.

Rescous, -se, obs. forms of RESCUE v.

Rescoure, -our, obs. ff. of RESCUE.

Rescow, **-e**, obs. forms of RESCUE.

Rescour, obs. form of RESCUE v.

Re-scream, v. To scream again.

Rescribe, v.

Rescribendary, Obs. rare⁻¹.

Rescript (rī·skript), sb.

Rescript, v.

Rescriptive, a.

Rescript, rare.

Re·scrible, a. Capable of being rescued.

Rescue (re·skiū), v. Forms: 4-7 rescowe, etc.

1. trans. To deliver (a person) from the attack of, or out of the hands of, assailants or enemies.

2. Law. To deliver or save (a person or thing) from some evil or harm.

3. absol.

4. refl. To save or deliver (oneself) in some respect.

Rescued (re·skiūd), ppl. a.

Re·sceneless, a. rare.

Rescuer (re·skiūə(r)).

Rescuing (re·skiū·iŋ), vbl. sb.

Recussor, Law. rare⁻¹.

Rescyve, obs. form of RECEIVE v.

Resdue, obs. form of RESIDUE.

Rese, sb. Obs.

†Rese, v.¹ Obs. Forms: 1 resan, 3 resen 3-5 rese, 4 reose (7 rise).

Research (rī·səɹtʃ), sb.

1. The act of searching (closely or carefully) for or after a specified thing or person.

2. A search or investigation directed to the discovery of some fact by careful consideration or study of a subject; a course of critical or scientific inquiry.

Research (rī·səɹtʃ), v.

Researcher. [f. RESEARCH v. + -ER¹.]

Re·seal, v.

Rese, v.²

Reseal, late variant of REOSE, to fall. Obs.

Reseal¹ (rī·sīl), v.

Research, sb.

Reseat (rī·sīt), v.

Re·secate, pa. pple. Obs. rare.

Resecrate, v.

Resect (rī·sekt), v.

Resection (rī·sekʃən).

Resedaceous, a.

Resee, v.

Reseek, v.

Reseek, v.

Reseech, sb.

Resect, pa. pple. Obs. rare.

Resectful, a.

Reseat, sb.

Resection (rī·sekʃən). [ad. L. *resectiōn-em*.]

Reseda (rī·sī·da).

Resedaceous, a.

Resee, v.

Reseek, v.

Reseize (rī·sī·z), v.

Reseizer, sb.

Resell, v.

Resemblable, a. Obs.

Resemblance (rī·zemblăns), sb.

1. The quality or being like or similar; likeness or similarity in appearance or any other respect; the fact of some likeness existing or being present.

2. A likeness, image, representation or reproduction of some person or thing.

Resemblance, *sb.* ... — [See RESEMBLE *v.*] Assembly.

Resemblance, *v.* ... To resemble. Hence **Resemblancing** *ppl. a.*

Resemblant (rĭzĕ·mblǎnt), *a.* and *sb.* [prec., pres. pple. of *resemble* to RESEMBLE; cf. SEMBLANT.]

A. *adj.* **1.** Similar, having resemblance or likeness, *to* something.

B. *sb.* **1.** A semblance: a show.

Resemble (rĭzĕ·mb'l), *v.* [ad. L. *resemblare* (see SEMINATE); in both equiv. after Ovid *Met.* — To reproduce as from seed.

Resen, obs. form of REASON *sb.*

Resenge, *v.* Obs. [f. RE- + SEMBLE *v.*; cf. ASSEMBLE and F. *rassembler*.]

Resent (rĭzĕ·nt), *v.* Also ? resent, resenct, resient.

Resent, *sb. Obs.* [ad. F. *resent-*, ...] A trace or flavour. To a grateful feeling.

Resentful (rĭzĕ·ntfᵘl), *a.* ... Full of resentment.

Resenter (rĭzĕ·ntə*r*). [prec. + -ER.]

Resentiment, *Obs. rare.* [ad. L. *resentiment-*, ...]

Resentive, *a. Obs. rare.*

Resentment (rĭzĕ·ntmĕnt). [ad. F. *ressentiment*, ...] A feeling of sorrow, etc.

Resequester, *v. Obs.* To sequester again. So **Resequestration**.

Reserate, *v. Obs.* [f. ppl. stem of L. *reserāre* to unbar, unbolt, open, f. RE- + *sera* a bar, bolt.] *trans.* To open up. Hence **Reserating** *vbl. sb.*

Reservable, *a.* [f. RESERVE *v.* + -ABLE.] That may be reserved.

Reserval (rĭzɔ·*r*val), *sb.* rare. [f. RESERVE *v.* + -AL.] A Reserve. *Obs.* **b.** Reservation.

Reservance, *sb. Obs. rare.* [-ANCE; cf. OF. *reservance*, It. *riserbanza*.] **1.** Reservation. *rare.*

Reservation (rezə*r*vēi·ʃən). Also 4 -cioun, 5 -cion. [a. OF. *reservation* (14th c.), or ad. late L. *reservātiōn-em*, n. of action f. *reservāre* to RESERVE.]

I. 1. *Eccl.* The action of reserving as a thing. **2.** *b.* The action, on the part of the Pope, of reserving to himself the right of filling up a vacant benefice.

3. *Mental* reservation, a qualification tacitly introduced in making a statement, taking an oath, etc.

4. *Reserve.* **5.** The action of keeping back or concealing.

Reservative, *a.* and *sb. Obs. rare.* [a. obs. F. *réservatif* (Cotg.), or ad. medL. *reservatīvus*: see RESERVE *v.* and -ATIVE.]

Reservatory (rĭzɔ·*r*vətəri), *sb.* [ad. med.L. *reservātōrium* store-house, f. *reservāt-*, ppl. stem of *reservāre* to RESERVE; cf. F. *réservatoire*.] **1.** A receptacle for food; a cupboard; a store-room or store-house.

Reserve (rĭzɔ·*r*v), *sb.* [ad. F. *réserve*, f. *réserver* to RESERVE.] **1.** Something reserved or kept back; a store or stock; an extra quantity.

II. 9. Self-restraint; self-control; imposition of restraint upon the expression of one's feelings.

RESERVE. — 513 — RESERVE. — RE-SERVE. — 514 — RESERVOIR.

b. Abstention from giving a full explanation or expressing one's mind freely; reticence; also *spec.* in casuistry, an intentional suppression of truth in cases where it might lead to inconvenience.

c. On *or* upon the reserve: (*a*) in a waiting attitude; (*b*) reserved; reticent. *Obs.*

d. *On the* reserve: (*a*) in a waiting attitude.

IV. intrb. or adj. Kept in reserve, constituting a reserve.

Reserve (rĕzŏ′rv), *v.* Also 4 rec-, 5 reas-, 4-5 *Sc.* reuerse. [ad. OF. *reserver* (mod.F. *ré-server*), ad. L. *reservāre*, f. re- RE- + *servāre* to keep, save: cf. PRESERVE.]

1. *trans.* To keep for future use or enjoyment; to store up *for* (to) some time or occasion; to refrain from using or destroying, etc.

2. To retain as one's own; to keep *to* or *for* oneself.

3. To set apart, keep (*t to* or) *for* another. Also *occas.* without *const.*

4. *Eccl.* a. To set apart, keep (cases for absolution) to be dealt with by a superior authority. Const. *to*, *for.* (Cf. RESERVATION 5 c.)

b. To set apart (benefices) for presentation by the Pope, *matr.-t.* (Cf. RESERVATION 5 b.)

5. a. To retain or secure (some right or profit).

RESERVOIR.

for oneself or another by formal stipulation; *t to* provide or stipulate (*that.* (Chiefly in legal use.)

6. To set *a* (thing) apart for some purpose or with some end in view; to keep *for* some use.

7. To retain or preserve alive; *t* exempt from slaughter; *to* save *from* death. Now *rare.*

b. To leave untouched or intact; to refrain from removing or destroying, etc.

8. To keep or maintain (a person or thing) in a certain state or condition. *Obs.*

Re-serve (rī′-), *v.* [RE- 5 a.] *trans.* To serve again, in various senses.

RE-SERVE.

subtyle reserved in syght.

Reserved (rĕzŏ′rvd), *ppl. a.* [f. RESERVE *v.*]

1. a. Excepted. Chiefly in prepositional use: With the exception of, except, save. *Obs.*

b. To retain (a person) in one's service. *Obs.*

2. a. To retain in store; to lay up as a store or stock; to deposit for preservation. *Obs.*

b. *absol.* or *intr.*

3. Averse to showing familiarity, or to open expression of thought or feeling; cold or distant; reticent, uncommunicative.

a. Of conduct, character, disposition, etc.

b. Of persons.

RESERVOIR.

Reserved List, in the remote contingency of the Active List being exhausted.

Reservedly (rĭzŏ′rvdli), *adv.*

Reservee, *rare.* [f. RESERVE *v.* + -EE.]

Reserveful, *a.* *rare* [f. RESERVE *sb.*]

Reserveless, *a.* [f. RESERVE *sb.*]

Reserver¹ [f. RESERVE *v.* + -ER¹.]

Reservery (rĭzŏ′rvori), *nonce-wd.* [f. RESERVE *sb.* + -ERY.]

Reserving, *ppl. a.* [-ING².]

Reservist (rĭzŏ′rvist), [f. RESERVE *sb.* + -IST.]

Reservoir (rĕ′zŏrvwār), *sb.*

RESERVOIR. — 515 — RESET. — RESETMENT. — 516 — RESIANT.

Reservoir (rĕzărvwā′r), *v.* [f. the *sb.*] *trans.* To store up, keep in a reservoir. *Obs.*

Reset (rĭset′), *v.¹* Forms: 3-5 reset, 4-5 recett(e, resset, 4-7 reset(t 5) reysatt, 4- reset. [a. OF. *recet*, *recept* (med.L. *receptum*), neut. pa. pple. of *recipere* to receive: cf. RECEIPT *sb.*]

1. *trans.* To receive, harbour, or shelter (a person, *esp.* an offender against the law). Now *arch.*

Reset (rĭset′), *v.²* Forms: 3-6 recette (5 recepte), 4-6 resette; 3-6 reset, 4- reset (6-ett). 5- reset (7 rett). Also as *pa. pple.* (Ogilvie, 1882.)

1. *trans.* To receive, harbour, or shelter (a person, *esp.* an offender against the law). Now *arch.*

Reset (rĭ′set), *sb.¹* Forms: 3-5 recett, 4-5 reette, 4-6 resett, 4-7 reset. [f. RESET *v.²*]

Resettable (rĭ-), *a.* [f. RESET *v.²*] Capable of being reset.

Resetter¹ (rī′se′taɹ). Forms: *a.* 4, 6 resset-tour, 4, 7 reettour, 5-our. 8, 5 resettry 6, resettar, 7 resettare, etc.; *b.* recetter, 6- resetter, [f. RESET *v.²*]

RESETMENT.

Reset (rĭ-), *v.* [RE- 5 a.] To settle over again; to make a new settlement of or in (something).

Resetment. In 5 recette-ment. [f. *Recettement* (Britton): see RESET *v.²* and -MENT.] The act or practice of unlawful receiving or harbouring.

Resettle (rĭset′l), *v.* [RE- 5 a.]

Resettlement (rī′set′lment). [RE- 5 a.]

Resew (rĭ-), *v.* [RE- 5 a.] To sew again.

Reship (rĭ-), *v.* [RE- 5 a.]

Reshipment (rĭ-). [RE- 5 a.] 1. The act of reshipping.

Reshoe (rĭ-), *v.* [RE- 5 a.]

Reshore (rĭ-), *v.* *Obs. rare.* [RE- 5 a.]

Reshow (rĭ-), *v.* [RE- 5 a.] To show again.

Reshuffle (rĭ-), *v.* [RE- 5 a.] *trans.* To shuffle again.

Re-sance (rĭ-), *sb.*

Reshape (rĭ-), *v.* [RE- 5 a.] To shape anew.

Reshine (rĭ-), *v.* [RE- 5 a.]

Reshod ppl.

Resiant (rĕ′-). Forms: 5 reande, reseant, -aunte, res-eant, 5-6 reseaunt, 6 resyaunt, -aunt, 6- resiant. [a. OF. *resseant*, *reseant*, pr. pple. of *reseeir*, *reseoir* (F. *résider*) to reside: cf. med.L. *resantisa*.]

A. *adj.* Resident, dwelling; abiding. In predicative use, *or* placed after the *sb.*, sometimes in *of* form. *Obs.* (Common c1450-1650.)

Resianty ... **Resiant** ... **Resicate** ... **Reside** ... **Residence** ...

Residence ... **Residencer, -ier** ... **Residenciarie, -y** ... **Residency** ... **Resident** ...

Resident ... **Residental** ... **Residenter** ... **Residentary** ... **Residentiary** ... **Residentiaryship** ... **Residenting** ... **Residently** ... **Residentship** ... **Residency** ... **Residentiarius** ...

Resider ... **Residual** ... **Residuary** ... **Residuation, residivation** ... **Residual** ... **Residing** ... **Residuum** ... **Residue** ...

Residuation ... **Residuum** ... **Residual class** ... **Resiance** ... **Residuous** ... **Resift** ... **Resign** ...

2. To give up, make over, abandon, consign *to* a person, thing, or condition.

c 1386 Chaucer *Man of Law's T.* 682 And therfor to the feend I the resigne, Let him endyten of thi treccherie. 1589 [? Nashe] *Almond for Parrat* 11 Whether he would haue the care of the commonwealth..resigned to the retorting of T. C. his unreuerent railings. 1667 Milton *P. L.* xii. 301 So Law appears..but giv'n With purpose to resign them in full time Up to a better Cov'nant. 1697 Dryden *Virg. Georg.* i. 124 The light Stubble, to the Flames resign'd, Is driv'n along, and crackles in the Wind. 1704 Swift *T. Tub* vi, His two Brethren..for ever discarded from his House, and resigned to the wide World. 1766 Goldsm. *Vic. W.* viii, Mr. Burchell..resigned her up to the chaplain. 1791 Mrs. Radcliffe *Rom. Forest* viii, Had I resigned you to his will I should have remained secure. c 1860 Bryant *A Sick-bed* xi, Then to the sleep I crave Resign me.

b. To yield up (oneself, etc.) with confidence *to* another for care or guidance.

c 1366 Chaucer *A.B.C.* 80 Myn hele in-to thyn hand al I resigne. c 1430 *Syr Gener.* (Roxb.) 1886 With louyng chere.. Hir hert to him she did resigne. c 1450 tr. *De Imitatione* iii. xlii. 113 Forsake þiself, resigne up þiself, & þou shalt fruisshe gret pes. 1642 Rogers *Naaman* 130 [She] will not..resigne up her selfe to God. 1667 Milton *P. L.* x. 148 Was shee made thy guide,..that to her Thou did'st resigne thy Manhood? 1751 Doddridge in *Paraph. Ch. Scot.* xliv. 5 To thee, as to our cov'nant God, We'll our whole selves resign. 1869 J. Martineau *Ess.* II. 79 He..vows to resign himself to her direction.

c. To make surrender of (one's will, reason, etc.), in reliance upon another.

1585 Jas. I *Ess. Poesie* (Arb.) 29 Amongst our hands, he must his witts resing, A holy trance to highest heauen him bring. 1647 Cowley *Mistr., The Soul* iii, If my Will do not resign All her Liberty to thine. a 1704 Locke (J.), Those who always resign their judgment to the last man they heard or read. 1781 Cowper *Retirem.* 130 To..Resign our own and seek our Maker's will.

d. To give (oneself, one's mind, etc.) up *to* some emotion, condition, or state.

1718 Pope *Iliad* xiii. 590 Æneas..for a space resign'd To tender pity all his manly mind. 1738 tr. *Guazzo's Art Convers.* 16 They did not so absolutely resign themselves up to a solitary Life, as to be entirely regardless of their neighbours. 1791 Cowper *Retired Cat* 61, I will resign myself to rest. 1815 Shelley *Alastor* 628 Yet a little, ere it fled, Did he resign his high and holy soul To images of the majestic past.

†3. To give over, desist or refrain from. *Obs.*

c 1374 Chaucer *Troylus* iii. 25 Thei dredyn shame, and vices thei resigne. c 1440 *Partonope* 2413* Of this and more ..Myne autor seyth which shall not fyne. Hem to reherse I will resyne. 1492 Ryman *Poems* xlix. 1. in *Archiv Stud. neu. Spr.* LXXXIX. 215 Now is tyme for to inclyne To vertue, and synne to resyne. 1590 Spenser *F. Q.* iii. xi. 5 Whom when the Gyaunt saw, he soone resinde His former suit, and from them fled apace.

†4. To cause (a person) to give up his place.

1674 *Essex Papers* (Camden) I. 280 That party made their braggs that they would resigne Arlington at his Returne.

II. *intr.* **5.** To give up an office or position; to retire; † to abdicate.

c 1450 *St. Cuthbert* (Surtees) 8289 At laste to reule it him thoght herd. He resygned and went away. a 1470 Gregory *Chron.* in *Hist. Coll. Cit. Lond.* (Camden) 76 And that yere ..he resynyd, and Edwarde his sone..was crounyd. 1530 Palsgr. 688/1 He is contented to resyne, but he demaundeth to great a pencyon. 1593 Shaks. *Rich. II*, iv. i. 190, I thought you had been willing to resigne. 1744 H. Walpole *Lett.* II. 3 Lord Granville has resigned: that is the term. 1818 Cruise *Digest* (ed. 2) III. 37 Where a clerk..entered into a general bond to the patron, to resign whenever the patron should require him. 1860 Warter *Sea-board* II. 7 If my Lord bishop wants to resign. 1876 Voyle & Stevenson *Milit. Dict.* 339/2 Non-commissioned officers..can resign when they find themselves unequal to perform the duties of their rank.

b. *U.S.* Const. *from.*

1885 J. Hawthorne *Love or a Name* 95 Is it true..that you have resigned from the Compensation Fund Commission? 1905 'M. E. Wilkins' *Debtor* 171 You would say at once they ought to be forced to resign from their offices.

6. To submit, to yield, *to* a person or thing. Now *rare.*

c 1450 tr. *De Imitatione* iii. xlii. 113 Somme resigneþ, but with som excepcion, for bei trust not fully to god. 1592 Shaks. *Rom. & Jul.* iii. ii. 59 Vile earth to earth resigne, end motion here. 1701 Collier *M. Aurel.* (1726) 19 That we should..resign to his wisdom, and adore his goodness. 1742 Richardson *Pamela* IV. 173, I will hope still the best, and resign to God's Will and his. 1805 Eugenia de Acton *Nuns of Desert* I. 288 Sophia and Emily Selwyn endeavoured to resign to their destiny. 1827 *Examiner* 325/2 The sun is resigning to the softer sway of the moon. 1861 Flor. Nightingale *Nursing* ii. (ed. 2) 23 People..take every disease as a matter of course, to be 'resigned to'.

7. To make surrender or relinquishment.

1738 Wesley *Ps.* cxxxix. ii, Thy Voice would break the Bars of Death, And make the Grave resign. 1871 R. Ellis tr. *Catullus* viii. 9 Now she resigns thee; child, do thou resign no less.

† Resi·gn, *v.*[2] *Obs. rare*⁻¹. [ad. L. *resignāre* to unseal: see prec.] *trans.* To disclose, reveal.

1595 B. Barnes *Div. Cent. Sonn.* xxi, Whome with thine angels manna thou didst feede,..When Moyses first thy statutes did resigne.

Re-sign (rī-), *v.* [Re- 5 a.] To sign again.

1805 W. Taylor in *Monthly Mag.* XX. 111 A monarch signs and resigns his name so often. 1855 Pusey *Doctr. Real Pres.* i. (1869) 155 The German copy of the Confession was..formally re-signed at subsequent periods.

† Resi·gnal. *Obs. rare*⁻¹. [f. Resign *v.*[1] + -al.] Resignation.

1634 Sanderson *Serm.* II. 283 A bold and just challenge of an old judge, made before all the people, upon his resignal of the government into the hands of a new king.

† Resi·gnant, *sb. Obs. rare.* [a. F. *résignant*, or ad. L. *resignant-*: see Resign *v.*[1] and -ant[1].] One who resigns.

1597 *Lawes Parlt. Scot.* Table, s.v. *Resignation*, The procuratorie suld be sealed and subscrived be the resignant. 1680 Brent tr. *Sarpi's Hist. Counc. Trent* viii. 792 The better sort were excluded by resignation, and hee onely preferred who pleased the resignant. 1693 Hackett *Life Abp. Williams* ii. 27 The good News came together, very welcome to the Resignant, that Sir Thomas Coventry should have that Honour.

Resignant, *a. Her.* ? *Obs.* [a. F. *résignant*: cf. prec.] (See quots.)

1572 Bossewell *Armorie* ii. 42 Their tayles forked,..resignante, reuerberaunte..and countercoloured. 1688 Holme *Armoury* ii. vii. 138/2 The tail resignant, is when the same is lost or gone, hath no tail, or maketh no shew of a Tail. c 1828 Berry *Encycl. Herald.* I. s.v., This term is sometimes applied to the tail of the lion when it is hid, as tail resignant.

Resi·gnatary. [ad. F. *résignataire*: see next and -ary[1].] One in whose favour something is resigned.

a 1768 Erskine *Inst. Law Scot.* ii. vii. § 18 Upon this act a notarial instrument is taken by him in whose favour resignation is made, called the resignatary. 1884 *Catholic Dict.* (1897) 788/1 A conditional resignation..is of five kinds, ..(3) with the right of resumption, if the resignatary should die before the resigner.

† Resignate, *v. Obs.*⁻¹ [f. L. *resignāt-*, ppl. stem of *resignāre*: see Resign *v.*[1] and -ate[3].] To resign. In *ppl. a.* **Resignating.**

1692 W. Marshall *Myst. Sanctif.* vi. (1764) 91 Their salvation is by faith, because sincere obedience is wrought in them..,and some call it the resignating act of faith.

Resignation (rezignēⁱ·ʃən). Also 4–5 -cio(u)n, 6 -tioun; 5–6 **resygnacyon.** [a. F. *résignation*, † *-acion* (14th c.), = Sp. *resignacion*, It. *risegnazione*, *rassegnazione*, med.L. *resignation-em*: see Resign *v.*[1] and -ation.]

1. The (*or* an) action of resigning an office, etc.

a. *Eccl.* (See quots. 1598 and 1680.)

1387 Trevisa *Higden* (Rolls) VIII. 309 Also he reserved to hym self þe firste benefice þat voyded by deeþ, by resignacioun, oþer by translacioun. 1467–8 *Rolls of Parlt.* V. 591/2 What so ever Prebende, that..by deth, resignation, dymyssion, or eny other cause..happeth to fall voide. 1562 *Bk. of Presidentes* 152 b, An Indenture vpon the resignacion of a benefice. 1598 [Rastell] *Termes Lawes* 173/1 Resignation, is where an incumbent of a Church resigneth or leaueth to the Ordinarie, which did admit him to it, or to his successours, and that differeth from surrender. 1611 Cotgr., *Regrés*, a resignation of a Benefice, vpon condition, that if during the Resignors life it become voyd by the resignation or death of the Resignee, it shall returne..vnto him. 1680 Godolphin *Rep. Can.* (ed. 2) xxv. § 3. 284 Resignation is *Juris proprii spontanea Refutatio*, or the voluntary yielding up of the Incumbent (into the hands of the Ordinary) his interest and right, which he hath in his Benefice. 1706 tr. *Dupin's Eccl. Hist. 16th Cent.* II. v. 91 That Resignations into the Pope's Hands are null, if the Resigner does not outlive his Resignation Twenty Days. 1765 Blackstone *Comm.* I. 476 Archbishopricks and bishopricks may become void..by resignation. All resignations must be made to some superior. 1818 Cruise *Digest* (ed. 2) III. 38 It was contended on the part of the bishop, that although there were several adjudged cases upon the subject of general bonds of resignation [etc.]. 1873 Phillimore *Eccl. Law* I. ii. xiii. 517 In this chapter the grave subject of the resignation of an office or benefice by a priest is considered.

attrib. 1680 Godolphin *Rep. Can.* (ed. 2) Index, Resignation-Bonds, whether good in Law.

b. In general use.

1412–20 Lydg. *Chron. Troy* i. 126 For whiche he made a resygnacion To his brother, next heyr by degre. 1494 Fabyan *Chron.* vii. 547 And for the sayde resygnacyon shuld haue his full force and strengthe, he..redde the scrowle of resygnacyon hymselfe. 1593 Shaks. *Rich. II*, iv. i. 179 The Resignation of thy State and Crowne To Henry Bullingbrooke. 1601 R. Johnson *Kingd. & Commw.* (1603) 101 Immediately vppon this resignation, with a loude voice he nominateth the partie, whome in his iudgement hee thinketh woorthy to succeede in his place. 1658–9 *Burton's Diary* (1828) IV. 237 Henry II. went thither and they made a resignation of their power to him. 1756 Nugent *Gr. Tour, Netherlands* I. 217 The chair of leather gilt, in which Charles V. performed the ceremony of his resignation. 1789 *Constitution U.S.* i. § 3 If vacancies [in the senate] happen by resignation or otherwise, the executive may make temporary appointments. 1848 W. H. Kelly tr. *L. Blanc's Hist. Ten Yrs.* I. 481 When..the ministers learned the step that had been taken.., they..gave in their resignation. 1898 *Green's Encycl. Sc. Law* X. 317 Resignation of Trustees.

2. *Sc. Law.* 'The form by which a vassal returns the fee into the hands of a superior' (Bell).

1555 *Sc. Acts Mary* (1814) II. 494/1 All resignationnis to be maid be vassallis..of thair propirteis in the superiouris handis. 1569 *Reg. Privy Council Scot.* I. 670 To dispone heretablie the landis of Strathnaver..for payment of the sowme of four thowsand markis, be resignatioun, to be haldin of the King. a 1768 Erskine *Inst. Law Scot.* ii. vii. § 17 The proper symbols of resignation are staff and baton. 1814 Scott *Wav.* lxxi, It will cost but a charter of resignation *in favorem*. 1838 W. Bell *Dict. Law Scot.* 858 Resignation is made in virtue of a procuratory of resignation.

3. A giving up *of* oneself (to God).

c 1450 tr. *De Imitatione* iii. xlii. 112 Of pure resignacion of a mannys self. 1504 Atkynson tr. *De Imitatione* iii. xlii. 231 If they make a hole resygnacyon & a dayly oblacion of them selfe. a 1664 Frank *Serm.* (1672) 212 A voluntary resignation of our selves and all that is ours to his choice, order, and disposing.

4. The fact of resigning oneself or of being resigned; acquiescence, submission, compliance.

1647 Clarendon *Hist. Reb.* i. § 106 Though he was not superiour to all other men in the affection, or rather resignation of the King,..he had a full share in his Master's esteem. 1736 Butler *Anal.* i. v. Wks. 1874 I. 109 The proper discipline for resignation is affliction. 1781 Gibbon *Decl. & F.* xxxi. (1787) III. 243 Proba supported, with Christian resignation, the loss of immense riches. 1838 Lytton *Leila* ii. ii, 'Our day is come' said the good knight Villena, with bitter resignation. 1881 Brooks *Candle of Lord* 98 You want to show him the possibility of a resignation and delight in suffering.

b. Const. *to* a person, his will, etc.

1663 Cowley *Cutter Colman St.* iv. iv, The same Obedience and Resignation to a Father's Will I found in my Aurelia. 1690 Locke *Hum. Und.* iv. xvi. § 4 A blind resignation to an authority which the understanding of man acknowledges not. 1711 Steele *Spect.* No. 153 ¶1 An abandoned Resignation to their Appetites. 1736 Butler *Anal.* i. v. 141 Passive submission or resignation to his will. 1812 Knox & Jebb *Corr.* II. 89 Resignation to God, whether in the way of obedience or of suffering, can be substantial, only so far as it grows out of knowledge and love.

Hence **Resigna·tionism.** (See quot.)

1898 *Contemp. Rev.* May 736 Nietzsche..distinguishes between the 'romantic pessimism'..and the 'Dionysiac pessimism'..He brands the former as Resignationism.

Resigne, obs. form of Raisin.

† Resi·gne, *a. Obs. rare*⁻¹. (See quot.)

14.. *Le Venery de Twety* in *Rel. Ant.* I. 151 When he [the hart] goth wexyng tyl he come to .xxxij. yere, than is he callyd an hert resygne, for cause his hed afiir that tyme wexith no further.

Resi·gned, *ppl. a.* [f. Resign *v.*[1] + -ed[1].]

†1. With *up.* Given up, abandoned, surrendered.

1654–66 Earl Orrery *Parthen.* (1676) 221 The receiving a resign'd up Mistriss, is like losing a life for a Friend. *Ibid.* 638 He shipt his Army for Italy in the resigned-up Fleet of the Pontick King.

2. Full of resignation; submissive, acquiescent.

1699 Collier *Def. Short View* 44, I wonder at his being so Resign'd. What, not care to have stark Nonsense found upon him! 1757 Gray *Mrs. Clarke* 7 In agony, in death resign'd. 1812 J. Wilson *Isle of Palms* iii. 276 Though ever lost to human kind And all they love, they are resign'd. 1855 Macaulay *Hist. Eng.* xviii. IV. 170 Anne..assumed the interesting character of a meek, resigned sufferer. 1894 Wolseley *Marlborough* I. 284 Sufficiently philosophical to be resigned, he was yet too ambitious to be contented.

Comb. 1856 Mrs. Carlyle *Lett.* II. 294 A sad, grey, resigned-looking, suffering woman.

b. Const. *to.*

1747 *Mem. Nutrebian Crt.* II. 91 Resigned to death with the heroick firmness of a primitive christian. 1781 Cowper *Charity* 151 To deep sadness sullenly resign'd. 1820 Byron *Mar. Fal.* i. ii. 43 Calm, but not overcast, he stood resign'd To the decree. 1838 Lytton *Alice* ii. ii, Evelyn.. had grown in some measure reconciled and resigned to her change of abode.

c. Characterized by resignation.

1749 Fielding *Tom Jones* vi. iii, He should insist on the most resigned obedience from his daughter. 1833 Tennyson *Two Voices* 98 Thought resign'd, A healthy frame, a quiet mind. 1885 J. K. Jerome *On the Stage* 111 A limp horse that..looked the picture of resigned misery.

3. That has retired from a position.

1896 *Daily News* 11 Mar. 4/7 A major..has threatened an action for libel against one of the resigned officers.

Resi·gnedly, *adv.* [f. prec. + -ly[2].] In a resigned manner; with resignation; submissively.

1671 Woodhead *St. Teresa* i. Pref. 19 She advised them, patiently, and resignedly, to bear this Cross. a 1700 Ken *Hymnotheo* Poet. Wks. 1721 III. 386 Lovers in their Arms resign'dly died. a 1721 Sheffield (Dk. Buckhm.) *Wks.* (1753) I. 79 Will any dog..Resin'dly leave his bitches and his bones, To turn a wheel? 1857 W. Collins *Dead Secret* (1861) 251 To face resignedly the duties and the sacrifices which the discovery of it imposed on them. 1887 *Cornh. Mag.* Mar. 277 The sports of the season..pass slowly and resignedly.

Resi·gnedness. [-ness.] Resignation.

a 1664 Frank *Serm.* (1672) 212 We begin our Christianity with the same resignedness. a 1695 Kettlewell *Chr. Obed.* (1715) 533 Our trust and dependence, submission and resignedness. 1748 Richardson *Clarissa* (1811) I. 139 The example which my mother sets of meekness, and resignedness to the wills of others. 1859 Geo. Eliot *Adam Bede* xxxix, The man..going forth with sad blind resignedness to an unreal sorrow.

Resignee. ? *Obs.* [f. Resign *v.*[1] + -ee[1].] One to whom anything is resigned.

1611 Cotgr. s.v. *Survivance*, That the Resignor may.. otherwise dispose of it if he happen to suruiue the Resignee. 1642 tr. *Perkins' Prof. Bk.* i. § 47. 22 An infant may be Grantee, Lessee, Obligee, Resignee.

Resi·gner. [-er[1].] One who resigns.

1555 *Sc. Acts Mary* (1814) II. 494/1 That the Instrument thairof be seilit with the seill of the resignar. 1611 Florio, *Risegnatore*, a resigner. 1706 [see Resignation 1]. a 1768 Erskine *Inst. Law Scot.* ii. vii. § 20 In resignations *ad remanentiam* made..by the resigner himself a special solemnity is introduced. a 1797 H. Walpole *Geo. II* (1822) I. 157 Of all the resigners, the Duke of Grafton had treated his master with the greatest decency. 1806 W. Taylor in *Monthly Mag.* XXII. 32 The resigners of livings, to be consistent, must maintain [etc.]. 1884 [see Resignatary].

Resi·gnful, *a. rare.* [f. Resign *v.*[1] + -ful.] Expressing resignation.

1876 Mrs. Whitney *Sights & Ins.* II. 419 The faint, tender little face, the sweet mouth, the resignful eyes.

Resigning (rīzəi·niŋ), *vbl. sb.* [f. Resign *v.*[1] + -ing[1].] Resignation.

1395 Purvey *Remonstr.* (1851) 144 Bi merciful dispensacioun aftir wilful resigning. c 1450 *Godstow Reg.* 202 Þat hir resininge & quite claiminge sholde be sure, she strengthid hit with be puttinge to of her seele. 1482 *Caxton's Chron. Eng.* ccliii. X 5 b, The peple wondred of the ceesing and resignyng of Felix to hym. 1530 Palsgr. 262/1 Resyning of a thyng. 1743 *Buccleuch MSS.* (Hist. MSS. Comm.) I. 407 His Lordship's resigning is of no loss to the service.

Resi·gning, *ppl. a.* [-ing[2].] That resigns.

1703 Collier *Ess. Mor. Subj.* ii. 99 Neither ought we to be too Implicit or Resigning to Authorities. 1710 Steele *Tatler* No. 198 ¶2 The peaceful, mild, resigning, humble Inhabitant, that animated her beauteous Body. 1894 R. Bridges *Humours Crt.* i. 109 The still fresh air of this October morning, With its resigning odours. 1899 J. W. S. Simpson *Mem. W. S. Simpson* 100 This resigning Choir found a home in the Church of St. Vedast.

Resi·gnment. Now *rare.* [f. as next + -ment.] The act of resigning; resignation.

c 1470 Harding *Chron.* clvii. iv, Then his title he sought By resignement and renunciacion. 1592 *Nobody & Someb.* in Simpson *Sch. Shaks.* (1878) I. 330 Give up thy state to these two princely youthes, And thy resignment shal preserve thy life. 1606 G. W[oodcocke] *Hist. Ivstine* xvii. 69 With his life [he] made resignement of the kingdome of Macedon. 1648 Boyle *Seraph. Love* (1660) 8 That Love.. which results from an entire Resignment to..the Lov'd Party. 1729 Butler *Serm.* Wks. 1874 II. 70 Time..begets in us that resignment of temper, which ought to have been produced by a better cause. 1825 Southey *Tale Paraguay* Poet. Wks. VII. 22 In this resignment to their hopeless case. 1891 *Q. Reg. Current Hist.* (Detroit) Feb. 10 It was feared that the Chancellor's resignment portended a precipitation of the inevitable war.

† Resi·gnor. *Obs. rare.* [f. Resign *v.*[1] + -or.] One who resigns.

1611 Cotgr. s.v. *Regrès*, If during the Resignors life it become voyd by the resignation or death of the Resignee.

Resile (rīzəi·l), *v.* [ad. obs. F. *resiler*, *resilir*, or L. *resilīre* to jump back, recoil, f. *re-* Re- 2 a + *salīre* to jump, leap: see Salient *a.*]

In senses 1–3 chiefly in Scottish use.

1. *intr.* To draw back *from* an agreement, contract, statement, etc.

1529 *State P. Hen. VIII*, I. 343 If the Quene wold heraftir resile and goo back from that, she semeth nowe to be contented with. 1671 [R. MacWard] *True Nonconf.* 231 Dare you..say, that the King and Parliament had power, either to resile, or to loose others, from the Bonds, which they themselves had thus established? a 1676 Bp. Guthrie *Mem.* (1702) 46 The next day he resiled from the Writing he had sign'd. 1830 Scott *Demonol.* ix. 293 Much pains was taken on her that she might resile from that confession. 1884 *Law Times Rep.* L. 643/1 Neither the company nor the landowner can, without the consent of the other, resile from the..contract.

b. Without const. To retract, draw back.

1662 J. Ellis *Retract.* 18, I was so weak as to resile and recal what I had said. 1754 Erskine *Princ. Sc. Law* (1809) 67 The party resiling is liable in damages to the other. 1814 Scott *Wav.* lxvi, A 'sma' minute, to prevent parties frae resiling'. 1845 Campbell *Chancellors* III. 565 But he thought it was too late to resile.

2. To draw back *from* a course of action, attitude of mind, etc.

1637 Gillespie *Eng. Pop. Cerem.* Epist. B, Let them resile from their violent proceedings. 1676 Row *Contn. Blair's Autobiog.* xii. (1848) 465 It has been said that I have resiled from my wonted zeal for Presbyterial Government. 1813 *Examiner* 22 Feb. 126/2 The noble family had too much real love of their country to resile from her service.

3. To shrink, recoil, retreat, *from* something with aversion or non-acceptance.

1697 Cleland *Poems* 79 (Jam.), Read Duram and Calvin well; If from their reasons you resile, I'le count you sots. 1776 Hume *My own Life* in *Ess.* I. 6 The more I resiled from their excessive civilities, the more I was loaded with them. 1813 Collinson *Key* iii. 60 Other persons resiling with abhorrence from unbelief. 1825 C. Butler *Bk. R. C. Ch.* 131 The pope resiled from the salutation. 1873 J. Hall *Questions of Day* viii. 101 So far from resiling from the prophecies..we regard the volume of evidence furnished by them as ever accumulating with the lapse of time. 1892 Bruce *Apologetics* ii. iii. 201 The modern mind has resiled from the pessimistic views of ethnic religions.

4. Of material things: To recoil or rebound after contact. Also const. *from.*

1708 Keill *Anim. Secretion* 43 The Particles which hit against one another do not resile, but unite together. 1738 Bayne *Gout* 102 An unequal velocity of particles will hinder and disturb their attractions, and by resiling from one another, cause an intestine motion which prevents their union. 1805 *Edin. Rev.* VII 81 The one by impinging on the other must be made to resile, according to the common laws of motion.

b. Of elastic bodies: To return to their original position after being stretched or compressed.

1709 *Phil. Trans.* XXVII. 81 There needs no more for stretching forth the Proboscis thus contracted, but the Fibres to resile to their former Position. 1853 Ure *Dict. Arts* (ed. 4) I. 362 The cake of caoutchouc, after being so condensed, resiles much more considerably than after the compressing action of the screw. 1898 Manson *Trop. Dis.* xxiii. 374 The drainage tube is allowed slowly to resile towards the fixed end.

5. a. To turn back from a point reached.

1887 Ferguson *Ogham Inscriptions* 97 Reading up to this digit..and resiling thence.

b. To return to one's original position.

1889 *Ch. Q. Rev.* XXVII. 351 It is impossible to specify any body of men of which so large a percentage has resiled as that of those who have become Roman Catholics during the period of which we are now speaking.

Hence **Resi·ling** *vbl. sb.* Also **Resi·lement.**

1644 Maxwell *Prerog. Chr. Kings* 102 The resileing of one partie contractor is not sufficient to void the contract. 1724 *Wodrow's Corr.* (1843) III. 146 A resiling from the declaration made by the Non-subscribers in the Synod. 1822 C. Butler *Reminisc.* (ed. 3) 181 Mr. Pitt's resiling from the coalition..will be mentioned in the pages of history with universal commendation. 1884 Ogilvie s.v. *Back* adv. 7, In withdrawal or resilement from an undertaking.

Resi·liate, *v. rare*⁻¹. [ad. F. *résilier.*] *trans.* To annul, cancel.

1881 *Daily News* 7 Mar. 6/1 Resiliating, at great cost to the State, the contracts with Heilbronner and other houses.

Resilience (rīzi·liĕns). [ad. L. type **resilientia*: see Resilient and -ence, and cf. It. *resilienza.*]

1. The (*or* an) act of rebounding or springing back; rebound, recoil. (See also quot. 1656.)

1626 Bacon *Sylva* § 245 Whether there be any such Resilience in Eccho's. 1656 Blount *Glossogr.*, *Resilience*, a leaping or skipping back, a rebounding; a going from ones word. ? 1799 Coleridge *Hymn to Earth*, Mightier far was the joy of thy sudden resilience. 1843 Carlyle *Past & Pr.* (1858) 79 The Heaviest..has its deflexions..nay at times its resiliences, its reboundings. 1866 J. Martineau *Ess.* I. 41 The heart does not always propel without resilience.

b. Revolt, recoil *from* something.

1858 Sears *Athan.* iii. ii. 267 Those smaller sects whose fierce resilience from Catholicism isolates them from the common reason. 1890 Garnett *Milton* 38 Nor can we doubt that the old Puritan fully approved his son's resilience from a church defined by Arminianism and prelacy.

c. Repugnance, antagonism.

1882 Mozley *Reminisc.* I. xii. 85 It was possibly a mutual resilience between him [Hartley Coleridge] and people of more orderly ways that prevented him from standing at Oriel till some years after.

2. Elasticity; the power of resuming the original shape or position after compression, bending, etc.

1824 Tredgold *Cast Iron* 82 The term modulus of resilience, I have ventured to apply to the number which represents the power of a material to resist an impulsive force. 1834 *Good's Study Med.* (ed. 4) I. 530 The natural elasticity or resilience of the lungs. 1867 C. T. F. Young *Fouling Iron Ships* 164 To bend back again.., if the metal possesses sufficient resilience to do so. 1897 *Allbutt's Syst. Med.* IV. 470 [The skin] giving a sensation of the loss of all elasticity or resilience.

fig. 1893 *Independent* (N. Y.) 19 Oct., The resilience and the elasticity of spirit which I had even ten years ago.

Resiliency (rīzi·liĕnsi). [Cf. prec. and -ency.]

1. Tendency to rebound or recoil.

1668 H. More *Div. Dial.* iii. xxiv. (1713) 238 There is the more strong and peremptory Resiliency from this sordid Region of Misery and Sin. 1676 — *Remarks* 143 The resiliency of the Quick-silver against the top of the Tube. 1751 Johnson *Rambler* No. 110 ¶7 The common resiliency of the mind from one extreme to another. 1826 [J. R. Best] *Four Yrs. France* 78 Disgusted with these appearances of distrust and resiliency.

2. Tendency to return *to* a state.

1778 *Phil. Surv. S. Ireland* 144 Such is the resiliency of all nature to its original state.

3. = Resilience 2.

1835–6 *Todd's Cycl. Anat.* I. 511/2 The resiliency by which the skin recovers itself after pressure. 1863 Wynter *Subtle Brains* 33 The process of vulcanization that gives such extraordinary resiliency to the material. 1890 W. J. Gordon *Foundry* 191 The advantage of combining the softening influence of the saccharine with the resiliency of the colloid.

4. Buoyancy, power of recovery.

1857 R. Tomes *Amer. in Japan* xvi. 379 Notwithstanding the calamities caused by the earthquake, there was shown a resiliency in the Japanese character which spoke well for their energy. 1888 *Leeds Mercury* 24 Feb. 4/7 The active properties of resiliency possessed by the Russian rouble.

Resilient (rīzi·liĕnt), *a.* [ad. L. *resilient-em*, pres. pple. of *resilīre* to Resile.]

1. Returning to the original position; springing back, recoiling, etc. Also, looking back.

1644 Bulwer *Chiron.* 43 The hand resilient or leapeing back to the Northward of the Body. 1706 Phillips (ed. Kersey), *Resilient*, leaping back, rebounding, or recoiling. 1822–34 *Good's Study Med.* (ed. 4) III. 191 Absorbing what he calls the resilient pulsations of sound. 1839–48 Bailey *Festus* xxx. 345 The soul in death resilient Looks back to whence its impulse came. 1880 Blackmore *Mary Anerley* III. iv. 60 Never yet looked horse through bridle, without at least one eye resilient towards the charm of headstall.

b. *Resilient escapement*, a form of lever escapement used in watches.

1879 *Cassell's Techn. Educ.* IV. 360/2 Another modification, called 'Cole's resilient', consists in the bending of the extreme points of the teeth back [etc.]. 1884 F. J. Britten *Watch & Clockm.* 150 Mr. J. F. Cole devised a resilient escapement without any banking pins.

2. Resuming the original shape or position after being bent, compressed, or stretched.

1674 Petty *Disc. Roy. Soc.* 122, I think it easiest to consider Elastic, Springing, or Resilient Bodies, as Laminæ, Laths, or Lines. 1767 Gooch *Treat. Wounds* I. 89 The fibrils of the resilient part of the nerve. 1859 *Todd's Cycl. Anat.* V. 287/2 The power of the heart is materially reinforced by the resilient structure which composes the parietes of the aortic bulb. 1873 *Contemp. Rev.* XXII. 181 His conscience consolidates itself, the original fibres grow firmer, more massive, and more resilient.

b. *Resilient stricture* (see quot.).

1874 Van Buren *Dis. Genit. Organs* 102 A resilient stricture is one which..is elastic, India-rubber like, contracting quickly after being dilated. 1891 Moullin *Surg.* ii. xxiii. 1273.

3. *fig.* Of persons, their minds, etc.: Rising readily again after being depressed; hence, cheerful, buoyant, exuberant.

1830 *Fraser's Mag.* II. 90 One vast receptacle for the abode of resilient and noisy saints like unto himself. 1859 S. R. Hole *Tour Irel.* 30 Nothing but..the resilient spirit of roving Englishmen could have induced us to sally forth. 1870 J. Hamilton *Moses, Man of God* viii. 150 Resolute and resilient is the stout heart of the sinner.

Hence **Resi·lientness,** 'rebounding Quality, Resiliency' (Bailey, vol. II, 1727).

† Resili·tion. *Obs.* [f. Resile *v.* + -ition.] The (*or* an) act of springing back; recoil, rebound, resilience.

1658 Phillips, *Resilition*, a rebounding, or leaping back. 1671 R. Bohun *Wind* 10 By Descension or Resilition, from the Middle Region. 1708 Keill *Anim. Secretion* 22 The greater their Elasticity, their Concussions and Resilitions will be the more sensible. 1727–38 Chambers *Cycl.*, *Recoil*, or *Rebound*, the resilition of a body, chiefly a fire-arm.

† Resil(i)ua·tion. *Obs.* [Erroneous for Recidivation. Cf. Residuation *sb.*[1]] Relapse.

1513 More in *Grafton's Contn. Harding* (1812) 488 There is, as phisicians saie, and as we also finde, double yᵉ perell in the resylynacion [*sic*: 1543 resiliuacion] yᵗ was in the firste syckenesse. 1577–87 Holinshed *Chron.* I. 178/2 The English kingdome..,as it had beene faine into a resiluation, came to extreame ruine. 1580 Lyly *Euphues* (Arb.) 316, I see now that as the resiluation of an Ague is desperate, and the second opening of a veyne deadly [etc.].

Re-si·lver (rī-), *v.* [Re- 5 a.] *trans.* To silver again; to replate with silver.

1856 *Orr's Circ. Sci., Pract. Chem.* 92 Re-silvering old articles. 1875 Bedford *Sailor's Pkt.-bk.* v. (ed. 2) 152 Directions for re-silvering sextant glasses when injured by damp or wet.

† Resimated, *ppl. a. Obs.*⁻¹ [f. L. *resim-us*, f. *re-* Re- + *sīmus* snub-nosed.] Turned up.

1681 Grew *Musæum* i. 73 These five Bones are resimated or bended upward, with some resemblance to a Saddle.

Resin, obs. f. Raisin; var. Reason *sb.*[2]

Resin (re·zin), *sb.* Forms: 4 **recyn(e, reyseu,** 4–6 **resyn,** 6–8 **resine,** 8– **resin** (9 **rezin**). [ad. F. *résine*, ad. L. *rēsīna* (Sp., Pg., and It. *resina*), cogn. with Gr. ῥητίνη. See also Rosin.]

1. A vegetable product, formed by secretion in special canals in almost all trees and plants, from many of which (as the fir and pine) it exudes naturally, or can be readily obtained by incision; various kinds are extensively used in making varnishes or adhesive compositions, and in pharmacy. (Cf. Gum-resin and Oleo-resin.)

1388 Wyclif *Jer.* viii. 22 Whether resyn is not in Galaad? *Ibid.* li. 8 Take ȝe recyn to the sorewe therof. c 1450 *M. E. Med. Bk.* (Heinrich) 225 Do þer to pouder recles, of resyn, & a party of virgyne wex, & boile hyt wel. 1538 Leland *Itin.* (1769) V. 91 The Wood of them in Burning savorith of Resine. 1744 Berkeley *Siris* § 18 A good pine might be made to yield resin every year. 1807 J. E. Smith *Phys. Bot.* 27 Here we find in appropriate vessels the resin of the Fir and Juniper. 1843 Holtzapffel *Turning* I. 30 In many of the more dense woods, we..find an abundance of gum or resin. 1876 Harley *Mat. Med.* (ed. 6) 409 Resin possesses the valuable quality of adhesiveness, and it is also slightly stimulant.

b. With *a* and *pl.* A particular kind of resin.

1801 *Med. Jrnl.* V. 366 Benzoic acid has been hitherto found in no other vegetable substance, except resins and balsams. 1837 M. Donovan *Dom. Econ.* II. 349 The aromatic portion of ginger is a resin, which constitutes about one tenth of the whole root. 1884 Bower & Scott *De Bary's Phaner.* 185 Resins are abundant, e.g. in the Euphorbias, and in Opium.

2. A resinous precipitate obtained by special treatment of certain vegetable products; a similar substance obtained from the bile of animals.

1681 tr. *Willis' Rem. Med. Wks.* Vocab., *Resine*, a chymical extraction of several druggs so called, being in substance like to rosine or resine. 1712 tr. *Pomet's Hist. Drugs* I. 29 The Resin or Magistery of Jalap is made with Spirit of Wine. 1826 Henry *Elem. Chem.* I. 401 The resin of bile may be obtained by the following process.. Berzelius, however,..denies that it is a true resin. 1880 J. W. Legg *Bile* 2 He also separated a resin or fat, to which he attributed in chief the colour and taste of the bile.

3. *attrib.* and *Comb.*, as *resin acid, candle, † gum, lac, -oil, -pot, soap, -wax*; **† resinasphalt,** = Retinasphalt; **resin-bush,** a South African shrub (see quot.); **resin-flux,** an excessive flow of resin, occurring as a disease in pine-trees; **resin gas,** illuminating gas made from resin; **resin opal,** a variety of opal (see quot.); **resin-plant** (see quot.); **resin-weed,** = *rosin-weed.*

1892 *Photogr. Ann.* II. 77 Rectified turpentine should always be used, since the crude oil contains *resin acids, formic acid, etc. 1811 Pinkerton *Petral* I. 595 In the strata of this substance, Mr. Hatchet also observed small masses approaching to the nature of the lignite of Cologne, and which he called *resinasphaltum*, or *resinasphalt. 1866 *Treas. Bot.* 479/2 *Euryops speciosissimus* is called *Resin-bush by the colonists, because of a gummy exudation often seen on the stem and leaves. 1849 James *Woodman* vii, Neither lamp nor taper, nor even a common *resin candle, gave light within. 1887 Garnsey & Balfour tr. *De Bary's Comp. Morph. Fungi* 384 The symptoms of disease which precede death in fir-trees are known as '*resin-flux' (' Harzsticken, Harzüberfülle'). *Note*, The word resin-flux is therefore introduced as indicating a prominent symptom of the disease, although it is not an exact rendering of the German terms. 1836–41 Brande *Chem.* (ed. 5) 556 *Resin Gas. 1856 *Orr's Circ. Sci., Pract. Chem.* 516 The liquor which is produced by the compression of resin-gas. 1382 Wyclif *Jer.* li. 8 Taketh *recyne gumme to his sorewe. 1839 Ure *Dict. Arts* 1097 The Hindus from time immemorial have possessed the *resin lac. 1856 *Orr's Circ. Sci., Pract. Chem.* 518 Seven and a quarter gallons of *resin-oil. 1868 Dana *Min.* (ed. 5) 198 *Resin opal (Wachsopal, Pechopal, *Germ.*), wax-, honey- to ochre-yellow, with a resinous lustre. 1884 Miller *Plant-n.* 115/1 *Resin-plant, Carana, *Bursera acuminata.* 1890 E. H. Barker *Wayfaring France* 40 The earthen *resin-pots fixed to the pines. 1875 *Ure's Dict. Arts* III. 850 Manufacture of Yellow or *Resin Soap. 1891 *Anthony's Phot. Bull.* IV. 299 Bringing their undersides in contact with the *resin-wax cement. 1869 Parkman *Discov. Gt. West* xvii. (1875) 206 The meadows spangled with the yellow blossoms of the *resin weed and the Rodbeckia.

b. *attrib.*, in terms denoting the parts of plants in which resin is secreted, as *resin-canal, -duct*, etc.

1854 *Q. Jrnl. Geol. Soc.* X. ii. 4 In form the amber is either like drops,..or as the casts of resin-ducts and cavities. 1875 Bennett & Dyer tr. *Sachs's Bot.* 77 The origin of resin and gum passages depends also on the formation of intercellular passages. 1884 Bower & Scott *De Bary's Phaner.* 357 In the angle of the Y lies a resin-canal. *Ibid.* 441 Among the *Coniferæ* all investigated species..have resin-passages or resin-reservoirs.

Resin (re·zin), *v.* [f. prec.] *trans.* To rub or treat with resin. Hence **Re·sined** *ppl. a.*

1865 *Spohr's Autobiog.* II. 69 The bow, which she had previously resined. 1884 Daniell *Princ. Physics* xiv. 395 A glass rod..rubbed longitudinally by a resined cloth..will produce a shrill sound. 1899 Beatr. Harraden *Fowler* 225 He resined his bow, and began.

Resinaceous (rezinēⁱ·ʃəs), *a. rare.* [ad. L. *rēsināceus*: see Resin *sb.* and -aceous.] That yields resin; resinous.

1669 Worlidge *Syst. Agric.* 275 *Resinaceous*, rosenny, or yielding Rosin. 1674 Blount *Glossogr.* (ed. 4), *Resinaceous*, of or belonging to Rozen. 1879 Lewis & Short *Lat. Dict.*, *Resinaceus*, resinous, resinaceous.

Resinate (re·zinĕt), *sb. Chem.* [f. Resin *sb.* + -ate[4]. Cf. F. *résinate.*] A salt formed by the action of a resinous acid on a base.

1838 T. Thomson *Chem. Org. Bodies* 530 The resinate of ammonia is easily formed... The resinates of the earths and metallic oxides are powders, insoluble in water, alcohol, and ether. 1868 Watts *Dict. Chem.* V. 79 *Resinates*, a general name for the salts of the acids obtained from turpentine.

Resinate (re·zineⁱt), *v.* [f. Resin *sb.* + -ate[3].] *trans.* To flavour or impregnate with resin.

1891 in *Cent. Dict.*

Resine, obs. f. Resign *v.*; obs. Sc. f. *risen*, pa. pple. of Rise *v.*

Resi·nein(e. *Chem.* [a. F. *résinéine* (Fremy): see Resin *sb.* and -in(e).] (See quots.)

1855 Ogilvie *Suppl.*, *Resineine*, an oil yielded by colophony. 1868 Watts *Dict. Chem.* V. 79 *Resinein*, or *Resinone*; this name is given by Frémy to a hydro-carbon (probably impure colophene..) obtained by the dry distillation of colophony.

† Re·sing, *vbl. sb. Obs.* [f. Rese *v.*[1] + -ing[1].] An attack, assault.

1387 Trevisa *Higden* (Rolls) III. 257 Half þe peple stood i-armed..for resynge and stekkynge of straunge naciouns. *Ibid.* V. 299 Seint Mammertus..ordeyned..letanyes.. aȝenst erþe schakynge..and peril of resynge of wylde bestes.

Resi·ng (rī-), *v.* [Re- 5 a.] *trans.* To sing again. Hence **Resi·nging** *vbl. sb.*

1618 Mynshul *Charac. Prison* Ep. Ded. 1, I come not now to re-sing, but to re-cant the errours both of my pen and iudgment. 1687 Beverley *Expos. Song of Songs* 54 That Song, that sprung In those first Times, is now, as new, Resung. a 1700 Ken *Hymns Festiv.* Poet. Wks. 1721 I. 209 Re-sing this Day the same Angelick Strain. 1885 *Manch. Exam.* 15 Apr. 3/1 *Apollo and Marsyas*..is..an imaginative resinging of the contending chants.

Resing, obs. Sc. form of Resign *v.*

Resinic (rezi·nik), *a.* [f. Resin *sb.* + -ic.] Of, belonging to, or derived from resin.

1895 in *Funk's Stand. Dict.*

Resiniferous (rezini·fĕrəs), *a.* [f. Resin *sb.* + -(i)ferous. Cf. F. *résinifère*, Sp., Pg., and It. *resinifero.*] Yielding or containing resin.

1673–4 Grew *Anat. Pl., Anat. Trunks* (1684) 110 The utmost are not Milk-Vessels, but Gum Vessels, or Resiniferous. 1676 — *Anat. Fl.* 156 As in Box, and Yew, as also Fir, and all Resiniferous Plants. 1797 *Encycl. Brit.* (ed. 3) XV. 3/2 The outmost are gum or resiniferous vessels, destined for the secretion of turpentine. 1881 *Scribner's Mag.* XXII. 834 The fragrance of wild honeysuckle and resiniferous trees.

Resinifica·tion. [a. F. *résinification*: see Resin *sb.* and -(i)fication.] The act or process of making resinous; the fact of becoming resinous.

1800 tr. *Lagrange's Chem.* II. 249 There is still a fourth operation in resinification. 1856 *Orr's Circ. Sci., Pract. Chem.* 493 Its liability to smoke..may arise..from a resinification of the camphine. 1875 *Ure's Dict. Arts* III. 448 The resinification of the drying oils may be effected by the smallest quantities of certain substances, which would act in the manner of ferments.

† Resinifluous, *a. Bot. Obs.* [f. Resin *sb.*, after *mellifluous.*] Producing resin.

1657 Tomlinson *Renou's Disp.* 388 The Pine-trees..are all tall, coniferous, resinifluous.

Resiniform (re·zinifǭɹm), *a.* [ad. F. *résiniforme*: see Resin *sb.* and -form.] Having the character of resin.

1811 Pinkerton *Petral.* II. 407 If I may be allowed to use the expression, it is what Dolomieu has called resiniform lava. 1852 Th. Ross tr. *Humboldt's Trav.* I. vi. 214 A resiniform matter, soluble both by alcohol and by water.

Resinify (re·zinifəi), *v.* [ad. F. *résinifier*: see Resin *sb.* and -fy.]

1. *trans.* To change into resin.

1816 Tingry *Varnisher's Guide* (ed. 2) 21 What is called frankincense is gallipot resinified. 1882 *Athenæum* 7 Oct. 469/2 Oxidized or resinified by the influence of the air.

2. *intr.* To become resinous.

1856 *Orr's Circ. Sci., Pract. Chem.* 476 Common nut oil.. is more apt to resinify and clog the wick than linseed. 1887 A. M. Brown *Anim. Alkaloids* 31 Parvoline resinifies readily on exposure to the air.

Resinite (re·zinəit). *Min.* [f. Resin *sb.* + -ite[1].] Retinasphalt.

1849 Dana *Geol.* x. (1850) 542 Some of the wood is beautifully opalized, though the greater part has the pitchy lustre of resinite.

Resinize (re·zinəiz), *v.* [f. Resin *sb.* + -ize.] To treat with resin. Hence **Re·sinized** *ppl. a.*

1878 Abney *Photogr.* (1881) 145 Another mode of producing a dull surface..is to use resinised paper.

Resi·nk (rī-), *v.* [Re- 5 a.] To sink again.

1612 J. Davies (Heref.) *Muse's Sacrifice* Wks. (Grosart) II. 29/2 Though there I vow'd.., I brake my vow and me re-suncke in sinne.

Resino-, combining form of Resin *sb.*, as in **resino-electric** *a.*, containing or exhibiting resinous or negative electricity (Webster, 1828–32, citing Ure); **resino-extractive** *a.*, designating extractive matter in which resinous matter predominates (*ibid.*); **resino-vitreous,** partaking of the characters of resin and glass.

1839 Ure *Dict. Arts* 40 The texture of amber is resino-vitreous, its fracture conchoidal, and lustre glassy.

Resinoid (re·zinoid), *a.* and *sb.* [f. Resin *sb.* + -oid. Cf. F. *résinoïde.*]

A. *adj.* Resembling resin.

1830 Lindley *Nat. Syst. Bot.* 232 A bitter resinoid matter, slightly soluble in water. 1894 *Westm. Gaz.* 18 June 8/1 Cyona Tincture is an alcoholic extract which has been found to contain a resinoid substance.

B. *sb.* A resinous substance.

1880 *Libr. Univ. Knowl.* VIII. 818 The resinoid extracted from it has the name of *leptandrin.* 1894 *Times* 11 Aug. 11/2 The woody fibre disappears first, leaving a residue richer in resinoids.

† Resinose, *a. Obs.*⁻¹ [ad. L. *rēsīnōs-us*: see next and -ose.] Resinous.

1712 Petiver in *Phil. Trans.* XXVII. 424 A Milk, which smells Resinose.

Resinous (re·zinəs), *a.* [ad. L. *rēsīnōs-us*: see Resin *sb.* and -ous. So F. *résineux*, Sp., Pg., and It. *resinoso.*]

1. Of the nature of resin.

1646 Sir T. Browne *Pseud. Ep.* 51 As all resinous bodies, Turpentine, Pitch, and Frankincense. 1694 Salmon *Bate's Dispens.* (1699) 229/1 This Tincture is only the resinous Parts of the Balsam dissolv'd in the Spirit of Wine. 1791 Hamilton *Berthollet's Dyeing* I. i. i. i. 15 It has been proposed to divide the colouring particles into extractive and resinous. 1838 T. Thomson *Chem. Org. Bodies* 288 Sulphuric acid..dissolves the corydalina, and leaves the green resinous matter. 1878 A. H. Green, etc. *Coal* i. 21 The resinous character also prevents the spores from being wetted.., and tends to preserve them from decay.

2. Of plants or their parts: Containing resin.

1656 Blount *Glossogr.*, *Resinous*, full of rozen or gum. 1673–4 Grew *Anat. Pl., Anat. Trunks* (1684) 110 The Barque of Oak it self is also somewhat Resinous. 1712 tr. *Pomet's Hist. Drugs* I. 146 The Fruit..more resinous, and falls easily when ripe. 1797 *Encycl. Brit.* (ed. 3) XVII. 692/2 Made of the most porous and resinous wood to be found. 1811 A. T. Thomson *Lond. Disp.* (1818) 35 The root is biennial, thick, fleshy, and resinous. 1858 Carpenter *Veg. Phys.* § 51 A peculiar form of woody fibre is found in the stems of resinous woods.

3. Of properties, etc.: Properly belonging to, or characteristic of, resin.

1811 A. T. Thomson *Lond. Disp.* (1818) 217 It is in brittle fragments of an almost black colour, having a shining, resinous fracture. 1838 T. Thomson *Chem. Org. Bodies* 550 Has a resinous and aromatic smell. 1884 Mrs. C. Praed *Zero* xiii, The atmosphere was pungent with a resinous odour.

4. Made or compounded of resin; affected or produced by the burning of resin.

1808 S. Young in *Med. Jrnl.* XIX. 567 A convenient slip of firm linen, uniformly covered by a resinous plaster. 1862 Dickens *Uncomm. Trav.* xxviii, I can smell the heavy resinous incense as I pass the church. 1871 B. Taylor *Faust* (1875) II. ii. iii. 140 The resinous atmosphere Gives hint of pitch. 1871 Tyndall *Fragm. Sci.* (1879) I. iv. 122 The resinous fumes slowly diminished.

5. *Electr.* = Negative *a.* 7.

1797 *Encycl. Brit.* (ed. 3) VI. 421/2 Mr Du Fay discovered the difference between positive and negative, or, as they were for some time called, the vitreous and resinous electricities. 1840 Carlyle *Heroes* (1858) 198 Thunder was not then mere Electricity, vitreous or resinous. 1860 Emerson *Cond. Life, Wealth*, The genius of reading and of gardening are antagonistic, like resinous and vitreous electricity. 1885 Watson & Burbury *Math. The. Electr. & Magn.* I. 94 A superficial electrification on the inner surface, the total amount of which will be resinous.

6. *Comb.*, as *resinous-like, -looking* adjs.

1807 T. Thomson *Chem.* (ed. 3) II. 449 It converts the drying oils into a yellow resinous-like mass. 1832 Brewster *Nat. Magic* xiii. 339 The dense fluid..quickly hardens into a transparent and yellowish resinous-looking substance.

Hence **Re·sinously** *adv.*, (*a*) with resinous electricity; (*b*) with an impregnation of resin. Also **Re·sinousness,** 'resinous or rosiny quality' (Bailey, vol. II, 1727).

1794 G. Adams *Nat. & Exp. Phil.* IV. xlvi. 264 Bodies electrified resinously repel each other. 1830 Lindley *Nat. Syst. Bot.* 53 Shrubs with alternate, toothed, resinously glandular, exstipulate leaves. 1873 Maxwell *Electr. & Magn.* (1881) I. 32 All electrified bodies are found to be either vitreously or resinously electrified.

Resiny (re·zini), *a.* [f. Resin.] Resinous.

1576 Newton *Lemnie's Complex.* (1633) 234 It is blacke like pitch, and shineth like to Jeat,..and as certaine resiny stuffe. 1847 in Webster. 1893 *Times* 13 Dec. 3/5 Shellac ..resiny blocky.

Resipiscence (resipi·sĕns). [a. F. *résipiscence*, or ad. L. *resipiscentia*, f. *resipiscĕre* to recover one's senses, come to oneself again, f. *re-* Re- + *sapĕre*: see Sapient.] Repentance for misconduct; recognition of errors committed; return to a better mind or opinion.

1570 T. Norton tr. *Nowel's Catech.* (1853) 177 Sinners.. have need of repentance, which some like better to call resipiscence or amendment. 1606 in Spottiswood *Hist. Ch. Scot.* vii. (1677) 499 Nothing had appeared in them but an obdured obstinacy, without any token of resipiscence. 1657 W. Morice *Cœna quasi Κοινὴ* xxiii. 231 If their return be upon the score of resipiscence, far be it from me to be such an one as Beza complains of. 1827 Hallam *Const. Hist.* (1876) II. viii. 67 They drew a flattering picture of the resipiscence of the Anglican party. 1864 Merivale *Conv. Rom. Emp.* 37 Full of horror at his own backsliding, full of hope for his tardy resipiscence. 1881 Saintsbury *Dryden* vi. 127 These prefaces and dedications show an ever-growing command of prose style, and, very soon, the resipiscence of Dryden's judgment.

So **† Resipi·scency.** *Obs.*

c 1540 tr. *Pol. Verg. Eng. Hist.* (Camden No. 36) 122 [Gildas] somtimes gentlie exorting them to goodnes and resipiscentie. 1672 Sir T. Browne *Let. to Friend* § 40 So closely shut up within the holds of vice and iniquity, as not to find some escape by a postern of resipiscency.

Resipiscent (resipi·sĕnt), *a.* [ad. L. *resipiscent-em*, pres. pple. of *resipiscĕre*: see Resipiscence.] Returning to a sound state of mind.

1872 F. Hall *False Philol.* 67 Grammar,..resipiscent and sane as of old. 1880 *Sat. Rev.* 26 June 821/2 Mr. Martin, at last resipiscent, and even like 'a prophet new inspired'.

Resist (rīzi·st), *sb.* [f. the vb.]

†1. Resistance. *Obs.*

1535 Stewart *Cron. Scot.* III. 411 Makand heirschip fra blude and fyre also, Without resist quhair euir tha list till go. 1584 Lodge *Forbonius & Prisc.* H j b, I make no resist in this my louing torment. 1608 Day *Hum. out of Breath* v. ii, Proud his assault, as proud be our resist. 1630 J. Lane *Contn. Sqr.'s T.* x. 437 (Ashm. MS.), Camball tooke (without resiste) the town.

2. In calico-printing, a preparation applied to those parts of the fabric which are not to be coloured, in order to prevent the dye from affecting them. Also *attrib.*

1836 *Penny Cycl.* VI. 156/1 White resist for deep blue, to be applied by the cylinder. *Ibid.*, After printing on the resist pastes, the goods should be hung up. 1860 Smiles *Self Help* ii, The process for producing what is called resist work in calico printing. 1890 W. J. Gordon *Foundry* 175 A style where a 'resist' is printed on the blank cloth, the 'resist' being a substance that is unaffected by the dye.

3. Any composition applied to a surface to protect it in part from the effects of an agent employed on it for some purpose. Also *resist-varnish.*

1839 Ure *Dict. Arts* 218 The copper is covered by a resist varnish while being heated by the transmission of steam through its axis. 1873 Spon *Worksh. Rec.* Ser. i. 199/1 [Steel] requires to be preserved against the action of the cleansing acids and of the graining mixture, by a composition called resist. 1890 *Pall Mall G.* 20 Feb. 3/1 When the 'resist' has been sufficiently applied, the instrument is again passed over the plate.

Resist (rīzi·st), *v.* Also 5 *Sc.* **rasyst,** 5–6 **resyst(e.** [ad. F. *résister*, † *resistir* (= It. *re-*, *risistere*, Sp. and Pg. *resistir*), or L. *resistĕre*, f. *re-* Re- + *sistĕre*, redupl. form of *stāre* to stand.]

1. *trans.* Of things: To stop or hinder (a moving body); to succeed in standing against; to prevent (a weapon, etc.) from piercing or penetrating.

c 1374 Chaucer *Boeth.* i. met. vii. (1868) 29 Þe fletyng streme..is arestid & resisted ofte tyme by þe encountrynge of a stoon. a 1533 Ld. Berners *Huon* lv. 186 Sorbryn.. strake..such a stroke that the buckles nor ony thynge elles coude resyste the stroke. 1658 Phillips s.v. *Resistence*, A solid body, which resisteth and opposeth whatsoever comes against it. 1667 Milton *P. L.* xii. 491 Spiritual Armour, able to resist Satans assaults. 1727–38 Chambers *Cycl.* s.v. *Respiration*, The air presses the lungs as much as the thorax resists them. 1797 *Encycl. Brit.* (ed. 3) VII. 363/1 They made the towers round instead of square, imagining this figure to be the strongest to resist the battering engines. 1860 Tyndall *Glac.* ii. xix. 332 It quite resisted the edge of a knife. 1894 H. S. Maxim in *Daily News* 4 June 5/7 It is quite true that I used a steel plate to resist my projectiles.

b. To withstand the action or effect of (a natural force or physical agency).

1567 Maplet *Gr. Forest* 2 b, It maketh it able to resist fire. 1687 A. Lovell tr. *Thevenot's Trav.* i. 6 A white soft Rock..does not long resist the Sea Winds..that eat it away. 1766 *Compl. Farmer* s.v. *Madder* 5 G 2/1 That which was dyed with the madder..resisted during thirty minutes a boiling which the other could not bear during ten. 1784 Cowper *Task* iii. 465 The stable yields a stercoraceous heap,..potent to resist the freezing blast.

c. Of immaterial things.

1726–31 Tindal *Rapin's Hist. Eng.* (1743) II. xvii. 31 If the interest and sollicitations of the King her Husband had not strongly resisted her zeal for her Religion. 1856 Emerson *Eng. Traits, Race* Wks. (Bohn) II. 21 But whilst race works immortally to keep its own, it is resisted by other forces.

2. Of persons: To withstand, strive against, oppose: **a.** a person, his will, etc.

1432–50 tr. *Higden* (Rolls) III. 333 This philosophre Demostines resistede the legates of the Molosynes commen to Athenes. c 1460 Fortescue *Abs. & Lim. Mon.* (1885) 115 Wherfor thai ben myghty, and able to resiste the aduersaries of this reaume. 1530 Palsgr. 688/1 He intendeth to take possessyon here agaynst my wyll, but he shall be resysted. 1593 Shaks. *3 Hen. VI*, ii. v. 79 Thou that so stoutly hath resisted me, Giue me thy Gold. 1651 Hobbes *Leviath.* ii. xxi. 110 Their Representative had the Libertie to resist, or invade other people. 1672 Petty *Pol. Anat.* (1691) 47 This Force I take to be sufficient to resist any number of men. 1717 Pope *Iliad* xi. 955 Shall Greece yet stand? Resists she yet the raging Hector's hand? 1771 *Junius Lett.* xliv. (1788) 248 They knew, that the present house of commons..were likely enough to be resisted. 1817 Shelley *Rev. Islam* x. xxviii, O King of Glory! thou alone hast power! Who can resist thy will? 1864 Bryce *Holy Rom. Emp.* xiii. (1875) 211 The Lombard league had successfully resisted Frederick's armies.

b. an attack, invasion, blow, or hostile action of any kind.

1533 Bellenden *Livy* iii. ii. (S.T.S.) I. 247 Þe Inemyis.. assaleȝet..þe Romane pussance, as Insufficient to resist þare Invasions. 1535 Coverdale *Matt.* v. 39, I saye vnto you: that ye resist not euell. 1585 T. Washington tr. *Nicholay's Voy.* ii. xiii. 48 Constantine..seeking to resist the courses and robberies which the Parthes dayly vsed towards the Romains. 1610 Shaks. *Temp.* i. ii. 465, I will resist such entertainment, till Mine enemy ha's more pow'r. 1667 Milton *P. L.* ii. 814 That mortal dint, Save he who reigns above, none can resist. 1840 Thirlwall *Greece* VII. 355 He felt himself unable to resist the attack. 1874 Green *Short Hist.* iv. § 3. 184 Pardon was freely extended to all who had resisted the invasion.

c. a moral or mental influence or suggestion.

1483 Caxton *G. de la Tour* f iij b, Be ye thenne strong ..to resist and ouercome them [temptations]. 1529 More *Dyaloge conc. Heresyes* i. Wks. 153/2 So muste reason not resyste faithe but walke with her. 1577 North *Guevara's Diall Pr.* 37 The favour that God wil geve you..no man can resist it. 1656 Jeanes *Fuln. Christ* 112 His grace.. can resist the strongest, and most restlesse temptations. 1670 Cotton *Espernon* iii. x. 522 With all these advantages he was not able to resist four words. 1717 Lady M. W. Montagu *Lett.* II. 35 The Greeks..resist, with incredible fortitude, the Conviction of their own eyes. 1786 Burns *To unco' Guid* viii, What's done we partly may compute, But know not what's resisted. 1817 Keatinge *Trav.* I. 81 It is hard to resist the surmise that Cæsar's account is drawn up with quite as much regard to effect as to reality. 1875 Jowett *Plato* (ed. 2) V. 33 Those who had never been taught to resist pleasure would be equally at the mercy of those who could.

d. something proposed to be done or likely to happen, a law or command, etc.

1593 Shaks. *Rich. II*, iv. i. 148 It will the wofullest Diuision proue..Preuent it, resist it, and let it not be so. 1607 — *Cor.* iii. i. 267 He hath resisted Law And therefore Law shall scorne him further Triall. 1771 *Junius Lett.* xliv. (1788) 254 If the process of the courts of Westminster-hall be resisted. 1781 Cowper *Expost.* 540 Thy parliaments ..Whate'er was asked, too timid to resist, Comply'd with. 1810 in Craufurd *Gen. Craufurd* (1891) 108 This arrangement..had before now been proposed to me, and I had resisted it. 1837 Dickens *Pickw.* v, The dismal man,..resisting Mr. Pickwick's invitation to breakfast.., walked slowly away. 1844 H. H. Wilson *Brit. India* II. 413 The disinclination of the native Princes to submit to, or their ability to resist, its dictation.

e. a natural force, weakness or disease, etc.

1593 Shaks. *3 Hen. VI*, iv. iii. 59 It boots not to resist both winde and tide. 1596 Spenser *F. Q.* iv. v. 43 Fleshly weaknesse, which no creature may Long time resist. 1806 *Med. Jrnl.* XV. 545 A case..where the inoculation was resisted till the twenty-ninth time.

†3. To prevent. Const. with inf. or *from.* *Obs.*

1500–20 Dunbar *Poems* xxvii. 105 To put this in rememberance, Mycht no man me resist. a 1586 Sidney *Arcadia* ii. (1605) 139 Beautifull trees, which resisted the sunnes darts from ouer-much piercing the naturall coldnesse of the River.

†4. To repel, affect with distaste. *Obs. rare*⁻¹.

1608 Shaks. *Per.* ii. iii. 29 These cates resist me, she but thought upon.

5. *intr.* **†a.** To stand *against*, to make opposition *to*, a person or thing. *Obs.*

c 1375 *Sc. Leg. Saints* xxii. (*Laurence*) 16 It has vertu.. fore to resyst a-gane fyre-slacht. *Ibid.* xxxiii. (*George*) 12 To resyst ay to sathane & to lordis of mykil mycht. c 1425 Wyntoun *Cron.* v. xi. 3548 Bot Valentynyane þe emperoure Resistyt ay til his erroure. 1483 Caxton *Cato* b ij b, Thou oughtest..to haue strengthe for to resiste ageynst alle aduersytees. 1538 Starkey *England* ii. i. 165 Except man wyth cure,..& labur, resyste to the same, they ouer-run reson. 1563 *Mirr. Mag.*, *Blacke Smyth* 175 b, That no man should resist agaynst his kyng. 1609 Bible (Douay) *Deut.* ix. 2 A great people and tal,..against whom no man is able to resist. 1651 tr. *De-las-Coveras' Don Fenise* 274 She forced herselfe to resist against the excesse of her affliction.

b. Without const. To offer resistance.

a 1547 Surrey *Ecclesiastes* iv. 31 What can he doo but yeld, that must resist aloone? 1582 Stanyhurst *Æneis* i. (Arb.) 21 Thee storme dyd conquoure, thee ships scant weaklye resisted. 1604 Shaks. *Oth.* i. ii. 80 Lay hold vpon him, if he do resist Subdue him, at his perill. 1653 Holcroft *Procopius, Goth. Wars* i. 30 The Horse-men,.. having nothing to resist with, are easily shot. 1771 *Junius Lett.* lxiii. (1788) 332 That the counsel did not resist, is true. 1822 Shelley tr. *Calderon's Mag. Prodig.* iii. 125 How wilt thou then Resist, Justina? a 1862 Buckle *Civiliz.* (1873) II. viii. 573 The nation not daring, and what was still worse, not wishing, to resist, gave way.

†c. To refuse *to* do something. *Obs. rare*⁻¹.

1539 *Act 31 Hen. VIII*, c. 4 In case it happen the Mayer ..make defaulte of paymente of the saide recompence & satisfaction, and resiste to paye the same.

†6. To stop; to rest. *Obs.*

c 1470 Henry *Wallace* viii. 1090 Bot I rasyst (*v.r.* desist) throw chargis off our consaill, The southmaist part off Ingland we sall se. 1556 *Aurelio & Isab.* (1608) O v, In yowere hande the goode and the ill of the ladies resistethe.

Hence **Resi·sted** *ppl. a.*

1713 M. Henry *Folly Despising* Wks. 1853 I. 179/1 The rejected Saviour and the resisted Sanctifier. 1753 Chambers *Cycl. Suppl.* s.v. *Resistance*, When the compression of the fluid is just sufficient to prevent a vacuum behind the resisted body. 1842 Gwilt *Archit.* 1024 The resisting and resisted parts are not only contiguous, but cohere.

† Resi·stable, *a. Obs.* [f. Resist *v.* + -able. Cf. Resistible.]

1. That may be resisted; resistible.

1608 Topsell *Serpents* (1658) 601 The Serpents of Europe are..more resistable for their weakness and strength. 1689 *Thoughts Gentlemen's Undertaking at York* 16 The Chimney-man that is Irresistable in his Office, is Resistable if he gather the Corn in the Town-fields. 1752 Carte *Hist. Eng.* III. 71 Henry thought Charles's power..scarce resistable by the rest of Europe.

2. Capable of resisting. Const. *of.* *rare*⁻¹.

1670 Pettus *Fodinæ Reg.* Introd., I speak of Fire, I might also Discourse of the strange nature of Bone-Ashes,..so resistable of that Element.

Hence **† Resistabi·lity; Resi·stableness.** *Obs.*

1622 K. Jas. *Direct. conc. Preachers* in Rushw. *Hist. Coll.* (1659) I. 65 The Universality, Efficacy, Resistability [1642 Resistibility], or Irresistibility of Gods Grace. 1784 J. Brown *Hist. Brit. Ch.* (1820) I. 205 The universality, efficacy or resistableness of God's grace.

† Resi·stal. *Obs. rare*⁻¹. [f. as prec. + -al.] Resistance.

1631 T. Heywood *Fair Maid of West* ii. iv. i, All resistals, Quarrels, and ripping-up of injuries, Are smothered in the ashes of our wrath.

Resistance (rīzi·stăns). Also 6 **-aunce,** 6 **resystaunce.** [a. F. *résistance*, later form of *resistence* Resistence: see Resist *v.* and -ance.]

1. The act, on the part of persons, of resisting, opposing, or withstanding. Const. *to*, † *of.*

1417 in Ellis *Orig. Lett.* Ser. ii. I. 59 To putt therwith a greate fortificacion aboute the same for resistance of the sayd enimies. 1535 Coverdale *Eccl.* iv. 12 One maye be ouercome, but two maye make resistaunce. 1560 Daus tr. *Sleidane's Comm.* 72 They tende to a publique peace, and to the resistaunce of Christes ennemies. 1651 Hobbes *Leviath.* ii. xxx. 175 Such is all resistance to the essentiall Rights of Soveraignty. 1687 A. Lovell tr. *Thevenot's Trav.* i. 229 They met with a stout resistance. 1729 Butler *Serm.* Wks. 1874 II. 93 Cases..in which sudden resistance is the only security. 1769 *Junius Lett.* xvi. (1788) 99 There is yet a spirit of resistance in this country, which will not submit to be oppressed. 1827 Southey *Hist. Penins. War* II. 596 The efforts..for organizing a civic and national resistance. 1874 Green *Short Hist.* viii. § 5. 499 The threat, however, failed to break the resistance of the Commons.

b. *Passive resistance*, simple refusal to comply with some demand, without active opposition.

In recent use *spec.* refusal to pay voluntarily the education rate imposed by the Education Act of 1902.

1819 Scott *Ivanhoe* xxiii, In this humour of passive resistance..Isaac sat in a corner of his dungeon. 1844 H. H. Wilson *Brit. India* I. 467 Their conduct was uniformly peaceable; passive resistance was the only weapon to which they trusted. 1869 Freeman *Norm. Conq.* (1875) III. 58 The resistance was probably passive.

attrib. 1845 Ld. Campbell *Chancellors* xc. (1857) IV. 227 By a partial scrutiny Pritchard, his passive-resistance competitor, was placed in the civic chair.

2. Power or capacity of resisting.

1590 Sir J. Smyth *Disc. Weapons* 4 b, If they were of diuerse lengths..and thereby..of lesse force and resistance. 1667 Milton *P. L.* vi. 838 They astonisht all resistance lost, All courage. 1703 Moxon *Mech. Exerc.* 256 When the Earth on which we would make Pillars or Piers is of [un]equal resistance, that is to say, not good. 1753 Chambers *Cycl. Suppl.* s.v., In the comparing together the resistances to all velocities. 1894 H. S. Maxim in *Daily News* 4 June 5/7 Provided he can produce something which has greater resistance for its weight than steel or copper bronzes. 1897 Mary Kingsley *W. Africa* 637 Not that these good people have a greater resistance to the fever than the Jamaica Christians.

3. Opposition of one material thing to another material thing, force, etc.

1625 N. Carpenter *Geogr. Del.* i. iv. (1635) 80 The Heauens in their motion find no resistance. 1645 Waller *My lady Isabella*, Musick so softens and disarms the mind, That not an arrow does resistance find. 1659 Hammond *On Ps.* lxxxix. 13 Above all the oppositions and resistances in nature. 1715 Gregory *Elem. Astron.* (1726) II. 710 They are stopp'd and repell'd by the Resistance of the neighbouring Vortices. 1838 *Civ. Eng. & Arch. Jrnl.* I. 374/2 Whereby he imparts great additional strength or power of resistance to the said metal rails and bars. 1880 Geikie *Phys. Geogr.* iv. 284 The rocks offering many varying degrees of resistance to erosion, they are worn down unequally.

b. *esp.* in the physical sciences, the opposition offered by one body to the pressure or movement of another.

1656 tr. *Hobbes' Elem. Philos.* (1839) 211, I define resistance to be the endeavour of one moved body..contrary to the endeavour of another moved body. 1690 Locke *Hum. Und.* ii. iv. § 3 All the Bodies in the World, pressing a drop of Water on all sides, will never be able to overcome the Resistance it will make. 1710 J. Clarke *Rohault's Nat. Philos.* (1729) I. 123 If I put my Finger to any of its Parts, I ought to feel the Resistance. 1777 Priestley *Matt. & Spir.* (1782) I. ii. 16 The cause of all resistance is repulsive power. 1831 Lardner *Hydrost.* ix. 192 The resistance of different fluids will be different according to their specific gravities. c 1860 Faraday *Forces Nat.* i. 41 The resistance of the air having been avoided. 1883 *Encycl. Brit.* XV. 751/1 Where the line representing the total resistance exerted at that joint intersects the joint.

pl. 1753 Chambers *Cycl. Suppl.* s.v., Though the hypothesis of a fluid..be of great use in explaining the nature of resistances. 1797 *Encycl. Brit.* (ed. 3) XVI. 92/2 Of all the resistances of bodies to each [other], there is..none of greater importance than the resistance or reaction of fluids. 1840 *Civ. Eng. & Arch. Jrnl.* III. 89/2 To overcome what are called the friction and resistances of the engine. 1855 J. R. Leifchild *Cornwall* 186 A steam pressure of 150 lbs, exclusive of engine resistances.

c. Hence *Line of resistance.*

1851 *Catal. Gt. Exhib.* 374 Forming a diagonal line of traction in the direct line of resistance. 1851 Ruskin *Stones Ven.* (1874) I. x. 122 This moral character of the arch is called by architects its 'Line of Resistance'.

4. Non-conductivity in respect of electricity, magnetism, or heat.

1860 G. Prescott *Electr. Telegr.* 279 A conductor, in fact, whose resistance is nothing. 1871 B. Stewart *Heat* (ed. 2) § 282 To determine the thermal resistance of various liquids. 1888 *Philos. Mag.* XXV. 422, I will now for a moment compare the case of magnetic resistance with a natural case of ordinary resistance.

b. A part of an electrical apparatus used to offer a definite resistance to a current.

1878 *Encycl. Brit.* VIII. 45/2 In the quicksilver agometer of Müller..the resistance is formed by a column of mercury of variable length. 1894 *Daily News* 6 Sept. 6/2 Lowering electric lights after the manner applied to gas, and without the use of resistances.

5. *Piece of resistance*, = F. *pièce de résistance* (see Pièce b).

1797 Burke *Regic. Peace* iv. Wks. IX. 7 Our appetite demands a *piece of resistance.* 1858 Hogg *Life Shelley* I. 459 The good girl liked a piece of resistance, a solid tome. 1894 Du Maurier *Trilby* I. 239 The pieces of resistance and plum-pudding and mince-pies.

6. *attrib.* and *Comb.*, as *resistance-attribute, pile*; **resistance-box,** *Electr.*, a box containing one or more resistance coils (Knight *Dict. Mech.* 1875); also *transf.*; **resistance coil** (see quot. 1873); so *resistance helix*; **resistance-piece,** = sense 5.

1862 H. Spencer *First Princ.* ii. iii. § 48 (1875) 166 The *resistance-attribute of matter must be regarded as primordial. 1899 *Allbutt's Syst. Med.* VII. 250 The great splanchnic area forms the *resistance box of the circulation. 1862 *Catal. Internat. Exhib., Brit.* II. No. 2867 *Resistance Coils, for testing the position of a fault in telegraph conductors from a distant station. 1873 Maxwell *Electr. & Magn.* (1881) I. 429 A Resistance Coil is a conductor capable of being easily placed in the voltaic circuit, so as to introduce into the circuit a known resistance. 1884 Knight *Dict. Mech.* Suppl. 752/2 Such unequal action is remedied by the provision of a high *resistance helix shunting the arc. 1895 C. Scott *Apple Orchards* 87 The *resistance piece was in the wicker basket. 1838 *Civil Eng. & Arch. Jrnl.* I. 374/1 What is called a *resistance pile, with one of the patentee's blocks or chairs.

† Resi·stancy. *Obs. rare*⁻¹. [f. as prec.: see -ancy and cf. Resistency.] Resistance.

1656 Jeanes *Fuln. Christ* 88 If we take the word (irresistably) in opposition unto a final, complete, and victorious resistancy.

Resistant (rīzi·stănt), *a.* and *sb.* [a. F. *résistant*, pres. pple. of *résister* to Resist. Cf. Resistent.]

A. *adj.* That makes resistance or opposition.

1610 Guillim *Heraldry* iii. xvii. (1611) 159 The rending and ruine of all that were resistant. 1668 Howe *Bless. Righteous* (1825) 52 There is no resistant principle remaining, when the love of God is perfected in it. 1768–74 Tucker *Lt. Nat.* (1834) II. 462 It is the essence of matter to be solid, that is, resistant and moveable. 1840 *Tait's Mag.* VII. 389 The aristocratic..elements..are become resistant, conservative, or inactive. 1860 Tyndall *Glac.* ii. v. 252 Each portion of the ice is surrounded by a resistant mass. 1884 *Contemp. Rev.* Oct. 528 The pressure of resistant wills now becomes incalculable.

B. *sb.* One who or that which resists; a resister. Now *rare.*

1600 W. Watson *Decacordon* (1602) 2 The thunder-bolt fell vpon the afflicted Priests.., striking all resistants with Ecclesiasticall censures. 1659 Pearson *Creed* vi. 577 According to the degrees of power in the Agent and the Resistant, is an action perform'd or hindered. 1828–32 in Webster. 1884 *Health Exhib. Catal.* p. liii/1 The most powerful resistant of acids or acid gases. 1903 *Westm. Gaz.* 3 June 7/1 To issue summonses against Nonconformist passive resistants.

b. In calico-printing, = Resist *sb.* 2.

1879 *Spons' Encycl. Manuf.* i. 50 The first crops of citric acid crystals..are used largely by the calico-printer as a 'resistant' for iron and alumina mordants.

Hence **† Resi·stantly** *adv.*, resistingly. *Obs.*⁻¹

1611 Speed *Theat. Gt. Brit.* x. (1614) 19/1 Brightrik..sent the Steward of his house to know their intents, whom resistantly they slew.

† Resi·stence. *Obs.* Also 5–6 **-ens, resyst-, recistence, -ens.** [a. OF. *resistence*, = Sp. and Pg. *resistencia*, It. *re-*, *risistenza*, ad. late L. *re-*

sistentia (Augustine), f. resistĕre to RESIST: see -ENCE.] = RESISTANCE. (In common use to c 1530.)

c 1374 Chaucer Troylus III. 990 Loue, a-yeyns þe which þat no man may Ne oughte ek goudly make resistence. c 1386 — Can. Yeom. Prol. & T. 356 Thise metales ben of so gret violence, Our walles may not make hem resistence. 1450 Rolls of Parlt. V. 200/2 For suche distres takyng, and yn resistens therof, ther is grete assembles. 1494 Fabyan Chron. VI. clxxi. 165 After many resistences by hym doon, to auoyde ye temptacion therof. 1512 Act 4 Hen. VIII, c. 20 Preamble, Theire adherentes made extreme resistens ayenst your said Beseecher. a 1548 Hall Chron., Hen. VIII 176 The Spaniardes so defended them with ordinaunce & resistences that they slew .v. or vi. M. Frenchmen. 1596 Spenser F. Q. VI. xi. 43 Where the bold knight Encountring him with small resistence slew. 1704 J. Harris Lex. Techn. I, Resistence of the Medium, is the opposition against, or hindrance of the Motion of any Body moving in a Fluid. 1727-38 Chambers Cycl. s.v., A greater weight is required to overcome their united resistence, than to overcome their several resistences one after another.

†**Resi·stency.** Obs. [ad. late L. resistentia: see prec. and -ENCY.] Resistance, repulsion.

1640 Wilkins New Planet ix. (1707) 250 It will easily follow, that these Bodies have resistency from one another. a 1688 Cudworth Immut. Mor. (1731) 77 We feel things at a Distance in the dark, by the Resistency which they make upon the further end of the Staff that we hold in our hands.

Resistent (rĭzi·stėnt), a. and sb. [ad. L. resistent-em, pres. pple. of resistĕre to RESIST.]

A. adj. = RESISTANT a.

1640 G. Watts tr. Bacon's De Augm. Sci. III. iv. 149 A Pestilentiall aire seizeth on bodies more open and lesse resistent. 1860 Tyndall Glac. II. xxvii. 377 The more resistent ones [sc. laminæ] stand out in ridges after the softer parts between them have been eaten away. 1887 W. G. Palgrave Ulysses 255 Native Indian tribes..resistent to the last..against every Argentine attempt at civilising..them.

†B. sb. = RESISTANT sb. Obs.

1600 W. Watson Decacordon (1602) 15 The foresaid resistance was not schisme in the Resisten[t]s. 1644 Digby Nat. Bodies xiii. § 5 The resistance..weakned by the thinnenesse of the resistent there.

Resister (rĭzi·stəɹ). Also 5 **resistour.** [f. RESIST v. + -ER 1.]

1. One who resists. Passive resister (see RESISTANCE 1 b).

1375 Barbour Bruce XVIII. 214 Quhen the feld wes clengit cleyne, Sa that na resisteris wes seyne. 1459 Rolls of Parlt. II. 370/1 Lyve and dye with the said Erle, ayenst his resistours. 1558 Goodman How to Obey 176 To counte your selues therin no rebells, but lawfull resisters. 1579 W. Wilkinson Confut. Fam. Love Heret. Affirm. bij b, Disputation..with the unwillyng ones and resisters. 1611 Speed Hist. Gt. Brit. IX. xxiv. (1623) 1158 [They] slew no small numbers of their resisters. a 1656 Hales Gold. Rem. (1677) 29 To resist the truth which is..believed by the resister himself is a direct contradiction. 1710 A. B. Answ. to Argts. Bp. Oxford's Resistance 18 That they never consider'd the Matter at all, and therefore assisted these Resisters. 1832 Examiner 97/1 The resisters of an exaction. 1873 Smiles Huguenots France vi. (1881) 100 The resisters of the policy were in both cases Calvinists. 1903 Westm. Gaz. 29 May 5/1 At Hastings, where the Passive Resisters are numbered by hundreds.

2. That which resists; a resisting body or force.

a 1586 Sidney Arcadia III. (1724) II. 575 Philoclea's shamefacedness and humbleness were as strong resisters as choler and disdain. 1596 T. Johnson Cornucopiæ B j b, Organy and Rue are great resisters of poyson. 1656 [? J. Sergeant] tr. T. White's Peripat. Inst. 73 If a Moveable be struck violently against a hard resister. 1686 Goad Celest. Bodies I. ix. 28 If Warmth be the producer of Moisture, Cold must be the Resister. 1759 Phil. Trans. LI. 84 You see, that animal, vegetable, and metallic bodies..are easily changed into resisters or non-conductors.

Resi·stful, a. [f. as prec. + -FUL.] Capable of, or inclined to, resistance.

1614 C. Brooke Rich. III, Poems (1872) 132 The wrong-incensed peeres, augment his band, And giue his weakenes, a resistfull force. 1846 Hawksley in Helps Friends in C. (1847) I. 134 The human constitution becomes gradually more resistful and..hardened. 1870 J. Hamilton Moses, Man of God vii. 120 The resistful only supplied victims.

Resistibi·lity. [f. as next + -ITY. Cf. F. résistibilité.]

1. The quality of being resistible.

1617 Donne Serm. cxxxii. Wks. 1839 V. 365 Resistibility and Irresistibility of Grace, which is every Artificers wearing now. 1642 [see RESISTABILITY]. a 1656 Hales Gold. Rem. (1688) 510 The Bremenses who handled the Head de gratia, & libero arbitrio in general, and in particular overthrew resistibility of Grace. 1850 J. Brown Disc. & Sayings Our Lord (1852) II. xx. 300 This character of resistibility the evidence in favour of Christianity possesses.

2. Power of offering resistance.

1646 Sir T. Browne Pseud. Ep. 3 Whether the resistibility of his reason did not equivalence the facility of her seduction. 1690 Locke Hum. Und. IV. vii. § 13 The complex Idea of Extension and Resistibility, or Solidity. 1820 Blackw. Mag. VIII. 251 Such was its innate and surpassing resistibility of temperament, that it could not be overwhelmed.

Resistible (rĭzi·stĭb'l). [f. RESIST v. + -IBLE. Cf. F. résistible, Sp. resistible]. Capable of being resisted; to which resistance can be made.

1643 Prynne Sov. Power Parl. III. (ed. 2) 121 Our Opposites must..make Kings as resistible, censurable, deprivable, as far forth as they. 1675 Baxter Cath. Theol. II. I. 172 They make Gods Grace a resistible thing, which Man can frustrate. 1759 Johnson Rasselas xxxi, Earthquakes themselves, the least resistible of natural violence. 1813 Sir R. Wilson Priv. Diary (1862) II. 235 A tempting booty, but I feel confident resistible, if not tangible with honour. 1884 Ch. Times 14 Nov. 858/4 A genuine outbreak ..would be no more resistible than James II found it.

Hence **Resi·stibleness; Resi·stibly** adv.

1674 Hickman Quinquart. Hist. (ed. 2) 125 God by his Spirit shall only resistibly, indifferently and remotely.. regenerate and renew our selves. 1847 Webster, Resistibleness. 1888 J. Martineau Study Relig. II. III. ii. 272 A dynamical resistibleness to a numerical law.

Resisting (rĭzi·stiŋ), vbl. sb. [f. RESIST v. + -ING 1.] The action of the vb. RESIST.

1482 Monk of Evesham (Arb.) 89 Chesyng rather to dyssymylle..than by her blamyng and resysting stere and moue agenste hem the wrathe..of suche euyl dysposyd persons. 1558 Goodman How to Obey 123 There is nothing in this saying..which can condemne lawfull resisting of vngodlie Rulers. 1614 Donne Βιαθανατος (1648) 110 The Devill is overcome by Resisting, but the World and the Flesh by running away. 1742 Richardson Pamela III. 86 This Passion had been heighten'd by my resisting of it. 1760-72 H. Brooke Fool of Qual. (1809) IV. 91 Here has been a large body of the gens d'armes sent for them, so that there was no resisting.

Resi·sting, ppl. a. [f. RESIST v. + -ING 2.] That resists or offers resistance. Resisting medium (see MEDIUM sb. 4).

Freq. in modern use as the second element in Combs., as cold-, disease-, dust-, fire-resisting, etc.

1593 Q. Eliz. Boeth. II. 25 These be not yet remedyes for thy disease, but serues for bellowes against the cure of thy resisting sorowe. 1595 Shaks. John II. i. 38 Against the browes of this resisting towne. 1625 K. Long tr. Barclay's Argenis I. xx. 60 Neither did lesse feare invade his resisting thoughts. 1694 Salmon Bate's Dispens. (1699) 402/1 It would be presently dull'd..by the resisting Sulphur. 1743 Emerson Fluxions 288 The Resistance of a Globe moving in a resisting Medium. 1798 Hutton Curs. Math. (1807) II. 357 The resisting force is equal to the weight that urges it. 1862 Spencer First Princ. II. v. § 56 (1875) 182 Uniform motion in a straight line, implies the absence of a resisting medium. 1863 Geo. Eliot Romola xl, But the resisting thoughts were not yet overborne. 1898 Allbutt's Syst. Med. V. 329 Anything which..tends to diminish the resisting power of the individual.

Hence **Resi·stingly** adv.

1548 Udall Erasm. Par. 1 John ii. 46 b, Doth not he, that lyueth after such sorte, resistingly denie Christ? 1905 Westm. Gaz. 1 July 17/2 The mob..fell back slowly and resistingly before the rifle volleys of the troops.

Resistive (rĭzi·stiv). [f. RESIST v. + -IVE.] Capable of or inclined to resistance.

1603 B. Jonson Sejanus II. i, Resistiue 'gainst the sunne, the raine, or wind. 1646 Sir T. Browne Pseud. Ep. IV. v. 191 The most vigorous part protecting it selfe, and protruding the matter upon the weaker and lesse resistive side. 1837 Carlyle Fr. Rev. III. VII. iii, Pardoning the submissive, cutting down the resistive. 1870 E. L. Hull Serm. Ser. II. 153 Every dark temptation makes us strong in resistive might. 1897 Allbutt's Syst. Med. III. 271 One man is more resistive than another, according to his strength of constitution.

Hence **Resi·stively** adv.; **Resi·stiveness.**

1803 W. Taylor in Monthly Mag. XIV. 491 Resistiveness, or the capability of becoming an object of sensation. 1864 A. Leighton Myst. Legends Edin. (1886) 238 Persistiveness draws, as it were, a power from the wearing out of resistiveness. 1887 Buck's Handbk. Med. Sci. IV. 649/1 Flexion and extension of the leg at the knee, either passively or resistively.

Resisti·vity. [f. prec. + -ITY.] Electr. The specific resistance of a substance.

1890 Nature 9 Oct. 577/2 The..diameter of any of the conductors..divided by its electric resistivity.

Resistless (rĭzi·stlės). [f. RESIST v. + -LESS.]

1. That cannot be resisted; irresistible.

1586 Marlowe 1st Pt. Tamburl. v. ii, So..Must Tamburlaine by their resistless powers..Conclude a league of honour. 1638 Mayne Lucian (1664) 390 It must be of a strong and resistlesse vertue. 1656 Jeanes Fuln. Christ 112 It can subdue the most raging, and resistlesse lusts. 1693 S. Harvey in Dryden Juvenal ix. (1697) 237 Try to Imprison the resistless Wind. 1748 Johnson Van. Hum. Wishes 137 Resistless burns the fever of renown. 1813 Parr Let. Wks. 1828 VIII. 496 So peerless, so resistless, and upon this occasion so guileless an advocate..as Mr. Burke. 1874 Geo. Eliot Coll. Breakf. P. 114 That resistless weight Obstinate, irremovable by thought.

2. Powerless to resist; unresisting.

1591 Spenser Muiopot. 436 He seized greedelie On the resistles pray. 1612 W. Parkes Curtaine-Dr. (1876) 44 Vpon whose breasts are charactred and insculpt the ensignes of weaknesse and resistlesse impotency. 1818 Keats Endym. III. 266 O misery of hell! resistless, tame; Am I to be burnt up? 1892 Cornh. Mag. May 559 She was quite resistless, quite gentle.

Resi·stlessly, adv. [f. prec. + -LY 2.] In a resistless manner; irresistibly.

1727 Blackwall Sacr. Class. (1740) I. 61 'Tis resistlessly plain, that the divine writers do not always confine themselves to plain and common grammar. 1813 T. Busby Lucretius II. 24 note (Jod.), He..displays to us in colours resistlessly strong one of the most dreadful instances of human affliction. 1852 Mrs. Stowe Uncle Tom's C. xl. 346 Had not this man braved him—steadily, powerfully, resistlessly? 1890 'R. Boldrewood' Col. Reformer (1891) 103 The chestnut..dropped with his mouth wrenched resistlessly from the rider's hold.

So **Resi·stlessness.**

1870 Echo 5 Dec., The self-confidence and resistlessness of the men in the road.

†**Resi·stment.** Obs. rare $^{-1}$. [f. RESIST v. + -MENT.] Resistance.

1605 Answ. Discov. Romish Doctr. 39 The resistment of this present King of that countrie, the Bull of Pius Quintus against Queene Elizabeth.

Resi·tting (rī-). [RE- 5 a.] A second sitting.

1661 J. Davies Civ. Warres 367 Lenthalls legal and conscientious objections against their re-sitting were never answered. 1754 H. Walpole Lett. (1846) III. 38 The grand juries are going to petition for the resitting of the Parliament. 1889 Anthony's Photogr. Bull. II. 385 The cost of the merchandise used in a resitting.

Resi·zer (rī-). [f. RE- 5 a + SIZE v. + -ER 1.] 'A tool for restoring an object, as a cartridge-shell, to its original size' (Funk's Stand. Dict. 1895). So Resizing-tool.

1882 Worc. Exhib. Catal. III. 57 Rifle with..resizing tools.

†**Reskippeson**: see SKIPPESON.

Reskus(e, variants of RESCOUS sb. Obs.

Resla·sh (rī-), v. [RE- 5 a.] To slash again.

1718 Ozell tr. Tournefort's Voy. II. 184 Leaves..slash'd into three principal parts, and reslash'd again almost like the other leaves.

Reslay· (rī-), v. [RE- 5 a.] To slay again.

1791 Anna Seward Lett. (1811) III. 49, I am not at all tempted..to..re-slay the already slain. 1839 Standard 24 Aug., Lord B— re-slew the slain in a speech of great brilliancy and sarcasm.

Resli·de (rī-), v. [RE-.] intr. To slide back.

1592 Wyrley Armorie, Ld. Chandos 29 Slow Lidian brooke,..Staying in doubt th'ocean t'enter in, Or to reslide where first it did begin.

Resme·lt (rī-), v. [RE- 5 a.] To smelt again. Also fig. Hence **Resme·lting** vbl. sb.

1839 Ure Dict. Arts 1248 Those of the third class c..are set apart, and re-smelted. 1858 Greener Gunnery 103 Thousands of tons have been..re-smelted by two adjoining iron-works. 1875 Stedman Victorian Poets (1887) 453 That magic transmutation which alone justifies a resmelting of the antique.

Resmi·le (rī-), v. [RE-.] To smile back.

1708 Ozell tr. Boileau's Lutrin (1730) III. 38 The smirking Barber brandishes on high A Bumper, which re-smiles with mutual Joy.

Resmoo·th (rī-), v. [RE- 5 a.] trans. To smooth again.

1830 Lytton P. Clifford iii, The treasury of Mrs. Lobkins resmoothed, as it were, the irritated bristles of his mind. 1847 Tennyson Princ. III. 225 And thus your pains May only make that footprint upon sand Which old-recurring waves of prejudice Resmooth to nothing.

Resnabel, -yl, obs. forms of RENABLE.

Resnu·b (rī-), v. [RE- 5 a.] To snub again.

1735 Hervey Mem. II. 35 And then carried the Queen to walk and be resnubbed in the garden.

†**Resoi·gn,** v. Obs. rare $^{-1}$. In 5 resoyngne. [ad. OF. resoignier, etc., f. re- RE- + soigner to be anxious, careful, f. soin care.] intr. To fear.

c 1500 Melusine 140 Our enmys..are come to assayll vs without cause vnto our right herytage and also we ought not to resoyngne ne dylaye therfore.

Resoi·l (rī-), v. [RE- 5 a and 5 c.]

1. trans. To soil or dirty again.

1591 Sylvester Du Bartas I. Ivry 29 Neither shall my Pen Re-purple Lisle; nor with dead Grease agen Re-soile the Soile at Courtras.

2. To cover again with soil. Hence **Resoi·ling** vbl. sb.

1842 Civil Eng. & Arch. Jrnl. V. 85/2 The top surface of cuttings and the seat of embankment are usually uncallowed for the purpose of resoiling the slopes. 1852 Wiggins Embanking 117 For soiling and re-soiling, 1d.

Resojourn (rī-), v. [RE- 5 a.] intr. To sojourn again.

1648 Herrick Hesper., To Dean-bourn, A people..rude (almost) as rudest Salvages, With whom I did, and may re-sojourne when Rockes turn to Rivers.

Reso·lder (rī-), v. [RE- 5 a: in early examples after F. resouder, † resoder, It. risaldare.] trans. To solder again. Also absol. and fig. Hence **Reso·ldering** vbl. sb.

1598 Florio, Risaldatura, a resoldring, a refastning. 1605 Sylvester Urania lxx, I'ld rather sing..the Bethanian Lazarus reuiuing, Then valiant Theseus Sonnes re-sodering. 1847 Tennyson Princ. v. 45 We twain, with mutual pardon ask'd and given For stroke and song, resolder'd peace. 1900 Hasluck Model Engineer's Handybk. 75 Turn the outer end of the cylinder true,..then reverse and resolder on the chuck.

Reso·le (rī-), v. [RE-.] trans. To furnish (a boot, shoe, etc.) with a new sole.

a 1853 Robertson No Church iv, His boots had come home, resoled and heeled. 1863 W. C. Baldwin Afr. Hunting iii. 65 A day employed in re-soling shoes.

Reso·lemnize (rī-), v. [RE- 5 a.] trans. To solemnize again.

1621 G. Sandys Ovid's Met. XIV. (1626) 283 His fathers funeralls re-solemniz'd, He puts to Sea, with ships well-nigh surpriz'd By Iris flames. 1654-66 Earl Orrery Parthen. (1676) 617 The Nuptials were re-solemnized.

Resoli·cit (rī-), v. [ad. It. risollecitare, = F. ressolliciter.] trans. To solicit again.

1641 Earl Monm. tr. Biondi's Civ. Wars III. 117 The second messengers, who with a herald were sent to re-sollicite him.

†**Resoli·citude.** Obs. rare $^{-1}$. [From the Fr. original.] Renewed solicitude.

1490 Caxton Eneydos xxvi. 92 Thou hast broughte me from solysitude, & remysed into resolysitude.

†**Reso·lidate,** pa. pple. Obs. $^{-1}$ [ad. med.L. resolidātus, pa. pple. of resolidāre to strengthen again.] Made solid again; reunited.

1485 Caxton St. Wenefryde 4 In the place of her necke where as her heede was smyten of and after by dyuyne operacion was sett on ageyn & resolydate.

Resoli·dify (rī-), v. [RE- 5 a.]

1. intr. To become solid again.

1861 Chambers's Encycl. II. 546/1 The C[amphor] sublimes and resolidifies in the interior upper part of the flask. 1875 Croll Climate & T. xxxi. 523 The moment that it parts with the heat received, it will of course resolidify.

2. trans. To make solid again.

1898 Westm. Gaz. 12 Dec. 9/2 Improving low grade butters by washing them in a melted state and then resolidifying them with buttermilk.

So **Re·solidifica·tion.**

1871 Tyndall Fragm. Sci. (1879) II. v. 66 Watch its subsequent resolidification.

Resolubi·lity. [f. as next + -ITY. Cf. F. résolubilité.] The quality of being resoluble.

1855 H. J. S. Smith in Oxford Ess. 123 In assigning reasons for his disbelief of the universal resolubility of nebulae. 1879 Encycl. Brit. X. 48/1 Researches on the resolubility of algebraic equations by radicals.

Resoluble (re·zǫliub'l), a. [ad. late L. resolūbilis (4th c.): see RE- and SOLUBLE, and cf. F. résoluble (1577).] Capable of being resolved, in various senses; resolvable.

1602 Fulbecke 2nd Pt. Parall. 62 Though the sale be pure and vnconditionall, yet it is resoluble and defeasible. 1660 R. Coke Justice Vind. 5 We see all things are in their individuals resoluble into their first composition. 1665-6 Phil. Trans. I. 204 The two first sorts are made of a matter easily resoluble. 1705 Berkeley in Fraser Life (1871) 421 Qu. if extension be resoluble into points it does not consist of? 1871 Earle Philol. Eng. Tongue § 649 The distinctiveness of all that which we call brogue, accent, &c. is ultimately resoluble into a speciality of modulation. 1871 Daily News 30 June, One of those mysteries resoluble only by a knowledge of the fact that [etc.].

Hence **Re·solubleness.**

1670 Boyle Tracts, Temp. Subterr. Reg. ix. 34 Many of them may be wrought on,..even by moist Air, which argues the resolublenesse of their Constitution.

Re-soluble (rīsǫ·liub'l), a. [RE- 5 a.] Capable of being dissolved again.

1839 Ure Dict. Arts 541 A solution that lets fall, with caustic soda, a precipitate partly re-soluble in carbonate of ammonia. 1846 Poe Willis Wks. 1865 III. 30 All which claims to be new..is re-soluble into the old.

Resolucion, obs. form of RESOLUTION.

†**Resolutative,** error for RESOLUTIVE a.

1582 Hester Secr. Phiorav. I. xliv. 54 The [remedy].. hath a penetratiue vertue and resolutative.

Re·solute, sb. rare. [See next.]

†1. A payment. Obs.

1534 Yorks. Chantry Surv. (Surtees) II. 512 In Resolutes yerely going forthe of the same vli ijs. 1573 Abp. Parker Corr. (Parker Soc.) 455 Subsidies, free rents, new-year's gifts, and other such resolutes cccc[l]. 1610 W. Folkingham Art of Survey IV. iv. 84 In this Rancke may be Marshalled al Resolutes, Dashes, Decrements.

2. A resolute or determined person.

1602 Shaks. Ham. I. i. 98 Young Fortinbras..Hath.. Shark'd vp a List of Landlesse Resolutes. 1799-1800 Coleridge tr. Schiller's Piccolomini I. iii. 62 Many a resolute, who now appears Made up to all extremes.

Resolute (re·zǫl[i]ūt), a. (and pa. pple.). [ad. L. resolūtus, pa. pple. of resolvĕre to RESOLVE. So It., Sp., Pg. resoluto, F. résolu.]

I. †1. Dissolved. Obs. rare $^{-1}$.

c 1420 Pallad. on Husb. I. 1119 For bathis hoot, ammoniak is tolde Right good, with brymstoon resolute.

†2. Of loose texture; friable. Obs. rare.

c 1420 Pallad. on Husb. III. 12 Now wold also thi puls be sowen there As thynne, & resolute..hit were. Ibid. IV. 51 Panyk & mylde in hoot & drie is sowe As now. Light resolute lond they desire.

†3. Morally lax, dissolute. Obs. rare $^{-1}$.

1432-50 tr. Higden (Rolls) III. 191 He wente to the cite of Crotines, resolute moche in vertues and in honeste, techenge men, wommen, and childer vertuous life.

†4. Relaxed, weak, infirm. Obs. rare $^{-1}$.

1607 Topsell Four-f. Beasts (1658) 148 The weak, resolute, or paralytike members being therewith anointed, they are much eased, if not recovered.

II. †5. Of rents: Paid, rendered. Obs.

c 1466 in Bedfordsh. N. & Q. (1886) I. 361 Rent resolute to our..lord the kyng, as to his manor of Bycleswade. 1534 Liber Regis (1786) p. ix, What annuell..rents..and Fees.. ben yerly accustumed to be resolute and paid. 1670 Act 22 Chas. II, c. 6 § 9 Allowances to be made of divers Pensions, Portions, Rents Resolute, or other Things of the like Nature.

III. †6. Determinate, decided, positive, absolute, final. Obs.

1501 Lett. Rich. III & Hen. VII (Rolls) I. 169 The same commissioners..promysid us..to shewe us the resolute mynde of the said king. 1532 More Confut. Tindale Wks. 524/2 Wherin what hys finall and resolute sentence is, ye shall..very scantly perceiue. 1597 Hooker Eccl. Pol. V. xlix. § 3 The answere of God was a resolute denyall of favour to them for whom supplication was made. 1606 Bryskett Civ. Life 122 His resolute opinion in that matter cannot be picked out of his writings.

†b. Esp. resolute answer. (Common in 16th c.)

1513 More Rich. III, Wks. 66/1 If he woulde geue them a resolute aunswere to the contrarye. 1581 J. Bell Haddon's Answ. Osor. 503 To satisfie this place of S. Paule, here is an easie and a Resolute aunswere. 1629 Massinger Picture IV. i, I expect now Your resolute answer: but advise maturely Before I hear it. a 1656 Hales Gold. Rem. (1688) 420 The Præses eagerly urged them to give their resolute answer.

†7. Of persons: Decided with regard to matters of doubt or opinion. Obs. rare.

1581 N. Burne Disput. in Cath. Tract. (S.T.S.) 148 Sua [they] vald be na mair resolut be the judgement of the bellis, nor thay var befoir. 1631 Weever Anc. Funeral Mon. 797 He..got the surname Doctoris resoluti, of Resolute or Resoluing Doctor.

8. Of persons, their minds, etc.: Determined, having a fixed resolve, constant, firm: a. Const. against, for, in, † to, † upon, and with inf.

1533 Bellenden Livy II. vii. (S.T.S.) I. 155 Þai war all resolute of ane mynde, to put ane end als sone to þare ciete as to þare liberte. 1579 Lyly Euphues (Arb.) 134 They would neuer haue ben so dissolute in their life, or so resolute in their owne conceipts. 1634 W. Tirwhyt tr. Balzac's Lett. 187, I am determined to continue resolute in well doing. 1670 Cotton Espernon I. I. 20 His Majesty..conceiv'd a mortal animosity against him, and was resolute to his ruine. 1715 De Foe Fam. Instruct. I. iv. (1841) I. 93 Are you so resolute against yourself? 1719 — Crusoe II. (Globe) 519 Seeing they were resolute for Mischief. 1838 Wordsw. Blest Statesman He, Him who holds his ministry, Resolute, at all hazards, to fulfil Its duties. 1874 Green Short Hist. vii. § 6. 406 If the Queen was resolute for peace, England was resolute for war.

b. Without const., in predicative or attrib. use.

1579-80 North Plutarch, Agis & Cleomenes (1657) 666 Agis..shewed himself in his counsell then, no rash, but a resolute and valiant man. 1588 Shaks. L. L. L. v. ii. 705 Clo. Ile do it in my shirt. Dum. Most resolute Pompey. 1604 T. Wright Passions III. ii. 84 In most vehement passions the resolutest minds are best prooued. 1652 J. Wright tr. Camus' Nat. Paradox 337 Liante..placed himself at the head of this resolute Party. 1729 Butler Serm. Wks. 1874 II. 100 A certain determination, and resolute bent of mind, not to be convinced or set right. 1817 Shelley Rev. Islam IX. ix, They were few, but resolute. 1863 Geo. Eliot Romola xxix, The simple, resolute man looked round him with grave joy.

9. Of actions, etc.: Characterized by determination or firmness of purpose.

1603 Shaks. Meas. for M. II. i. 12 That the resolute acting of [y]our blood Could have attain'd th' effect of your owne purpose. 1632 Lithgow Trav. II. 65 After a most resolute deliberation. 1784 Cowper Task v. 619 His master-lust Falls first before his resolute rebuke. 1813 Shelley Q. Mab III. 153 He..leads Invincibly a life of resolute good. 1874 Green Short Hist. ii. § 8. 101 Young as he was, Henry mounted the throne with a resolute purpose of government.

Resolute (re·zǫl[i]ūt), v. Now U.S. [orig. f. resolūt-, ppl. stem of L. resolvĕre to RESOLVE, but in mod. use a back-formation from resolution.]

†1. refl. To resolve, decide (oneself) upon a person. Obs. rare $^{-1}$.

a 1548 Hall Chron., Hen. VIII 184 b, After long debate the kyng resoluted him selfe vpon sir Thomas More [to be his Chancellor].

†2. trans. To resolve, dissolve into something.

1727 Bradley Fam. Dict., Hail, a cloudy Vapour resoluted into Water which in the Fall through..the Air is congealed, and so made Hail.

3. U.S. intr. To draw up or pass resolutions.

1860 in De Vere Americanisms (1871) 655 When you have done resoluting, you will only have lost your time. 1888 Bryce Amer. Commw. v. xc. III. 233 The discontented.. flocked every Sunday afternoon to cheer denunciations of corporations and monopolists, and to 'resolute' against the rich generally.

Resolutely (re·zǫl[i]ūtli), adv. [f. RESOLUTE a. + -LY 2.] In a resolute manner.

†1. Determinately, positively, definitely. Obs.

a 1548 Hall Chron., Hen. VIII 258 He tolde them resolutely that onelesse thei would yelde vp the toune franckly [etc.]. 1617 Moryson Itin. II. 225 Hee resolutely beleeuing they were intended for Ireland. 1661 Boyle Spring of Air III. xxxi, Possibly he would have spoken less resolutly if he had made all the trials.

2. With fixed purpose, boldly, determinedly.

1596 Shaks. 1 Hen. IV, I. ii. 38 A Purse of Gold most resolutely snatch'd on Monday night, and most dissolutely spent on Tuesday Morning. 1647 Clarendon Hist. Reb. I. § 40 Frankly and resolutely to enter into a war with Spain. 1728 Morgan Algiers II. iv. 271 He may be said to have deported himself rather resolutely than prudently. 1833 I. Taylor Fanat. vi. 183 note, To deny all connexion of causation is to be resolutely incredulous. 1868 E. Edwards Ralegh I. i. 9 Traditions which are resolutely..upheld by the inhabitants of the village.

Resoluteness (re·zǫl[i]ūtnės). [f. as prec. + -NESS.] The fact or character of being resolute; firm determination.

1593 G. Harvey Pierce's Super. 38 Pollicy deemeth that vertue a vice,..that resolutenes, dissolutenes. 1599 Sandys Europæ Spec. (1605) F iv, Men who with incessant industry and resolutenes incredible..leave no exploite..vnattempted. 1675 Brooks Gold. Key Wks. 1867 V. 169 A willingness and resoluteness to suffer for him when we are called to it. 1840 Arnold Hist. Rome II. 375 The plain resoluteness of his character..caused him to be elected tribune of the commons. 1890 Spectator 25 Jan., To make his resoluteness serve the purpose of extricating the great German from..a difficult and ambiguous crisis.

Resolution (rezǫl[i]ū·ʃən). Also 4-6 -cioun, 5-7 -cion, 5-6 -cyon. [a. OF. resolucion, -tion (14th c.; mod.F. résolution, = Sp. resolucion, It. re-, risoluzione), or ad. L. resolūtiōn-em, n. of action f. resolvĕre to RESOLVE.]

I. †1. a. = DISSOLUTION 8. Obs. rare.

1382 Wyclif 2 Tim. iv. 6 The tyme of my resolucioun [L. resolutionis], or deeth, is nyȝ. c 1449 Pecock Repr. I. xi. 57. 1582 N. T. (Rhem.) 2 Tim. iv. 6 The time of my resolution is at hand.

†b. A state of dissolution or decay. Obs. $^{-1}$

1533 Bellenden Livy II. xiv. (S.T.S.) I. 184 Þe membris ..brocht baith þame self and all þe body to extreme resolucioun [L. tabem].

2. The process by which a material thing is reduced or separated into its component parts or elements; a result of this. Also attrib.

1412-20 Lydg. Chron. Troy IV. xxxv, The flawme..queynt, that they ne myght se Nought but smoky resolucions. 1513 Bradshaw St. Werburge I. 3327 Our sauiour..preserued her body..Both hole and sounde from naturall resolucion. 1555 Eden Decades (Arb.) 239 It dooth preserue the same from resolution & putrefaction. 1626 Bacon Sylva § 400 The Immediate Cause of Death, is the Resolution or Extinguishment of the Spirits. a 1676 Hale Prim. Orig. Man. III. vi. (1677) 278 The Resolution or Maceration of Frogs and Worms will reproduce Individuals of the same species. 1707 Curios. in Husb. & Gard. 230 By their Resolution, or the true Anatomy I made of them, I found them to be compos'd of much Sulphur, a little Mercury, and less Salt. 1794 Hutton Philos. Light, etc. 297 The decomposition or resolution of phlogistic substances..is now well understood. 1822-34 Good's Study Med. (ed. 4) I. 12 The high temperature in the stomach produces a concretive resolution. 1881 Nature XXIV. 397/2 A simpler or fundamental group being the resolution product.

transf. 1856 Emerson Eng. Traits, Race, All our experience is of the gradation and resolution of races.

b. Const. to, into. Also, conversion into something else, or into a different form.

1519 Interl. Four Elem. in Hazl. Dodsley I. 12 Corruption of a body..Is but the resolution..Of every element to his own place. 1659 Hammond On Ps. xc. 3 The resolution of the body to dust, may be fitly exprest. 1812 Sir H. Davy Chem. Philos. 51 Their resolution into the supposed elements of the chemists of those days. 1867 H. Macmillan Bible Teach. vii. (1870) 134 Instances of the resolution of the stem into a rolled and compressed leaf may be seen in grasses and bulbous plants.

c. The effect of an optical instrument in making the separate parts of an object (esp. the stars of a nebula) distinguishable by the eye.

1860 Olmsted's Mech. Heavens 396 The resolution of this nebula. 1867 J. Hogg Microsc. I. ii. 72 Resolution, or the power of showing clearly minute details. 1868 Lockyer Guillemin's Heavens (ed. 3) 396 Each new triumph of optical skill results in a resolution of some nebulæ, before irreducible.

3. Med. †a. Dissolution or dispersion of humours or of morbid matter in the body. Obs.

1398 Trevisa Barth. De P. R. XVIII. lxxxvii. (Bodl. MS.), In somer [though] þere be grette resolucion of humours þer is grete wastinge þereof. c 1400 Lanfranc's Cirurg. 353 It wole make þe mater mollificatif, & make þe poris open to resolucioun. 1543 Traheron Vigo's Chirurg. II. 65 It causeth the humours to breath out wyth gentyll resolution, and sedation of payne. 1620 Venner Via Recta viii. 190 Through paruity of exercise, and resolution of superfluous matter by the pores many crude..humours are bred. 1778 K. James' Diss. Fevers (ed. 8) 7 To bring about a concretion or resolution of the humours which excited the fever.

†b. Conversion into purulent matter. Obs.

1597 A. M. tr. Guillemeau's Fr. Chirurg. 17 b/1 The suppuratione, or resolution to matter, beinge finished. 1676 Wiseman Surg. Treat., If..the Strumæ [be] recent and but moderately hard, the Resolution or Suppuration of them is seizable.

c. Disappearance of inflammation without coming to suppuration.

1783 W. Cullen First Lines § 249 Wks. 1827 II. 8 If an inflammation be cured while the state and texture of the part remain entire, the disease is said to be terminated by Resolution. 1833 Cycl. Pract. Med. II. 790/2 Resolution is not only the most favourable, but the most common termination of inflammation. 1853 Markham tr. Skoda's Auscult. 286 When resolution of the inflammation commences,..the bronchial respiration returns.

†4. Conversion to a fluid state. Obs.

1644 Digby Treat. Bodies I. x. 77 In the hoat springes of extreme cold countries, where the first heates are vnsufferable, which proceede out of the resolution of humidity congealed. 1686 Goad Celest. Bodies II. ii. 174 It must be caused by the resolution of the Snow which was dissolved the Week before.

5. Relaxation or weakening of some organ or part of the body. Now rare.

1547 Boorde Brev. Health cclxxi. 90 b, A palsey doth come..by resolucion or els compression of the nervous sinewes. 1558 Bp. Watson Sev. Sacram. xvi. c, What resolution, and as it were a meltinge of his bodie and bowelles. 1601 Holland Pliny II. 49 Those that haue the palsie or resolution of the nerues. 1661 Lovell Hist. Anim. & Min., Isagoge, Fear..causeth loosenesse, resolution of the muscles, and sometimes death with a small pulse. 1708 Brit. Apollo No. 45. 2/1 A Resolution of the Nerves may ensue, and this faltring of the Tongue be.. caused. 1779 Johnson Let. to H. Thrale 23 June, Weariness is itself a temporary resolution of the nerves. 1899 Allbutt's Syst. Med. VII. 618 Owing to the complete muscular 'resolution' the cheeks will be flaccid.

II. 6. The process of resolving or reducing a non-material thing into simpler forms, or of converting it into some other thing or form.

With quots. 1662 and 1677 compare 1656 in b.

1388 Prol. Wyclif Bible xv. (1850) 57 In translating into English, manie resolucions moun make the sentence open. Ibid., I Englishe it thus bi resolucioun. 1570 Billingsley Euclid I. prop. I. 9 The first principles and groundes, which are indemonstrable, and for theyr simplicity can suffer no farther resolution. 1662 Stillingfl. Orig. Sacræ II. iii. § 3 The infallible veracity of God in the Scriptures, as the last resolution of faith. 1677 J. Owen Reason of Faith Wks. 1852 IV. 114 Those of the Roman church who are the most averse from that resolution of faith which most Protestants acquiesce in. 1786 H. Tooke Purley (1829) I. 96 Though your method of resolution will answer

with most sentences, yet I doubt much whether it will with all. 1797 Encycl. Brit. (ed. 3) X. 193/2 Of the Composition and Resolutions of our Ideas, and the Rules of Definition thence arising. 1845 Proc. Philol. Soc. II. 167 This form furnishes a complete and intelligible resolution of the phrase. 1893 Chase in Archiv Stud. neu. Sprache C. 252 Resolution of contractions is denoted by italics.

b. Const. into or † in.

1530 Palsgr. 79 The pronownes derivatyves have thre accidentes,..by whiche their gendre and nombre is expressed, and resolucyon in to their primityves. 1597 Morley Introd. Mus. Annot., Black or halfe black ligatures,..with the resolution of the same in other common notes. 1656 Bramhall Replic. vii. 44 What that Catholick Church is, into the authority whereof they make the last resolution of their Faith. 1660 R. Coke Justice Vind. Pref. 12 This senseless resolution of all things into Reason. 1706 W. Jones Syn. Palmar. Matheseos 51 The Resolution of Powers into their Roots is called Evolution or the Analysis of Powers. 1837 Whewell Hist. Induct. Sci. (1857) I. 140 The Resolution of the apparent motions of the heavenly bodies into an assemblage of circular motions. 1875 Jowett Plato (ed. 2) III. 14 The resolution of justice into two unconnected precepts.

c. In prosody, the substitution of two short syllables in the place of a long one.

1884 Hadley & Allen Grk. Gram. § 1080 A tribrach stands by resolution in place of the first trochee.

7. †a. Math. and Logic. (See quots. and ANALYSIS 7, 8.) Obs.

1557 Recorde Whetst. Cc. ij, Proue theim bothe byresolution: and then shall you knowe, the reason of their agremente. 1570 Billingsley Euclid I. prop. I. 9 A demonstration a posteriori, or resolution is, when contrariwise in reasoning, we passe from the last conclusion made by the premisses.. til we come to the first principles and grounds. Ibid. XIII. prop. 5. 396 Resolution, is the assumption or taking of the thing which is to be proued, as graunted, and by thinges which necessarily follow it, to passe vnto some truth graunted. 1704 J. Harris Lex. Techn. I, Resolution (in Mathematicks) is a Method of Invention, whereby the Truth or Falshood of a Proposition..is discover'd, in an Order contrary to that of Synthesis, or Composition. 1727-38 Chambers Cycl. s.v., The business of resolution is, to..examine the truth or falshood of a proposition, by ascending from some particular known truth,..by a chain of consequences, to another more general one in question.

b. Logic. (See quot.)

1855 Abp. Thomson Laws Th. § 71 (1860) 118 Resolution, where the marks of the definitum are made its definition: as in 'a pension is an allowance for past services'.

8. Mus. †a. (See quots.) Obs. rare.

1727-38 Chambers Cycl., Resolution, in music, is when a canon or perpetual fugue is not written all on the same line, or in one part; but all the voices that are to follow the guida, or first voice, are written separately. 1811 Busby Dict. Mus. (ed. 3) s.v., Formerly also, a Canon was said to be resolved, or written in Resolution, when instead of being comprised in a single stave, all the parts were given on separate staves.

b. The process by which a discord is made to pass into a concord.

1727-38 Chambers Cycl. s.v. Discord, These discords.. must be succeeded by concords: which is commonly called the resolution of the discord. 1760 Sterne Tr. Shandy IV. vi, The preparation and resolution of the discord into harmony. 1838 Penny Cycl. XII. 50/1 Sometimes the resolution is brought about by the base, as in the instance of the discord of the 2nd. 1889 Prout Harmony ix. § 198 The interval of a seventh is always a dissonance, and therefore requires resolution—that is, to be followed by a consonance.

9. Mech. (See quots. 1798 and 1830.)

1798 Hutton Course Math. (1807) II. 137 The Resolution of Forces is the finding of two or more forces which, acting in any different directions, shall have the same effect as any given single force. 1830 Kater & Lardner Mech. v. 52 It is frequently expedient to substitute for a single force two or more forces, to which it is mechanically equivalent, or of which it is the resultant. This process is called 'the resolution of force'. 1882 Minchin Unipl. Kinemat. 124 The equations..expressing the components of the given strain with reference to a new set of axes..constitute the resolution of strain.

fig. 1852 Mrs. Stowe Uncle Tom's C. xxxii. 292 Legree ..governed his plantation by a sort of resolution of forces.

III. 10. The answering of a question; the solving of a doubt or difficulty. † Also, the supplying of an answer. Now rare. (Freq. in 17th c.)

1548 Geste Pr. Masse 103, I wyl addresse me to the ful answere and resolution of the same. 1577 Hanmer Anc. Eccles. Hist. v. xii. (1619) 85 Rhodion promised also to publish the resolutions of his Problemes. His Commentaries upon the six daies works are at this day extant. 1604 E. G[rimstone] D'Acosta's Hist. Indies II. xi. 106 Whoso woulde neerely consider the causes..shall finde them insufficient for the full resolution of this point. 1651 Baxter Inf. Bapt. 275 In resolution of the question of universall Redemption. 1705 Stanhope Paraphr. I. 350 For a resolution of this enquiry, the case of Abraham will be of great use to us. 1758 Johnson Idler No. 24 ¶ 2 Of this question ..we must be content to live without the resolution. 1845 Lewes Hist. Philos. III. ii, The resolution of that problem ..had left him unsatisfied. 1847 Miller First Impr. Eng. x. (1857) 164 Several antagonist theories have been promulgated in attempted resolution of the puzzle.

b. The solution of an arithmetical or mathematical problem. Now rare or Obs.

1579-80 North Plutarch (1676) 20 [He] gathered it out by certain accidents, as they do in the resolutions of certain Geometrical questions. 1636 Mellis Recorde's Gr. Artes 160 For the resolution whereof, and of all such other like, reduce 23 pound 8 shillings, all into shillings. 1715 tr. Gregory's Astron. (1726) I. 317 Concerning the Resolution of the most considerable Problems of the First Motion by Calculation. 1797 Encycl. Brit. (ed. 3) I. 431/2 Of the Resolution of Equations. 1817 H. T. Colebrooke Algebra 227 The resolution of these equations is so named, because it is in general effected by making the middle term..disappear from between two square terms. 1845 Encycl. Metrop. I. 543/1 The resolution of this equation gives the solution of the proposed problem. 1875 Encycl. Brit. I. 517/1 A problem subservient to the resolution of indeterminate problems of the first degree.

†c. Without const. An answer or solution. Obs. (Freq. in 17th c.)

a 1542 Wyatt in Tottel's Misc. (Arb.) 50 It liketh me (quod she) to haue hard your question, But, lenger time doth ask a resolucion. 1581 Pettie Guazzo's Civ. Conv. I. (1586) 6 Your resolutions, doe me content so well, That I delight..to aske. 1643 Sir T. Browne Relig. Med. I. § 9, I can answer all the objections..with that odde resolution I learned of Tertullian, certum est quia impossibile est.

†d. In phr. of..resolution, (hard or easy) to resolve. Obs. rare.

1658 Sir T. Browne Hydriot. I. (1736) 11 How the Romans left so many Coins seems of hard Resolution. 1675 Baxter Cath. Theol. I. I. 110 A strange dispute, and of most easie resolution.

11. A statement upon some matter; a decision or verdict on some point. Now rare or Obs.

1581 Marbeck Bk. Notes 1055 The Lord hath giuen a generall resolution, that no man can enter into the kingdome of heauen, vnles [etc.]. 1588 Fraunce Lawiers Log. I. iv. 25 Which last resolution of his I follow at this present. 1601 Holland Pliny I. 143 He speaketh so confidently thereof, as I will not altogether discredit his resolution in this behalfe. 1646 Sir T. Browne Pseud. Ep. I. i. (1686) 3 He hath reserved many things unto his own resolution. 1674 Essex Papers (Camden) I. 197 [He] promiseth to give his resolution about ye petitioners before his departure. 1818 Cruise Digest (ed. 2) VI. 506 The established law in cases of this nature was according to the resolution in the Duke of Norfolk's case.

b. A formal decision, determination, or expression of opinion, on the part of a deliberative assembly or other meeting; a proposal of this nature submitted to an assembly or meeting.

1604 Jrnls. Ho. Comm. 28 June, No Resolution or further Speech in it [a question] at that Time. 1651 Hobbes Leviath. II. xxii. 119 Present at all the Deliberations, and Resolutions of the Body. a 1715 Burnet Own Time (1897) I. 98 When these resolutions were passed with this protestation, a great many..met, and formed an association apart. 1771 Junius Lett. xlviii. (1788) 264 Yet now you confess that parliaments are fallible, and that their resolutions may be illegal. 1833 Ht. Martineau Manch. Strike iv. 41 To hold a meeting..in order to prepare resolutions to be laid before the masters. 1872 Freeman Eng. Const. iii. 155 The passing by the House of Commons of such a resolution as this.

c. A solution or settlement of a dispute.

1890 Spectator 15 Mar., The Italian Government, though it is strong, hardly hopes to see a resolution of its quarrel with the Papacy.

†12. An explanatory account of something. Obs.

1582 Reg. Privy Council Scot. III. 536 [The safeconduct had been obtained, and directed to him] togidder with a resolution of the forme and tyme appointit for his departing. 1658 Sir T. Browne Hydriot. 19 We much deplore the loss of that Letter which Cicero expected or received from his Brother Quintus, as a resolution of Brittish customes.

IV. †13. a. The removal of doubt on some point from a person's mind. Obs. rare.

1578 Lyte Dodoens To Rdr., For thy instruction and resolution in these matters I referre the to the same Authors. 1635 Pagitt Christianogr. III. (1636) 73 A German Monke adviseth him that doubteth of Purgatory, for his resolution to make his iourney into Scotland the greater. 1644 J. Cotton Keyes Kingd. Heaven iv. 18 The Church of Antioch sent messengers to Ierusalem for resolution and satisfaction in a doubt that troubled them.

†b. Confidence; conviction, certainty, positive knowledge. Obs. rare.

1590 Greene Never too Late Wks. (Grosart) VIII. 98, I haue such resolution in thy constancie, that [etc.]. 1605 Shaks. Lear I. ii. 108, I would vnstate my selfe, to be in a due resolution. a 1637 Holland (Webster), Little resolution and certainty there is as touching the islands of Mauritania.

14. The (or an) act of resolving or determining; anything resolved upon; a fixed determination.

1590 Greene Orl. Fur. (1599) 15 Trust me..I will sacke it, or on this Castle wall Ile write my resolution with my blood. 1617 Moryson Itin. I. 55 Suddenly al the passengers resolued to leaue the ships..; at which resolution the Masters of the ships stormed. 1647 Clarendon Hist. Reb. III. § 30 Mr. Pimm was looked upon as..not of those furious resolutions against the Church as the other leading men were. 1709 Steele Tatler No. 7 ¶ 24 He hopes they will come to a Resolution to send for no more Bulls to Rome. 1752 Johnson Rambler No. 193 ¶ 3 To be praised then every man resolves; but resolutions will not execute themselves. 1817 Jas. Mill Brit. India II. IV. v. 202 The Nabob,..fully persuaded of the resolution of the Council to depose him [etc.]. 1874 Green Short Hist. II. § 8. 104 Neither warning nor desertion moved the resolution of the Primate.

b. Const. for, of.

1633 Ford Broken Hrt. I. i, A resolution for a lasting league Betwixt your families, was entertained. 1647 Clarendon Hist. Reb. III. § 42 A sincere resolution of amity and unity between the two nations.

15. Determination; firmness or steadiness of purpose; unyielding temper.

1588 Shaks. Tit. A. III. i. 239 Thy griefes [are] their sports: Thy resolution mockt. 1592 — Lucr. 352 My will is back'd with resolution. 1636 E. Dacres tr. Machiavel's Disc. Livy II. 329 On each part he makes the Armyes equall for their order, valour, resolution, and number. 1667 Milton P. L. VI. 541 He comes, and settl'd in his face I see Sad resolution and secure. a 1703 Burkitt On N. T. Matt. iv. 10 A great temptation must be withs[to]od with great resolution. 1754 Johnson in Boswell, He was ..a coward, because he had not resolution to fire it off himself. 1819 Shelley Cenci I. iii. 173 Be thou the resolution of quick youth Within my veins. 1870 Dickens E. Drood vii, You seem to have resolution and power enough to crush me.

†16. A resolute person. Obs. rare $^{-1}$.

1643 Sir T. Browne Relig. Med. I. § 3 Those desperate Resolutions, who had rather venture at large their decayed bottome then bring her in to be new trim'd in the dock.

Re-solution (rīsǫl[i]ū·ʃən). [RE- 5 a.] Renewed or repeated solution.

1802 Phil. Trans. XCIII. 14 On re-solution in water, and crystallization, this saline matter proved to be..vitriol of zinc. 1850 Robertson Serm. Ser. III. v. (1872) 61 There are questions which, having been again and again settled, still from time to time present themselves for re-solution. 1874 Garrod & Baxter Mat. Med. (1880) 132 The former is dissolved out and crystallized, and purified by re-solution and crystallization.

Resolutioner (rezǫl[i]ū·ʃənəɹ). [f. RESOLUTION + -ER 1.]

1. Hist. A member of that party in Scotland which accepted the resolutions passed in 1650 for rehabilitating those persons who had not taken part in the struggle against Cromwell.

1693 Apol. Clergy Scot. 78 The Publick Resolutioners had made defection. a 1715 Burnet Own Time I. (1897) I. 97 Those who adhered to these resolutions were called the Public Resolutioners. Ibid. 111 The Resolutioners were known to have been more in the king's interests: so they were not so kindly looked on as the Protestors. 1816 Scott Old Mort. v, They had parted in some unkindness at the time when the kingdom of Scotland was divided into Resolutioners and Protestors. 1872 Contemp. Rev. XXI. 76 Resolutioners like Dickson and Protesters like Patrick Gillespie.

2. One who joins in or subscribes to a resolution.

1816 Southey Ess. (1832) I. 364 They say,..the said resolutioners of Bishopsgate-ward,..' We claim..a constitutional voice in the House of the people'. 1854 H. Miller Sch. & Schm. xxiv. (1858) 535 The parochial resolutioners, amounting in all to ten.

Resolutionist (rezǫl[i]ū·ʃənist). [f. as prec. + -IST.] One who makes, or joins in, a resolution.

1846 Life Guthrie in Lives Henderson & G. 145 This attack was unpalatable both to the courtiers, and the Resolutionist Presbyterians. 1856 Chamb. Jrnl. V. 136 [They] had declared their high resolves to confront the superstition..Simon..was the loudest among these resolutionists. 1891 Daily News 1 Jan. 3/4 My directors are as anxious as the resolutionists can be to secure for those in their service equitable conditions of labour.

Resolutive (re·zǫl[i]ūtiv), a. and sb. [ad. med.L. *resolūtīv-us (see RESOLUTE v. and -IVE), whence also It. and Sp. resolutivo, F. résolutif.]

A. adj. 1. a. Having the power to dissolve.

c 1400 Lanfranc's Cirurg. 334 Þan leie þervpon þe medycyn resolutif. Ibid., Of medicyns resolutiuis, summe ben simple. 1528 Paynell Salerne's Regim. dd iij, The .iiij. is baynyng specially resolutive, for that letteth bloud lettyng. 1566 Warde tr. Alexis' Secr. III. I. (1568) 49 A Repercussiue and Resolutiue oyntment against the Canker. 1601 Holland Pliny II. 557 Astringent it is, and yet resolutiue. 1651 Biggs New Disp. ¶ 133 There ariseth from the bottome a resolutive power. 1712 tr. Pomet's Hist. Drugs I. 196 Gum Tucamahaca is digestive, resolutive, neurotick. a 1774 Goldsm. tr. Scarron's Com. Rom. (1775) I. 309, I just now applied to him an anodyne and resolutive cataplasm on a livid tumour. 1873 R. Barnes Dis. Women xl. 517 So-called resolutive pessaries of iodine, made up into conical balls, with cocoa-nut butter or other ingredients.

b. Path. Terminating by resolution.

1861 Bumstead Ven. Dis. (1879) 544 The tubercular syphilide..disappears by interstitial absorption; hence, it has been called non-ulcerative or resolutive.

2. Law. a. Resolutive condition, a condition by the happening of which a contract or obligation is terminated.

a 1623 Swinburne Spousals (1686) 138 Forasmuch as this Condition is not suspensive, but resolutive or extinctive. Ibid. 144 [He] adviseth his Pupil to contract Matrimony conditionally,..under some like Resolutive Condition. 1832 Austin Jurispr. liii. (1879) II. 899 Rights subject to a contingency or condition resolutive. 1875 Poste Gaius III. 384 Conditions are Suspensive or Resolutive.

b. Resolutive clause, in Sc. Law, a clause extinguishing the right of the person who contravenes the conditions laid down in the deed.

1765 Act 5 Geo. III, c. 26 Preamble, [They] should convey, settle, and intail the lands..with all the proper, prohibitive, irritant, and resolutive clauses. 1838 W. Bell Dict. Law Scot. 164 By the resolutive clause, the right of the person contravening is resolved and extinguished. 1868 Act 31 & 32 Vict. c. 101 § 9 It shall not be necessary.. to insert..prohibitory, irritant, or resolutive clauses.

3. Logic. Analytical. ? Obs.

1654 Z. Coke Logick 4 It is delivered by an Analytical and Resolutive method, proceeding from the object and end foreknown. 1656 tr. Hobbes' Elem. Philos. (1839) 66 There is therefore no method, by which we find out the causes of things, but is either compositive or resolutive... And the resolutive is commonly called analytical method, as the compositive is called synthetical.

B. sb. A medical application or drug which serves to resolve or dispurse morbid matter.

c 1400 Lanfranc's Cirurg. 334 Rasis forbediþ þat þou schalt leie þerto no repercussiuis, ne noon resolutiuis but if þe mater be avoidid tofore. 1562 Bullein Bulwarke, Dial. Sorenes & Chir. 13 b, Whose cure must be in drawing forthe from the matter, with resolutiues, or softening medicenes. 1725 Bradley Fam. Dict. s.v. Tumour, You must neither use Convulsives nor Repercusives, but only gentle Resolutives.

1756 P. Browne Jamaica (1789) 121 The root is warm, and may be successfully administered as a resolutive, sudorific, or diaphoretic. 1873 R. Barnes Dis. Wom. xl. 519 It has been recommended to establish a seton in the vaginal portion as a derivative and resolutive.

Re·solutory, a. rare. [ad. late L. resolūtōri-us (cf. prec. and -ORY). Hence also Sp. and Pg. resolutorio, F. résolutoire (15th c.).]

†1. Explanatory, enlightening. Obs.

1609 Douland Ornith. Microl. 45 A Resolutorie Table, shewing the value of the Signes, by the beholding of every figure. 1669 Hopkins Serm. (1685) 24 Out of these distinctions, I shall form several propositions, resolutory, as I hope, to my subject in hand.

2. Law. RESOLUTIVE 2 a.

1818 Colebrooke Oblig. & Contr. 10 If an agreement bear, that the obligation shall have present operation and effect, but cease upon a certain event, that is a subsequent and resolutory condition; and the conditional obligation is called a resolutory one. 1875 Poste Gaius III. 384 Tradition, coupled with a Resolutory condition, operates two transfers of ownership.

Resolvabi·lity. [f. next + -ITY.] The capability of being resolved into parts.

1845 Herschel Ess. (1857) 661 The character of easy resolvability into separate and distinct stars. 1865 Masson Rec. Brit. Phil. 36 The resolvability of all Truth, or Knowledge..into Experience. 1871 Schellen's Spectr. Anal. § 41. 163 The D-line..is separated into two lines and shows besides a cloudy line of still further resolvability.

Resolvable (rĭzǫ·lvăb'l), a. Also 7-8 -veable. [f. RESOLVE v. + -ABLE. Cf. RESOLVIBLE.] Capable of being resolved, in various senses of the verb.

1646 Sir T. Browne Pseud. Ep. 316 The causes [are] surely best resolvable from observations made in the Countries themselves. 1688 Norris Love I. v. 60 All Love is not, as some pretend, resolvable into Self-love. 1755 Young Centaur ii. Wks. 1757 IV. 159 Want of faith. All is resolveable into that alone. 1770 Phil. Trans. LX. 435 The force of every particle, which impinges obliquely, is resolvable into two. 1816 Gilchrist Philos. Etym. p. xxi, All words are resolvable into a few primitives. 1877 E. R. Conder Bas. Faith ii. 55 Bold surmise..asks whether atoms may not themselves be resolvable into force.

b. Resolvable nebula, a nebula which admits of resolution by a powerful telescope.

1785 Herschel in Phil. Trans. LXXV. 251 Clusters of stars also may become resolvable nebulæ. 1853 Whewell Plur. Worlds 90 When we have thus to reckon as many galaxies as there are resolvable nebulae. 1870 Proctor Other Worlds xii. (1872) 291 The stellar nebulæ—resolvable and irresolvable.

Hence **Reso·lvableness** (Bailey, vol. II, 1727).

†**Reso·lvance.** Obs. rare $^{-1}$. [f. RESOLVE v. + -ANCE.] Resolve, decision.

1603 in Lismore Papers Ser. II. (1887) I. 45 To vnderstand their resoluance what they ment to do therin.

†**Reso·lvative,** a. Obs. rare $^{-1}$. [f. RESOLVE v. + -ATIVE.] = RESOLUTIVE a. 1 a.

1577 Frampton Joyful News II. (1596) 2 Copall..is resoluatiue, and softneth by some watrish partes that it hath.

Resolve (rĭzǫ·lv), sb. [f. the vb.]

1. A determination or resolution.

1592 Shaks. Rom. & Jul. IV. i. 123 Get you gone, be strong and prosperous In this resolue. 1600 W. Watson Decacordon (1602) 350 A catholike resolue for our Romane faith. 1667 Waterhouse Fire London 135 The common affection of Countrymen soders them into a common resolve of kindness each to other. 1700 Dryden Cymon & Iph. 526 Speak thy resolves; if now thy courage droop, Despair in prison. a 1794 Gibbon Misc. Wks. (1814) I. 125 My private resolves were influenced by the state of Europe. 1847 Helps Friends in C. (1851) I. 43 Mere stoicism, and resolves about fitting fortune to one's self. 1889 Jessopp Coming of Friars ii. 78 She made up her mind never to marry again, and she kept her resolve.

2. Firmness or steadfastness of purpose.

1591 Shaks. 1 Hen. VI, v. v. 75 A Lady of so high resolue, (As is faire Margaret). 1602 Marston Antonio's Rev. IV. v, We must be stiffe and steddie in resolve. 1789 Burns To Dr. Blacklock viii, Come, Firm Resolve, take thou the van. 1813 Shelley Q. Mab IV. 155 Man is of soul and body, formed for deeds Of high resolve. 1873 Symonds Grk. Poets ix. 296 We find in them no hesitancy and difficult resolve.

3. A determination of a deliberative body; a formal resolution. Now U.S.

1656 Burton's Diary (1828) I. 270 A short vote or resolve of this House..would haply give satisfaction for the present. 1657 Ibid. II. 94 The several resolves of Parliament touching the matter. 1713 Addison Cato II. i, Cæsar's approach has summon'd us together, And Rome attends her fate from our resolves. 1775 Franklin in Burke's Corr. (1844) II. 28, I hear your proposed resolves were negatived by a great majority. 1794 S. Williams Vermont 296 That part of the resolves in which the state was threatened. 1859 Bartlett Dict. Amer. (ed. 2) 362 Resolves are usually private acts, and are often passed with less formality. 1865 H. Phillips Amer. Paper Curr. II. 55 These resolves were ordered to be published.

†4. Answer, solution. Obs.

a 1625 Faithf. Friends II. ii, I crave but ten short days to give resolve To this important suit. 1643 Milton Divorce I. viii, In hope to give a full resolve of that which is yet so much controverted. 1670 W. Simpson Hydrol. Ess. 25 If you consult what I say..you may find a sufficient resolve thereof.

†5. Mus. (See quot.) Obs. rare $^{-1}$.

1721 Bradley Philos. Acc. Wks. Nat. 160 The progressive Tones from that Ground-Note to the Octave, which is the Resolve of the Ground-Note, declares the Key.

Resolve (rĭzǫ·lv), v. Also 4-7 **resolue.** [ad. L. resolvĕre, f. re- RE- + solvĕre to loosen, dissolve. Cf. It. re-, risolvere, Sp. and Pg. resolver, obs. F. resolver, -vir (mod.F. résoudre).]

I. †1. trans. To melt, dissolve, reduce to a liquid or fluid state. Obs.

For examples with const. into, to, see 6 and 9.

c 1374 Chaucer Boeth. IV. metr. v. (1868) 133 No man ne wondreþ whan þe weyȝte of þe snowe yhardid by þe colde is resolued by þe brennynge hete of phebus. 1388 Wyclif Job xxviii. 2 A stoon resolued, ethir meltid, bi heete, is turned in to money. c 1420 Pallad. on Husb. XII. 526 Whit wex is to resolue In fynest oil. 1530 Palsgr. 688/1 This metall can nat be resolved without a marvayllous sharpe fyre. 1555 Eden Decades (Arb.) 141 Cleopatra resolued a pearle in vineger & drunke it. 1609 Holland Amm. Marcell. 117 Euphrates was risen by reason of snow newly thawed and resolved. 1678 Dryden All for Love III. i, He could resolve his Mind, as Fire does Wax, From that hard rugged Image, melt him down [etc.]. 1732 Arbuthnot Aliments, etc. I. 270 Soaps which resolve solid Substances.

transf. 1582 Batman Barth. De P. R. XI. iii. 159 And the west winde..resolveth and unbindeth winter. 1638 Rawley tr. Bacon's Life & Death (1650) 5 The Drying caused by Cold, is but weak, and easily resolved.

2. To disintegrate; to break up or separate into constituent or elementary parts. Now rare or Obs.

1398 Trevisa Barth. De P. R. III. xix (1495) 63 The smoke that is resoluyd and comyth from the thynge that is smellyd. c 1400 tr. Secreta Secret., Gov. Lordsh. 68 Þe bodyes [of men]..ar resoluyd by kyndly hete, þat makes drye þe moystnes of þe body. c 1420 Pallad. on Husb. I. 365 The see grauel is lattest for to drye,..The salt in hit thi werkis wol resolue. 1577 B. Googe Heresbach's Husb. (1586) 17 b, A mellow ground that is fat, and will soone be resolved. 1584 Cogan Haven Health ccxviii. (1636) 251 The fumes and vapors of ale..cannot bee so soone resolved as those that rise up of wine. 1620 Venner Via Recta iii. 52 They will too soon resolue the iuyce of lighter meats. 1633 Earl Manch. Al Mondo (1636) 94 It is well for man that his bodie by death becomes putrid, resolved and crumbled to nothing. 1776 Bowden Farmer's Director 18 By the assistance of alternate rain and drought, to resolve and break the hard clods.

†b. To analyse, examine (a statement). Obs.

1594 Hooker Eccl. Pol. II. vii. § 9 Examine, sift, and resolve their alledged proofs, till you come to the very root whence they spring.

†c. Math. To solve (an equation). Obs.

1743 Emerson Fluxions 36 Then we had been obliged to substitute $a + z$ or $a - z$ for x in the given Equation before it could be resolved. 1798 Hutton Course Math. (1827) I. 269 The form that a cubic equation must necessarily have, to be resolved by this rule.

d. To analyse (a force or velocity) into its components. (Cf. RESOLUTION 9.)

1825 J. Nicholson Operat. Mechanic 5 Each of those portions may, by a similar process, be again divided, resolving the original force to infinity. 1866 Herschel Fam. Lect. Sci. 90 This force then being resolved in radial and tangential directions [etc.].

e. Of optical instruments (or persons using them): To separate, break up (an object) into distinguishable parts.

1785 Herschel in Phil. Trans. LXXV. 219 When he resolves one nebula into stars, he discovers ten new ones which he cannot resolve. 1868 Lockyer Elem. Astron. § 77 Star-clusters..so distant that even in telescopes of great power they could not be resolved. 1870 Emerson Soc. & Sol. Wks. (Bohn) III. 3 The remoter stars seem a nebula of united light; yet there is no group which a telescope will not resolve.

3. Med. To soften (a hard tumour); to disperse or dissipate (humours, swellings, etc.). ? Obs.

c 1400 Lanfranc's Cirurg. 210 If þou miȝt not wiþ repercussiuis do awei þe enpostym ne resolue him. Ibid. 353 Whanne þe mater þat þou wolt resolue is swiþe hard. 1541 Copland Galyen's Terap. Hh iv, When ecchymosis is all dygested & resolued, than it is parmytted to drye the broken flesshe. 1601 Holland Pliny II. 274 Those plasters which resolue or maturat any impostumed place. 1683 Salmon Doron Med. II. 427 For it resolves all hard humors. 1748 Hartley Observ. Man I. ii. § I. 127 Embrocations are of Use in resolving Obstructions. 1786 J. Hunter Ven. Dis. IV. vi. 404 This method of resolving buboes occurred to me at Belleisle in the year 1761.

absol. 1568 Turner Herbal II. (1568) 117 Oyl that is made of vnrype oliues..doth myghtely resolue. 1610 Markham Masterp. II. clxxiii. 483 It burneth, draweth, and resolueth, and is goode for scurfe. 1708 Brit. Apollo No. 93. 2/2 Green Tea..Resolves, and Attenuates.

†b. To dissipate or allay (pain, etc.). Obs. rare.

1573 Treas. Hid. Secrets xix, Oyle of Rue is hot, resolving pain. 1600 Surflet Countrie Farme II. xlviii. 306 An oyle..which hath power to resolue, soften, and appease the griefe of colde rheumes or distillations. a 1617 Bayne On Eph. (1658) 130 Fire..hath not onely heat resolving numbnesse,..but it hath light.

c. To remove (inflammation) by resolution.

1732 Arbuthnot Rules Diet in Aliments, etc. 321 Such a Fever is often resolv'd by a bleeding at the Nose. 1898 Allbutt's Syst. Med. V. 361 When empyema follows upon pneumonia, the pulmonary inflammation sometimes is never resolved.

†4. To slacken, relax (the limbs, etc.); to weaken. Obs.

1483 Caxton Fables of Æsop 3 By cause the water was hote and their stomake [was] resolued by the water. 1540-1 Elyot Image Gov. (1556) 30 Lyke as by the other the strengthe of bodie is resolvyd. 1588 Kyd Househ. Phil. Wks. (1901) 248 The night..[in which] we may sufficiently restore our bodies resolued with the..heate of the day. 1644 Bulwer Chiron. 35 The Hand collected, the Fingers looking downewards, then turned and resolved. 1715 Rowe Lady Jane Grey II, Every moving accent that she breathes Resolves my courage, slackens my tough nerves.

†b. To render lax in feeling or conduct. Obs.

c 1550 H. Rhodes Bk. Nurture in Babees Bk. (1868) 106 It is a very hard work of continence to repell the paynting glose of flatteringes whose wordes resolue the hart with plesure. 1611 B. Jonson Catiline III. iii, Each house [being] Resolved in freedom.

†c. To relax or withdraw (a law). Obs.

1537 State Papers Hen. VIII, VII. 706 The act made for money by exchange, the wiche,..onles it be resolvid, wilbe a great ocacion..to cawse a stey for salis of wolen clothis.

5. †a. To cause (discord) to pass away. Obs.

1526 Pilgr. Perf. (W. de W. 1531) 282 b, It resolueth discorde, reconsyleth ennemyes, & maketh them frendes.

b. Mus. To cause (a discord) to pass into a concord. (Cf. RESOLUTION 8 b.)

1727-38 Chambers Cycl. s.v. Discord, The discord is resolved by being immediately succeeded by a concord. 1797 Encycl. Brit. (ed. 3) XVI. 125/1 There is no possible manner of resolving a dissonance which is not derived from an operation of cadence. 1838 Penny Cycl. XII. 50/1 Most discords require to be prepared, and all must be resolved. 1868 Ouseley Harmony ii. (1875) 20 When the discords have thus been rendered agreeable to the ear, they are said to be resolved.

II. 6. To separate (a thing) into its component parts or elements; to dissolve into some other physical form. † Also const. in.

c 1430 Life St. Kath. 99 My body whyche aftur þe inevitable lawe of nature abydeth to be resolued into deþ. 1477 Norton Ord. Alch. v. in Ashm. (1652) 79 Liquors departeth Qualities asunder, Substance resolving in Attomes. 1533 Bellenden Livy I. xv. (S.T.S.) I. 85 Becaus þe stoupis and pillaris þareof war all of tre, they war haistelie brynt and resoluit in powder. 1598 Barckley Felic. Man (1631) 706 God will rayse up His worke that is resolved into dust. 1635 Swan Spec. M. v. § 2 (1643) 138 Green clouds..are altogether watery, and are that were resolved into water. 1668 Culpepper & Cole Barthol. Anat. I. xxvii. 65 The sooty Vapors are condensed, and being resolved into water, are [etc.]. 1781 Cowper Charity 562 He ordains things..To be resolv'd into their parent earth. 1817 Jas. Mill Brit. India I. II. x. 446 The Empire of the Mahrattas..would have been resolv'd..into its primitive elements. 1891 Spectator 4 July 5/2 A..campaign intended to break up Italy, or to resolve the German Empire back again into its elements.

b. In figurative contexts.

1526 Pilgr. Perf. (W. de W. 1531) 60 His herte shall yerne and melte,..& be hole resolued in to teares. 1568 Wilmot Tancred & Gismonda II. iii, A resolution that resolues my bloud Into the Ice-sie drops of Lethes flood. 1607 Shaks. Timon IV. iii. 442 The Seas a Theefe, whose liquid Surge, resolues The Moone into Salt teares.

c. To convert, transform, alter (a thing) into some other thing or form.

1570-6 Lambarde Peramb. Kent (1826) 327 A Towne called Horsmundene, which name (resolved into Saxon Orthographie) is [etc.]. a 1623 Swinburne Spousals (1686) 27 By the same means..are those Spousals by them contracted in their Minority..resolved or turned into Matrimony. 1641 Jrnls. Ho. Comm. 31 Dec., That the House be resolved into a Committee, to take into Consideration the Militia of the Kingdom. 1743 Tomlinson Prot. Birthright 13 Into whose Authority all Christians have resolved their Faith and Obedience. 1861 Dickens in All Year Round 1 June 221 The spectral figure..seemed all resolved into a ghastly stare. 1889 Standard 9 Apr., Emin..has seen islands resolved into headlands.

7. To reduce by mental analysis into more elementary forms, principles, or relations. † Also const. in.

1388 Prol. Wyclif Bible xv. (1850) 57 An ablatif case absolute may be resoluid into these thre wordis. 1570 Billingsley Euclid I. prop. 32. 42 Euery right lined figure is resolued in two triangles. 1628 T. Spencer Logick 284 When the causes doe argue the effect, the effect is resolued into the causes. a 1674 Clarendon Surv. Leviath. (1676) 8 He resolv'd all Wisdom and Religion itself into a simple obedience and submission to it. 1719 De Foe Crusoe I. (Globe) 204 After I had entertain'd these Notions, and, by long musing, had as it were resolv'd them all into nothing. 1774 Pennant Tour Scotl. in 1772, 233, I was for resolving this phænomenon into Ship-wrecks. 1841 Myers Cath. Th. IV. § 2. 184 Why may we not.. resolve Christianity into a system of practical Morality? 1875 Jowett Plato (ed. 2) IV. 239 All sensation is to be resolved into a similar combination of an agent and patient.

†b. To reduce or convert (a quantity) into some other denomination. Obs.

1571 Digges Pantom. I. xxi. G j b, Then resolue 20 foote into inches. 1669 Sturmy Mariner's Mag. II. vi. 66 The Degrees resolved into Hours and Minutes, is 1 Hour 49 Min. 1672 Petty Pol. Anat. (1691) 352 The victuals.., resolved into money, may be estimated 3s. 6d. per week.

8. refl. Of things: To pass, by dissolution, separation, or change, into another form or into simpler forms.

1602 Shaks. Ham. I. ii. 130 Oh that this too too solid Flesh, would melt, Thaw, and resolue it selfe into a Dew. 1614 Raleigh Hist. World I. i. § 7 (1634) 9 The Waters.. resolved their thinner parts into Aire. 1799 Southey Cool Refl. during Midsummer Walk, For the flesh upon them; It hath resolved itself into a dew. 1814 Chalmers Evidences ii. 46 The argument..resolves itself into four parts. 1868 Herschel in People's Mag. Jan. 63 Its pileus ..has the singular property of resolving itself..into a black liquid. 1879 Lubbock Addr. Pol. & Educ. iii. 44 His complaint resolves itself into two parts.

b. Of a deliberative body: To convert (itself) into a committee.

1710 Lond. Gaz. No. 4699/3 The House resolved it self into a Committee of the whole House. 1753 [see COMMITTEE 3]. 1818 Parl. Debates 1422/1 The house then resolved itself into a committee on the bill. 1885 Manch. Exam. 7 Oct. 5/3 The meeting unanimously resolved itself into a committee.

RESOLVE.

9. To reduce, transform, or change (a thing) *to* something else. *Also rare. Now rare.*

III. †10. To untie, loosen. *Obs.*

11. To answer (a question, argument, etc.); to solve (a problem of any kind).

12. To remove, clear away, dispel (a doubt, difficulty, or obscurity).

†13. To decide, determine, settle (a doubtful point).

†15. To free (one) from doubt or perplexity; to bring to certainty or clear knowledge. *Obs.* (Common in 17th c.)

†c. With dependent clause introduced by *where, which, why, etc.* (Passing into 17 b.) *Obs.*

†b. *Const.* of or in the matter of doubt. *Obs.*

IV. *intr.* †20. To take rise. *Obs. rare* —[1]

21. To melt, dissolve, become fluid. † *Obs.*

†c. With dependent clause introduced by *where, which, why, etc.* (Passing into 17 b.) *Obs.*

†16. To convince (one) of something. *Obs.*

b. With dependent clause (or equivalent) expressing the decision arrived at.

†c. To set down decisively as being of a certain character. *rare.*

†17. To inform, tell (a person) of a thing. *Obs.*

†d. To conclude, to settle (a thing) in one's mind. *Obs.*

†e. To resolve, determine. *Obs.*

14. To determine or decide upon (a course of action, etc.). *Also, with* oneself.

†c. To fix on, choose (a person). *Obs.*

16. To determine the action upon a certain resolution.

†b. To determine (a person) *on* a course of action. *Also with* it.

†c. To join oneself to another's opinion. *Obs.*

b. To adopt or pass as a condition by a resolution.

†c. To put (a person) *out of* a condition by a resolution.

†b. To determine (a person) *to* an action. *Obs.*

†18. To free (one) from doubt or perplexity.

22. To undergo dissolution or separation into elements; to pass *into*, return or change *to*, some form or state.

b. *Const.* with *for*, *to* against, *t* from, *t* of (=*on*).

22. To undergo dissolution or separation into elements.

b. *Of non-material things.*

†2. Convinced, satisfied. *Obs.*

23. To come to a determination; to make up one's mind; to take a firm purpose or decision.

†b. To determine (a person) *on* a course of action. *Also with* it.

b. To decide or setting out *for* a place. *Obs.*

†24. a. To be satisfied or convinced. *Obs.*

†c. Of the mind, etc.: Freed from doubt or uncertainty; fixed, settled. *Obs.*

d. *Law.* To lapse; to become void.

4. Of persons, the mind, etc.: Fully determined upon, deliberate.

RESOLVED.

1. Of persons I determined to an end, that, etc.

2. In a determined manner; resolutely.

Resolvedly, *adv.* [f. prec. + -LY[2].] 1. Definitely, determinately.

2. In a determined manner; resolutely.

Resolvedness. [f. as prec. + -NESS.] Resoluteness; determination; firmness, fixedness of purpose.

Resolver. [f. RESOLVE *v.* + -ER[1].] 1. One who resolves.

2. One who, or that which, answers a question, solves a doubt or difficulty, etc.

3. One who makes a resolve; one who supports a resolution.

Resolvible, a. [f. RESOLVE *v.* + -IBLE.] Capable of being resolved; resolvable.

RESOLVING. 531 RESORT.

Resolving (*rizɔ'lviŋ*), *vbl. sb.* [f. as prec. + -ING[1].] The action of the verb in various senses.

Resolving, *ppl. a.* [f. as prec. + -ING[2].] That resolves. (Chiefly *Med.*)

Reson, obs. form of REASON.

Reson, obs. forms of RAISIN, REASON *sb.*[1]

Resonance (*re'zɔnans*). Also ‡ *reson-ance* [a. OF. *resonance*, *resonnance* (15th c.; mod.F. *résonance*), — It. *risonanza*, Sp. and Pg. *reson-ancia*, ad. L. *resonantia* (adj. *resonant-*, *-sonare* to resound): see -ANCE.]

1. The reinforcement or prolongation of sound by reflection, or (esp. by synchronous vibration.

Resonancy (*re'zɔnansi*), *rare*. [See RESONANCE + -Y.] = RESONANCE.

Resonant (*re'zɔnant*), a. [ad. L. *resonant-*, *-ant-em*, pr. pple. of *resonare* to RESOUND: see -ANT.]

1. Of sounds: Re-echoing, resounding; continuing to sound or ring.

2. Of bodies: Echoing or resounding with sound.

3. Of places: Echoing or resounding with something.

Resonate (*re'zɔnat*), *v*. [f. L. *resonat-*, ppl. stem of *resonare*: see -ATE[3].]

1. *intr.* To produce or exhibit resonance. Hence **Re'sonating** *ppl. a.*

Resonator (*re'zɔnatə*), *rare*. [See RESONATE + -OR.] Producing resonance.

Resorb (*rizɔ'ɪb*), *v*. [ad. L. *resorbēre*, f. *re-* RE- + *sorbēre* to absorb again.]

Resorbent, *a*. [ad. L. *resorbent-, -entem*, pr. pple. of *resorbēre*: see prec.] Resorbing.

Resorption (*rizɔ'ɪpʃən*). [Noun of action, on L. type *resorptiōn-*.] So f. *-risorp'-tion*.] The fact or process of reabsorption, *spec.* of an organ, tissue, or secretion.

Resorptive, a. *rare*. [Cf. prec. and -IVE.] Pertaining to, or of the nature of, resorption.

RESORT.

Resorcin (*rezɔ'ɪsin*), *Chem.* Also -ine. [f. RES(IN) + ORCIN.]

A compound, formerly produced by the action of potash upon galbanum or other resins, now generally prepared synthetically.

Resorcinol (*rizɔ'ɪsinol*), *Chem.* = RESORCIN.

Resorcylic (*rezɔɪsɪ'lik*), *a. Chem.* [f. RESORC(IN) + -YL + -IC.] Pertaining to, derived from.

Resort (*rizɔ'ɪt*), *sb.*[1] Also -ort. [a. OF. *resort*, *resort*, f. *resortir*.]

1. That to which one has recourse for aid or assistance, or in order to accomplish some end.

b. Recourse or resource; chance or expedient of last resort. *Obs.*

2. The right or privilege of having final decision or appeal vested in one. *Obs.*

Resort (*rizɔ'ɪt*), *sb.*[2] Also 4-6 *resorte*, *r.* [a. OF. *resort*, resource, aid, spring, etc., f. *resortir*: see RESORT *v.*]

1. The act of resorting, or turning for aid or assistance. *Obs.*

†5. Concourse or assemblage of people. *Obs.*

b. An assemblage, gathering, throng, crowd.

2. a. The place, etc., to which one goes or turns.

b. *spec.* A place to which people resort, or are accustomed to resort, for some specified purpose.

RESORT. 532 RESORT.

c. *In the last resort* (after F. *en dernier ressort*), orig. as a judge or court from which there is no appeal; hence, as a last expedient, in the end, ultimately.

II. †B. A channel of an arm (of the sea). *Obs.* —[1]

†M. A spring. *Obs.*

†10. A mechanical spring. *Obs.* (Cf. RESSORT.)

5. *Without resort, without appeal. rare* —[1]

Resort (*rizɔ'ɪt*), *v*. Also 4-6 *resorte*, etc. [a. OF. *resortir*, -*ortir* (mod.F. *ressortir*) to rebound, retire, etc., f. *re-* RE- + *sortir* to issue, go out, etc., of obscure etymology.]

1. †a. To issue, to come out again, to be set free. *Obs.*

†2. a. To return to oneself; to revert to a former condition or state. *Obs.*

3. To go or betake oneself to some place or person.

b. *Of things resorting.* †Also *of.*

4. To frequent or betake oneself to some place or person.

5. To have recourse to; to repair or go, for some aid or assistance.

†3. To turn, direct one's course to (a place). *Obs.*

b. To repair, have recourse (to a person for aid, etc.). *Also* †*unto*.

c. To resort primarily or frequently to a place.

3. To repair, betake oneself to; to go to (a place).

b. With plural subject.

4. *To turn* or *apply oneself to; to come* or *go to a person.

5. To have recourse to; to repair or go, for some aid or assistance.

†6. To repair primarily or frequently to a place.

†7. To consort or associate with others. *Obs.* —[1]

b. To return (to a place, etc.).

†c. To return or go back to a former condition. *Obs.*

†d. To revert or fall to one's lot or share.

†8. Of blood: To flow to some part. *Obs.*

7. To proceed or go to (or *towards*) a place; to repair.

†8. To issue, to come out again. *Obs.*

Resparkle, v. [RE- 5 a.] To sparkle again.

Respass, obs. f. RASPIS [1], variant of RASPIS [2].

Respen, Sc. f. ...

Re-sort, v. ...

Resorter ...

Besorter ...

Resorting, vbl. sb. ...

Resortible, a. ...

Re-sound, v. [RE- 5 a.] To sound again.

Resounding, vbl. sb. ...

Resoundingly, adv. ...

† **Resour**. Obs. ...

Resource (rǐsō·rs), sb. ...

† **Resourd**, v. Obs. ...

Resourceful, a. ...

Resourcefully, adv. ...

Resourceless, a. ...

Resow, v. ...

Resowne, obs. form of REASON sb.

Resoyne ...

Resp., dial. ...

Respait ...

Respasse ...

Respect (rǐspe·kt), sb. [a. L. respect-us.]

Respect (rǐspe·kt), v. [f. L. respect-, ppl. stem of respicĕre to look (back) at, regard, consider.]

Respectability (rǐspektǎbi·lǐti) [f. RESPECTABLE: see -ITY.]

Respectable (rǐspe·ktǎb'l), a. and sb. [a. F. respectable.]

Respectableness ...

Respectably, adv. ...

Respectant (rǐspe·ktǎnt), a. ...

RESPECTED.

2. Looking backward.

Respected, *ppl. a.* [f. RESPECT *v.* + -ED¹.]
Held in respect.

Respecter (rispe·ktəɹ). [f. RESPECT *v.* + -ER¹.] One who respects a thing or person.

Respectful (rispe·ktfůl), *a.* [f. prec.] Full of, exhibiting, or marked by respect.

Respectfully, *adv.* [f. prec.] In a respectful or deferential manner.

Respectfulness. [f. prec. + -NESS.] The fact of being respectful.

Respectively, *adv.* [f. prec.]

Respective (rispe·ktiv), *a.* [ad. late L. *respectīv-us*: see RESPECT *sb.* and -IVE. Hence also F. *respectif,* Sp. and Pg. *respectivo,* It. *ri-, respettivo.*]

RESPECTIVELY.

†b. Of persons: Regardful, attentive, considerate, careful.

†a. Attentive to a person or thing.

b. Discriminating; partial.

†4. Worthy of respect or deference; respectable.

5. † **a.** Having relationship or reference to something; correspondent.

b. Without const. Relative. Now rare.

6. Properly pertaining to, or connected with, each individual, group, etc., of those in question; several.

RESPECTIVENESS.

Respectiveness. Now rare or Obs. [f. as prec. + -NESS.]

†1. Consideration of circumstances; care, attention, heedfulness.

†2. Deference; respect; respectfulness.

†Respiccion, *sb.* Obs. [Prob. a. L.]

Respectless (rispe·ktles), *a.* [f. RESPECT *sb.* + -LESS.]

Respectlessly, *adv.* [f. RESPECTIVE + -LY².] With respect to, in (their) several or particular respects.

Resper, var. RESPERSE *v.*

Respersion. [ad. L. *respersiōn-em*, n. of action f. *respergĕre*: see prec.] The action of sprinkling.

Respersive, *a. rare⁻¹.* [f. as prec.]

Respet(t)e, obs. forms of RESPITE.

†Respicient, *a.* Obs. rare. [ad. L. *respicient-em*, pres. pple. of *respicĕre* to RESPECT.]

Respirability (respirĭr·i·), [f. next.] The quality of being respirable.

Respirable (respi·răb'l, re·spĭrăb'l), *a.* [ad. F. *respirable* (14th c.), or ad. L. *respīrābilis* (Boeth.): see RESPIRE and -ABLE.]

RESPIRATO-

Respiration (respĭrē·ʃən). [ad. L. *respīrātiōn-em*, n. of action f. *respīrāre* to RESPIRE. So F. *respiration* (15th c.), Sp. *respiracion,* It. *re-, rispirazione.*]

Respirative (respi·rătiv), *a.* [f. L. *respīrāt-,* ppl. stem of *respīrāre* to RESPIRE + -IVE.]

Respirator (re·spĭrētəɹ). [a. L. type *respīritor,* agent-n. f. *respīrāre* to RESPIRE. Cf. F. *respirateur.*]

RESPIRATOR. 539 RESPITE. RESPITE. 540 RESPOND.

1. *Chem.* An apparatus used for testing the composition of exhaled air.

Respire (rispəi·əɹ), *v.* [ad. L. *respīrāre,* or a. F. *respirer* (13th c.), or a. late L. *respīrāre,* f. re- RE- + *spīrāre* to breathe. So Sp. and Pg. *respirar,* It. *respirare.*]

Respiring, *vbl. sb.* [f. next.] The action of breathing.

Respirit (rĭspi·rĭt), *v.* [f. RE- 5 a.] trans. To inspire with fresh spirit or courage.

Respite (re·spit, re·spait), *sb.* Forms: 3-7 respit, 6 respit(e) 4-6 respyt(e), 5 respyte, 7-8 respight. See also RESPECT [*sb.* 3. Cf. OF. *respit* (mod.F. *répit*)—L. *respect-us* RESPECT *sb.*]

I. **1.** *trans.* To grant a respite to.

I. **1.** Delay, or extension of time, asked or granted for some reason (orig. for further consideration of a matter). Also in *spite* to put *in respite.*

II. † **7.** Respect; regard; comparison.

II. **4.** Leisure; opportunity for doing something.

5. To delay, postpone, put off.

RESPOND.

Resplendently, *adv.* [f. prec. + -LY².] In a resplendent manner; brilliantly, brightly.

Resplendence (risple·ndens). [ad. late L. *resplendentia:* see next and -ENCE.]

Resplendency (risple·ndensi). [f. as next + -Y.] Resplendence.

Resplendent (risple·ndent), *a.* [ad. L. *resplendent-em,* pres. pple. of *resplendēre* to RESPLEND.] Shining with brilliant or splendid lustre.

Resplendish, *v.* Obs. [a. F. *resplendiss-,* lengthened stem of *resplendir* to RESPLEND.]

Resplendishing, *vbl. sb.* Obs. [f. prec. + -ING¹.]

Resplendishment, *a.* Obs. rare⁻¹. [f. prec. + -MENT.]

Resplent (risple·nt), *v.* rare. [ad. L. *resplendēre.*]

Respond (rispɔ·nd), *v.* [ad. L. *respondēre,* or a. OF. *respondre* (mod.F. *répondre*), f. re- RE- + *spondēre* to promise.]

1. *Eccl.* = RESPONSORY *sb.* 1 a. (See also quot. 1710.)

Respond (rĭspǫnd), sb.

Responde (rĭspǫnd). Sc. Law. [L., 2 sing. imp. of *respondēre*. Cf. RESPONSE.]

Respondence (rĭspǫndĕns), sb. [ad. L. respondentia, Sp. and Pg. respondencia, It. respondenza : see RESPONDENT and -ENCE.]

Respondency. [See prec. and -ENCT.]

Respondent (rĭspǫndĕnt), a. and sb.

Responder. [f. RESPOND v. + -ER 1.]

Respondentia. [mod.L.]

Respondent (rĭspǫndĕnt), sb.

Responsal (rĭspǫnsăl), sb. Obs. Also 4-sal.

Responsalis. [med.L.] = RESPONSAL sb.

Responsary, rare. [ad. med.L. responsārium.]

Response (rĭspǫns), sb.

Responsible (rĭspǫnsĭb'l), a. and sb.

Responsibility. [See next and -ITY.]

Responsion (rĭspǫnʃən). Also 6 -cion.

Responsive (rĭspǫnsĭv), a.

Responsively, adv.

Responsiveness.

Responsory (rĭspǫnsərĭ), sb.

Responsorial (rĭspǫnsō·rĭăl), a.

Responsory (rĭspǫnsərĭ), a.

Respread, v.

Respring, v.

Respue, v. Obs.

Respute, v. Obs.

Respunsory, a. Obs.

Respon'sor, var. RESPONSORY sb.

Responsorial, a. [ad. med.L. responsōriālis.]

Ressald, var. RISSOLE.

Ressaldar (resāldā·r). Also 8 rissalla, -dar, russala(h), russaldar. [Urdū (Arab.) رسالدار risāldār, f. Arab. arsala he sent.]

Ressort, v. Obs.

Ressaure, sb.

Resort, sb.

Resort, v.

Ressant, a. Obs.

Resat, v. Obs.

Resaisance, v.

Ressemble, v.

Ressant, sb.

Respite, v.

Resort, sb.

Resortment, sb.

Resorb, v.

Resorption.

Rest, sb.

Rest, sb.

Restant, a.

Restauration.

Restaurant.

Restauration.

†**1. a.** The reinstatement of man in the divine favour or in a state of innocence. *Obs.*

†**b.** The restoration of a person to a former status or position. *Obs.*

†**c.** *Hist.* = RESTORATION 2 a. *Obs.*

†**d.** The bringing back of the Jews to Palestine.

†**e.** The restoration of something material to its proper condition. Also, a restorative. *Obs.*

2. †a. The restoration of something lost or taken away; restitution. *Obs.*

b. The restoration of an institution, art, doctrine, etc., to its pristine condition.

†**c.** Reparation of defects, etc. *Obs. rare⁻¹.*

†**3.** Restoration of stolen goods. *Obs. rare⁻¹.*

4. A restaurant. [So G. *restauration.*]

†**Restaurant.** In 4–5 -if, 6 -iue. [a. OF. *restauratif*, -ive, or ad. med. L. *restaurātīvum.*]

†**Restaurator.** *Obs.* [ad. L. *restaurātor*, agent-n. from *restaurāre.*]

Restaurer. *Obs. rare⁻¹.* [Cf. obs. F. *restaureur*.] Restorer.

†**Restay**, v. *Int.* (Generan) *Epistle* viii, Iesus Christ...who shalde be...grace to men to be restaurer of the worlde.

1 *trans.* To check, restrain, keep back, hold in.

2. To stop, stay.

Rest-balk, sb. Also 4 rist-bauk. [f. REST sb.¹ or 2. + BALK sb. 3.] A ridge left unploughed between two furrows, *esp.* in the process of raftering or ribbing. Also *attrib.* or *Comb.*

Hence **Rest-balk** v. *trans.*, to plough (land).

Rest-day. [OE. *rest(e)dæg*, f. *rest(e* REST sb.¹ + *dæg* DAY. Cf. Du. *rustdag*, Da. *rastdag*, G. *rasttag.*] The day of rest; the Sabbath. Now *rare*.

Reste, var. of REST *sb.*¹

Rested, *ppl. a.* [f. REST v.¹ + -ED.] Refreshed by repose or sleep. Also used of land that has lain fallow for some time, and (*Sc.*) of a fire.

Rester¹. [f. REST v.¹ + -ER.] One who rests.

†**Rester².** [f. REST v.⁴ + -ER.] One who resists.

Resteth. Also 4 restenol. [f. REST sb.¹]

Restial, a. Also 4 resteol. [f. REST sb.¹]

Restible, a. *Obs. rare.* [ad. L. *restibilis*.]

Restiff, a. [See RESTIVE.]

Restie.

Restiff (re'stif), *a.* [a. OF. *restif*, *restive* (mod. F. *rétif*, rétive), f. *rest-* stem of *rester* to remain, stay:—L. *restāre*: see REST v.¹ and cf. RESTIVE, RESTY.]

1. Characterized by, of the nature of, productive of, rest or repose; free from strife or disturbance.

b. *transf.* Of persons.

2. Quiet; peaceful; lacking or enjoying rest.

Restie.

Hence **Resty** v. *trans.*, to plough (land)...

Rest-day.

Restfully, *adv.* [f. prec. + -LY².] In a restful manner; quietly, peacefully.

Restfulness. [As prec. + -NESS.] The state or quality of being restful.

Rest-harrow. [f. REST sb.³ or v.³ + HARROW: cf. med. L. *resta boāis*, OF. *reste bœuf.*] A field-shrub (*Ononis arvensis*), with tough roots, also called CAMMOCK.

Rest-house. [f. REST sb.¹] In India, a building in which travellers may obtain rest and shelter; a choultry, a dawk-bungalow.

Restiffness.

Restiff, *a.* See RESTIVE.

†Restiness.

Resting, *vbl. sb.¹* Also 4–6 restyng; 5 resteng. [f. REST v.¹ + -ING¹.]

1. Rest, repose, inactivity.

2. Remaining stationary.

Restingly, *adv.*

Resting-place. [f. RESTING *vbl. sb.¹*]

†Restitute, *pa. pple. Obs.* [ad. L. *restitūt-us*, pa. pple. of *restituĕre*: see REST sb. and STATUTE.] Restored.

Restitute (re'stitiūt), *v.* [f. ppl. stem of L. *restituĕre*.]

1 *trans.* To restore to a position or status; to reinstate, rehabilitate. Now *rare*.

Restituted, *ppl. a.*

Hence **Restituted** *ppl. a.*

Restitution (restitiū'ʃən). Also 5–6 resty-. [a. OF. *restitution*, -*cion* (13..), ad. L. *restitūtiōn-em*, n. of action f. *restituĕre*: see RESTITUTE v.]

1. The action of restoring or giving back something to its proper owner, or of making reparation to one for loss or injury previously inflicted.

b. Restoration of a thing or condition to its original state or form.

†**b.** Correction of an error. *Obs.*

6. †a. Repetition, replacement. *Obs. rare.*

b. Tendency to return to, or remain, a previous position by virtue of elasticity or resilience.

7. *Numism.* (See quot. 1742–58.)

Restitutional, *a.* [f. prec. + -AL.]

Restitutionism.

Restitutionist, -IST.

†**7.** Reparation of loss or injury.

Restitutive (re'stitiūtiv), *a.* [ad. L. type *restitūtīvus*, f. *restitūt-*, ppl. stem of *restituĕre*: see RESTITUTE v. and -IVE.]

†**1.** Of a character consequent or dependent on restitution, or restoration to a former status.

2. Tending or serving to make restitution.

Restitutor (re'stitiūtor). *Obs. rare.* [a. L. *restitūtor*, agent-noun from *restituĕre* to RESTITUTE. Cf. F. *restituteur*.]

Restitutory (re'stitiūtŏri), *a.* [f. as prec. + -ORY.] Of or belonging to restitution.

Restive (re'stiv), *a.* [Later form of RESTIF(F, assimilated to adjectives in -IVE.]

1. Inclined to rest or remain still; inactive, inert. Now *rare* or *Obs.*

2. Marked or characterized by unrest; affording or yielding no rest.

3. Of persons (or animals): Taking no rest; constantly stirring or active, or desirous to be so; averse to being quiet or settled.

Restiveness. [f. prec. + -NESS.] The quality or condition of being restive.

Restle, variant of RESTLE *sb.*

Restless (re'stles), *a.* [f. REST sb.¹ + -LESS. Cf. Fris. *restleas*, G. *rastlos* (Da. and Sw. *rastlös*).]

1. Deprived of rest; finding no rest; *esp.* uneasy in mind or spirit.

2. Of persons (or animals): Taking no rest; constantly stirring or active, or desirous to be so; averse to being quiet or settled.

Restlessly, *adv.* [f. prec. + -LY².] In a restless manner; without resting or pausing; unceasingly; uneasily.

Restlessness. [f. prec. + -NESS.] The state or character of being restless.

†Re-stock, *v.* [RE- 5 a.] *trans.* To stock again, to replenish.

Re-stock, *v.*² [RE- 5 a.] *trans.* To stock again.

Restorable (rɪstō'răb'l), *a.* [f. RESTORE v. + -ABLE.] That can be restored or brought back to a former condition.

Restoral (rɪstō'răl), *sb.* [f. RESTORE v. + -AL.] Restoration.

Restorance.

Restoration (restŏrē'ʃən). [f. RESTORE v. after RESTAURATION, and in part for earlier RESTAURATION.]

1. The action of restoring to a former state or position; the fact of being restored or reinstated. Also *const. to*.

2. *Hist.* The re-establishment of monarchy in England with the return of Charles II in 1660; also, the period marked by this event.

3. The action of restoring a person to health or consciousness; recovery of physical strength.

b. A restorative thing.

4. *Theol.* (Cf. RESTORATION 5.)

Restore (rǐstōᵘ·ɹ), v. Also 5 restour, -oyre. 6 Sc. -oir. [a. OF. restorer, -ir. ristorare : — L. restaurāre : see RESTAUR v.]

I. trans. To give back; to make return or restitution of (anything previously taken away or lost).

Restority. Obs. Also 5 restorite, 6 -ytee. [var. of RESTORATIVE.] A restorative.

Restour, obs. form of RESTORE v.

Restow, v. [RE- 5 a.] To stow again.

Restrain (rǐstrēᵃ·n), v. Forms: 4–7 re-strayne, 4–5 restreyn, 4–6 restreyne, 4–7 restreign; 4 rastrein (5–6 Sc. rastreyne), 6–7 restrayne, restreyne, 5–7 restrayn (6 re-straygne), 5 restrane, 5–6 strain. [a. OF. restrei-g·n-, restrai·gn-, stem of restreindre, restraindre (cf. Prov. restrenher, Sp. restreñir, It. ristringere) : see RESTRINGE v.]

I. trans. To check, hold back, or prevent (a person or thing) from some course of action.

Restorer (rǐstōᵘ·rəɹ). [f. RESTORE v. + -ER¹.] One who re-stores or re-establishes.

Restorement. Obs. [f. RESTORE v. + -MENT.] The act of restoring; restoration, restitution.

Re-sto·re, v. [RE- 5 a.] To store again.

Re·storation, variant of RESTAURY, Obs.

Restoring (rǐstōᵘ·riŋ), vbl. sb. [f. RESTORE v. + -ING¹.] That restores.

Re-strain (rǐ-), v. [RE- 5 a.] To strain again.

Restrainable (rǐstrēᵃ·nǎb'l), a. [f. RESTRAIN v. + -ABLE.] Capable of being restrained.

Restrained (rǐstrēᵃ·nd), ppl. a. [as prec. + -ED¹.] Checked; imprisoned; kept under control; confined; restricted.

Restrainedly (-ědli), adv. [f. prec. + -LY².] With restraint; restrictedly.

Restrainer. [f. RESTRAIN v. + -ER.] One who or that which restrains.

Restraining, vbl. sb. [f. as prec. + -ING¹.] The action of the verb, in various senses.

Restraining, ppl. a. [f. as prec. + -ING².] That restrains or checks; restringent.

Restrainment. Obs. [f. RESTRAIN v. + -MENT (cf. OF. restreignement).] The act of restraining; restraint.

Restraint (rǐstrēᵃ·nt), sb. Also 5–6 re-straynt, 6 -strainte, 5 restreinte, 6–7 restreint, 7 -streynt. [a. OF. restrainte, restrainct masc., verbal sb. f. restraindre to RESTRAIN.]

I. The action of restraining or checking a thing, operation, etc.; an instance of this; a stoppage.

Restrial, a. Her. Obs. [Of obscure origin.] Applied to a living dividing bands which extend to (or include) the point, the colour of the latter being that of the field.

Restrict (rǐstri·kt), v. Also 6–7 restrick. [ad. L. restrict- ppl. stem (cf. next) of restringĕre to RESTRINGE.]

1. trans. To confine (some person or thing) to or within certain limits; to limit or bound.

Restricted (rǐstri·kted), ppl. a. [f. RESTRICT v. + -ED¹.] Limited, confined.

Restriction (rǐstri·kʃən). Also 5 restric-cioun, 5–6 restrictioun, 6 -tion. [ad. L. restrictiōn-em, noun of action f. restring-ĕre to RESTRINGE. Cf. Sp. restriccion, It. ristrizione.]

Restrictionist. [f. prec. + -IST.] One who advocates the restriction of some practice, institution, etc.

Restrictive (rǐstri·ktiv), a. and sb. Also 6 -yf. [ad. L. restrictīv-us, or a. F. restrictif, -ive (14th c. in Godef. Compl.): see RESTRICT v. and -IVE.]

Restrictory, a. Obs. rare—¹. [irreg. f. RESTRICT v. + -ORY.] = prec. A.

Re·strik, obs. form of RESTRICT v.

Restriké, v. Obs. [Re- 5 a.] To strike again (a coin) afresh.

Restring (rǐ-), v. [RE- 5 a.] To string again.

Restringe (rǐstri·ndʒ), v. Obs. [ad. L. restringĕre to bind fast, confine, f. re- RE- + stringĕre to draw tight.]

Restringency. Obs. [f. next: see -ENCY.] The quality or property of being restringent.

Restringent (rǐstri·ndʒent), a. and sb. Obs. [ad. L. restringent-em, pres. pple. of restringĕre: see RESTRINGE v. and -ENT.]

A. adj. Having astringent or binding pro-perties; of an astringent nature; esp. tending to restrain the action of the bowels.

Restringing (continued)

c. Having an astringent taste. *rare*⁻¹.

Restrictive, etc.

Restring (riː-). To string again.

† **Restrigittive**, a.

Restrive (riː-). To strive again.

Restrude: see RESTRIKE v.

Restudy (riː-). To study again.

Restuff (riː-). *trans.* To stuff again or anew. Hence **Restuffing** *vbl. sb.*

Resty, a.² *Obs.* *exc. dial.* Also 6 restye, 6–7 re-, 7–9 resti, 7 -ey, *-y*.

Resty, a.³ *Obs.* A fresh substitution.

Resublimation.

Resublime (riː-). *trans.* To sublime again. Hence **Resubli·med** *ppl. a.*

Resubmission (riː-).

Resubmit (riː-). To submit again.

Resubstantiate (riː-). To change (a thing) back *into* the original form.

Resuccee'd, v. To succeed again.

Resuck (riː-). To suck back again.

Resudation.

Resu·ltate, v. *Obs. rare.*

† **Resuda·tion.** *Obs.*

Result (rizvlt), v. [ad. L. *result-* to spring or leap back, f. re- RE- + *saltare* to leap. So F. *résulter*, Sp. and Pg. *resultar*, It. *resultare*.]

1. *intr.* To arise as a consequence, effect, or conclusion from some action, process, etc.; to end or conclude *in* a specified manner.

† 2. A reflection (of light). Also *fig.* *Obs.*

3. That results, resulting; consequent.

4. To ensue as a result.

† 5. Resulting, resilient.

Resu·ltancy. [See prec. and -ANCY.]

1. = RESULTANCE 3 b.

Resu·ltant, a. (sb.) [ad. L. *resultant-em*, pres. pple. of *resultāre*: see RESULT v. and -ANT. So F. *résultant*, It., Sp., and Pg. *resultante*.]

Result (rizvlt), sb. [ad. L. *resultāt-um*, neut. of *resultāt-us*: see RESULT v. and -ATE.]

Resultance (rizvltăns). Now *rare.* Also 5 -aunce, -ans. [Prob. ad. med.L. *resultantia* (cf. Sp. and Pg. *resultancia*), f. *resultāre*: see RESULT v. and -ANCE.]

Resultful, a. [f. RESULT sb. + -FUL.] Rich or abounding in results. *rare.*

Resulting, *vbl. sb.* [f. RESULT v. + -ING¹.]

Resultive, a. *Obs. rare*⁻¹.

Resu·ltless, a. Devoid of, or without, result; ineffectual.

Resu·mability. [f. next + -ITY.] Capacity for, or possibility of, being resumed.

Resumable, a. [f. RESUME v. + -ABLE.] Capable of being resumed.

Resume (rizi·ūm), v. [ad. L. *resūm-ĕre*, f. re- RE- + *sūm-ĕre* to take up.]

1. *trans.* To assume, put on, or take on self anew (something previously lost, given up, or put aside).

Resume (continued)

5. To repeat (a sentence or word). *rare.*

Resu·mer. *rare.* [f. RESUME v. + -ER¹.] One who resumes.

Résumé (rezᵫme), v. to epitomize. *rare.*

Résumé (rezᵫme), sb. [Fr., pa. pple. of *résumer* to RESUME.] A summary, epitome.

Resu·mmon, v. To summon again.

Resu·mption (rizʊ·mpʃən), n. of action. [ad. L. *resumptiōn-em*, f. *resūmpt-*, ppl. stem of *resūmĕre* to RESUME. So Sp. *resunción*, It. *resunzione*.]

Resu·mptive, a. and sb. [ad. late L. *resumptīv-us* restorative.]

Resu·p. Forms of REASON.

Resu·pinate, a. [ad. L. *resupināt-us*, pa. pple. of *resupināre* to bend back.]

Resu·pination.

Resupine, a. [ad. L. *resupīn-us*.]

Resu·pply, v. To supply again or anew; to provide with a fresh supply.

Resu·rge, v. [ad. L. *resurg-ĕre*: see next.] *intr.* To rise again.

Resu·rgence, sb. The act of rising again. Also *fig.*

Resu·rgent, a. and sb. [ad. L. *resurgent-em*, pres. pple. of *resurgĕre* to RESURGE.]

Resu·rging, *ppl. a.* [f. RESURGE v. + -ING².]

Resurrect (rezŏre·kt), v. [Back-formation from RESURRECTION.]

1. *trans.* To raise (a person) from the dead or from the grave; to restore to life or to view again.

Resurrection (rezŏre·kʃən), sb. [a. F. *résurrection* (12th c.), ad. eccl. L. *resurrectiōn-em*, n. of action, f. *resurrect-*, ppl. stem of *resurgĕre*: see RESURGE.]

Resurrection plant, (a) a Californian plant, *Selaginella lepidophylla*, the dried fronds of which unfold again when moistened; (b) the Rose of Jericho, an Eastern plant having similar properties. Also called *resurrection flower*.

Resurrectionary, a. [f. prec. + -AL.] Relating to, or concerned with, resurrection.

Resurrectioner. [f. RESURRECTION + -ER] 1. Of the nature of resurrection; restorative.

Resurrectionism. [-ISM.] The practice of body-snatching.

Resurrectionist. [f. RESURRECTION + -IST.] 1. An exhumer and stealer of corpses; a resurrection man.

Resurrector. [f. RESURRECT v. + -OR.]

Resure-nder (ri-), v. [RE- 5 a.] To surrender or give up again.

Resure. [L. RESURRECTIONIST *v*.]

Resurvey (ri-), v. [RE- 5 a.] A fresh survey.

Resurvey (ri-), v. [RE- 5 a.] To examine or consider afresh.

Resu·scitate, *pa. pple.* (and *sb.*). *Obs.* [ad. L. *resuscitāt-us*, pa. pple. of *resuscitāre*: see next.]

Resurre·ctionize, v. [-IZE.] *trans.* To resurrect, in various senses.

Resuscitate, *v.* [f. ppl. stem of L. *resuscitāre*, f. RE- + *suscitāre* to raise, revive, etc.]

Resuscitation, *sb.* [ad. L. *resuscitātiōn-em*, n. of action f. *resuscitāre*: see RESUSCITATE.]

Resu·scitative, *a.* (See prec.)

Resuscitator. [f. as prec. + -OR.] One who resuscitates or revives.

Resu·scite, v. *Obs.* [ad. OF. *resusciter* or L. *resuscitāre*.]

Resweat, v. [RE- 5 a.] To sweat again.

Reswell, v. [RE- 5 a.] To swell again.

Ret, v.[1] *Obs.* In 4-5 rette (5 rettyn, rectyn); *pa.* t. 4 retted(e, -id, rett; *pa. pple.* 4 retted, 6 rected; 5 ret, 5-6 rette. [ad. OF. *retter*, *reter*, *retter*.—Prov., Sp., and Pg. *reptar* (mod. Sp. also *retar*).—L. *reputāre*: see REPUTE v. and cf. ARET v.]

Ret, n.[2] Forms: 4-5 rettyn, retyn, 9 ret; 8-6 rayte, 7- rate, *raite*. [Of somewhat obscure history.]

Retable (rĭtā·b'l). *Eccl.* [f. F. *rétable*, *retable* (16th c.), -. Sp. *retablo*, Pg. *retabolo*, -*tavolo*, med.L. *retabulum*.]

Retail, *sb.*[1] [a. AF. *retaille*, *-aile* (12th c.).]

Retail, *sb.*[2] *Obs. rare*[-1]. Retaliation.

Retail (rĭtā·l), v. [f. RETAIL *sb.*[1]]

[Lower section]

Retai·n, *sb. Obs. rare.* [f. the vb.] 1. Retention; retainment.

Retain (rĭtā·n), v. Forms: 5-6 reteign(e, 5 reteygne, 5-7 reteyn(e, 5-7 reteine, 7 reten(e. [f. AF., OF. *retein-*, tonic stem of *retenir*.—L. *retinēre*.]

Retai·nability. [See next and -ITY.] Capability of being retained.

Retai·nable, *a.* [f. RETAIN *v.* + -ABLE.] Capable of being retained.

Reta·inal. [f. RETAIN *v.* + -AL.] *Obs. rare.* In the retinal of the nobility.

Retai·nder. *Obs.* Forms: 5 retein-, 5-6 reteyn(d)er, -ander, 7 reteinder. [f. RETAIN *v.*, app. on the analogy of *attainder*, *remainder*. Cf. RETAINER[2].]

Retainer[1]. [f. RETAIN *v.* + -ER[1].] 1. One who or that which retains or holds; a maintainer, preserver.

Retainer[2] (rĭtā·naz). *Also* 4 reteyn-, retaynour, 6-7 reteyner, 7 -tayner, -teiner. [f. RETAIN *v.* + RET + -ER[4]. Cf.]

Retai·nership. *Obs. rare*[-1]. [f. RETAINER + -SHIP.]

Retai·nment. [f. RETAIN *v.* + -MENT.] 1. Retention; retaining.

Reta·ke (rī-), v. [RE- 5 a.]

Retaken, *ppl. a.* [f. RE- + TAKEN.]

Reta·ker. [f. prec. + -ER¹.] One who retakes.

Reta·king, vbl. sb. [f. RETAKE v. + -ING¹.] The action of the verb RETAKE in various senses.

Retaliate (rĭtæ·li̯e̯it), v.¹ [f. ppl. stem of late L. retāliāre (Gellius), f. re- RE- + tālis such-like: cf. tālio, -ōnis a punishment or penalty similar to the injury done.]

1. trans. To requite, repay in kind, make return for.

Retaliation (rĭtæli̯e̯i·ʃən). [See RETALIATE v.¹ and -ION.]

1. The action of retaliating; the return of like for like; repayment in kind; requital, reprisal.

Reta·liative, a. [f. RETALIATE v. + -IVE.] Tending to, or of the nature of, retaliation; vindictive, revengeful.

Reta·liator. [-OR 2.] One who retaliates.

Reta·liatory, a. Of the nature of, or pertaining to, retaliation.

Retal·iate, v.² [ad. L. retaliāre.] Retaliation.

Reta·liation, v.

Reta·lion.

Reta·lly, v. Obs. rare—¹.

Retama. [a. Sp. retama, ad. Arab. retám, pl. retaim.]

Retard (rĭtɑ̈·ɹd), sb. [a. F. retard (13th c., — Sp. and Pg. retardar, It. ritardare), f. retarder.]

Retard (rĭtɑ̈·ɹd), v. [a. F. retarder (13th c., — Sp., Pg. retardar, It. ritardare; or ad. L. retardāre, f. re- RE- + tardus slow.]

Retardation (rītāɹde̯i·ʃən). [ad. L. retardātiōn-em, n. of action f. retardāre to RETARD.]

Retar·date, a. Obs. rare. [ad. L. retardāt-us, pa. pple. of retardāre to RETARD.]

Retar·dative, a. [= F. retardatif, It. ritardativo: see RETARDATE v. and -IVE.] Tending or having power to retard.

Retar·datory, a. [f. prec. and -ORY.]

Retarded, ppl. a. [f. RETARD v. + -ED¹.] Checked; impeded; delayed.

Retar·dent, a. [ad. L. retardent-em, pr. pple.] Retardant.

Retar·der. [f. RETARD v. + -ER¹.]

Retar·ding, vbl. sb. [f. as prec. + -ING¹.] The action of RETARD v. in various senses.

Retar·ding, ppl. a. [f. as prec. + -ING².]

Retar·dingly, adv.

Retar·dment. [= F. retardement, Sp. retardamiento, It. ritardamento: see RETARD v. and -MENT.] The act of retarding; retardation; delay, check.

Retch (retʃ, rītʃ), v.¹ [Var. of REACH v.²]

Retch (retʃ), v.² [f. REACH v.¹, of which form the pron. (retʃ) properly belongs.]

Retch, sb.¹

Retch, sb.²

Rete (rī·tī). Pl. retia (rī·ʃĭa). [L. rēte a net, net-work.]

2. Anat. **Rete mirabile,** an elaborate network or plexus of blood-vessels.

Retea·ch, v. [RE- 5 a.] To teach again.

Reteck. [RE- 5 a.] One who retakes.

Rete·ne (retī·nē). Chem. [f. Gr. ῥητίνη resin + -ENE.] A hydro-carbon, polymeric with benzene.

Rete·ntion.

† Rete·cious, a.

† Rete·ction. Obs. rare. [ad. late L. retēctiōn-em, noun of action f. retĕgĕre to uncover, disclose.]

Retei·n, v.

Rete·nue, v. Obs. rare—¹. [a. F. retenue.]

Retene (retī·n). [a. F. retēne.]

† Rete·nt, sb. rare. [ad. L. retent-um, neut.]

Retention (rĭte·nʃən). [a. OF. retencion, -cioun, -sioun (F. rétention), ad. L. retentiōn-em.]

Retenti·onist, one who advocates the retention of something.

† Rete·ntist, one who advocates the retention of territory.

Retentive (rĭte·ntĭv), a. and sb. [a. OF. retentif, retentive, ad. L. retentiv-us.]

Retentively, adv. [f. as prec. + -LY².]

Retentiveness. [f. as prec. + -NESS.]

Rete·ntivity. [f. as prec. + -ITY.]

† Rete·nue, v.

Retention, sb. obs. variant of RETINUE.

Retire, obs. variant of RETIRE v.

Reto·rt.

Retothe, obs. form of ARITHMETIC.

Rethe, obs. variant of RATHE.

Rethe, a. (exc. Sc.)

Rethe·nesse, Obs. exc. Sc.

Rethmus, var. of RHYTHM.

Rethor, Rethoric, Rethorie, etc., obs. ff. RHETOR, RHETORIC, RHETORY, etc.

Rethrogate, obs. form of RETROGRADE v.

Rethrone, var. RE-ENTHRONE.

Reti·arius (rī̆ʃĭe̯·rĭɒs). [L. rētiārius, f. rēte net.] A Roman gladiator who carried a net with which to entangle his adversary.

Top row (pp. 569–570)

RETIARY.

Retiary (rīˈtjări). a. [as prec.]

Retiary (rīˈtjări), sb. [f. next and -ARY.]

Reticence (reˈtisĕns). Also 7, 9 -ence.

Reticent (reˈtisĕnt), a. [ad. L. reticent-em, pres. pple. of reticēre, f. re- RE- + tacēre to be silent.]

Reticency.

Reticle (reˈtik'l). [ad. L. rēticulum, dim. of rēte net: cf. RETICULE.]

Reticular (rēˈtikiŭlăr), a.

Reticulate (rēˈtikiŭlāt), a.

Reticulate (rēˈtikiŭlāt), v.

Reticulated (rēˈtikiŭlātĕd), ppl. a.

Reticulation.

Reticulato-, combining form of RETICULATE.

Reticule (reˈtikiŭl). [a. F. réticule, ad. L. rēticulum: see RETICULUM and -CULE.]

Reticuled.

Reticulo-, combining form of RETICULUM.

Reticulose.

Reticulum (rēˈtikiŭlŏm). [a. L. rēticulum, dim. of rēte net: cf. RETICULE.]

Retiform (rīˈtifōrm), a. [ad. mod.L. rētiform-is, f. rēte net: see -FORM.]

Retin-, combining form of RETINA.

Retina (reˈtĭnă). [a. med.L. retina, F. retine (1314).]

Retinacle.

Retinaculum (retināˈkiŭlŏm). Pl. -ula. [L.]

Retinal (reˈtĭnăl), a. [f. RETINA + -AL.]

Retinalite (reˈtĭnălăit). Min. [f. Gr. retine resin + -LITE.]

Retinasphalt (retināsˈfalt). Also -asphalt-.

Re-tinker (rī-). [RE- 5 a.]

Re-tinned (rī-).

Retinite (reˈtĭnăit). Min.

Retinoid (reˈtĭnoid), a.

Retinoscope.

Retinoscopic.

Retinoscopy.

Retinue (reˈtĭniŭ), sb.

Bottom row (pp. 571–572)

RETINUE.

Retinue (reˈtĭniŭ), sb. [a. OF. retenue, fem. of retenu, pa. pple. of retenir to RETAIN.]

Retiracy (rītăiˈrăsi). U.S.

Retiral (rītăiˈrăl). [f. RETIRE v. + -AL.]

Retire (rītăiˈăr), v. [a. F. retirer, -er, f. re- RE- + tirer to draw: cf. Sp. and Pg. retirar, It. ritirare.]

Retire (rītăiˈăr), sb.

Retired (rītăiˈărd), ppl. a. [f. prec. + -ED.]

RETIRE. / RETIRE. (pp. 571–572 continued)

RETIRE. RETIRED.

RETIREDLY.	573	RETORQUED.	RETORRID.	574	RETORT.

Retiredly, *adv.* [f. prec. + -LY².] In a retired or secluded manner; privately.

Retiredness. Also 7 retyr- [-NESS.] The state or quality of being retired; privacy, seclusion; reserve. (Very common in the 17th century.)

Retirement (rĭtəiə·rment). Also 6–7 retyre-.

Retiring (rĭtəiə·riŋ), *vbl. sb.* [-ING¹.]

Retiring, *ppl. a.* [-ING².]

Retiringness. [f. prec. + -NESS.]

Retirk, *v.* [Re- 5 a.] To decimate again.

Retomb, *v.* [Re- 5 a.] To entomb again.

Retorician, Retorik, obs. ff. RHETORICIAN, RHETORIC. **Retorne**, obs. f. RETURN.
Retornel, obs. f. RITORNELLO.

† Retoqued, *ppl. a.* Obs.⁻¹ [f. F. retorquer or L. retorquēre: see RETORT v.]
Turned backwards.

Retorsion (rĭtɔ·ɹʃən). Now *rare*. [a. F. retorsion (13–14th c.), or med.L. retorsiōn-em, var. of retortiōn-em RETORTION. So Sp. retorsion, It. ritorsione.] Retortion (of an argument, etc.).

Retort (rĭtɔ·ɹt), *sb.*¹ [f. RETORT v.]

Retort (rĭtɔ·ɹt), *sb.*² [a. F. retorte, pple. stem of retordre, L. re- RE- + torquēre to twist, turn.]

Retort (rĭtɔ·ɹt), *v.* [ad. L. retort-, ppl. stem of retorquēre to twist or turn back, hurl back, retaliate, f. re- RE- + torquēre to twist.]

I. 1. To throw or hurl back (a weapon); to turn back (a blow) upon the striker.

2. To make return (of something done to one, esp. an injury); to repay or pay back; to requite by retaliation.

3. *trans.* To make return of, give back in kind; to return (a charge, accusation, epithet, etc.). Freq. const. *on*.

4. To bend or turn back; to fold back, reflect.

Retort (rĭtɔ·ɹt), *v.*² [f. RETORT sb.²]

To purify (an amalgam, mercury, etc.) by subjecting to heat in a retort.

RETORT.	575	RETOUR.	RETOUR.	576	RETRACT.

† Retort, *pa. pple.* Obs.⁻¹ [ad. L. retort-us, pa. pple. of retorquēre: see prec.]

Retortable, *a.* [f. RETORT v.¹ + -ABLE.] Capable or admitting of retortion.

Retorted (rĭtɔ·ɹtĕd), *ppl. a.*¹ [f. RETORT v.¹]

Retorted, *ppl. a.*² [f. RETORT sb.²]
Refined or purified in a retort.

Retorter¹, *rare.* [RETORT v.¹ + -ER¹.] One who retorts.

Retorter² [f. RETORT v.²] One employed in retorting metals.

Retortion (rĭtɔ·ɹʃən). Also 6 -RETORTABLE.

Retorting, *vbl. sb.*¹ [f. RETORT v.¹] The action of bending or throwing back, etc.

Retorting, *vbl. sb.*² [f. RETORT v.²]
The action of treating in a retort.

Retortion (rĭtɔ·ɹʃən). [ad. med.L. retortiōn-em, noun of action: see RETORT v.¹ and cf. RETORSION.]
1. The action or fact of bending or turning backwards; an instance of this.

Retorial, obs. f. RETORT v.¹

Retortive (rĭtɔ·ɹtiv), *a. rare.* [f. L. retort-: see RETORT v.¹ + -IVE.]

Retorture, *v.* [RE- 5 a.]

Retoss, *v.* [RE- 5.] To toss back or again (esp. in phr. *tossed and retossed*).

Retouch (rĭtˈtʌtʃ), *sb.* [Prob. ad. F. retouche.]

Retouch (rĭtˈtʌtʃ), *v.* [ad. F. retoucher: see RE- and TOUCH v.]
1. *trans.* To touch again with a view to improving; to amend or improve by fresh touches; to touch up.

Retouching (rĭtʌ·tʃiŋ), *vbl. sb.* [f. prec.]

Retour (rĭtū·ɹ), *sb.* Chiefly *Sc.* [the sb.]

Retour (rĭtū·ɹ), *v.* Chiefly *Sc.* [the vb.]

Retrace (rĭtrē·s), *v.*¹ Also 6 *Sc.* retrak- *trahir* to draw, pull. So F. retracer.]
1. *trans.* To draw or pull (something) back.

Retrace (rĭtrē·s), *v.*² [f. RE- 5 + TRACE v.]
1. *trans.* To trace back to an origin or source; to trace through preceding stages.

Retract, v.

Retractable, a.

Retractation.

Retractatively, adv.

Retracted, ppl. a.

Retractible, a.

Retractile (rɪˈtraktil, -aɪl), a.

Retractility.

Retraction.

Retractive, a.

Retractor.

Retradition.

Re-tradition.

Re-traho, v.

Retrahent, a.

Retrahibition.

Retraict, sb.

Retrait, sb.

Retrait, v.

Retraitment.

Retraite.

Retraxit.

Retray, v.

Retreat, sb.

Retreat, v.

Retreatant.

Retreated, ppl. a.

Retreatful, a.

Retreating, vbl. sb.

Retreatment.

Re-treatment.

Re-treat, v.

Retreater.

Retrench, v.

Retrenched, ppl. a.

Retrenchment.

RETROGRADE.

6. As *quasi-adv.* In a backward or reverse direction.

2. A backward movement or tendency. *rare.*

Retrograd, obs. form of RETROGRADE *v.*

Retrograde (re'trogrēd, rītro-), *v.* [ad. L. *retrōgradī* or *retrōgradāre* (hence F. *rétrograder*, Sp. and Pg. *retrogradar*; It. *retro-, ritrogradare*); f. *retrō + gradī* to go.]

1. *trans.* To turn back, reverse, revert; to make, or cause to become, retrograde. Now *rare.*

2. *intr. astr.* Of the planets, etc.: To go backward (in apparent motion) in the zodiac; to seem to travel from east to west.

3. Of *gout*: To become retrocedent. *Obs.*

4. To move backwards, to take a backward course; to retire, recede, etc. Now *rare.*

Retrogradient. *rare⁻¹.* [ad. L. *retrōgradient-em*, pres. pple. of *retrōgradī*.] Astr. = RETROGRADE *a.* 1.

Retrogradism. *rare⁻¹.* [f. RETROGRADE *a.* + -ISM.] Adoption of reactionary principles.

Retrogradation. *Obs. rare.* [f. as prec.: see -ATION.]

Retrogradient. One who retrogrades.

Retrogress (rītro-, retrogres), *v.* [f. L. *retrogress-*, ppl. stem of *retrogradī* to RETROGRADE: see *intr.* To move backwards; to go back.

Retrogression (rītro-, retrogre'ʃən). [ad. L. type *retrōgressiōn-em*: see RETRO- and -GRESSION.]

1. *Astr.* = RETROGRADATION 1.

2. Movement in a backward or reverse direction. In early use *Math.*

3. The action or fact of going back in respect of development or condition; return to a less advanced state or stage; a case or instance of this.

b. Path. The disappearance of an eruption.

Retrogressional, *a.* Of a retrograde character.

Retrogressionist. One who is inclined to be retrograde.

Retrogressive (rītro-, retrogre'siv), *a.* and *sb.* [f. as RETROGRESS *v.* + -IVE.]

1. Working back in investigation or reasoning.

2. Characterized by, or situated at the back of, or behind, the pharynx.

Retrophraged, *a.* *Anat.* and *Path.* [See RETRO- 3 *b.*] Occurring or situated at the back of the pharynx.

Retropulsion. *See* RETRO- and PULSION. So F. *rétropulsion.*

1. Transference of an external disease to some internal part or organ. (Cf. REPULSION 2 *b.*)

2. *Retrogression*: tending to return to an inferior state; going back to a worse condition.

Retroversion (rītrovəɹ'ʃən). [ad. L. type *retroversiōn-em*: see RETRO- and VERSION *a.*]

1. A turning backward.

2. *Path.* The fact of (the uterus) becoming retroverted.

Retrovert (rītrovəɹt), *v.* [ad. L. *retrovert-ere*, f. RETRO- + *vertēre* to turn.] *intr.* and *trans.* To turn back.

Retroverted, ppl. *a.* Turned backwards; reverted.

Retrusion (rītrū'ʒən). *rare.* [ad. L. type *retrūsiōn-em*, n. of action from *retrūdēre* to thrust back.] The action of putting back or to an earlier date.

Retry (rī-), *v.* [RE- 5 *a.*] *trans.* To try again, in various senses of the verb.

Rette, obs. form of RATE *v.*²

RETURN.

Retteral, obs. form of RATE *v.*²

Retury. One engaged in retting.

Return (rītə·ɹn), *v.* Also 4-7 retorn, 5-6 retorne. [a. AF. *returner*, retorner, = OF. *retorner, returner* (mod.F. *retourner*), f. RE- + *torner*, tourner to TURN.]

I. *intr.* 1. The act of coming back to or from a place, position, or condition; coming back; arrival to come back.

II. 4. A side or part which falls away, usually at right angles, from the front or direct line of any work or structure.

b. The fact of bringing value in exchange.

I. The act of coming back again.

Supplement, p. 3873; Corrigenda, p. 4092; Spurious words, p. 4093; Books quoted, p. 4094

RETURN. | 589 | RETURN. | 590 | RETURN.

RE-TURN. | 591 | RETUSION. | RETUSO-. | 592 | REVALING.

| REVALENTA. | 593 | REVEILLE. | REVEILLE. | 594 | REVELATION. |

Revalenta. ... **Revalescence** ... **Revalescent** ... **Revalidate** ... **Revaluation** ... **Revalue** ... **Revamp** ... **Revary** ... **Revay** ... **Reveal**, v. ... **Reveal**, sb. ... **Revealable** ... **Revealableness** ... **Revealed** ... **Revealer** ... **Revealing** ... **Revealingly** ... **Reveille** ... **Reveille-matin** ... **Revel**, v. ... **Revel**, sb. ... **Revelability** ... **Revelable** ... **Revelant** ... **Revelation**

| REVELATIONAL. | 595 | REVENGE. | REVENGE. | 596 | REVENGEMENT |

Revelational ... **Revelationist** ... **Revelative** ... **Revelator** ... **Revelatory** ... **Revel-dread** ... **Revelent** ... **Reveller** ... **Revelling** ... **Revellous** ... **Revelly** ... **Revelment** ... **Revelous** ... **Revel-rout** ... **Revenant** ... **Revend** ... **Revendicate** ... **Revendication** ... **Revenewe** ... **Revenge** ... **Revengeable** ... **Revengeance** ... **Revengeful** ... **Revengefully** ... **Revengefulness** ... **Revengeless** ... **Revengement**

Revenger (rĕvĕnʤạr). Also 6 Sc. -eoure, -ear. [f. REVENGE v. + -ER. Cf. F. *revancheur*, + *revenchenr*, *revangeur*.] One who revenges; an avenger.

Revengeress, [f. prec. + -ESS.] A female revenger; an avengeress.

Revenging, *vbl. sb.* [f. REVENGE v.] The action of the verb, in various senses; vengeance.

Revenging, *ppl. a.* [f. REVENGE v.] That revenges; avenging.

Revengingly, *adv.* [f. prec. + -LY.] In a revenging manner.

†**Revengive**, *a. Obs. rare⁻¹.* [irreg. f. RE-VENGE v. + -IVE.] Revenging; vindictive.

†**Revent**, *sb.¹* [RE- 5 a.] To vent again.

†**Revent**, *sb.²* [RE-5 c.] *trans.* To provide (a cannon) with a new vent.

†**Revenuable**, *a. Obs. rare⁻¹.* [f. next + -ABLE.] A possible source of revenue.

Revenue (revĕniū). Forms: 4-6 revenu, 5- revenue ... [a. F. *revenu*, sb.]

†**Revengeance**, *Obs.* form of REVENGE *sb.*

Revenue office.

Reverb (rĕvə̆rb), *v.* [irreg. ad. L. *reverber-are*] ...

of this Lake is worth three hundred thousand duckets a-yeere ...

Reverberance.

Reverberant (rĕvə̆rbərănt), *a.* [a. F. *rever-berant*] ... Reverberating; resonant.

Reverberate, *v.* [f. L. *reverber-are*.]

Reverberate, *ppl. a.* [ad. L. *reverberat-us*.]

Reverberated, *ppl. a.* [f. the verb + -ED.]

Reverberating, *ppl. a.* [f. the verb + -ING².]

Reverberation (rĕvə̆rbərēiʃən). [ad. OF. *reverberation* (mod.F. *réverbération*)]

Reverberative, *a. rare.* [f. L. *reverber-are*] Reverberating.

Reverberator (rĕvə̆rbərēitər). [-OR 2.] A reflector; a reflecting lamp.

Reverberatory (rĕvə̆rbərătəri), *a.* and *sb.* [f. as prec.] So F. *réverbératoire*, It. *reverberatorio*.

Reverbitory, obs. form of REVERBERATORY *sb.*

Reverdure, *v. rare⁻¹.* To clothe again with verdure.

Revere (rĭvīəʳ), *v.* [ad. F. *révérer* or L. *reverēri*, f. re- + *verēri* to fear.]

Reverence (revĕrĕns), *sb.* Forms: 3-4 reuer-ence; 4-6 reu-, reverens; 3 -ense; 5-6 Sc. reu-, -erens ... [a. OF. *reverence* (mod.F. *révérence*)]

Reverence (revĕrĕns), *v.* [f. REVERENCE *sb.*]

Reverencer (revĕrĕnsəʳ), a respecter of some thing.

Reverend (revĕrĕnd), *a.* and *sb.* [a. F. *révérend*, fem. -ende, or ad. L. *reverend-us*, gerundive of *reverēri* to REVERE.]

pilgrim..flings crutch away, Or else appends it to the reverend heap Beneath you.

†**b.** Sacred, hallowed, holy. *Obs.*

1563 *Homilies* II. (1859) 445 When thou goest up to the reverend Communion to be satisfied with spiritual meats. 1631 HOWES *Stow's Annales* 999/1 Diuers Church-yards new layd apart, dedicated for reuerend places to bury the dead. 1693 CHEECH in Dryden *Juvenal* xiii. (1697) 332 Bold Sacriledge..destroys a Shrine, The Reverend Goblets, and the ancient Plate.

4. Connected with, characteristic of, belonging to, the clergy.

1645 MILTON *Tetrach.* Wks. 1851 IV. 229 As there is nothing more violent and boistrous then a reverend ignorance in fear to be convicted. 1742 (*title*) Ecclesiastical Transactions; or a Collection of Reverend Jokes. 1748 SMOLLETT *Rod. Rand.* lxii, This was a man in years, who wore a reverend periwig. 1842 MRS. BROWNING *Gk. Chr. Poets* Poems (1904) 603/1 So that reverend brows grew dark to hear women with musical voices sing them softly.

5. = REVERENT *a.* 2. Now somewhat *rare.* (In common use *c* 1590–1660.)

15.. in *Dunbar's Poems* (1893) 328 Inclyne befoir the Cristin Conquerour,..With reverend feir doun on ȝour facis ly. 1555 EDEN *Decades* (Arb.) 65 The reverende and thanckefull antiquite was accustomed to esteme those men as goddes. 1576 FLEMING *Panopl. Epist.* 116 There is in him singular honestie,..passing liberalitie towardes straungers, and plentie of reuerend behauiour. 1615 W. HULL *Mirr. Maiestie* 33 The minde beholdeth God with..ioy of heart, and reuerend admiration. 1686 PARR *Life Ussher* 85 From whence you may observe the reverend esteem he had for our Liturgy. 1748 RICHARDSON *Clarissa* (1811) III. 364 To see multitudes of well-appearing people all joining in one reverend act. 1796 R. BAGE *Hermstrong* xlv, Pray, good sir, said Miss Fluart, with a reverend curtsey [etc.]. 1818 SCOTT *Hrt. Midl.* xxxii, 'Ay, ay, we'se ha' reverend care on thee..', answered the man of constituted authority. 1855 FROUDE in *Oxford Ess.* 54 When nature shall be studied in a more reverend spirit. 1874 PUSEY *Lenten Serm.* 90 That reverend awe, amid which by God's grace we are..to work out our own salvation.

Hence **Re·verendize** *v.* (*nonce-wd.*)

1841 EMERSON in *Corr. Carlyle & Emerson* I. lvi. 320 You see the bookseller reverendizes me notwithstanding your laudable perseverance to adorn me with profane titles.

Reverendly (re·vĕrĕndli), *adv.* [f. prec. + -LY².]

†**1.** = REVERENTLY *adv. Obs.*

c 1375 *Sc. Leg. Saints* ii. (*Paul*) 396 Sone with worschipe þe body þai enclusit full reuerendly. *c* 1470 *Gol. & Gaw.* 331 Ressaue him reuerendly, as resoun in lyis. 1555 EDEN *Decades* (Arb.) 215 Men whom they reuerendely esteme. 1635 HEYLIN *Sabbath* (1636) II. 90 Reverendly kneeling on their knees, when they received the Sacrament of the Lords Supper. 1689 HICKERINGILL *Ceremony-Monger* i, My crafty Ceremony-Monger..passes most religiously for one of the Order, and Reverendly with a Mask does his Business. 1721 AMHERST *Terræ Fil.* No. 47 (1726) 252 Every undergraduate is bound to pay all becoming deference to a bachelor of arts..by..saluting him very reverendly.

2. In a way, to a degree, that inspires reverence.

a 1640 MASSINGER, etc. *Old Law* IV. ii, Thou'rt a man of sorrow, But reverendly becom'st it. 1699 GARTH *Dispensary* II. 19 Here, Mummies lay most reverendly stale.

Re·verendness. *rare*⁻¹. [f. as prec. + -NESS.] = REVERENTNESS b.

1639 F. ROBARTS *God's House & Service* ix. 65 By the reverendnesse of his behaviour in the worship of God.

Re·verendship. [f. as prec. + -SHIP.] Reverend or clerical character or standing. In early use with *your*, as a form of address.

1609 [BP. W. BARLOW] *Answ. Nameless Cath.* 203 Either your Reuerendships brother, or your Reuerend Brother. 1653 CHISENHALE *Cath. Hist.* Ep. Ded., And withal, give your Reverendships a view of the wilde Thistles that bear no Figgs. 1739 *Let.* in Whitefield *Life & Jrnls.* (1756) 222, I discouraged it before your Reverendship came to this town. 1870 *Pall Mall G.* 19 Aug. 5 A clergyman writing to a stranger should notify his reverendship in some manner, but how to do it is not clear.

Reverent (re·vĕrĕnt), *a.* [In sense 1, a. OF. *reverent* for *reverend*, or after med. L. *reverentissimus* = *reverendissimus*. In sense 2, ad. L. *reverentem*, pres. pple. of *reverērī* to REVERE: cf. Sp. and Pg. *reverente*, It. *re-*, *riverente*.]

1. = REVEREND *a.*, in various uses. Now *rare.* (Very common in 16–17th cent.)

c 1380 WYCLIF *Sel. Wks.* II. 229 Þat þe pope wole be clepid 'moost hooly fadir' here, and bishop 'moost reverent' man! *c* 1400 MAUNDEV. *Trav.* (1839) xxi. 230 In alle the remenant of the World, ne myghte a man fynde a more reverent man, ne highere in worschipe. *c* 1447 *Shillingford's Lett.* (Camden) 133 The suyt of the reverent fader in God Edmond Bysshop of Excestre. 1533 MORE *Apol.* 81 b, The sacred prynces and prestes. Agaynste any of whyche two reuerent orders [etc.]. 1584 *Mirr. Mag.* 36 Reuerent personages were in danger of dishonour, and innocentes in hazarde of death. 1615 G. SANDYS *Trav.* 216 This once famous Tyrus is now no other then an heape of ruines, yet haue they a reuerent respect. 1662 COKAINE *Ovid* III. ii, The more the merrier, my reverent Mo[ther]. 1796 MOSER *Hermit of Caucasus* I. 98 No harm is intended to the reverent sage of the mountain. 1860 WARTER *Seaboard* II. 443 Preach as did John Wesley at Winchelsea beneath some reverent tree.

2. Characterized by, exhibiting or feeling, reverence; deeply respectful.

1486 *Bk. St. Albans, Her.* a iv b, To be gracious to his presoner, to be reuerent and faythfull to his god. 1509 FISHER *Funeral Serm. C'tess Richmond* Wks. (1876) 302 He was herde of almyghtye god in his prayer and askynge.., for his reuerente behauoure. 1542 UDALL *Erasm. Apoph.* 80 b, Diogenes had muche reuerente attendaunce dooen to hym by the saied children. 1632 J. HAYWARD tr. *Biondi's Eromena* I. 38 Putting then his hat off in a reverent manner, he proceeded. 1667 MILTON *P. L.* III. 349 Lowly reverent Towards either Throne they bow. 1692 E. WALKER tr. *Epictetus' Mor.* xxxvii, 'Tis not likely you should have this Sense, These reverent Notions of their Providence. 1820 SHELLEY *Hymn Merc.* lv, Hermes and Apollo reverent stood Before Jove's throne. 1869 McLAREN *Serm.* Ser. II. x. 189 We shall exclaim with..more reverent wonder, 'What is man..that Thou visitest him?'

b. Const. *of* (the object revered).

1858 HAWTHORNE *Fr. & It. Note-bks.* II. 4 Reverent of the human soul. 1869 LOWELL *Cathedr.* 326, I entered, reverent of whatever shrine Guards piety and solace for my kind. 1890 HALL CAINE *Bondman* II. xiii, This rude chamber so reverent of law.

c. *U.S.* (See quot.)

1859 BARTLETT *Dict. Amer.* (ed. 2) 364 *Reverent*, strong; as, 'reverent whiskey', i.e. not diluted.

†**Re·verent,** *v. Obs. rare.* [f. prec., or by misreading of *-ence* as *-ente.*] *trans.* To reverence.

1565 *King Daryus* (Brandl) 698 We reuerent thee with fauour great For this thy foode and precyous meat. 1567 *Reg. Privy Council Scot.* I. 543 That thai..obey, serve, and reverent his Hienes.

Reverential (revĕre·nʃăl), *a.* (and *sb.*). [ad. med.L. **reverentiālis*, f. L. *reverentia* reverence: see -AL. So F. *révérenciel*, †*reverential*, Sp. and Pg. *reverencial*, It. *re-*, *riverenziale*.]

1. Of the nature of, inspired or characterized by, reverence; reverent.

c 1555 HARPSFIELD *Divorce Hen. VIII* (Camden) 148 He did it for a reverential fear he had of his father. *a* 1631 DONNE *Poems* (1650) 4 Wilt thou say. that oaths made in reverentiall feare of love..any may forsweare? 1676 GLANVILL *Ess. Philos. & Relig.* I. 26 Their Progress hath not been retarded by this reverential awe of former Discoveries. 1714 R. FIDDES *Pract. Disc.* II. 150 A filial and reverential fear of God is necessary. 1797 MRS. RADCLIFFE *Italian* xx, He was rather to be looked up to with reverential admiration. 1826 SCOTT *Woodst.* i, Their behaviour in the church was any thing but reverential or edifying. 1855 MACAULAY *Hist. Eng.* xix. IV. 377 The members..returned an answer in reverential and affectionate language. 1876 FREEMAN *Norm. Conq.* V. xxiv. 388 To change this reverential preference for the kingly stock into a definite rule of hereditary descent.

†**2.** = DIMISSORY *a.* 2. *Obs. rare*⁻¹.

1570 FOXE *A. & M.* (ed. 2) 1518/2 Desiring instantly.., accordyng to the lawes, letters reuerenciall or demissories, to bee geuen and deliuered vnto me in this behalfe.

3. Inspiring reverence; venerable, reverend. *rare.*

1654 GAYTON *Pleas. Notes* III. vi. 106 The Reverentiall Lady Meredina, and many more of her traine. 1656 *Artif. Handsom.* 187 Of which [a] fatherly, prolixe and reverentiall beard is a solemne sign and majestick Embleme. 1790 UMFREVILLE *Hudson's Bay* 24 Innumerable stars.., added to the beautiful appearance of the moon, make a most reverential and splendid appearance. 1804 EUGENIA DE ACTON *Tale without Title* II. 133 The office of a spiritual instructor..being so endearing as well as reverential.

b. *sb. pl.* Those attributes or qualities which command respect. *nonce-use.*

1740–1 RICHARDSON *Pamela* IV. 301 If she would lay Claim to her Reverentials, as I may say, and not endeavour to conceal her Age.

Hence **Reverentia·lity.**

1835 SIR H. TAYLOR in *Corr.* (1888) 68, I laughed inwardly at the reverentiality of the Editor of 'Blackwood'.

Reverentially (revĕre·nʃăli), *adv.* [f. prec. + -LY².] In a reverential manner; reverently.

1657 THORNLEY tr. *Longus' Daphnis & Chloe* 50 They would sit down by them reverentially in the Cave. 1664 H. MORE *Myst. Iniq.* viii. 24 Thus royally adorning and reverentially courting his Ape. *a* 1751 BOLINGBROKE *Ess., Hum. Knowledge* Wks. 1754 III. 459 He [Plato] made the system..as absurdly as many others, but more reverentially toward the supreme Being. 1834 L. RITCHIE *Wand. by Seine* 110 If the traveller is a Protestant, let him bend his head reverentially. 1881 *Macm. Mag.* XLV. 114/1 Not a voice but spoke lovingly and reverentially of him.

Revere·ntialness. [f. as prec. + -NESS.] The quality of being reverential.

1854 *Tait's Mag.* XXI. 520 Those essays..will be admired for the..reverentialness and sanctity of the spirit that breathes through them. 1890 *Spectator* 5 Apr., It suggests a total absence, not of reverentialness in the writer, but of the very capacity for being reverential.

Reverently (re·vĕrĕntli), *adv.* [f. REVERENT *a.* + -LY².] In a reverent manner; with reverence or profound respect.

1382 WYCLIF *Eccl.* viii. 12, I kneȝ that ther was good to men dredende God, that reuerentli dreden the face of hym. 1393 LANGL. *P. Pl.* C. IX. 44 In heuene..He worth raþer receyued and reuerentloker sette. *c* 1400 LOVE *Bonavent. Mirr.* (1908) 24 Gabriel..vppon his knees knelynge and.. reuerently bowynge. *c* 1489 CAXTON *Sonnes of Aymon* xvii. 397 They saluted hym reverently. 1538 STARKEY *England* I. ii. 55 Gyuyng also reuerently to theyr pryncys and lordys al humbul seruyce. 1599 NASHE *Lenten Stuffe* Wks. (Grosart) V. 228 Not any where is the word seuerer practised, the preacher reuerentlier obserued and honoured. 1635 A. STAFFORD *Fem. Glory* 143 Reverently and intentively look on him who descended from Heaven to Earth. 1688 PRIOR *Ode Exodus iii.* 95 Low, reverently low, Make thy stubborn Knowledge bow. 1792 BURKE *Let. to Sir H. Langrishe* Wks. I. 557 If the subject think so highly and reverently of the sovereign authority, as not to claim any thing of right. 1842 MIALL in *Nonconf.* II. 2 An authority to which sceptres must reverently bow. 1871 TYNDALL *Fragm. Sci.* (1879) II. vii. 94 It is the inner works of the universe which science reverently uncovers.

Re·verentness. *rare.* [f. REVERENT *a.* 1.] †**a.** Reverend personality or character. *Obs.* **b.** The quality of being reverent.

1566 STAPLETON *Ret. Untr. Jewel* IV. 36 Bicause your Reuerentnes shall easely see that this is not defined. 1584 *Mirr. Mag.* 25 b, Places, of much Honour,..as well, in respect of the Reuerentnesse of the Personages, which gouerne them, as (also) for the exercise of the Lawes.

Reverer (rɪvɪ⁰·rəɹ). [f. REVERE *v.* + -ER¹.] One who reveres; a reverent admirer.

1674 *Govt. Tongue* iii. 30 The Jews were such scrupulous reverers of it. 1825 COLERIDGE *Aids Refl.* (1848) I. 166 As often as I read what every reverer of Holy Writ..ought to read, his admirable *Vindiciæ Hebraicæ*. 1859 MEREDITH *R. Feverel* xxxviii, The reverer of the Royal Martyr. 1884 *Manch. Exam.* 27 Dec. 6/1 Upon which..the reverer of the poetic past might hang a serious homily.

Reverie (re·vĕri, re·vĕrī), *sb.* Forms: 4–5 reuerye, 5 -errye, -eri, 6 -ery; 5–6 reu-, reveray; 7– reverie, 8 réverie, rêverie, 8–9 revery; also 7–8 resuerie (8 resuery), resverie, -very (7 -fery). [In early use a. OF. *reverie* rejoicing, revelry, wantonness, wildness, rage, f. *rever* to revel, act or speak wildly: cf. RAVE *v.*¹ In 17th c. readopted from the later F. forms *resverie*, *rêverie*. The fully Anglicized form *revery* is comparatively rare.]

†**1. a.** A state of joy or delight. *Obs. rare*⁻¹.

The French text in Méon's ed. has *reverdie*, employed in an unusual sense, for which Chaucer may have read or substituted the more usual *reverie*.

a 1366 CHAUCER *Rom. Rose* 720 The swetnesse of her melodye Made al myne herte in reuerye [*Thynne* reuelrye].

†**b.** Wantonness; wildness. *Obs. rare.*

c 1386 CHAUCER *Reeve's T.* 85 And oonly for hire myrthe and reuerye Vp on the wardeyn bisily they crye. 1535 STEWART *Cron. Scot.* II. 370 Into Scotland thair wes richt mony lordis, ȝoung and wantoun, and full of reuery.

†**c.** A state of anger or irritation. *Obs. rare.*

1481 CAXTON *Godfrey* xxiv. 57 They had a Capytayne.. whiche brought them in suche reuerye [F. *enrederie*] and murmur that they spake largely and rudely ayenst the knyghtes. *Ibid.* cxvi. 174 Therle of tholouse, whiche, in a reuerrye wheryn he was, sayde that he wold not acquyte his part, ne gyue it ouer to noman lyuyng.

†**2. a.** Violent or rude language. *Obs. rare.*

c 1400 *Destr. Troy* 7651 Ephistafus hym presit with his proude wordes, As a ribold with reueray, in his Roide speche. *c* 1400 *Laud Troy Bk.* 14255 He at him hadde gret dispit For his wordes & his reueri Bothe of falsnes & losengeri That he on him bare.

†**b.** *Sc.* Noise, din. *Obs. rare.*

1513 DOUGLAS *Æneis* x. vii. 117 Than he..Behaldis quhou that the low dois mak deray, Blesand and crakand with a nice reuery. *Ibid.* XI. xiii. 32 The wemen rowtis baldly to the assay, With felloun bruyt, gret reveray, and deray.

c. *Sc.* A report or rumour. *rare.*

1787 W. TAYLOR *Sc. Poems* 59 This rev'rie spread about the Cummer. 1867 W. GREGOR *Banffsh. Gloss.* 143.

3. A fantastic, fanciful, unpractical, or purely theoretical idea or notion.

α. 1653 DOROTHY OSBORNE *Lett.* xxiii [xxvi], It may bee I dreampt it.., or Else it was one of the Resuery's of my Ague. *a* 1687 PETTY *Pol. Arith.* (1690) 65, I indeed desire Men to look upon [this] rather as a Dream or Resvery than a rational Proposition. 1710 PALMER *Proverbs* 325 The most Ridiculous Bigot thinks himself in the Right, and..Believes his Resveries acceptable to God. 1759 SARAH FIELDING *C'tess of Dellwyn* II. 29 The Moral of the Play seems to be.. that the most frantic Resverie is the highest Virtue.

β. 1758 CHESTERF. *Lett.* cccxlviii. (1792) IV. 156 This *rêverie* of mine, I hope, will be tried, and I wish it may succeed. 1774 J. BRYANT *Mythol.* I. 453 Some of them.. have rendered their works..little better than the reveries of Monsr. Voltaire. 1802 PLAYFAIR *Huttonian The.* 480 The author of this strange and inconsistent reverie is, nevertheless, an excellent observer. 1841 BREWSTER *Mart. Sci.* 143 Tycho delivered a course of lectures, in which he..defended and explained all the reveries of astrology.

4. A fit of abstracted musing; a 'brown study' or day-dream.

α. 1657 J. DAVIES tr. *Voiture's Lett.* I. 3, I am to learn whether the resueries of a soul so Elevated as yours is, are not too serious..to descend to any reflection on me. 1668 H. MORE *Div. Dial.* I. Publ. to Rdr., Men..obnoxious to Raptures and exalted Resveries. 1709 MRS. MANLEY *Secret Mem.* 121 Seeing her Cousin had left crying, and was fall'n into a profound Resuery. 1759 SARAH FIELDING *C'tess of Dellwyn* I. 268 At last a Petit-maitre, after having been in a long Resverie, crosses the Circle, and throws all into Confusion.

β. 1731 MEDLEY *Kolben's Cape G. Hope* (1738) I. 165 Their Drone of a Father, who lies stretch'd at his Ease in a profound *Reverie*. 1753–4 RICHARDSON *Grandison* (1781) VI. 28, I was sometimes ready to doubt whether I were not in a reverie. 1781 COWPER *Retirem.* 637 But reveries.. Attain not to the dignity of thought. 1820 IRVING *Sketch Bk.* I. 145 Walking about in a sad reverie,..unconscious of the world around her. 1871 BLACKIE *Phases Mor.* i. 14 Whether he would remain all night standing in that reverie.

b. With possessive pron.

α. 1711 SHAFTESBURY *Charact.* I. 162 If their Meditation and Resvery be obstructed by the fear of a nonconforming meen in Conversation. 1753–4 RICHARDSON *Grandison* V. 174 She never hinted at marriage in her resveries.

β. 1714 POPE *Lett.* (1735) I. *221 My *Rêverie* has been so deep, that I have scarce had an Interval to think myself uneasy. 1778 MISS BURNEY *Evelina* lx, I started from my reverie. 1820 H. MATTHEWS *Diary Invalid* 235, I endeavoured in vain to rouse him from his revery. 1853 C. BRONTË *Villette* vi, In my reverie, methought I saw the continent of Europe..far away.

c. *Mus.* An instrumental composition suggestive of a dreamy or musing state.

1880 MISS RITTER tr. *Schumann's Music & M.* 527 There is only one number among the reveries in which the composer has nearly refrained altogether from any mixture of virtuoso accessories.

5. The fact, state, or condition of being lost in thought or engaged in musing. Also *personif.*

1690 LOCKE *Hum. Und.* II. xix. (1695) 119 When Ideas float in our mind, without any Reflection or regard of the Understanding, it is that which the French call *Resvery*; our Language has scarce a name for it. 1755 GRAINGER *Solitude* iii. 7 Rapt earth-gazing *Resvery*, Blushing artless ..Modesty, Seek the solitary Wild. 1762 *Ann. Reg.* II. 19 His fits of reverie were..frequent. 1797 MRS. RADCLIFFE *Italian* i, He was lost in reverie on this subject. 1813 SCOTT *Rokeby* VI. xi, Mark with what flights Of wilder'd reverie he writes. 1889 MOLL *Hypnotism* iv. (1890) 193 There is often reverie independent of the will.

Hence **Re·verie** *v.*, to indulge in reveries.

1880 HAVERGAL *Mem.* vii. 98, I used to reverie about them.

Reverifica·tion (rɪ-). [RE- 5 a.] The action of verifying again.

1856 DOVE *Logic Chr. Faith* I. i. § 2. 63 May it not require many years of..re-verification? 1871 *Pall Mall G.* 23 Aug. 9 One set..is sent to the Standards Department for comparison and reverification within the prescribed periods.

Reve·rify (rɪ-), *v.* [RE- 5 a. Cf. F. *revérifier.*] *trans.* To verify (a thing) afresh, or again.

1611 COTGR., *Reverifier*, to reuerifie,..reapproue. 1842 CARLYLE in *FitzGerald's Lett.* (1889) I. 105, I have copied you my illegible pencil-notes, and re-verified everything. 1871 *Pall Mall G.* 23 Aug. 9 The illegal practice of locally reverifying county standards..after official verification.

Revering (rɪvɪ⁰·rɪŋ), *ppl. a.* [f. REVERE *v.* + -ING².] Reverent; paying reverence.

1639 S. DU VERGER tr. *Camus' Admir. Events* A 3 b, I make my addresse in the humble supplication of the first, or in a revering sence of the second. 1746 HERVEY *Medit.* (1818) 13, I have great reason to cry out with the revering patriarch, 'How dreadful is this place!' 1896 *Daily News* 18 Dec. 7/7 The dog barks from sheer sympathy with the delighted revering men and angels.

Reverist (re·vărist). *rare.* [f. REVERIE + -IST.] One who indulges in reveries; a dreamer.

1855 *Tait's Mag.* XXII. 81 Retrospections of a Reverist. 1884 BEECHER in *Chr. World Pulpit* XXV. 212 They were reverists, idealists.

‖**Revers** (rəvɛ̄ʳ). [F. *revers* REVERSE *sb.*] A part of a coat, vest, bodice, etc., of which the edge is turned back so as to exhibit the under surface; the material covering this reversed edge. (Most commonly used as a *pl.* Cf. REVER.)

1869 *Latest News* 5 Sept. 7 Very short veste, with revers of black velvet. 1889 *John Bull* 2 Mar. 150/2 The bodice made with revers of white velvet brocade. 1893 *The Lady* 10 Aug. 146 The Victorian revers are also partially covered with a frill of lace.

†**Reversable,** obs. variant of REVERSIBLE *a.*

1581 *Act* 23 *Eliz.* c. 3 § 2 No Fyne..shalbee reversed or reversable by any writte of Errour,..for false or incongrue Lattin, rasure [etc.].

Reversal (rɪvɜ̄·ɹsăl), *sb.* [f. REVERSE *v.* + -AL.]

1. *Law.* The act of reversing or annulling a decree, sentence, punishment, etc.; the fact of being reversed or annulled.

1488 *Rolls of Parlt.* VI. 413/1 The Acte of Restitution or Reversall, made in the said Parliament. 1503 *Ibid.* 526/2 Rehersyng the said Reversall, Repelle, Adnullacion and Avoydaunce, of this said Acte. 1562 *Act* 5 *Eliz.* c. 9 § 1 Upon every suche Reversall, the parties greeved to recover his or their Damages. 1622 BACON *Hen. VII* 12 The king likewise in the Reuersall of the Attainders of his Partakers ..had his will. 1640 in Rushw. *Hist. Coll.* (1692) I. III. 57 An Act for Reversal of a Decree made in Chancery. 1768 BLACKSTONE *Comm.* III. 284 Which reversal may be had by the defendant's appearing personally in court. 1797 *Month. Mag.* III. 552/2 The effect of the reversal of an outlawry in a civil action..has been before mentioned. 1818 CRUISE *Digest* (ed. 2) II. 328 It seems that the reversal of a fine by act of parliament will restore a contingent remainder destroyed by that fine. 1861 MAY *Const. Hist.* (1863) I. vii. 460 Believing the judgment of the court to be erroneous, they might have sought its reversal by a writ of error. 1884 *Law Rep.* 12 Q. B. Div. 439 The Queen's Bench Division reversed his decision, and the present case is an appeal from that reversal.

transf. 1818 G. S. FABER *Horæ Mosaicæ* I. 59 *note*, He cannot mean a reversal of any imaginary sentence of annihilation. 1869 HUXLEY in *Scientific Opinion* 21 Apr. 464/1 Whether they..appeal for a reversal of the sentence to that higher court of educated scientific opinion to which we are all amenable.

2. The act or process of reversing, in various senses of the verb; an instance of this.

1698 *Phil. Trans.* XX. 416 Tornadoes.., which made some small Reversal, though it was but for Two or Three Hours. 1794 SULLIVAN *View Nat.* II. 84 Doctor Franklin proved particularly..the effects of the reversal of the poles of magnets, as caused by lightning. 1814 CARY *Dante, Par.* XVII. 87 He shall cause Reversal of their lot to many people. 1833 HERSCHEL *Astron.* v. 197 The reversal of the seasons in the northern and southern hemispheres. 1880 HAUGHTON *Phys. Geogr.* iv. 187 The Monsoons are..produced by a reversal of the north-east trade winds.

attrib. 1698 *Phil. Trans.* XX. 415 Very high Lands, that of themselves doth most commonly give Reversal or Westerly Winds at Night.

3. Reversion *to* some practice, etc. *rare.*

1862 REICHEL *Cathedral 19th Cent.* 21 What I propose.. is no reversal to antiquated and unsuitable modes and forms of thought and worship. 1893 *Illustr. Lond. News* 1 Apr. 398/2 They had Nonconformity in the blood,..with occasional 'throwings back', or reversals, to Conformity.

†**Reve·rsal,** *a. Obs. rare.* [a. F. *réversal* or ad. med.L. *reversālis* (Du Cange).] Revocatory.

1656 HEYLIN *Surv. France* 77 Speciall letters reversall. *a* 1715 BURNET *Own Time* (1766) I. 439 After his death there were reversal letters found among his papers.

Reverse (rɪvɜ̄·ɹs), *sb.* Also 4–6 reuers (4 ry-), 5–6 reuerse (5 -ce, 6 -sse); 4–5 revers. [a. OF. *revers* masc. (so mod.F., = Sp. and Pg. *reverso*, It. *riverso*), or *reverse* fem., f. L. *revers-*, ppl. stem of *revertĕre* to REVERT.]

I. 1. The opposite or contrary of something.

1390 GOWER *Conf.* I. 356 Crist hath comanded love and pes, And who that worcheth the revers, I trowe his mede is ful divers. *c* 1393 CHAUCER *Gentilesse* 6 For vn-to vertue longeþ dignytee, And nouȝt þe reverse. *c* 1407 LYDG. *Reson & Sens.* 4160 Counsayl of the wyse Dooth profyte in many wyse,..As the revers dooth gret damage. 1425 *Rolls of Parlt.* IV. 269/1 Hit semeth..þat þis matier allegged for þe part of his Lord þe Erl of Warr, proveth rather for his Lord Erl Mareschall þan þe revers.

1716 BENTLEY *Serm.* xi. 373 The Heathen Poet in the Epigram teaches the down-right reverse. 1790 BURKE *Fr. Rev.* 90 The reverse also happens; and very plausible schemes.. have often shameful and lamentable conclusions. 1825 J. NICHOLSON *Operat. Mechanic* 224 In the horizontal castings ..the balance is in favour of the increased lengths; but in the vertical castings, it is the reverse. 1882 MINCHIN *Unipl. Kinemat.* 193 In this case the stream function..is single-valued. The reverse takes place in the case of a squirt.

b. *Card-playing.* (See quot. 1746.)

1742 HOYLE *Whist* 77 If you are weak in Trumps, you must play the Reverse. 1746 *Ibid.* (ed. 6) 69 Playing at any time the Reverse, means only the playing your Hand in a different manner.

†**c.** *On the reverse*, on the contrary. *Obs.*

1753 A. MURPHY *Gray's Inn Jrnl.* No. xxxvi, Mr. Such-a-one is a Man of very good Sense; or, on the Reverse,.. he has not common Sense. 1763 W. ROBERTS *Nat. Hist. Florida* 39 The general paid no regard to such remonstrances: On the reverse, he ordered all to hold themselves ready to march. 1786 MRS. A. M. BENNETT *Juvenile Indiscr.* IV. 214 On the reverse, if she would be ingenuous in her confession, he, Mr. Franklin, would be her protector.

2. The opposite or contrary *of* or *to* something specified. Also with possessive pron.

c 1386 CHAUCER *Nun's Pr. T.* 4167 Men may in olde bookes rede, Of many a man..That al the reuers seyn of this sentence. *c* 1392 — *Compl. Venus* 32 Al þe Reuers of any glaade felyng. *a* 1400 *Relig. Pieces fr. Thornton MS.* 29 Than it behufes þat þe riche hafe þe reuer[s]e of that benysone. *c* 1530 *Crt. of Love* 96 Of these the reverse may no wight approve.

1699 BENTLEY *Phal.* Pref. lxxxi, The candid part of mankind will rather believe the reverse of it. 1718 *Free-thinker* No. 29. 204, I found that the Town-Language was the very Reverse to mine. 1749 FIELDING *Tom Jones* V. i, For what demonstrates the beauty and excellence of anything but its reverse? 1771 *Junius Lett.* lix. (1788) 316 The present habit of our political body appears to me the very reverse of what it ought to be. 1834 SOUTHEY *Doctor* xiii. (1848) 34 The application which *Homo* makes of all this, is the very reverse to what his mother intended. 1876 VOYLE & STEVENSON *Milit. Dict.* 335/1 The front of the army forming a re-entering or enclosing angle, and the reverse of the salient formation.

b. Used with general terms or with adjectives to express more than a mere negation. (Common in recent use.)

1783 BURKE *Rep. Aff. India* Wks. II. 3 Against this evil large pecuniary interests were rather the reverse of a remedy. 1860 C. A. COLLINS *Eye-witness* vi. 81 [He] will..come in for certain remarks which are the reverse of complimentary. 1865 CARLYLE *Fredk. Gt.* XVIII. xi. (1872) VIII. 15 A cunctatory haggling mortal, the reverse of a General. 1875 JOWETT *Plato* (ed. 2) III. 33 Their tales are untrue, and the reverse of inspiring to heroes.

3. That side of a coin, medal, or seal which does not bear the main device or inscription; the back. (Opposed to OBVERSE *sb.* 1.)

a 1625 in Gutch *Coll. Cur.* I. 210 Upon the reverse King Solomon in a throne, visited by the Queen of Saba. 1658 SIR T. BROWNE *Hydriot.* (1736) 11 Silver Pieces..with a rude Head on the Obverse, and an ill formed Horse on the Reverse. 1711 ADDISON *Spect.* No. 59 ¶ 4 He placed the Figure of an Elephant upon the Reverse of the Publick Mony. 1788 PRIESTLEY *Lect. Hist.* IV. xxv. 193 To celebrate their exploits on the reverses of their coins. 1845 FORD *Handbk. Spain* I. 47 Every coin..has its reverse and every rose its thorn. 1853 HUMPHREY *Coin-coll. Man.* v. 39 The punch mark of the reverse assumed a somewhat regular form.

attrib. 1887 *Proclam.* in *Standard* 18 May 3/2 Every Sixpence should have the same obverse and reverse impression.

fig. 1868 G. DUFF *Pol. Surv.* 195 Then for the reverse of the medal you have Mr. Christie's *Notes on Brazilian Questions.*

b. The design, etc., on the reverse side.

1623 CAMDEN *Rem.* 170 As for the Romans, as they did set downe the Image and inscription of the Consul.., afterward of the Emperour on the one side, so they changed the reuerse alwayes vpon new euents. 1646 J. GREGORY *Notes & Obs.* (1650) 27 The Reverse a crocodile enchained to Palmetree. 1702 ADDISON *Dial. Medals* ii. 77 Our next reverse is an Oaken Garland. 1739 *Learned Wks.* I. 87 As appears by the Reverses of two curious Medals, struck by the Samians. 1817 in *Archæol.* XVIII. 457 Three ancient seals, with their reverses. 1841 ELPHINSTONE *Hist. Ind.* I. 471 The inscriptions, the figures, the reverses, and the workmanship are pure Greek.

c. The back or verso of a leaf (in a book).

1824 J. JOHNSON *Typogr.* I. 228 On the recto of the first leaf is a wood-cut of the Virgin and Child, and on the reverse a Crucifixion. 1885 *Antiquary* Sept. 89/1 On the reverse of the same folio, Meres goes on, 'So in England we have also these'.

d. In general use, as the correlative of *obverse.*

1831–47 [see OBVERSE *sb.* 2]. 1874 [see FACE *sb.* 13 a].

4. The back of a mountain, mound, etc.

1777 DONKIN *Milit. Coll.* 51 All military persons ought to know, that there are few mountains (be they ever so horrible) which have not reverses where men may pass. 1802 JAMES *Milit. Dict.* s.v. *Revers*, One or two banquettes are generally thrown up..in order that the trench guard may make a stand upon the reverse when it happens to be attacked by a sortie of the enemy.

5. The butt-end *of* a lance. *rare.*

1819 SCOTT *Ivanhoe* ix, Each touched slightly, and with the reverse of his lance, the shield of the antagonist to whom he wished to oppose himself.

6. *In reverse*: †**a.** Inverse. *Obs. rare*⁻¹.

1694 HOLDER *Harmony* 20 The Proportion by which the Frequency increaseth is..very near duplicate.., but is in reverse, *i.e.* as the Length increaseth, so the Vibrations decrease.

b. *Mil.* In the rear.

1781 HAMILTON *Wks.* (1886) VIII. 46 Two columns.., the left..destined to take the enemy in reverse, and intercept their retreat. 1834–47 J. S. MACAULAY *Field Fortif.* (1851) 303 One face [of a redoubt] is seen in reverse, and two are enfiladed; while one can neither be seen in reverse, nor enfiladed. 1897 *Cent. Mag.* June 203 Our troops were now exposed to attack both in flank and reverse.

c. Contrary to the usual manner.

1875 HELPS *Ess., Treatment Suitors* 79 Hope, an architect above rules, can build, in reverse, a pyramid upon a point. 1880 *Athenæum* 25 Dec. 873/1 The inedited manuscripts by Da Vinci, twelve in number, written in reverse, as was customary with the painter.

d. In contrast *to* something. *rare.*

1869 F. W. NEWMAN *Misc.* 163 The Hungarians..are not only tall and well grown, in reverse to the squat Huns, but are politically constitutional.

II. †**7.** A back-handed stroke or cut. *Obs.*

Cf. Egerton Castle *Schools & Masters of Fence* (1885) 72.

c 1489 CAXTON *Blanchardyn* xliii. 169 To whome he gaff a reuerse wyth his swerde. *a* 1533 LD. BERNERS *Huon* cx. 377 Huon..strake the Sarasyn with a reuerse that his hede flewe fro the body a great waye of. 1594 I. G. *Grassi's Art Def.* E e iv, When, after a right blowe, he would discharge a reuerse, he must encrease a slope pace. 1598 SHAKS. *Merry W.* II. iii. 27 To see thee passe thy puncto, thy stock, thy reuerse, thy distance. 1656 BLOUNT *Glossogr.* [copying Cotgrave].

fig. 1599 B. JONSON *Cynthia's Rev.* v. ii, You have your passages and imbrocatas in courtship; as the bitter bob in wit; the reverse in face or wry-mouth.

8. An adverse change of fortune; a disaster; esp. in mod. use, a defeat in battle.

1526 SKELTON *Magnyf.* 1509, I folowe in felycyte without reuersse. 1590 GREENE *Never too late* (1600) 61 Either ruminating passions or penance, either som old remembrance or some newe reuerse. 1646 SIR T. BROWNE *Pseud. Ep.* 77 The Arte of Pythagoras, who could read a reverse in the Moone. 1786 JEFFERSON *Writ.* (1859) I. 554 How comfortable a reflection will it be, to have prepared a refuge for him in case of a reverse. 1796 BURKE *Regic. Peace* Wks. II. 277 Some reverses which happened in the beginning of that war. 1815 J. W. CROKER in *C. Papers* 20 July, Buonaparte, great as he was in prosperity, was never able to bear up against a reverse. 1887 *Times* (weekly ed.) 9 Dec. 1/3 A serious encounter..in which the police encountered a sharp reverse.

b. Const. *of* fortune, etc.

1735 J. HUGHES tr. *Fontenelle's Dial.* I. vii. (ed. 3) 27 A terrible Reverse of Fortune! And pray who perform'd this noble Exploit? 1773 J. ALLEN *Serm. S. Mary's, Oxf.* 25 Let this reverse of things teach us not to be highminded. 1826 MISS MITFORD in L'Estrange *Life* (1870) II. 226 But what is his reverse of fortune compared with Napoleon's!

9. = REVERSAL *sb.* Now *rare* or *Obs.*

1589 PUTTENHAM *Eng. Poesie* III. xxiii. (Arb.) 282 This pleasant and speedy reuers of the former wordes holpe all the matter againe. 1602 MARSTON *Antonio's Rev.* III. iii, Since 'tis [*sc.* flesh] mixt together, Have at adventure, pel mell, no reverse. 1660 F. BROOKE tr. *Le Blanc's Trav.* 227 Engines..so drawne and bent by cordage and wheeles, fixt opposite, that the reverse was so vigorous, they would founder..a ship. 1698 *Phil. Trans.* XX. 414 The Reverse or Rebounding back of the Wind, which is occasioned by the calming of the Trade-Wind.

b. A complete change or alteration. ? *Obs.*

1728 VANBR. & CIB. *Prov. Husb.* v. ii, This promises a Reverse of Temper. 1781 MRS. INCHBALD *I'll tell you what* I. ii, The next time he insults me with his jealousy..I'll try a reverse of conduct.

c. *Mus.* An inverted phrase or passage. *rare*⁻¹.

1752 AVISON *Mus. Express.* 66 Such as admit of a Variety of Subjects,..and which, with their Imitations, Reverses, and other relative Passages, are conducted throughout the whole, in Subordination to their Principal.

d. = REVERS. *rare*⁻¹.

1859 THACKERAY *Virgin.* lxv, And what, pray, are lapels but reverses?

10. †**a.** = REVERSI 1. *Obs.*

1798 *Sporting Mag.* XI. 318 The game of reverse..is so called, because he that makes the least tricks wins the cards, which is the reverse of most other games.

b. *pl.* = REVERSI 2.

1886 *Sat. Rev.* LXII. 254/2 Reverses...It gets its name, as we suppose, from the continual turning over or reversing of the counters (or men) used in playing it.

11. The act of reversing in dancing.

1888 E. SCOTT *Waltz at a Glance* 21 The Reverse. 1892 — *Dancing* 200 He thinks, 'Now I will try the reverse'; then, dubious about a successful issue, he wavers [etc.].

Reverse (rɪvɜ̄·ɹs), *a.* and *adv.* Also 4 reuers, 4 (6) revers. [a. OF. *revers*, or ad. L. *revers-us*, pa. pple. of *revertĕre* to REVERT: cf. next.]

1. Opposite or contrary (*to* something else, or to each other) in character, order, succession, etc.

1303 R. BRUNNE *Handl. Synne* 11,112 Þese are þo yche twey verse, Þat to holynes are reuers. 1387–8 T. USK *Test. Love* III. iv. 84 Whych things ben more revers than commen and gone? 1390 GOWER *Conf.* I. 230 To feigne and schewe thing withoute Which is revers to that withinne.

1762 J. WOOLMAN *Wks.* (1840) 225 Others choose that which..proves utterly reverse to true happiness. 1792 BURKE *Corr.* (1844) IV. 37, I hear that the Bellingham story is the contrary to truth, and happened in the very reverse manner. 1826 *London's Gard. Mag.* (1828) I. 274 Observations on Reverse Grafting. 1836–41 BRANDE *Chem.* (ed. 5) 321 Decomposition of the iodide at *x* occurred, but in a reverse order. 1884 tr. *Lotze's Logic* 103 The mind.. employs them to form an inference which is just like the one described above, only in the reverse direction.

†**b.** Of winds: Contrary, adverse. *Obs.*⁻¹

1390 GOWER *Conf.* III. 49 Fro Troie as he goth hom ayein ..he fond the See divers, With many a wyndi storm revers.

c. Lying behind or to the back.

1851 MOGFORD *Preserv. Pict.* (ed. 3) II. 47 What would become of a fine Rembrandt..if subjected to violent blows on the reverse side from a weighty mass of iron?

†**2.** Of blows, etc.: Back-handed. *Obs.*

1591 FLORIO *2nd Frutes* 119 Hee will hit any man..with a right or reverse blowe,..even as liketh him. 1599 B. JONSON *Cynthia's Rev.* v. ii, Stooping over his shoulder, your hand on his breast,..You give him the reverse stroke. 1667 MILTON *P. L.* VI. 326 With swift wheele reverse, [the sword] deep entring shar'd All his right side.

3. a. *Arith.* = INVERSE *a.* 3 a. ? *Obs.*

1594 BLUNDEVIL *Exerc.* I. xix. (1636) 43 Proportion Reverse differeth nor from the Rule of Three, called *Regula reversa.* 1766 *Complete Farmer* s.v. *Surveying* 7 G 1/2 In the same manner you may, by the rule of three reverse, obtain your desire.

b. *Arch.* Inverted. (See note to CYMA 1.)

1730 A. GORDON *Maffei's Amphith.* 230 The Architrave is next divided into four Parts, two Stories, a Reverse Gula, and a List. *Ibid.* 234 Nor does it cause the reverse Gulæ to appear exceedingly narrow.

c. *Ent.* (See quot.)

1826 KIRBY & SP. *Entomol.* IV. 299 *Reverse*, when an object is viewed with its anus towards you.

4. *Mil.* **a.** Connected with, commanding, or facing towards, the rear.

1702–11 *Milit. & Sea Dict.* s.v. *Commanding-Ground*, A Reverse Commanding-Ground, an Eminence which plays upon the back of a Post. *Ibid.* s.v. *Reverse*, So we say, a Reverse View, a reverse Commanding Ground, a Reverse Battery. 1802 JAMES *Milit. Dict.* s.v. *Battery*, Reverse Batteries are those which play on the rear of the troops appointed to defend the place. 1879 *Encycl. Brit.* IX. 449/1 The ravelin has..8 casemated guns in its reverse battery of the salient. 1879 *Cassell's Techn. Educ.* II. 130/1 Reverse or counterscarp galleries..are placed under the glacis, their front wall being the counterscarp of the ditch.

b. *Reverse flank*: (see quots.).

1802 JAMES *Milit. Dict.* s.v., The reverse or outward wheeling flank; which is opposite to the one wheeled to or upon. 1803 *British Soldier's Guide* 40 The proper pivot flank is that which..forms the line in its proper order; the other is called the Reverse Flank. 1867 SMYTH *Sailor's Word-bk.* 571 The flank at the other extremity from the pivot of a division is termed the reverse flank.

c. *Reverse fire*: (see quots.).

(*a*) 1828 J. M. SPEARMAN *Brit. Gunner* (ed. 2) 209 The lunettes before the bastions should..be as little advanced as possible,..that they may..be themselves subject to a reverse fire from the flanks of those works. 1853 STOCQUELER *Mil. Encycl.* s.v., The Reverse fire is the fire on the enemy's rear, whilst he is engaging your army in front. 1879 *Cassell's Techn. Educ.* I. 223/1 Reverse fire is that which is brought to bear on the interior of a work by guns firing into it from the rear.

(*b*) 1834–47 J. S. MACAULAY *Field Fortif.* (1851) 43 Reverse fire [is] when the shot strikes the interior slope of the parapet at an angle greater than 30°. *Ibid.* 303 Two faces will be seen by slant and two by reverse fire.

5. Acting in a way contrary or opposite to that which is usual or customary.

a 1860 ALB. SMITH *Med. Student* (1861) 117 Having been squirted at through the keyhole five distinct times, with a reverse stomach-pump full of beer. 1880 *Marine Engin.* 2 Feb. I. 212/1 Reverse valves fitted on pipes leading from the boiler to the sea. 1888 *Lockwood's Dict. Terms* 285 *Reverse Keys*, keys..made and used not with the object of holding machine parts together, but for the purpose of driving them asunder.

6. *adv.* In a reverse way; reversely.

1434 MISYN *Mending Life* 120 Sum-tyme þa þat semys in þe hyar ar in þe lawar, & reuers. 1649 MILTON *Observ. Peace Ormond* Wks. 1851 IV. 580 The edg of their own Proverb falls reverse upon themselves. 1728 R. MORRIS *Ess. Anc. Archit.* 22 Some..act reverse to their own Ideas and Sentiments.

Reverse (rɪvɜ̄·ɹs), *v.*¹ Forms: 4–7 reuerse (5 -ce, -sse, 6 *Sc.* rewers); 4 revers(se, 4–6 reverce, 4– reverse. [a. F. *reverser*, †*reversser*, -*er* (12th c.), = Sp. *reve(r)sar*, Pg. *reversar*, *revessar*, It. *ri(n)versare*, f. L. *re-* RE- + *versāre* freq. of *vertĕre* to turn: cf. REVERT *v.*]

I. *trans.* †**1. a.** To bring back *to* or *into* a state or condition, a place, the mind, etc. *Obs.*

c 1315 SHOREHAM I. 446 Þanne gode, þat his so god, Anon his stronge makeþ,..And his god fey takeþ, Reuersed. *c* 1500 *Melusine* 316, I am..ouerthrowen & ayen reuersed in the greuouse and obscure penytence, where long tyme I haue be in. 1555 W. WATREMAN *Fardle Facions* Pref. 15 Some he reuersed into their former abuses and errours. 1570 FOXE *A. & M.* (ed. 2) 1040/1 From thence he was reuersed to Ville Franche, where he was condemned, degraded, and burned. 1590 SPENSER *F. Q.* I. ix. 48 The knight..to his..remembraunce did reverse The ugly vew of his deformed crimes.

†**b.** To send back *to* a place; to cause to revert *to* a person. *Obs. rare.*

1542 UDALL *Erasm. Apoph.* 189 b, At what tyme Alexander reuersed backe again to the sea..as many of the Macedonians as wer sickely. *Ibid.* 244 The young manne with a tryce reuersed the suspicion to the mother of Cæsar, or els to his sustur.

†**c.** To hand *over* by reversion. *Obs. rare*⁻¹.

1599 NASHE *Lenten Stuffe* 26 The newe fanglest raritie.. after three dayes gazing is reuerst ouer to children for babies to play with.

†**d.** To remove or put away; to divert or turn away. *Obs. rare.*

1590 SPENSER *F. Q.* III. ii. 48 That old Dame said many an idle verse, Out of her daughters hart fond fancies to reverse. 1592 GREENE *Philomela* Wks. (Grosart) XI. 136 A small resolution to reuerse your thoughts from this disordinat folly of loue. 1639 G. DANIEL *Ecclus.* ix. 17 Reverse thy burning Eye from the desir'd Obiect of Beautie, though to be admir'd.

†**2.** To overthrow, overturn, upset, or throw down (a person or thing). *Obs.*

1375 BARBOUR *Bruce* XV. 191 Schir Eduard..Reversit hym, and with a knyff Richt in that place him reft the liff. *Ibid.* XVI. 417 On hym arestit the Dowglas, And him reuersit. *c* 1400 *Laud Troy Bk.* 7415 How he the Gregeis ther reuerced, Helmes and hauberk how he persed. *c* 1477 CAXTON *Jason* 8 Pyritheon with somme other began to reuerse ther metes and tables fighting with hem with pottes and platters. *c* 1500 *Melusine* 142 They within the toune ..reuersed them fro the ladders vnto the botome of the dyches. *Ibid.* 241 Thenne..trompettes sowned, & knightes reuersed eche other. 1577–87 HOLINSHED *Chron.* III. 406/1 The prince..caused the walles to be vndermined, and quite reuersed into the ditch.

†**b.** To overthrow, cast down, bring to nought.

c 1375 *Sc. Leg. Saints* xxv. (*Julian*) 690 Þis cite hale I sal revers, & mak It for to bere corne. *c* 1400 *Rom. Rose* 5468 Froward Fortune..Whanne high estatis she doth reverse, ..Thus kan she maken high and lowe. 1402 *Pol. Poems* (Rolls) II. 61 In which ech religion perfitli is groundid, reversynge the soorie synnes notid of the postle. *a* 1618 SYLVESTER *Little Bartas* 207 How often hath Hee seen Empires reverst? 1638 SIR T. HERBERT *Trav.* (ed. 2) 103 Hee is convicted,..his honour reverst, himselfe manacled.

†**c.** To overthrow by argument, etc.; to confute. *Obs. rare.*

c 1380 WYCLIF *Wks.* (1880) 266 Þei seyn þat þe speche of holy writt is fals þat reuersiþ here owene fonnydnesse. *c* 1440 CAPGRAVE *Life St. Kath.* IV. 1396 There shal no man haue myght me to reuers, Though ȝe brynge a grettere multitude. 1581 MARBECK *Bk. Notes* 515 Afterward he doth reuerse the arguments and objections of the aduersaries, which he aunswereth by and by.

†**d.** To upset, disorder. *Obs. rare*⁻¹.

1760–72 H. BROOKE *Fool of Qual.* (1809) II. 95 A sudden sickness relaxed and reversed my whole frame.

3. To turn or place upside down; to invert.

1390 GOWER *Conf.* I. 3 Men se the world on every syde In sondry wyse so diversed, That it welnyh stant al reversed. *c* 1400 *Brut* ccix. 240 One Symunde of Redyng bifore ham bar her armes oppon a spere reuersede. *a* 1500 *Bernardus De Cura rei fam.* 282 Þan nedis thow nocht to rewerss hate na hude, To crafe þine awne hot haf it at þi wyl. *a* 1548 HALL *Chron., Hen. VIII*, 40 They make of hym an Image paynted reuersed with his heles upwarde. 1634 MILTON *Comus* 816 Without his rod revers't,..We cannot free the Lady. *a* 1700 B. E. *Dict. Cant. Crew*, *Revers'd*, a Man set (by Bullies) on his Head, and his Money turn'd out of his Breeches. 1708 J. CHAMBERLAYNE *St. Gt. Brit.* I. III. iv. (1710) 190 When a Knight is to suffer Death for any foul Crime..his Sword [is] taken away.., his Gauntlet pluckt off, and his Coat of Arms reversed. 1718 POPE *Iliad* XIII. 688 His shield revers'd o'er the fallen warrior lies; And everlasting slumber seals his eyes. 1781 COWPER *Hope* 468 No fertilizing streams your fields divide, That show, revers'd, the villas on their side. 1808 SCOTT *Marm.* I. xii, We saw ..On the gibbet-tree, revers'd, His foeman's scutcheon tied. 1842 TENNYSON *Will Waterproof* 159, I sit, my empty glass reversed, And thrumming on the table.

b. To hold or carry (a weapon) in the position contrary to that in which it is ready for use.

1650 R. STAPYLTON *Strada's Low C. Wars* X. 22 A Regiment of Foote..went before, with their Pikes and Muskets reversed. 1787 BURNS *Elegy J. H. Blair* vi, Revers'd that spear, redoubtable in war, Reclined that banner, erst in fields unfurl'd. 1833 *Reg. & Instr. Cavalry* I. 34 The officers' swords are reversed under the right arm. 1854 STOCQUELER *Milit. Encycl.* 232/2 Arms are said to be reversed when the butts of the pieces are slung or held upwards. 1864 TENNYSON *Voyage* 71 And now, the bloodless point reversed, She bore the blade of Liberty.

c. *Her.* (See quots.)

1656 BLOUNT *Glossogr.*, *Reversed*,..a term in Heraldry, when Arms, or any part of them, are turned the lower part upward. 1727–38 CHAMBERS *Cycl.* s.v. *Abatement*, In the case of treason,..the escutcheon is totally reversed, to intimate a total suppression of the honour. 1868 CUSSANS *Her.* (1893) 103 In the Arms of the See of Hereford the Lions' faces are Reversed, that is, turned upside down.

†**4.** To turn back or trim (a garment) *with* some other material. *Obs.*

1382 *Pol. Poems* (Rolls) I. 265 Somme frers beren pelure aboute, For grete ladys and wenches stoute, To reverce with thair clothes withoute. *a* 1400 *Morte Arth.* 3255 In a surcott of sylke..alle redily reversside with rebanes of golde. *c* 1420 *Anturs of Arth.* ii, Inne a gliderand gyde, that glemit so gay That was with rebans reuersut. 15.. *Jerusalem Reioss* 14 in *Dunbar's Poems* II. 322 Thre Kingis..All drest with dyamantis but dout, Reverst with gold in every hem. 1523 *Test. Ebor.* (Surtees) V. 172 To Elinor Studeley my sanguyne gowne reversid velvitt.

†**5. a.** To oppose, resist. *Obs. rare.*

c 1380 WYCLIF *Sel. Wks.* II. 75 Who woot how many persones assentiden to þis synne, and how myche helpe men hadden of oþers þat reversiden it? *c* 1380 — *Wks.* (1880) 286 For job seith in his book..þat no man reuersiþ god but ȝif he haue vnpees.

†**b.** To contradict (oneself). *Obs. rare.*

c 1380 WYCLIF *Sel. Wks.* II. 319 Siþ God, þat reversiþ not himsilfe, biddiþ þat men shulde love þer enemyes. 1402 *Pol. Poems* (Rolls) II. 86 Alas, Jak, for shame! whi art thou so fals, For to reverse thi silf in thin owne sawes?

6. To revoke, abrogate, annul (a decree, act, measure, etc.). †Also with personal object.

1395 PURVEY *Remonstrance* (1851) 46 The ij principle, A peere hath not power on his peere, is falsli applied to the lattere pope reuersinge the formere pope. *Ibid.*, Thanne the lattere pope..reuersith Goddis doom. *c* 1420 LYDG. *Assembly of Gods* 492 For a goddes wrytyng may nat reuersyd be. 1611 BIBLE *Num.* xxiii. 20, I haue receiued commandement to blesse: and hee hath blessed, and I cannot reuerse it. *a* 1656 HALES *Gold. Rem.* (1673) 100 It is not to be thought that St. Peter had revers'd with himself the confession that he had formerly made of Christ. 1703 POPE *Thebais* 396 Reverse, O Jove, thy too severe decree. 1727 DE FOE *Syst. Magic* I. iv. (1840) 112 But the Devil and he together were not able to reverse the blessing. 1836 THIRLWALL *Greece* III. 141 The enemies of Pericles believed that they might overthrow him, though they could not reverse his measures. 1869 TOZER *Highl. Turkey* II. 284 As she could not reverse the curse..she did what she could to mitigate it.

b. *esp.* in legal use, with reference to judgements, decrees, forfeitures, etc.

1485 *Rolls of Parlt.* VI. 290/2 The said Acte of Attaindre ..be..reversed, adnulled, void, and of noon effecte ne force. 1487 *Act* 3 *Hen. VII*, c. 10 Writtes of errour to adnulle and reverse the seid jugement. 1531 ELYOT *Gov.* II. v. Wherby, he fyndynge the poure woman to sustaine wronges, he reuersed his iugement. 1560 DAUS tr. *Sleidane's Comm.* 108 b, He desyreth that this sentence of outlawerye maye be reversed. 1666 PEPYS *Diary* 26 Aug., It was hoped by the party grieved, to get my Lord Chancellor to reverse a decree of his. 1689 LUTTRELL *Brief Rel.* (1857) I. 522 The earl of Macclesfeild hath revers'd his outlawry in the court of kings bench. 1754 SHERLOCK *Disc.* I. (1759) I. 45 They cannot reverse a Forfeiture once incurred. 1768 BLACKSTONE *Comm.* III. xxv. 411 Each court of appeal, in their respective stages, may..reverse, or affirm the judgment of the inferior courts. 1818 CRUISE *Digest* (ed. 2) VI. 212 Whereupon the judgment of the Court of King's Bench was reversed. 1855 MACAULAY *Hist. Eng.* xiv. III. 380 A bill for reversing the attainder of Lord Russell was presented to the Peers.

c. To undo (work).

1725 POPE *Odyss.* II. 118 The work she plied; but, studious of delay, By night reversed the labours of the day. 1816–60 WHATELY *Comm.-pl. Bk.* (1864) 91 All the work undone and reversed at which he had been labouring.

7. To turn the other way, in respect of position or aspect; to transpose, turn inside out, etc.

c 1380 *Lay Folks Catech.* (Lamb. MS.) 184 The furste word, þat is aue, reuersys þe name of Eua. *a* 1400 *Morte Arth.* 2070 He..Braydez owt his brande with a blyth chere, Reverssede it redelye, and awaye rydys.

1596 WARNER *Alb. Eng.* XII. lxxiii. (1602) 304 Reuerse the Cope. 1615 SANDYS *Trav.* 55 At which time they reuerse their faces, first ouer the right shoulder, and then ouer the left. 1669 STURMY *Mariner's Mag.* II. ii. 52 The Diameter of the Circle, or the Line of Sines Reversed. 1698 FRYER *Acc. E. India & P.* 319, I saw the Old Moon go out on the Hills at Lhor, and the Night following, the Horns reversed. 1784 COWPER *Tiroc.* 443 And he, that seem'd our counterpart at first, Soon shows the strong similitude revers'd. 1840 LARDNER *Geom.* 70 Because the position of the triangles on either side of the diagonal is reversed. 1878 ABNEY *Photogr.* (1881) 187 It will be found that as regards right and left the pictures will be reversed.

†**b.** To turn (the back). *Obs. rare*⁻¹.

1523 SKELTON *Garl. Laurel* 3 When Mars retrogradant reuersyd his bak.

8. To convert into something of an opposite character or tendency; to turn the contrary way; to alter or change completely.

c 1500 *Melusine* 316 Oure solace, playsire & joye ben reuersed in byttir teerys & contynuel wepynges. 1642 FULLER *Holy & Prof. St.* I. ii. 34, I like not this charitie reversed, when it begins farre off and neglects those at home. 1756 C. LUCAS *Ess. Waters* I. Pref., We have lived to see all this reversed. 1781 COWPER *Hope* 519 The wretch..Has wept a silent flood, revers'd his ways. 1827 D. JOHNSON *Ind. Field Sports* 231 This heaviness and want of appetite is soon reversed, and they become more than usually lively. 1841 MYERS *Cath. Th.* III. § 7. 23 It is only asking why the conditions of man's existence were not reversed before he was redeemed. 1875 GLADSTONE *Glean.* (1879) VI. 233 We fear it is not likely that the Court of Rome will reverse its policy.

b. To employ, perform, etc., in a way opposite to the former or usual method.

1728 R. MORRIS *Ess. Anc. Archit.* 113 Let us just remark on the reversing the Use of the Table. 1833 N. ARNOTT *Physics* (ed. 5) II. 53 On reversing the experiment, a pound of hot mercury will be cooled thirty degrees. 1873 RICHARDS *Operator's Handbk.* 53 Reversing the rule, from 4 inches diameter, with 4000 feet of cutting movement; deduct 750 feet of the movement [etc.].

9. To turn in the opposite direction; to send on a course contrary to the previous or usual one.

1509 HAWES *Past. Pleas.* XXXVII. (Percy Soc.) 193 At the last I did his body perce With my good swerde, he might it not reverce. 1530 PALSGR. 690/1 The thynge went forwarde a whyle marvayllously, but nowe it is reversed we wotte nat howe.

1781 COWPER *Retirem.* 327 The screws revers'd.., Ten thousand thousand strings at once go loose. 1824 R. STUART *Hist. Steam Engine* 49 The ingenious mode of consuming smoke by reversing the flame. 1860 PRESCOTT *Electr. Telegr.* 395 A peculiar arrangement, by which the direction of the current can be reversed by a single pressure of the finger. 1891 S. C. SCRIVENER *Our Fields & Cities* 5 Watch it approaching us without wind. The mighty stream is being reversed!

b. To cause (an engine, etc.) to work or revolve in the contrary direction. Also *absol.*

1860 *Merc. Mar. Mag.* VII. 274 Stopped the engines, and reversed full power. 1875 BEDFORD *Sailor's Pocket Bk.* (ed. 2) § iii. 65 She must stop and reverse if necessary. 1883 *Law Times Rep.* XLIX. 332/1 The engines of the *Clan Sinclair* were stopped and reversed full speed.

II. *intr.* **10.** To draw back or away; to move backwards. *rare.*

c 1430 *Pilgr. Lyf Manhode* II. cxix. (1869) 119 Adam.. mihte bi no wise taste it but he wente reuersinge [*en reculant*]; and reuerse miht he nouht but he hadde first the spore. *c* 1440 CAPGRAVE *Life St. Kath.* v. 529 The more benyngnely that we trete ȝow heere, As me semeth þe more ȝe reuers. 1509 HAWES *Past. Pleas.* xxii. (Percy Soc.) 158 With many mo that I do not rehearse; My time is short, I must from them reverse. 1692 *Capt. Smith's Seaman's Gram.* II. iv. 92 He ought to see..whether one Wheel be higher, or reverse faster than the other.

b. In dancing, *esp.* waltzing: To move or turn in a contrary direction.

1884 WALLACE *Man. Dancing* 32 The four Gentlemen walk round the outside, reversing when the Ladies reverse. 1892 E. SCOTT *Dancing* 198 It is comparatively easy for a lady to reverse if she will but remember to put her left foot forward instead of backward.

†**11.** To fall over, fall down. *Obs.*

c 1450 *Merlin* 157 Whan the kynge..saugh the kynge Tradelyuaunt reuerse to the erthe, he was right wroth. 1470–85 MALORY *Arthur* VI. xiii. 204 Syre launcelot charged so sore vpon hym that his hors reuersed vp so doune. *c* 1500 *Melusine* 227 The kynge..fell & reuersed deed fro his hors to the ground. *c* 1530 LD. BERNERS *Arth. Lyt. Bryt.* (1814) 290, I ensure you I shall make hym reuerse from his horse.

†**12.** To return *back* or *home*. *Obs. rare.*

c 1540 tr. *Pol. Verg. Eng. Hist.* (Camden No. 36) 198 Kinge Ethelwolphus, after hee hadd made his abode at Rome the greatest parte of the yeare, he reversed homewarde. 1591 SPENSER *Ruins Rome* 305 The bands of th' elements shall backe reverse To their first discord. 1647 H. MORE *Song Soul* III. App. ix, Transgressing souls are sorely scourged And back again are forced to reverse By Nemesis deep-biting whips well urged.

†**Reve·rse,** *v.*², incorrect form of *revess* REVESH *v.*, to revest. *Obs.*

13.. *Cursor M.* 10949 (Gött.), Zachari..reuersid him on his manere, Siþen he went vnto þe autere. *a* 1400 *R. Glouc. Chron.* 8392 (MS. Digby 205, lf. 110), Byschopes & prestes & men of religioun..Reuersede hom in Churche. *c* 1450 LOVELICH *Grail* xlvi. 234 Iosephes, that of the Cristene Maister was, him gan to Reversen In that plas.

Reversé, variant of REVERSI.

Reversed (rɪvɜ̄·ɹst), *ppl. a.* [f. REVERSE *v.*¹ + -ED¹.] Turned backwards, or placed the contrary way; inverted, etc.

a 1400 *Minor Poems fr. Vernon MS.* I. 281 Heore reuersede gydes on hem are streyt drawe.

1594 I. G. *Grassi's Art Def.* I i b, To discharge a thrust at the enimies thigh, the which withstandeth the fall of the reuersed blowe. 1610 GUILLIM *Her.* I. viii, Reuersed Coats for Treason. 1615 SANDYS *Trav.* 34 The darts not lighting in iest on their naked necks, and reuersed faces. 1669 STURMY *Mariner's Mag.* II. ii. 52 By the side thereof must be placed the Reversed six Northern Signs. 1766 *Complete Farmer* s.v. *Madder* 5 H 4/1 Underneath the floor should be a reversed pyramid, somewhat obtuse at bottom. 1799 *Naval Chron.* I. 342 She hoisted a reversed ensign as a signal of distress. 1855 MACAULAY *Hist. Eng.* xviii. IV. 242 Footguards with reversed arms escorted the hearse. 1880 HAUGHTON *Phys. Geogr.* iv. 188 The southwest monsoons.. are reversed Trades. 1892 *Photogr. Ann.* II. 95 Plates that are liable to fog..as a rule give reversed images with comparatively short exposures.

b. In various special uses: (see quots.).

1682 GIBBON *Ess. Blason* 141 In English he calls it a *Cross reversed, which Leigh terms Sarcelé. 1876 A. H. GREEN *Phys. Geol.* ix. § 4. 366 **Reversed fault*, when the hade or slope is not towards the down-throw side. 1871 TYLOR *Prim. Cult.* II. 133 An old-fashioned English conchologist's delight in a *reversed shell. 1888 ROLLESTON & JACKSON *Anim. Life* 108 When the spire of a shell turns in a direction opposite to what is normal, it is said to be 'reversed'. 1886 *Paul's Fish Culture* Dec. 120 A specimen of what is known as the '*reversed sole', one with the left side brown and the right side white. 1704 J. HARRIS *Lex. Techn.* I. s.v. *Talon*, The Talon consists of two Portions of a Circle, one without, and the other within; and when the Concave Part is uppermost, it is called *Reversed Talon. 1847 FREEMAN in *Ecclesiologist* VIII. 37 *Reversed Tracery, in which the piercings seem to hang down from the top towards the centre. 1822 *Hortus Anglicus* II. 271 *Reversed or Salamanca Trefoil. Heads of flowers roundish; flowers reversed.

Hence **Reve·rsedly** *adv.*

1777 BP. LOWTH *Life of William of Wykeham* (ed. 3) ix. 286 Over the direction, which now stands among the notes, intermixed reversedly with them, [he] noted from Dr. London's mouth the account, which he had to communicate. 1798 in Cockburn *Life Jeffrey* (1852) II. xviii, Dr. Thomas Brown and J— propose to travel in your track (only reversedly) through Cumberland.

Reve·rseful, *a. rare.* [f. REVERSE *sb.*] Full of reverses or vicissitudes.

1875 FORTNUM *Maiolica* iv. 39 He died from poison in 1538 at Pesaro, whither he had retired after a reverseful life and reign.

Reve·rseless, *a. rare.* [f. as prec. + -LESS.] Incapable of being reversed.

1796 ANNA SEWARD *To Thomas Erskine* xi, The urn, whence Fate Throws her pale edicts in reverseless doom!

Reversely (rɪvɜ̄·ɹsli), *adv.* [f. REVERSE *a.* + -LY².] In a reverse manner.

1659 PEARSON *Creed* (1839) 3 That..which is not..certainly to be collected, either antecedently by its cause, or reversely by its effect. 1752 J. LOUTHIAN *Form of Process* (ed. 2) 159 [They] battered on the Cross the said armorial Bearing reversely (which was the Top or Chief of the Shield undermost). 1797 *Gen. Hist.* in *Ann. Reg.* 166/2 This country and France have reversely consumed their capital of the present, and that of future generations. 1860 MILL *Repr. Govt.* (1865) 14/1 And, reversely, if their machinery is so badly constructed that they do their own particular business ill, the effect is felt in a thousand ways. 1879 H. GEORGE *Progr. & Pov.* III. ii. (1881) 153 Stated reversely, the law of rent is necessarily the law of wages and interest taken together.

Reve·rsement. Now *rare.* [a. F. *reversement* (14–15th c.), or f. REVERSE *v.* + -MENT.] The

act of reversing, or fact of being reversed, in various senses; reversal.

1575 FENTON *Gold. Ep.* (1582) 215 The others being transitorie suffer reuercement and dissolution. 1590 BARROUGH *Meth. Physick* I. xxxvi. (1639) 59 The like cure you shall use when the reversement of the eye-lids is caused of superfluity of blood. 1607 G. WILKINS *Miseries Enforced Marriage* I. in Hazl. *Dodsley* IX. 478 Sue for reversement, and say the deed was done under age. 1720 STUKELEY *Mem.* (Surtees) I. 60 Such a reversement of the order of Nature as succeeding ages can have no idea of. 1738 WARBURTON *Div. Legat.* I. 288 The Reversement of the Laws of Humanity. 1818 *Blackw. Mag.* III. 301 Which finds its harvest..in the reversement of the true bearings of objects and feelings.

Reverser (rɪvɜ̄·ɹsəɹ). [f. REVERSE *v.* + -ER¹.]

1. One who or that which reverses (in various senses of the transitive verb).

a 1743 LD. HERVEY in Dodsley *Collect. Poems* (1782) IV. 100 Dreams, the kind reversers of my pain. 1868 COFFIN tr. *Ligouri's Glories of Mary* 87 Reverser of misfortunes,.. listen to my prayers. 1874 THEARLE *Naval Archit.* 101 No reverser is required with this template. 1882–3 SCHAFF *Encycl. Relig. Knowl.* 1470 Manu, 'the great, the reverser of fate'.

2. *Sc. Law.* One who borrows money on security of land; a mortgager.

1754 ERSKINE *Princ. Sc. Law* (1809) 91 Wadsets, upon redemption by the reverser. *a* 1768 — *Inst. Law Scot.* II. viii. § 3 The debtor, who receives the money, and grants the wadset, is called the reverser because he is intitled to the right of reversion. 1838 W. BELL *Dict. Law Scot.* 1030 The lender is called the wadsetter, and the borrower the reverser.

Reve·rseways, -wise, *adv.* [f. REVERSE *a.*] In the reverse or opposite way or direction.

1792 SIBLY *Occult Sci.* I. 145 In a line reverseways to the order of the zodiac. 1855 DICKENS in Foster *Life* (1907) 674 The musket carried reversewise with the stock over the shoulder.

‖**Reversi** (rəvɛ̄rsi, rɪvɜ̄·ɹsi). Also reversé. [a. F. *reversi*, earlier *reversin* (1601), ad. It. *rovescino* (Sp. *revesino*), f. *rovescio* reverse, wrong side.

Cotgrave defines *reversi* as 'a kind of Trumpe (played backward, and full of sport) which the Duke of Savoy brought some ten yeares agoe into France'.]

1. An obsolete card-game in which the object was to avoid winning the tricks. (See also REVERSIS and REVERSE *sb.* 10 a.)

1815 *Paris Chit-chat* (1816) I. 189 Monsieur Descourtils.. is always ready for a hand at boston, whist, or reversi. 1826 MISS MITFORD *Village* Ser. II. (1863) 297 Trictrac superseded chess or backgammon, reversi took the place of whist. 1870 L'ESTRANGE *Life Miss Mitford* I. 11 *note*, These suppers..were followed by tric-trac and reversé. 1898 LADY MARY LOYD tr. *O. Uzanne's Fashion in Paris* ii. 24 The fair Parisian..loved to sit up late,..and play her game of bouillotte or reversi.

2. A game played upon a draught-board by two persons, with counters having one side different in colour from the other.

The object of the game is to enclose as many of the opponent's counters as possible between one's own, and by so doing to have the right to reverse them, so that they show the same colour and are 'taken' as one's own.

1888 *Daily Tel.* 23 Apr. 5/3 The issue was connected with the game called 'reversi', which was described as being analogous to draughts. 1898 HOFFMANN *Bk. of Card & Table Games* 633 Reversi is played upon an ordinary draught-board.

Reversibi·lity. [f. next + -ITY. Cf. F. *réversibilité*, Pg. *reversibilidade*, It. *riversibilità*.] The fact or condition of being reversible; capacity for, liability to, reversion or reversal.

1849 *Fraser's Mag.* XXXIX. 206 A subsequent treaty.. regulated the reversibility of Parma, Placentia, and Guastalla. 1869 TYNDALL *Notes Lect. Light* § 124 The principle of reversibility which runs through the whole of optics finds illustration here. 1876 TAIT *Rec. Adv. Phys. Sci.* v. 113 Reversibility is the sole necessary condition of the equivalence between two engines.

Reversible (rɪvɜ̄·ɹsɪb'l), *a.* and *sb.* [f. REVERSE *v.* + -IBLE. Cf. F. *réversible*, Sp. *reversible*, Pg. *reversivel*, It. *riversibile*.] Admitting of being reversed; capable of reversing.

1648 HAMMOND *Wks.* (1683) I. 81 The fate and state of this Kingdom might be a reversible mutable state. 1685 J. DUNTON *Lett. fr. New-Eng.* (1867) 18 If it was not Fate, and so might be reversible, then there was nothing certain in his Art. 1828 STARK *Elem. Nat. Hist.* I. 247 Tarsus short, the hind toe reversible. 1861 MISS BROMLEY *Woman's Wand. in West. World* 20 These benches have reversible backs; so that you may sit fronting the engine or not as you prefer. 1878 STEWART & TAIT *Unseen Univ.* iii. § 106. 118 That an engine whose cycle of operations is reversible is a perfect engine.

b. *sb.* A cloth which is faced on both sides, so as to allow of its being turned.

1892 *Daily News* 10 Aug. 2/7 For the country districts tweeds, serges, reversibles, and cheap ladies' materials are the most wanted.

Reversify (rɪ-), *v.* [RE- 5 a.] *trans.* To turn into verse again.

1804 SOUTHEY in *Ann. Rev.* II. 549 Thus the following sonnet is reversified from Mr. Bowles. 1826 — in *Corr. w. C. Bowles* (1881) 107 The Sherwood versification, and the mode of practice by translating or reversifying into it.

Reve·rsing, *vbl. sb.* [f. REVERSE *v.*¹ + -ING¹.] The action of the verb, in various senses.

1581 *Act* 23 *Eliz.* c. 3 § 3 Any Writ of Error..for the Reversing of any Fine or Recovery heretofore passed. 1610 GUILLIM *Heraldry* I. viii. (1611) 35 Reuersing is a preposterous manner of location of a Coat-armour, by turning of the whole Escocheon vpside downe, contrary to the vsuall forme of bearing. 1676 TOWERSON *Decalogue* 536 He who so desires..the reversing of the divine institution. 1727–38 CHAMBERS *Cycl.* s.v., Reversing is frequently practised in figurative counterpoint. 1855 MACAULAY *Hist. Eng.* xii. III. 202 By the reversing of old attainders, and by new creations, seventeen more Lords..were introduced into the Upper House. 1892 E. SCOTT *Dancing* 198, I would particularly caution the pupil not to attempt reversing in public until he has thoroughly mastered the art in private.

Reve·rsing, *ppl. a.* [f. as prec. + -ING².]

1. That reverses or causes reversal.

Freq. in technical use, of parts of machinery: see Knight *Dict. Mech.* (1875) and *Lockwood's Dict. Mech.*, etc. (1888).

1864 PERCY *Metall.* 709 Reversing rolls have been employed, so that immediately the iron has passed through, the motion of the rolls is reversed. 1870 ROSCOE *Spectrum Anal.* (ed. 2) 298 This has been partially accomplished by Zöllner in his reversing spectroscope. 1896 *Westm. Gaz.* 18 Mar. 8/2 During the trip the starboard reversing-gear broke down.

b. *Reversing layer* or *stratum*, a stratum of the solar atmosphere (first noticed in 1870), reversing the dark lines of the ordinary solar spectrum.

1873 *Proc. Roy. Soc.* XXI. 512 Strontium, cadmium,..and uranium would seem..to exist in the solar reversing layer. 1882 C. A. YOUNG *Sun* 83 This atmosphere, containing in gaseous form the substances whose presence is manifested by the dark lines of the ordinary spectrum—the sun's reversing layer, as it is now often called. *Ibid.* 280 Above the 'reversing stratum' lies the scarlet chromosphere.

2. Of the nature of, characterized by, reversal (of an action, process, etc.).

1878 ABNEY *Photogr.* (1881) 274 The red rays..have exerted a negative or reversing action on the sensitive plate. 1892 *Daily News* 5 April 7/5 The reversing process necessitated in ordinary engraving.

Reve·rsingly, *adv. rare*⁻¹. [-LY².] In a contrary or opposed manner.

c 1380 WYCLIF *Sel. Wks.* I. 360 And Crist wiste þat men shulden ordeyne reversingeli to Cristis dede.

Reversion¹ (rɪvɜ̄·ɹʃən). Forms: 5–7 reuersion (5 -syon, 6–7 *Sc.* -sioun), 5– reversion; 5–6 reu-, revercion (6 -cyon); 6 reu-, 6–7 revertion. [a. OF. *reversion*, -*cioun* (mod.F. *réversion*), = Sp. *reversion*, It. *re-*, *riversione*:—L. *reversiōn-em*, n. of action f. *revers-*, *revertĕre* to REVERT.

In legal use the word is found in AF. before 1300.]

I. 1. *Law.* The return of an estate to the donor or grantor, or his heirs, after the expiry of the grant; an estate which thus returns to the donor or his heirs.

Chiefly in legal definitions of the term, the common application in actual use being as in b.

1442 *Rolls of Parlt.* V. 42/2 Title and Interesse of reversion of Fee simple that bene fallen..be cause of the seide forfaiture, aftre the seide taillez dispended. 1523 FITZHERB. *Surveying* 11 If the gyfte were in the tayle and no remaynder in fe euer nowe the reuercyon resteth styll in ye donor. 1596 BACON *Max. & Use Com. Law* (1635) 49 The Reversion is an estate left in the giver, after a particular estate made by him for yeares, life, or intaile. 1628 COKE *On Litt.* 142 b, In such case..it behoueth that the reuersion of the Lands and Tenements be in the Donor or Lessor. 1727–38 CHAMBERS *Cycl.* s.v., A reversion is to himself, from whom the conveyance of the land, &c. proceeded, and is commonly perpetual as to his heirs also. 1766 BLACKSTONE *Comm.* II. 112 Vesting in the donor the ultimate fee-simple of the land, expectant on the failure of issue; which expectant estate is what we now call a reversion. 1841 *Penny Cycl.* XIX. 438/1 If a man seised in fee simple conveys lands to A for life, or in tail, he retains the reversion in fee simple. 1894 *Times* 6 Mar. 7/1 The Commissioners of Woods and Forests had failed to establish the right of the Crown to a reversion in the particular denominations mentioned.

b. An estate of this kind as granted or transferable to another party, esp. upon the death of the original grantee; hence, the right of succeeding to, or next occupying, an estate, etc.

1426 *E. E. Wills* (1882) 74, I will þat Richard, my brother, haue half þe Cok and þe garlond in Colmanstrete, þe terme of his life, and þe Reuersion to Richard Burdon,..the terme of his life. *c* 1460 FORTESCUE *Abs. & Lim. Mon.* xx. (1885) 156 Ellis importune suters wil gape vpon suche reuersiouns, and oftentymes asken hem or they befall. 1486 *Rec. St. Mary at Hill* (1905) 13, I bequethe to Beatrice my wyf the reuersion of all those londes & tenementes. 1529 WOLSEY in Ellis *Orig. Lett.* Ser. I. II. 13, I wold gladly..grawnte onto hym the revercion of such thinges as the lorde Sands hath ther. 1587 LADY STAFFORD in *Collect.* (O.H.S.) I. 209 A reversion of the best lease. 1650 R. STAPYLTON *Strada's Low C. Wars* II. 30 By the Kings procurement, Bishops were entituled to the reversions of Monasteries, after the abbots deceases. 1699 GARTH *Dispens.* v. 61, I give Reversions, and for Heirs provide. 1765 H. WALPOLE *Otranto* v. (ed. 2) 179 The principality of Otranto was a stronger temptation, than the contingent reversion of it with Matilda. 1837 LOCKHART *Scott* IV. vii. 211 The sudden death of his wife's brother,..who had bequeathed the reversion of his fortune to his sister's family. 1873 DIXON *Two Queens* XV. iii. III. 148 Henry showed a sense of his great services by granting him the reversion of three manors in Essex.

c. In phr. *in reversion*, conditional upon the expiry of a grant or the death of a person.

1557 *Order of Hospitalls* C iv b, That there be no Leases let in revertion but one year before the ould Lease be expired. 1727–38 CHAMBERS *Cycl.* s.v. *Covin*, As, if a tenant for life conspire with another..in prejudice to him in reversion. 1771 *Encycl. Brit.* I. 318/1 An annuity is said to be in reversion, when the purchaser..does not immediately enter upon possession. 1841 *Penny Cycl.* XIX. 430/1 A contract to pay 100*l.* at the death of a given individual is 100*l.* in reversion to the executors of that individual. 1858 LD.

St. Leonards *Handy-Bk. Prop. Law* ii. 72 The observation applies only to annuities, or interests for life, or interests in reversion.

d. A sum which falls to be paid upon the death of a person, esp. as a result of life-insurance.

1771 *Encycl. Brit.* I. 323/1 What is the reversion worth, reckoning interest at 4 per cent.? 1792 R. Price *Observ. Reversion. Paym.* (ed. 5) I. 281 Data for computing accurately the values of all life-annuities and reversions. 1841 *Penny Cycl.* XIX. 430/1 The value of a reversion depends in a very easy manner upon the value of the corresponding annuity. 1858 Ld. St. Leonards *Handy-Bk. Prop. Law* ii. 72 The Act already passed must give great satisfaction to purchasers of reversions.

2. *transf.* The right of succeeding to the possession *of* something after another is done with it, or simply of obtaining it at some future time; a thing or possession which one expects to obtain.

c 1530 Ld. Berners *Arth. Lyt. Bryt.* (1814) 93 Ye be but lytell worth..whan ye are fayne to take the reuersion of these ladyes olde clothynge. 1579 Gosson *Sch. Abuse* (Arb.) 39 The very hyerlings of some of our Players, which stand at reuersion of vi.*s.* by the weeke. 1596 Shaks. *1 Hen. IV*, iv. i. 53 Where now remaines a sweet reuersion, We may boldly spend, vpon the hope Of what is to come in. 1634 Sir T. Herbert *Trav.* 16 They haue all the trickes possible to disfigure themselues, and to proue their Patrimony and Reuersions in Acheron. 1690 Crowne *Eng. Frier* iii, Here are now several [ladies] wayting in their coaches to have the reversion of him. 1717 Pope *To Mem. of Unfort. Lady* 9 Is there no bright reversion in the sky, For those who greatly think, or bravely die? 1768–74 Tucker *Lt. Nat.* (1834) II. 352 He that suffers voluntarily in a righteous cause..purchases the reversion of an immense estate. c 1830 De Quincey *Dice* Wks. 1862 X. 307 The Medical Institute was in the habit of purchasing from poor people..the reversion of their bodies. 1871 Macduff *Mem. Patmos* xiii. 171 It assures..of a reversion of glory—a fulness of bliss and joy.

b. The right of succession to an office or place of emolument, after the death or retirement of the holder. Const. *of*.

1623 Webster *Duchess Malfi* iii. i, You have not been.. in prison, nor a suitor at the court, Nor begg'd the reversion of some great man's place. 1687 A. Lovell tr. *Thevenot's Trav.* ii. 158 Each Basha in his own life-time easily procuring the Reversion for his Son by means of good Presents. 1703 Pope *Thebais* 181 Impotent Desire to reign alone, That scorns the dull reversion of a throne. 1807 Syd. Smith *Lett. Catholics* (1808) 171 If Ireland is gone, where are jobs? where are reversions? 1879 *Cassell's Techn. Educ.* IV. 291/1 He wrote many letters, requesting his friend's permission to apply for a grant of the reversion of it, and even offered to resign in his favour.

Comb. 1809 E. S. Barrett *Setting Sun* III. 3 Can one of these reversion mongers stand forward, and assert without blushing, that his services merit even the place he holds in possession!

c. In phr. *in* (also *by*) *reversion.* (Cf. 1 c.)

1555 W. Watreman *Fardle Facions* ii. xii. 262 Simon Petre (to whom long afore he had surrendred the gouernaunce and chiefteinshippe of his Churche, as in reuercion aftre him). 1594 Nashe *Unfort. Trav.* 87 The soule which is in mee, is the verie soule of Iulius Cæsar by reuersion. 1601 Holland *Pliny* I. 161 The Queen..made ouer the kingdome and crown in succession and reuersion to whom she thought good. a 1680 Butler *Rem.* (1759) I. 408 A Cat, you know, is said to have nine Lives, that is eight in Reversion and one in Possession. 1709 Swift *Vind. Bickerstaff* Wks. 1751 IV. 222 Time..gives them a Lease in Reversion, to continue their works after their death. 1758 Johnson *Idler* No. 15 ¶ 1 The prospect of too good a fortune in reversion when I married her. 1801 *Lusignan* III. 44 Thinking she would be sooner reconciled to an event which had actually taken place..than to one in reversion.

3. *Sc. Law.* A right of redemption operative in the case of a legal adjudication or a wadset.

1563–4 *Reg. Privy Council Scot.* I. 262 To ressave the sowmes of money and lettres of tak contenit in the lettres of reversioun maid thairupoun. 1599 *Acts Sederunt* 3 Nov., Ane act anent the registering of seasingis, reversiounis, and sindrie utheris wreittis. 1681 Stair *Institut.* i. x. 148 In Sale there may be Earnest interposed, or Reversion granted. 1708 J. Chamberlayne *St. Gt. Brit.* ii. iii. v. (1710) 443 The Scottish Wadsets and Reversions answer to the English Mortgages and Defeasances. a 1768 Erskine *Inst. Law Scot.* ii. viii. § 2 Reversions are either legal, which arise from the law itself,..or conventional, which are constituted by the agreement of the parties. 1838 W. Bell *Dict. Law Scot.* 828 The power of redemption is not lost by the currency of the forty years, provided the right of reversion has been recorded in the register of sasines.

fig. c 1590 Montgomerie *Sonnets* xxxv. 8 Suppose my silly saull with sin be seasde, ȝit the reversiones rests that it redemes.

II. †**4.** The remains, that which is left over, of any dish, drink, or meal. *Obs.*

c 1440 *Alph. Tales* 247 He bad a childe go feche þe reuersion of a pulett þat was sett in a kiste, & giff hir it. *Ibid.* 364 When he felid þat it was venom, he garte hur drynke of þe reuercion. 1526 in *Househ. Ord.* (1790) 171 The said gentleman-usher, sewer,..& yeomen-ushers,..to have the reversion of the said service. 1548 Udall, etc. *Erasm. Par. Mark* vi. 48 After the feast was done, the Apostles.. gathered together the reuersion. 1615 Brathwait *Strappado* (1878) 1 Nor do I feare, But my poore fragments shall be made of there, For good reuersions by thy scrambling crew. 1650 Fuller *Pisgah* ii. vii. 159 The dogs eat her up to the reversion of her skull, palmes of her hands, and feet. 1816 Scott *Antiq.* ix, Let Lovel and me have forthwith the relics of the chicken-pie, and the reversion of the port. 1824 — *St. Ronan's* iv, Men who scorned that the reversion of one bottle of wine should furnish forth the feast of to-morrow.

†**b.** The rest, residue, or remainder *of* something; also, a remnant, small number. *Obs.*

c 1440 *Alph. Tales* 475 Sodanly þer come a grete wynd & blew all down, and efter þat þer come ane erde-quake & shuke down þe reuersyon. 1596 Lodge *Wits Mis.* & *Worlds Madn.* (Hunterian Cl.) 33 In his bosom he beares his handkerchiefe made of the reuersion of his old tablecloth. 1608 Topsell *Serpents* (1658) 595 That the reversions of their bodies should after death turn into Serpents. 1650 Fuller *Pisgah* 409 The..whole company of this Remnant, or rather, Reversion of the Jews.

†**5.** The action or fact of returning to or from a place. *Obs.*

1570 Foxe *A. & M.* (ed. 2) 219/2 After his reuersion home, [he] was spoyled also of al yᵗ he brought with him. 1696 Brookhouse *Temple Open.* 14 This..was the Sign of Dispersion, and it will..be the Sign of their Reversion. 1707 Hearne *Collect.* (O. H. S.) II. 17 The Bp...homeward made Reversion. 1741 tr. *Cicero's De Nat. Deorum* ii. 144 The Sun..every Year makes two contrary Reversions from the extreme Part.

b. The action or fact of returning to a certain condition, practice, or belief; an instance of this.

1582 Bentley *Mon. Matrones* 42 Christ rejoiced in the conversion of sinners, and I was not greeued to see their reuersion to sinne. 1661 K. W. *Charact. Conceited Coxcombs, Polititian*, That army, whose idle lives hate the mention of a reversion to their wonted druggery.

1860 Pusey *Min. Proph.* 24 It is not conversion only, but reversion too, a turning *back from* the unbelief and sins. 1865 *Sat. Rev.* 24 June 750 The intelligence..of two rather remarkable 'reversions' marks a critical point in the history of the Church of Rome. 1876 Mozley *Univ. Serm.* xv. 256 There is a sudden reversion, a reaction in the posture of his mind.

c. *Biol.* The fact, or action, of reverting or returning to a primitive or ancestral type or condition; an instance of this.

1859 Darwin *Orig. Spec.* v. (1860) 162 We could not have told, whether these characters in our domestic breeds were reversions or only analogous variations. 1868 Lyell *Princ. Geol.* (ed. 10) II. iii. xliii. 478 The power of re-growth of the supernumerary digits in man may be an instance of reversion to an enormously remote and multidigitate progenitor. 1890 *Rep. Brit. Assoc.* 973.

†**6.** The return *of* a courtesy. *Obs. rare*⁻¹.

1642–4 Vicars *God in Mount* (1844) 133 The Cavaliers were more wise and craftie, than to stay and wait upon their so eager enemies reversion of courtesie.

7. The act of turning something or fact of being turned the reverse way. Also *attrib.*

1677 Plot *Oxfordsh.* 230 A pretty stiff string..may turn the hand upon change of weather in the *punctum* of reversion. 1698 *Phil. Trans.* XX. 412 Which goes from the North to the South-East all the Year about; except where there are Reversions of Breezes, and In-Letts near the Land. 1727–38 Chambers *Cycl.* s.v. *Abatement*, Reversion is either turning the whole escutcheon upside-down; or the adding another escutcheon, inverted, in the former. 1802 Wollaston in *Phil. Trans.* XCII. 373 With heavy spar, the instances of reversion are very numerous. 1836–7 Sir W. Hamilton *Metaph.* xli. (1859) II. 416 By a total reversion of the whole analogy of his psychology. 1872 W. S. Symonds *Rec. Rocks* viii. 262 There is a fault along the course of the river and a reversion of dip takes place. 1885 Roscoe *Spectrum Anal.* (ed. 4) 160 Zöllner has examined these lines with his reversion-spectroscope.

b. *Math.* (See quots.)

1698 *Phil. Trans.* XX. 191 This Theorem may be applied to what is called the Reversion of Series, such as finding the Number from its Logarithm given; the Sine from the Arc. 1737 *Gentl. Mag.* VII. 135/1 When *v* is found by the Reversion of Series, and substituted in the first Equation. *Ibid.*, He himself has given us the Value of *v* above by Reversion. 1797 *Encycl. Brit.* (ed. 3) XVII. 297/2 Reversion of Series is the method of finding the value of the quantity whose several powers are involved in a series, in terms of the quantity which is equal to the given series. 1802 *Phil. Trans.* XCII. 102 What does reversion of series mean? Merely this; a certain method or operation, according to which, one quantity being expressed in terms of another, the second may be expressed in terms of the first. 1841 *Penny Cycl.* XIX. 437/1 If *y* be a given series of powers of *x*, the determination of *x* in a series of functions of *y* is not called inversion, but reversion.

Reve·rsion² (ri-). *rare*⁻¹. [Re- 5 a.] Translation back into the original language.

1814 W. Taylor in *Monthly Rev.* LXXIV. 311 The task of version and reversion is not to be recommended merely to the linguist, but also to the poet.

Reve·rsionable, *a. rare*⁻¹. [f. Reversion ¹.] Capable of reversion.

1681 H. Nevile *Plato Rediv.* 191 For it was proposed, that whatsoever Security we were to receive should be both Conditional and Reversionable.

Reve·rsional, *a.* [f. Reversion ¹ + -al.] = Reversionary *a.* 2.

1675 *Conn. Col. Rec.* (1852) II. 250 His deed of guift..so makeing over the reversionall distribution of his estate to posterity as that his present necessities canot be releiued. 1679 *Answ. Appeal from County to City* 36 They have their Reversionall prospects too. 1847 Clough *Poems*, etc. (1869) I. 285 Their lands come to them saddled with indefinite rent-charges, reversions, and reversional interests.

Hence **Reve·rsionally** *adv.*

1858 De Quincey *Wks.* VIII. 325 Modern Christendom, under which idea I comprehend Europe, and reversionally the whole continent of America.

Reversionary (rīvɜ·ɹʃənări), *a.* (and *sb.*). [f. Reversion ¹ + -ary.]

1. Entitled to the reversion of something. *rare.*

1651 Walton *Life Wotton* in *Reliq. W.* (1672) d 1 By which means, and quitting the King of his promised reversionary Officers, and a piece of honest policy,..he got a Grant of it from His Majesty. 1889 *Spectator* 9 Nov., The maritime Powers cannot settle..who shall be reversionary heir to the gateway of the Black Sea.

b. *sb.* A reversioner. *rare.*

1660 Pepys *Diary* 24 July, Baron had got a grant beyond sea, to come in before the reversionary of the Privy Seale. 1905 *Hibbert Jrnl.* Oct. 76 He becomes the reversionary therefore of all its claims on the race.

2. Of the nature of, connected with, a reversion.

1720 *Lond. Gaz.* No. 5864/4 Reversionary Annuities upon the 14 per Cents. 1753–4 Richardson *Grandison* (1781) I. xlii. 304 She has, it is true, reversionary expectations. 1818 Cruise *Digest* (ed. 2) IV. 215 It was argued, that this was a reversionary lease, to take effect after the determination of another lease then in existence. 1845 Ld. Campbell *Chancellors* lvi. (1857) III. 124 On his releasing a reversionary grant of the Mastership of the Rolls. 1876 Freeman *Norm. Conq.* V. xxii. 19 A Norman grantee..was not always ready to respect the reversionary rights of the church.

b. (Cf. Reversion ¹ 4.)

1816 Scott *Old Mort.* xix, Your person would be with me, and your mind with the cold meat and reversionary pasties.

3. *Biol.* Relating to reversion to type; tending to revert; atavistic.

1873 Darwin *Orig. Spec.* v. (ed. 6) 127 We cannot distinguish between reversionary and analogous characters. 1896 *Allbutt's Syst. Med.* I. 114 This is what may be termed reversionary degeneration.

Reversioner (rīvɜ·ɹʃənəɹ). [f. Reversion ¹ + -er ¹.] One who possesses the reversion to an estate, office, etc.; an heir in reversion. Also *transf.*

1614 Raleigh *Hist. World* ii. (1634) 450 It were the wisest way to designe by his authority not only his successour, but also the reversioner. 1678 Marvell *Growth Popery* 25 Might not his Reversioner justly expect to be put into present Possession of the Office? 1766 Blackstone *Comment.* II. 113 The grantee..by his alienation may bar the heir or reversioner. 1826 *Stat. Realm* II. 38 *marg.*, In case of Covin by the particular Tenant, the Reversioner shall recover the Land. 1885 *Law Times Rep.* LIII. 228/2 The Legislature intended to..put reversioners and remaindermen on the same level. 1891 *Times* 30 Jan. 9/1 In the interests of the nation—the ultimate reversioner of the tithe.

Reve·rsionist. [-ist.] = Reversioner.

1812 *Ann. Reg.* 33 The only two members who had spoken against the bill were two very principal reversionists. 1869 *Daily News* 20 Aug., Policy-holders, and more reversionists in expectancy, would be affected by its downfall.

‖**Reversis.** Now only *Hist.* [a. F. *reversis*, variant of *reversi*.] = Reversi 1.

1814 *Hoyle's Games* 163 (Stanf.), Reversis is played by four persons...For this game the tens must be taken out from a pack of cards. 1816 Singer *Hist. Cards* 266 Reversis is a French game, which, Bullet imagines, was invented in the Court of Francis the First. 1876 *Catal. Cards Brit. Mus.* 51 A game termed Mawe succeeded Primero, then came Gleek, Hombre, Quadrille, Reversis, and Bassett.

b. *To make the reversis* (see quot.).

1830 'Eidrah Trebor' *Hoyle Made Familiar* 40 When every trick is made by the same person, there is no party, and this is called making the Reversis.

†**Reve·rsive,** *a. Obs.* [ad. med.L. **reversivus*: see Reverse *v.* and -ive.] ? Retrahent.

c 1400 *Lanfranc's Cirurg.* 152 Þe senewe þat is clepid reuersif, þat is vndir boþe sidis of þe eere.

†**Reverso,** obs. variant of Riverso.

1598 B. Jonson *Ev. Man in Hum.* iv. vii, Your Punto, your Reuerso, your Stoccata, your Imbroccata.

Revert (rīvɜ·ɹt), *sb.* [f. the vb.; in sense 2 after *convert* and *pervert*.]

1. †**a.** *Mus.* (See quot. 1597.) *Obs.*

1597 Morley *Introd. Mus.* 85 The reuerting of a point (which also we terme a reuert) is, when a point is made rising or falling, and then turned to go the contrarie waie, as manie notes as it did yᵉ first. 1622 Peacham *Compl. Gent.* xi. 103 Hath not Musicke her figures, the same which Rhetorique? What is a Reuert, but her Antistrophe?

b. A return *to* some means, etc.

1895 *Daily News* 4 Jan. 5/3 A watery gravel will here be encountered, necessitating a revert to pneumatic pressure as a means of keeping out the water.

2. One who returns to his previous faith.

1655 Fuller *Ch. Hist.* ii. 84 An active promoter in making the East-Saxons Converts (or rather Reverts) to the Faith. 1880 *Church Times* 26 Feb. 143 Perversions are now few, and the percentage of reverts has been considerable. 1898 Zangwill *Dreamers of Ghetto* III. 96 The faith of the revert was quite fixed.

3. 'That which is reverted' (*Cent. Dict.* 1890).

Reve·rt, *pa. pple.* [irreg. f. next.] Reverted.

1632 Lithgow *Trav.* i. 5, I..strain'd to assume..A dying life, reuert in liuing death. 1854 S. Dobell *Balder* xxiii. 117 If who descried The deep sea-gulph, with sudden gaze revert, Sees..A great white cloud.

Revert (rīvɜ·ɹt), *v.* Also 4 **roverte**, 5–7 **reuerte**, 5 **reverte**, *Sc.* **rewert**; 5 **revart**, 6 *Sc.* **reuart, rewairt.** [a. OF. *revertir*, = Sp. and Pg. *reverter*, It. *re-*, *rivertere*:—L. *revertĕre* (*reverti*), f. *re-* Re- + *vertĕre* to turn.]

I. *intr.* †**1.** To recover consciousness; to come to oneself again. *Obs.*

13.. *K. Alis.* (7894) in *Rouland & Vernagu* (1836) p. xxiii, The king reuerted in this gredeinge, And gaf hem al comfortinge. c 1400 *Laud Troy Bk.* 3077 He lay in swone longe, or he spak ought,..But whan he reuerted and ros aȝeyn, 'Alas,' he seyde. c 1485 *Digby Myst.* (1882) iii. 782 A! no lengar now I reverte! I yeld vp þe gost! 1560 Rolland *Crt. Venus* i. 686 Ȝit for faintnes..The quhile befoir fra time he did reuert [etc.].

†**b.** To recover, recuperate. *Obs. rare*⁻¹.

c 1480 Henryson *Orph. & Eurydice* 365 War scho at hame..Scho wald rewert full sone in fax and face.

†**c.** Of plants, etc.: To spring up afresh. *Obs.*

c 1470 Harding *Chron.* xcv. xii, The grasse and corne, that wolked were afore.., waxed grene and gan reuert. 1500–20 Dunbar *Poems* x. 42 Now spring vp flouris fra the rute, Reuert ȝow vpwart naturaly. 1513 Douglas *Æneis* xii. Prol. 230 Throu kynd ilk thyng springis and revertis. c 1560 A. Scott *Poems* (S.T.S.) v. 5 May caussis curage frome the splene, And every thing in May revartis.

2. To return, to come or go back, to or from a place or position. Now *rare.*

c 1400 *Remedie of Loue* xiv. in *Chaucer's Wks.* (1561) 322 b, By the path of penaunce yet woll I reuert To the well of grace. c 1450 *Mankind* 405 in *Macro Plays* 15, I xall go fett corn for my londe; I prey yow of pacyence; Ryght sone I xall reverte. 1509 Hawes *Conv. Swearers* xviii, Come vnto my Joye and agayne reuerte Frome the deuylles Snare. 1568 Grafton *Chron.* II. 842 After that the Erle and he had commoned no long time together, he reuerted to his souldiors. 1579 Spenser *Sheph. Cal.* Nov. 191 Make hast..thether to reuert. 1608 Sylvester *Du Bartas* ii. iv. *Decay* 243 The Ten Tribes, transported To a far Clime (whence never they reverted) Sojourn in forreign soyl. 1642 H. More *Song Soul* ii. iii. iv. 33 I'll..force thy feeble feet back to revert, That cannot climb so high a mystery. a 1729 Congreve *Impossible Thing*, Old ocean ..The child of his own bed receives, Which oft as dipt new force exerts, And in more vig'rous curls reverts. 1765 *Univ. Mag.* XXXVII. 108/2 The lightning..reverted back through a strong wall.

1905 Garnett *Shaks.* 105 Needs must I follow this.., And then, unto my native place reverting [etc.].

†**b.** To recur; to happen again. *Obs. rare*⁻¹.

1678 B. R. *Let. Popish Friends* 4 The Fit will certainly Revert, as soon as the malignant Humours can gather Head.

3. *Law.* To return to the former possessor or his heirs. (Cf. Reversion ¹ 1.)

1447 *Rolls of Parlt.* V. 135/2 Al maner possessions.. shalle..descende and reverte to such persones or persone, as thay shuld doo and the saide Alianor were dede. 1495 *Act 11 Hen. VII*, c. 52 § 1 Hereditamentis whiche to him descended, remayned, or reverted. 1544 *Sel. Cas. Crt. Requests* (Selden Soc.) 108 After whose dethe the said cotage..reuertyd and came into the handes and possessyon of the said defendaunt.

1727–38 Chambers *Cycl.* s.v. *Formedon*, Whose land is entailed to certain persons, and their issue, with condition, for want of such issue, to revert to the donor, and his heirs. 1768 Blackstone *Comm.* I. 609 In this case their lands and tenements shall revert to the person, or his heirs, who granted them to the corporation. 1818 Cruise *Digest* (ed. 2) VI. 361 The said premises..should from thenceforth revert over and go to such of his grandchildren as should be living. 1876 Freeman *Norm. Conq.* V. xxiv. 379 It might be forfeited to the State by a process of law; it could not revert to a personal lord.

transf. 1647 Clarendon *Hist. Reb.* ii. § 103 The projects of Wine and Iron,..the entire profit of which allways reverted to himself. 1737 *Gentl. Mag.* VII. 503/2 Let nine parts of the Tythe revert From Gownsmen to the Poor. 1844 H. H. Wilson *Brit. India* II. 337 The management of the political interests..reverted to the functionaries in whom they had been vested at the beginning of the war. 1870 *Evening Stand.* 12 Nov., Alsace and all Lorraine are to revert to the conqueror.

4. To return to a person or party after estrangement or separation. Now *rare* or *Obs.*

c 1440 *Alph. Tales* 46 He askid hur husbond if he wold reverte agayn to Criste. c 1485 *Digby Myst.* (1882) ii. 502 Let vs departe, Hys deth to devyse, syth he wyl not revart. 1567 *Gude & Godlie B.* (S.T.S.) 126 The sinfull than to the reuart, Sall in to gudlie haist.

b. To return *to* a custom, practice, idea, etc.

1612 Bacon *Ess., Expense* (Arb.) 55 He that cleeres at once will relapse: For finding himselfe out of straught, hee wil reuert to his customes. 1836 Lane *Mod. Egypt.* II. 341 The Christians at that time had reverted to the habit of wearing the white turban. 1861 May *Constit. Hist.* (1863) I. i. 14 To revert to a policy under which kings had governed, and ministers had executed their orders. 1897 Mary Kingsley *W. Africa* 364 He reverted to his old idea, that he had had to abandon testing when leaving Brazzaville.

†**5.** To turn away again, so as to leave or desert one. *Obs. rare.*

a 1542 Wyatt in *Anglia* XVIII. 501, I trust to temper it so, not for to care which do revert; All shall be one. 1557 *Tottel's Misc.* (Arb.) 132 Truely to serue with all my hart, Whiles life doth last not to reuart. 1568 Grafton *Chron.* II. 527 The Magistrates,..knowing that the Duke of Britaine and his brother were reuerted and turned to the French partie, beganne..to mourne.

6. To go back, to recur, *to* a former subject of discourse.

1587 M. Grove *Pelops & Hipp.* (1878) 49 But leaue we them ..And reuert to the Pallace, where no wight doeth idle stand. 1632 Lithgow *Trav.* i. 26 This much in general.., and so I reuert to mine itinerary relation. 1660 F. Brooke tr. *Le Blanc's Trav.* 246 Now I will revert to the Town of Barua, which I left for this short digression.

a 1817 Jane Austen *The Watsons* (1879) 359 His attention was so totally engaged in the business,..as never to revert to what he had been saying before. 1844 H. H. Wilson *Brit. India* III. 31 In the mean time, it will be convenient to revert to the more recent occurrences on the confines of Chittagong. 1875 Jowett *Plato* (ed. 2) V. 70 Plato takes occasion to revert to his old proposal of the use of wine.

b. To return *to* a subject of thought.

1822 Scott *Peveril* vi, His ideas..naturally reverted to his neighbour. 1842 Tennyson *Day-Dream* 248 My fancy, ranging thro' and thro',..Perforce will still revert to you. 1895 C. Kernahan *God & the Ant* Apol. (ed. 4) 9 In my waking moments my thoughts reverted to my dream.

c. To look back. *rare*⁻¹.

1820 Lamb *Elia* i. *Oxford in Vac.*, What half Januses are we, that cannot look forward with the same idolatry with which we for ever revert.

7. To return *to* a former condition. Also *ellipt.*

1638 Sir T. Herbert *Trav.* (ed. 2) 219 The Persians kept it till the yeere of our Lord 1605,..when it reverted to Turkish thraldome. 1642 H. More *Song Soul* iii. App. xl. Wks. (Grosart) 122 But those of aire can easily convert Into new forms and then againe revert. 1723 Waterland *Serm.* Wks. 1823 VIII. 438 All things reverted to their primitive order and regularity, calm, quiet, and composed. 1786 *Ann. Reg., Hist.* 32/2 The United States..have reverted to the situation in which England was placed before the acquisition of Canada. 1842 L. Hunt *The Palfrey* iv. 27 They.. sit, one moment, bolt upright, But soon reverts each nodding crown.

b. To return *to* an earlier or primitive form; to reproduce the characteristics of an ancestral type.

1859 Darwin *Orig. Spec.* i. (1860) 14 That our domestic varieties, when run wild, gradually but certainly revert in character to their aboriginal stocks. 1870 Henfrey *Bot.* § 878 The plants revert..to the type of one or the other of the parents. 1892 *Gardeners' Chron.* 27 Aug. 236/3, I have endeavoured to raise it from seed many times, but it generally reverts to the White Broom.

c. To fall back into a wild state.

1884 Jefferies *Red Deer* (1892) 14 When ploughed and laid down to grass, unless broken up from time to time, the ground will revert and yield nothing but rushes.

II. *trans.* †**8. a.** To recall to mind. *Obs.*⁻¹

1340 *Ayenb.* 128 Þe holy gost..him brengþ ayen to himzelue, zuo þet he..him reuerteþ huet guodes he heþ uerlore and ine huet poverte he is y-ualle be his zenne.

†**b.** To cause to return, *esp.* to bring back or restore, to a person, place, etc. *Obs.*

c 1400 *Rom. Rose* 7188 That doth the synfulle folk converte, And hem to Ihesu Crist reverte. 1432–50 tr. *Higden* (Rolls) III. 197 The sawles begynne ageyne after dethe to wylle to be reuertede in to theire bodies. 1494 Fabyan *Chron.* vii. ccxxxix. 279 If the sayd yonge Henry dyed without issue.., than the sayd castellys and holdis to be reuerted vnto the crowne of Fraunce. 1545 Raynold *Byrth Mankynde* Hh vj, Physicions..set boxing glasses vnder the brestes, meanynge therby, to reuert and returne vpward, ye matter enclined to much downewarde. c 1560 A. Scott *Poems* (S.T.S.) ix. 44 Bot ȝour hairt to my hairt rewert, And send me hairt for hairt agane. 1651 Jer. Taylor *Serm. for Year* i. iv. 49 Those unprofitable and hurtful branches which..revert evil juice to the very root it self.

9. †**a.** To turn away, withdraw. *Obs.*

c 1560 A. Scott *Poems* (S.T.S.) xxiii. 31, I sall in tyme rewairt My luve frome hir agane. 1566 Painter *Pal. Pleas.* I. 89, I wyll giue ouer this vnsemely loue, and reuerting my mynde to some other wyght, I wyll [etc.].

†**b.** To turn, force, or drive back; also *transf.* to refute. *Obs. rare.*

1575 R. B. *Appius & Virg.* in Hazl. *Dodsley* IV. 129, I will not sure reverted be, my heart shall have no ruth. 1598 Florio, *Smentire*,..to confute, to reuert, to make one say 'toong, thou lyest!' 1649 G. Daniel *Trinarch., Hen. V*, ccxv, Firme-written destinie Reverts the Breath of Kings; and playes with it. 1664 [see Reverting *vbl. sb.*].

c. To turn (one's eyes or steps) back; to direct backwards.

1632 Brome *Northern Lasse* i. vii, And wearilie chance to revert a look Upon the price you gave for this sad thraldom. 1645 G. Daniel *Poems* Wks. (Grosart) II. 20 If you would behold A Beautie to Entice; Revert your pur-blind Eyes; Too blind, and yet too bold. 1716 Pope *Iliad* vi. 641 His princess parts with a prophetic sigh, Unwilling parts, and oft reverts her eye. 1729 Savage *Wanderer* ii. 117 In stedfast Gaze his Eyes her Aspect keep, Then turn away, a-while dejected weep; Then he reverts 'em; but reverts in vain. 1814 Cary *Dante, Inf.* x. 123 But I my steps toward the ancient bard Reverting, ruminated on the words. 1832 G. Downes *Lett. Cont. Countries* I. 98 On reverting our eyes, every step presented some new and admirable scene.

10. To turn the other way; to reverse, invert, turn up. Now *rare* or *Obs.*

?a 1400 *Morte Arth.* 2918 Thane sir Priamous..Presez to his penowne, and pertly it hentes, Reuertede it redily, and a-waye rydys. c 1500 *Melusine* 319 The lustes & playsirs that I was wonnt to haue shal be reuertid in tribulacions & grieuous penitences. 1659 Pecke *Parnassi Puerp.* 55 You deny Kisses unto None; none Kiss, But to their Mouths, your Cheek reverted is. 1688 R. Holme *Acad. Armoury* ii. xix. 481/2 Others [bear] a Leg in fesse, the Thigh couped and reverted. 1755 B. Martin *Mag. Arts & Sci.* 331, I apply my Finger..upon the Top of the Tube, and then invert it;..then I revert the Tube, or turn it up again. 1799 *Phil. Trans.* LXXXIX. 269 Since they express the nature and form of a quantity which, by involution or reverting the operation, reproduces it. 1801 Strutt *Sports & Past.* i. i. 1, I shall..revert the arrangement of those amusements, and begin with hunting. 1807–10 Tannahill *Poems* (1846) 36 In many a dogg'rel epitaph Our 'ahs!—alases!' raise the laugh, Revert the tide of pity.

b. *Math.* (Cf. Reversion ¹ 7 b.)

1737 *Gentl. Mag.* VII. 549 Find the Value of *z* in *v*, and then revert the Series. 1797 *Encycl. Brit.* (ed. 3) XVII. 297/2 Let it be required to revert the series $ax+bx^2+cx^3+dx^4+ex^5$, &c. $=y$. 1827 *Hutton's Course Math.* I. 223 Assume a series for the value of the unknown quantity, of the same form with the series which is required to be reverted. 1842 Brande *Dict. Sci.*, etc. s.v. *Reversion of Series*, The original series will be reverted on determining the coefficients A, B, C, D, etc.

†**11.** To reverse, revoke, recall, annul. *Obs.*

1544 tr. *Littleton's Tenures* (1574) 93 He shal reuert such outlawrye by writ of Error [etc.]. 1563 Foxe *A. & M.* 845 Which byl being red according to the order of the House, was reuerted. 1606 *Jrnl. Ho. Comm.* 11 Apr., Merchants the Guides of Princes for raising Customs:—When they devise it [imposition of customs] quiet; when it is reverted, they startle and stir. 1639 G. Daniel *Vervic.* 67 My name preserve By force of Numbers, which revert the Lawes Of Destinie.

†**12.** To turn over (in the mind). *Obs.*⁻¹

1751 Earl Orrery *Remarks Swift* (1752) 150 As I have often reverted in my mind certain particulars relating to my two poetical friends, I have always thought [etc.].

Reve·rtal. *rare*⁻¹. [f. prec.] Reversion.

1858 J. B. Norton *Topics* 192 As to any prospect of reversal to the village system at some future period [etc.].

Reve·rtant, *a. Her. rare*⁻⁰. [f. Revert *v.* + -ant.] (See quot. 1828.)

1688 Holme *Acad. Armoury* ii. 484/2. 1828 Berry *Encycl. Her.* I, *Revertant*, or *Reverted*, that is, flexed and reflexed, or bending in the form of an S; though it is sometimes used for a bending in the manner of a cheveron.

Reverted (rīvɜ·ɹtėd), *ppl. a.* [f. Revert *v.*]

1. Turned backwards or the wrong way; bent back; reversed.

1590 Shaks. *Com. Err.* iii. ii. 126 *Ant.* Where France? *Dro.* In her forhead, arm'd and reuerted, making warre against her heire. 1621 Quarles *Argalus & P.* i. Wks. (Grosart) III. 242/1 Downe each side of his reverted chinne A lock of black neglected haire. 1681 Grew *Musæum* ii. § iii. iv. 237 The lesser ground Mosse with Reverted Leaves. 1708 *Brit. Apollo* No. 91. 2/2 We may observe a Reverted Scene. 1765 *Treat. Dom. Pigeons* 112 Its feathers stand all reverted. 1845 *Encycl. Metrop.* II. 88 This reverted series..may be put under a very elegant and remarkable form. 1870 Henfrey *Bot.* § 880 In some cases it has been found that the reverted or pure shoots bore perfect seeds.

2. Of the eyes, etc.: Directed backwards.

1741–2 Gray *Agrip.* 198 Yielding modesty, And oft reverted eye. 1754 — *Pleasure* 28 With forward and reverted eyes. ?1815 Coleridge *Time, Real & Imag.* 7 Yet ever runs she with reverted face, And looks and listens for the boy behind. 1858 Longf. *Jew. Cemetery Newport* xiv, Thus for ever with reverted look The mystic volume of the world they read. 1870 Swinburne *Ess. & Stud.* (1875) 333 The bull.. looking back with reverted horn and earnest eye.

†**Reve·rtence.** *Obs.*⁻¹ [f. Revert *v.*] Return.

c 1470 Harding *Chron.* lxviii. 3 [They] Besought the Kyng they myght haue his lycence, To Germany to make their revertence.

Reverter ¹ (rīvɜ·ɹtəɹ). [f. Revert *v.* + -er ⁴.]

1. *Law.* Reversion (of lands, etc.).

1491 *Act 7 Hen. VII*, c. 2 § 4 Londes..which to theym be commen by discent, reverter or remaynder. 1544 tr. *Littleton's Tenures* (1574) 115 b, Hee in the reversion..is put to his action of Formedon in the reverter. 1618 J. Smyth *Lives Berkeleys* (1883) II. 416 This family was..enriched with the reverter of their Barony of Berkeley. a 1628 Sir J. Doderidge *Eng. Lawyer* 70 Never like to return to the Lord by Escheat or Donor by Reverter. 1768 Blackstone *Comm.* III. 192 A formedon in the reverter lieth, where there is a gift in tail, and afterwards..the reversion falls in upon the donor. 1818 Cruise *Digest* (ed. 2) VI. 287 A limitation of a term to one for life..leaves a possibility..of reverter in the executors of the testator. 1896 *Act* 59 & 60 *Vict.* c. 28 § 15 The property shall not be deemed..to pass by reason only of its reverter to the disponer in his lifetime.

†**2.** Return. *Obs. rare*⁻¹.

1667 Waterhouse *Fire London* 115 The advantage that accrewed to His Majesty upon his reverter.

Reverter ² (rīvɜ·ɹtəɹ). [f. Revert *v.*¹ + -er ¹.] One who or that which reverts.

1890 *Spectator* 15 Nov., An exact reverter to the wild type in both respects sometimes occurs.

Revertibi·lity. [f. next + -ity.] The quality of being revertible.

1816 F. H. Naylor *Hist. Germany* I. i. viii. 295 [His] dominions had been seized without any pretext, except that of their probable revertibility to the chief of the empire in quality of an imperial fief.

Revertible (revɜ·ɹtib'l), *a.* [f. Revert *v.*] Capable of reverting; admitting of reversion.

1472–3 *Rolls of Parlt.* VI. 162/2 As long as the said Grauntes or Giftes..stond and be in their force, and not determyned nor revertible to the Kyng. 1727–38 Chambers *Cycl.* s.v. *Revert*, All honours and royal fees, alienated, revert to the crown, or are revertible. 1801 Ranken *Hist. France* I. i. iii. 252 The whole lands of the Kingdom were still considered as revertible annually to the general assembly. 1807 Barrow *Life Macartney* I. 259 In prevailing upon some of the Company's servants to unite these offices for a time, the nabob..succeeded only upon a revertible contract.

Reve·rticle. *rare*⁻⁰. [ad. L. *reverticulum.*] 'A place to return unto' (Blount, 1656).

Reve·rting, *vbl. sb.* [f. Revert *v.* + -ing ¹.] The action of the verb, in various senses.

1559 W. Cunningham *Cosmogr. Glasse* 34 After this somerlye reuerting..: for which cause this circle is called a tropike (or circle of reuerting and turning back). 1597 Morley *Introd. Mus.* 85 The reuerting of a point (which also we terme a reuert). 1613 Selden *Illustr. Drayton's Poly-olb.* ii. This Eagle..foretold of a reverting of the Crown, after the Britons, Saxons, and Normans, to the first again. 1664 Evelyn *Kal. Hort.* (1729) 192 To apply the Collateral Branches as near as possibly he can (without Violation and unnatural bending and reverting) to the Earth or Borders.

Reve·rting, *ppl. a.* [-ing ².] That reverts or turns back.

1815 Shelley *Alastor* 395 Shall the reverting stress Of that resistless gulf embosom it? 1868 H. Law *Beacons Bible* (1869) 153 The reverting eye betrays the heart. 1887 Ruskin *Præterita* II. 59 At the top of a long flight of squarely reverting stair.

Reve·rtive, *a. rare*⁻¹. [f. Revert *v.* + -ive.] Retreating, turning back.

1727 Thomson *To Mem. Newton* 55 Till again The tide revertive, unattracted, leaves A yellow waste of idle sands behind.

Hence **Reve·rtively** *adv.*, 'by way of reversion' (Webster, 1847).

†**Reve·rture.** *Obs. rare.* [f. Revert *v.* + -ure: cf. Reverter ¹.] Reversion; return.

1495 *Act 11 Hen. VII*, c. 63 § 1 When the seid descent, remaynder or reverture shall mowe fall or growe. a 1529 Skelton *Death K. Edw. IV* 14, I slepe now in molde, as it is naturall That erth vnto erth hath his reuerture. 1602 Warner *Alb. Eng.* Epit. 372 From this present Reuerture of the English Diadem to the next Innouation.

Revery, variant of Reavery, Reverie.

Reveryng, obs. form of Rivering.

†**Reve·sh, reve·ss,** *v. Obs.* Forms: α. 5 **reuesche, reweash-,** 6 **reuessoh-**; 4 **reuysh-, revysah-,** 5 **rauasoh-,** 6 **rauisah-.** β. 5 **reuess-, reveso-,** *Sc.* **rawess,** 6 **revess-.** Cf. also Reverse *v.*² [Back-formation from next, the *t* being apprehended as a participial ending.] = Revest *v.* (Chiefly in pa. t. or pa. pple.)

α. c 1375 *Lay Folks Mass Bk.* (MS. B) 34 When þo auter is al dight, & þo preste is reuysht [*v.r.* re-wessbut] right. c 1400 *Melayne* 889 The Bischoppe sone gane hym reuesche. c 1420 *Chron. Vilod.* 4695 Þen twey prestes weron reuysshede at hurre byddyng. c 1450 Myrc *Festial* 61 Then segh scho a prest and too dekens honestly reueschet. 1513 Bradshaw *St. Werburge* i. 3424 The bysshops were reuesshed in pontificalibus. 1555 W. Watreman *Fardle Facions* ii. xii. 270 With the whiche aftre he hath rauisshed him selfe in the vestrie,..he commeth forth to the aultare.

β. a 1440 *Sir Degrev.* 1830 Solempnely a cardinal, Revescyd with a pontifical, Sang the masse ryal. c 1470 Henry *Wallace* viii. 1197 Maister Jhon Blar was redy to rawess. 1480 Caxton *Chron. Eng.* ccxliv. t vij b, There mette with hym xiiij bisshoppes reuessed and mitered. 1523 *Pleadings Duchy Lanc.* (1896) XXXII. 116 [The priest being] revessed at messe.

†**Reve·st,** *v.*¹ *Obs.* Forms: 3–6 **reueste** (4 **-en, -yn,** 5 *Sc.* **rauests**), 3–7 **reuest** (4 **reuist,** 5 *Sc.* **rew-, rawest**), 4– **revest.** [a. OF. *revestir, revistir* (mod.F. *revêtir*), = Sp. and Pg. *revestir*, It. *rivestire*:—late L. *revestire*, f. *re-* Re- + *vestire* to clothe. In ME. the stem is also employed as pa. t. and pa. pple. (see β), in addition to the normal forms in *-ed.* Cf. also prec.]

1. *trans.* **a.** In *pa. pple.* Of priests, etc.: Arrayed in ecclesiastical vestments, esp. for the purpose of performing mass or other office.

α. c 1290 *St. Brendan* 274 in *S. Eng. Leg.* I. 227 Monekes it weren ech-on, And yreuested faire and in queor-copes. c 1305 *St. Swithin* 139 in *E. E. P.* (1862) 47 To þe mynstre hi gonne wende Ireuested faire ynouȝ. c 1350 *Will. Palerne* 5047 Þe patriarkes & oþer prelates prestli were reuested. c 1425 Wyntoun *Cron.* v. x. 1891 Þe prest, rawestyt on his wysse For to ressaiff hir sacryfyce. 1481 Caxton *Godf.* cxl. 209 Emonge the men of armes were the men of the Chirche reuested with awbes and stooles. a 1548 Hall *Chron., Hen. VIII*, 90 b, The Cardinall beyng reuested to syng Masse, the Erle of Essex brought the Bason with water. 1588 Allen *Admon.* 14 She hath caused the Priests..to be caried in scornefull manner reuested through the streates. 1609 Bible (Douay) *Lev.* vi. 10 The priest shall be revested with the tunike.

β. 13.. *Seuyn Sag.* (W.) 3356 To kirk thai led that faire lady; A prieste was reuist hastily. 1338 R. Brunne *Chron.* (1810) 36 Þe bisshop Owald herd of þat miracle speke, Reuest [*printed* Renst; F. *revestu*] at þe toumbe, be tok vp þe bones. a 1400–50 *Alexander* 1500 Þou & þi prelatis & prestis of þe temple, Raueste [*Dubl.* Reuest] all on a raw. c 1475 *Rauf Coilȝear* 346 The gentill Bischop Turpine cummand thay se, With threttie Conuent of Preistis reuest at ane sicht. c 1530 Ld. Berners *Arth. Lyt. Bryt.* (1814) 402 The byshop of Pancopone, reuest in his pontificalibus, ..there dydde axe the banes betwene them. 1593 *Rites & Mon. Durham* (Surtees Soc.) 7 They were always revest in the same place.

b. In general use: To clothe, apparel, attire.

1480 Caxton *Faytes of A.* ii. iv. 98 Toke theyr garmentes fro them and reuested theyre owne folke with the same. 1513 Douglas *Æneis* vi. ix. 46 Tisiphone..In bludy caip revestit and oursyld. 1590 Spenser *F. Q.* ii. i. 22 Her nathelesse Th'enchaunter..Did thus revest, and deckt with dew habiliments. 1616 Middleton *Civitatis Amor* Wks. (Bullen) VII. 285 They departed..to be disrobed of their hermits' weeds, and were revested in robes of crimson taffeta. 1648 J. Beaumont *Psyche* xv. xcvi, He first revests his arms and breast, which by Their naked valour did his foes defy. 1664 Evelyn tr. *Freart's Archit.* ii. i. 91 Revested with the most rich and splendid Apparel which Art can invent.

transf. a 1547 Surrey in *Tottel's Misc.* (Arb.) 11 The pleasant plot reuested green with warme. 1590 Alex. Hume *Hymns*, etc. (Bann. Cl.) 45 Quhen darknes hes the heauen revest. 1601 Dolman *La Primaud. Fr. Acad.* (1618) iii. 647 The bodie it selfe..in the resurrection..shall be reuested with the nature of the soule. 1649 *Alcoran* 26 See the bones of thine Asse; I will recollect and revest them with flesh.

2. *refl.* To dress or apparel (oneself), esp. in ecclesiastical vestments. Also *fig.*

α. 1297 R. Glouc. (Rolls) 11,114 Þe godeman vor drede to churche wende..& reuestede him bi þe auter. c 1374 Chaucer *Troylus* iii. 51 Right so as thes holtes and thes hayes..Revestyn hem in grene whan that May is. a 1400 *Minor Poems fr. Vernon MS.* 347/726 Reuesten him þenne wole be wel Wiþ riche pal and sendel. a 1450 *Knt. de la Tour* (1868) 49 That signifiethe that ye had made mani preestes reuest hem, and synge masses for thaire soules. 1489 Caxton *Faytes of A.* iv. xvii. 280 Therfore it was ordeyned that religiouse should reueste and clothe hemself of the same. a 1533 Ld. Berners *Huon* lxiii. 219 He.. chargyd them..to reuest them selues with crosse and myter & copes. 1574 Hellowes *Gueuara's Fam. Ep.* (1577) 42 It is as necessarie that the knight doe arme, as the priest reuest himselfe. 1603 *Coronat. Jas. I* (1685) 5 The Arch-Bishop..revesteth himself. 1652 J. Wright tr. *Camus' Nat. Paradox* vi. 127 As hee was revesting himself in Almeria's Robes.

β. a 1300 *Cursor M.* 10949 Zachari..reuest him on his maner, Siþen he went vnto þe auter. c 1325 *Metr. Hom.* 78 This bisschope, als the manere es, Reueste him to synge his messe.

3. To invest or endow *with* property. *rare*⁻¹.

c 1500 *Melusine* 97, I enjoyne..that ye doo edefye..a pryorye with viii monkes, and that ye reueste them with rentes and reuenues.

4. To put on (attire) again. Also *fig.*

1591 Sylvester *Du Bartas* i. i. 440 Those..shall rise, and all revest The flesh and bones that they at first possest. 1605 — *Sonn. late Peace* iv, Revest (yee States) your Robes of dignitie. a 1639 Wotton *Ps.* civ. 10 Again, when Thou of Life renew'st the Seeds, The withered Fields revest their chearful weeds. 1645 *City Alarum* 4 If..I could awake all those..to shake off that frozen timidity,..and revest their wonted courage. 1867 Longf. *Dante, Inf.* xiii. 104 Like others for our spoils shall we return; But not that any one may them revest.

5. *refl.* and *absol.* To clothe oneself again.

1605 Sylvester *Du Bartas, Spectacles* viii, When Trees with Leaves and Blossoms them re-vest. 1660 F. Brooke tr. *Le Blanc's Trav.* 190 Being disrobed,..he receives from the Kings own hand certain stripes...Which done he revests.

Hence †**Reve·sting** *vbl. sb.*¹ *Obs.*

a 1500 in *Archaeol.* LII. 213 The Revestyng of the abbot of Westminster att evensong.

Revest (rīve·st), *v.*² [f. Re- 5 a + Vest *v.*]

1. *trans.* To reinvest (one) with power, ownership, or office; to reinstate.

1561 Pilkington *Burnynge Paules Ch.* K vj b, Because the kinge hais reuested and reseased me of the whole archbishopricke. 1570 Foxe *A. & M.* (ed. 2) 243/1 Commanding him yᵗ Anselme..should be reuested agayn into his archbishopricke. 1594 ? Greene *Selimus* 1497 We will thrust Selimus from his throne, And reuest Acomat in the Empirie. 1643 Prynne *Popish R. Favourite* 57 [Was not] then..the Pope revested in his long exploded usurped supremacie in our Realme?

2. To vest (something) again *in* a person, etc.

1697 Luttrell *Brief Rel.* (1857) IV. 195 The lords yesterday read the bill..for revesting the sinecure of Landinam in Wales in John Spademan in trust for Joseph Hill. 1799 *Public Characters* 58 A Bill to revest in the Universities the monopoly in Almanacks. 1823 J. Marshall *Const. Opin.* (1839) 267 The whole effect allowed to this judgment was to revest in the crown the powers of government. 1885 *Act* 48 & 49 *Vict.* c. 48 Preamble, To restore to and re-vest in him the lands belonging to the said ancient territorial earldom.

ellipt. 1826 Kent *Comm.* i. v. (1858) I. 112 If a captured ship escapes from the captor, or is retaken, or if the owner ransoms her, his property is thereby revested.

3. 'To lay out in something less fleeting than money; as, to revest money in stocks.'

1828–32 in Webster.

4. *intr.* To become reinvested (*in* one).

1651 Sir J. Davies *Abridg. Reports* i. 7 Had A been disseised, there the right remaines and the possession may revest. 1765 *Act 5 Geo. III*, c. 26 Preamble, The right of the said mines royal revested in his then Majesty King George the Second. 1766 Blackstone *Comm.* II. 434 [They] shall go to his executors or administrators,..and shall not revest in the wife. 1886 *Law Rep.* Weekly Notes 189/1 He obtained his discharge in March, 1883,..and the equity of redemption revested in him.

Hence **Reve·sting** *vbl. sb.*²

1766 Burrow *Rep.* II. 1214 Speculative Refinements.. concerning the Change or Re-vesting of Property.

†**Reve·st,** *v.*³, obs. f. Revet *v.* So **Reve·sted** *ppl. a.*; **Reve·stment.**

1684 tr. *Siege Luxembourg* 17 They have three stories of Battlements, with a revested Ditch,..in the Revestment whereof are *Caponieres*. 1745 *Nova Scotia Arch.* (1869) 150 Two Bastions have almost entirely been revested;..the old revestments..would in a little while longer have tumbled down.

†**Reve·ster,** *sb.*, obs. var. Revestry *sb.* 1.

1611 Speed *Hist. Gt. Brit.* vii. xii. § 5. 272 The Crosse of Lead..was kept in the Treasury or Reuester of Glastenbury Church..till the Suppression thereof.

†**Reve·ster,** *v.*¹ *Obs.*⁻¹ [Cf. prec. and Revestry *v.*] *trans.* To replace in the vestry.

1466 in *Archæol.* I. i. 49 To light þe tapers to the sensours and to see them borne or revesterid and the quier to be senced.

†**Reve·ster,** *v.*² *Obs.* [var. of Revest *v.*¹, after *vesture* or *vestry*.] *trans.* To array, robe, dress. Also *refl.*

1494 Fabyan *Chron.* vii. ccxxi. 243 Where the stole is worne nexte vnto the albe, whan the preest is reuestred to masse. 1533 Cranmer *Let.* in *Misc. Writ.* (Parker Soc.) 245 Which all revestred ourselves in our pontificalibus. c 1540 tr. *Pol. Verg. Eng. Hist.* (Camden No. 36) 80 Having a place feetlie selected for the plantinge of their tents, theye revestred their Yowthe in armowre.

Reve·stiary. [ad. F. *revestiaire* or med.L. *revestiārium*: see Revest *v.*¹ and Vestiary *sb.*] = Revestry.

c 1440 *Alph. Tales* 423 When he come in-to þe revestiarie, & saw þe stole and þe vestiment at was layd furth for þe dekyn. 1483 Caxton *Gold. Leg.* 357 b/2 Whanne he was secretely in the reuestyarye he hadde no chayer. 1605 Camden *Rem.* 27 The impious Iewes ascribed all miracles to a name..ingravened in the revestiarie of the Temple. [1715 M. Davies *Athen. Brit.* I. 297 The latter Rabinical Jews us'd to ascribe all Miracles to a Name which was engrav'd in the Revestiary of the Temple.] 1820 Scott *Monast.* xvi, We will..despatch a servant express to the keeper of our revestiary to send us such things as we may want.

Revestry (rīve·stri), *sb.* Forms: 5–6 **revestre,** 5 **rewystre,** 6 **reuestre**; 5 **reuestery**; 6–7 **reu-, revestrie** (6 **-rye**); 5–7 **reu-,** 5– **revestry.** [ad. OF. *revestiaire* (see prec.), after *vestry*: see also Revester *sb.* and Revesture.]

1. The vestry of a church († or temple).

In common use during the 15–17th centuries.

1412 *Catterick Ch. Contract* (Raine, 1834) 9 And the forsaide Richarde sall putte out tusses for the makyng of a Reuestery. 1484 *Churchw. Acc. Wigtoft, Linc.* (Nichols, 1797) 79 In makyng of the crosse tristles and settyng on a grete almery in the revestry. 1527 in Fiddes *Wolsey* (1726) II. 103 Oon man is not able both to attende and kepe the revestry and do all things in the churche. 1577–87 Holinshed *Chron.* III. 1185/1 One of the southdores of S. Dionise church..,with the dore of the reuestrie of the same church, were both striken through and broken. 1621 Bp. Mountagu *Diatribæ* 12 The Priest and Æditus..led the man along thorow Courts, Porches, Iles, Chancels, &c. into their inmost Reuestries. 1683 Cave *Ecclesiastici* Introd. p. xiv, The Commissioners enter'd every where into the Temples, and threw open the Doors of their most secret Revestries.

1844 Paley *Ch. Restorers* 106, I wish you could see the exquisite decorated revestry at Willingham near Cambridge. 1880 *Sat. Rev.* No. 1292. 135 The revestry, which had been walled up,..when again opened, disclosed the copes, albs, chasubles, and other garments of the priests.

attrib. 1539 *Lett. Suppress. Monast.* (Camden) 276 Item, the lytle cundyt standyng at the revestrye dore, sold to George Stonyng.

transf. 1513 Douglas *Æneis* vi. i. 154 To the, also, within our realmis, sal be Mony secret closet and revestre. a 1641 Bp. Mountagu *Acts & Mon.* (1642) 7 It is laid up with God in ἀποκρύφοις, in the Revestries of eternity.

†**2.** A vestry meeting. In quot. *attrib.* *Obs.*

1631 Brathwait *Whimzies, Questman* 79 Some orders.. which he purposeth the next revestrie day to present to the rest of his worshipfull brethren.

Hence †**Reve·stry** *v.*, to lay up. *Obs. rare*⁻¹.

1624 Bp. Mountagu *Gagg* 312 The Arke was revestried in the most holy place.

†**Reve·sture.** *Obs. rare.* [Cf. Revest *v.*¹ and Vesture.]

1. = Revestry 1. (Cf. Revester *sb.*)

1527 *Lanc. Wills* (Chetham Soc.) I. 16 My bodye to be bured wᵗin the white freris of Chester in thare Chansell affore the reuesture durr.

2. Vesture; vestments.

a 1548 Hall *Chron., Hen. VIII*, 73 b, The Aultars of this Chapell were hanged with riche reuesture of cloth of gold. 1621 Bp. Mountagu *Diatribæ* 554 The persons initiated were λάβοι. And so were the places and Reuestures in which they were initiated.

Revet, obs. form of Rivet.

Revet (rīve·t), *v.* [ad. F. *revêtir*: see next.] *trans.* To face (an embankment or wall) with masonry or other material, *esp.* in fortification.

1812 Wellington in Gurw. *Desp.* (1837) IX. 197 Works in earth are equally good, if not better..than those revetted in masonry. 1859 F. A. Griffiths *Artil. Man.* (1862) 250, 2 sappers, with 6 assistants, to revet the work. 1880 V. L. Cameron *Our Future Highway* II. 250 The face of the river bank was revetted with faggots of brushwood. 1884 *Milit. Engin.* I. ii. 26 In flying trench-work gabions are used to revet the interior slope of the parapet.

Revête (rīvê·t), *v.* Also **revete.** [ad. F. *revêtir*:—OF. *revestir*: see Revest *v.*¹] = prec.

1828 J. M. Spearman *Brit. Gunner* (ed. 2) 404 To find the Number of Turfs required to Rêvete [*sic*] a Work. 1832 Southey *Hist. Penins. War* III. 396 When they came to the escarpe, which was not revêted, the men scrambled up. 1841 *Penny Cycl.* XIX. 347/2 The exterior of the parapet and the escarp of the ditch are covered or reveted with sods. 1865 J. Fergusson *Hist. Archit.* I. 157 The great mass of the palace..was raised by artificial means to a height of 30 ft...and carefully revêted with stone.

‖**Revêtement** (rəvɛtmaṅ). Also **revetement.** [F. *revêtement*:—OF. *revestiment*, = Sp. *revestimiento*, Pg. *-mento*, It. *rivestimento*: see prec. and -ment.]

1. *Fortif.* = Revetment 1.

1771 *Encycl. Brit.* II. 620/1 s.v. *Fortification*, To prevent the earth of the parapet (which seldom has any revetement [1779 revetment]) from falling into the ditch. 1790 Beatson *Nav. & Mil. Mem.* II. 163 Having only a rampart, with a revetement flanked with redans. 1804 Wellington in Gurw. *Desp.* (1835) III. 277, I am inclined to be of opinion..that the revêtement would not bear those pieces of a heavy calibre. 1879 *Encycl. Brit.* IX. 443/2 A massive envelope,..formed of earth with thick masonry revêtements both in front and in rear.

2. *Civil Eng.* = Revetment 2.

1838 *Civil Eng. & Arch. Jrnl.* I. 380/2 In the backing of retaining-walls, revetements, &c., it [*sc.* concrete] may..be advantageously applied. 1886 *Daily News* 10 Dec. 3/4 The sea was yesterday..breaking over the revetements and pier in great quantities.

3. *Arch.* = Revetment 3.

1839 *Civil Eng. & Arch. Jrnl.* II. 244/1 The stone for the revêtement, or casing of the exterior [of the pyramid],..is a compact limestone. 1888 *New Princeton Rev.* V. 141 The absence of any fragments of columns, friezes, cornices, etc. (except terra-cotta revetements), confirms the theory that the Etruscan temple was built of wood.

4. *attrib.*, as *revêtement wall.*

1828 J. M. Spearman *Brit. Gunner* (ed. 2) 351 The manner of determining the strength of revêtement walls. 1889 *Harper's Mag.* June 92/1 Back of all this rises a stone revetement wall supporting the river street.

Revetment (rīve·tmĕnt). [ad. F. *revêtement*: see prec. and cf. Revet *v.*]

1. *Fortif.* A retaining-wall (of masonry or other material) supporting the face of an earthen rampart or the side of a ditch.

1779 [see Revêtement 1]. 1838 *Penny Cycl.* X. 375/2 The cordon..at the top of the revetment. 1863 Kinglake *Crimea* (1877) III. v. 365 The fort was surrounded by a ditch,..with revetments in masonry. 1876 Voyle & Stevenson *Milit. Dict.* 341/2 In field fortification, the materials used for the revetments are gabions, fascines, sandbags [etc.].

2. *Civil Eng.* A facing of masonry, concrete, sods, etc., supporting or protecting a bank or embankment.

1838 *Civil Eng. & Arch. Jrnl.* I. 338/1 B, revetment or sea wall. 1856 *Illustr. Lond. News* 2 Feb. 110/1 The revetment [of the dry dock] at top was 6 feet 8 inches broad. 1880 Ball *Jungle Life India* xi. 494 The site of the town of Cuttack..has necessitated costly revetments and other protective works on the river face.

3. *Arch.* A facing of stone or other hard material over a less durable substance.

1891 Sellers tr. *Schuchhardt's Schliemann's Excav.* 152 The slabs..were originally the mere outward revetment of a massive wall.

4. *attrib.*, as *revetment wall, system*, etc.

1838 *Penny Cycl.* X. 10/1 In large fortresses the escarp is the exterior surface of the revetment wall which supports the rampart. 1882 *Harper's Mag.* LXV. 612 The levee, jetty, and revetment system is not so simple. 1884 Knight *Dict. Mech.* Suppl. 755/2 The building of the revetment mattress at Council Bluffs.

Revette, obs. form of Rivet.

Reve·tted, *ppl. a.* [f. Revet *v.*] Provided with a revetment.

1879 *Cassell's Techn. Educ.* IV. 136/2 A deep ditch with a revetted escarp. 1888 H. D. Hutchinson *Field Fortif.* (ed. 2) 47 There being an embrasure with revetted cheeks in each gun-portion.

Reve·tting, *vbl. sb.* [f. Revet *v.*] **a.** The action of facing with masonry, etc.; also *attrib.* **b.** The materials used to form a revetment.

1880 in Knight *Dict. Mech.* Suppl. 755/1 The revetting should be put on so as to extend [etc.]. 1884 *Milit. Engin.* I. ii. 27 The revetting of this step is done after the parallel is completed. *Ibid.* 29 Revetting materials should not be made up in the park.

Revi·brate (ri-), *v.* [Re- 5 a.]

1. *intr.* To vibrate again.

a 1763 Shenstone *Economy* i. 46 This open'd soul, This boon companion, this elastic breast Revibrates quick. 1803 Jane Porter *Thaddeus* (1826) III. xiii. 294 The chord once touched, every note revibrated. 1839–48 Bailey *Festus* xix. 206 Which caused..earth revibrate to her inmost base.

2. *trans.* To cause to vibrate again.

1898 *Daily News* 13 Apr. 8/3 If the record of these vibrations were retraced over the needle it would re-vibrate the diaphragm.

So **Revibra·tion,** 'the act of vibrating back'.

1828–32 in Webster.

†**Revi·ct,** *v. Obs. rare*⁻¹. [f. *revict-*, ppl. stem of L. *revincĕre.*] *trans.* To recover.

a 1656 Bp. Hall *Specialities Life* Rem. Wks. (1660) 28 Lord Chancellor Ellesmere..adjudged these two sued for Prebends, clearly to be return'd to the Church, untill by common law they could..be revicted.

†**Revi·ction** ¹. *Obs. rare.* [ad. late L. *reviction-em*, n. of action f. *revincĕre*: see prec.]

1. Refutation, disproof.

1677 Gale *Crt. Gentiles* iii. 124 The invaliditie..of the evasion we have already in part demonstrated. But for a more satisfactory reviction thereof let us a little examine it according to rules both of Philosophie and Theologie.

2. Reconquest, recovery.

1679 Harby *Key Sacr. Script.* i. 9 To heal the Churche's almost deadly wounds..; and to procure the Peace, Conversion, and Reviction of all Sects and Nations.

†**Revi·ction** ², error for Reviviction. *Obs.*

1652 Bp. Hall *Gr. Myst. of Godliness* § 9 Do we live to see a reviction of the old Sadducisme, so long since dead and forgotten?

Revictual (rīvi·t'l), *v.* Forms: α. 6 **revitaille, revi-, reui-, reuytayle; revittell,** 6–7 **revittle.** β. 6–7 **reuictual, revictuall,** 7– **revictual.** [f. Re- 5 a + Victual *v.*]

1. *trans.* To supply (a place, fleet, etc.) with a fresh stock of provisions. Also *refl.*

α. 1523 Ld. Berners *Froiss.* I. ccxlii. 356 Perauenture ther be some that are comynge to reuitayle yᵉ castell. 1543 *State Papers* IX. 437 The Prynce wyth his armye, havyng revytayled Heynsborgh,..are retorned home. 1587 Fleming *Contn. Holinshed* III. 1402/1 When sir Richard Greenefield had..reuittelled himselfe, and laden his ships with horsses.

β. 1579 Fenton *Guicciard.* (1618) 246 [He] reuictualled Pisa continually with a Gallion and other Brigandines. 1603 Knolles *Hist. Turks* (1621) 1188 Having revictualled Buda, his purpose was for this yere to returne. 1693 Luttrell *Brief Rel.* (1857) III. 172 Orders are sent to the admiralls..to revictuall the smaller ships. 1750 Carte *Hist. Eng.* II. 722 The siege lasted several months; the place being revictualled, and the garrison relieved five different times. 1813 Sir R. Wilson *Priv. Diary* (1862) II. 139, I would sweep through Berlin, revictual the fortresses, and return via Magdeburg. 1861 Goldw. Smith *Lect. Mod. Hist.* iv. 16 This colony did not, like Virginia, require to be refounded, not even to be re-victualled. 1878 Bosw. Smith *Carthage* 107 The Roman fleet after it had been revictualled and repaired, stood right across the Mediterranean.

2. *absol.* To procure or take in a fresh supply of provisions.

1618 Raleigh *Let.* in *Rem.* (1661) 236 You shall hear from me..from the New-found Land, where I mean to make clean my Ships and revictual. 1656 Milton *Lett. of State* Wks. 1851 VIII. 351 In regard he had design'd to revittle in Portugal, from whence he was driven by contrary Winds. 1721 *Lond. Gaz.* No. 6000/2 A Frigate..is arrived at the Texel..to revictual. 1849–50 Alison *Hist. Europe* VII. xlii. § 39. 120 He watered and revictualled at Bahia. 1870 *Daily News* 25 Oct., An invading army..is therefore greatly harassed and cannot easily revictual.

Hence **Revi·ctualling** *vbl. sb.* and *ppl. a.* Also **Revi·ctualment.**

1525 Ld. Berners *Froiss.* II. clxix. 195 It was fournysshed with vytayles to haue been kepte seuen yere without any reuytaylynge. 1602 Carew *Cornwall* 236 No small quantitie for the revitailing of weather-driuen shippes. 1870 *Pall Mall G.* 7 Nov. 8 The Provisional Government made the revictualling of Paris..a *sine quâ non.* 1870 *Observer* 13 Nov., In return for the privilege of revictualment, the French authorities offered no kind of equivalent.

†**Revie·,** *sb. Obs.* Also 6–7 **reuie,** 7 **reuye.** [a. F. *renvi* (= It. *rinvito*, Sp. and Pg. *revite*), verbal sb. f. *renvier* Revie *v.*]

1. In card-playing, a higher stake ventured by a player against that proposed by an opponent.

1592 Greene *Conny Catch.* ii. Wks. (Grosart) X. 99 At last to maintain the main and to checke vies with reuies, he laide his horse in the hazard, and lost him. a 1618 J. Davies (Heref.) *Wittes Pilgr.* Wks. (Grosart) II. 38/1 Some Elders, for re-uies, passe Pare, and Post, When lo, the Yonger shares, or Doubles it. 1648 Gage *West Ind.* ix. 26 So the cards were handsomely shuffled, the vies and revies were doubled. *Ibid.*, Sometimes the vies and revies went round of twenty patacons. 1680 [see Revie *v.* 3].

fig. 1591 Greene *Conny Catch.* To Rdr., They haue their vies and reuies vppon the poore Cunnies backe, till [etc.].

2. *transf.* **a.** A return blow or thrust.

1589 Greene *Tullies Loue* Wks. (Grosart) VII. 202 In his owne minde hauing a boute or two with fancie, he gaue hir so deepe a reuie that hee held affection at the swordes point.

b. A repetition; a renewed inspection.

In quot. 1621 perh. associated with *review.*

1588 Greene *Metamorphosis* Wks. (Grosart) IX. 23 And here multiplying sigh vpon sigh with double and trebble reuies, shee ceased. 1621 Quarles *Esther* vi, He lik't them all, but when with strict reuye He viewed Ester's face, his wounded eye Sparkl'd.

†**Revie·,** *v. Obs.* Also 5–7 **reuye,** 6–7 **reuie, revy.** [ad. F. *renvier*, = Sp. and Pg. *revidar*, It. *rinvitare*, late L. *reinvitāre*, f. L. *re-* Re- + *invitāre* to invite.]

1. *trans.* To return (an invitation). *rare*⁻¹.

c 1430 *Pilgr. Lyf Manhode* iii. xliii. (1869) 159 If it bifalle that he drinke first, that oother wole drinke also, and seyth anoon, j reuye it.

2. To challenge in return. Also *intr.*, to make return of a challenge *on* another. *rare.*

c 1470 Harding *Chron.* clv. 2 For whose beautie it should the knyghtes moue In armes so echeone other to reuie, To get a fame in play of chiualry. *Ibid.* clxxviii. 20 Echeone on other of pride so reuied Without rule of marciall gouernaunce, Thei smored wer, by their contrariaunce.

3. In card-playing: To meet by venturing a larger stake than that proposed by an opponent. Also in fig. context.

1591 Florio *2nd Fruites* 69 *S.* I vye it, will you hould it? *A.* Yea sir, I hold it, and reuie it, but dispatch. 1591 Greene *Conny Catch.* (1859) 25 Ile vie and revie every card at my pleasure till eyther yours or mine come out. 1598 B. Jonson *Ev. Man in Hum.* iv. i, S'light, here's a trick vyed, and reuyed! 1635 Quarles *Embl.* ii. v. 3 Thy cunning can but pack the cards;..Thy game at weakest, still thou vy'st; If seen, and then revy'd, deny'st. 1680 Cotton *Compl. Gamester* (ed. 2) 66 The first or eldest says, I'le vye the Ruff, the next says, I'le see it, and the third, I'le see it and revie it: I'le see your revie, says the first.

transf. 1597 J. King *On Jonas* (1618) 282, I cal to minde an auncient historie of vowes vied and reuied between the citizens of Croto. 1609 Rowley *Search for Money* (Percy Soc.) 13 She vied and revied othes to the contrary that it was not so. 1654 Gayton *Pleas. Notes* iv. ix. 235 All this time the Knights play'd it at Dutch Gleek, and had so vied it, and revied it, that they were all Honours in their faces. 1673 [R. Leigh] *Transp. Reh.* 100 To vye him, and see him, and re-vye him in contradictions. This figure now is lost to any man that is not a gamester.

4. *intr.* To make a revie or revies.

1591 Greene *Conny Catch.* Wks. (Grosart) X. 27 So they vie and revie till some ten shillings bee on the stake. a 1618 J. Davies (Heref.) *Wittes Pilgr.* Wks. (Grosart) II. 38/1 Some, beeing Pa-riall,..Vy, and re-uy, and weene they all shall winn. a 1640 Jackson *Creed* x. xl. Wks. IX. 395 Like a wilful chafing gamester who after once he hath begun to vie upon or provoke his adversary resolves to revie upon him and to provoke him further. 1680 Cotton *Compl. Gamester* (ed. 2) 67 I'le see it and revie, saith one; I'le see it and revie, saith another.

fig. 1654 Gayton *Pleas. Notes* iii. v. 96 Where he plaied his cards so well, and vied and revied so often, that he had scarce an eye to see withall.

b. *transf.* To make counter-bids.

1602 Carew *Cornwall* 37 A farme..can no sooner fall in hand, then the Suruey Court shalbe waited on with many Officers, vying & reuying each on other.

c. To retort or retaliate.

a 1620 Babington *Wks.* (1622) 401 Not multiplying words with your husband,..vying and revying, and will he, nill he still hauing the last word. 1629 J. M. tr. *Fonseca's Devout Contempl.* 533 He that vpon the vying of an inimie will not ..reuie vpon him but let it passe. a 1734 North *Exam.* iii. vi. § 53 (1740) 462 The other revyed, and denied his Facts; and so too and fro, vying and revying with perpetual Contradiction, little less than giving each other the Lye.

Hence †**Revy·ing** *vbl. sb. Obs.*

1635 Quarles *Embl.* i. vi. 5 True rest consists not in the oft revying Of worldly drosse. 1680 Cotton *Compl. Gamester* (ed. 2) 67 For which seeing and revying they reckon but two, after that it is at once come to eight. 1689 *Tryal Bishops* 62 We must not have vying and re-vying, for then we shall have no end.

Review (rīviū·), *sb.* Also **re-view.** Also 6 **reveu,** 6–7 **rev-, reuiewe,** 7 **reuiew.** [a. older F. *reveue* (mod.F. *revue*), verbal sb. f. *revoir*, f. *re-* Re- + *voir*:—L. *vidēre* to see.]

I. 1. The act of looking over something (again), with a view to correction or improvement; a revision (of a book, etc.). Now *rare.*

1565 in *Lett. Lit. Men* (Camden) 27 We think so well of the first impression, and reviewe of those whiche have sithens travailed therin. 1622 Jaggard *Note to Brooke's Disc. Err. Catal. Nobility*, The sight alone of such a Reuerend man.. would do more good for keeping the presse in order then the view, and review of twentie proofes by himselfe. 1638 Junius *Paint. Ancients* A 3 Some things having passed therein, which..in the review..I wished might be altered. 1710 Wheatly *Bk. Com. Prayer* Pref., Some particular Alterations in after Reviews it will not be necessary to enter into the Detail of. 1790 Burke *Fr. Rev.* 354 What we have left standing in our several reviews and reformations, as well as to what we have altered or superadded.

†**b.** A revise in printing. *Obs. rare*⁻¹.

1622 Jaggard *Note to Brooke's Disc. Err. Catal. Nobility*, Though hee came not in person to ouer-looke the Presse, yet the Proofe, and Reuiewes duly attended him, and he perused them..in the maner he did before.

2. *Law.* Revision of a sentence, etc., by some other court or authority.

1654 Bramhall *Just Vind.* iii. (1661) 34 To render final justice, that is, to receive the last appeals of his own Subjects, without fear of any review from Rome. 1689 Burnet *Tracts* (1689) I. 79 The Decisions of this Court can never be brought under a second Review. 1706 *Act 6 Anne* c. 11 § 12 All reviews, reductions or suspensions of the sentences in maritime cases. 1765 Blackstone *Comm.* I. 11 Their sentence is final, decisive, irrevocable: no appeal, no correction, not even a review can be had. 1807 *Act 48 Geo. III*, c. 151 § 16 To submit the said Interlocutor..to the Review of the Division to which the said Lord Ordinary belongs. 1833 *Act 3 & 4 Will. IV*, c. 46 § 70 The decision of the magistrate shall be final, and not subject to review in any court. 1864 Pomeroy *Munic. Law* § 283 There is ample provision made for a review..of the rulings of law made by the judge at the trial.

b. *Bill of review*: (see quot. 1838).

1676 Duke *Moor's Law Charit. Uses* Table s.v. *Relief*, No relief upon a Bill of Review, after an Appeal, but in Parliament. 1768 Blackstone *Comm.* III. 454 A bill of review may be had upon apparent error in judgment, appearing on the face of the decree; or, by special leave of the court. 1818 Cruise *Digest* (ed. 2) III. 508 Upon a bill of review brought between 30 and 40 years after the decree pronounced. 1838 Story *Equity Pleadings* 15 A Bill of Review, which is brought to examine and reverse a decree made upon a former Bill, which has been duly enrolled, and thereby become a record of the Court.

c. *Commission, Court, of review*: (see quots.).

a 1633 Coke *Inst.* iv. lxxiv. (1648) 341 Upon a sentence given by the High Commissioners, a Commission of Review may be granted to and for the party grieved. 1766 Entick *London* IV. 33 The king has it in his power to grant a commission of review under the broad seal, for the delegates to consider and judge again, what has been decreed in the court of delegates. 1831 *Act 1 & 2 Will. IV*, c. 56 § 2 The said Judges or any Three of them shall..form a Court of Review,..and shall have Superintendance and Controul in all Matters of Bankruptcy. 1838 W. Bell *Dict. Law Scot.* 344 The court of review, in all questions connected with the representation of the peerage of Scotland, is the House of Lords.

3. A formal inspection of military or naval forces by the sovereign or other high personage, or by the general in command.

[1585 T. Washington tr. *Nicholay's Voy.* i. ii, We made ..reuiewe of the gentlemen, souldiers and other of our company.] 1683 *Lond. Gaz.* No. 1839/3 On Thursday last his Most Christian Majesty took a Review of the Cavalry. 1713 *Ibid.* No. 5106/3 Their Lordships will meet at the Horse-Guards..to finish the said Review. 1771 *Junius Lett.* xlii. (1788) 242 It is not probable that he would appear again before his soldiers, even in the pacific ceremony of a review. 1837 Dickens *Pickw.* iv, A grand review was to take place upon the Lines. a 1878 Princess Alice *Biogr. Sk. & Lett.* (1884) 164 The Sultan,..in whose honour a great naval review at Spithead was held.

attrib. 1876 Voyle & Stevenson *Milit. Dict.* 344/2 When a regiment or any larger body of men pass in review order before the sovereign or reviewing officer.

transf. 1762 Sterne *Tr. Shandy* vi. vii, At the great and general review of us all, corporal, at the day of judgment. 1796 *Grose's Dict. Vulgar T.* (ed. 3), *Review of the Black Cuirassiers*, a visitation of the clergy. 1840 Mrs. Trollope *Widow Married* i, She had made up her mind that day to have a general review of all her children's heads. 1865 Dickens *Mut. Fr.* i. vi, The guests filed out in the best order: Miss Abbey standing at the..door.., to hold a ceremony of review and dismissal.

b. In phr. *to march* or *pass in review.*

1728 Pope *Dunc.* iii. Argt., Some of the persons he causes to pass in review before his eyes. 1751 Johnson *Rambler* No. 170 ¶ 2 The little family passed in review before him. 1769 T. Nevile *Imit. Juvenal* 70 She sees him now in Sash and Solitaire March in Review.

4. An inspection, examination. *In review*, under examination.

1611 Cotgr., *Revisit*, a review taken by the King of his Officers accounts. 1765 *Museum Rust.* IV. iv. 23 At the end of May I make a second review, and if I find one branch ..stronger than the other, I cut..it off. 1793 Smeaton *Edystone L.* § 262 *note*, This bolt and shackle would necessarily be in review on getting in the bridle. 1833 Herschel *Astron.* viii. 276 Uranus was discovered by Sir W. Herschel in 1781,..in the course of a review of the heavens. 1863 Whyte Melville *Gladiators* I. 298 As the crowd pass the different combatants in review, none..have more backers than their old favourite.

5. A general survey or reconsideration of some subject or thing.

1604 Parsons *Review Ten Publike Disput.* Pref., I have thought good here to examine all together in this Re-view. 1613 Purchas *Pilgrimage* i. xiii. (1614) 71 Let vs take a little reuiew of some principall occurrents in the former Catalogue. 1715 M. Davies *Athen. Brit.* I. Pref. 1 To take a Review of the old and new Game of Pamphlets, play'd and penn'd by the meaner sort. 1736 Butler *Anal.* ii. iii. 380 They amount to a much higher degree of proof upon such a joint review. 1774 BURKE *Sp. Amer. Tax.* Pref., Wks. II. 348 He has taken a review of the effects of all the schemes which have been successively adopted. 1871 C. DAVIES *Metric Syst.* III. 178 The review of the proceedings in Great Britain and France..presents the general subject under two very different aspects.

b. Without article, esp. *in* or *under review.*

1729 BUTLER *Serm.* Wks. 1874 II. Pref. 6 Review and attention, and even forming a judgment, becomes fatigue. 1811 SHELLEY *St. Irvyne* x, It would unfold a tale of too much horror to trace, in review, the circumstances as they then occurred. 1878 BROWNING *La Saisiaz* 25 Passing lightly in review What seemed hits and what seemed misses. 1888 *Pall Mall G.* 7 Feb. 11/1 Passing under review the war dangers to which Germany and Prussia have been exposed.

c. Const. *of* (the agent).

1800 COLQUHOUN *Comm. Thames* Pref. p. vi, A variety of offences..have been brought under the review of the Reader. 1875 WHITNEY *Life Lang.* ii. 15 Directions given but not executed under the review of consciousness.

6. A retrospective survey of past actions, etc.

1673 *Rem. Humours Town* 20 The reviews of their own vertuous actions may give them content. 1773 JOHNSON *Let. to Mrs. Thrale* 27 Apr., I have lived a life of which I do not like the review. 1784 COWPER *Task* IV. 184 Mem'ry's pointing wand, That calls the past to our exact review. 1855 M. ARNOLD *New Sirens* xvii, Is the pleasure that is tasted Patient of a long review?

7. a. A general account or criticism of a literary work (esp. a new or recent one) either published separately or, more usually, as an article in a periodical or newspaper.

1649 R. BAILLIE (*title*), A Review of Doctor Bramble..his Faire Warning. 1712 HEARNE *Collect.* (O.H.S.) IV. 44 When I wrote last, I had not seen wt honour ye have done me in ye Review of Leland. 1772 WESLEY *Jrnl.* 11 July, I was presented with Mr. Hill's Review. 1824 W. E. ANDREWS (*title*), Critical Review of Fox's Book of Martyrs. 1850 THACKERAY *Pendennis* xlii, If a review of his work was very laudatory, it was a great pleasure to him to send it home to his mother at Fairoaks. 1898 L. STEPHEN *Stud. Biogr.* II. ii. 69 The fuller reviews, which in the Edinburgh supplanted the old meagre analysis of books.

b. A periodical publication consisting mainly of articles in which current events or questions, or literary works, are discussed or criticized.

1705 *Hudibras Redivivus* II. 10 No matter whether false or true, Take pattern by D[e] F[oe]'s Review. *a* 1721 PRIOR *Daphne & Apollo* 35 So do your Brother Quacks and Brother Beaus. Memorials only, and Reviews, write Prose. 1759 *Ann. Reg.* Pref. vi, Endeavouring to be as extensively useful as possible, we aimed at uniting the plan of the Magazines with that of the Reviews. 1813 SOUTHEY *March to Moscow* v, They all of them knew Mr. Jeffrey's Review, Which with Holy Writ ought to be reckon'd. 1865 *Sat. Rev.* 5 Aug. 169/1 There were no reviews in which he might either suggest his own improvements or be censured for his plagiarisms.

c. *attrib.* and *Comb.*

1781 COWPER *Let. to J. Newton* 17 Dec., I would not appear a dunce in matters that every Review-reader must needs be apprized of. 1807 SOUTHEY *Lett.* (1850) III. 115, I will seek more review employment,..and scribble verses for the newspapers. 1820–1 BYRON in *Westm. Gaz.* (1901) 5 Feb. 3/2 Your review people have no more right to kill, than any other footpads.

II. 8. A second or repeated view.

This would now be taken as *re-view* (rī-).

1665 SIR T. HERBERT *Trav.* (1677) 156 Abbas..having in that sort satisfied his passion, returned..to take a re-view of his cruel execution. 1683 KENNETT tr. *Erasm. on Folly* 37 That which at first blush seems alive, is in truth dead; and that again which appears as dead, at a nearer review proves to be alive. 1704 SWIFT *T. Tub* Ep. Ded. to Prince Posterity, Returning in a very few Hours to take a Review, they were all torn down, and fresh ones in their Places. 1705 ATTERBURY *Serm.* ii. (1726) II. 65 The Works of Nature will bear a Thousand Views, and Reviews, and will still appear new to us.

† b. The fact of seeing some place or person again. *Obs. rare.*

1652 J. WRIGHT tr. *Camus' Nat. Paradox* VI. 127 As the weary Pilgrim after a tedious travaill rejoyceth at the review of his Native Soil. 1660 F. BROOKE tr. *Le Blanc's Trav.* 211 Our fellows..found us at Carboran,..where you may imagine the joy this review diffused through all of us.

Review (rĭviū·), *v.* Also 6–7 **reuiew.** [f. RE- and VIEW *v.* (cf. prec.), after F. *revoir*, Sp. and Pg. *rever*, It. *rividere*, L. *revidēre.*]

† 1. *trans.* To see or behold again. *Obs.*

1591 *Troub. Raigne K. John* (1611) 28 Twise will I not reuiew the mornings rise, Till I haue torne that trophie from thy backe. 1613 PURCHAS *Pilgrimage* IX. iv. (1614) 842 Long it was before his longing could be satisfied to reuiew his Countrey and friends. 1725 POPE *Odyss.* VI. 347 Would'st thou soon review thy native plain? 1762 FALCONER *Shipwr.* I. 401 Where, anxious to review his native shore, He on the roaring wave embark'd once more. 1796 PEGGE *Anonym.* (1809) 4 Upon reviewing a place after an absence of some time, the several actions which formerly have passed there are wont to occur to the mind.

2. To view, inspect, or examine a second time or again. (In contrast to *view.*)

This would now be pronounced with (rī-) and usually written *re-view.*

1576 FLEMING *Panopl. Epist.* q v, To such a one I giue counsel..to view and reuiew..such weapons as he shall finde in this our Panoplie. 1591 SAVILE *Tacitus, Hist.* I. xliv. 24 No heade did he [Otho] view and reuiew so insatiably. 1616 R. C. *Time's Whistle* (1871) 2 Many hundred..eyes View, and review, each line, each word, as spies. 1653 GREAVES *Seraglio* 153 These slaves are bought, and sold, as beasts, and cattle are, they being viewed, and reviewed. 1762 STERNE *Tr. Shandy* VI. i, How they viewed and reviewed us as we passed over the rivulet! 1816 SCOTT *Old Mort.* xxv, [They] were on the battlements again, viewing and re-viewing the state of their preparations.

† 3. a. To look over or through (a book, etc.) in order to correct or improve; to revise. *Obs.*

1603 HOLLAND *Plutarch's Mor.* 1274 Dionysius had put into his hands a tragedy of his owne making, commanding him to review and correct the same. 1639 N. N. tr. *Du Bosq's Compl. Woman* I. B, This is certain, they have put the Author of this booke upon it, to review it well. 1695 J. EDWARDS *Perfect. Script.* 360 Ezra..reviewed the copies, and amended all errata's. *a* 1715 BURNET *Own Time* Pref., I am now beginning to review and write over again the History of my own time.

absol. 1622 JAGGARD *Note to Brooke's Disc. Err. Catal. Nobility*, He viewed, reuiewed, directed, corrected, or whatsoeuer els.

† b. To re-examine; to reconsider. *Obs. rare.*

1607 NORDEN *Surv. Dial.* I. 31 Euery Lord of a Mannor should cause his Lands to be duly seene, and truly surueyed and certifyed, and once in seuen or tenne yeares to haue it reuiewed. 1672 PETTY *Pol. Anat.* (1691) 18 Those who think 154,000 were so destroyed ought to review the grounds of their Opinion.

4. *Law.* To submit (a decree, act, etc.) to examination or revision.

1621 ELSING *Debates Ho. Lords* (Camden) 120 All my decrees have ben reviewed: yea, all my orders and peticions. 1771 *Junius Lett.* lx. (1788) 323 That parliament may review the acts of ministers is unquestionable. 1817 *Parl. Debates* 731 Praying that the Act.., regarding conveyancers, might be reviewed for the purpose of being repealed or amended. 1858 LD. ST. LEONARDS *Handy-Bk. Prop. Law* xii. 77 The order may be reviewed or may be appealed from. 1892 *Law Times Rep.* LXVII. 211/1 The court, on appeal, can review the exercise of his discretion by the County Court Judge.

5. To survey; to take a survey of.

c 1600 SHAKS. *Sonn.* lxxiv, When thou reuewest this, thou doest reuew, The very part was consecrate to thee. 1632 LITHGOW *Trav.* VIII. 347 After ten dayes feasting, reviewing Heidleberg, [we]..set forward. 1678 BUNYAN *Pilgr.* I. (1900) 26 The which [parlour], after he had reviewed a little while, the Interpreter called for a man to sweep. 1725 POPE *Odyss.* III. 127 Shall I the long, laborious scene review, And open all the wounds of Greece anew? 1787 JEFFERSON *Writ.* (1859) II. 291 When I review his dispositions, and review his conduct, I have little hope. 1800 MRS. HERVEY *Mourtray Fam.* I. 164 With his eyes seemingly cast down, he was employed in reviewing the charms of her lovely daughter. 1862 SIR B. BRODIE *Psychol. Inq.* II. i. 28 [He] reviews the whole of the facts..before he ventures to draw any conclusions from them. 1874 GREEN *Short Hist.* viii. § 2. 461 We must cursorily review the fortunes of Protestantism during the reign of Elizabeth.

absol. 1717 POPE *Ep. to Mr. Jervas* 21 How oft [do we] review; each finding like a friend Something to blame, and something to commend!

b. To look back upon; to regard or survey in retrospection.

1751 JOHNSON *Rambler* No. 141 ⁋ 2 Whoever shall review his life will generally find [etc.]. 1779 — *L. P., Duke* (1868) 205 Some of his compositions are such as he must have reviewed with detestation in his later days. 1807 WORDSW. *White Doe* II. 105 The past he calmly hath reviewed. 1850 THACKERAY *Pendennis* liv, As from a precipice down which he might have fallen,..he reviewed the Fanny Bolton snare, now that he had escaped out of it.

6. To make a formal inspection, to hold a review, of (troops, etc.).

1712–4 POPE *Rape Lock* III. 45 The skilful Nymph reviews her force with care. 1713 *Lond. Gaz.* No. 5106/3 The Lords ..have Reyiew'd the greater Part of the Out-Pensioners. 1727–38 CHAMBERS *Cycl.* s.v. *Order of battle*, In order to engage the enemy, or to be reviewed by the general. 1828 CAMPBELL *Departure of Emigrants for N. S. W.* 73 Hosts review'd in dazzling files and squares. 1840 DICKENS *Old C. Shop* lii, He charged the boy to run off and bring his schoolmates to be marshalled before their new master, and solemnly reviewed. 1889 *Infantry Drill* 443 When troops are reviewed in line of quarter columns, the brigadier only will accompany the reviewing general.

7. To write an appreciation or criticism of (a new literary work); also *absol.*, to write reviews; to follow the occupation of a reviewer.

1781 JOHNSON *Let. to Mrs. Thrale* 12 Nov., I would never review the work of an anonymous authour. 1783 COWPER *Let. to Unwin* Wks. 1836 II. 30, I am reviewed, and my book forwarded in its progress by a judicious recommendation. 1809 BYRON *Bards & Rev.* 549 See honest Hallam.. Resume his pen, review his Lordship's work. 1839 HALLAM *Hist. Lit.* IV. vii. § 24 The first book ever reviewed..was an edition of the works of Victor Vitensis and Vigilius Papsensis. 1892 DOBSON *18th Cent. Vignettes* 59 He drew up the 'Proposals' for a complete edition of her works, and he reviewed her repeatedly.

Hence **Review·ed** *ppl. a.*

1840 HOOD *Up Rhine* Introd. 3 It is the fashion now for the reviewed to retaliate on the reviewers.

Reviewable. [f. prec. + -ABLE.] That may be, capable of being, reviewed.

1846 in WORCESTER (citing Story). 1869 *Contemp. Rev.* XI. 153 The first and only reviewable part of his volume. 1891 *Sat. Rev.* 11 July 32/2 The Emperor..has reviewed most things reviewable.

Review·age. *rare.* [f. as prec. + -AGE.] Reviewing, or reviews, of books.

1807 W. TAYLOR in Robberds *Mem.* (1843) II. 214 Whatever you order down to me in the way of reviewage, I shall of course execute as speedily as may be. 1809 *Ibid.* 281 A quarterly magazine, wholly quit of reviewage.

Reviewal (rĭviū·ăl). [f. as prec. + -AL.]

1. The act of reviewing or revising; an instance of this.

1650 *Descr. Fut. Hist. Europe* 11 He that returns back in reviewall of the conjunctions and fiery Triplicities, may see how they have in part prognosticated the present troubles. 1665 BARROW in *Corr. Sci. Men* (1841) II. 45, I shall hardly ever induce myself to take the pains..requisite for the reviewal of them. 1844 SIR J. COLERIDGE *Dowling & Lowndes's Reports* 4, This Court will direct a reviewal of his [the master's] taxation. 1864 *Sat. Rev.* XVIII. 455/2 His reviewals of the findings of courts-martial, his observations on the faults of the British cavalry. 1885 *Law Times* LXXVIII. 340/2 A summons was taken out..to have a reviewal of the taxation of his bill of costs.

2. A review *of* a book. Also without article.

1798 W. TAYLOR in Robberds *Mem.* (1843) I. 229 How angry the Anti-jacobin Magazine is with a reviewal of D'Ivernois in the appendix to the Monthly! 1805 SOUTHEY *Let.* in *Life* (1850) II. 355, I perceive that the reviewals of Madoc have in a certain degree influenced you. 1834 *Blackw. Mag.* XXXVI. 273, I treat his offer of a reviewal of Mr. Hunt's London Journal with disdain. 1865 *Monthly Packet* Dec. 718 A fair subject for reviewal in a magazine.

Review·atory, *a. nonce-wd.* [f. as prec.] Of or pertaining to the writing of reviews.

1822 L. HUNT *Liberal* I. 70 It is the fault of the 'accursed critical spirit' that is the bane of these times, that we are obliged to be..base and reviewatory like the rest. 1831 *Fraser's Mag.* III. 101 A candour most unusual in persons of the reviewatory profession. 1837 *Ibid.* XVI. 666 He has passed unnamed by the ordinary guardians of the gates reviewatory.

Reviewer (rĭviū·əɹ). [f. REVIEW *v.* + -ER¹.]

† 1. One who revises; a reviser. *Obs.*

1611 FLORIO, *Risisore*, a reuisor, a reuiewer. 1710 BEVERIDGE *Wks.* (1846) VIII. 628 The composers and reviewers of the old translation. 1720 WHEATLY *Bk. Com. Prayer* (ed. 2) ii. § 5. 114 This Rubrick..may perhaps have slipt into the present Book thro' the Inadvertency of the Reviewers.

† 2. One who looks back upon something. *Obs.*⁻¹

1654 WHITLOCK *Zootomia* 517, I am ashamed of nothing more than the Crosse of Christ, as I believe those Reviewers are, whom the Prophet speaketh of, They shall look back on him whom they have peirced.

3. One who criticizes new publications; a writer of reviews. In early use, the author of a special pamphlet criticizing another work.

1651 R. WATSON *Second Faire Warning* Answ. Ep. Ded. 2 The præjudice the Reviewer would here..cast upon the person of the Bishop will advance his own reputation but a little. 1722 WODROW *Corr.* (1843) II. 660 You'll have heard of a printed letter by a Jacobite reviewer..upon my first volume. 1756 GRAY *Let.* in *Poems* (1775) 246 It has certainly worse nerves than mine, if your Reviewers have frighted it. *c* 1785 BURNS *Capt. Riddel* ii, Our friends, the reviewers, Those chippers and hewers. 1837 LYTTON *E. Maltravers* I. xii, The coteries cried him up and the reviewers adored him. 1871 TYNDALL *Fragm. Sci.* (1879) II. xv. 401 Free discussion should not be prevented, either by the ferocity of reviewers or the arm of the law.

Hence **Review·eress,** a female reviewer.

1830 CARLYLE in *Fraser's Mag.* I. 28 To review a revieweress of two literatures is not easy.

Review·ing, *vbl. sb.* [f. REVIEW *v.* + -ING¹.]

1. The action of the verb, in various senses.

1573 *Reg. Privy Council Scot.* II. 250 The revewing of ony decreittis or processis in that or the lyke caissis. 1598 FLORIO, *Recensione*, a rehearsing: a reuiewing or examination of an account or number. 1680 GODOLPHIN *Rep. Can.* (ed. 2) 119 Then such a Reviewing shall be final without further Appeal. 1719 LONDON & WISE *Compl. Gard.* 173 This reviewing must be continued for the following Months for all other Fruits; and in reviewing remove such as begin to rot. 1865 PUSEY *Truth Eng. Ch.* 67 The reviewing of the judicial sentences of its Bishops.

attrib. 1897 *Boston* (Mass.) *Jrnl.* 15 Jan. 6/5 The erection of reviewing-stands for spectators on the occasion of processions on the next inauguration day.

2. The act or practice of writing reviews.

1797 COLERIDGE *Lett.* (1895) I. 215 Fifty pounds you might ..gain by reviewing. 1819 SHELLEY *Peter Bell 3rd* VII. xvi, The Reviewers who were hired To do the work of his reviewing. 1888 *Athenæum* 19 May 631/3 In no case did I observe anything beyond..the customs of ordinary reviewing.

attrib. 1883 BLACK *Shandon Bells* xxx, We could not have one of our own reviewers abused in our own reviewing columns. 1894 *Idler* Sept. 165 'Reviewing' work is too badly paid for any reasonable being to think of making it either an art or a business.

Review·ing, *ppl. a.* [f. REVIEW *v.* + -ING².]

† 1. Looking backwards. *Obs. rare*⁻¹.

1643 DENHAM *Cooper's H.* 263 So fast he flies, that his reviewing eye Has lost the Chasers, and his ear the Cry.

2. Holding a review of troops, etc.

1735 SOMERVILLE *Chase* I. 273 Reviewing Generals his Merit own. 1769 *Junius Lett.* iii. (1788) 47 The reports of reviewing generals comprehend only a few regiments in England. 1832 *Regul. & Instr. Cavalry* III. 56 The Reviewing-General presents himself before the centre. 1876 [see REVIEW *sb.* 3]. 1889 [see REVIEW *v.* 6].

Review·ish, *a.* [f. REVIEW *sb.*] Characteristic of reviews (of books).

1835 R. H. FROUDE *Rem.* (1838) I. 416 M.'s [pamphlet] improves on acquaintance. The style is pedantic and reviewish.

Review·less, *a.* [f. REVIEW *sb.* 7 b.] Destitute of a review.

1849 SIR J. STEPHEN *Eccl. Biog.* II. 375 What is a party.. without a Review?..Reviewless, Clapham had scarcely been known beyond her own Common.

† **Revification,** erroneous form (perh. misprints) for REVIVIFICATION. (Cf. REVIVICATION.)

1677 CARY *Chron.* II. 143 In the revification of the Chaldæan Empire under Nabon-asser. 1712 STEELE *Spect.* No. 426 ⁋ 2 So long are these Medicines of Revification in preparing.

So † **Revify** *v.* = REVIVIFY.

1598 FLORIO, *Reuificare*, to reuiue, or reuifie.

Revi·gorate, *pa. pple. rare*⁻¹. [Cf. next.] Reinvigorated.

1814 SOUTHEY *Roderick* VII, The fire which seemed extinct Hath risen revigorate.

Revi·gorate, *v.* [Cf. F. *revigorer*, Pg. *revigorar*, med.L. *revigorare.*] To reinvigorate.

1611 COTGR., *Revigourer*, to reuigorate, reinforce. 1828–32 in WEBSTER. 1852 *Tait's Mag.* XIX. 52 His fellow-citizens..rose revigorated by the sparkling draught. 1861 *Times* 25 March 8/6 There are all the corn lands..which are revigorated by ages of fallow. 1886 *Pall Mall G.* 8 Nov. 13/2 He would have in every diocese a body of celibate clergy..to reinforce and revigorate the parochial system.

† **Revi·gour,** *v. Obs.* [See prec. and VIGOUR.]

1. *trans.* To restore to vigour.

c 1440 *Love's Bonavent. Mirr* (MS. e Musæo 35) lf. 213 The day in the which he badde receyue the forseide brede and was revigorede. 1447 BOKENHAM *Seyntys* (Roxb.) 200 Alle here spyrytys begunne to amende And were reuygguryd in wundyr wyse.

2. *intr.* To recover vigour.

1447 BOKENHAM *Seyntys* (Roxb.) 121 Dede men reuyguryn I dar wele seyn. *c* 1450 *St. Cuthbert* (Surtees) 5391 He reuygourd in strenth of cors.

† **Revi·le,** *sb. Obs.* Also **reveile.** [f. the vb.]

1. A reviling speech or remark.

1579 TOMSON *Calvin's Serm. Tim.* 985/2 Hee must heare threates, hee must suffer reuiles and tauntes. 1602 W. BAS *Sword & Buckler* C3ᵃ Whose busie tongues and lothing maw defiles Our honest sort with vomited reuiles. 1645 MILTON *Tetrach.* Wks. 1851 IV. 139 Since he waigh'd so little what a grosse revile that was to give his equall.

2. Revilement, reviling.

a 1603 T. CARTWRIGHT *Confut. Rhem. N. T.* (1618) 444 Their reveile of the worthy servant of God, M. Caluin, we will..lay vp with the Lord. 1650 EARL MONM. tr. *Senault's Man bec. Guilty* 316 Recreation..will always be innocent enough, if it can hinder revile and unchastity. 1684 BUNYAN *Pilgr.* II. (1862) 194 Render them not reviling for revile.

Revile (rĭvəi·l), *v.* [a. OF. *reviler*, f. *re-* RE- + *vil* VILE *a.* Cf. later F. *ravilir*, It. *ravvilire.*]

† 1. *trans.* To degrade, abase. *Obs. rare.*

1303 R. BRUNNE *Handl. Synne* 11546 Þou dysonourest hym yn þat outrage, And reuylyst hys feyre ymage. 1390 GOWER *Conf.* II. 221 Thou hast bothe hire and me beguiled And ek thin oghne astat reviled.

2. To subject to contumely or abuse; to assail with opprobrious or abusive language.

In early quots. more with reference to action than speech.

c 1330 R. BRUNNE *Chron. Wace* (Rolls) 11677 Þey..seye hit ys þer heritage To haue oure godes, & vs to reuille! 1390 GOWER *Conf.* III. 247 His fader and hise brethren bothe..Him hadde beten and reviled. 1432–50 tr. *Higden* (Rolls) VII. 97 Also he revilede moche and detracte seynte Edmunde. *c* 1460 *Wisdom* 989 in *Macro Plays* 68 By holy chyrch to be reconsylyde, Trustynge verely ye xall neuer be revylyde. 1530 PALSGR. 690/1 He is a marvaylouse hastye man in his fume, he revyled me and I had been a dogge. 1591 SPENSER *M. Hubberd* 365 The man..with reproachfull tearmes gan them revile. 1648 WILKINS *Math. Magic* I. xi. 69 He did not revile the gods of ingratitude. 1687 A. LOVELL tr. *Thevenot's Trav.* I. 219 [The Arabs] hate the Persians, they revile every thing that concerns them. 1729 SAVAGE *Wanderer* V. 411 They jar, accus'd accuse, revil'd revile, And wrath to wrath oppose. 1780 COWPER *Love of World* 33 Revil'd and lov'd, renounc'd and follow'd, Thus, bit by bit, the world is swallow'd. 1833 HT. MARTINEAU *Tale of Tyne* ii. 40 He reviled heaven and earth when he saw his wife sinking from want. 1875 JOWETT *Plato* (ed. 2) I. 185 Ctesippus then says that he is not reviling the two Sophists, he is only contradicting them.

fig. 1613 SHAKS. *Hen. VIII*, I. i. 126, I read in 's looks Matter against me, and his eye reuil'd Me as his abiect obiect. *a* 1616 BEAUM. & FL. *Bonduca* II. iv, No ill words! let his own shame first revile him.

3. *intr.* To use opprobrious language; to rail *at* a person or thing.

1526 TINDALE 1 *Pet.* ii. 23 When he was reviled, reviled not agayne. 1621 BRATHWAIT *Nat. Embassie* (1877) 141 This short Satyre..reuiling at the couetousnesse..of women. 1659 B. HARRIS *Parival's Iron Age* 58 It was then, that the doctrine of the Jesuits was carped, and reviled at. 1797 MRS. M. ROBINSON *Walsingham* III. 65 While the tithe-pamper'd churchman reviles at the poor. 1871 B. TAYLOR *Faust* (1875) I. xvii. 165 How scornfully I once reviled, When some poor maiden was beguiled.

Hence **Revi·led** *ppl. a.*

1855 KINGSLEY *Westw. Ho!* vii, The Lord's people were always a reviled people and a persecuted people.

Revilement (rĭvəi·lmĕnt). [f. REVILE *v.*]

1. The act of reviling; the fact or practice of employing abusive language.

1590 SPENSER *F. Q.* II. iv. 12 Yet n'ould she stent Her bitter rayling and foule revilement. 1618 T. TAYLOR *Comm. Titus* iii. 2 If any man prouoke thee by reuilement and reproaches, returne not euill for euill. 1649 tr. *Warn. fr. J. Bean* lviii. 25 He doth not push with the horn of revilement and scorne. 1780 BENTHAM *Princ. Legisl.* xviii. § 34 And thus we have two genera or kinds of offences against reputation merely; to wit, 1. Defamation and 2 Vilification or Revilement. 1881 *Harper's Mag.* LXIV. 216 It is devoted by custom to the particular revilement of Judas.

2. An instance of this; a reviling speech.

1637 R. HUMFREY tr. *St. Ambrose* I. 12 He was not..moved with whatsoever revilements. 1660 H. MORE *Myst. Godl.* VI. ii. 217 Christ will then vindicate himself from all those scorns and revilements. 1873 L. WALLACE *Fair God* VII. xiv, Again the people broke out in revilements. 1880 — *Ben Hur* VIII. x, Laughter and ribaldry and revilements, all for the Nazarene.

Reviler (rĭvəi·ləɹ). [f. as prec. + -ER¹.] One who reviles or abuses.

1598 HAKLUYT *Voy.* I. 553 [Those] who haue applied themselues..to shake off the yoke of railers & reuilers. *a* 1619 FOTHERBY *Atheom.* I. xi. § 4 (1622) 117 He maketh Diagoras (a knowne Reuiler of all their other gods) yet to be a true worshipper of the drunken God Bacchus. 1726 POPE *Odyss.* XXII. 498 The..base revilers of our house and name. 1748 SMOLLETT *Rod. Rand.* iv, Avaunt! unchristian reviler, avaunt! 1836 HOR. SMITH *Tin Trump.*, *Idleness*, Why do the revilers of the idle labour and toil with such perseverance? 1875 JOWETT *Plato* (ed. 2) V. 166 The reviler who indulges in anger..may be chastened by an elder.

Revi·ling, *vbl. sb.* [f. as prec. + -ING¹.] The action of the vb.; a reviling remark or speech.

1535 COVERDALE *Isa.* li. 7 Be not afrayde of their blasphemies & reuylinges. 1611 BIBLE *Ecclus.* xxvii. 15 Their reuilings are grieuous to the eare. 1641 J. JACKSON *True Evang. T.* II. 152 Breaches of charity..by the detraction, calumnie, and revilings of our tongues. 1693 DRYDEN *Disc. Satire* Ess. (ed. Ker) II. 45 Scoffs and revilings are of the growth of all nations. 1795 COLERIDGE *Plot Discovered* 15 An abusive fellow followed Pericles home with much panegyrical reviling. 1853 BP. WILBERFORCE in R. S. Wilberforce *Life* (1881) II. 182, I will not return any of your revilings. 1875 E. WHITE *Life in Christ* I. i. (1878) 5 A persistent reviling of the animals, and a resolute exaltation of humanity.

Revi·ling, *ppl. a.* [-ING².] That reviles; given to reviling; abusive.

1548 UDALL, etc. *Erasm. Par.* 1 *John* ii. 44 He gaue no reuilynge worde agayne to any man. *c* 1586 C'TESS PEMBROKE *Ps.* XLIV. viii, By reviling slaundring foe Inly wounded thus I languish. 1645 MILTON *Tetrach.* Wks. 1851 IV. 139 To smite so keenly with a reviling tongue. 1655 FULLER *Ch. Hist.* IX. 196 They came to bitterness, and reviling tearmes amongst themselves. *a* 1716 BLACKALL *Wks.* I. 230 The use of any sort of scurrilous or reviling language. 1833 TENNYSON *Two Voices* 220 He heeded not reviling tones.

Hence **Revi·lingly** *adv.*

1548 UDALL, etc. *Erasm. Par.* 1 *John* ii. 44 He prayed to the father for them that spake reuilyngly agaynste him. 1681 BAXTER *Acc. Sherlock* iii. 177 [They] talk revilingly of persons and things which they never knew.

Revin, obs. Sc. f. RAVEN *sb.*¹ and *riven* pa. pple. of RIVE *v.*

† **Revi·nce,** *v. Obs.* [ad. L. *revincĕre*, f. *re-* RE- + *vincĕre* to conquer, subdue.]

1. *trans.* To refute, disprove.

1529 MORE *Dyaloge* IV. Wks. 254/2 The king..effectually reuinced and confuted the..pestilent boke of Luther. 1570 FOXE *A. & M.* (ed. 2) 976/2 When he shoulde see his errour by manifest and sound testimonies of scriptures reuinced. 1640 G. WATTS tr. *Bacon's De Aug. Sci.* IV. i. 178 The opinion of Copernicus,..because it is not repugnant to the Phænomena, cannot be revinced by Astronomicall Principles. 1686 GOAD *Celest. Bodies* I. xii. 44 As if Astrology were a close and cunning Faculty, and afraid..to be revinced by ordinary experience.

2. To restore *to* a possession.

1584 *Sc. Acts Jas. VI* (1814) III. 355 The saidis personis.. to be consolidat and revincit, likas his hienes consolidatis and revincis thame to þe saidis beneficis.

† **Revi·ncible,** *a. Obs. rare*⁻¹. [f. prec., or ad. late L. *revincibilis.*] Refutable.

1633 T. ADAMS *Exp.* 2 *Peter* iii. 16 They are raised out of the Scriptures, though they be revincible by the same letters.

† **Revi·nct,** *pa. pple. Obs.*⁻¹ [ad. L. *revinct-us*, pa. pple. of *revincire.*] *trans.* Bound up, girt.

1650 BULWER *Anthropomet.* 191 Wherewith children in.. Summer revinct with swaith-bands, are as it were stew'd.

Revi·ndicate, *v.* [f. RE- and VINDICATE *v.*, after F. *revendiquer*. Cf. REVENDICATE and med.L. *revindicāre.*] *trans.* To vindicate anew; to reclaim, recover, or restore, as a rightful possession.

1828–32 in WEBSTER (citing Mitford). 1842 DE QUINCEY *Philos. Herodotus* Wks. 1858 IX. 179 Having thus said something towards revindicating for Herodotus his proper station [etc.]. 1864 BURTON *Scot Abr.* II. i. 52 There was no other country to which they could be revindicated. 1872 SWINBURNE *Ess. & Stud.* (1875) 27 In vain he..rebuked the untimely..haste of Paris to revindicate this right for herself.

Revindica·tion. [Cf. prec. and REVENDICATION.] The action of revindicating.

1643 [PRYNNE] (*title*), A Revindication of the anoynting and priviledges of faithfull subjects. 1652 COLLINGES (*title*), Responsoria ad Erratica Pastoris,..the Shepherds Wandrings discovered, in a Revindication of the Great Ordinance of God.

1818 COLEBROOKE *Obligations* 43 So as no injury be caused by unseasonable retraction and untimely revindication. 1851 GALLENGA *Italy* V. 288 The aim of all Italian revolution is the revindication of this natural frontier. 1877 E. CAIRD *Philos. Kant* iii. 28 The Renaissance was the revindication of nature and human nature.

Reving, obs. f. REAVING, REEVING *vbl. sbs.*

Revir, obs. Sc. form of RIVER.

† **Revire,** *v.*¹ *Obs. rare*⁻¹. [ad. L. *revirescĕre.*] *intr.* To recover freshness.

c 1420 *Pallad. on Husb.* II. 258 And when the list, in water hoote revire They wil, and taste ene as the list desire.

† **Revire,** *v.*² *Obs. rare*⁻¹. [a. F. *revirer*: see RE- and VIRE *v.*] *intr.* To swing back.

1456 SIR G. HAYE *Law Arms* (S.T.S.) 119 As the dure turnis about apon the herre,..and vyris and revyris.

Revire·scence. *rare.* [See next and -ENCE.] Return to a youthful or flourishing condition.

1741 WARBURTON *Div. Legat.* IV. iv. II. 112 A Serpent represented the Divine Nature, on account of its great Vigour and Spirit, its long Age and Revirescence. 1880 SWINBURNE *Stud. Shaks.* 126 A faded archaic style trying as it were to resume a mockery of revirescence.

Revire·scent, *a. rare.* [ad. L. *revirescent-em*, pres. pple. of *revirescĕre.*] Flourishing anew.

1644 R. HARWOOD *King David's Sanctuary* Ep. Ded., The True Religion..is Revirescent in your tender yeares. 1795 T. MAURICE *Hindostan* (1820) I. I. ix. 270 A snake, or serpent,..so universally venerated in the Asiatic world, both as an emblem of the sun, and of revirescent vigour.

Revis, obs. form of RAVISH *v.*

Revisable (rĭvəi·zăb'l), *a.* [f. REVISE *v.* + -ABLE. So F. *revisable.*] Capable of being revised; liable to revision.

1892 *Daily News* 16 Mar. 5/7 This is the ideal system—State ownership of the minerals with fair and revisable royalties. 1893 *Westm. Gaz.* 29 June 1/3 The tariff established by the treaty was to be revisable every 10 years.

Hence **Revi·sableness.**

1873 *Contemp. Rev.* XXI. 910 The revisableness of the Confession has always been an axiom.

Revisal (rĭvəi·zăl). [f. next + -AL.] The act of revising or looking over again; a revision, re-examination.

1612 J. DAVIES (Heref.) *Muse's Sacrifice* Wks. (Grosart) II. 18/2 Let me not enter in this strict reuisall of my Sinne and grace. 1672 MARVELL *Reh. Transp.* (1673) II. 289 The good inclination of my Lords the Bishops..as to a revisal of themselves. 1741 RICHARDSON *Pamela* III. 79 She has written a Letter to you, which passed Mr. Peters's Revisal before she had the Courage to send it. 1771 LUCKOMBE *Hist. Printing* 389 Titles should have the revisal of one that is allowed to have a good judgment. 1807 WRANGHAM *Serm. Transl. Script.* 29 Let these separate labours subsequently undergo the careful revisal..of the entire body. 1860 WHYTE MELVILLE *Mkt. Harb.* (1861) 36 A thorough revisal of gloves, neckcloths, etc., is soon made. 1873 BURTON *Hist. Scot.* VI. lxvi. 56 He had not submitted his dispatch to official revisal.

Revise (rĭvəi·z), *sb.* Also 6 **re-vise,** 7 **reuize.** [f. the vb.]

† 1. The fact of being seen again. *Obs.*⁻¹

1589 WARNER *Alb. Eng.* (1602) Prose Addit. 341 Of the drowning and Reuise of Palinurus..I omit.

2. The act of revising or reviewing; a revision, a looking over or examining again.

1591 SYLVESTER *Du Bartas* I. i. 487 We should not heedless-hastily bestow us In any Work, but patiently proceed With oft re-vises. 1615 JACKSON *Creed* V. x. Wks. IV. 84 The reflexed apprehension or revise..by which their examination should be tried. 1692 R. L'ESTRANGE *Josephus, Antiq.* ii. (1733) 306 They came to this Resolution, that the Book might be subjected to a careful Examination and Revise. 1710 *Acc. Distemper Tom Whigg* II. 50 Let it be the frequent Subject of your Revise and Meditation. 1811 GIFFORD in *M. Napier's Sel. Corr.* (1879) 4, I am greatly pleased with your additions, and indeed with the whole of your revise. 1832 BABBAGE *Econ. Manuf.* xxi. (ed. 3) 209 The corrections have been unusually large, and the revises frequent.

b. A revised version or form.

1894 *Current Hist.* IV. 283 Shortly after the revise of the Wilson bill came up..in the Senate on April 2.

3. *Typog.* A revised or corrected form of proof-sheet; a further proof submitted by the printer after having made the required corrections, alterations, or additions. Also *attrib.*

1612 T. JAMES *Corrupt. Scripture* III. 24 There was no sheete printed off, before either the proofe, or the reuize (as they call it) was brought vnto him. 1644 PRYNNE & WALKER *Fiennes' Trial* 56 When he read the printed proofe and revise. 1683 MOXON *Mech. Exerc., Printing* xvii. 264 After the Second or Third Proof he has a Revise, which is also a Proof-sheet. 1753 RICHARDSON *Grandison* VI. 417 He had hardly..composed any other Copy but first proofs, revises, &c., clandestinely obtained from England. 1778 JOHNSON in *Boswell* II. 345 Let me have the revises as soon as can be. 1816 SCOTT *Antiq.* xi, [He] pulled off the first proof as clear and free from errors, as if it had been a triple revise! 1887 RUSKIN *Præterita* II. 338 The revise of the last sheet was sent to printer. 1892 A. OLDFIELD *Man. Typog.* iii, When all the corrections have been made a *Revise Proof* will have to be pulled and submitted to the reader.

Revise (rĭvəi·z), *v.* [a. F. *reviser* (also *réviser*), f. *re-* RE- + *viser* to look at, aim:—pop. L. **visāre.* Cf. *advise, devise*, and L. *revisĕre.*]

† 1. *intr.* To look again or repeatedly *at*, to look back or meditate *on*, something. *Obs.*

1567 *Reception of Q. Eliz. at Cambridge* (Harl. MSS. 7037), The Queen following..and marvellously revising at the beauty of the chapel. 1627 LEVER *Q. Eliz. Teares* ix, Waking, or not, I oft reuise thereon. *a* 1640 JACKSON *Creed* X. xxxi. Wks. IX. 217 Surely the thoughts of a mere natural, civil or moral man are free..and able to revise and work upon these occurrences.

† 2. *trans.* To see or behold, to look at, again.

a 1618 SYLVESTER *Job Triumphant* II. 303 Th' Eye that hath seen him, shall not see him twise, Nor shall his Places him againe revise. 1687 BEVERLEY *Exposition Song of Songs* 66 So long forgotten, I by Love revis'd Would now from future Forfeiture Fore-pris'd, Stand sealed. 1727 FOXTON in Earbery *Burnet's St. Dead* App. 75 If any doubt it they may revise what we have there written. 1760–72 H. BROOKE *Fool of Qual.* (1809) II. 63 She reserves this..for her own..inspection; to revise it, to gaze and dwell upon it in secret.

3. To look or read carefully over, with a view to improving or correcting.

1611 BIBLE *Transl. Pref.* ⁋ 14 Neither did we disdaine to reuise that which we had done. 1693 FREKE *Sel. Ess.* Apol. 3 What I have done of late has been only to Correct and Revise them [*sc.* essays] a little for the Press. 1743 POPE *Let. to Warburton* 12 Jan., Whatever very little respites I have had..have been employed in revising the papers on the use of Riches. 1796 KIRWAN *Elem. Min.* (ed. 2) I. Pref. xii, Upon the decease of Mr. Leske, it was revised, corrected, and enlarged, by Mr. Karsten. 1828 D'ISRAELI *Chas. I*, I. iii. 30 The King carefully revised the

papers which he commanded others to write. 1847 DE QUINCEY *Sp. Mil. Nun* viii. Wks. 1853 III. 16 Pussy, however, saw no use in revising and correcting the text of papa's remembrances.

absol. 1749 FIELDING *Tom Jones* XV. xi, I am prevented from revising;—Perhaps I have said more than I meant.

b. To go over again, to re-examine, in order to improve or amend; † to condense by revision.

1596 BACON *Max. & Use Com. Law* (1630) Ep. Ded. 2 To revise the Romane lawes from infinite volumes..into one competent and uniforme corps of law. 1651 BAXTER *Inf. Bapt.* 120 That they would be pleased in the forementioned particulars to revise the Directory. 1764 BURN *Poor Laws* 274 There is great reason to revise the game laws, and to reduce them into some order and compass. 1768 BLACKSTONE *Comm.* III. 67 A commission sometimes granted ..to revise the sentence of the court of delegates. 1819 J. MARSHALL *Const. Opin.* (1839) 189 The opinion of the highest law tribunal of the state is to be revised. 1847 POWER *Law Qualif. & Registr.* 113 Every revising barrister is required to notify his appointment to the clerk of the peace of the county..where he has been appointed to revise. 1876 HOLLAND *Sev. Oaks* xi, People began to revise their judgments of the man whom they had..condemned.

Hence **Revi·sed** *ppl. a.*

Revised Version, the version of the Bible made in 1870–84 as 'a Revision of the Translation published in..1611, and commonly known by the name of the Authorised Version'.

1837 LOCKHART *Scott* II. vi. 223, I suspect this had been a revised edition. 1849 MACAULAY *Hist. Eng.* II. i. 159 There might be a revised liturgy which should not exclude extemporaneous prayer. 1880 N. T. (Revised Version) Pref., We forwarded to them the Revised Version in its final form.

Revisee·. [f. REVISE *v.* + -EE.] One whose work is subjected to revision.

1884 *Spectator* 4 Oct. 1289/1 We may by hypothesis want such an institution [*i.e.* a Second Chamber], even if the Revisers are inferior men to the Revisees.

Reviser (rĭvəi·zəɹ). [f. REVISE *v.* + -ER¹. Cf. REVISOR.] One who revises or makes corrections.

1694 SALMON *Bate's Dispens.* (1713) 475/2 The Commentator or Reviser, in his Notes upon the same. 1738 T. BIRCH *Life Milton* in *M.'s Wks.* 1738 I. 48 It is not improbable Milton trusted much to the Care of the Printer and Reviser. 1778 JOHNSON *L. P., Milton* I. 251 Verbal inaccuracies, which Bentley..imputed to obtrusions of a reviser. 1846 MASKELL *Mon. Rit.* II. 121 *note*, The Prymer of 1545 corrected it, and was followed in later years by the revisers of Q. Mary's Book. 1870 *Graphic* 25 June 703/3 The revisers of the authorised version of the New Testament met for the first time on Wednesday.

Revi·sership. [f. prec. + -SHIP.] The office of reviser, or *spec.* of a revising barrister.

1882 *Pall Mall G.* 5 July 4/1 Every kind of legal office in England—recorderships, reviserships, judgeships, &c.

† **Revi·sible,** *a.*¹ *Obs. rare*⁻¹. [RE- 5 a.] Visible again.

? *a* 1500 *Chester Pl.* (E. E. T. S.) I. 103 Here will I bide now in this place..; to be revisible in short space, yt is my will in this same hower.

Revi·sible, *a.*², variant of REVISABLE *a.*

1882 *Fraser's Mag.* XXV. 781 Any hold beyond that of expediency, revisible like all expediencies from time to time. 1898 *Daily News* 2 July 7/2 To insist that every arrangement between railway companies shall be revisible under the general law.

Revi·sing, *vbl. sb.* [f. REVISE *v.*] The action of the verb; revision.

1611 FLORIO, *Reuisione*, a reuising, or reuiewing. 1621 ELSING *Debates Ho. Lords* (Camden) 103 Moved, whether there may not be a newe revysing of this Bill to that purpose. 1673 S. PARKER *Reproof Reh. Transp.* 528 The authour had not the revising of the sheets.

Revi·sing, *ppl. a.* [f. REVISE *v.*] That revises. *Revising barrister*, a barrister appointed to hold local courts at stated periods for the purpose of revising the lists of parliamentary electors.

1832 G. PRICE *Compl. Election Guide* ix. (*heading*), Revisal of Lists of Voters, Appointment and Business of Revising Barrister. 1847 POWER *Law Qualif. & Registr.* 113 The like duty devolves upon the senior judge of assise on the summer circuit to appoint revising barristers to act for each circuit. 1875 E. WHITE *Life in Christ* Pref. (1878) x, In preparing the present edition I have been again much indebted to the revising accuracy of my friend. 1898 S. LEE *Life Shaks.* v. (1899) 59 In both these plays Shakespeare's revising hand can be traced.

Revision (rĭvi·ʒən). [ad. late L. *revīsiōn-em*, f. *revisĕre*: see REVISE *v.* So F. and Sp. *revision*, It. *re-*, *rivisione.*]

1. The action of revising or looking over again; esp. critical or careful examination or perusal with a view to correcting or improving.

1611 COTGR., *Revision*, a reuision, reuise, reuiew, reexamination, looking over againe. 1662 J. DAVIES tr. *Olearius' Voy. Ambass.* To Rdr. A 3 Considering this Revision, what is now publish'd is both a more curious, and more compleat Piece. 1771 JOHNSON in *Boswell* 29 Aug., I am engaging in a very great work, the revision of my Dictionary. 1797 MALONE *Mem. Reynolds* R.'s Wks. I. p. xxvii, Though they are only detached thoughts, and did not receive his final revision and correction, I am unwilling to suppress them. 1817 *Parl. Deb.* 14 Our commercial situation and system deserved and required revision. 1830 D'ISRAELI *Chas. I*, III. i. 12 Few letters or papers passed his revision without being returned with marginal notes. 1876 *Contemp. Rev.* June 96 Revision [of the New Testament] has..become a public question.

attrib. 1884 O. T. (Revised Version) Pref., The Rules laid down by the Revision Committee of Convocation for the guidance of the Revisers.

b. A product of revising; a revised version.

1845 KITTO *Cycl. Bibl. Lit.* (1849) II. 919/1 A revision of it..is now wanted, or rather, a new translation. 1880 N. T. (Revised Version) Pref., The English Version of the New Testament here presented to the reader is a Revision of the Translation published in..1611.

2. The fact of seeing some person or thing again.

1796 OWEN *Trav. Europe* II. 310, I was particularly gratified in this ascent by a revision of that prodigious rock, the Aiguille de Dru. 1838 S. JACKSON tr. *Strauss' Remin. Life Lutheran Clergym.* III. 286 Heaven and earth beheld each other, and seemed to be astonished at the revision. 1891 E. L. ARNOLD *Phra the Phœnician* xi, A sweet revision of Blodwin, my..British wife!

3. A retrospective survey.

1833 MACREADY *Remin.* Diary 3 Jan., Let my revision of this day enable me to be more resolute in my resistance of future temptations.

Hence **Revi·sional, Revi·sionary** *adjs.*

1828–32 in WEBSTER. 1856 W. H. THOMPSON in A. Butler *Hist. Anc. Philos.* I. 362 It probably would not have survived its author's revisionary criticism. 1859 I. TAYLOR *Logic in Theol.* 74 In explication of this revisional process in philosophic reasoning. 1882–3 SCHAFF *Encycl. Relig. Knowl.* I. 324 There arose in France a strong revisionary spirit,..which carried a great reform.

Revisionist (rĭvi·ʒənist). [f. prec. + -IST. Cf. F. *révisionniste* adj.]

1. One who advocates or supports revision.

1865 *Reader* No. 151. 567/3 The Revisionists and the ultra-Ritualists. 1884 *Spectator* 4 Oct. 1305/2 The more impatient political revisionists among ourselves should.. reflect,—and hesitate.

attrib. 1866 *Church Times* 17 Feb., The Revisionist party states its opinion [etc.]. 1888 *Times* 1 Oct. 5/4 The calling together of a Revisionist Congress.

2. *pl.* The revisers of the Bible.

1881 *Q. Rev.* Oct. 309 The result at which the Revisionists of the New Testament have arrived. 1885 FFOULKES *Prim. Consecration* ii. 16 The Revisionists much more correctly translate [etc.].

Revisit (rĭvi·zit), *sb.* [RE- 5 a.] A repeated or second visit.

1623 in Birch *Crt. & Times Jas. I* (1848) II. 385 So particular a relation of all their visits and revisits, that..it tells every step. 1665 SIR T. HERBERT *Trav.* (1677) 206 Albeit our Ambassadour in civility sent to visit him, he returned a slight thanks without a re-visit. 1699 R. L'ESTRANGE *Erasm. Colloq.* (1725) 13, I have been on a visit..to the famous Lady..in England (which in truth was a revisit). 1817 J. SCOTT *Paris Revisit.* (ed. 4) 307 The spirit of female intrigue..was very instrumental in bringing about the revisit from Elba. 1889 *Daily News* 10 May 2/2 The proposed revisit of the Russian pianist..has been abandoned.

Revisit (rĭvi·zit), *v.* [ad. F. *revisiter*, = Sp. and Pg. *revisitar*, It. *rivisitare*, L. *revīsitāre*, or f. RE- 5 a + VISIT *v.*]

† 1. *trans.* To revise, reinspect, re-examine. *Obs.*

1525 LD. BERNERS *Froiss.* II. ccxxiii. [ccxviii.] 691 They saye, that ye haue not dilygently reuisyted nor oversene the letters patentes. 1598 BARRET *Theor. Warres* IV. i. 105 To visit and reuisit all the before appointed matters and orders. 1712 J. JAMES tr. *Le Blond's Gardening* 156 You then revisit your Parterre from one End to the other, and new furnish with Box the Places that require it.

2. To visit again, to return or come back to (a place, person, etc.).

1602 MARSTON *Antonio's Rev.* III. iii, Now gapes the graves, and through their yawnes let loose Imprison'd spirits to revisit earth. 1633 P. FLETCHER *Poet. Misc.* 60 But then revisit our long-long'd-for Kent. 1667 MILTON *P. L.* III. 13 Thee I re-visit now with bolder wing. 1729 POPE *Let. to Harley* 24 Dec., I have been twice revisited with this distemper. 1776 GIBBON *Decl. & F.* xii. (1782) I. 405 It was time that the emperor should revisit Rome. 1817 SHELLEY *Rev. Islam* I. xlvi, My pale lip quivers When thought revisits them. 1847 C. BRONTË *J. Eyre* ii, I began to recall what I had heard of dead men..revisiting the earth. 1869 TOZER *Highl. Turkey* II. 324 The young mother longs to revisit the infant she has left behind her.

b. *absol.* To pay a visit or visits again.

1737 *Gentl. Mag.* VII. 312/2 Nanny revisits, and disgrac'd I fall. 1862 LYTTON *Str. Story* II. 73 Rejoiced, at least, that Margrave had not revisited at Mrs. Ashleigh's.

Hence **Revi·siting** *vbl. sb.*

1598 FLORIO, *Risisita*, a reuisiting, a reuiewing.

Revi·sitant, *a. rare*⁻¹. [f. prec. + -ANT.] Returning to a place.

1852 HAWTHORNE *Blithedale Romance* xxiii, A kind of medium fit for spirits departed and revisitant, like myself.

Revisita·tion (rī-). [a. obs. F. *revisitation* (Godef.), or f. REVISIT, after *visitation.*]

† 1. Revisal, revision. *Obs. rare.*

1549 PAGET in Strype *Eccl. Mem.* II. 258 We thought best to put you in mind of the confirmation and revisitation of the treaty. 1611 COTGR., *Revisitation*, a reuisitation; or..a reuising, reuiewing, recognizing,..overlooking againe.

2. The action or fact of visiting again.

1828–32 in WEBSTER. 1859 J. A. ALEXANDER *On Mark* vi. 6 A regular concerted plan of periodical revisitation. 1889 STEVENSON *Art Writing, Pref. Master Ballantrae* 145 There are few things more strange..than such revisitations.

† **Revi·sitor.** *Obs. rare.* [a. obs. F. *revisiteur* (Godef.), f. *revisiter* to REVISIT.] An examiner, inspector.

1594 R. ASHLEY tr. *Loys le Roy* 29 b, Controllers, reuisitors, and serchers. 1611 COTGR., *Revisiteur*, a reuisor, reuiewer, reuisitor, ouerlooker, ouerseer.

Revisor (rĭvəi·zəɹ). Also 7 **-our.** [See REVISE *v.* and -OR. So F. *reviseur*, Sp. and Pg. *revisor*, It. *revisore.*] One who revises; a reviser.

In quots. 1723 and 1891 after Russ. ревизоръ.

1598 FLORIO, *Riuisore*, a surueyer,..a reuisor. *c* 1620 Z. BOYD *Zion's Flowers* (1855) Introd. 23 Referring to the said revisours to make choose of such of my Workis. 1675 TEMPLE *Let.* Wks. 1720 II. 335 All Revisions should be made by Three of the first Judges, and Four Revisors joined with them. 1723 *Pres. St. Russia* II. 202 Brigadier and Revisor-General, Basili Zatoff. 1790 COWPER *Iliad* Pref., Mr. Fuseli ..voluntarily and generously offered himself as my revisor. 1825 JEFFERSON *Autobiog.* Wks. 1859 I. 45 The Revisors had adopted these opinions. 1850 FORSHALL & MADDEN *Wycliffe's Bible* I. Pref. p. xxxi, The revisor seems, as he proceeded, to have grown weary. 1891 *Pall Mall G.* 1 Apr. 2/3 The revisors of the population report..about 72,000 genuine Pagans in the Government province of Irkutsk.

Revisory (rĭvəi·zŏri), *a.* [f. REVISE *v.* + -ORY. Cf. med.L. *revisōrius* (Du Cange).] Having power to revise; engaged in, of the nature of, revision.

1846 in WORCESTER (citing Story). 1884 BRYCE in *Contemp. Rev.* Nov. 723 A revisory body is needed for all legislation. 1891 *Times* 29 Jan. 5/1 The law..conferred no revisory power upon the Supreme Court.

Revissar, -ing, obs. Sc. ff. RAVISHER, -ING.

Revitaliza·tion. [f. next.] The action of revitalizing, or the fact of being revitalized.

1872 NICHOLSON *Biol.* 16 This is a mere instance of revival and not of revitalisation. 1890 S. J. DUNCAN *Soc. Departure* 235 It was a revitalisation of a certain large round tin box associated with the home store-room.

Revi·talize (rī-), *v.* [RE- 5 a.] *trans.* To restore to vitality; to put new life into. Hence **Revi·talized** *ppl. a.*, **Revi·talizing** *vbl. sb.*

1858 BUSHNELL *Serm. New Life* 374 The returning sun.. sets them creeping forth, revitalized and re-empowered with life. 1862 REICHEL *Cathed. of 19th C.* 25 The regenerated and revitalized restoration or product of this century. 1869 *Microsc. Jrnl.* May 294 There are organisms which we can devitalise and revitalise—devive and revive—many times. 1892 *Daily News* 25 Oct. 6/2 This revitalising, if I may so express myself, in municipal life.

Revittle, obs. form of REVICTUAL.

Revivabi·lity. [f. next + -ITY.] The quality of being revivable.

1855 BAIN *Senses & Int.* II. ii. § 16 The property of mental persistence and revivability. 1868 SPENCER *Princ. Psychol.* (1872) I. II. v. 229 We have to inquire what determines this revivability.

Revivable (rĭvəi·văb'l), *a.* [f. REVIVE *v.* + -ABLE.] Capable of being revived.

1810 W. TAYLOR in Robberds *Mem.* (1843) II. 288 My zeals, however, though never lasting, are always revivable. 1860 *All Year Round* No. 43. 390 Living animalcules.. are revivable in this state. 1890 MAHER *Psychol.* 79 The very revivable and associable character of its sensations.

Hence **Revi·vably** *adv.*

1884 *Mind* IX. 350 What kind of agency can it..be..that revivably stores up the memory of departed phenomena?

Revival (rĭvəi·văl). [f. REVIVE *v.* + -AL.]

1. The act of reviving after decline or discontinuance; restoration to general use, acceptance, etc.; an instance or result of this.

1651 DAVENANT *Gondibert* III. iv. 68 The King has now his curious sight suffis'd With all lost Arts, in their revival view'd. 1693 DRYDEN *Disc. Satire* Ess. (ed. Ker) II. 29 Unnecessary coinage [of words], as well as unnecessary revival, runs into affectation. 1731–8 SWIFT *Polite Conv.* Introd. 58 The happy Revival of Masquerading among us. 1780 COWPER *Let. to Rev. J. Newton*, 12 July, I have often wished..for the revival of the Roman custom—*salutis* at top, and *vale* at bottom. 1865 FREEMAN *Hist. Ess.* Ser. I. vi. (1871) 160 The new German Empire is a fair revival of the old German Kingdom. 1874 MICKLETHWAITE *Mod. Par. Churches* 179 The modern revival of extempore preaching.

b. The act of restoring an old play to the stage, or of republishing an old literary work.

1664 J. WILSON *Cheats*, Another [prologue], intended, upon the revival of the Play, but not spoken. 1779 JOHNSON *L. P., Otway, Friendship in Fashion*..was, upon its revival ..in 1749, hissed off the stage. 1815 HASLEWOOD *Mirr. Mag.* Ded., The Mirror for Magistrates: A Popular Production of the Reign of Elizabeth which merited Revival. 1863 *Sat. Rev.* 16 May 633 The preservation of hundreds of plays, and names which deserve remembrance and justify revival. 1888 *Century Mag.* Feb. 544 *note*, Some of Mr. Daly's revivals have been beautifully costumed.

c. *Revival of learning, letters,* or *literature*, the Renaissance in its literary aspect.

1785 MARTYN *Rousseau's Bot.* Introd. (1794) 3 At the revival of learning, every thing disappeared to make room for the works of antiquity. 1812 SIR H. DAVY *Chem. Philos.* 20 Till the revival of literature in Europe there was no attempt at philosophical discussions in any of the Sciences. 1835 MACAULAY in Trevelyan *Compet. Wallah* (1866) 323 The great revival of letters among the Western nations at the close of the fifteenth and the beginning of the sixteenth century. 1872 MORLEY *Voltaire* (1886) 1 The names of the great decisive movements in the European advance like the Revival of Learning or the Reformation.

d. *Arch.* The reintroduction of Gothic Architecture towards the middle of the 19th century.

1850 SIR G. SCOTT *Anc. Churches* 20 One of the most discouraging features in the revival which has happily commenced among us. 1855 — *Sec. & Dom. Archit.* (1858) 17 We have so generally come to the conclusion that the best period of our national architecture was the latter half of the thirteenth and the beginning of the fourteenth centuries, that we have insensibly adopted that as the groundwork of our revival. 1872 EASTLAKE *Hist. Gothic Revival* 209 The year in which the foundation stone of the Parliament Houses was laid may be taken as a turning point in the History of the Revival.

2. a. Restoration to vigour or activity.

1752 MRS. DELANY *Life & Corr.* (1861) III. 151 A month's visit would have been such a revival to me! 1772 WESLEY *Jrnl.* 4 Sept., There had been a fresh revival of the work of God among them. 1783 BURKE *Rep. Aff. India* Wks. II. 33 The revival of trade in the native hands is of absolute necessity.

1866 G. MACDONALD *Ann. Q. Neighb.* (1878) 491 This was the first time he had shown such a revival of energy. 1874 J. SULLY *Sensation & Intuition* 153 Where a feeling is extremely simple..,its too frequent revival tends to exhaust it.

b. Restoration or return to life or consciousness.

1788 GIBBON *Decl. & F.* xlix. V. 134 On his revival from the swoon.., he recovered his speech and sight. 1810 CRABBE *Borough* XX. 253 His son suspended saw him, long bereft Of life, nor prospect of revival left. 1856 KANE *Arct. Expl.* II. xxiv. 240 Ohlsen was no more. He had shown, a short half-hour before, some signs of revival. 1875 JOWETT *Plato* (ed. 2) I. 446 And revival, if there be such a thing, is the birth of the dead into the world of the living?

c. *Chem.* Revivification.

1788 *Phil. Trans.* LXXIX. 14, I mentioned some instances of the revival of red precipitate in inflammable air.

d. The fact of renewing or raising again.

1885 *Act* 48 *Vict.* c. 15 § 1 Any notice..relating to the withdrawal and revival of objections.

3. A general reawakening *of* or *in* religion in a community or some part of one.

1702 C. MATHER *Magn. Chr.* III. 71 There was a notable Revival of Religion among them. 1757 E. WHEELOCK *Mem.* (1811) 215 We rejoice to hear of a revival of religion in the established church. 1793 *Baptist Reg. for 1794–7* II. 74 A short sketch of revivals in religion. *a* 1817 T. DWIGHT *Trav. New Eng.*, etc. (1821) II. 277 Four considerable revivals of Religion have taken place in Somers during his Ministry. 1821 *Universalist Mag.* 9 June 193/3 There has been of late, in Hartford and its vicinity, what is called a revival in religion.

b. *ellipt.* for prec.; freq. in depreciatory use in reference to the excitement and extravagance which tend to accompany such movements.

1818 J. PALMER *Jrnl.* 76 The Methodists of Cincinnati are very zealous, and have what they call 'a revival' in the country. 1849 C. BRONTË *Shirley* i, In the Methodist chapel down yonder, where they are in the thick of a revival. 1877 FROUDE *Short Stud.* (1883) IV. II. i. 166 The number of those who recollect the beginnings of the Oxford revival is shrinking fast.

attrib. 1843 J. C. in *Baptist Reporter* Feb. 56 A series of revival-meetings were held. 1859 STOFFORD *Work & Counter-work* 7 A bodily illness which has come to be co-existent with this revival movement.

Revivalism (rĭvəi·văliz'm). [f. prec. + -ISM.]

1. The state or form of religion characteristic of revivals. (Cf. prec. 3 b.)

1815 in Polwhele *Trad. & Recoll.* (1826) II. 679, I verily believe that Revivalism has had this effect in some degree. 1859 STOFFORD *Work & Counter-work* 37, I say, that hysteria, in connection with revivalism, is now commonly produced and propagated by man. 1883 *Pall Mall G.* 8 Nov., Revivalism in general and American revivalism in particular, is desperately vulgar.

2. Tendency or desire to revive what has gone out of use or belongs to the past.

1874 L. STEPHEN *Hours in Library* I. 245 However far the rage for revivalism may be pushed, nobody will ever want to revive the nineteenth century. 1876 F. HARRISON *Choice Bks.* (1886) 247 A whited sepulchre, where spruce revivalism is still scraping..the empty and ruined tombs.

Revivalist (rĭvəi·vălist). [f. as prec. + -IST.]

1. One who promotes, produces, or takes part in, a religious revival.

1820 R. POLWHELE *Introd. Bp. Lavington's Enthus. of Method. & Papists* p. cxiii, The Irish Shouters, the Welsh Jumpers, and the Cornish Revivalists. 1859 *All Year Round* No. 28. 33 Much stress has been laid by the Revivalists ..on the decrease of drunkenness..among the converted. 1889 JESSOPP *Coming of Friars* vi. 272 With the dawn of the thirteenth century came the great revivalists—the friars.

attrib. 1859 *All Year Round* No. 28. 33 During a Revivalist meeting. 1864 *Realm* 27 Apr. 2 'A lay teacher' appointed by some revivalist clergyman. 1890 *Times* 20 Dec. 9/3 The Salvation Army as a revivalist agency.

2. One who revives or reintroduces former conditions, methods, etc.

1856 MERIVALE *Rom. Emp.* lxviii. (1865) VIII. 364 The place they hold between the teaching of the earlier philosophers, and that of the revivalists of the third century. 1870 RUSKIN *Crown Wild Olive* II. (1898) 96 The Revivalist worshipped Beauty of a sort and built you Versailles and the Vatican. *a* 1878 SIR G. SCOTT *Lect. Archit.* (1879) I. 349 The error of the French revivalists in selecting an earlier type for their groundwork.

attrib. 1875 ROSSETTI *Hood's Poet. Wks.* Ser. II. Pref. p. xvii, A most astonishing example of revivalist poetry: it is reproductive and spontaneous at the same time.

Hence **Revivali·stic** *a.*

1882 *Macm. Mag.* XLVI. 413 What will be the position of this great revivalistic movement in the year 1900? 1886 *Century Mag.* XXXI. 438 Spiritual preaching is reviving; it is not necessarily revivalistic.

Revi·valize, *v.* [f. as prec. + -IZE.] *intr.* To conduct or bring about a religious revival.

1882 *Ch. Rev.* 73 Where Messrs. Moody and Sankey are revivalising.

† **Revi·ve,** *sb. Obs. rare.* [f. the verb.] **a.** Revival, restoration to life. **b.** A revival (of a play) on the stage.

1589 GREENE *Menaphon* (Arb.) 50 Hee is dead, and therefore grieue not thy memorie with the imagination of his new reuiue. 1663 PEPYS *Diary* 22 July, He grew very proud, and demanded 20*l.* for himself extraordinary..upon every new play, and 10*l.* upon every revive.

Revive (rĭvəi·v), *v.* Also 5 **revyfe,** 5–6 **reuyue, revyue,** 6 **revyve,** 6–7 **reuiue,** 7 **reviue.** [ad. F. *revivre* (10th c., = Prov. *reviure*, Pg. *reviver*, Sp. *revivir*, It. *rivivere*) or post-classical L. *revīvĕre*, f. *re-* RE- + *vīvĕre* to live. The trans. use (expressed in Italian by *rivivare*) probably originated in the conjugation of the perfect and past tenses with *is*, *was*, etc.]

I. *intr.* 1. To return to consciousness; to recover from a swoon or faint.

1432–50 tr. *Higden* (Rolls) VI. 477 Canutus..lay on the grownde as dedde; whiche revivynge, was gladde that he was reservede to lyfe [etc.]. 1530 PALSGR. 690/1 He is in suche a swounde that I wene he wyll never revyve agayne. 1611 BIBLE *Judg.* xv. 19 When he had drunke, his spirit came againe, and he reuiued. 1634 MILTON *Comus* 840 And through the porch and inlet of each sense [they] Dropt in Ambrosial Oils till she reviv'd. 1725 POPE *Odyss.* V. 507 As pious children joy..When a lov'd sire revives before their sight. 1769 BLACKSTONE *Comm.* IV. xxxii. 399 It is clear, that if, upon judgment to be hanged by the neck till he is dead, the criminal be not thoroughly killed, but revives, the sheriff must hang him again. 1852 MRS. STOWE *Uncle Tom's C.* xxviii. 268 St. Clare had fainted,..but as Miss Ophelia applied restoratives, he revived, opened his eyes. 1884 PAE *Eustace* 11 'She is reviving,' exclaimed Eustace.

2. To return or come back to life; to regain vital activity, after being dead; to live again.

1526 TINDALE *Rom.* xiv. 9 Christ therfore dyed and rose agayne and revived. 1567 MAPLET *Gr. Forest* 25 [Their parts] being once so discerped..can neuer after reuiue and quicken againe. 1591 SHAKS. 1 *Hen. VI*, I. i. 18 Henry is dead, and neuer shall reuiue. 1628 T. SPENCER *Logick* 128 The Sunne dyes by setting, and revives by rising, man dyes, but revives no more. 1659 PEARSON *Creed* (1839) 334 Nothing properly dieth but the body:..and nothing can revive but that which dieth. 1712–14 POPE *Rape Lock* V. 70 She smil'd to see the doughty hero slain, But, at her smile, the Beau reviv'd again. 1737 *Gentl. Mag.* VII. 113/2 Still the pale dead revives and lives to me. 1819 SCOTT *Let.* in *Lockhart* (1837) IV. ix. 284 Dr. Morris ought, like Nourjahad, to revive every half century, to record the fleeting manners of the age. 1861 TRENCH *Comm. Ep. Churches Asia* 11 Who revived at the touch of Elisha's bones.

fig. *a* 1661 HOLYDAY *Juvenal* (1673) To Rdr., The endeavor of such, as would prove that Martial..in his later age reviv'd into Christianity. 1888 *Pop. Sci. Monthly* XXXIII. 386 Emotionally we revive in our children.

b. *Chem.* To return to the metallic state.

1825 J. NICHOLSON *Operat. Mechanic* 765 When the lead revives, it separates the gold from the sand.

3. To assume fresh life or vigour after nearly dying or becoming extinct. Also *fig.*

1526 TINDALE *Phil.* iv. 10, I reioyse..greatly that now at the last ye are revived agayne to care for me. 1530 PALSGR. 677/1, I quycken, I revyve, as a thyng dothe ..that was wyddered, or almoste deed, and retourneth to lyfe agayne. 1592 SHAKS. *Ven. & Ad.* 338 Even as a dying coal revives with wind. 1611 BIBLE *Hosea* xiv. 7 They that dwell vnder his shadow shall returne: they shall reuiue as the corne. 1667 MILTON *P. L.* II. 493 If chance the radiant Sun..Extend his ev'ning beam, the fields revive. *a* 1763 SHENSTONE *Elegies* iii. 30 The sweetest bud that blows Revives less lovely from the recent show'r. 1776 GIBBON *Decl. & F.* xii. (1782) I. 396 The strength of Aurelian had crushed on every side the enemies of Rome. After his death they seemed to revive with an increase of fury and of numbers. 1821 SHELLEY *When passion's trance is overpast*, After the slumber of the year..All things revive in field or grove.

b. To resume courage or strength; to recover from depression.

1530 PALSGR. 677/1, I quycken or revyve, I take hert, *je deviens vif.* 1535 COVERDALE *Gen.* xlv. 27 Whan he sawe yᵉ charettes that Ioseph had sent to fetch him, his sprete reuyued. 1611 BIBLE 1 *Mac.* xiii. 7 As soone as the people heard these words, their spirit reuiued. 1667 MILTON *P. L.* XI. 867, I revive At this last sight, assur'd that Man shall live. 1817 SHELLEY *Rev. Islam* IV. xxxiii, My powers revived within me, and I went..Through many a vale. 1860 WARTER *Sea-board* II. 200 When this was done, his spirits seemed to revive.

4. Of feelings, dispositions, etc.: To become active or operative again.

1494 FABYAN *Chron.* V. cxv. 89 His olde condicions began in him to reuyue and quycken, soo that at length he retournyd to his olde accustomed vycys. 1526 TINDALE *Rom.* vii. 9 When the commaundement came synne revyved and I was deed. 1621 T. WILLIAMSON tr. *Goulart's Wise Vieillard* 69 There are sinnes, which doe not grow old, nor dye in old age, but commonly grow young, and reuiue againe. 1746 HERVEY *Medit.* (1818) 271 Anon, sin revives, and leads our souls into a transient, though unwilling captivity. 1779 COWPER *Human Frailty* 8 But Passion rudely snaps the string [of the bow], and it [*sc.* vice] revives again. 1814 SCOTT *Ld. of Isles* VI. ix, And Love, howe'er the maiden strive, Must with reviving hope revive! 1849 MACAULAY *Hist. Eng.* V. I. 544 Ambitious hopes which had seemed to be extinguished, had revived in his bosom. 1859 GEO. ELIOT *A. Bede* xxvi, The jealousy and fretfulness which had revived when Adam came to tell her that [etc.].

b. To return to a flourishing state; to assume fresh life or vigour after decline or decay; also in *Law*, to become valid again.

1565 COOPER *Thesaurus* s.v. *Resurgo*, *Maiestas Pop. Rom. resurrexit*, reuiued, or came to the olde state agayne. 1576 FLEMING *Panopl. Epist.* 124 Such is the kinde of your cause, that, together with the commonwealth,..it must of necessitie, as it were, revive. 1709 POPE *Ess. Crit.* 701 Then Sculpture and her sister-arts revive; Stones leap'd to form, and rocks began to live. 1709 STEELE *Tatler* No. 1 ⁋ 6 It is not now doubted but Plays will revive, and take their usual Place in the opinion of Persons of Wit and Merit. 1737 *Gentl. Mag.* VII. 3/2 Therefore I do not doubt..Trade will here again revive. 1771 *Encycl. Brit.* II. 910/2 Upon the vassals resignation, the superior's right of property revives. 1840 MACAULAY *Clive* Ess. (1897) 541 The abuses which he had suppressed began to revive. 1858 LD. ST. LEONARDS *Handy-Bk. Prop. Law* xix. 149 If..you desire the gift to the legatee to revive also, you should expressly declare such to be your intention. 1891 *Sat. Rev.* 24 Oct. 471/2 It looked as if speculation there was once more reviving; but it fell away again.

c. To return, come back again, after a period of abeyance.

1759 GOLDSM. *Polite Learn.* iii, Happy country, where the pastoral age begins to revive! 1809 SCOTT *Let.* in *Lockhart* (1837) II. v. 194 The days of William Wallace.. seem to be reviving there. 1881 STEVENSON *Lett.* (1899) I. 226 But the old time is dead also, never, never to revive.

II. *trans.* 5. To restore to consciousness; to bring back from a swoon or faint, or from a state of suspended animation.

In some instances with *was*, etc., perh. *intr.* (cf. etym. note).

c 1430 *Syr Gener.* (Roxb.) 9745 On swounyng she fel him beforn; When that she revived was, She called hir doghtre Lucidas. *a* 1533 LD. BERNERS *Huon* cl. 570 Huon and she ..fell downe bothe in a traunce..: then the lordes reuyued them. 1548 ELYOT, *Reminisco*, to be reuiued; to recouer life agayne. 1684 BUNYAN *Pilgr.* II. (1900) 176 They fetcht her a Bundle of Myrrh, and awhile after she was revived. 1719 DE FOE *Crusoe* I. (Globe) 243 This Water reviv'd his Father more than all the Rum or Spirits I had given him. 1737 WHISTON *Josephus, Antiq.* II. vii. § 5 Jacob almost fainted away at this..great joy; however Joseph revived him.

6. To restore to life; to resuscitate or reanimate; to bring back *from* death or the grave.

1470–85 MALORY *Arthur* XVI. xiii. 682 The blood that the grete foule bled reuyued the chyckens from deth to lyf. 1526 *Pilgr. Perf.* (W. de W. 1531) 139 b, Caused the spiryt of man after deth to returne to the body & reuyue the same. 1590 SPENSER *F. Q.* II. iii. 22 Hable to heale the sicke, and to revive the ded. 1603 *England's Welcome to Jas. I*, III. ix, He Lazarus reuiued from the graue. 1655 FULLER *Ch. Hist.* II. x. 129, I remember not in Scripture that God ever revived a brute Beast. 1700 DRYDEN *Pal. & Arc.* III. 877 Old Ægeus only could revive his son. 1711 STEELE *Spect.* No. 97 ⁋ 2 A Prince could not revive a Dead Man by taking the Life of him who killed him. 1818 SHELLEY *On a Faded Violet* 11, I weep,—my tears revive it not! I sigh, —it breathes no more on me.

absol. *c* 1440 *Found. St. Bartholomew's* (E.E.T.S.) 27 He roys vp hole And wente to his owne, yeldynge thankynges to God that mortifieth and revyuyth, smytyth and helyth.

transf. *c* 1450 *Cov. Myst.* (Shaks. Soc.) 256 Into this werd Goddys sone hath sowth For veray love man to revyfe. 1597 SHAKS. 2 *Hen. IV*, IV. i. 200 To end one doubt by Death Reuiues two greater in the Heires of Life. 1742 GRAY *Adversity* 45 The gen'rous spark extinct revive, Teach me to love and to forgive.

7. To restore from a languid, depressed, or morbid state; to infuse fresh life or vigour into. † Also const. with inf.

a 1547 SURREY in *Tottel's Misc.* (Arb.) 7 Reuiued with a glimse of grace olde sorowes to let fall. 1567 TURBERV. *Ovid's Ep.* 67 In fayth I was revivde At those thy cheerfull words. 1591 SPENSER *M. Hubberd* 756 He..with sweete delight Of Musicks skill revives his toyled spright. 1612 BRINSLEY *Lud. Lit.* 5 The Lord will reuiue you, I hope, and all of us also who labour in this toyling kinde. 1697 DRYDEN *Æneid* I. 633 What first Æneas in this place beheld, Reviv'd his courage, and his fear expell'd. 1712 BLACKMORE *Creation* IV. 446 Th' admitted Nitre..Revives the Fire, and referments the Blood. 1725 DE FOE *Voy. round World* (1840) 316 Our men were revived with this discovery. 1794 MRS. RADCLIFFE *Myst. Udolpho* V, St. Aubert was revived by rest, and by the serene air of this summit. 1806 *Med. Jrnl.* XV. 16 The turpentine revives the function of the liver. 1824 W. IRVING *T. Trav.* I. 251 Like a summer cloud, which..revives the fields over which it passes. 1898 J. GEIKIE *Earth Sculpt.* 306 The erosive energy of the rivers is renewed, and they are said therefore to be revived.

† b. To restore (persons) to a flourishing or thriving state. *Obs. rare.*

1560 DAUS tr. *Sleidane's Comm.* 304 b, Thus beyng againe revived [L. *auctus*], he forgot the benefit received. 1573 TUSSER *Husb.* (1878) 31 What helpes to reuiue the thriuing to thriue? Plough, fense, and store, aught else before.

c. To renew; to restore again from or after decline or decay.

1631 WEEVER *Anc. Funeral Mon.* 369 His Monument is lately reuiued by the Companie of the mystery of Mercers. 1633 P. FLETCHER *Purple Isl.* V. i, And Thirsil with night's death revives his morning lay. 1686 tr. *Chardin's Trav. Persia* 11 The War in Candy..encourag'd 'em to revive their Commerce in the Territories of the Grand Signior. 1731–8 SWIFT *Polite Conv.* Introd. 62 When Conversation appears in Danger to flag,..I took care to invent some sudden Question..to revive it. 1759 GOLDSM. *Polite Learn.* iii, Two poets in an age are not sufficient to revive the splendour of decaying genius. 1799 *Med. Jrnl.* II. 175 Those who are endeavouring so meritoriously to revive the reputation of digitalis. 1875 JOWETT *Plato* (ed. 2) V. 127 Plato is not disposed to encourage amateur attempts to revive religion in states.

8. To set going, make active or operative, again.

1494 FABYAN *Chron.* VII. ccxxiv. 250 Malcolyn departyd from the Kyng in great dysplesure, for the which..yᵉ warre atwene Englonde and Scotlande was reuyued. 1547 *Act* 1 *Edw. VI*, c. 7 Preamble, The Demandants..were compelled..to prosecute and sue Resummons..to revive their said Actions. 1598 MANWOOD *Lawes Forest* xxv. (1615) 257 The plees may be reuiued againe by the Kings writ of resummons. 1600 E. BLOUNT tr. *Conestaggio* 303 Yet the estates did not forbeare..to reuiue the demaunds made at the estates helde at Tomar. 1696 PHILLIPS s.v., To Revive an old grudge. 1727–38 CHAMBERS *Cycl.* s.v. *Revivor*, Praying the former proceedings may stand revived, and be put in the same condition as at the time of the abatement. 1845 S. AUSTIN *Ranke's Hist. Ref.* I. 349 Supported by the nation, he would have been able to revive the ancient opposition to the papacy. 1856 FROUDE *Hist. Eng.* (1858) II. vii. 176 The attempts which during that time were made to revive the feuds of the houses.

b. To re-enact (a law, etc.); to renew or revalidate; to reopen (an election).

a 1548 HALL *Chron.*, *Edw. IV*, 225 b, Suche Lawes..as kyng Henry the sixte had caused to be abrogated.., he again

reuiued and renouated. 1641 BAKER *Chron.* (1653) 226 A Parliament is holden, in which the Acts made in the eleventh year of king Richard were revived. 1655 *Clarke Papers* (Camden) III. 24 His Highnesse..hath past an ordinance for reviveing the former ordnance against horse races for 6 monthes longer. 1736 *Gentl. Mag.* VI. 301 The best Way to remedy this Grievance would be by reviving and pursuing the Design of the Act. 1747 *Col. Rec. Pennsylv.* V. 101 The last Act only [is] repealed, by which means the former stands revived. 1828 CRUISE *Digest* (ed. 2) II. 65 A writ of *scire facias*, for the defendant to shew cause why the judgement should not be revived. 1839 MONTAGU & NEALE *Law Parl. Elect.* I. 28 When once the poll is formally concluded by public announcement .. the election is complete, and cannot be revived. 1858 LD. ST. LEONARDS *Handy-Bk. Prop. Law* xix. 148 You may wish to revive your will after you have revoked it.

absol. 1838 STORY *Equity Pleadings* 393 In each of these cases, if the appropriate Bill is not brought by the party seeking to revive a demurrer will lie.

c. To reawaken (a desire, etc.).

1590–6 SPENSER *F. Q.* (J.), Noise of arms..Might not revive desire of knightly exercise. *a* 1771 GRAY *Dante* 4 Would'st thou revive the deep Despair. 1838 PRESCOTT *Ferd. & Is.* II. ix. III. 36 The beautiful specimens of pearls ..revived the cupidity of the nation. 1859 FITZGERALD *Omar* iv, Now the New Year reviving old Desires, The thoughtful Soul to Solitude retires.

9. To bring into existence or use, to set up, again; to restore or re-establish (something which has been discontinued or out of use).

1495 *Rolls of Parlt.* VI. 469/2 That the same Manours.. be reuiued and reannexed to the said Duchie of Cornwall. 1516 *Birgette* in *Myrr. Our Lady* (E. E. T. S.) p. l, And loo a meruaylous thyng, the olde myracle was reuyued. 1582 STANYHURST *Æneis* I. (Arb.) 24 Theare must thee kingdoom with Troian fame be reuiued. 1617 MORYSON *Itin.* II. 246 The end of our prosecution is to reforme the Kingdome, to reuiue Justice and order. *a* 1653 GOUGE *Comm. Heb.* x. 10 This demonstrateth the great danger.. of reviving Jewish ceremonies. 1712 PRIDEAUX *Direct. to Ch.-wardens* (ed. 4) 81 It may cost the Parish a Chancery Suit again to revive the Trust. 1776 GIBBON *Decl. & F.* x. (1782) I. 301 To execute this..arduous design, he first resolved to revive the obsolete office of censor. 1826 DISRAELI *Viv. Grey* v. xv, We might all retire to this valley, and revive the feudal times with great success. 1866 SEELEY *Ecce Homo* iii. (ed. 8) 28 In what new form he proposed to revive the ancient monarchy. *a* 1878 SIR G. SCOTT *Lect. Archit.* (1879) I. 348 If the revivers went on the principle of now reviving one style and now another.

b. To bring back again into knowledge, notice, or currency.

In quot. 1577 perh. used for *reviewed*, revised.

1509 HAWES *Past. Pleas.* I. (Percy Soc.) 9 Their great actes agayne to revive, In flaming tongues for to abyde on lyve. 1577 *Vicary's Anat.* (title-p.), Which work is newly reuyued, corrected, and published by the Chirurgions of the same Hospital. 1605 BACON *Adv. Learn.* II. vii. § 1 That..I may reviue and reintegrate the misapplyed..name of Natural Magicke. 1630 PRYNNE *Anti-Armin.* 124 It reuiues the old Pelagian Tenet. 1693 DRYDEN *Disc. Satire* Ess. (ed. Ker) II. 29 In my opinion, obsolete words may then be laudably revived. *c* 1730 SWIFT *Verses on Death of Dr. Swift* Wks. 1751 VII. 249 He'll treat me, as he does my Betters, .. Revive the Libels born to die. 1778 MISS BURNEY *Evelina* lxxvii, Have you, Madam, been prevailed upon to revive that ridiculous old story? 1837 LOCKHART *Scott* I. xi. 416 Scott's object and delight was to revive the fame of the Rhymer. 1882 AINGER *Lamb* vi. 99 The publishers brought out..a new monthly journal, reviving in it the name of an earlier, and extinct periodical.

c. To put (an old play) upon the stage again.

1823 *Examiner* 845/1 Do the managers 'revive' some of the standard plays? 1899 A. W. WARD *Eng. Dram. Lit.* I. ii. 248 *Thersytes*..was printed at some date not earlier than 1561; it may have been revived under Queen Elisabeth.

10. To bring again before the mind; to renew the memory of (a person or thing); to recall.

1638 SIR T. HERBERT *Trav.* (ed. 2) 160 The Citizens..send him a choking message reviving the cruelty done..his brother. 1670 PETTUS *Fodinæ Reg.* Ep. Ded., At every 70 Years some signal Occurrence revived them to our Memories. 1690 LOCKE *Hum. Und.* II. x. § 2 The mind has a power..to revive perceptions which it has once had. 1711 STEELE *Spect.* No. 192 ¶ 8 You cannot recal your Father by your Grief, but you may revive him to his Friends by your Conduct. 1759 DILWORTH *Pope* 85 Some of the letters served to revive past scenes of friendship. 1813 SHELLEY *Q. Mab* II. 246 The Spirit..felt All knowledge of the past revived. 1855 BAIN *Senses & Int.* III. i. § 8 Take first the recovery of feelings of energetic action, as when reviving the exploits and exertions of yesterday. 1860 TYNDALL *Glac.* I. iii. 24 The surrounding scene revived..all the impressions of my boyhood.

refl. 1774 JOHNSON *Let. to W. Hastings* 30 Mar., I cannot omit this opportunity of reviving myself in your memory.

b. To renew or freshen up, to bring back to one (the memory *of* some person or thing).

1592 NASHE *P. Pennilesse* 18 b, Vpbraiding me for reuiuing in an epistle of mine the reuerend memory of Sir Thomas Moore. 1665 BOYLE *Occas. Refl.* Pref. (1848) p. xxx, The Objects..do revive the Memory of those good Thoughts. 1713 STEELE *Guardian* No. 5 ¶ 2 This Conversation revives to us the Memory of a Friend. 1781 GIBBON *Decl. & F.* xxvii. (1787) III. 66 Every disgraceful moment of the unfortunate reigns of Arcadius and Honorius revived the memory of their irreparable loss.

11. *Chem.* To convert, restore, or reduce (a metal, esp. mercury) to or into its natural condition or form; to restore *from* a mixed to a natural state; to revivify.

1677 W. HARRIS tr. *Lemery's Course Chem.* 17 Thus Cinnaber and the other preparations of Mercury are Revived into Quick-silver. *a* 1691 BOYLE *Notes & Exper. Mercury* Wks. 1742 I. 645 Divers philosophical Spagyrists.. order it [mercury] to be..sublimed with acid salts or sulphurs, and then revived with alkalies. 1727–38 CHAMBERS *Cycl.* s.v. *Mercury*, By diluting the whole with an ounce of aqua stygia, the whole grain of mercury will be revived. 1784 *Phil. Trans.* LXXIV. 160 If a solution of luna cornea in volatile alkali be triturated with mercury, the silver will be revived. 1812 SIR H. DAVY *Chem. Philos.* 40 Bayen shewed that mercury converted into a calx or earth..could be revived without the addition of any inflammable substance. 1839 URE *Dict. Arts* 1116 Silver..was formerly called a perfect metal, because heat alone revived its oxide. 1878 *Encycl. Brit.* VIII. 114 It was observed..that certain metals could be 'revived' from solutions of their salts on the passage of a current of electricity.

12. a. To treat (faded clothing, etc.) with a reviver; to renovate. *rare.*

1836 DICKENS *Sk. Boz, Characters* x, It [*sc.* the hat] was as black as the coat. The truth flashed suddenly upon us—they had been 'revived'.

b. To restore to clearness; to bring out clearly.

1861 O'CURRY *Lect. on MS. Materials* 150, I took the necessary means of reviving the ink. 1875 SCRIVENER *Lect. Grk. Test.* 18 Attempts have been made to revive the faded characters.

Revived (rɪvəi·vd), *ppl. a.* [f. prec.]

1. Restored to life or health; brought up again, reintroduced; renewed or renovated; etc.

1615 CHAPMAN *Odyss.* IV. 127 So my heart were easde of sorrowes..by their reuiued breaths. 1667 MILTON *P. L.* IX. 440 Spot more delicious than those Gardens feign'd Or of reviv'd Adonis, or renownd Alcinous. 1728 POPE *Dunc.* I. 284 A vast, vamp'd, future, old, reviv'd, new piece, Twixt Plautus, Fletcher, Shakespear, and Corneille. 1748 RICHARDSON *Clarissa* IV. 228 How would the revived patient covet the physic! 1835 DICKENS *Sketches, Tales* i, The boy, who now appeared..in a revived black coat of his master's. *a* 1878 SIR G. SCOTT *Lect. Archit.* (1879) I. 351 Your revived style and its developments should.. be based on the earlier..half of Mediæval architecture. 1884 J. FISKE *Mem. Evolutionist* 327 A plexus of optical sensations with sundry revived states of mind.

2. *Chem.* Restored to the natural metallic state.

1666 BOYLE *Orig. Formes & Qual.* 279 The Whitenesse did not indeed appertain properly to the whole Mixture, but to a huge multitude of little Corpuscles of the reviv'd Concrete. 1797 *Encycl. Brit.* (ed. 3) XI. 465/2 The calcined matt is to be fused with litharge, and the silver incorporated with the revived lead. 1798 *Phil. Trans.* LXXXVIII. 451, I searched, but in vain, for traces of revived gold, in its reguline form and colour. 1849 NOAD *Electricity* (ed. 3) 203 The fused globules..serving as the continuation of the pole, until a wire or thread of revived silver..is produced.

Revi·vement. Now *rare.* [f. the vb. + -MENT.]

1. The (*or* an) act of reviving; revival.

1611 COTGR., *Remise*, a restorall, reuiuement, recouerie, setting vp againe. 1637 FELTHAM *Lusoria, Lett.* xvii. (1661) 84 We have the sacred Scriptures,..the purer Primitive Times, and the late Reformation, or Revivement rather, all on our side. 1670 G. H. *Hist. Cardinals* I. II. 54 It would be only a renovation and revivement of the memory of.. antient sorrows.

1843 *For. Q. Rev.* II. 351 The various and vaunted systems of Greece and Rome, and their modern German revivements and imitations.

2. A reviving or restoring influence.

1598–9 E. FORDE *Parismus* II. (1661) 114 All this while his beloved Lady was his physician..whose presence was more revivement to him than any thing else. 1628 FELTHAM *Resolves* I. xxiv, His with-drawings are our mi-series; his presence is joy, and revivement. *a* 1708 BEVERIDGE *Priv. Th.* I. (1730) 133 To lie down still and quiet, is a great Refreshment and Revivement to them.

Reviver (rɪvəi·vəɹ), *sb.*[1] [f. the verb + -ER [1].]

1. That which revives, restores, or invigorates; also *slang*, a stimulating drink.

1592 NASHE *P. Penilesse* 16 b, Hee saith, it [*sc.* learning] is..the reuiuer of vices, and mother of cowardize. 1638 SIR T. HERBERT *Trav.* (ed. 2) 344 The mirthfull sunne (the provoker and reviver of decayed nature). 1762 BEATTIE *Elegy* ii, Hail, kind reviver! that canst lull the cares, And every weary sense compose to rest. 1844 DICKENS *Mart. Chuz.* xxiii, 'Now, Mr. Tapley,' said Mark, giving himself a tremendous blow in the chest by way of reviver. 1876 BESANT & RICE *Gold. Butterfly* 63 It was but twelve o'clock, and therefore early for revivers of any sort.

b. A preparation for restoring a faded colour, polish, or lustre.

1836 DICKENS *Sk. Boz, Characters* x, It is a deceitful liquid that black and blue reviver. *Ibid.*, The transient dignity of the unhappy man decreased, in exact proportion as the 'reviver' wore off. 1885 LOCK *Workshop Rec.* Gen. Index, French Polish Reviver.

2. One who revives or restores that which has lapsed, become obsolete, or fallen into disuse.

1607 *Schol. Disc. agst. Antichr.* II. v. 2 The Magistrate must be a remoouer, or reviver of the Ceremonies controversed. 1673 MILTON *True Relig.* Wks. 1851 V. 410 The Authors or late Revivers of all those Sects or Opinions. 1741 MIDDLETON *Cicero* II. 479 The head and reviver of the Marian cause. 1797 GODWIN *Enquirer* I. vi. 38 We are indebted to the..revivers of letters for more than we can express. 1835 LYTTON *Rienzi* IV. i, To grace the palace of the Reviver of the old Republic. 1878 LECKY *Eng. in 18th C.* II. vii. 325 The first considerable reviver of Shakespeare.

b. (See quot. and cf. REVIVAL 3).

1824 W. E. ANDREWS *Crit. Rev. Fox's Bk. Mart.* I. 228 Religious frenzy, imbibed by her connexion with a sect of Methodists called Revivers.

c. One who touches up or renovates old clothes.

1864 *Times* 2 Nov. (Farmer), Revivers, who rejuvenate seedy black coats, and, for the moment, make them look as good as new.

† **Revi·ver,** *sb.*[2] *Obs.* [f. as prec. + -ER [4].]

1. Revival, restoration, re-establishment.

c 1617 BACON *Digest of Laws* (1629) 145 The Lawes of those three Law-Giuers had great Prerogatiues...The third, of a Spirit of Reuiuer; To bee often oppressed, and often restored. 1637 HEYLIN *Brief Answ.* 140 A reviver and continuance onely of the antient usages. 1641 — *Help to Hist.* (1671) 176 That act was totally repealed, and a reviver made of the said late dissolved Bishoprick.

2. *Bill of reviver*: (see quots. and REVIVOR [2] 2).

a 1631 DONNE *Lett.* (1651) 19 It was like a Bill of Reviver, by way of crosse-suits. 1704 J. HARRIS *Lex. Techn.* I, *Bill of Reviver*, is when a Bill hath been exhibited in Chancery, against one who answers, and before the Cause is heard, or if heard, before the Decree enrolled, either Party dies: In this case a Bill of Reviver must be brought, that the former Proceedings may stand revived, and the Cause be finally determined.

Revi·ver, *v.* *nonce-wd.* [f. REVIVER *sb.*[1] 1 b.] *trans.* To treat with a reviver; to renovate.

1861 SALA *Dutch Pict.* xxi. 337 Clothes good enough to be revivered..and sold..as superior second-hand garments.

Revive·scence, variant of REVIVISCENCE.

1794–6 E. DARWIN *Zoon.* (1801) III. 97 Does the revivescence of these affected parts, or their torpor, recurring at intervals, form the paroxysms of these fevers? 1875 H. ROGERS *Orig. Bible* (ed. 3) 147 The superstition on which this empire was founded had a curious property of revivescence.

Revive·scent, variant of REVIVISCENT *a.*

1801 SOUTHEY *Lett.* (1856) I. 183 The 'Anthology' is revivescent under the eye of Blind Tobin.

Revi·vicating, *ppl. a.*, for *revivificating*.

1814 MRS. J. WEST *Alice de Lacy* II. 171 The..sonorous trumpet, whose thrilling tone is even deemed significant of the revivicating summons of the Arch-angel.

Revivication, erroneous form, perhaps mispr. for REVIVIFICATION. Cf. REVIFICATION.

1831 HOWITT *Seasons* 70 If you plunge into their solitudes, there are symptoms of revivication under your feet. 1839 E. A. POE *Ligeia* Wks. 1865 I. 467 This hideous drama of revivication was repeated;..each terrific relapse was only into a sterner..death. 1844 STEPHENS *Bk. Farm* II. 428 Spring..is the season of revivication.

† **Reviviction.** *Obs. rare.* [irreg. f. L. *revivēre* or *reviviscĕre*.] Reviviscence.

1646 SIR T. BROWNE *Pseud. Ep.* III. xii. 134 If the Rabbines prophesie succeed [the phœnix] shall conclude its dayes, not in its owne, but the last and generall flames, without all hope of Reviviction. 1652 SPARKE *Prim. Devot.* (1663) 301 His bitter cup of death and crucifixion! Sweetned (you see) by speedy reviviction.

† **Revivificate,** *v.* *Obs. rare.* [ad. ppl. stem of late L. *revivificāre*: cf. REVIVIFY *v.*]

1. *trans.* To restore to life. Also const. *into*.

1660 H. MORE *Myst. Godl.* VI. vi. 231 The same individual Persons shall be revivificated body and soul, and made happy with Eternal life. 1685 — *Illustr.* 351 Much less were [they] revivificated into celestial bodies.

2. *intr.* 'To recover life again' (Bailey, 1727).

Revivification (rɪvi·vifikē^i·ʃən). [See prec. So F. *revivification*, Sp. *-acion*, It. *-azione*.]

1. Restoration or return from death to life.

1638 SIR T. HERBERT *Trav.* (ed. 2) 265 At the first sound [of the trumpet] will ensue a revivification of angells and men. 1675 WOODHEAD, etc. *Paraphr. S. Paul* 116 The soul owes its happy immortality as much to Christ's rising again, as the body doth its revivification. 1756 *Gentl. Mag.* XXVI. 213 The earthquake is said...immediately afterwards to be after their death and revivification. 1838 POE *A. G. Pym* Wks. 1864 IV. 77 A doubt that the apparition of Rogers was indeed a revivification of his disgusting corpse. 1875 E. WHITE *Life in Christ* II. ix. (1878) 96 Christ's own resurrection was the revivification even of the body which had died.

fig. 1807 E. S. BARRETT *Rising Sun* I. 192 As the revivification of nature from the death of winter had again brought round the season. 1848 DICKENS *Dombey* xxvii, The maid ..collected the ashes of Cleopatra and carried them away.., ready for to-morrow's revivification.

b. *Nat. Hist.* Recovery or awakening from a state of torpidity.

1801 *Encycl. Brit.* Suppl. II. 401/2 *Revivification*, in physiology, the recalling to life of animals apparently dead. 1815 KIRBY & SP. *Entomol.* I. ii. 72 The seeming revivification of the dead chrysalis. 1877 HUXLEY *Anat. Inv. Anim.* Introd. 3 This revivification may take place after months, or even years, of arrested life.

2. *Chem.* Reduction or restoration of a metal, etc., after combination, to its original state.

1643 SIR T. BROWNE *Relig. Med.* I. § 48, I have often beheld as a miracle, that artificiall resurrection and revivification of Mercury. 1680 BOYLE *Exp. Chem. Princ.* IV. 206 Salts or Sulphurs..when the Quicksilver is driven from them in the revivification. 1782 *Phil. Trans.* LXXVIII. 64 Which contributed to the revivification of a larger quantity of mercury. 1812 SIR H. DAVY *Chem. Philos.* 41 The same air is produced during the revivification of metallic calces by charcoal. 1839 URE *Dict. Arts* 1123 As soon as the revivification is complete, the casks must be filled with water.

b. (See quot.)

1881 LOCK *Spon's Encycl.* v. 1853 By 'revivification' of the [animal] charcoal, is meant the separation from it of those saccharine and other matters which it absorbs in the filtering process.

3. Revival, restoration; renewal of vigour or activity.

1756 C. LUCAS *Ess. Waters* III. 89 The milkiness and revivification of color ensued. 1812 SHELLEY *Proposals* Prose Wks. 1888 I. 280 One truth that has been discovered can never die, but will prevent the revivification of its apportioned opposite falsehood. 1863 HAWTHORNE *Our Old Home* 76 The revivification and improvement of its native manhood. 1880 DISRAELI *Endym.* lix, 'I am thinking of what is beneath all this,' replied Nigel. 'A great revivification.'

Revi·vified, *ppl. a.* [f. REVIVIFY *v.* + -ED [1].] **a.** Reduced to a metallic state; revived. **b.** Resurrected. **c.** Restored, renewed.

1727–38 CHAMBERS *Cycl.* s.v. *Antimony*, Revivified Antimony..is prepared of flowers of antimony and sal-ammoniac, digested in distilled vinegar. 1871 MACDUFF *Mem. Patmos* vi. 80 It is a life in which the raised and revivified body is married to the lost soul! 1892 GUNTER *Miss Dividends* (1893) 183 His pulse bounding with revivified hope.

Revi·vifier. *rare.* [f. REVIVIFY *v.* + -ER [1].] An apparatus used in the revivification of animal charcoal.

1881 LOCK *Spon's Encycl.* v. 1853 The black..descends into the driers.., enters the revivifiers..at about 90°.

Revivify (rɪvi·vifəi), *v.* [ad. F. *revivifier* (16th c.), = Sp. and Pg. *revivificar*, It. *re-, rivivificare*, or late L. *revivificāre*: cf. REVIVIFICATE *v.*]

1. *trans.* To restore to animation or activity; to revive or reinvigorate; to put new life into.

1675 COCKER *Morals* 53 Sleep..Revivifies the Brain, the Spirits chears. 1813 SHELLEY *Q. Mab* VI. 22 Will not the universal Spirit e'er Revivify this withered limb of Heaven? 1863 MISS BRADDON *J. Marchmont's Legacy* II. i. 3 Last night's festivities seem to have revivified me. 1883 H. WACE *Gosp. & its Witnesses* v. 102 We..can..revivify the nervous forces of life by galvanic currents.

transf. 1762–71 H. WALPOLE *Vertue's Anecd. Paint.* (1786) IV. 6 The arts, when neglected, always degenerate. Encouragement must keep them up, or a genius revivify them. 1859 THACKERAY *Virgin.* i, I have..endeavoured to revivify the bygone times and people.

absol. 1840 THACKERAY *Paris Sk.-bk.* (1872) 186 It is a food ..which when it does not revivify, smothers. 1879 H. GEORGE *Progr. & Pov.* x. v. (1881) 495 The struggle that must either revivify, or convulse in ruin, is near at hand.

2. To restore to life; to make alive again.

1744 STACKHOUSE *Hist. Bible* Apparatus p. xii, That the gross Matter, which they saw, laid in the Grave.., should ever be rais'd..and revivify'd. 1824 LAMB *Elia* Ser. II. *Blakesmoor in H—shire*, A germ to be revivified. *a* 1849 J. C. MANGAN *Poems* (1903) 85, I would spring up revivified, reborn, A living soul again. 1883 H. DRUMMOND *Nat. Law in Spir. W.* (1884) 86 The biologist cannot devitalise a plant or an animal and revivify it again.

3. *Chem.* = REVIVE *v.* 11.

1727–38 CHAMBERS *Cycl.* s.v. *Revivification*, Gold, and other metals, it is said, may be recovered or revivified into running mercury. 1770 *Phil. Trans.* LX. 221 If..a degree of heat be applied greater than is necessary to..revivify a metal. 1890 THORPE *Dict. Appl. Chem.* I. 171 A description of the kilns most generally in use for revivifying char.

b. *intr.* = REVIVE *v.* 2 b.

1727–38 CHAMBERS *Cycl.* s.v. *Revivification*, Having reduced it [mercury] into water,..into ashes, &c., it revivified, and resumed its first form. 1758 *Elaboratory laid open* 211 The operation should not be too much prolonged; lest the quicksilver revivify, or reassume its fluid state.

Hence **Revi·vifying** *vbl. sb.* and *ppl. a.*

1782 H. WALPOLE *Let. to Rev. Mr. Cole* 21 June, Swelled unreasonably with large collops of old authors, most of whom little deserved revivifying. 1818 BYRON *Ch. Har.* IV. lv, Thy decay Is still impregnate with divinity, Which gilds it with revivifying ray. 1878 STEVENSON *Inland Voy.* 192 Even the showers of rain had a revivifying effect.

Reviving (rɪvəi·viŋ), *vbl. sb.* [f. REVIVE *v.* + -ING [1].] The action of the vb., in various senses.

1486 *Hen. VII at York* in *Surtees Misc.* (1890) 57 New reviving in comforth to attaine your asstate. 1529 MORE *Dyaloge* I. Wks. x. 132/1 Cause can I se none, whye we shoulde of reason more meruaile of the reuyuyng of a dede man. 1577 HANMER *Anc. Eccles. Hist.* (1619) 79 This they did to the end they might..hinder the reviving of the Saints. 1612 BRINSLEY *Lud. Lit.* 3 This I thankefully acknowledge ..to give you likewise some reuiuing. 1677 W. HARRIS tr. *Lemery's Course Chem.* (1686) 138 Reviving of Cinnabar into Quick-silver. 1710 STEELE *Tatler* No. 118 ¶ 12, I shall not allow the reviving of any one Part of that antient Mode. 1741 J. EDWARDS in *Mem. E. Wheelock* (1811) 210 There has been a reviving of religion amongst us of late. 1824 ANN SMITH in *Life* (1851) 32 Return to thy Church in this corner. Grant some new revivings. 1865 *Cassell's Illustr. Fam. Paper* 15 Apr. 181/3 They are now past 'clobbering', 'reviving', or 'translating'.

attrib. 1839 URE *Dict. Arts* 1122 All ores which contain more than 7 lbs. of lead, or 1 lb. of copper, per cent., are excluded from this reviving operation.

Revi·ving, *ppl. a.* [f. REVIVE *v.* + -ING [2].]

1. That revives, or regains strength, vigour, or consciousness.

1592 SHAKS. *Ven. & Ad.* 977 For now reuiuing ioy bids her reioyce. 1667 DRYDEN *Prol. Tempest* 4 So, from old Shakespear's honour'd dust, this day Springs up and buds a new reviving Play. 1682 TATE *Abs. & Achit.* II. 64 Cherished by her bounty's plenteous spring, Reviving widows smile and orphans sing. 1782 COWPER *Heroism* 73 Increasing commerce and reviving art Renew the quarrel. 1789 H. WALPOLE *Lett.* (1858) IX. 200 Their King..may prove their tyrant if reviving loyalty does not in a new frenzy force him to be so. 1810 SCOTT *Lady of L.* II. i, All Nature's children feel the matin spring Of life reviving with reviving day. 1897 RHOSCOMYL *White Rose Arno* 125 With one hand upon the collar of the reviving man.

2. That refreshes, strengthens, or infuses fresh life; stimulating, reinvigorating.

1601 SHAKS. *Jul. C.* II. ii. 88 From you great Rome shall sucke Reuiuing blood. 1696 E. REYNER *Rules Government Tongue* 255 Comforts are reviving cordialls. 1709 MRS. E. SINGER *Love & Friendsh.* 4 While..closing Flowers reviving Odors yield. 1750 MRS. DELANY *Life & Corr.* (1861) II. 570, I don't pity you,..who have such trees to shade and such reviving cascades to cool you. 1878 STEVENSON *Inland Voy.* 79, I sat in a drift of rain by the side of the bank, to have a reviving pipe. 1881 MISS BRADDON *Asphodel* II. 253 After a reviving cup of tea.

b. Renewing an enactment.

1769 BLACKSTONE *Comm.* IV. 70 The suspending and repealing acts..and also the reviving act of 29 Hen. VI.

Hence **Revi·vingly** *adv.*

1847 in WEBSTER (citing Coleridge). 1886 MISS LINSKILL *Haven under the Hill* II. ix. 107 The south-west wind blew revivingly.

Reviviscence (revivi·sĕns). [ad. L. type *revīviscentia, f. pres. pple. of *revīviscĕre* to revive. So F. *réviviscence*, Pg. *reviviscencia*, It. *-enza*. See also REVIVESCENCE.]

1. Return to life or animation.

1626 DONNE *Serm.* lxxiii. 746 Corne that hath in nature a disposition to a Reviviscence and a Repullulation. 1669 BOYLE *Contn. New Exp.* II. (1682) 93 The Adder remained in the same state, and gave no hope of reviviscence. 1677 PLOT *Oxfordsh.* 197 The reviviscence of Anne Green, innocently condemned to die. 1748 *Phil. Trans.* XLV. 285 Some subtil vapour, issuing from their bodies, which might have been conducive to their reviviscence. 1774 *Ibid.* LXIV. 432 On the Reviviscence of some Snails kept 15 years. 1836–9 *Todd's Cycl. Anat.* II. 774/1 The calls of hunger are probably the principal cause of reviviscence.

transf. 1703 WHITBY *Acts* xvii. 32 Stoicks who asserted a Conflagration, and Reviviscence of the World. 1786 A. M'LEAN *Christ's Commiss.* Wks. 1846 II. 112 Our reviviscence, or resurrection to a new life of holiness.

2. Revival; restoration to a flourishing or vigorous condition.

1711 *Vind. Sacheverell* 94 If you can bury this in Oblivion, you think it would be a good Step to your own Reviviscence. 1782 R. CUMBERLAND *Anecd. Painters* II. 184 A spectator naturally regards these instances of reviviscence in the art with favour. 1814 BERINGTON *Lit. Hist. Middle Ages* I. (1846) 39 The encouragement which the Antonines gave to the Arts was..only that apparent reviviscence which is the precursor of death. 1844 in MacEwen *Life J. Cairns* (1895) 186 This spurious reviviscence of paganism is a blot upon the whole Munich School of Art. 1875 M. PATTISON *Casaubon* 379 The hagiological temper..which had enjoyed a forced reviviscence during the catholic reaction.

Revivi·scency. [See -ENCY.] = prec.

1659 PEARSON *Creed* (1839) 533 If we look upon it under the notion of reviviscency,..it proves as much; for nothing properly dieth but the body. 1682 H. MORE *Annot. Glanvill's Lux O.* 38 But the changing of our Earthly Body for an Aereal or Æthereal, this is not Death, but Reviviscency. 1788 *Trifler* No. 25. 322 Cases..where their vivifying power has actually caused reviviscency to those who had apparently sunk into everlasting slumber. 1816 KIRBY & SP. *Entomol.* xxvi. (1818) II. 446 Their [*sc.* bees] partial reviviscency, and consequent need of food in our climate, are owing to its..comparative mildness in winter.

Reviviscent (revivi·sĕnt), *a.* [ad. pres. pple. of L. *revīviscĕre*. So F. *réviviscent*, Pg. *reviviscente*. See also REVIVESCENT.]

1. Returning to life or animation; reviving.

1778 J. AIKIN *Thomson's Seasons* Ess. p. xxi, The poet.. begins with representing the reviviscent plants emerging.. in numbers. 1835 KIRBY *Hab. & Inst. Anim.* I. xi. 322 These pseudo-leeches..possess the same reviviscent powers. 1854 J. H. NEWMAN *Hist. Sk.* (1872) I. 51 How irrepressible was that desire, how reviviscent, how indestructible.

2. Causing renewed life.

1886 T. HARDY *Mayor Casterbr.* II. ix. 122 The piece of news acted as a reviviscent breath to that old view of his.

Revivi·scible, *a.* [f. L. *revīviscĕre*: see -IBLE.] Capable of returning to life.

1860 *All Year Round* No. 43. 389 Certain persons have gone so far as to credit the existence of reviviscible serpents.

Revi·vor[1]. *rare.* Also 6 reuiuour, 7 reuiuor. [f. REVIVE *v.* + -OR [1].] One who revives, renews, or restores; a reviver.

a 1540 BARNES *Wks.* (1573) 369 Hee hath therfore his reuiuour present with him, and dwellyng within hym. 1611 COTGR., *Renouvelleur*, a renewer,..reuiuor, beginner againe, of. 1841 S. FENTON *Salted Brandy* Pref. p. vii *note*, He positively denies himself to be either the inventor or revivor of it.

Revivor[2] (rɪvəi·vǫɹ). [f. REVIVE *v.* + -OR [2].]

† **1.** Renewal, revival. *Obs. rare.*

1602 WARNER *Alb. Eng.* Epit. 363 He commaunded that his whole Dominion heere should bee called Angel,..in Reuiuor of the name of the Countrie from which his Auncestors..scaled. 1741 T. ROBINSON *Gavelkind* v. 74 The Nature of Gavelkind Land cannot be entirely changed, nor the Custom extinguished beyond a Possibility of Revivor.

2. A proceeding for the revival of a suit or action abated by the death of one of the parties, or by some other circumstance. Chiefly in phr. *bill of revivor* (cf. REVIVER *sb.*[2] 2).

1727–38 CHAMBERS *Cycl.* s.v., In this case, a bill of revivor must be brought, praying the former proceedings may stand revived. 1768 BLACKSTONE *Comm.* III. 448 There may be also a bill of revivor, when the suit is abated by the death of any of the parties; in order to set the proceedings again in motion, without which they remain at a stand. 1828 LE MARCHANT *Rep. Claims to Barony of Gardner* 370 The bill of revivor brought after the death of Ann Smyth. 1884 *Law Times Rep.* LI. 333/2 Revivor was not allowed merely for the purpose of appealing against a decree.

Revle, obs. form of RULE. **Revlin,** variant of RIVELING. **Revly,** variant of RULY *adv.*

Re·vocabi·lity. [f. next + -ITY.] The property of being revocable.

1860 in WORCESTER (citing *N. Brit. Rev.*). 1883 *Law Rep.* 9 App. Cases 312/2 Revocability will not be taken away by delivery.

Revocable (re·vǒkab'l), *a.* [a. OF. *revocable* (mod.F. *révocable*, = Sp. *revocable*, Pg. *-avel*, It. *re-, rivocabile*), or ad. L. *revocābilis*: see REVOKE *v.* and -ABLE, and cf. REVOKABLE.] Capable of being revoked or recalled.

a 1471 FORTESCUE *Wks.* (1869) 484 Nothyng ellys but a commyssion revocable atte pleasir. 1568 GRAFTON *Chron.* II. 391 The Prelates were of lyke opinion,..that it [a charter] was reuocable. 1578 *Reg. Privy Council Scot.* III. 48 All the saidis alienationis..quhilkis of the law ar revocabill. 1612 T. TAYLOR *Comm. Titus* i. 2 The decree of God had been absolute, and so not revocable. 1660 R. COKE *Power & Subj.* 237 Any Grant or Lease..not revocable at the will and pleasure of the offender. 1748 RICHARDSON *Clarissa* (1811) III. 324 Give me leave to chide you..for your rash, and I hope revocable resolution. 1786 BURKE *Art. agst. W. Hastings* Wks. 1842 II. 212 Hastings..did maintain, that the acts done in consequence of that measure were not revocable by any subsequent authority. 1841 GLADSTONE *State in Rel. to Church* iv. (ed. 4) I. 200 Where the clergy are supported by annual and revocable votes. 1884 *Law Times* LXXVIII. 170/1 The deed having been executed by several creditors is not..revocable by the debtor.

Hence **Re·vocableness.** Also **Re·vocably** *adv.* 'in a revocable manner' (Webster, 1847).

1695 *Def. Vindic. Deprived Bps.* 97 [It] is expressly mentioned, even in our Modern Contracts,..purposely to prevent their revocableness. 1866 *Victoria Mag.* Nov. 4 The revocableness of conventual vows was another topic.

† **Re·vocate,** *pa. pple.* *Obs.* [ad. pa. pple. of L. *revocāre* to REVOKE.]

1. Recalled; brought back.

a 1400 *Add. Prologues* in *Wycliffite Bible* IV. 685^b, Aftir that Joon was reuocate fro the exile of Pathmos. 1432–50 tr. *Higden* (Rolls) III. 113 After whiche yeres he was reuocate to hym selfe, neuerthelesse he reignede not.

2. Repressed; rescinded.

c 1420 *Pallad. on Husb.* III. 256 About his thegh let no thyng growyng be, But if hit axe to be reuocate. 1533 BELLENDEN *Livy* III. vii. (S.T.S.) I. 273 Ilk thing þat was afore done..mycht þan be abrogate and revocate be public commites.

† **Re·vocate,** *v.* *Obs.* [ad. ppl. stem of L. *revocāre* to REVOKE.]

1. *trans.* To recall, call back.

1540 COVERDALE *Wks.* (Parker Soc.) II. 490 If it like your favour to revocate to your memory the godly communication. *a* 1548 HALL *Chron. Hen. VI.* 158 b, To appeace the furious rage,..and..to reuocate him into his olde estate.

2. To do away with, repress. *rare*[−1].

1547 BOORDE *Brev. Health* xlii. 21 b, To revocate this inordinate appetide I wolde that a cockrel or a pullet myght be sodyn or rosted.

3. To revoke, rescind.

1564 *Richmond Wills* (Surtees) 116, I do revocate and make frustrat all other wills and testaments. 1595 DANIEL *Civ. Wars* III. lxxxix, His successor..nullifies Many his patents, and did revocate And re-assume his liberalites.

Hence † **Re·vocating** *vbl. sb.* *Obs.*

1570 FOXE *A. & M.* (ed. 2) 1222/2 Vnles the kyng would recompense and requite the same by reuocatyng of such statutes as were made..in the hygh Courte of Parlament.

Revocation (revokē^i·ʃən). [a. OF. *revocacion, -ation* (mod.F. *révocation*, = Sp. *revocacion*, It. *re-, rivocazione*), or ad. L. *revocātio*, n. of action f. *revocāre* to REVOKE.]

1. The action of recalling; recall (of persons); a call or summons to return. Now *rare* or *Obs.*

In 17–18th cent. esp. the recall of a representative or ambassador from abroad; also in *letters of revocation*.

c 1420 LYDG. *Assembly of Gods* 1746 Then sesyd the Tyme of Deuyacion,..Entryng the Tyme of Reuocacion. 1432–50 tr. *Higden* (Rolls) V. 161 Themperour..callede Liberius from exile,..whiche beenge gladde of þat revocation..declinede hym selfe to þat heresy. 1570–6 LAMBARDE *Peramb. Kent* (1826) 179 They armed vessels to the Sea and sought to compell the King to their revocation. 1592 UNTON *Corr.* (Roxb.) 412, I perceave..howe willingly you vouchsaffe to assent to my revocation. 1612 *Buccleuch MSS.* (Hist. MSS. Comm.) I. 115 There may some stay be made of your revocation by reason of the necessary use of your presence there. *c* 1645 HOWELL *Lett.* I. xxxi. (1650) I. 87 Don Julian ..got letters of revocation, and came back to Spain. 1686 tr. *Chardin's Trav. Persia* 11 The whole Establishment.., had utterly gone to ruine, by the recalling of their Resident .., had they not been better advis'd then to make that Revocation. 1710 *Lond. Gaz.* No. 4713/1 The Envoy delivered his Letters of Revocation, and is preparing to leave this Court. 1782 JOHNSON *Let. to Dr. Taylor* 22 July, Sir Robert Chambers slipped this session through the fingers of revocation, but I am in doubt of his continuance.

b. *transf.* with reference to things.

1649 BP. HALL *Cases Consc.* I. iv. (1654) 29 The inconvenience or losse whereunto he is put upon the sudden revocation of that money. 1684 tr. *Bonet's Merc. Compit.* VI. 197 The Italians..apply Cupping-glasses to the lower parts, for revocation of the poisonous matter from the Heart. 1836–7 SIR W. HAMILTON *Metaph.* xxi. (1859) II. 25 The faculty of which this revocation is the energy, I call the Reproductive. 1881 *Nature* XXIV. 572/1 When the second patch is placed on an independent tube, where no such revocation is possible, phosphorescence actually appears, showing that the revocation is no mere supposition.

2. The action of revoking, rescinding, or annulling; withdrawal (of a grant, etc.).

c 1425 WYNTOUN *Cron.* V. ii. 281 Qwhen his procuratouris ordanyt he..Seyldyn reuocacion He made of þar commyssion. 1488–9 *Act 4 Hen. VII*, c. 5 This Act of adnullacion, resumpcion, revocacion, or voidaunce of lettres patentes. 1568 LD. SCROPE in Ellis *Orig. Lett.* I. II. 240 Synce thorow hyr pryvye revocation theroff within full aege they cowld not injoye the same by lawe. 1590 SWINBURNE *Testaments* 268 The former testament may be the more easily reuoked, without any such precise obseruation of speciall reuocation. 1639 FULLER *Holy War* IV. xix. (1840) 212 These [laws] were those of the grand charter, which admitted of no revocation. 1671 FLAVEL *Fount. Life* xii. 34 It expiates all fully without

Exception and finally without Revocation. 1710 PRIDEAUX *Orig. Tithes* i. 21 The Law of Tithes..could not cease without a particular revocation under the Gospel. 1788 *Gentl. Mag.* LVIII. 198/2 He foresaw the revocation of the edict of Nantz, several years before it happened. 1844 H. H. WILSON *Brit. India* I. 281 The persuasion that the revocation of the Government order would alone prevent a general and fatal insurrection. 1861 LD. BROUGHAM *Brit. Const.* xiv. 211 The Queen sent a message to promise a general revocation of all such grants.

† **3.** Recantation; withdrawal (of statements). *Obs.*

1532 MORE *Confut. Tindale* Wks. 510/2 When he wist wel his reuocacion could not saue his body: yet reuoked he his heresies..for to saue his soule. 1540 COVERDALE *Confut. Standish* Wks. (Parker Soc.) II. 345 What revocations ye make in men's names, they being absent, I cannot tell. 1612 BRINSLEY *Lud. Lit.* xiii. (1627) 181 Those figures of Sentences.., as of Exclamations, Revocations, Apostrophees. 1684 T. BURNET *The. Earth* I. 150, I affirm nothing therein but with a power of revocation, and a liberty to change my opinion when I shall be better inform'd.

† **4.** Reformation. *Obs. rare*[−1].

1579 FULKE *Heskins's Parl.* 484 Basil speaketh not of wicked men.., but of such as be not zealous and earnest ynough, to practise mortification, & reuocation.

Re·vocative, *a.* *rare.* [Cf. next and -IVE.] Possessing the power of recalling.

1836–7 SIR W. HAMILTON *Metaph.* xx. (1859) II. 16 The Reproductive or Revocative Faculty.

Revocatory (re·vǒkātəri), *a.* and *sb.* [ad. late L. *revocātōri-us*: see REVOCATE *v.* So F. *révocatoire* (1319), Sp., Pg., and It. *revocatorio*.]

A. *adj.* Tending or pertaining to, expressive of, revocation; esp. *revocatory letters*, after med.L. *litteræ revocatoriæ*.

1432–50 tr. *Higden* (Rolls) VII. 405 For diverse of those monkes, knowynge the wille of thabbot, purchasede letters revocatory of the pope. 1577–87 HOLINSHED *Chron.* III. 437/1 The king..directed his letters reuocatorie into euerie countie. 1590 SWINBURNE *Testaments* 267 The force and effect of these clauses derogatorie, and reuocatorie. 1611 SPEED *Hist. Gt. Brit.* IX. xii. § 67. 633 To these reuocatorie lines King Edward made this wise and noble answere. 1700 TYRRELL *Hist. Eng.* II. 899 The Pope..sent his Revocatory Letters to him. 1876 FR. A. KEMBLE *Rec. Girlhood* II. i. 33 Upon this view of her epistle,..she would (instead of rewriting it) tack on to it..a sort of revocatory codicil, in the shape of a postscript.

† **B.** *sb.* Revocation. *Obs. rare.*

1636 ABP. WILLIAMS *Holy Table* (1637) 66 To make Declaratories and Revocatories of their Common Law.

† **Revo·ce,** obs. variant of REVOKE *v.*

1528 *Test. Ebor.* (Surtees) V. 269 All testamentis and willes bifore maide..I revoce and utterly forsakes.

Revoi·ce (rɪ-), *v.* [RE- 5 a.]

1. *trans.* To voice again or in return. Hence **Revoi·cing** *ppl. a.*

1610 G. FLETCHER *Christ's Vict.* II. lxii, To the windes the waters hoarcely call, And Eccho back againe revoyced all. 1640 FULLER *Joseph's Coat* (1867) 219 The revoicing echo with replies Did descant on the plain-song of the cries.

2. 'To refurnish with a voice'; to readjust the tone of (an organ-pipe).

1847 in WEBSTER. 1898 ELLISTON *Organs & Tuning* (ed. 3) 112 If space permits, stops of too small scale may perhaps be shifted upwards one or two pipes, and be cut down and re-voiced.

Revokable (rɪvǭ^u·kăb'l), *a.* Also **revokeable.** [f. REVOKE *v.* + -ABLE.] = REVOCABLE *a.*

α. 1584 *Copie of Letter* 39 The Lord.., to do him good, no doubt, if he were reuokeable, hath laid his hand upon him. 1611 FLORIO, *Rinocabile*, reuokeable. 1648 ASHHURST *Reasons agst. Agreement* 9 A Magistrate with no power but such as is alterable and revokeable at the pleasure of any multitude. 1752 HUME *Ess. & Treat.* (1777) I. 68 A misguided prince arose who deemed all these privileges.. revokeable at pleasure.

β. 1596 BACON *Max. Com. Law* xx. (1630) 73 This is not simply revokable. 1644 BP. MAXWELL *Prerog. Chr. Kings* ii. 27 An ordinance by high authority not revokable, not repealable. 1670 *Conclave wherein Clem. VIII was elected Pope* 13 Which occasion being once omitted, would never be revokable. 1710 *Lond. Gaz.* No. 4668/3 Which Assignment is not revokable. 1750 CARTE *Hist. Eng.* II. 588 For they thought it revokable, and in every part of it erroneous.

Revoke (rɪvǭ^u·k), *sb.* [f. the vb.]

1. *Cards*, esp. *Whist.* An act of revoking; a failure to follow suit when a proper card can be played.

1709 *Brit. Apollo* No. 36. 2/1 If one side make a Revoke. 1742 HOYLE *Games* 8 No Revoke to be claimed 'till the Trick is turned. 1821 LAMB *Elia* Ser. I. *Mrs. Battle's Opinions on Whist*, She never made a revoke, nor ever passed it over in her adversary without exacting the utmost forfeiture. 1862 'CAVENDISH' *Whist* (1879) 2 The penalty for a revoke takes precedence of all other scores. 1874 H. GIBBS *Ombre* iv. 36 The other players have to show their hands, so that he may see that there has been no Revoke.

attrib. 1810 *Splendid Follies* III. 8 Spank flew another revoke card from the hand of Samuelina. 1862 'CAVENDISH' *Whist* (1863) 13 If they mix their tricks, the revoke penalty can be scored against them.

2. Revocation, recall.

a 1882 ROSSETTI *Soothsay* xi, How callous seems beyond revoke The clock with its last listless stroke!

Revoke (rɪvǭ^u·k), *v.* Forms: 4–7 reuoke (5 rewoke), 4– revoke (4 revokyn); 5 reuoque, 6 reuolk, *Sc.* rewolk, revolk, rewoik; 6–7 revock. [ad. OF. *revoquer* (mod.F. *révoquer*, = Sp. and Pg. *revocar*, It. *re-, rivocare*), or L. *revocāre*, f. *re-* RE- + *vocāre* to call.]

I. *trans.* † **1.** To recall, bring back, *to* a (right) belief, way of life, etc. Also without const. *Obs.*

1382 WYCLIF *Rom.* Prol., Thes reuokith the apostle to the verrey and the gospels bileue. 1412–20 LYDG. *Chron. Troy* II. 2509 To reuoke to þe riȝte weye Swiche as wrongly fro troube do forveye. 1532 MORE *Confut. Barnes* VIII. Wks. 811/1 Reuoking them that erred, setting vp agayne those that were ouerthrowen. 1577 *F. de Lisle's Legendarie* H iij, By this meanes may such be quailed and reuoked to their duties. 1687 *Assurance of Abbey Lands* 134 They had Conference, how the Kingdom of England might be revoked to the Unity of the Church.

† **b.** To recall, draw back or away, *from* some belief, practice, etc. (*esp.* a wrong or wicked one).

c 1400 *Three Kings Cologne* (1886) 122 In so mochel þat Preester Iohn and Patriark Thomas myȝt not revoke þe pepil from her heresyes. *c* 1450 tr. *De Imitatione* III. vii. 73 þat he [the devil] mowe..reuoke þe fro praier & holy redyng. 1542 UDALL *Erasm. Apoph.* 177 b, The woordes of Demaratus meaned to reuoke hym from ire and wrathe, to takyng better wayes. 1590 GREENE *Neuer too Late* Wks. (Grosart) VIII. 95 Hee was in loue..so deepely, that no perswasion might reuoke him from that alluring curtizan. 1603 SIR C. HEYDON *Jud. Astrol.* ii. 24 The Prophet euen here..reuoketh the Iewes from worshipping the heauenly bodies. *a* 1619 FOTHERBY *Atheom.* I. xii. § 3 (1622) 128 Visions, which God..sendeth him, to reuoke and deterre him from that his vngodlinesse.

absol. *c* 1440 *Alph. Tales* 464 When we synd, þou nowder reuokid with nowder gude wurde nor exsample.

† **c.** To induce (one) to desist or refrain *from* some purpose or action; to restrain or prevent *from* something. Also *refl.* *Obs.*

1491 CAXTON *Vitas Patr.* (W. de W. 1495) I. xxxvi. 33/1 All thyse thynges putt he in his mynde for to haue reuokyd hym from his good purpoos. 1494 FABYAN *Chron.* VII. 546 By whose polycies, not without great dyffycultee, they were reuokyd frome theyr euyll purpose. 1576 FLEMING *Panopl. Epist.* 36 You did..reuoke your selfe from continuing to the end, not unadvisedly. 1582 STANYHURST *Æneis* III. (Arb.) 92 From foloing oure ships thee fluds hye reuockt hym. 1600 HOLLAND *Livy* X. xlii. 384 He could not be revoked from battaile, albeit there was some question..about the auspice. 1608 WILLET *Hexapla Exod.* 732 He..commanded them hard things, to reuoke them from their intention.

† **d.** Without const. To check, restrain. *rare.*

1590 SPENSER *F. Q.* II. ii. 28 Yet she with pitthy words, and counsell sad, Still strove their stubborne rages to revoke. 1637 R. HUMPHREY tr. *S. Ambrose* I. 46 Abigael by her..deprecation pacified and revoked David and his army.

2. † **a.** To bring back *into* or *unto* life; to restore to consciousness. *Obs.*

c 1374 CHAUCER *Troylus* III. 1118 Him to revoken sche dide al hir peyne; And, at the last, he gan his breeth to drawe. 1528 ROY *Rede me* (Arb.) 40 Doynge all that ever he canne To revoke masse vnto lyfe agayne. 1613 PURCHAS *Pilgrimage* II. xxi. (1614) 221 Messias Ben Dauid with Elias shall reuoke into life that Messias Ben Ioseph. 1664 POWER *Exp. Philos.* I. 6 By virtue of the Sun..they [*sc.* flies] will be revoked into life and perform its functions again.

b. To call back to memory. Also const. *to*, *into*. Now *rare.*

1565 HAWKINS *Voy.* (Hakl. Soc.) 42 Reuoking to minde the former talke betweene the captaine and him. 1586 A. DAY *Eng. Secretary* I. (1625) 42 The man I know is not cleane out of your conceit, and therefore I will cease in further speeches at this present to revoke him. *a* 1618 SYLVESTER *Mottoes* 45 When Them I to my Minde revoke [etc.]. *a* 1716 SOUTH (Cent.), By revoking and recollecting ..certain passages. 1838 SIR W. HAMILTON *Logic* xxx. (1866) II. 121 If the faculty by which they [*sc.* cognitions] are revoked into consciousness be inert.

† **c.** To bring back into use; to revive. *Obs.*

1574 tr. *Marlorat's Apocalips* 47 Wicked Jezabel, which reuoked, stablished, and increaced the abhominable seruing of Baal. 1627 HERRICK *Hesper.*, *Dial. Horace & Lydia* v, Say our first loves we sho'd revoke, And sever'd joyne in brazen yoke. 1644 BULWER *Chiron.* 131 We are not to tread in their steps so far, as to revoke the whole Art of their obsolete Rhetorique.

3. To recall; to call or summon back:

a. a person, *esp.* from exile or from some office abroad. Now *rare.* (Common *c* 1540–1640.)

1521 *State Papers, Hen. VIII*, I. 10 Hys owne affayris doith not succede wyth thEmperour..and that therfore he intendith schortly to revoke the Mr. of the Rollys. 1535 in Ellis *Orig. Lett.* Ser. III. II. 361, I..trussed his male, and was cariying it to his horse, and he revoked me and seied [etc.]. *a* 1562 G. CAVENDISH *Wolsey* (1893) 48 Mistress Anne Bolleyn was revoked unto the court, where she florisshed after in great estimacion. 1617 MORYSON *Itin.* II. 8 Shortly after..Sir John Perrot being reuoked, Sir William Fitz-williams was sent Lord Deputy into Ireland. *a* 1661 FULLER *Worthies* (1840) III. 306 Had he not been suddenly revoked into England, he would have perfected the project. 1709 STRYPE *Ann. Ref.* Introd. I. 21 Now the English forces were revoked from the marches of Scotland. *Ibid.* xxxviii. 398 Sir Thomas Chaloner, being dangerously sick, without hope of recovery but by returning, was revoked. 1828–43 TYTLER *Hist. Scot.* (1864) III. 330 Sussex.. having assumed to himself some credit for revoking the army. 1887 *Pall Mall G.* 16 Feb. 2/1 The Directory would nominate and revoke the Ministers.

b. an animal or thing. Chiefly *fig.*

1576 FLEMING tr. *Caius' Dogs* (1880) 8 These Hounds.. being acquainted with their masters watchwordes, eyther in reuoking or imboldening them to serve the game. 1596 SPENSER *F. Q.* VI. iii. 28 The faint sprite he did revoke againe To her fraile mansion of mortality. 1599 DAVIES *Immort. Soul* Introd. xxxiv, Seas as troubled, when they do revoke Their flowing Waves into themselves again. 1648 HERRICK *Hesper.*, *Hock-cart*, Ye must revoke The patient Oxe unto the Yoke. 1784 COWPER *Task* VI. 25 How readily we wish time spent revok'd, That we might try the ground again.

† **c.** To refer (one) *to* some authority. *Obs. rare.*

1599 *Broughton's Let.* ix. 30 Thither you reuoke vs. 1602 [BP. W. BARLOW] *Defence* 181 Againe, he reuoketh us to Church and Councels.

† **d.** To reduce *to*, bring *into*, something. *Obs.*

1605 TIMME *Quersit.* I. xv. 78 What power or virtue soeuer is in the nature of medicines and of sicknesses,..the same is to bee reuoked to those three beginnings. 1652 J. WRIGHT tr. *Camus' Nat. Paradox* x. 246 Which clause was offensive to her Ears, as revoking into doubt her constancy.

4. To annul, repeal, rescind, cancel.

c 1380 WYCLIF *Sel. Wks.* III. 363 þe pope may graunte to day, and to morowe perseyve his folye, and revoke þe formere errour. *c* 1400 *Brut* clxxxvii, þe Kyng..bihight to þe peple of Engeland, þat þe exiling of þe forsaide Piers shulde bene reuokede. *c* 1449 PECOCK *Repr.* II. vi. 175 The gouernaunce of Laban..was not reuokid, as was the gouernaunce and lawe of the Iewis. 1489 CAXTON *Faytes of A.* IV. xii. 264 The prynces and lordes shuld not suffre to reuoque nor calle ayen theire sentences. 1578 T. N. tr. *Conq. W. India* 99 If by chaunce his Majestie had alreadie given the sayde office of Gouvernement to any other person, that it might please him to revoke it. 1590 SWINBURNE *Testaments* 268 Yet is þot the testament presumed to be reuoked by the course of so long time. 1615 G. SANDYS *Trav.* 143 Antipater the Idumoean procureth him to revoke his resignation. 1667 MILTON *P. L.* III. 126, I else must change Thir nature, and revoke the high Decree Unchangeable, Eternal. 1748 RICHARDSON *Clarissa* (1811) III. xvii. 109, I doubted not but the letter was to revoke or suspend your resolution. 1786 BURKE *Art. agst. W. Hastings* Wks. II. 162 Knowing, that the said Sullivan's appointment had been condemned and revoked by the court of directors. 1837 LOCKHART *Scott* II. v. 187 Her only son, who stood by, implored her to revoke the malediction; but in vain. 1873 SMILES *Huguenots France* I. i. (1881) 10 Louis XIV lived for thirty years after the Edict of Nantes had been revoked.

transf. 1534 WHITINTON *Tullyes Offices* I. (1540) 5 Where as profyte semeth to plucke and catch to hymselfe, honestie on the contrary parte semeth to revoke and reverse such thynges. 1655 STANLEY *Hist. Philos.* (1701) 99/2 Cicero.. saith, when Euripides made his Play *Orestes*, Socrates revoked the three first Verses.

† **b.** To break up, dismiss. *Obs. rare*[−1].

1675 HOBBES *Odyss.* (1677) 14 By Jove I you adjure and Themis, who Convokes assemblies, and revokes again.

† **5.** To retract, withdraw, recant. *Obs.*

1483 CAXTON *Gold. Leg.* 340 b/2 Whanne he seie this, He reuoked hit in his retractions. 1529 MORE *Dyaloge* II. Wks. 184/1 Therfore he bounde his preachers to stande thereby and not to reuoke his word for no pain. 1560 DAUS tr. *Sleidane's Comm.* 7 The Cardinall..at the fyrste metynge commaunded him to revoke his workes. 1581 G. PETTIE *Guazzo's Civ. Conv.* III. (1586) 141 Then revoke your first sentence, and conclude that the fault is in the father. 1611 BIBLE *Transl. Pref.* ¶ 13 The same S. Augustine was not ashamed to retractate, we might say reuoke, many things that had passed him. 1656 COWLEY *Pindar. Odes, To Dr. Scarborough* v, The first fam'd Aphorism thy great Master spoke, Did he live now he would revoke. 1671 MILTON *P. R.* III. 356 Prediction still In all things..supposes means, Without means us'd, what it predicts [it] revokes.

† **b.** To yield or give up. *Obs. rare*[−1].

1599 *Sir Clyom.* in *Peele's Wks.* (Rtldg.) 517/1 Take with thee that mortal blow or stroke The which shall cause thy wretched corpse this life for to revoke.

† **6.** To take back to oneself. *Obs.*

1526 *Pilgr. Perf.* (W. de W. 1531) 27 Suche sedes that we haue layde out of our spirituall barnes for his loue, let vs neuer reuoke or call agayne. 1557 *Tottel's Misc.* (Arb.) 144 Wherby is lost my libertie: Which by no meanes I may reuoke. 1560 DAUS tr. *Sleidane's Comm.* 425 Wherefore the Byshop..revoketh the suite to him selfe. 1600 E. BLOUNT tr. *Conestaggio* 94 Beseeching him to reuoke the cause vnto himselfe, and to be the onely iudge thereof.

† **b.** To draw back, withdraw. *Obs. rare.*

1590 SPENSER *F. Q.* III. viii. 39 Yet with his troncheon he so rudely stroke Cymochles twise, that twise him forst his foot revoke. 1644 BULWER *Chiron.* 41 Who..doe also revoke and bow back their whole body.

II. *intr.* **7.** To make revocation.

1500–20 DUNBAR *Poems* ix. 70, I rewoik in thir quhair I miswent. 1581 J. BELL *Haddon's Answ. Osor.* 411 It is.. an other thing to revoke in season, assoone as a man doth know his error. 1641 MILTON *Reform.* II. 81 To compasse sinister ends, and then revoke when they see their time. 1817 SELWYN *Law Nisi Prius* (ed. 4) II. 828 On the ground of an intention to revoke, to be presumed. 1819 CRABBE *T. of Hall* XII. 356, I make a promise, and will not revoke.

8. *Cards*, esp. *Whist.* To fail or neglect to follow suit when a proper card can be played.

1592 *Defence Conny Catch.* (1859) 6 As thus I stood looking on them playing at cros-ruffe, one was taken revoking. 1680 COTTON *Compl. Gamester* (ed. 2) 102 You must not revoke, if you do you pay all on the Table. 1742 HOYLE *Games* 8 A revokes; Query, what is the Penalty. 1851 J. T. HEWLETT *Parish Clerk* I. 261 A noisy rubber, in which Esau accused Jacob of having revoked. 1874 H. GIBBS *Ombre* 84 If either of the Adversaries revoke.., he who revoked pays his penalty.

fig. 1791 BURKE *App. Whigs* Wks. I. 535 And shall we Englishmen revoke to such a suit?

Hence **Revo·ked** *ppl. a.* Also **Revo·keless** *a.*

1461 *Rolls of Parlt.* V. 491/1 The pretended and revoked Parlement last holden at youre Toune of Coventre. 1628 LAYTON *Sion's Plea agst. Prelacy* (ed. 2) 20 According to that formerly revoked Statute of Henry 4. 1773 *Poetry* in *Ann. Reg.* 239 Why call us to revokeless doom?

† **Revo·kement.** *Obs. rare.* [f. prec. + -MENT.] The act of revoking; revocation.

1613 SHAKS. *Hen. VIII*, I. ii. 106 Let it be nois'd, That through our Intercession, this Reuokement And pardon comes. 1651 HOWELL *Venice* 137 The revokement wherof wold..utterly overthrow the very fundamentalls of the State.

Revo·ker. *rare.* [f. REVOKE *v.* + -ER [1].] *Cards.* One who revokes.

1886 *Field* 13 Mar. 313 If the stand hand loses, the revoker does not receive anything.

Revo·king, *vbl. sb.* [f. REVOKE *v.* + -ING [1].] The action of the verb, in various senses.

1547 J. C. (*title*), Melancthon's Epistle made unto..Kynge Henry the Eight for the revoking and abolishing of the Six Articles. 1680 SANDERSON *Serm.* I. 159 In the revoking of His threatnings, Gods mercy and His truth go hand in hand together. 1646 EVANCE *Noble Order* 2 Gods revoking of his promise. 1746 HOYLE *Whist* (ed. 6) 10 He can avoid it without revoking. 1830 'EIDRAH TREBOR' *Hoyle Made Familiar* 4 Renouncing or trumping suit..is in this case termed Revoking.

Revo·king, *ppl. a.* [-ING [2].] *Cards.* That revokes or has revoked.

1746 HOYLE *Whist* (ed. 6) 8 The revoking Party..must remain at 9. 1830 'EIDRAH TREBOR' *Hoyle Made Familiar* 12 If a revoke happens to be made, the adversaries may.. take tricks from the revoking party. 1862 'CAVENDISH' *Whist* (1879) 16 The revoking player and his partner may.. require the hand in which the revoke has been detected to be played out.

So **Revo·kingly** *adv.*, 'by way of revocation' (Webster, 1847).

Re·volant, *a.* *rare*[−1]. [ad. L. *revolant-em*, pres. pple. of *revolāre*.] Flying back.

1789 E. DARWIN *Bot. Gard.* II. (1791) 106 No refluent fin the unpeopled stream divides, No revolant pinion cleaves the airy tides.

Revolet, obs. variant of RIVULET.

Revolt (rɪvǭ^u·lt, rɪvǫ·lt), *sb.*[1] Also 6–7 reuolt, 6 revolte. [a. F. *révolte* (1501, = Pg. *revolta*, It. *rivolta*, Sp. *revuelta*), vbl. sb. from *révolter*: see REVOLT *v.*]

1. An instance, on the part of subjects or subordinates, of casting off allegiance or obedience to their rulers or superiors; an insurrection, rising, or rebellion. † *To give* (one) *the revolt*, to revolt against (one).

1560 DAUS tr. *Sleidane's Comm.* 310 *marg.*, A revolte. 1561 BRENDE *Q. Curtius* (1570) 184 For they had not lost the battaile at such tyme as the messengers were dispatched that brought the newes of their reuolt. 1567 *Satir. Poems Reform.* v. 109 Reuoltis hes bene ma nor fyftene. 1605 SHAKS. *Macb.* I. ii. 2 He can report, As seemeth by his plight, of the Reuolt The newest state. *Ibid.* v. iv. 12 Both more and lesse haue giuen him the Reuolt, And none serue with him. 1615 G. SANDYS *Trav.* 48 Whereby..the Empire [is] strengthened both against forraine inuasions, and reuolts of the subdued. 1667 MILTON *P. L.* I. 33 Who first seduc'd them to that fowl revolt? Th' infernal Serpent. 1737 WHISTON *Josephus, Antiq.* xx. vi. § 3 The authors of this revolt from the Roman government. 1838 THIRLWALL *Greece* V. 11 To engage the Macedonian towns in a revolt against their sovereign. 1841 R. H. DANA *Seaman's Man.* 245 Every person so offending..shall be deemed guilty of a revolt or mutiny and felony. 1871 FREEMAN *Norm. Conq.* IV. xvii. 75 William chose as his companions the men whose power he dreaded...In their absence revolts would be less to be feared.

b. An act of this nature on the part of an individual; a movement of strong protest against, or refusal to submit to, some condition, practice, etc.

1599 PEELE *David & Beth.* I. iii. 308 O prowd reuolt of a presumptuous man, Laying his bridle in the necke of sin. 1621 FLETCHER *Isl. Princ.* v. ii, 'Tis in their wills, their mercies,..And these revolts in you shew mere rebellions. 1710 STEELE *Tatler* No. 135 ¶ 4 We frequently see the Apostates turning from their Revolt toward the End of their Lives. 1788 GIBBON *Decl. & F.* xlix. V. 127 The images, the first cause of their [*sc.* the popes] revolt, were restored. 1844 EMERSON *New Eng. Reformers* Wks. (Bohn) I. 264 The revolt against the..inveterate abuses of cities did not appear possible to individuals. 1888 *Bibliotheca Sacra* Oct. 717 The iconoclasm of Protestantism was not a revolt against art, but against a misuse of art.

c. A change of sides, or of opinion; an emphatic withdrawal *from* a party, etc.

1596 WARNER *Alb. Eng.* XI. lxv. (1602) 280 She did obserue his soone Reuolt from friend to friend. *c* 1600 SHAKS. *Sonn.* xcii, Thou canst not vex me with inconstant minde, Since that my life on thy reuolt doth lie. 1668 DRYDEN *Dram. Poesy* Ess. (ed. Ker) I. 24 'Tis a revolt, without occasion, from your party.

2. The act of revolting or casting off allegiance; also, language tending to this (quot. 1611).

c 1586 C'TESS PEMBROKE *Ps.* LXXX. v, Then we preserv'd thy name shall magnify Without revolt. 1611 BIBLE *Isa.* lix. 13 Departing away from our God, speaking oppression and reuolt. 1781 COWPER *Hope* 181 Man is the genuine offspring of revolt. 1781 GIBBON *Decl. & F.* xxx. (1787) III. 173 The spirit of revolt, which had formerly disturbed the age of Gallienus, was revived. 1801 *Encycl. Brit.* Suppl. II. 404/1 They fixed upon the 20th of May as the day of revolt. 1854 MILMAN *Lat. Chr.* IV. vii. II. 158 An act of direct revolt, as prohibiting the payment of tribute by the Italian province.

b. *In revolt*, in a state of rebellion.

1602 MARSTON *Antonio's Rev.* v. i, They can scarce retaine from bursting foorth In plaine revolt. 1821 SHELLEY *Hellas* 580 The Christian tribes Of Lebanon and the Syrian wilderness Are in revolt. 1860 MRS. BROWNING *Little Mattie* iii, She will lie there in default And most innocent revolt.

† **c.** Revulsion of appetite. *Obs. rare*[−1].

1601 SHAKS. *Twel. N.* II. iv. 102 No motion of the Liuer, but the Pallat, That suffer surfet, cloyment, and reuolt.

† **Revo·lt,** *sb.*[2] *Obs.* [? ad. F. *révolté*, pa. pple. of *révolter*: see next.] A revolter or rebel.

1585 FETHERSTONE tr. *Calvin on Acts* vii. 1 He was accused as an Apostata or reuolt. 1600 HOLLAND *Livy* XLII. lxv. 1154 Having intelligence by a rennegate revolt, that the Romans were scattered all over the fields. 1627 W. SCLATER *Exp. 2 Thess.* (1629) 31 All equally suffer; as much Paganish Infants, as Christian Rebels or Reuolts.

Revolt (rɪvǭ^u·lt, rɪvǫ·lt), *v.* Also 6 reuolt(e, revolte. [ad. F. *révolter* (15–16th c.), = Pg.

revoltar, ad. It. *rivoltare*:—L. type *revolutāre, f. *re-* RE- + *volutāre* to roll, revolve, etc.]

I. *intr.* **1.** To cast off († or change) allegiance; to rise against rulers or constituted authority.

1548 ELYOT, *Deficio*, to go from one capitayne to an other, to reuolte. 1560 DAUS tr. *Sleidane's Comm.* 424 b, Al men..bycause they served against their wylles,..do revolte. 1573 P. MORE *Almanack & Prognost.* E iv b, Some noble men shall intende to reuolt. 1613 PURCHAS *Pilgrimage* IV. ix. (1614) 390 The sword signifieth death, if he reuolt againe. 1651 HOBBES *Leviath.* II. xxviii. 163 Such as are they, that having been by their own act Subjects, deliberately revolting, deny the Soveraign Power. 1727 DE FOE *Syst. Magic* I. iii. (1840) 71 Nor are the people we come to speak for, inclined to revolt or rebel. 1743 BULKELEY & CUMMINS *Voy. S. Seas* 183 If they should revolt at this Juncture, we shall stand a very bad Chance. 1836 THIRLWALL *Greece* xiv. II. 210 Aristagoras opened these singular credentials, and read an invitation to revolt. 1875 JOWETT *Plato* (ed. 2) V. 49 The youth revolted and refused to receive their own fathers.

fig. 1591 SHAKS. *Two Gent.* III. ii. 59 You are already loues firme votary, And cannot soone reuolt, and change your minde.

b. To fall away *from* a ruler, obedience, etc.; to rise *against* a person or authority.

1560 DAUS tr. *Sleidane's Chron.* 466 He sollicited the Emperour to make it frustrate: For he sawe how many revolted daily from his kingdome. 1610 HOLLAND *Camden's Brit.* (1637) 587 After he had revolted..from King Henry the Third. 1667 MILTON *P. L.* VI. 740, [I] shall soon..rid heav'n of these rebell'd..That from thy just obedience could revolt. *a* 1727 NEWTON *Chronol. Amended* (1728) 36 The Western nations..revolt from the Assyrians. 1768 *Swift's Hen. I*, S.'s Wks. IV. 285 The principal towns in Flanders revolted from him. 1838 THIRLWALL *Greece* xlii. V. 193 Pydna..had revolted from Archelaus. 1839 *Ibid.* VI. 105 Little encouragement could be necessary to induce him to revolt against the sovereign whom he had unpardonably offended. 1874 GREEN *Short Hist.* vii. § 8. 430 The national spirit of France revolted more and more from the rule of Spain.

transf. 1749 SMOLLETT *Gil Blas* (1750) II. 31 It was feared ..that he would revolt against the condition of the will.

c. To go over *to* a rival power, etc. † Also with *on* (one's side).

1560 DAUS tr. *Sleidane's Comm.* 202 He revolted unto the tentes of his adversaries. *Ibid.* 390 How much better were it, to abide thextreme peril, than..to revolte to the Romish Antichrist. 1593 SHAKS. *Rich. II*, II. ii. 89 The Commons they are cold, And will I feare reuolt on Herfords side. 1665 MANLEY *Grotius' Low C. Warrs* 224 The hopes of great plunder allured many to revolt to the Enemy. 1692 WASHINGTON tr. *Milton's Def. People Eng.* M.'s Wks. 1851 VIII. 232 To revolt to the common Enemy in their hearts is the worst sort of absence.

† **d.** In pa. pple. with *is*, *was*, etc. *Obs.*

1561 BRENDE *Q. Curtius* (1570) 10 b, He made al such feare him, as before were reuolted, and regarded him little. 1574 tr. *Marlorat's Apocalips* 37 As the mynd of man, whych is reuolted from God, is miserable or wretched. *a* 1618 RALEIGH *Mahomet* (1637) 128 Valentia was revolted from his obedience. 1664 MARVELL *Corr.* Wks. (Grosart) II. 124 When his Subjects were generally revolted, His Friends as it is usual most of them failed.

† **2. a.** To go over *to* another religion; to become a pervert (*from* some faith, etc.). *Obs.*

1560 DAUS tr. *Sleidane's Comm.* 36 If they revolte unto Papistrie. 1563 SANDYS in Strype *Ann. Ref.* (1709) I. xxxv. 356 He upon displesure departed from Mr. Goodrick, and revolted in religion. 1634 SIR T. HERBERT *Trav.* 135 Julian was first a Christian, but reuolted and became a most bitter and constant Persecutour to all that honoured Christ. 1673 CAVE *Prim. Chr.* I. ii. 19 Revolting from a way of Worship which had been universally received. 1681–6 J. SCOTT *Chr. Life* (1747) III. 132 All other Kings that were cotemporary with him were revolted to Idolatry.

† **b.** To draw back *from* a course of action, etc.; to return to one's allegiance. *Obs.*

1570 FOXE *A. & M.* (ed. 2) 155 It is better not to take good things in hand, than after they be begune to thinke to reuolte backe from the same againe. *c* 1590 MARLOWE *Faustus* xiii, Thou traitor, Faustus,..Revolt, or I'll in piece-meal tear thy flesh. 1610 G. CARLETON *Jurisdict.* 171 The Pope ..commanded the Archbishop to yeeld to the King without exception: whereupon hee did so, but afterward reuolted from that promise.

† **c.** To depart *from* the truth. *Obs. rare*[−1].

1585 FETHERSTONE tr. *Calvin on Acts* xv. 37 Paul might haue granted something to the importunatnesse of his fellow apostle and yet haue not reuolted from the trueth.

3. To feel revulsion or disgust *at* something.

1760–2 GOLDSM. *Cit. W.* cx[i]x, The observer revolts at this mixture of important and paltry claims. 1771 MRS. GRIFFITH *Hist. Lady Barton* III. 261 My heart revolted at the mean idea. 1802 BEDDOES *Hygeia* Advt. 7 Errors, at the grossness of which common sense..revolts. 1839 *Times* 27 July, Nature revolts at its complete infliction. 1878 BROWNING *La Saisiaz* 47 'Tis just the main assumption reason most revolts at!

b. To rise in repugnance *against* something.

1775 C. JOHNSTON *Pilgrim* 9 My heart revolted against eating at the same table with him. 1792 CHARLOTTE SMITH *Desmond* III. 10 A preference against the indulgence of which her principles must revolt. 1829 SOUTHEY *Sir T. More* (1831) II. 119 The heart instinctively revolts against the unnatural privations which are imposed upon it. 1860 HOLLAND *Miss Gilbert's Career* ix, Her whole nature, she felt, would revolt against the adverse judgment at once.

c. To turn in loathing *from* something.

1782 R. CUMBERLAND *Anecd. Painters* II. 87 The very eye that the hand of death was..closing..revolted with abhorrence from a disproportioned and ill-carved crucifix. 1796 SOUTHEY *Lett. fr. Spain* (1799) 299 How do we revolt from appearances, instead of from realities! 1806 H. SIDDONS *Maid, Wife, & Widow* I. 51 Every feeling of his heart and mind revolted from what he heard. 1863 GEO. ELIOT *Romola* III. xxiv, He knew well that her mind revolted from that means of escape.

† **4.** To return *to* a place. *Obs. rare*[−1].

1567 GOLDING *Ovid's Met.* x. 68 Shee..then reuolted too the place in which he had her found.

II. *trans.* † **5. a.** To turn back. *Obs. rare*[−1].

1590 SPENSER *F. Q.* III. xi. 25 As a thonder bolt..doth displace The soring clouds..; So to her yold the flames, and did their force revolt.

† **b.** To withdraw by revolting. *Obs. rare*[−1].

1607 DEKKER & WEBSTER *Sir T. Wyatt* Wks. 1873 III. 98 Then they reuolt the allegiance from my Daughter, And giue it to another.

† **c.** To cause to revolt. *Obs. rare.*

1574 HELLOWES tr. *Gueuara's Fam. Ep.* (1577) 236 Whether of vs is moste culpable, I in following and obeying the King, or you in altering and reuolting ye kingdome. 1624 BEDELL *Lett.* x. 136 Pope Constantine..reuolted Italie from the Greeke Emperours obedience.

6. To affect (a person, etc.) with disgust or repugnance; to nauseate.

1751 *Female Foundling* I. 170 From that time [I] avoided the low Name of Nancy, which revolted my Pride and Vanity. 1790 *Bystander* 284 Lest it should..revolt the feelings of the public to see it turn about so suddenly. 1828 SCOTT *F. M. Perth* xvii, Why, man, thy policy were enough to revolt a heathen divan. 1855 MILMAN *Lat. Chr.* VIII. viii. (1864) V. 32 Grave churchmen..who were revolted by these achievements in an ecclesiastic. 1867 FREEMAN *Norm. Conq.* (1877) I. vi. 496 The cruelties wrought on his captives deeply revolted the public opinion of the time.

b. *absol.* To cause revulsion.

1898 *Daily News* 24 Jan. 8/5 You may not treat of a subject until it disgusts and revolts.

Revo·lted, *ppl. a.* [f. prec. + -ED [1].]

1. That has cast off allegiance; rebel, insurgent.

1593 SHAKS. *Rich. II*, II. ii. 57 Why haue you not proclaim'd Northumberland And the rest of the reuolted faction, Traitors? 1611 — *Wint. T.* I. ii. 199 Should all despaire That haue reuolted Wiues, the tenth of Mankind Would hang themselues. 1667 MILTON *P. L.* IV. 835 Think not, revolted Spirit, thy shape the same. 1704 SWIFT *T. Tub* Introd., By the revolted and new-fangled Writers most perfidiously ascribed to the others. *a* 1781 WATSON *Philip III* (1839) 31 No other effectual remedy could be applied..but an accommodation with the revolted states. 1837 THIRLWALL *Greece* IV. 99 He restored the Athenian sovereignty in most of the revolted cities. 1871 FREEMAN *Hist. Ess.* Ser. I. viii. 213 The Emperor was leading an expedition against the revolted Bretons.

absol. 1653 (*title*), Legenda Lignea, with Pleadings to the Revolted to the Church of Rome.

† **2.** Torn or pulled out. *Obs. rare*[−1].

a 1668 DAVENANT *Poems* Wks. (1673) 314 Slender Ropes, on which instead Of Pearle, Revolted Teeth they thred.

3. Disgusted; outraged.

1819 SHELLEY *Cenci* I. i. 14 The deeds Which you scarce hide from men's revolted eyes. 1896 BLACK *Briseis* xvii, Her revolted judgment had hardly a word in reply.

Revo·lter. Also 6 reuolter. [f. as prec. + -ER [1].] One who revolts, or has revolted; a rebel, insurgent, or renegade.

1602 FULBECKE *Pandects* 46 Fugitiues, reuolters, rebels and traitors he may not bring with him. *a* 1641 BP. MOUNTAGU *Acts & Mon.* (1642) 469 The revolters with Jeroboam from the house of David. 1682 NORRIS *Hierocles* 31 Reclaiming the revolters from Vertue by the laws of his justice. 1749 SMOLLETT *Regicide* II. viii, There is no fame— no glory to be won From a revolter's brow. 1796 STEDMAN *Surinam* I. 76 These new revolters were now distinguished by the name of the Cottica Rebels. 1849 GROTE *Greece* II. xlv. V. 432 Their fleet, by invitation of the revolters, sailed up the Nile. 1868 FREEMAN *Norm. Conq.* (1877) II. x. 499 Harold tried in vain to reconcile the revolters to his brother.

Revo·lting, *vbl. sb.* [-ING [1].] The action of the verb; rebellion, insurrection.

1560 DAUS tr. *Sleidane's Comm.* 443 Fardinando alledgeth the revoltinge of..divers Townes from him. 1577 tr. *Bullinger's Decades* (1592) 478 Sundrie names, which do impart and signifie..a fault, an error, a reuolting. 1603 KNOLLES *Hist. Turks* (1638) 144 For which his reuolting, Othoman presently gaue him an ensigne. 1612 SELDEN *Illustr. Drayton's Poly-olb.* ix, After uncertain fortune of war, on both sides, and revolting of Southwales. 1898 *Daily News* 25 June 6/3 The peasant's revolting against the noble is easily explained.

Revo·lting, *ppl. a.* [-ING [2].]

1. That revolts or rebels; insurgent, rebellious.

1593 SHAKS. *Rich. II*, III. iii. 163 Our sighes..shall lodge the Summer Corne, And make a Dearth in this reuolting Land. 1595 — *John* III. i. 257 Let the Church our Mother breathe her curse..on her reuolting sonne. 1611 BIBLE *Jer.* v. 23 But this people hath a reuolting and a rebellious heart. 1842 MANNING *Serm.* (1848) I. xiii. 182 We..shall best spread His kingdom in an evil and revolting world. 1872 HANNA *Resurrection of Dead* 79 This last revolting province in the domains of the Most High.

2. That repels; repulsive, disgusting.

1806 A. KNOX *Rem.* (1844) I. 63 Nothing, having the Christian name, could be more uncouth or revolting. 1849 MAITLAND *Ess.* 67 There is, to us, something so revolting in the very idea. 1863 LONGF. *Wayside Inn, Robt. Sicily* 101 In the corner, a revolting shape, Shivering and chattering sat the wretched ape. 1890 *Sat. Rev.* 12 Apr. 446/1 The revolting inflictions which were abolished in 1814.

absol. 1888 STEVENSON *Pulvis et Umbra* i, This mountain mass of the revolting and the inconceivable.

Hence **Revo·ltingly** *adv.*

1835 HOOD *Poetry, Prose, & Worse* xxxiii, With gore made revoltingly florid. 1855 MILMAN *Lat. Chr.* XIV. ii. (1864) IX. 74 Its adoration in its intensity became revoltingly profane. 1876 MEREDITH *Beauch. Career* xxxii, A confused recollection..surged up in her mind revoltingly.

† **Revo·ltment.** *Obs.* [-MENT.] = REVOLT *sb.*

a 1572 KNOX *Hist. Ref.* Wks. 1846 I. 363 Sche had bruted

..that we sought nothing bot hir lyef, and a plane revoltment from the lawfull obedience dew to our Soverane. 1600 Holland Livy xxix. xvii. 721 The cause of our double revoltment and chaunge.

Revoltress. [Cf. Revolter and -ess.] A woman who revolts.
1868 Whitman Chants Democratic Poems 171 To a foiled Revolter or Revoltress. 1875 Dowden Shaks. vii. (1886) 342 The foiled revoltress against the law of sex.

†**Revolture.** Obs. [f. Revolt v. + -ure, or ad. It. rivoltura.] a. Reflow or return. b. Revolt.
1633 P. Fletcher Purple Isl. iv. xxiv, Three fair nymphs ..Draw down the stream which all the isle suffices, But stop back-ways, some ill revolture fearing. a 1660 — Father's Test. (1670) 55 After that by our treacherous revolture, and rebellion, we had broken Covenant.

Revolubility. [See next and -ity.] A tendency to roll back.
1835 Greswell Exp. Parab. II. 38 Nothing but the fatal revolubility of the stone itself.

Revoluble, a. rare. [ad. L. revolūbilis. So obs. F. revoluble.] Revolving; rolling.
1598 Chapman Iliad ii. 256 Us then, to whom the thrice three year Hath fill'd his revoluble orb since our arrival here. 1875 L. Morris Childr. of Street ix, Thus the revoluble Assonant echo Again they shout breathlessly.

Revolute (re·vǒliut), a. [ad. L. revolūt-us, pa. pple. of revolvĕre to Revolve. Cf. Pg. and It. re-, It. revoluto, F. révolu.]
†1. Having completed a full revolution. Obs.⁻¹
1432-50 tr. Higden (Rolls) IV. 275 From the xxv. day of December, is complete and finischede un to that tyme the yere revolute.
2. In scientific use (chiefly Bot.): Rolled backwards, downwards, or outwards.
1753 Chambers Cycl. Suppl. s.v. Leaf, Revolute leaf...a leaf, the upper part of which rolls itself downward. 1760 J. Lee Introd. Bot. i. xii. (1765) 28 Revolute, rowled back, as in Asparagus. 1785 Martyn Rousseau's Bot. xxii. (1794) 309 Garden Thyme is an erect plant, with its ovate leaves revolute. 1826 Kirby & Sp. Entomol. IV. 318 (Antennæ are) Revolute, when they roll outwards. 1846 Dana Zooph. (1848) 178 Margin of calicle not revolute, subacute. 1876 Harley Mat. Med. (ed. 6) 469 Leaves oblong, linear or lanceolate, entire, when young revolute.
So **Revoluted** ppl. a. rare⁻¹.
1797 Encycl. Brit. (ed. 3) III. 447 Revoluted, rolled backwards, having the edges on both sides rolled spirally, so as to be nearly met on the back of the leaf.

†**Revolute,** v.¹ Obs. rare. [f. ppl. stem of L. revolvĕre.] trans. and intr. To revolve.
1553 T. Wilson Rhet. 86 b, Ponderyng, expendyng, and reuolutyng with my self your ingent affabilitee..for mundane affaires. a 1630 Earl Pembroke Poems (1660) 50 Then he frames a second notion From the revoluting eyes.

Revolute (revǒliū·t), v.² [Back-formation from Revolution.] intr. To engage in revolution.
1890 'R. Boldrewood' Miner's Right (1899) 96/2 It looks bad when old Mark Thursby begins to 'revolute'. 1891 Sat. Rev. 5 Sept. 263/1 It is almost impossible to imagine a better arranged country for 'revoluting' in than Chili.

Revolution (revǒliū·ʃən), sb. Also 4-7 reu-, and -cion, 5 -cioun(e. [a. OF. revolucion, -tion (mod.F. révolution, = Sp. revolucion, It. re-, rivoluzione), or ad. late L. revolūtiōn-em, noun of action f. revolvĕre to Revolve.]
I. 1. Astr. The action or fact, on the part of celestial bodies, of moving round in an orbit or circular course; the apparent movement of the sun, stars, etc., round the earth.
1390 Gower Conf. II. 61 Per cas the revolucion Of hevene and thi condicion Ne be noght yit of on acord. 1413 Pilgr. Sowle (Caxton, 1483) v. xiii. 104 Suo thenne whan this Cercle hath made his reuolucion thenne they enforcen them to syngen and to ioyen. 1559 W. Cunningham Cosmogr. Glasse 24 In whiche the other Planetes, as well as the Sonne, do finyshe their reuolution and course according to their true tyme. 1576 Fleming Panopl. Epist. 211 To marke the course of starres, and viewe the reuolutions of the heauens. 1613 Purchas Pilgrimage ii. iv. (1614) 118 The whole reuolution of the Sunnes motion. 1678 Hobbes Decam. iv. 40 In what time do they make the whole Revolution through the Ecliptique of the Sky? 1715 tr. Gregory's Astron. (1726) I. 409 The Number of Revolutions of the Earth about the Sun made in the mean time. 1771 Encycl. Brit. I. 442/1 Jupiter's three nearest moons fall under his shadow, and are eclipsed in every revolution. 1812-16 Playfair Nat. Phil. (1819) II. 31 The cause of the apparent diurnal revolution of the heavens. 1878 Huxley Physiogr. xx. 337 A movement of revolution whereby it progresses through space, and is carried round the sun.
attrib. 1554 Brunswike tr. Montalmo's Facies Cœli C iij b, Because of Venus, beying impedite in the reuolucion figure in the sixte house.
b. The time in which a planet or other heavenly body completes a full circuit or course.
c 1391 Chaucer Astrol. ii. § 7 The day natural, þat is to seyn 24 houris, is the reuolucioun of the equinoxial. 1669 Sturmy Mariner's Mag. ii. 115 To count the Year or the Revolution of the Sun in even Days. 1696 Whiston The. Earth ii. (1722) 212 The Moon accompanies our Earth, and has her Annual Revolution exactly equal to that of the Earth. 1727 De Foe Syst. Magic i. i. (1840) 25 Who.. searched into and calculated all astronomical difficulties, the motions and revolutions of heavenly bodies. 1819 J. Wilson Dict. Astrol. 351 Revolutions, the time in which a star revolves round the Sun or the Earth.
2. The return or recurrence of a point or period of time; the lapse of a certain time. †By revolution, in due course of time.
14.. in Tundale's Vision (1843) 85 Hit befell then by revolucyon By just a cowntyng in the kalendere. c 1430 Lydg. Min. Poems (Percy Soc.) 24 By revolucion and turnyng of the yere, A gery march his stondis doth disclose. 1494 Fabyan Chron. 4 All suche actes as by Reuoluciowne In theyr dayes fyll. 1553 Brende Q. Curtius (1570) 78 b, They vnderstanding verie well the reuolutions of the time, and theire appointed courses. 1589 Pasquil's Ret. Diij b, From the day of the date heereof, to the full terme and reuolution of seuen yeeres next ensuing. 1601 Holland Pliny II. 349 To deliuer vnto the world those medicins which are not to be but once in the reuolution of a thousand yeres. 1662 Hopkins Funeral Serm. (1685) 48 The Naturalists affirm.. that the revolution of a few years gradually wears away the former body. 1741 Watts Improv. Mind Pref. (1801) 4 And did not increase half so much in the revolution of a year. 1822 Shelley tr. Calderon's Mag. Prodig. ii. 186 The winged years speed o'er the intervals of their unequal revolutions. 1842 H. Rogers Introd. Burke's Wks. I. 1 They recur..at long intervals; they depend on the slow revolutions of ages. 1889 Pop. Science Monthly XXXV. 573/1 The period for the 'revolution' of felling is fixed at forty years.
transf. 1605 Camden Rem. (1637) 199 All things runne round, and as the seasons of the yeare, so mens manners have their revolutions.
†b. A cycle, or recurrent period of time; an epoch. Obs.
1597 Hooker Eccl. Pol. v lxx. § 9 The day..changed in regard of a new reuolution begunne by our Sauiour Christ. 1667 Milton P. L. ii. 597 Thither..At certain revolutions all the damn'd Are brought: and feel by turns the bitter change Of fierce extreams. 1706 J. Logan in Pennsylv. Hist. Soc. Mem. X 164, I am sick of the world unless it would mend, which I scarce expect this revolution.
†c. The recurrence or repetition of a day, event, occupation, etc. Obs.
1669 Sturmy Mariner's Mag. ii. 121 The Change of the Moon..hapneth again upon the same Days, for several Revolutions of the Prime or Golden Number. 1670 Milton Hist. Eng. vi. Wks. 1851 III. 301 To fear from like Vices.. the Revolution of like Calamities. 1713 Guardian No. 147 At every revolution of her wedding day, she makes her husband some pretty present. 1751 Earl Orrery Remarks Swift (1752) 44 He seldom deviated many minutes, in the daily revolution of his exercises and employments. 1784 Cowper Task i. 462 It is the constant revolution..of the same repeated joys, That palls and satiates.
†3. A turn or twist; a bend or winding. Obs.
1541 R. Copland Guydon's Quest. Chirurg. Liij, Fyrste knyt it with two reuolucions. Secondly with one, & than cut the threde fer fro the knot. 1545 Raynold Byrth Mankynde 19 Vaynes infynytely intricate and writhid with a thousand reuolutions or tur[n]agayns. 1615 Crooke Body of Man 454 The braine..is foulded vp in so many conuolutions and revolutions. 1648 Wilkins Math. Magic i ix. 57 Continued by a helicall revolution about a Cylinder. 1729 Shelvocke Artillery iv. 361 The other [end]..is coiled around it, so as to have its Revolutions at a convenient Distance from each other. 1737 Whiston Josephus, Antiq. xv. x. § 1 For these roads are not strait, but have several revolutions.
†b. The action of turning something. Obs.⁻¹
1597 A. M. tr. Guillemeau's Fr. Chirurg. 15 b/1 When as in manner of revolutione we turne the needle, as the furriers doe.
4. The action, on the part of a thing or person, of turning or whirling round, or of moving round some point.
1664 Power Exp. Philos. iii. 157 They recoyl again, and return in a Vortical Motion, and so continue their revolution for ever. 1667 Milton P. L. x. 814 That fear Comes thundring back with dreadful revolution On my defensless head. 1714 R. Fiddes Pract. Disc. ii. 134 To cause a general revolution of the eyes or thoughts of the congregation. 1797 Bewick Brit. Birds I. 99 A sort of Vortex, in which the collective body performs an uniform circular revolution. 1877 R. J. More Under the Balkans xv. 216 Pausing on the completion of each revolution, to kiss the book of the Gospels. 1882 Vines tr. Sachs' Bot. 864 The shoot will retain its spiral form for a time, but will then straighten itself and recommence the revolution at its apex.
b. esp. Movement round an axis or centre; rotation.
1710 J. Harris Lex. Techn. II. s.v., In Geometry the Motion of any Figure quite round a fixt Line (which is called therefore its Axis) is called the Revolution of that Figure. a 1721 Keill Maupertuis' Diss. (1734) 51 The Diameter of the Equator would infinitely exceed the Axis of Revolution. 1831 Brewster Optics vi. 56 Part of a hyperboloid formed by the revolution of a hyperbola. 1840 Lardner Geom. 222 All the surfaces of revolution composing the same vessel having a common axis.
c. A single act of rotation round a centre.
1706 Phillips (ed. Kersey) s.v. Rota Aristotelica, A Wheel..moving..till it has made one entire Revolution. c 1790 Imison Sch. Arts I. 30 The number of revolutions a millstone 4½ feet diameter ought to have in a minute. 1825 J. Nicholson Operat. Mechanic 488 The pinion will make 10 revolutions while the wheel performs one. 1879 Cassell's Techn. Educ. IV. 358 The bobbin-wheel E would make..the same number of revolutions as the main shaft.
II. †5. a. The action of turning over in discourse or talk; discussion. Obs. rare.
1456 Paston Lett. I. 388, I pray you..bring not the matier in revolution in the open Courte. 1533 Bellenden Livy ii. xxiv. (S.T.S.) I. 228 The thing. be revolution of diuers tretyis was differrit to þe begynnyng of þe nixt ȝere.
†b. The action of turning over in the mind; consideration, reflection. Obs.
1586 A. Day Eng. Secretary ii. (1625) 17 In the revolution of the same you also doe grant that in all his behaviour you never saw so much as one suspect. 1599 B. Jonson Cynthia's Rev. v. ii, Answerable to any hourely or half-hourely change in his mistris reuolution. a 1610 Healey Cebes (1636) 160 To which ende you must continue an often reuolution thereof in your meditation. a 1792 Orme in Boswell Johnson an. 1775, Thoughts that by long revolution in the great mind of Johnson have been formed and polished like pebbles rolled in the ocean.
†c. An idea, opinion, notion. Obs. rare⁻¹.
1675 R. Burthogge Causa Dei 23 A Revolution and Hypothesis to which the Origenium is so like, that I believe it a Daughter.
III. 6. Alteration, change, mutation. rare.
c 1400 Rom. Rose 4366 It is I, that am come down Thurgh change & revolucioun! 1602 Shaks. Ham. v. i. 98 Heere's fine Reuolution, if wee had the tricke to see't. 1611 C. Tourneur Ath. Trag. i. i, Obseru'st thou not the very selfsame course Of reuolution, both in Man and Beast? a 1704 T. Brown Persius i. Prol., For thus, sir, modern revolution Has split the wits, t'avoid confusion. a 1718 Penn Maxims Wks. 1726 I. 841 Being, as to our Bodies, composed of Changeable Elements, we, with the World, are made up of and subsist by Revolution.
b. An instance of great change or alteration in affairs or in some particular thing.
c 1450 Lydg. Secrees 1196 Of Elementys the Revolucions, Chaung of tymes and Complexiouns. 1617 Moryson Itin. ii. 188 We haue vpon euery important reuolution of our businesse dispatched vnto your Lordships both our estate and desires. 1663 H. Cogan tr. Pinto's Trav. iii. 206 Whereby one may see, how great the revolutions of time and fortune are. 1685 Evelyn Diary 22 May, I chanc'd to pass just as execution was doing on him [Oates]. A strange revolution! 1707 Refl. upon Ridicule 104 There's a general Revolution in his Temper, he's grown haughty. 1751 Johnson Rambler No. 92 ⁋ 3 The changes which the mind of man has suffered from the various revolutions of knowledge. 1830 Lyell Princ. Geol. I. 461 He must feel at once convinced that, in the interval of ten centuries, a great revolution in the language had taken place. 1863 Froude Hist. Eng. VIII. 425 A vast intellectual revolution, of which the religious reformation was rather a sign than a cause. 1870 Yeats Nat. Hist. Comm. 3 This one material has been the main cause of a complete revolution in our national industry.
7. A complete overthrow of the established government in any country or state by those who were previously subject to it; a forcible substitution of a new ruler or form of government.
1600 E. Blount tr. Conestaggio 175 Assuring those quarters from all reuolutions that might be feared. 1655 Clarke Papers (Camden) IV. 303 Hee was very jealous of the intended revolucion of governm[t] to his Ma[ties] advantage. 1688 Evelyn Diary 2 Dec., The Papists in offices lay down their commissions, and fly..; it looks like a Revolution. 1726 Bolingbroke Study Hist. ii. (1752) 37 King James's maladministration rendered a revolution necessary and practicable. 1776 Gibbon Decl. & F. I. 281 The apprehensions of Saturninus were justified by the repeated experience of revolutions. 1837 Carlyle Fr. Rev. v. vii. (1872) I. 174 'Sire', answered Liancourt, 'it is not a revolt, it is a revolution'. 1855 Macaulay Hist. Eng. xi. III. 6 The most just and salutary revolution must produce much suffering. 1879 Froude Cæsar xiii. 171 Revolutions are the last desperate remedy when all else has failed.
b. Without article.
1796 tr. St.-Pierre's Stud. Nat. (1799) III. 668 Rebellion is the subversion of the laws, and Revolution is that of tyrants. 1819 Shelley Peter Bell 3rd iii. vi, There is great talk of revolution—And a great chance of despotism. 1861 Motley in Times 23 May, The right of revolution is indisputable...British and American history is made up of rebellion and revolution. 1892 Speaker 3 Sept. 278/1 In Uruguay it is said that revolution is kept down only by the army.
8. Eng. Hist. †a. The overthrow of the Rump Parliament in 1660, which resulted in the restoration of the monarchy. Obs.
a 1674 Clarendon Hist. Reb. xi. § 209 Many of these excluded members..forbore coming any more to the House for many years, and not before the revolution. 1725 B. Higgons Rem. Burnet i. Wks. 1736 II. 67 And now he approaches the Restoration,..at which not daring openly to repine, he vents all his Spleen on the happy Instrument [Monk] of that glorious Revolution.
b. The expulsion in 1688 of the Stuart dynasty under James II, and the transfer of sovereignty to William and Mary.
1688 Evelyn in Pepys Diary & Corr. (1879) VI. 163, I.. send on purpose..to know if, in any sort, I may serve you in this prodigious Revolution. 1689 Luttrell Brief Rel. (1857) I. 550 There has been also another addresse presented to his majestie from the tinners of Cornwall,..congratulating them on this great revolution. 1710 Steele Tatler No. 103 ⁋ 8 Upon Lady Autumn's disputing with him about something that happened at the Revolution, he replied with a very angry Tone. 1790 Burke Fr. Rev. Sel. Wks. II. 20 If ever there was a time favourable for establishing the principle, that a king of popular choice was the only legal king, ..it was at the Revolution. 1825 Macaulay Milton Ess. (1897) 15 The principles of the Revolution have often been grossly misrepresented. 1855 — Hist. Eng. xi. III. 15 The Revolution had..placed England in a situation in which the services of a great minister for foreign affairs were indispensable.
attrib. 1708 Reply to 'Bickerstaff Detected' Swift's Wks. 1755 II. i. 161 A Briton, born, a protestant astrologer, a man of revolution principles. 1738 Gentl. Mag. VIII. 485/2, I mean those Nominal Whigs, whose Principles destroy the old Revolution-Whiggism. 1756 Toldervy Hist. 2 Orphans II. 145, I..put a revolution crown into his hand, in order to his returning me the proper change, which he refused to do. 1827 Hallam Const. Hist. xiv. (1876) III. 90 The liberal principles..were necessarily involved in the continuance of the revolution-settlement. 1898 Payne Burke's Sel. Wks. II. 295 The Tories who supported the Hanoverian succession..called themselves 'Revolution Tories'.
9. French Hist. The overthrow of the monarchy, and establishment of republican government, in 1789–95.
1790 Ann. Reg. Pref., They will..be enabled to trace..the steps which have led to the late astonishing Revolution.

1801 Encycl. Brit. Suppl. II. 404/1 In all the turbulent days of the revolution, the women of Paris have never failed to act a conspicuous part. 1847 Emerson Repr. Men, Napoleon, The Revolution entitled..every horse-boy and powder-monkey in the army, to look on Napoleon, as flesh of his flesh. 1857 Buckle Civiliz. xii. (1903) II. 196 The people remained in slavery until the Revolution actually occurred.
10. Amer. Hist. The overthrow of British supremacy by the War of Independence in 1775–81.
1789 D. Ramsay Hist. Amer. Rev. II. 317 The Geography of the United States before the Revolution. 1797 Encycl. Brit. (ed. 3) XVIII. 928/1 Since the revolution the literature of the State [of New York] has engaged the attention of the legislature. 1833 Penny Cycl. I. 112/1 Samuel Adams was one of the firmest and most active patriots of the Revolution. 1882 Encycl. Brit. XIV. 201/1 This lad..presented himself to the Congress of the Revolution, then sitting in Philadelphia.
Hence **Revolu·tion** v., to revolutionize. rare.
1805 Southey in Robberds Mem. W. Taylor (1843) II. 117 It would not grieve me to see the Austrian dominions revolutioned. 1832 Examiner 803/1 England was revolutioned and all things turned topsy-turvy.

Revolutional (revǒliū·ʃənăl), a. [f. prec.]
†1. Astr. Pertaining to the revolution of the planets. Obs.
1658 Gadbury Doctr. Nativities 211 A perpetual Revolutional Table. 1693 W. Freke Sel. Ess. iv. 29 One tells you your Fortune by a Horary Question; another by a Revolutional Figure. 1696 Phillips, Lord of the Year, is that Planet that has most Testimonies of Fortitude in a Revolutional Figure.
†2. Pertaining to, approving or supporting, the Revolution of 1688. Obs.
1695 Rem. on some Late Serm. (ed. 2) 27 He hath made good..every Word of his Revolutional Declaration. 1733 (title), The Loyal: or Revolutional Tory. 1773 Gentl. Mag. XLIII. 438 Dr. Sherlock, then Master of the Temple, preached a most loyal revolutional sermon. 1785 Ann. Reg., Chron. 278/2, I was called forth as your representative, in support of revolutional principles.
3. Revolutionary.
1890 Fairbairn Cathol. Rom. & Angl. (1899) 285 Changes that were as to the English State constitutional, but as to the English Church revolutional.
Hence **Revolu·tionally** adv.
1839 Fraser's Mag. XIX. 127 He lived..with kings, monarchically; with the people, democratically;..with the revolution, revolutionally.

Revolu·tionariness, a. [f. next + -ness.] The quality or state of being revolutionary.
a 1866 J. Grote Exam. Utilit. Phil. (1870) 227 The same determined reformingness,..or, as it was considered by enemies, revolutionariness, belongs to all. 1884 Spectator 2 Aug. 1001 Lord Salisbury's fiercely superstitious belief in the aggressive revolutionariness of Mr. Gladstone.

Revolu·tionary, a. and sb. [f. Revolution sb. + -ary. Cf. F. révolutionnaire (1794), Sp. and Pg. revolucionario.]
1. Pertaining to or connected with, characterized by, of the nature of, revolution.
1774 Gouv. Morris in Sparks Life & Writ. (1832) I. 27, I think government should be founded on stationary and not revolutionary principles. 1796 Burke Regic. Peace Wks. IX. 95 Every thing we hear from them is new, and, to use a phrase of their own, revolutionary. 1827 Hallam Const. Hist. xv. (1876) III. 111 A new and revolutionary government is seldom fairly dealt with. 1838 Story Equity Pleadings x. 305 Which stock had been confiscated by the State during the Revolutionary war. 1874 Green Short Hist. vii. § 3. 362 The Calvinistic refugees were pouring back from Geneva with dreams of revolutionary change in Church and State.
b. sb. One who instigates or favours revolution; one who takes part in a revolution.
1850 Kingsley Alt. Locke Pref. (1879) p. xcviii, It is well ..for every student of history to know what manner of men they are who become revolutionaries. 1899 Allbutt's Syst. Med. VIII. 293 That this degree of enthusiasm has been ..reached by sane revolutionaries, history demonstrates.
2. Revolving; marked by rotation.
1832 Brewster Nat. Magic ii. 27 Cattle grazing in a field might make part of the revolutionary landscape. 1880 Sir E. Reed Japan II. 116 The Russian frigate..was spun round..and was thrown high and dry, a useless wreck, at the end of the revolutionary period.

Revolutionee·ring, vbl. sb. [See -eer.] The carrying out of revolutions.
1803 W. Taylor in Ann. Rev. I. 348 From no former experiment, therefore, can the philosophy of revolutioneering be expected to derive so important an improvement.

Revolu·tioner. [f. Revolution sb. + -er.]
1. a. A supporter or approver of the Revolution of 1688. Now only Hist.
1695 Whether Preserving Prot. Relig. etc. 22 Nor can his Majesty's Authority..be questioned by our Revolutioners and Abdicators themselves. 1706 in Maidment Bk. Scot. Pasquils (1868) 372 The staunch Revolutioners pretend all their care is securing religion. c 1728 Earl of Ailesbury Mem. (1890) 620 A member of the House of Commons, supported by all the revolutioners, brought thither the sermon in print. 1758 Smollett Hist. Eng. (1800) I. 175 The people were divided into three parties, namely, the Williamites, the Jacobites, and the discontented Revolutioners. 1896 J. Mackinnon Union Eng. & Scot. 374 The Jacobites..exulted in the unanimity of sentiment, which inspired Revolutioner and Cameronian alike.
b. One who took part in the American Revolution.
1835 D. Crockett Tour 52 General Morton is a revolutioner, and an officer in the society of old soldiers called the 'Cincinnati Society'.
2. A revolutionary.
1803 W. Taylor in Ann. Rev. I. 351/2 It is but too true, that there have been very honest revolutioners of the most exaggerated sentiments. 1831 Lincoln Herald 22 July 3/6 Take a Revolutioner from Belgium or France.

Revolu·tionism. [-ism.] Advocacy or spread of revolutionary principles.
1877 A. M. Sullivan New Irel. xiv. 164 He had seen the evil work which Revolutionism had wrought elsewhere. 1893 Current Hist. II. 374 The daily increasing growth of Revolutionism, Socialism, and Anarchy, is producing one result in Europe.

Revolu·tionist. [-ist.] An advocate or favourer of revolution; a revolutionary.
1710 Place (title), The True English Revolutionist. 1727 Warburton Tracts (1789) 104 The Title of Savage, restless, turbulent Revolutionists. 1790 Burke Fr. Rev. 83, I state here the doctrine of the Revolutionists. 1831 Sir J. Sinclair Corr. II. 97 There is no person at present, in whose favour the revolutionists would unite, and choose as a leader. 1856 Froude Hist. Eng. (1858) II. vi. 21 The Lollards had become political revolutionists as well as religious reformers. 1879 McCarthy Own Times xviii. II. 25 He was cast in the very mould of the genuine revolutionist.

Revolutionize (revǒliū·ʃənaiz), v. [f. Revolution sb. + -ize.]
1. trans. To bring (a country or state) under a revolutionary form of government.
1797 Rufus King in Life & Corr. (1895) II. 195 You will perceive by newspapers that all Italy will be overturned. Venice is no more; and Genoa has been completely revolutionized. 1797 Nelson 25 Jan. in Nicolas Disp. (1845) III. 238 Naples must be revolutionized unless the Emperor acts with vigour and speed. 1815 Wellington 5 Jan. in Gurw. Desp. (1838) XII. 237 He [Murat] knows he can revolutionize Italy, and will do so if it is necessary. 1849 Cobden Speeches 38 It was not an unnatural thing that men..should have been seized with the idea of revolutionising the country. 1868 G. Duff Pol. Surv. 30 The object of these invaders has been to revolutionize Bulgaria.
2. To convert into revolutionary forms; to infect with revolutionary principles or ideas.
1797 Earl Malmesbury Diaries & Corr. III. 380 They have not revolutionized..diplomatic forms and ceremonies. 1801 Southey Lett. (1856) II. 175 Sometimes the poet is called a Jacobin; at others it is said that his opinions are revolutionised. 1837 Ann. Reg., Hist. 255/2 Officers who had revolutionized their regiments and joined the rebels. 1870 Anderson Missions Amer. Bd. II. xii. 95 A reported threat..that..he would seize the prince and his sister, and revolutionize the government.
3. To change (a thing) completely or fundamentally; to reorganize or reconstruct upon altogether new lines.
1799 Southey in Life & Corr. (1850) II. 32 My father had ..revolutionised two adjoining cottages into a dwelling-house. 1822 Coleridge in Lit. Rem. (1836) I. 298 A violent motive may revolutionize a man's opinions and professions. 1861 M. Pattison Ess. (1889) I. 42 The opening of the Indies..revolutionized the channels and the direction of commerce. 1881 Froude Short Stud. (188.) IV. ii. i. 163 Mysteries..were now preached again..and had revolutionised the ritual in our churches.
absol. 1877 Owen Wellesley's Desp. p. xliv, He revolutionizes under the guise of conservative readjustment.
4. intr. To engage in revolutions.
1854 Semi-Centennial Anniv. Vermont 98 Boys like men will revolutionize, And put to straits the wisdom of the wise.
Hence **Revolutionized** ppl. a.; **Revolutionizing** vbl. sb. and ppl. a. Also **Revolu·tionizement**; **Revolu·tionizer.**
1815 Q. Rev. XIV. 54 The moral or political virtues of the *revolutionized part of that country. 1851 Gallenga Italy 331 Woe to him who teaches a revolutionized nation that there are two issues to an engagement! 1882 Standard 5 Oct. 3/2 To prevent..the *revolutionising and distracting of that country. 1861 G. Moore Lost Tribes 92 The 'revolutionizing influence of the Saxons who..took possession of..part of India. 1820 Ann. Reg., Chron. 503 A few days before the *revolutionisement of Venice. 1818 Blackw. Mag. IV. 308 The share of all ill-timed and unfortunate *revolutionizers. 1868 Boyd Less. Mid. Age 289 Conservatism is ever the wall to be battered: aggressive reformers or revolutionisers are the head of the battering-ram. 1895 Blackw. Mag. Feb. 181/1 Saint-Malo bore the revolutioniser of prose decades before any other town in France could boast a coadjutor to him.

Re·volutive, a. rare. [ad. F. révolutif or L. type *revolūtīv-us: see Revolute a. and -ive.]
†1. (See quot.) Obs. rare⁻⁰.
1611 Cotgr., Periodic, reuolutiue, comming or going by course, or fits.
†2. Contemplative, meditative. Obs. rare⁻¹.
1637 Feltham Lett. xvii. in Lusoria (1661), By being so conceived, aweth the inquisitive and revolutive Soul of man.
3. Bot. = Revolute a. 2.
1866 Treas. Bot. 968/1.

Revo·lvable, a. [f. Revolve v. + -able.] Capable of being revolved.
1889 Nature 3 Oct. 543/2 The upper cap of the mill is revolvable.

Revolve (rɪvǫ·lv), sb. [f. the verb.]
†1. Meditation, determination. Obs.
1595 Markham Sir R. Grinuile Diij, When Midelton saw Grinuills hie reuolue, Past hope, past thought,..Once more to moue him flie, he doth resolue.
2. Revolution; rotation.
1641 Crabtree in Phil. Trans. XXX. 608 If the Screws keep an exact Equality of Motion forward in each Revolve, it is a most admirable Invention. 1696 Whiston The. Earth ii. (1722) 110 In 365 Revolves the difference is scarce sensible. a 1806 H. K. White Time 279 Each revolve Of the recording sun conducts us on. 1822 B. W. Procter Two Dreams 43 The stars Went round and round, their circles lessening At each revolve.
fig. 1690 D'Urfey Collin's Walk i. 31 In all revolves and turns of State Decreed by (what dee call him) Fate.
3. Theat. (See quot.)
1900 Westm. Gaz. 18 May 4/2 In the course of the change a massive piece of scenery..is moved bodily from one side of the stage to the other. Nearly at the top of this 'revolve', as it is technically called, is the window.

Revolve (rɪvǫ·lv), v. Also 5-7 reuolue, 6-7 revolue (6 Sc. reuolfe). [ad. L. revolv-ĕre, f. re- Re- + volvĕre to roll, turn. So Sp., Pg., and obs. F. revolver, It. rivolvere.]
I. trans. †1. To turn (the eyes or sight) back or round. Obs.
1387-8 T. Usk Test. Love i. vii. (Skeat) l. 72 For if such men wolden their eyen of their conscience revolven, they shulden seen the same sentence they legen on other springe out of their sydes. 1523 Skelton Garl. Laurel 664 Then furthermore aboute me my syght I reuolde. 1695 Ld. Preston Boeth. iii. 147 Let him into himself revolve his Eye.
†2. To roll; to move by rolling. Obs. rare.
1412-20 Lydg. Chron. Troy i. 3919 And from þe hil þe water is revolvid Of snowys white, þat Phebus hath dissoluyd. 1541 Copland Guydon's Quest. Chyrurg. Piv b, Let them be applyed vpon the sayde places in reuoluynge them contynually from one place to another that they cleue nat to the fleshe.
†b. To bring round in course of time. Obs.⁻¹
a 1591 H. Smith Wks. (1867) II. 487 [I] yet desire to be dissolv'd (When my due date shall be revolv'd) As more happy far for me.
†3. a. To restore; to turn, bring, or roll back (into a place or state, or upon a person). Obs.
In the first quot. perh. an error for reuerld.
1430-31 Rolls of Parlt. IV. 371 Ye saide Prison..was throwen doune; and..revolved and made agayn in a better manner. 1622 Misselden Free Trade 127 The Current once diuerted will hardly bee reuolued into its genuine Source and Course againe. 1653 Milton Hirelings To Parl., The care and tuition of whose Peace and Safety..is now again by a new dawning of God's miraculous Providence among us, revolv'd upon your shoulders. 1665 Sir T. Herbert Trav. (1677) 53 And the four Elements..shall maintain a dreadful fight, so long and so fiercely..that at last all will be revolved into a dark confusion.
†b. To bring round again to some position. Obs.
1653 Manton Exp. James v. 17 This plainly revolveth you to the tenor of the old covenant, and maketh works the ground of your acceptance with God. 1675 Baxter Cath. Theol. i. iii. 32 As for predisposition, the question will be revolved to the same point.
4. To turn over (something) in the mind, breast, thoughts, etc.
c 1460 G. Ashby Dicta Philos. 125 So ye may Reuolue in cogitacion That here ther is no longe habitacion. 1474 Caxton Chesse 46 How be hit ye may reuolue hit in your mynde. 1513 Douglas Æneis v. xiii. 34 Venus,..Amyd hir breist revoluing mony a thocht, Spak to Neptune. a 1548 Hall Chron., Rich. III, 23 b, When he reuolued in his wauerynge mynde how greate a fountayne of mischiefe towarde hym shoulde sprynge. 1671 Milton P. R. i. 185 Musing and much revolving in his brest, How best the mighty work he might begin. 1704 Prior Let. to Boileau 128 The great Design revolving in his Mind. 1748 Anson's Voy. ii. vii. 210 The projects which the Commodore revolved in his thoughts. 1820 Shelley Hymn Merc. xi, Revolving in his mind some subtle feat Of thievish craft. 1859 Geo. Eliot A. Bede ii, The problem that Mr. Casson had been revolving in his mind for the last five minutes.
b. To consider, think over, ponder or meditate upon (something).
c 1425 Found. St. Bartholomew's (E.E.T.S.) 20 He, reuoluynge his relikys that he hadde of the Crosse,..depid them yn water, and wysshe the tonge of the pacient ther with. 1509 Hawes Conv. Swearers xlvi, I shall encrease And brynge you whiche reuolue inwardly This my complaynt to eternall glory. 1530 Lyndesay Test. Papyngo 507 Off Flodoun feilde the rewyne to reuolfe..I nyll, for dreid that dolour ȝow dissolfe. 1584 Cogan Haven Health ii. (1636) 17 For the residue of the day..[rather] to revolve things reade before, than to reade or muse of new. 1609 Holland Amm. Marcell. xxii. xvi. 216 If any man wil with a quicke understanding revolve the manifold introductions into the intelligence of Divinitie. a 1674 Clarendon Surv. Leviath. (1676) 134, And I cannot enough recommend Mr. Hobbes, that he will revolve his own judgment and determination in this chapter. 1718 Pope Iliad vi. 364 Here, as the queen revolved with careful eyes The various textures and the various dyes. 1756 Amory Buncle (1825) III. 76 While I revolved the case of these unfortunate young ladies. 1823 De Quincey Lett. Educ. i. (1860) 5 Even as I find, who have revolved the principal points almost daily for many years. 1856 Kane Arct. Expl. II. v. 61, I have plenty of time to revolve my most uncomfortable thoughts.
†c. To destine, purpose. Obs. rare⁻¹.
1513 Douglas Æneis i. i. 33 The fatale sisteres reuolue and schew, sche kend, Of Troiane blude ane peple suld descend.
5. To turn over, search through, study, or read (a book, or the works of an author). Now rare.
c 1480 Henryson Mor. Fab., Sheep & Dog 71 Of Ciuile Law volumis full mony thay reuolue. a 1533 Ld. Berners Gold. Bk. M. Aurel. Fiij b, As I reuolued the registers in the Capitol, I redde a ryght meruailous thynge. 1593 Nashe Christ's T. Wks. (Grosart) IV. 179 From thy byrth to thys moment of thine vnbeliefe, reuolue the diarie of thy memory. 1644 Milton Bucer on Divorce Wks. 1851 IV. 340 Of the clear judgment of your Royal Majesty I nothing doubt, revolving the Scripture so often as ye do. 1671 — P. R. i. 259 This having heard, strait I again revolv'd The Law and Prophets. 1718 Prior Solomon i. 46 Around my Throne the Letter'd Rabbins stand, Historic Leaves revolve, long Volumes spread. 1805 Richardson Poems & Plays I. 32,

I trim my lamp, revolve the page And scan the labours of the sage.
†6. To bind round, tie or wrap up. Also fig. Obs.
1599 A. M. tr. Gabelhouer's Bk. Physicke 21/1 A certayn kind of ligament, as is that wherwith we revolve a fracture of a Legge, that the one half therof cover the other. 1632 Lithgow Trav. vi. 250 These three reuolu'd in one, Points forth the Pope. Ibid. vii. 334 The commendation of which Cities rest reuolu'd in these following verses.
†7. To upset by revolution. Obs. rare.
1615 Wadsworth in Bedell's Lett. (1624) 10 His vnquietnesse and ambition, reuoluing the Commonwealth, and so vniustly expelling..the Bishop. [Hence 1624 Bedell Lett. x. 126 Caluin by his vnquietnes and ambition reuolued the State of Geneua.]
8. To cause (something) to travel in an orbit around a central point; to rotate (something) upon an axis.
1667 Milton P. L. vii. 381 Then in the East her turn she shines, Revolvd on Heav'n's great Axle. 1692 Bentley Boyle Lect. 220 There could not possibly arise in the chaos any vortices..either to form the globes of the planets, or to revolve them when formed. 1715 tr. Gregory's Astron. (1726) II. 473 The body, which is urg'd by a centripetal Force,..is revolv'd along with L. 1755 Man No. 50. 3 When he stretches out his arm it serves as a bar of defence, which, when he revolves it, acts as a sling. 1858 Greener Gunnery 15 Some mechanical adjunct for revolving the chamber. 1880 Encycl. Brit. XI. 312/2 It [the gun] is placed opposite the loading gear by revolving the turn-table.
II. intr. †9. To return to a person or place. Obs.
1586 J. Hooker Hist. Irel. in Holinshed II. 142/1 What should be the cause that they should thus rage, and so wickedlie and suddenlie reuolue, as dogs to their vomits, so they to their treasons. a 1700 Ken Hymnotheo Poet. Wks. 1721 III. 111 As soon might the Autumnal Sun To Libra, when its Course was run, Revolve, till it to Aries reel'd. 1726 Ayliffe Parergon 81 The Jurisdiction does ipso Jure revolve to the Judge a Quo. 1755 H. Walpole Let. to Mann 21 Dec., You will smile at seeing Doddington again revolved to the court.
†10. To deliberate or consider; to meditate or think upon something. Obs.
1601 Shaks. Twel. N. ii. v. 155 If this fall into thy hand, reuolue. 1622 J. Reynolds God's Revenge ii. ix. 157 With a hellish ratiocination ruminating and reuoluing on the manner thereof, hee..at last re-solves to poyson her. 1699 Pomfret Fortunate Compl. 3 As Strephon..Revolving lay upon his wretched state. 1785 Paley Mor. Philos. (1818) II. 247 To a mind revolving upon the subject of human jurisprudence.
11. To perform a circular motion; to move in a regular orbit about or round a fixed point.
1713 Berkeley Guardian No. 126 ⁋ 2 Those bodies that revolve round the sun. 1771 Encycl. Brit. I. 449/2 It will then be..forced to revolve about S in the circle BYTU. 1801 Charlotte Smith Lett. Solit. Wand. II. 84 Whose beams enlighten and cherish the unknown worlds which revolve around them. 1854 Brewster More Worlds iv. (1874) 93 Our Earth and Mars, Venus and Mercury...revolve nearest to the Sun. 1868 Lockyer Elem. Astron. § 142 The only satellite which takes a longer time to revolve round its primary than our Moon.
b. To rotate or move upon an axis or centre.
1727-38 Chambers Cycl. s.v. Earth, For a body, revolving on its axis, the parts..are continually endeavouring to recede from the centre. 1823 Scott Peveril xviii, The wheel appears to be again revolving. 1849 James Woodman ix, It was made to revolve upon hinges. 1885 Leudesdorf Cremona's Proj. Geom. 205 If a straight line f revolve round a fixed point E.
c. To wind spirally. Obs. rare⁻¹.
1772-84 Cook's 3rd Voy. iv. vii, From above and behind each eye arises an elegant yellowish-white crest, revolving backward as a ram's horn.
12. To come round again, to move round, in various senses.
1769 Burke Late St. Nat. Wks. II. 78 Publick accounts formerly printed and re-printed revolve once more, and find their old station in this sober meridian. 1787 Mme. D'Arblay Diary 3 Jan., My plan having long been revolving in my head, I had ventured..to hint at it [etc.] 1807 Crabbe Par. Reg. i. 1 The year revolves, and I again explore The simple annals of my parish poor. 1822-56 De Quincey Confess. (1862) 131 A world-wearied man could not do better than revolve amongst these modest inns.
Hence **Revo·lved** ppl. a.
1692 Ray Disc. iii. (1732) 14 The Sea with revolved Waves. 1760 P. Miller Introd. Bot. 35 When it is turned back or rolled.., [it is] a revolved leaf. 1825 J. Nicholson Operat. Mechanic 573 Roofs on circular bases..are called roofs of revolution or revolved roofs.

Revolvency (rɪvǫ·lvĕnsi). [f. prec. + -ency.] Tendency to revolve; capacity for revolution.
1784 Cowper Task i. 372 Its own revolvency upholds the world. 1839 Ure Dict. Arts 1033 Revolvency is the leading law in the system of the universe.

Revolver (rɪvǫ·lvəɹ). [f. Revolve v. + -er.]
1. A pistol provided with mechanism by which a set of loaded barrels, or (more usually) of cartridge-chambers, is revolved and presented in succession before the hammer, so as to admit of the rapid discharge of several shots without reloading.
1835 Colt in Abridgm. Patent Specif., Fire-arms (1859) 84. 1844 Dickens Mart. Chuz. xxxiii, Ripper, Tickler, and the revolvers, all ready for action on the shortest notice. 1848 A. Sedgwick in Life & Lett. (1890) II. 143 Bring your patent revolvers with you to take care of Lady H. 1861 T. L. Peacock Gryll G. 160 See the complications and refinements in modes of destruction—in revolvers and rifles. 1887 Besant & Rice Gold. Butterfly Prol. 1 If a search had been made, a revolver would have been found.
b. attrib. and Comb., as revolver cartridge, shot, etc.; revolver camera (see quot.).
1879 Cassell's Techn. Educ. I. 272/2 The old skin or paper revolver cartridge, which was in vogue until a few years ago. 1885 Sat. Rev. 17 Jan. 74/1 Revolver-carrying is fast becoming..a practice here. 1887 Pall Mall G. 23 Feb., Several revolver shots were fired at them. 1890 Woodbury Encycl. Photogr., Revolver Camera, a small instantaneous camera made in the form of a revolver.
2. A revolving furnace. Also attrib.
1879 Lock Spon's Encycl. i. 292 The 'revolvers' bid fair ..to supersede the old hand furnaces. 1880 Lomas Alkali Trade 4 A turn-out of at least 130 tons of salt-cake per week, with eight or nine hand-ball furnaces, or one revolver. 1880 Rep. Alkali Acts (1881) 63 On one occasion the escape of HCL from the Revolver chimney was high.
3. In miscellaneous uses: (see quots.).
1888 Lockwood's Dict. Mech. Terms 286 Revolvers, rotary pistons. 1899 tr. Jaksch's Clinical Diagnosis (ed. 4) x. 436 The tube of the microscope is provided with a 'revolver' or 'nose-piece', to which lenses of different magnifying powers are fixed.
Hence **Revo·lverer,** one who uses a revolver; **Revo·lvering** vbl. sb.
1885 Sat. Rev. 17 Jan. 74/1 The revolverer never reflects; he is moved by his own fears. 1889 Ibid. 23 Mar. 335/1 'Revolvering'..is nearly as great a curse of the present moment as democracy or anti-religious maundering.

Revolving (rɪvǫ·lviŋ), vbl. sb. [-ing¹.] The action of the verb, in various senses.
1387-8 T. Usk Test. Love ii. ix. (Skeat) l. 158 These transitory tymes that maketh revolving of your yeres thus stondmele. 1514 Barclay Cyt. & Uplondyshm. (Percy Soc.) 28 Processe of yeares, revolvynge of season, Bryngeth all these soone in oblyvyon. 1555 Eden Decades (Arb.) 106 They were greatly gyuen to..continuall reuoluinge of dyuers autours. c 1645 Howell Lett. (1650) II. 37 In my small revolving of Authors I find as high examples of vertue in Women as in Men. 1670 Clarendon Ess. Tracts (1727) 145 Without..many unnecessary revolvings which men of sharp and pregnant parts stand in no need of. 1867 Longf. Dante, Par. xiv. 24 The holy circles a new joy displayed In their revolving.

Revolving (rɪvǫ·lviŋ), ppl. a. [-ing².] Turning round; making revolutions; rotating: a. pr. Of time or seasons, or with reference to these.
1697 Dryden Æneid i. 386 An age is ripening in revolving fate, When Troy shall overturn the Grecian state. 1709 Watts in Sc. Paraph., Hymns iv. 2 The revolving skies had brought the third, th' appointed day. 1738 Wesley We lift our Hearts to Thee v, And live this short revolving Day As if it were our last. 1781 Cowper Heroism 25 Revolving seasons, fruitless as they pass. 1825 Waterton Wand. S. Amer. 152 For three revolving autumns. 1887 Bowen Virg. Æneid i. 269 Thrice ten glorious years of revolving months.
b. Of moving bodies, etc.
1715 tr. Gregory's Astron. (1726) II. 475 The point D (the Place of the Body describing the revolving Orbit). 1727-38 Chambers Cycl. s.v. Center, That point to which a revolving planet, or comet, is impelled. 1812-16 Playfair Nat. Phil. (1819) II. 235 The velocity of the falling body at L, as well as of the revolving body at P. 1822 Shelley tr. Calderon's Mag. Prodig. iii. 68 Thou Who gazest..On the sun's revolving splendour! 1867 J. Hogg Microsc. ii. i. 275 This little cell so well known to the older observers as the globe-animalcule or revolving-cell.
c. Of mechanical apparatus or parts of machinery. (Cf. Knight Dict. Mech.)
1814 Scott Diary 29 July in Lockhart, It [a beacon-grate] is to be abolished for an oil revolving-light. 1844 Dickens Mart. Chuz. xxxiii, He usually carried a brace of revolving pistols..., with seven barrels a-piece. 1892 Photogr. Ann. II. 60 A revolving wheel cutter for cushion or round shapes.
Hence **Revo·lvingly** adv.
1611 Cotgr., Periodiquement,..reuoluingly, by course or fits, or with a continuall, and interchanged course.

†**Revome,** v. Obs. rare⁻¹. [ad. L. revomĕre: see Re- 2 d.] trans. To swallow up again.
1596-7 in Hist. Croydon App. (1783) 153 This trenche revomed those small stones that lay in the court yarde.

Revo·mit, v. rare. [Re- 5 a. Cf. It. revomitare.] trans. To vomit up again.
1545 Joye Exp. Dan. vi. 87 Pillis, medecyns or pocions, which if yᵉ syke bodye reuomite there is no helth to be loked fore. 1601 Holland Pliny xiv. xxii. I. 426 Vomiting and revomiting twice or thrice together that which they have drunke.

Revon, obs. form of Raven sb.¹

Revo·te (rī-), sb. [Re- 5 a: cf. next.] A second or repeated vote; a renewed grant.
1865 Gladstone in Morn. Star 9 June, These are revotes of money granted on former occasions. 1891 Daily News 7 Apr. 3/1 The sum spent on the house was really a re-vote from last year.

Revo·te (rī-), v. [Re- 5 a.] trans. To grant, settle, or decree again by a new vote.
1865 Gladstone in Morn. Star 9 June, The Treasury should express its willingness, on a fair case being made out, to ask Parliament to revote the money. 1880 Burton Reign Q. Anne II. xii. 261 The signs of the times rendered it desirable to have that point settled by redebating and revoting the settlement of the throne. 1897 Pop. Sci. Monthly IV. 724 Certain expenditures..are not revoted every year.

Revow· (rī-), v. [Re- 5 a.] trans. To vow (something) again.
1748 Richardson Clarissa (1768) I. 248, I kneel not repenting of what I have vowed in such a case as that I have supposed. I revow it, at your feet. 1784 Unfortunate Sensibility I. 143 For the sake of..hearing him vow and revow ten thousand soft enchanting things.

Revu·lsant. Med. [ad. F. révulsant pres. pple. of révulser (see next), or L. type *revulsant-em.] A revulsive.
1875 H. C. Wood Therap. (1879) 560 The general law for deep-seated parts is that the revulsant should be put directly over the part. 1899 Allbutt's Syst. Med. VII. 42 Cups or leeches to the spine may be useful to some extent as revulsants.

†**Revu·lse,** v. Obs. rare. [f. L. revuls-, ppl. stem of revellĕre: see Revel v.² So F. révulser.] trans. To drag, draw, or pull back; to tear away.
1669 W. Simpson Hydrol. Chym. 78 This virulent acrimony..becomes by a retrograde motion revulsed into the veins. 1673 Harvey Anat. Exerc. ii. 123 To take away the blood..that it might be revulsed from the lungs. c 1690 Beverley Kingd. Christ 9 Any of the Ten, though if not Revuls'd from the Beast, they are in Prophetic Language, Horns of the Papacy.

Revu·lsent, variant of Revulsant.
1882 in Quain Dict. Med.

Revulsion (rɪvʌ·lʃən). Also 6-7 reuulsion, 6 revulsione, 7 -tion. [a. F. révulsion (16th c., = Sp. revulsion, It. revulsione), or ad. L. revulsio, noun of action f. revellĕre: see Revel v.²]
1. Med. The action or practice of diminishing a morbid condition in one part of the body by operating or acting upon another. (Cf. Derivation 1 c.)
1541 Copland Galyen's Terap. Gg iij, Yf the fluxyon be impetuous & great we shal make reuulsion in the contrary partyes. 1597 A. M. tr. Guillemeau's Fr. Chirurg. 40 b/1 As oltentimes as we desire to make any derivatione, revulsione, interceptione or evacuatione of anye matter. 1643 J. Steer tr. Exp. Chyrurg. v. 19 Let there be used..bloodletting, cupping, and other revultions. 1684 tr. Bonet's Merc. Compit. iv. 123 When a Looseness is cured by the use of a Bath, it is cured by revulsion. c 1720 Gibson Farrier's Guide ii. iii. (1738) 9 This Method of Revulsion has been safely practised among all Physicians. 1753 N. Torriano Gangr. Sore Throat 121 Her Throat had well nigh choaked her (notwithstanding the Revulsion of the Humour caused by the Blisters). 1833 Cycl. Pract. Med. I. 524/1 Derivation or revulsion is often found to occur independently of any artificial excitation. 1875 H. C. Wood Therap. (1879) 538 The process being called revulsion, or counter-irritation.
2. The action of drawing, or the fact of being drawn, back or away. In later use only fig.
1609 J. Davies Holy Roode cvii, That Head..vpon whose Crowne Depends the highest Heau'ns resplendant Roofe, By whose reuulsion It would soone fall downe. 1661 Boyle Examen (1682) 92 The repeated impulse and revulsion of the Sucker. 1687 Rycaut Hist. Turks II. 91 There necessarily followed a Revulsion of the Forces from Dalmatia. 1768 Sterne Sent. Journ., Remise Door, The blood and spirits, which had suffered a revulsion from her, crouded back to her. 1776 Adam Smith W. N. iv. vii. (1904) II. 116 Thrown out of employment by the revulsion of capital from other trades. 1850 Gladstone Glean. (1879) II. 106 For common speculative liberalism..he had a contempt as energetic even as his revulsion from theology.
†3. Recovery, restoration. Obs. rare⁻¹.
c 1760 in Etoniana (1865) 74 One of his..pupils speaks of the 'revulsion' of the fame of Eton 'owing to his able.. administration'.
4. A sudden violent change of feeling; a strong reaction in sentiment or taste.
1816 Scott Old Mort. xxxiv, The transition from the verge of the grave to a prospect of life had occasioned a dizzy revulsion in his whole system. 1853 Kingsley Misc. (1860) I. 289 There comes a natural revulsion from the baldness and puerility into which Wordsworth too often fell. 1867 Freeman Hist. Ess. Ser. 1 (1871) iii. 55 The cause of this strange..direction of popular feeling is to be found in a sort of generous revulsion of sentiment.
5. A sudden reaction or reverse tendency in trade, fortune, etc.
1812 Southey Ess. (1832) I. 147 To grow up..while the trade flourishes, and to be thrown out of employ..when it meets with any sudden revulsion. 1830 D'Israeli Chas. I, III. xiv. 321 In that great revulsion of fortune. the Archbishop was consigned to the hands of his old Sectarian. 1848 Mill Pol. Econ. III. 195 A state of business which, when pushed to an extreme length, brings on the revulsion called a commercial crisis.
Hence **Revu·lsionary** a.
1825 Coleridge Aids Refl. (1848) I. 298 That the tenet is not to be placed among the revulsionary results of the Scripture-slighting will-worship of the Romish Church. 1900 F. T. Bullen Idylls of the Sea 246 Recovering from that revulsionary paroxysm, all hands rushed upon the retreating mass.

Revulsive (rɪvʌ·lsiv), a. and sb. Med. [ad. L. type *revulsīv-us: see Revulse v. and -ive. So F. révulsif, Sp., Pg., and It. revulsivo.]
A. adj. Capable of producing revulsion; tending to revulsion.
1616 T. Adams Soul's Sickness i, Either by cutting a vein, purging, revulsive or local remedies. 1671 Salmon Syn. Med. iii. xxxviii. 522 Blood-letting..is also an operation revulsive and derivative. 1710 Floyer Physic. Pulse-Watch 462 This I call a revulsive Friction, to draw the Blood and Spirits towards the Limbs. 1753 N. Torriano Gangr. Sore Throat 7 Blisters..might have also been of great Service in this Case,..on account of their revulsive Effect. 1822-34 Good's Study Med. (ed. 4) III. 398 When cold, applied in this manner, takes off either clonic or entastic spasm, it is by a revulsive power. 1883-4 Med. Ann. 17/1 Its action is said to be sedative and revulsive.
B. sb. An application employed to produce revulsion. Also fig.
1661 J. Fell Life Hammond H.'s Wks. 1634 IV. 27 In his sicknesses..he never intermitted study, but rather re-inforc'd it..as the most frequent revulsive and diversion of pain. 1667 Decay Chr. Piety ix. ⁋ 17 Satan has in this instance found it a lucky Stratagem, it having proved the most powerful revulsive of his danger. 1831 Davies Mat. Med. 17 This is the effect we wish to produce when we administer remedies called revulsives. 1890 Times 11 Jan. 5/1 Towards 5 o'clock revulsives were applied to the head.

Hence **Revu·lsively** adv.
1856 Aird Poet. Wks. 145 His spirit with alternate change From pride to sorrow was compelled to range Revulsively.

Revy(e, obs. ff. Revie. **Revyn,** obs. f. Raven sb.¹, and riven, pa. pple. of Rive v. **Revyr,** obs. f. River. **Revyre:** see Revire v. **Revyssh,** obs. f. Ravish. **Revyue,** obs. f. Revive v.

Rew, sb.¹ Obs. exc. dial. Forms: 1 rǽw, réw, ráw, 3 reawe, 4-7 rewe, 5-7, 9 rew, 9 rue. [OE. rǽw, etc. (see 2 b), var. of ráw Row sb.]
†1. In adverbial phrases: a. By rew, in order, successively. Also in rew. Obs.
a 1225 Ancr. R. 336 Go so adunewardes bi reawe & bi reawe, uor tu kume to þe laste. 13.. R. Glouc. (Rolls) 6984 Þe bissopes ech on Bi rewe asoileden þe king of his gret trespas. c 1386 Chaucer Wife's T. Preamble 506 That feele I on my ribbes al by rewe. 1388 Wyclif Acts xviii. 23 He wente forth, walkinge bi rewe thorou the cuntrei of Galathie. c 1449 Pecock Repr. ii. xiv. 233 Whiche ij. textis, if thei ben considered as thei liggen to gidere in rewe, it schal be seen [etc.]. 1470-85 Malory Arthur ii. i. 77 Moost of.. the barons..assayed alle by rewe, but ther myght non spede. 1542 Udall Erasm. Apoph. 228 Before that thou shalt haue rekened vp by rewe one after other..the xxiiii. lettres. 1591 Spenser Tears of Muses 233 So rested shee; and then the next in rew Began her grievous plaint.
†b. On or in a rew, in a row or line. Obs.
Cf. arew adv. and OE. on ȝeræwe.
c 1290 St. Brendan 278 in S. Eng. Leg. I. 227 He ladde him and is monekus in-to a noble halle, And setten heom a-doun alle on a rewe. c 1384 Chaucer Ho. Fame 1692 Ther come the ferthe companye.., And gunne stonde in a rewe. c 1386 — Knt.'s T. 2008 To hakke and hewe The okes olde, and leye hem on a rewe. 1503 Hawes Examp. Virt. xiii. 254 All the ladyes..Stode on a rewe besyde the closette. 1590 Spenser F. Q. iii. vi. 17 She found the Goddesse with her crew..Sitting beside a fountaine in a rew. 1610 Holland Camden's Brit. ii. 99 Rugged rocks set orderly, as it were in a rew. 1615 Chapman Odyss. xxi. 173 On a rew [he] Set them, of one height, by a line he drew.
†2. A row or line of persons or things; a rank or series. Obs.
c 1290 St. Wulstan 224 in S. Eng. Leg. I. 77 Al along þe rewe þoruȝ þe queor he gan i-wiende. 1390 Gower Conf. III. 308 Than sen thei stonde on every side,..Of Peneonceals a riche rewe. c 1430 Two Cookery-bks. 53 Plante..a rew of on, & rew of a-noþer. c 1500 World & Child 532, I take recorde of this rewe My thedome is nere past. 1578 Lyte Dodoens 60 The floures..growing thicke togither in rewes by one side of the stem. 1601 [Br. W. Barlow] Defence 218 Registred in his rew of erroneous Doctors. a 1623 Ainsworth Annot. Ps. lxviii. 14 Betweene the two bankes or rewes, to wit, of stones made to hang pots and kettles on. 1664 Spelman's Gloss. s.v. Reia, A rew of muck or dung.
b. dial. A hedgerow.
OE. examples (hege-, wiþiȝrǽw) occur in Kemble Cod. Dipl. II. 54, III. 48, V. 275, etc.
1853 Cooper Sussex Gloss. (ed. 2), Rue, a row; a hedgerow. 1889 Nevill Old Cottages 115 (E.D.D.), The paving of this road is still very perfect in some of the wooded 'rews' at Coxland.
c. dial. (See quot.)
1886 Elworthy W. Som. Gloss., Rue, the row or ridge in which grass falls when cut with a scythe.
†3. A streak, stripe. Obs. rare.
c 1290 Beket 2177 in S. Eng. Leg. I. 169 A smal rewe þer was of blode, þat ouer his nose drouȝ. c 1400 Lanfranc's Cirurg. 304 [Water-leeches] þat han reed wombis & litil reed rewis in þe rigge medlid wiþ grene. 1611 Cotgr., Scrayer, to be full of rayes, rewes, or streakes. 1664 [see Rewey a.]
†4. A line in a book. Obs. rare.
1399 Langl. Rich. Redeles Prol. 54 Beholde þe book onys, And redeth on him redely rewis an hundrid.

†**Rew,** sb.² Sc. Obs. Also 6 reu. [a. F. rue.] A street; also, a village.
1375 Barbour Bruce xv. 71 Than wes the slauchter so felloune, That all the rewys ran of blude. c 1375 Sc. Leg. Saints ii. (Paulus) 575 Of þis towne pase til a rew, Quhare þat Iuda dwellis now. c 1425 Wyntoun Cron. v. ii. 350 Born of þe lande of Galile, In til þe rew of Bethsayda. c 1475 Rauf Coilȝear 351 Quhen thay Princis appeirit into Paris, Ilk Rew Ryallie with riches thame arrayis. 1533 Bellenden Livy i. xviii. (S.T.S.) I. 106 The place quhare þe deid was done is callit þe vnhappy and cursit rew. 1549 Compl. Scot. ix. 76 Aid ande ȝong ar slane on the reuis but mercy. 1590 in J. B. Pratt Buchan (1858) 101 The handbell passing throu the haill rewis.

†**Rew,** sb.³ Obs. rare⁻¹. [a. ON. ró: see Roove sb.] A form of burr for a rivet.
c 1440 York Myst. viii. 109 It sall be cleyngked..With nayles þat are both noble and newe...Take here a revette, and þere a rewe.

†**Rew,** a., ? obs. variant of Raw a. 6.
c 1440 Alph. Tales 211 Cristen men..fand þe child in þe ovyn, syttand open þe hate colis, right as [he] had syttyn opon fayr flowris; and hym as[k]d no rew sore.

†**Rew,** v. Obs. [Related to Rew sb.¹: cf. OE. ȝerǽwed striped, set in rows.] trans. To mark with lines or stripes. Hence †**Rewing** vbl. sb.
1553 in Feuillerat Revels Q. Eliz. (1908) 21, vi Turkye gounes of Crymesen rewed with golde threed. Ibid. 82, vi peces of laune rewed with counterfete cowlde. 1611 Cotgr., Poiler,..to rew; to dy or colour vnevenly. Ibid., Rayement,..a rewing. Rayer,..to rew, streake, or skore all ouer.

Rew, obs. form of Rue sb. and v.

Rew, to sift: see Ree v.

Rewa·ke (rī-), v. [Re- 5 a.] trans. and intr. To wake again. Hence **Rewa·king** ppl. a.
1593 Nashe Christ's T. Wks. (Grosart) IV. 53, I still assayed to rewake thee, & bring thee back againe to thy first image. a 1849 Mangan Poems (1903) 61 Then our silken-robed minstrels..Shall rewake the young slumbering blood of the land. 1885 Stevenson Prince Otto i. ii, 'I beg your pardon' cried the farmer, rewaking to hospitable thoughts. 1898 Daily News 25 Apr. 6/5 The subtle revelation of a rewaking love for the forgiving wife.

Rewa·ken, v. [Re- 5 a.] To waken again.
1638 Mayne Lucian (1664) 378 He thereby charmes up the Eyes of whom he lists, and rewakens them from sleep. 1850 Tennyson In Mem. xliii, And love will..at the spiritual prime Rewaken with the dawning soul. 1860 Ld. Lytton Lucile i. v. § 9. 15 Deem not it was with the thought Or your heart to regain, or the past to rewaken.

Rewall, obs. form of Rule.

Rewa·llow, v. [Re- 5 a.] To wallow again.
a 1700 Ken Hymnotheo Poet. Wks. 1721 III. 119 As clean-wash'd Swine return into their Sty, And in their stinking Mire re-wallowing lie.

†**Rewa·lt,** v. Obs. rare⁻¹. [app. f. Re- + Walt v.] trans. To overturn, throw down.
1587 Harrison England ii. xi. (1877) I. 225 Periurie is punished by the pillorie,..the rewalting of the trees growing vpon the grounds of the offendors.

Rewand, obs. Sc. f. Reaving ppl. a.

Reward (rɪwǭ·ɹd), sb.¹ Also 4-6 rewarde; 5 Sc. reuard, revard, ravard, 6 raward; 5-7 Sc. rewaird (6 reu-, rev-). [a. ONF. reward (rewart, reward, etc.), = OF. reguard, regard Regard sb.]
I. †1. Regard, consideration, heed. In phrases with have, take, or give. Obs.
a. 1338 R. Brunne Chron. (1810) 163 Þat I did dishonour, Sir, half it to no reward. 1390 Gower Conf. I. 291 For it sit every man to have Reward to love and to his miht. 1426 Lydg. in Pol. Poems (Rolls) II. 134 Havyng no reward..To suerte nor othe ymade toforne. a 1455 in Lett. Marg. Anjou & Bp. Beckington (Camden) 99 Summe of yoᶠ officers, having no rewarde therto, unadvisely toke..the horses of our said tenants.
b. c 1340 Hampole Pr. Consc. 1871 For þe dede til na man tas rewarde, Ne riche ne pover he spars. 1377 Pol. Poems (Rolls) I. 218 Therfore, gode sires, taketh reward Of ȝor douhti kyng that deyȝede in age. c 1400 Laud Troy Bk. 300 He schulde ay Holde him for a coward And neuere-more of him take reward. 1435 in Wars Eng. in France (Rolls) II. 577 Not havyng nor taking rewarde unto the clamour of the peple. c 1450 Lovelich Grail iv. 511 Owre lord..took Reward to his Good lyf.
c. c 1475 Rauf Coilȝear 630 Bot to his raifand word he gaue na rewaird.
2. In prepositional phrases:
†a. In reward of, in comparison with. Obs.
1340 Ayenb. 74 Vor al þet eure þoleden þe holy martires, ..ne ys bote a beþ ine chald weter to þe reward of þe fornayse. 1387 Trevisa Higden (Rolls) VII. 147 In reward of whiche flamme oure fire is but lewk. 1422 tr. Secreta Secret., Priv. Priv. 183 Therfor the Deuil may Iustifye hym in rewarde of extorcioner. 1460-70 Bk. Quintessence 2 As..[the] heuene of oure lord god, in reward of þe .iiij elementis, is yncorruptible & vnchaungeable.
†b. By reward of, by looking to. As to my reward, as seemed to me. Obs.
c 1380 Wyclif Wks. (1880) 21 Crist makeþ vs siker to dye for his lawe bi reward of þe blisse of heuene. 1426 Lydg. De Guil. Pilgr. 23435 And also (as to my reward,) hir hed was turned ek bakward.
†c. In reward of, at the discretion of. Obs.⁻¹
c 1400 Brut cxxvii, Y neuer him bitraede ne sloughe; and þerof y put me in rewarde of ȝour ccurt.
†d. At one's reward, in the place or places at table lying outward from one. Obs.
1551 Edw. VI Jrnl. (Roxb.) II. 363 She dined under the same cloth of estate, at my left hand. At her reward dined my cousen Fraunces and my cousen Magret. At mine sate the French embassadeur.
†3. a. Estimation, worth. Obs. rare.
c 1338 R. Brunne Chron. (1810) 101 He sent to kyng R[ichard] a stede for curteisie, On of þe best reward, þat was in paemie. 13.. E. E. Allit. P. A. 604 For þer is vch mon payed inliche, Wheþer lyttel oþer much be hys rewarde.
†b. dial. Colour, complexion. Obs.
1674 Ray N. C. Words 38 A Reward or good Reward; a good colour or ruddiness in the face, used about Sheffield.
II. 4. A return or recompense made to, or received by, a person for some (†favour,) service or merit, or for hardship endured.
13.. E. E. Allit. P. B. 208 Of alle þyse aþel aungeles [he was] attled þe fayrest, & he vnkyndely as a karle kydde a reward. c 1375 Sc. Leg. Saints xi. (Simon & Jude) 212 Þat he mycht gaynand reward mak to þame þat suthfaste fundyn war. c 1400 Destr. Troy 1579 For a riche reward of my ranke wille. All the soueranis by assent assignet me hir. 1422 tr. Secreta Secret., Priv. Priv. 130 Oone of his knyghtis for his Service askyd of hym a reward. c 1460 Fortescue Abs. & Lim. Mon. (1885) 113 Yf the kynge be pouere, he shall of necessite make his giftes and rewardes by asseignementes. 1534 More Treat. Passion Wks. 1304/1 Then was Judas rewarde the value of tenne shillings of our English money. 1553 Eden Treat. Newe Ind. (Arb.) 3 Wherin the diligent reader may see the good successe and rewarde of noble and honeste enterpryses. 1617 Moryson Itin. i. 244 My brother and my selfe treated with him by the way, to giue him a reward that he would dismisse vs. 1655 Fuller Ch. Hist. vii. 397 The King conferred the Manour of Exetland..on their Corporation, in reward of their loyalty and valour. 1710 Steele Tatler No. 124 ⁋ 6 He scorned to take a Reward for doing what in Justice he ought to do. 1758 Johnson Idler No. 6 ⁋ 6 She could at leisure gather her reward. 1832 Irving Alhambra I. 255 'Behold', cried the astrologer, 'my promised reward'. 1849 Macaulay Hist. Eng. iii. I. 326 The clergy had also lost the ascendency which is the natural reward of superior mental cultivation. 1876 Voyle & Stevenson Milit. Dict. 342/1 The most recent reward for military merit is the Victoria Cross.
attrib. 1820 F. Westley's Catal. 1 May, The following Catalogue of Reward-books.
†b. Hunting. Some part of the animal which has been caught and killed, given to the hounds on the spot. Also similarly in Hawking. Obs.
c 1410 Master of Game (MS. Digby 182) xxxiii, One shulde be rydy behynde to pulle away þe skynne, and let þe houndes come to þe rewarde. 1486 Bk. St. Albans eiij, Thay shall haue the bowyllis boyle with the brede Cast vppon the grownde ther the boore was slayne, And that is calde a Rewarde. 1575 Turberv. Venerie 132 Let him stand from the rewarde and suffer the Houndes to eate it. 1614 Latham Falconry i. iv. 15 If the pleasure which shee takes in her reward, be the only cause that moues a hawke to come vnto the man [etc.]. 1688 Holme Armoury ii. 188/1 Quarry, or Reward, is a gift or reward given the Hounds, being some part of the thing hunted.
†c. Remuneration (regular or extra). Obs.
1428 in Heath Grocers' Comp. (1869) 6 Mason's weages with maistre mason's rewarde... Carpenter's weages with the maistre carpenter's reward. c 1440 Promp. Parv. 431/2 Rewarde, for syngarys, and mynstrallys, siparium. 1466 Paston Lett. II. 267 To the baker for cccx. eggs, xixd. To him for hys reward, iiis. iiiid. c 1642 Twyne in Wood's Life (O.H.S.) I. 64 They were promised 5s. by the moneth for every man as a reward besides his daily paye. 1776 Adam Smith W. N. v. i. iii. (1904) II. 420 A little school, where children may be taught for a reward so moderate, that even a common labourer may afford it.
d. A sum of money offered for the capture or detection of a malefactor, discovery of a missing person, recovery of lost or stolen property, etc.
1593 Shaks. 3 Hen. VI, v. v. 10 Is Proclamation made, That who finds Edward, Shall haue a high Reward, and he his Life? 1702 Procl. in McCarthy Reign Q. Anne (1905) 60 Whoever shall discover the said Daniel De Foe..so as he may be apprehended shall have a reward of fifty pounds. 1722 De Foe Col. Jack ii, He should publish a reward for the encouragement of those that have them to bring them again. 1820 Shelley Hymn Merc. xliv, If you should promise an immense reward, I could not tell more than you now have heard. 1865 Dickens Mut. Fr. iv. xii, Julius Handford.., for intelligence of whom a reward had been publicly offered. 1907 Miss Braddon Her Convict v, I don't think there was any reward offered. Scotland Yard is against rewards.
5. Recompense or retribution for evil-doing; requital, punishment.
1388 Wyclif Isaiah lxvi. 6 The vois of the Lord ȝeldynge a reward to hise enemyes. c 1400 Brut cxcviii. 221 A, sire traitoure!..now shal ȝe haue þe reward þat longetyme ȝe haue disserued. c 1410 Sir Cleges 437 He sowght after the prowghd styward. For to yeve hym hys reward, Because he greved hym sore. 1535 Coverdale Ps. x[i]. 6 Vpon the vngodly he shal rayne..storme and tempest: this rewarde shal they haue to drynke. 1590 Spenser F. Q. iii. v. 14 He from daunger was releast,..Yet not escaped from the dew reward Of his bad deedes. 1610 Healey St. Aug. Citie of God i. xiv. (1620) 15 The just reward that our first parents received for their sinne. 1697 Dryden Virg. Georg. iv. 655 Thy great Misdeeds have met a due Reward. 1819 Shelley Cenci i. i. 73 That which the vassal threatened to divulge Whose throat is choked with dust for his reward. 1874 Stubbs Const. Hist. I. ii. 31 Hanging was the reward of treason and desertion.
†6. An extra supply or allowance of food; an extra dish. Obs.
c 1440 Promp. Parv. 431/2 Rewarde, at mete, whan fode fallythe [v.r. faylyth] of the seruyce. Ibid., Rewarde, yn þe ende of mete, of frutys, impomentum. c 1450 Bk. Curtasye iii. 423 Whenne brede faylys at borde aboute, The marshall gares sett withouten doute More brede, that calde is a rewarde. 1503 in Ann. Reg. (1758) 267/1 At dyner, a pese of beyf, a stroke of roste, and a rewarde at our said kechyn. 1530 Palsgr. 262/2 Rewarde of meate, entremetz.

†**Reward,** sb.² Obs. rare. = Rearward sb.
c 1440 Partonope 980 He sendith to his rewarde tho That they shull make hem redy And come hym to. 1515 Scottish Field 4.. in Chetham Misc. (1856) II. Thus the Reward in aray rayked ever after.

Reward (rɪwǭ·ɹd), v. Also 6 Sc. rewaird. [a. ONF. rewarder, = OF. reguarder, regarder to Regard.]
I. †1. trans. To regard, heed, consider; to look at or observe. Obs.
c 1315 Shoreham iii. 237 Þye senne schal ᵹe be, ȝyf þou rewardest þyne eldrynges nauȝt. 1338 R. Brunne Chron. (1810) 294 A child of þat land..Edward sauh him stand, þe Flemmynges to reward. 1377 Langl. P. Pl. B. xiv. 145 If ye riche haue reuthe and rewarde wel þe pore. 1422 tr. Secreta Secret., Priv. Priv. 217 Rewarde this figure and telle ve the qualyteis..of Suche a man as this figure Presentyth. c 1475 Partenay 2367 Hit you behouith rewarde and behold Ho shal this gouerne and rule this contre.
†2. To agree; to determine or decide. Obs.
c 1380 Sir Ferumb. 312 Hit ys rewardet oure two be twyne þat Oliuer schal wende & take þe batayl wiþ þe sond Sarsyne. Ibid. 3463 'Ȝus,' quaþ Roland, 'y wil it do, If ȝe rewardieþ it shel be so'. c 1440 Alph. Tales 359 And þan þe [the judge] rewardid at þe clew sulde be won of, & sho at said sothe of þe bothom sulde hafe it.
†3. intr. To look; to give heed. Obs. rare.
1382 Wyclif Job xxxix. 24 Feruent and gnastende he soupeth the erthe; and rewarde he not to the trumpe sounende trumping. 1422 tr. Secreta Secret., Priv. Priv. 174 He rewardid aboute, and Sawe an olde knyght quakynge for colde. c 1430 Bk. Hawkyng in Relq. Antiq. I. 296 If there be eny hawke, and she rewarde gladly to her game, ye shull say cast your hawke thereto.
II. †4. trans. To assign or give (to one) as a reward or recompense. Obs.
c 1320 Cast. Love (Halliwell) 1662 Receyvyth the blysfull joy anon That to ȝow byth rewarded withoutyn endenge. c 1370 Stacions Rome (Vernon MS.) 100 Pope Vrban þat holy syre So rewardede men beore huyre. 1393 Test. Ebor.

(Surtees) I. 185 It es my will that ye reward sumwhat to ilkane of my seruandes. 1426 Audelay Poems 13 He that is untreu to his lorde..The law wyl hym reward deth to his mede. 1475 Bk. Noblesse (Roxb.) 14 For whois raunson..king Edwarde rewarded the Prince xx. Ml. li. sterlinges. 1535 Coverdale Ps. xxxvii[i]. 20 They that rewarde me euell for good, speake euell of me. 1611 Bible 1 Sam. xxiv. 17 Thou hast rewarded mee good, whereas I haue rewarded thee euill. c1650 Metrical Ps. Scotch Ch. vii. 4 If I rewarded ill to him.

5. To repay, requite, recompense (one) for some service, merit, etc.

c1350 Will. Palerne 3840 What man vpon molde so may him me bring, I schal riuedli him rewarde. 1390 Gower Conf. II. 133 Bot he rewarde him for his dede, So as he mihte of his godhiede. c1400 Maundev. (Roxb.) xi. 49 Scho was wele rewarded, as scho was wele worthy. c1460 Fortescue Abs. & Lim. Mon. xi. (1885) 136 For lakke off money, the kyng than rewarded þam with lande. 1484 Caxton Fables of Æsop II. xix, I..praye the that thow wylt reward me of the grete seruyse whiche I haue done to the. a1533 Ld. Berners Huon lix. 204, I abandonyd to you all that I had; yll it hath ben employed without ye rewarde me better. 1588 Shaks. L. L. L. III. i. 134 There is remuneration, for the best ward of mine honours is rewarding my dependants. 1651 Hobbes Leviath. II. xxx. 183 To Reward those that aspire to greatnesse. 1685 Baxter Paraphr. N. T. Matt. xvi. 27 Then I will reward those that were faithful to me. 1744 Harris Three Treat. I. (1765) 3, I shall think myself well rewarded in the Labour of reciting. 1781 Cowper Truth 218 He..Consults all day your int'rest and your ease, Richly rewarded if he can but please. 1849 Macaulay Hist. Eng. vi. II. 83 Sir Edward publicly apostatized, and was rewarded with the command of a regiment of foot. 1872 Jenkinson Guide Eng. Lakes (1879) 224 The toil is forgotten when the highest point is attained, for a magnificent view rewards the traveller.

†**b.** Hunting and Hawking. (Cf. Reward sb.[1] 4 b.) Obs.

13.. Gaw. & Gr. Knt. 1610 With bred blent þer-with his braches [he] rewardez. c1410 Master of Game (MS. Digby 182) Prol., Whann the hert is spaied and dede he vndothe hym and maketh his kirre and enquirreth or rewardeþ his houndes. 1486 Bk. St. Albans b iiij, If she will forsake the fowle that she plumyth on,..then..rewarde yowre hawke with the Brayne and the necke. 1575 Turberv. Venerie 134 Call hir to your fist wyth meat.., and when she commeth rewarde hir well. Ibid. 174 How you shall rewarde your houndes when they haue killed an Hare. 1614 Latham Falconry I. v. 18 So reward her with cleanlie feed.

†**c.** To give (one) something out of a legacy.

1482 Paston Lett. III. 288, I wull that iche of myn other godchilder be rewarded by th' avyse of John Paston, my sone. 16.. in Mills Ordin. Isle of Man (1821) 47 Then the Ordinary shall make..his next of Kindred..to be lawful Executors: and the base begotten to be rewarded of Charity.

†**d.** To serve with food. Obs. rare.

c1440 in Househ. Ord. (1790) *38 When my lady is served of the seconde course,..the chamber is rewarded and the hall with breade and ale, after the discretyon of the usher.

6. †**a.** To make up for (a deficiency). Obs.[-1]

1398 Trevisa Barth. De P. R. xv. c. (Bodl. MS.), What lakkeþ in þis londe in quantite of space is rewarded & recouered in godenes of grounde.

b. To requite, to make return for (a service, merit, exertion, etc.).

a1533 Ld. Berners Huon lvi. 189 The grete seruyce..shall be euen ryght well rewarded. 1594 Carew Huarte's Exam. Wits xiii (1596) 201 Rome..did..reward..their temperancy in abstaining from wine. a1618 Raleigh Rem. (1664) 110 A crop of cares rewarding your labour with remorse. 1697 Dryden Virg. Georg. I. 72 That Crop rewards the greedy Peasant's Pains. 1748 Foote Knights Prol., The pious boy, his father's toil rewarding, For thousands throws a main at Covent-Garden! 1781 Cowper Hope 761 Still happier, if he till a thankful soil, And fruit reward his honourable toil. 1836 Random Recoll. Ho. Lords ix. 186 The discovery, when made, would not at all reward the labour expended in the search. 1862 Sir B. Brodie Psychol. Inq. II. iv. 113 The most upright and virtuous intentions are not always rewarded by happiness in proportion.

7. a. To requite or repay (one) for evil-doing; to punish, chastise.

1484 Caxton Fables of Æsop v. iv, Who so euer rendreth euylle for good he shalle therof iustly be rewarded. 1519 Fabric Rolls York Minster (Surtees) 269 One of them..sawe there were no dogges nor bryborse in ye Churche, bot tha wolde rewarde thame. 1560 Daus tr. Sleidane's Comm. 132 b, They were rewarded with the losse of their heades. 1611 Bible 2 Sam. iii. 39 The Lord shall reward the doer of euill, according to his wickednesse. 1671 Milton Samson 413 Servil mind Rewarded well with servil punishment!

b. To pay back (injury or wrong) to one; to visit upon one. rare.

c1420 Anturs of Arth. 525, I shal rewarde þe þi route, if I cone rede righte. 1535 Coverdale Judges ix. 57 All the euell of the men of Sichem, dyd God rewarde them vpon their heade. 1560 Bible (Genev.) Hosea iv. 9, I wil visit their wayes vpon them, and rewarde them their dedes.

8. absol. To make recompence.

1377 Langl. P. Pl. B III. 316 But after þe dede þat is don One dome shal rewarde. 1613 Chapman Mask Inns of Court, To employ with countenance, and encouragement, but reward with austerity and disgrace.

†**Rewa·rd,** pa. pple. Obs. [Irreg. from prec.] Rewarded.

1567 Pikeryng Horestes 491 (Brandl), Soffer him not for to depart, tyll well reward he be. 1574 R. Robinson Rewarde of Wickednesse S j b, All these I knewe and many moe,..That for their trauels were rewarde.

Rewardable (rǐwǭ·ɹdăb'l), a. [f. Reward v. + -able.] Capable of being rewarded; worthy or deserving of reward.

1534 More Comf. agst. Trib. I. Wks. 1153/2 We graunt..that no good woorke of man is rewardable in heauen of his own nature. 1594 Hooker Eccl. Pol. I. ix. § 1 Whether they bee in their own nature rewardable or punishable. 1621 Bp. Mountagu Diatribæ 71 Neither is Vertue rewardable, nor Vice punishable, except it be done..with intent of the will. 1680 Baxter Cath. Commun. (1684) 7 He is rewardable as he suffereth for fearing to disobey God. 1709 Stanhope Paraphr. IV. 108 The Actions were Voluntary and Rewardable in St. Paul. 1760 Wesley Jrnl. 20 Dec., Till you know the difference between meritorious and rewardable. 1829 I. Taylor Enthus. vii. (1867) 144 Christian philanthropy..is vicarious; obligatory; rewardable. 1868 Bain Ment. & Mor. Sci. (1875) 615 Virtue is in itself rewardable; vice is of essential demerit.

Rewa·rdableness. [f. prec. + -ness.] Capability of being rewarded; the state of being worthy of reward.

1654 J. Owen Doctr. Saints' Perseverance Wks. 1851 XI. 591 It will take away all rewardableness from their actings. 1705 Goodman Wint. Even. Conf. II. 159 What can be the Praise or Rewardableness of doing that which a Man cannot chuse but do? 1772 J. Fletcher Logica Genev. 32 She pleads for the rewardableness, which is all we understand by the merit of works. 1850 Robertson Serm. Ser. IV. vii. (1863) I. 43 The doctrine of the rewardableness of work.

Rewa·rdably, adv. [f. as prec. + -ly[2].] 'In a rewardable manner' (Webster, 1847).

Rewa·rded, ppl. a. [f. Reward v. + -ed[1].] Requited; recompensed.

1623 Wodroephe Marrow Fr. Tongue 318/2 From hired Preests, from rewarded Barbers, the Lord deliuer vs. 1728 Eliza Heywood tr. Mme. de Gomez's Belle A. (1732) II. 67 The Sweets of that Repose, which Virtue and rewarded Tenderness can never fail to afford.

Hence **Rewa·rdedly** adv.

1869 Browning Ring & Bk. IX. 741 Nay, and what if he gazed rewardedly On the pale beauty prisoned in embrace.

Rewarder (rǐwǭ·ɹdəɹ). [f. Reward v. + -er[1].] One who rewards or requites.

a1340 Hampole Psalter iv. 6 God is rewardere of goed and ill. 1382 Wyclif Hebr. xi. 6 He is rewarder of men ynsekinge him. c1450 tr. De Imitatione III. iii. 67, I am rewarder of all gode men. 1526 Pilgr. Perf. (W. de W. 1531) 187 That he is the rewarder of all good dedes. 1594 Shaks. Rich. III, I. iii. 124 A liberall rewarder of his Friends. 1680 Fletcher Chances III. ii, Whose hard heart never Slew those rewarders. 1670 G. H. Hist. Cardinals II. III. 182 He is..no great rewarder of his Servants. c1705 De Foe in Lett. Lit. Men (Camden) 324 The unknown rewarders of my mean performances. 1772 Priestley Inst. Relig. (1782) I. 106 God is..the most munificent rewarder of real worth. 1865 M. Arnold Ess. Crit. ix. (1875) 373 The belief that God is..a rewarder of them that seek him.

Rewa·rdful, a. [f. Reward sb. + -ful.] Yielding or producing reward.

1595 Spenser Col. Clout 187 Whose grace was great, and bounty most rewardfull. 1846 D. Jerrold Chron. Clovernook Wks. 1864 IV. 381 Blessings rewardful of their piety. 1903 Ainger Crabbe xi. 198 What is best and most rewardful in the study of Crabbe.

Hence **Rewa·rdfulness.**

1873 Scribner's Mag. VI. 30 Of the beauty, the rewardfulness of the place, I cannot trust myself to speak.

Rewa·rding, vbl. sb. [f. Reward v. + -ing[1].] The action of the verb, in various senses.

a1340 Hampole Psalter lviii. 18 In rewardinge of endles bliss. 1390 Gower Conf. I. 333 Thanne I scholde in such a wise In rewardinge of my servise Be ded. c1410 Master of Game (MS. Digby 182) xxxiii, Also if þe lorde be þere alle þinge shulde be doo of þe abay and rewardynge, as before is seyde. 1422 tr. Secreta Secret., Priv. Priv. 230 Tho that in lokynge or in rewardynge ficchyth hare syght and hit holdyth stabill. 1561 T. Norton Calvin's Inst. III. 262 The rewardinges which ar sayd to be prepared for the keper of the law. 1582 Stanyhurst Æneis IV. (Arb.) 95 Wyl ye not haue children, nor sweete Venus happye rewarding's? 1650 J. Hall in Harrington's Oceana (1700) 10 Their generous and indiscrete rewarding of Virtue.

Rewa·rding, ppl. a. [-ing[2].] That rewards.

1697 Collier Ess. Mor. Subj. II. (1703) 131 Hope..is sometimes so sprightly and rewarding a quality. a1708 Beveridge Thes. Theol. (1710) I. 40 This is what we call His distributing or rewarding justice. 1871 Meredith H. Richmond xxxvi, My grandfather's praise of her she received with a rewarding look back of kindness.

Hence **Rewa·rdingly** adv.

1850 Browning Christmas Eve xviii, Which fact pays the damage done rewardingly.

Rewa·rdless, a. [f. Reward sb. + -less.] Devoid of reward; unrewarded.

a1470 Tiptoft Tulle on Friendship (Caxton, 1481) b vij, For Vertue is neyther uncurtoyse ne rewardless, ne prounde. 1552 Huloet, Rewardles, as for thankes onely, or vnhiered. 1687 Shadwell tr. Juvenal x. 213 Virtue's less thirsted for than Fame, for who, Her, for her self, Rewardless will pursue? 1827 Pollok Course T. I, Yet haply not rewardless we shall trace The dark disastrous years of finished Time. 1886 Ruskin Præterita I. xii. 424 Wasted affection, and rewardless semi-virtue.

†**Rewa·rdon.** Obs. rare. [a. ONF. rewardon, rewerdon, var. of reguerdon.] = Reguerdon sb.

1338 R. Brunne Chron. (1810) 96 For riche rewardons to Roberd [they] gan loute. Ibid. 143 Inglis & Normant, knyghtes for rewardoun, With Richard ere in conant.

Rewa·rdress. rare[-1]. [f. Rewarder + -ess.] A female rewarder.

1613-16 Browne Brit. Past. (1625) To Rdr., The great Rewardresse of a Poet's pen, Fame.

Re-wa·rehouse (rī-), v. [Re- 5 a.] To warehouse again. Hence **Re-wa·rehousing** vbl. sb.

1833 McCulloch Dict. Commerce (1834) 1221 Goods may be removed to any Ports to be rewarehoused. Ibid., Bond to rewarehouse. 1863 Olver Shilling Tariff 40 On the re-warehousing after the expiration of five years [etc.].

‖**Rewa-rewa** (rī·wa-rī·wa). [Maori, f. the verb rewa to float.] A tall handsome flowering tree common in New Zealand, yielding a light easily-split wood which is used for furniture. Also called honeysuckle.

1843 C. Holtzapffel Turning I. 41 The Rewa-rewa (Knightia excelsa), from New Zealand. 1878 Trans. New Zealand Inst. XI. 73 Dry rewarewa wood being used for the charring. 1880 Ibid. XIII. 53 The boy went into the forest.., and brought back with him a seed-pod of the rewarewa tree.

Rewa·rm (rī-), v. [Re- 5 a.] To warm again.

1608 Sylvester Du Bartas II. iv. III. Schisme 490 His spirits (rewarm'd) with-in his artir's tremble. 1673 Harvey Anat. Exerc. II. 120 Unless..new, warm and spirituous blood flowing in do foment and re-warm the parts. 1861 Olmsted Journ. & Expl. in Cotton Kingd. I. 160 Coffee evidently made the day before, and half re-warmed.

Rewa·sh (rī-), v. [Re- 5 a.] To wash again.

1725 Bradley Fam. Dict. s.v. Tin, After this they rewash it, as before, and then dry it a little. 1805 Med. Jrnl. XIV. 449 It will be adviseable to rewash with milk afterward. 1874 Raymond Mines & Mining 21 [As much] as would justify their being rewashed for these substances alone.

Rewate, Sc. variant of Realty[1] Obs.

Rewa·ter (rī-), v. [Re- 5 a.] To water again; to place in water again.

1612 J. Davies Muse's Sacrifice Wks. (Grosart) II. 64/2 The Vrchin of the Sea, in pieces rent, Re-water'd, ioynes, and liues incontenent!

Rewbarb(e, obs. ff. Rhubarb. **Rewbarbative:** see Rubarbative. **Rewde,** obs. f. Rude a.

†**Rew·den,** a. Obs. dial. 'Made of Rood or Reed, that is of combed Straw' (Exmoor Gloss.).

a1746 Exmoor Scolding (1879) 34 Why dest thee, than, tell me 'Isterday o' losing my Rewden Hat in the Rex-bush.

Rewðe, rewðful, obs. ff. Ruth, -ful. **Rewe,** obs. f. Reave v. and Rew, row; obs. pa. t. of Row v.; obs. f. Rue sb. and v.

Reweave (rī-), v. [Re- 5 a.] To weave again. In quots. fig.

c1700 Congreve Ovid's Met. x, Let me again Eurydice receive, Let Fate her quick-spun thread of life re-weave. 1860 Ld. Lytton Lucile II. I. § 19. 1 'So!' he thought, 'they meet thus: and reweave the old charm!' 1882 Miss Woolson Anne 349 [It] will rend this filmy fabric of imagination immediately, never to be rewoven again.

refl. 1877 Ruskin Laws of Fesole vi. (1907) 84 It is a web which re-weaves itself when you tear it.

Rewe·d (rī-), v. [Re- 5 a.] To wed anew.

1839-48 Bailey Festus 49 Industry, and commerce,..Rewedding those the Deluge once divorced.

Reweful, obs. form of Rueful.

Re-weigh (rī-), v. [Re- 5 a.]

1. trans. To weigh again. Also absol.

1812 J. Smyth Pract. Customs (1821) 400 Order for re-weighing Pimento, to be taken from the Pile. 1849 Ansted Gold-seeker's Man. 74 Weigh it first in air...Immerse it and re-weigh it in water. 1892 E. Reeves Homeward Bound 308 We re-weighing and opening in presence of English Post Office clerk.

2. intr. To amount to (so much) on being weighed again.

1812 J. Smyth Pract. Customs (1821) 405 Ten boxes of foreign clayed Sugar,..weighing, on delivery there, thirty-four hundred-weight and fifteen pounds, and re-weighing here thirty-four hundred-weight one quarter.

Hence **Re-weighing** vbl. sb. Also **Re-weigher.**

1812 J. Smyth Pract. Customs (1821) 361 The Warehouse-keeper..subscribes the re-weighing Note. 1820 Ibid. (1821) 360 The necessary order for the re-weighing of three Casks of Currants. 1878 Olver & Midlane Imperial Tariff (1879) 82 The date of re-weighing or re-examination. 1883 Cable Dr. Sevier i. Cotton factors, buyers, brokers, weighers, re-weighers, etc.

Re-weight. [Re- 5 a.] Weighing again; also, the weight ascertained by re-weighing.

1812 J. Smyth Pract. Customs (1821) 399 Increase by re-weight. Ibid. Reweight of the Bags. 1841 Ellis Laws & Reg. Customs II. 310 If any deficiency be found between such re-weights and the original landing weights, the duty is to be paid on such deficiency.

Rewel, obs. f. Rowel, Rule. **Rewel-bone:** see Ruel-bone. **Rewele(r,** obs. ff. Rule(r. **Rewelich, -ly,** obs. ff. Ruly.

Rewe·nd (rī-), v. rare[-1]. [Re- 5 a.] To wend or turn again.

1616 J. Lane Contn. Sqr.'s T. IV. 344 Wheare in hee trottes, vnto the pathes farr ende, but theare, on thinder heeles turnes to rewend.

Rewene-cheese: see Rowen. **Rewengeance,** var. Revengeance Obs. **Rewer(e,** obs. ff. Ruer. **Rewese,** obs. f. Ravish v.

†**Rewet.** Obs. rare[-0]. [a. F. rouet, f. roue wheel.] (See quot.)

1706 Phillips (ed. Kersey), Rewet, the Lock of a Harquebuss, or other Gun. [Hence in Bailey and later Dicts.]

Re-we·t (rī-), v. [Re- 5 a.] trans. To make wet again.

1844 H. Stephens Bk. Farm I. 241 The wet bulb..will last a considerable time wet, and be rewetted when required. 1889 Westgarth Austral. Progress 50 This gum tasted abominably, if you licked it for re-wetting.

Rewet, variant of Ruet Obs.

Reweth, Rewepe, obs. ff. Ruth.

†**Rew·ey,** a. Obs. rare. [app. f. Rew sb.[1] 3 + -y.] (See quots.)

1601 Act 43 Eliz. c. 10. § 1, The same Clothes being put

in Water, are found to shrink, be rewey, pursey, squally, cockling, bandy, light, and notably faulty. 1684 Manley Cowell's Interpr., Rewey.., it is as much as unevenly wrought, and full of Rewes.

Rewful(li, etc., obs. forms of Rueful(ly.

†**Rewhe·lp,** v. Obs. rare[-1]. [Re- 5 a.] trans. To bring forth (young) again.

1591 Sylvester Du Bartas I. vi. 318, I fear the Beast..which thousand times (almost) Re-whelps her whelps.

Rewhi·rl (rī-), v. [Re- 5 a.] To whirl again.

1799 W. Taylor in Monthly Mag. VII. 140 Now at the witches sabbath may attend Long-absent I—rewhirl the airy reel.

Rewhi·sper (rī-), v. [Re- 5 a.] To whisper again or in reply.

1782 Miss Burney Cecilia IX. vi, 'Surely he will not come in here?' re-whispered Cecilia. 1894 Bliss Carman Low Tide, Afoot, And the Mother there once more Will re-whisper her dark word.

Rewhi·ten (rī-), v. [Re- 5 a.] To whiten or whitewash again.

1790 J. Williams Shrove Tuesday in A Cabinet, etc. (1794) 27 Sooner may ye re-whiten the chaste Snow..Than wipe the odium from a nymph beguil'd. 1854 tr. Mary. de Custine's Russia 158 These men..seem to support themselves like insects against the edifices which they rewhiten.

Rewile, -ill, obs. Sc. forms of Rule sb.

Re-wi·n (rī-), v. [Re- 5 a.] trans. To win back or again; to recover.

1608 Sylvester Du Bartas II. iv. Vocation 339 Either of which a hundred times a minute Doth lose a Souldier, and as oft re-win it. 1611 Speed Hist. Gt. Brit. IX. xxiv. § 54 Your Father, noble King, rewan it to his Crowne. a1814 Apostate II. iv. in New Brit. Theatre III. 319, I am not worthy of fair Mora's love, Reclaim her yet, re-win her for thyself. 1888 Pall Mall G. 20 Jan. 2/3 Desert your comrades in their great battle to re-win the lands of their fathers.

Rewin, obs. Sc. form of Riven, Ruin.

Re-wi·nd (rī-), v. [Re- 5 a.] To wind again.

trans. 1717 Eusden Claudian II. (R.), Clotho shall rewind the clue. 1839 Ure Dict. Arts 1115 The throwster re-winds and re-twists it upon the spinning mill. 1868 Rep. U.S. Commissioner Agric. (1869) 289 Trams and organzines are then rewound upon bobbins.

intr. 1862 Lytton Str. Story lv. II. 115 The path was rugged..and painfully rewinding up the ascent.

Hence **Re-wi·nding** vbl. sb.

1839 Ure Dict. Arts 1115 The cost of..re-winding and re-twisting, after it [raw Novi silk] has been dyed, [is] about 5s. 1881 C. A. Young Sun 13 A process precisely equivalent to the daily rewinding of the clock.

Re-winder (rīwəi·ndəɹ). [Re- 5 a.] One who or that which winds again.

1842 Encycl. Brit. (ed. 7) VI. 774 We shall..describe a few [scapements] of a different class, which are called remontoirs or rewinders. 1881 Census Instruct. (1885) 67 Winder, Filler of Shute, Re-winder, Picker-up.

Rewine, obs. Sc. pa. pple. of Rive v.; obs. f. Ruin. **Rewinus,** obs. f. Ruinous a. **Rewis,** obs. f. Ravish v.

†**Rew·ish,** a. Obs.[-0] [ad. Du. reeuwsch.]

1617 Minsheu Ductor, Rewish, vehement in copulation, spoken of the Pigeon. [Hence in Blount and Phillips.]

Re-wi·sh (rī-), v. [Re- 5 a.] To wish again.

1635 Quarles Embl. v. xi. 280 These in few hours Re-wish what late their wishes did obtain.

Rewl(e, obs. forms of Rule. **Rewlar, -er,** obs. ff. Ruler. **Rew(le)less,** obs. ff. Ruleless. **Rewli(che, -lik, -ly(che,** variants of Ruly a. **Rewll(e,** obs. ff. Rule. **Rewmatick(e,** obs. ff. Rheumatic. **Rewm(e,** obs. ff. Realm, Rheum.

†**Rewness.** Obs. [See Rue sb. and v.] Repentance; sorrow; pity, compassion.

c950 Lindisf. Gosp. Mark i. 4 Iohannes..bodade fulwiht hreowinises on forȝefnisse synna. a1225 Ancr. R. 144 note, Þe muchele reounesse of þe lure of þe muchele blisse of heouene. c1300 Havelok 502 He þe knaue nouth ne slou, But for rewnesse him wit-drow. Ibid. 2227 He hauede reunesse of þe knaue.

Rewo·rd (rī-), v. [Re- 5 a.]

1. trans. To put into words again; to repeat.

1602 Shaks. Ham. III. iv. 143 Bring me to the Test And I the matter will re-word. 1874 Tennyson in Mem. (1897) II. 159, I bolted out a long metaphysical term which he could not re-word to me. 1885 Yeats Song of Happy Shepherd Poems (1899) 186 They thy comforters will be, Rewording in melodious guile Thy fretful words.

2. To re-echo. Also **Rewo·rding** ppl. a.

1597 Shaks. Lover's Compl. 1 Off a hill whose concaue wombe reworded A plaintfull story from a sistring vale. a1650 T. May Life Satyrical Puppy (1657) 42 Farwell the lowde Trumpet with whose voyce rewording Ecchoes scolde.

3. To put into different words.

1892 Proc. Amer. Mission Assoc. 73 The reports..lead me to believe that my subject needs if not to be re-worded, to be defined. 1894 Daily News 1 Sept. 6/2 Titles are reworded, re-arranged, perhaps curtailed, or expanded.

Hence **Rewo·rding** vbl. sb.

1849 Sears Regeneration III. i. (1859) 126 The wording and rewording of liturgies is not prayer.

Rewo·rk (rī-), v. [Re- 5 a.] To work again.

1842 Civil Eng. & Arch. Jrnl. V. 392/2 The whole of the walls, arches, and aisle vaults have been reworked. 1855 J. R. Leifchild Cornwall Mines 254 Thus a great and profitable tin mine seemed to wear out by degrees. It may, however, be successfully re-worked. 1891 Law Times Rep. LXV. 562/2 Butterine.., if intended for exportation to London,..was reworked at the Drummoyne factory.

Hence **Rewo·rking** vbl. sb.

1873 Whitney Oriental & Ling. Stud. 267 There has been no thorough reworking of those parts of the lecture. 1891 Law Times Rep. LXV. 562/2 Of these ninety-five kegs three were lost in the reworking.

Rewo·rship (rī-), v. [Re- 5 a.] trans. † To restore to former honour and dignity.

1562 Legh Armory 122 b, These..may be reworshipped agayne, with somethynge of mettall sette vpon them.

Rewou·nd (rī-), v. [Re- 5 a.] To wound again. Hence **Rewou·nded** ppl. a.

1621 Quarles Argalus & P. I. Wks. (Grosart) III. 244/1 Demagoras, whose rewounded heart Had newly felt the unexpected smart. 1817 Hogg Dram. Tales I. 250 Do not Re-wound that kind and virtuous heart.

Rewri·te (rī-), v. [Re- 5 a.]

1. trans. To write back; to reply in writing.

1567 Drant Horace, Ep. vi. D ij, Straighte waye when he had searched his house rewrytte agayne this mome, That [etc.].

2. To write again, esp. in a different form.

1730 Young Ep. to Pope II. 137 Write and re-write, blot out and write again. 1806 Southey Let. in Life (1850) III. 8, I acknowledge no fault..., except the struggle of the women.., which is clumsily done, and must be rewritten. 1845 M. Pattison Ess. (1889) I. 2 Every generation..demands that the history of its forefathers be rewritten from its own point of view. 1880 Swinburne Stud. Shaks. 103 The two tragedies..were thoroughly recast and rewritten from end to end.

Hence **Rewri·ting** vbl. sb.

1863 Sat. Rev. 4 Apr. 446 There is nothing in them that cannot easily be remedied by a little re-writing. 1892 Athenæum 9 Apr. 468/3 'The Foreign Policy of Pitt'..is hardly a rewriting of history.

Rewri·tten, ppl. a. [Cf. prec.] Written over again.

1828-32 in Webster. 1875 Poste Gaius Pref. p. v, The palimpsest or rewritten manuscript originally contained 129 folios. 1882 Athenæum 7 Jan. 27/3 Mr. Byron's rewritten burlesque of 'Pluto' follows.

Rewth(e, etc., obs. ff. Ruth. **Rewth(e)full, -volle,** obs. ff. Ruthful a. **Rewtheles(se,** obs. ff. Ruthless a. **Rewve,** obs. f. Rue. **Rewvine,** obs. Sc. f. Ruin sb. **Rewych,** obs. f. Ravish v. **Rewyll(e,** obs. ff. Rule. **Rewyn,** obs. f. Raven sb.[1], Riven. **Rewyne, Rewynus,** obs. ff. Ruin, Ruinous. **Rewys,** obs. f. Ravish v.

†**Rex**[1]. Obs. Also 7 recks. [Of obscure origin: see Reaks. In sense 2 evidently associated with L. rex, but the evidence does not show clearly that this is the source.]

1. = Reaks. Usu. to play...rex, to play pranks.

1566-76 [see Revel sb.[1] 4]. 1596 Spenser State Irel. Wks. (Globe) 659/2 To suffer such a caytiff to play such Rex. 1615 Armin Val. Welshm. (1663) C iv b, The Bastard plays his Rex, whose ancient sore Begins to fester. a1638 Mede Wks. (1672) 657 Another [king]..should bring down or humble three Kings, and play those recks which follow in the Text. 1642 Rogers Naaman 304 The Lord Jesus will one day judge you for your prankes and rex that you haue plaid in your Services.

2. To play rex, to act as lord or master; to domineer.

1578 Foxe in Bk. Chr. Prayers 28 b, Needs would haue..an Italian stranger, the Bishop of Rome to play Rex ouer them. 1597 Beard Theatre God's Judgem. (1612) 529 The Scots that were so curbed in his fathers dayes, now played rex through his negligence. 1608 Sylvester Du Bartas II. iv. Decay 412 Then playes hee Rex: tears, kils, and all consumes. 1651 N. Bacon Disc. Govt. Eng. II. xxxvii. (1739) 168 The Prelacy..played Rex all the while with the people. 1692 Washington tr. Milton's Def. People Pref., Consider with your selves,..who it was, that but lately began to play Rex in your Country.

b. So to play the rex.

1570 Foxe A. & M. (ed. 2) 67/1 This Theodorius..began to playe the rex, placing and displacing the Bishops at hys pleasure. 1593 G. Harvey Pierce's Super. Wks. (Grosart) II. 126 Roome for a roister,..that will suffer none to play the Rex, but himselfe.

‖**Rex**[2]. rare. [L. rex.] A king. Also attrib.

1617 Moryson Itin. I. 284 They had Rex groats so called of the Kings of England, after they had the stile of Kings of Ireland. a1653 G. Daniel Idyll II. 101 'Tis not the fatall Rex, doth only Sting; A Commonwealth's a Tirant, as a King. 1883 Besant All in Garden fair I. xii, He will be the leader, dictator, rex, imperator.

Rex, obs. f. recks, Reck v. **Rex-doller,** obs. f. Rix-dollar. **Rexen,** dial. pl. of resh Rush sb.

Rey, obs. f. Ray, Re sb.[1], Roe (deer). **Reyal(ly,** varr. Real a.[1], Really adv.[1] **Reycetter,** obs. f. Receipter. **Reyche,** obs. f. Reach v.[1] **Reycive,** obs. f. Receive. **Reyd,** obs. f. Rede v., Reid[1]. **Reye,** obs. f. Ray. **Reyes,** obs. f. Reis (Portuguese money). **Reyff,** obs. Sc. f. Reave v. **Reyflake:** see Reflac. **Reygalle,** obs. f. Regal sb.[2] **Reygh(e, reyh(h)e,** etc.: see Reigh. **Reygne,** var. Raign v.; obs. f. Reign sb. and v. **Rey-grass,** obs. f. Ray-grass.

†**Reȝhel-boc.** Obs. rare[-1]. [f. OE. reȝol rule + bōc Book.] A book of monastic rules.

c1200 Ormin Ded. 8 Þurrh þatt witt hafenn takenn ba An reȝhellboc to follȝhenn.

Reyie·ld (rī-), v. [Re- 5 a.] To yield again.

1562 Phaer Æneid IX. Cc iv b, Some should soone repent If Turnus from the Troians loftie walles did not reyeelde.

Reyingsife: see Reeing vbl. sb. **Reyjoysse,** obs. f. Rejoice v. **Reyk(e,** obs. ff. Raik sb. and v., Reach v.[1], Reek sb.[1] **Reyle, reyll(e,** obs. ff. Rail, Reel. **Reyme,** obs. Sc. f. Ream sb.[2], Realm. **Reyn,** var. Raign v. Obs. **Reyn,** obs. f. Rain, Reign, Rein.

Reynard (re[i]·năɹd). Forms: α. 4 reniarde, 5, 8 ren-, 5 reygnard (-art, reynart), 6 raynard(e, 6-7 rain-, 5, 7- reynard. β. 4 renaud; 6 rayn-, 7 rein-, 6-7 reynold (9 -olds); 7 rein-, reynald. [Orig. a. OF. Renart, Renard, Regnart (see Regnard), etc., the name of the fox in the celebrated Roman de Renart, repr. the OHG. personal name Reginhart. The β-forms show assimilation to ME. Reinaud, Raynold, Reynold, OF. Renaud, = G. Rein(h)old (OHG. Reginolt). The later form Reynard is that used by Caxton (along with Reynart, etc.) to render the MDu. Reynaerd-, Reynaert of his original.] A quasi-proper name given to the fox; also occas. used as an ordinary noun.

As a proper name written either with or without capital.

α. 13.. Gaw. & Gr. Knt. 1728 Ofte he was runnen at, when he out rayked, & ofte reled in aȝayn, so reniarde was wylé. c1430 Pilgr. Lyf Manhode II. cxxiii. (1869) 121, I do as Renard dide that made him ded in the weye, for to be cast in to the carte. [1481 Caxton Reynard (Arb.) 5 Alle the beestis grete and smale cam to the courte sauf reynard the fox.] 1562 Legh Armory (1597) 82 b, Hee beareth Or, a Saltier Sable, between foure Rainardes passant proper. 1592 Nashe P. Penilesse 10 b, Raynard, the Fox, may well beare vp his taile in the Lion's denne. 1616 R. C. Times' Whistle (1871) 136 So Aesops crow whom crafty rainard spide With prey in bill, was easily by him deceivde. 1622 Fletcher Beggars' Bush III. iii, Prick ye the fearefull hare through crosse wayes, sheep walks; And force the craftie Reynard climb quicksets. 1700 Dryden Cock & Fox 492 Before the break of Day, Saint Reynard through the Hedge had made his way. 1709 Dykes Eng. Prov. & Refl. (ed. 2) 46 Let Reynard loose after five or six Years taming,..and I would not be a Goose in his Way, for the Kingdom. 1793 Bloomfield Farmer's Boy, Spring 158 Where prowling Reynard trod his nightly round. 1842 J. Wilson Christ. North (1857) I. 39 After the first Tally-ho, Reynard is rarely seen, till he is run in upon. 1873 Tristram Moab ix. 168 A foxhunt after a reynard who started under our horses' feet.

β. 13.. Gaw. & Gr. Knt. 1898 Renaud com richchande þurȝ a roȝe greue, & alle þe rabel in a res, ryȝt at his helez. 1591 Spenser M. Hubberd 917 Such as hath a Reynold to his man, That by his shifts his Master furnish can. 1667 in J. Playford Mus. Comp. 67 Acteon shall eccho my Hounds and my Horn; Ne Reynold shall 'scape, though he run by the way. 1875- in dialect use (see Eng. Dial. Dict.).

†**Reyne.** Obs. [? a. MDu. reen, reyn shooting-range, etc., identical with Rain sb.[2]] pl. Lists.

c1440 Partonope 6511 Two fayre Reynes ordeyned haue he Where in these lordys shuld turneye. Ibid. 6526 And after cometh Gaudyn..In to the Reynes rydyng avysely.

Reyne, obs. form of Rain, Reign sb., Rein sb.[1] **Reynes,** var. Raines; obs. f. Reins. **Reyng,** obs. f. Reign, Ring. **Reynge,** var. Renge sb.[2] Obs. **Reynge-net,** obs. f. Ring-net. **Reyngne,** obs. f. Reign v. **Reyng syff:** see Reeing vbl. sb. **Reyni(e,** obs. ff. Rainy a. **Reynke,** var. Rink Obs. **Reyny,** obs. f. Rainy a. **Reynyez,** obs. f. Reins. **Reynyssh,** obs. f. Rhenish a.

Reyo·ke (rī-), v. [Re- 5 a.] To yoke again.

1813 Hogg Queen's Wake 193 Scarce had the Pleiades cleared the main, Or Charles reyoked his golden wain. 1862 Stretton Chequered Life II. 223 Dinner over, and the pipes smoked, we began to re-yoke the beasts.

Reyose, obs. form of Rejoice v.

Reyou·ng (rī-), v. rare[-1]. [Re- 5 a.] trans. To make young again; to rejuvenate.

1605 Sylvester Du Bartas II. iii. III. Lawe 955 A plenteous stream,..proud, that his glass, Gliding so swift, so soon re-youngs the grass.

Reyou·th (rī-), v. [Re- 5 a.] refl. To make (oneself) young again.

1834 Lytton Pompeii I. iv, From the young hearts of my victims I draw the ingredients of the caldron in which I re-youth myself. 1836 E. Howard R. Reefer xxiii, He re-youthed himself.

Reyoyse, obs. f. Rejoice v. **Reys,** obs. f. Raise v., Reis, Rese, Rice. **Reysbuto,** obs. f. Rajpoot. **Reyse(n,** obs. ff. Raise v. **Reysen,** obs. f. Resin. **Reysin(ge,** obs. f. Raisin. **Reyson(e,** obs. ff. Raisin, Reason. **Reyst(e,** obs. ff. Rest sb.[3] **Reyster,** var. Reister Obs. **Reysyn,** obs. f. Raise v. **Reysyn(ge,** obs. ff. Raisin. **Reyte,** var. Reit Obs. **Reyter,** obs. f. Reiter sb. **Reyuer, -our,** obs. ff. Reaver.

†**Reyve,** v. Obs. rare[-1]. [a. ON. reifa to disclose, to sum up. Cf. Rave v.[3] and Reave v.[2]] trans. To disclose, make clear.

1338 R. Brunne Chron. (1810) 294 Oþer were perceyued, þat þer ȝede disceite, Bot ȝit was it not reyued, so Edward pouht him streite.

Reyve, obs. f. Reeve sb.[1] **Reȝȝn,** obs. f. Rain sb.[1] **Reȝȝsenn,** obs. f. Raise v.

‖**Rezai** (rĕzai·). Anglo-Ind. Also rezai(ee, rosei, rozye. [Urdū razāi, of obscure origin.] A quilted counterpane or coverlet.

1834 Col. Mountain Mem. (1857) 137 The saddle bears the coarse blanket of the animal and the resai of the master. 1859 Lang Wand. India 139 The Sepoy covered his head over with his resaiee (counterpane), and lay as still as possible. 1884 'Edna Lyall' We Two xxvi, All that she

could do was to..throw herself, half-dressed, on the bed, draw the rezai over her, and yield to..slumber.

Reze, obs. f. Raise v. **Rezen,** obs. dial. f. Reason sb.[2]

Rh, a consonantal digraph used in Latin, and hence in English, French, and other languages, to represent Gr. initial ῥ (with spiritus asper); in English it has the same phonetic value as the simple r. In med.L., OF., and consequently in ME., the h was frequently dropped (see Rhetoric, Rheum[1]), and in a few instances (e.g. Rachis, Raphe) custom has sanctioned its omission in mod. English. Gr. medial ρρ (formerly often printed ῤῥ) is normally represented by rrh (as in diarrhœa).

While OE. initial hr is rarely represented in later periods by rh, a large number of variant spellings are found with rh where it is etymologically inappropriate (cf. Rhine[1]).

†**Rha.** Obs. [late L., a. Gr. ῥᾶ, said to be from the ancient name 'Pā of the river Volga. See also Rhabarbarum, Rhapontic.] Rhubarb.

1578 Lyte Dodoens III. x. 329 Rha is hoate in the first degree, and dry in the second. 1597 Gerarde Herbal II. lxxviii. 313 The root [of Bastard Rhubarb] is..verie like vnto the Rha of Barbarie.

Rhaading, obs. form of Raiding vbl. sb.

†**Rha·barb.** Obs. Variant f. Rhubarb; cf. OF. rhabarbe, and med.L. rhabarbarum.

1646 Sir T. Browne Pseud. Ep. IV. xiii. 230 Of this sort [sc. gentle purgatives] are Aloe, Rhabarbe, Senna, &c. 1657 Tomlinson Renou's Disp. 6 Simples..as Cassia, Rhabarb, Polipody. 1698 Fryer Acc. E. India & P. 377 Rhabarb, Turbith, and Scammony, are dreadful to them.

Rhabarbarate (răbā·ɹbărĕt), a. and sb. [f. med.L. Rhabarbarum + -ate.] †**A.** adj. 'Impregnated or tinctured with rhubarb' (J.).

1696 Floyer Anim. Hum. xii. 151 The Salt Humours must be evacuated by the Sennate, Rhabarbarate, and sweet Manna Purgers, with Acids added, or the Purging Waters.

B. sb. A salt of rhabarbaric acid. Also -erate.

1840 Pereira Mat. Med. 818 Metallic rhabarberates and tannates.

Rhabarbaric (ræbaɹbæ·rik), a. Chem. Also -eric. [f. med.L. rhabarbarum (see next) + -ic. Cf. rhubarbaric, -arin.] = Chrysophanic. So **Rhaba·rbarin** [-in[1]], chrysophanic acid.

1839 Royle Bot. Himalayan Mts. I. 317 Rhabarbarin. 1840 Pereira Mat. Med. 817 Pfaff's rhabarberin consists of uncrystallizable sugar, extractive, resin, rhabarberic acid, and tannin. 1853 W. Gregory Outl. Chem. II. 455 Rhabarberine..the yellow acid of rhubarb, now called chrysophanic acid. 1850 Chem. Gaz. VIII. 100 It [sc. erythrose] is almost entirely soluble in alcohol and in æther, which on evaporation furnish rhabarbaric or erythrosic acid.

‖**Rhabarbarum** (răbā·ɹbărŏm). [med.L., = rha barbarum 'foreign Rha' (cf. Rhapontic).] Rhubarb-root.

[1533 Elyot Cast. Helthe (1541) 58 Reubarbarum by it selfe from two drammes unto foure, infused or stiped in [ycour.] 1597 Gerarde Herbal II. lxxix. 317 It is called..in shops Rhabarbarum: in English Rubarbe, and Rewbarbe. 1598 Sidney Def. Poesie 502 If one should begin to tell them the nature of the Alloes or Rhabarbarum they should receiue. 1660 Bk. Rates (Act 12 Chas. II, c. 4), Rhabarbarum or Rubarb ye pound. 1693 [see Rhapontic 2].

¶ The Lat. word (with its var. rheubarbarum: see Rhubarb) is widely represented in the Romanic and Germanic langs., and hence various forms appear in Eng. translations of foreign books (see quots., and cf. MLG., MDu. rebarber, MDu., Du. rabarber, G. rhabarber).

1525 tr. Jerome of Brunswick's Surg. xiii. R iij, Take Rebarbere [orig. rebarbara] one dragma. 1578 Lyte Dodoens III. x. 328 Of Reubarbe, or Rhabarba. 1597 A. M. tr. Guillemeau's Fr. Chirurg. 49/1 An ounce of Cassia, with halfe a dragma of Rabarber. 1598 W. Philip tr. Linschoten lxxxi. 126 Rhabarbo, Manna, and such like costlie Apothecaries ware.

Rhabdal (ræ·bdăl), a. Zool. [f. Rhabdus + -al.] Pertaining to a rhabdus.

1888 Sollas in Challenger Rep., Zool. XXV. 345 Disc..sometimes notched by a rhabdal sinus.

Rhabdite (ræ·bdəit). [f. Gr. ῥάβδος rod + -ite.]

1. Zool. One of the homogeneous rod-like bodies found in the integument of turbellarian worms.

1885 L. von Graff in Encycl. Brit. XIX. 170/2.

2. Ent. One of the three pairs of organs forming the ovipositor of some insects.

1890 in Cent. Dict. 1898 Packard Text-bk. Entom. [167 Morphologically the ovipositor is composed of three pairs of unjointed styles (rhabdites of Lacaze-Duthiers, gonapophyses of Huxley). Ibid.] 168 Two pieces forming the outer pair of rhabdites.

3. Min. (See quots.)

1881 Jrnl. Chem. Soc. XL. 690 The phosphide [of iron] found in a Branau meteorite by G. Rose, who gave to it the name rhabdite. 1892 Dana Min. 31 Rhabdite...A phosphide of iron and nickel.

‖**Rhabditis** (ræbdəi·tis). [mod.L., f. Gr. ῥάβδος rod.] A genus of minute nematode worms of the family Anguillulidæ; a worm of this genus.

1876 van Beneden's Anim. Parasites (1883) 156 This worm is evidently a Rhabditis. 1884 Sedgwick tr. Claus' Text-bk. Zool. I. lx. 350 Numerous generations of the Rhabditis form may succeed one another.

Hence **Rhabdi·tic, Rhabdi·tiform** adjs., characteristic of, or of the form of, Rhabditis.

1890 Cent. Dict., Rhabditic. 1897 Allbutt's Syst. Med. II. 1040 Development proceeds under certain circumstances so rapidly that in one to two days a rhabditiform embryo..is born. Ibid. 1088 The various species are heterogamous, each species including a free, bisexual, and rhabditic form.

Rhabdo- (ræ·bdo, ræbdǫ·), combining form of Gr. ῥάβδος rod, occurring in a few technical terms (chiefly zoological): **Rha·bdocœl(e** [Gr. κοῖλος hollow] a., having a straight digestive cavity, as turbellarian worms; sb., a worm of this kind; one of the Rhabdocœla. **Rhabdocœ·lian, -cœ·lous** adjs., = prec. adj. **Rhabdocre·pid** a. [Gr. κρηπίς foundation], belonging to the group Rhabdocrepida of lithistid sponges having desmas of various forms. **Rha·bdocyst,** a rod-like cell. **Rha·bdolith** [Gr. λίθος stone], one of the rod-like bodies forming the armature of a rhabdosphere. **Rha·bdomere** [Gr. μέρος], one of the rod-like constituents of a rhabdom. ‖**Rha:bdomyo·ma,** a myoma involving the striped muscular fibres (Dunglison Dict. Med. 1876). ‖**Rhabdone·ma** [Gr. νῆμα thread], a minute slender worm living in the duodenum. **Rha·bdophane, Rhabdo·phanite** [Gr. -φανής appearing], see quots.: identified with scovillite. **Rha·bdopod,** one of the clasping organs of the Ephemeridæ. ‖**Rhabdosarco·ma** (see quot.). **Rha·bdosphere,** a name given to certain spherical bodies found in abundance on the surface of the waters in warm seas.

1877 Huxley Anat. Inv. Anim. iv. 194 The *rhabdocœle Turbellaria. 1883 Q. Jrnl. Microsc. Sci. XXIII. 353 Graff's Rhabdocœl family of the Proboscida. Ibid. 355 Phylogenetically related to the separate proboscis of certain Rhabdocœls. 1864 T. S. Cobbold Entozoa I. 10 *Rhabdocœlian group [of Planarians]. 1877 Huxley Anat. Inv. Anim. iv. 178 The higher *rhabdocœlous Turbellaria. 1887 Sollas in Encycl. Brit. XXII. 416/2 *Rhabdocrepid desma. Ibid. 422/1 A distinct passage can be traced from the Tetracladose to the Rhabdocrepid group. 1888 Rolleston & Jackson Anim. Life 332 In the Turbellaria very similar structures are met with in the *rhabdocysts or rod-cells. 1885 Challenger Rep., Narr. Cruise I. I. 394 In all the deposits the carbonate of lime consisted chiefly of pelagic Foraminifera, Coccoliths, and *Rhabdoliths. 1883 Q. Jrnl. Microsc. Sci. XXIII. 211 The compound hard-piece formed in the axis of a retinula by the union of the laterally formed *rhabdomeres of its constituent nerve-end cells. 1897 Allbutt's Syst. Med. II. 1088 The mature *rhabdonema lives in the intestinal mucus of the duodenum. 1878 Jrnl. Chem. Soc. XXXIV. 652 A specimen in the Mineralogical Collection, Oxford, labelled Cornwall blende, was found..to consist essentially of didymium and erbium phosphates. The name *Rhabdophane has been given to this very rare mineral. 1892 Dana Min. 890 *Rhabdophanite. Rhabdophane...Scovillite. 1898 Packard Textbk. Entom. 179 The cercopods and *rhabdopods in the Trichoptera. 1891 Moullin Surg. 131 In the *rhabdo-sarcomata the muscle takes the form of transversely striated fibrils, or of elongated spindle-cells, also striated. 1885 Challenger Rep., Narr. Cruise I. I. 218 The occurrence of the following organisms was noted during the trip...*Rhabdospheres, Coccospheres.

Rhabdoid (ræ·bdoid), a. (sb.). Also ra-. [ad. mod.L. rhabdoīdēs (Blancard), a. Gr. ῥαβδοειδής, ῥαβδώδης, f. ῥάβδος rod: see -oid.] Resembling a rod; rod-like. Also sb. (Bot.): see quot. 1900.

1858 Mayne Expos. Lex., Rhabdoides,..rhabdoid. Anat. An old epithet of the sagittal suture. 1885 E. R. Lankester in Encycl. Brit. XIX. 849/2 The siliceous skeleton..may become discoid, rhabdoid, or irregular. 1900 B. D. Jackson Gloss. Bot. Terms, Rhabdoid, a rod-shaped body found in the cells of the tentacles of the Drosera.

So **Rhabdoi·dal** a.

1855 Ogilvie Suppl., Rabdoidal. 1864 Webster, Rhabdoidal, the same as Rabdoidal.

Rhabdology (ræbdǫ·lŏdʒi). Also rabdo-. [ad. mod.L. r(h)abdologia (Napier, 1617), f. Gr. ῥάβδος rod + -λογία -logy. Cf. F. rhabdologie.]

1. The act or art of computing by Napier's bones (or rods). Now Hist.

1667 Leybourne Art of Numbering I. 1 Rabdologie is the Art of Counting by Numbering Rods. 1671 Phil. Trans. VI. 3044 In the Rabdology of the Noble Nepper, the multitude and embarassment of those sticks..proved long and tedious. 1700 Moxon Math. Dict. 144 Rhabdology. 1841 Penny Cycl. XIX. 228/2 Rabdology.

¶**2.** Used for Rhabdomancy.

1855 Leifchild Cornwall 134 One or two remarkable instances of the supposed efficacy of the rod are on record...I find that some learned men believed in this science, called rabdiology.

Hence **Rhabdolo·gical** a.: (see quot.).

1825 Ann. Philos. Feb. 147 A box of rods, named the Rhabdological Abacus...These rods were invented by Mr. Goodwyn for the purpose of facilitating the multiplication of long numbers of frequent occurrence.

Rhabdom (ræ·bdǫm). Ent. Also -ome. [ad. late Gr. ῥάβδωμα, f. ῥάβδος rod.] One of the rods supporting the crystalline lenses in a faceted eye.

1878 Bell tr. Gegenbaur's Comp. Anat. 264 The rods..become united, and form a special structure, the 'rhabdom', in the long axis of a group of combined retinal cells. 1888 Rolleston & Jackson Anim. Life 460 Two to four rhabdomeres fuse into a rhabdome.

Rhabdomancer (ræ·bdomænsəɹ). [f. next: see -er[1].] One who professes or practises rhabdomancy; a dowser.

1817 Edin. Rev. XXVIII. 184 No proprietor will..dig down in trace of the metallic effluvia, which reach the subtle senses of the Rabdomancer above.

Rhabdomancy (ræ·bdomænsi). Also 7 rhadomoncie, 7, 9 rabdomancy. [ad. late L. rhabdomantia, a. Gr. ῥαβδομαντεία, f. ῥάβδος rod + μαντεία (see -mancy).] Divination by means of a rod or wand; spec. the art of discovering ores, springs of water, etc., in the earth by means of a divining-rod.

1646 Sir T. Browne Pseud. Ep. v. xxi. 271 A..peculiar way of Rhabdomancy is that which is used in Minerall discoveries, that is, with a forked hazell. 1649 G. Daniel Trinarch., Rich. II, cxxxv, The Hassle soe will bend (A Rhadomoncie was observ'd of old) Stretch'd on the Earth, vnto a Mine of Gold. 1727-38 Chambers Cycl. s.v. Divination. 1817 Edin. Rev. XXVIII. 184 note, The doctrines of Rabdomancy still retain their ground in various parts of the Continent. 1856 De Quincey Confess. 85 note, Whatever science or scepticism may say, most of the tea-kettles in the vale of Wrington are filled by rhabdomancy. 1871 E. B. Tylor Prim. Culture I. iv. heading, Rhabdomancy, Dactyliomancy, Coscinomancy.

fig. 1856 De Quincey Confess. 84 The memorable rhabdomancy or magical power of evocation which Christianity has put forth.

So **Rhabdoma·ntic** a., pertaining to rhabdomancy or the use of the divining-rod (in recent Dicts.); **Rha·bdomantist,** = Rhabdomancer.

1856 De Quincey Confess. 85 note, The remedy is—to call in a set of local rhabdomantists. These men traverse the adjacent ground, holding the willow rod horizontally.

Rhabdome (ræ·bdōᵘm). Zool. [ad. late Gr. ῥάβδωμα (see Rhabdom).] The shaft of a rhabdus of which one ray is branched.

1887 Sollas in Encycl. Brit. XXII. 417/1 A particular case of the cladose rhabdus, but one of the most frequent occurrence, is the triæne; in this form one ray of a rhabdus ends in three branches, which diverge at equal angles from each other. The rhabdus then becomes known as the shaft or rhabdome. 1900 Minchin Sponges 132.

Rhabdo·sophy. [See Rhabdo- and -sophy.] (See quot.)

1820 L. Hunt Indicator No. 33 I. 262 There is an undoubted Rhabdosophy, Sceptrosophy, or Wisdom of the Stick, besides the famous Divining Rod...It supplies a man with inaudible remarks, and an inexpressible number of graces.

‖**Rhabdus** (ræ·bdŭs). [mod.L., a. Gr. ῥάβδος.]

1. Bot. The stipe of certain fungi.

1866 Treas. Bot. 968/2.

2. A sponge spicule of the monaxon biradiate type.

1887 [see Rhabdome]. 1900 Minchin Sponges 116.

Rhachi(o)-, Rhachis: see Rachi-, Rachis.

Rhadamanthus (rædămæ·nþŭs). Also anglicized 6-7 Rhadamant, 7 -manth. [L., a. Gr. Ῥαδάμανθος.] In Greek mythology, a son of Zeus and Europa and one of the judges in the lower world. Hence used allusively for: An inflexible judge; a rigorous or severe master. Also transf.

1582 Stanyhurst Æneis, etc. (Arb.) 155 In wisdom Salomon,..For iustice Radamanthus: in equitye woorthye Lycurgus. 1599 Nashe Lenten Stuffe 67 Petty diuels, and cruell Rhadamants. 1603 S. Daniel Def. Ryme H, For who hath constituted him to be the Radamanthus thus to torture sillables, and adiudge them their perpetuall doome? 1634 Massinger Very Woman II. (1655) 26 Yirk him soundly. 'Twas Rhadamanths sentence. 1656 Blount Glossogr., Rhadamant, taken for a severe Judge. 1879 Geo. Eliot Theo. Such xvii. 300 A wondrously delicate machine for testing sovereigns, a shrewd implacable little steel Rhadamanthus, that..lifts and balances each in turn.

Comb. 1828 Eng. in France II. 337 A certain Rhadamanthus-looking personage, who listened..with all the impartial and unmeaning suavity of the bench.

Hence †**Rhadama·nthean,** †**-ian, Rhadama·nthine** adjs., resembling or characteristic of Rhadamanthus; inflexibly rigorous or severe. So **Rhadama·nthously** adv., with the severity of a Rhadamanthus.

1655 J. Owen Vind. Evang. xxiii. 484 The Heathens Apprehension of Rhadamanthean Righteousnesse. 1833 Fraser's Mag. VII. 4 Rejecting whatever deserves such a fate with Rhadamanthian sternness of purpose. 1840 Thackeray Paris Sk.-bk. Wks. 1900 V. 220 Severe Rhadamanthine judges are not to be melted by such trumpery. 1859 Dr. John Brown Lett. (1907) 129 All this will come before you and you will deal with it Rhadamanthously. 1878 Browning Poets Croisic 38 Rhadamanthine law.

Rhada-, Rhadomontade, obs. ff. Rodomontade. **Rhadar, Rhadorage:** see Rahdar, Rahdarage. **Rhadish,** erron. obs. f. Radish.

Rhætian (rī·ʃăn), a. and sb. Also Rhe-. [f. Rhætia (see next) + -ian.] = Rhæto-Romanic.

1779 Coxe Trav. Switzerland III. lxxix. 281 The Rhetian, or as it is more commonly called the Romansh, which is the vernacular tongue among the greatest part of the Grisons. 1828 Encycl. Metrop. (1845) XIX. 756/1 The Romansh, or ancient Rhætian. 1880-1 Trans. Philol. Soc. 403 The Rhætian language is also spoken in the large district of the Engadin.

Rhætic (rī·tik), a. Geol. Also Rhe-. [ad. L. Rhætic-us, adj. of Rhætia, ancient name of a district of the Alps.] Applied to strata, extensively developed in the Rhætian Alps, regarded as passage-beds between the lias and trias; belonging to or characteristic of these. Also sb., the Rhætic formation; pl., Rhætic series of strata.

1861 Q. Jrnl. Geol. Soc. 22 May 496 The Kössen stage, or, as it is now proposed to be termed by Mr. Gümbel the State-Geologist of Bavaria, the Rhætic formation,—a designation recognized by Professor E. Suess. 1881 Nature 15 Sept. 474/2 The green marls agreed with underlying beds in the Keuper, but differed markedly from the overlying Rhætics. 1896 Guide Fossil Rept. Brit. Mus. 103 Semionotus and Colobodus are Triassic and Rhætic;..and Lepidotus ranges from the Rhætic to the Wealden.

Rhætizite (rī·tizəit). Min. Also rhe-; erron. rhœ-. [ad. G. rhätizit (1815), f. Rhætia: see prec. and -ite.] A white variety of cyanite.

1816 Jameson Syst. Min. (ed. 2) II. 424 Rhaetizite...It occurs at Pfizsch in the Tyrol. 1837 Dana Min. 319 A milk-white variety of Rhœtizite. 1864 Webster, Rhetizite.

Rhæ·to-Roma·nic, a. and sb. Philology. Also Rhe-. [f. Rhæto-, combining f. L. Rhætus Rhætian + Romanic.] Applied to those dialects of the Romance family which are spoken in south-eastern Switzerland and the Tyrol; sometimes particularly to the Rumansch of the Grisons or the Ladin of the Engadine. Also **Rhæ·to-Roma·nce.**

1867 Whitney Language iv. 167 The Rhæto-Romanic of southern Switzerland. 1878 Encycl. Brit. VIII. 699/2 Ladin (Rumonsh, Rumansh, Rheto-Romance). 1880-1 Trans. Philol. Soc. 402 The district in which the Rhæto-Romanic language is spoken comprises a large..part of the canton of Bünden, otherwise..Graubünden or Grisons.

‖**Rhagades** (ræ·gădīz), sb. pl. Path. Also 7 -ies. [late L., a. Gr. ῥαγάδες, pl. of ῥαγάς rent, chink.] Chaps or fissures of the skin.

1601 Holland Pliny II. 169 The rhagadies, fissures, and chaps in the feet. 1772 McBride Physic 541 Dry fissures called Rhagades. 1835-6 Todd's Cycl. Anat. I. 184/1 These fissures or rhagades are attended with pain in defæcation. 1879 St. George's Hosp. Rep. IX. 744 In winter she has rhagades in the hands and elsewhere.

Rhagite (ræ·gəit). Min. [ad. G. rhagit (1874), f. Gr. ῥαγ-, ῥάξ grape: see -ite.] Hydrous arsenate of bismuth, occurring in yellowish-green concretions with grape-like arrangement.

1874 Jrnl. Chem. Soc. XXVII. 667.

Rhagon (ræ·gǫn). [mod.L., f. Gr. ῥαγ-, ῥάξ grape.] A type occurring as a stage in the development of some sponges, so called from the botryoidal form of its flagellated chambers. Hence **Rha·gose** a., having the characters of a rhagon.

1887 Sollas in Encycl. Brit. XXII. 422/1 The eurypylous Rhagon type. Ibid., The flagellated chambers are eurypylous and rhagose. 1900 Minchin Sponges 125 The Rhagon is a little sponge organism, in shape like a cake or bun, being usually slightly flattened and spread out.

Rhaim, variant of Rame sb.[3]

Rhamadan, -azan(i: see Ramadan.

Rhame, variant of Rame sb.[3] and v.[1]

Rhamn (ræm). Also 4 rammyn, ramne, 6 ram(me, 7 rhamne, rham. [ad. late L. Rhamnus.] The buckthorn; also, the buckthorn berry.

a1340 Hampole Psalter lvii. 9 Rammyn, þat þai call thefthorne. 1388 Wyclif Judg. ix. 14 The ramne [gloss ether theue thorn]. 1562 Turner Herbal II. 115 The fruyt or rounde ramnes. 1597 Gerarde Herbal III. xxvi. 1153 Christes Thorne or Ram of Lybia. 1601 Holland Pliny II. 197 Among the diuers kinds of brambles, is reckoned the Rhamne...This Rham beareth many flours. 1633 Johnson Gerarde's Herbal III. xxviii. (1636) 1334 White floured Ram-thorne. 1697 Potter Antiq. Greece (1715) II. Index, Rhamn fixed on sick Persons Doors. 1807 Robinson Archæol. Græca v. ii. 416. 1895 F. T. Elworthy Evil Eye 446 Rhamn or Christ-thorn.

Rhamnad (ræ·mnæd). Bot. [f. Rhamnus + -ad.] Lindley's name for a plant of the N. O. Rhamnaceæ. So **Rha·mnal** a., belonging to the 'alliance' Rhamnales of plants allied to N. O. Rhamnaceæ; sb., a plant of this 'alliance'.

1846 Lindley Veget. Kingd. 576 Rhamnales.—The Rhamnal Alliance. Ibid., The compound ovary of Rhamnals. Ibid. 581 Spurgeworts are allied to Rhamnads. 1866 Treas. Bot., Maimunna, a fruit-bearing rhamnad of Afghanistan.

Rhamnegin (ræ·mnĭdʒin). Chem. [arbitrarily f. Rhamnus: see -in[1].] A glucoside obtained from buckthorn berries.

1872 Watts Dict. Chem. Suppl. s.v. Rhamnus.

Rhamneous (ræ·mnĭəs), a. [f. mod.L. Rhamneus, f. Rhamnus: see -eous.] Belonging to or resembling the genus Rhamnus.

1847 Nat. Encycl. I. 959 Brogniart, in his memoir on Rhamneous plants. 1858 Mayne Expos. Lex. s.v. Rhamneus.

Rhamnetin (ræ·mnĭtin). Chem. Also -ine. [Arbitrarily f. Rhamnus: see -in[1].] A yellow crystalline substance obtained from rhamnin.

1858 Gellatly in Edin. New Phil. Jrnl. (N. S.) VII. 257 The pale yellow matter separated by boiling with the dilute mineral acids, according to the nomenclature in use.., should receive the name of Xanthorhamnetine, but..I propose to..call it simply Rhamnetine. 1861 Jrnl. Chem. Soc. XIII. 327 Rhamnetin.

So (in the names of chemical substances, chiefly crystallizable principles, obtainable from Rhamnus): **Rha·mnin** (also -ine); **Rha·mnite; Rha·mno-,** used as combining form of Rhamnus, in rhamnoxanthin, etc.; **Rha·mnose.**

1843 Ann. Chym. & Pharm. L. 407 While the juice of the [buckthorn] berries is undergoing fermentation, a portion of *rhamnin gathers on the surface of the liquid. 1844 Chem. Gaz. II. 430 Rhamnine, under the influence of oxydising agents,..becomes of a dark yellow colour. 1894 Morley & Muir Dict. Chem., *Rhamnite $C_6H_{14}O_5$...Formed by reducing isodulcite with sodium-amalgam in a solution kept nearly neutral by H_2SO_4. 1854 Chem. Gaz. XII. 129 *Rhamnoxanthine is dissolved by ammonia and the fixed alkalies with a purple-red colour. 1868 Watts Dict. Chem., Rhamnocathartin,..the uncrystallizable bitter principle of buckthorn berries...Rhamnotannic acid,..obtained in the preparation of rhamnocathartin. 1890 Jrnl. Soc. Chem. Industry IX. 1141/2 Rhamno-hexose..is obtained by reducing a solution of the lactone of rhamnohexonic acid by 2½ per cent. sodium amalgam. 1888 Ibid. VII. 578/1 All alcoholic solutions of crystalline *rhamnose are lævo-rotatory. 1890 Ibid. IX. 1141/1 Rhamnose is a methyl pentose.

‖**Rhamnus** (ræ·mnŏs). [late L., a. Gr. ῥάμνος.] Formerly, the buckthorn (R. catharticus) or Christ's thorn (Paliurus aculeatus); now only the name of a genus of shrubs typical of the N. O. Rhamnaceæ and comprising the buckthorns. Also attrib.

1562 Turner Herbal II. 114 b, Rhamnus..hath twigges that grow right vp, and sharpe prickes. 1578 Lyte Dodoens VI. xxix. 696 The leaues of Rhamnus do cure Erysipelas. 1610 Fletcher Faithf. Sheph. II. i, Ramnus [early edd. mispr. Ramuus, Ramuns] branches..stucke..about the barre That holds the dore, kill all inchantments. 1672 Petty Pol. Anat. 355 As for wild and green weeds [for dyeing], they find enough, as also of Rhamnus-berries. 1755 Gentl. Mag. XXV. 408/1, I have two female rhamnus's in my garden. 1872 Watts Dict. Chem. Suppl. s.v., The constituents of rhamnus berries have..been examined by W. Stein.

b. Bastard rhamnus: the sea-buckthorn, Hippophae rhamnoides. 1760 J. Lee Introd. Bot. App. 324.

Rhamphoid (ræ·mfoid), a. Math. Also ram-. [f. Gr. ῥάμφος beak + -oid.] Rhamphoid cusp, a cusp at which the two branches of the curve lie on the same side of the common tangent.

1852 Todhunter Diff. Calc. § 301. 1873 [see Keratoid 1].

Rhanny, obs. form of Ranee.

Rhantism, -ize, varr. Rantism[1], Rantize v.

1843 Baptist Rep. Jan. 16 The holy Gospel says, Baptizing; these vile magicians must of necessity say, (Rhantizing) sprinkling and pouring. Ibid. 61 Unless they wash their hands clean of 'Infant Rhantism'. 1894 Freeman 20 July 486/1 We believe that all the monarchs of England up to Queen Elizabeth were baptized, but none have been since—only rhantized.

Rhaphe, Rhaphis, varr. Raphe[2], Raphis.

Rhapontic (răpǫ·ntik), sb. (a.). Also 6 rha ponticke, 7 rha-pontick(e, 7-8 rhapontick, 8 r(h)aphontic, 9 rapontic; also in L. form 7 rapontica, 7-8 -icum. β. 6 rewponticke, rupontike, reu-, 7 ruponti(c(k. [ad. mod.L. (1) rhaponticum, = rha Ponticum (see Rha and Pontic a.[1], and cf. radix Pontica, Celsus); (2) r(e)uponticum (altered form corresp. to reubarbarum Rhubarb). Cf. OF. reupontic, r(h)eu-, repontique, mod.F. rhapontic, It. reupontico, MLG. repontik.]

†**1.** Greater Centaury, Centaurea Rhapontica. Obs.

1548 Turner Names Herbes (E. D. S.) 24 Centaurium magnum..is called of the Poticaries Ruponticum, and in Englishe Rupontike. c1550 H. Lloyd Treas. Health R viii, Rewponticke is a singular remedye agaynst Feuers. 1601 Holland Pliny XXVI. viii. II. 250 The greater Centaurie, commonly called Rhapontick. 1627 Mosan Gen. Pract. Phys. and Table, It is..called with vs pontish Rubarbe, to distinguish it from the roote of the great Centorie, which we do commonly call Rapontica.

2. A species of rhubarb, Rheum Rhaponticum, or its root. Also applied to other species.

1578 Lyte Dodoens III. x. 329 The roote of Rha Pontické..cureth the vile white scurffe. 1583 Rates Custome Ho. E b, Rhaponticum the pound ii s. 1609 Holland Amm. Marcell. XXII. vii. 198 Neere unto this is the river Rha, on the sides whereof groweth a comfortable and holsom root so named [marg. Rha-Ponticke: and not Rhabarbarum or Rhewbarbe]. 1693 Phil. Trans. XVII. 933 That the Rhabarbarum of Alpinus, which in our Gardens is called Rubarb, is the true Rupontick. 1724 Index Mat. Med. 49 True Raphontick, or English Rhubarb. 1763 S. T. Janssen Smuggling laid open 114 This Rhapontick..is a Root so very much resembling Rhubarb..that it is very common to export the same as Rhubarb. 1802-3 tr. Pallas's Trav. (1812) I. 138 Our rhapontic, or rhubarb of the steppe, is no other than the Rheum Ribes. 1819 Pantologia s.v. Rhaponticum, The rhapontic..is more astringent than rhubarb. 1838 Lindley Flora Med. 358 There is no difficulty in recognising it by..its smell of 'rhapontic'.

†**3.** Mountain rhapontic: monk's rhubarb. Obs.

1727-38 Chambers Cycl. s.v. Rhaponticum, The mountain rhapontic, or monk's rhubarb. 1737 [see Monk's rhubarb].

4. attrib. or adj.

1758 Elaboratory laid open 371 The true rhubarb may be distinguished from the rhapontic..by the grain and colour. 1820 Hooper Med. Dict., Rheum rhaponticum, the systematic name of the rhapontic rhubarb. 1860 Darlington Amer. Weeds, etc. 285 Rhapontic Rheum..Pie Rhubarb.

Hence **Rhaponticin** (răpǫ·ntisin) Chem. [-in[1]], a yellow principle extracted from the root of Rheum Rhaponticum. 1840 Pereira Mat. Med. 817.

Rhapsode (ræ·psōᵘd). [ad. Gr. ῥαψῳδός, f. ῥάπτειν to stitch + ᾠδή song, Ode.] = Rhapsodist 2.

1834 H. N. Coleridge Grk. Poets (ed. 2) 95 These rhapsodes were indigent persons, who gained their livelihood by reciting the Homeric poetry. 1846 Grote Greece I. xxi. II. 173 The expulsion of the rhapsodes from Sicyôn, by the despot Cleisthenês in the time of Solôn. 1907 T. W. Allen in Class. Quart. I. 135 The rhapsode, Socrates says, should also interpret his poet.

transf. 1867 Swinburne Ess. & Stud. (1875) 116 There has been since Chaucer no second teller of tales, no second rhapsode, comparable to the first.

†**Rhapsoder.** Obs. rare. [f. as prec. + -er[1].] = Rhapsodist 1.

1610 Donne Pseudo-martyr 16 These Rhapsoders, and fragmentary compilers of Canons. a1624 — Βιαθανατος (1644) 32 Those definitions of sinne, which the first Rhapsoder Pet. Lombard hath presented out of ancient learning. 1711 Shaftesb. Charac. (1737) I. 224 Let a nation remain ever so rude or barbarous, it must have its poets, rhapsoders, historiographers.

Rhapsodic (ræpsǫ·dik), a. [ad. Gr. ῥαψῳδικός, f. ῥαψῳδός Rhapsode or ῥαψῳδία Rhapsody.]

1. = Rhapsodical 2.

1782 V. Knox Ess. xv. (1819) I. 88 Many books of devotion, are written in that rhapsodic style, which wearies by its constant efforts to elevate the mind to ecstacy. 1787 Mme. D'Arblay Diary 16 Feb., I begged him to rise, and be a little less rhapsodic. 1879 Geo. Eliot Theo. Such viii, There is a fable that when the badger had been stung all over by bees, a bear consoled him by a rhapsodic account of how he himself had just breakfasted on their honey.

2. Consisting of the recitation of rhapsodies.

1846 Grote Greece I. xxi. II. 188 note, It appears that there had once been rhapsodic exhibitions at the festivals of Dionysus.

Rhapsodical (ræpsǫ·dikăl), a. [f. as prec.]

†**1.** Of a literary work: Consisting of a medley of narratives, etc.; fragmentary or disconnected in style. Obs.

1659 E. Martin His Opinion Let. i. (1662) 17 Dr. Heylin's Confutation of Fuller's Rhapsodical stories of the Church of England. 1692 Wood Ath. Oxon. II. 315 [Prynne's works] are looked upon to be rather rapsodical and confus'd, than any way polite or concise. 1759 Sterne Tr. Shandy (1760) I. xiii. 75 It is so long since the reader of this rhapsodical work has been parted from the midwife, that it is high time to mention her again to him.

2. Characteristic of or of the nature of rhapsody (sense 4); exaggeratedly enthusiastic or ecstatic in language, manner, etc.

1783 Blair Rhet. xxxix. II. 359 The Odes of Jean Baptiste Rousseau have been..justly celebrated...They are animated, without being rhapsodical. 1844 Disraeli Coningsby v. vii, We..alternate between a supercilious neglect of genius and a rhapsodical pursuit of quacks. 1847 Longf. in Life (1891) II. 97 A very striking, rhapsodical, forcible..sermon. 1885 J. Payn Talk of Town I. 213 The whole composition strikes me as rather rhapsodical.

3. Of the rhapsodist. rare.

a1822 Shelley Ion Prose Wks. 1888 II. 126 Does it belong to the medical or rhapsodical art, to determine whether Homer speaks rightly on this subject?

Rhapso·dically, adv. [f. prec. + -ly[2].] In a rhapsodical manner; † disconnectedly.

a1608 Dee Relat. Spir. I. (1659) 423 Thus much very rhapsodically, (yet faithfully),..I thought good to commit to the safe..conveyance of a young Merchant here. 1787 Hawkins Life Johnson 129 Pitt's [speech] void of argument, but rhapsodically and diffusively eloquent. 1819 Lamb Lett. (1888) II. 25 My pen goes galloping on most rhapsodically. 1853 Fraser's Mag. XLVII. 560 He breaks out rhapsodically in its praises.

Rha·psodism. rare[-1]. [f. Rhapsodist: see -ism.] The recitation of poems by rhapsodists.

1829 E. H. Barker Parriana II. 763 The preservation of poems by rhapsodism and oral tradition.

Rhapsodist (ræ·psŏdist). Also 7 rap-. [f. Gr. ῥαψῳδός Rhapsode + -ist. Cf. F. rhapsodiste.]

†**1.** A collector of literary pieces. Obs.

1646 Sir T. Browne Pseud. Ep. I. viii. 31 Plinius Secundus..was the greatest Collector or Rhapsodist of all the Latines. 1671 J. Webster Metallogr. i. 4 The Catholick Transcriber and Rhapsodist Athanasius Kircherus.

2. Antiq. In Ancient Greece, a reciter of epic poems, esp. one of a school of persons whose occupation it was to recite the Homeric poems.

1656 Blount Glossogr., Rhapsodists, the Interpreters or Rehearsers of Homers verses. 1669 Gale Crt. Gentiles I. III. i. 15 The Rapsodists, holding a Rod, or branch of Laurel, in their hands. 1763 J. Brown Poetry & Mus. § 6. 117 The Rhapsodists, whose Profession it was to sing the Poems of Homer and Hesiod. 1795-1814 Wordsw. Excurs. IV. 733 The gross fictions chanted in the streets By wandering Rhapsodists. a1854 H. Reed Lect. Eng. Lit. iv. (1878) 153 When the earliest poetry of Greece had no surer abiding place than the memories and tongues of the Rhapsodists. 1880 Mahaffy Hist. Grk. Lit. I. 26 It was believed in old times that both poems were written down by Homer, and then transcribed and preserved by schools of rhapsodists. 1886 J. B. Jevons in Jrnl. Hellenic Stud. VII. 294 Before rhapsodists existed, the Iliad was.

b. transf. and gen. A reciter of poems.

1765 Percy Reliq. I. Pref. x, The artless productions of these old rhapsodists [sc. our ancient English Minstrels]. 1831 Carlyle Sterling III. iv, The same populace sit for hours.., listening to rhapsodists who recite Ariosto. 1869 Tozer Highl. Turkey II. 229 In his character of rhapsodist he passes from village to village.

3. One who rhapsodizes or uses rhapsodical language: in early use, with implication of want of argument or fact.

1741 Watts Improv. Mind I. x. § 11 (1801) 90 Let me ask our rhapsodist, 'if you have nothing else, Sir, but the beauty and excellency, and loveliness of virtue to preach and flourish upon.' 1786 Gentl. Mag. LVI. I. 305 He complains of some other ranters and rhapsodists. 1817 Coleridge Biog. Lit. xxiv, The grief with which I read this rhapsody of predetermined insult had the rhapsodist himself for its whole and sole object. 1873 Dixon Two Queens II. ii. I. 78 'Granada', cried her rhapsodists, with Oriental flush of metaphor, 'has no equal on the earth'. 1889 Spectator 26 Oct. 556/2 Like Burns, he was a satirist..and a rhapsodist of Nature, animate and inanimate.

Rhapsodize (ræ·psŏdəiz), v. Also 7 rap-. [f. Rhapsody + -ize.]

†**1.** To piece (miscellaneous narratives, etc.) together; to relate disconnectedly. Obs.

1607 Walkington Opt. Glass Ep. Ded. ¶ 6 Looke not on these rapsodized lines, I pray you, with a pittying eie. 1762 Sterne Tr. Shandy VI. xxi, To rhapsodize them, as I once intended, into the body of the work. 1765 Ibid. vii. xxviii, I am..in a handsome pavilion.., where I now sit rhapsodizing all these affairs.

2. To recite in rhapsodies. Also absol.

a 1822 Shelley Ion Prose Wks. 1888 II. 130 How is it.. that..you continually go about Greece rhapsodising, and never lead our armies? 1846 Grote Greece i. xxi. II. 173 That the Thebais and the Epigoni were then rhapsodised at Sicyôn as Homeric productions. 1886 F. B. Jevons in Jrnl. Hellenic Stud. VII. 307 We do know on good external evidence that the Iliad was rhapsodised.

3. intr. To utter rhapsody; to talk rhapsodically.

1806 H. K. White Let. to J. Charlesworth 22 Sept., I.. shall be happy to spend a few days with you at Clapham, and to rhapsodize on your common. 1855 Smedley H. Coverdale xliv. 303 Thinking the gallant Hibernian had been rhapsodising. 1862 Thornbury Turner I. 250 He never rhapsodized about scenery. 1887 Marzials Dickens v. 66 [Little Nell] has been etherialized, vapourized, rhapsodized about, till the flesh and blood have gone out of her.

† 4. trans. To exalt, carry aloft. Obs.

(? Suggested by Rapt pa. pple.)

1616 R. C. Times' Whistle v. 1925 But for the rest, whose vertuous operation..Doth rapsodize the soules intelligence Above the levell of inferiour sence.

Hence **Rha·psodizing** vbl. sb. and ppl. a.

1872 Miss Braddon R. Ainsleigh II. xii. 171, I took you for a beggarly native; and here have you been listening to my rhapsodizing. 1874 Mahaffy Soc. Life Greece iv. 94 He specially inveighs against rhapsodising bards.

Rha·psodomancy. [f. Gr. ῥαψῳδός Rhapsode + μαντεία -mancy.] (See quot.)

1727-38 Chambers Cycl., Rhapsodomancy, an antient kind of divination performed by pitching on a passage of a poet at hazard, and reckoning on it as a prediction of what was to come to pass.

Rhapsody (ræ·psŏdi). Also 7 rapsody, -idy, -idie. [ad. L. rhapsōdia (applied by Nepos to a book of Homer), a. Gr. ῥαψῳδία, related to ῥαψῳδός Rhapsode. Cf. F. r(h)apsodie.]

1. An epic poem or part of one, e.g. a book of the Iliad or Odyssey, suitable for recitation at one time.

1542 Udall Erasm. Apoph. 76 The grammarians in olde tyme spent moste of their studie and were moste famyliare in the rhapsodies of Homerus. 1640 B. Jonson Horace A. P. 11 A Rhapsody of Homers [L. Iliacum carmen]. 1713 Bentley Freethinking vii. (1743) 26 Poor Homer..wrote a sequel of Songs and Rhapsodies, to be sung by himself for small earnings. 1727-38 Chambers Cycl. s.v., Those [verses] of Homer, which..were at length, by Pisistratus's order, digested into books, called rhapsodies. 1886 F. B. Jevons in Jrnl. Hellenic Stud. VII. 298 The Διομήδους ἀριστεία, which seems to have been a favourite rhapsody.

transf. 1813 Scott Let. to Byron in Lockhart (1837) III. ii. 101 Those who have done me the honour to take my rhapsodies for their model. 1817 Moore Lalla Rookh 293 The youth..proposed to recite a short story, or rather rhapsody.

2. † a. The stringing together of poems. Obs.—⁰

1603 Holland Plutarch's Mor. Explan. Words, Rhapsodie, a sowing together or conjoining of those Poems and verses ..which before were loose and scattered. 1616 Bullokar Eng. Exp., Rapsodie, a ioyning of diuerse verses together.

b. The recitation of epic poetry. rare.

a 1822 Shelley Ion Prose Wks. 1888 II. 119 A man professing himself a judge of poetry and rhapsody.

† 3. A miscellaneous collection; a medley or confused mass (of things); a 'string' (of words, sentences, tales, etc.). Obs.

1574 Life Abp. Parker To Rdr. C iv b, Certaine Rapsodies, and shredes off olde forworne storyes, allmost forgotten. 1580 J. Hay in Cath. Tractates (S.T.S.) 34 The doctreine..is na other thing bot other the inuention of Iohne Caluin, or ane rapsodie of awld condamned heresies. 1602 Shaks. Ham. iii. iv. 48 Such a deed, As..sweete Religion makes A rapsidie of words. 1665 Glanvill Def. Van. Dogm. 72 A meer rhapsody and confused ramble of they knew not what. 1699 Bentley Phal. Pref. p. lxxvii, His whole Book..is nothing else but a Rhapsody of Errors and Calumnies. 1711 Addison Spect. No. 46 ⁋ 1 That would look like a Rhapsody of Nonsense to any Body but myself. 1765 H. Walpole Otranto ii. 59 Have done with this rhapsody of impertinence. 1837 Hallam Hist. Lit. I. i. vii. § 20. 399 The treatise of Agrippa on occult philosophy is a rhapsody of wild theory and juggling falsehood.

† b. A literary work consisting of miscellaneous or disconnected pieces, etc.; a written composition having no fixed form or plan. Obs.

1602 Davison (title), A Poetical Rapsody Containing, Diuerse Sonnets,..and other Poesies, both in Rime, and Measured Verse. 1603 Holland Plutarch's Mor. 207 Some old ragged rapsodies and overwoorne discourses. 1685 Cotton tr. Montaigne (1877) I. 56 There is no subject so frivolous that does not merit a place in this rhapsody. 1710 T. Smith Let. in Hearne Collect. (O. H. S.) III. 53, I have lately got A. Wood's Rhapsody [sc. Athenæ Oxonienses]. 1764 Chron. in Ann. Reg. 51 A treatise entitled Droit le roy, a rhapsody of all the prerogatives at any time attributed to the kings of England.

† c. A collection (of persons, nations). Obs.

1647 Sanderson Serm. II. 217 A cento and a rhapsody of uncircumcised nations. 1654 Vilvain Epit. Ess. iv. 90 The Queen of Woors had a large rapsody. 1689 Def. Liberty agst. Tyrants 120 According to the saying of Saint Augustine, those Kingdoms where Justice hath no place, are but a rapsody of freebooters. 1701 De Foe True-born Eng. 21 Which Medly canton'd in a Heptarchy A Rhapsody of Nations to supply.

4. An exalted or exaggeratedly enthusiastic expression of sentiment or feeling; an effusion (e.g. a speech, letter, poem) marked by extravagance of idea and expression, but without connected thought or sound argument. Also without article.

1639 Quarles Embl. iv. xv, O then my brest Should warble Ayres, whose Rapsodies should feast The eares of Seraphims. 1711 Steele Spect. No. 30 ⁋ 2 To turn all the Reading of the best and wisest Writings into Rhapsodies of Love. 1771 Junius Lett. liv. (1772) II. 232 If he means any thing more than a pompous rhapsody, let us try how well his argument holds together. 1784 Cowper Task v. 677 Spend all the pow'rs Of rant and rhapsody in virtue's praise. 1802 Mrs. E. Parsons Myst. Visit IV. 187 'Upon my word, a fine rhapsody,' said she, with a disdainful smile. 1839 James Louis XIV, II. 353 After some wild and vehement rhapsodies..he was easily persuaded to retire. 1879 Gladstone Glean. II. ii. 101 This looks like mere rhapsody.

5. Mus. An instrumental composition enthusiastic in character but of indefinite form.

1880 F. Hueffer in Grove Dict. Mus. II. 147/2 The fifteen Hungarian Rhapsodies [of Liszt]. 1894 Sir G. Parker Transl. Savage xii, Marion was seated at the piano, playing a rhapsody of Raff's.

Rhatania, obs. form of Ratanhia.

Rhatany (ræ·tăni). Also rat(t)any, ratanhy. [ad. mod.L. rhatania, ad. Ratanhia.] The South American shrub Krameria triandra; the astringent extract of its root, used in adulterating port-wine and medicinally. Also attrib.

Savanilla rhatany, Krameria Ixina of New Granada.

1808 Reece Dict. Dom. Med. s.v., Tincture of Rhatany. Take of Rhatany root bruised, three ounces. 1846 Lindley Veget. Kingd. 378 The Kramerias,..called Rhatany-roots. 1861 Bentley Man. Bot. 487 Our supplies at present being chiefly derived from an unknown species, a native of New Granada, and which is called Savanilla Rhatany. 1879 Cassell's Techn. Educ. I. 215/1 The roughness and flavour of the red wines are..often communicated to them by the addition of astringents, such as rhatany. 1879 St. George's Hosp. Rep. IX. 565 Rhatany lozenges..will..relieve the symptoms. Ibid. 576 The cases..were treated..by astringents, such as rhatany, locally.

b. False rhatany: the astringent extract of the Seaside Grape, Coccoloba uvifera.

1839 Penny Cycl. XIII. 237/2 In the West Indies the juice of the Coccoloba uvifera is called..false rhatany extract. 1873 Hooker tr. le Maout & Decaisne's Syst. Bot. 635.

Rhe, variant of Ree sb.[1]

Rhea[1] (rī·ă). [mod.L. generic name (Möhring, 1752), a use of the mythological name L. Rhea, Gr. Ῥέα.] The South American or three-toed ostrich; the genus to which this bird belongs.

[1797 Encycl. Brit. (ed. 3) XVIII. 38/2 According to the new classification of Dr. Latham, it [sc. struthio] forms, along with the dodo, cassuarius, and rhea, a separate order.] 1801 Latham Gen. Syn. Birds Suppl. II. 292 American Rhea. 1860 Gosse Rom. Nat. Hist. 201 The rheas, which are the representatives of the ostrich in South America, inhabit regions presenting many of the characteristics of the African plains. 1884 G. Allen in Longman's Mag. Jan. 293 The South American rheas have real wings with real feathers in them.

Rhea[2] (rī·ă). Also rheea. [Assamese.] = Ramie. Also attrib.

1853 J. G. Marshall in Royle Fibrous Pl. India (1855) 354 Cultivated Rheea...Rheea fibre. 1855 Royle Ibid. 363 The Ramee or Rheea Nettle. 1861 Bentley Man. Bot. 636 Bœhmeria speciosa (Wild Rhea)...Ibid., Caloee Hemp or Rhea fibre, one of the strongest known fibres.

Rheadic, -ine, varr. Rhœadic, -ine. **Rheam**, obs. f. Ream sb.[3] **Rhebarb, Rhebuck**: see Rhubarb, Reebok.

Rheda·rious, a. rare—⁰. [f. L. rhēdāri-us (rhæ-), f. rhēda four-wheeled carriage.]

1656 Blount Glossogr., Rhedarious, of or serving for a Cart or Chariot.

Rheeboc, -bok, -buck, variants of Reebok.

1834 Penny Cycl. II. 80/1 The Rheebok (Antilope capreolus). 1850 R. G. Cumming Hunter's Life S. Afr. I. i. 18 The rhooye-rheebok, or red rheebuck.

Rheem, dial. form of Ream v.[1]

Rheen, variant of Reen, Rhine[1].

Rheic (rī·ik), a. Chem. [f. Rhe-um[2] + -ic, after F. rhéique.] Rheic acid = Rhein.

1847-54 Webster, s.v. Rhein. 1868 Watts Dict. Chem.

‖ **Rheim** (rīm), sb. Variant of Riem. Cf. Reim. Also attrib., as rheim-chain. Hence **Rheim** v., to secure with a rheim. Also **Rheimpy** (rī·mpi) [a. Du. riempje, Cape Du. rimpi], = Rheim sb.

1850 R. G. Cumming Hunter's Life S. Afr. I. ii. 25 Each pair of oxen is strongly coupled by the buffalo rheims..: a rheim is a long strip of prepared hide with a noose at the end. Ibid. iii. 45 Having rheimed or secured the two hind wheels by means of the drag-chains. Ibid. xvi. 384 A wide-awake hat, secured under my chin by 'rheimpys', or strips of dressed skin. 1863 W. C. Baldwin Afr. Hunting iv. 96 With its assistance and two rheim chains we reached the bottom in safety. 1880 P. Gillmore On Duty 348 Fastening them taut with a fresh rheim to the cantle of the saddle.

Rhein (rī·in). Chem. Also -ine. [f. Rhe-um[2] + -in[1], after F. rhéine.] An orange-coloured principle obtained from rhubarb; rheic acid.

1838 Thomson Chem. Org. Bodies 160. 1857 Miller Elem. Chem., Org. (1862) III. 603.

Hence **Rhei·nic** a., = Rheic (1897 Syd. Soc. Lex.).

Rhein, variant of Rhine[1], ditch.

† **Rhein-berry.** Obs. Also Rheyn-, Rheine-. [ad. MDu. rijnbesie, f. Rijn Rhine[3] + besie berry.] The buckthorn berry. Also attrib.

1578 Lyte Dodoens vi. xxx. 697 The fruite of the same thorne [sc. buckthorn] is called..in English, Rheyn beries, because there is much of them founde alongst the riuer Rhene. 1611 Cotgr., Nerprun, buck-thorne, way-thorne, Rhein-berries. 1635 J. Hayward tr. Biondi's Banish'd Virg. 153 Aurora..painting with her more lively colours the Rheineberry or full-ripe Cherry. 1671 Skinner Etym. Bot., Rhein-berries, Spina Cervina. 1706 Phillips (ed. Kersey), Rhamnus,..the Rhein-berry Bush.

Rhematic (rimæ·tik), a. and sb. rare. [ad. Gr. ῥηματικός, f. ῥηματ-, ῥῆμα word, verb.]

A. adj. a. Pertaining to the formation of words.

1856 Max Müller Chips (1867) II. 9 This period, during which expressions were coined for the most necessary ideas, ..forms the first in the history of man,..and we call it the Rhematic Period. 1882 L. Campbell Life Clerk Maxwell 379, I think a good deal may be learned from the names of colours,..and I think it is remarkable that the rhematic instinct has been so much more active..on the less refrangible side of primary green.

b. Formed on verbs.

1877 F. Hall Adjs. in -able 47 Such [adjectives in -ble] as are derived from verbs deserve the precedence. And these, to avoid the ambiguousness of the term verbal, I shall take leave to denominate rhematic.

B. sb. The science of sentences or propositions.

1830 Coleridge Table-t. 23 Sept., The object of rhetoric is persuasion,—of logic, conviction,—of grammar, significancy. A fourth term is wanting, the rhematic, or logic of sentences.

Rheme, obs. form of Ream sb.

Rhemish (rī·miʃ), a. [f. Rhemes, former Eng. spelling of Rheims + -ish.] Of or pertaining to Rheims in the north-east of France: the specific designation of an English translation of the New Testament by Roman Catholics of the English college at Rheims, published in 1582.

1589 W. Fulke Text of N. T. Ep. Ded., Discharged.. from any further dealing against these Rhemish glosses. 1610 C. Hampton Serm. (1611) 24 Our Rhemish Seminaries, say Luther, Caluin, &c. came out of their Church, not they out of ours. 1753 Chambers Cycl. Suppl. s.v. Bible, The second [version] by the papists at Rheims in 1584, called the Rhemish bible, or Rhemish translation. 1841 Bagster's Eng. Hexapla 144 The chief agent in causing the Rhemish version to be made was..Cardinal Allen. Ibid. 146 The Rhemish translators.

Rhemist (rī·mist). Also 6 Remist. [f. as prec. + -ist.] One of the authors of the Rhemish translation of and commentary on the New Testament.

1596 Harington Metam. Ajax C 2 b, We call it very wel Circumcision, and vncircumcision, though the Remists (of purpose be like to vary from Geneua) will needs bring in Prepuse. a 1620 Bp. Hall Hon. Marr. Clergy i. § 18 It is a cunning tricke of the Rhemists, and their Vulgar, in stead of Their Wiues, to reade, The Women. 1753 Chambers Cycl. Suppl. s.v. Bible, Dr. Fulke..who refuted the Rhemists with great spirit and learning. 1849 Stovel Canne's Necess. 67 Cartwright's answer to the Rhemist's Testament.

b. Comb.: † Rhemist-English, = Rhemish.

a 1653 Gouge Comm. Heb. xiii. 4 The manifest mistake of the Vulgar Latine and Rhemist-English translation.

Rhen, Rhendeer: see Rein sb.[2], Reindeer.

Rhene, variant of Rhine[1].

Rhenish, obs. form of Renish a.

1596 Nashe Saffron Walden Wks. (Grosart) III. 201 Chute,..that hold me with nothing but Rhenish furie.

Rhenish (re·niʃ), a. and sb. Forms (formerly often with small initial letter): 4 Raynysh, Rynys, -is, Rinische, Renys, -is, -yche, 5 Reynyssh, Rynisch, -yssh(e, 6 Reinnishe, Reinish, Rennish, Rheynisshe, 6-7 Renish, 7 Reanish, Rhinish, Rhennish, 6- Rhenish. β. Sc. 5 Rynche, Ryns, 6 Rens, Ranche. [Orig. partly a. or ad. OF. rinois, rynois, rainois, AF. reneis (from 13th c.):—med.L. type Rhēnensis, f. Rhēnus; partly ad. continental Germanic forms (MHG. rīnisch, G. rheinisch, also monosyllabic MHG., MLG. rīnsch, MDu. rijnsch, rinsch, rijns, Du. rijnsch): see -ish. The mod. spelling is due to L. Rhēnus or early mod. Eng. Rhene, = Rhine[3].]

A. adj.

1. Of or belonging to the river Rhine, or the regions bordering upon it.

1545 Rates Custome Ho., Glasses, Reinish. 1676 Phil. Trans. XI. 587 As green as the Rhinish glasses were heretofore tinged. 1837 Alison Hist. Europe (1847) III. 318 Soldiers trained in the regular wars on the Rhenish frontier. 1856 Bryce Holy Rom. Emp. viii, The three Rhenish archbishops.

† b. Applied to the gulden formerly current in Germany and the Netherlands. Obs.

Cf. MDu. rijnsch gulden, MLG. rinsche gulden.

1479 in Cely Papers (1900) 19, xxx Rynysche iiij[s] iiij[d] sum ..vj[li] xv[s] fls. c 1485 [see Guilder]. 1617 Moryson Itin. i. 286 A Rhenish Gold Gulden was worth seuen and twenty silver Groshen. 1756-7 [see Guilder]. 1787 Maty tr. Riesbeck's Trav. through Germany III. 104 One million one hundred and fifty thousand Rhenish guilders, or about one hundred and fifteen thousand pounds.

c. = Rhineland.

1832 Encycl. Amer. XI. 11 Rhenish or Rhinland Foot. 1858 Homans Cycl. Commerce 1949/1 Engineers and surveyors use the Rhenish foot and inch.

2. Rhenish wine: wine produced in the Rhine region; Rhine wine.

1375-6 Durh. Acc. Rolls 582 Ryniswyne. Ibid., Rinischewyn. 1390-1 Earl Derby's Exp. (Camden) 80 Pro xij stopis de Rynyswyn. ? a 1400 Morte Arth. 203 Rynisch wyne and Rochelle, richere was neuer. c 1490 Paston Lett. III. 361, I sen my lady a lytyll pes of Renysch wyne of the best. 1528 Paynell Salerne's Regim. R ij, Mustis, that haue bytynge lies, as moche reinnishe muste. 1596 Shaks. Merch. V. i. ii. 104 A deepe glasse of Reinish-wine. 1607 Englishman's Docter in Regimen Salern. (1830) 133 New Rhennish-wine stirs vrine. 1660 Bk. Rates (Act 12 Car. II, c. 4), Rhinish wines brought into any Port the Awme, j li. 1787 Maty tr. Riesbeck's Trav. through Germany III. 189 The little village of Hocheim, from whence the English give all kinds of Rhenish wine the name of Hock. 1840 L. Playfair Liebig's Org. Chem. 287 The aroma which distinguishes Rhenish wine.

attrib. 1700 Congreve Way of the World iii. i. F 4 b, That goodly Face, which in defiance of her Rhenish-wine Tea, will not be comprehended in a Mask. 1707 Mortimer Husb. (1721) II. 291 The Underleaf [apple] hath a Rhenish-Wine flavour.

β. 1468 Burgh Rec. Edin. (1869) 23 Rynche wyne. 1546 Ibid. (1871) 125 The Rens wyne xx[ti] d. the pynt. 15.. Aberd. Reg. (Jam.), Ane greit peis of Rance wyne.

B. sb. Rhenish wine. Now rare. Also attrib.

[1596 Shaks. Merch. V. iii. i. 44 There is more difference betweene..your bloods, then there is betweene red wine and rennish.] 1602 — Ham. i. iv. 10 As he dreines his draughts of Renish downe. 1638 T. Whitaker Blood of Grape 52 Adolescency..may not feare either White, Claret, or Rhenish. 1685-8 Dryden Let. to Sir G. Etherege 45 Then Rhenish rummers walk the round, In bumpers every king is crowned. 1756 Johnson Let. to Miss Boothby 3 Jan., I took Rhenish and water, and recovered my voice. 1820 Keats Eve of St. Agnes xxxix, Drown'd all in Rhenish and the sleepy mead. 1828 Scott F. M. Perth v, If sack, or rhenish, or wine of Gascony can serve, why, say the word.

† **Rhenite** (rī·nəit). Min. Obs. [f. L. Rhēn-us Rhine + -ite.] Pseudomalachite.

c 1830 H. J. Brooke in Encycl. Metrop. (1845) VI. 488/1 Hydrous Phosphate of Copper. Rhenite.

Rheo- (rī·ŏ, rīǫ·), also reo-, used as comb. form of Gr. ῥέος stream, current, chiefly in names of electrical apparatus: **Rhe·ochord, -cord**, a wire used in measuring the resistance or reducing the strength of an electric current. † **Rhe·ocline** [Gr. κλίνη couch], a form of air-bed. **Rhe·o-ele·ctric** a., producing electric currents. **Rhe·omotor**, an apparatus by which an electric current is generated. **Rhe·ophore** [F. rhéophore; Gr. -φορος bearing], (a) Ampère's name for the connecting wire of a voltaic cell; (b) one of the poles of a voltaic battery; an electrode; hence **Rheopho·ric** a. **Rhe·otome** [Gr. -τομος cutting], a device for interrupting an electric current; = Interrupter b. **Rhe·otrope** [Gr. -τροπος turning], an instrument for reversing an electric current.

1865 Tyndall Heat § 508 It was only necessary, by means of the tangent compass and *rheocord, to keep the current constant. 1890 in Phil. Trans. (1892) CLXXXII. 326 note, The rheochord readings are in decimals of a volt. 1851 Hooper Physician's Vade-Mecum 315 The water-bed or the *rheiocline, should be resorted to in the more severe class of cases. 1860 Flor. Nightingale Nursing viii. 46 An iron bedstead, with rheocline springs, which are permeable by the air up to the very mattress. 1843 J. Nott in Rep. Brit. Ass. Notices & Abstr. (1844) 16, I insulated the ring, and connected it with the resinous conductor of the *rheo-electric machine. 1843 Wheatstone in Phil. Trans. 306, I shall..employ the word *Rheomotor to denote any apparatus which originates an electric current. 1873 F. Jenkin Electr. & Magn. (1881) xxii. § 2 The sending battery, or other rheomotor. 1843 Wheatstone in Phil. Trans. 307 The word *Rheophore was employed by Ampère to designate the connecting wire of a voltaic apparatus as being the carrier or transmitter of the current. 1880 M. Mackenzie Dis. Throat & Nose I. 421 To carry out this treatment, either the double laryngeal rheophores or my single electrode may be used. 1843 Wheatstone in Phil. Trans. 307 The method of obtaining the constants of a *rheophoric circuit. Ibid., *Rheotome. 1879 G. Prescott Sp. Telephone 117 One of the numerous apparatus called rheotomes, or cut currents. 1843 Wheatstone in Phil. Trans. 307 *Rheotrope. 1884 Sprague Electr. (ed. 2) 636 Rheotrope. —A reversing commutator.

Rheometer (rīǫ·mĭtəɹ). [f. Rheo- + -meter.]

1. Electr. An instrument for measuring the force of an electric current.

1843 Wheatstone in Phil. Trans. 307. 1852 Lardner Handbk. Nat. Phil. ii. 384 In certain researches a differential reometer is found useful. 1884 Sprague Electr. (ed. 2) 630 Rheometer.—A galvanometer.

2. An instrument for measuring the force or velocity of (a) a water-current, (b) the blood-flow.

1877 M. Foster Text-bk. Physiol. Index, Rheometer of Ludwig, for measuring blood pressure. 1881 Nature 26 Jan. 290/2 A rheometer, for measuring currents at different depths in water.

Hence **Rheome·tric** a., pertaining to a rheometer or rheometry; **Rheo·metry**, the measurement of electric currents, as by a rheometer.

1850 A. Secchi (title), Researches on Electrical Rheometry. 1852 Lardner Handbk. Nat. Phil. ii. 383 Such an apparatus would be reoscopic, but not reometric.

Rheoscope (rī·ŏskoup). Electr. Now rare. [f. Rheo- + -scope.] (See quot. 1843.)

1843 Wheatstone in Phil. Trans. 307 A Rheoscope is an instrument for ascertaining merely the existence of an electric current. 1852 Lardner Handbk. Nat. Phil. ii. 380 Reoscopes and Reometers. 1881 S. P. Thompson Electr. & Magn. 161 note.

Hence **Rheosco·pic** a., (a) pertaining to the rheoscope; (b) applied to preparations of certain nerves of a frog for showing the variation of electric currents; so rheoscopic frog, muscle.

1852 [see Rheometric]. 1877 M. Foster Text-bk. Physiol. 44 The method known as 'the rheoscopic frog', in which the natural current of one nerve, or the negative variation of that current, is used as a stimulus to another nerve. Ibid. 107 note, The absence of tetanus in a rheoscopic muscle.

Rheostat (rī·ŏstæt). Electr. [f. Rheo- + στατός, vbl. adj. of ἱστάναι to stand.] (See quot. 1843.)

1843 Wheatstone in Phil. Trans. 309 As the principal use of this instrument is to adjust or regulate the circuit so that any constant degree of force may be obtained I have called it a rheostat. 1896 Allbutt's Syst. Med. I. 369 The rheostat is again brought into use to lower the current.

attrib. 1850 A. Secchi Res. Electr. Rheometry 35 Coiling the rheostat wire on the wooden cylinder. 1879 Noad & Preece Electr. 207 The rheostat cylinder.

So **Rheosta·tic** a. [ad. F. rhéostatique, 1877], the name of an electric machine invented by Planté, by which continuous static effects are produced.

1878 Chem. News XXXVII. 184/2 Effects of the Rheostatic Machine.—G. Planté.

Rheostatics (rīǫstæ·tiks), sb. pl. ? Obs. [f. Rheo- + Statics.] The statics of fluid bodies.

1753 Chambers Cycl. Suppl., Rheo-statics, is used by some for the statics, or the science of the equilibrium of fluids. [Hence in recent Dicts.]

Rheotannic (rīǫtæ·nik), a. Chem. [f. Gr. ῥῆον Rheum[2] + Tannic.] The name of a variety of tannic acid found in rhubarb.

1883 Encycl. Brit. XX. 530/1 The chief chemical constituents of Chinese rhubarb are chrysophan ($C_{15}H_{10}O_4$), rheotannic acid ($C_{26}H_{26}O_{14}$) [etc.].

‖ **Rhesis** (rī·sis). [a. Gr. ῥῆσις word, speech.] A set speech or discourse.

1871 Browning Balaust. Wks. 1896 I. 629/2 Any who could speak A chorus to the end, or prologize, Roll out a rhesis. 1906 Athenæum 31 Mar. 383/2 The discourse (or rhesis) put into the mouth of Martin.

‖ **Rhesus** (rī·sŏs). [mod.L., arbitrary use of L. Rhēsus, Gr. Ῥῆσος, a mythical king of Thrace.] In full, Rhesus monkey: one of the macaques, Macacus rhesus, an Indian monkey.

1839 Penny Cycl. XIV. 236/1 [The tail] rather more developed in the Wanderoo and Rhesus than in the Magot and Papio niger. 1841 Ibid. XIX. 448/2 Rhesus Monkey, a species of Simiadæ. 1859 Wood Illustr. Nat. Hist. I. 52.

Rhetian, etc.: see Rhætian, etc.

Rhetor (rī·tǫɹ). Forms: 4-6 rethor, 5 rether, 5-6 -our, 6- rhetor. [a. L. rhētor (in med.L. often rethor), a. Gr. ῥήτωρ. Cf. F. rhéteur.]

1. A teacher or professor of rhetoric; a rhetorician.

c 1375 St. Augustin 71 in Horstm. Altengl. Leg. (1878) 62/2 Austin þe doctour..was a philosofre and a rethor. c 1386 Chaucer Sqr.'s T. 30 A Rethor excellent, That koude hise colours longynge for that Art. 1500-20 Dunbar Poems lxiii. 5 Divinouris, rethoris, and philosophouris. 1611 H. Broughton Require of Agreement 47 Aristides, the Rhetor Sophister. 1643 Hammond Serm. Wks. 1683 IV. 514 Your Hearing,..what is it but as of a Rhetor at a Desk, to commend or dislike? 1750 Warburton Julian Introd. p. xxxiii, From the teaching Rhetors they learnt the art of reasoning by similitudes and analogies. 1847 Grote Greece ii. xxxvi. IV. 454 Themistoklês had received no teaching from philosophers, sophists and rhetors, who were the instructors of well-born youth in the days of Thucydidês. 1879 Farrar St. Paul (1883) 386 The..city..was full of professors, rhetors, tutors,..grammarians.

† b. transf. A master of eloquence or literary expression. Obs.

? 1409-11 Lydg. Life our Lady xxxiv. (Caxton) e vij b, And eke my master chauceris now is graue The noble rethor poete of brytayne. ? c 1450 in Lydg. Temple Glas (1891) 78 Moral gower, lydgate, Rether and poete. 1508 Dunbar Gold. Targe 253 O reuerend Chaucere, rose of rethoris all.

2. An orator, esp. a professional one. Sometimes in depreciatory use: A rhetorical speechifier, a mere rhetorician.

1588 Fraunce Lawiers Log. i. v. 31 b, This were an affect of an extemporall Rhetor to salute a man by name without premeditation. 1807 W. Taylor in Ann. Rev. V. 577 He must be pacing about in his rhetor's cassock, watching its turgid folds. 1821 Jefferson Autobiog. Writ. 1892 I. 140 The rhapsodies of Rhetor Burke. 1860 A. L. Windsor Ethica vii. 383 Not that Chatham was a mere sophistical rhetor. 1874 Lewes Probl. Life & Mind I. 29 Those rhetors who declaim against it.

† **Rheto·reulist.** rare. [f. L. dim. *rhētorculus (see -culus) + -ist.] A petty rhetorician.

1609 [Bp. W. Barlow] Answ. Nameless Cath. 25 Many restraints were made vnder seuere penalties, which this Rhetorculist himselfe confesseth. Ibid. 201.

† **Rhetorial**, a. Obs. rare—¹. [f. Rhetor or Rhetory + -(i)al.] Rhetorical.

1513 Bradshaw St. Werburge, Balade (1887) 201 O frutefull histore...Enbawmed with doctrine of virtues infinite, With termes exquised and sence retoriall.

† **Rheto·rian**, sb. and a. Obs. In 4-5 rethorien, -yen, 5 retoryan. [a. OF. rethorien (rect-), f. med.L. *rethoria Rhetory: see -ian.]

A. sb. = Rhetorician.

c 1374 Chaucer Boeth. ii. pr. iii. (1868) 38 Þou rethorien or pronouncere of kynges preysinges. c 1430 Life St. Kath. (1884) 54 And sent out lettres..vnto alle rethoriens and gramariens. 1447 Bokenham Seyntys (Roxb.) 41 The fresh rethoryens Gowere, Chauncere & now Lytgate. 1483 Cath. Angl. 305/2 Retoryan, rethor, rethoricus.

B. adj. = Rhetorical. [So OF.]

c 1374 Chaucer Boeth. ii. pr. i. (1868) 30 Þe suasioun of swetnesse Rethoryen.

Rhetoric (re·tŏrik), sb.[1] Forms: 4 [rethorice,] rettorike, 4-6 ret(h)orik(e, -yk(e, 5-7 rethorick (4 -ikke, 5 -ykk, -yque, retherique, 6 rethoric, -ique, -icke, rhet(h)orike, 7 rhet'rique, reth'rick), 6-7 rhetorique, -icke, rhetorick, -ique, 7-8 rhetorick, rhet'ric, 7- rhetoric. [a. OF. rethorique (mod.F. rhétorique), or ad. L. rhētorica, -icē (med.L. reth-), a. Gr. ῥητορικὴ (sc. τέχνη), fem. of ῥητορικός Rhetoric a.]

1. The art of using language so as to persuade or influence others; the body of rules to be observed by a speaker or writer in order that he may express himself with eloquence.

In the Middle Ages rhetoric was reckoned one of the seven 'liberal arts', being comprised, with grammar and logic, in the 'trivium'.

13.. Senyn Sag. 186 (W.), Geometrie, and arsmetrike, Rettorike, and ek fisike. 1387 Trevisa Higden (Rolls) III. 361 Aristotle..tauȝte eloquence..as it is specialliche i-sene ..in his Dyalogus of Poetis and in Tretys of Rethorik. 14.. Bewte will shewe 69 in Pol., Rel., & L. Poems, Was neuer clerk, by retoryk or science, Cowde all hyr verteus reherse to þis day. 1475 Bk. Noblesse (Roxb.) 25 The famous clerke of eloquence Tullius seithe in his booke of retherique [etc.]. 1481 Caxton Myrr. i. ix. 34 The therde of the vii sciences is called Rethoryque. 1553 T. Wilson Rhet. 1 Rhetorique is an art to set furthe by utteraunce of wordes matter at large. 1586 A. Day Eng. Secretary i. (1625) 10 Many excellent Figures and places of Rhetorique. 1656 Stanley Hist. Philos. v. (1687) 176/2 Rhetorick is conversant in singulars, not in universals. 1741 Watts Improv. Mind xx. § 33 (1801) 193 Rhetoric in general is the art of persuading. 1836 Penny Cycl. V. 280/1 Having lectured successively in grammar, rhetoric,..humanity, and moral philosophy. 1843 Mill Logic Introd. § 3 The communication of those thoughts to others falls under the consideration of Rhetoric.

b. fig. or with personification.

[c 1374 Chaucer Boeth. ii. pr. i. (1868) 30 And wiþ Rethorice com forþe musice a damoisel of oure house.] 1423 Jas. I Kingis Q. cxcvii, Gowere and chaucere, that on the steppis satt Of rethorike. c 1430 Lydg. Min. Poems (Percy Soc.) 11 And Retoryk had eke in her presence Tulyus, callyd 'Mirrour of Eloquence'. 1530 Lyndesay Test. Papyngo 11 For quhy the bell of Rethorick bene roung Be Chawceir, Goweir, and Lidgate laureate. 1642 Fuller Holy & Prof. St. ii. vii. 73 Some condemn Rhetorick as the mother of lies. 1742 Pope Dunc. iv. 24 There, stript, fair Rhet'ric languish'd on the ground.

c. A treatise on, or 'body' of, rhetoric.

1565 Cooper Thesaurus s.v. Rhetoricus, In primo Ciceronis rhetorico.., in the firste booke of Ciceroes rhetorike. 1580 G. Harvey in Three Proper Lett. 32 To bring our Language into Arte, and to frame a Grammer or Rhetorike thereof. 1581 Lambarde Eiren. i. xi. 63 It is a good Counsell (which Aristotle giueth in his Rhetorikes ad Theodectem). 1654 T. Blount (title), The Academie of Eloquence, Containing a Compleat English Rhetorique. 1712 Addison Spect. No. 297 ⁋ 17 Aristotle himself has given it a place in his Rhetorick among the Beauties of that Art.

d. The top class or the second class (from the top) in certain English Roman Catholic schools and colleges. So † to make one's rhetoric.

1599 in Foley Rec. Eng. Prov. S. J. (1879) V. 569, I have made my rhetoric in these parts. c 1620 in Mem. Stonyhurst Coll. (1881) 8 They go down two by two with their books under their arms, and first those in Rhetoric, into the Refectory. 1908 Stonyhurst Mag. in Tablet 25 Apr. 646/2 We are informed that any boy from Rhetoric down to Elements may join the class.

2. † a. Elegance or eloquence of language; eloquent speech or writing. Obs. b. Speech or writing expressed in terms calculated to persuade; hence (often in depreciatory sense), language characterized by artificial or ostentatious expression.

c 1386 Chaucer Clerk's Prol. 32 Fraunceys Petrak,..whos Rethorik sweete Enlumyned al Ytaille of poetrie. 1426 Lydg. in Pol. Poems (Rolls) II. 133 Alle be that I in my translacioun..Of rethoryk have no maner floure. 1562 Winȝet Cert. Tractates Wks. (S.T.S.) I. 25 As I persaue rethorik thairof verray small, swa I can espy na thing thairin abhorring fra the treuth. 1570 Dee Math. Pref. 46 Nor your faire pretense, by such rashe ragged Rhetorike, any whit, well graced. 1615 Brathwait Strappado (1878) 24 Heere is no substance, but a simple peece Of gaudy Rhetoricke. 1671 Milton P. R. iv. 4 And the perswasive Rhetoric That sleek't his tongue. 1733 Swift Lett. (1766) II. 189 The one word from you, is of much more weight than my rhetoric. 1784 Cowper Task iv. 491 Modern senators..Whose oath is rhet'ric, and who swear for fame! 1825 Macaulay Ess., Milton, The sublime wisdom of the Areopagitica and the nervous rhetoric of the Iconoclast. 1837 Landor Pentameron 33 Escape from rhetoric by all manner of means. 1880 Swinburne Stud. Shaks. 269 The limp loquacity of long-winded rhetoric, so natural to men and soldiers in an hour of emergency.

† c. pl. Elegant expressions; rhetorical flourishes. Also, rhetorical terms. Obs.

1426 Lydg. De Guil. Pilgr. 19774 That poete, Wyth al hys rethorykes swete. 1543 Bale Yet a Course 26 Neuer coude tolwyn throughlye knowe what these rhetoryckes ment, as are denuncyacyon, deteccyon, and presentacyon. 1589 Puttenham Eng. Poesie iii. ii. (Arb.) 151 Graue and wise counsellours..do much mislike all scholasticall rhetoricks. 1628 Wither Brit. Rememb. 42 b, Their fantastique Rhetoriques, Who trim their Poesies with schooleboy-tricks.

d. in ironical or jocular use.

1580 Spenser in Three Proper Lett. 14 Like a drunken man, or women (when their Alebench Rhetorick commes vpon them). 1595 W. S. Locrine iii. iii, I think you were brought up in the university of Bridewell, you have your rhetoric so ready at your tongue's end. 1613 Purchas Pilgrimage iii. xiv. (1614) 315 Some of them vpbraiding both him and other Christians with the names of dogs, Ethnickes, vnbeleeuers, and the like zealous Rhetorick. 1742 Fielding J. Andrews i. xviii, The rhetoric of John the hostler, with a new straw hat, and a pint of wine, made a second conquest over her. c 1750 Shenstone Ruin'd Abbey 10 Fearless he of shouts Or taunts, the rhet'ric of the wat'ry

crew. 1849 Macaulay Hist. Eng. iv. I. 450 He [Jeffreys] acquired a boundless command of the rhetoric in which the vulgar express hatred and contempt.

e. transf. and fig., said esp. † (a) of the expressive action of the body in speaking; (b) of the persuasiveness of looks or acts.

1569 Sanford tr. Agrippa's Van. Artes xxi, This daunsinge or Histrionical Rhetorike in the ende beganne to be lefte of all Oratours. 1587 Greene Euphues his Censure Wks. (Grosart) VI. 252 For he considered with himselfe,.. that liberality was the soundest rethoricke. 1588 Shaks. L. L. L. iv. iii. 60 The heauenly Rhetoricke of thine eye. 1597 Breton Wit's Trenchmour Wks. (Grosart) II. 15/1 Silence can best talke with wooden Rethoricke. 1644 J. B. (title), Chironomia: Or, The Art of Manuall Rhetorique. 1647 Cowley Mistr., Rich Rival ii, Whilst thy sole Rhetorick shall be Joynture, and Jewels, and Our Friends agree. 1669 Stillingfl. Six Serm. iii. 127 Every part of the Tragedy of his [the Son of God's] life, every wound at his death,.. were designed by him as the most prevailing Rhetorick, to perswade men to forsake their sins. 1712 Gay Trivia iii. 318 Mov'd by the Rhet'rick of a Silver Fee. 1851 Ruskin Stones Venice I. i. 11 His larger sacred subjects are merely themes for the exhibition of pictorial rhetoric,—composition and colour.

† 3. Skill in or faculty of using eloquent and persuasive language. Obs.

c 1440 Partonope 5835 These lordis are chosyn be myn assent. The fyrst ys the kyng of affryke For his grete wytte and his retoryke. 1509 Barclay Shyp of Folys (1570) 17 Though he be wise and of might meruailous, Endued with Rhethorike and with eloquence. 1634 Milton Comus 790 Enjoy your deer Wit, and gay Rhetorick That hath so well been taught her dazling fence. 1680 H. More Apocal. Apoc. Pref. 7 The highest Encomium..that the Wit and Rhetorick of men or Angels can invent. 1711 Addison Spect. No. 171 ⁋ 12 Joseph..endeavoured, with all his Art and Rhetorick, to set out the Excess of Herod's Passion for her. 1750 Gray Long Story 117 But soon his rhetorick forsook him.

4. attrib. and Comb.

1656 Earl Monmouth tr. Boccalini's Advts. from Parnass. ii. lxxxviii. (1674) 240 To Declaim..publickly in the Rhetorick-School. 1806 H. K. White Let. to Bro. Neville 30 July, The Rhetoric Lecturer sent me one of my Latin Essays to copy for the purpose of inspection. 1884 Punch 23 Feb. 87 To unmask His rhetoric-shrouded weakness.

† **Rhetoric**, sb.[2] In 4 rethorik, -ique, 4-5 retorike. [ad. L. rhētoric-us (med.L. reth-), subst. use of adj. (see next).] = Rhetorician.

a 1350 St. Catherine 159 in Horstm. Altengl. Leg. (1881) 166 All þe maisters of clergy, Both retorikes and gramarione. 1390 Gower Conf. III. 48 Tullius the rethorique. a 1450 R. Spalding St. Kath. in Anglia (1907) 540 Fyfti fyue retorikes in hast þei hem hent.

Rhetoric (rĭte·rik), a. rare. Also 5-6 reth-, 6 ret-, rheth-. [a. F. rhétorique (OF. also reth-), or ad. L. rhētoric-us (med.L. reth-), f. rhētor: see Rhetor and -ic.] Rhetorical; † eloquent.

? 1400 Lydg. Serp. Devision (1590) C iij b, The first that euer elumined our language with flowers of rethorick eloquence: I mean..Chaucer. 1484 Caxton Fables of Alfonce vii, This fable..of a rethoryque man or fayr speker. 1517 Watson Shyppe of Fooles Prol., It was translated..out of Latyn in to rethoryke Frensshe. 1542 Boorde Dyetary Pref. (1870) 228 With eloquent speche & rethorycke termes. 1678 Gale Crt. Gentiles iv. iii. vi. 180 With many rhetoric flourishes and pompose triumphs. 1866 Kingsley Herew. ii. I. 81 note, The crude matter, too little..ornate by the care of any trained intellect, or by dialectic and rhetoric enigmas. 1889 Pater G. de Latour (1896) 104 Helping himself indifferently to all religions for rhetoric illustration.

Rhetorical (rĭtǫ·rĭkăl), a. Forms: as in prec. [f. L. rhētoric-us: see prec. and -ical.]

1. † a. Eloquent, or eloquently expressed. Obs. b. Expressed in terms calculated to persuade; hence (often in depreciatory use), composed or expressed in artificial or extravagant language; of the nature of mere rhetoric (as opposed to sober statement or argument).

1476 in Antiq. Rep. (1808) II. 385 A Colacyon made by Metre in Rhetorical Terms. 1509 Barclay Shyp Folys (1570) 222 Other with their wordes hye and retoricall Their sentences paynt. ? 1554 Coverdale Hope of Faithful Pref., If one should barely, and wyth oute all rhetorical amplificacions, but reherce only the great pompe..[etc.] of myghtye men and rulers. 1589 Puttenham Eng. Poesie i. iv. (Arb.) 24 It [sc. metrical speech] is beside a maner of vtterance more eloquent and rethoricall then the ordinarie prose. 1613 Purchas Pilgrimage viii. i. (1614) 719 But easier it was for him, with a Rhetoricall flourish..to dash this opinion out of countenance. a 1660 Hammond Wks. (1684) IV. 564 A degree of stupidity..that neither the iniquity of Sodom,.. nor the Rhetoricall'st Phrase almost in the very Scripture can express. 1783 Ld. Hailes Antiq. Chr. Ch. iv. 127 There is no rhetorical exaggeration in this passage of Josephus. 1852 Mrs Stowe Uncle Tom's C. xvii. 163 If these words had been spoken by some easy, self-indulgent exhorter, from whose mouth they might have come merely as pious and rhetorical flourish. 1869 Buckle Civiliz. III. v. 347 The facts..were more intended to persuade than to prove. They were rather rhetorical than logical.

c. Applied to the rhythm of prose as distinguished from metrical rhythm.

1727-38 Chambers Cycl. s.v. Numbers, Rhetorical, or prosaic Numbers, are a sort of simple unaffected harmony, less glaring than that of verse. 1832 Encycl. Amer. XI. 591 Rhetorical rhythm is satisfied with a pleasing cadence of syllables.

d. Rhetorical accent: (see quots.).

1727-38 Chambers Cycl. s.v. Accent, The rhetorical Accents [in Hebrew] are said to be Euphonic; inasmuch as they tend to make the pronunciation more sweet and agreeable. 1866 Chamb. Encycl. VIII. 243/1 There is also an irregular or rhetorical accent in music called emphasis.

e. Rhetorical question: (see quots.).

1843 T. K. Arnold Latin Prose Comp. § 442 Non is often used without ne in vehement questions, especially, of course, questions of appeal, or, as Reisig calls them, rhetorical questions. 1884 Bradley's Aids to Lat. Prose § 150 Questions that do not require an answer, but are only put in the form of a question in order to produce a greater effect,..are called rhetorical questions.

2. Of, belonging to, concerned with, or comprised in the art of rhetoric.

1530 Palsgr. 322/2 Rethoricall, belongynge to rethoricke, rethoricque. 1533 Frith Answ. More E 4, I expounde my minde by a rethoricall correction and saye, Imo recordationem sacrificij. 1608 D. T. Ess. Pol. & Mor. 27 b, Such is the force of the Rhetoricall Enthymems. 1657 North's Plutarch, Add. Lives (1676) 39 [Charlemagne] was instructed in the Rhetorical, Dialectical, and Astrological Arts. 1791 Mackintosh Vind. Gallicæ Wks. 1846 III. 77 It would have been quoted by Quintilian as a splendid model of rhetorical common-place. 1837 Hallam Lit. Eur. I. 3 The rhetorical works of Cicero and Quintilian. 1871 R. F. Weymouth Euphuism 13 Irony or climax or hyperbole or any other rhetorical figure.

3. Of persons: Given to the use of rhetoric.

1651 H. More Enthus. Tri. (1712) 18 Melancholy, as well as Wine, makes a man Rhetorical or Poetical. 1656 Blount Glossogr., Rhetorical, skilful in Rhetorick, that speaks eloquently. 1882 Farrar Early Chr. I. 406 note, St. Paul is often rhetorical, i.e. he writes with a passion which finds natural expression in the most forcible figures of speech.

Rheto·rically, adv. In a rhetorical manner.

1543 Bale Yet a Course 44 b, My lorde hath rhetorycallye begonne hys proposycyon to wynne hys audytorye,..in callynge them good peple. 1646 Sir T. Browne Pseud. Ep. 135 Many others cannot be drawne into Argument as writing Poetically, Rhetorically, Enigmatically, Hieroglyphically. 1788 Wesley Wks. (1811) IX. 110, I could.. write..floridly and rhetorically. 1831-3 E. Burton Eccl. Hist. xxii. (1845) 459 Tertullian..perhaps speaks rhetorically, when he says, that the Gospel had penetrated into.. countries, which had not as yet submitted to the Romans.

b. With reference to the art of rhetoric.

1828 Whately Rhet. in Encycl. Metrop. (1845) I. 270/1 Some passions may be, Rhetorically speaking, opposite to each other, though in strictness they are not so.

So **Rheto·ricalness**, 'eloquentness' (Bailey, vol. II, 1727).

Rhetoricaster. rare—¹. [f. L. rhētoric-us Rhetoric sb.[2] + -aster.] A poor rhetorician.

1591 Fraunce Ctess Pembr. Ivychurch i. ii. iii, Trope-turned tale, or ryming ditty, deryued from foole-hardy Poets, or vaine-head Rhetorica-sters.

† **Rheto·ricate**, v. Obs. [f. ppl. stem of L. rhētoricārī, f. rhētoricus Rhetoric.] intr. To speak rhetorically; to use rhetorical language. Hence **Rheto·ricating** vbl. sb. and ppl. a.

1617 Collins Def. Bp. Ely i. i. 87 It was easie for Leo to rhetoricate at Rome, in the praise of Peter. a 1648 Digby Closet Opened Pref., There needs no Rhetoricating Floscules to set it off. 1676 Cudworth Serm. 1 Cor. xv. 57 A faculty of Rhetoricating and extemporizing with zeal and fervency. 1681 Colvil Whigs Supplic. (1710) 166 I'le use no Speech with Art besprinkled,..Without Rhetoricating Fond shows [etc.]. 1719 Waterland Vind. Christ's Div. 382 Strange, that They should all Rhetoricate in a Matter of Faith, of so great Weight. 17.. — Doctr. Holy Trin. Add., Wks. 1823 V. 357 To magnify another kind of guilt, as still greater according to their way of reasoning, or rather rhetoricating.

† **Rhetorica·tion.** Obs. Also 7 ret-. [ad. L. rhētoricātiōn-em, n. of action f. rhētoricārī to Rhetoricate.] The action of speaking or writing rhetorically; usually with a and pl., a piece of rhetoric, a rhetorical flourish.

1607 Schol. Disc. agst. Antichr. i. ii. 105 These were but rhetorications in the Fathers. 1664 Power Exp. Philos. iii. 192, I think it is no Rhetorication to say, That all things are Artificial. a 1697 Aubrey Lives (1898) I. 253 It was a two-handed rhetorication, but the citizens tooke it in the best sense. 1732 Waterland Christ. Vind. 9 Take but away their Rhetorications and equivocal Expressions,..and their Cause will be left in a manner destitute. 1793 C. Boettiger Let. in A. Dalzel Hist. Univ. Edin. (1862) I. 107 Blair's blooming rhetorications.

Rhetorician (retŏri·ʃăn). Forms: 5-6 reth-, 6 ret-, 6-7 rheth-; 5 -icyen, -ycien, -ian, -icion, 5-6 -icien, 6 -ycyne, -icyan, -ian, -ycyne, 5-7 -ician, 6-7 -itian; 5 retricion, retrycyan; 6- rhetorician. [a. OF. rethoricien (rett-, rest-), mod.F. rhétoricien, f. L. rhētoricus Rhetoric a. and sb.[2] or rhētorica Rhetoric sb.[1]: see -ician.]

1. A professor or teacher of the art of rhetoric (esp. in Ancient Greece and Rome); a professional rhetor or orator.

1412-20 Lydg. Chron. Troy ii. 176 After þe maner of gramariens, Nor lyke þe stile of rethoricyens, I toke nat on me þis story to translate. 1432-50 tr. Higden (Rolls) V. 261 Victorius the rethoricion. 1581 Sidney Apol. Poetry (Arb.) 25 And the Rethorician, and Logitian, considering what in Nature will soonest proue and perswade, thereon giue artificial rules. 1680 T. Granger Div. Logike 148 The figure Imago of the vulgar Rhetoricians. 1663 Butler Hud. i. i. 89 For all a Rhetoricians Rules, Teach nothing but to name his Tools. 1711 Addison Spect. No. 231 ⁋ 4 Rhetoricians have recommended it [sc. modesty] to their Disciples as a Particular in their Art. 1838 Thirlwall Greece V. 239 Isocrates was a Rhetorician by profession: the framing of sentences, and turning of periods, was the great business of his long life. 1869 Lecky Europ. Mor. I. ii. 329 A curious contrast to the Cynic was the philosophic rhetorician.

2. † a. An eloquent or elegant writer. Obs. b. One who uses rhetorical language or expression; esp. (often in depreciatory use) a public speaker who indulges in rhetoric.

1412-20 Lydg. Chron. Troy Prol. 57 O thou Calliope,.. that wyth thyn hony swete Sugrest tongis of rethoricyens. c 1440 — Hors, Shepe & G. 185 Whan Rethoriciens han doon ther besy peyn Fressh Epistolis & lettris to endite. 1561 T. Norton Calvin's Inst. i. 16 When that rough..simplicitie doeth raise vp a greater reuerence of it self than any Rhetoricians eloquence. 1588 J. Udall Diotrephes (Arb.) 25 It is a thing incident vnto a rethorician to be girding. 1630 Brathwait Eng. Gentlem. (1641) 8 Whoever intendeth his care rather to find out words than matter may bee holden for a verball Rhetorician, but no serious orator. 1839 Hallam Lit. Eur. IV. 170 No one would call Bourdaloue a rhetorician. 1861 London Rev. 20 Apr. 431/2 The finances of England are in the hands of a rhetorician, who, in place of acts, seeks to dazzle the people with fine promises. 1874 Green Short Hist. x. § 1. 731 Passionate as was Pitt's eloquence, it was the eloquence of a statesman, not of a rhetorician.

3. In English Roman Catholic schools, a scholar in the class of Rhetoric (see Rhetoric 1 d).

1790 in Mem. Stonyhurst Coll. (1881) 30 Academical exhibition in which the new President was finely complimented by the Rhetoricians.

4. attrib. or as adj.

1712 Blackmore Creation iii. 140 Pyrrhonians..Boldly presum'd, with Rhetorician Pride, To hold of any Question either side. a 1864 Landor Imag. Conv., Pollio & Calvus Wks. 1876 II. 451 Asiatic never was Cicero, although he sometimes wore at the bottom of his rhetorician robe a flounce too many.

Hence **Rhetori·cianism**, the style of a rhetorician.

a 1849 Poe Wks. (1864) III. 143 'Deep calleth unto deep' is a great improvement upon his previous rhetoricianism.

† **Rhe·toricly**, adv. Obs. In 5 rethorikly, retoriquely. [f. Rhetoric a. + -ly[2].] Rhetorically.

1423 Jas. I Kingis Q. vii, So full of fruyte, and rethorikly pykit. 1481 Caxton Tulle of Olde Age e 7 The poet Ennius callys him his swete hony, by cause that his boke was so retoriquely made.

† **Rheto·riously**, adv. Obs. In 5 reth-. [f. *rethorious (f. Rhetor or Rhetory + -(i)ous) + -ly[2].] With 'colours' of rhetoric.

c 1475 Partenay 6611 Now ye all that shall thys..rede.., Remembreth myn unconnyng simplesse; Thought rethoriously peinted [it] be not in-dede,..yut excusith me.

† **Rhe·torism.** Obs. [ad. mod.L. rhētorismus: see next and -ism.] Rhetorical language or action.

1569 Sanford tr. Agrippa's Van. Arts xxi. heading, Of Rhetorisme, or of the Rhetoricall Daunsinge [orig. De Rhetorismo].

Rhe·torize, v. ? Obs. [ad. late L. rhētorizāre (Bede), a. Gr. ῥητορίζειν, f. ῥητορ-, ῥήτωρ Rhetor: see -ize.] intr. To use rhetorical language.

1608 Hieron Defence iii. 65 The Ancient Fathers have.. been pleased thus to rhetorise, in commendation of the Sacrament. 1611 Cotgr., Rhetoriquer, to rhetorize it, play the Rhetorician. 1624 Bp. Mountagu Immed. Addr. 206 Gregory Nazianzen hath taught Saint Hierome also how to Rhetorize. 1834 Southey Doctor xlvi. (1848) 108 After having rhetorised in praise of sacred music. 1841 Tait's Mag. VIII. 484 There is another [kind of art] which, by.. rhetorizing, assumes to itself the false importance of an end.

Hence † **Rhe·torized** ppl. a., addressed rhetorically.

1642 Milton Apol. Smect. 8 To write a Letter to a prosopopœa, a certain rhetoriz'd woman whom he calls mother.

† **Rhe·tory.** Sc. Obs. Also 5-6 r(h)ethorie, retory. [ad. late L. *rethoria, *rhetoria, a. Gr. ῥητορεία, f. ῥήτωρ Rhetor.] Rhetoric; eloquence.

c 1480 Henryson Mor. Fab. Prol. 3 Thair polite termis of sweit Rhetorie [v.rr. rethorie, retory] Richt plesand ar vnto the eir of man. 1500-20 Dunbar Poems lxv. 10 The eloquence of ornat rethorie. 1501 Douglas Pal. Hon. i. i, Schaw thy endite reprufe of rethoryis.

Rheubarb, obs. form of Rhubarb.

Rheum (rūm), sb.[1] Now arch. Forms: 4-6 rewme, 4-7 reume (5 reem, 6 ryme), 6-7 r(h)ewm, rhewme, r(h)ume, 8 rhum, 6- rheum. [a. OF. reume (13th c.), mod.F. rhume, = Pr., Sp., It., Pg. reuma, ad. L. rheuma, a. Gr. ῥεῦμα flow, stream, f. root ῥευ- to flow.

With the forms reem (Promp. Parv. 429/1), ryme (Palsgr. 263/1), cf. med.L. ri(h)ema (It. rema), obs. F. ryme, rime.]

1. Watery matter secreted by the mucous glands or membranes, such as collects in or drops from the nose, eyes, and mouth, etc., and which, when abnormal, was supposed to cause disease; hence, an excessive or morbid 'defluxion' of any kind.

1398 Trevisa Barth. De P. R. v. xiii. (1495) h j, The nose is..lette..of to grete constreynynge & closyng that comyth of colde, as it faryth ofte in a rewme that fallyth to the breste. c 1400 Lanfranc's Cirurg. 220 It fallib sumtyme þat for reume þat fallib adoun of a mannis heed, þer wexiþ in þe rote of þe tunge a maner round þing. c 1410 Master of Game (MS. Digby 182) xii, Also houndes haue an oþer sikenes þat cometh to hem of þe reume. 1565 Cooper Thesaurus, Branchos, the rewme fallynge downe by the cheekes or throte. 1591 Sparry tr. Cattan's Geomancie ii. viii. 113 The disease commeth of a rheume or watrishnes. 1596 Shaks. Merch. V. i. iii. 118 You that did voide your rume vpon my beard. 1613 Purchas Pilgrimage (1614) 839 They..haue continually a leafe thereof [sc. tobacco] along the mouth betweene the lip and teeth, the rheume running out at the lip-hole. 1699 Garth Dispens. i. 68 Eyes in rheum, thro' midnight watching drown'd. 1733 Cheyne Eng. Malady iii. i, A constant Ptyalism, or spitting thin Rheum. 1784 Cowper Task ii. 728 His sparkling eye Was

quench'd in rheums of age. 1850 J. P. Kennedy Rob of the Bowl xii. 127 A laugh..brought the rheum from his eye down his cheek. 1897 Allbutt's Syst. Med. III. 1 The [rheumatic] pain being attributed to rheum flowing down from the brain and settling in the affected part.

b. poet. Used for: Tears.

1593 Shaks. Rich. II, i. iv. 8 The Northeast wind.. Awak'd the sleepie rhewme, and so by chance Did grace our hollow parting with a teare. 1607 — Cor. v. vi. 46 A few drops of Womens rhewme, which are As cheape as Lies. 1803 Southey Eclogues ix. Alderman's Funeral, A good March wind Were to be prayed for now, to lend their eyes Some decent rheum. 1818 Keats Endym. iii. 286 Had he, though blindly contumelious, brought Rheum to kind eyes? 1833 H. Coleridge Poems I. 42 Stoic eyes with foolish rheum o'erflow.

† c. Moisture 'distilled' from the sky. Obs.

1599 Nashe Lenten Stuffe 10 To canopie their heads in from the rheume of the heauens.

† d. transf. and fig. Applied to pernicious moisture or humour, or something resembling it.

1501 Douglas Pal. Hon. Prol. 39 The dasy and the maryguld..lay with their leuis happit, Thame to reserue fra rewmes pungitiue. 1591 Lyly Endym. iv. ii. 71 He is resolued to weep some three or foure payle-fuls, to auoyde the rume of loue that wambleth in his stomacke. 1607 Dekker & Marston Westw. Hoe ii. i, A mastic patch upon some womens temples hath been the very rheum of beauty. 1650 Milton Eikon. (ed. 2) i. 14 If from his Divines he have borrow'd nothing, nothing out of all the Magazin, and the rheume of their Mellifluous prayers.

2. spec. A mucous discharge caused by taking cold (sometimes distinguished as hot or cold rheum); hence, a cold in the head or the lungs; catarrh. Chiefly pl. (occasionally used = Rheumatic pains).

1377 Langl. P. Pl. B. xx. 82 Crampes, and tothaches, Rewmes, & radegoundes. c 1450 M. E. Med. Bk. (Heinrich) 184 Hyt ys good for þe toþ ache of cold rewme. 1486 Bk. St. Albans c v b, When ye se yowre hauke cloose her Eyghen, and shakith hir hede, then hath she the Reume in the hede. 1533 Elyot Cast. Helthe (1541) 69 b, Fleume hath moste puissance in wynter,..whereby are ingendred Catarres or reumes. 1615 Crooke Body of Man 644 In Rheumes and Murrhes the Voyce is hoarse, because the Larynx is dewed with too much moysture. 1656 Evelyn Mem. (1819) I. 297 A mist falling as I returned, gave me such a rheume as kept me within doores neere a whole moneth after. 1667 Milton P. L. xi. 485 [488] Dropsies, and Asthma's, and Joint-racking Rheums. 1752 Hume Ess. & Treat. (1777) II. 197 Old men..endeavour, as long as possible, to conceal their blindness and deafness, their rheums and gouts. 1807 Med. Jrnl. XVII. 475 He..was affected with a rheum for a few days after his arrival. 1864 N. & Q. Ser. iii. VI. 452/2, I provided myself against the contingencies of colds and rheums with military leggings and padded knee-caps.

3. attrib. and Comb., as rheum-cough, -distilling, purging; † rheum-cap (see quot. 1655).

1655 Culpepper, etc. Riverius i. i. 7 The Brain is also strengthened by outward application of..*Rhewm-Caps [orig. cucufæ], by which it is comforted and made warm. 1553 P'cess Mary in Strype Eccl. Mem. (1721) II. ii. xxii. 424 Your Highness late *Rheum-Cough. 1615 Brathwait Strappado (1878) 33 Nose-dropping, *rhewme-destilling, drivelling mouth. 1770 Armstrong Misc. I. 131 The shivering clown..With livid cheeks and rheum-distilling nose. 1612 Drayton Poly-olb. xiii. 200 Heere finds he on an oake *rheume-purging Pollipode.

Hence † **Rheum** v. intr., to 'void rheum'.

1602 2nd Pt. Return fr. Parnass. ii. vi. 968 A meere scholler, is a creature that can..put on a pair of lined slippers, sit rewming till dinner [etc.].

‖ **Rheum** (rī·ŏm), sb.[2] Bot. [mod.L., ad. Gr. ῥῆον.] The generic name for the Rhubarbs.

1753 Chambers Cycl. Suppl. App., Rheum, in botany, the name given by Linnæus to Rhubarb. 1811 A. T. Thomson Lond. Disp. (1818) 334 Rheum undulatum...This species of rheum was supposed by Boerhaave to be the true Chinese rhubarb. 1841 Penny Cycl. XIX. 451/1 What is termed Monk's rhubarb is not the produce of any species of rheum, but of the Rumex alpinus.

Rheumate (rū·mēt). [f. as Rheum-ic + -ate[1] 1 c.] A salt of rheumic acid. 1815 [see Rheumic].

Rheumatic (rumæ·tik), a. and sb. Forms: 4-6 r(e)um-, 4-7 rewm-, 7 rhewm-; 4-6 -atyk(e, 4-7 -ike, -icke, 6 -eticke, -iticke, -atique, 7-8 -atick; 6- rheumatic. [a. OF. ru-, reumatique (mod.F. rhumatique), or ad. late L. rheumaticus, a. Gr. ῥευματικός, f. ῥευματ-, ῥεῦμα Rheum sb.[1] Cf. It., Sp. reumatico, Pg. rheumatico.] A. adj.

† 1. Consisting of or of the nature of rheum or watery secretion or discharge. Obs.

1398 Trevisa Barth. De P. R. iv. iii. (1495) e vj b/2 For somtyme reumatyk humours comyth to þe spirytuel partyes & stoppe þe wayes of þe spyryte. 1547 Boorde Brev. Health (1557) cxix, A reumatyke humour suppressyng the brayne. 1594 Nashe Unfort. Trav. Wks. (Grosart) V. 16 After hee had..spunged..all the rumatike driuell from his ill fauoured Goates beard. 1606 Dekker Newes fr. Hell Wks. (Grosart) II. 121 More salt Rewmatick water runnes out of them, than would pickle all the Herrings that shall come out of Yarmouth. 1696 Floyer Anim. Humours xiii. 158 The Blood taken away looked very Sizie or Rheumatic.

† 2. Full of or dropping with watery mucus.

1599 Nashe Lenten Stuffe 47 Shee..had rumatique sore eyes that ran alwaies. 1601 Holland Pliny II. xx. xx. 69 Rheumaticke ulcers. 1607 Walkington Opt. Glass 71 He was wiping his rheumatick nose. c 1630 Risdon Surv. Devon (1810) 8 It is good to cure rheumatic eyes.

3. Of persons, their bodies: † a. Suffering from a 'defluxion of rheum' or catarrh. Obs.

1574 Hellowes tr. Guevara's Fam. Ep. (1577) 122 By sleeping in an ayrie place, you haue bene very rumatike. 1592 Shaks. Ven. & Ad. 135 Were I hard-fauourd, foule, or wrinckled old,..Ore-worne, despised, reumatique, and cold. 1655 tr. Sorel's Com. Hist. Francion viii. 19 A defluction which fell upon my lungs did make me very rheumatick. 1661 Culpepper London Disp. 13/1 They are good for Rhewmatick people to chew in their mouth, for they draw forth much water.

b. Affected with, suffering from, or subject to rheumatism or rheumatic pain.

1727-38 Chambers Cycl. s.v. Rheumatism, The urine of rheumatic people does not afford above the thirtieth part of the alcaline salt found in that of healthful persons. 1834 E. Barlow in Cycl. Pract. Med. III. 608/1 We have seen leeches when applied to a rheumatic joint prematurely.. exasperate every symptom. 1852 S. Thomson Dict. Dom. Med. 442/2 Many rheumatic patients find their chief protection in an underdress of chamois leather.

4. Of a disease, symptom: † a. Characterized by rheumy or catarrhal 'defluxion'. Obs. b. Of the nature of or characteristic of rheumatism. Rheumatic fever, an acute non-infectious febrile disease marked by inflammation and pain of the joints.

1563 T. Gale Antidot. ii. 82 Thys woode hath a synguler propertie..agaynste many other moyste and rumiticke sicknesses. 1590 Shaks. Mids. N. ii. i. 105 The Moone (the gouernesse of floods)..washes all the aire; That Rheumaticke diseases doe abound. 1688 Holme Armoury ii. 136/1 Rewmatick, or the Slavering Madness. 1704 F. Fuller Med. Gymn. (1705) 118 An excessive Dose of Millepedes in an odd kind of a Rheumatick Case. 1711 Swift Jrnl. to Stella 19 Sept., She is lame in one of her legs with a rheumatic pain. 1782 Miss Burney Cecilia ix. v, The poor woman, whose disease was a rheumatic fever, was already much better. 1783 J. C. Smyth in Med. Commun. I. 152 A kind of arthritis vaga (or what is vulgarly called rheumatic gout). 1797 Jane Austen Sense & Sens. viii, A slight rheumatic feel in one of his shoulders. 1836-9 Todd's Cycl. Anat. II. 518/2 We are acquainted with no disease which more frequently produces deformity of the hand and fingers than chronic rheumatism (chronic rheumatic arthritis). 1845 R. Williams in Encycl. Metrop. VII. 681 In scarlatina the joints are often the seat of the severest rheumatic inflammation. 1887 Brit. Med. Jrnl. 5 Mar. 510/2 Rheumatic pyrexia.

† c. transf. and fig. (a) Tearful. (b) Phlegmatic.

a 1625 Fletcher Nice Valour ii. i, The Rhumaticke story of some loving Chandler. a 1680 Charnock Attrib. God (1682) 762 We present him with a sleepy, sickly, rheumatick service.

5. Of weather, places: Inducing or having a tendency to produce † (a) catarrhal affections, (b) rheumatism. (Cf. Rheumy 3.)

1565 Abp. Parker Corr. (Parker Soc.) 250 If any offence be taken for my not attending, and to come over the reumatike Tempsis. 1589 Peele Eglogue Grat. Earl of Essex xxxviii, And evening air is rheumatick and cold. 1598 Shaks. Merry W. iii. i. 47. 1609 Dekker Gull's Horn-bk. ii. 11 The Sun..hath..refind that thicke tobacco-breath which the rheumaticke night throwes abroad. 1856 F. E. Paget Owlet of Owlst. 23 Church towers are..warmer and less rheumatic than hollow trees. 1879 Mrs. A. E. James Ind. Housh. Managem. 14 India is a very rheumatic country.

B. sb.

1. pl. Rheumatic pains, rheumatism. colloq.

1789 Burns To the Toothache ii, When fevers burn, or ague freezes, Rheumatics gnaw, or cholic squeezes. 1803 Mary Charlton Wife & Mistress IV. 166 John's hands were so contracted by the rheumatics that had settled in them. 1852 S. Thomson Dict. Dom. Med. 439/2 The acute form of rheumatism..is popularly named the 'rheumatics', whilst the chronic form..is known..in vulgar parlance as 'the rheumatiz'. 1897 Allbutt's Syst. Med. III. 57 The 'rheumatics' so often complained of by elderly patients.

2. A rheumatic patient. rare.

1884 Harper's Mag. Aug. 439/2 Rheumatics, who so largely preponderate among the invalided visitors.

Hence **Rheuma·ticness**, rheumatic condition or tendency. So **Rheuma·tical** a., rheumatic; **Rheuma·tically** adv., by or with rheumatism.

1702 R. Pitt Crafts of Physick Expos'd 154 An Acrid Collection of Humours..causing the Rheumatical Pains. 1727 Bailey, vol. II, Rheumaticalness, subjectness to be afflicted with a Rheumatism. 1747 Wesley Prim. Physick (1762) 92 note, Rheumatical pains are generally most violent as soon as you are warm in bed. 1852 S. Thomson Dict. Dom. Med. 440/2 The heart in a child may become affected rheumatically.

Rheumaticky (rumæ·tiki), a. colloq. [f. Rheumatic + -y.] Suffering from rheumatism.

1852 Tait's Mag. XIX. 343 [She] netted with her own fair and rheumaticky fingers a handsome silk purse. 1886 B. Roosevelt Copper Queen II. x. 175 A rheumaticky man knows when it is going to rain.

Rheumatism (rū·mătiz'm). [ad. late L. rheumatism-us, a. Gr. ῥευματισμός, f. ῥευματίζειν (see Rheumatize). Cf. F. rhumatisme (16th c.).]

† 1. A 'defluxion of rheum'. Obs.

1601 Holland Pliny II. 133 Fluxes, called by the Greekes Rheumatismes.

2. A disease of which inflammation and pain of the joints are prominent features. In early use commonly with a and pl., an attack of this disease. Acute (articular) rheumatism, the same as rheumatic fever. Muscular rheumatism, myalgia.

Formerly supposed to be caused by a 'defluxion of rheum'. In popular use the word is applied to various kinds of painful articular and muscular affections.

1688 Salmon Phylaxa Med. (ed. 2) 14/1 Tartarous Diseases, as the Scurvy, Pox, Dropsy, Jaundice, Gout, Rheumatism. 1699 Bentley Phal. Introd. 24 That common story, that Epictetus was lame of one Leg..by a Rheumatism. 1700 Dryden Pal. & Arc. iii. 407 And rheumatisms I send to rack the joints. 1749 R. James Diss. Fevers Add. 62 This Medicine [sc. James's Powder] has been found..to be most effectual in a Rheumatism. 1845 Budd Dis. Liver 43 Diseased heart, consequent on rheumatism. 1859 Geo. Eliot A. Bede xviii, On wet Sundays, or whenever he had a touch of rheumatism, he used to read the three first chapters of Genesis. 1899 Allbutt's Syst. Med. VII. 476 A girl..had post-scarlatinal 'rheumatism' at nine years of age.

3. attrib.: rheumatism root, the root of (1) some species of Jeffersonia, (2) Dioscorea villosa; the plants themselves; rheumatism weed, a name for some species of Pyrola.

1798 Nemnich Polygl. Lex., Rheumatism weed, Pyrola minor. 1855 Dunglison Dict. Med. Sci., Rheumatism Weed, Pyrola maculata, P. umbellata. 1857 Ibid., Rheumatism Root, Jeffersonia Bartoni. 1866 Treas. Bot., Rheumatism-root, Jeffersonia diphylla. 1887 Bentley Man. Bot. 706 The rhizome of D[ioscorea] villosa,..commonly known as 'rheumatism root'.

Hence **Rheumati·smal** [cf. F. rhumatismal], † **Rheumatisma·tic** adjs., rheumatic; **Rheumati·smoid** a., resembling rheumatism.

1695 Phil. Trans. XIX. 19 Those sharp and pungent Pains which Rheumatismatick Persons so generally complain of. 1855 Jrnl. R. Agric. Soc. XVI. i. 11 A rheumatismal inflammation. 1858 Mayne Expos. Lex., Rheumatismoid,..resembling rheumatism:..applied to symptoms of diseases which resemble those of rheumatism.

Rheumatiz (rū·mătiz). dial. and vulgar. Also -ize, -ise, etc. (see E. D. D.). Rheumatism.

1760 Foote Minor i. (1767) 32 My old di-order, the rheumatise. 1816 Scott Old Mort. v, Robin's ill o' the rheumatize, and he's to his bed too. 1830 Marryat King's Own xxvi, Our first-lieutenant was..on his beam-ends, with the rheumatiz. 1852 [see Rheumatic B. 1].

Rheumatize (rū·mătəiz), v. [ad. med.L. rheumatisāre to snuffle, or Gr. ῥευματίζειν, f. ῥευματ-, ῥεῦμα Rheum[1]: see -ize.]

† 1. a. To bring 'rheum' or tears to (the eyes). 1593 Nashe Christ's T. 27 b, What should I..rumatize my Readers eyes, with the sadde tedious recitall? 1598 Tofte Alba (1880) 17 Whilst I my Readers eyes do rumatise With brinish drops to heare this wofull Tale.

† b. 'To shed tears' (Cockeram, 1623). Obs.

2. trans. To make rheumatic, affect with rheumatism. Hence **Rheu·matizing** ppl. a.

1852 Meanderings of Mem. I. 57 Raw November's rheumatizing grass. 1862 G. H. Kingsley Sport & Trav. (1900) 379 London..with its..cold,..rheumatising winds. 1876 Smiles Sc. Natur. xiii. (ed. 4) 276 It is not the cold, so much as the damp, that rheumatises the muscles.

Rheu·mato-, combining form of Gr. ῥευματο-ς, ῥεῦμα Rheum[1], used in the sense of 'rheumatic' or 'rheumatic and . . .'.

1843 R. J. Graves Syst. Clin. Med. xxvii. 340 Gastro-rheumatic and rheumato-nervous fevers. 1858 Mayne Expos. Lex., Rheumolymphokeratoditis,..rheumatolymphatic inflammation of the cornea.

Rheumatoid (rū·mătoid), a. [f. Gr. ῥευματ-, ῥεῦμα Rheum[1] + -oid.] Having the characters of rheumatism. Also, suffering from rheumatism.

Chiefly in rheumatoid arthritis, a chronic disease of the joints characterized by changes in the synovial membranes, etc., and resulting in deformity and immobility.

1859 A. B. Garrod Gout xv. 534 Although unwilling to add to the number of names, I cannot help expressing a desire that one might be found for this disease, not implying any necessary relation between it and either gout or rheumatism. Perhaps Rheumatoid Arthritis would answer the object. 1866 Tanner Index of Diseases 233 Rheumatoid Arthritis...Synon. Rheumatic Gout; Chronic Rheumatic Arthritis. 1871 Practitioner VII. 87 The judicious practitioner will regulate the action of the bowels of his rheumatoid patient by proper diet. 1876 Bartholow Mat. Med. (1879) 224 The joints become the seat of rheumatoid pain.

So **Rheumatoi·dal** a., **Rheumatoi·dally** adv.

1889 Lancet 9 Nov. 947/2 Repeated rheumatic attacks may beget a condition commonly called rheumatoidal. Ibid., It is of such sufferers that we constantly ask ourselves..is this case going off rheumatoidally?

Rheumed (rūmd), ppl. a. [f. Rheum[1] + -ed[2].] = Rheumy 2.

1819 Keats Otho iv. ii. 83 No rheumed eyes, no furrowing of age. 1831 Trelawny Adv. of a Younger Son III. 231 Rheumed, glassy, blood-shot eyes. 1877 Lanier Poems (1892) 161 An aged Ram...Rheum'd, wind-gall'd, rag-fleec'd.

Rheumic (rū·mik), a. Chem. [irreg. f. Rheum[2] + -ic.] Rheumic acid: a. J. Henderson's name for an acid discovered by him in the stem of garden rhubarb, but subsequently identified as oxalic acid. b. An acid obtained by treating rheotannic acid with dilute acids.

1815 J. Henderson in Thomson's Ann. Philos. (1816) VIII. 250, I am now convinced that the rheumic acid exists in the plant under the form of rheumate of ammonia. 1883 Encycl. Brit. XX. 530/1 Rheumic acid is a reddish-brown powder, sparingly soluble in cold water.

Rheumin (rū·min). Chem. [ad. F. rheumine (Hornemann), irreg. f. Rheum[2]: see -in.] = Rhein.

[1839 Hooper Med. Dict. s.v. Rheum, M. Hornemann has found a principle which he calls rheumine.] 1858 Mayne Expos. Lex., Rheumin, the same as Rhein.

Rheumy (rū·mi), a. [f. Rheum[1] + -y.]

1. = Rheumatic a. 1.

1592 Greene Upst. Courtier Wks. (Grosart) XI. 242 The filthy reumicast of his bloodshotten snowt. 1596 Barrough Meth. Physick vii. v, Sirupes laxatiue for the purging.. of matter that is rheumic and filthie. 1842 A. de Vere Song of Faith 197 Blear eyes scalded in their rheumy flood.

2. = Rheumatic a. 2. Also Comb.

1591 SYLVESTER *Du Bartas* I. ii. 158 Too-much Cold.. Withers his face, hollows his rheumy eyes. 1624 — *Tobacco Battered* 414 Base rheumy rascals. 1700 DRYDEN *Ovid's Met.* I. 269 His head, and rheumy eyes distil in show'rs. 1837 CARLYLE *Fr. Rev.* IV. iv. (1872) I. 127 The rheumy soberness of extreme age. 1842 TENNYSON *Vision of Sin* xxiii, Till..the glow-worm of the grave Glimmer in thy rheumy eyes. 1895 ZANGWILL *Master* II. ix, A rheumy-eyed stonemason.

3. Moist, damp, wet; *esp.* of the air (cf., however, RHEUMATIC 4 a).

1601 SHAKS. *Jul. C.* II. i. 266 And will he steale out of his wholsome bed To..tempt the Rhewmy and vnpurged Ayre, To adde vnto his sicknesse? 1715 ROWE *Lady Jane Grey* v. i, The night..with her raw And rheumy damps infests the dusky air. 1866 J. B. ROSE tr. *Ovid's Met.* 12 Forthwith, on rheumy pinions [orig. *madidis alis*] hieth he. 1876 T. HARDY *Ethelberta* I. 287 The two sisters walked..into the rheumy air.

Rhewbarb, obs. form of RHUBARB.

‖ **Rhexia** (re·ksiă). [mod.L. (Linnæus), = late L. *rhexia* (Pliny).] A genus of North American plants of the N. O. *Melastomaceæ*; a plant of this genus, meadow-beauty or deer-grass.

1833 WHITTIER *Toussaint L'Ouverture* 19 The rhexias dark, and cassia tall.

Rhigolene (ri·golīn). *Chem.* [f. Gr. ῥῖγος cold + L. *ol-eum* oil + -ENE.] The lightest and most volatile liquid obtained from petroleum, used to produce local anæsthesia.

1866 *Chem. News* XIII. 244/2 Rhigolene, a Petroleum Naphtha for Producing Anæsthesia by Freezing, by Henry J. Bigelow, M.D.

Rhime: see RHYME, RIME.

Rhinal (rəi·năl), *a.* [f. Gr. ῥιν-, ῥίς + -AL.] Belonging to or connected with the nose.

1864 in WEBSTER. 1875 HUXLEY in *Encycl. Brit.* I. 755/2 From the ventral face, just behind the truncated anterior end of the chondrocranium [of a frog's skull] spring two slender cartilages...These may be termed the rhinal processes. 1884 M. MACKENZIE *Dis. Throat & Nose* II. 252 The rhinal mirror should then be carried to the back of the throat. 1897 *Allbutt's Syst. Med.* IV. 717 A rhinal or rhino-pharyngeal irritation.

‖ **Rhinarium** (rəinē°·riŏm). [mod.L., f. Gr. ῥιν-, ῥίς nose + -ARIUM. Cf. F. *rhinarion*.] **a.** *Ent.* The space between the anterior edge of the nasus and the lip. **b.** In mammals, the extremity of the nose, esp. when hairless and habitually moist.

1826 KIRBY & SP. *Entomol.* xxxiv. III. 455 The under side of..the *rhinarium* is lined with a quadrangular fleshy cushion. *Ibid.* xlv. IV. 254 The *rhinarium* or nostril-piece. 1900 W. SCLATER *Mammals S. Africa* I. 156 Cephalophinæ. Antelopes of small or medium size; rhinarium well developed.

Rhind: see RIND.

Rhind-mart, var. spelling of RYNMART.

1788 J. RUSSELL *Conveyancing* Pref. p. viii, A word often made use of in the reddendo of charters in the North country, a *Rhind Mart*.

Rhine[1] (rīn). *south-west. dial.* Also 7 **royne**, 9 **rhyne, rhoyne**; β. **rheen, rhene, rhein.** [app. repr. OE. *ryne* (see RUNE), but the spelling is difficult to account for; cf. REEN.] A large open ditch or drain.

1698–9 *Act 10 Will. III*, c. 26 The present Roynes and Water Courses are not sufficient to Drain the same [*sc.* Sedgemoor]. 1724 J. FORTESCUE-ALAND *Note in Fortescue's Abs. & Lim. Mon.* 104 In Somersetshire they call the Streams and Rivulets between their Moors, which on Floods rise high, Rhines to this Day. 1800 *Phil. Trans.* XC. 548 So much..is this flat cut up with rhynes and ditches, that [etc.]. 1849 MACAULAY *Hist. Eng.* v. I. 608 But between them and the enemy lay three broad rhines filled with water and soft mud. 1886 *Weston-super-Mare Gaz.* 27 Nov., One of the footpaths in the parish of Brent Knoll was reported to have fallen into the rhyne.

β. 1801 W. COXE *Hist. Tour Monm.* I. 72 The water.. runs in perpetual streams called rheens. 1878 SMILES *G. Moore* vii. 112 He had a run of about an hour and a quarter during which we had to cross about 20 rheins, or water jumps. 1891 *Field* 7 Mar. 332/3 The country intersected with rhenes, most of which take some doing.

Rhine[2] (rəin). Also 7–9 **rine**, 8 **ryne**, 9 **rhyne.** [orig. *rine hemp*, ad. G. *reinhanf*, lit. 'clean hemp'. The form was influenced by association with the river Rhine; cf. G. *Rheinhanf*.] The name of a fine quality of Russian hemp. Usually *Riga rhine* (*hemp*).

1641 S. SMITH *Herring-Busse Trade* 13 The best Rine and Rushand are these, Hempe brought in by the Eastland Merchants from the parts of Leiffeland and Prussia. 1765 *Museum Rust.* IV. xxiii. 108, I have seen very good hemp, the growth of that country [*sc.* North America], not inferior to the best Riga ryne. 1794 *Rigging & Seamanship* 94 Bolt Rope should be well made, of fine yarn, spun from the best Riga rhine hemp well topt. 1812 Rhyne [see OUTSHOT *ppl. a.* 3]. 1873 *Beeton's Dict. Comm.*, *Rine-Hemp*.

Rhine[3] (rəin). The name of the chief river of Germany, used *attrib.* to designate wines made from grapes growing in the Rhine valley. Cf. RHENISH.

1843 *Penny Cycl.* XXVII. 455/2 We find the most renowned of the Rhine-wines produced between 50° and 51°. 1866 *Chambers's Encycl.* VIII. 235/2 The red Rhine-wines ..are not nearly so much prized as the white.

Rhine, variant of RIND, hoar-frost.

Rhinegrave (rəi·ngrēiv). Also 6 **Rin-**, 7–9 **Rhingrave.** [a. MDu. *Rijngrave* (mod. *-graaf*), G. *Rheingraf*: see RHINE[3] and GRAVE *sb.*[4]] A count whose domain borders on the river Rhine.

Hence **Rhi·negravess, Rhi·negravine** (= Du. *Rijngravin*, G. *Rheingräfin*).

1548 T. FISHER in Ellis *Orig. Lett.* Ser. III. III. 293 Monsieur Dessie..sending for the Ringrave to mete him with his band. 1676 *Lond. Gaz.* No. 1114/3 The Rhingrave is slightly wounded in the Cheek. 1762 tr. *Busching's Syst. Geogr.* V. 504 Juliana, ..Wildgravess and Rhinegravess of Grumbach. 1821 JEFFERSON *Autobiog.* Writ. 1892 I. 106 The States had appointed the Rhingrave of Salm their Commander-in-chief. 1894 Rhinegravine [see PALSGRAVINE].

† **Rhinehurst.** *Obs.* Also **rine-.** [ad. Du. *rhynseharst* (Nemnich), ad. G. *rheinharz*, f. *Rhein* RHINE[3] + *harz* resin.] Burgundy pitch.

1724 *Bk. Rates* (Act 11 Geo. I, c. 7), Rinehurst, the C. wt. containing 112 lb. 1*s.* 1774 BURROW *Bk. Rates* 240 Rhinehurst. 1820 *Act 59 Geo. III*, c. 52.

Rhineland (rəi·nlænd). Also 7 **Rhyn(e-**, 8–9 **Rhinland.** [= Du. *Rijnland*, G. *Rheinland*.] The country around the river Rhine: used as a spec. designation in *Rhineland foot*, etc. (see quots.). Hence †**Rhinelandish** *a.*, in same sense.

1675 *Phil. Trans.* X. 269 The Rhynland (or Leyden) Foot. 1688 HOLME *Armoury* III. xvi. (Roxb.) 98/1 A Rhyneland foot, is the measure by which all fortifications are made by. 1706 PHILLIPS (ed. Kersey), *Rhine-Land Rod*, a Measure of two Fathom, or twelve Foot; us'd in Fortification by Dutch Engineers. 1712 DESAGULIERS tr. *Ozanam's Curs. Math.* V. 105, 295566 Rods, or Verges of the Rhine, each of 12 Rheinlandish Feet. 1832 [see RHENISH *a.* 1 c].

‖ **Rhinencephalon** (rəinense·făl̩n). *Anat.* [f. Gr. ῥιν-, ῥίς nose + ENCEPHALON.] The olfactory lobes of the brain. Hence **Rhinencepha·lic** *a.*, pertaining to or consisting of the rhinencephalon.

1851 CARPENTER *Gen. & Comp. Phys.* (ed. 3) Index, Rhinencephalon. *Ibid.* § 320 *i*, These segments [of the skull] are named (proceeding from behind forwards) the Epencephalic, the Mesencephalic, the Prosencephalic, and the Rhinencephalic, according to the divisions of the brain to which they respectively correspond. 1870 ROLLESTON *Anim. Life* 41 The optic lobes..are,..like the prosencephalon and rhinencephalon, paired. 1880 GÜNTHER *Fishes* 86 Rhinencephalic arch, composed of vomer, prefrontal, and nasal. 1899 *Allbutt's Syst. Med.* VI. 753 The great rhinencephalon of macrosmatic mammals.

Rhinestone (rəi·nstōun). [f. RHINE[3] + STONE *sb.*, after F. *caillou du Rhin*.] **a.** A variety of rock crystal. **b.** A colourless artificial gem of paste or strass, cut to imitate a diamond.

1890 in *Century Dict.* 1895 *Daily News* 20 Apr. 3/6 A buckle of Rhinestones. 1906 L. CLAREMONT *Gem-Cutter's Craft* xx. 228 Fancy names..applied to rock crystal..'Cornish Diamond', 'Brighton Diamond', 'Rhine Stone', etc.

Rhineurynter (rəi·niurintəɹ). *Med.* [f. Gr. ῥιν-, ῥίς nose + εὐρύνειν to broaden.] An inflatable elastic bag for plugging the nose.

1876 DUNGLISON *Dict. Med.* 903/1. 1876 tr. *von Ziemssen's Cycl. Med.* IV. 164 Belloc's canula or the rhineurynter.

Rhinish, obs. var. RHENISH.

Rhinitis (rinəi·tis). [f. Gr. ῥιν-, ῥίς nose + -ITIS. Cf. F. *rhinite*.] Inflammation of the nose.

1884 MACKENZIE *Dis. Throat & Nose* II. 295. 1887 *Brit. Med. Jrnl.* 2 Apr. 730/1 Rhinitis with Spasmodic 'Snorting'.

Rhino[1] (rəi·no). *slang.* Also 7 **ry-**, 7–8 **rino.** [Origin unknown.] Money. (Often *ready rhino*.)

1688 [see RHINOCERICAL 2]. 1699 DUNTON *Convers. in Irel.* in *Life & Errors* (1818) 564 It was pretty to see the Squire choused out of so fair an estate with so little ready rhino. 1747 *Gentl. Mag.* 147 When they come to shew their hoard, And tell the Rino on the board. 1796 J. ANSTEY *Pleader's Guide* vii, Not one of all the trade that I know E'er fails to take the Ready rino. 1805 *Sporting Mag.* XXV. 201 His [Geo. Morland's] impatience for the ready rhino. 1834 MARRYAT *P. Simple* ii. 22 Now that I see you look so sharp after the rhino, it's my idea that you're some poor devil of a Scotchman. 1851 MAYHEW *Lond. Labour* I. 384/2 You shall have it cheap, for me and my mate are both short of rhino.

Rhino[2] (rəi·no). Colloq. abbrev. of RHINOCEROS.

1884 *Graphic* 30 Aug. 229/3 A magnificent rhino lazily eating some rich herbage. 1888 J. INGLIS *Tent Life in Tigerland* 1 The opportunities for sport—from rhino and tiger-shooting, down to ortolan and plover.

Rhino- (rəi·no, rəinǫ·), combining f. Gr. ῥινο-ς, ῥίς nose, used in the formation of various scientific terms: ‖ **Rhinobyon** (rəinobəi·ǫn) [Gr. βύειν to stuff], a nose-plug: see quot. 1884. **Rhi·nocaul** [L. *caulis* stalk]: see quot. ‖ **Rhinodon, -dont** (rəi·nodǫn, -dǫnt) [Gr. ὀδοντ-, ὀδούς tooth], a gigantic shark common in the Indian Ocean. **Rhi·nolith**, a nasal calculus; hence **Rhinoli·thic** *a.* ‖ **Rhinolithi·asis**, a condition characterized by rhinoliths. **Rhinolo·gical** *a.*, pertaining to rhinology or the study of the nose. **Rhino·logist**, a student of rhinology. **Rhino·logy**, the study of the nose; that part of pathology dealing with nasal diseases. **Rhi:no-phary·ngeal** *a.*, pertaining to the rhino-pharynx. ‖ **Rhino-pha·rynx**, = *naso-pharynx*. **Rhi·nophor(e**, an external olfactory organ; *spec.* in certain molluscs (see quot. 1878). ‖ **Rhinorrhœ·a** [Gr. ῥοία flow], discharge of blood from the nose. ‖ **Rhino-scleroma** (see quot. 1876). ‖ **Rhinothe·ca**, the horny sheath of the beak in birds.

1858 MAYNE *Expos. Lex.*, *Rhinobyon. 1884 M. MACKENZIE *Dis. Throat & Nose* II. 278 [The] 'rhinobyon' consists of three parts, viz., a small syringe; a tube opening at its distal end into an india-rubber bag; and a small pilot sound. 1889 *Buck's Handbk. Med. Sci.* VIII. 525/2 The less frequently mentioned supports of the olfactory bulbs may be called olfactory crura or *rhinocauls. 1850 F. MASON *Nat. Prod. Burmah* 327 *Rhineodon Shark. The natives describe to me a species like rhineodon, 'with the mouth placed at the tip of the snout'. 1887 *Sci. Amer.* 26 Feb. 130 The great rhinodon, the largest living fish, measuring 70 feet in length. 1859–62 RICHARDSON, etc. *Mus. Nat. Hist.* II. 165/2 Rhinodonts (*Rhinodontidæ*). This family is represented by a single known species (*Rhinodon typicus*), which frequents the seas round the Cape of Good Hope. 1866 TANNER *Index of Diseases* 234 *Rhinolithes...Concretions of phosphate and carbonate of lime, magnesia, and mucus. 1884 M. MACKENZIE *Dis. Throat & Nose* II. 544 Rhinoliths generally owe their origin to the accidental impaction of small foreign bodies around which the salts of the pituitary secretion collect. 1887 *Brit. Med. Jrnl.* 26 Feb. 467/2 *Rhinolithiasis and lupus of the nose. 1891 *Jrnl. Chem. Soc.* LX. II. 1279 Analyses of four *rhinolithic calculi. 1838 *Blackw. Mag.* XLIII. 654 Notwithstanding the ingenuity of your *Rhinological arguments. 1889 *Med. Directory* 374 British Laryngological and Rhinological Association.— Established 1888. 1838 *Blackw. Mag.* XLIII. 654 Veneration..was at first thought by the French *Rhinologist to reside in the tip..of the nasal apparatus. 1897 *Allbutt's Syst. Med.* IV. 689 The growths for which the name polypus is now reserved by rhinologists. 1838 *Blackw. Mag.* XLIII. 653, I am a Professor..of *Rhinology, or the science of divining characters by the dimensions of the nose. 1888 *Brit. Med. Jrnl.* 18 Aug. 361/1 A..course of laryngology and rhinology. 1897 *Allbutt's Syst. Med.* IV. 715 The *rhino-pharyngeal affection. *Ibid.* 724 The back of the uvula and soft palate, and the *rhino-pharynx should be examined with the rhinoscope. 1878 BELL tr. *Gegenbaur's Comp. Anat.* 352 In the Opisthobranchiata the hinder pair of tentacles (*rhinophor) appear to have the function of an olfactory organ. 1866 TANNER *Index of Diseases* 234 *Rhinorrhœa...Nasal Gleet. 1884 M. MACKENZIE *Dis. Throat & Nose* II. 315 In rhinorrhœa..the lining membrane is usually pale and sodden. 1876 DUHRING *Dis. Skin* 412 *Rhinoscleroma consists of a circumscribed, irregularly-shaped, flattened, tubercular growth,..having its seat about the region of the nose. 1891 MOULLIN *Surg.* 858 Rhinoscleroma is a very rare disease. 1866 COUES in *Proc. Philad. Acad.* May 172 By Illiger the tubulation of the *rhinotheca has been made indicative of a tube.

Rhinobatid (rəinǫ·bătid). *Ichth.* [ad. mod.L. *Rhinobatidæ*, f. ῥίνη shark + βάτος ray.] A shark-like ray of the family *Rhinobatidæ* (see quot.).

1859–62 RICHARDSON, etc. *Mus. Nat. Hist.* II. 167 Rhinobatids (*Rhinobatidæ*). The ventrals in this group are close behind the pectorals, which pass imperceptibly into the snout.

Rhino·ceral, *a. slang.* = RHINOCERICAL 2.

1860 *Slang Dict.* (ed. 2) 199 *Rhinoceral*, rich, wealthy, abounding in rhino.

Rhinoce·rial, *a.* [f. RHINOCER-OS + -IAL.] Pertaining to or resembling the rhinoceros (1828–32 in Webster, citing *Tatler*, where the true reading is *rhinocerical*: see next).

† **Rhinoce·rical**, *a. Obs.* [f. RHINOCER-OS + -ICAL; in sense 2 with reference to RHINO[1].]

1. a. Heavy or unwieldy as a rhinoceros.

1689 *Muses Farewell to Popery* 18 Prodigious Guts, no Brains at all, But very Rhynocerical.

b. Of a nose: Like a rhinoceros' horn; retroussé. (Cf. quot. 1712 s.v. RHINOCEROS 1.)

1710 *Tatler* No. 260 ₱3 These Gentlemen were formerly marked out and distinguished by the little Rhinocerical Nose.

2. *slang.* Having plenty of 'the rhino'; rich.

1688 SHADWELL *Sqr. Alsatia* I. i, The Ready, the Rhino; thou shalt be rhinocerical, my Lad. 1796 *Grose's Dict. Vulgar T.* (ed. 3), *Rhinocerical*, rich: the cull is rhinocerical.

Rhinocerine (rəinǫ·serəin), *a.* [f. RHINOCER-OS + -INE.] Infesting the rhinoceros.

1879 COBBOLD *Parasites* 401 The rhinocerine stomach-bot (*Gastrophilus rhinocerontis*, Owen).

† **Rhino·cerite.** *Obs.* App. an alteration of RHINOCEROT for the sake of rhyme.

1659 PECKE *Parnassi Puerp.* 127 Will the debonair Rhinocerite For Cæsar's pleasure rush into a fight? *Ibid.* 130.

Rhinoceroid (rəinǫ·seroid), *a.* [f. RHINOCER-OS + -OID.] Rhinocerotic.

1879 NICHOLSON *Palæont.* II. xlii. 329 The molars are not at all of the Rhinoceroid pattern.

Rhinocero·ntine, *a.* [f. mod.L. *rhinoceront-* (see next) + -INE.] Rhinocerotic.

1857 LIVINGSTONE *Trav.* i. 22 The rhinocerontine family.

Rhinoceros (rəinǫ·serǫs). Forms: 4, 6 **rinoceros** (7 **-as**), 5 **rynoseros**, 5, 7 **-ceros**, 7 **rhenoreno-**, **r(h)ynoceros**, **rhonoserous**, **renoceros**, 6– **rhinoceros.** Also 6 **renocero**, 7 **rinocere.** *Pl.* 6, 9 **rhinoceros**, 6 **-ons**, **-ontes**, 7 **-ceroes**, **-cero's**, 8– **-ceri**, **-ceroses**; also 6–7 **-cerotes** (see RHINOCEROT). [a. late L. *rhinocerōs* (also med. and mod.L. *rhinoceron*, gen. *-ontis*), a. Gr. ῥινόκερως, f. ῥινο-, ῥίς nose + κέρας horn. Cf. F. *rhinocéros*, It., Sp. *rinoceronte*, Pg. *rhinoceronte*, *-ceros*.]

1. A large, unwieldy quadruped of a genus now found only in Africa and Southern Asia, having a horn (or, in some species, two horns) on the nose and a very thick skin disposed in plates and folds.

The chief of the one-horned species are the Indian Rhinoceros (*Rhinoceros unicornis*) and the Javan Rhinoceros (*R. sondaicus*); of the two-horned species, the African Rhinoceros (*R. bicornis*).

13.. *K. Alis.* 6514 (Bodl. MS.), Anoþer beeste also þer is þat hat Rinoceros. *a* 1400–50 *Alexander* 4133 And sa þai willid in-to a wod was full of wild bestis, Rynoceros, as I rede, þe romance þam callis. 1553 EDEN *Treat. Newe Ind.* (Arb.) 16 This Rhinoceros hath two hornes, whereof the one is of notable bignes. 1555 — *Decades* (Arb.) 385 A great

region which bryngeth furth.. the beastes cauled Rhinocerontes. 1589 PUTTENHAM *Eng. Poesie* I. xvii. 29 Their baitings of wild beasts, as Elephants, Rhinocerōs, Tigers, Leopards. 1596 RALEIGH *Discov. Guiana* 61 A beast.. all barred ouer with small plates somewhat like to a Renocero. 1606 J. COPRARIO *Funeral Teares Earl Devonsh.* Introd., Rhinoceroes some by their arm'd snowtes I deem'd. 1623 COCKERAM III, *Rinocere*, a beast as bigge as an Elephant. 1680 MORDEN *Geog. Rect.*, *Ganges Penins.* (1685) 412 The Forests..are full of Rhinocero's. 1753 HANWAY *Trav.* (1762) I. VII. xcv. 440 Rhinoceroses of the size of a large dog. 1799 KIRWAN *Geol. Ess.* 68 The remains of elephants and rhinoceri accompanied by marine vegetables. 1850 R. G. CUMMING *Hunter's Life S. Afr.* I. xi. 247 *note*, There are four varieties in South Africa,..the borèlé or black rhinoceros, the keitloa or two-horned black rhinoceros, the muchocho or common white rhinoceros, and the kobaoba or long-horned white rhinoceros. 1863 W. C. BALDWIN *Afr. Hunting* viii. 327, I saw four rhinoceros drinking at the fountain.

Phrase. 1712 ADDISON *Spect.* No. 275 ₱8 When they talk of a Man's cocking his Nose, or playing the Rhinoceros.

b. *transf.* A large, unwieldy person.

1885 J. PAYN *Talk of Town* I. 160 What is the tune which has set this rhinoceros a dancing?

†**2.** = *rhinoceros-beetle*, *-bird*. *Obs.*

1613 PURCHAS *Pilgrimage* VII. v. (1626) 742 Andrea Corsali..mentioneth also a bird, called the Rhinoceros of the ayre.., hauing..a horne betweene the eyes. 1658 ROWLAND tr. *Moufet's Theat. Ins.* Ep. Ded., The greater Beetle, the Indian Rhinoceros. 1822 LATHAM *Gen. Hist. Birds* II. 306 The bill of the Rhinoceros in no instance we have seen is more than twelve [inches].

3. *attrib.*, as *rhinoceros bull, calf, cow, horn, hump, hunt, skin, spoor*; also = 'resembling that of a rhinoceros', as *rhinoceros build* (cf. 1 b), *hide*; **rhinoceros auk**, the bird *Ceratorrhina monocerata*, having a horn at the base of its beak; **rhinoceros beetle**, a kind of beetle having a horn; **rhinoceros bird**, †(*a*) the Indian bird *Buceros rhinoceros*; (*b*) the African Beef-eater or Ox-pecker, genus *Buphaga*, which rids the rhinoceros' skin of ticks; **rhinoceros-bush** [= Cape Du. *renoster-bos*], a shrub *Elytropappus rhinocerotis*, said to be the food of the rhinoceros; **rhinoceros-chameleon**, the Malagasy *Chamæleon rhinoceratus*; † **rhinoceros cup**, a cup of rhinoceros horn; **rhinoceros hornbill**, = *rhinoceros bird* (*a*); **rhinoceros leg**, elephantiasis (*Syd. Soc. Lex.* 1897); † **rhinoceros nose**, = L. *nasus rhinocerotis* (Martial), used as descriptive of a sneer; **rhinoceros puff-adder** (see quot.).

1681 GREW *Musæum* I. § vii. ii. 162 The *Rhinoceros Beetle..hath only one Horn upon the Nose standing almost upright. 1711 PETIVER *Gazophyl.* 12 Black Luzone Rhinoceros's Beetle. 1826 KIRBY & SP. *Entomol.* xxix. III. 90 The Rhinoceros beetle (*Oryctes nasicornis*). 1651 EVELYN *Diary* 23 May, The head of the *rynoceros bird, which was very extravagant. 1678 [see RAVEN *sb.*[1] 1 b]. 1783 MARSDEN *Sumatra* 98 Engang, or rhinoceros bird. 1885 *Harper's Mag.* Feb. 422/2 Although called the rhinoceros-bird, it does not confine its beneficent attentions to that animal. 1865 DICKENS *Mut. Fr.* I. v, He was of an overlapping *rhinoceros build, with folds in his cheeks, and his forehead,..and his lips. 1863 W. C. BALDWIN *Afr. Hunting* ix. 410 One white *rhinoceros bull. 1786 tr. *Sparrman's Voy.* I. 232 The *Rhinoceros-bush, which the cattle always pass by and leave untouched. 1795 *Thunberg's Trav.* (ed. 2) I. 247 Such horns as were taken from a young *rhinoceros calf..were said to be the best. 1876 *Encycl. Brit.* V. 382/1 The *Rhinoceros Chameleon, the male of which has a horn-like tubercle at the end of the muzzle. 1863 W. C. BALDWIN *Afr. Hunting* iv. 105 An old *rhinoceros cow. 1649 *Inv.* in *Archæol.* (1806) XV. 284 A *rinoceras cupp graven with figures. 1863 W. PHILLIPS *Sp.* iii. 48 The *rhinoceros hide of a Webster. 1876 G. B. GOODE in *Smithsonian Coll.* XIII. vi. 84 Rhinoceros-hide used for shields, targets, whips. 1625 PURCHAS *Pilgrims* I. IV. ii. 394 *Renosceros horne. 1657 TOMLINSON tr. *Renou's Disp.* III. xxi. 457 To others I prescribe Rhinoceros, and Hartshorn. 1841 *Penny Cycl.* XIX. 473/2 Clubs of Rhinoceros horn about three feet in length had been obtained from Western Africa. 1887 RIDER HAGGARD *Allan Quatermain* i, The rhinoceros-horn handle of his axe. 1781–7 LATHAM *Gen. Synopsis Birds* I. 341 *Rhinoceros Hornbill. 1812 SHAW *Zool.* VIII. I. 3 The general size of the Rhinoceros Hornbill is that of a hen turkey. 1863 W. C. BALDWIN *Afr. Hunting* vi. 190, I breakfasted this morning on *rhinoceros hump. 1849 *Mammalia* III. 33 His animated account of a *rhinoceros-hunt. 1555 EDEN *Decades* (Arb.) 398, I haue not..byn very curious To auoyde the scornes of *Rhinoceros nose. 1870 GILLMORE tr. *Figuier's Reptiles & Birds* iii. 83 The *Rhinoceros Puff Adder (*Clotho nasicornis* of Guinea) has the scales over the nostrils of the male produced into a long re-curved spine. 1681 GREW *Musæum* I. § ii. ii. 30 A piece of a great *Rhinoceros-Skin, tann'd. 1863 W. C. BALDWIN *Afr. Hunting* ix. 380 There is plenty of *rhinoceros spoor, but we have not found them.

Rhinocerot (rəinǫ·serǫt). Now *rare.* Also 7 **rin-**; 6–7 **-ote.** [ad. L. *rhinocerōt-*, *-cerōs* (see prec.); med.L. also *rinocerota*.] = RHINOCEROS.

† *Rhinocerot's nose* = 'rhinoceros nose' (see prec. 3).

1573 L. LLOYD *Marrow of Hist.* (1653) 44 Tygers, Panthers, Rhinocerots and such wild..beasts. *a* 1637 B. JONSON *Epigr.* I. xxviii, Don Surly..speakes to men with a Rhinocerotes nose. 1673 RAY *Journ. Low C.* 28 We saw the whole Skin of a young Rhinocerot stuft. 1694 *Acc. Sev. Late Voy.* Introd. p. xiv, Towards the Gulf of Bengal, Elephants, Rhinocerots, Lions. 1905 *Athenæum* 22 Apr. 489/1 Suicidally-minded rhinocerots.

¶ The form *rhinocerotes*, orig. representing L. *rhinocerōtēs*, Gr. ῥινοκέρωτες, serves as a pl. for both RHINOCEROS and (*c* 1550 to 1700) RHINOCEROT.

c 1554 in Hakluyt *Voy.* (1599) II. II. 20 [332] The beastes called Rhinocerotes. 1601 HOLLAND *Pliny* I. 548 The Rhinocerotes whet their horns against the rockes. 1613 PURCHAS *Pilgrimage* v. v. 400 In Bengala are found great numbers of *Abadas* or Rhinocerotes. 1694 MOTTEUX *Rabelais* IV. lvii. (1737) 237 Lions, Rhinocerotes. 1845 KITTO *Cycl. Bibl. Lit.* II. 607/1 In general structure so much lighter than other rhinocerotes. 1869 GRAY *Catal. Carniv. Mammalia Brit. Mus.* 301 Camper..pointed out that there were two Asiatic one-horned Rhinocerotes with upper incisors.

† **b.** **rhinocerot bird**, = *rhinoceros bird* (*a*).

a 1672 WILLUGHBY *Ornith.* (1678) 127 The horned Indian Raven or Topau, called the Rhinocerot Bird.

Rhinocerotic (rəinǫserǫ·tik), *a.* [ad. late L. *rhinocerōtic-us*, f. *rhinocerōt-*, *-ōs*.] Of, belonging to, characteristic of, or resembling the rhinoceros.

1755 *World* No. 130 V. 84 Martial in one of his epigrams, calls this kind of nose the rhinocerotic nose [= *nasus rhinocerotis*]. 1868 B. L. GILDERSLEEVE *Ess. & Stud.* (1890) 427 Some demagogue's rhinocerotic smeller-face. A paragon of never-ceasing snufflecdom. 1883 *Nature* XXVIII. 579/2 The rhinocerotic features of the skull. 1887 HEILPRIN *Distrib. Anim.* 368 The somewhat rhinocerotic Amynodon.

So **Rhino·cerotine, Rhino·cerotoid** *adjs.*

1845 KITTO *Cycl. Bibl. Lit.* II. 607/1 A Rhinocerotine animal, in form lighter than a wild bull. 1891 C. F. HOLDER *C. Darwin* 206 A rhinocerotoid, or a tapiroid animal.

Rhinodon to **Rhinophore**: see RHINO-.

Rhinoplastic (rəinoplæ·stik), *a.* and *sb. Surg.* [See RHINO- and PLASTIC *a.*] Pertaining to the plastic surgery of the nose; connected with rhinoplasty. Also *sb.* (*sing.* and *pl.*), = RHINOPLASTY.

1832 *Encycl. Amer.* XI. 18 *Rhinoplastic*...The art of restoring the nose, when lost by disease or external injury, was early practised. 1833 J. S. BUCHNAN tr. *Dieffenbach's Surg. Obs.* (title), Surgical Observations on the Restoration of the Nose,..With the history and physiology of rhinoplastic operations. 1842 W. FERGUSSON *Pract. Surg.* IV. vii. 455 Dieffenbach.., whose skill in rhinoplastics seems to be such that he will repair or rear up this most important feature with all the genius of a Telford. 1870 EMERSON *Soc. & Solit.* vii. 131 The rhinoplastic treatment. 1887 MORLEY *Stud. Lit.* (1891) 85 A false tooth, or a rhinoplastic nose.

So **Rhi·noplasty**, the rhinoplastic operation.

1855 OGILVIE Suppl., *Rhinoplasty*. 1862 *Syd. Soc. Year-bk.* XV. 252 A short historical account of rhinoplasty.

Rhinoscope (rəi·noskōup). [See RHINO- and -SCOPE.] An instrument for examining the nasal cavity. So **Rhinoscopic** (rəinoskǫ·pik) *a.*, pertaining to rhinoscopy; performed by means of the rhinoscope; **Rhinoscopy** (rəinǫ·skŏpi), examination of the nasal cavity; use of the rhinoscope.

1861 G. D. GIBB tr. *Czermak's Laryngoscope* 73 The method which I invented and called 'Rhinoscopy'. *Ibid.* 74 In rhinoscopic examinations, the success depends principally on the sufficiency of the distance between the soft palate and posterior wall of the pharynx. *Ibid.* 79 The undoubted utility of the rhinoscope in cases where the tumours attain such a large size. 1897 *Allbutt's Syst. Med.* IV. 671 Anterior rhinoscopy is the name applied to the examination of the anterior nares and posterior rhinoscopy to the examination of the naso-pharynx and posterior nares.

Rhipidoglossate (ri:pidoglǫ·sēⁱt), *a.* [f. Gr. ῥιπιδο-, ῥιπίς fan + γλῶσσα tongue + -ATE[2].] Having upon the radula several median and many marginal teeth; belonging to the *Rhipidoglossa*, a division of molluscs having these characteristics.

1883 *Encycl. Brit.* XVI. 660/2 The Pneumonochlamyda.. have..a complex rhipidoglossate or tænioglossate radula.

Rhipipterous (ripi·ptĕrəs), *a. Entom.* [f. *Rhipiptera* (irreg. f. Gr. ῥιπίς fan + πτερόν wing) + -OUS.] Fan-winged; belonging to the *Rhipiptera*, the eleventh order of insects in Latreille's classification; strepsipterous. So **Rhipi·pteran** *a.*, rhipipterous; *sb.*, a rhipipterous insect.

1855 HYDE CLARKE *Dict.*, *Rhipipteran*. 1876 *Van Beneden's Anim. Parasites* 257 When the rhipipterous insect is six millimètres in length, it changes its skin the second time.

Rhithm, obs. form of RHYTHM.

Rhizanth (rəi·zænþ). *Bot.* [ad. mod.L. *Rhizantheæ*, f. Gr. ῥίζα root + ἄνθος flower.] A plant of the class *Rhizantheæ*, producing (apparently) only a root and flowers. So **Rhiza·nthous** *a.*, flowering (apparently) from the root.

1840 PEREIRA *Mat. Med.* 578 Rhizantheæ,.. Rhizanths. 1849 BALFOUR *Man. Bot.* § 252. 1856 HENSLOW *Dict. Bot. Terms*, *Rafflesiaceæ*,..an order of flowering rhizanthous parasites.

Rhizic (rəi·zik), *a. Math.* [f. Gr. ῥίζα root.] Pertaining to or concerning the root of an equation.

1871 W. WALTON in *Q. Jrnl. Math.* XI. 91 The two curves *P* = 0, *Q* = 0, referred to rectangular axes of co-ordinates *u* and *v*, I propose to call rhizic curves, in virtue of their relation to the roots of the equation *f*(*x*) = 0. 1874 CAYLEY in *Trans. Camb. Phil. Soc.* XII. II. 395 Cauchy's rhizic theorem.

‖ **Rhizina** (rizəi·nă). *Bot.* [f. Gr. ῥίζα root + -ina = -ινη.] = RHIZOID. Also **Rhizine** (rəi·zin).

1839 LINDLEY *Introd. Bot.* I. ii. 109 The terms *rhizina* and *rhizula* have been given by Link to the young roots of mosses and lichens. 1873 HOOKER *le Maout & Decaisne's Bot.* 941 The lower layer, or hypothallus..is..covered with rootlike hairs, which have been called rhizines. 1807 W. PHILLIPS *Brit. Discomycetes* 40 The rhizinæ are coarse fibres occupying the greater part of the under surface.

Rhizo- (rəi·zo, rəizǫ·), combining f. Gr. ῥίζα root, used in the formation of many scientific (chiefly botanical) terms: **Rhi·zocarp** [Gr. καρπός fruit], a plant of the group *Rhizocarpeæ* (= *Marsileaceæ*). **Rhizocarpean** *a.*, belonging to the *Rhizocarpeæ*. **Rhizoca·rpic, -ca·rpous** *adjs.*, having a perennial root but perishing stems. ‖ **Rhizoce·phala** *sb. pl.* [Gr. κεφαλή head], an order of parasitic hermaphrodite crustaceans closely related to the cirripedes; also *sing.* ‖ **Rhizoce·phalon**, a crustacean of this order; hence **Rhizoce·phalous** *a.*, belonging to the Rhizocephala. **Rhi·zodont** [Gr. ὀδοντ-, ὀδούς tooth] *a.*, having teeth with branching fangs anchylosing with the jaw, as a crocodile; *sb.*, a rhizodont reptile. **Rhizodo·ntropy** [Gr. ὀδοντ-, ὀδούς tooth, τροπή turning], 'pivoting an artificial crown on the root of a tooth' (*Syd. Soc. Lex.* 1897). **Rhizodo·ntrypy** [Gr. τρυπᾶν to bore], 'perforation of the root of a tooth for the discharge of fluid' (Dunglison, 1876). **Rhi·zogen**, (*a*) a plant parasitic on the roots of another plant; *spec.* one of the *Rhizantheæ*, Lindley's group of plants of fungoid habit parasitic on rootstocks; (*b*) a part from which a root or roots grow; **Rhizogene·tic, -ge·nic** *adjs.*, root-producing. ‖ **Rhizoma·nia**, an abnormal development of roots (*Treas. Bot.*). **Rhi·zomorph**, ‖ **Rhizomo·rpha**, a mycelial growth, such as occurs in various fungi, preying on the roots of higher plants. **Rhizomo·rphoid, -mo·rphous** *adjs.*, root-like; resembling a rhizomorph. **Rhizo·phagous** *a.*, feeding on roots. ‖ **Rhizo·stoma** [Gr. στόμα mouth], a genus of discomedusan hydrozoans having root-like oval arms; an animal of this genus (also **Rhi·zostome**); hence **Rhizosto·matous, Rhizo·stomous** *adjs.* ‖ **Rhizota·xis, Rhi·zotaxy**, arrangement or disposition of roots. **Rhizo·tomist** [Gr. ῥιζοτόμος; cf. *Rhizotome*, name of Gargantua's page-apothecary in Rabelais I. xxiii], a collector of roots for medicinal purposes.

1875 BENNETT & DYER tr. *Sachs' Bot.* 391 The Branching of *Rhizocarps is similar to that of Ferns. 1888 J. W. DAWSON *Geol. Hist. Plants* 48 The curious aquatic plants known as Rhizocarps. [*Note.* Or, as they have recently been named by some botanists, 'Heterosporous Filices'.] *Ibid.* 41 The shallow waters filled with aquatic or amphibious *Rhizocarpean plants. 1858 MAYNE *Expos. Lex.*, *Rhizocarpicus*,..*rhizocarpic. 1832 LINDLEY *Introd. Bot.* 402 **Rhizocarpous*, or those whose root endures many years, but whose stems perish annually; as herbaceous plants. 1865 DARWIN in *Life & Lett.* (1887) III. 38 Until reading your book I knew nothing of the *Rhizocephala. 1869 W. S. DALLAS tr. *F. Müller's Facts for Darwin* 139 The Cirripede had become a *Rhizocephalon. 1894 W. BATESON *Mat. Study of Variation* I. ii. 95 Males..inhabited by the *Rhizocephalous parasite *Sacculina*. 1879 ROSSITER *Dict. Sci. Terms*, **Rhizodont*. Teeth with branching fangs, which anchylose with the jaw. 1900 *Nature* 20 Sept. 505/2 The Rhizodont genera *Tristichopterus* and *Eusthenopteron*. *Ibid.* 506/1 We are..justified in considering the Holoptychians..a newer type than the Rhizodonts. 1876 T. BRYANT *Pract. Surg.* I. 561 The performance of *rhizodontropy [*read* -trypy], coupled or not with a direct opening into the abscess to evacuate the pus. 1846 LINDLEY *Veget. Kingd.* 83 *Rhizogens all agree in being of a fungus-like consistence. 1849 BALFOUR *Man. Bot.* § 64 [Lenticels] are considered, by Decandolle..,as being the points where young roots are produced in certain circumstances, and on that account they have been called Rhizogens. 1884 BOWER & SCOTT *De Bary's Phaner.* 398 Those rows of the next outer cortical layer, which lie in front of the *rhizogenetic rows. 1885 GOODALE *Physiol. Bot.* iii. 115 *note*, The mother-cells of this layer (the so-called *Rhizogenic cells). 1848 WATTS tr. *Gmelin's Handbk. Chem.* I. 188 *Rhizomorphs shine more brightly in oxygen gas than in common air. 1830 LINDLEY *Nat. Syst. Bot.* 335 No inconsiderable number of the Fungi of botanists are.., as various *Rhizomorphas, the deformed roots of flowering plants growing in cellars, clefts of rocks, and walls. 1883 *Harper's Mag.* Jan. 191/2 The rhizomorpha —a curious organism resembling long, thin, dark-colored roots, sometimes expanding into a membraniform production. 1871 COOKE *Handbk. Fungi* I. 307 *Odontia fimbriata*.., traversed by *rhizomorphoid threads. 1858 MAYNE *Expos. Lex.*, *Rhizomorphus*,..*rhizomorphous. 1831 CARLYLE *Sart. Res.* III. x, All Poor-Slaves are *Rhizophagous (or Root-eaters). 1856–8 W. CLARK *van der Hoeven's Zool.* I. 404 Larvæ smooth, with 16 feet, subterranean, rhizophagous. 1841 *Penny Cycl.* XIX. 119/2 Certain **Rhizostomata* acquire a considerable development, so as to reach nearly a foot and a half in diameter. 1843 OWEN *Compar. Anat., Invertebrates* 103 It may be asked, why the Cyanæa should have intestines and vents, whilst the Rhizostoma has neither. *Ibid.* 104 The very remarkable..system of nutrition in the *Rhizostome. 1836–9 *Todd's Cycl. Anat.* II. 407/2 The young..in the *Rhizostomatous species [are excluded] through the ramified canals of the pedicle. 1858 MAYNE *Expos. Lex.*, *Rhizostomus*,..*rhizostomous. 1876 *Encycl. Brit.* IV. 95/1 Different forms of *rhizotaxis. 1870 HENFREY *Bot.* Index, *Rhizotaxy (arrangement of roots). 1836 *Penny Cycl.* V. 247 Some sorts [of roots]..are to be cut against the wind, others after the body of the *rhizotomist has been well oiled. 1837 WHEWELL *Hist. Induct. Sci.* (1857) III. 221 The drug-sellers and the rhizotomists.

Rhizoid (rəi·zoid), *a.* and *sb. Bot.* [f. Gr. ῥίζα root + -OID.] **A.** *adj.* Resembling a root. *rare*—°.

1858 MAYNE *Expos. Lex.*, *Rhizoides*,..resembling a root; rhizoid. 1866 *Treas. Bot.* 974/1.

B. *sb.* A root-hair or filament.

1875 BENNETT & DYER tr. *Sachs' Bot.* 317 The Root-hairs (Rhizoids) play an..important part in the Economy of Mosses. *Ibid.*, In Atrichum and other Polytrichaceæ, the stouter rhizoids coil round one another.

So **Rhizoi·dal, Rhizoi·deous** *adjs.*, root-like; also, of the nature of a rhizoid.

1866 *Treas. Bot.*, *Rhizoid*, or *Rhizoideous*, resembling a root. 1875 BENNETT & DYER tr. *Sachs' Bot.* 282 The rhizoidal tubes are segmented by only a few septa which lie far below the growing apex.

‖ **Rhizoma** (rəizōu·mă). *Bot.* Pl. **rhizo·mata, rhizo·mas.** [mod.L., a. Gr. ῥίζωμα, f. ῥιζοῦσθαι to take root, f. ῥίζα root.] = RHIZOME.

1830 LINDLEY *Nat. Syst. Bot.* 253 Aquatic plants..with a fleshy rhizoma which is eatable. 1841 *Penny Cycl.* XX. 312/1 The rhizomata of many of the species [of *Sagittaria*] contain amylaceous matter. 1877 F. G. HEATH *Fern World* 18 From various parts of the upper side of the creeping rhizomas spring the fronds.

Hence **Rhizo·matous** *a.*, consisting of or of the nature of a rhizoma; having rhizomata.

1847 W. E. STEELE *Field Bot.* 210 *Filiceæ.* Leafy, perennial plants, often rhizomatous. 1872 OLIVER *Elem. Bot.* II. 186 In germinating the radicle [of mistletoe] penetrates the bark, forming a kind of rhizomatous root.

Rhizome (rəi·zōum). *Bot.* [Anglicized f. RHIZOMA, and now more usual.] A prostrate or subterranean root-like stem emitting roots and usually producing leaves at its apex; a rootstock.

1845 LINDLEY *Sch. Bot.* i. 4 If prostrate and rooting into the ground..[the stem] is a rhizome, as in the Iris. 1862 *Jrnl. Roy. Soc. Dubl.* Apr. 346 Whilst ferns have nutritive rhizomes. 1875 BENNETT & DYER tr. *Sachs' Bot.* 411 Similar rudimentary leaves..occur also on the ordinary rhizome-shoots. 1882 VINES tr. *Sachs' Bot.* 228 Phanerogams in which lateral branches with foliage-leaves spring from a rhizome clothed only with scales.

‖ **Rhizophora** (rəizǫ·fŏră). *Bot.* [mod.L. (sc. *planta*), f. Gr. ῥίζα root + -φόρος -bearing: see -A 2.] A genus typical of the N.O. *Rhizophoraceæ*; a tree of this genus, a mangrove.

1832 MACGILLIVRAY *Trav. Humboldt* xxi. 306 A forest of rhizophoræ, intermixed with euphorbiæ..and other plants. 1870 KINGSLEY *At Last* xiii, The common Rhizophoras, or black mangroves. 1876 R. F. BURTON *Gorilla L.* I. 31 The rhizophora is the growth of shallow brackish water.

Rhizophore (rəi·zofōəɹ). *Bot.* [f. as prec.: see -PHORE.] A structure in the genus *Selaginella* that bears the roots. So **Rhizo·phorous** *a.*, root-bearing (Ogilvie, 1882).

1875 BENNETT & DYER tr. *Sachs' Bot.* 411 The Rhizophores of Selaginella.

Rhizopod[1] (rəi·zŏpǫd). *Zool.* [ad. mod.L. RHIZOPODA.] An animalcule of the class *Rhizopoda*.

1851 OWEN *Gen. & Comp. Phys.* (ed. 3) § 285 From the polythalamous shells of Cephalopods..those of Rhizopods may be distinguished [etc.]. 1859 GREENE *Protozoa* ii. 3 The most easily procured of all Rhizopods is, perhaps, the *Amœba*. 1869 SPENCER *Princ. Psychol.* III. iv. (1870) I. 307 In many Rhizopods the tactual surface and the absorbing surface are co-extensive.

Rhizopod[2] (rəi·zŏpǫd). *Bot.* Also **-pode**, and in L. form. [ad. mod.L. *rhizopodium*, f. Gr. ῥίζα root + ποδ-, πούς foot.] The mycelium of fungi.

1858 MAYNE *Expos. Lex.*, *Rhizopodium*,..a rhizopode. 1866 *Treas. Bot.* 975/2 Rhizopod, or Rhizopodium.

‖ **Rhizopoda** (rəizǫ·pŏdă), *sb. pl. Zool.* [mod. L., f. Gr. ῥίζα root + ποδ-, πούς foot: see -A 4.] The lowest class of Protozoa comprising animalcules having pseudopodia.

1859 GREENE *Protozoa* ii. 3. 1876 tr. *Wagner's Gen. Pathol.* 111 Rhizopoda which are partly naked, partly provided with shells. 1904 *Brit. Med. Jrnl.* 10 Sept. 569 A wide zoological field ranging from the lowly rhizopoda to the highest mammals.

Hence **Rhizopodal** (rəizǫ·pŏdăl), **Rhizopodic** (-pǫ·dik), **Rhizopodous** (-ǫ·pŏdəs) *adjs.*, belonging to or characteristic of the Rhizopoda.

1866 *Rep. Brit. Ass., Trans.* (1867) 63 The Rhizopodal Fauna of the Hebrides. 1869 *Monthly Microsc. Jrnl.* 1 Jan. 39 Of the animal of *Eozoon* we know..little beyond its having been recognized by Professor Carpenter as distinctly of a Rhizopodous type. 1871 T. R. JONES *Anim. Kingd.* (ed. 4) 17 No rhizopodic extensions are in these organisms protruded externally.

‖ **Rhizula** (rəi·ziŭlă). *Bot.* [mod.L., f. Gr. ῥίζα root: see -ULE.] = RHIZOID.

1839 [see RHIZINA]. 1858 HENSLOW *Dict. Bot. Terms*.

Rhoade, obs. form of ROAD.

Rhodalite (rōu·dăləit). *Min.* [f. Gr. ῥοδαλός (f. ῥόδον rose) + -ITE.] A clayey rose-red mineral found in Ireland.

1836 T. THOMSON *Min., Geol.*, etc. I. 354 *Rhodalite*. I give this name to a mineral from Ireland, which I got in the autumn of 1834 from Mr. Doran. 1843 J. E. PORTLOCK *Geol.* 223 Rhodalite occurs associated with Chabasie and carbonate of lime in the cavities of Amygdaloid at Ballintoy.

Rhodanate (rōu·dănēⁱt). *Chem.* [irreg. f. Gr. ῥόδον rose + -AN + -ATE[1].] = SULPHOCYANATE. **Rhodanic** (rodæ·nik) *a.*, = SULPHOCYANIC. **Rhodanide** (rōu·dănəid), = SULPHOCYANIDE.

1867 BRANDE & COX *Dict. Sci.*, etc., *Rhodanic acid*. 1868 WATTS *Dict. Chem.*, *Rhodanides*, a name applied to sulphocyanates, on account of the red colour which they produce with ferric salts. 1872 THUDICHUM *Chem. Physiol.* 3 Rhodanate or sulphocyanate (also termed rhodanide or sulphocyanide) of potassium and sodium.

Rhodate (rōu·dēⁱt). *Chem.* [f. Gr. ῥόδον rose + -ATE[1].] A salt of rhodic acid.

1858 MAYNE *Expos. Lex.*, *Rhodate*,..a combination of rhodic oxide with a salifiable base.

Rhoddon, variant of RODDEN, rowan.

Rhodeoretin (rōudĭ,ǫ·rĕtin). *Chem.* [ad. G. *rhodeoretin*, f. Gr. ῥόδεος roseate (f. ῥόδον rose) + ῥητίνη resin.] = CONVOLVULIN. Hence **Rhodeoreti·nic** *a.*, obtained from rhodeoretin; **Rhodeore·tinol**, = CONVOLVULINOL; **Rhodeoretinoˈlic** *a.* = CONVOLVULINOLIC.

1845 W. GREGORY *Outl. Chem.* II. 454 When rhodeoretine is acted on by hydrochloric acid, it is resolved into grape sugar..and an oily liquid rhodeoretinole. 1853 *Chem. Gaz.* XI. 23 Rhodeoretinic acid is insoluble in æther. *Ibid.* 24 Rhodeoretinolic acid is very sparingly soluble in pure water.

Rhodes-wood (rōu·dz,wud). [app. after F. *bois de Rhodes*, which however = rhodium-wood.] The wood of the West Indian tree *Amyris balsamifera*; candle-wood. 1866 *Treas. Bot.* 976/1.

Rhodian (rōu·diăn), *a.* and *sb.* [f. L. *Rhodi-us*, f. *Rhodos*, *-us*, = Gr. Ῥόδος Rhodes: see -IAN.]

A. *adj.* **a.** Of or belonging to the order of the Knights of Rhodes or Hospitallers.

1592 ?KYD *Soliman & Pers.* III. i. 67 This is Erastus, the Rhodian worthie. 1843 BROWNING *Return of Druses* I. 3/2 A Rhodian eight-point cross of white flame.

b. Belonging to or inhabiting the island of Rhodes in the Ægean Sea off the south-west coast of Asia Minor. *Rhodian law* (see quot. 1866).

1697 R. COLLIER *Essays on Moral Subjects* II. (1703) 5 The Rhodian Colossus. 1796 MORSE *Amer. Geogr.* II. 454 The Rhodian law was the directory of the Romans in maritime affairs. 1839 *Civil Eng. & Arch. Jrnl.* II. 435/1 Variegated marbles...Rhodian, with golden or pyritic spots. 1866 *Chambers's Encycl.* VIII. 230/2 *Rhodian Law* is the earliest system of marine law known to history, said to be compiled by the Rhodians after they had by their commerce and naval victories obtained the sovereignty of the sea, about 900 years before the Christian era. 1880 *Jrnl. Hellenic Stud.* I. 308 Mediæval Rhodian love-poems.

B. *sb.* **a.** A Knight of Rhodes; a Hospitaller.

1550 COKE *Deb. betw. Heralds* § 168 (1877) 107 Armytes, anceres, rodianes, and other disguised harlottes. 1551 BALE *Eng. Votaries* II. 47 b, Rhodyanes, Templers, Hospyteler[s].

b. An inhabitant or native of Rhodes.

1593 LODGE *Life & Death Will. Longbeard* (Hunter. Cl.) 63 Sicilians, Rhodians, Athenians. 1660 JER. TAYLOR *Duct. Dubit.* III. i. 42 Some of the Rhodians had mov'd that they might help Perseus the King of Macedonia, in case peace could not be obtained for him. 1799 CAMPBELL *Pleas. Hope* II. 73 When first the Rhodian's mimic art arrayed The queen of Beauty in her Cyprian shade. 1831 A. SUTHERLAND *Achievements of Knights of Malta* II. 3 Anthony Meligalle, a Rhodian of noble birth, who had once worn the cross of the Order. 1866 *Chambers's Encycl.* VIII. 239/2 The Rhodians rose upon and expelled the intruders.

† **Rhodian-wood.** *Obs.*—° Englishing of mod. L. *lignum rhodium*: see RHODIUM[1] 1.

1727–38 CHAMBERS *Cycl.*, *Rhodium lignum*, rhodian-wood.

Rhodic (rōu·dik), *a. Chem.* [f. RHODIUM[2] + -IC.] Containing rhodium in smaller proportions, relatively to oxygen, than the rhodous compounds.

1842 PARNELL *Chem. Anal.* (1845) 56 The solutions of rhodic oxide in hydrochloric and concentrated sulphuric acid have a yellow colour. 1858 GRAHAM *Elem. Chem.* II. 410 Protochloride of rhodium, RCl, is obtained by heating the protosulphate (precipitated from rhodic salts by hydrosulphuric acid) in a steam of chlorine.

Rhodiene (rōu·di,īn). *Chem.* [f. RHODIUM[1] + -ENE.] (See quot.)

1872 J. H. GLADSTONE *Jrnl. Chem. Soc.* Ser. II. X. 3, I would suggest the following...Hydrocarbon from Rosewood, Rhodiene.

Rhodings (rōu·dinz), *sb. pl. Naut.* (See quot.)

c 1850 *Rudim. Navig.* (Weale) 141 Rhodings of the pumps, &c., the brass cleats on which the axles work.

Rho:dio-chlo·ride. *Chem.* [irreg. f. RHODIUM[2] + CHLORIDE.] A double chloride of rhodium and one of the alkali metals.

1842 LIEBIG & GREGORY *Turner's Chem.* 671 Rhodiochlorides... Dirhodio-chloride of Potassium... Trirhodio-chloride of Sodium.

Rhodium[1] (rōu·diŏm). [mod.L. (sc. *lignum* wood), neut. of *rhodius* rose-like (f. Gr. ῥόδον rose), which has been sometimes associated with *Rhodius* RHODIAN.]

1. *Rhodium-wood* [partial translation of mod.L. *lignum rhodium*; cf. RHODIAN-WOOD], the sweet-scented wood of two species of Convolvulus, *C. floridus* and *C. scoparius*, of the Canary Islands.

1661 CULPEPPER *London Disp.* 73 Wood of...Rhodium encreases milk in Nurses. 1741 *Compl. Fam.-Piece* I. iv. 249 Take...Rhodium Wood, Yellow Saunders, each 6 Drams.

2. *Oil of rhodium* [= mod.L. *oleum rhodii*]: oil obtained from rhodium-wood; rosewood oil.

1678 PHILLIPS, *Lignum Rhodium*, or *Aspalathus*, a certain sweet Wood; of which, the Oyl of Rhodium much used in Perfumes is made. 1764 *Museum Rust.* I. 397 To the above-mentioned means of alluring by trailing..is added another of very material efficacy, which is, the use of oil of Rhodium. 1844 H. STEPHENS *Bk. Farm* III. 1296 A mixture of wheaten-flour and sugar..flavoured with the oil of rhodium. 1846 J. BAXTER *Libr. Pract. Agric.* (ed. 4) II. 371 To entice Rats. Oil of Rhodium, twenty drops [etc.].

Rhodium[2] (rōu·diŏm). *Chem.* [f. Gr. ῥόδον rose + -IUM.] A very hard white metal of the platinum group, discovered by Wollaston (see quot. 1804). Symbol Rh, formerly Ro.

1804 WOLLASTON in *Phil. Trans.* XCIV. 419, I design in the present Memoir to prove the existence..of another metal, hitherto unknown, which may not improperly be distinguished by the name of Rhodium, from the rose-colour of a dilute solution of the salts containing it. 1836 T. THOMSON *Min., Geol.*, etc. II. 460 Rhodium is a white metal, of so difficult fusion, that hitherto it has been obtained only in grains. 1880 CLEMINSHAW *Wurtz' Atom. Theory* 223 Iridium and rhodium..form well-characterised trichlorides and sesquioxides.

b. *attrib.*, as *rhodium salt*; **rhodium-black** (see quot.); **rhodium-gold**, native gold containing rhodium; so *rhodium ingot*; **rhodium pen**, a steel pen tipped with rhodium.

1883 *Jrnl. Chem. Soc.* 849 *Rhodium black, obtained by the action of formic acid on rhodium hexchloride and sodium chloride. 1868 WATTS *Dict. Chem.*, **Rhodium-gold*. 1882 DANA *Min.* 110 A rhodium-gold from Mexico. 1895 *Daily News* 2 May 3/1 A *rhodium ingot. 1839 URE *Dict. Arts*, etc. 1028 The inalterable nibs of the so-named *rhodium pens. 1853 W. GREGORY *Inorg. Chem.* 261 The *rhodium salt [is] insoluble in alcohol.

Rhodizite (rōu·dizəit). *Min.* [ad. G. *rhodizit* (Rose), f. Gr. ῥοδίζειν to be red, from ῥόδον rose.] Borate of aluminium and potassium: so called because it colours the blowpipe-flame red.

1836 T. THOMSON *Min., Geol.*, etc. I. 679 Rhodizite dissolves with great difficulty in muriatic acid. 1882 DANA *Min.* 206 Rhodizite,..supposed to be a lime-boracite.

Rhodizonic (rōdizǫ·nik), *a. Chem.* [f. Gr. ῥοδίζειν to be red, f. ῥόδον rose, after G. *rhodizonsäure* (Heller, 1837).] The name of two acids (so named because their salts are red) obtained from carboxide of potassium. Hence **Rhodizo·nate**, a salt of rhodizonic acid.

1839 R. D. THOMSON in *Brit. Ann.* 346 Rhodizoic [*sic*] acid may be isolated from the potash salt. *Ibid.*, Rhodizoate of potash. 1842 GRAHAM *Elem. Chem.* 934 Rhodizonic Acid..was first observed by L. Gmelin, and recognised as a new acid by Heller. *Ibid.*, A red solution..containing rhodizonate of potash. 1860 BRODIE in *Q. Jrnl. Chem. Soc.* XII. 272 The rhodizonate appears as a red insoluble powder. 1868 WATTS *Dict. Chem.* s.v., It will be convenient to designate the acid originally obtained by Heller..as α-rhodizonic, and that obtained by Brodie as β-rhodizonic acid.

Rhodo- (rōu·do), combining f. Gr. ῥόδον rose, used chiefly in names of mineral and chemical substances: **Rho·dochrome** [Gr. χρῶμα colour], a rose-coloured variety of penninite. **Rhodochro·site** [Gr. ῥοδόχρως], carbonate of manganese occurring in rose-red crystals. **Rhodocri·nite**, a rose-like encrinite. **Rhodophy·llite** [Gr. φύλλον leaf], = *rhodochrome* (Watts *Dict. Chem.* 1868). **Rhodo·psin** [Gr. ὄψις sight], visual purple. **Rho·dosperm** [Gr. σπέρμα seed], a seaweed of the class *Rhodospermeæ* characterized by rose-coloured spores. **Rhodospe·rmin**, the colouring matter of the red algæ of the group *Florideæ*. **Rhodospe·rmous** *a.*, having red seeds or spores; belonging to or characteristic of the group *Rhodospermeæ* of algæ. **Rhodota·nnic** *a.*, in *rhodotannic acid*, tannic acid obtained from the leaves of *Rhododendron ferrugineum*. **Rhodoxa·nthin**, rhodotannic acid.

1854 R. D. THOMSON *Cycl. Chem.* 410/2 **Rhodochrome*,..a variety of serpentine...It contains sesquioxide of chromium. 1836 T. THOMSON *Min., Geol.*, etc. I. 512 Carbonate of Manganese. Dialogite, *rhodochrosite, and..allagite, photizite, rhodonite. 1882 OGILVIE, **Rhodocrinite*. 1886 *Jrnl. Chem. Soc.* L. 375 After a frog has been poisoned by pilocarpin, the regeneration of *rhodopsin in the dark after exposure to light is hastened. 1866 *Treas. Bot.* 978/1 The *Rhodosperms form one of the three great divisions of *Algæ*. 1875 BALFOUR in *Encycl. Brit.* I. 505/2 *Chondrus* (*Sphærococcus crispus* and *C. mammillosus*, two Rhodosperms. 1875 BENNETT & DYER tr. *Sachs' Bot.* 31 In dried specimens of other Florideæ.. Klein observed colourless crystalloids of a different form. These formations may all be comprised in the name first given by Cramer,—*Rhodospermine. 1856 W. L. LINDSAY *Hist. Brit. Lichens* 2 The *rhodospermous seaweed. 1858 MAYNE *Expos. Lex.*, *Rhodospermus*,..rhodospermous. 1853 *Chem. Gaz.* XI. 41 *Rhodotannic acid in the anhydrous state has..the composition represented by the formula $C^{14}H^{5}O^{8}$. *Ibid.* 45 That [substance] obtained from the pure [rhodotannic] acid, to which the author [R. Schwartz] gives the name of *rhodoxanthine.

† **Rhododa·phne.** *Obs.* [late L., a. Gr. ῥοδοδάφνη, f. ῥόδον rose + δάφνη laurel, DAPHNE.] The rose-bay or oleander.

1548 [see OLEANDER]. 1581 MAPLET *Diall of Destiny* 67 Among hearbs he [*sc.* Saturn] holdeth Sanoury...And Hemlocke...And Rhododaphne, which beinge taken inwardly poysoneth. 1591 SPENSER *Virg. Gnat* 673 Fresh Rhododaphne, and the Sabine flowre. 1601 [see RHODODENDRON 1]. 1628 LE GRYS tr. *Barclay's Argenis* 121 A whole Wood of Pomegranates, Rhododaphne [etc.].

‖ **Rhododendron** (rōudŏde·ndrǫn). Plural: **Rhododendrons, -dendra.** [late L., a. Gr. ῥοδόδενδρον, f. ῥόδον rose + δένδρον tree.]

†**1.** = RHODODAPHNE. *Obs.*

1601 HOLLAND *Pliny* I. 469 As for the Oleander, although it be called the Sabine herb, yet it commeth from the Greeks, as may appeare by the name Rhododendron. Some haue called it Nerion; others Rhododaphne. 1607 TOPSELL *Fourf. Beasts* 611 Sauine,..Rhododendron, or Rose-tree.

2. A genus of showy ericaceous shrubs or low trees, akin to the azaleas, much cultivated for their evergreen foliage and profusion of large, beautiful flowers; a plant or flower belonging to this genus.

The garden varieties are derived mainly from *R. ponticum*, a native of Pontus and the Caucasus.

1664 EVELYN *Kal. Hort.* Sept., Flowers in Prime, or yet lasting...Rhododendron white and red [etc.]. 1785 MARTYN *Rousseau's Bot.* xix. (1794) 268 Andromedas, Rhododendrons,..and a few others, have regular monopetalous

corollas. 1828 *Q. Jrnl. Sci.* XXVI. 165 The fine mountain Rhododendron of India, with scarlet flowers. 1843 THACKERAY *Bluebeard's Ghost* in *Fraser's Mag.* Oct. 415/1 Polyanthuses, rhododendra, ranunculuses, and other flowers..with the largest names and of the most delightful odours. 1867 H. MACMILLAN *Bible Teach.* iv. (1870) 85 Luxuriant thickets of rhododendrons lighting up the green recesses with their gorgeous crimson flowers.

3. *attrib.*, as *rhododendron bush, thicket, tree*, etc.

1855 KINGSLEY *Westw. Ho!* xix, Through woods of wild plantain, and rhododendron thickets. 1859 LANG *Wand. India* 409 Some of the hills are literally covered with rhododendron trees, fifty or sixty feet high. 1876 GEO. ELIOT *Dan. Der.* II. xiii, Lightly whipping the rhododendron bush in front of her.

Rhodomantade, -montad(e, -ide, -ado, obs. ff. RODOMONTADE, -ADO.

† **Rhodomel.** *Obs.* Also 5 **rodomelle.** [mod. L., ad. late L. *rhodomeli*, a. Gr. ῥοδόμελι, f. ῥόδον rose + μέλι honey.] Honey of roses.

1398 TREVISA *Barth. De P. R.* XIX. xliv. (Bodl. MS.), Rodomel is made of þe Iuce of rose & hony medled. *c* 1420 *Pallad. on Husb.* VI. 217 And xl dayes to biholde on heuen, In Iuce of rose a sester that wel smelle, A pound hony, and name hit rodomelle. 1657 TOMLINSON tr. *Renou's Disp.* III. v. 102 Rhodomel prepared without colature.

Rhodonite (rōu·dŏnəit). *Min.* [ad. G. *rhodonit*, f. Gr. ῥόδον: see -ITE[1] 2 b.] Silicate of manganese, of a rose-pink colour when pure; manganese-spar, rose manganese.

1823 W. PHILLIPS *Introd. Min.* (ed. 3) 247 The Rhodonite appears to occur both compact and of a fibrous texture. 1883 *Scotsman* 9 May 7/5 Tables, vases, and columns of malachite,..rhodonite—a lovely red crystalline stone.

† **Rhodostauro·tic**, *a. Obs. rare*—[1]. A rendering into Greek form of ROSICRUCIAN (f. Gr. ῥόδον rose + σταυρός cross).

1625 B. JONSON *Masque Fort. Isl.*, The Castle in the aire, where all the Brethren Rhodostaurotick live.

Rhodous (rōu·dəs), *a. Chem.* [f. RHODIUM[2] + -OUS.] Containing rhodium in larger proportions, relatively to oxygen, than the rhodic compounds.

1842 GRAHAM *Elem. Chem.* 634 Rhodium is the most oxidable of the platinum metals...It appears to form two oxides, the rhodous and the rhodic.

Rhœadic (rīˌæ·dik), *a. Chem.* Also **rhe-.** [f. Gr. ῥοιαδ-, ῥοιάς a kind of poppy + -IC.] *Rhœadic acid*, a principle found in the flowers of the red poppy (*Papaver Rhœas*). So **Rhœa·dine**, a crystalline alkaloid found in the red poppy; **Rhœa·genine** (see quot. 1872).

1845 *Chem. Gaz.* IV. 193 Pure rhœadic acid is a shining dark red amorphous mass. 1858 MAYNE *Expos. Lex.*, *Rhœadin*,..term by Riffard for the colouring matter of the *Papaver rhœas*. 1872 WATTS *Dict. Chem.* 1st Suppl., *Rhœagenine*, a base isomeric with rhœadine.

Rhomb (rǫmb, rǫm). Also 6 **rombe**, 7 **rhombe, romb, roumb**, 8 **rumb.** [ad. L. *rhombus* RHOMBUS. Cf. F. *rhombe* (1542 in Hatz.-Darm.).]

1. *Geom.* A plane figure having four equal sides and the opposite angles equal (two being acute and two obtuse). Also, a lozenge-shaped object or formation; *Nat. Hist.*, etc., a part, disposition of parts, marking, etc., of this shape.

Pectinated rhomb: a hydrospire.

c 1578 in Hakluyt *Voy.* (1600) III. 43 We builded a little house..and garnished it with many kinds of trifles, as Pinnes, Points, Laces, Glasses, Rombes. 1597 MORLEY *Introd. Mus.* Annot. ₱4 The semibriefe was at the first framed like a triangle,..but..it grew afterward to the figure of a rombe or losing. 1671 MILTON *P. R.* III. 309 See how in warlike muster they appear, In Rhombs and wedges, and half moons, and wings. 1696 PHILLIPS, *Rhomb*, or *Roumb*. 1726 SWIFT *Gulliver* III. ii, If they would..praise the Beauty of a Woman, or any other Animal, they describe it by Rhombs, Circles,..and other geometrical Terms. 1727–38 CHAMBERS *Cycl.* s.v. *Neper's bones*, By adding the several numbers occurring in the same rhomb together. 1794 KIRWAN *Elem. Min.* (ed. 2) I. 257 Garnet..presenting either 12 rhomboidal planes, or 24 trapezoidal, or 36 planes, of which 12 are rhombs. 1818 KIRBY & SP. *Entomol.* xv. (ed. 3) I. 489 For the solution of this problem the geometrician..found that the great angles of the rhombs should be 109° 26′, and of the small angles 70° 34′. 1849 H. MILLER *Footpr. Creat.* iii. (1874) 32 The more amply imbricated tile-like rhombs of the Dipterians and Palæonisci. 1854 MURCHISON *Siluria* ix. 217 A pair of pectinated rhombs. 1855 in *Orr's Circ. Sci.*, *Inorg. Nat.* 300 The rhombic dodecahedron is a solid, bounded by twelve equal and similar four-sided figures, called rhombs. 1859 DARWIN *Orig. Spec.* viii. (1860) 229, I have noticed half-completed rhombs at the base of a just-commenced cell.

2. *Cryst.* A solid figure bounded by six equal and similar rhombic planes; a rhombohedron.

1800 tr. *Lagrange's Chem.* I. 305 [It] will crystallize..in the form of a rhomb. 1813 BAKEWELL *Introd. Geol.* (1815) 48 Calcareous stalactites..cleave into regular rhombs. 1831 BREWSTER *Optics* xvii. 145 A rhomb of Iceland spar. 1869 TYNDALL *Notes Lect. Light* § 419 When a small aperture through which light passes is regarded through a rhomb of Iceland spar two apertures are seen.

b. *Fresnel's rhomb*: see quot.

1854 *Pereira's Polarized Light* (ed. 2) 105 Fresnel effected the circular polarization of light by means of a parallelopiped of St. Gobin (crown) glass.., whose acute angles B and C are about 54° and consequently whose obtuse ones A and D are about 126. This apparatus is commonly called Fresnel's rhomb.

† **3.** A circle; a magic circle. *Obs. rare.*

1656 BLOUNT *Glossogr.* [after Cotgr.], *Rhomb*, a Spinning Wheel, Reel, or Whirle. 1667 MILTON *P. L.* VIII. 134 That swift Nocturnal and Diurnal rhomb suppos'd, Invisible else above all Starrs, the Wheele Of Day and Night. 1697 ABELL in Potter *Antiq. Greece* IV. x. 269 [tr. Ovid *Amores* I. viii. 7–8], She knows the Rhomb, what Feats in Magick are From th' pois'nous Issue of a lustfull Mare.

† **4.** ? A turbot. *Obs. rare.*

1720 STRYPE *Stow's Surv.* II. xxvii. 366/2 [transl. statute for buying fish], A Piece of Rumb, gross and fat, for 4*d.*

5. *Conch.* (See quot. and cf. *rhomb-shell*.)

1815 E. J. BURROW *Conch.* 200 *Porphyria*. Large clouded Rhomb or Camp Olive. *Oliva*, Yellow Rhomb; Olive. *Paupercula*, Zebra Rhomb.

6. *attrib.* and *Comb.*, as *rhomb-marked*, *-shaped* adjs.; **rhomb-dodecahedron**, a rhombic dodecahedron; **rhomb-ovate** *a.*, partly rhomboid and partly ovate; **rhomb-porphyry**, a porphyry enclosing crystals of orthoclase of a rhombic outline (Cassell); **rhomb-shell**, *Conch.*, a volute; **rhomb-solid**, a solid figure consisting of two equal right cones joined together at their bases and generated by the revolution of a rhomb upon a diagonal; **rhomb-spar** [G. *rhomboidalspath*], see quot. 1837.

1895 MASKELYNE *Crystallogr.* 195 Diamond, gold, and electrum are among the substances that occur in *rhomb-dodecahedra. 1877 *Nature* XV. 326/2 Three *Rhomb-marked Snakes (*Psammophylax rhombeatus*) from South Africa. 1793 MARTYN *Lang. Bot.* (ed. 2), *Rhombeum folium*, a Rhombed or *rhomb-shaped leaf. 1796 WITHERING *Brit. Plants* (ed. 3) II. 483 Petals rhomb-shaped. *c* 1711 PETIVER *Gazophyl.* 8/1 A White Indian *Rhomb-shell finely speckled with black. 1815 E. J. BURROW *Conch.* 200 *Voluta*, Rhomb Shell or Cylinder. 1704 J. HARRIS *Lex. Techn.* I, **Rhombe Solid*. 1804 JAMESON *Syst. Min.* I. 516 Calc Genus. Seventh Species. *Rhomb-spar. 1837 DANA *Min.* 197 The names Rhomb spar and Bitter spar, have been applied to the perfectly crystallized specimens [of dolomite], excepting those with curved faces and a pearly lustre, which have been designated Pearl spar.

Rhombarsenite (rǫmbā·ɹsĕnəit). *Min.* [f. RHOMB + ARSENIC + -ITE.] = CLAUDETITE.

1887 in *Cassell's Encycl. Dict.* 1892 DANA *Min.* 199.

Rhombed (rǫmbd), *a. rare*—°. [f. RHOMB + -ED[2].] Rhomboid.

1793 [see RHOMB 6]. 1814 LUNAN *Hortus Jamaic.* II. 384/2 *Rhombeum*, rhombed.

Rho·mbeous, *a. rare*—°. [f. mod.L. *rhombeus*, f. RHOMBUS: see -EOUS.] Rhomboid.

1797 *Encycl. Brit.* (ed. 3) III. 442/1 Rhombeous, or rhomboidal. 1858 MAYNE *Expos. Lex.*, *Rhombeus*,..presenting four parallel sides, two by two, forming two acute angles and two obtuse..; rhombeous.

Rhombic (rǫ·mbik), *a.* [f. RHOMB + -IC.]

1. Of the form of an oblique equilateral parallelogram; rhomb-shaped.

1701 [see RHOMBOID A. 1]. 1798 GREVILLE in *Phil. Trans.* LXXXVIII. 426 The Abbé Haüy, by measuring the rhombic plane of Corundum, found its two diagonals to be as two to three. 1816 P. CLEAVELAND *Min.* 444 Dodecaedrons with rhombic faces. 1849 D. CAMPBELL *Inorg. Chem.* 50 Sulphur occurs in nature crystallized in acute octohedrons with rhombic bases. 1888 ROLLESTON & JACKSON *Anim. Life* 577 Grooves pierced by pores which form a rhombic figure.

b. *Zool.* Lozenge- or diamond-shaped, often with the corners somewhat rounded.

1815 E. J. BURROW *Conch.* 76 The form differs much, being subglobose, reniform, cordate, or rhombic. 1851 WOODWARD *Mollusca* 69 *Loligo Vulgaris*:..body tapering behind..; fins terminal, united, rhombic. 1870 GILLMORE tr. *Figuier's Reptiles & Birds* iii. 109 Strobilosaura have the scales of the back and sides imbricate, generally rhombic.

c. *Bot.* Oval but angular at the sides.

1857 A. GRAY *First Less. Bot.*, Gloss. 1870 HOOKER *Stud. Flora* 318 Atriplex patula,..sepals rhombic or deltoid.

2. Of solid figures: **a.** Having a rhomb for its base or section plane; also, bounded by equal and similar rhombs; *Cryst.* = ORTHORHOMBIC.

1670 *Phil. Trans.* V. 2041 The Figure of this Chrystal stone is like a Rhombick or Rhomboid Prisme. 1802 PLAYFAIR *Illustr. Hutton. Th.* 246 The spar taking the form of rhombic crystals. 1841 BRANDE *Man. Chem.* 123 The rhombic dodecaëdron contained between twelve equal rhombic planes. 1842 FRANCIS *Dict. Arts*, *Rhombic spar*, Iceland spar, or the doubly-refractive carbonate of lime. 1869 ROSCOE *Elem. Chem.* (1874) 153 Rhombic or common neutral sodium phosphate. 1879 RUTLEY *Stud. Rocks* ix. 84 In the rhombic system the three axes of elasticity coincide with the three crystallographic axes.

b. In the specific names of minerals.

1788 J. H. DE MAGELLAN tr. *Cronstedt's Syst. Min.* (ed. 2) I. 198 Rhombic Quartz, *Spatum Scintillans*. Feltspatum. 1844 DANA *Min.* 322 Rhombic Mica. 1867 HUNT & RUDLER *Descr. Guide Mus. Pract. Geol.* 101 Marcasite occurs in a series of prismatic forms, which have suggested the name of rhombic pyrites.

3. *Comb.*, as *rhombic-based*, *-scaled* adjs.; also with adjs. = 'partly rhombic (and partly ...)'.

1828 STARK *Elem. Nat. Hist.* I. 395 Body rhombic-ovate, slightly lengthened. 1870 HOOKER *Stud. Flora* 317 Leaves rhombic-triangular. *Ibid.* 319 Lower leaves opposite rhombic or rhombic-hastate. 1895 MASKELYNE *Crystallogr.* 331 A rhombic based prism. 1896 *Guide Fossil Reptiles Brit. Mus.* 105 The Eugnathidæ are the rhombic-scaled forerunners of the modern *Amia*.

Rhombifer (rǫ·mbifəɹ). *Ichthyol.* [ad. mod.L. *Rhombifera*, neut. pl. of *rhombiferus*, f. *rhombus* RHOMBUS + *-ferus* (see -FER).] A ganoid fish, characterized by rhomboidal scales.

1863 DANA *Man. Geol.* 279 Rhombifers, or Ordinary Ganoids. *Ibid.* 280 The Pycnodonts are Rhombifers.

Rhombiferous (rǫmbi·ferəs), *a.* [In sense 1, after F. *rhombifère* (Haüy); in sense 2, f. mod.L. *Rhombifera* (see prec.).]

1. *Cryst.* (See quot.)

1816 R. JAMESON *Char. Min.* (ed. 2) 217 The Rhombiferous rock-crystal,..which is a six-sided prism, acuminated on both extremities with six planes, which are set on the lateral planes, and slightly truncated on the alternate angles; the truncating planes are rhombs.

2. *Ichth.* Having rhomboidal scales.

1855 in *Orr's Circ. Sci.*, *Org. Nat.* III. 67 The Rhombiferous Ganoid Fishes.

Rhombiform (rǫ·mbifǫɹm), *a.* [f. RHOMB(US + -(I)FORM.] Rhomb-shaped; see also quot. 1826.

1826 KIRBY & SP. *Entomol.* xlvi. IV. 266 Rhombiform.., whose horizontal section is rhomboidal. 1858 [see RHOMBO-].

† **Rhombite.** *Obs.* [ad. mod.L. *rhombites*, f. RHOMBUS: see -ITE.] An alleged precious stone.

1688 HOLME *Armoury* II. 41/2 The Rhombite, is a stone after the figure of the Mathematitians Rhombus.

Rho·mbo-, comb. form of Gr. ῥόμβος RHOMBUS, used to denote (1) 'rhombic', as in *rhombo-dodecahedron*; (2) 'forming a rhombus' (and another figure), as in *rhombo-quadratic*, *-rectangular*.

1839 URE *Dict. Arts* 954 Phosphorus..crystallizing in *rhombo-dodecahedrons out of its combination with sulphur. 1858 MAYNE *Expos. Lex.*, *Rhombododecahedrum*,..a body with twelve rhombiform sides: a rhombododecahedron. 1841 J. J. GRIFFIN *Syst. Cryst.* 67 Forms of the Equators of Pyramids...A *Rhombo-Quadratic Equator is one whose sides, when extended till they meet, form both a square and a rhombus. A *Rhombo-Rectangular Equator is one whose sides, when extended till they intersect one another, form both a rhombus and a rectangle. 1872 *Jrnl. Bot.* X. 194 Cells..rhombo-rectangular at base.

Rhombogen (rǫ·mbodʒĕn). [f. Gr. ῥόμβος RHOMBUS + -GEN.] In the *Dicyemidæ*, the form which produces infusoriform embryos. Hence **Rhomboge·nic** *a.*

1885 [see NEMATOGENIC]. 1888 ROLLESTON & JACKSON *Anim. Life* 815 The Rhombogen and secondary Nematogen are successive phases in the life-history of one and the same individual.

Rhombohedral (rǫmbohī·drăl), *a.* [f. next + -AL.] Pertaining to or having the form of a rhombohedron; *Cryst.*, denoting a system in which all the forms are derivable from the rhombohedron; also, belonging to this system.

1830 H. J. BROOKE in *Encycl. Metrop.* (1845) VI. 432/1 The rhombohedral [system of Mohs] consists of the rhomboid. 1837 WHEWELL *Hist. Induct. Sci.* (1857) II. 293 The rhombohedral calc-spar; or..Iceland spar. 1854 [see next]. 1881 *Nature* XXIV. 355 Prof. Tschermak has adopted the four-plane axial system in the rhombohedral system.

So **Rhombohedric** (-he·drik), *a.*

1854 *Pereira's Polarized Light* 165 The rhombohedric or rhombohedral system. 1855 J. SCOFFERN in *Orr's Circ. Sci.*, *Elem. Chem.* 77 Crystals not having 3 rectangular axes...Rhombohedric, Pyramidal, Prismatic.

Rhombohedron (rǫmbohī·drǫn). *Cryst.* Pl. **-hedra.** Also **rhomboedron.** [f. Gr. ῥόμβος RHOMBUS + ἕδρα base.] A solid figure bounded by six equal rhombs; a crystal of this form.

1836 MRS. SOMERVILLE *Connex. Phys. Sci.* xiv. 128 All the hundreds of forms of carbonate of lime split into six-sided figures called rhombohedrons. 1850 DAUBENY *Atom. The.* vi. (ed. 2) 171 The metals arsenic and antimony both crystallizing in the form of an acute rhomboedron. 1880 J. W. LEGG *Bile* 11 Glycocoll forms large rhombohedra which are easily soluble in water.

Rhomboid (rǫ·mboid), *a.* and *sb.* Also 7 **romboid.** [(1) ad. F. *rhomboïde* or late L. *rhomboīdēs* RHOMBOIDES; (2) ad. mod.L. RHOMBOIDEUS.]

A. *adj.* **1.** Having the form of a rhomb; *spec.* in *Bot.* (see quot. 1839).

a 1693 *Urquhart's Rabelais* III. xlix. 398 Some of these Plants are..Romboid. 1701 GREW *Cosmol. Sacra* I. iii. 14 Many other sorts of Stones are regularly figured;..the Selenites, of Parallel Plates, as in a Deck of Cards; and they are of a Rhombick Figure; Talk, of such as are Rhomboid. 1729 WOODWARD *Fossils* I. I. 70 A large Rhomboid Selenites. 1824 J. E. SMITH *Eng. Flora* II. 11 Red Goosefoot. Leaves triangular, somewhat rhomboid. 1839 LINDLEY *Introd. Bot.* 457 *Rhomboid*, oval, a little angular in the middle. 1877 W. H. DALL *Tribes of N. W.* 59 Artistic implements of rhomboid or semi-lunar form.

b. *Comb.*, as *rhomboid-oblong*, *-ovate*, *-ovoid* adjs.

1824 J. E. SMITH *Eng. Flora* II. 13 White Goosefoot. Leaves rhomboid-ovate. 1845 LINDLEY *Sch. Bot.* vii. (1858) 123 Fruit rhomboid-oblong. 1870 HOOKER *Stud. Flora* 315 Leaves..rhomboid-ovoid.

2. *Cryst.* = RHOMBIC 2. Now *rare.*

1870 [see RHOMBIC 2]. 1845 G. E. DAY tr. *Simon's Anim. Chem.* I. 37 Prisms of the right rhomboid system.

3. *Anat.* **a.** *Rhomboid muscle*, = RHOMBOIDEUS. **b.** *Rhomboid ligament*: the costo-clavicular ligament.

1834 J. FORBES *Laennec's Dis. Chest* (ed. 4) 21 So that the rhomboid and trapezius muscles are made quite tense. 1848 QUAIN *Anatomy* (ed. 5) I. 202 *marg.*, Rhomboid ligament. *Ibid.* 296 To expose the rhomboid muscle and the levator scapulæ, the trapezius must be removed.

B. *sb.* **1.** A quadrilateral figure having only its opposite sides and angles equal.

1570 DEE *Math. Pref.* a iiij b, Rhombe, Rhomboid, Lunular, Ryng, Serpentine, and such other Geometricall figures. 1672 BOYLE *Virtues of Gems* 91 Geometrically figur'd Bodies, shap'd like *Rhombus's* or *Rhomboides*. 1789 MRS. PIOZZI *Journ. France* I. 139 The hall of Justice..is two hundred and fifty-six feet long, and eighty-six broad; the form of it

Supplement, p. 3873; Corrigenda, p. 4092; Spurious words, p. 4093; Books quoted, p. 4094

Rhomboidal (rǫmboi·dăl), a. [ad. mod.L. *rhomboidāl-is*: see RHOMBOID and -AL.]

Rhomboides (rǫmboi·dīz). Now *rare* or *Obs.* Also 6 ombds, -oyades, -oeides.

Rhomboidal-ite (rǫmboi·dălăit). [...]

Rhomboideus (rǫmboi·diǫs). [...]

Rhomboidly, adv. rare.

Rhombus (rǫmbŏs). Also 6-8 rombus. Pl.

rhombuses (-s -us·z); 8 rhombi [l., a. rhombos.]

Rhophography [...] Painting in still life.

Rhotacism (rǫ·tăsiz'm). [...]

Rhotacize [...]

Rhotacsmando, obs. f. RODOMONTADO.

Rhubarb (rū·bärb). Forms: 4-7 rubarbe, [...] Also RHABARB.

Rhubarbaric, a. [...]

Rhubarbarate, *rare*−1. [ad. Gr. [...]]

Rhubarby (rū·bärbi), a. [f. RHUBARB + -Y.] Resembling rhubarb or that of rhubarb.

Rhyme (rǎim). v. Also 7-9 rime. [Graphic variant of RIME v.]

Rhymed (rǎimd), a.

Rhymeless (rǎi·mles), a.

Rhymer (rǎi·mǝr). [variant of RIMER sb.]

Rhymester (rǎi·mster). Also rhime-.

Rhymic, *rare*−1.

Rhymical, *rare*.

Rhymist, *rare*−1.

Rhynchocephalian (riŋkoˌsefā·liǎn).

Rhynchocele [...]

Rhynchonella [...]

Rhynchophorous (riŋkǫ·fǫrǝs), a. [...]

Rhynchophore (ri·ŋkofǫǝr). [...]

Rhyncosaur (ri·ŋkosǫǝr). [...]

Rhynchosaurian (riŋkosǫ·riǎn), a.

Rhyme [...]

Rhyming (rǎi·miŋ), vbl. sb.

Rhyming, ppl. a.

Rhyolite (rǎi·olǎit). [...]

Rhyparographer [...]

Rhyparography [...]

Rhyptic, *rare*−1.

Rhysimeter (risi·mītǝr). [...]

Rhythm (riðm). Forms: 6-7 rithme, rithm, 7-9 rythm, 8 rhithm, 7- rhythm. [...]

Rhythmed (ri·ð'md, ri·þ'md), a.

Rhythmic, -ical (ri·ðmik, -ikǎl). adj.

Rhythmist (ri·ðmist). [...]

Rhythmize (ri·ðmǎiz), v.

Rhythmless, a.

Rhythmic

d. *transf.* and *fig.*

Rhythmical, *a.*

Rhythmically, *adv.*

Rhythming, *vbl. sb.*

Rhythmist.

Rhythmize, *v.*

Rhythm-meter.

Rhythmopoeia.

Rhythmopee-tic, *a.*

Rhythmus.

Rhythmy.

Rhyton.

Rial, *sb.*[1]

Ri'a. *Geol.*

Rial (raiˑəl).

Rial, *a.*

Rialm. *Obs.*

Rial-ty, *Obs.*

l. Royalty; regal state or dignity.

Riancy.

Riant (raiˑənt, rǐ'ãn), *a.*

Rib, *sb.*[1]

Rib, *v.*[1]

Ribald, (riˑbald), *sb.* and *a.*

Ribaldish. *Obs.*

Ribaldize. *Obs.*

Ribaldly. *Obs.*

Ribaldous. *Obs.*

Ribaldry, *Obs.*

Ribaldrous. *Obs.*

Ribald-like.

Ribaldry.

Ribaldous, *a.*

† **Ribaldric** *a.*, **Ribaldrious** *a. Obs.* = next.
1633 Prynne *1st Pt. Histriom.* 68 Playes..purged from all Ribaldrious, Amorous, Vnchast, and filthie passages. 1796 *Mod. Gulliver* 205, I published a strain..of ribaldric, metaphoric, abusive invective.

Ri·baldrous, *a.* Now *Obs.* or *arch.* Also 6 **riba(u)drous.** [f. Ribald *sb.* + -(r)ous.] Of ribald character; ribald.
1565 Cooper *Thes.*, *Carmina obscœna*, ribaudrous verses. 1592 Greene *Disput.* Wks. (Grosart) X. 247 He..could gawll out many quaint and ribadrous Ligges and songs. 1622 T. Robinson *Anat. Eng. Nunnery* 13 They sing him ribaldrous Songs and jigs. 1633 Prynne *1st Pt. Histriom.* 65 Such Christians whose tongues are tipt, and hearts delighted with Ribaldrous Songs. 1794 *Gentl. Mag.* LXIV. II. 1133/1 What is thine but noisy strife.., Ribaldrous and vacant laugh! 1839 Hallam *Hist. Lit.* II. iv. § 28 The usual fault—vulgar and ribaldrous invective. *Ibid.* III. vii. § 35 If he turns to invective..it is mere ribaldrous vulgarity blended with pedantry.

Ribaldry (ri·băldri). Forms: α. 4 **riboud-**, 4–6 **ri-**, **rebaud-**, 4–7 **ribaud-**; 5 **rebawd-**, 5–6 **ri-**, **rybawd-**. β. 5 **ry-**, 6–7 **ribauld-**; 5–6 **ry-**, **rebald-**, 6 **ribaldry** (7 **ribb-**). Also 4 **-ri**, 4–5 **-rye**, 4–7 **-rie**; 5 **-ery.** [a. OF. *re-*, *ribau(l)derie* (= Sp., Pg., and It. *ribalderia*): see Ribald *sb.* and -ry. So MDu. *ribauderie.*]

† 1. Debauchery, lasciviousness, vice. *Obs.*
α. 13.. *E. E. Allit. P.* B. 184 For þefte, & for þrepyng, vn-þonk may mon haue; For roborrye, & riboudrye. *c* 1386 Chaucer *Pars. T.* ⁋ 390 Schewyng of vice and rybaudrie and seruage of synne. 1474 Caxton *Chesse* 20, I shal say that I haue slayn you for your rybaudrye. 1547 *Bk. of Marchantes* d v, The desyre to norishe well..their rybawdry or (as thei saye) their estate. 1567–9 Jewel *Def. Apol.* (1611) 345 Take Harlots away from among men, and ye fill all the Country with ribaudrie and villanie. 1635 Pagitt *Christianogr.* I. iii. (1636) 207 A Jew maide..turned..Christian that she might freely exercise the art of Ribaudrie.
β. *c* 1425 Wyntoun *Cron.* v. iv. 708 Al his men he lewit for þi In til al tyme oysse rebaldry, And alkyn wicis at þar wil. 1483 Caxton *Cato* A vi b, Dame harlote ye come from your rybauldrye as ye ben acustomed. 1577 tr. *Bullinger's Decades* (1592) 200 Let him punish dishonestie, ribauldrie, filthy lust. 1610 Healey *St. Aug. Citie of God* 56 Their beastly stage plaiers acted such ribauldry as was a shame [etc.]. 1645 Milton *Tetrach.* Wks. 1851 IV. 198 A little purer then the prerogative of a legal and public ribaldry.

2. Obscenity or coarseness of language, †a coarse tale, a rude composition; in later use, scurrilous or irreverent jesting; coarse or wanton mockery.
α. 13.. *Cursor M.* 23856 (Gött.), Bot war a ribaudri vs tald, Of a fantum.., þat suld we hald in herte stable. 1393 [see Ribald *sb.* 4]. *c* 1460 *Vrbanitatis* 76 in *Babees Book* (1868) 15 Lawȝe þou not with no grette cry, Ne Rage þou not with Rybawdry. *c* 1460 *Stans Puer ad Mensam* 44 *Ibid.* 24 Swere none othes, speke no ribawdrye. 1514 Barclay *Egloges* ii. (1570) B ij, On eche side soundeth foule speche of ribawdry. 1592 Greene *Disput.* Wks. (Grosart) X. 270, I..still delighted in iangling Ditties of rybaudrie. 1606 Holland *Sueton.* 250 So skurrile and filthy, that he could not so much as forbeare words of ribaudrie.
β. 1501 Douglas *Pal. Hon.* Epil., Ressaue this roustie rurall rebaldrie. 1589 Nashe *Anat. Absurd.* Wks. (Grosart) I. 43 Tender youth ought to bee restrained for a time from the reading of such ribauldrie. 1601 B. Jonson *Poetaster* III. iv, We haue as much ribaldrie in our plaies, as can bee. 1682 Sheffield (Dk. Buckhm.) *Ess. Poetry*, Bare ribaldry, that poor pretence to wit. 1711 Steele *Spect.* No. 36 ⁋ 8 To the great Offence of chaste and tender Ears, they learn Ribaldry, obscene Songs, and immodest Expressions. 1759 Goldsm. *Polite Learn.* x[ii], The piece..pleases the galleries because it has ribaldry. 1827 Hallam *Const. Hist.* ii. (1876) I. 93 The ribaldry which vulgar protestants uttered against their most sacred mystery. 1886 Ruskin *Præterita* I. 329 An article in Blackwood's..of sufficiently telling ribaldry.
personif. 1781 Cowper *Table-T.* 729 Satire has..done his best, and curst And loathsome ribaldry has done his worst.

† 3. a. Rabble, canaille. *Obs. rare.*
1550 J. Coke *Eng. & Fr. Heralds* (1877) § 190. 112 The sayde rybaldry callyng them selves Hungariens. *Ibid.* § 201. 115, I dare let slyp a .C. good yomen of England or Wales to .Vᵉ. of such ribaldry.
† b. A trumpery toy. *Obs. rare*⁻¹.
1594 Carew *Huarte's Exam. Wits* (1596) 183 To make clocks, pictures, poppets and other ribaldries which are impertinent to mans service.

† 4. *attrib.* or as *adj.* Obscene, indecent. *Obs.*
1519 Horman *Vulg.* 62 b, I consayle the refrayne thy selfe fro such foule and rebaudry wordes. 1547 Boorde *Brev. Health* clxiii. 58 b, With out swerynge or slaunderynge, and rybaldry speaking. 1592 Nashe *Four Lett. Confut.* Wks. (Grosart) II. 247 Such a ribauldry Don Diego as thou art. 1633 Prynne *1st Pt. Histriom.* 225 Not onely Drunkennesse, Luxury, Playes, and ribaldry Songs. 1638 Junius *Paint. Ancients* 124 It hath been pleasing..to drinke in ribauldrie abominations.

† **Ri·baldy**, *sb. Obs.* Forms: 4 **ribod-**, 5 **rybod-**, **reboud-**; 3–5 **ri-**, 4–5 **rybaud-**; 5 **re-**, **ribawd-**; 5 **rybbald-**, 8 **ribbaldy.** Also 3–4 **-ie** (4 **-i**, **-e**), 4–5 **-ye.** [a. OF. *ribaudie*, *-auldie* (= med.L. and Pg. *ribaldia*): see Ribald and -y. So MDu. *ribaudie.*] Ribaldry.
c 1290 *St. George* 30 in *S. Eng. Leg.* I. 294 Þov schalt in oþere ribaudies sone daiȝes beo i-do. 13.. *K. Alis.* 21 (Bodl. MS.), Wel fele..Beeþ yfounde..Þat hadden leuer a ribaudye þan here of god. *c* 1386 Chaucer *Pard. T.* Prol. 38 Nay, lat hym telle vs of no ribaudye. *c* 1440 *Jacob's Well* 217 Whanne þou openyst þin erys to here flatereris, or lyerys, bacbyterys, or rybaudye. 1482 *Monk of Evesham* (Arb.) 74 They that spake wordis of reboudye..were ponysshte.

† **Ri·baldy**, *a. Obs. rare.* Also 5 **ribaudy.** [f. Ribald + -y.] Ribald.
1430–40 Lydg. *Bochas* vii. viii. (1554) 171 They wer proud, ribaudy, lecherous, Cruel. 1600 O. E. (M. Sutcliffe) *Repl. Libel* v. 124 Hath not..a ribaldy lying frier..sought to dishonour her Maiestie?

Riband (ri·bănd), *sb.* Now *arch.* Forms: α. 4–6 **ryban** (5 **-anne**), **reban** (6 **-en**), 4–7 **riban**, 5, 7 **ribban**; 4–5 **ribane**, 5 **ry-**, **rebane**, **rebayn**; 5, 7 **riben.** β. 5–6 **ryband**, 6 **re-**, 6– **riband**; 6 **ri-**, **ry-**, **reabande**; 5 **ribawnde**, 6 **rebaund**; 5 **re-**, 6 **rybende.** γ. 6–9 **ribband.** See also Ribbon and Ruban. [a. OF. *riban*, *ruban* (13th cent.), of obscure origin: possibly a Teutonic compound of which the second element is *band.*]

1. = Ribbon *sb.* 1. a. Without article.
α. 139. *Earl Derby's Exped.* (Camden) 285 Pro reban aureo pro domino. 1411 *Close Roll* 13 *Hen. IV*, 2 li. Ryban et Frenges. 1463 *Mann. & Housch. Exp.* (Roxb.) 238 For a gyrdyll off reban, ij.s. 1520 *MS. Acc. St. John's Hosp., Canterb.*, Payd for reban to mend ij vestmentis. 1525 *Will of J. Williams* (Somerset Ho.), Ryban of silk. 1712 Steele *Spect.* No. 478 ⁋ 7 Bows of Riban.
β. *c* 1440 *Promp. Parv.* 432/2 Ryband, of a clothe (*K.* ribawnde or liour..), *limbus.* 1477–9 *Rec. St. Mary at Hill* (1905) 80 Rebende of diuerse colowris, iiij *s.* 1534 *Inv. Wardr. Kath. Arragon* in *Camden Misc.* (1855) 40 Three bookes..tyed with grene reabande. 1581 in Feuillerat *Revels Q. Eliz.* (1908) 344–5 Ribande of silk of sondrye Colours. 1592 Shaks. *Rom. & Jul.* III. i. 32 Did'st thou not fall out..with another, for tying his new shooes with old Riband? 1870 Dickens *E. Drood* xiii, The housemaids had been bribed with various fragments of riband.
γ. 1784 Cowper *Task* I. 537 In cloak..trimm'd With lace, and hat with splendid ribband bound. 1822 Imison *Sci. & Art* II. 100 Any substance, as a piece of ribband.

b. With *a* and *pl.*
α. 1377 Langl. *P. Pl.* B. II. 16 Hire robe..of red scarlet engreyned, With ribanes of red golde. *c* 1384 Chaucer *H. Fame* 1318 Many ryban and many frenges Were on her clothes. *c* 1400 *Land Troy Bk.* 8049 Here hodes dyght with gold ribanes,—Better weres non among the Danes. 1455 *Rolls of Parlt.* V. 325/1 Wrought Silk throwen, Rybens, and Laces falsly..wrought. 1471 *Exch. Rolls Scot.* VIII. 120 Pro..iij unciis de ribbanys. 1520 *Test. Ebor.* (Surtees) V. 119 To Marjory Conyers a yolow ryban. *a* 1674 Clarendon *Hist. Reb.* VIII. (1703) II. 408 They had marched, from the time they left Oxford, with Orange-Tawny Scarfs and Ribbans.
β. *c* 1475 *Pict. Voc.* in Wr.-Wülcker 792 *Hic limbus*, a rebant. 1503 *Cal. Doc. Scot.* IV. 346 Garnysshed with ryngs and rebaunds convenable. 1535 Coverdale *Song Sol.* iv. 3 Thy lippes are like a rose coloured rybende. 1592 Greene *Groat's W. Wit* (1617) 14 She..returned him a silke Riband for a fauour. 1604 Shaks. *Ham.* IV. vii. 79 (Q. 2), A very riband [*pr.* ribaud] in the cap of youth. *c* 1611 Chapman *Iliad* XXII. 408 Her Coronet, Call, Ribands, Vaile. 1768–74 Tucker *Lt. Nat.* (1834) I. 619 The wearing a particular coloured riband upon a certain festival. 1778 Miss Burney *Evelina* x, They recommended caps and ribands. 1810 Wellington in Gurw. *Desp.* (1837) VII. 40 Whether they might not wear the riband of the medal at the button hole. 1848 Layard *Nineveh* ix. (1850) 218 Ornamented with long ribands or streamers. 1885 Runciman *Skippers & Sh.* 1 The wake coiled away like a pale riband.
γ. 1596 Spenser *F. Q.* IV. x. 8 On which this shield..Was hangd on high with golden ribbands laced. 1611 Bible *Num.* xv. 38 Bidde them..that they put vpon the fringe of the borders a ribband of blew. 1643 Chas. I *Wks.* (1662) II. 341 [They] should have been all killed..that had not such a Word or wore not such a Ribband. 1711 Steele *Spect.* No. 4 ⁋ 5 She has stolen the Colour of her Ribbands from another. 1784 Cowper *Task* IV. 541 Her head, adorn'd with lappets pinn'd aloft, And ribbands streaming gay. 1828 Scott *F. M. Perth* xi, A small scrip, suspended..by a blue silk ribband, hung on her left side.

c. = Ribbon *sb.* 2.
1766 H. Walpole *Let. to Sir H. Mann* 29 Feb., You have seen this divinity [i.e. the Duke of York], and have prayed to it for a Riband.

2. *Her.* = Ribbon *sb.* 3.
1562 Leigh *Armorie* 110 b, He beareth Or, a Riband, Gueules. This conteineth in bredeth, the eight parte of yᵉ bende, and viii. of these make a bende. 1572 Bossewell *Armorie* 12 A Ribande..is of it selfe mettall, and so beyng it is a secret. 1610 Guillim *Heraldry* II. v. (1660) 61. 1727–38 Chambers *Cycl.* s.v. *Bend*, A cost, which is the fourth part of a bend; and a ribband, which is the moiety of a cost. 1797 *Encycl. Brit.* (ed. 3) VIII. 448/1 Argent, a Ribband Gules. 1868 Cussans *Her.* (1893) 57 The Riband does not extend to the extremities of the shield; its ends being couped, or cut off.

3. † a. *St. Johnston's riband*, a halter. *Sc. Obs.*
1774 Adamson *Muse's Threnodie* 119 Hence of Saint Johnston's ribband came the word In such a frequent use, when with a cord They threaten rogues.
b. *pl.* Reins. = Ribbon *sb.* 4 b.
1840 Barham *Ingol. Leg.* Ser. I. *St. Odille*, If once she contrives To get hold of the ribands. 1857 Moncrieff *Bashful Man* II. iv, Shouldn't have any objection..to let you handle the ribands for a stage or two.

4. a. A narrow strip *of* something; an object resembling a ribbon in form; = Ribbon *sb.* 5 d.
1801 *Encycl. Brit.* Suppl. II. 517/2 It is upon this stripe or riband of cotton wool that the operation of spinning begins. 1834 McMurtrie *Cuvier's Anim. Kingd.* 271 The branchiæ form a single tube or riband. 1837 W. Irving *Capt. Bonneville* II. 223 Upon the narrow riband of ice that bordered the shore. 1890 W. J. Gordon *Foundry* 21 The long steel tube..is wrapped round and round by a riband of steel.
b. *pl.* Torn strips; shreds, tatters.
1818 Mrs. Shelley *Frankenst.* i. (1865) 42 The tree was not splintered by the shock, but entirely reduced to ribands of wood. 1840 Dickens *Barn. Rudge* xlix, With their clothes hanging in ribands about them. 1865 Kingsley *Herew.* vi, The clouds tore up into ribands.
c. *spec.* (See quot.)
1886 *Amer. Nat.* July 675 *Riband*, a term applied to the stripes painted on arrow-shafts, generally around the shaftment. These ribands have been called clan-marks,..etc.

5. *attrib.* and *Comb.* a. Attrib., in sense 'made of ribbon, resembling a ribbon', as *riband cockade, lace, ligature, wick.*
1585 T. Washington tr. *Nicholay's Voy.* II. vii. 37 [They] fasten their sleeues aboue with silk ryband lace of diuers colours. 1793 *Phil. Trans.* LXXXIV. 98 A very excellent common lamp, with a riband wick. 1802 James *Milit. Dict.* s.v., The Riband Cockade, which is given to recruits, is commonly called colours. 1826 S. Cooper *First Lines Surg.* (ed. 5) 104 The history of the broad tape, or riband ligature.
b. Misc., as *riband-like, -shaped, -wreathed* adjs.; *riband-maker, -manufacturer, -weaver.*
c 1515 *Cocke Lorell's B.* 10 Golde sheres, keuercbef, laundis, and reben makers. 1615 Chapman *Odyss.* IV. 329 Their riband-wreathed wiues brought fruit and cakes. 1722 De Foe *Plague* (1884) 31 Ribband Weavers. 1826 Ribband manufacturer [see Broad *a.* 1 c]. 1836–9 *Todd's Cycl. Anat.* II. 203/2 A strip of continuous riband-shaped membrane. *a* 1843 Southey *Comm.-pl. Bk.* (1849) Ser. II. 604 We perceived in the water..a sort of riband-like object,..which had the direct form and figure of a snake.
c. Special combs.: **riband coal, conspiracy, cream, -fish, -grass, gurnard, jasper, snail, snake, -stone, wave, weed** (see quots. and cf. Ribbon *sb.* 9 d, 10).
1796 Kirwan *Elem. Min.* (ed. 2) II. 56 Fifth Variety [of coal] from Irwine.., black, presents layers in contrary directions, hence often called *Riband Coal. 1858 *Illustr. Times* 4 Dec. 381 The *Riband conspiracy is extensively revived. 1769 Mrs. Raffald *Eng. Housekpr.* (1778) 250 To make *Ribband Cream. Take eight quarts of new milk [etc.]. 1751 Edwards *Nat. Hist.* IV. 210 The *Ribband Fish. 1836 Yarrell *Brit. Fishes* I. 224 Red Bandfish, Snakefish, Ribbandfish. 1854 Badham *Halieut.* 232 Leaving the Mackerel family, we come next to that of the Tænioides, or riband-fish. 1793–8 Nemnich *Polyglot Lex.* v. 957 *Ribband grass, *arundo picta.* 1854 Adams, etc. *Man. Nat. Hist.* 101 *Riband-Gurnards (*Lepidosomatidæ*). Body anguilliform, sword-shaped. 1809 Kidd *Outl. Min.* I. 207 It is called *ribband jasper from the striped disposition of these [colours]. 1852 Th. Ross tr. *Humboldt's Trav.* III. xxvi. 93 Some fine pieces of riband jasper, or Egyptian pebbles. 1900 E. S. Dana *Text-Bk. Min.* 327 Striped or riband jasper has the colors in broad stripes. 1752 J. Hill *Hist. Anim.* 192 The horn-coloured, depressed, fasciated cochlea. The Jamaica *Ribband-snail. 1815 Burrow *Conchol.* 204 *Helix Zonaria*, Ribband Snail. 1791 W. Bartram *Carolina* 271 The *ribband snake is another very beautiful innocent serpent. 1883 Gresley *Gloss. Coal-mining* 203 **Riband-stone*, sandstone in thin layers alternating in colour, generally light and dark grey. 1832 J. Rennie *Consp. Butterfl. & M.* 142 The *Ribband Wave (*Acidalia aversata*, Stephens) appears in June, July, and beginning of September. 1866 *Treas. Bot.* 981/2 **Riband-Weed*, the common name in some districts of the ordinary form of *Laminaria saccharina.*

Ri·band, *v.* Now *arch.* Also 5–9 **ribband**; and *pa. pple.* 4 **i-rybaunt**, 5 **ribaned**, 6 **ribband.** [f. the sb., or ad. F. *rubaner.*] *trans.* To adorn or trim with (or as with) ribands.
α. 1362 Langl. *P. Pl.* A. II. 13 In Red Scarlet heo Rod I-Rybaunt with gold. *c* 1400 *Rom. Rose* 4752 Ragges, ribaned with gold, to were. *c* 1430 *Pilgr. Lyf Manhode* II. civ. (1869) 113, I make hoodes purfyled with silke and ribaned with gold aboute. *c* 1480 Henryson *Garment of Gude Ladies* v, Her gown suld be of gudliness, Weill ribband with renowne.
β. 1642 Howell *For. Trav.* (Arb.) 65 Others by a phantastique kind of ribanding themselves..do make themselves knowne to have breathed forraine ayre. 1833 L. Ritchie *Wand. by Loire* 182 A cap, laced and ribanded in all manner of zig-zags. 1837 *Penny Cycl.* IX. 451/1 Species which have..the whorls of the spire flat and ribanded. 1840 H. Ainsworth *Tower of London* 9 A cloak of crimson satin,..ribanded with nets of silver.
γ. 1485 *Rutland Papers* (Camden) 23 A surcote of purpill velwet..ribbanded with gold at the colar, hands, and speris. 1599 B. Jonson *Cynthia's Rev.* v. ii, Your mistris appeares..ribbanded with greene and yellow. 1795 Burke *Regic. Peace* iv. Wks. IX. 46 Now they are..powdered and perfumed and ribbanded and sashed and plumed. 1812 *Examiner* 12 Oct. 652/2 So to ribband, to fur,..and to fringe..men is..degrading their humanity. 1880 Gosse in *Ward's Eng. Poets* II. 126 Ribbanding the may-pole as though it were the cone-tipped rod of Dionysus.
Hence **Ri·banded** *ppl. a.*
1598 Marston *Sco. Villanie* 167 Castilios,..court-boyes, spanish blocks, Ribanded eares. *a* 1625 Fletcher, etc. *Fair Maid Inn* III. i, One that..has miraculously purchast a ribanded wastcote.

Riband, variant of Ribband *sb.* and *v.*

Ri·banding. Also **ribb-**; and **rib(b)aning.** [f. Riband *sb.* or *v.*] Ribbons; ribbon-work.
? *a* 1366 Chaucer *Rom. Rose* 1077 A robe..With orfrays leyd was everydel, And portrayed in the ribaninges Of dukes stories, and of kynges. *c* 1600 Chalkhill *Thealma & Cl.* (1683) 51 White Buskins lac'd with ribbanding they wore. 1648 Herrick *Hesper.*, *To the Maids to walke Abroad*, What gloves we'l give, and Ribanings. *Ibid.*, *Temple*, The Trout-flies curious wings, Which serve for watched Ribbanings. 1855 Ld. Lytton *Poet. Wks.* 1867 I. 100 That windeth in and windeth out, Under those bright ribandings.

Ri·bandism. *rare.* = Ribbonism.
1848 *Edin. Rev.* LXXXVII. 230 Roman Catholic bigotry, or Orangeism, or Ribbandism. 1888 *Times* (weekly ed.) 13 Apr. 7/2 A place..notorious as a centre of Land League ribandism.
So **Ri·bandist**, a Ribbonman.
1883 *Ann. Reg.* 61 The judge dismissed both Orangemen and Ribandists.

Ri·bandman. *rare.* = Ribbonman.
1880 *Lond. Mag.* Mar. 356/2 The detachment of police stationed at Ballintubber succeeded..in apprehending four riband-men. 1858 *Illustr. Times* 4 Dec. 381 The calculations of the Ribandmen.

Ri·bandry. *rare.* [f. Riband *sb.* + -ry.] Ribbons collectively.
1823 Byron *Age of Bronze* ix. 430 The show is rich in ribandry [1824 ribbonry] and stars. 1828 *Blackw. Mag.* XXIV. 49 The leghorn has fallen back, with its flaunting ribbandry.

Ribaud(e, obs. forms of Ribald.

† **Ribau·dekin.** *Obs.* In 5 **-kyn**, **rebawdkin**, **rybawdekyn.** [a. OF. *ribaudequin*, *-kin*, = MDu. *ribaudekijn*, *-kin*, app. a dim. of *ribaud* Ribald. Sp. *ribadoquin* is prob. from French.] A kind of cannon used in mediæval warfare.
1443 *Acts Privy Counc.* V. (1835) 257 The ribaudekyns desirede in particles. 1450 *Ibid.* VI. (1837) 94 Item v. grete rebawdkins..with x. chambres, & price the pece iiij. li. 1489 Caxton *Faytes of A.* I. xxvii. 82 Semblable engyns as ben thoo that now be called rybawdekyns.

Ribaudery, obs. form of Ribaldry.

[**Ribaudred**, a corrupt reading in Shaks. *Ant. & Cl.* III. x. 10 which has not yet been satisfactorily emended.]

Ribaudri(e, **Ribauld(e**, **Ribawd(ry**, etc., obs. forms of Ribald(ry.

‖ **Ribazuba.** *Obs.* Also **ribzuba.** [f. Russ. рыба *ruiba* fish + зубъ *zub'* tooth.] Walrus ivory.
1591 Fletcher *Russe Commonw.* (Hakl. Soc.) 13 The fishe tooth (which they cal ribazuba)... The fish that weareth it is called a morse. 1665 Sir T. Herbert *Trav.* (1677) 298 The hilts are without wards, being..sometimes of the Ribzuba or Morses teeth.

Ribband (ri·bănd), *sb.* Also 8–9 **rib-band**, 9 **riband.** [Taken as f. Rib *sb.*[1] + Band, but possibly a transferred use of *ribband*, var. of Riband *sb.*: cf. Ribbon *sb.* 8.]
1. In shipbuilding, a long narrow flexible piece of timber, of which a number are nailed or bolted externally to the ribs of a ship from stem to stern, to keep them temporarily in position.
1711 W. Sutherland *Shipbuild. Assist.* 163 Ribbons, or Rib-bands; so called from binding the Ribs or Ship's Timber together. 1769 Falconer *Dict. Marine* (1780) s.v., The ribbands, being judiciously arranged with regard to their heighth and distance from each other,..will compose a kind of frame [etc.]. *c* 1850 *Rudim. Navig.* (Weale) 141 The difference between cant ribands and square or horizontal ribands is that the latter are only ideal, and used in laying off. 1874 Thearle *Naval Archit.* 23 The ribbands are sometimes placed just below the lines of the sirmarks. ..The ribband is made of 5 in. or 6 in. fir quartering.
b. *attrib.*, as *ribband batten, carvel, line, nail* (see quots.).
1797 *Encycl. Brit.* (ed. 3) XVII. 378/1 *Ribband lines*, are curves on a ship's bottom by the intersection of a plane inclined to the plane of elevation. *c* 1850 *Rudim. Navig.* (Weale) 141 *Riband lines*, the same as diagonal lines. *Ibid.* 134 *Riband nails* are similar to weight nails, with this difference, that they have large round heads, so as to be more easily drawn. 1874 Thearle *Naval Archit.* 27 The ribbands..are simply checked with breadth staffs and marked with ribband battens. 1879 *Outing* XXX. 225/1 The hull is of ribband-carvel construction.
2. In launching vessels, a square timber fastened on the outer side of the bilge-ways, to prevent the cradle from slipping outwards.
1779 *Phil. Trans.* LXX. 106 From this fore and aft piece or ribband to the ship's side, and from it to the uprights in the middle, were placed two rows of diagonal shores. 1879 *Cassell's Techn. Educ.* IV. 223/2 The ribbands are secured to the sliding-ways, and strongly shored to the sides of the ship, in order to prevent the bilge-ways from moving farther apart.
3. *Mil.* A wood scantling used in the construction of a gun or mortar platform.
1859 F. A. Griffiths *Artil. Man.* (1862) 256 The planks may be confined by two ribbands (which are pieces of wood of the same length, but weaker scantling than the sleepers). 1879 *Man. Artill. Exerc.* 81 Five..sleepers, held down by eye-bolt or coach screws, with or without ribands.
4. A light spar used in the construction of a pontoon-bridge.
1899 *Westm. Gaz.* 8 Dec. 2/1 Across these are placed planks called 'chesses', which are secured in their places by long and light spars termed 'ribands'.
Hence **Ri·bband** *v.*, to secure with ribbands.
c 1850 *Rudim. Navig.* (Weale) 113 The frames are ribanded and shored.

Ribband, var. Riband *sb.* and *v.*; Ribbin *Obs.*

† **Rib-baste**, *v. Obs.*⁻⁰ [f. Rib *sb.*[1] + Baste *v.*[3]] (See quots.) Hence † **Rib-basting** *vbl. sb.*
1598 Florio, *Stringare*, to beate, to bang or ribbaste one. 1611 — *Rifrustare*, to beat, to bang, to swadle, or rib-baste with rod or cudgell. 1659 Torriano, *Rifristo*, a swadling or rib-basting with a rod or cudgel.

Ribbauld(e, obs. forms of Ribald.

Ribbed (ribd), *ppl. a.* Also 6 **rybbed.** [f. Rib *sb.*[1] or *v.*[1]]
1. With qualifying word prefixed: Having ribs of a specified kind or number, or arranged in a certain way.
1523 Fitzherb. *Husb.* § 75 The .ix. propertyes of an oxe. The fyrste is, to be brode-rybbed. 1601 Holland *Pliny* XXV. x. II. 231 For otherwise ribbed they be and full of veins, as like as may be to Plantaine. 1602 Marston *Antonio's Rev.* v. i, I am as gant as leane ribd famine. 1603 Shaks. *Meas. for M.* III. i. 123 In thrilling Region of thicke-ribbed Ice. 1684–88 [see Flat *a.* 14]. 1707 *Lond. Gaz.* No. 4391/4 A bay gelt Horse,..well made and well ribb'd. 1753 Chambers *Cycl. Suppl.* s.v. *Plantago*, The three-ribbed mountain-plantain. 1828 Sir J. Smith *Eng. Flora* II. 118 Calyx-leaves ..obscurely five-ribbed. 1857 Henfrey *Bot.* § 85 Straight-ribbed leaves occur not unfrequently in Dicotyledons. 1874 Raymond *Statist. Mines & Mining* 39 These are either very close-ribbed, or else simply perforated [etc.].
b. Having ribs *like* something specified.
1698 Fryer *Acc. E. India & P.* 178 A Leaf of the like Bigness, but ribbed like our Plantain.
2. Having ribs or ridges; marked with ribs:
a. Of leaves, plants, shells, etc. *Ribbed grass*, = Rib-grass.
1742 Shenstone *Schoolmistr.* 103 Radish..And plantain ribb'd that heals the reaper's wound. 1752 J. Hill *Hist. Anim.* 145 The ribbed Music-shell. 1784 Twamley *Dairying Exemp.* 113 Ribwort, ribbed grass. 1796 Withering *Brit. Plants* (ed. 3) I. 248 The permanent involucrum..is egg-shaped, compressed, ribbed. 1851 Woodward *Mollusca* I. 46 Races of Neritina,..with whorls ribbed or keeled. 1861 Bentley *Man. Bot.* 153 These ribbed leaves have frequently a great resemblance to parallel-veined leaves. 1871 T. R. Jones *Anim. Kingd.* (ed. 4) 65 The interior of the capsules has a slightly ribbed or striated appearance.
Comb. 1846 Dana *Zooph.* (1848) 175 Calicles remotely ribbed-angular, not dentato-echinate.
b. Of knitted or woven fabrics.
1787 *Phil. Trans.* LXXVII. 397 It is ribbed longitudinally like a ribbed stocking. 1834–6 *Encycl. Metrop.* (1845) VIII. 748/1 Ribbed stocking-frame.., employed for working stripes or ribbed stockings. 1840 Dickens *Old C. Shop* xlvi, A waistcoat of ribbed black satin. 1882 Caulfeild & Saward *Dict. Needlework* 125/1 Ribbed Stitch.—This stitch is also called Russian Stitch.
c. In miscellaneous applications.
1798 Coleridge *Anc. Mar.* IV. i, Thou art long, and lank, and brown, As is the ribb'd sea-sand. 1815 J. Smith *Panorama Sci. & Art* I. 163 The ribbed roofs, which are rich without being gorgeous. 1862 Burton *Bk.-hunter* 56 Their dwarfish ribbed backs like those of ponderous folios. 1887 Furnivall *R. Brunne's Chron. Wace* (Rolls) Introd. p. xix, Two manuscripts,..of the old ribbed paper of about the middle of the fourteenth century.
d. **Ribbed-nose baboon**, the mandrill.
1771 Pennant *Synop. Quad.* 103 Ribbed-Nose B[aboon]. 1862 Kearley *Links in Chain* 261 The huge Mandrill (*Cynocephalus mormon*), or ribbed-nose Baboon,..is a native of the western coast of Africa. 1894 *Pop. Sci. Monthly* XLIV. 516 The ribbed-nose or mandrill baboon.
3. Furnished with ribs.
1814 Cary *Dante, Inf.* x. 74 Nor moved the neck, nor bent his ribbed side.
b. Of horses: (see quot. 1831).
1831 Youatt *Horse* 164 Some horses are what is called ribbed home; there is but little space between the last rib and the hip-bone. 1850 Smedley *Frank Fairleigh* xxi, Rather inclined to be cow-hocked...Not ribbed home. 1861 H. Kingsley *Ravenshoe* I. 231 The horse was not so well ribbed up as he should be.
Hence **Ri·bbedly** *adv.*
1886 Ruskin *Præterita* I. iv. 123 The paper pure white, and ribbedly gritty.

Ri·bber[1]. *Pugilism.* [f. Rib *sb.*[1] + -er[1].] A blow on the ribs.
1814 *Sporting Mag.* XLIII. 69 B. gave a tolerable ribber. 1819 *Blackw. Mag.* IV. 727 While ribbers rung from each resounding frame.

† **Ribber**[2]. *Obs.* (Doubtful: see quot.)
14.. *Lat.-Eng. Voc.* in Wr.-Wülcker 575 *Costa*, a ryb (*et est instrumentum pistoris*, a rybbere). [This may be the source of Halliwell's '*Rib*, a scraper or rasp for bread'.]

Ribbet, variant of Rybat.

† **Ribbie.** *Obs.* ? for *ribbe* Rib *sb.*[2]
? *a* 1500 *Chester Pl.* (E. E. T. S.) VII. 22 Of henbane, and horehound, Ribbie, raddish, and Egremond, which be my hearbes, safe and sound.

† **Ri·bbin.** *Obs. Cant.* Also 9 **ribband.** [Perh. identical with Ribbon.] Money.
a 1700 B. E. *Dict. Cant. Crew*, *Ribbin*, money. 1796 *Grose's Dict. Vulgar T.* (ed. 3), The ribbin runs thick; i.e. there is plenty of money. 1812 J. H. Vaux *Flash Dict.*, *Ribband*, money in general.

Ribbin, obs. variant of Ribbon.

Ri·bbing, *vbl. sb.* [f. Rib *v.*[1] + -ing[1].]
1. The action of the verb. (See quots.)
1765 A. Dickson *Treat. Agric.* (ed. 2) 312 A method of plowing, used in some places, called ribbing. This method of plowing is performed by making furrows about two feet distant from each other. 1812 Sir J. Sinclair *Syst. Husb. Scot.* I. 403 Ribbing, by which half the land was left untilled. 1844 H. Stephens *Bk. Farm* I. 481, I have mentioned a mode of ploughing called ribbing. In its best form it is usually performed in spring with the small plough. 1883 Gresley *Gloss. Coal-mining* 203 *Ribbing*..enlarging a heading or drift. 1893–4 Heslop *Northumbld. Wds.* s.v. *Ribbin*, A sound thrashing is often called 'a good ribbin'.
2. *concr.* Ribs collectively (in various senses).
1564 *Wills & Inv. N. C.* (Surtees, 1835) 219, I geue him..a payre of lynnen shetes wᵗʰ a silk ribbing thorow them, a rode, and a pilleber. 1703 [see 3]. 1823 P. Nicholson *Pract. Build.* 131 Sometimes the ribbing of circular roofs consists of only several principal axal ribs. 1861 S. Thomson *Wild Flowers* I. (ed. 4) 38 Throughout plants generally, the ribbing or veining is arranged according to two..plans. 1880 *Plain Hints Needlework* 28 The size of ribbing is a matter of individual taste.
3. *Comb.*, as *ribbing-nail, -needle, -plough.*
1703 T. N. *City & C. Purchaser* 212 *Ribbing-nails..are ..us'd to fasten the Ribbing, to keep the Ribs of Ships in their place in Building. 1867 Smyth *Sailor's Word-bk.* 571 *Ribbing-Nails*, similar to deck-nails, but not so fine. 1881 *Encycl. Brit.* XII. 299/2 A set of *ribbing-needles placed at right angles to Lee's plain needles. 1832 *Scoresby Farm Rep.* 4 in *L. U. K.*, *Husb.* III, The *ribbing-plough was first introduced into this neighbourhood..about twenty years ago.

† **Ribbing-skin.** *Obs. rare*⁻⁰. = Ribskin.
14.. *Voc.* in Wr.-Wülcker 601 *Pellicula*, a rybbyngskyn. 1483 *Cath. Angl.* 306/2 A Rybbynge skyn, *nebrida.*

† **Ribbis.** *Obs.*⁻¹ (See quot.)
1688 Holme *Armoury* III. 348/1 The Ribbis is a piece of Plate Iron, cut with Teeth like a Saw; with it the Cloth Worker lays the Wool of the Cloth by drawing it over the same.

Ribbit, variant of Rybat.

Ribble (ri·b'l), *v.* [? f. Rib *sb.*[1] + -le.] (See quot. 1847.) Hence **Ri·bbling** *vbl. sb.*
1765 *Museum Rust.* III. lxxiv. 318 First ploughing, a clean earth...Second ditto, ribbling it close overwart. 1847 *Jrnl. R. Agric. Soc.* VIII. II. 288 Another system of fallowing is adopted by many, namely, that of 'ribbling'; this is done by turning a furrow to the unploughed land, and, in returning, to turn over this furrow and the earth upon which the first furrow was laid. *Ibid.* 296 Others again scarify or ribble after the fold, and drill the barley on one earth.

Ribble, error for Ribible.

Ribble-rabble (ri·b'l-ræ·b'l), *adv.* and *sb.* Also 5 **rebylle rable**, 7 **rible rable**, 9 *Sc.* **ribble rabbill.** [A reduplication of Rabble *sb.*[1], of the same type as *fiddle-faddle, gibble-gabble*, etc.]
A. *adv.* In great confusion. *rare.*
c 1460 *Play Sacram.* 598 Here master master, ware how ye tugg..for yt gooth rebylle rable. 1882 in *Jamieson's Sc. Dict.* IV. 25.
B. *sb.* 1. Confused meaningless language; rigmarole, gibble-gabble. Now *arch.*
1601 Munday *Downf. Earl of Hunt.* in Hazl. *Dodsley* VIII. 110 High time 'tis for me, To leave off my babble And fond ribble-rabble. 1668 R. L'Estrange *Vis. Quev.* (1708) 202 Then with a certain Ribble Rabble of Mysterious Words, he proceeds to his Calculation. 1677 Cary *Chronol.* II. II. vii. 219 That other Rible Rable..of that other Annotatour upon Clement. 1737 Byrom *Rem.* (1856) II. I. 142, I saw the name of Mademoiselle Bourignon, and ribble rabble, fiddle faddle. 1883 Hall Caine *Cobw. Crit.* ii. 44 The ribble-rabble of the Examiner's poetical animosity.
attrib. 1598 Florio, *Fanfaluche*,.. flim flam tales, old wiues fables, a ribble rabble discourse. 1601 Munday *Downf. Earl of Hunt.* IV. ii. in Hazl. *Dodsley* VIII. 185 You fall into your vein Of ribble-rabble rhymes Skeltonical. 1655 tr. *Sorel's Com. Hist. Francion* I. 11, I cry God mercy..if thou gratest my eares any more with thy ribble rabble discourse.
2. = Rabble *sb.*[1] 2.
1635 Shirley *Traitor* v. iii, My ends are compassed: hang the ribble rabble! 1653 Urquhart *Rabelais* I. xxi, Perpetual drinking in a rible rable like ducks. 1769 *Trinculo's Trip* 41 Wrangling with the ribble-rabble. 1771 Smollett *Humph. Cl.* 18 July iii, A mischievous mob of colliers, and such promiscuous ribble rabble. 1819 Tennant *Papistry Storm'd* (1827) 105 A gabble O' tongues.. Frae that wine-flister't ribble-rabbill. 1854 Miss Baker *Northampt. Gloss.* s.v., What a set of ribble-rabble there are about!
attrib. 1600 Lane *Tom Tel-troth* 110 So will I leaue to write Against this popish ribble rabble route.
So † **Ribble-row**, a rigmarole. *Obs. rare.*
1664 Cotton *Scarron.* IV. Wks. (1715) 106 This Witch a Ribble-row rehearses Of scurvy Names in scurvy Verses. 1685 — tr. *Montaigne* (1877) I. 458 Superscribing them with a long ribble-row of qualities and titles.

Ribbon (ri·bən), *sb.* Forms: α. 6 **rybben**, **rybbon**, 7 **ribbin**, 7– **ribbon.** β. 6 **rebond**, 7 **ribond**, 6–8 **ribbond.** [Later form of *riban* Riband. In the 16th–18th c. the French form Ruban was also frequent.]
I. 1. A narrow woven band of some fine material, as silk or satin, used to ornament clothing or head-gear, or utilized for other purposes: a. Without article, as a material.
α. 1545 *Fabric Rolls York Minster* (Surtees) 136 For sylke rybben, 16*s.* 1572 in Feuillerat *Revels Q. Eliz.* (1908) 159 Rybbon for Laces. 1781 Cowper *Flatting Mill* 6 It appears, Like a loose heap of ribbon, a glittering show. 1810 Clark *Trav. Russia* (1839) 138 Half a dozen bits of ribbon strung in a line across the breast. 1864 Tennyson *Enoch Ard.* 750 From her lifted hand Dangled a length of ribbon. 1901 *Lady's Realm* X. 616 Orange ribbon of a soft kind, and sold now under the name of giant ribbon, is laid down in Vandykes.
β. 1527 *Churchw. Acc. St. Giles, Reading* (ed. Nash) 31 For rebond & silk for the reperacon of vestiments. 1555 W. Watreman *Fardle Facions* I. v. 59 Girding them selues.. with brode Ribbond of sarsenet. 1727 Pope, etc. *Art of Sinking* in *Swift's Wks.* 1751 V. 129 And knots of scarlet ribbond deck his Mane.
b. With *a* and *pl.*: A piece or length of this. Also, a particular kind or make of it.
α. 1611 Shaks. *Wint. T.* IV. iv. 205 Hee hath Ribbons of all the colours i'th Rainebow. *Ibid.* 236 The bondage of certaine Ribbons and Gloues. 1650 T. B[ayley] *Worcester's Apoph.* 22 At the last I spide a young man, who had a ribbin in his hat. 1697 Dryden *Virg. Georg.* III. 734 The Victim Ox,.. Trim'd with white Ribbons, and with Garlands drest. 1718 *Free-thinker* No. 149. 325, I find Four Parchments tyed together with a Ribbon. 1758 Johnson *Idler* No. 16 ⁋ 5 He had..innumerable boxes of antiquated ribbons. 1820 Scott *Monast.* xvi, Four suits.., every one having a treble, and appropriate change of ribbons, trimmings, and fringes. 1835 Ure *Philos. Manuf.* 244 A great house engaged in the trade of ribbons and broad silks. 1876 Planché *Cycl. Costume* I. 416 It is not till the sixteenth century that ribbons in the present sense are..heard of.
β. *a* 1631 Donne *Poems* (1650) 264, I beg nor ribbond wrought with thine owne hands.. Nor Ring. 1676 Etherege *Man of Mode* I. i, That a mans excellency should lie

in Neatly tying of a Ribbond, or a Crevat! 1712 Steele *Spect.* No. 410 ⁋ 1 She was dressed in a black Tabby Mantua and Petticoat, without Ribbonds.
2. The badge of an order of knighthood; also *transf.*, high distinction in anything.
1651– [see Blue Ribbon]. 1725– [see Red *a.* 19]. 1726 Young *Instalment*, See, Britain, see thy Walpole shine from far, His azure ribbon, and his radiant star. 1835 Ure *Philos. Manuf.* 404 Grandees..may be indulged in their learned play-things, as in the ribbon and the star. 1863 Kinglake *Crimea* (1876) I. i. 14 Down to the giving of trinkets and ribbons he was not forgetful. 1879 *London Soc.* Christmas No. 64/1 There were one or two stars and ribbons.
3. *Her.* A sub-ordinary, in width one eighth of the bend, and one half of the cost, usually borne couped. (Cf. Riband *sb.* 2.)
1704 J. Harris *Lex. Techn.* I. s.v. *Ribbon*..; it is born a little cut off from the out-lines of the Escutcheon. 1722 Nisbet *Her.* I. xiii. 90. 1838 *Penny Cycl.* XII. 141/1 The Bend has four diminutives; the Bendlet, the Garter, the Cost, and the Ribbon. 1880 *Encycl. Brit.* XI. 695/1 The ribbon is used as a difference, and is sometimes couped or cut short, when it becomes a bâton.
4. † a. *Cant.* A bell-pull. *Obs.*⁻⁰
a 1700 B. E. *Dict. Cant. Crew*, *Pluck the Ribond*,..ring the Bell at the Tavern.
b. *pl.* Reins. (Cf. Riband *sb.* 3 b.)
1813 *Sporting Mag.* XLI. 129 Their adroitness in the use of the ribbons..excited universal admiration. 1843 Le Fevre *Life Trav. Phys.* III. III. iv. 124, I was surprised to see my factotum mount the box, and take the ribbons in his hand. 1890 'R. Boldrewood' *Col.-Reformer* (1891) 187 Brandon held the ribbons, while Parklands took the box-seat.
c. *Cant.* Gin, spirits.
1823 Egan *Grose's Dict. Vulg. T.*, The cull lushes the blue ribbon; the silly fellow drinks common gin. 1874 *Slang Dict.* 269 *Ribbon*, gin, or other spirits.
5. a. A long, thin, flexible strip of metal, etc.
1763 W. Lewis *Phil. Comm. Arts* 45 The ribbon [gold leaf] is divided by compasses and cut with sheers into equal pieces. 1843 Holtzapffel *Turning* I. 223 The twisted barrels [of muskets] are made out of long ribbons of iron wound spirally around a mandrel. 1871 B. Stewart *Heat* (ed. 2) § 80 If a straight ribbon or bar be made of two metals.
b. A continuous band of untwisted fibre; a sliver. (Cf. Riband *sb.* 4 a, quot. 1801.)
1842 *Penny Cycl.* XXII. 349/1 It is necessary..to lay the fibres or filaments parallel with each other, so as to form them into a soft continuous ribbon or cord. 1879 *Cassell's Techn. Educ.* IV. 273/1 The cotton..issues a soft pure ribbon, technically called a sliver.
c. One of the long thin strips or films into which wax is separated for bleaching after being melted and cleansed.
1838 T. Thomson *Chem. Org. Bodies* 445 To free it from these impurities, it is melted in water, and cast into thin ribbons. 1856 *Orr's Circ. Sci.*, *Pract. Chem.* 460 The melted wax, running in small streams upon the revolving wet drum, is floated off..in the form of exceedingly thin strips or flakes, called ribbons.
d. A narrow strip of anything; = Riband *sb.* 4 a.
1857 Dufferin *Lett. High Lat.* 220 A ribbon of beach not more than fifteen yards wide. 1872 O. W. Holmes *Poet Breakf.-t.* i, A long ribbon of bark [was] torn away. 1889 *Proc. Phys. Soc.* X. 181 A second plate shows four flashes [of lightning]...None of these flashes are ribbons. 1893 Stevenson *Catriona* 4 At the top only a ribbon of sky showed in.
6. a. *Anat.* and *Zool.* A tissue or structure having the form of a ribbon. *Lingual ribbon*, = Odontophore. *Nidamental r.*, in certain molluscs, the string of eggs with the connecting secretion of the nidamental gland.
1803 *Med. Jrnl.* IX. 260 He perceived a kind of vascular ribbon, which he feared to divide, from an apprehension of hæmorrhage. 1851 [see Nidamental 1]. 1851–6 [see Lingual *a.* 2]. 1861 J. R. Greene *Man. Anim. Kingd.*, *Cœlent.* 224 At each extremity of the ribbon the marginal and medial canals anastomose with one another.
b. *Bot.* A leaf, branch, or other structure, resembling a ribbon.
1855 Kingsley *Glaucus* (1878) 63 The delicate green ribbons of the Zostera. 1882 Vines tr. *Sachs' Bot.* 362 Transverse divisions arise, and irregularly branched cellular ribbons are formed.
7. *pl.* Torn strips of anything; tatters, shreds.
1820 Shelley *Vision of Sea* 2 The rags of the sail Are flickering in ribbons within the fierce gale. 1848 Ld. G. Bentinck in *Croker Papers* (1884) III. 165 He cuts Cobden to ribbons; and Cobden writhes and quails under him. 1883 *Cent. Mag.* XXVI. 244/1 The sails hung in ribbons from the yards.
8. A ribband; a wale or strip of wood.
See etym. note to Ribband.
1711 W. Sutherland *Shipbuild. Assist.* 26 Then hang up a Ribbon at the Floor Sirmark, and..nail that Ribbon, and shore it with very able Pieces of Timber. 1739 Labelye *Short Acc. Piers Westm. Bridge* 25 A Ground-Timber or Ribbon 14 Inches wide and 7 Inches thick. 1776 G. Semple *Building in Water* 102 Such Piles..may be cut off level, and a Ribbon run along the outside of them. 1875 Knight *Dict. Mech.*, *Ribbon*,..a long, thin strip of wood or a series of such strips connecting a number of parts.
II. *attrib.* and *Comb.*
9. In sense 1. a. Objective or obj. genitive, as *ribbon-maker, -manufacturer; -pulling, -weaving.* Also Ribbon-weaver.
1611 Cotgr., *Rubennier*, a ribbon maker, head-band maker. 1782 *Encycl. Brit.* (ed. 2) IX. 6711/2 On the well-ordering of these cords chiefly depends the art of ribbon-weaving. 1818 *Parl. Papers* IX. 27 The respectful Address of the Weaver..to the Ribbon Manufacturers of the City of Coventry. 1873 Leland *Egypt. Sketch Bk.* 61 His tricks were of the commonest kind of old-fashioned hankypanky,.. ribbon-pulling and fire-blowing.
b. Instrumental, as *ribbon-bound, -marked*, etc.
1786 Cowper *Gratitude* 2 This cap..With ribbon-bound tassel on high. 1871 *Figure Training* 124 As the pupil reaches one end of the ribbon-marked path the movement is reversed. 1897 Watts-Dunton *Aylwin* (1900) 74/1 The ribbon-bedizened hat which prosperous Gypsies once used to wear.
c. Attrib. (in various uses), as *ribbon-block, cotillon, factory, -front, -knot, -loom, rose, -streamer.*
1884 *Pop. Sci. Monthly* XXV. 111 He would sit for hours, with a board two or three feet long resting on his knees, and rub *ribbon-blocks over it in various ways. *c* 1874 *Ball Room Guide* 84 The *Ribbon Cotillon...Each dancer selects a ribbon. When all have chosen, those which have selected the same colour dance together. 1850 Thackeray *Pendennis* lxxvi, The enterprising head of the *ribbon factory in Clavering. 1812 *Sporting Mag.* XXXVII. 304 *Ribbon-fronts are more in request than those of brass. 1725 Ramsay *Gentle Sheph.* I. ii, With *ribbon-knots at his blue bonnet lug. 1782 *Encycl. Brit.* (ed. 2) IX. Pl. cclviii, *Ribbon-Loom. 1835 Ure *Philos. Manuf.* 245 In our single-hand ribbon-loom, the weaver can make but a piece and a half a week. 1604 Terilo *Friar Bacons Brazen-heads Prophesie* lxix, And *Ribon Roses take such place, That Garden Roses want their grace. 1755 E. Young *Centaur not Fabulous* 174 Beautiful Fillies with flounc'd Trappings, *Ribbon-streamers, and braided Manes.
d. *Ribbon Society*, a Roman Catholic secret society or league formed in the north and north-west of Ireland early in the nineteenth century to counteract the Protestant influence, and associated with agrarian disorders. So *Ribbon association, pass-word, system, work.*
1818 in *Edin. Rev.* (1899) Jan. 171 A great deal of Ribbon work is carrying on at Ballycastle. 1839 Carleton *Fardorougha* xviii, He was accosted in the significant terms of the Ribbon pass-word of that day. 1857 *Parl. Papers* XXVI. 11 It can hardly be necessary to imitate the vices of the Ribbon system in order to counteract it. 1866 *Chambers' Encycl.* VIII. 244/2 The class of men with which the Ribbon societies were recruited. *Ibid.*, The Ribbon association was divided, like the Orange, into lodges.
10. Attrib., in sense 'resembling a ribbon or ribbons', 'forming a long narrow strip or strips', etc., as *ribbon border, -bordering, -borer, coil, conductor, -edge, flash, -isinglass, -letter, lightning, map, saw, -steel.* Also *ribbon-like, -shaped* adjs.
1892 *Dixon's Seed Catal.* 36 Specially suited for *ribbon borders. 1875 Miss Braddon *Hostages to Fortune* ii, Whether it went in for *ribbon-bordering and bedding-out plants, or essayed the classical. 1881 Raymond *Mining Gloss.*, **Ribbon-borer*, a boring-tool consisting of a twisted flat steel blade. 1849 Noad *Electricity* (ed. 3) 409 Instead of a *ribbon coil, a helix containing two thousand..yards of fine insulated wire. 1896 Bedell *Princ. of Transformer* 306 Conductors may be made of a number of wires in parallel, although *ribbon-conductors are preferable. 1753 Hogarth *Anal. Beauty* v. 68 Called by the carvers 'the stick-and-ribbon ornament'; and, when the stick through the ribbon is omitted, it is called 'the *ribbon-edge'. 1889 *Proc. Phys. Soc.* X. 176 Photographs of lightning have frequently been obtained showing banded, *ribbon or double flashes. 1888 Goode *Amer. Fishes* 361, $450,000 worth of *ribbon-isinglass. 1870 E. Peacock *Ralf Skirlaugh* III. 190 The *ribbon-letters in which they were carved. 1888 *Q. Jrnl. Meteor. Soc.* XIV. 227 The following appear to be some of the most typical forms of Lightning flashes:—..6 *Ribbon Lightning. 1808 Eleanor Sleath *Bristol Heiress* V. 135 The..Derwent..poured down from the heights by *ribbon-like torrents. 1897 Mary Kingsley *W. Africa* 610 The pretty, long, ribbon-like town of Victoria. 1866 (*title*), Coloney and Fairchild's *Ribbon Map of the Father of the Waters. 1843 Holtzapffel *Turning* I. 751 The mode adopted in joining the ends of this elastic blade, or *ribbon saw. 1890 W. J. Gordon *Foundry* 155 There are ribbon saws—endless tapes of metal working over pairs of rollers. 1861 J. R. Greene in Nicholson *Man. Zool.* xvi. (1875) 151 A flat, *ribbon-shaped body, three or four feet in length. 1875 Sir T. Seaton *Fret Cutting* 67 He must now procure a bit of *ribbon-steel.
b. Marked with bands or stripes, as *ribbon agate, jasper* (cf. Riband *sb.* 5 c), *onyx.*
1778 *Phil. Trans.* LXIX. 26 Such is the Saxon jasper, called ribbon agate. 1804 Jameson *Syst. Min.* I. 235 The common name ribbon jasper is not appropriate. 1867 Brande & Cox *Dict. Sci.*, etc., *Ribbon Jasper*..is, in general, a result of the alteration of argillaceous strata by contact with igneous rocks. 1877 W. Jones *Finger-ring* 383 A Roman gold finger-ring, set with an intaglio in ribbon onyx.
c. In names of plants, as **ribbon-fern, -gum, -laver, -tree, -wood.** Also Ribbon-grass.
1892 *Garden* 27 Aug. 185 Of the *Ribbon Ferns (Pteris serrulata) there are many varieties of great beauty. 1889 Maiden *Useful Native Pl.* 429 A variety of E[ucalyptus] *amygdalina* growing in the south coast district of New South Wales, goes by the name of '*Ribbon Gum'. 1793–8 Nemnich *Polyglot Lex.* v. 869 *Ribbon laver, *Ulva linza.* 1866 *Treas. Bot.* 981 *Ribbon-Tree, *Plagianthus betulinus.* 1874 *Ibid.* Suppl. 1338/1 *Ribbon-wood of Otago, *Hoheria populnea.* 1898 Morris *Austral Eng.* 386 All species of Plagianthus and Hoheria are to the colonists Ribbonwood, especially *Plagianthus betulinus*..and *Hoheria populnea.*
d. In names of animals, fishes, etc., as **ribbon gurnard** (see Riband *sb.* 5 c), **seal, snake, worm.**
1881–2 Goode *Fish. Indust. U.S.* 67 Almost nothing appears to have been yet recorded respecting the habits of the *Ribbon Seal. 1711 Petiver *Gazophyl.* vii. 69 Sir Walter Rawleigh's *Ribbond Snake. 1736 *Phil. Trans.* XXXIX. 256 *Anguis gracilis, fuscus*: the Ribbon-Snake. 1808 Ashe *Trav.* II. 287 The conversation..turned on the serpent tribe and we called the following at least to our recollection.., Brown Snake, Ribbon ditto. 1860 F. Mason *Burmah* 317 Ribbon Snake. This tree snake is grass-green all over.., excepting under the lips and throat. 1855 *Orr's Circle Sci.*, *Org. Nat.* II. 275 The family of *Nemertidæ*, or **Ribbon-worms.* 1870 Nicholson *Man. Zool.* xxvi. (1875) 198 The *Nemertida*, or 'Ribbon-worms', agree in most essential respects with the *Planarida.*

Ribbon (ri·bən), *v.* [f. the sb.]
1. *trans.* To adorn with ribbon or ribbons; also *transf.*, to mark or stripe in a way resembling ribbons. Usually in *pa. pple.*
1716 Lady M. W. Montagu *Lett.* I. v. 15 Like a poor town lady of pleasure, painted and ribboned out in her headdress. 1858 G. P. Scrope *Geol. Central France* (ed. 2) 16 Numerous calcareo-volcanic strata..ribboned with different colours. 1869 Blackmore *Lorna Doone* xlviii, I could see all the inland valleys ribbon'd with broad waters. 1885 *Daily News* 13 Feb. 3/1 Baskets..very much ribboned with broad white silk bows.
b. To separate into thin narrow strips; to tear into ribbons.
1856 *Orr's Circle Sci.*, *Pract. Chem.* 460 They are also melted and ribboned once or twice during the process. 1897 Mary Kingsley *W. Africa* 174 Your hair being torn out and your clothes ribboned by others.
2. *intr.* Of melted soap, wax, etc.: To form into 'ribbons'. Also with *out.*
1895 *Funk's Stand. Dict.*

Ribboned (ri·bənd), *a.* [f. Ribbon *sb.* or *v.*]
1. Adorned with a ribbon or ribbons.
1743 J. Brown *Honour* 7 in Dodsley *Coll. Poems* (1748) III. 286 Oft' Honour, perching on the ribon'd breast, Sneers at weak justice. 1812 Byron *Ch. Har.* I. lxx, Some o'er thy Thamis row the ribbon'd fair. 1847 Disraeli *Tancred* II. xvi, A blue frock coat with a ribboned button-hole. 1873 'Ouida' *Pascarel* I. 19 Ribboned playthings of the pageantry were all showered upon them.
2. Having ribbon-like markings or stripes.
1790 White *Voyage N. S. Wales* App. 245 The Ribboned Lizard. 1837 Whewell *Hist. Induct. Sci.* (1857) III. 456 It shews this character..by a ribboned structure. 1878 Ramsay *Geol. & Geogr. Gt. Brit.* i. (ed. 5) 21 Ancient lavas ..often still possess a slaggy and ribboned structure.

Ri·bbon-fish. *Zool.* [f. Ribbon *sb.*] A fish having a very long, slender, flattened body, as those of the genera *Cepola* and *Regalecus.* (See also *riband-fish*, s.v. Riband *sb.* 5 c.)
1793–8 Nemnich *Polyglot Lex.* v. 869 Ribbon fish, *Cepola tænia.* 1860 Gosse *Rom. Nat. Hist.* 354 There are, however, the ribbon-fishes; and some of these, as the hair-tail, the Vaegmaer, and the Gymnetrus, are of large size. 1866 *Proc. Zool. Soc.* 147 The recent capture of *Gymnetrus banksii*, the Great Ribbonfish. 1885 C. F. Holder *Marvels Anim. Life* 101 These ribbon fishes are deep water forms.

Ri·bbon-grass. [f. Ribbon *sb.*] A grass having long slender leaves, esp. a variegated variety of *Phalaris.*
1786 Abercrombie *Gard. Assist.*, *Arrangem.* 63 Arundinaceous striped-leaved, or ribbon-grass. 1827 Clare *Sheph. Cal.* 58 With marjoram knots, sweet-brier, and ribbon-grass. 1846–50 A. Wood *Class-bk. Bot.* 607 *Phalaris picta* is the well-known striped or ribbon grass, with beautifully variegated leaves longitudinally striped in endless diversity. 1882 'Ouida' *Maremma* v. I. 115 Rock pools..filled with green ribbon-grasses and red sea-foliage.

Ri·bboning, variant of Ribanding.
1609 T. Cocks *Diary* (1901) 80 Paide for 3 yardes di. of viij *d* ribboninge, ij *s* ij *d.*

Ri·bbonism. [See Ribbon *sb.* 9 d.] The principles or policy of the Ribbon Society.
1848 [see Ribandism]. 1857 *Parl. Papers* XXVI. 10 The Orange Society was a protective society against Ribbonism and other secret societies amongst the Roman Catholics. 1869 *Daily News* 13 Dec., The Roman Catholic farmers and labourers who have not yet joined the ranks of Ribbonism.

Ri·bbonman. [Cf. prec. and Ribandman.] A member of the Ribbon Society.
1813 *Chron.* in *Ann. Reg.* 41/1 A shocking affray..between a party of Orangemen and a party of Ribbonmen. 1842 S. C. Hall *Ireland* II. 121 Their society has been revived under the name of Ribbonmen. 1869 *Pall Mall G.* 13 Oct. 3/1 Our close allies the Ribbonmen have recently disposed of many an obnoxious landowner and agent.

Ri·bbonry. = Ribandry.
1824 [see Ribandry]. 1883 Howells *Woman's Reason* (1884) II. 151 She is pandering to a very depraved taste in ribbonry.

Ri·bbon-weaver. [f. Ribbon *sb.*] One engaged in the weaving of ribbons.
1655 Marq. Worcester *Cent. Invent.* § 75 How a Tape or Ribbon-weaver may set down a whole discourse without knowing a letter. 1676 Shadwell *Virtuoso* v, They are Ribbon-weavers, who have been informed, that you are he that invented the Engine-Loom. 1704 *Lond. Gaz.* No. 4026/4 John Stillington,..both Ribbon-Weaver and Cobler. 1818 *Parl. Papers* IX. 7 Is there more than one class of ribbon weavers in Coventry?—Yes, two. 1835 Ure *Philos. Manuf.* 257 They were persecuted for their pains by the ribbon-weavers of the old school. 1876 Goode *Anim. Res. U.S.* 51 Manufacture of ribbon weaver's bone.

Ri·bbony, *a.* [f. Ribbon *sb.* + -y.] Abounding in, decked with, ribbons; resembling a ribbon or ribbons. **Ribbony gum** (see quot. 1889).
1839 *Civil Eng. & Arch. Jrnl.* II. 452/1 White and reddish brown, ribbony or festoony. 1858 Carlyle *Fredk. Gt.* VII. vi. (1872) II. 301 Some questionable quaint procession, ribbony, perhaps musical. 1889 Maiden *Useful Native Pl.* 527 In Southern New South Wales it [*Eucalyptus viminalis*] bears the name of 'Ribbony Gum'. 1890 *Harper's Mag.* June 5/1 Rank rushes, with their long ribbony leaves.

Ri·bby, *a. rare*⁻¹. [f. Rib *sb.*[1] + -y. Cf. G. *rippig.*] Full of ribs; having prominent ribs.
1849 *Florist* 50 Yellow [dahlia], tipped with white; constant, but ribby.

Ribe, obs. variant of Ruby.

Ribel, obs. variant of Rebel *sb.*

† **Riberry.** *Obs.*⁻¹ [For *ribe-berry.*] = next.
1676 *Phil. Trans.* XI. 628 But I never saw any of our English Currants, (Riberries) there.

‖ **Ribes** (rəi·bīz). Now *Bot.* Also 6 **rybes**; 9 *erron.* **rhibes.** [a. med.L. *ribes* (whence also F., Sp., and It. *ribes*, Da. *ribs*), ad. Arab. ريباس *rībās* (also *rībās*, *rīwās*, Pers. *rībāj*), sorrel.
The meaning of the Arab. word was retained in med. L.: *a* 1387 *Sinon. Barthol.* 36 '*Ribes*, acedula'; *c* 1450 *Alphita* 2 '*Acedula*, *ribes*,..sourdocke'. Cf. also the mod. botanical name *Rheum Ribes*, a species of rhubarb.]
† 1. As *pl.* (Red, Black, or White) Currants. *Obs.*
1562 Turner *Baths* 15 b, A littell bread stieped in the juyce of Pomegranates, Berberies, or Ribes. *Ibid.* 17 The syrope of rybes or berberis. 1578 Lyte *Dodoens* 683 In Englishe, Redde Gooseberies..and common Ribes... In English, Blacke Gooseberies, or blacke Ribes. 1620 Venner *Via Recta* vii. 124 Ribes, which with vs are commonly knowen by the name of Red Currants. 1657 Purchas *Pol. Flying-Ins.* I. xv. 94 Bees gather of these flowers following...In April, Ribes, white, red.
2. *Bot.* A genus of plants comprising the currants and gooseberry.
1731 Miller *Gard. Dict.*, *Ribes*, the Currant-Tree. 1753 Chambers *Cycl. Suppl.* App., *Ribes*, in botany, a general name given by Linnæus to the gosberry and currant bushes, which he makes one genus of plants, called by others *Grossularia.* 1807 J. E. Smith *Phys. Bot.* 392 Thus *Ribes*, the Currant and Gooseberry genus,..stands in the fifth class. 1817 J. Bradbury *Trav. Amer.* 74, I found a species of *Ribes*, or currant. 1873 Miss Broughton *Nancy* I. 97 'It is the colour of this,' pointing to a branch of red rhibes.

Ribet, variant of Rybat.

Rib-grass (ri·bgrɑs). Also 6 **rybgyrse**, 9 *dial.* **ribgirse**, 6 **ryb-**, **ribgrasse**; 8–9 **rib-grass**, **rib grass.** [f. Rib *sb.*[1] + Grass.]
1. = Ribwort.
1538 Turner *Libellus*, *Plantago*, Majorem vulgus appellat waybred aut Plantane. Minorem vero Rybwort, rybgyrse, aut Lancell. 1548 — *Names Herbes* (E.D.S.) 63 The other is called Rybwurte, or Rybgrasse. 1562 — *Herbal* II. 94 The lesse Kynde [of plantain]..is called..in many places rybgrasse. 1775 *Ess. Agric.* 434 The narrow-leaved plantain, or rib-grass, is well liked by horses and cattle. 1799 J. Robertson *Agric. Perth* 213 If the rotation admits of the grass lands lying a few years in pasture, there is commonly some white or yellow clover or rib-grass added. 1830 *Kyle Farm Rep.* 38 in *L.U.K.*, *Husb.* III, Those sown on this farm besides rye grass, the clovers, and rib grass (*plantago media*), are timothy, and cocksfoot. 1855 Miss Pratt *Flower. Pl.* IV. 261 Modern farmers term it Rib-grass, including it among those plants which they distinguish as artificial grasses.
attrib. 1830 Lindley *Introd. Bot.* 194 The Rib-Grass Tribe.
2. The Native Plantain (*Plantago varia*) of Australia and Tasmania.
1898 in Morris *Austral Eng.* 387/1.

† **Ribibe**, *sb. Obs.* Forms: 5 **rybybe**, **ribup(e**, 6 **rybibe.** [ad. OF. *rubebe*, *rebebe* (hence MDu. *rebebe*), It. *ribebba* (Florio), ad. Arab. رباب *rebāb.*]
1. = Rebeck *sb.*[2]
The Cambr., Petw., and Lansd. MSS. read *rubybe*, *rybibe*, and *rebibe* in Chaucer *Miller's T.* 145, where the correct reading is *rubible*: see Ribible.
c 1425 *Voc.* in Wr.-Wülcker 667 *Hec uetella*, rybybe. *c* 1440 *Promp. Parv.* 433 Rybybe, *vitula.* *c* 1450 Holland *Howlat* 759 The rote, and the recordour, the ribupe, the rist.
2. An opprobrious or abusive term for an old woman. (Cf. Rebeck *sb.*[1])
It is probable that both Skelton and Jonson took the word from Chaucer.
c 1386 Chaucer *Friar's T.* 79 (Corpus MS.), This somnour ..Rode for to somne an old wijf, a ribibe. *a* 1529 Skelton *E. Rummyng* 492 There came an old rybybe; She halted of a kybe. 1616 B. Jonson *Devil an Ass* I. i, Some good Ribibe, about Kentish Towne, Or Hogsden, you would hang now, for a witch.
Hence † **Ribibe** *v.*, to play on the ribibe. *Obs.*
14.. in *Rel. Ant.* I. 81 The sow..harpyd Robyn-Howde; The fox fydylyd, tho ratton rybybyd.

Ribi·ble. *Obs.* exc. *Hist.* Forms: 4 **rouwe-**, **row-**, 5 **ru-**, **ribible.** [ad. OF. *rubebe* (see prec.); the ending may have been influenced by the musical terms *trible, quadrible, quinible.*] = Ribibe *sb.* 1.
13.. *Pol. Songs* (Camden) 327 He..rat on the rouwe-bible and on other look no mo. *c* 1386 Chaucer *Miller's T.* 145 In twenty manere koude he trippe and daunce..And pleyen songes on a small Rubible. *c* 1386 — *Cook's T.* 32 (Ellesm. MS.), Al konne he pleye on gyterne or Ribible. *a* 1450 *Knt. de la Tour* (1868) 159 The said Sir piere..axed hym, where was his fedylle or hys Ribible or suche an instrument as longithe vnto a mynstralle. ? *c* 1475 *Sqr. lowe Degre* 1071 There was myrth and melody With harpe, getron and sautry, With rote, ribible and clokarde.
1844 James *Agincourt* II. 52 'Yes and the ribible too,' answered Ella Brune. 1853 Rock *Ch. of Fathers* III. x. 469 Gleemen played on harp and ribible.

† **Ribibour.** *Obs.* In 5 **rybibour**, **ribibor.** [f. Ribibe *sb.*] One who plays on a ribibe.
1362 Langl. *P. Pl.* A. v. 165 A ribibor [*v.r.* rybibour], a ratoner, a rakere of Chepe.

Ribie, obs. variant of Ruby.

Ribless (ri·bles), *a.* [f. Rib *sb.*[1] + -less. Cf. G. *rippenlos.*] Destitute or devoid of ribs.
1794 Coleridge *To a Young Ass* 30 Where Toil shall call the charmer Health his bride, And Laughter tickle Plenty's ribless side! 1796 Withering *Brit. Plants* IV. 101 Flat wedge-shaped, ribless, thick, very succulent. 1828 J. E. Smith *Eng. Flora* II. 3 Seeds ribless, rough. 1854 *Orr's Circle Sci.*, *Org. Nat.* I. 216 The eight cervical vertebræ are free, moveable, and ribless. 1886 *Pall Mall G.* 28 July 11/3 Are they flexible, like elastic, or ribless, like a coiling snake, those lumbering vessels?

Ri·blet (riblet). [f. Rib *sb.*[1]] A small rib.
1880 *Jrnl. Linn. Soc.* XV. 101 The following whorls are beset with..more numerous riblets. 1887 *Geol. Mag.* IV. 451 The surface has longitudinal ridges which..are connected by transverse riblets.

Riblet: see Rivulet. **Ribosa**, var. Rebozo.

Riboudry(e, obs. forms of Ribaldry.

† **Ri·b-roast**, *sb. Obs.* [f. next.]
1. Beating, cudgelling.
1595 *Maroccus Extaticus* p. iii, Such a peece of filching is..punishable with ribroast. 1630 J. Taylor (Water P.) *Navy of Land Ships* Wks. I. 83/2 Her Mariners doe..endure much hardnesse,..yet many times they are allowed more Lamb and Ribroste then they would have. 1665 Brathwait *Comment Two Tales* (1901) 57 Truth is, he was shrewd to me, and gave me store of rib roast.
2. *fig.* A damaged part.
1654 Gayton *Pleas. Notes* III. i. 69 There is no flaw, no shoulder-spraine, hip-shot, nor rib-rost in thy credit.

Ri·b-roast, *v.* Now *arch.* [f. Rib *sb.*[1] + Roast *v.*] *trans.* To belabour with a cudgel; to beat severely; to thrash. Also *fig.*
1570 North *Doni's Mor. Philos.* IV. 100 After he had well fauouredly ribbe rosted his poore innocent wife. 1589 [Nashe] *Almond for Parrat* 11 Ile ribroste my brother Martin a little, for obiecting..the not answering of his bookes. 1599 — *Lenten Stuffe* 12 Not a victualer..but was rib-roasted or had some of his ribbes crusht. 1618 Rowlands *Night Raven* (1620) Diij, Tom, take thou a cudgell, and rib roast him. 1694 Motteux *Rabelais* v. xxvii. (1737) 121 Who us'd to baste, rib-roast, swaddle, and swinge them well-favour'dly. 1740 tr. *De Mouhy's Fort. Country Maid* (1741) II. 289 He was rib-roasted according to his Merits. 1796 *Grose's Vulgar T.* (ed. 3) s.v., I'll rib-roast him to his heart's content. 1809 W. Irving *Knickerb.* (1861) 119 Impounding horses, and sometimes grievously rib-roasting their owners. 1890 'R. Boldrewood' *Col.-Reformer* (1891) 188 Brandon..was engaged..in rib-roasting Darkie to make him 'come out of that'.
Hence **Ri·b-roasted** *ppl. a.*; **Ri·b-roaster**, a severe blow on the ribs.
1755 Smollett *Quix.* (1803) I. 43 The peasant staid till it was quite dark, that the poor rib-roasted knight might not be seen in such a woful condition. 1854 'C. Bede' *Verdant Green* II. 16 There's a regular rib-roaster for you.

Ri·b-roasting, *vbl. sb.* [f. prec.] A beating, cudgelling. Cf. Rib-roast *sb.*
1613 Purchas *Pilgrimage* II. xvii. 203 The woman gave me of the tree (to wit a sound rib-roasting) and I did eate. 1664 Butler *Hud.* II. i. 248 He..Departs not meanly proud, and boasting, Of his magnificent Rib-roasting. 1718 Motteux *Quix.* (1733) III. 37 Among my Master's Rib-roastings he has not forgot mine. 1817–18 Cobbett *Resid. U. S.* (1822) 301 There are..the slashings and the rib-roastings to undergo. 1837 W. Irving *Capt. Bonneville* (1849) 193 This sturdy ribroasting calmed the fury of the Crows.

Ribrusch, obs. form of Rubbish.

† **Ribskin.** *Obs.* Also 5–6 **rybbeskynne**, **rybskyn**, 5 **rybschyn.** [f. Rib *v.*[2] + Skin *sb.* Cf. LG. *ribbelap*, *-lappe(n* in the same sense.] A leather apron, worn by women while engaged in 'ribbing' flax.
c 1440 *Promp. Parv.* 432/2 Rybbe skynne (rybskyn, *H.P.*), *melotula.* *c* 1475 *Pict. Voc.* in Wr.-Wülcker 794 *Hic fusus*, a spyndylle. *Hec pellicula*, a rybschyn. *Hec nebryda*, *idem est.* *a* 1529 Skelton *E. Rummyng* 209 They layde to pledge theyr wharrowe, Theyr rybskyn and theyr spyndell, Theyr nedell and theyr thymbell.

Ri·bspare. *Obs.* exc. *dial.* Also 7 **-sparre.** [So MLG. *ribbesper*, LG. *ribbspeer*, G. *rippspeer.*] = Sparerib.
1654 Gayton *Pleas. Notes* III. iv. 91 The remainder of the Dons morning draught, and drench for his rib-sparre or split (choose you which). 1736 Pegge *Kenticisms* s.v. *Fore-right*, So, in Kent, to *wrong-take* a person is to take him wrong, ..and a *ribspare* is a spare rib. 1887 Parish & Shaw *Kentish Gloss.*, *Ribspare*, the spare rib.

Ri·bston. Also **Ribstone.** [f. *Ribston* Park, between Knaresborough and Wetherby in Yorks.]
1. Used *attrib.* with *pippin* as the name of a choice variety of dessert apple, originally introduced from Normandy about 1707.
See A. Amherst *Gardening* (1895) 226.
1769 Hargrove *Hist. Knaresbro.* vi. (1798) 246 This place is remarkable for the produce of a delicious apple, called the Ribstone-Park Pippin. 1796 C. Marshall *Gardening* (1813) 280 Ribstone pippin. 1836–7 Dickens *Sk. Boz*, *Charact.* i, About the size and shape of a reasonable Ribstone pippin. 1860 R. Hogg *Fruit Manual* 22 Ribston Pippin,..the king of English dessert apples. 1872 H. Macmillan *True Vine* v. 197 The English Ribston Pippin assumes in the hotter parts of India, a fastigiate or pyramidal aspect.
2. *ellipt.* The (or a) Ribston pippin.
1844 M. Paterson *Manse Garden* 106 The Ribston as a tree thrives better in the orchard. 1878 T. Hardy in *Belgravia* Apr. 234 Now a few russets...He used to like them almost as well as ribstones.

Ribup(e, variants of Ribibe *sb. Obs.*

Ri·bwork. [f. Rib *sb.*[1]] Any work or arrangement presenting the appearance of ribs.
1892 Dana *Syst. Min.* (ed. 6) 271 The crystals..affording a rectangular rib-work on the cross-section. 1894 H. Barber *Furness & Cartmel Notes* 140 The gateway..resting upon a deep arch decorated by rib-work. 1895 *Outing* XXVII. 18/2 Over the rib-work thus formed, long strips of canvas are stretched.

Ribwort (ri·bwɔ̄rt). Also 5–6 **ribbe-**, **rybbe-**, **ryb-**; 3 **-uurt**, 6 **-wurte**, 7 **-wurt**; 5–7 **-worte**, 6 **-woorte.** [f. Rib *sb.*[1] or *sb.*[2] + Wort. Cf. MLG. *ribbewort*, *ribwort*; G. *rippenwurz.*] The Narrow-leaved Plantain (*Plantago lanceolata*); ribgrass.
c 1440 *Promp. Parv.* 433/1 Rybbeworte, herbe, *lanciola.* *c* 1450 *M. E. Med. Bk.* (Heinrich) 126 Take þe jus of weybrode & of rybbewort. 1530 Palsgr. 262/2 Rybbe worte, an herbe. 1548 [see Ribgrass 1]. 1597 Gerarde *Herbal* II. xiii. 341 Ribwoorte or small Plantaine, hath many leaues flat spred vpon the ground. 1629 Parkinson *Paradisi* lxxxv. 352 Rose Plantane..is in all things like vnto the ordinary Plantane or Ribworte. 1671 Salmon *Syn. Med.* III. xxii. 424 Ribwort..stops Fluxes and the Termes and is of the nature of Plantain. 1763 Mills *Pract. Husb.* III. 345, I do not know that the narrow leaved plantain, or ribwort (*Plantago angustifolia*) hath ever been cultivated purposely for the food of cattle. 1784 Twamley *Dairying Exemp.* 113 Ribwort, ribbed grass, black plantain or cock plant. 1813 Vancouver *Agric. Devon* 220 Ribwort, white clover, and many other valuable grasses, are found to grow for the first period of perhaps two or three years.
attrib. 1711 Petiver *Gazophyl.* 9/1 Cape Cats-foot with Ribwort-leaves. 1849 Balfour *Man. Bot.* § 978 *Plantaginaceæ*, the Ribwort Family. 1861 Bentley *Man. Bot.* 616 *Plantaginaceæ*.—The Ribwort Order.
b. So *Ribwort Plantain.*
1597 Gerarde *Herbal* II. xiii. 341 *Plantago quinquenervia*, Ribwoorte Plantaine. 1611 Cotgr., *Lancelée*, Ribwort Plantaine, Lambes-tongue. 1696 Floyer *Anim. Humours* x. 129 Plantane boiled in Broths, and Ribwort Plantane. 1805 R. W. Dickson *Pract. Agric.* II. 836 Ribwort Plantain..is a plant much relished by neat cattle and horses. 1872 Oliver *Elem. Bot.* II. 222 Ribwort Plantain.. is a common plant of pastures.
c. A plant belonging to the N.O. *Plantaginaceæ.*
1846 Lindley *Veg. Kingd.* 642 There is nothing to distinguish the corolla of Ribworts from the part so called in other plants except its..want of vascular texture.

-ric, *suffix*, in *abbotric, bishopric*, etc.: see these words and Riche *sb.*

Ricardian (rĭkā·diăn), *a.* and *sb.* [f. the name *Ricardo*: see def.]
A. *adj.* Of, pertaining to, or accepting the doctrines of the political economist David Ricardo (1772–1823).
1863 Fawcett *Pol. Econ.* II. iii. 118 Political economists of the Ricardian type. 1878 F. A. Walker *Money* I. iv. 86 The Ricardian economist..declares that he sees no advantage in an increase of money above its former level. 1887 Ashley *Eng. Woollen Indust.* Pref. 9 The truth or falsehood of the main Ricardian doctrines.
B. *sb.* A follower or adherent of Ricardo.
1886 *Encycl. Brit.* XX. 294/1 In his great work he kept clear of the exaggerated abstraction of the Ricardians.
Hence **Rica·rdianism.**
1887 *Pall Mall G.* 18 Oct. 3/2 Mr. Henry George with his revolutionary Ricardianism.

Ricardon: see Richardine. **Ricche**, obs. f. Reach *v.*[1], Rich *a.* **Ricchedom**, var. Richdom *Obs.* **Ricchesse**, var. Richesse *Obs.*

Rice[1] (rəis). *Obs.* exc. *dial.* Forms: 1 **-hrīs**, 3, 6 **ris** (5 **risse**), 4–7 **rys**, 5–6, 9 **ryss**; 3–6, 9 **rise**, 5–7, 9 **ryse** (9 **ryze**), **ryce**, 6– **rice**; 9 **reis(s**, **reise**, **reyce.** [Common Teutonic: OE. *-hrīs* (in comb. *gelǣafhrīs*), = Fris. *riis*, *rys*, MDu. and Du. *rijs*, OS. **hrīs* (dat. *rīse*), OHG. *hrīs* (MHG. *rīs*, G. *reis*), ON. *hrís* (Norw., Sw., and Da. *ris*): the stem may be an ablaut-variant of that represented by Goth. *hrisjan* to shake.]
† 1. *collect.* a. Without article: Twigs or small branches on growing trees or bushes. *Obs.*
c 1205 Lay. 740 Ich eou wile leden forð to mine lauerde iþon wode rime, þer he vnder rise lið. *c* 1305 *Land Cokayne* 8 What is þer in paradis, Bot grasse and flure and grene ris? 13.. *Gaw. & Gr. Knt.* 1698 Rocheres roungen bi rys, for rurde of her hornes. *c* 1480 Henryson *Mor. Fab.* 1327 The rosis reid arrayit on rone and ryce [*v.r.* rys]. 1501 Douglas *Pal. Hon.* Prol. 35 Baith foullis, flouris, and rice Recomfort was. 15.. *Tayis Bank* 109 Quhair ron & ryss raiss in aray.
† b. So with *the.* *Obs.*
a 1250 *Owl & Night.* 1664 Foweles..sungen al so uale wise þat blisse wes among þe ryse. *c* 1450 Holland *Howlat* 89 The Howlet wylest in wyce, Raikit vnder the rys. *c* 1500 *World & the Child* 268, I am ryall arayde to reuen [? read rennen] vnder the ryse. 1535 Stewart *Cron. Scot.* III. 233 With buglis blast quhill rairdit all the ryce.
2. *collect.* Twigs, small branches, or brushwood, cut and used for various purposes. *Stake and rice* (see Stake *sb.*).
a 1225 *Ancr. R.* 100 Leswe þine ticchenes bi heordmonne hulen of ris & of leaues. *a* 1250 *Owl & Night.* 586 Þar þornes boþ & ris i-draȝe, Bi hegge & bi þicke wode. 1471–2 *Durh. MS. Cell. Roll*, Pro le fellyng del Ryss pro emendacione sepium, ij *s.* 1535 Stewart *Cron. Scot.* III. 227 Trynchis [he] gart mak..And stoibbit thame with ryce. 1594 in *N. & Q.* (1881) 6th Ser. III. 428 None shall gett Ryce in Bardengill on paine of xijᵈ a burthen. 1612 *Naworth Househ. Bks.* (Surtees) 37 For cutting ryse at Netherton, and dyking. 1669 Worlidge *Syst. Agric.* 330 *Rice*, the shrouds or tops of Trees, or fellings of Coppices. 1789 Davidson *Seasons* 51 Now weir an' fence o' wattl'd rice, The hained fields inclose. 1821 Carlyle *Early Lett.* (1886) II. 13 As a man cutting rice would wish to do. 1829 J. Hunter *Hallamsh. Gloss.*, *Rice*, sticks used in gardens to support pease or any deciduous plants. 1894 Heslop *Northumb. Gloss.* s.v., The brushwood used to bed in with stones in the weiring of rivers is called *rice.*

b. The stems of peas or beans. (E. Anglian.)
1889 Macm. Mag. Sept. 360 Olly..pulled the rice..and I sat and stripped the peas.

3. A single twig or small branch.
a 1250 Owl & Night. 1636 Þe nihtegale iherde þis An hupte uppon on blowe ris. 13.. Cursor M. 5614 (Gött.) A kist of rises did scho be wroght. 1507-8 Durh. Acct. Rolls III. 660 Pro fossacione ejusdem, cum les Stakes et Ricez. 15.. Christ's Kirk xv. in Bann. MS., Heich Hucheoun with a hissill ryss, To red can throw thame rummill. 1578 Lyte Dodoens 473 Garden Smilax hath long and small branches ..taking holdfast when they be succoured with rises or long poles. 1814 Scott Wav. lviii, I saw him whisk away through amang the reises. 1839 Wilson Tales Borders V. 322 (E.D.D.), Like a squirrel, swinging frae ae ryss to anither. 1894 Heslop Northumb. Gloss. s.v., When tall hedges are cut down a rice is generally run alongside.

†b. Without article, in phr. on (or in) rice. Obs.
c 1300 in Wright Lyric P. v. 26 Hire rode is ase rose that red is on rys. ?a 1366 Chaucer Rom. Rose 1015 As whyte as lylye or rose in rys. a 1400 Pistill of Susan 72 Þe rose ragged on rys. c 1470 Gol. & Gaw. 854 The blude of thair bodeis.., As roise ragit on rise, Our ran thair riche vedis.

†c. So upon, on, or in the rice. Obs.
c 1386 Chaucer Miller's T. 138 He hadde a gay surplys, As whit as is the blosme vpon the rys. a 1500 London Lickpenny ix, Hot pescods.., Strabery rype, and cherryes in the ryse. 1513 Douglas Æneis xii. Prol. 237 The cowschet crowdis and pirkis on the rys. c 1560 A. Scott Poems (S.T.S.) i. 4 Welcum, oure rubent roiss vpoun þe ryce!

†**4.** A reel or winder. Obs. (Cf. Reed sb.¹ 9 a.)
1611 Florio, Naspo, a rice or reele for silke or yarne. 1611 Cotgr., Tournette, a Rice, or Yarwingle to wind yarne on. 1688 Holme Armoury iii. xxi. (Roxb.) 265/2 Upon this Barrell the wyer is turned as it is drawn of the Rice through the seuerall degrees of holes.

5. attrib., as rice-bloom, -bush, -dike, -hedge, -wood; †**rice-bank**, a mound faced with brushwood; **rice-knife** (see quot. 1894).
1508 Dunbar Tua Mariit Wemen 524 Than..rakit [they] hame to ther rest, through the rise blwmys. 1642 Rel. of Action bef. Cirencester 4 The streets were barricadoed up with..waggons of bavins or Rise-bushes. 1665 Manley Grotius' Low-C. Warr 424 For taking the Bridge,..he raised against the Wall a Tower, which is called a Rice-Bank. 1847 Halliw. s.v. Rise, Rise-dike, a hedge made of boughs and twigs. Ibid., Rise-wood, small wood cut for hedging. 1881 N. & Q. 6th Ser. IV. 53/2 When a fence is made of stakes with dead thorns twined in, it is called a 'rice-hedge'. 1894 Heslop Northumb. Gloss. s.v., Rice-knife, a light slasher with a hooked point, used for cutting hedges.

Rice² (rais). Forms: α. 3-6 **rys**, 5 **ryss**, **rysz**, 5-6 **ryse**, **rysse**; 4-5 **ris**, 6-7 **rise**, **rize**. β. 5-7 **ryce**, 6- **rice**. [ME. rys, etc., = Fris. rys, Du. rijst, †rijs, rys, MLG. riis, rîs, MHG. rîs (G. reis), MSw. riis (Sw. and Da. ris), a. OF. ris (F. riz), ad. It. riso, repr. L. *orizum, var. of oriza, oryza, a. Gr. ὄρυζα (also ὄρυζον), probably of Oriental origin. Sp. and Pg. arroz is from Arab. aruz(z, uruz(z.]

1. The seeds of the plant Oryza sativa, forming one of the important food-grains of the world.
α. 1234 Close Roll 18 Hen. III (1905) 381 Dimidiam centenam de rys; et j. centenam piperis. 1299 Durh. MS. Burs. Roll, In C et v li. de Rys, xxjs. vjd. 1390 Earl Derby's Exped. (Camden) 22 Pro vj lb. floure de rys. c 1400 Maundev. (Roxb.) xxx. 134 Þai ete milet and rysz. c 1420 Liber Cocorum (1862) 16 Take ryse and wasshe and grynde hem smalle. 1535 Coverdale Gen. xxv. 34 Then Iacob gaue him bred and that meace of ryse. 1555 W. Watreman Fardle Facions ii. viii. 166 Their drincke is a bruage that thei make sometyme of Rize, sometyme of Barlie. 1626 Bacon Sylva § 49 Rice is in Turky and other Countries of the East, most fed upon. 1653 Greaves Seraglio 22 Broth of Rise and pulse dressed after divers fashions.
β. c 1420 Liber Cocorum (1862) 14 Floure of ryce þou grynd. c 1440 Promp. Parv. 433/1 Ryce, frute, risia, vel risi. 1541 Elyot Cast. Helthe 13 Ryce with almond milk. 1582 Munday Eng. Rom. Life vi. 65 One to fetch milke, an other to make ready Rice for the pottage. 1638 Sir T. Herbert Trav. (ed. 2) 240 Wot you forsooth why Rice is so generally eaten and so valuable? 1698 Fryer Acc. E. India & P. 35 For Corn, they have Rice the Staff of the Land. 1732 Arbuthnot Rules of Diet in Aliments, etc. i. 250 Rice, nourishing, good in Hæmorrages. 1801 Encycl. Brit. Suppl. II. 462 Rice is a favourite substitute for bread in years of scarcity. 1867 H. Macmillan Bible Teach. v. (1870) 103 Rice..furnishes the chief article of diet for the largest proportion of the human race.

2. The rice-plant, Oryza sativa.
1562 Turner Herbal ii. (1568) 41 Nether cocle nor tares are in any poynt like unto ryse. Ibid. 72 b, Rys is to looke to lyke vnto Lolium or darnel. 1753 Chambers Cycl. Suppl. App., Rice, the English name of a genus of plants, known among botanists by that of Oryza. 1785 Martyn Rousseau's Bot. xviii. (1794) 232 The Rice is almost the only plant to be found in the second order of this class. 1832 Tennyson Palace of Art 114 Many a tract of palm and rice. 1866 Treas. Bot. 326/1 The Common Rice is a marsh-plant.

3. With pl. A kind or variety of rice.
1681 Knox Ceylon iii. 9, I have hitherto spoken of those Rices that require to grow in Water. 1826 Ainslie Mat. Indica I. i. 340 Supposing the rices of different crops to have very different effects.

4. a. Wild rice, = Canada or Indian Rice.
1814 Lunan Hort. Jamaic. II. 242 The seeds..are a good substitute for rice, and for this reason it is called wild rice in America. 1858 Homans Cycl. Comm. 1633/2 The wild rice, or water oat, Zizania aquatica, which grows along the muddy shores of our tide-waters. 1874 J. W. Long Amer. Wild-fowl viii. 135 Almost the entire surface is covered with the dense growth of the wild oats or rice.

b. Petty rice (see Petty a. 5).

5. attrib. **a.** In sense 'made, prepared, or derived from rice', as rice-arrack, -beer, -bread, -broth, etc.
1875 Encycl. Brit. II. 628 A nauseous and unpalatable spirit.., which goes by the name of *rice arrack. 1795 tr. Thunberg's Trav. (ed. 2) IV. 76 The Seuki Colic, which proceeds from the use of Sacki, or *Rice-beer. 1898 Westm. Rev. May 514 The women made rice-beer for their partners to drink. 1704 in Churchill's Voy. II. 187/2 They are very eager after our Wheat or *Rice Bread. 1796 New Ann. Reg. 147 In this manner pure rice-bread may be made. 1867 Anne Bowman New Cookery Bk. 533 Wheat and Rice Bread. 1707 Floyer Physic. Pulse-Watch 250 They first forbid Eggs,..but allow *Rice-Broth. 1683 P. Lorrain tr. Muret's Rites Funeral 241 This being done, all the company sit down to eat *Rice-cakes in the Church it self. 1769 Mrs. Raffald Eng. Housekpr. (1778) 269 To make Rice Cake. 1862 S. St. John Forests of Far East II. 42 A particular kind of rice-cake sent in very hot. 1665 May Accomplish'd Cook 285 To make *Rice Cream. 1747 tr. Astruc's Fevers 241 Let him eat of rice-cream, that nothing may be wanting to nourish him properly. 1866 Chambers's Encycl. VIII. 248/2 The refuse of R[ice], which..is known as Rice-meal and *Rice-dust. 1769 Mrs. Raffald Eng. Housekpr. (1778) 269 Put in half a pound of *rice flour. 1849 Diss. Silkmanuf. (Shanghai) 38 Mix also some rice-flour with their food. 1854 Simmonds Comm. Products Veg. Kingd. 303 *Rice-meal is commonly used for feeding pigs. 1681 Grew Musæum ii. § i. iv. 200 From the Kernel it self..they press out a Milk, which they always mix and eat with their *Rice-Meats. 1728 E. Smith Compl. Housew. (ed. 2) 89 To make *Rice Pancakes. c 1592 Marlowe Jew of Malta iii, Will you poison her with a mess of *rice porredge? 1579 Langham Gard. Health (1633) 528 *Rice pottage made with good milk..is of easie digestion. 1594 Handmaids Kitchin 34 The Almonds..strained to make the Rice pottage withal. 1853 Soyer Pantroph. 349 The Dauphin took for his dinner a rice pottage. c 1500 Respublica iii. iii, Whares *Rice-puddingcake? [= Respublica]. 1728 E. Smith Compl. Housew. (ed. 2) 82 A Rice Pudding. 1837 Lockhart Scott IV. viii. 259 He sat at table while we dined, but partook only of some rice pudding. 1854 Pereira's Polarized Light (ed. 2) 155 Wheat-starch, Portland arrow-root, and *rice-starch. 1861 Bentley Man. Bot. 697 Starch of good quality, known as ..Patent Rice Starch,..prepared from rice. 1845 Encycl. Metrop. XXV. 1290/2 The Chinese make *rice wine perfumed. 1894 Outing XXIV. 207/1 Their faces showed signs of rice wine.

b. In sense 'producing rice', 'used for growing rice', as rice-country, -field, -ground, etc.
1776 Adam Smith W. N. i. xi. (1904) I. 182 Rice in some *rice countries, the common and favourite vegetable food of the people. 1704 in Churchill's Voy. II. 263/1 A..Valley, full of *Rice-fields. 1776 Adam Smith W. N. i. xi. (1904) I. 181 A rice-field produces a much greater quantity of food than the most fertile corn-field. 1875 Knight Dict. Mech. 1937/1 The watered rice-fields of 'the East'. 1625 Purchas Pilgrimage II. 1764 marg., *Rice grounds. 1756-7 tr. Keysler's Trav. (1760) I. 371 The roads adjoining to the rice grounds. 1840 Buel Farmer's Comp. 197 Water meadows and rice grounds profit by periodical floodings. 1776 Adam Smith W. N. i. xi. (1904) I. 182 The rent of *rice lands cannot regulate the rent of the other cultivated land. 1880 Encycl. Brit. XIII. 574/2 The rising grounds which skirt the rice-land are tilled by the hoe. 1797 Ibid. (ed. 3) VII. 694 The funds..chiefly in *rice plantations and negroes. 1831 Audubon Ornith. Biog. 286 The rice plantations of the Carolinas. 1874 J. W. Long Amer. Wild-fowl ii. 49 When two persons are hunting in company in a *rice-pond. 1779 Ann. Reg. 31 A bluff, rising considerably above the level of the *rice-swamp. 1843 Whittier Christian Slave xiv, From the low rice-swamp..Rises to Heaven that agonizing cry.

c. Miscellaneous, as rice-bag, -basket, -boat, -corn, -crop, -harvest, -mill, -plant, -straw, etc.
1897 Mary Kingsley W. Africa 20 Red flannel petticoat, or *rice-bag drawers. 1854 Zoologist XII. 4269 The *rice-basket is invaded. 1755 Acts Gen. Assembly Georgia (1881) 53 That this Act do not extend to decked Pettiaguas or *Rice Boats. 1681 Knox Ceylon iii. 11 Thus much concerning *Rice-corn. 1813 Ainslie Mat. Med. Hindostan 271 An almost continual succession of *rice crops throughout the year. 1732 Barbot Churchill's Voy. V. iii. xiii. 197/2 The *rice-harvest is usually in September. 1881 Encycl. Brit. XII. 747/2 In British Burmah there is but a single rice harvest in the year. 1842 Bonar & M'Cheyne Mission to Jews (1843) 58 We visited a *Rice-mill which is in the course of erection. 1778 in Pinkerton's Voy. (1811) IX. 716 The *rice-plant grows to the height of three or four feet. 1840 Penny Cycl. XVII. 45/2 The Rice plant is therefore an undoubted native of India. 1719 De Foe Crusoe I. (Globe) 208 A Place where I had laid a great Parcel of *Rice Straw. 1887 Moloney Forestry W. Afr. 451 In many districts rice-straw is almost the only food which cattle have.

6. Comb. **a.** With agent-nouns, denoting persons, implements, or machines, as rice-cleaner, -eater, -grower, -huller, -miller, -planter, -seller, -stirrer.
1858 Simmonds Dict. Trade, *Rice-cleaner, one who husks paddy, and sifts and prepares it for sale as rice. 1859 Cornwallis New World I. 307 The Chinese immigrants consisted entirely of males...So much for the *rice-eaters. 1863 Trevelyan Compet. Wallah (1866) 145 Informing us that the Chinese *rice-growers even now cast their bread on the waters. 1875 Knight Dict. Mech. 1937/2 Ewbank's *rice-huller (English patent, 1819). 1851 in Illustr. Lond. News 5 Aug. (1854) 119/3 *Rice..miller. 1856 Olmsted Slave States 409, I left town yesterday..with a letter..to Mr. X., a *rice-planter. 1875 Knight Dict. Mech. 1938/1 Rice-planter, an implement for sowing rice. 1871 C. Kingsley At Last vi, Old Coolies..find it convenient to turn *rice-sellers. 1900 Proc. Zool. Soc. Dec. 861 On *rice-stirrers and other articles of household use.

b. With vbl. sbs. or ppl. adjs., as rice-chewing, -cleaning, -eating, -growing, -pounding.
1884 Sat. Rev. 7 June 752/1 The ordeal of *rice-chewing is applied to priests accused of unchastity. 1839 Ure Dict. Arts 1068 *Rice cleaning. Various machines have been contrived for effecting this purpose. 1841 Penny Cycl. XIX. 500/1 Several large rice-cleaning establishments. 1840 Ibid. XVII. 46/1 The natives..have rather a contempt for *rice-eating districts. 1873 Drury Useful Pl. India (ed. 2) 324 The most fertile province for *rice-growing. 1875 Knight Dict. Mech. 1938/1 *Rice-pounding Machine.

7. Special combs.: **rice-bunting**, the rice-bird or bobolink; **rice-Christian**, a Hindu convert; **rice cut-grass**, **rice embroidery** (see quots.); **rice-flower**, (a) an East Indian plant; (b) one or other of the various species of the Australian genus Pimelea; **rice-grains**, Astr., granular markings observed on the surface of the sun; **rice grass** (see quots.); **rice-hamster** (see quot. and Hamster); **rice-rat**, an American rodent feeding upon rice; **rice-sand** (see quot.); **rice sapper**, an Indian beetle injurious to growing rice; **rice-shell** (see quot.); †**rice sparrow**, = Rice-bird 2; **rice-stitch**, **-troopial**, **-weevil**, **-wheat** (see quots.).
1783 Latham Gen. Synopsis Birds II. i. 188 *Rice Bunting, Emberiza oryzivora. 1893 Newton Dict. Birds i. 46 What is commonly called in books the Rice-Bunting, Dolichonyx oryzivora. 1816 Q. Rev. XV. 352 We are sneeringly told, that these Missionaries only make *rice-Christians in India. 1836 Col. Wiseman Lect. Cath. Relig. (1847) I. 226 It is a well-known fact that the new Christians in India are called Rice-Christians. 1874 A. Gray Less. Bot. 607 Leersia oryzoides,..*Rice Cut-grass. 1882 Caulfeild & Saward Dict. Needlework 424/1 *Rice Embroidery ..is a white Embroidery upon washing materials, in which the principal stitch used is..Rice Stitch. 1704 in Churchill's Voy. II. 326/2 The *Rice-flower is called..from its Scent, which is like Rice when it comes boiling hot out of the Pot. 1898 Morris Austral Eng. 387/1 The Rice-flowers are beautiful evergreens about three feet high, and bear rose-coloured, white, and yellow blooms. 1878 Newcomb Pop. Astron. iii. ii. 239 This structure of the *rice-grains has been seen only by Professor Langley. 1884 Proctor in Longman's Mag. Apr. 590 We may describe the solar rice grains, in fact, as mighty metallic clouds. 1889 Maiden Useful Native Pl. 93 Leersia hexandra,..'*Rice Grass'. A rough-leaved species, common along the watercourses of Queensland. Ibid. 94 Microlæna stipoides,..'Weeping Grass', 'Meadow Rice Grass'. 1792 Kerr Anim. Kingd. 245 *Rice Hamster, Mus Cricetus phæus. 1797 Encycl. Brit. (ed. 3) XII. 461/1 The phæus, or rice-hamster, has the upper parts of the body of a hoary ash-colour. 1884 Encycl. Brit. XVII. 5/1 The *Rice-rat of America. 1883 Sunday Mag. Aug. 510/2 Then another bed [of sand].., rough and large-grained, called '*rice-sand', and exactly like unboiled rice. 1889 E. T. Atkinson Indian Insect Pests 1 The *Rice Sapper (Leptocorisa acuta)...In Tinnevelly it is called the munju vandu, or rice-juice sucker or sapper. 1855 Ogilvie Suppl., *Rice-shell, the species of the genus Oliva. 1898 Morris Austral Eng. 387/1 Rice-shell..in Australia..denotes the shell of various species of Truncatella, a small marine mollusc. 1704 in Churchill's Voy. II. 357/2 The *Rice Sparrows are no bigger than our ordinary Sparrows. 1882 Caulfeild & Saward Dict. Needlework 424/1 *Rice Stitch..resembles Rice loosely scattered over a flat surface. 1836 Penny Cycl. V. 29/2 The 'rice-bunting' of Pennant and of Wilson, '*rice-troopial' of authors. 1815 Kirby & Sp. Entomol. vi. (1818) I. 174 The *rice-weevil (Calandra Oryzæ, F.) is very injurious to the useful grain after which it is named. 1879 E. A. Ormerod in Entomologist XII. 51 The history of its near ally the Sitophilus oryzæ, or rice weevil. 1879 Encycl. Brit. X. 451/1 To these [crops] in some districts are added spelt, buckwheat, millet, *rice-wheat (Triticum dicoccum).

-rice: see -trice.

†**Rice-balking**: see Rest-balk v.
1787 W. Marshall Rural Econ. Norfolk Gloss., Rice-balking, a particular method of ploughing.

Rice-bird. [Rice².]
†**1.** An East Indian bird (see quot.). Obs.
1704 in Churchill's Voy. II. 357/1 The Rice-Bird is of the bigness of one of our Pullets,..with brown feathers on the Body, a red Head, and very large Claws; they live among the Rice.
2. The Paddy bird or Java sparrow.
1743 Edwards Nat. Hist. Birds I. i. 41 The Cock Padda or Rice-Bird..is about the Size of a Green-Finch, or rather bigger. 1777 Forster Voy. round World II. 568 Rice-birds, commonly called paddies (loxia oryzivora). 1841 Penny Cycl. XIX. 500/2. 1904 Blackw. Mag. Jan. 243 Java sparrows, rice-birds, and those squawking mynahs.
3. The reed-bird or bobolink.
1747 Phil. Trans. XLIV. 438 Flights of Rice-Birds..go to Carolina annually at the time Rice begins to ripen; and, after growing fat with it, return South back again. 1769 Bancroft Guiana 178 The Rice Bird of Guiana has a bill like the former,..and is of nearly the same size. 1832 Veg. Subst. Food Man 94 The cultivators of rice in America.. suffer..from the depredations of the rice-bird. 1884 Harper's Mag. Mar. 620/1 The mouse-hawk..interrupts the flocks of bobolinks or rice-birds in their depredations.

Rice-milk. [Rice².] Milk boiled and thickened with rice and other ingredients.
1600 Venner Via Recta v. 90 Rice-milke. There is also the like kinde of pottage,..made of Rice accurately depilated and boyled in milke. 1674 Eng. & Fr. Cook. 441 A dish of hot Rice-Milk. 1731 Swift Let. to Gay 29 June, One of them..refused to beg my pardon upon her knees, for once neglecting to make my rice-milk. 1786 Med. Comment. II. 117 Rice-milk for supper. 1851 Mayhew Lond. Labour I. 193 Rice-milk is always sold at stalls arranged for the purpose. 1904 Windsor Mag. Jan. 268/2 Sometimes the butter is omitted, and then the bread is served..with rice-milk.

Rice-paper. [Rice².] (See quots. 1857 and 1872.)
1822 Edin. Jrnl. Sci. (1825) II. 176 The rice-paper consists of long hexagonal cells, whose length is parallel to the surface of the film. 1849 Balfour Man. Bot. § 852 Some say that a species of Desmanthus is the source of the cellular substance called Rice-paper. 1857 Henfrey Bot. 311 The substance called Rice-paper, prepared by the Chinese, consists of thin slices of the pith of Aralia papyrifera. 1872 Oliver Elem. Bot. ii. 185 Rice-paper is prepared from the pith of Aralia papyrifera, a tree of Formosa; the pith is cut spirally and unrolled into small squares.

b. attrib. in rice-paper plant or tree, the shrub Aralia or Fatsia papyrifera; also the sola-plant of India (Æschynomene aspera).
1832 Lindley Introd. Bot. i. ii. 61 As in the Horse Chestnut, the Rice-paper plant, and many others. 1849 Balfour Man. Bot. § 75 In the Rice-paper plant..the interior of the stem is occupied almost entirely by cellular tissue. 1882 Garden Apr. 236/3 There is a wide ascending pathway, edged with Rice-paper plants.

Rice-water. [Rice².]
1. A liquid, for drinking or other purposes, prepared from rice boiled in water.
1797 Underwood Disorders Childhood III. 88 Thin tapioca, or if a purging attends, rice-water. 1856 Orr's Circ. Sci., Pract. Chem. 167 Rice-water is commonly recommended as the vehicle, on account of the starch it contains. 1877 A. B. Edwards Up Nile xxi. 666 The drinks throughout were plain water, rice-water, and lemonade.
2. Used attrib. to describe the evacuations of cholera-patients.
1866 J. R. Reynolds Syst. Med. I. 150 The name of rice-water stool has been given to the genuine unmixed cholera evacuation...When the rice-water evacuations appear, cramps generally set in. 1876 Bristowe The. & Pract. Med. (1878) 241 The rice-water fluid, as found in the intestines, is alkaline. 1883 Fortn. Rev. Aug. 181 The rice-water purgings and cramps.

Ri·cey, a. [f. Rice² + -y.] Of or pertaining to rice; resembling rice.
1776 Mickle tr. Camoens' Lusiad 463 Where end the ricey groves that crown the shore. 1883 Philadelph. Tel. XL. 1 Also, the flavors [of the wheat] are too ricey.

Rich, obs. form of Reek sb.¹

Rich (ritʃ), a., adv., and sb. Forms: α. 1-2 **rice** (also 1 comp. **ricore**, sup. **ricoste**), 2-6 **riche**, 3 **ri(c)hche**, 3-5 **ricche**, 4-6 **ryche** (5 **ryiche**), 6 **reche**, **rytche**, **rutche**; 4 **rycch**, 5-6 **rych**, 6 **rytch**, **ritch**, 4- **rich**. β. 4-5 **rik(e**, 5-6 Sc. **ryk(e**, 6 Sc. **ryik**. [Com. Teut.: OE. rice, = OFris. rîke, rîk (mod. Fris. ryk, rik-, †rijck), MDu. rijke, rijck, etc. (Du. rijk), OS. rîki (MLG. rike, LG. rîk), OHG. rîchi, rîche (G. reich), ON. ríkr (Norw. and Sw. rik, Da. rig), Goth. reiks, believed to represent an early Teutonic adoption of Celtic rīx = L. rēx king.
In ME. the use of the word may have been reinforced by F. riche (= Sp. rico, It. ricco), itself of Teutonic origin. This would help to explain the early disappearance of the northern form rike.]

I. adj. †**1.** Of persons: Powerful, mighty, exalted, noble, great. Obs.
In many OE. and ME. passages it is difficult to decide whether this or sense 2 is mainly intended.
a 900 O. E. Martyrol. 27 Dec., Rice hæðene men hine snidon þæt he drane attor. c 900 tr. Baeda's Hist. iv. xxviii. (1890) 368 Se..cyning sylfa, & se halga bysceop..& monige oðre æfæste weras & rice [L. potentes]. c 1000 Ælfric Saints' Lives i. 12 Ne on-dret he him nanes þinges, for ðan þe he næfð nenne riccran. a 1122 O. E. Chron. (Laud MS.) an. 1087 Swa þæt þa riceste Frencisce men..wolden swican heora hlaforde. 1129 Ibid. an. 1129 Þa ricceste men of Rome. c 1205 Lay. 27232 Ich æm richest alre kinge vnder gode seolue. a 1275 Luue Ron 97 in O. E. Misc. 96 He is richest mon of londe,..Alle heo beoþ to his honde. a 1300 Cursor M. 9 O kyng arthour þat was so rike. c 1330 R. Brunne Chron. Wace (Rolls) 2685 Bot whoso myghte, of oþer wan; Þat rycchest were, most bar þem stout. a 1400-50 Alexander 197 In reuerence of þe riche kyng at had þer rewme gydid. Ibid. 351 As arly as þe riche qwene was resyn fra slepe. c 1470 Gol. & Gaw. 412 He is the riallest roy, reuerend and rike. 1535 Stewart Cron. Scot. III. 7 King Henrie passit into France With mony rynk that ryall wes and ryke In plane battell.

†**b.** Of things: Powerful, strong. Obs.
a 1000 Daniel 457 Wæron hyra rædas rice, siððan hie rodera waldend..wið þone hearm gescylde. c 1000 Sax. Leechd. II. 106 Of ȝeal adle..cymeþ great yfel; sio biþ ealra adla ricust. c 1205 Lay. 26736 Walwain..ridende igrap Petreium on richen his [c 1275 his gode] steden. c 1470 Henry Wallace vi. 547 With rych hors the Scottis befor thaim raid. Ibid. ix. 18 Aryet the hot syng coloryk, In to the Ram, quhilk had his rowmys ryk.

2. Having large possessions or abundant means; wealthy, opulent.
α. c 900 tr. Baeda's Hist. iii. v, Þa feoh þe him rice men sealdon [L. a divitibus]. c 1000 Ælfric Hom. I. 204 Þæs rican mannes welan sind his sawle alysednyss. c 1175 Lamb. Hom. 53 Þes riche men þe habbeð þes mucheles weorldes ehte. a 1225 Ancr. R. 66 Þe wreche peoddare more noise he makeð..þen a riche mercer. 1297 R. Glouc. (Rolls) 495 Corn & frut hom wax inouȝ. so þat hii were riche inou in a stounde. c 1375 Cursor M. 27830 (Fairf.), Bot maste riche men rewes me, þat of þe pouer has na pite. 1390 Gower Conf. II. 214 Sche per cas that richest is And hath of gold a Milion. c 1450 Merlin 3 Whiche yaf to hym all her part of that she hadde, and here lord was right a ryiche man. 1538 Starkey England i. iii. 98 When the fermys of al such pasturys..are brought to the handys of a few and rychar men. 1580 Lyly Euphues (Arb.) 228 To bee rich is the gift of Fortune, to bee wise the grace of God. 1624 Massinger Renegado iii. ii, Rich sons forget they ever had poor fathers. 1651 Hobbes Leviath. ii. xxvii. 161 To Robbe a poore man, is a greater Crime, than to robbe a rich man. 1707 J. Stevens tr. Quevedo's Com. Wks. (1709) 310 There is no doubt but that you imagin'd me to be as rich as Crœsus. 1770 Goldsm. Des. Vill. 142 He was..passing rich with forty pounds a year. 1802 Mar. Edgeworth Moral T. (1816) I. ix. 71 You cannot be rich and poor at the same time. 1862 Ruskin Unto this Last iv. 128 The persons who become rich are, generally speaking, industrious.
fig. 1828 Carlyle Misc. (1857) I. 218 Hume was too rich a man to borrow. 1841 Macaulay in Trevelyan Life (1876) II. 101 At present I consider myself as one of the richest men of my acquaintance. 1871 Cayley Heart-Thoughts 31 Would you grow rich toward God? Then learn to give.
β. a 1300 Cursor M. 12492 And was þar wonnand in þat wik, þat hight iosep, a burges rik. c 1375 Sc. Leg. Saints xlvi. (Anastas) 287 God had sel al þe gudis þat I had, & gif pure men, & nocht ryk. c 1425 Wyntoun Cron. viii. xxxviii. 5868 The land had rest, the folk ware ryke. 1535 [see 11 b].

b. Of places, countries, etc.: Abounding in wealth or natural resources.
c 1250 Gen. & Ex. 1280 Doȝ it was noȝt is kinde lond; Richere he it leet ðan he it fond. 1377 Langl. P. Pl. B. iii. 207 That is þe richest rewme þat reyne ouer houeth. 1585 T. Washington tr. Nicholay's Voy. iii. xviii. 104 b, They doe lodge themselues..in the best and richest house. 1596 Spenser F. Q. iv. xi. 22 Those warlike women, which so long Can from all men so rich a kingdome hold! 1666 Dryden Ann. Mirab. cxliii, With cord and canvas from rich Hamburg sent His navy's moulted wings he imps once more. 1742 Richardson De Foe's Tour Gt. Brit. III. 285 A Town which, in its flourishing State, was said to be the richest in Christendom. 1787 Maty tr. Riesbeck's Trav. Germany III. 238 The monks fare particularly well in so rich a Country. 1802 Pinkerton Mod. Geogr. (1811) 634 New Spain is by far the richest mineral country in the world. 1859 Tennyson Elaine 1321 That shrine which then in all the realm Was richest.

3. With preps.: Wealthy in, having abundance †of, amply provided with, some form of property or valuable possessions.
c 1200 Ormin 6384 Laban wass an riche mann I werelldþingess sellþe. Ibid. 12084 Þeȝȝ hafenn mikell fe & sinndenn riche off ahhte. c 1205 Lay. 4063 Heo weoren richere of golde & of garisume. 1382 Wyclif Gen. xiii. 2 He was forsothe ful riche in possessioun of siluer and of gold. 14.. Theophilus i, Wyse clerk & a man of myȝt And riche of gold & fee. 1470-85 Malory Arthur iii. xv. 118 Them that were of londes not ryche he gaf them londes. 1530 Palsgr. 322/2 Ryche of substance, riche, opulent. 1596 [see b]. 1604 E. G[rimstone] D'Acosta's Hist. Indies iii. xx. 186 High rockes, the which are very rich in mines. 1697 Dryden Æneid vi. 1181 He moves with manly grace, how rich with regal spoils! 1756 Smart tr. Horace, Ep. vi, The king of the Cappadocians, though rich in slaves, is in want of coin. 1802 Pinkerton Mod. Geogr. (1811) 632 note, The mines ..not less rich in gold and silver. 1843 Penny Cycl. XXVI. 230/1 Like most other Venetian churches, [it is] rich in paintings.

b. transf. or fig. in various applications.
c 1205 Lay. 18529 Ich am on rade rihchest alre monnen. a 1300 Cursor M. 11312 For pouert thar naman mislik Quils he es in god truth rike. c 1386 Chaucer Prol. 479 Riche he was of holy thoght and werk. 1500-20 Dunbar Poems lxiv. 3 Sweit roiss of vertew.., Richest in bontie. 1596 Drayton Legends i. 826 They rich in Gold, he onely rich in Wounds. a 1691 Boyle Hist. Air (1692) 55 Nature is much more rich in things, than our dictionaries are in words. 1750 Gray Elegy 50 Her ample page, Rich with the spoils of time. 1791 Mrs. Radcliffe Rom. Forest i, Rich with wood, and fading away in blue and distant mountains. 1845 M. Pattison Ess. (1889) I. 1 Our own immediate age is confessedly rich in works of the historical class. 1878 Huxley Physiogr. 126 The river-water..is usually rich in organic impurities.

4. Valuable; of great worth or value.
c 1250 Gen. & Ex. 3937 Balaac sente richere and mo Medes, and oðer men to ðo. a 1300 Cursor M. 5120 Als he gaue þam giftes rik. c 1330 Arth. & Merl. 4055 (Kölbing), Þe siluer to part & þe gold & mani oþer riche þinges. 1377 Langl. P. Pl. B. ii. 16 With ribanes of red golde and of riche stones. a 1400-50 Alexander 1572 With releckis..þe richest on þe auutere. 1470-85 Malory Arthur iv. vii. 126 He kepeth from hym a ful fair maner and a ryche. 1560 Daus tr. Sleidane's Comm. 414 b, There is a very ritch promotion ecclesiasticall whiche he had sued for manye moneths. 1595 Raleigh Discov. Guiana (1887) 120 The great, good, and rich trade with England may be possessed of thereby. 1642 Fuller Holy & Prof. St. v. xviii. 430 Counting themselves the petty-Landlords of the times, to whom rich fines and heriots would accrue upon every exchange. 1699 Dampier Voy. II. i. 145 Some of the Portuguese..put their richest Goods into a Boat, ready to take their flight on the first Alarm. 1738 Gray Tasso 61 In one rich mass unite their precious store. 1788 Gibbon Decl. & F. xlix. V. 136 The first fruits were paid in rich offerings to the shrine of the apostle. 1871 Freeman Norm. Conq. (1876) IV. xviii. 142 A rich harvest for Norman spoilers.

b. Of non-material things.
c 1290 S. Eng. Leg. I. 23/53 Huy bi-heten him þe loye of heouene þat so riche was and is. c 1330 Arth. & Merl. 4058 (Kölbing), Arthour bouȝt gode afin þe riche conseyl of Merlin. 1612 Bacon Ess., Of Despatch (Arb.) 244 True dispatch is a rich thing. 1859 Tennyson Elaine 1223 As much fairer—as a faith once fair Was richer than these diamonds.

†**c.** Choice; good of its kind. Obs. rare.
c 1315 Shoreham i. 1575 By-tuixe god and holy folk Loue hys wel trye and ryche. c 1330 Arth. & Merl. 523 (Kölbing), Loke, þat tre & ston be riche, Þe tour langge & depe þe diche.

5. Of dress, etc.: Splendid, costly; of expensive or superior material or make.
c 1200 Trin. Coll. Hom. 33 A man..bicam uppe þeues, and hie him bireueden alle hise riche weden. a 1300 Cursor M. 5167 He..sagh þam cled in pall sa rike. 1393 Langl. P. Pl. C. iii. 14 Hure robe was ryccher þan ich rede couthe. c 1450 St. Cuthbert 812 Þai se þe woman in ryche wedis. 1508 Dunbar Gold. Targe 83 Thare saw I Nature present hir a goun Rich to behald. a 1548 Hall Chron., Edw. IV, 210 b, His high cap of estate..garnished with twoo riche Crounes. 1591 Spenser M. Hubberd 582 The Mule all deckt in goodly rich aray. 1617 Boyle in Lismore Papers (1886) I. 157, I gave Sir Robert Steward a ritch pair of gloves. 1662 J. Davies tr. Mandelslo's Trav. 119 On each side of the head Pendants as rich as can be imagined. 1718 Lady M. W. Montagu Let. to C'tess of Mar 10 Mar., I don't doubt these rich habits were purposely placed in light. 1761-2 [see Habit sb. 1 b]. 1807 Crabbe Par. Reg. ii. 338 Silks beyond price, so rich, they'd stand alone. 1866 Kingsley Herew. vi, His handsome palfrey, furry cloak, rich gloves and boots.

b. Of buildings, furniture, etc.: Made of, or adorned with, valuable materials; also, elaborately ornamented or wrought.
c 1205 Lay. 4286 In are riche temple mid golde he hine bi-tunden. a 1300 Cursor M. 415 To þis palais at was so rike..he fordestend tuin creature. 1377 Langl. P. Pl. B. xx. 180 Gode herte he hente, And rode so to reuel a ryche place and a merye. c 1400 Destr. Troy 9085 To be entriely in a toumbe riche, As bi-come for a kyng, þat kythe riche. 1430 Lydg. in Parker Dom. Archit. (1859) III. 125 The ryche coynyng of ryche tablementis. 1506 in Ld. Hen. VII (Rolls) 285 Which was richly hanged with cloth of arras and a great rich bed in the same chamber. 1553 Wriothesley Chron. (Camden) I. 19 She herself rid in a rytch chariott covered with cloath of silver. 1617 Moryson Itin. i. 262 The roofe is beautified with pictures of that painting which Italians call alla Mosaica. 1815 [see Ribbed ppl. a. 2 c]. 1848 Rickman Styles Archit. Engl. The whole of the interior of the richer buildings of this style, is more or less a series of panels. 1864 D. G. Mitchell Sev. Stor. 220 An ancient bronze knocker..of rich Venetian sculpture.

†**c.** In a more general sense: Fine, splendid, magnificent. Obs.
c 1205 Lay. 11159 Þa læuedi Elene..to Jerusalem heo wende mid richere genge. 13.. Coer de L. 5809 That castel was strong and ryche, In the world was non it lyche. c 1400 Rom. Rose 4184 The tour was rounde maad in compas; In alle this world no riccher was. c 1400 Tourn. Tottenham in Hazl. E. P. P. III. 91 Alle the wyues of Totenham come..To fech home thaire husbondis..; that was a riche sight. c 1470 Gol. & Gaw. 248 Apone that riche river.. side-wallis war set. 1578 Lyte Dodoens v. xxxiii. 593 In her most ryche and pleasant gardens.

d. Of feasts, etc.: Sumptuous, luxurious.
1297 R. Glouc. (Rolls) 10977 Richard..made so noble fest, Þat of alle þat me wuste it was þe richoste & þe beste. c 1330 Arth. & Merl. 6521 (Kölbing), In halle þai hadden riche seruise. c 1375 Cursor M. 3532 (Fairf.), His moder he fande sone in siȝt A riche soper for to diȝt. 1604 E. G[rimstone] D'Acosta's Hist. Indies v. xxviii. 411 They called it Capacrayme, which is to say, a rich and principall feast. 1757 Gray Bard 78 The rich repast prepare. 1785 Cowper Task iv. 113 He..spreads the honey of his deep research At his return—a rich repast for me. 1813 Byron Corsair ii. iv, Methinks he strangely spares the rich repast.

6. Of choice or superior quality; esp. of articles of food or drink with reference to their stimulating or nourishing effects; also, composed of choice ingredients; containing plenty of fat, butter, eggs, sugar, fruit, etc.
c 1330 Sir Beues 732 Riche baþes ȝhe let him make. c 1400 Leg. Rood (1871) 151 At many a betyr wownde, þe riche blod out spronge. a 1400-50 Alexander 4822 Þare fand þai Revers,..ricchest of þe werd..; Was neuir no medecyne.. milke so mild. 1508 Dunbar Tua Mariit Wemen 14 Thai ..raucht the cop round about full off riche wynis. 1633 Massinger New Way i. iii, There came, not six days since, from Hull, a pipe Of rich Canary. 1697 Dryden Virg. Georg. iii. 789 He never..surfeited on rich Campanian food. 1714 Pope Hor. Satire ii. vi. 202 That Jelly's rich, this Malmsey healing. 1781 Cowper Truth 364 As lean as mine supplies the richest wine. 1824 Miss Ferrier Inher. xxxv, The richest of cakes, and the strongest and sweetest of wines. 1844 Stephens Bk. Farm II. 169 A great favourite..on account of the pieces of rich fat in it. Ibid., The nap or shin is..rich and fine. 1856 Kane Arct. Expl. II. x. 106 Every man with a bowl of rich gravy-soup between his knees. 1861 Beeton All about Cookery 352 Richer rolls may be made by adding 2 or 3 eggs and a larger proportion of butter.

b. Of colour: Strong, deep, warm.
c 1330 Arth. & Merl. 5641 (Kölbing), His pensel was of riche colour, Alle he was couched wiþ azur. c 1375 Cursor M. 17867 (Fairf.), Brighter thanne þe sonnys beme Se his purpour here is non. 1387-8 T. Usk Test. Love ii. (Skeat) l. 14 Some men there ben that peynten with colours riche. c 1400 Destr. Troy 9130 Hir face..was red as the Roses, richest of coloure. c 1450 Merlin 384 Ther myght oon haue seyn..many a fressh banere of riche colours wavinge in the wynde. a 1520 Douglas K. Hart i. 90 Richer than rose..In ruby colour reid most ryck of hew. 1657 R. Ligon Barbadoes (1673) 81 A rich green, with stripes of yellow intermixt, as hardly to be discerned where they are. 1742 Gray Cat 17 Their scaly armour's Tyrian hue, Thro' richest purple, to the view Betray'd a golden gleam. 1830 Tennyson Arab. Nts. 82 A sudden splendour from behind Flush'd all the leaves with rich gold-green. 1889 Sat. Rev. 16 Mar. 326/1 The celebrated Monarque, who was a rich bay.

†**c.** Of the nose or face: Highly inflamed. Obs.
1610 Boys Wks. (1629) 528 At last his house doth spue him out at the doore, having nothing rich excepting his nose. 1638 Brathwait Barnabees Jrnl. i. (1818) 41 Let Bacchus' bush bee Barnabee's rich nose. 1796 Grose's Dict. Vulg. T. (ed. 3), Rich Face or Nose, a red pimpled face.

d. Of musical sounds: Full and mellow in tone. Also fig.
1592 Shaks. Rom. & Jul. ii. vi. 27 Let rich musickes tongue Vnfold the imagin'd happinesse. 1754 Gray Poesy 7 Now the rich stream of music winds along. 1760 Sterne Tr. Shandy iv. xxv, Up started an air in the middle of it, so fine, so rich, so heavenly. 1836 Dubourg Violin ix. (1878) 268 The Amati family..constructed instruments of a soft and rich tone. 1859 Geo. Eliot A. Bede li, The boy's flute-like voice has its own spring charm; but the man should yield a richer, deeper music.

e. Of odours: Full of fragrance.
1599 B. Jonson Cynthia's Rev. v. ii, Is the perfume rich in this jerkin? 1707 Pope Winter 47 No rich perfumes refresh the fruitful field. 1810 [see Perfume sb. 1 a]. 1833 Tennyson Song, 'A spirit haunts,' etc., ii, The moist rich smell of the rotting leaves.

7. Plentiful, abundant, ample.
c 1450 Merlin 400, I se ther my baners that brynge vs riche socour. 1588 Shaks. L. L. L. v. ii. 199 Our duetie is so rich, so infinite, That we may doe it still without accompt. 1741 Watts Improv. Mind i. iii. § 2 In order to furnish the mind with a rich variety of ideas. 1745 Scot. Trans. & Paraph. v. ii, In rich Effusion on his Soul My Spirit's Pow'rs shall flow. 1833-4 Encycl. Metrop. (1845) VI. 655/1 It yields a most rich supply of molluscous remains. 1867 P. Schaff Hist. Church (1888) VI. v. lxxvii. 459 The event was a rich theme for scandal.

b. Of a full, ample, or unstinted nature; highly developed or cultivated.
1561 Winjet Wks. (S.T.S.) I. 5 Ȝour nurissing of pure studentis, of ryche ingynis. 1678 Cudworth Intell. Syst. 364 This sence, we chose rather to follow, as more Rich and August, than that other Vulgar one. 1759 B. Martin Nat. Hist. Eng. I. 78 A very thick and delicious Compound, greatly admired by People of a rich Taste. 1781 Cowper Expost. 166 What nation will you find, whose annals prove So rich an int'rest in almighty love? 1820 Keats Ode Melancholy ii, If thy mistress some rich anger shows, Emprison her soft hand. 1858 Hawthorne Fr. & It. Note-bks. I. 138 This idea..would develop itself into something very rich. 1884 Ruskin Pleas. Eng. 43 The richest fighting element in the British army and navy is British native.

c. Rich rhyme: (see quots.).
1656 Cowley Pindar. Odes, To Dr. Scarborough Note 2, Find, Refind: These kind of Rhymes the French delight in, and call Rich Rhymes. 1727-38 Chambers Cycl. s.v. Rhyme, Double Rhymes, by the French called rich rhymes, are those where the two words terminate alike through the whole two last syllables. 1866 Chambers' Encycl. VIII. 233/2 Complete identity in all the parts of the syllables constitutes what the French call rich rhime.

d. Highly entertaining or amusing; also, preposterous, outrageous.
1760 Sterne Tr. Shandy iv. vii, O Garrick!—what a rich scene of this would thy exquisite powers make! 1836 Fonblanque Eng. under 7 Administr. (1837) III. 313 This is marvellously rich. Sir O. Mosley thinking work on the Sabbath a sin, compounds for obliging servants to commit it. 1842 S. Lover Handy Andy xxi, The scene was rich: the gravity with which the Doctor carried on the quiz was admirable. 1863 Cowden Clarke Shaks. Char. iv. 97 But what a rich set of fellows those 'mechanicals' are! 1889 L. B. Walford Stiff-necked Generation xxix, If it really is so, it would be the richest thing I ever knew in my life.

8. Of mines or ores: Yielding a large quantity or proportion of the precious metals. Also rich conduit (see quot. 1839).
1555 Eden Decades (Arb.) 177 Rytcher golde mynes are founde in Cuba. 1604 E. G[rimstone] D'Acosta's Hist. Indies iv. v. 218 They call that poore which yields least silver,..and that rich which yields most silver. 1670 Pettus Fodinæ Reg. 9 Where the Oar digged from any Mine doth yield..so much Gold or Silver,..then it is called rich Oar or a Mine Royal. 1758 Reid tr. Macquer's Chym. I. 398 The oldest and richest mine of Mercury is that of Almaden in Spain. 1839 Ure Dict. Arts 816 The conduit or water-course is divided into three portions.., called the rich conduit, the middle conduit, and the inferior. Ibid. 1124 The argentiferous or rich lead is treated in Germany by the cupellation furnace. 1877 Raymond Statist. Mines & Mining 236 This enables capitalists to buy up the richest ores of men who produce but comparatively few tons.
fig. 1638 Junius Paint. Ancients 46, I cannot see what helpe there is in study without a rich veine.
Comb. 1877 Raymond Statist. Mines & Mining 42 The rich-ore bodies, however, seem to occur in lenticular masses.

b. Of soil, lands, etc.: Abounding in the qualities necessary to produce good vegetation or crops.
1577 B. Googe Heresbach's Husb. i. (1586) 30 It is cast into very riche grounde or wel manured. 1697 Dryden Virg. Georg. ii. 130 The Thasian Vines in richer Soils abound. 1703 Maundrell Journ. Jerus. (1732) 3 We came into a very rich Valley. 1786 Abercrombie Gard. Assist. 69 Earth the beds..with rich, light, dry earth. 1813 Sir H. Davy Agric. Chem. (1814) 183 Such soils merit the appellation which is commonly given to them of rich soils. 1865 Kingsley Herew. Prel., Its herds of mares and colts, which fed with the cattle and the geese in the rich grass-fen. 1888 Bryce Amer. Commw. III. xci. 256 One of the richest wheat-growing districts on the continent.
Comb. 1889 Westgarth Austral. Progress 187 The flats and rich-soil marshes had much of the New Zealand flax.

c. Of sand (see first quot.) or lime.
1838 J. T. Smith tr. Vicat's Mortars 44 This powder renders the sand 'rich', or, in other terms, susceptible of a certain cohesion, when tempered with water. Ibid. 186 The known absence of action of the hydrate of rich lime upon quartz.

II. adv. and Comb. (Cf. Richly adv.)
9. a. With pa. pples. used predicatively.
13.. K. Alis. 4166 (Bodl. MS.), Þer weren coupes riche ywrouȝth. a 1450 Knt. de la Tour (1868) 39 Welle arraied with riche clothinge, and riche atyred of perles and presious stones. 1595 T. Edwards Cephalus & Procris L'Envoy, Adon deafly masking thro Stately troupes rich conceited. 1606 Sylvester Du Bartas ii. iv. ii. Magnificence 270 Not far from her, comes Wealth, all rich-bedight. 1667 Milton P. L. i. 538 Th' Imperial Ensign..With Gemms and Golden lustre rich imblaz'd. 1671 — P. R. ii. 352 In order stood Tall stripling youths rich clad. 1718 Blackmore Alfred iii. (1723) 88 Whither rich-laden num'rous Fleets resort.

b. With pa. pples., forming attrib. combs.
1591 Shaks. 1 Hen. VI, i. vi. 25 The rich-iewel'd Coffer of Darius. 1593 — Lucrece 1524 The shining glory Of rich-built Ilion. 1608 Sylvester Du Bartas ii. iv. Decay 213 The rich-perfumed royall Carrion. 1611 Shaks. Cymb. iv. ii. 226 Those rich-left-heyres, that let their Fathers lye Without a Monument. 1634 Milton Comus 556 A steam of rich distill'd Perfumes. 1663 Wood Life (O.H.S.) I. 493 A rich imbroidered purse. 1776 Mickle tr. Camoens' Lusiad 70 Rich-figured tap'stry now supplies the sail. 1807 Crabbe Par. Reg. iii. 386 A rich-bound Book of Prayer the Captain gave. 1848 W. S. Mayo Kaloolah (1850) 170 The merchants..with rich-laden camels.

c. In parasynthetic combs.
1590 Spenser F. Q. i. ii. 16 As when two rams..Fight for the rule of the rich fleeced flocke. a 1756 Collins Ode Poet. Char. 39 Thou rich-hair'd youth of morn. 1820 Keats Isabella xiv, Many..stood, To take the rich-ored driftings of the flood. 1850 Tennyson In Mem. lxxv, What..voice the richest-toned that sings, Hath power to give thee as thou wert? 1889 Pater G. de Latour (1896) 17 He hunted the rich-fleshed game of La Beauce through the..corn.

10. With verbs. rare⁻¹.
c 1375 Sc. Leg. Saints xiii. (Mark) Prol. 82 Sa sancte Iohnne, quhene he spekis, to godis godhed rycheste rekis.

b. With pres. pples., forming attrib. combs.
a 1586 Sidney Arcadia (1622) 351 So fitly did the rich-growing marble serue to beautifie the vault of the first entry. 1839 Ure Dict. Arts 963 This coal has been found to afford ..a very rich-burning gas. 1842 Is. Williams Baptistery i. v. (1874) 58 What I thought rich-glittering spoil, Was but the [serpent's] scales. 1881 Macm. Mag. XLIV. 86 Mrs. Osmond's warm, rich-looking reception-rooms.

III. absol. or as sb.
11. Those who are rich; rich persons as a class.
a. With the.
c 888 K. Ælfred Boeth. xxxviii. § 7 Þæm wære mare ðearf..þæt him mon þingode to þæm ricum. c 1000 Ags. Gosp. Luke i. 52 He awearp þa rican of setle. c 1205 Lay. 2364 Þa riche he makede wrecchas. c 1275 — 11378 He ..sloh þe Romleode, þe pore and þe riche. 1362 Langl. P. Pl. A. i. 149, I rede þe riche haue reuþe on þe pore. 1426 Audelay Poems (Percy Soc.) 16 The pore schul be made domysmen Apon the ryche at domysday. c 1475 [see Poor a. 7]. 1738 Wesley 'O Thou, whose Wisdom' ii, The Rich, the Poor, the Mean, the Great Are link'd by thy strong Hands. 1781 Cowper Hope 18 The rich grow poor, the poor become purse-proud. 1817 Scott Let. in Lockhart (1837) IV. ii. 75 The rich..do not, in general, require to be so much stimulated to benevolence.
Comb. 1609 J. Davies (Heref.) Humours Heauen on Earth ccxlv. Wks. (Grosart) I. 29/2 The working woes of th' idle-curious; Of the Rich-couetous.

b. Without article.
c 1200 Ormin 16139 Acc stanndeþþ upp biforenn follc, Biforenn riche & kene. a 1300 Cursor M. 1796 All tok a right, bath pouer and Rike, All hade a dom, bath riche and pour. c 1375 Sc. Leg. Saints i. (Catherine) 17 Þat þai suld cume, bath gret & small,..bath poure & Rik. 1433 Rolls of Parlt. IV. 476/2 Do right as well to poure as to ryche. 1535 Stewart Cron. Scot. II. 445 Pluralitie of meit and drink siclike, Forbiddin wes bayth for puir and ryke. 1567 Gude & Godlie B. (S.T.S.) 13 As we forgeue all Creature Offendand vs, baith ryche and pure. 1622 Drayton Poly-olb. xxii. 536 Then [Cade] goodly London took, There ransoming some rich. 1850 Tennyson In Mem. cvi, Ring out the feud of rich and poor.

12. One who is rich; a rich person.
c 1205 Lay. 24967 Þa iherde Arður..and þus spac þe riche wið raȝen his folke. 1390 Gower Conf. III. 37 The riche ayeinward cride tho: 'O Habraham' [etc.]. c 1412 Hoccleve De Reg. Princ. 4885 Þe worlde fauorith ay þe riches sawe, Þow þat his conseil be noght worth an hawe. c 1470 Gol. & Gaw. 1265 Yone riche cummis arait in riche robbing. 1611 Bible Prov. xiv. 20 The poore is hated euen of his owne neighbour: but the rich hath many friends.

†**Rich**, v.¹ Obs. Also 4 **reche**, 4-5 **ryche**, 4-6 **riche**, 6 **ritch**. [ME. riche(n, = OFris. rîkia, MDu. rîken, rijcken, OHG. rîhhan, rîchan to become rich, MLG. rîken, ryken to make rich.]
1. trans. To enrich, make rich.
a 1300 Cursor M. 7481 Þe man þat him wald fight a-gain,..I suld him riche in all his lijf. 1390 Gower Conf. II. 77 Thanne he schal be riched so, That it mai faile neveremo. 1422 tr. Secreta Secret., Priv. Priv. 186 For y-now be hath, that Is appayet of that, that he i-richet is. 1483 Act 1 Rich. III, c. 8 Preamble, Youre Realme..hath greatly ben encresed and riched. 1515 St. Papers Hen. VIII, II. 10 Who richeith the Kinges treasor, and repayreith his cofers..,saue the Comyns? 1567 Drant Horace Ep. ii. i. H iiij, To ritch his cuntry let his words lyke flowing water fall. 1610 Heywood Gold. Age iv. i, Those barren Kingdomes I haue richt with spoiles. 1657 W. Burton Comm. Itin. Antoninus (1658) 162 Thus richt, thus populous, thus great.
absol. 13.. Pol., Rel., & L. Poems 260 Hit resteþ and hit quemeþ; hit richeþ and hit demeþ. 1382 Wyclif 1 Sam. ii. 7 The Lord makith pore, and richeth.
2. intr. To become rich.
c 1350 Will. Palerne 3014 Wiþ richesse i wol ȝou reward forto riche for euer. 1362 Langl. P. Pl. A. iii. 74 Þei.. recheþ þorw Regratorie and Rentes hem buggeþ. c 1450 in 3rd Rep. Hist. MSS. Comm. 280/1 The Frensshe partie & the Duke of Suffolk riched, the trewe subjects lost her londe. 1721 Kelly Scot. Prov. 24 As the Carle riches, he wratches.
Hence †**Ri·ching** vbl. sb. Obs.
c 1380 Wyclif Wks. (1880) 445 O cause is dowing of þe chirche & riching þer-of ouer cristis wille. c 1449 Pecock Repr. iii. viii. 327 It wolde folewe that thilk riching of the aungel was vicioseli doon of God.

†**Rich**, v.² Obs. Forms: 4-5 **rijch-**, **rich-**, **ricch-**, **riche(n**. [Perh. repr. an OE. *ryccan, = MDu. and MLG. rucken (Du. rukken), OHG. rucchen (G. rücken), ON. rykkja (Sw. rycka, Da. rykke) to tug, pull.
The evidence for the word appears to be entirely limited to the alliterative poems cited below. A variant form ruche also occurs in Gaw. & Gr. Knt.]
1. trans. To draw, pull (a rein).
c 1400 Destr. Troy 1231 Þe king..Ricchis his reynys & the Reenke metys. Ibid. 1258 He Richet his Reynes and his roile stroke.
2. refl. To address (oneself) to a place, or to do something.
13.. Gaw. & Gr. Knt. 8 Riche Romulus to Rome ricchis hym swyþe. Ibid. 1309 He ryches hym to ryse, & rapes hym sone. a 1400-50 Alexander 5056 He risis vp belyue, Riches him radly to ride & remows his ost.
b. intr. To take one's way; to run.
13.. Gaw. & Gr. Knt. 1898 Þer as he herd þe howndes,.. Renaud com richchande þurȝ a roȝe greue.
3. refl. To dress or array (oneself).
13.. Gaw. & Gr. Knt. 1130 Gestes þat go wolde..trussen her males, Richen hem þe rychest, to ryde alle arayde. Ibid. 1873 When he was gon, sir G. gerez hym sone, Rises, & riches hym in araye noble.
4. trans. To direct, advise.
13.. Gaw. & Gr. Knt. 1223 Ȝe schal not rise of your bedde, I rych yow better.
5. To arrange, prepare (a thing).
13.. Gaw. & Gr. Knt. 2206 Þat gere as I trowe, Is ryched at þe reuerence, me renk to mete.
6. To adjust, settle, set right, restore.
c 1400 Destr. Troy 1736 Thes redurse to riche..Hit were sittyng, me semys. Ibid. 2059 To wreke hym of wrathe & his wrong riche. Ibid. 13149, I..Restid me rifely, ricchit my seluyn.

†**Ri·chard.** Obs. rare. ? = Richardine.
1648 Hexham ii, Ritsart-boom, Apple Richard. 1707 Mortimer Husb. 540 The Arier Apple, a constant bearer, making a strong and lasting Cyder; some call them Richards, some Grange Apples.

†**Ri·chardine.** Obs. Also 5 **ric(h)ardon**. [f. the personal name Richard: cf. OF. richars, ricars pl., ellipt. for pommes de Richard, so named, acc. to Benoit, from Richard, Duke of Normandy (see Godef.).] A kind of apple.
c 1430 Lydg. Min. Poems (Percy Soc.) 15 Costardes, etiam wardons, And other many [fruits] fulle faire and ffresshe to see; The pome-watyr, and the gentylle ricardons. [a 1513 Fabyan Chron. vii. 605 Costardes, wardens, pomewardons, richardons.] 1600 Surflet Countrie Farme iii. xviii. 465 Graft the graftes of an apple tree vpon a sowre peare & vpon the Richardine apple tree, and you shall haue apples of a yellow or straw colour.

Richardso·nian, a. and sb. [See def.]
A. adj. Pertaining to, resembling, etc., the works or style of the novelist Samuel Richardson (1689-1761).
1831 Macaulay in Trevelyan Life (1883) I. 216 When my Richardsonian epistles are published, there must be dull as well as amusing letters among them. 1836-7 Dickens Sk. Boz, Tales x, To demonstrate that the Richardsonian principle was the best on which love could possibly be made.
B. sb. An admirer of Richardson.
1888 Stevenson Some Gentlemen in Fiction ii, My own investigation of a kindred quarter of the globe (Clarissa Harlowe) has led me to set a high value on the Richardsonians.

Richas, **richchesse**, varr. Richesse Obs.
Rich-dollar, obs. form of Rix-dollar.

†**Ri·chdom.** Obs. rare. Forms: 1 **ricedóm**, 3 **richedom(e**, 6 **rychedom(e**. [Common Teutonic: OE. ricedóm, = OFris. rîkedôm, MDu. rijcdoem (Du. rijkdom), OS. rîkidôm (MLG. rikedom), OHG. rîh-, rîchtuom (G. reichtum), ON. ríkdómr (Sw. rikedom, Da. rigdom): see Rich a. and -dom.]
a. Royal power; kingdom. **b.** Wealth, riches.
In latest quot. introduced from Flemish or LG.
a 1023 Wulfstan Hom. (1883) 125 Þin ricedom ofer us rixie symble. c 1205 Lay. 6555 Wha se hæfde richedom, he hine makede wræcche mon. c 1230 Hali Meid. 3 Þe richedom þat tes lauedis hauen. c 1275 Lay. 7283 Hii neme of þan londe richedomes stronge.
c 1511 1st Eng. Bk. Amer. (Arb.) p. xxx, Pope Iohn whose myghtynes and rychedome amounteth aboue all prynces of the world. [He] hathe vnder hym well xl. kynges rychedom.

†**Riche**, **rike**. Obs. Forms: α. 1-2 **rîce**, 2-4 **riche**, 3-4 **ryche**. β. 4-5 **rik(e**, 5 **ryk(e**. [Common Teutonic: OE. rîce, = OFris. rîke, rîk (mod. Fris. ryk), MDu. rike, rijc, ric (Du. rijk), OS. rîki (MLG. rike, ryke, LG. rîk), OHG. rîchi, rîhhi, etc. (G. reich), ON. ríki (Norw. and Sw. rike, Da. rige), Goth. reiki, a derivative from the stem of reiks Rich a.] A kingdom, realm, royal domain; also, royal power or estate, sovereignty.
α. Beowulf (Z.) 1390 Aris, rices weard; uton hraþe feran. c 897 K. Ælfred Gregory's Past. C. l. 391 He him sealde ricu oðerra kynrena. 971 Blickl. Hom. 187 Ure bisceopas geond eal Romana rice. c 1000 Ælfric Saints' Lives xviii. 13 God..hine of his rice awearp. a 1122 O. E. Chron. (Laud MS.) an. 1102, Se hæfde þone eorldom..& micel rice þær to. c 1200 Ormin 7011 Himm ȝifenn wass þatt riche. a 1225 Leg. Kath. 47, I þe moderburh of Alixandres riche. 1390 Gower Conf. I. 118 To sechen al the worldes riche, Ther was no womman forto liche.
β. a 1300 Havelok 290 Sho was þe rithe eyr Of engelond, of al þe rike. 13.. Cursor M. 24821 (Edinb.), Til erlis and baruns of þat rik Þan gaf he serkin giftis rik. c 1400 Rule St. Benet 2238 Þen sal þe bisschop of þat rike Swilk a priores sone depose. c 1470 Henry Wallace ii. 359 Bot Wallace..In Ingland fer socht battaill on that rik.
b. The kingdom of God or of heaven.
α. a 900 O. E. Martyrol. 7 Mar., He..gesohte þa heofonlice rico. a 900 Cynewulf Crist 1527 Bið þonne rices Weard ..yrre ond egesful. 971 Blickl. Hom. 31 Se þe stiȝeþ ofer þa þrym-setl heofona rices. c 1175 Lamb. Hom. 59 His riche is al þis middeleard, Eorðe & heofene. c 1200 Trin. Coll. Hom. 67 Cumeð ȝe blescede, and underfoð þat riche þat ȝiu is iȝarked. c 1220 Bestiary 732 Hise loðe men sulen to helle faren, hise leue to his riche. a 1310 in Wright Lyric P. xxxiii. 94 Bring us to thin riche ther is joie most. 1377 Langl. P. Pl. B. xiv. 179 Conforte þi careful..in þi ryche.
β. 13.. Cursor M. 11979 (Gött.), Þu wast neuer ne es worthi Mi faþer rike part of to gete. a 1340 Hampole Psalter xvii. 31 Takand me out of þis lif in til þi rike. c 1375 Sc. Leg. Saints ii. (Paul) 209 Þane paule þam prechit..of crist,..of his gret Joy, and of his ryk. c 1440 Bone Flor. 1809 [She] preyed god..That he wolde bryng hur to that ryke.

Riche, obs. form of Reach v.¹

Richel bird. [Of obscure origin.] The Lesser Tern.
1802 Montagu Ornith. Dict. (1833) 419.

Richelees, obs. f. Reckless. **Richelich(e**, **-ly**, obs. ff. Richly adv. **Richelle**, var. rechels Rekels, incense.

Richen (ri·tʃ'n), v. [f. Rich a. + -en⁵.]
1. trans. To make richer or more intense.
1878 P. Brooks Myst. Iniq. xv. (1893) 270 The old truth of covenant between man and God..is richened and deepened. 1897 Daily News 24 Apr. 6/3 Delicate greys and greeny whites and black, richened with touches of red.
2. intr. To become richer.
1888 Black In Far Lochaber xxiii, As the afternoon wanes, and the skies richen in intensity.
Hence **Ri·chening** vbl. sb.
1881 P. Brooks in Atlantic Monthly XLVIII. 550 The softening and richening of opinions. 1896 'Ian Maclaren' Kate Carnegie 38 'Marget,' began Kate, not with a blush, but rather a richening of colour.

Riches (ri·tʃɛz). Also 4-6 **ryches** (5 **rychches**, 6 **rytches**); 5 **ricches**, **risches**, 6 **ritches**; 5 **re(c)ches**, **-ez**. [var. of next, assuming the form of a pl., and finally construed as such.
The conversion into the pl. form may have been assisted by L. divitiæ. In older Sc. texts, where the usual ending of the pl. is -is, the form riches properly belongs to next.]
1. Abundance of means or of valuable possessions; wealth. Also, in certain constructions, the possession of wealth, the condition of being rich.
c 1205 Lay. 8091 Was at-foren þan wæfde imaked an wunlic fur; þe king warp riches þer in. a 1300 Cursor M. 8123 Þe riches þat þai wit þam ledd, þai offerd in þat ilk stedd. c 1330 Amis & Amil. 761 No be thou neuer so pouer of kinde, Riches anough Y may the finde. c 1380 Wyclif Wks. (1880) 369 Þe temporal lordis ben not in noumbre and in ryches lyke as þai wer sum tyme. c 1400 Maundev. (Roxb.) v. 17 A full faire citee and full of riches. c 1491 Chast. Goddes Chyld. 63 Riches and worshippes ben but lente to man for a tyme. 1531 Tindale Exp. 1 John (1537) 101 Here is not forbidden to haue riches. 1560 Daus tr. Sleidane's Comm. 117 b, He had a good witte, &..had attayned to great ryches. 1610 Holland Camden's Brit. (1637) 428 In processe of time..their riches turned to their ruine. 1671 Milton P. R. ii. 427 Get Riches first, get Wealth, and Treasure heap. 1741-2 Gray Agrip. 78 The riches of the earth, the train of pleasures. 1776 A. Smith W. N. i. xi. (1904) I. 196 With the greater part of rich people the chief enjoyment of riches consists in the parade of riches. 1851 Helps Comp. Solit. iii. (1874) 34 Their riches furnished forth abundant armies. 1862 Ruskin Unto this Last iii. 103 The attraction of riches is already too strong.
personif. 1704 Swift Batt. Bks. Wks. 1751 I. 189 War is the Child of Pride, and Pride the Daughter of Riches.
b. transf. or fig.
1586 Spenser Astrophel 62 On her he spent the riches of his wit. 1646 H. P. Medit. Seige 136 Another kinde of riches, the riches of thy glory, and the riches of thy mercie. 1721 Swift Propos. Use of Irish Manuf., People are the Riches of a Country. 1765 Museum Rust. V. 122 To lead out the riches of a pond..which had been..never thoroughly cleaned during near thirty years. 1824 Landor Imag. Conv., Milton & Marvel, The writings of the wise are the only riches our posterity can not squander.
†**2.** Construed as a sing. Also, a particular form of wealth. Obs.
c 1330 Arth. & Merl. 3583 (Kölbing), Of ich riches & deinte, Certes, þer was gret plente. a 1400-50 Alexander 3931 Þare reches was of redde gold & many riche gemes. c 1449 Pecock Repr. iii. viii. 326 That ricches is not cause of eny synne mai be proued thus. 1545 Brinklow Compl. iii. (1874) 14 The riches of men hath helpyd many an honest man to his death. 1586 T. B. La Primaud. Fr. Acad. i. 69 All riches is of it selfe blinde, and bringeth no light to the soule. 1632 Massinger City Madam i. iii, Not that riches Is, or should be, contemn'd, it being a blessing Derived from heaven. 1657 Waterhouse Fire London 30 This riches..was as well devoured by the Suburbian thieves.
†**b.** transf. or fig. Obs.
1513 Bradshaw St. Werburge i. 318 Bytwyx them descended a precyous ryches: The blessyd Ermenylde. 1586 T. B. La Primaud. Fr. Acad. (1589) 51 This pretious and inestimable riches, I meane of vertue. c 1600 Shaks. Sonn. lxxxvii, For that riches where is my deseruing? 1622 Wither Philarete (1633) 714 Floras riches in a row Doth in seemely order grow.
3. Construed as a plural.
c 1374 Chaucer Boeth. ii. met. ii. (1868) 35 As many recches [L. tantas opes] as þe see turneþ vpwardes sandes. 1535 Coverdale Prov. xix. 4 Riches make many frendes. 1559 Mirr. Mag., Hen. VI, xvii, In heaven wer my ryches heapt. 1612 Bacon Ess., Riches (Arb.) 231 As Salomon saith; Riches are as a strong hold. 1691 Locke Lowering Interest 8 Riches do not consist in having more gold and silver. 1732 Pope Ep. Bathurst 169 Riches, like insects,..Wait but for Wings. 1755 Young Centaur iii. Wks. 1757 IV. 165 There are two kinds of expence; in both, riches make themselves wings, and fly away. 1838 Dickens Nich. Nick. i, That riches are the only true source of happiness and power.
†**4.** Richness; great worth. Obs. rare.
1547 Bk. of Marchauntes b vj b, Yet wyl it not..laugh nor stier at the beautie of the cloth nor at the riches of the crosse. a 1548 Hall Chron., Hen. VIII, 74 There lacked neither Pearles nor Stones of riches.

†**Richesse.** Obs. Forms: 3 **richeis(s)e**, 4 **richeyse**, 4-5 **richess** (5 **-eese**); 3 **rich-**, 4 **rychesce**; 3-7 **richesse** (4 **richch-**, 4-5 **ricch-**), 4-6 **rychesse** (4 **ryhch-**, **rychch-**); 3-7 **richess** (5 **richas**, 5-6 Sc. **riches**). [a. OF. richeise, -esce, -ece, -esse, f. riche Rich: see -ess².]
1. Wealth; opulence.
c 1200 Trin. Coll. Hom. 51 Hie..hadden þe fulle of wurldes richeisse. c 1230 Hali Meid. 31 Þu seides þruppe, þat ter walde wakenen..richesce & worldes weole. 1297 R. Glouc. (Rolls) 409 Brut & corineus..astored hom aboute mid richesse & chateus. c 1330 R. Brunne Chron. Wace (Rolls) 2196 Anor..was ful curteyse, & well couþe demeyne richeyse. 1377 Langl. P. Pl. B. ii. 17 Hire arraye me rauysshed, suche ricchesse saw I neuere. c 1412 Hoccleve De Reg. Princ. 1316 Than schal men see, how in his world, I gesse, Richesse is pouert, and pouert richesse. 1460 Capgrave Chron. (Rolls) 164 The Jewis..with her usure encresed hemselve to grete richesse. 1509 Hawes Joyf. Med. 11 Gadryinge grete rychesse of this his regyon. 1555 Eden Decades (Arb.) 54 The Phenician marchauntes..got great rychesse therby. 1609 Holland Amm. Marcell. xiv. ix. 67 The Germanes..got away their wives,..together with the corne and barbarous richesse. 1687 Rycaut Hist. Turks II. 97 England's Richess depends absolutely on her Foreign Trade.
personif. ?a 1366 Chaucer Rom. Rose 1033 Bisyde Beaute yede Richesse, An high lady of greet noblesse. 1508 Dunbar Gold. Targe 176 Wnto the pres persewit Hie Degree,.., Richesse, Fredome, and eke Nobilitee. 1590 Spenser F. Q. ii. vii. 24 Betwixt them both was but a litle stride, That did the house of Richesse from hell-mouth divide.
transf. c 1400 Love Bonavent. Mirr. xxix. (1908) 149 Gostly richesse of vertues and conforte of the holy goost. 1590 Spenser F. Q. ii. ii. 41 In her the richesse of all heauenly grace In chiefe degree are heaped up on hye.
b. The choice or flower of anything.
c 1391 Chaucer Compl. Venus 12 For grace haþe wolde so ferforthe him avaunce, Þat of knighthoode he is parfyt Rychesse.
2. In plural form. Cf. Riches.
a 1225 Ancr. R. 168 Þu leauedest to oðre men alle richesses. a 1300 E. E. Psalter xxxvi. 16 Better is litel to right, with wele, Over richesses of sinful fele. 1387 Trevisa Higden (Rolls) IV. 55 To gilde up..al þe gold and selver and oþere richesses. c 1449 Pecock Repr. ii. iv. 295 Men that trusten in richessis. ?1485 Caxton St. Wenefryde 2, I am a kynges sone whiche haue plente of rychesses. c 1532 Du Wes Introd. Fr. in Palsgr. 1030 Dyverse other maner of love, as of richesses. 1601 Dolman La Primaud. Fr. Acad. (1618) iii. 666 All the beauties and richesses of the Vniuers. 1677 Gale Crt. Gentiles iv. 199 To be furnished with Richesses and other necessaries.
transf. 1382 Wyclif Eph. iii. 16 That he ȝyue to ȝou, vp the richessis of his glorie, vertu for to be strengthid. 1539 Tonstall Serm. Palm Sund. (1823) 95-6 So for these ii. rychesses, the one the rychesse of faythe, the other the rychesse of good workes, we shoulde chiefly studye.
3. An alleged name for a number of martens.
Quot. 1486 is the original source of all later references.
1486 Bk. St. Albans f vj, A Richesse of Martronys. 1575 Turberv. Venerie 235 Trystram addeth, a Richesse of Marternes. 1598 Manwood Lawes Forest iv. (1615) 44 The Foresters doe call a companie of Marternes, a Richesse of Marternes. 1610 Guillim Heraldry iii. xiv. (1660) 167 Skilfull Forresters and good Woodmen Do use to say, a Riches of Marternes. a 1700 B. E. Dict. Cant. Crew, Richess, (of Marterns) a Company. 1801 Strutt Sports & Past. i. i. 17.

†**Ri·chestly**, adv. Obs. rare. Most richly.
1506 Paston Lett. III. 405 The Kynges of Castylle chamber, whych is the rychestly hangyd that ever I sawe. c 1540 Pilgr. T. 330 in Thynne Animadv. (1875) 86 The woman.. Was gorgiously be-seyn as she rod, in purple, with stons set so well, most rychestly, chast with margarites.

†**Ri·chful**, a. Obs. rare⁻¹. Wealthy.
c 1460 Ashby Dicta Philos. 949 A fornicatour may not be preised, Ner a Ireful man to be meche gladful,..nor couetouse [to be] richeful.

Ri·chish, a. rare⁻¹. Somewhat rich.
1877 Carlyle in Lett. Mrs. Carlyle I. 153 A richish country living.

Ri·chling. rare. [f. Rich a. + -ling.] (With contemptuous force.) A rich person.
a 1500 Inscript. in Yarnton Church, Oxon, Greete, greete, richlyng, greete. ?1667 O. Heywood Heart-Treasure vii. Wks. 1825 II. 62 O how much better is a poor soul than such a self-deluding richling, that thinks he is something, yet he is nothing!

Richly (ri·tʃli), adv. Forms: α. 1 **ríclíce**; 3 **richelike**, 3-4 **-lich(e**, 4 **-leche**, 5 **-lych**; 3 **rycheliche**, 5 **-liche**. β. 4-6 **riche-**, **rychely**; 4 **richli**, **-ley**, 4-6 **-lie**, 6 **-lye**, 6- **richly**; 6 **rychly**, **ry(t)chlie**, **rechlie**. [OE. ríclíce, = MDu. rikelike, etc. (Du. rijkelijk), MLG. rîk(e)lîken, OHG. rîh-, rîchlîcho (G. reichlich), ON. ríkulega (Sw. rikligen, Da. rigeligt): see Rich a. and -ly².]
†**1.** With great authority or power. Obs.
c 897 K. Ælfred Gregory's Past. C. xix. 144 Ȝe budon swiðe riclice & swiðe agendlice. c 1000 Ælfric Hom. II. 128 On ðam dagum rixode Æþelbyrht cyning on Cantwarebyrig riclice.
2. In a rich, sumptuous, or splendid manner.
α. c 1000 Ags. Gosp. Luke xvi. 19 Sum welig man wæs, & he.. dæghwamlice riclice [L. splendide] gewistfullude. c 1205 Lay. 2728 Siluius..richeliche he nom his sonde & sende to Ebrauke. 1297 R. Glouc. (Rolls) 7725 Festes he wolde holde so nobliche..& so richeliche. c 1330 Arth. & Merl. 2160 (Kölbing), Aurilisbrosias out þai souȝt & richelich in erþe him brouȝt.
β. a 1300 Cursor M. 21604 Wit-in þe kirc of saint soffie þar ha þai sett it richelie. 1338 R. Brunne Chron. (1810) 35 Þe abbey of Rumeye he feffed richely, With rentes fulle gode & kirkes of pris. c 1385 Chaucer L. G. W. 1037 Dido, This fresche lady..Stod in the temple in hire estat ryal So rychely. c 1400 Destr. Troy 13630 Ermonia, þe myld,..Þat Orestes þe rynke richeli had weddit. c 1450 Merlin 188 The Duke hym contened in this maner richely as ye haue herde. 1484 Caxton Fables of Æsop i. xii, Better worth hit is to lyue in pouerte surely than to lyue rychely beynge euer in dauger. a 1542 Wyatt in Tottel's Misc. (Arb.) 85 Richely she fedes, and at the richemans cost. 1583 Stubbes Anat. Abus. ii. (1882) 4 They might liue richly and in abundance of all things. 1633 Ford Broken Heart iv. iv, For requital I will report thee to thy mistress richly. 1651 French Distill. v. 126 To make a Spirit of Amber-gryse that a few drops thereof shall perfume a pint of Wine most richly. 1754 Gray Poesy 90 Whose colours clear Richly paint the vernal year. 1797 Coleridge This Lime-Tree Bower, Richlier burn, ye clouds! 1819 Scott Anne of G. ii, He is mountain-bred, and I will reward him richly.
b. With pa. pples. used predicatively.
α. c 1320 Sir Tristr. 1434 His armes weren al newe, Þat richeliche were wrouȝt. 1390 Gower Conf. II. 47 What ben thei, that now riden hiere, And ben so richeliche arraied? c 1450 Lovelich Grail xxxv. 321 A lytel hows..Whiche was som tyme Richelych dyht.
β. c 1320 Sir Tristr. 1662 Þe coupe was richeli wrouȝt, Of gold it was, þe pin. c 1350 Will. Palerne 1931 No man vpon molde schuld mow deuise Men richlier a-raid. c 1400 Maundev. (Roxb.) ii. 6 Þe coroune lyes in a vessell of cristall, wele dight and richely. 1470-85 Malory Arthur iv. vi. 125 They..founde hit..rychely behanged with clothe of sylke. a 1533 Ld. Berners Huon lxxxiii. 259 He was rychely apareylyd in cloth of golde. a 1572 Knox Hist. Ref. (1587) 192 With promise that they should be rechlie rewarded for their good seruice. 1637 Heywood Royall King iv. xiii, I have not seene a Modell richlier fram'd. 1670 12th Rep. Hist. MSS. Comm. App. V. 21 The under petticoatt very richly laced with two or three sorts of laces. 1709 Steele Tatler No. 6 ¶ 11 Seventeen Volumes, very richly bound. 1756-7 tr. Keysler's Trav. (1760) III. 187 Under this hangs another, richly set with jewels. 1794 Sullivan View Nat. I. 25 His memory was richly stored. 1825 J. Neal Bro. Jonathan I. 74 It may have been richly sculptured. 1880 C. R. Markham Peruv. Bark 120 Large pictures..in frames of carved wood, richly gilt.
c. With pa. pples., forming attributive combs.
1656 Earl Monm. tr. Boccalini's Advts. fr. Parnass. i. lxxxvii. (1674) 116 The most magnificent, and richliest adorn'd Palace in all Parnassus. 1822 Scott Pirate xxxvii, A lofty, well-proportioned, and richly-ornamented Gothic window. 1849 Macaulay Hist. Eng. iii. I. 369 Tobacco in any other form than that of richly scented snuff was held in abomination. 1874 Micklethwaite Mod. Par. Churches 61 In richly-furnished churches all the upper row of seats may be stalls, i.e. separated by elbows.
d. In comb. with adjs. or pres. pples.
1606 Sylvester Du Bartas ii. iv. Magnificence 9 The glorious Temple, Builded richly-rare. Ibid. 1018 His saffron'd Ruffe is edged richly-neat With burning Carbuncles. 1848 Buckley Iliad 83 The fences of the richly-blooming fields. 1850 Thackeray Pendennis xxiv, One asked for a lock of his hair, which was long and in richly-flowing ringlets.
3. So as to be rich.
c 1400 Maundev. (Roxb.) vi. 18 He wald hafe maried me richely with a grete prince doghter. c 1440 Alph. Tales 246 Gyff me all þi gudis, at þurgh þame I may richelie be marid. 1613 Purchas Pilgrimage iii. xv. (1614) 321 She was faire and noble..and richly married to Sinatus the Tetrarch. a 1814 Fam. Politics i. i. in New Brit. Theatre II. 194, I hoped to see her greatly, richly married. 1876 Miss Yonge Womankind xxxi, Their mothers..cherish wishes that their girls may 'marry well'; i.e. richly.
4. With possession of riches. rare⁻¹.
1588 Greene Perimedes 31 Poorely content is better then richlye couetous.
5. Amply, fully, thoroughly.
1617 Moryson Itin. i. 179 Which made me repent the buying of him, though otherwise he was richly worth my money. 1694 Gibson in Lett. Lit. Men (Camden) 236 It seems to me to be richly worth the money. 1709 Steele Tatler No. 7 ¶ 17 So richly does he seem to deserve his Chastisement. 1854 Doran Habits & Men 178 She richly merited the well-earned benedictions. 1856 Hawthorne Eng. Note-bks. (1879) I. 270 The Aquarium..was richly worth inspecting. 1884 Manch. Exam. 14 May 5/2 If they did so they would richly merit the severest censure.
6. Of colour: Intensely, deeply.
a 1601 ?Marston Pasquil & Kath. (1878) i. 298 Her face as richly yellow as the skin of a cold Custard. 1785 Burns Scotch Drink ii, Whether thro' wimplin worms thou jink, Or, richly brown, ream owre the brink. 1792 S. Rogers Pleas. Mem. ii. 153 The bald veteran..Richly bronz'd by many a summer-sun.

†**Richman.** Obs. [f. Rich a. and Man: formerly as a comb. (cf. Goodman), now only as separate words.] A wealthy man.
In quot. 1643 a rendering of med.L. ricomines (= OSp. ricos omes).
1154 O. E. Chron. (Laud MS.) an. 1137, Æuric riceman his castles makede. 1297 R. Glouc. (Rolls) 8839 To saui pouere men vram richemenne vnriȝt. a 1542 Wyatt in Tottel's Misc. (Arb.) 85 Richely she fedes, and at the richemans cost. 1567 Drant Horace, Ep. i. xviii. Fiiij, Him hates the ritchman, that ritchman doth hate him dedely sore. 1575 Turberv. Venerie Pref., The needie neighbors grudge to see the rychman thryue. 1643 Prynne Sov. Power Parl. App. 76 Let them be devided not only between the Rich-men, but likewise between the soldiers and infantry.

Richness (ri·tʃnės). [-ness.] The state or quality of being rich, in senses of the adj.
1338 R. Brunne Chron. (1810) 155 My sister Aleyse.. is now forsaken For on of mor richenesse of Nauer þou has taken. 14.. Nom. in Wr.-Wülcker 714 Hic census, rychenes. c 1500 Communycacyon C iij, Thou shalte haue in my palesse..No pouerte but all rychenesse. c 1530 Compl. of them that been to late Maryed (Collier, 1862) 18 Rychenes in youth, with good governaunce, Often helpeth age. 1583 Golding Calvin on Deut. xxxix. 234 For the true richnesse..is the blessing of God. 1649 Blithe Eng. Improv. Impr. (1653) 23 The water..leaving her Thickness, Soyl or Filth, which I call Ricnness, among the Grass. 1699 Bentley Phal. 361 The Tragic Ornaments were so famous for their Richness. 1718 Lady M. W. Montagu Lett. II. xlvi. 33 The mosques..only differ in largeness and richness of material. 1796 Morse Amer. Geogr. I. 158 This tract of land is reckoned equal in richness and fertility to any in America. 1814 Scott Diary 25 Aug.

riddle, more or less coarse, is the arrowy Maine forest..relentlessly sifted,..till it comes out boards, clapboards [etc.].

b. *To turn* (or *cast*) *the riddle* (*and shears*), to practise a mode of divination mainly employed for the discovery of theft. *Sc.* and *north. dial.*

For a description of the process, see Jamieson.

1570 *Durham Depos.* (Surtees) 117, I, Allice Swan,..used by the space of certen yeres to cast or tourne the riddle and sheares. 1573 *Ibid.* 251 Ther was a wyff in Newcastell..that culd torne the ryddle [etc.]. 1589 in Lawson *Bk. Perth* (1847) 191 Whilk day Violet Brown..was accused for turning of the riddle with sheers. 1709 [see 4].

c. *A riddle of claret*: (see quot. 1889).

1831 Wilson in *Blackw. Mag.* XXX. 413, I bet you a riddle of claret. 1889 *N. & Q.* 7th Ser. VIII. 13 A riddle of claret is thirteen bottles, a magnum and twelve quarts. The name comes from the fact that the wine is brought in on a literal riddle.

2. *To make a riddle of*, to pierce with holes.

1817 J. Bradbury *Trav. Amer.* 19 He was instantly pierced with arrows so numerous, that, to use the language of Colter, 'he was made a riddle of'. 1842 Lever *J. Hinton* li, I was to be made a riddle of if I attempted to escape.

3. A board or metal plate set with pins, used in straightening wire.

1843 Holtzapffel *Turning* I. 425 The riddle is a piece of wood or metal with sloping pins, which lean alternately opposite ways, so as to keep the wire close down on the board. 1866 *Tomlinson's Cycl. Usef. Arts* II. 912/2 Hard-drawn and unannealed wires..are straightened..by drawing them through a riddle.

4. *attrib.* and *Comb.*, as *riddle-frame, -maker, manufactory, sieve*; *riddle-turning* (see 1 b).

1709 in W. Andrews *Bygone Ch. Life Scot.* (1899) 124 The horrid sin of the hellish art of riddle-turning. 1747 *Gentl. Mag.* XVII. 311 The greatest part of the corn, which falls thro' this riddle sive, is at once clear from chaff and huzzes. 1818 J. Palmer *Jrnl. Trav.* 48 One wire weaving and riddle manufactory. 1844 H. Stephens *Bk. Farm* II. 332 That part of the sides that form[s] the riddle-frame lies horizontally. 1858 Simmonds *Dict. Trade, Riddle-maker*, a manufacturer of large coarse wire sieves.

Riddle, *sb.*[3] *nonce-wd.* [f. Riddle *v.*[2]] A hole made by a bullet.

1880 E. Marshall *Troublous Times* I. 82 My mother..had dropped a tear over the riddle of a bullet in the flap.

Riddle, *sb.*[4], variant of Reddle or Ruddle.

1681 Chetham *Angler's Vade-m.* iv. § 7 (1689) 34 Riddle or red Oker (with which People in Lancashire use to mark their sheep). 1886 *Gloss. Rochdale.*

†**Riddle**, *sb.*[5], obs. variant of Raddle *sb.*[1]

1695 Kennett *Par. Antiq., Gloss.* s.v. *Cladus*, A hurdle..in Kent is sometime call'd a Riddle, Raddle, or Ruddle: ..as riddle-wall, a riddle-basket.

Riddle, *v.*[1] Also 7 ridle. [f. Riddle *sb.*[1]]

1. *intr.* To speak in riddles, or enigmatically; also, to propound riddles.

1571 Golding *Calvin on Ps.* xlix. 4 That is to say, Riddle thou in riddle. 1590 Shaks. *Mids. N.* ii. iii. 53 Lysander riddles very prettily. 1649 Carlell *Deserving Favorite* ii. ii, What, do you riddle me? Is she contracted, And can I by your counsell attaine my wishes? 1660 Shirley *Merchant's Wife* iii. iii, Madam, you riddle strangely. 1748 Melmoth *Fitzosborne Lett.* (1749) I. 8 That he who knows not how to riddle, knows not how to live. 1888 Gilbert *Yeomen* i, I can riddle you from dawn of day to set of sun.

2. *trans.* To interpret or solve (a riddle or question). **a.** In imp. phr. *riddle me a* (or *my*) *riddle*; or *riddle me this, that, why*, etc.

1588 *Marprel. Epist.* (Arb.) 11 Riddle me a riddle, what is that his grace threatened to send Mistris Lawson to Bridewell? 1641 Br. Mountagu *Diatribæ* 526 Riddle me a riddle, what is this? 1661 Holyday *Juvenal* (1673) 38 Riddle me this: what's he, that to Rome came [etc.]? 1668 Davenant *Man's the Master* iii. i, Riddle my riddle, what's this? 1773 Goldsm. *Stoops Conq.* v. ii, Riddle me this then. What's that goes round the house, and round the house, and never touches the house?

b. Redupl. *riddle me, riddle me.*

1590 Nashe *Pasquil's Apol.* B b, Riddle me, riddle me, what was he? 1631 P. Fletcher *Piscatory Eclog.* I. iv b, I have another play within to doe, Riddle me, Riddle me, what's that? 1673 Hickeringill *Father Greybeard* 199 Riddle me, riddle me what it is. [1842 Chambers *Pop. Rhymes Scott.* (1870) 109 Riddle me, riddle me, rot-tot-tot, A little wee man in a red red coat.]

c. In general use. Also *absol.*

1627 Drayton *Agincourt, Moon-Calf* 176 The tale our Gossip Red-cap told before, You so well ridled, that there can no more Be said of it. 1654 Trevor in Carte *Collect.* (1735) 266 The affaire..is now understood and that mystery riddled to be a bragge. 1820 Scott *Abbot* xxiii, Were I as wise a warlock as Michael Scott, I could scarce riddle the dream you read me. 1824 Miss Ferrier *Inher.* xxvii, Promise that you will riddle me right, and tell me why poverty is the greatest misfortune in the world.

d. With adverbs, as *to riddle forth, out.*

1624 Quarles *Job Militant* xiv. 84 You understand To riddle forth man's Fortunes by his Hand. 1642 H. More *Song of Soul* ii. ii. lxv, So might we riddle out some mystery. 1685 — *Par. Prophet.* xii. 91 The Time-eaten names of the Consuls in that Monumentum Ancyranum above-mentioned, as riddled out by T. L.

3. To be a riddle to (a person); to puzzle. *rare.*

1818 Scott *Rob Roy* xviii, I think it will riddle him or he gets his horse ower the Border again.

Riddle (ri·d'l), *v.*[2] Forms: 3 ridlen, 4 rydelyn; 4 5 ridile, 4–6 ridele (6 redyle), 4–8 ridle, 4– riddle. [f. Riddle *sb.*[2]]

1. *trans.* To pass (corn, gravel, etc.) through a riddle; to separate with a riddle; to sift. Also const. *out, in.*

a 1225 *Ancr. R.* 234 Satan is ȝeorne abuten uorto ridlen þe ut of mine corne! 1382 Wyclif *Dan.* xiv. 13 Thei brouȝten to ashe, and by al the temple he ridlide [it] byfore the kyng. — *Luke* xxii. 31 Sathanas hath axid ȝou, that he schulde ridele [you] as whete. c 1440 *Promp. Parv.* 433/2 Rydelyn, *cribro, capisterio.* 1523 Fitzherb. *Husb.* § 146 The bolles of flaxe, whan they be ripeled of, must be rideled from the wedes. 1570 Levins *Manip.* 116 To Riddle, *cribrare.* 1603 Owen *Pembrokeshire* xi. (1892) 90 Two ridlers, who ridle the coales when it is aland. 1688 [see Riddling *vbl. sb.*[2] 1]. 1707 Mortimer *Husb.* (1721) II. 244 The finest sifted Mould that can be got, which must be..rather ridled in than pressed down. 1789 Walkden *Diary* 12 Sept. (1866) 41, I owed..3*d.* to his son, due for riddling and blending lime. 1764 *New Spectator* No. 10. 5 As ridiculous as Hercules with the distaff, or a Duchess ridling cinders! 1833 J. Holland *Manuf. Metal* II. 203 The ashes, on falling, are riddled or sifted through the grating. 1844 Stephens *Bk. Farm* II. 281 The shrivelled beans and other refuse being riddled out. 1890 W. J. Gordon *Foundry* 16 One is sifting or 'riddling' the old sand to make it ready for another casting.

absol. 1616 B. Jonson *Love Restored* Wks. (Rtldg.) 588/2 Robin Goodfellow, he that sweeps the hearth.., riddles for the country maides, and does all their other drudgery. 1844 H. Stephens *Bk. Farm* II. 282 Very few people who profess to work in the barn can riddle well.

b. *transf.* and *fig.*

1613 Jackson *Creed* ii. 468 Appointed to riddle out some good meaning. 1630 Davenant *Cruel Brother* iii. i, Thus thy years do riddle grief away. 1649 Blithe *Eng. Improv. Impr.* (1653) 23 The Goodness of the Water is as it were Ridled, Screened, and Strained out into the Land. 1831 Carlyle in Froude *Life* (1882) II. 146 That mind which must all be riddled monthly to see if there are any grains in it. 1863 Torrens *Life Sir J. Graham* I. 235 His power of sifting evidence, and riddling the truth out of reluctant or evasive witnesses.

2. To pierce with holes like those of a riddle; to render sieve-like by perforation (*with* bullets or the like); to shatter by missiles.

1849–50 Alison *Hist. Europe* IV. xxi. § 62. 195 Above 100,000 cannon-balls, and 25,000 bombs,..had riddled all its defences. 1874 Green *Short Hist.* iv. § 3. 186 Edward riddled the Scottish ranks with arrows. 1886 *Law Times* LXXX. 213/2 Worms will riddle the wood-work of a ship.

fig. 1888 Bryce *Amer. Commw.* III. lxxxvii. 165 Proposals..which the criticism of opinion riddled with its unceasing fire.

b. *esp.* in pa. pple. *riddled* (*with* holes, etc.).

1817 J. Scott *Paris Revisit.* (ed. 4) 211 The door was riddled through and through with all sorts of shot. 1865 Gosse *Land & Sea* (1874) 31 An interior riddled with holes like a honeycomb. 1884 *Cassell's Fam. Mag.* Mar. 220/1 Steep banks of sandstone, riddled with the holes of the sand-martin.

fig. 1897 Ouida *Massarenes* viii, They are as poor as Job and riddled with debts.

c. *intr.* To penetrate. *rare*[−1].

1856 Kane *Arct. Expl.* II. x. 99 Blanket-bags are nearly useless below—30°, in a gale of wind; it riddles through them.

d. With cogn. obj.: To make (one's way) by penetration. *rare*[−1].

1892 G. Hake *Mem.* 80 *Yrs.* lxiii. 259 An enemy could cross a moat; could he riddle his way through the countless canals of Venezia?

Riddle-bread, -cake. *north. dial.* (See quots.)

1674 Ray *N. C. Words* s.v. *Bannock, Riddle-cakes*, thick Sour-cakes, from which differs little that which they call *Hand-hoven Bread*, having but little leaven, and being kneaded stiffer. 1797 *Monthly Mag.* III. 33/1 The bread used is made of oatmeal, and by some is called riddle bread. It is slightly baked in thick cakes, being previously leavened. 1828 Carr *Craven Gloss.*, *Riddle-bread*, oat cake which is riddled or shaken on a chequered board, before it is thrown on an iron plate over the fire, called a bakestone.

Riddled, *ppl. a.*[1] *rare*[−1]. [f. Riddle *v.*[1] + -ed [1].] Made enigmatical.

c 1586 C'tess Pembroke *Ps.* xlix. i, I will..ridled speech to tuned harp accord.

Riddled, *ppl. a.*[2] [f. Riddle *v.*[2]]

1. Passed through a riddle; sifted, winnowed.

1844 H. Stephens *Bk. Farm* II. 273 While the unwinnowed heap is becoming less,..the riddled one increases in bulk. 1891 *Times* 5 Oct. 4/4 Slacks can be bought at 5*s.* 6*d.* to 6*s.* 6*d.*..and ordinary riddled nuts at 8*s.*..per ton.

2. Pierced with holes, as by bullets; shattered.

1862 *Index* 25 Sept., He bore aloft the riddled flag of the 3rd Alabama. 1871 *Daily News* 14 Aug., The world at large associates it with long runs, riddled wickets [etc.].

Riddled, variant of Rideled *a. Obs.*

Riddle-like: see Riddle *sb.*[1] 4 b.

Riddlemeree·, riddle-me-ree.

1. A fanciful variant of the phrases *riddle me a riddle, riddle my riddle*, etc. (See Riddle *v.*[1] 2.)

1710 Addison *Whig Examiner* No. 1 ⁋ 3 Riddle my ree, what is this? c 1730 *Royal Remarks* 50 They argued it upon it in the familiar Phrase of Riddle my Riddle my Ree [etc.].

2. Rigmarole; nonsense.

1736 tr. *Ruggle's Ignoramus* i. 10 It is, as the Law says,—in Nubibus—'tis riddle me re—'tis something, and nothing. 1785 *European Mag.* VIII. 463 By this quaint riddle-meree, I suppose it is meant that [etc.]. 1806 Surr *Winter in Lond.* III. 233 Pray, Lady Roseville, what riddle-me-ree is this? 1818 Keats *Wks.* (1889) III. p. cxxxvii, Not omitting..any little choice conversation or riddle-me-ree between him and his nursery maid. 1848 *Blackw. Mag.* Oct. 461 Her style is all riddle-ma-ree.

So †**Riddlemy riddlemy.** *Obs. rare*[−1].

1641 Brome *Joviall Crew* i. Wks. 1873 III. 353, I would be drunk A thousand times to bed, rather then dream Of any of their Riddlemy Riddlemies.

Riddler[1]. [f. Riddle *v.*[1] + -er [1].] One who speaks or deals in riddles.

1610 Donne *Pseudomartyr* 363 Were this..springing out of the spirituall authoritie as the Popes ridler makes his authoritie to bee? 1671 Aphra Behn *Forc'd Marriage* iii. i, Prethee be not thou a Ridler too. 1728 Pope *Dunc.* iii. 157 Each Songster, Riddler, ev'ry nameless name. 1757 Home *Douglas* iii, Thou riddler, speak Direct and clear. 1838 *New Monthly Mag.* LIV. 247 His elevation as a puzzler and riddler among men.

Riddler[2]. Also 7 ridler. [f. Riddle *v.*[2] + -er [1].] One who uses a riddle.

1603 [see Riddle *v.*[2] 1]. 1771–2 *Ess. fr. Batchelor* (1773) II. 50 With shaking nought remains but coals, To warm the riddler's breast. 1844 H. Stephens *Bk. Farm* II. 273 The corn begins to accumulate amongst the riddlers' feet. 1853 R. S. Surtees *Sponge's Sp. Tour* (1893) 83 Riddling lime—an unpleasant occupation..when the wind veers capriciously, and the riddler is inexpert at 'dodging'.

Riddle-wise: see Riddle *sb.*[1] 4 a.

Ri·ddling, *vbl. sb.*[1] [f. Riddle *v.*[1] + -ing [1].] The propounding of a riddle or riddles; also, an instance of this, †a riddle. Also *attrib.*

1483 *Cath. Angl.* 307/2 A Rydellynge (*A.* Ridyllynge), *enigma.* 1611 Middleton & Dekker *Roaring Girl* D.'s Wks. 1873 IV. 184 What..meanes this ridling? 1671 Milton *Samson* 1064 Be less abstruse, my riddling days are past. 1812 *Sporting Mag.* XXXIX. 110 The laughable exercises of blindman's buff, riddling, and question and command. 1872 Tennyson *Gareth & Lynette* 279 Know ye not then the Riddling of the Bards?

Ri·ddling, *vbl. sb.*[2] [f. Riddle *v.*[2] + -ing [1].]

1. The action of sifting or separating by means of a riddle. Also *fig.*

1603 Owen *Pembrokeshire* xi. (1892) 90 Then the seconde ridlinge with a smaler Ridle. 1688 Holme *Armoury* iii. 74/1 Ridling, is a sifting the corn from the chaff. 1839 Ure *Dict. Arts* 814 This operation by the hand-sieve, is called riddling in the tub, or riddling by deposit. 1850 Carlyle *Latter-d. Pamph.* i. (1872) 39 By manœuvring of ballotboxes, and riddling of the popular clamour. 1891 *Athenæum* 15 Aug. 223/1 Some day..some patient person will take these six volumes, and, by severe riddling first and compressing afterwards, get them into one or two.

2. *pl.* The coarser or less valuable parts which are separated by the riddle; siftings, screenings.

1600 Surflet *Countrie Farme* i. xxv, By that part of increase which the farmer spareth in his fodder, siftings, ridlings, and such other things. a 1796 Burns *Poet. Wks.* (W. S. Douglas) p. lxxi, God has riddled the hale creation, and flung the riddlings on Ellisland! 1824 T. Hogg *The Carnation* 34 The coarse parts or riddlings..would not pass through the sieve. 1844 H. Stephens *Bk. Farm* III. 1125 The riddlings, or small potatoes, are used on the farm. 1866 Blackmore *Cradock Nowell* xxxvi, Small-coals men..buy the crushings and riddlings by the sack. 1894 *Labour Commission Gloss.*, Riddlings, the portions of lime rejected from the slaking because they are too coarse or strong or ill-burned.

transf. 1824 Galt *Rothelan* III. 117 It was in truth an epitome of the world—the riddlings of all nations. 1851 Madden *Shrines & Sepulchres* II. 544 The riddlings of society in the sea-ports, and the capitals.

3. = Reckling.

1850 *Jrnl. R. Agric. Soc.* XI. ii. 598 There is generally one small pig in every litter, called the riddling.

Ri·ddling, *ppl. a.* [f. Riddle *v.*[1] + -ing [2].]

1. Speaking in riddles; uttering or dealing in riddles; ambiguous or enigmatic in expression.

1591 Shaks. 1 *Hen. VI*, ii. iii. 57 This is a Riddling Merchant for the nonce. 1592 — *Rom. & Jul.* ii. iii. 56 Ridling confession, findes but ridling shrift. 1655 Fuller *Ch. Hist.* x. xvii. 37 That ridd'ling Letter brought him the first notice thereof. 1748 Melmoth *Fitzosborne Lett.* (1749) I. 10 Your grave friend..who reproached you..for your riddling genius. 1838 J. Sterling *Ess.*, etc. (1848) I. 205 He intimated the state of the case in these riddling lines. 1869 Tennyson *Coming Arthur* 401 He [Merlin] laugh'd.., and answer'd me In riddling triplets of old time.

2. That is or presents a riddle; dark, enigmatic, obscure, puzzling.

1627 Donne *Serm.* v. 45 Under that..Riddling Distemper. *Ibid.* 47 Riddling and entangling Perplexities of the Schooles. 1654 Whitlock *Zootomia* 558 When the most intricate and ridling Articles of our Creed shall shine in glorious and undoubted satisfactions. 1718 Rowe tr. *Lucan* vii. 27 Perhaps, the riddling Visions of the Night With Contrarieties delude our Sight. 1789 T. Twiss *Treat. Poetry* (1812) II. 325 *note*, Dante has a riddling metaphorical expression of the same kind. 1837 C. Wordsw. *Misc.* (1879) I. 5 Mural arabesques of Japanese jugglery, or riddling hieroglyphics. 1856 R. S. Vaughan *Mystics* (1860) II. xiii. i. 251 Its material, remote and riddling to the lower apprehension of common minds.

3. That expounds riddles; divining.

1590 Spenser *F. Q.* iii. xi. 54 She..could not construe it By any ridling skill, or commune wit. 1827 Hood *Midş. Fairies* lviii, Purblind men..In riddling wonder his great bones survey. 1865 Swinburne *Chastelard* i. ii. 31 A..riddling skill at love.

Hence **Ri·ddlingly** *adv.*

1593 Donne *Sat.* ii. 8 Wks. (Grosart) I. 29 Poetry..like the Pestilence or old fashion'd loue It [doth] ridlingly catch men and doth remove Neuer. a 1631 — *Lett. Persons of Honour* (1651) 79, I..am riddlingly subject to two contrary wracks, sinking and oversetting. 1875 Browning *Aristoph. Apol.* 296 Heyday! How riddlingly that hint returns.

Riddock, -uck, obs. variants of Ruddock.

Riddour, variant of Reddour *Obs.*

Riddyl(l, variants of Ridel *sb. Obs.*

Ride (raid), *sb.*[1] [f. Ride *v.*

ME. *ride* (only in *Gen. & Ex.* 3950) is app. to be taken as a derivative from the stem *rīd-*: cf. Du. *rit*, MLG. *rid, rit*, G. *ritt*, Da. *ridt*.]

1. a. An excursion or journey in some vehicle or conveyance, now esp. a public one; † a drive.

1779 Mrs. Harris in *Priv. Lett. Ld. Malmesb.* (1870) I. 433 Your father and I intend driving every day to the camp. 'Tis a fine ride. 1800 Helena Wells *Constantia Neville* II. 15 Taking a ride with the nurse and child. 1808 Eleanor Sleath *Bristol Heiress* I. 54 Miss Williams should..take a ride thither in Lady Harcourt's carriage. 1840 Thackeray *Catherine* vii, A ride in a 'bus to Richmond. 1894 S. Fiske *Holiday Stories* (1900) 30 To..enjoy his company during my car-ride up town.

b. A turn or spell of riding.

1815 Scott *Guy M.* ix, He had often promised the child a ride upon his galloway. 1859 Tennyson *Elaine* 827 'Alas,' he said, 'your ride hath wearied you. Rest must you have'. 1898 Florence Montgomery *Tony* 10 A few hours' bicycle ride in the country.

c. One of the districts into which a coast is divided for purposes of excise. Also *ride-officer.*

1858 Simmonds *Dict. Trade, Ride-officer*, an exciseman. 1885 *Civilian* 3 Jan. 133/1 The breaking of Rides and Divisions affects no grade in the Service to the same extent as Assistants.

d. (See quot.)

1851 Mayhew *Lond. Labour* I. 175/2 The trotting butcher is..not likely to be succeeded by any in the same line, or—as I heard it called—'ride' of business.

e. *U.S.* (See quot.)

1859 Bartlett *Dict. Amer.* (ed. 2) 365 A stream is said to be 'out of ride' when it is past fording [on horseback].

2. a. A road or way made for riding on horseback, esp. through a wood; a riding. **b.** *spec.* The riding-course in Hyde Park, London.

a. 1805 *Trans. Soc. Arts* XXIII. 139 Each separate division of the wood..including fences, rides, and bog. 1856 'Stonehenge' *Brit. Rural Sports* i. i. vii. 64/1 In flying,..they may always be seen to take the same ride or break in the trees. 1864 J. Payn *Sir Massingberd* 14 Coming slowly along a long, broad 'ride',..was a youth of seventeen. 1898 Hewlett *Forest Lovers* xvi, She..crossed open rides in fear what either vista might set bare.

b. 1814 *Sporting Mag.* XLIII. 220 The ride being intended for the recreation of Noblemen, Gentlemen, &c. 1869 M. Arnold *Epil. Lessing's Laocoön*, We..reach'd the ride Where gaily flows the human tide.

3. A batch of mounted recruits.

1833 *Regul. & Instr. Cavalry* i. 51 The Ride moves forward, preserving the dressing. 1896 *Daily News* 17 Jan. 3/3 The primary object of Lord Wolseley's visit was to inspect the 'rides'. *Ibid.*, Four selected rides of first-class recruits, who negotiated the jumps..with their arms folded.

4. A saddle-horse; a mount.

1787 W. Marshall *Rur. Econ. Norf.* (1795) II. 386 Gloss., *A Ride*, a common name for a saddle-horse. 1904 *County Gentleman* 16 July 2096/3 Messrs. Ward's Stella, who in her day was a beautiful ride.

5. *transf.* A surging motion.

1821 Ainslie *Land of Burns* 207 The rack an' the ride o' the restless tide.

Ride (raid), *sb.*[2] *dial.* [Perh. f. Ride *v.*: see sense 10.] The band or strap of a hinge for a door, gate, etc., fitting on to the hook.

1522 *MS. Acc. St. John's Hosp., Canterb.*, Paied for a lytyll ryde for a hasse. 1591–2 in *Archæol. Cantiana* XVI. 186 For makinge a newe doore..the rydes, nayles and Woork. 1703 T. N. *City & C. Purchaser* 245, 10 pair of Hooks and Rides for Doors. 1838 Holloway *Prov. Dict.*, *Rider*, the iron hinges fixed on a gate by means of which the gate is hung on the hooks in the post. 1853–87 in dial. glossaries (Kent, Surrey, Sussex).

Ride, *sb.*[3] *dial.* [See Wride *sb.*] (See quot. 1669.)

1669 Worlidge *Syst. Agric.* 275 A Ride of Hazel, or such like Wood, is a whole plump of Sprigs or Frith, growing out of the same Root. 1890– in dial. glossaries (Yks., Glouc., E. Anglia).

Ride, obs. f. Reed; var. Rithe, stream.

†**Ride**, *a.*[1] *Obs. rare.* Also **ryde.** [Of obscure origin: poss. for Unride, but cf. also MLG. *ryde* violent (Theutonista).] Of blows: Violent, severe.

In *Bruce* vi. 288 the Edinb. MS. has *roid* by mistake for *ride.* It is doubtful whether *rydde men* in the alliterative *Morte Arthur* 4117 belongs here.

1375 Barbour *Bruce* xii. 557 Ther men mycht se..mony a riall rynmyll ryde Be roucht thair apon athir syde. c 1400 *Land Troy Bk.* 9271 Then myȝt men se strokes ride, Gregeis feld on eche a syde. c 1470 *Gol. & Gaw.* 500 Yit sall I..reve thame thair rentis, with routis full ride.

†**Ride**, *a.*[2] *Obs.*[−1] [f. by substitution of *not* for *un-* in Unride.] Small, slight.

c 1462 *Wright's Chaste Wife* 524 As he cam by hys hows syde He herd noyse that was nott ryde.

Ride (raid), *v.* [Common Teutonic: OE. *rīdan* (*rād, ridon, geriden*), = OFris. *rīda* (mod. Fris. *ride*), MDu. *rīden* (Du. *rijden*), OS. *-rīdan* (MLG. *rīden, ryden*), OHG. *rītan, rîten* (G. *reiten*), ON. *rīða* (Norw. and Sw. *rida*, Da. *ride*). The pre-Teut. stem *reidh-* is represented by OIr. *riadaim* I travel, *riad* journey, Old Gaulish *rēda* chariot. OF. *rider, ryder* (Godef.) is prob. from Flemish.]

A. Inflexional forms.

1. *Inf.* (and *Pres.*). 1 rīdan, 2–4 riden, 3–5 ryden, 5 rydyn; 3–7 ryde (4 ryede), 5–7 *Sc.* ryd (6 rid), 3– ride.

c 900 tr. *Bæda's Hist.* iv. iii, Heht hine Theodor biscop ridan. a 1000 *Riddles* lxxx. 7 (Gr.), Hwilum ic on wloncum wicge ride. c 1205 Lay. 432 Þa lette he riden vnirimed folc. c 1330 R. Brunne *Chron. Wace* 14818 An hauene hit is, schipes in to ryde. c 1350 *Ipom.* 1164 Where thou shalte goo or ryede. 1390 Gower *Conf.* I. 53 On his bunting as he cam ride. c 1440 *Promp. Parv.* 433/2 Rydyn, *equito.* 1483 *Cath. Angl.* 307/2 To Ryde, *equitare.* 1533 Gau *Richt Vay* 36 He sal rid apone ane ass. 1585 T. Washington tr. *Nicholay's Voy.* i. viii, Camels..they doe..lade, and ryde vppon. 1601 Shaks. *Twel. N.* iii. iv. 318 Marry Ile ride your horse as well as I ride you. 1639 *Sc. Acts Parl.* (1814) V. 249 To ryde solemnlie to Parliament.

b. 3 *sing. pres. ind.* 1–5 rit, 4–5 rytt, 4 ritt.

c 888 K. Ælfred *Boeth.* xxxiv. § 7 Nan mon forðy ne rit [etc.]. c 1000 Ælfric *Gram.* v. (Z.) 10 Hwa rit into ðam port? a 1225 *Hali Meid.* 18 Þe deofle..rit ham. 13.. *Sir Beues* (A.) 1260 In is wei forþ a rit. 1393 Langl. *P. Pl.* C. i. 186 Wher he ryt oþer rest. c 1400 [see B. 4].

2. *Pa. t.* **a.** 1 rád, 2–5 rad (3 ræd), 3– rade, 5– raid (5–6, 9 red, 6 rayde, 9 rayd, raidd, reayde, reead, ryad, etc.).

After 1300 these forms are only northern and Scottish.

a 900 tr. *Bæda's Hist.* iii. ix, Sum mon rad be þære stowe. c 1123 *O. E. Chron.* (Laud MS.) an. 1123, Se king rad in his der fald. c 1205 Lay. 19516 Octa him ut ræd. a 1300 *Cursor M.* 11425 Quer þai rade [*v.r.* rad] or yode. 1375 Barbour *Bruce* xiv. 329 Toward Odymsy syne thai rayde. c 1440 *Alph. Tales* 310 He rade his ways. 1535 Stewart *Cron. Scot.* III. 533 He raid ouir all Scotland. 1594 in Dalziel *Scot. Poems 16th C.* II. 347 Back wt him I red. 1615 Sir W. Mure *Misc. Poems* xiv. 4 Quhill he liued, to Pluto [he] raid post. 1785 Burns *Mauchline Lady*, Where'er I gaed, where'er I rade. 1816 Scott *Old Mort.* xxvii, They..rade through the country, couping and selling a' that they gat.

β. 3–8 (9 *dial.*) rod, 4–5 rood, 6 roode, rodde, 6–7 road(e, 4– rode (9 *dial.* raud, rwode).

c 1200 *Trin. Coll. Hom.* 89 Ure helende rod þerone. c 1275 in *O. E. Misc.* 39 He..rod vppe on asse. 1390 Gower *Conf.* I. 202 He tok his hors and rod anon. c 1420 *Sir Amadace* (Camden) vi, Amadace..Rode furthe opon his way. 1536 Wriothesley *Chron.* (Camden) I. 51 Then she roode to Hunsdone agayne. 1565 Cooper *Thes.* s.v. *Alcoranum*, The asse, that Jesus rodde on. 1570–6 Lambarde *Kent* (1826) 359 He roade to London. 1653 Holcroft *Procopius, Goth. Wars* ii. 51 As the Romans rod back. a 1700 Ken *Hymnoth.* Poet. Wks. 1721 III. 42 On a pale Horse lean as himself, he rod. 1761 Gray *Odin* 3 Down the yawning steep he rode. 1863 W. C. Baldwin *Afr. Hunting* 324 We rode a weary way.

γ. *pl.* 1 ridon(e, rid-, riod-, reodan, 3 reoden, 3–5 riden, 4 rydden; (also *sing.*) 5–6 ryd(de, 7 rydd, 6–7 ridde, 6– rid; 6 rydyde.

Beowulf 3170 Þa ymbe hlæw riodan hildedeore. c 900 *O. E. Chron.* (Parker MS.) an. 871, Þæs ymb iii. niht ridon ii. eorlas up. c 1127 — (Laud MS.) an. 1127, Hi ridone on swarte hors. c 1205 Lay. 5507 Þat Romanisce floc riden [c 1275 reoden] heom bi-hinden. 13.. *Coer de L.* (W.) 4025 These rydden in the vawmewarde. c 1374 Chaucer *Troylus* i. 473 Wher-so men wente or riden. c 1489 Caxton *Blanchardyn* 83 So longe rydde blanchardyn. 1523 Ld. Berners *Froissart* I. xii. 12 And so [they] ryd forth on theyr iourneis. 1599 Hakluyt *Voy.* II. i. 15 His troopes..rid backe vpon the spurre. 1627 *Lisander & Cal.* ii. 33 The same footman..also ridde. 1714 Steele *Lover* No. 11 He rid an Hour and a half. 1823 Byron *Juan* xiii. xxiii, Henry rid Well, like most Englishmen. 1852 Thackeray *Esmond* ii. v, He rid to the end of the village.

3. *Pa. pple.* **a.** 3 (h)iriden, 4–5 riden (5 -in, -yn), 5 rydin, -yn, reden, -yn(e, -yng: 5 *Sc.* ryddin, 6 rydden, *Sc.* ridne, 6–7 *Sc.* riddin(e, 5– ridden (9 *dial.* rudden).

c 1205 Lay. 24855 Heo beoð hider iriden. 1375 Barbour *Bruce* xiv. 326 Scottis men..in the forest War ryddin. c 1400 Maundev. (Roxb.) 3, I hafe many tymes..riden it. 1461 *Paston Lett.* II. 4 My brother is redyn to Yarmowth. 1568 Grafton *Chron.* II. 328 We haue ridden so nere. 1596 Dalrymple tr. *Leslie's Hist. Scot.* x. 406 Four myl scho had not ȝit ridne. 1639 *Sc. Acts Parl.* (1814) V. 254 These who..have..riddine before him. 1649 Milton *Eikon.* 5 A natural sottishness fit to be abus'd and ridd'n. 1741 Berkeley in Fraser *Life* (1871) 274 To be ridden and hood winked by the Pope. 1839 Fr. A. Kemble *Resid. Georgia* (1863) 265, I have ridden ..over it in every direction.

β. 4 i-ride, y-ride, 5 i-ryde; 4 ride, 4–6 ryde; 4, 6–7 ridde, 4–6 ryd, 7– rid (9 *dial.* red).

c 1330 *Arth. & Merl.* 3093 (Kölbing), Þei he fer hadde yride. 1390 Gower *Conf.* III. 181 This Consul..was into the feldes ride. c 1450 *Solomon's Bk. Wisdom* 250 So fer to haue iryde. 1568 Grafton *Chron.* II. 306 They had not ryd halfe a league. 1664 H. More *Exp. 7 Epist.* 130 They have not rid upon white Horses. 1703 Farquhar *Inconstant* i. i, We have rid a swinging pace. 1798 Jane Austen *Northang. Abbey* x, He has rid out this morning with my father.

γ. 6– rode, 7 (9 *dial.*) rod.

1597 Shaks. 2 *Hen. IV*, v. iii. 98 Helter skelter haue I rode to thee. a 1699 Lady Halkett *Autobiog.* (Camden) 10 And had Rod up and downe that part of the country. 1788 *Trifler* No. 18 We might in a few years behold a sweepstakes rode by women. 1835 Moore *Mem.* (1856) VII. 92 Tom having rode thither direct. 1856 Emerson *Eng. Traits, Result*, The swarms which..have sailed, and rode, and traded.

B. Signification.

I. *intr.* **1.** To sit upon, and be carried by, a horse or other animal; to move about, make one's way, or journey upon horseback (or, in mod. use, on a cycle).

Freq. const. *on, upon*, †*of*, the horse, etc., and with prepositional or adverbial complements, as *at, against, over, to*; *away, forth, on, out, up*, etc.

Beowulf 1893 Landweard..him toȝeanes rad. a 900 tr. *Baeda's Hist.* iii. xxviii, Nalæs ridende on horse, ac..on his fotum gangende. c 1000 *Ags. Gosp.* Matt. xxi. 5 Þin cyning..rit uppan tamre assene. 1154 *O. E. Chron.* (Laud MS.) an. 1137, Ȝif twa men oþer iii. coman ridend to an tun. c 1200 Ormin 6966 Þatt follc rideþþ onn a der Þatt iss Dromeluss nemmnedd. c 1250 *Gen. & Exod.* 3953 Ðus rideð forð ðis man for-loren. c 1320 *Sir Tristr.* 179 Þo rouland to hem rade, Oȝain him gun þai ride. c 1380 *Sir Ferumb.* 1548 Alday þai riden & noȝt ne aliȝt. c 1430 *Syr Gener.* (Roxb.) 129 What knight is yon That rideth of Gwynanes stede? 1470–85 Malory *Arthur* ix. xxviii. 382 He rydeth wel that neuer fylle. 1553 T. Wilson *Rhet.* (1562) 72 And so ridde awaie, as faste as his horse could cary him. a 1599 Spenser *F. Q.* vii. vii. 43 Lastly came cold February, sitting In an old wagon, for he could not ride. 1617 Moryson *Itin.* i. 240 We..rode over the place of burial of the Turks. 1658 Franck *North. Mem.* (1821) 146 He carelessly rid along to view the country. 1722 De Foe *Hist. Plague* (1754) 181 The Aldermen in Person, and on Horseback frequently rid to such Houses. 1782 Cowper *J. Gilpin* 251 And, when he next doth ride abroad, May I be there to see! 1825 Scott *Talism.* i, The long steel-headed lance,..which, as he rode, projected backwards. 1850 R. G. Cumming *Hunter's Life S. Afr.* (ed. 2) I. 98 At which time they can easily be ridden into. 1894 A. Morrison *M. Hewitt* iii, Osmond, I believe, was better than any man riding now.

fig. 1393 Langl. *P. Pl.* C. iii. 184 And ich my-self cyuyle and symonye my felawe Wollen ryden vp-on rectours. 1529 Skelton *Bouge of Court* 472, I hate these wayes..: Were I as you, I wolde ryde them full nere. 1581 Burne *Disput.* 156 Ye Ministeris in Scotland ryd als neir thame [the Anabaptists] as ye may. 1613 Purchas *Pilgrimage* (1614) 216 Riding on quite through the Alphabet. c 1742 Gray *Hymn to Ignorance* 28 She [Ignorance] rode triumphant o'er the vanquish'd world. 1803 Jane Porter *Thaddeus* xxii, A young guardsman, who had just rode into her heart. 1869 Hughes *Alfred* 160 A desire to ride off on side issues.

b. In pa. pple. with *is, was*, etc. Now *arch.* or *Obs.*

c 1205 Lay. 19495 Alle heo..þat hider beoð iridenen. 1375 Barbour *Bruce* xix. 596 His men..War rydyn in-till a randoune. 1390 Gower *Conf.* III. 181 This Consul..was into the feldes ride. 1461 *Paston Lett.* II. 4 My brother is redyn to Yarmowth. 1599 Shaks. *Hen. V*, iv. iii. 2 The King himselfe is rode to view their Battaile. 1633 Ford *Love's Sacrifice* ii. ii, Now when the duke is rid abroad. 1742 Richardson *Pamela* III. 308 My Brother..and Mr. H. are all rid out together. 1761 Mrs. F. Sheridan *S. Bidulph* II. 296 One of the gentlemen is rid off for a surgeon. 1778 Miss Burney *Evelina* lxiii, Is he rode out this morning?

c. With sbs. denoting the rate of progress, as *to ride a* (*good*) *pace, gallop*, etc.

Also *to ride whip and spur*: see Whip *sb.*

13.. *Coer de L.* 2773 Our men..gunnen to ryde swythe gret randoun. c 1374 Chaucer *Troylus* v. 60 Forth she rit..a pas. a 1425 *Cursor M.* 11657 (Trin.), Marie folewed ridyng good paas. 1470–85 Malory *Arthur* i. xxii. 69 He rode a grete wallop tyll he cam to the fontayne. 1523 Ld. Berners *Froissart* I. 228 He..rode forthe a gret galoppe. 1549– [see Post *adv.*]. 1617 [see Gallop *sb.* 3 a]. 1703 Farquhar *Inconstant* i. i, We have rid a swinging pace from Nemours. 1749 Fielding *Tom Jones* xvi. ii, He..rode a full gallop. 1788 Clara Reeve *Exiles* II. 3 Adam..rode full speed up to the house.

d. With other complements, as *to ride bodkin, booty, pillion*, etc. *To ride for a fall*, to ride recklessly, so as to be liable to a fall; usu. *fig.*

To ride grub: (see Grub *sb.* 3 b).

1631 Shirley *Love's Cruelty* iii. ii, Would you durst no better ride booty at the horse-match! 1654 Whitlock *Zootomia* 424 If Fortune had been one of the Jockeys, and rid booty, the three to one hath lost the Prize. 1760 Sterne *Tr. Shandy* iv. xvi, To have so many jarring elements..riding triumph in every corner of a gentleman's house. 1861 Pycroft *Agony Point* I. xix. 294 Her maid by special agreement riding bodkin all the way. 1895 *Pall Mall Mag.* Mar. 520 Roy Branton, who rode pillion, had an opportunity of studying his pilot's pretty hair. 1898 *Allbutt's Syst. Med.* V. 910 Her husband..has ridden for his falls.

e. To serve in a cavalry regiment.

1711 Steele *Spect.* No. 152 ⁋ 3, I remember two young Fellows who rid in the same Squadron of a Troop of Horse. 1796 *Grose's Dict. Vulgar T.* s.v. *Ride*, He rode private, i.e. was a private trooper. 1806 M. Noble *Hist. Eng.* III. 314 Wishing to have a commission he rode as a private in the guards. 1849 Macaulay *Hist. Eng.* ix. II. 516 The military ardour which he had felt twenty-eight years before, when he rode in the Life Guards.

f. Of persons: To weigh when mounted.

1836 Sir G. Stephen *Search of Horse* i, Be it known, then, that I ride rather more than twelve stone. 1857 G. Lawrence *Guy Liv.* iii, He rode little under fourteen stone.

g. To sit on and manage a horse properly.

1881 Miss Braddon *Asphodel* I. 167 He can stick in his saddle somehow,..but he can't ride.

2. *spec.* To go on horseback upon a warlike expedition; to go upon, take part in, a raid or foray. In later use *Sc.* and now *arch.*

c 1205 Lay. 432 Þa lette he riden vnirimed folc. c 1330 R. Brunne *Chron. Wace* (Rolls) 2583 Þou may haue hit..To ride ȝyf þat þou wile bygynne. c 1386 Chaucer *Prol.* 45 Fro the tyme that he first bigan To riden out, he loued chiualrie. 1412–20 Lydg. *Chron. Troy* i. 603 Alysaundre..Rood in his conqueste..With al his hooste. c 1420 *Brut* (E.E.T.S.) 321 Þe Frensshe men breken þe pees..ryding on the Kinges ground. 1523 Skelton *Garl. Laurel* 196 Theis people..ryde and rinne from Carlyll to Kente. 1550 *Reg. Privy Council Scot.* I. 86 That nane of thame tak upoun hand to ryde in Ingland or to mak ony perturbatioun thairintill. 1561 *Ibid.* 186 Gif it be thocht expedient..that ony persone..be riddin on and invadit be fyre and swerd. a 1639 Earl Monm. *Mem.* (1759) 119 Not so few as two hundred..that were ever ready to ride with them to all actions. 1802 Scott *Border Minstrelsy* (1869) 249 The rapacity of this clan, and of their allies, the Elliots, occasioned the popular saying, 'Elliots and Armstrongs ride thieves all'. 1824 — *Redgauntlet* let. xi, As if a tenant could have helped riding with the Laird. 1897 Ld. E. Hamilton *Outl. Marches* 7 Others of the Scots rode into England.

b. To go in procession on horseback. In later use *Sc.* (cf. 13 b).

1466 *Cal. Rec. Dublin* (1889) I. 324 For procession and pylgrymage, and hors for rydyng at Corpus Christi. 1495–6 in *Rep. Hist. MSS. Comm.* IV. 212 All they of the xxxiiij that hath be maire shall ride in scarlett ayenste the Kynge.

1530 *Ibid.* 216 Mr. Mayer and all his brethern shall ride on Seynt Osmundy's evyn..in maner folowyng. 1606 *Sc. Acts Parl.* (1814) IV. 279 The haill Estaittis of Parliament will convene and ryd with thair honouris with crowne, sword, and sceptour. 1637–50 Row *Hist. Kirk* (Wodrow) 223 Mr. David Lindesay..and Mr. Johne Spotiswood..did ryde in Parliament as commissioners fra the Kirk. *Ibid.*, At Perth the Parliament did not ryde.

3. To mount the female; to copulate. (Cf. 16.)

Now only in low and indecent language.

a 1250 *Owl & Night.* 494 He ne rekþ of clennesse,..Ac euerich vp oþer rideþ. 1377 Langl. *P. Pl.* B. xi. 329 As whan þei hadde ryde in rotey tyme. 1393 *Ibid.* C. xiv. 154 Man and his make..out of reson..ryde. 1523 Fitzherb. *Husb.* § 37 He maye suffre his rammes to goo with his ewes ..to blyssomme or ryde whan they wyll. a 1659 Osborn *Charac.* Wks. (1673) 664 In case any ride double, he proclaims them Man and Wife. 1719 D'Urfey *Pills* IV. 141, I will..find out a Russet-coat Wench and a Hay-cock, And there I will ride Tan-tivee.

4. To be conveyed, to travel or journey, *in* a wheeled or other vehicle. (Cf. Ride *sb.*[1] 1 a.)

Now chiefly of travelling in public vehicles: see Drive *v.*

a 1300 *Cursor M.* 4657 To ride ai quar in kinges char. 1362 Langl. *P. Pl.* A. iv. 27 On a wayn witti and wisdame I-feere Folweden hem..And Riden faste. c 1400 Maundev. (1839) 241 He rytt in a Charett with 4 Wheles. a 1548 Hall *Chron., Hen. VIII*, 238 b, Her Grace..alyghted out of her Chariot in the whych she had rydden all her long iourney. 1634 Milton *Comus* 135 Stay thy cloudy Ebon chair, Wherin thou rid'st with Hecat', and befriend Us thy vow'd priests. 1667 Pepys *Diary* 13 Feb., I rid with my sword drawn in the coach. 1746 H. Walpole *Lett.* (1846) II. 132 The Duke has given Brigadier Mordaunt the Pretender's coach, on condition he rode up to London in it. 1788 Mrs. Hughes *Henry & Isabella* IV. 165, I am going to send the coach to town.., and..you may ride in it. 1810 *Splendid Follies* II. 19, I never rode with such a disagreeable driver in my life. 1844 S. R. Maitland *Dark Ages* 307 Gerard.. always rode in a carriage, reading his own books. 1886 Elworthy *W. Somerset Wordbk.* s.v., You can jump in the train and ride so var's [= far as] Norton.

b. To be carried or drawn about (*on* or †*in* a cart, hurdle, rail, etc.) as a punishment. (Cf. Cart *v.* 2.)

1556 *Chron. Grey Friars* (Camden) 70 A tayler of Fletstret & hys syster rydde in a carte abowte London..for avoutre. 1632 Massinger *City Madam* iii. i, I'll hang you both, you rascals! I can but ride! 1777 Sheridan *Sch. Scand.* ii. i, Ah! many a wretch has rid on a hurdle who has done less mischief. 1872 De Vere *Americanisms* 194 Riding on a rail..is a savage punishment inflicted by an excited crowd upon a person who has exasperated a community by some real or fancied outrage.

c. *Mining.* (See quots.)

1860 *Eng. & Foreign Mining Gloss.* (ed. 2) 61 *Ride*, to ascend up the pit. 1883 Gresley *Gloss. Coal-mining*, *Ride*, to be in a cage or bowk whilst descending or ascending a pit-shaft.

5. To sit or be carried *on* or *upon* something after the manner of one on horseback; †to hang *on* the gallows, *in* a rope, etc.

Beowulf (Z.) 2446 Swa bið ȝeomorlic gomelum ceorle to ȝebidanne þæt his byre ride ȝiong on galȝan. c 888 K. Ælfred *Boeth.* xxxvi. § 6 Ða cild ridað on hiora stafum. 1500–20 Dunbar *Poems* xxxv. 34 Jonet the weido on ane bussome rydand. a 1585 Montgomerie *Flyting* 96 Goe ride in a raipe for this noble new ȝeir. 1596 [see Fiddlestick 1]. 1605 Shaks. *Mach.* iv. i. 138 Infected be the Ayre whereon they ride. 1610 — *Temp.* ii. i. 115, I saw him beate the surges vnder him, And ride vpon their backes. 1667 Milton *P. L.* ii. 663 The Night-Hag, when call'd In secret, riding through the Air she comes. 1697 Dryden *Virg. Georg.* ii. 212 Nor in so vast a length our Serpents glide, Or rais'd on such a spiry Volume ride. 1834 Mudie *Brit. Birds* (1841) I. 109 The bird rides lightly on the wind. 1892 Rider Haggard *Nada* 7 She carried my little sister Baleka riding on her hip.

fig. 1601 Shaks. *All's Well* iii. ii. 112 O you leaden messengers, That ride vpon the violent speede of fire. 1784 Cowper *Task* i. 369 Constant rotation of th' unwearied wheel That nature rides upon. 1812 Byron *Ch. Har.* i. xxxviii, Death rides upon the sulphury Siroc. 1816 *Ibid.* iii. xliv, Their breath is agitation, and their life A storm whereon they ride.

6. a. Of horses, etc.: To admit of being ridden; to carry a rider; to 'go'.

1470–85 Malory *Arthur* ii. vi. 82 Thenne he..was ware of a damoysel that came ryde ful fast as the hors myghte ryde. 1598 Rous *Thule* O 3, The horse whose back the tamer oft bestrides, At length with easie pace full gently rides. 1632 Lithgow *Trav.* vi. 298 The Dromidory..will ride aboue 80. miles in the day. 1692 *Lond. Gaz.* No. 2792/4 A Chesnut Gelding,..rideth gracefully, paceth a little. 1714 *Ibid.* No. 5195/4 Commonly Rides with her Tongue out of her Mouth. 1805 *Spirit Publ. Jrnls.* IX. 352 Can you get me a nag That will ride very quiet?

b. Of a stream: To allow of crossing on horseback. *Sc.*

17.. *Jock o' the Side* xxvii, Honest man, will the water ride? 1890–1 in *Eng. Dial. Dict.*

c. Of land: To be of a specified character for riding upon; to bear riding upon.

1864 M. J. Higgins *Ess.* (1875) 200 Its soil..rode quite as clean and sound as the Nottinghamshire dukeries ride. 1889 Crommelin & Brown *V. Vyvian* III. xii. 207 Rain..made the ground ride soft.

II. 7. Of vessels: To lie *at* (or †*on*) anchor; also *to* (or †*at*) *an anchor.*

Beowulf 1882 Sægenga bad aȝendfrean, se þe on ancre rad. 1390 Gower *Conf.* I. 197 This grete Schip on Anker rod. 14.. *Sailing Directions* (Hakl. Soc.) 15 A man that ridith in the way of odierne at an ankre. 1447 Bokenham *Seyntys* (Roxb.) 175 He the shypmen preyid hertyly..To rydyn on ankyr a whyl ther by. 1598 [see Anchor *sb.*[1] 6 a]. 1624 Capt. Smith *Virginia* (1629) 56 Long they shot, we still ryding at an anchor without there reatch. 1698 T. Froger *Voy.* 4 The next day we likewise rode at anchor. 1745 P. Thomas *Jrnl. Anson's Voy.* 276 We rid fast at an Anchor. 1812 J. Wilson *Isle of Palms* ii. 185 He sees a stately vessel ride At anchor in a bay. 1894 Hall Caine *Manxman* iii. x. 160 A schooner riding to an anchor in the bay.

fig. 1824 Scott *Redgauntlet* ch. iii, This..snug little road-stead, where I thought to ride at anchor for life.

b. *ellipt.* in the same sense. Also with compl., as *to ride across, a-peak, hawse-full*, etc. (see these words).

a 1300 *K. Horn* 146 Bi þe se side Hi leten þat schup ride. c 1385 Chaucer *L. G. W.* 968 *Dido*, But forth they gon & lafte his schepis ryde. 14.. *Sailing Directions* (Hakl. Soc.) 13 Yif ye be bounde to Caleis haven and Ride in the Doowns. 1497 *Naval Accts. Hen. VII* (1896) 252 In Portesmouth haven..the seid Ship rode betwyxt the Towre & the dokke. 1555 Eden *Decades* (Arb.) 381 In the rode yow shall ryde in .xiij. or .xiiij. fadomes, good owes & sande. 1627 Capt. Smith *Seaman's Gram.* ix. 45 To ride betwixt wind and tide, is when the wind and tide are contrary and of equall power. 1668 *Lond. Gaz.* No. 286/4 Sir Thomas Allen with his squadron is still riding at Spithead. 1712 W. Rogers *Voy.* (1718) 244 Capt. Dampier..never rode where we did, which is the best and only good road in the island. 1793 Smeaton *Edystone L.* § 148 The Buss had rode perfectly easy in the gale of wind. 1832 Marryat *N. Forster* xiii, The shipping..with a heavy strain on their cables were riding to the S.E. gale. 1867 Smyth *Sailor's Word-bk.* 39 Ground which is suitable..for ships to ride safely upon.

fig. 1666 *Third Advice to a Painter* 27 Well George, in spite of them thou safe dost ride.

†**c.** In phr. *to ride admiral. Obs.*

1660 Hickeringill *Jamaica viewed* (1661) 72 He's unfit to ride Admiral of a Fleet, that cannot carry the Flag at home. 1697 *Phil. Trans.* XIX. 597 The Ambassador was Complemented by Sir Jeremy Smith, then riding Admiral.

fig. 1689 Shadwell *Bury Fair* i. i, What lady rides Admiral here at Bury. 1713 M. Henry *Admonit. Drunkards* Wks. 1853 I. 95/2 When reason is sunk and drowned, rage and passion will ride admiral.

8. To float or move upon the water; to sail, esp. in a buoyant manner.

a 1000 *Genesis* (Gr.) 1392 He þæt scip beleac. Siððan wide rad wolcnum under ofer holmes hrincg hof seleste. a 1300 *Cursor M.* 1843 On þe streme þat arche can ride. 13.. *Propr. Sanct.* (Vernon MS.) in *Herrig's Archiv* LXXXI. 112/82 Whil crist in þat hul abod, Þe schip a-midde þe see rod. c 1400 Maundev. (Roxb.) xxii. 102 Fra þis citee may men ride in schippe or in bate by þat riuer. c 1420 *Chron. Vilod.* 3486 [They] reden hamewarde fast wt seylle & hore. 1555 Eden *Decades* (Arb.) 66 Saylinge by the coastes of Iohanna..he rode lyttell lesse then eyght hundreth miles. 1643 *Jrnl. Ho. Comm.* 13 Apr., To appoint a Ship to ride Northward, for the Relief of Berwick. 1688 Prior *Ode Exodus* iii. ii, Yet cease to hope thy short-liv'd Bark shall ride Down spreading Fate's unnavigable Tide. 1757 Gray *Bard* 72 While proudly riding o'er the azure realm, In gallant trim the gilded vessel goes. 1839 *Civil Eng. & Arch. Jrnl.* II. 450/2 This is effected by what is called riding on the wave. 1850 Thackeray *Pendennis* l[i]x, It has been prosperous, and you are riding into port. 1887 Bowen *Virg. Æneid* v. 862 Not less safely and swiftly the fleet rides over the wave.

9. Of things: To move in any way, to be carried or supported, after the manner of one riding.

In fig. uses hardly distinct from sense 5.

a 1586 Montgomerie *Misc. Poems* xxviii. 41 The busteous blast..Quhilk ramping ouer his riggis ryds. 1600 Surflet *Countrie Farme* iii. liii. 553 A droppe of oile dropped vpon your hand, if there be any moisture,..it will swim and ride aloft vpon the same. 1674 Fairfax *Bulk & Selv.* 196 None of those rayes of other atoms..come riding or drilling through both. 1771 Luckombe *Hist. Print.* 322 That the Carriage may ride so far out, as that the irons of the Tympan may just rise free. 1840 *Civil Eng. & Arch. Jrnl.* III. 5/2 The eccentrics are then brought into the position shown in the drawing, riding clear of the rails. 1862 *Catal. Internat. Exhib., Brit.* II. No. 2466 By means of the straps..[they] can be carried on the shoulders, where they ride the lightest.

fig. 1593 Shaks. 3 *Hen. VI*, iii. iii. 18 But let thy dauntlesse minde still ride in triumph, Ouer all mischance. 1605 — *Lear* i. ii. 198 On whose foolish honestie My practises ride easie. 1679 Dryden *Troil. & Cress.* iv. ii, Hinder us not,..My blood rides high as his. 1770 Jenner *Placid Man* i. iv, Philosophy and love for his brother had so long rode triumphant. 1848 Mrs. Gaskell *M. Barton* ix, The distress which was riding..among the people.

b. Of the heavenly bodies: To appear to float in space. Freq. with *high.*

1632 Milton *Penseroso* 68 To behold the wandring Moon, Riding neer her highest noon. 1667 — *P. L.* i. 769 In spring time, when the Sun with Taurus rides. 1727 Dyer *Grongar Hill* 11 While Phœbus, riding high, Gives lustre to the land and sky. 1825 Scott *Talism.* xii, The moon rode clear and high in heaven. 1871 C. Kingsley *At Last* i, To see Sirius ..riding high in a December heaven.

fig. 1821 Shelley *Hellas* 273 The lamp of our dominion still rides high.

10. To rest or turn *on* or *upon* something of the nature of a pivot, axle, or protuberance.

1597 Shaks. 1 *Hen. IV*, v. ii. 84 If life did ride vpon a Dials point. 1606 — *Tr. & Cr.* i. iii. 67 Strong as the Axletree In which the Heauens ride. 1665 *Phil. Trans.* I. 10 Between the Fore-leggs and the Hinder-leggs was a great Stone on which the Calf rid. 1683 Moxon *Mech. Exerc.*, *Printing* xvi, He..tries whether or not the Lyner ride upon the part that was extuberant. 1805 Dickson *Pract. Agric.* I. Pl. xi, An Improved Harrow, with running bulls: By this contrivance the harrows are prevented from riding on each other. 1844 H. Stephens *Bk. Farm* I. 170 Try by a searching motion of the legs and feet whether any of the stones ride upon others.

b. To extend or project *over* something.

1601 Holland *Pliny* II. 594 To bind the stones wel, they ought in alternatiue course to ride and reach one ouer another halfe. 1634 T. Johnson *Parey's Chirurg.* xv. viii. (1678) 332 You must have a care [in fracture] that the bones ride not one over another. 1880 Huxley *Crayfish* 98 The pleura ..even ride over the posterior edges of the branchiostegites.

c. *ellipt.* in previous senses. Also *Naut.* of a rope (see quot. 1769).

1683 Moxon *Mech. Exerc.*, *Printing* xvi, To know which of them it is that Rides, or is extuberant, he uses the Liner. 1741 *Phil. Trans.* XLI. 564 In oblique Fractures of the Thigh, where the Bones are apt to ride. 1769 Falconer *Dict. Marine* (1780) s.v. *Riding*, A rope is said to ride, when one of the turns by which it is wound about the capstern or windlass lies over another, so as to interrupt the operation of heaving. 1784 J. Barry in *Lect. on Art* (1848) 141 Their toes are even pressed close together, and ride, as is seen in the feet of those that have been accustomed to wear tight shoes. 1844 H. Stephens *Bk. Farm* I. 170 When the stones ride, they have not been properly bedded in mortar. 1862 *Catal. Internat. Exhib., Brit.* II. No. 2799 It prevents the chain from riding, in paying out or heaving in. 1888 Jacobi *Printer's Voc.* s.v., When leads are pieced in wide measures they sometimes shift and overlap each other. They are then said to 'ride'.

11. a. *dial.* (See quot.)

1736 Pegge *Alph. Kent* (E. D. S.) 43 The raddishes 'ride', i.e. rise upon the stomach. 1887–93 in Kent and Surrey glossaries.

b. Of a dress, etc.: To work *up* so as to form folds or creases; to ruck.

1854 Miss Baker *Northampt. Gloss.* s.v., A badly made gown rides up more in one place than another. 1881 Mrs. P. O'Donoghue *Ladies on Horseback* 253 Short-skirted hunting-habits frequently ride up.

III. *trans.* **12.** To traverse on horseback; to ride over, along, or through: **a.** a certain distance. Also with cognate accusative, as *to ride a race, course, circuit, match*, etc.

c 1290 *S. Eng. Leg.* I. 49/80 He ne rod bote wel luyte wei, are he feol to grounde. a 1300 *Cursor M.* 11385 Elles moght not kinges thre Haf raght to ride sa ferre wai. c 1400 *Avow. Arth.* xxxii, Gawan hase my rawunsun made For a course that he rode. 1596 Shaks. 1 *Hen. IV*, iii. iii. 222 [We] haue thirtie miles to ride yet ere dinner time. 1599 in Fowler *Hist. C. C. C.* (O. H. S.) 352 The Fellows whom the rest appoint for the time to ride the circuit with the President. 1617 Sir E. Mountagu in *Buccleuch MSS.* (Hist. MSS. Comm.) I. 231 My brother..rid in two days a hundred miles. 1736 Pegge *Alph. Kent* (E. D. S.) 43 *To ride tythe*, ..to ride about for that purpose [of collecting tithes]. 1778 Foote *Cozeners* i, But were you to see him on the turf, at Newmarket,..Why, he has rid matches. 1782 Cowper *Gilpin* 115 He rides a race! 'Tis for a thousand pound! 1808 Scott *Marmion* i. xxii, We can neither hunt, nor ride A foray on the Scottish side. 1853 G. J. Cayley *Las Alforjas* II. 152 These poor wretches, who have to ride three or four hundred miles on end without stoppage of more than two hours.

b. a road or way, a street, a stretch of ground or country, etc.

1377 Langl. *P. Pl.* B. iv. 42 Þanne resoun rode faste þe riȝte heiȝe gate. ? a 1400 *Morte Arth.* 52 Whene he thys rewmes hade redyne and rewlyde the popule. 1464 *Paston Lett.* II. 145 It is seid that the Kyng wold ride Sussex, Kent, Essex, Suffolk, and Norffolk, and so to the Parlement. 1525 Ld. Berners *Froissart* II. 181 The duke rode the fronters of Galyce. 1592 Marlowe *Massacre Paris* i. iv, The Lord High Admiral, Riding the streets, was traitorously shot. 1648 *Lanc. Tracts Civil War* (Chetham Soc.) 263 Twelve miles of such ground as I never rod in all my life. 1706 Baynard *Cold Baths* ii. 376, I rode, quoth he, the cold Hills every Morning. 1787 'G. Gambado' *Acad. Horsem.* (1809) 43 In riding the road, observe [etc.]. 1850 Mrs. Browning *Rime of Duchess May* lxv, May the sweet Heavens hear thee plead If he rides the castle-wall. 1876 Morris *Sigurd* iv. 309 Three days they ride that country.

c. a boundary, etc., for the purpose of maintaining or reviving a clear knowledge of it. (See also quot. 1877.)

1421 *Cov. Leet-bk.* 33 Hit is ordenyd that the fraunches of this Cite be Ryden this yere within the monyth of May. 1476 *Rental-bk. Cupar-Angus* (1879) I. 204 He sal kep and defend our marchis as tha war redyng at the last ridyng. 1572 in W. H. Turner *Select. Rec. Oxford* (1880) 341 The francheses of this Cytie shalbe ryd according to auncient custom. 1733 W. Crawford *Man. agst. Infid.* (1836) 106 To ride the marches between good and evil. 1798 *Statist. Acc. Scot.*, *Dunkeld* XX. 441 It is customary to ride the marches, occasionally, so as to preserve in the memory of the people the limits of their property. 1816 in Picton *L'pool Munic. Rec.* (1886) II. 316 The day on which the Liberties were rode. 1877 *N. Linc. Gloss.* s.v., The surveyor of the court of sewers is said to ride the drains when he goes to overlook them.

d. a river or water. Also in *fig.* use.

1501 Douglas *Pal. Hon.* ii. xxxix, We raid the swift riuer Sparthiades. a 1670 Spalding *Troub. Chas. I* (1850) I. 198 They could not ride the water, it being great. 1774 D. Jones *Jrnl.* (1865) 18 Several ferries are kept on it, tho' it may frequently be rode in the summer season. 1790 Scott *Let.* 6 Aug. in *Lockhart*, The servant was waiting there with our horses, as we were to ride the water. 1896 *E. Durh. Gloss.*, He's not safe to ride the water with.

13. a. To pursue, proceed upon (one's way, etc.) on horseback.

In OE. with genitive, as *þonne rideð ælc his weȝes* (Ælfred *Oros.* i. i. 21).

a 1300 *Cursor M.* 11427 Þir kinges rides forth þair rade. 1390 Gower *Conf.* I. 94 Ryd thanne forth thi wey. c 1450 *Merlin* 202 Thei rode so her iournes till thei com to Tarsaide. 1509 Hawes *Past. Pleas.* xxxv. (Percy Soc.) 184, I..made me ready for to ride my waye. 1642 Slingsby *Diary* (1836) 83 He rode up..and shot a towsman on ye neck..., and so rid his ways.

b. *Sc.* and *north.* To open (Parliament, a fair) by a procession (cf. 2 b). Now only *Hist.*

[a 1557 *Diurnal Occurrents* 13 Vpoun the xvj day of Maij (1529), thair was ane greit conventione..and raid all the Parliament to the tolbuith.] 1604 *Reg. Privy Council Scot.* VII. 2 Act ordaining the Estates to attend the Earle of Montrose, Commissioner, for ryding the Parliament. a 1670 Spalding *Troub. Chas. I* (1850) I. 40 The Parliament wes riddin agane by the King and his thrie estaitis. 1826 Hone *Every-day Bk.* II. 1655 A procession moves from the principal alehouse for the purpose of riding the fair, as they call it. 1838 A. Shortreed *Let.* in Lockhart *Scott* vi, The honest burghers of Jedburgh..have suffered the ancient privilege of 'riding the Fair', as it was called.., to fall into disuse.

14. *To ride out.* Of a ship: To sustain (a gale or storm) without great damage or dragging anchor.

1529 [implied in b]. 1603 Knolles *Hist. Turks* (J.), The sea was grown so rough, that the admiral was not able longer to ride it out with his gallies. a 1674 Clarendon *Hist. Reb.* xv. § 53 That Fleet had rode out all the Winter Storms before Cadiz. 1748 *Anson's Voy.* iii. ii. 318 The wind blew..with such fury, that we..despaired of riding out the storm. 1790 Beatson *Nav. & Mil. Mem.* I. 183 His Majesty's ship, the Rippon, alone rode out the gale. 1840 R. H. Dana *Bef. Mast* xiii. 31 The ship Lagoda..rode out the gale in safety. 1854 G. B. Richardson *Univ. Code* v. (ed. 12) 58 Ride it out if possible.

b. In fig. contexts. Also, to endure or sustain successfully, to last to the end of, †to spend, pass.

1529 More *Dyaloge* ii. Wks. 195/1 [He] went ouer the sea..to se flaunders, & France, and ryde out one somer in those countrees. 1597 Sir W. Slingsby in Sir H. Slingsby *Diary* (1836) 251, I thank God my brother and myself ride it out at an anker. 1622 Malynes *Anc. Law-Merch.* 99 If this man will not ride out (as they say) the time of the payment of the Bills. 1646 H. P. *Medit. Seige* 4 He that rides out a Seige, and gives his Enemy the check, beares away the greatest honour. a 1676 Hale *Prim. Orig. Man.* (1677) 86 It could not be, for then he could never have ridden out an eternal period. 1710 Palmer *Proverbs* 64 A courtier should ..foresee a storm, know whether he is able to ride it out [etc.]. 1808 Jefferson *Writ.* (1830) IV. 112 We shall have safely rode out the storm. 1877 Spurgeon *Serm.* XXIII. 254 That our faith may ride out every storm of doubt.

c. With ellipsis of *out. rare.*

1718 Steele *Fish Pool* 165 She..rid the storm, and our trusty pilot jumped into the river and took her up. 1799 *Hull Advt.* 17 Aug. 4/2 The ship was riding flood, and the wind from the southward. 1885 *Western Mail* 23 Feb. 3/5 A large sailing vessel was sighted dismasted, riding the storm.

transf. 1814 Scott *Wav.* lxvi, He will of course repair to the Duchran without loss of time, there to ride quarantine for a few weeks.

IV. *trans.* **15.** To sit or be carried upon, to go or travel upon (a horse, or other animal of burden); to manage or control while seated on.

a 1225 *Hali Meid.* 13 Þa ilke sari wrecches..beoð þe deueles eaueres, þat rit ham & spureð ham to don al þat he wile. c 1440 *Ipomydon* 1005 The whiche, I say,...Will..many an hors ryde to dede. Or I come there, þat me most nede. c 1440 *Alph. Tales* 510 Som tyme a man had ane ass, & he rade hur. 1508 Dunbar *Tua mariit wemen* 331, I wald haif ridden him to Rome. 1542 Udall *Erasm. Apoph.* 230 By his ieoperdyng to ride the vnbroken horse Bucephalus. 1601 Holland *Pliny* I. 221 The Sarmatians..prepare their horses two daies before,..and thus they will ride them gallop 150 miles an end. 1665 Boyle *Occas. Refl.* iii. viii, Upon the taking up his Horses from Grass, and giving them Oats before they were to be Ridden a Journey. 1718 Lady M. W. Montagu *Let. to Mrs. Thistlethwayte* 1 April, I never rid a horse so much at my command in my life. 1774 Goldsm. *Nat. Hist.* (1862) I. i. 252 They are rid generally in a snaffle, without spurs. 1863 Kingsley *Water-Bab.* 10 Grimes rode the donkey in front. 1872 Tennyson *Holy Grail* 642 He dash'd across me—mad, And maddening what he rode.

fig. 1590 Shaks. *Mids. N.* v. i. 119 Lys[ander]. He hath rid his Prologue, like a rough Colt. 1610 — *Wint. T.* i. ii. 94 Our prayses are our Wages. You may ride's With one soft Kisse a thousand Furlongs. 1647 Ward *Simp. Cobler* 36 There is a set of Bishops..Will ride the Devill off his legs, and break his wind. 1700 T. Brown tr. *Fresny's Amusem.* 52 When any Humour Takes in London, they Ride it to Death before they leave it. 1804 G. Rose *Diaries* (1860) II. 111 Mr. Hiley Addington rode him hard with fulsome eulogiums. 1887 *Spectator* 9 Apr. 491/2 The dangers of such a method when ridden to death by inferior imitators.

b. *Racing.* To urge (a horse) to excessive speed; to 'squeeze'.

1853 *Sat. Rev.* 23 May 657 When Fordham had charge of Buckstone in the St. Leger, it was said that he began to 'ride' his horse too soon. 1888 *Pall Mall G.* 2 July 5/2 He will pretend to be 'riding' (that is squeezing) his horse.

16. To mount or cover (the female). (Cf. 3.)

1500–20 Dunbar *Poems* xxxii. 6 Syne till his breist did hir imbrace, And wald haif riddin hir lyk ane rame. 1607 Topsell *Four-f. Beasts* (1658) 473 Partitions wherein..they may easily abide alone..., and especially that one may not ride another. 1665 Sir T. Herbert *Trav.* (1677) 173 These ..in shallow plashes croak and ride one another outrageously. 1694 Motteux *Rabelais* v. (1737) 222 They will not be ridden, tupp'd, and ramm'd. 1808 *Compl. Grazier* (ed. 3) 16 It not unfrequently happens that cows (after taking the bull) will ride each other.

17. a. Of the nightmare, witches, etc.: To sit upon (a person); to use (one) as a horse.

1597 Shaks. 2 *Hen. IV*, ii. i. 83, I will haue some of it out againe, or I will ride thee o' Nights, like the Mare. 1601 Holland *Pliny* II. 283 The black grains..help those that be ridden with the night-mare. 1649 in Campbell *Balmerino* (1899) 386 Margaret Boyd..declares that hir goodman..went to deathe with it, that Elspeth Seith and other two did ryde him to deathe. 1693 C. Mather *Wond. Invis. World* (1862) 169 The Men they commonly laid asleep at the place, whereto they rode them. 1880 [see Nightmare *sb.* 1]. 1865 Tylor *Early Hist. Man.* 7 Such expressions as being ridden by a hag, or by the devil.

fig. 1775 Burke *Sp. Concil. Amer.* Wks. 1842 I. 195 All the while, Wales rid this kingdom like an *incubus*; it was an unprofitable and oppressive burthen.

b. To have the mastery of (one); to manage at will; to oppress or harass; to tyrannize over; to dominate completely.

Partly transf. from prec., and partly from sense 15.

1583 Babington *Commandm.* (1590) 265 Their weaknes.. haunting them and riding them as wee vse to speake in euery corner. 1589 Puttenham *Eng. Poesie* iii. xix. (Arb.) 218 When with proud and insolent words, we doo vpbraid a man, or ride him as we terme it. 1664 Pepys *Diary* 13 Aug., The Duke [of York]..did cry..' All the world rides us, and I think we shall never ride anybody'. 1680 Otway *Orphan* ii. i, I have seen enough to..ride him to advantage as I please. 1731 Bowman *Serm. Vers.* 9 The ambitious giddy priesthood Rides you, as you the tamest beast wou'd. 1806–7 J. Beresford *Miseries Hum. Life* ii. Concl., Rogues! they are ridden by prejudices. 1837 Emerson *Wks.* (Bohn) II. 175 The tradesman..is ridden by the routine of his craft. 1903 *Strand* Nov. 511/2 Grim fear rode him day and night.

18. To sit upon, to be carried or borne along upon (something).

Also in various phrases denoting forms of punishment, as *to ride the cowl-staff, hatch, horse, mare, stang*, etc. (see the sbs.).

1597 Shaks. *Lover's Compl.* 22 Some-times her leueld eyes their carriage ride, As they did battry to the spheres intend. 1629 H. Burton *Babel no Bethel* Pref. Ep. 11 To perswade them, that they ride Peters ship, wherein they may safely arriue at the holy Land. 1781 Cowper *Retirement* 535 Till he that rides the whirlwind checks the rein. 1782 J. Wolcot (P. Pindar) *Ode to R. A.'s* i, That easy.. thing Rid by the Chancellor, yclep'd a Sack. 1816 Byron *Prisoner of Chillon* xiii, The eagle rode the rising blast. 1839 *Civil Eng. & Arch. Jrnl.* II. 450/2 A passage boat.. riding the wave. 1890 *St. Nicholas* May 584 Not infrequently the boys will 'ride' a log down the current.

b. Of things: To rest upon, esp. by projecting or overlapping.

1713 *Phil. Trans.* XXVIII. 189 Its Root Leaves deeply cut, and those which ride the Stalk whole and round. 1754 Smellie *Midwifery* I. 84 Sometimes the *Vertebræ* which compose the *Sacrum* ride one another, and form a large protuberance. 1801 J. Wolcot (P. Pindar) *Tears & Smiles*, Of spectacles that rode his nose. 1899 *Allbutt's Syst. Med.* VI. 230 Very often an embolus is caught in an arterial bifurcation, which it rides with a prolongation extending into each branch.

19. *To ride down*: To exhaust (a horse) by excessive riding; to overtake by pursuit on horseback; to charge, or collide with, so as to overthrow.

1709 *Lond. Gaz.* No. 4580/1 The Czar was very active.., and rid down four Horses. 1850 Thackeray *Pendennis* xxxix, He..was on the point of riding down a large old roomy family carriage. 1856 C. J. Anderson *Lake Ngami* 266 The ostrich is also at times ridden down by a single horseman.

fig. 1670 Eachard *Cont. Clergy* 111, I could procure hundreds, that should ride both sun and moon down, and be everlastingly yours. 1840 R. H. Dana *Bef. Mast* xvii, When officers are once determined to 'ride a man down', it is a gone case with him. 1874 Green *Short Hist.* ix. § 9. 700 The support of the Commons..enabled Harley to ride down all resistance.

b. *Naut.* (See quot. 1867.)

1841 R. H. Dana *Seaman's Man.* 120 To bend or bear down by main strength and weight; as, to ride down the main tack. 1867 Smyth *Sailor's Word-bk.*, *Riding-down*, the act of the men who throw their weight on the head of a sail to stretch it.

20. To cut (an animal) *off* or *out* from the herd by skilful riding.

1843 *M. A. Richardson's Historian's Table-bk., Leg. Div.* I. 14 The horsemen rode off the bull from the rest of the herd until he stood at bay. 1850 R. G. Cumming *Hunter's Life S. Afr.* (ed. 2) I. 253, I have often ridden the best bull out of the herd. 1863 W. C. Baldwin *Afr. Hunting* 262, I shortly came across another troop of bulls...I rode out one with beautiful long teeth.

b. *Polo.* To edge *off* (an opponent).

1897 *Outing* XXX. 487/1 Play into your comrades' hands, and watch out to edge or ride-off an adversary.

c. To hunt (an animal) on horseback.

1889 Baden-Powell *Pigsticking* 2 It became usual to get up a sweepstake before starting to ride a boar.

21. To cause (one) to ride.

1711 *Fingall MSS.* in *10th Rep. Hist. MSS. Comm.* App. V. 160 Ginckle designed to ride his cavalry into the breach when made. 1876 'Mark Twain' *Tom Sawyer* x, The villagers had a strong desire to..ride him on a rail for body-snatching. 1895 Crockett *Cleg Kelly* xli, Gin the wives noo-adays had ony spunk in them ava', ye wad be mobbed and ridden on the stang, my man!

b. To convey in a cart or other vehicle. Chiefly *U.S.*

1687 *Ann. of Albany* (1850) II. 97 It is very requisite that there be fyre-wood rid to ye indian houses. 1692 *Ibid.* 121 Ye sheriffe..is required to see each trader ride a load of wood to the said house. 1837 S. R. Maitland *Vol. Syst.* 287 If he is a rich man, he may ride his family away, every Sunday. 1859 Bartlett *Dict. Amer.* (ed. 2) 364, I heard a witness..testify that he had 'rode some hogs from the wharf to the store'.

c. To keep (a ship) moored; to secure or maintain at anchor.

1726 Shelvocke *Voy. round World* 267 Having nothing to ride the bark with, we were obliged to keep the sea. 1793 Smeaton *Edystone L.* § 254 The buss was now rode by this buoy. 1803 Nelson 22 Dec. in Nicolas *Disp.* (1845) V. 326 Bays to ride our Fleets in.

d. To run *up* (a sail). *rare*[−1].

1880 *Daily Telegr.* 7 Sept., Waiting for the flash from the commodore's boat to tell them that they can ride up the mainsail.

V. *intr.* **22. Ride and tie.** Of two (or three) persons: To travel with one horse by alternately riding and walking, each one riding ahead for some distance and tying up the horse for the one who comes behind.

1742 Fielding *J. Andrews* ii. ii, They were both setting out, having agreed to ride and tie; a method of travelling much used by persons who have but one horse between them. 1791 Boswell *Johnson* an. 1737, Both of them used to talk..of this their first journey to London. Garrick, evidently meaning to embellish a little, said one day in my hearing, 'We rode and tied'. 1866 Carlyle *Remin.* (1881) I. 176, I never rode and tied (especially with three) before or since. 1868 Holme Lee *B. Godfrey* xxiii, Mervyn and Olive were to ride and tie.

fig. 1805 H. Macneill *Poems* (1844) 114 When folk are sair put, they maun e'en 'ride and tie'.

b. As *sb.* or *adv.* (Sometimes hyphened.) Also *fig.* (see quots. 1826 and 1830).

1791 T. Paine *Rights of Man* i. (ed. 2) 64 It is like what the country people call 'Ride and tie—You ride a little way, and then I'. 1826 Syd. Smith *Wks.* (1859) II. 124/1 It must absolutely be ride-and-tie with them; the butcher must hear the baker in the morning [etc.]. 1830 Miss Mitford *Village* Ser. iv. (1863) 225 Dinah having given to each of the four the half of a year's schooling, upon the principle of ride and tie, little Lucy going one day, and little Patty the next. 1893 Stevenson *Catriona* xiii, We were travelling 'ride and tie'.

c. Used attributively. (With hyphens.)

1809 Malkin *Gil Blas* v. i. ⁋ 9 We journeyed on the ride-and-tie principle. 1824 *Examiner* 434/1 It is a ride-and-tie system with him. 1885 *Scribner's Mag.* XXX. 388/2 By the 'ride-and-tie' method, a horse was yet further economised.

23. *Ride-and-drive*, used attributively.

1865 *Cornh. Mag.* May 558 A good, useful,..ride-and-drive horse. 1900 *Westm. Gaz.* 2 Jan. 5/1 The 'ride and drive' system necessary in the Royal Artillery.

Ri·deable, *a.* Also ridable. [f. Ride *v.*]

1. Capable of being ridden through, over, etc.

1637 Rutherford *Lett.* cxxii. (1664) 234 Till the water fall and the foord be ridable. 1709 J. Lister *Autobiog.* (1842) 45 A man..who had..known when the water was rideable. 1860 C. S. Forbes *Iceland* 103 As for the road, it was..in some places more rideable than in others. 1891 *Field* 19 Dec. 957/1 The grass pastures..were far from rideable.

2. Capable of being ridden or used for riding.

1611 Cotgr., *Chevauchable*, rideable; easie to be rid on. 1820 L. Hunt *Indicator* No. 26 (1822) I. 207 So built with muscle was his chest, So rideable his back. 1850 Smedley *F. Fairleigh* xxxvii, Is there anything rideable to be hired in Hillingford? 1897 *Cyclist Touring Cl. Gaz.* Sept. 358 The tyre when pumped remained rideable for two or three hours.

Hence **Rid(e)abi·lity.**

1899 *Hub* 8 July 322/2 The relation of an up gradient to a down as regards ridability.

Ri·ded, *a. rare.* [f. Ride *sb.*[1] 2 + -ed [2].] Provided with ridings or 'rides'.

1896 Mordaunt & Verney *Warw. Hunt* I. 7 Coughton Park has always been well rided. *Ibid.* 8 Chesterton Wood ..is beautifully rided.

Ri·del, ri·ddel, *sb.* Now only *arch.* Forms: α. 4 rudel, 4–5 ridel(le, rydel(le, 5 rydyl, rydal. β. 4–5 riddell(e, 5 (9) riddel, -yl(l, ryddyll, 6 ryddel. γ. 4–5 redell, 5 redel(e. [a. OF. *ridel*, mod.F. *rideau*.] A curtain; in later use *esp.* an altar-curtain.

α. 13.. *Gaw. & Gr. Knt.* 857 Rudelez rennande on ropez, red golde ryngez. c 1380 *Sir Ferumb.* 2537 Florippe drow a ridel þan þat stod be-fore þe frount. 1395 *E. E. Wills* 5, I bequethe..alle the rydelles and trussynge cofres..that longeth to my chapelle. 1466 in *Archaeologia* L. 42 Item j Rydyl steyned, with a chalix. 1483 *Cath. Angl.* 307/2 Rydelle, *vbi* a curtyn.

β. 1368–9 *MS. Hosteler's Roll, Durham*, In iij Riddell' et i Selour emp. pro uno lecto. 1466 in *Archaeologia* L. 44 Item j Ryddyll of blewe bokrame be hynd the Vicares in the quere. 1517 in Kerry *St. Lawrence, Reading* (1883) 111 Also ij staynyd clothis wt ryddels to þe same.

1908 *Ch. Times* 21 Feb. 241/2 A new high altar..has been erected.., furnished with dossal and riddels, and angels carrying candles, in correct English style.

γ. 1382–3 *Durh. Acct. Rolls* 389 Le Redell' pro magno altari. a 1400–50 *Alexander* 4930 Þe renke within þe redell þan raxsilis his armes. 1466 in *Archaeologia* L. 35 Item j long Redell with ij smalle Redyll[es] at the trinite aucter.

†**Ri·del**, *v.*[1] *Obs. rare.* [a. OF. *rideler* to flow (of blood).] *intr.* To fall, drop.

13.. *E. E. Allit. P.* B. 953 Þe rayn rueled adoun, ridlande þikke, Of felle flaunkes of fyr.

†**Ri·del**, *v.*[2] *rare.* In 5 rydely. [a. OF. *rideler*, f. *ride* wrinkle, fold.] *intr.* To make folds or pleats in (cloth). (Cf. next.)

14.. *Lat. Eng. Voc.* in Wr.-Wülcker 614 *Supero, i, pannum rugare*, to rydely.

†**Ri·deled**, *pa. pple.* and *ppl. a. Obs.* Forms: 4 rydelid, 6 ryddylled; 5 red-, rydlyd, rid-, rydled, 6 riddled. [a. OF. *rideled* (later *ridelé*), pa. pple. of *rideler*: see prec.]

1. Pleated, gathered, arranged in folds.

? a 1366 Chaucer *Rom. Rose* 1235 Lord, it was ridled fetysly. *Ibid.* 1243 The whyte roket rydled faire. 1380 in *Rel. Ant.* I. 41 With her hornes, lockis,..filettis, and wymplis, and rydelid gownes, and rokettis. 1444 *Pol. Poems* (Rolls) II. 217 Lyk a materas redlyd was his coote. *Ibid.* 220 The kevel wroot in his rydlyd coote.

2. Wrinkled.

1530 Palsgr. 447/1 It is a goodly syght to se an olde ryddylled queene to beholde herselfe in a glasse. 1596 Nashe *Saffron Walden* 110 His skin riddled and crumpled like a peice of burnt parchment.

†**Rideling**, *ppl. a.* In 4 rydelande. (Of obscure origin and meaning: cf. Ridel *v.*[1])

13.. *E. E. Allit. P.* C. 254 Thenne he swenged & swaynes to þe se boþem, Bi mony rokkeȝ ful roȝe & rydelande strondes.

Supplement, p. 3873; Corrigenda, p. 4092; Spurious words, p. 4093; Books quoted, p. 4094

† Rideman. *Obs.* [f. RIDE *v.*, or its stem.] A riding bailiff.

Recorded only in Latin form *ridemannus*, pl. *-manni*, rendered by *rideman*, *-men*, in the modern translation accompanying the text.

1258 in *Sel. Pleas Manorial Courts* (Selden Soc.) II. (1888) 53 Idem Rogerus affidavit quod pl[egia] inveniet Ridemanno. 1293 *Ibid.* 72 Unde Ridemanny conqueruntur quod ponunt ibi districtiones. 1294 *Ibid.* 77 Districtus est per tres equos ut Ridemannus testatur.

Rident (rai·dənt), *a. rare.* [f. L. *rīdent-*, *rīdens*, pres. pple. of *rīdēre* to laugh.] Radiantly cheerful, riant.

1609 *Ev. Wom. in Hum.* I. i. in Bullen *O. Pl.* IV, Then most rydent starre, faire fall ye. 1855 THACKERAY *Newcomes* xxiv, A smile so wide and steady—so exceedingly rident, indeed, as almost to be ridiculous. 1859 — *Virgin.* lxxvii, Hetty was radiant and rident.

† Ri·deout. *Obs.*[−1] [f. RIDE *v.* + OUT *adv.*] A bagman; = RIDER 6.

1752 FIELDING *Covent Gard. Jrnl.* No. 33 He was a sort of rider, or rideout to a linendraper at London.

Rider (rai·dəɹ). Forms: 2–4 **ridere** (3 **ridære**, **-are**, **-eare**), 4–5 **rydere**, 5 **rydare**; 3– **rider** (4 **ridir**, 5 **ridar**, 7 ? **ridder**), 4–9 **ryder**; 5–6 *Sc.* **ridar**, **rydar**. [Late OE. *ridere*, = Fris. *rider*, † *rijder*, MDu. *rider(e*, Du. *rijder*), MLG. *rîder*, *ryder*, OHG. *rîtari* (MHG. *rîtære*, *rîter*, G. *reiter*), ON. *ríðeri*, *ríðari*: see RIDE *v.* and -ER[1]. It is uncertain how far the forms were independently developed in these languages.]

I. † 1. a. A knight; a mounted warrior. *Obs.*

c 1085 *O.E. Chron.* (Laud MS.) an. 1085, Se cyng..dubbade his sunu Henric to ridere þær. c 1090 *Ibid.* an. 1090, He beȝeat ma castelas..& þær inne his rideras ȝelogode. c 1205 LAY. 5495 Heo ȝærkeden..twa þusend rideres [c 1275 ridares]. *Ibid.* 9288 Hamun þe ridere smat his aȝene ifere. 1382 WYCLIF *Exod.* xiv. 23 Al the horsyng of Pharao, his chares, and his ryders [1388 knyȝtis; L. *equites*]. a 1400–50 *Alexander* 1054 He fande..Na ridars [*v.r.* ryders] in þa regions, ne rebell bot littill. 14.. *Sir Beues* (E) 1746 He took hys scheeld & hys spere, As it semyd a good rydere. 1596 DALRYMPLE tr. *Leslie's Hist. Scot.* VI. 312 Thay namet him..a noble rydar, frome this stock is the Erle of Rothose.

b. A mounted reaver or raider, a moss-trooper. Cf. *rank rider*, s.v. RANK *a.* 3 b. Now *arch.*

1549 *Compl. Scot.* viii. 74 Sum of ȝou ar be cum neutral men, lyik to the ridars that dueillis on the debatabil landis. a 1639 EARL MONM. *Mem.* (1759) 92, I had intelligence that there was a great match made at foote-ball, and the chiefe ryders were to be there. a 1649 DRUMM. OF HAWTH. *Hist. Jas. V*, Wks. (1711) 99 In Ewsdale eight and forty notorious Riders are hung on growing Trees, the most famous of which was John Armstrong. 1806 SCOTT *Fam. Lett.* 23 Nov., Executions..thinned..the Border riders who had subsisted by depredation.

2. One who rides a horse or other animal (also in mod. use, a cycle); a mounted person. See also ROUGH-RIDER.

a 1300 *Cursor M.* 22015 Neder in strete, waitand hors to stang in fete, to do þe rider fall bi þe wai. 1362 LANGL. *P. Pl.* A. XI. 208 Now is Religioun a ridere and a rennere aboute. c 1440 *Promp. Parv.* 433/1 Rydare, horsman, *equester*. c 1470 HENRY *Wallace* V. 287 Or he was horst, ridaris about him kest. 1583 [see HORSEMAN 1]. 1596 SPENSER *F.Q.* IV. iii. 39 Two grim lyons..Now made forget their former cruell mood, T' obey their riders hest, as seemed good. 1601 R. JOHNSON *Kingd. & Commw.* (1603) 152 Yet euery one is not to be accounted a horse of seruice, no more then euery horseman a rider. 1671 MILTON *P. R.* III. 314 In Mail thir horses clad, yet fleet and strong, Prauncing their riders bore. 1732 LEDIARD *Sethos* II. x. 381 They ran with all their might to see the rider and the horse. 1783 W. THOMSON *Watson's Philip III* (1839) 293 Two hundred and twenty horses, with their riders, miserably perished in one sudden conflagration. 1841 BORROW *Zincali* I. v, I am a bad rider, and to save myself expense, I always walk. 1881 FROUDE *Short Stud.* (1883) IV. II. i. 170 In his younger days he had been a hard rider across country. *transf.* or *fig.* a 1586 MONTGOMERIE *Misc. Poems* xlviii. 184 Neptunus ryders begouth also to ryis. 1588 SHAKS. *L. L. L.* II. i. 121 *Ber.* Your wit..will tire. *Rosa.* Not till it leaue the Rider in the mire. 1658 ROWLAND tr. *Moufet's Theat. Ins.* 929 They [*sc.* bees] carry a most cruel rider on their backs. 1887 MORRIS *Odyss.* I. 8 They ate up the beasts of the Sun, the Rider of the Air.

† b. (See quot.) *Obs.*

1796 *Grose's Dict. Vulgar T.*, *Rider*, a person who receives part of the salary of a place or appointment from the ostensible occupier, by virtue of an agreement with the donor, or great man appointing.

c. *Sc. Law.* A creditor having a 'riding interest'.

1826 BEVERIDGE *Forms of Process* I. 384 As much of the sum..as will pay the debt and claim of the rider. *Ibid.*, A competition may..ensue among these riders.

d. *Rider's bone*, a form of ossification (see quot.).

1891 MOULLIN *Surg.* III. v. 331 The best known example is what is called rider's-bone, developing in the tendon of the adductor longus in those who are accustomed to rough riding.

3. A gold coin, having the figure of a horseman on its obverse, formerly current in Flanders and Holland; also, a gold coin first struck by James II of Scotland and current in Scotland during the 15–16th centuries. (After Du. and Flem. *rijder*.)

1479 in *Cely Papers* (1900) 20 An gylden rydar, iijs vjd. 1482 *Ibid.* 126 Item vj Rydars vjs iiijd, xxxviijs. 1488 *Inv. R. Wardr.* (1815) 1 Item, in ridaris nyne score & aucht ridaris..Item, fyftene Flemis ridaris. 1540 in Pitcairn *Crim. Trials* I. *301 Deliverit to þe said Johnne, in Ridaris, Angelnobillis, and Rois-nobillis. 1617 MORYSON *Itin.* I. 289 Also they coyne gold Lyons, called Riders, whereof each is worth four Flemmish Guldens and a halfe. 1660 in J. Simon *Irish Coins* (1749) 126 The several species, sorts and kinds of coins following, *viz.* The Golden Rider, the Half golden Rider. 1688 HOLME *Armoury* III. 30/1 The Scotch Gold Coin,..a Scotch Rider, or Horseman..; they call it also a Ten Mark Peece. 1727 W. MATHER *Yng. Man's Comp.* 236 Holland Rider, 6s. 10d. 1783 *Ann. Reg.* 193 The states general of Holland..offered a reward of 1000 golden ryders. 1875 JEVONS *Money* 189 In former days many large gold coins, such as..the double ryder, were current.

4. † a. A riding-master; a horse-trainer. *Obs.*

a 1568 ASCHAM *Scholem.* I. (Arb.) 43 Wise riders, by ientle allurementes, do breed vp in them, the loue of riding. 1600 SHAKS. *A. Y. L.* I. i. 14 They are taught their mannage, and to that end Riders deerely hir'd. 1607 TOPSELL *Four-f. Beasts* (1658) 259 The Riders of Ferdinand the first, told him there was a Horse in their Masters stable of seventy year old. 1678 J. WILLIAMS *Hist. Gunpowder Treason* 21 A Gentleman in those parts..broke open the Stables of one Benock, a Rider of great Horses.

b. A jockey or riding lad.

1805 Patent (No. 2809) to Samuel Chifney, of Newmarket, rider. 1810 *Sporting Mag.* XXXVI. 239 William Wilkinson, rider and training groom to Sir Sitwell Sitwell, Bart.

† 5. A ranger of a forest. *Obs.*

1450– [implied in RIDERSHIP]. 1647 HAWARD *Crown Rev.* 50 Rider of the Forrest. c 1710 CELIA FIENNES *Diary* (1888) 40 There is also a Rider of ye Forest who is to see yt all things are secure and well done, and ye timber kept and deer.

† 6. A commercial traveller, a bagman. *Obs.*

1752 [see RIDEOUT]. 1754 SHEBBEARE *Matrimony* (1766) II. 216 Jack Goodfellow, a Rider to Mr. Buckram, a very eminent Haberdasher..in the City. 1791 'G. GAMBADO' *Ann. Horsem.* (1809) 87 That very numerous and brilliant fraternity, called London Riders, or Bagsters; who..make so smart a figure in a country town. 1800 HELENA WELLS *Constantia Neville* (ed. 2) III. 125 The last comer was a rider to a wholesale warehouse in the city. 1837 T. HOOK *Jack Brag* ii, Either a rider to some respectable house in the button line, or a small dealer.

7. A horse (of a specified kind) for riding on; *dial.* a saddle-horse.

1856 OLMSTED *Slave States* 59, I have some horses—none on 'em very good ones, though—rather hard riders. 1887 *Kentish Gloss.* s.v., He kips several riders.

8. *Curling.* A stone driven so as to dislodge other stones blocking the tee.

1891 H. JOHNSTON *Kilmallie* II. 112 This shot,..in curling phrase, was a 'rider', for it cannoned on two of the enemy's stones, and drew in softly to the tee.

II. 9. *Naut.* a. *pl.* An additional set of timbers or iron plates used to strengthen the frame of a ship internally or externally (see quots.).

1627 CAPT. SMITH *Seaman's Gram.* ii. 5 Great ships haue a tier of beames vnder the Orlop..and great posts and binders called Riders from them to the keele. 1688 R. HOLME *Armoury* III. xv. (Roxb.) 37/1 The Riders are great tymbers..which are not properly in the building of the ship but put in to make it the more stronger. 1711 W. SUTHERLAND *Shipbuilder's Assist.* 163 Riders; Pieces fixed on the Inside of the Ship on the In-board Plank, something imitating the Ships Timbers or Ribs. 1769 FALCONER *Dict. Marine* (1780), *Riders*, a sort of interior ribs, fixed occasionally in a ship's hold..,and reaching from the kelson to the beams of the lower-deck, and sometimes higher, in order to strengthen her frame. 1810 *Naval Chron.* XXIII. 112 Standards, top and breadth riders. 1840 *Civil Eng. & Arch. Jrnl.* III. 277/2 Wherever there is an athwartship bulk-head, there is a system of riders worked on the inner surface of this diagonal frame. c 1860 H. STUART *Seaman's Catech.* 67 The frames are bound together diagonally, by a series of iron plates called 'riders', which are let into the timbers and bolted to them. 1874 THEARLE *Naval Archit.* 34 By Lloyd's rules, riders, termed diagonal iron plates, are fitted on the outside of the frames of fir built ships of more than 600 tons.

attrib. 1691 T. H[ALE] *Acc. New Invent.* 47 The heads of the Ryder-bolts.

b. *pl.* A second or upper tier of casks in a hold.

1846 YOUNG *Naut. Dict.* 251 The term Riders is applied also to any tiers of casks stowed above the ground-tier or above any other tier in a vessel's hold. c 1860 H. STUART *Seaman's Catech.* 61 How will you proceed? By stowing the lower or ground tier of tanks, then riders or upper tier.

c. A rope, or turn of one, overlying another.

1841 R. H. DANA *Seaman's Man.* 42 Pass five, seven, or nine turns..directly over these, as riders. The riders are not hove so taut. 1875 KNIGHT *Dict. Mech.* 1939/1.

10. *Mining.* a. = HORSE *sb.* 11. Also *attrib.*

1653 MANLOVE *Lead Mines* 258 Soletrees, Roach, and Ryder. 1747 HOOSON *Miner's Dict.* K iv, Rider-joynt runs along as the Vein, and varies according as the Rider grows thicker or thinner. 1813 BAKEWELL *Introd. Geol.* (1815) 279 There is generally what is called a rider or mass of mineral matter between the ore of very strong rake veins. 1867 SMYTHE *Coal* 25 When they here and there meet a 'rider' inclined the other way, they form a loose mass of coal, very dangerous to unwary colliers.

b. A thin seam of coal or deposit of ore overlying a principal seam or lode.

1875 KNIGHT *Dict. Mech.* 1939/1. 1883 GRESLEY *Gloss. Coal-mining* 203.

c. (See quot.)

1883 GRESLEY *Gloss. Coal-mining* 203 *Rider*, a guide-frame for steadying a bowk in a sinking pit.

11. An additional clause tacked on to a document after its first drafting; *esp.* a supplementary and amending clause attached to a legislative Bill at its final reading. † In early use *rider-roll*.

1669 Nov *Rep. & Cases* (ed. 2) 84 That which is certified shall be annexed to the Record, and is called a Rider-roll. 1684 MANLEY *Cowell's Interpr.* s.v. *Roll*, A Ridder-roll is a Schedule, or small piece of Parchment, added to some part of a Roll or Record. a 1734 NORTH *Exam.* III. vi. § 60 Colonel B—h..carried a Rider as it is called, being a Clause to be added at the last Reading. 1765 BLACKSTONE *Comm.* I. 182 If a new clause be added, it is done by tacking a separate piece of parchment on the bill, which is called a ryder. 1833 HT. MARTINEAU *Manch. Strike* 34 If ever Parliament passes a Bill to regulate wages, we must have a rider put to it. 1888 BRYCE *Amer. Commw.* I. xviii. I. 251 The House..tried to coerce the Senate into submission by adding 'riders', as they are called, to appropriation bills.

b. A corollary or addition supplementing, or naturally arising from, something said or written.

1813 BRAND *Pop. Antiq.* ii. 237 He only inflamed the rage for the Toast, to which they afterwards tacked the following Rider. 1829 *Examiner* 252/2 Such a 'rider' to his work would be inestimable to young students. 1868 HELPS *Realmah* xvii, The rider which Sir John Ellesmere was good enough..to add to the title of my essay. 1885 *Law Times* LXXIX. 93/1 This then is the inseparable rider to the rule that the death of the master dissolves the contract of apprenticeship.

c. *Math.* (See quot. 1851.)

1851 F. J. JAMESON *Solution Of Senate-House 'Riders'* Introd. v, The Board conceives that these Examples, or Riders, to use the more familiar term, afford a searching test of the merits of the candidates. *Ibid.* vi, Riders we define to be original questions arising either directly or indirectly out of the propositions to which they are appended. 1887 *Camb. Local Exam.*, 29*th Rep.* 18 A large number of candidates sent up correct solutions of the easier riders.

d. A clause added as a corollary to a verdict.

1884 *Daily News* 2 Sept. 3/2 The jury returned a verdict ..with a rider that some restrictions ought to be placed on the indiscriminate sale of revolvers. 1886 G. ALLEN *Maimie's Sake* xxix, The jury..added a rider condemning the use of paraffin lamps..in the Hospital.

e. *transf.* of material objects. *nonce-use.*

1859 SALA *Gas-light & D.* xxx, A curiously-bladed knife with a boat-hook and a corkscrew by way of rider.

12. An object bestriding or surmounting another. In various technical uses:

† a. A leaden pipe opening out of a larger one and running parallel with it above. *Obs.*[−1] b. *Agric.* A bar of wood for connecting two or more harrows. c. = RIDE *sb.*[2] d. *U.S.* The top bar of a zigzag fence. e. A small sliding piece of aluminium or other metal placed upon the beam of a precision balance and used to determine minute differences of weight. f. *Typog.* (see quot.). g. *Med.* In a tintometer: (see quot.). h. *Med.* A clot (of blood) obstructing a bifurcated vessel.

a. 1726 *Phil. Trans.* XXXIV. 79 From the Middle of the Leaden Pipe. (call'd a Rider, from its being laid along on the Main or Conduct Pipe) there goes another Leaden Pipe.

b. 1793–1813 *Rep. Agric.* 69 (E.D.D.), All the harrows being fastened together with a lay over, provincially a rider. 1799 J. ROBERTSON *Agric. Perth* 97 In some places of the Carse of Gowrie and Stormont the harrows have what are called riders...Wherever the double coupling iron is used, there is no need of these riders. 1844 *Jrnl. R. Agric. Soc.* V. I. 171 Two or three harrows are kept together by a rider, or overlay, and the horses draw abreast.

c. 1833 LOUDON *Encycl. Archit.* § 1805 The door to the coal-place to be 1½-inch proper ledged; hung with hooks and riders (bands), fixed in the wall.

d. 1836 *Backwoods of Canada* 188 Breachy cattle..will even toss down a fence with stakes and riders for protection. a 1862 THOREAU *Cape Cod* ix, Birchen riders, highest of rails. 1885 *Harper's Mag.* Apr. 702/2 The 'riders' of his fences were always heavy and straight.

e. 1875 *Encycl. Brit.* III. 263/1 The rider in this case must, of course, form part and parcel of the beam. 1886 CUMMING *Electricity treated Exp.* 44 A rider reading thousandths of an ounce on the beam of a grocer's balance.

f. 1890 in *Cent. Dict.* 1891 POWELL *Southward's Pract. Print.* lii. 463 Riders, i. e., rollers working on rollers, materially assist distribution and good inking.

g. 1898 *Allbutt's Syst. Med.* V. 433 The riders are small squares of tinted glass provided for the reading of the degrees between each standard gradation...For the reading of the units nine riders are required.

h. 1899 *Allbutt's Syst. Med.* VI. 234 Cylindrical, elongated, or flat emboli are usually caught as riders at an arterial bifurcation.

13. *Gardening.* A standard tree used temporarily to cover the upper part of a wall. *Sc.*

1826 in Loudon *Encycl. Gard.* (ed. 2) 479 Against low walls, currants, gooseberries, and raspberries may be placed instead of riders. 1824 LOUDON *ibid.* 478 Dwarfs are understood to be the permanent trees, and riders merely temporary plants introduced to fill up the upper part of the wall. 1860 N. PATERSON *Manse Garden* (ed. 9) 65 Let the whole be interspersed with riders, if your wall be eight feet high.

14. *Artillery.* (See quot.)

1802 JAMES *Mil. Dict.*, *Rider*, in artillery carriages, a piece of wood somewhat higher than broad, the length equal to that of the body of the axle-tree, upon which the side-pieces rest, in a four-wheel carriage.

15. *attrib.*, as † *rider millstone*, the upper millstone; *rider-bolt* (see 9 a), *-joint* (see 10 a, quot. 1747), *-kelson* (see KELSON 1 b), *-roll* (see 11, quots. 1669–84), *-stone* (see quot. 1686). Also *rider-like* adv.

1548 THOMAS *Ital. Dict.*, *Macina*, the rider milstone. 1686 ROBT. PLOT *Nat. Hist. Staffordshire* iv. § 17. 159 About Dudley where the Iron-stone lyes..of a considerable thickness, it is divided..into divers measures of different denominations....4. The Rider-stone. 1879 MRS. H. B. PAULL tr. *Swiss Fam. Robinson* xxi, Fritz sat rider-like on the now tamed onager.

Ridered (rai·dəɹd), *a.* [f. prec.]

1. *Geol.* Of rocks: Traversed by riders.

1833–4 PHILLIPS *Geol.* in *Encycl. Metrop.* (1845) VI. 771/1 A rock thus penetrated by strings is sometimes said to be ridered. *Ibid.*, In many rocks these ridered parts are very greatly altered from their original state.

2. *U.S.* Of a fence: Strengthened with riders.

1890 C. L. NORTON *Political Americanisms* 95 Such a fence is 'staked and ridered' when stakes are driven in the

angles and a rider laid on top of them. 1891 *Harper's Mag.* Mar. 544/2 The staked and ridered rail-fence.

Ri·deress. *rare.* [f. RIDER + -ESS.] A female rider; a horsewoman.

1849 THACKERAY *Out of Town* vi, Where are the dear rideresses, above all? 1881 *Contemp. Rev.* Oct. 545 Freyja ..once was a Cloud Rideress and a Swan Virgin.

Riderless, *a.* [-LESS.] Having no rider.

1847 in WEBSTER. 1862 H. KINGSLEY *Ravenshoe* liv, He caught a riderless horse, and the cornet mounted. 1883 GILMOUR *Mongols* xxv. 304 His horse arrives riderless, and he is found dead on the plain.

fig. 1874 LISLE CARR *J. Gwynne* v, Excluding for a time all dreamy wanderings of the riderless mind.

Ri·dership. *rare.* [f. RIDER + -SHIP.] The position or office of a rider; † rangership (*obs.*).

1450 *Rolls of Parlt.* V. 192/1 The office of Ridership within the Forest of Delamare. 1485 *Ibid.* VI. 382/1 The Office of Rydership or Maister Forster of the Forest or Chase of Dertmore. 1821 W. TAYLOR in *Monthly Rev.* XCIV. 493 He ventured to propose the abolition of all riderships.

† Ride-way. *Obs.*[−1] [Cf. MSw. *ridhvägh* (Sw. *ridväg*), G. *reitweg*, Du. *rijweg*.] A bridle-path.

c 1435 *Torr. Portugal* 598 A lytyl whyll be-fore the day He toke in to a Ryde-wey Hyme self to meche care.

Ridge (ridʒ), *sb.*[1] Forms: α. 1 **hrycg**, **hrygc** (**hryg-**, **hryc-**), 3–4 **rug**, 4 **reg**; *dat.* 1 **hrycge**, 3–6 **rugge** (3, 5 **ruge**), 6 (9 *dial.*) **rudge**, 4–5 **regge**. β. 1 **hricg**, **hric(c)**, **hrig-**, **ricg**, **rihg**; *dat.* **hricge**, **hrigge**, **rh-**, 4–6 **rigge**, **rygge** (5 **ryge**), 5–6 **rydge**, 6–7 **ridg**, 5– **ridge**. See also RIG *sb.*[1] [Common Teut.: OE. *hrycg*, = OFris. *(h)reg* (mod. Fris. *rêch*, *rich*), MDu. *ruc* (Du. *rug*), *ric*, *rec*; also *rugge*, *rigge*, *regge*, MLG. *rugge* (LG. *rügge*, *rüg*), OHG. *hrucci*, *rucki*, etc. (MHG. *rucke*, *rücke*, G. *rücken*), ON. *hryggr* (Norw. and Sw. *rygg*, Da. *ryg*):—Teut. **hrugja-z*, of uncertain relationship.

The normal ME. representative of OE. *hrycg* is *rigge* (later *ridge*), with the variants *rugge* (= *rudge*) in south-western dialects, and *regge* (= *redge*) in Kentish. The northern and Sc. form is RIG *sb.*[1] In some cases it is uncertain which form is denoted by the spelling *rigge*.]

† 1. The back or spine in man or animals. *Obs.*

α. c 897 K. ÆLFRED *Gregory's Past. C.* i. 28 Ðonne ȝebiʒð ðæt folc hira hrycg to hefeȝum byrðenum. c 1000 ÆLFRIC *Saints' Lives* xxxiv. 1047 Ða ȝeseah se halga wer þæt þær sæt an deofol on þære cu hrycge. c 1205 LAY. 540 Þa Grickes ..wenden him þeo rugges. *Ibid.* 1912 Corineus..breid Geomagog þat him þe rug for-berst. c 1290 *Beket* 1156 in *S. Eng. Leg.* I. 139 Opon is rugge is cope he bar. 1340 *Ayenb.* 116 Huanne þe uondere ous knokeþ ope þane reg..ase þe ilke þet ope þe regge of þe guode knyȝte smit [etc.]. 1387 TREVISA *Higden* (Rolls) II. 177 Þe depnesse þat is from þe rugge to þe wombe. 1463 ASHBY *Prisoner's Refl.* 27 Puttyng on me many fals lesyng, Whyche I must suffyr and bere on my ruge.

β. c 1000 *Sax. Leechd.* I. 290 Ȝif hors on hricge oððe on þam boȝum awyrd sy. *Ibid.* III. 120 On þan hrigge. c 1205 LAY. 6718 Þe king aras..and burne he warp on rigge. a 1325 *Prose Psalter* xlix. 18 Þou kest my wordes byhynde rygge. 1393 LANGL. *P. Pl.* C. XXII. 287 Sholde no curiouse clope come on hus rygge. c 1425 *Leg. Rood* (1871) 202 All is rede, Ribbe and rigge, þe bak bledeþ aȝens þe borde. 1470–85 MALORY *Arthur* v. iv. 165 The dragon..smote the bore on the rydge whiche was x foote large fro the hede to the taylle. 1578 LYTE *Dodoens* 391 Let the backe or ridge be anoynted therewithal before, or at the first comming of the fittes of the Ague. 1581 MULCASTER *Positions* xxxvii. (1887) 157 Neither refusing the saddle on his ridg, to be rid on, neither the bit in his mouth. 1607 TOPSELL *Serpents* (1658) 599 Their gall..is forced to the mouth by certain veins under the ridge or back-bone. 1678 BUTLER *Hud.* III. iii. 673 They rob'd me, and my Horse, And stole my Saddle,.. And made me mount upon the bare-ridge.

2. The top, upper part, or crest *of* anything, esp. when long and narrow. a. Of the sea, waves, rising ground, hills, etc.

In pl. passing into sense 4.

Beowulf (Z.) 471 Sende ic..ofer wæteres hrycg ealde madmas. c 1000 *Ags. Ps.* (Thorpe) lxviii. 2 Com ic on sæs hricg. 14.. *Tretyce* in *Walter of Henley's Husb.* (1890) 47 Þe corne þt is in þe ryge off þe lande. 1523 FITZHERB. *Husb.* § 16 Make a depe holowe forowe in the rydge of the lande. 1555 EDEN *Decades* (Arb.) 155 The rydgies also of these mountaynes are diuided with..valleis. 1593 SHAKS. *Rich. II*, I. i. 64, I would..meete him, were I tide to runne afoote Euen to the frozen ridges of the Alpes. *1665 SIR T. HERBERT *Trav.* (1677) 11 Dancing upon the ridge of dreadful waves. 1669 WORLIDGE *Syst. Agric.* 275 The Ridge, the upper edge of a Bank, or other rising Land. 1737 [S. BERINGTON] *Mem. G. de Lucca* (1738) 89 We were almost on the Ridge of Africa, which made it cooler than one can well believe. 1788 GIBBON *Decl. & F.* xlix. V. 123 The Pentapolis..advanced into the midland country as far as the ridges of the Apennine. 1839 THIRLWALL *Greece* xiv. II. 215 They..hastily retraced their march over the ridge of Tmolus. 1879 BROWNING *Pheidippides* 57 Such my cry as, rapid, I ran over Parnes' ridge.

fig. 1678 DRYDEN *All for Love* II. i, Is this the Man who ..Drives me before him, To the World's Ridge, and sweeps me off like Rubbish? 1823 BYRON *Juan* XI. xxiii, Night was on the ridge Of twilight. 1878 SPURGEON *Treas. Dav.* Ps. cxxx. 5 As of one on the ridge of a journey, looking onward on his way.

b. Of the back, or other parts of the body.

c 1550 H. LLOYD *Treas. Health* T i, Mingle the joyce therof with oyle to anoynte the rigge of the backe. 1580 BLUNDEVIL *Horsemanship* III. 24 b, Drawe his backe with a hot iron right out on both sides of the ridge of his backe. 1602 MARSTON *Ant. & Mel.* v. Wks. 1856 I. 60 A bush of furs on the ridge of his chinne. 1641 BEST *Farming Bks.* (Surtees) 1 Close tuppes are such as have both the stones in the ridge of the back. 1690 S. BLANCARD *Lex. Med.* 339 *Isthmus* .., the ridg of the nostrils. 1759 JOHNSON *Idler* No. 82 ¶ 5 The line that forms the ridge of the nose. 1774 GOLDSM. *Nat. Hist.* (1776) III. 185 The short bristles..gradually encrease in length, as they approach the ridge of the back. 1876 SWINBURNE *Erechtheus* 1374 The ridge of their necks as the wind-shaken mane on the ridges of waves. 1888 *Harper's Mag.* July 186, I made out the horns, neck, and the ridge of the back of a tremendous old bull.

fig. 1671 WOODHEAD *St. Teresa* I. xx. 129 This kind of Soul is..upon the very top, or ridge, as one may say, of itself.

3. The horizontal edge or line in which the two sloping sides of a roof meet at the top; the uppermost part or coping of a roof.

c 1000 *Ags. Gosp.* Luke iv. 9 Ða lædde he hyne..& ȝesette hine ofer þæs temples hricg [*Hatton* ricg]. 1503 HAWES *Examp. Virt.* x. 178 A lytell brydge Not halfe so brode as a hous rydge. 1556 RECORDE *Castle Knowl.* 114 A three cornered forme like the rygge of an house where tone syde lyeth flatte, and the other two leane a slope. 1607 SHAKS. *Cor.* II. i. 227 Leades [are] fill'd, and Ridges hors'd With variable Complexions; all agreeing In earnestnesse to see him. 1662 GERBIER *Principles* 9 A Chimney some two Foote higher than the Ridges of the Roof of a Building. 1726 SWIFT *Gulliver* II. v, Here I sat for some Time,..expecting every Moment..to fall..and come tumbling..from the Ridge to the Eves. 1833 LOUDON *Encycl. Archit.* § 849 To cover the whole of the roofing with old sound plain tiles.., the hips, ridges, and eaves in mortar. 1876 W. P. BUCHAN *Plumbing* iii. 16 Zinc ridges are made of sheet zinc. 1884 *Law Times Rep.* LI. 161/2 The attachments to buildings were made..by a bolt screwed into the lead of the ridge.

Prov. 1562 HEYWOOD *Prov. & Epigr.* (1867) 50 A man may loue his house well, Though he ryde not on the rydge.

b. *Fortif.* (See quot.)

1853 STOCQUELER *Mil. Encycl.*, *Ridge*..is the highest part of the glacis proceeding from the salient angle of the covered way. 1875 KNIGHT *Dict. Mech.* 1939/1.

4. A long and narrow stretch of elevated ground; a range or chain of hills or mountains.

938 in Birch *Cartul. Sax.* II. 431 Anlang hryeges to ðære eorðburh. 941 *Ibid.* 498 West ðonan on ðone hrycg. a 1000 *Ibid.* I. 229 Ærest of sæ upp on Hængestes ricg;..swa norð andlang rihges. 1538 LELAND *Itin.* (1769) VII. 10 There is a grete Hill or Rigge, that stretchethe..from Glassenbyry on to within 2 Miles of Bridgewater. 1574 HELLOWES *Gueuara's Fam. Ep.* (1577) 367 This hill or ridge ioyneth vnto the citie. 1604 E. G[RIMSTONE] *D'Acosta's Hist. Ind.* III. xx. 184 There are two ridges of mountaines which runne..in one altitude. 1671 *New York Col. Doc.* (1853) III. 195 They saw a Ridge of Mountains lyeing N. and S. 1737 [S. BERINGTON] *Mem. G. de Lucca* (1738) 158 Vast ridges of Mountains in the Heart of the Country. 1774 GOLDSM. *Nat. Hist.* (1776) I. 136 In Holland, which is all a flat, they shew a little ridge of hills, near the sea-side. 1815 ELPHINSTONE *Acc. Caubul* (1842) I. 129 There are three branches, which stretch from the great ridge at right angles to the inferior ranges. 1880 HAUGHTON *Phys. Geogr.* v. 208 The Kenia ridge has deprived the Equatorial lakes of fully one-half of their natural rainfall supply.

fig. 1784 COWPER *Task* IV. 57 Here runs the mountainous and craggy ridge That tempts ambition.

b. A line or reef of rocks.

1695 *Phil. Trans.* XIX. 35 The Riff or Ridge..descending a little towards the Eastward. 1769 HOME *Fatal Disc.* II, Fast, on a ridge of rocks, a wreck appear'd. 1867 SMYTH *Sailor's Word-bk.* 572.

c. *Meteorol.* (See quots.)

1883 *Daily News* 15 Sept. 2/7 The 'ridge' of high pressure which lay over our islands on Thursday. 1887 *Ibid.* 10 Jan. 3/5 A 'ridge' lay over that region, and the sky was clear.

5. *Agric.* A raised or rounded strip of arable land, usually one of a series (with intermediate open furrows) into which a field is divided by ploughing in a special manner. (Cf. LAND *sb.* 7.)

† *To spare neither ridge nor furrow*: see FURROW *sb.* 1.

c 1380 *Sir Ferumb.* 1565 Þay..Ne spared rigges noþer vores til þay mette þat pray. c 1440 *Pallad. on Husb.* I. 1151 Lete se the litel plough, the large also, the rigges [*v.r.* londes] forto enhance. 1523 FITZHERB. *Husb.* § 7 He seeth not whether the plough go in rydge or rayne. 1577 B. GOOGE *Heresbach's Husb.* I. (1586) 23 b, As we leaue betwixt two Furrowes a Ridge, for the drie keeping of the graine like a Garden bedde. 1649 BLITHE *Eng. Improv. Impr.* 79 Consider thy Land how it lyeth, whether round with Ridg and Furrow [etc.]. 1697 DRYDEN *Virg. Georg.* I. 168 Th' aspiring Off-spring of the Grain O'ertops the Ridges of the furrow'd Plain. 1733 TULL *Horse-Hoeing Husb.* 120 *note*, This Observation was before I planted my Rows on high Ridges. 1787 WINTER *Syst. Husb.* 276 A few buts or short ridges, which were planted with a proportion of one bushel to an acre. 1844 H. STEPHENS *Bk. Farm* I. 465 Heavy land is formed into narrow ridges, to allow the rain to flow quickly into the open furrows. 1884 ALLEN *Amer. Farm Bk.* 103 The depth of the furrow should be about one-half its width, and the land or ridges as wide as can conveniently be made.

transf. 1667 MILTON *P. L.* VI. 236 Each Warriour..expert When to..turn the sway Of Battel, open when, and when to close The ridges of grim Warr.

Comb. 1851 *Art Jrnl. Hist. Exhib.* 22/2 Among other striking examples of the ingenuity of the originators and constructors of the Crystal Palace is the ridge-and-furrow roof. 1871 KINGSLEY *At Last* ii, Gullies sawn in the slopes ..giving..a ridge-and-furrow look to this and most other of the Antilles.

b. Used as a measure of land.

The size of ridges varied greatly in different parts of the country; cf. Stephens *Bk. Farm* (1844) I. 465.

967 in Birch *Cartul. Sax.* III. 486 Þæt lytle linland eal butan anan hrycge, þæm westmæstan tweȝen æceras. 1439 *Brasenose Coll. Munim.* C[2] 7, 4 rygges of meadow in Cropredy. 1631 *Indenture, Bucks*, 3 ridges or butts. 1688 HOLME *Armoury* II. ii. § 32 Smaller parcells according to that quantity of ground it containeth,..Ridges, Butts, Flats, Stitches or small Butts, Pikes. 1716 *Lond. Gaz.* No. 5487/4 Also four or five Ridges of Arable Land, and one Ley. 1875 MAINE *Hist. Inst.* iv. 114 Such was their numbers that they used not to get but thrice nine ridges for each man.

c. *Hort.* A raised hot-bed on which cucumbers or melons are planted.

1725 *Family Dict.* s.v. *Melon*, To make Ridges for you. Melons and Cucumbers, of the same kind of Dung with the Seed-Bed. 1796 C. MARSHALL *Gardening* xiv. (1798) 194 The hot-bed, or ridge made in May, for hand-glass, should be sunk in a dry soil. 1847 MRS. LOUDON *Amateur Gardener* 86/2 The cucumbers raised from seed last month should now be planted out on ridges.

6. A narrow elevation or raised part running along or across a surface.

1523 FITZHERB. *Husb.* § 4 A reste-balke is where the plough ..leaueth a lyttell rydge standynge betwene. 1677 YARRANTON *Eng. Improv.* 41 At last I found in the Sea great quantities of Iron Stones lye in a Ridge. 1693 EVELYN *De La Quint. Compl. Gard.* II. 94 Strawberries being likewise order'd in double ridges, in Baskets made on purpose. 1726 SWIFT *Gulliver* IV. i, They had Beards like Goats, and a long Ridge of Hair down their Backs. 1757 W. WILKIE *Epigoniad* VII. 228 A tempest..began to blow And rear in ridges high the deep below. 1796 WITHERING *Brit. Plants* (ed. 3) II. 293 Seeds small, with 5 membranaceous ridges. 1810 CRABBE *Borough* xxii. 71 None could the ridges on his back behold. 1846 DANA *Zooph.* (1848) 154 In a few species, the cells are confluent also across the ridges. 1872 YEATS *Techn. Hist. Comm.* 347 Dead-smooth files are..of so fine a cut that the unaided eye cannot discern the ridges.

b. = BAR *sb.*[1] 7 a.

1728 CHAMBERS *Cycl.* s.v., It is commonly in the third or fourth Ridge that the Farriers strike, in order to bleed a Horse whose Mouth is over heated. [1831 YOUATT *Horse* 133 The hard palate, composed of a firm dense substance divided into several ridges called bars.] 1847 T. BROWN *Mod. Farriery* 198 The palate, divided into ridges and bars. 1876 HUXLEY in *Nature* XIV. 34/1 The valleys between the various ridges are not filled up with cement.

c. A raised line, bank, bed, or strip *of* something.

1763 MILLS *Pract. Husb.* IV. 364 The French vine-dressers ..lay along that side of the vineyard..a ridge of dry litter. 1800 WORDSW. *Brothers* 31 The snow-white ridge Of carded wool which the old man had piled. 1852 MRS. STOWE *Uncle Tom's C.* xiv. 123 From behind some dusky cotton-bale, or ..over some ridge of packages. 1878 HUXLEY *Physiogr.* 168 A ridge of chalk runs across the island.

7. *attrib.* and *Comb.* a. In sense 3 (or related uses), as *ridge-beam*, *-board*, *-cap*, *-crest*, etc. Also RIDGE-PIECE, -POLE, -TILE, -TREE.

1578 BANISTER *Hist. Man* I. 18 The composition of the Vertebres compared to the *ridgbeame of a shippe. 1875 KNIGHT *Dict. Mech.* 1939/1 *Ridge-beam*, a beam at the upper ends of the rafters beneath the ridge. 1833 LOUDON *Encycl. Archit.* § 1301 The *ridge-board, 8 inches and a half by 1 inch and a half, [to be] of red deal. 1881 YOUNG *Every Man his own Mechanic* § 970 The rafters may abut after the manner of rafters against the ridge-board or pole of a span roof. 1787 W. MARSHALL *Prov. Norf.* (1795) II. 387 *Roofing*, the *ridge-cap of thatched roofs. 1849 *Ecclesiologist* IX. 161 There are rich but over large *ridge-crests to the chancel. 1856 KANE *Arct. Expl.* II. xvi. 170 A neat housing of light canvas was stretched upon a *ridge-line sustained fore and aft by stanchions. 1850 PARKER *Gloss. Arch.* (ed. 5) 388 *note*, The longitudinal *ridge-rib runs along the apex of the main vault; the transverse ridge-rib crosses this and runs along the apex of the cross vault. 1879 BARING-GOULD *Germany* II. 355 English architects alone used the ridge rib, running the whole length of the church and uniting the keys. 1833 LOUDON *Encycl. Archit.* § 1301 The *ridge roll (a piece over which the lead is turned on ridges and hips). 1883 HARDWICK *Phot. Chem.* 299 Many operators prefer to work in what is called a *ridge-roof studio. 1833 LOUDON *Encycl. Archit.* 1130/1 **Ridge-spikes*, nails with broad heads for fastening on lead. 1535 COVERDALE *Ezek.* xlvi. 23 There went a *rygge wall rounde aboute them all foure.

b. In sense 5, as *ridge-are* (EAR *v.*[1]), *-breadth*, *-furrow*, *-hoe*, *-method*, etc.

Also *ridge-drill*, *-harrow*, *-plough* (Knight *Dict. Mech.*). For *ridge-and-furrow* see sense 5.

1649 BLITHE *Eng. Improv. Impr.* 79 If it be Lands & great Balkes together, then for the Lands Plough them as you please, that is, whether *Ridge-Are [etc.]. 1806 J. GRAHAME *Birds of Scot.* 141 A *ridge-breadth round The partridge nest. 1805 R. W. DICKSON *Pract. Agric.* II. 666 Rendering them drier by deepening the *ridge-furrows. 1858 SIMMONDS *Dict. Trade*, *Ridge-hoe, a field implement for row-culture, of which there are several combinations. 1805 R. W. DICKSON *Pract. Agric.* II. 687 In setting the plants out, in the *ridge method, it is necessary to have them placed in lines as regularly as possible. 1817–8 COBBETT *Resid. U.S.* (1822) 71 The *ridge-sowing method, or the broad-cast method. 1786 ABERCROMBIE *Gard. Assist.* 11 Blending the whole together into an heap *ridgeways. 1725 *Family Dict.* s.v. *Mushroom-beds*, The Dung should be well mix'd.. and thrown into the Trench two Foot up *Ridge-wise. 1765 *Museum Rust.* III. 88 The manner of performing the *ridge-work, or laying up the soil for the winter.

c. Misc., as *ridge-form*, *-like*, *-line*, *-nose*, etc.

1703 *Lond. Gaz.* No. 3945/4 A black Cart Gelding..with.. a ridge Nose. 1805 R. W. DICKSON *Pract. Agric.* I. Pl. 31 A white-thorn hedge,..cut..in the ridge form, or broad at bottom and narrow at the top. 1816 COLERIDGE *Lay Serm.* (Bohn) 379 A few..whose ample foreheads, with the weighty bar, ridge-like, above the eyebrows, bespoke observation. 1833 HERSCHEL *Astron.* iii. 156 The bottoms of valleys and the ridge-lines of hills. 1877 BRYCE *Transcaucasia* i. 35 Looking from one of these billowy ridge-tops across the vast expanse.

8. Special combs.: **ridge-fillet**, **ridge myrtle** (see quots.); **ridge stone**, (*a*) a curb-stone for a well; (*b*) a coping-stone for the ridge of a house; **ridge stay**, *dial.*, a ridge-band; **ridge-tackle** (see quot.); **ridge-washed** *a.* (see quot.); **ridge-with** (**ridgeworth**, etc.), *dial.*, a ridge-band (cf. RIG-WITH).

1875 KNIGHT *Dict. Mech.*, **Ridge-fillet*, 1. (Architecture), the fillet between two channels of a pillar. 2. (Founding), the runner or principal channel. 1889 MAIDEN *Useful Native Pl.* 276 *Melaleuca genistifolia*..'*Ridge Myrtle'. Called 'Ironwood' in Queensland. 1838 HOLLOWAY *Prov. Dict.*, **Ridge stay*. 1694 in Picton *L'pool Munic. Rec.* (1883) I. 320 Some *ridg stones may be sett round the mouth of the well. 1889 *Glover's Hist. Derby* I. 91 At Pentrich common quarry, ridge stones are prepared, sawed out like an angular trough. 1899 MACKAY *Introd. to Lindesay of Pitscottie's Chron.* (S.T.S.) 34 A few of the ridge stones were unearthed some years ago. 1794 *Rigging & Seamanship* 177 *Ridge Tackle is composed of a double block and a single block, strapped with an eye: it is used to suspend the awning in the middle. 1823 CRABB, **Ridge-washed-kersey* (Mech.), kersey-cloth made of fleece wool, washed only on the sheep's back. 1552 HULOET, *Ridgwyth for a cart. c 1700 KENNET in *MS. Lansd.* 1033, fol. 322 A *Ridge-with*, the rope that is fastned to the rods, and goes over the saddle of the Fillar. Chesh. 1854– in Lanc., Chesh., and Northampton glossaries.

† Ridge, *sb.*[2] *Obs. Cant.* [Origin obscure.] Gold; gold coin. Also **† Ridge-cully**, a goldsmith.

1665 R. HEAD *Eng. Rogue* I. iv, *Ridge-cully*, a Goldsmith. [Hence in B. E. *Dict. Cant. Crew* (a 1700), and later Dicts.] 1796 *Grose's Dict. Vulgar T.*, *Ridge*, a guinea. 1812 J. H. VAUX *Flash Dict.*, *Ridge*, gold, whether in coin or any other shape..; *a cly-full of ridge*, a pocketfull of gold. 1834 H. AINSWORTH *Rookwood* III. v, My thimble of ridge [= gold watch].

Ridge (ridʒ), *v.* Forms: 5 **ryge**, **rigge**, 6 **rygge**, **rydge**, 6– **ridge** (6 **ridgg**, 7 **ridg**). [f. RIDGE *sb.*[1] An OE. *hrycigende* occurs as a gloss to L. *resulcans*.]

1. *trans.* To provide (a building) with a ridge, or a proper covering for this; to make or renew the ridge of (a house, etc.). Cf. RIG *v.*[1] 1.

1445 in *5th Rep. Hist. MSS. Comm.* (1876) 528/1 Paid William Brownflet for rygyng the house with turfs, 3*d.* 1496 *Will of Pimpe* (Somerset Ho.), Whereas the roffe of the body of the said churche is now Rigged wt Rigge tile I will that it be rigged wt leede. 1595 in *Sheffield Gloss.* (1888) 328 That the copyholders of this manor shall..moss and ridgg the west end of the mylne. 1610 HEALEY *St. Aug. Citie of God* xv. xvii. 569 The fittest forme for to keepe of the rayne and weather was to bee ridged downe a proportioned descent from the toppe downeward. 1686 PLOT *Staffordsh.* 115 As in Oxfordshire..they use it [*sc.* turf] frequently to ridg and head their meaner houses.

2. To break or throw up (land, a field, etc.) into ridges. Freq. with *up*. Cf. RIG *v.*[1] 2.

1523 FITZHERB. *Husb.* § 13 In the begynnynge of Marche, rydge it vppe agayne. *Ibid.*, Than let hym caste his barleyerthe, and shortly after rygge it agayne. 1549 LATIMER *Ploughers* (Arb.) 19 The ploughman..breaketh it in furroughes, and sometime ridgeth it vp agayne. 1580 HOLLYBAND *Treas. Fr. Tong*, *Seillonner vne terre*, to ridge a ground. 1677 PLOT *Oxfordsh.* 239 Ridging it up twice or thrice for every casting tilth. 1733 TULL *Horse-Hoeing Husb.* xviii. 121 The Soil is equally rich, whether it be plowed plain or ridged up. 1805 R. W. DICKSON *Pract. Agric.* I. 366 The land may be again ridged up by means of the plough. 1859 R. F. BURTON *Centr. Afr.* in *Jrnl. Geog. Soc.* XXIX. 397 The fields are neatly ridged with the hoe. 1884 ALLEN *Amer. Farm Bk.* 103 A stiff clay is sometimes ridged up by turning a double furrow.

fig. 1549 LATIMER *Ploughers* (Arb.) 20 Nowe ridgynge them vp agayne, with the gospel.

absol. 1868 *Rep. U.S. Comm. Agric.* (1869) 248 The safest course is to ridge before the 10th of November.

3. To mark with or as with ridges; to raise ridges or ripples upon (a surface).

1671 MILTON *Samson* 1137 Bristles..like those that ridge the back Of chaf't wild Boars. 1816 L. HUNT *Rimini* I. 204 The branching veins ridging the glossy lean. 1830 TENNYSON *Arab. Nts.* 35 A motion from the river won Ridged the smooth level. 1886 RUSKIN *Præterita* I. 242 The kind of breeze that drifts the clouds, and ridges the waves.

refl. 1880 J. LEGGE *Mem.* 262 The placid sea may ridge itself in mountains.

4. To plant (*out*) in ridges or hot-beds.

1731 MILLER *Gard. Dict.* s.v. *Cucumis*, The common Allowance for ridging out the earliest Plants, is one Load to each..Hole. 1786 ABERCROMBIE *Gard. Assist.* 31 To have a proper supply for ridging or planting into large hot-beds. *Ibid.* 32 Melons.—Sow in hot-beds,..ridge out into strong hot-beds. 1851 *B'ham & Midl. Gard. Mag.* Apr. 45 Sow in frame on hot bed,..Ridge Cucumbers [etc.]. 1868 *Rep. U.S. Comm. Agric.* (1869) 248 The young plants make a more uniform growth when ridged.

b. To cover *in*, by raising ridges.

1827 STEUART *Planter's G.* (1828) 496 The practice usually is, to dig in Farm-yard Dung..; or sometimes to ridge in the dung. 1868 *Rep. U.S. Comm. Agric.* (1869) 422 The dressings were sown..in drills, which were then ridged in.

c. To arrange in ridges.

1821–30 LD COCKBURN *Mem.* (1874) iv. 220 It ran over the sky-lines of people ridged on all the buildings.

5. *intr.* To form ridges; to rise (*up*) in ridges.

1864 TENNYSON *En. Ard.* 525 The Biscay, roughly ridging eastward, shook And almost overwhelm'd her. 1891 MEREDITH *One of our Conq.* III. x. 194 Dartrey's forehead ridged with his old fury. 1899 *Pall Mall Mag.* Jan. 9 The veins ridged up upon his forehead.

Hence **Ri·dging** *ppl. a.*

1828 TENNYSON *Lover's Tale* 55 The slowly-ridging rollers on the cliff Clash'd, calling to each other. 1885–94 R. BRIDGES *Eros & Psyche* Apr. xxix, Hid from earth by ridging summits twain, They came upon a valley.

Ri·dge-band. Now *dial.* Also 5 **rigebound**. [f. RIDGE *sb.*[1] + BAND *sb.*[1]] = BACKBAND.

1418 in Rymer *Fœdera* (1709) IX. 543/1 Rigeboundes, Bellibondes, & Shotyng-ledders. 1611 COTGR., *Dossiere*, the part of a draught horses harnesse which runnes orecrosse his backe, we call it the ridgeband. 1775 in *E. Angl. Gloss.* (1895). 1838 in Holloway *Prov. Dict.* 1854– in dial. glossaries (Northampton, Shropsh., Heref., Sussex).

Ri·dge-bone. Forms: 1 **hrycgbán**, 4–5 **rugge-**, 4–6 **rygge-**, **rigge-** (5 ? **ragge-**), 5–6 **rydge-**, 5– **ridgebone** (6 **ridg-**); also 4 **-boon**, 5 **-boone**, 4–5 **-bon**. [OE. *hrycgbán*, = OFris. *regben*, MDu. *rig(ge)-*, *rug(ge)been* (Du. *ruggebeen*), MLG. *ruggebên* (LG. *rügge-*, *rügbên*), OHG. *rukkipein* (MHG. *rückbein*, G. *rückenbein*), Norw. *ryggbein*, Sw. *-ben*, Da. *rygben*.] The spine or back-bone. Now *rare* or *Obs.* (common c 1380–1610). For northern and Sc. examples, see RIG-BONE.

a 1000 *Ags. Ps.* (Lamb.) xxxi. 4 Ȝewend ic eom on..yrmðum minum, þanne tobrocen bið hrycgban. 13.. *Gaw. & Gr. Knt.* 1344 So ryde þay of by resoun bi þe rygge bonez, Euenden to þe haunche. 1387 TREVISA *Higden* (Rolls) II. 383 Perdix..made it i-toþed as a rugge boon of a fissche. c 1400 *Lanfranc's Cirurg.* 226 A greet boch þat comeþ of þe passioun of þe riggeboon. c 1425 *Eng. Conq. Irel.* 142 My fyngyr ys gretter than was my faders ryggebone. 1485 *Bk. St. Albans* f iij b, Than schall ye kyt the skyrtis..And after the Ragge boon cuttis euen also. 1547 BOORDE *Brev. Health* cccxxii. 104 b, The backe bone or the rydge bone the which may have many diseases. 1581 MULCASTER *Positions* xxvii. (1887) 105 It helpeth the ridgebone, by stowping, bending, and coursing about. 1651 *Raleigh's Ghost* 85 Throughout the whole spine or ridge-bone of the back. 1765 J. L. JACKSON *Riding* 7 The rider ..sitting with his body erect, his ridge bone answering to the ridge bone of the horse. 1828 SCOTT *F. M. Perth* viii, The saddle and the man were girthed on the ridge-bone of a..Flemish mare.

Ridged (ridʒd), *ppl. a.* [f. RIDGE *sb.*[1] or *v.* Cf. ME. *broke-rugget* broken-backed.] Rising in a ridge or ridges; marked by a ridge or ridges.

c 1410 *Master of Game* (MS. Digby 182) iv, He renneth with leepes and with rygged and stondyng heere. 1551 ROBINSON tr. *More's Utop.* I. (1895) 31 Afterwarde they founde shyppes wyth rydged kyeles. 1578 LYTE *Dodoens* 313 A certayne fruit like unto small peares, saving they be ridged alongest the sydes. 1622 DRAYTON *Poly-olb.* xxvii. 11 So lowd the Ecchoes cry'd, that they were heard to shreeke To Fournesse ridged Front. 1681 GREW *Musæum* I. iii. 51 A kind of a Ridged Tail or Epiphysis. 1687 A. LOVELL tr. *Thevenot's Trav.* I. 136 A great Room.. with a Ridged Roof. 1726 LEONI *Alberti's Archit.* I. 15/1 Sloping or ridged like ordinary mean Houses. 1789 T. WRIGHT *Meth. Watering Meadows* (1790) 25 A field that has been..left by the plow in a ridged state. 1830 TENNYSON *Sea Fairies* 39 When the sharp clear twang of the golden chords Runs up the ridged sea. 1870 HOOKER *Stud. Flora* 329 Seeds ridged and wrinkled.

Ridged, obs. variant of RIGID *a.*

Ridgel (ri·dʒĕl). Now *dial.* Forms: 6–7 **ridgell**, 8–9 **ridgel**, 9 **rudgel**; 7–9 **ridgil** (8 **-ill**, 9 **-ul**); also 7 **rigele**, **-ell(e**, **-il**. [App. f. RIDGE *sb.*[1] 1 (cf. 2 b, quot. 1641), the testicle being supposed to remain near the animal's back, instead of descending into the scrotum.

The northern forms answering to *ridgel* and *ridgeling* (see below) are RIGGALD and RIGLIN(G: cf. also RIG *sb.*[3], RIGGON, and RIGGOT[1].]

An animal which has been imperfectly castrated († or spayed), or whose genital organs are not properly developed; *esp.* a male animal (ram, bull, or horse) with only one testicle. Also *attrib.*

1597 in *Sheffield Gloss.* (1888) 328 That no persone..shall put any ridgell tupp upon the moore..upon payne for euery ridgell so found xij*d.* 1641 BEST *Farm. Bks.* (Surtees) 154 One branded rigelle whye, and a little blacke rigele stot. 1664 COTTON *Scarron.* IV. (1741) 64, I hate a base cowardly Drone Worse than a Rigil with one Stone. 1697 DRYDEN *Virg. Past.* IX. 31 O Tityrus tend my Herd..And 'ware the Libyan Ridgils butting Head. 1723 DR. WHARTON *True Briton* No. 59, When they make Ridgels, I have known as unlikely things hit off. 1779 *Phil. Trans.* LXIX. 290 Nearly as large..as those of the ridgill, the bull whose testicles never come down. 1811 *Sporting Mag.* XXXVIII. 210 He would not give so much for a ridgil as for a clean-cut horse. 1884– in dial. glossaries (Chesh., Notts., Worc., Glouc.). 1886 *Trans. Amer. Philol. Assoc.* XVII. 42 *Ridgling* or *ridgil*..is still used in Tennessee and the West.

transf. a 1625 FLETCHER *Women Pleased* II. vi, A pox of yonder old Rigell The Captaine, the old Captaine.

Ri·dgelet. Also **ridglet**. [f. RIDGE *sb.*[1] + -LET.] A small ridge, esp. of earth.

1778 [W. MARSHALL] *Minutes Agric.* 17 Oct. 1774 Observ., Opened the potatoe-ridgelets with a plow. 1787 — *Norfolk* I. 234 If the land lie in narrow work, the ridglets are split. 1805 R. W. DICKSON *Pract. Agric.* II. 592 To plough the land into ridglets of about two feet six inches in width. 1852 DANA *Crust.* I. 249 One of the ridgelets or rugæ extends inward. 1863 — *Man. Geol.* 723 It should be remembered that mountains are relatively to the size of the earth but little ridgelets on its surface.

Ri·dgeling. Now *rare.* Also 6 **redge-**, 7–9 **ridgling**. [-ING or -LING: cf. RIGLIN.] = RIDGEL.

1555 W. WATREMAN *Fardle Facions* II. xi. 259 Greate menne, that cannot alwaie haue their wiues in their own eye, appoincte redgelinges, or guelte menne to awaite vppon them. 1682 D'URFEY *Royalist* Prol., Yet who here would refuse a kind Intrigue; Faith none; who does it, is a Ridgling Whig. 1684 DRYDEN *Theocritus*, *Idyl* iii. 5 O Tityrus, tend them well,..And 'ware the Ridgling with his butting head. 1886 [see RIDGEL]. 1891 *Hartland Glossary* s.v. *Ridger*. A ridgel or ridgeling, an animal half castrated.

Ridgeling *adv.*: see RUGLING.

Ri·dge-piece. [RIDGE *sb.*[1] 3.] (See quots. 1823 and 1850.)

1611 COTGR. s.v. *Enfaisture*, *Pieces d'enfaisture*, sparres, rafters, ridge-peeces of timber. 1823 P. NICHOLSON *Pract. Build.* 128 A ridge-piece is a beam at the apex of a roof. 1833 LOUDON *Encycl. Archit.* § 83 Ridge pieces, nine inches deep.., rounded on the top for lead. 1850 PARKER *Gloss. Arch.* (ed. 5) 388 A piece of timber called the ridge-piece, upon which the upper ends of the rafters rest. 1863 BARING-GOULD *Iceland* 270 Then the men pulled at the gable ends, heaved the ridgepiece aside, and broke it asunder.

Ri·dge-pole. [RIDGE *sb.*[1] 3.]

1. The horizontal pole of a tent.

1788 FALCONBRIDGE *Afr. Slave Trade* 5 The sailors first lash the booms and yards from mast to mast, in order to form a ridge-pole. 1828 J. M. SPEARMAN *Brit. Gunner* (ed. 2) 391 Captain's Marquee. Ridge-pole, length 6 ft. 11 in. 1855 LONGF. *Hiaw.* XIII. 155 Tied him fast..To the ridge-pole of his wigwam. 1894 A. ROBERTSON *Nuggets*, etc. 27 The sun was..shining cheerily through the thin canvas. Three magpies were chattering on the ridge-pole.

fig. 1788 J. MAY *Jrnl. & Lett.* (1873) 29 We..began to ascend Alleghana...At ten o'clock we were on the ridge-pole.

b. *attrib.* in *ridge-pole pine* (see quot.).

1885 ROOSEVELT *Hunting Trips* 306 The forest was composed mainly of what are called ridge-pole pines, which.. do not branch out until the stems are thirty or forty feet from the ground.

2. A horizontal timber at the ridge of a roof, into which the rafters are fastened.

1833 LOUDON *Encycl. Archit.* § 1940 The ridge pole of such a roof is made exactly like one of the main ribs of the principals. 1863 HAWTHORNE *Our Old Home* (1879) 80 They are mostly of the timber-and-plaster kind, with bowed and decrepit ridge-poles. 1881 YOUNG *Every Man his own Mechanic* § 1332. 614 The rafters are notched on to the wall plates..at their lower end, while the upper end of each is rested against the ridge-pole.

Hence **Ri·dge-poled** *a.*

1861 RUSSELL in *Times* 10 July, A few ridge-poled tents, pitched under the shade of some trees.

Ri·dger. *rare.* [RIDGE *sb.*[1] or *v.*]

1. *dial.* = RIDGE-BAND.

1838 HOLLOWAY *Prov. Dict.* 1854 MISS BAKER *Northampt. Gloss.* s.v. *Ridge-band*, Ridge-band..in Suffolk..is called ridger;..and ridge-rope in London and its vicinity.

2. A ridging implement.

1875 *Encycl. Brit.* I. 315/2 An implement which he calls a Ridger and Subsoiler. By means of it the soil..is thrown into 36-inch ridges. a 1890 *Sci. Amer.* LXII. 181 (Cent. Dict.), A small ridger or subsoiler extending below to form a small furrow into which the seed is dropped.

Ri·dge-rope. [RIDGE *sb.*[1]]

1. *dial.* = RIDGE-BAND.

1611 COTGR., *Surselle*, a broad and great band,..fastened on either side of a thill, and bearing vpon the..saddle...About London it is called the Ridge-rope. 1854 [see RIDGER 1].

2. *Naut.* (See quots. 1769 and 1867.)

1769 FALCONER *Dict. Marine* (1780), *Sauve-gardes*, the ridge-ropes which extend the nettings of a ship's head. 1846 YOUNG *Naut. Dict.*, Ridge-ropes (or Man-ropes). 1857 LD. DUFFERIN *Lett. High Lat.* (ed. 3) 22, I, guessing we were in for it, sent down the topmasts,..rove the ridge-ropes, and reefed all down. 1867 SMYTH *Sailor's Word-bk.*, *Ridge-ropes* are of various kinds. Thus the centre-rope of an awning, and those along the rigging to which it is stretched, the man-ropes to the bowsprit, safety lines from gun to gun in bad weather—all obtain this name.

Ri·dget. *rare.* [RIDGE *sb.*[1]] = RIDGELET.

1791 W. MARSHALL *W. England* (1796) II. 278 A wrested plow..forcing up the ridgets. 1796 *Ibid.* I. 190 The rows or ridgets of soil and clods, forced up by the plow.

Ri·dge-tile. Also **ridge tile** (5 **rigge**, 7–8 **tyle**). [RIDGE *sb.*[1]] A tile used for roofing the ridge of a building.

The northern form *rig-tile* is found a little earlier: see RIG *sb.*[1] 5.

1496 [see RIDGE *v.* 1]. 1611 COTGR., *Renfester vne maison*, to put new ridge-tyles on it. 1677 PLOT *Oxfordsh.* 64 Laid on Mud-walls, and the tops of Houses, in the place and manner of these we call Ridge-tiles. 1726 SWIFT *Gulliver* II. v, The Monkey..let me drop on a Ridge Tyle, and made his Escape. 1837 CARLYLE *Fr. Rev.* IV. vii. (1872) III. 164 All prisons and Houses of Arrest in French land are getting crowded to the ridge-tile. 1851 *Ord. & Regul. R. Engin.* xix. 100 The Ridges being covered with lead, or Ridge Tiles.

Ri·dge-tree. [RIDGE *sb.*[1]] = RIDGE-POLE 2.

1641 BEST *Farm. Bks.* (Surtees) 148 They will sowe downe theire thatch in fower places,..lastly, aboute a yard or more belowe the ridge-tree. 1793 SMEATON *Edystone L.* § 100 Planks being well spiked down upon the ridge-tree and upon the sills on each side. 1844 H. STEPHENS *Bk. Farm* I. 187 If a slated roof is adopted, there should be a ridge-tree 10 inches broad by 2 inches thick. 1879 *Cassell's Techn. Educ.* II. 100.

Ri·dgeway. [OE. *hrycgweg*: see RIDGE *sb.*[1] 4 and WAY *sb.*] A way or road along a ridge, esp. one following the ridge of downs or low hill-ranges. Also *attrib.*

938 in Birch *Cartul. Sax.* II. 431 Þanon on þone norðmystan hryc weȝ. a 1000 in Kemble *Cod. Dipl.* III. 427 On ðone beorh to ðem ricgweȝe; ðonne east andlang hricgweȝes. 1565 COOPER *Thesaurus* s.v. *Plaga*, An high ridge way paued with marble. 1778 *Eng. Gaz.* (ed. 2) s.v. *Childrey*, The ridge-way, called Ickleton, part of the Roman Icknild-street, runs just above this place. 1861 SMILES *Engineers* I. 157 In some districts they are called trackways or ridgeways, being narrow causeways usually following the natural ridges of the country. 1882 JESSOPP *Arcady* 72 Across ridgeway plantations, furze breaks, and short cuts.

Ridgeways, -wise, *adv.*, see RIDGE *sb.*[1] 7 b.

Ridgid, Ridgil(l: see RIGID, RIDGEL.

† Ridgill-backed. *Obs.*[−0] (See quot.)

1611 COTGR. s.v. *Asne*, *A Dos d'asne*,..ridgill-backed; bowed, boughtie, or bowing; highest in the middle.

Ri·dging, *vbl. sb.* [f. RIDGE *v.* + -ING[1].]

1. The action of making or covering the ridge of a house; the ridge itself. Also *attrib.*, as *ridging grass* (see quot. 1864), *stone*, *tile*, *tree*.

1458 *Visitat. St. Paul's Churches* 96 Orreum indiget reparacioni cum stramine et in ryggyng. 1611 COTGR., *Enfaisture*, a ridge, or a ridging; or the frame of a ridge, roofe, or house top. 1752 RAY *Hist. Reb.* 311 The spy was hanged on what they call the ridging-tree of a house. 1844 H. STEPHENS *Bk. Farm* I. 198 The droved angular freestone ridging-stone..costs 6d. a lineal foot. 1862 *Catal. Internat. Exhib.*, *Brit.* II. No. 2286 Ridging, roofing, and flooring tiles. 1864 GRISEBACH *Flora W. Ind. Isl.* 787 Ridging grass, *Anatherum bicorne*.

2. The action of ploughing in ridges, or of rising up in ridges. Also with *up*.

1523 FITZHERB. *Husb.* § 13 The whiche ryggynge maketh the lande to be drye. 1805 R. W. DICKSON *Pract. Agric.* II. 647 The ridging up of the land may be of utility. 1834 *Penny Cycl.* II. 224 Sometimes two ridges are set up against each other, which is called ridging or bouting. 1897 GEIKIE *Anc. Volcanoes Gt. Brit.* I. 12 The ridging up of any part of the terrestrial crust.

attrib. 1875 KNIGHT *Dict. Mech.* 1939/2 A ridging-plow, the wings of which are expanded or contracted by segmental racks and a pinion.

Ri·dgingly, *adv. rare*[−0]. [f. RIDGE *v.*]

1552 HULOET, *Ridgynglye*, or after the maner of rydges.

Ridgy (ri·dʒi), *a.* [f. RIDGE *sb.*[1] + -Y.] Rising in ridges, or after the manner of a ridge.

1697 DRYDEN *Virg. Georg.* I. 599 Ridgy Roofs and Tiles. — *Æneid* III. 739 To Heav'n aloft on ridgy waves we ride. 1718 ROWE tr. *Lucan* IV. 251 Long rows of ridgy mountains run behind. 1783 W. F. MARTYN *Geogr. Mag.* II. 139 Cleves..is said to derive its name from its ridgy situation. 1791 W. BARTRAM *Carolina* 182 A very ridgy horny cartilage. 1820 CRABBE *Borough* i. 182 Faint, lazy waves o'ercreep the ridgy sand. 1849 RUSKIN *Sev. Lamps* iii. § xxii. 89 A low ridgy process is seen emerging along the outer edge of the cylindrical shaft. 1880 MISS BIRD *Japan* I. 314 The back bones of all [the horses] are ridgy.

Comb. 1872 JENKINSON *Guide Eng. Lakes* 334 To the right of Skiddaw is..the ridgy-fronted Blencathara.

Hence **Ri·dgyness**.

1872 C. KING *Sierra Nevada* v. 100 The eye..took cognizance of a certain ridgyness of surface.

† Ridibu·ndal, *a. Obs.*[−1] [f. L. *rīdibund-us*, f. *rīdēre* to laugh.] Inclined to laughter.

1652 URQUHART *Jewel* Wks. (1834) 231 With no less impetuosity of ridibundal passion..she fell back in a swoon.

† Ri·dicle. *Obs. rare.* = next.

1570 FOXE *A. & M.* (ed. 2) 194/1 So was the comming & assaulting of their enemies to the people..but a trifle, to the king but a ridicle. *Ibid.* 942/1 So minde I to leaue it stil vnto them selues, with other their apishe toyes and ridicies, as thinges worthy to be laught at.

Ridicule (ri·dikiul), *sb.*[1] [a. F. *ridicule* or ad. L. *rīdiculum*, neut. of *rīdiculus*: see RIDICULE *a.*]

1. A ridiculous or absurd thing, feature, characteristic, or habit; an absurdity. Now *rare*.

1677 GALE *Crt. Gentiles* III. 201 In this Masse-Sacrifice what a world of ridicules are there. 1690 *Andros Tracts* I. 143 The purchasing of the Natives Right, was made nothing of, and next to a Ridicule. 1762 GIBBON *Misc. Wks.* (1814) IV. 139 Monarchs..have their private life, and may not the ridicules of it be displayed upon the stage? 1785 'C-T-SS OF R.' *Ess.* II. 33 The English have taken it into their heads to assume all the ridicules of their neighbours. 1802 MAR. EDGEWORTH *Moral T.* (1816) I. viii. 51 Not that any folly or ridicule escaped his keen penetration. 1850 MACAULAY in Trevelyan *Life* (1875) II. 273 He marked every fault of taste, every weakness, every ridicule. 1867 *Q. Rev.* July 16 This comedy..summed up..the vices and ridicules..of the 'great' of the present time.

† b. A subject of ridicule; a laughing-stock.

1680 *Honest Cavalier* 7, I am so far from making a Ridicule (as you call it) of that Worthy Person that [etc.]. 1694 WOOD *Life* 23 June, Imposing upon a generous person and making him a ridicule to the company.

2. Ridiculous nature or character (*of* something).

1711 ADDISON *Spect.* No. 18 ¶ 6 It does not want any great Measure of Sense to see the Ridicule of this monstrous Practice. 1761 HUME *Hist. Eng.* xxix. II. 147 Leo was fully acquainted with the ridicule and falsity of the doctrines. 1824 MISS FERRIER *Inher.* lx, He..seemed quite unconscious of the ridicule of such a supposition. 1859 J. C. HOBHOUSE *Italy* I. 148 Cicognara luckily saw the ridicule of such a project, and stopped it. a 1864 HAWTHORNE *Amer. Note-bks.* (1879) I. 69 The man seemed too simple..to comprehend the ridicule of his situation.

b. That which is ridiculous; ridiculousness.

1712 ? HUGHES *Spect.* No. 467 ¶ 1 We rather delight in the Ridicule than the Virtues we find in others. 1729 LAW *Serious C.* i. (1732) 3 We see such a mixture of Ridicule in the lives of many people. 1769 GOLDSM. *Hist. Rome* (1786) I. 423 A desire of uniting in himself incompatible qualities, which gave an air of ridicule to his greatest actions. 1804–6 SYD. SMITH *Mor. Philos.* (1850) 365 If a nation of savages were to see such a drama acted, they would see no ridicule in it at all.

3. The act or practice of making persons or things the object of jest or sport; language intended to raise laughter against a person or thing.

1690 TEMPLE *Ess. Poetry* Wks. 1720 I. 240 Another Vein which has enter'd, and help'd to corrupt our Modern Poesy, is that of Ridicule; as if nothing pleas'd but what made one laugh. 1712 ADDISON *Spect.* No. 291 ¶ 8 A Man who has the Gift of Ridicule is apt to find Fault with any thing that gives him an Opportunity of exerting his beloved Talent. 1736 BUTLER *Anal.* Introd., The system of Religion..is not a subject of ridicule. 1798 FERRIAR *Illustr. Sterne*, etc. 6 Which give an appearance of extravagance to what was once correct ridicule. 1844 THIRLWALL *Greece* VIII. 117 He had to sustain a storm of reproach and ridicule from his own people. 1873 HELPS *Soc. Press.* iii. 56 Such a proposal is just one of those things which admits of great ridicule.

b. *To turn* (*in*)*to ridicule*, to make ridiculous.

1673 DRYDEN *Marr. à la Mode* III. i, Methinks I'm to be turn'd into ridicule by all that see me. 1702 ADDISON *Dial. Medals* Wks. 1736 III. 11 The very naming of them is almost sufficient to turn them into ridicule. 1784 COWPER *Task* v. 689 'Tis a change That turns to ridicule the..stately tone of moralists.

† 4. A piece of derisive mirth or light mockery.

1710 ADDISON *Whig Exam.* No. 1 ¶ 14 That..piece of raillery..appears a pleasant ridicule to an ignorant Reader. 1755 H. WALPOLE *Let. to Bentley* 17 Dec., There never was so good a ridicule of all the formal commentators on Shakspeare. 1774 EARL PERCY *Lett.* (1902) 45, I have sent you enclosed a Ridicule upon the Genl Congress.

Ri·dicule, *sb.*[2] *Obs.* exc. *dial.* [a. F. *ridicule*, perversion of *réticule*.] = RETICULE 2.

1805 HARRAL *Scenes of Life* II. 105 Angela instantly drew the paper from her ridicule. 1824 CREEVEY in *C. Papers* (1904) I. 78 Having deposited and left upon the counter her ridicule. 1838 DICKENS *O. Twist* xlii, 'Pockets, women's ridicules, houses, mailcoaches..,' said Mr. Claypole.

† Ri·dicule, *a. Obs.* [a. F. *ridicule*, ad. L. *ridiculus*, f. *rīdēre* to laugh.] = RIDICULOUS *a.* 1.

1672 MARVELL *Reh. Transp.* I. 54 Our Author having undertaken to make Calvin and Geneva ridicule. 1674 *Case of Bankers & Creditors* vii. 31 It was thought very pleasant and ridicule. 1683 D. A. *Art Converse* 28 Let us not discover by a suddain fit of anger our ridicule ambition.

Ri·dicule, *v.* [f. prec. or RIDICULE *sb.*[1]]

† 1. To render ridiculous. *Obs. rare.*

1684 N. S. *Crit. Enq. Edit. Bible* xxvi. 238 Save only when he..Preaches, Cants and ridicules himself. 1735 POPE *Prol. Sat.* 110 One dedicates in high heroic prose, And ridicules beyond a hundred foes.

2. To treat with ridicule or mockery; to make fun of, deride, laugh at.

a 1700 B. E. *Dict. Cant. Crew*, *Ridicule*, to Railly or turn any thing to a Jest. 1705 CLARKE *Nat. & Revealed Relig.* Introd. xv. § 2 They indeavour to ridicule and banter all Humane as well as Divine Accomplishments,..all learning and knowledge. 1726 SWIFT *Gulliver* III. iv, His Countrymen ridiculed and despised him for managing his Affairs no better. 1790 BURKE *Fr. Rev.* 101 Humanity and compassion are ridiculed as the fruits of superstition and ignorance. 1838 LYTTON *Calderon* i, This tale,..ridiculed by most, was yet believed by some. 1874 L. STEPHEN *Hours in Library* (1892) II. ii. 46 The old-fashioned pastorals ridiculed by Pope and Gay.

Hence **Ri·diculed** *ppl. a.*; **Ri·diculing** *vbl. sb.*

1701 NORRIS *Ideal World* I. vi. 305 Those whom he exposes under the ridiculing title of meditative men. 1710 BERKELEY *Princ. Hum. Knowl.* I. § 11 That antiquated and so much ridicul'd Notion of *Materia Prima*. 1887 *Athenæum* 19 Feb. 253/1 There is a good deal of very excellent ridiculing of the early days of Royat.

Ri·diculer. [f. prec.] One who ridicules.

1705 CLARKE *Nat. & Revealed Relig.* Introd. xv. § 4 They are generally Ridiculers of all that is truly excellent. 1748 RICHARDSON *Clarissa* (1811) V. 115 A ridiculer or scoffer at an institution which all sober people reverence. 1812 D'ISRAELI *Calam. Authors* (1867) 115 The wisest men have been some of the most exquisite ridiculers. 1896 *Godey's Mag.* Apr. 396/1 A group..in the midst of which were several of my chief ridiculers.

† Ridi·culize, *v. Obs. rare*[−1]. [Cf. F. *ridiculiser* (1666).] *trans.* To make ridiculous.

1615 CHAPMAN *Odyss.* XXIII. 333 My heart still trembling lest the false alarms That words oft strike up should ridiculize me.

Ridiculo·sity. *rare.* [See next and -ITY.] A ridiculous matter; ridiculousness.

1725 BAILEY *Erasm. Colloq.* (1878) I. 120 Bring..all your witty Jests..and all your Ridiculosities. 1876 *Quiver* XI. 701 Look at the ridiculosity of ladies' dresses behind.

Ridiculous (ridi·kiuləs), *a.* Also 6 **ridyculouse**; β. 6–8 **rediculous**. [ad. L. *rīdiculus* (see RIDICULE *a.*) or *rīdiculōsus*; cf. F. *ridiculeux*.]

1. Exciting ridicule or derisive laughter; absurd, preposterous, comical, laughable.

α. 1550 BALE *Eng. Votaries* II. S j b, A subtile enemye was it..that prouided hym so ridyculouse and obprobriouse a falle. 1570 FOXE *A. & M.* (ed. 2) 1615/2 It is ridiculous & a very fond aunswere [1563 It is an answere to be laughed at]. 1617 MORYSON *Itin.* I. 258 We all obeyed this ridiculous custome, not to offend them. 1655 STANLEY *Hist. Philos.* (1701) 243/2 You are not unreasonable as some are, who think good advice ridiculous. 1711 J. GREENWOOD *Eng. Gram.* 16 We..send our Boys and Girls to learn French, a Custom..very ridiculous and nonsensical. 1745 ELIZA HEYWOOD *Female Spect.* No. 21 (1748) IV. 155 The thing appeared to her so very ridiculous, that..she could not forbear bursting into a loud laughter. 1817 J. SCOTT *Paris Revisit.* (ed. 4) 331 No tale was too ridiculous for momentary belief, if it accorded with the national anger. 1848 W. H. BARTLETT *Egypt to Pal.* x. (1879) 228 Gazelles sometimes occur, with ridiculous magnitude of horns. 1886 MABEL COLLINS *Prettiest Woman* x, It was ridiculous to hurry away like a thief.

Comb. 1859 J. WHITE *Hist. France* (1860) 106 A ridiculous-looking hollow mass composed of plates of iron.

β. 1579 G. HARVEY *Letter-bk.* (Camden) 63 You see nowe what homely and rediculous stuffe I still sende abroade. 1610 SHAKS. *Temp.* II. ii. 169 A most rediculous Monster, to make a wonder of a poore drunkard. 1663 GERBIER *Counsel* 14 Rediculous Ornaments. 1691 L. EACHARD *Descr. Irel.* 24 With great out-Crys, and abundance of rediculous Expostulations.

b. *dial.* (and *U.S.*). Outrageous, scandalous, shameful, etc.

1839 [SIR G. C. LEWIS] *Hereford Gloss.*, *Ridiculous*, scandalous, morally wrong. 1842 C. H. HARTSHORNE *Salop. Antiq.* 547 *Ridiculous*, taken frequently in the sense of indelicate. 1886 *Trans. Amer. Philol. Assoc.* XVII. 43 In the South we often say, 'That's a ridiculous affair,' when we really mean outrageous. 1893 COZENS-HARDY *Broad Norfolk* (ed. 2) 98, I never heard of such conduct. I call it right down ridiculous.

2. a. *absol.* with *the*: That which is ridiculous.

1742 FIELDING *J. Andrews* Pref., The only source of the true Ridiculous..is affectation. 1795 PAINE *Age of Reason* (ed. 2) II. 22 One step above the sublime, makes the ridiculous. 1858 O. W. HOLMES *Aut. Breakf.-t.* iv, It is a very dangerous thing for a literary man to indulge his love for the ridiculous. 1863 *Sat. Rev.* 13 June 755 If there is an air of the ridiculous in the business.

b. As *adv.* Ridiculously, absurdly. *dial.*

1830 GALT *Lawrie T.* III. ix, It was ridiculous strong.

3. Derisive, mocking. *rare*[−1].

1771 LUCKOMBE *Hist. Printing* 132 Scurrilous pamphlets wrote..in a snarleing and ridiculous manner.

Ridi·culously, *adv.* [f. prec. + -LY[2].] In a ridiculous manner; absurdly.

α. 1570 FOXE *A. & M.* (ed. 2) 1383/1 So foolishly and ridiculously seeking holes and corners to hyde them selues in. 1580 G. HARVEY in G. G. Smith *Eliz. Crit. Ess.* (1904) I. 119 We are..not to deuise any..Accent of oure owne, as manye..haue corruptely and ridiculouslye done in the Greeke. 1601 R. JOHNSON *Kingd. & Commw.* (1603) 34 They most ridiculously pretended, that in a vniversall deluge, mankinde was preserued in themselues onely. 1662 STILLINGFL. *Orig. Sacræ* III. iv. § 3 It could not bee then any particular deluge.., as some have ridiculously imagined. 1713 BERKELEY *Hylas & Phil.* III. Wks. 1871 I. 335 Whether it be not ridiculously absurd to misapply names contrary to the common use of language. 1753 HOGARTH *Anal. Beauty* viii. 40 In some it would be ridiculously losing time. 1822 SCOTT *Peveril* iv, If the Puritan was..ridiculously precise in his manners. 1885 *Manch. Exam.* 18 Feb. 3/3 The ridiculously high prices given for violins.

β. 1606 G. W[OODCOCK] *Lives Emperors, Hist. Ivstine* F f 6, Being redicolously left off, he followed swarmes of flies. 1638 SIR T. HERBERT *Trav.* (ed. 2) 65 Rediculously supposed ..[to be] Seth, Enosh and Methuselah.

Ridi·culousness. [f. as prec. + -NESS.] The state or quality of being ridiculous; absurdity.

1603 BP. HALL *Serm.* Wks. 1837 V. 13 The Church of Rome shall vie..with them, whether for number or for ridiculousness. 1661 BOYLE *Style of Script.* (1675) 178 Designed by their ridiculousness to make their readers sport. 1735 BOLINGBROKE *On Parties* 118 They would prove that the Form of our Government is defective to a Degree of Ridiculousness. 1753 HANWAY *Trav.* (1762) I. VII. xciii. 428 Frugality to a degree of ridiculousness. 1843 MIALL in *Nonconf.* III. 744 A certain air of ridiculousness and burlesque. 1875 G. MACDONALD *Malcolm* II. xix. 254 Florimel..attempted a laugh at the ridiculousness of her late situation.

Riding (rai·diŋ), *sb.* Forms: α. 1 ? **þrihing**, **trehing**, 1, 3 **treing**; 1 **treding**, 3 **trething**, **trithing**, **triding**. β. 3 **redyng**, 5 **rithyng**, **-ing**, 6 **rydding**, **rydinge**, 7 **rideing**, 6– **riding**. [Late OE. type **þriðing* or **þriding* (recorded only in Latin contexts or forms), ad. ON. *þriðjung-r* third part, f. *þriði* third: see -ING[3]. The initial consonant was subsequently absorbed by the preceding *t* or *th* of *east*, *west*, *north*.

a 1066 *Laws Edw. Conf.* 31 (Lieberman), Erant etiam potestates super wapentagiis quas trehingas uocabant, scilicet super terciam partem prouincie. 1086 *Domesday Bk.* (1783) 375 Treding dicit quod non habet ibi nisi ix acras et dimid. 1215 *Magna Charta* § 25 Omnes comitatus, hundredi, wapentakii, et trethingii, sint ad antiquas firmas.]

1. One of the three administrative districts into which Yorkshire is divided (the East, West, and North Ridings).

1295–6 *Rolls of Parlt.* I. 227 In Westredyng, In Estredyng, In Northredyng. *Ibid.* 241/2 In Comitatu Ebor'..& in supradictis tribus Trithing. 13.. in Birch *Cartul. Sax.* III. 676 Four Threue..Of ilk a plowgh of Estriding. 1474 *Rolls of Parlt.* VI. 113/1 The Shire of York, in the Estrithyng, Northrithyng, and Westrithyng of the same. 1495 *Act* 11 *Hen. VII*, c. 59 § 1 Within the Westrithing, the Estrithing or the Northrithing of your seid Countie. 1514 FITZHERB. *Justyce of Peace* (1538) 96 Inhabitauntes of the shyre, or rydding, within which the sayde brydge shalbe. 1595 NORDEN *Spec. Brit.*, *Cornwall* (1728) 29 Euerye Shyre or Countye hath his lesser diuisions, as Kente hath Lathes: Sussex Rapes:..and Yorkshire for the greatnes of the circuit hath Rydinges. 1610 HOLLAND *Camden's Brit.* (1637) 689 This whole Shire is divided into three parts..The West-Riding, The East-Riding, and The North-Riding. 1678 PHILLIPS *Suppl.*, Ridings of York-shire, the three Divisions of that County, *viz.* East, West and North. 1704 *Lond. Gaz.* No. 4066/4 The North Riding of the County of York. 1735 *Act* 8 *Geo. II*, c. 6 Preamble, Whereas the Lands in the North Riding of the County of York are generally Freehold [etc.]. a 1845 HOOD *The Desert-Born* 77 If mine had been the luck in Yorkshire to be born, Or any of its ridings. 1872 E. W. ROBERTSON *Hist. Ess.* 120 These districts..have long faded out of recollection except in the great shire of York with its three Ridings.

2. A similar division of other counties or districts in the United Kingdom or its Colonies.

1675 in J. Easton *Narr.* (1858) 79 That the Indyans of the north and west Ridings of Long Island shall..have their Guns restored to them. 1848 *Times* 10 Nov. 6/4 State of Tipperary. The journals of both ridings of this ill-fated county [etc.]. 1867 *Act* 30 & 31 *Vict.* c. 3 § 40 Ontario shall be divided into the Counties, Ridings of Counties, Cities,..and Towns, enumerated in the First Schedule to this act. 1882 *Encycl. Brit.* XIV. 655 The primary divisions of Lincolnshire are three trithings or ridings.

Riding (rai·diŋ), *vbl. sb.* [f. RIDE *v.* + -ING[1].]

I. 1. The action or fact of sitting or travelling on horseback, etc.; a journey or expedition made in this way; † a mounted combat.

a 1300 *Cursor M.* 14992 Mismay yow noght, Bot mas mi

RIDING.

riding *vbl. sb.* ...

A. *adj.* **1.** Of common or frequent occurrence; widespread. **a.** Of hurtful or obnoxious things or conditions; in later use *esp.* of infectious diseases or epidemics.

Bi-ding-school. [RIDING *vbl. sb.*] A school or establishment where riding is taught; *esp.*, a school for training troopers in horsemanship.

Ri·ding-hood. [RIDING *vbl. sb.*] A large hood originally worn while riding, but in later use forming an article of out-door costume for women and children.

Ri·ding-horse. Now *Obs.* or *arch.* [RIDING *vbl. sb.*] A large building specially erected for practising riding in.

Ri·ding-master. [RIDING *vbl. sb.*] A teacher of riding or horsemanship; *esp. Mil.*, an officer having charge of the instruction of troopers in a cavalry regiment.

Ri·ding-officer. A mounted revenue-officer.

Ri·ding-rhyme. Also 6–7 ryme, rime, 7 rhime.

Ri·ding-habit. [RIDING *vbl. sb.*] A dress or costume used for riding; now *spec.* a riding-dress worn by ladies, consisting of a cloth skirt worn with a double-breasted tight-fitting jacket.

Ri·ding-school. [RIDING *vbl. sb.*] A school or establishment where riding is taught.

Ri·dotto (ridō·to), *sb.* Also 8 ridotta. [It.]

Rid-work: see RID *sb.*

Rie, variant of RYE.

Riem (rīm), S. African. [Du. *riem*, G. *riemen*]

Rie·ve, variant of REEVE *sb.*

Ri·facimento (rǐfatʃime·nto). Also 8 refacimento, 9 refaci-, rifacci-mento, rifac(c)i-mento.

Rife (raif), *a.* (*sb.*) and *adv.* Forms: 2 ryfe, 3–5 rif, rif (4 rijf), 5 ryif, ryif, 5–6 ryue, ryve, 5 rif, 6–7 ryfe, ryf, 5–7 ryf, rive, riif, rive, ryyf, 5–6 ryfe, ryffe, 5–7 ryf, 3 rife, rif, 6–7 reef, 7 rief. [Late OE. *rýfe* (*ryfe*), *ryfe*, rife, rive.]

Rife, *v.* Obs. [f. prec.]

Riff-raff. Obs. Forms: 4 ruelic, -li, -ly, 5 ryuely, 7 rivelie, 4 ryfly, 6 rafly, 5 riuely, ryfely, 7 rifraffe (MSw. *riffkaja*, MDa. *rivelige*.)

Riff-raff, *sb.* Obs. rare. [var. of Rif *sb.*]

Riffle, dial. variant of RIPPLE *sb.*

Riffle, *v.* *rare.* [Of obscure history: perh. partly a variant of RUFFLE *v.*, and partly f. *rifle*; cf. also *rir raffle* (see RIPPLE *v.*)]

Riffler. [a. F. *riffler* (16th c. in Godef.), f. *rifler* to scrape, f. OF. *riffler* ...]

Riff-raff, *sb.* Also rif-raff, rif-raffe, riffraff. [ME. *rif and raf*.]

Rifle (rai·f'l), *sb.*[1] Also 7 ryfle. [In sense 1 corresponding to ON. *rifa* to tear, rive; cf. RIVE *v.*]

Rifle (rai·f'l), *sb.*[2] Forms: 4–9 rifil, 4–7 ryfle, 6 riffle, 6 riffel, 6–9 ryfyll, 4–6 ryfle, riffle, 6 riffell. [a. OF. *rifler*, *riffler* to graze, scratch, strip, plunder, etc., of obscure origin (cf. F. *raifler*, *rafler*), and HAVELOK Flem. *rijffelen* 'rapere' (Kilian).]

Rifle, *v.*[1] To search, plunder, or rob a thorough fashion; *esp.* by searching his pockets or clothes; to search (one) thoroughly with intent to rob.

Rifle, *v.*[2] To groove (a gun-barrel with the object of giving to the projectile a rotatory motion for the sake of ...

and putting into it, what he had rifled. a 1648 Ld. Herbert Hen. VIII (1683) 68 They kill'd some, chased the rest and rifled his Goods. 1747 Smollett Regicide IV. iii, Shall he rifle all thy sweets, at will? 1765 Goldsm. Double Transf. 79 The small pox,..rifling every youthful grace, Left but the remnant of a face. 1821 Clare Vill. Minstr. I. 196 Wert thou but a rose..And I a bold bee for to rifle its bloom. 1850 Robertson Serm. Ser. III. xxi. 281 The bodies have been rifled from their mausoleum.

† 4. absol. Of a hawk: (see quot.). Obs.
1486 Bk. St. Albans a vij b, When he shulde Nomme a fowle he seesith bot the federis, and as ofte as he doos so he Rifiith.

† 5. trans. To affect strongly or injuriously; to break or strip off. Obs.
The precise sense in some cases is not quite clear; with latest quots. cf. Riffle v. 2.
1604 Hieron Wks. I. 480 We can be content to heare the word vntill it rifle vs. 1641 Milton Church Govt. II. iii, That lightning which harms not the skin, and rifles the entrals. 1649 Taylor Gt. Exemp. Ad Sect. xii. § 6 Conversation..does too much rifle the ligaments and reverence of spiritual authority. 1655 Stanley Hist. Philos. (1701) 558/2 Where neither blasting Frost, nor hoary Snow Rifle the place; but Heaven is ever bright. 1762 Phil. Trans. LII. 510 The detached side-shootings of this flash only rifling the plaister in several places. 1770 Ibid. LXI. 72 At the same time the roof of the church was rifling.

Hence **Ri·fling** ppl. a.
1611 Speed Hist. Gt. Brit. IX. xxiv. (1632) 1225 A number of rifeling Robbers.

Ri·fle, v.2 Obs. exc. dial. Also 6 **rifel, ryfle, ryffle**, 7 **riffel, riffle**. [ad. Du. rijfelen (in Kilian), obscurely related to F. rafler Raffle v.1, and Sp. rifar, It. arriffare. The vbl. sb. (q. v.) is found somewhat earlier, as in Dutch.]

1. intr. To play at dice; to gamble or raffle (for a stake).
1590 Lodge Rosalynde (Hunterian Cl.) 17 Let him reade on Galen while thou riflest with gold. 1598 Chapman Blinde Beg. Alexandria Wks. 1873 I. 15 Weele..call people together, put crownes a peece, lets rifle for her. 1610 B. Jonson Alch. I. i, He would haue..a familiar, To rifle with, at horses, and winne cups. a 1633 W. Austin Medit. (1635) 111 These Theeves cast Lotts, and rifled for it. 1673 Dryden Amboyna V. i, We will divide their greatest Wealth by Lots, While wantonly we rifle for the rest. 1891 in Hartland (Devon) Gloss.

2. trans. To dispose of by raffling; to gamble away.
1607 Dekker & Marston Northw. Hoe V. D.'s Wks. 1873 III. 74 If you like not that course, but do intend to be rid of her, rifle her at a tauern. 1608 Dekker Lanth. & Candle Lt. Wks. (Grosart) III. 276 In the verie morning when hee is to bee rifled away amongst the Gamsters in Smithfield.

Rifle (rəi·f'l), v.3 [In sense 1 ultimately repr. F. rifler to scratch, scrape; whence obs. Flem. rijffelen 'fricare, radere, scalpere, terere' (Kilian), LG. rifeln, G. riefeln, Da. rifle, Sw. reffla to groove, chamfer, etc. It is not clear whether the special application originated in England or abroad. In sense 2 from Rifle sb.3 2.]

1. trans. To form spiral grooves in (the barrel of a gun or the bore of a cannon).
1635 Patent in Scott Brit. Army (1868) II. 286 To rifle, cutt out, and screwe barrels, as wide, or as close, or as deepe, or as shallowe, as shalbe required. 1769 Falconer Dict. Marine (1776) P 3 The carabine is a sort of musquetoon, the barrel of which is rifled spirally from the breech. 1797 Nicholson's Jrnl. Nat. Phil. I. 382 The effect which is produced by rifling musquetry. 1860 All Year Round No. 73. 548 The same gun rifled..has a recoil two feet less. 1879 Man. Artill. Exerc. 42 R.M.L. guns, up to the 7-inch inclusive, are rifled with a uniform spiral.
transf. 1855 Brit. Ass. Rep. 206 The author pronounced the principle of rifling the shot instead of rifling the gun.. to be absolutely necessary for large [projectiles].

2. To shoot with a rifle. Also intr. with at.
1821 Welby Visit N. Amer. 85 We kept a good look out, a little apprehensive of being rifled at from behind the trees. Ibid. 95 Instances are not infrequent of individuals among them being 'rifled' for having rendered themselves obnoxious. 1901 Sir H. Smith Autobiogr. I. 248 All my Rifle education was required to protect myself from being rifled.

Rifle-ant. [? f. Rifle v.1 Cf. Raffle-ant.] ? The foraging ant.
a 1818 Lewis Jrnl. W. Indies (1834) 251 The rifle-ant.. was imported for the purpose of eating up the ants of the country;..but into the bargain they eat up everything else.

Ri·fle-bird. [f. Rifle sb.3 The precise reason for the name is uncertain: see Newton Dict. Birds 789 and Morris Austral Eng. 387.] An Australian bird of the genus Ptilorrhis (esp. P. paradisea).
1831 Swainson Fauna Bor.-Amer. II. 321 Such a form we..see in..the Rifle-bird of the Australian colonists. 1837 — Nat. Hist. & Classif. Birds II. 144 There is an evident connection between..the Paradise birds..and the rifle-bird of New Holland. 1841 Encycl. Brit. (ed. 7) XXI. 717/1 The rifle-bird is nearly the size of a jay, its bill long and sickle-shaped, and colour a rich dark green, like velvet. 1869 Macgillivray in Gould Birds Austral. Suppl. pl. 50 On one of the Barnard Isles..I found the Victoria Rifle Bird [P. Victoriæ] in considerable abundance. Ibid. pl. 51 This fine Rifle Bird [P. magnifica] inhabits the densest of the brushes in the neighbourhood of Cape York.

Rifled (rəi·f'ld), ppl. a.1 [f. Rifle v.1]
† 1. Disordered, disarranged, ruffled. Obs.
1637 Davenant Madagascar (1638) 37 The Plume a Captive weares, Whose rifled Falls are steept i' th teares Which from his last rage flow. 1677 Otway Titus & Berenice 27 Your rifl'd dress let me in order place.

2. Plundered, pillaged, ransacked.
1719 Young Busiris I. i, While he aloft displays his impious state, With half their rifled kingdoms o'er his brow. 1748 Shenstone Visit to a Lady of Quality iv, Tho' rifled groves and fetter'd streams But ill befriend a poet's dreams. a 1839 Praed Poems (1864) II. 288 The hoarded vengeance and the rifled spoil. 1871 Macduff Mem. Patmos 92 The rifled and deserted dwelling.

Rifled (rəi·f'ld), ppl. a.2 Also 7 rifald, 8 riffled. [f. Rifle v.3 1.]
1. Of firearms: Having a spirally grooved bore.
1689 Spalding Cl. Misc. II. 297 He, with a pocket rifald pistoll, shot the President in at the back. a 1751 B. Robins Math. Tracts (1761) I. 328 Of the Nature and Advantages of Rifled Barrel Pieces. Ibid. 331 Bullets discharged from rifled pieces. 1777 H. Brown tr. Euler's Princ. Gunnery 46 The riffled barrel..is known to carry much farther than a barrel not riffled. 1844 Regul. & Ord. Army 107 The prices for repairs of the Rifled Muskets. 1868 U.S. Rep. Munitions War 93 A four-pounder rifled breech-loading field-piece of crucible steel.

2. Of balls, shells, etc.: † a. Grooved. Obs. b. Having projecting studs or ribs which fit into the grooves in the bore.
The precise sense in the first quot. is not clear.
1760-72 H. Brooke Fool of Qual. (1809) I. 98 Your wound has been made by a rifled ball, and it may cause you some pain to extract it. 1797 Nicholson's Jrnl. Nat. Phil. I. 382 Rifled Shot. 1879 Man. Artill. Exerc. 47 All rifled shells, except segment and common for B.L. field guns.

Ri·fle-gun. Now arch. Also rifle gun. [f. Rifle sb.3 1.] = Rifle sb.3 2.
1776 Ann. Reg. 148 Some experiments were tried at Woolwich..with a rifle gun upon a new construction. 1814 Scott Diary 20 Aug. in Lockhart, I saw a pair of large eagles, and if I had had the rifle-gun might have had a shot. 1868 U.S. Rep. Munitions War 151 We have no desire to decry improvements, or to undervalue heavy rifle-guns. 1890 Henty With Lee in Virginia 105 The grand army numbered 55,000 men, with..49 rifle-guns.

Rifleite (rəi·f'lˌəit). [f. Rifle sb.3 2 + -ite.] A special slow-burning powder used in certain kinds of rifles.
1891 Pall Mall G. 12 Oct. 7/2 The powder 'Rifleite' for the Lee rifle..burns so slow that it cannot be used in the Martini larger bore. 1894 Times 23 July 6/1 The talk of the respective merits of cannonite, cordite, rifleite, and Walsrode has been incessant.

Ri·fleman. [f. Rifle sb.3 2.]
1. A soldier armed with a rifle; formerly the name of a member of certain specially raised regiments or companies, as in the American Revolution; one who shoots with a rifle.
1775 Almon's Remembrancer I. 132/1 The Congress have ordered one thousand more markesmen, or, as we call them, rifle-men, to be raised. 1792 Gentl. Mag. LXII. I. 175 Gen. Scott has proceeded towards Fort Jefferson with 1500 mounted militia and rifle-men. 1802 James Mil. Dict., Mounted Riflemen, a corps of riflemen in the British service, dressed like hussars. 1836 W. Irving Astoria (1849) 158 The loss of two..prime riflemen was a serious affair to the party. 1860 G. H. K. Vac. Tour 140 Popping their heads round for an instant to fire a bark at you, and then dodge back like riflemen.

2. Ornith. a. = Rifle-bird. Also attrib.
1826 Lesson & Garnot Voy. Coquille, Zoologie I. 663 Nous nous procurâmes un très-bel individu de l'epimaque royal à Sydney...Il..portait dans la colonie le nom vulgaire de riffle-man, pour rappeler que ce fut un soldat de la garnison qui le tua le premier. 1886 Newton in Encycl. Brit. XX. 553/1 Rifleman-bird, or Rifle-Bird.
b. A diminutive New Zealand bird (Acanthidositta chloris).
1888 Buller Birds N. Z. (ed. 2) I. 113 The Rifleman is the smallest of our New-Zealand birds.

Rifler 1 (rəi·fləɹ). Now rare. Also 4 **rifflere**, 4-5 **ryfeler**, 5 **rifeler, -or, ryflar**; 4 **riflowr**, 5 **ryflowre**. [f. Rifle v.1]
1. A robber, plunderer, spoiler.
1326 Ann. Paulini (Rolls) I. 321 Vocabatur tunc temporis hujusmodi robaria 'Rifflinge'; et prædones appellabuntur 'Riffleres'. a 1350 in Reliq. Antiq. II. 121 [Death is] Riche mannis riflowr, Povere mannis purveyowr, Old mannis somenowr. 1393 Langl. P. Pl. C. VII. 316 Roberd þe ryfeler on reddite lokede. 1399 — Rich. Redeles III. 197 Robbers and riffleris of peple. c 1420 Lydg. Assembly of Gods 688 Robbers, reuers, rauenous ryfelers. c 1440 Promp. Parv. 433/2 Ryflowre (ryflar or rifelor, P.), depredator, spoliator. 1591 Greene Conny-catch. II. Wks. (Grosart) X. 87 In Prigging Law. The towler, the Rifler. 1611 Florio, Raffatore, a rifler. 1643 Quarles Loyall Convert Wks. (Grosart) I. 144/2 Cromwell, that profest defacer of Churches ..and Rifler of the Monuments of the dead. 1750 Carte Hist. Eng. II. 379 The riflers..committed depredations on the most irreproachable persons, when any booty was to be got.
2. A hawk that 'rifles'. Obs. exc. arch.
1486 Bk. St. Albans a vij b, As ofte as he doos so be Rifiith; therfore such hawkys been called Rifeleres if they doo ofte so. 1607 Heywood Wom. Kill'd w. Kindn. Wks. 1874 II. 104 She did discomfit Some of her feathers; but she brake away. Come, come, your hawk is but a rifler. 1828 Scott Br. Lamm. xxix, She's going to prove, after all, nothing better than a rifler. 1820 — Abbot vii, I would rather have a rifler on my perch than a false knave at my elbow.

Rifler 2. [f. Rifle sb.3 2.] = Rifleman 1.
1776 McIntosh in Sparks Corr. Amer. Rev. (1853) I. 169 The two armed vessels..were attacked by parties of riflers ordered for that purpose. 1807 J. Barlow Columb. V. 626 Morgan in front of his bold riflers towers.

Ri·fle-range. [f. Rifle sb.3 2 + Range sb.1]
1. The distance that a rifle-ball will carry. Cf. Rifle-shot 1.
1850 R. G. Cumming Hunter's Life S. Afr. (ed. 2) I. 192 He kept feeding just out of rifle-range. 1863 Sat. Rev. 8 Aug. 187 Their skirmishers came within rifle-range of Fort Wagner.
2. A place for practising rifle-shooting. (Cf. Range sb.1 11 c.)
1885 Act 48 & 49 Vict. c. 36 Title, Land held by..a Volunteer Corps for an Artillery or Rifle Range.

Ri·fle-shot. Also rifleshot. [Rifle sb.3 2.]
1. Such a distance as may be covered by a shot from a rifle.
1840 Dickens Old C. Shop li, The Wilderness..was within rifle-shot of his bachelor retreat. 1871 Kingsley At Last xvii, Threading our way between them, sometimes not a rifle-shot from the cliffs.
2. One skilled in shooting with a rifle.
1850 R. G. Cumming Hunter's Life S. Afr. (1902) 18/1, I have always been reckoned..to be a very fair rifle-shot. 1869 Ruskin Q. of Air i. § 36 If there be any good rifleshots here, they know something about Athena's parrying.
3. A shot fired with a rifle.
1875-6 Stevenson Ess. Trav. (1905) 167 Out of the thick of the trees, comes the jar of rifle-shots.

Ri·fling, vbl. sb.1 [f. Rifle v.1] The action of the vb.; plundering, sacking; an instance of this.
1326 [see Rifler 1]. 1377 Langl. P. Pl. B. v. 238, 'I wende ryflynge were restitucioun,' quod he. 1532 More Confut. Tindale Wks. 585/2 After many soules sent vnto the deuill by theym, they shoulde..fall to ryfling, robbery, murdre, and manslaughter. 1568 Grafton Chron. II. 84 Such as resisted them in their rifelynges and spoyles. 1633 Heywood Eng. Trav. II. i, Here comes some, that it seems were at the rifling of the dead carcases. a 1662 Heylin Laud I. (1671) 181 Found in the rifling of his Study amongst the rest of his Papers. 1748 Anson's Voy. II. xiv. 285 They still remember ..the sacking of their cities, the rifling of their convents. 1862 S. St. John Forests Far East I. 58 The rifling of the place of interment has often given great and deserved offence to the relations. 1870 Disraeli Lothair vi, Hexham House..has escaped the rifling arts of speculators in furniture.

† **Ri·fling**, vbl. sb.2 Obs. [f. Rifle v.2 Cf. MDu. rijffeling.] The action of raffling or dicing; an instance or occasion of this.
1569 in Ellis Orig. Lett. Ser. I. II. 255 Theare was none used but one onlie Game, called Riflinge, by which..diverse persons weare spoyled and utterlie undon. 1581 Burford Reg. in Hist. MSS. Comm., Varr. Collect. I. 68 They have used certeine games called Trolemadame and ryffling for disshes and platters,..being unlawfull and cossyning games. 1609 Dekker Gull's Horn-bk. vii, To conclude, [they] count it an honour, either to inuite or be inuited to any Rifling. 1611 Cotgr., Ballotage, a rifling, or lotterie.

Ri·fling, vbl. sb.3 [f. Rifle v.3] The operation of making grooves in the bore of a fire-arm; the grooving itself, or the nature of this.
1797 Nicholson's Jrnl. Nat. Phil. I. 382 The method of rifling consists in cutting..spiral grooves [etc.]. 1839 Ure Dict. Arts 477 The operation of grooving is repeated till the whole number of riflings is completed. 1859 F. A. Griffiths Artil. Man. (1862) 1 The Rifling is 3 grooves and one turn in 6 ft. 6 in. 1897 Q. Rev. Jan. 199 Rifling, projectiles, sights have all been revolutionized.
attrib. 1839 Ure Dict. Arts 476 After the barrel is bored, and rendered truly cylindrical, it is fixed upon the rifling machine. 1862 Catal. Internat. Exhib., Brit. II. No. 2612 The pitch, or rifling turn, is one in 20 inches.

Rifraf, rif raf, rifraff(e, obs. ff. Riff-raff.

† **Rift**, sb.1 Obs. Also ryft, hryft. [OE. rift (ryft) neut., = ON. ript fem., ripti neut.] a. A cloak. b. A veil.
c 725 Corpus Gloss. (Hessels) L 80 Laena, rift. Ibid. P 126 Palla, rift. c 950 Lindisf. Gosp. Matt. xxvii. 31 [Hi] ongeredon hine by ryfte. c 1000 Ælfric Lev. iv. 17 Nime se sacerd his blod..and sprenge..on þæt ryft. c 1205 Lay. 28476 Me hire hafd bi-weide mid ane hali rifte.

Rift, sb.2 Also 5-6 **ryft(e**, 4-5 **rifte**, 5 **reft**. [Of Scand. origin: cf. Da. and Norw. rift, a cleft, chink, etc., OIcel. ript breach of contract. The stem is that of the vb. Rive, to split.]
† 1. An act of tearing or rending; a splitting, riving. Obs.
a 1300 Cursor M. 8220 Sua depe þair rote þai samen kest, Þat moght þam naman þeþen win, Wit-vten rift for ani gin. c 1400 Destr. Troy 12697 Þe remnond..Herd þe rurde & þe ryfte of þe rank schippis. c 1440 Promp. Parv. 433/2 Ryfte, or ryvynge of cloþe, or cuttynge, scissura.
2. A cleft, fissure, or chasm in the earth, a rock, etc. (Cf. Reft sb.2, Riff sb.5)
13.. E. E. Allit. P. B. 964 Þe grete barrez of þe abyme he barst vp at onez, Þat alle þe regioun to-rof in riftes ful grete. c 1400 Maundev. (Roxb.) xi. 43 Þe roche clafe in twa, and in þat rift he hidd him. c 1425 Wyntoun Cron. IV. x. 1204 Sa hugsum þar þat oppynnynge fel Þat throw þat rift men mycht se hell. 1511 Guylforde's Pilgr. (Camden) 26 Whiche ryfte gothe downe thorughout the Rok of Caluery. 1606 Shaks. Ant. & Cl. III. iv. 32 As if the world should cleaue, and that slaine men Should soader vp the Rift. 1639 Ainsworth Annot. Ps. lx. 4 Earthquakes, rifts and chinkes appeare. 1725 Family Dict. s.v. Garden, But you must above all things remove Stones out of your Garden Ground, and leave no Rifts therein. 1799 Kirwan Geol. Ess. 29 Some few petrifactions have been found in the rifts even of granitic mounts. 1814 Scott Ld. of Isles III. xvi, Yonder peak..That to the evening sun uplifts The griesly gulfs and slaty rifts. 1856 Ruskin Mod. Painters IV. v. xix. § 27 The rocks above are torn by their glaciers into rifts and wounds that are never healed. 1876 Smiles Sc. Natur. viii. 134 The rift in the glen is almost overhung by the ruins of the ancient Church of Aberdour.
b. An opening or break in clouds or mist.
a 1400-50 Alexander 1756 Riȝt as a flaw of fell snawe

ware fallyn of a ryft. 1513 Douglas Æneis VIII. vii. 47 We se The schynnand brokin thunderis lychtning fle Wyth subtill fyry stremis throu a ryft. 1671 Milton P. R. IV. 411 The Clouds From many a horrid rift abortive pour'd Fierce rain with lightning mixt. 1863 Jean Ingelow Honours II, A soul-mist, through whose rifts familiar stars Beholding we misname. 1874 Symonds Sk. Italy & Greece (1898) I. xiii. 282 Through their rifts the depth of heaven is of a hard and gemlike blue.
c. A split, crack, rent, or chink in any object or article. Now somewhat rare.
c 1400 Rom. Rose 2661 Than shal thou go the dore bifore, If thou maist fynde any score, Or hole, or reft [etc.]. c 1440 Promp. Parv. 433/2 Ryfte, in a walle, or boord, or oþer lyke,..rima. 1513 Douglas Æneis I. iii. 51 Salt watter stremis Fast bullerand in at every ryft and boir. 1578 Banister Hist. Man I. 15 This great rift is that which [is] in the lower part of the roundell of the eye. 1626 Bacon Sylva § 556 [A seed] which falling upon the bough of a tree that hath some Rift, putteth forth Misseltoe. 1693 Evelyn De la Quint. Compl. Gard. 3 This Yellowness appearing in some part of it or other, and not seldom with some Rift, or little Casm's about the Stalk. 1725 Family Dict. s.v. False Quarter, The Chink..must be opened to the Quick with a drawing Iron, and the Rift filled with a Rowl of Hurds. 1859 Tennyson Vivien 240 It is the little rift within the lute.
† d. A chap or crack in the skin. Obs.
1553 Eden Treat. Newe Ind. (Arb.) 16 Theyr skinne is very rowghe & full of chappes & riftes like the bark of a tree. 1598 Gerarde Herbal I. xxxvii. 54 The meale thereof healeth all the rifts of the fundament. 1614 Markham Cheap Husb. I. xliii, Bloody rifts..are chaps or rifts in the palate of the horses mouth. [Hence in Dict. Rust. (1704) s.v. Chops; (1726) s.v. Rifts.]
e. fig. or in fig. contexts.
1627 Jackson Chr. Obed. Wks. XII. 190 Nothing but this bred that lamentable schism or rift in the walls of God's house. 1642 Fuller Holy & Prof. St. V. xviii. 4 Through the rifts and chinks of their several aims and ends. 1879 Farrar St. Paul II. 122 The needless widening of the rift which separated them.
3. Oak timber rent or split into strips or boards, in place of being sawn. ? Obs.
1577 Harrison England II. xii, Lattise..made either of wicker or fine rifts of oke in chekerwise. 1670 R. Coke Disc. Trade 22 Rift bearing about a third penny more price then if it were sawn into planck.
b. So rift timber. (Cf. Reft ppl. a.2)
1875 Temple & Sheldon Hist. Northfield, Mass. 14 Oak, or rift timber, as it was called, i.e., timber that could be easily split into clap-boards and shingles.
4. Comb. **Rift-valley**, a valley with steep parallel walls, formed by the subsidence of a part of the earth-crust.
1894 J. W. Gregory in Geogr. Jrnl. IV. 295 The famous Yosemite valley may be taken as a well-known type of these 'rift valleys', as they may conveniently be called. 1900 H. R. Mill Internat. Geog. (ed. 2) 53 The..lowered masses..give rise..to rift-valleys, such as the upper Rhine plain or the great rift-valleys of the Dead Sea.

Rift, sb.3 Now Sc. and north. dial. [f. Rift v.2] An act of belching, an eructation.
c 1425 Wyntoun Cron. V. iii. 53 He thoucht to ordane.. Be statute qwhen men sulde lat ga Out of þar bodeis riftis of wynde. 1570 Levins Manip. 118 A Rift, belch, ructus. 1790- in dial. texts and glossaries (see Eng. Dial. Dict.).

Rift, sb.4 U.S. [? Alteration of riff, obs. var. of Reef sb.1]
1. A rapid, a cataract; esp. one formed by the protrusion of rocks in the bed of a stream.
1755 L. Evans Middle Brit. Col. 27 The River is full of Falls and Rifts for forty Leagues. 1778 T. Hutchins Descr. Virg. 21 The Muskingum is muddy, and not very swift, but no where obstructed with Falls or Rifts.
2. The wash of the surf on a beach or shore.
1869 Stedman Lyrics & Idylls, Surf iii, Light falls her foot where the rift follows after.

† **Rift**, sb.5 Obs. rare—0. (See quot.)
1728 Chambers Cycl. s. v. Horse, The Hoof is call'd the Horn,..the Ball of the Foot, the Frog; the Part to be pared or cut off the Hoof when overgrown, the Rift.

Rift, v.1 Also 6 ryft(e. [Of Scand. origin: cf. ON. ripta to break (a bargain, etc.); also MDa. ryftæ, MSw. rypta to tear or break up.]
1. intr. a. To form fissures or clefts; to gape open, to split. ? Obs.
a 1300 Cursor M. 22633 Þe erth þai sal do for to rift. 1530 Palsgr. 691/1, I ryft, as bordes that gape a sonder, je me desbrise...This bordes wyll ryfte, if they be nat taken hede of. 1611 Shaks. Wint. T. V. i. 66 Then I'ld shrieke, that euen your eares Should rift to heare me. 1626 Bacon Sylva § 843 When Ice is congealed in a cup, the Ice will swell instead of Contracting; and sometimes Rift. 1664 Evelyn Sylva 61 It is certain, that it never rifts, or cleaves, but with great violence.
b. To break through something. rare—1.
1859 Miss Mulock Rom. Tales 319 Rifting through the harmonious cloud, let there be a sunburst of melody.
2. trans. To rend apart or asunder, split, cleave.
1566 Drant Horace, Sat. I. i. A vj b, With grounded axe cutte him in twaine, And rifted him throughoute. 1590 Spenser F. Q. II. vii. 23 A song of bale..That hart of flint asonder could have rifte. 1610 Shaks. Temp. V. i. 45 To the dread ratling Thunder Haue I giuen fire, and rifted Ioues stowt Oke With his owne Bolt. 1671 Milton Samson 1621 At sight of him the people with a shout Rifted the Air. 1743 Blair The Grave 48 Some rift half down Their branchless trunks. 1793 G. White Nat. Hist. Selb. lxxxvii, Some hillocks..were rifted in every direction. 1820 Shelley Let. to Peacock 20 Nov., The loftiest Apennines..are here rifted to their base. a 1861 Palgrave Norm. & Eng. (1864) III. 337 Giving a temporary support to the walls which they have split and rifted.
b. dial. To break up (grass-land) with the plough. Also new-rift, adj.
c 1636 Strafford in Browning & Forster Life (1892) 186, I know right well the profits of those new rift grounds. 1829 in Brockett N. C. Gloss.
c. To form or force by cleaving. Also fig.
1849-50 Alison Hist. Europe II. lxxvi. § 74. 481 Whether the rugged chasm..had been rifted from the hillside by an earthquake. 1854 Thoreau Walden, Where I lived, The intellect..rifts its way into the secret of things.

Rift, v.2 Now Sc. and north. dial. Also 4 **rifte**, 5 **ryfte**. [a. ON. rypta, repta (cf. MSw. rāpta), f. a stem rup-, which appears also in ON. ropi belching, Icel. ropa to belch.]
1. trans. To belch out (wind, etc.). Also fig., to utter (words, etc.) in a manner suggestive of this.
a 1300 E. E. Psalter xliv. 1 Mi hert riftet [L. eructavit] gode worde. Ibid. cxviii. 171 Rifte sal [L. eructabunt] mine lippes ympne. a 1340 Hampole Psalter xliv. 1 As he þat is ful of wickidnes riftis an ill worde. 1601 Holland Pliny II. 16 If a man take them with vnripe oliues condite, he shall neither belch or rift wind so much. 17.. Ramsay The Lure 33 Nor spat he fire, or brimstone rifted. 1880 Beattie John Arnha' (1882) 39 Spewin' reek an' riftin' fire.
2. intr. To break wind upwards from the stomach; to belch.
a 1340 Hampole Psalter xviii. 2 Bi riftynge he takyns fulnes of wit, for wha sa riftes it semes þat he is ful. 1483 Cath. Angl. 308/1 To Ryfte, ructare. c 1500 Droichis Part of Play 51 in Dunbar's Poems (1893) II. 316 The hevin reirdit quhen scho wald rift. 1535 Lyndesay Satyre 4353 Scho riftit..Till scho had castin ane cuppill of quarts. 1631 R. H. Arraignm. Whole Creature xiii. 169 Let a mans stomacke be so full of Winde, till he belch againe, and Rift, and breake wind. 1669 W. Simpson Hydrol. Chym. 103 It is not enough to make one rift or belch. 1721 Ramsay Lucky Spence i, Three times the carline grain'd and rifted. 1797 Brydges Hom. Trav. II. 153 His stomach is so full of ire That when he rifts he belches fire. 1821- in dial. texts and glossaries (see Eng. Dial. Dict.).
b. With up. To rise upon the stomach; hence fig., to come back unpleasantly to the memory.
1636 Rutherford Lett. (1862) I. lxxii. 186 In the resurrection..our yesternight's sour drink and swinish dregs shall rift up upon us. 1877 in Holderness Gloss. (E. D. S.).
c. To boast or brag.
1786 Har'st Rig xxxv, Some carle that's weel ken'd to rift, Declares, whan in a blasting tift [etc.].
Hence **Ri·fting** vbl. sb. and ppl. a.
a 1340 [see the vb., sense 2]. 1581 Mulcaster Positions x. (1887) 56 Weaknesse or pewkishnesse of stomacke, with vomiting or bytter rifting. 1597 Lowe Chirurg. (1634) 53 Sleeping in the day..hindereth the concoction, of the which commeth ganting, rifting,..and divers sicknesses. 1824 Mactaggart Gallovid. Encycl. 334, I envy not your fu' broth-pot, Your beefy, bursen, rifting lot.

Rifted, ppl. a. [f. Rift v.1] Split, cleft, cloven; broken by a rift or rifts.
1602 Marston Antonio's Rev. II. ii, Defyance to thy power, thou rifted jawne. 1634 Milton Comus 518 Rifted Rocks whose entrance leads to hell. 1725 Pope Odyss. xxiv. 9 The cavern of some rifted den, Where flock nocturnal bats. 1797 Southey Joan of Arc VI. 17 Breaking through a rifted cloud The moonlight show'd. 1863 Longf. Wayside Inn, Saga K. Olaf II. 21 The rifted Streamers o'er him shook and shifted. 1877 Tennyson Har. I. ii. 58 The rifted pillars of the wood.

Riftless, a. [f. Rift sb.2 + -less.] Having no rift or rifts.
1890 Universal Rev. 15 June 295 Miss Winterbotham was really and after all riftless, completely sound. 1892 Jane Barlow Irish Idylls 102 The dark riftless cloud-canopy.

Rift-valley: see Rift sb.2 4.

Ri·fty, a. [f. Rift sb.2] Having rifts, full of rifts or chinks.
1637 Rutherford Lett. (1862) I. cxx. 299 Nothing but glory will make tight and fast our leaking and rifty vessels. 1796 Kirwan Elem. Min. (ed. 2) I. 110 These are rifty, and present numerous distinct concretions. 1811 Pinkerton Petral. II. 250 [It] may become rifty, and thus split by the weather.

† **Rifty tufty**, adv. Obs.—1 Helter-skelter.
1592 Breton Pilgr. Parad. Wks. (Grosart) I. 16/2 To sweare, and stare, vntil we come to shore, Then rifty tufty, each one to his skore.

Rig, sb.1 Also 4-6 **ryg**, 6 **rigge**, 7- **rigg**. [Northern and Sc. form of Ridge sb.1]
1. The back, in man or animals; = Ridge sb.1 1.
a 1300 Havelok 1775 Bernard stirt up, þat was ful big, And caste a brinie up-on his rig. a 1352 Minot Poems (ed. Hall) vii. 81 Ilk Inglis man on oþers rig Ouer þat water er þai went. a 1400-50 Alexander (Dubl.) 775* Som þar riggez owt rytte & som þar ribbez rent. c 1450 Holland Howlat 835 The Tuchet gird to the Golk,..Raif his taile fra his rig. 1513 Douglas Æneis XI. xv. 104 His taill, that on hys ryg befor tymes lay, Vnder hys waymb [he] lattis fall. 1581 Rec. Elgin (New Spald. Cl.) I. 162 That all flescheris.. present their haill fleschis to the mercat haill oncuttit in the rig or ony vther part. 1718 Ramsay Christ's Kirk Gr. III. xii, To try the pith o's rigg and reins, They gart him cadge this pack. 1846- in northern dial. glossaries. 1889 Mabel Peacock Taales Linkisheere 59 If I'd wool upo' my rig, saame as sheep hes.
2. = Ridge sb.1 4 (4 b). Freq. in place-names in the north of England and south of Scotland.
[c 1190 Liber de Melros I. 46 Pratum..in feudo de Innerwic subtus Brunrig. a 1250 Ibid. 219 Usque ad fossatum de Grenrig.]
1375 Barbour Bruce XIX. 308 Our ane hye ryg thai saw rydand Toward thame evyn a batteil braid. 1513 Douglas Æneis Wks. 1874 II. 284 Thar lyis.., amyd the sey, a hirst or ryg of craggy rolkis. 1587 Fleming Contn. Holinshed III. 968/1 Entering with the same into Scotland, [he] was incountered at Halidon rig by the earle of Arraine. 1708 Thoresby Diary (1830) I. 380 The Roman rig or ridge, which passeth by it in its course. 1715 Pennecuik Tweeddale at Then..below Kirkhouse..The Riggs and the Know of Traquair. 1788 W. Marshall Rur. Econ. Yorksh. II. 348 Rigg,..a long narrow hill. 1817 Scott Rob Roy xviii, I hae taen the bent ower the Otterscrape-rigg. 1896 Snowden Web of Weaver i, The black crags upon the moor rig.
3. Agric. = Ridge sb.1 5 (cf. corn-rig, harvest-rig, lea-rig). Also, the elevation between each pair of plough-furrows in a ploughed field.
For examples of the phrases rig and balk, rig and furrow, rig and rean, etc., see Eng. Dial. Dict.
1513 Douglas Æneis VI. xiv. 96 Quhair thow thi riggis telis for to saw. 1573 Satir. Poems Reform. xlii. 729 Quhidder were it better..Till labour ane of them onlie...Or in ilk steding teill ane Rig. 1639 Horn & Rob. Gate Lang. Unl. xxxii. § 391 As he layeth it up into rigs, with the one hand hee holdeth the plough-handle.., with the other the plough-staffe. 1681 Colvil Whigs Supplic. (1751) 72 Thistles with corn grow on the riggs, And rogues may lurk among the Whigs. 1783 Burns Rigs o' Barley ii, I kiss'd her owre and owre again, Amang the rigs o' barley. 1820 Blackw. Mag. VII. 265 Dibbled in rigs and furrows like beans and potatoes. 1834 Penny Cycl. II. 224/1 Ploughing..in lands or stitches, as they are called in England, and, in Scotland, riggs. 1881 Blackmore Cristowell xxxiii, Mrs. Sage was glad indeed to see Betty Cork come up the rigs.
b. As a measure of land. = Ridge sb.1 5 b.
1541 Rec. Elgin (New Spald. Cl.) I. 59 William Malcome protestit that he hes rycht to ane rig of land liand on the vast syid of Merevall. 1589 Wills & Inv. N.C. (Surtees, 1860) 167, I give to..my servantt, thre buttes or rigges of land. 1681 Sc. Acts, Chas. II (1814) VIII. 295 Other two Riggs of land thereof lyand contigue in the field called the Gallowbank. 1720 Ramsay Rise & Fall of Stocks 51 Some lords and lairds sell'd riggs and castles. 1724 — Tea-t. Misc. (1733) II. 122 Woods and parks And castles and riggs. a 1796 Burns Country Lassie 33 Gear will buy me rigs o' land. 1814 Scott Wav. lxvii, I now wish..I could have left Rose the auld hurley-house, and the riggs belonging to it. 1884 Pall Mall G. 10 May 1/2 A cottar..paying perhaps five or ten shillings to the crofter for the use of a 'rig' or two of potatoes.
c. The shearers engaged in reaping a ridge.
1786 Har'st Rig xxiii, The next rig redds them to take care To cut their fur. 1897 Pryde Queer Folk 168 Each rig or company..of shearers tries to get before the others.
4. a. The centre line of a web of cloth, along which it is folded; the line of a fold in cloth, as contrasted with the free edge.
1469 Sc. Acts, Jas. III (1814) II. 95 It is thocht expedient þat in tyme cummyn all wolen claith be met be the Rig, and nocht be þe selwich. 1862 C. C. Robinson Dial. Leeds Gloss. s.v., When cloth is folded, or doubled up, and cuttled, the two extremities are called respectively the 'rig' and the 'list'.
b. The top of a roof; = Ridge sb.1 3.
1570 Levins Manip. 118 Ye Rig of a house, culmen. 1854 Miss Baker Northampt. Gloss., Rig or Rig-Piece, the top of a roof, the ridge of a building. a 1864 Clare Rem. (1873) 215 The sparrow on the cottage rig.
† c. The shoulder of an arrow-head. Obs.—1
1545 Ascham Toxoph. (Arb.) 149 To drawe..alwayes after one fashion vntil you come to the rig or shouldring of ye head, is best.
d. A rib in a stocking; esp. in rig and fur (transf. from 3), used attrib. or as adv.
1822 Galt Sir A. Wylie x, He had on a pair o' dark-blue ..rig-and-fur..worsted stockings. 1838 Holloway Prov. Dict., Rig,..a rib in a stocking. 1854 Miss Baker Northampt. Gloss., Rig and Fur, ribbed; as 'rig and fur'd stockings'. 1855 Robinson Whitby Gloss. 154 'Do you knit your stockings rig and fur?' that is, with an alternate rib and indent longways.
5. Comb., as **rig-back**, the back; **rig-band**, = Ridge-band; **rig-length**, the length of a ridge of land; **rig-piece** (see 4 b); **rig-rope** (see quot. c 1700); **rig-tile**, = Ridge-tile; **rig-tow**, = rig-rope; **rig-tree**, = Ridge-tree.
For other combs. in dial. use see Eng. Dial. Dict.
1796 Lauderdale Poems 62 To lay Britannia flat On her *rig back. c 1817 Hogg Tales & Sk. VI. 134 He..struck a third on the rigback, where no leister can pierce a fish. 1408-9 Durham Acc. Rolls (Surtees) 607 Cartcharnas,..belybandes et *Rygbandes. 1661 Sc. Acts, Chas. II (1814) VII. 225/2 The said burgh..is within a *rig lenth to the same old and rwinous burgh. 1790 Morison Poems 6 (E. D. D.), He'll wi' ease a rigg length rin. c 1800 A. Carlyle Autobiogr. (1860) 138 That part of it..was divided into three shots, as they were called, or rigg lengths. c 1700 Kennett in MS. Lansd. 1033 fol. 323 A *Rig-rope, the rope that is fastned to the rods of a cart or waggon and goes over the saddle of the Fillar horse. Westmorl. 1805 Stagg Epit. Burns xvi, A rig-reape, braugham, pair o' heams. c 1460 Fabric Rolls York Minster (Surtees) 35 In lx *rygtiell emptis de eodem Willelmo, 20 d. 1484 Nottingham Rec. III. 230, iij rigg tyles þat were tiled apon the Mercerie. c 1310 Durham Acc. Rolls (Surtees) 511 Pro carecta Prioris et viij Wambtoues et *Rigtoues. 1313-4 Ibid. 512 Rigtowes et Wambetowes. 1672 O. Heywood Diaries (1882) I. 289 We had busy work in laying our *rig-tree. 1703 Thoresby Let. to Ray (E.D.S.) s.v. Bawks, A prick-post under the rig-tree. 1889 Tennyson Owd Roä lviii, When the rigtree was tummlin' in.

Rig, sb.2 Now dial. Also 4 **ryg(e**, 7-9 **rigg**. [? a. ON. hregg storm and rain.] A storm, tempest, strong wind. In later use chiefly in Michaelmas rigs.
13.. E. E. Allit. P. B. 354, I sende out by-lyue Such a rowtande ryge þat rayne schal swyþe. Ibid. 382 For neuer cowþe stynt þe roȝe raynande ryg & þe raykande wawez. 1603 Owen Pembrokeshire (1892) 74 Vpon springe tydes, or after great Riggs of the sea. Ibid. 75 With Tempest, and Riggs of the sea. 1745 Mrs. Delaney Life & Corr. (1861) II. 374 As Michaelmass 'riggs' (or winds) have an ill name,

we think it best to defer our journey to October. 1796 Burke Regic. Peace III. Wks. VIII. 331 Appearing..before the riggs of old Michaelmas were yet well composed, and when the inclement storms of winter were approaching. 1836 Wilbraham Chesh. Gloss. (ed. 2), Rig, a strong blast of wind. The storms which usually prevail about the time of the autumnal equinox are called Michaelmas Riggs.

Rig, sb.3 Also **rigg**. = Ridgel, Riggald. Also attrib., as rig-horse.
c 1430 Lydg. Min. Poems (Percy Soc.) 54 Late at eve thou wolt unspere the gate, And grope at morwe if riggis bak be wett. 1578 Nottingham Rec. IV. 181 No butcher shalle put in enye rigges into ye medows. 1702 Lond. Gaz. No. 3852/4 One side of his Cod looks like a Rig. 1705 Ibid. No. 4125/4 A light black Rig Horse, one Stone come down on the near side of his Cod. 1851 Jrnl. R. Agric. Soc. XII. II. 431 Three out of the four [sheep]..were, indeed, what are termed 'riggs', or were only half-castrated. 1881 Greener Gun 509 Ox-deer, or 'heaviers', and rigs are in season with the yeld-hinds till the end of January.

Rig, sb.4 Now dial. Also 6 **ryg, rigg**, 6-7 **rigge**. [Of obscure origin: cf. Rig v.4] A wanton girl or woman.
1575 Gamm. Gurton III. iii, Nay, fy on thee thou rampe, thou ryg, with al that take thy part. 1598 E. Guilpin Skial. (1878) 49 My Muse shall play the rig Once in her dayes, but shee shall quittance thee. a 1618 J. Davies (Heref.) Wittes Pilgr. Wks. (Grosart) II. 49/2 The most voluptuous ouerwanton Rigge, Proud Plentie, scornes meeke Pieties Woman-hood. 1650 Fuller Pisgah IV. vi. 110 Let none condemn them for Rigs, because thus hoiting with boys. 1694 Motteux Rabelais, Prognost. v, Those whom Venus is said to rule, as Punks, Jills, Flirts,..Misses, Cats, Riggs. 1829 Brockett N. C. Gloss. (ed. 2), Rig, a female light in her carriage, a wanton. 1886 Elworthy W. Somerset Word-bk. s.v., Proper rig her is, an' no mistake.

Rig, sb.5 slang or colloq. [Of obscure origin. For dialect variations of meaning and phrasing see the Eng. Dial. Dict.]
1. Sport, banter, ridicule. Chiefly in phr. to run (one's) rig(s) upon (another), to make sport or game of, to banter unsparingly. Now dial.
1725 New Cant. Dict., Rig, Game, Diversion, Ridicule. 1753 A. Murphy Gray's Inn Jrnl. No. 25 You have been very facetious all Night,—you have run your rig upon me. 1802 Spirit Publ. Jrnls. VI. 113 I'll tell thee, Dear Jack, without nonsense or rig, Why I'm constantly seen in this old flaxen wig. 1814 in Nichols Lit. Anecd. 18th C. (1816) VIII. 543 You are always running your rig upon me, and calling me stupid. 1840 Thackeray Yellowpl. Mem. (1869) 330 Mr. Deuceace, don't you be running your rigs upon me.
2. A trick, scheme, or dodge; a method of cheating or swindling. (Cf. Racket sb.3 3.) Rig sale, a sale by auction under false pretences.
1775 in Farmer Musa Pedestris (1896) 55 I'm up to all your knowing rigs. 1796 Grose's Dict. Vulgar T. (ed. 3) s.v., I am up to your rig; I am a match for your tricks. c 1830 Frauds of London 12 (Thimble-riggers) The rig is practised at fairs, at races, or on public roads. 1851 Chamb. Jrnl. XV. 102 The 'Rig' Sale. Ibid. 105 Sometimes the Rig..is only confined to one or two rooms, or to a certain species of goods. 1894 Maskelyne Sharps & Flats 194 The 'rig is worked'; or in other words, the swindle is perpetrated, by means of a dealing-box.
b. = Corner sb. 14.
1877 Giffen Stock Exch. Sec. 46 The operations of such syndicates are usually accompanied by market manœuvres which are described generically by the name of 'rigs'. 1897 Westm. Gaz. 9 April 2/3 When a man first gets into his hands the whole stock of any particular article and then goes into the market and secures contracts for more than exists, that is what is called a 'rig' or a 'corner'.
3. A frolic or prank; an act of a mischievous or wanton kind; a 'game'.
1811 Sporting Mag. XXXVII. 75 War cannot..be styled a sporting rig; why then, I answer, it is a fashionable rig. a 1845 Barham Ingol. Leg. Ser. III. Wedding-Day, Don't grudge them their jigs, And their frolics and 'rigs'. 1866 Cornh. Mag. Nov. 620 Everybody says that she is as proud as Lucifer; and, after all, nobody knows what rigs she has been up to.
b. In phr. to run a (or the) rig, to run (one's) rigs, to play pranks, to run riot.
1782 Cowper Gilpin xxv, He little dreamt, when he set out, Of running such a rig! 1797 B. Hamilton in Beddoes Contrib. Phys. & Med. Knowl. (1799) 315 To run the rig with the boys in the street in place of going on my errand. 1818 Scott in Lockhart Life IV. 185 While Tom marks out a dyke or drain.., She's fancy may be running its ain riggs in some other world. 1885 Mrs. Lynn Linton Paston Carew xxv, When I'm gone I sha'n't be none the wiser if you go wrong and run your rigs as you have done.

Rig, sb.6 [f. Rig v.2 Cf. Norw. and Swed. rigg, which may be from English.]
1. Naut. The arrangement of masts, sails, etc., on a vessel.
1822 Scoresby in Brewster Nat. Magic vi. (1832) 144, I could distinguish by a telescope every sail, the general rig of the ship, and its particular character. 1856 'Stonehenge' Brit. Rural Sports II. VIII. i. § 4. 462/2 The rig suited to very small river boats. 1897 F. T. Bullen Cruise 'Cachalot' 3 As old-fashioned in her rig as in her hull.
fig. 1878 Emerson Misc. Wks. (Bohn) III. 399 More forward and forthright [are] his whole build and rig than the Englishman's.
2. colloq. Costume, outfit, style of dress. Also rig-up and Rig-out.
1857 Hughes Tom Brown I. v, You'll do very well as to rig, all but that cap. 1884 G. Allen Philistia II. 28 Two sturdy British holiday-seekers, in..regular Alpine climbing rig. 1896 Mrs. Caffyn Quaker Grandmother 283 Either she's mad or in a peck of trouble, to come..in this rig-up.
3. U.S. a. Apparatus for well-sinking.
1875 Knight Dict. Mech. III. s.v. Well-boring Tools. 1883 Cent. Mag. July 329/2 [The boiler] usually stands at some distance from the derrick, so that it will not be injured in case the rest of the 'rig' is destroyed by fire. 1885 Encycl. Brit. XVIII. 716/2 A..'rig' is built, which consists of the derrick itself and a small house for an engine.
b. An equipage; a horse vehicle.
1885 Trans. Amer. Philol. Assoc. XVI. 110 One part of the team (or 'rig', as they say west of the Hudson). 1894 C. L. Johnstone Canada 64, I hired a 'rig' or 'buckboard' for 3 dollars to take me as far as Carlton. Ibid., Springless vehicles, these rigs.

Rig, v.1 Also 4-5 **rygg-**. [f. Rig sb.1]
1. trans. = Ridge v. 1.
1379 Mem. Ripon (Surtees) III. 102 In coopertura et tractacione dicti straminis cum eodem ryggand. c 1440 Promp. Parv. 433/2 Ryggyn howsys, porco. 1678 O. Heywood Diaries (1881) I. 187 Willm. Clay points, rigs his house. 1690 Burgery of Sheffield 246 Paid for poynting and rigging the Almshouse, 7s. 7d.
2. = Ridge v. 2. Also absol.
1853 W. Watson Poems 82 (E.D.D.), Her fertile braes are rigget by the ploughman lad. 1886 S. W. Linc. Gloss. s.v., They're beginning to rig for swedes.

Rig, v.2 Also 5-6 **ryg(ge**, 5-7 **rigge** (6 Sc. **reg**), 7-8 **rigg**. [Of obscure origin. Norw. and Sw. rigga, Da. rigge, in nautical use, are prob. from English, but Norw. has also rigga to bind or wrap up, and Sw. dial. rigga på to harness (a horse); the precise relationship of these to the Eng. word is doubtful. Cf. also Reek v.2]
1. trans. To make (a ship) ready for the sea; to fit out with the necessary tackle.
c 1489 Caxton Blanchardyn liv. 221 He rigged certaine ships, wherein he and his Lordes embarqued themselues. 1530 Palsgr. 691/2 He intendeth or it be aught longe to make sayle, for his shyppe is rygged all redy. 1575 Turberv. Venerie 2 Then did hee cause to be rygged and trimmed a greate nomber of shippes. 1608 E. Grimstone Hist. France (1611) 454 Hee rigges a great fleet of gallies to seize vpon the Islands. 1653 H. Cogan tr. Pinto's Trav. vi. 14 After that he caused some of the vessels of the fleet to be rigged. 1738 Johnson London 247 Lest ropes be wanting ..To rig another convoy for the king. 1769 Falconer Dict. Marine (1780) s.v. Girt-line, The girt-line is therefore the first rope employed to rig a ship. 1870 Bryant Iliad I. II. 68 He rigged a fleet of ships and led on board A numerous host.
fig. 1637 Milton Lycidas 101 That fatall and perfidious Bark Built in th'eclipse, and rigg'd with curses dark.
b. Const. with forth, out, up.
1567 Reg. Privy Council Scot. I. 546 To reg furth how mony schippis thai sall think meit. 1570-6 Lambarde Peramb. Kent (1826) 109 At ech time that the King passeth over the sea, the Portes ought to rig up fiftie and seaven ships. 1593 Lodge Will. Longbeard (Hunterian Cl.) 52 Rigging out two warlike Gallies, he sailed with them into the great sea. 1626 Middleton Anything for Quiet Life I. i, Your lordship, minding to rig forth a ship To trade for the East Indies. 1665 Manley Grotius' Low-C. Warres 544 With a greater Fleet, which was to be built and rigged up in Spain. 1737 [S. Berington] Mem. G. de Lucca (1738) 29 He had made a Shift to rig out a small Vessel.
c. In passive sense: To be rigged; to get rigged (afresh).
1614 in Birch Crt. & Times Jas. I (1849) I. 337 Eight of the king's ships are rigging and making ready for sea. 1688 3rd Coll. Papers rel. to Pres. Juncture of Affairs 1 Two of the Prince's principal Men of War were forced to new Rigg at Helversluse. 1794 Rigging & Seamanship 229 Ship's Pinnaces..sometimes..rig with a sliding-gunter. 1805 Collingwood 28 Oct. in Nicolas Disp. Nelson (1846) VII. 218 In the gale the Royal Sovereign and Mars lost their foremasts, and are now rigging anew.
† 2. To make ready (an army). Obs.—1
a 1513 Fabyan Chron. VII. ccxliv. 285 Wherefore he rygged his army, & drewe towarde theym.
3. To dress, clothe, fit out or provide with clothes. Now colloq. or slang.
1534 More Comf. agst. Trib. II. Wks. 1201/1 When he beholdeth him self richly appareled & ye beggar rygged in his ragges. 1625 B. Jonson Staple of N. II. v, P. Iu. Your Fortunate Princesse, Vncle, is long a comming. P. Ca. She is not rigg'd, Sir. 1689 Chancellor's Prep. for Trial in Harl. Misc. (1746) VIII. 603/1 New Liveries of the best Irish Frize, completely to rig a whole Regiment of his new-raised Teagues. 1721 Swift Epil. to Play Wks. 1751 VII. 182 We'll rig in Meath-Street Ægypt's haughty Queen. 1774 Westm. Mag. II. 429 If they can't rigg a Captain— a Frenchman they'll dress. 1821 Sporting Mag. VIII. 111 The gentlemen were neatly rigged, and looked the thing to a T. 1854 Miss Baker Northampt. Gloss. s.v., 'I'll board him, but I can't rig him,' is often said by a master of his apprentice.
refl. 1662 Pepys Diary 7 Apr., While he was rigging himself, he bid his man listen at the door. 1693 Humours Town 24 She hastens home, washes, new riggs, and seats herself. 1819 J. H. Vaux Mem. I. 241 The liberty-men were busily employed in rigging themselves..in their best togs. 1845 Alb. Smith Fort. Scattergood Fam. xxxi, Our hero rigged himself afresh in some rough nautical habiliments.
absol. 1813 Moore Twopenny Post Bag II. 50 Else, though the P—— be long in rigging [etc.]. 1831 Anne Royall Southern Tour 235 He told her..that she must rig up a little, while he went for me.
b. Const. with out.
c 1616 Beaum. & Fl. Four Plays, Triumph of Time Prol., All occupations..That serve to rig the body out with braverie. 1676 Wycherley Pl. Dealer IV. i, You shall see, how I have rigg'd my Squire out, with the remains of my shipwrack'd Wardrobe. 1730 Swift Death & Daphne Wks. 1751 X. 156 A Consult of Coquets below Was call'd, to rig him out a Beau. 1807-8 W. Irving Salmag. (1824) 47 Take of..ribands, and artificial flowers, as much as will rig out the congregation of a village church.' 1885 Lady Brassey The Trades 504 Great were the efforts made to 'rig-out' the performers.
refl. 1673 R. Head Canting Acad. 107 She riggs her self out in the best manner she can. 1688 Penton Guardian's Instruction (1897) 28 He riggs himself out in a new Suit. c 1735 Fielding Fathers I. i, Once in seven years came up Madam in the stage coach, to..rig out herself and family. 1818 Lady Morgan Autobiog. (1859) 46 Intending to rig myself out in Paris, I have had to set myself up with an evening dress. 1888 Baring-Gould Crt. Royal xi, I allow you a quarter of an hour for rigging yourself out.
4. To furnish or provide, to fit or fix up, with something. Also rarely without const.
1594 Nashe Unfort. Trav. Wks. (Grosart) V. 164 Therupon..her wardrop was richly rigd,..and presented she was ..to the countesse. 1619 Fletcher Mons. Thomas III. i, Your noble heart..Rigd round about with vertue. 1688 Holme Armoury III. xviii. (Roxb.) 140/2 Termes used by Gunners..Rigging a peece, is to haue it fitted with all thing necessary for service. 1713 Derham Phys. Theol. 189 In others [the mouth is] strongly rigged with Jaws and Teeth; to gnaw, and scrape out their Food. 1820 Combe Syntax, Consol. II, He would rig With friz and curl the Doctor's wig. 1841 Col. Hawker Diary (1893) II. 198, I rigged up Charley Page of Hurst with powder and shot. 1876 Besant & Rice Celia's Arb. xxi, The Captain went round rigging up the curtains with brighter ribbons.
b. To fit out in some way.
1679 Alsop Melius Inq. II. iv. 286 The same Cardinal from these words..found out a Masse compleatly rigged out for Service. 1816 Scott Bl. Dwarf ii, And ye'll rig out the auld tower a bit? 1885 Manch. Exam. 16 June 4/6 It would be easy for Lord Salisbury to rig out half a dozen Administrations.
5. To adjust or fix; to set in proper order for working. Chiefly Naut.
1627 Capt. Smith Seaman's Gram. v. 18 It is proper to say, The Mast is well rigged, or the Yard is well rigged,.. when all the Ropes are well sised to a true proportion of her burthen. 1745 P. Thomas Jrnl. Anson's Voy. 23 He..got down the broken Main-top-sail Yard, and got up and rigg'd another in its Place. 1748 Anson's Voy. III. viii. 378 The Spaniards in a bravado rigged their sprit-sail-yard fore and aft likewise. 1836 Marryat Pirate iv, We must rig the pumps. 1860 All Year Round No. 66. 384 We rigged the machine, and set hotly to work. 1876 Voyle & Stevenson Milit. Dict., To Rig,..an expression made use of in fitting up a gyn or capstan for working, &c.
b. Naut. To run out, draw in, a boom or stay.
1769 Falconer Dict. Marine (1780) s.v. Horse, The sailors..are loosing, reefing or furling the sails, rigging out the studding-sail booms, &c. 1841 R. H. Dana Seaman's Man. 14 When the breast-backstays are to be rigged in, cast off the lanyard. Ibid. 22 Rig the boom out until the inner sheave-hole is clear of the cap. 1882 Nares Seamanship (ed. 6) 212 The boom is rigged in immediately the sail is canted clear.
intr. 1867 Smyth Sailor's Word-bk. 575 A boom called a ring-tail boom, which rigs in and out upon the main or driver boom.
6. To fit up, esp. as an expedient or makeshift.
1829 Marryat F. Mildmay xv, I rigged jury-masts: I made sail on them. 1850 W. Scoresby Cheever's Whalem. Adv. iv. (1859) 60 An ingenious Frenchman..once rigged swivels in the heads of his boats. 1883 F. M. Crawford Dr. Claudius xvii, I have managed to rig a sort of table in my cabin at last.
b. Const. out or up.
1823 J. Badcock Dom. Amusem. 69 Ships holds are well ventilated..by means of a sail, rigged out from the deck to below, like a funnel. 1841 B. Hall Patchwork II. v. 65 As if they had been rigging up a stage for Pantaloon. 1861 Hughes Tom Brown at Oxf. iii, Outside these windows, Drysdale had rigged up hanging gardens.

† **Rig**, v.3 Also 6 **rigge**. [Of obscure origin.]
1. a. intr. To make search, to ransack.
1565 Golding Ovid's Met. I. (1593) 5 Eft they gan to digge, And in the bowels of the ground unsatiably to rigge For riches coucht and hidden. 1616 Chapman Homer's Hymn Hermes, Thou..Hast beene besieging house and man together, Rigging and rifeling all waies.
b. trans. To search, ransack, rifle (a house, etc.).
1579 Gosson Sch. Abuse (Arb.) 54 If he presume to enter our house, and rig euery corner, searching more then belongs to his office, we..turne him away. 1610 Women Saints 22 Her house..was rigged by them [sc. Goths]. 1635 R. N. tr. Camden's Hist. Eliz. II. 151 Whereas I saw all things to be curiously searched and rigged, I commanded that Packet to be burnt.
2. To make free with (another's goods); to take or carry away.
1573 Tusser Husb. (1878) 33 Some rigs thy plow, some milks thy cow. Ibid. 43 Some prowleth for fewel, and some away rig fat goose and the capon.
3. To rob or despoil (one) of something.
1629 Wadsworth Pilgr. vii. 73 Some Chambermaids which hauing beene..well rigd of their maidenhead,..are sent ouer..to do penance.

Rig, v.4 Now dial. Also 6 **rigge**, 9 **rigg**; 8-9 **riggy** (8 **riggee**). [Cf. Rig sb.4] intr. To play the wanton; to romp or climb about.
1570 Levins Manip. 119 To Rigge, lasciuire puellam. 1592 Lyly Midas I. ii, Indeed if thou shouldest rigge vp and downe in our jackets, thou woudst be thought a very tomboy. 1598 Florio, Treccolare, to rig vp and downe as a gixie wench. 1691 Ray N. C. Words (ed. 2) 59 Renl, to be rude: to behave one self unmannerly, to Rig. 1746 Exmoor Scolding (E.D.S.) 56 Thee wut..colty, and hobby, and riggy, wi' enny Kesson Zoul. 1815 Hist. J. De Castro II. 12 Will you never leave off galloping, dancing, rigging, and romping amongst the boys and girls? 1838 Holloway Prov. Dict., To rig, to climb about; to get up and down a thing in wantonness or sport. 1876- in dial. glossaries (esp. of south-western counties).
transf. a 1613 Overbury A Wife, etc. (1638) 271 A young

Pullet, who often rigging from her nest makes hot and cold beget rottennesse.

† **Rig**, v.5 Obs.—1 (See quot.)
Perh. the same as Brockett's 'Rig, to perform the act of supersaliency only, to back'.
1619 Fletcher Wild Goose Chase III. i, That this Bilbo-Lord shall reap that Maiden-head That was my due; that he shall rig and top her!

Rig, v.6 slang or colloq. [f. Rig sb.5]
1. trans. To hoax, play tricks on, befool.
Common in dialect use: see Eng. Dial. Dict.
1823 Examiner 652/1 One of the party..announced himself at the several houses of those who were to be rigged (as the phrase elegantly expresses it) in the quality of footman.
2. To manage or manipulate in some underhand or fraudulent manner.
1851 Chamb. Jrnl. XV. 105/1 Frequently the plate is rigged; more frequently the pictures. 1885 Pall Mall G. 30 May 2/1 It is agreed to vote only for those names, and thus secure their return: this is what is termed 'rigging the committees'.
3. To rig the market, to cause an artificial rise (or fall) of prices with a view to personal profit.
1855 T. Taylor Still Waters 13 We must rig the market. Go in and buy up every share that's offered. 1875 Jevons Money xvii. 210 About ten years ago it became the practice to rig the market as regards the shares of particular joint-stock banking companies.
b. To send up (prices) artificially.
1884 Pall Mall G. 14 Feb. 5/2 Mexican Railway stock.. is rigged up to a ridiculous extent.

Riga (rəi·gă), the name of a Russian seaport, situated in the Baltic Provinces, used attrib. in the names of certain products exported from there, as Riga deal, fir, hemp, oak, etc. Riga balsam, an essential oil (also called Carpathian balsam) obtained by distillation from Pinus Cembra.
1765-94 [see Rhine 1]. 1802 W. Coxe Trav. Russia in Pinkerton's Voy. VI. 712 The Riga hemp is chiefly used for shrouds and stays of men of war. 1840 Civil Eng. & Arch. Jrnl. III. 128/1 The fixtures are of riga oak. 1842 Gwilt Archit. § 1706 Red Riga deal, or pine wood, would endure as long as oak in all situations. 1849 Balfour Man. Bot. § 932 Benzoin..exists also in other empirical remedies, such as Riga balsam. 1861 Bentley Man. Bot. 659 P[inus] sylvestris, the Scotch Fir, which yields the timber known as Dantzic or Riga Fir.

Rigadig. [Imitative.] (See quot.)
1851 H. Melville Whale xxvii, He would hum over his old rigadig tunes.

Rigadoon (rigădū·n), sb. [a. F. rigaudon, rigodon, of doubtful origin.
'I have heard a dancing-master say that the name of this dance came from that of its inventor, who was called Rigaud.'—Rousseau Dict. de mus. s.v. Mistral states that Rigaud was a celebrated dancing-master at Marseilles.
The French forms are more closely represented in the following examples:—a 1701 Sedley Grumbler II. i, Will you have a minuet, Sir? The trocanny, tricotez, rigadon? Come, choose. 1706 Lond. Gaz. No. 4213/4 With an Addition of the English Rigaudon and French Bretagne.]
1. A lively and somewhat complicated dance for two persons, formerly in vogue.
1691 Satyr agst. French Ep. A 2 It is an original, I assure you, and drawn as near to the Life as a Limner could take the Features of one dancing the Rigadoon. 1715 Addison Freeholder No. 36 He..gained a great Reputation, by his Performance in a Rigadoon. 1751 Eliza Heywood Betsy Thoughtless I. 85 The gentleman-commoner..led her some steps of a minuette, then fell into a rigadoon. 1829 Marryat F. Mildmay i, He taught us the rigadoons of his own country. a 1845 Barham Ingol. Leg., House-Warming, Sir Christopher..skips away with much glee in his best rigadoon. 1872 Holmes Poet Breakf.-t. iv, She would dance you a rigadoon..very respectably.
attrib. 1709 Steele Tatler No. 34 ℙ 4 Damia made her utterly forgot by a gentle sinking, and a Rigadoon Step.
2. The music for such a dance.
1731 (title), Instructions upon the Hautboy; together with a curious collection of Marches, Minuets, Rigadoons, and Opera Airs. 1797 Encycl. Brit. (ed. 3) XII. 551/2 The rigadoon has two times in a bar, is composed of two strains, each to be repeated. 1812 W. Tennant Anster Fair IV. xc, The puissant Piper, Rob, Whose bagpipe wak'd so hot a rigadoon From his well-managed bag. 1874 Ouseley Musical Form 32 Gavottes, Corantos, Rigadoons, Jiggs, and other old-fashioned dance-tunes.
attrib. 1844 L. Hunt Blue-stocking Revels ii. 245 With Hall he developed the rigadoon organ.
Hence **Rigadoo·n** v., to dance a rigadoon.
1803 Poet. Petit. agst. Tractorising Trumpery 14 So fam'd Aldini..Led dead folks down a contra dance And made them rigadoon and chassée. 1860 O. W. Holmes Elsie V. vii, The Doctor looked as if he should like to rigadoon and sashy [= chassé] across as well as the young one.

† **Rigald.** Obs. Also α. 4 **rigold, regal(d, reggalt**, 5 **rygald**. β. 4 **righolt**, 5 ? **richolt, ryghold**. [The β-forms are prob. the more original, and appear to represent MLG. regel-, rigelholt (MDu. righelhout), f. regel rail, spar, + holt wood. In the α-forms there may be some confusion between the simple word and the compound.] A rail or spar of wood.
α. 1338 in Sir N. H. Nicholas Hist. Navy (1847) II. 476, cc waynscots,..ij novelx lollers, v regaldes. 1344-5 Durham Acc. Rolls (Surtees) 544 In vij melis emp. pro Bracina et xiij Rigaldis, vs. 9d. c 1357 Ibid. 560 Et in cc. bord. de Waynscot et c. Reggalt'. 1369-70 Norwich Sacrist's Roll, Pro tabula de rigold. 1392 Exped. Earl Derby 157 Pro xxxiij deles.., pro vi regal.., pro xiij oken sparres. 1415-6 Durham Acc. Rolls (Surtees) 406 In factura hostii capituli, sc. pro xij rygald, xij s., et pro ligaturis et clavis, x s. iiij d.
β. 1399 York Fabric Rolls (Surtees) 16 In sarracione meremii righolts et waynscots,..38 s. 10 d. 1405 in Hakluyt Voy. (1599) I. 173 For ech hundreth of bowstaues & boords called Waghenscot, 2 d.; for euery hundreth of boords called Richolt, 4 d. ? 1460 York Fabric Rolls (Surtees) 35 In sarracione meremii ryghold, waynskot,..100 s. 10 d.

† **Ri·galding**, vbl. sb. Obs.—0 [Cf. Riggal, and Rigol v.] (See quot.)
1688 Holme Armoury III. 111/1 By Free Masons and Stone-Cutters..Rigalding is to set in the Wedges.

Rigall, groove: see Riggal.

Rigalle, obs. form of Regal sb.2

† **Rigate**, v. Obs.—1 [f. ppl. stem of L. rigāre: cf. irrigate.] trans. To moisten.
1657 Tomlinson Renou's Disp. 396* Bole-arminack..may be rigated by humid things.

† **Riga·tion.** Obs. [ad. L. rigātio: see prec. and -ation.] Irrigation; moistening.
1651 Raleigh's Ghost 57 The said mediterranean Countries would be continually scorched with the Sun, and be deprived of all rigation and watering. 1657 Tomlinson Renou's Disp. 239 This delights in siccity and perishes by frequent rigation. 1733 Tull Horse-Hoeing Husb. xv. (Dubl.) 203 They found something else more necessary to employ them in, than the Sarritions, Runcations, and Rigations of the Medica. 1779 Swinburne Trav. Spain xvi. 119 In dry years, every field that has not some spring or aqueduct, to furnish it with repeated rigations, is sure to fail in its crop.

Rigatt, variant of Riggot 2.

Ri·g-bone. Now Sc. and north. Forms: α. 4 **rigbon**, 5-6 **ryg-**, 6 **rigbone**. β. 5 **rygbane**, 6, 9 Sc. **rigbane** (9 north. **-baan, -beean, -beyan**). [f. Rig sb.1] = Ridge-bone.
a 1330 Syr Degarre 450 Some he brekketh the nekke anon, And of some the rig-bon. c 1400 Song of Roland 736 His shulder smot he quyt asundur, rent out the rigbon. 1495 Trevisa's Barth. De P. R. (W. de W.) v. xxxi. 142 The joyntes of the rygbone and of the breste bone. a 1510 Douglas King Hart II. 112 Ane fellounn rout he layde on his rig-bone. 1828 Carr Craven Gloss., Rig-Baan, the back bone. 1894 P. H. Hunter J. Inwick 183 It was men like me wha were the rig-bane o' the Leeberal pairty.

Rigby, obs. variant of Rigsby.

Rigel (rəi·dzĕl, rəi·gĕl). Astr. Also 8 regel. [a. Arab. رجل rijl foot.] The star β in the constellation Orion.
1592 Hues Treat. Globes (Hakl. Soc.) 59 That which is in his left foote..[is called] Rigel Algeuze or Algibbar. 1659 Moxon Tutor Astron. II. 66 Orions foot, Rigel. 1764 Ann. Reg. I. 47/2 To the east of Rigel, a star of the first magnitude in the left foot of Orion. 1840 Penny Cycl. XVII. 18/1, α and β, of the first magnitude, were frequently called Betelgeuse..and Rigel, corruptions from Arabic names. 1868 Lockyer Guillemin's Heavens (ed. 3) 323 Two of the stars of the quadrilateral, named Betelgeuse and Rigel, are of the first magnitude.

† **Rigent**, a. Obs.—1 [ad. L. rigent-, rigens, pres. pple. of rigēre to be stiff.] Stiff, rigid.
c 1440 Pallad. on Husb. XII. 453 Elm & asshe ydried beth rigent.

Rigescence (ridʒe·sĕns). [f. L. rigescĕre to become stiff.] Stiffening.
1768 Woman of Honor III. 5 Such particles..increase the obstructions and rigescence..natural to that time of life. 1846 Trench Mirac. xxvii. 362 note, The stiffness and starkness, the unnatural rigescence of the limbs.

Rige·scent, a. Bot. [ad. pres. pple. of L. rigescĕre.] Tending to be rigid or stiff.
1873 M. C. Cooke Man. Bot. Terms (ed. 2), Rigescent, approaching a rigid or stiff consistence.

Riget(t, obs. forms of Riggot 2.

† **Rigg.** ? error for Rugg sb.
1769 Dublin Mercury 16-19 Sept. 2/2 Poplins, riggs and riggs-royal, stuffs, camblets.

Ri·ggage. rare—1. [f. Rig v.2] Rigging.
1627 Capt. Smith Seaman's Gram. v. 18 Riggage or Cordage.

Ri·ggal. Obs. exc. dial. Also 6 **rigall**, 7 **riggald**, 9 dial. **riggle**. [ad. F. rigole: see Rigol sb. and Regal sb.3]
1. A groove in wood or stone.
1555 in Hardwicke Misc. State Papers (1778) I. 71 The handle of the same [saw] is kept in a rigall of wood from swerving. 1609 Holland Amm. Marcell. XXIII. iv. 221 There lyeth foorth farther out a fouresquare beame or spire, made hollow with a direct and streight passage of a narrow riggall or trough. 1639 in J. J. Cartwright Chapters Hist. Yorks. (1872) 339 A great waightie block wth riggalds for those ribbs to shoote in. 1886 [see Regal sb.3].
† 2. A ring-like mark. Obs. rare—1.
1714 Lond. Gaz. No. 5233/4 Two white Riggals round her Ears.

Riggald. dial. Forms: α. 6 **rigolde, reg-, rigald**, 8-9 **riggald** (9 **-old**); 7, 9 **riggilt**. β. 7 **regle, riggall**, 8-9 **riggil**, 9 **reggil, roggel**. [Northern var. of Ridgel: see also Riggon and Riggot.] A ridgel. Also attrib.
1584 Vestry Bks. (Surtees) 18 A weather, a rigolde, and a lame. 1588 Invent. of T. Carppnell, Kendal (Somerset Ho.), Im liiijor weythers; tuppe and regalds. 1596 Invent. in Archaeologia XLVIII. 151 Item Tupp lambes...Item Rigald lambes. 1615 Crooke Body of Man 244 Many creatures haue their Testicles within tyed to their backs,.. as some Tuppes or Ramines called Riggall Tuppes. 1617 Moryson Itin. III. 115 The stones of Rammes and Regles (vulgarly Granella) are esteemed great dainties, especially in Tuscany. 1691 Ray N. C. Words (ed. 2), A Riggilt, a Ram with one Stone. 1703 Thoresby Let. to Ray (E.D.S.), Riggald,..abusively apply'd to men as well as to cattle. 1788 Marshall Rur. Econ. Yorks. II. 348 Riggil, ridgil. 1828- in many dial. glossaries (Northumb., Yorks., Lanc., Derby, Shropsh., Glouc.).

Riggan, dial. variant of Rigging sb.1

Riggat(e, -att, variants of Riggot 2.

Rigged, a.1 [f. Rig sb.1] Of cattle: Having a white streak along the back.
Other dialect uses are given in the Eng. Dial. Dict.
1555 Knaresb. Wills (Surtees) I. 69 A browne rigged cowe. 1789 Sillar Poems 118 Your Quey an' rigget Cow. 1811 Aiton Agric. Ayrsh. 425 When a stripe of white run along the ridge of her back, she got the name of a rigged cow.

† **Rigged**, a.2 Obs.—1 (Of doubtful meaning; perh. from Rig sb.3)
1598 Bp. Hall Sat. IV. ii. 96 The young Elephant, or two-tayl'd steere, Or the rig'd Camell, or the Fidling Frere.

Rigged (rigd), ppl. a.1 [f. Rig v.2]
1. Naut. Equipped with rigging. (Chiefly predicative, with adverbs.)
1494 Fabyan Chron. II. xxix. 21 When he had theym newely Rygyd & vytayled. 1502-9 Lett. Rich. III & Hen. VII (Rolls) I. 417 Their barges..weale and pompously rigged and adressed. 1600 Holland Livy XXVI. xxxvi. 611 That the people of Rome may be..furnished of a fleete rigged and trimmed. 1610 Shaks. Temp. V. i. 224 Our Ship..Is tyte, and yare, and brauely rig'd. 1671 Milton Samson 200 My Vessel trusted to me from above. Gloriously rigg'd. 1704 J. Harris Lex. Techn. I. s.v. Rigging, A Ship is well Rigged, when all her Ropes are of their fit size in proportion to her Burden. 1841 R. H. Dana Seaman's Man. 132 The sail so carried at the mainmast of a full-rigged brig. 1879 Beerbohm Patagonia 7, I seemed to behold some strangely rigged vessels lying close to me in the bay.
b. As the second element in combs., denoting the kind of rig carried by a vessel.
1769 Falconer Dict. Marine (1780), Vergue en borte dehors, the main-boom of a sloop-rigged, or schooner-rigged vessel. 1780 in Naval Chron. II. 518 They were two Spanish Xebec Ships, polacre rigged. 1799 Ibid. 519 The third vessel..was a xebec latine-rigged. 1834 [see Fore and aft B]. 1860 Merc. Mar. Mag. VII. 148 She was a two-masted vessel,..and snow-rigged. 1880 [see Lateen].
2. Dressed, clothed. Also with out.
1722 Ramsay Three Bonnets iii. 47 Bawsy rises, quickly dresses..: Now rigg'd [etc.]. 1757 Foote Author I. Wks. 1799 I. 136 He's very young, and exceedingly well rigg'd. 1821 Sporting Mag. IX. 27 Lenny showed afterwards equally well rigged-out. 1878 M. A. Brown tr. Runeberg's Nadeschda 36 Prince Woldmar looks around and sees The strangely rigged-out girl again.
transf. 1727 Philip Quarll 96 Her Husband stands in the way rigg'd in all those engaging Qualifications which did win her Affection.

Rigged (rigd), ppl. a.2 [f. Rig v.6] Fraudulently contrived; fictitiously enhanced in value.
1879 Dickens Dict. Lond. 12/3 It..is known..as a 'rigged sale', consisting of articles vamped up or originally manufactured for the purpose. 1901 Westm. Gaz. 10 Oct. 9/1 The natural result of..made markets, rigged shares, paid puffs in the newspapers, and all the other scandals.

Rigger 1 (ri·gəɹ). [f. Rig v.2]
1. Naut. One who rigs ships.
1611 Cotgr., Galefretier, a rigger, trimmer, mender of ships. 1703 Lond. Gaz. No. 3929/4 Wife of William Holcroft, Rigger in Her Majesty's Yard at Deptford. 1772 Hertford Merc. Suppl. 18 Sept. 3/1 One of the Riggers belonging to his Majesty's Dock-yard. 1840 R. H. Dana Bef. Mast xxxv, Riggers' seizings and overhand knots in place of nice seamanlike work. 1884 Manch. Exam. 21 Apr. 5/1 The crosstree fell some 80 feet on to the deck, carrying with it a rigger, who was picked up dead.
2. Mech. A band-wheel. Also attrib.
1797 Trans. Soc. Arts XV. 282 Which rollers are turned from the outside by the riggers or ratchet-wheels. 1825 J. Nicholson Operat. Mechanic 371 The knife is kept moving ..by means of a band passing round the small rigger. 1838 Civil Eng. & Arch. Jrnl. I. 357/2 Certain Improvements in Rigger Pulley Bands, for driving Machinery. 1894 Labour Commission Gloss. s.v., In the mill-sawing industry the band wheels revolving on the shafting are called riggers.
3. (See quot. 1883.)
1883 M. E. James How to Decorate 12 A very long-haired sable brush (technically called a rigger)..derives its odd name from marine painters, who with such brushes delineate the cordage of ships. 1887 Art Jrnl. 341 Some prefer..to use the long-pointed sable brush, known to the dealers in artists' materials as a 'rigger'.
4. A vessel with a specified rig.
1897 Kipling Capt. Cour. ix. 229 They're square-riggers, mother; iron built an' well found.
5. Colloquial abbrev. of Outrigger 3.

Rigger 2 (ri·gəɹ). [f. Rig v.6] A thimble-rigger; one who rigs the market, etc.
c 1830 Frauds of London 12 The rig is practised at fairs, at races [etc]...The rigger offers to bet sovereigns, crowns, half-crowns, and so on. 1859 Athenæum 31 Dec. 883 The name of Solomons is suggestive of..auction-mart 'riggers', second-hand garments, and the slums of Aldgate. 1883 Pall Mall G. 31 Oct. 5/1 A great cotton cornerer has gone the way of most of those great financial market 'riggers'.

Rigget(t, variants of Riggot 2.

Rigging (ri·giŋ), (vbl.) sb.1 Sc. and north. dial. Also 4 **ryggyng**, 5-6 **-ynge**, 6 **riggyng (riging)**, 7 **-inge**; 6 **riggein**, 6, 8-9 **riggen**, 7 **-ine, -an**, 8-9 **riggin**. [f. Rig sb.1 or v.1: cf. Ridging vbl. sb.]
1. The ridge or roof of a building; also, the making of a ridge or ridges (rare).
1399 Mem. Ripon (Surtees) III. 130 In salario j hominis temporantis lutum pro ryggyng pro prædicta domo. c 1440 Promp. Parv. 433/2 Ryggynge of howsys, porcacio. 1513 Douglas Æneis XII. iii. 48 The hicht and hedis of the towris,

The wallis all and howsis ryggyngis. 1533 BELLENDEN *Livy* v. x. (S.T.S.) II. 176 Seand þe stanis and sclatis cassin be þe wemen & servandis of þe riggingis of þe housis. 1641 BEST *Farm. Bks.* (Surtees) 60 On the toppe of all hee layeth noe thatch, but onely loose strawe, which hee calleth the rigginge. 1724 RAMSAY *No my ain House* i, This is no my ain house, I ken by the rigging o't. 1785 BURNS *Vision* 18, I sat..And heard the restless rattons squeak About the riggin. 1861 QUINN *Heather Lintie* (1863) 155 Oor wa's are only ae brick thick, Rent frae the riggin' doon. 1894 CROCKETT *Lilac Sunbonnet* 277 Up to the rigging of the house he went and then along it.

fig. 1821 SCOTT *Pirate* vii, Though my master be a stranger, and no just that tight in the upper rigging.

b. *attrib.*, as *rigging-stone*, *-tree*.

1573 *Satir. Poems Reform.* xxxix. 96 Of Daueis toure.. Thay *riggein stanes cum tumland ouir the trinschis. *a* 1670 SPALDING *Troub. Chas. I* (1851) II. 398 He took doun the rigging stanes, cyngzie stanes, with the rest. 1829 J. HUNTER *Hallamsh. Gloss.*, *Rigging-Stones*, slates. 1896 *Newcastle Courant* 21 Mar. (E.D.D.), Covering..the houseleek on the rigging-stone. 1788 MARSHALL *Rur. Econ. Yorks.* II. 348 **Riggen-tree*, a piece of timber laid along the ridge of a roof to support the heads of the spars. 1855 ROBINSON *Whitby Gloss.* s.v., 'The man astride the riggin tree,' the person who holds a mortgage on the premises.

2. The ridge or top of an elevated stretch of ground or raised path. Also *attrib.*

1540 *Sc. Acts Jas. V* (1814) II. 379 As þai ly towart þe north to þe heid of þe bank riggin. 1574 *Cal. Laing Charters* (1899) 225 Thaireftir plat north the riggen of the nethir quhyt hill. 1599 *Extr. Aberd. Reg.* (1848) II. 201 The rigging stane of the calsey that passis fra the croce towardis Johne Kemptis land. 1888 ADDY *Sheffield Gloss.* 190.

3. The back.

1513 DOUGLAS *Æneis* XIII. Prol. 148 Syne to me wyth his club he maid a braid, And twenty rowtis apoun my rigging laid. *a* 1585 MONTGOMERIE *Misc. Poems* xxviii. 41 The rok,..With watring wauis and huge, Quhilk ramping ouer his rigging ryds. *c* 1690 *Roxb. Ball.* (1888) VI. 616 The Butter-box got many knocks, the riggans pay'd for a' then. 1721 RAMSAY *Lucky Spence* ix, Wild hangy's tawz ye'er riggings saft Makes black and blae. 1814 in Hone *Every-day Bk.* II. 1115 The colt..scampered off sneering, with his tail on his 'riggin'. 1898 LD. E. HAMILTON *Mawkin* x, It would maybe be more to my liking to bonnilie reesle the limmer's riggin with a stirrup leather.

Rigging, (*vbl.*) *sb.*[2] [f. RIG *v.*[2]]

1. *Naut.* The action of equipping a vessel with the necessary shrouds, stays, braces, etc.

1486 *Naval Accs. Hen. VII* (1896) 16 Expenses & labor xiiij daies in rigging of the Kyngs said Ship. 1502 ARNOLDE *Chron.* (1811) 133 He was of councell of beyng of the sayde ship and of vitayling and rigging of her to the see. 1585 T. WASHINGTON tr. *Nicholay's Voy.* I. ii, His Lieuetenant had giuen order for the ful rigging of his gallies. 1624 CAPT. SMITH *Virginia* VI. 209 The building and rigging of ships of any proportion. 1726 LEONI *Alberti's Archit.* I. 91/1 The right construction and rigging of the Vessels. 1803 *Naval Chron.* IX. 243 The rigging of the Plantagenet..goes on briskly.

2. The ropes or chains employed to support the masts (*standing rigging*), and to work or set the yards, sails, etc. (*running rigging*).

1594 MARLOWE & NASHE *Dido* v. i, I want both rigging for my fleet, And also furniture for these my men. 1626 CAPT. SMITH *Accid. Yng. Seamen* 3 All the Cordage,..and saile-cloth, and rigging of the shippe. *a* 1674 CLARENDON *Hist. Reb.* XIII. § 163 They were not able to give them farther chase, till their sailes and rigging could be repaired. 1715 *Lond. Gaz.* No. 5360/5 All their standing and running Rigging was mostly shot away. 1762 FALCONER *Shipwr.* II. 102 The flying rigging all aloft belay'd. 1836 W. IRVING *Astoria* I. 136 A shed for the reception of the rigging, equipments, and stores of the schooner. 1869 GIBBON *Robin Gray* vii, The wind was whistling shrilly through the rigging.

fig. 1670 DRYDEN *Conq. Granada* II. Prol. 18 That done, [he] bears up to th' prize, and views each limb, To know her by her rigging and her trimm. 1884 *Pall Mall G.* 17 Oct. 11/2 We do not want to know how their lower rigging [=skirts, etc.] is placed and set up.

3. *transf.* Clothing, dress. Also with *out*.

1662 J. WILSON *Cheats* I. i, I ha'n't seen her since my last mischance; Must ev'n to her for new riggings. 1691 *Satyr agst. French* 6 So many sorts of Rigging dress the Elf, Himself sometimes does hardly know himself. 1729 GAY *Polly* I, She is in most charming rigging; she won't cost you a penny, Sir, in clothes at first setting out. 1768 *Phil. Trans.* LX. 122 We who stayed at the factory began to put on our winter rigging. 1821 SCOTT *Pirate* viii, I have saved..my clothes—that the tall old woman in the dark rigging managed for me. 1865 W. G. PALGRAVE *Arabia* I. 5 Salim's own rigging out was of the same description.

4. Equipment, outfit.

1849 THOREAU *Week Concord Riv.* Sunday 68 They had teams with rigging such as is used to carry barrels. 1877 RAYMOND *Statist. Mines & Mining* 63 This claim has a splendid hydraulic rigging.

5. *attrib.* or *Comb.*, as *rigging house*, *mat*, *room*, *time*, *victuals*, *wages*; *-cutter*, *-stopper* (see quots.).

c 1599 in Bree *Cursory Sk.* (1791) I. 217 For the rigging wages of 200 men. *Ibid.*, For rigging-victuals of 200 men. 1662–3 PEPYS *Diary* 7 Jan., Commanders did never heretofore receive any pay for the rigging time, but only for sea-time. 1669 R. EASTWOOD in *St. Papers, Dom.* 1668–9, 593 We will lay the floor of the rigging-house this week. 1794 *Rigging & Seamanship* 181 Rigging is..prepared..in a rigging-house. 1863 P. BARRY *Dockyard Econ.* 108 Eleventh in order stand the rigging-houses. 1867 SMYTH *Sailor's Word-bk.*, *Rigging-Mats*, those which are seized upon a vessel's standing rigging, to prevent its being chafed. *Ibid.*, *Rigging-stoppers*..are used when the shrouds, stays, or backstays are stranded in action, or in a gale [etc.]. 1870 *Pall Mall G.* 17 Oct. 6 The fire broke out..in the fitting and rigging rooms. 1884 KNIGHT *Dict. Mech.* Suppl., *Rigging Cutter*, an apparatus invented to cut the rigging of sunken vessels.

6. Rigging-loft. a. (See quot. 1867.)

1821 SCOTT *Pirate* xviii, I love to see my rigging-loft well stocked with goods. 1867 SMYTH *Sailor's Word-bk.*, *Rigging-Loft*, a long room or gallery in a dockyard, where rigging is fitted..to be in readiness for the ship. 1894 *Labour Commission Gloss.*, *Rigging lofts*, the workshops on shore, in which the ship's gear is fitted for use.

b. The space above a theatre-stage from which the scenery is manipulated. *U.S.*

1883 *Harper's Mag.* Nov. 879 Rigging Loft 90 ft. above stage. 1888 *Scribner's Mag.* Oct. 438 Looking upward from the floor of the stage, he would call them [the beams] the gridiron; standing on them, he would speak of them as the rigging-loft.

Riggish (ri·giʃ), *a.* Now *dial.* [f. RIG *sb.*[4]] Wanton, licentious. (See also quot. 1881.)

1570 LEVINS *Manip.* 145/38 Riggish, *licentiosus*. 1581 PETTIE tr. *Guazzo's Civ. Conv.* II. (1586) 115 In their outward behaviour, they shew themselues foolish, riggish, and retchless. 1606 SHAKS. *Ant. & Cl.* II. ii. 245 For vildest things Become themselues in her, that the holy Priests Blesse her, when she is Riggish. 1634 BP. HALL *Contempl.*, *N. T.* IV. iv, The wanton gesticulations of a virgin in a wild assembly of gallants warmed with wine, could be no other than riggish and unmaidenly.

1869 in *Lonsdale Gloss.* 1881 *Isle of Wight Gloss.* (E.D.S.), *Riggish*, usually applied to cattle or sheep..breaking through fences; also, wanton.

Ri·ggite. *rare*[−1]. [f. RIG *sb.*[5]] One who makes game or fun of others.

1788 FRANKLIN *Autobiog.* Wks. 1840 I. 61 My being esteemed a pretty good *riggite*, that is a jocular verbal satirist, supported my consequence in the society.

Riggle, dial. variant of RIGGAL, groove.

Riggle, variant of WRIGGLE *sb.* and *v.*

Riggmonrowle, obs. form of RIGMAROLE.

†Ri·ggon. *Obs. rare.* (See quot. and next.)

1641 BEST *Farm. Bks.* (Surtees) 1 Riggon tuppes are such as have one stone in the codde, and the other in the ridge of the backe. *Ibid.* 2 A riggon weather is such an one as hath formerly beene a riggon tuppe.

Ri·ggot[1]. *dial.* Also 6 **rygett**, 9 **riggit** (**ricket**). [var. of RIGGALD: cf. prec.] = RIDGEL.

1559 *Richmond Wills* (Surtees) 135, xxij[tie] tupes and rygetts. 1814 PEGGE *Suppl. Grose*, *Riggot*, a half-gelded horse. *Lanc.* 1825- in northern dial. glossaries (Northumb., Durh., Yorks.).

Ri·ggot[2]. Now *dial.* Forms: 7 **riget(t**, 9 **-att**, **-ot(t**; 7 **riggett**, 7, 9 **rigget**, 9 **riggat(e**, **-att**, **-ut**; 7 **riggott**, 8–9 **riggot**. [Related to *riggald* RIGGAL, REGAL *sb.*[3]] A groove, furrow, or channel; in mod. *dial.* a water-channel, surface-drain, gutter, rain-spout.

1634–5 BRERETON *Trav.* (Chetham Soc.) 32 Some of the seats of the windows gilded in the riggott that is planed. 1688 HOLME *Armoury* III. 99/1 Channelling the sole is making a riggett in the outer sole for the Wax thread to ly in. *Ibid.* 111/2 A flat in a Cornice, with a Channel or Rigget at the bottom inwards. 1747 HOOSON *Miner's Dict.* s.v. *Blasting*, This Plug has a Riggot made in it down the Side. *Ibid.* P ij b, Upon one of which Edges the Riggot is made for the Priming of it. 1826- in dial. glossaries (Lanc., Chesh., Derby, Leic., Shropsh.).

Righe, Righolt: see REIGH, RIGALD.

Right (rəit), *sb.*[1] Forms: 1 **riaht**, **reoht**, **reht**, **rict**, 1–5 (6) **riht**, 3 **rih(te**, **rihht**, 3–4 **rihtt**; 3 **riþt**, 4 **rith**, **ȝit**, 5 **rite**; 2, 5– *Sc.* **richt** (4 **-te**), 4–5 **riȝt(e**, 4 **riȝtt**), 5 **reght**, **righte**, 4– **right**; 1, 4 **ryht** (4 **rythe**, **ryte**), 5–7 *Sc.* **rycht**; 4–5 **ryȝt(e**, 4–6 **ryght** (4–5 **rygth**, **ryghth**), 5–6 **ryghte**. [OE. *riht*, *ryht*, etc., = OFris. *riucht* (mod. Fris. *rjucht*), OS., OHG. *reht* (Du. and G. *recht*), ON. *réttr* (Da. *ret*, Sw. *rätt*), related to RIGHT *a.*]

I. †1. The standard of permitted and forbidden action within a certain sphere; law; a rule or canon. *Obs.*

c 900 *Bæda's Hist.* IV. v. (1890) 276 Licade us efencuman æfter þeawe arwyrðra rehta [L. *iuxta morem canonum venerabilium*]. 971 *Blickl. Hom.* 135 Þa men þe..wiðerwearde wæron Godes beboda & þæs gastlican rihtes. *c* 1000 ÆLFRIC *Gloss.* in Wr.-Wülcker 114 *Fas*, Godes riht. *Jus*, mennisc riht. *Ibid.* 115 *Rodia lex*, scipmanna riht. *c* 1200 ORMIN 7202 Herode king wass grill..whannse he seþ þatt Godess rihht & Godess laȝhe riseþþ. 1483 CAXTON *Gold. Leg.* 427/1 Ful of grete scyence bothe in ryght cyuyl and in cannon. 1610 WILLET *Dan.* 356 These doe not distinguish betweene the ceasing of the sacrifices in right and in fact.

†2. That which is proper for or incumbent on one to do; one's duty. *Obs.*

c 897 K. ÆLFRED *Gregory's Past. C.* xxi. 159 Ðæt ðonne bið ðæs recceres ryht ðæt he ðurh ða stemne his lariowdomes ætiewe ðæt wuldor ðæs uplican eðles. *a* 1000 *Cædmon's Gen.* 1 (Grein), Us is riht micel, ðæt we rodera weard..wordum herigen. *a* 1225 *Ancr. R.* 134 Ichulle deien i mine neste, & beon as dead þerinne: vor þet is ancre rihte: & wunien uort heo deie þerinne. *Ibid.* 142 Vor þet is ancre rihte, muchel uor to wakien.

3. That which is consonant with equity or the light of nature; that which is morally just or due. (Often contrasted with *might* and *wrong*, and in ME. freq. coupled with *reason* or *skill*.)

Beowulf 1700 Þæt la mæg secgan, se þe soð & riht fremeð on folce. *c* 888 K. ÆLFRED *Boeth.* xxxviii. § 7 Ne þæt nis nan riht þæt mon þone yflan hatige. *c* 1000 ÆLFRIC *Hom.* II. 48 Ȝif se lareow riht tæce, do ȝehwa swa-swa he tæcð. *c* 1123 *O. E. Chron.* (Laud MS.) an. 1123, He sæde þone cyng þæt hit wæs togeanes riht þæt man scolde setten clerc ofer muneces. *a* 1225 *Leg. Kath.* 961 Hit is aȝein riht,..þæt godd, þe is undedlich mahe deð drehen. *c* 1250 *Owl & Night.* 950 Þe heorte..so uorleost al his lyht, Þat ho ne syhþ soþ ne riht. *a* 1300 *Cursor M.* 29 Þe wrang to here o right is lath. 13.. *E. E. Allit. P.* A. 622 Ay þe ofter, þe alder þay were, Þay laften ryȝt & wroȝten woghe. 1390 GOWER *Conf.* I. 351 If ther were..such a knyht That wolde sein it was no riht, I wole it with my bodi prove. *c* 1470 *Gol. & Gaw.* 1219 Now wil I be obeyand, And make the manrent with hand, As right is, and skill. 1500–20 DUNBAR *Poems* l. 52, I cry him Lord of everie fuill,..And, verralie, that war gryt rycht. 1567 GOLDING *Ovid's Met.* IX. 119 Too age it dooth belong To keepe the rigor of the lawes and search out ryght from wrong. 1606 SHAKS. *Tr. & Cr.* I. iii. 116 Force should be right, or rather, right and wrong..Should loose her names. 1667 MILTON *P. L.* VIII. 572 Self-esteem, grounded on just and right Well manag'd. 1737 *Gentl. Mag.* VII. 131/1 You must acknowledge a Distinction betwixt Right and Wrong, founded in Nature,..by which Actions may be call'd just or unjust. 1757 W. WILKIE *Epigoniad* IV. 118 So let their blood be shed, who scorning right, Shall impiously dare its ties to slight. 1832 TENNYSON *Œnone* 147 Because right is right, to follow right Were wisdom. 1884 W. C. SMITH *Kildrostan* 46 We judge a stranger by our home-bred ways, Who, maybe, walks by other rule of right.

Comb. 1865 RUSKIN *Sesame* ii. § 90 Rex et Regina,..'Right-doers'. 1874 W. P. MACKAY *Grace & Truth* 202 Many moral, unconverted men are specimens of the highest external right-doing. 1896 MORLEY in *Westm. Gaz.* 7 Nov. 4/2, I am for a safe England,..a just England, a right-doing England.

b. The fact or position of being in the right (cf. 6 b). Chiefly in phr. *to have right*. Now *rare*.

c 1369 CHAUCER *Dethe Blaunche* 1282 Whan I had wrong and she ryght, She wolde alwey so goodely For-yeve me. *c* 1430 *Syr Gener.* (Roxb.) 5534 Right maketh a feble man strong. 1456 SIR G. HAYE *Law Arms* (S.T.S.) 74 Had the pape Clement had rycht his folk had nocht bene in bataill disconfyte. *c* 1500 *Melusine* 128 We haue good right in oure caas; they are come vpon vs without cause. 1565 COOPER *Thesaurus* s.v. *Jus*, The indifferent judge attributed victorie to him..to whome right appeared. 1604 T. WRIGHT *Passions* (1620) 117 Whether you have right or wrong, I knowe you must have the last word. 1822 SCOTT *Peveril* xxix, The bigots have some right when they affirm that all is for the best. 1865 KINGSLEY *Hereward* xxvii, 'The king has right!' cried Hereward. 'Let them take the plunder' [etc.].

c. Consonance with fact; correctness.

1796 BURKE *Regic. Peace* ii. (1892) 126 Whether..there was some mixture of right and wrong in their reasoning. 1849 RUSKIN *Sev. Lamps* iv. § xxviii. 118, I can but rapidly name the chief conditions of right. 1867 — *Time & Tide* x. § 51 And yet..there was something of right in the terrors of this clerical conclave.

4. Just or equitable treatment; fairness in decision; justice. Freq. in phr. *to do* (one) *right*.

c 900 in Thorpe *Dipl. Angl. Sax.* (1865) 140 Þa cwædon ealle þa weotan þæt mon uðe þære cyrcan rihtes swa wel swa oðerre. *c* 1205 LAY. 2511 Heo was swa swiðe wel bi-þouht, þat ælche monne heo dude riht. *c* 1250 *Gen. & Ex.* 52 Ðat wise wil, ðat weldet alle ðinge wit riȝt and skil. *a* 1300 *Cursor M.* 1796 All tok a right, bath pouer and Rike; All hade a dom, bath riche and pour. 1375 BARBOUR *Bruce* XVI. 598 The gilt spuris..He suld in hy ger hew ȝow fra; Richt vald with cowardis men did swa. 1413 *Pilgr. Sowle* (Caxton, 1483) I. ii. 3 Come byfore the Iuge and he shal do the ryght. *c* 1450 BURGH *Secrees* 2051 Ryght and the Kyng as brethryn owen to be. 1535 COVERDALE *2 Chron.* vi. 23 Then heare thou from heauen, and se y[t] thy seruaunt haue righte. 1565 COOPER s.v. *Jus, Nundinatio iuris*, sellyng of right and iustice. 1589 LODGE *Scillaes Metam.* (Hunterian Cl.) 20 Which spectacle of care made Thetis..call on Glaucus, and command her Sonne To yeelde her right. 1642 FULLER *Holy & Prof. St.* I. xi. 34, I can do her memorie no better right, then to confesse she was wrong in somethings. 1691 T. H[ALE] *Account New Invent.* 86 In right to his Majesty and his Service, no less than to it and themselves. 1735 SOMERVILLE *Chase* II. 71 Oh! were a Theban Lyre not wanting here, And Pindar's Voice, to do their merit right! 1828 SCOTT *F. M. Perth* xx, To petition the King, as a matter of right, that the murder of their fellow-citizen should be inquired into. 1842 BROWNING *Cavalier Tunes* II. i, King Charles, and who'll do him right now?

†b. With reference to drinking, in phr. *to do* (one) *right*. (Cf. REASON *sb.*[1] 15 b.)

1597 SHAKS. *2 Hen. IV*, v. iii. 76 Why now you haue done me right. 1605 CHAPMAN *All Fools* v. i, Come in when they haue done the Ladyes right. *Ibid.*, Fill's a fresh pottle, by this light, Sir Knight, You shall do right. 1624 MASSINGER & FIELD *Bondman* II. iii, These Glasses containe nothing; doe me right As e're you hope for liberty.

5. In prepositional phrases, *with*, *by*, or *of right*, = rightfully, properly, with reason or justice.

†a. *With* (or *mid*) *right*. *Obs.*

863 *Charter* in *O. E. Texts* 439 Sue ðer mid riahte to ðem lande limpað. 971 *Blickl. Hom.* 123 Seo mennisce ȝecynd ..mæg mid rihte þæm Scyppende lof & wuldor secȝean. *c* 1127 *O. E. Chron.* (Laud MS.) an. 1127, Þa forlæs he þæt mid rihte forþi þæt he hit hæfde ærор beieten mid unrihte. *c* 1200 ORMIN 1395 Forr enngless haffdenn heoffness ærd Forrlorenn all wiþþ rihhte. *c* 1290 *St. Brandan* 53 in *S. E. Leg.* I. 221 He..seide þat we ouȝten Ihesu crist þonki suyþe wel with riȝte. *c* 1315 SHOREHAM I. 1656 He spekeþ of þyng þat his to come, Þat scholde be myd ryȝte Of treuþe. *a* 1400 in *Relig. Pieces fr. Thornton MS.* 22 With gud ryghte þay loue þe, and onoures þe,..all thy creatures.

b. *By right*; in mod. use *by rights*.

c 1315 SHOREHAM I. 1671 Þet compleþ þet spoushod..Þat hyt ne may be ondon..By ryȝte. 1387–8 T. USK *Test. Love* II. iii. (Skeat) l. 83 On you by right ought these shames and these reproves al hoolly discende. *a* 1425 *Cursor M.* 4589 (Trin.), God haþ þe shewed fair warnyng, Þerfore owe þou by riȝt To honoure him. 1535 COVERDALE *Luke* xxiii. 41 And truly we are therin by right, for we receaue acordinge to oure dedes. 1567 *Gude & Godlie B.* (S.T.S.) 143 Haly is his name be richt. 1600 SHAKS. *A. Y. L.* IV. iii. 177, I should haue beene a woman by right.

1818 KEATS *Let.* Wks. 1889 III. 159, I should not, by rights, speak in this tone to you. 1853 WHEWELL in *Life* (1881) 429 By rights he ought to leave his work and go play. 1884 RIDER HAGGARD *Dawn* vii, I suppose that I should not by rights have told you.

†c. *Of right*. *Obs.*

1413 *Pilgr. Sowle* IV. xxx. (Caxton, 1483) 78 To lesen his lyf as to a fals traitour of good right and reason belongeth. *a* 1450 *Knt. de la Tour* (1868) 85 For the wiff of right owithe to honoure her husbonde. *c* 1500 *God spede the Plough* 17 (Skeat), And so shulde of right the parson praye, That hath the tithe shefe of the londe. 1560 DAUS tr. *Sleidane's Comm.* 345 Seinge the case standeth thus, ther can no rebellion of right be obiected unto us. 1681–6 J. SCOTT *Chr. Life* (1747) III. 277 They are all of Right his Subjects.

6. *The right*: that which is right; righteousness, justice, truth; *esp.* the cause of truth or justice.

c 1000 ÆLFRIC *Deut.* xvi. 20 Filiȝe rihtlice þam rihte, þæt þu lybbe lange on þam lande, þe drihten..þe sylð. *c* 1205 LAY. 19941 Woh him wes wunder lað, and þat rihte a leof. *a* 1300 *Cursor M.* 4370 O þe haf i nakin might, For elles it war a-gain þe right. *c* 1420 *Anturs of Arth.* xxi, We ..That riche rewmes ouer rynnes agaynes the ryghte. 1535 COVERDALE *Ps.* xvi[i]. 1 Heare ye right (O Lorde), considre my complaynte. *c* 1560 A. SCOTT *Poems* (S.T.S.) ii. 63 The harralde cryd, 'God schaw the rycht'. 1593 SHAKS. *2 Hen. VI*, II. iii. 55 Here let them end it, and God defend the right. 1611 BIBLE *Isa.* x. 2 To take away the right from the poore of my people. 1690 W. WALKER *Idiomat. Anglo-Lat.* 376 The right itself shineth of itself. 1774 GOLDSM. *Retal.* 40 Too fond of the right to pursue the expedient. 1849 MACAULAY *Hist. Eng.* v. I. 561 The liberty of governing himself..according to his own sense of the right and of the becoming. 1865 LINCOLN *2nd Inaug. Address*, With firmness in the right, as God gives us to see the right.

b. In phr. *to have the right* (cf. 3 b).

c 1430 *Syr Gener.* (Roxb.) 5533, I haue the right and he the wrong. *a* 1585 MONTGOMERIE *Cherrie & Slae* 892 Ȝea, he suld rather die than ȝield, Though Reason had the richt. 1828 SCOTT *F. M. Perth* ii, It is not my part..to decide who had the right or wrong in the present brawl.

c. *To be in the right*, to have justice, reason, or fact upon one's side.

c 1489 CAXTON *Sonnes of Aymon* xxvi. 554 Ye shall take vengaunce of thyse traytours, For ye ben in the right and they in the wronge. 1523 LD. BERNERS *Froiss.* I. ccclxxvi. 626 Ye be in the ryght of this warre. 1594 SHAKS. *Rich. III*, v. iii. 275 He was in the right, and so indeed it is. 1603 — *Meas. for M.* II. i. 167 He's in the right (Constable), what say you to it? 1680 OTWAY *Orphan* I. iv, Your Sex Was never in the right, y're always false, Or silly. 1710 [see REVERIE *sb.* 3 a]. 1782 MISS BURNEY *Cecilia* v. ii, She knew all the time she was in the right. 1815 SCOTT *Let.* in *Lockhart* (1837) III. 365 They are in the right, however, to enforce discipline and good order. 1855 MACAULAY *Hist. Eng.* xviii. IV. 125 A historical question about which they were in the right.

II. 7. Justifiable claim, on legal or moral grounds, to have or obtain something, or to act in a certain way.

Chiefly in various phrases, as *writ* (etc.) *of right*, *in right*, *to have* (good) *right*, etc.

c 888 K. ÆLFRED *Boeth.* xiii, Forðæm hi mid nanum ryhte ne magon ȝearnigan þæt ȝe heora wundrien. *a* 1000 *Cædmon's Gen.* 2152 (Gr.), Nelle ic þa rincas rihte benæman. *c* 1205 LAY. 28776 For he hefde rihte to þissere kineriche. 1297 R. GLOUC. (Rolls) 7496 Þus lo þe englisse folc..come to a nywe louerd þat more in riȝte was. 1338 R. BRUNNE *Chron.* (1810) 57 To coroune kyng Edward, Als he þat had gode right vnto þe regalte. 1375 BARBOUR *Bruce* I. 46 Off kingis, that aucht that reawte, And mayst had rycht thair king to be. 1414 *Rolls of Parlt.* IV. 59/2 Oure Lord, by the Kynges Writ of right enclosed. 1425 *Ibid.* 271/1 He þat hath verray title of right in eny thing. 1461 *Ibid.* V. 467/2 Any of the Kynges in dede and not in right. *c* 1510 *Gesta Rom.* (E.E.T.S.) 432 As moche ryght haue I in this tree as ye. 1579 FULKE *Heskins' Parl.* 89 A writ of right being brought against him, prescription of possession will not serue him. *a* 1600 HOOKER *Eccl. Pol.* VIII. ii. § 8 In case it do happen that without right of blood a man in such wise be possessed. 1642 FULLER *Holy & Prof. St.* II. x[i]x. 123 Nor doth it follow that he hath the best in right, who hath the best in fight. 1671 MILTON *Samson* 310 Who made our Laws to bind us, not himself, And hath full right to exempt Whom so it pleases him. 1727 SWIFT *Baucis & Phil.* 134 Against Dissenters [he] would repine, And stood up firm for Right divine. 1771 *Junius Lett.* (1788) 239 [He] rejects with indignation the claim of right, which his adversary endeavours to establish. 1828 SCOTT *F. M. Perth* xix, But here comes one has good right to do our errand to him. 1868 J. H. BLUNT *Ref. Ch. Eng.* I. 191 It was might, not right, which had put her in the position she occupied. 1897 *Daily News* 11 Dec. 5/7 Right, in its personal application, is indeed never but the underside of duty; turn it uppermost, and everything becomes topsy-turvy.

b. In phr. *in right of* (a person or thing).

1439 *Rolls of Parlt.* V. 26/2 Noght seised of Lond or rentes.., bot in right of þeire Wyves. 1613 PURCHAS *Pilgrimage* IV. viii. (1614) 379 Solimanbee,..who made challenge to the State in right of his wife. 1704 SWIFT *T. Tub* Ded., I should now, in Right of a Dedicator, give your Lordship a List of your own Virtues. 1726 — *Gulliver* I. vi, I allow he preceded me in Right of his Post. 1859 JEPHSON *Brittany* xvi. 258 Claiming the dukedom in right of his wife. 1887 RIDER HAGGARD *Allan Quatermain* i, Nought have I brought save this mine axe; in right of which once I ruled the people of the axe.

c. So *by right* (also *†rights*) *of*.

1600 E. BLOUNT tr. *Conestaggio* 89 They succeeded by right (as they call it) of consanguinitie. 1611 BIBLE *Tobit* iii. 17 She belongeth to Tobias by right of inheritance. 1660 PEPYS *Diary* 9 Jan., He said that..he did it by rights of his office. 1789 COWPER *On the Queen's Visit to London* 3 By right of worth, not blood alone, Entitled here to reign! 1833 TENNYSON *Palace of Art* 207 Hers by right of full-accomplish'd Fate. 1865 KINGSLEY *Hereward* xxi, Pack up the Englishman's plate-chest, which we inherited by right of fist.

8. In prepositional phrases denoting justifiable title or claim to something:

a. *With right*. (In OE. *mid rihte*.)

Beowulf 2056 [He] þone maðþum byreð, þone þe ðu mid rihte rædan sceoldest. *c* 888 K. ÆLFRED *Boeth.* vii. § 3 Hi me habbað benumen mines naman þe ic mid rihte habban sceolde. *c* 1290 *St. Gregory* 29 in *S. Eng. Leg.* I. 356 Ȝif þat lond is swuch ase þe men beoth, name it hauez with riȝte. *c* 1470 *Gol. & Gaw.* 1314 Thoght I myght reif thame with right, rath to my handis. 1599 SHAKS. *Hen. V*, I. ii. 96 May I with right and conscience make this claim?

b. *Of right*.

1375 BARBOUR *Bruce* I. 159 The kynryk ȝharn I nocht to have, Bot gyff it fall off rycht to me. *c* 1410 *Master of Game* (MS. Digby 182) xxxiii, Lete þe houndes comme too and eete þe flessh..for þat is hir rewarde of reght. 1526 *Pilgr. Perf.* (W. de W. 1531) 117 He that of very ryght owed ye cappe. 1576 FLEMING *Panopl. Ep.* 391 He may (of right) chalenge to him self this singular title. 1656 EARL MONM. tr. *Boccalini's Advts. fr. Parnass.* II. xxi. (1674) 169 He ought of right to have precedency. 1667 MILTON *P. L.* IX. 611 To come..and worship thee of right declar'd Sovran of Creatures. 1827 COBBETT *Prot. Reform.* § 330 Those great estates, which of right belonged to the poorer classes. 1874 GREEN *Short Hist.* x. § 4. 791 While England repelled the claims of the Prince of Wales to the Regency as of right, Ireland admitted them.

c. *By* (*good*) *right*; also in mod. use *by rights*.

1377 LANGL. *P. Pl.* B. x. 343 Þei han heritage in heuene, and bi trewe riȝte. *Ibid.* xx. 95 By riȝte he it claymed. 1466 in *Archaeologia* (1887) L. I. 52 Askynge..their Casuallys and other thynges þ[t] long to hem be right ameabully. 1560 DAUS tr. *Sleidane's Comm.* 78 [He] affirmed the kyngdome to be his by good right. 1594 SHAKS. *Rich. III*, I. iii. 172 This Sorrow that I haue, by right is yours. *c* 1616 SIR W. MURE *Misc. Poems* xx. 10 Pretending tytyls..By ry[ch]t hereditar to serve thy grace. 1671 MILTON *P. R.* II. 325 Owe not all Creatures by just right to thee Duty and Service? 1855 KINGSLEY *Westw. Ho!* ii, Days when the gentry of England were by due right the leaders of the people. 1868 DICKENS *Uncomm. Trav.* xxvii, Any little matters which ought to be ours by rights.

9. A legal, equitable, or moral title or claim to the possession of property or authority, the enjoyment of privileges or immunities, etc.

Freq. with qualifying word, as *civil*, *natural*, *real rights*: see the various adjs. *Declaration* or *Bill of Rights*, 'a Bill declaring the Rights and Liberties of England, and the Succession to the Crown' (Burnet), passed in 1689.

a 900 CYNEWULF *Elene* 909 (Gr.), Nu cwom elþeodig.. hafað mec bereafod rihta ȝehwylces. *c* 900 in Thorpe *Dipl. Angl. Sax.* (1865) 140 Þa sona wæs Eþelwald þæs wordes, þæt he no þes rihtes wiðsacan wolde. *a* 1300 *Cursor M.* 3544 Þou sal neuer..In þi forbirth do claim na right. 1375 BARBOUR *Bruce* I. 78 He suld that arbytre disclar,..And lat him ryng that had the rycht. 1491 *Act 7 Hen. VII*, c. 20 § 7 All such right, title, interesse, clayme..as they.. have in any of the premisses. 1525 LD. BERNERS *Froiss.* II. lii[i]. 188 Let the ryght go to the ryght. 1544 tr. *Littleton's Tenures* (1574) 96 b, The donee to whom the release was made then had nothinge in the land, but onely a righte. 1641 *Termes de la Ley* 129 b, For when the Right, which is the foundation and the principall, is released, by consequence the Action..is also released. 1681 STAIR *Instit.* (1693) II. i. 161 All Real Rights are either that original Community of all Men,..Or the Interest which Possession giveth, or Property. 1706 STANHOPE *Paraphr.* III. 334 After all our boast of Settlements and Estates, nothing is or can be settled, but the Fee and Original Right in the great universal Lord. 1768 STERNE *Sent. Journ.* (1778) I. 1 Strange! ..that one and twenty miles sailing..should give a man these rights. 1818 CRUISE *Digest* (ed. 2) I. 172 The husband is entitled to all those rights and privileges which his wife would have had if she were alive, and which were annexed to her estate. *a* 1853 ROBERTSON *Lect.* (1858) 747 Rights are grand things,..but the way in which we expound those rights..seems to me to be the very incarnation of selfishness. 1893 TRAILL *Soc. Eng.* Introd. p. xiii, Association, however, necessarily creates rights and duties; from rights and duties spring law and government.

Comb. *a* 1816 BENTHAM *Offic. Apt. Maximized, Introd. View* (1830) 17 A civil, or say a right-conferring code.

b. Const. *to* (*† unto*, rarely *† for*), with following sb. (or equivalent construction).

c 1205 LAY. 26411 Oðere londes monie, Þe Julius hafde an honde, Þat he naueð nane rihte to. 1297 R. GLOUC. (Rolls) 7495 A fals king þat nadde no riȝt to þe kinedom. *a* 1300 *Cursor M.* 26511 To couer þe right til heuen blis. 14.. GAYTRYGE in *Hampole's Wks.* (1896) I. 109 Robes and Rychesce..þat we haf na gud titil ne na ryght to. 1567 *Satir. Poems Reform.* viii. 9 War ȝour richt reknit to þe croun It mycht be laid with litill menss. *a* 1643 LD. FALKLAND, etc. *Infallibility* (1646) 99 The Turkes..are sensible of the right the Christians..haue for the free exercise of their Religion. *c* 1680 BEVERIDGE *Serm.* (1729) I. 71 When he hath given it to us, we have a civil right to it. 1709 MRS. MANLEY *Secret Mem.* (1720) III. 28 He..is not permitted to fill those Vacancies (to which by the Law of War, he has an indisputed Right). 1789 BENTHAM *Princ. Legisl.* xviii. § 25 *note*, On various occasions you have a right to the services of the magistrate. 1855 BREWSTER *Newton* II. xv. 40 He asserted his own right to the discovery of the differential calculus. 1882 FARRAR *Early Chr.* II. 536 [St. Paul] maintained against them his independent right to the highest order of the Apostolate.

c. Const. *to* with inf. Chiefly in phr. *to have a* (or *no*) *right to* (do something), which in dialect use is also employed with reference to obligation (see quots. under *b*).

?*a* 1400 *Morte Arth.* 1275 Thane salle we rekkene..whatt ryghte þat he claymes, Thus to ryot þis rewme! 1591 SPENSER *M. Hubberd* 524 Some good Gentleman, that hath the right Unto his Church for to present a wight. 1662 J. DAVIES tr. *Olearius' Voy. Ambass.* 194 A Palisadoe..to hinder the fishing of those that have no right to fish. 1681 DRYDEN *Abs. & Achit.* I. 409 If not, the people have a right supreme To make their kings. 1711 STEELE *Spect.* No. 145 ¶ 4 He has no Right to act here as if he were in an empty Room. 1784 J. POTTER *Virtuous Villagers* II. 128 Women claim a right to inspect into the indiscretions of their husbands. 1803 SIR J. MACKINTOSH *Wks.* (1846) III. 242 He has a right to expect from me a faithful, a zealous, and a fearless defence. 1887 RIDER HAGGARD *Allan Quatermain* xvi, We were officers.., and in that capacity had a right to come and go unquestioned.

(*b*) 1771 SMOLLETT *Humph. Cl.* 24 May ¶ 7, I have no right to maintain idle vagrants. 1808 ELEANOR SLEATH *Bristol Heiress* I. 209, I don't see as how women have any right to be trampled on. 1829 J. HUNTER *Hallamsh. Gloss.* s.v., 'I have no right to pay at that toll-bar,' means, I am not obliged to pay there. 1854 MISS BAKER *Northampt. Gloss.* s.v., 'I have no right to pay': i.e. I ought not to be compelled to pay. 1892 M. C. F. MORRIS *Yorks. Folk-talk* 82 'To have a right' is equivalent to 'ought' or 'in duty bound', in such a phrase as this—'He' gotten a weyfe an' bairns, and he's a right to keep 'em.'

d. Const. *of* (in early use = *to*), with sbs. or gerunds. See also RIGHT OF WAY.

1463–4 *Cal. Rec. Dubl.* (1889) I. 315 Apon the varyaunce of the ryght and tytle of the office of Recorder. 1559 BALDWIN in *Mirr. Mag.* e ij, Earle Richard..had the right of Salysbury in holde. 1585 T. WASHINGTON tr. *Nicholay's Voy.* IV. xxxiii. 155 b, [He] wold not permit these..to enjoy the right of Burgesie. 1611 BIBLE *Tobit* vi. 11, I wil speake for her, that she may be giuen thee for a wife. For to thee doth the right of her appertaine. 1641 *Termes de la Ley* 129 b, Right of entrie. 1702 H. DODWELL *Apol.* § 15 in S. Parker *Cicero's De Finibus*, Authority..had undoubtedly the Right of Life and Death. 1768 BLACKSTONE *Comm.* III. 178 The alienee..hath not only a bare possession, but also an apparent right of possession. 1842 W. SPALDING *Italy & It. Isl.* I. 81 A certain part of the senators..possessed votes without the right of addressing the assembly. 1889 *Law Times Rep.* LVIII. 163/2 The right of using this road constituted an easement of the farm.

e. A document substantiating a claim or title. *Miner's right*: see MINER[1] 6.

1545 *Reg. Privy Council Scot.* I. 9 The said Thomas.. hes promittit to bring with him sik rychtis as tha will use quharby tha clame the sadis landis to pertene to thame. 1637 RUTHERFORD *Lett.* (1862) I. lxxvii. 198 The man who will not be content with rights to bought land, except he get also the ridges and acres laid upon his back to carry home with him. 1890 [see MINER[1] 6].

10. With possessive pron. or genitive: The title or claim to something properly possessed by one or more persons. Also *transf.*

c 1129 *O. E. Chron.* (Laud MS.) an. 1129, Þæt hi scolden ealle cumen to Lundene.., & þær scolden sprecon of ealle Godes rihtes. *c* 1250 *Gen. & Ex.* 3714 Burȝes stronge and folc vn-friȝt, stalwurði to weren here riȝt. *a* 1290 *Beket* 229 in *S. Eng. Leg.* I. 113 Swyþe wel bi-gan þis Ercedekne boli churche bi-lede, And stifliche heold op hire riȝte. *a* 1300 *Cursor M.* 26320 Þou þi right fordon has þan. 1389 in *Eng. Gilds* (1870) 30 Þey schal saue þe kynge hys rythe, and non prejudys don a-geyn his lawe in þes ordenaunce. 1425 *Rolls of Parlt.* IV. 273/1 Þe pretensed ryght of my said Lord. 1483 CAXTON *G. de la Tour* h vj, Whanne the kyng was dede, somme wold haue taken her ryght fro her. 1558 GOODMAN *How to Obey* 180 It is..a great discouraging to the people..when they are not defended..in their right and title. 1590 SHAKS. *Mids. N.* I. i. 92 Lysander, yeelde Thy crazed title to my certaine right. 1638 BAKER tr. *Balzac's Lett.* (vol. II.) 194, I yeeld up my right in all the good I receive from you. 1670 HOBBES *Dial. Comm. Laws* (1681) 37 My Right is a Liberty left me by the Law to do any thing which the Law forbids me not. 1757 W. WILKIE *Epigoniad* I. 14 In vain for Polynices' right they bled. 1799 HAN. MORE *Fem. Educ.* (ed. 4) I. 147 To these have been opposed, with more presumption than prudence, the rights of woman. 1819 MACKINTOSH *Parl. Suffrage* Wks. 1846 III. 232 The enlightened friends of the rights of the people. 1855 MACAULAY *Hist. Eng.* xii. III. 222 Human nature at last asserted its rights. 1878 DALE *Lect. Preach.* ix. 291 Respect the rights of the past: assert the rights of the present.

b. In phr. *in* (*the*) *right of*, *in one's* (*own*) *right*.

1472 *Rolls of Parlt.* VI. 15/2 In the possession of the same Richard and Anne his wyfe, as in the right of the same Anne. 1540 *Act 32 Hen. VIII*, c. 48 The castell of Douer, wherof the kinges maiesty is verye owner in the right of the imperial crowne of this his realme. 1568 GRAFTON *Chron.* II. 53 Wherefore king Henry havyng now maryed the sayde Alianor claymed as in her right the Erledome of Tholose. 1599 THYNNE *Animad.* (1875) 26 Alice, the wyfe of Richarde Neuille, (erle of Sarisbery in the righte of the same Alice). 1628 BOLTON *Florus* III. xvii. (1636) 225 The gentrie..robbed the commonweale in their own right. 1749 FIELDING *Tom Jones* I. x, Where they might enjoy almost the same advantages of a liberal fortune as if they were entitled to it in their own right. 1766 BLACKSTONE *Comm.* II. 435 The only method he had to gain possession of it, was by suing in his wife's right. 1838 DICKENS *Nich. Nick.* iv, She has a little money in her own right. 1885 *Law Times Rep.* LIII. 526/1 Property which should come to the wife, or the husband in her right.

11. That which justly accrues or falls to any one; what one may properly claim; one's due.

c 897 K. ÆLFRED *Gregory's Past. C.* 397 Ȝiȝife se wer his wife hire ryht on hira ȝesinscipe. *c* 970 in Thorpe *Laws* I. 258 Do ðam ðeofe his riht, swa hit ær Eadmundes cwide wæs. *c* 1200 *Trin. Coll. Hom.* 179 Unneðes hie winnen ȝiet here louerdes rihtes. *c* 1275 LAY. 7906 Ich hou segge, enihtes, Rome his oure rihtes [*c* 1205 eowre irihte]. *c* 1330 R. BRUNNE *Chron. Wace* (Rolls) 6755 Ȝe..waytes vs wyþ sum tresons, For to wyþ-halden vs oure right. *c* 1380 WYCLIF *Sel. Wks.* III. 328 Þei ben þevys,..and cursed, for þei wiþdrawen riȝttis of holy Chirche. *c* 1400 *Destr. Troy* 7987, I shall..our ground to þe grekes graunt as for right. 1535 COVERDALE *Jer.* xxii. 16 Yee when he helped ye oppressed and poore to their right, then prospered he well. *a* 1586 *Answer to Cartwright* 55 Wee shoulde not take our ryghte on a thyefe, to iustyfie his theeuerye. *a* 1625 FLETCHER *Nice Valour* v. iii, Honour and admiration are

her rights. 1652 NEEDHAM tr. *Selden's Mare Cl.* 11 Observing the Laws and paying the Rights of the Countrie. 1655 MOUFET & BENNET *Health's Improv.* (1746) 81 Let us not but give the Devil his right. 1782 MISS BURNEY *Cecilia* x. iii, He has been advised by his friends to claim his rights. 1832 HT. MARTINEAU *Life in Wilds* iii. 41 Our provisions are the right of those who work for them. 1875 JOWETT *Plato* (ed. 2) IV. 35 We cannot help acknowledging that what is right for us is the right and inheritance of others.

fig. 1810 SCOTT *Lady of L.* III. xviii, Grief claim'd his right, and tears their course.

†b. A territory, estate, dominion. *Obs. rare.*

1338 R. BRUNNE *Chron.* (1810) 10 Whan he had regned foure ȝere, one ryued vpon his right. 1596 SPENSER *F. Q.* v. viii. 26 Sir Artegall..taking with him, as his vanquisht thrall, That Damzell, led her to the Souldans right.

†c. (Usu. *pl.*) The last sacraments of the Church.

a 1330 *Roland & V.* 372 Þer fel a miracle of a kniȝt, Wiche þat was to deþ y-diȝt,..Er he dyd he hadde his riȝt. *c* 1400 *Brut* 134 Oppon seynt Iohnes day..þe Kyng vnderfonge his rightes of holy cherche, as falliþ to euery Cristen man. [*c* 1450 *Contin. Brut* (E. E. T. S.) 493 When he saw he shold dye, he made his testament, and..receyved al þe rightes of holy churche.] 1470–85 MALORY *Arthur* XIII. xiii. 630 But bere me vnto the Abbay..that I may be confessyd and haue my ryghtes. 1509 HAWES *Past. Pleas.* XLI. (Percy Soc.) 204 Of holy church with all humilite My rightes I toke.

†d. *pl.* That part of the quarry given to the hounds as their share or due. *Obs.*

c 1410 *Master of Game* (MS. Digby 182) xxxiii, When þe houndes beth þus enquyrered, þe lymmers shulde haue both þe shuldres for þeire reghtes. *a* 1533 LD. BERNERS *Huon* lii. 177, I can chase the herte & the wyld bore, and blowe the pryce, and serue the houndes of theyr ryghtes.

e. *pl.* A stag's full complement of antlers, consisting of the brow, bay, and tray.

c 1410 *Master of Game* (MS. Digby 182) xxiv, Fourched on þe reght syde and lacke nought of reghtes bynethe. *Ibid.*, If hym lacke any of his reghtes benethe, ye muste abate so many in þe toppe. 1611 COTGR. s.v. *Marque*, A deere, which hath more rights, or branches, on th' one side then on th' other. 1637 B. JONSON *Sad Shepherd* I. ii, A head, Large, and well beam'd: with all rights somm'd, and spred. 1677 *Gentl. Recr.* in *Encycl. Metrop.* (1845) XX. 416/2 You must say he beareth..a false Right on his near horn, for all that the Beam bears are called Rights. 1856 'STONEHENGE' *Brit. Rural Sports* I. x. 82 The three first are termed the rights; the two points, the crockets. 1884 JEFFERIES *Red Deer* ii. 142 To be runnable or warrantable, a stag..must bear his 'rights' (that is, brow, bay, and tray), and two on top.

III. †12. a. *On*, *of*, or *by right*, = ARIGHT *adv.*

Beowulf 1555 Rodera rædend hit on ryht ȝesced. *c* 888 K. ÆLFRED *Boeth.* vii. § 1 Ȝif ic þine unrotnesse on riht ongieten hæbbe. 971 *Blickl. Hom.* 45 Se biscop sceal.. þrafian þa mæsse-preostas..þæt hie healdan Godes æwe on riht. *c* 1250 *Gen. & Ex.* 2226 Alle he woren ðanne sori ofriȝt; Iacob ðus him bi-meneð o-riȝt. *a* 1300 *Cursor M.* 1566 Sua blind þai war in þair insight, Þat reckining cuth þai nan o right. 13.. *E. E. Allit. P.* B. 1513 Þer was ryngíng, on ryȝt, of ryche metalles. *c* 1400 *Destr. Troy* 344 And all fowles in Fether fell þere vppon, For to reckon by right, þat to ryuer haunttes. *c* 1420 *Avow. Arth.* xxxiii, Quat is the rawunsun opon ryȝte, The sothe thou me sayn?

†b. *At right* (rarely *rights*), properly, aright. *Sc. Obs.*

1375 BARBOUR *Bruce* XIV. 171 That nycht the Scottis cumpany War wachit richt weill, all at richt. *c* 1470 HENRY *Wallace* IV. 278 Syne restit thar at rycht In a forest. 1513 DOUGLAS *Æneis* III. vi. 22 All..godlie wychtis Schew we suld haue a prosper rais at rychtis. 1535 LYNDESAY *Satyre* 414 Placebo, rewll our Roy at richt.

†c. *At their right*, to the full, completely. *Obs. rare.*

c 1410 *Master of Game* (MS. Digby 182) vi, So þat hir teth be waxe vp alle at hire ryght. *Ibid.*, Þen oþer teth commeth to hem alle newe...And whan þei be wexe vp agaynn at hir right, þen þei..gothe at hir aventure.

†13. *At* (or *to*) *all rights* (also *Sc. right*), at all points, in every respect. *Obs.*

13.. *Coer de L.* 3123 He was armyd to alle ryghtes. *c* 1325 *Orfeo* 134 Ther come to me two fair knyghtes, Wele arayde at alle ryghthis. 1375 BARBOUR *Bruce* x. 312 The castele..wes varnyst vondir wele With men and wittale at all richt. *c* 1386 CHAUCER *Knt.'s T.* 2102 An hundred knyghtes Wel armed for the werre at alle rightes. 1470–85 MALORY *Arthur* VIII. vi. 281 Syr Trystram commaunded his seruaunt..to..dresse his harneis at al manere of ryghtes. *c* 1475 *Rauf Coilȝear* 686 Greit Squechonis on hicht.. Reulit at all richt Endlang the hall.

14. *To rights*: **a.** (Also rarely *to right*, *† to the rights*, *at rights*.) In a proper manner (*obs.*); to or into a proper condition or order. In later use chiefly with *bring*, *put*, or *set*.

c 1330 R. BRUNNE *Chron. Wace* (Rolls) 4127 He mayntende þe lond to ryght, He was curteys & doughty knyght. 1340–70 *Alisaunder* 846 With þe gaie golde ring graue too-rightes. *Ibid.* 1222 That bolde borou Byzance þat buyld was to-rihtus. *c* 1350 *Will. Palerne* 53 A-greþed ful riche, wiþ perrey & pellure pertelyche to þe riȝttes. *Ibid.* 1632 Þemperour & eueri man were esed to riȝttes. 1472–3 *Rolls of Parlt.* VI. 59/1 That all Wolles..be sufficiauntly, trewly and indifferently pakked to rights, within the Royalme of Englond. 1535 COVERDALE *Luke* vi. 10 Then was his hande restored him to right, euen as whole as the other. 1627 CAPT. SMITH *Seaman's Gram.* ix. 43 Bring the ship to rights, that is, againe vnder saile as she was. *a* 1641 BP. MOUNTAGU *Acts & Mon.* (1642) 481 To set all things at rights as at first they were being no work..for the arme of man. 1662 PEPYS *Diary* 30 Jan., Employed all the afternoon in my chamber, setting things and papers to rights. 1706 LOGAN in *Pennsylv. Hist. Soc. Mem.* X. 146 When once puzzled he can with difficulty bring himself to rights. 1748 RICHARDSON *Clarissa* Wks. 1883 V. 487 Sense of shame ..may make rifled rank get up, and shake itself to rights. 1767 FRANKLIN *Let.* Wks. 1887 IV. 23, I received the watch chain, which you say you send to be put to rights. 1821 JEFFERSON *Autob.* Writ. 1892 I. 109 How the good should be secured, and the ill brought to rights, was the difficulty. 1842 G. S. FABER *Prov. Lett.* I. 55 Call in Mr. Maitland, ..and he will speedily set all to right. 1859 MRS. CARLYLE *Lett.* III. 8 A good sleep would have put me to rights. 1888 BRYCE *Amer. Commw.* III. 216 The lists of voters..were set to rights.

b. At once, straightway (now *U.S.*); also, † completely, altogether. Formerly freq. in phr. *† to sink to rights*.

(*a*) 1663 PEPYS *Diary* 8 June, Mr. Coventry and us two did discourse with the Duke a little.., and so to rights home again. 1683 TRYON *Way to Health* 390 The King..ordered him to be carried to rights, to the Tower. 1702 S. PARKER tr. *Cicero's De Finibus* v. 303 When Indigent People are ready ..to suffer any Thing rather than die to Rights. 1835 MAJOR DOWNING *Lett.* 129 So to rights the express got back, and brought a letter.

(*b*) 1673 DRYDEN *Amboyna* III. iii, The vessel rifled, and the rich hold rummaged, they sink it down to rights. 1695 WOODWARD *Nat. Hist. Earth* III. i. (1723) 150 The whole Tract..sinks down to rights into the Abyss underneath. 1726 SWIFT *Gulliver* II. viii, The Hulk.., by Reason of many Breaches.., sunk to Rights. 1731 MEDLEY *Kolben's Cape G. Hope* I. 34 The poor fellow, in a most piteous condition, and his heart sinking to rights under the melancholy notion he had of it.

†15. *Hunting.* The scent, the track. *Obs.*

c 1410 *Master of Game* (MS. Digby 182) xiii, A bolde hounde shulde neuer pleyne nor yowle, but if he were oute of þe reghtes. And also he shulde agayne seche þe rightes.

16. The true account or interpretation *of* a matter. Now *pl.*

1749 FIELDING *Tom Jones* XVIII. ii, There hath been a terrible to do. I could not possibly learn the very right of it. 1751 ELIZA HEYWOOD *Betsy Thoughtless* III. 147, I verily believe thou hast hit upon the right. 1846 MARRYAT *Valerie* viii, I have never heard the rights of that story. 1853 WHYTE MELVILLE *Digby Grand* I. vi. 166 Those ladies who dearly love the last bit of news..and who are never satisfied without learning what they call the rights of it.

IV. 17. a. = RIGHT HAND 2.

a 1240 *Sawles Warde* in *O. E. Hom.* I. 257 Þe middel sti bituhhe riht ant luft. *a* 1300 *Cursor M.* 2463 Queder þou ches, on right or left, I sal ta me þat þou haues left. 1382 WYCLIF *Prov.* iv. 27 Ne bowe thou doun to the riȝt, ne to the lift; turne awei thi foot fro euel. 1667 MILTON *P. L.* VI. 558 Vangard, to Right and Left the Front unfould. 1707 FREIND *Peterborow's Cond. Sp.* 211 Take to the Mountains on the right with all your Men. 1764 GOLDSM. *Trav.* 105 Far to the right, where Apennine ascends. 1823 F. CLISSOLD *Ascent Mont Blanc* 11 A precipitous declivity, which shelved down, upon our right, in one plane of smooth rock. 1894 MRS. H. WARD *Marcella* II. 306 Benny appeared.. elbowing the Jewesses to right and left.

b. The right wing of an army, etc.; the right-hand extremity of a line of men.

1707 *Lond. Gaz.* No. 4334/4 Our right was then at Louvignies, and our Left at Naast. 1743 in *Buccleuch MSS.* (Hist. MSS. Comm.) I. 401 Their right reaching to the village called Keldersbach. 1828 SCOTT *F. M. Perth* xxxiv, Four of them occupied the right of the first line. *Ibid.*, The Chief occupied the centre of the middle rank, instead of being on the extreme right. 1865 KINGSLEY *Herew.* xxxiii, There are the French, close on our right. 1896 BADEN POWELL *Matabele Campaign* viii, The Cape Boys had worked their way round to the enemy's right.

c. The right-hand way or road.

1764 *J. Kirby's Suffolk Trav.* (ed. 2) 278 At 2 m. take the Right which goes to Sutton Church,..at 3 m. 6 f. the Right goes to Sutton.

d. *Politics.* In Continental legislative chambers, the party or parties of conservative principles. (See CENTRE *sb.* 15.)

1887 *Harper's Mag.* Jan. 180/1 The political differences between the two great parties, the parliamentary Right and Left.

18. a. A boot or shoe for the right foot; a glove for the right hand.

1825 HONE *Every-day Bk.* I. 515 It belonged to the left foot of the wearer; so..this is proof that 'rights and lefts' are only 'An old, old, very old' fashion revived. 1864 F. LOCKER *My Mistress's Boots* vii, Cinderella's lefts and rights To Geraldine's were frights. 1884 *Harper's Mag.* Dec. 117/1, I didn't want two rights [*sc.* gloves].

b. (See quots.)

1846 HOLTZAPFFEL *Turning* II. 911 Nail scissors are made in pairs, and formed in opposite ways, or as 'rights and lefts', so that they may suit the respective hands. 1889 C. T. DAVIS *Bricks & Tiles* (ed. 2) 73 Bricks..are termed 'rights' and 'lefts' when they are so moulded or ornamented that they cannot be used for any corner.

c. A blow given with the right hand.

1898 *Daily News* 24 Nov. 7/3 Sharkey put over a straight right on Corbett's nose, seeming to bring blood.

†19. The direct road or way. *Obs. rare.*

1535 LYNDESAY *Satyre* 4189, I man pas to the King of Farie, Or ellis the rycht to hell. 1595 SHAKS. *John* I. i. 170 Something about a little from the right, In at the window or else ore the hatch.

20. A facet (of a diamond). *Obs. rare.*

1675 *Lond. Gaz.* No. 1050/4 A short hart Diamond,..4 Rights and the Coller pollished, the Stone being about half made.

Right, *sb.*[2], erron. spelling for RITE *sb.*

1590 SHAKS. *Mids. N.* (1600) IV. i. 138 No doubt they rose vp early, to obserue The right of May. 1634 MILTON *Comus* 125 Com let us our rights begin, 'Tis onely day-light that makes Sin. 1655 STANLEY *Hist. Philos.* (1687) 405/1 Being initiated into the Orphick Solemnities, the Priest telling him, that they who were initiated into those Rights [etc.]. 1700 PRIOR *Carm. Sec.* 36 Numa the Rights of strict Religion knew; On ev'ry Altar laid the Incense due. 1768–74 TUCKER *Lt. Nat.* (1834) I. 463 Worship the immortal gods according to the rights of thy country. 1865 LEVER *Luttrell* i, He'll give her the rights. *Ibid.*, I sent for you to administer to her the rights of her Church. [Cf. RIGHT *sb.*[1] 11 c.]

Right (rəit), *a.* Forms: 1 **reht** (**rect**), **reoht**, **ræht**; 1–4 **riht**, 3 **rihht**, **rihet**, 2–3, *Sc.* 6– **richt**; 3–5 **riȝt(e**, 4 **riȝtt**, **riȝht**, **riȝth** (4–5 **rith**), 3– **right**; 1, 4 **ryht** (4 **-te**), 5–6 *Sc.* **rycht**; 4 **ryȝht**, 4–5 **ryȝt** (4 **-tte**, 5 **-te**); 4 **rygth**, 5 **rygt**, **ryth**, 4–6 **ryght** (5–6 **-te**); also *dial.* 8–9 **reet**, 9 **reeght**, **reight**, **raight**. [Common Teutonic: OE. *reht*, *riht*, *ryht*, = OFris. *riucht* (mod. Fris. *rjucht*), MDu. *recht*, *richt* (Du. *recht*, † *regt*), OS. *reht* (MLG. and LG. *recht*), OHG. *reht* (MHG. and G. *recht*), ON. *réttr* (Norw. *rett*, Da. *ret*, Sw. *rätt*), Goth. *raihts*; related to L. *rectus*, the base being the root *reg-* to make or lead straight.

In OE. *riht* frequently forms the first part of a compound instead of having adjectival flexion.]

I. 1. †a. Straight; not bent, curved, or crooked in any way. Also *right with*, in a line with. *Obs.*

c 950 *Lindisf. Gosp.* Matt. iii. 3 Ræhta doeð *vel* wyrcas stiga his [*Hatton* Doð hys syþas rihte]. 971 *Blickl. Hom.* 207 Nalas..þæt þa waxas wæron rihte, ac ȝit swiðor on scræfes onlicnesse þæt wæs æteowed. *c* 1000 *Sax. Leechd.* I. 316 Ðeos wyrt..hafað leaf swylce winȝeard & rihte stelan. *a* 1122 *O. E. Chron.* (Laud MS.) an. 656, v. mile to þe rihte æ þe gað to Ælm & to Wisebece. *c* 1175 *Lamb. Hom.* 7 Þenne make we ham [his paths] rihte ȝef we haldet his beode. *c* 1205 LAY. 7830 Þa Bruttes..nomen longen ræftres, stronge & rihte. *c* 1220 *Bestiary* 86 Siðen wið his riȝte bile [he] takeð mete ðat he wile. *c* 1330 *Assump. Virg.* 666 As soone as he hadde seide þis bede,..Alle his lymes bi come ful ryȝt. ?*a* 1366 CHAUCER *Rom. Rose* 1701 The stalke was as risshe right. 1422 tr. *Secreta Secret., Priv. Priv.* 233 He hath..the body al holle and wel y-mesurid, ryght estature. *c* 1430 *Hymns Virgin* (1867) 46 Crokid & creplis he makiþ riȝt. 1578 LYTE *Dodoens* I. lxxii. 107 The stem of this herbe..is right and straight. 1589 R. TOMSON in Hakluyt *Voy.* 587 The said Citie of Mexico hath the streetes made very broad, and right. 1607 TOPSELL *Four-f. Beasts* (1658) 457 It hath a mane standing up in the upper part right or direct, but hollow or bending before. 1669 STURMY *Mariner's Mag.* II. viii. 73 Hold the Instrument..with the Foot AB right with the Horizon level. 1704 J. HARRIS *Lex. Techn.* I. s.v., Right Muscles of the Head.

Phr. *a* 1327 in *Rel. Antiq.* II. 19 Stod y in my stirop streyt,..As ryt as ramis orn. *c* 1430 LYDG. *Min. Poems* (Percy Soc.) 172 Conveyede by lyne ryght as a rammes horne. *c* 1522 SKELTON *Why nat to Court* 87 Do ryght and do no wronge, As ryght as a rammes horne. 1678 RAY *Prov.* 288.

†b. Of a way or course: Direct, going straight towards its destination. *Right range* (see quot. 1669). *Obs.*

With *way*, the adj. passes into the sense 'correct, proper' (cf. 9), and in ME. it is sometimes uncertain which meaning is intended.

c 825 *Vesp. Psalter* cvi. 7 Dryhten..ut-alaedde hie in weȝ rehtne, ðæt hie eoden in cestre eordunge. *a* 900 tr. *Baeda's Hist.* I. xii. (1890) 46 Þæt hi ȝemænelice fæsten ȝeworhten.. stænene weal rihtre stiȝe fram eastsæ oð wæstsæ. *c* 1000 *Guthlac* iii. (1848) 20 He ðan rihtestan weȝe ðyder to geferde. *c* 1200 ORMIN 11093 Þatt newe sterrne þatt.. shollde ledenn hemm Till himm þe rihhte weȝȝe. 13.. *Coer de L.* 3894 Ful ryght way wenten [they] to Archane. *c* 1350 *Will. Palerne* 5322 He rides..to-wardes rome þo' riȝtes gates. *c* 1386 CHAUCER *Frankl. T.* 504 Vpon the morwe.. To Britaigne tooke they the righte way. *c* 1400 MAUNDEV. (Roxb.) xiv. 62 Now will I tell ȝow þe rightest way and þe schortest to Ierusalem. *c* 1470 HENRY *Wallace* v. 3 The day faillit, throu the rycht cours worthit schort. 1535 LYNDESAY *Satyre* 1929 Wische me the richt way till Sanct-Androes. 1555 EDEN *Decades* (Arb.) 162 A newe & ryghter way founde of late. 1600 FAIRFAX *Tasso* XIX. cxvi, Many follow'd that enquest, But these alone found out the rightest way. 1620–55 I. JONES *Stone-Heng* (1725) 60 Ermin-street ..led the right Way into the Northern Countries. 1669 STURMY *Mariner's Mag.* v. xii. 69 To shoot in a Right-Range..is, as far as the Bullet doth go in a Right-line at any Degree of Elevation. 1704 [see RANGE *sb.*[1] 11 b].

†c. In fig. contexts. *Obs.* (Cf. 9.)

c 888 K. ÆLFRED *Boeth.* xxiii. § 2 Þu ne meahtes ȝyt ful rihtne weȝ aredian to ðæm soðum ȝesælðum. 971 *Blickl. Hom.* 109 Þa men þe bearn habban..him tæcean lifes weȝ & rihtne gang to heofonum. *c* 1200 ORMIN 5507 Þatt rihhte weȝȝe..þatt ledeþþ þa till heoffness ærd. *c* 1300 *Harrow. Hell* 211 Þou sendest me þe ryhte wey into helle. *c* 1380 WYCLIF *Wks.* (1880) 58 Also it is a gret werk of mercy to teche men þe riȝtte weie to heuene. *c* 1440 *Jacob's Well* 258 Kepyth þe ryȝte weye in myddys of þe x. comaundementys. 1451 CAPGRAVE *Life St. Aug.* (E. E. T. S.) 2 He was cause..with his bokis þat many a soule is ledde þe rith weye to heuene. 1538 STARKEY *England* I. ii. 39 We must now seke out..the veray true commyn wele, seyng that we haue therby thus found..the ryghtyst way therto. 1590 SPENSER *F. Q.* I. x. 10 All..take delight With many rather for to goe astray,.. Then with a few to walke the rightest way.

†d. Of lineage, descent, etc.: Direct, legitimate.

1387–8 T. USK *Test. Love* II. ii. (Skeat) l. 115 Who is discended of right bloode of lyne fro king Artour? 1448–9 METHAM *Wks.* (E. E. T. S.) 79 This knyght despousyd had a lady, Hauyng decens be ryght lynage Off that wurthy and excellent stok lyneally, That Poolys men clepe. 1570 *Satir. Poems Reform.* xiii. 117 Ane teinfull tratour of rycht succession.

†e. *transf.* Keeping a straight course. *Obs.*

1603 DANIEL *Def. Rhime* in G. G. Smith *Eliz. Crit. Ess.* (1904) II. 372 Discretion is the best measure, the rightest foote in what habit soeuer it runne. 1626 [see FOOT *sb.* 29 c]. 1640 FEATLY *Abbot* in Fuller *Abel Rediv.* (1867) II. 282 All their children, treading in their holy steps, walked with a right foot to the Gospel.

†f. (After L. *rectus*.) Nominative. *Obs.*[−1]

1654 Z. COKE *Logick* 20 Always absolutely in the right (that is the nominative) Case.

2. *Right line*, a straight line. (Cf. LINE-RIGHT.)

1551 RECORDE *Pathw. Knowl.* I. Defin., Of lynes there bee two principall kyndes,..a right or straight lyne, and..a croked lyne. 1570 BILLINGSLEY *Euclid* I. def. 5. 2 One right lyne cannot be righter then an other. 1658 SIR T. BROWNE *Hydriot.* iv. (1736) 43 Circles and Right Lines limit and close all Bodies. 1715 tr. *Gregory's Astron.* (1726) I. 146 A Body which is not urged by a Force tending to a Centre, will not describe a Circle, but a Right line. 1812 DAVY *Chem. Philos.* 69 Supposing that there is a certain unknown matter always moving through the universe in right lines. 1898 TOUT *Empire & Papacy* xvii. (1901) 425 The right lines and measured regularity of an American city.

Comb. 1715 tr. *Gregory's Astron.* (1726) II. 466 An uniform progressive Motion in a Right-line Tangent to its Orbit. 1875 KNIGHT *Dict. Mech.* 1943/2 *Right-line Pen*, a drawing-pen.

transf. 1697 DRYDEN *Ded. Æneid* Ess. (ed. Ker) II. 165 Pulci, Boiardo, and Ariosto, would cry out, 'make room for the Italian poets, the descendants of Virgil in a right line'.

3. Formed by or with reference to a right line or plane perpendicular to another right line or plane.

a. *Right circle*, *horizon*, *sphere*: (see quots. and the sbs.).

c 1391 CHAUCER *Astrol.* II. § 27 This is the conclusioun to knowe the Assenciouns of signes in the riht cercle. *c* 1391, 1549 [see HORIZON *sb.* 3]. 1551 RECORDE *Cast. Knowl.* (1556) 209 In the Righte Sphere. 1559 W. CUNNINGHAM *Cosmogr. Glasse* 15 The sphere is deuided into a right sphere and into an oblique or crokyd sphere. *Ibid.* 20 This Picture sheweth the fourme of a right Horizont. 1594 BLUNDEVIL *Exerc.* III. xvii. (1636) 313 When is the Horizon said to be right, and thereby to make a right Spheare? 1700 MOXON *Math. Dict.* 158 A Right or Direct Sphere hath both the Poles of the World in the Horizon, and the Equinoctial transiting the Zenith. 1715 tr. *Gregory's Astron.* (1726) I. 221 For either the Horizon of the Place is right to the Equator,..or it is oblique. 1795 HUTTON *Math. & Phil. Dict.* II. 375/1 Right Sphere, is that where the equator cuts the horizon at Right angles; or that which has the poles in the horizon, and the equinoctial in the zenith. 1846 GWILT *Archit.* Gloss., *Right Circle*, a circle drawn at right angles with the plane of projection. 1868 LOCKYER *Elem. Astron.* 147 Parallel, Right, and Oblique Spheres.

b. In miscellaneous uses: *† Right corner*, a right angle. *Right sailing* (see quots. 1704 and 1867). *Right sine*: (see SINE *sb.*).

1548 ELYOT, *Orthogonius*, that hath ryght corners. 1551 RECORDE *Pathw. Knowl.* I. Defin., The square angle, whiche is commonly named a right corner, is made by twoo lynes meetyng together in fourme of a squire. 1579 J. STUBBES *Gaping Gulf* F iv b, The very rightest perpendicular downfal that can be imagined from the point. 1655 STANLEY *Hist. Philos.* (1701) 250/2 Simple, local Motion is twofold: circular..and right: the right is either upwards from the center, or downwards to the center, and both these either simply, or κατὰ τι. 1667 MILTON *P. L.* IV. 541 The setting Sun..with right aspect..Leveld his eevning Rayes. 1704 J. HARRIS *Lex. Techn.* I., *Right Sailing*, is when a Voyage is perform'd on some one of the four Cardinal Points. 1748 H. ELLIS *Hudson's Bay* 93 The land trenched away from East by North to North by West, making right Points of the Compass. 1840 *Civil Eng. & Arch. Jrnl.* III. 232/1 It is a common idea that the oblique is weaker than the right arch. 1867 SMYTH *Sailor's Word-bk.*, *Right sailing*, running a course on one of the four cardinal points, so as to alter only a ship's latitude, or longitude.

c. *Right ascension*: (see ASCENSION 3). Also *† Right descension* (see DESCENSION 5).

1594 BLUNDEVIL *Exerc.* II. (1636) 114 Knowing the Sunnes place, you shall learne the right ascention thereof thus. 1651 C. BROOKES *Sphær. Triang.* 24 It is required to find out the Right Adscension and Declination of both those starres severally. 1690 LEYBOURN *Curs. Math.* 367 Such is the Sun's Right Ascension when he is in 29 deg. of Taurus. 1755 B. MARTIN *Mag. Arts & Sci.* 185 The same Thing which on the terrestrial Globe and Maps is called Longitude, is, on the celestial Globe and Sphere, called Right Ascension. 1812–16 PLAYFAIR *Nat. Phil.* (1819) II. 79 The parallax in right ascension is nothing when a body is on the meridian. 1882 *Knowledge* No. 15. 317 Transit observers have to determine the declination of a star as well as what is called the right ascension.

d. Of solid figures: Having the ends or base at right angles with the axis.

1674 JEAKE *Arith.* (1696) 524 If a Right Cylinder have the Diameter 14, and the Height..as much; then shall the Area of each Base be 154. 1795 HUTTON *Math. & Phil. Dict.* II. 375/1 Right Cone, or Cylinder, or prism, or pyramid. 1805–17 R. JAMESON *Char. Min.* (ed. 3) 140 All the faces of the right quadrangular prism are equal and similar. 1854 *Pereira's Polarized Light* (ed. 2) 218 In this system are included the right rhombic prism, the right rhombic octohedron [etc.]. 1887 [see CYLINDER 1 b].

†4. a. Of the eyes, etc.: Directed straight forwards. *Obs.*

c 1410 *Master of Game* (MS. Digby 182) xxxi, Þere oþer beloweth with a reght musell byfore hem. 1616 J. LANE *Contn. Sqr.'s T.* IV. 73 Wrest the streight crooked, the right eyes besquint.

†b. Of a blow: Direct, forward. *Obs.*

c 1470 HENRY *Wallace* II. 62 The tothir fled,..Bot a rycht straik Wallace him gat that tyd. 1591 FLORIO *2nd Fruites* 119 Hee will hit any man..with a right or reverse blowe. 1594 I. G. *Grassi's Art Def.* E eiv, When, after a right blowe, he would discharge a reverse.

II. 5. Of persons or disposition: Disposed to do what is just or good; upright, righteous. Now *rare*.

c 825 *Vesp. Psalter* xxiv. 8 Swoete & reht [is] dryten. *Ibid.* xxxi. 11 Wuldriað alle rehte on heortan. *a* 900 CYNEWULF *Crist* 18 Eala þu Reccend ond þu riht Cyning. *c* 1320 *Cast. Love* 398 Þi douȝter..I am, I wot bi þon, For þou art kyng, riht domes-mon. *a* 1340 HAMPOLE *Psalter* vii. 10 When he sees oure hert in heuen..þan he makis vs mare right and helpis vs. 1382 WYCLIF *Ps.* lxxviii. 37 The herte forsothe of hem was not riȝt with hym. 1567 *Gude & Godlie Ball.* (S. T. S.) 28 Thow, God, the quhilk is onlie richt, Thow saif me fra the Deuillis net. 1576 FLEMING *Panopl. Epist.* 360 Execute this office simply, justly, and according to the rule of a right conscience. 1652 *Nicholas Papers* (Camden) II. 307, I believe he hath a very right heart for the K[ing]. 1667 MILTON *P. L.* IX. 352 But God left free the Will, for what obeyes Reason, is free, and Reason he made right. 1770 BURKE *Corr.* (1844) I. 237 He is a right man, and, I make no doubt, much yours. 1871 MORLEY *Crit. Misc.* Ser. I. (1878) 23 Hence, in right character there is no struggle at all.

6. Of actions, conduct, etc.: In accordance with what is just or good; equitable; morally fitting. In later use chiefly predicative.

c 825 *Vesp. Psalter* xxxii. 4 Forðon reht is word dryhtnes & all werc his in ȝeleafan. *c* 888 K. ÆLFRED *Boeth.* iii. § 4 Is þis nu se cwide þe þu me ȝeo sædest þæt se wisa Plato cwæde,..þæt nan anweald nære riht butan rihtum þeawum? *c* 1000 *Ags. Gosp.* Luke xii. 57 Hwi ne deme ȝe of eowsylfum þæt riht is. *c* 1200 ORMIN 18773–4 Unnderr Cristess rihhte dom, & inn hiss rihhte wræche. *a* 1250 *Owl & Night.* 179 And fo we on myd rihte dome. *a* 1300 *E. E. Psalter* xviii. 9 Right wisenesses ofe lauerd [are] right, hertes fainand. 13.. *Cursor M.* 3394 (Gött.), Abraham..Tok a wijf, for sua was riht. *a* 1400 *Pistill of Susan* 265 Alle my werkes þou wost, þe wrong and þe riht. 1445 in *Anglia* XXVIII. 267 Al that right is thou grauntyst soon. 1542 UDALL *Erasm. Apoph.* 145 That he maye learne to liue in a right trade of vertue and honestee. 1579 *Poore Knt.'s Palace* G iij b, No freendship hath withdrawe his minde to leve the rightest part. 1600 HOLLAND *Livy* XXII. xxxix. 457 b, That right and true dealing may well be sicke, but it shall not die. 1667 MILTON *P. L.* XII. 16 With some regard to what is just and right [they] Shall lead thir lives. 1745 BUTLER *Serm.* Wks. 1874 II. 276 Religion is the principal security of men's acting a right part in society. 1753–4 RICHARDSON *Grandison* (1781) VII. 126, I sincerely think this is the rightest measure you can now pursue. 1828 SCOTT *F. M. Perth* xviii, The patrons by whose direction they expected to obtain it [revenge] in right and legal fashion. 1852 MRS. STOWE *Uncle Tom's C.* xix. 187 Don't you..ever do anything that you did not think quite right?

Comb. 1598 SYLVESTER *Du Bartas*, *Eden* 563 False guiding paths,..And right-wrong errors of an end-less Maze.

b. In phr. *it is right to* or *that*.

c 888 K. ÆLFRED *Boeth.* xxxix. § 12 Forðæm hit is riht þæt ða goodan hæbben good edlean hiora godes [etc.]. *c* 950 *Lindisf. Gosp.* Luke xx. 22 Is reht us to seallanne þæt ȝeafel ðæm caseri? 971 *Blickl. Hom.* 35 Riht þæt is þæt ealle ȝeleaffulle men [etc.]. *a* 1023 WULFSTAN *Hom.* lviii. (1883) 304 Þonne is hit rihtast þæt he þanonforð buton ælcum wife wunige. *c* 1200 ORMIN 2532 Þatt iss rihht onn eorþe, Þatt mannkinn be till Drihhtin Godd Herrsumm onn alle wise. *a* 1340 HAMPOLE *Pr. Consc.* 6837 It es right þat þai duelle þare, In þat hidus myrknes ever-mare. *c* 1375 *Cursor M.* 3126 (Fairf.), Doun our lorde to erþ he liȝt to fonde abraham him þoȝt riȝt. 1535 COVERDALE *Acts* iv. 19 Whether it be right before God, that we shulde be more obedient vnto you, then vnto God. *c* 1560 A. SCOTT *Poems* (S. T. S.) xx. 31 Þairfoir it is bot rycht That thow indure þe pane. 1663 BUTLER *Hud.* I. iii. 953 They thought it was but just and right, That [etc.]. 1667 MILTON *P. L.* IX. 570 It is..right thou shouldst be obeyd. 1819 SHELLEY *Peter Bell 3rd* II. iii, Like some one whom it were not right To mention. *a* 1832 BENTHAM *Wks.* (1843) II. 522 It is right that men should be as near upon a par with one another.. as they can be made.

7. Agreeing with some standard or principle; correct, proper. Also, agreeing with facts; true.

c 888 K. ÆLFRED *Boeth.* xxxv. § 1 Forþan hit is swiðe ryht spell þæt Plato se uðwita sæde. *a* 1000 *Colloq. Ælfric* in Wr.-Wülcker 88 Hwæt rece we hwæt we sprecan buton hit riht spræc sy? *a* 1122 *O. E. Chron.* (Laud MS.) an. 627, He sende Scottum ȝewrit þæt hi scoldon ȝecerran to rihtum Eastrum. *c* 1200 ORMIN 7264 Þatt wass baþe rihht & wel Þatt Crist wass borenn þære. *c* 1250 *Gen. & Ex.* 4148 Him lestede hise siȝte briȝt, And eueriłc toð bi tale riȝt. 1340 *Ayenb.* 252 Ase ich habbe aboue ysewed, sobrete ne is oþer þing bote to loky riȝte mesure ine alle þinges. *c* 1400 in Turner *Dom. Archit.* (1859) III. 86 Who so dispyse this lesson ryȝt, At borde to sitt he hase no myȝt. 1500–20 DUNBAR *Poems* xxiii. 37 Ane raknyng rycht cumis of ane ragment small. *a* 1568 ASCHAM *Scholem.* II. (Arb.) 136 The knowledge of the tonges..was manifestly contemned: and so, ye way of right studie purposely peruerted. 1588 SHAKS. *L. L. L.* v. ii. 522 A right description of our sport, my Lord. *c* 1630 SANDERSON *Serm.* II. 301 To bring us, by a righter understanding of our selves, to a better knowledge of God. 1678 CUDWORTH *Intell. Syst.* 274 He contends, that the Pagans did entertain righter Opinions concerning the Supreme God, than the Jews themselves. 1709 J. PALMER *Latter Day Glory* 117 Time..will discover which is the rightest way of counting. 1762 FOOTE *Orators* I. i, The perfectioning of our countrymen in..the right use of their native language. 1779 BURKE *Corr.* (1844) II. 275 What you say about his engaging in parties may be right, for any thing I know to the contrary. 1861 FLOR. NIGHTINGALE *Nursing* (ed. 2) 32 This simple question..(not, how can I always do this right thing myself? but), how can I provide for this right thing to be always done? 1875 JOWETT *Plato* (ed. 2) V. 70 In the next book, Plato pursues further his notion of educating by a right use of pleasure.

b. Of belief: Orthodox, true; that ought to be accepted or followed.

?*c* 825 *Vesp. Hymns* (Sweet) xi. 9 Se rehta ȝeleafa mid haetu walle. 971 *Blickl. Hom.* 77 Þæt hie sceolan þurhwunian on rihtum ȝeleafan. *c* 1200 ORMIN 13005 Forr þatt teȝȝ wolldenn þære att himm þe rihhte trowwþe lernenn. *a* 1225 *Leg. Kath.* 2438 Wið luue & rihte bileaue. 13.. *Coer de L.* 284 Them to noye..That be not in the ryght byleve. 1362 LANGL. *P. Pl.* A. XI. 297 Arn none raþere yrauisshid fro þe riȝte beleue þanne arn þise grete clerkis. *c* 1380 WYCLIF *Sel. Wks.* III. 520 Þe riȝtte feiþ of Cristene men. 1548 ELYOT *Orthodoxus*, a man of a right opinion, faith, or belefe. 1648 HEXHAM II, *Recht-geloovigh*, of the True and Right faith, or Orthodoxall.

c. With agent-nouns: Correct, exact.

a 1568 ASCHAM *Scholem.* II. (Arb.) 154 He requireth a learned Reader, and a right considerer of him. 1589 PUTTENHAM *Eng. Poesie* (Arb.) 242 This manner of speech is by the figure *Dialogismus*, or the right reasoner. 1611 FLORIO, *Rettimetra*, a right measurer. 1650 FULLER *Pisgah* II. xii. 157 Whose inhabitants were..right shooters (at an haires breadth and faile not) but unrighteous livers.

d. Leading in the proper direction or towards the place one wishes to reach. Also *transf.*

1814 D. H. O'BRIEN *Captiv. & Escape* 95 Happening to hit the right road, I resolved to follow it for some time. 1835 MACAULAY *Mackintosh* Ess. (1897) 324 Were their faces set in the right or in the wrong direction? 1861 BUCKLE *Civiliz.* II. i. 85 The change was slight, but it was in the right direction.

8. Fitting, proper, appropriate; exactly answering to what is required or suitable.

c 900 tr. *Baeda's Hist.* v. xxi. [xix.] (1890) I. 468 Þæt hi Eastran heoldan & wurðedon butan heora rihtre tide. *c* 960 *Canons Edgar* in Thorpe *Laws* II. 254 We lærað þæt man on rihtne timan tida ringe. *c* 1175 *Lamb. Hom.* 13 Ȝif ȝe mine bibode healded, þenne sende ic eou rihte widerunge. *c* 1200 ORMIN 216 Mine wordess, Þatt filledd shulenn ben þurrh Godd Att heore rihhte time. 1390 GOWER *Conf.* I. 42 For ther may noman finde The rihte salve of such a Ser. 1584 *Three Ladies Lond.* I. in Hazl. *Dodsley* VI. 254 Huff! once aloft, and I may hit in the right vein. *a* 1720 SEWEL *Hist. Quakers* (1795) I. i. 1 Thou, O Lord, alone knowest the right times and seasons to open the eyes of the people. 1809 MALKIN *Gil Blas* I. xii, God knows if his heart lay in the right place. 1854 STANLEY *Mem. Canterb.* iii. (1857) 145 That happy art of saying the right thing to the right person. 1883 V. STUART *Egypt* 7 Her Commander's knack of being in the right place at the right time, and doing the right thing.

Comb. 1895 K. GRAHAME *Golden Age* 44 Nature, in providing water-rats, had furnished right-sized stones.

b. *Mr. Right*, *Miss Right*, the right person, the destined husband or wife. *colloq.*

1860 SALA *Baddington Peerage* xviii, I suppose I'm not the Mr. Right of her affections. 1891 KIPLING *Light that Failed* 164 But..couldn't you take and live with me till Miss Right comes along?

9. *Right way* (cf. 1 b and 1 c): **a.** The way of moral rightness or spiritual salvation.

c 825 *Vesp. Psalter* cxlii. 10 Gast ðin god ȝelaedeð mec in weȝe rehtum. *c* 897 K. ÆLFRED *Gregory's Past. C.* ix. 58 Naðer ne hie selfe on ryhtne weȝ gan noldon, ne oðrum ȝeðafian. *a* 1023 WULFSTAN *Hom.* x. (1883) 75 Ȝebringan on rihtweȝe þa ðe ær dweledan. *c* 1200 ORMIN 16501 Crist.. wollde turrnenn hemm Inntill þe rihhte weȝȝe. *c* 1330 *Spec. Guy Warw.* 22 Ne for loue to god, ne for his eiȝe, To gon out of þe rihte weye. *c* 1380 *St. Augustine* 164 in Horstm. *Altengl. Leg.* (1878) 64/2 For hire sone þat he schulde preye Þat he weore broubt in to rihte weye. 1412–20 LYDG. *Chron. Troy.* II. 2509 To reuoke to the riȝte weye Swiche as wrongly fro trouþe do forveye. 1781 COWPER *Truth* 17 Grace leads the right way: if you choose the wrong, Take it, and perish. 1816 SCOTT *Old Mort.* xiii, 'But you are a presbyterian..?' 'I am, sir; praised be the light that shewed me the right way', replied the landlady.

b. The correct method, or that most conducive to the end in view.

1561 T. NORTON *Calvin's Inst.* I. 9 This is the rightest way and fittest order to serve God. *a* 1577 SIR T. SMITH *Commw. Eng.* (1609) 134 To see who hath taken righter, truer, and more commodious way to gouerne the people as well in warre as in peace. *a* 1637 B. JONSON *Discov.* Wks. (Rtldg.) 743/1 If they would venture their industry the right way. 1670 MILTON *Hist. Eng.* I. Wks. 1738 II. 10 [He] took the right way to be depos'd. 1705 ADDISON *Italy* 390 What Miracles of Architecture they would have left us, had they only been instructed in the right way. 1828 SCOTT *F. M. Perth* xvi, Thou mayst do the Smith a kind turn, an thou takest this matter the right way.

c. As *adv.* In the proper direction.

1704 *Compl. Servant Maid* (ed. 7) 60 Rub your Sarsnet well, the right way of the Sarsenet. *a* 1756 MRS. HEYWOOD *New Present* (1771) 256 Let it be a constant rule to scrub the boards the right way of the grain; that is lengthways.

d. The facts or truth *of* a matter.

1887 ANNIE S. SWAN *Gates of Eden* xvii, I really cannot speak with any certainty, for nobody seems to know the right way of it.

10. *Right side*: **a.** That side of anything which is regarded as the principal, or is naturally turned towards one; the face or upper side.

1511–2 *Act 3 Hen. VIII*, c. 6 § 1 The Walker..shall not rowe..Clothe..with any Cardes on the right side nor of the wrong side. 1704 *Compl. Servant Maid* (ed. 7) 61 Smooth them..upon the right side of the Sarsenet. 1728 CHAMBERS *Cycl.* s.v. *Cloth*, All the sheerings must be on the right Side, except the two last. 1851 MAYHEW *Lond. Labour* I. 350 What the street medal-sellers call the 'right-side'—I speak of the 'penny' medal.—presents the Crystal Palace.

fig. 1872 *Routledge's Ev. Boy's Ann.* 11/2 This..smuggling pedlar (with whom I hope to be right sides uppermost before I die). 1897 *Daily News* 17 Mar. 2/1 To the power of presenting a case systematically and clearly he united that of putting it, as it has been expressed, 'right side up'.

b. The party or principle of which one approves.

1649 JER. TAYLOR *Gt. Exemp.* Ep. Ded. 6 Oftentimes they choose the wrong side, and they that take the righter, doe it so by contingency. 1816 SCOTT *Old Mort.* xxxv, Cuthbert ..himself..[is] more for the hand than the head, and might be drawn to the right side.

c. (With *on*.) The better or more commendable aspect of anything.

1713 ADDISON *Guardian* No. 113 ¶ 4 The Lady has been disappointed on the right side. 1855 KINGSLEY *Westw. Ho!* xxvii, At all events,..it's a fault on the right side.

d. The safe, advantageous, appropriate, desirable (etc.) side *of* anything.

1700 T. BROWN tr. *Fresny's Amusem.* 98 He Swears it, and Swears like T. O. on the right side of the Hedge. 1809 MALKIN *Gil Blas* x. x. ¶ 35 A widow on the right side of thirty. 1865 M. ARNOLD *Ess. Crit.* vi. 197 We are all of us the right side of the door. 1889 JESSOPP *Coming of Friars*

iii. 153 Confinement..was..relaxed if one of the brethren could manage to get the right side of the abbot.

11. Properly pertaining or attached to a person or thing.

c 1200 *Trin. Coll. Hom.* 179 Ʒiet ne wile þe louerd ben paid mid his rihcte mol. *c* 1250 *Gen. & Ex.* 2539 Pharao kinges riȝte name. 1377 LANGL. *P. Pl.* B. v. 226 Rose þe regratere was hir riȝte name. *c* 1475 *Rauf Coilȝear* 239 Wymond of the Wardrop is my richt Name. 1567 *Gude & Godlie Ball.* (S.T.S.) 23 Thow..gaif thy self to plaige, Me Catiue to conuoy To my rycht heritage. 1599 SHAKS. *Much Ado* v. ii. 56 Thou hast frighted the word out of his right sence. 1602 — *Ham.* v. ii. 95 Put your Bonet to his right vse, 'tis for the head. 1610 B. JONSON *Alch.* IV. v, Error! Guilt, guilt, my sonne. Giue it the right name.

12. Of the mind or mental faculties: Normal, natural, sound, whole. Chiefly in phr. *to be in one's right mind* or *senses*.

c 1200 ORMIN 3838 Ʒiff he seoþ þe mann forrdredd, He wile..ræfenn himm hiss rihhte witt. 1487 *Test. Ebor.* (Surtees) IV. 23, I, beyng in my right witte and mynde.., hole and not seke. *c* 1510 *Gesta Rom.* (W. de W.) L iij, Fader, quod he, it semeth yt thou arte out of thy ryght mynde. 1535 COVERDALE *Mark* v. 15 And they..sawe hym which was possessed..,that he sat, and was clothed, and in his right mynde. 1599 SHAKS. *Hen. V*, IV. vii. 49 So also Harry Monmouth being in his right wittes, and his good iudgements, turn'd away the fat Knight. 1601 — *Twel. N.* v. 305 Prethee read i' thy right wits. 1735 BERKELEY *Free-think. in Mathematics* § 8 Wks. 1871 III. 306 By such as are in their right mind. 1818 SHELLEY *Julian & Maddalo* Pref., He was evidently a very cultivated and amiable person when in his right senses. 1875 JOWETT *Plato* (ed. 2) I. 47 He is not in his right mind, said Ctesippus; he is talking nonsense, and is stark mad.

13. Of persons: **a.** Mentally normal or sound; sane. Chiefly with negatives, and freq. in colloq. phr. *right in one's* (or *the*) *head*.

1662 STILLINGFL. *Orig. Sacræ* III. ii. § 6 The World was not generated as Plants or Animals are; and who ever right in his wits asserted that it was? 1680 SIR J. LAUDER *Decisions* (1759) I. 85 He was of a weak judgment, and not very right. 1808 JAMIESON s.v. *Richt*, *He's quite richt now*, he has come to his senses: *No richt*, insane. 1854 MISS BAKER *Northampt. Gloss.* s.v., He's not right in his head. 1895 J. HOCKING *Mist on the Moors* ii, We've got an old aunt of mine in the carriage who isn't exactly right.

b. In good health and spirits; sound, well, comfortable. Also in various colloq. phrases, as *right as my glove, ninepence, a trivet*, etc.

1837 DICKENS *Pickw.* l, 'I hope you are well, sir.' 'Right as a trivet, sir,' replied Bob Sawyer. 1873 MRS. BROOKFIELD *Not a Heroine* II. 194 'Are you quite well enough?' her mother asked, 'you really don't look right yet.' 1875 B. MEADOWS *Clin. Obs.* 40 This medicine soon put her right. 1889 'R. BOLDREWOOD' *Robbery under Arms* xx, We both felt as right as the bank. 1890 [see NINEPENCE 1].

c. *To set* or *put* (one) *right*, to correct or direct (one); also, to justify (oneself).

1699 BENTLEY *Phal.* 280, I'll set you right in your opinion of Minos. 1710 *Managers' Pro & Con* 35 Sacheverell's part was to set right (as they cant) the young Clergy. *a* 1734 NORTH *Life Ld. Kpr. North* (1742) 26 The more mistaken he found himself, the more violent was he in his Proceedings; as if, by that Means, he was to set himself right. 1902 MASON *Four Feathers* xiv, He looks as if he had lost his way. I will go on and put him right.

d. Having a proper disposition *towards*, or relations *with*, another.

1754 CHATHAM *Lett. Nephew* iv. 25 If you are not right towards God, you can never be so towards men. 1876 J. PARKER *Paracl.* I. viii. 124 The Holy Ghost teaches that we cannot be right with one another until we are right with God.

14. Of persons: Judging, thinking, or acting in accordance with truth or the facts of the case; correct in opinion, judgement, or procedure.

1597 SHAKS. 2 *Hen. IV*, v. ii. 102 You are right, Iustice, and you weigh this well. 1599 SANDYS *Europæ Spec.* (1632) 197 That negative and contradictory humour, of thinking they are then rightest, when they are unlikest the Papacie. 1665 BAXTER *Quaker's Catech.* Pref. C iij b, I would ask you whether in all these great Points you think the Papists are righter then the Reformed Churches? 1716 HEARNE *Collect.* (O. H. S.) V. 320 He observes that Hollenshede is righter than Parker. 1781 COWPER *Conversat.* 96 'Tis hard if all is false that I advance—A fool must now and then be right, by chance. 1817 KEATS *Let.* Wks. 1889 III. 95, I think he is right, and yet I think Hazlitt is right, and yet I think Wordsworth is rightest. 1890 *Law Times Rep.* LXIII. 735/1, I think that the learned judge was right in applying that rule, in the present case.

b. *Right!* = You are right; you say well. Also, in recent slang use, *Right you are!*

1588 SHAKS. *Titus A.* IV. ii. 24 *Chi.* O 'tis a verse in Horace, I know it well...*Moore.* I iust, a verse in Horace: right, you haue it. 1634 FORD *Perk. Warbeck* I. ii, She's ..A princess of the blood, and I a subject. *Hunt.* Right; but a noble subject. 1698 BOYLE, etc. *Bentley Exam.* (ed. 2) 178 Right! it sometimes happens that a Word is Older than the Thing to which it is apply'd. 1732 POPE *Hor. Sat.* II. ii. 111 'Right,' cries his Lordship, 'for a rogue in need To have a Taste is insolence indeed'. 1781 COWPER *Hope* 397 Right, says an ensign; and, for aught I see, Your faith and mine substantially agree. 1818 SCOTT *Rob Roy* xxvii, 'I will certainly..be entirely guided by your experience.' 'Right, Mr. Osbaldistone—right.' 1874 *Slang Dict.* 269 *Right you are*, a phrase implying entire acquiescence in what has been said or done. 1888 CHURCHWARD *Blackbirding* 110, I said 'Right you are; I don't think I'll go up'.

15. In a satisfactory or proper state; in good order. *To get..right*, to set in order. *To make it right*, to square or settle matters.

In earliest quots. app. *transf.* from sense 1.

1662 WILSON *Cheats* II. iv. (1664) 26 All's well, and as right as my Leg. 1702 FARQUHAR *Sir H. Wildair* I. i, All right as my leg. 1719 DE FOE *Crusoe* I. (Globe) 281, I..desir'd him to..keep all right in the Ship. *c* 1800 T. J. DIBDIN *Snug Little Island*, It's a snug little island! A right little, tight little island! 1822 SHELLEY *Faust* II. 374 That was all right, my friend. 1889 HISSEY *Tour Phaeton* 213 We made it 'right' by the expenditure of half-a-crown. 1891 'J. S. WINTER' *Lumley* xi, It will be all right, as right as right can be, if all goes well. 1892 MRS. H. WARD *David Grieve* II. v, Don't mix up my silks, Lucy; I shall never get them right again.

b. In phr. *to come (all) right*.

1844 DICKENS *Mart. Chuz.* xvii, Their mother, who looked ..more faded than she ought to have looked; and their grandmother,..who seemed to have got past that stage, and to have come all right again. 1885 MRS. LYNN LINTON *Chr. Kirkland* III. vi. 194 Perhaps on a second trial things would come more right than before. 1888 MCCARTHY & PRAED *Ladies' Gallery* II. 56 All will come right in the end.

c. *All right*, used to express acquiescence or assent.

1837 DICKENS *Pickw.* xxxviii, 'Stand firm, Sam,' said Mr. Pickwick, looking down. 'All right, sir,' replied Mr. Weller. 1887 *Courier* 7 July 5/4 Witness told Treadwell what Wright had told him, and he replied, 'All right'.

III. 16. Having due title or right; rightful, legitimate, lawful. Now *arch.*

a 900 tr. *Baeda's Hist.* IV. xxvi[i]. (1890) 360 Heora riht cyning Wihtred. *a* 1122 *O. E. Chron.* (Laud MS.) an. 1100, Margareta þære goda cwæne Eadwardes cynges magan & of þan rihtan Ængla landes kyne kynne. 13.. *K. Alis.* 1140 (Bodl. MS.), He is biknowe he is his son And þat he is rigth heir After hym to regne veir. 1338 R. BRUNNE *Chron.* (1810) 56 Right heyre of þe lond. 1433 *Rolls of Parlt.* IV. 441/2 John Duc of Norfolk, fader unto your said Warde, as right enheriter. 1492 *Ibid.* VI. 450/1 To the right heyres of the same Elizabeth. 1519 *Knaresb. Wills* (Surtees) I. 9 To the use of my right heires. *a* 1564 BECON *Fl. Godly Prayer* Pref., They slew their right king and set up three kings. 1660 F. BROOKE tr. *Le Blanc's Trav.* 3 Twenty Souldiers..took good order to see the commodities dryed, and restored to the right owners. 1731–8 SWIFT *Pol. Conv.* 62 He has a great Estate, only the Right Owner keeps him out of it.

17. Justly entitled to the name; having the true character of; true, real, veritable. **a.** Of persons, their character or position.

c 1000 ÆLFRIC *Hom.* I. 238 Se hyra, seðe nis riht hyrde, ..he forlæt ða scep. *c* 1000 *Canons Ælfric* in Thorpe *Laws* II. 344 Ne mæsse-preost, ne diacon, ne nan riht canonicus, næbbe on his huse nænne wifman. *a* 1300 *Cursor M.* 14022 If þis man war right prophet,..He aght to wijt al quat sco were. 1384 CHAUCER *L. G. W.* 2628 *Hypermnestra*, My ryght doghter, tresoure of myn hert. 1481 *Paston Lett.* III. 278 She is ryght systyr, of fader and modyr, to Herry Ynglows. 1526 TINDALE *John* i. 47 Beholde a right hisraheliite, in whom is no guile. 1579 LYLY *Euphues* (Arb.) 191 A right Gentleman is sooner seene by the tryall of his vertue than blasing of his armes. 1614 B. JONSON *Barth. Fair* I. iii, She'll ha' conuey'd her state, safe enough from thee, an' she be a right widdow. 1662 J. DAVIES tr. *Olearius' Voy. Ambass.* 221 He went to the sepulchre of their great Saint ..where he did his Devotions as a right Mahumetane. 1711 STEELE *Spect.* No. 144 ¶ 7 If you describe a right Woman in a laudable Sense, she should have gentle Softness, tender Fear. 1727 SWIFT *Gulliver* IV. iii, The Houyhnhnms.. could hardly believe me to be a right Yahoo, because my Body had a different Covering from others of my Kind. 1813 SCOTT *Rokeby* I. xii, Right English all, they rush'd to blows. 1885 GRANT ALLEN in *Dict. Nat. Biog.* II. 215 To mark him [Athelstan] out, in spite of his illegitimacy, as a right ætheling.

transf. 1864 LOWELL *Fireside Trav.* 286 It is not often that we can..enjoy a day of right Chaucer.

b. Of qualities or things. Also of some animals, esp. *right whale*: see WHALE *sb.*

a 900 tr. *Baeda's Hist.* II. ii. (1890) 98 Ond he ða ongon.. heo monian & læran, þæt heo rihte sibbe & lufan him betweonum hæfden. 971 *Blickl. Hom.* 109 Þa men þe bearn habban, læran hie þam rihtne þeodscipe. *c* 1200 ORMIN 9868 Þa staness þatt he spacc þæroff, Þezz wærenn rihhte staness. *c* 1290 *St. Michael* 391 in *S. Eng. Leg.* I. 311 Þe riȝte put of helle is a-midde þe eorþe. *c* 1340 HAMPOLE *Pr. Consc.* 4150 Þai sal turne þe Iewery Until right cristendom halely. *c* 1400 *Destr. Troy* 1756 It reuys me my rest & my right hele. 1528 TINDALE *Obed. Chr. Man* To Rdr., Prosperity is a right curse, and a thing that God giveth to His enemies. 1590 C'TESS PEMBROKE *Antonie* 1425 Is not this folie right? 1612 BACON *Ess.*, *Wisdom for Man's Self* (Arb.) 182 It is a poore Centre of a mans actions, himselfe. It is right earth. 1623 CAMDEN *Rem.* 284 A right woman and Lady like disdaine may be obserued in the same Author. 1771 WESLEY *Jrnl.* 27 Aug., We crept through a right Welsh road. 1817 SCOTT *Let.* in *Lockhart* (1837) IV. ii. 42 Some of the Scotch Whigs, of the right old fanatical leaven, have waxed wroth with Jedediah. 1834 CUNNINGHAM *Wks. Burns* VII. 170 The words instanced against him, 'cootie' and 'heugh', are right old Scottish. 1875 WHYTE MELVILLE *Katerfelto* xxix, He's a right deer, I tell ye.

c. Of material substances, fabrics, etc.: Genuine, not counterfeit or spurious.

1466 in Grose *Antiq. Repertory* I. 12 To paye for his Ransom thre yardes of Right Sattin to the Taker. 1529 MORE *Dyaloge* III. Wks. 237/1 Some man..canne perceyue by hys owne eye whether a stone bee righte or counterfet. 1582 N. T. (Rhem.) *John* xii. 3 Marie therfore tooke a pound of ointement of right spikenard. 1662 J. DAVIES tr. *Mandelslo's Trav.* 32 Michael Boyen..sayes, that the right Musk is made..of that Animal which he calls Hiam. 1681 GREW *Musæum* III. iv. 282 Rough Diamonds ..: a mark to know a right one by. 1711 STEELE *Spect.* No. 134 ¶ 2 By the Application of your Medicines, taken only with half an Ounce of right Virginia Tobacco. 1769 ENTICK *London* IV. 278 It is well pewed, and wainscotted with right wainscot. 1821 SCOTT *Pirate* xxxi, I will bestow some thought on the matter, with the help of a right pipe of Trinidado. 1869 RUSKIN *Q. of Air* I. § 32 Whenever you draw a pure, long, full breath of right heaven, you take Athena into your heart, through your blood.

†d. *Bot.* Rightly so called; true, genuine. *Obs.*

1548 TURNER *Names Herbes* (E.D.S.) 34 Dictamnus maye be named in englishe righte Dittany, for some cal Lepidium also Dittany. *Ibid.* 72, I neuer sawe the ryghte Melilote yet in England. 1578 LYTE *Dodoens* IV. lxi. 522 The right Artechoke hath great long broade leaues. 1611 COTGR., *Dictame blanc*..called also, bastard, or false Dittanie; and oft mistaken..for the right Dittanie.

IV. 18. The distinctive epithet of the hand (see RIGHT HAND) normally the stronger; by extension also of that side of the body, its limbs, their clothing, etc.; hence *transf.* of corresponding parts of other objects. *Right bank* (of a river), that on the right of a person facing down the stream. (Cf. LEFT *a.* 3.)

c 1205 LAY. 28040 Ich hæld to grunden, þat mi riht ærm to-brac. *c* 1300 *Havelok* 2408 Godard..smot him þoru þe rith arum. *c* 1330 R. BRUNNE *Chron. Wace* (Rolls) 6960 Whan Guncelyn byheld þe knyght, þe hand he lyfte þat was þe ryght. 1382 WYCLIF *Rev.* x. 2 He putte his riȝt foot on the se. *c* 1400 *Song Roland* 102 Redely the right ere he pullid from the hed. *c* 1440 *Promp. Parv.* 434/1 Ryghte parte of a beest, *dexter*. 1513 MORE in Grafton *Chron.* (1568) II. 758 Richarde..was..crooke backed, his left shoulder much higher than his right. 1523 FITZHERB. *Husb.* § 10 Whan the ryght fote ryseth, than cast them fro the. 1577–87 HOLINSHED *Chron.* I. 35/2 There was..no square battell,no right wing, nor anie other prouision appointed. 1611 BIBLE 2 *Kings* xi. 11 From the right corner of the Temple. 1670 EACHARD *Cont. Clergy* 47 He..makes a pitch'd battel of it, dividing it into the right-wing and left-wing. 1703 FARQUHAR *Inconstant* III. i, The secret flew out of the right pocket of your coat. 1797 *Encycl. Brit.* (ed. 3) VIII. 457/2 The Virgin Mary crowned, with her Babe in her right arm. 1816 SCOTT *Old Mort.* xxxii, Monmouth..might be discovered on the top of the right bank of the river. 1850 R. G. CUMMING *Hunter's Life S. Afr.* (1902) 123/1 When within seventy yards I sent my right ball through his shoulder.

Comb. 1675 BROOKS *Gold. Key* Wks. 1867 V. 51, I desire nothing more..than that God would pull out right-eye sins. 1711 PETIVER *Gazophyl.* VIII. 72 Right-nosed Limington Fossile Oyster. 1879 *St. George's Hosp. Rep.* IX. 198 A small right-inguinal hernia. 1891 SIR D. WILSON *Right Hand* 169, I believe about four were left and four right-footed.

†19. *Right half.* **a.** The right-hand side. *Obs.*

a 1175 *Lamb. Hom.* 141 Þer stod a richt halue and a luft alse an castel wal. *c* 1200 ORMIN 144 Godess enngell comm himm to O rihht hallf bi þatt allterr. *c* 1290 *Beket* 2176 in *S. Eng. Leg.* I. 169 Bote fram þe riȝt half of is frount toward þe left chinne A smal rewe þere was of blode. *a* 1325 *Prose Psalter* xl[i]v. 11 Þe quene stode at þy ryȝt half in gildan cloþyng. 1382 WYCLIF *Matt.* xx. 21 Seie that..my sonys sitten, oon at thi riȝthalf, and oon at thi lefthalf, in thi kyngdam. *c* 1400 LOVE *Bonavent. Mirr.* (1908) 249 Joseph gooth vppe on the laddre stondynge on the riȝt half.

†b. The right hand. *Obs.*

a 1325 *Prose Psalter* cxliii. [cxliv.] 9 Whaus mouþe spake vanite, her riȝthalf is riȝthalf of wickednes. 1382 WYCLIF *Prov.* iii. 16 Lengthe of dais in his riȝt half, and in the left half of it richessis and glorie. 1388 — *Ps.* xv[i]. 10 Delityngis ben in thi riȝthalf til in to the ende.

20. *Right side.* **a.** The right-hand side; the right-hand quarter or region. † Also *righter side* (quot. 1565).

a 1340 HAMPOLE *Psalter* xl[i]v. 11 Þe quene vpstode at þi rightside in gilt clathynge: vmgifen with sernes. *c* 1380 WYCLIF *Sel. Wks.* I. 362 How Crist sittiþ on þe riȝt side of his Fadir. *c* 1410 *Master of Game* (MS. Digby 182) xxxiii, Þenne þe lorde shulde take vppe þe hertes heede by þe reght syde. *c* 1440 *Astron. Cal.* (MS. Ashm. 391), Þan goo toward þe right side til ye finde your dominical lettre. 1513 MORE in Grafton *Chron.* (1568) II. 761 The king..layd him downe on his right side. 1565 GOLDING *Ovid's Met.* I. (1593) 2 Two Zones do cut the heaven upon the righter side, And other twaine upon the left likewise the same divide. 1728 CHAMBERS *Cycl.* s.v. *Starboard*, When the Man at the Helm should put the Helm to the Right Side of the Ship. 1771 *Encycl. Brit.* I. 55/1 The earth..will be thrown on the right side of the sheath. 1828 SCOTT *F. M. Perth* ii, He came on the right side of Catharine,..and slackened his pace. 1887 RIDER HAGGARD *Allan Quatermain* v, Let them make their way one to the right side of the kraal and one to the left.

attrib. 1815 J. SMITH *Panorama Sci. & Art* I. 68 A right side tool, with two cutting edges. 1846 HOLTZAPFFEL *Turning* II. 518 The right side tool..is thus named because it cuts from the right hand towards the left.

†b. The right hand (of a person). *Obs. rare.*

1377 LANGL. *P. Pl.* B. III. 74 Lat nouȝte þi left half..Wyte what þow worchest with þi riȝt syde. 1382 WYCLIF *Prov.* xxvii. 16 The oile of his riȝt side he shal cleepe.

c. *To rise*, or *get out of bed, on one's right side*, used with allusion to the supposed luckiness of the practice, or its effect on one's temper.

1562 J. HEYWOOD *Prov. & Epigr.* (1867) 51 You rose on your right syde here right. 1575 *Gamm. Gurton* II. i, Thou rose not on thy right side, or else blest thee not well. 1608 MACHIN *Dumb Knight* IV. i. H ij, Sure I said my prayers, ris'd on my right side. 1678 RAY *Prov.* (ed. 2) 268 He rose on his right side.

Right (rəit), *v.* Forms: 1 rihtan (rehtan), 3–5 rihten (3 rihhtenn, rehtten, risten), 3–4 rihte, 9 *Sc.* richt; 3–5 riȝte(n, 4 riȝtyn, riȝtte), 4–5 righte, 4– right (7 wright); 1 ryhtan, 3–4 ryhte(n, 5 ryhtyn, rythyn, *Sc.* rycht; 4–5 ryȝte(n, 5 ryghte(yn; also *dial.* 7–9 rect, 9 reight, raight. [Common Teutonic: OE. *rihtan, ryhtan, rehtan*, = OFris. *riuchta* (mod.Fris. *rjuchtsje*), MDu. (and Du.) *richten, rechten*, OS. *rihtian* (MLG. *richten, rechten*), OHG. *rihtan*, *rihten* (G. *richten*), ON. *rétta* (Norw. *retta*, Sw. *rätta*, Da. *rette*), f. *reht* RIGHT *a.*]

I. *trans.* **†1.** To make straight (a path, way, etc.); to straighten. *Obs.*

c 950 *Lindisf. Gosp.* John i. 23 Ic [am] stefne cliopppendes in uoestern, 'rehtas woeg drihtnes'. *c* 1200 ORMIN 9201 Gab till, & rihhteþþ wiþþ wel Drihhtiness narrwe stighess. *Ibid.* 9206 All þatt ohht iss wrang & crumb Shall effnedd beon & rihhtedd.

†2. To guide, direct (movements, etc.). *Obs.*

c 888 K. ÆLFRED *Boeth.* xxxv. § 3 He riht & ræt eallum ȝesceaftum, swa swa god stiora anum scipe. *c* 950 *Lindisf. Gosp.* Luke i. 79 To rehtanne foet usra in we[ȝ] sibb[es]. *a* 1300 *E. E. Psalter* v. 9 Ryght my wai in syghte þine. *Ibid.* cxviii. [cxix.] 133 Right my steppes after þi speche. *a* 1340 HAMPOLE *Psalter* xxxvi. 24 Mannys gangynge til heuen..sall be rightid of god. 1390 GOWER *Conf.* II. 29 He scholde se the liht brenninge, Wherof he mihte his weies rihte To come wher sche was. *c* 1440 *Jacob's Well* 234 In alle þi thowȝtys thynke on þi god, & he schal ryȝten þi weyis.

refl. *c* 1430 *Pilgr. Lyf Manhode* IV. lxv. (1869) 207, I wolde ..þat bi þe meetinge þat j haue seyn alle pilgrimes ryghteden hem and kepten hem from forueyinge.

†3. To guide as ruler; to govern, rule, judge.

971 *Blickl. Hom.* 191 Þurh þe Ic þys eowde styran & rihtan nu ne mæg. *c* 1205 LAY. 6254 Heo sculleð eow þet lond bitaken..and eower laȝen setten to rihten eore leoden. *a* 1225 *Ancr. R.* 2 Þeos riwle is euere wiðinnen & rihteð þe heorte. *a* 1300 *Cursor M.* 7747 He þat al rightes wit na ros Sal ilk man yeild after he dos. 1390 GOWER *Conf.* III. 170, I finde a tale..Of him that whilom Achab hihte, Which hadde al Irahel to rihte. *a* 1400 *Prymer* (1891) 24 Thou demest peplis in euenhed, and folkes in erthe throw riȝtest. 1512 *Helyas* in Thoms *Prose Rom.* (1858) III. 149 He was so good and so prue to right and governe the welth publyke.

†b. *intr.* To go right, to act rightly. *Obs.*[-1]

1390 GOWER *Conf.* I. 262 Whan that holi cherche wrongeth, I not what other thing schal rihte.

II. 4. To set up, establish (*obs.*); to raise, rear, erect, set upright. Now *dial.*

a 1000 *Cædmon's Gen.* 749 (Gr.), [He] mid handum his eft on heofonrice rihte rodorstolas. *c* 1205 LAY. 14882 Þas biscopes ferden ȝeond þis lond..& þene cristindom heo rihten. *Ibid.* 23531 Walles heo gunnen rihten. *c* 1489 CAXTON *Sonnes of Aymon* xx. 444 He made to be broughte there a longe ladder, and righted it to the walles. *Ibid.* xxii. 481 Thenne he made hym to be brought whereas the galohous were righted. 1864 MRS. LLOYD *Ladies of Polcarrow* 163 Ever since Government has ordered great white stones to be righted up along cliff, for we to see in the dark.

†5. a. To set (one) upright; to raise (*up*), esp. after a fall; to lift *up* (the head). *Obs.*

c 1230 *Hali Meid.* 25 Þe þat art i wit iwraht to godes ilicnesse, & i-riht, ba bodi up and heaued toward heuene. *a* 1340 HAMPOLE *Psalter* xix. 9 Þai ere obligid and þai fell, bot we rase and we ere rightid [L. *erecti sumus*]. *Ibid.*, *Comm. Cant.* 526 Thoro takyng in kynde, he riȝttyd vs out of deth. *c* 1400 *English Conquest Irel.* (E.E.T.S.) 44 [When] holy chyrche..redy was to falle, wyth hys blode he ryght hyr vp. *c* 1489 CAXTON *Sonnes of Aymon* xiv. 316 He righted his hede vp.

†b. *refl.* To assume an upright position. *Obs.*

c 1280 *Bestiary* 152 If he cloðed man se, cof he waxeð, For up he riȝteð him. *a* 1225 *Ancr. R.* 18 Rihteð ou up þer efter, & siggeð 'Domine, labia mea aperies'. *a* 1300 *Cursor M.* 5439 Iacob vp in bedd him right. *Ibid.* 11604 'Rise vp,' he said, 'and right þe nu'. *a* 1400–50 *Alexander* 839* Þat oþer renishit renke hym rightes in þe sadyll. *c* 1489 CAXTON *Sonnes of Aymon* x. 259 He righted hymself vpon his buttocke.

6. a. *To right the helm*: (see quot. 1627).

1627 CAPT. SMITH *Seaman's Gram.* ix. 37 Right your Helme, that is, to keepe it in the mid ships, or right vp. 1669 STURMY *Mariner's Mag.* I. ii. 16 Right your Helmnes. 1769 FALCONER *Dict. Marine* (1780), *Righting*, when expressed of the helm, implies the replacing it in the middle of the ship, after having produced the required effect. 1794 *Rigging & Seamanship* 292 Right the helm, and haul up the mizen. 1841 R. H. DANA *Seaman's Man.* 66 Get the main tack down and sheet aft, and right your helm. 1867 SMYTH *Sailor's Word-bk.*, *Right the Helm*, the order to put it amidships, that is, in a line with the keel.

b. To bring (a ship) back into a vertical position.

1748 *Anson's Voy.* III. vii. 367 They righted her again, to set up anew the careening rigging. 1751 *Narr. of H.M.S. Wager* 18 The Gunner..got the Cutter righted. 1834 MARRYAT *P. Simple* (1863) 357 They were forced to cut away the masts to right her. 1861 *All Year Round* 13 July 365 The crew of the galley righted her with great speed.

fig. 1817 SCOTT *Let.* in *Lockhart* (1837) IV. ii. 46 The mass of property has the same effect on our Constitution, and is a sort of ballast which will always right the vessel, to use a sailor's phrase, and bring it to its due equipoise.

refl. 1861 HUGHES *Tom Brown at Oxf.* ii, [The boat] righted herself, and glided swiftly into the still water.

c. *intr.* Of a ship, etc.: To recover or reassume a vertical position.

1745 P. THOMAS *Jrnl. Anson's Voy.* 24 She providentially righted again, tho' slowly. 1762 FALCONER *Shipwr.* II. (1819) 181 The lab'ring ship may bend, ne'er more to right. 1834 MARRYAT *P. Simple* (1863) 107 The ship righted, trembling fore and aft. 1878 STEVENSON *Inland Voy.* 112 The Arethusa..whipped under the tree, righted, and went merrily away down stream.

d. *refl.* To recover one's balance or equilibrium; to recover one's footing; to correct a false step. Also *fig.*

1805 WORDSW. *Prelude* III. 623 Till 'mid this crowded neighbourhood of things..The head turns round and cannot right itself. 1830 *Chron.* in *Ann. Reg.* 137/1 He leaned forward 'to right himself in the saddle'. 1864 M. EYRE *Lady's Walks S. France* xxiv. (1865) 263 The pony righted himself, and she rode on..unhurt.

fig. 1896 MRS. CAFFYN *Quaker Grandmother* xxii, Mrs. Ince righted herself instantaneously and superbly.

e. To restore to the proper position after a fall, overturn, break-down, etc.

1823 *Blackw. Mag.* XIII. 442 Leaving the guides to remount him, and right him in his seat. 1841 CAPT. B. HALL *Patchwork* III. vii. 132 By the help of some..peasants.. we soon righted the carriage. 1867 HOWELLS *Ital. Journ.* 192 To bring out the baggage and right the fallen diligence.

7. To do justice or make reparation to (a person); to redress the injuries of; to avenge.

c 900 in Thorpe *Dipl. Angl. Sax.* 139 Heo smeadan hu heo..mehton monige men ryhtan,..ȝe on londum ȝe on ma þara þinga þe heo onforhaldne weran. 1483 *Cath. Angl.* 308 To Ryghte, *iustificare*. 1592 *Nobody & Someb.* in Simpson *Sch. Shaks.* (1878) 314 Let his sonne Be righted; give him backe the government You tooke from him. 1599 TYRONE *Let.* in Moryson *Itin.* (1617) II. 58 Oneale will spend to see you righted in all your affaires. 1621 SIR D. NORTON in *Lismore Papers* Ser. II. (1888) III. 24, I..do appeale to your own noblenes..to right me as you would be righted if my case were your own. 1656 S. H. *Gold. Law* 23 [He] righted his individual wrong'd brother. 1720 POPE *Iliad* XIX. 192 'Tis the chief Praise that e'er to Kings belong'd To right with Justice, whom with Pow'r they wrong'd. 1782 ELIZ. BLOWER *Geo. Bateman* II. 164 I'll see thee righted, or I'll know the reason why! 1834 MARRYAT *P. Simple* (1863) 30 Mrs. Trotter..reminded him that he had the protection of Lord this and Sir Thomas that, who would see him righted. 1891 *Spectator* 21 Feb., He thinks that when he is wronged, it is the business of the ruler..to right him at once.

refl. 1588 SHAKS. *L. L. L.* v. ii. 734, I haue seene the day of wrong, through the little hole of discretion, and I will right my selfe like a Souldier. *c* 1645 HOWELL *Lett.* III. xxiii, In case of non-performance,..to right himself by war. 1733 SWIFT *Legion Club* 210 Wks. 1751 X. 227 Bind them fast, or..They will come, and right themselves. 1828 SCOTT *F. M. Perth* xxx, He that cannot right himself by the hand, must use his head. 1874 L. STEPHEN *Hours in Library* (1892) I. i. 25 In that case..the injured person would be always coming back to right himself.

†b. Const. *of, on*, or *upon* (a person). *Obs. rare.*

1668–9 PEPYS *Diary* 29 Jan., [He] condemns him to pay both their victuals and wages, or right himself of the purser. 1670 DRYDEN *Conq. Granada* I. i, My Hands shall right your King on him I seize. 1694 CROWNE *Regulus* I. 3 I'll try To right my countrymen upon all of you.

c. To vindicate, set right, justify. Chiefly *refl.*

1390 GOWER *Conf.* II. 229 Wher kinde wole himselve rihte, ..Ther mai no wiht be therayein. 1617 HEYWOOD 1st *Pt. Fair Maid* IV. i, I'll complain And right myself before the magistrate. 1621 QUARLES *Argalus & P.* (1678) 6 If my ruder Tongue, To right it self, should do your patience wrong. *a* 1691 BOYLE *Theodora* (1703) xi. 181 Expressing more than she said, without injuring her Modesty she righted her Gratitude. 1864 BURTON *Scot Abr.* I. iii. 112 The most likely cause..was, the necessity felt by Bournerel to right himself at once at court.

8. To avenge or redress (an injustice or injury).

1399 LANGL. *Rich. Redeles* Prol. 13 Whom all þe londe loued..And ros with him rapely to riȝtyn his wronge. 1588 SHAKS. *Tit. A.* v. ii. 4, I am Reuenge sent from below, To ioyne with him and right his hainous wrongs. 1642 FULLER *Holy & Prof. St.* v. vi. 381 He objects that none righteth the wrongs of Gods people. 1816 W. TAYLOR in *Monthly Mag.* XLI. 527 'Twas well with England, when..Men dar'd to right their wrongs. 1876 GEO. ELIOT *Dan. Der.* VII. lvii, There is no injury that could be righted in that way.

III. †9. To correct or amend (a person, one's life, etc.). *Obs.*

971 *Blickling Hom.* 63 Þa deman..þæt hie him selfum heora synna bebeorgaþ, ȝe eac oþre syngiende rihtaþ. *a* 1000 *Laws Wihtræd* (Liebermann) 12 Ælтheodiȝe mæn, ȝif hio hiora hæmed rihtan nyllað, of lande..ȝewiten. *c* 1200 ORMIN 10361 Itt maȝȝ hemm bringenn onn To rihhtenn þeȝȝre dede. *c* 1275 *Pass. Our Lord* 544 in *O. E. Misc.* 52 Iesus crist bet..com in-to þis myddenerd sunfulle men to ryhte. *c* 1315 SHOREHAM VI. 11 Þou hast y-ryȝt þat was amys, Y-wonne þat was y-lore. *c* 1375 *Cursor M.* 26779 (Fairf.), To þe prest þai make a hiȝt þaire synne for-sake, þaire life to riȝt. *c* 1440 *Promp. Parv.* 434/1 Ry(g)hteyn, or make ryghte, *rectifico*.

10. To bring into accordance with truth; to correct or render exact (accounts, etc.); to set right or inform (a person) correctly. Also with *up*.

1027–34 *Sec. Laws Cnut* ix. (Liebermann) 314 Ȝemeta and ȝewihta rihte man ȝeorne. *c* 1400 *Destr. Troy* 69 The whiche bokes..A Romayn ouerraght & right hom hym-seluyn. 1578 J. JONES *Preserv. Bodie & Soule* I. xxxvii. 77 Prudence righteth vnderstanding, Fortitude Courage. *a* 1603 T. CARTWRIGHT *Confut. Rhem. N. T.* (1618) 39 Augustine..might heere haue righted you up, if you had not willingly closed your eyes. 1677 CARY *Chron.* II. II. § 3. xiv. 251 The true reading of Josephus as to these Numbers, righted by D. Vossius. 1690 W. WALKER *Idiomat. Ang.-Lat.* 5 He said he was righting his accounts. 1706 FARQUHAR *Recruiting Officer* v. vii, 'Tis time to right all mistakes. 1863 W. PHILLIPS *Speeches* vi. 151 Endeavor to right the public mind.

11. To set in order, to adjust, to set or put right. Now somewhat *rare.*

a 1100 *Gerefa* in *Anglia* IX. 262 A he mæiȝ on byriȝ betan,..oððe hus godian, rihtan, & weoxian. *c* 1205 LAY. 25732 Heo lihten of heore steden, and ihten heore iweden. *Ibid.* 30921 Heo rihten heore loues and up droȝen seiles. *c* 1290 *St. Edmund* 45 in *S. Eng. Leg.* I. 298 Huy benden heore bouwene and stoden a-feor, and heore Arewene riȝten. *c* 1330 R. BRUNNE *Chron. Wace* (Rolls) 12055 Þer myghte men se þe mariners..Ropes to righte, lynes to leye. 1390 GOWER *Conf.* III. 262 Hire clothes with hire hand sche rihte. 1413 *Pilgr. Sowle* (Caxton, 1483) III. i. 49 Somme blewe the fyre, somme with yron forkes ryghted the brondes. 1470–85 MALORY *Arthur* I. xvi. 60 Thenne they amended their harneys and ryghted theire sheldes and tooke newe sperys [etc.]. 1594 CAREW *Huarte's Exam. Wits* (1616) 113 The Schollers who haue their bookes well righted, and their Chamber well dressed, and cleane kept. 1611 SPEED *Theat. Gt. Brit.* (1614) 5/2 The kings of England..sate in person in the seate of justice to right the greater affayres of their subjects. 1793 SMEATON *Edystone L.* § 275 After righting all matters to our satisfaction. 1807 VANCOUVER *Agric. Devon* (1813) 140 These ridges are also looked over and righted with the mattock. 1863 W. C. BALDWIN *Afr. Hunting* 365 An excellent omelette for breakfast..has already righted me considerably. 1899 *Allbutt's Syst. Med.* VIII. 416 Much in the same way the other systems are righted.

†b. To cure of distortion. *Obs. rare.*

c 1205 LAY. 19502 Sa me scal lacnien his leomes..and his ban rihten mid bitele stelen. *c* 1330 *Assump. Virg.* 748 (BM. MS.), Ihesu, þorw his mochil myȝt, Here feet and handes gan to ryȝt. *c* 1375 *Sc. Leg. Saints* xl. (*Ninian*) 1308 Mystrowand he wald gif me mycht þi lath lymmys for to rycht.

c. To mend or do *up*, to clear or clean *up*, to set *up* again. Now *dial.* and *U.S.*

a 1656 USSHER *Ann.* (1658) 391 Having there new wrighted up such ships of his as had been any wayes bruised in the fight, he put over from thence to Phocaea. 1702 in G. Sheldon *Hist. Deerfield, Mass.* (1895) I. 283 That ye Town fort shall forthwith be Righted vp Voted affirmatively. 1824 MRS. SHERWOOD *Waste Not* I. 10 There is a kitchen maid wanted, just to wash dishes, and right up the kitchen after the cook. 1856 OLMSTED *Slave States* 78 After righting up an old door that had fallen from one hinge, and setting a rail against it to keep it in its place, we returned to the house.

12. *refl.* To return to a proper or normal condition. (Cf. 6 d.)

1833 HT. MARTINEAU *Berkeley the Banker* I. viii. 159 Convertibility ensures the ultimate balance of the currency, —provides that it shall right itself from time to time. 1838 DE QUINCEY *Lamb* Wks. 1859 IX. 160 Slowly all things right themselves. 1867 TROLLOPE *Chron. Barset* II. xlix. 51 Had he not resolved to go, things might even yet have righted themselves.

Right (rəit), *adv.* Forms: 1 rehte, 1–3 rihte, 1–5 riht (3 rihht, 4 rith, 4–5 rit), 5–6 rich(e, 5– *Sc.* richt; 3–5 riȝt (3 rigt, 4 riȝth, 5 reȝt), 4–5 riȝte, 5–6 righte, 3– right (5 reght, 9 *dial.* reet); 1 ryhte, 4–5 ryht, 5 ryth(e, 5–6 *Sc.* rycht; 4–5 ryȝt (5 -te), 5 rygth, rygh, 5–6 ryghte (5 ryte), 4–6 ryght (6 ryt). [OE. *rehte, rihte, ryhte*, = OFris. *riuchte* (mod.Fris. *rjucht*), MDu. *recht(e, richte* (Du. *recht*, †*regt*), OS. *rehto, reht* (MLG. *rechte, recht*), OHG. *rehto, rechto* (G. *recht*), ON. *rétt* (Norw. *rett*, Da. *ret*, Sw. *rätt*), f. *reht, riht* RIGHT *a.*]

I. 1. Of motion or position: Straight; in a direct course or line. In later use chiefly with preps. or advbs., as *right forth, forward, on(ward), from, to*, etc.

c 897 K. ÆLFRED *Gregory's Past. C.* xi. 64 Stæppað ryhte; ne haltigeað leng. *a* 1000 *Boeth. Met.* v. 14 Swa oft aspringe ut awealleð of clife harum.., & ȝereclice rihte floweð. *c* 1205 LAY. 1395 Heo ferden from Spaine riht toward Brutaine. *Ibid.* 27345 Forð he wolde riden from Lengres to Auste: swa læi his weie rihte. *a* 1300 *Cursor M.* 12957 He..tok his flight To tun o ierusalem ful right. 1375 BARBOUR *Bruce* x. 82 And thai that mycht eschap, perlay, Richt till ane vattir held thair vay. *c* 1400 MAUNDEV. (1839) iv. 29 Men myghte go more right to that havene. *c* 1450 *Godstow Reg.* 21 Lede us þederward, as ryght as a lyne, Seynt Myghel! To þat heuenly kyngdome. *c* 1485 *Digby Myst.* (1882) III. 1592 Lede hyr to þe prynssys chambyr ryth. 1530 PALSGR. 827/1 Ryght forthe, *tout droyt avant*. 1571 DIGGES *Pantom.* I. xiv. E b, Now go right from that staf some space at pleasure. *a* 1586 SIDNEY *Arcadia* (1622) 51, I thought nothing could shoot righter at the marke of my desires. 1611 BIBLE *Prov.* iv. 25 Let thine eyes looke right on, and let thine eye lids looke straight before thee. 1623 BINGHAM *Xenophon* 29 Holding on right forth, by sunne-set he reached to the villages. 1667 MILTON *P. L.* VI. 831 Hee on his impious Foes right onward drove. 1716 B. CHURCH *Hist. Philip's War* (1865) I. 159 The Captain ordered one man to..show himself. Upon which the Indian ran right to him. 1748 *Anson's Voy.* III. vi. 345 We had a constant gale blowing right upon our stern. *c* 1800 FOSTER in *Life & Corr.* (1846) I. 170 He is like an African buffalo— sees rightforward. 1818 SCOTT *Rob Roy* xxiv, It was left to me, therefore, to do honour..to his tea, right from China. 1855 MACAULAY *Hist. Eng.* xii. III. 236 Then the Mountjoy took the lead, and went right at the boom. 1876 GEO. ELIOT *Dan. Der.* I. ii, She would be put into the ladies' compartment and go right on. 1884 *Harper's Mag.* Dec. 87/1, I'm going right home now.

b. In the proper course.

c 1330 R. BRUNNE *Chron. Wace* (Rolls) 15720 He sailed al day, & on þe nyght, Vmwhile boþe wrong & ryght, Til he com in-til an ilde. 13.. *Cursor M.* 25681 (Gött.), Leuedi.., þu lede þaim right þar þai ga wrang. *a* 1400 *Minor Poems fr. Vernon MS.* 497/131 Þou schalt..þi weyes wende þe Rihtore, Þorwh him þat mihtes may. 1567 *Gude & Godlie Ball.* (S.T.S.) 45 To leide vs in his Law full richt. 1611 BIBLE *Ecclus.* xlix. 9 He..directed them that went right. 1843 CARLYLE *Past & Pres.* (1858) 235 Compel him to go a little righter.

c. *Right up*, straight up, upright. Now *dial.*

c 1440 in *Househ. Ord.* (1790) 434 Dresse hit forthe, and almondes or paynes fryed, and styk hom right up therin. 1552 HULOET s.v. *Bowghe*, Bowghes of trees or bushes whych do grow streight out, but not ryght vp. 1562 TURNER *Herbal* II. 114 b, Rhamnus..hath twigges that grow right vp. 1627 CAPT. SMITH *Seaman's Gram.* ix. 37 Right your Helme, that is, to keepe it in the midships, or right vp. 1854 MISS BAKER *Northampt. Gloss.*, *Right on end, Right up*, upright.

2. In a straight or direct course leading quite up *to* a place, person, or thing; hence, all the way *to, into, round, through*, etc.; also with advbs. as *down, along, in, back*.

a 1122 *O. E. Chron.* (Laud MS.) an. 656, Ðas is se ȝife fram Medeshamstede to Norðburh..& swa æl se feon riht to Esendic. *c* 1200 ORMIN 6623 Þa kingess..Fundenn forrþrihht tatt steorrneleom, Þatt ledde hemm rihht to Criste. *a* 1300 *Cursor M.* 3780 In slepe he sagh stand vp a sti Fra his heued right to þe ski. *c* 1385 CHAUCER *L. G. W.* 738 *Thisbe*, This wal..Was cloue a two ryght from the cop a-doun. *c* 1400 MAUNDEV. (Roxb.) xxxiii. 149 Þase desertez laste riȝt to Paradyse terrestre. 1530 PALSGR. 827/1 Ryght downe, *tout droyt embas*. 1535 STEWART *Cron. Scot.* II. 74 All the landis..Fra Forth streikand recht on to Eskis mouth. *c* 1560 A. SCOTT *Poems* (S.T.S.) ix. 8 Quhen I behald it rycht till end. 1667 MILTON *P. L.* X. 398 You two this way..right down to Paradise descend. 1758 S. THOMPSON *Diary* (1896) 8, I marched up to ye Lake with 10 men, and came back to the Halfway Brook, and right back to ye Lake again. 1766 W. STORK *Acc. E. Florida* p. xviii, The strong current that constantly runs from the east..right into the gulph of Mexico. 1836 BROWNING *Johannes Agricola in Medit.* 2 There's heaven above, and night by night I look right through its gorgeous roof. 1865 CAMERON *Malayan India* 75 The broad verandah which runs right round the house. 1887 RIDER HAGGARD *She* 2 The hair grew right down on his forehead. 1899 LT.-COL. BALDOCK *Cromwell* 202 Goring..pushed a cavalry raid right up to Farnham.

b. Quite or completely *off, out, round*, etc.

c 1400 *Sege Melayne* 329 At þe erthe he smate righte of his hede. 1665 PEPYS *Diary* 4 Dec., The King..hath justified my Lord Sandwich to the highest degree, and is right in his favour to the uttermost. 1877 SPURGEON *Serm.* XXIII. 8 This looks to me like taking the door right off the hinges. 1894 H. NISBET *Bush Girl's Rom.* 115 We will, Captain, blot them right out. 1894 *Idler* Sept. 116 He's turned right round, and he's staring at her like anything.

3. a. Immediately *after* some event.

c 1200 ORMIN 2799 Rihht affterr þatt tin greting word Wass cumenn i min ære. 1597 BEARD *Theatre God's Judgem.* (1612) 496 Hieronymus..began right after the death of his father Hiero..to shew forth his arrogancie. 1872 O. W. HOLMES *Poet Breakf.-t.* iii, Come in,—said he, —come in right after breakfast.

b. †*Right forth*, straightway, at once. *Obs.* So *right off, right away*, immediately, without delay. Originally *U.S.*

(*a*) 1440 *Sc. Acts, Jas. II* (1814) II. 55 Oure..lord will.. gerr deliuer þe Castel of kildrummy to þe said lord of Erskyne Richt furthe in al gudely haste. *c* 1500 *Melusine* 275. I ryght foorth shall departe to assayll them. (*b*) 1790 R. TYLER *Contrast* II. ii. (1887) 39, I was glad to take to my heels and split home, right off. 1849 WEBSTER *Priv. Corr.* (1857) II. 339 We will go to that place and shut ourselves up in the office..and do the work right off. 1884 *Harper's Mag.* Oct. 789/1 He wasn't [sick] long. Had a kind of a fit this noon, and died right off. (*c*) 1818 H. B. FEARON *Sk. Amer.* 5, I have been slick in going to the stand right away. 1842 DICKENS *Amer. Notes* ii, I saw now that 'Right away' and 'Directly' were one and the same thing. 1897 'MARK TWAIN' *More Tramps Abroad* lxxi, A round man cannot be expected to fit a square hole right away. He must have time to modify his shape.

c. *U.S.* Straight (with temporal connotation).

1849 LONGF. *Kavanagh* xxix, If you don't go right about your business, I will come down. 1852 MRS. STOWE *Uncle Tom's C.* xxii, I'll go right in the house, for paper and ink. 1901 *Munsey's Mag.* XXIV. 800/1 Yes, I'll be right down.

4. *Right out*, = OUTRIGHT *adv.* 3, 4; also *dial.*, completely.

1610 SHAKS. *Temp.* IV. i. 101 Her waspish headed sonne.. Swears he will shoote no more, but play with Sparrows, And be a Boy right out. 1622 S. WARD *Woe to Drunkards* (1627) 18, I haue seene one slaine right out with the timber he stole halfe an houre before. 1692 WASHINGTON tr. *Milton's Def. People Eng.* Wks. 1738 I. 493 The house.. they fired about his ears, and at last killed him right-out. 1854 MISS BAKER *Northampt. Gloss.*, *Right-Out*, completely, throughout.

II. 5. Precisely, exactly, just, quite, altogether, to the full. Now *dial.* or *arch.*

In ME. poetry sometimes a mere rime-tag.

c 893 K. ÆLFRED *Oros.* II. iv. 74 Seo burȝ..is swiþe ryhte feowerscyte. *c* 1000 *Ags. Ps.* (Th.) cxxxviii. 6 Ȝif ic on helle ȝedo hwyrft ænigne, þu me æt-byst efne rihte. *c* 1200 ORMIN 414 Ȝȝþerr heore sexe ȝeer swa Rihht affterr Godess lare. *c* 1250 *Gen. & Ex.* 2951 Ðis wreche, in al egypte riȝt, Lestede fulle seuene niȝt. 13.. *K. Alis.* 2998 (Bodl. MS), It was rigth after þe tenure Þat first spaak þe Emperoure. *c* 1386 CHAUCER *Prol.* 804, I wol my self goodly with yow ryde Right at myn owene cost. *c* 1410 HOCCLEVE *Mother of God* 125 Vn-to oon of yow seide he Right in this wyse. 1551 RECORDE *Pathw. Knowl.* I. Defin., Other their corners bee all sharpe,..other iȝ. sharpe and one right square. 1598 B. JONSON *Ev. Man in Hum.* (Q.) v. 67 My wife hath spoyld her, She takes right after her. 1633 HEYWOOD *Eng. Trav.* III. i, To talk of borrowing, lending, and of use! The usurer's language right. 1705 *Lond. Gaz.* No. 4118/4 Pure Venice-Treacle, in Tin Pots, right as it came over. 1854 MISS BAKER *Northampt. Gloss.* s.v., He's not right sharp.

6. Qualifying adverbs (or adv. phrases) of time, esp. *right now*, † *then* or † *tho*, † *anon*. Now *arch.*

c 888 K. ÆLFRED *Boeth.* vii. § 2 Swylce hi wæron rihte ða hi ðe mæst ȝeolectan, swilce hi nu sindon. *c* 1200 ORMIN 11046 Rihht o þatt daȝȝ uppo þe ȝer Þatt twellfte daȝȝ iss nemmnedd. *a* 1225 *Ancr. R.* 54 Heo þet was riht þo imaked mid Godes honden. *a* 1300 *Cursor M.* 3547 For hunger loo i dei right now. *c* 1375 *Sc. Leg. Saints* II. (*Paul*) 298 Mony ane Richt þane þe cristine treutht has tane. *c* 1386 CHAUCER *Knt.'s T.* 550 And right anon he chaunged his array. *a* 1400–50 *Alexander* 431 Riȝt in þe dawyng of day a diuinour he callis. 1426 LYDG. *De Guil. Pilgr.* 10729 Quod rudententement ryht tho. 1470–85 MALORY *Arthur* x. xix. 443 Remembre ye of the shame ye dyd to me ryght now. 1535 COVERDALE *John* ix. 27 He answered them: I tolde you right now. 1594 O. B. *Quest. Profit. Concernings* 9 b, Wit, arte, and counsell, which you spake of right now. 1624 BEDELL *Lett.* xi. 139 Haue you forgotten what you said right now? 1650 FULLER *Joseph's Coat* (1867) 85 Right at this time there raged and reigned in the church of Corinth an epidemical disease.

1897 LORD E. HAMILTON *Outlaws* 130, I can put my hand on the quean right now.

†b. Placed after the adv. or phrase, esp. *now right*. *Obs.*

c 950 *Lindisf. Gosp.* Matt. xxvi. 53 Woenæs ðu þæt..fader min [ne mæge] sella me nu reht mæ ðon tuelf hergas engla. 971 *Blickl. Hom.* 225 He..sæȝde, þæt hit ða rihte wære þæt he of ðisse worlde sceolde. *c* 1000 ÆLFRIC *Exod.* ix. 19 Send nu rihte and ȝegadera ealle þine nytenu. 1297 R. GLOUC. (Rolls) 7072 Þis tueye breþeren gode frend were þo riȝt. *Ibid.* 8910 Þis was endleue hondred ȝer, & in þe niþe ȝer riȝt. *c* 1375 *Cursor M.* 19651 (Fairf.), Noȝt he ete þre daies riȝt. *c* 1420 *Chron. Vilod.* 2772 For ioy of a sweuene þat y haue mette now ryȝt.

7. With preps. or advbs. of place, as *right at, in, on*, etc.

c 893 K. ÆLFRED *Oros.* I. i. 16 Ryhte be eastan him sindon Bæme. *c* 1200 ORMIN 6554 Rihht i þe land off Ȝerrsalæm. *a* 1250 *Gen. & Ex.* 1604 He lay.., A ston under hise heued riȝt. *c* 1300 *Havelok* 2495 Sket cam a ladde with a knif, And bigan rith at þe to For to ritte. *c* 1400 *Rom. Rose* 3076 Right nygh the botoun pullede he A leef al grene. *c* 1440 *Pallad. on Husb.* IV. 27 Into the lond let synke A reed right by. 1481 CAXTON *Godfr.* clxxiii. 256 In theyr comyng on they toke the barbycannes that were right ayenst them. 1535 COVERDALE *Josh.* viii. 14 He made haist ..to mete Israel..euen righte before the felde. 1589 PUTTENHAM *Eng. Poesie* III. i. (Arb.) 150 Vpon a Ladies lips, or right in the center of her cheekes. 1632 MILTON *L'Allegro* 59 Right against the Eastern gate, Wher the great Sun begins his state. 1669 STURMY *Mariner's Mag.* I. ii. 18 The Wind is right in our teeth. 1722 DE FOE *Col. Jack* (1840) 84 He was set right against me. 1775 ROMANS *Hist. Florida* App. 28 Right abreast of this spot..is a very fine anchorage. 1826 J. WILSON *City of Plague* II. iii. 55 Sitting..Right o'er St. Paul's Cathedral. 1891 C. E. NORTON *Dante's Hell* xxviii. 156 When it was right at the foot of the bridge, it lifted its arm high.

b. With *here, there*. Now chiefly *U.S.* Cf. HERE-RIGHT and THERE-RIGHT.

c 1290 *Beket* 126 in *S. Eng. Leg.* I. 110 I-porueid it was.. þat heo scholde i-cristned beo riȝt þare. *a* 1300 *Cursor M.* 6542 Þe tables þat in hand he bare To pees he þam brak right þar. 1399 *Rolls of Parlt.* III. 424/1 On Moneday.. ryght here in this Chaumbre..ȝe renounsed and cessed of the State of Kyng. *c* 1450 *Merlin* xiv. 202 Right here, seith the frensch booke, that [etc.]. 1483 CAXTON *Gold. Leg.* 442 b/2 Ryght there he retourneth hymself and salueth the peple. 1530 PALSGR. 822/2 Ryght there, *droyctement la*. 1866 LOWELL *Biglow P.* Ser. II. Introd., 'Right here,' a favorite phrase with our orators and with a certain class of our editors. 1893 FULLER *Lit. Courtship* x. 98, I may as well say, right here, that I, for my part, had a rousing good time. 1896 *Westm. Gaz.* 2 Jan. 3/1, 'I got on the trail right there,' pursued Mr. Stanley, with a momentary relapse into American idiom.

8. Qualifying *as* or *so* († *also*) in various constructions. Now *arch.*

c 1175 *Lamb. Hom.* 67 He fondede god solf mid his wrenche..and his apostles riht al swa. *c* 1200 ORMIN 1188 Rihht all swa summ þe shep onfoþ Meoclij, þatt mann itt clippeþþ. *a* 1300 *Sarmun* xli. in *E. E. P.* (1862) 5 Riȝt as he com he sal wend in wo and pine and pouerte. *c* 1340 HAMPOLE *Pr. Consc.* 1696 Als þe body..Es ded when þe saule es passed out, Þe saule of man es ded ryght swa, When God es departed þarefra. *c* 1385 CHAUCER *L. G. W.* 1555 *Hypsipyle*, Ryght as hym-selfe now dothe, ryght so did he. 1413 *Pilgr. Sowle* (Caxton) IV. xxix. (1859) 62 Euery good kynge is..known therby, ryght as a man is known by his visage. 1497 BP. ALCOCK *Mons Perfect.* A iij, Ryght as ye erthe can brynge forth no fruyte without ye dewe of heuen ..Right so without the grace of God [etc.]. 1535 COVERDALE 1 *Kings* vi. 35 So made he also..palme trees and floures, right as it was appoynted. 1589 PUTTENHAM *Eng. Poesie* I. xix. (Arb.) 54 Right so no kinde of argument..doth better perswade..then example. 1615 CROOKE *Body of Man* 401 Right so is it (sayth he) in the heart of a man the heate boyleth vp the bloud. 1633 BP. HALL *Hard Texts, N. T.* 594 Right so as God threatened to deale with us according to our doings, even so hath he done. 1648 HEXHAM II, *Recht of het soo waere*, right as if it were so. 1871 ROSSETTI *Staff & Scrip* ix, Right so, he knew that he saw weep Each night through every dream The Queen's own face.

9. With intensive force (cf. FULL *adv.* 1): Very. Now *arch.* **a.** With adverbs.

c 1200 ORMIN 6281 Þuss mihht tu ledenn her þatt lif Rihht wel, wiþþ Godess hellpe. 1375 BARBOUR *Bruce* xv. 82 Schir Iohne Steward..Wes voundit throu the body thair With a sper that richt scharply schair. 1399 LANGL. *Rich. Redeles* Prol. 16 Thus tales me troblid..And amarride my mynde rith moche. *c* 1450 *Cursor M.* 17413 (Laud), Ye diddyn hym vnder lok and sele That he awey shuld not stele But ye hym myssid right sone. 1477 EARL RIVERS (Caxton) *Dictes* 2 He trusted I shulde lyke it right wele. 1503 HAWES *Examp. Virt.* I. xvii, Though thou ryght by do oft assende. 1590 SPENSER *F. Q.* I. x. 7 A gentle Squyre..Right cleanly clad in comely sad attyre. 1600 J. PORY tr. *Leo's Africa* III. 165, I know right well how tedious I haue beene in the description of this citie. 1663 BUTLER *Hud.* I. ii. 953 To him the Squire right nimbly run. 1784 COWPER *Task* VI. 662 The simple clerk..did rear right merrily, two staves. 1826 DISRAELI *Viv. Grey* III. iv, The portrait of him she loved right dearly. *a* 1862 THOREAU *Yankee in Canada* v. (1866) 93, I should like right well to make a longer excursion on foot. 1885 *Mag. Art* Sept. 452/1 They conquered it right royally.

b. With adjectives.

c 1200 ORMIN 5563 Þe sexte ȝife off Haliȝ Gast Iss an rihht god reowwsunge. *Ibid.* 7133 An child..þatt shall ben þiss Judisskenn king All þurrh rihht aþell kinde. 1375 BARBOUR *Bruce* x. 84 Ane vattir..That..wes rycht styth, bath deip & wyde. *c* 1386 CHAUCER *Prol.* 288 A Clerk ther was..And he nas nat right fat. *c* 1430 *Two Cookery-bks.* 5 Take hem and presse hem on a fayre bord, an hew hem ryght smal. 1470–85 MALORY *Arthur* II. ii. 78, I am ryght wrothe for your departyng. *Ibid.*, Ye shal be ryght welcome to..my barons. 1521 WARHAM in Ellis *Orig. Lett.* Ser. III. I. 239, I doubt not but it is to your good Grace right pensiful hearing. 1589 [? LYLY] *Pappe w. Hatchet* (1844) 24 At his table, where he sate..right like a superintendant. 1611 B. JONSON *Catiline* II. i, I should be right sorry To have the means so to be venged on you. *a* 1661 FULLER *Worthies* (1840) III. 296 Yet is their surname right ancient in the place. 1704 SWIFT *Mech. Operat. Spir.* Misc. (1711) 289 Those illustrious and right eloquent Pen-men, the Modern Travellers. 1765 GRAY *Shaks.* 3 Willy begs, once a right proper man. 1800 COLERIDGE *Lett.* (1895) 336, I was right glad.. to see your writing again. 1851 FITZGERALD *Lett.* (1889) I. 276 He is a right good little Fellow, I do believe. 1877 LYTTELL *Landmarks* III. viii. 142 And right interesting it is to observe [etc.].

c. In titles or forms of address. (See also HONOURABLE, REVEREND, WORSHIPFUL.)

c 1390 *Rec. Coldingham Priory* (Surtees) 65 Richt honorabylle fadyr in Crist, God have yhow in kepynge. 1420 WATERTON in Ellis *Orig. Lett.* Ser. I. I. 6 Ryght excellent hegh and ryght myghty Prynce. *c* 1489 CAXTON *Blanchardyn* iv. 20 O my rightbeloued sonn,..who moued you to leue me, and to parte soo? 1512 *Helyas* in Thoms *Prose Rom.* (1858) III. 148 Right noble chylde and my deare frende. 1565 *Reg. Privy Council Scot.* I. 400 The rycht excellent, rycht heich and illustir Princessis. 1599 SHAKS. *Much Ado* I. i. 84 He is most in the company of the right noble Claudio. 1640 GLAPTHORNE *Wit in Constable* I, And pray right witty, and right honor'd sir, What may your businesse seeme to be i th' city? 1674 *Essex Papers* (Camden) I. 197 Right Trusty and Right Welbeloved Cousin and Councellour, Wee greet you well. 1826 DISRAELI *Viv. Grey* VI. i, Noble and right thirsty lords. 1828 SCOTT *F. M. Perth* xxx, Will you indeed prefer me to your right royal consort's service?

†10. With negatives: At all; whatever. *Obs.*

c 1200 ORMIN 680 Niss he rihht nohht forrfæredd. *Ibid.* 18961 Acc hemm ne cumeþþ rihht na god. *a* 1300 *Cursor M.* 28794 Vr lauerd..receues he right nan Almus þat o wrang es tan. *c* 1385 CHAUCER *L. G. W.* 1325 *Dido*, But al this thing auayleth hire ryght nought. *c* 1450 *St. Cuthbert* (Surtees) 6223 Ryght noȝt þan he felde. 1484 CAXTON *Fables of Æsop* II. xi, Thow shalt haue ryght nought of me. 1571 GOLDING *Calvin on Ps.* xlv. 11 To acount whatsoever we set most store by, to be but as dung or as rightnought.

†11. With *a.* Indeed, assuredly. *Obs.*

c 1400 MAUNDEV. (Roxb.) iii. 8 Constantinople is riȝt a faire citee. *c* 1450 *Merlin* 141 Þat is right a worthi man. 1483 CAXTON *G. de la Tour* a iij, It is moche fayre and ryght a noble thyng for to see..thauncient hystoryes. 1523 LD. BERNERS *Froiss.* I. ccxxxv. 330 The prince graunted hym with ryght a good wyll his requeast. *Ibid.* ccclxxiv. 619 He accorded to that his men hadde done with right an yuell wyll.

III. 12. In accordance with justice or righteousness; righteously, uprightly; in harmony with the moral standard of actions.

c 888 K. ÆLFRED *Boeth.* xxxix. § 12 Se scippend..rehte ȝesceop eall þæt he ȝesceop. 971 *Blickl. Hom.* 43 He him symle rihte deme, ȝif he wille syl Godes domas ȝedeȝan. *c* 1000 *Ags. Ps.* (Th.) cxxxix. 13 Scylan eard niman.., þa mid ræde her rihte lifiȝeað. *a* 1200 *Moral Ode* 109 Ne mei him na Mon alsa wel demen ne alswa rihte. 1611 BIBLE *Ps.* ix. 4 Thou satest in the throne iudging right. 1667 MILTON *P. L.* III. 155 Father, who art Judge Of all things made, and judgest onely right. 1736 BUTLER *Anal.* II. viii, They act right or wrong. 1746 CHESTERF. *Lett.* cxii. (1792) I. 303, I am convinced that you will act right.

†b. Rightly; by right. *Obs.*

1508 KENNEDIE *Flyting w. Dunbar* 386 The Erl of Murray bure that surname ryght.

13. In a proper or fitting manner; in the required or necessary way; properly; duly, aright.

Beowulf 1696 Swa wæs..þurh runstafas rihte ȝemearcod ..& ȝesæd hwam þæt sweord ȝeworht..wære. *c* 888 K. ÆLFRED *Boeth.* xxvi. § 2 Ȝenoh ryhte þu spyrast; swa hit is swa þu seȝst. *a* 1000 *Battle of Maldon* 29 (Gr.), Byrhtnoð ..bæd þæt [hie] hyra randan rihte heoldon. *c* 1200 ORMIN 5505 All hu mann birrþ follȝhenn itt Forr Drihhtin rihht to þeowwtenn. *c* 1230 *Hali Meid.* 5 Hwil ha riht lued him wið soðe bileaue. *c* 1300 *Harrow. Hell* 24 Moyses þe holy whyt, Þe heuede þe lawe to ȝeme ryht. *a* 1310 in Wright *Lyric P.* vii. 30 Thou rew ant red me ryht. *a* 1350 *St. Thomas* 211 in Horstm. *Altengl. Leg.* (1881) 23 He bad hym reuerence right A maumet þat þai cald 'god of light'. 1535 COVERDALE *Judges* xii. 6 They bad him saye: Schiboleth, & he sayde: Siboleth, & coulde not speake it righte. 1595 SHAKS. *John* II. i. 139 Ile smoake your skin-coat and I catch you right. 1642 H. MORE *Song of Soul* III. III. xlviii, Hence phancie, sight, And memory in age do not their functions right. *a* 1684 ROSCOMMON *Ess. on Verse* 5 With strict Discipline instructed right. 1693 LOCKE *Educ.* § 160 The first thing should be taught him is to hold his Pen right. 1705 tr. *Bosman's Guinea* 419 Were not these Villains right served? 1764 GOLDSM. *Hist. Eng. in Lett.* (1772) I. 278 You counsel right, my friend. 1851 MRS. BROWNING *Casa Guidi Wind.* II, A people, to speak right, Must speak as soft as courtiers.

b. In due or proper order.

c 1330 R. BRUNNE *Chron. Wace* (Rolls) 12060 Roberes, helmes, right for to stande. *a* 1586 SIDNEY *Ps.* xix. 2 Day unto day, doth it display,..And night to night succeeding right. 1603 SHAKS. *Meas. for M.* IV. iv. 37 When once our grace we haue forgot Nothing goes right. 1876 HARDY *Ethelberta* (1890) 253 Everything is going on right there, and you have no occasion to be anxious about them.

c. In colloq. phrases *all right, right enough*.

1844 FITZGERALD *Lett.* (1889) I. 124, I got your letter all right. 1885 ANSTEY *Tinted Venus* 7 You'll enjoy yourself, Bella, right enough when you get there.

14. In accordance with facts or the truth of the case; accurately, correctly, exactly.

c 950 *Lindisf. Gosp.* Luke vii. 43 He cuoeð him, 'Rehte ðu doemdest'. *c* 1000 *Ags. Gosp.* Luke x. 28 Þa cwæð he, 'Rihte þu andswarodest'. *c* 1200 ORMIN 13811 Natanæl,.. Þatt I þe sahh unnderr fictre, Þu cnawest rihht & trowwesst. *a* 1225 *Leg. Kath.* 1079 Ah beo nu soð cnawes, ȝef ich riht segge. *c* 1394 *P. Pl. Crede* 372 And men ryȝt lokede, Þer is more pryue pride in prechours hertes Þan [etc.]. *c* 1450 HOLLAND *Howlat* 162 A college of cardinalis come syne in a lyng, That war Crannis of kynd, gif I richt compt. 1549 RIDLEY in *Liber Cant.* (1855) 245 Alexander, if I do right remember the history. 1581 SIDNEY *Apol. Poetrie* (Arb.) 32 The lawyer seeketh to make men good,..or to say righter, .. that their euill hurt not others. 1690 LOCKE *Hum. Und.* IV. viii. § 10 A man, accustom'd to..regular Experiments,..shall be able to..guess righter at their..Properties. 1709 POPE *Ess. Crit.* 22 The lines, tho' touch'd but faintly, are drawn right. 1763 *Priv. Lett. Ld. Malmesbury* (1870) I. 103 The affair of Wilkes and Dun is related right in the papers. 1857 KINGSLEY *Misc.* (1859) II. 320 It was on the Tuesday or Wednesday after, if I recollect right. 1878 HARDY *Ret. Native* VI. iii, Yes, you guess right. It is going to be after all.

phr. 1642 J. EATON *Honey-c. Free Justif.* 202 Reason agrees with them no righter than a Rammes horne.

15. On or towards the right side (*of*). See also RIGHT AND LEFT.

a 1300 *Cursor M.* 21639 Ouer and vnder, right and left, In þis compas godd all has left. *c* 1511 *1st Eng. Bk. Amer.* (Arb.) p. xxix/2 As we stande ryght of yat poynt. *a* 1796 BURNS *Sic a Wife as Willie had* iii, She's twisted right, she's twisted left. 1816 'QUIZ' *Grand Master* II. 50 'Tention eyes right!' The serjeant calls with all his might. 1828 SCOTT *F. M. Perth* xii, As he spoke thus, he looked neither right nor left. 1869 FREEMAN *Norm. Conq.* (1875) III. 146 The force of all the lands right of the Seine gathered under the banners of Guy and Odo.

IV. *Comb.* **16. a.** With pa. pples., as *right-born, -bred, -framed, -made, -shapen*, etc. Also in parasynthetic combs., as *right-believed, -headed*.

971 *Blickling Hom.* 167 Eal rihtȝelyfed folc sceal ȝefeon. *c* 1200 ORMIN 1645 All birrþ itt offredd ben wiþþ skill..Off rihhtbiȝetenn ahhte. *a* 1225 *Leg. Kath.* 2377 Lauerd, leome & lif of alle riht bileafde. 1398 TREVISA *Barth. De P. R.* XIII. ix. (Tollemache MS.), This ryuer..departeþ þe contrey of ryȝt-bileuid men fro þe contrey of misbileuid men. 1526 TINDALE *Prol. Ep. Romans*, That the ryghte shapen workes abyde not behynd, but accompanye fayth. 1553 in Strype *Eccl. Mem.* (1822) III. I. 76 If ye saw them [the Bishops]..ye would say, they were the Pope's right-shapen sons. 1571 GOLDING *Calvin on Ps.* xxxix. 5 Within a while after hee will intermedle holy and right framed prayers. 1659 THORNDIKE *Wks.* (1846) II. 653 The right born, debasing..his birth, shall slide down. 1680 ALLEN *Peace & Unity* Pref. p. xxxiii, It does agree with every right made publick prayer whatsoever. 1706 E. WARD *Wooden World Diss.* (1708) 18 What Discouragement gives not this to right-bred Tars from entering Volunteers? 1791 'G. GAMBADO' *Ann. Horsem.* (1809) 69 Such a right-headed Reverend Gentleman. 1829 SCOTT *Jrnl.* 25 Apr., I assured him that a man who had been wrong in the head all his life would scarce become right-headed after death. 1891 ATKINSON *Last of Giant-killers* 170 Some even say that a right-shaped twig of any tree will do just as well.

b. With pr. pples., as *right-aiming, -believing, -feeling, -meaning*, etc.

971 *Blickling Hom.* 185 On eallum rihtȝelyfendum on me. *c* 1420 *Master of Game* (MS. Digby 182) i, The hare that rennyth with right stondyng eers is but litell aferde. 1483 *Cath. Angl.* 308/2 Ryghte trowande, *ortodoxus*. 1565 T. STAPLETON tr. *Bede's Hist. Ch. Eng.* 131 Whome we following in good,..godly, and rightbeleuing maner [etc.]. 1583 GOLDING *Calvin on Deut.* x. 59 They which haue sought him with a true and rightmeaning heart. 1611 BIBLE *Wisd.* v. 21 Then shal the right-aiming thunder bolts goe abroad. 1813 BAKEWELL *Introd. Geol.* (1815) 284 In Cornwall and Devonshire, and in the mines of Northumberland and Durham, the principal metallic veins range nearly east and west. In the former counties they are called lodes, in the latter right running veins. 1829 GEN. P. THOMPSON *Exerc.* (1842) I. 156 There is always a way that all right-thinking people fall into. 1850 THACKERAY *Pendennis* lxiii [lxiv], He thought Blanche..the most pious, gifted, right-thinking, fascinating person he had ever met. 1885 C. J. LYALL *Arab. Poet.* 90 A heart still and stedfast, right-walking, honest.

†c. With vbs., as *right-rule, -participate*.

1382 WYCLIF *Isa.* liv. 17 Eche vessel that is mad aȝen thee, shal not be riȝt reulid. *Ibid.*, *Jer.* vii. 5 If ȝee wil euene riȝt reulen ȝoure weies, and ȝoure studies. 1591 SYLVESTER *Du Bartas* I. iii. 397 Teaching thy wealthy Neighbours..How, When, and Where to right-participate Their streams of Comfort.

17. With adverbs, forming attributive combs., as *right-away, -forward, -onward, -out*.

1593 NASHE *Christ's T.* (1613) 62 It is not my intent to runne a right out-race through all the accidents of their reprobation. 1648 HEXHAM, *Een Rechte strate*, a Right-out streete. 1794 COLERIDGE *Lett.* (1895) I. 114 The well-disciplined phalanx of right-onward feelings. 1826 SCOTT *Jrnl.* 1 Mar., The work of an uncompromising right-forward Scot of the old school. 1830 GALT *Lawrie T.* III. xv, With his wonted, right-away activity. 1877 *Daily News* 9 Oct. 5/3 The anticipation of a good honest right-away race was not disappointed.

-right, *suffix*, representing OE. *riht* adj. and *rihte* adv., which are employed as suffixes in OE. *forðriht, -rihte* FORTHRIGHT, and *upriht, -rihte* UPRIGHT. A few other compounds of the same type appear first in early ME., as † *adownright*, † *anonright*, DOWNRIGHT, † *evenright*, OUTRIGHT, and somewhat later FORERIGHT, OVERRIGHT.

Rightable (rəi·tăb'l), *a.* [f. RIGHT *v.* + -ABLE.] Capable of being righted.

1891 *Star* 31 Dec. 2/6 The one unfairness is in a measure rightable, and the other is not. 1893 *Field* 25 Feb. 297/2 Though she [the boat] may be quickly righted in inland waters,..she probably would not be rightable in open, rough tidal waters.

Right about, *sb., adv.* (and *a.*). Also **right-about, rightabout.** [f. RIGHT *sb.*[1] 17 a + ABOUT *adv.* 6; orig. as two separate words.]

A. *sb.* **1.** *Mil.* In phr. *To the right about*, a command to turn towards the right so far as to face the opposite way (now simply *right about*). Hence with vbs., as *go, face*, etc. (Cf. FACE *v.* 9 b.)

1700 FARQUHAR *Constant Couple* I. ii, To the right about as you were; march, colonel! 1749 FIELDING *Tom Jones* VIII. ix, To give it you in the military phrase then,..as we are soldiers; To the right about. Let us return the way we came. 1766 in W. Smith *Bouquet's Exped.* (1868) 132 The rear goes to the right about. 1844 *Regul. & Ord. Army* 31 When General Officers..pass in the rear of a Guard, the Officer is..not to face his Guard to the right-about. 1889 *Infantry Drill* 11 When the soldier has previously turned about, he will always front by the right about.

b. In general use.

1773 GOLDSM. *Stoops to Conq.* I. ii, You are to turn..to the left, and then to the right about again. 1775 J. JEKYLL *Corr.* (1894) 12 After [dessert]..all rise, turn to the rightabout and.. then return to the drawing-room. 1828 SCOTT *F. M. Perth* viii, The strong inclination which prompted him to wheel Jezebel to the right about. 1883 E. PENNELL-ELMHIRST *Cream Leicestersh.* 376 Their fox took the opportunity to swing to the rightabout.

fig. 1828 MOIR *Mansie Wauch* xxii, Whenever I chose, I could make them wheel to the right about.

c. With *the* omitted. *rare.*

1778 TICKELL & SHERIDAN *Camp* II. iii, I wish I was ordered to right about.

2. In phr. *To send to the right about*: **a.** To cause (troops) to turn and retreat or flee.

1814 SCOTT *Wav.* xxxv, Six grenadiers of Ligonier's.. would have sent all these fellows to the right about. 1860 RUSSELL *Diary India* II. i, This, and the sight of the Carabineers bearing down on them, rapidly sent the sowars flying to the right-about.

b. To send packing; to dismiss or turn away unceremoniously. (Also with *turn*.)

1831 LYTTON *Eugene Aram* I. ii, Send verses to the right-about. 1850 THACKERAY *Pendennis* lv[i], Mamma comes and turns Fanny to the right-about. 1861 MRS. H. WOOD *East Lynne* (1888) 326 One of the members was unseated with ignominy and sent to the right-about.

B. 1. *adv.* = A. 1; usually as a command with additional word, as *wheel, face, turn*.

1796 *Instr. & Reg. Cavalry* (1813) 222 Right about wheel! 1833 *Reg. & Instr. Cavalry* I. 13 Right about, face—1st. Place the ball of the right foot against the left heel...2nd. Raise the toes, and turn to the right about on both heels. 1840 HOOD *Up Rhine* 205 She..wheeled right-about with the alacrity of a Prussian soldier,..and was soon out of sight. 1889 *Infantry Drill* 10 Right about—Turn.

b. Hence *right about face* as a compound vb. or adv.

1815 W. H. IRELAND *Scribbleom.* 26 Southey, who once wrote for freedom—egad, True turn-coat, can right about face, pliant lad. 1840 THACKERAY *Catherine* i, Show those fellows, Corporal, how to rightabout face. *a* 1894 STEVENSON *St. Ives* 309 She had whipped right-about face and was gazing towards the kitchen garden.

2. *attrib.* or as *adj.* with *face* or *turn*. Also in fig. use, denoting a complete change of front; an entire reversal of principles or policy.

1862 THACKERAY *Wks.* (1872) X. 154, I take the rebuke, and turn a soft right-about face. 1891 *Daily News* 3 Feb. 3/4 Will any body deny the Tory right-about-face? 1897 *Westm. Gaz.* 22 Apr. 4/2 If the words were actually used they are intended to prepare the European mind for a right about turn as shameless as it is incredible.

Right and left, right-and-left, *adv.* (*v*), *a.*, and *sb.*

A. *adv.* **1.** On or towards the right and the left; on both sides, in both directions.

[*a* 1300 *Cursor M.* 21639 Ouer and vnder, right and left.] 1829 *Examiner* 196/1 He would lay about him right and left, what havoc he would make! 1855 KINGSLEY *Westw. Ho!* xxv, The Spaniards recoiled right and left. 1865— *Herew.* xiv, Right and left of her..sat the other great ladies.

b. *transf.* On all hands; on all sides.

1893 F. F. MOORE *Gray Eye or So* II. 221 He is being robbed right and left.

2. *ellipt.* as *v.* To turn right and left; to dodge.

1855 DICKENS *Little Dorrit* vii, It took him a matter of ten weeks to set to his creditors, lead off, turn the Commissioners, and right and left back to his professional pursuits.

B. *adj.* Of or pertaining to the right and the left hand, side, etc.; turning to the right and the left; fitting the right and left hand or foot respectively. *Right-and-left screw*, one having the threads at the two ends running opposite ways.

1854 WOODWARD *Mollusca* II. 280 They are essentially unsymmetrical, and right-and-left valved. 1863 W. C. BALDWIN *Afr. Hunting* viii. 342, I missed having an excellent right-and-left shot at wild dogs this morning. 1871 *Figure Training* 117 Comfort..is easily attained by wearing right and left stockings and boots made on strictly anatomical principles. 1877 RAYMOND *Statist. Mines & Mining* 288 Through these the coal is forced by a right-and-left screw.

C. *sb.* **1.** A method of beating the drum. *rare*[-0].

1688 HOLME *Armoury* III. xix. (Roxb.) 154/2.

2. A right-and-left shot.

1856 'STONEHENGE' *Brit. Rural Sports* I. I. v. 52/1 In many cases very wild birds will allow him to come up and get 'a right and left'. 1886 *Pall Mall G.* 27 Aug. 5/1 With single 'right-and-lefts', however, our crack marksmen are no longer inclined to rest content. 1892 GREENER *Breech-Loader* 191 In taking a double rise from traps, or in making a right and left at game.

Right angle. *Math.* [f. RIGHT *a.* 3 + ANGLE *sb.*[2]] An angle of 90°; = RECTANGLE *sb.* 2.

c 1391 CHAUCER *Astrol.* II. § 26 This forseid rihte orisonte ..diuideth the equinoxial in-to riht Angles. 1551 RECORDE *Pathw. Knowl.* I. Defin., A blunt or brode corner is greater then is a square angle, and his lines do parte more in sonder then in a right angle. 1570 BILLINGSLEY *Euclid* I. post. iv. 6 All right angles are equall the one to the other. 1611 FLORIO, *Retto angolo*, a right angle or corner. 1726 SWIFT *Gulliver* III. ii, Their Houses are very ill built, the Walls bevil, without one Right-Angle in any Apartment. 1798 HUTTON *Course Math.* (1799) I. 331 These planes make with each other two angles whose sum is equal to two right angles. 1880 MACCORMAC *Antiseptic Surg.* 11 The right leg was at a right angle with the thigh when the limb was extended.

attrib. 1884 KNIGHT *Dict. Mech.* Suppl., *Rightangle Prism*, an attachment to the microscope stand for throwing light upon an object.

b. *At right angles*, † *in right angle*, perpendicularly (*to* another line, etc.); so as to form an angle of 90°.

1679 MOXON *Math. Dict.* (1701) 23 Cutting the Horizon at Right Angles. 1687 A. LOVELL tr. *Thevenot's Trav.* II. 145 There are six figures on each side..and as many on the border in right Angle. 1734–96 [see AXIS[1] 7]. 1837 LOCKHART *Scott* III. iii. 128 [His] residence was then in George Street, situated very near to, and at right angles with, North Castle Street. 1892 *Speaker* 3 Sept. 289/2 The high road..runs at right-angles to..the lane.

Right-angled, *a.* [f. RIGHT *a.* 3 + ANGLED *a.*]

1. a. Of geometrical figures, etc.: Containing or forming a right angle or right angles; rectangular.

1571 DIGGES *Pantom.* I. B iij, A Rightangled Triangle is suche a one as hath one Righte Angle. *Ibid.* II. xii. N ij b, Rightangled Parallelogrammes. 1608 TOPSELL *Serpents* (1658) 785 Some are made with all sides equall, but yet not right angled or cornered like a quarry of Glasse. 1651 C. BROOKES *Sphær. Triangles* 4 Any right-angled or quadrantal triangle proposed. 1750 FRANKLIN *Opin.* Wks. 1887 II. 189 Bring this on your plate..in such a manner as that the right-angled part may be first raised. 1778 C. HUTTON *Bridges* 77 It is least of all in the triangle..when right-angled. 1831 BREWSTER *Optics* xxix. 244 The apophyllite from Faroe generally crystallises in right-angled square prisms. 1857 THOREAU *Maine W.* (1894) 85 The remains of a gray rabbit, skin, bones, and mould closely fitting the right-angled corner of one side [of the box]. 1883 *Cent. Mag.* Oct. 818/2 Long lines of olive orchard, and right-angled walls of eucalyptus trees shutting in wheat-fields.

transf. 1791 T. PAINE *Rights of Man* I. (ed. 2) 85 The graceful pride of truth knows no extremes, and preserves, in every latitude of life, the right-angled character of man.

b. Of a hyperbola: (see RECTANGULAR *a.* 4).

1743 EMERSON *Fluxions* 61 The right angled Hyperbola, whose semi-transverse is R.

c. Lying at right angles *to* something.

a 1817 T. DWIGHT *Trav. New Eng.*, etc. (1821) II. 218 The streets are both parallel, and right-angled to the river.

2. Characterized by right angles.

1833 MOTLEY *Corr.* (1889) I. ii. 28, I am settled in this most right-angled of cities. 1834 *Tait's Mag.* 381/1 A letter of his written with every character, sturdy, firm and right-angled. 1891 MOULLIN *Surg.* III. vi. 365 Tonic shortening of the gastrocnemius (the so-called right-angled contraction of the tendo Achillis).

3. That deals with right angles. *rare*[-1].

1828 MOORE *Pract. Navig.* 38 Solution of the Six Cases in Right-angled Trigonometry.

So **Right-a·ngle** *v. trans.*, to cross or cut at right angles; **Right-a·ngledness**, rectangularity.

a 1847 ELIZA COOK *My Murray Plaid* ii, The lines of purple deeply spread, Right-angled with the stripes of red. 1805 *Harper's Mag.* Feb. 344/1 This crossing right-angled a deep railroad. 1891 *Athenæum* 15 Aug. 215/1 The surviving Etruscan L's do not on the whole suggest right-angled-ness.

Right-a·ngular, *a.* *rare*[-1]. [f. RIGHT *a.* 3 + ANGULAR *a.*] = RECTANGULAR *a.* 3.

1769 FALCONER *Dict. Marine* (1780), *Courbes d'equerre*.., knees which are right-angular.

Right-away *a.* (See RIGHT *adv.* 17.)

Right boys. Also **Right-boys, Rightboys.** [See quot. 1787.] An irregular association formed in the south-west of Ireland in 1785–6, and connected with political or agrarian disorders in the later years of the 18th century.

1787 *New Annual Reg.* I. 43/2 A person very early distinguished himself among them,..whose real or assumed appellation was that of captain Right; and from him they soon became known by the denomination of Right Boys. 1808 COBBETT *Weekly Reg.* XIII. 126 White Boys, Right Boys, and various other denominations, and combinations of lawless nocturnal insurgents associated. 1819 SCOTT *Let.* in *Lockhart* (1837) IV. ix. 301 Ireland..has never been without White Boys, or Right Boys,..or some wild association or another for disturbing the peace of the country. 1842 S. C. HALL *Ireland* II. 121 In 1785, however, they [the Whiteboys] re-appeared under the name of 'Right-boys'.

Right close. *Law.* Now *Hist.* [tr. AF. *dreit clos* (Britton), close right or law.] *Writ of right close*, a writ applicable only to the court of the lord of a manor, in regard to cases concerning the tenants of the manor. Also *ellipt.*

1533 in Leadam *Sel. Cas. Crt. Requests* (Selden Soc.) 37 All the Tenauntes within the seid manour haue vsid..to plede..within the same manour by pety writte of righte close for all maner of pleys towching their landes. 1607 COWELL *Interp.* s.v. *Recto*, A writ of right close..lieth for those which hould their lands..by charter in fee-simple.., or in dower, if they be eiected out of such lands. 1614 SELDEN *Titles Hon.* 335 In the writ of Right Close, the Tenure must not be laid *per liberum seruitium*, because.. no Free man may bring that writ. 1651 tr. *Kitchin's Jurisd.* (1657) 193 Copy-holder of base tenure shall not have a Right Close. 1768 BLACKSTONE *Comm.* III. 195 There is likewise a little writ of right close,..which lies for the king's

tenants in antient demesne,..to try the right of their lands and tenements in the court of the lord exclusively. 1865 Nichols *Britton* II. 338 *marg.*, Writ of right close not removable.

† **Right-cornered,** *a.* *Obs.* [f. Right *a.* 3.] Right-angled, rectangular.

1551 Recorde *Pathw. Knowl.* I. No. 21 Therfore turne that into a right cornered triangle, accordyng to the worke in the laste conclusion. 1611 Cotgr., *Orthogonal*, orthogonall, right cornered. 1617 Moryson *Itin.* III. 267 Each weare a right cornerd crosse upon his Armes.

Right-down, *adv.* and *a.* Also **right down, rightdown.** [f. Right *adv.* + Down *adv.* Cf. Downright.]

A. *adv.* †**1.** With verbs: Positively; without any limitation or reserve; right out. *Obs.*

1644 J. Goodwin *Innoc. Triumph.* 81 This being so, Mr. Prynnes comparison or parallel halts right-downe. 1646 Bp. Maxwell *Burd. Issach.* 9 They threatned the Ministerie Right downe, That if they persisted in that course [etc.]. 1709 J. Johnson *Clergym. Vade M.* II. 194 They that used evasion, and did not right down subscribe the abnegation.

2. With pples. or adjs.: Thoroughly; out and out.

1648 J. Beaumont *Psyche* XVII. lxix, Who has no power to be Right-down displeas'd at whatsoever sounds From those beloved lips. 1683 Kennett tr. *Erasm. on Folly* 97 They..were right down honest well meaning people. 1832 Mrs. Trollope *Manners Amer.* (1901) II. 63 That's right down well done. 1838 Dickens *O. Twist* vi, Yer mother was a regular right-down bad 'un. 1888 'R. Boldrewood' *Robbery under Arms* i, He was real rightdown sorry for me.

B. *adj.* Positive; thorough, complete.

1623 in Rushw. *Hist. Coll.* (1659) I. 121 The Earl of Bristol made a more benign construction thereof, the Duke a right-down conclusion. 1648 J. Beaumont *Psyche* XXIII. cciv, Degenerating into Sorrows and Rightdown Vexations, rather than impart One Taste of Joy. 1670 Eachard *Cont. Clergy* 16 Such pretended favours and kindnesses as these, are the most right down discourtesies in the world.

1875 Sir T. Seaton *Fret-Cutting* 1 Such fellows..get into all kinds of mischief, and become right-down scamps. 1890 'R. Boldrewood' *Col. Reformer* (1891) 221 Not a sheep near the place..; all good right-down cattle work to look forward to.

Right-drawn, *a.* [f. Right *sb.*[1] 6.] Drawn in a rightful or just cause.

1593 Shaks. *Rich. II*, I. i. 46 What my tong speaks, my right drawn sword may proue.

Righten (rəi·t'n), *v. rare.* [f. Right *a.* + -en[5]. Cf. ON. *rétlna* to become straight.] *trans.* To put or set right, in various senses.

a 1340 Hampole *Psalter* xxiv. 5 Righten me in þi sothfastnes, and lere me.

1597 J. King *On Jonas* (1618) 368 For I shall see the day, when the Lord shall..righten my wrongs, [and] finish my sorrowes. 1611 Bible *Isa.* i. 17 Learne to doe well, seeke iudgement, relieue [*marg.* Or, righten] the oppressed. 1635 J. Hayward tr. *Biondi's Banish'd Virg.* 32 A long silver bodkin, wherewith she used to righten her haire.

1852 M. Arnold *Empedocles* I. ii. 320 How our own minds are made,..How righten'd, how betray'd. 1871 B. Taylor *Faust* II. iii. (1875) II. 136 Thy stubborn mind will not be rightened.

absol. 1887 H. S. Holland *Christ or Eccles.* (1888) 96 God ..would put out His strength to correct, to righten, to redeem.

Hence **Ri·ghtening** *vbl. sb.*

1674 N. Fairfax *Bulk & Selv.* 174 For the rightning of all which there is nothing in the world to be brought forth but this. 1869 Eadie *Galatians* 231 The whole of that rightening which a sinner needs and through faith enjoys.

Righteous (rəi·tyəs, rəi·tʃəs), *a.*, *adv.*, and *sb.* Forms: 1 **reht-**, 1–4 **riht-**, 3–5 **riȝt-** (etc., as Right *a.*); also 1–6 **-wis**, 3–6 **-wise** (5 *Sc.* **-vise**), **-wys(e**, 5 **-wijs**), 4–5 **-wiss, -wyss** (5 **-wisse**, *Sc.* **-uis**), 5–6 **-wes** (5 **-wesse**), 5–6 **-wos** (5 **-wose**), 5–6 **-uous(e**, 6 *Sc.* **-uus**), 6 **-ous** (*Sc.* **-us**). [OE. *rihtwis*, *ryhtwis*, f. *riht*, *ryht* Right *sb.*[1] + *wis* Wise *a.* (or Right *a.* + *wis*, *wise* way, manner, Wise *sb.*): cf. ON. *réttviss* (Da. *retvis*, Sw. *rättvis*), perh. from OE., and OHG. *rehtwîsig*.

The orig. spelling *rightwise* remained in use till the 16th cent. (in some late examples perhaps confused with *right wise*); the obscured endings *-wos(e*, *-uous* appear in the 15th, and *righteous* in the first half of the 16th.]

1. Of persons: Just, upright, virtuous; guiltless, sinless; conforming to the standard of the divine or the moral law; acting rightly or justly.

a. *c* 825 *Vesp. Psalter* x. 8 Forðon rehtwis [is] dryhten. *c* 888 K. Ælfred *Boeth.* xxvii. § 2 Se Wisdom ȝedeð his lufiendas..ȝeþyldiȝe & rihtwise. *Ibid.* xxxix. § 13 He is cyning & dryhten..& rihtwis dema. 971 *Blickl. Hom.* 95 Uton beon eaþmode & mildheorte..& beon rihtwise on urum mode wiþ oþre men. *c* 1100 *O. E. Chron.* (MS. D) an. 1067, Ful oft se ungeleaffulla wer bið ȝehalȝad..þurh þæt rihtwise wif. *a* 1175 *Cott. Hom.* 231 He haueð ȝerimed rihtwisan mannan infer to his rice. *c* 1200 Ormin 2880 Josæp wass rihhtwis, & tatt iss tunnderrstanndenn Forr þatt hiss trowwþe wass full god. *c* 1250 *Gen. & Ex.* 516 Lamech [was born] of matusalé, And of lamech riȝt-wise noé. 13.. *E. E. Allit. P.* A. 675 Þe ryȝt-wys man schal se hys face. *c* 1385 Chaucer *L. G. W.* 905 *Thisbe*, And ryght-wis god to euery lover sende..moore prosperite Than ever hadde Piramus. *c* 1400 Maundev. (Roxb.) xi. 46, I hafe synned, betrayand riȝtwyse biude. *a* 1425 *Seven Sag.* (P.) 2754 Syre, ryghtwys emperour, Thou dost thy selven lytyl honour. 1509 Barclay *Shyp of Folys* (1570) 205 None rightwiser then he Is in the worlde, nor of more noblenes. 1577 *St. Aug. Medit.* A v b, But Christ is iust In hym haue trust And hys iustice Makes thee rightwise.

β. *c* 1440 *Partonope* 5806 He ys a ryghtwos man and full sage. 1486 *Hen. VII at York* in *Surtees Misc.* (1890) 54 Most reverend, rightwose regent of this rigalitie. 1523 [Coverdale] *Old God* (1534) K iij b, Unto the euerlastynge ryghtuous, moost good..god. 1596 Dalrymple tr. *Leslie's Hist. Scot.* v. 308 A Prince maist godlie and rychtuous.

γ. 1526 Tindale *Matt.* xxiii. 35 From the bloud of righteous Abell, vnto the bloud of zacharias. 1561 Daus tr. *Bullinger on Apoc.* (1573) 69 b, There is nothyng better,.. righteouser, or holyer, than he. 1607 Shaks. *Timon* IV. ii. 4 Let me be recorded by the righteous Gods, I am as poore as you. 1671 Milton *P. R.* I. 425 What but thy malice mov'd thee to misdeem Of righteous Job? 1736 Butler *Anal.* I. iii, A righteous government..which necessarily implies a righteous governor. 1797 Mrs. Radcliffe *Italian* x, 'To what do you allude, righteous father?' inquired the astonished Marchesa. 1864 Pusey *Lect. Daniel* (1876) 523 A righteous intercessor for man. 1875 Jowett *Plato* (ed. 2) V. 92 He who is righteous in the treatment of his slaves.. will sow in them the seed of virtue.

absol. *c* 825 *Vesp. Psalter* cxxiv. 3 Ne forleteð dryhten ȝerd synfulra ofer hlet rehtwisra. *c* 1000 Ælfric *Hom.* II. 322 And rihtwisra siðfæt is swilce scinende leoht. *c* 1400 *Cursor M.* 25246 (Cott. Galba), In þis point also we pray For all rightwiss on domesday. *a* 1530 *Myrr. our Ladye* 159 Of men, and of aungels, of ryght wyse and of synners.

b. *absol.* (in sing. or pl.) with *the*.

c 825 *Vesp. Psalter* v. 13 Ðu bledsas ðone rehtwisan. *c* 888 K. Ælfred *Boeth.* iii. § 4 Ȝesihst þu nu þæt þa rihtwisan sint laðe & forþrycte. *c* 1000 Ælfric *Hom.* I. 350 Ȝif se rihtwisa ȝecyrð fram his rihtwisnysse. *c* 1200 *Trin. Coll. Hom.* 67 Ure louerd..shodeð þe rihtwise an his rihthalue and wurðeð hem. *c* 1250 *Gen. & Ex.* 1043 Salt ðu noȝt ðe riȝt-wise weren, Or for hem ðe toðere með beren? *a* 1300 *Cursor M.* 23343 Þe right-wis blith sal be Quen he sal wrak on sinful se. 1382 Wyclif *Isa.* i. 26 Aftir these thingus thou shalt ben clepid the cite of the riȝtwis. 1535 Coverdale *Matt.* ix. 13, I am not come to call the righteous, but yᵉ synners to repentaunce. 1611 Bible *Ps.* lxxii. 7 In his dayes shall the righteous flourish. 1641 Hinde *J. Bruen* xxxiv. 108 The life of the righteous findes never any worse end than the death of the righteous. 1738 Wesley *Ps.* IV. ii, Madly against the Righteous fight And follow after Lies. 1781 Cowper *Truth* 506 Th' atonement a Redeemer's love has wrought Is not for you—the righteous need it not. 1827 Pollok *Course T.* x, The righteous saved, the wicked damned, And God's eternal government approved. *c* 1850 Neale *Hymns East. Ch.* (1866) 107 When Thou.. The righteous from the sinners shalt divide.

† **c.** As *sb.* A righteous person. *Obs.*

c 1000 *Ags. Gosp.* Matt. x. 41 And se þe under-fehþ rihtwisne on riht-wises naman he onfehþ riht-wises mede. *a* 1300 *Cursor M.* 12915 Als bedel gais be-for iustis, Als come þou be-for þat rightwis. 1382 Wyclif *Isa.* li. 5 Nyȝ is my riȝtwis, gon out is my saueour. 1435 Misyn *Fire of Love* 62 Truly god more displesis a ryghtwys prowd þen a synnar meyk. 1667 Milton *P. L.* XI. 697 Hee..whom thou beheldst The onely righteous in a World perverse.

2. Of actions, etc.: Characterized by justice or uprightness; morally right or justifiable.

a. 971 *Blickl. Hom.* 73 Se Gǒdes man sceal beon fulfremed on rihtwisum weorcum. *a* 1300 *Cursor M.* 10744 Quik man þat his wand suld blome Suld maria haf wit rightwis dome. *c* 1375 *Sc. Leg. Saints* xxiii. (*George*) 440 Quhethire þat it mare richtwis be til honoure god..þane appolline. 1444 *Rolls of Parlt.* V. 112/1 To delay the rightwys and true Suytes of suche Defendantz or Plaintiffs. 1523 [Coverdale] *Old God* (1534) K ij b, The Pope, whiche is your god.., what soeuer he doethe is ryghtwyse. 1549 Coverdale, etc. *Erasm. Par. Rom.* 25 Callyng man to rightwyse life he therin sheweth his bounteous mercy & goodnes.

β. 1470–85 Malory *Arthur* X. xiv. 436 By mysauenture kynge Marke smote Amant thorugh the body, And yet was Amant in the ryghtuous quarel. *a* 1533 Frith *Answ. More* (1548) C vj b, Zuinglius..was slayne..in defendinge hys citye.., which cause was moost rightuous. 1596 Dalrymple tr. *Leslie's Hist. Scot.* I. 71 Strukne with a richtuous and true terrour.

γ. *a* 1548 Hall *Chron.*, *Hen. VI*, 96 Edmond erle of Marche ..made hys title and righteous clayme. 1590 Spenser *F. Q.* III. xi. 9 What booteth then the good and righteous deed, If goodnesse find no grace? 1651 Hobbes *Leviath.* III. xxxiv. 214 Instructing men in the way of righteous living. 1667 Milton *P. L.* VI. 804 Faithful hath been your Warfare, and of God Accepted, fearless in his righteous Cause. 1727 De Foe *Syst. Magic* I. iv. (1840) 94 Nor would it have been righteous in Noah to have done so. 1789 Cowper *Ann. Mem.* 44 The symbol of a righteous reign Sat fast on George's brows again. 1808 Southey *Lett.* (1856) II. 86, I devoted a week to the corrections, weeding them with righteous relentlessness. 1853 Kingsley *Hypatia* xxvi, Her righteous wrath was too deep for upbraidings.

† **3.** Chiefly *Sc.* Rightful, lawful, legitimate.

1375 Barbour *Bruce* II. 159 He come to mak homage Till him as till his rychtwis king. 1456 Sir G. Haye *Law Arms* (S.T.S.) 28 Thai..dar nocht..say othir wayis, bot that he was rychtwis pape. *c* 1489 Caxton *Sonnes of Aymon* i. 20 He is your ryght-wyse lorde. 1535 Stewart *Cron. Scot.* III. 141 Robert.., Quhilk in that tyme alledgit for to be The richteous air. 1596 Dalrymple tr. *Leslie's Hist. Scot.* II. 131 His eftircumeris.., quha war rychteous Kingis of Scottis.

† **b.** *Sc.* Rightfully belonging to one. *Obs.*

1474 [see Righteously *adv.* 4].

† **4.** Right, genuine; correct, exact. *Obs. rare.*

1543 *Extr. Aberd. Reg.* (1844) I. 187, vj barrallis of salmond, full reid and sueit, of the rychtus kynd of this toun. 1605 Verstegan *Dec. Intell.* 52 The truth-trying Logyk.., The righteous Geometrie. 1614 W. Barclay *Nepenthes* A iv b, Avarice and greedines of gaine haue moued the Marchants to apparell some European plants with Indian coats, and to enstall them in shops as righteous and legittime Tabacco.

† **5.** As *adv.* Righteously; rightfully. *Obs.*

a 1300 *Cursor M.* 28232 Þe lagh is þeron laid, Þat biddes al þat rightwys liue Til oþer alle þaire gilt for-giue. *c* 1430 *Anturs of Arth.* xxv, For him that ryȝtewis rest, and rose on the rode. *c* 1470 Henry *Wallace* VII. 374 And ye ar her ..Als rychtwis born..As euir was I.

† **6.** *Comb.*, as *righteous-maker*, *-making*; also **righteous-doomous**, right-judging. *Obs.*

?*a* 1400 in *Sel. Wks. Wyclif* (1871) III. 208 For soþly to be riȝtwisdomous man it fallith [etc.]. 1535 Coverdale *Jer.* xxiii. 6 This is the name that they shall call him: euen the Lorde oure rightuous maker. — *Baruch* ii. 17 For the deed..ascribe vnto the Lorde nether prayse ner rightuousmakynge. 1553 *Short Catech.* 40 Fayth..doth..perceyue our righteousmakyng to be geuen vs of God freely. 1560 Becon *Christian Kt.* Wks. II. 149 In my self I am a sinner, but in Christ, my righteous maker, I am righteous.

† **Ri·ghteous,** *v.* *Obs.* Forms: 1 (ȝe)reht-, rihtwisian, 4 rightwis(h)e, -wyse, 6 ryghtous. [f. *rihtwis* Righteous *a.*] *trans.* To set right; to justify; to do justice to; to make righteous.

c 825 *Vesp. Ps.* xviii. 10 Domas godes [sind] soðe, ȝerehtwisade in him seolfum. *Ibid.* lxxxi. 3 Heanne & ðearfan ȝerehtwisiað. *c* 1000 *Ags. Gosp.* Luke xvi. 15 Ȝe synt þe eow sylfe beforan mannum ȝerihtwisiaþ. *a* 1300 *E. E. Psalter* xviii. 10 Domes of lauerd soth er ai, And rightwished in þar-selfe er þai. *Ibid.* lxxxi. 3 Meke and poure rightwises swa. *a* 1340 Hampole *Psalter* lxi. 6 He calles me, he rightwises me and glorifies me. 1387–8 T. Usk *Test. Love* I. viii. (Skeat) l. 35, I shal sustayne my ladyes wrathe which I have deserved, so longe as my Margarite hath rightwysed my cause. 1543 Bale *Romish Fox* 62 b, Canne we meryte grace with synne? or deserue to be ryghtoused by folye?

Hence **Ri·ghteousing** *vbl. sb. rare.*

a 1340 Hampole *Psalter* cxviii. 5 God gif rightid be my wayes: forto kepe þi rightwisyngis. 1865 Bushnell *Vicar. Sacr.* III. vii. (1868) 432 They had their righteoussing in God.

Ri·ghteouser. *rare.* [Cf. prec.] One who makes righteous; a justifier.

1865 Bushnell *Vicar. Sacr.* III. vii. (1868) 421 That he might be righteous and the righteouser of him that believeth.

† **Ri·ghteoushead, -hood.** *Obs. rare.* [f. Righteous *a.*] Righteousness.

c 1250 *Gen. & Ex.* 936 Abram leuede ðis hot in sped; dat was him told to riȝt-wished. *a* 1300 *Cursor M.* 26528 For suilk es crist reght-wis-hede Þat metes ilk man his mede. *c* 1470 Harding *Chron.* XC. xii, That he wolde then of his ryghtwyshode [*v.r.* rightfulhode] Do euery man ryght without more abode.

So † **Ri·ghteouslaik.** *Obs. rare.*

c 1200 Ormin 2521 All full off hallȝhe mahhtess, Off herrsummleȝȝc, off rihhtwisleȝȝc.

Ri·ghteously, *adv.* Forms: see Righteous *a.*; also 1 **-lice**, 3 **-liche** (5 **-lyche**), 4 **-lyke** (*comp.* **-liker**), **-li**, 5 **-lye**, 6 **-lie**. [OE. *riht-*, *ryhtwíslice*: cf. ON. *réttvisliga* (MDa. *retviselige*, MSw. *rätvisliga*, Sw. *rättvisligen*).]

1. Justly, uprightly; in a righteous manner; with due regard to what is right.

a. *c* 888 K. Ælfred *Boeth.* xxxv. § 1 Hu mæȝ..æniȝ man ryhtwislice & ȝesceadwislice acsigan [etc.]. *a* 1225 *Leg. Kath.* 753 Þu,..keiser, nauest nawt þis strif rihtwisliche idealet, þæt dest fifti meistres to motin wið a meiden. *a* 1300 *Cursor M.* 9708 Of vs four sett es a-sise Rightwisli to do iustise. *c* 1375 *XI Pains of Hell* 348 in *O. E. Misc.* 221 He þat leuys here ryȝtwysly..His soule neuer paynd schal be. *c* 1400 Maundev. (Roxb.) xi. 44 Þat he wald here þaire praier and graunt þat þai asked riȝtwisely. 1474 Caxton *Chesse* 29 To thende that the Sone shold iuge rightwysly. *c* 1510 Barclay *Mirr. Gd. Manners* (1570) G v, But a famous merchaunt,..riche, and haboundant, And rightwisely dealing, is not vituperable. 1523 Fitzherb. *Husb.* § 156 Doo well, and worke ryghtwysly.

β. 1526 *Pilgr. Perf.* (W. de W. 1531) 5 b, All the chyldren of Israel that dyed ryghtuously vnder the lawe of Moyses. 1533 Gau *Richt Vay* 85 Supposing thow may richtuslie be ane scherp iuge.

γ. 1526 Tindale *Titus* ii. 12 That we shuld live sobre mynded, righteously and godly in this..worlde. 1556 Lauder *Tractate* 52 Geue thay haif rewlit rychteuslie. 1611 Bible *Isa.* xxxiii. 15 He that walketh righteously, and speaketh vprightly. 1684 *Contempl. St. Man* II. ii. (1699) 147 Let us..Live so Righteously and Holily, that we may be thought worthy of that Crown. 1757 W. Wilkie *Epigoniad* v. 150 Against the foe I'll [never] lift a hostile hand; Till, righteously fulfil'd, the truce expires. 1829 Lytton *Devereux* I. i, And he solaced himself by righteously governing domains worthy of a prince. 1875 Jowett *Plato* (ed. 2) III. 693 They righteously administered their own land and the rest of Hellas.

b. = Religiously *adv.* 3.

1863 Kinglake *Crimea* (1877) IV. 398 They did not slip their cable, but righteously got up their anchor. 1868 *Ibid.* V. 122 As Scarlett had led, so his front line righteously followed.

† **2.** Correctly, rightly; aright. *Obs.*

a 1300 *Cursor M.* 3742 Right-wisli es iacob his nam, Þat es to sai, wit right langage, Supplanter als of heritage. 13.. *E. E. Allit. P.* A. 709 Ryȝt-wysly quo con rede, He loke on bok & be awayed. *c* 1425 Wyntoun *Cron.* I. x. 844 Next lyis þe landis of Medy, Off Medus kyng callit richtwisly. 1470–85 Malory *Arthur* VII. xxvi. 253 Yet sir kay ..named hym more righteously than he wende. 1531 Frith *Upon Tracy* Wks. (1573) 78 Therfore he doth both righteously and godly deduce his resurrection by Christes. 1561 Brende *Q. Curtius* (1570) 302 Considering Alexander rightuously, wee must impute all his vertues to hys owne nature, and hys vyces eyther to hys youth, or to the greatnes of hys Fortune. 1600 Shaks. *A. Y. L.* I. ii. 14 If the truth of thy loue to me were so righteously temper'd, as mine is to thee.

3. Rightfully, properly, deservedly. Now *rare.*

1413 *Pilgr. Sowle* (Caxton) I. xix. (1859) 19 Than thou bere thy peyne as thou hast ryghtwysly deseruyd. 1504 Lady Margaret tr. *De Imitatione* IV. xvii. 281 Benediccions ..without ende, whiche rightwisly be due vnto the. 1548–9 (Mar.) *Bk. Com. Prayer, Litany*, Those euilles that we moste righteously haue deserued.

c 1840 Sir W. Hamilton *Logic* (1860) II. App. 264 It is material and precarious, and has righteously been allowed

to drop out of science. 1855 Macaulay *Hist. Eng.* xiii. III. 248 William saw that he must not think of paying to the laws of Scotland that..respect which he had wisely and righteously paid to the laws of England.

† **4.** *Sc.* By legal right; lawfully. *Obs.*

1456 Sir G. Haye *Law Arms* (S.T.S.) 131 Here speris the doctour gif a man may for his temporale gudis rychtwisly conquest mak defensable were. 1474 in *Acc. Fam. of Innes* (1864) 82 With all..richtwis pertinentis to the forseidis landis pertening or that richtwisly may pertene. 1596 Dalrymple tr. *Leslie's Hist. Scot.* Prol. 17 Ilke hes rychteouslie from age to age succeidet till vther. *Ibid.* II. 137 Reuther is rychtuouslie sett in his place.

Ri·ghteousness. Forms: see Righteous *a.*; also 1 **-nysse**, 1, 4 **-nys**, **-nisse**; 1–7 **-nesse**, 1, 4–7 **-nes** (5 *Sc.* **-nese**), 5 **-nasse**. [OE. *reht-*, *riht-*, *ryhtwísnisse*: see Righteous *a.* + -ness.]

1. Justice, uprightness, rectitude; conformity of life to the requirements of the divine or moral law; virtue, integrity.

a. *c* 825 *Vesp. Ps.* iv. 6 Onseċȝað onseȝdnisse rehtwisnisse [L. *justitiæ*]. *Ibid.* xcvii[i]. 9 Doemæð ymbhwyrf eorðan in rehtwisnisse. *c* 897 K. Ælfred *Gregory's Past. C.* xlix. 380 Dryhten,..ðine ryhtwisnesse ic ne diȝle on minre heortan. *c* 1000 *Ags. Gosp.* Matt. xxi. 32 Iohannes com on rihtwisnesse weȝe, and ȝe ne ȝelyfdon him. *a* 1122 *O. E. Chron.* (Laud MS.) an. 1086, Hi nellað lufian God & rihtwisnesse. *c* 1200 *Trin. Coll. Hom.* 109 Of þe is arisen þe sunne of rihtwisnesse. *c* 1230 *Hali Meid.* 41 Þe uertuz þat be streoneð in þe þurh his swete grace, as rihtwisnesse. *a* 1300 *Cursor M.* 1640 Þe erth wit sin and scham es schent, Al rightwisnes awai es went. 1387 Trevisa *Higden* (Rolls) V. 7 For so greet riȝtwisnesse it semeþ þat Seint Gregorie wan his soule out of helle. *c* 1400 Maundev. (Roxb.) xv. 67 Godd þan had done agayne his riȝtwisnesse for to suffer swilk ane innocent die withouten gilt. 1482 *Monk of Evesham* (Arb.) 64 He sofryd by cause that often tymes he peruerted ryghtwesnes as a man myghty in wordys takyng gestys. 1535 Coverdale *Rev.* xix. 11 He..was called faithfull and true, & in rightewesnes dyd judge. 1577–87 Holinshed *Chron.* III. 1174 Wrong decaieth still, and rightwisenesse vp stands.

β. 1523 [Coverdale] *Old God* (1534) E viij, Justinianus.. was so great a louer of iustice and rightuousness, that [etc.]. 1596 Dalrymple tr. *Leslie's Hist. Scot.* VI. 326 *marg.*, He is a manteiner of pietie and richtuousnes.

γ. 1535 Coverdale *Deut.* vi. 25 It shall be righteousnes vnto vs before the Lorde oure God. 1556 Olde *Antichrist* 105 Christ expresseth him selfe to be our only righteousnesse. 1628 Wither *Brit. Rememb.* v. 780, I finde a better righteousness imputed Then I have lost. 1667 Milton *P. L.* XII. 550 Ages of endless date Founded in righteousness. 1738 Wesley *Ps.* ii. 7 All my Powers shall join to bless The Lord, my Strength and Righteousness. 1781 Cowper *Truth* 576, I never..hop'd, but in thy righteousness divine. 1858 Trench *Par.* xii. (1877) 241 What this guest wanted was righteousness both in its root of faith and its flower of charity. 1875 J. P. Hopps *Princ. Relig.* ix. 28 Righteousness is obedience to law, observance of duty, and fidelity to conscience.

personif. *c* 825 *Vesp. Psalter* lxxx[i]v. 14 Rehtwisnis biforan him gongeð & seteð in weȝe gongas his. *a* 1225 *Ancr. R.* 324 On oðer half stont rihtwisnesse, þet no reouðe nis mide, dredful & grureful uorto biholden. *a* 1300 *E. E. Psalter* lxxx[i]v. 11 Rightwisenes and pais kissed ere swa. 1377 Langl. *P. Pl.* B. XVIII. 197 Aȝeines resoun, I, riȝtwisnesse, recorde þus with treuth, Þat her peyne be perpetuel. *c* 1420 Lydg. *Assembly of Gods* 795 At the furst corner was Ryghtwysnes that tyde. 1653 Milton *Ps.* lxxxv. 53 Before him Righteousness shall go His Royal Harbinger.

† **b.** *pl.* Particular acts of justice; righteous deeds. *Obs.*

c 825 *Vesp. Psalter* cxviii. 16 In ðinum rehtwisnissum ic smegu. *c* 1000 Ælfric *Hom.* II. 532 Hwi bodast ðu mine rihtwisnyssa and mine gecyðnysse þurh þinne muð? *a* 1300 *E. E. Psalter* xviii. 9 Rightwisenesses ofe lauerd [are] right, hertes fainand. *a* 1340 Hampole *Psalter* x. 8 Rightwis is lord, and he lufid rightwisnes-is. *a* 1400 *Prymer* (1891) 19 Riȝtwysnesses of the lord. 1535 Coverdale *Baruch* ii. 12 We haue behaued oure selues vngodly in all thy rightuousnesses. 1611 Bible *Isa.* lxiv. 6 We are al as an vncleane thing, and all our righteousnesses are as filthy ragges.

† **2.** Fitness; propriety. *Obs. rare.*

1481 Caxton *Myrr.* I. ix. 34 Rethoryque whyche conteyneth in substaunce, rightwisnes, Rayson and ordynaunce of wordes.

Righter[1] (rəi·tər). [See Right *v.* and -er[1]. Cf. OFris. *riuchtere*, MDu. *rechter(e*, *richter(e*, Du. *rechter*, † *regter*), MLG. *richter(e*, OHG. *rihtâri* (G. *richter*), ON. *réttari* judge, executioner.]

† **1.** One who arranges or regulates. *Obs.*

c 888 K. Ælfred *Boeth.* v. § 3 Ic wat ðætte God rihtere is his aȝenes weorces. 1593 Q. Eliz. *Boeth.* IV. pr. i. 75 When the Righter of all thing is good.

† **2.** An executioner, headsman. *Obs.*[−1]

1483 Caxton *Gold. Leg.* 88/1 The rightar brandysshid hys swerd ouer their heedes.

3. One who settles or sets right (*esp.* wrongs, grievances, etc.); a redresser, vindicator.

1598 Florio, *Giudice*, a iudge, a commissarie, a righter of causes. [Hence 1611 Cotgrave s.v. *Iuge*.] 1612 Shelton *Quix.* I. iv. 26 Know that I am the valorous Don-Quixote of the Mancha, the righter of wrongs, and vndoer of iniuries. 1711 'J. Distaff' *Char. Don Sacheverellio* 9 Behold in me the Righter of Injuries. 1822 Scott *Peveril* x, The times demand righters and avengers, and there will be no want of them. 1876 Morris *Sigurd* IV. 328 The righter of wrongs, the deliverer.

Ri·ghter[2]. [f. Right *sb.*[1]] An advocate of (some one's) rights.

1897 *Globe* 11 Mar. 3/4 She is what one might call an early specimen of a woman's righter.

† **Right-forth,** *adv.* and *a.* [f. Right *adv.* + Forth *adv.* Cf. Forthright.]

A. *adv.* Straight forward; in a straight course.

1382 Wyclif *Ps.* ci. 29 The sed of hem in to the world shal be riȝtforth reulid. 1587 Golding *De Mornay* xiv. (1592) 218 Reason certifieth vs that they runne rightfoorth with equall distance one from another.

B. *adj.* Direct; straight-forward.

1540 Hyrde tr. *Vives' Instr. Chr. Wom.* (1592) vj, All shall be simple and right forth, demure, sober. 1561 Eden *Arte Nauig.* I. vi, The earth dyd moue..not by a ryght forth motion, but circulerly about.

Rightful (rəi·tfŭl), *a.* (*sb.* and *adv.*). Forms: see Right *a.*; also 3–4 **-fol(le**, **-vol(le**, 4–5 **-fulle**, 4–6 **-full**, 5 **-fful**. [Late OE. *rihtful*, f. *riht* Right *sb.*[1] + -ful.]

1. Of persons: Disposed to do right; upright, just. (Cf. Righteous *a.* 1.) Now *rare* or *Obs.*

a 1122 *O. E. Chron.* (Laud MS.) an. 1100, Eall þet þe Gode was lað & rihtfullan mannan..wæs ȝewunelic on þisan lande. *c* 1275 Lay. 10100 Luce was kinebore..and he was swiþe rihfolle. 1297 R. Glouc. (Rolls) 1606 Emperour [Trajan] was þe nobloste þat miȝte be,..So riȝtuol he was. 1362 Langl. *P. Pl.* A. IX. 17 Seue siþes a day..sungeþ þe rihtful mon. *c* 1380 *Lay Folks Catech.* (Lamb. MS.) 531 This god is..most ryȝtful, and most ful of goodnesse. 1422 tr. *Secreta Secret.*, *Priv. Priv.* 189 He ryghtfull to al men, Slow to be wroth, Redy to mercy. 1483 Caxton *Gold. Leg.* 66/4 Thenne said Saul, I haue synned..Thou arte rightfuller than I am. 1529 Rastell *Pastyme* (1811) 20 The moost ryghtful and indyfferent juge that euer was. 1596 Shaks. *Merch. V.* IV. i. 301 *Por.* The Court awards it, and the law doth giue it. *Iew.* Most rightfull Iudge. 1611 Cotgr., *Iuste*,..incorrupt, rightfull, vpright, sincere. 1819 Shelley *Cenci* III. i. 179 Mighty death! Thou double-visaged shadow! Only judge! Rightfullest arbiter!

† **b.** *absol.* (Cf. Righteous 1 b and 1 c.)

a 1325 *Prose Psalter* xxxvi[i]. 25 Whan þe riȝtful haþ fallen, he ne shal nouȝt ben hirt. 1377 Langl. *P. Pl.* B. III. 241 Alle þat helpeth þe innocent and halt with þe riȝtful. *a* 1425 *Cursor M.* 17315 (Trin.), Euel haue ȝe done wolde ȝe be knowen Of þat riȝtful þat ȝe dud honge.

2. Of actions, etc.: In conformity with what is right or just; equitable, thoroughly fair.

1297 R. Glouc. (Rolls) 2876 Hii binome him is kinedom & þat is a riȝtuol dede. *Ibid.* 5391 Lawes he made riȝtuolore & strengore þan er were. 1340 *Ayenb.* 44 Þe oþre manere is huanne me heþ riȝtuolle wyȝtes and riȝtuolle mesures and zelleþ ontreweliche. 1377 Langl. *P. Pl.* B. Prol. 127 Crist,..leue þe lede þi londe, so leute þe louye, And for þi riȝtful rewlyng be rewarded in heuene! 1422 tr. *Secreta Secret.*, *Priv. Priv.* 145 Hoppe is a ryghtfull tryste for a ryghtfull Werke. 1481 Caxton *Reynard* (Arb.) 103 The quarel that I haue is rightful. *a* 1533 Ld. Berners *Huon* lxxxi. 249 Let me haue ryghtfull and trewe iugement. 1590 Spenser *F. Q.* I. xii. 28 For truth is strong her rightfull cause to plead. *c* 1630 Milton *Upon Circumc.* 17 For we by rightfull doom remediles Were lost in death. *a* 1721 Prior (J.), The smiling hours; Such as with friendly care have guarded Patriots and kings in rightful wars. 1813 Scott *Rokeby* V. xxi, He that sings the rightful cause. 1859 I. Taylor *Logic in Theol.* 201 Can it be rightful..to enact in India.. that which was enacted for the Roman world?

3. Legal, lawful, legitimate: **a.** Of persons, in respect of position or claims.

c 1330 *Arth. & Merl.* 2804 (Kölbing), Euerichon..maden solempne bisecheinge For to haue a riȝtful kinge. 1390 Gower *Conf.* III. 4122 So were thei for everemo..Departed fro the rihtfull heir.

1590 Spenser *F. Q.* II. vii. 19 But those didst these goods bereave From rightfull owner by unrighteous lott. 1591 Shaks. *1 Hen. VI*, II. v. 80 In this haughtie great attempt ..to plant the rightfull Heire, I lost my Libertie. 1605 Camden *Rem.* 3 Her vndoubted and rightfull successor. 1667 Milton *P. L.* V. 815 Every Soule in Heav'n Shall.. Confess him rightful King. 1724 Welton *Chr. Faith & Pract.* 215 A due obedience to our rightful governors. 1784 Cowper *Task* III. 749 The legitimate and rightful lord Is but a transient guest. 1849 Macaulay *Hist. Eng.* vii. II. 161 The common people..regarded him as their rightful head. 1855 *Ibid.* xxi. IV. 684 How a rightful and lawful possessor is to be distinguished from a possessor who has the exclusive right by law [etc.].

Comb. 1856 Lever *Martins of Cro' M.* 623 A daughter— an illegitimate one—but worthy to be the rightful-born child to the first man in the land.

b. Of inheritance, possessions, etc.

1377 Langl. *P. Pl.* B. XIV. 291 Selde is any pore riche, but of riȝtful heritage. 1399 Gower *Conf.*, *To Hen. IV*, 59 To cleime and axe his rightful heritage In alle places wher it is withholde. 1483 [see Heritage *sb.* 2]. 1612 Drayton *Poly-olb.* xii. 359 His..son, By..stepdame's hate, to death was lastly done, To set his rightful Crown upon a wrongful head. 1736 *Gentl. Mag.* VI. 434/1 The rightful undisturbed Possession of it will add vastly to the Power of France. *c* 1792 Burns *Extempore on Thomson* 8 Th' unfading garland.., Thy sair-won, rightful spoil. 1856 Hawthorne *Eng. Note-bks.* (1870) II. 69 This unparalleled Englishman declined taking anything beyond his rightful halfpenny. *a* 1859 Macaulay *Hist. Eng.* xxv. V. 294 An innocent boy, who was kept out of his rightful inheritance by an ambitious kinsman.

† **4.** Straight. *Obs. rare.*

1382 Wyclif *Matt.* iii. 3 Make ȝe redy the wayes of the Lord; make ȝe riȝtful the pathes of hym. [Also *Heb.* xii. 13.]

5. Proper, fitting; correct. Now *rare.*

?*a* 1366 Chaucer *Rom. Rose* 405, I trowe that she Was fair sumtyme,..Whan she was in hir rightful age. 1393 Langl. *P. Pl.* C. IV. 377 Relacion rect is a ryhtful custome. 1422 tr. *Secreta Secret.*, *Priv. Priv.* 240 Of the ryghtfull houris and tymes of ettynge and drynkynge. *a* 1586 Sidney *Ps.* XLI. vi, Triumph well may I, whome thou did'st stay In my sound rightfull way. 1591 Spenser *M. Hubberd* 704 Such is the rightfull Courtier in his kinde. 1676 Marvell *Wks.* (Grosart) II. 537 If they have no share by right in the government of themselves, by their certain rightful times of parliaments. 1704 Prior *Let. to Boileau* 111 Danube scarce retains his rightful Course. 1839 J. Very *Poems* 42 (Cent.), The hand and foot that stir not, they shall find Sooner than all the rightful place to go. *a* 1853 Robertson *Lect.* i. (1858) 30 You have surely proceeded in the rightful order.

† **6.** As *adv.* Rightfully, properly. *Obs.*

13.. *Cursor M.* 3742 (Gött.), He has me done ful mekil schame, Rihtful was iacob cald his name. 1422 tr. *Secreta Secret.*, *Priv. Priv.* 167 The Powere of a prynce that is not ryghtfull demenyt.

Hence † **Ri·ghtfulhood.** *Obs.*[−1]

c 1470 [see Righteoushood].

Rightfully (rəi·tfŭli), *adv.* Forms: see Rightful *a.*; also 4 **-lych(e** (*comp.* **-lokest**), 4–5 **-liche**, 5 **-lich**; 4 **-li**, 6 **-lie**, **-lye**. [f. Rightful *a.* + -ly[2].]

1. In accordance with, with due regard for, what is right or just; justly, equitably, fairly.

1297 R. Glouc. (Rolls) 1872 Constantin..ladde is kinedom Riȝtuolliche & suiþe wel. *c* 1330 *Arth. & Merl.* 2048 (Kölbing), It nis no riȝt, þat þou me werne, Riȝtfulliche þat y wil ȝerne. *c* 1380 Wyclif *Sel. Wks.* III. 328 Where he be wrongly cursed or riȝtfully. *c* 1400 *Rom. Rose* 6630 Ne I ne were not, sikerly, That they may have it rightfully. 1495 *Act 11 Hen. VII*, c. 64 § 12 Other enberitamentis perteynyng rightfully to dyverse the Kingis true lieges. 1545 Brinklow *Lament.* 6 The plages of Egipte, which ye haue already rightfully deserued. 1568 Grafton *Chron.* II. 350 The realme of Fraunce, the whiche rightfully did apperteyne vnto them. 1658–9 *Burton's Diary* (1828) IV. 124, I should be glad they could make it out by law, that they sit here rightfully. 1695 *Anc. Const. Eng.* 5 This [kingly] power cannot rightfully be acquired without the people's consent. 1809–10 Coleridge *Friend* (1865) 14 No man can rightfully be condemned without reference to some definite law. 1885 *Law Times Rep.* LI. 747/1 The goods were rightfully sold under the bill of sale.

2. Rightly, properly, correctly.

1340 *Ayenb.* 196 Yef hi weren riȝtuolliche milde, hi ssolden bere louie þe uelaȝrede of poure men [etc.]. 1362 Langl. *P. Pl.* A. I. 52 For rihtfolliche Resoun schulde rulen ou alle. *c* 1430 *Pilgr. Lyf Manhode* III. xiv. (1869) 142 For rihtfulliche j may be cleped an ape clogged. 1548 Udall, etc. *Erasm. Par. John* xv. 90 b, They that are vnder Moses law be rightfully called seruauntes. 1591 Spenser *Teares Muses* 52 None but you..Can rightfully aread so dolefull lay. 1831 Coleridge *Table-t.* 12 Sept., I show to each system that I fully understand and rightfully appreciate what that system means. 1854 Thoreau *Walden* (1884) 112 Books.. stand naturally and rightfully on the shelves of every cottage. 1884 *Manch. Exam.* 24 Nov. 6/3 He rightfully distrusted such a frail-looking craft.

Rightfulness (rəi·tfŭlnės). Forms: see Rightful *a.*; also 4–6 **-nes**, 4–7 **-nesse**. [-ness.]

† **1.** = Righteousness 1. *Obs.*

Until *c* 1400 the Vulg. *justitia* was frequently translated as 'rightfulness'.

1303 R. Brunne *Handl. Synne* 600–1 Yn þe touþer werlde ..Þere ys but ryȝtfulnes of dome; Þere ys al ryȝtfulnes at þe last ende. *a* 1325 *Prose Psalter* xxxix. [xl.] 13 Y ne hyd nouȝt þy ryȝtfulnes in myn hert. 1388 Wyclif *Gen.* xviii. 19 That thei kepe the weie of the Lord, and..do riȝtfulnesse and dom. 1422 tr. *Secreta Secret.*, *Priv. Priv.* 147 The Ryghtfulnes of workis or of dedis comyth and rysyth of Ryghtfulnesse of wille. *c* 1460 Metham *Wks.* (E. E. T. S.) 94 The fourthe lyne..sygnyfyith ryteffulnes and enduryng in gode werkes..and vertu. 1532 Hervet *Xenophon* (1768) 58 Do you in dede take vpon you to teach them that iustice and ryghtefulnes? *a* 1586 Sidney *Ps.* XXXIII. i, Rejoyce in God, O ye That..cherish rightfullnesse. 1594 Carew *Huarte's Exam. Wits* (1616) 204 The rightfulnesse and singlenesse of the vnderstanding, which admitteth no doublenesse.

personif. *a* 1325 *Prose Psalter* lxxx[i]v. 14 Ryȝtfulnes shal go to-fore hym, and shal sett his goings in his waie. *a* 1470 H. Parker *Dives & Pauper* (W. de W. 1496) 329/2 Ryghtfull dome is tourned bacwarde, & ryghtfulnesse stode from ferre. *c* 1557 Abp. Parker *Ps.* XXV. 59 Let perfectnes and rightfulnes both guide and wayte on mee.

† **b.** *pl.* = Righteousness 1 b. *Obs.*

a 1325 *Prose Psalter* xviii. [xix.] 9 Þe ryȝtfulnesses of our Lord ben makand ioyful ryȝtlich þe hertes. 1388 Wyclif *Deut.* iv. 5 Y tauȝte ȝou the comaundementis and riȝtfulnessis, as my Lord God comaundide to me.

† **2.** Of stature: Erectness, uprightness. *rare*[−1].

1387 Trevisa tr. *Higden* (Rolls) II. 213 In mannis body was..riȝtfullnesse of stature, fairenesse of schappe.

3. The fact of being right or just; the justness or equity *of* something.

1676 Towerson *Decalogue* 265 The rightfulness of princes pleas. 1736 *Plea for Sacram. Test* 48 None of their Tenets ..will incline them to dispute the Rightfulness of the present Civil Settlement. 1882 Coleridge *Lett.*, *Convers.*, etc. II. 36 Those women..who feel the rightfulness of their own claim to be loved with honor. 1879 McCarthy *Own Times* xxviii. II. 334 The men who are to carry on a war must have no doubt of its rightfulness of purpose.

Right hand. Also **right-hand, righthand.** Forms see Right *a.* and Hand *sb.* [f. Right *a.* 18. Cf. Fris. *rjuchterhân*, (M)Du. *rechter hand*, G. *rechte hand*.]

1. That hand which is normally the stronger of the two. (Opposed to Left hand.)

c 1000 *Nicodemus* xxi, Se Hælend..be ðære ryht handa me ȝenam. *c* 1200 Ormin 8181 And himm wass sett inn hiss rihht hannd An dere kineȝerrde. *c* 1290 *S. Eng. Leg.* I. 11 His riȝt hond he liet of-smite. *a* 1300 *Cursor M.* 1618 Be his right hand he suar his ath. 1340–70 *Alisaunder* 1174 He raught forthe his right hand & his rigge frotus. *a* 1400–50 *Alexander* 784* With hys right hande hym rodely [he] straker. *c* 1475 *Rauf Coilȝear* 150 He..hit him vnder the eir with his richt hand. 1535 Coverdale *Tobit* vii. 13 So he toke the righthande of his daughter, and gaue her in to the right hande of Tobias. *c* 1585 R. Browne *Answ. Cartwright* 3 This he shoulde houlde in his right hande. 1635–56 Cowley *Davideis* I. 2 That right hand which held the

Crook before. 1670 C. Gataker in *Gataker's Antid. Errour* To Rdr. B ij b, Whom I desire to receive with the right hand, that which is offered with the right hand. 1710 *Lond. Gaz.* No. 4784/1 On Condition that he should give the Right Hand to the Marquis de Prié in his own House. 1781 Cowper *Anti-Thelyphth.* 169 To horse! he cried, or by this good right hand..I smite you. 1808 Scott *F. M. Perth* xix, She let her right hand fall on his shoulder. 1879 Browning *Halbert & Hob* 4 Right-hand with left-hand linked,—He faced his son submissive.

attrib. 1675 Brooks *Gold. Key* Wks. 1867 V. 51, I desire nothing more..than that God would pull out right-eye sins, and cut off right-hand sins. 1680 Roscommon *Poems* (1780) 78 Give my exalted soul a place Among thy chosen right-hand race. 1762 Sterne *Tr. Shandy* V. xxix, He set his right-hand thumb upon the bow of the saddle. 1805 Southey *Madoc in W.* xi, The Prince..gave to Caradoc the right-hand pledge. 1884 *Harper's Mag.* Dec. 114/2 She started from home with two right-hand gloves.

b. *transf.* as a symbol of friendship or alliance. (Rendering L. *dextræ*.)

1591 Savile *Tacitus*, *Hist.* I. liv. 31 The Lingones..had sent giftes to the Legions, Right-hands in token of mutual loue. 1598 Greneway *Tacitus*, *Ann.* II. xiv. (1622) 53 Calling to mind their friendship..with the Romans, and desiring that they might renew right hands.

c. *transf.* A person of usefulness or importance; an efficient or indispensable helper or aid.

c 1528–37 Ld. J. Butler in Ellis *Orig. Lett.* Ser. II. II. 48 O Connor..who hath maried the erle of Kildare's doghter, is his right hand. 1581 G. Elliot (*title*), A very true Report of the apprehension..of that arch-Papist Edmund Campion, the Pope his right hand. 1615 J. Stephens *Satyr. Ess.* 329 A Lawyers simple Clarke Is his Masters right hand, if hee bee not left-handed. 1665 Pepys *Diary* 22 July, It is strange to see how poor..Backewell is like to be put to it in his absence, Mr. Shaw, his right hand, being ill. 1713 Steele *Guard.* No. 5 ⁋ 4 For Mrs. Jane is the Right-hand of her Mother. 1765 Welldon (*title*), The Smith's Right Hand, or a Complete Guide to the Various Branches of all sorts of Iron Work. 1846 Grote *Greece* (1869) I. 57 [Hêphaestos] is indispensable as the right-hand and instrument of the gods. 1847 Tennyson *Princess* III. 21 Lady Psyche was the right hand now, And she the left, or not, or seldom used.

2. a. The right side. **b.** The direction towards the right. = Right *sb.*[1] 17 a.

c 1205 Lay. 14734 Heo iseȝen an heore riht hond a swiþe feier æit-lond. *a* 1240 *Creed* in *O. E. Hom.* I. 217 Þer he sit o godes rithond feder al-mihti. *a* 1300 *Cursor M.* 6325 He loked als on his righthand. *a* 1340 Hampole *Psalter* cxli. 5, I byheld til þe righthand. *c* 1420 Lydg. *Assembly of Gods* 1769 The iiiᵈᵉ on the ryght hande here bit ys to the tolde. 1470–85 Malory *Arthur* I. xv. 56 Syr Arthur.. stered his hors here & there on the right hand & on the lyft hand. *a* 1548 Hall *Chron.*, *Edw. IV*, 26 He left the right way toward Pomfret,..and toke the way on the right hand. 1596 Shaks. *Merch. V.* II. ii. 42 Turne vpon your right hand at the next turning. 1661 Pepys *Diary* 23 Apr., My wife [was] in one little one, on the right hand. 1687 T. Brown *Saints in Uproar* Wks. 1730 I. 82 *Pluto.* Two martyrs, say'st thou? Where the devil are they? *Pope.* On my right-hand. 1720 De Foe *Capt. Singleton* (1907) 99 They might continue as far to the right hand, and to the left as far. 1837 G. Phillips *Syriac Gram.* 1 The Syrians in common with many other Eastern nations, read from the right-hand to the left. 1863 Mary Howitt tr. *F. Bremer's Greece* I. 2 On the right hand we discern Mount Athos.

attrib. 1592 Kyd *Sp. Trag.* I. i, Three waies there were: that on the right hand side Was ready way unto the foresaid fields. *a* 1600 *Flodden F.* v. (1664) 46 In Right-hand wing did warlike wend. 1667 Milton *P. L.* II. 633 Som times He scours the right hand coast. 1757 W. Wilkie *Epigoniad* II. 33 [It] struck the right-hand courser to the ground. 1839 De la Beche *Rep. Geol. Cornw.*, etc. x. 305 What the miner terms a 'right hand heave'. 1887 Rider Haggard *Allan Quatermain* ii, I made out several dark heads gliding away towards the right-hand bank.

† **b.** The position of honour. *To take the right hand of*, to take or assume precedence of. *Obs.*

1652 *Seas. Exp.* 9 If..the time..be made Umpier of Precedency, Geneva must take the right hand of You. 1682 *News fr. France* 2 It is true, the Precedence was then granted to the Bishops of Rome,..and the Empire carrying its name from Rome, no wonder if the Bishop..had the Right-hand still reserved to him. 1704 N. N. tr. *Boccalini's Advts. fr. Parnass.* I. 188 The Scotch Nobility..said 'twas a very hard Case, that a poor Scholar..should afterwards by Virtue of a Bishoprick..not only assume as good a Title as his Master, but even pretend, upon some Occasions, to take the Right-hand of him.

c. Of errors: *On the right hand*, on the right side, in the right direction. Also *attrib.* ? *Obs.*

1693 Dryden *Persius* vi. (1697) 490 One Error, tho' on the right hand, yet a great one, Is, That they are no Helps to a Virtuous Life. 1785 Wesley *Wks.* (1872) XIII. 95 Miss Cooke leans to the right-hand error—It is safer to think too little than too much of yourself.

3. *Right-hand man*: † **a.** A soldier holding a position of responsibility or command on the right of a troop of horse. *Obs.* **b.** = sense 1 c.

a. 1665 Pepys *Diary* 4 Dec., Not only..being admitted into the Duke of Albemarle's guards..but also..put as a right-hand man, and other marks of special respect. 1710 Steele & Addison *Tatler* No. 253 ⁋ 1 Mr. Alexander Truncheon, who is their Right-Hand Man in the Troop [of horse guards]. 1721 *Lond. Gaz.* No. 5925/3 He..was lately a Right Hand Man in the 4th Troop of Horse-Guards.

b. *a* 1802 *Earl Richard* xxiii. in Scott *Border Minst.* (1869) 362 O wha has slain my right-hand man, That held my hawk and hound? 1809 Malkin *Gil Blas* VII. vi, I am in want of a secretary..: he shall be my right-hand man. 1841 Marryat *Poacher* xxii, Little Peter was her right-hand man. 1890 'R. Boldrewood' *Col. Reformer* (1891) 145 He will go with me as stockman and right-hand man generally.

4. *Right-hand (-laid) rope*: (see quot. 1867); *right-hand screw*, one with the thread turning to the right; *right-hand lock* (see quot. 1875).

1841 Dana *Seaman's Man.* 8 Parcel the score of the dead-eye, and heave the shroud taut round it, turning in with the sun, if right-hand-laid rope. *Ibid.* 34 Right-hand rope must be coiled with the sun. 1859 F. A. Griffiths *Artil. Man.* (1862) 89 A metal fuze with a right-hand screw. 1867 Smyth *Sailor's Word-bk.*, *Right-Hand Rope*, that which is laid up and twisted with the sun, that is to the right hand. 1875 Knight *Mech. Dict.* 1340/2 The right-hand and left-hand locks are for doors to swing to the right or to the left.

Right-handed, *a.* (*adv.*). [f. prec. + -ed[1].]

1. Having the right hand or arm stronger or more useful than the left; using the right hand by preference; = Dextrous *a.* 6. Also *transf.*

1398 Trevisa *Barth. De P. R.* v. xxviii. (Bodl. MS.), A womman is nought right handed and lifte handed. 1581 Mulcaster *Positions* xix. (1887) 81 Double right handed which vse both the handes a like. 1585 T. Washington tr. *Nicholay's Voy.* III. vii. 80 A ranke [of archers] on the right side, whiche are lefthanded, and another vpon the left being right handed. 1629 Sir W. Hope *Fencing-Master* *4 If you are a Right-Handed Man. 1646 Sir T. Browne *Pseud. Epid.* 191 Some are..ambidexterous or right handed on both sides. 1833 Nyren *Yng. Cricketer's Tutor* 68 If bowling to a right-handed hitter, his ball would twist from the off-stump into the leg. 1885 Myers in *Proc. Psychical Res.* Jan. 58 The following formulæ will represent the graphic automatism of a right-handed man.

b. *fig.* Skilful, dexterous. *rare.*

a 1661 Fuller *Worthies* (1840) I. 424 He was right-handed in the Cyclopædia of all arts. *Ibid.* III. 372 He was.. right-handed to any great employment.

2. On the right side; of the right kind.

1656 Bramhall *Replic.* I. 8 Yet these [schisms] were not about the essentials of Religion, but about a right-handed error, even too much admiration of their Pastors. 1822 T. Mitchell *Aristoph.* II. 295, I this last conclusion draw, That for smart right-handed wisdom none my equal ever saw.

3. In various uses: **a.** Pertaining or belonging to the right hand. **b.** Of a blow: Delivered with the right hand. **c.** Of implements, etc.: Fashioned for the right hand.

1700 T. Brown tr. *Fresny's Amusem.* Wks. 1709 III. 28 A London Alderman, who sold a Jew five Fatts of Right-handed Gloves, without any Fellows to them. ?1820 *Debtor & Creditor* 41 If you resent that, it's ten to one but you're complimented with a right-handed facer. 1828 Scott *F. M. Perth* v, I..am sorry for that poor lover who will never wear right-handed chevron again. 1891 Sir D. Wilson *Right Hand* 138 It is a right-handed implement.

4. *Conchol.* † **a.** Sinistral; reversed. *Obs.* **b.** = Dextral *a.* 2.

1776 Da Costa *Elem. Conchol.* 119 Right-handed shells are such, whose whirls or convolutions turn from right to left, or contrary to the most general manner of turbinated univalves. 1838 *Penny Cycl.* XII. 108/2 Shell cylindrical, very spiral;..right or left-handed (dextral or sinistral). 1851 Woodward *Mollusca* I. 99 Nearly all the spiral shells are dextral, or right-handed.

5. In scientific and technical uses: Characterized by rotation or direction towards the right. Also as *adv.* (quot. 1841).

1825 J. Nicholson *Operat. Mechanic* 146 We have represented..the grinding surface of the upper mill-stone, upon the supposition that it moves from east to west, or for what is called a right-handed mill. 1841 Dana *Seaman's Man.* 34 Ropes..of three strands, laid right handed, or, as it is called, with the sun. 1846 Holtzapffel *Turning* II. 604 An..imperfect expedient for producing a left-handed screw from a right-handed tap. 1875 Bedford *Sailor's Pocket Bk.* x. (ed. 2) 360 Running rigging is hawser-laid, right-handed. 1876 Preece & Sivewright *Telegraphy* 52 Electromagnets are almost invariably wound with the right-handed helix.

b. Of rotatory polarization: (see quot. 1854).

1827–8 Herschel in *Encycl. Metrop.* (1845) IV. 550 The liquids in which he observed a right-handed rotatory property. 1854 *Pereira's Polarized Light* (ed. 2) 254, I shall adopt Biot's nomenclature, and designate the polarization right-handed or left-handed, according as we have to turn the analyzing prism to the right or to the left. *c* 1865 Wylde *Circ. Sci.* I. 84/2 Such bodies have what is called right-handed polarisation.

c. Producing right-handed polarization.

1827–8 Herschel in *Encycl. Metrop.* (1845) IV. 550 The index of rotation in a right handed crystal. 1831 Brewster *Optics* xxvi. 218 Hence, in reference to this property, quartz may be divided into right-handed and left-handed quartz. 1869 Roscoe *Elem. Chem.* 396 Dextrose, or right-handed glucose.

6. In the direction of the right; rightward. Also as *adv.*, to the right. *rare.*

1900 *Westm. Gaz.* 19 Jan. 3/1 A right-handed turn brought the hunt near Billesdon. *Ibid.* 30 Nov. 4/3 Turning right-handed short of Norton Brook.

Hence **Right-ha·ndedly** *adv.*, **-ha·ndedness.**

1855 Scofferin in *Orr's Circ. Sci.*, *Chem.* 82 The amount of right-handedness or left-handedness displayed by the solution. 1876 D. Wilson *Preh. Man* (ed. 3) I. 107 The question of right-handedness, as a natural or acquired practice peculiar to man, has a special interest. 1882 *Encycl. Brit.* XIV. 613/1 The motion takes place in one direction (say right-handedly) in the circle.

Right-ha·nder. [f. Right hand + -er[1].]

1. A blow struck with the right hand. (Cf. Left-hander c.)

1857 Hughes *Tom Brown* II. v, Tom..is..deposited on the grass by a right-hander from the Slogger. 1860 Dickens *Uncomm. Trav.* vii, One of the combatants, receiving a straight right-hander with the glove between his eyes. 1883 C. Reade in *Harper's Mag.* Dec. 132 The carter..received a dazzler with the left, followed by a heavy right-hander.

2. One who naturally uses the right hand; a right-handed person. (Cf. Left-hander a.)

1885 Myers in *Proc. Psychical Res.* Jan. 42 There are.. some right-handers..who, if they try to write with their left hands, instinctively produce *Spiegel-Schrift*.

† **Righthead.** *Obs. rare*[−1]. [f. Right *a.* + -head.] Rightness.

a 1340 Hampole *Psalter* xxxv. 11 Þi rightwisnes, þat is, righthed of life.

Ri·ghting, *vbl. sb.* [f. Right *v.* + -ing[1].]

† **1.** The action of guiding or directing aright; also, setting right. *Obs.*

c 960 Æthelwold *Rule St. Benet* (Schröer, 1885) 61 Ne scylen hy beon butan reȝole, þæt is lifes rihtinge. *c* 1000 Ælfric *On N. T.* (Gr.) 21 Þonne mann wisdom spreceð maneȝum to þearfe and to rihtinge. *a* 1300 *E. E. Psalter* xcvi[i]. 2 Rightwisenes and dome als-swa, Rightinge of his sete ere þa. *a* 1325 *Prose Psalter* cxviii. [cxix.] 80 Be myn hert made vnfiled in þy riȝtinges, þat ich ne be nouȝt confounded. *a* 1400 Hylton *Scala Perf.* (W. de W. 1494) II. xxxiv, The ryghtyng of a synfull soule thorugh foryeuenesse of synnes.

2. Reparation or redress *of* wrongs, injuries, etc.

1566 *Acts & Constit. Scot.* To Rdr., The Lawis..ar the.. decreit of wyse men, the amending and rychting of forthocht and suddane faultis. 1681 College in Wood *Life* (O. H. S.) II. 553/2 Leave the righting of my wrongs to God Almighty. 1828 Scott *F. M. Perth* vii, The Duke..will make our petition for righting of our wrongs the pretence for squeezing money out of us. 1883 Sime *All-Israel* 107 Private righting of injury is not allowed.

b. Re-establishment *of* oneself or another in a due or rightful position; vindication.

1611 Cotgr. s.v. *Iustice*, Jurisdiction vsurped by diuers Lords..for the righting of themselues in the recouerie of duties withheld from them. 1642 C. Vernon *Consid. Exch.* 81 For concluding of this point concerning the righting of Sheriffes. 1685 Baxter *Paraphr. N. T.* v. 38 Prefer not the righting of your selves before the winning of him by Love. 1831 E. Irving *Exp. Rev.* I. 64 The judging, righting, and rewarding of his servants the prophets, the saints, and them that fear his name.

3. The action of mending *up* something.

1615–6 *Sarum Churchw. Accs.* (Swayne, 1896) 166 Righting vpp of two pewes for Joyners worke and nayells, 4*s*.

4. Of vessels or vehicles: Restoration or return to the usual upright position. Also *attrib.*

1769 Falconer *Dict. Marine* (1780), *Righting*, the act of restoring a ship to her upright position, after she has been laid on a careen. 1841 Dana *Seaman's Man.* 76 The sails may be trimmed to help her in righting. 1885 *Athenæum* Mar. 411/1 The maximum stability of the Captain is attained at an angle of 21°, where the righting lever is only 102 inches.

transf. 1869 *Daily News* 16 Dec., Cavour..had the greatest confidence in what we may call the 'righting power' of the Italian intelligence.

† **Rightleche,** *v.* *Obs.* Forms: 1 **rihtlæcan**, 2 **-lecen**, **-lachen**, 2–3 **-leche(n**, 3 **ryht-**); 4 **riȝt(e)-**, **ryȝtleche**, **riȝtlyche**. [OE. *rihtlǽcan*, f. *riht* Right *a.*]

1. *trans.* To set right, rectify, amend; to order aright. Also *refl.*

c 960 Æthelwold *Rule St. Benet* (Schröer, 1885) 46, Ȝif he þonne swa ne bete and rihtlæce, he sy of ðam ealdorscype aworpen. *a* 1023 Wulfstan *Hom.* (1883) 277 Se þe ær þysum misdyde, þæt he..hit ȝeorne ȝebete and rihtlæce hine sylfne. *c* 1175 *Lamb. Hom.* 17 Gif he him nule rihtlechen for preoste na for halie chirche, hald hine þenne swilche mon þe beo bute laȝe. *c* 1200 *Trin. Coll. Hom.* 69 Ute wei þe we shule leten is ure liflode þe we shule rihtleche. *c* 1275 *Wom. Samaria* 57 in *O. E. Misc.* 86 Hwenne he cumeþ he wyle vs alle ryhtleche. *a* 1400 *Prymer* (1891) 28 Blessed trinite delyuere us, saue us, and riȝteleche us.

2. To rule or govern.

c 1350 *Will. Palerne* 1310 [They] nomen omage in his name ..Forto riȝtleche þat reaume. 1398 Trevisa *Barth. De P. R.* v. i, The yen ryȝtlecheþ and reuleþ þe neþer membris.

Rightless (rəi·tlės), *a.* [f. Right *sb.*[1] + -less. Cf. MDu. *rechtelɔos*, MHG. *reht(e)lôs* (G. *rechtlos*).]

† **1.** Wrongful, lawless. *Obs.*

1596 Dorrell in *Willobie's Avisa* Apol. K 4 If any..continue the errour of their vnsatisfied minds they must for euer rest in the rightlesse erring. 1613 Purchas *Pilgrimage* IX. iv. (1614) 837 Howsoeuer they exercise..mutuall disagreements, yet agree in like barbarous and rightlesse Rites. *a* 1618 Sylvester *Job Triumphant* III. 555 If Tithe-lesse, Taxe-lesse, Wage-lesse, Right-lesse, I Have eat the Crop, or caused the Owners dye.

2. Devoid or deprived of rights.

1823 Scott *Quentin D.* xxii, For this thou..hast deserved to be declared outlawed and fugitive, landless and rightless. 1897 Maitland *Domesday & Beyond* 42 One may be born to serve without being born rightless.

Hence **Ri·ghtlessness.**

1895 *19th Cent.* Jan. 57 It is ordinarily assumed that the social and legal position under Islam is one of extreme degradation and absolute rightlessness.

Right-lined, *a.* [f. Right *a.* 2 + Line *sb.*[2] 9.] = Rectilinear *a.*

1551 Recorde *Pathw. Knowl.* I. No. 17 To make a likeiamme equal to any right lined figure, and that on an angle appointed. 1570 Billingsley *Euclid* I. def. ix. 3 If the lines which containe the angle be right lynes, then is it called a rightlyned angle. 1670 R. Coke *Disc. Trade* 74 If a right lined Angle be not space, it is nothing; yet nothing but two right lines comprehend it. 1764 Reid *Inquiry* vi. § 9 Wks. I. 148/1 The properties..of visible right-lined triangles are not the same with the properties of plain triangles. 1769 *Phil. Trans.* LIX. 64 To determine whether the force of an explosion was..diminished by being diverted from a right-lined course. 1808 J. Webster *Nat. Philos.* 14 The body will be either accelerated or retarded in a right-lined

direction. 1834 *Tait's Mag.* I. 42/1 London rain,..a true right-lined, continuous, equable outpouring of water pellets from above. 1840 Lardner *Geom.* 81 The sum of all the angles of any right-lined figure.

fig. 1792 Burns *Let. to W. Nicol* 20 Feb., From the luminous path of thy own right-lined rectitude thou lookest benignly down on an erring wretch.

Rightly (rəi·tli), *adv.* Forms: 1–3 **rihtlice** (1 **ryht-**, **reht-**), 2 **richtlice**, 3 **ri(c)htliche**, 5 **ryghtlyche**; 1 **rihtlic**, **re(c)htlic**, 4 **riȝtlich**; 4–5 **riȝtli** (4 **riȝtly**, 5 **ritli**), 4 **rightli**; 4, 6 **ryghtely**, 6 *Sc.* **rychtly**, **richtlie**, 7 **rightlie**; 4– **rightly.** [OE. *reht-*, *riht-*, *ryhtlíce*, = MDu. *rechtelike* (Du. *rechtelijk*), MLG. *rechtliken*, etc., G. *rechtlich*, ON. *rétt(i)liga* (Sw. *rätteligen*): see Right *a.* and -ly[2].]

1. In accordance with equity or moral rectitude; justly, fairly, uprightly; in conformity with right conduct or procedure.

805 *Charter* in *O. E. Texts* 442 Ðæt wiorð ȝedæle [he] fore hiora gastas suæ ælmeslice & suæ rehtlice suæ he him seolfa ..geleornie. *c* 897 K. Ælfred *Gregory's Past. C.* xxii. 172 Beoð simle ȝearwe..to forȝifonne ælcum ðara þe eow ryhtlice bidde. 971 *Blickl. Hom.* 75 Þæt is þonne, þæt we sceolan god weorc wyrican, & rihtlice libban. *c* 1000 Ælfric *Hom.* II. 322 Ȝe manna bearn, demað rihtlice. *a* 1122 *O. E. Chron.* (Laud MS.) an. 1083, Ða munecas..beadon hine þæt he sceolde healdan hi rihtlice. *c* 1200 *Trin. Coll. Hom.* 9 Ure lif we ledeð richtliche togenes ure louerd ihesu crist, ȝif we forbereð al þat, þat him is unqueme. 1303 R. Brunne *Handl. Synne* 1433 Þo men þat loue to do ryghtely..shal passe þere sauely Into þat blesful cuntre. *c* 1375 *Cursor M.* 21480 (Fairf.), Þe lauedi..ho bad vs riȝtli dome to giue. 1567 *Satir. Poems Reform.* vi. 104 Godly men..Quha..can Judge the people rude, And rychtly reule ouer thame. 1613 Purchas *Pilgrimage* III. iv. (1614) 251 Euery one who-so-euer liueth rightly..shall vndoubtedly obtaine Diuine fauour. 1706 E. Ward *Hud. Rediv.* (1710) 20 To rightly Judge without the Laws, The Person, or his doubtful Cause. 1741 in *Col. Rec. Pennsylv.* IV. 488 Until such prohibited Goods are rightly and lawfully proceeded against. 1829 D'Israeli in *Croker Papers* 28 Jan., Many papers..which rightly should have been deposited at the State-paper Office. 1873 Symonds *Grk. Poets* vii. 227 Make not fine speeches, but be rightly minded! 1874 Motley *Barneveld* II. xix. 283 His moral constitution made him incapable of..acting rightly on any vital subject.

Comb. 1768–74 Tucker *Lt. Nat.* (1834) II. 326 Calculating their systems for a few contemplative, rightly-disposed persons.

2. Properly; in the right or proper manner.

c 825 *Vesp. Psalter* xviii. 9 Rehtwisnisse dryhtnes rehtlice [L. *recte*] blissiende heortan. *c* 900 tr. *Baeda's Hist.* IV. ii. (1890) 260 Þa he Ceddan biscop mid wordum þreade, þæt he rihtlice ȝehalȝad na wære. *c* 950 *Lindisf. Gosp.* Mark vii. 35 And sona..un-bunden wæs ȝebend tungæs his & spreccend wæs rehtlice. *c* 1200 *Trin. Coll. Hom.* 27 Þe godfrihte..lueð rihtliche alle liuiende men, and ben hersume alle godes hese. *a* 1340 Hampole *Pr. Consc.* 1104 Na man may serve rightly Twa lordes to-gedir, þat er contrary. 1382 Wyclif *Mark* vii. 35 Anon..the bond of his tunge is unbounden, and he spak riȝtly.

a 1586 Sidney *Ps.* II, They that in him their only trust do rest, O, they be rightly blest! 1611 Cotgr., *Legitime*, legitimate..; rightly born, truly begot. 1631 Gouge *God's Arrows* III. § 36. 246 They who rightly and duly subject themselves, procure good to themselves. *Ibid.* IV. § 12. 390 This is rightly and truly to be content with things present. *a* 1653 Binning *Serm.* (1845) 53 If thy soul rightly discover God, it cannot but abase thee.

3. In accordance with truth or fact; correctly, exactly, accurately, † precisely.

c 897 K. Ælfred *Gregory's Past. C.* xxi. 156 Swiðe ryhtlice hit wæs awriten æfter ðæm nietenum ðæt ða hearȝas wæron atifrede. *c* 950 *Lindisf. Gosp.* Luke x. 28 And cuoeð him, Rehtlice ðu ȝoond-suaredes; ðis do þætte ðu ȝelifiȝe. *c* 1055 *Byrhtferth's Handboc* in *Anglia* VIII. 298 Oðra þinga þe man mæȝ rihtlice todælan onfeower. *a* 1122 *O. E. Chron.* (Laud MS.) an. 1107, Ðis wæs rihtlice ymbe vii. ȝear þæs þe se cyng Henri cynedomes onfeng. *a* 1300 *Cursor M.* 42 Þis fruit bitakens alle our dedis, Both gode and ille qua rightly redis. *c* 1380 *Antecrist* in Todd *Three Treat. Wyclif* (1851) 116 Wher it is not riȝtly understonden what is to be coveiten or desiren, or what is to be fled. *a* 1425 *Cursor M.* 7122 (Trin.), He het þe men to ȝyue hem mede If þei coude it riȝtly rede. 1549 Coverdale, etc. *Erasm. Par. 1 Tim.* 5 A perfite synceree loue telleth a great deale ryghtelyer, what is to be doen, than any constitucions. 1581 Mulcaster *Positions* xxxix. (1887) 202 The generall skill to iudge..most things rightly. 1611 Bible *Gen.* xxvii. 36 Is not he rightly named Iacob? 1632 Milton *Penseroso* 170 Where I may sit and rightly spell Of every Star that Heav'n doth shew. 1675 Baxter *Cath. Theol.* II. x. 213 The determining which of you doth rightliest expound the Scripture is not my business. 1712 Addison *Spect.* No. 265 ⁋ 1 One of the Fathers, if I am rightly informed, has defined a Woman [etc.]. 1754 Edwards *Freed. Will* I. ii. (1762) 12 Whether I have been so happy, as rightly to explain the Thing wherein consists the Strength of Motives or not. 1858 Carlyle *Fredk. Gt.* x. iii. (1865) III. 241 He cannot see rightly, and shoots always with help of an opera glass. 1875 Freeman in W. R. W. Stephens *Life* (1895) II. 93 If I read your question rightly.

Comb. 1768–74 Tucker *Lt. Nat.* (1834) II. 511 A rightly-aimed intention will prove a guidance both in the manner and measure of our religious duties. 1863 W. C. Baldwin *Afr. Hunting* 177 This rightly-named *thirst* land.

b. Properly or correctly speaking.

1785 Burns *2nd Ep. J. Lapraik* 39 I've begun to scrawl, but whether In rhyme, or prose,..Or some hotch-potch that's rightly neither, Let time mak proof.

c. With good reason; justifiably.

1883 *Manch. Guard.* 3 Nov. 7/3 We rightly judge of people by the company they keep.

† **4.** Directly, straightly. *Obs.*

c 1350 *Will. Palerne* 232 Riȝtly þenne þemperour wendes him euene tille. 1548 Elyot, *Directe*,..an adverbe signifyinge rightly or streightly. 1559 W. Cunningham *Cosmogr. Glasse* 25 The zodiack goeth ouerthwarte them, and not rightly as th'equinoctiall and the right Horizont doth. 1593 Shaks. *Rich. II*, II. ii. 18 Like perspectiues, which rightly gaz'd vpon Shew nothing but confusion, ey'd awry, Distinguish forme. 1635 Swan *Spec. M.* (1670) 293 The Optick Masters confess and prove, that the forms of the Stars are comprehended of the sight reflectly, and not rightly.

† **5.** At right angles; so as to form a right angle. *Obs. rare.*

1594 Blundevil *Exerc.* III. i. (1636) 272 There be also certain Sphericall..Angels..which do crosse one another in some point, either rightly or obliquely: if rightly, then they make right angles.

Right-minded, *a.* [f. Right *a.* + Mind *sb.*[1]]

1. Having a mind naturally inclined or disposed towards what is right.

1585–6 Hooker *Serm.* III. Wks. 1888 III. 601 There is no incongruity in terming them right-minded men. 1791 Ld. Auckland *Corr.* (1861) II. 396 The public prosperity is great, and the nation is right-minded. 1833 *Tracts for Times* No. 10. 3 All well-disposed, right-minded people. 1860 Pusey *Min. Proph.* 488 The good and right-minded have power to fulfil what is to the glory of God. 1885 Ruskin *Præterita* v. § 102 As all right-minded apprentices and good shopmen do.

2. *colloq.* Sane; of sound mind.

1877 Blackmore *Cripps* vi, That his sister was not 'right-minded'—that she dreamed things, and imagined things.

Hence **Right-mi·ndedness.**

a 1817 Jane Austen *Persuasion* i, With her had died all such right-mindedness. 1830 H. N. Coleridge *Gk. Poets* (1834) 153 She possessed a right-mindedness towards the really beautiful, which was then..rare in France. 1870 Lowell *Study Wind.* 174 That simple confidence of his in the right-mindedness of his fellow-men is very touching.

Rightness (rəi·tnės). Forms: 1 **rehtnisse**, 1–2 **-nise** (2 **-nis**), 1–3 **rihtnesse** (3 **rist-**), 4 **ryȝ-**, **riȝtnesse**, **-nisse**, 6–7 **rightnes**, **-nesse** (6 **righte-**), 7– **rightness.** [OE. *rehtnisse*, *rihtnesse*, etc., = MDu. *rechtenesse*, OHG. *rehtnissa*: see Right *a.* and -ness.]

1. Uprightness, integrity, moral rectitude; the quality or condition of being right in respect of character or conduct.

c 1000 *Ags. Ps.* (Thorpe) xcvii. 9 He..his syndrig folc on rihtnesse ræde gebringeð. *c* 1300 *Beket* 1629 Oure Louerd loveth soth and Rightnesse. *c* 1380 Wyclif *Sel. Wks.* II. 53 So alle creaturis shal dampne him þanne, and witnesse to Cristis dome þat it is fulli riȝtnesse. 1530 Palsgr. 263/1 Rightnesse, *rectitude*. 1646 H. Lawrence *Comm. Angells* 125 Sincerity is immixednesse, and rightnesse of ends. 1650 W. Brough *Sacr. Princ.* (1659) 414 A rightness in religion and conversation perfect a good man. *a* 1716 South *Serm.* (J.), It is not necessary for a man to be assured of the rightness of his conscience [etc.]. 1834 Chalmers *Const. Man* II. 89 A rightness which..hath had everlasting residence in the character of the Godhead. 1860 Pusey *Min. Proph.* 415 Pride and independence of God are the centre of the want of rightness. 1891 H. Jones *Browning* 74 The meaning of the universe is moral, its last might is rightness.

personif. 1340 *Ayenb.* 265 Ryȝtnesse zayþ, 'Lybbe we sobreliche, ry[ȝt]uollyche an bonayrelyche.'

b. Sincere attachment *to* a party. *rare*[−1].

1654 *Nicholas P.* (Camden) II. 95 His rightnes to our cause I take up upon my implicite faith of Sir E. Hide.

† **2.** Straightness; the fact of being straight. *Obs.*

c 1050 *Voc.* in Wr.-Wülcker 522 *Perpendicula*, walðræd, þæt is rihtnes. *c* 1200 *Trin. Coll. Hom.* 219 Ȝerde rihtnesse he heuede on hire liflode, for he ne turnde naht on hire to dointe..nan þer þinge þe he leten solde. 1610 Guillim *Heraldry* II. iii. (1611) 43 Rightnesse is a propertie of a line whereby it is carried levelly or equally throwout the Escocheon without either rising or falling. 1626 Bacon *Sylva* § 201 Which neverthelesse is not caused by the Rightness of the Line, but by the shortness of the distance.

† **3.** Reckoning; account. *Obs. rare.*

c 950 *Lindisf. Gosp.* Matt. xxv. 19 Æfter monige tides cuom drihten ðeana ðara & sette rehtnise mið him. *c* 1275 Lay. 14 Hit com him on mode..þat he wolde of Engelond þe ristnesse telle.

4. Correctness, accuracy; fitness, appositeness.

1561 T. Norton *Calvin's Inst.* Pref., Accordyng to the rightenesse that they haue bothe of witt, judgement and mynde. 1657 Fuller *Comm. Jonah* (1868) 190 The rightness of the way..maketh our going pleasing to God. 1666 Bunyan *Grace Abound.* § 188 The fitness of the word, the rightness of the timing of it,..was marvellous to me to find. 1690 Locke *Hum. Und.* II. xxxii. (1695) 214 It is in our Ideas, that both the Rightness of our Knowledge, and the Propriety or Intelligibleness of our Speaking consists. 1787 Jefferson *Writ.* (1859) II. 240 Your own reason is the only oracle given you by heaven, and you are answerable, not for the rightness, but uprightness of the decision. 1865 Ruskin *Sesame* ii. § 70 That poet who is distinguished..from all others—not by power, but by exquisite *rightness*. 1885 *Law Times Rep.* LIII. 199/1, I..followed it without expressing any opinion as to the rightness of the decision.

b. An instance of this.

1872 Ruskin *Fors Clav.* xiv. 20 The rightnesses only perceived; the felicities only remembered.

5. The condition or character of being on the right-hand side. *rare.*

1887 W. James in *Mind* Jan. 14 Rightness and leftness, upness and downness, are again pure sensations differing specifically from each other.

Right of way. Also **right-of-way.**

1. The legal right, established by usage, of a person or persons to pass and repass through grounds or property belonging to another.

1768 Blackstone *Comm.* III. 241 When a person..is obstructed by inclosures, or other obstacles,..by which means he cannot enjoy his right of way. 1818 Cruise *Digest* (ed. 2) III. 115 Where a person has a right of way over another's close, and he purchases such close, his right of way is extinguished by the unity of seisin and possession. 1843 *Penny Cycl.* XXVII. 153/1 The proper origin of a private right of way is, a grant from the owner of the soil, whose means of enjoying his own property are abridged thereby. 1890 *Spectator* 30 Aug., Lord Salisbury..insisted upon rights-of-way being established between the British lane and the coast.

fig. 1877 E. R. Conder *Basis Faith* ii. 62 Denying our right of way in this inquiry.

2. A path or thoroughfare which one may lawfully make use of, *esp.* one traversing the property of another.

1855 Macqueen *Rep. Sc. Appeals* 451 That the terminus of a public right of way need not itself be a public place. 1894 A. Robertson *Nuggets*, etc. 177, I went into a right-of-way, and showed about a hair-breadth of my right eye in the direction of the shop.

Right-rule, *v.* (see Right *adv.* 16 c).

† **Rights,** *adv.* *Obs.* [OE. *rihtes*, gen. sing. neut. of *riht* Right *a.*] Of direction: Straight, direct, right.

c 1205 Lay. 2659 He nom his folc & ferde forð & droh him rites norð. *c* 1275 — 15549 Tweie verden anne way þat west rihtes him lay. *c* 1400 *Sowdone Bab.* 2278 The Sowdon.. Sente iij hundrid of knightis, To kepe the brigge and the waye Oute of that Castil rightis.

b. Of time: Precisely, just.

13.. *E. E. Allit. P.* B. 427 Of secounde monyth þe seuenþe day ryȝtez. *c* 1400 *Land Troy Bk.* 14144 Armed knyȝtes That haue sclayn youre men now rightes.

-rights, *suffix*, an occasional ME. variant of -right, as in *anonrights*, *duvelrights*, *forthrights*.

Ri·ghtship. *dial.* [f. Right *sb.*[1] + -ship.] Rightness, justness.

1873 in *Eng. Dial. Dict.* 1899 Raymond *No Soul* i, He spoke with firm conviction, as if the rightship of this to any English understanding must be beyond doubt.

Ri·ght-side, *v.* Chiefly *dial.* [f. Right *a.* + Side *sb.*] *trans.* To put right, set in order.

1865 W. White *E. Eng.* I. 46 'When last come last,' said a rustic to whom I spoke about the devastation, 'it'll take years to right side it'. 1874 W. E. Forster in Reid *Life* (1888) II. 57, I have very nearly right-sided my papers.

Right-sided, *a.* [f. Right *a.* + Side *sb.*]

1. *Path.* Of diseases, etc.: Situated in, or affecting, the right side of the body.

1876 *Clin. Soc. Trans.* IX. 96 After he had been at his duties for about two hours, intense right-sided vertigo suddenly set in. 1881 *Obstet. Soc. Trans.* XXII. 103 The great majority of the tumours twisted were right-sided tumours.

2. Having a tendency to use the limbs on the right side of the body.

1884 J. Le Conte in *Nature* XXIX. 452/2 In my own case the whole body is right-sided, so far as dexterity is concerned.

Hence **Right-si·dedness.**

1884 H. T. Wharton in *Nature* XXIX. 477/2 In discussing right-sidedness..we must not forget that prize-fighters normally strike with the left hand. 1891 Sir D. Wilson *Right Hand* 169 Dr. Brown-Sequard affirms that right-sidedness affects the arms much more than the legs.

† **Ri·ghtsomes,** *adv.* *Obs.*[−1] [Cf. Leftsomes *adv.*] Towards the right.

1398 Trevisa *Barth. De P. R.* IX. i. (Tollemache MS.), Strayte and forþryȝt meuynge is riȝtsomis oþer lyftesomis, forþwarde oþer bakwarde, upwarde oþer dounwarde.

Right-thinking *a.* (see Right *adv.* 16 b).

Right-up, *a.* ? *Obs.* [f. Right *adv.* + Up *adv.* Cf. Upright *a.*]

1. Steep; rising straight up.

1511 *Guylforde's Pilgr.* (Camden) 52 It is very daungerous to go vp vnto the hyghte of this mounte..for the perillous, step and right vp passage. 1604 E. Grimstone *Siege Ostend* 87 This house was in the right-vp-street. 1838 Ht. Martineau *West. Trav.* I. 120 Utica, the most extempore place we had seen. The right-up shops, the daubed houses.

† **2.** Upright; honest. *Obs.*

1545 *Primer of Hen. VIII*, DD ij b, Then shal I with a ryght vp hart..extolle and magnifie thy holy name. *c* 1557 Abp. Parker *Ps.* cxix. 343 A rightup man of perfect wayes is blest and blest agayne.

Ri·ghtward, *adv.* and *a.* [f. Right *a.* + -ward. Cf. Leftward.]

A. *adv.* **1.** On the right hand. Also *to rightward of*. *rare.*

1814 Scott *Ld. of Isles* VI. xxiv, To rightward of the wild affray The field show'd fair and level way. *a* 1843 Southey (Ogilvie), Rightward and leftward rise the rocks.

2. In the direction of the right hand; towards the right. Also *to rightward*. Somewhat *rare.*

1814 Cary *Dante*, *Purg.* XI. 49 Along the bank to rightward come with us. 1886 W. R. Evans *Walking Routes* Ser. I. 20 Where the lane bends rightward, you see before you a park-gate. 1889 *Cornh. Mag.* May 552 The face..looks rightward.

B. *adj.* Tending or directed towards the right.

1825 Gleig *Subaltern* xvi, The..division took a rightward course. 1885 Myers in *Proc. Psychical Res.* Jan. 59 A hypnotic subject who..has been accustomed to write with her left-hand in ordinary rightward script.

So **Ri·ghtwards** *adv.*

1865 Masson *Rec. Brit. Philos.* 275 There has similarly been a drift rightwards.

Right whale, -whaleman, etc., see Whale, etc. **Rightwis(e, -ly(e, -nes(se,** etc., obs. varr. Righteous, Righteously, Righteousness.

Rigid (ri·dʒid), *a.* and *sb.* Also 6 **regyd**, 7 **rigide**, **riged**, **ridgid**, 8 **ridged**. [ad. L. *rigidus*,

f. *rigēre* to be stiff; cf. F. *rigide*, Sp., Pg., It. *rigido*.]

A. *adj.* **1.** Stiff, unyielding; not pliant or flexible; firm; hard.

1538 Starkey *England* I. ii. 40 Master Lvpset, you euer bryng in some regyd knottys in communycatyon. 1615 Crooke *Body of Man* 211 Being alwayes rigid or stiffe it woulde haue beene..vncomely. 1631 Vicars *Eng. Hallelujah* Ps. cv. 22 And then the rigid Rockes he rent, From whence did Floods of Water flow. 1667 Milton *P. L.* vi. 83 With upright beams innumerable Of rigid Spears. 1728 Chambers *Cycl.* s.v. *Marble*, Rigid Marble [is] that which, being too hard, works with difficulty, and is liable to splinter. 1796 Withering *Brit. Plants* (ed. 3) I. 177 The cup becoming more rigid, contains the seeds. 1832 Babbage *Econ. Manuf.* xxvii. (ed. 3) 263 Metals are not perfectly rigid but elastic. 1862 Darwin *Orchids* iii. 116 It is nearly rigid and appears fibrous. 1873 Richards *Operator's Handbk.* 115 The saws have to be at least one-third thicker in order to be rigid enough for their work.

fig. 1708 J. Philips *Cyder* I. 592 Cressy Plains..confess What the Silures Vigour unwithstood Cou'd do in rigid Fight. 1710 Palmer *Proverbs* 82 There is a rigid horror and chagrin in envy, malice, and revenge. 1822 Hazlitt *Table-t.* Ser. II. vi. (1869) 139 We have none of the hardy spirit or rigid forms of antiquity. 1888 Bryce *Amer. Commw.* (1890) I. 477, I propose to call it a Rigid Constitution, i. e. one which cannot be bent or twisted by the action of the legislature.

Comb. 1816 J. Scott *Vis. Paris* (ed. 5) 34 The thin-faced rigid-nerved men. 1870 Morris *Earthly Paradise* I. 460 That..melody, He drew from out the rigid-seeming lyre. 1882 *Nature* XXVII. 201 The ordinary lunar irregularities which are recognised in rigid-body astronomy.

b. *spec.* in plant-names (see quots.).

1859 Miss Pratt *Brit. Grasses* VI. 33 Rigid Sedge. *Ibid.* 164 Rigid Three-branched Polypody. *Ibid.* 179 Rigid Fern. 1871 Cooke *Handbk. Fungi* I. 190 *Cortinarius..rigens*, Rigid Cortinarius. 1877 F. G. Heath *Fern World* 359 The Rigid Buckler Fern, *Lastrea rigida*.

2. Of cold, etc.: Severe, hard, rigorous. *rare.*

1611 B. Jonson *Catiline* I. i, As when rigid frosts Have bound up brookes and rivers. 1726 Shelvocke *Voy. round World* 72 One would think it impossible that any thing living could subsist in so rigid a climate.

3. Rigorous, harsh, severe, inflexible, strict: **a.** Of actions, conduct, etc.

1624 Massinger *Renegado* II. iv, All tortures that A flinty hangmans rage could execute, Or rigide tyranny command with pleasure. 1660 R. Coke *Power & Subj.* 72 The violent and rigid execution of laws against all offenders. 1729 Butler *Serm.* Wks. 1874 II. 126 We shall [not] be able to say..where rigid right and justice ends, and oppression begins. 1769 Bancroft *Guiana* 367 Rigid treatment.. renders them content. 1807 J. Barlow *Columb.* III. 3 They rule with rigid but with generous care. 1840 Thirlwall *Greece* VII. 155 A very rigid inquiry was instituted. 1868 Freeman *Norm. Conq.* (1877) II. 487 Rigid justice, untempered by mercy, easily changes into oppression.

b. Of persons or disposition.

1634 Habington *Castara* I. (Arb.) 13 If my rigid friend question superciliously the setting forth of these Poems. 1665 Brathwait *Comment. Two Tales* (1901) 97 The clear and weighty Judgments of the Strictest and Rigidest Censors. 1710 Steele *Tatler* No. 175 ¶ 2 The young Man is under the Dictates of a rigid Schoolmaster. 1752 Young *Brothers* IV. i, O rigid gods! and shall I then fall down! 1775 De Lolme *Eng. Const.* I. iii. (1784) 48 A prince of a more rigid disposition.

4. Strict in opinion or observance; scrupulously exact or precise in respect of these.

1598 B. Jonson *Ev. Man in Humour* III. iii, H'is no precisian..Nor rigid Roman-catholike. 1657 *Penit. Conf.* iii. 23 Marvel not at the rigid Penitents of that age. 1687 A. Lovell tr. *Thevenot's Trav.* I. 53 He was a very riged Man, as I understood at a Visite which the French Ambassadour..made to him. 1707 Potter in *Lett. Lit. Men* (Camden) 271 Knox, a rigid presbyterian. 1790 Bruce *Source Nile* II. 579 David was a rigid adherent to the church of Alexandria. 1827 Lytton *Pelham* xiv, In the theory of philosophy he was tolerably rigid. 1849 Macaulay *Hist. Eng.* ii. I. 170 He had indeed some reason to dislike the rigid sect. 1874 Green *Short Hist.* vii. § 4. 378 The Lennoxes had remained rigid Catholics.

b. Of life, conduct, etc.

1634 Milton *Comus* 450 Rigid looks of Chast austerity. 1738 T. Shaw *Trav. Barbary* 306 Their Marabbutts..are generally Persons of a rigid and austere Life. 1753 R. Clayton *Jrnl. fr. Cairo to Mt. Sinai* 22 A cave, in which two kings sons spent their lives in performing rigid penances. 1872 *Routledge's Ev. Boy's Ann.* 296/1 The most rigid principles of honesty.

c. Of observances or practices.

1736 Butler *Anal.* II. i, The rigid Observance of the Sabbath. 1751 Earl Orrery *Remarks Swift* (1752) 105 The history of Brutus may instruct us, what unhappy effects the rigid exercise of superior virtue..may produce. 1782 Miss Burney *Cecilia* II. iv, A rigid seclusion from company was productive of a lassitude as little favourable to active virtue as dissipation itself. 1842 Combe *Digestion* 324 If such a change can be effected, by rigid adherence to rules, in the course of two or three months. 1861 Ld. Brougham *Brit. Constit.* xiv. 193 His avaricious habits inclined him to rigid parsimony.

5. Exact, precise, in respect of procedure or method; admitting or allowing of no deviation from strict accuracy.

1646 Sir T. Browne *Pseud. Ep.* 14 All deductions from metaphors, parables, allegories, unto reall and rigid interpretations. 1676 Towerson *Decalogue* 47 Those descriptions..rather as emblems and pictures than as rigid definitions of his nature. 1713 Berkeley *Hylas & Phil.* Pref., To observe the most rigid laws of reasoning. 1729 Law *Serious C.* xxii. (ed. 2) 440 This is as strictly true, in the most rigid sense. 1805 Foster *Ess.* III. iii. II. 40 The rigid laws of time and distance. 1860 Tyndall *Glac.* I. i. 5 The fossils which they contained were subjected to rigid scrutiny. 1869 — *Notes Lect. Light* § 214 For it has been demonstrated, by the most rigid experiments, that the velocity of light diminishes as the index of refraction increases.

B. *sb.* A strict or precise person. *rare.*

1712 Steele *Spect.* No. 492 ¶ 4 If you do not take measures for the immediate Redress of us Rigids, as the Fellows call us. 1749 W. Douglass *Summary* I. 444 The Rigids generally seceded from the more moderate, and removed with their teachers or ministers without the limits or jurisdiction of the colony.

Rigi·dify, *v. rare.* [f. prec. + -(I)FY.] **a.** *trans.* To make rigid. **b.** *intr.* To become rigid.

1842 J. Cairns *Let.* in *Life* (1895) 137 The muscles of the mind..are rigidified by frost and unstrung by heat. 1879 Baring-Gould *Germany* I. 300 Education restrains, rigidifies the organ of voice. *Ibid.* 301 The muscles rigidify.

Ri·gidist. *rare.* [f. Rigid *a.* + -IST.] One who holds strict views; a rigorist.

1716 M. Davies *Athen. Brit.* II. 254 Not that those ancient Orthodox Rigidists..would have the Arians..to be downright persecuted. 1793 tr. *Gresset's Ver-Vert* IV. (ed. 2) 43 *note*, Two celebrated rigidists of the last century.

Rigidity (ridʒi·diti). [ad. L. *rigiditās* (Vitruvius): see Rigid *a.* and -ITY. So F. *rigidité* (17th c.), It. *rigidità, -tade, -tate*.]

1. The state of being rigid; stiffness, hardness.

1624 Wotton *Arch.* in *Reliq.* (1672) 56 Which severe Observation of Nature..must needs produce..a kind of Rigidity. 1731 Arbuthnot *Aliments* (1735) 162 Rigidity of the Vessels and Organs must necessarily follow from Rigidity of the Fibres. 1794 G. Adams *Nat. & Exp. Philos.* III. xxix. 192 Its endeavour to overcome the rigidity of the cooled oil. 1805 Saunders *Min. Waters* 146 Where it has left..a rigidity or impaired action in the seat of the disease. 1859 Lang *Wand. India* 134 They were lying dead, but still warm, and their limbs, as yet, devoid of rigidity. 1882 Minchin *Unipl. Kinemat.* 121 The motion may be one which is consistent with perfect rigidity.

2. Strictness, severity, harshness, inflexibility; an instance of this.

a 1653 Binning *Serm.* (1845) 572 Will rigidity, severity.. and such like, ever conciliate the hearts of Men? 1699 Burnet 39 *Art.* Pref. 8 Till the Lutherans abate of their Rigidity. 1761 Hume *Hist. Eng.* lv. (1806) IV. 149 This assertion..displeased the house by shewing a stiffness and rigidity in the king. 1829 I. Taylor *Enthus.* x. 262 Disqualified from free and energetic action by rigidities and scruples and divisions. 1847 Lewes *Hist. Philos.* (1867) I. 344 The spasmodic rigidity and unnatural exaggeration of the Stoics. 1884 Courthope *Addison* 10 Though many of them were connected with the Presbyterian system, their common sense made them revolt from its rigidity.

Rigidly (ri·dʒidli), *adv.* [f. Rigid *a.* + -LY [2].]

1. In a rigid manner; severely, strictly.

1639 Fuller *Holy War* II. iv. 47 It is a greater fault rigidly to censure, than to commit a small oversight. 1699 Bentley *Phal.* 468 If we examine this rigidly, the computation cannot be true. 1748 Hartley *Observ. Man* I. iv. 461 Covetous Persons are often rigidly just in paying. 1791 Boswell *Johnson* I. 255 Johnson, though he could be rigidly abstemious, was not a temperate man. 1836 Thirlwall *Greece* II. 9 The founder of a government which was, for many centuries after him, rigidly aristocratical. 1859 Darwin *Origin Spec.* iv. 83 He does not rigidly destroy all inferior animals. 1875 Ouseley *Mus. Form* ii. 9 A melody need not be kept rigidly in one key.

2. With material stiffness or rigidity.

1861 Holland *Less. Life* vi. 84 His elevated rectangular elbows cut rigidly against the air on either side. 1863 Mary Howitt tr. *F. Bremer's Greece* II. xvi. 144 In the north the mountain masses ascend ever more rigidly. 1871 B. Stewart *Heat* (ed. 2) § 34 This axis carries a cross piece A B rigidly attached to it.

Rigidness (ri·dʒidnės). [f. Rigid *a.* + -NESS.] The state of being rigid; rigidity.

1642 Fuller *Holy & Prof. St.* II. ix. 81 That his rigidnesse frighted people from consulting with him. 1653 Firmin *Sober Reply* 1 Mr. Cawdrey did justly taxe me with rigidnesse. 1680 *Nation's Interest rel. to Dk. York* 30 Rigidness, Censuring and the Sword Inflame and Harden. 1796 Morse *Amer. Geogr.* I. 333 *note*, His high idea of virtue giving him a rigidness, which makes it difficult for him to accommodate himself to those intrigues. 1853 Maurice *Proph. & Kings* i. 9 The unchangeableness of God is not to be confounded with the rigidness of a rule or a system.

Rigi·dulous, *a. rare*—°. [ad. mod.L. *rigidulus*.] Somewhat stiff; rather stiff.

1858 Mayne s.v. *Rigidulus*. 1882 in Ogilvie.

† **Rigled,** *a. Obs.*—[1] (Meaning uncertain.)

1630 Davenant *Cruel Brother* v. i, But where's the rigled Hag? the incestuous lump of heat? where is she?

Riglet, variant of Reglet.

Ri·glin(g. *Sc.* (and *north.*). Also 7–8 **riglen,** 9 **-lan.** [Northern var. of Ridgeling.] = Ridgel.

1662 in Pitcairn *Crim. Trials* III. 603 Paddokis did draw the plewgh, as oxen: qwickens wer sowmes, a riglen's horne wes a cowter. 1697 *Lond. Gaz.* No. 3316/4 A bay Horse.. quite blind, a Scar on the near Whirle Bone, and a Riglin. 1703 *Ibid.* No. 3929/4 A Dun Horse, a Riglin, wall Eyed. 1724 *Ibid.* No. 6283/3 Stolen.., a bright bay Rigling, 14 Hands high. 1787 W. Taylor *Poems* 66 A Riglen, Ram, an' thirty yowes. 1844 H. Stephens *Bk. Farm* II. 472 They are already too well aware of the plague of even a single riglin or chaser on a farm.

† **Rig-marie.** *Sc. Obs.* A coin of small value.

'Supposed to have originated from one of the billon coins struck during the reign of Queen Mary, which had the words *Reg. Maria*, as part of the legend' (Jam.).

a 1682 F. Sempill *Banishment Poverty* 96 No *Reg. Marie* was in my purse. 1807 Ruickbie *Wayside Cottager* 189 (E.D.D.), Wha valued not your college spither A rigmarie.

Rigmarole (ri·gmărōl), *sb.* (and *a.*). Also 8 **riggmonrowle, rig-my-role, -roll, rig-me-role, rigmarol.** [App. a colloquial survival and alteration of Ragman roll (sense 2); the latter seems to have gone out of literary use about 1600.]

1. A succession of incoherent statements; an unconnected or rambling discourse; a long-winded harangue of little meaning or importance.

1736 Pegge *Kenticisms*, *Rigmarole*, a long story; a 'tale of a tub'. 1746–7 Mrs. Delany *Life & Corr.* Ser. I. II. 454 At first she could not tell what to make of such a *rig-my-role*, but at last fixed it on Greene and the duke. 1757 Foote *Author* II, You are always running on with your riggmonrowles. 1766 Mrs. Delany *Life & Corr.* Ser. II. I. 77 How I have run on! Burn this rig-me-role instantly, I entreat your ladyship. 1779 Mme. D'Arblay *Diary* 20 Oct., That's better than a long rigmarole about nothing. 1814 Scott in *Lockhart* (1839) IV. 274 She repeated a sort of rigmarole which I suppose she had ready for such occasions. 1859 Meredith *R. Feverel* xi, You never heard such a rigmarole. 1883 *Times* 2 Nov. 2/3 A long rigmarole was told how the journalist's hat had fallen into the Seine.

b. Without article: Language of this kind.

1809 W. Irving *Knickerb.* VII. vi. (1820) 488 They were exactly the same that..may be classed in rhetoric under the general title of Rigmarole. 1818 Byron *Juan* I. clxxiv, His speech was a fine sample, on the whole, Of rhetoric, which the learn'd call 'rigmarole'. 1887 Jessopp *Arcady* iii. 88 Scraps of paper..scribbled over with rigmarole.

2. *attrib.*, passing into *adj.* Incoherent; having no proper sequence of ideas; rambling.

1753–4 Richardson *Grandison* VI. xxv. 141 You must all of you go on in one rig-my-roll way; in one beaten track. 1791 Boswell *Johnson* I. 191 *note*, In that manner vulgarly, but significantly, called rigmarole. 1806–7 J. Beresford *Miseries Hum. Life* (1826) VI. xviii, Their rigmarole wonderings..at the number of miles which you have travelled out of your way. 1839 Miss Maitland *Lett. fr. Madras* (1843) 242 Probably the performance will be so queer and rigmarole that nobody will read it. 1857 S. Osborn *Quedah* xi. 138 He began a long rigmarole story about Malaymen not liking to clean copper. 1870 Miss Bridgman *R. Lynne* II. x. 213 What a rigmarole letter!

Hence **Ri·gmarole** *v. intr.*, to talk rigmarole; **Rigmaro·lery,** rigmarole discourse; **Rigmaro·lic** *a.*, of the nature of rigmarole.

1831 *Blackw. Mag.* XXX. 330/2 Ridgway rigmaroled, and Brougham vapoured. 1839 *Ibid.* XLV. 466 Sentimental rigmarolery and practical benevolence seldom go together. *a* 1849 Poe *Wks.* (1864) III. 576 'What is Poetry?' notwithstanding Leigh Hunt's rigmarolic attempt at answering it, is a query [etc.].

Rigmaro·lish, *a.* [f. Rigmarole *sb.* + -ISH.[1]] Somewhat akin to rigmarole.

1827 J. W. Croker in *C. Papers* (1884) I. 369, I have been betrayed into this rather rigmarolish note by an expression in your note which [etc.]. 1842 Lover *Handy Andy* xvii, He's going to..read some long rigmarolish old records. 1885 *Daily Tel.* 16 Mar. (Cassell), His rambling rigmarolish way.

Hence **Rigmaro·lishly** *adv.*

1841 *Fraser's Mag.* XXV. 240 We will proceed rigmarolishly by first speaking..of..a real Simon Pure.

Rigne, obs. form of Reign *v.*

Ri·gol, *sb. Obs.* exc. *dial.* Also 6–7 **rigoll.** [ad. F. *rigole* water-course, gutter, furrow, drill, groove: see Riggal and Regal *sb.*[3] for variant forms in English.]

† **1.** A ring or circle. *Obs. rare.*

App. derived from the application of the word to a groove running round a thing: cf. sense 3 and Rigol *v.*, also Riggal 2 and Regal *sb.*[3] (quot. 1886). The possibility that in both passages it may be an error for *ringol*, var. of Ringle *sb.*[1], appears to be very slight.

1593 Shaks. *Lucrece* 1745 About the mourning and congealed face Of that blacke bloud, a watrie rigoll goes, Which seemes to weep vpon the tainted place. 1597 — *2 Hen. IV*, IV. v. 36 This is a sleepe, That from this Golden Rigoll hath diuorc'd So many English Kings.

2. † **a.** A small furrow or drill for seeds. *Obs.*—[1]

1599 Gardiner *Kitchin Garden* 16 His sowing in Rigols doth saue the better halfe of the seedes.

b. *dial.* A small channel or gutter.

1879 Miss Jackson *Shropshire Word-bk.* 352 I've made a bit of a rigol to carry the waiter off the posy-knot.

3. *dial.* A groove.

1879 Miss Jackson *Shropshire Word-bk.* 352 Look at the dirt i' the rigol round the table.

† **Ri·gol,** *v. Obs. rare*—°. [f. *rigol* (cf. prec.), var. of Riggal and Regal *sb.*[3] F. *rigoler* (now dial.) is app. not recorded in this sense.] *trans.* To furnish (a barrel) with a groove at the top, into which the head fits.

1580 Hollyband *Treas. Fr. Tong*, *Enjabler*, to rigoll a tunne, hogshead, or barrell, and to putte the heade vnto it. 1611 Cotgr., *Enjabler*, to rigoll a peece of caske; or, to make the Crowes. *Ibid.*, *Renjabler*, to new-rigol a peece of caske.

Rigolage, variant of Recolage *Obs.*

Rigold(e, variants of Rigald, Riggald.

† **Rigole,** *v. Obs. rare*—[1]. [a. OF. *rigoler*: see Recolage.] *trans.* To indulge wantonly.

1390 Gower *Conf.* II. 175 So dede in the same wise Of Rome faire Neabole, Which liste hire bodi to rigole.

† **Rigolice.** *Obs. rare*—°. [ad. F. *regolisse*, obs. var. of *réglisse*.] Liquorice.

1580 Hollyband *Treas. Fr. Tong*, *Ragalice, regalice*, or *riglice*, rigolice.

Rigoll, obs. f. Regal *sb.*[2]

‖ **Rigor** (rəi·gǫɹ, ri·gǫɹ). *Path.* Also 5 **rigoor.** [L. *rigor* numbness, stiffness, related to *rigēre* to be stiff, *rigidus* Rigid *a.*]

1. A sudden chill, *esp.* one accompanied with fits of shivering which immediately precedes certain fevers and inflammations. (Cf. Rigour 7.)

c 1400 *Lanfranc's Cirurg.* 120 A rigor is no þing ellis, but as it were a prickynge of nedelis, or ellis of netlis in þe fleisch, & if þis rigor come wiþ a feuere, or ellis without feuere, it is þe worste signe tokene of deeþ. 1615 Crooke *Body of Man* 76 If it be goaded by any sharpe humor, it causeth a rigor or shivering. 1693 tr. *Blancard's Phys. Dict.* (ed. 2), *Rigor*, a Vibration and Concussion of the Skin and Muscles of the whole Body, accompanied with Chilness. 1732 Arbuthnot *Rules of Diet* in *Aliments*, etc. I. 261 Extreme Cold stimulates, producing first a Rigor, and then a glowing Heat. 1776–84 Cullen *First Lines Physic* I. i. Wks. 1827 I. 483 The patient's sense of cold increasing, produces a tremor in all his limbs, with frequent succussions, or rigors of the trunk. 1822–34 *Good's Study Med.* (ed. 4) I. 698 It may be employed at the very onset of the fevers during the rigors. 1899 *Allbutt's Syst. Med.* VIII. 936, I have also observed five cases of rigors..occurring immediately after an injection of serum.

attrib. 1898 P. Manson *Trop. Diseases* ii. 50 The rigor stage is relatively less marked.

2. *Rigor mortis*, the stiffening of the body following upon death.

1839–47 Todd *Cycl. Anat.* III. 524/1 Passive contraction is a vital act, for it ceases with the *rigor mortis*. 1873 T. H. Green *Introd. Pathol.* (ed. 2) 13 The more healthy and vigorous this [nutrition of the muscles] is,..the longer it is before the rigor mortis supervenes.

Rigor, variant of Rigour.

† **Rigo·rious,** *a. Obs. rare.* [Alteration of Rigorous *a.*] Fierce, stern, severe.

1509 Hawes *Past. Pleas.* I. (Percy Soc.) 10 He brake first horses wilde and rigorious. *a* 1548 Hall *Chron.*, *Hen. VIII*, 160 b, The Almaynes..demaunded money of hym, in suche rigoriouse manier, that he was fayne..to flee.

Hence † **Rigo·riously** *adv. Obs. rare.*

a 1533 Ld. Berners *Huon* lxxxi. 247 He began to speke rygoryously to haue occacyon of some stryfe betwene vs. 1535 Fisher *Wks.* (1876) 373 And yet he..did not..reuenge him selfe vppon you rigoriously.

Rigorism (ri·gŏriz'm). Also **rigourism.** [f. L. *rigor* Rigour + -ISM. Cf. F. *rigorisme*, Sp. and Pg. *rigorismo*.]

1. The principles and practice of a rigorist; austerity, stringency; extreme strictness.

1704 *Gentl. Instructed* VI. iii. (ed. 2) 124 Your Morals have a Flavour of Rigorism. 1716 M. Davies *Athen. Brit.* II. 253 Biam'd for too great a Rigorism in their over zealous Orthodoxy against the Arians. 1860 W. G. Ward *Nat. & Grace* I. 353 [The Church] has been no less watchful against any intrusion of rigorism and harshness. 1875 Lightfoot *Coloss. & Phil.* (1876) 98 She [Phrygia] was the mother of Montanist enthusiasm, and the foster-mother of Novatian rigorism. 1896 *Academy* 22 Feb. 150/3 The sermons are remarkable for their uncompromising rigorism.

2. *R. C. Theol.* The doctrine of the rigorist school of moral theology.

1882 *Encycl. Brit.* XIV. 636/1 The line he draws is not.. an intermediate one between rigorism and laxity.

Rigorist (ri·gŏrist). Also **rigourist.** [f. as prec. + -IST. Cf. F. *rigoriste*, Sp. *rigorista*.]

1. One who favours or insists upon the severest or strictest interpretation or enforcement of a law, precept, principle, or standard of any kind.

1714 Mandeville *Fab. Bees* (1733) II. p. xx, He had a strong aversion to rigorists of all sorts. 1789 Bentham *Princ. Legisl.* ii. § 8 Those deluded rigorists who..first laid themselves under that idle obligation by a vow. 1804 *Edin. Rev.* III. 405 The propositions may appear exceptionable ..to the rigorists in geometry. 1823 *New Monthly Mag.* VII. 33, I am apt to doubt the virtue of an obtrusive Puritan and rigourist. 1882 Farrar *Early Chr.* II. 64 If they were rigorists in the minutiæ of Levitism instead of examples of ideal righteousness.

attrib. 1876 Plummer tr. *Döllinger's Hippolytus & Callistus* 237 Origen..shared the rigorist principles of Hippolytus. 1890 [see Laxist].

2. *R. C. Theol.* One who holds that in doubtful cases of conscience the strict course is always to be followed. Also *attrib.*

1715 M. Davies *Athen. Brit.* I. Pref. 65 Of the Popish Church-Rigorists and Laxarists. 1768 Maclaine tr. *Mosheim's Eccl. Hist.* (ed. 2) IV. 379 The Jansenists are not undeservedly branded by their adversaries with the denomination Rigourists. 1864 Newman *Apologia* (1865) 276 A priest might write a treatise which was really lax on the subject of lying,..and yet in his own person be a rigorist. 1882 *Encycl. Brit.* XIV. 637/1 When such a text-book.. comes to be ranked amongst rigorist works.

† **Rigoro·sity.** *Obs.*—[1] In 6 **rugorosyte.** [ad. med.L. *rigorōsitas* (Du Cange): see next and -ITY.] Austerity, rigour.

c 1531 Boorde *Let.* in *Introd. Knowl.* (1870) 47, I am nott able to byd þe rugorosyte off your relygyon.

Rigorous (ri·gŏrəs), *a.* Also 5 **ryger-, rygour-, rygor-**; 5 **regor-, rigur-,** 5–6 **riger-,** 6 **rygur-,** 6–7 **rigourous**; 5 **-is,** 5–6 **-us**; 5 **-use,** 5–6 **-ouse.** [a. OF. *rigorous* (mod.F. *rigoureux*), = Sp., Pg., It. *rigoroso*, med.L. *rigorōsus*: see Rigour and -ous.]

1. Characterized by rigour; rigidly severe or unbending; austere, harsh, stern; extremely strict: **a.** Of laws, procedure, etc.

c 1380 Wyclif *Sel. Wks.* II. 346 Þis lawe hadde þree parties; ..þe secounde part.., ȝif it be to rigorous,..shal ceesse on sutil maner. *c* 1430 Lydg. *Min. Poems* (Percy Soc.) 163 Lat mercy modefie rigerous correccioun. 1483 *Rolls of Parlt.* VI. 250/1 To forbere the said rigorouse punysshement. *a* 1533 Ld. Berners *Huon* lxv. 222 Fynde sum rygurus wordes to hym, & make as though ye were dyspleasyd with hym. 1590 Shaks. *Com. Err.* I. i. 9 Our well-dealing Countrimen..Haue seal'd his rigorous statutes with their bloods. 1657 *Penit. Conf.* vii. 188 As the injunction itself is too rigorous, so the limitation is too ridiculous. 1678 Butler *Hud.* III. *Lady's Answ.* 333 Nor can the rigourousest Course Prevail, unless to make us worse. 1748 *Anson's Voy.* II. vi. 197 He,..far from insisting on a rigorous equivalent,..might be satisfied with some live cattle. 1781 Gibbon *Decl. & F.* xxvii. (1787) III. 54 The rigorous conditions of peace and pardon were accepted. 1816 W. Duncan *Sel. Orat. Cicero* iii. 101 He is searching for the most rigorous precedents. 1863 Geo. Eliot *Romola* II. ii, He wanted a refuge from a standard disagreeably rigorous.

b. Of persons.

c 1430 Lydg. *Minor Poems* (Percy Soc.) 81 A rigorous juge..Withe hate and rancour dothe his vertu dresse. 1456 Sir G. Haye *Law Arms* (S.T.S.) 243 Gif a king be a rigorous man, and wele sett to kepe law and justice, is nane so grete bot he will sare drede till offend him. 1509 Hawes *Past. Pleas.* xxxIII. (Percy Soc.) 162 There is a gyaunte bothe fyerce and rygorous That wyth his might shall hym soune overthrowe. 1577 tr. *Bullinger's Decades* (1592) 186 Jehu a verie iust, although a rigourous prince. 1649 N. Bacon *Disc. Govt. Eng.* II. xxii. (1739) 102 Coming in by the people's favour, he was obliged to be rather remiss than rigorous. 1685 Baxter *Paraphr. N. T.* 1 Tim. iii. 3 A Bishop must be..one that by lenity taketh all things in the best sense, and is not rigorous. 1776 Sir D. Dalrymple *Annals Scotl.* I. 148 Adam Bishop of Caithness, a rigorous exacter of Tithes. 1780 Johnson *Let. to Mrs. Thrale* 4 July, I..hope she will not be too rigorous with the young ones.

2. Of the weather, etc.: Severe; bitterly cold. † Of heat: Excessive, violent (*obs.*).

1513 More in Grafton *Chron.* (1568) II. 705 Beyng letted for lacke of prosperous wind, and encombered with so much rigorous tempest. 1604 Drayton *Moses Map Mirac.* 13 If the fleet winde by some rigorous gale Seem'd to be mou'd. 1630 *R. Johnson's Kingd. & Commw.* 3 All moderne Navigators, who..have found..the regions situated under the Tropikes to bee tormented with more rigourous heat. 1647 Cowley *Mistr.*, *Bathing* iv, When rigorous Winter binds you up with Frost. 1748 *Anson's Voy.* I. i. 9 The delays.. confined his passage round Cape Horn to the most rigorous season of the year. 1774 Pennant *Tour Scotl. in 1772*, 175 The cold is very rigorous. 1867 Lyell *Princ. Geol.* III. xxxix. (1875) II. 361 These excursions usually precede a rigorous winter. 1896 Workman *Algerian Mem.* 159 The climate is more rigorous than that of the coast.

3. Scrupulous, unswerving, strict. *rare.*

1641 Milton *Reform.* II. Wks. 1851 III. 47 Well knows every wise Nation that their Liberty consists in manly and honest labours, in sobriety and rigorous honour to the Marriage Bed. 1847 Mrs. Jameson *Sacr. & Legendary Art* (1850) 193 Leading a life of such rigorous abstinence that his health sank under it.

4. Severely exact, rigidly accurate.

1651 Hobbes *Leviath.* I. viii. 34 In Demonstration..and all rigourous Search of Truth, Judgement does all. 1659 Pearson *Creed* (1839) 327 Not if it be taken in a strict, rigorous, proper, and formal sense. 1732 Berkeley *Alciphr.* IV. § 2 Truth and convenience are very different things to the rigorous eye of a philosopher. 1774 Mitford *Ess. Harmony Lang.* 273 The short syllables shortened without regard to their rigorous natural value. 1795 Ld. Auckland *Corr.* (1862) III. 301 Many members insist on a rigorous account of the debt by a secret committee. 1838 Emerson *Lit. Ethics* Wks. (Bohn) II. 214, I think that we have need of a more rigorous scholastic rule. 1879 Thomson & Tait *Nat. Phil.* I. I. § 89 The second order of infinitely small quantities may be with rigorous accuracy neglected.

† **5.** Accompanied by rigors. *Obs.*—[1]

1579 Langham *Gard. Health* (1633) 474 Drinke the root with wine against the rigorous fits of old feuers.

Ri·gorously, *adv.* [f. prec. + -LY [2].]

1. With rigour or severity.

1375 Barbour *Bruce* IV. 88 To the castell [they] went in hy, And assegit it rygorusly. *Ibid.* VI. 136 He smat the first sa rygorusly Vith his spere. *c* 1407 Lydg. *Reson & Sens.* 6628 Rygorously to denovnce Hys curse vpon the folkys all Which that in the sentence fall. 1442 in *Proc. Council Irel.* (Rolls) 276 He hath so rigorously entreted your pouere people of your said londe. 1484 Caxton *Fables of Alfonce* xiii, The mayster came to his seruaunt Medius and rygorously sayd to hym [etc.]. 1509 Barclay *Shyp of Folys* (1570) 126 Justice ought to be wayed..By egall measure, all fauour set aside, Not rigorously for..displeasaunce. 1576 Fleming *Panoplie Epist.* 280 Some..plucked their haires up by the rootes most rigorously. 1604 E. G[rimstone] *D'Acosta's Hist. Indies* v. xvii. 374 They did whip themselves rigorously in the maner aforesaid. *a* 1661 Fuller *Worthies* (1840) II. 508 It brake his heart, that the queen..rigorously demanded the present payment of some arrears. 1788 Gibbon *Decl. & F.* lxiv. VI. 311 The tribute was rigorously collected. 1803 Mackintosh *Def. Peltier* Wks. 1846 III. 295 The horrible consequences of enforcing rigorously principles of law..against political writers. 1867 Smiles *Huguenots Eng.* x. (1880) 158 The provisions of the Edict of Revocation were rigorously put in force.

b. Without any exception or allowance.

1858 Carlyle *Fredk. Gt.* XIV. iii. (1865) V. 179 As a primary measure, Belleisle keeps those orders of his rigorously secret. 1885 *Law Times Rep.* LIII. 319/2 An ambulance station..from which the public is rigorously excluded. 1891 *Law Times* XCI. 21/2 The City Sittings..must be rigorously protected against the invasion of rubbish of this description.

2. Strictly, scrupulously.

1613 Purchas *Pilgrimage* II. xviii. (1614) 211 Their fast on the 17. of the fourth Moneth for the destruction of their Citie is rigorously kept. 1662 J. Davies tr. *Olearius' Voy. Ambass.* 26 The Fast which the Muscovites very rigorously observe before Christmas. 1750 *Student* I. 48 He is.. rigorously just in discharging the duties of his station. 1792 Burke *Corr.* (1844) IV. 23 We must do right, and do it simply and rigorously, and trust to Providence for the rest. 1859 Geo. Eliot *A. Bede* xi, She was too rigorously truthful for benevolent invention. 1866 Liddon *Div. Our Lord* i. (1875) 40 The worship of Christ is rigorously due to Our Lord from all Christians.

3. With severe or close accuracy; exactly.

1651 Hobbes *Leviath.* II. xxv. 133 He may interrupt him, and examine his reasons more rigorously. 1662 J. Davies tr. *Olearius' Voy. Ambass.* 394 To speak rigorously, there is no haven in those parts. 1748 Hartley *Observ. Man* I. iii. 365 They ought always to be defined, the Definitions rigorously kept to. 1794 G. Adams *Nat. & Exp. Philos.* IV. xlv. 242 When therefore the motion of two bodies..is considered rigorously, the central body should not be regarded as fixed. 1834 Mrs. Somerville *Connex. Phys. Sci.* xvi. (1840) 152 They have been predicted and computed rigorously by the laws of mechanics. 1879 Thomson & Tait *Nat. Phil.* I. I. 498 A solution which will be more and more nearly rigorously correct the oftener we pass it through the machine.

† **4.** In literal sense: Stiffly. *Obs.*—[1]

c 1425 *Found. St. Bartholomew's* (E. E. T. S.) 45 The extremyteis of his fyngers were so rigorisly contracte in the synowys that he myght vnneith put mete to his moweth.

Ri·gorousness. [f. as prec. + -NESS.] Rigorous action, procedure, or temper; rigour.

1526 *Pilgr. Perf.* (W. de W. 1531) 54 Yf our iustyce begyn to extende it selfe so farre that it turne in to inordynate zele or rygorousnes,..temper it with mercy. 1542 *Lament. & Piteous Treatise* in *Harl. Misc.* (Malh.) I. 245 Whiche tempest vsed no lesse rygorousnes with the shippes of the Rhodyans. 1642 H. More *Song of Soul* I. III. xv, Oppression-of-the-poore, Fell-rigourousnesse. 1694 Kettlewell *Comp. Penitent* 31 The Rigorousness and Unrelenting hardness of my own Dealings towards them. 1882–3 Schaff *Encycl. Rel. Knowl.* 2324 The rigorousness, not to say cruelty, with which he enforced his various measures against image-worship.

† **Rigorousté.** *Obs.* Also 5 **rigorousete, rigourstee.** [See Rigorous *a.* and -TY.] Rigour.

1399 *Rolls of Parlt.* III. 452/1 If it were so taken and construed to the beghest sentence and most rigorouste. ? *c* 1470 G. Ashby *Active Policy* 502 Vndur drede of the lawe is Rigourstee. *Ibid.* 804 Ye shul moe people hertis conquere Bi compassion..Than bi crueltee, & rigoroussete.

Rigot(t, variants of Riggot [2].

Rigour (ri·gəɹ). Forms: 4–6 **rygour(e,** 6 **r(e)ygur,** 5–7 **rygor** (5 **-ore**); 5–6 **rigoure** (5 **rigur**), 4– **rigour,** 4–9 (now *U.S.*) **rigor.** [a. OF. *rigor, rigour* (13th c.; mod.F. *rigueur*), = Sp. and Pg. *rigor*, It. *rigore*, ad. L. *rigor* Rigor.]

I. 1. Severity in dealing with a person or persons; extreme strictness; harshness.

c 1386 Chaucer *Frankl. T.* 47 Pacience..venquysseth.. Thynges þat rigour sholde neuere atteyne. 14.. in *Tundale's Vis.* (1843) 97 Sothfast kyng..To repentaunt by rygour not vengeable. *c* 1460 Sir R. Ros *La Belle Dame* 720 What vayleth you to schew so gret rygour? 1495 *Act* 11 *Hen. VII*, c. 2 Preamble, Of his pitie intending to reduce theym theruntto by softer meanes then by such extreme rigour. 1555 Eden *Decades* (Arb.) 193 Their rygour and fiercenesse ageynst suche as stoobernly contemned them. 1597 Hooker *Eccl. Pol.* v. lxxvi. § 8 If..they haue tempered rigour with lenitie. *a* 1648 Digby *Voy. Medit.* (Camden) 30 Such is the effect of gentlenesse and faire wordes after rigour vpon a iust ground, with the vulgar. 1690 Locke *Gov.* II. vi. § 67 There is little Fear that Parents should use their Power with too much Rigor. 1757 in Ellis *Orig. Lett.* Ser. II. IV. 395 Some of high rank in the Navy..declare they will not serve under the rigor of so hard and unequitable a law. 1776 Gibbon *Decl. & F.* vii. (1782) I. 226 The rigour of the one was tempered by the other's clemency. 1822 Scott *Peveril* viii, His rights as a creditor, he had hitherto used with gentleness; but if he should employ rigour [etc.]. 1878 Macdonald *Ann. Q. Neighb.* xii, Rigour was past, and tenderness had not come.

b. An instance of this; a harsh or severe action or proceeding.

a 1548 Hall *Chron.*, *Edw. IV*, 16 b, This was a greate rigor and extremitie, for the seruaunt to vse agaynst the Master. 1578 Fenton *Guicciard.* I. (1618) 50 The remembrance of many rigors which his father Ferdinand had vsed against them. 1672 Marvell *Reh. Transp.* I. 33 At that time the Ecclesiastical Rigours here were in the highest ferment. *a* 1734 North *Examen* I. iii. § 164 Many affect Rigors, and will apply them in all Cases, but of themselves and their Partisans. 1786 Burke *Art. agst. W. Hastings* Wks. II. 122 All the rigours practised upon the chief ministers..being found ineffectual. 1847 Emerson *Repr. Men, Napoleon*, Those who smarted under the immediate rigours of the new monarch, pardoned them. 1874 S. Cox *Pilgr. Ps.* 107 By the rigours of bondage they might be constrained to repent.

2. The strict terms, application, or enforcement *of* some law, rule, etc.

1427 *Rolls of Parlt.* V. 409/2 That thenne the rygour of the Statut be executed. *c* 1430 Lydg. *Minor Poems* (Percy Soc.) 77 Almesdede shal make acheuisaunce, T'exclude by grace the rigour of vengeaunce. 1489 Caxton *Faytes of A.* III. xxi. 221 Suche a man..ought not to be spared, but al rygoure of rudnesse be doon to hym. 1552 Abp. Hamilton *Catech.* (1884) 25, I haif determit to use agains thame the rigour of jugement. 1620 Heywood *Gold. Age* I. i, One louely boy Hath felt the rigor of that strict decree. 1673 *Essex P.* (Camden) 89 Should there be any Lands of yᵉ Northumberland family wᶜʰ, in rigor of law, revert to yᵉ Crowne upon yᵉ failure of an Heir Male. 1791 Burke *App. Whigs* Wks. 1808 VI. 9 They never intended to execute those declarations in their rigour. 1821 Lamb *Elia* I. *Mrs. Battle's opinions on whist*, A clear fire, a clean hearth, and the rigour of the game. 1837 Carlyle *Fr. Rev.* III. I. ii.

Let 'Domiciliary visits', with rigour of authority, be made to this end.

b. *esp.* in phr. *the (..) rigour of the law.*

1479 *Paston Lett.* III. 239 To shew un to yow the rigur of the lawe. 1553 T. Wilson *Rhet.* 58 b, With mercie to mitigate all rigor of the lawe. 1593 Shaks. *2 Hen. VI*, I. iii. 199, I doe beseech your Royall Maiestie. Let him haue all the rigor of the Law. 1637 R. Humphrey tr. *St. Ambrose* I. 18 Ful performance of duty according to the extreme rigour of the law. 1669 Sturmy *Mariner's Mag.* Summary N 2 b, Not to take the just rigour of the Law of England, ..but take reasonable satisfaction. 1831 in Picton *L'pool Munic. Rec.* (1886) II. 330 The party offending should..be proceeded with to the utmost rigour of the law.

† **c.** *ellipt.* in the same sense. *Obs.*

1456 Sir G. Haye *Law Arms* (S.T.S.) 88 Be the rygour he has tynt his hede. *Ibid.*, The prince..may do him sum favour that he be nocht all punyst be the rigour. 1700 *Pennsylv. Arch.* I. 137, I will have him proceeded against.. to yᵉ utmost Rigour. *a* 1715 Burnet *Own Time* (1724) II. 415 The setting fines on their husbands to the rigour would make all the estates of the country be at mercy.

† **3.** Hardness of heart; obduracy. *Obs.*—[1]

c 1460 *Play Sacram.* 822 Thowgh we haue be vnryghtfulle, forgyf vs our rygore.

4. Of weather or climate: Severity; extremity or excess of cold; † violence (of storms).

a 1548 Hall *Chron.*, *Hen. V*, 26 b, Such is the power of the wynd, and suche is the rigoure of the tempest. *Ibid.*, *Hen. VI*, 181 A Croune whiche did hang in the middell.., without touche of any creature, or rigor of wynd, sodainly fell doune. 1601 R. Johnson *Kingd. & Commw.* (1603) 147 The snowe..keeping it warme from the rigor of the frost. 1665 Boyle *Occas. Refl.* (1675) 67 In Winter, when it needs their shelter from the Rigors of that cold season. 1741–2 Gray *Agrip.* 109 The rigour Of bleak Germania's snows. 1771 *Ann. Reg.* 99/2 The present severity and extreme rigour of the weather is..very remarkable. 1851 Carlyle *Sterling* III. iv. (1872) 197 The rigours of spring were always dangerous to him in England. 1878 Bosw. Smith *Carthage* 209 From regions of Arctic rigour.

b. Extreme distress or hardship.

1769 *Charact.* in *Ann. Register* 13/2 By this time, the besieged endured the utmost rigour of famine. 1836 7 Dickens *Sk. Boz* (C. D. ed.) 223 Alleviating the rigour of her condition by pecuniary donations for her comfort.

5. Strictness *of* discipline, etc.; austerity of life; an instance of this.

c 1440 *Alph. Tales* 11 Sho..kepyd diligentlie emang hur susters þe rigur of disciplyne. 1526 *Pilgr. Perf.* (W. de W. 1531) 262 b, That it is impossyble for vs to perseuer and contynue in suche rygour & streytnesse of lyuyng. 1579 Lyly *Euphues* (Arb.) 79 Seeing I cannot by reason restraine your importunate suite, I will by rygour done on my selfe, cause you to refraine the meanes. 1674 Brevint *Saul at Endor* 223 The Holy Fathers did lay on him several Degrees of Rigors, before they would take him in again. 1684 Burnet tr. *More's Utopia* 91 To undergo much Pain, many Hardships, and other Rigours. 1705 Addison *Italy* 524 This Prince..liv'd in this Convent with all the Rigor and Austerity of a Capucin. 1833 L. Ritchie *Wand. by Loire* 130 The rigour of the monastic discipline speedily terminated her life.

b. Puritanic severity or strictness; rigorism; † an instance of this.

1597 *Dowland's First Bk. Songs* in Arb. *Garner* IV. 39 The ice of her indurate heart, Whose frozen rigour..Feels never any touch of my desert. 1634 Milton *Comus* 107 Rigor now is gon to bed, And Advice with scrupulous head, ..Age, and..Severity, With their grave Saws in slumber ly. 1650 Trapp *Comm. Deut.* ii. 5 It is therefore a rigour, to say, the wicked are usurpers of what they have. 1748 Richardson *Clarissa* (J.), Rigour makes it difficult for sliding virtue to recover. 1784 Cowper *Task* II. 321 What vice has it [satire] subdu'd? whose heart reclaim'd By rigour, or whom laugh'd into reform? 1835 Thirlwall *Greece* I. ix. 352 The emergencies of the war had induced the Spartans to relax the rigour of their principles.

6. Strict accuracy, severe exactitude.

1565 Cooper *Thesaurus* s.v. *Accipio*, *Ad verbum accipere*, to take the rigour of the woorde: to take the woorde as it lyeth. 1594 R. Parsons *Confer. Success.* I. vi. 132 As this man in rigour is not truly mayor,..nor the other is properly Emperor. *a* 1614 Donne *Βιαθανατος* (1644) 127 Our soule..in rigour is murdered by every sinne consented unto. *a* 1665 J. Goodwin *Filled w. the Spirit* (1867) 215 This word, in the rigour of the grammatical signification of it, is not always used for interceding for another. 1774 Mitford *Ess. Harmony Lang.* 271 Either the value of the syllable is taken with the utmost rigor, or with latitude. 1836–7 Sir W. Hamilton *Metaph.* iii. (1877) I. 61 Sciences which the term philosophy exclusively denotes, when employed in propriety and rigour. 1879 Thomson & Tait *Nat. Phil.* I. I. § 77 Hence we may with perfect rigour conclude that even the extreme case..is included in the general theorem.

II. 7. = Rigor 1.

1541 Elyot *Cast. Helthe* 48 In palseys, or apoplexies, or agaynst the rigour, whiche hapneth in feuers. 1543 Traheron tr. *Vigo's Chirurg.* 96 b/1 Whyche cause rigours, fieuers, spasmes. 1676 Wiseman *Surg. Treat.* VI. App. ii. 444 The Part is first benummed,..and a Horrour and Rigour seizeth upon the Patient. 1754 Smellie *Midwifery* III. 180 A fever intervened, with irregular horrors and rigours. 1776 Sir G. Baker in E. S. Thompson *Influenza* (1890) 80 Some few had, in the beginning, successive rigours. 1890 Stevenson *Let. to Dr. Scott* 20 Jan., I find it at once produces a glow, stops rigour.

transf. 1859 Sala *Gaslight & D.* xxvi. 297 Shall the young lady in the apartment next to mine string my nerves into the rigours?

† **8.** Of material objects: Stiffness, hardness. *Obs.*

1578 Banister *Hist. Man* VII. 90 That so, the outer might defend the inner Membran..from the rigour of the ribbes. 1667 Milton *P. L.* x. 297 The rest his look Bound with Gorgonian rigor not to move. 1700 Dryden *Ovid's Met.* I. 539 The stones..Did first the rigour of their kind expel, And suppled into softness as they fell.

† **Ri·gourest,** obs. form of superl. to Rigorous *a.*

a 1653 Gouge *Comm. Heb.* vi. § 42 They disgrace his Gospel; they persecute his members, and that in the sorest and rigourest manner that they can.

Rig-out. *colloq.* [f. Rig *v.*[2] 3 b.] An outfit; a suit of clothes; a costume. (Cf. Rig *sb.*[6] 2.)

1823 Moncrieff *Tom & Jerry* I. iv, This toggery of yours will never fit—you must have a new rig-out. 1834 Medwin *Angler in Wales* I. 28 A rig-out enough to frighten all the fish out of their skins. 1874 W. Simpson *Meeting the Sun* xxiii. 313 An Inverness cape and a Glengarry bonnet is a favourite rig-out with many.

† **Rigruff.** *Obs.*—° (See quot.)

1611 Cotgr., *Mal mort*, a running scab, or thicke morphew, which couering all ouer the vlcers that bee vnder it, seemes wholly dead: Some Northerne people call it, the Rigruffe (in beasts).

Ri·gsby. Also 6 **rigby.** Now *dial.* [Cf. Rig *sb.*[4] and *v.*[4], and see -BY 2.] A wanton; a romping lad or lass.

1546 Langley tr. *Pol. Verg. de Invent.* VII. vi. 140 These ..be so light fingered and suche rigbies Children that they wil fynde two thynges, afore they lose one. 1607 R. C[arew] tr. *Estienne's World of Wonders* A 2 Here dwels that towring and terrible Nimrod, that hunting rigsby Semiramis. 1691 Ray *N. C. Words* (ed. 2) 59 A Reuling Lad; a Rigsby. 1814 Pegge *Suppl. Grose*, *Rigsby*, a romping girl. York. 1838 Holloway *Prov. Dict.*, *Rigsby*, a hoyden. 1877 *Holderness Gloss.*, *Rigsby*, a romping child.

Rigsdollar, obs. form of Rix-dollar.

Rig-up: see Rig *sb.*[6] 2.

Rig-veda (rig₁vē·dă). Also 8 **Reig Beid**; 8–9 **Rigvéda.** [Skr. *rigveda*, f. *ric* praise + *veda* knowledge: see Veda.] The principal of the Vedas or sacred books of the Hindus.

1776 Halhed *Gentoo Laws* Pref. p. xxxii, The Style of this Writer is clear, but very concise; a Specimen of it is here offered, in his Explanation of the first chapter of the Reig Beid. 1788 *Asiatic Res.* I. 340 The Rigvéda consists of five sections. 1796 Sir W. Jones tr. *Inst. Hindu Law* 104 The Rigvéda is held sacred to the gods. 1805 *Asiatic Res.* VIII. 374 Tradition, preserved in the Purāṇas, reckons sixteen Sanhitas of the Rigvéda. 1840 H. H. Wilson *Oxford Lect.* I. 5 The text also..of one of the Vedas, the Rig-Veda, has been printed. 1899 Monier-Williams *Sanskrit-English Dict.* Introd. p. xxi, Vedic literature begins with the Rig-veda (probably dating from about 1200 or 1300 B.C.).

transf. 1895 Salmond *Doctr. Immort.* I. v. 80 These ancient Accadian hymns, which Lenormant has named the Chaldæan Rig-Veda.

Ri·gwiddy. *Sc.* († and *north.*) Forms: 5 **rygwythi,** 5 **rigwethy,** 6, 8 **-widdy** (9 **-widdie, -wuddie**), 8–9 **rigwoodie.** [f. Rig *sb.*[1] + Withy: cf. next.] A back-band or ridge-band for a carthorse, orig. one made of twisted withes or twigs.

1419–20 *Durh. Acc. Rolls* (Surtees) 407 In reparacione sellarum, frenorum..et j rygwythi. *Ibid.* 636, j Crowpour, j rigwethy novum. 1513 *Acc. Ld. High Treas.* IV. 514 For xxiiij stane of towis to be thetis, soumes and rigwiddeis. 1709 *Rec. Elgin* (New Spalding Cl.) I. 381 Ilk dozen rigwoodies, 2*d.* 1752 *Ibid.* I. 465 Sowms, thramels, rigwoodies, tethers, wallropes, thrawn wawns and all other wood or work of wood, straw, bent or rushes. 1799 J. Robertson *Agric. Perth* 100 What are called coup-carts, i. e. when..the contents can be discharged, without lifting the shafts or rig-widdy. 1808 Jamieson s.v., The rigwiddie, in the Highlands, is to this day made of twisted twigs of oak. 1894 Latto *T. Bodkin* ix, A cadger bodie..gettin's rigwoodie mendit.

b. *attrib.* as an abusive epithet.

1790 Burns *Tam O'Shanter* 160 Wither'd beldams, auld and droll, Rigwoodie hags, wad spean a foal. 1828 Buchan *Rigwoodie Carlin* i, Faer ye gaun, ye rigwoodie carlin? *c* 1860 W. Anderson in Edwards *Mod. Scot. Poets* (1881) II. 236 A rigwoodie deil was Jean Findlater's loon.

† **Rigwith(e.** *Obs.* [f. Rig *sb.*[1] + Withe *sb.* Cf. *ridgewith* s.v. Ridge *sb.*[1] 8.] = prec.

c 1340 *Nominale* (Skeat) 880 *Dosser, biletz de fut*..Rigwith, dractepynnes. 14.. *Lat. Eng. Voc.* in Wr.-Wülcker 593 *Limo*, a rygwythe. 1570 Levins *Manip.* 150 A Rigwith, *dorsualis*.

Riht(e, obs. ff. Right. **Rihȝe:** see Reigh.
Riif(e, Rijf,e, obs. ff. Rife. **Rijp,** obs. f. Reap *sb.*[2], Ripe *a.* **Rik(e,** obs. or dial. f. Reke *sb.*[1], *v.*[1] **Rike,** *sb.*, kingdom: see Riche.

† **Rike,** *v. Obs. rare.* [ad. ON. *rikja*, f. *riki* kingdom.] *intr.* To reign.

a 1300 *E. E. Psalter* xcii. 1 Lauerd riked; fairhed schred he to se. *Ibid.* xcv. 9 Þat god riked, in genge sai yhe.

Rike, Sc. var. Reach *v.*[1] **Rikelot:** see Kikelot. **Rikels,** var. Rekels *Obs.* **Riken(i,** obs. ff. Reckon *v.* **Riksha,** var. Ricksha(w.

‖ **Rilawa** (ri·lāwā). *Zool.* [Cingalese *rilawā*: cf. Rillow.] The Toque Macaque (*Macacus pileatus*) of Ceylon.

1859 Sir J. E. Tennent *Ceylon* I. 129 The little graceful grimacing *rilawa*..is the universal pet and favourite of both natives and Europeans. 1897 H. O. Forbes *Handbk. Primates* II. 35 Knox, in his interesting account of the island, gives an accurate description of the Rilawas.

Rile (rəil), *sb.* [var. of Roil *sb.*[2]] A thick or muddy condition of water or other liquid.

1848 Lowell *Biglow P.* Ser. I. Poems 1890 II. 124 'T 'll take more fish-skin than folks think to take the rile clean out on't. 1859 Beecher *Life Thoughts* Ser. II. 7 The muddy bottom sends its rile through all the waters.

Rile, dial. variant of Roil *sb.*[1] and *v.*[1]

Rile (rəil), *v.* Chiefly *U.S.* and *colloq.* Also **ryle.** [Later form of Roil *v.*[2]]

1. *trans.* To make (a liquid) thick or turbid by stirring up the sediment; to muddy.

1838 Holloway *Prov. Dict.*, To *rile* or *roile*, to stir up liquor and make it thick by moving the sediment. 1838 J. C. Neal *Charcoal Sketches* (Bartlett), No doubt existed in the minds of Mr. Dobb's fellow-boarders, that the well of his good spirits had been riled. 1896 *Strand Mag.* XII. 348/2 At spring tides the water becomes too 'riled-up' to dive with any degree of success.

2. To excite, disturb, to vex, annoy, make angry.

1825 J. Neal *Bro. Jonathan* I. 158 Bein' afeared he might ryle my blood. 1836 Haliburton *Clockm.* Pref. (1862) 7 Fair play's a jewel, and I must say I feel ryled and kinder sore. 1850 Smedley *F. Fairleigh* viii, I like to rile Cumberland sometimes because he's so soft and silky. 1863 W. C. Baldwin *Afr. Hunting* vii. 273 It riles me to hear them everlastingly talking of getting home. 1889 R. Buchanan *Heir of Linne* xxi, Don't get riled.

b. *absol.* with *up.* To get angry.

1844 Dickens *Mart. Chuz.* xvi, They rile up, sometimes; but in general we have a hold upon our citizens. 1863 Brierley *Waverlow* 156 The little fellow riled up at this.

Hence **Riled** *ppl. a.* (Cf. Roiled *ppl. a.*)

1839 J. Very *Poems* 163, I thirst for one cool cup of water clear, But drink the riled stream of lying breath.

Riley (rəi·li), *a. U.S.* Also **ryley, rily.** [f. prec. + -Y: cf. Roily *a.*]

1. Thick, turbid, muddy.

1825 J. Neal *Bro. Jonathan* I. 369 A gallon o' ryley water ..right out o' the spring. 1828 Cunningham *N. S. Wales* II. 55 An American landlord brought in a jug of water, and apologised for its being so riley. 1850 Pangborn *Diary* in *Amer. Hist. Rev.* (1903) IX. 105 Got more black rily Coffee and eat sea Bread. 1861 Catlin *Life among Indians* 16 The mud and water in the 'Lick' still riley with their recent steps.

2. Angry; irritable, bad-tempered.

1847 Robb *Squatter Life* 64 (Bartlett), The boys and gals were laughin' at my scrape.., that I gin to get riley. 1867 *Blackw. Mag.* Oct. 404 The Americans..speak of an ill-tempered person as being riley. 1872 De Vere *Americanisms* 534 An ill-tempered, cross-grained person is apt to be called 'a rily fellow'.

Rilievo, variant of Relievo.

Riligioun, obs. form of Religion.

Riling (rəi·liŋ), *ppl. a. colloq.* [f. Rile *v.*[2]] Annoying, aggravating.

1870 Simmons *Oakdale Grange* 291 You know it's such a riling thing to have said of one. 1894 F. S. Ellis *Reynard Fox* 212 But was it not a little riling, To bear this infamous reviling?

Rill (ril), *sb.*[1] Also 6 **rylle,** 7 **ril(le.** [Agrees in form and meaning with mod.Du. and Fris. *ril*, LG. *ril, rille*, G. *rille*: the precise nature of the connexion is not clear.]

1. A small stream; a brook, runnel, rivulet.

1538 Leland *Itin.* (1768) I. 37 There is a rylle that cummith by the Towne. 1598 Stow *Surv.* 13 Diuers rilles or rillets to the Riuer of Thames. 1637 Milton *Lycidas* 24 We..Fed the same flock, by fountain, shade, and rill. 1694 Addison *Poems, Virgil* Misc. Wks. 1726 I. 17 And shallow rills run trickling through the grass. 1725 De Foe *Voy. round World* (1840) 253 Innumerable rills and brooks of water. 1784 Cowper *Task* I. 192 Rills that slip Through the cleft rock. 1829 Lytton *Devereux* III. v, I have some remembrance of the green sod, and the silver rill. 1850 Tennyson *In Mem.* xxxvii, Go down beside thy native rill. 1878 Huxley *Physiogr.* 176 A mere rill of warm water running over the surface of the sea.

b. *transf.* and *fig.*

1698 Farquhar *Love & a Bottle* III. ii, Our knives cut passage clean Through rills of fat, and deluges of lean. 1704 Fuller *Med. Gymn.* (1711) 95 There must be a continual Rill of these temperate Juices into the Blood. 1784 Cowper *Task* IV. 64 Here rills of oily eloquence in soft Meanders lubricate the course they take. 1864 Lowell *Fireside Trav.* 214 The exiguous rill of a discourse. 1891 E. Peacock *N. Brendon* I. 85 His was a tiny rill of conversation, not a tidal wave of thought.

c. *attrib.* and *Comb.*, as *rill-mark, -way*; *rill-like* adj.; *rill-wise* adv.

1862 F. Hall *Hindu Philos. Syst.* 238 The water of a reservoir..enters the fields rillwise. 1863 Dana *Man. Geol.* 94 Rill-marks, mud-cracks, and rain-drop impressions. 1876 Meredith *Beauch. Career* xxxv, The ripple crease and rill-like descent of the turf. 1886 A. Winchell *Walks Geol. Field* 51 Obviously, the roadside slime has descended the rill-ways from the middle of the street. 1888 Dawson *Geol. Hist. Pl.* 32 The beautiful branching rill-marks produced by the oozing of water out of mud and sand-banks left by the tide.

2. A small narrow trench; a drill. Now *dial.*

1658 Evelyn *Fr. Gard.* (1675) 244 Lay them in the bottom of the rills. 1664 — *Sylva* 6 Immediately before you sow, cast, and dispose it [the ground] into Rills, or small narrow Trenches of four, or five inches deep. 1706 London & Wise *Retir'd Gard.* I. 314 To succeed in planting Anemones,.. draw a Rill from one End of the Bed to the other. 1725 *Family Dict.* s.v. *Candy-Tuft*, When you have drawn Rills Length-ways, and Cross-ways, you may sow the Seed. 1871 *W. Morning News* May (E.D.D.), Potatoes which were up in rills looking healthy and promising.

3. *Astr.* = Rille. Also *attrib.*

1888 J. A. W. Oliver *Astron.* 70 On the south-east of this bright little crater there is an easy rill. *Ibid.* 73 This ring-plain is associated with one of the most remarkable rill-systems on the moon.

† **Rill,** *sb.*[2] *Obs. rare*—°. In 5 **rylle.** [Of obscure origin.] (See quots.)

c 1440 *Promp. Parv.* 434/1 Rylle, thynne clothe, *ralla*. *Ibid.* 491/1 Thynne clothe, that ys clepyd a rylle, *ralla*.

Rill (ril), *v.*[1] [f. Rill *sb.*[1]]

1. *intr.* To flow in a small stream.

1610 [see the *ppl. a.*]. 1651 Biggs *New Disp.* ¶ 144 The profuse sweat, that rills through..the pores. *c* 1709 Prior *2nd Hymn Callim.* 153 The wholesome Draught from Aganippe's Spring..gently rilling Adown the Mountains. 1821 Clare *Vill. Minstr.* I. 106 May showers never fail.., Nor suns dry the fountain that rills by its side. 1855 Bailey *Mystic* 44 Time's sand-dry streamlet through its glassy strait Rilled restless. 1884 Sala in *Illustr. Lond. News* 30 Aug. 195 A small fountain rills from the rockwork.

2. *trans.* **a.** To form by flowing. **b.** To utter in liquid notes.

1845 Hood *Stag-eyed Lady* xiv, Then closed the wave, and then the surface rill'd A ring above her, like a water-knell. 188. Scollard *Summer Song* ii. (Funk), The brook is dry; its silver throat Rills song no more.

3. To make drills in (a garden bed). *rare*—[1].

1658 Evelyn *Fr. Gard.* (1675) 244 For this you may make use of the houe, rilling the bed where you would set them.

Hence **Ri·lling** *ppl. a.*

1610 W. Folkingham *Art of Survey* I. ii. 40 The grauelly colde of rilling fountaines. 1797 F. Baily *Tour* (1856) 260 Vortices, which..cause a rilling, murmuring sound. 1853 F. W. Newman *Odes of Horace* 207 What boy these cups of hot Falernian Tempers quick with rilling water?

† **Rill,** *v.*[2] *Obs.*—[1] In 5 **ryll.** (App. meaning 'to roar or bellow', but perhaps an error.)

c 1400 *Song of Roland* 421 Your knyghtis be-hind haue som bores fond, or Among the holtis I-herd ryll som hertis.

Rille (ril). *Astr.* [a. G. *rille*: see Rill *sb.*[1]] One of the long narrow trenches or valleys observed on the surface of the moon. (Cf. Rill *sb.*[1] 3.)

1868 Lockyer *Elem. Astron.* § 226 The rilles, of which 425 are now known, are trenches with raised sides more or less steep. 1878 — *Stargazing* 350 Hours may be spent in examining the craters, rilles, and valleys on the surface.

Rillet (ri·lėt). Also 6 **ryllet.** [f. Rill *sb.*[1] + -ET or -LET.] A small rill or rivulet; a brooklet.

1538 Leland *Itin.* (1769) V. 37 Ther cummith a litle Ryllet by this square Toure... There be other smaulle Ryllettys yn Molesdale. 1598 Stow *Surv.* 13 Diuers rilles or rillets to the Riuer of Thames. 1612 Drayton *Poly-olb.* i. 264 Those rillets that attend proud Tamer and her state. 1678 Hobbes *Decam.* v. 55 A thousand small Rillets of melting Snow fall down into it.

1830 Tennyson *Arab. Nts.* 48 From the green rivage many a fall Of diamond rillets musical. 1871 Meredith *H. Richmond* xlv, A single tent stood in a gully.., near an iron-red rillet. 1890 H. M. Stanley *Darkest Africa* I. ix. 223 A score of lazy, oozy rillets.

Comb. 1868 Browning *Ring & Bk.* x. 1476 Let the world's praise or blame run rillet-wise Off the broad back.

b. *transf.* and *fig.*

1621 Burton *Anat. Mel.* To Rdr. (1651) 14 This by-stream, which as a rillet, is deducted from the main chanel of my studies. 1626 Shirley *Brothers* I. i, Francisco and Fernando are two rillets from one spring. 1885 Meredith *Diana* II. xiii. 310 Then was heard such a rillet of dialogue..as nowhere else in Britain.

Rille·tt(e)s. [a. F. *rillettes* pl.] A tinned preparation of minced ham, chicken, fat, etc.

1896 *Southampton Times* 11 Jan. 6/1 Charged with stealing 4 lbs. of rillets. *Ibid.*, He identified the..tins of rilletts as the property of the company.

† **Ri·lling,** *sb. Sc. Obs.* Also 6 **relyng, ryll-ing.** [var. of Riveling [1]. Cf. Rullion.] A shoe made of undressed hide. Also *transf.*

1508 Dunbar *Flyting* 243 Rank beggar.., ruch rilling. 1513 Douglas *Æneis* VII. xii. 118 Ane rouch rylling of raw hyd and of hayr. 1535 Stewart *Cron. Scot.* III. 268 The Scottis..Tha rouch rillingis..behind thame than left thair. 1570 *Henry's Wallace* I. 219 Rouch rillingis [1489 rewlyngis] upon thi harlotis fete. *c* 1700 Kennet in *MS. Lansd.* 1033, fol. 323 b, The Scotch now call a Shoe that hath a sole with the hair to the ground a *Rough Rilling*.

Ri·lling, *vbl. sb. rare.* [f. Rill *v.*[1]] † The formation of a rill or runnel; a furrow or drill.

1610 W. Folkingham *Art of Survey* II. ii. 50 Dyking, drayning,..rilling, brooking, riuaging, foording. 1725 *Family Dict.* s.v. *Springs*, Smaller Fowl..that uses to feed in wet..Grounds, and amongst Water Furrows, or Rillings.

Ri·llock. *rare.* [f. Rill *sb.*[1] + -OCK.] A rillet.

1893 *Nat. Observer* 18 Nov. 17/2 She dabbled her feet in the rillock. 1903 R. M. Gilchrist *Beggar's Manor* 161 A stream—or rather a rillock—runs from end to end.

† **Ri·llow.** *Zool. Obs.* [ad. Cingalese *rilawā*, pl. *rilaw*.] = Rilawa. *Bonneted rillow*, the Bonnet Macaque of Southern India.

1681 R. Knox *Rel. Ceylon* vi. 26 This sort of Monkeys have no beards, white faces, and long hair on the top of their heads...They call these Rillowes. 1792 Kerr *Anim. Kingd.* 69 Rillow. *Ibid.*, Bonneted Rillow. 1797 *Encycl. Brit.* (ed. 3) XVII. 498/1 The rillow, cercopithecus sinicus, or Chinese bonnet...Inhabit[s] Ceylon.

Ri·lly, *a.* [f. Rill *sb.*[1]] Abounding in rills.

1727 in Bailey, vol. II. 1791 J. Learmont *Poems* 123 How sweet 's the windin's o' the rilly flood.

Rily: see Riley.

Rim, *sb.*[1] Forms: 1 **rimo, rima,** 5 **reme,** 5, 7, 9 **rime,** 6–7 **ryme**; 5–7 **rym,** 6 **rymme,** 7 **rimme,** 7–8 **rimb,** 7– **rim.** [OE. *rima* wk. masc., = ON. *rime, rimi* (Norw. *rime*) a raised strip of land, a ridge. There are app. no parallel forms in the other Teutonic languages.

The evidence for the OE. word chiefly rests on the compounds *dægrima* Day-rim, *sǽrima* Sea-rim, and *ticrima* gums. The *Corpus Gloss.* however has the entry '*Crepido*, rimo' (Hessels, C 898), which is repeated in a later vocabulary (*c* 1050, in Wr.-Wülcker 366) as '*Crepido*, rima'. In early ME. the evidence appears to be limited to *day-rim* and *sea-rim*, *wood-rim* in Laȝamon 740, and perhaps *way-rim* (text *weie reme*) in the *Prov. Ælfred* 617.]

1. The peripheral portion or outer ring of a wheel, connected with the nave or boss by spokes or by a web.

In wooden wheels the rim does not include the metal tyre protecting it. In the metal wheels of locomotives, cycles, or machinery it is usually grooved or flanged.

a 1400–50 *Alexander* 1850 We riden on þe rime [*v.r.* reme] & on þe ringe seten of þe qwele of Fortoun. *c* 1440 *Promp. Parv.* 434/1 Rym, of a whele, *timpanum, circumferencia*. 1513 Douglas *Æneis* XII. Prol. 162 The payntit povne.. Kest vp his taill, a provd plesand quheil rym. 1530 Palsgr. 263/1 Rymme of a whele or stabbe, *peav*. 1688 Holme *Armoury* III. 331/1 The Cart Wheel hath the Rim set with round Nails. 1704 J. Harris *Lex. Techn.* I, *Rim*, in a Watch or Clock, is the Circular part of the Ballance thereof. 1794 W. Felton *Carriages* (1801) I. 113 The patent wheel has the rim of one entire piece. 1873 Richards *Operator's Handbk.* 140 Procure pulleys of 30 to 36 inches diameter with 8 inches face, the rims heavy and turned true inside and out. 1886 *Cyclist Touring Cl. Gaz.* Dec. 474/2 A fairly deep rim is important. Whether the advantage of the hollow rim is paid for or not should depend a great deal on the character of the general riding.

b. The hoop-shaped piece of wood which forms the outer frame of a sieve, etc. Also *dial.* a hoop.

1660 *Bk. Rates* in *Stat. Realm* V. 196 Rims for Sives. 1674 Ray *Coll. Words* 122 The sand, earth and other dross, flows over the rimme of the sierce with the water. 1707 Mortimer *Husb.* (1721) II. 33 The Drum-maker uses it for Rimbs. 1844 Stephens *Bk. Farm* II. 281 A wheat-riddle of wood..with an oak rim. 1888 *Sheffield Gloss.* s.v., A child's hoop, used as a plaything, is called a *rim*.

c. A circular mark or object.

1860 Reade *Cloister & H.* lii, They have all the Dutch rim under their bright eyes, that comes of dwelling in eternal swamps. 1873 W. H. Dixon *Two Queens* III. XIII. iii. 18 He besought the king to crown his brother Henry with that golden rim.

2. *Naut.* The surface *of* the water.

1602 Carew *Cornwall* 106 In the hotest Summer weather, they swimme with the ryme of the water, and in the Winter, keepe the depth. 1622 R. Hawkins *Voy. S. Sea* (1847) 72 The sword fish placeth himselfe under the belly of the whale, and the thresher upon the ryme of the water. *Ibid.* 116. 1887 J. T. Brown in Goode *Fisheries of U.S.* II. 264 If the whale is swimming 'top-water', the harpooner has a better target to dart at; but if swimming under the 'rim of the water',..he must make the best use of his time.

3. The edge, border, or margin *of* an object, esp. one which has more or less of a circular form. Also *fig.* (quot. 1603).

1603 Breton *Dial. of Pithe & Pleasure* Wks. (Grosart) II. 13/1 By her that came out of him, euen a part of himselfe, the Rimme of his whole selfe. 1667 *Phil. Trans.* II. 437 The Sight of the Quadrant being slid along the Rimb of it. 1698 *Ibid.* XX. 112 The Verge or Rime of the outward Ear seem'd to be crimp'd. 1753 Chambers *Cycl. Suppl.* s.v. *Mushroom*, The rims of the tender umbels in these kinds clap themselves quite close to the stalks. 1768–74 Tucker *Lt. Nat.* (1834) II. 596 We..garnish the rims of our dishes with dabs of chewed greens. 1796 Withering *Brit. Plants* (ed. 3) I. 335 Anthers forming a hollow cylinder as long as the floret, with 5 teeth at the rim. 1817 Keats *I stood tip-toe* 113 The moon lifting her silver rim Above a cloud. 1855 Macaulay *Hist. Eng.* xxi. IV. 620 Few pieces were exactly round; and the rims were not marked. 1885 Watson & Burbury *Math. Electr. & Magn.* I. 137 The disc [becomes] a spherical bowl, whose rim is a circle at right angles to the axis. *Ibid.*, The colatitude of that rim.

b. The verge *of* the horizon, sea, hills, etc. Chiefly *poet.*

1842 Tennyson *Day-dream* 170 Across the hills, and far away Beyond their utmost purple rim. 1850 B. Taylor *Eldorado* i. (1862) 3 The far rim of the horizon seemed as if it would never break into an uneven line. 1858 Longf. *M. Standish* I. 56 The steel-blue rim of the ocean.

fig. 1862 'Shirley' (J. Skelton) *Nugæ Crit.* ii. 97 The desolate and unpeopled unknown which lies beyond the rim of our life. 1863 Tyndall *Heat* xiv. (1870) 502 Having exhausted science and reached its very rim.

4. An edge, margin, or border; *esp.* a raised or projecting one upon something having a circular form.

1669 Boyle *Contn. New Exp.* I. (1682) 165 A Wooden plug, ..furnished with a Rimme or Lip. 1824 R. Stuart *Hist. Steam Engine* 69 A projecting rim rising above the highest point to which the piston is elevated. 1832 H. Martineau *Life in Wilds* iii. 30 One little boy complained..that there was no rim to his plate. 1875 Darwin *Insectiv. Plants* xiv. 324 A narrow rim of the broad flat exterior part of each lobe is turned inwards. 1896 *Daily News* 19 Dec. 6/4 A rim of chinchilla finished the edges of this novel sleeve.

b. A verge or margin of land, sea, etc.; a narrow strip.

1781 Cowper *Hope* 49 The blue rim, where skies and mountains meet. 1833 Tennyson *Palace of Art* 75 The ragged rims of thunder brooding low. 1864 — *Aylmer's F.* 147 Where the brook Vocal, with here and there a silence, ran By sallowy rims. 1878 Huxley *Physiogr.* xv. 254 Inside the rim of land there is a shallow lake or lagoon.

fig. 1858 Froude *Hist. Eng.* xix. IV. 185 Having fringed the Tweed with a black broad mourning rim of havoc.

c. *Naut.* (See quot.)

c 1850 *Rudim. Navig.* (Weale) 141 *Rims*, those pieces which form the quarter-galleries between the stools. Also a cast-iron frame in which the dropping palls of a capstan traverse and bring up the capstan.

5. *Orkney dial.* A rocky bottom in the sea.

Cf. Norw. dial. *rimm* (*rimb*), *rimme*, = *rime* ridge.

1795 *Statist. Acc. Scotl.*, *Orkney*, *Birsay* XIV. 315 As to rocks, we have three of what we call rims, which are generally occupied by our fishermen as their best fishing grounds ..; the rim shoals deepen from 20 to 40 fathom, or upwards.

6. *Comb.*, as **rim-base** (see quots.); **rim-brake,** a brake operating on the rim of a wheel; **rim-cap** (see quot.); **rim-face,** the outer surface of a wheel-rim; **rim-fire,** of a cartridge, having the detonating substance disposed round the edge (opp. to *centre-fire*); hence of a gun, adapted for cartridges of this kind; **rim-ignition,** = prec.; **rim-iron,** iron intended to form the rim of a wheel; **rim-lock,** a lock having a metal case which stands out from the face of the door (opp. to *mortise-lock*); **rim-rock,** *U.S.* (see quot. 1882); **rim-shaft,** the shaft of a rim-wheel; **rim-wheel,** a fly-wheel.

1864 Webster, **Rimbase*, a short cylinder connecting a trunnion with the body of a cannon. 1867 Smyth *Sailor's Word-bk.*, *Rim-Base*, the shoulder on the stock of a musket. 1875 Knight *Dict. Mech.* 447/1 The trunnions.. support the gun on its carriage, the width of which is determined by the distance between the rim-bases. 1899 *Fortn. Rev.* LXV. 120 Of the *rim-brakes there are several varieties. 1884 Britten *Watch & Clockm.* 47 The *rim cap encloses the space between the plates or frame [of a watch]. 1863 P. Barry *Dockyard Econ.* 243 The fly-wheel is 25 feet in diameter, 15 inches broad on the *rim-face. 1868 *Rep. to Govt. U.S. Munitions War* 28 In the Spencer rifle magazine,..it is impossible to explode the *rim-fire cartridges, except by a concussion made by the hammer. 1881 Greener *Gun* 136 The cartridge is rim-fire. 1868 *Rep. to Govt. U.S. Munitions War* 19 The comparative merits of central-fire and *rim-ignition cartridges. 1841 *Civil Eng. & Arch. Jrnl.* IV. 29/1 A faggot of wrought iron bars are worked and..drawn out..under the hammer upon an anvil, having a groove to form the flanch, into the state of *rim iron. 1844 H. Stephens *Bk. Farm* I. 218, 8-inch Scotch made iron *rim-lock for back-door. 1872 Raymond *Statist. Mines & Mining* 84 Two small mills of eight stamps each were erected in 1868 and inclines sunk on the *rim-rock. 1882 *U.S. Rep. Prec. Met.* 621 'Rim-rock' is such portion as remains of the country-rock which formed the sides or banks of the ancient rivers. 1839 Ure *Dict. Arts* 370 A second band, which had..lain upon its loose pulley, upon a small driving pulley of the *rim-shaft. *Ibid.* 369 For one revolution of the great *rim or fly wheel of the mule, the front roller makes about 6-tenths of a turn.

Rim, *sb.*[2] Now *dial.* Forms: 1 **réoma, réama,** 4 **reme**; 4–6 **rym(e, rime,** 6 **rysme, rism(m)e**; 6–7 **rimme, rymme,** 7 **rimm,** 7– **rim.** [OE. *rēoma* (*rēama*), = MDu. *rieme* (Du. *riem*), OS. *reomo* (MLG. *rēme*; hence prob. ON. *reim*, Sw. and Da. *rem*), OHG. *riumo, riomo* (MHG. *rieme*, G. *riemen*), a leather strap or thong: see Riem, Reim, etc. The later forms of the Eng. word appear to have been influenced by Rim *sb.*[1]]

† **1.** A membrane, pellicle, caul. *Obs.*

c 1000 *Sax. Leechd.* III. 146 Þonne bið þæt bræȝen utan mid reaman bewefen. *c* 1050 *Voc.* in Wr.-Wülcker 380/1 *Cartilago*, se reoma þæs brægenes. *c* 1340 *Nominale* (Skeat) 306 *Poi vaut le crut del oef*, lityl is worth the reme of an ey. *c* 1340 Hampole *Pr. Consc.* 520 A rym [*v.r.* reme] þat es ful wlatsome, Es his garment when he forth sal com, Þat es noght bot a blody skyn. 13.. *Gaw. & Gr. Knt.* 1343 Verayly þerafter Alle þe rymez by þe rybbez radly þay lance. *c* 1500 Kennedie *Passion of Christ* 768 Fra heid to fute þai brak baith hid and ryme [= *rim*]. 1545 Elyot, *Meninges*, the rysme wherin the brain is inclosyd. 1553 Eden *Treat. Newe Ind.* (Arb.) 35 A thinne skinne or rimme like a nette, encompassing the shell of a nutte. 1601 Holland *Pliny* I. 342 Certain pellicles or rims of the Midriffe, which the Latines call *Præcordia*.

† **b.** A scale or film upon the eyes. *Obs.*

1382 Wyclif *Tobit* vi. 9 The galle is worth to eȝen to ben enointid, in the whiche were rime. *Ibid.* xi. 14 The ryme of his eȝen began, as the fellis of an ey, to go out. 1580 Frampton *Yron & Steele* in *Joyful News* (1596) 158 b, The pouder made of yron..taketh away the Rime from the eye.

† **c.** *Rim-side*, the flesh-side of a skin. *Sc. Obs.*

1474 *Records Burgh Edinb.* (1869) 29 Brekand schepe skinnis on the ryme sidis.

2. *Rim of the belly* (*womb, paunch*, etc.), the peritoneum. Now *dial.*

[1545 Raynold *Byrth Mankynde* 8 Vnder the last muskle of the belly..succedyth a certayn thyn ryme, kell, or skyn, named in latin Peritoneum.] 1565 Cooper *Thesaurus* s.v. *Ascites*, When betweene the rimme of the beally and the guttes is gathered..much watry humour. *a* 1585 Montgomerie *Flyting* 329 The rotten rim of thy wombe with rooke shall bee reivin. 1601 Holland *Pliny* I. 321 Even as the rim of the paunch, which is called in Latine *Centipellio*. 1621 Burton *Anat. Mel.* Democritus to Rdr. (1651) 27, I thinke he would breake the rimme of his belly with laughing. 1718 Pope *Iliad* XIV. 521 Struck thro' the Belly's Rim, the Warrior lies Supine. 1757 Burke *Abridgm. Eng. Hist.* Wks. X. 411 The rim of his belly was wounded; and this wound..proved fatal. 1804 *Med. Jrnl.* XII. 258 A slight degree of anasarca extended to the rim of the belly. 1838 Holloway *Prov. Dict.*, *Rim-of-the-body*, the membrane lining the abdomen and covering the bowels. 1893 Heslop *Northumbld. Gloss.* s.v., The rim of the belly is said to be broken when its muscles are lacerated or violently sprained.

b. *ellipt.* in the same sense.

1599 Shaks. *Hen. V*, IV. iv. 15, I will fetch thy rymme out at thy Throat, in droppes of Crimson blood. 1607 Markham *Caval.* II. (1617) 94, I opened her with mine owne hands,..and I found that her rimme was broken, her call cleane consumed. 1621 Burton *Anat. Mel.* I. i. II. iv. 25 The second [concavity] of the Navell and Flancks, diuided from the first by the Rimme.

Rim, *sb.*[3] *north. dial.* [= ON. *rim* (Norw. *rim, reem*) a rail or rung; cf. also Fris. *rim* shelf, LG. *rimm* cross-beam.] A rung of a ladder.

1788 W. Marshall *Yorksh.* II. 348 *Rims*, the steps or staves of a ladder. 1876 *Mid Yorks. Gloss.*, *Rim*, a spoke, or 'rung' of a ladder.

Rim, sb.¹ variant of RIEM.

Rim, sb.¹ [OE. rim, rima] trans. To furnish with a rim; to border, edge, or encircle in some way.

Rim, v. U.S. [var. of RIME v.¹] trans. To slush (mackerel) in the process of curing.

Rim, dial. variant of RHYME sb.⁴

Rima (raiˈmă). Physiol. The rima, a fissure, cleft, chink.

Rimate (raiˈmeit), a. rare⁻¹. [See prec. and -ATE.] Chinky, cleft.

Rimble-ramble, a. Obs. [Echoic reduplication of RAMBLE sb.¹]

Rimbomb, v. nonce-wd. [ad. It. rimbombare.] intr. To re-echo, ring, resound.

Rim-burst, en, a. dial.

Rime, raim, sb.¹ Forms: 1 hrim, 3-4 rim, etc.

Rime, sb.² Obs. [OE. rīm] number, reckoning.

Rime, raim, sb.³ Forms: 4-7, 9 ryme, etc.

Rime, v.¹ [ad. OF. rimer] To rhyme.

Rime, v.² [ad. OE. *hrīman]

Rime-frost, sb.

Rimed, ppl. a.¹

Rimed, ppl. a.² rare⁻¹.

Rimer (raiˈmə), sb.¹

Rimer, variant of REAMER.

Rimester (raiˈmestə).

Riming, vbl. sb.

Rimless, a. Without rim; unrimmed.

Rimless (raiˈmld), a.

Rimmed, ppl. a.

Rimmer (riˈmə), sb.

Riming, vbl. sb.

Rimose (raiˈməus), a.

Rimous (raiˈməs), a.

Rimple, sb.

Rimple, v.

Rin, dial. var. of RUN.

Rinabout, Sc.

Rina'trix, Obs.

Rind (raind), sb.¹ Forms: 1-4, 7, 9 rind, etc.

Rind, sb.²

Rind (raind), v.¹

Rind (raind), v.²

Rindle (rindˈl), sb.

Rindle, variant of RENDLE.

Rindled, ppl. a.

Rindy (raiˈndi), a.

Rine, obs. f. RIND, RUN.

†Rine, obs. Forms: 1 rínan, 3-4 rine, ryne. *Pa. t.* 1, 3 rinde; 1 rán. 4 roon, rone. [OE. *rínan* (*rígnan* = ON. and Icel. *rigna*, Goth. *rignjan*), *f.* *regn* RAIN *sb.*¹ Properly a weak vb.; the strong conj. is no doubt most immediately due to the analogy of *scínan*.]

Rine, obs. form of RIND *sb.*, RINE.

Riner, *dial.* [f. RINE *v.*] (See quots.)

R'inforce, variant of REËNFORCE *ppl. a.*

Ring (riŋ), *sb.*¹ Forms: 1 hring (hringo), 3-ring, 4-7 ringe; 3-6 ryng (4 rynk, 5 rynge)–4-6 yreng; 4-5 reng, 5 reyng. [Comm. Teut.: OE. *hring*, = OFris. *hring*, *ring* OS. *hring* (MLG. *rink*, *ring*, LG. OHG. *hring* (MHG. *rinc*, *ring*; G. *ring*), OHG. *hring*, ON. *hringr* (Sw., Da. *ring*). The pre-Teut. stem **kreng ho-* appears in Umbrian *krenkatrum* 'cingulum', and with dental-variation in OSl. *kragŭ* circle.]

Ring (riŋ), *sb.*² Also 6-7 ringe, 6 ryng. [f. RING *v.*²]

1. A set or peal of bells.

Ring (riŋ), *sb.*³ Also 5-6 rynge, 7-9 ringe. [f. RING *v.*³]

Ring, obs. f. WRING *v.*

ring-digger, a drunkard; ring-plate, (*a*) a plate with a ring attached for supporting a pipe (Knight); (*b*) an iron plate underlying a door-ring; ring-post, a post used in the construction of scaffolding; †ring-rathe (*q.f.*), ...

Ring (riŋ), *v.*¹ Also 5-6 rynge, 6 rynge. [f. RING *sb.*¹]

Ring (riŋ), *v.*² Also 5-6 ryngen, 7-9 ringe. Pa. t. and pa. pple. **ringed**, 5-6 *pres.* rong. [OE. *hringan*.]

Ring (riŋ), *v.*³ Also 5-6 rynge, *pa. t.* and *pa. pple.* **rung**, 7-9 *rang*. [OE. *hringan*.]

Ring-bone. *Farriery.* Also ringbone, ring bone. [f. RING *sb.*[1] + BONE, G. and Norw. *ringben*, MSw. *ringben.* One example of an OS. *Arngiden* appears in the following gloss.] 1. A deposit of bony matter on the pastern-bones of a horse.

2. The growth of such bony matter, as a specific disease of horses.

Ring-dance. [f. RING *sb.*[1] Cf. Du. *ringdans*, MLG. *ringedans*, G. *ringtanz*, Da. *ringdans*, Sw. *-dans*, Icel. *hringdans*.] A dance in which the dancers move round in a ring or form a ring.

Ring-dial. [f. RING *sb.*[1]] A portable kind of sun-dial consisting of a ring.

Ring-dove. [f. RING *sb.*[1] + DOVE. Cf. Du. *ringduif*, G. *ringtaube*, Da. *ringdue*.] 1. The wood-pigeon, cushat, or quest (*Columba palumbus*); also called ring-pigeon.

Ring-bark, *v.* [f. RING *sb.*[1] 9 b.] *a. intr.* To remove rings of bark from trees, in order to kill them. *b. trans.* To bark (trees) in this way.

Ring-bolt. Also ringbolt, ring bolt. [f. RING *sb.*[1] + BOLT.] A bolt with an eye at one end, to which a ring is attached.

Ring-dropper, dropping : see RING *sb.*

Ringe (rindʒ), *sb.*[1] *dial.* Also 8 rindge.

RINGE. 695 RINGING. 696 RINGLET.

Ringe, *sb.*[2] *dial.* [Of obscure origin.]

Ringe, variant of RENGE *v. Obs.*

Ringed (riŋd), *ppl. a.* [f. RING *sb.*[1] and *v.*[1]] 1. Of armour : Made of rings. rare.

2. Of persons : Wearing a ring or rings; also, wedded with a ring.

Ringer[1] (riŋə(r)). [f. RING *sb.*[1] + -ER[1].]

Ringer[2]. [f. RING *v.*[2]] A crow-bar.

Ring-fence, *sb.* [RING *sb.*[1]] A fence completely enclosing an estate, farm, or piece of ground.

Ring-finger. [RING *sb.*[1] + FINGER.] The third finger of the hand, especially of the left hand.

Ringing (riŋiŋ), *vbl. sb.*[1] [f. RING *v.*[1]]

Ringing, *vbl. sb.*[2] [f. RING *v.*[2]]

Ringing, *ppl. a.* [f. RING *v.*[1]]

Ringle (riŋ'l), *sb.* Now *dial.* Also 5 rengel, 6 ryngel, 7 ringel. 8 b ringoll, 7 -ol.

Ringle-eye. *Sc.* In form *-o*, *-e*.

Ring-leader. 6-9 ryngledere, -ledor, -leder; ringe-leader, leader. 1. One who leads a dance.

Ring-leadership.

Ringleading, *vbl. sb.*

Ringleading, *ppl. a.* [f. RINGLEADER.]

Ringleader. 6-9 ryngledere, -lodor, -leder; ringe-leader, leader. 1. One who takes a leading place or conducts a body or number of persons.

Ringed, *a.* rare. [f. RING *sb.*[1] + -ED[2].] provided with rings; marked by circular bands.

Ringlet (riŋlet). [f. RING *sb.*[1] + -LET.] 1. A small ring made of metal or other material.

Ringlet-straw. *dial.* [RINGLET.]

Ringletstones. *dial.* [RINGLET.]

Ringleted (riŋlĕted), *a.* Also -letted. [f. prec. + -ED[1].]

Ringlet-ed.

Ringlety, *a. rare.*

Ringly, *a. rare.*

Ring-man. [f. RING *sb.*[1]]

Ring-master. Also ringmaster. [f. RING *sb.*[1]]

Ring-neck, *a. sb.* [f. RING *sb.*[1]]

Ring-necked, *a.* [f. RING *sb.*[1]]

Ringol (riŋ·ŏl). Also ring-gol. [f. RING *sb.*[1]]

Ringoll, obs. form of RINGLE *sb.*[1]

Ring-goose. *rare —.*

Ring-rock, *for ring-root:* see ERYNGO.

Ringster, *U.S.* [f. RING *sb.*[1] b + -STER.]

Ring-straked, *a.* Also 6 -strieked. [f. RING *sb.*[1]]

Ring-streaked, *a.* Also 6 -streaked.

Ring-tail, *a. sb.* Also ringtail. [f. RING *sb.*[1]]

Ring-tailed, *a.* [f. prec.]

Ring-ousel. Also -ouzel. [f. RING *sb.*[1]]

Ringtaw. *U.S.* [f. RING *sb.*[1] b + -STER.]

Ring-walk. *sb. exc. arch.* [f. RING *sb.*[1]]

b. *Austr.*—JACKAROO *sb.*

Ring-necked, *a.* [RING *sb.*[1]]

Ring-net. [f. RING *sb.*[1]]

Ringal, ringall, ringol.

Ringingall, ringtail, ringtall.

1. A wall completely surrounding or encircling a Jackan area. (Cf. RING-FENCE.)

2. *techn.* (See quots.)

+ Ringwood. *Obs.* Ale brewed at Ringwood in Hampshire.

Ringworm (riŋ·wɔɹm).

1. A skin-disease usually manifesting itself in circular patches, and frequently affecting the scalp in childhood; *tinea.*

b. The golden eagle or kite's third year. Usually *ring-tail.*

2. *attrib.* and *Comb.*

Ring-worm bush *or* **shrub,** a tropical American shrub (*Cassia alata*).

Ring·y, *a.* [f. RING *sb.*[1] + -Y.]

Rink (riŋk). *sb.* Also 5 *renke,* 4-6 ryke, 6 rinke, 9 rynk. [OE. rinc = OS. rinc, ON. rekkr: the stem is app. an ablaut-variant to that of RANK *a.*]

Rink, *sb.*[2] Also 4-6 (9 *dial.*) rynk; 6 rynk. [App. a. OF. renc row, rank, RENK *sb.*]

Rinking, *vbl. sb.* [f. RINK *sb.*[2] + -ING.]

Rink·er, *a.* [f. RINK *sb.*[2] + -ER.]

Rinkist. [f. RINK *sb.*[2] + -IST.]

Rinkle, obs. variant of WRINKLE *sb.*

Rinkoma·nia. [f. RINK *sb.*[2] + -MANIA.] A passion for rink-skating. So **Rinkoma·niac.**

Rinner, -ing, *dial.* variants of RUNNER, -ING.

+Rinnet. *sb.* In 6 rinet, 7 rynnet. Variant of RENNET or RUNNET *sb.*[2] used figuratively.

Rino, obs. var. RHINO *sb.*[2]

Rinoceros, obs. var. RHINOCEROS.

Rinology, variant of RHINOLOGY.

Rinse (rins), *sb.* Also rinse, rince, ringe, reenge. [f. RINSE *v.*]

1. A small bundle of twigs (esp. of heather) used for cleaning out pots or other vessels. Hence **rinse-heather,** the variety of heather used for making this.

2. A rinsing; a final application of water to remove impurities; *colloq.* a wash.

Rinsed.

Rinse-pitcher.

Rinser, *rare.* Also 7 rencer, reinser, rensor. [f. RINSE *v.*] One who rinses.

Rinsing (rinsiŋ), *vbl. sb.* [f. RINSE *v.* + -ING.]

b. *attrib.,* as **rinsing appliance, machine,** etc.

2. The liquid or liquor with which anything has been rinsed out. Chiefly *pl.*

b. To treat (clothes or textile fabrics) in this way; *spec.* to put through a clean water in order to remove the soap used in washing.

+Rin-spindle. *Obs. rare.* In 3 -spindel, -dil, ryaspyndell, -dle. [App. f. RIN RUN *v.* + SPINDLE *sb.*] A boring instrument used for cutters and in the surgical treatment of a broken skull.

Rin-there-out; see RINY.

+Ri·ny, *a. Obs. rare —[1].* [f. rine, var. of RIND *sb.*[1] Cf. RINDY *a.*] Bearing the rind or skin.

Rioal, variant of RIOLL, RIAL *a. Obs.*

Riolly, Riol., variants of RIAL(LY, RIALTY.

Riot (rai·ǎt), *sb.* Forms: 3-7 riote, 4-riot, 4-6 ryott, 5 riote, riat, 6 riat, riett; 4-6 ryote (3 rayate), 4-7 ryot, 5-7 ryotte, 6-ryote; 4 ryatt. [a. OF. *riote* (XII), *ryote,* Pr., It. *riotta,* of obscure origin.]

I. **1.** *intr.* To live in a wanton, dissipated, or unrestrained manner; to revel; to indulge to excess in something. Now somewhat *rare.*

+ b. *trans.* To attack (persons or property).

Rioter (rai·ǎtəɹ). Forms: 4-7 riot(t)our, 4-6 ryot(t)our; also -er, etc. [a. OF. *riotour, *riotter,* f. *riote* RIOT *sb.*]

1. One who leads a disorderly or licentious life, or who indulges in debauchery; a dissolute person; a reveller. *Obs. exc. arch.*

2. One who takes part in a riot or rising against constituted authority.

Rioting, *vbl. sb.* [f. RIOT *v.* + -ING.]

1. Dissoluteness of life, debauchery, revelry.

b. Noisy, tumultuous, seditious, or violent conduct.

+Rio·tise, *Obs.* Also 6-7 -yse, 7 -ise. [f. RIOT *sb.* + -ISE.] Riotous life or conduct.

Ri·otous, *a.* (and *sb.*) Forms: 4-6 riotous (4-nouse), 5 ryotouse, ryoteux, ryoutous (5-6 ryotous, 4-5 riotous, 5 riatous), 4-7 riotous. [a. OF. *riotous, riotos,* f. *riote* RIOT *sb.*]

1. Troublesome, difficult. *Obs.*

2. Of persons: Given to wantonness, revelry, or dissolute life; prodigal, extravagant. Now *rare.*

b. Of things: Characterized by, proceeding from, or involving unrestrained revelry.

3. Of persons, their actions, etc.: Marked by or exhibiting wanton disregard of restraint; unbridled, unruly, wild.

4. Characterized or marked by rioting or disturbance of the peace; taking part in or inciting to a riot or tumult; turbulent.

Ri·otously, *adv.* [f. prec. + -LY[2].] In a riotous manner.

Ri·otousness.

Riotously (rai·ətəsli), adv. Also 5 riot(e)s-, 6 ryot(e)sous-, ryotous-, riotte-us-, riat, to(e)s-, riotously. [f. prec. + -LY².]

1. a. In a wanton or unrestrained manner.

b. With revelry or debauchery; in a prodigal or spendthrift manner; extravagantly.

c. Most angrily or profusely. *Obs.*⁻¹

2. In a turbulent or seditious manner.

Riotousness (rai·ətəsnes). Also 5 ryotousnesse. [f. as prec. + -NESS.] The state or condition of being riotous.

Rioty (rai·əti). Also 4 ryotye, rioterie. [f. RIOT v. + -Y.] Formed afresh in 18th cent.] Rioting, riotous conduct, riotousness; also, riotous persons (quot. 1786).

Rip, *sb.¹* Also 7 ripp. [Of obscure origin.]

1. A wicker basket or pannier, esp. one used for carrying fish.

2. An inferior horse.

3. A worthless, dissolute fellow; a rake.

Rip, *sb.²* Also 7 ripp, 6 rype. [Of obscure origin.]

In some western counties the form is *ripe.*¹ A strickle for a scythe. Also *rip-stick.*

Rip, *sb.³* Also 8 ripp. [f. RIP v.²] Cf. Flem. *rip* in sense 1.]

1. A rent made by ripping; a laceration, tear.

2. ellipt. A rip-saw. In comb. *half-rip.*

3. dual, or collog. A rapid rush; a quick run.

Rip, *sb.⁴* [? Related to RIP v.²]

1. A disturbed state of the sea, resembling breakers; an overfall. (See also *tide-rip.*)

2. A stretch of broken water in a river.

Rip, *sb.⁵* [Perh. a later form of REP.¹ If this is an abbreviation of *reprobate*, the appearance of sense 1 earlier than sense 2 is prob. accidental.]

1. An inferior, worthless, or worn-out horse.

2. A worthless, dissolute fellow; a rake.

3. a person or thing of little or no value.

Rip, obs. form of REAP *sb.²* and *v.²*

Rip, obs. form of RIPE *sb.³*, *a.*, and *v.¹*

Rip, *sb.⁶* Also 5 *Sc.* Also 8 ripp, 6 ryp, 6 rype. [Perh. f. RIP *v.²*]

The vowel is against connexion with REAP *sb.¹*]

A handful of unthreshed grain or hay; also *spec.* the last handful of grain remaining to be cut in a harvest-field.

Rip, *v.¹* Also 7 ripp. [Of obscure origin.]

Rip, *v.²* Also 7 ripp. [Of obscure origin.]

1. trans. To cut, pull, or tear (anything) away from something else in a vigorous manner.

2. To cut or tear apart in a rough or slashing fashion.

b. To tilt up or raise.

Rip, *v.³* [Perh. a. North. repp'r.]

1. An inferior, worthless, or worn-out horse.

Ripa (rəi·pă). *rare.* [Sw. ripa, pl. ripor; see KYPE *sb.*] Ptarmigan.

Riparial (rai·peə·riəl), *a.* [f. L. ripari-us (see RIPARIAN) + -AL.] = RIPARIAN *a.¹*

Riparian (rai·peə·riăn), *a.¹* and *sb.¹* [f. as prec.] Of or pertaining to, or situated on, the banks of a river; riverine.

Riparian (rai·peə·riăn), *a.²* and *sb.²* = RIPUARIAN.

Ripa·rian *a.²* and *sb.²* = KIPUARIAN.

Ripary, *sb.* Obs. [ad. med.L. *riparia*, fem. of L. *riparius*: see prec.] A stream.

Ripe (rəip), *sb.¹* Forms: 1 ripe (hripp), 4, 4 rip (4-5 rip), 3-4 rype, 4 ryp (4-5 rype), 5-7 ripe. [OE. *ripe.*]

Ripe (rəip), *sb.²* Now *rare.* [a. (ad.? and adv.), Also 3-7 rype, 4 ripe, *rip.*] The bank of a river; the shore.

Ripe (rəip), *a.* Forms: 1 ripe, 2-3 ripe, 4 rype (4-5 ripe), 3-4 ripe, 5 ryppe. [OE. *rīpe*.]

Ripe (rəip), *v.¹* Forms: 1 ripian, 4 rypen, 5 ripen, 5-7 rype, 6-9 ryply (4-7 -lie, 6 -lye), 7 reape. [OE. *ripian*, v.¹: Fris. *rīpje*, MDu. *rīpen*; related to Goth. *raupjan*, OHG. *roufen* (G. *rausfen*) and to LG. *ruppen*, G. *rupfen* to pluck, pull. After OE. to change in to ripe.

Ripe (rəip), *v.²* Also 6-7 ripe, 7 ryppe. [Of somewhat obscure origin and history; it is not quite certain that all the senses really belong to the same word.]

1. To cut, pull, or tear (anything) away from something else.

b. To search into, examine. Now *rare.*

Ripe, *obs. form of* RIPPLE *v.¹*

Ripely (rəi·pli), *adv.* Also 6 ryply. [f. RIPE *a.* + -LY².]

1. Quickly, immediately. *Obs. rare.*

I thought I saw it glancin.

Ripen (rəi·p'n), *v.* Also 6 rypen. [f. RIPE *a.* + -EN⁵.]

1. intr. To grow ripe; to come to maturity.

2. To make (corn, etc.) ripe; to mature.

Ripened (rəi·p'nd), *ppl. a.* [f. prec. + -ED¹.] Advanced to ripeness, maturity, or full development.

Ripener (rəi·p'nəɹ). Also 6 rypener. [f. RIPEN *v.* + -ER¹.]

1. One who, or that which, causes ripening.

Ripeness (rəi·pnes). [f. RIPE *a.* + -NESS.] The state of being ripe. In various senses; maturity, mellowness.

Ripening (rəi·p'niŋ), *vbl. sb.* [f. RIPEN *v.* + -ING¹.]

Ripening, *ppl. a.* [f. prec. + -ING².]

Hence **Ri·peningly** *adv.*
1894 *Temple Bar* CII. 142 The sun..shone ripeningly upon the mellow clusters.

Riper [1]. *rare.* [f. Ripe *v.*[1]] Ripener.
c 1400 *Lanfranc's Cirurg.* 6 Of Maturatiuis, þat buþ Ripers. 1572 Bossewell *Armorie* ii. 124 That mighty planet, Luna, the riper and encreaser of fruites.

Riper [2] (rai·pəɹ). Now *dial.* Also 1 rýpere, 2 rupere. [f. Ripe *v.*[2]]
†1. A robber, plunderer. *Obs.*
a 1023 Wulfstan *Hom.* xxxiii. (1883) 159 Us stalu and cwalu..and rypera reaflac derede. 1027–34 *Sec. Laws Cnut* vii. in Liebermann *Gesetze* 312/1 Ryperas and reaferas Godes graman habban. *c* 1175 *Lamb. Hom.* 15 Þas ruperes and þas reueres and þas þeues.
2. *dial.* (See quot.)
1894 Heslop *Northumb. Gloss.*, *Riper*, an iron prong used for clearing dirt and dust out of the oilholes in machinery.

†**Ri·per** [3]. *Obs.* [? cf. Rip *v.*[2] 2 b, quot. 1688.] An instrument used by arrow-makers.
1659 Howell *Vocab.* li, A thwitting knife, nocksaws a rasp, a riper, a share.

Rip-hook, dial. var. of Reap-hook.
Current in southern and south-western counties.
1872 'Agrikler' *Rhymes* 105 (E. D. D.), I handled the rip-hook and zive. 1881 Blackmore *Cristowell* xxii, A shortish old man with..a rip-hook swinging in one hand.

Ripi·colous, *a.* *rare*⁻⁰. [f. L. *ripa* bank + *-colus* inhabiting.] Riparious. (Mayne.)

Ripidolite (raipi·dŏlait). *Min.* [f. Gr. ῥιπιδο-, ῥιπίς fan + -lite; named by Kobell in 1839.] = Clinochlore.
1850 Daubeny *Atom. The.* xii. (ed. 2) 412 Silicates with hydrates. Ripidolite (chlorite). 1857 Dana *Man. Mineral.* (1862) 145 Chlorite...This species has lately been subdivided on chemical grounds, and the name *Ripidolite* applied to the new species instituted. 1880 *Libr. Univ. Knowl.* (N. Y.) XIII. 155 [Sapphire] is found..in granular limestone in New Jersey, and in the ripidolite of North Carolina.

Ripienist (ripyē·nist). [f. next + -ist.] 'A performer who only assists in the ripieno parts'.
1876 Stainer & Barrett *Dict. Mus. Terms.*

‖ **Ripieno** (ripyē·no), *a.* and *sb.* *Mus.* Also 7 repieno, 7–8 -piano. [It., f. *ri-* Re- + *pieno* full.]
1. Supplementary, re-enforcing. (Cf. quots.)
1724 *Short Explic. For. Wds. Mus. Bks.* 63 *Repieno*, or *Repiano*, signifies Full; and is used to distinguish those Violins in Concerto's, which play only now and then to fill up, from those which play throughout the whole Concerto. 1811 Busby *Dict. Mus.* (ed. 3), *Ripieno*..is used in orchestral compositions, to distinguish those parts which are only occasionally introduced to fill up and supply the chorus. 1879 in Grove *Dict. Mus.* I. 153 Handel's scores contain few bassoon parts, and those..mostly of a ripieno character.
b. *sb.* A supplementary player or instrument.
1753 Chambers *Cycl. Suppl.* s.v., There are..two kinds of the ripieno: one plays the part of the little chorus exactly, and does not, therefore, increase the harmony or number of parts. 1789 Burney *Hist. Mus.* III. 560 Twelve concertos for a violino principale, with two *ripienos.* 1873 H. C. Banister *Music* (1885) 248 The subordinate stringed instruments in an Orchestra are sometimes termed Ripieni, as distinguished from the Principals.
2. *transf.* Serving to fill up; supernumerary.
1811 L. M. Hawkins *C'tess & Gertr.* I. 52 An oriental Crœsus and his beautiful lady, one or two ripieno characters, and the observing party. *Ibid.* 135 In the..re-adjustment of the treasury-balance, he got a *ripieno* appointment.

Ripier, variant of Rippier.

Riping (rai·piŋ), *vbl. sb.*[1] Now *rare.* [f. Ripe *v.*[1]] The process or fact of becoming ripe.
c 825 *Vesp. Psalter* cxviii. 147 Ic forecom in ripunge [L. *in maturitate*]. *c* 960 Æthelwold *Rule St. Benet* (Schröer) 126 Seo ripung his ʒestæþþignesse sy swylc, þæt hine ne worian..lyste. *c* 1055 *Byrhtferth's Handboc* in *Anglia* VIII. 312 Se þridda tima ys Autumnus on lyden ʒecweden, ..boceras ʒetrahtniað þæne naman for þære ripunge. 1398 Trevisa *Barth. De P. R.* viii. xliv. (Tollemache MS.), [An eclipse] tarieþ rypynge of frute, and of corne. *c* 1450 Lydg. *Secrees* 1371 Euery thyng drawith to his Rypyng. 1523 *St. Papers Hen. VIII*, VI. 131 The Ambassadour, for his more parfite knowlege and ripyng in this matier, shal understand [etc.]. 1544 Phaer *Pestilence* (1553) P iij, It is better..to breake the sore by times, than to tary for yᵉ riping long. 1596 Shaks. *Merch. V.* ii. viii. 40 Stay the very riping of the time. 1627 Hakewill *Apol.* (1630) 140 The uncertaine and unkindely riping of fruites. 1899 *Daily News* 30 Dec. 6/1 Has the rotting followed so fast after the riping?

Ri·ping, *vbl. sb.*[2] [f. Ripe *v.*[2]] The action of searching († or plundering).
a 1100 in Napier *O. E. Glosses* 84 *Prouscriptionem*, i. *fraudationem*, fordeminge, rypincge. 1815 Scott *Guy M.* xlv, An unco ranging and ripeing they have had a' gates seeking for her.

Ri·ping, *ppl. a.* [f. Ripe *v.*[1]] Ripening.
c 1550 H. Lloyd *Treas. Health* H vij, Use outwardly.. drawynge and ryping medicines. 1590 Greene *Never too Late* Wks. (Grosart) VIII. 225 The riping corne growes yeolow in the stalke. 1863 Lancaster *Praeterita* 57, I scent A riping vintage from the Cretan hills.

Riple, obs. form of Ripple *v.*[1] **Riply,** obs. f. Ripely. **Ripman,** variant of Reapman *Obs.* **Ripnes,** obs. f. Ripeness. **Ripon**: see Rippon.

‖ **Riposte** (ripǭ·st), *sb.* Also 7 risposte, 9 ripost (cf. Repost *sb.*). [F. *riposte*, earlier *risposte*, ad. It. *risposta* response, reply.]
1. *Fencing.* A quick thrust given after parrying a lunge; a return thrust. Also *attrib.*
1707 Sir W. Hope *New Method Fencing* iv. 85 For the Riposte, it is impossible for a Man to give it, until his Adversary..offers to launch in a Thrust. *Ibid.* vi. 171 To defend himself well from his Adversary's Risposte Thrusts, or Blows. 1809 Roland *Fencing* (1823) 104 The party standing on the defensive, is not allowed to make any riposte. *Ibid.* 142 By not fearing the riposte upon you, it will render your mode of attack more precise. 1893 *Fencing* (Badminton Libr.) (ed. 3) iv. 82 To meet this riposte: parry second or septime while rising.
2. *transf.* A counterstroke; an effective reply by word or act.
1865 *Pall Mall G.* 19 June 1 The thrust..was an ugly one, but the ripost which he has succeeded in planting is uglier still. 1877 Morley *Crit. Misc.* Ser. ii. 107 The Feast of the Supreme Being..was designed as a triumphant ripost to the Feast of Reason. 1886 N. L. Walford *Parl. Gen. Civil War* 74 To us the 'riposte' of Charles appears to have been a fair one.

‖ **Riposte** (ripǭ·st), *v.* Also 8 risposte, 9 ripost (cf. Repost *v.*). [ad. F. *riposter*, earlier *risposter*: see prec.]
1. *Fencing.* To make a riposte. Also *trans.* with personal object.
1707 Sir W. Hope *New Method Fencing* iv. 96 Nothing can be more dangerous, because of the Opportunity it gives a Man's Adversary to Risposte him. 1809 Roland *Fencing* (1823) 115 B. Parries Tierce smartly, and ripostes straight over the arm. 1885 *New Bk. Sports* 121 Smartly raising the knee..and riposting with a quick downward movement.
2. *transf.* To reply or retaliate; to answer (one).
1851 Kingsley *Lett. & Mem.* (1877) I. 267 If you do not think our mutual 'honour' satisfied..., you will riposte at the first opportunity. 1871 Meredith *H. Richmond* xlviii, Riposte me—have you too many? 1883 Wingfield *Abigel Rowe* I. iii. 57 The other side dared not ripost with the real report. 1893 Lang *St. Andrews* v. 128 The Cardinal riposted by an interdict.
Hence **Ripo·sted, Ripo·sting** *ppl. adjs.*
1707 Sir W. Hope *New Method Fencing* iv. 96 To come off safe, from an Exchanged and Risposted Thrust. *Ibid.* vi. 173 Give him a Risposted Blow. 1893 *Fencing* (Badminton Libr.) (ed. 3) iv. 83 The riposting fencer must..deliver his thrust with the hand inclined towards pronation.

Ripp(e, obs. forms of Reap *sb.*[2] and *v.*[1]

Ripper (ri·pəɹ). [f. Rip *v.*[2] + -er [1]. Cf. Fris. *ripper* a poor knife.]
1. One who rips. Chiefly in technical uses.
1611 Cotgr., *Descouseur*, a ripper, vnsower; vndooer of. 1674 Ray *Coll. Words*, *Wirework* 133 Then the Rippers take them and draw them into wire through two or three holes. 1833 J. Holland *Manuf. Metal* II. 332 Where the rippers, as the workmen are called, care little about modern improvements. 1852 J. C. Brown tr. *Arboussat's Narr.* 127 A number of rippers at once cast off their garments, and began by cutting off the head of the animal. 1892 *Daily News* 8 Mar. 6/1 The 'ripper' clears off the roof to a height sufficient for the passage of the horses with their loaded 'corves'. 1896 in *Eng. Dial. Dict.* s.v., Wanted..: good rippers for coppice.
2. That which rips; a tool or apparatus intended for ripping; esp. (*a*) a tool used in removing old slates; (*b*) a rip-saw.
1793 O'Keeffe *London Hermit* ii. v, *Tom P.* I'll quicken him with a touch of the rippers...(Tom Pranks spurs him.) 1823 P. Nicholson *Pract. Build.* 400 The ripper is formed of iron..with a very thin blade...This tool is used for lifting up and removing the nails out of old slating. 1842 Gwilt *Archit.* § 2115 The half ripper is used also for dividing wood in the direction of the fibres. 1875 Knight *Dict. Mech.* 1945/2 *Ripper*, a tool for ripping seams of garments. 1876 *Encycl. Brit.* IV. 43/2 The first process in the preparation of the cloth cases is cutting the millboard. This is now effected by a rotary cutting-machine or 'ripper'.
attrib. 1892 *Pall Mall G.* 4 Apr. 6/3 A huge steel saw that will cut through a nickel-steel armour plate just as easily as an ordinary ripper saw will go through a pine board.
3. *slang.* a. Something especially good.
1851 Mayhew *Lond. Labour* I. 301 Sarah was a cock, sir, and a ripper. 1859 Lang *Wand. India* 144 'But, he is a ripper, nevertheless,' said the Lieutenant, touching the animal very gently with the whip. 1892 Boyd *25 Yrs. St. Andrews* I. ii. 28 When a graduate stated that 'every lecture was a ripper', I understood he meant very high praise indeed.
b. One who pursues a reckless course.
1877 *Temple Bar* May 109 If the ripper rips for the benefit of his party,..the turning out by no means follows.

Ripper, obs. or dial. f. Reaper; var. Rippier.

Rippet (ri·pėt). *Sc.* Also 6 repet, repit, rippett, 6, 9 rippit. [Perh. of imitative origin.] Tumult, uproar, disturbance, noisy dispute.
1508 Dunbar *Tua Mariit Wemen* 193 He ralis, and makis repet with ryatus wordis. 1513 Douglas *Æneis* viii. xii. 104 Off riot, rippett, and of reveling. 1535 Stewart *Cron. Scot.* I. 221 Sic ane repit, rumour, and sic ane reird, Was neuir hard befoir into this eird. 1596 Dalrymple tr. *Leslie's Hist. Scot.* i. 76 Sik a rippet is amang thame. *c* 1800 Jamieson *Water Kelpie* iii, And Prosen proud, with rippet loud, Cums ravin' frae his glen. 1887 Service *Life Dr. Duguid* v. 31 Some rippit getting up at the other end of the schule.

Rippier (ri·piəɹ). *Obs.* exc. *Hist.* Forms: α. 6 repier, repar, repayre, repear, rypear, 6–7, 9 ripier. β. 6–8 rippier, 7 ryppier. γ. 6–7 ripper, 6 rippar. [f. Rip *sb.*[1] + -(i)er. In old statutes latinized as *riparius*, and supposed by Cowell and others to be derived from L. *rīpa* bank, shore.] One who carries fish inland to sell.
α. *a* 1513 Fabyan *Chron.* (1516) 169 b/1 Repiers and other Fisshers commynge with Fysshe from Rye and Wynchylsee. *c* 1530 in *Songs, Carols*, etc. (E.E.T.S.) 159 This yere..the rypears sold fish at London Hall in þe Lent. 1538 Leland *Itin.* (1769) V. 77 A poore Market, much standing by Repears that cary Fische from the Quarters of Cairmardine to the lowers Partes of Wales. 1591 Savile *Tacitus, Hist.* ii. lxii. 89 The hyewaies from both the seas sounded of nothing els but of caters and ripiers. [1880 *Archæol. Cant.* XIII. 206 The cess upon the Ripiers (or as they would now be termed 'long-shore-men').]
β. 1589 ? Lyly *Pappe w. Hatchet* L.'s Wks. 1902 III. 405 With the cloak cast ouer each shoulder like a rippier. 1598 Florio, *Mutade*, panniers or paddes, such as Rippiers bring fish in. 1607 Chapman *Bussy d'Ambois* iii. ii, Like a Rippiers legs rowl'd vp In bootes of haie ropes. *c* 1640 J. Smyth *Hund. Berkeley* (1885) 302 A common Inne in this village addes fame thereto, by the constant customary baytes of the Ryppiers and their horses. 1709 in *Sussex Archæol. Coll.* (1848) 144 The horses on which the rippiers..shall ride going on or towards London. 1778 *Eng. Gazetteer* (ed. 2) s.v. *Rye*, They trowl for soles, plaise,..brills, &c. which are carried up every day by the rippiers (as the fishermen are called).
γ. 1530 in W. H. Turner *Select. Rec. Oxford* (1880) 87 Who wold never suffer rippers to sell ther owne fische. 1598 Stow *Surv.* 147 The Rippars of Rie..solde their fresh fish in Leaden hall market. 1622 Fletcher *Beggar's Bush* v. i, But what's the action we are for now? ha: Robbing a Ripper of his fish? 1674 Ray *S. & E. C. Words* 75 A *Ripper*: a Pedder, Dorser or Badger, Suss. [Hence in Pegge, Grose, Holloway, etc.]

Rippill, obs. form of Ripple.

Ripping (ri·piŋ), *vbl. sb.* [f. Rip *v.*[2] + -ing [1].]
1. The action of the vb. in various senses: a. In lit. or technical uses. Also *concr.*, that which is ripped off.
1532 [see Rip *v.*[2] 2 b]. 1611 Cotgr., *Descousure*, a ripping, vnsowing, vndoing of. 1615 W. Lawson *Country Housew. Gard.* (1626) 16 Here you must be carefull, not to hurt your tree when you gather them, by ripping amongst the roots. 1678 R. L'Estrange *Seneca's Mor.* (1705) 482 The Ripping of a Hang-nail is sufficient to Dispatch us. 1801 Coleridge in Mrs. Sandford *T. Poole & Friends* (1888) II. 27 When your Ripping [of oak-bark] is over you will come, or, at furthest, immediately after hay harvest. 1833 J. Holland *Manuf. Metal* II. xiv. 331 These rods were afterwards further reduced by an ingenious operation, called by the workmen in this country *ripping* or *rumpling*. 1894 *Labour Commission Gloss.*, *Ripping*, that portion of the roof which is cut down in the roadways to make sufficient height for men and horses to travel.
b. In fig. uses. Const. *up*.
1576 Fleming *Panopl. Epist.* 55 With the ripping up of ciuil commutations and chaunges. 1596 Spenser *State Irel.* Wks. (Globe) 629/1 This ripping up of auncient historyes, is very pleasing unto me, and indeede savoureth of good conceite. 1617 Hieron *Wks.* II. 267 Indeuour the ripping vp of thy heart. 1674 *Essex Papers* (Camden) 254 If..there should be now a ripping up of Crimes,.. no man can see where it will stop. 1843 J. W. Croker in *C. Papers* 5 Dec. (1884), I cannot..understand what authority can exist for such a ripping up of private life. 1863 *Sat. Rev.* 12 Sept. 352 Five years ago, there was a great ripping-up of the skirts of society.
2. *attrib.*, as *ripping-bed*, *-cut*, *-gauge*, *-hook*, *-iron*, *-tool*. Also Ripping-chisel, -saw.
1850 Holtzapffel *Turning* III. 1206 For cutting slabs of marble into narrow pieces..a machine called a *ripping bed is employed. 1823 P. Nicholson *Pract. Build.* 220 If planks are sawed longitudinally, through their thickness, the saw-way is called a *ripping-cut. 1875 Knight *Dict. Mech.* 1945/2 The *ripping-gage..is screwed to the table, and, by means of a thumb-nut, is adjusted to cut square or beveling. 1825 Knapp & Baldw. *Newgate Cal.* IV. 57/2 The instrument called a *ripping-hook. 1846 A. Young *Naut. Dict.*, **Ripping-Iron*, a tool used in stripping copper, or thin wood-sheathing, off a vessel's bottom. 1867 Smyth *Sailor's Word-bk.*, *Ripping-Iron*, a caulker's tool for tearing oakum out of a seam. 1875 Knight *Dict. Mech.* 1946/1 **Ripping-tool*, one for following a seam and cutting stitches without slitting the fabric.

Ri·pping, *ppl. a.* [f. as prec. + -ing [2].]
1. That rips or tears; also *fig.*, cutting.
1714 Arbuthnot *Let. to Ford* 19 Oct., It is necessary for him to do that..., else there will be a ripping answer, as you say. 1827 Cobbett *Prot. Reform.* (1899) § 351 Ripping-knives. 1845 J. Coulter *Adv. Pacific* xv. 230 The bark of the various trees also showed many a sign of the ripping passage, or graze of a bullet. 1894 T. Pinkerton *Blizzard* 106 With a ripping slash she cut into a wicker stand.
2. *slang.* Excellent, splendid; rattling.
1826 *Sporting Mag.* XVII. 319 They had slipped away down wind, at a ripping pace. 1858 Thomson *Alma Matres* i. 3 Some a little encouraged by the ripping Burton which the Scouts took care to ply liberally. 1887 Miss Braddon *Like & Unlike* i, We killed on Hagley Heath after a ripping half-hour over the grass. 1894 Doyle *S. Holmes* 57 Old Coxon gave me a ripping good testimonial.
Hence **Ri·ppingly** *adv.*, splendidly.
1892 H. Nisbet *Bushranger's Sweetheart* xxvi. 209 'How are you getting on with her?' 'Rippingly as far as she is concerned'.

Ripping, dial. variant of Reaping.

Ri·pping-chisel. (See quots.)
a. 1659 Howell *Vocab.* li, A maul, a mallet, a chizel, a rippin chizel. 1679 Moxon *Mech. Exerc.* vii. 124 The Ripping-Chissel..is about an Inch broad, and hath a blunt Edge...Its Office is..to rip or tear two pieces of Wood fastned together from one another. *Ibid.*, Most commonly Carpenters use an old cast off Chissel for a Ripping Chissel. 1842 Gwilt *Archit.* 949 There are various kinds of chisels; the principal ones used in carpentry and joinery are..the socket chisel, and the ripping chisel.
b. 1812 *Ann. Reg.*, *Chron.* 5 The ripping-chisel or crow-bar, about three feet long. 1823 P. Nicholson *Pract. Build.* 220 To cut or break a hole in brick-work, with the ripping-chisel.
c. 1875 Knight *Dict. Mech.* 1945/2 *Ripping-chisel* (Woodworking), a crooked chisel for cleaning out mortises.

Ri·pping-saw. (See quots. and Rip-saw.)
1825 J. Nicholson *Operat. Mechanic* 584 The ripping-saw, for dividing boards into separate pieces, in the direction of the fibres. 1860 Tomlinson *Arts & Manuf.* Ser. ii. *Saws* 32 A ripping-saw..is a hand-saw with a blade twenty-eight or thirty inches long, and having large teeth for ripping, or cutting out stuff coarsely and quickly. 1881 W. E. Dickson *Pract. Organ Build.* i. 4 The usual saws, the ripping saw, the panel saw,..will be required.

Ripple (ri·p'l), *sb.*[1] Also 5 ryppyll, repylle, 6 reple. [Corresponds to Fris. *ripel* (*roepel*, *rûpel*), Du. *repel*, MLG. *repel(e*, LG. *repel*, *rapel*), OHG. *rifila* (G. *riffel*): see Ripple *v.*[1] A shorter form appears in Flem., older Du., and MLG. *repe*, G. *riffe*.] An implement toothed like a comb, used in cleaning flax or hemp from the seeds.
1660 Sharrock *Vegetables* 22 They get out the seeds [of flax] by drawing it through an engine like an iron double tooth combe, which they call a Ripple. 1766 *Compl. Farmer* s.v. *Hemp* Z 4/2 The seed..which remains in the heads of the hemp..is got out by combing the heads on the teeth of a ripple. 1807 Hoare *Tour Irel.* 324 If the seed [of flax] is to be saved, it is drawn through an iron comb, fastened in wood, called a ripple. 1846 Sproule *Flax* 20 The operation in this case not being performed by the ripple, but by repeated strokes of a stick. 1875 *Encycl. Brit.* I. 380 Lifting each handful separately and pulling the top through a ripple or iron comb fixed upon a piece of plank.
b. *attrib.*, as *ripple-stock*, *-comb* (also as *vb.*).
Perhaps properly combs. of the verbal stem.
c 1475 *Pict. Voc.* in Wr.-Wülcker 795 *Hoc rupeste*, a repyllestok. 1499 *Wills & Invent.* (Surtees) I. 104 A hekyll, ..a ryppyll came,..a payr of wool cames. 1581 *Invent.* in *Best's Farm. Bks.* (Surtees) 171 One peare of reple comes. 1615 Markham *English Housew.* ii. v. (1668) 132 You must take ripple combs, and ripple your flax over. 1899 *Academy* 11 Feb. 184/1 Flax was grown, dried, ripple-combed, cleaned.

Ri·pple, *sb.*[2] *north. dial.* Also 7 rippill. [f. Ripple *v.*[2]] A slight cut, scratch, or mark.
1666 *Depos. Cast. York* (Surtees) 141 He..opened his buttons, and gave him some rippills with his knife on his breast. 1869 Peacock *Lonsd. Gloss.*, *Ripple*, a slight scratch. 1876 C. C. Robinson *Mid-Yorksh. Gloss.* s.v., A mark across the grain of wood, as if where a saw had just grazed, would be called a *ripple*.

Ripple (ri·p'l), *sb.*[3] [f. Ripple *v.*[3]]
1. a. *U.S.* A piece of shallow water in a river where rocks or sand-bars cause an obstruction; a shoal. (Cf. Riffle *sb.* 4 and Rippling *vbl. sb.*[3] 2.)
1755 *New Hampshire Prov. Papers* (1872) VI. 431 Swift water falls and Ripples that they were oblig'd to wade and carry all day. 1789 J. May *Jrnl. & Lett.* (1873) 131 The river so low that it is impossible to get over the shoal places, 'ripples,' as they are called here. 1808 Ashe *Trav.* I. 92 The river is full of eddies, ripples, rapids, rocks, and other dangers. 1855 W. Sargent *Braddock's Exped.* 218 Forming a gentle rapid or ripple, and easily fordable at almost any point. 1872 De Vere *Americanisms* 532 In Pennsylvania..the more grievous obstructions are riffles, the slighter ones ripples.
b. *Naut.* (See quot. and Rippling *vbl. sb.*[3] 1.)
1869 A. R. Wallace *Malay Archip.* I. 239 What seamen call the 'ripples' are also very violent in the straits, the sea appearing to boil and foam and dance like the rapids below a cataract.
2. A light ruffling of the surface of water, such as is caused by a slight breeze; a wavelet.
1798 Coleridge *Anc. Mar.* vi. xi, Its path was not upon the sea, In ripple or in shade. 1814 Scott *Diary* 15 Aug. in *Lockhart*, The channel now seems like a Highland loch; not the least ripple on the waves. 1843 Ruskin *Mod. Paint.* ii. v. i. § 11 (1851) I. 330 If water be rippled, the side of every ripple next to us reflects a piece of the sky. 1873 Black *Pr. Thule* iii, The wash of the ripples along the coast could be heard in the stillness.
attrib. 1848 Lowell *Fable for Critics* Poet. Wks. (1884) 166/1 Like ripple-shades netting the bed of a brook. 1856 Sorby in *Edinb. New Phil. Jrnl.* III. 114 The direction of a current can also be ascertained from the ripple marks; from that modification of them for which I have proposed the term 'ripple drift'.
fig. 1838 Emerson *Address* Wks. (Bohn) II. 201 See how nations and races flit by on the sea of time, and leave no ripple to tell where they floated or sunk. 1859 Geo. Eliot *A. Bede* iii, Mere waves and ripples in an unfathomable ocean of love and beauty. 1872 Holmes *Poet Breakf.-t.* viii, It always seems to me that talk is a ripple and thought a ground swell.
b. *transf.* A mark, appearance, or movement resembling or suggestive of a ripple on water.
1843 Holtzapffel *Turning* I. 39 The fibres..will be found to be wavy, on the face, at right angles to that on which the ripple is observed. 1850 Thackeray *Pendennis* iv, Her black hair waved..with a natural ripple. 1881 *Truth* 19 May 686/2 The dress..was of pink silk,..the front being covered with ripples of white lace. 1891 Hardy *Tess* xxxii, A glistening ripple of gossamer webs was visible.
attrib. 1870 *Daily News* 12 May, The Princess, who in her..new 'ripple' fashion of hairdressing never looked more lovely. 1899 R. Munro *Preh. Scot.* v. 107 The execution of what is known as ripple-flaking.
c. *ellipt.* A ripple-mark.
1852 Lyell *Elem. Geol.* (ed. 4) ii. 20 This ripple is not entirely confined to the beach between high and low water mark, but is also produced on sands which are constantly covered by water. *Ibid.*, In sandstones..also, as now on the sea-coast, we may often detect two systems of ripples interfering with each other.
3. A sound as of rippling water.
1859 Hawthorne *Marb. Faun* xvii, Talking in the quick, short ripple of the Italian tongue. 1882 Miss Braddon *Mt. Royal* III. vi. 97 A ripple of laughter floated from the hall. 1889 Ruskin *Præterita* III. 63 Presently I was aware of a little ripple of brighter converse going round the table.
4. = Riffle *sb.* 5. Also *attrib.*
1857 Borthwick *3 Yrs. California* vi. 121 The earth and small gravel falls with the water through the sieve into the 'ripple-box'. 1879 Atcherley *Trip Boërland* 114 Half-way down the box is a little ledge termed a 'ripple', about 2 inches in height. 1886 *Pall Mall G.* 18 June 5/2 What is called a 'quicksilver ripple', a solid bit of wood with three troughs cut along it about two inches deep, each a little lower than the other.

Ri·pple, *sb.*[4] ? An attack of the Ripples.
1785 Burns *Let. Goudie* iii, Auld Orthodoxy lang did grapple, But now she's got an unco ripple.

Ripple (ri·p'l), *v.*[1] Also 5–6 rypel (6 ripel, repeyl), 5 rippil (7 -el), 8 riple. [Corresponds to Fris. *ripelje* (*roep-*, *rûpelje*), MDu. (and Du.) *repelen*, MLG. *repelen* (LG. *repeln*, *räpeln*), OHG. *rifilôn* (G. *riffeln*); cf. Ripple *sb.*[1], Du. and MLG. *repen* (whence Sw. *repa*) in the same sense.]
1. *trans.* To draw (flax or hemp) through a kind of comb (see Ripple *sb.*[1]) in order to remove the seeds; to clean from seeds in this manner.
c 1340–[see Rippling *vbl. sb.*[1]]. 1523 Fitzherb. *Husb.* § 146 Howe it [flax] shulde be sowen, weded, pulled, repeyled, watred. 1615 [see Ripple *sb.*[1] b]. 1649 Blithe *Eng. Improv. Impr.* (1653) 262 It is indifferent whether you ripple it, or take off the boles of it, as soone as you bring it home, or when you intend to use it. 1694 Westmacott *Script. Herb.* 75 Then ripple it [flax] through a double tooth'd Iron Comb. 1763 *Museum Rust.* I. 11, I ripple it and water it, and, if I have leisure, proceed to dress it. 1780 Young *Tour Irel.* I. 164 They..immediately ripple it to get the seeds off. 1846 Sproule *Flax* 18 As soon as the capsules containing the seed are dried.., the flax is ready for being rippled.
2. To remove or take *off* (the seeds) by this process.
c 1480 Henryson *Mor. Fab.* viii. (*Preach. Swallow*) xxx, The carle pullit the lyne, Rippillit the bollis, and in beitis set. 1523 Fitzherb. *Husb.* § 146 The bolles of flaxe, whan they be ripeled of, must be rideled from the wedes. 1805 R. W. Dickson *Pract. Agric.* II. 740 It is likewise the practice..to ripple off the seed-pods before the business of watering is commenced. 1861 *Times* 10 Oct., The bolls are rippled off and kiln-dried for very superior cattle-food.
Hence **Ri·ppled** *ppl. a.*
1851 H. Stephens *Bk. Farm* (ed. 2) II. 322/1 The rippled plants should be tied in sheaves. 1879 *Encycl. Brit.* IX. 294/2 The rippled stalks are tied in small bundles.

Ri·pple, *v.*[2] Now *north. dial.* Also 5 reple, repul-. [Of Scand. origin. Cf. Norw. *ripla* to scratch, make strokes in, frequentative or diminutive from *ripa* (Sw. *repa*), of similar meaning.]
1. *trans.* To scratch slightly; to graze or ruffle.
14.. *Guy Warw.* (Caius MS.) 9942 The Duke..smote to Gye...He replid [*v.r.* repulde] hys face and hys chyn. 1570 Levins *Manip.* 128 To Ripple, *rescindere*. 1609 Holland *Amm. Marcell.* xxv. iii. 264 An horsemans javelin.. having slightly rippled the skinne of his left arme, pierced within his short ribs. 1670 Cotton *Espernon* ii. x. 512 The others that had pass'd before him had only rippled up the skin. 1681 — *Wonders of Peak* Wks. (1741) 339 Sans hurt or Blemish, save a little strip Of Hair and Skin rippled upon her Hip. 1781 Hutton *Tour to Caves* Gloss. (ed. 2) 95 *Ripple*, to scratch. 1828 *Craven Gloss.*, *Ripple*, to scratch gently, as with a pin, or to gore slightly. 1855 in *Whitby Gloss.* 1869 in *Lonsd. Gloss.*
2. To break up (ground) slightly.
1764 *Museum Rust.* II. lxxiv. 247 The former only slightly plough, or ripple, their fallows the first year. 1790 W. Marshall *Rur. Econ. Midl. Co.* II. 368 By way of experiment, —Rippled the vacant places of the Bank, at the time of cutting this hedge.

Ri·pple, *v.*[3] Also 7–8 riple. [Of obscure origin. App. distinct from prec., and not obviously related to any sense of Rip *v.*[2]]
1. *intr.* To have or present a ruffled surface; to be covered with small waves; to form ripples.
1670–1 Narborough *Jrnl.* in *Acc. Sev. Late Voy.* i. (1694) 18 The Sea ripled in many places. 1748 *Anson's Voy.* iii. viii. 383 The sea had a very dangerous aspect, for it rippled and foamed, as if it had been full of breakers. 1836 R. H. Froude *Lyra Apost.* (1849) 99, I watch the waves that rippling still Chase one another o'er the marble shore. 1878 Abney *Photogr.* (1881) 9 The interstellar ether in which these waves ripple is assumed to permeate every body. 1887 'Stuart Cumberland' *Queen's Highway* 15 Between the pines, little lakes sparkle and ripple in the sun.
transf. and *fig.* 1844 Emerson *Ess.*, *Nature*, Acres of houstonia, whose innumerable florets whiten and ripple before the eye. 1877 A. B. Edwards *Up Nile* xxi. 605 The young barley rippling for miles in the sun.
b. To flow in ripples.
1769 Gray *Let. to Dr. Wharton* 18 Oct., Along the vale of Eeman, which runs rapidly on near the way, rippling over the stones. 1824 W. Irving *T. Trav.* I. 322 Watched the silver waves rippling through the arches of the broken bridge. 1855 Tennyson *Maud* ii. iv. vi, The rivulet at her feet Ripples on in light and shadow. 1894 Winsor *Cartier to Frontenac* 177 Southward, the sources of the Delaware and Susquehanna rippled onward to the great bays.
transf. and *fig.* 1858 *Sat. Rev.* 20 Nov. 506/2 Saying that Mr. Jones..ripples out in a level current of poetical talk. 1873 Symonds *Grk. Poets* x. 312 Stone walls..fragrant with gadding violets that ripple down their sides. 1889 A. J. C. Hare *Story Life* (1900) VI. 182 Life ripples by so quickly.
c. Of sound: To flow in a sprightly manner.
1879 Dowden *Southey* iv. 85 The *carillons* ripple from old spires. 1892 Sladen *Japs at Home* xvi, Nearly two minutes had elapsed before the last faint wave of sound rippled away.
2. *trans.* To form little waves upon (the surface of water); to agitate lightly.
1786 tr. *Beckford's Vathek* (1868) 96 The water..was violently rippled by the flutter of their fins. 1817 J. Scott *Paris Revisit.* (ed. 4) 16 The vessel rippled the transparent water as she inclined easily on her way. 1840 R. H. Dana *Bef. Mast* xvii, A cool sea-breeze came rippling and darkening the surface of the water. 1887 Rider Haggard *Jess* 62 The great wind..does but ripple the shallow pool as it passes.
fig. 1854 Thoreau *Walden, Solitude*, Like the lake, my serenity is rippled but not ruffled. 1884 *Fortn. Rev.* Apr. 567 Hardly a single event of consequence has rippled the still surface of the financial world during the past month.
b. To mark with or as with ripples; to cause to undulate slightly.
1860 Emerson *Cond. Life, Beauty*, There are faces so.. flushed and rippled by the play of thought, that we can hardly find what the mere features really are. 1891 Meredith *One of our Conq.* II. ii. 29 Mademoiselle rippled her shoulders. 1897 *Geogr. Jrnl.* IX. 280 The finest variety of the assorted sands was also quickly rippled.
c. To turn *out* with a rippling sound.
1890 W. J. Gordon *Foundry* 192 The ordinary notion of printing—a man sitting at a piano and rippling out types.

Ri·ppled, *ppl. a.* [f. prec.] a. Marked with ripples. b. Of hair: Wavy.
1833 Lyell *Princ. Geol.* III. 176 The rippled surface of the hills of blown sand near Calais. 1842 Tennyson *Godiva* 47 She shook her head, And shower'd the rippled ringlets to her knee. 1872 W. S. Symonds *Rec. Rocks* iii. 70 On the west may be seen grand sheets of rippled rocks. 1883 *Science* I. 521/1 Rippled cirrus clouds may have a similar origin.

Ri·pple-grass. *Sc.* and *U.S.* [f. Ripple *sb.*[2]] Rib-leaved plantain.
1824 Mactaggart *Gallovid. Encycl.*, *Ripplegirse*, a broad-leaved herb, which labourers put on cuts. 1856 A. Gray *Man. Bot.* (1860) 269 Ribgrass, Ripplegrass, English Plantain. 1880 in *Antrim & Down Gloss.*

Ri·ppleless, *a.* [f. Ripple *sb.*[3] + -less.] Without a ripple; free from ripples; calm.
1838 Miss Pardoe *River & the Desert* I. 116 The sea lies rippleless like a sheet of lead. 1849 *Zoologist* VII. 2542 Surveying the calm heavy rippleless swell of the sea. 1887 W. Rye *Norfolk Broads* 54 The moonlight slept on the rippleless water.

Ri·pple-mark. [f. Ripple *sb.*[3]] A wavy surface, line, or ridge on sand, mud, or rock, formed by the action of waves or the wind, or by both. Chiefly *Geol.*
1833 Lyell *Princ. Geol.* Index III. 102 Ripple marks formed by the winds on dunes. 1854 *Bakewell's Geol.* 41 The ripple marks of the sea on the shore are very frequently preserved. 1888 *Jrnl. Derbysh. Archæol. Soc.* X. 7 The ripple-marks, rain-pittings and footprints so well known in certain sandstones.
fig. 1876 Lowell *Among my Bks.* Ser. ii. 243 The very ripple-marks on the remotest shores of being.
So **Ri·pple-marked** *a.* Also *transf.*
1841 *Penny Cycl.* XX. 19/1 We find ripple-marked strata among the rocks of every geological age. 1898 *Allbutt's Syst. Med.* V. 919 'Ripple-marked' thickening of the endocardium due to the strain of aortic regurgitation.

Rippler (ri·pləɹ). [f. Ripple *v.*[1] + -er [1].] One who ripples flax; also, an implement for rippling.
1743 R. Maxwell *Sel. Trans.* 328 This Comb separates the Seed from the Lint, with much more Ease to the Ripplers. 1765 *Museum Rust.* IV. 457 Which gives the flax sufficient air, and keeps the handfuls separate and ready for the rippler. 1847 *Jrnl. R. Agric. Soc.* VIII. ii. 375 The ripplers strike the flax through alternately. 1879 *Encycl. Brit.* IX. 294/2 The best rippler..consists of a kind of comb [etc.]. *Ibid.*, Two ripplers sitting opposite each other,..work at the same time.

Ripples. *Sc.* Also 6 rippillis, 7 riples. [? Connected with Ripple *sb.*[2]] 'A weakness in the back and reins, said to be attended with shooting pains' (Jamieson).
c 1500 *Rowlis Cursing* 58 in Laing *Anc. Poet. Scot.* 212 Rimbursin, rippillis or belly-thra. 1586 *Indictment* in *Scott's Minstr. Scot. Bord.* (1869) 457 That the bishop of St. Andrews laboured under sindrie diseases, sic as the ripples. 1681 Colvil *Whigs Supplic.* (1751) 43 Priests diseased of the Riples, Hirpling through the streets like criples. 1728 Ramsay *Advice to Mr.* — 8 For warld's wasters, like poor cripples, Look blunt with poverty and ripples. 1787 Taylor *Scot. Poems* 143 It tempered weel our mony-plies, Ca'd ripples frae our backs. 1898 Ld. E. Hamilton *Mawkin* xvi. 218 I'm never the same man since the ripples took me.

Ripplet (ri·plėt). [f. Ripple *sb.*[3] + -et.] A small ripple; a wavelet.
1846 in Worcester. 1866 Neale *Sequences & Hymns* 144 While to her quays and wharves..Creep up the ripplets. 1880 *Time* II. 12 The broad, calm, and limpid river, with its riplets and currents.

Ri·ppling, *vbl. sb.*[1] [f. Ripple *v.*[1]] The action or process of cleaning flax, etc., from seeds.
c 1440 *Promp. Parv.* 434/2 Rypelynge, of flax, or oþer lyke, *avulsio*. 1660 Howell *Parly of Beasts* 14 There must be..rippling, braking,..and heckling of Hemp. 1765 *Museum Rust.* IV. 456 When the flax grows crooked, it is more liable to be hurt in the rippling and swingling. 1805 R. W. Dickson *Pract. Agric.* II. 739 The operation of rippling should be performed as soon as possible after the crops have been pulled. 1846 Sproule *Flax* 17 The interval between pulling and rippling should not be great.
b. *attrib.*, as *rippling-comb*, *-machine*, *-stick*.
c 1340 *Nominale* (Skeat) 545 Swangulstoke, riplingcombe, swyngilwande. 1483 *Cath. Angl.* 306/2 A Ripplyng stoke. 1721 Kelly *Scot. Prov.* 95 Every Thing has its time, and so has the Rippling-comb. *a* 1796 Burns *Had I the Wyte?* 29 He claw'd her wi' the ripplin-kame. 1837 *Flemish Husb.* (L.U.K., III.) 44 Drawing the flax through a rippling machine, which is a kind of comb with blunt iron teeth. 1847 *Jrnl. R. Agric. Soc.* VIII. ii. 375 Four men, with two rippling-combs, will take the seed off rather more than an acre in the day.

Ri·ppling, *vbl. sb.*[2] *rare.* [f. Ripple *v.*[2]] A scratch or graze; the action of grazing a surface.

c 1430 *Syr Gener.* (Roxb.) 5750 Yet it hurt not the king, Vnethes but a litle rippling. *a* 1661 Fuller *Worthies*, *Wales* Pref., Like a Ball cast down and deaded on a soft Floor,.. without the least Ripling or Rebounding.

Ri·ppling, *vbl. sb.*[3] Also 7–8 ripling, 8 repling. [f. Ripple *v.*[3]]
1. The formation, or appearance, of ripples on the surface of water; *spec.* a strong ruffling of the sea caused by conflicting currents or tides.
1669 Sturmy *Mariner's Mag.* iv. i. 138 The Ship is carried away by unknown Currents,..discovered by their Ripplings. 1699 Dampier *Voy.* II. 494, I found by the rippling of the Sea, that there was a strong Current against us. 1726 Shelvocke *Voy. round World* 299, I took all imaginable precaution to discover any ripling, or discoloured water. 1744 J. Philips *Jrnl. Anson's Exped.* 30 *note*, A Replin is a Meeting of two Currents, which creates a cockling in the Sea, and makes it appear like shallow Water. 1779 Forrest *Voy. N. Guinea* 127 Many calms and ripplings of currents. 1820 W. Scoresby *Acc. Arc. Regions* I. 287 This occasions ripplings in the water. 1850 McCosh *Div. Govt.* iv. ii. (1874) 486 Like the rippling on the surface of a stream made by winds opposed to the current. 1860 Maury *Phys. Geogr.* (Low) ix. § 445 The tiny ripplings of this feeble tide.
fig. 1891 *Spectator* 22 Aug., Agitated by the vivid rippling of all sorts of changeful sympathies.
2. *U.S.* = Ripple *sb.*[3] 1.
1751 J. Bartram *Observ. Trav. Pennsylv.* etc. 47 Half a mile farther we came to a rippling, which carried us with prodigious swiftness down the stream. 1755 L. Evans *Middle Brit. Colonies* 26 At Hart's Rock, the River [Ohio] makes..a very sharp Rippling, where the Boatmen are obliged to wade and hawl up near the Rocks.
3. The sound made by water in motion.
1769 Falconer *Dict. Marine* (1780), *Rippling*, a broken and interrupted noise, produced by a current. 1810 Crabbe *Borough* i. 290 Now walking silent, by the river's side, The ear perceives the rippling of the tide. 1899 Rodway *Guiana Wilds* 226 In the direction from which the rippling of a stream could be heard.

Ri·ppling, *ppl. a.* [f. Ripple *v.*[3]] That ripples; flowing in ripples.
1670 Boyle *Tracts*, *Bottom of Sea* 6 He perceived the Water to make a rippling noise (as the Sea-men call it). 1781 Cowper *Anti-Thelyphth.* 24 Inconstant as the beams that play On rippling waters in an April day. 1801 Foster in *Life & Corr.* (1846) I. 133 The rippling course of a rill. 1852 Longf. *Warden of Cinque Ports* ii, The red autumn sun..glanced on flowing flag and rippling pennon. 1859 Geo. Eliot *A. Bede* i. xv, It was not heavy, massive, merely rippling hair, but soft and silken. 1877 L. Morris *Epic of Hades* ii. 145 Streams Laughed with a rippling music.
Hence **Ri·pplingly** *adv.*
1844 *Fraser's Mag.* XXX. 433 A rill which ran ripplingly over the pebbles.

Ripply (ri·pli), *a.* [f. Ripple *sb.*[3] + -y [1].] Marked or characterized by ripples.
1775 J. Melvin *Jrnl.* (1857) 13, I proceeded down Chaudeur river,..and came to a riply place, which was very dangerous, the rocks standing up all over the river. 1807 J. Barlow *Columb.* iv. 546 The moonbeam..Silvers with trembling tints the ripply tide. 1842 Tennyson *E. Morris* 98 We..ran By ripply shallows of the lisping lake. 1875 Grant *One of the '600'* ix, Undoing her hair, she cut a long and ripply tress.

Ri·ppock. *Sc.* [Origin obscure: cf. Rittock.] The Common Tern.
1813 Montagu *Ornith. Dict.* Suppl., [In] the Orkney and Zetland Islands..they are known by the..names of Tarrock, ..Rittock or Rippock. 1825 Fleming *Brit. Anim.* 143.

Ri·ppon. *Obs.* exc. *Hist.* The name of a town in Yorkshire (now written *Ripon*), used *attrib.* or *ellipt.* as a designation of spurs, for the manufacture of which it was formerly renowned.
1625 B. Jonson *Staple of N.* i. iii, There's an angel, if my Spurres Be not right Rippon. 1636 Davenant *Wits* v. i, With rowels of Sharp Rippon spurs. *a* 1661 Fuller *Worthies*, *Yorks.* (1662) 190 As true Steel as Rippon Rowels. 1704 Swift *Mech. Operat. Spir.* Misc. (1711) 299 The former, while it is in the State of a Rider, wears huge Rippon Spurs. 1835 W. Irving *Abbotsford* § 5 Around were hung..a Highland broadsword from Floddenfield; a pair of Rippon spurs from Bannockburn. 1850 Fairholt *Costume* (ed. 3) II. 349 *Rippons*, spurs.

Rip-rap (ri·p,ræp), *sb.* Also 6 ryprap, riprapp. [f. Rap *sb.*[1] or *v.*[1], with usual change of *a* to *i* in the first syllable; but senses 2 and 3 may be partly of different origin.]
†1. An imitation of the sound caused by a rapid succession of blows; hence, a sharp blow. *Obs.*
c 1580 J. Jeffere *Bugbears* Epilog, With hyffa, with huffa, with ryprap, poff, puffa, and sprityng go we! 1582 Stanyhurst *Æneis* iv. (Arb.) 59 With rip rap bouncing thee ram to the chapter is hurled. *c* 1600 Ruggle *Club Law* i. iv, Hee tooke me such a riprapp on the head.
b. A kind of detonating firework.
1894 Hall Caine *Manxman* 257 A few fireworks, a riprap or two, and some general illumination.
2. *Naut.* (See quots.)
1669 Sturmy *Mariner's Mag.* iv. xviii. 214 Dongeness, Dover, Ripraps, The South Foreland. 1699 Dampier *Voy.* II. ii. 10 Near this Island we always find a great ripling which Seamen call the Rip-raps. 1784 Pennant *Arct. Zool.* Introd. (1792) III. p. iii, Between Bologne and Folkstone ..is..a narrow submarine hill, called the Rip-raps. 1885 C. F. Holder *Marvels Anim. Life* 224 The rip-rap, as they call the tide agin' the wind.
3. *U.S.* Loose stone thrown down in water or on a soft bottom to form a foundation for a breakwater or other work.
1847 in Webster. 1875 Knight *Dict. Mech.* 1946/2 s.v., Charleston Harbor, and Plymouth Breakwater, England, are founded on rip-raps. 1899 *Rep. Iowa Geol. Surv.* IX. 435 Limestone weathering to a most irregular face, of no value except for rip-rap.
attrib. 1886 C. D. Warner *Their Pilgr.* v. (1888) 120 Broken, ragged, slimy rocks, as if they had been dumped there for a rip-rap wall.
So **Ri·p-ra·p** *v.*, to found upon, or cover with, a deposit of loose stone. Hence **Ri·p-ra·pped** *ppl. a.*, **Ri·p-ra·pping** *vbl. sb.* *U.S.*
1848 in Bartlett *Dict. Amer.* (1859) s.v., If, in constructing a bulkhead, it should be determined to rip-rap to low-water mark,..the cost for rip-rapping..would be about eighty thousand dollars. 1883 *American* VI. 297 The stream will be confined within permanent barriers by rip-rapped banks and levees. 1884 *Harper's Mag.* Sept. 621/2 The face slope ..and the rear..are riprapped with stone.

Rip-reyue: see Reap-reeve.

Riproa·rious, *a.* *U.S.* Also -rorious. [f. Rip *v.*[2], after *uproarious*.] Boisterous, violent.
1855 Haliburton *Nature & Human N.* I. 58 That's because you..never saw a riprorious hurricane in all your life. 1890 *Harper's Mag.* Apr. 796/2 His waning buzz of rip-roarious approbation.

Ripsack (ri·psæk). [f. Rip *v.*[2] + Sack *sb.*[1] (cf. quot.).] The Californian Grey Whale.
1860 *Merc. Marine Mag.* VII. 213 It being difficult to capture them, they have a variety of names among whalemen, as 'Ripsack',..'Devil-fish'.

Ri·p-saw, *sb.* [f. Rip *v.*[2]] A saw used for cutting wood in the direction of the grain.
1846 Holtzapffel *Turning* II. 708 The rip-saw has the coarsest teeth, and which are of slight pitch...The half-rip is similar, but a little finer. 1875 *Carp. & Join.* 14 Hand saw, divided into the largest or rip saw, intermediate or half-rip, and smallest. 1883 *Harper's Mag.* Jan. 198/2 Dawson's lumber was cut over pits by means of a rip-saw.
Hence **Ri·p-saw** *v.*, to cut with a rip-saw.
1885 *Cent. Mag.* Nov. 33, I ripsawed the lumber up here.

Rip-stick: see Rip *sb.*[3]

Ripstone, incorrect form of Ribston(e.
1837 Dickens *Pickw.* vi, A little hard-headed, Ripstone pippin-faced man. *Ibid.* lx, The officiating clerk peeled and ate three Ripstone pippins.

Rip-sulwer: see Reap-silver.

[**Rip-towel.** 'The gratuity or reward given to customary Tenants, when they have reaped their Lord's Corn'.
1701 Manley *Cowell's Interpreter* s.v. *Reap-towel* (and hence in later Dicts.), citing *MS. Cott. Nero* A. xii. fol. 104 b (*c* 1350). The word in the MS. is *ripetowel* and the meaning uncertain.]

Ripuarian (ripiu,ē·riăn), *a.* and *sb.* [f. med. L. *Rīpuāri-us* (also *Ribuāri-us*); that this is a derivative of L. *rīpa* is very doubtful.]
A. *adj.* 1. The distinctive epithet of the ancient Franks living on the Rhine between the Moselle and Meuse.
1839 Keightley *Hist. Eng.* I. 129 Lands were given to those who were named the Limitanean and Ripuarian soldiery, the latter from their location on the banks of the great frontier rivers. 1861 J. G. Sheppard *Fall Rome* iv. 190 A great multitude..burst over the Rhine, easily overcoming the feeble resistance offered by the Ripuarian Franks.
2. The distinctive epithet of the code of law observed by the Ripuarian Franks.
1781 Gibbon *Decl. & F.* xxxviii. (1787) III. 585 *note*, The Ripuarian law declares..this indulgence in favour of the plaintiff. 1804 Ranken *Hist. France* III. iii. iii. 292 By the consuetude of Roman and Gothic law in the south and west counties: of the Salic, Ripuarian, and Burgundian, on the north and east. 1875 Maine *Hist. Inst.* x. 284 Under the Ripuarian Law he goes through the expressive formality of standing at his door with a drawn sword.
B. *sb. pl.* The Ripuarian Franks.
1781 Gibbon *Decl. & F.* xxxviii. (1787) III. 584 Within the same period, the customs of the Ripuarians were transcribed and published. 1862 *Chambers's Encycl.* IV. 494/2 The Ripuarians..on both sides of the Rhine as far up as the Main. 1882–3 Schaff *Encycl. Relig. Knowl.* I. 513 In the hands of the Franks the city was the metropolis of the Ripuarians until the time of Charlemagne.

Ripuary (ri·piuări), *a.* *rare.* [ad. med.L. *Rīpuāri-us*.] = Ripuarian *a.* 2.
1622 Malynes *Anc. Law-Merch.* 475 The auncient Gaules termed all their lawes either Ripuarie or Salique. 1801 Ranken *Hist. France* I. i. 24 Clovis seems to have occupied himself..in revising and improving the Salic and Ripuary laws. 1843 Brougham *Pol. Phil.* i. 367 The Ripuary law was apparently of later date than the Salic. *Ibid.* 368 The Burgundian Law..is..more refined than the Salic or Ripuary codes.

Ris, obs. variant of Rice [1]; Rise *v.*

‖ **Risagallo.** *Obs.*⁻¹ [It. *risagallo*, obs. var. of *risigallo*: see Resalgar.] Arsenic.
1610 Markham *Masterp.* ii. cxxx. 432 Other Farriers vse the powder of Risagallo, or Risagre, but it is a great deale too strong a fretter.

† **Risagon.** *Obs. Med.* Also 7 rysagone (8–9 -gon), risagon. [Orig. obscure.] = Cassumunar.
1679 J. Pechey (*title*), Some Observations made upon the Root Cassumuniar called otherwise Rysagone. 1681 Grew *Musæum* 386 Rizagon, a Root brought from Bengala, of good use. 1748 W. Lewis *Pharmacop.* 20 Cassumuniar, the root. Risagon. 1850 Pereira *Mat. Med.* II. i. 1121.

Risagre, obs. variant of Resalgar.

† **Risbank.** *Obs.* [ad. Du. *rijsbank*, f. *rijs* Rice [1]. Hence also G. *rissbank*, F. *risban*.] An artificial bank, properly one faced or strengthened with brushwood.
Earlier in the form *rice-bank*: see Rice [1] 5.
1731 *Hist. Litteraria* I. 515 The Art of constructing Sluices, Dykes, Piles, Moles, Risbanks, Light-houses, Docks. 1758 Borlase *Nat. Hist. Cornwall* 325 This Risbank, or mound, ranges up-hill and down-hill indifferently. 1761 Hume *Hist. Eng.* (1770) IV. xxxvii. 482 The fleet battered the risbank, which guarded the entry of the harbour.

† **Riscalda·tion.** *Obs.*⁻¹ [ad. It. *riscaldazione*.] The action of warming or heating.
1599 Linche *Anc. Fiction* E iv, From the ouer-vehement ardour and riscaldation of his beames.

Risch(e, obs. forms of Rush (the plant).

‖ **Ri·sco.** *Obs.* [a. older It. *risco* (Florio), var. of *risico*, *rischio*: see Risk *sb.*, and cf. Risgo.] Risk.
1657 R. Ligon *Barbadoes* 1 Having been censured by some that I should..undertake to run so long a Risco from England to the Barbadoes. 1682 Scarlett *Exchanges* Pref. A 3 b, To consider..their great Labour and Expences, the Risco that they run [etc.]. 1707 tr. *Wks. C'tess D'Anois* (1715) 431 The King had run a thousand Risco's since his confinement in the Cage.

† **Risconter.** *Obs.*⁻¹ [ad. It. *riscontro*: see Rescounter *sb.*] Meeting, encounter.
1592 Wotton in *Reliq.* (1685) 659 The Cardinal had only signified the Fact, as suspecting (belike) the risconter of the Pope's Courriers.

Rise (raiz), *sb.* Forms: 5 ryse, ryese, 6 rys, 6– rise. [f. the vb. Cf. LG. *rîs*.]
I. †1. The act, on the part of a hare, of finally rising to return to its form. *Obs.*⁻¹
c 1410 *Master of Game* (MS. Digby 182) i, And there she shall crosse wayes x. or xii. tymes and then she shal make hir ryses.
†2. a. A spring or bound upwards; *esp.* one made with the help of a run at the outset of a long leap. *Obs.*
1600 Kemp *Nine Daies Wonder* B ij b, At length comming to a broad plash of water and mud, which could not be auoyded I fetcht a rise. 1642 Fuller *Holy & Prof. State* iv. iii. 251 A long leap from York to Rome, and therefore he needed to take a good rise. 1681 W. Robertson *Phraseol. Gen.* (1693) 480 He runs far back that means to leap a great way; He takes his rise far.
†b. A start or aid towards rising in a leap; a place from which to rise or soar. *Obs.*
1639 Ld. Digby *Lett. conc. Relig.* (1651) 85 There might be a man so disposed as (having a good rise, and with a convenient career) to leap at once from England to Rome. 1648 Boyle *Seraph. Love* (1700) 170 Having Piled them up together, have made that heap but a Rise to take our soaring flight from. 1697 Creech tr. *Manilius* i. 6 Rais'd so high, from that convenient rise She took her flight, and quickly reacht the Skies. 1728 Chambers *Cycl.* s.v. *Step*, The Step, properly, puts a Horse on the Hand, and gives him a Rise to Leap.
3. The coming of the sun (moon, or planets) above the horizon; hence also, the region of sunrise, the east. (Now usually *rising*.)
1599 Shaks., etc. *Pass. Pilgr.* 194 The morning rise Doth cite each moving sense from idle rest. 1635–56 Cowley *Davideis* iv. 6 Moab..Up with the Sun arose, and..With lifted Hands bow'd towards his shining rise. 1665 Sir T. Herbert *Trav.* (1677) 44 Truly many Sun-Idolaters I have seen, all which worship his rise, but none his setting. 1712 Blackmore *Creation* 98 Th' adventurous merchant thus pursues his way Or to the rise, or to the fall of day. 1865 Sir J. K. James *Tasso* xii. xc, To her at rise, to her at sunset hour. 1885–94 R. Bridges *Eros & Psyche* March xxiii, She..Lookt left and right to rise and set of day.
fig. 1671 Milton *P. R.* i. 294 So spake our Morning Star then in his rise. 1738 Wesley *Hymns*, '*The Sun of Righteousness appears*' iv, In vain the Stone, the Watch, the Seal Forbid an early Rise. 1781 J. Morison in *Scot. Paraphr.* xix. 2 To hail thy rise, thou better Sun, the gathering nations come.
4. Upward movement; ascent; transference to a higher level. Also *fig.*
1573–9 G. Harvey *Letter-bk.* (Camden) 69 If once to heaven we take our rise. 1640 W. Stryle *Antisco's Span. Gallant* A 10 b, Like Birds for want of ayre we faint: Lye still and cannot make our rise. 1659 *Instructions Oratory* 11 Which it cannot so easily mount unto at the first, without taking, by the way, this meaner rise. 1788 *Trifler* No. 16. 216 He was on the rise to treat more largely on the folly of parental officiousness. 1808 Scott *Marm.* vi. xv, The steed along the drawbridge flies, Just as it trembled on the rise. 1847 *Illustr. Lond. News* 10 July 27/3 The balloon..now and then took a rise out of the hands of the stalwart men who held it. 1872 Jenkinson *Guide Eng. Lakes* (1879) 173 Beyond Gosforth a steep rise is made.
b. Capacity for or power of rising.
a 1716 South (Cent.), These were sublimities above the rise of the apostolic spirit. 1848 *Jrnl. R. Agric. Soc.* IX. ii. 574 There is no rise or spring in them. 1881 W. E. Dickson *Organ-Build.* vi. 73 The reservoir may have a rise or play of about 10 inches or a foot.
5. Elevation in fortune or rank.
1632 Massinger *City Madam* v. i, Many..Have written 'Ladies of Honour', and some few Have higher titles; and that's the furthest rise You can in England hope for. 1654 Gayton *Pleas. Notes* iii. x. 132 Duke Ricards Letter..He bid me read, my Rise was laid. 1706 E. Ward *Wooden World Diss.* (1708) 87 All Admirals, as well as Captains, are oblig'd to begin their Rise there. 1781 Justamond tr. *Priv. Life Lewis XV*, I. 99 We have seen the beginning of this fortunate man's rise. 1841 Spalding *Italy & It. Isl.* II. 243 The rise of the Medici and other wealthy Florentine families, furnished liberal patrons to art. 1866 G. Macdonald *Ann. Quiet Neighb.* xiii. (1878) 255 It was considered a rise in life.
b. An occasion or means of rising (in fortune or rank).

c 1680 G. Dallas *Stiles* (1697) 89 The eminent Parts with which the Lord has Endued your Lordship..have been no small Rise to your Noble Family in this Age. 1773 Foote *Bankrupt* i. Wks. 1799 II. 101 Don't you consider, that her ruin, as you call it, will be your rise?
c. Upward course; advance towards a flourishing or prosperous condition, etc.
Not always distinguishable from sense 17 or 19.
1721 Berkeley *Prev. Ruin Gt. Britain* Wks. 1871 III. 211 Our ancestors during their rise and greatness. 1727 De Foe *Syst. Magic* i. iii, A great many useful and agreable speculations offer themselves in the rise and progress of the thing itself. 1869 J. Martineau *Ess.* II. 173 This period of rise and of decline. 1888 Bryce *Amer. Commw.* II. liii. 335 The second period in the annals of American parties, which ..include the rise and fall of the Whig party.
6. *Angling.* The movement of a fish to the surface of the water to take a fly or bait; an instance of this.
1651 T. Barker *Art of Angling* (1653) 5 If you can attain to angle with one haire, you shall have the more rises. 1860 Russell *Diary India* II. 199, I tried every fly that I could think of; but not a sign of a rise. 1867 F. Francis *Angling* i. (1880) 6 Let him then note where these rises are the thickest, and choose that place.
b. *To get*, *have*, or *take a rise out of* (one), to make a butt of, raise a laugh at, by some form of pretence or dissimulation.
1834 Medwin *Angler in Wales* I. 113 We will have a rise out of Charters at our *noctes*. 1840 Thackeray *Catherine* vii, Oh but it was a rare rise we got out of them chaps. 1882 Blackmore *Cristowell* xviii, It would be worth a hundred pounds to me, to have a rise taken out of him.
c. *To make a rise*, to succeed in striking gold by mining.
1890 'R. Boldrewood' *Miner's Right* (1899) 24/1 You've got to work till you make a 'rise', for my sake.
7. The act of rising from the dead (also *rise-again*), or *from* some condition.
1738 Wesley *Easter Hymn* iii, Death in vain forbids His rise; Christ hath opened Paradise. 1839–52 Bailey *Festus* 30 The grave hath no pride, nor the rise-again. 1868 Lynch *Rivulet* cli. iv, Thy word..insure[s] Our rise from shame.
†8. A revolt, rising. *Obs.*⁻¹
1768 Boswell *Corsica* (ed. 2) 109 The Genoese, eager to repress the rise of 1734.
II. 9. A piece of rising ground; a hill.
1639 Fuller *Holy War* i. ii. (1840) 3 The Jews..were forbidden to enter into Jerusalem, or so much as to behold it from any rise or advantage of ground. 1654 Earl Monm. tr. *Bentivoglio's Wars Flanders* 206 It hath on one side an eminent Rise, which Commands the whole Town. 1700 Dryden *Baucis & Philemon* 17 Two neighb'ring Trees.. Stand on a mod'rate Rise. 1708 J. Philips *Cyder* i. 6 If therefore, thou incline To deck this Rise with Fruits of various Tastes. 1816 Byron *Ch. Har.* iii. lvi, On a rise of gentle ground There is a small and simple pyramid. 1856 Ruskin *PræRaphaelitism*, etc. (1906) 231 Distant cumuli, heavy with rain, hanging on the rises of the moorland. 1878 B. Taylor *Deukalion* i. v. 40 Yonder, on the rise, Who leans with folded arms against the stone?
10. An upward slope or direction, *esp.* of strata, coal-beds, veins of ore, etc.
1698 G. Thomas *Pensilvania* 46 Some of their Noses having a rise like the Roman. 1708 J. C. *Compl. Collier* (1845) 40 It is always look'd upon to be of good Advantage to the Colliery, to have a rise in the Thill, and of the Coal as we work. 1731 W. Halfpenny *Perspective* 31 Draw Lines..parallel to the line SF, which shews the Perspective Rise of every Member. 1839 Ure *Dict. Arts* 984 This gas being lighter than common air, always ascends to the roof or to the rise of the galleries. 1856 Whyte Melville *Kate Coventry* xii, The ground is now..on the rise. 1878 Huxley *Physiogr.* xviii. 313 A very sharp rise leads from the Pacific to the range of the Andes.
attrib. 1768 *Gen. Hist.* in *Ann. Reg.* 63 There are two other fire-engines of a pretty large size, working on the rise-part of this colliery. 1839 Ure *Dict. Arts* 964 Where the coal-measures are horizontal, and the faults run at a greater angle than 45° to the line of bearing, they are termed dip and rise faults. 1883 Gresley *Gloss. Coal-mining* 204 *Rise Split*, a proportion of the ventilative current sent into a rise district of a mine. *Ibid.*, *Rise Workings*, underground workings carried on to the rise or high side of the shafts.
b. *Mining.* An excavation or working on the up side of a shaft. (Cf. Rising *vbl. sb.* 12 c.)
1839 *Penny Cycl.* XV. 241/1 Should the ore extend far enough..levels may be driven from the 'rises' to render it more accessible. 1861 G. Harris in *Athenæum* 19 Jan. 82 Here were ends Cut through hard marble by the miners' skill, And winzes, stopes and rises. 1884 R. Hunt *Mining* 912 *Rise*, this is the same meaning as stope, or excavation in the back of a level. 'I belong (*viz.* I work) up in the rise.'
11. The vertical height of a step, an arch, an inclined surface or object, etc., measured from the base or springing-line to the highest point.
1663 Gerbier *Counsel & Adv. to Builders* 100 The rise, width, and depth of steps, shall not need to be repeated, since they have been described [etc.]. 1739 Labelye *Short Acc. Piers Westm. Bridge* 74 The prick'd Lines shew what would be the Rise of Stone Arches, and the Disposition of their Joints. 1825 J. Nicholson *Operat. Mechanic* 539 The height, or rise of the arch, is a line drawn at right angles from the middle of the chord..to the intrados. 1839 *Civil Eng. & Arch. Jrnl.* II. 81/2 The two side arches 156 feet span, and 15½ feet rise. 1874 Micklethwaite *Mod. Par. Churches* 89 The rise of the steps will vary according to circumstances.
†b. The pitch of a screw. *Obs. rare.*
1683 Moxon *Mech. Exerc.*, *Printing* xi. ¶ 1, I shew'd..the manner of making a Screw..; but assigned it no particular Rise;..Therefore its assigned Rise being two Inches and an half in a Revolution [etc.].
12. a. A flight *of* steps.
c 1710 Celia Fiennes *Diary* (1888) 258 The queen being come up to her table wᶜʰ was a great rise of stepps. 1848 B. Webb *Cont. Ecclesiol.* 45 There is a rise of steps at the east end of the nave. *Ibid.* 400.
b. = Riser 7.
1711 W. Sutherland *Shipbuild. Assist.* 65 The Steps.. have no Rises nor Stiles. 1793 Smeaton *Edystone L.* § 227 It was stopped by the rise of the third step, against which it seemed abutted. 1879 *Cassell's Techn. Educ.* I. 329/2 The flat surface of a stair is called the tread, and the upright face is termed the rise.
III. 13. An increase in height of the sea, streams, or water, by tides, floods, etc., or of a liquid in a vessel; the amount of this increase.
1626 Bacon *Sylva* § 889 Experiment..Touching the Rise of Water, by Meanes of Flame. 1662 Dryden *To Ld. Chancellor Clarendon* 142 The hill..mounts, but so as billows play, Whose rise not hinders but makes short our way. 1743 Bulkeley & Cummins *Voy. S. Seas* 120 We ran in before the Wind for about two Leagues, expecting every Rise and Fall of the Sea to be a Wreck. 1771 *Jrnl. Cook's Voy. World* 119 We observed the whole rise of the tide did not exceed four feet. 1797 *Encycl. Brit.* (ed. 3) XVIII. 406 That the rise and fall of the mercury [in a thermometer] may be better seen. 1830 Lyell *Princ. Geol.* I. 264 The perpendicular rise and fall of the spring-tides is fifteen feet, and at neap-tides, eight feet. 1847 Grote *Greece* IV. xxv. 14 He is preserved by the sudden rise of a river. 1860 *Merc. Mar. Mag.* VII. 339 South-westerly wind will follow, especially if the barometer rise is sudden.
transf. 1713 Steele *Guard.* No. 149 The head-dress receives frequent rises and falls every year. 1868 Tennyson *Lucretius* 10 His mind..fancy-borne perhaps upon the rise And long roll of the Hexameter.
14. *Mus.* An increase of pitch in a tone or voice.
1626 Bacon *Sylva* § 105 In the ordinary Rises and Falles of the Voice,..there fall out to be two Beemols..betweene the Vnison and the Diapason. 1867 MacFarren *Harmony* (1892) 73 A complete chord may be suspended when the progression of roots is by the rise of a 4th or fall of a 5th. 1879 Grove *Dict. Mus.* I. 43 The..graces peculiar to old English music..include the Plain-beat or rise.
15. An increase in amount.
a 1699 Temple (J.), The rise or fall that may happen in his constant revenue by a Spanish war. 1811 A. T. Thomson *Lond. Disp.* (1818) 664 By the sudden rise of temperature.. a considerable waste of product also takes place. 1817 Jas. Mill *Brit. India* II. v. vii. 591 On the same terms, excepting a small rise in the annual payment. 1871 B. Stewart *Heat* (ed. 2) § 91 This heat is..absorbed by the ice without producing any rise of temperature.
b. *colloq.* An advance in wages or salary.
1836–7 Dickens *Sk. Boz*, *Scenes* i, The receipt of seven shillings a-week, with the prospect of an early rise to eight.
c. *U.S.* (See quot.)
1859 Bartlett *Dict. Amer.* (ed. 2) 367 The phrase 'and the rise', is used in some parts of the South to mean 'and more';..'I should think there were a thousand and the rise', i.e. a thousand and more.
16. An increase in the value or price *of* a thing.
1691 Locke *Money* Wks. 1727 II. 87 The Market-price of any thing, and so of Bullion, is to be taken..not from the extraordinary Rise of two or three Market-days in a Year. 1723 Swift *Agst. Enlarging Power Bps.* Wks. 1751 IX. 23 The Bishops have had some Share in the gradual Rise of Lands. 1790 Washington *Writ.* (1892) XII. 1 The progress of public credit is witnessed by a considerable rise of American stock abroad as well as at home. 1821 Clare *Vill. Minstr.* I. 17 'Bout work being slack, and rise and fall of bread. 1885 *Law Times Rep.* LII. 648/2 A great rise had taken place in the value of the Sydney property.
b. *On the rise*, becoming more valuable or dearer.
1808 *Times* 23 Feb., Colonial produce is on the rise. 1884 *Illustr. Lond. News* 13 Dec. 570/3 'Sheep,' for five years, have been steadily 'on the rise'.
IV. 17. An origin or source; a beginning; a start. Freq. in phr. *to have* or *take one's rise*.
1630 Prynne *Anti-Armin.* 115 Which by this meanes take their rise and being from the creature. 1664 Power *Exp. Philos.* i. 60 If you take Nature at the rise, and critically observe her in her imperfect and obscure beginning. 1690 Locke *Govt.* ii. i, He..must..find out another rise of Government, another original of political power. 1738 Wesley *Ps.* xci. iii, Nor Plague of unknown Rise that kills In Darkness. 1763 J. Brown *Poetry & Mus.* v. 77 He..sung the Generation of the World and the Rise of Things. 1847 Yeowell *Anc. Brit. Church* iii. 25 Intimately acquainted with the rise of all churches. 1878 Browning *La Saisiaz* 33 Ask the rush if it suspects Whence and how the stream which floats it had a rise.
†b. *To take one's rise* (*from*), to start, begin with, in narration. *Obs.*
1647–8 Cotterell *Davila's Hist. Fr.* (1678) 14 Taking his rise from the fortunes of the House of Lorraine. 1697 J. Sergeant *Solid Philos.* 63, I take my Rise from the remotest Principles that can concern that Point, and these are my Thoughts. 1716 J. Collier tr. *Gregory Nazians.* 60 Let us take our rise a little from the Original of things.
†18. An occasion; a ground or basis. *Obs.* (Common *c* 1650–90.)
1641 *Triumph of K. Chas.* in *Harl. Misc.* (Malh.) V. 101 We had two humble petitions to present to both their Majesties, and we had the rise and encouragement to both, from that which his Majesty was pleased to deliver to us. 1669 R. Montagu in *Buccleuch MSS.* (Hist. MSS. Comm.) I. 431, I will write a letter which he may show the King, and shall be a rise for him to ask the King to do the business. 1688 Boyle *Final Causes* iv. 111 These Celestial bodys may..give man a rise to admire and praise the greatness and power of the Divine Maker. 1759 Sterne *Tr. Shandy* ii. v, The reason, or rather the rise of this sudden demigration was as follows. 1820 Jodrell s.v. *Manteau*, Mantua in Italy may have given the rise of its etymology.
b. *To give rise to*, to occasion, to bring about, to cause. (See also Give *v.* 48.)
1705 Addison *Italy* 132 His Reputation..gave Rise to the Republick that calls it self after his Name. 1774 Goldsm. *Nat. Hist.* (1776) I. 256 This shallowness and narrowness in many parts of the sea, give also rise to a peculiarity in the tides. 1830 R. Knox *Béclard's Anat.* 304 When this action has been very long and violent, it gives rise to a painful sensibility. 1873 Symonds *Grk. Poets* 417 The strangest misconception to which religious prejudice has ever given rise.
19. The act of coming into existence or notice.
1656 Earl Monm. tr. *Boccalini's Advts. fr. Parnass.* i. xvii. (1674) 19 Remedies..whereby stoutly to resist vice in its rise. 1664 Power *Exp. Philos.* i. 78 Which practical part of Opticks is but yet in the rise. 1737 Whiston *Josephus, Antiq.* ix. x. § 2 Upon the rise of a most terrible storm. 1777 Sir W. Jones *Ess. Poet. Eastern Nat.*, The rise of a poet in their tribe. 1869 J. Martineau *Ess.* II. 52 It is manifestly concurrent with the rise of new questions.

Rise, obs. variant of Rice [1] and [2].

Rise (raiz), *v.* Pa. t. rose. Pa. pple. risen. [Common Teutonic: OE. *rísan*, = OFris. *rīsa* (mod.Fris. *rize*, *ryzje*), MDu. *rīsen* (Du. *rijzen*), OS. *rīsan* (MLG. *rīsen*), OHG. *rīsan*, *risen* (G. *reisen*, of the sun), ON. and Icel. *rísa* (Norw. and MSw. *risa*), Goth. (*ur*)*reisan*. No related forms have been traced outside of Teutonic.
In OE., as in OS., the simple *rīsan* is extremely rare, the common form being the compound *arīsan* Arise *v.* In early ME. the use of *rise* for *arise* is prominently northern, and may be mainly due to the influence of ON. *rísa*.
The causative forms related to *rise* are Raise and Rear, but *rise* itself has to a certain extent (esp. in later use) assumed the functions of a transitive verb.]
A. Inflexional forms.
1. *Inf.* (and *Pres.*). 1–2 rísan, 3–4 risen (3 -enn, 4 -in, 5 -yn), 4 rijsen, 4–5 rysen (5 -yn); 3– rise, 4 rijse, 4–6 (8 *Sc.*) ryse (6 rysse, reyse), 6 rize; 3–4 ris, rys, 5 riss, 5–6 ryss, 6 *Sc.* ryis(s.
c 1000 *Ags. Ps.* (Thorpe) lviii. 1 Fram laðum, þe me..on risan willað. *c* 1200 *Trin. Coll. Hom.* 103 Ich ne mai wið-uten þin elp risen. *c* 1250 *Gen. & Ex.* 4039 Of ðe sal risen sterre briȝt. *a* 1300 *Cursor M.* 14495 All þe werld mon wit him rijs. *c* 1340 Hampole *Pr. Consc.* 4810 Þai shalle with þam rys ogayn. 1382 Wyclif *Ps.* xciii. 16 Who shal al rijsen to me aȝen the warieris? *c* 1440 *Promp. Parv.* 435/1 Rysyn erly. 1483 *Cath. Angl.* 309/2 To Ryse be fore day. 1550 Crowley *Epigr.* 626 Fewe..do vse to rise earelye. 1556 *Chron. Gr. Friars* (Camden) 59 Thoys that dyd rysse in dyvers places. 1567 *Gude & Godlie B.* (S.T.S.) 234, I do call on all men mortall To ryis. 1590 Spenser *F. Q.* i. iii. 19 Nohe durst rize..him in to lett.
b. 3 *sing. pres. ind.* 4–5 rist(e, ryst(e.
13.. *K. Alis.* 2158 (Bodl. MS.), Now rist grete tabor betyng. *c* 1330 R. Brunne *Chron. Wace* (Rolls) 15597 Þer kynde so ryst on heyghte. *c* 1385 Chaucer *L. G. W.* 887 *Thisbe*, Tysbe ryst vp with-outyn ony bost.
2. *Pa. t.* α. 3–5 ras (5 rase), 3–4 (9) raas, 5–9 rase, 9 raze; 4–6 (8) rais, 5–6 raiss (6 raisz), 5 rays, 6 rayis; 5 rayse, 5–9 raise, 8 raaize, 9 raaise; 7, 9 rease, 9 reaise, reaaze.
After 1300 these forms are only Sc. and northern.
c 1200 Ormin 4341 Crist ras upp off dæþe. *a* 1300 *E. E. Psalter* xix. 9 We raas, and rightid are. *c* 1340 Hampole *Pr. Consc.* 4308 Als he fra dede rase. *c* 1425 Wyntoun *Cron.* i. xvi. 1542 Agayn his fadyr..Þan he [Jupiter] rase. *c* 1470 Henry *Wallace* v. 966 Rays neuir agayne quhat ane at he hyt rycht. 1533 Gau *Richt Vay* 68 Mony bodis of sanctis ..raisz wp. 1567 *Gude & Godlie B.* (S. T. S.) 111 Quhen men rais in our contrairie. *c* 1680 A. Hume *Brit. Tongue* (1865) 18 Ther rease..a hoat disputation betuene him and me. 1718 Ramsay *Christ's Kirk Gr.* iii. iii, To see the young fouk ere they raise. 1785 Hutton *Bran New Wark* (E. D. S.) 367 Up as she raaize. 1816 Scott *Old Mort.* xxvii, To..sit by the chimley when the reek rase. 1881 Sargisson *Joe Scoap* 105 When t'sun reaaze an set. 1883 R. M. Fergusson *Rambl. Sk. Far North* 143 The water raise an' raise.
β. 3–5 ros, 4–6 roos; 4– rose (5 rosse), 4–5 roose (5 *pl.* rosyn, roosen), 6 roase, rhose, 9 roze, *dial.* rause, rauze, rawse, ruse, ruz.
c 1250 *Gen. & Ex.* 4152 Swilc prophete..Ros non. *c* 1300 *Beket* 1082 He ros him up and bihuld. 1377 Langl. *P. Pl.* B. v. 234, I roos whan þei were arest. *c* 1385 Chaucer *L. G. W.* Prol. 112 (Tanner MS.), The son that roose as rede as rose. *c* 1410 *Sir Cleges* 194 He..rosse upe in that stede. *c* 1449 Pecock *Repr.* v. iii. 497 [There] roosen also manye untrewe sectis. 1568 Grafton *Chron.* II. 382 Then roase the streete, namely the youth. *a* 1591 H. Smith *Wks.* (1867) I. 444 Thou..hast rebelled more since thou rosest. 1637 Milton *Lycidas* 30 The Star that rose..bright. 1732 Berkeley *Alciphr.* i. § 1 Next morning Euphranor rose early. 1804 R. Anderson *Cumbld. Ball.* (*c* 1850) 68 Fast flew the hours—now ruse the muin.
γ. *pl.* 2, 4–5 risen, 4–5 rysen, 5 resyn, reson, rison; *sing.* (and *pl.*) 6 rysse, 6–7 risse; 6 ryse, 6–8 rise, 7 rizze; 7, 9 *dial.* riss (7 riss', ris'), ris, riz.
1154 *O. E. Chron.* (Laud MS.) an. 1135, Agenes him risen sona þa ricemen. 1362 Langl. *P. Pl.* A. v. 176 Þei Risen vp Raply. 1382 Wyclif 1 *Sam.* xxiv. 8 Dauid..suffrede hem not, that thei rysen into Saul. *a* 1440 *Sir Eglam.* 284 Hertys reson on eche a syde. 1556 *Chron. Gr. Friars* (Camden) 45 Thys yere..rysse a gret tempest. 1590 Lodge *Rosalynde* (Hunterian Cl.) 55 He rise vp and went to him. 1609 Tourneur *Funeral Poem* 2 From thy spirit rizze thy worthy fame. 1611 B. Jonson *Catiline* v. vi, As he riss', the day grew black. 1654 Earl Monm. tr. *Bentivoglio's Wars Flanders* 136 As the Tide rise, the Enemies Boats drew nearer. 1676 Hobbes *Iliad* 379 Achilles..sat upon the seat from whence he ris. 1715 M. Davies *Athen. Brit.* I. 154

solemnity of drinking out of a cup, ritually composed, deckt, and fill'd with countrey liquor. 1657 TRAPP *Comm. Ezra* vi. 20 'All of them were pure'—Ritually at least, if not really. 1752 WARBURTON *Serm.* Wks. 1788 V. 79 The rest of the sons of Adam; who, because ritually unholy and prophane, were deemed to be naturally unrelated to them. 1770–4 A. HUNTER *Georg. Ess.* (1804) IV. 291 Besides the mistletoe, the Druids ritually gathered the Selago. 1847 *Ecclesiologist* May 200 Chancel..is ritually confined to that part of the church where the Clerici celebrate the lesser offices. 1892 BRUCE *Apologetics* II. ii. 184 Obligations to be holy, not ritually only but really.

† **Ri·tuous**, *a. Obs.*$^{-1}$ = RITUAL *a.*

1604 HIERON *Wks.* I. 569 Whence had you all that rituous store Vs'd in the masse, and nam'd before?

Riuage, Riual, obs. ff. RIVAGE, RIVAL. **Riue**, obs. f. RIFE, RIVE. **Riuel**, obs. f. RIVEL. **Riuele**, obs. f. RULE. **Riuelet**, obs. var. RIVULET. **Riueling, -yng**, obs. ff. RIVELING[1]. **Riuely**, obs. f. RIFELY. **Riuen**, obs. f. RIVEN. **Riuer(e**, obs. ff. REAVER, RIVER. **Riuersa**, var. RIVERSO *Obs.* **Riuulet**, obs. var. RIVULET.

Rivage (rəi·vėdʒ). Also 4–6 **ryuage, -vage**; 5–7 **riuage**. [a. F. *rivage* (12–13th c.): see RIVE *sb.*[1] and -AGE. So It. *rivaggio*; med.L. *rivagium* (esp. in sense 3).]

1. A coast, shore, or bank. Now only *poet.*

13.. *Reinbroun* xxix. 10 Þe cite on þe riuage hii sye. 1390 GOWER *Conf.* III. 329 The hihe festes of Neptune Upon the stronde at the rivage..Sollempneliche thei besihe. c 1400 *St. Alexius* (Laud 622) 592 He gan to shippen atte Ryuage; Wynde aroos wiþ wood rage. 1483 CAXTON *Cato* D vij, A good holy man which was on the ryuage of the see. 1490 — *Eneydos* vii. 30 Dydo..arryued vpon the Ryuage of affryque for to repayre hir shyppes. 1523 CROMWELL in Merriman *Life & Lett.* (1902) I. 40 Sum other Contraye in the possession of his enemye vpon the Ryvage of the see. 1596 SPENSER *F. Q.* IV. vi. 20 The golden sand, The which Pactolus..Throwes forth upon the rivage. 1609 HOLLAND *Amm. Marcell.* XIV. ii. 5 Having imbattelled themselves neere unto the rivage. 1658 W. BURTON *Itin. Anton.* 161 The River full of Ships,..the rivage full of sea-faring men. 1661 EVELYN *Fumifugium* Misc. Writ. (1805) I. 208 The scent of the orange flowers from the rivage of Genoa. 1814 CARY *Dante, Inf.* XXIX. vii, So mov'd she on, against the current, up The verdant rivage. 1855 SINGLETON *Virgil* II. 100 The dreadful rivages, and brawling floods.

attrib. 1509 HAWES *Past. Pleas.* XXXVI. xvi, Ryght by anone the rivage syde, She cast an anker. 1513 DOUGLAS *Æneis* VI. v. 44 This sorofull boitman..sum..maid to stand Fer from the rivage syde upon the sand.

†2. Arrival at, landing on, a shore. *Obs.*

13.. *K. Alis.* 6079 Kyng Alisaunder, and his baronage, Haveth y-take god ryuage. c 1475 *Partenay* 2734 Hys brother..At vavuent that day riuage gan purchas. c 1500 *Melusine* 114 The patrons made theire recommendacions to god..that by hys benygne grace he wyl graunte to them good ryuage.

†3. Shore or river dues. *Obs.*

Quot. 1598 is translated from a charter of 1278.

1598 HAKLUYT *Voy.* I. 117 So that they shall be free..from all lastage, tallage, passage, cariage, riuage. [1706 PHILLIPS (ed. Kersey), *Rivage*,..a certain Toll, or Duty anciently paid to the King, in some Rivers, for the Passage of Boats, or Vessels.]

Hence † **Ri·vaging**, the act of making up or repairing the bank of a stream. *Obs.*

1610 W. FOLKINGHAM *Art Surv.* II. ii. 50 Sewaging, rilling, brooking, riuaging, foording.

† **Rival**, *sb.*[1] *Obs.* Forms: 4–5 **riuale**, 5 **riuayle**, 6 **rivaile**; 5 **ryuaile, -ayle, ryvaille, -aylle**, 6 **ryual(e**. [a. OF. *rivaille*, f. *rive* RIVE *sb.*[1]]

1. A bank, shore, landing-place. Also *port rival.*

1338 R. BRUNNE *Chron.* (1810) 153 Þe kynges moder Richard Arived at þat riuale. c 1400 tr. *Secreta Secret., Gov. Lordsh.* 52 He þat spendys his good ouyr mesure shal sone come to þe better riuale of pouert. c 1450 LYDG. *Secrees* 1328 Walkyng by Ryvaylles, holdyng ther passage On plesaunt hylles. 1502 in Arnolde *Chron.* (1811) 217 That noo Man be distreyned too make Bruggis ne Ryuals. 1594 GREENE & LODGE *Looking Gl.* (Hunterian Cl.) 57 As I was comming alongst the port ryuale of Niniuie.

2. Landing; arrival at a port.

1412–20 LYDG. *Chron. Troy* II. 8110 To Grekis pleinly þis ryvaille So mortal was & so infortunat. 15.. *Piers of Fulham* 316 in Hazl. *E. P. P.* II. 13 To make his rivaile to be know, At redclif in his saile to show.

Rival (rəi·văl), *sb.*[2] and *a.* Also 6–7 **riual**, 7 **riu-, rivall**. [ad. L. *rīvāl-is*, orig. one living on the opposite bank of a stream from another, f. *rīvus* stream. Hence also F. *rival* (15th c.), Sp. and Pg. *rival*, It. *rivale.*]

A. *sb.* **1.** One who is in pursuit of the same object as another; one who strives to equal or outdo another in any respect.

1577 tr. *Bullinger's Dec.* (1592) 106 To mingle poison priuily..Or else in armour openly to worke his riuals death. 1590 SHAKS. *Mids. N.* III. ii. 156 You both are Riuals, and loue Hermia; And now both Riuals to mocke Helena. 1648–9 *Eikon Bas.* xxvi. (1662) 127 The Independents think themselves manumitted from their Rivals service. 1694 ADDISON *Virg.* Wks. 1726 I. 20 So let the royal insect rule alone And reign without a rival in his throne. 1712 STEELE *Spect.* No. 306 ¶ 1 My Lovers are at the Feet of my Rivals, my Rivals are every Day bewailing me. 1769 ROBERTSON *Chas. V*, IX. III. 173 He beheld a prosperous rival receiving those ensigns of dignity of which he had been stripped. 1835 THIRLWALL *Greece* x. I. 436 Chalcis and Eretria were long rivals. 1853 C. BRONTË *Villette* xv, Come, we will not be rivals, we will be friends. 1899 MISS HARRADEN *Fowler* 128, I believe the medical name for a rival is 'colleague'.

Comb. 1597 SHAKS. *Rich. II*, I. iii. 131 (Q.[1]), The Egle-winged pride Of skie aspiring and ambitious thoughts, With riuall hating enuy.

transf. 1871 FREEMAN *Norm. Conq.* (1876) 211 That long line of low hills,..which seems like a feeble rival of the loftier ranges of the West.

2. One who, or that which, disputes distinction or renown with some other person or thing.

1646 CRASHAW *Sospetto d'Herode* iv, That neither Rome nor Athens can bring forth A Name in noble deeds Rivall to thee! 1667 MILTON *P. L.* II. 472 And so refus'd might in opinion stand His rivals, winning cheap the high repute. 1770 *Junius Lett.* xxxvi. (1788) 194 The successor of one Chancellor might well pretend to be the rival of another. 1776 R. CHANDLER *Trav. Greece* 81 This stadium..is extolled as without a rival, and as unequalled by any theatre. 1855 BREWSTER *Newton* II. xxvii. 400 A man who has had no rival in the times which are past. 1874 GREEN *Short Hist.* vii. § 6. 403 The Spanish generals stood without rivals in their military skill.

B. *adj.* Holding the position of a rival or rivals.

1590 SHAKS. *Mids. N.* IV. i. 139, I know you two are Riuall enemies. 1619 DRAYTON *Lady Geraldine to Surrey* 11 Nor euer did suspitious riuall Eye Yet lye in wait my Fauours to espie. 1697 DRYDEN *Virg. Georg.* III. 28 The Rival Chariots in the Race shall strive. 1712 POPE *Ep. to Miss Blount* 15 Ev'n rival Wits did Voiture's death deplore. 1784 COWPER *Task* V. 123 Thus nature works..in defiance of her rival pow'rs. 1830 D'ISRAELI *Chas. I*, III. v. 62 These Ministers of State attempted..to restrain or abolish, a rival minority. 1886 RUSKIN *Præterita* I. vii. 227 He was perfectly..candid in appraisement of the wine of rival houses.

Comb. 1802–12 BENTHAM *Ration. Judic. Evid.* (1827) IV. 47 The principle..may be termed the double-shop, or rival-shop principle.

† **Ri·val**, *sb.*[3] *Obs.*$^{-1}$ [? ad. L. *rīvulus*, dim. of *rīvus*; cf. RIVEL *sb.*[3]] A small stream.

1600 W. WATSON *Decacordon* (1602) 68 A faire seeming..fountaine..deuided into two armes or riuals from the head.

Rival, obs. form of RIVEL *v.*[1]

Rival (rəi·văl), *v.* [f. RIVAL *sb.*[2]]

1. *trans.* To enter into competition with; to contend or vie with; to strive to equal or excel (another).

1609 W. M. *Man in Moon* (1849) 43 He watcheth and prayeth for her,..sobbing like a silly sot if he be rivald and put besides her. 1637 RUTTER *Cid* III. iv, Shall I Love where I am so rivall'd? No, my heart. 1697 DRYDEN *Virg. Past.* V. 10 Your Merit and your Years command the Choice: Amyntas only rivals you in Voice. 1711 STEELE *Spect.* No. 91 ¶ 1 These Beauties Rival each other on all Occasions. 1787 *Generous Attachment* I. 25 You will have one half of the gay world to rival, and the other to approve your choice. 1824 BP. HEBER *Life Jer. Taylor* p. ccx, A work..which contending sects have rivalled each other in approving. 1875 JOWETT *Plato* (ed. 2) I. 432, I had no idea of rivalling him or his poems.

b. *transf.* of things.

1784 COWPER *Task* I. 431 The cheering fragrance of her dewy vales, And music of her woods—no works of man May rival these. 1841 W. SPALDING *Italy & It. Isl.* II. 370 A host of writers, whose numbers rivalled, if they did not surpass, those of the sixteenth century. 1860 TYNDALL *Glac.* I. v. 38 A crash which rivalled thunder. 1880 HAUGHTON *Phys. Geogr.* v. 208 A desert region, rivalling..the bare and repulsive features of the Sahara.

2. *intr.* To act as a rival, be a competitor.

1605 SHAKS. *Lear* I. i. 194 We first addresse toward you, who with this King Hath riuald for our Daughter. 1654 Z. COKE *Logick* Pref., Every Colon & Column of your lives..[will] cause your Names (Rivalling with time) to survive on Earth. 1862 *Vacation Tour.* 1861, 271 Even Christianity has not been able to uproot an idea which Poetry and Art have rivalled to perpetuate. 1898 TOUT *Empire & Papacy* xvii. (1901) 427 The Lombard and Cahorsin usurers, who had now begun to rival with the Israelites in finance.

†b. So with *it. Obs.*

1656 S. H. *Gold. Law* 65 Silver and gold rival'd it in number and weight with the stones in the street. *Ibid.* 68 His [Joshua's] rivalling it with his master in dividing of Jordan's Rivers, Red Sea-like.

Hence **Ri·valled** *ppl. a.*; **Ri·valling** *vbl. sb.*

1606 SYLVESTER *Du Bartas* II. iv. *Magnificence* 76 Whom, with-out Force, Uproar, or Rivaling, Nature and Law, and Fortune make a King. a 1649 CRASHAW *Carmen Deo Nostro, Flaming Heart* 44 Give Him the vail; that he may cover The Red cheeks of a rivall'd lover. a 1748 THOMSON *Hymn on Solitude* 24 As..she,..Amid the long withdrawing vale, Awakes the rival'd nightingale.

Ri·valess. [f. RIVAL *sb.*[2] + -ESS.] A female rival or competitor.

1680 MORDEN *Geog. Rect.* (1685) 465 Once formerly Romes great Rivaless. 1707 tr. *Wks. C'tess D'Anois* (1715) 434 She got to her Rivaless's Throne: where she stood upright, leaning against a Pillar. 1740 RICHARDSON *Pamela* (1824) I. lxix. 414 For, oh, my happy rivaless! if you tear from me my husband,..I cannot help it.

Rivalet, obs. form of RIVULET.

‖ **Riva·lis.** *Obs.*$^{-1}$ [L. *rīvālis.*] A rival.

1600 B. JONSON *Cynthia's Rev.* v. ii, Your Riualis..dispatcheth his lacquay to the chamber, early, to know what her colours are for the day.

Ri·valism. *rare.* [-ISM.] Rivalry.

1879 FARRAR *St. Paul* I. 32 Where Christian brotherhood and mutual esteem have taken the place of wretched rivalism.

Rivality (rəivæ·liti). [ad. L. *rīvālitas*: see RIVAL *sb.*[2] and -ITY. So F. *rivalité*, It. *rivalita*, Sp. *rivalidad*, Pg. *-ade.*] = RIVALRY 1.

1582 STANYHURST *Æneis*, etc. (Arb.) 140 Dame Venus and kingdooms can no riualitye suffer. 1606 SHAKS. *Ant. & Cl.* III. v. 8 Cæsar..denied him riuality, would not let him partake in the glory of action. 1648 BP. HALL *Old Relig.* (1686) 107 Whatever worship more than mere humane is imparted to the creature, sets it in rivality with our Maker. a 1684 LEIGHTON *Comm. 1 Pet.* Wks. (1868) 236 Loyalty can admit of no rivality. 1781 *Characters* in *Ann. Reg.* 31/1 The rivality between the two nations will last. 1796 BURNEY *Mem. Metastasio* I. 318, I wish this rivality to be strongly marked. 1803 [see RIVALRY 2]. 1830 W. TAYLOR *Hist. Surv. Germ. Poet.* II. 63 It..stimulates the exertions of rivality without hazarding its disappointments. 1876 'OUIDA' *Winter City* x, Society is a Battle of the Frogs, for rivality in dress and debt.

Rivalize (rəi·vǎləiz), *v.* [f. RIVAL *sb.*[2] + -IZE. Cf. F. *rivaliser*, Pg. *-izar*, Sp. *-izar.*] *intr.* To enter into rivalry, to compete, *with.*

1802–12 BENTHAM *Ration. Judic. Evid.* (1827) IV. 337 Being..the delegates of a spiritual authority, rivalizing with the temporal authority of the king. 1839 *Blackw. Mag.* XLV. 385 These steps I took, not with the intention of rivalizing with M. Daguerre in the perfection of his processes.

Ri·valless, *a.* [f. RIVAL *sb.*[2] + -LESS.] Without a rival; having no rival.

1822 *Blackw. Mag.* XI. 69 When his young eye was bright as her rivalless star. 1856 RUSKIN *Mod. Paint.* III. IV. xvii. § 27 Leaving Fleur de Marie and Virginia rivalless.

Rivalrous (rəi·vălrəs), *a.* [f. next + -OUS.] Of the nature of rivalry.

1812 W. TAYLOR in *Monthly Mag.* XXXIV. 415 These would tend to independency, to rivalrous competition. 1853 G. J. CAYLEY *Las Alforjas* II. 45 Celebrated..for their rivalrous animosity in lecture-room.

Rivalry (rəi·vălri). [f. RIVAL *sb.*[2] + -RY.]

1. The act of rivalling; competition, emulation.

1598 MARSTON *Sco. Villanie* III. xi. 230 Who enuies him? not I, For well he may, without all riualrie. 1633 BP. HALL *Occas. Medit.* (1851) 82 Forsaking all the base and sinful rivalry of the world. a 1719 ADDISON (J.), Those antagonists, who, by their rivalry for greatness, divided a whole age. 1759 JOHNSON *Rasselas* xxix, From those early marriages proceeds likewise the rivalry of parents and children. 1816 SCOTT *Antiq.* xvi, Jealousies, rivalries, envy, intervene to separate others from our side. 1850 KINGSLEY *Alt. Locke* xxxix, The innate selfishness and rivalry of human nature. 1875 JOWETT *Plato* (ed. 2) V. 403 Let them have conflict and rivalry in these matters in accordance with the law.

2. A body of rivals.

1803 W. TAYLOR in *Monthly Mag.* XIV. 114 The appearance of Ulysses among the suitors of Penelope disappointed the *rivality* of the whole *rivalry.*

Rivalship (rəi·vălʃip). [f. RIVAL *sb.*[2] + -SHIP.] The state or character of a rival; emulation, competition, rivalry.

1632 B. JONSON *Magn. Lady* II. i, He hath confess'd To me in private that he loves another..; therefore Secure you of rivalship. 1664 POWER *Exp. Philos.* I. 11 That proud Madam which Pallas, for her Rivalship, transform'd into the Spider. 1700 FARQUHAR *Constant Couple* I. i, I was beginning to mistrust some rivalship in the case. 1761 HUME *Hist. Eng.* xxix. II. 161 The emulation and rivalship which had so long subsisted between these two monarchs. 1818 COLEBROOKE *Import Colonial Corn* 198 The necessity must exist so long as rivalship continues among independent states. 1870 W. R. GREG *Polit. Probl.* 224 Permanence is necessary to good government, and..our system of party rivalship forbids permanence.

† **Ri·valty.** *Obs. rare.* [-TY.] Rivalry.

1644 [H. PARKER] *Jus Populi* 21 This does absolutely destroy that opinion, which places the good of Kings in any rivalty with the good of States. 1662 *Eikon Bas.* in *Chas. I, Wks.* 136 They are divided to so high a rivalty [*ed.* 1648 rivalry] as sets them more at defiance against each other then against their first Antagonists.

† **Rive**, *sb.*[1] *Obs.* Forms: 3–5 **ryue**, 4–6 **ryve**, 4, 6 **riue**. [a. OF. *rive*:—L. *ripa* bank.]

a. The sea-shore. **b.** The bank of a river.

a 1300 *K. Horn* 142 Bliþe beo we on lyue, Vre schup is on ryue. c 1330 *Sir Tristr.* 1369 Now bringeþ me atte riue Schip and oþir þing. 1390 GOWER *Conf.* III. 49 Whan they herde hou Uluxes Is londed ther upon the ryve. c 1477 CAXTON *Jason* 79 b, In alle parties along by the Ryue of the cite. 1480 — *Ovid's Met.* XI. ii, To wesche and purge hym, he must goo ayenst the ryve of a flood or ryver.

† **Rive**, *sb.*[2] *Obs. rare.* In 5 **ryue, riue.** [App. ad. L. *rīvus* stream.] A stream or rill.

1489 CAXTON *Faytes of A.* I. xvii. 49 Somtyme..an ost must passe ouer grete watres & ryues. 1533–4 *Act 25 Hen. VIII*, c. 7 Anie streites, riuers, riues, or brokes, salte or freshe within the realme.

† **Rive**, *sb.*[3] *Obs. rare*$^{-0}$. In 5 **ryve.** [= MDu. *rive* (Du. *rijf*), Fris. *riuwe*, ON. and Icel. *hrífa* (Norw. *riva*, Sw. *rifva*, Da. *rive*).] A rake.

c 1440 *Promp. Parv.* 435/1 Ryve, or rake, *rastrum.*

Rive (rəiv), *sb.*[4] [f. RIVE *v.*[1]] A pull, tug, tear, rent, crack, etc.

1527 ANDREW *Brunswyke's Distyll. Waters* A iij, And so ordred laye it to the ryue of the glasse standynge upon the fyre. 1808 JAMIESON, *Rive*, a rent, or tear. 1822 HOGG *Perils of Man* II. vii. 246 A little hollow place in a wild moor,..where our horses get nothing but a rive o' heather. a 1878 AINSLIE *Land of Burns* (1892) 223 Sair's the rive that breaks the twist Which binds our hearts in ane. 1895 CROCKETT *Men Moss-Hags* lii, With one rive he tore it from its fastenings.

Rive, obs. form of RIFE *a.*

Rive (rəiv), *v.*[1] [a. ON. and Icel. *rífa* (Norw. *riva*, Sw. *rifva*, Da. *rive*), = OFris. **rīva* (in pa. pple. *eriven*). It is doubtful whether these are to be identified with MLG. *rīven*, Du. *rijven*, G. *reiben* to rub, grate, rasp, etc.]

A. Inflexional forms.

1. *Inf.* (and *Pres.*). α. 3–7 **riue**, 4–6 **ryue** (6 *Sc.* **rywe, ryiue**); 4–7 (9 *Sc.*) **ryve** (5 **ryvyn**), 4– **rive.**

For examples of these see B. 1. 10. and 11.

β. 4 **rijf**, 4–5 **ryf** (5 **ryff**), **rife**, 5–6 **ryfe**; *Sc.* 5–6 **rif**, 6 **riff(e, ryffe.**

c 1340 HAMPOLE *Psalter* cxxiii. 5 Þai had na myght to ryfe vs. 1375 BARBOUR *Bruce* XX. 255 Thair mycht men se men rif thar hare. ? a 1400 *Morte Arth.* 362, I salle..ryfe it in sondyre. c 1460 *Towneley Myst.* ii. 153 To were my shoyn & ryfe my hose. 1500–20 DUNBAR *Poems* lxxii. 91 Ane rude speir..did his precious body ryff. a 1578 LINDESAY (Pitscottie) *Chron. Scot.* (S.T.S.) I. 108 To ryfe the lyfe out of my bodie.

2. *Pa. t.* α. 3–5 **rof**, 4–5 **rofe, roff** (5 **roffe**), **roof** (5 **roofe**), 4–6 **roue**, 7 (9) **rove**, 9 *dial.* **rov.**

c 1275 LAY. 26566 Þe spere..rof þorh þan swere. 1303 R. BRUNNE *Handl. Synne* 9288 Hys rolle to-braste and rofe. c 1385 CHAUCER *L. G. W.* 661 *Cleopatra*, He..roof hym-self anoon. c 1400 *Destr. Troy* 10208 Þai..Rofe hit full Roidly. 1470–85 MALORY *Arthur* II. vi. 82 She..rofe her self thorow the body. 1535 COVERDALE *1 Kings* xiii. 5 Yᵉ altare roue. 1807 in *Allan's Tyneside Songs* (1891) 90 Aw..Rove my breeks.

β. 4–5 **raf(e**, 5 **raffe** (5–6 *Sc.* **raeff, raif(f, raife**); 4–6 **raue** (5–6 *Sc.* **rawe**), 5– **rave** (7 *Sc.* **raive**), 9 *dial.* **raeve, reave.**

a 1300 *Cursor M.* 7510, I þair chaffies raue in tua. *Ibid.* 9110 He wald men raf it al to dust. c 1375 *Sc. Leg. Saints* xxi. (*Clement*) 93 Scho..grat, & rawe hir hare. c 1440 *Alph. Tales* 55 With þer hornys & þer tethe þai rafe his flessh. c 1450 *St. Cuthbert* (Surtees) 4683 Þai raue þair clathes. 1525 LD. BERNERS *Froiss.* II. xlvii. 160 It raue clene in sondre. 1535 LYNDESAY *Satyre* 623 Wind, that raif the sails in sunder. 1603 *Reg. Privy Counc. Scotl.* VI. 589 [He] raive and distroyit it. 1728 RAMSAY *Christ's Kirk Gr.* III. xvii, Wi' her nails she rave his face. 1819 W. TENNANT *Papistry Storm'd* (1827) 190 [They] rugg't and rave them out. 1828 P. BUCHAN *Ballads* (1875) II. 249 Meggie reave her yellow hair.

γ. 4–5 **ref**, 5 **refe.**

13.. *Cursor M.* 24420 (Gött.), Þe temple fra þe rof it ref. a 1425 *Ibid.* 7809 (Trin.), Þourȝe his body my swerd I ref. c 1460 *Play Sacram.* 48 The ovyn refe a sondre.

δ. 6 **ryued, ryved, riued, yriv'd**, 7– **rived**, 8 **riv'd.**

a 1513 FABYAN *Chron.* VII. (1811) 249 The wynde..ryued..ouer the nomber of vi. hundred howses. 1547 J. HARRISON *Exhort. Scottes* b iij b, It riued a sunder theyr kyngdome. 1591 SPENSER *Astrophel* 120 That it both bone and muscles ryved quight. 1596 — *F. Q.* IV. vi. 15 That all his mayle yriv'd. 1727 DE FOE *Protestant Monastery* 14 She..used me in such a Manner as has riv'd my..Heart. 1791 COWPER *Iliad* XX. 475 Achilles drove his spear, And rived his skull. 1887 HALL CAINE *Deemster* xxxvii, [I] rived them [*sc.* rabbits] asunder.

3. *Pa. pple.* α. 4–6 **ryuen** (5 **ryuyn**), 5–6 **ryven**, 5 *Sc.* **rywen, -ine**; 4–7 **riuen** (4 **riuin**); 5 **rifen**; 5– **riven** (7 *Sc.* **rivin**).

a 1300 *Cursor M.* 4165 He riuen es Wit beistes wild. c 1375 *Sc. Leg. Saints* xxxviii. (*Adrian*) 346 Þane wes he..rywine & rente. c 1400 *Ywaine & Gaw.* 3539 Thair sheldes war shiferd, and helms rifen. 1483 *Cath. Angl.* 310/1 To be Ryven, *fatiscere.* 1566 in Peacock *Eng. Ch. Furniture* (1866) 48 Torn, broken, and ryven in peces. 1621 BP. MOUNTAGU *Diatribæ* 323 A rough knot, not riuen out. 1746 THOMSON *Cast. Indol.* II. lxix, The brand by which the rocks are riven. 1870 HUXLEY *Lay Serm.* xiv. (1874) 342 Riven by the lightenings.

β. 4 (6 *Sc.*) **reuin**, 5 **reuen**, 5, 7 **reven**; 9 *dial.* **reaven**; *Sc.* 5 **refyn(e, rewyn, rewine**, 5–6 **reuyn**, 6 **rewin, revin, reivin, reiuen.**

13.. *Cursor M.* 22636 (Gött.), Þat erd þat sal be reuin. c 1375 *Sc. Leg. Saints* i. (*Petir*) 25 He wald haf refyn [him] sone. c 1400 *Laud Troy Bk.* 13320 Ther schal be reuen many a scheld. c 1425 WYNTOUN *Cron.* v. x. 1898 His westment rewyn al in raggis. 1549 *Compl. Scotl.* vii. 69 This mantil..vas reuyn. 1596 DALRYMPLE tr. *Leslie's Hist. Scot.* IV. 251 Quhair thay war reiuen in duigis.

γ. 5 **ryue, reve**, 6 **rive**, 9 *dial.* **riv.**

a 1425 *Cursor M.* 1855 (Trin.), Ofte þei wende her shippe wold ha ryue. 1430 *Syr Gener.* (Roxb.) 6001 The sheld that was reue. 1596 SPENSER *F. Q.* V. xi. 5 That seem'd a marble rocke asunder could have rive. 1895 A. PATTERSON *On the Broads* 22 Years ago, afore laths was riv'.

δ. 6 **ryued**, 7 **riv'd**, 7– **rived.**

a 1513 FABYAN *Chron.* II. (1811) 249 Yᵉ rofe..was also ryued. 1601 SHAKS. *Jul. C.* I. iii. 6 When the scolding Winds Haue riu'd the knottie Oakes. 1681 FLAVEL *Meth. Grace* ii. 39 The tree..was rived asunder. 1782 ELIZ. BLOWER *Geo. Bateman* I. 216 My heart is rived with agony!

B. Signification.

In standard English the word is now somewhat rare, being most frequently employed in sense 4, and chiefly in the pa. pple. *riven* (riv'n).

I. *trans.* **1.** To tear apart or in pieces by pulling or tugging; to rend or lacerate with the hands, claws, etc.; to pull asunder.

a 1300 *Cursor M.* 4161 His kyrtil sal we riue and rend. c 1340 HAMPOLE *Pr. Consc.* 888 Wormes sal ryve hym in sondre. 14.. *Tundale's Vis.* 283 Ychon..with oder dyd stryve And with her naylys her chekys dyd ryve. c 1450 HOLLAND *Howlat* 815, I sall ryiue the Ravyne, baith guttis and gall. c 1500 *World & Child* 529, I praye you, syr, ryue me this cloute. a 1572 KNOX *Hist. Ref.* Wks. 1846 I. 329 Monsieur Dosell and the Capitanis.., efter the reading of thame, began to ryve thair awin beardis. 1596 DALRYMPLE tr. *Leslie's Hist. Scot.* Prol. 20 Thay sett vpon thame, and..thame onlie thay ryue with thair teith. 1638 BAILLIE *Lett. & Jrnls.* (1841) I. 76 They sett on him in church, ryves his gowne,..and so..dismisses him. 1697 CONGREVE *Mourn. Bride* III. vi, Then will I..disfigure And dash my Face, and rive my clotted Hair. c 1715 in Maidment *Pasquils* (1868) 393 Dee'l ryve and burst him. 1824 SCOTT *Redgauntlet* ch. xxiii, What are ye pooin' me that gate for?—Ye will rive my coat. 1862 C. C. ROBINSON *Dial. Leeds* Gloss. 394 Rive us that sheet o' paaper i' two.

fig. c 1380 WYCLIF *Sel. Wks.* I. 103 ȝif rychesse liken þe fleishe, nebeles þei ryven þe soule. c 1460 *Wisdom* 175 in *Macro Plays* 41 Ye Godis ymage neuer xall ryve. 1572 *Satir. Poems Reform.* xxxiii. 44 The malice greit, that ilk to vther beiris, Dois ryfe my bowells. c 1785 BURNS *2nd Ep. to Davie* iv, I'm on Parnassus' brink, Rivin the words to gar them clink. 1863 W. PHILLIPS *Sp.* xvi. 349 It went through the land,..riving sects.

refl. 1830 GALT *Lawrie T.* I. xi, It was a sad sight to see that mother and that daughter rive themselves asunder.

†b. To tear up (a letter, document, etc.), so as to destroy or cancel. Chiefly *Sc. Obs.*

1415 SIR T. GREY in 43 *Rep. Deputy Kpr. Rec.* 583, I redde hit and rofe hit and kest hit in a govnge. 1480 *Acta Dom. Conc.* (1839) 73 The said dauid bowy tuke it again, rafe & distruyt it, but þe said dauid westis consent. 1527 [see RIVING *vbl. sb.*[1] 1]. 1566 *Reg. Privy Council Scot.* I. 471 That..thair Comptrollar..at the first sycht and presentatioun of thame ryve and cancellat sic writtingis. a 1650 CALDERWOOD *Hist. Kirk* (1843) II. 506 Their armes were rivin at the Croce, in presence of the regent and the lords.

2. With various advs. and preps.:

a. To tear or pull *off* or *away.*

13.. *Cursor M.* 9099 (Gött.), Of his robe be gan to riue. c 1480 HENRYSON *Mor. Fab.*, *Wolf & Wether* xiii, Ane breir busk raif rudelie of the skyn. 1500–20 DUNBAR *Poems* lxxii. 60 The claith that claif to his clene hyde, Thai raif away with ruggis rude. 1680 H. MORE *Apocal. Apoc.* 136 Excommunication, that rives off a member from the church. c 1784 BURNS *Ep. to Rankine* iii, Your curst wit..Rives 't aff their back.

b. To tear, wrench, or pluck roughly away *from* (a person or thing).

a 1340 HAMPOLE *Psalter, Comm. Cant.* 518 Deuyls, þe whilk cruelly ryuys saules fra god. a 1400 *Sir Perc.* 2157 Hir clothes ther scho rafe hir fro. c 1450 HOLLAND *Howlat* 835 The Tuchet..Raif his taile fra his rig. 1554 KNOX *Faythf. Admon.* C v, That God..haue much to do to ryffe or plucke any man backe from their forefathers footesteppes. 1816 BYRON *Corsair* III. vi, They loved one from thee riven. 1863 BARING-GOULD *Iceland* 129 The cold hands came down on Grettir's arms, riving them from their hold.

c. To pull *down*, or *to* the ground; to tear, drag, or pull *up* or *out.*

c 1375 *Sc. Leg. Saints* v. (*John*) 305 He þe tempil suld in hy of dame diane gere Ryve done. c 1400 *Destr. Troy* 4783 Robbet was þis ronke hold & ryuyn to ground. 1470–85 MALORY *Arthur* XII. iii. 596 The bore torned hym nemly & rafe out the longes & the hert of the hors. 1535 COVERDALE *Zeph.* ii. 14 The bordes of Cedre shalbe ryuen downe. 1545 ASCHAM *Toxoph.* I. (Arb.) 93 Plowing..rieuth and plucketh vp by the rootes, all thistles, brambles and weedes. c 1585 MONTGOMERIE *Sonnets* lv. 12 Rigour ryvis the hairt out by the root. 1621 BP. MOUNTAGU *Diatribæ* 323 An hard and a rough knot, not riuen out by the Author of the History. 1680 OTWAY *Caius Marius* v. i, As storms let loose That riue the trunks of tallest cedars down. 1754 T. GARDNER *Hist. Dunwich* 161 John Arnold..gave Order to..the Sexton to rive it out for the Plumber's Use. 1873 GIBBON *For Lack of Gold* xxi, I would rive the heart out of my breast.

3. To sever, cleave, or divide, by means of a knife or weapon; † to pierce or thrust.

13.. *Gaw. & Gr. Knt.* 1341 Syþen britned þay þe brest, &..Ryuez hit vp radly, ryȝt to þe byȝt. c 1385 CHAUCER *L. G. W.* 1351 *Dido*, With his swerd she rof hyre herte. 1426 LYDG. *De Guil. Pilgr.* 14944 The sharpe sperys hed..Rooff that lord vn-to the herte. 1483 CAXTON *Gold. Leg.* 316 b/2 He sayd yf it be trewe..late a swerd ryue me thurgh my body. a 1592 GREENE *Selimus* 592 Vpon my swords sharpe point standeth pale death Readie to riue in two thy caitiue brest. 1659 [see RIFE *sb.*[1]]. 1668 HOPKINS *Serm.* (1685) 57 What torments the conscience feels, when God causes his sword to enter into it, to rive it. 1791 COWPER *Iliad* XX. 475 Achilles drove his spear, And rived his skull.

refl. c 1384 CHAUCER *H. Fame* 373 She rofe hir selfe to the herte. 1430–40 LYDG. *Bochas* VI. xiii, Scipion..rofe hymselfe to the heart and so died. 1474 CAXTON *Chesse* 21 With a swerde..she roof her self vnto the herte. 1612 DRAYTON *Poly-olb.* vii. 187 Marcely,..Inrag'd and mad with griefe, himselfe in two did riue.

†b. To drive (a weapon) *through* (the heart, etc.); to thrust *into* (the body). *Obs.*

c 1385 CHAUCER *L. G. W.* 1793 *Lucrece*, This swerd thour out thyn herte shal I ryue. a 1425 *Cursor M.* 7809 (Trin.), Þourȝe his body my sword I ref. 1483 CAXTON *Gold. Leg.* 69/1 Eche toke other by the heed and roof their swerdes in to eche other sydes.

†c. To make (a way) by piercing. *Obs.*$^{-1}$

1600 FAIRFAX *Tasso* XII. lxxxii, You deere lims.., Through which my cruell blade this flood-gate roue.

4. To rend or split by means of shock, violent impact or pressure, etc.; to strike asunder; † to break or crack (a dish).

a 1300 *Cursor M.* 22636 Þe deuels vte sal be fordriuen O þat erth þat sal be riuen. 1338 R. BRUNNE *Chron.* (1810) 148 Ten schippes wer dryuen, þorgh ille auisement, þorgh a tempest ryuen. 1526 *Pilgr. Perf.* (W. de W. 1531) 256 b, This deth..dyd ryue the myghty & stronge wall of yᵉ [temple]. a 1548 HALL *Chron., Hen. VI*, 9 b, [They] shot..great stones.., the strokes whereof..shaked, crushed and ryued the walles. 1596 [see A. 3 γ]. 1625 PURCHAS *Pilgrimes* II. 1637 If a dish happen to be a little riven or crackt, they eat no more in it. 1653 H. COGAN tr. *Pinto's Trav.* lxxi. 288 After this, he..caused all the lesser Ordnance to be rived asunder, and the greater..to be cloyed. 1748 THOMSON *Cast. Indol.* II. lxix, Repentance..quells the brand by which the rocks are riven. 1768 BEATTIE *Minstrel* I. xlviii, Like yonder blasted boughs by lightening riven. 1803 HEBER *Palestine* 55 Where the tempest rives the hoary stone. 1860 TYNDALL *Glac.* I. ii. 20 The Rhone glacier,..where it is greatly riven and dislocated.

fig. c 1460 *Towneley Myst.* xiv. 296 Those lurdans wote not what thay say; Thay ryfe my hede. 1591 SHAKS. *1 Hen. VI*, IV. ii. 29 Ten thousand French haue tane the Sacrament, To ryue their dangerous Artillerie Vpon..English Talbot. 1837 CARLYLE *Fr. Rev.* III. vii. (1857) II. 242 With fire-words the exasperated rude Titan rives and smites these Girondins.

b. To split or cleave (wood, stone, etc.) by appropriate means. Also with *up, off.*

c 1440 *Promp. Parv.* 435/1 Ryvyn, or clyvyn, as men doo woodde, *findo.* 1530 PALSGR. 692/2, I ryve wodde in to byllettes, or splentes, or suche lyke, *je fends.* 1567 MAPLET *Gr. Forest* 16 Nitrum is a stone..easie to be riuen. 1622 BP. HALL *Contempl., O. T.* XVII. i, That wood which a single iron could not rive, is soon splitted with a double wedge. 1670 EACHARD *Cont. Clergy* 22 As for him that rives blocks, or carries packs, there is..no great intellectuall pensiveness. 1793 WINDHAM in *Burke's Corr.* (1844) IV. 190 The progress of the northern armies must, of necessity, be slow; they are there riving the block at the knotty end. 1830 SOUTHEY in *Q. Rev.* XLIII. 22 When this politic purpose had been sufficiently answered, it was riven up for fuel. 1891 MISS DOWIE *Girl in Karp.* 258 It is a stake of pine wood..commonly speaking rived off at an early period.

absol. 1622 *Relat. Eng. Plantation in Plymouth* 24 We went on shore. Some to fell tymber, some to saw, some to riue, and some to carry.

transf. 1875 KINGLAKE *Crimea* (1877) V. i. 127 The taller horsemen who were riving it [*sc.* the column] deeper and deeper.

c. *techn.* To make (laths) by splitting wood along the grain into thin narrow strips.

1610 [implied in *lath-river*: see LATH *sb.* 4]. 1618 *Nottingham Rec.* IV. 359 For ij men to rive lathes. [1892 *Eastern Morn. News* (Hull) 16 Feb. 2/8 The lath-riving in Sweden.] 1895 [see A. 3 γ].

5. *Sc.* and *north.* To plough (untilled ground); to break *up* with the plough. Also with *out.*

1536 *Reg. Magni Sig. Scot.* (1883) 394/2 To ryfe out, breke, and teill yeirlie 1000 acris of thair..landis. 1572 *Satir. Poems Reform.* xxxiii. 271 Now mon thay..Ryue out the Mures, the bestiallis gers intak. 1590 *Reg. Privy Council Scot.* IV. 515 [The bailies and council] had revin out and sawin ane pairt thairof this present yeir. 1610–53 [see RIVING *vbl. sb.*[1] 1]. 1785 BURNS *Death & Dr. Hornbook* xxiii, His braw calf-ward whare gowans grew, Sae white an' bonie, Nae doubt they'll rive it wi' the plew. 1787 in Cudworth *Manningham*, etc. (1896) 330 That they will not..plow, grave, or rive up any Part of the Close of Land. 1816 SCOTT *Bl. Dwarf* i, Ill wad he hae liked to hae seen that braw sunny knowe a' riven out wi' the pleugh.

absol. 1856 G. HENDERSON *Pop. Rhymes Berwick* 70 Where the scythe cuts, and the sock rives.

6. To rend (the heart, soul, etc.) with painful thoughts or feelings.

a 1300 *Cursor M.* 26015 Þarfor agh sinful man and wijf On þis maner þair hert to rijf. c 1400 tr. *Secreta Secret., Gov. Lordsh.* 93 He schall ryue þe hert of his subgitz, þat ys to say,..his subgitz shall fele hym at þaire hertes. 1647 H. MORE *Exorcismus* Wks. (Grosart) 177 What's this that..Rives my close-straitned heart? 1713 ADDISON *Cato* II. v, Why will you rive my heart with such expressions? 1795 MACNEILL *Scotland's Skaith* xlii, Jean's condition Rave his very heart in twa. 1822 MRS. NATHAN *Langreath* III. 186 Deeply drawn sighs, which seemed to rive the agonized bosom from whence they issued. 1896 HOUSMAN *Shropshire Lad* xlviii, All thoughts to rive the heart are here, and all are vain.

II. *absol.* **†7.** To pierce, cut, or shear *through* or *into* (the body). *Obs.*

c 1275 LAY. 26566 Beofs..smot hine..þat þe spere deore rof þorh þan swere. *Ibid.* 27685 Þe brunie gan to berste, þat þe spere þorh rof. 1388 WYCLIF *2 Sam.* ii. 23 Abner smoot him with the spere..,and roof thorouȝ, and he was deed. c 1400 *Destr. Troy* 5907 He bere to þe bold with a big sworde, And rof þurgh the Ribbes right to þe hert. c 1477 CAXTON *Jason* 102 b, Iason toke his swerd and roof into the paunche of the dragon.

8. To commit spoliation or robbery; to reave; to take away *from.* Now *dial.*

1489 *Barbour's Bruce* XVI. 551 (Edinb.), On west half, towart Dunferlyng, Tuk land; and fast begouth to ryve. 1513 MORE in Hall *Chron., Edw. V* (1548) 9 b, There deuyse they newe robberies nightely and steale oute and robbe, riue, and kyll menne. 1559 *Mirr. Mag., Glendour* ix, Bent my selfe to rob and ryue. 1816 [see RIVING *vbl. sb.*[1] 1]. 1858 RAYSON *Poems* 7 I've nought but sarvants riving frae me.

†b. *trans.* To rob or despoil (a person). *Obs.*

1582–8 *Hist. & Life Jas. VI* (1804) 85 The people..were become of sic dissolut..actiones, that nane was in account bot he that wald ather kill or ryve his nybour.

9. To tear voraciously; to tug *at* something.

1552 LYNDESAY *Test. Papyngo* 1148 The Rauin began rudely to rugge and ryue, Full gormoundlyke his emptie throte to feid. 1818 SCOTT *Hrt. Midl.* xlvii, Twa precious saints might pu' sundry wise, like twa cows riving at the same hay-band. 1829 BROCKETT *N. C. Gloss.* (ed. 2) 248 *Rive*, to tear membrane from membrane, to eat voraciously without knife or fork. 'See how he's riving and eating'. 1865 DICKENS *Mut. Fr.* I. xiii, Standing..roared and riven at by the wind. 1867 A. DAWSON *Rambling Recoll.* (1868) 8 His neighbour was 'riving' at an obstinate sinew.

III. *intr.* **10.** To part asunder; to cleave, split, crack, open up, etc.

a 1300 *Cursor M.* 1767 Þe see [gan] to ris, þe erth to riue. c 1330 *Arth. & Merl.* 448 (Kölbing), Mani schaft þer gan riue. c 1400 *Ywaine & Gaw.* 636 Thair sheldes sone bigan to ryve, Thair shaftes cheverd. 1480 *Robt. Devyll* 133 in Hazl. *E. P. P.* I. 224 They feared that the house woulde ryue a sonder. 1527 ANDREW *Brunswyke's Distyll. Waters* a iij, A lutynge for a glasse that ryveth upon the fyre. 1563 SACKVILLE *Induct., Mirr. Mag.* lxxix, As though the heauens riued with the noyse. 1578 LYTE *Dodoens* 762 A thinne barke the which will soone rive, or cleeve asunder. 1616 SURFL. & MARKHAM *Country Farme* v. viii. 537 All sorts of ashes, either of Wood or Coale, is a good manure,..for ground that is apt to chap or riue. a 1661 FULLER *Worthies* (1840) I. 110 The oak..may be called cowardly, as riving and splitting round about the passage of the bullet. 1805 SCOTT *Last Minstrel* Note

xlviii, Sutor Watt, ye cannot sew your boots; the heels risp, and the seams rive. 1877 TENNYSON *Harold* II. ii. 426 Why let earth rive, gulf in These cursed Normans.

fig. 1549 *Compl. Scotl.* i. 21 Lucan..said that the vecht of rome suld gar it ryue in mony partis. 1589 NASHE *Martin Marprelate* Wks. (Grosart) I. 78 Theyr Religion like an ancient building, worne with..age, riues and threatens ruine on euery side.

b. Of wood or stone: To admit of splitting or cleaving.

1699 *Phil. Trans.* XXI. 437 A Tree we call Cypress..; it is soft and spungy, will not Rive. 1772 *Ann. Reg.* 119 The body of the willow tree rives into pales. 1811 PINKERTON *Petral.* I. 432 All like sorts of stone that are composed of granules, will cut and rive in any direction. 1831 JOHN HODGSON in Raine *Mem.* (1858) II. 212 They rive, according to the term of the quarry-men, into thin..laminæ.

11. In hyperbolical or figurative use:

a. Of the heart: To break or burst with sorrow.

c 1400 *Rom. Rose* 5718 She fighteth with hym ay, and stryveth, That his herte asondre ryveth. c 1460 *Towneley Myst.* iii. 399 Me thynk my hert ryfis..To se sich stryfis. 1550 LEVER *Serm.* (Arb.) 23 Thys playne worde..wold make..oure hertes to ryue in peces. c 1595 J. DICKENSON *Sheph. Compl.* (1878) 13 This said, he sighd, as though his heart would riue. 1620–6 QUARLES *Feast for Wormes* 1635 O kill me (Lord) or lo, my heart will riue. 1870 ROSSETTI *Poems, Sister Helen* xxvii, He prays you, as his heart would rive,..To save his dear son's soul alive.

b. Denoting the effect of repletion, excessive laughter, etc.

1586 D. ROWLAND *Lazarillo* (1653) E j, My stomack began to rive for hunger. a 1682 F. SEMPILL *Blythsome Wedding* 72 There will be meal-kail and castocks With skink to sup till ye rive. 1715 RAMSAY *Christ's Kirk Gr.* II. xiv, Jock, wi' laughing like to rive. 1785 BURNS *To a Haggis* iv, Then auld Guidman, maist like to rive, Bethankit hums. 1827 *Kinloch's Ballad Bk.* 68 Ye wad hae riven for laughter. 1884 D. GRANT *Lays* 20, I winna drink anither drap! My head is like to rive.

† **Rive**, *v.*[2] *Obs.* Forms: α. 4 **riue, ryue**, 5–6 **ryve** (5 **ryvyn**). *Pa. t.* 4 **riuede**, 5 **ryuede, revede**, (and *pa. pple.*) 3–4 **riued**, 4–5 **ryued**, 4–6 **ryved**, 5 *Sc.* **rywit**, 6 **riude.** β. *Pa. t.* 4 **roue, raue**, 5 **raffe.** γ. *Pa. pple.* 4 **(y)ryuen**, 5 **ryven, reuyn, revyn.** [ad. OF. *river*, aphetic form of *arriver* ARRIVE *v.* Common in the 14th cent.] *intr.* To arrive, to land. Freq. with *up.*

α. a 1300 *K. Horn* 162 And sey..þat iche..On londe am riued here. c 1330 *Sir Tristr.* 2190 Til ingland wil y riue. 1387 TREVISA *Higden* (Rolls) VII. 85 Wiþ a grete navey he ryved up at Cornwayle. c 1430 LYDG. *Min. Poems* (Percy Soc.) 63 To the haven of dethe whan we gan to ryve. c 1440 *Promp. Parv.* 435/1 Ryvyn to londe, as schyppys or botys, fro water, *applico, appello.* 1483 *Cath. Angl.* 310/1 To Ryve vp, *appellere, applicare.* 1530 PALSGR. 692/2 In shorte space they ryved at Calays. 1592 WYRLEY *Armorie* 134 We there were riude with vigerous entent With him to fight.

β. c 1350 *St. Mary Magd.* 478 in Horstm. *Altengl. Leg.* (1881) 86 Þe weders fand þai gude and gayne, So þat þai raue up in Romayne. 1387 TREVISA *Higden* (Rolls) VII. 87 Þe navy of Danes rove up at Sandwyche, and robbed Kent. a 1440 *Sir Eglam.* 1297 + 15 (Linc. MS.), This fayre navé Alle in lykynge passed the see, In Artasse up thay raffe.

γ. c 1400 *Chron. R. Glouc.* (Rolls) 362 (MS. B), Þo he was ware, Þat such folk was y-armed..& ryuen vp hys lond. 14.. *Guy Warw.* 4244 So longe þe wynde haþ þem dreuyn: At Almayne they be vp reuyn. *Ibid.* 8476 In Awfryke well soone þey be yryuen. c 1435 *Torr. Portugal* 1438 Sith we be ryven on this lond, To nyght wylle I ryde.

† **Rive**, *v.*[3] *Obs.*$^{-0}$ [Related to RIVE *sb.*[3] Cf. Du. *rijven*, Fris. *riuwje.*] *trans.* To rake.

c 1440 *Promp. Parv.* 435/1 Ryvyn, or rakyn, *rastro.*

Rived (rəivd), *ppl. a.* [f. RIVE *v.*[1] + -ED[1].] Riven, rent. Also *fig.*

1631 FLETCHER *Piscatory Eclogs* iii, To break the rived heart with fear and fright. 1799 SHERIDAN *Pizarro* I. i, Thou, all-powerful!..whose lightnings can pierce to the core the rived and quaking earth. 1838 ELIZA COOK *I thank Thee, God!* vii, So in the rived heart there'll be Mercy that never flowed before.

† **Rived**, *a. Obs. rare.* [f. *rive*, early form of RIFE *a.* The ending is irregular.] = RIFE *a.*

a 1300 *Joseph & Jacob* 18 Forþi sende oure Louerd Noees flod...Hi floten swiþe riued bi dich & bi pulle. a 1400–50 *Alexander* 1740 So..riued [*v.r.* ryfe] is oure rewme þat þou may reȝt lycken þe store strenthe of oure stoure to sternes of þe heuen. *Ibid.* 1779 So riued is þe rede gold oure regions with-in. 1513 BRADSHAW *St. Werburge* II. 168 Couetise, pride, lechery were ryued alway.

† **Ri·vedly**, *adv. Obs.* In 4 **riuedlich(e, -li.** [f. RIVED *a.* + -LY[2].] = RIFELY *adv.*

a 1300 *Fall & Passion* 103 in *E. E. P.* (1862) 15 Þe..iii. dai he ros to liue; is lore riuedlich he send. c 1350 *Will. Palerne* 2113 For missing of þat mariage al murþe was seced, riuedliche þurth rome & reuþe bi-gunne. *Ibid.* 3840, I schal riuedli him rewarde to be riche for euer.

Riveir, obs. Sc. form of RIVER *sb.*[1]

† **Rivel**, *sb.*[1] *Obs.* Forms: 4–6 **ryuel** (4 **reuel**), 5 **ryvel**, 6–7 **riuel**, 7 **riuil, -ell, rivel.** [Perh. repr. an OE. **rifel*, whence *rifelede* RIVELLED *a.*] A wrinkle or fold upon the skin (*esp.* of the face) or on the rind of a fruit.

1382 WYCLIF *Job* xvi. 9 My ryuelis seyn witnesse aȝen me. 1387 TREVISA tr. *Higden* (Rolls) I. 257 He haþ a large ryuel, as it were a bagge, vnder þe chynne. 1398 — *Barth. De P. R.* XVII. lxi. (Bodl. MS.), It is iseide þat figes doþ awei reuels of olde men ȝif þei ete wele þerof. 1426 LYDG. *De Guil. Pilgr.* 24273 Thou mayst se, by my lokkes hore, and by ryvels of my visage, How that I am called 'Age'. 1545 RAYNOLD *Byrth Mankynde* 11 Though that the matrix..be full of ryuelles or wrinkles by the reason that it is so contract from a great amplytude. 1601 HOLLAND *Pliny* XII. vii, It wanteth the due parching and ripening against the sunne: and by that meanes commeth short of the rivels and blacknesse that the outlandish pepper hath. *Ibid.* XVIII. xii, It causeth the skin to looke cleare and white, and without any rivels or wrinkles. 1632 SHERWOOD, A riuell, *ride.*

fig. 1598 E. GUILPIN *Skial.* (1878) 43 And leauing it their lothsome playstered skins, Shall shew the furrowed riuels of their sins.

† **Ri·vel**, *sb.*[2] *Obs.*$^{-1}$ [Cf. RIVEL *v.*[2]] A ravel or tangle.

? a 1630 JACKSON *Wks.* (1673) II. 513 You haue perhaps already espied..a knot or rivel, wherewith your beliefs..may be entangled.

Ri·vel, *sb.*[3] *rare*$^{-1}$. A rivulet.

1886 LEIFCHILD in *Contemp. Rev.* July 90 'Tis A full-fed rivel lapsing by.

Ri·vel, *v.*[1] Now *rare.* Forms: 4 **rivele**, 5 **ryvel**, 6 **ryvell**, 7 **rivell**, 8 **rival**, 4– **rivel**; 4, 6 **ryuel**, 4–7 **riuel.** [Cf. RIVELLED *a.*]

1. *intr.* To become wrinkled or shrivelled; to form wrinkles or small folds.

c 1325 *Old Age* in *Rel. Ant.* II. 211, I rivele, I roxle, I rake, I rouwe. 1390 GOWER *Conf.* I. 98 Hire chekes ben with teres wet, And rivelen as an emty skyn Hangende doun unto the chin. c 1400 *Rom. Rose* 7262 And highe shoes, knopped with dagges,..Or botes riveling as a gype. 1530 PALSGR. 692/2, I ryvell, as ones vysage dothe for age, *je ride.* 1540 HYRDE tr. *Vives' Instr. Chr. Wom.* (1592) F iij, The tender skinne will ryvill the more soone, and all the favour of the face waxeth old. 1610 HOLLAND *Camden's Brit.* I. 357 Some will last a whole yeare and not wither and rivell. 1657 C. BECK *Univ. Charac.* K v b, To rivell or wrinckle.

2. *trans.* To cause (the skin) to wrinkle or pucker; to shrivel *up.*

1583 STUBBES *Anat. Abus.* I. (1879) 95 It riueleth the face. 1585 R. PARSONS *Chr. Exer.* II. iii. 268 Quickly commeth on olde age, which riueleth the skinne. 1609 N. F. *Fruiterers Secr.* 15 Neither layed in a windy colde roome, for feare of shrinking and riueling them. 1638 BURTON *Anat. Mel.* III. ii. VI. iii. (1651) 561 Raging time, care, rivels her upon a sudden. a 1704 T. BROWN *Sat. agst. Woman* Wks. 1730 I. 55 Till the devouring heat..Rival thy body, and distort thy mind. 1868 BROWNING *Ring & Bk.* I. 1279 And death came, death's breath rivelled up the lies. 1893 *S.E. Worc. Gloss.* s.v., He rivelled 'is brow.

absol. 1543 TRAHERON *Vigo's Chirurg.* II. vi. vii, This pouldre..dryeth, riveleth, or wrynkleth, and incarneth not a lytle.

† **Ri·vel**, *v.*[2] *Obs.* Also 4 **ryuel, reuel**, 6 **ryvell.** [ad. obs. F. *river* (Walloon *rifler*) to ravel. Cf. RIVEL *sb.*[2]]

1. *intr.* **a.** To become entangled.

c 1330 R. BRUNNE *Chron. Wace* (Rolls) 4629 Ropes ryueled and swerued [*Petyt MS.* reueld & snarled] in lyne.

b. To ravel or fray *out.*

1530 PALSGR. 692/2, I ryvell out, as sylke dothe, *je riule.*

2. *trans.* To open *out* by unravelling.

1650 ELDERFIELD *Civil Right Tythes* 297 'Tis in the hands of all men, and rivels out the generall subject into many particulars.

Rivelet, obs. form of RIVULET.

Riveling[1] (ri·vəliŋ). Now *dial.* and *Hist.* Forms: 1 **rifeling**, 3 **riueling** (4 **-yng**), 4 **ryve-**, (9) **riveling**; 5 **revelyng(e**, *Sc.* **rewelyn, rewlyng, raweling**; 9 *dial.* **rivilin, riv(e)lin**, etc. [OE. *rifeling*, perh. related to RIVEL *sb.*[1], RIVELLED *a.* ON. *hriflingr* and MHG. *ribbalin*, occurring only in the Perceval legend, represent OF. *revelin* (*rov-*, *rouvelin*), which was no doubt from early ME. The mod.F. *rivelin* a shop-worn shoe (Littré) may be the same word.]

1. A shoe of raw hide. = RILLING *sb.*

c 1000 ÆLFRIC *Gloss.* in Wr.-Wülcker 125 *Obstrigelli*, rifelingas. ? a 1300 *MS. Digby 172*, fol. 146 b/1 *Perone* .i. anglice 'riueling'. c 1300 in Langtoft *Chron.* (Rolls) II. 264 Somme is left na thing, Bot his rough ryveling To hippe tharynne. 1338 R. BRUNNE *Chron.* (1810) 282 Þou getes no þing, but þi riuelyng, to hang þer inne. c 1425 WYNTOUN *Cron.* VIII. xxix. 4421 Hys knychtis weryd revelyngs Off hydis or off hart hemmynys. c 1470 HENRY *Wallace* I. 219 Ane Ersche mantill it war thi kynd to wer;..Rouch rewlyngis apon thi harlot fete. 1483 *Cath. Angl.* 305/2 A Revelynge, *pero.* 1837 R. DUNN *Ornith. Ork. & Shetl.* 13 A kind of shoe of the untanned skins of the ox and seal, which are called rivilins. 1880 *Times* 21 Sept. 10/5 At Symbister we note that most of the boatmen wear 'rivilins'.

†2. *transf.* A wearer of rivelings; a Scot. *rare.*

c 1300 in Langtoft *Chron.* (MS. Fairf. 22) If. 4 Tprut! skot riueling, In vnseli timing Crope þu out of cage. a 1352 MINOT *Poems* ii. 19 Rughfute riueling, now kindels þi care.

† **Ri·veling**[2]. *Obs.* In 7 **riuel(l)ing.** [Perh. based upon *rivelet*, obs. form of RIVULET.] A rivulet or rill.

1615 BRATHWAIT *Strappado* (1878) 5 Hypocrenes pure riuelings of wit. 1621 — *Nat. Embassie* (1877) 61 Ninus Tombe, Erected neare a Christall riueling. 1622 DRAYTON *Poly-olb.* xxviii. 256 Swale bonny Codbeck brings, And Willowbeck with her, two pretty Riuellings.

Rivelled (ri·v'ld), *a.* Forms: α. 1 **rifelede**, 4 **riuelede**, 4, 6–7 **riueled** (5 **rieu-**), 4, 6– **riveled** (5–id), 6– **rivelled**, 6–7 **riueld, rivel(l)d**; 5 **ryuelyd**, 6 **ryu-, ryvyled, ryu-, ryvelled**, 5 **ryuelde**, 6 **ryuilde**, 7 **ryveld.** β. 5 **reuylde**, 5–6 **reueled** (5 **-lid**), 6 **reuyled, reveld.** [OE. *rifelede*, app. f. **rifel* (see RIVEL *sb.*[1]), of obscure etym. Formerly in freq. use; now *dial.* or *arch.*]

1. Wrinkled; full of wrinkles or small folds; corrugated, furrowed: **a.** Of the skin, face, etc. (Very common c 1530–1720.)

α. a 1100 in Napier *O. E. Glosses* 187/2 *Rugosus*, rifelede. c 1380 *Barlaam & Josaphat* 248 in Horstm. *Altengl. Leg.* (1875) 218/2 An old Mon he saiȝ, wᵗ a riueled fas. 1390 GOWER *Conf.* III. 370 Al my face With Elde I myhte se deface, So riveled and so wo besein. c 1425 *Found. St. Bartholomew's* (E. E. T. S.) 27 By and by his senowys were contracte, pale and lene and ryvelyd abowte the moweth all discolouryd. c 1450 *Merlin* 262 He lefte vp his heed that was lothly and rivelid. 1513 MORE *Chron., Rich. III* (1883) 54 Now is she old..and dried vp, nothing left but ryuilde skin and hard bone. 1566 DRANT *Wailings Jer.* K viij, Their ryveled skinnes, clongde to their bones unseparable be. 1620 VENNER *Via Recta* ii. 40 The colour of the face becommeth pale and riu'led. 1658 ROWLAND tr. *Moufet's Theat. Ins.* 1023 Where ever it finds a rivled pleated skin, it will cause very great pain. 1711 ADDISON *Spect.* No. 86 ¶ 2 When I see a Man with a sour rivell'd Face, I cannot forbear pitying his Wife. 1784 COWPER *Task* II. 488 From the rivel'd lips of toothless, bald Decrepitude. 1820 C. R. MATURIN *Melmoth* (1892) III. xxviii. 117 His rivelled and toothless mouth. 1879 MISS JACKSON *Shropsh. Word-bk.* 353 Martha begins to shewn age—'er neck an' 'ands bin all rivelled an' s'runk.

fig. and *transf.* 1546 J. HEYWOOD *Prov. & Epigr.* (1867) 41 That ye herein awarde me to forsake Beggerly beautie, and riueld riches take. 1609 SHAKS. *Tr. & Cr.* V. i. 26 (Q.[1]), The riueled fee simple of the tetter.

β. 1430–40 LYDG. *Bochas* I. xx. (MS. Bodl. 263), Ther reuelid skin abrod to drawe & streyne, Froward frounces to mak hem smothe & pleyne. 1509 BARCLAY *Shyp of Folys* (1874) I. 288 Theyr face and vysage stande awry And all to reuylde.

b. Of fruit (dried or stored up).

1565 COOPER *Thesaurus*, *Acina rugosa*, riueled grapes, or reasons. 1601 HOLLAND *Pliny* XV. xiv, The ragged apples Pannucea take this name, for that..they soonest be riveld. 1678 DRYDEN *All for Love* Prol. 40 Take in good part from our poor poet's board Such rivelled fruits as winter can afford.

c. Of bark, leaves, etc.

1594 NASHE *Terrors of Night* Wks. (Grosart) III. 257 The riueld barke or outward rynde of a tree. 1601 HOLLAND *Pliny* XIII. xxi, The leaves..be somewhat longer..,with long cuts or lines wrinkled and riveled throughout. *Ibid.* XVI. xxxi, Ordinarily, all old trees have more riveled barkes and furrowed, than the younger. 1665 REA *Flora* 70 If it [the root] appear rivelled or crumpled on the outside.

2. Shrunken, shrivelled, esp. by heat.

1629 MAXWELL tr. *Herodian* (1635) 417 As for the leather and wood it was all burnt and riveld. a 1640 DAY *Peregr. Schol.* (1881) 53 Upon the barren trees..hung fruite..shrunk up and riveld like scrowles of scortcht parchment. 1697 DRYDEN *Virg. Georg.* IV. 616 The sultry Dog-star..Scorch'd Indian Swains, the rivell'd Grass was dry. 1712–4 POPE *Rape Lock* II. 132 Or Alum styptics with contracting pow'r Shrink his thin essence like a rivel'd flow'r. 1784 COWPER *Tiroc.* 596 Ev'ry worm..weaves And winds his web about the rivell'd leaves. 1886 BARNES *Dorset Gloss.*, *Rivelled*.., shrivelled as grass.

fig. 1842 LYTTON *Zanoni* (1860) 100 Its power is rivelled as a leaf which the first wind shall scatter.

b. With *up.*

1627 HAKEWILL *Apol.* (1630) 80 They shall passe away with a noyse,..like the bissing of parchment, riveled up with heat. 1686 F. SPENCE tr. *Varillas' Ho. Medici* 440 The Spleen was..straitu'd and rivell'd up. 1700 DRYDEN *Flower & Leaf* 378 The fading flowers..hung the head, And rivell'd up with heat, lay dying in their bed.

†3. Pleated or gathered in small folds. *Obs.*

1480 CAXTON *Trevisa's Higden* II. xxxv. (1527) 90 This was the fyrst kyng of Romayns that ware purpure, a maner reed clothynge of kynges and broudred and ryuelde. 1515 BARCLAY *Egloges* i. (1570) A ij b/1 Their reuilde shirtes of cloth white, soft and thin. ? 1523 *Rec. St. Mary at Hill* (1905) 36 Playne Surplices for Men...Reveld Surplices for Men. 1583 STUBBES *Anat. Abus.* F v b, Some [capes] are pleated, and ryueled down the back wonderfully.

4. Twisted; coiled. *rare.*

1594 MARLOWE & NASHE *Dido* 754 Ile giue thee tackling made of riueld gold. 1835 BROWNING *Paracelsus* I. 481 He points, smiling, to his scarf Heavy with riveled gold.

† **Ri·velling**, *vbl. sb. Obs.* Forms: 5 **ryueling, -yng(e, reuel-, revelynge, ryvullyng(e.** [f. RIVEL *v.*[1] + -ING[1].]

1. A wrinkle (on the skin).

c 1380 WYCLIF *Sel. Wks.* III. 194 Not havynge wem ne revelynge ne ony siche filþe. 1388 — *Job* xvi. 9 My ryuelyngis seien witnessyng aȝens me.

2. The action of the verb.

1398 TREVISA *Barth. De P. R.* v. xxx. (Bodl. MS.), By chaungyng of ham, schrinking, and reueling, he bodith and tokeneþ deying. *Ibid.* lxiv, Reueling þat comeþ of wasting of substancial moisture. c 1440 *Pallad. on Husb.* XI. 258 Chiries in the sonne ydried take And kepe, as they bygynne in rivullynge. a 1470 H. PARKER *Dives & Pauper* (W. de W. 1496) VIII. xvi. 343/2 Many tokenes of warnynge, ..as age, sekenesse,..rymplynge or reuelynge of the skynne.

So † **Ri·velling** *ppl. a. Obs.*

a 1470 TIPTOFT *Tulle on Friendsh.* (Caxton, 1481) f iv, The whyte heris & the ryvillyng [*pr.* ryvikyng] chier of the body of an olde man.

Rivel-ravel, variant of RIBBLE-RABBLE.

1709 *High German Looking-Glass* in Wright *Prov. Dial.*, A great deal more of such rivel-ravel, of which they knew no more than the man in the moon. 1876 in *E. D. D.*

Riven (ri·v'n), *ppl. a.* Forms: α. 4 **rivyn, ryffen**, 5–6 **ryven**, 6–7 **ryuen, riuen**, 4, 6– **riven.** β. 5–6 **revyn**, 6 **reven**, *Sc.* **reuin.** [Pa. pple. of RIVE *v.*[1]]

1. Split, cloven, rent, torn asunder.

1307–27 *Pol. Poems* (Camden) 307 Sum es left na thing Boute his rivyn riveling To hippe thar-hinne. 1457 *Fabric Rolls York* (Surtees) 69 Pro c long revyn burdes, prec. pece, 2d. c 1460 *Towneley Myst.* ii. 141 For had I giffen away my goode, then myght I go with a ryffen hood. 1563 WINȜET *Wks.* (S.T.S.) I. 114 Auld and reuin ornamentis. 1590 SPENSER *F. Q.* I. viii. 9 Through riven cloudes and molten firmament. *Ibid.* 10 Like fresh water streame from riven rocke. 1619 T. TAYLOR *Comm. Titus* ii. 14 We may not, like riuen vessels, let this doctrine slip. 1667 MILTON *P. L.* VI. 449 He stood..Sore toild, his riv'n Armes to havoc hewn. 1720 POPE *Iliad* XX. 328 O'er him high the riven Targe extends. 1784 COWPER *Task* IV. 444 The well-stack'd pile of riven logs and roots. 1815 SHELLEY *Alastor* 347 The little boat..pausing on the edge of the riven wave. 1877 W. BLACK *Green Past.* xxxvii, A series of majestic peaks, their riven sides sparkling with sunlit snows.

fig. 1817 SHELLEY *Revolt Islam* III. 1300 The caverns dreary..Of the riven soul. 1849 MISS MULOCK *Ogilvies* xxxvi, To cast out from his riven heart the very ashes of this bitter love.

†2. Ornamentally slashed. *Obs. rare.*

c 1450 *Songs on Costume* (Percy Soc.) 65 So many ryven shertes..And so many lewed clerkes, Say I never. a 1548 HALL *Chron., Hen. VIII*, 57 b, One Shynynge, Mayre of Rochester, set a young man on the Pillory for wering of a ryuen shert.

River (ri·vəɹ), *sb.*[1] Forms: α. 4 **riuere, rivere**, 4, 6–7 **riuer**, 5– **river** (6 *Sc.* **-eir**); 5–6 **ryuere** (*Sc.* **-were**), 5 **-yre**; 4–6 **ryuer** (5 **-eer**), **ryver** (6 *Sc.* **ryuir, ryvir, rywir**). β. 4–5 **reuere** (5 **-ire**), 4–6 **revere** (5 **-yre**); 4–5 **reuer** (5 **-ir**, 6 *Sc.* **-ar**), 5 **revyr**, 5–6 **rever** (5 *Sc.* **-eir, -ar**, 5–6 **-ir**). [a. OF. *rivere*, *riviere*, *reviere* (mod.F. *rivière*), = Prov. and Pg. *ribeira*, Sp. *ribera*, It. *riviera*, med.L. *rivera*, *riveria*:—pop. L. **rīpāria*, f. *rīpa* bank. From OF. are also MDu. *riviere* (Du. *rivier*), MHG. *rivier* (G. *revier*), MLG. *rivēr*, *revēr*, obs. Da. *revier*, *rever.*]

I. 1. A copious stream of water flowing in a channel towards the sea, a lake, or another stream.

In some ME. examples the OF. sense of 'river-bank' appears to be possible.

α. 1297 R. GLOUC. (Rolls) 487 Gret plente hii founde of fiss,..Of wodes & of riuers, as is in þe contreie. c 1320 *Sir Tristr.* 1884 His gle al for to here Þe leuedi was sett onland To play bi þe riuere. 1390 GOWER *Conf.* I. 232 Upon a Rivere as he stod, That passe he wolde over the flod Withoute bot. *Ibid.* II. 161 In the valleie, Wher thilke rivere..made his cours. c 1430 LYDG. *Min. Poems* (Percy Soc.) 26 The Theban legeon,..At Rodomus ryver was expert there corage. c 1470 *Gol. & Gaw.* 248 Apone that riche river..The side-wallis war set. 1526 *Pilgr. Perf.* (W. de W. 1531) 6 b, Than shall there be neyther..ryuer ne fysshe, castell ne towne. 1587 GOLDING *De Mornay* i. (1592) 11 As the River leadeth thee to his head, shal not the heade lead thee to the originall spring thereof? 1625 N. CARPENTER *Geogr. Del.* II. ix. (1635) 142 All Riuers haue their first originall from the Sea. 1667 MILTON *P. L.* IX. 514 A Ship by skilful Stearsman wrought Nigh Rivers mouth or Foreland. 1727 GAY *Fables* I. xxv. 9 'Tis like a rolling river, That murm'ring flows, and flows for ever! 1779 FORREST *Voy. N. Guinea* 178 The bar of the river Tamantakka..makes that river's access less safe than the Pelangy's. 1823 SOUTHEY *Hist. Penins. War* I. 599 The crowd still continued on both sides the river. 1842 ALISON *Hist. Europe* lxxviii. X. 1017 The great rivers of the world have now become the highways of civilization and religion. 1880 HAUGHTON *Phys. Geogr.* v. 203 A river may be defined to be the surplus of rainfall over evaporation.

fig. c 1380 WYCLIF *Sel. Wks.* I. 14 Þese fisheris of God shulden waishe þere nettis in þis ryver. 1432–50 tr. *Higden* (Rolls) I. 29 And soe this presente story is smyten in to vij. ryuers [*text* ryuerers]. 1535 COVERDALE *Ps.* xxxv[i]. 8 Thou shalt geue them drynke of the ryuer of thy pleasures. 1576 FLEMING *Panopl. Epist.* 180 They..throwe themselues into riuers, nay, mayne seas of errours. 1602 SHAKS. *Ham.* I. ii. 80 The fruitfull Riuer in the Eye. 1816 BYRON *Fragment*, Could I remount the river of my years. 1832 E. REEVES *Homeward Bound* 13 It is amusing to note how stout conservatives have drifted down this river of socialism.

β. 13.. *Cursor M.* 5922 (Gött.), For þe rott þat þar-on fell, Bath it stanc, reuer and well. 1387 TREVISA *Higden* (Rolls) II. 327 Whan reueres wexeþ ouer mesures þey dooþ..harme. a 1400–50 *Alexander* 5279 Þare ran a reuire..vndire þat riche hame. c 1450 HOLLAND *Howlat* 12, I raikit till ane Reveir That ryally apperd. 1500–20 DUNBAR *Poems* xxv. 52 To eit..pertrik and plever, And every fische that swymis in rever. 1567 *Gude & Godlie Ball.* (S.T.S.) 109 God turnit the craig in fresche reueir.

b. Const. *of* (the name of the river). Now somewhat *rare.*

c 1375 *Sc. Leg. Saints* xxxvi. (*Baptist*) 285 Criste..come to sancte Iohne howine to be in-to þe rywere of Iordane. c 1400 MAUNDEV. (1839) i. 7 This Ryvere of Danubee is a fulle gret Ryvere. c 1425 WYNTOUN *Cron.* IV. iii. 199 Þe rywere of Ewfrate. a 1548 HALL *Chron., Hen. V*, 33 Borne at Monmouth on the River of Wye. 1565 in Marsden *Sel. Pl. Crt. Adm.* (Selden Soc.) II. 55 Honnefleur and Rouen and other ports in the revere of Seine. 1606 SHAKS. *Ant. & Cl.* II. ii. 192 She purst vp his heart vpon the Riuer of Sidnis. 1652 NEEDHAM tr. *Selden's Mare Cl.* 218 Those words concerning the River of Rhine. 1710 J. CHAMBERLAYNE *St. Gt. Brit.* II. I. 323 It's watered with the pleasant River of Clyde. 1753 CHAMBERS *Cycl. Suppl.* s.v. *Rivers*, The river of St. Lawrence..pours forth nearly as much as this. 1817 SCOTT *Rob Roy* xxviii, The river of Forth forms a defensible line.

c. *transf.* A copious stream or flow *of* (something). Also *fig.*

1382 WYCLIF *Job* xxix. 6 Whan I wesh my feet with buttere, and the ston helde to me ryueres of oile. 1526 TINDALE *John* vii. 38 He that beleveth on me,..out of his belly shall flowe ryvers of water of lyfe. 1588 SHAKS. *Titus A.* II. iv. 22 A Crimson riuer of warme blood. 1611 BIBLE *Ps.* cxix. 136 Riuers of waters runne downe mine eyes. 1767 *Ann. Reg.* IX. I. 98 The lava is really tremendous, the river of fire being..four miles in length. 1776 A. ADAMS in *Fam. Lett.* (1876) 144 In peacable possession of a town which we expected would cost us a river of blood. 1855 KINGSLEY *Westw. Ho!* xxi, Beneath that long shining river of mist. 1898 MEREDITH *Odes Fr. Hist.* 29 You away sweep Rivers of horse, torrent-mad, to the shock.

d. *Astr.* The constellation Eridanus or Fluvius.

1551 RECORDE *Cast. Knowl.* (1556) 268 A greate tract of starres, which represent the forme of a Riuer: and therefore are they called the Ryuer. 1771 *Encycl. Brit.* I. 487 Eridanus, the River.

e. Used euphemistically for the boundary between life and death.

Compare the use made of this figure by Bunyan in his *Pilgrim's Progress.*

1790 BURNS *Elegy Capt. Henderson* xv, And hast thou crost that unknown river, Life's dreary bound? 1843 in Quincy *Life W. L. Garrison* (1889) III. 79 She had gone down with him [*sc.* her late husband] to the brink of the River, and..he had gone over and she returned. 1892 *The Week* (Toronto) 660 [Whittier] had at last crossed the river, on whose brink he had been so long waiting.

†2. A stream, or the banks of a stream, as a place frequented for hawking. Hence, the sport of hawking. *Obs.*

c 1330 R. BRUNNE *Chron. Wace* (Rolls) 3135 Brenne..coube of chas & of ryuere, Inow of game of here manere. 1338 — *Chron.* (1810) 94 Neuer on Friday to wod þou go to chace. Þe riuer salle þou forsake on Friday ilka dele. c 1386 CHAUCER *Sir Thopas* 26 (Ellesm.), He koude..ride on haukyng for Riuer With grey goshauk on honde. c 1400 *St. Alexius* (Laud 622) 968 He was to þe Emperoure ysent, to..lernen chiualrie, Of huntyng, & of Ryuere. 14.. *Guy Warw.* 856 (Cambr. MS.), Wyth howndys we wyll chace dere And wyth hawkes to the ryuere. 1513 DOUGLAS *Æneis* v. Prol. 4 The very hunter to fynd his happy pray, The falconer the riche riveir our to flene. 1615 MARKHAM *Country Contentm.* I. v, To make your Hawk fly at fowl, which is called the flight at the River. a 1625 BEAUM. & FL. *Woman's Prize* III. ii, He must..send me..by all means, Ten cast of hawkes for th' river.

†3. The coast or littoral (of Genoa). *Obs.*

After It. *la riviera di Genoa.*

1549 THOMAS *Hist. Italie* 185 He..gatte Sauona and Voragine in the ryuer of Genoa. 1693 SIR T. P. BLOUNT *Nat. Hist.* 25 [These vessels] are built all along the River of Genoa, being very swift.

II. *attrib.* and *Comb.*

4. a. Attrib. in the sense of 'situated in, on, or beside a river', as *river-bar, -beach, -board*, etc.

1874 RAYMOND *Statist. Mines & Mining* 20 The gravel taken from the gulches and *river-bars. 1895 KIPLING *2nd Jungle Bk.* 242 The dholes rushed up the *river-beach in a wave. 1866 CONINGTON *Æneid* 221 When the Trojans moored Their fleet on Tiber's *river-board. 1535 COVERDALE *Jos.* xvii. 9 Then commeth it downe..towarde the south syde of the *ryuer cities. 1509 HAWES *Past. Pleas.* XXXVI. xvii, By the *ryuer coast. 1830 LYELL *Princ. Geol.* I. 91 Marine currents, preying alike on *river-deltas, and continuous lines of sea-coast. 1862 *Luck of Ladysmede* II. 282 The chime of the abbey bells came to them over the *river-flats. 1820 SHELLEY *Hymn Merc.* 447 He right down to the *river-ford had driven. 1865 DICKENS *Mut. Fr.* I. vi, This description applies to the *river-frontage. 1861 W. F. COLLIER *Hist. Eng. Lit.* 122 Shadowy *river-glade and rolling plough-land. 1610 HOLLAND *Camden's Brit.* (1637) 617 A *River-Island, insulated within waters. 1836 *Penny Cycl.* V. 359/1 S. Anna [is] perhaps the largest river island in the world. 1781 S. PETERS *Hist. Connecticut* 242 One acre commonly yields..from 40 to 60 bushels [of Indian corn] on *river land. 1899 T. NICOL *Rec. Archæol. Bible* x. 168 The fertile plains..of the Eastern River-land. 1820 SHELLEY *Hymn Pan* 20 The edge of the moist *river-lawns. a 1876 M. COLLINS *Pen Sketches* I. 72 The little lawn by the *river-marge. 1838 T. L. MITCHELL *Three Exped.* (1839) II. 89 It appeared to belong to the *river margin. 1859 LD. LYTTON *Wanderer* (ed. 2) 211 Lady Eve..dwells beside The *river-meads, and oak-trees tall. 1832 LYELL *Princ. Geol.* II. 130 An extensive moor, or a great *river-plain. 1846 MCCULLOCH *Acc. Brit. Empire* (1854) I. 326 Rivers and *River Ports. 1842 TENNYSON *Gardener's Daughter* 259 The balmy glooming, crescent-lit, Spread the light haze along the *river-shores. 1846 HOR. SMITH *Tor Hill* (1838) III. 321 The adjoining market and *river-stairs. 1852 LYELL *Elem. Geol.* (ed. 4) 85 *River Terraces and Parallel Roads. 1712 SWIFT *Jrnl. to Stella* 7 Aug., Pray observe the cherry-trees on the *river-walk. 1837 *Civil Eng. & Arch. Jrnl.* I. 12/1 The whole to be surrounded by a *river wall, 30 feet high. 1884 C. DAVIES *Norf. Broads & Rivers* xv. 110 Between the river-wall and the water is always a strip of land.

b. With words denoting the course, or some part of the course, of a river or rivers, as *river-basin, -channel, -course, -head*, etc.

1878 HUXLEY *Physiogr.* 19 A map..completely divided into *river-basins. 1833–4 *Encycl. Metrop.* (1845) VI. 705/2 By the waste of the uplands..the *river-channels are raised. *Ibid.* 705/1 This fluctuation of the *river-courses is excessively irregular. 1685 in Dryden *Misc.* II. 408 It..Then to our Springs and *River heads ascends. 1872 TENNYSON *Gareth & Lynette* 999 When they touch'd the second *river-loop. 1865 KINGSLEY *Herew.* xxii, Hereward lay outside the *river mouth, his soul..black with disappointment. 1859 MEREDITH *R. Feverel* xiv, Across sheets of *river-reaches, pure mirrors to the upper glory. 1887 STEVENSON *Merry Men* ii. 77 Looking down the *river shed and abroad on the fat lowlands. 1834 *Penny Cycl.* II. 468/1 Extensive terraces, through which the great *river-systems descend to the low lands. 1841 *Ibid.* XX. 24/1 The basins which occur in these *river-valleys. 1878 HUXLEY *Physiogr.* 138 Our river-valleys are mainly the result of work performed by rain, river, and similar agents of denudation. 1888 *Pall Mall G.* 13 Apr. 4/2 We fear..that the Zambesi *riverway is practically doomed.

c. In the sense of 'used or operating upon a river', as *river-artillery, -boat, -craft*, etc.

1860 SPOTTISWOODE *Vac. Tour* 88 The fifteenth [district] maintaining a battalion of *river artillery. 1801 NELSON 10 Aug. in Nicolas *Disp.* (1845) IV. 452 The defence of our numerous landing-places is better adapted to our *River-Barges, than any other which we could adopt. 1565 COOPER *Thesaurus*, *Fluuiatiles naues*, *riuer or fresh water boates. 1841 *Penny Cycl.* XIX. 460/2 The Lippe..is navigated..by small river-boats. 1892 C. ROBERTS *Adrift Amer.* 16 This was the first time that I ever saw a real Mississippi river boat. 1840 *Penny Cycl.* XVI. 259/2 The Waveney is now navigable..to Bungay..for *river-craft. 1863 HAWTHORNE *Our Old Home* (1879) 280 A crowd of river craft are generally moored in front of it.

d. Miscellaneous, as *river-boar* (BORE *sb.*3), *-breeze, -bud*, etc.; **river-pay, -risk** (see quots.).

1856 MISS MULOCK *J. Halifax* iv, I've often seen it on Severn...We often call it the *river-boar. 1864 TENNYSON *Aylmer's F.* 454 The soft *river-breeze which fann'd the gardens. 1820 SHELLEY *Sensit. Pl.* I. 46 Starry *river-buds glimmered by. 1851 KINGSLEY *Yeast* iii, The *river-damps are God's sending. 1863 RAMSAY *Phys. Geogr.* 106 The old system of *river-drainage. 1626 BACON *Sylva* § 596 Pond-earth, or *River-earth,..is a very good Compost. 1819 SHELLEY *Cyclops* 50 Here..the *river-eddies meet In the trough beside the cave. 1841 *Penny Cycl.* XX. 26/2 The importance of a *river fishery. 1855 LYNCH *Rivulet* LXXXII. v, A *river-fount unsealing In our dry hearts. 1863 *Sat. Rev.* 1 Aug. 162 He has..attempted to classify all the chief *river-names of Europe. 1809 R. LANGFORD *Introd. Trade* 134 **River-pay*, a month's wages advanced to sailors with other allowances. 1681 GREW *Musæum* I. § iii. 52 With some ash-colour intermixed; so as to look like a *River-pebble. 1859 TENNYSON *Merlin & V.* 807 The rotten branch Snapt in the rushing of the *river-rain. 1867 SMYTH *Sailor's Word-bk.* 576 **River-Risk*, a policy of insurance from the docks to the sea, at any port. 1856 'STONEHENGE' *Brit. Rural Sports* I. I. viii. 70/2 For pond and *river-shooting, these guns may be from 12 to 16 lbs. 1876 PAGE *Adv. Text-bk. Geol.* ix. 171 The gigantic bird-bones found in the *river-silts of New Zealand. 1822 SHELLEY *Fragm. Unfinished Drama* 62 How oft we two Have sate..near the *river springs. 1842 *Encycl. Metrop.* (1845) V. 393* The theory of *river-tides. 1855 TENNYSON *Maud* II. iv. 67 In drifts of lurid smoke On the misty river-tide. 1893 *Dict. Nat. Biogr.* XXXIV. 153 He..excelled in *river-views. 1839 DE LA BECHE *Rep. Geol. Cornw.*, etc. xiii. 406 Among wood, moss, leaves, and nuts,..described as *river-wash. 1865 KINGSLEY *Herew.* Prel., To form, from the rain and *river washings of eight shires, lowlands of a fertility inexhaustible.

e. With names of persons, as *river-boy, -consul, -deity*, etc. Also *river-rat, -wolf* in fig. use.

1613 PURCHAS *Pilgrimage* VI. i. (1614) 561 Some imagined him to be Nilus the Riuer-deitie. 1697 DRYDEN *Æneid* Notes 627 The Poet here records the Names of Fifty River Nymphs. 1791 E. DARWIN *Bot. Gard.* I. 117 Or sport in groups with River-Boys, that lave Their silken limbs amid the dashing wave. 1835 MRS. HEMANS *Water-Lily* Poems (1875) 608 Oh! beautiful thou art, Thou..stately river-queen. 1835 *Court Mag.* VI. 33/1 They were river wolves, seizing upon every canoe which floated on those broad blue waters. 1859 BARTLETT *Dict. Amer.* (ed. 2) 368 *River-Thief*, one of a class of thieves in New York city who in boats prowl about vessels at night and plunder them. 1884 *Harper's Mag.* 513/1 Observe the river-rats clustering about the groggeries.

f. With agent-nouns, as *river-carrier, -farmer, -keeper*, etc.

1851 MAYHEW *Lond. Labour* II. 147 The dredgermen of the Thames, or river finders. 1856 'STONEHENGE' *Brit. Rural Sports* I. I. viii. 67/1 They afford better sport to the puntsman than to the river-shooter. 1865 DICKENS *Mut. Fr.* I. i, He could not be a lighterman or river-carrier. 1888 GOODE *Amer. Fishes* 434 For the benefit of our river fishermen I quote two recipes. 1894 C. H. COOK *Thames Rights* 127 To every honorary assistant river-keeper they give a ticket to fish from the weirs.

g. Comb. with pa. pples., as *river-blanched*, etc.

1788 COWPER *Mrs. Montagu* 8 The Cock his arch'd tail's azure show, And, river-blanch'd, the Swan his snow. 1796 W. MARSHALL *W. Eng.* II. 49 A narrow flat of river-formed land. 1820 SHELLEY *Hymn Pan* 3 The river-girt islands, Where loud waves are dumb. 1832 TENNYSON *Œnone* 112 From many a vale And river-sunder'd champaign clothed with corn. 1864 RAINE *Hexham* (Surtees) I. Pref. 6 Heavy..with grain and grass which that river-given soil produces. 1883 *Archæol. Cant.* XV. 92 On the terraces are found river-worn implements lying in the old gravel.

5. Attrib. with the names of fishes or animals (freq. contrasted with *sea-*), as **river bass** (*U.S.*), the black bass (*Micropterus*); † **river boar**, a kind of fish (L. *aper*); † **river bull**, ? the rhinoceros; **river bullhead**, the miller's thumb, *Cottus gobio*; **river carp**, the common carp, *Cyprinus carpio*; **river chub** (*U.S.*), the horny-head or jerker, *Ceratichthys biguttatus*; **river crab**, any crab which inhabits rivers, freshwater pools, or swamps; also, a crayfish; **river dog**, † (*a*) the river otter; (*b*) *U. S.*, = HELLBENDER; **river dolphin**, (*a*) = DOLPHIN 2; (*b*) the Gangetic dolphin (*Platanista*); † **river dragon**, the crocodile (with allusion to Pharaoh of Egypt); **river duck** (see quot.); **river eel**, the common freshwater eel (see EEL 1); **river garfish**, an Australian fish belonging to the genus *Hemirhamphus*, inhabiting freshwater streams; † **river gilt** (see quot.); † **river hawk** (see quot.); **river hen**, = WATER-HEN; **river herring**, *U.S.*, = ALE-WIFE[2]; **river hog**, (*a*) the capybara or water-hog; (*b*) a South African hog of the genus *Potamochœrus*; **river**

Supplement, p. 3873; Corrigenda, p. 4092; Spurious words, p. 4093; Books quoted, p. 4094

ibis (see quot.); **river jack (viper)**, a West African viper having a flat head and a somewhat long horn on either side of the snout; **river lamprey**, a freshwater lamprey, *Petromyzon fluviatilis*; **river limpet**, a pulmonate gasteropod of the genus *Ancylus*, found in rivers; **river mussel**, a freshwater shellfish, *Unio pictorum*; †**river nightingale** (see quot.); **river otter**, the common otter, *Lutra vulgaris*; **river pearl mussel**, a fluviatile mussel bearing pearls; **river perch**, the common perch, *Perca fluviatilis*; **river porpoise**, a species of dolphin; **river salmon**, the ordinary freshwater salmon; **river seal**, *U.S.*, a seal which ascends rivers; **river-shell**, a shell found in freshwater streams; **river-shrew**, = *Otter-shrew*; **river snail**, a kind of snail (*Paludina vivipara*), found in lakes and rivers; †**river soldier** (see quot.); **river swallow**, †(*a*) the bleak; (*b*) the bank-swallow or sand-martin; **river tern**, the common tern; **river tortoise**, the ordinary freshwater tortoise; **river trout**, a freshwater trout; **river turtle**, = *river tortoise*; †**river whale**, ?the sheat-fish; †**river whisker** (see quot.); **river wolf**, †(*a*) the pike; (*b*) a kind of otter (*Lutra Brasiliensis*) found in South America.

1877 JORDAN *N. Amer. Ichth.* in *Smithson. Coll.* XIII. I. 20 *River-Bass, *Lepomis*. 1601 HOLLAND *Pliny* I. 353 What will they say then to the water-Goat & the *river-Bore, which in the river Achelous do evidently grunt. 1639 FULLER *Holy War* II. xiii, Strange creatures bred therein [sc. in the Nile], as *river bulls, horses and crocodiles. 1776 PENNANT *Brit. Zool.* (ed. 4) III. 189 *River Bullhead, *cottus gobio*. 1842 H. MILLER *O. R. Sandst.* iii. 77 The river bull-head, when attacked by an enemy,..erects its two spines. 1896 tr. *Boas' Text Bk. Zool.* 390 In the rivers of Great Britain is found the small River Bull-head. 1653 WALTON *Angler* xii. 236 [Bait] for a *River Carp. 1726 *Gentl. Angler* 63 Carp spawn generally in May, or the beginning of April, especially the River-Carp. 1729 *Dampier's Voy.* III. 412 The River-Carp [of Central America]. Its shape, colour and taste resemble ours. 1884 JORDAN *Fish. U.S.* in *Senate Misc.* VI. I. 617 The 'Horny-head', '*River Chub', or 'Jerker' is one of the most widely diffused of fresh-water fishes. 1861 HULME tr. *Moquin-Tandon* III. iii. 96 The *River Crab or Cray-fish (*Astacus Fluviatilis*) is a decapod crustacean. 1866 *Chambers's Encycl.* VIII. 275/2 River-Crab (*Thelphusa depressa*). 1610 HOLLAND *Camden's Brit.* I. 206 Otterey, that is, The River of Otters, or *River-Dogs, which we call Otters. 1646 SIR T. BROWNE *Pseud. Epid.* 114 Ætius..prescribeth the stones of the Otter, or River-dog, as succedaneous unto Castoreum. 1876 GOODE *Anim. Res.* in *Smithson. Coll.* XIII. 13 *Proteida.* (River-dogs, hell-benders.) 1781 PULTENEY *View Writings Linnæus* 95 *Coryphæna*,..*River Dolphin. 1667 MILTON *P. L.* XII. 191 Thus with ten wounds This *River-dragon..submits To let his sojourners depart. 1837 SWAINSON *Nat. Hist. & Classif. Birds* II. 189 The *Anatinæ*, or *river ducks, show the typical perfection of the whole family [etc.]. 1872 COUES *N. Amer. Birds* 285 River ducks..are not by any means confined to fresh waters, and some species constantly associate with the sea-ducks. 1769 J. WALLIS *Nat. Hist. Northumb.* I. 391 The *River-Eel is frequently taken from two to three feet long in our alpine stony rivers. 1883 E. P. RAMSAY *Food-Fishes N.S. Wales* 28 The two species..*Hemirhamphus intermedius* (the sea gar-fish), and *H. regularis* (known as the *river gar-fish). 1729 *Dampier's Voy.* III. 413 The *River-Gilt [of Central America] hath small scales with a Blush of Gold towards the Back. 1611 COTGR., *Faulcon riuereux*, that preyes on ..riuer fowle; a *riuer Hawke, or Hawke for the riuer. 1894 G. PARKER *Trail of Sword* xi, The cries of herons, loons, and *river-hens. 1884 *Cent. Mag.* Apr. 909/2 The different townships on Cape Cod protect the ..'*river herring'. 1729 *Dampier's Voy.* III. 400 The *River-Hog [of Central America] feeds on Grass and divers Fruits, can swim and dive well. 1868 DARWIN *Anim. & Pl.* II. 150 Even the Red River hog (*Potamochærus penicillatus*).. has bred twice in the Zoological Gardens. 1879 J. G. WOOD *Waterton's Wand. S. Amer.* 402 The *River Ibis (*Ibis infuscatus*) is found..on the rivers of Guiana. 1877 *Nature* Oct. 531/2 A *River Jack Viper (*Vipera rhinoceros*) from West Africa. 1836 SIR J. RICHARDSON *Fauna Bor. Amer.* III. 294 *Petromyzon Fluviatilis* (Linn.), *River Lamprey. 1880–4 DAY *Fishes Gt. Brit.* II. 362 It has been questioned whether this fish [*Petromyzon branchialis*] is not the young form of the river lamprey. 1778 DA COSTA *Brit. Conch.* 1/1 The Limpet, *River. 1864 *Chambers's Encycl.* VI. 138/1 In *Ancylus* (River Limpets) it is limpet-shaped. 1769 J. WALLIS *Nat. Hist. Northumb.* I. 402 The fresh-water shell-fishes,..or *River-Muscles, are plentiful in most of our rivers. 1776 DA COSTA *Elem. Conch.* 295 The Pearl River Muscle. 1851 RICHARDSON *Geol.* (1855) 435 A fresh-water deposit containing the shells of *Unio*, a river mussel. 1611 COTGR., *Rousserole*, the *Riuer Nightingale; a kind of Kings-fisher. 1840 *Penny Cycl.* XVII. 63/2 The Otters.. consist of two forms nearly allied: the first, including the *River Otters..; the second, the Sea Otter. 1896 tr. *Boas' Text Bk. Zool.* 315 The River Mussel (*Unio*) and the *River Pearl Mussel (*Margaritana margaritifera*), which are common in England, are allied forms. 1836 SIR J. RICHARDSON *Fauna Bor. Amer.* III. 1 This fish [*Perca flavescens*, (Cuvier), American perch] has a close resemblance to the *river Perch [*Perca fluviatilis*] of Europe. 1884 JORDAN *Fisheries U.S.* in *Senate Misc.* VI. I. 279 'River Perch' (*Hysterocarpus Traski*, Gibbons). 1849 EASTWICK *Dry Leaves* 97, I saw several *river-porpoises, of the kind the natives call the Bolan. 1888 GOODE *Amer. Fishes* 440 *River-salmon, not anadromous. 1851 *Zoologist* IX. 3298 The fur-seal and *river-seal are found. c1711 PETIVER *Gazophyl.* x. § 99 A thin-rib'd Luzone *River-shell. 1816 T. BROWN *Elem. Conch.* 130 River and land shells are mostly thinner than those of the sea. 1776 DA COSTA *Elem. Conch.* 201 The Planorbis *River Snail. 1859–62 RICHARDSON *Mus. Nat. Hist.* II. 339/2 The species of River Snails, amounting to upwards of sixty. 1729 *Dampier's Voy.* III. 416 The *River Souldier [of Central America]. It's mail'd somewhat like the Sturgeon, the Meat good. 1653 WALTON *Angler* xvi. 205 There is also a Bleak, a fish that is ever in motion, and therefore called by some the *River-Swallow. 1817 T. FORSTER *Nat. Hist. Swallow Tribe* (ed. 6) 79 *Hirundo Riparia*, Sandmartin, Sand-swallow, Bankmartin, or River Swallow. 1831 *Wilson's Amer. Ornith.* IV. 358 *River tern, *Sterna fluviatilis*. 1839 SWAINSON *Nat. Hist. Fishes*, etc. II. 344 *Emydæ*. *River Tortoises. 1843 *Penny Cycl.* XXV. 74/2 Potamians, or River Tortoises,..live constantly in the water, only coming out occasionally. 1884 *St. James's Gaz.* 23 Feb. 5/2 A big *river-trout will lie quietly head to stream. 1802 WILLICH *Domest. Encycl.* IV. 232/2 The *orbicularis*, or common *river-turtle, inhabits the milder climates of Europe. 1895 SWETTENHAM *Malay Sk.* 212 The river-turtle is a great deal smaller than the sea-turtle. 1601 HOLLAND *Pliny* I. 242 In some..riuers..there be fish found full as bigge: and namely, the *riuer-Whale called Silurus, in Nilus. 1681 GREW *Musæum* I. § v. ii. 103 The Head of the River-Whale. 1729 *Dampier's Voy.* III. 418 The *River Whisker. Has long black Whiskers but no Scales: it tastes well, and is frequently eaten. 1655 MOUFET & BENNET *Health's Impr.* (1746) 279 Pikes or *River-wolves are greatly commended..for a wholesome Meat. 1840 *Penny Cycl.* XVII. 66/2 This is the *Lobo de rio* (River Wolf) of the colonists.

6. Attrib. with names of trees, plants, etc., as *river-flag, -reed, sponge*; **river birch**, the red birch, *Betula nigra*; **river black-oak**, an Australian tree (see quot.); **river gum**, the red gum-tree, *Eucalyptus rostrata*; **river lettuce**, a kind of weed, very common in tropical rivers and streams; the water lettuce, *Pistia stratiotes*; **river mangrove** (see quot. and MANGROVE[1] 2); **river oak**, an Australian tree of the genus *Casuarina*; **river pear**, = ANCHOVY-PEAR; **river poisonous tree**, a shrub of the genus *Excæcaria* (see quot.); **river poplar** (see quot.); **river she-oak**, a tree of the genus *Casuarina* (cf. SHE-OAK); **river tea-tree**, the broad-leaved tea-tree, *Callistemon salignus*; **river tree** (see quots.); **river white gum** (see quot.).

1889 MAIDEN *Usef. Native Pl.* 122 *Casuarina suberosa*, ..'*River Black-oak'. 1855 KINGSLEY *Westw. Ho!* ii, A car wherein sate, amid reeds and *river-flags, three or four pretty girls. 1889 MAIDEN *Usef. Native Pl.* 431 This particular specimen was collected by Sir William Macarthur, and called by him '*River Gum of Camden'. He describes it..as a small, quick-growing species, very elegant when in blossom. 1897 MARY KINGSLEY *W. Africa* 378 Great floating masses of *river lettuce (*Pistia stratiotes*). 1889 MAIDEN *Usef. Native Pl.* 370 *Ægiceras majus*,..'*River Mangrove'. A shrub or small tree. Wood of light colour, close-grained, and easily worked. 1838 T. L. MITCHELL *Three Exped.* (1839) I. 39 [The] banks were overhung by the dense, umbrageous foliage of the *casuarina*, or '*river-oak' of the colonists. 1696 PLUKENET *Opera Bot.* II. 32 *Anona Americana*,..Anchovie Pear, & *aliquando* *River Pear, *Nostratibus nuncupatur*. 1889 MAIDEN *Usef. Native Pl.* 187 *Excæcaria Agallocha*,..'*River Poisonous Tree'. ..It produces..an acrid, milky juice. 1885 *Encycl. Brit.* XIX. 512/1 The *P[opulus] canadensis* of Michaux..in New England..is sometimes called the '*River Poplar'. 1855 SINGLETON *Virgil* I. 134 By the banks the *river-reed is cut. 1889 MAIDEN *Usef. Native Pl.* 398 *Casuarina glauca*, ..'*River She-oak'. 1712 J. MORTON *Northampt.* vi. § 22. 367 The brittle-branched *River Spunge. 1889 MAIDEN *Usef. Native Pl.* 390 *Callistemon salignus*,..'*River Tea-tree'. 1705 PLUKENET *Opera Bot.* IV. 176 *Potamodendron, arbor..amnicola, Barbadensibus* *River Tree *nuncupata*. 1729 *Dampier's Voy.* III. 436 River Tree. Because it always grows on its Banks, and shoots its Roots on the Water; it bears a beautiful Umbel of small 5 leaved scarlet Flowers. 1838 T. L. MITCHELL *Three Exped.* (1839) II. 51 A line of yarra river-trees. 1889 MAIDEN *Usef. Native Pl.* 430 A variety of this gum (*E. radiata*) is called in New South Wales 'White Gum' or '*River White Gum'.

River (rai·vəɹ), *sb.*[2] Also 5–7 (9) **ryver**, 6 *Sc.* **rivere**, 6–7 **riuer**. [f. RIVE *v.*[1] + -ER[1].]

1. One who rives, rends, or cleaves. Also in combs., as *block-, girnel-, lath-river*.

1483 *Cath. Angl.* 310/1 A Ryver, *lacerator*. 1508 [see GIRNEL *sb.* b]. 1610 [see LATH *sb.* 4]. 1611 COTGR., *Fendeur*, a cleauer, slitter; a riuer. 1671 EACHARD *Obs. Answ. Cont. Clergy* 22 An honest Block-River, with his Beetle, heartily calling. 1865 W. WHITE *Eastern Eng.* I. 146 These women are known as 'ryvers', because they rive or rend the gills with their thumbs to make way for the stick. 1884 *Good Words* June 395/1 Men have to serve seven years in the quarries..before they get full wages. They then become 'rivers' or 'trimmers'.

†**2.** One who robs; a reaver. *Obs.*

1513 MORE *Chron. Rich. III*, Wks. 40/1 Robbers and riuers walking at libertie vncorrected. 1535 STEWART *Cron. Scot.* II. 341 Ane multitude..Off theif and riuer.. hereit all the landis of Kyntyre. 1568 *Henryson's Cock & Fox* 180 (Bann. MS.), Nay, murther theif and rivere, stand on reir. *Ibid.* (ed. 1631), No, false riuer and theefe, stand not mee neere.

River (ri·vəɹ), *v. rare.* [f. RIVER *sb.*[1]] *trans.* †To wash (wool or sheep) in a river.

1531–2 *Act* 23 *Hen. VIII*, c. 17 § 1 No maner person.. [shall] winde..any fleesse of wolle beinge not sufficiently riuered or washed. *Ibid.*, To riuer or washe their sheepe afore they be shorne. 1724 [see RIVERING *vbl. sb.*].

Riverain (ri·vərēⁱn), *a.* and *sb.* [a. F. *riverain*, f. *rivière* RIVER *sb.*[1]]

A. *adj.* **1.** Pertaining to a river or its vicinity.

1858 *Times* 1 Dec. 9/3 The eddies..which the men wise in riverain mining assert to have drawn the greater quantity of gold to this bank. 1882 *Nature* 23 Nov. 97/1 Special riverain surveys will in future be made.

2. Situated on the banks of a river; dwelling near a river; = RIVERINE *a.* 1.

1870 HUXLEY in *Contemp. Rev.* 515 The riverain population of the North Sea. 1872 M. COLLINS *Two Plunges* III. iii. 70 He..climbed the narrow riverain path. 1883 'OUIDA' *Wanda* I. 61 A whole riverain town on the Danube.

B. *sb.* One who dwells on the banks or in the vicinity of a river.

1864 *Temple Bar* Feb. 337 Take the riverain of the Strand or the environs of Westminster Abbey. 1867 *Standard* 10 Jan. 4/4 Being riverains of the Scheldt, they were free to use it with all its tributaries and outlets.

Ri·ver-bank. [f. RIVER *sb.*[1] + BANK *sb.*[1]] The raised or sloping edge or border of a river; the bank or ground adjacent to a river.

1565 COOPER *Thesaurus* s.v. *Margo*, The brimmes of the riuer banke. 1697 DRYDEN *Virg. Georg.* IV. 764 With his last Voice, Eurydice, he cry'd; Eurydice, the Rocks and River-banks reply'd. 1710 SHAFTESB. *Adv. Author* I. i. 9 A great Frequenter of the Woods and River-Banks. 1764 *Skeffling Inclosure Act* 13 In case the said river Humber shall..destroy the present river-bank. 1843 *Penny Cycl.* XXV. 75/1 The females..seek out on the river-banks sandy spots for the deposit of their eggs. 1864 TENNYSON *Aylmer's F.* 451 He ran Beside the river-bank.

Ri·ver-bed. [f. RIVER *sb.*[1] + BED *sb.* 9.] The bed or channel in which a river flows.

1833 TENNYSON *Mariana in the South* v, The riverbed was dusty-white. 1862 STANLEY *Lect. Jewish Church* v. 116 The delicious water from the sediment of the river-bed. 1899 *Q. Rev.* July 61 The country from the river-bed to hill-top was densely cultivated.

Ri·ver-bottom. *U.S.* [f. RIVER *sb.*[1] + BOTTOM *sb.* 4 b.] Low-lying alluvial land situated along the banks of a river.

1814 BRACKENRIDGE *Views Louisiana* 29 The river bottoms being generally fine. 1843 CAPT. MARRYAT *M. Violet* xxviii, Between the upland and the little ridge..there was a river-bottom. (*Note.* River bottom is a space, sometimes of many many miles in width, on the side of the river, running parallel with it.) 1895 WINSOR *Mississ. Basin* 26 The luxury of the river bottoms and their timber margins.

Ri·ver-drift. *Geol.* [f. RIVER *sb.*[1] + DRIFT *sb.* 10.] Ancient alluvia of rivers in which early palæolithic remains are found. Also *attrib.*, as *river-drift gravel, man.*

1839 DE LA BECHE *Rep. Geol. Cornw.*, etc. xiii. 403 The whole probably being the accumulation of river-drift during a long period of time. 1865 LUBBOCK *Preh. Times* 239 Neither the mammoth, nor the..rhinoceros have been found in any stratum anterior to the river-drift gravels. 1880 DAWKINS *Early Man Brit.* v. 99 The last and most important addition to be made to this list is the man of the river deposits, or the River-drift man. 1892 [see DRIFT *sb.* 10].

River-driver. *U.S.* [f. RIVER *sb.*[1] + DRIVER 2.] (See quot. 1848.)

1848 BARTLETT *Dict. Amer.* (1859) 368 *River-Driver*, a term applied by lumbermen in Maine, to a man whose business it is to conduct logs down running streams, to prevent them from lodging upon shoals or remaining in eddies. 1864 LOWELL *Fireside Trav.* 141 This was M.., a famous river-driver, and who was to have fifty men under him next winter. 1893 *Scribner's Mag.* June 714/1 Every river driver wore a long red sash.

Rivered (ri·vəɹd), *ppl. a.* [f. RIVER *sb.*[1] + -ED[2].] Watered by rivers; furnished with a river or rivers. Chiefly in combs., as *best-, deep-, slow-rivered*; †*muddy-rivered*, living in muddy rivers.

1655 MOUFET & BENNET *Health's Improv.* (1746) 279 If fenny or muddy-river'd Fishes be unwholesome, the Pike is not so good as Authors make him. 1673 E. BROWNE *Trav. Hungaria*..is..the best Rivered Country in Europe. 1796 W. MARSHALL *W. Eng.* I. 279 The ground is..strongly featured; being there divided by deep rivered vallies. 1892 LD. LYTTON *King Poppy* IV. 74 On either side The river'd glen..rear'd Steep crags abrupt. 1899 *Echo* 20 Feb. 1/7 Russia being flat, windy, and slow-rivered.

Riveret (ri·vərèt). Now *rare* or *Obs.* [ad. OF. *riverete, riv(i)erette* (F. *rivièrette*): see RIVER *sb.*[1] and -ET.]

1. A small river or stream; a rivulet, rill, or brook. (Common c 1600–1660; now *rare*.)

1538 LELAND *Itin.* (1768) I. 106 The Castelle of Nottingham stondith on a rokky Hille.., and Line Riveret goith by the Rootes of it. 1577 HARRISON *England* II. i, Caue.. which is no great water nor quick streame.., and yet is it a prety riueret. 1600 HOLLAND *Livy* Pref. p. vi, A little rill, which..is maintained with fresh springs and new riverets. 1633 GERARD *Descr. Somerset* (1900) 1 On the utmost edge of this County Ore a little riverett gusheth out under a large Oak. 1670 DENTON *Desc. N. York* (1845) 5 The South-side is not without Brooks and Riverets, which empty themselves into the Sea. 1807 G. CHALMERS *Caledonia* I. I. i. 46 Waters..such as form pools, in their course, like the riverets above mentioned.

transf. 1594 ? GREENE *Selimus* Wks. (Grosart) XIV. 242 The channels run like riuerets of blood.

fig. c 1616 S. WARD *Coal from Altar* (1627) 28 May not he iustly disdaine, that the lest Riueret should be drained another way? 1623 LISLE *Ælfric on O. & N. Test.* To Rdr. 22 So much better they thought it for men to draw.. religion from the Lord's fountaine, than from creekes and riuerets of men. 1641 HINDE *J. Bruen* lxii. 209 Being as it were broken open by afflictions, the riverets of grace and truth did issue out amayne.

2. *transf.* A surface vein. Also *attrib.*

1603 DRAYTON *Bar. Wars* VI. lvi, Her fair breasts.. Whose violet veins in branched riverets flow. 1658 W. SANDERSON *Graphice* 42 A fair breast,..interlaced with Riveret-azur-veines.

b. A small blood-vessel.

1615 CROOKE *Body of Man* 172 If onely the riuerets or channels of the Hollow-vein did containe Alimentary blood. *Ibid.* 254 From the same braunch of the Hypogastricall Veine come small riuerets to the bladder.

Ri·ver-fish. Also **river fish.** [f. RIVER *sb.*[1] Cf. Du. *riviervisch*.] Any fish that has its habitat in a river or stream; a freshwater fish.

1398 TREVISA *Barth. De P. R.* XIII. xii. (Bodl. MS.), Laye fissche..beþ nouȝt so goode as ryuer fissches. 1587 HARRISON *England* III. iii. (1878) 18 Pike, carpe, and some other of our riuer fishes are solde by inches of cleane fish. 1617 MORYSON *Itin.* III. 95 They have little plenty of River fish, excepting onely Eales. 1630 *R. Johnson's Kingd. & Commw.* 376 It yeeldeth Wine and Wheat.., and affordeth Cattell, Horse, and River-fish. 1753 CHAMBERS *Cycl. Suppl.*, *Lampern*, a river fish of the lamprey kind found in many parts of England. 1888 GOODE *Amer. Fishes* 6 Worthy among river fish to be compared with sea fish.

Ri·ver-god. *Mythol.* [f. RIVER *sb.*[1] + GOD *sb.* I. Cf. Du. *riviergod*.] A tutelary deity supposed to dwell in and to preside over a river.

1661 COWLEY *Of Greatness*, The water every whit as clear.., as if it darted from..the Urn of a River-God. 1713 GAY *Rural Sports* 7 The River-Gods and Nymphs about thee throng To hear the Syrens warble in thy Song. 1775 R. CHANDLER *Trav. Asia M.* (1825) I. 163 The river-god is represented on the Ephesian medals with this aquatic as one of his attributes. 1832 TENNYSON *Œnone* 37, I am the daughter of a River-God. 1859 GEO. ELIOT *A. Bede* xiii, It was as if she had been wooed by a river-god, who might any time take her to his wondrous halls below a watery heaven.

Ri·verhood. [f. RIVER *sb.*[1] + -HOOD.] The state of being a river; the office or duty of a river.

1841 *Blackw. Mag.* XLIX. 302 Expanding into the.. ambitious promise of the youthful river; and anon, swelling forth in the stately majesty of full-grown riverhood. 1847 H. MILLER *First Impr. Eng.* ix. (1857) 144 The dull mound cuts off the Stour from its sorely-tasked term of useful riverhood.

Ri·ver-horse. [f. RIVER *sb.*[1] + HORSE *sb.* 5. Cf. MDu. *rivierpeert* (Du. *-paard*).]

1. The hippopotamus. Cf. WATER-HORSE.

1601 HOLLAND *Pliny* II. 316 As touching the riuer-horse called Hippopotamus, there is a great affinitie..betweene him and the crocodile. 1667 MILTON *P. L.* VII. 474 Ambiguous between Sea and Land The River Horse and scalie Crocodile. 1759 JOHNSON *Rasselas* xxxviii, The crocodiles and river-horses are common in this unpeopled region. 1843 LONGF. *Slave's Dream* vi, The river-horse, as he crushed the reeds. 1898 BOSW. SMITH *Carthage* 39 The Senegal River, a river abounding, then as now, with crocodiles and riverhorses.

2. The water-kelpie: see KELPIE.

1851 THORPE *Northern Myth.* II. 22 He secured the assistance of the water-kelpie or river-horse.

Riverine (ri·vərəin), *a.* and *sb.* [f. RIVER *sb.*[1]]

A. *adj.* **1.** Situated or dwelling on the banks of a river; riparian.

1860 *Chamb. Jrnl.* XIV. 40 Swampville was in reality a riverine town. 1888 INGLIS *Tent Life* 22 Such villages are common enough in these..riverine plains, all over India. 1898 G. W. STEEVENS *With Kitchener to Khartum* 78 Like all riverine peoples he is more clean than bashful.

2. Of or pertaining to a river.

1871 *Graphic* 29 April 382 The view at high water on the riverine curve is hardly surpassed in any European city. 1876 S. BIRCH *Rede Lect.* 24 The riverine navies of Egypt floated to the scene of action. 1898 *Pall Mall Mag.* May 9 Great riverine improvements..effected at great cost.

B. *sb.* The banks or vicinity of a river.

1895 SWETTENHAM *Malay Sk.* 215 All the dwellers on the riverine.

Ri·vering, *vbl. sb.* [Cf. RIVER *v.*] †**a.** Pursuit of game on the banks of rivers. *Obs.* †**b.** Washing (of wool or sheep) in a stream. *Obs.* **c.** Sailing, rowing, etc., on a river.

13.. *K. Alis.* 678 (Weber), Now con Alisaundre..In grene wode of huntyng, And of reveryng, and of haukyng. 1532 *Act* 23 *Hen. VIII*, c. 17 This Act concerning riuering and washing of any wooll. 1724 *Lond. Gaz.* No. 6264/2 By not sufficiently Rivering, or Washing of Sheep, before they are shorn. 1891 MISS DOWIE *Girl in Karp.* 139 We got under weigh, and had the next two hours in the open, with a good deal of rivering.

Ri·verish, *a. rare*[—1]. [f. RIVER *sb.*[1] + -ISH.] Giving rise to rivers; abounding in rivers.

1570 DEE *Math. Pref.* *j b, Easy wayes are made, by which the zelous Philosopher, may wyn nere this Riuerish Ida, this Mountayne of Contemplation.

Ri·verless, *a.* [f. RIVER *sb.*[1] + -LESS.] Destitute or devoid of rivers.

1860 MAURY *Phys. Geogr.* vii. § 404 That sea lies, for the most part, within a rainless and riverless district. 1870 YEATS *Nat. Hist. Comm.* 108 The region of Patagonia, riverless and hilly, is dry, cold, and barren.

Ri·verlet. *rare.* [f. RIVER *sb.*[1] + -LET.] A small river; a brook, stream, or rivulet.

1674 *N. Eng. Hist. & Gen. Reg.* (1850) IV. 34, I give to my son..my house and home lot on the South side of the riverlet. 1883 MISS BROUGHTON *Belinda* I. vii, Here by the riverlet sits the floury mill.

Ri·ver-like, *adv.* and *a.* [f. RIVER *sb.*[1] + -LIKE.]

A. *adv.* In the manner of or like a river.

1646 J. BENBRIGGE *Usura Acc.* 18 Thankfulnesse to God, River-like, returnes unto the Ocean of his glory, those streames of blessings [etc.]. 1868 BROWNING *Ring & Bk.* III. 165 Prosperity rolled river-like.

B. *adj.* Characteristic of or resembling a river.

1830 MISS MITFORD *Village* Ser. IV. (1863) 252 Where the ..brook winds away..until it spreads into a river-like dignity. 1839–48 BAILEY *Festus* xiv. 137 If I could ever think to wrong A love so riverlike, deep, pure, and long. 1878 STANLEY *Dark Cont.* I. xvi. 425 These watercourses, though called rivers, show no running stream, but only river-like marshes.

Ri·verling. *rare.* [f. RIVER *sb.*[1] + -LING[1] 2.] = RIVERLET. Also *fig.*

1591 SYLVESTER *Du Bartas* I. iii. 133 Of him she also holds her silver Springs, And all her hidden Crystall Riverlings. *Ibid.* vi. 755 Sent as from the lively Spring Of his Divineness, some small Riverling.

Ri·verly, *a. rare.* [f. RIVER *sb.*[1] + -LY[1].] Resembling a river; river-like.

1858 *Times* 27 Aug. 8/4 We found the river..broad, deep, and flowing with riverly strength.

Ri·verman. [f. RIVER *sb.*[1]] A waterman.

1722 DE FOE *Hist. Plague* (1756) 254 The Seamen had no communication with the River-Men. 1880 W. NEWTON *Serm. for Boys & Girls* 410 A weather-beaten river man. 1898 *Pall Mall G.* 19 Jan. 4/3 He is a frozen-out riverman, connected with the heavy lighter trade.

Ri·ver-sand. [f. RIVER *sb.*[1] and SAND *sb.* Cf. Du. *rivierzand*.] Sand procured from the bed of a river or stream.

1563 HYLL *Art Gard.* (1593) 19 If you set any young Trees in that grounde, let that there-about bee mixed with a quantitie of sweete Earthe and Riuer sand. 1703 *Moxon's Mech. Exerc.* 242 Also to River or Sea-Sand, if you put a third part of Powder of Tiles.., it works the better. 1726 LEONI *Alberti's Archit.* I. 35 There are three sorts of Sand, Pit-sand, River-sand, and Sea-sand. 1834–6 *Encycl. Metrop.* (1845) VIII. 475/2 The manufactories are restricted to the use of the commonest kind of sea or river sand. 1870 tr. *Baron von Richthofen's Lett.* (1874) 4 River-sand, of which probably millions of tons are yearly carried over these places.

Ri·verside. Also **river-side.** [f. RIVER *sb.*[1] + SIDE *sb.*] The side or bank of a river; the ground adjacent to, or stretching along, a river.

?a 1366 CHAUCER *Rom. Rose* 134 Tho gan I walke through the mede, Dounward ay in my pleying, The river-syde costeying. c 1410 *Master of Game* (MS. Digby 182) xii, Men shulde leed hem oute euery day..vpon a..hard path by a Ryuerside. c 1480 HENRYSON *Mor. Fab., Frog & Mouse* i, Ane litill mous come to ane reueir syde. c 1500 *Melusine* 361 The peple vpon the ryuere syde had grete merueyll & were al abasshed. 1523 LD. BERNERS *Froiss.* I. 19 The ost lodged them in a wodde by a lytle ryuersyde. 1597 BRETON *Wit's Trenchmour* Wks. (Grosart) II. 7/1 Narcissus, or some of his kindred, had been so in loue with theyr owne shadowe, that hee could not goe from the Riuer side. 1611 BIBLE *Acts* xvi. 13 On the Sabboth we went out of the citie by a riuer side. 1662 J. DAVIES tr. *Mandelslo's Trav.* 35 He commonly lurks in the high grass on the river side. 1725 POPE *Odyss.* x. 192 Casting on the river-side The bloody spear, his gather'd feet I ty'd. 1774 GOLDSM. *Nat. Hist.* (1824) II. 182 This animal..seldom ventures from the river side. 1834 MARRYAT *P. Simple* (1863) 160 We..walked along the river-side till we fell in with a small craft. 1865 J. H. INGRAHAM *Pillar of Fire* (1872) 411 Instantly the woman..hurried to the river-side.

b. *attrib.*, as *riverside inn, situation, villa*, etc.

1799 *Hull Advertiser* 15 June 2/4 A warehouse..desirable for any purpose where a river-side situation is required. 1849 J. FORBES *Physician's Holiday* (1850) 1 The river-side inns of Wales or Scotland. 1863 BARRY *Dockyard Econ.* 280 Mr. Stewart has now extensive river-side premises. 1889 C. C. R. *Up Season* 277 A lawn, and a riverside villa.

Hence **Riversi·der.**

1889 C. C. R. *Up Season* 282 Few but will say Something kind of the old riversider.

‖**Riverso.** *Obs. rare.* Also 6 **riuersa.** [a. It. *riverso* 'a back-blow' (Florio).] = REVERSE *sb.* 7. (See also REVERSO.) Also *fig.*

1595 SAVIOLO *Practise* I. 11, I would not aduise any freend of mine..to strik neither mandrittaes nor riuersaes. *Ibid.* L 3 b, If you see he keepes his dagger winding towardes his right side, thrust a riuersa at his face. 1600 O. E. (M. SUTCLIFFE) *Repl. to Libel* I. iii. 81, I haue thought good to bestow on them these Riuersoes, and Tramazzones.

Ri·verward, *adv.* and *a.* [f. RIVER *sb.*[1]]

A. *adv.* Toward a river; in the direction of a river. Also *to riverward of*.

1833 RITCHIE *Wand. by Loire* 62 Looking riverward, the vista is terminated..by a village church. 1872 M. COLLINS *Princess Clarice* II. xvii. 204 Skolinson and Clarice went off wordlessly riverward. 1896 *Atlantic Monthly* May 598/1 The first rising-ground to riverward of the hollow.

B. *adj.* Facing or directed toward a river.

1889 *Daily News* 7 Oct. 2/2 The outside embankments are being actively made, and the river-ward sides faced with strong rubble walling.

So **Ri·verwards** *adv.*

1870 LOWELL *Study Wind., Gard. Acquaint.*, A pair or two..every evening fly over us riverwards.

Ri·ver-water. Also **river water.** [f. RIVER *sb.*[1] + WATER *sb.* Cf. Du. *rivierwater*, G. *revierwasser*.] Water in, forming, or obtained from, a river or stream.

1398 TREVISA *Barth. De P. R.* XIII. iii. (Bodl. MS.), Ryuer water is beeste þat renneþ esteward.., and þe reuer water þat renneþ westward is lasse worthie. 1565 COOPER *Thesaurus* s.v. *Aqua*, Runnyng or riuer water. 1600 J. PORY tr. *Leo's Africa* III. 160 Engins, for the conueying of riuer-water ouer the said walles into cesternes. 1620 VENNER *Via Recta* Introd. 9 Riuer-water hath the third place of goodnes. 1707 *Curios. in Husb. & Gard.* 350 A wooden Trough, fill'd with River-Water. 1762 MILLS *Syst. Husb.* I. 483 The Spaniards..steep them in river water and salt till that bitterness is gone. 1835 LYELL *Princ. Geol.* (ed. 4) I. 345 The area over which the river-water is spread. 1849 NOAD *Electr.* (ed. 3) 220 Common river-water was employed to fill the basin, and to knead the pipe-clay.

Ri·ver-weed. [f. RIVER *sb.*[1] + WEED *sb.*]

1. A weed naturally growing in rivers.

1671 SKINNER *Etym. Bot.*, River-weed, *Conferva Plinii.* 1704 *Dict. Rust.* s.v. *Sea*, Sea and River Weeds. 1805 R. W. DICKSON *Pract. Agric.* II. 643 The dung of rabbits, pigeons, and poultry,..river weeds, and other similar matters. 1895 *Jrnl. R. Agric. Soc.* Mar. 12 He..advised river-weeds and sedge as a manure for them.

2. An American aquatic plant, the threadfoot (*Podostemon ceratophyllus*).

1856 A. GRAY *Man. Bot.* (1860) 384 *Podostemon*, River-weed. *Ibid.*, *Podostemaceæ*, River-weed Family.

Ri·very, *a. rare.* [f. RIVER *sb.*[1] + -Y.]

†**1.** Resembling a river; river-like. *Obs.*[—1]

1612 DRAYTON *Poly-olb.* x. 94 Thy full and youthful breasts, which..Are branch'd with rivery veins.

2. Abounding in streams or rivers; pertaining to a river, etc.

1828 WILSON in *Blackw. Mag.* XXIV. 302 As woody, as lochy, and as rivery a parish. 1859 *All Year Round* No. 28. 29 Upon the artificial peninsula.., transport a bit of rivery Orientalism.

Rivet (ri·vėt), *sb.*[1] Forms: 5 **ryvette**, 6 **ryuet(te, ryvet(t**; 6–7 **riuet**, 6 **-ett**, **rivette**, 6–**rivet**; 5–6 **revette**, 6 **-ett**, **reyvett**, 6, 8 **revet.** [a. OF. *rivet*, f. *river* to fix, clinch, of uncertain origin.]

1. A short nail or bolt for fastening together metal plates or the like, the headless end of which is beaten out after insertion.

[The following quot. is doubtful, but cf. the OF. pl. *rivés*. ?a 1400 *Morte Arthur* 1764 That alle þe rowte ryngez, Of ryues and raunke stele, and ryche golde maylez.]

14.. *Lat. Eng. Voc.* in Wr.-Wülcker 573 *Cnusticium, quedam pars sotularis*, a Ryvette. c 1440 *York Myst.* viii. 109 It sall be cleyngked euer-ilka dele With nayles...Take here a revette, and þere a rewe. 1511 *Nottingham Rec.* III. 332 Neyles and revettes to ye boote. 1599 SHAKS. *Hen. V*, IV. Prol. 13 The Armourers accomplishing the Knights, With busie Hammers closing Riuets vp. 1669 STURMY *Mariner's Mag.* II. vii. 73 Let the Index be fastned to the Center with a Brass Rivet. 1781 COWPER *Conversat.* 64 They fix attention..With oaths, like rivets, forc'd into the brain. 1819 SHELLEY *Cyclops* 391 He flung one against the brazen rivets Of the huge caldron. 1851 RUSKIN *Stones Ven.* Pref., Bars and rivets instead of mortar for securing stones. 1884 W. H. GREENWOOD *Steel & Iron* xvii. 400 The rivet is to be capable of bending hot without fracture.

b. *fig.* or in fig. contexts.

1672 WYCHERLEY *Love in a Wood* I. i, You are the rivet of sanctified love. 1693 DRYDEN *Persius* I. 127 The Verse in fashion, is..So smooth and equal, that no sight can find The Rivet, where the polish'd Piece was join'd. 1742 YOUNG *Nt. Th.* II. 534 This carries friendship to her noon-tide point, And gives the rivet of eternity. 1862 MERIVALE *Rom. Emp.* lxiv. (1865) VIII. 90 The lack of religious and moral principle..loosened the rivets of Pagan society.

†**c.** = ALMAIN-RIVETS. *Obs.*

a 1548 HALL *Chron., Hen. VIII*, 25 Ouer his riuet he had a garment of white cloth of gold with a redde crosse. 1577 EDEN & WILLES *Hist. Trav.* 300 Theyr horsemen are armed with pykes, Ryuettes, Mases of yron, and arrowes.

d. A burr or clinch upon a nail. *rare.*

1634–5 BRERETON *Trav.* (Chetham Soc.) 88 Made of thin plates nailed together, and strong square rivets upon the nail heads. 1753 CHAMBERS *Cycl. Suppl.*, *Rivet*, in the manege, is the extremity of the nail that rests or leans upon the horn when you shoe a horse.

2. *attrib.* and *Comb.*, as *rivet-bolt, -head, -hole, -hoop, iron, machine(ry, -shank*, etc.

1844 H. STEPHENS *Bk. Farm* II. 314 The *rivet-bolts are inserted and riveted down in the red-hot state. 1840 *Civil Eng. & Arch. Jrnl.* III. 351/1 Not a single rivet started nor a *rivet-head flown off. 1832 BABBAGE *Econ. Manuf.* xiii. (ed. 3) 121 Tools, by which the expense of punching the *rivet-holes of each tank was reduced. 1686 PLOT *Staffordsh.* 169 They binde it..with a joynted hoop of Iron, which they call a *Rivet-hoop. 1861 FAIRBAIRN *Iron* 204 Staffordshire bridge plates,..for *rivet iron, bearing a strain of 24 tons before breaking. 1841 *Civil Eng. & Arch. Jrnl.* IV. Index, Stocker's *Rivet Machine. *Ibid.* 56/1 Nail, Pin, and *Rivet Machinery. 1869 SIR E. REED *Shipbuild.* xvii. 328 The dies by which the *rivet-shank is held.

Rivet (ri·vėt), *sb.*[2] [Of obscure origin.] Bearded or cone wheat. Also in pl. form *rivets*.

1573 TUSSER *Husb.* (1878) 49 White wheat or else red, red riuet or whight, far passeth all other, for land that is light. 1764 *Phil. Trans.* LII. 530 This family have been used to buy two bushels of clog-wheat, or rivets, or bearded-wheat, (as it is variously called in this county) every fortnight. 1799 *Monthly Rev.* XXX. 182 Bearded wheat is called in some counties Cone wheat, in others Rivets, and in Nottinghamshire it is called Yeogrove. 1813 BATCHELOR *Agric.* 362 (E. D. D.), Cone wheat, or rivets, is very little used. 1851 LAWSON *Veg. Prod. Scot.* I. No. 146 Common Rivet. Ear smaller and less compact than that of the Cone Rivet.

b. Used *attrib.* with *wheat*.

1707 MORTIMER *Husb.* (1721) I. 126 There are several sorts of Wheat, as red Straw-wheat, Rivet-Wheat. 1805 R. W. DICKSON *Pract. Agric.* I. 540 There are two sorts of rivet wheat, the white and brown. 1886 BRITTEN & HOLLAND *Plant Names* 403 Rivet-Wheat is a well-known variety.

†**Rivet,** *sb.*[3] *Obs. rare.* Also 6 **ryvet.** [Of obscure origin.] The liver of a fish.

1530 PALSGR. 722 Slyt this pykes belly and take out this ryvet [F. *sa gresse*]. 1736 BAILEY *Houshold Dict.* 355 Cut the rivet or liver of the pike small and chop some oisters. 1741 *Compl. Fam.-Piece* I. ii. 128 Your Milts, Spawn and Rivets, must be laid on the Top.

Rivet (ri·vėt), *v.* Also 5 **reuet(t**, 5–7 **revet**, 7 **reuit**; 6 **ryvet**, 6–7 **riuet**, 7 **rivit.** [f. RIVET *sb.*[1] Cf. mod.F. *riveter*.]

1. *trans.* To secure (a nail or bolt) by hammering or beating out the projecting end of the shank into a head or knob; to clinch. Also with *down*.

c 1430 *Syr Gener.* (Roxb.) 87 With a grete hamour of stele The nales he reueted wele. 1530 PALSGR. 690/1, I revet a nayle, *je rive*. Ryvet this nayle and than it wyll holde faste. 1611 COTGR., *River*, to riuet or clench; to fasten or turne backe the point of a nayle. 1677 MOXON *Mech. Exerc.* ii. 24 When you rivet a Pin into a Hole. 1683 — *Printing* xi. ¶ 19 This small Shank is fitted into a small Hole made near the end of the Plate, and Revetted on the other side. 1769 FALCONER *Dict. Marine* (1780), *River un clou*, to rivet a nail. 1834–6 *Encycl. Metrop.* VIII. 299/1 Pins are sometimes inserted.., being also rivetted at each end. 1875 KNIGHT *Dict. Mech.* 1506/1 Rose-clinch nail; ..either clinched or riveted down on a washer or rove.

2. To secure or fasten with or as with rivets. Also with *down, in, together*.

c 1430 *Pilgr. Lyf Manhode* I. cxvii. (1869) 61 With the nailes with whiche was nayled the sone of the smith..the mailes weren enclowed and rivetted. 1485 [see RIVETING 1.] 1530 PALSGR. 692/2, I ryvet peces of yron togyther. 1582 STANYHURST *Æneis* III. (Arb.) 84 A braynsick prophetesse.. whom dungeon holdeth In ground deepe riueted. 1603 DRAYTON *Bar. Wars* II. xx, Their Greaues, and pouldrons others riuet fast. 1663 GERBIER *Counsel* 96 Nor do provident builders rivet locks only at the one side. 1771 LUCKOMBE *Hist. Print.* 305 The plates..[are] rivetted down through the bottom and top-sides of the frame. 1814 SCOTT *Lord of Isles* v. vii, Warriors, who, arming for the fight, Rivet and clasp their harness light. 1834–6 *Encycl. Metrop.* VIII. 298/2 The next process..is to have the coaks rivetted in. 1893 *Archaeologia* LIII. 559 The statue had been broken in ancient times and afterwards carefully riveted together again.

fig. a 1631 DONNE *Select.* (1840) 86 Sin entrenched and barricadoed in sin, sin screwed up, and rivetted with sin. 1654 tr. *Scudery's Curia Pol.* 132 They are bonds and chains of their absolute obedience, riveted by their tongues. 1796 MORSE *Amer. Geogr.* II. 606 The Turks have rivetted the chains of barbarous ignorance which they imposed. 1837 LOCKHART *Scott* IV. xi. 346 [It] served to rivet the bonds of affection and confidence, which were to the end maintained between him and them. 1868 FREEMAN *Norm. Conq.* (1877) II. 332 A war for no object but to rivet the yoke of outlandish men about their necks.

b. Const. *to, into*, or *in* something. Also *fig.*

1650 FULLER *Pisgah* IV. iii. 51 Who violently brake off their ear-rings, even such as were riveted in their skin with long wearing. 1669 STURMY *Mariner's Mag.* IV. xvi. 200 A Libal or Index to be rivetted to the Center. 1713 ADDISON *Cato* II. v, I've seen you..stooping from your Horse Rivet the panting savage to the ground. 1765 A. DICKSON *Treat. Agric.* (ed. 2) 203 A plate of iron..riveted fast into it by bolts. 1802 PLAYFAIR *Huttonian Theory* 334 The mountain of Goatfield which I have mentioned above as..rivetted..to the superincumbent rock. 1833 MRS. BROWNING *Prometh. Bound* 61 Seize him,..Rivet him to the rock.

c. Const. *on* or *upon*.

1679 MOXON *Mech. Exerc.* ix. 161 Instead of Nailing the Hindges upon the Door, they Rivet them on, for more strength. 1698 FRYER *Acc. E. India & P.* 39 A Coronal Arch, on whose Vertex a Globe is rivited by an Iron Wedge. 1797 *Encycl. Brit.* (ed. 3) V. 69/1 By means of the fork.. rivetted on the palettes.

d. *nonce-use.* To marry, join in wedlock.

1700 CONGREVE *Way of the World* I. i, We drove round to Duke's Place; and there they were rivetted in a trice.

3. *transf.* To fix, fasten, or secure firmly.

1639 WOTTON in *Reliq.* (1672) 568 It is none of the least ends of my going to rivet that business. 1672 MARVELL *Reh. Transp.* I. 36 All her Excesses and Errors were further rivited and confirmed. 1768–74 TUCKER *Lt. Nat.* (1834) I. 658 The ideas of precausation and fatality..are so strongly rivetted together in men's minds. 1788 MME. D'ARBLAY *Diary* June, I am wholly ignorant in what manner..his first attachment may have rivetted his affections. 1839 HALLAM *Hist. Lit.* IV. iii. § 103 It is evident that until objects are truly classified, a representative method of signs can only rivet and perpetuate error. 1861 MILL *Utilit.* 46 He never conceives himself otherwise than as a member of a body; and this association is riveted more and more.

b. Const. *to* or *into* something.

1596 SHAKS. *Merch. V.* v. i. 169 A thing stucke on with oathes vpon your finger, And so riueted with faith vnto your flesh. 1611 — *Cymb.* II. ii. 46 Why should I write this, downe, that's riueted, Screw'd to my memorie. 1655 FULLER *Ch. Hist.* II. 107 He riveted the Archbishoprick into the City of Canterbury. 1727 GAY *Begg. Op.* I. xiii, My hand, my heart,..is so riveted to thine that I cannot unloose my hold. 1792 ALMON *Anecd. Pitt* I. x. 203 Great Britain was ..every day more closely rivetted to the continent by fresh engagements. 1817 SCOTT *Rob Roy* xxxviii, Astonishment actually riveted my tongue to the roof of my mouth. 1847 C. BRONTË *J. Eyre* ii, My seat, to which Bessie and the bitter Miss Abbot had left me riveted, was a low ottoman.

c. Const. *in* a practice, the mind, etc.

1618 T. TAYLOR *Comm. Titus* ii. 12 Thou reuitest thy selfe in thy sinne, and wilt not be reclaimed. 1667 WATERHOUSE *Fire Lond.* 11 It is riveted in the corrupt nature of man to revenge injuries. 1709 BERKELEY *Th. Vision* § 51 The prejudice is confirmed and riveted in our thoughts by a long tract of time. 1761 HUME *Hist. Eng.* II. xl. 402 A prince who..appeared not to be rivetted in any dangerous animosities. 1849 ROBERTSON *Serm.* Ser. I. x. (1866) 179 Things become riveted in the memory. 1897 MARY KINGSLEY *W. Africa* 211 Riveting him in the practice of polygamy.

d. Const. *on* or *upon*.

1829 GEN. P. THOMPSON *Exerc.* (1842) I. 162 Bribery attracts men's decision from the right; persecution rivets it upon the wrong. 1830 D'ISRAELI *Chas. I*, III. vii. 139 The affections of Henrietta were riveted on those of her royal husband. 1870 HOWSON *Metaph. St. Paul* 122 The lesson is riveted for ever on the church.

4. To fix intently (the eye or the mind); to command or engross (the attention).

1602 SHAKS. *Ham.* III. ii. 90 Giue him needfull note, For I mine eyes will riuet to his Face. 1621 G. SANDYS *Ovid's Met.* VII. (1626) 129 Her eger eyes she riuets on his face. 1760–72 H. BROOKE *Fool of Qual.* (1809) III. 144 While his attention was thus rivetted. 1791 COWPER *Odyss.* XXIII. 107 She rivetted her eyes on his. 1821 SCOTT *Pirate* xxxi, The attention..of Bunce..was riveted to the armed sloop. 1852 M. ARNOLD *The Future* 6 He..Rivets his gaze on the banks of the stream. 1878 BOSW. SMITH *Carthage* 298 That march riveted the attention of the world.

b. To engross the attention of (a person).

1762 FALCONER *Shipwr.* III. (1819) 23 In dire amazement rivetted they stand. 1861 STANLEY *East. Ch.* xii. (1869) 381 We are riveted by this strange apparition in foreign lands. 1883 PATTISON *Mem.* (1885) 33, I..was riveted by the book.

Hence **Ri·veting** *ppl. a.*

1677 W. HUGHES *Man of Sin* II. iii. 54 A clinching, riveting Argument, I trow! 1899 *Dict. Nat. Biog.* LVII. 178/1 His brilliant, original, riveting, but most censorious conversation.

Ri·veted, *ppl. a.* Also 7– **rivetted.** [f. RIVET *v.* + -ED[1].] Fastened with rivets; clinched. Also in *Combs.*, as *close-, double-, single-riveted*.

1606 SHAKS. *Ant. & Cl.* IV. iv. 22 A thousand Sir, early though 't be, haue on their Riueted trim. 1753 CHAMBERS *Cycl. Suppl.* s.v. *Shoe*, A shoe for all [equine] feet, is one that is cut at the toe into two equal parts, which are joined by a riveted nail. 1861 FAIRBAIRN *Iron* 208 The strength of the parts in riveted joints is reduced. *Ibid.*, The strength of the double riveted joint will be 68. And that of the single riveted joint 46. 1898 *Daily News* 8 Sept. 4/7 The old artillery with riveted wheels and huge wooden axles.

b. *fig.* Firmly fastened, established or settled, rooted; fixed, intent.

1670 W. SIMPSON *Hydrol. Ess.* 72 Some menstruums may dissolve..the close rivetted parts of some..bodies. 1706 BAYNARD *Cold Baths* II. 301 To persevere in..Drunkenness, until a riveted Disease entails his Folly..on his Blood. 1748 RICHARDSON *Clarissa* (1811) VIII. 6, I have a rivetted hatred to him. 1822 HAZLITT *Table-T.* II. vii. 165 Casts a pensive, rivetted look downwards to the modest flowers. 1879 *Cassell's Techn. Educ.* IV. 3/2 Few works..have destroyed more riveted and deeply-rooted errors.

Ri·veter. Also **rivetter.** [f. RIVET *v.* + -ER[1].]

1. One who rivets.

1800 *New Ann. Direct.* 34 Saddle-tree-maker and Rivetter. 1853 URE *Dict. Arts* II. 556 The average work that can be done by two riveters, with one 'holder on' and a boy. 1894 *Labour Commission, Gloss.*, After the boot has been sewn the rivetter again takes the boot and hammers the sole out to make it level.

2. A riveting machine.

1884 *Machinery & Eng.* I. 88/1 Compressing machines, such as steam hammers,..riveters, forging presses.

Ri·veting, *vbl. sb.* Also 7– **rivetting.** [f. RIVET *v.* + -ING[1].]

1. The action of the vb., in lit. and fig. uses.

1485 in Sharp *Cov. Myst.* (1825) 189 Payd for revettyng of þe plats, & for þe iiij boultes, xs. ob. 1611 COTGR., *Rivement*, a riueting, a clenching. 1663 GERBIER *Counsel* 96 A thief..makes that single riveting of no use as to security. 1706 M. HENRY *Wks.* (1853) II. 528/1 He prayed with them partly for..the riveting of the things he had said in their minds. 1779 T. HUTCHINSON *Diary* 1 Dec. II. 299, I think we may beat the French fleet, but if we should, it will be the rivetting of this damned Ministry. 1845 R. W. HAMILTON *Pop. Educ.* ix. (ed. 2) 257 The development of national mind may be but the riveting of a prejudice. 1870 *Spectator* 19 Nov. 1373 To prevent the rivetting of this ascendancy on the neck of Europe.

b. With qualifying word prefixed.

1874 THEARLE *Nav. Archit.* 104 The Liverpool rules require chain riveting for all double and treble riveted joints and butts. *Ibid.*, In edge or butt riveting the space between two consecutive rows of rivets must not be less than one and a half times their diameter.

2. *attrib.*, as *riveting hammer, machine, nail, plate, set, tool.*

See also KNIGHT *Dict. Mech.* (1875) and *Suppl.* (1884).

a 1642 SIR W. MONSON *Naval Tracts* III. (1704) 345/2 Clinch-bolts are clinched with a Rivetting Hammer. 1688 HOLME *Armoury* III. 321/1 The Rivetting Hammer..is very rarely used at his Forge, unless the Work be very small. 1769 FALCONER *Dict. Marine* (1780), *Clous à river*, a rivet, or riveting-nail to be clenched at both ends. 1802 JAMES *Milit. Dict.*, *Riveting-plates*, in gun-carriages, small square thin pieces of iron, through which the ends of the bolts pass, and are riveted upon them. 1843 HOLTZAPFFEL *Turning* I. 387 A rivetting-set or punch for the heads of rivets. 1843 *Civil Eng. & Arch. Jrnl.* VI. 115/2 The Patent Riveting Machine..constructed by Mr. Fairbairn, of Manchester. 1866 *Tomlinson's Cycl. Usef. Arts* III. 611/2 The strong semicircular bracket carrying the fixed riveting tool.

†**Rivia·tion.** *Obs. rare*[—1]. Fishing.

a 1676 HALE *De Jure Maris* I. ii. in *Hargrave's Tracts* (1787) I. 7 The writ..which anciently was directed to the sheriff to prohibit riviation in any rivers in his bailiwick.

‖**Rivière** (rivyę̄r). [a. F. *rivière* (RIVER *sb.*[1]) in same sense.] A necklace of diamonds or other gems, esp. one consisting of more than one string.

1880 DISRAELI *Endym.* xxxviii, Myra was amused as she watched their dazzling tiaras and flashing rivières. 1887 *Pall Mall G.* 29 June 13/3 Buying a diamond for £12,000 and ordering it to be set in her rivière as the centre stone.

Rivilin, variant of RIVELING[1].

Rivina (rivəi·nă). *Bot.* [mod.L., f. the name of Aug. Q. *Rivinus*, a German botanist (1652–1723).] An American plant belonging to the same family as Phytolacca.

1819 *Pantologia* s.v., Three [species]..are cultivated... Downy rivina...Smooth rivina...Climbing rivina. 1882 *Garden* 5 Aug. 112/1 Rivinas..are eminently deserving of more general cultivation than they meet with at present.

Riving (rəi·viŋ), *vbl. sb.*[1] [f. RIVE *v.*[1]]

1. The action of the vb.; rending, tearing, etc.

a 1400–50 *Alexander* 747* (Dubl. MS.), A store..stede stalwortly bondyn;..In rapes fast for ryfyng of bernes. c 1440 *Pallad. on Husb.* XII. 140 Fro rotyng & ryuing they be byraft. c 1450 *St. Cuthbert* (Surtees) 2368 Cuthbert wayued his hand on þaim, Fra ryvyng of thak þaim to reclaym. 1527 *Accs. Ld. High Treas. Scot.* V. 320 To underly the law for the ryving of the Kingis lettres. 1578 *Reg. Privy Council Scot.* III. 57 Taking of the saidis letters perforce fra him and ryving of thame all in pecis. 1609 SKENE *Reg. Maj.* 68 The injurie done to her,.. and also the ryving of her claiths. 1619–53 in Heslop *Northumbld. Gloss.* (1894) 580 Edward Dobson for riving out of twoe ridges of land [etc.]. 1816 SCOTT *Antiq.* xxiv, In the auld times o' rugging and riving through the hail country. 1863 GEO. ELIOT *Romola* v, Power was to be won by other means than by rending and riving. 1875 F. W. MYERS *Poems* 91 Where wilt thou find a riving or a rending?

b. *spec.* Splitting or cleaving of wood.

1471–2 *Durham Acc. Rolls* (Surtees) 94 Pro le ryvyng et sharpyng M[l]D del stakes. 1543 *Fabric Rolls York* (Surtees) Gloss. s.v. *Revyn*, Ryving of fyerwoode in Frankelyn for my lorde. 1576 FLEMING *Panopl. Epist.* 356 Let us take the axe, the wedge and the beetle, and settle our selues to cleauing and riueing. 1634 W. WOOD *New Eng. Prosp.* (1865) 19 The Horne-bound tree..requires so much paines in riving as is almost incredible. 1831 J. HOLLAND *Manuf. Metal* I. 331 The rude practice of riving was soon superseded by the more effective operation of the saw.

Comb. 1875 KNIGHT *Dict. Mech.* 1950/2 *Riving-knife*, a tool used in splitting balks for staves, clapboards, shingles, etc. *Ibid.*, *Riving-machine*, a machine for splitting wood in the direction of the grain.

2. *concr.* A fissure, cleft, or rent. *rare.*

c 1450 METHAM *Wks.* (E. E. T. S.) 41 'Come to the ryuyng off this same walle'...'The ryuyng?' quoth he, 'qwere ys that?' 1591 PERCIVAL *Sp. Dict.*, *Abertura*, opening, cleft or ryuing of any thing. 1859 SALA *Gas-light & D.* ii. 29 He contemplates the rents and rivings, the rags and tatters.

†**Ri·ving,** *vbl. sb.*[2] *Obs. rare.* [f. RIVE *v.*[2] + -ING[1].] Arriving; landing.

1338 R. BRUNNE *Chron.* (1810) 70 At his riuyng þe lond non him forbedde. c 1440 *Promp. Parv.* 435/1 Ryvynge vp to lond, fro water, *applicacio, applicatus.*

Ri·ving, *ppl. a.* [f. RIVE *v.*[1] + -ING[2].] That rives; rending, tearing.

a 1300 *Cursor M.* 20976 Paul..suffurd..Bath mang men and riuand beist. c 1400 *Sc. Trojan War* II. 445 [An eagle] Wytht hys rywand and sharpe tallons..The forseyde bowelles..toke. 1642 H. MORE *Song of Soul* I. vii. Wks. (Grosart) 14 Riving tortures spight,..To good the soul doth nearer reunite. 1781 COWPER *Hope* 640 Nature opposes, with her utmost force, This riving stroke. 1827 PRAED *Arminius* vi, The riving axe and burning brand Rent forests. 1877 BRYANT *Song Sower* iii, The pelting hail and riving blast.

Rivlin, variant of RIVELING[1].

‖**Ri·vo.** *Obs.* [App. of Spanish origin; perh. Sp. *arriba* up, upwards.] An exclamation used at revels or drinking-bouts.

c 1592 MARLOWE *Jew of Malta* IV. (1633) H iv, Hey, *Riuo Castiliano*, a man's a man. 1596 SHAKS. *1 Hen. IV*, II. iv. 124 *Rivo*, sayes the drunkard. 1600 *Look about You* Liv, And *Ryuo* will he cry and *Castile* too. 1607 MARSTON *What You Will* II. i, Weele quaffe or any thing; *Riuo*, Saint Marke.

Rivo·se, *a.* *Ent.* [ad. late L. *rīvōs-us*, f. *rīvus* stream.] (See quot.)

1826 KIRBY & SP. *Entomol.* xlvi. IV. 271 *Rivose*, when furrows do not run in a parallel direction and are rather sinuate.

Ri·votite. *Min.* [f. the name of Professor L. E. *Rivot* of Paris.] 'An amorphous mineral, of yellowish-green colour, containing antimony, copper, and carbon di-oxide' (Chester).

1874 *Geol. Mag.* 367 Under the name of Rivotite..a new Spanish mineral is described by M. Ducloux. It occurs..on the western slope of Sierra del Cadi, in the province of Lerida.

†**Ri·vule,** *v.* *Obs.*[—1] [f. L. *rīvul-us*, dim. of *rīvus* stream.] *trans.* To break up or divide *into* (channels).

1628 FELTHAM *Resolves* (1677) II. lxxxiv. 340 Rivuled into petty Issues running thick corruption.

Rivulet (ri·viulėt). Forms: α. 6–7 **riuelet**, **rivlet**, 7 **riulet**, **riuilet**, **rivelet.** β. 6–7 **riuolet**, 7 **rivolet**, **reu-**, **revolet**, **rivalet.** γ. 7 **riuulet**, 7– **rivulet.** [Perh. ad. It. *rivoletto*, dim. of *rivolo*, dim. of *rivo* :—L. *rīvus* stream: cf. prec. and -ET.]

1. A small stream or river; a streamlet.

α. 1587 HARRISON *England* I. xi. I. 52 Meeting with sundrie other riuelets by the waie. *Ibid.* 55 A pretie riuelet rising about Michelneie. 1596 WARNER *Alb. Eng.* XII. lxxv, Of that huge Sea let's through a Riblet [1612 Riulet] waide. 1624 CAPT. SMITH *Virginia* IV. 108 Two new Forts..vpon a pleasant plaine, and neare a little Riuilet. 1641 J. JACKSON *True Evang. T.* I. 8 As naturall a fluxe..as the water in the rivelet hath from the fount. 1671 *New York Col. Doc.* (1853) III. 196 They past this day several brave brookes and small Rivelets.

β. 1615 G. SANDYS *Trav.* 22 There being sundry riuolets that descend from the mountains. 1660 STANLEY *Hist. Philos.* IX. IV. ix, A tender Olive set In a lone place, near a smooth Rivolet. 1700 ASTRY tr. *Saavedra-Faxardo* I. 123 The most noted Rivers take their rise and beginning from the smallest Rivolets.

γ. 1613–6 W. BROWNE *Brit. Past.* I. ii, Triton..call'd the neighb'ring Nymphs each in her turne To poure their pretty Riuulets from their Urne. 1667 MILTON *P. L.* IX. 420 By Fountain or by shadie Rivulet He sought them both. 1726 SWIFT *Gulliver* III. iii, The Dews and Rains..are conveyed in small Rivulets towards the Middle. 1779 FORREST *Voy. N. Guinea* 320 These clouds feed the rivulets which run from the hills. 1815 ELPHINSTONE *Acc. Caubul* (1842) I. 157 The water of the lake is salt, as is that of some of the rivulets which join it. 1897 MARY KINGSLEY *W. Africa* 364 He discovered one of the sources of the Ogowé at a point where it formed a mere rivulet of water.

b. *transf.* and *fig.*

α. 1660 WINSTANLEY *Eng. Worthies* Ep. Ded. 4 A Nobler confluence of so many Loyal Purple Rivelets of Honour.

β. 1589 GREENE *Menaphon* Wks. (Grosart) VI. 42 The woman ceased not from streaming foorth riuolets of teares. 1600 *Look about You* L, Looke how the furrowes of his aged cheeke Fild with the reuolets of wet eyde mone. 1670 W. PENN *Truth Rescued fr. Imposture* 60 England's Fountain of Justice was clear and wholesom, although the Rivolets or lesser Streams might be troubled.

γ. 1639 LD. DIGBY *Lett. conc. Relig.* (1651) 86 There cannot be admitted..unto the avowed channell of the Church, any corrupt Rivulet of erroneous Doctrine. 1710 T. FULLER *Pharm. Extemp.* 37 Steel..causes the Blood to run.. through all the minutest Canals and Rivulets of the Body. 1758 JOHNSON *Idler* No. 7 ¶ 4 The rivulets of intelligence which are continually trickling among us. 1860 SANGSTER *Hesperus* 44 A rivulet of song..Welled free and sparkling.

2. *attrib.* and *Comb.*, as *rivulet-bed, -side*; also in specific names, as *rivulet carp, dipper, salmon* (see quots.).

1744 J. WILSON *Synop. Brit. Plants* 10 By the rivulet side. 1804 SHAW *Gen. Zool.* V. I. 65 Rivulet Salmon [*Salmo Rivalis*]. *Ibid.* 245 Rivulet Carp [*Cyprinus Rivularis*]. 1811 COOKE *Thames* I. 1* b, From its source it flows on in a rivulet character, till it reaches Cricklade. 1819 TURTON *Conchol. Dict.* 27 *Bulla fluviatilis*. Rivulet Dipper. 1896 *Sunday Mag.* Nov. 621 The rivulet-bed in which you walk is dry.

3. A name of several geometrid moths of the genus *Emmelesia*.

1832 J. RENNIE *Conspect. Butterfl. & M.* 137 The Rivulet ..appears in June on shrubs. *Ibid.*, The Small Rivulet.. appears the end of June. *Ibid.* 138 The Grass Rivulet.

Rivulo·se, *a.* *Bot.* [f. L. *rīvul-us* + -OSE.] Marked with irregular sinuous lines or stripes.

1871 COOKE *Handbk. Fungi* I. 257 Pileus pulvinate, silky, soft, then rivulose. 1887 W. PHILLIPS *Brit. Discomycetes* 94 Cup..externally blackish-brown, rivulose.

Riwell: see REUALL. **Riwle,** obs. f. RULE.

Rix, dial. variant of *rish* RUSH *sb.* (plant).

†**Rixa·tion.** *Obs.*[—0] [f. L. *rixārī* to quarrel: see -ATION.] Scolding, brawling.

1623 in COCKERAM. [Hence in later Dicts.]

Rix-baron. [ad. G. *reichsbaron*.] A baron of the German Empire.

a 1849 MANGAN *Poems* (1859) 138 Thou knowest him well, The proud Rix-baron.

Rix-dollar (ri·ksdǫlaɹ). Now *Hist.* Forms: α. 6 **reekes** (7 **reichs**) **doller**, 7 **rexdolar, dollar, dol(l)er.** β. 7 **rix(e dollar, rixdoller, rix doller, ricksdoller**, 8 **rycksdollar**, 7– **rix dollar, rix-dollar, rixdollar.** γ. **rich dollar.** [ad. older Du. *rijcksdaler* (Kilian; mod.Du. *rijksdaalder*, Fris. *ryksdaelder*), = Sw. *riksdaler*, Da. *rigsdaler*, G. *reichsthaler*: see RICHE and DOLLAR.] A silver coin and money of account, current from the latter part of the 16th to the middle of the 19th century in various European countries (as Holland, Germany, Austria, Denmark, Sweden) and in their commerce with the East, etc.; the value varied from about 4s. 6d. to 2s. 3d.

α. 1598 W. PHILLIP tr. *Linschoten* I. vi. 17 Each pardauwe, accounted as much as a Reekes Doller, Flemish money. [1617 MORYSON *Itin.* I. 286 The silver Doller of the Empire (called Reichs Doller) is of the standard of ten ounces or thereabouts.] 1640 *Bk. War Committee Covenanters* 2 For fornishing thairof, ordaines to be given xx rex dollares. 1654 *Nicholas Papers* (Camden) II. 76 The King..has givin him in landis to the valew of 100,000 Rex dolers. 1690 *Burgh Rec. Lanark* (1893) 234 Thrie rex dollars.

β. 1622 in Birch *Crt. & Times Jas. I* (1848) II. 306 He cometh for his army with great store of rix dollars. 1658 *Cal. Domest. State Papers* 313 The Turks demand 75,000 rix dollars for the provisions. 1700 S. L. tr. *Fryke's Voy. E. Ind.* 6 The Surgeons 28 Gilders, and Diet, and on Shoar 3 Ricksdollers. 1753 HANWAY *Trav.* (1762) I. VII. xciv. 434 The par is reckoned one hundred and twenty-five Saxon dollars, for one hundred rix dollars current in Amsterdam. 1803 *Med. Jrnl.* IX. 539 At all other times they would receive the regular salary of thirty rix-dollars monthly. 1842 BISCHOFF *Woollen Manuf.* II. 168 The price which was charged me..was about five rix dollars and three quarters.

γ. c 1645 HOWELL *Lett.* VI. i, So I left my Lord at Glukstad,..being com hither to take up 8000 rich Dollars upon Mr. Burlamachs Bils.

†**Ri·xle,** *v.* *Obs.* Forms: 2 **rixlan**, 2–3 **rixlen**, 3 (*Orm.*) **rix(s)lenn**, **rixlien**, **rixli**, **rixly(e**, 3–5 **rixle**, 5 **ryxle.** [f. OE. *rīx-ian* to rule + -LE.]

1. *intr.* To reign, bear sway; to rule, have dominion; to prevail.

c 1175 *Lamb. Hom.* 25 From þan helle..us bureȝe þe lauerd þe is..wuniende and rixlende on worlde a buten ende. c 1200 ORMIN 8304 Onn hiss fiftende ȝer fra þatt þatt he bigann to rixlenn I Rome riche. a 1225 *Leg. Kath.* 226 He ane is to herien, þurh hwam & under hwam alle kinges rixleð. c 1400 *Chron. R. Glouc.* (Rolls) App. H. 207 After him Rixlede o king, Rime ihote was. c 1400 *Destr. Troy* 221 Whyle þou rixlis in this Reame no riot we drede.

fig. c 1200 ORMIN 4253 Þurrh all þatt fele kinne gillt..I þa limess rixsleþþ. a 1225 *Ancr. R.* 82 Eresie, God beo iþoncked, ne rixleð nout in Engielond. *Ibid.* 374 Þus, lo! in eueriche stat rixleð bitternesse. c 1400 *Destr. Troy* 2726 Envy..Ryxles full Ryfe in her ranke hertes.

2. To deal masterfully *with* (a person).

c 1400 *Destr. Troy* 13891 With the remnond full rade he rixlit vnfaire,..Cast hom ouer clanly at the cloise brigge.

3. To conduce, lead *to*.

c 1400 *Destr. Troy* 5129 Sely is the kyng, þat kepis the for counsell clene for hym-seluyn, þat well con..rede hym to redurs, þat rixles to shame.

Hence †**Ri·xling** *vbl. sb.* *Obs.*

c 1175 *Lamb. Hom.* 111 Elles ne bið his rixlunge ne fest ne lonsum. c 1200 *Trin. Hom.* 27 *Adueniat regnum tuum*, cume þi rixlinge. a 1225 *Ancr. R.* 248 Alle þe holie haluwen ouercumen þuruh bileaue þes deofles rixlunge.

†**Rixo·sous,** *a.* *Obs.*[—0] [ad. L. *rixōsus*.] 'Full of brabbles' (Cockeram, 1623).

Riyf, obs. f. RIFE. **Riz,** dial. f. RISE *v.* **Rizagon,** var. of RISAGON. **Rize,** obs. f. RISE *v.*

Rizom(e, varr. of RISOM.

Rizzar (ri·zəɹ), *sb.*[1] *Sc.* Also 7 **rasour, rizer**, 8 **rizzer**, 9 **rizzart, rizar.** [Of obscure origin; perh. f. *rid* RED *a.* on the analogy of GROSER.] The red currant; also *attrib.*, as *rizzar-berry, -bush.*

1679 CUNNINGHAM OF CRAIGENDS *Diary* 9 July (S.T.S.) 112 For razour-berries in a yeard. 1684 J. ERSKINE *Jrnl.* 27 June (1893) 67, I did eat some straw and rizer berries. 1703 BRAND *Orkney* 80 There are also at Scalloway some Goose and Rizzer-berrie bushes. 1899 JAS. COLVILLE *Scot. Vernacular* 12 Round the garden ran a high, flat-topped wall, clad on the sunny side with rizzars.

Ri·zzar, *sb.*[2] *Sc.* Also **rizar.** [f. the vb.]

1. 'A drying by means of heat, properly that of the sun' (Jamieson, 1808).

2. A rizzared haddock.

1834 J. WILSON *Noct. Ambr.* xxxiv, Loaves and fishes! Rizzars! Finnans! Kipper!

Ri·zzar, *v.* *Sc.* Also 9 **rizar, rizzer, -or.** [See next.] *trans.* To dry or parch (esp. haddocks) in the sun.

a 1818 MACNEILL *Poems* (1844) 88 Haddies caller at last carting, Or rizzered sweet. 1893 STEVENSON *Catriona* xii, He engaged the goodwife..with some compliments upon the rizzoring of our haddocks.

Rizzared (ri·zəɹd), *ppl. a.* *Sc.* Also 8 **rizzerd**, 9 **riz(z)ard, -art, rizzered.** [ad. obs. F. *ressoré* 'parched, scorched, dryed, or burnt vp, by the sunne' (Cotgr.), f. *re-* RE- + *sorer* 'to reeke; to drie, or make red': see SORE *a.*] Dried up by exposure to the sun: **a.** Of haddocks.

1798 *Monthly Mag.* VI. 436/1 *Rizerd haddocks*, dried haddocks. 1819 SCOTT *Leg. Montrose* xiii, Strung up by the head like rizzered haddocks. 1854 *Phemie Millar* II. 107 Mr. Millar..discussed his newspapers silently along with tea and rizzered haddie. 1880 *Blackw. Mag.* Mar. 360 Anything from Scotch collops to rizzard haddocks.

b. Of soil.

1844 H. STEPHENS *Bk. Farm* III. 744 After the soil on the top of the drills has become a little browned with the sun, or rizzared as it is technically phrased.

Rizzim, -om, -um, variants of RISOM.

†**Ro,** *sb.* *Obs.* Forms: α. 3–5 **ro**, 4–5 **roo**, 4 **rou**, 5 **rowe.** β. *Sc.* 5 **ruf, ruff**, 6 **rufe, ruve, rove, roif.** [a. ON. and Icel. *ró* (Norw., Sw., and Da. *ro*, Fær. *rógv*), = OE. *rów* (once), Fris. *rouwe*, MDu. *rouwe, roe*, (M)LG. *rouwe, rôwe, rou(e, rô(e*, OHG. *ruowa* (MHG. *ruow(e*, later *ruw*) and *rôa* (MHG. *ruo, rue*, G. *ruhe, ruh*), regarded as cognate with Gr. ἐρωή cessation, rest. With the Sc. forms *rufe, ruve*, etc. (= rö̆v), compare ROOVE rivet-burr :—ON. *ró*, CRUIVE var. of CROO, and the northern *grofe, grove* (:—ON. *grôa*), obs. variants of GROW *v.*] Rest, repose, peace.

α. c 1200 ORMIN 7042 Cristess resste & Cristess ro & Cristess swete slæpess. a 1225 *Juliana* 77 Ich aȝeoue þe mi gast,..& do bit, blisfule godd,..to ro & to reste. a 1300 *Cursor M.* 1007 Paradis is a..land o liue, o ro, and rest. 13.. *Coer de L.* 7135 God geve us alle good endyng, And hys soule reste and roo! c 1375 *XI Pains of Hell* 299 in *O. E. Misc.* 220 Al þe fest of þe sunundai..Þai schal haue rou and rest perpetualy. c 1440 *York Myst.* iv. 38 Nowe ar we brought Bothe vnto rest and rowe [*rimes* to, doo]. c 1450 *St. Cuthbert* (Surtees) 4880 Þar durst na paynym eftirward Assayle,..Bot lete þaim rest in ro.

β. c 1450 HOLLAND *Howlat* 14 This riche Revir down ran, but resting or ruf, Throwe ane forest. c 1470 HENRY *Wallace* VI. 60 Now at vnes, now in to rest and ruff. c 1560 A. SCOTT *Poems* (S.T.S.) 5 His mynd sall moif, But rest or ruve. *Ibid.* xxxvi. 85 As wes, is, salbe ay, but roif. c 1570 MONTGOMERIE *Misc. Poems* vi. 20 To run that race but ather rest or rove.

b. In asseverative phrases, as *so have I ro!*

c 1375 *Sc. Leg. Saints* xlii. (*Agatha*) 134 Þat I for-think, sa haf I ro. c 1400 *Laud Troy Bk.* 17568 Sithen ȝe it say I wol also Aȝeyn my wille—so haue I ro! c 1460 *Towneley Myst.* iii. 237 Full well may we mys the, as euer haue I ro. ?a 1500 *Chester Pl.* (E. E. T. S.) vii. 40 As ever haue I rest or rowe, much he spake of glasse.

†**Ro,** *v.* *Obs. rare.* Also 4 **rone**, 6 *Sc.* **rufe, ruve.** [f. RO *sb.* With sense 1 cf. MSw. *roas* to rest oneself, Sw. *roa* to amuse, Norw. *roa* to bring to rest; and with sense 2, MSw. *roa*, MDu. *r(o)uwen*, MLG. *r(ou)wen*, OHG. *ruowon* (MHG. *ruowen*, G. *ruhen*), to rest.]

1. *refl.* To recreate (oneself). *rare*[—1].

a 1300 *Cursor M.* 3351 Ysaac him yode to rone [*Gött.* went him forto ro], Thoȝt on thing he had to done [*Gött.* to do].

2. *intr.* *Sc.* To have or take repose.

c 1560 A. SCOTT *Poems* (S. T. S.) xxx. 19 That thay ma nowþir rest nor rufe, Till thay mischeif þair sellis. a 1568 MONTGOMERIE *Misc. Poems* lii. 14 My mad misfortoun dois me so commuve, That I may nowthir rest nor ruve.

Ro, obs. f. ROE. **Roab(e,** obs. ff. ROBE.

Roach (rōutʃ), *sb.*[1] Also 4–7 **roche**, 6–8 **roch.** [a. OF. *roche* (13th c. in Godef.), *roce*, also *roque*, *rocque*, of uncertain origin.]

1. A small freshwater fish (*Leuciscus rutilus*) of the Carp family, common in the rivers of northern Europe. *Blue roach* = AZURINE. In *U.S.* also applied to various small fishes resembling, or mistaken for the roach.

1314 in *Wardrobe Acc.* 8 *Edw. II*, 21 Dars, roches, et pik, 2s. 8d. 1390 *Earl Derby's Exp.* (Camden) 53 Cuidam homini de Lettowe pro roches ab ipso emptis apud le Haff, vs. iiij d. 1391 *Ibid.* 73 Pro tenches et roches. c 1400 in *N. & Q.* 3rd Ser. VI. 4/1 Yᵉ gutts of a roche is good for a roch:, and so furth of all other fysshys. c 1430 *Two Cookery-bks.* 21 Take Trowtys, Rochys,..an make hem clene. c 1500 *For to serve a Lord* in *Babees Bk.* (1868) 372 Roches in sotelte, Playce in sotelte. 1577 B. GOOGE *Heresbach's Husb.* IV. (1586) 173 b, Some againe delight in both, as the Pike..and the Roach. 1612 PEACHAM *Gentl. Exerc.* III. i. (1634) 153 Of fishes you shall finde in Armes..the Trout, Barbel, Turbot, Herring, Roach. 1653 WALTON *Angler* 206, I might now tell you how to catch Roch and Dace. 1738 SWIFT *Printer sent to Newgate*, If a Gudgeon meet a Roach, He dare not venture to approach. 1787 BEST *Angling* (ed. 2) 56 The Roach is as foolish as the carp is crafty. 1802 BINGLEY *Anim. Biog.* (1813) III. 84 The Roach..is found chiefly in deep still rivers, where it is often seen in large shoals. 1868 PEARD *Water-farm.* xvi. 170 No fish thrives better in confinement, or breeds more rapidly than the roach. 1883 *Fish. Exhib. Catal.* (ed. 4) 107 Collection of Stuffed..Azurine or Blue Roach. 1888 GOODE *Amer. Fishes* 129 The Spot..is known ..in the Chesapeake region also as the..'Roach'.

b. In phrase *as sound as a roach*, = F. *sain comme un gardon* (cf. *plus sain qu' un gardon* in Cotgrave).

1655 MOUFET & BENNET *Health's Improv.* (1746) 280 Roches..are esteemed..uncapable of any Disease, according to the old Proverb, As sound as a Roch. 1667 DENHAM *Direct. Paint.* I. 32 Till some judicious Dolphin might approach, And land him safe and sound as any Roach. 1700 T. BROWN tr. *Fresny's Amusem.* 135 My Father.. turn'd of Seventy, and as yet he's as sound as a Roach still. a 1732 GAY *New Song on New Similies* viii, Hearts, sound as any bell or roach. 1825 J. NEAL *Bro. Jonathan* III. 297 My health is capital—constitution ditto—sound as a roach. 1895 'F. ANSTEY' *Lyre & Lancet* IX. 92 Sickly..? Not a bit of it—sound as a roach!

2. *attrib.* and *Comb.* **a.** In similative combs., as *roach-back, -backed, -bellied, -bent.*

1575 TURBERV. *Venerie* 15 The ridge or chine of the backe rochbent, and the hamme streight, betoken swiftnesse. 1668 *Lond. Gaz.* No. 272/4 A Baye Mare,..flat ribb'd, Roach back'd. 1833 LOUDON *Encycl. Archit.* § 1277 Laths...of cast iron,..four feet long, roach-bellied, that is, forming the segment of a circle on the under side. 1847 YOUATT *Pig* vi. 74 The real Irish pig was a huge,..roach-backed, coarse-boned, grisly brute. 1881 GRANT *Bush Life Queensland* I. vii. 88 The flocks of sheep..return bare, leggy, roach-backed-looking objects. a 1884 JARVIS in Allen *New Amer. Farm Bk.* 410 The Nigretti flock..were not handsomely formed, being rather flat-sided, roach-back [etc.].

b. Attrib., etc., as *roach-angler, -fisher, -fishing, -hook, -net, -pie, -tackle, -weel.*

1661 WALTON *Angler* (ed. 3) xvii. 218 About London, where I think there be the best Roch-Anglers. 1704 *Dict. Rust.* s.v. *Roach-fishing*. They add 12 strong links of Hair, with Roach-Hooks at them. 1725 *Family Dict.* s.v., The Roach-Pie may be made, as that of Tunny-Pie. 1823 in Hofland *Brit. Angler's Man.* (1841) 247 A barbel, caught with roach-tackle. 1867 FRANCIS *Bk. Angling* 18 The Thames, Lea, and Colne are eagerly sought by shoals of roach-fishers. *Ibid.* 19 Roach-fishing is very pretty sport. 1877 — *Angling* 27 One of the finest roach rivers within fifty miles of London. 1883 *Fish. Exhib. Catal.* 366 Roach Weel, from the Province of Bleking. *Ibid.* 376 Roach Net.

Roach (rōutʃ), *sb.*[2] Also 8 **roch.** [var. of ROCHE *sb.*[1], as the usual or only spelling in certain special senses.]

1. *Mining.* (See quot. 1836.) ? *Obs.*

1653 MANLOVE *Lead Mines* 258 Soletrees, Roach, and Ryder. 1747 HOOSON *Miner's Dict.* Q ij b, I have likewise heard of other Veins discovered after the same manner; as also in Fields of Grass lying near the Roch. 1836 FURNESS *Astrologer* II, Roach, Rag-pump, Rider. *Ibid.* Gloss., *Roach*, ore found on the side of the main vein and divided from it by rock or rither.

†**2.** A seam or bed of coal. *Obs.*

1677 *Phil. Trans.* XII. 896 It was found upon the rising grounds (where the signs of the Cole, and the Cole it self came near the day) that there lay another Roach of Cole at a certain depth under it. 1686 PLOT *Staffordsh.* 137 In working the roach of coal 5 yards thick. *Ibid.* 147 He shewed me a level of 35 yards of roach. 1704 *Lond. Gaz.* No. 4008/4, 220 Acres, in which are great Quantities of Roch of Coal, now open.

†**3.** *Peter in roach*, = ROCHE-PETRE. *Obs.*

1692 *Capt. Smith's Seaman's Gram.* II. xxxi. 150 Take of ..Peter in Roach one pound; Peter in Meal one pound.

4. **a.** (See quots. and cf. ROCHE *sb.*)

1831 J. HODGSON in Raine *Mem.* (1858) II. 213 The same sort of conglomerate rock as that at the foot of Ulswater, and which the country people there [in 1799] called roach. *Ibid.* 215 The old red sandstone of the Mellfell district is through all that country called roach or roche.

b. A variety of Portland stone (see quots.).

1829 WEBSTER in *Geol. Trans.* 2nd Ser. II. 42 The bed below this [= School Cap] is the first which is worked for freestone, and is called Roach...It is entirely oolitic..and contains marine shells. 1839 *Civil Eng. & Arch. Jrnl.* II.

Roach (rōtʃ). The new Church in the island, built...of a variety of the Portland stone through the island.

Roach (rōtʃ), *sb.*[1] *Naut.* [Of obscure origin.] 'An upward curve in the foot of a square sail.'

Roach, *sb.*[4], abbrev. form of COCKROACH.

Roach, variant of ROCHE, ROTCHE.

Roach (rōtʃ), *v.*[1] [f. ROACH *sb.*[3]]
1. *trans.* To cut (a tail) with a roach.
2. *U.S.* To clip or trim (a horse's mane) so that the hair stands on end.

Roach alum, variant of ROCHE ALUM.

Roached (rōtʃt), *a.* [f. ROACH *sb.*[3] or *v.*] Having an upward curve.

Roaching (rōtʃiŋ), *vbl. sb.* [f. ROACH *sb.*] Fishing for roach.

Road (rōd), *sb.* Forms: 1 rád, 3–5 (7 *dial.*) rode, 3–7 roade (6 rhoade), 6– road. See also RAID *sb.*

1. † 1. The act of riding on horseback; also, a spell of riding; a journey on horseback. *Obs.*

2. A sheltered piece of water near the shore where vessels may lie at anchor in safety; a roadstead.

3. In pregnant uses: a. *On, upon, the road*, travelling, journeying, upon or during a journey, etc.; on tour. *To take the road*, to set out.

b. *The road*, the highway. In phrases, *to go upon*, or *take to, the road*, to become a highwayman; *gentleman, or knight, of the road*, a highwayman. Now *arch.*

4. *a.* A way or direction taken or pursued by a person or thing; a course followed in a journey. Freq. with possessive pronouns.

Miscellaneous; as *road-cut*, *-hill*, *-cess*, *-chart*; *road-worthy*.

10. *a.* Attrib., with words denoting persons, or a course of action, connected with the making or control of roads, as *road-authority*, *-gang*, *-master*, *-party*, *-police*, *-trust*, *-trustee*; also *road-acquaintance*, *-fellow*, *-pilgrim*, etc.

b. With agent-nouns, as *road-builder*, *-cutter*, *-improver*, *-mender*, *-surveyor*, etc.

c. *dial.* Way, manner; esp. in phrases *no road*, *some road*.

d. *attrib.* and *Comb.* (chiefly in sense 4.)

Road (rōd), *v.*[1] Also 7 rode. [f. ROAD *sb.*]

Roa'ding, *ppl. a.*

Road, *v.*[2] (to clear of weeds): see RODE *v.*

Road, *v.*[3] (of woodcock or wild fowl): see RODE *v.*[2]

Road-book. Also *road-book*. [ROAD *sb.* 4.] A book exhibiting or describing the roads of a district or country.

Road-less, *a.* [f. ROAD *sb.* 4. + -LESS.] Destitute of roads.

Road-maker. [ROAD *sb.* 4 and *a.*]

Road-making, *vbl. sb.* [ROAD *sb.* 4.] The act of constructing a road; the practice of making roads.

Road-man. [ROAD *sb.* 4.] 1. A workman engaged in the making or upkeep of roads.

Road-side. Also *road-side.* [ROAD *sb.* 4.]
1. The side next to the road. *rare.*[-1]
2. The side, or border, of the road; wayside.

Road-stead (rōd'sted). Forms: 4 radestede, 5 rode-stede, 6–9 roadstead; 7 rodestead, 8 road-, 8 roadsted. [ROAD *sb.* 3.] A place where ships may conveniently or safely lie at anchor near the shore.

Road-worthy, *a.* [ROAD *sb.*] Fit for the road; in a suitable condition for road use.

Roadster (rōd'stǝr). Also 7 road-ster.
1. *Naut.* A vessel lying, or able to lie, at anchor in a road; a roadster.
2. A horse for riding (or driving) on the road.
3. One who is accustomed to the road; a coach-traveller.
4. A bicycle for use on the road.

Road-way. [ROAD *sb.* 4.]
1. A way used as a road; a highway.

Roak, -y, *dial.* variants of ROKE, -Y.

Roall, Roalte, obs. forms of ROYAL(TY).

Roam (rōm), *sb.* [f. the vb.] The act of wandering or roaming; a ramble.

Roam (rōm), *v.* Forms: 4–5 romen, -yn, 4–6 rome, 5–6 roome, 6 roame, etc. [Of obscure origin.]

Roamer (rō'mǝr), *sb.* Also 5 rome, 6 rome. [f. ROAM *v.* + -ER.] One who roams or wanders.

Roaming (rō'miŋ), *vbl. sb.* [f. ROAM *v.* + -ING.] The action of the verb; a wandering journey. Also *fig.* and *attrib.*

Roaming, *ppl. a.* [f. ROAM *v.* + -ING.] That roams or wanders.

Roam'ingly, *adv.* [f. prec.]

Roan (rōn), *a.* and *sb.*[1] [a. F. *roan*, earlier *rouen*, *rouan*.]

Roan, *sb.*[2] A soft flexible leather made of sheepskin, used in bookbinding as a substitute for morocco.

Roan, variant of ROWAN, ROWAN-BERRY.

Roan-berry, variant of ROWAN-BERRY.

Roa'ned, *a.* *Obs.* Of a roan colour.

Roany (rō'ni), *a.* [f. ROAN *a.* + -Y.]

Roar (rōǝr), *sb.* Also 4–7 rore; 5–7 roare. [f. ROAR *v.*]

Roar (rōǝr), *v.* Forms: 1 rárian, 3–7 rore, 4–7 roare, 5–6 rawre, 6– roar. [OE. *rárian* = MDu. *reeren*, OHG. *rêrên*.]

Roar, *sb.* ...

Roar (rōⁱ), *v.* Forms: α. 1 rárian, 3 rarin, 4–6, 8 rare (5 rar), 5– rair (5 rayr), 9 *dial.* rear. β. 4 roren, 5 rory ... 7– roore, 6– roar. [OE. rárian = MDu. rēren, reren (still in that use), MLG. rôren (LG. raren, reren, raren), OHG. rêrôn (MHG. rêren, G. *röhren*), probably of imitative origin.]

Roarer[1] (rōⁱ'ra²). [f. ROAR v. + -ER[1].]

Roaring, *vbl. sb.* [f. ROAR v.]

Roaring, *ppl. a.* [f. ROAR v. + -ING[2].]

Roaring-basket ...

Roaringly, *adv.*

Roaring, obs. form of RORY 2.

Roaring, *ppl. a.* [ROARING *ppl. a.* and MEG.]

Roar-worthy, *a. nonce-word.*

Roary, *a.* and *sb.* [f. ROAR v.]

Roast (rōst), *v.* Forms: 4–7 roste, 5–6 rost, 4–6 rooste, 5–7 roost; 6–8 roaste. Also *pa. t.* 5 roste, 9 *dial.* roust, roost, Sc. rostin. [ad. OF. *rostir* (mod.F. *rôtir*) ...]

Roast (rōst), *ppl. a.* [Obs. *pa. pple.* of ROAST *v.* Cf. ROAST *sb.* 2.]

Roast (rōst), *sb.* Forms: 4 roste, 5–6 rosty, 4–6 rooste, 5–7 roost; 5–6 rooste. Also *pa. t.* 5 roste, *pa.* 4 roost[e], 6 roaste. [f. ROAST *v.*]

Roast-table, *a. rare*—. [f. ROAST *v.* + -ABLE.] That may be roasted.

Roast-beef, *sb.* Also roast-beef. [ROAST *ppl. a.*]

Roast-beef-dress (see quot. 1867); roast-beef plant, the fetid iris, *a.* Iris foetidissima ...

Roasted (rōs'ted), *ppl. a.* [f. ROAST v. + -ED[1].]

Roaster (rōs'tə²). [f. ROAST v. + -ER[1]. Cf. Sw. *rostare*, G. *röster*.]

Roasting (rōs'tiŋ), *vbl. sb.* [f. ROAST v.]

Roasting, *ppl. a.* [f. ROAST v. + -ING[2].]

Roasting-iron, *sb.* = ROAST-IRON.

Roasting-jack ...

†Roast-iron. Forms: 4 roast-iron, 5– yren, 7–yren, *pa.* roaste-iron(e, -iryn, -yren, 9 *dial.* roasting-iron. A gridiron.

Roast meat. Also roast-meat. [f. ROAST *ppl. a.*] 1. Meat cooked by roasting.

Rob (rǫb), *v.* Forms: 3–5 robbe, 4– rob; 5 robben. [a. OF. *rober* (mod.F. *dérober*) ...]

Rob (rǫb), *sb.*[1] Also 6 robbe, 8–9 rhob, robe, 7 rob, robb; also 7 rhob, 8–9 rob. [ad. med.L. *rob*, a. Arab. *rubb* ...]

Roba. *Obs.* — BONA-ROBA.

Roband. *Naut.* Also 8-9 robin.

Robardesmen, variant of ROBERDSMEN.

Robbare, obs. form of ROB sb. and v., ROBE.

Robbe, obs. form of ROB v., ROBE.

Robbed (rpbd), *ppl. a.* [f. ROB v.]

Robber (rpbəɹ). Forms: α. 2 rubbere, 3 robbere, 3-7 robbere, 4-5 robbore, 5-6 robur, -ere, 5 rubbere, 4 robboure, -e, 4-5 roboure, -ure, 4-5 robbour, 4 robeur, -our. β. 4 robour, 5-6 robbowre, -eur. [The...]

Robbery (rpbəri). Forms: α. 2-4 roberie, 4 roborye, 5-6 robere, 5-7 roborie; 3-5 robberie, 4-erye, 5-6 robberie, -ery, 4-5 robery, -rie, 4-6 robry(e, -rie.

Robbin. *Naut.* Now *rare* or *Obs.*

Ro'bbin. *Naut.* Now *rare* or *Obs.*

Robbing, vbl. sb. [f. ROB v.]

Ro'bbing, vbl. sb. [f. ROB v. + -ING¹.]

Robble, Robble-hobble.

Robe (rəub), sb. Also 5 roob(e, 6 robbe, 6-7 roab(e; Sc. 5-7 rob, 5 rowb. [a. OF. robe (robbe, roube) = Prov. rauba, Catal. and It. roba.]

Robe de chambre (rɔb də ʃãbr). Also 7-8 robe de chamber.

Robe, the legal profession.

Robe, *sb.* U.S. and Canada.

Robe (rəub), v. [f. ROBE sb.]

Roberd, obs. form of ROBERT.

† **Roberdavy**, **Rob-o-Davy.** *Obs.*

Roberdsmen, obs. forms of ROBBERSMEN.

Robere, obs. form of ROBBERY.

Robert. [A personal name, a F. Robert, ultimately of Teutonic origin.]

Robert(e)s-men, variants of ROBERDSMEN.

Robeux, obs. f. RUBBISH.

† **Robigineous,** a. *Obs.*

Robin¹ (rɔbin). Forms: 4-5 Robyn, 6 Roben, 5. Robene, Robeen, 7 5. Robbin, 5- Robin. [a. OF. Robin, a dim. or familiar form of the personal name ROBERT.]

Robin², *Commerce.* Also robbin. [a. Fr. robin.]

Ro'bin³, *Chem.* [irreg. f. ROBINIA + -IN¹.]

Robin⁴. *Chem.* Also ROBIN. [F.]

Robin Goodfellow (rɔbin gu'dfeloʊ).

Robin Hood (rɔbin hud). Forms: 4 Robyn hood, 6 Robyn hode, 5 Robyn Hude, 6 Robene Hude, 6-Robin hood, 6-hoode, 6- Robin Hood.

Robin Hog. † a constable.

Robin redbreast. [Cf. ROBIN¹ and REDBREAST.]

Robing, vbl. sb. [f. ROBE v. + -ING¹.]

Robinia (rɔbi'niă). *Bot.* [mod.L. (Linnæus).]

Roble (rɔ'ble). [Sp. and Pg. roble.]

Roborant (rɔ'bŏrănt), a. and sb. *Med.* [ad. L. robŏrant-, -rans, pres. pple. of roborare.]

Roborate, v. *Obs.* [f. L. roborāt-, ppl. stem of L. roborāre to strengthen, f. robur, robŏris strength.]

Roboration. *Obs.* [ad. L. roborātiōn-, -ātiō.]

Roborean, a. *Obs.*

Roboreous, a. *Obs.* Also robor-ous.

Robur, obs. form of ROUBLE.

Roburite (rɔ'bŏrəit). [f. L. robur + -ITE.]

Robybke, obs. form of RUBRIC.

Roburnean, a. *Obs.* Of or belonging to Oak [Blount, 1656].

Robust (rob┐st), a. Also 6–7 robuste. [ad. L. robust-us, f. robur strength.]

1. Of persons: Strong and hardy in body or constitution; possessed of rude strength; strongly and stoutly built; of a full and healthy habit.

Ro·bustic, a. Obs. Also 7–8 -ick. [f. robust.]

Robu·stical, a. Obs. [f. as robustic + -al.]

Robu·sticity. rare. [f. as robustic + -ity.]

Robu·stious, a. [f. robust + -ous.]

Robu·stiously, adv. Now rare. [f. robustious.]

Robu·stiousness. Now rare. [f. robustious.]

Robu·stly, adv. [f. robust + -ly.]

Robu·stness. [f. robust + -ness.]

Robustuous, a. Obs. [f. robust + -ous.]

Robu·stuous, a. Obs. = robustious.

Robwort, 7 variant of ribwort.

Roc (rpk). Also 7 rock, 9 roukh. Forms: 7 rock, 9 roo (rokh). B. 6–7 rue, roch, ruck(e, 9 rukh(kh. [ad. Arab. رخّ rokh, rukh(kh : hence Sp., Pg. ruc (ruch). The older plural form in the account of Madagascar in Marco Polo (In. clxxxv.° et l'appellent les genz de ces isles ruc°; in mod. use it is partly from the Arabian Nights.]

A mythical bird of Eastern legend, imagined as being of enormous size and strength.

Rocambole (rɒ·kămbōl). Forms: 7 roccombo, roukombo(l, 7) 8 rockenbole, rockcombo; 7 roomboll, rocombole, rocombo; 8–9 rocambole. [a. F. rocambole, of obscure origin:

Roccellate (rɒkse·lĕt). Chem. [as next + -ate.] A salt formed by the action of roccellic acid upon a base.

Roccellic (rɒkse·lik), a. Chem. (See quots.)

Roccellin (rɒ·kselin). Chem. Also -ine, + -in, -ine². [f. roccella + -in (-ine²).] A coal-tar colour used in dyeing, derived from the orchil lichens.

Roccellinic (rɒkse·lini·k), a. Chem. [f. prec.] 'A crystalline substance obtained from Roccella tinctoria' (Watts).

Rocelin, -ine, obs. var. roccellin.

Rocer, obs. form of rosary.

Roch, obs. f. ratch sb¹; roach; Roche.

Roche (rəʊtʃ). Forms: 4 roche, 5–6 roch, 7–8 roach. Also 5 roach. [a. OF. roche.]

Rochet (rɒ·tʃet). Forms: 4 rokett, 5–6 rochett (5 -yt, -ete, rogett), 6 8 roch-ete; 6–8 rotchet (6 -ette); Rochet. [a. OF. rochet.]

Rochet (rɒ·tʃet). Forms: 4 roket, 5 ruget, 5 roget, 6 roschett, 6–9 rochet; 6 rotchet. [a. OF. rochet, a. OHG. rochon, roc.] The Red Gurnard.

Rochet, obs. form of ratchet.

Rochetta, obs. f. var. rochetta.) = Polverine. Also attrib.

Ro·cheting, vbl. sb. Also 7, 9 roach-ing. [f. roch vb.]

Rochet, -eted, etc.

Ro·chy, a. Obs. var. rocky.

Rock (rɒk). Forms: 4–6 rokke, 6 rokke, 5 roc, 5–6 rok(e, 6 rocke, 4–7 rocke, 5 roo, rok. [a. OF. roque, var. roc.]

I. A large rugged mass of stone forming a cliff, crag, or natural prominence on land or in the sea.

Rock, sb.¹ [f. Rock v.¹] A movement or swaying to and fro, or a spell of this.

Rock, sb.² Forms: 1 roccian, 3, 5 rokken, 5 rokken; 4 rocky, rokky; 4–7 rocke, 6 rook. [OE. roccian, app. f. the Teutonic stem rukk-...] 1. A distaff. Now arch. or Hist.

Rock, v.¹ Forms: 1 roccian, 3–6 rok(k, 6–rock; 4–5 rokke, 4–7 rocke. [OE. roccian...] 1. trans. To move (a child) gently to and fro in a cradle, in order to soothe or send it to sleep. Also in fig. contexts.

Rock cod. [Rock sb.¹] A cod found on rocky sea-bottoms or ledges. Chiefly Sc. and north.

Rock, v.² [f. Rock sb.¹] 1. trans. To encompass or wall with or as with rocks. Obs. rare.

Rockamony, U.S. Also 8 roccahomony, rockahomonie, –homine. [Algonquin Indian, –rokat... to grind, with the termination tula. See Nata & Cawn (1906) 28 Apr. 326.] = HOMINY.

Rock-alum, variant of ROQUELAURE.

Rock alum. [Rock sb.¹] (See ALUM 1 and ROCHE ALUM.)

Rockalow, variant of ROQUELAURE.

Rock crystal. [Rock sb.¹] 1. Pure silica or quartz in a transparent and colourless form, most usually occurring in masses, generally with hexagonal pyramid ends.

Rock crew, [Rock sb.¹] A plant of the genus Arabis.

Rock cry'stal, var. prec.

Rockamboy, rockamboro'; see ROCAMBOLE.

Rockat, obs. form of ROCKET.

Rockaway (rọ'kăwē), U.S. [f. Rock v.¹] A four-wheeled carriage, open at the sides, with two or three seats and a standing top, used in the United States.

Rock-basin. [Rock sb.¹] A basin-shaped hollow in a rock, esp. one of natural origin; in Geol. a large depression in a rocky area, attributed to the action of ice-masses.

Rock-bed. [Rock sb.¹] A floor or base of rock; a rocky bottom or under-stratum; often fig. (Cf. Bed-rock, s.v. Bed 16, 18.)

Rock-bird. [Rock sb.¹] A bird that haunts rocks; esp. a puffin. b. A bird of the genus Rupicola; a 'cock of the rock'. c. U.S. (See quot.)

Rock-birth. [Rock sb.¹] Constructed of, built with or upon, rocks.

Rock. v.³ [f. Rock sb.³, and of Roc, Roke 15.] **Rock**, sb.³ v.¹ Forms: 1 roccian, 3, 5 rocken, 5 rokken; 4 rocky... = Roke.

Rocked, ppl. a. [f. Rock v.¹ + -ED¹.] Curved like a rocker.

Rockelay, variant of ROQUELAURE.

Rockenbole, obs. form of ROCAMBOLE.

Rocker¹ (rọ'kər). Also 5–6 rokker(e, 6 rokke.) [f. Rock v.¹ + -ER¹.] 1. a. A nurse or attendant charged with the duty of rocking a child in the cradle. Now arch. or Obs.

Rocker² [f. Rock sb.¹ + -ER¹.] = ROOKER.

Rocker³, St. rare⁻¹. [f. Rock v.¹] One who takes part in a rocking.

Rockery (rọ'kəri). 1. An artificial heap or pile of rough stones and soil used for the ornamental growing of ferns and other plants. Also transf.

Rocket¹ (rọ'ket), sb.¹ Now rare. Forms: 3–5 roket (5 –ett, –ette, –ytte, 6 –it), 5 rocad, 6 rokkat, –et; 4 –rocket (9 –at), 5–6 rockets, 6 rokkats, –et; 4 rocket (9 –at), roc(q)uet, northern variant of ROCKET. Also Flem. roket.

Rocket² (rọ'ket), sb.² [ad. It. rocchetta, rochetta (Florio rocchetto)...] 1. An apparatus consisting of a cylindrical case of paper or metal containing an inflammable composition, by the ignition of which it may be projected to a height or distance.

Rocket, sb.³ [? f. Rock sb.¹] Some species of dog.

Rocket, sb.⁴ [? var. of Racket sb.]

† Rocket, sb.[3] Obs. rare. In 6 rokket, pl. rokettes. [f. Rocket sb.[1] or of F. roquette (Picard roketé).] A small rock.

† Rocket, sb.[4], var. of, or error for, Rocket sb.[2]

Rocket (ṛ̓kĕt), v. [f. Rocket sb.[3]]

1. trans. To discharge rockets at; to bombard with rockets.

2. intr. a. Of a horse (or rider). To spring or bound up like a rocket; to dart like a rocket.

b. Of game-birds: To fly up almost vertically when flushed; to fly fast and high overhead.

Rocketeer, rare.—[f. Rocket sb.[3] + -eer.] A discharger of rockets.

Rocketer (ṛ̓kĕtǝɹ). Also 9 rocketter. [f. Rocket v. 2 b + -er.] A game-bird that 'rockets'.

Ro·cketing, ppl. a. [f. Rocket v. + -ing.] That rockets, in the senses of the verb.

Ro·cketing, vbl. sb. [f. as prec.] Acting like a rocket; flight.

Rock-fish. [Rock sb.[1]]

1. A fish frequenting rocks or rocky bottoms.

Rock-hewn, a. [Rock sb.[1]] Cut out of the rock.

Ro·ckier, dial. [f. Rock sb.[1] + -ier.] The rock-dove.

Ro·ckiness. Also 7 rookiness, 9 rockyness. [f. Rocky a.[1] + -ness.] The quality of being rocky; rocky character.

Rocking, vbl. sb.[1] [Rock v.[1]] A social gathering (originally a spinning party) of a kind formerly held on winter evenings in the country districts of Scotland.

Rocking, vbl. sb.[2] [Rock v.[1] + -ing.]
1. The action of swaying or swaying to and fro, or causing such motion.
2. The operation of using the rocker or cradle in engraving. Also attrib.

Rocking, ppl. a. [Rock v.[1] + -ing.]

Rockinge, obs. f. Rocken.

Ro·ckish, a. [Rock sb.[1] + -ish.] Resembling a rock; hard as rock.

Rockit, obs. f. Rochet, Rocket.

Rockle, var. of, or error for, Ruckle.

Rockling. [Rock sb.[1] + -ling.]
1. That rocks; swaying, oscillating; also, causing to rock.

Rockman. [Rock sb.[1]]
1. Sc. One who bakes birds on rocks or cliffs.
2. In slate quarries, a skilled workman who gets out the slate rock.

Rocking-chair. [f. Rock v.[1]] A chair mounted on rockers; also, a chair having a rock-ing seat attached to the base by springs.

Rocking-horse. [Rocking ppl. a.] A wooden horse mounted on rockers for children to ride upon with a rocking motion.

Rocking-stone. [Rocking ppl. a.] A large stone or boulder so poised on a limited base as to be easily swayed to and fro; a logan-stone.

Rock-pigeon.
1. A species of dove (Columba livia) inhabiting rocks and believed to be the source of the domestic pigeon; the rock-dove.

Rockle, Rochelle, rockes; rockinesse.

Rockie, Also 6 rockynes, of Rokeley.

Rockless (ṛ̓klĕs). Devoid of rocks; without rocks.

Ro·cklike, a.

Ro·cklike, a. Resembling a rock; hard as rock.

Rock-oil. [Rock sb.[1]] Native naphtha.

Rock-ousel. [Rock sb.[1]] The ring-ouzel.

† Rock-petre. Obs.—[Rock-petre.]

Rock-salt. [Rock sb.[1]] Salt found in a state disposed in strata, and capable of being extracted in large lumps.

Rock-shaft. [Rock v.[1]] A shaft which merely rocks or oscillates about its axis in place.

Rock-plant. [Rock sb.[1]]

Rock-ribbed, a. Having ribs of rock.

Rock-rose. [Rock sb.[1]]
1. A variety of Daphne Cneorum. Obs.

Rock-ruby. Obs. [Cf. Rock sb.[1] 6 c.]

Rock-water. [Rock sb.[1]] Water issuing from a rock, naturally clear and cold.

Rock-weed. [Rock sb.[1]] A seaweed, esp. one growing on the rocks.

Rock-work. [Rock sb.[1]]
1. A natural mass or group of rocks or stones.

Rock-shaft. [Rock v.[1]]

Ro·shaft, obs. form of Rod v.[1]

Rocky (ṛ̓kĭ), a.[1] Also 5–6 rokky, 6 rokki, 7 rokie, 7–8 rookey. [f. Rock sb.[1] + -y.]
1. Full of, abounding in, rocks; consisting or formed of rock; having the character of rock.

Rock-salt, etc.

Rockard, adv. [Rock sb.[1] + -ward.]

Ro·cky (ṛ̓kĭ), a.[2] Also 5–6 rokky, 6 rokki, 7–8 rookey. [f. Rock sb.[1] + -y.]

6. *Brewing.* (See quot.)

Ro·cky, obs. form of Rock v.[1]

Rococo (rǝkō·kō), a. and sb. Also rococco. [a. F. rococo, supposed to be a fanciful formation on the stem of rocaille pebble- or shell-work.]
A. adj. 1. Old-fashioned; antiquated.
B. sb. The style of architecture, art, etc., having rococo characteristics.

Rocquet, Obs. rare. Also 7 roquet [Adaptation of a native name.] (See quots.)

Rocou, variant of Roucou.

† Rocquet, Obs.—form of Rocket sb.[1]

Rod (ṛ̓d), sb. [f. Rod sb.[1]]

1. A straight, slender shoot or wand, growing upon or cut from a tree, bush, or shrub.

II. 8. † a. The shaft of a spear. Obs. rare.

Rode, var. of Rood.

Rod (ṛ̓d), v. [f. Rod sb.[1]]
† 1. trans. To furnish with rods or laths. Obs.

2. U.S. To fit with lightning-conductors.

Rod, obs. and dial. pa. t. and pa. pple. of Ride v.

Rod, obs. or dial. pa. t. of Ride v.

Rodde, obs. pa. t. of Ride v.

Ro·dded, ppl. a. [f. Rod sb.[1] or v. + -ed.]

Rodden, sb.[1] Sc. Also 6 roddyne, 6–9 roddin, 9 rodan, 7 b)oddon. [Of obscure formation.]

Rodden-flike. Sc. Also roddin-flike. [Perh. f. Rodden sb.[1] + Fluke.]

Rodde-fluke. Sc.

Rodden, a. Obs. rare.—[f. Rod sb.[1]]

Roddikin. Sc. Also 6 rodekin, 8 -ikin, 9–9 roddin, 9 roddan, 7 b)oddon. [Of obscure formation.]

Roddin(g, Sc., a path: see sheep-rodding.

Rodding, vbl. sb. [f. Rod v.]

Rodding, sb.[1] Sc.

Roddle, variant of Raddle sb.[1]

Ro·ddy, a. Obs.—[f. Rod sb.[1] + -y.]
Roddy, obs. form of Ruddy a.

Rode, sb.[1] Obs. [Prob. a. Du. roede measuring-rod (ten feet long): see Rood sb.[1]] A certain length of rope.

Rode, sb. Also 7–8 road(e, 9 rhode. [Of obscure origin.] A rope, esp. one attached to a boat-anchor for travel.

Rode, sb. Also 7 road. [Prob. ad. older Du. *roden* (Kilian).]

Rode, v. Also 7 road. [Of obscure origin. Sense 2 is evidently related in some way to *cock-rode*, *road*.]

Rodeo, sb. [a. Sp. *rodeo*.] A place or enclosure where cattle are brought together for any purpose.

Rodomel, Obs. [a Spanish personal name.]

Rodewort, Obs. variant of ROOD-TREE.

Rodge, variant (of error for) RADGE.

Rodges-blast, variant of ROGER'S BLAST.

Rodian, obs. form of RHODIAN.

Roding. [f. ROD sb.] An anchor rope.

Rodion, Obs. (See quot.)

Rodney (rǫdni). [Of obscure origin.]

1. *Coal-mining.*

2. An idler or loafer; a casual worker; a disreputable character. Also *attrib.*, hulking, rough.

Rodomontade (rǫdǫmǫntēid). Also rodo-, rhodo-. [f. prec.]

Rodomonta·der. Also rhodo-. [f. prec.]

Roe, sb.[1] Forms: a. 5–6 a(h)buke, 6 rayboke, 6–7 royboke, 6 roebuck, 6 rawbuck, 9 roebuck. [OE. *rā* (gen. *rāh-).] 1. The roe-deer; a male roe.

Roe, sb.[2] Having roe; full of spawn. Also in comb. *full-*, *hard-*, *soft-roe*.

Roe-deer. Forms: 1 rah-, 2 roadeor; 6 rowdeare, 7 roa deere, 8–9 roe-deer.

Roer (rūər). [Du. *roer*, ad. G. *rohr*.]

Rofe, obs. pa. t. of RIVE v.[1]; obs. ff. ROOF.

Rofis (rōfis). Also 8 rofear, 9 roffia. [Malagasy.]

Rog (rǫg), v. Obs. exc. dial. Also 4–6 rogge, 5 roggyn. [Of obscure origin.]

Rogatian, (rǫgā·tian). [f. *Rogatus*, the leader of the sect, who flourished in the 4th century.]

Rogation (rǫgē·ʃǫn). Forms: 4–6 roga-tioun, 5–6 -cioun, 5 -cyon.

So Roga·tianist, *rare*[-].

Rogatory (rǫ·gatǫri), *a.*

Rogerian (rǫdʒī·riǎn), *a.* (See quot.)

Rogative *rare*[-]. [ad. Sp. *rogativa*.]

Rogatory, *a. rare*. [ad. L. *rogatōri-us*, f. *rogāt-*: see prec.]

Roger (rǫ·dʒər), sb.[1] *rare.* An early canting word.

Roger[2] (rǫ·dʒər). [A personal name of men, a. OF. *Roger*, *Rogier*, of Teut. origin,—OHG. *Ruadgēr*, *Hrodgar*.]

Roger of Coverley (rǫ·dʒər ǫv kǫ·vǫli).

Roger's blast. [Evidently a survival of Lydgate's RODION, with assimilation to the personal name.]

Rogue (rōug), sb. Also 6 roge, rogge, rooge, 6–7 roag, roag(e, roague. [One of the numerous canting words introduced about the middle of the 16th cent.]

Roguery (rōu·gǫri). [f. ROGUE sb. + -ERY.]

1. Conduct or practices characteristic of rogues; knavishness, rascality; trickery, vagrancy.

Rogueship. [f. ROGUE sb.] Also 7 **roguehipp.** The state of being a rogue; also as a mock title in 7 your rogueship, etc.

Roguing, vbl. sb. [f. ROGUE v.] †1. The action of wandering about the country; tramping from one place to another as a rogue or vagrant; also, an instance of this.

Roguing, ppl. a. [f. ROGUE v. + -ING.] Wandering, living, or acting like a rogue.

Roguish, a. [f. ROGUE sb. + -ISH.] 1. Pertaining or appropriate to, characteristic of, rogues (†or vagrants); disreputable.

2. Given to roguery; knavish or rascally in conduct.

3. Playful; mischievous; waggish.

4. Of plants: Inferior, degenerate.

Roguishly, adv. [f. prec. + -LY.] In a roguish manner (variously): mischievously.

Roguishness. [f. prec. + -NESS.] The state or character of being roguish; knavery, roguery; also in later use, playfulness, archness.

† **Roguy,** a. [f. ROGUE sb. 6-7 roguie, 7-8 roguey, [f. ROGUE + -Y.] 1. = ROGUISH a. 1 and 2.

Rohun, Med. [Hindi] Rohun bark (see quots.).

Rohuna, Bot. [Hindi rohunha.] (See quots.)

Roid, obs. form of ROUGHLY adv.

Roil, rally, etc., obs. ff. ROYAL(LY, etc.

Roid, a. Obs. rare. Also 7 roide, royd(e, rode (rode). [a. OF. roide, royde (mod.F. raide), -L. rigid-um RIGID a., but in some cases (esp. 7 rode Sc. texts) perh. a variant or scribal alteration of RUDE a.] 1. Stout, strong; violent, rough.

2. To move about vigorously. Obs. rare.

3. dial.: To play or frolic, esp. in a rough manner; to romp, rampage (to frisk).

† **Roil,** sb.2 Obs. rare. In 4-5 royle, [a. OF. roillier, roeillier, etc. (see Godefroy s.v. roeillier), related to roeille roil.] 1. intr. Of a stream: to flow.

Roil (roil), v.1 Forms: 2-5 royle, 5-7 (9-9 dial) royl(e, 7 (9 dial.) roile. 8- roil. See also RILE v. [Of obscure origin. F. ruiler, to mix up mortar, is cited by Godefroy.]

1. trans. To render (water or any liquid) turbid or muddy by stirring up the sediment; hence esp. fig., to perturb, disquiet, disorder. Cf. RILE v. 1.

2. To disturb in temper; to vex, irritate, make angry. Cf. RILE v. 2.

Roil, v.2 Also royl. [Of doubtful origin: connexion with prec. is not clear.] To salt (fish).

Roiled (roild), ppl. a. Also 7 royled. (See prec.) 1. Rendered turbid by stirring of sediment; also fig. of the passions.

Roiler, Obs. [f. ROIL v.1] One who roams idly or dissolutely.

Roily (roi'li), a. Chiefly U.S. and dial. [f. ROIL v.1] Muddy, turbid.

† **Roin,** v.1 Obs. In 4-5 royne, (noyne, rungne). [a. OF. roignier, -L. roniare or (*rotundiare) rotundiare, to pare away; to clip; to cut round.] 1. trans. To pare away; to clip; to cut round.

† **Roin,** sb.1 Obs. In 4, 6-7 royne. Forms: 4 royne (runne), rynne. [a. OF. roigne (cf. rungier in Godef. VII. 238/2), var. of grugnie GROIN sb.1] 1. scab, scurf; also fig.

Roin, v.2 [f. prec.] 1. trans. To make scurvy or scabby; hence, to befoul, make dirty or filthy.

† **Roiner; Roining** vbl. sb. Obs.

Roil, pa. t.: see ROUGHLY adv.

Roister (roi'stər), sb. Now arch. Also 7 (9 arch.) royster. [Back-formation from ROISTER vb.1] A swaggering or noisy reveller. Cf. ROISTER sb.1 2.

Roister (roi'stər), v. Now arch. Also 7 royster. [f. OF. rustre (*ruistre), 'a ruffin, royster, hacster, swaggerer' (Cotgr.), var., with excrescent r, of ruste -L. rustic-um RUSTIC a.] 1. A swaggering or blustering bully; a riotous fellow; a rude or noisy reveller.

2. intr. To revel noisily; to swagger. Also royster.

Roistering, vbl. sb.1 Obs. [f. ROISTER v.1] T' action or practice of roving or roaming about.

Roistering, ppl. a.1 [f. ROISTER v. + -ING.] 1. Blustering, boisterous; associated with noisy revelling; uproarious, wild.

Roisterer (roi'stərər). Also 6-7 royster. [f. ROISTER v. + -ER.] A swaggering reveller. Cf. ROISTER sb.1 1.

Roistering, vbl. sb.2 [f. ROISTER v.2] The conduct of roisterers; a revel or racket.

Roisterly, a. Obs. rare. [f. ROISTER sb.1 + -LY.] Resembling, characteristic of, a roisterer.

Roisterous, a. Also 6 roysterus, 7, 9 -ous.

† **Roisting,** vbl. sb. Obs.

Roistingly, adv. Obs.

Roiston crow, variant of ROYSTON CROW.

† **Roit,** sb.1 Obs.1 In 5 royt, or royt, ydyle walkynge aboute... discourse, vagabie, vagilias.

Roit, sb.2 Sc. rare. Also royt. [? Related to ROIT v.] An attire named to persons or cattle (see quot. 1825).

Roit, v. Now Sc. and dial. 7 5 roytyn, royt.e, 9 Sc. royt. [Of obscure origin.] 1. intr. To wander about idly or aimlessly.

Roke, sb.1 Now rare. [Of obscure origin.] Also 5 rok. [Related to ROIT sb.1] (See quot.)

Rokkat, obs. form of ROCKET.

Roke (rōk), sb.1 Now dial. Also 6 roik, royk, rook; plad. 8 rocke, 9 roke, roke. [Prob. a. ON. reykr. Also 6 ROKE, ROWK. [Prob. of Scand. origin.] The variants roke, rouk, rowk would normally arise from an Oscand. *reuk(o)-, which has been superseded by a form with umlaut.

Roke, v. Now dial. Also 6 Sc. roik, royk, rouk; plad. 6 rocke, 9 rooc, royok. rawk, rauk. See also ROOK, ROWK. [Prob. of Scand. origin. The variants roke, rouk, rowk would normally arise from an Oscand. *reuk(o)-.

Roke, a scratch, flaw, etc.: see ROKE.

Roke, obs. form of ROCK, ROCKY.

Roko (rōk), var. of ROKE sb.

Roland (rō'land). Also 4 Rouland (Rau-), Rouland, 5 Rowlande, 5-6 Rowlande, 6-9 Rowland. [Of obscure meaning.] The legendary nephew of Charlemagne, celebrated in the Chanson de Roland and many other romances (frequently together with his comrade Oliver); hence, one comparable to Roland in respect of courage or warlike deeds; one who is a full match for another.

Roll (rōl), sb. Forms: 3-7 rolle, 5-7 rol, rowle, 6-8 rowl, 6-7 roole (6 roull), 7-8 roul, 6-7 (9 roole 7 roale), 7- roll. [a. OF. rolle, roole, roul, roll (mod.F. rôle), -L. rotulus, var. of rotula ROTULA, dim. of rota wheel.] I. 1. A piece of parchment, paper, or the like, which is written upon or intended to contain writing, etc., and is rolled up for convenience of handling or carrying; a scroll.

2. spec. Such a piece of parchment, paper, etc., inscribed with some formal or official record, a document or instrument in this form.

a. Master (or Clerk or Keeper) of the Rolls: one of the three ex-officio judges of the Court of Appeal and a member of the Judicial Committee, who has charge of the rolls, patents, and grants that pass the great seal, and of all records of the Court of Chancery.

b. Rolle sometimes attrib.: the rolls, the former buildings in Chancery Lane in which the records in the custody of the Master of the Rolls were preserved (now represented by the Public Record Office).

3. A register, list, or catalogue of names, deeds, etc.; also pl. roll of honour.

4. A list of names used to ascertain whether each one of a set of persons is present; esp. Mil.

II. 6. A quantity of material (esp. cloth), a cylindrical form, sometimes forming a definite measure. Also, a paper of papers, etc., rolled together.

a. The Rolls, the former buildings in Chancery Lane in which the records in the custody of the Master of the Rolls were preserved.

7. Something rolled up in a cylindrical form.

a. gen. A cylindrical body.

b. A quantity of tobacco leaves rolled up into a cylindrical mass; tobacco in this form.

8. † a. A round cushion or pad of hair or other material, forming part of a woman's head-dress.

b. A small loaf of bread, properly one which has been rolled or doubled over before baking.

9. a. A cylinder or roller.

10. A small loaf of bread, properly one which has been rolled or doubled over before baking.

11. A part which is rolled or turned over.

12. attrib., as roll-board, -collar, etc.

13. attrib., in sense '-keeping the form, made up in, a roll,' as roll-bread, brimstone, cake, tobacco, etc.

Roller-gin. [ROLLER *sb.*[1] 9.] A cotton-gin in which the cleaning was effected by rollers.

Roller-skate. [ROLLER *sb.*[1] 7.] A skate mounted on small wheels or rollers, usually two pairs, instead of a metallic blade, for use in skating on smooth flooring, etc.

Hence **Ro'ller-skater**, one who skates on roller-skates; **Ro'ller-skating** *vbl. sb.*

Rolley (rɒ'li). Also *rully*. [Of obscure origin: perh. connected with ROLL *v.*[1], but cf. RULLEY.]
1. *Mining.* A kind of truck without sides, formerly much in use for carrying corves along underground horse-roads or upon rails to the shaft.

Rollick (rɒ'lik), *sb.* [f. ROLLICK *v.*]
1. Exuberant gaiety or joviality; a very gay and jovial tone.

Rollick (rɒ'lik), *v.* Also *rollic*, *roolick*. [Of obscure origin.]
1. To frolic, sport, or romp, in a joyous, careless fashion; to go off, move along, enter, etc., in this manner.

Roller. (rɒ'lər.) *sb.*[1]
21. Attrib. with names of persons, as **roller-boy**, **-coverer**, **-joiner**, **-maker**, **-man**, etc.
b. in sense 'fitted with, coiling up on, a roller', as **roller-blind**, **-curtain**, **-map**, etc.
c. In sense 4 c, as **roller-bus**, **-competition**, **-knock**, **-stock**, etc.
d. in sense 6, as **roller-arm**, **-frame**, **-movement**, **-peg**. Also **ROLLER-BOARD**.
22. Objective, as **roller-carrier**, **-carrying** adj., **-making**.
23. a. Objective, as **roller-carrier**, **-carrying** adj., **-making**.

Ro'ller-board. [ROLLER *sb.*[1] 6.] The board carrying the rollers in an organ. Also *attrib.*

Ro'lling, *ppl. a.* [f. ROLL *v.*[1]]
An enrolling, enrolment; an entering upon a roll.

Rolling (rɒ'liŋ), *vbl. sb.* [f. ROLL *v.*[2]]
The sense in one case is 'rolling something over and over, or of causing it to roll'; bowling.

Rolling-mill. [ROLLING *vbl. sb.* 2.]
A machine or set of machines in which metal, etc., is rolled out or flattened.

Ro'lling-pin. [f. as prec.]
1. A cylindrical piece of wood round which a batter may be rolled to prevent creasing.

Rolling-press. [f. as prec.]
1. A copper-plate-printer's press in which the plate passes in a bed under a revolving cylinder.

Ro'lling stock. [ROLLING *ppl. a.*]
The locomotives, wagons, carriages, or other vehicles, used on a railway.

Ro'lling stone. [f. as prec.]
1. A rolling stone gathers no moss.

Roloway. *Obs.* [Of obscure origin: perh. a misapplication of Roloway monkey.]

Rolster, error. form of ROSTER.

Roly, abbrev. of ROLY-POLY *sb.* 5.

Roly-poly (rō'lipō'li), *sb.*, *a.*, and *adv.*
Also *rolypoly*. Forms: 7 rowle-powle, 7–8 (9 *dial.*) rowly-powly; 8–9, *dial.*, poly-, rowley-powley; 8 roly-powly, 9. rowlie-powlie, 8–9 rolly-pooly, -poly, 9 rol(l)y-pol(l)y, *etc.*

Romal, -aul. *Obs.* Chiefly *Sc.* Also 5 rolment, 5 rolmond, 7 rowmont. [a. OF. *rollement* (= EMBULLMENT):]
1. The bringing or winding of a roll.

Romaika (rōmai'ka). Also 7–9 romaica, 7 Romanica, 9 Romany(e). [mod.Gr. Ῥωμαίϊκα, neut. pl.]
A modern Greek national dance.

Roman (rō'man), *a.* and *sb.* Forms: 1 *Romane*, 3–7 *Romayn(e*, 4 *Romaigne*, etc.
A. *adj.*
1. Forming, composed of, pertaining to, etc., the vernacular language of modern Greece.
B. *sb.*
1. A native or inhabitant of ancient Rome; one belonging to the Roman state or empire.

ROMAN.

II. 8. A member or adherent of the Roman Catholic Church; a Roman Catholic.

Roman, sb.[2] = ROMANZ [2]

Roman (rōu·măn), a.[2] and sb.[3] Forms: 1-4 Romasin, syn, 6 syne; 1-6 Romayn, 6 ayne; 4-7 Romain(e, 5-7 Romane, 6- Roman. [In early use a. OF. Romain, -ayn, subsequently ad. L. Rōmān-us: see ROMAN sb.[1]]

I. 1. Of persons: Inhabiting, belonging to, or originating from the ancient city of Rome or its territory; holding the position of a citizen or member of the ancient republic or empire of Rome.

2. Of or pertaining to, connected with, ancient Rome, its inhabitants or dominion; practised or used by, current or usual among, the Romans, etc.

II. 10. Pertaining to Rome in its ecclesiastical aspect; belonging to, connected with, etc., the Church of Rome. Cf. ROMAN CATHOLIC a.

III. 13. Of or pertaining to medieval or modern Rome or its inhabitants; printed at Rome, etc.

16. A Roman school, the school of painting of which Raphael is the leading representative.

18. *Roman alum*, a reddish native alum found in Italy, or a manufactured imitation of this.

Romance (rǒmæ·ns), sb. and a. Forms: 4, 7 roman, romaunce, 4-6 (8-9) romaunce, 5-6 romaunse, romance, -ounce, 4-romaunce, 5-6 romaunt; 6- (8- ROMAUNT) ; so-pl. 7 romaunce adv. ...

Romancize, v. To make Roman, to Romanize.

Romancy, sb. [Alteration of ROMANCE sb.; perh. after Sp. romance or It. romanzo.]

Romancy, a. [f. ROMANCE sb. + -Y.] Associated with, or redolent of, romance; romantic.

Romanian, a. and sb. = ROMANIAN.

Romanic, a. and sb. = ROMANIC.

Romanism (rōu·mǎniz'm). [f. ROMAN a.[2]]

1. The Roman Catholic religion or doctrines; Roman Catholicism.

Romanite, rare[-1]. [f. ROMAN a.[2] + -ITE.]

Romanity (romǎ·niti). [f. ROMAN a.]

Romanization, **Romanian**, **Romanic** ...

Romaniser, **Romanizing**, **Romanism**, **Romanist** ...

Romanly, **Romano-**, **Romans**, **Romansh** ...

Roman-nosed, **Romantic** (romæ·ntik), a. and sb.

Romantical, **Romanticalness**, **Romanticality**, **Romantically** ...

Romanticalness, **Romanticism**, **Romanticist** ...

Romanticity, **Romanticize**, **Romanza** ...

Rome (rōm), sb.

Romance, **Romant**, **Romanism** ...

Rome-raker, **Rome-runner**, **Romic** ...

Rome-scot, **Romeward**, **Romish** ...

Romized, **Rommack**, **Romp** ...

Romping, **Rompish**, **Rompy** ...

Ron, **Roncador**, **Rond**, **Ronde**, **Rondache**, **Rondeau** ...

Rondel (rǫ'ndĕl). Also **rondelle.**
[a. F. *rondel*, dim. of *rondel* Rondel 2.] A short rondeau. (Cf. Roundel.)

Rondo (rǫ'ndo). [It. *rondo*, a. F. *rondeau*.]
Mus. A piece of music having one principal subject, to which a return is always made after the introduction of other matter (Grove).

Ring v. **Ronge**, variant of Rounge v. *Obs.*

Rongue, obs. f. Rung sb. **Ronk'o**, obs. f. Ronco.

Ronneagate, obs. f. Runagate.

Ronnelless, obs. var. Rendless, rennet.

Ronnen, obs. pa. pple. of Run v. Ronner, obs. f. Runner. Sc. var. Runnet sb.

Rood (rūd). Forms: 1 hrof, 3 hrof.

Rood, v. [var. of Roud, rudd, etc.: see Redi sb.] *dial.* The heavier fish rood on the deeper runs.

Rood-day. Now only *Hist.* [Rood sb. 2.]
a. The Exaltation of the Cross (14 September).
b. The Invention of the Cross (3 May).

Roof (rūf). Forms: α. 1 hrof, 3 hrof, 1–6 rof, 4–6 roff, 5 roffe; 4–7 roof, 7 roofe, 6 roofe rough, 6–7 roufe, rowfe, 6–7 ruffe, 6 pl. ruvis, 6 8–9 ruif (7 ruff), 9 roef. OE. *hróf*, *hróf*-, roof, roof.

Roofer. [f. Roof sb. or v. + -er.] One who constructs or repairs roofs.

Roof-tree. Also 5 roff tyle, rofte, roffe tyle; 6 roofe tyle.

Roof-ward (rūf), a. [f. ROOF sb. + -WARD.] Toward, in the direction of, the roof.

Roofy (rū·fi), a. [f. ROOF sb. + -Y.]
1. Furnished with a roof.
2. Abounding in roofs.
3. transf. High-pitched.

Roofye, variant of RUFFY.

Roog, obs. form of ROGUE.

Roog, obs. form of ROOK sb.

Rook (ruk), sb.¹ Forms: a. 1 hrooc, hroc, 3 rok, 3–6 roke, 5–7 rooke, 5– rook. β. Sc. (and north.) 5–6 ruke, 6 rwk, 6–7 ruik e. In comb. 8–9 MDu. roec, rook-, rouk- (Du. and Fris. rook), MLG. rôk (LG. rôk, rôke, rauk, rauck), OHG. (Du. Du. rag), OHG. druak (MHG. ruoch (g. ruck); cf. also MSw. rôka, Sw. råka, Da. roage. The name may be of imitative origin.]

Rook (ruk), sb.² Chess. Forms: 4–5 rok, 5–6 roke (5 rooke), 6–7 rook ; 7–9 rook.

Rook (ruk), sb.³ Sc. and north. dial. [Var. of ROKE or ROUK : the difference in the vowel is unusual.] Mist, fog.

Rook, v.¹ [f. ROOK sb.¹]
1. trans. To cheat ; to defraud, esp. in gaming ; to clean of money by fraud, extortion, or other means ; to charge exortionately.
2. intr. To practise cheating. Obs.

Rooker¹, rare⁻¹. [f. ROOK v.¹ + -ER¹.] One who rooks or cheats.

Rooker², obs. form of ROKER.

Rook, v.² [f. ROOK sb.¹] Of or pertaining to rooks; resembling a rook.

Rookie, v., dial. var. of ROOTLE v. Hence **Rookier** sb.

Rook-ling, dial. [f. ROOK sb.¹ + -LING.] A young rook.

Rookly, variant of ROOKLALY.

Rookship. [f. ROOK sb.¹] A mock title applied to a clergyman.

Rookster. [f. ROOK sb.¹] A cheat.

Rooky, sb. slang. A raw recruit.

Rooky, a.¹ [f. ROOK sb.¹] Full of, abounding in, consisting of, rooks; also fig.

Rooky, a.² [f. ROOK sb.³] Foggy, misty. Cf. ROKY a.

Rool, v. rare. (See quots.)

Room (rūm), sb.¹ Forms: (see below). [Common Teut.: OE. rūm masc., = MDu. ruum, ruym, rūm (Du. ruim), MLG. rûm (LG. rûm), OHG. rûm (Du. ruim), OHG. rûm (G. raum), ON. rúm (Sw. and Da. rum), Goth. rûm. The relationship to forms outside of Teutonic is uncertain.]

A. Illustration of forms.

B. Signification.

I. Space; dimensional extent.

Room (rūm), sb.² Obs. Forms: (see below). [Common Teut.: OE. rûm, 1 rum, 3 rume; 4–5 roume (4 roume), 4–6 rowm(e, 5 rowme; 4–6 rome, 6– room.]

Room, adv. Obs. Forms: 1 rume, 4–6 rome, 4–7 rowme(e. Comp. 5 rowmer. [OE. rûme, f. rûm adj., = OS. and OHG. rûmo.]

Room, v. Now dial. or arch. [OE. rûmian, 3–6 rumen, 4–5 rowm, 5 rowme; 4–5 rome, 6– room.]

Roomed (rūmd), ppl. a. [f. ROOM sb.¹ + -ED.] With defining word prefixed: Having rooms of a specified number or kind, as one-, double-, many-roomed; also wide-roomed, + spacious.

Room-age, U.S. rare. [f. ROOM sb.¹ + -AGE.] Space; internal capacity; accommodation.

Roomer, U.S. [f. ROOM v.² + -ER¹.] A lodger who occupies a room or rooms without board.

Roomery. rare⁻¹. [ad. Sp. romería, f. Roma Rome.] A pilgrimage.

Room-free, Sc. and north. Also 3–4 rum-.

Room-handed, Sc. and north. Obs. rare.

Room-handed-house, see ROOM a.

Roomie, a. [f. ROOM sb.¹ + -Y¹.] Capacious, roomy.

Roominess. [f. ROOMY a. + -NESS.] The quality of being roomy or spacious; capaciousness.

Roomly, sb. [f. ROOM sb.¹ + -LY².] As much or as many as a room will hold.

Roomly, adv. Obs. rare. [f. ROOM sb.¹ + -LY².] Capaciously, amply, roomy.

Roomliness. Obs. rare. [f. ROOMLY a.] Lacking room or space; strait, confined.

Roomlet, dial. Evans. Par. Nat. ij. 18 The shyppe wherein Jesus preached it was very narowe and not cleane and ruffull. A small room.

Roominess. Obs. rare. [f. ROOMLY a.]

Roomly, adv. [OE. rûmlîce (see ROOM a. and ROOMLY).] Liberally, largely, abundantly.

to hire comen..for seoluere & for golde, & heo rumliche hit ȝef. *a* 1300 *E. E. Psalter* xxx. 30 And roum-like sal he yhelde in land To þus þat ere pride doand. *c* 1425 Wyntoun *Chron.* ix. ix. 1136 (Royal MS.), Til lordis rowmly he landis gave; His swnnys he mad rych and mychty.

Roo·m-mate. *U.S.* [f. Room *sb.*[1]] One who lodges in or occupies the same room or rooms with another; a fellow-lodger.

1838 J. L. Stephens *Trav. Russ. & Turk. Emp.* I. 251 With a Frenchman and a Greek for my room-mates. 1849 W. S. Mayo *Kaloolah* (1850) 107 My interesting room-mates were so far recovered as to be able to take the air upon deck. 1899 Whiteing *5 John St.* 210 Little Nance, the chum and room-mate of Tilda.

† Roo·msome, *a. Obs.* In 6 romesome, 6–7 roomesome, 7 rowmsome, roomsom. [f. Room *a.*] Ample, capacious, roomy.

1581 Pettie tr. *Guazzo's Civ. Conv.* I. (1586) 22 b, I know by this your exposition of this worde (*Ciuile*) the field wee haue to enter into is verie wide and roomesome. 1598 Florio *Dict.* To Rdr., A more..vnweildie and more roomesome vessell then the biggest hulke on Thames. 1602 J. Davies (Heref.) *Mirum in Modum* xxiii. Wks. (Grosart) I. 7 The Cells..Are made by right more rowmsome then the rest. *a* 1642 Sir W. Monson *Naval Tracts* III. (1704) 357/1 She is Roomsom for her Men. 1671 Evelyn *Diary* 16 Oct., An old house..made..capable and roomesome.

Roo·mstead. Now *rare* or *Obs.* Also 7 roomesteade, 8 room stead. [f. Room *sb.*[1]] A compartment or division; a certain space or length.

1641 Best *Farm. Bks.* (Surtees) 47 The greate roomesteade in the northende of the rye-barne helde all our winter corne this yeare. *Ibid.*, As much as could possibly be layed in that roomsteade. 1691 J. Gibson in *Archæologia* XII. 188 Dr. Uvedale of Enfield... His greens take up six or seven houses or roomsteads. 1718 in *Trans. Cumb. & Westm. Archæol. Soc.* (N.S.) III. 200 Benjamin Farish hath one firehouse containing two room steads..to lett. 1764 *Sheffling Inclosure Act* 9 The pieces, parts, or roomsteads of the earth-bank. 1800 Tuke *Agric.* 93 A roomstead (i. e. one post and two rails), being 1*s.* 7*d.* including carriage. 1820 W. Scoresby *Acc. Arctic Reg.* II. 461 The carpenters had completely cleared the roomstead. *Note*, Roomstead is the space between any two ribs or frames of timber in a ship.

† Roo·mster. *Obs.*[−1] An occupant of space.

1674 N. Fairfax *Bulk & Selv.* 181, I being at no agreement with this same hideous Roomster.., I may..have my harmless mistake paid home by a vile mischance.

Roomth (rūmþ). Now *dial.* Also 6 rumeth, 6–7 rometh(e, roometh; 6 romth(e, rompth; 7 roumth, roomthe. [f. Room *a.* + -th: cf. Færöese *rúmd*. The earlier form is Rimth.]

1. Space; *esp.* ample or unconfined space. † *To make roomth*, to make way.

1540 Bible (Cranmer) 2 *Sam.* xxii. 20 For he brought me out into roumth, he delyuered me, because he had a loue vnto me. 1559 Aylmer *Harborowe* E iv b, All histories and monumentes canne not be conteined in so lytle rometh. 1575 *Gammer Gurton* II. iv, Make here a little romth. 1612 Drayton *Poly-olb.* vi. 122 But Rydoll,..Not finding fitting roomth upon the rising side, Alone unto the West directly takes her way. 1643 Trapp *Comm. Gen.* xliii. 25 A mans gift makes roomth for him. 1881– in dial. glossaries (Leic., Warw., Sheff.).

† **b.** Space occupied by an object; extent, bulk.

1603 Drayton *Bar. Wars* vi. xxviii, Whose romth but hinders others that would grow. 1622 Malynes *Anc. Law-Merch.* 40 Pease grinded weigh more than corne, the roundnesse giveth cause to have more roomth. 1674 N. Fairfax *Bulk & Selv.* 54 Having seen what the Worlds lastingness and roomth is.

† **c.** Extent; jurisdiction. *Obs.*[−1]

1601 Bp. W. Barlow *Defence* 188 Lastly, that the Church haue roometh vniuersally extended.

† **2.** Sufficient space or scope *for* or *to* do something. *Obs.*

a 1540 Barnes *Wks.* (1573) 296 The false brethren..unto whom S. Paule gaue no romthe as concernyng to bee brought into subiection. 1596 Drayton *Legends* iv. 209 Where now my Spirit got roomth it selfe to show. 1615 W. Lawson *Country Housew. Garden* (1626) 10 So there be sufficient roomth left for walkes. 1639 H. Ainsworth *Pentateuch* Gen. ix. 27 'Inlarging' also, is not only of roomth to dwell in.., but oftentimes of the heart.

† **b.** A sufficient occupation. *Obs.*[−1]

1585 Dyer *Prayse of Nothing* C ij, It were a romth for some idle bodye, to looke into the accedents of euery state, which hath been diuersly afflicted for nothing.

† **3.** A defined or limited space. *Obs.*

1550 *Nottingham Rec.* IV. 98 In the est end of the Spyces Chamber a romthe for a p[r]esse. 1579 Twyne *Phis. agst. Fortune* I. 6 b, This narrowe roomth, and place of necessitie, is knowne without Astrologicall coniecture. 1596–7 S. Finche in *Hist. Croydon* (1783) 155 We..are now fillinge the voyde rometh therin with earth and rubbishe. 1639 H. Ainsworth *Pentateuch* Num. ii. 27 So many thousand tents as Israel had could not be pitched in a little roomth.

† **b.** A chamber, apartment. *Obs.*

1579 Fenton *Guicciard.* 415 A fire kindled..in their stoare house called the Arzenale, euen in the rometh where was their saltpeter. 1635 *Maldon Doc.* (Bundle 80, No. 2), viz. viii*d.* for dressing up the said moote-hall, counsell chamber, and other the Romethes there this yere.

† **4.** An office, function, or dignity. *Obs.*

1504 Lady Margaret tr. *De Imit.* IV. v. 267 By the puttynge to of the handes of the Byssboppe thou arte admyttyd vnto that hye rometh. *a* 1530 in Ellis *Orig. Lett.* Ser. III. II. 153 Very gladde I wolbe that he in that romethe myght doo your most excelent Grace service. 1586 in *10th Rep. Hist. MSS. Comm.* App. V. 439 The credytt, vocacion, rompth, promocion and callinge of Bayliefes. *a* 1604 Hanmer *Chron. Irel.* (1633) 57 He preferred one Iohn his Deacon and disciple, to the roomth.

† **b.** A position or office pertaining to a person; one's place. *Obs.*

1544 A. Cope *Hannibal & Scipio* 40 They commanded to let the old Senatours go free, and use their romthes. 1573 Twyne *Virgil* Life ¶ j b, When his voice failed him at eny time, Mecænas supplied his romth in readynge. 1600 S. Finche in *Hist. Croydon* (1783) 154 b, Margaret her daughter is in good hope to supplie her mothers romthe.

† **c.** *In the roomth of*, in the place of, instead of. Also with possessives. *Obs.*

1533 Wriothesley *Chron.* (Camden) I. 21 The Lorde William Howarde as deputie..in the romth of the Marshall of Englande. 1578 J. Stockwood *Serm.* 24 Aug. 78 It were farre better that they were vtterly remoued, and able Pastors put in theyr roomths. 1615 W. Lawson *Country Housew. Garden* (1626) 6 Our old fathers can tell vs, how woods are decaied, and people in the roomth of trees multiplied. 1624–5 *Nottingham Rec.* (1889) IV. 393 Annother Counceller to be elected in his roomthe.

† Roo·mthily, *adv. Obs.*[−1] [f. Roomthy *a.*] In respect of space; spatially.

1674 N. Fairfax *Bulk & Selv.* 103 God by making of a body and real space with it,..is thereby..no more roomthily there than he was before.

† Roo·mthiness. *Obs.* Also 7 roomethinesse, roomthyness(e. [f. Roomthy *a.*] Roominess.

1553 Grimalde *Cicero's Offices* (1556) 55 Likewise in a noble mannes howse..ther must be made a provision for roomethinesse. 1570 T. Norton tr. *Nowel's Catech.* 60 Neither is there any thyng or place that is not enuironed and enclosed with the roomthinesse of heauen. 1627 Drayton *Agincourt* 8 Tents and Pauillions in the fields are pitcht, (E'r full wrought vp their Roomthynesse to try). 1674 N. Fairfax *Bulk & Selv.* 23 The everlasting time and boundless roomthiness. *Ibid.* 82 There is roomthiness between that and the other boundary or term.

† Roo·mthsome, *a. Obs.*[−1] In 6 romth-. [f. Roomth.] Spacious, roomy.

1599 Nashe *Lenten Stuffe* 42 A cage or pigeon house, romthsome enough to comprehend her and..her nurse.

Roomthy (rū·mþi), *a.* Now *dial.* Also 6 romthie, romthy, room(e)thie, roomethy. [f. Roomth + -y.]

1. Spacious, ample, roomy.

1578 Banister *Hist. Man* I. 30 With a slacke or romthy kynde of knitting. *Ibid.* 33 These bones in women [are]..much more ample, and romthy. 1612 Drayton *Poly-olb.* i. 210 After whom, cleere Enian in doth make, In Tamer's roomthier bankes their rest that scarcely take. 1655 Fuller *Ch. Hist.* II. 104 Because England was richer and roomthyer then their own Countrey. 1676 Hubbard *Happiness People* 55 God will rather have his people..pent up in a corner, then roomthy, and swoln with pride. 1726 S. Sewall *Lett.-bk.* (1886) II. 202 He has a situation roomthy and beautifull enough to build the New-Jerusalem in. 1854– in dial. glossaries (Northamp., Warw., Oxf.).

† **2.** Pertaining to space; occupying space. *Obs.*

1674 N. Fairfax *Bulk & Selv.* 21 Time had not been if God had not made timesome beings, nor room if he had not made roomthy.

† Roo·mward, *adv. Naut. Obs.* Also 7 roome-. [f. Room *adv.*] = Room *adv.* 3.

1611 Cotgr., *Bouter au vent*, to beare roomeward; or, to fill the sayles with wind. 1647 W. Browne tr. *Polexander* II. III. 214 My Pilot was constrained to goe Roome-ward to Sea. *Ibid.* 226 This Fleet..put roome-ward to Sea, as soone as they had descried us. 1658 Earl Monm. tr. *Paruta's Wars Cyprus* 140 Having fallen much Roomeward at the beginning of the fight,..they kept aloof from the great gallie.

So † **Roo·m-way** *adv. Obs.*[−1]

1627 Capt. Smith *Seaman's Gram.* ix. 44 When she would not come neere the land, but goeth more Roome-way than her course, wee say she beares off.

Roomy (rū·mi), *a.* and *adv.* Also 7 roumy, rommy. [f. Room *sb.*[1] + -y. Cf. MLG. *rumich*, *ruymich*, G. *räumig*.]

A. *adj.* **1.** Of ample dimensions; capacious, large; wide.

1627 Capt. Smith *Seaman's Gram.* xi. 52 This makes a Ship more roomy. *a* 1656 Bp. Hall *Rem. Wks.* (1660) 64 A place both more publick, roomy, and chargelesse. 1697 Dryden *Virg. Georg.* II. 388 Let thy Vines in Intervals be set, Indulge their Width, and add a roomy Space. 1743 Blair *Grave* 267 His roomy chest by far too scant To give the lungs full play. 1773 *Life N. Frowde* 199 He agreed..to accommodate us all on board his Ship, which was a very fine and roomy one. 1807 G. Chalmers *Caledonia* I. I. ii. 101 In this roomy currach, St. Cormac sailed into the north sea. 1855 Thackeray *Newcomes* viii. I. 77 A gentleman of bland aspect with a roomy forehead. 1883 J. Gilmour *Mongols* xxvii. 320 The outer garment of both sexes is a wide roomy coat which reaches down to the ground.

fig. 1693 Dryden *Juvenal* Ded. (1697) p. lxxxii, This sort of Number is more roomy: The Thought can turn it self with greater ease in a larger compass. 1827 Pollok *Course T.* (1834) 280 A roomy life, a glowing relish high.

2. Of female animals: Of large proportions internally.

1796 W. H. Marshall *W. Eng.* II. 202 Some roomy good cows. 1853 *Jrnl. R. Agric. Soc.* XIV. II. 430 A well-proportioned roomy cow. 1853 Stonehenge *Greyhound* 174 A large roomy bitch..will most probably 'throw' a lot of undersized greyhounds. 1894 *Field* 9 June 846/1 [A mare,] a fine, roomy daughter of Lincolnshire Lad II.

† **B.** *adv. Naut.* = Room *adv.* 3. *Obs.*

1624 Capt. Smith *Virginia* 192 At last she bore up rommy for the Sea, and we heard of her no more. *Ibid.* 224 The next was a ship of Holland...She was put roomy. 1626 — *Accid. Yng. Seamen* 18 Beare vp the helme, goe roumy.

Roon (rōn). *Sc.* Also roen, roond, and Rund. [Of obscure origin.] A piece of the list or selvage of cloth; a strip or shred. Also *roon-shoon* (see quot. 1824).

1785 Burns *To W. Simpson* Postscr. iii, They thought the Moon, Just like a sark, or pair o' shoon, Woor by degrees, till her last roon Gaed past their viewin. 1808 Jamieson, *Roon*, a shred, a remnant,..also *roond*. 1824 Mactaggart *Gallovid. Encycl.*, *Roon-shoon*, shoes made of the roons, or selvages of cloth. 1862 Hislop *Prov. Scot.* 179 The best o' wabs are rough at the roons.

Roonde, obs. f. Round. **Roone,** obs. f. Roan.

Roong, obs. pa. pple. of Ring *v.*[1]

Roop (rūp), *sb.*[1] [var. of Roup *sb.*[3]] Hoarseness; a hoarse sound.

1674 Ray *N. C. Words* 39 A *Roop*, a Hoarseness. 1788– in northern dial. glossaries (Yks., Northumb.). 1898 *Daily News* 22 Feb. 3/3 That touch of noble hoarseness..like the roop of the bow on the string of a violoncello.

Roop, *sb.*[2], in northern and Sc. phrase *stoop and roop*, completely: see Stoop *sb.*

Roop, *v. rare.* [Cf. Roop *sb.*[1]] *intr.* To utter a hoarse note or sound.

1894 Crockett *Love Idylls* (1901) 182 A sleepy hen rooped lazily in a hole under the hedge. 1894 — *Raiders* (ed. 3) 234, I only rooped like a rough-legged fowl.

Roop(e, obs. ff. Rope; variants of Roup.

Rooped, *a. Sc.* and *north. dial.* Also 7 roopt, 9 roopit, -et, and Rouped. [f. Roop *sb.*[1]] Hoarse.

1677 Nicolson in *Trans. R. Soc. Lit.* (1870) IX. 316 *Roopt*, hoarse with bawling. 1822 Scott *Nigel* xv, He had something of a catarrh, and spoke as hoarse as a roopit raven. 1881 J. L. Robertson in Edwards *Mod. Sc. Poets* III. 35 The minister grew hearse and roopit.

Roopee, obs. form of Rupee.

Roope-sicke: see Rope-sick *a.*

Roopy (rū·pi), *a.* Chiefly *dial.* See also Roupy *a.*[2] [f. Roop *sb.*[1]] Hoarse.

1825– in dial. glossaries (Northumb., Durh., Yks., Berks, Hants). 1850 Dickens *D. Copperfield* vii, He had observed I was sometimes hoarse—a little roopy was his exact expression. 1864 Miss Braddon *J. Marchmont's Legacy* III. 179 The lonely hen set up a roopy cackle.

Roopy, variant of Roupy *a.*[1]

Roor, obs. form of Roar.

Roorback (rū·rbæk). *U.S.* Also -bach. [A fictitious personal name: the accounts of its origin differ widely from each other.] A false report or slander invented for political purposes.

1864 Webster, *Roorbach*, a forgery or fictitious story published for purposes of political intrigue. [*Note.* The word originated in 1844, when such a forgery was published, purporting to be an extract from the 'Travels of Baron Roorbach'.] 1884 *Boston* (Mass.) *Jrnl.* 6 Sept., The Herald and Globe abound in roorbacks which are designed to influence the vote in Maine.

Roore, obs. form of Roar.

Roos, obs. form of Rouse *sb.*

Roosa, rusa (rū·sā). Also roussa, rusha. [Hindi *rūsā*.] *Roosa grass*, an Indian grass (*Andropogon Schœnanthus* or *Cymbopogon Martini*), from which *roosa oil* is distilled.

1853 T. C. Archer *Pop. Econ. Bot.* 279 Oil of Indian Grass, Roosa Oil, or *Roosa-ke-til*, is distilled from the leaves of *Andropogon Calamus aromaticus*. 1858 Simmonds *Dict. Trade*, Roosa-Grass Oil. 1885 Watt *Econ. Prod. India* 249 This is the roussa paper grass, abundant everywhere in the Deccan. *Ibid.* 250 Perhaps the name by which it is most generally known is rusa oil. *Ibid.*, Rusha oil.

Roose, *sb.* ? *Obs.* Forms: α. 3–5 ros, 4 rose, 4–5 roos, 5 roys(e. β. 4–6 rous, 7 rowze. γ. *Sc.* 4–6, 9 ruse, 5 rus(s, 6 ruys, ruiss(e. δ. S-roose. [a. ON. *hrós* (Icel. *hrós*, Fær. *rós*, Norw., Sw., and Da. *ros*): cf. Roose *v.*]

1. Boasting, vainglory; an instance of this, a boast, brag, vaunt.

α. *c* 1200 Ormin 4910 All idell ȝellp & idell ros þu cwennkesst i þe sellfenn. *a* 1300 *Cursor M.* 11948 Nu þat i do þou it for-dos, And þar-of sal þou mak na ros. 13.. *Minor Poems fr. Vernon MS.* 505 Such þing as þou seyst and doos, Þi Neiȝebor wol þerof make Roos. *c* 1400 *Song Roland* 650 Shall none of you mak your rose or ye go furþre. *c* 1450 *Cast. Perseverance* 1068 Þerfore do as no man dos,..& of þi-self make gret ros. 1486 *Bk. St. Albans* e vj b, The master to his man makyth his Roys That be knowith be kynde what the hert doys Att huntyng.

β. 1303 R. Brunne *Handl. Synne* 5158 Ne be nat proude þogh þou weyl dous, yn þyn herte to make a rous. 1463 G. Ashby *Poems* 11 Goo forth, lytyll boke, mekely, without rous. 16.. *Sir Lambewell* 304 in *Percy's Folio MS., Ball. & Rom.* I. 154 Shee warned me be-forne, of all things that I did vse, of her I shold neuer make my rowze.

γ. *c* 1470 *Gol. & Gaw.* 98 Bot thow mend hym that mys... Thow sall rew in thi ruse. 1513 Douglas *Æneis* VIII. Prol. 50 Sum makis a tume ruse. *a* 1572 Knox *Hist. Ref.* Wks. 1846 I. 242 What thei receaved we can nott tell; but few maid ruse at thare returnyng. 1596 Dalrymple tr. *Leslie's Hist. Scot.* II. 242 Johne Moydert..maid meikle ruse that he him selfe was the cheif of Makdonelis kynd. 1808 Jamieson, *To mak a tume ruse*, to boast where there is no ground for it, but the reverse.

δ. 1718 Ramsay *Christ's Kirk Gr.* III. iv, Wha wins syn may make roose, Between you twa. 17.. *Maggie's Tocher* in Herd *Coll. Sc. Songs* (1776) II. 78 We'll nae mair toom roose.

† **2.** Commendation, praise. *Obs.*

a 1300 *Cursor M.* 13896 Quen he his aun roos has soght, In his muth sothfast es noght. *a* 1350 *St. Nicholas* 87 in Horstm. *Altengl. Legend.* (1881) 12 Noght for no ruse of erthli thing Bot allone vnto goddes louyng. *c* 1375 *Sc. Leg. Saints* xli. (*Agnes*) 114 þe prefet begane to spere.. quhat man it wes..þat agnes þe ruse of mad. *c* 1470 *Gol. & Gaw.* 1241 All erdly riches and ruse is noght in thair garde.

Roose, obs. form of Rose *sb.*

Roose (rūz, *Sc.* rōz), *v.* Now *Sc.* and *north. dial.* Forms: α. 3 rosenn, 4 ros, 4–5 (9 *dial.*) rose, 5 roys. β. 4–9 ruse, 5–6 rus(s, 6 rws, ruis, 7–9 ruze; 6 reuse, 7 reouse, reuze; *Sc. dial.* 8 reese, rease, 8–9 reeze. γ. 6 rowse, 7–9 rouse. δ. 7– roose (*dial.* 8 rooyse, 9 rooze, roois). [a. ON. *hrósa* to boast of, praise (Icel. *hrósa*, Fær. *rósa*, Norw. and Sw. *rosa*, Da. *rose*): cf. Roose *sb.*]

† **1.** *intr.* To boast or be proud *of* something. *Obs.*

c 1200 Ormin 4906 Þatt iss hæfedd sinne..To rosenn off þin haȝherrleȝȝc. *c* 1475 *Rauf Coilȝear* 481 Of that Ryall array that Rolland in raid, Rauf rusit in his hart of that Ryall thing.

† **2.** *refl.* **a.** To boast oneself; to vaunt. Const. *of*, *that* with clause, or infin. **b.** To praise or commend oneself. *Obs.*

α. *a* 1300 *Cursor M.* 28102 Ic ha me rosed in my mode bath o my werkes wyc and gode. *a* 1340 Hampole *Psalter* xxxi. 3, I cried all þe day rosand me of rightwisnes.

β. 13.. *SS. Peter & Paul* 152 in Horstm. *Altengl. Leg.* (1881) 78 Simon..rusid him þan þat he might raise Dede men to lyue. *c* 1340 Hampole *Prose Tr.* 12 Noghte ruysand hyme of his reghtwesnes. *c* 1400 *Melayne* 936 So mot I spede, He sall noghte ruysse hym of this dede. *c* 1460 *Towneley Myst.* xxiii. 492 He has hym rused of great prophes. 1508 Dunbar *Tua Mariit Wemen* 191 He.. makis repet with ryatus wordis, Ay rusing him of his radis. 1533 Gau *Richt Vay* 75 Mony spekis mekil and rwsis thayme of faith. *c* 1560 A. Scott *Poems* (S. T. S.) iii. 21 Reuse nocht ȝour self, latt vþiris preiss ȝour rentis.

γ. *c* 1440 *York Myst.* xxix. 271 Oure stiffe tempill,..This rebalde he rowses hym it rathely to rayse.

δ. 1637–50 Row *Hist. Kirk* (Wodrow Soc.) 476 Alledging that honest ministers that went to the Bishop roosed themselves little of it.

3. *trans.* To praise, extol, commend, flatter.

α. *a* 1300 *Cursor M.* 2417 Sua þai rosed hir to þe king þat he þam did befor him bring. 13.. *E. E. Allit. P.* B. 1371 To rose hym in his rialty rych men soȝtten. *c* 1460 *Towneley Myst.* ii. 95 What gifys god the to rose hym so? *Ibid.* xii. 234 Here is..the leg of a goys, With chekyns endorde, pork, partryk, to roys. 1877 *N. W. Linc. Gloss.*, *Rose*, to praise, to flatter.

β. *c* 1460 *Towneley Myst.* xxi. 33 For if other men ruse hym, we shall accuse hym. *c* 1475 *Rauf Coilȝear* 80 Thank me not ouir airlie,..For I haue seruit the ȝit of lytill thing to ruse. 1513 Douglas *Æneis* I. ix. 84 This ilk Tewcer his enemyis of Troy Rusit and lovit. 1570 *Satir. Poems Reform.* xii. 132 Be my saule, my self culd neuer ruse ȝow. 1603 *Philotus* xxxiv, Bot be it gude ȝe do not spair, As royallie to ruse it. 1677 Nicolson in *Trans. R. Soc. Lit.* (1870) IX. 316 *Ruze*, to flatter. 1691 Ray *N. C. Words* 59 To *Reuze*, to extol or commend highly. 1715 Ramsay *Christ's Kirk Gr.* II. viii, They rus'd him that had skill. *a* 1800 in Skinner *Misc. Poet.* 110 There's nane that reads them...But reezes Robie. *a* 1800 *Young Alian* ii. in Child *Ballads* IV. 378 Some there reasd their hawk, their hawk, And some there reasd their hound. 1879 John White *Jottings* 225 (E.D.D.), I've rus'd ye for yer head and heart.

γ. 1549 Coverdale, etc. *Erasm. Par.* 1 *Cor.* 27 If such let passe nothing undone and unsuffered and all to be rowsed and commended of the lewde people. *a* 1553 Udall *Royster D.* I. i, Prayse and rouse him well, and ye haue his heart wonne. 1766 A. Nicol *Poems* 104, I right fickle was and fain To be sae rous'd. 1842 Clark *Rhymes* 23 Wi' flattery I'll no rouse thee.

δ. 1703 Thoresby *Yorkshire Wds.* (E. D. S.), *Rooyse*, to extol. 1723 Ramsay *Fair Assembly* ix, These modest maids inspire the muse, In flowing strains to shaw Their beauties, which she likes to roose. 1785 Burns *1st Ep. to J. Lapraik* 94 Friends an' folk that wish me well, They sometimes roose me. 1786 — *Ded. to G. Hamilton* 3 A fleechan, fleth'ran Dedication, To roose you up, an' ca' you guid. 1834 A. Smart *Rambl. Rhymes* 162 Let poets in their idle lays Roose up auld Scotland's early days. 1865 Waugh *Lanc. Songs* 30 Aw roos't her, poor lass.

b. In various proverbs and sayings.

1710 Ruddiman *Gloss. Douglas Æneis* s.v., Every body ruses the ford as he finds it. 1721 Kelly *Scot. Prov.* 210 If it be ill, it is as ill rused. *Ibid.* 282 Ruse the fair Day at Night. 1818 Scott *Rob Roy* xxvii, Let ilka ane roose the ford as they find it.

Roo·ser. *Sc. rare.* Also rusar, ruser. [f. Roose *v.* Cf. ON. *hrósari*.] A boaster, braggart.

1535 Stewart *Cron. Scot.* III. 440 [It] hapnis oft ane vanter to be liear,..And ane gude rusar [is] seindill ane gude rydar. 1721 Kelly *Scot. Prov.* 36 A great ruser was never a good rider.

Rooser, variant of Rouser, a sprinkler.

Roo·sing, *vbl. sb.* [f. Roose *v.*] **a.** Boasting, vaunting, vainglory. **b.** Commendation, praising.

c 1200 Ormin 4564 Ȝæn rosinng, & ȝæn idell ȝellp. *Ibid.* 4902 Rosinng & all idell ȝellp..iss hæfedd sinne. *a* 1300 *Cursor M.* 28524 Þer-of haf i made rosyng. *c* 1340 Hampole *Pr. Consc.* 7070 What avayld us pryde,..rosyng of ryches or of ryche aray? *c* 1350 *St. John* 318 in Horstm. *Altengl. Leg.* (1881) 38 Þe sext teches..To refuys riches for ruseing. *a* 1800 *Redesdale & Wise William* in Child *Ballads* IV. 383 There fell a roosing them amang.

Roosing, obs. form of Rousing.

Roost (rūst), *sb.*[1] Forms: 1 hrost, 4 rooste, 5 roist, 6 roust, rowst, ruste (7 roest), 6– roost. [OE. *hróst*, = MDu. and Flem. *roest*, and prob. OS. *hróst* the spars of a roof (cf. sense 3). The further relationship is uncertain.]

1. A perch for domestic fowls; also *gen.* a perching- or resting-place of a bird.

a 1100 *Gerefa* in *Anglia* IX. 262 On odene cylne macian —ofn & aste & fela ðinga macian sceal to tune—ȝe eac henna hrost. 1398 Trevisa *Barth. De P. R.* XII. xvii. (Bodl. MS.), [The cock] setteþ nexte to hym one rooste þe henne þat is moste fatte and tendre. 1530 Palsgr. 264/1 Roost for capons or hennes, *juchoir*. 1565 Harding *Confut. Apol.* 17 b, Gete ye now vp into your pulpettes, like bragging cockes on the rowst, flappe your winges, and crow out alowde. 1593 Drayton *Ecl.* iii. 46 Since good Robin to his Roost is gone. 1607 Topsell *Four-f. Beasts* 151 In a Dogge [the power of smell] is that sence which searcheth out and descryeth the routes, fourmes, and lodgings of Wilde Beasts. 1700 Dryden *Cock & Fox* 46 Sooner than the matin-bell was rung, He clapp'd his wings upon his roost, and sung. 1751 Johnson *Rambler* No. 138 ¶ 12 When she is to see the hogs fed, or to count her poultry on the roost. 1820 W. Irving *Sketch Bk.* II. 359 The sudden rustling in the thicket of birds frightened from their roost. 1884 Allen *Amer. Farm Book* 491 Swabbed along the roosts and laying boxes..it has proved destructive to these vermin.

b. A hen-house, or that part of one in which the fowls perch at night.

1580 Hollyband *Treas. Fr. Tong*, *Gelinier*, a hen house, a roust. 1589 *Hay any Work* 36 He sleepeth belike in the top of yͤ roust. 1671 Milton *Samson* 1693 As an ev'ning Dragon came, Assailant on the perched roosts, And nests in order rang'd Of tame villatic Fowl. 1784 Cowper *Task* v. 58 Now from the roost, or from the neighb'ring pale,..Come trooping..The feather'd tribes domestic. 1821 Clare *Vill. Minstr.* I. 18 Sad deeds bewailing of the prowling fox; How in the roost the thief had knav'd his way. 1839 *Lincoln Gaz.* 12 Feb. 3/4 The rogues went to another roost adjoining the house. 1855 D. J. Browne *Amer. Poultry Yard* 83 The dormitory, or roost, should be well ventilated. *Ibid.*, To let air or light into the roost.

c. A collection or number *of* fowls, etc., such as may occupy a roost.

1827 Col. Hawker *Diary* (1893) I. 303, I killed a roost of small birds.

d. *fig.* A resting-place; a lodging, bed.

1858 O. W. Holmes *Aut. Breakf.-t.* (1883) 122 The world has a million roosts for a man, but only one nest. 1864 Lowell *Fireside Trav.* 110 The only roost was in the garret, which..contained eleven double beds, ranged along the walls. 1891 C. Roberts *Adrift Amer.* 23, I selected what appeared to me to be about the best spot for a roost, and..made a fairly comfortable bed.

2. Without article, in various phrases:

a. *To go*, etc., *to roost*. Also *fig.* of persons: To retire to rest. (Cf. Flem. *te roest gaan*.)

a 1529 Skelton *E. Rummyng* 191 The hennes ron in the mashfat; For they go to roust Streyght ouer the ale ioust. *a* 1631 Drayton *Noah's Flood* 383 When the crowned cock ..Comes to roost by him. 1648 Hexham II, *Roesten*, to Jugge, or goe to Roost, as Hens, Patridges, &c. 1797–1808 Vince *Astron.* xxi. 228 The birds went to roost. 1836 Macgillivray *Trav. Humboldt* viii. 109 These birds go to roost long before night. 1867 'Ouida' *Castlemaine's Gage* (1879) 20 The swallows were gone to roost amidst the ivy.

fig. 1829 Scott *Jrnl.* II. 314 So to roost upon a crust of bread and a glass of small beer, my usual supper. 1852 Thackeray *Esmond* I. xiii, 'Tis time for me to go to roost. I will have my gruel a-bed. 1879 Stevenson *Travels in Cevennes* (1886) 212 Half an hour later, and I must have gone supperless to roost.

b. *At roost*, roosting, perched. Also *to take roost*, to perch.

1692 Sir R. L'Estrange *Fables* ccclii, A Fox spy'd a Cock at Roost with his Hens about him. 1713 Derham *Phys.-Theol.* VII. ii, The Breast, and its Bone, made like a Keel..to counterpoise the Body, and support and rest it upon at Roost. 1848 Lytton *Harold* VII. ii, Where the falcon took roost. 1864 Browning *Mr. Sludge*, While you cling by half a claw To the perch whereon you puff yourselves at roost.

c. *To come home to roost*, to come back upon the originator.

1810 Southey *Kehama* Motto, Curses are like young chickens: they always come home to roost. 1838 Lytton *Alice* 340 The curse has come home to roost. 1887 Lowell *Democr.* 173 All our mistakes sooner or later surely come home to roost.

3. In various local applications (see quots.).

1790 Morison *Poems* 105 (E. D. D.), Frae the roost a rung she drew. 1808 Jamieson, *Roost*,..the inner roof of a cottage, composed of spars of wood reaching from the one wall to the other...It is also vulgarly used to denote a garret. 1856 Morton *Cycl. Agric.* II. 725/2 *Roost*, (Lancas.), the upper part of a cow-house; loft over stable.

4. *attrib.*, as *roost-time*, *-tree*; *roost lay* (see quot.).

1780 G. White *Selborne* xciv, They happened to be suddenly roused from their roost-trees. 1823 Egan *Grose's Dict. Vulg. T.*, *Roost Lay*, stealing poultry. 1884 Jefferies *Life of Fields* (1908) 97 A loud..clamour of rooks and daws, who have restlessly moved in their roost-trees. 1889 — *Open Air* 216 The partridges may run through to join their friends before roost-time on the ground.

Roost (rūst), *sb.*[2] Also 7–9 roust, 8–9 rost, 9 rust. [a. ON. *rǫst* (Norw. *rost*), in the same sense.] A tumultuous tidal race formed by the meeting of conflicting currents off various parts of the Orkney and Shetland Islands.

1654 Blaeu *Atlas, Scotia* 150 Exiguis scaphulis quas facile maris æstus ac fluctus, quem *Roosts* appellant, absorbet. 1693 J. Wallace *Orkney* 93 *Roust*, a very tempestuous tide. 1774 Low *Orkney* (1879) 14 Where the water breaks on Stroma, it goes off in vast whirls, and forms a roust by the dancing of the stream. 1821 Scott *Pirate* i, The current of a strong and furious tide, which..is called the Roost of Sumburgh. 1841 *Penny Cycl.* XXI. 384/1 The majestic cliffs and towering headlands that tower over the dark and stormy seas and *rousts*. 1868 D. Gorrie *Summers & W. Orkneys* v. 161 The roosts are in their wildest state of agitation with ebb tides and westerly swells.

Roost, obs. form of Roast *sb.* and *v.*

Roost (rūst), *v.* Forms: 6 rust(e, roste, 6–7 roust(e, rowst, 7– roost. [f. Roost *sb.*[1] Cf. Flem. *roesten* (Kilian).]

1. Of birds: To settle on a perch or the like for sleep or rest; to settle for sleep, go to rest.

1530 Palsgr. 696/1 These capons ruste whan it draweth towardes nyght, they be wyser than men be. 1577 B. Googe *Heresbach's Husb.* IV. (1586) 166 After the seuenth moneth, you may put them to roust in the house with the other Peacockes. 1600 Surflet *Countrie Farme* I. xv. 96 By hauing rousted vpon the trees in the open aire. *a* 1682 Sir T. Browne *Tracts* (1683) 29 Sitting, roosting, covering and resting in the boughs. 1748 *Anson's Voy.* III. i. 400 The greatest part of the birds..were such as are known to roost on shore. 1791 Cowper *Yardley Oak* 52 Time hath made thee what thou art—a cave For owls to roost in. 1852 M. Arnold *Empedocles* II. 432 On the cliff-side, the pigeons Roost deep in the rocks.

transf. 1567 Turberv. *Epit.*, etc. 36 No sooner stirres Auroras Starre,..But they that rousted were in rest..Do pack apace to labours left. *a* 1661 Fuller *Worthies* (1840) I. 106 Verres..never saw the sun either to rise or set, as roosted after or before.

b. Of persons: To seat oneself, to perch. *colloq.*

1816 Scott *Antiq.* viii, Down to the flat shelf on which the sufferers had roosted. 1852 Mrs. Stowe *Uncle Tom's C.* vi, About a dozen young imps were roosting, like so many crows, on the verandah railings. 1897 Flandrau *Harvard Episodes* 60 She is the woman who, when you call, roosts discreetly at the extreme end of a long sofa.

2. To lodge, harbour, make one's abode or quarters. In mod. use: To pass the night.

1593 Nashe *Christ's T.* Wks. (Grosart) IV. 95 Banisht he was, and longer in Ierusalem might hee not roust. 1610 Holland *Camden's Brit.* (1637) 366 A rabblement of Danes rousted heere one whole yeare. [1664 J. Webb *Stone-Heng* (1725) 206 Camden finds him and his Danes roosting afterwards for one whole Year at Cirencester.] 1716 B. Church *Hist. Philip's War* (1865) I. 161 It was hard to tell where to find Annawon, for he never roosted twice in a place. 1813 Sir R. Wilson *Priv. Diary* (1862) II. 486, I am most anxious to be on the wing, and again roosted. 1855 Thackeray *Newcomes* xxxix, Stopped to roost at Terracina. 1883 J. A. Symonds *Shaks. Predec.* v. (1900) 166 These vagrants wandered up and down the country, roosting in hedge-rows.

b. *fig.* or in fig. contexts.

c 1554 Coverdale *Hope of Faithful* Pref. A iij, It vnknowne, all vices swarm and roste in vs. 1598 Marston *Sco. Villanie* I. ii. 178 Modestie is rousted in the skyes. 1607 S. Hieron *Wks.* I. 262 Men haue euen determined with themselues, that, let the word of the kingdome roust where it will, sure with them it shall not harbour. 1660 Bonde *Scut. Reg.* 108 So great ignorance cannot roust in their pates, who are so worldly wise. 1730 Young *1st Ep. to Pope* 10 Where speculation roosted near the sky. 1793 Burns *Address spoken by Miss Fontenelle* 5 So [I] sought a Poet, roosted near the skies.

3. *trans.* To afford a resting-place to (one); to accommodate, harbour. Also *fig.*

1854 S. Dobell *Balder* iii. Poet. Wks. 1875 II. 17 They defy the storms of heaven, and roost The weary-winged Ages. 1873 Carleton *Farm Ball.* 43 You have often slept in pens; I've a mind to take you out there now, and roost you with the hens!

Roo·st-cock. Now *rare.* [f. Roost *sb.*[1]] A domestic cock.

1606 H. Parrot *The Mous-Trap* (Halliw.), Gallus, that greatest roost-cock in the rout. 1627 E. F. *Hist. Edw. II* (1680) 88 The old Roost-cock in his Country-language. 1668 Charleton *Onomast.* 75 Gallus Gallinaceus,..the House, or Roost-Cock. 1736 Ainsworth II, *Gallinaceus*,..a roost-cock, a cockerel. *c* 1750 [Mrs. Palmer] *Devonsh. Dial.* (1837) 18 Their blowzy faces as rid as roost-cocks. 1789 G. White *Selborne* cv, Roost-cocks, which had been silent, began to sound their clarions. 1858 Polson *Law & Lawyers* 116 A beautiful roost-cock flew upon his head and crowed three times.

Rooste, obs. form of Roast *sb.* and *v.*

Roo·sted, *a. rare.* [f. Roost *v.* or *sb.*[1]] Perched on a roost. Also *fig.*

1748 Thomson *Castle Indol.* II. xl, Yet oft his anxious eye Mark'd them, like wily fox who roosted cock doth spy. 1779 Sheridan *Critic* II. ii, Is't thus your new-fledged zeal And plumed valour moulds in roosted sloth?

Rooster (rū·stəɹ). Chiefly *U.S.* and *dial.* [f. Roost *sb.*[1] + -er[1].]

1. A cock.

1822 J. Flint *Lett. fr. Amer.* 264 Rooster, or he-bird.—Cock, the male of the hen. 1836 *Backwoods Canada* 308 The produce of two hens and a cock, or *rooster*, as the Yankees term that bird. 1847 H. Melville *Omoo* lxvi, With a rooster's quill, therefore, a bit of soiled paper, and a stout heart, he set to work. 1882 *Garden* 20 May 348 At sunrise I was awakened by a sturdy old rooster.

b. *transf.* of persons.

1871 G. Meredith *H. Richmond* II. 214 Hang..your talk of a fine girl, like my Janet, as a piece of poultry, you young rooster! 1881 *Philad. Rec.* No. 3428. 2 It is not..in the nature of things that a rooster in the Legislature should quietly submit to be lectured by a rooster outside of the legislature. 1897 Barrère & Leland *Dict. Slang* II. 136 *Queer rooster* (American thieves), a man that lodges among thieves to pick up information for the police.

2. *U.S.* (See quot.)

1871 in De Vere *Americanisms* 262 Rooster..indicates a bill, or proposed law, which will benefit the legislators—and no one else.

Roo·sting, *vbl. sb.*[1] [f. Roost *v.*]

1. Perching for rest; places for perching.

1604 Drayton *Owle* Poems (1619) 413 By all signes..The Birds therein their nightly roosting made. 1713 Derham *Phys.-Theol.* VII. i. § 5 The Legs all curved for their easy Perching, Roosting, and Rest. 1820 Scott in *Lockhart* (1837) IV. 376 A great deal of valuable fir planting, which you may remember; fine roosting for the black game.

2. *attrib.*, as *roosting-cage*, *-house*, *-time*, etc.

1621–3 Middleton & Rowley *Changeling* IV. i, At roosting time a little lodge can hold 'em. 1840 *Penny Cycl.* XVIII. 477/1 The first roosting-perch..should be placed lengthways. 1844 H. Stephens *Bk. Farm* I. 153 An opening..in the outer wall of the roosting-house. 1874 J. W. Long *Amer. Wild-fowl* ix. 161 In the evening the ducks will be seen coming from the roosting-ponds. 1879 Jefferies *Wild Life* 281 They [*sc.* rooks] stretch from here to the roosting-trees.

b. Esp. *roosting-place*; also *fig.*

1725 *Fam. Dict.* s.v. *Poultry*, Being wont in a Morning early, to go out of the Hen-House or Roosting-Place. 1789 G. White *Selborne* cvi, The poultry dared not to stir out of their roosting-places. 1809 Malkin *Gil Blas* I. xiii. ¶ 6, I..slunk to my roosting-place, where I fell asleep. 1844 Alb. Smith *Adv. Mr. Ledbury* iii, Jack quitted his roosting-place amongst the baggage. 1874 J. W. Long *Amer. Wild-fowl* xxiv. 245 When their feeding-grounds and roosting-places are near together.

† Roo·sting, *vbl. sb.*[2] *Obs.*[−1] In 6 roostynge. [Cf. Roost *sb.*[2]] Turbulent flow or turmoil.

1555 Eden *Decades* (Arb.) 382 We mette northerly wyndes and greate roostynge of tydes.

Roo·sting, *ppl. a.* [f. Roost *v.*] That roosts or perches; going to roost.

1798 Bloomfield *Farmer's Boy*, *Autumn* xlii, From each bough The roosting Pheasant's short but frequent crow Invites to rest. 1813 Scott *Rokeby* v. ii, Hoarse into middle air arose The vespers of the roosting crows. 1886 *Daily News* 24 Sept. 5/2 They..startle from its crumbling recesses the roosting doves.

Root (rūt), *sb.*[1] Forms: α. 1, 5 rot, 3–6 rote, 4 rotte, 5 roth, roytt, rowte, 6 rott, roite, rout(e, rowth, 9 *dial.* roit; 4–7 roote, 5– root. β. *Sc.* 5–6 rut, 6 ruite, rwit, 5– rute, 6– ruit, 9 reet, rit; *north.* 9 reut, rut, re(e)at. [Late OE. *rót*, a. ON. *rót* (Icel. and Fær. *rót*), Norw. and Sw. *rot* (MSw. *root*), Da. *rod* († *rood*), NFris. *rôt*, *rut* (prob. from ODa.), LG. *rut*. The original stem **wrôt-* is connected on the one hand with L. *rādīx*, and on the other with OE. *wyrt*: see Wort. The usual OE. words for 'root' are *wyrttruma* and *wyrtwala*.]

I. 1. That part of a plant or tree which is normally below the earth's surface; in *Bot.*, the descending axis of a plant, tree, or shoot, developed from the radicle, and serving to attach the plant to and convey nourishment from the soil, with or without subsidiary rootlets or fibres; also applied to the corresponding organ of an epiphyte, and to the rootlets attaching an ivy to its support.

a 1150 in Napier *Contrib. O.E. Lex.* 54 Se Godes freond cwæð þæt he leofode be weode & be wyrtan roten & be wæteres drence. *Ibid.*, He leofode be wyrtan rotan. *a* 1175 in *Hist. Holy Rood-tree* 4 An fet..wæs ifylled of þæt ylce watere & þa ȝyrdæ þeron asette, forþan ðe he wolde þæt ða roten fordruȝode wæron. *c* 1200 Ormin 10064 Þatt axe shollde þa beon sett Rihht att te treowwess rote. *a* 1300 in *E. E. P.* (1862) 10 Þer nis..no tre in erþ so fast, mid al har rotis so fast ipiȝt, þat [etc.]. *a* 1300 *Cursor M.* 1346 Þis tre was of a mikel heght.., And to þe rotte [*Gött.* rote] he kest his he. 1362 Langl. *P. Pl.* A. VII. 96 Mi plouh-pote schal be my pyk, and posshen atte Rootes. 1390 Gower *Conf.* I. 7 Now stant the crop under the rote. *c* 1440 *Promp. Parv.* 437/2 Rote, of a thynge growynge, *radix*. 1483 *Cath. Angl.* 314/2 A Rute, *radix*, *radicula*. 1513 Douglas *Æneis* IV. viii. 80 Als far his ruite doith spreid Deip ondir erth. 1573 Tusser *Husb.* (1878) 98 Get..a parer..to pare away grasse and to raise vp the roote. 1613 Shaks. *Hen. VIII*, I. ii. 97 Though we leaue it with a roote thus hackt, The Ayre will drinke the Sap. 1672 3 Grew *Anat. Pl.* (1682) 128 What the Mouth is to an Animal; that the Root is to a Plant. 1750 Gray *Elegy* 102 Yonder nodding beech, That wreathes its old fantastic roots so high. 1792 J. Belknap *Hist. New Hampsh.* III. 108 When the roots have been loosened by the frost, they are..cut and dug out of the ground. 1815 Shelley *Alastor* 531 Ancient pines Branchless and blasted, clenched with grasping roots The unwilling soil. 1846 J. Baxter *Libr. Pract. Agric.* II. 383 In transplanting walnuts..great care should be taken that their roots be as little injured as possible. 1884 Bower & Scott *De Bary's Phaner.* 438 In the growing-point of the stem, branches, and roots, and in young rudimentary leaves.

b. In phr. *by the root(s)*, denoting the complete pulling up of a plant or tree. (Cf. 9 c.)

c 1385 Chaucer *L. G. W.* 2613 *Hypermnestra*, The floure, the lefe, ys rent vp by the rote To maken garlandes. *c* 1400 Maundev. (Roxb.) xvii. 79 So þat þai be taken vp by þe rutes. *c* 1440 *Promp. Parv.* 131 Drawe vp by þe rote, *eradico*. 1526 *Pilgr. Perf.* (W. de W. 1531) 23 He..plucketh vp the breers, wedes and grasse by the rotes. 1593 Shaks. 3 *Hen. VI*, v. iv. 69 Yonder stands the thornie Wood, Which ..Must by the Roots be hew'ne vp yet ere Night. 1648 Milton *Ps.* lxxx. 54 The tusked Boar out of the wood Up turns it by the roots. 1667 — *P. L.* II. 544 As when Alcides..tore Through pain up by the roots Thessalian Pines. 1765 A. Dickson *Treat. Agric.* (ed. 2) 112 The weeds themselves must be pulled up by the root. 1833 Ht. Martineau *Briery Creek* ii. 26 They could pull up a tall tree by the roots.

c. Used without article; also in phrases as *to take root*, to settle properly in the ground, *to make root*, *strike root*.

c 1386 Chaucer *Squire's T.* 153 Euery gras that groweth vp on roote. 1432–50 tr. *Higden* (Rolls) I. 265 For a tree may not take þer [L. *ibi*] roote for saltenes of the erthe. *c* 1440 *Promp. Parv.* 437 Rotyn, or take rote, as treys, *radico*. *c* 1480 Henryson *Fables*, *Trial Fox* xxx, Ouer Ron and Rute thay ran togidder raith. *c* 1560 A. Scott *Poems* (S. T. S.) xxxv. 9 He sall haif brute, as tre on rute Endlang the rever plantit. 1573 Tusser *Husb.* (1878) 83 Thy garden plot..Well clensed and purged of roote and of stone. 1611 Bible *Ps.* lxxx. 9 Thou..didst cause it to take deepe root, and it filled the land. 1707 Mortimer *Husb.* 7 This will cause it to strike fresh Root. 1725 *Fam. Dict.* s.v. *Root-grafting*, Which Piece of Root will draw in Sap, and nourish the Graft. 1738 Wesley *Ps.* lxxx. xi, Water'd with Blood, the Vine took Root. 1826 Glenny *Everyday Bk.* 203 The object of this is to let them make root when inclined, but not to grow any until wanted. 1878 Browning *La Saisiaz* 29 Fruit Others reap and garner, heedless how produced by stalk and root.

2. The permanent underground stock of a plant from which the stems or leaves are periodically produced; also, by extension, a plant, herb.

c 1200 *Trin. Coll. Hom.* 161 [It] is cleped..wildernesse ȝef þare manie rotes onne waceð. 1596 Dalrymple tr. *Leslie's Hist. Scot.* I. 26 The herb gude to give the cattel against the rute that thay cal trifoly. 1599 Shaks. *Hen. V*, II. iv. 39 As Gardeners doe with Ordure hide those Roots That shall first spring, and be most delicate. 1664 Evelyn *Kal. Hort.* April (1671) 48 Transplant such Fibrous roots..as Violets, Hepatica, Primroses. 1786 Abercrombie *Gard. Assist.*, *Arr.* 81 The propagation of bulbous and tuberous roots for general supply. 1847 Mrs. Loudon *Amateur Gard. Monthly Cal.* 22/1 Others succeed pretty well by buying imported roots from the nurseryman every year. 1858 Kingsley *Poems* 137 That roots, which parch in burning sand, May bud to flower and fruit again.

3. The underground part of a plant used for eating or in medicine; now *spec.* in *Agric.*, one of a fleshy nature, as the turnip or carrot, and by extension, any plant of this kind.

a 1150 [see sense 1]. *c* 1200 Ormin 3213 Hiss drinnch wass waterr.., Hiss metewilde rotess. *c* 1205 Lay. 31885 Þat folc.. lufeden bi wurten, bi moren and bi rote. 13.. *Cursor M.* 4711 (Gött.), Þe wrecched pore miht find na fode,..Þat soght þaim rotis als þe suyn. 1393 Langl. *P. Pl.* C. XVI. 244 Bestes [live] by gras & by greyn and by grene rotes. *c* 1400 Maundev. (Roxb.) viii. 30 Þai liffe with dates and rutes and herbes. *c* 1489 Caxton *Blanchardyn* xxi. 70 He hath in his house a rote that..shal gyf me help. *a* 1533 Ld. Berners *Huon* xxi. 63, I haue eten none other thynge but rootes & frutes. 1551 Turner *Herbal* (1568) 21 It is euidently knowen that water wyll wexe thycke, if this roite be brused and put in it. 1605 Shaks. *Macb.* I. iii. 84 Or haue we eaten on the insane Root, That takes the Reason Prisoner? 1617 Moryson *Itin.* I. 34 Corne fields set with cabbages and roots. 1671 Milton *P. R.* I. 339 We here Live on tough roots and stubs, to thirst inur'd More then the Camel. 1704 F. Fuller *Med. Gymn.* (1711) 94 These Roots may be so manag'd by a good Hand as to eat as Food. 1763 *Museum Rust.* I. 332 This root would..fill them up with flashy fat. 1801 *Farmer's Mag.* Jan. 113 Very few turnips are with us this season; this root having generally failed. 1817 Shelley *Rev. Isl.* v. lvi. 5 Melons, and dates, and figs, and many a root Sweet and sustaining. 1879 *Cassell's Techn. Educ.* IV. 237/1 Cattle require their 'roots' to be carted from the field to the homestead.

b. With defining words: (see quots.).

1787 *Gentl. Mag.* Nov. 963/1 The Mangel Wurtz..or Root of Scarcity. 1789 *Trans. Soc. Arts* VII. 33 The cows fed on the Common Turnep gave most milk..and those on the Root of Scarcity the least. 1801 *Farmer's Mag.* Jan. 87 In the mean time, all, rich and poor, have the greatest abundance of the root of plenty, potatoes.

4. a. The imbedded or basal portion of the hair, tongue, teeth, fingers, nails, or other members or structures of the body.

a 1225 *Leg. Kath.* 2121 [To] þurhdriuen hire tittes wið irnene neiles, & renden ham up hetterliche wið þe breoste roten. *c* 1320 *Sir Tristr.* 1185 His tong hab he ton And schorn of bi þe rote. 1398 Trevisa *Barth. De P. R.* v. xxviii. (Bodl. MS.), Þese boones stonde of twey ordres in þe oone side with þe rootes of þe fingres. 1508 Kennedie *Flyting w. Dunbar* 374 The ravyns sall ryve na thing bot thy tong rutis. 1523 Fitzherb. *Husb.* § 91 If they be not kilde, they wyl..eate the rotes of the horse eares, and kil hym. 1580 Blundevil *Horsem.* IV. cxvii. 54 A malander..hath long haires with stubborne roots. 1607 Shaks. *Timon* v. i. 136 Each false [word] Be as a Cantherizing to the root o' th' Tongue. 1681 Grew *Musæum* I. v. i. 85 Beneath, close by the Root of the Saw, are two oblique Nostrils. 1710 *Lond. Gaz.* No. 4672/4 A..Spanish Dog, with..one large Liver colour Spot at the Root of his Stern. 1798 Coleridge *Anc. Mar.* II. xiii, Every tongue, through utter drought, Was withered at the root. 1817 Kirby & Sp. *Entomol.* xix. (1818) II. 145 The rightful queen..seized her with her jaws near the root of the wings. 1856 Stonehenge *Brit. Rural Sports* 479/2 The root of the thumb should be brought close up to the ribs. 1898 *Allbutt's Syst. Med.* V. 131 Most frequently it starts from the root of the lung.

b. The more or less 'muddy' base of a crystal or gem, esp. of an emerald.

1695 Woodward *Nat. Hist. Earth* IV. (1723) 192 Their Root, as the Jewellers call it; which is only the Abruptness at that End of the Body whereby it adhered to the Stone. 1867 Billing *Sci. of Gems* 126 A large piece of veiny, cloudy root of amethyst, 2¼ inches by 2 inches (not good enough to rank as a jewel).

c. That part of anything by or at which it is united to something else.

1632 Lithgow *Trav.* I. 22 The breadth of Italy at the roote and beginning thereof,..from the Adriaticke coast, to the riviera di Genoa. 1840 *Civil Eng. & Arch. Jrnl.* III. 237/1 A wooden jetty has been run out from the root of the pier. 1869 Sir E. Reed *Ship Build.* xx. 430 The angle iron..is liable to open at the root under very heavy blows. 1884 F. J. Britten *Watch & Clockm.* 289 In watches the roots of all the wheels and pinions are left square except the roots of the barrel or great wheel teeth and the roots of the centre pinion leaves.

5. The bottom or base *of* something material; *esp.* the foot of a hill.

c 1386 Chaucer *Clerk's T.* 58 At the West syde of Ytaille, Doun at the roote of Vesulus the colde. 1483 Caxton *Gold. Leg.* 59 b/2 Whan moyses had brouht them forth unto the rote of the hylle they stode there. 1553 Eden *Treat. New Ind.* (Arb.) 20 Mountaynes..at the rootes wherof are found Rubines, Hiacinthes. 1579 *Reg. Privy Council Scot.* III. 189 That na thing remane within the clois about the rute of the tour bot the dur thairof. 1635–56 Cowley *Davideis* I. Poems (1905) 261 Numbers which still encrease more high and wide From One, the root of their turn'd Pyramide. 1687 Lovell tr. *Thevenot's Trav.* II. 74 A rock .., at the root whereof there is a little spring of Water. 1726 Leoni *Alberti's Archit.* I. 11/1 That Stream..continually undermining and eating away the Root of the Mountain. 1817 Shelley *Rev. Isl.* VII. xi. 3 A burst of waters driven As from the roots of the sea. 1844 Mrs. Browning *Drama of Exile* Poems 1850 I. 85 Split the charnel earth To the roots of the grave. 1897 Geikie *Anc. Volcanoes Grt. Brit.* I. 12 There will thus be a constant pressure of the molten magma into the roots of volcanoes.

II. 6. The source or origin *of* some quality, condition, tendency, etc. Also occas. without const.

Freq. with fig. context directly referring to sense 1.

c 1200 Ormin 4976 Forr niss nan mahht tatt bettre maȝȝ þe winnen eche blisse Þann allre mahhte rote maȝȝ. *a* 1225 *Ancr. R.* 54 Biginnunge & rote of þis ilke reouðe was a liht sihðe. *a* 1300 *Cursor M.* 28744 Þou þain þe rotes as þou mai O þis man sin to do awai. 1390 Gower *Conf.* III. 197 Pite, men sein, is thilke roote Wherof the vertus springen alle. 1423 Jas. I *Good Counsel* 2 Wertew floure and rut is of noblay. 1467–8 *Rolls of Parlt.* V. 622/2 It was shewed.. that Justice was grounde well and rote of all prosperite. 1525 Ld. Berners *Froiss.* II. clxxviii. [clxxiv.] 535 This rote and foundacion of hatred multyplyed greatly after. 1589 *Pasquil's Return* C iij b, This is the roote of all the mischife. 1611 Shaks. *Wint. T.* II. iii. 89 The Root of his Opinion, which is rotten, As euer Oake or Stone was sound. 1639 S. Du Verger tr. *Camus' Admir. Events* 34 To cut up the roote of all these fooleries in her sonne. 1711 Steele *Spect.* No. 48 ¶ 4, I have several Follies which I do not know the Root of. 1720 Ramsay *Prosp. Plenty* 145 Malicious envy! root of a' debates. 1821–2 Shelley *Chas. I*, I. i. 103 The root of all this ill is prelacy. 1884 tr. *Lotze's Metaph.* 513 The root of all these difficulties seems to be a confusion in our idea of..an acting force.

b. Predicated of persons or material things.

1377 Langl. *P. Pl.* B. xv. 98 Prestes, and prechoures.., That aren rote of þe riȝte faith. *c* 1386 Chaucer *Can. Yeom. T.* 516, I wol it verifie In this Chanoun, roote of alle trecherie. *c* 1400 *Beryn* 4015 Saff the Burgeysis of the town, of falshede þat were rote. *c* 1485 *Digby Myst.* (1882) III. 1671 O blyssyd womman, rote of ower savacyon. 1549 Latimer *2nd Serm. bef. Edw. VI* (Arb.) 64 These flattering clawbackes are originall rotes of all mischyue. 1590 Spenser *F. Q.* II. vii. 12 All otherwise..I riches read, And deeme them roote of all disquietnesse. 1667 Milton *P. L.* IX. 645 To the Tree Of prohibition, root of all our woe.

7. A source of some quality, etc.; *esp.* a virtue or vice giving rise to some condition or action.

c 1200 Ormin 11658 Alle fule lusstess Biginnenn þære & springenn ut Off gluterrnessess rote. *a* 1310 in Wright *Spec. P.* xviii. 57 Suete Jhesu,..In myn huerte thou sete a rote Of thi love. *c* 1380 Wyclif *Wks.* (1880) 173 This [covetousness] is a venymous rote þat makiþ here seruyce..not acceptable to god. *c* 1400 *Apol. Loll.* (Camden) 91 Wene we not þe gospel to be..in þe leuis of wordis, but in rot of resoun. 1564 *Reg. Privy Council Scot.* I. 291 Hir Majestie wald nocht that ony rute were left behind, quhilk mycht engender ony new displesour or grudge betuix thame. 1603 H. Crosse *Vertues Commw.* (1878) 26 Considering those inconueniencies that rise out of the roote of aboundance. 1671 Milton *Samson* 1032 Or was too much of self-love mixt, Of constancy no root infixt. 1781 Cowper *Expost.* 111 Faith, the root whence only can arise The graces of a life that wins the skies. 1823 Moore *Loves Angels, 3rd Angel's Story* x, Humility, that low, sweet root From which all heavenly virtues shoot. 1876 Mellor *Priesth.* ii. 77 The root of bitterness out of which all this strife has grown is simple.

† **b.** *To take root*, to spring *from* something.

a 1300 *Cursor M.* 43 Vr dedis fro vr hert tas rote, Quedur þai be worthi or bale or bote.

8. A person or family forming the source of a lineage, kindred, or line of descendants.

13.. *Seuyn Sages* 1072 (W.), I ne mai do thi sone no bot, But yif I wite the sothe rot, Of what man hit was biyete. *c* 1375 *Cursor M.* 10162 (Trin.), Ioachim bringere of bote, he was comen of dauid rote. 1388 Wyclif *Isaiah* xi. 1 And a ȝerde schal go out of the roote of Jesse. 1555 Harpesfield in Bonner *Hom.* 6 For as much as they two were the very route, where of all men must ryse. 1582 Stanyhurst *Æneis* I. (Arb.) 17 Thence flitted thee Latin ofspring. Thee roote of old Alban. 1605 Shaks. *Macb.* III. i. 5 It was saide ..that my selfe should be the Roote, and Father Of many Kings. 1667 Milton *P. L.* II. 383 To confound the race Of mankind in one root. 1766 Blackstone *Comm.* II. 217 This taking by representation is called a succession *in stirpes*, according to the roots; since all the branches inherit the same share that their root, whom they represent, would have done. 1818 Cruise *Digest* (ed. 2) III. 409 It was introduced with a view to discard the son; and that the father should become the *propositus* or *root*, to whom Nº 10 is exactly in the same relation as Nº 11 is to the son. 1873 Dixon *Two Queens* I. i. I. 4 Among the deputies were many who had sprung from Oriental roots.

transf. *a* 1653 Gouge *Comm. Heb.* vii, Shem was the root of the Church.

b. A scion, offshoot. (Chiefly Biblical.)

13.. *Guy Warw.* (1883) 442 Þei be þe deuels rote, Y schal nouȝt fle him a fot. 1382 Wyclif 1 *Macc.* i. 10 And there wente out of hem a roote of synne, Antiochus the noble. — *Rev.* xxii. 16. 1526 Tindale *Rev.* v. 5 A lion beinge off the tribe off Juda, the rott of David, hath obtayned to open the boke. 1611 Bible *Isaiah* xi. 10 In that day there shall bee a roote of Iesse, which shall stand for an ensigne of the people. 1632 Lithgow *Trav.* x. 435 The plants of their Parishes, being the rootes of meere Irish. 1745 W. Robertson in *Trans. & Paraph. Scot. Ch.* vi. 13 So in this cold and barren World That sacred Root arose.

9. That upon or by which a person or thing is

established or supported; the basis upon which anything rests.

In 19th cent. use common in the phr. *to have (its) root(s) in* (something).

1340 *Ayenb.* 116 [To] strengþi his roten ine þe erþe of libbende. 1377 Langl. *P. Pl.* B. xx. 53 Antecryst cam þanne and al þe croppe of treuthe Torned it vp so doune and ouertilte þe rote. 1523 Coverdale *Old God & New* (1534) D iv, By so moche the more the christen fayth waxed stronge and gathered fast rotes. 1563 Winȝet *Wks.* (S. T. S.) I. 127 Sen it hes the grund and deip ruitis in the Scriptuir. 1612 Selden *Illustr. Drayton's Poly-olb.* xvii. (1876) II. 250 Some have referred the utmost root of the Lancastrian title to Edmund,..eldest son to Henry III. 1679 Ness *Antichrist* 180 Two..is the lowest number (for one is but the root of numbers). 1730 Ozell *Vertot's Rom. Rep.* II. xi. 179 Cato..fell into Pompey's Hands, who to cut up the Root of the Civil War, put him to Death. 1784 Cowper *Task* v. 353 Our love is principle, and has its root In reason. 1787 — *Stanzas Bills Mortality* 24 A worm is in the bud of youth, And at the root of age. 1820 Shelley *Prometh. Unb.* II. iii. 42 The nations echo round, Shaken to their roots, as do the mountains now. 1849–50 Alison *Hist. Europe* II. vi. § 63. 57 This prodigious change..laid the axe to the root of the aristocracy. 1874 Stevenson *Ess. Trav.* (1905) 245 A high wind under a cloudless sky.. seems to have no root in the constitution of things.

b. Of qualities, esp. with reference to their hold upon persons.

1340 *Ayenb.* 34 Of þe rote of auarice guoþ out manye smale roten. *c* 1400 *Sc. Trojan War* II. 396 In þe which dame Auaryce Festned hyr rotes at dewyce. 1556 J. Heywood *Spider & Fly* xxxix. 17 Where honestnes or vertuesnes bearth rout. 1570 Dee *Math. Pref.* *iiij b, What rotes..vertue had fastened in his brest. 1605 Shaks. *Macb.* IV. iii. 85 This Auarice..growes with more pernicious roote Then Summer-seeming Lust. 1781 Cowper *Table Talk* 15 With a courage of unshaken root, In honour's field advancing his firm foot. 1841 Trench *Parables* xii. (1877) 241 Righteousness, both in its root of faith and its flower of charity.

c. In phrases denoting completeness or thoroughness, as *to the root(s)*, *by the root(s)*, etc. (Cf. 1 b.)

1388 Wyclif *Ps.* li[i]. 7 Therfor God schal distrie thee in to the ende, he schal drawe thee out bi the roote. 1560 Daus tr. *Sleidane's Comm.* 93 b, Wherby these newe spronge up sectes maye be plucked up by the rotes. 1599 B. Jonson *Cynthia's Rev.* v. v, That so she might, more strictly, and to root, Effect the Reformation she intende. 1611 Shaks. *Cymb.* I. i. 28 What's his name, and Birth? I cannot delue him to the roote. 1640–1 in Rushw. (1721) III. I. 187, I wonder not at all..that they would have them [Bishops] up by the Roots. 1781 Cowper *Truth* 574 Since the dear hour that..cut up all my follies by the root. 1818 Cruise *Digest* (ed. 2) III. 12 This argument was quite cut up by the roots by the determination of the House of Lords in the case of Tong v. Robinson. 1860 Ruskin *Unto this Last* i. § 22 He [the merchant] has to understand to their very root the qualities of the things he deals in. 1894 Fenn *Real Gold* 89 As if he were enjoying himself right down to the roots.

10. The bottom or real basis, the inner or essential part, of anything.

The root of the matter, a literal rendering of Heb. *shōresh dābār* in Job xix. 28.

c 1386 Chaucer *Can. Yeom. T.* 908 (Ellesm. MS.), Telle me the roote..Of that water, if it be youre wille. 1393 Langl. *P. Pl.* B. xv. 64 [He] þat þorw resoun wolde þe rote knowe Of god and of his grete myȝtes, his graces it letteth. 1426 Lydg. *De Guil. Pilgr.* 10033 Yiff the roote be wel out souht, Strengere than thow, that ys be nouht. 1565 Cooper *Thesaurus*, *Stirps quæstionis*, the roote, and foundation of a question. 1611 Bible *Job* xix. 28 Seeing the root of the matter is found in me. 1674 N. Fairfax *Bulk & Selv.* 168 That everlastingness which the soul has in the root.. is of the same kind. 1735 *Col. Rec. Pennsylv.* IV. 45 Until he advisedly looketh into the Roots of it and tries it by the Rule of Law. 1850 Robertson *Serm.* Ser. III. v. (1872) 61 In every such case it may be taken for granted that the root of the matter has not been reached. 1875 Swinburne *Ess. & Stud.* 274 His resolute desire to get at the roots of things, and deeper yet if deeper might be.

† **b.** The bottom *of* the heart, in various figurative uses. *Obs.*

For earlier examples see Heart-root 1. In latest examples perh. an alteration of *rote*.

1485 Caxton *Paris & V.* (1868) 11 In hym I haue putte the rote of myn entyere herte. 1508 Dunbar *Poems*, *Tua Mariit Wemen* 162, I sall a ragment reveil fra the rute of my hert. *c* 1560 A. Scott *Poems* (S. T. S.) xv. 1 Vp, helsum hairt! thy rutis rais, and lowp. 1607 Shaks. *Cor.* II. i. 202 A Curse begin at very root on's heart. 1607 Chapman *Bussy D'Ambois* Plays 1873 II. 82 As illiterate men say Latine praiers By roote of heart, and daily iteration. 1684 Bunyan *Pilgr.* II. 11 That thou read therein to thy self, and to thy Children, until you have got it by root-of-Heart.

c. *At (the) root*, at bottom, essentially.

1855 Kingsley *Westw. Ho!* ii, He was, at root, a godly and kind-hearted pedant enough. 1857 Borrow *Rom. Rye* xvi, At the root mad.

11. a. *To take* (or *strike*) *root*, to obtain a permanent footing or hold; to settle down *in* a place, etc.

1535 Coverdale 2 *Kings* xix. 30 And the doughter Iuda ..shall from hence forth take rote beneth, and beare frute aboue. 1560 Daus tr. *Sleidane's Comm.* 92 b, No suche sectes can take roote or remayne emonges them. 1605 Camden *Rem.* (1613) 10 This warlike..Nation, after it had as it were taken roote here. 1784 Cowper *Task* II. 568 Prejudice in men of stronger minds Takes deeper root, confirm'd by what they see. 1809 Malkin *Gil Blas* x. xi. ¶ 5 As soon as I had taken root in my new soil. 1840 Dickens *Barn. Rudge* xlviii, The cause has taken a deep root, and has spread its branches far and wide. 1899 Gardiner *Cromwell* 36 The idea struck root.

† **b.** A hold upon a person's affections, confidence, or favour. *Obs.*

a 1715 Burnet *Own Time* (1724) I. 207 Such an attempt.. would give him a faster root with the King. 1756 Home *Douglas* II, Let not thy jealousy attempt to shake And loosen the good root he has in Randolph.

c. A strong link or attachment.

1854 Kingsley *Lett.* (1878) I. 431 The awful feeling of having the roots which connect one with the last generation seemingly torn up.

12. *Root-and-branch*: see Branch *sb.* 6 b.

For *root and crop*, *root and rind*, in similar uses, see Crop *sb.* 5 and Rind *sb.*[1] 2.

1642 Sir E. Dering *Sp. on Relig.* 94, I never gave my name in to take away both root and branch.

b. In adverbial use: Completely, utterly.

1640 Slingsby *Diary* (1836) 66 Some do petition to reform them, others to abolish them root and branch. 1650 R. Stapylton *Strada's Low C. Wars* v. 141 Constantly to endeavour the extirpation of it, Root and Branch. 1777 J. Adams *Fam. Lett.* (1876) 299 If our people do not turn out now and destroy Burgoyne's gang, root and branch. 1829 Scott *Rob Roy* Introd., Cutting off the tribe of MacGregor root and branch. 1887 *Times* (weekly ed.) 23 Sept. 17/3 You may look forward..to local government being dealt with by Parliament root and branch.

† **c.** *ellipt.* The policy of total abolition. *Obs.*

1679 Evelyn *Sylva* (ed. 3) 2 Professing themselves against Root and Branch.

d. In attributive use, of persons or things.

1737 *Gentl. Mag.* VII. 479 These are Root and Branch Men, and strike at the Foundation of all our National Happiness. 1788 *Ann. Reg.*, *Misc.* 143, I have hit upon a plan which will make root and branch work of it, and do the business effectually. 1816 *Edin. Rev.* XXVII. 167 We have seen that our root-and-branch Reformer went a great deal farther. 1858 J. Payn *Foster Brothers* xv, The boy had become at heart a root-and-branch democrat. 1887 *Dict. Nat. Biog.* IX. 249/2 The so-called root-and-branch bill for the total extinction of episcopacy.

III. † **13.** *Astrol.* = Radix 2. *Obs.*

c 1386 Chaucer *Man of Law's T.* 314 Of viage is ther noon eleccioun,..Noght whan a roote is of a burthe yknowe? *c* 1391 — *Astrol.* ii. § 54 Consider thy rote furst, the wyche is made the begynnyng of the tabelis. 1575 F. Wither tr. *Indagine's Chiromancy* III. N iv, They which haue Venus in the rote of their natiuity. 1603 [see Radix 2]. 1647 Lilly *Chr. Astrol.* clvii. 654, I oft am enforced to name the Root of the Nativity, it were more proper to say the Radix, for our English doth not well expresse the sense of the words.

14. *Math.* **a.** A number, quantity, or dimension, which, when multiplied by itself a requisite number of times, produces a given expression. *Cube* (or *third*) *root*: see Cube *sb.* 3. *Square* († *quadrate*) or *second root*: see Square *a.*

1557 Recorde *Whetstone* C iv, Thei onely haue rootes, whiche bee made by many multiplications of some one number by it self. 1571 Digges *Pantom.* I. xxv. H j b, The roote quadrat of the whole number, is the desired distance or line Hypothenusal. 1660 Barrow *Euclid* Expl. Signs, The Side or Root of a Square. 1679 Moxon *Math. Dict.* 38 *Cube Root*, the Root or Side of the third Power: So if 27 be the Cube, 3 is the Side or Root. 1706 W. Jones *Syn. Palmar. Matheseos* 47 The Root or First Power being taken as a Side, the Second Power will be a Square. 1753 *Chambers' Cycl.* Suppl. s.v., The extraction of the roots of algebraic quantities. *Ibid.*, Impossible Root is not only the square root of a negative quantity, but any other root denominated by any even number. 1798 Hutton *Course Math.* (1799) I. 80 Roots are sometimes denoted by writing the character √ before the power, with the index of the root against it. 1859 B. Smith *Arith. & Algebra* (ed. 6) 190 The Square Root of any proposed quantity. 1898 G. Chrystal *Introd. Algebra* (1902) 5 Special cases are the second root written $\sqrt{a}$; the third root or cube root [etc.].

b. The value or values of an unknown quantity which will satisfy a given equation.

1728 Chambers *Cycl.* s.v. If the Value of x be Negative, e.gr. $x = -5$, the Root is said to be false. 1798 Hutton *Course Math.* (1799) I. 249 To find the root of the cubic equation $x^3 + x^2 + x = 100$, or the value of x in it. 1826 in *Encycl. Metrop.* (1845) I. 544/2 Both members of an equation may be raised to the same power, or the same root of them may be extracted. 1885 Watson & Burbury *Math. Th. Electr. & Magn.* 179 The three roots are always real. The equation is the same as that [etc.].

15. *Philol.* One of those ultimate elements of a language, that cannot be further analysed, and form the base of its vocabulary; † a primary word or form from which others are derived.

1530 Palsgr. *Introd.* 31 His thre chefe rotes, that is to say, his theme, his preterit participle, and his present infynityve. 1599 *Broughton's Lett.* xii. 39 Recourse must be had to the Hebrew, euen to a false roote. 1615 Bedwell *Index Ass.* O iij, The theame or roote, as they call it, from whence it is deriued, is..*Kara*, to reade. 1631 Gouge *God's Arrowes* I. § 11. 15 The word..is derived from the same roote. 1740 Chesterf. *Lett.* lxiii. (1792) I. 177 The shortest and best way of learning a language is to know the roots of it; that is those original primitive words, of which many other words are made. 1760 Sterne *Tr. Shandy* IV. xxix, As it is a fault only in the declension, and the roots of the words continue untouch'd. 1837 G. Phillips *Syriac Gram.* 20 The simplest forms of nouns are those which consist only of the letters composing the root. 1856 Stanley *Sinai & Pal.* (1858) 260 Sharon, a name of the same root as that used to designate the table-lands beyond the Jordan. 1883 Morfill *Slavonic Lit.* ii. 39 A Slavonic root, meaning dwelling.

b. With punning allusion to sense 1.

1663 Butler *Hud.* I. i. 59 Hebrew Roots, although th' are found To flourish most in barren ground, He had such plenty. 1812 Combe *Syntax*, *Picturesque* xxiii. 20 What though by toil and pain, I know Where ev'ry Hebrew root doth grow. 1831 Carlyle *Misc.* (1857) II. 318 No Greek Roots grew there.

16. *Mus.* (See quot. 1889.)

1811 Busby *Dict. Mus.* (ed. 3), *Root*, a term applied by theorists to the fundamental note of any chord. 1818 — *Gram. Mus.* 314 The Triad may have its mediant either two whole tones, or a tone and a semitone, above its Root. 1867 Macfarren *Harmony* (1892) 51 The inversion of a chord is the placing one of its other notes, instead of the root, in the bass. 1889 Prout *Harmony* iii. § 58 Much trouble is sometimes caused to students from the word *Root* being used in two senses by theorists—as the lowest note of any combination of thirds, and also as the fundamental tone in the key from which the combination is harmonically derived.

IV. *attrib.* and *Comb.*

17. Attrib. in sense 1, with words denoting some part, appendage, or feature belonging to a root, as *root-bark*, *-bud*, *-cap*, *-fibre*, etc.

1832 *Planting* 7 in *Husb.* III. (L.U.K.), Should the soil be dry.., the bark in question is gradually converted into *root-bark. 1805 R. W. Dickson *Pract. Agric.* II. 603 They are enabled to propagate their subterraneous wires or *root-buds. 1875 Huxley & Martin *Elem. Biol.* 71 Its lower end is covered by the *root-cap of the ultimate termination of the principal root. 1805 R. W. Dickson *Pract. Agric.* II. 779 It is quite necessary that the sets have formed *root-fibres at the bottoms before they are removed. 1874 Cooke *Fungi* 9 A stray fragment of a *root-fibril. 1875 Huxley & Martin *Elem. Biol.* vi. 41 Appendages, consisting of leaves, branches, *root-filaments, and reproductive organs. 1882 *Garden* 25 Feb. 133/1 *Root fungus frequently attacks the Rose. 1707 Mortimer *Husb.* 513 *marg.*, *Root grafting. *c* 1820 *Edin. Encycl.* XI. 196/1 Recourse is sometimes had to root-grafting. 1868 *Rep. U.S. Commiss. Agric.* (1869) 249 The large amount of *root-growth in the deeper, central parts of the ridge. 1857 A. Gray *First Less. Bot.* (1866) 31 The absorbing surface of roots is very much greater than it appears to be, on account of the *root-hairs. 1849 Balfour *Man. Bot.* § 963 They [broomrapes] attach themselves to the roots of various plants, and are hence called *Root-parasites. 1883 *Science* I. 369/2 The cause of the *root-rot in grape-vines. 1805 R. W. Dickson *Pract. Agric.* I. 550 Different new lateral stems or *root-scions are sent off. 1848 Lindley *Introd. Bot.* (ed. 4) II. 183 *Root secretions are now regarded as unimportant. 1805 R. W. Dickson *Pract. Agric.* II. 620 The branching out of the stringy *root-shoots or wires. 1742 *Lond. & Country Brewer* IV. (ed. 2) 258 The *Root-spire..will be so many Tails to increase the Measure. 1804 J. Grahame *Sabbath* (1827) 82 When the wren..from the *root-sprig trills her ditty clear. 1805 R. W. Dickson *Pract. Agric.* II. 731 The earth being well laid upon the hills round the *root-stems of the plants. 1875 Bennett & Dyer tr. *Sachs' Bot.* 608 The cut surface of the *root-stump remains at first quite dry. 1786 Abercrombie *Gard. Assist.* 17 To clear away all *root-suckers. 1805 R. W. Dickson *Pract. Agric.* II. 625 The continued propagation of potatoes by subterraneous buds, or *root-wires.

b. In the sense 'made of roots'.

1853 Lowell *Moosehead Jrnl.* Prose Wks. 1890 I. 9 Sometimes a root-fence stretched up its bleaching antlers. 1864 Atkinson *Stanton Grange* 7 On the garden side, a root-bench was constructed against the bole of the tree. 1895 *Outing* XXVI. 389/2 The grass needs time to weave the deep, tough, root carpet so essential for sure footing.

c. Misc., as *root-beset*, *-built*, *-inwoven*; *root-bitten*, *-bound*, *-stricken*, *-torn*; *root-devouring*, *-digging*, *-eating*, *-feeding*; *root-like*.

1897 Mary Kingsley *W. Africa* 554 A narrow, slippery, muddy, *root-beset bush-path. 1872 Tennyson *Gareth & Lynette* 445 Wan-sallow as the plant that feels itself *Root-bitten by white lichen. 1634 Milton *Comus* 662 As Daphne was *Root-bound, that fled Apollo. *a* 1763 Shenstone *Economy* I. 167 Suffice the *root-built cell, the simple fleece, ..the crystal stream. 1817 Kirby & Sp. *Entomol.* xvi. II. 5 The males of another *root-devouring beetle. 1877 tr. *Tiele's Hist. Relig.* 17 Lowest in the scale stands the religion of the *root-digging Australians. 1882 *Garden* Mar. 147/2 The Cabbage fly is much of the same size as the *root-eating fly. 1892 Lubbock *Beaut. Nat.* 67 Others collect *root-feeding Aphides into their nests. 1792 S. Rogers *Pleas. Mem.* I. 79 Yon *root-inwoven seat. 1832 Lindley *Introd. Bot.* III. v. 351 Generally the root or *root-like bodies are to be excluded from all characters higher than those of species. 1860 Christina Rossetti *Poems* (1904) 191/1 Thou, *root-stricken, shalt not rebuild thy decay On my bosom for aye. 1871 R. Ellis *Catullus* lxiv. 288 Tall *root-torn beeches.

18. In sense 3, as *root-boat*, *-cellar*, *-crop*, *-culture*, etc.; also *root-eater*, *-gatherer*, *-pedlar*, *-woman*.

For names and descriptions of various implements or machines, as *root-bruiser*, *-cutter*, *-digger*, etc., see Knight *Dict. Mech.* (1875) and *Suppl.* (1884).

1636 *Maldon Borough Deeds* (Bundle 110, fol. 2), March 13. Re[ceived] for the groundage of a *Root boate at barrow hills, 4*d.* 1822 Loudon *Encycl. Gard.* 378 The *root-cellar may have a few divisions on the ground to keep the different roots apart. 1834 *Husb.* II. 381 (L. U. K.), Regarding *root crops, Mr. Cuthbert Johnson also mentions [etc.]. 1847 W. C. L. Martin *Ox* 115/1 Of all these root-crops, it appears that the least exhausting to the land is that of the beet. 1840 Buel *Farmer's Comp.* 163 The advantages of *root culture to the soil. 1807 T. Young *Lect. Nat. Phil.* II. 208/2 Scythes, chaff cutter, *root cutter. *a* 1735 Arbuthnot *Misc. Wks.* (1751) I. 212 Any Daughter of a Waterdrinker and *Root-eater. 1562 Turner *Herbal* II. 56 b, Theyr *root gatherers digged not theyr rootes hole out of grounde. *Ibid.*, Yͤ Duche *roote pedlers of Antwerp. 1699 Evelyn *Acetaria* App. P 5 b, So have you a Composition for any *Root-Pudding. 1820 W. Tooke *Lucian* I. 306 You are nothing but a *rootscraper and a mountebank. 1851 Mayhew *London Lab.* I. 130/1 The *'root-sellers' (as the dealers in flowers in pots are mostly called). 1802 Willich *Dom. Encycl.* III. 503/2 *Root-Steamer, an useful machine..for steaming potatoes, carrots, and other roots, with the view of feeding cattle. 1886 C. Scott *Sheep-Farming* 80 A *root store, a small hay shed,..and a comfortable hut for the shepherd, are all requisites of the lambing fold. *Ibid.* 66 Corn boxes do not need to be so large as the *root troughs. 1898 *Allbutt's Syst.*

Rosat. ...

Rosate, *ppl. a. Obs.* [ad. L. *rosātus*: cf. prec.]

1. Crowned with a chaplet of roses.

2. ? Treated with oil of roses.

Roscius (rǫ'ʃiǫs), *a.* [f. the name of Quintus Roscius Gallus (†62 B.C.), a famous Roman actor.] Characteristic of Roscius as an actor; famous or eminent in respect of acting.

Roscid (rǫ'sid), *a.* Now *rare. Also poetic.* [ad. L. *rōscid-us* dewy, f. *rōs* dew: cf. ROSID.] Dewy, moist, damp; resembling or falling like dew.

+ **Roscidating,** *ppl. a. Obs.* [f. as prec.] Having a dewy or cooling effect.

Rose (rǫʊz), *sb.* and *a.* Forms: 1- rose, 5 roos, 5-6 roose, ross, 5-7 roose, 6 rois, 6-7 roze, 5-6 rois, royz; 6- rose. [OE. *rose* str. and wk. fem., and also (northern) *rose* ... f. L. *rosa* (It., Sp., Pg. *rosa*, F. *rose*); in ME. reinforced from French. Cf. MDu. *rose* (Du. *roos*), Fris. *rose*), LG. *rose*, OHG. *rôsa* (G. *rose*), ON. *rōsa* (MSw. *rosa*, Da. *rose*), Icel. *rós*, Sw. *ros*). L. *rosa* is prob. an adoption of Gr. *ῥόδεα* 'Rhodian' ... Greek and Italian dialects (Brugmann, I. 684).]

I. *sb.* The flower or plant.

1. A well-known beautiful and fragrant flower which grows upon a shrub of the genus *Rosa*, usu. of a red, white, or yellow colour, and cultivated in most civilized countries.

II. In allusive, emblematic, or figurative uses.

4. **a.** The flower as distinguished by its surpassing beauty, fragrance, or rich red colour.

III. As designation of colour.

8. A delicate red or light crimson colour.

IV. A figure or representation of the flower.

12. **a.** *Her.* A conventional design or figure representing this flower, usu. consisting of five lobes or petals.

VII. ... Red granite, hornblende and rose, ...

Roseal (rǫ'zĭal), *a.* Now *arch.* Also 6-7 roseall, rosiall, 7 rosial. [L. *roseālis* ...]

1. Having the pink of light crimson hue of roses; rose-coloured, rosy.

Roseate (rǫ'zĭět), *a.* Also 6-7 roseat, 7 rosiat. [f. L. *rose-us* + -ATE[2]]

1. Having the pink or light crimson hue of roses; rose-coloured, rosy.

Roseately, *adv. rare.* [f. prec.] In a roseate manner; rosily.

Rosed, *ppl. a.* [f. ROSE *sb.*] Flushed or tinged with the colour of roses.

Rose-bay. [ROSE *sb.* + BAY *sb.*[3]]

1. The oleander or rose-laurel, *Nerium Oleander.* Also *rose-bay tree.*

Rose-breasted, a. [f. ROSE sb.] Having a breast of a rosy or carmine hue. In the names of various birds, as *rose-breasted cockatoo*, *finch*, *fly-catcher*, *grosbeak*, etc.

Rose-bush. [f. ROSE sb. + BUSH sb.] A bush of the rose plant.

Rose-cake. [f. ROSE sb.] A compaction of rose-petals in the form of a cake, used as a perfume, etc. *Obs.*

Rose-chafer. *Ent.* Also 8 schaffer. A beetle of the genus *Cetonia* (esp. *C. aurata*), of a burnished green or copper colour, frequenting roses and in the grub-state very destructive to vegetation.

Rose-cheeked, a. Having rosy or rose-coloured cheeks; rosy-cheeked.

Rose-colour, sb. Also rose colour. [f. ROSE sb. & 4.]

Rose-coloured, a. attrib.

Rose-drop.

Rose-leaf. [f. ROSE sb.] The leaf of a rose; usually, a rose-petal.

Roseless, a. [f. ROSE sb.] Without or destitute of roses; pale, colourless.

Roselet.

Roselite, sb. [Named after *roselite*, a German mineralogist (1798–1873) + -LITE.] A rare hydrous arsenate of cobalt and calcium, of vitreous

Rose-engine. [f. ROSE sb.] An appendage to a turning-lathe by means of which curvilinear or intricate patterns can be engraved.

Rose-like, a. [f. ROSE sb. + -LIKE 1.] Resembling a rose in colour, appearance, or fragrance.

Rose-lipped, a. [f. ROSE sb.] Having lips of a rosy hue.

Rose. Also rose, rosee. [ad. OF. *rose*, f. rose ROSE sb.] A dish flavoured with rose-petals.

Rosemary (rōu'zmări). Forms: 5 rose mary, 6 rosemarie (6 -ye), 7 rose mary: 6 rosemary. [An alteration of ROS-MARINE, ad. L. *ros marinus* or late L. *rosmarinus* ...] An evergreen shrub (*Rosmarinus officinalis*) of the N.O. Labiatae, native to the south of Europe.

Rose-mallous, variant of RASAMALA.

Rose-nail. [f. ROSE sb.] A wrought nail having a round head made with, or cut into, triangular facets.

Rosella[1]. [App. for *Rose-hiller*, f. Rose-hill, Parramatta near Sydney.] The rose parakeet of Australia, *Platycercus eximius*.

Rosella[2], rose-lle. Also roselle. [Perth, a corruption of the French name *l'oseille* (sorrel) *Hibiscus sabdariffa*.] The red or Indian sorrel.

Roseine. [f. ROSE sb.] One of the red salts derived from rosaniline; *spec.* acetate of rosaniline.

Rosen, a. Obs. Also 9-rosyne, rosyne.

Rose noble. [f. ROSE sb. + NOBLE sb.] A gold coin current in the fifteenth and sixteenth centuries, bearing a figure of the noble with the figure of a rose stamped upon it, and varying in value at different times and places.

Roseo-. Combining form, repr. L. *rose-us* in the sense 'rose-coloured', in names of various salts, alkalis, etc., as *roseo-nitrate*, *chromic*, *chromium*, *cobalt*, *cobaltous*, *rhodium*.

Rose of Jericho. [Cf. *Ecclus.* xxiv. 14.] A small annual cruciferous plant (*Anastatica hierochuntica*), native to the arid deserts of Southwest Asia and North-east Africa, the dried fronds of which unfold under the influence of moisture: the resurrection plant, Mary's flower, or rose of the Virgin.

Rose of Sharon (*Syrn*-). [Heb. *shārōn*, the name of a fertile tract traversing the coast of Palestine between Joppa and Mount Carmel.]

Rose-pink, sb. and a. [f. ROSE sb. + PINK sb.]

Rose-rash. *Path.* [f. ROSE sb. + RASH sb.]

Rose-red, a. and sb. [f. ROSE sb. + RED a. or sb.]

Roseola (rōzī'ōla). *Path.* [mod.L., f. *rōse-us* rosy + dimin. suffix -ola; cf. F. *roséole*.] A rash of rosy spots or eruptions occurring in measles and similar diseases; also, false or German measles.

Roseolar, a. *Path.* [f. prec. + -AR.] Of or pertaining to, or of the nature of, roseola.

Roseolous, a. *Path.* [-OUS.]

Roseous, a. [f. L. *rose-us* + -OUS.] Rosy, rose-coloured.

Rose-rial. *Obs.* A gold coin of the value of thirty shillings, having the figure of a rose upon one side, coined by James I.

Roset, sb. *Bot.* [var. of ROSSET.] 1. One of certain related herbaceous plants, esp. of the mullein family.

Roset[2], Sc. Also 6 rosset, 7 rossit. [Based upon ROSIN sb.] Rosin.

Rose-scented, a. [f. ROSE sb.] Having the perfume of a rose.

Rose-tree. [f. ROSE sb.] A rose-bush or -tree of large size.

Rosette (rōzet'). [a. F. *rosette*, dim. of rose ROSE sb.; see -ETTE.]
1. A decoration consisting of a bunch or knot of ribbons, leather strips, worsted or the like, concentrically disposed so as to resemble a rose, and worn as an ornament or badge.

Rose-water (rōu'z-wŏ'tă). *sb.* [f. ROSE sb. + WATER sb. Cf. MDu. *rose(n)water*, Du. *rozenwater*), MLG. *rōsenwater*, MHG. *rōsenwazzer* (G. *rosenwasser*), MSw. *rōsenwater* (Sw. *rosenvatten*).]
1. Water distilled from roses, or impregnated with essence of roses, and used as a perfume, etc.

Rose-window, sb. *Archit.* [f. ROSE sb. + WINDOW sb.] A circular window, divided into compartments by mullions radiating from a centre, or filled with tracery suggestive of the form of a rose; a Catherine or marigold window.

Rosewood. [f. ROSE sb. + WOOD sb.]
1. One of several kinds of valuable, fragrant, close-grained cabinet-wood, chiefly that yielded by tropical leguminous trees of the genus *Dalbergia* (esp. *D. nigra*) and *Machaerium*; also, a tree yielding this wood.

[This page is a column from the Oxford English Dictionary. The entries are set in extremely small type across multiple columns and include the following principal headwords:]

Rosewood. — **Rose-wort.** — **Rosial.** — **Rosiar.** — **Rosical.** — **Rosicler.** — **Rosicrucian.** — **Rosied.** — **Rosier.** — **Rosily.** — **Rosin.** — **Rosinante.** — **Rosined.** — **Rosiness.** — **Rosing.** — **Rosinous.** — **Rosiny.** — **Rosy.**

Rostel. — **Rostellar.** — **Rostellate.** — **Rostelliform.** — **Rostellum.** — **Rostrate.** — **Rostrated.** — **Rostriferous.** — **Rostriform.** — **Rostrous.** — **Rostrulate.** — **Rostrulum.** — **Rostrum.** — **Rosulate.** — **Rosy.** — **Rot.**

Rosmarine. — **Rosmarine.** — **Rosminian.** — **Rossals.** — **Rosse.** — **Rossel.** — **Rosselled.** — **Rosset.** — **Rosolic.** — **Rosolio.** — **Rosoignal.** — **Rossen.** — **Rosser.** — **Rossignol.** — **Rossiing.** — **Rossel.** — **Rosting-machine.** — **Rosslynge.** — **Rot.** — **Rossome.** — **Rossy.**

Rosyrusian. — **Rosy-fingered.** — **Rosyn.** — **Rot.**

Alch. 69 Abusing himself in all blasphemies, riot and excess, in due time the Rot, or the Pox overtook them. 1836 Encycl. Brit. (ed. 7) XIV. 510/2 The disease called grinder's rot, an incurable consumption. 1898 [see Grinder 9].

† b. In the imprecation Rot on or upon. Obs.

1604 Heywood Captives II. ii. in Bullen O. Pl. IV, Rott on that villeyne! no. 1638 Cowley Love's Riddle I, A rott upon you; you must still be humoured. Ibid. IV, Rot on your possibles.

4. Decay in timber or other vegetable products, stone, etc. See also Dry-rot.

1830 Lyell Princ. Geol. I. 217 The rock may with propriety be said to have the rot, for it crumbles to pieces in the hand. 1841 Emerson Man the Reformer Wks. (Bohn) II. 240 Every species of property is preyed on by its own enemies, as iron by rust, timber by rot. 1868 Rep. U. S. Comm. Agric. (1869) 214 Low, wet soils almost invariably produce rot in the berry. 1882 De Windt Equator 85 Enormous holes in the bamboo flooring occasioned by rot.

5. slang. Nonsensical rubbish; trash, bosh.

1848 Shilleto in Whibley In Cap & Gown (1890) 228 Your Natural-rot, your Moral-bosh. 1857 Hughes Tom Brown vi, Let's stick to him and talk no more rot. 1882 Miss Braddon Mt. Royal III. i. 13 You are just the sort of woman to believe in that kind of rot.

6. Cricket. A rapid break-down or fall of wickets during an innings. Also transf.

1884 Lillywhite's Cricket Ann. 64 After this came the rot, and the total only reached 118. 1901 Westm. Gaz. 24 Apr. 2/3 It is to be hoped that something can be done (as cricketers would say) to 'stop the rot'.

7. Comb., as rot-disease, epidemic, -proof, -proofed, -stricken; † rot-bean (see quot.); rot-grass, one or other of several plants supposed to cause rot in sheep (see quots.); rot-heap, a rubbish-heap; rot-steep (see quot. 1838); rot-stone, = rotten-stone.

1726 Petiveriana I. 180 Barbadoes *Rot-bean,..Jetaiba Barbad. lobis minoribus. 1864 T. S. Cobbold Entozoa 173 The main facts relating to the origin..of the *rot-disease. Ibid. 172 The *rot epidemic of 1824. 1631 R. H. Arraignm. Whole Creature ix. 69 They are as *rot grasse to sheepe. 1794 Hutchinson Hist. Cumb. I. App. 39 Pinguicula vulgaris, Rot-grass, supposed highly injurious to sheep, on moist grounds. 1844 H. Stephens Bk. Farm I. 330 Melica cærulea,..fly-bent or rot-grass. 1863 Prior Brit. Plants 192 Rot-grass, from its being supposed to bane sheep, a grass in the sense of herbage, Pinguicula vulgaris. 1881 Miss Ormerod Man. Injurious Ins. 43 Burning the infested old cabbage-stocks.., instead of throwing them into *rot-heaps. 1870 Daily News 19 Aug. 2 Blocks of wood on end, with gravel pounded between, the whole made permanently waterproof and *rotproof. 1884 Health Exhib. Cat. 90/1 Rotproof Non-poisonous Wall Linings. Ibid. 104/2 Hammock Awnings, comprising also *Rotproofed specimens. 1838 T. Thomson Chem. Org. Bodies 396 The cloth is steeped in a weak alkaline ley to remove the weaver's dressing. This is technically called the *rot steep. 1874 W. Crookes Dyeing & Cal.-printing 45 The 'rot steep', so called because the flour or size with which the goods were impregnated was formerly allowed to ferment and putrefy. 1819 Scott Leg. Montrose vi, The soldier, who was..burnishing his corslet with *rot-stone and shamois-leather. 1897 Month June 638 One who..had allowed human beings to perish like *rot-stricken sheep.

† **Rot**, sb.[2] Obs. [a. Du. rot neut., or G. rotte fem., a. OF. rotte, rote, route, Rout sb.[1]] A file (of soldiers). Cf. Rat sb.[5] Also attrib.

1635 Barriffe Mil. Discipl. cxx. (1643) 417 The other thirty two rots of Muskettiers belonging to the middle squadron. 1637 Monro Expedit., etc. II. Abridgm. Exerc. 183 There must be nine Rots of Pikemen, which have the Right hand, and twelve Rots of Musketiers on the left hand. Ibid., Two are esteemed as Leaders, being a Corporall a Rot-master or Leader, and an under Rot-master.

† **Rot**, a. Obs. [f. Rot v. Cf. Du. rot, LG. röt, rot.] Rotten; decayed.

1598 Bp. Hall Sat. IV. iv. 118 Byting on Annis-seede, and Rose-marine, Which might the Fume of his rot lungs refine. 1620 Westward for Smelts (Percy Soc.) 19 Her teeth were rot, Her tongue was not. 1631 R. H. Arraignm. Whole Creature xiv. 235 Those things..are as rot as our Irish bogs, or English Quagmires. 1707 Mortimer Husb. (1721) I. 189 A good quantity of..well-rot Dung and Earth mixt together.

Rot (rɒt), v. Forms: 1 rotian, 3 rotien, 3–4 rotie, 3–5 rotye, 5 rootye; 3–5 roten, 5 rotyn (rooton); 4 roote, 4–5 root, 5 royt; 4–6 rote, rotte, 4– rot. [Common Teut.: OE. rotian, = Fris. rotsje, MDu. roten, rotten (Du. rotten), OS. rotôn (MLG. roten, LG. rötten), OHG. rozzên; Icel. rota (trans.), obs. Da. rodde, røde: see Rotten a., and cf. the etym. note to Ret v.[2]]

1. intr. Of animal substances: To undergo natural decomposition; to decay, putrefy, through disease, mortification, or death.

c 897 K. Ælfred Gregory's Past. C. xxi. 153 Swa se læce, ðonne he on untiman lacnað wunde, hio wyrmseð & rotað. c 1000 Sax. Leechd. II. 264 Manegum men lungen rotað. c 1055 Byrhtferth's Handboc in Anglia VIII. 299 Mid þam man smyrað ricra manna lic þæt hiꝫ rotian ne maꝫon. c 1200 Ormin 4773 He warrþ all..secnedd, Swa swiþe þatt hiss bodiꝫ toc To rotenn bufenn eorþe. c 1275 Serving Christ 72 in O. E. Misc. 92 Boþe him schal rotye þat body and þe bon. 13.. Sir Beues 1697 Her I legge al to-blowe, And roteþ me flesch fro þe bon. 1387 Trevisa Higden (Rolls) I. 363 Þere is an ilond, þere no dede body may roty. c 1440 Jacob's Well 125 Þanne fell on his fote a maladye, þat it rotyd. c 1520 L. Andrew Noble Lyfe L ij, Than the fedders of the goshawke rote of yᵉ dounge of ardea as far as it toucheth. 1548 Udall, etc. Erasm. Par. Acts ii. 9 b, Although his bodye was laid in graue voyde of all lyfe, yet ther it did not rotte or putrify. 1602 Shaks. Ham. v. i. 179 How long will a man lie i' th' earth ere he rot? 1737 Gentl. Mag. VII. 117/2 The rest are stark dead, and may rot when they list. 1791 Cowper Iliad IV. 212 Where he left his brother's bones to rot. 1887 Morris Odyss. XII. 46 Dead men rotting to nothing.

b. Similarly of other substances liable to natural decay, as timber, fruit, vegetable matter, etc.

c 897 K. Ælfred Gregory's Past. C. xxii. 171 Of ðæm treowe sethim, ðæt næfre ne rotað. c 1000 Ælfric Exod. xvi. 24 Hit [sc. the manna] ne rotode. c 1200 Vices & Virtues 91 Hier is igadered swilch timber ðe nature rotien ne mai. c 1250 Gen. & Ex. 3342 It [the manna] wirmede, bredde, and rotede ðor. a 1300 Cursor M. 23893 Þat þat besaunt rote noght in hord. 1382 Wyclif Isaiah xl. 20 The stronge tree, and the vnable to roten, ches the wise craftes man. c 1400 Maundev. (Roxb.) ii. 5 Cedre may noȝt rote in erthe ne in water. 1470–85 Malory Morte Arth. XVII. vi. 698 She lete make a..clothe of sylke that shold neuer rote for no maner of weder. 1530 Palsgr. 694/1 This peare wyll rotte if you eate it nat betyme. 1581 Mulcaster Positions vi. (1887) 40 Like corne not reaped, but suffered to rotte by negligence of the owner. 1630 R. Johnson's Kingd. & Commw. 540 Yet..the Grasse groweth at least one yard high, and rotteth..upon the ground. 1687 A. Lovell tr. Thevenot's Trav. I. 136 Sycamore-Wood..that does not rot so soon as other Wood. 1726 Leoni Alberti's Archit. I. 34/1 There will be some small unconcocted Stones in it, which afterwards coming to rot, throw out little Pustules. 1748 Anson's Voy. II. iv. 219 Several of her casks had rotted. 1822 Shelley When the Lamp iv, From thy nest every rafter Will rot. 1858 Glenny Everyday Bk. 203/2 Piled in a stack, till the grass and fibre all rot together. 1876 J. Saunders Lion in Path i, Still year after year the fruit has rotted and dropped.

c. In pa. pple. used predicatively.

c 1290 St. James 301 in S. Eng. Leg. I. 43 Þis ȝoungue Man sixe and þritti dawes heng up-on þe galu-treo Are is fader a-ȝein to him come, þat i-roted he auȝte to beo. c 1350 Will. Palerne 4124 For many a day hade i be ded & to dust roted, nadde it be goddes grace. 1387 Trevisa Higden (Rolls) VI. 475 Whan here body was i-take up of þe erþe it was i-founde al i-roted and i-torned into powder. 1419 in Ellis Orig. Lett. Ser. II. I. 69 The Kele..is rotyt and must be chaungyd. 1561 Hollybush Hom. Apoth. 27 If the iaundis were rotted in a man. 1593 Shaks. Lucr. 823 The branches of another roote are rotted. 1668 [see next]. 1726 Leoni Alberti's Archit. I. 7/1 Stones..in Buildings, if their Tops are..rotted, shew the Intemperature of the Air. 1872 Bushnell Serm. Living Subj. 369 They are humbled to a point so low by their idols, rotted into falsehood, buried in lust and shame.

d. With away, off, out.

c 1440 Alph. Tales 64 Þer happend a surans for to fall in hys lymbe, þat his fute rotid off. a 1548 Hall Chron., Rich. III, 28 Myles Forest, at saint Martyns le graunde by pece meale miserably rotted awaye. 1607 Shaks. Timon IV. iii. 63 Thy lips rot off. 1668 Culpepper & Cole Barthol. Anat. III. ix. 149 Some Scythians, whose earlets ar mortified and rotted of with cold. 1678 Illingsworth (title), A Just Narrative, or Account of the Man whose Hands and Legs rotted off in the Parish of Kingswinford. 1802–12 Bentham Ration. Judic. Evid. (1827) I. 398 Say, you wish your tongue may rot off,..if you ever saw any such thing. 1849 Lyell 2nd Visit U. S. II. 137 Some of the trunks must have rotted away to the level of the ground.

2. fig. in various contexts, chiefly denoting decay of a moral or abstract kind.

a 1225 Ancr. R. 84 Þeo þet rotieð and stinkeð al ine fulðe of hore sunnen. 1382 Wyclif Jer. xiii. 9 Thus to roten Y shal make the pride of Juda. 1393 Langl. P. Pl. C. VI. 151 Ryght so religion roteþ and sterueth. 1460 Rolls of Parlt. V. 377/2 Though right for a tyme rest and bee put to silence, yet it roteth not ner shall not perissh. 1594 T. B. La Primaud. Fr. Acad. II. 271 If wee staye and as it were rotte in these base, brutish and supposed pleasures. 1707 M. Henry Serm. Wks. 1853 II. 597/1 It is true of prayer, what we say of winter, that it never rots in the skies. 1838 Lytton Alice VI. v, Take the history of any civilised state before she rotted back into second childhood. 1870 Lowell Study Windows 25 If they are cheated, it is, at worst, only of a superfluous hour, which was rotting on their hands. 1891 Spectator 13 June, A kind of society..which always ends, sooner or later, by rotting down.

3. Of persons: To become affected with some putrescent or wasting disease, esp. as the result of confinement in jail.

1340 Ayenb. 32 Þe ilke anlikneþ þane ssrewe þet heþ leuere rotye in a prison [etc.]. 1393 Langl. P. Pl. C. XIV. 22 Lo, how pacience..brouhte hem al aboue þat in bale rotede. 1542–3 Act 34 & 35 Hen. VIII, c. 8 § 1 Many rotte, and perishe to death for lacke of helpe of surgery. 1587 Golding De Mornay xxvii. (1592) 437 If I in the meane whyle do rotte there [in prison]. 1692 Covenant of Grace 11, I might use extremity towards you, cast you into Prison, and there let you Rot. 1758 Johnson Idler No. 22 ¶ 5 Some will confess their resolution that their debtors shall rot in gaol. 1784 Cowper Task III. 805 He..Can dig, beg, rot, and perish. 1889 Jessopp Coming of Friars i. 6 The civil authorities took no account of them as long as they quietly rotted and died.

b. Of sheep: To become affected with the rot.

1523 Fitzherb. Husb. § 66 If thou waine thy calues with hey,..the rather they wyll rotte whan they come to grasse. 1596 Harington Metam. Ajax (1814) 3 The poor sheep would eat him without salt (as they say); but if they do, they will soon after rot with it. 1637 Milton Lycidas 127 The hungry Sheep..Rot inwardly, and foul contagion spread. 1683 Tryon Way to Health 88 Over-wet Weather will corrupt them, and cause them to Rot in moist low Grounds.

4. trans. To affect with decomposition, putrescence, or decay; to corrupt, make rotten.

c 1386 Chaucer Cook's T. 43 Wel bet is roten Appul out of hoord, Than þat it rotie al the remenaunt. 1557 North Guevara's Diall Pr. 442 Let an apple have never so little a broose, that broose is ynough to rotte him quickely. 1572 Bossewell Armorie II. 118 Her dung is poyson to the Hauke, and rotteth her fethers. 1604 Hieron Wks. I. 504 He shewed His justice in rotting it at the other time. 1672 Marvell Reh. Transp. I. 132 A Dart, that where it does but draw blood, rots the person immediately to pieces. 1726 Leoni Alberti's Archit. I. 58/1 To keep the mortar from rotting the Timber. 1733 Tull Horse-hoeing Husb. 68 It is long continual Rains that Rot or Chill the Blossoms. 1820 W. Scoresby Acc. Arctic Reg. I. 271 The salt in the sea.. destroys the tenacity of the bay-ice.., and, in the language of the whale-fisher, completely rots it. 1889 Anthony's Photogr. Bull. II. 241 It is necessary to rot or sweat ink after it is ground from ten to twenty-four hours.

refl. 1606 Shaks. Ant. & Cl. I. iv. 47 This common bodie ..Goes too, and backe,..To rot it selfe with motion. 1649 Blithe Eng. Improv. Impr. (1653) 113 Many of your Cold, Sowr, Rushy Pastures, Rot themselves though never plowed.

b. fig. Also const. with off, out.

1567 Trial Treas. in Hazl. Dodsley III. 284 The Ruler of all rulers will..rot their remembrance off from the ground. 1579 Tomson Calvin's Serm. Tim. 116/2 We shall see these vermine that seeke nothing else but to rotte or venime the Church of God. 1628 Ford Lover's Mel. I. ii, Why shouldn't I..snarl at the vices Which rot the land. 1848 Lytton Harold IX. ii, Better that we had rotted out our lives in exile. 1871 Carlyle in Daily News 4 Jan., This I lay at the door of our spiritual teachers.., who thereby incalculably rot the world.

c. spec. To ret. Cf. Rotting vbl. sb. 2.

1835–6 Encycl. Metrop. (1845) VIII. 702/1 The operation of rotting, or as it is most commonly called, water-retting, flax and hemp.

5. To affect (sheep) with the rot. Also absol.

c 1380 Wyclif Wks. (1880) 408 Þanne be lediþ his sheep wel in hool pasture þat wole not rote. 1523 Fitzherb. Husb. § 54 It is necessary that a shepeherde shoulde knowe what thynge rotteth shepe. 1588 Shaks. Tit. A. IV. iv. 93 More dangerous Then baites to fish, or hony stalkes to sheepe, When as the one is wounded with the baite, The other rotted with delicious foode. a 1656 Vines Lord's Supper (1677) 221 No shepherd would call his sheep into such pastures as will certainly rot them. 1725 Ramsay Gentle Sheph. I. ii, Blashy thows..may rot your ews. 1794 Trans. Soc. Arts XII. 235 Produce of the land..very rushy,..and always rotted sheep. 1854 Jrnl. R. Agric. Soc. XV. I. 234 Apparently sound pastures..have rotted sheep this Season.

6. Used in imprecations against a person or thing, sometimes merely an outburst of irritation or impatience.

1588 Shaks. Titus A. V. i. 58 But vengeance rot you all. 1611 — Cymb. II. iii. 136 The South-Fog rot him. 1664 Cotton Scarronides I. Wks. (1715) 37 Where once your what shall's call'ums—(rot em, It makes me mad I have forgot 'em), Liv'd a great while. 1682 Dryden Prol. to Southerne's Loyal Brother 5 Both pretend love, and both (plague rot 'em!) hate. 1709 Steele Tatler No. 73 ¶ 2 Rot you, Sir, I have more Wit than you. 1756 Foote Engl. fr. Paris II, I'll be rot if we don't make them caper higher. 1767 S. Paterson Anoth. Trav. II. 52 Rot the name of the first post! I have forgot it. 1817 Keats Lett. Wks. 1889 III. 74 For, rot it! I forgot to bring my mathematical case with me. 1859 Dickens T. Two Cities II. v, 'She was the admiration of the whole Court!' 'Rot the admiration of the whole Court!'

7. slang. To chaff severely. Also absol., to talk nonsense. (Cf. Rot sb.[1] 5.)

1890 Lehmann H. Fludyer at Cambridge 106 Everybody here would have rotted me to death. 1899 Phillpotts Human Boy 169 Freckles, who was an awfully sportsman-like chap really, said he was only rotting all the time.

Rota (rōu·tă). [a. L. rota wheel.]

1. A political club, founded in 1659 by J. Harrington, which advocated rotation in the offices of Government; also, a society of this type.

1660 Harrington (title), The Censure of the Rota upon Mr. Milton's Book, entituled, The Ready and Easie way to Establish A Free Common-wealth. 1662 in J. Ogilby King's Coronation (1685) 3, I..With Common-wealths and Rota's fill their heads. a 1680 Butler Characters, Politician, A speculative Statesman,..that did all his Exercises in the late Times of cursed Memory at the Rota, but is not yet admitted to practise.

attrib. 1664 Butler Hud. II. iii. 1108 As full of tricks, As Rota-men of Politicks. 1673 Character Coffee-House in Harl. Misc. (1745) VI. 429 A Coffee-House is ..a Rota Room, that, like Noah's Ark, receives animals of every Sort. 1691 Wood Ath. Oxon. II. 439 Dr. Will. Petty was a Rota-man and would sometimes trouble Ja. Harrington in his Club.

2. A rotation (of persons, etc.); a round or routine (of duties, etc.); † a rote.

1673 Ray Journ. Low C. 425 These [councillors] are taken out of the great Council, and go round in a rota. 1710 Palmer Proverbs 95 Such Formal Devotions that are nothing but a Rota. 1751 R. Paltock P. Wilkins (1884) I. 186 The..occurrences which happened during this period.. consisted chiefly of the old rota of fishing, watering [etc.]. 1800 Colquhoun Comm. Thames 631 Perambulating the River..agreeably to a rota which is laid down. 1844 in Ribton-Turner Vagrants & Vagrancy (1887) 254 The experience of those managers who have taken their rota of duty in the office. 1868 Rogers Pol. Econ. xiii. (1876) 10 According to a rota to be agreed on between each other.

b. A list of persons acting in rotation; a roster.

1856 Hughes Tom Brown I. vii, The senior fag who kept the rota. 1878 Stubbs Const. Hist. III. xx. 419 Pleas of debt, which required the attendance of the parties to suits and the rota of qualified jurors. 1882 Keary Outl. Prim. Belief ix. 437 They heard names called over and voices answering as if by rota.

3. R. C. Ch. The supreme court for ecclesiastical and secular causes. (Cf. Rote sb.[5] 2).

1679 Burnet Hist. Ref. I. 50 At that time Staphileus Dean of the Rota was there. 1685 Lond. Gaz. No. 2081/1 The Republick of Venice have named four Persons for the Pope to chuse one, to fill the Place of Auditor of the Rota. 1728 Chambers Cycl. s.v., The Rota consists of twelve Doctors, chosen out of the four Nations of Italy, France, Spain, and Germany. 1765 Blackstone Comm. I. Introd. 15 To tell the king's courts at Westminster, that their practice is..conformable to the decrees of the Rota or Imperial Chamber. 1845 S. Austin Ranke's Hist. Ref. III. 149 He also claimed the holidays of the Roman rota for himself. 1877 D. Lewis tr. Sander's De Schism. Anglica Introd. p. lxxiv, The next day was the day of the Conference with the Dean of the Rota. 1908 Westm. Gaz. 6 July 5/1 A special law for regulating the working of the ancient tribunals, the Rota, and the Segnatura.

Rotacism, -ize, variants of Rhotacism, -ize.

Rotal (rōu·tăl), a. [ad. late L. rotāl-is wheeled, or f. rota (see prec.) + -al.]

1. Pertaining to a wheel or wheels. Also fig.

1656 Blount Glossogr., Rotal, of or belonging to a wheel [ed. 1674 adds, also inconstant, now up, now down]. 1881 Illustr. Lond. News 5 Nov. 439/2 The Cannebière is in a chronic state of vocal and rotal tumult.

2. Pertaining to rotation or circular motion.

1855 Ogilvie Suppl., Rotal action of affinity, a term applied to the inductive action of affinity, as exhibited in the voltaic circle, in which it assumes a circular direction or return upon itself.

3. R. C. Ch. Connected with the Rota.

1907 Cath. Weekly 8 Nov. 8/2 On November 12 the Sacred Congregation of Rites will hold a rotal meeting.

Rotalian (rotēⁱ·liăn), sb. and a. Zool. [f. mod.L. Rotalia (Lamarck, 1809), neut. pl. of late L. rotālis: see prec.]

A. sb. A foraminifer of the genus Rotalia.

1869 Monthly Microsc. Jrnl. 303 If one of the simple Rotalians were thickened and drawn out at the umbilici. 1879 Carpenter in Encycl. Brit. IX. 380/2 The..spiral mode of growth differs entirely from that of ordinary Rotalians.

B. adj. Of or belonging to the genus Rotalia.

1862 Carpenter Microsc. (ed. 3) 517 The two great series which may be designated (after the leading forms of each) as the Textularian and the Rotalian. 1879 — in Encycl. Brit. IX. 380/1 This intermediate skeleton..completely envelops the original rotalian shell.

Rotalid (rōu·tălid), sb. and a. Zool. [See prec. and -id.] a. sb. A foraminifer of the family Rotalidea. b. adj. Belonging to this family.

1888 Rolleston & Jackson Anim. Life 886 Exceptions to this rule however occur among the Rotalid Tinoporinae. Ibid. 892 There appear within the adult minute young with calcareous tests,..three-chambered in the Rotalid.

Rota·liform, a. Zool. [See prec. and -form.] Having the typical form of the genus Rotalia.

1888 Rolleston & Jackson Anim. Life 895 Typically spiral and 'Rotaliform', i. e. coiled so that the whole of the segments are visible on the superior surface.

Rotaline (rōu·tăləin), a. and sb. [ad. mod.L. Rotalina: see Rotalian.]

A. adj. Of or belonging to the Rotalina, a sub-family of Rotalidea.

1862 Carpenter, etc. Introd. Foraminif. 212 It is in the true Rotalinæ..that we meet with the highest development of the Rotaline type. 1888 Rolleston & Jackson Anim. Life 889 Calcareous spicules..make up its Rotaline test.

B. sb. A member of the Rotalina.

1862 Carpenter, etc. Introd. Foraminif. 200 Certain shells ranked by D'Orbigny under the genus Valvulina are true Rotalines. 1879 H. A. Nicholson Palæont. I. 116 One of the earliest representatives of the Rotalines.

† **Rotan.** slang. Obs.—⁰ (See quot.)

1725 New Cant. Dict., Rotan, a Coach, or Waggon, any thing that runs upon Wheels; but principally a Cart.

Rotang (rotæ·ŋ). Also 7 rottang. [ad. Malay rōtan: see Rattan. So F. and G. rotang, F. rotin, Du. rotting.] One of the rattan palms. Also attrib. with cane, palm.

[1598 W. Phillip tr. Linschoten I. xvi. 28 There is another sorte of the same reeds which they call Rota: these are thinne like twigges of Willow for baskets.]

1662 J. Davies tr. Mandelslo's Trav. 134 From their Neighbours they fetch Timber to build withall, Rottang, that is, cordage of Cocoe. 1697 Phil. Trans. XIX. 590 Anchors of Iron and Wood, Cables of Rotang Canes. 1771 Encycl. Brit. II. 8/1 There is but one species [of calamus], viz. the rotang, a native of India. 1846 Lindley Veget. Kingd. 135 The Calami, or Rotangs, and the siliceous secretions of their leaves, indicate an affinity with Grasses. 1884 Longman's Mag. June 191 Spindle-trees grew side by side with prickly Rotang palms.

Rotary (rōu·tări), a. and sb. [ad. late L. rotāri-us (Quicherat), f. rota wheel: see -ary.]

A. adj. 1. Of motion: Circular; taking place round a centre or axis.

1731 Bailey, vol. II, Rotary, of or pertaining to a wheel; whirling or turning round, as a rotary motion. 1815 J. Smith Panorama Sci. & Art I. 330 A rotary motion is very frequently transmitted by means of an endless strap. 1853 Kane Grinnell Exped. xv. (1856) 113 During its rotary oscillations against the bottom of the sea. 1867 Denison Astron. 10 But the rotary motion of the earth is of no use for measuring latitude.

Comb. 1883 Wheel World Mar. 185 The 'Orbi-cycle', a rotary-motioned front steerer.

2. Operating by means of rotation; rotative.

Used spec. to designate a large number of machines in which the action depends on the rotation of some part.

1799 Repertory Arts X. 303 Similar effects may be produced..by a rotary cutter. 1838 Civil Eng. & Arch. Jrnl. I. 139/1 The expansive principle would not answer for rotary or double engines. 1844 Grove Contrib. Sci. 351 Two sets of magnets are employed, the one set stationary, and the other rotary. 1884 J. Burroughs Locusts & Wild H. 118 All our general storms are cyclonic in their character, that is, rotary and progressive.

3. Of persons: Acting in rotation.

1862 Congregationalist 30 May (Cent.), Several years since they..became an Independent Presbyterian church with a rotary board of elders.

B. sb. A rotary machine or apparatus.

1888 Jacobi Printer's Vocab. 115 Rotary, a short term for rotary printing machines. 1890 W. J. Gordon Foundry 203 This machine gives twice the speed of the early rotaries.

Ro·tascope. [f. L. rota wheel: see -scope.] A kind of gyroscope.

1832 W. R. Johnson in Silliman's Jrnl. XXI. 265 Description of an Apparatus called the Rotascope, for exhibiting several phenomena and illustrating certain laws of rotary motion. 1873 Spon's Dict. Engin. VII. 2440 The gyroscope or rotascope, an instrument illustrating the tendency of rotating bodies to preserve their plane of rotation.

Rotatable (rotēⁱ·tăb'l), a. [f. Rotate v. + -able.] Capable of being rotated; admitting of rotation or rotatory movement.

1875 Knight Dict. Mech. 1926/1 Sims's uterine repositor consists of a short metallic sounder, rotatable on a long shaft. 1889 Sci. Amer. LX. 306/3 The rotatable blade is designed to do the general work of the pressman in making forms ready.

Rotate (rōu·tēⁱt), a. Bot. [f. L. rota wheel + -ate[2].] Wheel-shaped; esp. of a monopetalous corolla with a short tube and spreading limb.

1785 Martyn Rousseau's Bot. xii. 129 This genus is easily known by the monopetalous, rotate or wheel-shaped corol. 1830 Lindley Nat. Syst. Bot. 206 Corolla superior, monopetalous or polypetalous, rotate or tubular. 1872 Oliver Elem. Bot. II. 211 A perennial herb, with..scorpioid cymes of rotate bright-blue flowers.

† **Rotate**, pa. pple. Obs. [ad. L. rotāt-us, pa. pple. of rotāre: see next.] Revolved.

1471 Ripley Comp. Alch. II. viii. in Ashm. (1652) 137 Thyngs into thyngs must therfore be rotate, Untyll dyversyte be brought to parfyt unyte.

Rotate (rotēⁱ·t), v. [f. L. rotāt-, ppl. stem of rotāre to turn or swing round, whirl about, roll round, revolve, f. rota wheel.]

1. intr. To move round a centre or axis; to perform one or more revolutions.

1808 Med. Jrnl. XIX. 899 Permitting the corresponding part of the bone to rotate upon it. 1853 Kane Grinnell Exped. xxxvii. (1856) 339 Our brig had..rotated considerably to the northward. 1858 Lockyer Elem. Astron. § 104 The Sun, like the Earth or a top when spinning, turns round, or rotates, on an axis.

2. trans. To cause (a thing) to turn round or revolve on a centre or axis.

1831 Knox Cloquet's Anat. 366 It brings the thigh toward that of the opposite side, bends it a little, and carries it outward by rotating it. 1844 G. Dodd Textile Manuf. i. 38 The warper..rotates the vertical wheel or frame..by means of the wheel..and the rope. 1878 Huxley Physiogr. 193 Sometimes the masses of lava are rotated in their flight.

3. To change, or take, in rotation.

1879 J. Hawthorne S. Strome I. iii. 36 She could mow a field, drain it, plough it, and rotate its crops. 1894 Sperry Talks w. Young Men 159 It is wise to alternate, or rotate the various forms of life's duties so as to secure daily, restful change, both physical and mental.

4. To put out in turn.

1881 Harper's Mag. LXIII. 265 Both, after a brief service, were rotated out of office.

Hence **Rota·ted** ppl. a.

1844 A. Dods (title), Pathological Observations on the rotated or contorted Spine,..called Lateral Curvature.

† **Rotated**, a. Bot. Obs. = Rotate a.

1753 Chambers' Cycl. Suppl. App. s.v. Petal, The second class is of the plants with..rotated, or wheel-like flowers. 1797 Encycl. Brit. (ed. 3) III. 442/2 The figure of Solids is either..Rotated, wheel-shaped, plain [etc.].

Rotating (rotēⁱ·tiŋ), ppl. a. [f. Rotate v.]

1. a. Turning round on a centre or axis.

1854 Emerson Lett. & Soc. Aims, Resources, Our Copernican globe is a great factory or shop of power with its rotating constellations. 1863 Tyndall Heat i. 10 The edge of a swiftly rotating wheel. 1875 Bedford Sailor's Pocket Bk. iv. (ed. 2) 82 If the veering of the former, and the marked fall of the latter prove the gale to be rotating, or cyclonic.

b. Causing rotation; rotatory.

1883 J. Millington Are we to read backwards? 67 The rotating muscles have a much more numerous amount of contractions to effect.

2. Acting in rotation; rotative.

1884 Athenæum 19 Jan. 82/3 Four rotating regents conducted the classes of philosophy or arts.

Rotation (rotēⁱ·ʃən). [ad. L. rotātiōn-em, n. of action f. rotāre: see Rotate v. and -ation. So F. rotation, Sp. rotacion, It. rotazione.]

1. The action of moving round a centre, or of turning round (and round) on an axis; also, the action of producing a motion of this kind.

1555 Eden Decades (Arb.) 185 The rotation or impulsion of the heauens. 1594 Plat Jewell-ho. II. 37 A trew & philosophicall rotation whereby the inwarde fire of nature may be stirred vppe in euery vegetable. 1605 Timme Quersit. I. ii. 8 By the yearly and continual rotation and reuolution of the right heauen,..all thinges might be well gouerned. 1661 Glanvill Van. Dogm. 158 [A] puzled Candidate,..being ask'd what a circle was, describ'd it by the rotation of his hand. a 1680 Butler Rem. (1759) I. 318 All Rotations and Wheelings cause a kind of Giddiness in the Brain. 1720 Welton Suffer. Son of God I. viii. 200, I see..all Things..as if they were whirl'd about by the Quick Rotation of a Wheel. 1784 Cowper Task III. 160 Some.. tell us whence the stars;..what gave them first Rotation. 1815 J. Smith Panorama Sci. & Art I. 559 His diurnal rotation is believed to be performed in 10 hours, 16 minutes, 2 seconds. 1851 Woodward Mollusca I. 64 Eyes fixed, incapable of rotation. 1876 Tait Rec. Adv. Phys. Sci. xii. (ed. 2) 294 This property of rotation may be the basis of all that to our senses appeals as matter.

fig. 1647 May Hist. Parl. I. i. 4 The perpetuall Rotation of fortune. 1700 Congreve Way of World II. iv, She has that everlasting rotation of tongue. 1710 Palmer Proverbs 245 A jest keeps an ill story alive and in countenance, and gives it a rotation.

2. The fact of coming round again in succession; return or recurrence; a recurring series or period.

1610 Healey St. Aug. Citie of God XXI. 17. 858 That rotation, and circumvolution of misery and blisse, which he [Origen] held, that all mankind should run in. a 1676 Hale Prim. Orig. Man. (1677) 150 That by a kind of circulation or rotation Arts have their successive invention and perfection. 1756 C. Lucas Ess. Waters I. 172 Medicines..suffer a rotation of fashions like our cloaths. 1765 A. Dickson Treat. Agric. (ed. 2) 47 It observes a constant rotation, and is conveyed regularly from the earth to the air, and from the air to the earth. 1779 J. Moore View Soc. Fr. (1789) I. xxix. 244 There is a constant rotation of society at Ferney. 1847 W. C. L. Martin The Ox 33/1 It is not.. until the close of the third [year] that the [teeth] next in rotation succeed. 1890 W. J. Gordon Foundry 127 The Earl of Seafield's forest.., which is regularly planted and felled so as to cut a thousand acres annually on a rotation of sixty years.

b. Regular and recurring succession in office, duties, etc., of a number of persons. Freq. in phr. by or in rotation.

The recent adoption of this sense in general use is noticed in the British Mag. for April 1763 (IV. 542), and ascribed to 'advertisements from the Police relating to the justices sitting by rotation, the felony-rotation in Bow-street', etc.

1656 Harrington Oceana (1700) 54 Equal Rotation is equal vicissitude in Government, or succession to Magistracy confer'd for such convenient terms..as take in the whole body by parts. 1660 Milton Free Commw. Wks. 1851 V. 439 A numerous Assembly of them all form'd and conven'd on purpose with the wariest Rotation. a 1721 Sheffield (Dk. Buckhm.) Wks. (1753) II. 180 This is no small advantage in Republicks, where a sort of rotation is necessary, by which men are seen under several capacities. 1762 Falconer Shipwr. II. 483 So the brave mariners their pumps attend, And help incessant by rotation lend. 1800 Colquhoun Comm. Thames xiii. 366 Five of the twenty-one Directors shall go out of office by rotation every year. 1833 Ht. Martineau Manch. Strike 73 Three members.. sit daily,..viz., the treasurer, secretary, and one of the other members in rotation. 1888 Bryce Amer. Commw. (1890) II. 88 In America..the tendency is towards 'rotation' in office.

c. Agric. A change or succession of crops in a certain order on a given piece of ground, in order to avoid the exhaustion of the soil.

1778 [W. Marshall] Minutes Agric. Digest 76 A regular rotation of Crops and Fallow is, perhaps, more convenient than profitable. 1792 Young Trav. France 346 The effects derived from the rotation of crops. Ibid., The miserable rotations commonly practised in France. 1845 McCulloch Taxation II. vi. (1852) 247 By narrowing the demand for barley, and obliging the farmers to adopt imperfect rotations. 1874 Stubbs Const. Hist. I. iii. 50 The proper rotation of crops and fallow might be observed.

3. attrib. and Comb., as rotation-movement, -tide; † rotation-office (see sense 2 b, note); rotation grasses, grasses sown in a rotation of crops.

1768 Ann. Reg., Chron. 57/2 The sitting Magistrates..at the Rotation-office in Whitechapel. 1812 Sporting Mag. XL. 283 At the Leeds Rotation-office this month, John Waddington, of Farnley.., was convicted..for shooting a hare. 1865 Proc. Amer. Phil. Soc. X. 165 Evidences of rotation-tides. 1886 Daily News 11 Dec. 6/3 As temporary pastures, that is to say, rotation grasses (including clover), are included in the arable area, one would naturally look for a proportional diminution in rotation grasses. 1899 Allbutt's Syst. Med. VII. 883 The balancing, nodding, and rotation movements are more especially likely to preserve a definite rhythm.

Rotational (rotēⁱ·ʃənăl), a. [f. prec. + -al.] Acting in rotation; of or belonging to rotation.

1852 De Morgan in Graves Life Hamilton (1889) III. 394 Members to go out by rotation each year...The rotational electors to be distributed through the year. 1870 Proctor Other Worlds v. 111 The energies indicated by mere velocity of motion, whether orbital or rotational, must be equally disregarded. 1886 Ball Story Heavens 534 In a similar manner we find the rotational moment of momentum for each of the other planets.

Rotative (rōu·tătiv), a. [f. L. rotāt-, ppl. stem of rotāre: see Rotate v. So F. rotatif, -ive.]

1. Rotating, turning round like a wheel; acting or operating by circular motion.

1778 Pryce Min. Cornub. 313 He completed both a reciprocating and a rotative or wheel engine. 1799 Repertory Arts X. 295 How, by means of a rotative saw, to shape a piece from the rough. 1822 New Monthly Mag. VI. 267 By means of rotative machinery, connected with.. a steam-engine, or other rotative power. 1877 Encycl. Brit. VI. 499/2 No rotative engine had yet been erected at Manchester.

b. Produced by rotation; producing, connected with, rotation.

1823 P. Nicholson Pract. Build. 443 Mouldings, which may be generated by planes carried round their axis' in those planes, are called rotative mouldings. 1824 W. Taylor in Monthly Rev. CIII. 193 He first advanced..the rotative doctrine. 1879 Newcomb & Holden Astron. 211 The rotative forces acting on A and B are as it were distributed.

c. Of the nature of rotation.

1846 Holtzapffel Turning II. 522 The general practice ..is to give the tool a constant rotative shuffling motion. 1868 Lockyer Elem. Astron. § 359 As the Earth's rotative movement is uniform.

2. Acting or coming in rotation; recurrent.

1813 T. Busby Lucretius II. v. Comm. p. xxv, By the rotative course of nature [the earth] is now enabled to bring forth some things which she did not yield at her beginning. 1864 R. A. Arnold Cotton Famine 372 Cotton was cultivated in India as a rotative and not as a special crop.

Rota·to-, used as combining form of mod.L. rotātus Rotate a. in rotato-dentate, -plane.

1760 J. Lee Introd. Bot. I. xiii. (1765) 34 Rotato-dentate, wheel-shaped and indented. Ibid. III. 7 Rotato-plane, wheel-shaped and flat.

Rotator (rotēⁱ·təɹ). [a. L. rotātor, agent-n. from rotāre to Rotate. Cf. F. rotateur.]

1. Anat. A muscle by which a limb or part can be moved circularly.

1676 Wiseman Surg. Treat. VII. viii. 494 The Triceps, together with the Levidus, and the four little Rotators. 1744 tr. Boerhaave's Inst. III. 254 There was no other Place where the Rotators of the Thigh could be fixed, which draw it partly outwards. 1808 Barclay Muscular Mot. 389 In rolling the arm, the rotators radial co-operate with the muscles called supinators; the rotators ulnad, with the pronators. 1893 A. S. Eccles Sciatica 74 The action will only be carried to the extent possible without using the external rotators of the thigh.

attrib. 1744 tr. Boerhaave's Inst. III. 254 The Rotator Muscles insert their Tendons into the Protuberant Process. 1899 Allbutt's Syst. Med. VIII. 31 The spasmodic action shifted from one rotator muscle to another.

2. A thing, apparatus, part, etc., which has a rotatory motion or action.

1772 Scots Mag. XXXIV. 186/2 A..machine, which he [William Kenrick] says he has contrived and denominated a Rotator. 1803 Naval Chron. X. 191 The spring part..is fixed to a rotator, or revolving apparatus. 1875 Bedford Sailor's Pocket Bk. v. (ed. 2) 161 The rotator [of a log] is a continuation of the part that holds the wheelwork. 1884 W. H. Greenwood Steel & Iron xi. 214 In the front end of the rotator are the slag-holes.

3. One of the Rotatoria; a rotifer.

1876 Beneden's Anim. Parasites 36 An animal..which is only an imperfectly described Rotator.

4. Math. (See quot.)

1879 Thomson & Tait Nat. Phil. I. i. § 345 The reciprocal of this time we shall call..the rapidity of the system, for convenience of comparison with the frequency of a vibrator or of a rotator, which is the name commonly given to the reciprocal of its period.

Rotatory (rōu·tătəri), a. and sb. [See Rotate v. and -ory.]

A. adj. 1. a. Of the nature of rotation; connected with rotation.

1755 Johnson, To Wheel,..to have a rotatory motion. 1777 Phil. Trans. LXVII. 266 A new Theory of the Rotatory Motion of Bodies affected by Forces disturbing such Motion. 1794 G. Adams Nat. & Exper. Phil. III. xxxii. 308 The obstacles in the rough road cause this rotatory motion in the wheel. 1833 Herschel Astron. vii. 234 By a sufficient rotatory velocity. 1845 Todd & Bowman Phys. Anat. I. 145 A rotatory movement at the hip-joint. 1882 Minchin Unipl. Kinematics 22 The theory of the rotatory polarisation of quartz.

b. Rotating; working by means of rotation.

1812 H. & J. Smith Rej. Addr. 89 Pure child of Chance, which still directs the ball, As rotatory atoms rise or fall. 1837 Brewster Magnet. 112 Trying if the magnetic needle would be dragged along by the rotatory plates. c 1850 Rudim. Nav. (Weale) 67 The track of five..rotatory storms. 1892 Stevenson Across the Plains ii. 93 Urging their horses with cries..and cruel rotatory spurs.

c. Causing rotation.

1828 Stark Elem. Nat. Hist. II. 444 Rotatory organ quadrilobed. 1871 T. R. Jones Anim. Kingd. (ed. 4) 476 A small oval orifice situated near the sinuated disk formed by the rotatory organs. Ibid., The rotatory apparatus.

2. Going round, or coming, in rotation.

1824 W. Taylor in Monthly Rev. CIII. 193 This principle of frequent rotatory election. 1832 W. Godwin Thoughts Man 97, I become..wearied with the repetition of rotatory acts and every-day occurrences.

B. sb. A rotifer. (Cf. Rotator 3.)

1835 Kirby Hab. & Inst. Anim. I. iv. 154 The Rotatories, to which the wheel-animalcules belong.

† **Rotch.** Sc. Obs. In 6 roche, rotche. [Of obscure origin. For later examples see Ratch sb.[1] 1.] A gun or gun-barrel.

1571 Bannatyne Jrnl. (1806) 147 There was in her..thre or foure last of powder, some croslettis, and roches of small ordinance. 1598 Reg. Privy Council Scot. V. 438 Sic peceis as salbe of the lenth of ane elne in the rotche at the leist.

Rotch(e, variants of Roche sb.[1]

Rotche (rɒtʃ). Ornith. Also rotch, roach, and Rotchie. [A later form of Rotge, but the precise source is not clear.] The little auk.

α. 1809 Edmonston Zetland Isl. II. 274 Alca Alle, Rotche, Greenland Rotche. 1843 Yarrell Brit. Birds III. 358 The Little Auk, or Common Rotche,..is only a winter visiter to the British Islands. 1894 Newton Dict. Birds 797 In Smith Sound the Rotche is said not to breed below lat. 68° or above 79°.

β. 1820 W. Scoresby Acc. Arctic Reg. I. 536, I..have observed it in pursuit of the rotch. 1831 Rennie Montagu's Ornith. Dict. 438 The Rotch has sometimes been found dead very remote from the sea. 1841 Proc. Berw. Nat. Club I. 255 The Mergulus alce, rotch, a species that breeds in very high latitudes.

γ. 1820 W. Scoresby Acc. Arctic Reg. I. 528 Alca Alle, the Little Auk, or Roach. 1823 — Jrnl. 143 An immense quantity of roaches..flew past the ship towards the west.

† **Rotchet**, obs. form of Ratchet.

1764 Ann. Reg. I. 78/2 Barrel and main spring...Great wheel and rotchet.

Rotchet(te, obs. forms of Rochet.

Ro·tchie. Ornith. = Rotche.

1831 Rennie Montagu's Ornith. Dict. 438. 1859 MacClintock Voy. 'Fox' 139 The rotchie or little auk lays its single egg upon the bare rock.

Rote (rōut), sb.[1] Now only Hist. [a. OF. rote (rothe, route), = Prov. and med.L. rota, rotta; also MDu. rote, MLG. rotte, rode, MHG. rote, rott(e, OHG. rota, rotta. The original form was prob. *hrotta, an early Teutonic adoption of the Celtic word recorded by Venantius Fortunatus (6th cent.) as chrotta, on which see Crowd sb.[1]] A mediæval musical instrument, probably of the violin class.

a 1300 Cursor M. 7408 Dauid cuth on sere-kin note, Bath he cuth on harpe and rote. 13.. E. E. Allit. P. B. 1082 Organes & pypes, & rial ryngande rotes & þe reken fybel. 1390 Gower Conf. III. 303 He tawhte hir til sche was certein Of Harpe, of Citole and of Rote. c 1407 Lydg. Reson & Sens. 2394 He kan..Touche be crafte, and nat be rote, Harpe and lute, fythel and Rote. c 1450 Holland Howlat 759 The rote, and the recordour,..The trumpe, and the talburn. 1590 Spenser F. Q. II. x. 3 Argument worthy of Mæonian quill; Or rather worthy of great Phoebus rote. 1596 Ibid. IV. ix. 6 There did he find..The faire Pœana playing on a Rote.

1814 Scott Ld. of Isles III. xxiii, The lad can deftly touch the lute, And on the rote and viol play. 1823 Roscoe tr. Sismondi's Lit. Eur. (1846) I. v. 128 Psaltry, symphony, and rote, Help to charm the listening throng. 1859 Jephson Brittany vii. 93 To converse, or sing ancient Breton lays to the rote. 1884 Heron-Allen Violin Making 62 The only difference between the earliest crwths..and the latest rotes..seems to be the addition of the bow and finger-board.

Rote (rōut), sb.[2] Also 4–5 roote, 5–6 root, 5 rot, 5–7 roat(e. [Of obscure origin; there is no evidence to confirm the suggestions that it is a. OF. rote, route route, way, or ad. L. rota wheel.]

† 1. a. Custom, habit, practice. Obs.

c 1315 Shoreham III. 210 Þy wykked rote, Wanne þou ne halst þy maseday, As god hyt haþ y-hote. 1390 Gower Conf. III. 45 Thilke art which Spatula is hote, And used is of comun rote Among Paiens. Ibid. 50 He..broght hem into such a rote, That upon him thei bothe assote. c 1440 Promp. Parv. 437/2 Root, of vse and custome.

† b. Mechanical practice or performance; regular procedure; mere routine. Obs. (Cf. sense 2.)

1581 Mulcaster Positions xli. (1887) 242 By the meere shadow, and roat of these sciences. 1693 Evelyn De La Quint. Compl. Gard. I. 3 A presumptuous Pratling Ignorance, upheld by some wretched Rote. 1712 J. James tr. Le Blond's Gardening 80 Experience, Tryal upon the Ground, and a certain Rote,..necessary to this End. 1768 Woman of Honor II. 81 His education had proceeded in the common rote through school and college. Ibid. II. 189 He took the rote of forms to be the very quintessence of affairs.

† c. A rigmarole. Obs. rare.

14.. Sir Beues (MS. S) 1191 Men seye. in olde roote þat wimmannes bolt is sone schote. 1681 Peace & Truth 14 The Church of Rome hath turned Prayer into a meer Rote or Charm of unintelligible Words.

2. By rote, in a mechanical manner, by routine, esp. by the mere exercise of memory without proper understanding of, or reflection upon, the matter in question; also, † with precision, by heart.

a. With say, sing, play, etc.

The meaning of the first quot. is not clear.

13.. Gaw. & Gr. Knt. 2207 Þat gere as I trowe, Is ryched at þe reuerence, me renk to mete, bi rote. c 1394 P. Pl. Crede 377 A ribaut..þat can nouȝt wel reden His rewle ne his respondes, but be pure rote. 1444 Pol. Poems (Rolls) II. 217 Suych labourerys synge may be roote, 'Alle goo we stille, the cok hath lowe shoon'. 1526 Pilgr. Perf. (W. de W. 1531) 160 Yf it were, than I myght..saye my seruyce by rote and custome. 1577–82 Breton Toyes Idle Head Wks. (Grosart) I. 27/1, I did not sing one noate, except it were by roate. 1628 Earle Microcosm., Shop-keeper (Arb.) 54 Hee tels you lyes by rote. 1662 Playford Skill Mus. II. (1674) 110 To learn to play by rote or ear without Book. 1715 De Foe Fam. Instruct. I. vi. (1841) I. 112 We can all repeat the Commandments by rote. 1773 Han. More Search after Happiness ii. 141, I talk'd by rote the jargon of the schools. 1833 Ht. Martineau Hill & Valley vii. 111 The young ladies..played their duet more by rote than con amore this night. 1860 Hawthorne Eng. Note-bks. (1870) II. 160 This guide..did his business less by rote..than any guide I ever met. 1878 Bosw. Smith Carthage 436 The college..where little boys learn to repeat by rote the Koran from end to end.

b. With know, get, learn, etc.

c 1386 Chaucer Prol. 329 Ther-to he koude endite, and make a thyng,..And euery statut koude he pleyn by rote. — Prioress' T. 1712 He..herkned ay the wordes and the noote, Til he the firste vers koude al by rote. c 1440 Partonope 3215 The maner of spyces I know by rote. 1531 Tindale Prol. Ep. Rom. Wks. 39, I thinke it meete that euery christen man..know it, by rote and without the boke. 1596 Spenser F. Q. IV. ix. 6 Singing all her sorrow to the note, As she had learned readily by rote. 1624 Heywood Gunaik. VIII. 375 The Psalmes of David which shee had almost ad unguem and by roat. 1663 Butler Hud. I. i. 135 All which he understood by Rote, And as occasion serv'd, would quote. 1709 Steele Tatler No. 38 ¶ 12 He has by Rote, and at Second-hand, all that can be said of any Man of Figure, Wit, and Virtue in Town. 1781 Cowper Conversat. 7 Words learn'd by rote a parrot may rehearse. 1840 Carlyle Heroes (1858) 321 Their commonplace doctrines, which they have learned by logic, by rote, at secondhand. 1874 L. Stephen Hours in Library (1892) II. iii. 102 In time we learn by rote the lessons which we had to spell out in our youth.

3. attrib., as rote knowledge, -learning, -lesson, -work; rote-learned adj.; also, † by-rote babble, lesson.

1598 E. Guilpin Skial. (1878) 45 T' heare a Parrat cry Her by-roate lesson of like curtesie. 1641 Milton Animadv. Wks. 1851 III. 201 To pray in his own words without being ..fescu'd to a formal injunction of his rote-lesson. 1669 Penn No Cross Wks. 1782 II. 107 A little by-rote-babble, with..an hour's talk in other men's words. 1848 Eliza Cook To Charlotte Cushman iii, No rote-learned sighing. 1862 G. P. Marsh Orig. & Hist. Eng. Lang. 25 A rote-knowledge of paradigms and definitions. 1864 Knight Passages Work. Life I. i. 23 The dreary life of a day-school.., for the education was altogether rote-work. 1876 Grant Burgh Sch. Scot. II. xiii. 401 The rote-learning of rules once so universal.

† **Rote**, sb.[3] Obs.—¹ [a. OF. rote, var. of route Rout sb.[1] Hence also MDu., MLG., MHG., MSw. rote, MDa. rode.] A company, squadron.

1387 Trevisa Higden (Rolls) I. 311 [Creta] was þe firste lond þat..tauȝte horse men to ryde in rotes [L. turmas].

† **Rote**, sb.[4] Obs. rare. [ad. med.L. rota (Du Cange).] A certain measure or weight.

c 1400 tr. Secreta Secret., Gov. Lordsh. II. lxvii. 84 Take ..þe Ferthe party of a Rote, and put all in x Rotes of swete water. Ibid. 85.

Rote (rōut), sb.[5] Now rare. Also 6 root. [ad. L. rota Rota, or (in sense 2) a. F. rote.]

† 1. A wheel used as an instrument of torture or punishment. Obs.

1526 R. Whytford Martiloge (1893) 43 All theyr membres & hole body stretched vpon a rote or turnyng whele. a 1575 Diurn. Occurr. (Bann. Cl.) 250 James Cadder..being..tane in Striueling in maner foirsaid, wes brokin on the root.

† 2. R. C. Ch. = Rota 3. Obs.

1528 Gardiner in Burnet Hist. Ref., Rec. (Pocock) I. 106 One Jacobus Symonet, dean of the rote. 1529 More Dyaloge III. Wks. 216/1 Sauyng the premunyre, we myghte haue it tryed in the rote at Rome. 1787 Charlotte Smith Romance Real Life II. 130 At the court of Rome, the department called the Rote, allowed the validity of her marriage.

3. Rotation; turn. rare—¹.

1831 Fraser's Mag. III. 508 They at first resolved That each should govern in diurnal rote.

Rote (rōut), sb.[6] Now U.S. [See Rut sb.[3]] The roaring of the sea or surf.

1610 R. Niccols England's Eliza cclxx. 837 While the seas rote doth ring their doleful knell. 1682 Flavel Fear 24 Such a noise as the rote of the sea. 1855 Haliburton Nature & Human N. 210 When..the rote is on the beach, it tells me it is the voice of the south wind giving notice of rain. 1864 Lowell Fireside Trav. 193 X. walked away, rumbling inwardly like the rote of the sea heard afar. 1869 T. W. Higginson Oldport Romance xviii, She could only distinguish the rote on the distant beach.

† **Rote**, a., obs. variant of Rotten a.

c 1386 Chaucer Sec. Nun's T. 17 (Cambr. MS.), Ȝit seen men weel..That ydilnesse is rote slogardye. Ibid. 228 Neuere mo ne schal they rote be.

Rote (rōut), v.[1] Also 7 roat. [f. Rote sb.[2]]

1. trans. To repeat, to run over, to rattle off, from memory. Also absol.

1593 Drayton Ecl. i. 16 Ravish'd to heare the warbling Birds to roat. 1630 — Muses Eliz. Nymphal ii. 121 If by chance a Tune you roate, 'Twill foote it finely to your note. 1682 Baxter Answ. Dodwell iv. 57 Did you think that your roteing over the name to them that deny the thing, would make a wise man change his Religion? 1816 J. Gilchrist Philos. Etym. 134 It is really to be wished that authors would think more and rote less. Ibid. 140 The usual violations of usage might be put into a sixpenny piece to be roted off by the grammatical disciple. 1838 Tupper Proverb. Philos., Of Memory iii, Memory is not wisdom: idiots can rote volumes.

† 2. To learn or fix by rote. Obs. rare.

1607 Shaks. Cor. III. ii. 55 Now it lyes you on to speake to th' people..with such words That are but roated in your Tongue. 1775 T. Sheridan Art Reading 283 Not..able to repeat even what is perfectly roted on the memory.

Hence **Ro·ting** vbl. sb. and ppl. a.

1816 J. Gilchrist Philos. Etym. 186 Can our roting, repeating scholar make Latin as Cicero made it? 1817 — Intell. Patrimony 15 You will witness much reading, roting and repeating among those who pretend to learning.

Rote (rōut), v.[2] [ad. L. rotāre, f. rota wheel.]

† 1. trans. To rotate. Obs.

1578 Banister Hist. Man I. 27 When the cubit is at furthest extended, the posteriour and great Processe thereof, is roted and wheled.

2. intr. To go out or in by rotation or turn.

a 1697 Aubrey Lives, J. Harrington (1898) I. 291 Now this modell upon rotation was:—that the third part of the Senate should rote out by ballot every yeare. 1806 W. Taylor in Ann. Rev. IV. 240 Of three County Members one might rote out yearly. 1860 Gen. P. Thompson Audi Alt. clxxi. III. 199 Here the only way seems to be, that instead of roting out, as was the device of our ancestors, men should for once in a way rote in.

† **Rote**, v.[3] Obs. [Cf. Rottle v.] ? To flutter.

c 1330 Arth. & Merl. 3867 (Kölbing), Þer miȝt men se þe baners roten, Þe stedes forþ wel ȝern schoten.

Rote, obs. f. Root, Rot, Rout, Rut.

† **Ro·ted**, a. Obs. rare—¹. [app. f. Rote sb.[2]] Skilled, practised, experienced.

1470–85 Malory Morte Arth. X. xxxvi. 472 This malgryne was an olde roted knyghte, and he was called one of the daungerous knyghtes of the world to doo bataille on foot.

Roted, obs. f. Rooted, Rotted. **Rotel**, obs. f. Rottle v.

† **Rote-master.** Obs.—¹ [ad. Du. rotmeester, G. rottmeister: see Rot sb.[2]] One in command of a company of gunners.

1523 Lett. & Pap. Hen. VIII, III. II. 1526.

Roten, obs. f. Rotten a.

† **Ro·ter** [1]. Obs.—¹ [a. OF. rotier, variant of routier, Router sb.[1]] A robber, highwayman.

1297 R. Glouc. (Rolls) 6032 Aboute heruest þis deneis as roters [v.r. rotours, rotors] arnde Bi chilterne & to oxenford.

Roter [2] (rōu·təɹ). [f. Rote v.[1]] One who repeats by rote.

1624 Bp. Mountagu Gagg 301 Such Roters as these, are the men that talk of Fathers amongst their Gossips and Proselytes. 1816 J. Gilchrist Philos. Etym. 217 A canting, mystical, visionary race of roters, eternally saying after consecrated authorities. 1817 — Intell. Patrimony 102 The sole reason must have been, that he was less of a reader and roter.

Rotey-time: see Rutey sb.

Rotge(e. Ornith. [Given by Martens (1675) as the name current among Dutch or Frisian sailors, with the statement that it is derived from the bird's cry rottet tet; but perh. a misunderstanding of Fris. rotgies, pl. of rotgoes, brent-goose.] The little auk. See also Rotche.

1694 Martens' Voy. Spitzbergen in Acc. Sev. Late Voy. II. 76 The old Lumbs have a very tough and dry Flesh, not to disparage the Rotges, Kirmews and young Lumbs when boiled. Ibid. (1711) 91 The calling or crying of the Rotges amongst one another. 1859 Cornhill Mag. I. 109 Passing Cape Dudley Diggs, we landed at a breeding-place of rotges (little auks). 1882 Nature XXVI. 387 Many rotgees had their young among the basaltic columns.

Ro·t-gut, ro·tgut. [f. Rot v. + Gut sb.]

1. An adulterated or unwholesome liquor; spec. bad small beer, or (in U.S.) inferior whiskey.

1633 Heywood Eng. Trav. IV. Wks. 1874 IV. 72 Let not a Teaster scape To be consum'd in rot-gut. 1666 G. Harvey Morb. Angl. xxviii. (1672) 76 They overwhelming their panch daily with a kind of flat Scarbier, or Rot-gut; we with a bitter dreggish small liquor. 1715 Addison Drummer v. Wks. 1830 II. 208 Sir George. Drink nothing but smallbeer for a fortnight——. But. Smallbeer! Rot-gut! 1831 Lover Leg. 222 To the divil I pitch sitch rot-gut. 1867 P. Fitzgerald 75 Brooke St. II. 67 What is it to me..if you fill your cellars with all the 'rotgut' in the kingdom? 1892 Henley & Stevenson Deacon Brodie I. iv, What brings the man from stuff like this to rotgut and spittoons at Mother Clarke's.

2. attrib. or as adj. Of liquor: Unwholesome, deleterious, injurious to the system.

1706 T. Baker Tunbridge Walks III. i, Damn rotgut Rhenish: we'll have Mrs. Motion's health in a bumper of Barcelona. 1767 S. Paterson Anoth. Trav. II. 42 Their only drink was a cursed rot-gut stuff, which they called wine. 1830 Marryat King's Own xxxiv, The rotgut French wines had given him a pain in the bowels. 1871 Daily News 19 Jan., To take glass after glass of rotgut rum, schnapps, or arrack.

b. spec. (See quot.) U.S.

1888 Goode Amer. Fishes 432 Its flesh spoils very quickly after the fish is taken from the water, hence the name 'Rotgut Minnow', applied to it in Alabama.

Roth, obs. form of Root sb.[1]

† **Rothe**, v.[1] Obs.—¹ [ad. ON. ræða, = OE. rǽdan: see Rede v.] trans. To counsel, advise.

c 1300 Havelok 2817 And siþen shal ich under-stonde Of you..Manrede, and holde oþes boþe, Yif ye it wilen, and ek rothe.

† **Rothe**, v.[2] Obs.—¹ [Of obscure origin.] intr. ? To talk nonsense.

c 1440 York Myst. xvii. 122 Kyng! in þe deuyl way, dogges, Fy! Now I se wele ȝe roþe and raue.

† **Ro·thel**, v. Obs. rare. (Of obscure origin and doubtful meaning.)

13.. E. E. Allit. P. B. 59 Al is roþeled & rosted ryȝt to þe sete, Comeȝ cof to my corte, er hit colde worþe. Ibid. 890 Þenne vch tolke tyȝt hem þat hade of tayt fayled, & vchon roþeled to þe rest þat he reche moȝt.

‖ **Rötheln** (rö·teln). [G. rötheln, röteln pl., f. rot(h) red.] German measles.

1873 F. T. Roberts Handbk. Med. 179 Hybrid of Measles and Scarlatina—Rötheln. 1877 Ibid. (ed. 3) I. 147 Rötheln has been regarded either as a mild form of measles or scarlatina. 1889 E. Smith Pract. Treat. Dis. Children (ed. 2) ii. 32 An attack of rötheln is then, as a rule, a very insignificant matter.

Rother (rɒ·ðəɹ). Obs. exc. dial. Forms: α. 1 hriðer, hryþer, 1–2 hryðer, 4 riþer. β. 2–3 reðer, 4 reþer, 5–6 rether. γ. 2–3 roðer, 3 roþer, 3– rother, 5 rodder, 6 rowder. δ. 1 hruðer, 3 ruðer, ruþer, 4, 6 ruther, 5 rudder. [OE. hriðer, hrȳðer, = OFris. (h)rither, reder (NFris. ridder, redder young ox, WFris. rier heifer), a derivative from the stem hriþ- (found in hriðfald, -hiorde), = OS. hrîth, for earlier *hrinþ-, which is also represented by OHG. hrind (G. rind), MLG. and MDu. rind-, rint (Du. rund). The shortening of the vowel before the ending -ther (as in mother, brother) prob. took place in later OE., with subsequent variation due to the influence of r.

It is not clear whether OE. hrȳðer is a mere variation of hriðer, or represents an original ablaut variant *hrunþ-.]

1. An ox; an animal of the ox kind; pl. oxen, cattle, neat.

α. 805–31 Charter in O. E. Texts 444 An hriðer duȝunde. 971 Blickl. Hom. 199 He..ongan sceotan wiþ þæs þe he geseah þæt hryþer stondan. c 1000 Sax. Leechd. II. 200 Ȝenim cealfes scearn oþþe ealdes hryþeres wearm & leȝe on. c 1050 Voc. in Wr.-Wülcker 341 Armenta, hryðera heorde. a 1122 O. E. Chron. (Laud MS.) an. 1012, Hi.. hine þa þær oftorfodon mid banum & mid hryðera heafdum. c 1400 Trevisa's Higden (Rolls) III. 205 Senewes of schepe and of reþeren [β. riþeren].

β. c 1200 Trin. Coll. Hom. 37 Ðet oref..beð shep and reðeren and get and swin. a 1290 Leben Jesu (Horstm.) 853 Fond he þer inne..Schep and reþren, and coluerene eke. c 1306 Pol. Songs (Camden) 220 Upon a retheres hude forth he wes y-tuht. 1387 Trevisa Higden (Rolls) II. 13 Þis ilond..bringeþ forþ..reþeren and oþer bestes. a 1400–50 Alexander 1239 Meliager with his men..Raschis with rethere & rydis bot a quyle [etc.]. 1509 Will of Myll (Somerset Ho.), Duos Retheres et viginti oues.

γ. c 1225 Leg. Kath. 60 Þe riche reoðeren & schep.. brohten to lake. c 1290 S. Eng. Leg. I. 300/11 Garganes reoþeren and oþure bestes I-nowe..to heore lesewe heom drowe. 13.. K. Alis. 4719 Men to beom threowe drit and donge, With foule ayren, with rotheres lunge. 1398 Trevisa Barth. De P. R. XVIII. i. (Bodl. MS.), Bestes þat eteþ grete gras and herbes as roþeren. 1474 Waterf. Arch. in 10th Rep. Hist. MSS. Comm. App. V. 311 Rodders or ony othre marchaundise. 1607 Shaks. Timon IV. iii. 12 It is the Pastour Lards the rothers [em. for Brothers] sides. 1875 Parish Dict. Sussex Dial., Rother,..a horned beast.

δ. c 1050 in Kemble Cod. Dipl. IV. 275 Þæron næs orfcynnes nan mare buton vii hruðeru. c 1205 Lay. 8106 Islaȝene weoren to þon mele twælf þusend ruðeren. 1297 R. Glouc. (Rolls) 1209 King cassibel..sacrefise to hor godes ..Vourti þousend of ruþeren. 1485 Waterf. Arch. in 10th Rep. Hist. MSS. Comm. App. V. 319 The said bouchers bye the same rudders in thar names. 1518 in Trans. Kilkenny Arch. Soc. Ser. II. IV. 112 An Indentur..vpon ij rudders to be payed..yerly to Gerald Erle of Kildare.

2. attrib. and Comb., as rother-cattle, -driver, -herd, -soil.

c 1000 Ælfric Gen. xlv. 10 Eowre sceap and eower hryðerheorda. c 1000 — Hom. I. 322 Amos hatte sum hryðer-hyrde. c 1175 Lamb. Hom. 97 Amos het a reoðer heorde. 1396 Chancery Warrants file 560 Quatre boefs, pris de quarante soulds, [stolen] de Johan ap Jakke, retherdryver. 1578 Lyte Dodoens 752 The leaves of Elme are good fodder for rother cattell. 1602 Carew Cornwall 23 Beastes seruing for meate onely, are Pigs, Goates, Sheepe, and Rother cattell. 1670 Blount Glossogr. (ed. 3) s.v., Hence Rother-soyle, also used in Hereford shire, for the soyle or dung of those beasts.

Rother, obs. form of Rudder.

† **Rother-beast.** Obs. = Rother 1.

α. 1483 in Somerset Wills (1901) 254 Also tow oxen..and all my rother bestes. 1533 in Weaver Wells Wills (1890) 61 Every child of my son Thos. a Rother beste. 1567 Golding Ovid's Met. VII. 89 b, The cruell Beare to fall Upon the herdes of Rother beastes had now no lust at all. 1630 R. Johnson's Kingd. & Commw. 78 You shall see Heards of Rother Beasts and Horses, and Flocks of Sheepe. c 1640 J. Smyth Hund. Berkeley (1885) 19 Lands which suffice for the breedinge of an horse beast or Rother beast. 1670 Blount Glossogr. (ed. 3), Rother-beasts (a word used both in our old Statutes, and still in the North of England).

β. 1561 Hollybush Hom. Apoth. 25 The mary of Hertes, Roes, or rudder beastes. 1596 Harington Metam. Ajax Prol. A viij, The ruther beastes that eate too greedily hereof wil swell til they burst. 1610 Guillim Heraldry III. xiv. (1660) 163 The Bull is the ringleader amongst ruther beasts. 1698 Fryer Acc. E. India & P. 244 The Ruther Beasts with distended Bags grazing in the Meadows.

† **Ro·theren**, a. Obs. Forms: 1 hryþeren, 4–5 reþeren (5 -erne), rotheren (roþerne), rutheren. [OE. hrȳðeren, f. hrȳðer Rother. Cf. OS. hrîtherin, MLG. rindern.] Of or belonging to oxen or cattle. Retheren tongue, bugloss.

c 1000 Sax. Leechd. II. 186 Ȝenim hryþeren flæsc gesoden on ecede. 1387 Trevisa Higden (Rolls) II. 309 It was a grete abhomynacioun among þe Egipcians to sle reþeren or ete reþeren flesche. 1398 — Barth. De P. R. XVIII. i. (Bodl. MS.), Roþeren flesche and gote flesche is better sode þanne rosted. c 1400 Trevisa's Higden (Rolls) VII. 504 The Danes ..slouȝ him with stones and with rotheren bones. 14.. MS. Sloane 5 lf. 5/2 Buglossa,..lingua bouis. gallice, Lange de boef. Anglice, reþerne tounge.

Rotherham (rɒ·ðərăm). Also **Rotheram.** The name of a parish and township in Yorkshire, formerly used attrib. to designate an improved form of plough introduced (app. from Holland) about the middle of the 18th century.

1762 Mills Syst. Husb. I. 255 The Rotheran [sic], or patent plough,..deserves the husbandman's particular attention. 1763 Museum Rust. I. 24 To stir the intervals,.. the Rotheram plow may be used. 1805 R. W. Dickson Pract. Agric. I. 7 An intelligent farmer..assures us, that the rotheram-plough..goes very light, and is very useful. 1844 H. Stephens Bk. Farm I. 406 About the middle of the past century, the Rotherham plough appears to have been partially introduced into Scotland.

† **Ro·therish**, a. Obs.—¹ [f. Rother + -ish.] Resembling oxen.

c 1200 Trin. Coll. Hom. 37 Sume men..winned wið þe eorðe, and tiliȝet michel to oðre mannæs bihofþe, and þese men beð icleped ruðerishse men. Of þese shepishse and ruðerishse men specð þe prophete.

Rothesay (rɒ·þsĕⁱ). Also 5 Roth(is)say, 6 Rothsay. The name of an ancient castle in Scotland, used attrib. in Rothesay herald, one of the six Scottish heralds. Also ellipt.

1401–2 Exch. Rolls Scot. (1880) III. 552 In partem pensionis.., videlicet Rothesay heraldo. 1488 Sc. Acts Parl. (1814) II. 214/1 The lettrez brocht fra him be Rothisay herrald. 1507 Acc. Ld. High Treas. Scot. III. 371 Item, to Blewmantill, now callit Rothsay, for to pas in France. 1581 Sc. Acts Parl. (1814) III. 286/1 His said office of Rothesay herauld. 1642 Reg. Privy Council Scot. VII. 331 The other two [were charged] by John Spence, Rothesay Herald,..to render their houses. 1742 A. Nisbet Syst. Heraldry II. IV. xvi. 171 Rothsay has his Name and Title from the Castle of Rothsay,..an antient Residence of our Scots Kings in the Isle of Bute. 1863 [see Ross sb.[1]].

† **Rothly**, a. Obs.—¹ (Meaning uncertain.)

a 1400 Pistill Susan 341 Þo þat roþly cherl ruydely rored, And seide bi-fore þe prophete: 'þei pleied bi a prine'.

† **Rothun.** Obs.—¹ (Meaning uncertain.)

13.. E. E. Allit. P. B. 1009 Suche a roþun of a reche ros fro þe blake, Askeȝ vpe in þe ayre & vsellez þer flowen.

Rotie, obs. form of Rot v.

Rotifer (rōu·tifəɹ). [mod.L. (Leeuwenhoek, 1702), f. L. rota wheel + -fer bearing.] An animalcule belonging to the class Rotifera.

1793 T. Beddoes On Calculus 250 The phænomena displayed by the rotifer..appear inexplicable. 1835–6 Todd's Cycl. Anat. I. 608/2 Singular experiments on the apparent resuscitation of the Rotifer. 1846 Dana Zooph. ii. (1848) 11 Polyps are..even less complex in structure than the minuter Rotifers. 1872 Nicholson Biol. 15 The Rotifers are minute mostly microscopic creatures which inhabit almost all our ponds and streams.

‖ **Rotifera** (roti·fĕră). [mod.L., neut. pl. of rotifer(us): see prec.] A class of minute (usually microscopic) animalcules, having rotatory organs which are used in swimming.

1830 R. Knox Béclard's Anat. 18 Other animals somewhat more compound, as the rotifera..and the polypi. 1848 Carpenter Anim. Phys. ii. (1872) 112 The group of Rotifera or Wheel-Animalcules, which is one of great interest to the Microscopist. 1896 tr. Boas' Text-bk. Zool. 157 The Rotifera lay two different kinds of eggs.

Hence **Roti·feral** a., **Roti·ferous** a., of or belonging to the Rotifera.

1835–6 Todd's Cycl. Anat. I. 607 The..rotatory or wheel-like organs of the Rotiferous Infusoria. 1871 T. R. Jones Anim. Kingd. (ed. 4) 463 In the rotiferous animalcules. 1886 Encycl. Brit. XXI. 8/1 Possessing undoubtedly Rotiferal characters.

† **Ro·tified**, ppl. a. Obs.—¹ [f. Rote sb.[2]] Repeated by rote.

1719 D'Urfey Pills V. 242 Let 'em tire all that pass with their rotified Cant, 'Will you buy any Shoes, pray see what you want'.

Ro·tiform, a. rare—⁰. [ad. mod.L. rotiformis, f. L. rota wheel.] (See quots.)

1855 Ogilvie Suppl., Rotiform, shaped like a wheel. 1864 Webster, Rotiform,..having a very short tube, and spreading limbs;—said of a monopetalous corolla.

Rotine, obs. form of Routine.

Roting, obs. form of Rooting, Rotting.

‖ **Rotl** (rɒ·t'l). Forms: 7 rethel, rotte (?rotle), rotal, 9 rotol, rottle, rattle, rutl, rotl. [a. Arab. رطل, retl, ratl, which is supposed by some to be an alteration of Gr. λίτρα.] An eastern weight, varying in different places and for different commodities, but usually something between one and five pounds. Cf. Rotolo.

1615 W. Bedwell Arab. Trudgman s.v., An hundred Rethels do make a Cantar. 1685 Pococke Comm. Hosea iii. 2 It contained the weight of seventy-two thousand drachms, that is, five hundred common rotals. 1687 A. Lovell tr. Thevenot's Trav. I. 262 The Quintal contains 150 Rottes, the Rotte 12 ounces. 1825 Milburn's Oriental Commerce I. 88 [At Judda] 15 Vakias make 1 Rattle; 2 Rattles 1 maund. 1836–7 Encycl. Metrop. (1845) XVIII. 438/2 The Greek rotl = 180 dirhems is used in weighing cotton thread; the common rotl = 144 dirhems. 1836 Lane Mod. Egypt. II. 8 The rutl is about 15⅞ oz.

Rotle, obs. form of Rottle v.

† **Ro·tness.** Obs.—¹ [Cf. Rot a.] Rottenness.

1387 Trevisa Higden (Rolls) VII. 149 Seint Laurence, whos chirche dissolved and lowsed þoruȝ longe rotnes [L. caric] be reparailde.

† **Roto·cracy.** Obs. [f. rot(ten): see Rotten a. 7 c and -ocracy.] The body of persons who had the control of rotten boroughs.

1831 Examiner 81/2 Why have a constituency, if the constituency is passively to subserve to the Rotocracy?—(we thank The Times for the word). 1831 Fonblanque Eng. under 7 Administr. (1837) II. 101 Lest the Rotocracy should imagine..that it has been the cause of the progress of society.

Rotograph (rōu·tŏgræf). [f. L. rota wheel + -graph.] A photographic print (esp. of a page in a book or manuscript) made by exposing the object through a lens and prism, so that its reversed image is thrown upon part of a roll of sensitive paper. Also attrib.

1898 in Trade Marks Jrnl. No. 1098 (1899) 408. 1903 H. S. Ward's Fig. Photogr. (ed. 3) 95 'Rotograph' Papers. Ibid. 183 'Rotograph' formulæ. 1906 Oxford Univ. Press Circular (24 Nov.), Rotary Bromide Prints, or Rotographs.

‖ **Rotolo** (rɒ·tŏlo). Forms: 7 rottala, rotola, rotello, 8 rottel(l)o, 8–9 rotolo, 9 rottolo; also pl. 7 rottollies, 8–9 rotoli, 9 rottolis. [a. It. rotolo (pl. rotoli), ad. Arab. ratl.] = Rotl.

1625 Purchas Pilgrims I. iv. 347 The weight..is two Rottalas, a Rottala is a pound of their weight. Ibid. II. VII. 1188 Three hundred and sixtie Rottollies of Moha. Ibid. IX. 1644 Eight and twentie Rotellos of this place. 1698 Fryer Acc. E. India & P. 207, 1 Rotola is 16 Ounc. or 1 l. Averd. 1727 W. Mather Yng. Man's Comp. 399 In Aleppo, some [commodities] are weighed by the Rotolo of 680 Drachms; some by that of 700, and others by that of 720 Drachms. 1765 Ann. Reg. I. 75 At Brundisi, a hundred rotoli (a weight of about 33 ounces English) of Roman silver denarii were lately discovered. 1853 W. B. Barker Lares & Penates 75 From a rotolo of coffee, or a few rotolos of rice,

Supplement, p. 3873; Corrigenda, p. 4092; Spurious words, p. 4093; Books quoted, p. 4094

Rotombe, variant of ROTUMBE *Obs.*

Rotonda: see ROTONDO.

Rotor (rǝu·tǝʳ). [Irreg. for ROTATOR.]

Rotonda, *a. Obs. rare.* [ad. It. *rotondo* or L. *rotund-us*: see ROTUND *a.*] Round.

Rotour, *Obs. rare.* (a. OF. *rotor*, *rote(e)ur*, f. *rote* ROTE *sb.*¹] A player on the rote.

Rotship, *Obs. rare.* [f. ROT *a.*] Rottenness.

Rotous = see ROTTEN *sb.*¹

Rottack = see ROTTOCK.

Rottan (rǝ·tn), *n.* Now *Sc.* and *dial.* Also 6, 8–9 rottane, 6 rottane. [var. of RATTON.]

Rotter (rǫ·tǝʳ). [f. ROT *v.*]

Rottenish, *a. rare.* [f. ROTTEN *a.* + -ISH.] Somewhat rotten or decomposed.

Rottenly, *adv. rare⁻⁰.* [-LY².] In a rotten manner; unsoundly.

Rottenness (rǫ·t'nnes). Forms: 4–5 rotenesse; 5 rotynes⟨s⟩e; 6 rottinesse, rottinnesse, 6–7 rotten⟨n⟩esse, 7, 9 rotteness; 7- rottenness. [f. ROTTEN *a.* + -NESS.]

Rotten Row. [App. f. ROTTEN *a.* + ROW *sb.*¹]

Rotten-stone. Also rottenstone. [f. ROTTEN *a.* + STONE *sb.*]

Rottock. Now *Sc.* Forms: 4 rottok, 9–azk, -iok. [? f. ROT *v.*]

Rotula (rǫ·tiǔlǎ). Pl. aus. **rotulæ** (rǫ·tiǔlī·). [L. *rotula*, dim. of *rota* wheel.]

Rotular (rǫ·tiǔlǎʳ), *a.* [See prec. and -AR.] Of or pertaining to the rotula or knee-cap.

Rotule (rǫ·tiūl). [a. F. *rotule*, ad. L. *rotula* ROTULA.]

Rotulet (rǫ·tiǔlet). [f. *rotul-us* roll + -ET.]

† **Rotund**, *v. Obs.* [f. next.] To make round.

Rotund (rǫtǫ·nd), *a.* Now *rare.* [Subst. use of next.]

Rotund (rǫtǫ·nd), *a.* [ad. L. *rotund-us*, related to *rota* wheel: cf. ROTOUND *a.* and ROUND *a.*]

Rotundity (rǫtǫ·nditi). [ad. L. *rotunditas*, f. *rotundus*: see ROTUND *a.*]

Rotundly, *adv.* [f. ROTUND *a.* + -LY².]

Rotundo. Now *rare* or *Obs.* [Alteration of ROTUNDA.]

† **Rotundal**, *a. Obs.⁻¹* [f. ROTUND *a.* + -AL.] Round, circular.

Rotundant. *Obs.⁻¹* [ad. L. *rotundant-em*, after *quadrant*.] A round thing.

Rotundate (rǫtǫ·ndǝt), *a.* [ad. L. *rotundat-us*, pa. pple. of *rotundāre*.] Rounded off.

Rotundo-, combining form of L. *rotundus*, used in a few scientific terms.

Roturier (rǫtyʳǝi), *sb.* and *a.* Also 7 roturer, and 8–9 rot-, -iero (-yē⁻). [F., f. *roture*: see prec. and -IER.]

Roture (rǫtiū·ǝʳ), *sb.* Now *rare.* [a. F. *roture*.]

Roucou (rū·kū), *sb.* Also 7 roccou, 7 roccou, 8 rocou, 9 roucu, 8 rowcu, roucoua. [a. F. *roucou*, *rucou*, ad. Brazilian (Tupi) *urucú*.]

Roucote. *Obs.⁻¹* Some kind of fish.

Roud, *sb. dial.* [Cf. next and KUD (the fish).]

Roud (rūd), *v. intr.* To spawn.

Roudes, variant of RUDAS *Sc.*

† **Roudou**. *Obs. rare.* [Of obscure origin.] Some kind of coarse cloth.

Rouen (rū·ǎn). The name of a city in Northern France, used to designate various things in commerce.

Rouge (rūʒ), *sb.* [F. *rouge* red.]

Rouge (rūʒ), *v.* [f. ROUGE *sb.*]

Rougeing, variant of ROUGING.

Rough (rʌf), *a.* Forms: 3 ruhe, 4 roȝ, 5, 7 roughe, 6– rough, 9 ruff; *Sc.* 6, 9 roch. [OE. *rūh*.]

fury the greatest execration they use to rap out, is [etc.]. 1725 Vanbrugh Prov. Wife iv. iii, Justice...Does he not use you well? Sir John. A little u on the rough sometimes. 1801 Mar. Edgeworth Contrast Wks. 1832 V. 134 His new foreman bore the rough well. 1861 Gen. P. Thompson Audi Alt. clvii. III. 164 When he is brought into court, and trailed through all the rough of calling a spade a spade. 1893 C. G. Leland Memoirs I. 31 When doing rough and tough in West Virginia.

b. Used in contrast to smooth. Also pl.

1612 Buccleuch MSS. (Hist. MSS. Comm.) I. 126, I truly delivered as well the rough as the smooth of all my speech. 1822 Irving Bracebr. Hall (1890) 147 Through the rough and the smooth, the pleasant and the adverse. 1829 Sir T. Lawrence in D. E. Williams Life (1831) II. 519 The boys ..must encounter the rough and the smooth of weather, as of life. 1900 J. K. Jerome Three Men on Bummel 190 One must take a little rough with one's smooth.

pl. 1804 Europ. Mag. XLV. 334/1 In this manner had Blair and his horse Pocket..travelled, and taken the roughs and the smooths of the world together. 1862 Thackeray Philip ix, You and I will take..the roughs and the smooths of this daily existence.

7. A man or lad belonging to the lower classes and inclined to commit acts of violence or disorder; a rowdy.

1837 Barham in Life & Lett. (1870) II. 39 There'll be lots of new policemen, To control the rogues and roughs. 1847 Illustr. Lond. News 27 Nov. 339/1 Will you let the jury know what 'Roughs' are? I believe it is an electioneering name for ruffians. 1853 Croker Papers (1884) III. 268 To be stoned by some of the thousand roughs with which the accesses to Parliament will be thronged. 1883 Ld. R. Gower Reminisc. II. 108 She is educating and civilising a little colony there of roughs and vagabonds.

8. colloq. Short for Rough-rider.

1899 Daily News 23 Feb. 6/2 The Roughs swore by Roosevelt. 1900 Westm. Gaz. 17 July 8/1 The 'Roughs' and the 'Sharps' of the 18th Battalion Imperial Yeomanry.

III. 9. Rough or refuse matter in the working of minerals. Cf. Row sb.[5] 2.

1677 Yarranton Eng. Improv. 59 In the Forest of Deane ..iron is made at this day of Cinders, being the rough and offal thrown by in the Romans time. 1778 Pryce Min. Cornub. 223 The rough that is carried back with the stream, by drawing it over again, may be rendered merchantable at a lower rate than the crop; and the rough of this rough, is thrown aside to make leavings. 1839 Ure Dict. Arts 1244 The ore, on issuing, deposits its rough in the first basin. 1875 J. H. Collins Met. Mining 111 Material of a mixed nature, called 'dredge', or 'roughs', or 'rows'. 1881 Raymond Mining Gloss., Roughs,..coarse, poor sands, resulting from tin-dressing. 1887 P. M'Neill Blawearie 174 Then it was indeed difficult to detect the foul from the roughs of the main coal.

b. Agric. (See quot. 1853.)

1844 H. Stephens Bk. Farm II. 267 A second woman is required to riddle the roughs from the foul spout into a heap by itself. 1853 Encycl. Brit. II. 282/2 The unthrashed ears and broken straw called roughs or shorts.

10. a. A rough draft. rare[−1].

1699 S. Sewall Diary 23 Sept., Agree for 15l. and draw a rough of it and take his hand to it.

b. The rough state or material of anything; the rough outline of a spoon, etc.; hence rough-maker.

1799 Repertory Arts X. 295 How, by means of a rotative saw, to shape a piece from the rough. 1879 Cassell's Techn. Educ. IV. 413/2 The 'rough-maker'..smooths off the burr left by the stamp, strikes up finally the under side, and bends down the little curve at the end of the handle.

c. Unhusked rice; paddy. (Cf. Rough a. 21.)

1837 Civil Eng. & Arch. Jrnl. I. 51 An Improved Mortar for Dressing Rough or Paddy, or Redressing.

11. In the rough: a. In a rough, imperfect, or unfinished state; in a preliminary sketch or design.

1823 P. Nicholson Pract. Build. 159 Every kind of surface is first formed in the rough, and then finished by means of tools. 1848 Mill Pol. Econ. II. xvi. § 4 (1876) 259 We must never forget that the truths of political economy are truths only in the rough. 1879 B. Taylor Germ. Lit. 99 An unlettered minstrel, with great qualities in the rough.

b. In an untidy state; in disorder; in an every-day condition.

1825 Mrs. Cameron Seeds of Greediness 3 'We are all in the rough to-day, Sir,' answered the woman; 'for I am very busy with this job'. 1844 Dickens Mart. Chuz. xxiii, 'You'll have a party?' said Crimple. 'No, I won't,' I said; 'he shall take us in the rough'. 1865 — Mut. Fr. II. i, I wish you'd come with me, and take her in the rough, and judge her for yourself.

c. Approximately, roughly.

1868 Rogers Pol. Econ. iii. (1876) 29 In the rough, it may be said that the cost of producing a pound Troy of gold [etc.].

† **Rough**, sb.[2] Obs. Forms: 2 **ruhha, roche**(?), 3 **rohȝe**, 5 **rowhe, rowe, rowghe**, 6 **roughe**. [? late OE. rukha, ME. type roȝe, = MDu. rock(e, rockghe, rogghe (Du. rog, Fris. roch), MLG. roche, ruche (hence Da. rokke, Sw. rocka), G. roche, † rock. Obscurely related to OE. reohhe Reigh.] The fish called the Ray.

c 1110 in Napier Contrib. O.E. Lex. 60 Fannus, suhha [? read ruhha]. a 1200 Voc. in Wr.-Wülcker 543 Fannus, ro(che). c 1275 Lay. 29557 Hii..nemen rohȝe tayl..and honge(de on h)is cope. c 1440 Promp. Parv. 438/1 Rowhe, or reyhe, fysche (K. rowe-fysshe, P. rowghe), ragadies. 1530 Palsgr. 264/1 Roughe fysshe.

Rough, obs. var. of Ruff (the fish); see also Roughy.

Rough (rʊf), a. Forms: (see below). [OE. rûh, rûg-, = Fris. rûch (pl. rûge), † ruwg, MDu. ruuch (rugh-), ruych (Du. ruig), MLG. rûch, rûge (LG. rûg; hence Da. † rug), OHG. rûuh, rûh, rûch, ruoch (G. rauh). Varying notation of the vowel and final guttural gives rise to a large number of spellings in ME. In OE. the stem rûg- also appears (by a normal change) as rûw-, whence ME. and later Row a.]

A. Forms.

α. 1–3 **ruh** (1 **hruh**, 3 **ruhh**), 3 **ruhe, ruchȝe**, 1, 4, 6, 8 Sc. **ruch**, 5 Sc. **roucht**, 6 Sc. **rwch**; 4 **roh, rohu, rohw**, 5–7 Sc. **roche**, 6 Sc. **rocht**, 5, 8–9 Sc. **roch**; 5 **rouh, rowh**, 5–9 Sc. **rouch**, 6 Sc. **rouche, rowch**; 6 **routh, rowth**.

c 1000 Saxon Leechdoms III. 170 Þæt he habbe ruh lic. a 1100 in Napier O. E. Glosses 3250 Nodosi cippis ruches.. stocces. Ibid. 5189 Hirsutas lanas, hruhge wulla. c 1200 Ormin 9663 Ruhh & harrd & sharrp. 12.. Ancr. R. 184 (MS. C.), Of þi ruchȝe sunnen. 13.. Cursor M. 21962 (Edin.), Þe toþir sal be ful ruch and reþe. c 1450 Holland Howlat 616 The rouch Wodwyss wyld. 1477 Paston Lett. III. 186 Fixid so fast with hys prikks rowh. 1523 Skelton Garl. Laurel 803 Florisshyng of flowris, With burris rowth. c 1560 A. Scott Poems (S. T. S.) v. 58 Quhair the gait is ruch. 1596 Dalrymple tr. Leslie's Hist. Scot. I. 28 A rouch rock or craig. 17.. Ramsay Vision ii, The air grew ruch. 1808 Jamieson s.v., A rouch hass, or throat. 1872 W. Alexander Johnny Gibb viii, Your fader—the roch dyker.

β. 1 **ruȝ**, 3–5 **ruȝ(e**, 5 **ruȝhe**; 4 **roȝ(e**; 4–5 **rouȝ, rowȝ(e**, 5 **rouȝe**.

? a 1000 Gloss. in Wr.-Wülcker 243 Ȝebuf ficbeam,..uel ruȝ. 13.. E. E. Allit. P. B. 1545 Þe honde..rasped on þe roȝ woȝe. 1382 Wyclif Gen. xxv. 25 And al in maner of a skyn rowȝ. 1398 Trevisa Barth. De P. R. v. xxiii. (Bodl. MS.), Ȝif þey been rouȝe and..brode. a 1425 Cursor M. 21962 (Trin.), Þe toþer shal be wondir rowȝe.

γ. 4 **rug(g**, 4–7 (9 Sc.) **rugh** (5 **rughh, rught**); 4–6 **rughe** (4 **rughȝe**, 6 **ruyghe**); 4–6 **rogh(e**, 5 **roght**; 4–5 **rowgh**, 5–6 **rowghe**; 5–7 **roughe** (5 **rought**), 4– **rough**.

a 1300 Cursor M. 3489 Þe first..was rogh as hare,..He þat was rugh was rede wit-als. 13.. Ibid. 24838 (Edin.), Þe wedir..bigan be rug and reþe. a 1340 Hampole Psalter lxviii. 14 Wiþ þe haire þat is rughe & sharpe. c 1400 Destr. Troy 6632 With a rught batell. c 1400 Maundev. xxviii. (1839) 285 Thei beren gret Wolle and roughe. c 1440 Promp. Parv. 437/2 Rowghe, scharp or knotty. 1495 Trevisa's De P. R. IV. iii. 82 The thynge is rough. 1559 W. Cunningham Cosmogr. Glasse 45 The bodye..beyng a rough stone.

δ. 6 **rouf, roffe**, 6–7 **ruffe**, 7–8 **ruff**.

1577 B. Googe Heresbach's Husb. I. (1586) 28 b, The blades of both kindes are ruffe. 1665 Sir T. Herbert Trav. (1677) 20 Winds and ruff Seas. 1683 Pettus Fleta Minor I. (1686) 9 It was ruffe and sharp. a 1738 Swift To Dr. Sheridan 12 Compar'd with which..A Smoothing-Ir'n itself is ruff. 1787 Minor 53 Saw away the ruff corners of your mind.

B. Signification.

I. 1. Having a surface diversified with small projections, points, bristles, etc., so as to be harsh or disagreeable to the touch; not even or smooth.

a 1000 Riddles xxvi. 5 Staþol min is steap,..neoþan ruh nathwær. c 1000 Sax. Leechd. I. 254 Ðeos wyrt..hafað leaf neah swycle mistel; þa beoð ruȝe & brade. a 1225 Ancr. R. 284 Nis þet iren acursed þet iwurðeð þe swarture & þe ruhure so hit is ofture & more iviled? 13.. E. E. Allit. P. B. 1724 Þe fyste..rasped renyschly þe woȝe with þe roȝ penne. 13.. Gaw. & Gr. Kt. 745 Þe hasel & þe haȝ-þorne..With roȝe raged mosse rayled ay-where. a 1400–50 Alexander 3815 Þai..findis all þe strandis Full of Redis.. rughere þan thornes. c 1460 Wisdom 1055 in Macro Plays 70 Tyll þi nakyde body were all rought, Ande evyn rent to þe bonys bare. 1526 Skelton Magnyf. 453 Whan the noppe is rughe, it wolde be shorne. 1553 Eden Treat. New Ind. (Arb.) 16 Theyr skinne is very rowghe and full of chappes, and riftes like the barke of a tree. 1667 Milton P. L. v. 342 Fruit of all kindes, in coate, Rough, or smooth rin'd. 1670 in 12th Rep. Hist. MSS. Comm. App. V. 15 The silke.. will soone grow rough, gather dust and sullie. 1774 Goldsm. Nat. Hist. (1776) III. 221 The tongue is rough, and beset with prickles. 1781 Cowper Retirement 230 Rough elm, or smooth-grain'd ash, or glossy beech. 1820 Shelley Prometh. Unb. III. iii. 21 The rough walls are clothed with long soft grass. 1873 J. Richards Operator's Hdbk. 135 The lumber is guided by its rough surface before coming in contact with the cutters.

b. Of cloth: Coarse.

a 1000 Agz. Hymn. (Surtees) 103 Ruhne wæfels, yrcum tegimen. c 1000 Ælfric Gloss. in Wr.-Wülcker 125 Amphibalum, ruhhrægel. 1426 Lydg. De Guil. Pilgr. 17168 Off rowh frese, she hadde..A garnement shape lyk a sak. 1530 Palsgr. 322/2 Roughe as course clothe is, rude. 1611 Bible Zech. xiii. 4 Neither shall they weare a rough garment to deceiue. 1648 Hexham II, Rouw laken, Rough, or Course cloth. 1886 C. D. Warner Their Pilgr. 3 A gentleman clad in a perfectly-fitting rough travelling suit.

c. A rough bone, one with meat on it. Sc.

1826 Scott Woodst. xx, A hungry tyke ne'er minds a blaud with a rough bane.

2. Having the skin covered with hair; hairy, shaggy, hirsute. In later use spec. unclipped, unshorn; having a rough coat of hair.

c 1000 Ælfric Gen. xxvii. 11 Esau min broður ys ruh and ic eom smeðe. a 1225 St. Marher. 12 [She] sette hire fot uppon his ruhe necke. a 1250 Owl & Night. 1013 Hi goþ bi-tiȝt mid ruȝe uelle. 13.. K. Alis. 5956 He was rughher than any ku. 1382 Wyclif 2 Kings i. 8 A rowȝ man, and with an bery gyrdyl gyrd to the reenys. c 1400 Maundev. (Roxb.) xxxii. 147 Þe folk er all full of feþers and rugh. 1481 Caxton Myrr. II. viii. 83 Men and wymmen alle naked and also rowhe as beeres. 1565 Cooper Thesaurus s.v. Horridus, Sus horridus, a rough hogge with bristles standynge vp. 1610 Shaks. Temp. II. i. 250 Till new-borne chinnes Be rough, and Razor-able. 1637 Milton Lycidas 34 Rough Satyrs danc'd, and Fauns with clov'n heel. 1708 Lond. Gaz. No. 4421/8 Both are Rough, having lain at Grass all the Winter. 1875 Encycl. Brit. I. 396/1 Few fat sheep are now sent to market rough after the 1st of April. 1897 Daily News 2 Feb. 9/4 Fat bulls and rough cows were a difficult sale.

† b. Of hides: Undressed, untanned. Also of shoes, etc.: Made of undressed hide. Obs.

c 1050 Voc. in Wr.-Wülcker 468 Pero, hemming i. ruh sco. a 1300 Cursor M. 3677 Wit a rugh skin sco hidd his hals. c 1375 Sc. Leg. Saints xxxvi. (John Baptist) 279 With a belte of reucht skine made. 1432–50 tr. Higden (Rolls) I. 265 Hauenge clothes of the ruȝhe skynnes of bestes. 1489 Caxton Faytes of A. II. xxxv. K j b, All rounde aboute are nayled rowhe hydes and all wete and fresshe. 1508– [see Rilling sb.]. 1588–9 Reg. Privy Council Scot. IV. 365 Rouch hydis and barkit leddir. 1645 Rec. Elgin (1903) I. 179 Sex roche hyddes pertaining to the said Johne.

3. Of ground: Difficult to traverse; uneven, rugged, broken; uncultivated, wild.

c 1000 Life St. Guthlac (1848) 20 Ða ferdon begen þurh ða ruȝan fennas. c 1200 Ormin 9211 Whærse iss all..sharrp, & ruhh, & gatelæs þurrh þorrness & þurrh breress. 13.. Gaw. & Gr. Kt. 1898 Renaud com richchande þurȝ a roȝe greue. 1387 Trevisa Barth. De P. R. xvii. cxxvii. (Bodl. MS.), Paliurus is a þistel..& growiþ in rowȝ londe and vntelied. 1526 Tindale Luke iii. 5 And the rought wayes shalbe made smoth. 1553 Eden Treat. New Ind. (Arb.) 14 This region is rough with mountaynes. 1593 Shaks. Rich. II, II. iii. 4 These high wilde hilles, and rough vneeuen waies, Drawes out our miles. 1611 Bible Deut. xxi. 4 The Elders of that citie shall bring downe the heifer vnto a rough valley. 1686 tr. Chardin's Trav. Persia 386 The Road is somewhat crooked and rough. 1719 De Foe Crusoe I. (Globe) 297 We had some rough Way to pass yet. 1791 Cowper Odyss. VII. 346 The shore presented only roughest rocks. 1820 Shelley Sensit. Pl. II. 44 Into the rough woods far aloof. 1865 Ruskin Sesame i. § 26 Most men's minds are indeed little better than rough heath wilderness. 1885 Law Rep. Weekly Notes 146/2 A small cottage and some 22 acres of rough land held therewith.

fig. 1671 Milton P. R. I. 478 Hard are the ways of truth, and rough to walk. 1741–2 Gray Agrip. 53 Gain the rough heights, and grasp the dangerous honour. 1821 Shelley Epipsych. 72 She met me, Stranger, upon life's rough way.

II. 4. a. Of the sea or water: Running high, agitated, turbulent.

13.. E. E. Allit. P. C. 147 Hit reled on round vpon þe roȝe yþes. c 1400 Destr. Troy 3693 With a ropand rayne rugh was the se. 1470–85 Malory Arthur XIV. v. 648 He came to a rough water the whiche roryd. 1553 Eden Treat. New Ind. (Arb.) 33 The sea was very rough. 1593 Shaks. Rich. II, III. ii. 54 All the Water in the rough rude Sea. 1615 G. Sandys Trav. 17 The winds grew contrary: and the seas..too rough to be brooked by so small a vessell. 1662 J. Davies tr. Mandelslo's Trav. 117 The sea is rough at all times, there is no Landing without danger. 1743 P. Francis tr. Hor., Odes III. xii. 9 When he rises with vigor from Tiber's rough waves. 1808 Jamieson s.v. Heis, One is said to get a heisie in a rough sea. 1862 Miss Braddon Lady Audley x, She had always been..afraid of a rough sea.

fig. a 1596 Sir T. More II. iii. 27 A quiet ebb will follow this rough tide. 1769 Sir W. Jones Palace Fortune Poems (1777) 23 And rough with tempests [is] his afflicted breast. 1887 Times (Weekly ed.) 16 Dec. 1/3 He will find rough waters very soon.

b. Of weather, wind, etc.: Stormy, tempestuous, violent; rigorous, severe.

13.. Cursor M. 24838 (Edin.), Þe wedir als in somer smeþe Son bigan be rug and reþe. 13.. E. E. Allit. P. C. 139 Roȝ rakkes þer ros with rudnyng an-vnder. 1470–85 Malory Arthur XX. i. 797 Wynter with his rouȝ wyndes and blastes. 1530 Palsgr. 669/2, I pull in the sayle of a shyppe, as marryners do in a roughe wether. 1565 Cooper Thesaurus, Dies turbidus, a foule rough day. 1605 Shaks. Macb. I. iii. 147 Time, and the Houre, runs through the roughest Day. 1663 Cowley Verses & Ess. (1669) 108 The roughest season of the sky. 1764 Goldsm. Trav. 166 Turn we to survey Where rougher climes a nobler race display. 1784 Cowper Task III. 441 That no rough blast may sweep His garlands from the boughs. 1818 Scott Let. in Lockhart (1837) IV. iv. 123 Should the weather be rough,...do not think of riding. 1852 M. Arnold Empedocles I. ii. 246 Nor is the wind less rough that blows a good man's barge.

c. Of a voyage or journey: Accompanied or attended with, performed in, rough weather.

1854 Doyle Brown, Jones & R. 2 After a rough passage, ..landed at Ostend. 1877 [see Passage sb. 4].

5. Of actions, etc.: Violent; marked by violence towards, or harsh treatment of, others.

a 1300 Cursor M. 21962 His first comme it was ful smeth, þe toþer sal be rugh and reth. c 1400 Destr. Troy 10161 With a rumour full roide & a roght hate. Ibid. 13002 The ruerde wax ranke of þat rught fare. 1591 Shaks. 1 Hen. VI, IV. vii. 8 Rough deeds of Rage, and sterne Impatience. 1611 — Cymb. IV. i. 22 Her Father..may (happily) be a little angry for my so rough vsage. 1635–56 Cowley Davideis IV. 83 Nor was their Lust less active or less bold, Amidst this rougher search of Blood and Gold. 1756 tr. Keysler's Trav. (1760) IV. 446 The elector..seemed highly provoked at this rough usage. 1861 Hughes Tom Brown at Oxf. ix, There might be some reason for the rough handling he had got. 1881 Stevenson Virg. Puerisque (1903) 65 Those who have..not learnt the rough lessons that youth hands on to age.

b. Of places or times: Riotous, disorderly; attended with, or marked by, rowdiness.

1863 Mrs. Gaskell Sylvia's Lovers iv, The town was rough with a riot between the press-gang and the whaling-folk. 1884 Western Daily Press 2 June 3/1 In the language of the police the Derby Day was the 'roughest' which they had ever experienced.

c. Troublous, unpleasant.

1891 F. Paget Spirit of Discipline 164 Things promised a rough time for the Church at Ephesus.

6. Of language or expression: Harsh, over-bearing; uncivil, rude; angry, passionate.

c 1400 Destr. Troy 2031 Antenor..rekont by row all þere rogh speche. 1535 Coverdale 1 Kings xii. 13 The kynge gaue the people an harde rough answere. a 1548 Hall Chron., Rich. III, 14 b, Letters of a more rougher and hawter sort, not without minatorie termes. 1599 Shaks. Hen. V, V. ii. 313 Our Tongue is rough, Coze, and my Condition is not smooth. 1617 Moryson Itin. I. 84 Austine Barbadici.., by faire and rough tearmes, kept the league unbroken. 1647 Clarendon Hist. Reb. I. § 27 The Duke, by his rougher Dialect, in the end prevailed. 1709 Steele Tatler No. 31 ¶ 2 [He] called him..Lyar, Dog, and other rough Appellatives. 1754 Chatham Lett. Nephew v. 39 Towards Servants, never accustom yourself to rough and passionate language. 1848 Thackeray Van. Fair lix, The landlady reproached herself bitterly for ever having used a rough expression to her. 1891 Bp. W. How Lighter Moments (1900) 22 He answered with a rough 'Yes'.

fig. 1611 Shaks. Wint. T. III. iii. 55 Thou'rt like to haue A lullabie too rough.

b. So of features or looks.

1595 Shaks. John III. i. 104 The grapling vigor, and rough frowne of Warre. 1849 James Woodman v, My friend,.. whose looks are rougher than his intentions.

7. Of persons, their disposition, etc.: Inclined to be violent, harsh, rude, or ungentle.

To cut up rough: see Cut v. 59 l.

1530 Palsgr. 322/2 Roughe, boystous in dealyng, royde. 1535 Coverdale Wisdom xviii. 15 As a rough man of warre. 1593 Shaks. 2 Hen. VI, IV. ix. 44 Be not to rough in termes, For he is fierce. 1600 E. Blount tr. Conestaggio 23 Fearing more the Kings choler, by reason of his rough inclination. 1607 Shaks. Cor. III. ii. 25 You haue bin too rough, somthing too rough: you must returne, and mend it. 1746 P. Francis tr. Horace, Ep. II. i. 384 The bards..Who dare not trust the rough, contemptuous stage. 1802 Mar. Edgeworth Moral T. (1816) I. xvii. 142 So rough in my manner to him ..that he thinks I have no feeling. 1867 Princess Alice Mem. (1884) 170, I am so afraid they will be too rough with her. 1875 Jowett Plato (ed. 2) I. 231 Nay,..do not be rough; good words, if you please.

transf. 1671 Milton Samson 1066 A rougher tongue Draws hitherward, I know him by his stride. 1742 Gray Spring 38 Brush'd by the hand of rough Mischance. 1821 Shelley Dirge for the Year 9 So White Winter, that rough nurse, Rocks the death-cold Year to-day.

b. The rougher sex, the male sex.

1781 Cowper Conversat. 843 Divest the rougher sex of female airs. 1822 Scott Nigel Introd. Epist., I must abide by the general opinion, that he is of the rougher sex.

c. Of horses: Not properly broken in; not easy to ride on. rare.

1590 Shaks. Mids. N. V. i. 119 He hath rid his Prologue, like a rough Colt. 1685 Cotton tr. Montaigne I. xlviii, The Prince of Sulmona, riding a rough horse at Naples. 1797 Encycl. Brit. (ed. 3) VIII. 666/1 The more he trots, and the more he rides rough horses, the better.

8. Of remedies, medicines, etc.: Violent in effect; strong, powerful.

a 1674 Clarendon (J.), He..forced him to a quicker and rougher remedy. 1705 Arbuthnot Coins, etc. (1727) 234 His Purgative Medicines are generally very rough and strong.

9. colloq. a. Bearing or falling hardly on a person, etc.

1870 Bret Harte Luck Roaring Camp 2 Sandy Tipton thought it was 'rough on Sal'. 1887 Besant Kath. Regina iv, She is a governess somewhere, I believe. It's rough on her, isn't it?

b. Severe on, 'down' on, a person.

1870 Bret Harte Luck Roaring Camp 15 They're mighty rough on strangers. 1895 Hardy in Harper's Mag. Mar. 579 The management had..been rough on cousins ever since.

10. dial. Unwell, sick, ill.

a 1893 Story of Dick viii. 85 (Wilts. Gloss.), She was took rough as it might be uv a Monday.

III. 11. Of sounds: Discordant, harsh.

c 1400 Lanfranc's Cirurg. 197 Also her vois is rowȝ, ouþer sumtyme it is wondirly scharp. c 1450 Holland Howlat 215 The Ravyne, rolpand rudly in a roche ran. 1580 Spenser Let. Harvey in H.'s Wks. (Grosart) I. 35 Rough words must be subdued with Vse. 1608 Shaks. Per. III. ii. 88 The rough and woeful music that we have. 1683 Kennett tr. Erasm. on Folly (1709) 16 The delivery of Achilles was rough, harsh, and hesitant. 1751 Johnson Rambler No. 92 ¶ 12 It requires very little skill to make our language rough. 1845 Proc. Philol. Soc. II. 139 In general it will be found to have affected broad, rough sounds. 1876 Bristowe Th. & Pract. Med. (1878) 503 The roughest and most grating murmurs.

b. Gram. Aspirated.

1736 Ainsworth Lat. Dict. II. s.v. H, The original softer א and ה,..and the rougher ח and ח the parent of H. 1746 [see Breathing vbl. sb. 9]. 1785 Ess. Punctuation 153 That the letters over which it [ʽ] is placed, should be pronounced with a rough breathing. 1880 Encycl. Brit. XI. 355/1 H still remained as the rough breathing.

12. Sharp, acid, or harsh to the taste, esp. of wine or cider.

1545 Elyot, s.v. Asper, Asperum uinum, a rough wyne. 1583 Stubbes Anat. Abus. II. (1882) 25 Harshe, rough, stiptike, and hard wine. 1606 Shaks. Ant. & Cl. I. iv. 64 Thy pallat the[n] did daine The roughest Berry on the rudest Hedge. 1743 P. Francis tr. Horace, Odes I. xx. 6 'Twas rack'd into a Grecian cask, Its rougher juice to melt away. 1800 Med. Jrnl. IV. 252 Six pounds and a half of syrup, which had rather an unpleasant rough taste. 1834 Good's Study Med. (ed. 4) IV. 110 New and rough port-wine, diluted with an equal quantity of cold water. 1892 Sat. Rev. 15 Oct. 435/2 That..attraction that West-country folk find in rough cider.

13. Of diction, style, etc.: Wanting grace or refinement; rude, unpolished, rugged.

1535 Stewart Cron. Scot. I. 5 Thocht thi langage be bayth rouche and rude, Ȝit neuirtheles the sentence is richt gude. 1599 Shaks. Hen. V, Epil. 1 Thus farre with rough and all-vnable Pen, Our bending Author hath pursu'd the Story. 1638 Junius Paint. Ancients 27 The Art of Painting hath been about the time of her infancy..rough and poore. 1709 Pope Ess. Crit. 338 Most by Numbers judge a Poet's song; And smooth or rough, with them is right or wrong. 1751 Chatham Lett. Nephew I. 1 Your translation..is very close to the sense of the original.., the numbers not lame, or rough. 1818 Scott Hrt. Midl. xxxii[i], Gifted with a sort of rough eloquence which raised him above his companions. 1881 Jowett Thucyd. I. Introd. p. viii, The old version of Hobbes ..is very rough and inaccurate.

14. Of persons, their disposition, etc.: Lacking in culture or refinement; uncultivated; having rude manners or ways.

1588 Shaks. L. L. L. V. ii. 306 Their shallow showes,..And their rough carriage so ridiculous. 1688 Penton Guardian's Instruction (1897) 20, I was pleased to see the ruff boyish humour filed a little. 1709 Addison Tatler No. 108 ¶ 4 A plain, rough, honest Man, and wise, tho' not learned. 1781 Gibbon Decl. & F. xix. (1787) II. 134 Who, under the semblance of a rough soldier, disguised the most artful insinuation. 1821 Shelley Epipsych. 440 The mossy tracks.. (Which the rough shepherd treads but once a year). 1842 Miall in Nonconf. II. 249 A rougher earnestness than is at present fashionable. 1888 F. Hume Mme. Midas I. Prol., The man at his feet was a rough, heavy-looking fellow.

absol. 1784 Cowper Tiroc. 341 Great schools suit best the sturdy and the rough.

b. Rough and round or tough: cf. Rough and ready.

1825 Scott Jrnl. 18 Dec., I love the virtues of rough and round men. 1848 Dickens Dombey ix, A blundering young rough-and-tough boy like me.

c. Unrefined (but kindly or friendly).

1848 Dickens Dombey xxxii, The generous..youth, whom he had loved, according to his rough manner. 1864 Tennyson Aylmer's F. 591 Being much befool'd..By the rough amity of the other. 1873 Black Pr. Thule (1874) 9 Mackenzie offered them a rough and hearty welcome.

15. Of occupations or exercises: Requiring or associated with rude energy or strength.

1717 Lady M. W. Montagu Let. to Pope ¶ 5 The softness and warmth of the climate forbid..all rough exercises. 1797 Encycl. Brit. (ed. 3) VIII. 665/2 This rough work, all at once, is plainly..detrimental at first. 1865 Ruskin Sesame ii. § 68 The man, in his rough work in open world, must encounter all peril and trial. 1906 Temple Bar Jan. 6 Living in a native hut and maintaining himself by the roughest labour.

IV. 16. Of materials: In a natural or crude state; undressed, unwrought; not brought by working into a finished condition or form.

1434 in Dugdale Monast. (1846) VI. 1414/1 All the inner side of rough stone, except the bench-table-stones. 1435 Coventry Leet Bk. 181 Here is a ston of rough-iron, the whiche must be tendurly cherysshet. 1485 Nott. Rec. III. 231, vj. lode of rugh plaster vnbrenned. 1545 Bk. of Rates d ij b, Blowynge hornes the dossen...Roughe hornes the M. 1582 in Trans. Jewish Hist. Soc. (1903) IV. 93 For everie quintall of rough Copper he made (being cxij li.) he must have vij. Kebulls of Copper ure. 1601 Act 43 Eliz. c. 10 § 2 Other Engine to stretche or straine any roughe and unwroughte Woollen Clothe. 1670 Pettus Fodinæ Reg. 5 In these Veins..are often found Loadstones,..Rough pearl and Soft diamond. 1766 Compl. Farmer s.v. Queen-bee, The intestines of these bees are found at times to be more or less distended with honey, and with rough wax. 1788 Gibbon Decl. & F. l. V. 227 A chair or pulpit of rough timber. 1839 Ure Dict. Arts 704 The bloom or rough ball, from the puddle furnace. 1897 Henty On the Irrawaddy 131 As they [sc. jewels] were in the rough state, he had no idea what size they would be when cut.

† b. Sc. Raw, uncooked. Obs.[−1]

1793 T. Scott Poems 351 Nae mair a rive o' gait, or fowl, Ha'f rough, ha'f roastet on a coal, But guid sirloin.

17. Made in a general way without detailed minuteness; having an approximate accuracy or adequacy; rudely sufficient; also, in a preliminary form, to be further improved or elaborated.

1607 Shaks. Timon I. i. 43, I haue in this rough worke, shap'd out a man [etc.]. a 1766 G. Colman Posth. Lett. (1820) 336, I have drawn out the above rough sketch, merely to enable you to think in the same train with me. 1801 Farmer's Mag. Jan. 21 A subject susceptible only of a rough guess. 1819 Scott Let. in Lockhart (1837) IV. viii. 255, I add a rough drawing of the arms. 1866 Rogers Agric. & Prices I. xxiii. 601 The possible produce was in a rough way understood and attained. 1882 Floyer Unexpl. Baluchistan 70 The inhabitants seemed capable of a rough division into three classes.

b. Rough draft, draught (cf. Draught sb. 32).

1699 Temple Ess. Pop. Discontent Wks. 1720 I. 263, I shall..trace upon this Paper the rough Draught of some such Notions as I have had long and often in my Head. 1706 E. Ward Wooden World Diss. (1708) To Rdr. A vj b, This rough Draught of my untutor'd Pencil. 1712 Steele Spect. No. 272 ¶ 1 The rough Draught of the Marriage Settlement. 1831 [see Draught sb. 32]. 1879 Froude Cæsar xiii. 173 His Agrarian law, the rough draft of which had been already discussed.

c. Rough copy (cf. Copy sb. 6).

1781 Cowper Table-T. 614 A rough copy of the Christian face Without the smile, the sweetness, or the grace. 1811 Miss L. M. Hawkins C'tess & Gertr. (1812) I. 259 She could not always read his rough copy. 1888 M. Robertson Lombard St. Myst. xxii, The supposed deeds were only rough copies.

18. Not very good or perfect.

1812 Examiner 7 Sept. 563/2 Barley rather a rough sample. 1862 Miller Elem. Chem., Org. (ed. 2) 337 Red liquor, a rough acetate of alumina used by the calico-printer. 1868 Joynson Metals 22 The iron..run into rough moulds or channels made in sand.

b. London slang. Coarse or stale (food).

1851 Mayhew Lond. Labour I. 53/1 The 'dropped' and 'rough' fish is bought chiefly for the poor. 1859 Slang Dict. 82 'Rough fish', bad fish.

c. Lacking in comfort or refinement.

1859 Jephson Brittany i. 5 Who can put up with rough accommodation on an emergency. 1881 R. Buchanan God & the Man II. v, The rough fare of the ship's crew.

19. Comprising or requiring only the ruder degrees or processes of workmanship or skill.

1680 Moxon Mech. Exerc. xi. 211 We will not suppose that the Grooves are of equal depth with the Rough-working of the Gouge. 1704 Fuller Med. Gymn. Pref., We know..their Pharmacy was Rough and Barbarous. 1746 P. Francis tr. Horace, Sat. II. iii. 34 Here the rude chisel's rougher strokes I trac'd. 1803 Med. Jrnl. X. 90 To avail themselves of those methods, however rough and unsightly they may appear, which experience shews to possess great power. 1845 Penny Cycl. Suppl. I. 674/1 After the first or rough boring the interior is fine-bored. 1860 Tomlinson Arts & Manuf. 2 Ser. Cutlery 61 The first, which is called rough buffing, is with Trent sand, and the second, gloss buffing.

b. Ignoring, or incapable of, fine distinctions; not entering into minutiæ or details.

1819 Scott Ivanhoe xliii, The natural and rough sense of Robin Hood. 1855 Pusey Doctr. Real Presence Note B 43 Such a rough, indefinite mind as Luther's. 1873 Hamerton Intell. Life XI. ii. 405 In this rough justice of the world there is a natural distribution of rewards.

20. Sc. Having abundance or plenty, esp. of a homely or plain sort. Also rough and round, coarse but plentiful.

1721 Kelly Sc. Prov. 145 He has a Hole under his Nose that will never let him be rough. 1808 Jamieson s.v., A gude rouch house, a house where there is abundance of provisions. 1818 Scott Hrt. Midl. xlv[i], Plenty of all the requisites for 'a rough and round dinner'.

V. 21. In special collocations, as **rough arch**, a discharging arch; **rough band**, dial., a band playing 'rough music'; † **rough bear**, a Scottish variety of barley; **rough bine**, a prickly hop-bine (see quot.); **rough book**, Naut. (see quot.); **rough bounds**, (a) the Scottish Highlands; (b) part of western Inverness-shire; **rough coal** (see quots.); **rough coat**, the first coat of plaster on lath; **rough coating**, = Rough-cast sb. 2; **rough Epsom** (see quot.); **rough file**, a file with a deep-cut face; **rough house**, U.S., a disturbance, row; **rough-knots**, 'unsophisticated seamen' (Smyth); **rough-mast, mortar, plate, -rendering** (see quots.); **rough rice**, unhusked rice, paddy; **rough-scuff**, U.S. (see quots.); † **rough setter**, a rough-stone mason; **rough-skins**, U.S. (see quot.); **rough-slant**, U.S., a lean-to, a rude shelter; **rough-stoning**, scouring with rubbing-stone; **rough strings** (see quots.); **rough stuff**, (a) the bottom stuff for boots and shoes; (b) coarse paint used before the final coat; **rough timber** (see quot. 1711); † **rough wall**, rubble work; **rough-waller**, a builder of rough-stone walls.

1833 Loudon Encycl. Archit. § 1075 All the doors, windows, etc., to be saved with *rough arches (to have discharging arches) over the same. 1854 Wilts. Arch. Mag. I. 88 The procession was in each instance headed by what is called a '*rough band'. 1771 Encycl. Brit. I. 61/1 The common barley,..the Highland barley, more commonly called *rough bear [etc.]. 1846 J. Baxter Libr. Pract. Agric. (ed. 4) I. 398 What is commonly called 'white bine', tolerably free from the rough barbs which are often found on the under part of the leaves, which constitute a '*rough bine'. 1867 Smyth Sailor's Word-bk. 580 *Rough Books, those in which the warrant officers make their immediate entries of expenditure. 1814 J. Grant Orig. Gael 288 The people or Gael of the mountains, expressed in English by *rough bounds. 1830 Encycl. Metrop. (1845) XXI. 54/1 The most rugged district is that..between Argyleshire, Loch Lochy, and the sea, and generally called the Rough-bounds. 1862 Skene Introd. Dean of Lismore's Bk. p. xv, The Garbh chriochan or rough bounds, consisting of Arisaig, Moydart, Moror and Knoydart. 1789 J. Williams Min. Kingd. I. 244 *Rough, roch, or rock coal,..is a free coal of various degrees of strength and hardness, commonly of a good black colour. 1839 Ure Dict. Arts 962 The open-burning cubical coals are known by several local names; the rough coal or clod coal, from the large masses in which they may be had. 1855 J. Phillips Man. Geol. 204 The coal is partly 'splint', partly 'rough' or 'cheery'. 1875 Knight Dict. Mech. 1993/2, *Rough-coat,..the first coat on lath. On brick it is termed laying..; on masonry, rendering. 1791 W. H. Marshall W. Eng. (1796) II. 297 Stucco is analogous to the materials of a dam,..*Rough Coating, to the puddle of Canal Makers. 1853 Ure Dict. Arts I. 57 The alum mothers are boiled down to a crystallizing point, and afford a crop of '*Rough Epsom', which is a sulphate of magnesia and protoxide of iron. 1834–6 Encycl. Metrop. (1845) VIII. 275/2 Files of the very coarsest sort are called rubbers, and the next in order to these are called *rough files. 1895 Harper's Mag. Mar. 540/2 They might be goin to hev considerable *rough house—a fuss, I mean, sir. 1867 Smyth Sailor's Word-bk. s.v. Mast, *Rough-mast, or rough-tree, a spar fit for making a mast. 1775 Ash s.v. Roughcasting, The *rough mortar on the surface of a building. 1823 Crabb Technol. Dict., Rough mortar, a sort of sand which, when mixed with mortar, makes it look as red as blood. 1883 J. D. Weeks Rep. Manuf. Glass 20 *Rough plate is the crude plate-glass as it comes from the annealing oven. 1823 P. Nicholson Pract. Build. 393 *Rough-rendering .. means one coat rough. 1763 Ann. Reg. I. 92, 776 bushels of *rough rice. 1859 Bartlett Dict. Amer. (ed. 2) 371 *Rough-Scuff, the lowest people; the rabble. 1864 Webster, Rough-scuff, a rough, coarse fellow.

1435 in Dugdale Monast. (1846) VI. 1415/1 Will. Horwode shall nether set mo nor fewer free masons, *rogh setters ne leyes thereupon. 1859 Bartlett Dict. Amer. (ed. 2) 371 *Roughskins, a gang of Baltimore bullies. 1855 Mrs. Gaskell North & S. xii, There had been *rough-stoning done in the middle of the floor. 1823 P. Nicholson Pract. Build. 189 The pieces of timber which are thus placed under the steps are called *rough strings. 1842 Gwilt Encycl. Arch. § 2026 The framed timbers which support the steps of a staircase..generally consist of two pieces inclined to the pitch of the stairs, called the rough strings. 1889 Charity Organis. Rev. Jan. 7 Clickers cut out the leather for the uppers, *rough-stuff cutters that for the soles and heels. 1607 Nott. Rec. IV. 284 The marketts of sawen and cloven tymber..exceptinge all *rough tymber. 1711 W. Sutherland Shipbuild. Assist. 163 Rough Timber; that which is only cut down, and the Boughs lop'd off. 1398 Hist. Dun. Script. Tres (Surtees) p. clxxx, Exterius de puro lapide vocato achiler.., interius vero de fracto lapide vocato *rogh-wall. 1864 C. W. King Gnostics 174 The common workman who ran up the body of the wall..was called the '*Rough-waller'. 1885 Westall Old Factory i, He was a first-rate hedger and ditcher and rough waller.

b. In names of animals, esp. fishes and reptiles, as **rough aphrodite, bullhead, dab**, etc. Also **rough-tail, -wing**.

1783 Barbut Vermes 43 Aphrodita Scabra, the *Rough Aphrodite. 1803 Shaw Gen. Zool. IV. 259 *Rough bull-head, Cottus Scaber...Native of the Indian seas. 1840 Cuvier's Anim. Kingd. 323 P[leuronectes] leminoides, the Long, or *Rough Dab. 1843 R. T. Lowe Fishes Madeira I. 55 Trachichthys pretiosus, *Black-mouthed affonsin or *Rough-fish. 1883 Day Fishes Gt. Brit. II. 342 Fuller's ray,..*Rough flapper, Edinburgh. 1802 Shaw Gen. Zool. III. I. 229 *Rough lizard. Lacerta Stellio...This species is remarkable for the unusually rough..appearance of its whole upper surface. 1769 Pennant Brit. Zool. (1776) III. 75 *Rough Ray...The upper part of the body..entirely covered with small spines. 1883 Day Fishes Gt. Brit. II. 346 The Homelyn ray: rough ray: sandy ray. 1781 Pennant Hist. Quadrup. II. 524 *Rough Seal...Perhaps what the Newfoundland Seal-hunters call Square Phipper. 1866 Chambers's Encycl. VIII. 535/1 The Rough .. Seal (P. hispida) frequents quiet bays on the coasts of Greenland. 1802 Shaw Gen. Zool. III. II. 494 *Rough snake, Coluber Scaber. 1803 Ibid. IV. II. 408 *Rough sparus, Sparus Dentex. 1661 Lovell Hist. Anim. & Min. 234 *Rough-taile [= the horse mackarel]..is a dry fish and engendreth thick juyce. 1887 Encycl. Brit. XXII. 192/1 s.v. Snakes, Family 3. Uropeltidæ (Rough Tails). 1877 Nature 3 May 18/1 A *Rough Terrapin (Clemmys punctularia) from the Upper Amazons. 1802 Shaw Gen. Zool. III. I. 55 *Rough tortoise, Testudo scabra! 1819 G. Samouelle Entomol. Compend. 408 Tortrix rugosana, the *Rough-wing. 1832 J. Rennie Consp. Butterfl. & M. 154 The Rough-Wing..appears the beginning of June on hedges. Ibid. 180 The Grey Rough-Wing. 1648 Hexham II, Een Steen-worm, a *Rough-worme in a mans foote, or a Lope.

c. In names of plants, as **rough bindweed, bristle-grass, cadlock**, etc.

1601 *Rough-bindweed [see Bindweed 2]. 1611 Cotgr., Liset picquant, Rough Bindweed. 1823 Crabb Techn. Dict., Rough Bindweed,..the Smilax aspera of Linnæus. 1859 Miss Pratt Brit. Grasses 82 *Rough Bristle-grass. 1611 Cotgr., Langue de bœuf,.. Ox-tongue, *rough or small Buglosse. 1790 W. H. Marshall Midl. Gloss. (E. D. S.), Cadlock, *Rough,..wild mustard. 1859 Miss Pratt Brit. Grasses 73 Tufted Hair-grass..is also termed *Rough-caps, from its long, narrow, rough, twisting leaves. Ibid. 63 *Rough Cat's-tail. 1849 Craig, *Rough-chervil, the plant Anthriscus vulgaris. 1562 Turner Herbal II. 26 a, Lagopus maye be called in Englishe Haris foot or *rough clauer. 1611 Cotgr., Treffle bas, hares-foot, rough Clauer. 1772 Encycl. Brit. II. 304/1 Dactylis ..glomeratus, or *rough cock's-foot grass. 1805 R. W. Dickson Pract. Agric. II. 831 Rough Cock's-foot Grass .. is a coarse, rough grass, but very hardy and productive. 1859 Miss Pratt Brit. Grasses 97 Rough Cock's-foot. 1889 Maiden Useful Native Pl. 143 Trema aspera,..'*Rough Fig'...This shrub is firmly believed by some to be poisonous. 1886 Britten & Holland Plant-n., *Rough Grass, Dactylis glomerata. 1833 Sturt S. Australia I. iii. 118 The *rough-gum abounded near the creek. 1898 Morris Austral Eng. 180 1 Rough-barked or Rough Gum, Eucalyptus botryoides. 1784 Cullum Hist. Hawsted 4 *Rough Horse-tail, or Shave-grass (Equisetum hyemale) in woods. 1861 Bentley Man. Bot. 703 Equisetum hyemale, Rough Horse-tail, which is largely imported from Holland under the name of Dutch Rushes. 1883 Almondbury Gloss. s.v. Kex, There are two sorts of kex—Shiny Kex, Angelica sylvestris; and *Rough Kex, Heracleum spondylium. 1877 E. Leigh Cheshire Gloss., *Rough-nut, the sweet or Spanish chestnut. 1548 Turner Names Herbes (E. D. S.) 76 It may be called in englishe Cow-persnepe or *rough Persnepe. 1797 Billingsley Agric. Somerset 116 The sorts [of potatoes] cultivated are the kidney,..*rough red, purple, and silver-skin. 1886 Britten & Holland Plant-n. 408 *Rough Robin, Lychnis Flos-cuculi. 1548 Turner Names Herbes (E. D. S.) 46 It maye be named in englishe *rough Trifoly or harefote. 1885 Britten & Holland Plant-n., *Rough Weed, Stachys palustris.

22. With sbs. used attrib., as rough-board, -edge, -weather.

1862 Burton Book-hunter I. 13 He was not a black-letter man,..or a rough-edge man. 1865 Dickens Mut. Fr. II. xii, Rough-weather nautical clothes. 1893 Outing XXII. 122/1 Curiosities without number hide the rough-board walls.

23. Comb., forming parasynthetic adjs., as rough-backed, -bearded, -edged, -faced, and sbs. derived from these, as rough-handedness, -heartedness; also rough-looking.

1837 Penny Cycl. IX. 396 Any other *rough-barked plant. 1612 Webster White Divel v. i, No *rough-bearded comet Stares on thy mild departure. 1828 J. E. Smith Engl. Flora II. 49 Leaflets ovate, pinnatifid, *rough-edged. 1895 F. M. Crawford Casa Braccio xvii. The lower story was built of *rough-faced blocks of travertine stone. 1849 D. J. Browne Amer. Poultry Yd. (1855) 243 One short, squat, *rough-feathered, ill-marked goose. 1611 Cotgr., Perche de mer, the sea Perch; a wholesome, *rough-find, and tongue-lesse, rocke-fish. 1703 J. Philips Splendid Shilling 128 Walnut in *rough-furrow'd Coat secure. 1704 Dict. Rust. (1726) s.v. Oak, The *rough-grain'd Body of a stubbed Oak. 1840 Dickens Old C. Shop xv, A gentle hand—rough-grained and hard though it was. 1548 Elyot, Hispidus, bristled, or *rough heared. 1648 Hexham II, Ruydigheydt, Scabbinesse, Scurvinesse, or Rough-haired. 1793 Martyn Lang. Bot., Hirtus, rough-haired. 1863 Life Normandy II. 224 A couple of big rough-haired deer-hounds. a 1680 Butler Charact., A Bumpkin (1908) 41 He is never without some *rough-handed Flatterer, that rubs him, like a Horse, with a Curry-Comb. 1870 J. B. Brown Eccles. Truth 269 The age of conquest and rough-handed violence. 1889 Gretton Memory's Harkback 22 One instance as well as a hundred will tell my babyism and their *rough-handedness. 1856 Lever Martins of Cro' M. 244 To rub shoulders with the coarse-minded, the *rough-hearted, and the vulgar. 1615 Byfield Coloss. iii. 12 The first is fear.., as it is opposed unto boldness, conceitedness, *rough-heartedness. 1860 Ruskin Unto this Last iv. § 79 These *rough-jacketed, rough-worded persons. 1826 Surr Winter in London III. 226 A *rough-looking sea-faring man, about four-and-thirty years old. 1630 R. Johnson's Kingd. & Commw. 279 More *rough mannerd than the Silesians and Bohemians. 1594 Nashe Unfort. Trav. Wks. (Grosart) V. 104 Boulstered out with *rough plumed siluer plush. 1690 Norris Beatitudes (1692) 83 The World is made for the bold and violent, the *rough-spirited and turbulent. 1593 Nashe Christ's T. Wks. (Grosart) IV. 248 Hee wil sende a *rougher stringed scourge amongst vs. 1533 *Rough-tasted [see Apple 1]. 1731 Miller Gard. Dict. s.v. Wines, Of the same Sort are certain austere or rough-tasted Substances. 1872 Tennyson Gareth & Lynette 885 *Rough-thicketed were the banks and steep. 1598 Marston Sco. Villanie III. ix. 217 Higher straines Then well beseemes a *rough-tongu'd Satyres part. 1855 Kingsley Heroes, Argonauts v. 165 They were rough-tongued. 1728 Chambers Cycl. s.v. File, Some cutting faster, as the *rough-tooth'd file. 1818 Keats Endym. II. 864 No longer did he wage A *rough-voic'd war against the dooming stars. 1865 Morris Jason XVII. 79 The shout Of rough-voiced sea-folk endeth every song.

b. In specific names of animals, birds, etc.

1890 Cent. Dict. s.v., The *rough-backed cayman, Alligator or Caiman trigonatus, of South America. 1785 Latham Gen. Synop. Birds VI. 586 *Rough-billed Pelican. 1803 Shaw Gen. Zool. IV. II. 191 *Rough-finned band-fish, Cepola Trachyptera. 1843 R. T. Lowe Fishes Madeira I. 155 Mugil corrugatus, Common or *Rough-lipped Grey Mullet of Madeira. 1887 Cassell's Encycl. Dict., *Rough-necked jacare..from Demarara. 1758 Borlase Nat. Hist. Cornw. 276 *Rough-ridged limpet. c 1711 Petiver Gazophyl. vi. 58 *Rough-scaled Cape Lizard. 1802 Shaw Gen. Zool. I. I. 134 *Rough-Tailed Bat. 1871 Darwin Desc. Man II. xii. (1890) 332 The rough-tailed stickleback (G. trachurus). 1838 Audubon Ornith. Biog. IV. 593 *Rough-winged Swallow, Hirundo Serripennis. Ibid. 595 In its general appearance ..the Rough-winged Swallow is extremely similar to the Bank Swallow. 1872 Coues N. Amer. Birds 114 Stelgidopteryx, Rough-winged Swallow.

c. In specific names of plants.

1882 Proc. Berwick Nat. Club IX. 430 There is a fine cluster of *rough-barked Spanish chestnuts among the oaks. 1889 Maiden Useful Native Pl. 441 The former [was called] by the colonists 'Rough-barked Bloodwood'. Ibid. 85 Echinopogon ovatus,..*Rough-bearded Grass. 1833 Proc. Berwick Nat. Club I. 29 Hieracium prenanthoides—*Rough-bordered Hawkweed. 1753 Chambers' Cycl. Suppl. s.v. Tithymalus, The wart-Spurge, or *rough-fruited Spurge. 1822 Hortus Anglicus II. 7 P. Argemone, Long *Rough-headed Poppy. 1789 J. Pilkington View Derbysh. I. 443 Lathyrus hirsutus, *Rough podded Vetchling, or Pease-everlasting. 1796 Withering Brit. Plants (ed. 3) III. 640 Ervum hirsutum, Rough podded Tare. 1822 Hortus Anglicus II. 246 L. Hirsutus, Rough-podded Lathyrus. Ibid. 463 T. Dactyloides, *Rough-seeded Tripsacum. 1805 R. W. Dickson Pract. Agric. II. 826 The Common or *Rough-stalked Meadow Grass. 1854 H. Miller Sch. & Schm. (1858) 398 The characteristic vegetable is the *rough-stemmed tangle—Laminaria digitata.

Rough (rʊf), adv. Also 7–8 **ruff**; Sc. 6 (8) **ruch**, 9 **rouch, roch**. [f. the adj. Cf. the earlier form Row adv.]

1. In a rough manner; roughly, rudely; without special care or accuracy, etc.

1560 Rolland Seven Sages Prol. iii, Scho..Merueillit at me how I durst..Aganis wemen to speik sa ruch and rude. 1610 Holland Camden's Brit. (1637) 739 The river Cam, which running rough upon stones, cutteth through it. 1680 Otway Orphan II. iv, Should you charge me rough I should but weep. 1687 Lond. Gaz. No. 2289/7 A plain brown cropt Nag,..Walks and trots well, gallops rough. 1762 Mills Syst. Husb. I. 92 Before the land is plowed rough for a spring crop. 1780 Mirror No. 97 They should be taught..to speak their own language rough and round. 1858 Kingsley Poems 62 As we pledge the health of our general, Who fares as rough as we. 1897 Outing XXX. 481/2 In polo, a man rides rough all the time.

b. To lie (or sleep) rough (see quots.).

1697 Dryden Virg. Georg. III. 357 Rough upon the flinty Rock he lyes. a 1700 B. E. Dict. Cant. Crew, To lie Rough, in one's Clothes all Night. 1796 Grose's Dict. Vulg. T. (ed. 3), To lie rough,..to sleep on the bare deck of a ship. 1824 Scott Redgauntlet ch. xii, Job will take you to a place where you may sleep rough till he calls you. 1893 Wiltshire Gloss., 'To sleep rough', or 'lay rough', to sleep about out of doors like a vagabond.

2. Comb. a. With verbs, as rough-bore, to bore roughly, rough-enter, -hull, -lay, etc.

1565 Cooper Thesaurus, Crustare parietes,..to rough lay; to pariette walles. 1593 Nashe Christ's T. Wks. (Grosart) IV. 69 Now the raine wil rough-enter through the crannies of theyr wauering. 1679 Moxon Mech. Exerc. ix. 155 They generally Rough-plain their Boards for Flooring. 1776 G. Semple Building in Water 3 They..could not conveniently get the Ruins at that Time removed, therefore, they only just rough-levelled them. 1793 Smeaton Edystone L. § 81, I immediately rough-turned a piece of wood. 1812 Sir J. Sinclair Syst. Husb. Scot. II. App. 50 After kiln-drying the barley, it is put into the mill, and rough hulled. 1829 A. Cunningham Lives Brit. Painters I. 111 Having received an agreeable letter from Dr. Franklin he rough-wrote an answer. 1881 Miss Braddon Asphodel II. 66 [He] had rough-ploughed a thousand acres or so of his best land. 1890 W. J. Gordon Foundry 18 At first it is rough bored, should it not have been cast hollow.

b. With pa. pples. used attributively or predicatively, as rough-bedded, -clad, -cut, etc.

1593 Shaks. Lucrece 1249 As in a rough-grown grove. 1612 Drayton Poly-olb. I. 52 Thou Jersey, bravely crown'd With rough-imbattl'd rocks. 1683 Moxon Mech. Exerc., Printing xiii. ¶ 3, I have Fil'd the Face..with a Rough-Cut-File. 1727–46 Thomson Summer 1761 A savage..with the unfashioned fur Rough-clad. 1793 Smeaton Edystone L. § 148 The second step rough bedded. 1818 Scott Rob Roy xix, The crowd..forced its way up a steep and rough-paved street. 1864 Tennyson Enoch Arden 95 His face, Rough-redden'd with a thousand winter gales. 1877 R. J. More Under the Balkans 215 A small bit of woollen carpet laid on the red rough-plastered floor. 1887 Ruskin Præterita II. 400 Floors and partitions all of rough-sawn larch.

c. With pres. pples., as rough-blustering, -clanking, -living, -rising.

1605 Sylvester Du Bartas II. iii. Lawe 1003 Rough-blust'ring Boreas nurst with Riphean snow. 1729 Savage Wanderer II. 15 Rough-rising from yon sculptur'd wall, Bold prophets nations to repentance call! Ibid. v. 460 His chains rough-clanking to discordant groans. 1743 Francis tr. Hor., Odes III. vii. 28 The rough-swelling tides. 1808 Jamieson s.v. Rouch, A profane swearer, a drunkard, &c. is called a rouch, or a rouch-living man.

d. With vbl. sbs., as rough-boring, -locking, -rolling.

1853 Ure Dict. Arts (ed. 4) II. 509 Shingling..costs, in wages, 1s. 9d. per ton; and rough-rolling, 1s. 2d. 1859 Marcy Prairie Trav. iii. 93 Rough-locking is a very safe method of passing heavy artillery down abrupt declivities. 1890 Rep. Brit. Assoc. 939 The mild steel..is after forging and rough-boring subjected to the process of oil-hardening.

Rough (rʊf), v.[1] Also 8 **ruff**. [f. the adj.]

I. 1. trans. † a. To raise a nap on (cloth); = Row v.[1] Obs.

1483–4 Act 1 Rich. III, c. 8 § 13 Tayntours..for evenynge of cloth onely after it commeth from the Mille and before it be roughed [AF. text rougher].

b. To turn, pull, scrape or rub up, so as to make rough. Also fig.

1763 Mills Pract. Husb. III. 123 The wheat..felt a little rough in the hand, because, not having been stirred for six years, the little hairs that are at the extremity of the grain, and the particles of the bran, were roughed up. 1850 Holtzapffel Turning III. 1121 The face of the polisher is roughed up, or thoroughly scraped with an old razor blade or knife. 1879 Jefferies Wild Life 124 If the hurricane roughs up the straw on all the ricks in the parish. 1884 — Life of Fields (1891) 171 It roughs them up the wrong way.

c. To make rough; to ruffle.

1844 Mrs. Browning Dead Pan x, Thine eagle, blind and old, Roughs his feathers in the cold. 1875 R. Browning Aristoph. Apol. 114 Go ask my rivals..how they roughed my fleece. 1887 Daily News 29 Sept. 3/1 The salt water caused it to blister and roughed her bottom.

d. spec. (See quots.)

1825 Jennings Dial. W. Eng. p. xviii, To Rough, to roughen; particularly a horse's shoes. 1838 Holloway Prov. Dict., To rough, to put long headed nails into a horse's shoes to make them rough, and so prevent the horse from slipping in frosty weather. 1889 Gretton Memory's Harkback 152 The ordinary remedy was to 'rough' your horse; that is, to turn up the heels of the shoes, and fasten them with great-headed nails.

2. a. To offend, grate upon (the ear).

1623 H. Sydenham Serm. (1637) 133 Those eares which have been stockt hitherto with the supple dialect of the Court..will not be rough't now with the course phrase of a reproofe.

b. To use rough language to (a person); to ruffle (one).

1861 Hughes Tom Brown at Oxf. iii, [He] lost no chance of roughing him in his replies. 1883 Cent. Mag. Sept. 737, I didn't mean to rough you when I said that. I don't want to hurt your feelings.

c. To deal roughly with, ill-use (one).

1868 Pall Mall G. 5 Oct. 4 This year a band of these Hungarians..were considerably roughed and mishandled. 1869 T. B. Aldrich Story Bad Boy 191 How tenderly the years touched him..!—all the more tenderly..for having roughed him so cruelly in other days.

3. intr. a. To become rough or stormy. rare[−1].

1876 Capt. R. F. Burton Gorilla L. I. 21 The cruel crawling sea began to rough, purr, and tumble.

b. To bristle or ruffle up.

1904 Sladen Lovers Japan xii, When a snake is drawn backwards, its scales rough up like cogs and hold it.

II. 4. To rough it, to face or submit to hardships, rough or casual accommodation, etc.; to do without ordinary conveniences or luxuries; to live in a rough way.

1768 J. Byron Narr. Patagonia 205 We were obliged to ruff it the whole passage. 1796 Washington Writ. (1892) XIII. 341 Never having been accustomed to shift or rough it. 1826 Scott Jrnl. 20 Nov., The expense of travelling has mounted high. I am too old to rough it. 1879 Geo. Eliot Theo. Such ii. 37 Roughing it with them under difficulties.

b. To rough (it) out: (see Out adv. 7 b).

1821 Scott Pirate xxix, We have no other course for it but to..rough it out as well as we can. 1833 Marryat P. Simple (1863) 404. I determined, to use a nautical expression, to rough it out. 1836 Backwoods of Canada 41, I might..have roughed out a year or so.

5. trans. a. To break in (a horse).

1802 James Mil. Dict., To Rough Horses, a word in familiar use among the dragoons to signify the act of breaking in horses, so as to adapt them to military purposes.

b. To expose (an animal) to rough weather and hard or scanty fare.

1858 Jrnl. R. Agric. Soc. XIX. I. 147 The idea..that 'roughing' calves (which means exposing them to cold and hunger) makes them hardy.

III. 6. With various advs. a. To trim or work off in a rough fashion.

1789 G. Keate Pelew Isl. 96 Timber..which being cut down at the back of the island and roughed off, they could easily manage to bring round.

b. To shape or cut out roughly; to plan or sketch out roughly.

1793 Smeaton Edystone L. § 144 The two new steps..and all the dovetails were roughed out. 1820 W. Scoresby Acc. Arc. Reg. I. 232 In the formation of these lenses, I roughed them out with a small axe. 1843 Holtzapffel Turning I. 168 The stone is first roughed out with a point and mallet. 1875 Carpentry & Join. 113 He will rough out these at his own saw pit with the usual felloe saw.

c. To fill or work in, to sketch in, roughly.

1864 Blackmore Clara Vaughan xxi, I had just roughed in my outline. 1891 Kipling Light that Failed (1900) 129, I must rough 'em in with the pencil.

d. To work down (iron) into rods.

1839 Ure Dict. Arts 707 A steam engine of thirty-horse power can rough down in a week 200 tons of coarse iron.

e. Mus. To tune up roughly.

1889 Grove's Dict. Music IV. 554 As much proficiency in tuning as enabled him to 'rough up', the technical term for the first tuning of a pianoforte.

f. To dig out in a rough manner.

1887 Daily News 8 Feb. 6/3 Miners rough out the clay in the first place with pick and shovel, and .. machinery finishes the circular cutting with mathematical accuracy.

7. To work or shape in a rough preliminary fashion.

1815 Scoresby in Mem. Wernerian Soc. II. 270, I roughed them with a small axe. 1839 Ure Dict. Arts 596 The piece of glass is now roughed into a circular form. 1850 Holtzapffel Turning III. 1034 The alabaster is roughed, or roughly ground on what the lapidary terms a roughing or lead mill. a 1890 E. L. Wilson Quarter Cent. Photogr. 35 (Cent.), In the grinding of a lens the first operation consists in roughing it, or bringing it approximately to the curvature it is ultimately to assume.

b. To clean (grain) roughly.

1851 Jrnl. R. Agric. Soc. XII. II. 412 He..'chaffs' or 'roughs' the corn once over with a roughing-machine.

c. To heckle (flax) roughly. See also Ruff v.

1882 Encycl. Brit. XIV. 665/1 In the case of heckling by machinery, the flax is first roughed and arranged in stricks, as above described under hand heckling. 1902 Brit. Med. Jrnl. 31 May 1341 The process of roughing, sorting, and hackling the flax.

† **Rough**, v.[2] Obs. Forms: 4 **rouwen**, 5 **row(w)hyn, rewyn**, 5–6 **rough**. [ME. type *roȝen (rowen), corresponding in form to OHG. and MHG. rohen (ruhen) to roar, and in meaning to (M)Du. rochelen, G. röcheln.] intr. To cough, to hawk, to clear the throat.

13.. Old Age in Reliq. Antiq. II. 211, I rivele, I roxle, I rake, I rouwe. c 1440 Promp. Parv. 249/1 Hostyn, or rowhyn, or cowghyn (H., rowwhyn..), tussio. a 1470 H. Parker Dives & Pauper (W. de W. 1496) IV. iv. 164/1 He cought & roughed so, that his sone..myght haue no reste by hym in the chambre. a 1529 Skelton Col. Cloute 1223 Let hym cough, rough, or sneuyll.

Rough, obs. var. of Roe, Roof; var. of Ruff v.

Roughage. dial. and U.S. [f. Rough a. + -age.] The less useful or refuse part (of crops); rough grass or weeds.

1883 Encycl. Amer. I. 98 The 'roughage' of crops has been neglected, the entire straw and stalks being burned. 1890 Glouc. Gloss., Roughage, rubbish; the clearings off the land or out of ditches would be so called.

Rough-and-ready, a. Also unhyphened.

1. Of things: Not elaborately or carefully ordered, contrived, or finished; just good enough to serve the purpose.

1810 F. J. Jackson in Sir G. Jackson Diaries & Lett. (1873) I. 120 A more rough and ready state of things..than we had before been accustomed to. 1858 R. S. Surtees Ask Mamma xlv, The hunting establishment was of the rough and ready order. 1893 Sir R. Ball Story of Sun 222 The rough-and-ready compass so invaluable to the navigator.

Comb. 1856 Stonehenge Brit. Rur. Sports 414/1 Sharp spurs are on the heels—rough and ready-looking prads these.

2. Of persons: Ready to take things as they come; not finical or particular; working in a rough but prompt and effective manner.

1849 E. E. Napier Exp. S. Afr. I. 163 If you can catch a sober, rough-and-ready 'Totty', who is able to..put his hand to any thing. 1870 W. Thornbury Tour round Eng. I. ii. 44 In a few days his rough and ready hand was on their collars. 1894 Mrs. F. Elliot Roman Gossip iv. 94 A sort of leer, as of a rough-and-ready cynic.

3. Of manner, etc.: Roughly efficient or effective, without entering into minutiæ or observing a regular procedure.

1860 Emerson Cond. Life ii. (1861) 39 The rough and ready style which belongs to a people of sailors, foresters, farmers, and mechanics. 1868 Freeman Norm. Conq. (1877) II. 493 A rough and ready way of repaying themselves. 1897 Allbutt's Syst. Med. II. 880 Instead of all this rough-and-ready turbulence, relays of attendants should be..organized.

Rough-and-tumble, a., sb., and adv. Also unhyphened. [Orig. boxing slang.]

A. adj. 1. Characterized by rough informality or disregard of usual rules; having the character of a scuffle or scramble; rude and disorderly.

1832 J. P. Kennedy Swallow B. xv. (1860) 138 Rough-and-tumble fights in which they were often engaged. 1859 Bartlett Dict. Amer. (ed. 2) 371 A rough and tumble fight is said to be one in which all the laws of the ring are discarded. 1872 O. W. Holmes Poet. Breakf.-T. x, That circle of rough-and-tumble political life where the fine-fibred men are at a discount. 1887 Stevenson Underwoods I. iv. 7 Their rough-and-tumble play they shared.

transf. 1899 Callow Old Lond. Tav. i. 3 There was always a more or less rough-and-tumble air about the place.

2. Of persons: Practising irregular or informal methods of boxing, etc.; inclined to be rough or violent.

1848 B. D. Walsh Aristoph. 137 note, The victories of.. wrestlers, boxers, and rough-and-tumble gentlemen. 1860 O. W. Holmes Elsie Venner (1887) 39 The rough-and-tumble fighters all clinch. 1890 F. W. Robinson Very Strange Family 18 Rough-and-tumble lads, with no fine feelings.

3. transf. Riotous, disorderly, forming a confused mass or group.

1858 O. W. Holmes Aut. Breakf.-t. (1883) 237 Dare-devil impudence of rough-and-tumble vegetation. 1879 Stevenson Trav. Cevennes (1886) 49, I..found..another marish bottom among rough-and-tumble hills.

B. sb. 1. Haphazard or random fighting, struggling, or adventure; scuffle, scramble.

1810 Edin. Rev. XV. 447 When two persons fight, it is generally 'according to the rule of rough and tumble'. 1840 R. H. Dana Bef. Mast xxviii. 92 The old brig..in which I had spent nearly a year, and got the first rough and tumble of a sea-life. 1875 Whyte-Melville Katerfelto i, The Cornish hug, the Devonshire shoulder-grip, and the West Somerset rough-and-tumble.

2. With a. A random or free fight or set-to.

1821 Southey in Q. Rev. XXIV. 494 The Coalheaver.. closed with him at once for a rough-and-tumble. 1887 Rider Haggard A. Quatermain viii, He had been successful in his rough and tumble with the Elmoran.

C. adv. In a rough, informal manner.

1818 J. Palmer Jrnl. Trav. 131, I understand the question is generally asked, will you fight fair, or take it rough and tumble? 1825 J. Neal Bro. Jonathan III. 270 A bit of clear tussle with a redhot Mohawk or so—rough an' tumble—would be a relief to me.

Hence **Rough-and-tumbling**. nonce-wd.

1808 Ashe Trav. I. 296 No fighting, no racing, no rough and tumbling, or anything to be observed but industry.

Rough-board, v. [Rough a. 21.] trans. To cover with rough boards.

1849 D. J. Browne Amer. Poultry Yd. (1855) 87 Rough-board it from the apex downward by the sills to the ground.

Rough-cast, roughcast (rʊ·fkɑst), ppl. a. and sb. Also 7 **ruff-cast**. [f. Rough adv. and a. See Cast v. 57, 45, and sb. 25.]

I. 1. ppl. a. Of walls, etc.: Roughly coated with a mixture of lime and gravel.

1519 Horman Vulg. 241 Some men wyll haue theyr wallys plastered, some pergetted.., some roughe caste. 1617 Moryson Itin. I. 188 The building of the City is..of unpolished stone with the outside plastered, and rough cast. 1655 Fuller Ch. Hist. I. 7 As white-limed houses exceed those which are only rough cast. 1704 Swift T. Tub xi, He rubbed..against a rough-cast Wall. 1830 Miss Mitford Village Ser. IV. (1863) 239 A low, white, irregular, rough-cast building. 1861 Neale Notes Dalmatia 97 Arbors running along the top of rough-cast walls.

b. transf. or fig. Also const. with.

1606 Sylvester Du Bartas II. iv. Magnificence 1266 Where Wals are rough-cast wth the richest Stones. 1655 Vaughan Silex Scint. I. Regeneration, My walke a monstrous, mountain'd thing, Rough-cast with rocks and snow. 1681 Grew Musæum I. iv. iv. 76 The Shell underneath or within is white: without, it is all over rough-cast.

2. sb. A composition of lime and gravel, used as a plastering for the outside of walls.

1590 Shaks. Mids. N. III. i. 71 Let him haue some Plaster, or some Lome, or some rough cast about him, to signifie wall. 1622 Mabbe tr. Aleman's Guzman d'Alf. I. 39 The face of her..looked like an old wall all to bedawbed with rough-cast. 1663 Gerbier Counsel 79 Rough-cast upon Lath being very well done, is worth eighteen pence the yard. 1789 M. Madan tr. Persius (1795) 120 note, The plaster, parget or rough cast of a wall. 1810 Wordsw. Prose Wks. (1876) II. 277 The house must be covered with rough-cast, otherwise it cannot be kept dry. 1850 Ecclesiol. XI. 74 Both tower and spire are covered with rough-cast. 1883 Mrs. Banks Forbidden to Marry I. v. 85 Black beams intersecting..the weather-stained roughcast.

b. transf. or fig. Also with a.

1609 J. Davies (Heref.) Holy Roode D 2 b, A Rough-cast of thicke Gore his Body shrouds. 1648 J. Beaumont Psyche XXII. ccxcix, Her scurfy Roughcast scaled off, and all Her Skin to fresh and tender smoothness left. 1658 Rowland tr. Moufet's Theat. Ins. 922 [The wasp's nest is] well fenced above with a certain rough-cast to keep off all wind and weather.

c. attrib. Consisting of rough-cast. Also fig.

1599 Nashe Lenten Stuffe Wks. (Grosart) V. 201 With light cost of rough cast rethoricke it may be tollerablely playstered ouer. c 1670 Wood Life (O. H. S.) I. 280 Two or three stones, and some rough-cast stuff were blown from off the tower. 1828 Lights & Shades II. 122 A decent-looking inn with a rough-cast coating.

II. † 3. sb. A rough sketch or outline. Obs.

Properly in two words, as in the earlier quots.

1579 Gosson Sch. Abuse (Arb.) 24 To show you that in a rough cast, which I see in a cloude. 1641 Milton Ch. Govt. I. vii, If we look at his native towardlinesse in the rough cast without breeding. 1644 Digby Nat. Bodies a iv b, A loose modell and roughcast of what I designe to do.

4. ppl. a. Roughly or rudely contrived, designed, or made; of a rough, imperfect type.

1591 Nashe Prognostication Wks. (Grosart) II. 151 Vttering in their furye such rough cast eloquence. 1635–56 Cowley Davideis I. 811 He smooth'd the rough-cast Moons imperfect mold. 1693 Dryden Disc. Satire Ess. (Ker) II. 55 This rough-cast unhewn poetry was instead of stage-plays for the space of an hundred and twenty years together. 1714 R. Fiddes Pract. Disc. II. 367 This brightest jewel and ornament of human nature is so rough cast. 1880 Stallybrass tr. Grimm's Teut. Myth. I. 103, I can only look upon Cæsar's statements as a half-true and roughcast opinion. 1892 J. Tait Mind in Matter (ed. 2) 159 The rough-cast 'goodness' of the bonus homo of Christianised heathenism.

Rough-cast (rʊ·fkɑst), v. Also 7 **rogh-, roof-**. [f. Rough adv. + Cast v. Cf. prec.]

1. trans. To coat, cover, or fill in, with rough-cast.

1565 Cooper Thesaurus, Incrusto, to parget, or to roughe cast. 1584 in Willis & Clark Cambridge (1886) I. 294 To Parkes seruant for roughcasting and filling the place behind the armes and Creast. 1639 [see Parget sb. 1]. 1757 Phil. Trans. L. 199 The steeple is..roughcasted on the outside. 1797 Mme. D'Arblay Let. July 27 Our cottage is now in the act of being rough cast. 1833 Loudon Encycl. Archit. § 478 It is brought to an even surface by rough-casting it with a mixture of lime and fine gravel. 1875 W. M'Ilwraith Guide Wigtownshire 31 Some of the houses have been carefully rough-cast and white-washed.

transf. and fig. 1593 Nashe Christ's T. Wks. (Grosart) IV. 210 With blacke boyling Pitch, rough cast ouer her counterfeite red and white. 1609 J. Davies (Heref.) Hum. Heauen on Earth Wks. (Grosart) I. 43/2 Rogh-cast the skin of smooth-fac'd glozing Guile With burning blisters to consume the same. 1640 Bastwick Lord Bishops ii. C, Thus did they incrustare vitia, parget, or roughcast their vices.

2. To mould, fashion, or shape roughly; to prepare in a rough form.

The first quot. may belong to sense 1.

1586 T. B. La Primaud. Fr. Acad. I. Ep. Ded., This Platonical Academie & schoole of moral philosophy, which..was raised up & set togither in France, & is newly rough-cast (as you see) by an English workman. a 1613 Overbury Characters, Taylor, Wks. (1856) 78 A Taylor is a creature made up out of threds, that were pared off from Adam, when he was rough-cast. a 1658 Cleveland Poems (1677) 58 Nor bodily, nor ghostly Negro could Roughcast thy Figure in a sadder mold. 1751 Warburton & Hurd Lett. (1809) 85, I have so imperfect an idea of my subject, and rough-cast my composition so loosely, that my works, if they escape damning, are yet in a state of purgatory. 1835 W. Irving in Life & Lett. (1866) III. 72, I have commenced, and have rough-cast several of the chapters.

Hence **Rou·gh-caster**, a workman who puts on rough-cast.

1594 in Antiquary XVII. 211 Itm. to the roughcaster, xxvjs., viijd. 1855 in Ogilvie Suppl.

Rou·gh-casting, vbl. sb. [f. Rough-cast v.]

1. The action of coating with rough-cast.

1565 Cooper Thesaurus, Tectorium, the plaisterynge, pargettynge, or rough castyng of walles. 1611 Cotgr., Crespissement, a pargetting, rough-casting. 1703 R. Neve City & C. Purchaser 236 River-sand is very good for Rough-casting of Walls. 1795 W. H. Marshall W. Eng. II. 296 An admirable theory of the operation of roughcasting. 1833 Loudon Encycl. Archit. § 529 Roughcasting, or Harling as it is called in Scotland, is a mode of outside finishing well calculated to protect walls from the weather.

2. concr. = Rough-cast sb. 2.

1703 Art's Improvement i. 8 Of a Serviceable and useful Plaster.., the which they call Rough-casting. 1823 P. Nicholson Pract. Build. 380 Rough-casting is an outside finishing cheaper than stucco. 1875 W. M'Ilwraith Guide Wigtownshire 80 On the inside of the walls the plaster still clings here and there,—coarse, however, as modern rough-casting.

Rou·gh-coated, a. [Rough a.] Having a rough coat. Chiefly of animals.

1687 Lond. Gaz. No. 2303/4 A large grey Gelding,..rough Coated. 1742 De Foe's Tour Gt. Brit. III. 257 Rough-coated Fish, such as Rousses, Haus, &c. the coarsest of all. 1843 Holtzapffel Turning I. 89 Lance-wood..is called one of the rough-coated woods. 1852 C. W. H[oskins] Talpa 133 His hot and rough-coated nag jumped with some alacrity.

Rou·gh-draft, v. [Cf. Rough a. 17 b.] trans. To draft in a rough form.

1879 Miss Braddon Cloven Foot x. 101, I am ready to rough-draft any form of settlement you dictate.

Rou·gh-draw, v. ? Obs. [Rough adv.] trans. To draw, draft, or design roughly. Hence **Rou·gh-drawn** ppl. a.

1672 Dryden Conq. Granada I. II. i, His Victories we scarce could keep in view, Or polish 'em so fast as he rough-drew. 1679 — Troil. & Cress. Prol., In this my rough-drawn Play, you shall behold Some Master-strokes. 1716 M. Davies Athen. Brit. II. 21 The Author of such Legal Formularies, tho' they had been rough-drawn by his Clerk or some Body else. 1779 Johnson L. P., Cowley, 'The Guardian,' a comedy which Cowley says was neither written nor acted, but rough-drawn by him.

Rou·gh-dry, v. [Rough adv.] trans. To dry (clothes) without smoothing or ironing.

1837 Dickens Pickw. xvii, The process of being washed in the night-air, and rough-dried in a close closet.

So **Rou·gh-dry** a.

1890 Cent. Dict., Rough-dry, dry but not smoothed or ironed: as, rough-dry clothes.

Roughed (rʊft), ppl. a. [f. Rough v.[1]]

1. Plastering. (See quot. 1823.)

1823 P. Nicholson Pract. Build. 393 Rendered, Floated,

Supplement, p. 3873; Corrigenda, p. 4092; Spurious words, p. 4093; Books quoted, p. 4094

Roughen (rŏ'f'n), a. [f. ROUGH a. + -EN.]

Roughen (rŏ'f'n), v. [f. ROUGH a. + -EN.]
1. trans. To render or make rough; to bring into a rough state. Also with up.

Rough-grind, v. trans. To grind roughly or so as to leave an unsmoothed or uneven surface.

Hence **Rough-grinder**; **Rough-grinding** vbl. sb.

Rough-head. Sc. and US. Dialect.

Roughened (rŏ'f'nd), ppl. a. [f. ROUGHEN v.] That has been made rough, in various senses.

Rough-hew, v. trans. To hew (timber, etc.) roughly; to shape out roughly, give crude form to; to work or execute in the rough.

Rough-hewer (rŏ'f,hiu·ər), a.

Rougher (rŏ'f·ər), sb. [f. ROUGH v. or a. + -ER.]

Rough-hewn (rŏ'f·hiūn), ppl. a. [ROUGH + HEW v.]
1. Roughly hewn or shaped out, roughly wrought; lacking the finishing process.

Roughet: see ROUCHET.

Roughie, -y. Sc. and north. [Var. of ROKE sb., and of ROUK sb.]

Roughings (rŏ'f·iŋz), sb. pl. [See quots.]

Rough-hound, esp. of the large and small spotted species.

Roughling (rŏ'f·liŋ), vbl. sb. [f. ROUGHLE v.]

Ronghish (rŏ'f·iʃ), a. [f. ROUGH a. + -ISH.]
Somewhat rough.

Rough mason (Obs.) [ROUGH a.] A mason building only with unhewn stone.

Rough leaf. [ROUGH a.]

Rough-leaved, a. [ROUGH a.] Having rough leaves.

Rough music: see MUSIC sb. 9 b. Hence **Rough-music** v.

Rough-leaved, a. [ROUGH a.] Having rough leaves.

Rough-legged, a. [ROUGH a.] Having hairy or feathered legs; esp. of birds: having the tarsi feathered.

Roughly (rŏ'f·li), adv. Forms: 4 ruchli, rohli; 6 Sc. roughly; 4 rugli, 6, 7 rughly, 6 roughlli; 6-7 roughli; 7 ruffly. [f. ROUGH a. + -LY.]

Roughling, obs. form of RUFFLING a.

Roughness (rŏ'f·nes). Forms: 4 rownes, 6 rowgnes; 5-7 roughnes, 6 rowghe-, roughnesse; 6-7 rouf-, ruffenesse; Sc. 6 rochnes, 6 ro(u)chnesse. [f. ROUGH a. + -NESS.]
1. The quality of being rough to the touch.

Roun-ride, v. [Back-formation from ROUGH-RIDER.] intr. To ride an unbroken horse.

Roun-rider (rŏ'f·rəidər), sb. Also **rough-ryder.** [ROUGH a.]
1. A horse-breaker.

Rough-riding (rŏ'f·rəidiŋ), vbl. sb.

Roughshod (rŏ'f·ʃod), a. and adv. ppl.
1. Of horses: Having shoes with the nail-heads projecting; chiefly fig. in the phr. to ride roughshod over, to domineer or tyrannize over, to treat without any consideration.

Rough-skinned, a. [ROUGH a.] Having a rough skin or bark.

Rough-spoken, a. [ROUGH adv.] Blunt or rough in speech.

Rough-spun, a. Sc. and north. dial. [ROUGH adv.]

Roughsome (rŏ'f·səm), a. [-SOME.]

Rought (rout), obs. pa. t. of REACH, RECK, WORK; obs. f. ROUGH, ROUT, RUTH.

Roughty, a. Obs.—¹ [? 5 roghtsisse.]

Rough-wrought, pa. pple.

Rough-tree, sb. slang. [f. ROUGH a.] An informal encounter or bout. A trial race.

Rough-up. slang. [f. ROUGH a.]

Rougy (rau'gi), a. [Cf. RUTTY.]

Rou ghy: An Australian fish (Arripis georgianus).

Rouging (rūʒiŋ), vbl. sb. Also rougeing.
The action or practice of applying rouge to the face.

Rougy (rū'ʒi), a.

Rouk (ruuk, ruk), sb. Sc. and north. [Var. of ROKE sb., and of ROUK sb.]

Rouk, obs. form of ROOK.

Roukery: see ROOKERY.

Rouky (rū'ki), a. and north. [f. ROUK sb. + -Y. Cf. ROKY and ROOKY.]

Roulade (rulāːd), sb. Mus. [F., f. rouler to roll.]

Roulette (rulet). Also 8-9 roulet, 8-9 roulette.
1. A number of gold coins made up into a cylindrical packet.

Roulé, obs. f. ROLE, ROLL.

Rouleau (rulō'). Also 8-9 roleau. Pl. rouleaux, -eaux. [F., repr. OF. rolel (cf. roleaus), f rôle roll.]
1. A number of gold coins made up into a cylindrical packet.

Roulette (rulet). sb. [F., prec.]
1. A game of chance played on a table with a revolving centre, on which a ball is set in motion, and finally drops into one of a set of numbered compartments.

Rouleting, vbl. sb.
So **Rouletting** vbl. sb.

Roulier (rū'liər), sb.

Rouman (rū'man), sb. and a.

Roumelitote (Poumelit-ot), sb. and a.

Roun, obs. forms of ROON.

Rounant, var. ROUNDING.

Roumanian (rūmē·niən), sb. and a. Also **Rumanian.** [See prec. and -IAN.]
A. sb.
1. A native of Roumania.
2. The language of Roumania.

Roumansch, var. of ROMANSH. **Roumbill**, obs. f. RUMBLE. **Roume**, obs. f. ROOM.

Roumy, **Rouncy**: see ROOM sb., ROUNCY.

Round (round), sb.¹ Forms: 4 roonde, 5-6 rounde, 5 round, 6-9 rownde; 5 rounde, 5-6 rowned(e, 6-7 roonde, round. [a. OF. ronde, roonde, -e, rond, rounde, rund (mod.F. ronde), fem. of rond, round.]

Rounce (rauns), sb.¹ Typog. [ad. Du. ronds(e, var. ronse in the same sense.]

Rouncival (rau'nsivăl), sb. and a. Also -ceval, -sival, etc., and in 6 rouncy-, roncy-, etc.

Rouncy (rau'nsi), sb. Obs. exc. arch. Forms: 4 runci, runce, runcy; 5-6 rouncy, runsy; 6 rouncey, ronsey, 5-6 rouncey, 7 rounce; 5 ar(o)ched. [a. OF. ronci, roncin, runcin (mod.F. roussin).]

Rouncy, var. ROUNCIVAL.

Round (round), sb.² Forms: 4 roonde, 5 roun(e, 5-6 round(e, 6-7 rounde, round. [a. OF. ronde, rounde.]

Round (round), a. Forms: 4 roonde, rounde, 5 roun(d, 5-7 rounde, 6-9 rownde, round. [a. OF. rond, ront, round.]
1. Used attrib. as the specific designation of a large variety of patent or of leaf.

Round-armed. (Also as adv.)

Round-bow. …

Round-dealing. …

Round-eared. [ROUND a.] Having round ears, or ear-like appendages.

Rounded, ppl. a. [f. ROUND v.]

Roundel, …

Roundelay (round'ēlā). …

Round hand. [f. ROUND a. + HAND sb.]

Roundhead, round-head (round'hed). —Head, Round head.

Roundheadism. rare⁻¹.

Round-house, sb.

Rounding, ppl. a.

Roundish, a. [f. ROUND + -ISH.]

Roundle. [var. of ROUNDEL.]

Round-leaved, -leafed. [ROUND a. 16 c.] Having round leaves.

Round-mouthed, a.

Roundness (round'nes). Also 4 rond(e, 5 roundenes, -nys.

I returned this rough answere...For which roundnes, though I have sufficient warrant.., yet it may be I should have spared some part of the harshnes.

†7. Energy, activity; thoroughness. *Obs.*

1629 *Decl. Apprehension Bp. Chalcedon* 36 [That] they and every of them proceed with all diligence and roundness ..against the said Smith. 1709 Strype *Ann. Ref.* I. iv. 83 Had it not been for Cecyl's Wisdom, Diligence, and Interest with the Queen, in all likelihood it had not proceeded with that Roundness it did.

Round-nosed, *a.* [Round *a.* 16.] Having a round nose. Chiefly of tools (cf. *round-nose*, s.v. Round *a.* 17).

1611 Cotgr. s.v. *Teste*, A kind of blunt, and round-nosed Porpose. 1677 Moxon *Mech. Exerc.* i. 5 Plyers are of two Sorts, Flat Nos'd, and Round Nos'd. 1766 *Compl. Farmer* s.v. *Surveying* 7 G 1/2 Good iron-wire and curtain-rings to make it of, and a sharp-edged file, and round-nosed plyers to make it with. 1875 Knight *Dict. Mech.* 1742/2 Pliers with peculiarly shaped or proportioned jaws are called long-nosed pliers, round-nosed pliers,..etc. 1898 *Archaeol. Jrnl.* V. 270 Among the relics were a few stone hammers or polishers, a number of 'round-nosed' chisels of bone.

†**Rou·ndo.** *Obs.* Also 8 **Round O.** [Anglicized form of F. *rondeau*.] = Rondeau.

1710 Pope *Lett.* (1735) I. 94 The vulgar spelling and pronouncing it Round O, is a manifest Corruption. 1751 Earl Orrery *Remarks Swift* (1752) 55 On Roundos hereafter your fiddle-strings spend, Write verses in circles, they never shall end. 1765 Percy *Reliq.* II. 11 The versification is of that species, which the French call Rondeau, very naturally englished by our honest countrymen Round O.

Round O: see Round *a.* 15.

Round-off, *a.* [f. Round *v.*[1] + Off *adv.*] *Round-off file*: (see quot.).

1846 Holtzapffel *Turning* II. 826 Nicking and piercing files..are called round-off files, and are used for rounding or pointing the teeth of wheels. 1875 Knight *Dict. Mech.*

Round Ro·bin. Also round robin.

†1. (See quots.) *Obs.*

1546 Coverdale tr. *Calvin's Treat. Sacr.* Pref. Aij, Certayne fonde talkers..applye to this mooste holye sacramente, names of despitte and reproche, as to call it Jake in the boxe, and round roben, and suche other not onely fond but also blasphemouse names. 1555 Ridley in Foxe *A. & M.* (1570) 1924/2 There were at Paules..fixed railing bils against the Sacrament, terming it Jacke of ye boxe, the sacrament of the halter, round Robin, with lyke unseemely termes.

†2. Applied to persons. *Obs.*

1592 Greene *Conny Catch.* Wks. (Grosart) X. 36 There in faith round Robin his deputie, would make them, like wretches, feel the waight of his heauiest fetters. 1636 R. N. in *Ann. Dubrensia* (1877) 66 Thou art he in whom All the brave Robins meet to make vp one, Round-Robin. *a* 1671 Hacket *Abp. Williams* II. (1692) 177 These Wat Tylers and Round-Robins being driven or persuaded out of Whitehall.

3. A document (esp. one embodying a complaint, remonstrance, or request) having the names of the subscribers arranged in a circle so as to disguise the order in which they have signed.

Originally used by sailors, and frequently referred to as a nautical term.

(*a*) 1731 *Gentl. Mag.* I. 238 The Method used by Sailors when they mutiny, by signing their names in an orbicular manner, which they call a round Robin. 1742 J. Campbell *Lives Admirals* (1750) II. 98 The sailors on board the fleet, signed, what is called by them, a round Robin, that is, a paper containing..their names subscribed in a circle, that it might not be discerned who signed first. 1828 *Lancet* 21 June 382/2 If thirteen physicians..had written what seamen call a round robin to an authority. 1847 H. Melville *Omoo* xx, I proposed that a 'Round Robin' should be prepared and sent ashore to the consul. 1870 Thornbury *Tour rd. Eng.* I. 192 [He] so tormented his crew that they signed a round robin, and sent it to the Admiralty.

(*b*) 1755 Chesterf. in *World* No. 146 ¶ 8 If I thought it could be of any use, I could easily present them with a round robin to that effect of above a thousand..names. 1791 Sir W. Forbes in *Boswell* (Oxf. ed.) II. 60, I enclose the Round Robin. This *jeu d'esprit* took its rise one day at dinner at our friend Sir Joshua Reynolds's. 1829 *Farmer's Jrnl.* Oct. 330 Last week the whole of the tenants..sent a round-robin to his lordship's steward. *a* 1859 Macaulay *Biog.* (1867) 217 He tried to induce a large number of the supporters of the government to sign a round robin desiring a change. 1896 J. D. Coleridge *Eton in the Forties* 133 The headmaster suggested our signing and sending a round robin of congratulation.

transf. 1816 Coleridge *Lay Serm.* (Bohn) 349 Such a round robin of mere lies, that you knew not which to begin with.

†4. (See quot.) *Obs.*—[0]

1688 Holme *Armoury* III. 97/2 *Round Robins*, narrow Rufls only about the Doublet Collar.

5. *Mech.* (See quots.)

1794 W. Felton *Carriages* (1801) II. 195 The round Robin is a broad rim fixed to the end of the axletree bed, to prevent dirt falling in to injure the Arms of the Axletree. 1875 Knight *Dict. Mech.* 669/1 *Cuttoo-plate*,..otherwise called a dirt-board, or round robbin.

6. a. *U.S.* The fish *Decapterus punctatus*.

1876 Goode *Fishes Bermudas* 46 The Round Robin is seined in great numbers in Hamilton Harbor.

b. The angler-fish, *Lophius piscatorius*.

1880 *E. Cornwall Gloss.* (E. D. S.).

7. *Devon dial.* a. A small pancake.

1847 Halliwell.

b. Herb Robert; Ragged Robin.

1882 *Devonsh. Plant Names.*

Round-shouldered, *a.* [Round *a.* 16.] Of persons: Having round shoulders; round-backed.

1586 Wynkfeilde in *Trial*, etc. *Mary Q. of Scots* (1889) 2 Y^e^ Q. of S. being of stature tall and bodie corpulent, round shouldered. 1682 *Lond. Gaz.* No. 1737/4 A middle sized man, a little round shouldered. 1753 Hanway *Trav.* (1762) II. xvi. i. 437 *note*, The oriental people generally are round-shouldered, arising from their manner of sitting. 1825 J. Neal *Bro. Jonathan* I. 191 He stood..regarding his vulgar ..round-shouldered brother opposite. 1865 Dickens *Mut. Fr.* I. v, A broad, round-shouldered, one-sided old fellow in mourning.

transf. 1895 Rider Haggard *Heart of the World* xiv, To the right and left of us the huge, round-shouldered mountains stretched in a majestic sweep.

Ro·undsman. [f. Round *sb.*[1]]

1. A labourer in need of parochial relief, who was sent round from one farmer to another for employment, partly at the expense of the farmer and partly at the cost of the parish.

1795 Eden *State of the Poor* (1797) II. 384 Persons working in this manner are called rounds-men, from their going round to village or township for employ. 1820 Syd. Smith *Wks.* (1859) I. 302/2 The system of roundsmen is much complained of. 1830 Cobbett *Rur. Rides* (1885) II. 350 The labourers here who are in need of parochial relief, are formed into what are called roundsmen. 1854 *Jrnl. R. Agric. Soc.* XV. II. 262 The surplus labourers are employed in turns by the farmers..: these odd men were called 'rounds-men'.

attrib. 1834 *Tait's Mag.* I. 37/2 At present the roundsman system is a wasteful and unequal tax.

2. One who makes rounds of inspection; esp. *U.S.* a police-officer in charge of a patrol.

1883 *Daily News* 18 Oct. 3/2 A roundsman and five patrolmen were present to preserve order. 1888 *Pall Mall G.* 9 Mar. 2/3 Shortly before the Emperor left the palace two roundsmen and two detectives patrolled the road.

3. A person employed by a tradesman to go the round of his customers for orders and the delivery of goods.

1884 *Weekly Notes* 29 Nov. 216/2 The defendant agreed to serve the plaintiff as 'roundsman' and assistant.

Round Table, *sb.* Also Table Round.

1. a. The table, celebrated in mediæval legend, round which Arthur and his chosen knights were supposed to have sat, and which was made round so that there might be no pre-eminence or rivalry.

The earliest mention of the table is that in Wace's *Roman de Brut* (1155). From at least the 15th century (see quot. 1485) the name has been given to a large circular table preserved at Winchester, bearing the names of Arthur and his most famous knights.

a 1300 *Cursor M.* 14 O kyng arthour þat was so rike,..O ferlys þat hys knythes fell, Þat aunters sere I here of tell,.. For to were þe ronde tabell. *c* 1330 R. Brunne *Chron. Wace* (Rolls) 10525 For his barons þat were so bolde..Dide Arthur ordeyne þe round table [F. *la roonde table*] | at ȝit men telle of many a fable. 1470–85 Malory *Arthur* III. i. 101 For I shalle gyue hym the table round, the whiche Vtherpendragon gaue me. 1485 Caxton *Malory's Arthur* Pref., In dyuers places of Englond many remembraunces ben yet of hym...At wynchester the rounde table. 1589 Nashe *Anat. Absurd.* Wks. (Grosart) I. 14 The feyned no where acts of Arthur of the rounde table. 1612 Drayton *Poly-olb.* iv. 299 Then sing they how he first ordain'd the Circled-board, The Knights whose martial deeds far fam'd that Table-round. 1728 Chambers *Cycl.* s.v. *Table*, The Round Table..was an Invention of that Prince, to avoid Disputes about the upper and lower End. 1802 Ritson *Metr. Rom.* I. p. xlvi, Neither..does this impostour [Geoffrey of Monmouth] ever mention the round table.

b. In *Knight* (etc.) *of the Round Table*.

c 1330 *Arth. & Merl.* 6518 (Kölbing), Next hem, wiþ outen fable, Sat þe kniȝtes of þe rounde table. ? *a* 1400 *Morte Arth.* 17, I salle telle ȝow a tale..Off the ryealle renkys of the Rowunde Table. 1430–40 Lydg. *Bochas* VIII. xxv. (1494) E ij, Arthure..Amonge his knyghtes of the round table. *Ibid.* E ij b, By othe and promyse bounde To brotherhede of the table rounde. 1470–85 Malory *Arthur* IV. iv. 124 By my hede said Arthur he is best worthy to be a knyght of the rounde table of ony that ye haue rehereed. 1589 Puttenham *Eng. Poesie* I. xix. (Arb.) 57 Old adventures and valiaunces..of king Arthur and his knights of the round table. 1671 Phillips, Knights of the Round-Table, or King Arthur's Knights. 1728 Chambers *Cycl.* s.v. *Table*, Paulus Jovius says, 'twas under the Empire of Frederic Barberosa, that the Knights of the Round Table first began to be talk'd of. 1781 Gibbon *Decl. & F.* xxxviii. (1787) III. 619 The gallantry and superstition of the British hero,..and the memorable institution of his Knights of the Round Table. 1802 Ritson *Metr. Rom.* III. 240 Queen Guinever, ..with certain knights of the round-table, clothe'd all in green. 1859 Tennyson *Geraint* 3 The brave Geraint,..one Of that great Order of the Table Round.

c. The body of knights of this order.

c 1330 *Arth. & Merl.* 2196 (Kölbing), Afterward..Our king bigan þe rounde table..Of kniȝtes, þat men wist best In þis warld. ? *a* 1400 *Morte Arth.* 93 That thow bee redy at Rome with alle thi Rounde Table. 1470–85 Malory *Arthur* IX. i. 339 All your courte and alle your Round table is by sire launcelot worshipped..more than by ony knyghte now lyuynge.

1842 Tennyson *Morte d'Arth.* 234 But now the whole Round Table is dissolved.., And I, the last, go forth companionless.

†d. A meeting or assembly of Arthur's knights and nobles. *Obs.*

1297 R. Glouc. *Chron.* (Rolls) 3916 Þer nas bituene þis & spayne no prince wiþoute al þis, Þat nas at þis rounde table, & at is feste ywis. ? *a* 1400 *Morte Arth.* 53 Whene he thys rewmes hade redyne.., Then rystede that ryalle and helde the Rounde Tabylle. *Ibid.* 74 Thus one ryalle araye he helde his Rounde Table. *c* 1470 Harding *Chron.* lxiii. 25 He [*sc.* Arthur] held his houshold, and the rounde table, Some time at Edenburgh, some tyme at Striueline.

e. *attrib.*, as *Round Table cycle, hero, knight, legend*, etc.

1700 Dryden *Wife of Bath's T.* 352 Is this the custom of King Arthur's court? Are all Round-Table Knights of such a sort? 1798 C'tess Purgstall *Let.* in Lockhart *Scott* (1837) I. ix. 288 Don't..give him a name out of your list of round-table knights. 1883 *Encycl. Brit.* XV. 523/1 He [Walter Map] was..one of the principal creators of the Round Table legends. 1886 *Ibid.* XX. 646 Pedigree of the Round-Table Heroes. 1897 Amours *Scot. Allit. Poems* (S. T. S.) p. lxxii, One of the stock stories so common in the Round Table cycle.

2. An imitation of Arthur's Round Table as an institution; an assembly of knights for the purpose of holding a tournament and festival, esp. that instituted by King Edward III in 1345.

The statements in Dugdale, Warton, etc., in regard to the tournament held by Mortimer at Kenilworth in 1279 are based on misunderstandings of the older authorities (see Wykes in *Ann. Monast.* (Rolls) IV. 281–2 and Rishanger *Chron.* 94).

[1232 *Patent Rolls* (1903) 492 De rotunda tabula prohibenda.—Rex omnibus fidelibus suis qui conventuri sunt ad rotundam tabulam, salutem. *c* 1330 *Ann. Lond.* in *Chron. Edw. I & II* (Rolls) I. 46 Tabula rotunda apud Waldene, ubi Ernulphus de Mounteneye a Rogero de Leyborne lancea interfectus est.] *c* 1400 *Brut* (1908) 296 When þe Iustes were don, King Edward made a grete soper, in þe wiche he ordeyned feest, and bygan þe Rounde Table, & ordeyned & stefastyd þe day of þe forsaide Rounde Table to be holde þer at Wyndissore in Whitesen-wike euermore after erly. 1483 Caxton *G. de la Tour* C ij, A good lady that gat a grete blame at a grete feste of a round table atte Joustes. 1523 Ld. Berners *Froiss.* I. c. 120 The king of Englond toke pleasure to newe reedefy the Castell of Wyndsore,..and ther firste begonne the table rounde. 1552 in *Archaeologia* (1863) XXXIX. 34 To the knights of the Round Table (if I do it not in my lifetyme) xxs. to be spent at Myle end. 1765 Percy *Reliq.* I. 35 Any king was said to 'hold a round table' when he proclaimed a tournament attended with some peculiar solemnities. 1803 Godwin *Life Chaucer* I. 133 Edward III..purposing from the knights whose prowess on this occasion should be the most approved, to select the members of his new order, to be styled knights of the Round Table. 1846 *Archaeologia* XXXI. 106 The feast of the Round Table..in March, 1345.

†b. (See quot.) *Obs.*

The quotation is a direct translation from Walsingham *Historia Brevis* (1574) 154.

1592 Stow *Ann.* (1595) 367 King Edward [III in 1345] caused to be called together a great many Artificers, to the Castell of Windsore, and beganne to builde an house, which was called the round Table.

3. A name applied locally to various natural or artificial antiquities, freq. reputed to have associations with King Arthur.

1375 Barbour *Bruce* XIII. 379 Beneth the castell [of Stirling] went thai soyne, Richt by the Rownde Tabill thair way. 1530 Lindesay *Test. Papyngo* 634 Adew, fair Snawdoun, with thy touris hie, Thy Chapell royall, Park, and tabyll rounde! 1612 Selden *Illustr. Drayton's Poly-olb.* iv. 302 In Denbighshire..is a circular plain, cut out of a main rock, with some twenty-four seats unequal, which they call Arthur's Round Table. 1813 Scott *Trierm.* I. vii, He pass'd red Penrith's Table Round, For feats of chivalry renown'd. 1836 *Penny Cycl.* VI. 106/2 A space of ground [at Caerleon], which it is believed was a Roman amphitheatre, is commonly called Arthur's Round Table. 1872 Hardwicke *Trad.*, etc. *Lancs.* 216 Several circular mounds in various parts of England..are..honoured with the name of 'King Arthur's Round Table'.

4. Used generally (alone or as *attrib.* phrase) to denote a number of persons seated round a circular table, or imagined as forming a gathering of this kind.

1826 Miss Mitford *Village* Ser. II. (1863) 342 For cards she had no genius. Even the noise and nonsense of a round-table could not reconcile her to those bits of painted pasteboard. 1852 *Life in Bombay* 33 The snug round-table dinner-party. 1885 *Encycl. Brit.* XVIII. 656/2 Those four hundred poets who formed the famous 'Round Table' in the sultan's..palace. 1889 *Pall Mall G.* 6 Nov. 4/1 The 'New Round Table' is a symposium on Home Rule—a collection of remarks..from persons of various standpoints.

Hence **Round-table** *v.*, to take part in a round-table conference; **Round-tabler.** *nonce-uses.*

1887 *Pall Mall G.* 3 Feb. 1 When Mr. Goschen goes over to the Tories on one side, Mr. Chamberlain round-tables on the other. 1889 *Ibid.* 6 Nov. 4/1 Other round tablers are Mr. Andrew Reid.., Lord Monkswell.., and others.

Round-top. Also roundtop. [f. Round *a.*]

1. *Naut.* A platform (formerly circular) about a mast-head.

1706 Phillips (ed. Kersey), *Top-Armours*, are a kind of Clothes, &c., set about the Round-tops of the Masts. 1722 De Foe *Col. Jack* xi, A man on the roundtop cried out, Au voile, a sail. 1769 R. Wood *Ess. Genius Homer* p. xxxi, As I looked from the round-top of the main mast, the fresh water appeared like an immense muddy pond. 1855 Kingsley *Westw. Ho!* xxi, The fog was up to our round-tops at sunrise this morning. 1876 Bancroft *Hist. U. S.* VI. xl. 242 Jones could use only their nine-pounders and muskets from the round-tops.

2. *attrib.* Having a rounded top.

1825 J. Nicholson *Operat. Mech.* 644 [A railway] known ..by the denomination of the edge rail, round-top rail, fish-backed rail, &c.

Round-towner. [f. Round *prep.*] One who loafs about a town.

1778 [W. Marshall] *Minutes Agric.* 10 Oct. 1775, I hope I shall never pay-off another 'Round Towner. *Ibid.*, Digest 36 The Roundtowners are wholly ineligible as in-door Servants.

Round-up. [See Round *sb.*[2] and *v.*[1]]

1. *Ship-building.* (See quot. 1846.)

1769 Falconer *Dict. Marine* (1780) s.v. *Transom*, The

former of these is called..the round-up, and the latter the round-aft. *Ibid.*, *Touture des baux*, the round-up, or convexity of a ship's beams. 1833 Richardson *Merc. Mar. Arch.* 8 Short curved line for the round-up and round-aft of the wing transom. 1846 A. Young *Naut. Dict.*, *Round-up* of the Transoms; the segment of a circle to which they are sided; of beams, that to which they are moulded. 1869 Sir E. Reed *Shipbuilding* xx. 431 While the frames and keel of the ship are in progress, beam moulds, with the round-up and lengths marked on them, are given out to the workmen to guide them in making beams.

2. *U.S.* (and *Austr.*). The driving of cattle, etc., together or into an enclosure, usually for the purpose of registering ownership, counting, etc.

1882 Baillie-Grohman *Camps Rockies* xii. 339 To collect these stragglers and to take a census,..the annual 'round-up' is held. 1887 T. R. *Ranche Life Montana* 160 When they have gone some miles, the captain of the round-up tells them to spread out into a wide half-circle, driving-in all the horses.

b. A meeting or social gathering of acquaintances or friends; a reunion.

1887 A. A. Hayes *Jesuit's Ring* 270 We'll have a round-up of your old friends. 1895 *Daily News* 16 Sept. 6/4 The good bishop had a family reunion or 'round up' on the lawn of one of his estates.

3. *U.S.* A settlement, clearance.

1886 *Philadelphia Times* 3 May (Cent.), That exception ..will probably be included in the general round-up to-morrow.

Roundure (rau·ndiūı). Also 7 **rowndure.** [f. Round *a.* Cf. Rondure.] Roundness; rounded form or space.

In Shaks. *K. John* II. i. 259 the reading of the first folio is *rounder*.

1600 Dekker *Fortunatus* Dram. Wks. 1873 I. 90 Your cries to me are Musicke, And fill the sacred roundure of mine eares With tunes more sweete then moving of the Spheres. 1620 — *Dream* Wks. (Grosart) III. 40 Were all the Rowndure betwixt Hell and Heauen One Clowd condens'd, and into blackness driuen. 1623 Favine *Theatr. Honour* I. ii. 12 The frightfull eye of the Gyant Polyphemus, great and wide as the roundure of the Sunne. 1818 Keats *Wks.* (1889) III. p. cxxxix, You might suppose that the fair roundure of her fingers reached back to heaven.

Rou·ndward, *a.* and *adv.* *nonce-word.* [f. Round *adv.*] In a circular direction.

1893 *Scribner's Mag.* XIII. 376/1 There was a bolt..rearward, roundward, upward, downward. *Ibid.* 376/2 There was the same rearward, roundward bolt.

Rou·ndway, *a.* *rare.* [f. Round *a.* 17.]

1. ? Having a round passage-way.

1862 *Catal. Internat. Exhib. Brit.* II. No. 2409 Improved extra strong round-way screw-down bib and stop cocks.

2. Moving round in the arena.

1875 Morris *Æneid* VIII. 636 From concourse of the hollow seats where roundway games were wrought.

Rou·ndways, *adv.* *rare.* = Roundwise.

1644 Digby *Nat. Bodies* xxvi. § 5. 236 The second, go crosse or roundwayes about the ventricles within the hart. 1769 Mrs. Raffald *Eng. Housekpr.* 9 Skin and cut roundways in slices six large Spanish onions.

Round-winged, *a.* [f. Round *a.* 16.]

†1. *Arch.* = Peripteral *a.* *Obs. rare*—[1].

1715 Leoni *Palladio's Archit.* (1742) II. 8 This prospect is call'd *Peripteros*, that is, wing'd round.., the same round-wing'd prospect remaining..to every one that saw the Temple in flank.

2. *Ent.* In the names of moths, as round-winged muslin, (white-)wave (see quots.).

1832 J. Rennie *Consp. Butterfl. & M.* 273/1 Round-Winged Wave [114, The Round Wing, *Cabera rotundaria*]. 1869 E. Newman *Brit. Moths* 27 The Round-winged Muslin (*Nudaria Senex*). 1887 *Cassell's Encycl. Dict.* s.v., Round-winged white-wave, a British geometer moth, *Cabera exanthemaria*. 1907 R. South *Moths Brit. Isles* Ser. I. 175 The Round-winged Muslin (*Comacla senex*)..; the wings of this moth are rounder in outline than those of the Muslin.

3. Applied to certain hawks, as those of the genera *Accipiter* and *Astur*. 1890 in *Cent. Dict.*

Rou·ndwise, *adv.* and *a.* Now *rare.* [f. Round *a.* + -wise.]

1. *adv.* In a circular form, disposition, or arrangement; circularly.

1577 Harrison *Eng.* II. xxv. (1877) 364 King Edward the first..did first coine the penie and smallest peeces of siluer roundwise. 1609 Bible (Douay) *Lev.* xix. 27 Neither shal you cut your heare roundwise; nor shave your beard. 1675 Han. Woolley *Gentlewoman's Comp.* 146 Take Apples sliced thin round-wise. 1725 *Fam. Dict.* s.v. *Larch-Tree*, It produces its Branches roundwise, at some equal Distance from each other.

2. *adj.* Circular, round. *rare*—[1].

1633 P. Fletcher *Purple Isl.* II. xxviii, The form (as when with breath our bagpipes rise, And swell) round-wise, and long, yet long-wise more.

Round-wood: see Rowan[1].

1857 Thoreau *Maine W.* (1894) 79 Mountain-ash, or round-wood, as the Maine people call it.

Round-worm. *Zool.* Also round worm. [f. Round *a.* + Worm *sb.* In early examples only descriptive, later a specific name.] A parasitic worm of a rounded form infesting the human intestines: a. A worm of the genus *Lumbricus* or *Ascaris*, esp. *A. lumbricoides*.

1565 Cooper, *Lumbricus*, a longe rounde woorme..in mans body. 1611 Cotgr., *Ascaride*, a kind of small round worme, which breeds in the bowels. 1658 *Moufet's Theat. Insects* II. xxxii, Round worms [breed] only in the small guts, Ascarides in the Longanum, the Gourd-worms..in all. 1683 *Phil. Trans.* XIII. 154 The *Lumbricus teres*, that common Round Worm which Children usually are troubled with. 1797 *Encycl. Brit.* (ed. 3) XI. 343/1 The long round worms seem to be the most dangerous which infest the human body, as they often pierce through the stomach and intestines. 1822 Good *Study Med.* (1829) I. 345 The head of the long round worm is slightly incurved. 1829 Cooper *Ibid.* 344 It is calculated one-half of the total number of children have either the round, or thread-worm. 1896 tr. *Boas' Text Bk. Zool.* 160 The Common Round-worm (*Ascaris*), often of considerable size.

b. A nemathelminth, or a nematode worm.

1836–9 *Todd's Cycl. Anat.* II. 116/2 *Nematoidea*,.. Round-worms...Body elongated, rounded, elastic. 1864 *Chambers's Encycl.* VI. 704/1 The N[ematelmia] are sometimes termed *Round-worms*, just as the Platyelmia..are called *Flat-worms*. 1896 tr. *Boas' Text Bk. Zool.* 158 *Nemathelminthes* (Round-worms).

Rou·ndy, *a.* Now *dial.* [f. Round *a.*]

1. Rounded; of a round shape.

a 1586 Sidney *Arcadia* (1891) 310 Her roundy sweetly swelling lippes a little trembling. 1821 Clare *Vill. Minstrel* II. 55 Welcome, red and roundy sun, Dropping lowly in the west.

2. *dial.* Of coals: (see Round *a.* 15).

1868– in northern dial. glossaries.

Roune, var. of Roun *sb.*, Round *v.*[2]; obs. f. Rune *sb.*[2]

†**Rou·ner.** *Obs.* Forms: 1 runere, 4–6 rowner (5 -ere, 6 *Sc.* -ar), 5 rouner (6 *Sc.* -ar, roundar). [OE. *rúnere*, f. *rúnian* to whisper, Round *v.*[2] Cf. MDu. *runer* (*ruyner*, *runaer*, etc.), MLG. *runer*, OHG. *rûnari* (G. *rauner*).] A whisperer; a tatler, tale-bearer.

c 1000 Ælfric *Gram.* xxxvi. (Z.) 217 *Hic susurro*, ðes runere oþþe wroht. 1388 *Pol. Poems* (Rolls) I. 271 Rowners and flatreres. *c* 1425 Lydg. *Assembly of Gods* 687 Rowners, uagaboundes, forgers of lesynges. *a* 1470 H. Parker *Dives & Pauper* (W. de W. 1496) IV. v. 199/2 A preuy rowner, that pryuely telleth false tales amonges the people. 1500–20 Dunbar *Poems* xx. 33 Be thow not ane roundar in the nwke. *Ibid.* xxvi. 52 With..rownaris of fals lesingis. 1551 Abp. Hamilton *Catech.* 71 Of thame that ar quysperaris, rowkaris and rounaris.

Roung, obs. Sc. pa. pple. of Reign *v.*; obs. f. Rung *sb.*

†**Rounge,** *v.* *Obs.* Also 6 *Sc.* runge, ronge, rownge. [ad. OF. *roungier*, *rungier*, *rongier* (mod.F. *ronger*): of obscure formation.]

1. *intr.* To roar, cry out.

a 1375 *Joseph Arim.* 361 He roungede an heiȝ, and rorede so harde, his eiȝen flowen out of his hed.

2. *intr.* and *trans.* To gnaw; to champ.

1390 Gower *Conf.* I. 177 For evere on hem I rounge and gknawe And hindre hem al that evere I mai. *c* 1400 *Pilgr. Sowle* (Caxton) I. xx. (1859) 20 Lyke a worm I am woned to byte and to rounge them that wronge theym selue. *c* 1430 *Pilgr. Lyf Manhode* I. lv. (1869) 33 It wolde neuer stinte to rounge [*printed* raunge] so michel til it hadde slayn his mayster. *Ibid.* II. cxxxvi. 129 As the wolf that hath strangled the shepe..and hath rounged his chekes. 1513 Douglas *Æneis* III. iv. 93 With ȝour chaftis to gnaw ȝe sall be fane, And rounge ȝour tabillis all and burdis. *Ibid.* IV. iv. 11 Hir fers steid stude stamping,..Rungeand the fomy goldin bitt.

b. *intr.* To chew the cud.

c 1410 *Master of Game* (MS. Digby 182) xxxiv, For euermore she [the hare] fumeth and croteth and roungeth and bereth talowe and grece. 1486 *Bk. St. Albans* e iij b, All [beasts] that bere skyne and talow and Rounge..shall be flayne safe the hare.

3. *trans.* To clip (coin). *Sc.*

1540 *Sc. Acts Jas. V* (1814) II. 373 Þat na maner of man tak vpoun hand for to Ronge the croun of wecht. 1619 in C. Innes *Sk. E. Scot. Hist.* App. (1861) 522 Thair wes tuo of the xx mark peceis rounged and far les then the thrid wes.

Hence †**Rounged** *ppl. a.* *Obs.*

a 1572 Knox *Hist. Ref.* Wks. 1846 I. 404 Thair clyppit and rowngeit Soussis..ar commandit to have course in this realme. 1622 W. Scot *Course Conformitie* x. 43 To attaine thirteen rounged and dilapidate Bishoprickes.

†**Rou·nger.** *Obs.* Also 5 roungere, roundgar. [f. Rounge *v.* 3, or ad. AF. *roungere, OF. *rongeur*.] A clipper of coins.

1338 R. Brunne *Chron.* (1810) 238 Edward..wille wite certeyn, who schent has his mone. Of clippers, of roungers [F. *roygnurs*], of suilk takes he questis. *c* 1430 *Pilgr. Lyf Manhode* III. xvii. (1869) 144 This hand is an..vnhelere and brekere of cofres, and a roungere of floreyns. *a* 1600 in Drake *Eboracum* I. vi. (1736) 189 Roundgars of gold, washers of gold.

†**Rou·ning,** *vbl. sb.* *Obs.* Also 1 runung, 3 runing, roning; 4–6 rounyng(e, 5 rounn-, rovn-); 4–6 rownyng(e, 5 rowyn-), 5–6 rowning(e, 6 rowening). See also Rounding *vbl. sb.*[2] [f. OE. *rúnian*, ME. *rounen*: see Round *v.*[2]] Whispering; private conversation or consultation, etc.

c 1000 Ælfric *Hom.* (ed. Assmann) vi. 161 Hi..on synderlicum runungum þæt riht eall rædon. *c* 1205 Lay. 14070 He wolde wið þan kinge holden runinge. *c* 1275 — 3249 Þe Scottene king and þe duk..mid hire stille runing nemen heom to reade. 13.. *K. Alis.* 7604 (Laud MS.), After þis queynt rounyng Alisaunder spedde in þis doyng. *c* 1384 Chaucer *H. Fame* III. 1960 And ouer alle the houses Angles Ys ful of rovnynges. *c* 1450 tr. *De Imitatione* III. i. 64 Blessid be þo eres þat receyueþ of goddys rounynge, & takiþ non hede of þe rounyng of þis worlde. *c* 1475 in *Babees Bk.* (1868) 4 Withe-oute lowde lauhtere or langelynge, Rovnynge, lapynge, or other Insolence. 1533 More *Apol.* 240 Castyng abrode a suspicyouse bablynge, of gatheryng, and assemblynge, and rownynge, and talkynge.

†**Rou·ning,** *ppl. a.* *Obs.* Also 1 runiende, 4 rownande, rownende. [Cf. prec.] Whispering, murmuring.

c 1050 *Voc.* in Wr.-Wülcker 441 *Musitantes*, þa runiendan. 13.. *E. E. Allit. P.* A. 112 Swangeande swete þe water con swepe, Wyth a rownande rourde raykande aryȝt. 1382 Wyclif *Ecclus.* xxi. 31 The rownende gruccher shal defoule his soule.

Hence †**Rou·ningly** *adv.*, in a whisper. *Obs.*

c 1380 Wyclif *Wks.* (1880) 328 Sum confessioun is made to man, and þat may be on many maneres; outher opynly & generaly..or priuely & rownyngly. 1406 Hoccleve *La Male Regle* 172 Cloos kepte I me; no man durste I depraue But rownyngly; I spak no thyng on highte.

Rounsefal, obs. form of Rouncival.

†**Rou·nsepike.** *Obs. rare.* In 5 rounse-, rownsepyk. [Of obscure origin: cf. Rampike and Rampick.] A leafless branch.

1470–85 Malory *Arthur* VI. xvi. 209 Ouer his hede he sawe a rownsepyk, a bygge bough leueles. *Ibid.*, Syr Launcelot putte aweye the stroke with the rounsepyk.

Rounseval, obs. form of Rouncival.

Rounsy, obs. form of Rouncy.

†**Rount,** *a.* *Obs.*—[0] Roan.

1688 Holme *Armoury* II. 155/1 Colours of Horses... Rount, is a kind of flesh colour, or a Bay intermixt with white and gray; a Roan-colour. *Ibid.*, Grissel, is a light Rount.

Rountree, obs. variant of Rowan-tree.

Roup (raup), *sb.*[1] *Sc.* and *north.* Also 7 roop, 8 roupe, 9 *north.* raup. [f. Roup *v.* 2.] An auction; the act of selling or letting by auction.

1693 Stair *Instit.* I. xvi. (ed. 2) 135 A Roup at the half or major part of the Owners against the rest. 1698 A. Fletcher *Two Disc. Aff. Scot.* 36 The letting of Farms.. by Roop or Auction. 1700 Law *Council of Trade* (1751) 9 All other effects that shall be sold by public roupe in this kingdom. 1785 Mrs. Grant *Lett. fr. Mountains* (1813) II. 114 Every article of cattle and furniture was sold. The roup lasted a week. 1833 *Act* 3 & 4 *Will. IV*, c. 46 § 70 The said collector is..to sell by public roup..such part of the said goods and effects. 1878 C. Gibbon *For the King* i, Bauldy's chief business had been to announce roups.

attrib. and *Comb.* 1785 Mrs. Grant *Lett. fr. Mountains* (1813) II. 110 Roups, then, are a source of great amusement here and a very expensive one to the roup-makers. 1829 Hogg *Sheph. Cal.* ii, This cow..is valued in my roup-roll at fifteen pounds. 1890 Service *Notandums* 5 Shall I reprint the roup bills o' my ryegrass parks?

Roup (rūp), *sb.*[2] Forms: 6 roupe, 6–7 roope, 7 rup, roupp, 6– roup, 7– roop. [Of obscure origin.] A disease in poultry characterized by morbid swellings on the rump.

1551 Turner *Herbal* I. B v, Garlyke..is also good for the pype or roupe of hennes and cockes, as Pliny wryteth. 1578 Lyte *Dodoens* 638 They cure the pipe or roupe of Pultrie and Chickens with Garlyke. 1614 Markham *Cheap Husb.* (1623) 141 The roupp is a filthy bile or swelling on the rumpe of Poultrie, and will corrupt the whole body. 1765 *Treat. Dom. Pigeons* 34 The wet roop next falls under our consideration. 1805 R. W. Dickson *Pract. Agric.* II. 1210 The Roup is shown by the rump becoming swelled and enlarged. *c* 1858 Eliz. Watts *Poultry Yard* 167 Inflammation and Intumescence of the Rump Gland..To this affection the term 'roup'..is often applied.

attrib. and *Comb.* 1748 Richardson *Clarissa* (1768) VI. lxxvi. 324 Thou droopest like a pip or roup-cloaking chicken. *c* 1858 Eliz. Watts *Poultry Yard* 168 Baily's roup pills are almost universally known and appreciated.

Roup (rūp), *sb.*[3] Also 8 roupe, and Roop *sb.*[1] [Prob. of imitative origin.]

1. *Sc.* and *north.* Hoarseness, huskiness; †some disease affecting the throat.

a 1585 Montgomerie *Flyting* 323 The rot, the roup, and the auld rest. 1674– [see Roop *sb.*[1]]. *c* 1770 Beattie *To Alex. Ross* iii, O may the roupe ne'er roust thy weason. 1773 Fergusson *Poems* (1789) II. 77 To fleg frae a' your craigs the roup, Wi' reeking het an' creeshy soup. 1811– in northern dial. glossaries.

2. A form of purulent catarrh affecting domestic poultry.

1808 Jamieson, *Roup*..also denotes a disease which affects hens in the mouth or throat. 1849 D. J. Browne *Amer. Poultry Yd.* (1855) 267 The symptom most prominent in the roup, is difficult and noisy breathing, beginning with what is termed the gapes, as in the pip. *c* 1877 L. Wright *Bk. Poultry* 200 In very aggravated cases of roup the entire throat is sometimes filled with the diseased secretion.

Roup (raup), *v.* *Sc.* and *north.* Also 4 roupe, 5–6 rolp, 6 rowp, 9 *north.* raup, rawp, etc. [Of Scandinavian origin: cf. Icel. *raupa* (Fær. *reypa*) to boast, brag, MSw. *rōpa* to shout, Da. *røbe* to disclose, reveal.]

1. *intr.* To cry, shout, roar; to croak. Now *arch.*

13.. *St. Alexius* 566 in Horstm. *Altengl. Leg.* (1881) 187 Scho beganne to roupe & rare. *c* 1450 Holland *Howlat* 215 The Ravyne, rolpand rudly in a roche ran. 1513 Douglas *Æneis* IX. viii. 44 Taikand..na maner schame, Sua amangis men to ryn, and roup or rame. 1535 Lyndesay *Satyre* 3075 Thir ruiks thay roupit wonder fast. 1571 *Satir. Poems Reform.* xxviii. 89 Rowpand for riches..Sum benefice I bocht or euer it vaikit.

1841 Lytton *Nt. & Morn.* (1851) 111 There they were, romping and rouping in the garden, like a couple of gaol birds. 1892 Mrs. Stuart Menteath *Lays Kirk & Covenant* 24 Let heretics both rave and roup.

†b. *trans.* To proclaim or utter with a loud voice. *Obs.*

1513 Douglas *Æneis* III. i. 129 The lattir halsing syne

lowde [we] schowtit thrise, Rowpand at anis, adew! *Ibid.* IV. viii. 129 Or lyk Orestes,..Rowpit and sung quhow he his modir fled. *a* 1572 Knox *Hist. Ref.* Wks. 1846 I. 96 These slaves of Sathan..rowped as thei had bein ravinis, yea, rather thei yelled and rored as devillis in hell, 'Heresy! heresy!'

†c. To invoke loudly. *Obs. rare.*

1513 Douglas *Æneis* IV. ix. 75 Thre hundreth goddis with hir mouth rowpit sche. *Ibid.* xi. 51 Thow Proserpyne, quhilk, by our gentile lawis, Art rowpit hie, and ȝellit lowd by nycht.

2. To sell or let by auction.

1568 Lauder *Minor P.* II. 37 Iustice is rowpit, as vtheris waris; This is most plane, and nocht obscure. 1574 *Reg. Privy Council Scot.* II. 391 To caus rowp the said croft and myre. 1590 *Ibid.* IV. 534 That the small custumes ..micht be yeirlie roupit and sett to the best availl. 1637 Rutherford *Lett.* (1862) I. lxxxviii. 225 If men and angels were rouped and sold at the dearest price. 1693 Stair *Instit.* I. xvi. (ed. 2) 135 Either to take his part at such a rate,..or Roup his own part when he pleases. 1733 P. Lindsay *Interest Scot.* 213 Those poor Fishermen..must pay it,..or have their Houshold furniture distrained and roupt for the Payment of it. 1827 Scott *Jrnl.* 11 Apr., The parks were rouped for £100 a year more than they brought last year. 1879 *Scotsman* 22 Mar., The Linlithgow town and bridge customs were rouped yesterday. 1889 Barrie *Window in Thrums* 90 His effects were rouped before I knew him.

b. To sell up (a person).

c 1817 Hogg *Tales & Sk.* VI. 61 He has since heard..that they had been rouped out at the door. 1824 Mactaggart *Gallovid. Encycl.* 342 Squire Kirtle..May roup his farmers. 1871 C. Gibbon *Lack of Gold* viii, It was not Angus's fault that he was rouped.

Hence **Rou·ping** *ppl. a.*

1530 Lyndesay *Test. Papyngo* 1083 The rowpand Reuin said: sweit syster, lat se ȝour holy intent.

Rouped, *a.* *Sc.* and *north.* Also 8–9 roupet, -it, and Rooped. [f. Roup *sb.*[3] + -ed.] Affected with hoarseness; hoarse.

1677– [see Rooped *a.*]. 1786 Burns *Earnest Cry & Prayer* ii, Alas! my roupet Muse is haerse! 1806 A. Douglas *Poems* 29 Is your throat no dry an' roupit Whistlin a' day loud an' sweet? 1897 Beatty *Secretar* xli, He had a voice like a roupet craw.

Roupee, obs. form of Rupee.

Rouper (rau·pəɹ). *Sc.* Also 6 rowper. [f. Roup *v.* + -er[1]. Cf. Icel. *raupari* braggart.]

1. One who cries or shouts.

a 1585 Polwart *Flyting w. Montgomerie* 757 Ragged rowper like a raven.

2. One who sells goods by auction.

1799 W. Thom *Wks.* 447 A rouper is pursuing his interest when he pays the bell-man to intimate his roup.

Roupie, obs. form of Rupee.

Rouping (rau·piŋ), *vbl. sb.* *Sc.* and *north.* Also 6 rowp-, 7 roupeing, roping. [f. Roup *v.*]

1. The action of selling or letting by auction; also, an auction, a roup.

1593 *Sc. Acts Jas. VI* (1816) IV. 30 The commoun guid and patrimonie of all Burrowis within this Realme,.. efter the ȝeirlie rouping and setting thairof, as vse is. 1646 R. Baillie *Anabaptism* (1647) 17 One..in a public roping did seem to use some couzenage in buying of a house. 1685 *Min. Bk. New Mills Cloth Manuf.* (1905) 85 Appoynts [that] a roupeing be called upon Monday. 1785 Fraser Tytler *The Lounger* No. 79 ¶ 4 Was you ever at a sale,—a rouping you call it in this country? 1818 Scott *Hrt. Midl.* xlii, After the rouping is ower, and the bills paid. 1888 Barrie *Auld Licht Idylls* ii, Then took place the rouping of seats in the parish church.

b. *Comb.*, as **rouping-clerk**, an auctioneer's clerk; †**rouping-wife, -woman**, a woman who holds auctions, or who buys at auctions for the purpose of selling again.

1782 Sir J. Sinclair *Observ. Scot. Dial.* 127 *Rouping-wife*, a female auctioneer. 1785 *Gentl. Mag.* LV. I. 201 The furniture of the house being previously sold to a rouping-woman, as she called it. 1818 Scott *Hrt. Midl.* iv, His neighbour the rouping-wife, or saleswoman. 1882 J. Walker *Jaunt to Auld Reekie* 180 Would'st [thou] be degraded to a rouping clerk.

2. Crying, yelling.

c 1865 S. S. Jones *Northumb.* 115 Ilka bairnie spite o' its roupin' an' skirlin' had gotten washed an' busked up.

Roupy (rū·pi), *a.*[1] Also 9 roopy. [f. Roup *sb.*[2]] Of poultry: Affected with the roup (inflammation of the rump-gland).

1722 De Foe *Plague* (Bohn) 165 The breath of such a person would poison..even a cock or hen:..it would cause them to be roupy, as they call it. 1823 *New Monthly Mag.* VIII. 501 Fast he sat as roopy turkey-poult. 1830 'B. Moubray' *Poultry* (ed. 6) 73 Imposthume upon the rump is called roup. *Ibid.* 74 Roupy hens seldom lay.

Roupy (rū·pi), *a.*[2] [f. Roup *sb.*[3]]

1. Hoarse, husky.

1808 Jamieson s.v. *Roup*, A peculiar sense,..denoting.. hoarseness of voice, as the adj. *roupy* is now used. 1872 F. W. Robinson *Bridge of Glass* II. i, The sheep grew wheezy and roupy and unnaturally dispirited. 1898 Munro *J. Splendid* iv. 48 The crows..complained in a rasping roupy chorus.

2. Of poultry: Affected with the roup (purulent catarrh). Also, pertaining to the roup.

1830 'B. Moubray' *Poultry* (ed. 6) 32 Cocks..are liable to become aguish,..perhaps, in the end, turning roopy or glandered. *Ibid.* 74 When the malady becomes confirmed, with running at the nostrils, swollen eyes, and other well-known symptoms, they are termed Roupy. *c* 1877 L. Wright *Bk. Poultry* 199 The characteristic roupy discharge.

fig. 1863 Quinn *Heather Lintie* 64 Wi' dark, bedimmed, dull roupy e'en..We slowly staumer on.

Roupy, obs. form of Rupee.

Rourde, variant of Rerd(e *sb. Obs.*

†**Rous,** *sb.* *Sc.* *Obs.*—[1] [Of obscure origin: cf. next.] A heavy fall or crash.

1535 Stewart *Cron. Scot.* III. 135 His hors hapnit to snapper and to fall, With sic ane rous quhill that him self flew wnder.

Rous (raus), *adv.* *rare.* Also 9 rouse. [Echoic.] With a bounce or bang.

1672 Villiers (Dk. Buckhm.) *Rehearsal* III. ii, 'Slife, Sir! you should have come out in choler, rous upon the Stage, just as the other went off. 1888 Elworthy *W. Somerset Word-bk.* s.v., Down come the roof, rouse.

Rous, variant of Rouse *a.*, red. *Obs.*

Rousant (rau·zănt), *a.* *Her.* [f. Rouse *v.*[1] + -ant[1].] (See quot. 1780.)

1688 Holme *Armoury* II. xix. 479/1 A Falcon rowsant to the Sinister, is the Crest of Falckenstein of Bavaria. 1780 Edmondson *Compl. Body Her.* II, *Rousant*, a term given by some Heralds to a bird rising, as if preparing to take wing. 1868 Cussans *Heraldry* (1893) 95 *Rising*, or *Rousant*. ..This term is usually employed in blazoning Swans.

Rousch, obs. form of Rush *v.*

†**Rouse,** *sb.*[1] *Obs.* [Of obscure origin.] Mirth.

c 1400 *Beryn* 1669 The todir burgeyse rose hym vp, for to make Rouse, And axid of his felawe [etc.]. *Ibid.* 3610 Beryn & his feleshipp wer within the house, And speken of hir answer, & made but litill rouse.

Rouse (rauz), *sb.*[2] Also 6–7 rowse. [f. Rouse *v.*[1]]

†1. A shake (of the feathers, etc.). *Obs.*

1589 Puttenham *Eng. Poesie* III. xxiii. (Arb.) 272 These fowles in their moulting time, when their feathers be sick, and be so loase in the flesh that at any little rowse they can easilie shake them off. 1600 Breton *Melanch. Humours* Wks. (Grosart) I. 14/1 But all in feare to make so farre a flight, Vntill his pennes were somewhat harder growne; He gaue a rowse. 1614 Latham *Falconry* (1633) 53 If her stomacke..be cold and dull, she will flie wilde and carelesly, and on plains and rowses. 1672 Josselyn *New Englands Rarities* 17 The Porcupine.., a very angry Creature and dangerous, shooting a whole shower of Quills with a rowse at their enemies.

2. *Mil.* The signal for arousing; the réveille.

1802 James *Milit. Dict.*, *Rouse*, one of the bugle-horn soundings for duty. 1821 Joanna Baillie *Metr. Leg.*, *Wallace* xxxvii, No more again the rouse of war to hear. 1863 *Cornh. Mag.* VII. 446 The first notes of the rouse are dismal,..but they are succeeded by a few others of an encouraging and lively character. 1894 Wolseley *Marlborough* II. 198 When the 'rouse' had sounded that morning.

3. A violent stir.

1824 W. Irving *T. Trav.* I. 61 He revolutionized the whole establishment, and gave it such a rouse that the very house reeled with it.

Rouse (rauz), *sb.*[3] Now *arch.* Also 7 rouce, rouze, 7, 9 rowse. [Prob. an aphetic form of *carouse*, due to the phrase *to drink carouse* having been apprehended as *to drink a rouse*.

It has been suggested that the word is ad. Da. (also Sw. and Norw.) *rus*, = Du. *roes*, LG. *rūse*, G. *rausch* intoxication, drunken fit; but both form and meaning are more easily accounted for by the above explanation. 'The Danish rowsa' in Dekker *Gull's Hornbook* may be simply due to the passages in Shaks. *Hamlet*.]

1. A full draught of liquor; a bumper.

1602 Shaks. *Ham.* I. ii. 126 And the Kings Rouce, the Heauens shall bruite againe. 1626 J. Taylor (Water P.) *Trav.* Wks. (1630) III. 80/2 Because death should not terrifie him, they had giuen him many rowses and carowses of wine and beere. 1640 Glapthorne *Wallenstein* V. ii, My Lord, ..take me off This lusty rowse to your owne health.

1820 Shelley *Let. to Maria Gisborne* 65 Then all quaff Another rouse, and hold their sides and laugh.

2. A carousal or bout of drinking.

1602 Shaks. *Ham.* II. i. 58 There was he gaming, there o'retooke in's Rouse. 1619 Fletcher *Mons. Thomas* I. ii, She has heard..The gambols that you plaid.., your several mischiefs, Your rowses and your wenches. 1654 Gayton *Pleas. Notes* IV. viii. 217 After a good rouze, or good dose of *Nepenthe*, they are in a trance.

1855 Kingsley *Westw. Ho!* viii, Amyas..invited..his old schoolfellows..to a merry supper and a 'rowse' thereon consequent. 1863 Cowden Clarke *Shaks. Char.* v. 131 It was natural that a free, open-hearted soldier should welcome the arrival of his brother-officers with a rouse.

3. In the phrases *to take one's rouse*, *have a rouse*, *give a rouse*.

(*a*) 1602 Shaks. *Ham.* I. iv. 8 The King doth wake to night, and takes his rouse. 1616 *Marlowe's Faustus* (Rtldg.) 122/2 He took his rouse with stoops of Rhenish wine. 1623 Massinger *Dk. Milan* I. i, Your lord, by his patent, Stands bound to take his rouse.

(*b*) 1609 B. Jonson *Sil. Wom.* III. vi, We will haue a rouse in each of him, anon, for bold Britons, yfaith. 1667 Davenant & Dryden *Tempest* IV. iii, I long to have a rouse to her grace's health. 1815 Scott *Guy M.* xxxiv, Rambling up and down this d—d vault, and thinking about the merry rouses we have had in it. 1842 Tennyson *Vision of Sin* IV. ix, Fill the cup, and fill the can: Have a rouse before the morn. 1864 Burton *Scot Abr.* II. 181 Patrick's neighbour,..with whom..he has a merry rouse.

(*c*) 1604 Shaks. *Oth.* II. iii. 66 'Fore heauen, they haue giuen me a rouse already. 1609 Healey *Discov. New World* 84 Giue me one rouse, my freind, and get thee gone. 1842 Browning *Cavalier Tunes* II. i, Give a rouse: here's, in Hell's despite now, King Charles!

†**Rouse,** *a.* *Obs.* Also 5 rous, rowse. [a. OF. *rous* (mod.F. *roux*):—L. *russum*, acc. of *russus* red.] Red-haired. (Only in personal names.)

c 1400 *Ywaine & Gaw.* 1146 Pray to hir..That sho forgif the, in this stede, Of Salados the rouse ded. *c* 1400 *Brut* cxxxiv. 138 After þis William Bastard regnede his sone William [þe] Rous. *c* 1425 in Maskell *Mon. Rit.* (1847) III. 345 For the soules of the kyngis William Rowse, Herry the firste [etc.]. 1531 Elyot *Gov.* I. xii, William called Rouse.

Rouse (rauz), *v.*[1] Also 5–8 rowse, 6–8 rowze, 6–9 rouze (7 rouz), 7, 9 *Sc.* roose. [Orig. a technical term in hawking and hunting, and so presumably of AF. or OF. origin, but the precise source is obscure. In general use common after *c* 1585, and freq. strengthened by *up*. Cf. also Arouse *v.*[1]]

I. †1. *refl.* a. Of a hawk: To shake the feathers. *Obs. rare.* Cf. sense 9.

1486 *Bk. St. Albans* A vi, And whanne she hathe doone she will rowse hire myghtyly. [1825 Scott *Betrothed* xxiii, The..vigour with which they pruned their plumes, and shook, or, as it was technically termed, roused themselves.]

†b. (See quot.) *Obs. rare.*

1530 Palsgr. 694/2, I rowse, I stretche my selfe, as a man dothe whan he gothe to prove a maystrye, *je me coppie*. It was a sporte to se him rowse him selfe and stretche out his armes, or ever he began to wrestyll.

2. *trans.* To cause (game) to rise or issue from cover or lair. Cf. Raise *v.*[1] 4 b.

1531 Elyot *Gov.* I. xviii, If they wold use but a fewe nombre of houndes, onely to harborowe, or rouse, the game. 1575 Turberv. *Venerie* 106 The huntesman.. shall then go before them and rowze the Deare. 1596 Shaks. 1 *Hen. IV*, I. iii. 198 The blood more stirres To rowze a Lyon, then to start a Hare. 1627 Taylor (Water P.) *Armado* Wks. (1630) I. 93 So hath this Woodmanship diuers and sundry tearmes of Art..as you must say, Rowse a Bucke, Start a Hare, and vnkennel a Foxe. 1697 Dryden *Virg. Georg.* III. 624 Thou mayst..Rouze from their Desart Dens, the bristled Rage Of Boars. 1709 Prior *Henry & Emma* 307 To beat the woods, and rouse the bounding prey. 1774 Goldsm. *Nat. Hist.* (1776) III. 121 The chief huntsman, entering with his hounds within the lines, roused the game with a full cry. 1831 Scott *Cast. Dang.* vi, He proposes to go to rouse the wild cattle. 1858 Kingsley *Poems* 160 They roused a hart,..A hart of ten.

fig. 1589 Greene *Menaphon* (Arb.) 15 When they want certaine liquid sacrifice, to rouze her [the muse] foorth her denne. 1593 Shaks. *Rich. II*, II. iii. 128 To rowze his Wrongs, and chase them to the bay.

†3. a. To raise or set up, to ruffle. *Obs.*

1590 Spenser *F. Q.* I. xi. 9 An Eagle, seeing pray appeare, His aery plumes doth rouze. *Ibid.* II. iii. 35 He.., standing stoutly up, his lofty crest Did fiercely shake, and rowze as comming late from rest. 1604 Drayton *Owle* 732 As he stands proudly rowzing up his Plumes.

†b. To raise or lift up. Also *fig.* *Obs.*

1597 Shaks. 2 *Hen. IV*, IV. i. 118 Henry Bullingbrooke and hee Being mounted, and both rowsed in their Seates. 1633 P. Fletcher *Purple Isl.* XI. xxix, She strives..to.. rouze her fainting head, which down as oft would fall. 1650 Earl Monm. tr. *Senault's Man bec. Guilty* 310 When he heard the comfort of birds or the noyse of the waters he rowsed up his soul to his Creator.

refl. 1599 Shaks. *Hen. V*, I. ii. 275, I will..shew my sayle of Greatnesse, When I do rowse me in my Throne of France.

4. To cause to start up from slumber or repose; to awaken from sleep, meditation, etc. Also with *up*, *out*.

1593 Shaks. *Rich. II*, I. iii. 134 Rouz'd vp with boystrous vntun'd drummes. 1601 — *Twel. N.* II. iii. 60 Shall wee rowze the night-Owle in a Catch? 1632 Milton *L'Allegro* 54 The Hounds and horn Chearly rouse the slumbring morn. 1711 Addison *Spect.* No. 55 ¶ 1 A young Fellow who was rouzed out of his Bed, in order to be sent upon a long Voyage. 1757 W. Wilkie *Epigoniad* VII. 231 The stars descend; and soon the morning ray Shall rouse us to the labors of the day. 1819 Shelley *Cenci* IV. iv. 18, I must rouse him from his sleep, Since none else dare. 1853 Kingsley *Hypatia* xxviii, At last a low whistle roused her from her dream. 1896 Baden-Powell *Matabele Campaign* iii, Here I roused out Pyke, the officer in command. *Ibid.* xvi, At 2.30 we were roused up.

absol. 1846 Trench *Mirac.* xiv. (1862) 244 Christ rouses from the bier as easily as another would rouse from the bed.

b. To disturb, chase away (sleep). *rare.*

1667 Milton *P. L.* III. 329 The cited dead Of all past Ages to the general Doom shall hast'n, such a peal shall rouse thir sleep.

5. *fig.* a. To awaken or startle (one) from a state of ease or security.

1594 T. B. *La Primaud. Fr. Acad.* II. 577 Although some men..fall sometimes into this senslesnesse, yet..God afterwards rowseth them vp well enough. 1627 Drayton *Agincourt* 100 And in vpon Northumberland doth breake, Rowzing the Sluggish villages from sleepe. 1650 Hubbert *Pill Formality* 90 It rowsed him out of his security. *a* 1740 Waterland *Serm.* xxxiii. Wks. 1823 IX. 412 His present fears, rather than any thing of true penitence, roused him up, and made him have recourse to God. 1770 Pitt in Almon *Anecd.* (1810) II. xxxix. 104, I mean to rouse, to alarm the whole nation—to rouse the Ministry, if possible, who seem awake to nothing but the preservation of their places.

b. To stir up, excite to vigorous action or thought, to provoke to activity.

c 1586 C'tess Pembroke *Ps.* LV. iv, Purple morn,..and midday cleare, Shall see my praying voice to God enclin'd, Rowzing him up. 1612 T. Taylor *Comm. Titus* i. 16 When the holy Ghost would rowse vp the slothfull seruant, he threateneth him his portion with hypocrites. 1678 R. L'Estrange *Seneca's Mor.* (1702) 120 Philosophy..rouzes, us where we are faint and drouzy. 1710 Steele *Tatler* No. 2 ¶ 2 The Emperor is rouzed by this Alarm. 1777 Watson *Philip II* (1793) II. XIII. 173 The Spaniards, rouzed by the danger which threatened them,..made a bold and vigorous resistance. 1808 *Med. Jrnl.* XIX. 161 Emetics..I thought might rouse the liver from its state of torpor. 1860 Tyndall *Glac.* I. xxvii. 197 Vainly the postilion endeavoured to rouse them [*sc.* horses] by word and whip. 1888 Bryce *Amer. Commw.* II. 413 To excite the voters by..the sense of a common purpose, rousing them by speeches or literature.

c. Const. *to* or *into*.

1701 De Foe *Trueborn Eng.* 45 Till Pity rowz'd him from his soft Repose, His Life to unseen Hazards to expose. 1715 Pope *Iliad* II. 94 Unite, and rouze the sons of Greece to arms. 1743 R. Blair *Grave* 319 Enough to rouse a dead man into rage. 1831 Sir J. Sinclair *Corr.* II. 151 They roused the population to action, and armed them. 1847 Martin *Ox* 130/2 The animal is roused to fury. 1863 Geo. Eliot *Romola* vi, His pride was roused to double activity.

d. To provoke to anger.

1843 *P. Parley's Ann.* IV. 355 He felt a delight..in plaguing the nursemaid, and in rousing the cook.

6. *refl.* in senses 4 and 5.

1590 Lodge *Rosalynde* (Hunterian Cl.) 85 With that his Brother began to stirre, and the Lion to rowse himselfe. 1606 Shaks. *Tr. & Cr.* III. iii. 222 Sweete, rouse your selfe; and the weake wanton Cupid Shall from your necke vnloose his amorous fould. 1656 Sanderson *Serm.* (1689) 141 Rowzing up himself and his spirits with zeal as hot as fire. 1726 Swift *Gulliver* IV. ii, I roused myself, and looked about me in the Room where I was left alone. 1794 Mrs. Radcliffe *Myst. Udolpho* iv, He seemed by an effort to rouse himself. 1842 Tennyson *Ld. of Burleigh* 21 From deep thought himself he rouses.

b. Const. *to*.

1587 Golding *De Mornay* Pref. (1592) p. vi, That reason rowseth up her selfe to rest vpon truth. 1606 Shaks. *Ant. & Cl.* V. ii. 287, I see him rowse himselfe To praise my Noble Act. 1693 Owen *Holy Spirit* 114 Let such Souls rouze up themselves to lay hold on him. 1746 P. Francis tr. *Horace, Epist.* I. ii. 48 Will you not rouse you to preserve yourself? 1848 Dickens *Dombey* xxxii, The Captain..roused himself to a sustained consciousness of that gentleman's presence. 1880 Mrs. Forrester *Roy & V.* I. 2 He too rouses himself to acknowledge the general homage.

7. To stir up, agitate, put into motion, bring into an active state.

1582 Stanyhurst *Æneis* II. (Arb.) 50 Thee water is rowsed, they doe frisk with flownse to the shoare ward. 1667 Milton *P. L.* II. 287 The sound of blustring winds, which all night long Had rous'd the Sea. 1728 T. Sheridan tr. *Persius* vi. (1739) 84 In rouzing the Strings of the Lyre. 1785 Burns *Ep. to Rev. J. M'Math* 11 Lest they shou'd blame her, An' rouse their holy thunder on it. 1810 *Sporting Mag.* XXXVI. 277 All the charges which they and the prosecutor had roused up against him. 1836 *Backwoods of Canada* 79 The landlady..led me to a blazing fire, which her damsels quickly roused up.

b. To stir up, excite, inflame (a feeling).

1589 Greene *Menaphon* (Arb.) 68 He began thus to rowze vp his furie. 1637 Heylin *Answ. Burton* 184 You call upon the nobles to rowze up their noble Christian zeale. 1666 Dryden *Ann. Mirab.* cxc, But sharp remembrance..And shame..Rouse conscious virtue up in every heart. 1752 Hume *Ess. & Treat.* (1777) I. 12 The spirit of the people must frequently be rouzed. 1777 Robertson *Hist. Amer.* II. (1778) I. 116 Those unprovoked injuries rouzed their courage. 1841 Elphinstone *Hist. Ind.* II. 605 This crime only roused the indignation of the Marattas, without weakening their power. 1875 Jowett *Plato* (ed. 2) IV. 156 The passions of religious parties have been roused to the utmost.

c. To stir (a liquid, *esp.* beer while brewing).

1823 J. Badcock *Dom. Amusem.* 101 Having poured boiling water on the suspected sample, rouse it well. 1839 Ure *Dict. Arts* 118 Rouse the beer as the hops are gradually introduced. 1876 *Encycl. Brit.* IV. 275/2 This is done by 'rousing' the gyle every two hours with a utensil made for the purpose.

8. *Naut.* To haul *in*, *out*, or *up* with force.

c 1625 *Nomenclator Navalis* (MS.), *Rowse in* is a worde they use particulerlie when as a Cabell or Hawser doth lie slack in the water and they would have him made tawght. *Ibid.*, To keepe it [the cable] stiff and tawght, they will hale in soe much as lies slack, and this they call Rowsing-in the Cabell or Rowse-in the Hawser. [Hence in various 17th cent. nautical works.] 1769 Falconer *Dict. Marine* (1780), *Recouvrer*, to rowse-in, or haul any rope into the ship. 1832 Marryat *N. Forster* v, You and the boy, rouse the cable up.., and bend it. 1841 R. H. Dana *Seaman's Man.* xv. 85 Rouse the cable out through the hawse-hole. 1885 J. M. Caulfeild *Seamanship Notes* 3 Rouse out reef pendant.

transf. 1890 'R. Boldrewood' *Col. Reformer* (1891) 193 You cut a straight sapling while we rouse out the saddle-straps for a splice.

II. *intr.* †9. Of hawks or other birds and animals: To shake the feathers or body. *Obs.*

1486 *Bk. St. Albans* C viij, She Rousith when she shakith all hir federis. 1575 Turberv. *Faulconrie* 149 Then suffer hir until she rowse or mewte, and when she hath done either of them unhode hir. 1639 T. de Grey *Compl. Horsem.* 216 You shall perceive him either to shake his head, or to winch with his tayle, to rouze, or shake. 1657 R. Ligon *Barbadoes* (1673) 4 The Turtles..there, mute, prune, and oyl their feathers; rouse, and doe all their offices of nature. 1678 Phillips, *Rowze*, in Faulconry is when a Hawk lifteth up, and shaketh her self.

10. Of game: To rise from cover. *rare.*

1575 Turberv. *Venerie* 106 All the horsemen must quickly cast abrode about the couert, to discouer ye Harte when he rowzeth and goeth out of his hold. 1590 Sir T. Cockaine *Treat. Hunting* C iv b, This done, you may begin to tuft for a Bucke, and finding him single, especially if he rouse foorth of a great brake, put your hounds softly upon. 1826 Hone *Every-day Bk.* II. 1031 A red buck roused, then crossed in view.

11. To move with violence; to rush. *rare.*

1582 Stanyhurst *Æneis* I. (Arb.) 19 A king he placed, throgh whose Maiestical Empyre Theese blasts rouze forward, or back by his regal apoinctment. 1818 *Sporting Mag.* II. 279 The Paddington boy..tried again to rouse in upon Doly's victualling-office.

†12. To rise up, stand on end. *Obs.*—[1]

1605 Shaks. *Macb.* V. v. 12 My Fell of haire Would at a dismall Treatise rowze, and stirre As life were in't.

13. To get up from sleep or repose; to waken up.

1605 Shaks. *Macb.* III. ii. 52 Good things of Day begin to droope, and drowse, Whiles Nights black Agents to their Prey's doe rowse. 1642 Milton *Apol. Smect.* Wks. 1851 III. 266 Up, and stirring,..with the Bird that first rouses. 1682 Creech *Lucretius* (1683) 131 And softer Curs, that lie and sleep at home, Do often rouse, and walk about the Room. 1707 J. Stevens tr. *Quevedo's Com. Wks.* (1709) 229 Day came, and we all rouz'd. 1719 De Foe *Crusoe* II. (Globe) 488 Rouzing..from Sleep with the Noise, I caus'd the Boat to be thrust in. 1882 Floyer *Unexpl. Baluchistan* 99, I gradually roused up on hearing this, and..put my head out of the tent door. 1890 *Illustr. Lond. News* 13 Dec. 746/1 When I roused, the yellow sun was pouring in at my lattice.

b. *fig.* To become active; to bestir oneself, take heart or courage, etc.

1589 L. Wright *Hunting of Antichrist* 13 Shortly after began to rowse our noble and valiant Lion of England, Henrie the eight of famous memorie. 1611 Speed *Hist. Gt. Brit.* VII. xxxvi. (1623) 386 Hubba that had harried the English, and now rouzed upon the newes of King Elfred's victory and life. 1624 Quarles *Job Militant* xix. 6 Rouze up, fond man, and answere my replies. 1740 *Johnson's Debates* (1787) I. 91 It is surely time for this nation to rouse from indolence, and to resolve to put an end to frauds that have been so long known. 1791 Cowper *Iliad* IV. 498 Be it ours to rouse at once To action. 1831 Scott *Cast. Dang.* xiii, In God's name, rouse up, sir; let it not be said that [etc.].

c. Of qualities or feelings.

1671 Milton *Samson* 1690 His fierie vertue rouz'd From under ashes into sudden flame. 1759 Adam Smith *Moral Sent.* (1804) I. 181 Our indignation rouses and we are eager to refute..such detestable principles. 1850 Thackeray *Pendennis* lxxi, Arthur..felt his anger rousing up within him.

Rouse (rauz), *v.*[2] Also *Sc.* and *north.* roose, rooze. [Aphetic form of Arrouse *v.*]

1. *trans.* To sprinkle (herring, etc.) with salt in the process of curing.

17.. in *Lauder's Suppl. Decis. Lds. Council* IV. 845 His charter not mentioning that it was for export, he was not bound to rouse them with salt upon salt. 1800 *Chron.*, *Ann. Reg.* 110/2 Herrings sprinkled (or as it is termed 'roused or corned') with a moderate quantity of salt will continue perfectly good at least two months. 1854 H. Miller *Sch. & Schm.* (1858) 43 We could see..the curers going about rousing their fish with salt, to counteract the effects of the dog-day sun. 1894 R. Leighton *Wreck Golden Fleece* 57 While I go below and roose the fish.

2. To cause (water) to overflow (see quot.).

1794 Davis *Agric. Wilts* 38 In the catch-meadows..the great object is to keep the 'works of them' as dry as possible between the intervals of watering; ..care is necessary to make the most of the water by catching and rousing it as often as possible.

†**Rouse,** *v.*[3] *Obs. rare.* [Of obscure origin.] ? To rest, settle.

1563 Foxe *A. & M.* 1393/2, I was caryed to my Lordes Colehouse agayne, where I with my syxe fellowes do rouse together in the straw, as cherefullye..as other doo in theyr beds of downe. 1616 *Rich Cabinet* 153 The maister of the house began to rouse his shoulders in a rich chaire.

Rouseabout (rau·zăbaut). [f. Rouse *v.*[1]]

1. *dial.* (See quots. 1778 and 1886.)

1746 *Exmoor Scolding* (E. D. S.) 30 A rubbacrock, rouze-about..swashbucket. 1778 — *Gloss.*, *A Rouzabout*, a restless Creature never easy at Home, but roaming from Place to Place. Also, a Sort of large Pease [etc.]. 1886 Elworthy *W. Somerset Word-bk.* 633 *Rouse-about*..implies coarseness, roughness, awkwardness, yet withal bustling activity.

2. *Austr.* A man or boy employed on a sheep station; an odd man on a farm. Cf. Roustabout.

1881 *Chamb. Jrnl.* Mar. 157 Rouseabouts are men and boys who pen the sheep, pick up the fleeces as they are shorn, sort and pack the wool [etc.]. 1890 *Melbourne Argus* 20 Sept. 13 6 The shearers hold themselves as the aristocrats of the shed, and never associate with the 'rouse-abouts'. 1893 J. A. Barry *S. Brown's Bunyip* 280 The everlasting drudgery of the rouseabout.

3. *Rouse-about block*, a large snatch-block.

1875 Knight *Dict. Mech.* 2230/1.

Roused (rauzd), *ppl. a.*[1] [f. Rouse *v.*[1] + -ed[1].] Disturbed; aroused, awakened.

1590 Spenser *F. Q.* III. i. 62 The whole family..Rashly out of their rouzed couches sprong. 1602 Shaks. *Ham.* II. ii. 510 So after Pyrrhus pause, A rowsed Vengeance sets him new a-worke. 1716 *Loyal Mourner* 10 And rouz'd Sea-Monsters in the Tempest play. 1820 Shelley *Witch Atl.* l, The flagging wing Of the roused cormorant. 1856 Stonehenge *Brit. Rural Sports* 129/1 The fine fresh scent of a newly-roused fox. 1894 Mrs. H. Ward *Marcella* II. 245 He leant over her in his roused strength.

Roused, *ppl. a.*[2] (See Rouse *v.*[2] 1.)

1899 *Shetland News* 22 July (E. D. D.), Two small cargoes of 'roused' herrings were sent south from Lerwick.

†**Rousee.** *Obs.* [a. OF. *rousee*, *rosee* (mod.F. *rosée*), ultimately f. L. *rōs*.] Dew.

1481 Caxton *Godfrey* cxl. 208 How oure men reioysed them of a dew or rousee descendyng thenne fro heuen. *Ibid.*, Thenne began to falle a rayne or a dewe, so swete a rousee was neuer seen.

Rousement (rau·zmĕnt). *U.S.* [f. Rouse *v.*[1] + -ment.] A rousing up of religious excitement.

1883 *Congregationalist* 27 Sept. (Cent.), Deep strong feeling, but no excitement. They are not apt to indulge in any more rousements. 1885 *Home Missionary* Apr. 473 The 'rousement' as the religious excitement was called, was not long in coming.

Rouser (rau·zəɹ). [f. Rouse *v.*[1] + -er[1].]

1. One who, or that which, rouses or stirs up.

1611 Cotgr., *Esveilleur*,..a rowser, a raiser from sleepe. 1612 Shelton *Quix.* I. III. vi, All this which I have depainted to thee, are inciters and rowsers of my mind. 1783 J. Young *Crit. Gray's Elegy* (1810) 44 The rousers to morning labour are also enumerated as four. 1801 Scott *Glenfinlas* xxxv, Within an hour return'd each hound; In rush'd the rousers of the deer. 1898 Monson *Trop. Dis.* xii. 212 A fine stream of iced water poured on the forehead from an elevation will act as a stimulant and rouser.

b. An implement or apparatus used for stirring (*esp.* beer in brewing).

1830 M. Donovan *Dom. Econ.* I. 165 A vertical rod plunges down the copper...This rod terminates in a horizontal bar, carrying an extended chain, called, on account of its duty, a *rouser*. The rod and rouser are both kept in continual motion. 1839 Ure *Dict. Arts* 585 The intermixture may be effected either by lading the glass out of one pot into another..or by stirring it up with a rouser. 1854 Ronalds & Richardson *Chem. Technol.* (ed. 2) I. 287 The contents can be constantly agitated by the rouser.

attrib. 1839 Ure *Dict. Arts* 116 The rouser shaft may be lifted by means of the chain.

2. One who, or that which, is remarkable in some respect.

1859 Bartlett *Dict. Amer.* (ed. 2) 372 *Rouser*, something very exciting or very great. Thus an eloquent speech or sermon, a large mass-meeting, or a big prize-ox, is a rouser. 1868 *Putnam's Mag.* Jan. 70 He's a rouser to make punch, I assure you. 1895 Crockett in *Cornh. Mag.* Dec. 578 For a' the leers in the pairish—and there are some rousers—ye beat them clean.

b. An outrageous falsehood.

1825–9 Brockett *N. C. Gloss.* s.v. *Ruze*. 1838 Holloway *Prov. Dict.*, *Rouser*, or a Rousing Lie, is such a monstrous lie as rouses the wonder and astonishment of every one who hears it. 1873 Leland *Egypt. Sketch-Bk.* 176, I like a man to tell a rouser while he is about it.

3. A loud noise; a noisy person, song, etc.

1731 Swift *Strephon & Chloe*, He..Let fly a Rouzer in her Face. 1872 De Vere *Americanisms* 225 The rouser is ..a man who talks very loud and occasionally yells. 1893 Milliken *'Arry Ballads* 64 (Farmer), We made the whole place ring a rouser, till Julter implored us to stop.

4. *Austr.* = Rouseabout 2.

1902 H. Lawson *Children of Bush* 241, I must get some more money for the rouser from some of those chaps.

Rousette, variant of Roussette.

Rousing (rau·ziŋ), *vbl. sb.*[1] [f. Rouse *v.*[1] + -ing[1].] The action of the verb in various senses.

c 1580 Jeffere *Bugbears* Epil., With sowcynges, with rowsynges, with bownsynges. 1587 Golding *De Mornay* xvii. (1617) 290 A rouzing of her feathers & a vaine flapping of her wings. 1627 Capt. Smith *Seaman's Gram.* vii. 31 Rousing is..pulling the slacknesse of any Cables with mens hands into the Ship. 1634 W. Burton (*title*), The Rowsing of the Sluggard. Deliuered in seuen Sermons. 1719 Baynard *Health* (1740) 19 Ferments in the body pent, which early rowzing may prevent. 1756 Burke *Subl. & B.* Wks. I. 265 That without this rousing they would become languid and diseased. 1823 J. Badcock *Dom. Amusem.* 22 The addition of lime to the pyrolignous acid..is done in a large vessel by frequent rousings up. *c* 1870 Stubbs *Lect. Europ. Hist.* II. x. (1904) 253 A sort of rousing appears to take place.

Rou·sing, *vbl. sb.*[2] [f. Rouse *v.*[2]] The action of sprinkling, etc.

1706 A. Boyer *Ann. Q. Anne* IV. 51 The clause relating to the rousing of herrings with foreign salt. 1842 J. Wilson *Voy. Scotl.* II. 158 The necessities of gutting and rousing. 1887 Moloney *Forestry W. Afr.* 177 It is recommended that new resins should be subject to a rough sifting and rousing in common soda-and-water.

Rousing (rau·ziŋ), *ppl. a.* [f. Rouse *v.*[1]]

In the following quotation the precise sense is not clear.

1606 *Wily Beguiled* E ij, He..wrap me in a rousing Calueskin suite, and come like some Hob-goblin, or some Diuell Ascended from the grisly pit of Hell.

1. That rouses, awakens, or stirs up.

1641 Milton *Animadv.* Wks. 1851 III. 230 Against negligence or obstinacy will be requir'd a rousing volie of Pastorly threatning. 1665 Boyle *Occas. Refl.* IV. ix. (1848) 222 The careless Sensualists, that fly a rowzing Sermon. 1755 *Connoisseur* No. 92 ¶ 8 Justice Silence..has no sooner swallowed the rouzing cup, than he roars out a catch. 1791 Mrs. Radcliffe *Rom. Forest* ii, He gave the fire a rousing stir. 1889 *Spectator* 14 Dec. 830 He was the most rousing of our poets.

transf. 1799 Robertson *Agric. Perth* 181 A rousing furrow should be given to it, and the rough stubble turned down.

2. a. Of a lie: Outrageous, gross.

1664 H. More *Myst. Iniq.* viii. 133 It were likewise a good rousing lie, and bigger then belief, that a certain Holy House..should be carried out of Palestine into Italy. 1677 Coles *Eng.-Lat. Dict.*, A rousing lye, *mendacium magnificum*. 1706 Phillips (ed. Kersey), *Rousing Lie*, a whisking great one. 1791 Burns *Death & Dr. Hornbook* i, Ev'n Ministers, they hae been kenn'd..A rousing whid, at times, to vend. 1828 *Carr Craven Gloss.*

b. Of a fire: Roaring, blazing strongly.

1682 Tate *Abs. & Achit.* II. 547 For our wise rabble ne'er took pains to inquire, What 'twas he burnt, so it made a rousing fire. 1760–72 H. Brooke *Fool of Qual.* (1809) II. 151 The weather was very cold.., and I had a rousing fire. 1838 Dickens *Lett.* (1880) I. 9 A rousing fire halfway up the chimney. 1887 R. N. Carey *Uncle Max* vi, Come into the parlor: there is a fine rousing fire that will soon warm you.

c. Of trade, etc.: Brisk, lively.

1767 Sterne *Tr. Shandy* IX. v, A Jew..had the ill luck to die of a strangury, and leave his widow in possession of a rousing trade. 1895– in *Eng. Dial. Dict.* in various contexts.

Rove, sb., Forms: 5-7 roue, 6 roaue, 6-8 roue, 5-rove. [Of doubtful origin: possibly a Midland form of RAVE sb.¹ to stray (cf. note to ROVE v.¹]

Rove, v.¹

Rove, v.² and clinch (nails), to provide with roves for clinching. Obs.

Rove, sb.² Obs. Also 5-8 roove. [ad. F. arrove, obs. var. arrobe, ad. Sp. and F. arroba.]

Rove, v.³

Rove, v.⁴

Rove, v.⁵

Rove-beetle. [f. ROVE v.¹] A beetle of the family Staphylinidæ.

Roveison. Obs. rare. In 4 roueiso(u)n, royson. [a. OF. roveison, etc. :—L. rogātiōn-em: see ROGATION]

Roven, var. pa. pple. REVE v.¹

Rover¹ (rōu·vəɹ). Also 5-7 rouer, 6 roauer, rowar, 5-7 rouer [= REAVER.]

Rover², Obs. rare.

Rover³ (rōu·vəɹ).

Roverry, rare.— [f. ROVER.] Piracy.

Roving (rōu·viŋ), vbl. sb.¹ [f. ROVE v.¹]

Roving (rōu·viŋ), vbl. sb.² [f. ROVE v.⁴]

Roving (rōu·viŋ), vbl. sb.³ [f. ROVE v.⁵]

Rovery² rare.— [f. ROVER³.] Piracy.

Rovingly, adv. [f. ROVING ppl. a.]

Row, sb.¹ Forms: 1, 4-5 (6-9 north. and Sc.) raw (-e), 3-5 (6 Sc.) rawe. 8-9 rowe, 9 roo, 6 roo. [OE. ráw (late sense 8 b), var. of ráw Rów sb.², which may be related to MDu. (h)rie (in MDu. rij), MHG. rige (G. reihe).]

Row, sb.² Obs. [ad. F. arrobe. See also ROVE sb.²]

Row, sb.³ [f. ROW v.¹] A spell of rowing; a journey on the water in a rowing-boat.

Row, sb.⁴ Obs. rare. [OE. rōw, ON. rá.]

Row, sb.⁵ rare. Obs. [OE. row, ON. rá.]

Row, sb.⁶ [? cf. Row v.²]

Row, sb.⁷ Obs. Also 6 rowe. [Cf. Row¹.] A rove of wool or cotton.

Row, a.¹; cf. MDu. and MLG. ruw, ru (Du. ruw). See also Row sb.⁶

1. Rough, in various senses. (Common from c 1200 to 1450.)

Row, a.² Now north. dial. Forms: 1 hréow, 5-6 rowe, 5-7, 9 rou, 9 dial. roo. [OE. hréow, etc., an ablaut-variant of Aw or Raw v. Raw, uncouth, untamed, etc. Also rou-nosed.]

Row (rau), v.¹

Row (rau), v.² Now north. dial. [OE. rōwan, ON. róa.]

Row, v.³

Supplement, p. 3873; Corrigenda, p. 4092; Spurious words, p. 4093; Books quoted, p. 4094

royal: —I., regtī-em Regal a. in ME. the variants Real (a.) and Rial were also in common use. The French origin of the word may still be shown by the adj. being placed after the noun.

adj.

I. Of blood, etc.: Originating from, connected with a king or line of kings.

1. Of persons: Having the rank of king or queen; belonging to the royal family.

2. Of rank, etc.: Of or pertaining to a sovereign, or the dignity or office of a sovereign.

3. So of insignia or emblems of royalty.

4. *Royal Burgh*, a Scottish burgh which derives its charter directly from the Crown.

5. *Royal Society*, a Society incorporated by Charles II in 1662 for the pursuit and advancement of the physical sciences.

6. Founded or established by, under the patronage of, a sovereign or royal person.

II. Belonging to, occupied or used by, a king or kings; forming part of the possessions or property of the crown.

7. Proceeding from, performed by, a (or the) sovereign.

II.8. Befitting, appropriate to, a sovereign; esp. stately, magnificent, splendid.

9. Of persons: Having the character proper to a king; noble, majestic; generous, munificent.

10. In various military and related uses.

sb.

1. *s.a.* A king or prince.

2. A kingly or royal personage.

3. A royal of the royal family; a royal personage.

15. In various special collocations, as *royal antler*, etc.

ROYALET. 851 ROYALTY. ROYALTY. 852 RUB.

Royalet. A royal boat or vessel. *Obs.*

Royalism (roi'aliz'm), *n.* Attachment or adherence to the monarchy or to the principle of monarchical government.

Royalist (roi'alist), *sb.* and *a.*

Royalize (roi'alaiz), *v.* To render royal; to invest with a royal character or standing.

Royally (roi'ali), *adv.* Also 4–7 royalliche.

Royalty (roi'alti), *sb.* Forms: 4–6 roialte, 5–6 (royalte), 6–7 -tie, 6 royalty.

Roylet: *obs. forms of* Roil, Royalet.

Royster, *obs. form of* Roister.

Royston crow (roi'st'n). Also 7 Roiston. [f. the place-name *Royston* on the borders of Hertfordshire and Cambridgeshire.] The hooded or grey crow (*Corvus cornix*).

Rub (rʌb), *sb.[1]*

Supplement, p. 3873; Corrigenda, p. 4092; Spurious words, p. 4093; Books quoted, p. 4094

Rubbishing, a.

Rubbishly, a.

Rubbishy, a.

Rubble, sb.

Rubble-stone.

Rubble-work.

Rubbly, a.

Rubbidge.

Rubbish, v.

Rubbisher.

Rubbling.

Rubble, v.

Rubbler.

Rubefacient, a. and sb. Med.

Rubefaction.

Rubefy, v.

Rubeola, sb. Path.

Rubeolar, a.

Rubella, sb. Path.

Rubellan.

Rubellite, sb. Min.

Rubelle.

Ruben, sb.

Rubeoid, a.

Ruberythric acid.

Rubescence.

Rubescent, a.

Rubescence, rare.

Rubian, Chem.

Rubianic, a.

Rubicelle, sb.

Rubicon, sb.

Rubicund, a.

Rubicundity.

Rubidine, Chem.

Rubidic, a. Chem.

Rubidium, Chem.

Rubied, ppl. a.

Rubific, a.

Rubify, v.

Rubification.

Rubificative, a.

Rubiginose, a.

Rubiginous, a.

Rubine, sb.

Rubineous, a.

Rubious, a.

Rubric, sb. and a.

Rubrical, a.

Rubrically, adv.

Rubricate, v.

Rubricated, ppl. a.

Rubrication.

Rubricator.

Rubrician.

Rubricist.

3. A rubricator.

Rubricity (rubri·siti). [f. as prec. + -ITY.]

1. Assumption of a red colour.

2. Adherence to liturgical rubrics.

Rubricked, Rub, ppl. a. rare. [f. RUBRIC v. + -ED.] Rubricated.

Rubris, sb. Sc. form of ROBBERY.

† Rubrify, v. Obs. [See RUBRIFF and -FIC.] Conferring a red colour.

Rubrification. In 6 rubryfycacyon. [ad. med.L. *rubrificātio*: see RUBRIFY.]

† Rubrificative, a. [f. as next.]

† Bu·briform, a. [Cf. next and -FORM.] Of red nature.

† Rubrify, v. Obs. [f. RUBR- + -FY, prob. after a med.L. *rubrificāre*.]

Rubrish, sb. Obs. Forms: 4-5 rubrich(e, roberych (6 ribrusch); 5 rub-, 6 robrishe; 5-6 rubryssh, &c.

† Bu·brish, v. Obs.

† Bu·bster. Obs. Forms: 6 rub, 9 dial. rubster. [f. RUB v.¹ + -STER.] A means of rubbing.

Rubstone, sb. [f. RUB sb.¹ + STONE sb.]

Ruck, sb.¹ Forms: 4-5 ruke, 6 rowke, 6 rouk, rook, &c.

Rubus, uncle, sb. also forms of RUBBISH.

Ruby (rū·bi), sb. and a. Forms: 4 ruby, 4-6 rubye, 5-7 ruble, rubey; 5 ro(o)by, rube (6 ruby.

1. I. A very rare and valuable precious stone.

2. Crystalline, as ruby P., v. 25.

3. A red pimple on the face.

b. With **a** and **pl.**

II. attrib. and **Comb.**

3. Attributive, as **ruby chain, cylinder, hale, mine, ring, rock, roller, spark, stone.**

Ruby-tail, a. [RUBY a.] — attrib. — next. **b.**

Ruby-tailed, a. [RUBY a.]

Ruby-throat, sb.

Ruby-throated, a. [RUBY a.]

Ruo, obs. form of Roc.

Rucervine (rūsə·vəin), a. Zool.

Ruch, sb. f. ROUGH a. and RUCK.

Buche (rūʃ, Fr. rʏʃ), sb. Also rouche. [F. *ruche*, *rusche*, bee-hive, and (sense 3) frill.]

† Ruche (rūtʃ), sb.²

Ruchet, sb., variant of ROCHET².

Ruching (rū·ʃiŋ). [f. RUCHE sb. + -ING.]

Buchy (rū·ʃi), a. [f. RUCHE sb.]

Ruck (rɒk), sb.³ Forms: a. 3 ruke, 5 roke, 5-6 rouk, 6-7 rowke, 9 dial. rook, rouk.

Ruck (rɒk), v.¹ dial. Forms: a. 5 Lewis HENRI-ford, 6 ruckt.

Ruckle (rɒ·k'l), sb.¹ Sc. and north. dial.

Buche (rūʃ), sb.¹

Buckle (rɒ·k'l), v.¹ [f. RUCK sb.³]

Ruck (rɒk), v.² [f. RUCK sb.¹] Cf. Norw. *rukka* in the same sense.

1. intr. To slip up or work into creases or ridges; to become creased or wrinkled.

2. trans. To crease; to wrinkle or cause to work up into ridges.

3. To draw or gather into small folds.

Buck, v.³ dial. [Cf. RUCK sb.² or v.²] To crouch.

† Buck, v.⁴ Obs. [f. RUCK sb.² or v.²]

Ruckle (rɒ·k'l), sb.²

Rucksack (rʊk·sæk), sb.

Bucky (rɒ·ki), a. rare. [f. RUCK sb.³]

† Ruot, v. Obs. rare. [ad. F. *ructer.*]

† Ructate, v. Obs.

† Ructation. Obs.

Ruction (rɒk·ʃən). dial. or colloq.

Ructuation. Obs.

† Buctuous, a. rare. [f. L. *ructuōsus.*]

Rucup, sb., obs. form of RICKUP.

Ruel, sb., obs. form of RUELLE.

Ruoul (Palladius): see RUKEL.

Rud (rɒd), sb.¹ and a.

1. Red or ruddy colour; redness, ruddiness.

2. Colour or mark with ruddle.

† Rud, v. Obs. [f. RUD sb.¹]

Rud (rɒd), sb.²

1. The spawn of frogs or toads.

2. The act of spawning.

3. The act of spawning. Also **t ruction.**

Rud (rɒd), sb.³

Rudas (rū·das), sb. and a. Sc. Forms: 8 routhes, 9 rudass. [Of obscure origin.]

Rud, sb.⁴

Budas (rū·das), sb.

Budd (rɒd), sb. [A freshwater cyprinoid fish related to RUD.]

† Budden, v. Obs. [f. RUD sb.¹]

Budde, v., obs. form of RUD.

Rudder (rɒ·dəɹ), sb.¹ Forms: a. 1 rother, rothor, róðor; pl. roðra; 3 rothere.

Ruddered (rɒ·dəɹd), a. [f. RUDDER sb.]

Budder-fish. [RUDDER sb.]

Budderless, a. [f. RUDDER sb. + -LESS.]

† Rudderman. Obs.

Budderless, a.

Buddily (rɒ·dili), adv. [f. RUDDY a. + -LY.]

Buddiness (rɒ·dines), sb. [f. RUDDY a. + -NESS.]

Ruddle (rɒ·d'l), sb.¹ Also 6 ruddel, 6-7, 9 ruddle. [Related to RUD sb.¹ and v.]

Ruddle (rɒ·d'l), v. Also 6 ruddel, 6-7 ruddle. [f. RUDDLE sb.]

Ruddle (rɒ·d'l), sb.²

Ruddle, *sb.* [Of obscure origin.] (See quots.)

Ruddle (rʌd'l), *sb.* [f. RUDDLE *sb.*] *trans.* To mark, smear, or paint with ruddle.

Ruddock (rʌd'ɒk). Forms: 1 rudduc, 5 (*dial.*)-uck; 4 ruddoke, 4-5 -ok (5 rodd-d:ok), 5-6 -oke, 5-7 -ocke, 6 -ruddock (7 rudoke), 8-9 *dial.* ruddick, 8 *dial.* hirdick; 7 reddocke (9 *dial.* -ock, -ok), reddocks. [OE. *rudduc*, related to RUD *sb.*]

Ruddy (rʌd'i), *a.* [f. RUDDY *a.* + -ISH.] Somewhat ruddy.

Ruddy (rʌd'i), *v.* [f. RUDDY *a.*]

Ruddyish *a.* *Obs.*—¹ In 5 rodylose.

Rude (riud), *a.* and *sb.* Forms: 4 ruide, 4-5 rowde (5 -Sc. royde), 5 ruyd, 5 roude, 5-6 rewde; 4-5 rude.

Rudely (riud'li), *adv.* Forms: 5 ruydlyche, -ely; 4 rudli, 5-6 *Sc.* -ly, 6 -lie, 7 -lye; 5 rewdly; 5 rudeli(che, 6 -lie, 7- rudely; [f. RUDE *a.* + -LY².]

Rudeful, *a.* *Obs.* In 5 RUDE *a.*] Full of sorrow.

Rudeness (riud'nes). Forms: 4-7 rudeness, 5 -nes, 6-7 rudenesse, 5 rudnes, rudes, 6-7 rudness. [f. RUDE *a.* + -NESS.]

Rudent, *a.* *Obs.* In 7 rudent; [ad. L. *rudent-*, *rudens* rope.]

Rudenture, *Arch.* [f. F. *rudenture* (16th c.).]

Rudera. *Obs.*—¹ [a. L. *rúdera*, pl. of *rúdus* broken stone.] Fragments or ruins of a building.

Ruder-, also **rudder-**, comb. form.

Rudesby. *Obs.* [f. rude + -BY.] An insolent, unmannerly, or disorderly fellow.

Rudesheimer (rū'deshaimər). *also* **Rudes-**. Also **Rudesheimer**. A white German wine produced at Rüdesheim on the Rhine.

Rudeship. *Obs.*—¹ [f. RUDE *a.* + -SHIP.] Roughness, unmannerliness.

Rudge. *Obs.* In *Dial.*, in various senses.

Rudi-, prefix. In various senses.

Rudiment (rū'dimĕnt), *sb.* [ad. L. *rudimentum*, f. RUDIS rude.]

Rudimental (rūdimĕn'tal), *a.* [f. RUDIMENT + -AL¹.] Rudimentary.

Rudimentary (rūdimĕn'təri), *a.* [f. RUDIMENT + -ARY¹.] Cf. *rudimentaire*.

Hence **Rudime·ntariness.**

1899 W. JAMES *Talks to Teachers* (1904) 233 No modern person ought to be willing to live a day in such a state of rudimentariness and denudation.

Rudish (rū·diʃ), *a.* [f. RUDE *a.* + -ISH.] Somewhat rude.

1774 FOOTE *Cozeners* III. ii, For man and wife to quarrel before folks is rather rudish, I own. 1822 *Blackw. Mag.* XI. 163 For most are but rudish. 1881 CARLYLE *Remin.* II. 158 Nothing but rudish hands, rude though kind enough, being about.

† **Ru·dity.** *Obs. rare.* [ad. obs. F. *rudité* or late L. *ruditas*: see RUDE *a.* and -ITY.] Rudeness.

1592 NASHE *Four Lett. Confut.* Wks. (Grosart) II. 236 Yea, rather than faile, Maister Bird shall..meeter it mischieuously in maintenance of their scurrilitiship and ruditie. 1609 T. BELL *Dial. Theoph. & Remigius* 51 Such things as he had reserued by reason of their rudity and imperfection in conceiuing heauenly doctrine.

Rudle, obs. and dial. f. RUDDLE *sb.*

Rudli(che, etc., obs. forms of RUDELY.

Rudnin, -nyng: see RUDDEN *v.*

Rudock, obs. form of RUDDOCK.

Rudolphine (rudǫ·lfəin), *a.* [f. the name *Rudolph* (see def.) + -INE[1].] *Rudolphine tables* (*numbers*), a series of astronomical calculations published by Kepler in 1627 and named after his patron the Emperor Rudolph II.

1656 tr. *Hobbes' Elem. Philos.* (1839) 292 The strait line..is found..to be somewhat greater than that which is exhibited by the Rudolphine numbers. 1728 CHAMBERS *Cycl.* s.v. *Table*, And Kepler, likewise,..in 1627, publish'd the Rudolphine Tables, which are now much esteem'd. 1761 *Ann. Reg.* 192 The imperfect state of the Rudolphine tables was the cause that the transit was expected in 1631. 1839 *Penny Cycl.* XIII. 201/1. 1882 *Encycl. Brit.* XIV. 47/2.

† **Ru·dstay.** *Obs.*[−1] [? for *rudge-stay*, f. *rudge* RIDGE *sb.*[1]] (See quot.)

1688 HOLME *Armoury* III. xviii. (Roxb.) 139/1 The thill hookes, to this is fasned the rudstay which goes ouer the horse back.

Rudyr, obs. form of RUDDER *sb.*

Rue (rū), *sb.*[1] Now *dial.* or *arch.* Forms: 1 **hreow**, 3 **reowe**, 4–6 **rewe**, 5–6 *Sc.* **rew**, 7– **rue.** [OE. *hrēow*, = Fris. *rou*, MDu. *rou(w)*, *rouwe*, *rauwe* (Du. *rouw*), MLG. *rouwe*, *ruwe* (LG. *rou*, *rau*, *ro*, etc.), OHG. *(h)riuwa* (MHG. *riuwe*, G. *reue*), related to OE. *hrēowan* RUE *v.*[1]]

1. Sorrow, distress; repentance; regret.

Beowulf 2130 Þæt wæs Hroðgare hreowa tornost. *c* 897 K. ÆLFRED *Gregory's Past. C.* liii. 415 Ðæt beswicene mod ..wyrð..amierred from ðære incundan hreowe. *a* 900 CYNEWULF *Christ* 1674 Eart nu tidfara to þam halȝan ham þær næfre hreow cymeð. 971 *Blickl. Hom.* 35 Don we urum Drihtne sobe hreowe & bote. *c* 1400 *Song Roland* 555 He may walk homward with hert-rew. *c* 1440 *Partonope* 3052** Allas he thought I am but rewe To hur that is my soverayne lady. 1581 *Satir. Poems Reform.* xliii. 211 Of rasche decreitis cums rew and may not mend it. 1628 WITHER *Brit. Rememb.* II. 1142 His Physicke must be Rue (ev'n Rue for Sinne). 1848 LONGSTREET *Georgia Scenes* 29 I'm a man that, when he makes a bad trade, makes the most of it...I'm for no rues and after-claps. 1893 LESLIE KEITH *'Lisbeth* xxii, The heart's rue for that which it had scarce possessed, and yet had lost. 1896 HOUSMAN *Shropshire Lad* liv, With rue my heart is laden For golden friends I had.

b. *Sc.* In phr. *To take the rue*, to repent.

1789 *Shepherd's Wedding* 10 (E. D. D.), I own, indeed, I've ta'en the rue, My mind is fairly alter'd. 1816 SCOTT *Old Mort.* xxviii, Tam Halliday took the rue, and tauld me a' about it. 18.. in Nimmo *Songs Clydesdale* (1882) 145 She wanted him to break the marriage, for she had ta'en the rue.

2. Pity, compassion.

a 1250 *Owl & Night.* 1445 Ne mai ich for reowe lete,.. Þat ich of murȝþe him ne singe. *c* 1300 *Beket* 1051 Nou God beo this holi manes help, for he hadde ther lute Rewe. 1867 JEAN INGELOW *Story of Doom* v. 102, I was good—Had rue on thee a tender sucking child. 1900 ELLIS *Rom. Rose* I. 12 Till every eye that saw her grew Bedewed with tears of pitying rue.

Rue (rū), *sb.*[2] Forms: 4–5 **ruwe**, 5–6 **rewe**, 5–7 **rew**, 6 *Sc.* **reu**; 4– **rue** (5 **rwe**). [a. F. *rue*, for earlier *rude* (cf. OE. *rūde*), = Prov., Sp., Pg. *ruda*, It. *ruta*:—L. *rūta*, ad. Gr. *ῥυτή*, orig. a Peloponnesian word.]

1. A perennial evergreen shrub of the genus *Ruta*, esp. *Ruta graveolens*, having bitter, strong-scented leaves which were formerly much used for medicinal purposes.

α. 1382 WYCLIF *Luke* xi. 42 Woo to ȝou, Pharisees, that tythen mynte, and ruwe. *a* 1400 *Pistill of Susan* 112 With Ruwe and Rubarbe, Ragget ariht. *c* 1440 *Promp. Parv.* 438/2 Ruwe, herbe, *ruta*.

β. *a* 1400 *Stockholm Med. MS.* ii. 846 in *Anglia* XVIII. 328 Rewe bitter, a worthy gres, Mekyl of myth & vertu is. *c* 1450 *M. E. Med. Bk.* (Heinrich) 198 Tak & grynde fenel & rewe, & boyle hem in water. 1533 ELYOT *Cast. Helthe* (1539) 21 Two drye nuttes, as many fygges, and .xx. leaues of Rewe. 1570 *Satir. Poems Reform.* xv. 25 Cum, Nettillis, thornie breiris, & rew, With all foull filthie weid. 1617 *Salerne's Regiment* 46 From Garlicke, Nuttes, Hearb-grace, or Rew.

γ. *c* 1400 *Lanfranc's Cirurg.* 104 Anoynte his nolle & his necke wiþ..oile of rue. *c* 1450 METHAM *Wks.* 49 Modyrwort, rwe, red malwys. 1562 TURNER *Herbal* II. (1568) 123 The iuice of Rue..is good for the ake of the eares. 1578 LYTE *Dodoens* 260 There be two sortes of Rue, that is garden Rue, and wilde Rue. 1608 SYLVESTER *Du Bartas* II. iv. *Decay* 425 As one same ground indifferently doth breed..The fragrant Rose, and the strong-senting Rue. 1667 MILTON *P. L.* XI. 414 Then purg'd with Euphrasie and Rue The visual Nerve, for he had much to see. 1712 tr. *Pomet's Hist. Drugs* I. 189 A Shrub whose Leaves have a great resemblance to those of Rue. 1789 MRS. PIOZZI *Journ. France* I. 417, I perceived all the company..stop their noses with rue. 1813 SCOTT *Rokeby* v. xiii, When villagers my shroud bestrew With pansies, rosemary, and rue. 1846 LINDLEY *Veget. Kingd.* 470 Common Rue, and another species, are said to be emmenagogue, anthelmintic, and sudorific. 1875 H. C. WOOD *Therap.* (1879) 537 The influence of rue upon the system is similar to, but less decided than that of savine.

fig. 1830 SCOTT *Demonol.* vi. 186 Persons who, upon this subject, purged their eyes with rue and euphrasie. 1862 WHITTIER *Waiting* v, For one shall..drink life's rue, and one its wine.

b. With punning allusion to RUE *sb.*[1]

1500–20 DUNBAR *Poems* lxiv. 10 Leif nor flour fynd could I nane of rew. 1583 GREENE *Mamillia* II. Wks. (Grosart) II. 297 Least time and triall make thee account Rue a most bitter hearbe. 1606 J. DAVIES (Heref.) *Select Sec. Husband* Wks. (Grosart) II. 8/1 So shalt thou But beare thine own Harts-ease, and neuer Rue. 1721 KELLY *Scot. Prov.* 284 Rue in Thyme should be a Maiden's Posie. 1825 WATERTON *Wand. S. Amer.* III. 238 They did all in their power to procure balm for me instead of rue. But it would not answer.

2. a. With qualifying word prefixed, applied to various plants:

Aleppo rue, a species of *Ruta*. **Black rue** (see quot.). **Dog's rue**, figwort, *Scrophularia*. **Goat's rue** (see GOAT 4 c). **Meadow rue** (see MEADOW *sb.* 4 c). **Syrian rue** (see SYRIAN *a.*). Also WALL-RUE.

1731 MILLER *Gard. Dict.* s.v. *Ruta*, The two Aleppo Rues and the Wild Rue are somewhat tenderer than the common Sort. *Ibid.* s.v. *Scrophularia*, Figwort, commonly called Dogs Rue. 1874 *Treas. Bot.* Suppl. s.v., Rue, Black (N. Zeal.), *Podocarpus spicata*.

b. With *pl.* A species of rue.

1731 MILLER *Gard. Dict.* s.v. *Thalictrum*, Some Botanists have classed this Plant with Rues. 1753 *Chambers' Cycl.* Suppl. s.v. *Ruta*, The rues would seem to belong properly to the plants, with cruciform not rosaceous flowers. 1842 *Penny Cycl.* XXIV. 278/1 Herbs which have..a fetid smell like rue, and hence are called meadow rues.

3. *attrib.* and *Comb.*, as *rue-juice*, *-leaf*, *-oil*, *-water*; *rue-like* adj.

1558 WARDE tr. *Alexis' Secr.* 37 Rue water, Rose water. 1617 *Salerne's Regiment* 133 Rew-water sprinckled in the house, kils all the fleas. 1681 GREW *Musæum* II. v. ii. 248 Of a russet colour, and as it were all over pounced, somewhat after the manner of a Rue-Leaf. 1725 *Fam. Dict.* s.v. *Ranunculus*, The Yellow Ranunculus, with Rue-like Flowers. 1799 G. SMITH *Laboratory* II. 449 Put into very strong vinegar, verdigrise, rue-juice. 1863 PRIOR *Brit. Pl.* 193 Its rue-like much divided leaves. 1866 *Treas. Bot.* 807/2, *Rue oil*, a volatile stimulant oil obtained from the shoots of *Ruta graveolens*.

b. In plant-names, as **rue anemone**, an American species of *Thalictrum*; † **rue maiden-hair**, wall-rue; **rue-weed** (see quot. 1796).

1611 COTGR., *Rue de muraille*, wall rue, Rue Maiden haire. 1796 WITHERING *Brit. Pl.* (ed. 3) II. 501 *Thalictrum alpinum*, Mountain Rue-weed. *T. flavum*, Meadow Rue-weed. *T. minus*, Lesser Rue-weed. 1802 WILLICH *Domest. Encycl.* s.v., Common Meadow-rue, Spurious Rhubarb, or Rue-weed. 1846–50 A. WOOD *Class-bk. Bot.* 148 *Thalictrum anemonoides*,..Rue Anemone. 1884 *Harper's Mag.* May 934/2 Burt now appeared with a handful of rue-anemones.

c. *Rue family, order, -worts*, the natural order *Rutaceæ*.

1846 LINDLEY *Veget. Kingd.* 470 The Cneoreæ..seem to be a form of this Order of Rueworts. 1849 BALFOUR *Man. Bot.* § 827 *Rutaceæ*, the Rue Family. 1857 HENFREY *Bot.* 266 *Rutaceæ*, the Rue order. 1875 *Encycl. Brit.* III. 111/1 A sub-order of the Rutaceæ or rue family.

† **Rue**, var. of (or error for) REE *sb.*[2], REEVE *sb.*[2]

1696 *Phil. Trans.* XIX. 349 We have Ruff and Rue, the former being the Cock, the other the Hen.

Rue, dial. variant of REW *sb.*[1]

Rue (rū), *v.*[1] Forms: *Inf.* 1 **hreowan**, 2 **reouwen**, **reuwe**, **rowe**, 2–4 **reowe**; 2–4 **rewen**, 3–6 **rewe** (4 **riewe**), 4–7 **rew** (6 **reew**); 3–4 **ruwe** (5 **ruwyn**), 4 **rywe**; 4–5 **reue**, 4 **reu**, **ru**, **rwe**, 4– **rue**; also 3 *sing. pres.* 1 **hriwð**, 2 **reouð**, **rieweð**. *Pret.* 1 **hreaw**, 2–3 **ræw**, **reu**, 3 **rew**, **rev**, 4 **rewe**; 4 **reud(e**, **reued**, **rwed**, 4–6 **rewed**; 5–6 *Sc.* **rewit**, 5 **ruet**, **ruit**, **rwyt**, etc. [OE. *hrēowan* (a strong vb. with pa. t. *hrēaw*) = OFris. *riowa* (Fris. *rouwe*, *rouje*), MDu. and Du. *rouwen* († *rauwen*, *ruwen*), OS. *hrewan*, pa. t. *hrau* (MLG. *rouwen*, *ruwen*, *ruen*, LG. *rouen*, *rauen*, *roen*, etc.), OHG. *(h)riuwan*, pa. t. *hrau*, *rou*, pl. *ruwun* (MHG. *riuwen*, *ruwen*, G. *reuen*), related to OE. *hrēow* RUE *sb.*[1] and to the adj. OE. *hrēowe*, OS. *hriwi* sad, sorrowful. There are also slight traces of an OE. weak vb. *hrēowian*, = OS. *hriwôn*, *hreuuôn*, OHG. *(h)riuwôn*. Related forms in ON. are *hryggr* (stem *hryggv-*, for earlier **hriww-*) adj., *hryggva*, *hryggja* weak vb., *hryggð* fem., sorrow.]

† I. *trans.* With dat. (or acc.) of the person, and usually with impersonal subject. *Obs.*

The various constructions illustrated under sense 2 occur also with senses 1, 3, and 4.

1. To affect (a person) with penitence or contrition (for sins or offences committed).

c 888 K. ÆLFRED *Boeth.* xxxvi. § 7 Ne bið se cwuca ðonne nyttra ðe se deada, ȝif him his ȝfel ne hreowð. *c* 1000 in Thorpe *Laws* II. 260 Ȝif þu ongite þæt him his synna hreowen. *c* 1200 ORMIN 3976 Ȝiff..þat he missdoþ Onn aniȝ kinne wise, Itt reoweþþ himm. *a* 1300 *Cursor M.* 28676 Þis man sais..þat him reuys his sinnes sare. *c* 1375 *Lay Folks Mass-Bk.* (MS. B) 359 Gyue me grace for to etchewe to do þat þing þat me shulde rewe.

2. To affect with regret (for some act); to make (one) wish one had acted otherwise.

c 897 K. ÆLFRED *Gregory's Past. C.* xxxix. 286 Ne do ðu nan wuht butan ȝeðeahte, ðonne ne hriwð hit ðe, ðonne hit ȝedon bið. *c* 1250 *Prov. Alfred* A. 111 þe þat nule one youhþe yeorne leorny,..þat him schal on elde sore rewe. *a* 1300 *Cursor M.* 16465 Þan him reued of his res, and went him-self [to] wrei. 1338 R. BRUNNE *Chron.* (1810) 237 Þe Walssh wer alle day slayn, now rewes þam þer res. *c* 1420 *Avow. Arth.* xxii, Ȝette Menealfe, or the mydnyȝte, Him ruet alle his rees. *c* 1440 *York Myst.* xiii. 36 Þe bargayne I made þare, Þat rewes me nowe full sare.

b. With clause as subject, usually *me* (or *him*) *rues that*, etc.

a 1000 *Genesis* 1276 Hreaw hine swiðe, þæt he folcmægþa fruman aweahte. *a* 1300 *Cursor M.* 1602 Me reus þat euer made i man. *c* 1386 CHAUCER *Epil. Merch. T.* 14 Me rewith sore I am unto hir teyd. *c* 1440 *York Myst.* xlviii. 8 Þerfore me rewis þat I þe worlde began.

c. With *it* as subject (also followed by *that*).

a 1200 *Moral Ode* 354 Þe blisse for ðos for-lat, it him mai reuwe sore. 13.. *E. E. Allit. P.* B. 290 Sore hit me rwez þat euer I made hem my self. 1382 WYCLIF *2 Cor.* vii. 8 If I made ȝou sori in a pistle, now it rewith me not. *c* 1412 HOCCLEVE *De Reg. Princ.* 754 It rewiþ me if I yow haue disesyd.

3. To affect with sorrow; to distress, grieve.

In some cases with approximation to sense 2 or 4.

a 900 CYNEWULF *Christ* 1414 Ða mec ongon hreowan þæt min hondȝeweorc on feonda ȝeweald feran sceolde. *a* 1000 *Genesis* 819 Me nu hreowan mæȝ æfter to aldre, þæt ic þe minum eaȝum ȝeseah. *c* 1175 *Lamb. Hom.* 149 If he ne mei..his neode ibete, þet him sare roweþ. *c* 1200 ORMIN 5576 Himm reoweþþ þatt he dwelleþþ her Swa swiþe lange onn eorþe. 13.. *Sir Beues* 1220 Wel sore me reweþ þat tiding. *a* 1450 *Le Morte Arth.* 1029 Me Rewith the deth of hyr for his sake. 1548 PATTEN *Exped. Scotl.* B v b, It would haue rued any good huswiues heart, to haue beholden ye..murder.

4. To affect with pity or compassion.

c 1200 ORMIN 5592 Himm reoweþþ ec of alle þa þatt follȝhenn deofless lare. *c* 1320 *Cast. Loue* 540–1 Ful sore þe prisun reweþ me: For-þi he reweþ me wel þe more, For Merci euere clepeþ þin ore. *c* 1400 *Laud Troy Bk.* 3367 Alas, me rewes of Priamus. *c* 1555 HARPSFIELD *Divorce Hen. VIII* (Camden) 136 It pitieth and rueth every good man..to remember the same. 1590 SPENSER *F. Q.* I. ii. 21 Deare dame, your suddein overthrow Much rueth me.

II. *trans.* With personal subject.

5. To repent of (wrongdoing); to feel penitence, remorse, or contrition for (sin, etc.).

c 1200 *Trin. Coll. Hom.* 95 Armheorted is þe man þe swiðere reoweð his sinne. *a* 1300 *Cursor M.* 7965 In takening sare he reud his sake, An orisun sun can he make. *a* 1450 MYRC 2016 Ȝef þow hyt fynde no wey myȝte, Þrytty dayes þow rewe hyt ryȝte. 1596 DRAYTON *Legends* ii. 549 Ruing the spoile done by his fatall hand. 1628 WITHER *Brit. Rememb.* 240 Nor shall I live to view Thy sorrows ended, if thou do not rue Thy sins with speed. 1771 BEATTIE *Minstr.* II. xiv, But now, with pangs of keen remorse, I rue Those years of trouble and debasement vile. 1813 SCOTT *Rokeby* I. ii, Conscience, anticipating time, Already rues the enacted crime. 1846 KEBLE *Lyra Innoc.* (1873) 139 Lest thou in sevenfold guilt thy heart's backsliding rue.

6. To repent of (some act or course of action); to regret and wish undone or altered, on account of the consequences.

Frequently with implication of suffering or punishment following upon the act.

a 1300 *Cursor M.* 4138 Þat Baret rede i noght yee bru, Þat yow mai euer after ru. *c* 1375 *Sc. Leg. Saints* xxvii. (*Machor*) 972 Bot he in þame ruit his teching, For..þai na tyme for to scorne hym fane. *c* 1470 HENRY *Wallace* VIII. 857 The layff raturnyt..And rwyt full sar that euer furth coud found. *a* 1548 HALL *Chron., Edw. IV*, 201 b, Whiche vnmercifull acte, the Welshemen sore ruied the next daie or night. 1611 SIR W. MURE *Misc. Poems* ii. 51 Too lait, I feir, thow rew thou did espy him. 1726 POPE *Odyss.* XIX. 371 Whoe'er neglects to pay distinction due, The breach of hospitable right may rue. 1828 SCOTT *F. M. Perth* ii, Well, my princess..., I will teach you to rue this. 1874 DEUTSCH *Rem.* 248 Rome has had to rue many a too hasty step. 1885–94 R. BRIDGES *Eros & Psyche* May xxviii, And yet..no sooner was alone, Than she for loneliness her promise rued.

b. Freq. in phr. *to rue it*.

a 1300 *Sarmun* xxxvii. in *E. E. P.* (1862) 5 Bot þou nelt þench her apan,..Þou salt hit rew bitter and sore. *a* 1400–50 *Alexander* (Dubl.) 1975 Remefe agayn to þi realm or þow sall it rewe. 1593 SHAKS. *3 Hen. VI*, I. i. 94, I remember it to my griefe, And by his Soule, thou and thy House shall rue it. 1642 ROGERS *Naaman* 160 Examine thy selfe about this now, one day thou wilt else rue it. 1795 BURKE *Corr.* Wks. 1842 II. 459 Admitting..the enormous and unpardonable magnitude of this their crime, they rued it in their persons. 1841 JAMES *Brigand* xliii, If they hurt a hair of his head they shall rue it. 1871 B. TAYLOR *Faust* (1875) I. xxv. 210 If longer here thou stayest, We shall be made to dearly rue it.

c. In phr. *to rue the day, hour*, etc.

Differing from 7 b only by referring to some act committed by the party rueing.

1595 SHAKS. *John* III. i. 325 France, thou shalt rue this houre within this houre. 1708 *Bickerstaff detected* in *Swift's Wks.* (1751) IV. 205, I am alive..to make him rue the hour he ever affronted a man of Science and Resentment. 1782 ELIZ. BLOWER *G. Bateman* II. 170 Ye shall rue the day ye took it. 1818 SCOTT *Br. Lamm.* ii, You'll rue the day that clogs me with this answer. 1881 'RITA' *My Lady Coquette* ii, It will go hard with me if I don't make you rue the day you wrote or said it.

7. To regard or think of (an event, fact, etc.) with sorrow or regret; to wish that (something) had never taken place or existed.

1297 R. GLOUC. (Rolls) 10127 So þat hii ne com nammore To þe croune of engelond, and þat was to rewe sore. 1390 GOWER *Conf.* Prol. 164 To make of thilke werre an ende, Which every day now groweth newe, And that is gretly forto rewe. *c* 1430 *Hymns Virgin* (1867) 47 Oonys he bad me 'go, foule sathan!' Euere-more þat repreef y rewe. 1557 *Tottel's Misc.* (Arb.) 230 It was the day on which the sunne..To rew Christ's death amid his course gaue place vnto ye night. 1648 J. BEAUMONT *Psyche* XII. cxlviii, Both Sence and Reason rue that tyranny. 1796 BURKE *Regic. Peace* iii. Wks. VIII. 223 The world will have cause to rue this iniquitous measure. 1813 SCOTT *Rokeby* IV. xiv, Redmond now alone must rue The love he never can subdue. 1826 HOOD *Last Man* xii, I promis'd myself an hour should come To make him rue his birth.

b. In phr. *to rue the day, hour*, etc. (Cf. 6 c.)

1593 SHAKS. *3 Hen. VI*, V. vi. 43 Orphans, for their Parents timeles death, Shall rue the houre that euer thou was't borne. 1714 GAY *Sheph. Week* Thursday 5, I rue the day, a rueful day I trow,..When Lubberkin to Town his cattle drove. 1807 J. BARLOW *Columb.* IV. 389 Nor think the native tribes shall rue the day That leads our heroes o'er the watery way. 1887 HALL CAINE *Son of Hagar* III. vi, Take him away, before I rue the day I saw him.

† 8. To regard with pity or compassion; to feel sorry for (a person, etc.). *Obs.*

c 1200 *Trin. Coll. Hom.* 95 Mildheorted beð þe man þe reouð his nehgebures unselðe. 1375 BARBOUR *Bruce* XVI. 280, I trow thar is na man That he will rew a woman than. *c* 1400 *Pilgr. Sowle* (Caxton, 1483) IV. xx. 68 That ye ne reweth hym myn herte it sleeth. 1555 PHAER *Æneid* II. 43 Mine own band shall my deth obteyn, my foo will rue my plight. 1590 SPENSER *F. Q.* I. i. 51 Die is my dew; yet rew my wretched state. *c* 1611 CHAPMAN *Iliad* XXI. 72, I kiss thy knees, divine Æacides! Respect me, and my fortunes rue.

III. *intr.* 9. To be penitent or contrite; to feel repentance or remorse. Also const. *for*.

[*c* 950 *Lindisf. Gosp.* Mark i. 15 Hreowigas & ȝelefes to godspell.]

13.. *Cursor M.* 19014 (Gött.), Þair hert gan tru, And als for þair misdedis þai ru. *c* 1430 *Hymns Virgin* (1867) 69, I wole biþinke me on my werkis biforn, Do almes dede, praie, & rewe. 1500–20 DUNBAR *Poems* lxxiii. 5 O wreche, be war! ..Remeid in tyme, and rew nocht all to lait. 1580 GIFFORD *Poems* (1870) 75 Ah! Jesus! how then my heart did rue Because I had folowed them, as true! 1768–74 TUCKER *Lt. Nat.* (1834) I. 219, I shall find perpetual cause, if not to repent, at least to rue sufficiently for my misconduct. 1871 R. ELLIS tr. *Catullus* xxx. 12 Hereafter again honour awakes, causeth a wretch to rue.

10. To be repentant, or full of regret and dissatisfaction, in respect of some act (in mod. Sc. use *esp.* of a bargain or promise, and freq. with implication of consequent withdrawing from it).

c 1374 CHAUCER *Troylus* V. 1070 (Harl.), Syn I se..þat to late is now for me to rue To dyomede algate I wol be trewe. 1390 GOWER *Conf.* I. 334 Men sen alday that rape reweth. 1426 AUDELAY *Poems* 42 After here werkus worche ȝe never a dele, Ellus schul ȝe reue. *a* 1586 SIDNEY *Ps.* XVIII. xii, They do faile, and in their mazed corners rue. 1603 J. DAVIES (Heref.) *Microcosmos* Wks. (Grosart) I. 41/1 Thus when our Teares doe testifie our ruth, We neede not rue, or of them be asham'd. *c* 1706 in Calderwood *Dying Testimonies* (1806) 186 That none may think..I am rueing. 1790 SHIRREFS *Poems* 87 Aft has he promis'd, that he wad be true; But, now, I find my lad begins to rue. 1830 GEN. P. THOMPSON *Exerc.* (1842) I. 235 The caution of the nurse is, 'Avoid green gooseberries, or you will have cause to rue'. 1884 *Harper's Mag.* Mar. 655/1 B—issued a license for the marriage of John Murphy and Mary Manning...But the intended bride 'rued'.

† b. Const. *of* (the act). *Obs. rare.*

a 1400–50 *Alexander* (Dubl. MS.) 871 Then rewys hym þe riche kyng of hys vnrode werkez. *Ibid.* (Ashm. MS.) 1975 Remowe agayne to þi rewme, & rew of þi werkis. 1631 RUTHERFORD *Lett.* (1862) I. xix. 79 Do ye believe that our Lord will..rue of the bargain and change His mind?

11. To feel sorrow or grief, *esp.* by reason of suffering from some fact or event; to lament.

13.. *K. Alis.* 3944 (Laud MS.), Þer miȝth man in herte rewe, Hou noble kniȝttes ouer þrewe. *c* 1400 *Melayne* 197 Bot þe peris take a concelle newe That made alle fraunce ful sore to rewe. *a* 1548 HALL *Chron., Rich. III*, 9 b, I remembred an olde prouerbe.., that often ruithe the realme, where chyldren rule, and woman gouerne. 1643 TRAPP *Comm. Gen.* ix. 22 The whole race of Religious persons must rue for it. 1663 BUTLER *Hud.* I. i. 252 Like Sampson's Heart-breakers, it grew In time to make a Nation rue.

† b. To be sorry, feel reluctant, *to* do something.

1583 BABINGTON *Commandm.* To Gentl., I rew to thinke it, there are witnesses moe, than I would there were, that know it. 1607 in *Harington's Nugæ Ant.* (1804) II. 138 This church, the ruins whereof I rue to behold even in wryting theis lynes. 1630 R. *Johnson's Kingd. & Commw.* 559 How long every particular Prince reigned..I rue to record, and meane not to relate.

12. To have, take, or feel pity or compassion:

† a. With *of*.

c 1200 ORMIN 14782 Moysæs ræw off þatt follc Þatt swa wass haldenn harrde. 1297 R. GLOUC. (Rolls) 6747 Louerd, wiþ draw þin hond,..and reu of engelond. *c* 1374 CHAUCER *Anel. & Arc.* 287 God so wisseyly of my soule ruwe As verrayly ye slen me with þe peyne. *c* 1475 *Babees Bk.* 54 (1868) 3 Off myn vnkunnynge, swete lady, now Rewe. 1578 WHETSTONE *Promos & Cass.* II. v. iii, Rue of my teares from true intent which flowe.

b. With *on* or *upon*. Now *arch.*

1297 R. GLOUC. (Rolls) 9229 He wep & cride on is men, þat hii ssolde on him rewe. 13.. *Cursor M.* 4738 (Gött.), To ioseph went þai criand þan,' þu reu on vs, þu blisful man'. 1423 JAS. I *Kingis Q.* ci, Haue pitee now..Off ȝour pure man, and rew on his distresse. *a* 1547 SURREY *Æneid* IV. 410 Rue on this realme, whoes ruine is at hand. 1579 W. WILKINSON *Confut. Fam. Love* 53 b, As many as rue upon the state of the poore seduced soules. 1632 RUTHERFORD *Lett.* (1862) I. xxi. 85 Till your Dear Lord come and loose the pawn, and rue upon you. 1788 BURNS *Turn again*, Rue on thy despairing lover! Canst thou break his faithfu' heart? 1865 SWINBURNE *Poems & Ball.*, *Masque of Q. Bersabe* 365 Lord, thou rue on me.

† c. Without const. Also with *inf.*, to spare.

a 1300 *Cursor M.* 6784 Qua þat anurs godds neu, Him to sla sal naman reu. *a* 1300 *E. E. Ps.* xxxvi. 27 Alle daie he rewes, and lenes his þinge. *c* 1430 *Pol., Rel., & L. Poems* (1903) 177 Þouȝ he me wraþþe in diuerse wise,..ȝit muste y rue til þat he rise. 1530 PALSGR. 690/2, I rewe, I pytie or have compassion of one. *c* 1560 A. SCOTT *Poems* (S. T. S.) ix. 30 It is ane hairt..set in to sabill, Ane wofull hairt, bot gif ȝe rew.

† **Rue**, *v.*[2] *Obs. rare.* Also 6 **rewe.** [ad. L. *ruere*.] *intr.* To fall, decline. Hence **Rueing** *ppl. a.*

1557 *Tottel's Misc.* (Arb.) 256 Of lofty ruing towers the fals the feller be. 1576 GASCOIGNE *Steele Gl.* (Arb.) 54 This is the cause (beleve me now, my Lorde) That Realmes do rewe from high prosperity. *a* 1591 H. SMITH *Wks.* (1867) II. 477 So, lowly rest; so, lofty rues.

Rue, to sift: see REE *v.*

Rue-bargain. Chiefly *dial.* [RUE *v.*[1]] A bargain one repents of or breaks; also, the forfeit paid for withdrawing from a bargain.

1649 G. DANIEL *Trinarch.*, *Hen. IV*, cclxxii, The King.. could haue beene well-pleas'd To quitt, if a Rue bargaine may be put In state. 1814– in northern dial. glossaries. 1818 SCOTT *Rob Roy* xxvii, He said it would cost him a guinea of rue-bargain to the man who had bought his pony, before he could get it back again. 1844 BAMFORD *Traveller* 130 (E. D. D.), Give him a shilling or two for a rue-bargain.

Rued, obs. form of REED.

Rueful (rū·fŭl), *a.* Forms: 3 **reowful**, 3–5 **rewful(l**, 4–5 **reweful**; 3–4 **reuful**, 4–5 **-ful(l**, 5 **rouful**; 4–8 **ruful(l**, 5 **rufol**, 6 **ruifull**, 7– **rueful.** [f. RUE *sb.*[1] + -FUL.]

1. Exciting sorrow or compassion; pitiable, lamentable; doleful, dismal.

In the contexts illustrated under b, c, d, the sense passes into 'expressive of sorrow or dejection'.

a 1240 *Ureisun* in *O. E. Hom.* I. 187 Bitweone þine rewfulle earmes on þe rode. 1297 R. GLOUC. *Chron.* (Rolls) 6703 Þe erl godwine..let smite of hor alre heued, & made a reuful dom. *c* 1330 *Arth. & Merl.* 6232 (Kölbing), Þe kniȝtes of þe rounde table..Com to þis reweful bataile. *c* 1385 CHAUCER *L. G. W.* 1838 *Lucrece*, She hem tolde This rewful case. *c* 1449 PECOCK *Repr.* I. xvi. 86 In this wise.. bifille the rewful and wepeable destruccioun of the worthi citee and vniuersite of Prage. 1470–85 MALORY *Morte Arth.* X. viii. 425 Hit is an honderd parte more reufullyr than my herte can vtter. 1559 *Mirr. Mag.*, *Jack Cade* xxi, All men reioicing at the rufull sight. 1582 STANYHURST *Æneis* II. (Arb.) 55 Euery house, eech temple with ruful slaughter aboundeth. 1613 PURCHAS *Pilgr.* (1614) 546 Grinding the face of their poore tenants in ruefull manner. 1687 *Death's Vision* ix, The Rufull Ills and World from whence I Came! 1742 BLAIR *Grave* 12 How dark Thy long-extended realms, and rueful wastes! 1797 MME. D'ARBLAY *Let.* 8 Jan., Our adventures in coming back..were rather rueful. 1812 J. WILSON *Isle of Palms* II. 90 Not even one rueful plank is seen, To tell that a vessel hath ever been. 1885 *Manch. Weekly Times* 20 June 5/5 The Conservative Opposition..was in a rueful plight, crushed by a great defeat.

b. Of cries or utterance.

a 1225 *Leg. Kath.* 162 Þeotinde unþuldeliche wið reowfule reames. *a* 1300 *Cursor M.* 20129 Til him scho cald wit reufull steuen. 1387 TREVISA *Higden* (Rolls) I. 317 In þat place beeþ..i-herd reweful voys and gronynge. *c* 1400 *Pilgr. Sowle* (Caxton, 1483) III. iii. 52 Myn Aungell speke to these spirites that maden this reuful crye. 1572 BOSSEWELL *Armorie* II. 56 b, [The cat] maketh a rufull noyse, and a gastefull, when one proferth to fighte with another. 1593 BRETON *Daff. & Prim.*, *Asp.* Wks. (Grosart) I. 21/1 But yow that rede this ruifull verse, consider of his care. 1648 J. BEAUMONT *Psyche* VIII. ccli, In vain the skies And stones they rent with rufull Exclamations. 1671 MILTON *Samson* 1553 The accident was loud, & here before thee With rueful cry. 1748 THOMSON *Cast. Indol.* II. xliv, Alarm'd, the inferior demons of the place Rais'd rueful shrieks and hideous yells around.

c. Of looks, features, or actions.

a 1300 *Cursor M.* 14301 Lazar freindes..cried and mad a reuful chere. *c* 1400 *Beryn* 3525 He stode al abasshid,.. And lokid oppon the Steward with a rewful cher. *a* 1547 SURREY *Æneid* II. B ij, Before mine eies, me thought, With rufull chere I sawe where Hector stood. 1636 E. DACRES tr. *Machiavel's Disc.*, *Livy* II. 492 They usd to accompany them in a rufull manner, clad in blacke, and all sorrowfull. 1684 OTWAY *Atheist* II, That face..o'er grown with rueful beard. 1728 POPE *Dunc.* II. 142 Piteous of his case, Yet smiling at his rueful length of face. 1781 MME. D'ARBLAY *Diary* 2 June, He suddenly called out, and with a most rueful face,—'Oh, certainly' [etc.]. 1806 J. BERESFORD *Miseries Hum. Life* V. i, As you had augured from the rueful bow of the speaker. 1835 W. IRVING *Tour Prairies* 136, I looked after him with a rueful eye as he limped off. 1877 BLACK *Green Past.* xliii, With a rueful smile.

d. Of persons.

c 1386 CHAUCER *Knt.'s T.* 2028 Of wepyng Emelye, The rewfullest of al the companye. 14.. *Pistill of Susan* 341 (I.), Þen þat rewful charle began for to rore. *c* 1440 *Promp. Parv.* 439/1 Rufulle, and fulle of peyne and desese, *Anglice*, a caytyf,..*dolorosus*, *penosus*. 1526 *Pilgr. Perf.* (W. de W. 1531) 306 b, Now may I take and drawe out of thy moost rewfull brest the paynfull drynke of sorowe. 1650 MILTON *Eikon.* (ed. 2) 14 Those ruefull Preists whom Eliah mock'd. 1692 WALKER tr. *Epictetus* lv, Joy in a nimble moment ends its Race And rueful, pale Repentance takes its Place. 1742 YOUNG *Nt. Th.* II. 144 And all mankind,.. Rueful, aghast! cry out at his career. 1759 GOLDSM. *Bee* No. 8 ¶ 16 This rueful figure frightens a child into the palpitation of the heart. 1807 WORDSW. *White Doe* II. 23 Full soon to be uplifted high, And float in rueful company. 1855 MOTLEY *Dutch Rep.* V. v. (1866) 752 'Take them away; take them home again' said the rueful burgomaster. 1863 KINGSLEY *Water Bab.* v, Very rueful they looked.

transf. 1697 DAMPIER *Voy.* (1699) 415 The Sky looked very black and rueful.

Comb. 1844 KINGLAKE *Eothen* iii, Some rueful-looking fellows came rapidly shambling down the steps.

† 2. Full of pity or compassion. *Obs.*

a 1300 *E. E. Psalter* cxi[i]. 4 [God is] Mildeherte and rewfulle and rightwis. *a* 1325 *Prose Psalter* cxl[i]v. 8 Our Lord is rewful and merciable. 1377 LANGL. *P. Pl.* B. XIV. 148 Criste..shal..rewarde alle dowble ricchesse, þat reuful hertes habbeth. *a* 1400 *Cast. Love* 378 (H.), Mercies herte so rufull is. *c* 1440 *Promp. Parv.* 439/1 Ruful, or ful of ruthe and pyte, *pieticus*, *compassiuus*.

Hence † **Ruefulhead**, compassion. *Obs.*[−1]

1338 R. BRUNNE *Chron.* (1810) 263 Þorgh pite mykelle he les, & reufulhed of herte.

Ruefully (rū·fŭli), *adv.* Forms: 3 **reufulike**; 4 **rew-**, **reu-**, **rufullich(e**, **-ych)**; 4 **rew-**, **reufully**, 4–5 **reufulli**, 5–7 **rufully** (6 **-lie**), 6– **ruefully.** [f. RUEFUL *a.* + -LY[2].]

1. In a doleful or dismal manner; sorrowfully, dejectedly, regretfully.

c 1220 *Bestiary* 652 [The elephant] remeð reufulike on his wise. 13.. *E. E. Allit. P.* A. 1180 Rewfully þenne I con to reme. 1377 LANGL. *P. Pl.* B. XVII. 235 So wole þe fader forȝif folke..þat reufulliche [*v.r.* rufulliche] repenten. *a* 1400–50 *Alexander* 3083 With þat reufully [*v.r.* rewfully] he rase & renkis out he sendis. *a* 1450 *Le Morte Arth.* 3423 To the kynge spake he full styll, Rewffully as he myght than Rowne. 1509 HAWES *Past. Pleas.* XIV. (Percy Soc.) 54 Of the fall of pryncés...He did endyte.., Folowynge his auctoure Bocas rufully. 1581 MULCASTER *Positions* iii. (1887) 14 She would oftimes be brought into a miserable plighte, and looke rufully vpon it. 1657 REEVE *God's Plea* 4 Would it not grieve thee..that they should cry rufully in a sad desolation, which have cryed mightily unto their God? 1809 W. IRVING *Knickerb.* (1861) 105 It was a piteous sight to behold the late valiant burgomasters..peeping ruefully out of their hiding-places. 1850 THACKERAY *Pendennis* i, He..ruefully wrote off refusals to..all his entertainers. 1888 FERGUS HUME *Madame Midas* I. ii, Slivers looked ruefully at the bottle.

† 2. In a pitiable or lamentable fashion. *Obs.*

a 1300 *Cursor M.* 1825 Noe..praid to godd for þam alsua ..Sin þai ware ded sua reufulli, þe saulus he wald haf of merci. 1377 LANGL. *P. Pl.* B. XII. 48 Rosamounde riȝt so reufully bysette, Þe bewte of hir body in badnesse she dispended. *c* 1450 *St. Cuthbert* (Surtees) 4692 Þou ert reufully fra vs reft. *c* 1485 *Digby Myst.* (1882) IV. 71 How rewfully he hinges here, That set you first in ceile! 1526 *Pilgr. Perf.* (W. de W. 1531) 254 Se there the sone of god so rewfully and piteously deformed and arayed for thy saluacion. 1590 SPENSER *F. Q.* III. viii. 30 Those pittifull outcries he heard Through all the seas so ruefully resownd. 1634 SIR T. HERBERT *Trav.* 199 All the wounded body..rots and consumes most rufully.

Ruefulness (rū·fŭlnės). Also 3 **reou-**, **reow-**, 5 **rew-**, 7 **rufulnesse.** [f. RUEFUL *a.* + -NESS.]

† 1. Compassionateness, pitifulness. *Obs.*

a 1225 *Ancr. R.* 368 Þet oðer þing is heorte þeauwes, deuociun, reoufulnesse, merci, pite of heorte. *c* 1230 *Hali Meid.* 41 Þolemodnesse & reowfulnesse of euch monnes sorhe. *c* 1440 *Rel. Pieces Thornton MS.* (1867) 51 Rewfulnes sall make the fermorye. *c* 1557 ABP. PARKER *Ps.* cxxx. 383 Let Jacob wayt the Lord so gent, Because with God is rufulnes.

2. Dismalness, dolefulness, dejection.

1590 SPENSER *F. Q.* I. iv. 25 He..well could daunce; and sing with ruefulnesse. 1595 HUBBOCKE *Apol. Infants Unbaptized* 26 Haue we so learned Christ? are his lawes so ful of ruefulnes? 1613 PURCHAS *Pilgrimage* IV. xv. (1614) 420 The rufulnesse of this sight was seconded with a more dismall euent. 1751 SMOLLETT *Per. Pic.* lvi. (1779) II. 152 He could not..vanquish the ruefulness of his countenance. 1842 DICKENS *Amer. Notes* (1868) 131 Some, growing bold in ruefulness, predicted that we should land about the middle of July. 1894 MRS. DYAN *Man's Keeping* (1899) 299 'Not exactly,' said Lanyon, with hesitating ruefulness.

Rueing (rū·iŋ), *vbl. sb.* [f. RUE *v.*[1] + -ING[1].] Repentance, sorrow, regret.

a 1300 *Cursor M.* 27341 Wit suet and luueli sermoning, He lede penant to half-reuing. *c* 1440 *Promp. Parv.* 439/1 Ruynge, for a thynge, *penitudo*, *penitencia*. 1559 ASCHAM in *Babees Bk.* (1868) 361 Cause of greife and sorrowe to your selfe, of chideing and rueing to your lord. 1611 SIR W. MURE *Misc. Poems* i. 106 Þe poysonous potioune of late rewing. *a* 1618 SYLVESTER *Woodman's Bear* xii. Wks. (Grosart) II. 308 Who the eager game pursuing, Lost her Ladies in the chase, Till shee heard the wretche's ruing. 1730 T. BOSTON *Mem.* App. 35 Stand to the bargain and check yourselves for any semblance of rueing. 1844 *Cath. Weekly Instructor* 42 Weep, sire, with shame and ruing! Weep for thy child's undoing! 1844 MRS. BROWNING *Lost Bower* xxxii, Did she pause in tender rueing Here of all her sylvan scorn? 1891 T. HARDY *Tess* xxviii, A step which might afterwards cause bitter rueing to her husband.

Rue·ing, *ppl. a. rare.* [-ING[2].] a. Penitent.

b. Compassionate, pitying.

c 950 *Lindisf. Gosp.* Luke *Intr.* 9/4 Ðæm hræwende broder..heht þætte were forȝefen. *a* 1300 *Cursor M.* 27153 Preist agh be skilwis, soft, and meke, Reuand, rightwis, luuelili speke. 1637 RUTHERFORD *Lett.* ccvii. (1675) 387 Christ's love..must be a ruing, a pitiful, a melting-hearted love. *a* 1814 *Witness* II. i. in *New Brit. Theatre* I. 16 Like the ruing prodigal reclaim'd.

† **Ruel**, *sb. Obs. rare.* In 4 **ruwal.** [a. AF. *roal*, Norman *rohal*, *rochal* (Godef.), Latinized as *rohallum*, *rohaulum* (Du Cange), in all probability

a Scandinavian word of which the second element is *hval* whale.] = RUEL-BONE.

[*a* 1250 *Vie St. Auban* 3 De peres preciuses, de ivoire ne roal.] *c* 1314 *Reinbrun* lxxix. in *Guy Warw.* (1891) 657 Þe walles were of cristal, Þe heling was of fin ruwal Þat schon swiþe briȝte.

† **Ruel**, *v. Obs.*[−0] [perh. a. OF. *rueler*, *roeler*, *rouler* to roll.] *intr.* To fall.

13.. *E. E. Allit. P.* B. 953 Þe rayn rueled adoun, ridlande þikke, Of felle flaunkes of fyr.

Ruel, obs. form of ROWEL *sb.*, RUELLE.

† **Ruelberd.** *Obs.*[−1] (Meaning doubtful.)

Perh. f. OF. *ruele* wheel: cf. BEARD *sb.* and BRED.

1424 *Court Roll Grt. Waltham* 18 Dec., Rota dicti molendini indiget ruelberd et molendinum vocatum *Champeneys mell* indiget quoddam instrumentum vocatum *le Nedele*.

† **Ruel-bone.** *Obs.* Forms: 4–5 **rouwel**, **rowel**, **roelle**, **ruel(l**, **rewel(l**, **reuyll bone** (**boon**). [f. RUEL *sb.* + BONE *sb.*] Ivory (possibly that of the narwhal).

13.. *Leg. Pope Gregory* (Schulz) 994 Briȝter þan þe rouwel-boon. *c* 1350 *Ipomadon* 6456 A sadull all off sylke, The sege off rewell bone. *c* 1386 CHAUCER *Sir Thopas* 167 His sadel was of rowel [*varr.* rewel, ruel] boon. *a* 1400 *Sir Degrev.* 1429 [The chamber] was buskyd above With besauntus ful bryȝth All off ruel bon. *a* 1400 *Tourn. Tottenham* 83 in Hazl. *E. P. P.* III. 86 A garland on hir hed full of ruell bones. *c* 1425 *Thomas of Erceld.* (Thornton) 49 Hir selle it was of roelle bone [*Camb.* reuyll bone].

Ruele, obs. form of RULE *sb.*

Rue-leaved, *a.* [f. RUE *sb.*[2]] Having leaves similar to, or resembling, those of the common rue.

1744 T. BIRCH *Life of Boyle* B.'s Wks. 1772 I. p. cxlvii, Rue-leaved whitlow grass. 1777 JACOB *Catal. Plants* 102 *Saxifraga tridactylites*.., Rue-leaved Saxifrage, or Whitlow-grass. 1822 *Hortus Anglicus* II. 46, *I. Thalictroides*. Meadow Rue-leaved Isopyrum. *Ibid.* 52 *A. Thalictroides*. Meadow Rue-leaved Anemone. 1862 ANSTED *Channel Isl.* II. viii. 183 The rue-leaved spleen-wort (*A. ruta muraria*), grows abundantly in both islands on walls and churches.

Ruell(e, obs. forms of ROWEL, RULE.

‖ **Ruelle** (rü̱ˌe·l). Also 4, 7–8 **ruel.** [F. *ruelle*, dim. of *rue* street, passage.]

1. The space between a bed and the wall; the part of a bed next the wall.

1393 LANGL. *P. Pl.* C. X. 79 Wo in winter-tyme, with wakynge a nyghtes To ryse to þe ruel to rocke þe cradel. 1688 *Engl. Prot. Mem. to Prince & P'cess of Orange* 21 There was a private door within the ruel of the bed into a room. 1751 ELIZA HEYWOOD *Betsy Thoughtless* II. 173 Miss Flora had thrown herself on a carpet by the bedside, her head leaning on the ruelle. 1824 tr. *Duchesse d'Orleans' Mem. Crt. Louis XIV* 273 A number of plates were found in the ruelle of his bed.

2. A bedroom, where ladies of fashion in the seventeenth and eighteenth centuries, especially in France, held a morning reception of persons of distinction; hence, a reception of this kind.

1676 ETHEREDGE *Man of Mode* IV. ii, I have his own fault, a weak voice, and care not to sing out of a ruelle. 1697 DRYDEN *Ded. Æneid* Ess. (ed. Ker) II. 161 The poet who flourished in the scene is damned in the ruelle. 1704 SWIFT *T. Tub* ii, No approaching the Ladies Ruelles without the Quota of Shoulder-Knots. 1749 BOLINGBROKE *Lett. on Patriotism* 221 The forms of a drawing room, the regulation of a ruelle, the decoration of a ball. 1763 C. JOHNSTONE *Reverie* II. 16 How can you intrude so rudely into a lady's ruelle? You see I have set out my toilet. 1812 SCOTT *Let.* in *Lockhart* (1837) II. xii. 390 Acquainted with all the intrigues and tracasseries of the cabinets and *ruelles* of foreign courts.

‖ **Rue·llia.** *Bot.* [mod.Latin: named after the French botanist Jean *Ruel* (1479–1539).] A genus of acanthaceous plants, chiefly tropical, natives of Asia and America.

1753 in *Chambers' Cycl.* Suppl. 1846 LINDLEY *Veget. Kingd.* 679 Plants of great beauty, especially the species of Justicia, Aphelandra, and Ruellia. 1848 *Chambers' Inform.* I. 106/2 A valuable deep blue dye is said to be obtained from one of the East Indian Ruellias.

† **Ruen.** *Obs.* Also 6 **rewene**, **rowen**, 7 **ruin.** [Of obscure origin: cf. RUENING.]

1. = RENNET *sb.*[1] 1.

1558 WARDE *Alexis' Secr.* I. I. (1568) 28 b, Take the ruen of a Hare, and having frayed and consumed it in hote water, give it the woman to drinke. 1565 COOPER *Thesaurus*, *Coagulum*, a curde or creame: the ruen of a beast that turneth milke. 1609 BIBLE (Douay) *Ps.* lxvii. comm., Ruen turneth liquide milke into curde, and so into cheese.

2. *Ruen cheese*, a soft kind of cheese.

1539 ELYOT *Cast. Helthe* (1541) 67 b, Mylke hot from the udder,..ruen chese, sweete almondes. 1542 BOORDE *Dyetary* xii. (1870) 266 Yet besyde these .iiii. natures of chese, there is a chese called a rewene chese. 1565 COOPER *Thesaurus*, *Caseus mustens*, greene cheese, or softe & rowen cheese. 1655 MOUFET & BENNET *Health's Improv.* 131 We may feed liberally of ruin Cheese.

† **Rue·ness.** *Obs.* Forms: 1 **hreo(w)nis**, **-nys**, **hreu(w)nis**, **hreawnis**, 3–4 **reunes(se.** [f. OE. *hrēowe* adj. (see RUE *v.*[1]).]

1. Repentance.

c 950 *Lindisf. Gosp.* Matt. iii. 11 Ic fulwa iuih in wætre in hreonisse [*Rushw.* hreunisse]. *Ibid.* xxi. 29 Æfter ðon..mid hreawnise ȝecerred [he] ȝe-eade. *c* 1000 in Thorpe *Laws* II. 170 Æfter his dædbote hreownysse.

2. Pity, compassion.

a 1300 *Cursor M.* 3134 Moght na reunes do him reu, þat he wald leuer his child cole þan of his lauerd wrath to thole. *c* 1300 *Havelok* 2227 God him wolde wel haue saue, He hauede reunesse of þe knaue.

† **Ru·ening.** *Obs. rare.* = RUEN 1.

1398 TREVISA *Barth. De P. R.* XVIII. lviii. (Bodl. MS.), His ruennynge is cheife medicine in venyms. *Ibid.* XVIII. lxvii, In no beeste wiþ teeþ in aiþer iowe is ruennynge ifounde but in þe hare.

Ru·er. *rare.* Also 4 **rewer(e**, **reewer.** [f. RUE *v.*[1] + -ER[1].]

1. One who pities or feels compassion.

a 1300 *E. E. Psalter* lxxxv. 14 Þou, laverd, rewer and mildeherted. 1382 WYCLIF *Isaiah* xlix. 10 The rewere of them shal gouerne them. *Ibid.* liv. 10 The bond of my pes shal not be moued, seide the Lord, thi reewer.

2. One who repents.

1721 KELLY *Scot. Prov.* 284 Reavers should not be Ruers.

Rue-raddy, *sb.* [Of obscure origin.]

1. A belt or rope passed over the shoulder in order to drag something by it.

1856 KANE *Arct. Expl.* I. 112 Each man had his own shoulder-belt or rue-raddy as we used to call it, and his own track line. 1880 *Standard* 20 May 3 One section of the men are armed..with long knives and a 'rue raddy', or drag rope, slung across the shoulders.

2. *transf.* One who drags by means of a belt or rope passing over the shoulder.

1856 KANE *Arct. Expl.* II. xix. 190 An additional burden, but a necessary one, for our weary rue-raddies.

Hence **Rue-raddy** *v.*, to attach by means of a shoulder rope.

1856 KANE *Arct. Expl.* I. xv. 181 Five men were then rue-raddied to the track-lines.

† **Rue·someness.** *Obs.*[−1] In 2 **reowsum-.** [f. RUE *sb.*[1] Cf. mod. Yorks. dial. *ruesome* 'sorrowful, pitiable'.] Repentance.

c 1175 *Lamb. Hom.* 21 Bute he hine driue a-wei mid soðe dedbote his sunne bi reowsumnesse.

† **Ruet.** *Obs.* Also 5 **ruett**; 4 **ruwet**, **rewet**, **ryuet**, 6 **rivette.** [Of obscure origin.] A small horn or trumpet. Also *fig.*

13.. *K. Alis.* 1638 (Laud MS.), A-rovme he drouȝ quyk iwys And sett a Ruet to his mouþe. *Ibid.* 3699 A litel ruet [*v.r.* ruwet] a loude he blewe. 1362 LANGL. *P. Pl.* A. V. 193 Gloten..bleuh the ronde ruwet [*varr.* rewet, ryuet] atte rugge-bones ende. *c* 1400 *Laud Troy Bk.* 5987 Ector bar a litel ruet, Vnto his mouth his horn he set. *c* 1420 *Master of Game* (MS. Digby 182) xxi, Ther beth dyueres maneres of hornes, þat is to say: buglys,..ruetes, smale forsters hornes. 1483 *Cath. Angl.* 313/2 A Ruett, *lituus*. *c* 1580 JEFFERIES *Bugbears* I. ii, Stope downe a low & kisse my round rivette.

Ruet, obs. variant of ROWET *dial.*

Rueth, obs. form of RUTH.

Ruf, obs. form of ROOF, ROUGH, RUFF.

Ruf(e, Sc. variants of RO, rest. *Obs.*

† **Rufe**, *sb. Obs.*[−1] [ad. L. *rūfus*.] Rufous.

1477 NORTON *Ordin. Alch.* v. in Ashm. (1652) 56 Theis two Colours Rufe and Citrine, Be meane Colours betweene White and Red.

† **Rufe**, *a. Sc. Obs. rare.* Also 6 **ruf.** (Of doubtful origin and meaning; identity with OE. *rōf* valiant, stout, strong, is phonetically possible.)

c 1475 *Rauf Coilȝear* 109 Ane Ryall rufe het fyre war my desyre. 15.. *Peebles to Play* vi. in Sibbald *Chron. Sc. Poet.* (1802) I. 131 He cleikit up ane hie ruf sang.

Rufe, obs. or dial. form of ROOF.

Rufe·scence. *rare*[−1]. [See next and -ENCE.] Tendency to rufous or reddish colour.

1874 COUES *Birds N. W.* 478 A slight rufescence of the under plumage, may frequently be observed until October.

Rufescent (rufe·sĕnt), *a.* and *sb.* [ad. L. *rūfescent-*, *rūfescens*, pres. pple. of *rūfescĕre*, f. *rūfus* reddish.] Of a colour tending to reddish; somewhat rufous.

1817 KIRBY & SP. *Entomol.* xvii. (1818) II. 77 The rufescent ants do not leave their nests to go upon these expeditions..till [etc.]. 1823 W. SCORESBY *Jrnl.* 417 Back grey.. lower parts rufescent. 1874 COUES *Birds N. W.* 304 The same rufescent phase occurs in other species of Owls.

b. *ellipt.* as *sb.* An ant of this colour.

1817 KIRBY & SP. *Entomol.* xvii. (1818) II. 81 When the rufescents, laden with pillage, retire, they do it in close order.

Ruff (rʊf), *sb.*[1] Forms: 5 **rowe**, **roffe**, **ruf**, 5–9 **ruffe**, 7– **ruff**; 7 **rough.** [Possibly f. ROUGH *a.* Cf. the mod.L. name *aspredo* given to the freshwater fish by Dr. Caius, who drew attention to it about the middle of the 16th cent.]

† 1. A sea-bream or other sparoid fish. *Obs.* (Cf. RUFFLE *sb.*[3])

14.. *Lat.-Eng. Voc.* in Wr.-Wülcker 612 *Sparrus*, a rowe. *c* 1440 *Promp. Parv.* 438/2 Ruffe, fysche, *sparrus*. 1647 HEXHAM I. (Fishes), A Ruffe or a Sea Breame, *een Zeebraessem*. 1668 CHARLETON *Onomast.* 140 *Synodon*..Ruff, with dogs Teeth.

2. A small freshwater fish (*Acerina cernua*) of the perch family, of olive-brown colour with brown and black spots, and having rough prickly scales.

a 1450 *Fysshynge w. Angle* (E. D. S.) 15 The bleke and the gogyn & þe Roffe. 1496 *Ibid.* 29 The ruf is ryght an holsome fysshe: And ye shall angle to him..in the same wise as I haue tolde you of the perche. 1538 ELYOT Additions, *Melanurus*, a kynde of perches, callydde Ruffes. 1577 B. GOOGE *Heresbach's Husb.* IV. (1586) 173 b, Some sorts..delighting onely in Grauellie, Stonie, and Sandie Waters, as ..Gudgins, Bulheads, Ruffes, Trowtes. 1608 SYLVESTER *Du Bartas* II. iv. *Schisme* 1010 Like as a Roach, or Ruff, or Gudgeon, born By some swift stream into a Weer..Frisks to and fro. 1653 WALTON *Angler* xi. 204 There is also another fish called a Pope, and by some a Ruffe;..it is much like the Pearch for his shape, but will not grow to be bigger than a Gudgion. 1740 R. BROOKES *Art of Angling* I. xv. 44 The Ruff or Pope..is found in most of the large Rivers in England. 1797 *Encycl. Brit.* (ed. 3) XIII. 102/1 The Yare has a fish peculiar to it called the ruffe. 1836 YARRELL *Brit. Fishes* I. 18 The Ruffe is common to almost all the canals and rivers of England, particularly the Thames, the Isis, and the Cam. 1882 *Blackw. Mag.* Jan. 105 Great quantities of ruffs are caught at times, and the men's fingers get pricked with their sharp spines.

† 3. A sea-urchin. *Obs.*[−0]

1591 PERCIVALL *Sp. Dict.*, *Erizo*, an hedgehog,..also a fish called a Ruffe. 1706 STEVENS *Span. Dict.*, *Erizo de mar*, a deform'd Shell-fish call'd a Ruff.

Ruff (rʊf), *sb.*[2] Also 6–7 **ruffe**; 6 **rouffe**, *Sc.* **ruiff**, 7 **rooffe.** [? f. ROUGH *a.* Cf. RUFFLE *sb.*[1] and *v.*[1]]

† 1. A circular outstanding frill on the sleeve of a garment; a ruffle. *Obs.*

1523 FITZHERB. *Husb.* § 151 They haue suche pleytes vpon theyr brestes & ruffes vppon theyr sleues, aboue theyr elbowes. 1591 [see HAND-RUFF 1]. 1607 HEYWOOD *Fayre Mayde Exch.* F j, Ruffes for your hands, wast-cotes wrought with silke. 1647 HEXHAM I, Full of ruffes and foldes, *vol rimpelen, ployen ofte vouwen*.

2. An article of neck-wear, usually consisting of starched linen or muslin arranged in horizontal flutings and standing out all round the neck, worn especially in the reigns of Elizabeth and James I.

1555 EDEN *Decades* (Arb.) 320 The collars and ruffes bysette with lyttle rounde baules lyke beades. 1583 STUBBES *Anat. Abus.* II. (1882) 35 They not only continue their great ruffes still, but also vse them bigger than euer they did. *c* 1618 MORYSON *Itin.* IV. 418 They desyre to haue..falling bands rather then Rooffes, Caps of taffety rather then hatts. 1644 QUARLES *Sheph. Orac.* VIII. 47 That heath'nish Ruffe of thine, that perks Upon thy stiffe-neckt coller. 1728 YOUNG *Love of Fame* IV. 122 He shews on holidays a sacred pin, That touch'd the ruff, that touch'd queen Bess's chin. 1752 HUME *Ess. & Treat.* (1777) I. 263 Must we throw aside the pictures of our ancestors, because of their ruffs and fardingales? 1822 SCOTT *Nigel* x, My grey beard falls on a cambric ruff, and a silken doublet. 1880 'OUIDA' *Moths* II. 375 She wore black velvet with a high ruff of old Flemish lace.

transf. 1633 P. FLETCHER *Purple Isl.* XXX, As a virgin Rose..Whom too hot scorching beams quite disarayes Down flags her double ruffe.

b. (See quot.)

1858 J. PURCHAS *Direct. Anglic.* 21/1 Under this 'tippet' is worn what is called by University robe-makers 'the Ruff'. *Note.* This ruff is simply a breadth of silk of about two yards long...It is *gathered* round the neck.

3. A collar of projecting or distinctively coloured feathers or hair round the neck of various birds and animals.

1698 FRYER *Acc. E. India & P.* 56 Monkeys with white Ruffs, and black shagged Bodies. 1760–72 tr. *Juan & Ulloa's Voy.* (ed. 3) I. 58 A little aboue the beginning of the crop, they haue a ruff of white feathers. 1781 [see 6 below]. 1802 BINGLEY *Anim. Biogr.* (1805) II. 475 The male bird does not acquire his ruff till the second season. 1856 BRYANT *Old Man's Counsel* 49 The grouse that wears A sable ruff around his mottled neck. 1871 DARWIN *Desc. Man* II. xvii. 267 The broad ruff round the throat and chin of the Canadian lynx is much longer in the male than in the female. 1887 *Standard* 28 May 1/2 Lost, a black and Tan Colley Dog, with white ruff.

b. An artificial variety of the domestic pigeon resembling the jacobin.

1735 J. MOORE *Columbarium* 49 The Strain of Jacobines has been much vitiated..in Order to improve their Chain by the Length of the Ruff's Feathers. 1765 *Treat. Domest. Pigeons* 119 The ruff, if attentively examined, will be found larger than the jack, with a longer beak, and a larger head. 1854 MEALL *Moubray's Poultry* 285 The similarity between the Ruff and the Jacobine obviates the necessity for describing it. 1881 J. C. LYELL *Fancy Pigeons* 199 Moore describes a pigeon known as a ruff.

† 4. *The wooden ruff*, the pillory. *Cant. Obs.*

1685 *Roxb. Ball.* (1885) V. 605 The Tories to spight us,.. With a damn'd Wooden-Ruff will bedeck our Friend Titus. *a* 1700 B. E. *Dict. Cant. Crew* s.v. *Wooden*, *He wore the Wooden-ruff*, he stood in the Pillory.

5. A circular object resembling a ruff.

1693 EVELYN *De la Quint. Compl. Gard.* II. 107 You must raise small Shavings out of the Wood of the Branch.. and make them hang like a kind of Ruff on the Extremity of that Bark. 1742 POPE *Dunciad* IV. 407 Soft on the paper ruff its leaves I spread. 1864 WEBSTER, *Ruff*,..an annular ridge formed on a shaft, or other piece, to prevent it from moving endwise. Ruffs are also sometimes loose rings.

6. *attrib.* and *Comb.*, as *ruff band*, *sleeve*; *ruff-like*, *-necked* adjs.

1558 in Feuillerat *Revels Q. Eliz.* (1908) 28 Imployed wholye in to twoo greate gounes with Ruff Sleves. 1591 FLORIO *2nd Fruites* 9 Eight ruffe bands with their hand cuffs wrought with silke. 1639 *Knaresb. Wills* (Surtees) II 167 To Sibbill Hudsonne one ruffe band. 1781 LATHAM *Gen. Synop. Birds* I. I. 269 Ruff-necked Parrot...When it erects the neck feathers, it makes the appearance of a ruff round the head. 1782 *Ibid.* II. 785 Ruff-necked Humming Bird. 1838 AUDUBON *Ornith. Biog.* IV. 555 Ruff-Necked Humming Bird. *Trochilus Rufus*. 1854 MEALL *Moubray's Poultry* 286 A compact mass of ruff-like feathers.

Ruff (rʊf), *sb.*[3] Also 6–7 **ruffe.** [ad. OF. *roffle*, *rouffle*, earlier *romfle*, *ronfle* (1414), = It. *ronfa* (Florio), a certain card-game, perh. a popular corruption of F. *triomphe*, It. *trionfo*: see TRUMP.

Godefroy also cites a F. dial. *roufe* as meaning 'the highest of two cards which one returns along with the trump-card in the game of quarante'. Pg. *rufa* and *rifa* denote a set of cards of one suit.]

† 1. A former card-game. Also *ruff and honours*.

Literary allusions occur chiefly between 1590 and 1630.

1589 NASHE *Martin Marprelate* Wks. (Grosart) I. 161 Leauing the auncient game of England (Trumpe) where euerie coate and sute are sorted in their degree, [they] are running to their Ruffe where the greatest sorte of the sute carrieth away the game. 1600 ROWLANDS *Lett. Humours Blood* iv. 64 At Ticktacke, Irish, Noddie, Maw, and Ruffe. 1611 DAVIS *Panegyrick Verses* in *Coryat's Crudities*, Of that tongue he so hath got the Body That he sports with it at Ruffe, Gleeke, or Noddy. 1674 COTTON *Compl. Gamester* (1680) 81 Ruff and Honours (alias Slamm) and Whist, are Games..commonly known in England in all parts thereof. 1688 HOLME *Armoury* III. xvi. (Roxb.) 72/1 Ruffe and Honors and Whisk, which are generally among the Vulgar termed Trump.

† 2. (See later quots.) *Obs.*

1611 COTGR., *Triomphe*, the Card-game called Ruffe, or Trump; also, the Ruffe, or trump at it. 1651 *Royal Game of Picquet* 11 After they have done discarding,..they then begin to look after the Ruffe, and to see how much each of them can make of a suit. 1674 COTTON *Compl. Gamester* (1680) 66 Next you speak for the Ruff, and he that hath most of a suit in his hand wins it, unless some of the Gamesters have four Aces, and then he gains the Ruff.

3. [f. RUFF *v.*[2] 2.] The act of trumping at cards, esp. in whist, when one cannot follow suit.

1856 *Handbk. Games* (Bohn) 176 You may suspect the lead was from a single card, and with a view to a ruff. 1856 LT.-COL. B. *Whist-player* (1858) 31 You obtain the desired ruff to a certainty.

Ruff (rʊf), *sb.*[4] [Perh. from RUFF *sb.*[2] 3, but this leaves the similarity to REEVE *sb.*[2] unexplained.] The male of a bird of the sandpiper family (*Tringa* or *Machetes pugnax*), distinguished during the breeding-season by a ruff and ear-tufts.

1634, 1648 [see REEVE *sb.*[2]]. 1663 DRYDEN *Wild Gallant* I. iii, I have a delicate dish of ruffs to dinner. 1752 HILL *Hist. Anim.* 475 We call the male the ruff and the female the reeve. 1768 PENNANT *Brit. Zool.* II. 363 The males or Ruffs assume such variety of colors in several parts of their plumage, that it is scarce possible to see two alike. 1839 STONEHOUSE *Isle of Axholme* 66 Those very curious and beautiful birds, the ruffs, are now seldom to be met with. 1843 YARRELL *Brit. Birds* II. 574 The Ruff...may be considered only as a summer visiter to this country. 1863 *Sat. Rev.* 284 The extension of drainage has banished the avoset, and the ruff, and the godwit from our eastern marshes.

Ruff (rʊf), *sb.*[5] Also 7 **roofe.** [? Imitative.]

1. = RUFFLE *sb.*[4] (Hence perh. Pg. *rufo*.)

1688 [see ROLL *sb.*[2] 2]. 1706 FARQUHAR *Recruiting Officer* V. ii, The drum beats a ruff, and so to bed. 1726 SHELVOCKE *Voy. round World* 137 At the turning of every glass during the night we beat 3 ruffs on the drum. 1811 BOSWELL *Sir Albon Poet.* Wks. (1871) 102 Quicker than the drum-boy's ruff His horse hoofs clatter'd hard and tough.

2. *Sc.* An expression of applause by making a noise with the feet. 1801– in *Eng. Dial. Dict.*

† **Ruff**, *sb.*[6] *Obs.* Also 6–7 **ruffe.** [Of obscure origin. Cf. Sw. *ruff* spirit, go.] *Obs.*

1. The highest pitch or fullest degree *of* some exalted or excited condition. Usu. *in the ruff of*.

1549 LATIMER *2nd Serm. bef. Edw. VI* (Arb.) 49 Wher is all thy ruffe of thy gloriousnes become? 1592 G. HARVEY *Four Lett.* Wks. (Grosart) I. 199 He, which in the ruffe of his freshest iollity, was faine to cry [etc.]. 1622 FOTHERBY *Atheom.* II. vii. § 1. 261 When they view themselues in the ruffe of their greatnes, they are vtterly ashamed, to thinke of their first littlenesse. 1692 L'ESTRANGE *Fables* (1694) 39 How many Emperours and Princes..in the Ruff of all their glory have been taken down.

2. An exalted or elated state; elation, pride, vainglory: a. With possessive pronouns, esp. in phr. *in his* (or *their*) *ruff*. (Very common from *c* 1570 to 1675).

a 1548 HALL *Chron.*, *Hen. IV*, 30 The duke of Burgoyn beyng now in his ruffe..toke upon him the hole rule and governance of the realme. 1568 V. SKINNER tr. *Montanus' Inquisit.* 46 b, Such is their ruffe in that triumph. 1581 J. BELL *Haddon's Answ. Osorius* 319 Which would undertake so weerysome a course for his Rhetoricall ruffe. 1615 W. HULL *Mirr. Maiestie* 51 What came ye out to see? a mere mortall man in the huffe of his ruffe? 1653 J. CARTER *Tombstone* 107 They think in their ruffe and gallantry that none can pluck them down; they vaunt, who shall us controule? *a* 1679 GOODWIN *Creatures* II. x. Wks. 1683 II. 96 When the Saints shall be in their ruff and glory.

b. Without article, esp. in phr. *in* (*great, jolly, rash*, etc.) *ruff*.

1555 J. PROCTOR *Hist. Wyat's Rebellion* 30 Where thei.. displaied their Ensignes brauelie: seeming to be in great ruffe. 1556 J. HEYWOOD *Spider & Fly* lvii, Who that (in rash roofe) beginneth to contende, He repenth beginning, ere be cum to ende. 1567 GOLDING tr. *Ovid's Met.* XII. 318 In jolly ruffe he passed straight. 1581 MULCASTER *Positions* xiv. (1887) 68 Against all..with whom all vertues be voluntarie, when reason is in ruffe. 1600 W. WATSON *Decacordon* (1602) 34 He tooke vpon him the defence of the Sea Apostolike in managing with huffe and ruffe this foisted in authoritie. [1624 J. GEE *Hold fast* 30 A vigorous Iesuite.. attired like a Gallant of none of the lowest ruffe.]

c. In phr. *in the* (*high*) *ruff*.

1600 HOLLAND *Livy* XXVIII. xxviii. 690 Being in the ruffe and iollitie upon their fresh and late victorie. 1607 R. C[AREW] tr. *Estienne's World of Wonders* 352 Whilest the folly of the former abuses was in the ruffe. 1690 *Andros Tracts* II. 64 Methods that must be taken to unite England, ..and subdue France, (now in the high Ruff).

3. *Her.* Of a ship: *In her ruff*, in full course.

1562 LEGH *Armory* 178 b, He beareth Or, a Shippe vnder Saile in her ruffe Sable. 1586 FERNE *Blaz. Gentrie* 38 You haue heard of two thinges, a ship in her ruffe and a fayre lady..most worthye of sight. 1610 GUILLIM *Heraldry* III. xxii, The Dolphin..outstrippeth a Ship under sayle, in her greatest ruffe and merriest winde, in swiftness of course. 1688 HOLME *Armoury* III. xv. (Roxb.) 33/1 He beareth Argent, a Ship in her Ruffe, vnder full Saile and Streamers flying, all proper.

4. Excitement, passion, fury. Freq. *in a ruff*.

1567 GOLDING *Ovid's Met.* XIII. (1593) 296 In the mids of all His bloodie ruffe I coupt with him. 1604 PARSONS *3rd Pt. Three Convers. Eng.* 112 All ignorant Craftesmen of Kent, but yet sett in such a ruffe with the heate of new opinions. 1611 J. DAVIES (Heref.) *Scourge Folly* Wks. (Grosart) II. 76 Such Stuffe (As might put plainest Pacience in a Ruffe). 1641 HINDE *J. Bruen* lii. 173 There was a Gentleman, who..in his heat and ruffe sent his man to this Gentleman with this message, &c.

† **Ruff**, *sb.*[7] *Obs.*[−0] [Of obscure origin.] A candle or candle-wick.

c 1440 *Promp. Parv.* 439/1 Ruffe candel, *hirsepa*, *funale*. 1570 LEVINS *Manip.* 183 Ye Ruffe of a candle, *finale*.

† **Ruff**, *sb.*[8] *Obs.*[−1] (See quot.)

1601 HOLLAND *Pliny* I. 243 Moreover in the river Donow, there is taken the Mario, a fish much like to a Ruffe or Porpuis [L. *porculo marino simillimus*].

† **Ruff**, *sb.*[9] *Obs. rare.* A blockhead.

1606 *Choice, Chance & Change* (1881) 66 The next was on a fool, on a swaggering ruffe. 1674 N. FAIRFAX *Bulk & Selv.* Ep. Ded., Though it may seem but a wooden come off, and like that of the sorry numb-skull'd Ruffes.

Ruff, var. ROUGH *sb.*[1]; Sc. var. RO, rest. *Obs.*

† **Ruff**, *a. Obs. rare.* (Meaning not clear, but perh. only a variant spelling of ROUGH *a.*)

1651 T. BARKER *Art of Angling* (1653) 15 When your grid-iron is hot you must coole it with ruff suet. 1676 WORLIDGE *Cyder* (1691) 161 Let your murc or chaff..abide in the must..more or less ruff or tinctured.

Ruff, obs. f. ROUGH *a.* and *adv.*

Ruff (rʊf), *v.*[1] Now *rare.* Forms: 6–7 **ruf**, **ruffe**, 6– **ruff.** [? f. RUFF *sb.*[2] Cf. RUFFLE *v.*[1]]

1. *trans.* To form into a ruff or ruffs; to provide with a ruff or ruffs. Also with *up*.

Chiefly in pa. pple.; cf. RUFFED *ppl. a.*[1] 3.

a 1548 HALL *Chron.*, *Hen. VIII*. 134 b, His base and bard wer cloth of siluer, and blacke velvet ruffed and not plain. 1571 A. JENKINSON *Voy. & Trav.* (Hakl. Soc.) I. 39 The sleeues thereof very long, which he weareth on his arme ruffed up. 1592 GREENE *Def. Conny Catch.* Wks. (Grosart) XI. 95 The round hose bumbasted close to the breech, and ruft aboue the necke with a curle. 1647 HEXHAM I, To ruffe, or gather into a ruffe, *rimpelen ofte fronsen vergaderen*. 1834 PLANCHÉ *Hist. Brit. Cost.* 238 The sleeves were also ruffed or ruffled at the hand.

2. † a. Of a bird: To ruffle (the feathers). *Obs.*

1590 SPENSER *F. Q.* III. ii. 27 Thenceforth the fether in her lofty crest, Ruffed of love, gan lowly to availe. *Ibid.* XI. 32 The proud Bird, ruffing his fethers wyde. 1597 DRAYTON *Heroical Ep.* 67 b, The siluer swannes..Ruffing their plumes, come glyding on the lake.

b. To make rough; to disorder. *rare.*

1817–8 COBBETT *Resid. U.S.* (1822) 338 To return to the thatching: Straw..., in very high winds,..is liable, if not reeded, to be ruffed a good deal.

† 3. *Falconry.* Of a hawk: To strike (the quarry) without securing it. *Obs.*

1575 TURBERV. *Falconry* 122 Your Falcon wyll stowpe hir and ruffe hir, vntyll the dogges maye take hir. 1620–6 QUARLES *Feast for Wormes* 103 If in her downy Soreage, she but ruffe So strong a Doue, may it be thought enough. 1646 G. DANIEL *Poems* Wks. (Grosart) I. 97 Give her way to kill The Harpie She has ruff't; for I dare say She has earn'd her Bells, to bring downe such a prey.

Ruff (rʊf), *v.*[2] Forms: 6– **ruff**, 7 **ruffe**, 8–9 **rough.** [Related to RUFF *sb.*[3]]

† 1. *intr.* (See quot. 1674.) *Obs. rare.*

1598 FLORIO, *Ronfare*,..also to ruff or trump at cards. 1674 COTTON *Compl. Gamester* (1680) 82 He that hath the Ace of that (i.e. trumps) Ruffs; that is, he takes in those four Cards, and lays out four others in their lieu.

2. *trans.* To trump (a card, etc.) when unable to follow suit. Freq. *absol.*

1760 MURPHY *Way to Keep Him* III. i, Sir George, why did not you rough the spade? 1837 DICKENS *Pickw.* xxxv, Why Mr. Pickwick had not..roughed the spade, or finessed the heart. 1856 LT.-COL. B. *Whist-player* (1858) 36 A suit being so frequently ruffed third round. 1885 PROCTOR *Whist* 49 The state of the score might render it advisable to take the trick lest second round should be ruffed.

absol. 1781 HUTTON *Tour to Caves* Gloss. (ed. 2) 95 *Rough*, to renounce at cards. 1865 LOWELL *Thoreau* Prose Wks. 1890 I. 372 He wishes always to trump your suit and to ruff when you least expect it. 1885 PROCTOR *Whist* 71 Ruff at every opportunity if so weak in trumps that you cannot hope to disarm the enemy.

Ruff (rʊf), *v.*[3] *Sc.* [f. RUFF *sb.*[5] Cf. Pg. *rufar*.]

1. *trans.* To beat a ruff or ruffle upon (a drum). Also *intr.* of a drum: To be thus beaten.

1827 W. TAYLOR *Poems* 65 (E. D. D.), He..ruff'd the drum at ilka door. 1828 MOIR *Mansie Wauch* xiv. 206 The drum ruffed, and off set four of them.

2. *trans.* and *intr.* To applaud by making a noise with the feet.

1826 WILSON *Noct. Ambr.* Wks. 1855 I. 243 A' the crowd ruffin the exploit. 1842 VEDDER *Poems* 104 They ruffed, and for the duty clamoured. 1877 in J. A. Chalmers *Tiyo Soga* 419 He was..heartily ruffed by his fellow-students.

† **Ruff**, *v.*[4] *Obs.* Also 7 **ruffe**, **ruf.** [f. RUFF *sb.*[6]]

1. *intr.* To swagger, bluster, domineer. Also with *it* and *out*.

1600 W. WATSON *Decacordon* (1602) 65 This foundation thus laid, then to huffe and ruffe it out, a Councell of women must be called to set cocke a hoope. 1618 T. JAMES *Jesuits Downefall* 65 He is now become that learned counseller, that must rule, ruffe, and range through every estate. 1683 *Songs Lond. Prentices* (Percy Soc.) 77 Rufing thus, They gave him words opprobrious.

2. To brag or boast *of* a thing.

1600 W. WATSON *Decacordon* (1602) 107 [A letter] to be huffed, ruffed and vanted of.

Ruff (rʊf), *v.*[5] [var. of ROUGH *v.*[1]]

1. *trans.* To heckle (flax) with a ruffer.

1853 URE *Dict. Arts* (ed. 4) I. 741 He seizes the ruffed part of the strick.., and proceeds by similar treatment to 'ruff' the top end.

2. To work the beaver felt into (a hat-body).

1845 [see RUFFING *vbl. sb.*[2]]. 1868 J. THOMSON *Hatmaking & Felting* 37 The known impossibility of napping or ruffing a hat by any means with machinery.

Ru·ff-coat. ? *Obs.* [prob. f. *ruff* ROUGH *a.*] The caddis-worm.

1653 WALTON *Angler* xii. 232 There is also another Cadis called by some a Straw-worm, and by some a Ruffe-coate. 1787 BEST *Angling* (ed. 2) 20 Another sort..is found..in rushes, water-weeds, straw, &c. called ruff Coats, or straw worms. 1833 J. RENNIE *Alph. Angling* 34 The grubs which are known by the name of caddis-worms, case-worms, cad or cod bait and ruff coats.

Ruffe, obs. form of ROOF, ROUGH, RUFF.

Ruffed (rʊft), *ppl. a.*[1] Also 6 **ruft.** [f. RUFF *sb.*[2] or *v.*[1]]

1. Wrinkled, curled. *rare.*

1578 LYTE *Dodoens* V. vi. 553 Ruffed, or curled Colewurtes. *Ibid.* 554 The fourth kind of red Cole, is called..in Englishe Wrinckled or ruffed Cole.

2. Ruffled. *rare*[−1].

1591 SPENSER *Teares Muses* 402 Thy gay Sonne, that winged God of Love, May now goe prune his plumes like ruffed Dove.

3. Wearing a ruff; provided with ruffs.

1586 T. B. *La Primaud. Fr. Acad.* I. (1589) 207 What would he have said of our Courtiers, so finely curled, ruft, and perfumed? 1810 CRABBE *Borough* ii. 98 That marble arch, our sexton's favourite show, With all those ruff'd and painted pairs below. 1859 KINGSLEY *Misc.* II. 134 If we met such a ruffed and ruffled worthy as used to swagger by hundreds up and down Paul's Walk.

b. In names of birds and animals: Having a ruff-like collar or markings, as *ruffed bustard*, *grouse*, *heathcock*, *pigeon*; *ruffed lemur*, *macaco*.

1783 LATHAM *Gen. Synop. Birds* II. II. 805 *Ruffed Bustard. 1819 STEPHENS in *Shaw's Gen. Zool.* XI. 448 Ruffed bustard..inhabits Arabia and the northern parts of Africa. 1782 *Phil. Trans.* LXII. 397 *Ruffed Grous, *T. Umbellus*. 1785 PENNANT *Arct. Zool.* II. 301 *Ruffed Grous*, Grous with a great ruff on the hind part of the neck. 1812 A. WILSON *Amer. Ornith.* VI. 45 The Pinnated Grous was seen in great numbers, but none of the Ruffed. 1872 COUES *N. Amer. Birds* 235 *Ruffed Grouse*...Sides of the neck with a tuft of numerous..broad, soft, glossy-black feathers. 1752 EDWARDS *Glean. Nat. Hist.* I. 79 The *Ruffed Heath-cock, or Grous. 1840 *Cuvier's Anim. Kingd.* 63 One beautiful species, the *Ruffed Lemur (*L. macaco*, Lin.), is varied with large patches of black on a pure white ground. 1897 H. O. FORBES *Hand-bk. Primates* I. 69 The Ruffed or Variable Lemur [*Lemur Varius*]. 1771 PENNANT *Syn. Quadrup.* 138 *Ruffed maucauco. 1797 *Encycl. Brit.* (ed. 3) IX. 785/2 The..ruffed maucauco, (the *Vari* of Buffon), is also an inhabitant of Madagascar. 1611 COTGR., *Pigeon chaperonné*, a *ruffed, or copped, Pigeon.

Ruffed (rʊft), *ppl. a.*[2] [f. RUFF *v.*[5]] a. Covered with beaver felt. b. Heckled with a ruffer.

1846 MCCULLOCH *Acc. Brit. Empire* (1854) I. 763 Few beaver or ruffed hats meet the English manufacturer in the markets referred to. 1853 URE *Dict. Arts* (ed. 4) I. 741 When this is finished the 'ruffed' work is taken to the tool called a 'common 8'. *Ibid.* [see RUFF *v.*[5] 1].

Ru·ffer[1]. *rare*[−0]. [f. RUFF *v.*[2]] (See quot.)

1611 FLORIO, *Ronfatóre*,..a ruffer or trumper at cardes.

Ru·ffer[2]. [f. RUFF *v.*[5]] = ROUGHER 3.

1853 URE *Dict. Arts* (ed. 4) I. 741 The pins..are much closer placed than those of the ruffer. 1882 [see ROUGHER 3].

Ruffet, variant of ROUGHET.

Ruffian (rʊ·fiăn), *sb.* and *a.* Forms: α. 6 **rufian**, **ruffyan(e**, **ruffiane**, **-ion**, 6– **ruffian.** β. 6 **rouffyn**, **ruffyne**, 6–7 **ruffin**, **ruffen**, 7 **ruffon.** [a. OF. *rufyen*, *-ien*, *ruffien*, *ruffian* (mod.F. *rufien*, *rufian*), = Prov. *rufian*, *rofian*, Catal. *rufia*, Sp. *rufian*, Pg. *rufião* (*rafião*), It. *ruffiano*, med.L. *ruffianus*: the ultimate origin of these forms is obscure, there being no evidence to support any of the conjectures which have been offered. French is also the source of MDu. *roff-*, *ruffiaen* (Du. *roffiaan*), MLG., MHG., and mod.G. *ruffian*.]

1. A man of a low and brutal character; one habitually given to acts of violence or crime; a cut-throat villain.

α. 1531 ELYOT *Gov.* II. xii. (1880) II. 156 A commune and notable rufian or thefe, whiche had robbed and slayne a man. 1568 GRAFTON *Chron.* II. 119 Assemblyng together a greate rowte of Ruffians and Robbers. 1633 G. HERBERT *Church Militant* 163 The old debauched ruffian would turn writer. 1664 H. MORE *Myst. Iniq.* 413 Their beginnings being helped on by a rabble of Ruffians and Robbers. 1727–46 THOMSON *Summer* 274 Near the dire cell the dreadless wanderer oft Passes, as oft the ruffian shows his front. 1754 YOUNG *Brothers* IV. i, Stab me yourself, nor give me to the knife Of midnight ruffians. 1820 BYRON *Mar. Fal.* I. ii, With common ruffians leagued to ruin states! 1848 MRS. JAMIESON *Sacr. & Leg. Art* (1850) 64 It is not a fiend, but a degraded prosaic human ruffian. 1868 FREEMAN *Norm. Conq.* (1877) II. 68 The courts of ruffians like Harold and Harthacnut.

β. 1553 T. WILSON *Rhet.* 99 Not a common ruffin, but a most cruell cut throte. 1576 BP. WOOLTON *Chr. Man.* I v b, Some tyme lyke Routters, some tyme lyke Rouffyns, but

Ruffiandom.

Ruffianing, vbl. sb.

Ruffianish, a.

Ruffianism.

Ruffianosity, nonce-wd.

Ruffianry.

Ruffianship.

Ruffin, variant of RUFFY sb.

Ruffin.

Ruffian-like, a. and adv.

Ruffiano.

Ruffianly, a.

Ruffianry (repr.).

Ru-ffian, sb.

Ruffle, sb.¹

Ruffle, sb.²

Ruffle, sb.³

Ruffle, v.¹

Ruffling, vbl. sb.¹

Ruffle, v.²

Ruffle, v.³

Ruffled, ppl. a.

Ruffled grouse.

Ruffler.

Ruffless, a.

Ruffly, a.

Ruffmans, sb.

Ruffler.

Ruffling, vbl. sb.²

Ruffling, ppl. a.

Ruffly, adv.

Ruffy, sb.¹

Ruffy, a.

Ruffy-tuffy, a.

Rufi-, comb. form of L. rufus red.

Bufo-, comb. form of L. rufus.

Rufescent, a.

Rufous, a.

Rufter-hood.

Rug, sb.¹

Rug, sb.²

Rug, v. To pull forcibly, violently, or roughly; to tear, tug.

Rug, sb. [Of Scand. origin: cf. Swed. dial. *rug* in the same sense.] Prob. related to *rag* mist, rime, common in northern Eng. dialects. Drizzling rain.

Ruga (rū′gǎ). Pl. **rugæ** (rū′dʒī). *Zool.*, *Anat.* A wrinkle, fold, or ridge.

Rugate (rū′gĕt), a. [ad. L. *rūgātus*.] Having rugæ; wrinkled.

Rugged, a. Also *north. dial.* Rough, uneven, broken; full of stones, rocks, abrupt rises or declivities, etc.

Ruggedly, adv. In a rugged manner.

Ruggedness. The state or character of being rugged; roughness, unevenness.

Rugger, slang or colloquial alteration of Rugby (in the sense of 'Rugby football').

Rugging, sb. [f. RUG sb.²] (See quot.)

Rugging, vbl. sb. [f. RUG v.¹] Pulling, tugging.

Rugine (rū′dʒīn), sb. A surgeon's rasp.

Rugose (rū′gōs), a. [ad. L. *rūgōsus*, f. *rūga* wrinkle.] Wrinkled; marked by rugæ or wrinkles; ridged.

Rugosity (rūgŏ′sĭtĭ). The state of being rugose or wrinkled.

Rugosous, a. Obs. rare. = next.

Rugous (rū′gǎs), a. [ad. L. *rūgōsus*.] Rugose, wrinkled.

Rug-saw. A wide-toothed saw.

Rugulose (rū′gĭulōs), a. Minutely rugose.

Rugulous (rū′gĭuləs), a. = prec.

Ruh(e, Ruhh, obs. forms of ROUGH.

Ruid, Ruif, etc. Sc. forms of ROOD, RIDE, ROOF, etc.

Ruin (rū′in), sb. Also 6–8 ruine, 6 ruyne, 7 ruin.

I. 1. The act of giving way and falling down.

Ruin (rū′in), v.

Ruinable, a. rare. [f. prec. + -ABLE.] That may be ruined; perishable.

Ruinate (rū′inĕt), v.

Ruinate (rū′inĕt), ppl. a. [ad. med.L. *ruinat-us*, ppl. stem of *ruinare*.] Ruined, ruinous.

Ruinated (rū′inĕtĕd), ppl. a. [f. prec. + -ED.] Ruined; fallen into ruin.

Ruinating, vbl. sb. [f. RUINATE v. + -ING.]

Ruination.

2. Falling to ruin; decaying.

Ruination (rūinā′·ʃən). [f. RUINATE v. + -ATION.] The action of ruining; the fact or state of being ruined.

Ruining, ppl. a. [f. RUIN v. + -ING²]

Ruinous, a. U.S. [f. prec. and -OUS.] Ruinous.

Ruinator. One [Agent-noun, on L. types, f. RUINATE v.] One who ruins.

Ruined (rū′·ind), ppl. a. [f. RUIN v. + -ED¹.]

Ruiner (rū′·inəɹ). [f. RUIN v. + -ER¹.] One who or that which ruins.

Ruini-ferous, a. nonce-word. Rich in ruins.

Ruini-form, a. Min. rare. [? ad. F. ruini-forme.] Presenting the appearance of ruins.

Ruining, vbl. sb. [f. RUIN v. + -ING¹.] The action of bringing to ruin; the result of this.

Ruinousness. [f. prec. + -NESS.]

2. The condition of being in ruins.

Ruin-tail, -tailed. rare.

Ruissel. Obs. Forms: 5 ruys(c)el, rais-h(e)oul. [a. OF. ruisel, ruisseau, etc. (mod.F. ruisseau), a. L. rivus stream.] A rivulet, brook.

Ruiter. Obs. [a. OF. ruit, rupt, in the same sense.] Noise, disorder.

Ruk, sb. Obs. rare. Also ij rukul, ruoul. [ad. med.L. rucula, for *eruculla, dim. of L. erūca; cf. ERUCA and ERUKE.] The rocket (Eruca sativa).

Rukelen, obs. f. RUCKLE v.¹

Rukh variant of ROC, RUKH, v. Rukh.

Rulable (rū′·lăb'l), a. Also ij reule-, ruil-able. [f. RULE sb. and v. + -ABLE.]

1. Capable of being ruled, controllable. ? Obs.

b. Almost obliterated. Obs.

2. Brought to, sunk into, ruin or decay. rare.

3. Bringing or tending to ruin; disastrous, destructive, pernicious.

4. Fertaining to a fall or crash. rare⁻¹.

Ruinously, adv. [f. prec. + -LY².] In a ruinous manner or degree; in a way, or to an extent, ruinous.

laid his of rule aside.

b. With a, the, that, etc.

2. Admissible as a rule. rare⁻¹.

3. U.S. colloq. Allowable by rule; permissible.

Rule (rūl). Forms: 1 riwle, 3-4 riule; 3 ruile, 4-5 ruwle, rewle, 5-6 rewill, 6 rewle; 4 rule, 4-7 reule, reull, 4-5 rewyl, 5 rewill, ruyle, rule. [a. OF. riule, reule, rule, etc. (see later form), etc.]

1. A principle, regulation, or maxim governing individual conduct.

Rule over (one); see quot. Cont.

ruele, 7 ruil; 4 rulen, rulye, 5 rulyn, roul(e, (see Godefroy), etc. to regulate, of which OF. regler (mod.F. régler).

I. I. trans. To control, guide, direct, exercise sway or influence over (a person, his actions, life, etc.).

Of ne seurte wio met pat rulede be kyngdom of Perse.

decide, determine, declare formally. In later use cont. that, or with and of.

Ruled (rūld), ppl. a. [f. RULE v.]

8. To lay down judicially or authoritatively;

2. To convey, restrain, curb (one's appetites, etc.) by the exercise of self-control.

RUN.

may run thus, An Host shall be given [etc.] ...

33. To have a specified character, quality, arrangement, form, etc. Const. with preps. and *adj.*

II. Transitive senses.

To traverse, accomplish, aim at or avoid, etc., by running.

34. To pursue or follow (a certain way or course) in running, sailing, etc. †*To run one's way*; to run away, make off hurriedly.

b. Hunting. To pursue, follow up (a scent). Also †*to run one's country* (see quots. 1611).

35. To traverse or cover by running, sailing, etc.: a. a specified distance.

b. a defined stretch or space.

36. To perform or accomplish by running or riding; as a course (on horseback or foot), career, etc. Freq. in *fig.* contexts.

To run the gauntlope or *gauntlet*: see GANTLOPE, GAUNTLET.

37. a. To go upon (an errand or message).

b. *Run descent, division* (q.): see DESCANT sb. 6, 7, and DIVISION sb. 7. Now only *arch.*

38. To be or escape from (a place, country, etc.); to desert from (a ship).

40. a. *Run it*, or *a voyage* (see quot. 1838).

41. To couple, chase, hunt.

42. To cause or force (a horse or other animal) to go rapidly, esp. when riding it. †Also *ad ride*.

43. To cause a (horse or other animal) to run rapidly, or extend.

44. To incur or undergo (risk, danger, etc.)

45. To cause (a boat or ship) to move rapidly or easily forwards, esp. towards or against the land.

46. To carry through, smuggle (contraband goods).

47. To run into a certain state, affect in a certain way, by running. Chiefly *refl.* and in phrases (see quots.)

48. To drive or cause (one's head, etc.) to strike forcibly against (a person or thing).

49. To carry, pass, or suspend (a line or rope) into or through something.

*** To cause to flow or come together.**

54. To give forth, to flow with (a specified kind of liquid).

52. a. *Run one's face for*; to get (an article) on credit. *U.S.*

53. † a. To prolong (a note) in singing. *Obs.*

b. *Run the line(s)*, to determine, fix, or mark (a line).

55. To cause to coagulate, or to unite in a viscid mass. Also *const. b.*

56. To convert (ore or metal) into sheets, bars, etc., by allowing to flow into moulds.

57. a. To cause (a substance, etc.) to pass into or through something.

b. To unite or combine.

58. To let water escape through or from (a sluice, pool, etc.); esp. *runn dry* (also *refl.* and *fig.*)

59. *Run across*, to meet or fall in with.

60. *Run after* — a. To endeavour to gain the companionship or society of; to pursue with admiration or attentions.

61. *Run against* — a. To dash rapidly and forcibly against (a person or thing); to encounter suddenly or casually.

62. *Run before* —, to keep ahead of; to anticipate (a time, subject, etc.)

63. *Run in* — † a. To incur, involve oneself in (blame, penalties, etc.)

64. *Run into* —

† a. To run through or squander (property). *Obs.*

a. To incur (blame, displeasure, loss, etc.); to involve oneself in (debt, expenses, etc.)

65. *Run on* —

66. *Run out of* —

67. *Run over* —

a. To take a mental review of; to think over.

b. To glance or look over; to survey, scan, peruse or read, rapidly.

c. To repeat or recite quickly; to tell over again; to recapitulate.

d. To pass by change or transformation, to develop, into (something).

e. To go on, advance, into (something); to mount up or amount to.

f. To fall into; to tend towards; to be displayed in.

g. To dash into or collide with, esp. by accident.

68. *Run through* —

a. To examine, inspect, peruse, treat of or deal with, rapidly.

b. Of plants: To tend to the development of (seed, straw, etc.)

69. *Run up* —

70. *Run upon* —

† a. *Run through* (a person): To run through, impel, or thrust.

b. To have a tendency to, a favour or craving for, to seek much after (something).

RUN.
905

RUN.
906

RUN.
907

RUN.
908
RUNAWAY.

Runcation. *Obs.* ... the course which the runaway is taking.

2. An act of running away; *spec.* an elopement, a runaway snatch (see 3 b).

II. *attrib.* and *adj.*

3. *attrib.* Running: having run away; given to running away; fugitive.

4. Of horses, etc.: Escaped; or given to escaping, from the control of the rider or driver.

5. *Sporting.* Easily won; one-sided.

6. *Sporting.* Easily won; one-sided.

† Runcation. *Obs.* ad. L. *runcātiō*, f. *runcāre* to weed.] The action of weeding.

Runch (rɒnʃ). *Sc.* and *north.* [Orig. obscure.]
a. Charlock or wild mustard, *Brassica Sinapistrum.* **b.** Wild radish, *Raphanus Raphanistrum.*

Runchie. *Sc.* (See quots. and compare prec.)

† Runcation. *Obs.* ad. L. *runcātiō*, f. ...

Runcival, obs. form of ROUNCIVAL.

† Runcle. *Obs. rare.* [ad. G. *runkel*, also *runkel-rübe*, of obscure origin.] A variety of beet.

Rund (rɒnd). *Sc.* and *north.* Also *ruind, rind,* etc. [Of obscure origin. — ROON.]

Rundale (rɒ·ndēl). Also 6 *ryndale, rindaill,* 8 *rendal, rennal,* -el. [f. KUN u + DALE.]

Rundel. *Obs.* exc. *dial.* Also 6–7 *rundel.*

† Rundel[e. *Her.* — ROUNDEL 2 (b, c, d).

† Rundelet, Rundlet, etc. ...

Rundle (rɒ·nd'l). Also 4–7 (9 *dial.*) *rundel,* 6–7 *rundell,* 9 *dial.* -el. [var. of ROUNDLE.]

Rundle[2. Now *dial.* Also 6–7 *rundel.*

† Bundle 3. *Obs. rare.* — 1 *roundele, rundelis,* 6 *roundelles,* 7 *rundell.*

† Rundled, *ppl. a.* *Obs.*

Rundlet, rundele. See ROUNDLET.

Run-down, *ppl. a.* [RUN 2.]
1. Downtrodden, oppressed. *rare*−1.

† Rune 1. *Obs.* Forms: 1, 4 *ryne, rene.* 2 *rine,* 3 *rune.* [Com. Teut. ...]

Rune 2, obs. form of ROON.

† Runer. *Obs.* A writer of runes.

Rune (rūn). [In origin the same word as ROUN, mystery, etc., but in sense 1 adopted in the 17th cent. (through Danish writers on Northern antiquities) from ON. and Icel. *rún*, pl. *rúnar* ...

1. A letter or character of the earliest Teutonic alphabet ...

The original runic alphabet dates from at least the second or third century, and was formed by modifying the letters of the Roman or Greek alphabet so as to adapt them to hard wood or stone.

2. A Finnish poem, or division of a poem, of Kalevala. Also incorrectly applied to old Scandinavian poems.

3. *attrib.* and *Comb.,* as *Rune-stone,* ... *Rune-carver,* -*carver,* -*rister* (= cutter), -*writer* ; *rune-bearing adj.* ...

Hence **Run-down-able** ... **Run-down-ness** ...

Rune-staff. Also 8 *runstaff.* [f. RUNE *sb.*2 + STAFF.] A runic calendar or clog-almanac.

Runes-taves. Now only *Hist.*

Rune-stave. *Obs.*

Rung, *ppl. a.* [f. RING v.1]
1. Having a ring inserted in the nose. **b.** Ring-necked.

Rung, *ppl. a.2* [f. RING v.2] Made to ring or resound.

Runge (rɒndʒ). 16. *dial.* Also 9 *ronge.* [Of obscure origin.] A kind of tub (cf. RINGE *sb.* and PLASKET 1 d).

Rung (rɒŋ), *sb.* [Com. Teut. Forms: 1 *hrung,* 5– *rung* (7 *wrong*), 2 *roung,* 4, 6 *ronge,* etc.]

1. A stout stick of a rounded form, *esp.* one used as a rail (in a cart, etc.), cross-bar, or spoke.

2. *†a.* An incantation or charm denoted by magic signs. *Obs.*

Rung-head. *Shipbuilding.* *Obs.*

† Runian. *Obs. rare.* (See quot.)

† Runic, *a.* and *sb.* ...
A. *adj.* **1.** Consisting of runes.
2. Carved or written in runes; — etc.

Runie-like ...

Runish (rū·niʃ), *a.* *Obs.* [var. RENISH *a.*] Fierce, violent, rough.

Runkle (rɒŋk'l), *sb.* *Obs.* exc. *north.* Forms: 1 *runcle,* 7 *runkle,* *runckle,* 9 *runkle,* 6 *runkle,* dim. of *rukka,* ON. *hrukka* (see RUCK *sb.*2)] A wrinkle, crease.

Runkle (rɒŋk'l), *v.* *Obs.* exc. *north.* [f. prec. *sb.*] *trans.* To wrinkle, rumple.

Runkled (rɒŋk'ld), *ppl. a.* *north.* Wrinkled, rumpled.

Runkly (rɒŋkli), *a.* *Obs.* exc. *dial.* Also 6–9 *runkly.* Full of wrinkles; rumpled.

† Runlet 1. *(rɒ·nlet).* *Obs.* [var. RUNDLET.] **1.** Forms: ...

† Runlet 2. *(rɒ·nlet).* *Obs.* Now only *dial.* A small run or stream; a runnel.

Runnable (rɒ·nab'l), *a.* Of deer: Proper for the chase; warrantable.

Runnel (rɒ·nel), *sb.* Also 6–7 *runnel,* 7 *rundle,* etc. A small stream of water; a brook, rivulet, rill, or trickle.

Runner (rɒnə·). Forms: 1 *iornere,* *irnere* ; ... [f. RUN v. + -ER 1.]

1. One who, or that which, runs; a runner.

II. 9. *a.* A strainer.

Supplement, p. 3873; Corrigenda, p. 4092; Spurious words, p. 4093; Books quoted, p. 4094

Runner-up. A dog that takes the second prize, losing only the final course to the winner.

Runnet. Now *dial.* Also *5-6* runnett, *9* rennet. Var. of RENNET *sb.*

† Runnet *Obs. rare.* Also *-ett.* [f. RUN *v.*]

Runnet, obs. variant of RENNET *sb.*

Running (rvˈniŋ), *vbl. sb.* [f. RUN *v.* + -ING 1.] **I.** The action of the vb. RUN (in sense 1): rapid motion on foot; racing; an instance of this.

Running (rvˈniŋ), *ppl. a.* [f. RUN *v.* + -ING 2.]

I. Of water, streams, etc.: Flowing.

Runo-, comb. form of mod.L. *runa* RUNE, used in a few forms, as **Runogra·phic** *a.*, pertaining to runic writing; **Runo·logist,** one versed in runology; **Runo·logy,** the study or science of runes.

Run-off. [RUN *v.* + OFF.] Also *attrib.*

Runrig (rvnˈrig). *Sc.* Also **rynrig, -rig, 6 ryndge, 6-9 runrig, rin-, run-ridge.** [f. RUN *v.* + RIG *sb.*]

A ridge of land lying among others held by joint tenants, *etc.*

landis callit the fourt rinrig of the Sandy hill. 1875 *Sc. Acts* XII. Index s.v., The heritors may apply..for division of the run-rigs according to their respective interests.

2. A form of land-tenure, = RUNDALE 1.

a 1583 SIR J. BALFOUR *Practicks* (1754) 536 Landis lyand togidder in rin-rig, and swa pertenand and occupyit be divers and sindrie persounis. 1733 P. LINDSAY *Interest Scot.* 47 The arable Land or Grounds for Tillage are divided by Runrig equally amongst them. 1791 NEWTE *Tour Eng. & Scot.* 239 Every tenant should have his farm, not in the way of runrigg, but by itself. 1845 MCCULLOCH *Acc. Brit. Empire* (1854) I. 287 Several of the landlords..having..divided the lands held in common, or in run-rig, into separate possessions. 1880 CARMICHAEL in Skene *Celtic Scotl.* III. 379 In Uist and Barra the arable land is divided, in part into crofts, and in part worked in runrig.

3. As *adv.* In separate ridges cultivated by different occupiers.

1695 *Sc. Acts* IX. 421/1 Act anent Lands lying Run-rig. 1751 MCDOUALL *Inst. Laws Scot.* I. 220 The possession of lands lying run-rig..is most prejudicial to the policy of the nation. 1814 SCOTT *Diary* 4 Aug., There are several obstacles to improvement, chiefly the undivided state of the properties, which lie run-rig.

4. *attrib.* Held or characterized by this mode of tenure.

1751 MCDOUALL *Inst. Laws Scot.* I. 220 Lands are run-rig, where one heritor has one ridge or rig, and another the second, and so on interchangeably over the whole parcel of land. 1765–8 ERSKINE *Inst. Law Scot.* III. iii. § 59 The division competent to landholders..is not in practice confined to runrig lands in a strict sense of the word. 1792 *Stat. Acc. Scot.* III. 217 This runrig disposition of lands in Scotland. 1805 BARRY *Orkney* (1808) 356 Unless these commons be divided, and runrig possessions abolished, agricultural improvements are impracticable. 1874 *Act* 37 & 38 *Vict.* c. 94 § 35 A decree of division of commonty or of common property or runrig lands. 1880 CARMICHAEL in Skene *Celtic Scotl.* III. 382 A wet or a dry season affects..the tenant of the combined system more than the tenant of the runrig system.

Hence **Ru·nrigged** *ppl. a.*, portioned out on the runrig system.

1683 M. MACKAIL *Orkney* in MacFarlane *Geogr. Collect.* (S.H.S.) III. 1 The Earles and Bishops lands were runrig'd through Orkney and Shetland. 1765 *Forfeited Est. Papers* (S. H. S.) 71 To measuring the runrigged lands on the Lovat estate. 1805 FORSYTH *Beauties Scotl.* II. 443 [The land] was often run-rigged or mixed property.

Runsh, obs. variant of RUNCH.

† **Runsik,** obs form of RANSACK *v.*

c 1470 HENRY *Wallace* VII. 120 My witt vnabill is To runsik [*v.r.* ransik] sic, for dreid I say off myss.

Runsy, obs. form of ROUNCY.

Runt (rɒnt), *sb.* Also 6 **ront(e, 7 runte.** [Of obscure origin. It seems unlikely that sense 2 is at all connected with MDu. *runt* (Du. *rund*) ox.]

1. An old or decayed stump of a tree. Also *attrib.*, as *runt-tree, -wood*, and *fig.* (quot. *a* 1585). Now *dial.*

1501 DOUGLAS *Pal. Hon.* I. iii, Not throw the soyl bot muskane treis sproutit,..Auld rottin runtis quhairin na sap was leifit. *a* 1585 POLWART *Flyting w. Montgomerie* 789 Iock Blunt, deid runt! I sall dunt whill I slay thee. 1601 HOLLAND *Pliny* XVI. xxxix. I. 480 Neither yong poles nor old runts are fit for durable building. 1603 — *Plutarch* 399 Like unto old runt-trees or dodils, which repining as it were at others, do manifestly hinder and take away the spring and growth of young poles and plants which come up under them, or grow neere about them. 1710 *Tusser Redivivus* in *Tusser's Husb.* (1878) 78 Few Pollards perish for want of it [lopping], but Runt-wood will. 1841 HARTSHORNE *Shropsh. Gloss.* 552 *Runts*, decayed stumps of trees.

b. *Sc.* and *north.* A hardened stem or stalk of a plant, *esp.* of a cabbage (cf. *kale-runt*, KALE 3).

1785 BURNS *Halloween* iv, Poor hav'rel Will..pow't, for want o' better shift, A runt was like a sow-tail Sae bow't that night. 1786 — *Ordination* vi, Lapfu's large o' gospel kail..An' runts o' grace. 1807–10 TANNAHILL *Poems* (1846) 117 They got naething for crowdy, but runts boiled to sowdie. 1829 BROCKETT *N. C. Gloss.*

2. An ox or cow of a small breed or size, esp. one belonging to the small breeds characteristic of Wales and the Highlands of Scotland.

1549 *Act* 3 & 4 *Edw. VI*, c. 19 § 1 Any manner of Oxen, Steres, Rontes, Kyen, Heighfers or Calves. 1579 SPENSER *Sheph. Cal.* Feb. 5 My ragged rontes all shiver and shake, As doen high Towers in an earthquake. 1620 MIDDLETON *Chaste Maid* IV. i, She's full of cattle, some two thousand runts. 1649 BLITHE *Eng. Improv. Impr.* (1652) 184 That year may put up three midling Runts upon an Acre and feed them up. 1700 J. BROME *Trav.* I. (1707) 23 Multitudes of Oxen, which they call Runts. 1768 PENNANT *Brit. Zool.* I. 18 The Welsh runts are much larger: the black cattle of Cornwall are of the same size with the last. 1825 COBBETT *Rur. Rides* 253 The cattle here are chiefly Welsh, black and called runts. 1847 W. C. L. MARTIN *Ox* 100/1 From the midland and western counties, 230 Herefords, runts, Devons, &c. 1886 *Daily News* 14 Dec. 2/5 Welsh Runts were in good force, and maintained a prominent rank in the exhibition.

attrib. 1884 *W. Sussex Gaz.* 25 Sept., 25 Scotch Cows and Heifers, 16 Runt Steers. 1886 *Daily News* 15 Sept. 2/4 Prime sides of English runt beef.

b. An old cow or ox. Now *dial.*

1638 LAUD *Wks.* (1857) VI. 538 Your hung beef..was..as hard as the very horn the old runt wore when she lived. 1808 JAMIESON. 1823 E. MOOR *Suffolk Wds.* 1877 *Cumb. Gloss.*

c. A small or inferior horse.

1725 *Portland Papers* (Hist. MSS. Comm.) VI. 90 We met a parcel of Scots horses..I should let them pass unremembered but for the extravagant value I thought they set upon one of their runts. 1895 *Westm. Gaz.* 7 Sept. 2/1 He ..drove a little ole runt that couldn't go seven mile a hour.

d. A small pig, esp. the smallest in a litter. *dial.* and *U.S.*

1841 HARTSHORNE *Shropsh. Gloss.* 552 *Runt, Runtling*, the smallest in a litter of pigs. 1886 *Cent. Mag.* XXXII. 107 While the runt is the weakest and most forlorn of pigs [etc.]. 1887 in *Kent. Gloss.*

3. *transf.* **a.** An ignorant, uncouth, or uncultivated person.

1614 B. JONSON *Barth. Fair* IV. vi, Sir, you are a welsh Cuckold, and a prating Runt, and no Constable. *a* 1658 CLEVELAND *Sir J. Presbyter* 24 Reforming Tweed Hath sent us Runts even of her Churches breed. 1719 D'URFEY *Pills* II. 77 Shone a Welch Runt, and Hans a Dutch Boor. 1723 MRS. CENTLIVRE *Artifice* III. i, This City spoils all Servants. I took a Welsh Runt last Spring. 1830 GLEIG *Country Curate* II. iii. 62 Things have come to a pretty pass, when a set of beggarly Welsh runts use threats to their betters.

b. An old woman, esp. an ill-favoured or ill-conditioned one; a hag. Now *Sc.* or *dial.*

a 1652 BROME *Eng. Moor* III. iii, Sure some old runt with a splay-foot hath crost him. 1676 COLES *Eng.-Lat. Dict.*, An old runt, *vetula*. 1769 *Herd's Songs* (1904) 159, I think the auld runt be gone mad. 1787 W. TAYLOR *Scot. Poems* 26 At last brave Jess..Did had Dad's hands, till the auld runt, Wi' boilin broe, John Ploughman brunt. 1823 E. MOOR *Suffolk Wds.*, *Runt*,..an ill-conditioned woman. *a* 1856 G. OUTRAM *Annuity* in *Lyrics* (1874), Catch the doited runt To ca' for her annuity. 1899 S. R. CROCKETT *Kit Kennedy* 40 The auld runt Babby is fell fond o' ye.

c. A person of low but thick-set build; a stunted or undersized person; a dwarf.

a 1700 *Dict. Cant. Crew*, *Runt*, a little, short, truss Man. 1828 CARR *Craven Gloss.*, *Runt*, a person of a strong though low stature. 1854 MISS BAKER *Northampt. Gloss.*, *Runt* or *Runty*, a dwarfish person; particularly a child stunted in its growth by short food or over work. 1890 L. C. D. D'OYLE *Notches* 65 My brother Bill..was a fine, tall fellow —not a little bit of a 'runt' like me.

d. A dwarfish or diminutive object.

1845 *Punch* VIII. 224 You work in that little runt of a garden of yours for half-an-hour or so before breakfast. 1873 CARLETON *Farm Ball.* 43 Takin' all the biggest apples, leavin' all the littlest runts. 1900 R. BARR *Unchanging East* 258 This insignificant runt of a Turkish steamer.

attrib. 1874 COUES *Birds N. W.* 36 In a large number examined, little 'runt' eggs are sometimes found.

4. a. A domestic pigeon of a breed characterized by size and stoutness of build, of which there are a number of varieties.

1661 WALTON *Angler* (ed. 3) iv. 73 Of the tame [pigeons] there be Cropers, Carryers, Runts. 1668 CHARLETON *Onomast.* 77 *Columbæ Russicæ*, Runts. 1725 *Fam. Dict.* s.v. *Pigeon*, Of Runts are different Sorts, one called Spanish Runts, generally of a Blood Red, or Mottled Colour. 1735 MOORE *Columb.* 44 There are other Sorts of Runts, as the Roman Runt.., and the Smyrna Runt. 1840 DICKENS *Barn. Rudge* i, The wheeling and circling flights of runts, fantails, tumblers, and pouters, were perhaps not quite consistent with the grave and sober character of the building. 1881 J. C. LYELL *Fancy Pigeons* 104 In appearance runts are like huge common pigeons.

attrib. and *Comb.* 1688 HOLME *Armoury* II. 244/1 The Runt Pigeon, or Russian Dove,..are large Pigeons as big as young Hens. 1854 MEALL *Moubray's Poultry* 249 In the head and bill the Archangel is very Runt-like. *Ibid.* 252 In size it would seem to be the smallest of the Runt family.

† **b.** A canary-bird over three years old. *Obs.*

a 1700 B. E. *Dict. Cant. Crew.* 1704 *Dict. Rust.* (1726) s.v. *Canary-birds*, The several Names of these Birds at different Times and Ages: Such as are above 3 years old are called Runts.

† **Runt,** *v. Obs.*[−1] In 5 **runte, ront.** [Cf. ARUNT *v.*] *trans.* To reprove, rate.

c 1440 CAPGR. *Life St. Kath.* III. 96 Euyr hys body wold he chyde & runte [*v.r.* ront]: 'What eylyth þe now?'

Ru·nted, *a. Obs.* exc. *dial.* [f. RUNT *sb.* + -ED[2].] Stunted in growth, undersized, dwarfish.

1681 *Lond. Gaz.* No. 1651/4 The other is a middle aged Runted Ox, all Black, his Horns turn a little round. 1783 BURNS *Mailie's Elegy* vi. (orig. text), She was nae get o' runted rams. 1879 MISS JACKSON *Shropsh. Wd.-Bk.*

Ru·ntish, *a.* [f. RUNT *sb.* + -ISH.]

1. Of animals: Stunted; dwarfish.

1641 BEST *Farm. Bks.* (Surtees) 5 These usually that fall to grasse over soone, proove short runtish sheepe. 1738 *Briton Described* 60 The Cattle, we saw most legible on their Mountains, were Goats and Heifers, a runtish Sort of Animals. 1805 R. W. DICKSON *Pract. Agric.* II. 1124 This same kind of runtish coarse breed continues all the way to the Frith of Forth.

† **2.** Like a runt (pigeon).

1765 *Treat. Dom. Pigeons* 137 It is of a runtish make, and has a gravel eye.

Hence † **Ru·ntishly** *adv. Obs.*

1735 J. MOORE *Columb.* 45 The Trumpeter is a bird much about the size of a Laugher, and very runtishly made.

Ru·nty, *a. U.S.* and *dial.* [f. RUNT *sb.*]

1. Dwarfish, undersized; small and ill-made; of low, thick-set build.

1807 W. IRVING *Salmagundi* (1824) 86 A trio of as odd, runty, mummy-looking originals as ever Hogarth fancied in his most happy moments. 1834 BURGON in Goulburn *Life* (1892) I. 81 These runty little thick-set Yorkshire men seem to consider me as a wild beast escaped from some show. 1891 T. N. PAGE *Ole Virginia* 42 Sometimes you see a weevly runty pig in a right good litter.

2. *dial.* Surly, ill-tempered, obstinate.

a 1825–66 in dial. glossaries (E. Anglia, Linc., Northampt.).

Run-up. [f. RUN *v.*]

1. The act of running up to a certain point; esp.

a. *Coursing.* The race between two greyhounds up to the first turn or wrench of the hare.

1834 THACKER *Courser's Comp.* I. 134 One dog is sometimes behind the other in the first run up to the hare. 1853 'STONEHENGE' *Greyhound* 358 The first cote constitutes what is sometimes called the run up, or speed to the hare. 1884 *Field* 6 Dec. (Cassell's), Pious Fraud scored the run-up from Alone.

b. The act of taking or sending a ball up to the goal or into a position for final play.

1897 *Outing* XXX. 484/1 Foster.., after a clean run from 'way down the field, puts the ball through the uprights... The excitement of the run-up has been intense. 1901 *Scotsman* 9 Sept. 4/7 Vardon, after being short in his run up, missed the hole for a 3.

2. *Bookbinding.* (See quot. 1875.) Also *attrib.*

1875 KNIGHT *Dict. Mech.* 2004/2 *Run-up*, a fillet-mark which runs from head to tail on the back, without mitering with the horizontal cross fillets on the panels. 1880 ZAEHNSDORF *Bookbinding* 131 With a 'run-up' back, the edge of the leather round the end papers is to..have a roll run round it in gold.

Runway (rɒ·nwēⁱ). Chiefly *U.S.* [f. RUN *v.*]

1. a. The customary track or run of an animal (*esp.* of deer) or a fish.

1873 *Forest & Stream* I. 178/2 We crossed the runway where the deer and pack had passed. 1894 *Outing* XXIV. 186/2 Sometimes we followed a 'runway' or deer's path for a distance, and then it was mostly easy going. *Ibid.* 453/1 After a minute's rest, to let him settle in his runway, I made a cast.

b. A place for fowls to run in.

1886 *Pall Mall G.* 27 Aug. 14/1 The incubators, hatching houses, brooding houses and runways have a capacity to keep 5,000 eggs in process of hatching all the time.

c. A running-path.

1889 *Pall Mall G.* 19 Jan. 7/1 The field [in baseball] consists of a continuous runway of clay-covered paths.

2. Any artificial (sloping or horizontal) track or gangway made for convenience of passage or carriage.

1888 *Scribner's Mag.* Oct. 444 If there is a 'runway', which is an elevation like the rocky ascent in the second act of Die Walküre.., it is 'built' by the stage-carpenters.

3. A groove in which anything slides, *esp.* one of the grooves in the casing of a sash-window.

1890 in *Cent. Dict.* 1900 R. BARR *Unchanging East* 309 Its runway was so smooth..that a man of ordinary strength could roll it backward and forward.

4. The bed or channel in which a stream runs.

1879 in WEBSTER *Suppl.*

† **Runy,** *a. Obs. rare.* [Of doubtful origin: cf. RUNISH *a.*[2]] Fierce, furious.

c 1205 LAY. 1545 Corineus heom rasde to, swa þe runie [*c* 1275 wilde] wulf. *Ibid.* 20123 Arður..gon to rusien swa þe runie [*c* 1275 wode] wulf.

† **Ruoken,** *v. Obs.*[−1] [Cf. note to ROCK *v.*[1] 5 b.] *trans.* ? To clean by rubbing.

c 1205 LAY. 22287 Heo ruokeden burnen [*c* 1275 hii rollede wepne]; bonneden helmes.

Rupee (rūpī·). Forms: α. 7 **rupia**, 7–8 **ropia**, 8 **roupia**; 7 (9) **rupeia**. β. 7 **roopee, rowpee, roupy**, 7–8 **roupie**; 7 **rupeye, rupie**, 7– **rupee**. [ad. Urdū روپيه *rūpiyah*, f. Skr. *rūpya* wrought silver.] The monetary unit of India, represented by a silver coin now valued at 1*s.* 4*d.*

The silver rupee was introduced by Shir Shah in 1542, and varied in weight at different times and places between 170 and 192 grains; from 1836 the weight in British India has been 180 grains, but the value has diminished considerably since 1875. A slightly heavier rupee was in use in Bengal: see SICCA. The gold rupee mentioned in quot. 1678 is properly called a MOHUR.

α. 1612 N. WITHINGTON *Trav.* (1735) 289 Givinge mee 200 Rupeias, everye Rupie containinge 2*s.* 6*d.* 1613 PURCHAS *Pilgrimage* V. xvii. (1614) 544 The Kings reuenue of his Crown-land is fiftie Crou of Rupias. 1665 *Phil. Trans.* I. 104 They now sell us a Maon of 6 pounds for two Rupias. 1704 *Collect. Voy.* (Churchill) III. 578/2, 1000 of them weigh not above 20 Ropias, and cost about 60 Ropias. 1728 CHAMBERS *Cycl.* s.v. *Money*, A Lacre of Roupias is a hundred thousand Roupias. [1841 ELPHINSTONE *Hist. Ind.* II. 245 Shír Sháh changed the name of tankha to that of rupeia, or rupee, which was adopted by Akber.]

β. 1615 SIR T. ROE *Jrnl.* Hakl Soc.) I. 95 *note*, A rupee is 2*s.* 3*d.* starling. 1638 SIR T. HERBERT *Trav.* (ed. 2) 62 Thirty, sometime twenty tack make one roopee; a roopee is two shillings three pence. 1678 J. PHILLIPS tr. *Tavernier's Trav.* II. 2 The Roupy of Gold weighs 2 Drams and a half, and 11 Grains, and is valued..at 14 Roupies of Silver. 1712 E. COOKE *Voy. S. Sea* 164 Forty Roupies to be allow'd James Stretton in India, as Smart-Money. 1761 *Ann. Reg., Hist.* 55 Sixteen roupies (half-crowns) had been paid for the flesh of a dog. 1842 BISCHOFF *Woollen Manuf.* II. 312 The usual price demanded for such a pair of shawls is 3000 rupees. 1893 SIR W. HUNTER *Ind. Empire* (ed. 3) 506 The rupee, which formerly was nearly equal to two shillings, has fallen to nearly fourteen pence.

attrib. 1727 A. HAMILTON *New Acc. E. Ind.* II. 42 Rupee Silver, which has no Alloy in it, will bear twenty eight per Cent. of Copper alloy. 1884 *St. James's Gaz.* 10 May 7/1 There was a sharp rise yesterday in rupee paper. 1887 *Pall Mall G.* 7 Nov. 11/1 The rupee prices in India of commodities exported to..England.

Rupelian (rupī·liăn), *a. Geol.* [a. F. *Rupelien*, f. *Rupel*, the name of a small tributary of the river Scheldt.] A division of the oligocene of Belgium, lying above the tongrian.

1852 *Jrnl. Geol. Soc.* VIII. 296 They [shells] are referred by M. Dumont to part of his Rupelian system. 1883 *Science* II. 16/1 The oligocene system shows two principal divisions

(tongrian, rupelian), which stretch across the lower part of the river Escaut.

† **Rupellary,** *a. Obs.*[−1] [irreg. f. L. *rūpes* rock.] Rocky.

a 1700 EVELYN *Diary* 27 Feb. 1644, In this rupellary nidary do the fowle lay eggs and breede.

Rupert's drop, metal: see DROP *sb.* 10 h, and PRINCE *sb.* 12.

Rupestral (rupe·străl), *a.* [f. mod.L. *rupestris*, f. L. *rūpes* rock + -AL.] Growing on rocks.

1847 H. C. WATSON *Cybele Brit.* I. 340 Native. Rupestral and Pascual. Frequent on the Highland mountains. 1854 J. H. BALFOUR *Outl. Bot.* 527 Rupestral and mural plants are those found on rocks and walls, such as species of Saxifrage, Sedum, Draba,..Lichens and Mosses.

So **Rupe·strean, Rupe·strine,** *adjs.*

1786 ABERCROMBIE *Arr.* in *Gard. Assist.* 66 Rupestrean or rock stone-crop sedum. 1890 *Cent. Dict.*, *Rupestrine*, rock-inhabiting; living or growing on or among rocks.

‖ **Rupia** (rū·piă). *Path.* [mod.L. (Bateman), f. Gr. ῥύπος dirt, filth.] A skin disease characterized by an eruption of broad, flattish, scattered vesicles, succeeded by thick ulcerating scabs.

Good *Study Med.* (1822) points out that the spelling *rhypia* would have been more in accordance with analogy. 1815 BATEMAN *Delin. Cutaneous Dis.* Pref. p. v, With the exception of the representations of Impetigo, Porrigo,.. Rupia [etc.]. 1834 *Cycl. Pract. Med.* III. 632 Rupia may be considered as altogether a constitutional affection, being only seen in the aged, or..debilitated. 1878 T. BRYANT *Pract. Surg.* I. 27 Constitutional sores..originating in some ulcerating skin eruption, such as ecthyma or rupia.

Hence **Ru·pial** *a.*, pertaining to, of the nature of, affected with, rupia.

1861 BUMSTEAD *Ven. Dis.* (1879) 541 The small rupial eruption begins either about the face or on the inner and outer surface of the forearms. 1879 *St. George's Hosp. Rep.* IX. 603 On the left shin he had a rupial sore.

‖ **Rupica·pra.** *Zool.* [L., f. *rūpes* rock + *capra* she-goat.] The chamois (*Rupicapra tragus*).

1693 SIR T. P. BLOUNT *Nat. Hist.* 385 Some beasts and birds we find live upon the highest tops of the Alps,..as the Ibex, and Rupicapra, or Chamois. 1728 CHAMBERS *Cycl.*, *Chamois Leather*..is prepar'd from the Skin of the Chamois, a kind of Rupi-Capra, or wild Goat.

Hence **Rupica·prine** *a.*

1827 GRIFFITH tr. *Cuvier* IV. 281 The Rupicaprine Group. 1876 *Encycl. Brit.* V. 384/1 The only Antelope found in Western Europe, and..the type of the Rupicaprine or goatlike group of that family. 1891 FLOWER & LYDEKKER *Mamm.* 349 Rupicaprine section [of the Bovidæ].

Rupi·coline, -colous, *adjs.* (See quots.)

1858 MAYNE *Expos. Lex.*, *Rupicolus*, living in or among rocks..: rupicolous. 1890 *Cent. Dict.*, *Rupicoline*,..rock-inhabiting; growing on rocks; living among rocks.

Rupi·tic, *a. Path. rare*[−1]. [irreg. f. RUPIA.] Pertaining to, characterized by, rupia.

1878 HAMILTON *Nerv. Dis.* 38 There were three rupitic phlegma on the head, each of which contained a little pus.

Rupo·graphy. *rare.* [f. G ῥύπος sealing-wax: see -GRAPHY.] The art of taking an impression of a coin or medal upon sealing-wax. Hence **Rupogra·phical** *a.*

1838 *Jrnl. Asiat. Soc. Bengal* VII. 415 As a first specimen, then, of the capabilities of this art of rupography I select a coin, or rather medal [etc.]. *Ibid.*, The rupographical process may be safely confined to the first stage, or simple impression on sealing-wax.

Rupontike, obs. form of RHAPONTIC.

Rupt, obs. form of RUT *sb.*[2]

† **Rupt,** *v. Obs.*[−1] [f. L. *rupt-*, ppl. stem of *rumpĕre* to break.] *trans.* To break, nullify.

1726 AYLIFFE *Parergon* 32 When the Will which he has made is rupted and made void by the Birth of a Posthumous Issue.

† **Ru·ptic,** *a. Obs.*[−1] [f. as prec. + -IC.] Breaking; causing (a sore) to break.

1541 R. COPLAND *Guydon's Quest. Chirurg.* O iij b, Whose operacions..appereth afterward as they that be made with brenning or ruptycke medecines.

Ru·ptile, *a.* Now *Bot.* [ad. mod.L. *ruptilis* or F. *ruptile*: cf. prec. and -ILE.] (See quots.)

1721 BAILEY, *Ruptile*, easy to be broken. 1858 MAYNE *Expos. Lex.*, *Ruptilis*, applied to an organ that..opens in an irregular manner by the enlargement of the parts it contains..: ruptile. 1866 *Treas. Bot.* 999/1 *Ruptile*, bursting irregularly, not in the line of union of parts in cohesion.

Ruption (rɒ·pʃən). Now *rare.* Also 5 rupcioun, 6 -cyon, -tioun. [ad. obs. F. *ruption*, or late L. *ruptio*, noun of action f. *rumpĕre* to break.]

1. Breach of the peace; disturbance. *rare.*

1483 in *Lett. Rich. III & Hen. VII* (Rolls) I. 51 How beit that oft tyme afore certain rupcioun, breke and distroblaunce, has been betwixt the realmes of Ingland and Scotland. 1893 HESLOP *Northumbld. Gloss.* s.v. *Ruction*, *Ruption*, a turmoil, as in cleaning; a disturbance, a row.

2. Breaking or rupture of some membrane or tissue of the animal body.

1541 R. COPLAND *Galyen's Terap.* 2 A ij b, The solution of contynuyte..commeth most often with concussyon and ruption. 1578 BANISTER *Hist. Man* V. 80 Membrans, and Fibers, toughe..and able, not in prompt to euery ruption. 1655 CULPEPPER, etc. *Riverius* II. v. 74 The Tunicle..is obnoxious to divers diseases, and especially to Ruption, Distortion, Dilatation, and Constriction. 1676 *Phil. Trans.* XI. 607, I found..I could easily enough unravel that cluster to a considerable length,..before ruption. 1855 HALIBURTON *Nature & Human Nat.* (1902) 218 You can't cure it, for it's a ruption of an air vessel, and you can't get at it to sew it up.

fig. 1650 ELDERFIELD *Civ. Right Tythes* 343 When mens greedy affections are also checked, their lusts crossed, and their tender ruptions touched to danger of offence.

Ru·ptive, *a. rare.* [f. L. *rupt-* (cf. next) + -IVE.] Causing, or tending to cause, breaking.

c 1425 tr. *Arderne's Surgery* (E.E.T.S.) 83 Witte þou þat auripigment is desiccatyue,..ruptyue and cauteriatyue. *a* 1890 *Engineer* LXIX. 492 (Cent.), The action of a torsional ruptive force on rounding curves.

† **Ru·ptor.** *Obs. rare.* [a. L. *ruptor*, agent-noun f. *rumpĕre* to break.] (See quot.)

1656 BLOUNT *Glossogr.*, *Ruptor*, a breaker or tearer in peeces, a destroyer, he that violates.

† **Ru·ptory,** *sb. Med. Obs.* [ad. med.L. *ruptōrium*: cf. prec. and -ORY. So obs. F. *ruptoire*, Sp. and Pg. *ruptorio*, It. *rottorio*.] An application which causes a swelling to come to a head and break.

c 1400 *Lanfranc's Cirurg.* 292 Manye lewid lechis haue I seen þat coude on ruptorie, & þei supposide..bi þis maner ruptorie for to surmounte Galien in worchinge. *c* 1425 tr. *Arderne's Surgery* (E.E.T.S.) 14 Þer shewed ane bolnyng vnderneþe,..whiche I opned wiþ a ruptorie. 1544 PHAER *Pestilence* (1553) P j, Some..breake the forsaid botche with a strong ruptorie. 1597 A. M. tr. *Guillemeau's Fr. Chirurg.* 42/1 To prævent that the *Escara* of the cauteryes or ruptoryes be not to harde. 1603 LODGE *Treat. Plague* (Hunterian Cl.) 68 Insteed of the actuall cautery.. you must proceede with familiar ruptories, of which the best is that which is made of ashes and quicke lime boyled together. 1684 tr. *Bonet's Merc. Compit.* XII. 388 Then apply the Ruptory..till all the superfluous flesh be consumed. *c* 1720 W. GIBSON *Farrier's Guide* II. (1738) 121 The same author also recommends the use of *Retoires* or Ruptories.

So † **Ru·ptory** *a. Obs. rare.* [Cf. obs. F. *oingnement ruptoire.*]

c 1425 tr. *Arderne's Surgery* (E.E.T.S.) 14, I putte on his testiculez oon oyntement ruptorye. *c* 1720 W. GIBSON *Farrier's Dispens.* II. (1734) 91 It has the effect of a..Ruptory plaister without any considerable swelling.

Ru·pturable, *a.* [f. RUPTURE *v.* + -ABLE.] Capable of being ruptured or broken.

1898 W. JAMES *Human Immortality* 35 The veil of nature can grow thin and rupturable enough for such effects to occur.

Rupture (rɒ·ptiŭı), *sb.* Also 5 ruptur, 6 *Sc.* ruptor. [a. F. *rupture*, or ad. L. *ruptūra*, f. *rupt-*, ppl. stem of *rumpĕre* to break: see -URE.]

1. † **a.** Breach *of* a covenant, intercourse, or the peace. *Obs.*

1481 *Coventry Leet Bk.* 475 Wherby the seid trewes & other conuencions..myght fall in vyolacion or Ruptur in any wyse. 1496 *11th Rep. Hist. MSS. Comm.* App. III. 13 His requeste for to have..entrecours of merchandise..is gretly to our honour seing that the ruptur and discontinuaunce therof hathe not stand by us. 1535 *Act 27 Hen. VIII* c. 5 § 1 Manifolde robberies,..ruptures of his peace & many other malfaites. 1551 *Reg. Privy Council Scot.* I. 118 Providing alwayis that the said Lord do, nor procure to be done,..that may tend to the ruptor of the peace. *c* 1645 HOWELL *Lett.* I. IV. xxvii, Which was promis'd upon the rupture of the Treaties with Spain.

b. A breach of harmony or friendly relations between two persons or parties.

1583 STUBBES *Anat. Abus.* II. (1882) 115 Making schismes, ruptures, breaches, and factions in the church of God. *c* 1645 HOWELL *Lett.* I. III. xxvii, For we that have business to negotiate here are like to suffer much by this rupture. 1674 *Essex Papers* (Camden) I. 236 Who have declared a war..by open Acts of Hostilitie; and also those of Algier, Tripoly, and Tunis have offered faire for a Rupture. 1759 ROBERTSON *Hist. Scot.* VI. Wks. 1813 I. 461 This rupture contributed..to render the Duke still more odious to the nation. 1788 H. WALPOLE *Reminis.* vii. (1818) 50 She was safe while under the royal roof, even after the rupture between the king and prince. 1838 PRESCOTT *Ferd. & Is.* (1846) II. xviii. 164 He at first threw out hints of an immediate rupture. *a* 1862 BUCKLE *Civiliz.* (1869) III. ii. 93 The rupture between Church and State was now complete.

Comb. 1810 CRABBE *Borough* VI. 90 The litigious rupture-stirring race; Who to contention as to trade are led.

† **c.** Breach of continuity; interruption. *Obs.*

1639 FULLER *Holy War* I. xxiii, Some eminent particulars ..which constant tradition without rupture hath entailed on Posteritie. 1640 LD. DIGBY in Rushw. *Hist. Coll.* (1692) III. 147 A truer cause than the Ruptures and Intermission of Parliaments.

† **d.** The act of breaking out *into* arms. *Obs.*

1647 CLARENDON *Hist. Reb.* V. § 91 [He] believed..that the preserving that Magazine..would likewise prevent any possible rupture into Armes.

2. *Path.* Abdominal hernia; a case of this.

1539 ELYOT *Cast. Helthe* 49 b, Than shal ensue to hym that exerciseth, no peryll of obstruction or rupture. 1581 MULCASTER *Positions* XV. (1887) 69 The holding of ones breath vnadvisedly and with to much strayning causeth ruptures. 1615 CROOKE *Body of Man* 79 Which inward membrane if it be broken, and the externall dilated,.. causeth the one kinde of rupture or the other. 1662 R. MATHEW *Unl. Alch.* 126 Who said, that he had been troubled with a Rupture for ten or eleven years. 1706–7 FARQUHAR *Beaux' Strat.* I. i, She cures rheumatisms, ruptures, and broken shins in men. 1796 STEDMAN *Surinam* (1813) II. xviii. 63 Two fine young officers arrived, unfit for service by ruptures. 1818 CANNING *Sp. Indemnity Bill* Speeches (1838) VI. 33 That he had been cured of a rupture at the public expense. 1880 *Encycl. Brit.* XI. 752/2 Rupture is either congenital or acquired. *Ibid.*, Ruptures are most frequent at the extremes of life.

b. *attrib.* and *Comb.*, as *rupture-cutter, -doctor, -quack, -surgeon.*

1654 WHITLOCK *Zootomia* 436 A rare Oculist, Operator, Stone, or Broke, or Rupture-cutter, &c. 1763 *Ann. Reg.* 57 Another trial..wherein a rupture surgeon was plaintiff. 1783 POTT *Chirurg. Wks.* II. 48 That positive assertion which all rupture-quacks make use of. *Ibid.* 65 *note*, Some of these rupture-doctors have been largely rewarded. *a* 1843 SOUTHEY *Comm.-pl. Bk.* (1851) IV. 589 There were itinerant rupture-surgeons.

3. † **a.** A break in a surface or substance, such as the skin, flesh, etc. *Obs.*

c 1550 H. LLOYD *Treas. Health* R iij, Agaynst the chopping or ruptures. The Causes. Muche goynge in cold wyndes and drynesse. 1607 ROWLANDS *Earl of Warwick* (Hunterian Cl.) 78 He lent him such a powerful stroke It made wide ruptures in the Giant's flesh. 1673–4 GREW *Anat. Pl.*, *Trunks* I. iii. 120 The Pith,..as the Plant grows up,..hath divers openings or Ruptures made in it.

b. A break in the surface of the earth, etc.; a ravine, chasm, gorge, rift.

1555 EDEN *Decades* (Arb.) 212 In the riuers or ruptures or breaches of water. 1594 GREENE & LODGE *Looking Gl.* G.'s Wks. (Rtldg.) 132 What..malevolent Conspiring power..Hath made the concave of the earth unclose, And shut in ruptures lovely Radagon? 1609 BIBLE (Douay) *Zech.* xiv. 4 The mount of olives shal be cloven..with a stiepe rupture exceding great. 1684 T. BURNET *Theory Earth* II. 50 At this chasm or rupture we suppose the fire wou'd gush out. 1703 MAUNDRELL *Journ. Jerus.* (1732) 142 There is a very great rupture in the side of Libanus. 1853 KANE *Grinnell Exp.* xxxvii. (1856) 344 The sea has dwindled to a narrow lane, flanked by the heavy hummocks, whose rupture formed the sides.

4. The act of breaking or bursting; the fact of being broken or burst.

1647 LILLY *Chr. Astrol.* xxxvi. 215 It's probable..your Water-course will be subject to ruptures or breaking downe of the Banks. 1667 MILTON *P. L.* VII. 419 The Egg that soon Bursting with kindly rupture forth disclos'd Thir callow young. 1731 ARBUTHNOT *Nat. of Aliments* (1735) 157 A Lute-string will bear a hundred Weight without Rupture. 1739 S. SHARPE *Surg.* 137 The Rupture of the Vessels of the Brain. 1799 KIRWAN *Geol. Ess.* 97 The rupture of the isthmus that joined Calais and Dover was probably effected by an earthquake at a later period. 1839 G. BIRD *Nat. Philos.* 276 A rapid succession of powerful currents being at each rupture of contact sent through the long coil. 1860 TYNDALL *Glac.* I. vi. 44 The rupture of the ice by the expansion of the air-bubbles. 1878 T. BRYANT *Pract. Surg.* I. 607 Rupture of the diaphragm is an accident that occurs in practice, but difficult to diagnose.

fig. 1642 FULLER *Holy & Prof. St.* III. i. 153 If with feasting him thou breakest thyself, he will not cure thy rupture. 1648 BOYLE *Seraph. Love* xi. (1700) 63 The glad Heart..to make room for such Guests, would stretch unto a Rupture. 1745 *De Foe's Eng. Tradesm.* (1841) I. vii. 46 Nor can a man be supposed, in the rupture of his affairs, to receive any comfort.

Rupture (rɒ·ptiŭı), *v.* [f. prec.]

1. *trans.* **a.** To break, burst (a vessel, membrane, etc.).

1739 S. SHARPE *Surg.* 136 [If] the Vessels of the Brain and Membranes..are ruptur'd, they absorb the extravasated Blood again. 1797 M. BAILLIE *Morb. Anat.* (1807) 446 The vessels of the brain under such circumstances of disease, are much more liable to be ruptured than in a healthy state. 1834 J. FORBES *Laennec's Dis. Chest* (ed. 4) 143 We observe..that some of the cells are simply dilated, while others are ruptured. 1875 DARWIN *Insectiv. Pl.* iii. 57 Here and there a few cells both in the glands and in the pedicels had escaped being ruptured.

b. To cause a breach of; to sever.

1854 MRS. JAMESON *Comm. Pl. Book* 256 The first [marriage], though perhaps unhappy or early ruptured. 1869 GOULBOURN *Purs. Holiness* vi. 53 My filial relationship to Him cannot be ruptured by my sin.

c. To affect (a person) with hernia.

1818 [see RUPTURED *ppl. a.* 2]. 1907 *Westm. Gaz.* 15 July 3/2 A printer..stated that he had been put in irons and had been thereby ruptured.

2. *intr.* To suffer a break or rupture.

1863 SPENCER *Ess.* II. 25 *note*, Instead of a nebulous ring rupturing at one point and collapsing into a single mass. 1876 BRISTOWE *Theory & Pract. Med.* (1878) 556 Aneurysms ..are very apt to rupture at an early period into the pericardial cavity.

Ru·ptured, *ppl. a.* [f. prec. + -ED[1].]

1. Broken, burst.

1747 tr. *Astruc's Fevers* 292 The heat may be so great, as to..form a scab or crust on these ruptured pustules. 1813 J. THOMSON *Lect. Inflam.* 209 Fractured, torn, or ruptured surfaces. 1860 MOTLEY *Netherl.* V. I. 163 The patriots.. now erected a sconce..upon the ruptured dyke of Borght. 1887 D. MAGUIRE *Art Massage* iii. (ed. 4) 44, I will treat of ruptured tumours while on therapeutics.

2. Affected with rupture or hernia.

1818 CANNING *Sp. Indemnity Bill* Speeches (1838) VI. 32 With all the pomp of eloquence..was introduced, the revered and ruptured Ogden.

Ru·pturewort. *Bot.* [f. RUPTURE *sb.* 2.]

1. A plant of the genus *Herniaria*, esp. *Herniaria glabra*, formerly supposed to be efficacious in curing rupture or hernia.

1597 GERARDE *Herbal* II. clxxii. 569 A kind of knot grasse called Rupture Woorte. 1611 COTGR., *Boutonnet*, Rupturewort, Burstwort. 1671 SALMON *Syn. Med.* III. xxii. 403 *Herniaria Millegrana*, Rupture-wort,.. cures Ruptures, the Jaundies, Fluxes. 1713 *Phil. Trans.* XXVIII. 35 This seems to differ from the common hairy Rupture-wort, in having more twiggy Branches. 1775 J. JENKINSON tr. *Linnæus' Brit. Pl.* 38 Smooth Rupturewort. Found in gravelly places. *Ibid.*, Rough or hairy Rupturewort. In gravelly places, but not common. 1828 SIR J. E. SMITH *Eng. Flora* II. 8–9. 1848 JOHNS *Week at Lizard* 304 *Herniaria glabra*, variety *subciliata*, Fringed Rupturewort,..is a plant peculiar to the district. 1866 *Treas. Bot.*

2. (See quots.)

1760 J. LEE *Introd. Bot.* App. 325 Rupture-wort, Least,

Linum. 1777 JACOB *Catal. Plants* 92 *Linum Radiola*... The least Rupture-wort, or All-seed.

3. A West Indian plant (see quot.).

1864 GRISEBACH *Flora Brit. W. Ind.*, Colonial Names 787/1 Rupture-wort, *Alternanthera polygonoides*.

Ru·pturing, *vbl. sb. Bot.* [f. RUPTURE *v.* + -ING[1].] (See quot. 1839.)

1839 LINDLEY *Introd. Bot.* 226 Rupturing consists in a spontaneous contraction of a portion of the pericarp, by which its texture is broken through. 1862 DARWIN *Orchids* i. 12, I will not affirm that the rupturing of the exterior membrane of the rostellum takes place spontaneously.

Rural (rū·răl), *a.* and *sb.* Also 5 **rurale**, 5–7 **rurall**, 6 **-ell.** [a. F. *rural, -ale* (14th cent.), or ad. L. *rūrāl-is*, f. *rūr-*, *rūs* country: cf. RUSTIC *a.*]

In early examples there is usually little or no difference between the meanings of *rural* and *rustic*, but in later use the tendency is to employ *rural* when the idea of locality (country scenes, etc.) is prominent, and *rustic* when there is a suggestion of the more primitive qualities or manners naturally attaching to country life.

A. *adj.* **1.** Of persons: Living in the country; having the standing, qualities, or manners of peasants or country-folk; engaged in country occupations; agricultural or pastoral.

1412–20 LYDG. *Chron. Troy* (E. E. T. S.) 618 Ful likly is þat al þe gentil blood Þoruȝ-out þe world shal distroied be; And rural folke..Shal han lordshipe & holy gouernaunce. 1430–40 — *Bochas* IV. xv. (MS. Bodl. 263), Agothodus of berthe ful rurall Promooted was vnto estat roiall. *c* 1480 *St. Ursula* (Roxb.) A vij, The rurall rebelles aspyed her with her spouse. 1509 BARCLAY *Shyp of Folys* (1570) 152 A rurall man, rude and of simplicitie. 1547 BOORDE *Introd. Knowl.* v. (1870) 140 They do dyffer..as well in theyr apparel as in theyr maners, for they be rurall and rusticall. 1606 SHAKS. *Ant. & Cl.* V. II. 233 Heere is a rurall Fellow, That will not be deny'de your Highnesse presence. 1697 DRYDEN *Virg. Georg.* I. 11 Ye Fawns, propitious to the rural Swains, Join in my Work. 1784 COWPER *Task* I. 281 Not all its pride secures The grand retreat from injuries impress'd By rural carvers. 1837 LOCKHART *Scott* I. ii. 76 It was a system which bound together the various classes of the rural population in bonds of mutual love and confidence. 1876 MISS BRADDON *J. Haggard's Dau.* II. 16 Perhaps to keep company—odious phrase—with some rural swain.

absol. 1611 SPEED *Hist. Gt. Brit.* IX. xix. (1632) 931 Hee lulled the rural to thinke that his like had neuer raigned in England.

b. Presiding over, haunting, the country. *rare*[−1].

1582 STANYHURST *Æneis* III. (Arb.) 71 Thee sweete Nymphs rural I woorshipt.

c. Applied to a moth (see quot.).

1832 J. RENNIE *Butterfl. & M.* 53 The Rural Dart.. appears in August...Huntingdonshire and Kent.

2. a. *Rural dean, deanery*: (see DEAN[1] 5).

c 1450 HOLLAND *Howlat* 809 The dene rurale, the Ravyn, reprovit him than. 1534 *Const. Provinc.* 2, 3 deanes rurall. *c* 1628 in Foley *Rec. Eng. Prov. S. J.* I. i. 137 Vicaires Generalis,..deanes, archdeacons, rurall deanes. 1642 SIR E. DERING *Sp. on Relig.* 91 The rurall Deanery. 1697–1765 [see DEAN[1] 5]. 1867 TROLLOPE *Chron. Barset* xlvii, Such a preliminary inquiry..need not be done by the rural dean at all. *Ibid.*, You will select two [clergymen] yourself out of your rural deanery.

b. Employed or stationed in country districts.

1840 BARHAM *Ingol. Leg.* Ser. I. *Bagman's Dog*, It's your uncle, or one of the 'Rural Policemen'. 1870 E. PEACOCK *Ralf Skirl.* III. 142 There were no rural messengers in those days.

3. Of or pertaining to, characteristic of, peasants or country-folk; rustic.

1513 DOUGLAS *Æneis* I. Prol. 316 And ȝit persaif I wele, be my consait, The king of poetis ganis nocht for rurale estait. 1617 MORYSON *Itin.* III. 200 The inhabitants [of Jutland] keeping their enemies out, long preserved a rude or rurall liberty. 1634 MILTON *Comus* 952 All the Swains that there abide, With Jiggs, and rural dance resort. 1770 GOLDSM. *Des. Vill.* 398, I see the rural virtues leave the land. 1784 COWPER *Task* IV. 557 Scenes rarely grac'd with rural manners now! 1874 GEO. ELIOT *Coll. Breakf.-P.* 368 In a sleek and rural apathy.

† **b.** = RUSTIC *a.* 1 c. *Obs.*[−1]

1560 DAUS tr. *Sleidane's Comm.* 99 The state of christendom was troublesome..for the late sedition and rurall warre, and for disobedience within the Empyre.

4. Of poetry, music, etc.: Natural or appropriate to the country or to country-people; unpolished, plain, simple.

c 1470 HENRY *Wallace* XI. 1431 All worthi men at redys this rurall dyt, Blaym nocht the buk. 1552 LYNDESAY *Monarche* 6333 All gentyll Redaris hertlye I Implore For tyll excuse my rurall rude Indyte. 1579 SPENSER *Sheph. Cal.* Jan. 64 Shee deignes not my good will, but doth reprove, And of my rurall musicke holdeth scorne. 1634 MILTON *Comus* 547, I..began..To meditate my rural minstrelsie. 1738 *Gentl. Mag.* VIII. 152/1 The Stile [of Comus], as it is rural, is more simple and plain than that of his Paradise Lost.

b. Similarly of musical instruments.

1610 WILLET *Daniel* 96 It was a kind of rurall harpe [sackbut]. 1717 LADY M. W. MONTAGU *Let. to Pope* 1 Apr., I have often seen them..playing on a rural instrument, perfectly answering the description of the ancient fistula, being composed of unequal reeds. 1797 MRS. RADCLIFFE *Italian* xiii, They were amusing themselves by playing upon these rural instruments.

5. Of, pertaining to, or characteristic of the country or country life as opposed to the town.

1590 SPENSER *F. Q.* III. vi. 15 In the countrey she abroad him sought, And in the rurall cottages inquired. 1611 SHAKS. *Wint. T.* IV. iv. 449 If euer henceforth, thou These rurall Latches to his entrance open. 1638 R. BAKER tr. *Balzac's Lett.* (vol. II.) 129, I see..that our rural pleasures are not worthy so much as to amuse so great a spirit. 1667 MILTON *P. L.* IX. 451 Each rural sight, each rural sound. 1746 FRANCIS tr. *Horace, Ep.* I. xvii. 12 By my advice retreat To the calm raptures of a rural seat. 1784 COWPER *Task* III. 625 So manifold,..All healthful, are th' employs of rural life. 1810 *Sporting Mag.* XXXVI. 167 Innocent country amusements called Rural Sports. 1841 W. SPALDING *Italy & It. Isl.* II. 32 Where a rural lane strikes off from the Appian Way towards the Grotto of Egeria. 1884 *Standard* 29 Feb. 2/4 The smaller tradesmen scattered throughout our rural towns.

b. Of occupations, labour, etc.

1608 WILLET *Hexapla Exod.* 11 They wrought..in all manner of rurall workes. 1667 MILTON *P. L.* V. 211 On to thir mornings rural work they haste Among sweet dewes and flours. 1725 POPE *Odyss.* XIV. 28 Of four assistants who his labour share, Three now were absent on the rural care. 1835 THIRLWALL *Greece* I. 405 To force a part of the population to quit the capital, and seek subsistence in rural occupations. 1875 RUSKIN *Fors Clav.* lviii, They can work ..better than their labourers at all rural labour.

transf. 1774 GOLDSM. *Nat. Hist.* (1776) VIII. 87 How they are treated..belongs rather to the rural œconomist, than the natural historian.

6. Of a rustic form or make. *rare.*

1624 WOTTON *Architecture* in *Reliq.* (1672) 23 The Tuscan is a plain, massie, rural Pillar, resembling some sturdy well-limb'd Labourer, homely clad. 1875 KNIGHT *Dict. Mech.* 2004/2 *Rural Lock*, a cheap kind of lock with a wooden case. 1885 R. BUCHANAN *Annan Water* xi, She came to the rural bridge above Annan Water.

B. *sb.* **1.** An inhabitant of the country; a countryman, rustic. Now *rare.*

a 1513 FABYAN *Chron.* VII. (1811) 497 Sir Thomas punysshed the sayd vyllages and ruralls by greuous fynes. *a* 1575 tr. *Pol. Vergil's Eng. Hist.* (Camden No. 36) 41 The ruralls and common people bie the entercourse..are made verie civill. 1602 J. DAVIES (Heref.) *Mirum in Modum* ccxlii, The Cittizens the outward Sences bee, The Ruralls be the Bodies rare. 1657 G. THORNLEY *Daphnis & Chloe* 47 Every rural began to be busie in the fields. 1831 *John Bull* Aug. 250 This delightful place continues the resort of the *élite* of the town; nor are the 'rurals' less liberal in their patronage.

b. A rural policeman.

1860 *Illustr. Lond. News* 26 May 506/2 Sir Richard Mayne's picked A's, and the ever-meddling Surrey 'rurals'.

† **2.** *pl.* = GEORGIC B. 2 b. *Obs.*

1589 A. FLEMING *Virg. Georg.* 3 First beginning with his Bucoliks or Pastoralls,..then his Georgiks or ruralls went in hand, as he fell in loue with good husbandrie.

Ru·ralism. [f. prec. + -ISM.]

1. Rural quality or character; country life.

1864 WEBSTER, *Ruralism*, the state of being rural; ruralness. 1879 MRS. HUNGERFORD *Airy Fairy Lilian* II. 208 Addicted to City pursuits and holding country life and ruralism generally in abhorrence. 1894 MRS. H. WARD *Marcella* I. 51 The agricultural world as it is,—no stage ruralism, but the bare fact.

2. A country idiom or expression; a rusticism.

1882 *Ogilvie's Imp. Dict.* (Annandale).

Ru·ralist. [f. as prec. + -IST.]

1. A countryman, peasant.

1739 H. COVENTRY *Philemon to Hydaspes* III. 66 An Image, which must have pleaded so strongly with our Egyptian Ruralists for a direct and unqualified Adoration of the solar Orb. 1756 AMORY *Buncle* (1770) II. 272 The Egyptian ruralists, without a creed and without a philosophy. 1822 LAMB *Elia* I, *Distant Correspondents*, Four poor elms, from whose smoke-dyed barks, the theme of jesting ruralists, I picked my first lady-birds. 1892 *Temple Bar* June 176 His childish faith..and absence of all hypocrisy make him [the Russian peasant] one of the most interesting ruralists in Europe.

2. An advocate of country as opposed to town life; one who leaves the town for the country.

1828 *Blackw. Mag.* XXIV. 326 The London season is over. Spite of the showery weather, the ruralists carry the day. 1889 WHITTIER *Prose Wks.* II. 248 The mere dilettante and the amateur ruralist may as well keep their hands off.

Rurality (ruræ·lĭti). [f. RURAL *a.* + -ITY, perh. after F. *ruralité* (med.L. *ruralitas*).]

1. Rural quality or character, rusticity; country life, manners, or scenery.

1730 BAILEY (folio), *Rurality*, Ruralness, Country-likeness, Clownishness. 1778 [W. H. MARSHALL] *Minutes Agric.*, *Digest* 1 A few years acquaintance with the World had convinced him, that Nature, Rurality, Contemplation and Happiness, are nearly allied. 1809 PINKNEY *Trav. France* 236 It has..an animation, an air of cleanness and rurality which seldom belong to a populous city. 1853 SURTEES *Sponge's Sp. Tour* (1893) 11 The full rurality of grass country, sprinkled with fallows and turnip-fields. 1883 W. BESANT *All in Garden Fair* I. ii, The rurality of the place, to one fresh from town, seems overdone.

2. With *a* and *pl.* A rural characteristic, feature, or topic; a rural object, locality, landscape, etc.

1823 SCOTT *Fam. Lett.* (1894) II. xix. 171 The 12th of July dismisses me to my ruralities for four months. 1844 R. P. WARD *Chatsworth* I. 17 The Regent's Park ruralities of Marienbad; the Primrose-hill prettiness of Kissingen. 1893 *Athenæum* 9 Dec. 813/2 Spottiness and..slight opacity ..have long beset his pleasant ruralities.

Ruraliza·tion. [f. next + -ATION.] Going into, transference to, the country.

1859 SALA *Tw. round Clock* (1861) 198 Turnham Green and Kew were places where citizens took their wives to enjoy the perfection of ruralisation. 1892 *Standard* 10 June 5/2 This ruralisation of the great Metropolitan schools.

Ruralize (rū·rălǝiz), *v.* [f. RURAL *a.* + -IZE.]

1. *trans.* To render rural or rustic in character.

1805 WORDSW. *Prel.* I. 89 Casting then A backward glance upon the curling cloud Of city smoke, by distance ruralised. 1883 STEVENSON *Silverado Sq.* 29 This tardy favourite of fortune..—thoroughly ruralized from head to foot.

2. *intr.* To go into the country; to sojourn in the country, to rusticate.

1822 MRS. E. NATHAN *Langreath* I. 15 A large party, whom he intended bringing from London to ruralize during the autumn. 1843 F. E. PAGET *Warden of Berkingholt* 139 It will be found that they have been ruralizing with Dr. Wiseman at Oscott. 1866 *Lond. Rev.* 23 June 697/2 In these days a man won't ruralize without publishing.

Hence **Ru·ralizing** *vbl. sb.*

1837 *New Monthly Mag.* LI. 341 A few days' ruralizing in the forest on such primitive fare. 1895 *Daily News* 4 June 3/5 The ruralising of parts of the metropolis through opening new grounds.

Rurally (rū·răli), *adv.* [-LY[2].] In a rural or country-like manner.

1792 WAKEFIELD *Mem.* (1804) I. 80 Jesus College is rurally situated at some distance from the body of the town. 1799 J. ROBERTSON *Agric. Perth* 476 In a situation warmly sheltered and rurally picturesque. 1845 J. COULTER *Adv. Pacific* xvii. 267 The houses are all so rurally concealed, that [etc.]. 1871 B. TAYLOR *Faust* II. III. (Chandos) 299 Rurally quiet [do thou] Brighten the plain.

Ru·ralness. *rare*[−0]. [-NESS.] 'Country-likeness, clownishness' (Bailey, 1730).

† **Ru·ralty.** *Obs.*[−1] [-TY.] Agricultural or country population.

c 1640 J. SMYTH *Lives Berkeleys* (1883) II. 287 None other guests but the gentlemen and ruralty of the County.

† **Ru·rate.** *Obs.*[−1] (Apparently f *rur-al*, after *curate*; but perh. an error for *jurate.*)

c 1560 *Phylogamus* in *Skelton's Wks.* (1843) I. p. cxvi, O poet rare and recent.., Sparyng no priest or curate, Cyuylyan or rurate.

Rurd(e, obs. variants of RERD(E.

† **Rure.** *Obs.* Forms: 1 **hryre**, 2 **rere**, 3 **rure.** [OE. *hryre*, f. *hrur-*, *hrus-*, weak grade of *hrēosan* REOSE *v.*] Fall; ruin.

Beowulf 1681 Hit on æht ȝehwearf æfter deofla hryre. *c* 888 K. ÆLFRED *Boeth.* xvi. § 4 We witon..hwilce hryras ..se unrihtwisa kasere Neron weorhte. *c* 1000 ÆLFRIC *Hom.* I. 144 Þis cild is ȝesett maneȝum mannum to hryre. *c* 1160 *Hatton Gosp.* Mark v. 13 On mycelen rere se heord warð on sæ bescofen. *a* 1250 *Owl & Night.* 1154 Þu singst aȝen eiȝte lure, Oþer of summe frondes rure.

† **Ru·ric,** *a. Obs.*[−1] In 5 **ruryk.** [Cf. med.L. *ruricus* (Du Cange).] Rustic.

c 1470 HENRY *Wallace* VII. 398 Thocht ruryk folk tharoff haff litill feill, Na deyme na lord, bot landis be thair part.

Ruri·colist. *rare*[−0]. [f. L. *rūricola*.] A husbandman (Bailey, 1730). So **Ruri·colous** *a.*, 'living in the country or fields' (Mayne, 1858).

Ruridecanal (rūride·kănăl, -dĭkēⁱ·năl), *a.* [f. L. *rūri-*, combining form of *rūs* country, + DECANAL.] Of or pertaining to a rural dean or deanery.

1861 J. A. PHILLIPS *Missionary Pupils* 10 Members of each Ruri-decanal chapter should find a Missionary-candidate and raise funds for his education. 1888 BURGON *Lives 12 Gd. Men* II. x. 280 A revival of Ruridecanal action throughout the diocese had preceded.

† **Ru·rify,** *v. Obs.*[−1] [See prec. and -FY.] *trans.* To countrify.

1593 R. HARVEY *Philad.* 77 His grace is lost, his maiestie diminished, and hee euen rurified like a priuate subiect.

† **Ru·rigene.** *Obs.*[−0] (See quot. and next.)

1656 BLOUNT *Glossogr.*, *Rurigene*, born in, dwelling or abiding in the Country; country people. [Hence in Phillips, Bailey, etc.]

Ruri·genous, *a. rare.* [f. L. *rūrigen-a* + -OUS.] Born or dwelling in the country; rustic.

1730 in BAILEY (folio). 1799 E. DU BOIS *Piece Family Biog.* II. 119 Rurigenous cook-maids, and automatical bankers' clerks may take care of their autography. 1807 G. CHALMERS *Caledonia* II. 936 The word runchies, for weeds, is generally known to rurigenous people.

Rus, abbrev. of RUSTICATION 3.

a 1890 SIR R. F. BURTON in Lady Burton *Life* (1893) I. 90 I was singled out..by an especial recommendation not to return to Oxford from a Rus.

Rusa (rū·să). [mod.L. (C. Hamilton Smith, 1827), a. Malay روس *rūsa*: cf. BABIROUSSA.] **a.** A genus of large East Indian deer, including the sambur and rusa proper. **b.** A deer belonging to this genus, esp. the Javanese *Rusa hippelaphus*. Also *attrib.*

1827 C. H. SMITH in Griffith tr. *Cuvier* IV. 104 The Rusa Group. This group consisting of Stags entirely Asiatic, is distinguished from all other Deer, by having round horns with a brow antler, but no median or bezantler. *Ibid.* 105 The Great Rusa (*Cervus Hippelaphus*). *Ibid.* 116 Although the true Axines have horns of similar form with the Rusas, their structure is more slender. 1862 BEVERIDGE *Hist. India* I. Introd. 11 The Saumer, or black rusa of Bengal. *Ibid.*, The great rusa stag, nearly as large as a horse. 1877 *Nature* 26 Apr. 562/1 The additions..during the past week include a Rusa Deer (*Cervus rusa*) from Java.

Rusa, variant of ROOSA.

† **Rusband.** *Obs.*[−1] [Perhaps a misprint for *Rusland* Russia.] Some kind of hemp.

1641 S. SMITH *Herring Buss Trade* 13 The best Rine and Rusband are these, Hempe brought in by the Eastland Merchants from the parts of Leiffeland and Prusia.

Ruscan, variant of RUSKIN[2] *Obs.*

Rusche, obs. form of RUSH *sb.* and *v.*

Ruschew, variant of RISHEW *Obs.*

† **Ru·scled,** *a. Obs.*[−1] [Of obscure origin.] ? Wrinkled, rugged.

? *a* 1400 *Morte Arth.* 1096 Bullenekkyde was þat bierne, and brade in the scholders,..Ruyd armes as an ake with rusclede sydes.

‖ **Ruscus** (rɒ·skɒs). [med.L., for class. L. *ruscum.*] The plant butcher's broom or knee-holly.

1578 [see BUTCHER'S BROOM]. 1753 *Chambers' Cycl.* Suppl. s.v. *Bonifacia*, The broad-leaved ruscus, or butcher's-broom, commonly called the Alexandrian bay. 1882 'OUIDA' *Maremma* I. 250 Where the tombs of the Tyrrhenes were hidden away behind the fence of thorny ruscus. 1899 *Allbutt's Syst. Med.* VIII. 517 Birch tar (often sold as oleum rusci, but not made from the ruscus).

Ruse (rūz), *sb.* [a. F. *ruse* (14th c.), vbl. sb. from *ruser*: see next.]

† **1.** *Hunting.* A detour; a doubling or turning of a hunted animal to elude the dogs. *Obs.*

c 1410 *Master of Game* (MS. Digby 182) ii, Somtyme he goth away with hem and þen he maketh a ruse in some side. *Ibid.* xxx, Alle his blenches and his ruses beforeseyde.

2. A trick, stratagem, artifice, 'dodge'.

1625 in *Buccleuch MSS.* (Hist. MSS. Comm.) I. 261 The ruse of the bill of plague will start men to come up that are in the country. 1670 *Ibid.* 473 This might have been a ruse of the French. 1692 RAY *Creation* (ed. 2) 128 The wiles and ruses, which these timid creatures [hares] make use of to save themselves. 1746 G. TURNBULL tr. *Justin* XXI. iii, When there was no more opportunity for rapine, he outreached the whole city by this cunning ruse. 1823 J. BADCOCK *Domestic Amusem.* 33 The double ruse of decyphering the despatches, and then forwarding them by another hand. 1845 M. PATTISON *Ess.* (1889) I. 14 They.. endeavoured by some clumsy expedient, or grotesque ruse, to evade it. 1879 FARRAR *St. Paul* (1883) 173 The asserted conversion might be only a ruse to enable Saul to learn their secrets.

b. Without article.

1815 W. H. IRELAND *Scribbleomania* 120 Ruse ever ranks with the Cloth as Fair Game. 1863 *Sat. Rev.* 4 Apr. 447 Seizing by ruse the game that evaded other snares.

† **Ruse,** *v.*[1] *Obs.* Also 4 **ruyse**, 5 *Sc.* **rus.** [a. OF. *ruser, ruiser* (mod.F. *ruser*): see RUSH *v.*[2]]

1. a. *trans.* To drive back in battle.

c 1330 R. BRUNNE *Chron. Wace* 4658 Þeyr egre comyng þe Romayns a-boden,..& ruysed þe Brutons abak in feld. 1375 BARBOUR *Bruce* XII. 527 The Scottis men fast can thame payne Thair fais mekill mycht to rus. I trow thai sall no payne refus [etc.].

b. *intr.* To give way, retreat.

c 1450 *Merlin* xviii. 288 As soone as Gawein was come he be-gan to do so well that the saisnes rused and lefte place.

2. Of a hunted animal: To make a detour or other movement in order to escape from the dogs.

c 1369 CHAUCER *Dethe Blaunche* 381 So at þe last This hert rused & stale away Fro al þe houndis a prive way. *c* 1410 *Master of Game* (MS. Digby 182) ii, Þenne he begynneth to shewe his wiles and ruseith to and fro. *Ibid.*, Þen he shall ruse oute of þe wey for to stalle or qwatte to rest hym.

Hence † **Ru·sing** *vbl. sb. Obs.*

c 1410 *Master of Game* (MS. Digby 182) xxxiii, He seeth þat betynge vppe þe ryueres and brokes,..nor rusyng to and froo vpon hymselfe.., ne may not helpe.

Ruse, *v.*[2] *dial.* Variant of ROSE *v.*[2]

1847 HALLIW., *Ruse*, to slide down a declivity with a rustling noise. *Devon.* 1874 MRS. WHITCOMBE *Bygone Days Devon & Cornw.* 91 Hold up your mare, for just here the cliff roozed down last week. 1888 ELWORTHY *W. Som. Word-bk.* s.v. *Ruse* and *Rusement.*

Ruse, obs. form of ROOSE *sb.* and *v.*

Ruset-offal: see RUSSET *sb.* 5.

Rusewale, variant of RUSSWALE *Obs.*

Rush (rɒʃ), *sb.*[1] Forms: α. 1 **risc** (**hrisc**), **risce**, 3 **riges** (?), 4–5 **rische** (5 **rissche**), 4–6 **risshe**, 4–7 **rishe** (5 **riche**), 4–7 (9 *dial.*) **rish**; 4–5 **rysche** (5 **rysch, ryche**), 5–6 **rys(s)he**, **rysse** (5 **ryse**), 6 **ryesh, rysh**; also 1 (8–9 *dial.*) **rix**, 1 **rixe.** β. 1 (**h**)**rysc-**, 2 **rysse-**, **russe-**, 4 **rusche, ruysshe**, 4–6 **russhe** (5 **russh**), 6 **rushe**, 5– **rush**; 5 **roysche, rossh**, 6 **roche.** γ. 1 **resce**, 4 **ress(e, ressche, reisshe, reysshe**, 5 **resch(e, ressch**, 5–6 (9 *dial.*) **resh** (6 **reshe**), 9 *dial.* **reish**; also 8–9 *dial.* **rex** (**rexen**). δ. 6 *north.* and *Sc.* **rasch, rashe, raiche**, 8– **rash.** [The remarkable variations in the vowel of this word make its precise history far from clear. The OE. *risc* (*rix*) and *risce* (*rixe*) correspond to MDu. *risch*, MLG. *risch(e, rysse*, and *risk, rysk*, LG. *risch(e, risk(e*, WFris. *risk*, and it is no doubt these forms, rather than *rysc*, which are represented by ME. *risch(e*. The evidence for OE. *rysc* is very slight, but is strengthened by the existence of continental forms with *u*, as Du. *rusch* (16th cent.), MLG. *rusch*, MHG. *rusch(e*, G. *rusch*, LG. and WFris. *rusk* (LG. also *rüsschen, rüsken*, etc.); whether ME. *rusch(e* is merely a dialectal representative of OE. *rysc*, or is due to foreign influence, is not clear. The continental forms, however, are prob. the source of OF. *rusche, rousche, rouche* (mod.F. dial. *rouche, rouce*), rush, reed, or sedge, which may have had some effect in ME. The OE. *resce* (found only once) appears to have no parallel in the cognate languages; the northern and Scottish *rash* is probably a variant of this, as in the case of *nash* for NESH *a.*

All the forms might have arisen as natural variants from an ablaut series **resc-*, *rasc-*, *rusc-*, but the disturbing effect of both *r* and *sh* on adjacent vowels makes it uncertain how far this is really the case. The German adj. *rasch* has an almost parallel series of variants, and some ultimate connexion between this and the sb. is not impossible. The suggestion that the Teutonic word is an early adoption, with complete change of meaning, of L. *ruscum*, butcher's broom, is in the highest degree improbable.]

1. A plant of the order *Juncaceæ*, having straight naked stems or stalks (properly leaves) and growing in marshy ground, or on the borders of rivers or ponds; a single stem or stalk of this, either as growing, or as cut and used for some purpose.

Down to the 17th century green rushes were commonly employed for strewing on the floors of apartments.

α. *c* 725 *Corpus Gloss.* I 530 *Juncus*, risc. *c* 900 tr. *Baeda's Hist.* III. xxiii, In þæm cleofum..wære upyrnende grownes hreodes & rixa. *c* 1000 ÆLFRIC *Hom.* II. 402 Spyrte bið..of rixum gebroden. *Ibid.*, Rixe weaxst gewunelice on wæteriȝum stowum. *c* 1250 *Gen. & Ex.* 2595 In an fetles, of rigesses wrogt..ðis child wunden ghe wulde don. 13.. *Coer de L.* 6038 Kyng Richard garte al the Ynglys Schere rysches in the marys. ? *a* 1366 CHAUCER *Rom. Rose* 1701 The stalke was as risshe right, And theron stood the knoppe upright. *c* 1400 *S. Eng. Leg.* (MS. Bodl. 779) in Herrig's *Archiv* LXXXII. 335 Vppon a bed of risschen.. his body he gan reste. 1483 *Act 1 Rich. III*, c. viii. § 4 The seid Diers..upon the lystes of the same Clothes festen and sowe great Risshes called Bull Risshes. 1529 MORE *Dyaloge* IV. Wks. 286/1, I haue laid you the places ready with ryshes betwene the leaues. 1562 TURNER *Herbal* II. (1568) 104 It hath leues lyke succory and stalkes lyke rysshes. 1601 HOLLAND *Pliny* XIX. ii, The Greekes in old time emploied their rishes in drawing of ropes. 1778 *Exmoor Scolding* Gloss. (E. D. S.), *Rex* or rather *Rix*, a Rush; *Rixen*, Rushes. 1828 CARR *Craven Gloss.*, *Rish*, rush. 1831 LOVER *Leg.* 182, I..was peepin' out iv a turf o' rishes.

β. ? *c* 1000, *a* 1200 [see 5 a]. 1393 LANGL. *P. Pl.* C. x. 81 To rubbe and to rely, russhes to pilie. 1426 LYDG. *De Guil. Pilgr.* 14673 And placys ful off old ordure, I kan strowhe with Rosshys grene, That ther ys no Felthe sene. *c* 1475 in Wr.-Wülcker 786 *Hic cirpus*, a roysche. 1513 T. MORE in Grafton *Chron.* (1568) II. 765 The Queene..sate alone alowe on the rushes all desolate. 1561 in *Record of Caernarvon* (1838) 298 Permitting the rushes..and the roots of the same to stand and growe. 1635–56 COWLEY *Davideis* I. 696 The Scholars far below upon the Ground, On fresh-strew'd Rushes place themselves around. 1697 DRYDEN *Virg. Past.* I. 66 Tho' Rushes overspread the Neighb'ring Plains. 1756–7 tr. *Keysler's Trav.* (1760) I. 379 A wretched country, all overgrown with heath and rushes. 1796 H. HUNTER tr. *St.-Pierre's Stud. Nat.* (1799) III. 416 It was lighted by a window shut by a texture of rushes. 1839 URE *Dict. Arts* 836 The miner requires a powder-horn, rushes to be filled with gunpowder. 1848 *Jrnl. R. Agric. Soc.* IX. II. 556 The rush should at all times be tied only in a slip knot. 1869 RUSKIN *Queen of Air* § 79 The rushes differ wholly from the sedge and grass in their blossom structure.

γ. *a* 1100 in Wr.-Wülcker 324 *Juncus*, *uel scyrpus*, resce. *a* 1300 [see 2 a]. 1340 *Ayenb.* 253 Þet byeþ ylich þan þet zekþ þe crammeles ine þe russoles..oþer þane knotte ine þe resse. 1382 WYCLIF *Job* viii. 11 Whether a ressche may liuen withoute humour? *a* 1400–50 *Alexander* 4126 Þare fand þai bernys & bridis..resild as a resch & roghe as a bere. 1489 *Accs. Ld. High Treas. Scotl.* I. 118 For resschis to the Haw off Lythqow the tyme of the Imbassatouris. 1570 LEVINS *Manip.* 91 A Resh, *iuncus*. 1778 [see α]. 1855 [ROBINSON] *Whitby Gloss.*, *Reshes*, the wire rush, the seaves of the moors and wastes. 1886 ELWORTHY *W. Somerset Wd.-Bk.*, *Rexen*, rushes. One of the very few words which retain the *en* plural.

δ. ? 15.. *Song* in *Compl. Scot.* (1872) vi. 64 Cou thou me the raschis grene. 1548 TURNER *Names Herbes* (E. D. S.) 71 Scirpus..is called..in english a rishe or a rashe. 1554 *Extr. Burgh Rec. Edinb.* (1871) 283 For beireing of burds and trestis to the Queenis luging..and for flouris and raichis. ? *a* 1700 *Bessy Bell & Mary Gray* i. in Child *Ballads* IV. 76/2 They bigget a bower..And theekit it oer wi rashes. 1795 MACNEILL *Scotland's Skaith* I. viii, Light he bare her,..Plac'd her on the new-mawn rashes. 1827 *Peril & Captivity* (Constable's Misc.) 133 See these hurdles of reeds.., this bed of rashes.

b. Used for burning; also *ellipt.*, a rush-light.

14.. in Wr.-Wülcker 722 *Hic lichinus*, a weke.. *Hec secula*, a rysch. 1499 *Promp. Parv.* 456/2 Synke, of a lampe (*P.* holdinge the risshe), *mergulus*. 1572 BARET *Alv.*, The rushe, weeke, or match, that mainteyneth the light in the lampe. 1775 G. WHITE *Selborne* lxviii, A good rush, which measured in length two feet four inches and a half, being minuted, burnt only three minutes short of an hour. 1840 HOOD *Up Rhine* 206 Without the glimmer of a farthing rush! 1884 *Leisure Hour* Feb. 79/2 A long tallowed rush, which preserved an economical flame.

† **c.** Used for making a finger-ring: cf. RUSH-RING. *Obs.*

c 1449 PECOCK *Repr.* II. v. 166 It is weel allowid..that he make a ring of a rische and putte it on his fynger. 1589 GREENE *Menaphon* (Arb.) 88 Twas a good world..when a ring of a rush woulde tye as much Loue together as a Gimmon of golde. 1601 SHAKS. *All's Well* II. ii. 24 As fit..as Tibs rush for Toms fore-finger.

† **d.** In reference or with allusion to the practice of strewing fresh rushes for visitors. *Obs.*

1562 J. HEYWOOD *Prov. & Epigr.* (1867) 48 Greene rushes for this straunger, strawe here. 1589 GREENE *Menaphon* (Arb.) 35 When you come you shall haue greene rushes, you are such a straunger. 1602 BRETON *Wonders worth Hearing* Wks. (Grosart) II. 5 Greene rushes, M. Francisco, it is a wonder to see you heere in this Country. 1617 FLETCHER *Valentinian* II. iv, Rushes, Ladys, rushes, Rushes as green as Summer for this stranger. 1731–8 SWIFT *Pol. Conv.* 7 If we had known of your Coming, we would have strown Rushes for you.

e. Without article, as a material or species of plant.

1728 CHAMBERS *Cycl.* s.v. *Shuttle*, A little Tube of Paper, Rush, or other Matter. 1847 C. BRONTË *J. Eyre* xxviii, It showed no variation but of tint: green, where rush and moss overgrew the marshes. 1879 TENNYSON *Lover's T.* IV. 141 A flat malarian world of reed and rush! 1907 *Athenæum* 14 Dec. 772/2 The body should be wrapped in rush, or bast, or grass, or hemp, and placed in a cage.

2. a. Used as a type of something of no value or importance, esp. in negative phrases as *not to care a rush, not worth a rush.*

(*a*) *a* 1300 *Cursor M.* 21441 O ranscun namar þan a ress Wald he of her [= hear] bot of his flesche. *c* 1374 CHAUCER *Troylus* III. 1161 He seide,..Not I not what, al dere ynow a rische. 1390 GOWER *Conf.* II. 284 Only the value of a reysshe Of good in helpinge of an other. *a* 1450 *St. Cuthbert* (Surtees) 6077 Noȝt harmed þe valu of a resch. *a* 1568 ASCHAM *Scholem.* (Arb.) 54 To be able to raise taulke, and make discourse of euerie rishe. 1581 J. BELL *Haddon's Answ. Osor.* 423 It forceth not of a rush what you do there. 1841 MIALL in *Nonconformist* I. 17 It matters not a rush. 1884 *Western Daily Press* 11 July 8/1 It does not signify a rush whether they can find..a precedent for what they ask.

(*b*) 1362 LANGL. *P. Pl.* A. III. 137 Heo þat ben curset in constorie counteþ hit not at a russche. 1390 GOWER *Conf.* II. 97 For til I se the daies spring, I sette slep noght at a risshe. *c* 1440 *Generydes* 1680 Of all his payne he wold not sett a rissh. 1543 GRAFTON *Contn. Harding* 533 He should then bee hable to matche with theim well ynough, and not to care a rushe for theim. 1584 R. SCOT *Discov. Witchcr.* VI. iii. (1886) 93 Night-walking sprites..Esteeme them not twoo rushes. 1622 MASSINGER & DEKKER *Virg. Martyr* II. iii, I weigh thee not a rush. 1658 BRAMHALL *Consecr. Bps.* viii. 194 Whose unjust Judgement we doe not value a rush. 1712–3 SWIFT *Jrnl. to Stella* 9 Mar., People will grumble; but Lord Treasurer cares not a rush. 1759 STERNE *Tr. Shandy* I. xvi, He did not mind it a rush. 1848 J. GRANT *Aide-de-C.* xxiv, He would not value his ducats..a rush. 1883 F. M. CRAWFORD *Dr. Claudius* vii, Claudius did not care a rush whether the night were beautiful or otherwise.

(*c*) *c* 1422 HOCCLEVE *Min. Poems* xxiv. 193 They can nat keepe conseil worth a risshe. 1577 B. GOOGE *Heresbach's Husb.* I. (1586) 14 Without whiche, he is not woorth a rushe. 1627 HAKEWILL *Apol.* (1630) 296 They esteem not worth a rush any of our actions or manners. 1674 W. POPE in *Flatman's Poems* 2 Friends Applauses are not worth a Rush. 1768 GOLDSM. *Good-n. Man* IV, My master's bill upon the city is not worth a rush. 1858 LINCOLN in Herndon *Life* (1892) II. 116 Not one of them is worth a rush if you deny it.

(*d*) 1563 FOXE *A. & M.* 1367/2 Tush! a rushe for holy bread! *c* 1610 ROWLANDS *Terrible Battell* (Hunterian Cl.) 38 A figge for the whole world. A rush for thee. 1632 VICARS *Virgil* XI. 335 Brave sirs, our main work done,..A rush for what remains.

b. In various fig. or allusive phrases.

With quot. 1649 cf. the phrase *to seek a knot in a rush*, s.v. KNOT *sb.*[1] 14 b.

1525 LD. BERNERS *Froiss.* II. lviii. 198 They..were redy for waggyng of a rysshe to make debate and stryfe. 1579 FULKE *Heskins' Parl.* 289 It hangeth on a rush that M. Hes. concludeth. 1611 BIBLE *Isaiah* ix. 14 The Lord will cut off from Israel head and taile, branch and rush in one day. 1629 H. BURTON *Babel no Bethel* 103 They are all head and taile, branch and rush, one intire Papall faction. 1649 JER. TAYLOR *Gt. Exemp.* iii. § 14 The Lawyer being captious made a scruple in a smooth rush, asking what is meant by Neighbour. 1844 H. STEPHENS *Bk. Farm* I. 191 The larch.. shoots up, as straight as a rush, to a great height. 1889 'R. BOLDREWOOD' *Robbery under Arms* xiii, She was always as straight as a rush.

3. † **a.** One of the branchlets springing from the stem of Equisetum. *Obs.*

1578 LYTE *Dodoens* 100 The stemmes..do bringe forth rounde about every knot or joynt divers little, small, slender, and knottie rushes.

b. *U.S.* The horsetail. (Cf. DUTCH *a.* 3 c.)

1817 J. BRADBURY *Trav.* 15 On the islands which we passed there is abundance of *Equisetum hyemale*, called by the settlers *rushes*.

4. With specific epithets:

a. Denoting various species of *Juncus*.

See also *moss-* (MOSS *sb.*[1] 6 b), *sea-*, *toad-*, and *wood-rush*.

1753 *Chambers' Cycl.* Suppl. s.v. *Juncus*, The species of rush, enumerated by Mr. Tournefort, are these: The sharp or pointed Rush... The smooth or soft Rush [etc.]. 1796 WITHERING *Brit. Pl.* (ed. 3) II. 345 Trifid Rush... Round-headed Rush...Soft Rush. Common Rush [etc.]. 1855 MISS PRATT *Flower. Pl.* V. 295 Lesser Bog Rush, or Little Bulbous Rush. *Ibid.* 296 Clustered Alpine Rush, or Black-spiked Rush.

b. *Flowering rush*: (see quots.).

1731 MILLER *Gard. Dict.*, *Butomus*,..the Flowering Rush or Water Gladiole. 1760 J. LEE *Introd. Bot.* App. 325 Rush, Lesser flowering, *Scheuchzeria*. 1858 BAIRD *Cycl. Nat. Sci.*, *Butomus umbellatus*, the flowering rush, is considered the handsomest herbaceous plant of the British flora.

c. Applied to many plants of different genera more or less resembling the rush, as *bog-*, *club-*, *Dutch*, *hare's-tail-*, *nut-*, *paper-*, *scouring*, *shave-*, *sweet*, *twig-*, *wood-rush* (see these words).

5. *attrib.* **a.** Denoting the growth or prevalence of rushes, as *rush-bed, -drain, -land, -plat, -tuft.*

The second element in *rush-aisle* and *-hylle* appears to be the Lanc. dial. *hile* a cluster.

956 in Earle *Land Charters* 192 Of ðam broce..on þæt riscbed; of ðam riscbedde on ðone weȝ. ? *c* 1000 in Birch *Cartul. Sax.* I. 183 Of þam streame on rysch-alas middewearde. *a* 1200 *Ibid.* III. 189 Fram gryndelessylle to russemere, fram ryssemere to bælȝenham. 1483 *Cath. Angl.* 309/2 A Rysche hylle, *cirpetum*. 1736 AINSWORTH *Eng.-Lat. Dict.*, A rush bed, *juncetum*. 1800 BEWICK *Hist. Quad.* 354 A Hound bitch..pupped four whelps during a hard chase, which she carefully covered in a rush aisle. 1821 CLARE *Vill. Minstr.* I. 58 The rush-tuft gone that hid

Rush, sb.² Also 5 russche, 5–6 rusche, 6 russhe, rushe. [f. RUSH v.²]

1. The act, or an act, of rushing; a sudden or tumultuous movement; a charge, an onslaught; a. Of persons or animals.

b. Of material things.

c. Similnative, as *rush-leaved*, *-stemmed*; *rush-looking*. See RUSHLIKE.

7. Special combs., as *rush-broom*, (a) Spanish broom; (b) a yellow-flowered Australian shrub.

†**Rush**, sb.³ ... a (migratory) flock or flight of birds.

†b. To pull out hastily, drag off violently. *Obs.*

3. a. *refl.* To move with speed and force (*obs.*); to impel (oneself) heedlessly, violently, or hurriedly upon or on something. *Obs.*

8. *Mining.* (See quot.)

9. b. To tie up, work or make with rushes.

2. *intr.* To gather rushes.

Rush (rɒʃ), v.¹ Forms: 4 ruschen, 4–6 rusche (5 russch-, rusch-), 4–6 rushe (6 russhe, 6 rosshe), 4–6 rush. [a. AF. *russher*, var. of *russer*, ...]

Rush-bearing. [RUSH sb.¹] An annual ceremony in northern districts of carrying rushes and garlands to the church and strewing the floor or decorating the walls with them; usually made the occasion of a general holiday.

Rush-buckler. [f. RUSH v.²] A swashbuckler.

Rush-bush, ... 5 rechebush, 6 rysshe-bush, 8–9 *dial.* rez-bush; 8–9 rysshe-, rasoh(e)-bush, rush-bush. [f. RUSH sb.¹ Cf. G. *rischbusch*.] A tuft of rushes.

Rush-candle. [RUSH sb.¹] A candle of feeble power made by dipping the gift of a rush in tallow or other grease; a rushlight.

Rushed, ppl. a. [f. RUSH sb.¹ or v.¹] Overgrown or strewn with rushes.

Rushen (rɒʃ'n), a. Also 4 rischen, 4 russchen, 8–9 Sc. rashen. [OE. *riscen*, f. *risc* RUSH sb.¹] Made of rushes, or of a rush.

†**Rusher**¹. *Obs.* [f. RUSH sb.¹] One who strews rushes on a floor.

Rusher² (rɒʃəɹ). [f. RUSH v.²] One who or that which rushes; one who acts precipitately or without deliberation.

2. *U.S.* One who takes part in a rush to a new gold-field or to new territory.

3. *U.S. Football.* A forward.

Rushet, obs. or erron. form of RUSSET.

Rush-grown, a. [RUSH sb.¹]
1. Having the slender tapering form of a rush.
2. Overgrown with rushes.

Rushiness, *rare* —⁰. [f. RUSHY + -NESS.] A being full of or having rushes.

Rushing, *vbl. sb.* [f. RUSH v.¹] The action of running or moving with great speed or force; the noise produced by some rapid violent movement. Also in fig. uses.

Rushing, *ppl. a.* [f. RUSH v.¹] That rushes; moving or acting with rapidity or impetuosity.

Rushingly, *adv.* In a rushing manner; rapidly or impetuously.

†**Rushle**, v. *Obs. rare.* [perh. f. RUSH v.² + freq. suf. of RUSTLE v.] To rush. Hence †**Rushling** *ppl. a. Obs.*

Rushlight. Also *rush-light*. [RUSH sb.¹]

Rushlike, a. [f. RUSH sb.¹] Resembling a rush.

Rusk¹ (rɒsk). *rare.* [ad. Scand. origin: cf. Icel., Sw., Norw., MSw. *ruska*, Da. *ruske*, in the same or related senses.]
†1. *trans.* To disturb violently; to shake; to tear or tug up. *Obs.*

Rusk² (rɒsk). Also 4 reoskh, 5–6 russhy, 6 rusk. [f. RUSK sb.¹]

Rushy (rɒʃi), a. Also 4 reoshi, 5–6 rushy, 6–7 roushy. [f. RUSH sb.¹ + -Y.]

Rusine (rū'sɒin), a. *Zool.* [See RUSA sb.] Of, belonging to, or characteristic of the cervine genus *Rusa*.

Rusk¹, sb.¹ [ad. Sp. or Pg. *rosca* a twist, turn, coil, screw, and spec. a twisted roll of bread (Sp. *rosca de mar* sea-rusk).]
1. Bread in the form of small pieces which have been re-fired so as to render them hard and crisp; formerly much used on board ships.

Ruskin (rɒskɪn). The surname of John Ruskin (1819–1900), distinguished as a writer on art and social subjects; used *attrib.* in *Ruskin linen*, a kind of hand-woven linen produced near...

Ruskinade (rɒskɪneɪd). [f. RUSKIN² + -ADE.] A basket for holding meal or seed-corn, made of twigs and straw; a bee-hive of straw or rushes, a coarse straw-hat.

Ruskinian (rɒskɪniən), a. and sb. [f. RUSKIN + -IAN.] The style of art or architecture associated with or characteristic of Ruskin; *sb.*, a follower of Ruskin; *intr.*, to advocate or adopt Ruskinian principles.

Ruskinism. The principles and views of Ruskin.

Rusky (rɒski). *Sc.* Also *ruskie*, *-key*. [ad. Gael. *rusgan*: see RUSKIN² .] A basket for holding ...

Rusma (rɒzmə). Also 9 rhusma. [app. ad. Turk. رسمه *khirisma*, ad. Gr. χρίσμα ointment.] A depilatory composed of lime and orpiment, once chiefly used in the East.

Russ (rɒs), sb. and a. Also attrib. [Early 6th Russe. (1598) ...] A Russian. Now *rare*.

Russe, *bad.* in Hakluyt Voy. (1598). 1. 1. 396 Certaine Russe ...

†**Russel**¹. *Obs. rare.* Also 5 russell. [f. OF. *roussel*, -*sselle*, in the same sense.] A kind of woollen fabric formerly used for articles of attire, esp. in the 16th century.

Russel², f. OF. *roussel*: see RUSSEL¹. The French form of the name is still in use.

†**Russet**, *sb.* and *a.* Also 3–7 russet, 4 rosset, 6–9 *dial.* russit, etc. [a. OF. *russet*, -*sette*, rousset (mod.F. *rousset*), dim. of *roux*, red: ...]

1. A coarse homespun woollen cloth of a reddish-brown, grey or neutral colour, formerly used for the dress of peasants and country-folk; also such stuff of, a similar colour worn at particular seasons.

2. The Russian language.

Russet (continued) ...

Russeting. Also 6-7 russetting, 7 roasset(t)ing, 7 russeten, 7-9 russetin, 6-9 russetine. ...

Russet clothing. Obs. ...

Russet coat [Russet a.] A coat of russet cloth or colour, typical of a humble or rustic condition. ...

Russet-coated, a. [Russet a. 1 e. Cf. also prec.] Wearing a russet coat; rustic, homely. ...

Russian (rʒ'ʃən), sb. and a. Also 4 colloq. Roos(h)ian. ... [med.L. Russiān-us, f. Russia : see Russ, Russi-a.]

Russia (rʒ'ʃa), sb. [med.L., f. Russi the Russ. ...]

Russet, variant of Russwale Ob.

Russet, rare[-]. [f. the adj.]

Russetting ... (continued)

Russianism (rʒ'ʃəniz'm), sb. [f. Russian + -ism.]
1. Tendency to favour Russia. ...
2. Prevalence of Russian ideas or spirit. ...
3. An idiom of the Russian language. ...

Russianization. [f. next + -ation.] The action or process of Russianizing. ...

Russianize (rʒ'ʃəniz), v. [f. Russian a. + -ize. Cf. F. russianiser.] trans. To render Russian in character; to Russify. ...

Russic, a. Obs.[-1] In 7 Russick. [f. Russ sb. + -ic.]

Russie, obs. form of Rustle.

Russiniak, sb. and a. Also Russniac, Russniak. [f. the native name Rusnyák, Rusnák. ...] A member of the Little Russian or Ruthenian race inhabiting Galicia; also, the language of this people. ...

Russo- (rʒ'so), combining form (on Greek analogies) of Russ a. Used appositively with terms denoting peoples or countries, as Russo-Caucasian, -Greek, -Polish, -Turkish, etc.

Russophile, **Russophil.** ...

Russophobe, ... -pho'bia, -pho'bian, -pho'bist, -pho'bism. ...

Russo- ... **Russophilism** ...

Russniak ...

Russule, obs. form of Rustle.

Russwale. Obs. Forms: 4 russhewale, 4-5 russe-, 5 russe-wale ... [Russ sb. + Wale.] A kind of ...

Rust, sb. [OE. rúst = OFris. rost, rust, Du. roest, LG. rust, rüst, OHG. and G. rost ...]

Rust, v. [OE. rústian.] ...

Hence **Ru'sticating** vbl. sb. and ppl. a. Also **Ru'sticater**, one who is rusticating.

Rustica'tory, a. nonce-wd. [f. RUSTICATE v. + -ORY.] Pertaining to rustication.

Rusti-dial, a. pseudo-arch. — RUSTICAL a.

Ru'sticism. rare⁻¹. [f. RUSTIC a. + -ISM.] Rustic quality; rusticity.

Rusti'city (rŏstivĭti). Also 6 rustycyte, 6-7 **rusticitie**. [ad. L. rusticitā(t-em) or L. rustic: see RUSTIC and -ITY.]

Rustica'tion (rŏstikēⁱʃən). [ad. L. rusticātiōn-em, n. of action f. rusticārī: see RUSTICATE v.]

Ru'sticate (rŏstikēⁱt), v. [ad. L. rusticā- ppl. stem of rusticārī to dwell in the country.]

Ru'sticated, ppl. a. [f. prec. + -ED.]

Ru'sticate, sb. rare. one who is rusticating.

Rustle (rŏs'l), v. [f. the vb.]

Rustle (rŏs'l), sb. [f. the vb.]

Rustling (rŏsliŋ), vbl. sb.

Rustling, ppl. a. [f. RUSTLE v.]

Rustled (rŏs'ld), ppl. a.

Ru'stler (rŏslə'). [f. RUSTLE v. + -ER.]

Rusty (rŏsti), a.¹

Rusty, a.² [Also of doubtful origin.]

Rust-bred ppl. a., furnished with rusts.

Hence **Ru'sticate**, furnished...

Rut (rŏt), sb.¹ Forms: 5-6 rutte (ruthe), 5-7 rutt, 7 rute; 6- rut. [a. OF. rut, ruit — rut —root.]

Rut (rŏt), sb.² [app. related to ROUT v.⁶]

Rut (rŏt), sb.³ Now S.c. and dial. [Of doubtful origin: cf. the variant ROTE sb.³]

Rut, v.¹ [f. RUT sb.¹]

Rut, v.² Now Sc. [f. RUT sb.³]

Ruta-baga (rūtăbē¹gă). Now rare. Also 9 rootabaga. [Sw. dial. (W. Götland) rotabagge.] The Swedish turnip, Brassica campestris, var. rutabaga.

Ruth (rūþ). [ME. reuthe, f. reowen to RUE v.¹ + -TH¹.]

Ru'tate. [f. RUTIC + -ATE.]

Rutin, sb. [f. RUTA + -IN.]

RUTH.

my reuthe is pe mare. ... **Ruthenian** (rŭþī·nian), sb. and a. [See prec.] ... **b.** Of sounds, actions, etc. (passing into the sense 'expressive of grief or sorrow'). ... **Rutic** (rū·tik), a. Chem. [f. L. rūta rue + -IC.] Rutic acid, a colouring matter discovered by Weiss in the common rue: capric acid. ... **Rutted** (rŭ·ted), ppl. a. [f. RUT v.⁴ or sb.²] Furrowed with ruts; broken, cut up, or marked, with ruts.

Ruth. ... **Ruthe**, obs. variant of RUT sb. — **Ruther**, variant of RIDDER sb.¹, RUDDER sb. — **Ruthe.** ... **Ruthness** ... **Rutic.** ... **Rutyl.**

Rutylene. Chem. [f. prec. + -ENE.] ... **Ryb(b)aud, Rybawd** — see RIBALD. — **Ryb-beck.** slang. ... **Rye-flour.** ... **Rye-grass.** ... **Ryze.**

Ryacolite, Ryakolite, erroneous f. RHYACOLITE.

Rybat (rai·băt). Sc. Forms: 6 rebatt, 9 rybbat, rebat, 9 ribbet, 9 ribbit, reabat. [prob. a variant of RABBET sb., REBATE sb.², but used in the same sense as REVEAL sb.²] A polished stone reveal (side-piece) for windows, doors, etc. Also attrib.

S.

S (es), the nineteenth letter of the English and other modern alphabets, and the eighteenth of the ancient Roman alphabet, derives its form (through the ϟ and Ϛ, Σ of early Latin and Greek inscriptions) from the Phœnician W (Hebrew ש *shin*), which represented a voiceless sibilant: in some of the Semitic langs. (s), in others (ʃ). (Each of these phonetic symbols is intended to represent a class of sounds the articulatory positions of which vary considerably; the difference between the two classes is acoustically very recognizable, but the nature of the essential difference in formation is still obscure.) In ancient Greek and Latin the value of the letter is believed to have been always (s). In late L. *s* between vowels was in most instances pronounced (z), a sound which was not separately represented in the Latin alphabet. Hence when the Roman letters were adopted in OE., the letter S was used to represent both the unaltered Germanic (s), and the (z) which had been developed from that sound in certain positions.

In OE. *s* was pronounced (s) initially and finally, and medially when it was either contiguous with a voiceless consonant or began the second element of a compound; medially between voiced sounds it was pronounced (z). The southern dialect had in ME., and possibly in late OE., the peculiarity of voicing the initial *s* (in native words) as well as the initial *f* and *þ*. This phonetic habit extended to Kent as late as 1340, as is shown by spellings like *zenne* (OE. *synn*, sin) in the *Ayenbite of Inwyt*; it is now confined to the south-western dialects.

In mod. English the general rule is that *s* is pronounced (s) at the beginning of a word or of the second element of a compound, and when doubled or in contact with a voiceless consonant. Between vowels, and when phonetically final, a single *s* is mostly (z). But there are many anomalies and uncertainties, especially in classical derivatives: cf., e.g., *absurd* (æbsɜ̄·ɹd), *observe* (ǫbz-); with regard to some words usage is divided, as in *absolve* (æbs-, æbz-), and the words in *-ive*, e.g. *effusive*, *evasive*. Even *ss* is in some words sounded (z), as in *dissolve* (against *dissent*, *dissect*, etc.), *dessert*, *possess*.

The phonetic combinations (sy), (zy), when rapidly pronounced, are very similar in acoustic effect to the simple consonants (ʃ), (ʒ), the position of the tongue for these being intermediate between the positions for (s) or (z) and (y). Hence in some words where earlier Eng. had (sy) or (zy), written either as *s* (before diphthongal *u*) or as *si*, the modern language has (ʃ) or (ʒ), so that the letter has acquired these two new values. Examples are *sure*, *sugar*, *censure*, *mission* (mi·ʃən), *Asia* (ē̆·ʃă), *treasure* (-ʒŭı, -ʒəı), *evasion* (-ʒən). In some varieties of vulgar speech this tendency is carried much further, as in the pronunciations (ʃū), (prĭʒū·m) for *sue*, *presume*.

S is silent in a few words adopted from Old French, as in *aisle*, *isle* (hence also pseudo-etymologically in *island*); in the Law French *mesne*, *demesne*, a silent *s* was inserted by false analogy.

1. The letter and its sound.

c 1000 Ælfric *Gram.* ii. (Z.) 6 *Semivocales* syndon seofan: *f, l, m, n, r, s, x.* c 1460 *Pol. Rel. & L. Poems* 2 An S. for Salisbery, without any avision. 1709 Steele *Tatler* No. 77 ⁋ 1 Some [lispers] never uttered the letter H; and others had as mortal an Aversion for S. 1842 *Gentl. Mag.* May 480/2 The letter S was the device of Henry of Lancaster.

2. The shape of the letter; an object having this shape.

1426 Lydg. *De Guil. Pilgr.* 17952 Every .s. y-crokyd is, lyche a crose highe in the top. 1614 B. Jonson *Barth. Fair* ii. ii, I doe water the ground in knots, as I goe like a great Garden-pot, you may follow me by the S. S.s I make. 1688 R. Holme *Armoury* iii. xvi. (Roxb.) 58/1 The seuerall parts of a Viol...The S'es of the belly or round holes. 1894 *Outing* (U.S.) XXIII. 407/1 Make an S of wire, sharpened at one end. 1898 Haweis *Old Violins* 77 One 'ʃ' is a shade lower than the other, a practice so common with Strad... that it must have been intentional. 1899 *Blackw. Mag.* 331/2 Round the great S the river made She battled her blind way.

b. *Collar of S, S's, SS.,* or *Esses*: see Collar *sb.* 3 c.

c. *attrib.* and *Comb.*, as *S-necked*, *-shaped* adjs.; *S-curve*, *-hook*, *-perforation*, *-piece*.

1839 *Civil Eng. & Arch. Jrnl.* II. 139/1 He is compelled to connect by a *S curve. 1844 *Ibid.* VII. 152/1 An *S hook of iron must be fitted into the eye of the valve. 1896 *Royal Nat. Hist.* V. 89 The foregoing assemblage of *S-necked or Cryptodiran tortoises. 1851 D. Wilson *Preh. Ann.* (1863) I. ii. iv. 391 Produce the appearance of an *S or Ogee perforation. 1891 Kipling *Light that Failed* viii, Uncouth brick and zinc mysteries supported by iron stanchions and clamped by *S-pieces. 1837 Kirby *Richardson's Fauna Bor.-Amer.* iv. 8 The third becoming a broken or *S-shaped band.

3. Used like the other letters of the alphabet to denote serial order; applied e.g. to the nineteenth (or more usually the eighteenth, either I or J being omitted) group or section in classification, to the eighteenth sheet of a book or quire of a MS., etc.

4. Abbreviations. **a.** S. = various proper names, as Samuel, Sarah, etc.; = Saint; so SS. = Saints; † = Sir (prefixed to the name of a knight or a priest); = Society (L. *societas*), as in F.R.S., Fellow of the Royal Society, F.S.A., Fellow of the Society of Antiquaries, S.P.G., Society for the Propagation of the Gospel, etc.; *Mus.* = Solo; *Chem.* = Sulphur; *Anat.* and *Zool.* = sacral (vertebra); *Her.* (also *l.c.*) = Sable; = snow (in ship's log-book). S. B. = smooth bore (gun). S. M. = Silver Medallist (in shooting competition). S.S. = Steam ship.

a 1400 *Wyclif's Bible* IV. 690 S. Lucie virgyn. 1535 Joye *Apol. Tindale* (Arb.) 4 His felowe called Hijpinus pastour of .s. nicholas parisshe in Hambourg. 1549 Latimer *6th Serm. bef. Edw. VI* (Arb.) 166, I am goynge to S. Tomas of Acres to the sermon. 1591 Harington *Orl. Fur.*, *Apol. Poetrie* ⁋ vij b, If S. Philip Sidney had counted this a fault. 1648 Sir J. Campbell in *Thanes of Cawdor* (Spalding Cl.) 271, I rest, your loueing father S. J. Campbell of Calder. 1648 Herrick *Hesper.* 172 (*title*), To his Valentine, on S. Valentines day. 1724 *Explic. Foreign Words Mus.* 66 The letter *S* is used as an Abbreviation of the Word Solo. 1828–40 Berry *Encycl. Herald.* I, S. This letter...signifies sable, or black. 1885 *Daily News* 12 May 5/1 The Society for the Propagation of the Gospel, familiarly known as the S.P.G. 1899 *Ibid.* 21 July 11/1 Who...was to have the honour of figuring in future records, with the letters 'S. M.' attached to his name. 1903 Sir M. G. Gerard *Leaves fr. Diaries* iv. 104 In 1870 our armament was still the old 12-pr. S. B. gun and 24-pt. howitzer.

b. S. = South; also S.E., SE., South-east, etc. Also † S.S. = South Sea (Company).

1708 *Lond. Gaz.* No. 4418/3 The Wind was, this Morning ...at 10, at S. and S.S.E. 1720 De Foe *Capt. Singleton* xvi (1840) 273 After that it blew...S. W. by S. then S. W. by W. 1768 *Ann. Reg.* 178 Transferring 50*l.* new S. S. annuities,...at the S. S. house, as if it had been his own. 1840 Marryat *Olla Podr.* III. 10 [The wind] is S. W. and by W. ½ W. 1884 H. A. Moriarty in *Encycl. Brit.* XVII. 277/1 A point of destination bore W. S. W. 10 miles; a current ran S. E. by S. 4 miles an hour.

c. s. = L. *solidus* and so used for shilling(s; † = Scilicet; = second (of time).

1387 *E. E. Wills* (1882) 1 Also y be-quethe genet my dowter xl. s. a 1450 Myrc *Festial* lxxiv. 300 Ther was a man on a time þat lant to anothur man iiii s of money to an certeyn day. 1540 Palsgr. *Acolastus* Prol. B iij b, Suche as opteyne vyctory (s. in some great enterpryse). a 1548 Hall *Chron., Hen. VIII* 241 b, A Subsedy, of twoo .s. of landes. 1579 E. K. *Gloss. Spenser's Sheph. Cal.* July 33 Lurdanes s. Lord Danes. 1664 Pepys *Diary* 4 July, My wife...have lain out 25s. upon a pair of pendantes for her eares. 1702 De Foe *Shortest Way w. Dissenters* 21 To talk of 5*s.* a Month for not coming to the Sacrament, and 1*s.* per Week for not coming to Church, this is such a way of converting People as never was known. 1848 Thackeray *Van. Fair* xxxviii, The best coals at — *s.* per chaldron. 1884 H. A. Moriarty in *Encycl. Brit.* XVII. 274/1 The chronometer showed 9ʰ 43ᵐ 15·5ˢ as a mean. 1884 F. J. Britten *Watch & Clockm.* 24 It [*sc.* a watch] is found to have lost 8 s.

'S, a euphemistic shortening of *God's* in certain oaths (now *Obs.* or *arch.*); written continuously with the following word, as in 'Sblood, 'Sdeath, 'Sfax, 'Slife, etc.

s', a colloquial shortening of *sal*, northern dialect form of Shall *v.* when occurring in unstressed positions. Written continuously with the preceding noun or pronoun, usually in the incorrect form **'s**.

's, representing a shortened pronunciation of various monosyllables when unstressed. (Written continuously with the preceding word.)

1. = *is*: see Be *v.* Now only *colloq.* and *poet.*

1584 Lyly *Sappho* iii. ii. 75 Whats he so swaegers in the Van? O! thats a roring Englishman. 1611 Beaum. & Fl. *Philaster* i. i, But I'le suppress him, he's a factious spirit. 1699 Dampier *Voy.* (1729) II. i. 19 In some Places there's very strong Clay. 1741 Richardson *Pamela* II. 356 The Devil's in't if we are not agreed in so clear a case. 1821 Byron *Sardan.* iii. i. 401 Again the love-fit's on him.

2. = *has*: see Have *v. colloq.*

a 1845 Hood *Parental Ode* 38 He's got a knife!

3. = *Us pron.* Now *dial.* exc. in *let's* = let us (*colloq.*).

1588 Shaks. *L.L.L.* v. i. 158 If you desire to dance, let's hold more chat. 1634 Milton *Comus* 5.9 But come let's on. 1662 Cokaine *Trag. Ovid* v. v, Let us go home, send for a Priest of Hymens, And presently each Couple on's be married. 1741 Richardson *Pamela* II. 300 But come, I must love him! Let's find him out. 1893 Crockett *Stickit Minister* 100 What'll ye gie's?

4. = His *poss. pron.*, q.v. *Obs.* exc. *dial.*

5. = As. *Sc.* and *north. dial.*

1718 Ramsay *Christ's Kirk* iii. 49 I've done my best...As well's I may. 1786 Burns *To a Haggis* i, A grace As lang's my arm. 1861 Quinn *Heather Lintie* (1863) 85 Let us crack the news As soon's we greet.

-s, *suffix*, forming adverbs, was originally *-es*, identical with the suffix of the genitive singular of many neuter and masculine sbs. and adjs. Several of the adverbs in *-es* that existed in OE. are genitives either of sbs. (neut. or masc.) as *dæges* by day, *nédes* Needs, *þances* voluntarily, or of neuter adjs., as *sóþes* truly; on the analogy of these, *-es* was added, with adv.-forming function, to feminine nouns, as in *nihtes* by night, *endebyrdes* in order. OE. had also advs. compounded of *tó* prep. and a genitive governed by it, as *tó-gegnes* (see To-gains), *tó-middes* (see To-mids); side by side with these there existed parallel and synonymous advs. like *on-gegn* Again, *on-middan* Amid, in which the dat. or accus. was governed by a prep. Hence there arose in early ME. mixed forms such as *ayeines*, *amiddes*; and the frequent coexistence of the two forms of the same adv., one with and the other without *s*, led to the addition of *s* to many advs. as a sign of their function. In some instances the extended form prevailed, as in *eftsoons*; in others it survived only in dialects, as in *oftens*, *gaylies* (Sc.). See also the articles -ling², -li(n)gs, -ward, -wards, -way, -ways.

In *once*, *twice*, *thrice*, *hence*, *since*, etc., the suffix is written differently. In Againsт, Alongst, Amongst, Amidst, and the dialectal *onst* (see Once), the original *-es*, *-s* has become *-st*.

Sa, obs. f. See *v.*, Soe *sb.*; obs. or dial. f. So.

Sa', obs. var. of Save *v.* in *God sa' me* and similar phrases.

1604 Dekker *Honest Wh.* A 4, Yet so god sa mee shees mine owne sister. *Ibid.* G 3 b, Thats all so god sa me, I thirst after. 1668 Shadwell *Sullen Lovers* iv. 61 As God shall sa'me, she is a very ingenious Woman. 1819 Scott *Ivanhoe* xxxiv, Friend Isaac, will you pleasure us in this matter, and our day shall be truly kept, so God sa' me?

Sa. *Her.* Abbreviation of Sable *sb.*²

1780 Edmondson *Heraldry* I. *Arms Abbies* etc., Augustine's [St.] Monastery, Canterbury. Sa. a cross ar. 1828–40 Berry *Encycl. Herald.* II, *Abbersbury*...or, a fesse embattled sa. 1871 Burke *Peerage*, etc. 195/2 Sa., a naked man, ppr.

Saa(e, Saac(ke, obs. ff. Soe, Sake.

Saad(e, obs. forms of Sad; pa. t. of Say *v.*, q.v.

Saaf(e, saaff, obs. ff. Safe and Save *prep.*

Saage, Saake, obs. f. Sage *a.*, Sack *sb.*

Saald, obs. pa. t. of Sell *v.*

Saale, Saand, obs. ff. Sale *sb.*, Sand *sb.*

Saap(pe, obs. forms of Sap *sb.*

Saar, Saara, obs. forms of Sore *adv.*, Sahara.

Saarce, -cyn, obs. forms of Searce, -cing.

Saat(e, obs. forms of pa. t. of Sit *v.*

† Sab. *Her. Obs.* Abbreviation of Sable *sb.*²

1660 M. Carter *Honor redív.* 249 Bernards Inne Beareth party per pale indented Ermin and Sab. a Cheveron Gul. fretty.

Sab, obs. form of Sahib.

Sabadilla (sæbădi·lă). [a. Sp. *cebadilla*, dim. of *cebada* barley.] = Cevadilla. Also *attrib.*

1812 J. Smyth *Pract. of Customs* (1821) 208 Sabadilla seed, Indian Caustic Barley, very useful in Medicine. 1836 J. M. Gully *Magendie's Formul.* (ed. 2) 71 Boil the seeds of the sabadilla with alcohol. 1876 Duhring *Dis. Skin* 596 Powdered sabadilla...may be sprinkled throughout the hair with good result.

Hence **Sabadi·llia, Sabadi·lline**, *Chem.*, an alkaloid obtained from sabadilla seeds.

1836 J. M. Gully *Magendie's Formul.* (ed. 2) 70 M. Couerbe ...has severally named them [*i.e.* the principles in sabadilla] sabadilline, veratrin [etc.]. 1857 Miller *Elem. Chem.* (1862) III. 503 Three other poisonous bases, sabadillia, colchinia, and jervia, are found, along with veratria, in the *Veratrum album*. 1887 A. M. Brown *Anim. Alkaloids* 29 Anemonine, peltierine, sabadilline.

Sabæan, Sabean (săbī·ăn), *a.* and *sb.* [f. L. *Sabæ-us*, Gr. Σαβαῖ-ος (f. *Saba*, Σάβα, Arabic سبا *Saba'* = Heb. שׁבא *Sh'bā*, the ancient name of the

people of Yemen; by Gr. and Roman writers imagined to be the name of the capital city) + -an.

In one passage (Isa. xlv. 14) the Eng. Bible, following the LXX and the Vulgate, uses *Sabeans* for the quite different tribal name סְבָאִים *S'bāīm*. Another instance of this is in Ezek. xxiii. 42, but the marginal reading in 1611 is *drunkards*, which the Revised Version (1884) adopts in the text.]

A. *adj.* Of or belonging to the ancient population of Yemen in Arabia. In poetic use, often with allusion to the ancient renown of the spices brought from Yemen.

a 1586 Sidney *Ps.* xlv. iv, The fragrant riches of Sabean grove, Mirrh, Aloes, Cassia. 1623 Massinger *Bondman* iv. iii, Whole Hecatombes or Sabæan Gums. 1698 Fryer *Acc. E. India & P.* 115 Two skins of Sabæan Asses. 1700 Dryden *Cinyras & Myrrha* 323 Sabæan Fields afford her needful Rest. 1830 Tennyson *Adeline* v, Dripping with Sabæan spice On thy pillow. 1883 I. Taylor *Alphabet* I. 345 The Himyaritic or Sabean Alphabet.

B. *sb.* One of the ancient inhabitants of Yemen.

1607 Topsell *Four-f. Beasts* 239 The Sabeans by reason of continual vse of Mirrhe and Frankinsens, grow to a loathing of that sauour. 1611 Bible *Joel* iii. 8 They shall sell them to the Sabeans, to a people farre off.

Sabæan, erroneous form of Sabian.

Sabahdaur, variant of Subadar.

Sabaism (sē̆·bĕ,iz'm). Also 8–9 **Zabaism**, 9 **Sabeism, Sabiism, Sabism, Tsabaism, Sabæism.** [f. Heb. צבא *çābā* host (after the presumed etymology of Sabian) + -ism. Cf. F. *sabéisme*, *sabaïsme*, *sabisme*.] The worship of 'the host of heaven'; star-worship. Also sometimes used for Sabianism in its various historical applications.

1727–41 Chambers *Cycl.* s. v., *Sabaism* consisted in the worship and adoration of the stars. 1794 Sullivan *View Nat.* II. xliv. 281 The first variation from the purer zabaism consisted in the ophilatreia, or worship of the serpent. 1839 Yeowell *Anc. Brit. Ch.* xiii. (1847) 148 The worship of the celestial bodies, or Sabæism, as it is termed. 1841 *Penny Cycl.* XX. 295/2 The religious books of Tsabaism were written in Syriac. 1859 J. M. Arnold *Ishmael* 36 The more corrupt form of superstition, which in a measure co-existed with Sabeism. 1878 A. Fornander *Polynesian Race* I. 36 Glimpses of Cushite Zabaism.

Sabalo (sæ·bălo). *U.S.* [a. Sp. *sábalo* shad.] The tarpon, *Megalops atlanticus*.

In recent U. S. Dicts.

‖ **Sabaoth** (sæ·beɪ,ǭþ). Also 6 **sabbaoth**. [L. *Sabaōth* (Vulg.), a. Gr. Σαβαώθ (LXX. and New Testament), a. Heb. צְבָאוֹת *ç'bāōth* pl. of צבא *çābā* army.] A Hebrew word (lit. 'armies', 'hosts'), retained untranslated in the English New Testament (as in the original Greek and in the Vulgate) and the *Te Deum*, in the designation *The Lord of Sabaoth*, for which in the original Old Testament passages the English versions have the rendering 'The Lord of Hosts'.

The Gr. and L. forms being indeclinable, and therefore not easily recognizable as genitives, a frequent early form in Eng. was *The Lord Sabaoth*.

a 1325 *Prose Psalter, Te Deum* 6 Holy! holy! holy! Lord God Sabaoth. 1398 Trevisa *Barth. De P. R.* ix. xxviii. (1495) 364 On the saterdaye in Albis...in the gospell we ben taughte to traueylle in the vyneyerde of our lorde Sabaoth. 1535 Coverdale *Rom.* ix. 29 The Lorde of Sabbaoth [1611 Sabaoth]. — *Jas.* v. 4 The cryes of them which haue reped, are entred in to the eares of the Lorde Sabaoth [1611 the Lord of Sabaoth].

¶ Confused with *sabbath*. (See also Sabbath β.)

1596 Spenser *F. Q.* vii. viii. 2 But thence-forth all shall rest eternally With Him that is the God of Sabaoth hight: O! that great Sabaoth God, graunt me that Sabaoths sight.

Sabarcane, variant of Sarbacane.

Sabat(e, -tille, obs. ff. Sabbath; Sapodilla.

† Sa·batine. *Obs.* In quots. **sab(b)atyne.** [a. Pr. *sabatina*, dim. of *sabata*: see Sabaton and -ine.] A kind of buskin.

c 1460 in *Archæologia* XVII. 295 First ye must set on sabatynes and tye them upon the shoo. c 1538 *Ibid.* XLIII. 248 A payr of sabbatynes; and a payre of syndalls.

Sabatine, obs. variant of Sabbatine.

† Sabaton. *Obs.* Also 4–5 **sabatoun**, 5 **sabatton**, 9 **sabbaton**. [a. Pr. *sabató* (mod. Pr. *sabatoun* shoe), augmentative of *sabata* = F. *savate*, Sp. *zapata* boot (also *zapato* shoe), Pg. *sapata*, It. *ciabatta* shoe. Cf. med.L. *sabbatum*.

The ultimate origin of the Rom. word is obscure. It exists in Arabic (*sabbât*, *çabbât*, etc., Dozy II. 625), in Berber (*sappat*, ibid.), and in Basque (*zapata*), but is prob. in all these a loan-word from Spanish.]

A broad-toed armed foot-covering worn by warriors in armour.

c 1330 R. Brunne *Chron. Wace* (Rolls) 10026 Hym self was armed fynly wel Wyþ sabatons [Wace *cauces de fer*], & spores, & iaumbers of stel. 13.. *Gaw. & Gr. Knt.* 574 Þenne set þay þe sabatounz vpon þe segge fotez. c 1420 Lydg. *Assembly of Gods* 346 Gauntlettes on hyr handys, & sabatouns on hyr fete. c 1450 J. Metham *Wks.* (E.E.T.S.) 36 This forsayd knyght Blak sabatouns weryd. 1485 *Mattrials Reign Hen. VII* (Rolls) II. 21 For making of a paire of sabatons of clothe of golde iiii s. 1543 Grafton *Contn. Harding* 594 The hernayes...was all ouer gylte frome the heade peece to the sabatons. 1869 Boutell *Arms & Arm.* x. (1874) 206 At the commencement of the 16th century, the pointed sollerets were succeeded by broad sabbatons, cut off square or rounded at the toes.

‖ **Sabbat** (saba). In 7–8 **sabat.** [Fr.; a special application of *sabbat* Sabbath.] A 'witches' sabbath'; see Sabbath 3. Also *attrib.*, and *fig.*

1652 J. Wright tr. *Camus' Nat. Paradox* vii. 153 In this Desart corner, which...seemeth onely fit for a Sabat or Assembly of Sorcerers. 1658 tr. *Bergerac's Satyr. Char.* xiii. 54 As to the sabat-voyages, this is my beliefe; they noint themselves with some somniferous oyles, and as while they wake they easily fancy to be carried astride upon a broome through the chimny, into a Hall, where is feasting, dancing, and where they kisse the Goate's brich. 1763 H. Walpole *Let. to Montagu* 15 Aug., My youthfullity, which bears me out even at a sabat. I dined last week at Lady Blandford's, with her, the old Denbigh, the old Litchfield, and Methuselah knows who. 1861 Lytton *Str. Story* xxvi, I could have fancied myself at a witch's sabbat. 1893 Leland *Mem.* I. 75 The book was a perfect Sabbat of devilry and dramatic horrors.

Sabbatarian (sæbătē̆·riăn), *a.* and *sb.* [a. L. *sabbatāri-us* (Sp. *sabatario*, Pg. *sabbatario*), f. *sabbatum* Sabbath: see -arian.] **A.** *adj.* † **a.** Of or pertaining to the Sabbath or its observance. *Obs.*

b. Having relation to the tenets of the Sabbatarians.

a 1631 Donne in *Select.* (1840) 105 A sabbatarian righteousness is no righteousness. 1654 H. L'Estrange *Chas. I* (1655) 129 The rigour and strictnesse of Sabbatarian Ministers, in denying People recreations on the Sunday. 1668 Wells (*title*) The Practical Sabbatarian or Sabbath Holiness crowned with Superlative Happiness. 1733 Neal *Hist. Purit.* II. 250 These Divines, instead of softening some excesses in Bradbourne's Sabbatarian strictness, ran into the contrary extreme. 1796 Morse *Amer. Geog.* I. 436 These are called Sabbatarian, or Seventh day Baptists. 1837 Whewell *Hist. Induct. Sci.* (1857) I. 224 With references to Jewish Sabbatarian notions. 1859 Mill *Liberty* 161 Another important example of illegitimate interference with the rightful liberty of the individual...is sabbatarian legislation. 1863 A. Blomfield *Mem. Bp. Blomfield* I. vi. 154 He entertained rather strict, or what would now be called 'Sabbatarian' notions.

B. *sb.*

1. A Jewish observer of the (Saturday) Sabbath.

1613 Purchas *Pilgrimage* (1614) 149 The word *Masbothæi*, Scaliger saith, signifieth Sabbatists or Sabbatarians, because they professed to haue learned the obseruation of the Sabbath from Christ, and therein differed from the other Iewes. a 1641 Bp. Mountagu *Acts & Mon.* (1642) 454 These Esseni were yet further, more, and most rigid Sabbatarians, beyond all other sects and schismes amongst the Jewes. 1830 D'Israeli *Chas. I*, III. xv. 330 Sabbatarians, became a term of reproach for the Jews with the Polytheists.

2. A Christian who regards the Lord's Day as a Sabbath, deducing its obligation from the Fourth Commandment. Also, and more commonly, one whose opinion and practice with regard to Sunday observance are unusually strict.

1620 J. Dyke *Counter-poyson* 15 He is none of your precise Sabbatarians. 1656 Heylin *Extraneus Vapulans* 110 We are now come unto the business of the Lords day, in which our Author sheweth himself a stiffe Sabbatarian. 1728 Hickes & Nelson *J. Kettlewell* iii. xxiv. 237, I don't know whether you are a Strict Sabbatarian. 1864 Eastwick *3 Years in Persia* I. 4, I am not a Sabbatarian, I showed it by travelling on Sunday.

3. A member of a Christian sect founded towards the close of the sixteenth century, the members of which maintained that the Sabbath should be observed on the seventh and not on the first day of the week; a Seventh-day Baptist. Cf. Sabbatary *sb.*, Sabbatharian.

1645 Pagitt *Heresiogr.* (1647) B j, The Sabbatarians affirme the old Jewish Sabbath to be kept, and not the Lords day. 1710 Steele & Addison *Tatler* No. 257 ⁋ 12 Præ-Adamites, Sabbatarians, Cameronians, Muggletonians...and the like. 1820 *Trav. Cosmo III* 445 Robert Dogs, a coal-man in London, was the first founder of the sect of Sabbatarians.

Sabbatarianism (sæbătē̆·riăniz'm). [f. prec. + -ism.] Sabbatarian principles or practice.

1673–4 Bp. Ward *Case of Joram* 34 [Laws] against Prophanation of the Lord's Day (I do not mean tending to Judaism or Sabbatarianism). 1876 Gladstone *Glean.* (1879) II. 360 The rather judaical Sabbatarianism of Scotland... was simply a form of Protestant tradition. 1894 Max O'Rell *J. Bull & Co.* 54 Narrow Sabbatarianism is neither Protestant nor Christian: it is a Jewish institution.

† Sa·bbatary, *a.* and *sb. Obs.* Also 6–7 **sabbatharie.** [ad. L. *sabbatārius*, f. *sabbatum* Sabbath: see -ary. Cf. F. *sabbataire*.]

A. *adj.* Pertaining to the Sabbath.

1613 Purchas *Pilgrimage* (1614) 204 They are of opinion, that themselues haue a superfluous Sabbatharie soule, which on that day is plentifully sent in to them, to inlarge their heart. 1635 Heylin *Sabbath* ii. (1636) To Rdr., This sabbatarie soule, may be a Pythagoricall μετεμψύχωσις. 1641 H. L'Estrange *God's Sabbath* Pref., Had they left us no other demonstrations of their excellency that way then their Sabbatary Tracts, they should never have attained so high a repute amongst us. 1674 Jeake *Arith.* (1696) 663 Seven...is sometime called the Sacred and Quiet, or Sabbatory [*sic*] Number.

B. *sb.* A Christian who observes the Jewish (seventh-day) Sabbath.

1596 Bell *Surv. Popery* i. iii. v. 112 The sabbatharies contend with tothe and nail. 1621 *Three Quest. Answ. conc. 4th Commandm.* 3 The Sabbataries, which heretofore would haue vs Christians obserue the Iewes Sabbath.

Sabbath (sæ·băþ). Forms: α. 1, 3–5 **sabat**, (3 *pl.* **sabaz**), 3 **sabadt**, 4 **sabath**, **-aat**, 4–5 **sabate**, 4–6 **sab(b)ot**, 4–7 **saboth**, 5 **sabott(e**, **sabbate**, **-atte**, **-ott**, 5–6 **sabote**, 5–7 **sabboth**, 6 **sabett**, **-att**, **-otte**, **othe**, *Sc.* **sabbuth**, 6– **sabbath**; β. (*erron.*, by confusion with Sabaoth) 4–8 **sabaoth**, 6 **sabaothe**, **sabbaoth**. See also Sabbat. [ad. L. *sabbatum* (partly through OF. *sabbat*, *sabat*, mod.F. *sabbat* = Pr. *sabbat*, Sp. *sábado*, Pg. *sabado*, It. *sabbato*), Gr. σάββατον, ad. Heb. שַׁבָּת *shabbāth*, f. root שׁבת *shābath* to rest. Cf. Goth. *sabbatus*, *-o*, MDu. *sabaet*, *sabbet*, *sabbat*, Du. and G. *sabbat*.

The Sp., Pg., and It. forms are the ordinary names in those langs. for Saturday; but Pr. used *dis-sapte* (:–L. *diēs sabbati*) in that sense. A popular Latin nasalized form *sambatum (of oriental origin) appears in F. *samedi* (:–*sambati diēs*), OHG. *sambaztac* (mod. G. *samstag*) Saturday.

The confusion with Sabaoth was not peculiar to England; it occurs in MHG. and in med.Latin.

The word is now very often written (like the names of the days of the week and of festivals) with initial capital.]

1. a. In the original use: The seventh day of the week (Saturday) considered as the day of religious rest enjoined on the Israelites by the fourth (or in mediæval reckoning the third) commandment of the Decalogue. Phrases, *to keep*, *break the Sabbath*.

The word was never in England, as in some continental countries, a vernacular synonym for Saturday, though English writers of med.Latin used *dies Sabbati* as frequently as *dies Saturni*.

α. c 950 *Lindisf. Gosp.* Matt. Capitula Lectionum § 87 From efernes sabates [L. *a vespere sabbati*]. c 1230 *Hali Meid.* 17 Low, godd him seolf seið þurh þe prophete: 'þeo þe hableð from ham forcoruen flesches lustes, & haldeð mine sabaz'. 13.. *Cursor M.* 11987 (Cott.) And o lame o þaa lakes selue Wit handes made he sparus tuelue, Apon þair sabadt þus he did. 1340 *Ayenb.* 7 Þe þridde heste is þellich: 'Loke þet þou halȝi þane day of þe sabat (Zeterday)'...Þis word, zeterday, þet þe iuïe clepeþ sabat, is ase moche worþ ase reste...And ine þe stede of þe sabat...zet holi cherche þane sonday to loky ine þe newe laȝe. c 1380 Wyclif *Serm.* Sel. Wks. I. 41 And Jesus spake to wyse men of þe lawe, and to Pharisees where it were leveful to hele in þe Sabot. 1382 — *Acts* i. 12 Thanne thei turneden aȝen to Jerusalem, fro the hil that is clepid Olyuete, the which is bisydis Jerusalem, hauynge the iurney of a saboth. 1432–50 tr. *Higden* (Rolls) IV. 267 Oure Savioure Criste was borne ...in the nyȝhte of the holy Sabotte [orig. *sancti Sabbati*]. 1596 Shaks. *Merch. V.* iv. i. 36 By our holy Sabbath haue I sworne To haue the due and forfeit of my bond. 1649 Jer. Taylor *Gt. Exemp.* ii. Disc. ix. 119 The Primitive Church kept both the Sabbath and the Lords day. 1727–41 Chambers *Cycl.* s.v. *Week*, The Days of the Week were denominated by the Jews, from the order of their succession from the sabbath. 1871 R. W. Dale *Commandm.* iv. 106 The Christian Sunday and the Jewish Sabbath are absolutely different institutions.

β. 13.. *Cursor M.* 11987 (Gött.) Apon þar sabaoth þus he did. c 1520 Nisbet *N. Test. in Scots* (S.T.S.) I. 11 [Jesus] Healith the ydropysie vponn the sabaothe. c 1610 *Women Saints* 171 Of the Iewes, hating Circumcision, yet with them keeping their Sabaoth. 1658 Phillips, *Sabaoth*,...a celebration of the seventh day of the week.

b. Since the Reformation, often applied to 'the Lord's day', i.e. the first day of the week (Sunday) observed by Christians in commemoration of the resurrection of Christ. This use was originally connected with the opinion that the sabbatic law of the Decalogue remains in force under the Christian dispensation, the date of the 'Sabbath' having by Divine appointment been changed from Saturday to Sunday; but it occasionally appears in writers who did not hold this view. In Scotland it is still very common. (Phrases as in 1 a.)

The notion that the Lord's day is a 'Christian Sabbath', or, more commonly (as in quot. 1340 under a) a substitute for the Sabbath, occurs in theological writings from the 4th c. onwards, but was not popularly current before the Reformation. In English, *Sabbath* as a synonym for 'Sunday' did not become common till the 17th century.

[c 1440: see Sabbath-day.]

α. 1509 Barclay *Ship of Foole* (1874) II. 175 Amonge the whiche preceptis this was one The sabbot to Worshyp and sanctyfy alway The seuenth day of the weke called the sonday. 1594 Shaks. *Rich. III*, iii. ii. 113 *Hast.*...Come the next Sabboth, and I will content you. *Priest.* Ile wait vpon your Lordship. 1607 Hieron *Wks.* I. 150 Thou art laboured with from sabboth to sabboth...that thou maist be prepared for Christ. 1654 Trapp *Comm. Ps.* xxiv. Introd., The first day of the week...which is now the Christian Sabboth. 1717 *Wodrow Corr.* (1843) II. 237 Mr. John Adamson, Sabbath was fortnight, intruded on the ministry. 1809 Syd. Smith *Serm.* I. 74 Prayer should be offered up eminently, and emphatically...on the Sabbath. 1863 Hawthorne *Our Old Home* II. 100 Severe and sunless remembrances of the Sabbaths of childhood. 1888 *Ch. Times* 9 Nov. 977/2 The British Sabbath is now-a-days always on its trial. 1897 *Q. Rev.* Jan. 66 The term Sabbath as applied to the Lord's Day is unknown to the Articles, the Canons, and the Prayer-book of the Church of England.

β. 1583 Stubbes *Anat. Abus.* i. Pref. (1879) 11 To the prophanation of the Lord his sabaoth. 1591 Sylvester *Du Bartas* i. ii. 940 Common Blaspheming of God's Name in Oaths; Usuall profaning of his Sabbaoths. 1621 Elsing *Debates Ho. Lords* (Camden) 3 The Bill for Sabaoth.

c. *gen.* Applied occas. to the day of the week set apart for rest or worship by any religious body, e. g. to the Friday as observed by Mohammedans.

1613 Purchas *Pilgrimage* (1614) Table, Sabath...of Saracens on Friday..; of Peguans on Monday. 1704 J. Pitts *Acc. Mohammetans* 42 Friday is their Sabbath, or Gemague.

d. Applied to the sabbatical year of the Israelites.

1382 Wyclif *Lev.* xxv. 4 The seuenthe forsothe ȝeer of the loond shal be the saboth of the restynge of the Lord. [So in later versions.]

2. *transf.* and *fig.* A time or period of rest; a cessation from labour, trouble, pain and the like.

α. 1591 Sylvester *Du Bartas* i. vii. 446 He would, this Sabbath should a figure be Of the blest Sabbath of Eternity. 1611 Bible *Heb.* iv. 9 There remaineth therefore a rest [*marg.* keeping of a Sabbath] to the people of God. 1681 Dryden *Abs. & Achit.* 913 He...safe enjoys the Sabbath of his Toils. 1737 Pope *Hor. Ep.* i. i. 3 Why will you break the Sabbath of my days? 1795 Southey *Pauper's Funeral* 8 Yes, I will weep; but not that thou art come To the cold sabbath of the silent tomb. 1854 Neale *Hymn*, '*Oh, what the joy*', Those endless Sabbaths the blessed ones see. 1860 Tyndall *Glac.* i. ii. 20 It was Sunday, and the scene was itself a Sabbath, with no sound to disturb its perfect rest.

β. 1398 Trevisa *Barth. De P. R.* ix. xxviii. (1495) 364 Whan we come to the Sabaoth of endles rest thenne we shall haue joye. 1598 Sylvester *Du Bartas* ii. ii. iv. *Columnes* 132 Th'eternall sacred Sabbaoth. 1610 G. Fletcher *Christ's Vict.* i. vi, To keep an everlasting Sabbaoths rest.

3. A midnight meeting of demons, sorcerers and witches, presided over by the Devil, supposed in mediæval times to have been held annually as an orgy or festival. Often more explicitly *witches' sabbath*. Also Sabbat.

α. 1660 F. Brooke tr. *Le Blanc's Trav.* 312 Divers Sorcerers ...have confessed that in their Sabbaths,...they feed on such fare. 1735 Pope *Ep. Lady* 239 As Hags hold Sabbaths, less for joy than spite, So these their merry, miserable Night. 1860 J. A. Hessey *Bampton Lect.* 399 Here malignant spirits have held their sabbath or hellish revelries. 1883 *Harper's Mag.* 831/2 It might have been...a veritable Witches' Sabbath.

β. 1857 B. Taylor *North. Trav.* xi. 115 It would be far more picturesque to describe a sabaoth of Lapland witches than a prayer-meeting of shouting converts.

4. *attrib.* and *Comb.*: simple attrib., as *Sabbath devotion*, *dress*, *evening*, *morning*, *music*, *rite*, *season*, *service*, *sound*, *work*; *Sabbath-like* adj.; objective and objective genitive, as *Sabbath-breach* (rare⁻¹), *-breaker*, *-breaking* sb. and adj., *-keeper*, *-keeping* sb. and adj. Also † **Sabbath-ceased** *a.*, discontinued during the Sabbath; **Sabbath-school**, *a*) = Sunday-school; (*b*) a Jewish school held on the Saturday for giving religious instruction to children.

1784 Cowper *Task* iv. 653 To show at home By lewdness, idleness, and *sabbath-breach, The great proficiency he made abroad. 1607 Hieron *Wks.* I. 234 It cutteth the *sabboth-breaker, to begin his prophanenesse still cried out vpon. 1738 *Gentl. Mag.* VIII. 658/2 The excellent Laws against Tippling Houses, Tipplers, Sabbath-Breakers, &c. 1853 Card. Wiseman *Ess.* I. 636 They tax Papists with being habitual Sabbath-breakers. 1651 *Petition in Proc. Parl.* No. 85. 1303 Acts past against Blasphemies, prophan cursing and swearing, *Sabbath breaking, &c. 1714 Mandeville *Fab. Bees* (1733) I. 92 In the commission of the peace,...he becomes...the...constant plague to sabbath-breaking butchers. 1769 Blackstone *Comm.* IV. 63 Profanation of the lord's day, or sabbath-breaking. 1593 Nashe *Christ's T.* 3 Theyr vnrespited, and not so much as *Saboth-ceased blood-shed. 1613 Zouch *Dove* To Rdr. E 6 b, Poetry...in which diuers haue shewed their thoughts not vnfit for solemne, yea *Sabaoth devotions. 1825 J. Wilson *Poems* II. 94 Smiling in their *Sabbath-dress. 1820 Southey *Wesley* II. 87 Having...spent a *sabbath evening at an inn. 1854 Neale *Hymn*, '*Oh, what the joy*', There dawns no Sabbath, no Sabbath is o'er; These *Sabbath keepers have one, and no more. 1897 Mary Kingsley *W. Africa* 403 His rigid *Sabbath-keeping. 1824 Miss Mitford *Village* Ser. i. 28 A *sabbath-like pause of work and play, rare on a work-day. 1878 B. Harte *Man on Beach* 74 An almost Sabbath-like stillness prevailed. 1863 Geo. Eliot in Cross *Life* (1885) II. 355 Your letter was a welcome addition to our sunshine this *Sabbath morning. 1807 Wordsw. *White Doe* vii. 1761 When the bells of Rylstone played Their *sabbath music—'*God us ayde*'. 1784 Cowper *Task* i. 746 Till *sabbath-rites Have dwindled into unrespected forms. 1845 R. W. Hamilton *Pop. Educ.* vi. (ed. 2) 133 The *Sabbath school generally supplies the sanctuary with its most intelligent hearers. 1864 Skeat *Uhland's Poems* 14 Nature's *Sabbath-season reigns. 1617 Hieron *Wks.* II. 365 John...neglected not the spirituall part of the *sabbath-seruice, though hee was restrained from the outward. 1855 Longf. *My Lost Youth* 49 The early loves Come back with a *sabbath sound. 1625 Bacon *Ess.*, *Truth* (Arb.) 500 His *Sabbath Worke, euer since, is the Illumination of his Spirit.

Sabbathaism (sæbăþē̆·iz'm). [f. *Sabbathai* + -ism.] The doctrines of Sabbathai Zebi (Heb. *Shabb'thai Ç'bi*), a false Messiah born at Smyrna A.D. 1626.

1882–3 *Schaff's Encycl. Relig. Knowl.* II. 1129 Two Polish rabbis, who travelled extensively to propagate Sabbathaism.

Sabbatharian (sæbăþē̆·riăn). *Hist.* [f. Sabbath + -arian. Cf. Sabbatarian.] **a.** = Sabbatarian *sb.* 3. **b.** A member of the religious sect founded by Joanna Southcott in 1801–14.

1719 Ozell tr. *Misson's Mem. & Observ.* 235 These Sabbatharians are so call'd because they will not remove the Day of Rest from Saturday to Sunday. 1882–3 *Schaff's Encycl. Relig. Knowl.* III. 2083 Sabbatharians or New Israelites,...a religious sect founded by Joanna Southcott.

Sabbathariе, -y, variant forms of Sabbatary.

Sa·bbath-day. Forms: (see Sabbath).

1. = Sabbath 1 a.

a 1300–1400 *Cursor M.* 17355 (Laud) After that sabot-day was gon Thedir come they euery-chon. c 1380 Wyclif *Wks.* (1880) 58 He belid a sik man vpon þe sabaat day. 1432–50 tr. *Higden* (Rolls) IV. 327 Whiche peple keped theire Sabbatte day [orig. *Sabbatum*], and hade hyt in so grete veneracion, that thei wolde not ordeyne meyte þat day. 1534 More *Treat. Passion* Wks. 1308/1 So do...their sabbot dayes begynne in the euenyng, and endure to the euenynge folowynge. 1562 Cooper *Answ. Def. Truth* ix. 75 By necessitie of their enemies constreined they [*sc.* the Jews] ...fought on the Sabboth day. c 1610 *Women Saints* 156 He...with the Iewes kept the Saboth day,...yet refused Circumcision. 1709 J. Johnson *Clergym. Vade M.* ii. 104 Christians must not Judaize and rest on the Sabbath-day; but work on that very day; and give the preference to the Lord's day. 1726 J. Henley *Prim. Liturgy* 10 Feasts, are all Lords-days, all Sabbath-days, or Saturdays [etc.].

b. *Sabbath day's journey*: the distance (2,000 *ammôth* or 'ells' = 1225 yards) which (according to Rabbinical prescription in the time of Christ) was the utmost limit of permitted travel on the Sabbath.

1526 Tindale *Acts* i. 12 Mount olivete which is neye to Jerusalem...conteynynge a saboth dayes iorney. 1628 Earle *Microcosm.*, *Shee Precise Hypocr.* (Arb.) 63 Her oftest Gossipings are Sabaoth-dayes iourneyes.

2. = Sabbath 1 b.

The first two quots. may perhaps not be rightly placed here, as it was the common view that the commandment 'to keep holy the Sabbath-day', in its Christian interpretation, related to the festivals of the Church in general, and not to Sunday only or eminently.

c 1440 *Gesta Rom.* x. 30 (Harl. MS.) Hope we hit is our lord ihesu crist, þe which hath ordeyned for lawe, þat ech man shold kepe þe saboth day. 1513 Bradshaw *St. Werburge* ii. 879 A woman which brake the commaundement Of god and holy churche hye sabbot-day dyd violate Vnlaufully wurkynge. 1575 Laneham *Let.* (1871) 12 On munday: the forenoon occupied (az for the Sabot day) in quiet and vacation from woork, & in diuine seruis. 1605 *Vestry Bks.* (Surtees) 284 There shall be no meetinges as concerning any business about upon the Sabbath day. 1651 *St. Andrews, Newcastle-on-Tyne Par. Reg.* in *N. & Q.* 8th Ser. I. 273 Robard Fenwick, which was drowned in the Bares myll dam wher he went to swim on the Saboth day. 1715 De Foe *Fam. Instruct.* i. iii. (1841) I. 63 As soon as they come home next Sabbath-day from the sermon. 1810 Wordsw. *Prose Wks.* (1876) II. 33 The sensations of pious cheerfulness, which attend the celebration of the sabbath-day in rural places. 1830–2 Carleton *Traits Irish Peasantry* (1860) I. 146 (*Priest*) On the Sabbath day too, without my leave!

3. = Sabbath 1 c.

1704 J. Pitts *Acc. Mohammetans* 42 The Hattech, i.e. a Priest which is above the *Emaum*, officiates on their Sabbath-day.

4. *gen.* A Sabbath, day of sacred rest.

1755 Pope *Prol. Sat.* 12 No place is sacred, not the Church is free; Ev'n Sunday shines no Sabbath-day to me.

Sabbathine (sæ·băþəin), *a.* [f. Sabbath + -ine¹.] Affecting or pertaining to the Sabbath.

1850 T. M'Crie *Mem. Sir A. Agnew* viii. (1852) 194 The Sabbathine rules enjoin the Sons of Abraham to prepare for the Feast, by laying in a stock of provisions the day before.

Sabbathize (sæ·băþəiz), *v.* [Altered form of Sabbatize after Sabbath.] *intr.* To observe or keep a Sabbath or period of rest.

1609 Bible (Douay) *1 Esdras* i. 58 The land quietly kept her sabbathes, al the time of her desolation she sabbathized in the application of seventie yeares. 1622 Ainsworth *Annot. Pentat.* Gen. ii. 2 Rested: or Sabbathised, that is, kept Sabbath. 1633 W. Struther *True Happiness* 75 This dwelling in God is our spiritual sabbathizing, the type of the eternall. 1705 Hickeringill *Priest-cr.* i. Wks. 1716 III. 52 The Solemn League and Covenant...Mr. Knox did...bring into Scotland, where it is rampant to this day, and more rigid than the Inquisition in Spain, with the additional Bigotism of Sabbathising.

Sabbathless (sæ·băþlĕs), *a.* [f. Sabbath + -less.] Observing no Sabbath.

1605 Bacon *Adv. Learn.* ii. xxiii. § 46 This incessant and Sabbathlesse pursuit of a mans fortune leaueth not tribute which we owe to God of our time. a 1656 Hales *Gold. Rem.* (1688) 178 Prayer itself is Sabbathless, and admits no rest, no intermission at all. 1820 Lamb *Sonn.*, '*Who first invented work*', Sabbathless Satan! he who his unglad Task ever plies. 1888 *Pall Mall G.* 31 Oct. 2/2 In 1885 Austria-Hungary in response to the bitter cry of Sabbathless toilers enacted a stringent Sunday law.

Sabbathly (sæ·băþli), *a.* [f. Sabbath + -ly¹.] Recurring every Sabbath.

1822 Galt *Sir A. Wylie* III. xvii. 139 It was a Sabbathly theme of regret.

Sa·bbathly, *adv.* [f. Sabbath + -ly².]

1. Every Sabbath; Sabbath by Sabbath. *Sc.*

1627 in Cramond *Ann. Banff* (1893) II. 34 Their absenceis fra the Kirk Sabbothlie at the direction of the bailyies and elderis. 1671 *Rec. Presbyt. Inverness* 29 Mar. (S. H. S. 1896) 9 They were refreshed very much by him Sabbathly. 1820 *Blackw. Mag.* VII. 467 As the Rev. Mr. F——. Sabbathly says, in the peroration of his sermons.

2. In a manner befitting the Sabbath.

1891 C. James *Rom. Rigmarole* 110 The Squire was Sabbathly solemn and imposing.

Sabbatian (săbē̆·ʃiăn), *sb.*¹ [f. *Sabbati-us* (see below) + -an.] A member of a sect founded by Sabbatius (originally a convert from Judaism), who seceded from the Novatianists before 380, having adopted Quartodeciman views.

1708–22 Bingham *Orig. Eccles.* xx. iii. § 5 The Marcianists ...kept the Sabbath also a fast. So did also the Sabbatians, Lampetians [etc.]. 1727–41 Chambers *Cycl.* s.v., The Sabbatians are recorded by ecclesiastical historians, as having a great abhorrence of the left-hand. 1882–3 *Schaff's Encycl. Relig. Knowl.* III. 2090 By his followers, the Sabbatians, he was honored as a martyr.

Sabbatian (sæbē̆·ʃiăn), *a.* and *sb.*² [f. *Sabbatius* (mod.L. form of *Shabbethai*: see Sabbathaism) + -an.] **A.** *adj.* Pertaining to Sabbathaism.

1892 tr. *Grätz's Hist. Jews* V. 151 The Sabbatian mystics.

B. *sb.* A believer in Sabbathaism.

1892 tr. *Grätz's Hist. Jews* V. 159 At Venice...a quarrel broke out between the Sabbatians and their opponents.

Hence **Sabba·tianism** = Sabbathaism.

1892 tr. *Grätz's Hist. Jews* V. Index, Sabbatianism, revival of, v. 219. 1898 Zangwill *Dreamers Ghetto* vi. 205 Sabbatianism did not play much part in my early life.

Sabbatic (săbæ·tik), *a.* and *sb.* [ad. F. *sabbatique* (= Sp. *sabático*, Pg., It. *sabbatico*), ad. med.L. *sabbaticus, a. Gr. σαββατικός, f. σάββατ-ον Sabbath: see -ic.] **A.** *adj.* Of or pertaining to the Sabbath; resembling or appropriate to the Sabbath. *Sabbatic year* = *sabbatical year* (Sabbatical *a.* 2 a).

1649 Jer. Taylor *Gt. Exemp.* ii. Disc. ix. 119 Strict and necessary rest...was one great part of the Sabbatick rites. 1650 *Vind. Hammond's Addr.* § 16. 6 The servant...is to be set free from that servitude...in the seventh, or sabbatick year. 1660 Jer. Taylor *Duct. Dubit.* ii. ii. rule vi. § 46 They kept their first Sabbatick rest upon the very day in which their redemption was completed. a 1711 Ken *Preparatives* Poet. Wks. 1721 IV. 30 Sabbatick Dawn, a Priest of old, By sound of Trumpet told. 1737 Whiston *Josephus, War* vii. v. § 1 They call it the sabbatick river. 1861 Lewin *Jerusalem* 87 Provisions in the little garrison from the effect of the sabbatic year, began to run short. 1882 J. Parker *Apost. Life* I. 49 Grant Sabbatic peace to every soul.

† **B.** *sb.* A sabbatic year. *Obs.*

1650 *Vind. Hammond's Addr.* § 16. 6 The Jubilee, which is the great Sabbatick (made up of seven times seven).

Sabbatical (săbæ·tikăl), *a.* Also 8 **sabbathical.** [f. med.L. *sabbatic-us (see prec.) + -al.]

1. Pertaining to or appropriate to the Sabbath.

1645 *City Alarum* 20 The formerly mentioned are but our working dayes abuses, now followes our seventh and Sabbaticall errour, wherein we seeme to rest. 1799 Cobbett *Sat. Lond.* (1803) 94 The Curate is so far from being prepared for his sabbatical avocation, that he is engaged during the week in some worldly pursuit. 1849 H. Miller *Footpr. Creat.* xv. (1874) 295 It seems, besides, to throw light on the prominence of the Sabbatical command. 1877 Mrs. Oliphant *Carita* II. xxxi. 201 This, too, was a kind of solemn sabbatical exercise. 1892 A. Birrell *Res Judic.* ii. 38 A sabbatical calm results from the contemplation of his labours.

b. *Sabbatical river*: an imaginary river celebrated in Jewish legend, which was said to observe the Sabbath. Similarly *Sabbatical pool*: see quot. 1649.

The legend of the 'sabbatical river' existed in two discrepant forms: cf. quots. 1671 (after Josephus) and 1849.

1613 Purchas *Pilgrimage* (1614) 519 This was the issue of their Pilgrimage to the Sabbaticall streame, which they supposed to finde in this Persian Gulfe. 1649 Jer. Taylor *Gt. Exemp.* iii. xiv. 51 The sabbaticall pool in Judea, which was dry six dayes, but gushed out in a full stream upon the sabbath. 1671 Stillingfl. *Serm.* viii. (1673) 151 The famous Sabbatical River...which for 6. days bear's all before it..: the admirable nature of that River is, that it keeps the Sabbath and rests all that day. 1849 Longf. *Kavanagh* xi. (1857) 221 And must my life, then, be always like the Sabbatical river of the Jews, flowing in full stream only on the seventh day?

c. Of the nature of a Sabbath or period of rest.

1836 Sir H. Taylor *Statesman* xi. 79 It were to be wished that he should set apart from business, not only a sabbatical day in each week, but if it be possible a sabbatical hour in each day!

2. a. *Sabbatical year*: the seventh year, prescribed by the Mosaic law to be observed as a 'Sabbath' in which the land was to remain untilled and all debtors and Israelitish slaves were to be released. Also *allusively*.

1635–56 Cowley *Davideis* ii. Note 8 From hence contracts, and the account of Sabbatical years and Jubilees bare date. 1705 Hickeringill *Priest-cr.* i. Wks. 1716 III. 24 Neither Seventh Days...nor Sabbath Days, nor Sabbathical Years...is now any more obligatory to us. 1828 E. Irving *Last Days* p. viii, May it prove unto us as a sabbatical year of rest!

b. *Sabbatical millenary*, *millennium*: the last of the seven thousands of years which (on the analogy of the seven days of the creation) were supposed to form the destined term of the world's existence.

1646 Sir T. Browne *Pseud. Ep.* vi. i. 278 He conceaveth the Elementall frame shall end in the seventh or Sabbaticall millenary. 1814 J. Christie *Ess. Early Idol.* 11 The supposed continuance of this earth as many thousand years, the last thousand of which, it was reported, would be a Sabbatical Millenium.

Hence **Sabba·tically** *adv.*, **Sabba·ticalness.**

1727 Bailey vol. II., *Sabbaticalness*, the Being of the Nature or Quality of a Sabbath. 1847 Disraeli *Tancred* ii. xv, He sabbatically abstains from the debate or the rubber.

Sabbatine (sæ·bătain), *a.* *Hist.* [ad. med.L. *sabbatin-us* (and Sp. *sabatino*), f. *sabbat-um* Sabbath, Saturday.] **a.** *Sabbatine preacher*: one appointed to preach on Saturdays. **b.** *Sabbatine bull*: a bull of Pope John XXII, proclaiming, as a reward for the wearing of the scapular, a plenary indulgence available on the first Saturday after the death of him who gains it. So *Sabbatine indulgence*.

1772 Nugent tr. *Hist. Fr. Gerund* I. 437 Friar Gerund appeared a Priest *in facie ecclesiæ*, and Sabatine Preacher in full form. 1826 T. Coleman *Indulgences, etc., Order Mt. Carmel* 13 That the so celebrated name of the Sabbatine Bull might not be forgotten. 1886 *Month* Dec. 473 The second of these privileges is...the Sabbatine Indulgence. It is a plenary...Indulgence...available on the first Saturday after the death of him who gains it, releasing him then and there from Purgatory and admitting him straightway to the joys of Heaven.

Sabbatism (sæ·bătiz'm). *rare.* [ad. late L. *sabbatismus*, Gr. σαββατισμός, n. of action f. σαβ-

βατίζειν to keep the Sabbath, f. σάββατ-ον Sabbath: see -ism.]

1. A sabbatical rest: in allusions to Heb. iv. 9.

1582 N. T. (Rhem.) *Heb.* iv. 9 Therefore there is left a sabbatisme [Vulg. *sabbatismus*, Gr. σαββατισμός; Wycl. 1382 a saboth halowynge; 1611 a rest; 1881 *Revised* a sabbath rest] for the people of God. 1647 J. Cotton *Sing. Ps.* iii. 11 There is now remaining to us another Sabbatisme, or day of rest, now in the dayes of the Gospel, different from the seventh day of rest. 1885 S. Cox *Expositions* II. xxvii. 376 This Divine sabbatism, this pure eternal rest.

2. The formal observance of the Sabbath.

1611 Broughton *Require of Agreement* 13 In the Iubilee the Maiestie of God will be a remission, and redemption, and ending of Sabbatisme to Israell. a 1711 Ken *Preparatives* Poet. Wks. 1721 IV. 29 Sabbatism. To a Seventh Day God Jews restrain'd, For Joy, Rest, Praise ordain'd. 1879 Farrar *St. Paul* (1883) 117 Sabbatism had been elevated above faith and purity.

Hence **Sabbati·smal** *a.*, characterized by holy rest.

1881 J. C. Burns in *J. Bruce's Serm.* Biog. 102 Very peaceful, Sabbatismal, these years were.

Sabbatist (sæ·bătist). [f. L. *sabbat-um* Sabbath + -ist.] Sabbatarian.

1857 Baden Powell *Chr. without Judaism* 161 Some Sabbatists...keep holy the seventh day of the week. 1865 J. Gill tr. *Rovet's Banished Count* xxi. 222 The Sabbatists observed the Seventh day of the week instead of the first.

Sabbatization (sæbătəizē̆·ʃən). [f. next + -ation.] The action of sabbatizing: **a.** Observance of the Sabbath, Sabbath-keeping. **b.** The conversion (of Sunday) into a Sabbath.

1644 Laud *Troub. & Tryal* xxxv. (1695) 345 Those Men who stand so strictly upon the Morality of the Sabbath, do by a gross and carnal Sabbatization, three times out-go the Superstition of the Jew. 1837 G. S. Faber *Orig. Expiat. Sacr.* 202 He actually mentions the non-sabbatization of the patriarchal religionists as a circumstance quite indisputable. 1882 *Ch. Times* 11 Aug. 544 The Sabbatization of Sunday came in comparatively late.

Sabbatize (sæ·bătəiz), *v.* Also Sabbathize. [ad. L. *sabbatiz-āre*, ad. Gr. σαββατίζειν, f. σάββατον Sabbath: see -ize. Cf. F. *sabbatiser*.]

1. *intr.* To keep the Sabbath; to observe a specified day as a day of rest.

1608 Willet *Hexapla Exod.* 247 They are also commanded to keepe the Sabbaths rest, to Sabbatize. a 1716 Blackall *Wks.* (1723) I. 214 We do not so Sabbatise as we should do, if we give only one Day of the Week to God, and the other six Days to the Devil. 1881 Blackie *Lay Serm.* ii. 105 A Samaritan...made it a point...in whatever attitude the first moment of the day had found him, in that position to remain..: if sitting, then to Sabbatise in the sitting attitude.

b. *fig.* To enjoy or undergo a period of rest analogous to a Sabbath.

1382 Wyclif *1 Esdras* i. 58 At the time of ther forsaking he [*i.e.* the land] sabatisede, in the apliyng of seventi ȝer. 1596 Bell *Surv. Popery* i. iii. v. 109 Although the mind regenerate do sabbatize in the Lord. 1625 Gill *Sacr. Philos.* ii. 140 But if there were no incarnation...neither our understanding, nor our sences could have any object wherein to rest and sabbatize. a 1711 Ken *Edmund* Poet. Wks. 1721 II. 89 It was the Day which Jesus canoniz'd, When he from all his Dolours sabbatiz'd.

2. *trans.* To observe or keep as a Sabbath; to assimilate to a Sabbath.

1609 Bible (Douay) *Lev.* xxv. 2 Thou shalt sabbatize the sabbath to the Lord. 1880 *W. Smith's Dict. Chr. Antiq.* II. 1052/2 The tendency to sabbatize the Lord's day is due chiefly to the necessities of legal enforcement. 1906 H. Begbie *Priest* xvi. 256 Silvia is inclined to Sabbatize the week-days.

† 3. To give sabbatical rest to. *Obs. rare*⁻¹.

1701 Beverley *Apoc. Quest.* 8 For the Type is Sacrifice Honourably Sabbatiz'd, and at Rest in the Antitype, Our Lord Jesus Christ, our great Sacrifice Sabbatizing All Sacrifice by the sacrifice of Himself.

Hence **Sa·bbatizing** *vbl. sb.* Also **Sa·bbatizer**, in quot. one who observes the Jewish Sabbath.

1613 Purchas *Pilgrimage* (1614) 122 The Jewes on their Sabbaths...did vse...to drink somwhat more largely (a Sabbatising too much, by too many Christians imitated). 1683 Hickes *Case Inf. Bapt.* 61 Let the Adversaries of Infant-Baptism consider..Whether rejecting of it...they do not teach others, especially Atheists, pure Deists, and Sabbatizers...a way to deny all the rest. a 1711 Ken *Preparatives* Poet Wks. 1721 IV. 20 Wear Jesus Yoke,...'Twill prove a Sabbatising to your Mind. 1742 J. Glas *Lord's Supper* ii. (1883) 76 Our sabbatizing, or resting from our own works on the first day of the week is a sign of the truth of the promise of entering into his rest. 1855 *People's Sunday* 5, I shall, therefore, further show the complete absence of scripture authority for the doctrines of our Sabbatizing brethren.

Sabbaton, -tyne: see Sabaton, Sabatine.

‖ **Sabbe·ka.** *Antiq. rare*⁻¹. [Biblical Aramaic סַבְּכָא or שַׂבְּכָא *sabb'kā*.] An ancient musical instrument mentioned in the Book of Daniel; in the English Bible erroneously called Sackbut, q. v.

1845 Whittier *Ezekiel* ix, They listen, as in Babel's throng The Chaldeans to the dancer's song, Or wild sabbeka's nightly play.

‖ **Sabdariffa** (sæbdări·fă). [mod.L.; in Lobel *Plantarum Hist.* (1576) 375; of obscure origin.] An East Indian rose-mallow, *Hibiscus Sabdariffa* (Linnæus 1759), cultivated for its acidulous calyxes.

1866 *Treas. Bot.* 1002/2 Sabdariffa. *Hibiscus Sabdariffa*, called Red Sorrel in the West and Rozelle in the East Indies, where it is used in tarts, jellies and salads, and to form a cooling drink.

Sabe: see Savey.

Sabean, Sabeism: see Sabæan, Sabaism.

Sabel, obs. form of Sable.

† Sabeline, *sb. Obs.* Also 3 **sablyne**, 7 **sabelline.** [a. OF. *sabeline* (12th c. in Godef.), ad. med.L. *sabelina* (*pellis*), sable (fur), f. *sabellum* Sable *sb.*¹ Cf. Zibeline.] The fur of the sable.

a 1200 *Moral Ode* 364 (Egerton MS.) Ne scal þer beo fou ne grei ne cunig ne ermine ne ocquerne ne martres cheole ne bever ne sabeline [c 1275 *Jesus MS.* sablyne]. ? 1700 *Cruel Mother* in Child *Ballads* (1882) I. 221/2 We neither wore the silks nor the sabelline. 1876 Planché *Cycl. Costume* I. 439 *Sable*, *sabelline*, the skin of an animal of the weasel or marten kind.

Sabeline: see Sabelline *a.*¹

‖ **Sabella** (săbe·lă). *Zool.* [mod.L. (Gmelin *Linnæus Syst. Nat.*, ed. 12, 1788), perh. f. *sabulum* sand.] A tubicolous annelid of the family *Sabellidæ*.

a 1851 Dalyell *Powers Creator* (1853) II. 175 Different species or varieties of the Sabella are found on the shores and in the seas of Scotland. *Ibid.*, *Sabella alveolaria*.—The Honeycomb Sabella. 1851 Medlock tr. *Schoedler's Bk. Nature* ii. 530 There are besides, the Sabellas, or *pencil*, *fan*, and *comb-worms* (Sabella). 1863 Wood *Illustr. Nat. Hist.* III. 699 We now come to another pretty tube-inhabiting annelid, which is called Sabella, because it lives in the sand and forms its tube of that substance. Several species of Sabella are found on the British coasts, the most common of which is the Shore Sabella (*Sabella alveolaria*).

Sabellian (săbe·liăn), *a.*¹ and *sb.*¹ *Theol.* [ad. eccl. L. *Sabelliān-us*, f. *Sabelli-us* (see B): see -an.]

A. *adj.* Pertaining to the Sabellians (see B) or their doctrine.

1577 Hanmer *Anc. Eccl. Hist.* vii. v. 126 Of the Sabellian heresie...The Sabellian heretickes. 1720 Waterland *Eight Serm.* 4 Under the Sabellian Interpretation I include all that belongs to Men of Sabellian Principles. 1848 R. I. Wilberforce *Doctr. Incarnation* ix. 259 The Sabellian theory is, that there exists no real diversity of Persons in the Ever-Blessed Trinity.

B. *sb.* One who accepts the view of Sabellius (an African heresiarch of the third century) that the Father, Son, and Holy Spirit are merely different aspects or modes of manifestation of one Divine person. Cf. Modalist.

1402 *Pol. Poems* (Rolls) II. 92 He is callid an heretike that heresies sowith, as Arrians, Wyclyfanes, Sabellyanes, and other. 1556 Clement in Strype *Eccl. Mem.* III. App. lxi. 214 From all Arians, Eutichians, Manichians, Sabellians...and all other heretikes. 1685 Rycaut tr. *Platina's Lives Popes* 52 The Sabellians...asserted that the Father, Son, and holy Ghost were but one Person. 1702 Echard *Eccl. Hist.* (1710) 619 Tho' those who then held this opinion were call'd Sabellians, yet the heresie itself was more ancient than Sabellius. 1850 Robertson *Serm.* Ser. iii. iv. (1877) 45 Sabellians, or worshippers of one person under three different manifestations.

Sabellian (săbe·liăn), *a.*² and *sb.*² *Hist.* [f. L. *Sabell-us* + -ian.] **a.** *adj.* Pertaining to a group of related peoples who inhabited certain parts of ancient Italy, comprising the Sabines, Samnites, Campanians, and others. **b.** *sb.* A person belonging to any of these peoples.

In Latin poetry *Sabelli* is commonly used as a synonym of *Sabini*. The use of *Sabellian* by modern writers is somewhat arbitrary.

1601 Holland *Pliny* I. 64 Of Samnites, whom the Greekes called Sabellians and Saunites, The Colonie Bouianum, the old. 1841 W. Spalding *Italy & It. Isl.* I. 277 The territory of those Sabellian tribes [*sc.* the Sabines, Marsians, Pelignians, Vestinians, and Samnites], which are here classed together, includes the central heights and valleys of the Apennines. 1880 *Encycl. Brit.* XIII. 445/2 Oscan is...a useful term to designate the nation or group of tribes composed of the Samnites, together with their descendants or offshoots, the Campanians, Lucanians, and Bruttians. The name Sabellians, used by the Roman poets, has been employed by some modern writers in much the same signification.

Sabellianism (săbe·liăniz'm). [f. Sabellian *a.*¹ and *sb.*¹ + -ism.] The doctrinal conception of the Trinity as held by the followers of Sabellius; belief in the Sabellian doctrine of the Trinity.

1668 H. More *Div. Dial.* Schol. (1713) 549 Sabellianism, which allows the Consubstantiality or Coequality in the Trinity. 1852 Robertson *Serm.* Ser. iv. xi. (1876) 104 A heresy known by the name of Sabellianism or Modal Trinity. 1907 Illingworth *Doctr. Trin.* vii. 127 To avoid Tritheism on the one hand,...and Sabellianism on the other.

Sabellianize (săbe·liănəiz), *v.* [f. Sabellian + -ize.] *intr.* To adopt Sabellian views.

1833–40 J. H. Newman *Church of Fathers* (1842) 171 We have bid farewell to contentious deviations of doctrine,...neither Sabellianizing nor Arianising. 1833 — *Arians* v. i. (1876) 356 Not only did he [Athanasius] reluctantly abandon his associate, the unfortunate Marcellus, on his Sabellianizing but [etc.].

Sabellic (săbe·lik), *a.* [f. L. *Sabellus* Sabellian *a.*² + -ic.] Pertaining to the language or the nationality of the Sabellians.

1880 *Encycl. Brit.* XIII. 126/1 The Sabellic inscriptions. 1902 Giles in *Encycl. Brit.* XXXIII. 898/2 The Sabellic alphabet,...found in a few inscriptions.

Sabellid (săbe·lid), *a.* and *sb. Zool.* [f. Sabella + -id.] **A.** *adj.* Pertaining to or connected with the family *Sabellidæ*, of which the genus *Sabella* is the type.

1900 *Nature* 6 Dec. 140/1 A paper...on the sabellid worms collectively designated as Polychætes.

B. *sb.* An individual of the family *Sabellidæ*.

1893 *Jrnl. Mar. Zool.* Nov. 13 On the method of dispersion and fertilization of ova in some sabellids. 1896 Benham in *Camb. Nat. Hist.* II. 286 The beautiful branchial crowns of various Sabellids.

Sabelline (săbe·ləin), *a.*¹ Also (in Dicts.) **sabeline.** [ad. med.L. *sabellīnus*, f. *sabellum* Sable *sb.*¹] Of the colour of sable fur.

1888 *Longm. Mag.* July 297 Bird and beast must assume alike the uniform grey sabelline tint of external nature.

Sabelline (săbe·ləin), *a.*² *Zool.* [f. Sabella + -ine¹.] Pertaining to the genus *Sabella* or to the family *Sabellidæ* (Cent. Dict. 1891).

Sabelline, variant of Sabeline *Obs.*

Sabellite (săbe·ləit). *Zool.* [f. Sabella + -ite¹.] A fossil sabella, or some similar worm (*Cent. Dict.* 1891).

Sabelloid (săbe·loid), *a.* and *sb. Zool.* [f. Sabella + -oid.] **a.** *adj.* Of or resembling the annelidan *Sabellidæ* (Cent. Dict. 1891). **b.** *sb.* One of the *Sabellidæ* (ibid.).

Saber, obs. or U.S. form of Sabre.

Sabian (sē̆·biăn), *sb.* and *a.* Also 7–8 **Zabian**, 7–8 **Sabean**, 8 **Zabæan**, **Tsabæan**, 8–9 **Sabæan**, **Tsabian.** [f. Arab. صابى *çābi'* + -an.

According to Nöldeke, the word represents the pr. pple. of the Aramaic צבע *ç'ba'* to baptize (the ע being changed into א as is usual in the Mandæan and cognate dialects). In the actual form in which the word occurs in Arabic, it has the appearance of being derived from the same root as the Hebrew צבא *çābā* host (see Sabaoth); hence, as certain sects claiming the name of Sabians were alleged to be worshippers of the stars, the name was (already by Maimonides in the 12th c.) interpreted as referring to 'the host of heaven'.]

A. *sb.*

1. An adherent of a religious sect mentioned in three passages of the Koran (ii. 40, v. 73, xxii. 17), and by later Arabian writers.

In the Koran the Sabians are classed with Moslems, Jews, and Christians, as believers in the true God. On account of the toleration extended by Moslems to them, the name of Sabians was, some centuries after Mohammed, assumed not only by the Gnostic half-Christian Mandæans (whose religion is perhaps akin to that of the true Sabians), but also by certain actual polytheists. The statement of some Arabic writers is that the Sabians were professedly Christian, but secretly worshippers of the stars. (Cf. Sabaism.)

1661 Boyle *Style of Script.* (1675) 35 For want of knowing the Religion of the antient Zabians...Of those Zabiists...I find a deep and general silence in Classick Authors. 1797 *Encycl. Brit.* (ed. 3) X. 462/1 The fourth [*sc.* apartment of hell] named *al Sair*, [Mohammedans assign] to the Sabians. 1841 *Penny Cycl.* XX. 295/2 That the unity of the Deity was however still acknowledged in the religious system of the Tsabians is manifest from the way in which this religion is spoken of in the Korân.

b. Used for Mandæan (see quot. 1883).

1797 *Encycl. Brit.* (ed. 3) X. 458/2 The Sabians have several books which they attribute to some of the antediluvian prophets. 1883 K. Kessler *ibid.* (ed. 9) XV. 467/2 *note*, In their dealings with members of other communions the designation they [*i.e.* the Mandæans] take is Sabians.

2. In erroneous use: A worshipper of 'the host of heaven'; a star-worshipper.

1716 Prideaux *O. & N. Test. Connected* i. iii. (1718) I. 140 The remainder of this sect still subsists in the east under the same name of Sabians...That which hath given them the greatest credit among the people of the east is, that the best of their astronomers have been of this sect...For the stars being the gods they worshipped, they made them the chief subject of their studies. 1864 Col. Greenwood in *Athenæum* 23 July 115/3 Bishop Cumberland and Bishop Warburton...agree that Cain...and his descendants were Sabæans. Abraham and Moses were Sabæans till Jehovah revealed himself to them.

B. *adj.* Pertaining to the Sabians (in the various applications of the name: see A).

1796 Morse *Amer. Geog.* II. 571 The Sabean Christians have, in their religion, a mixture of Judaism and Mahometanism. 1859 J. M. Arnold *Ishmael* 35 In a Sabian Almanac ...it is stated: 'They fast in it seven days...in honour of the great Lord, the Sun, the Lord of all Good.' 1886 *Encycl. Brit.* XXI. 128/1 It is quite inappropriate to call star-worshippers in general Sabians or Zabians or to speak of a distinct Sabian religion, as older writers do.

Sabianism (sē̆·biăniz'm). Also 9 **sabæanism.** [f. prec. + -ism.] The religion of the Sabians; chiefly in erroneous use, worship of 'the host of heaven', star-worship. Cf. Sabaism.

1788 Gibbon *Decl. & F.* V. l. 194 Sabianism was diffused over Asia by the science of the Chaldæans and the arms of the Assyrians. 1826 G. S. Faber *Orig. Pagan Idol.* I. 31 Astrolatry or Sabianism; that is to say, the worship of the Sun, the Moon, and the Host of Heaven. 1871 Proctor *Light Sci.* 333 Sabæanism, or star-worship.

Sabicu (sæbikū·). A timber tree, *Lysiloma Sabicu*, native of Cuba, the wood of which is greatly valued for its hardness and durability; the wood of this tree. Also *attrib.*

1866 *Treas. Bot.* 704/1 The valuable hard timber known as Sabicù, Savacù or Savicù wood. *Ibid.*, Sabicu timber is imported...from Cuba. 1875 *Encycl. Brit.* I. 68/2 *Acacia formosa* supplies the valuable Cuba timber called sabicu. 1879 *Man. Artillery Exerc.* 588 A number of 5-in. sabicu shifting rollers.

Sabiism: see Sabaism.

Sabill, obs. f. Sable. **Sabin(e**, var. ff. Savin.

Sabine (sæ̃·bəin), *a.* and *sb.* *Hist.* [ad. L. *Sabīnus* adj. and sb.] **A.** *adj.* Of or pertaining to the Sabines: see B.

Sabine, obs. form of SABINE *Bot.*

Sabino (sæbī·no), [app. altered form of Sp. *sabina* SAVIN.] The bald or deciduous cypress, *Taxodium distichum* (Treas. Bot., Suppl., 1874).

Sabir: see SABIR.

Sable (sæ̃·b'l), *sb.*[1] Forms: *a.* 4 sabylle, 5 sabulle, 5–6 sabill, 5–7 sabel, 6 sabel(l)e, *β.* sabell, 5–6 sabel. [a. OF. *sable*, *sabel*; *sable* fur, also quasi-*adj.* in *martre sable* ('sable marten') as the name of the animal and its fur.]

b. sable-mouse (= Ger. *zobelmaus*) = LEMMING.

Sable (sæ̃·b'l), *sb.*[2] Also *4–5* sabyl(l)e, *5–6* sabill. [*f. a.* *sable sb.*[1] is commonly assumed]

A.
I. Her. Black, as one of the heraldic colours.

2. The colour black; black clothing, also, esp. as a symbol of mourning. *poet.* and *rhetorical.*

† b. Blackness, darkness. *Obs.*

3. *Mournful.* *Obs.*

† b. sable, *sb.*[3] Also *pl.* sables, *7–8* sabel; and see SABLE. *Obs.* [a. F. *sable*: see SABLE.]

‡ Sable, *sb.*[4] *Chiefly poet.* [f. SABLE *a.*] *trans.* To blacken or darken. Also, to clothe in 'sables'. Now *rare.*

Sableness (sæ̃·b'l·nes). [f. SABLE *a.* + -NESS.] Blackness; mournfulness.

†Sablière[1]. *Arch. Obs.* [a. F. *sablière*, of obscure origin.] A piece of wood as long as a beam but not so thick (Phillips 1696).

†Sablière[2]. *Arch. Obs.* [a. F. *sablière* sand-pit, f. *sable* sand:—L. *sabulum*.] A sand-pit or gravel-pit.

Sably (sæ̃·bli), *adv.* [f. SABLE *a.* + -LY[2].] Darkly, blackly.

Sablyne, variant of SABELINE *Obs.*

Sabot (sæ·bo), *sb.* [F. (OF. in 13th c. *cabot*, mod. *Picard chabot*) prob. related in some way to *savate* shoe, Pr. *sabata*: see SABATON.]

b. *Mech.* Also in *sabot-cartridge*.

Saburra (sæbɵ·ră). *Med.* [L. *saburra* sand, ballast.]

Hence Sa·burral *a.*, pertaining to or consisting of saburra.

Sabulose (sæ·biŭlōus), *a.* [ad. L. *sabulōsus*, f. *sabulum*: see prec.] Sandy.

Sabulosity (sæbiŭlŏ·siti). Sandiness.

Sabulous (sæ·biŭləs), *a.* [ad. L. *sabulōsus*, f. *sabulum*: see prec.] Sandy; consisting of or abounding in sand; arenaceous.

Saccharide (sæ·kăroid, -id). *Chem.* [f. med. L. *sacchar-um* sugar + -IDE.]

Saccharification (sækærĭfĭ·keɪʃən). *Chem.* [f. SACCHARIFY: see -FICATION.] The natural process by which starch and gum become converted into sugar.

Saccharify (sækæ·rĭfəɪ), *v.* [f. med. L. *sacchar-um* sugar + -(I)FY.] *trans.* To convert (starch) into sugar.

Saccharimeter (sækărĭ·mĭtər). *Chem.* [f. sacchari- (see SACCHARINE) + -METER.]

Saccharin (sæ·kărĭn). *Chem.* [f. med. L. *sacchar-um* + -IN[1].]

Saccharine (sæ·kărəin, -in), *a.* and *sb.* [Formed as prec. + -INE[1].]

Saccharoid (sæ·kăroid), *a.* and *sb.* [f. Gr. *σάκχαρ* sugar + -OID.]

Saccharoidal (sækăroɪ·dăl), *a.* [Formed as prec. + -AL[1].] = SACCHAROID *a.*

Sacculina (sækiŭləɪ·nă). *Zool.* [mod.L., *saccul-us*: see SACCULUS.] A genus of degenerate cirripeds parasitic on crabs; an animal of this genus.

Saccule (sæ·kiūl). *Anat.* [ad. L. *sacculus*, dim. of *saccus* sac.] A little sac or bag.

Sacculus (sæ·kiūləs). Pl. **sacculi** (-ləi). *Anat.* [L., dim. of *saccus* sac.] A little sac.

Sacellum (săse·lĕm). Pl. **sacella** (-lă). [L., dim. of *sacer* sacred.]

Sacerdotage. *jocular.* [f. L. *sacerdōt-* priest + -AGE.]

Sacerdotal (sæsərdōu·tăl), *a.* [a. F. *sacerdotal*, ad. L. *sacerdōtāl-is*, f. *sacerdōt-* priest.]

Sacerdotalism (sæsərdōu·tălĭz'm). The spirit or principles of the priesthood; sacerdotal character or religion.

Sacerdote. *rare.* [a. F. *sacerdote*, ad. L. *sacerdōt-em* priest.]

SACERDOTALISM.

sacerdōt-, sacerdōts, f. *sacri-, -sacer* holy, sacred (nent. pl. *sacra* sacrifices) + *dō-* ablaut-var. of *dare* to give. The etymological sense of the sb. is thus 'one who offers sacrifices'.]

A. adj.

1. Of or belonging to the priests or priesthood; of or pertaining to a priest; befitting or characteristic of a priest; priestly.

Sacerdote, *nonce-wd.* In 7 **sacerdott.** [ad. L. *sacerdōt-em.*]

Sacerdotical, a. Obs. rare⁻¹. [f. L. *sacerdōt-em* + -ICAL.] = SACERDOTAL.

Sacha, obs. form of SAC¹.

Sachem (sē'tʃem). Also **sacheem, sachim, -hem, sachin,** 9 **saquem.** [a. Narragansett *sâchim* = Delaware *sakima,* Micmac *sakumow,* Penobscot *sagum* (whence SAGAMORE).]

The supreme head or chief of some American Indian tribes.

b. Holding the office of a priest.

Hence **Sacerdo'tally** adv., **†Sacerdo'talness.**

Sacerdotalism (sæsædōu'tāliz'm). [f. SACERDOTAL + -ISM.]

1. The sacerdotal spirit or system; the principles or practice of the priesthood.

Sacerdotalist (sæsædōu'tālist). [f. SACERDOTAL a. + -IST.] One who advocates or defends sacerdotalism.

Sacerdotalize (sæsædōu'tālaiz), v. [f. SACERDOTAL a. + -IZE.] *trans.* To make subservient to sacerdotalism. Hence **Sacerdo'talized** ppl. a., **Sacerdo'talizing** vbl. sb.

Sachet (sæʃe'). Fr. *sachet* (from 12th c.; in ONF. *saguet* = see SACKET), dim. of sac L. *saccum* (see SACK sb.¹).

Sachem-maker [app. a derivative or corruption of *sachama* (*Sachem* = SACHEM, SAGAMORE.

Sachere, obs. form of SACRE.

Sachel, -ell, obs. forms of SATCHEL.

Sack (sæk). *sb.¹* Forms: 1 *sæc, sacc,* 3-4 *sac, soc, sæc,* (3 *soo,* 6 *north. seik*), 3 *sakke,* 3-7 *sacke,* 4-5 *sak, sekke,* 4-6 *sek,* (5 *sac, cek, sacke, sake, seocke,* Sc. *seck,* 7 *sek,* 5-*sack.* [OE. *sacc,* masc. (also L. *sacc-us* lang. ... = ON. *sekk-r*]

Sack (sæk). *sb.²* = SACK *sb.¹* cf. L. *saccare* to strain through a bag (med.L. also to put into a bag), MDu. *sacken* (Du sakken), G. *sacken* to put into a bag.]

Sackage (sæ'kēdʒ). *sb.* Now rare. Also 6-7 **sacrage.** [f. SACK v.² according to IIats.-Darm.]

Sachet (sæʃe'). Fr. *sachet* ... = SACKET.

Sach-chego, *sb.* Obs. [a. F. *sac-cage.*]

Sackbut (sæ'kbʌt). Forms: 6-7 *saghut, -bot,* 6 *sagbout, sagebut,* 7 *sagbuth, 7-8 shagbush, 7 -but), 6 sackbut,* 7 *-buck, shagbush, 8 -sackut, 7 sac-but. [a. F. *saquebute, sacqueboute, -boute, -botte,* etc.]

Sack (sæk), *sb.³* cf. L. *saccare* ... G. *sacken* to put into a bag.]

Sackage (sæ'kēdʒ). *sb.* Now rare.

Sackcloth (sæ'kklɒθ). Forms: cf. SACK *sb.¹* and CLOTH.]

Sacked (sækt), *ppl. a.* [f. SACK *v.¹* + -ED¹.] Garments of sackcloth.

Sacking (sæ'kiŋ), *vbl. sb.¹* [f. SACK *v.¹* + -ING¹.]

Sacked (sækt), *ppl. a.* [f. SACK *v.²* + -ED¹.]

Sacking (sæ'kiŋ), *vbl. sb.²* [f. SACK *v.²* + -ING¹.]

Sacked Friar. = SACK-FRIAR.

Sackbutter, a player on the sackbut.

†Sa'ck-bush. Obs. rare. [f. SACK *sb.¹* + BUTT *sb.²*] A butt of sack.

Sacker. One who sacks or plunders.

Sacker, variant of SAKER.

Sacket. 1 *sakett,* 6 *sakket,* 9 *sakit.* [a. 1 *sag.* Obs. exc. dial.

Sackless (sæ'klēs). *a.* Forms: 1-3 *sacléas,* 3-4 *sacleas,* ... [OE. *sacléas.*]

Sack-friar. Also **Sacked Friar.** [SACK *sb.¹*]

Sackful (sæ'kful). *sb.* [f. SACK *sb.¹* + -FUL.]

Sacrament, ...

SACRAL.

Sacral (sē'kral), a.¹ [f. L. *sacr-um* SACRUM + -AL.] Anat. Pertaining to the sacrum.

Sacral (sē'kral), a.² [f. L. *sacr-* (sacer sacred) + -AL.] Pertaining to sacred rites.

Sacrament, ... Also mod.L. *Sacra-...*

Sacre, obs. form of SACRIFICE.

Sacred (sē'kred), *ppl. a.* and *a.* [f. *sacre-n* SACRE *v.* + -ED¹.]

Sacrify, var. SACRIFY.

Sacral, ...

Sacredness.

Sacrifice, leger, legie, obs. ff. SACRILEGE.

Sacreng, Sacret, obs. ff. SACRING, SAKERET.

Sacri, sacrid: see SACRE v.

† Sacrificeal. Obs.

† Sacriferous, a. Obs. rare.

Sacrifice (sæ·krifəis), sb.

Sacrifice (sæ·krifəis), v.

† Sacrifical, a.

Sacrificable, a.

Sacrification. rare.

Sacrificator.

Sacrificature.

Sacrifice (sæ·krifəis), sb.

Sacrifice (sæ·krifəis), v.

Sacrificable, a.

† Sacrificeable, a. Obs.

Sacrificed, ppl. a.

Sacrificing, ppl. a.

Sacrificer.

† Sacrificial, a. Obs.

Sacrificial (sækrifi·ʃəl), a.

Sacrificing, vbl. sb.

† Sacrificulist.

† Sacrifico, v. Obs.

Sacrifier.

Sacrify, v.

Sacrilege (sæ·krilédʒ), sb.

Sacrilege.

Sacrileger (sæ·kriledʒər).

Sacrilegious (sækrilī·dʒəs), a.

Sacrilegiously, adv.

Sacrilegiousness.

† Sacrilegist. Obs.

† Sacrilege. Obs.

Sacring (sēi·kriŋ), vbl. sb.

Sacring-bell.

Sacripant.

Sacrist (sēi·krist).

Sacristan (sæ·kristən).

Sacristy (sæ·kristi).

Sacro-.

Sacro-sciatic.

Sacrosanct (sæ·krosæŋkt), a.

Sacrosanctity.

Sacrum (sēi·krəm).

Sacry, obs.

Sad (sæd), a.

A. adj.

I. Of persons and immaterial things.

Sad.

be used [for scouring fire irons] for it makes sad work. 1819 SHELLEY Peter Bell 3rd VI. xii, All Peter did on this occasion Was, writing some sad stuff in prose. 1819 BYRON Juan II. cxxvii, Heaven knows what cash he got or blood he spilt, A sad old fellow was he, if you please. 1835 J. MACDONALD in Tweedie Life iii. (1849) 240, I am a sad coward. 1836–7 DICKENS Sk. Boz, Charact. vii, The sad-dog sort of feeling came strongly upon John Dounce. 1892 Daily News 25 Jan. 5/3 Unpolished granite..is a sad harbourer of soot and dust.

II. In various physical senses.

7. Of material objects. †a. Solid, dense, compact; massive, heavy. Obs. [So early mod.G. satt.]

13.. K. Alis. 5587 Two grete ymages..of golde sad. c 1330 R. BRUNNE Chron. (1810) 198 With iren nayles sad..his fete was schod. 1340 HAMPOLE Pr. Consc. 3189 Þe mast veniel syns sal þar bryn langly, Als wodde brinnes, þat es sadde and hevy. c 1350 Will. Palerne 1072 No strengþe him wiþstod of sad stonen walles. 1388 WYCLIF Exod. xxxviii. 7 Forsothe thilke auter was not sad [Vulg. solidum], but holowe. c 1440 Promp. Parv. 440/1 Sad, or hard, solidus. c 1450 Cov. Myst. xxiv. (Shaks. Soc.) 236 In feyth it is an holy ston, Ryth sad of weyth and hevy of peys. 1513 DOUGLAS Æneis XI. xi. 47 The schaft was sad and sound, and weill ybaik. 1587 HARRISON England III. i. (1878) II. 2 The flesh of buls..is of sadder substance and therefore much heauier as it lieth in the scale. 1611 COTGR., Fourmage de taulpe, heauie or sad cheese. 1625 LISLE Du Bartas, Noe 29 This kind of timber..growes so sad and hard that it cannot rot. c 1638 STRAFFORD in Browning Life (1891) 219 To those that..tell you..I am but as a feather, I shall be found sadder than lead. 1641 BEST Farm. Bks. (Surtees) 147 Short barley strawe..is the best for stoppinge of holes ..because it is sadder, and not soe subjeckt to blowe out with everie blast of winde, as other light and dry strawe is. fig. c 1400 Rom. Rose 6907 For sadde burdens that men taken Make folkes shuldres aken. c 1400 Apol. Loll. 45 Wo worþ 3ow þat ti3en mynt, aneis, & comyn, & ilke herbe, & leuen þe sadder þings of þe lawe, dome, feiþ, & mercy. c 1485 Digby Myst. (1882) IV. 1328 The wordes of Andrewe beyn sadd & ponderose. 1611 BEAUM. & FL. Knt. Burn. Pestle IV. i, Damsel right faire, I am on many sad adventures bound, That call me forth into the wildernesse.

†b. Solid as opposed to liquid. Obs.

c 1380 WYCLIF Serm. Sel. Wks. II. 259 Þer mete was þer bileve þat þei hadden of sadde þingis, and þer drynke was þer bileve þat þei hadden of moist þingis. 1382 — Heb. v. 13 To whom is nede of mylk, and not sad mete [Vulg. solido cibo].

†c. Firmly fixed. Obs. exc. dial.

1338 R. BRUNNE Chron. (1810) 305 St[r]ength suld non haf had, to perte þam þorgh oute, So wer þei set sad with poyntes rounde aboute. a 1375 Joseph Arim. 258 Þenne he seos Ihesu crist in a sad Roode. 1382 WYCLIF 2 Tim. ii. 19 But the sad foundement [Vulg. firmum fundamentum] of God stondith. a 1400 Leg. Rood (1871) 137 Beo a staf stondeþ sad, Whon 3e fongen flesch in godes hous, Þat staf is Cristes Crouche.

d. Of soil: Stiff, heavy. ? Obs. exc. dial.

1340–70 Alex. & Dind. 912 For to sowe & to sette in þe sad erthe. c 1420 Pallad. on Husb. II. 173 Vynes preueth best yf they Be sette anoon aftir the spade or plough, Er then the lond be woxen sadde or tough. 1600 SURFLET Country Farm v. xviii. 702 Nauets and turneps delight in a light and fine mould, and not in a churlish and sad ground. 1707 MORTIMER Husb. (1721) I. 66 Chalky Lands are naturally cold and sad. 1712 J. MORTON Nat. Hist. Northampt. 44 The Clay-land..is the toughest, or most tenacious, and the most dense of all our Soils; upon this Account, on the Thrapston Side, they call it Sad-land. 1889 N. W. Linc. Gloss. s.v., Land is sad when the frosts of winter have not mellowed it.

e. Of bread, pastry, etc.: That has not 'risen' properly; heavy. Now dial.

1688 R. HOLME Armoury III. 317/1 Bakers Terms in their Art...Sad, heavy, close Bread. 1747–96 MRS. GLASSE Cookery xiii. 191 It makes the crust sad, and is a great hazard of the pie running. 1824–9 LANDOR Imag. Conv. Wks. 1846 I. 82 Let him place the accessaries on the table lest what is insipid and clammy, and (as housewives with great propriety call it) sad, grow into duller accretion and inerter viscidity the more I masticate it. 1889 SKRINE Mem. E. Thring 51 Of what meagre straw and doughy brick was our weekly batch! It was what bakers call 'sad'.

†f. Of a number of persons or things: Forming a compact body. Obs.

a 1400–50 Alexander 2614 Þe multitude ware to me meruaile to reken, Þat sammed was on aiþir side many sadd thousand. Ibid. 5559 Þai sett in a sadd sowme & sailid his kni3tis. c 1430 Chev. Assigne 119 Of sadde leues of þe wode wrow3te he hem wedes.

8. Of colour: Dark, deep. In later use, influenced by sense 5: Not cheerful-looking; neutral-tinted, dull, sober.

The Ger. satt and MDu. sat (Du. zat) have the sense 'dark' or 'deep' as applied to colours, as a direct development from the primary sense 'full' (see sense 1 above).

c 1412 HOCCLEVE De Reg. Princ. 695 And where be my gounes of scarlet, Sanguyn, murreye, & blewes sadde & lighte. c 1425 Cast. Persev. (Stage direction) in Macro Plays 76 Þe iiij dowteris schul be clad in mentelys;..Trewthe in sad grene, & Pes al in blake. c 1483 CAXTON Dialogues 14/36 Yelow, reed, Sad blew [Fr. entrepers], morreey. a 1539 in Archæologia XLVII. 53 Noo more to use rede stomachers but other sadder colers in the same. 1578 HUNNIS Hyvesf. Hunnye xxxvii 92 Colours lyght and sad. 1600 SURFLET Country Farm VI. xxii. 802 Russet wines: In the number wherof, are contained the red wines, or sad, and light red. 1609 C. BUTLER Fem. Mon. (1634) 105 The second Summer, this light yellow is changed to a sad. 1658 ROWLAND tr. Moufet's Theat. Ins. 936 Long and slender shanks of a very sad black colour. 1686 PLOT Staffordsh. 201 First of a dark greenish colour, growing sadder by degrees as the plant decays, till it approaches a black. 1799 G. SMITH Laboratory II. 311 Dubbing, of the down of a sad grey cat. 1836 Backwoods of Canada 241 The leaves are of a sad green, sharply notched, and divided in three lobes. 1855 BRIMLEY Ess., Tennyson 99 Sad greys and browns. 1867 O. W. HOLMES Guard. Angel iii, She had always..been dressed in sad colors. 1883 STEVENSON Treas. Isl. xiii, The general colouring was uniform and sad.

†b. Dark-coloured, sober-coloured. Obs.

1560 BECON Catech. VI. Wks. I. 536 If they be olde women and maryed: not lyght apparell, but sad raiment pleaseth a godly husband. 1590 SPENSER F. Q. I. xii. 5 Arayd in antique robes downe to the grownd, And sad habiliments. 1668 PEPYS Diary 24 Aug., My wife is upon hanging the long chamber..with the sad stuff that was in the best chamber. 1711 Lond. Gaz. No. 4919/4 A Man..between 20 and 30 years of Age, pale Visage and sad Hair.

†9. Of sleep: Sound, deep. Obs.

a 1350 St. Nicholas 329 in Horstm. Altengl. Leg. (1881) 15 Sodanly he fell on full sad slepe. 1377 LANGL. P. Pl. B. V. 4 Þanne waked I of my wynkynge and wo was with-alle, Þat I ne hadde sleped sadder and yseijen more. c 1400 Destr. Troy 679 Medea..Persauyt..Þat all sad were on slepe. c 1450 Mankind 585 in Macro Plays 22 3e may here hym snore; he ys sade a-slepe. 1485 CAXTON St. Wenefr. 20, I couerd my hede and fylle in to a sadde slepe.

†10. Of blows: Heavy, delivered with vigour. [So early mod.G. satt.]

c 1350 Will. Palerne 2775 He..set hire a sad strok so sore in þe necke, þat sche top ouer tail tombled ouer þe hacches. c 1400 Destr. Troy 1263 One caupet with hym kenely,.. And set hym a sad dynt. 1470–85 MALORY Arthur XI. iv. 576 And there they dasshed to gyders many sadde strokes. 1503 HAWES Examp. Virt. XI. xix, But I my swerd in my hand had Strykynge at hym with strokes sad. a 1578 LINDESAY (Pitscottie) Chron. Scot. (S. T. S.) I. 222 The strampe of Mr Patrickis was so sade wpoun his brotheris footte.

†b. Of a fire: Violent. Obs.

c 1420 Chron. Vilod. 1911 Hurre thou3t þat hurre chaufere ..Was set ouer a feure bothe gret & sadde.

†c. Of rain: Heavy. Obs.

1638 SIR T. HERBERT Trav. (ed. 2) 30 Heaven it self at that instant weeping so abundantly, that I never saw a sadder raine and of lesse continuance. c 1645 HOWELL Lett. (1650) I. 184 In a sad shower of rain.

III. 11. Comb. in many adjs., chiefly parasynthetic, as sad-avised (quasi-arch. after BLACK-A-VISED), -coloured, -eyed, -faced, -hearted, -natured, -paced, -seeming, -tuned, -voiced; **sad-cake** dial. and U.S., an unleavened cake.

1878 BESANT & RICE Monks Thelema III. 124 She did not writhe as she walked; she was not *sad-avised. 1889 J. NICHOLSON Folk Sp. E. Yorksh. 79 *Sad keeaks and dip form a favourite breakfast. 1660 BLOUNT Boscobel II. (1680) 27 His Majesty..cloathed in a short Juppa of *sad coloured cloath. 1818 SCOTT Hrt. Midl. iv, A decent suit of sad-coloured clothes. 1599 SHAKS. Hen. V, I. ii. 202 The *sad-ey'd Iustice with his surly humme. 1588 — Tit. A. V. iii. 67 You *sad facde men, people and sons of Rome. 1593 — 3 Hen. VI, II. v. 123 *Sad-hearted-men, much ouergone with Care. a 1568 ASCHAM Scholem. I. (Arb.) 36 This *sadde natured, and hard witted child. 1599 MARSTON Sc. Villanie I. Proem., Stay his quick iocund skips, and force him runne A *sad pas't course. a 1633 AUSTIN Medit. (1635) 131 So all is Joy againe; till this *Sad-seeming Tydings come. 1597 SHAKS. Lover's Compl. 4 And downe I laid to list the *sad tun'd tale. 1844 MRS. BROWNING Wine of Cyprus vi, I am *sad-voiced as the turtle Which Anacreon used to feed.

B. adv. Obs. exc. poet.

†1. Firmly, strongly, fixedly. Obs.

c 1380 Sir Ferumb. 353 Loke þat þou be armed sad & hele þy bare scolle. c 1400 Destr. Troy 2078 He þat set is full sad on a soile euyn,..Hym þar not hede to be hurt with no hegh falle. c 1440 Pallad. on Husb. VII. 59 Nowe potage ware in askes mynge, & kepe In oil barelles or salt tubbis done; Saad cleyed wel, they saaf beth leyd to slepe. c 1475 Partenay 3859 Adieu, my suete loue prented in hert sad!

†2. Heavily, with force. Obs.

?a 1400 Arthur 605 Þey fow3t euer sore & sadde; Men nyst ho þe betere hadde. c 1400 Avow. Arth. xxv, He stroke him sadde and sore. 1629 Z. BOYD Balme of Gilead 41 (Jam.) The longer the stroake be in comming it commeth down the sadder. a 1743 RELPH Misc. Poems (1747) 4 Up flew her hand to souse the cowren lad, But ah, I thought it fell not down owr sad.

†3. Steadfastly. Obs.

c 1440 Partonope 1863 These covenauntis to holde surely and sadde. a 1450 MYRC Instr. Par. Priests 260 Teche hem alle to leue sadde, Þat hyt þat ys in þe awter made, Hyt ys verre goddes blode.

†4. Seriously, soberly, discreetly. Obs.

14.. How Gd. Wyfe taught Dau. 198 in Q. Eliz. Acad. (1869) 50 And þus thi frendes wylle be glade þat thou dispos þe wyslye and sade.

†5. Thoroughly, truly, certainly. Obs.

c 1380 WYCLIF Serm. Sel. Wks. I. 56 Maister, þei seiden, we witen wel þat þou art sad trewe. c 1400 Destr. Troy 3605 In sorow may be sene who is sad wise. c 1475 Partenay 874 Ful wel thay sad knew it the fayry was. Ibid. 950 Merueles,..I se ful sad; Neuer humain ey saw to it egal!

6. Sorrowfully.

1667 MILTON P. L. IV. 28 Sometimes towards Eden..his grievd look he fixes sad. 1819 KEATS Lamia II. 49 Why will you plead yourself so sad forlorn?

b. Comb. = sadly-.

1593 SHAKS. Lucr. 1590 Which when her sad beholding husband saw. 1613 W. BROWNE Brit. Past. II. iv, Their sad-sweet glance.

Sad (sæd), v. Forms: see the adj. [f. SAD a. Cf. SADE v.]

1. trans. To make solid, firm, or stiff; to compress. Obs. exc. dial. Cf. SADDEN v. 1.

1382 WYCLIF Acts iii. 7 And anoon the groundis and plauntis of him ben saddid to gidere [Vulg. consolidatæ sunt]. 1398 TREVISA Barth. De P. R. VII. lviii. (1495) 272 The matere is thycked and sadded and not obedyente to dygestyon. 14.. Tretyce in Walter of Henley's Husb. (1890) 47 Sowe your wyntur corne tymely so þt your lande may be sadid & your corne rotyd afore þe grete wyntur com. c 1440 Promp. Parv. 440/1 Saddyn, or make sadde, solido, consolido. 1496 Dives & Paup. (W. de W.) VI. xxi. 268/2 The fende by suffraunce of god may sadde the ayer and make hym a bodye of the ayer. 1807 HOGG Mtn. Bard, Sandy Tod 111 Sandy..Then the hay, sae rowed an' saddit, Towzled up that nane might ken.

†2. To make steadfast, establish, confirm (in).

1377 LANGL. P. Pl. B. X. 242 Austyn þe olde here-of he made bokes, And hym-self ordeyned to sadde vs in bileue. c 1425 Orolog. Sapient. i. in Anglia X. 333/2 Þe sowle þat is not 3it fullye saddete and stablete in þe moste parfyte degre of loue. c 1450 tr. De Imitatione III. l. 120 My mynde is saddid [orig. solidata est] in god, & groundid in crist.

†3. To darken (a colour). Obs.

1573 Art of Limming 4 Two parts azure and one of cerewse and sadded with the same azure or with blacke incke. 1634 J. B[ATE] Myst. Nat. 124 You may alay your Orpment with chalke, and sadde it with browne of Spain [etc.].

†4. To make sorrowful; to sadden. Obs.

1602 MARSTON Antonio's Rev. IV. iii, May it not sad your thoughts. 1643 PRYNNE Sov. Power Parl. I. (ed. 2) 24 The Lords hearing of these proceedings were much sadded. 1692 Covt. Grace Conditional 73 The Hearts of your Friends [are] exceedingly sadded. 1810 The Age: A Poem 3 When nature's visage sads the sight.

†b. To make dull or gloomy. Obs.

1620 G. FLETCHER Christ's Vict. I. ix, As when a vapour ..sads the smiling orient of the springing day.

†c. intr. To sad it: to talk in a sad manner.

1663 KILLIGREW Parson's Wedd. II. v. 95 While you sad it thus to one.

Sad, obs. form of SAID, SHED.

Sadaiceus, obs. pl. of SADDUCEE.

†**Sa·dded**, ppl. a. Obs. [f. SAD v. + -ED[1].] In senses of the verb: a. Solidified; compacted. b. Confirmed, strengthened. c. Saddened, made sorrowful.

c 1520 NISBET N. T. in Scots, Rom. xv. 1 Bot we saddit men aw to sustene the febilnes of seek men, and nocht pleise to our self. 1610 G. FLETCHER Christ's Tri. I. xxxviii, The sadded aire hung all in cheerlesse blacke. 1654–66 EARL ORRERY Parthen. (1676) 693 The sadded Soldiers marched in the first Ranks. 1680 LACY Prol. to 'Love Lost in the Dark', Which keeps our sadded Hearts in deep suspence.

Saddell, -ly, obs. forms of SADLY.

Sadden (sæ·d'n), v. [f. SAD a. + -EN.]

1. trans. To make solid, firm, or stiff; to compress, render cohesive; to press or beat down into a compact mass. Now dial.

1600 G. PLAT in Worlidge Syst. Agric. (1669) 44 Also the roots of the Corn will spread better..if the ground be saddned a little in the bottom of every hole. 1641 BEST Farm. Bks. (Surtees) 77 Hee woulde have the water sattle away, and the grownd somewhat saddened. 1649 BLITHE Eng. Improv. xvii. 102 For your Lime after it is once Slacked, and Melted, it is of a very cold Nature; for it will sadden your Land exceedingly. 1688 R. HOLME Armoury III. 73/1 Treading it [sc. Hay] is to sadden it down either in the Mow or Rick, &c. 1707 MORTIMER Husb. (1721) I. 94 If Marle sadden Land, or make it stiff or binding, you must dung it well. 1813 T. BATCHELOR Gen. View Agric. Bedf. 342 (E. D. D.), The soil below will, instead of being brought up, be trampled and saddened.

†b. intr. To become stiff or solid. Obs.

1641 BEST Farm. Bks. (Surtees) 77 If there bee any winds aloft without raine, the grownd will sadden and the fields waxe dry. 1764 Museum Rust. I. xcii. 407 After which the ground began to sadden. 1764 ELIZA MOXON Eng. Housew. (ed. 9) 117 Then take them off the fire and let them stand a little to sadden.

2. trans. To render sad or sorrowful; to depress in spirits. Also, to give a sad appearance to.

1628 FELTHAM Resolves II. [I.] lviii. 166 He smarts, and pines, and sadneth his incumbred soule. 1717 POPE Eloisa to Abelard 167 Her gloomy presence saddens all the scene. 1797 MRS. RADCLIFFE Italian i, With a heart saddened by disappointment. 1824 W. IRVING T. Trav. I. 28 Its beauty was saddened by care and anxiety. 1863 GEO. ELIOT Romola xx, Her round face much paled and saddened since he had parted from it. 1884 Graphic 4 Oct. 358/2 It saddens me to enter a Government bureau at the present day.

b. intr. To become sad or gloomy.

1728 POPE Iliad XIV. 558 Troy sadden'd at the View. 1727–46 THOMSON Summer 979 And Mecca saddens at the long delay. 1751 SMOLLETT Per. Pic. xviii, Her countenance saddened in a moment. 1818 KEATS What the Thrush said 12 He who saddens At thought of idleness cannot be idle. 1859 FITZGERALD tr. Omar xxxix, Better be merry with the fruitful Grape Than sadden after none, or bitter, Fruit. fig. 1795 COLERIDGE Æolian Harp 7 And watch the clouds, that late were rich with light, Slow saddening round.

3. Dyeing and Calico-printing. To tone down (colours) by the application of certain chemicals.

1791 HAMILTON Berthollet's Dyeing II. II. III. v. 196 These substances however saddened the crimson colour and gave it less lustre than alum. 1866 Chamb. Encycl. VIII. 414/2 Saddening, a peculiar method of applying certain mordants in dyeing and printing cloths, so as to give duller shades to the colours employed. 1873 E. SPON Workshop Receipts Ser. I. 30/2 Winch 30 minutes, and lift for saddening. 1874 SIR W. CROOKES Handbk. Dyeing & Calico-print. 53 For saddening olives, drabs, clarets, &c...it [sc. copperas] has been generally discarded in favour of a nitrate of iron.

Saddened (sæ·d'nd), ppl. a. [f. SADDEN v. + -ED[1].] Made sad.

1700 DRYDEN Iliad I. 768 The Limping Smith observ'd the sadden'd Feast. 1842 MANNING Serm. xi. (1848) I. 146 There is something peculiarly touching in the saddened tone of these few words. 1874 LISLE CARR Jud. Gwynne I. ii. 47 A bright flush swept over her..rather saddened face. 1879 FARRAR St. Paul (1883) 58 The Resurrection of Christ had scattered every cloud from their saddened souls.

Saddening (sæ·d'niŋ), ppl. a. [-ING[2].]

†1. That saddens or renders stiff. Obs.

1653 BLITHE Eng. Improv. Impr. 135 In..working it [lime] into the Land..it seems & appeares to be Coldest, and most sadning of Land of any Soyl whatsoever.

2. Causing sadness.

1742 COLLINS Oriental Ecl. IV. 24 And shrieks and sorrows load the saddening wind. 1804 J. GRAHAME Sabbath 705 He never longs to read the saddening tale Of endless wars. 1856 FROUDE Hist. Eng. (1858) II. vii. 190 The circumstances under which this session opened were..grave and saddening. 1884 Chr. Commw. 23 Oct. 21/3 It is saddening to hear that the Sunderland engineers have been on strike for 60 weeks.

Saddil, obs. form of SADDLE.

†**Sa·dding**, vbl. sb. Obs. [f. SAD v. + -ING[1].] The action of making sad.

1643 W. GREENHILL Axe at Root 35 Those Nations are remisse in Justice: besides the sadding of those are innocent, they abound in Delinquents and dangers. 1645 RUTHERFORD Tryal & Tri. Faith xxiv. 277 There is a sadding of the spirit,..which is forbidden.

†**Sa·dding**, ppl. a. Obs. [f. SAD v. + -ING[2].] a. That makes sad. b. Becoming sad.

1650 BAXTER Saints' R. IV. vi. § 7 (1654) 154 Are these such sadding and madding thoughts? a 1839 GALT Demon Destiny v. (1840) 34 Alas! my son, the sadding matron cried.

Saddish (sæ·diʃ), a. [f. SAD a. + -ISH.] Somewhat sad (see the adj.). Also Comb.

1647 W. BROWNE Polex. II. 265 Our Heroe..put off aswell all his saddish Ornaments, as his triumphant. 1686 Lond. Gaz. No. 2192/4 A saddish coloured stuff Sute. 1848 J. H. NEWMAN Loss & Gain 336 His companion..in a hesitating, saddish voice, said that he was an Englishman.

Saddle (sæ·d'l), sb. Forms: 1 sadol, 3–6 sadel, 4–6 sadill, 5–6 sadell, sadil, 5 saddill, sadille, -yl, -yll(e, -elle, -ul, 5, 9 Sc. saidle, 5–7 sadle, 6– saddle. [Com. Teut.: OE. sadol, -ul masc. = MDu. sadel (mod.Du. sadel, zaal), OHG. satal, -ul (MHG. satel, mod.G. sattel), ON. sǫðull (Sw., Da. sadel):—OTeut. *sadulo-z.

Possibly adopted in OTeut. from some other Indogermanic language, and if so perh. a derivative of the root *sed-, ablaut-var. of *sed- (see SIT v.), whence the synonymous L. sella (:-*sedla), OSl. sedlo (Russian сѣдло sĕdlo, Pol. siodło). No known language, however, has a corresponding derivative from the o grade of the root.]

I. 1. A seat for a rider to be used on the back of a horse or other animal; esp., a concave seat of leather having side flaps and fitted with girths and stirrups. Also an analogous kind of seat for use on a cycle.

For the saddle, for riding purposes. In the saddle, on horseback. To lose one's saddle, to become unhorsed.

Beowulf 1038 (Gr.) Eahta mearas..þara anum stod sadol ..þæt wæs hildesetl heahcyninges. c 1205 LAY. 6473 Æt his sadele an æx. c 1250 Gen. & Ex. 3949 Vp-on hise asse his sadel he dede. c 1330 Arth. & Merl. 3871 (Kölbing) Mani in sadles held hem stille, & mani al so of hors felle. c 1385 CHAUCER L. G. W. 1199 Vpon a thikke palfrey paper white With sadel rede..Sitte Dido. 1484 CAXTON Chivalry 65 Lyke as by the sadyl a knyght is sure upon his hors. 1596 SHAKS. 1 Hen. IV, II. i. 6, I prethee Tom, beate Cuts Saddle, put a few Flockes in the point. 1640 tr. Verdere's Rom. of Rom. III. 182 [They] let fly..with such a force, that they had almost lost their saddles. 1650 FULLER Pisgah IV. v. § 31. 91 Yea, such was his persevering beauty (fair in the Cradle and Saddle too)—that it lasted unto his old-age. 1672 PETTY Pol. Anat. (1691) 56 The 16,000 Families have for the Coach and Saddle near 40 M. Horses. a 1745 SWIFT Direct. Servants, Groom, Contrive that the Saddle may pinch the Beast in his Withers. 1837 W. IRVING Capt. Bonneville I. 113 Taking a couple of horses, one for the saddle, and the other as a pack-horse. 1859 TENNYSON Elaine 96 Sir King, mine ancient wound is hardly whole, And lets me from the saddle. 1887 BURY & HILLIER Cycling (Badm. Libr.) 340 A suitable saddle is a necessity for the comfort of the cyclist. fig. 1630 R. Johnson's Kingd. & Commw. 42 Nothing awes a great River so much as a bridge;..a bridge is the saddle to ride the Sea-horse.

b. With qualifying word indicating a particular kind of saddle; esp. great saddle, a saddle for the 'great horse' (see HORSE sb. 21).

For hunting, pad, portmanteau, running, war saddle, etc. see the first element. Also PACKSADDLE, SIDE-SADDLE.

1508 Acc. Ld. High Treas. Scotl. IV. 119 Item, for v French sadilles to giff away; ilk sadill xxviijs. 1581 Will of Wylteshire (Somerset Ho.), Scottissh sadell. 1598 FLORIO, Scrignuto naso, a camoset, a flat-nose, a nose like a scotch-saddle. 1607 MARKHAM Cavelarice VI. ix. 49 [margin] The great horse saddle. Ibid. 50 Next vnto this saddle is the Morocco saddle.., and these two Saddles for seruice in the warres, are..sufficient. 1644 EVELYN Diary 1 Apr., The designe is admirable, some keeping neere an hundred brave horses, all managed to ye great saddle. 1665 SIR T. HERBERT Trav. (1677) 314 Saddles..high and close, like our great Saddle. 1688 R. HOLME Armoury III. 345/1 A Burford Saddle, hath the Seat plain, and the Skirts plain and streight. 1701 P. WARWICK Mem. Chas. I, 66 He rid the great horse very well; and on the little saddle he was ..a laborious hunter, or field-man.

†c. Saddle curule [nonce-use, tr. L. sella curulis], the curule chair.

1533 BELLENDEN Livy I. iii. (S.T.S.) I. 47 He cled him with riche & riall abil3ementis, þat he was wourthy to sett in þe sadill curall. Ibid. 25, 181.

2. Figurative phrases. a. In the saddle, in a position of active management and guidance of affairs, in office; also, in readiness for work. Similarly to get into the saddle. To cast out of saddle, to deprive of office or position.

1660 PEPYS Diary 3 Mar., He told me he feared there was new design hatching, as if Monk had a mind to get into the saddle. 1675 tr. Machiavelli's Prince vii. (Rtldg. 1883) 52 Such as by the favour of fortune..have got into the saddle. 1738 NEAL Hist. Purit. IV. 225 The Presbyterians being now again in the saddle. 1819 SCOTT Ivanhoe xxv, I have known when my bare word would have cast the best man-at-arms among ye out of saddle and out of service. 1879 19th Cent. 668 All the states of Italy accepted the new Pope; and Rodrigo Borgia, once in the saddle, was not a man to be easily dislodged. 1881 R. G. WHITE Eng. Without & Within xiv. 323 The phrase 'in the saddle'—as an expression of readiness for work, is a peculiarly English phrase. 1891 S. C. SCRIVENER Our Fields & Cities 28 Otherwise the happy-go-lucky..system of production could not keep itself in the saddle to any durable extent.

b. †To be beside the saddle: to be beside the mark. (Cf. CUSHION sb. 10 b.) †To put or set beside the saddle: to put 'out of the running', to defeat the plans or ruin the career of. (Cf. CUSHION sb. 10 c.) †To sit beside the saddle: ? to abandon oneself to despair.

1568 GRAFTON Chron. II. 873 The French king..fearing least when he had almost runne his race, King Henry would put him beside hys sadell, whome he did halfe suspect to be a back friend of hys. 1579–80 NORTH Plutarch, Tiberius & Caius (1656) 693 If he could obtain it [sc. the Consulship], he was fully bent to set Caius beside the saddle. a 1590 GREENE Metamorph. Wks. (Grosart) IX. 81 Well, howsoeuer it be, Lucidor shall be mine, hee shall haue my heart, and I his, or else I will sit beside the saddle. 1644 VICARS God in Mount (1844) 19 As that no power either of Prince or Parliament, shall ever be able to set us, hereafter, beside the saddle. 1664 J. WEBB Stone-Heng (1725) 36 This Doctor is besides the Saddle, what is now in Use is not our Enquiry.

c. (I will) either win the saddle or lose the horse (or vice versa): said by one engaging in an adventure of which the issue will be either highly profitable or ruinous. Hence in various similar phrases.

1579 W. WILKINSON Confut. Fam. Love 62 b, He hath both ieoperded the horse, and lost the saddle. 1594 NASHE Unfort. Trav. Wks. 1883–4 V. 131 Whatsoeuer two resolute men will goe to dice for it, and win the bridle or lose the saddle. 1596 SPENSER F. Q. IV. v. 22 But Blandamour..little prays'd his labours evill speed, That for to winne the saddle lost the steed. 1603 BRETON Packet Mad Lett. 7 But my state being so downe the winde..I wil..thrust my selfe into some place of seruice in the warres, where I will either winne the Horse, or lose the Saddle. 1678 CUDWORTH Intell. Syst. I. v. § 42. 894 They..resolve either to 'win the saddle or loose the Horse'.

d. To lay or set the saddle upon the right horse (and similar phrases): to lay the blame on the right person.

1635 in Sainsbury Cal. of Court Min. E. I. Co. (1907) 15 [Resolving how they might] sett the saddle upon the right horse. 1652 COLLINGES Caveat for Prof. (1653) ii. C 1, You have laid the saddle upon the wrong Horse. a 1653 GOUGE Comm. Hebr. xi. 37 To remove this scandal, the apostle setteth the saddle on the right Horse, and sheweth, that [etc.]. 1690 WOOD Life 25 July (O.H.S.) III. 336 E. G. with child, layd on the tapster, who said that 'set the saddle on the right horse'. 1727 DE FOE Syst. Magic I. iii. (1840) 83 But let us bring things to a right understanding, do Satan justice, and set the saddle upon the right devil. 1752 MRS. C. LENNOX Female Quixote (1820) II. VII. xii. 154 I'll clear myself, and put the saddle upon the right horse! 1839 HOOD Tale of a Trumpet xlviii, And the cat at last escapes from the bag—And the saddle is placed on the proper nag.

e. To put (one) to every corner of or to all the seats of (one's) saddle: to compel to try every expedient. Sc.

1825 SCOTT in Lockhart Life (1837) VI. 24, I have the dregs of Abbotsford House to pay for..so I must look for some months to be put to every corner of my saddle. 1825 JAMIESON Dict. s.v., To put one to a' the seats o' the Saddle, to nonplus, to gravel one, S.

f. In proverbial similative phrases.

1566 KNOX Hist. Ref. Wks. (1846) I. 242 Als seimlye a sight..as to putt a sadill upoun the back of ane unrewly kow. 1663 Aron-bimn. 88 But for this pretence of pulling down Antichrist, it is a saddle that will fit any back. 1677 W. HUGHES Man of Sin II. xii. 215 That becometh him as handsomely (according to our Proverb) as A saddle doth a Cowes back.

3. That part of the harness of a shaft-horse which takes the bearing of the shafts (see quot. 1851); a cart- or gig-saddle.

[1377: see cartsaddle vb., CART sb. 6. c 1425 Voc. in Wright-Wülcker 665/33 Hoc dorsilollum, cartsadylle.] 1794 [see HOUSING sb.[2] 2 b]. 1837 MARRYAT Olla Podr. xxxvi, The shaft horse neither felt his saddle nor his belly-band. 1851 H. STEPHENS Bk. of the Farm (ed. 2) I. 430 The shaft-horse requires bridle, collar, haims, saddle, and breeching, to be fully equipped...The saddle—as saddle and breeching together are commonly called—is placed on the horse's back immediately behind the shoulder. 1856 'STONEHENGE' Brit. Rural Sports III. III. iv. 543/1 The supporting and backing part [of gig harness] consists of the Pad or Saddle...This has two rings for the reins, called the Terrets, and a Hook for the bearing rein. 1875 [see PAD sb.[3] 2 b]. 1882 J. PHILIPSON Harness 25 The pad is sometimes used instead of a saddle for single harness.

II. Something resembling a saddle in shape or position.

4. Physical Geogr., Mining, etc. a. A depression in a hill or line of hills. [So G. sattel.] b. A long elevation of land with sloping sides; a ridge, esp. one connecting two hills; also, a similar formation of ice or snow.

1555 EDEN Decades 350 A lowe longe lande, and a longe poynt, with a saddle through the myddeste of it. 1697 DAMPIER Voy. (1699) 267 A very high Hill..with a Saddle or bending on the top. 1779 FORREST Voy. New Guinea 159 (We) discerned other land, bearing from N. W. to W. N. W. forming in saddles and hummocks. 1833 M. SCOTT Tom Cringle xix, There was a long narrow saddle or ridge of limestone about five hundred feet high. 1839 MURCHISON Silur. Syst. I. 134 The carboniferous strata are thrown into partial saddles and curvatures. 1860 TYNDALL Glac. I. xvi. 108 The glacier..being terminated by a saddle which stretches across from mountain to mountain. 1862 MERIVALE Rom. Emp. (1865) V. xl. 23 The Palatine is connected with the Esquiline by the low ridge or saddle of the Velia. 1871 L. STEPHEN Playgr. Eur. (1894) 130 We stepped at last on to the little saddle of snow. 1876 GREEN Phys. Geol. ix. § 3. 347 When the beds have been bent into the form of arches these are called Anticlinals or Saddles.

5. In mechanical uses. a. Naut. A block of wood, hollowed out above and below, fastened to a spar to take the bearing of another spar attached to it.

1512–13 Acc. Ld. High Treas. Scot. IV. 463 Item..for viij greit treis to mak the sadillis to the greit schip and Margret..xlviij s. 1769 FALCONER Dict. Marine (1780), Saddle, a small..wooden block..nailed on the lower yardarms, to retain the studding-sail booms in a firm and steady position. 1882 NARES Seamanship (ed. 6) 178 To get the heel of the boom..down in the saddle.

b. Bridge-construction. (a) A block on the top of a pier to carry the suspension cables. (b) A frame used in the construction of a pontoon-bridge (see quot. 1853).

1831 J. HOLLAND Manuf. Metal I. 108 On the extreme height of the suspension piers are placed the cast iron blocks or saddles. 1853 SIR H. DOUGLAS Milit. Bridges (ed. 3) 30 The Saddle [of a pontoon bridge] is a frame of fir timber, which is placed centrally over the axis of a pontoon..and serves to receive the ends of the balks. 1868 Daily Tel. 14 Apr., A fresh pontoon was brought alongside, fresh saddles were lashed to it, another length of balks..was dropped into the saddle. 1876 Encycl. Brit. IV. 301/2 Suspension Bridges.—The chains where they pass over the piers rest on saddles.

c. A 'seat' or support on which a gun is placed for bouching.

1862 F. A. GRIFFITHS Artil. Man. (ed. 9) 190 Saddle [for Armstrong gun], with Tightening Screws. 1875 in KNIGHT Dict. Mech.

d. (See quot. 1888.)

1888 Lockwood's Dict. Mech. Engin. s.v., The seatings or supports which carry horizontal cylindrical boilers..are called saddles. 1899 Daily News 9 Mar. 5/3 The saddles that held the six thirty-ton boilers in place broke.

e. Telegraphy. A bracket to support the wire on the top of a pole or ridge.

1867 R. S. CULLEY Pract. Telegr. (ed. 2) 122 The saddle or bracket must be fixed with screws. 1885 Ibid. (ed. 8) 148 At the top of the pole a galvanised iron roof is fixed, and over it a cast-iron saddle, into which the insulator bolt fits. 1884 Law Times Rep. LI. 161/2 The attachments to buildings were made..by means of standards or ridge saddles attached to the roofs.

f. Railways. (? U.S.) (a) The bearing resting on the journal of an axle in the axle-box. (b) A chair for a rail. 1875 in KNIGHT Dict. Mech. 459, 2011.

g. In various machines: The base of a slide rest, drilling head, etc., which slides along its support.

1869 W. J. M. RANKINE Cycl. Mach. & Hand-Tools Plate H 8 The self-acting motion for the saddle is arranged as follows. 1869 Eng. Mech. 24 Dec. 355/1 The saddle (which carries the wood) is drawn to the hand-wheel end of the machine. 1879 Cassell's Techn. Educ. IV. 264/2 The lower part of the slide-rest is termed the 'saddle'. 1888 Lockwood's Dict. Mech. Engin., Saddle, the base of a slide rest. ..Similarly, the sliding plate which carries the drill spindle and gear wheels of a radial drill.

h. (a) A saddle-shaped electrical conductor. (b) A concave pad to be applied to a limb that is to be electrified.

1838 FARADAY Exper. Researches (1844) II. 5 A plate of copper..was bent into a saddle shape,..a jacket of sheet caoutchouc was put over the saddle. 1849 NOAD Electricity (ed. 3) 492 If, then, we wish to administer direct shocks to a paralytic limb, say the leg, we apply a sponge director or saddle..to the hip.

i. In various applications: see quots.

1750 BLANCKLEY Nav. Expositor, Saddles are used by the Smiths to turn Thimbles hollow on. 1833 LOUDON Encycl. Arch. 492 To pebble-pave the byres..with proper cribstone and saddle (the former partitions off the crib; and the latter the gutter behind). 1856 MORTON Cycl. Agric., Provincialisms, Saddle, (Fife), that part of stall between manger and grip. 1873 E. SPON Workshop Receipts Ser. I. 61/2 [Varnish making.] A saddle, which is a sheet of plate-iron, or tin, 12 in. broad, and turned up 1½ in. at each side..to prevent the spilling of the varnish during the time of taking..out. 1875 T. SEATON Fret Cutting 76 There are two very efficient aids to the saw...The first is the bench saddle...It is a piece of wood with reverse shoulders; the under shoulder hooks against the side of the bench,..the upper shoulder catches any piece of wood laid against it for sawing. 1884 W. S. B. MCLAREN Spinning 250 Saddles, the steel bars in a gill box on which the fallers travel. 1887 Archit. Publ. Soc. Dict., Saddle, a term used in Suffolk for a thin piece of wood fixed on the floor between the jambs of a door and under it.

6. Cookery. In full saddle of mutton. A 'joint' of mutton, venison, etc., consisting of the two loins and conjoining vertebræ.

1747 MRS. GLASSE Cookery 4 The Saddle of Mutton (which is the two Loins). Ibid. 24 To French a Hind Saddle of Mutton. It is the two Rumps. 1789 MRS. PIOZZI Journ. France II. 338 A saddle of mutton, or more properly a chine. 1806 PIKE Sources Mississ. (1810) 75 Hams and saddles of venison. 1844 H. STEPHENS Bk. of the Farm II. 99 When cut double, forming the chine or saddle. 1859 All Year Round No. 20. 57 Nowhere can the equal of a

Sussex haunch or saddle be obtained. 1890 L. C. D'OYLE Notches p. ix, They took merely the skins and 'saddle' of the antelope they killed.

7. Applied to certain parts of animals. a. A natural saddle-like marking on the back of the Harp Seal. Cf. SADDLE-BACK sb. 4 c.

1784 PENNANT Arctic Zool. I. 165 The Newfoundland Seal-hunters call it the Harp, or Heart Seal, and name the marks on the sides the saddle. 1884 GOODE, etc. Nat. Hist. Aquatic Anim. 62.

b. Conchol. †(a) A saddle-oyster (see 10); (b) see quot. 1851.

1815 S. BROOKES Introd. Conchol. 116 Saddle, Anomia Sella. 1851 WOODWARD Mollusca 78 The shell..is an extremely elongated cone,..divided into cells or chambers by a series of partitions (septa)...When they are folded, the elevations are called 'saddles'. 1894 Geol. Mag. Oct. 436 Shell (cast) discoidal, with somewhat inflated whorls;..outer saddle only partly known.

c. (See quot.)

1872 L. WRIGHT Poultry xvii. 205 Saddle, the posterior part of the back, reaching to the tail, in a cock, answering to the cushion in a hen; often, however, applied to both sexes, cushion being more restricted to a great development, as in Cochins, while 'saddle' may be applied to any breed.

8. Bot. A ridge separating the fovea and foveola in the leaves of Isoetes.

1882 VINES tr. Sachs' Bot. 475 Above the fovea and separated from it by the 'saddle', lies a smaller depression.

III. attrib. and Comb.

9. Simple attrib., as saddle-flap, -girt, -girth, -horn (HORN sb. 21 b), -lap, -lashing, -nail, †-panel (PANEL sb.[1] 1), -place, -pommel, -soap, -spring, -strap, -stuffing, -tack, -withers; saddle-like adj.; with the sense 'used for riding', as saddle-ass, -colt, -horse, mare, -ox, pony; with the meaning 'saddle-shaped', as saddle flange, key; in the names of affections incident to the use of the saddle, as saddle-bruise, raw, soreness; also appositive, as (sense 5 a) saddle-crutch, (sense 4) -glacier, (sense 5 g) -piece; objective, as saddle-maker, -making.

1657 J. WATTS Vind. Ch. Eng. 112 God once opened the mouth of Balaams *Saddle-asse. 1709 Lond. Gaz. No. 4523/4 He had..a white Spot on his Back, that came by a *Saddle-bruise. 1707 MORTIMER Husb. (1721) I. 208 The first Year *Saddle-Colts should only be walked. 1867 SMYTH Sailor's Word-bk. s.v. Saddles, We have a *saddle-crutch for the main or driver boom on the taffarel. 1888 Lockwood's Dict. Mech. Engin., *Saddle Flange, a curved flange hollowed out to fit a boiler, a pipe, or other cylindrical vessel. 1844 H. STEPHENS Bk. of the Farm II. 219 The *saddle-flaps should be sponged clean of mud. 1813 J. C. HOBHOUSE Journey (ed. 2) 712 We..found the stream as high as the *saddle-girts. 1813 SCOTT Rokeby VI. xxxiii, And, bursting in the headlong sway, The faithless *saddle-girths gave way. 1884 Pall Mall G. 10 June 11/1 The summit of the [Kangla] pass..is crowned by a noble *saddle glacier. 1890 L. C. D'OYLE Notches 73, I..threw the rein of his horse up over the *saddle-horn. 1662 GERBIER Principles 32 To accustome the Neapolitan great *Saddle-Horse to raise their Neck. 1867 TROLLOPE Chron. Barset I. xxvii. 238 He hired a saddle-horse..and started after breakfast. 1888 Lockwood's Dict. Mech. Engin., *Saddle Key, a key whose inner face is hollowed to fit its shaft. 1803 Scott's Minstrelsy III. 266 He louted owr his *saddle lap, To kiss her ere they part. 1822 A. CUNNINGHAM Tradit. Tales, Last Ld. of Helvellyn (1887) 217 My fathers have fought to the saddle-laps in English blood for the men of the house of Maxwell. c 1860 H. STUART Seaman's Catech. 1 The muzzle and *saddle lashings of guns. 1784 J. KING Cook's Voy. III. VI. iii. 238 On each side of this break the land is quite low; beyond the opening rises a remarkable *saddle-like hill. c 1500 Melusine 43 Raymondyn sent for a *Sadlemaker, to whom he said: 'My frend..ye muste cutte this hyde in fourme of a thonge'. 1886 Encycl. Brit. XXI. 142/1 The saddle-maker has to consider the ease and comfort of both horse and rider. Ibid., *Saddle-making and the cutting and sewing of bridles. 1707 Lond. Gaz. No. 4312/3 Lost..a bay *Saddle Mare. 1875 KNIGHT Dict. Mech., *Saddle-nail, a short nail having a large, smooth head, used in making saddles. 1824 W. J. BURCHELL Trav. S. Africa Index, s.v. Oxen, *Saddle Oxen: their rate of travelling. 1465–6 Durh. Acc. Rolls (Surtees) 90 Pro ij *Sadillpanell empt. pro le ffissheman, ij s. iiij d. 1725 BRADLEY Fam. Dict. s.v. Saddle, Some stuff their Saddle-Pannels with well dry'd Moss. 1825 J. NICHOLSON Operat. Mechanic 322 When the screw is turned round, the *saddle-piece will slide uniformly along the triangular bar. 1890 SLINGO & BROOKER Electr. Engin. xvii. 600 The channelling [for underground cables] consists of blocks of bituminous concrete made in six-foot lengths and jointed by a saddle-piece of the same material. 1707 MORTIMER Husb. (1721) I. 209 Whoever..takes not off his [horse's] Saddle 'till he is cold, and then rubs the *Saddle-place well. 1593 MARKHAM Horsemanship B 3 b, Casting the raynes thereof ouer the *Saddle pomell. 1900 H. SUTCLIFFE Shameless Wayne xxiv. (1905) 308 His return blow..grazing the Lean Man's saddle-pummel as it fell. 1887 ANSTEY in Macm. Mag. Feb. 261/2 My riding was interrupted for a while. Brutus was discovered..to have a *saddle-raw. 1889 Field 7 Dec. LXXIV. 793/2 The *saddle soap made by Messrs. B——. 1907 Daily Chron. 1 Mar. 7/5 *Saddle soreness is provoked if every stroke of the pedals extends the leg to the utmost. 1887 BURY & HILLIER Cycling (Badm. Libr.) 340 The combined *saddle-springs recently introduced. 1753 CHAMBERS Cycl. Supp., *Saddle-straps ..are used to hold the girths fast to the saddle. 1890 'R. BOLDREWOOD' Col. Reformer (1891) 193 Cut a straight sapling while we rouse out the saddle-straps for a splice. 1871 KINGSLEY At Last xiii, We saw the husk carded out ..for..*saddle-stuffing. 1821 Blackw. Mag. IX. 132 Hogg should purchase a pennyworth of *saddle-tacks, and..nail the ears of the Gude Grey Catte to his stable-door. 1725 BRADLEY Fam. Dict. s.v. Saddle, The *Saddle-Withers should be low.

10. Special comb., as **saddle-band** Sc., ? the band of a pedlar's pack; **saddle-bar**, (a) Glazing, each of the small horizontal iron bars (fitting over the upright stanchions) to which the lead panels are secured; (b) Saddlery (see quot. 1875); **saddle-billed** a., an epithet applied to the stork Ephippiorhynchus senegalensis, from the recurved shape of its bill; †**saddle bitten** a., galled with a saddle; **saddle-blanket** U.S., a small blanket used, folded, as a saddle-cloth; **saddle boiler**, a boiler of concave form for use with heating apparatus; **saddle-bracket**, (a) a receptacle for a saddle when not in use; (b) Telegr. = 5 e above; **saddle carp** (see quot.); **saddle-carpenter**, one who makes the frames or trees of saddles; **saddle-case**, †(a) the housing of a saddle (obs.); (b) a travelling case for a saddle; †**saddle-charge**, ? a saddle load; **saddle clip** (see quot.); †**saddle drum**, ? a small drum carried on the saddle; **saddle-eaves** pl., jocularly used for the side of a saddle; **saddle-fast** a., firmly seated in the saddle; **saddle-gall**, a sore produced on the back of a horse by the chafing of the saddle; **saddle-galled** a., chafed with the saddle; affected with saddle-gall; **saddle-grafting** (see quot.); †**saddle-hill**, a saddle-back hill; **saddle-house**, †(a) a saddle-cloth (obs.); (b) a building in which saddlery is kept; **saddle-iron** Sc., a stirrup; **saddle-joint**, (a) Mech. (see quot. 1875); (b) Building (see quot. 1901); (c) Anat. (see quot. 1897); **saddle leaf** U.S., the saddle-tree, or American tulip-tree (Cent. Dict. 1891), **saddle-leather**, the leather composing a saddle; also, leather specially prepared for saddle-making; **saddle-mat**, a mat used in the Western U. S. as a saddle-cloth; **saddle-nose**, (a) a flat or snub-nose; (b) see quot. 1897; **saddle-nosed** a., having a saddle-nose; also, of a bird 'having a soft nasal membrane saddled on the bill' (Cent. Dict.); **saddle-oyster**, a name given to certain anomioid bivalves, the shape of which resembles that of a saddle; **saddle-pin**, the pin of a cycle saddle which fits into a socket on the cycle frame; **saddle pistol**, a holster pistol; **saddle-plate**, the bent plate which forms the arch of the furnace in steam boilers of the locomotive type (Cent. Dict.); **saddle-quern** (see quot.); **saddle-rack** = saddle-bracket (a); **saddle-rail**, **-reed** (see quots.); †**saddle-rings**, circular marks on the back of a horse caused by the abrasion of the saddle; **saddle-roof**, a saddleback roof; **saddle-room**, a room in which saddlery is kept when not in use; **saddle-rug**, a saddle-cloth made of carpeting (Cent. Dict.); **saddle sealing**, hunting and catching the saddleback seal; **saddle seat** dial., a horse for riding purposes; **saddle-shaped** a., resembling a saddle in shape; Geol., anticlinal; **saddle-shell** = saddle-oyster; **saddle-sick** a., Sc., indisposed through riding; †**saddle side**, the concave lower side (of the liver); **saddle-skirts** pl., the lowermost parts of a saddle; also, the part of a horse's flanks covered by these; **saddle-sore** a., chafed with the saddle; †**saddle-speck**, a mark caused by the abrasion of the saddle; **saddle spot** = prec.; hence **saddle-spotted** a.; **saddle-stead** poet., the place of the saddle; **saddle-stone**, (a) Arch., the stone forming the angle at the summit of the coping of a gable; (b) 'an old name for a variety of stone containing saddle-shaped depressions' (Cent. Dict.); **saddle-stool** = saddle-bracket (a); **saddle-tank** (see quot. 1871); also attrib. as **saddle-tank engine** (see quot. 1888); †**saddle tore** (see quot.); **saddle wire** Telegr., the wire running along the tops of telegraph posts. Also SADDLE BACK, -BAG, -BOW, -CLOTH, -TREE.

a 1604 in Row Hist. Kirk (1842) 463 It [sc. the ministrie] will die in thy hand Therefor the backe shall beare the *sadle-band. 1825 J. NICHOLSON Operat. Mechanic 638 Frames [in lead-work] intended to receive these lights are made with bars across, to which the lights are fastened.. called *saddle-bars. 1874 MICKLETHWAITE Mod. Par. Churches 293 It is now most common to place the saddle-bars outside the glass. 1875 KNIGHT Dict. Mech., Saddle-bar, the side-bar, side-plate, or spring-bar of a saddle-tree, one on each side connecting the pommel and cantle. 1877 Nature 17 May 54/1 The additions to the Zoological Society's Gardens..include..a *Saddle-billed Stork. 1592 GREENE Conny Catch. II. Wks. (Grosart) X. 80 He..made him spotted in the backe, as if he had been *saddle bitten. 1885 B. HARTE Maruja vi, His quick eye was attracted by a *saddle-blanket. 1881 Encycl. Brit. XII. 228/2 The *saddle boiler is very efficient in form, steady and sure in its working. 1885 Bazaar 30 Mar. 1254/2 Wanted, saddle boiler ..to heat small greenhouse. 1844 H. STEPHENS Bk. of the Farm I. 190 The riding-horse-stable should have *saddle-brackets. 1876 PREECE & SIVEWRIGHT Telegraphy 210 If a wire is to be run along the top of the pole, brackets.. named saddle-brackets, or simply saddles, are..used. 1888 G. B. GOODE Amer. Fishes 416 When there is a row of large scales down the back it [sc. the King Carp] is called the '*Saddle Carp'. a 1720 W. GIBSON Dict of Horses viii. (ed. 3) 125 A Country where there is perhaps the most expert *Saddle-Carpenters and Saddlers in the World. 1753 CHAMBERS Cycl. Supp., *Saddle-case. See the article Housing. 1895 Army & Navy Co-op. Soc. Price List 497 Tin-lined Saddle Cases for Ladies' Saddles. a 1500 Lat. & Eng. Voc. in Wr.-Wülcker 609/35 Sauma, a *Sadyl-charge. 1884 KNIGHT Dict. Mech. Suppl., *Saddle Clip, a clip which holds together the spring and axle. 1617 PURCHAS Pilgrimage (ed. 3) 593 *Saddle drummes of gold set with stones, vsed in Hawking. 1663 BUTLER Hudibras I. i. 412 But after many strains and heaves, He got up to the *saddle-eaves. 1805 SCOTT Last Minstr. III. vi, Still sate the warrior *saddle-fast. 1726 Dict. Rust. (ed. 3), *Saddle-gall. 1831 YOUATT Horse 169 For saddle galls there is no better application than [etc.]. 1680 Lond. Gaz. No. 1555/4 One brown bay Nag..having been lately *Saddle-galled. 1898 DOYLE Trag. Korosko i, The saddle-galled donkeys. 1824 LOUDON Encycl. Gard. § 2032 *Saddle-grafting is performed by first cutting the top of the stock into a wedge-like form, and then splitting up the end of the scion; it is then placed on the wedge, embracing it on each side. 1773 Cook's 1st Voy. II. vii. in Hawkesworth's Voy. III. 419 There is,..very near the shore, a remarkable *saddle-hill. 1431 2 Durh. Acc. Rolls (Surtees) 231 Et in j nova hakney-sadyll et j nova *Sadyllehouse. 1799 Hull Advertiser 12 Oct. 1/1 A very excellent Mansion House with coach house, saddle house and stabling. 1870 E. PEACOCK Ralf Skirl. III. 101 The Squire sought out Bob in the saddle-house. 1822 GALT Gilhaize i. 3 His father having a profitable traffic in *saddle-irons and bridle-rings among the gallants of the court. 1875 KNIGHT Dict. Mech., *Saddle-joint, a form of joint for sheet-metal...One portion overlaps and straddles the vertical edge of the next. 1897 Syd. Soc. Lex., Saddle-joint, a joint in which the articulating bony surfaces are convex in one direction and concave in the other. 1901 R. STURGIS Dict. Archit. s.v. Joint, Saddle Joint. In a weathered course of masonry,..a joint formed between two adjoining stones whose ends are cut higher than the surface of the weathering between. These projections at the ends are usually sloped or rounded away from the joint ..so as to shed water from the mortar. 1832 TENNYSON Lady of Shalott III. iii, Thick-jewell'd shone the *saddle-leather. 1883 Century Mag. Aug. 523/1 Mats, called 'cocas',..are much sought after by California ranchmen as *saddle-mats. 1626 BACON Sylva § 27 The Raising gently of the Bridge of the Nose [of an infant], doth preuent the Deformity of a *Saddle Nose. 1897 Syd. Soc. Lex., Saddle-nose, a nose the bridge of which has sunk, in consequence of necrosis of the nasal bones. 1598–9 HAKLUYT Voy. I. 101 His wife..had cut and pared her nose betweene the eyes, that she might seeme to be more flat and *saddle-nosed. 1742 C. JARVIS Quix. I. III. ii. 86 An Asturian wench, broad-faced, flat-headed, and saddle-nosed. 1856 WOODWARD Mollusca 256 P[lacuna] sella, called, from its shape, the '*saddle-oyster', is remarkably striated. 1896 Westm. Gaz. 28 Apr. 5/2 He carried the despatches in the *saddle-pin of his bicycle. 1881 GREENER Gun 376 The Double-grip *Saddle Pistol. Side-lever action Saddle Pistol. 1872 J. EVANS Anc. Stone Impl. x. 226 The name of *saddle-quern has been given to this form of grinding apparatus [sc. a bed-stone slightly hollowed on its upper surface and a large oval pebble for a muller]. 1890 A. T. FISHER Through the Stable xii. 93 *Saddle-racks are usually fixed to the walls of a saddle-room. 1875 KNIGHT Dict. Mech., *Saddle-rail, a railway rail which has flanges straddling a longitudinal and continuous sleeper. Ibid., *Saddle-reed, small reeds used in the place of cord to form the edges of gig-saddle sides. 1694 Lond. Gaz. No. 3017/4 Stolen..a brown bay Mare with a bald Face, *Saddle-rings [etc.]. 1875 KNIGHT Dict. Mech., *Saddle-roof, a double gabled roof. 1883 B'ham Weekly Post 18 Aug. 8/6 He procured a loaded gun from the *saddle-room. 1888 Encycl. Brit. XXIV. 527/1 The majority of the vessels, after prosecuting the '*saddle' sealing at Newfoundland or Greenland, proceed direct to Disco. 1895 'HUGH HALIBURTON' Dunbar 70 Farmers that hed a *saddle seat,..Keep nae beast noo but cats an' mice. 1833–4 J. PHILLIPS Geol. in Encycl. Metrop. (1845) VI. 594/2 The limestone is uplifted into a *saddle-shaped or anticlinal ridge. 1870 ROLLESTON Anim. Life 17 Being concave from side to side and therefore saddle-shaped. 1900 B. D. JACKSON Gloss. Bot. Terms, Saddle-shaped, applied to such valves of Diatoms as those of Coscinodiscus. 1863 J. G. WOOD Nat. Hist. III. 419 *Saddle-shell, Anomia ephippium. 1823 GALT Entail vii, Weel do I ken what it is to be *saddle-sick mysel'. 1844 MRS. CARLYLE Let. 7 July, New Lett. & Mem. 1903 I. 140 The girls were dreadfully saddle-sick. For me, my old habit of riding, I suppose, had saved me. 1615 CROOKE Body of Man 1 The inward face of the Liuer which is the lower, is..hollow, vnequall, and is called the Simus or *saddle side, that it may giue way to the stomacke strutting..with plenty of meat. 1610 MARKHAM Maister-p. II. xliv. 286 Of Wennes or Knobs growing about the *saddle skirts. a 1656 USSHER Ann. vi. (1658) 153 Pharnabazus..rid his horse into the very sea, up to his saddle-skirts. a 1725 THORESBY Diary (1830) I. 295 We missed the deepest of the Wash..though we rode to the saddle-skirts for a considerable way. 1907 Daily Chron. 22 Oct. 8/4 Nicholas *saddle-sore by this time, and the mare too weary to shy. 1685 Lond. Gaz. No. 2062/4 Lost a black Coach Mare.., hath a small *Saddle-speck. 1668 Ibid. No. 272/4 A Baye Mare, no white, save some *Saddle spots. 1676 Ibid. No. 1098/4 Stolen.., a large brown bay Coach Gelding,..*saddle-spotted. 1876 MORRIS Sigurd II. 133 And his war-gear clanged and tinkled as he leapt to the *saddle-stead. 1843 Civil Eng. & Arch. Jrnl. VI. 320/1 Modern gables too are generally awkwardly terminated at the eaves by..*saddle-stones. 1856 'STONEHENGE' Brit. Rural Sports 583/2 Hooks and *saddle-stools, or brackets, for the saddles or harness. 1871 Young Gentleman's Ann. Dec. 28 Other engines of this class [sc. tank-engines], however, carry their water in a tank (called a *saddle-tank) which rests on the top of the boiler. 1888 Lockwood's Dict. Mech. Engin., Saddle Tank Engine, a locomotive engine in which the water tank envelops the top and sides of the boiler. 1681 COLVIL Whigs Supplic. (1741) 13 A Pistol..at either *Saddle tore. Note. Saddle tore, Saddle Bow. 1876 PREECE & SIVEWRIGHT Telegraphy 253 The most important circuit is generally worked upon the *saddle wire.

Saddle (sæ·d'l), v. Forms: 1 sadolian, sadelian, 3–6 sadel, (6 -ell), 4–5 sadyl(l, (5 -ylle), 4–7 sadle, (5 sadulle, sadil, 6 -ill), 6– saddle. [OE. sadolian, f. sadol SADDLE sb.; cf. MLG. sadeln, MDu. sadelen, Du. zadelen, OHG. satalôn (MHG. satelen, mod.G. satteln), ON. sǫðla (Sw. sadla, Da. sadle).]

1. trans. To put a riding-saddle upon (a horse or other animal); also to saddle up. Also absol.

c 1000 ÆLFRIC Gram. xxviii. (Z.) 165 Sterno..ic sadelige hors. c 1205 LAY. 13512 Fortiger hæhte his sweines sadeli his blonken. a 1300 K. Horn 763 (Cambr. MS.) Horn sadelede his stede. c 1320 Sir Beues 757 (MS. A.) Beues let sadlen is ronsi. 1388 WYCLIF 1 Kings xiii. 13 And he seide to hise sones, Sadle 3e an asse to me. And whanne thei hadden sadlid, he stiede, and 3ede after the man of God. c 1420 Sir Amadace (Camden) xxviii, Quen Sir Amadace hade etun, To sadulle his horse was no3te for3etun. 1485 Rutland Papers (Camden) 4 A spare coursar lad in hand.. sadlet with a saddell of estate. 1587 TURBERV. Trag. T. iv. 69 b, He sadled vp his horse, and roade in post away. 1637 J. WILLIAMS Holy Table 206 What needs the Writer saddle up his Horse. 1761 GRAY Odin 2 Uprose the king.. And saddled strait his coal-black steed. 1839–55 W. IRVING Wolfert's Roost 47, I almost determined..to..saddle my horse, and ride off. 1901 Daily Chron. 27 Aug. 5/5, I then asked him to saddle-up my horse while I was dressing.

†b. intr. or absol. To inure a colt to the saddle.

1656 Markham's Perfect Horseman 19 When to Saddle.

c. To saddle and bridle fig., to subject to control.

1864 LOWELL Fireside Trav. 133 The cover [of the kettle] was chattering with the escaping steam, which had thus vainly begged of all men to be saddled and bridled, till James Watt one day happened to overhear it.

†2. trans. To ride, bestride (an animal). Also transf. Obs.

1550 BALE Eng. Votaries II. 18 b, Take that benefyce to you (sayth he to the priest) but saddle nomore the nonne. 1585 JAS. I Ess. Poesie (Arb.) 68 Vpon Alhallow ene, Quhen our gude nichtbors rydis..Some sadland a sho ape, ..Some hotcheand on a hemp stalk. 1598 R. DALLINGTON Meth. Trav. X 2 b, No maruell then, the bridle being left in their owne [French wives'] hands, though sometimes they be saddled, and their husbands know not. 1713 PETIVER in Phil. Trans. XXVIII. 184 Its lower Leaves are like the Garden Poppy, which higher saddle or ride the Stalk.

3. intr. To get into the saddle. In Colonial use to saddle up.

1835 BURNES Trav. Bokhara (ed. 2) II. 198 We dressed ourselves..and saddled at three P.M. 1849 E. E. NAPIER Excurs. S. Africa II. 12 Another term of Colonial import is that of 'saddling-up', and 'off-saddling'. 1863 W. C. BALDWIN Afr. Hunting ii. 33 We saddled and went in pursuit. 1865 KINGSLEY Herew. I. i. 61 Ay, every churl who owns a manor, must needs arm and saddle and levy war. 1890 'R. BOLDREWOOD' Col. Reformer (1891) 206 Bothwell, myself, and the six troopers, saddled up and departed.

4. trans. To charge or load with (a burden); now only fig. to load with (something) as a burden.

1693 DRYDEN Persius v. 207 The Slaves thy Baggage pack, Each saddled with his Burden on his Back. 1728 VANBRUGH & CIBBER Prov. Husb. I, His Estate..was left him saddled with two Joyntures, and two weighty Mortgages upon it. 1731 BAILEY vol. II. s.v., To saddle,..to embarrass, as to saddle a Cause. 1767 A. YOUNG Farmer's Lett. to People 162 But Mr. Justice saddles the parish with whatever burthen he thinks proper. 1775 SHERIDAN Duenna I. iv, I'll saddle him with this scrape. 1837 LOCKHART Scott (1839) III. ix. 295 The earnest wish of Scott and Ballantyne to saddle the publisher of the new poem with part of their old 'quire stock'. 1858 SURTEES Ask Mamma xliv. 196 The chances then, are, that he is saddled with a sort of old man of the sea. 1874 L. STEPHEN Hours in Library (1892) I. iv. 157 We are perhaps inclined to saddle Scott unconsciously with the sins of a later generation. 1895 Law Times Rep. LXXIII. 691/1 Otherwise a testator would be able to saddle people with duties of an onerous description.

b. ? To secure for (a burdensome task). rare[—1].

1826 SCOTT Jrnl. 25 Oct., Sotheby..endeavoured to saddle me for a review of his polyglot Virgil.

5. To put (a burden) upon (another's back).

1808 COBBETT Pol. Reg. XIV. 547 The men..who, if they serve us but for a few years, are saddled upon our devoted ass-like backs for life. 1812 Sporting Mag. XL. 153, I should not wonder if that Bully Mitchell saddles this poisoning upon me. 1880 L. J. JENNINGS in Croker Papers I. vi. 158 The whole of the Bergami family had..been saddled upon the Princess. 1881 BESANT & RICE Chapl. Fleet III. 248, I found her only too eager to marry anyone upon whom she could saddle her debts.

6. a. Masonry. To work (a joint) so as to form a 'saddle' projecting above the horizontal surface of the stones joined. b. Carpentry. To join or fit together by HALVING.

1823 P. NICHOLSON Pract. Build. 311 A process by workmen called saddling the joints. 1897 Westm. Gaz. 3 Sept. 2/1 These consist of one log laid upon another, saddled in at the corners.

7. To bend downwards in the middle.

1803 Sporting Mag. XXI. 327 Saddling the cards..is bending the sixes, sevens, eights, and nines, in the middle longways. 1880 Standard 10 Dec., Walls are cracked and roofs 'saddled' in every direction.

8. (See quot.)

1731 BAILEY vol. II. s.v., To saddle,..to furnish, as to saddle a spit.

†9. Comb.: **Saddle-goose**, a nickname for a fool; **saddle-nag**, a stable-boy, groom. Obs.

1526 SKELTON Magnyf. 1834 Sym Sadylgose was my syer, and Dawcocke my dame. 1646 J. HALL Poems 7 Who would employ his Sadle-nagg to come And hold a trencher in the Dining-roome?

Saddleback (sæ·d'lbæk), sb. and a. [f. SADDLE sb. + BACK sb.] A. sb.

1. †a. Archery. A saddle-backed feather. Obs. b. A saddle-backed hill. (Cf. SADDLE-BACKED a. 1.)

1545 ASCHAM Toxoph. II. (Arb.) 133 The swyne backed fashion..gathereth more ayer than the saddle backed, and therefore the saddle backe is surer for daunger of wether. 1869 E. A. PARKES Pract. Hygiene (ed. 3) 289 A saddleback is usually healthy..so are positions near the top of a slope. 1907 Gentl. Mag. Mar. 247 A regular saddleback of grey Silurian blocks the wayfarers path.

†2. A back (of an animal) having a depression in the middle of it. Obs.

1625 PURCHAS Pilgrims II. 1694 Certaine beasts..much like unto a Deere, hauing a Saddle-backe like unto a Camell.

3. Arch. A roof of a tower, having a gable at two opposite sides connected by a ridge-roof; a packsaddle roof.

1849 FREEMAN Archit. 238 The gabled tower..does not seem to occur; but we meet with the form usually called a saddle-back. 1861 BERESF. HOPE Eng. Cathedr. 19th C. 243 The due and moderate use of the gabled tower of the German style..may be adopted,..so too may the saddle-back. 1893 C. HODGES in Reliquary Jan. 15 The finish of the tower was what is generally known as a saddle-back, a form common in Normandy, but rare in England.

4. A name of various birds and fishes. a. The Grey or Hooded Crow, Corvus cornix; also called saddleback crow. b. The adult of either of the Black-backed Gulls, Larus marinus and L. fuscus; also saddleback gull. c. The male of the Greenland or Harp Seal (Phoca grœnlandica) when three years old; in full saddleback seal. d. The Creadion carunculatus, a bird of New Zealand. e. A variety of the goose (see quot. 1885). f. A kind of oyster (see quot. 1876).

1847 COL. HAWKER Diary (1893) II. 275 A huge saddle-back gull. 1856 KANE Arct. Expl. I. ii. 22 The valued furs of the saddle-back seal. 1864 ATKINSON Prov. Names Birds, Saddleback Crow..Hooded Crow. Corvus cornix. Ibid., Saddle-back, Saddleback Gull..Great Blackbacked Gull. Larus marinus. 1868 W. BULLER Ess. Ornithol. in Trans. N. Z. Inst. I. 5 (Morris) The Saddle-back (Creadion carunculatus) of the North is represented in the South by C. Cinereus, a closely allied species. 1872 Daily News 23 Aug., The decrease of the gulls would be attended with certain loss to fishermen who were often directed and piloted to the shoals by the keen-eyed saddle-back. 1872 COUES Key N. Amer. Birds 312 Great Black-backed Gull. Saddle-back. 1876 Weale's Dict. Terms, Saddle-backs, in fishery, a name given to a bastard kind of oyster by the fishers; they are considered unfit for human food. 1885 Encycl. Brit. XIX. 647/1 The common variety [of the goose] frequently marked with dark feathers on the back, and hence termed 'saddlebacks'. 1895 P. H. EMERSON Birds etc. of Norf. Broadland xlix. 140 A useful bird is the handsome but sluggish 'saddle-back' [i.e. the grey crow]. 1896 LYDEKKER Brit. Mammals 136 It is not till the third year that the males (then called 'Saddle-backs') assume the characteristic dark harp-shaped markings.

5. a. Coal-mining (see quot.). b. Geol. An anticlinal (Cassell's Encycl. Dict. 1887).

1883 GRESLEY Coal-mining Terms, Saddleback, a depression or valley in strata.

B. adj.

1. = SADDLE-BACKED a., in various senses.

1677 Lond. Gaz. No. 1257/4 Stolen or strayed.., one dapple gray Gelding..a little saddle-back. 1696 Ibid. No. 3202/4 A brown Mare,..Saddle Back, well risen on the Crest. 1862 Ecclesiologist XXIII. 252 Gabled or saddle-back towers. 1876 Encycl. Brit. IV. 472/1 [Coping] sloping to both sides from the middle..is technically termed saddle-back coping. 1897 Daily News 3 May 7/3 The Greek troops occupied..a saddleback hill. 1904 Westm. Gaz. 2 Sept. 4/1 A high saddle-back peak. 1906 Edin. Rev. Jan. 114 A plain..building.. with two low gable or 'saddle-back' roofs.

2. Saddleback crow, gull, seal: see A. 4.

3. Mech. (See quot.)

1844 Civil Engin. & Arch. Jrnl. VII. 236/2 At the bottom of the hopper there is a number of angular or 'saddle back bars', placed transversely..; the 'saddle back bars' will have the effect of dividing the ores. 1888 Lockwood's Dict. Mech. Engin., Saddle Back Rail, or Barlow Rail, a rail whose sides curve rapidly outwards and downwards.

4. Geol. (See quot.)

1854 PAGE Introd. Textbk. Geol. § 31 When strata dip in opposite directions from a ridge or line of elevation..the axis is termed anticlinal or saddleback.

5. Path. (Cf. saddle-nose, SADDLE sb. 10.)

1897 Allbutt's Syst. Med. IV. 686 As a result of cicatricial contraction of the connective-tissue..the so-called 'saddle-back' nose may be formed.

6. Put for 'horse-back'. Also advb.

1899 'ZACK' On Trial xiv. 124 If 'tworn't that I can trust 'ee saddle-back..I should hold you had done the mare a mischief. 1904 Westm. Gaz. 29 Feb. 1/3 His love of saddle-back exercise.

Saddle-backed (sæ·d'lbækt), a.

1. Having the back, upper surface, or edge curved like a saddle; having a concavely curved outline; spec. in Archery (see quot. 1545).

1545 ASCHAM Toxoph. II. (Arb.) 129 Fourthly in couling or sheryng [the feather of a shaft],..whether somewhat swyne backed (I must vse shoters wordes) or sadle backed, whether rounde, or square shorne? 1599 HAKLUYT Voy. II. II. 126 It is a hill sadlebacked..: and..we saw a row of hils sadlebacked also. 1601 HOLLAND Pliny I. 238 They (dolphins) are saddle-backed. Ibid. 492 The Walnut tree wood soone bendeth, and is saddle-backt as it lieth. 1884 G. ALLEN Philistia I. 235 A saddle-backed hill.

2. Of a horse: see quot. 1831.

1675 Lond. Gaz. No. 967/4 Strayed or stolen.., a bright Bay Gelding,..a little Saddle-back'd. 1753 CHAMBERS Cycl. Supp. 1831 YOUATT Horse 166 Some horses have a very considerable hollow behind the withers. They are said to be saddle-backed. 1895 Westm. Gaz. 29 July 2/3 A thorough-bred Arab..should be..very slightly saddle-backed. To be 'saddle-backed' is to have a depression where the saddle would naturally come.

3. Arch. a. Of coping: see quot. 1842. b. Of a tower: Having a SADDLEBACK.

1842 GWILT Archit. s.v. Coping, Coping thicker in the middle than at the edges is called saddle-backed coping. 1870 F. R. WILSON Ch. Lindisf. 23 A small straight saddle-backed tower.

4. An epithet applied to birds having saddle-like markings on the back, as saddle-backed crow, the Grey Crow, Corvus cornix.

1838 HOLLOWAY Provinc., Saddle-backed crow, the Royston, or sea-crow, so called from its mixture of black and grey feathers. Sussex. 1894 R. B. SHARPE Birds Gt. Brit. I. 12 The Hooded, or Saddle-backed Crows. 1895 J. G. MILLAIS Breath from Veldt vii. 142 Here also are a big flock of saddle-backed Jabiru storks (Mycteria senegalensis).

Sa·ddle-bag.

1. A bag carried at the saddle; esp. one of a pair laid across the back of a horse, behind the saddle.

1796 MORSE Amer. Geog. I. 542 Manufactures of leather ..holsters, saddle-bags [etc.]. 1841 LANE Arab. Nts. I. 43 He..put his hand into his saddle-bag, and eat a morsel of bread and a date which were among his provisions. 1856 STANLEY Sinai & Pal. i. (1858) 67 The great saddle bags act like sails to the camels. 1857 HUGHES Tom Brown I. i, A visit..which the Squire made on his horse with a pair of saddle-bags containing his wardrobe.

2. attrib. Used to designate a fine quality of carpeting, made in sizes and designs imitating the saddle-bags carried in the East by camels; now chiefly employed as a covering for cheap classes of dining-room furniture.

1882 Daily News 30 May 5/7 Settees and easy-chairs upholstered in what is known as the Persian saddle-bag pattern. 1900 FLO. WARDEN Plain Miss Cray 80 There was ..a saddle-bag couch and two big easy-chairs. 1903 MCNEILL Egregious English 125 A saddle-bag suite.

Sa·ddle-bow. Now arch. or poet. [BOW sb.[1] Cf. OHG. satilpogo (MHG. satelboge, mod.G. sattelbogen).] The arched front part of a saddle-tree or of a saddle.

c 725 Ags. Voc. in Wr.-Wülcker 11/17 Carpella, sadulboga. a 1250 Prov. Alfred 229 in O. E. Misc. 116 If þu hauest seorewe, ne seye þu hit nouht þan arewe, seye hit þine sadel-bowe [a 1275 seit þin sadilbowe] and ryd þe singinde forþ. c 1330 Arth. & Merl. 8148 (Kölbing) Wawain him 3aue a dent of howe & cleued him to þe sadel bowe. 1470–85 MALORY Arthur IX. xvi, And the lady of the lake took vp her heed and henge it vp by the heyre of her sadel bowe. 1592 SHAKS. Ven. & Ad. 14 Vouchsafe, thou wonder, to alight thy steed, And rein his proud head to the saddle-bow. 1658 tr. Porta's Nat. Magick XIV. 314 We use to hang up Turkies alive by the bills, at the saddle-bow, when we ride. 1757 BURKE Abridgm. Eng. Hist. Wks. X. 411 The beast ..plunged, and threw his rider violently on the saddle-bow. 1805 SCOTT Last Minstr. I. v, Steeds..Barb'd with frontlet of steel, I trow, And with Jedwood-axe at saddlebow. 1879 'OUIDA' Cecil Castlemaine's Gage 7 He lifted his hat, and bowed down to his saddle-bow as he passed her.

Saddle-cloth. Forms: see SADDLE and CLOTH; also 5 sadylclow. A cloth placed on a horse's back beneath the saddle; †in early use = foot-cloth, housing-cloth.

1481–90 Howard Househ. Bks. (Roxb.) 222 Item,..paied.. for ij. yerdes and di. and di. qrter of blak cloth, for a sadylclow for my Lord. 1523 FITZHERB. Husb. § 142 Spere, male, hode, halter, sadelclothe, spores. 1683 Lond. Gaz. No. 1786/4 A bay Mare, with..a black Saddle, and a green Saddle-Cloth. 1776 BOSWELL Johnson II. 349, I observed them [at Lichfield] making some saddle-cloths. 1818 SCOTT Hrt. Midl. v, The Laird..has had his running footman here..to see when the broidered saddle-cloth for his sorrel horse will be ready. 1845 FORD Handbk. Spain I. 31 There is no bed like the saddle-cloth. 1867 S. W. BAKER Nile Trib. Abyssinia v. 111 We were requested to mount two superb white hygeens, with saddle-cloths of blue Persian sheep-skins.

Saddled (sæ·d'ld), ppl. a. [f. SADDLE v. + -ED[1].]

1. Furnished with a saddle.

1002 in Kemble Cod. Diplom. VI. 147 Ic 3eann minum hlaforde..feower hors twa gesadelod and twa ungesadelode. 1890 Daily News 15 Feb. 2/5 A saddled horse was seen in a field without a rider.

2. As the epithet of fishes, insects, etc., having saddle-like markings.

1803 SHAW Zool. IV. 467 Saddled Sparus. Sparus Ephippium. Ibid. 596 Saddled Mackrel. Scomber Equula. 1880 SWINTON Insect Variety 162 The common Saddled Leaf-cricket of the Vine (Ephippigera vitium) has especially thick cup-shaped elytra.

Saddleless (sæ·d'l₁lės), a. [f. SADDLE sb. + -LESS.] Without a saddle; esp. of a horse, not furnished with a saddle. Also rarely of a rider: †(thrown) out of the saddle.

14.. Sir Beues 253–8 (MS. C.) The erle, amonge them all To the grounde he ys falle And ys sadulles. c 1489 CAXTON Sonnes of Aymon 268 But he had no sadel upon his horse. ..Whan Reynawd sawe brayforde sadilles, he called to oger, & sayd [etc.]. a 1500 Prophecy in Bernard. de cura rei fam. (E. E. T. S.) 18 The Egyll and þe antelope...And Sadilles horse. 1886 G. GISSING Isabel Clarendon I. ii. 33 She had learned her riding on a saddleless colt.

Saddler (sæ·dlər). Forms: 4–5 sadelere, 5 sadel(l)er, 5–8 sadler, (5 sedler, sadlare), 5

Supplement, p. 3873; Corrigenda, p. 4092; Spurious words, p. 4093; Books quoted, p. 4094

| SADDLERY | 25 | SADLY. | SADNESS. | 26 | SAFE. |

Saddlery, -yl(1)ər, 5–6 *Sc.* **sadillar,** 6 **sadiller,** *Sc.* **saiddlair, saidlar,** 7–**saddilar.** [f. SADDLE sb. + -ER 1. Cf. MLG. *sadeler, sedeler,* MDu. *sadelare, sadelaar,* OHG. *satilari* (MHG. *sateler,* mod.G. *sattler*).]

Saddling (sæ·dliŋ), *vbl. sb.* [f. SADDLE v. + -ING 1.] The action of the vb. SADDLE.

·Sa·ddling (sæ·dliŋ), *ppl. a.* [f. SADDLE sb. + -ING 1.]

Sadducaic (sædikē·ik), *a.* [f. Gr. Σαδδου-

Sadducean, Sadducæan (sædiniə·ən), *a.* and *sb.* Also 6 **Saducian, Saducœan,** 6–7 **Saducean, Sadducean.**

Sadducee (sæ·didiū̆·), *sb.* Forms: *pl.* 1 sad(d)u-cēas, 2–5 Saduceus, 3 Saduceis, 4 Sadduces; (also 4 Saducey repr. L. *Saduceni*); *sing.* 6–Saducee, 8 late Sad-.

Saddle-tree.

Safe (sēf), *a.* Also 5 **save.** [Originally *save*, f. *Save v.; later assimilated to Safe a.*]

Sa·d-iron.

·Sa·d·ful, a. Obs. rare⁻¹. [+ -FUL.] Sorrowful.

Sadism (sæ·dizm), [f. F. *sadisme,* f. the name of the Count (usually called 'Marquis') de Sade (1740–1814).]

Sadly, adv. Also 4 **sadliche,** 3–4 **sad-lyk, sa·dly,** 4–5 **sadeli, sadliche, lyche,** 4, 6 **sadely,** 6 **sadlich, sadlie, -ye,** 4 sadly. Also 4 *comp.* **sadloker.** [f. SAD a. + -LY 2.]

Sa·d-tree.

Sae: see SAW, Save, SEA, SEE, SO, SOE.

Saecular: see SECULAR.

Saer, Saet, obs. ff. SAFETY, SEAL 2.

Saer, obs. form of SAWYER, SEAR.

Sadness (sæ·dnes), [f. SAD a. + -NESS.] The condition or quality of being sad.

| SAFE | 27 | SAFE. | SAFE-CONDUCT. | 28 | SAFE-GUARD. |

Safe-conduct (sē·fkŏndŏkt), *sb.* Forms: 5–7 **saufconduit** (13th c.), 5 **saufcon-duct, sauf conduct,** 5–6 **safe conduct,** 6 **safconduct.** Also 5 *attrib.*

·Safe-conduct, v. Obs. [prec. sb.] *trans.* To lead, convoy, or conduct safely.

Safe-guard (sē·fgārd), *sb.* Forms: 5–6 **saufgarde,** 6 **saufe garde,** 6 **saffegarde, save-garde** (13th c. in Hatz.–Darm.), 5 *savve* **fem.** of *sauf* **Safe** + *garde* **guard.** Cf. It., Sp. *salva-guardia,* Pg. *salvaguarda.*

Safeguard (sǣ·fgard), v. [f. prec. sb. Cf. F. sauvegarder, which Littré and Hatz.-Darm. call a 'néologisme'.] trans. To keep secure from danger or attack; to guard, protect, defend. Now chiefly with immaterial obj. (e.g. interests, rights).

Hence **safeguarding** vbl. sb. and ppl. a. Also **Safeguarder**.

Safe-hold. [f. Hold sb.[1]: cf. stronghold.] A place of safety.

Safe-keeper. rare⁻¹. [cf. next.] A protector.

Safe-keeping, vbl. sb. The action of keeping safe; reservation, preservation; custody.

Safely (sǣ·fli), adv. Forms: 3–4 sauueli, 3–5 saueliche, 4–5 safliche, -lich, 4–6 saueliche, -like. [f. Safe a. + -ly².]

1. Without harm or injury occasioned or received. Often with verbs of coming, going, keeping, and the like, where the adj. might be used (see Safe a. 1).

2. In a manner free from danger or hazard; securely, without risk.

Safer, obs. form of Saviour, Savour.

Safer ic. = for safe a.: see Safe.

Safer-g, Saferay, obs. ff. Sapphire, Savory.

Saffron (sæ·frn). Forms: 3–4 saueroun, sauron, 4–5 savrone, or safron, -roun, 4–6 saffroun(e, saffyron, safforn, saffern, saffron, safron, saffrun, sauffroun, safran, sauffran, saffern, 4–7 saffran, 5 savfran, 5–6 saffern, saffrone, 6 saffyn, 6–7 saphron, 7– saffron. [a. F. safran (= Pr. safran, Sp. azafran, Pg. açafrão, It. zafferano, med.L. safranum, etc.; cf. med.G. saffran (mod.G. safran).]

Saffron, variant of Sapphire.

Saffron (sæ·frn). Forms: a. 5 saffran, 4–5 saffron, saf(f)ron, 4–6 saphron, saffroun(e, 7 saffran, 5– saffron.

Saffron (sæ·frn), v. [f. prec. sb.] 1. trans. To colour or flavour with saffron.

Saffron bag. †To sink or depress a saffron with the jaundice.

2. The Autumnal Crocus, Crocus sativus, which produces saffron.

b. Bastard Saffron = Safflower 2; called also American, Dyer's, or Mock Saffron. Meadow or Wild Saffron, Colchicum autumnale. Spring Saffron, + Saffron of the Spring, Crocus vernus. African or + Cape Saffron, Lyperia crocea.

3. The orange-yellow colour of saffron (sense 1).

4. Old Chem. = Crocus 3.

5. Special attributives: † saffron butterfly, see B. b.

6. attrib. and Comb. a. simple attrib., as saffron broth, colour, head, knife, ointment yellow (adj.).

b. objective, as saffron-gatherer; parasynthetic, as saffron-coloured, -hued adjs.

c. Special combinations: † saffron-bag, in which saffron is kept; † saffron cake, (a) a cake flavoured with saffron; (b) (see quot. 1867, cf. cake 7); † saffron cordial, a cordial made with saffron.

Saffron, obs. form of Sapphire.

Saffrony (sæ·frni), a. [f. Saffron sb. + -y.] Of a colour somewhat resembling saffron.

Saffry, obs. form of Sapphire.

Safir, Saflin, obs. forms of Sapphire, Saffron.

Safranin (sæ·fran). Chem. Also -ine, [f. F. safran Saffron + -in.] A yellow colouring matter of saffron.

Saft, northern and Sc. form of Soft.

Sag (sæg), sb.[1] Now dial. Also 4–7 sagge.

Sag (sæg), v. Forms: 4–5 saggen, 5 sagge, 4–6 sag. [Of Scand. origin: cf. Sw. sacka to settle down, sink, Norw. sakka to subside.]

1. intr. Of a beam, floor, rope, etc., extended between two points of support: To hang down in the middle, from its own weight or superincumbent pressure.

2. To tend to one side; to lean, incline. Chiefly dial.

3. trans. To cause to sag.

Sag, variant of Seg (rush).

Saga (sɑ̄·gə). [a. ON. saga fem., story; cogn. w. Saw sb.[2]]

1. Any of the narrative compositions in prose that were written in Iceland or Norway during the middle ages; in English use often applied also to those which embody the traditional history of Icelandic families or of Norway.

Sagacious (sagē·ʃəs), a. [f. L. sagāci-, sagax + -ous.]

1. Of animals: Intelligent.

2. Gifted with acuteness of mental discernment; having special aptitude for the discovery and right judging of what is wise or fitting; shrewd, discerning.

Sagacity (sagæ·siti). [ad. F. sagacité, ad. L. sagācitāt-em, f. sagāci-em Sagacious a.: see -ITY.]

1. Acuteness of mental discernment.

SAGAMITÉ. ... Also **sagamity**, **sagamitie**, **sagamity**. [a. F. *sagamité* ...

Sagan, obs. form of CIGAR and SAKER [1].

Sagathy (sæ·gaþi). Obs. exc. Hist. Also **Sagathee**, **sagathie**. ...

Sagbut (sæ·gbʌt). ...

†Sage, a. Her. Clothed in a mantle.

Sage, sb. [1] ...

Sage, sb. [2] ...

Sagar, obs. form of CIGAR and SAKER [1].

†Sagate, a. Her. [L. type *sagatus*]

Sagamore (sæ·gəmōɹ). Also [various forms], sagamo, sagomore, sagamores, sagamour, sagomore.

†Sagamore § sachemore. ...

†Sagan (sē·gæn). Jewish Antiq. Also § sogan.

†Sage (sēdʒ), sb. [1] ...

†Sagapen (sæ·gəpen), Pharm. ...

†Sagapenum (sægəpī·nŏm) ...

Sago (sē·gō). ...

Sagittarius ...

Sagittary (sæ·dʒitəri), sb. and a.

Sagittate (sæ·dʒiteit), a. [ad. mod.L. *sagittatus*, f. L. *sagitta* arrow: see -ATE [2]]

Sagittiform (sædʒi·tifɔɹm), a. [ad. mod.L. *sagittiformis*, f. L. *sagitta* arrow + -FORM]

†Sagittipotent, a. Obs. rare [ad. L. *sagittipotent-em*, f. *sagitta* arrow + *potent-em*]

†Sagittiferous (sædʒiti·fərəs), a. rare. [f. L. *sagittifer* ... + -OUS]

Sagitt·le. Obs. rare [ad. mod.L. *sagittella*, dim. of *sagitta* arrow.]

Sagittocyst (sædʒi·tosist). Zool. [f. L. *sagitta* arrow + CYST sb.]

Sago (sē·gō). Forms: 6-7 sagu, (7 sago, sagou), 7-8 saggo, 9 sago. ... [Malay *sāgū*.]

Sagomo(re, obs. forms of SAGAMORE.

Sagon, obs. form of SAGOIN.

Sagoin (sæ·gɔin). Also 7-9 **sagouin**, (8 **saguyn**), 9 (in Dicts.) **saguin**, 8 **sagouin**.

Sagomin, obs. form of SAGOIN.

Sagoon, obs. form of SAGOIN.

†Sa·goize, v. Obs. rare [1]

Sagre, obs. f. SAKER.

†Sagree. The Picked Dogfish. [Connected with SHA-GREEN.]

SAGGED.　　34

†Sagate, a. Her. Clothed in a mantle.

Sage (sēdʒ), a. and sb. [2] Also 6 saage. Sc. saige, seage. ...

Sagely (sēdʒli), adv. [f. SAGE a. + -LY [2]]

Sageness (sēdʒnes). [f. SAGE a. + -NESS.]

Sagged (sægd), ppl. a. rare. [f. SAG v. + -ED [1].]

Saggar, **Sagger** (sæ·gəɹ). Forms: 7 [various], 8-9 saggar, seggar, 9 sagger. [Prob. a contraction of SAFEGUARD sb.]

Sagene (sæ·gēn). Also 8 sajen, 9 sazhine, saahine, sajene, saajen, [Russian сажень.] A measure of length used in Russia, equal to seven English feet.

Saginate (sæ·dʒineit), v. Obs. [f. L. *sagināt-*, ppl. stem of *saginare* ...]

Saggard, var. SAGGAR.

Sagitta (sædʒi·ta). [L., lit. an arrow.]

SAGGING.　　35　　　　　　　　　　　　　　　　　　　　　　　　SAID.

Sagging (sæ·giŋ), vbl. sb. [f. SAG v. + -ING [1].] The action of the verb SAG in various senses.

Sagging (sæ·giŋ), ppl. a. [f. SAG v. + -ING [2].]

Saggy (sæ·gi), a. [f. SAG v. + -Y [1].]

Saghe, obs. form of SAW.

Saghte, -il, etc., var. f. SAUGHT, -LE, etc.

†Saginary. Obs. rare [ad. L. *saginari-us*, *sagina* ...]

Saginate (sæ·dʒineit), v.

Sagination (sædʒinē·ʃən). rare [ad. L. *sagination-em*, n. of action f. *saginare*: see prec.]

Sagitta (sædʒi·ta). [L., lit. an arrow.] 1. Astr. A northern constellation.

Sagittal (sæ·dʒitæl), a. [ad. mod.L. *sagittalis*, f. L. *sagitta*: see -AL [1].]

Sagittarius (sædʒitē·riəs). [L. *sagittarius*, f. *sagitta*.]

Sagittary (sæ·dʒitəri), sb. and a.

SAGOIN.　　36

Sagittary (sæ·dʒitəri), sb. and a.

†Saginate, v.

Sago (sē·gō).

Sagoin.

Sagomo(re, obs. forms of SAGAMORE.

Saguin.

Sagun, obs. f. SAGOIN.

SAID.

Sahib (sā·ib, sāb). Also 7 **saheb**, 8-9 **saïb**, **saheb**, **sahob**, 9 **saïb**, **saeb**. [Urdu, ad. Arab. *ṣāḥib* lord, master, friend.]

Sahibah, **Sahiba** (sā·iba). [From *Sahib*.] A lady; a mistress.

Sahme, var. SHAME.

Sahras, obs. f. SAHARA.

Sahlite (sā·lait). Min. Also **salite**. [a. G. *sahlit*, named in 1800, f. *Sahla* (*Sala*) in Sweden ...]

Sagwire (sæ·gwaiɹ). Forms: 7 **sagowar**, 8 **sagwire**, 9 **saguery**, 9 **saguire**, 9 **saguer**, etc. [ad. F. *saguier* ...] The Indian Archipelago ... *Arenga saccharifera*, of the Indian Archipelago.

Sahib, see above.

Sahidic (sāhi·dik), a. [f. Arab. *ṣaʿīd*, with article *aṣ-ṣaʿīd*, lit. 'the Fortunate', a name ...] Belonging to the dialect of Coptic spoken in Thebes and Upper Egypt, in which a version of the Bible is extant. Also *quasi-sb.*, the Sahidic language, or the Sahidic version of the Bible.

Saïle, var. f. SAKE.

Saif, Sc. var. of SAFE, SAVE.

SAIGA.

Saifare, saiffer, obs. Sc. forms of SAVER.
Saife, saiffe, obs. Sc. forms of SAFE.
Saffor, obs. form of SAPPHIRE.
Saifte, -tie, obs. Sc. forms of SAFETY.

Saiga (səi'gə, sai'gä). [a. Russ. *saĭga*. Cf. F. *saïga*.] A kind of antelope (*Saiga tartarica*) of the steppes of Russia. Also *saiga antelope*.

Saige, obe, f SURGE. **Saih**, obs. pa. t. of SEE.
Saik, obe, Sc. form of SAKE.
Saikles, obe, obs. Sc. forms of SACKLESS.
Sailkyr, obe, Sc. form of SAKER (cannon).

Sail (sēil), *sb.*[1] Forms : 1 **segel, segl**, 3 **seille, seyl**, 3–4 **seil, seyl**...

SAIL.

Sail (sēil), *v.*[1]

SAIL-FISH.

SAILFUL.

†Sai·lful, *sb. rare.* [f. SAIL *sb.*[1] + -FUL[1].]
Enough of wind to fill the sails.

Sailie, var. SAILY *sb.*[1], *Sc.*, no project.

Sailing (sēi'liŋ), *vbl. sb.*[1] [f. SAIL *v.*[1] + -ING[1].]

SAILOR.

Sailor (sēi'ləł). Also 7 *saylor.* [An altered spelling of SAILER, prob. assimilated to *-or*...]

Sailoress. [f. SAILOR + -ESS.] A female sailor.

Sailoring (sē·lǝriŋ), vbl. sb. [f. SAILOR + -ING.] The work of a sailor.

Sailorly (sē·lǝli), a. [f. SAILOR + -LY.] Befitting a sailor; having the characteristics of a sailor.

Sailory. Obs. rare⁻¹. [f. OF. sailloir, f. saillir to dance: see SAIL v.] A place to dance in.

Sail-worthy, a. Obs. rare. [f. SAIL sb.¹ + WORTHY.] Of weather: Admitting of the use of sails.

Saily, a. Obs. [f. SAIL sb.¹ + -Y.] Having the appearance of a sail or sails.

Sailyard (sē·ljārd). Forms: see SAIL and YARD. [f. SAIL sb.¹ + YARD sb.]

Sail·lyie, sail·ȝie, v. Sc. Obs.

Saim, dial. and obs. form of SEAM (lard).

Saimiri (saimī·ri). Also 8 samiri in Dicts.

Sain (sēn), v. Now arch. and dial. Forms:

Sains, the plural of SAINT.

Sainfoin (sē·nfoin). Forms: 7 S. Foyne, Saint-, St. Foin, saint-foin, santfine, -foyne, 7-8 St. Foyne, 8 foin, sainfoine, 6 saintfoin, 7- sanfoin, 8- sainfoin. [a. F. sainfoin, also 7 saintfoin (cf. 6b., 6n.).]

Saing fayle, variant of SANSFAIL.

+ Sainse, Saynsure, obs. ff. CENSE v.¹ and CENSER.

Saint (sēnt, unstressed sǝnt, snt), sb. a. and sb. Forms: a. 2–6 seint, 3–6 seinte, seynte, sainte, a–5 sayn, 3 seinte, 3 seinte, 6 seynt, sayn(e, 4–6 saynt, 5 saint, seynte, &c. β. (prefixed to a name beginning with a cons.) 3–4 sein, 4 san, sen, 4–6 sayn, 5 sayne, sain, syn. γ. 3–5 saunt, 4–6 sawnt (6 -e), 5 seant, 5 sante, 6 saunct.

Saint (sēnt), v. [f. prec.]

Sainted (sē·nted), ppl. a. Also 6 sancted. [f. SAINT v. + -ED.]

Sainthood (sē·nthud). [f. SAINT sb. + -HOOD.]

Saintify, v. rare. [f. SAINT sb. + -FY.]

Saintish, a. rare. [f. SAINT sb. + -ISH.]

Saintism. Obs. rare⁻¹. [f. SAINT sb. + -ISM.]

Saintless, a. [f. SAINT sb. + -LESS.]

Saintlike, a. [See -LIKE.] Resembling a saint or that of a saint; of a saintly life, character, etc.

Saintlily (sē·ntlili), adv. [f. next + -LY.] In a saintly manner.

Saintliness (sē·ntlinǝs). [f. SAINTLY + -NESS.] The condition or quality of being saintly.

Saint, sb. (continued)

Saint-errant. ironical. [Modelled on KNIGHT-ERRANT.] A saint who travelled in quest of spiritual adventures.

Saint-errantry. [See prec.] The character, practice, or spirit of a saint-errant.

Saintess (sē·ntes). [f. SAINT sb. + -ESS.] A female saint.

Sainting (sē·ntiŋ), vbl. sb. [f. SAINT v. + -ING.]

Saintish, **Saintism:** see above.

Saintdom (sē·ntdǝm). [f. SAINT sb. + -DOM.]

Saintling (sē·ntliŋ). [f. SAINT sb. + -LING.] A little or petty saint.

Saintly (sē·ntli), a. [f. SAINT sb. + -LY.]

Saintly, adv. [-LY².] Holily.

Saintologer: [f. SAINT sb. + -OLOGER.] a hagiologist.

Saintology. [f. SAINT sb. + -OLOGY.]

Saintrel. [a. OF. saintrel, dim. of saint.] Cf. SANTREL.

Saintess, **Saint-seeming:** see above.

Saintship (sē·ntṣip). [f. SAINT sb. + -SHIP.] The condition or status of a canonized saint.

Saintuary, obs. form of SANCTUARY.

+ Sainty, a. Obs. [f. SAINT sb. + -Y.] Saintly.

Saip, Sc. var. SOAP. **Saipheron** (sē·), var. SAFFRON. **Sair,** Sc. var. SAVOUR, SERVE v., SORE. **Saircoteit,** obs. form of SURCOAT. **Sais,** var. SAY and SEE v., viz. SIZE. **Saise, Saison,** etc., obs. ff. SAIN, Indian antelope. **Saisin,** variant of SASIN, Indian antelope.

Saith, Sc. Forms: 7 sheath, 7–9 seath, 8 seeth, 8– saithe. [Cf. Icel. seiðr.] A fish of the cod kind, the coal-fish or coal-fish.

Saite (sē·it), a. [ad. L. Saītē-us sb.] and adj., a. Gr. Σαΐτης.] of, pertaining to Saïs, the ancient capital of Lower Egypt.

Saiva, var. SHAIVA.

Saivo, Sc. var. of SAFE.

Saix, variant of SAX (a slater's tool).

Sajou (sǝ·ʒū). [F., variant of sajouassou.] One of various small South American monkeys.

Sak, obs. form of SACK.

Sakawinki (sǝkawī·ŋki). [Corruptly a Du. negroslang] A South American monkey, the White-headed Saki, Pithecia pithecia or capillamentosa.

Sake (sēk), sb.¹ Forms: 1 sacu, 3 sak, 4–5 sak(e, 5 saak, 6 saick, 6 saick, 4–6 sake. [OE. sacu fem.]

Saké, Saki (sā·ki), sb.² In 6 seynty. ?A mock-affectionate formation on SAINT sb.

SAKE.

(Dictionary entries under SAKE, including senses relating to cause, account, purpose; phrases "for the sake of," "for God's sake," "for goodness' sake," etc.)

Sake, sb. Aphetic form of FORSAKE.

Sake, obs. form of SAO¹, SACK sb.¹, SHAKE.

Saki (saˈkɪ). Forms: 7 saquo, 8 saki, 9 saki, saky, sacki, sakie. [a. F. *saki.*] A small S. American monkey of the genus *Pithecia*.

Sakeret (saˈkərɛt). Obs. or arch. Forms: 5 sacreto, 5-7 sacret, 6 sagaret, 7 saker, caret, sakeret, 8- sakeret. [a. F. *sacret*, dim. of *sacre* SAKER.] The male of the saker.

Sakerfyse, obs. form of SACRIFICE.

Sakering, -ryng, obs. forms of SACRING.

Saketi, obs. form of SACKET.

†Sakful, a. Obs. [OE. *sacfull*, f. *sacu* SAKE + -FUL.] Contentious, quarrelsome.

Saki, variant of SAKÉ.

Sakia (saˈkɪə). Forms: 7 saki, 8 sakieh, 9 sakie, sackiyeh, saqueer, sakhyia, sah, 9 sakiah, sakies. [Arab. *sāqiya*, fem. pr. pple. of *saqā* to water.] A machine for raising water for irrigation.

Sakieh, Sakiyeh, variants of SAKIA.

Sakret, variant of SAKERET.

Sakre, obs. form of SAKER, SACRE.

†Sakre, v. Obs. rare. Also *sacre, sakar.* [f. SAKER sb.] To make a saking or sacring sound.

Sakring, variant of SACRING.

Sal¹ (sæl). *Chem., Alch., and Pharm.* [L. (masc. and neut.) = salt.] Salt (in various senses). Obs.

Sal² (sæl). *Bot.* Also *saul.* [Hindī *sāl* = Skr. *śāla.*] A valuable timber tree of India, *Shorea robusta*; also the timber. Also *attrib.*

Sal³ (sæl). A hall or large apartment; *spec.* a dining-hall.

Sala¹ (sæˈlə). [Sp., Pg., It. *sala* = OF. *sale*, SALLE.]

†Sala² (sæˈlə). Obs. rare. [Hindī, Skr. *śālā* house.] An Indian rest-house or inn.

Salad (sæˈləd). Forms: 4- salad, 5-7 sallad, 5-9 sallet, 7-9 sallad. [a. OF. *salade* (mod.F. *salade*, It. *salata*, Sp. *ensalada*, med.L. *salata*).] A cold dish of herbs or vegetables.

SALADINE. 47 SALAMANDER. SALAMANDER. 48 SALBAND.

Salade, var. form of SALLET, helmet.

Saladin (sæˈlədɪn). Obs. Also *saladyne, -o.* [ad. L. *Saladinus.*]

Saladine, sb. Obs. var. of CELANDINE.

Saladin¹, sb. Obs. ? = CELIDONY.

Saladine² (sæˈlədɪn). [f. *Saladin*.]

Salading (sæˈlədɪŋ). Forms: see SALAD; also 7 salleting, 8 salleting. [f. SALAD + -ING¹.] Herbs and vegetables used for salad.

Salad-oil. Olive oil of superior quality.

Salal (sæˈlæl). [Chinook Jargon *salal* = Chinook *kl-kwu-shā-la*.] An evergreen shrub (*Gaultheria Shallon*) of California and Oregon.

Salamander (sæˈləmændə). Forms: 4 *salamandre*, etc. [a. F. *salamandre.*]

Salamandrian (sæləˈmændrɪən), a. and sb.

Salamandrid (sæləˈmændrɪd). [ad. mod.L. *Salamandridæ.*]

Salamandriform (sæləˈmændrɪfɔːm), a.

Salamandrine (sæləˈmændrɪn), a.

Salamandroid (sæləˈmændrɔɪd), a. and sb.

Salamandry, a. and sb. Obs. rare.

Salamon, Salmon, cant. name for the mass.

Salamstone (sæˈləmstəʊn). *Min.* A blue variety of sapphire.

Salangane (sæˈlæŋɡeɪn). *Zool.* Also 8 *saligan, 9 salagane.* [a. F. *salangane.*]

Salary (sæˈlərɪ), sb. Forms: 4- salary, 4-8 salarie, 4 salari, 5 saleri, solary, etc. [a. AF. *salarie* = OF. *salaire*, ad. L. *salārium* orig. money allowed to Roman soldiers for salt.] Fixed payment made periodically to a person as compensation for regular work.

Salary, v.

Salband (sælˈbænd). *Geol.* Also *salbande, salband.* [G. *salband* selvage, OHG. *selbende*, i.e. self-end.]

SALD. — 49 — SALEABLE. — SALEABLENESS — 50 — SALIC.

SALICACEOUS — 51 — SALIENT. — SALIFEROUS — 52 — SALIRETIN.

Salited, ppl. a. ? Obs. [f. L. salīt-us, pa. pple. of salīre to salt + -ED¹.] Impregnated with salt.

Sali-tion, rare. [ad. late L. salītiōn-em, n. of action f. salīre to leap.] Leaping.

Salitre (sal-). See SALTPETRE; Sodium nitrate.

Salitrose, a. Sp. salitroso. [f. Sp. salitre (see quot.)] Saltpetrous.

Saliva (sălăi·vă). [a. L. salīva.] Spittle; the mixed secretion of the salivary glands and of the mucous glands of the mouth, a colourless liquid, having normally an alkaline reaction, which mixes with the food in mastication.

Salival (sălăi·văl), a. and sb. Now rare. [ad. mod.L. salīvāl-is, f. L. salīva: see prec. and -AL. Cf. OF. salival.] A. adj. Salivary.

Salivant, a. and sb. rare. [ad. L. salīvant-em, pres. pple. of salīvāre, f. salīva SALIVA.]

Salivarious, a. Obs.—⁰ [f. L. salīvāri-us + -OUS.] (See quot.)

Salivary (sæ·lĭvări), a. [ad. L. salīvāri-us, f. salīva: see SALIVA and -ARY¹.] Secreting or conveying saliva.

Salivate (sæ·līveit), v. [f. L. salīvāt-, ppl. stem of L. salīvāre, f. salīva SALIVA.]

1. trans. To produce an unusual secretion of saliva in (a person), generally by the use of mercury; to produce ptyalism in.

2. intr. To secrete or discharge saliva. Also Sally-man.

Salivation (sælīveɪ·ʃən). [ad. L. salīvātiōn-em, n. of action f. salīvāre: see prec.]

Salive, obs. form of SALIVA.

Salivous (sælăi·vəs), a. Obs. [f. L. salīv-us + -OUS.] Causing a flow of saliva; salivant.

Salix (sei·liks). Pl. salices. [L., willow.]

Sall, obs. form of SHALL.

Salle (sal). [Fr.] A hall, room.

Sallet, -man, obs. forms of SALLOW, SALLOW-MAN.

Sallow, sb.¹ [OE. sealh (Anglian salh)—prehistoric *salho-z masc.; cogn. w. OHG. salaha wk. fem.]

A plant of the genus Salix, a willow; chiefly, in narrower sense, as distinguished from 'osier' and 'willow', applied to several species of Salix of a low-growing or shrubby habit.

Sallow, a. [OE. salo = MDu. salu, saluw-coloured, dirty (Du. †zaluw), OHG. salo, salaw-dark-coloured (MHG. sal, salw-), mod.Ger. dial. sal).]

1. Of complexion: Having a sickly yellow or brownish yellow colour.

2. b. transf. and of things personified.

3. trans. To make sallow.

Sallowish, a. [f. SALLOW a. + -ISH.] Somewhat sallow in hue.

Sallowness (sæ·ləunes). [f. SALLOW a. + -NESS.]

Sallowy (sæ·ləuí), a. [f. SALLOW sb.¹ + -Y¹.]

Sally, sb.¹ Forms: sallie, salie, sally, salley, sallye, 8 sallly, 7-9 sally. [ad. F. saillie, sb., a sortie; esp. in the phrase to make a sally.]

1. A sudden rush (out) from a besieged place upon the enemy; a sortie; esp. in the phrase to make a sally.

2. b. A place whence a sally may be made; a sally-port. Obs.

3. A going forth, setting out, excursion, expedition (of one or more persons).

4. A breaking forth from restraint; an outburst or transport (of passion, delight, or other emotion); a flash (of wit); a flight (of fancy).

Sally, sb.² [Of obscure origin.] Bell-ringing. Also 9 sallie.

Sally, v.¹ Obs. rare. Forms: 5 salyyn, 6 saly, 7 sally; [irreg. ad. F. saillir: see SALLY sb.¹]

1. intr. To leap, bound, prance.

2. trans. Of a horse: To leap (a mare).

Sally, v.² [f. SALLY sb.¹]

1. intr. Of a warlike force: To issue suddenly from a place of defence or retreat in order to make an attack; spec. of a besieged force, to make a sortie. Also to sally out.

Sally-man, Sally rover: see SALLEE-MAN.

Sallyport. [f. SALLY sb.¹ + PORT sb.²] A kind of tee-cake (see quot. 1892).

Sally Lunn. [app. a proper name.] A kind of sweet tea-cake or bun.

Salm, obs. form of PSALM.

Salmagundi (sælmăgɒ·ndi). Forms: 7-8 salmagundy, 8 salamongundy, (salled-magundy), Solomon Gundy, salmi-, salmongundy, salmon-, 9 salmagundi (in the dict. c. salmigundie, salmingondin), of obscure origin.]

1. A dish composed of chopped meat, anchovies, eggs, onions with oil and condiments.

2. fig. A heterogeneous mixture; a miscellany; a medley.

Salmi (sæ·lmi). Also 8 salmy. [a. F. salmi, according to Hatz.-Darm. shortened from salmigondi: see SALMAGUNDI.] A ragoût of partly roasted game, stewed with sauce, wine, bread, and condiments (Garrett's Encycl. Cookery 1893).

Salmiac (sæ·lmiæk), contraction of L. sal ammoniacum. Native sal-ammoniac.

Salmody, obs. form of PSALMODY.

Salmon (sæ·mən), sb.¹ and a. Forms: 4-5 saumoun, -own (5, 6 samoun, -on, -one, sawmoun), -mund, (5 samond), 6-7 sammon, samon, salmond (6, 5 salmone, salmon), 5 salmone, 7 salmon, 7- salmon. [a. AF. saumun, OF. saumon, salmon (mod.F. saumon), ad. L. salmōn-em.]

A large fish belonging to the genus Salmo, family Salmonidae, esp. Salmo salar, comprising the largest fish of this family, which when mature are characterized by having red flesh, and a silvery skin marked with large black and red spots.

Salmonid (sæ·lmɒnid), a. and sb. [ad. mod.L. Salmonidae.] A fish of the family Salmonidae.

Salmon-coloured, a. = SALMON a.

Salmonet (sæ·lmɒnet). Also 6 samonet.

Salmony (sæ·lmɒni), a. [f. SALMON sb.¹ + -Y¹.]

Salmoniform, *a.*

Salmonine (sæˈmoˌnaɪn), *a.*

Salmonoid (sæl·mɒnɔɪd), *a.* and *sb.*

Sal-monoseuse, *a.*

Salmon-trout.

Sal-nitre. *Obs.*

Salni·tral, *a.*

Salol (sæ·lɒl). *Chem.*

Salod, *var.* **Salute** 2. *Obs.*

Salomene. *Obs.*

Salometer (sæˈlɒmɪtə(r)).

Salomonic.

Salon (sælɒn). Also **8 saloon.** [Fr.]

Saloon (səˈluːn). Also **8 salon.**

Saloonist.

Saloop (səˈluːp).

Salopettes.

Salp (sælp).

Salpa (sæ·lpa).

Salpian (sæˈlpiːən).

Salpicon.

Salpian (sæ·lpiːən).

Salpiglossis (sælpɪˈglɒsɪs).

Salpingitis (sælpɪnˈdʒaɪtɪs).

Salpingo- (sælˈpɪŋgo).

Salpinx (sæ·lpɪŋks).

Salse (sæls).

Salsify (sæˈlsɪfɪ).

Salsilla (sælsɪ·lla).

Salsolaceous (sælsəˈleɪʃəs).

Salsa, *obs. Sc. form of* **Sauce.**

Salster. *Obs.*

Salsuginous (sælˈsjuːdʒɪnəs), *a.*

Salsure. *Obs.*

Salt (sɔːlt), *sb.*[1]

Salt, *sb.*[2]

Salt (sɒlt), *a.* Also 6 saute.

Salt, *sb.1*

Saltant (sæ·ltănt), *a.* [ad. L. *saltant-em*, pres. pple. of *saltāre* to SALT.]

Saltation (sæltēiˑʃən), *n.* [ad. L. *saltātiōn-em*.]

Saltatoric (sæltătɒˑrik), *a.* Path.

Saltatorious (sæltătōuˑriŏs), *a.*

Saltatory (sæˑltătəri), *a.*

Salter (sɒˑltəɹ), *sb.1*

Saltbush.

‖Saltarello (saltărēˑlo).

Salter, -tartre: see SALT 2.

‖Saltant (sæˑltănt), *a.*

‖Saltator (sæltēiˑtŏr), *sb.*

Saltatorial (sæltătōuˑriăl), *a.*

‖Saltatress. *Obs. rare−1.*

Saltatrix. *rare.*

Salting, *vbl. sb.*

Salt-cat.

Salt-cellar. Forms: 5–6 saler, (5 sellere, seler, 6 celar); 5, 6 seller, 6–7 sellar, 7 sallar.

‖Salt-cote, -coat. *Obs.*

Salted, *ppl. a.*

Salten, *a. Obs.*

Salter, *sb.2*

Saltern (sɒˑltəɹn), *sb.*

Salting (sɒˑltiŋ), *vbl. sb.*

Saltier, variant of SALTIRE.

Saltant, var. of SALTANT.

Saltigrade (sæˑltigrēid), *a.* and *sb. Zool.*

Saltimbanco (sæltimbæˑŋko), *sb.* Also 7 saltinbanco, (erron. salta-banco), and 7, 9 saltimbank.

Saltire (sæˑltəɹ), *sb.* Her.

Saltish (sɒˑltiʃ), *a.* [f. SALT *sb.1* + -ISH.]

Saltless (sɒˑltles), *a.*

Saltly (sɒˑltli), *adv.*

Saltness (sɒˑltnes).

Salton. *Obs. rare−1.*

Saltion (sɒˑlʃən).

Saltire (sæˑltəɹ), *sb.*

Saltireways, -wise, *adv.*

Saltish.

Saltitant, *a. Obs. rare−1.*

Saltless, *a.*

Saltly, *adv.*

Saltness.

Salt-lick.

Saltly (sɒˑltli), *adv.*

Salt-marsh (sɒˑltmɑɹʃ), *sb.*

Saltory (sɒˑltəri).

Saltou, obs. f. *shalt thou*: see SHALL.
Saltoyre, obs. form of SALTIRE.
Sa·lt-pan. [Cf. Du. *zoutpan*, G. *salzpfanne*.] **a.** (Usually *pl.*) A shallow depression near the sea into which sea-water is allowed to flow, where it evaporates, leaving a deposit of salt; in Africa, applied (after Du. *zoutpan*) to dried-up salt lakes or marshes. **b.** A shallow vessel in which brine is evaporated in salt-making; *pl.*, a salt-works.

1493 *Newminster Cartul.* (Surtees) 195, iiij salt pannes standynge vp on the north syde of yᵉ water of Blyth. 1533 BELLENDEN *Livy* App. (S.T.S.) II. 263 *note*, Salynis ar callit certane places besyd þe se quhair þe salt Is made. We call þame salt pannys. 1573 *Reg. Privy Council Scot.* II. 265 Havand commissioun of the rest of awnars of the salt pannis of Dysert. 1708 J. C. *Compl. Collier* (1845) 11 The best Coals are best for the Salt Pans and Salt too, and make most and best Salt. 1748 BROWNRIGG *Art of Making Salt* 52 The salt pans are made of an oblong form, flat at the bottom, with the sides erected at right angles. 1785 G. FORSTER tr. *Sparrman's Voy. Cape G. Hope* II. 14 A good mile and a half from the river, we met with the capital *Zout-pan*, or Salt-pan. 1857 LIVINGSTONE *Trav.* iv. 78 In every salt-pan in the country there is a spring of water on one side. 1883 F. DAY *Indian Fish* 9 (Fish. Exhib. Publ.) The salt used there costing about threepence per 82⅔ lb. weight, whereas in the contiguous British territory it stood at the salt-pans at about four shillings.

Saltpetre (sǫltpīˑtəɹ). Also 6–9 (now *U.S.*) **-peter, 6 petir, -ur, 7 -ar, 6–7 peeter.** [Alteration of SALPETRE after SALT *sb.*¹ (see sense 5 b).]

1. Potassium nitrate; = NITRE *sb.* 1 b. *Chili* or *cubic saltpetre*: sodium nitrate.

Saltpetre is a white crystalline substance having a saline taste; it is the chief constituent of gunpowder, and is used medicinally.

1501–2 *Acc. Ld. High Treas. Scot.* II. 139 For ij pund salt petir to the leich. 1528–9 *Acc. St. Mary at Hill* 347 The tyme that the kyng caused Salte peter to be made in the said house. 1590 GREENE *Never too late* (1600) 21 Like Saltpeeter, that fiereth at the first, and yet proueth but a flash. 1612 WOODALL *Surg. Mate* Wks. (1653) 209 Salt-Peeter..is of excellent use for medicine. 1669 STURMY *Mariner's Mag.* v. xii. 80 The Shot is driven forth..by the Air's exaltation, or Wind, caused through the Salt-Peter. 1722 *Phil. Trans.* (abr. ed.) III. 371 The pendent Rocks were glazed with Salt Peter. 1768 BOSWELL *Corsica* i. (ed. 2) 52 There are also mines of allum, and of salt-petre, in several parts of Corsica. 1837 M. DONOVAN *Dom. Econ.* II. 241 On account of the property which saltpetre possesses of giving a pleasing redness to beef, it is always an ingredient in the brine with which meat is preserved. 1846 GREENER *Sci. Gunnery* 21 Gunpowder is an explosive propellant compound, consisting of saltpetre or nitre, charcoal, and sulphur. 1877 [see CUBIC *a.* 1 b]. 1886 *Encycl. Brit.* XXI. 235/2 A large quantity of saltpetre is now prepared from Chili saltpetre, the nitrate of soda.

†b. *Oil of saltpetre* [? error for *oil of* PETRE]: petroleum. *Spirits of saltpetre*: nitric acid. *Obs.*

1685 BOYLE *Salubr. Air* 95 The Spirits of Salt-peter will readily corrode silver. 1692 in *Capt. Smith's Seaman's Gram.* II. xxxi. 144 Fill these with good Powder dust, moistned with Oyle of Salt-Peter.

2. *attrib.* and *Comb.*, as *saltpetre-boiler*, *-boiling*, *cave*, *crystal*, *earth*, *-maker*, *work(s)*, *-worker*; **saltpetre flour** (see quot.); **saltpetre house**, (*a*) a building in which saltpetre is made or stored; (*b*) = F. *la Salpêtrière*, a hospital for aged and infirm women at Paris; formerly a prison for women; **saltpetre-lye**, 'a liquid obtained by the treatment of saltpetre with water' (*Syd. Soc. Lex.* 1897); **†saltpetre man**, a man appointed to find saltpetre for the manufacture of gunpowder; **saltpetre paper** = TOUCH-PAPER; **saltpetre rot**, white efflorescence which forms on new or damp walls, caused by saltpetre working through to the surface; **†saltpetre salt** (see quot. 1683).

1580 *Faversham Par. Reg.* (MS.), Edward Hale, a *saltpeeter boyller. 1683 PETTUS *Fleta Min.* I. 333 Some Salt-Petre Boylers (who sell the raw unpurified Earth-Petre). *Ibid.* 338 A true large Instruction of the *Salt-Peter boyling. 1868 *Rep. U.S. Commissioner Agric.* (1869) 397 *Saltpeter Caves in the South. 1878 GURNEY *Crystallogr.* 7 These beautiful rods which we call *saltpetre crystals. 1601 HOLLAND *Pliny* I. Index, *Saltpetre earth good for plants. 1699 DAMPIER *Voy.* II. II. i. 8 Probably there may be Salt-Petre-Earth in other Places. 1848 *Knapp's Chem. Technol.* I. 373 The saltpetre is obtained as a snow-white powder, consisting of fine crystalline needles—'*saltpetre-flour'. 1683 PETTUS *Fleta Min.* I. 340 The fore-part of the *Salt-Petre House, wherein the Lee Tubs do stand. 1767 *Ann. Reg.* 77 A woman..condemned to be branded and confined to the saltpetre-house for nine years. 1683 PETTUS *Fleta Min.* I. 321 How the weak *Salt-Petre Lee is to be made richer and boil'd to greater profit. 1799 G. SMITH *Laboratory* I. 49 Saw-dust, boiled in saltpetre-lye. 1611 COTGR., *Salpestrier*, a Salt-peter-man, or *Salt-peter-maker. 1843 *Civ. Eng. & Arch. Jrnl.* VI. 424/1 In 1627 the saltpetre-makers were authorized to take away the ground of all dove houses, stables, lairs, or other places where cattle were kept. 1578 *Acts Privy Council Eng.* XXVIII. 382 For chardges of William Shill and John Tyrret, *saltpeter-men. 1589 NASHE *Martins Months Minde* Ep. Ded., Wks. (Grosart) I. 147 That haue chosen a Saltpetre man for their foreman, and a gunne powder house..for their printing shop. 1617 MIDDLETON & ROWLEY *Fair Quarrel* I. i, They are saltpetre-men...And they bring commission, the king's power indeed. *a* 1691 BOYLE *Hist. Air* (1692) 43 We seldom find Salt-peter in the earth, but that there is sea-salt mixed with it, which puts the salt-peter-men to a great deal of trouble to separate it. 1832 BREWSTER *Nat. Magic* xiii. 320 The heat of the wire is always sufficient to kindle a piece of German fungus or *saltpetre paper. 1848 *Knapp's Chem. Technol.* I. 351 A flocculent, white, crystalline efflorescence..which is called *salt-petre rot. 1682 J. COLLINS *Salt & Fishery* 126 *Salt-Petre Salt as to goodness hath no great Repute. 1683 PETTUS *Fleta Min.* I. 337 The black or grey Salt-Petre Salt, which is found (in boyling Salt-petre) below in the Kettle and slender Tub. 1753 CHAMBERS *Cycl. Supp.* s.v. *Mortar*, The finest of all kinds of Mortar for *salt-petre work, is such as is had from the ruins of old buildings in a low situation. *Ibid.*, The common managers of the saltpetre-works. *Ibid.*, The *salt-petre workers in France using the Mortar of old buildings.

b. quasi-*adj.* Explosive.

1598 E. GUILPIN *Skial.* C 3, Tearms of quick Camphire & Salt-peeter phrases.

Hence **Saltpe·treing**, the formation of saltpetre rot; **†Saltpe·trish**, **† -pe·trous** *adjs.*, pertaining to, of the nature of, or impregnated with, saltpetre.

1662 J. DAVIES tr. *Mandelslo's Trav.* 54 Their Salt-petrous Earth. 1683 PETTUS *Fleta Min.* I. 322 The ..Clay of very old Walls..where the Earth it self is Salt-Petrish. 1885 *Spons' Mech. Own Bk.* 602 The surfaces of walls are often covered with an efflorescence of an unsightly character, formed by a process known as 'saltpetreing'.

Sa·lt-pit. A pit where salt is obtained.

1398 TREVISA *Barth. De P. R.* XVI. xciv. (Bodl. MS.), [It] is somtyme idrawe oute of salte pittes and isode. 1535 COVERDALE *Zeph.* ii. 9 Moab shalbe as Sodome, and Ammon as Gomorra: euen drie thorne hedges, salt pittes and a perpetuall wyldernes. 1560 DAUS tr. *Sleidane's Comm.* 338 b, The daye before he died, he released the customes which he had imposed upon Salt pits. 1625 PURCHAS *Pilgrims* III. I. i. 3 Out of those Salt-pits Baatu and Sartach haue great Reuenues. 1769 FALCONER *Dict. Marine* (1789), *Salt-pits*, reservoirs on a coast, to contain sea-water for the purposes of making salt. 1889 *Helps Study Bible* xlii. 125 A ridge of salt-rock runs into that sea [*i.e.* the Dead Sea], and there are salt-pits, and a plain of salt.

Sa·lt-pond. A natural or artificial pond into which sea-water is run in order to be evaporated: cf. SALT-PAN a.

1697 DAMPIER *Voy.* I. 40 On the South side..is a good Salt-pond, where Dutch Sloops come for Salt. 1748 *Anson's Voy.* I. vi. 69 We..sent an Officer on shore to the salt-pond..to procure a quantity of salt. 1836 EARL CARNARVON *Portugal & Gallicia* II. 38 The salt-ponds, which are situated in the immediate neighbourhood of the sea. 1883 MOLONEY *W. African Fisheries* 48 (Fish. Exhib. Publ.) The many 'salt ponds' [*Note*, Brackish inlets or salt-water lakes] adjacent to the African coast line.

Salt rheum. [See SALT *a.*¹ 1 b.]

†1. An irritating discharge of mucus from the nose; a running cold. *Obs.*

1590 SHAKS. *Com. Err.* III. ii. 131. 1604 — *Oth.* III. iv. 51, I haue a salt and sorry Rhewme offends me.

2. *U.S.* **a.** A popular name for 'almost all the non-febrile cutaneous eruptions which are common among adults, except perhaps ringworm and itch' (Webster 1854).

1828–32 WEBSTER (citing MINER). 1855 DUNGLISON *Dict. Med.*, *Rheum, Salt*, a popular name..for various cutaneous affections of the eczematous and herpetic forms more especially. [Also in recent U. S. dicts.]

b. *attrib.* **Salt-rheum weed**, *Chelone glabra*, which is supposed to be a remedy for herpes.

1846–50 A. WOOD *Class-bk. Bot.* 400.

Saltry, obs. form of PSALTERY.

†Sa·lt-stone. *Obs.* [OE. *sealtstān*: see SALT *sb.*¹ and STONE *sb.* Cf. Du. *zoutsteen*, MHG. *salzsteyn* (G. *-stein*), ON. *saltsteinn*.]

1. Rock-salt; a mass of rock-salt.

In early use chiefly in allusions to the fate of Lot's wife.

a 1000 *Cædmon's Gen.* 2564 (Gr.) Heo on sealtstanes sona wurde anlicnesse ætre siððan. *c* 1000 *Sax. Leechd.* I. 374 Fenim geoluwne stan & salt stan & pipor. *a* 1300 *Cursor M.* 2835 In a salt stan men seis hir stand. *c* 1475 *Pict. Voc.* in Wr.-Wülcker 768/2 *Hic cautes*, a salt-stone. 1535 FISHER *Wayes to perfect Religion* Wks. (1876) 370. 1585 HIGINS *Junius' Nomencl.* 409 *Sal natiuus vel fossilis*,..Saltnaturall, or that is digged out of the earth: saltstone. 1677 PLOT *Oxfordsh.* 37 Besides its saltness it [*sc.* the water] has such a stink, that it equals the salt stone. 1680 MORDEN *Geog. Rect., Hungary* (1685) 94 The colour of the Saltstone is somewhat gray.

attrib. 1638 JUNIUS *Paint. Ancients* 91 The woman..keeping still her old posture in the same salt-stone image.

2. A salt-cat for pigeons.

1425 in Kennett *Par. Antiq.* (1818) II. 255, i saltstone empt. pro columbario. 1584 in Rogers *Agric. & Prices* VI. 575/1, 4 saltstones for the dovecot at 1/9. 1646 SIR T. BROWNE *Pseud. Ep.* III. xxii. 165 Pigeons delight in salt stones.

Saltsage, obs. form of SAUSAGE.

†Sa·ltuary. *Obs.* [ad. med.L. *saltuāri-us*, f. *saltus* woodland, forest-pasture.] (See quot.)

1674 BLOUNT *Glossogr.* (ed. 4), *Saltuary*, a Forrester, Woodward, or Ranger.

†Sa·lture. *Obs.* [ad. mod.L. *saltūra*, f. *salt-*, *salire* to leap.] (See quot.)

1655 BLOUNT *Glossogr.*, *Salture*, a leaping or dancing.

Saltus (sæ·ltŏs). [L. = leap.] A 'leap' or sudden transition; a breach of continuity.

1665 HOOKE *Microgr.* 228 No Experiment yet known to prove a Saltus, or skipping from one degree of rarity to another. 1875 WHITNEY *Life Lang.* xiv. 291 These would be the real analogues of speech, and would bridge the saltus of which some are so afraid.

Salt water, *sb.* and *a.* [SALT *a.*¹ Cf. LG. *salt-wat(t)er*, MDu. *sout-water*, G. *salz-wasser*.]

A. *sb.* (stressed *salt wa·ter*). Water impregnated with salt; sea-water.

a 1000 *Ags. Ps.* (Th.) lxxvi. 13 Sweȝ micel sealtera wætera. *c* 1200 *Trin. Coll. Hom.* 151 Þe wop þe man wepeð for his aȝene sinne is swiðe biter alse saltwater. *c* 1440 *Promp. Parv.* 441/1 Salt water, or see water, *Nereis*. 1497 *Naval Acc. Hen. VII* (1896) 129 Gonnepoudre wett in saltwater. 1530 PALSGR. 263/1 Saltewater, *saulmerre*. 1580 LYLY *Euphues* (Arb.) 296, I laboured no otherwise, then..he that hauing sore eyes rubbeth them with salt water. 1610 HOLLAND *Camden's Brit.* (1637) 268 Salt-waters, out of which they boile salt. 1669 WORLIDGE *Syst. Agric.* 5 By watering the place with brine or Salt water. 1706 E. WARD *Wooden World Diss.* (1708) 8 Seeing his Spot of Territory incircl'd with Salt-water. 1841 *Penny Cycl.* XX. 368/2 Hot parts of the world where the soil is saline or there is salt water in the vicinity.

fig. *a* 1450 MYRC *Festial* xxvii. 120 When he passyth þrogh þe salt-watyr of payne of deþe.

b. Applied humorously to tears. (See SALT *sb.*¹ 2 e.)

c 1400 *Laud Troy Bk.* 15691 He wepis..Many a tere of salt watir. 1592 SHAKS. *Rom. & Jul.* II. iii. 71 How much salt water throwne away in wast, To season loue that of it doth not tast. 1612 WEBSTER *White Devil* K, 'Faith, for some few howers salt water will runne most plentifully in euery Office o' th Court. 1833 L. RITCHIE *Wand. by Loire* 128 Let us hear what all this salt water is about.

c. Applied to the sea. Hence, a jocular form of address to a sailor.

1839 H. AINSWORTH *Jack Sheppard* I. vi. 111 'Hark'ee, Ben', said the old sailor,..'you may try, but dash my timbers if you'll ever cross the Thames to-night'. 'And why not, old saltwater?' inquired Ben. 1843 MARRYAT *M. Violet* xv, When this sun will have disappeared behind the salt-water.

B. *attrib.* as *adj.* (stressed *sa·lt-water*). Of, pertaining to, consisting of, or living in salt water.

1528 *Lett. & Pap. Hen. VIII*, IV. II. 2232 The warffs gittes and saltwater banckes, beginning at Calais and continuing to Graveling. 1601 SHAKS. *Twel. N.* v. i. 72 Notable Pyrate, thou salt-water Theefe. 1796 WITHERING *Brit. Plants* (ed. 3) IV. 129 Salt water ditches between Greenwich and Woolwich. 1810 SCOTT *Let. to Miss J. Baillie* 19 July in *Lockhart*, The salt-water loch called Loch an Gaoil. 1858 O. W. HOLMES *Aut. Breakf.-t.* i, It does not follow that I wish to be pickled in brine because I like a salt-water plunge at Nahant. 1859 DARWIN *Orig. Spec.* xii. 384 Salt-water fish can with care be slowly accustomed to live in fresh water. 1892 GUNTER *Miss Dividends* I. iv, The train..crossing the Harlem, skirts that pretty little salt water river.

b. In specific names of sea animals.

1828 SIR H. DAVY *Salmonia* (1840) 72 The salt-water louse adheres to his sides. 1888 GOODE *Amer. Fishes* 405 The bluefish, which is called the 'Salt water Tailor'. 1892 *Chamb. Encycl.* s.v. *Terrapin*, The terrapin *par excellence* is the *Malacoclemmys palustris*, the diamond-back salt-water terrapin.

Hence **Salt-watery** *a.*

1812 *Sporting Mag.* XL. 167 All very greasy, blowsy, dauby, dusty, salt-watery, and so on.

Sa·lt-well. [OE. *sealtwielle, -wylle* (Northumb. *-wælle*).] A salt spring, well, or pit; now, a bored well from which brine is obtained for salt-making.

c 950 *Lindisf. Gosp.* Prol. 1 Of saltwælla ðone æne in-dranc. [1042 in Kemble *Cod. Dipl.* IV. 70 Ðer ofer ða stræt æfter ðam gemære in saltwyllan; of saltwyllan in segchæma gemær.] 1398 TREVISA *Barth. De P. R.* XIX. liii. (1495) 894 Some lycoure comyth of veynes of the erth: as water of salt welles. *a* 1647 HABINGTON *Surv. Worcs.* in *Proc. Worcs. Hist. Soc.* II. 296 The freashe water with excedynge fluddes overflowethe the banckes and for a season drownethe the salt-wells. 1656 SMITH & WEBB *Vale-Royal Engl.* I. 19 The Salt-wells, which they call Brine-pits; out of the which, they make yearly a great quantity of fine white Salt. 1756 C. LUCAS *Ess. Waters* II. 30 Salt was..made in Cappadocia from salt wells. 1848 *Knapp's Chem. Technol.* I. 260 Salt wells..are..frequently found ready formed in nature, wherever a spring, during its course, has come in contact with a bed of rock-salt. 1891 JACKSON in Lee *Hist. Columbus* (Ohio) I. 791 While working in the saltwells of Virginia.

Hence **†Saltweller**, one who works at salt-wells.

1624 *Maldon, Essex, Borough Deeds* Bundle 108 lf. 2 Samwell Smyth, saltweller.

Sa·lt-works. Formerly also **-work.** [Cf. G. *salzwerk*.] A salt manufactory.

1565 ABP. PARKER *Corr.* (Parker Soc.) 258 Your letters requesting timber and firewood for your salt-works. 1674 BOYLE *Saltness of Sea* 29 A friend of mine that is Master of a Salt-work. 1697 *Lond. Gaz.* No. 3307/4 At the Salt-Works of Samuel Acton in Namptwich. 1712–13 SWIFT *Jrnl. to Stella* 21 Feb., Griffin..says he knows nothing of a salt-work at Recton. 1796 MORSE *Amer. Geog.* II. 242 Gallicia is famous for its immense salt-works at Wielitzka. 1848 *Knapp's Chem. Technol.* I. 261 The salt-works at Salzhausen.

Sa·ltwort. *Bot.* [prob. after Du. *zoutkruid*; cf. G. *salzkraut*.] A name for several maritime and salt-marsh plants. Cf. GLASSWORT.

1. Any plant of the genus *Salsola*, spec. *S. Kali* (Common or Prickly Saltwort); = KALI 1.

1568 TURNER *Herbal* III. 37 Kali..hath no name in English...But lest this herbe shoulde be without a name, it maye be called Saltwurt, because it is salt in taste. 1671 SKINNER *Etymol. Ling. Angl.*, *Bot.*, *Salt-wort*, Kali. 1712 tr. *Pomet's Hist. Drugs* I. 101 A Plant..which the Botanists call Kali, and we Salt-wort. 1810 CRABBE *Borough* i. 41 Here sampire-banks and salt-wort bound the flood. 1828 J. E. SMITH *Eng. Flora* II. 18 *Salsola fruticosa*. Shrubby Saltwort. 1862 ANSTED *Channel Isl.* II. viii. 177 The saltwort or glass-wort (*Salsola kali*), grows freely on most of the shores. 1884 [see KALI 1].

2. Black Saltwort, *Glaux maritima*. = MILKWORT 2.

1597 GERARDE *Herbal* II. clix. 447 Of blacke Salt woort.

1760 J. LEE *Introd. Bot.* App. 326. 1861 MISS PRATT *Flower. Pl.* IV. 234 Sea Milkwort, or Black Saltwort. 1867 SOWERBY *Eng. Bot.* (ed. 3) VII. 154.

3. A plant of the genus *Salicornia*, esp. *S. herbacea*; = GLASSWORT a.

1597 [see GLASSWORT]. 1760 J. LEE *Introd. Bot.* 326. 1785 MARTYN *Rousseau's Bot.* xvii. (1794) 233 *note*, Marsh Sampire, called also jointed Glasswort or Saltwort. 1845 LINDLEY *Sch. Bot.* (ed. 14) 110 b, *Salicornia annua* (Saltwort). 1864 GRISEBACH *Flora W. Ind. Islands* 787.

Salty (sǫ·lti), *a.*¹ [f. SALT *sb.*¹ + -Y.]

1. Containing or impregnated with salt; tasting of salt; = SALT *a.*¹ 1.

c 1440 *Promp. Parv.* 441/1 Salt, or salti..*salsus*. 1563 HYLL *Art Garden.* II. liv. (1608) 133 Infused in warm and salty water for a season. 1634 SIR T. HERBERT *Trav.* 65 Sand and salty Desarts. 1657 TOMLINSON *Renou's Disp.* 161 Any convenient humour, whether bitter, acerb, salty, or oyly. 1670 W. SIMPSON *Hydrol. Ess.* 53 This yellow green salty liquor. 1860 R. C. A. PRIOR *Danish Ball.* I. 5 Launching over the salty sea. 1872 J. HATTON *Valley Poppies* II. i. 27, I smell the salty breath of the wind. 1875 LANIER *Symphony* 222 Her eyes with salty tears are wet. 1889 A. T. PASK *Eyes Thames* 49 From this sandy salty loam is made the best Portland cement.

†2. Consisting of salt. *Obs. rare.*

1605 WILLET *Hexapla Gen.* 219 God could turne a womans bodie into a saltie piller. 1633 T. ADAMS *Exp. 2 Peter* ii. 7 [Lot's wife] was turned into a material salty pillar. 1665 NEEDHAM *Med. Medicinæ* 393 If the Salty part becomes extravagant for want of the Spirit and Sulphur to restrain..it.

3. Piquant; racy.

1866 *Athenæum* 10 Mar. 332/2 This..only makes the books more salty; and we must add, that the piquancy is not diminished by [etc.].

†Sa·lty, *a.*² *Obs.* [f. SALT *sb.*² or *a.*² + -Y.] Of a bitch: In heat.

1603 SIR C. HEYDON *Jud. Astrol.* xx. 416 A bitch..is 9. daies saltie, goeth 9. moneths with whelps, and hath her whelps 9. daies blind. 1796 PEGGE *Derbicisms* Ser. I. 59 (E.D.S.) *Salty*, of a bitch, when she is proud, or in her heat.

Saltyr, Salu: see SALTIRE, SALUE *v.*

†Saluberrime, *a. Obs. rare*⁻¹. [ad. L. *salūberrim-us*, superl. of *salūbris*: see SALUBRIOUS.] Highly salubrious.

1509 WATSON *Ship of Fools* lx. (1517) O v b, All vacabondes.., the which gothe beggynge from dore to dore..come vnto me and I shall gyue you an almesse saluberryme.

Salubrify (sălʹū·brifəi), *v. rare.* [f. L. *salūbri-s* (see next) + -FY.] *trans.* To render salubrious.

1842 *Jrnl. R. Agric. Soc.* III. II. 407 The rain..washes out from the subsoil those noxious ingredients.., sweetens and salubrifies it to the depth of the drains.

Salubrious (sălʹū·briəs), *a.* [f. L. *salūbri-s* (f. *salū-s* health) + -OUS.] Favourable or conducive to health.

a. Of food, medicine, etc. Now *rare*.

1547 BOORDE *Brev. Health* 121 b, I myghte here shewe of many salubriouse medecines. 1667 FLAVEL *Saint Indeed* (1754) 121 The Unicorn's horn..in the Apothecaries shop, where it is made salubrious or medicinal. 1709 W. KING *Art of Love* VIII. 1065 Give the salubrious draughts with your own hand; Persuasion has the force of a command. 1748 *Anson's Voy.* II. viii. 220 A species of food so very palatable and salubrious as turtle. 1842 A. COMBE *Physiol. Digestion* (ed. 4) 341 The more slowly they [ices] are eaten, the more refreshing and salubrious will they become. 1871 NAPHEYS *Prev. & Cure Dis.* I. ii. 68 Fish..In the hot months all kinds are less salubrious than in cold weather.

b. Of air, climate, places, etc.

1615 G. SANDYS *Trav.* 8 The forraine merchants here [Zacynthus] resident..by their frequent deaths do disprove the aire to be so salubrious as is reported. 1774 PENNANT *Tour Scotl. in 1772*, 175 In summer the air is remarkably salubrious. 1807 G. CHALMERS *Caledonia* I. I. iv. 164 The Roman officers seem to have had many villas along its salubrious shore. 1833 HT. MARTINEAU *Berkeley the Banker* I. i. 3 Foreseeing the possibility of his having four or five Masters Cavendish as boarders in his salubrious..establishment. 1875 BROWNING *Inn Album* 2 Hail calm acclivity, salubrious spot!

c. Of an occupation. *rare*.

1675 WORLIDGE *Syst. Agric.* xii. (ed. 2) 253 Angling; a moderate, innocent, salubrious, and delightful exercise.

d. Of physiological processes: = SALUTARY.

1855 RAMSBOTHAM *Obstetr. Med.* 70 The salubrious change which the fœtal blood undergoes, is accomplished in the placental mass.

e. *transf.* and *fig.*

1659 HAMMOND *On Ps.* xcvii. 485 Dispensed by the divine providence for many salubrious and beneficial ends. 1737 THOMSON *To Mem. Ld. Talbot* 147 In Senates, He to Freedom firm, Enlighten'd Freedom, plann'd salubrious Laws. *a* 1780 H. BLAIR *Serm.* II. 31 If that fountain [the heart] be once poisoned, you can never expect that salubrious streams will flow from it. 1809 CAMPBELL *Gertr. Wyom.* I. ix, And dwells in day-light truth's salubrious skies No form with which the soul may sympathise? 1855 LANDOR *Imag. Conv.*, *A. Pollio & L. Calvus* II. Wks. 1876 II. 443 Religions, like the sun, take their course from east to west: traversing the globe, they are not all equally temperate, equally salubrious; they dry up some lands, and inundate others.

Hence **Salu·briously** *adv.*; **Salu·briousness.**

1677 W. HUBBARD *Narrative* I In the..salubriousness of the Air..most resembling the Country from whence it borrowed its appellation. 1790 BURKE *Fr. Rev.* 238 Does not the sweat of the mason and carpenter..flow as pleasantly and as salubriously, in the construction and repair of the majestic edifices of religion, as in the painted booths and sordid sties of vice and luxury. 1888 *Schaff's Encycl. Relig. Knowl.* 1391 The salubriousness of their climate.

Salubrity (sălʹū·briti). [ad. L. *salūbritās*, f. *salūbri-s* SALUBRIOUS.]

1. The quality of being salubrious or healthful. **a.** Of the air, a country, etc.

1432–50 tr. *Higden* (Rolls) I. 75 Paradise..hath salubrite [orig. *Habet enim salubritatem*] and wholsomnesse. 1604 R. CAWDREY *Table Alph.*, *Salubritie*, wholesomeness. 1685 BOYLE (*title*) An Experimental Discourse of some unheeded Causes of the Insalubrity and Salubrity of the Air. 1767 *Byron's Voy. rd. World* 57 The salubrity of the air had a surprizing effect in strengthening both the appetite and digestion. 1799 *Monthly Rev.* XXX. 400 In many instances, salubrity will be promoted by inclosures. 1870 YEATS *Nat. Hist. Comm.* I. ii. 12 Penzance and Torquay, in mildness and salubrity, resemble Madeira. 1876 A. J. EVANS *Through Bosnia* ii. 73 This decrease of salubrity is attributed..to the great destruction of forests.

†b. Of food, etc.: Wholesomeness. *Obs. rare.*

1620 VENNER *Via Recta* iii. 69 The heart of a fat Calfe is for pleasantnes of taste,..and salubrity of iuyce, the best. 1733 TULL *Horse-hoeing Husb.* v. (Dublin) 41 What can we say then to the Salubrity of those Roots themselves, bred up and fatten'd amongst these Toads and Corruption?

†c. *fig. Obs.*

c 1643 *Observ. his Maj. late Answ. & Expresses* 8 A..proofe of the integrity, and salubrity of that publick advice.

¶2. Healthy condition, health. (Also *fig.*) *rare.*

1654 [see SALVIFICAL *a.*]. 1786 *Pogonologia* 58 This bushy hair on man's face must have an influence on the salubrity of the neighbouring parts. 1822–34 *Good's Study Med.* (ed. 4) II. 63 The feet..ulcerated and healed, with a speedy return of general salubrity.

Salud, var. pa. t. of SALUE *v. Obs.*

‖**Saludador.** Spanish form of SALUTATOR.

1685 EVELYN *Diary* 16 Sept.

†Salue·, *sb. Obs. rare.* Also **salew.** [a. OF. *salu* (in mod.Fr. written *salut*: see SALUTE *sb.*¹) = Sp. *saludo*, It. *saluto*, a Com. Rom. vbl. sb. f. *salūtāre* SALUTE *v.*] A salutation.

c 1430 LYDG. *Min. Poems* (Percy Soc.) 8 They..Goyng owtward gave the kyng salue [*rime* dewe]. *c* 1450 *Merlin* xxvii. 506 The quene..seide thei were welcome, and thei dide yelde hir a-gein hir salew debonerly. 1485 CAXTON *Paris & V.* (1868) 32 Parys rendred hys salewes ayeyn moche humbly.

†Salue·, *v. Obs.* Forms: **4–5 saluwe, saliewe, salwe, 4–6 salew, 5 salowe, 6 salu, 4–7 salue**; *pa. t.* **4 salewede, saluet, 4–5 salu(e)de, salewed, salwed, saluwed, saluyd, 5 salut(e, ?salit, salod, -ud, saylut, salowed, -id, saluid, saluyed, 6 salewd, 4–7 salued.** [a. F. *saluer* = Pr., Sp. *saludar*, Pg. *saudar*, It. *salutare*:—L. *salūtāre* to SALUTE.]

1. *trans.* = SALUTE *v.*

c 1300 *Harrow. Hell* 868 (MS. Sion) To Ierusalem come on a day Thre prestes of þe Iewery, Tille þe temple held þai streke þe way And saluede þe clergy. *c* 1330 R. BRUNNE *Medit.* 1076 Anone come petyr, with wepyng chere, And salude Mary and Ion yn fere. *c* 1374 CHAUCER *Troylus* II. 1619 (1668) Eleyn in al hire goodly soft wyse Gan hym salue and wommanly to pleye. *c* 1386 — *Frankl. T.* 781 And he saleweth hire with glad entente. 1387 TREVISA *Higden* (Rolls) V. 101 Þey emperoures þat were to fore hym were i-salwed as iuges. *c* 1400 *Destr. Troy.* 4981 Þai salut not þat souerain with no sad wordes. *c* 1420 *Sir Amadace* (Camden) xi, Ho sayd, 'Sir, welcum most ȝe be!' A[nd] salit him anon ryȝte [Weber's ed. l. 112 And salod hym anon ryght]. *Ibid.* xxxvii, He saylut him anon ryȝte [Weber 409 Bot salud hym full ryght]. *c* 1430 LYDG. *Min. Poems* (Percy Soc.) 242 The amerous fowlys with motetys and carollys, Salwe that sesoun every morwenyng. *c* 1440 *Gesta Rom.* xxiii. 83 (Harl. MS.) Thei fille doun on kne..and salowid him, as thei aught to do to themperour. 1481 CAXTON *Godeffroy* xiii. 40 He..salewed hym in the name of the Patriarke ..of Surye. 1502 ARNOLDE *Chron.* (1811) 159 Salu me highly with honorable salutacions to the honorable Lordis. 1542 UDALL *Erasm. Apoph.* 122 Diogenes..salued or hailed hym wᵗ this verse of homere. 1596 SPENSER *F. Q.* IV. vi. 25 Glaucè ..her salewd with seemely bel-accoyle, Joyous to see her safe after long toyle. 1601 HOLLAND *Pliny* II. 297 Euen Tiberius Cæsar..required in that manner to be salued and wished well vnto, whensoeuer he sneezed.

fig. 1606 WARNER *Alb. Eng.* XIV. xci. 369 Great'st Ladies with their women, on their Palfries mounted faire,..Which now in Coches scorne to be salued of the aire.

b. *absol.*

13.. *Gaw. & Gr. Knt.* 1473 Þe lady noȝt forȝate, Com to hym to salue. *c* 1386 CHAUCER *Pars. T.* ⁋ 333 Yet is ther a priuee spece of pride, that waiteth first to be salewed er he wole salewe [*Harl. MS.* to be saluet er he saliewe]. 1596 DRAYTON *Leg. Cromw.* 827 Peace, the good Porter,..prayes him God to saue, And after saluing, kindly doth demand What was his will.

2. By confusion = *salve*, SAVE *v.*

1484 CAXTON *Fables of Æsop* v. ix, The lyon ansuerd to hym God salewe the swete frend come nyghe me and kysse me.

Salue, written for *salve*, obs. form of SAVE.

Salufer (sæ·liŭfəɹ). [irreg. f. L. *salū-s* health (see SALUTARY) + *-fer* producing.] Silicofluoride of sodium, used as an antiseptic. Hence **Salu·ferize** *v.*, to cleanse or purify with 'salufer'.

1894 *Times* 5 May 6/1 Mr. Thomson, the successor of Playfair..at the Manchester Royal Institution Laboratory. He has a plan of attacking the mud in the bottom of the canal with a powerful antiseptic compounded of sodium, silicon, and fluorine. Salufer the mixture is named. *Ibid.*, It may be requisite to saluferize not only the canal water, but that of the river for some distance higher up. 1905 *Brit. Med. Jrnl.* 27 May 1147 The ear was syringed once or twice daily with a solution of salufer in boiled water.

Salugh, obs. form of SALLOW *sb.*

Saluid, var. pa. t. of SALUE *v. Obs.*

†Salu·ing, *vbl. sb. Obs.* [f. SALUE *v.* + -ING¹.] The action of the verb SALUE; a salutation.

c 1374 CHAUCER *Troylus* II. 1519 (1568) Lat vs of hire saluynges pace. *c* 1386 — *Knt.'s T.* 791 Ther nas no good day ne no saluyng. *c* 1430 *Syr Gener.* (Roxb.) 916 Make him noo privey salewing, But openlie afore hem all Profre youre seruice in the hall. *c* 1489 CAXTON *Blanchardyn* v. 23 The knyght, right humbly and wyth a right lowe voyce,..rendryd hym ayen his salewyng.

Salumin (sæ·liŭmin). [f. SAL(ICYLATE) + (AL)UMIN(IUM).] Salicylate of aluminium used in nose and throat diseases. 1897 in *Syd. Soc. Lex.*

Salure, variant of SALER, salt-cellar.

†Salus, *sb. Obs.* Also **saluz.** [Perh. a. early OF. *saluz*, *salus*, subj.-case sing. or obj.-case pl. of *salu*: see SALUE *sb.*] A salutation.

a 1225 *Ancr. R.* 388 And wrot mid his owune blode saluz to his leofmon, of luue gretunge. *a* 1400–50 *Alexander* 4647 To Alexander..salus & ioye. *c* 1400 *Destr. Troy* 3640 Let vs send to hom salus solemli by letre, Praiand hom..To helpe vs in hast our harmys to venge. *c* 1450 *St. Cuthbert* (Surtees) 5923 Þe schipmen wendys to þe priour, And haylsid him with honour, he said saluz agayne. *c* 1475 *Partenay* 896 The Erle ther saluz yilding ryght goodly Vnto euery man.

†Salus, *v. Sc.* and *north. Obs.* Also **5 salose, 6 saluse, saluis.** [f. prec. sb.] *trans.* = SALUTE *v.* Hence **Salusing** *vbl. sb.*, greeting.

1375 BARBOUR *Bruce* IV. 509 Than went thai to the kyng in hy, And hym salusit full curtasly. *c* 1440 *Gesta Rom.* lxix. 318 (Harl. MS.) And so she come to him, and worshipfully she salusid him. *c* 1450 *St. Cuthbert* (Surtees) 3419 The abbot salust him on hyght. *c* 1470 HENRY *Wallace* x. 593 Thar salusyng was bot boustous and thrawin. *c* 1500 *Lancelot* 1309 Nothir of thi salosing, nor the, Ne rak I nocht. 1500–20 DUNBAR *Poems* xlvi. 18 With notis glaid..This joyfull merle so salust scho the day. 1528 LYNDESAY *Dreme* 149 Me thocht ane lady..Did salus me, with benyng contynance. 1533 BELLENDEN *Livy* I. vii. (S. T. S.) I. 41 And Incontinent all þe remanent pepil salust him as king and fader of þe romane ciete. *Ibid.* xviii. 105 Scho..was þe first þat salust him king. 1560 ROLLAND *Crt. Venus* I. 290 Greit salusingis, with gretingis full of gloir. *Ibid.* II. 37 [He] saluist thame on his best wayis anone.

absol. *c* 1470 HENRY *Wallace* v. 576 Quhen Wallace saw that thai war ma than he, Than did he nocht but salust curtasle.

Salus, salut: see SALUTE *sb.*² *Obs.*

Salut, variant pa. t. of SALUE *v. Obs.*

†Salutaire, *a. Obs. rare.* Forms: **5 saluter, 6 salutaire.** [a. F. *salutaire*, ad. L. *salūtāris* SALUTARY.] Salutary.

c 1450 *Mirour Saluacioun* 1234 And marie wombe flovred & broght forth fruyt saluter to mankynde. 1593 A. HUME *Treat. Conscience* v. in *Poems*, etc. (S.T.S.) App. A. 108 Sicknes may be healed, by the application of salutaire medicaments. 1600 J. HAMILTON *Facile Traictise* Ep. Ded. 3 For the reduction of dissauit people in maters of religion, to the salutaire vnion..of Christs halie Catholik kirk.

Salutarily (sæ·liŭtărili), *adv.* [f. SALUTARY *a.* + -LY².] In a salutary manner.

1532 R. COPLAND in *Prymer of Salysbury vse* 27 b, The maner to lyue well, deuoutly and salutarily. 1846 in WORCESTER (citing *Ed. Rev.*). 1861 SALA *Dutch Pict.* xii. 175 Very many vagrants..were salutarily scourged by the parish constable. 1882–3 *Schaff's Encycl. Relig. Knowl.* 1275 [Lanfranc] says that those who unworthily partake..receive the essence of the body and blood of Christ, without, however, being salutarily affected thereby.

Salutariness (sæ·liŭtărinės). [f. SALUTARY *a.* + -NESS.] The property of being salutary.

1727 BAILEY vol. II. 1755 JOHNSON, *Salutariness*, wholsomeness; quality of contributing to health or safety. 1873 M. ARNOLD *Lit. & Dogma* (1876) 98 The desire felt by the pious Israelites for some new aspect of religion such as Jesus Christ presented, is..the best proof of its..salutariness. 1879 H. SPENCER *Data of Ethics* iii. 41 Insistence on the salutariness of a state in which the wills of slaves and citizens are humbly subject to the wills of masters and rulers.

Salutary (sæ·liŭtări), *a.* (and *sb.*) [ad. F. *salutaire* (see SALUTAIRE) or its source L. *salūtāris*, f. *salūt-em*, *salūs* health, well-being: see -ARY¹.]

1. Conducive to health; *chiefly*, serving to promote recovery from disease, or to counteract a deleterious influence.

1649 JER. TAYLOR *Gt. Exemp.* I. Ad. § 1. 15 Abana and Pharpar..were not so salutary as the waters of Jordan to cure Naamans leprosie. 1685 BOYLE *Eng. Notion Nat.* 225 Experience hath oblig'd Physicians to divide Crises's..into Salutary, that quite deliver the Patient, and Mortal, that destroy him. 1751 JOHNSON *Rambler* No. 83 ⁋ 5 The man that first..climbed the mountains for salutary plants. 1771 SMOLLETT *Humph. Cl.* 8 June, At Brambleton Hall, I..breathe a clear, elastic, salutary air. 1810 E. D. CLARKE *Trav. Russia* xv. (1839) 69/1 When a current sets in from the sea, it [the water of the Sea of Azof] is more salutary. 1872 T. BRYANT *Pract. Surg.* 119 When due to plethora of the vessels from any cause, it [*sc.* epistaxis] is often salutary.

2. Conducive to well-being; calculated to bring about a more satisfactory condition, or to remedy some evil; beneficial, 'wholesome'. Often with figurative notion of sense 1.

In early instances often = 'bringing salvation'.

1490 CAXTON *Eneydos* xii. 43 Consideringe the waye salutary to reuerte sone her sorow in to gladnesse. 1541 R. COPLAND *Guydon's Quest. Chirurg.* Q ij, The sayd dissease is penaunce salutary for the saluacion of theyr soules. 1729 STACKHOUSE *Body Divin.* IV. i. § 2 (1776) II. 422 The blessings of Christ's salutary passion. 1741 MIDDLETON *Cicero* II. xii. 569 Cicero's [virtue] will be found..always beneficial, often salutary to the Republic. 1760–72 H. BROOKE *Fool of Qual.* (1809) III. 154 The French..I look upon to be our natural and salutary enemies. They..hold us in exercise, and keep quarrelsome people from falling out among themselves. 1855 MACAULAY *Hist. Eng.* xix. IV. 360 The plot which ruined Bohun..produced important and salutary effects.

1865 LIVINGSTONE *Zambesi* ii. 45 The natives having a salutary dread of the guns.

†3. *absol.* as *sb. pl.* (See quot.) *Obs.*

1823 CRABB *Technol. Dict.*, *Salutaries* (*Med.*), such diseases as admit of an easy cure, and are supposed to have a salutary effect on the constitution.

Salutation (sæliŭtēⁱ·ʃən). Forms: **4–5 salutacioun, 4–6 -acion, -acyon, 5 -acioune, 6 -atioun, -atyon, -asyon, 6– salutation.** [a. OF. *salutacion* (mod. F. *salutation*), ad. L. *salūtātiōn-em*, n. of action f. *salūtāre* to SALUTE. Cf. Sp. *salutacion*, It. *salutazione*.]

1. The action, or an act, of saluting; a manner of saluting; an utterance, form of words, gesture, or movement, by which one person salutes another.

1382 WYCLIF *Luke* i. 41 As Elizabeth herde the salutacioun of Marie, the ȝonge child in hir wombe gladide. *c* 1386 CHAUCER *Shipman's T.* 8 Swiche salutacions and contenaunces Passen as dooth a shadwe vp on the wal. 1387 TREVISA *Higden* (Rolls) IV. 307 Þanne a poore sowtere fondede to teche a chouȝhe to speke and seie þe same salutacioun. 1471 CAXTON *Recuyell* (Sommer) II. 352 Whan hercules sawe the salutacion..of this man, he toke hym by the hande [etc.]. *a* 1533 LD. BERNERS *Huon* lviii. 201 When all the company had made there salutasyons one to an nother. 1610 SHAKS. *Temp.* III. iii. *Stage Direction*, Enter seuerall strange shapes, bringing in a Banket; and dance about it with gentle actions of salutations. 1620 *Westward for Smelts* (Percy Soc.) 23 He..kissed her..., after this salutation, he said [etc.]. 1650 JER. TAYLOR *Holy Living* ii. § 3 (1686) 101 In all publick meetings, or private addresses..use those forms of salutation..which..[are] usual amongst the most sober persons. 1706 J. POTTER *Antiq. Greece* IV. xix. (ed. 2) II. 374 The most common Salutation was by the conjunction of their right Hands. 1756–7 tr. *Keysler's Trav.* (1760) I. 88 The commonalty of late are, by their salutation, come to be immediately known, whether they are protestants or papists. Sixtus V..granted an indulgence of one hundred days to the salutation, 'Praised be Jesus Christ', and the answer, 'For ever or amen'. 1821 SCOTT *Kenilw.* xix, Out into the yard sallied mine host himself also, to do fitting salutation to his new guests. 1851 HAWTHORNE *Ho. Sev. Gables* vii. (1852) 76 He made a salutation, or, to speak nearer the truth, an ill-defined, abortive attempt at courtesy. 1851 DIXON *W. Penn* iv. (1872) 32 He had bowed his head and taken off his hat in salutation. 1867 LADY HERBERT *Cradle L.* vii. 202 Their usual salutation was—'welcome'.

transf. 1594 SHAKS. *Rich. III*, v. iii. 210 The early Village Cock Hath twice done salutation to the Morne.

b. *The Angelic(al salutation*, †*the salutation of our Lady*, etc.: the AVE MARY (see Luke i. 29). Also a representation of the Annunciation.

1459 in *Archæologia* XXI. 37 A Tablet of gold of yᵉ Salutacion of our Lady. 1534 in Peacock *Eng. Ch. Furniture* (1866) 197 A masar..with a prynt in the bothom of siluer & gilte of the salutacion of our lady. ? *c* 1600 SOUTHWELL *Rosary* xiii. 19 Next after our Lords praier the Angells Salutation is vsually saide. *Ibid.* xi. 170 The Angelicall Salutation. 1852 MRS. JAMESON *Leg. Madonna* Introd. (1857) 25 Towards the end of the tenth century the custom of adding the angelic salutation, the 'Ave Maria', to the Lord's prayer, was first introduced.

c. Applied to certain liturgical formulas of greeting between the minister and the people.

1450–1530 *Myrr. our Ladye* 294 The preste..sayeth *Dominus vobiscum*...The quier answereth, *Et cum spiritu tuo*, And with thy spirite. In this salutacion of the preste, and answere of the people, or of the quier, the preste prayeth that oure lorde be with them, & they pray that oure lorde be with hym. 1832 W. PALMER *Orig. Liturg.* I. 161 Then followed the salutation and kiss of peace; after which the priest read the collect, 'ad pacem'.

d. *Naut.* The action of saluting by firing of guns, lowering of flags, etc.; an instance of this, a salute. Now *rare*.

1585 T. WASHINGTON tr. *Nicholay's Voy.* I. xv. 13 b, The chaines of the hauen being opened with salutation accustomed of the one side & other. 1652 NEEDHAM tr. *Selden's Mare Cl.* Ep. Ded. 13 That egregious attempt upon your Shipping, under pretence of a friendly salutation. 1727–41 CHAMBERS *Cycl.* s.v. *Salutation*, Saluting with the flag, is performed two ways; either by holding it close to the staff, so as it cannot flutter, or by striking it so as it cannot be seen at all, which is the most respectful salutation. 1808 SCOTT *Marm.* VI. xxiii, And distant salutation past From the loud cannon's mouth.

2. Elliptically for 'I offer salutation'. *arch.*

1535 COVERDALE *Ezra* vii. 12 Vnto Esdras..peace and salutacion. 1588 SHAKS. *L. L. L.* v. i. 38 Most millitarie sir salutation. 1600 — *A. Y. L.* v. iv. 39 Salutation and greeting to you all. 1871 ALABASTER *Wheel of Law* 224 The donor says: 'Salutation to this land with its produce, salutation to the priest to whom I give it'.

3. *Antiq.* A visit of ceremony paid to a Roman in his house.

a 1700 DRYDEN tr. *Horace, Epode* ii. 17 And court and state, he wisely shuns, Nor brib'd with hopes, nor dar'd with awe, To servile salutations runs. 1741 JOHNSON *Life Morin* Wks. IV. 478 It is easy to conceive that a man of this temper was not crouded with salutations; there was only now and then an Antony that would pay Paul a visit.

¶4. *nonce-use.* (Cf. SALUTE *v.* 5.)

c 1600 SHAKS. *Sonn.* cxxi, For why should others false adulterat eyes Giue salutation to my sportiue blood?

5. *attrib.* or passing into *adj.*

1713 ADDISON *Guardian* No. 137 ⁋ 5, I have seen him in every inclination of the body, from a familiar nod, to the low stoop in the salutation sign. 1899 *Allbutt's Syst. Med.* VIII. 106 Thus a patient may be constantly making bowing movements (salutation spasm). 1903 SIR H. C. MAXWELL-LYTE in *Cal. Charter Rolls* (1903) I. Pref. 5 In form, a Charter is distinguished from Letters Patent by the salutation clause addressed to Archbishops, Bishops, Abbots, Earls, Barons and so forth..by the *quare volumus* clause.

Hence **Saluta·tional**, **Saluta·tionless** *adjs.*

1855 *Household Words* XII. 388, I would not advise the shooting of squires for breaches of salutational reciprocity; only, if his worship did not take off his hat to me in return, I would never again take off mine to his worship. 1885 HOWELLS *Silas Lapham* II. 116 The two came out together, and parted in their salutationless fashion.

‖**Salutator** (sæliŭtēⁱ·təɹ). *Hist.* [eccl. L., use of L. *salūtātor* one who salutes, agent-n. f. *salūtāre* to SALUTE.] The designation given to a class of persons in Spain who professed to work miraculous cures in the name of St. Catherine. See also SALUDADOR, SALUTER.

1668–72 M. CASAUBON *On Credulity & Incred.* 147 The Salutators of Spain.

Salutatorian (sălʹū·tătō·riăn). *U. S.* [f. next + -AN.] In American schools and colleges the student who delivers the 'salutatory' oration at the annual commencement day exercises.

1847 in WEBSTER. 1887 *Harper's Mag.* Sept. 636 The graduating class were the heroes of the hour. The valedictorian, the salutatorian, the philosophical orator, walked on air.

Salutatory (sălʹū·tătəri), *a.* and *sb.* [ad. L. *salūtātōrius*, f. *salūtāre* to SALUTE.] **A.** *adj.* Pertaining to, or of the nature of, a salutation.

1895 *Critic* 19 Jan. 57/2 Henry Ward Beecher's salutatory editorial. 1898 J. R. HARRIS in *Expositor* Sept. 175 Jowett's argument for the authenticity of the Epistle is based on the salutatory formulae.

b. *U. S.* The distinctive epithet of the address of welcome (usually in Latin), which introduces the exercises of commencement in American colleges.

It is delivered by the senior of second highest position in his class for four years, or sometimes by a junior who has the highest position in his class. Cf. *valedictory*.

1702 C. MATHER *Magn. Chr.* IV. Introd. (1852) 13 These exercises were, besides an oration usually made by the President, orations both salutatory and valedictory. 1846 WORCESTER (citing Kirkland), *Salutatory*, containing salutations; greeting, as 'a salutatory oration' (U. S.).

c. *Gram.* [tr. L. *salutatorius casus*.] *Salutatory case*: the vocative case.

1818 STODDART *Gram.* in *Encycl. Metrop.* (1845) I. 32/2 The fifth case is the vocative or salutatory.

B. *sb.*

†1. [= med.L. *salūtātōrium*.] An audience-chamber; *spec.* in a church or monastery, a chamber where visitors were received to give their salutations.

1641 MILTON *Reform.* II. Wks. 1851 III. 63 Coming to the Bishop with Supplication into the Salutatory, some out Porch of the Church, he was charg'd by him of tyrannicall madnes against God, for comming into holy ground. 1656 BLOUNT *Glossogr.*, *Salutatory* (*salutatorium*), a place where men stand to salute a Prince.

2. *U. S.* **a.** An address or greeting to the reader of the first number of a newspaper or magazine.

1880 *Scribner's Mag.* July 455 Its salutatory is worth quoting as a piece of brave crowing. 1887 *Lit. World* (U.S.) 25 June 206/2 In his salutatory the editor declares his paper to be 'a very modest effort to assist in a practical way the "Literary Movement in Chicago"'.

b. The 'salutatory oration' (see A. b) delivered at 'commencement' in American colleges.

a 1851 *Amherst Indicator* II. 96 (Hall *College Words*) We ask our friends..not to ask if he had the Valedictory or Salutatory.

Hence **Salu·tatorily** *adv.* (*rare*), by way of greeting or salutation.

1847 in WEBSTER. 1863 MRS. WHITNEY *Faith Gartney's Girlh.* vi, 'Well, Melindy', said Mrs. Griggs, salutatorily.

Salute (sălʹū·t), *sb.*¹ Also **5–6 salut**, (**6 saluyte**). [a. F. *salut* masc., of twofold origin: (1) = Sp. *saludo*, It. *saluto*, vbl. sb. f. Common Rom. (L.) *salūtāre* to SALUTE; (2) originally fem., = Sp. *salud*, Pg. *saude*, It. *salute*:—L. *salūt-em* (nom. *salūs*) health, safety, salvation.]

I. An act of saluting.

1. An utterance, gesture, or action of any kind by which one person salutes another; a salutation. Now chiefly used with reference to other than verbal modes of saluting: cf. the following senses.

a 1400–50 *Alexander* 1490 'I bringe þe bodword of blis ser bischop' he said, 'With salutis of solas I am sent fra þe trone'. 1483 CAXTON *Gold. Leg.* 430/1 The preest..tourneth hym toward the peple & saleweth them sayeng Dominus vobiscum and that sygnefyeth salut whyche our lorde gafe to his appostles after his blessyd resurrexyon. *c* 1511 *1st Eng. Bk. Amer.* (Arb.) Introd. 35/1, I Pope Iohn ..gyue saluyte the Emperour of Rome..& also the kinge of France. 1597 DRAYTON *Heroic Ep.*, *Mortimer to Q. Isabel* 1 As thy saluts my sorrowes doe adiourne, So backe to thee their interest I returne. 1633 FORD *Broken H.* v. i. I 3 b, The doublers of a Hare, or, in a morning, Salutes from a splay-footed witch,..Are not so boading mischiefe as thy crossing My priuate meditations. 1671 MILTON *P. R.* II. 67 O what avails me now that honour high To have conceiv'd of God, or that salute Hale highly favour'd, among women blest. 1702 ADDISON *Dial. Medals* II. Wks. 1766 III. 35, I shall not trouble myself nor my Reader with the first salutes of our three friends. 1790 J. BRUCE *Source Nile* I. 18 We passed near enough, however, to give them the usual salute, *Salam Alicum*. 1794 MRS. RADCLIFFE *Myst. Udolpho* iv, He waved his hand, and Valancourt..returned the salute and started away. 1859 TENNYSON *Geraint & Enid* 723 Last, coming up quite close, and in his mood Crying, 'Take my salute', unknightly with flat hand, However lightly, smote her on the cheek. 1878 BROWNING *La Saisiaz* 16 From no far mound Waved salute a tall white figure. 1879 — *Pheidippides* 111 So, to this day, when friend meets friend, the word of salute Is still 'Rejoice!'

2. A kiss, by way of salutation. (Cf. SALUTE *v.* 2 e.)

1590 GREENE *Never too late* (1600) 93 To her hee goes, and after his wonted salute sat downe by her. 1684 EARL ROSCOMMON *Ess. Transl. Verse* 314 There, cold salutes, But here, a Lovers kiss. 1688 R. HOLME *Armoury* III. 169/1 In Dances,..a Salute, a Kiss, or Kiss of the hand with a bow of the Body. 1719 D'URFEY *Pills* (1872) V. 80 With a kind Salute, and without Dispute, He thought to gain her for his own. 1782 MME. D'ARBLAY *Diary* 26 Oct., Dr. Johnson..received me..with a salute so loud, that the two young beaux..have never done laughing about it. 1828 SCOTT *Fair M. Perth* xix, He folded the fair maiden in his arms, and was permitted to take the salute which she had refused to bestow. 1906 H. WALES *Mr. & Mrs. Villiers* vii, She extricated his right arm also, and was rewarded by the complimentary salute on the left cheek.

3. *Mil.* and *Naut.* **a.** A discharge of cannon or small arms, display of flags, a dipping of sails, a cheering of men, manning the yards, etc., as a mark of respect, or as military, naval, or official honour, for a person, nation, event, etc.

A salute is said to be of as many guns as there are volleys fired.

1698 FRYER *Acc. E. India & P.* 107 Their way of Salutes are with Even, as ours with Odd Guns. 1727–41 CHAMBERS *Cycl.* s.v. *Salutation*, Father Fournier has an express treatise of sea-salutes and signals. 1744 J. PHILIPS *Jrnl. Exped. Anson* 181 He saluted us with eleven Guns, and we returned the salute with three. 1832 R. & J. LANDER *Exped. Niger* III. xx. 232 As we passed Forday's town, a salute of seven guns was fired off. 1838 J. L. STEPHENS *Trav. Russia* 88 A frigate..was firing a salute. 1876 VOYLE & STEVENSON *Milit. Dict.* (ed. 3) s.v., In firing salutes 10 seconds is to be allowed between each round. 1883 'OUIDA' *Wanda* I. 307 The culverins on the keep fired their salutes.

transf. 1719 DE FOE *Crusoe* II. (Globe ed.) 569 As we found them [the enemy] within Gun-shot, our Leader ordered the two Wings to advance swiftly, and give them a Salvo on each Wing with their Shot... And indeed that Salute clogg'd their Stomach, for they immediately halted.

b. (See quot. 1876.)

1832 LYTTON *Eugene A.* I. v, 'Beg pardon, Squire,' said he, with a military salute. 1876 VOYLE & STEVENSON *Milit. Dict.* (ed. 3) s.v., A salute is made by an inferior meeting or passing his superior, when in uniform and even out of uniform, by raising his hand to his cap or chaco.

c. The position of the sword, rifle, hand, etc., or the attitude assumed in saluting. Phrase, *to stand at (the) salute*.

1833 *Regul. & Instr. Cavalry* I. 36 Officers recover their swords.., and drop them to the 'Salute'.

4. *Fencing.* A formal greeting of swordsmen when about to engage, consisting of a conventional series of guards, appels, thrusts, parries, parades, etc.

1809 J. ROLAND *Fencing* 130 The salute of *carte* and *tierce* is practised on the same principle. 1889 POLLOCK, etc. *Fencing* (Badm. Libr.) 98 The Salute, or prelude to the Assault.

†II. 5. Safety, well-being, salvation. *Obs.*

1471 CAXTON *Recuyell* (Sommer) I. 275 She shall dye for the salute and helthe of troye. 1483 — *Gold. Leg.* 430/2 As the auncyente tholye gaue to them admonestyng of salut techyng them ouer alle thynges to drede god. 1509 WATSON *Ship of Fools* Argt. A j, This booke compyled for the felycyte & salute of all the humayne gendre.

†b. Used *ellipt.* (= L. *salutem*) in epistolary salutations. *Obs.*

a 1533 LD. BERNERS *Gold. Bk. M. Aurel.* Let. iv. (1535) 107 b, Marke oratour Romayn..to the Domitian of Capue, salute and consolacion of the goddis. 1549 *Compl. Scot.* xiv. 116 Pausanias duc of spart, to the kyng xerses salut.

Salu·te, *sb.*² *Obs.* exc. *Hist.* Forms: **5–8 salut, 6, 9 salute**; *pl.* **5 saluz, salutz, salews**, (**salux**), (**5, 8 salus**). [a. OF. *salut*, *saluyt*, pl. *saluts*, *saluz*, *salus*, a special use of *salut* salutation, SALUTE *sb.*¹] A gold coin bearing a representation of the salutation of Gabriel to the Virgin Mary; struck by Charles VI of France, and also by Henry V and Henry VI of England for circulation in their French dominions.

1488 *Acc. Ld. High Treas. Scot.* I. 79 Item, in Hari nobilis and salutis fourti and ane. 1455 *Paston Lett.* I. 360 For the value and denombrement of iiij. mˡ. saluz of yerly rent. 145. *Rolls of Parlt.* V. 181/1 Oon obligation of the Duchesse of Burgoyne of XV m. salutz. 1475 *Bk. Noblesse* (Roxb.) 19 Johan..paied to the said regent duc of Bedforde for his raunson and fynaunce allone clx. M. salux. *c* 1483 CAXTON *Dialogues* 17 Ryallis nobles of englond, Salews of gold lyons, Olde sterlingis pens. *a* 1548 HALL *Chron.*, *Hen. V* 75 The kyng of England..caused a new coyne to be made called the Salute, where in wer the Armes of Fraunce, and the Armes of England and Fraunce quarterly. 1577 HARRISON *England* II. xxv. (1877) I. 363 We haue yet remaining, the riall..the salut, the angell [etc.]. 1580 STOW *Chron.* 618 King Henry [VI] caused a peece to be stamped called a Salus, worth two and twentie Shillings and Blans of eyghtpence a peece. 1653 URQUHART *Rabelais* I. xlvi, The summe of three score and two thousand saluts (in English money fifteen thousand and five hundred pounds). 1688 R. HOLME *Armoury* III. 29/1 The Salute of England, worth six shillings ten pence. 1716 M. DAVIES *Athen. Brit.* III. 79 Hen. 5's Golden Coyns were Rose-Nobles, Half-Nobles and Farthings, and Salus. *Ibid.*, Hen. 6. brought in the Rials, or Royals, Angels, Angellets and Salut. 1837 *Penny Cycl.* VII. 331/1 To these [coins].. Henry V. [added] salutes, and half-salutes. Henry VI. coined salutes, angelots, and francs in gold.

Salute (sălʹū·t), *v.* Also **5 salewt.** [ad. L. *salūtāre*, f. *salūt-em*, *salūs* health. (Cf. SALUE *v.*) It is possible that this may have coalesced with an independent formation on SALUTE *v.*]

1. *trans.* To accost or address with words expressive of good wishes, respect, or homage, esp. with some customary formula of that import; to greet in words.

c 1380 WYCLIF *Sel. Wks.* II. 9 Marie..went mekeli in hast to salute her cosyn. 1387 TREVISA *Higden* (Rolls) II. 193 He saluted and grette þe senatoures, and spak to eueriche of þe peple þat come aboute hym by his owne name. 14.. *Sir Beues* 1283 + 291 (Camb.) [He] saluted þe kyng on þys manere, As ye may aftur here. *c* 1430 LYDG. *Min. Poems* (Percy Soc.) 78 With ave or kirye salute a kyng. 1483 CAXTON *Cato* A v, Thou sholdest salewt and grete the peple gladly. 1526 *Pilgr. Perf.* (W. de W. 1531) 180 Forgete not to salute her with this swete word Aue. *a* 1533 LD. BERNERS *Huon* xxi. 60 He drew thedyr & salutyd yᵉ olde man in yᵉ name of god. 1592 SHAKS. *Rom. & Jul.* II. iii. 32 *Rom.* Good morrow Father. *Fri.* Benedicite. What early tongue so sweet saluteth me? 1711–12 SWIFT *Jrnl. to Stella* 22 Jan., T'other day at the Court of Requests Dr. Yalden saluted me by name. 1845 M. PATTISON *Ess.* (1889) I. 22 Being admitted to his presence they saluted him in the queen's name. 1875 JOWETT *Plato* (ed. 2) IV. 160 He saluted me as an acquaintance whom he remembered from my former visit.

b. *I salute you*: used as itself a formula of salutation. Similarly in the 3rd person, of one who 'sends greeting'. [So L. *salutare*.] *arch.*

1599 SHAKS. *Hen. V*, v. ii. 22 You English Princes all, I doe salute you. 1834 LYTTON *Pompeii* I. ii, 'Fair Julia, we salute thee', said Clodius. *c* 1850 *Arab. Nts.* (Rtldg.) 252 'My mistress', said she, 'salutes you, and I come from her to beg you to deliver this letter to the prince of Persia'. 1881 TENNYSON *To Virgil* x, I salute thee, Mantovano, I that loved thee since my day began.

†c. *Salute me* used for: Give my greeting (*to*). Cf. *remember me to...* REMEMBER *v.* 8 c. *Obs.*

1700 PENN in *Pa. Hist. Soc. Mem.* IX. 5 Salute me to the commissioners.

d. To hail or greet (as king, etc.).

1560 DAUS tr. *Sleidane's Comm.* 101 b, All people saluted hym with the tytle of the Emperour Auguste. *Ibid.* 423 He is saluted Prynce Electour. 1593 SHAKS. *2 Hen. VI*, II. ii. 61 Be we the first, That shall salute our rightfull Soueraigne With honor of his Birth-right to the Crowne. 1595 — *John* II. i. 30 Till that vtmost corner of the West Salute thee for her King. 1617 MORYSON *Itin.* II. 2 King Henrie..for the time was saluted Lord of Ireland. 1642 MILTON *Apol. Smect.* 40 Now they heare it as their ord'nary surname, to be saluted the Fathers of their countrey. 1755 W. DUNCAN *Cicero's Sel. Orat.* xi. (1841) 217 It was but lately that L. Torquatus..was, at my instance, saluted emperor from this province.

e. In extended sense: To accost or address (whether courteously or otherwise).

c 1420 ? LYDG. *Assembly of Gods* 438 On a rewde maner he salutyd all the rout, With a bold voyse, carpyng wordys stout. 1639 S. DU VERGER tr. *Camus' Admir. Events* 303 Adiuste..being returned to towne, saw himselfe saluted by a letter of defiance.

f. *poet.* Of birds, etc.: To hail or greet (the sun, the dawn) with song.

1682 CREECH tr. *Lucretius* II. 39 The Morning climbs the Eastern Skies, And tuneful birds salute her early rise. 1700 DRYDEN *Pal. & Arc.* II. 38 The Morning-Lark, the Messenger of Day, Saluted in her Song the Morning gray. 1821 SHELLEY *Hellas* 941 Victorious Wrong, with vulture scream, Salutes the rising sun, pursues the flying day!

2. To greet with some gesture or visible action conventionally expressive of respect or courteous recognition.

c 1440 *Gesta Rom.* xxiii. 83 (Add. MS.), All his [the emperor's] knyghtes and other men, whan thei sawe hym, worshipfully thei saluted hym. *a* 1533 LD. BERNERS *Huon* lxii 216 Huon approchyd & salutyd hym humbly. *a* 1585 SIDNEY *Arcadia* I. Ecl. i. (1598) 82 When that noble toppe doth nodd, I beleeue she salutes me. 1590 SPENSER *F. Q.* I. i. 30 He faire the knight saluted, louting low. 1593 SHAKS. *Rich. II*, III. ii. 6 Deere Earth, I doe salute thee with my hand. 1655 STANLEY *Hist. Philos.* III. (1687) 80/1 As soon as the Sun arose, [he] saluted it, and retir'd. 1727–41 CHAMBERS *Cycl.* s.v. *Salutation*, In England, we salute one another by uncovering the head, inclining the body, &c. The orientals salute by uncovering their feet, laying their hands on the breast, &c. 1760–2 GOLDSM. *Cit. W.* lxxix, One curtsies to the ground, the other salutes the audience with a smile. 1762 KAMES *Elem. Crit.* (1763) III. xx. 67 Among the ancients, it was customary after a long voyage to salute the natal soil. *a* 1859 MACAULAY *Hist. Eng.* xxiii. V. 93 Were they to stand erect and covered while everybody else saluted him?

b. *absol.* and *intr.* To perform a salutation.

1589 PUTTENHAM *Eng. Poesie* III. xxiv. (Arb.) 292 With them [the men of the East] to congratulat and salute by giuing a becke with the head, or a bende of the bodie, with vs here in England, and in Germany..to shake hands. 1600 SHAKS. *A. Y. L.* III. ii. 50 You told me, you salute not at the Court, but you kisse your hands. 1617 MORYSON *Itin.* III. 174 They..salute by bending the body and laying their left hand on their right side.

c. *spec.* in *Mil.* and *Naval* use. (*a*) *trans.* To pay respect to (a superior) by a prescribed bodily movement, the presenting of arms, or the like. (*b*) Of a ship, a body of troops, a commander: To honour or ceremoniously recognize in the customary manner, by a discharge of artillery or small arms, by lowering of flags, or the like. (*c*) *absol.*, and *intr.* To perform a salute.

1582 N. LICHEFIELD tr. *Castanheda's Conq. E. Ind.* I. ii. 5 b, They came to sight of their Captaine Generall,..and saluting him with many shot of ordinaunce, and with sound of Trumpets, they spake unto him. 1706 PHILLIPS (ed. Kersey) s.v., The Colours also salute Princes and Generals, which is done by Bowing them down to the Ground. 1725 DE FOE *Voy. round World* (1840) 94 We saluted the Spanish flag. 1727–41 CHAMBERS *Cycl.* s.v. *Salutation*, In the army, the officers salute by certain orderly, studied motions of the half-pike, &c. *Ibid.*, *Saluting with the Sails*, is performed by hovering the topsails half way of the masts.—Only those vessels which carry no guns, salute with the sails. 1744 J. PHILIPS *Jrnl. Exped. Anson* 148 We saluted the Governor of Macao with 11 Guns. 1769 *Regul. Sea-Service* in Falconer *Dict. Marine* (1780) K k 4, When a captain salutes an admiral..he is to give him fifteen guns. 1802 C. JAMES *Milit. Dict.* s.v., When a regiment is to be reviewed by..the king, or his general,..the officers salute one after another, pointing their swords downwards. The ensigns salute together, by lowering their colours, when his Majesty, or any of the royal family, are present. 1803 NELSON in Nicolas *Disp.* (1845) V. 139 You are not to salute the Fort of his Catholic Majesty, unless you receive a positive assurance that an equal number of guns will be returned. 1844 *Regul. & Ord. Army* 32 Officers wearing Hats, are not on any occasion to take them off in saluting; but when their Swords are not drawn, they are to salute, by bringing up the right hand to the forehead horizontally, on a line with the eyebrow. 1877–81 VOYLE & STEVENSON *Milit. Dict.* Suppl. (ed. 3) s.v., Her Majesty the Queen as Empress of India is saluted in India with 100 guns; the viceroy and governor-general of India with 31 guns. 1878 D. KEMP *Man. Yacht Sailing* 341 The ensign is lowered or dipped as a means of saluting a commodore, &c. or member of a club. 1889 *Infantry Drill* I. 24 When a soldier is about to pass an officer, he will salute with the further hand on the third pace before reaching him, and will lower the hand on the third pace after passing him.

d. *Fencing. intr.* To perform the salute used in fencing. See SALUTE *sb.*¹ 4.

1809 J. ROLAND *Fencing* 135 As it is understood when you salute, that it is a compliment you pay to the company, you should, while forming the parade of carte, turn your face to the spectators. *Ibid.* 136 Although I have directed that in saluting you should, in general, do it in *carte first*, and tierce *afterwards*.

e. *trans.* To kiss, or greet with a kiss. *arch.*

1716 ADDISON *Drummer* III. (1722) 31 You have the prettiest Tip of a Finger—I must take the Freedom to salute it. *Ibid.* IV. 37 *Ab.* Ay! but you han't saluted me. *Fan.* That's right; Faith I forgot that Circumstance. [*Kisses her.*] 1766 GOLDSM. *Vic. W.* v, He..was going to salute my daughters as one certain of a kind reception. 1773 JOHNSON *Let. to Mrs. Thrale* 30 Sept., I had the honour of saluting the far famed Miss Flora Macdonald. 1849 THACKERAY *Pendennis* viii, He once more saluted the tips of Mrs. Pendennis's glove.

intr. 1629 DAVENANT *Albovine* III. i, It is a piece of courtship to salute at parting.

†f. To honour (a person) *with* a present, gift, etc. Cf. GREET *v.* 3 d. *Obs.*

a 1592 GREENE *George a Greene* (1599) C 1 b, And first I saluted her with a greene gowne. 1601 ? MARSTON *Pasquil & Kath.* II. 249 Wouldst haue a Ballet to salute her with? 1632 LITHGOW *Trav.* VIII. 346, I saluted the Princesse Palatine, with certayne rare Relickes of the Holy Land.

g. *ironically* used for: To assail.

1607 ROWLANDS *Famous Hist.* 60 Here is a weapon that must do me right. So draws his sword, salutes him with the same About the head, the shoulders, and the side.

†h. *To salute Tyburn*: jocularly, to be hanged.

1640 SOMNER *Antiq. Canterb.* 205 Conspired with the Holy Maide of Kent..and saluted Tiburne for his paines.

†3. To pay one's respects to; to pay a complimentary visit to. *Obs.*

1585 T. WASHINGTON tr. *Nicholay's Voy.* I. xi. 13 The Ambassadour sent to salute the Caddy. 1591 SHAKS. *Two Gent.* I. iii. 41 To-morrow..Don Alphonso, With other Gentlemen of good esteeme Are iournying, to salute the Emperor, And to commend their seruice to his will. 1638 *Hamilton Papers* (Camden) 26 Eayrlie in the morning they sent their commissioners doune to salut me. 1698 FRYER *Acc. E. India & P.* 367 Having not saluted the Temple Twelve times since he began to Reign.

†4. *fig.* To begin acquaintance with. *Obs.*

1648 BP. HALL *Breathings Devout Soul* (1851) 190 Methusalah..did not more truly live; than the child, that did but salute and leave the world. 1722 WOLLASTON *Relig. Nat.* iii. (1733) 60 Every one, who has but just saluted the mathematics and philosophy, must be convinced, that [etc.].

5. *transf.* and *fig.* Of inanimate things, in various applications: †To bow or incline towards (*obs.*); to appear or come forth as if in welcome of; to approach, come into contact with; † (in Shaks.) to affect or act upon in any way (*obs.*).

c 1440 *Pallad. on Husb.* XII. 62 And there let bowis multiplie, And afterlong on euery side hem plie, Salutyng eest & west, & north & south. 1588 SHAKS. *Tit. A.* II. i. 5 As when the golden Sunne salutes the morne. 1595 — *John* II. i. 590 Not that I haue the power to clutch my hand, When his faire Angels would salute my palme. 1613 — *Hen. VIII*, II. iii. 103 Would I had no being If this salute my blood a iot. 1660 WALLER *To King on Return* 88 Like Ears of Corn when wind salutes the field. 1830 J. G. STRUTT *Sylva Brit.* 59 It [the elm] is the first tree that salutes the early spring with its light and cheerful green. 1880 SHORTHOUSE *J. Inglesant* (1882) II. 119 A land bathed in sunset light, overarched by rainbows, saluted by cool zephyrs.

b. Of a sound or sight: To strike (the eye or ear).

a 1586 SIDNEY *Arcadia* II. (Sommer) 117 Her eyes were saluted with a tuft of trees. *c* 1586 C'TESS PEMBROKE *Ps.* LXXXVIII. x, And ere the light Salute my sight. 1665 BOYLE *Occas. Refl.* IV. ii. (1848) 173 Our Ears were saluted with the melodious Musick of a good number of Larks. *a* 1668 LASSELS *Voy. Italy* (1698) I. 100 You may look..a huge way into their gardens, which even from thence will salute your eye with a fair prospect. 1771 SMOLLETT *Humph. Cl.*, *To Dr. Lewis* 28 Apr., The first object that saluted my eye was a child, full of scrofulous ulcers. 1791 COWPER *Retired Cat* 89 A long and melancholy mew, Saluting his poetic ears. 1805 T. J. DIBDIN *All's Well* 14 Some well known voice salutes his ear.

Hence **Salu·ted** *ppl. a.* In quots. used *absol.*

1658 MANTON *Exp. Jude* 1. Wks. 1871 V. 9 This first verse presenteth us with the two first circumstances, the saluter and the saluted. 1864 W. HANNA *Earlier Years Lord's Life* 293 The Ruler..who..might have counted on being the saluted rather than the saluter, does not hesitate to address him thus: 'Rabbi, we know' [etc.].

Salute, var. pa. t. of SALUE *v. Obs.*

Saluter (sălʹū·təɹ). [f. SALUTE *v.* + -ER¹.]

1. One who salutes or greets.

1542 UDALL *Erasm. Apoph.* 250 b, We have enough of suche saluters as this at home alreadie. 1611 COTGR., *Bailleur de bons iours*, an ordinarie saluter of euery one he sees, or meets. 1730 WALL *Crit. Notes N. T.* 295 Both he [*sc.* Aristarchus] and Epaphras are mentioned as saluters. 1753 CHAMBERS *Cycl. Supp.* s.v. *Salutation*, The women too had their crowds of saluters attending them every morning. 1834 L. RITCHIE *Wand. by Seine* 69 With a great lady, the saluter fell upon his knees, and kissed the hem of her gown.

2. = SALUTATOR.

1586 ROWLAND *Lazarillo* C vj *marg.*, A Saluter is a kinde of drunken prophets in Spaine which take vpon them the healing of mad dogges. 1591 PERCIVALL *Sp. Dict.*, *Saludador*, a saluter, a charmer, *Salutator, incantator*. 1738 [G. SMITH] *Curious Relat.* II. v. 152 The Saluters (a certain Order in Spain) make the People believe, that by uttering the Name of St. Catharine, they have Power to heal Wounds.

†Salutifere, *a. Obs. rare*⁻¹. In 6 **salutiffere.** [a. OF. *salutifere* (*salutiffere*), ad. L. *salūtifer*: see next.] Salutiferous.

1549 *Compl. Scot.* Epist. 1 It bringis furtht salutiffere & hoilsum frute of honour.

Salutiferous (sæliŭti·fĕrəs), *a.* Also 6 **salutiferus.** [f. L. *salūtifer* (f. *salūt-* health, safety, salvation + *-fer* bringing) + -OUS: see -FEROUS.]

1. Promoting or conducive to health.

1604 F. HERING *Mod. Defence* 35 Safe, wholesome and salutiferous Medecins. 1696 TRYON *Misc.* Pref. 4 The pleasant influences and salutiferous Breezes of Wind in a hot season. 1747 *Gentl. Mag.* 77 Such exercise is not much less salutiferous than riding. 1752 C. SMART *Hop-Gard.* I. 41 Tunbridgia's salutiferous hills. 1824 SCOTT *St. Ronan's* xxviii, As soon as the ancient priestess had handed him his glass of the salutiferous water. 1865 CARLYLE *Fredk. Gt.* XXI. iv. (1872) X. 41 Forcing-on his salutiferous drains and fruitful canals through the morasses of the Weichsel.

2. Conducive to well-being, safety, or salvation. (Very common in the 17th c.)

c 1540 tr. *Pol. Verg. Eng. Hist.* (Camden) I. 209 The fowntaine beetokened the salutiferus water of baptisme. 1629 H. BURTON *Truth's Triumph* 253 The sweet and salutiferous streames of the waters of life. 1636 BRATHWAIT *Rom. Emp.* 139 France: Which he furnished with things necessary, salutiferous, good Lawes and customes. 1756 C. LUCAS *Ess. Waters* II. 63 He means to instruct us in following his salutiferous steps. 1760 SARAH FIELDING *Ophelia* I. xxx. 266 Her Ladyship thought Fasting and Mortification most salutiferous for my Soul.

Hence **Saluti·ferously** *adv.*

1678 CUDWORTH *Intell. Syst.* 509 The Chief Prince of this great City..who governeth all things salutiferously. 1696 TRYON *Misc.* v. 142 [The] Preparations [of Corn Food]..are very wholsom and salutiferously used in many Countries.

†Saluti·gerous, *a. rare*⁻⁰. [f. L. *salūtiger* (f. *salūt-em* health + *-ger* carrying) + -OUS.] 'That brings commendation from another, or that is sent with *How-d'yees*' (Blount *Glossogr.* 1656).

Saluting (sălʹū·tiŋ), *vbl. sb.* [f. SALUTE *v.* + -ING¹.] The action of the verb SALUTE.

1533 *Mystik Rosary* A j b, The saluting of the wounde of the right fote of our Lorde. *a* 1617 CORYAT in Purchas *Pilgrims* II. 1824 The Turke doth neuer at the saluting of his friend..put off his Turbant (as wee Christians doe our Hats one to another). 1811 W. R. SPENCER *Poems* 139 One day, Good-bye met How-d'y-do, Too close to shun saluting.

b. *attrib.*, as *saluting-colour*, *-ground*, *-point*.

1894 *Times* 19 May 10/1 The Queen then quitted the saluting-point. 1895 *Funk's Stand. Dict.*, *Saluting-color*, *Mil.*, a camp-flag, distinguished by a transverse cross. 1902 *Westm. Gaz.* 11 Aug. 7/2 The saluting-ground. 1905 *Ibid.* 13 Sept. 3/2 The grim guns are disclosed as the artillery rattle past the saluting-point.

Saluting (sălʹū·tiŋ), *ppl. a.* [f. SALUTE *v.* + -ING².] That salutes.

1800 *Chron.* in *Asiat. Ann. Reg.* 46/2 His suite arrived at this Presidency, under a salute of thirteen guns from the saluting battery. 1885 *Athenæum* 11 July 44/3 The English pilgrim passed to the palace between bewildered boys and saluting soldiers.

Salutz, obs. pl. form of SALUTE *sb.*²

Saluwe, variant of SALUE *v. Obs.*

Saluy(e)d, var. ff. of pa. t. of SALUE *v. Obs.*

Saluyte, obs. form of SALUTE *sb.*¹

Saluz, obs. var. SALUS; obs. pl. f. SALUTE *sb.*²

Salvability (sælvăbi·liti). *Theol.* [Formed as next + -ITY.] Capability of being saved.

1654 WARREN *Unbelievers* 52 We have only a salvability by Christ, but no certainty of salvation. *a* 1663 SANDERSON *Five Cases Consc.* (1666) 4 Holding that there is no Salvability but in the Church. 1700 J. H. *Salvab. Heathen* 3 You and I do believe a Salvability for some Heathen. 1868 *Contemp. Rev.* VII. 355 Chillingworth makes good use of the concessions of his opponent as to the salvability of Protestants.

Salvable (sæ·lvăb'l), *a.*¹ [ad. L. *salvābilis, f. salvāre* to SAVE: see -ABLE.]

1. *Theol.* Capable of being saved, admitting of salvation.

1667 *Decay Chr. Piety* viii. ⁋ 6. 167 Our wild Phancies about Gods Decrees have in event reprobated more than those Decrees,..and have bid fair to the damning of many, whom those left salvable. 1734 WESLEY *Wks.* (1872) XII. 50 He is not in a salvable state. 1839 BAILEY *Festus* xxiii. (1848) 294 If God be Love, Or man a being salvable. 1858

SALVABLE.

G. MACDONALD *Elect Lady* 253 It was enough to be a Christian like other good and valuable Christians.

2. Of a ship, cargo, etc. : That can be salved or salvaged.

Hence Sa'lvableness; Sa'lvably *adv. rare* —⁰.

† Sa'lvable, *a.²* *Obs.* rare⁻¹. That can be met, explained or cleared up (*see* SALVE v.² 3).

2. Of 'phenomena' : *see* SALVE v.² 2.

Salvage (sæ'lvedʒ), *sb.* Also 7 *silvage*. [ad. med.L. *salvagium* or 2. OF. *salvage*, *-aige* (in sense 1), f. L. *salvāre* to SAVE: *see* -AGE.]

1. A payment or compensation to which those persons are entitled who have by their voluntary efforts saved a ship or its cargo from impending peril or rescued it from actual loss; e.g. from shipwreck or from capture by the enemy (called respectively *civil* and *military* or *hostile* salvage).

Salvation (sælvē'ʃən). Forms : 2. *salva-ciun, 4-5 sauacion, -acioun, savacion, -acyon, 4 savacion, 5 sauation, (sauacyon)-un, -acyoun, savacy-oun); 4-5 salvacion, -acyon, -acioun, 5 -acioun, -acyon, (salvatioun),-a-salvation.*

Salvation Army. An organization, or a quasi-military model, founded by the Rev. William Booth for the revival of religion among the masses in this and other countries.

Salva'tional, *a.* [-AL.] Relating to or concerned with salvation.

Salva'tionism [-ISM.] A Religious teaching which lays prime stress on 'salvation' or the saving of the soul. The principles or methods of the Salvation Army.

Salva'tionist, [-IST.] A member of the Salvation Army.

† Salvatory (sæ'lvătəri), *sb.* Also 7-8 *salva-tor*(e. [ad. med.L. *salvatōrium* of preservation (only spec. *a.* fishpond), f. *salvāre* to SAVE.]

† A box for holding ointment. *Obs.*

2. gen. A repository for safe storage. *rare*.

Salvatory (sæ'lvătəri), *a. rare.* [f. L. *salvātōri-us see* prec.] Saving, imparting safety or health.

† Salvatrice, *a.* *rare.* [ad. med.L. *salvā-tric-em* (nom. *-trix*), f. *salvātor* SAVIOUR.]

Salve (sāv), *sb.¹* Forms : 1 *sealb, salf, saalf, sealfe, 3 sealfe, 3-7 (9 *dial.*), *saalve, (salf)-5 sauue, sawe, 6c. aaeve, 5 Sc. saufe, 4-5 salue, salfe, (6 saue), 5 salve, sauf, 5- salve.* [OE. *sealf*, *salf* . . . OHG. *salba*, *salba* lemm., *salb*.]

Salve (sāv), *v.¹* Forms : 1 *sealfian, 3 (meredith, 5 salfen), 6 saufe, 6 savve, 4 *Sc. saue, 5 sawe*, . . . [OE. *sealfan*.]

1. *trans.* To anoint (a wound, wounded part) with salve or healing unguent.

SALVE.

3. To render tenable, obviate the objections to (an opinion) ; to vindicate from incredibility (an alleged fact).

Salver (sæ'lvər), *sb.¹* Also 7 *salvor*. [Formed (with suffix *-er* after *platter* or some other word of like meaning) on F. *salve* (1666 in Hatz.-Darm.), a tray used for presenting certain objects to the king.]

Salver, *sb.²* = SALVOR.

Salver-shaped *a.* [*Bot.*] = HYPOCRA-TERIFORM.

Salverform (sæ'lvəɔfɔ:m), *a. Bot.* [SALVER + -FORM.] = HYPOCRATERIFORM. (Cf. SALVER *a.*)

Salvia (sæ'lviə), *sb. Bot.* and *Gardening*. [L. *salvia* SAGE *sb.¹*] A large genus (Tournefort 1700) of *Labiatæ*, including the common sage; a plant of this genus.

Salving (sæ'lviŋ), *vbl. sb.¹* [SALVE v.¹ + -ING¹.] The action of anointing with salve (*lit.* and *fig.*).

Salving (sæ'lviŋ), *ppl. a.¹* [SALVE v.¹ + -ING¹.] Healing as with salve, soothing.

Salvia'nia (sælvī'niə), *sb. Bot.* [mod.L. named by Micheli in 1729 after Antonio Maria Salviani (1653-1729), a Greek scholar of Florence.] The typical genus of the N.O. *Salviniaceæ* of small cryptogamous plants ; a plant of this genus.

Hence Salvinia'ceous *a.*, pertaining to the N.O. *Salviniaceæ*.

Salviol (sæ'lviɒl), *sb. Chem.* [f. SALV(IA + -OL.]

Salvo, *sb.¹* *Chiefly pl.* [ad. It. *salva* (whence F. *salve* = Originally

Salvo, *sb.²* *pl.* *salvoes*, *-os*. [f. L. *salvo*, abl. sing. of *salvus* safe : see SAVE *a.*]

SAM.

Sam (sæm), *sb.¹* *Obs. exc. dial.* [Origin uncertain.]

1. *Upon my Sam*, a jocular mode of asseveration.

2. *Upon my Sam* : a jocular mode of asseveration.

Sam, *sb.² Obs. exc. dial.*

For the ME. forms descending from OE. *sęmnian*, see †SOMNE v.[1] The β forms exhibit the same simplification of final *mn* to *m* that appears in the pronunciation of *damn*, *limn*, *contemn*.]

†**1.** *trans.* To assemble (persons). *Obs.*

a1000 *Daniel* 228 Þa he þyder folc samnode. a1300 *Cursor M.* 2515 Quen he herd þan o þis tyþand; He did to-geder samen his men. 1338 R. BRUNNE *Chron.* (1810) 100 Whan he had samned his oste of folk fer & nere. a1400–50 *Alexander* 1732 For þou has samed [*Dubl.* sampned], as men sais a selly nounbre Of wrichis & wirlingis out of þe west endis. c1400 *Land Troy Bk.* 3232 To alle the lordes that there were Were redy dyght and samed there With ther meyne. c1440 *York Myst.* xxxiv. 43 Oure gere behoues to be grayde, And felawes sammed sone.

†**b.** To bring together, join (in marriage, friendship, love, etc.). *Obs.*

c1200 ORMIN 322 Þatt Dawiþ kingess kinness menn Off weress oþþr off wifess Wiþþ Aaroness kinness menn Off siþþe wærenn sammnedd. a1340 HAMPOLE *Psalter* cxxi. 7 Þat neghburs & breþere be samynd in charite.

refl. a1300 *Cursor M.* 2239 Þis fol folk þam sammen þan Brathli þai þis werk bigan. a1300 *E. E. Psalter* xlvi. 10 Princes of folke þai samened þam With þe God of Abraham.

†**c.** *intr.* for *refl.* To assemble, come together.

[a1000 *Ags. Ps.* (Spelman) xxx. 17 Hi ʒederedon *vel* somnodon samod togeanes me.] c1200 ORMIN 2412 Ʒa mihhte ʒho sket affterr þatt Wiþþ hire macche sammnenn. c1250 *Gen. & Ex.* 434 He ches a stede toward eden, And to him sameden oðer men. c1330 R. BRUNNE *Chron. Wace* (Rolls) 1932 Þe names of contres Ben chaunged..Als straunge folk han hider y-samed.

2. *trans.* To bring together, collect (things); now only *dial.* (Yorks., Lancs., etc.), chiefly with *together*, *up*. †Also in occasional senses: To bring together the edges of (a wound), *OE.*; to join or fasten together; to amass, hoard up; to fill full *of*.

Modern dialectal uses (for which see E. D. D.) are *to sam up*, to pick up eagerly; *to sam hold of*, to clutch, grasp.

c1000 *Sax. Leechd.* II. 22 Þonne samnað hio þa wunde & hælð. c1200 ORMIN 1552 Þu sammnesst all þin mele inn an & cnedesst itt togeddre. 13.. *Gaw. & Gr. Knt.* 659 Vchone..Ne samned neuer in no syde, ne sundred nouþer. a1400–50 *Alexander* 1520 He plyes ouire þe pauement with pallen webis, Mas on hi3t ouire his hede for hete of þe sone, Sylours of sendale to sele ouire þe gatis, And sammes [*Dubl.* sampnez] þaim on aithire side with silken rapis. *Ibid.* 5250 Þan scho laches him be-lyfe & ledis him forthire, In-to a clochere with a kay þe clennest of þe werde, Was sammed all of sipris & seder-tables. c1400 *Cursor M.* 27762 (Cott. Galba) Slewth oft samnes sorow strang, and þat vnmekely lastand lang. 1893 SNOWDEN *Tales Yorksh. Wolds* 163 We sammed together all we could find.

3. To coagulate († const. *together*). Now only *dial.*, to curdle (milk) for cheese; also *absol.*

1615 CROOKE *Body of Man* 263 There is nothing to be seene but the seede coagulated or sammed together. *Ibid.* 429 Whereby those things which otherwise could hardly be sammed together might receiue their conglutination. 1691 RAY *N. C. Words* (ed. 2), *To samme Milk*, to put the running to it, to curdle it. 1788 W. MARSHALL *Yorksh.* II. 349 'When do you sam?' When do you set your milk? or, When do you make cheese?

Sam (sæm), *v.*[2] *Leather Manuf.* [Of doubtful origin: the explanation in quot. 1870 may point to derivation from some word with SAM- *prefix*.] See quots. Cf. SAMMY *v.*

1870 *Eng. Mech.* 11 Feb. 534/2 Hang until about half dry, or, technically speaking, 'Sammed'. 1883 R. HALDANE *Workshop Receipts* Ser. II. 367/1 The skins are allowed to drain,..and after 'samming', or damping with cold water, are staked.

†**Sam,** *adv. Obs.* Forms: 3–5 **same**, 4–6 **samme, sam.** [Shortened form of SAMEN *adv.*] Together; mutually.

For *in sam(e*, see INSAME, I-SAME. For *to sam*, see TO SAME.

13.. *Sir Beues* (A.) 4561 Þe maide & Miles wer spused same In þe toun of Notinghame. 13.. *Cursor M.* 9750 (Gött.), I sal crie pes in lande i-wiss, And dome and pes do sam [*Cott.* samen] þen kis. 13.. *Gaw. & Gr. Knt.* 363 Syþen þay redden alle same, To ryd þe kyng wyth croun. 1390 GOWER *Conf.* II. 240 Doun thei seten bothe same. c1430 *Syr Tryam.* 1127 They seyde, 'God be at yowre game!' He seyde, 'Welcome, alle same!' c1450 *St. Cuthbert* (Surtees) 4895 Þe scottys were gadird sam. c1460 *Towneley Myst.* xii. 179 Now god gyf you care foles all sam. 1513 DOUGLAS *Æneis* VII. iv. 59 And heyr full oft at buyrdis by and by The heris wer wont togiddir syt all sam. c1525 *Tale of Basyn* 8 in Hazl. *E. P. P.* III. 44 Off a parson ʒe mowe here,..And of his brother that was hym dere, And louyd well samme. 1579 SPENSER *Sheph. Cal.* May 168 For what concord han light and darke sam? a1600 *Flodden F.* ii. (1664) 18 When they were all assembled Sam The town of Edenbrough before, Fifty great Lords there were of Fame. *Ibid.* vii. 68 All Sam the souldiers then replied.

Sam- (sæm) *prefix. Obs.* exc. *dial.* [OE. *sam-*, repr. (with vowel-shortening usual in compounds) prehistoric **sǣm-*:—W.Ger. **sāmi-* (e.g. in OS. *sâmquik*, OHG. *sâmiqueck* = OE. *samcucu* 'half-quick', *semianimis*):—OTeut. **sǣmi-*:—Indogermanic **sēmi-*: see SEMI-.] = HALF-, in various adjs. as *sam-crisp, -dead, -red, -ripe*; **sam-hale**, 'half-whole', in poor health; **sam-sodden**, half cooked, half done; also *fig.* 'half baked', stupid.

c1425 *Eng. Conq. Irel.* xxxix. 98 Yolowe her & *sam-crysp. 1297 R. GLOUC. (Rolls) 3416 Ʒut ichabbe leuere *samded hom ouercome Þan hol & sound be ouercome. a1023 WULFSTAN *Hom.* l. (Napier) 273 Nu ne beoþ naht fela manna ætsamne, ðæt heora sum ne si seoc and *samhal. a1300 *Cursor M.* 5153, I mai noght rise, i am sam-hale. *Ibid.* 13262 Þe sam-hale fast til him þai soght. 1393 LANGL. *P. Pl.* C. IX. 311 Chiboles and chiruylles and chiries *sam-rede [MS. M. *sam-ripe]. c1425 *Eng. Conq. Irel.* xxi. 54 (Dubl. MS.) He was samroed, with grey eghen. c1440 *Ibid.* xxxvi. 89 (Rawl. MS.) The kynge henry the othyr, was a man same rede [*Dubl. MS.* saunrede]. a1000 *Ecgberti Confessionale* § 40 Ʒif man awiht blodiges þicge on healf-sodenum [MSS. X. Y. *sam-sodenum] mete. 1825 JENNINGS *Obs. Dial. W. Eng.* 85 Any thing heated for a long time in a low heat so as to be in part spoiled, is said to be zamzodden. 1891 'Q.' (Quiller-Couch) *Noughts & Cr.* 97, I'm afeard you'm o' no account,..but sam-sodden if I may say so.

Samaca, samakade: see SAMBOCADE.

‖**Samara** (sæ·mără). *Bot.* [mod.L. use of L. *samara* or *samera* seed of the elm.] The indehiscent winged fruit of the elm, ash, sycamore (etc.).

1577 B. GOOGE *Heresbach's Husb.* II. (1586) 103 He that will plante a Groue of Elmes, must gather the seede called Samara. 1731 *Gentl. Mag.* I. 40 Sow the Sameria [*sic*] of the Elm, and Bay-berries, all which come up the first Year. 1830 LINDLEY *Nat. Syst. Bot.* 131 Its ovarium..finally changes into a samara which is 1-celled and 1-seeded by abortion.

Samaria: see SAMARIUM.

Samariform (sămæ·rifǭɹm), *a. Bot.* [f. SAMARA + -(I)FORM.] Having the form of a samara.

1891 in *Century Dict.*

Samarin: see ZAMORIN.

Samaritan (sămæ·rităn), *sb.* and *a.* Also 6 **Samerytane**, 6–8 **Samaritane**. [ad. late L. *Samarītānus*, f. Gr. Σαμαρείτης Samaritan, f. Σαμαρεία Samaria.] **A.** *sb.* A native or inhabitant of Samaria, a district of Palestine named from its chief city, anciently the capital of the kingdom of Israel; *esp.* one who adheres to the religious system which had its origin in Samaria.

c1000 *Ags. Gosp.* Matt. x. 5 Ne ga ʒe innan samaritana ceastre. 1377 LANGL. *P. Pl.* B. XVII. 48 Þanne seye we a samaritan sittende on a mule. c1511 *1st Eng. Bk. Amer.* (Arb.) Introd. 31/2 There be some crystened that in the holy land is namyd samerytanes. 1577 HANMER tr. *Eusebius' Eccl. Hist.* IV. xxi. 70 Sundry sectes among the children of Israell..the Samaritans: the Sadduces: the Pharises. 1799 *Med. Jrnl.* I. 439 The Samaritans who, in a life of solitude and retirement, incessantly contemplating the deity, abstained from the use of flesh. 1841 *Penny Cycl.* XX. 376/1 Samaritans are still found in their old country, especially at Nablous, near Sichem, and also in Egypt.

b. *fig.* with reference to the 'good Samaritan': see Luke x. 33.

Samaritan's balsam, 'a mixture of wine and oil, formerly used in treating wounds' (*Cent. Dict.* 1891); **Samaritan hospital,** a hospital specially devoted to the sick poor; **Samaritan schools,** 'common name in the United States for ambulance classes' (*Syd. Soc. Lex.* 1897).

1644 (*title*) The compassionate Samaritane: Vnbinding the Conscience, and powring oyle into the wounds which have beene made upon the Separation. 1649 P. CHAMBERLEN (*title*) The Poore Mans Advocate, or, Englands Samaritan. 1823 SCOTT *Quentin D.* ii, The bonny Scot had already accosted the younger Samaritan. 1846 LD. ASHBURTON in *Croker Papers* III. xxiv. 77, I wish some good Samaritan of a Conservative with sufficient authority could heal the feuds among our friends. 1887 HALL CAINE *Deemster* xxxix, The Samaritans laughed and bade them not to think of price or money until their captain should return.

B. *adj.* Of or pertaining to Samaria or the Samaritans; used by the Samaritans.

Samaritan Pentateuch: a recension of the Hebrew Pentateuch used by the Samaritans; the MSS. are written in 'Samaritan' (i.e. archaic Hebrew) characters.

1382 WYCLIF *Luke* x. 33 Forsoth sum man Samaritan, makynge iourney, cam bisydis the weye. 1624 in *Abp. Ussher's Lett.* (1686) 311 The five Books of Moses in the Samaritan Character. *Ibid.* 321, I also told him of your Samaritan Pentateuch. 1641 MILTON *Animadv.* 21 As little doe wee esteem your Samaritan trumpery, of which people Christ himselfe testifies, Yee worship you know not what. 1858 G. F. NICHOLLS (*title*) A grammar of the Samaritan language. 1889 *Harper's Mag.* Sept. 582/1 The greatest of the Samaritan festivals, the Passover, is still celebrated on the top of Gerizim.

b. *absol.* (quasi-*sb.*) in various contextual uses, e.g. the Aramaic dialect formerly spoken in Samaria; the character in which this is written; the Samaritan text of the Hebrew Pentateuch.

1627 ABP. USSHER *Let. to Selden* 30 Nov. *Lett.* (1686) 383 In the numbering of the Years of these Fathers..there is not the like consent betwixt the LXX, and the Samaritan, as was before. 1653 *Ibid.* 588 The Persian Pentateuch.. being translated not out of the Original, but out of the Chalde and the Hebrew Samaritan. 1770 [LUCKOMBE] *Hist. Printing* 159 Pica Samaritan. 1787 *Printer's Gram.* 300 Long Primer Samaritan. 1797 J. PRATT *Prospectus New Polyglot Bible* 8 Printing the Samaritan and Syriac in a character familiar to the Hebrew scholar. 1886 *Encycl. Brit.* XXI. 648/2 The false notion that Samaritan is a mixture of Hebrew and Aramaic.

†**Sama·ritanish,** *a. Obs.* [f. SAMARITAN + -ISH.] Belonging to Samaria; Samaritan.

[c1000 *Ags. Gosp.* Luke x. 33 Sum samaritanisc man] 1532 MORE *Confut. Tindale* Wks. 693/2 Of thys ye haue an ensample John .iiij. of yᵉ Samaritanish wyfe.

Samaritanism (sămæ·rităniz'm). [f. SAMARITAN + -ISM.]

1. The religious system of the Samaritans. In the 17th c. often *transf.*

a1641 BP. MOUNTAGU *Acts & Mon.* (1642) 474 All these consented to the generall Samaritanisme, of receiving Moses his Law. 1683 L. MILBOURNE (*title*) Samaritanism Reviv'd. 1693 *Consid. Explic. Trinity by Dr. Wallis*, etc. 32 What the Mystical Divines teach, cannot be called an Explication; they deny all Explications: we must say therefore 'tis Samaritanism; for what our Saviour says of the Samaritans, by way of Reproof and Blame, that these Gentlemen profess concerning themselves, that they worship they know not what. 1886 *Encycl. Brit.* XXI. 244/1 Before that time Samaritanism cannot have existed in a form at all similar to that which we know.

2. An idiom or form of expression belonging to the Samaritan dialect of Aramaic.

1889 *Harper's Mag.* Sept. 582/1 Insertions of foreign passages, alterations, Samaritanisms, and changes in support of Samaritan doctrine.

3. Imitation of the 'good Samaritan'.

1843 SYD. SMITH in Lady Holland *Mem.* (1855) II. 522 Mankind are getting mad with humanity and Samaritanism. 1863 'OUIDA' *Held in Bondage* (1870) 348 A shrew's vituperations rewarded him for his Samaritanism.

Samarium (samē·riŏm). *Chem.* [f. SAMAR(SKITE) + -IUM.] An alleged metallic element, the existence of which rests only on spectroscopic evidence; the bands supposed to indicate its presence were first found in the spectrum of samarskite. Hence **Sama·ria** [*-a* after *potassa*, etc.], the hypothetical oxide of samarium.

1883 *Athenæum* 14 Apr. 480/3 This metal is proved by the author to be samarium. 1898 SIR W. CROOKES *Addr. Brit. Assoc.* 23 The persistence of the samarium spectrum in presence of overwhelming quantities of other metals, is almost unexampled in spectroscopy: thus one part of samaria can easily be seen when mixed with three million parts of lime. 1907 *Athenæum* 31 Aug. 244/3 A sulphide of calcium containing a trace of the rare element samarium.

Samaroid (sæ·măroid), *a.* [f. SAMARA + -OID.] Resembling a samara.

1830 LINDLEY *Nat. Syst. Bot.* 111 Fruit either consisting of 3 samaroid carpella, or berried with from 1 to 3 cells.

Samarr, variant of SIMARRE.

‖**Samarra** (sămæ·ră). *Hist.* Also 8 **samarre**. [med.L.: see SIMARRE.] A kind of cassock, painted with flames, etc., worn on the way to execution by persons condemned by the Inquisition to be burnt.

1731 CHANDLER tr. *Limborch's Hist. Inquis.* II. IV. xli. 295 They [prisoners designed for the fire] are..cloathed with the Sackcloth, or kind of Mantle, which some call the Sambenito, others the Samarra or Samaretta. 1736 — *Hist. Persec.* 265 The infamous Samarre. 1841 BARHAM *Ingold. Leg.* Ser. II. *Auto-da-fé*, Each clothed in a garment more frightful by far, a Smock-frock sort of gaberdine, call'd a Samarra.

Samarskite (samā·ɹskəit). *Min.* [Named by H. Rosé in 1847, after Colonel *Samarski*: see -ITE.] A complex columbate of uranium and other bases.

1849 in J. NICOL *Man. Min.* 285. 1884 *Brit. Almanac & Comp.* 164 A few exceedingly rare minerals—..samarskite.

Sambenit, -benita, -i, -o: see SANBENITO.

Samber, sambhar, sambhur, var. ff. SAMBUR.

Samble, var. SEMBLE *sb. Obs.*, assembly.

Sambleblie, obs. form of SEMBLABLY.

Sambo (sæ·mbo). Pl. **-bos, -boes.** Forms: 8 **samboe**, 9 **zambo**, 8– **sambo**. [a. Sp. *zambo*. applied in America and Asia to persons of various degrees of mixed negro and Indian or European blood; also, a name for a kind of yellow monkey; perh. identical with *zambo* bandy-legged (according to Diez repr. L. *scambus*).]

1. (See quot. 1884.)

1748 *Earthquake Peru* iii. 240 Sambo de Mulatto, sprung from Negroes and Mulattos. *Ibid.*, Sambo de Indian, sprung from Negroes and Indians. 1796 STEDMAN *Surinam* (1813) I. xiii. 340 A Samboe is between a mulatto and a black. 1833 MARRYAT *P. Simple* xxxi, A quadroon looks down upon a mulatto, while a mulatto looks down upon a sambo, that is, half mulatto half negro. 1884 *Encycl. Brit.* XVII. 319/2 *Zambo*: any half-breed, but mostly the issue of Negro and Indian parents; in the United States, Peru, and West Indies of Negro and Mulatto.

attrib. 1748 *Earthquake Peru* iii. 240 Giveros, the Offspring of Sambo Mulattos and Sambo Indians.

2. (With capital S.) A nickname for a Negro. [Perh. a different word; it has been suggested that it may be the Foulah *sambo* uncle.]

1860 BARTLETT *Dict. Amer.* (ed. 3), *Sambo*, a term often applied to negroes. 1866 W. REED *Hist. Sugar* 32 Sambo tells him the skip is ready; but it would never do for the sugar master to seem to be taught by Sambo.

†**Sambocade.** *Cookery. Obs.* Also in corrupt forms: 5 **samakade, samaca, samaka, semaka, samata, samartard**, 6 **semeca**. [f. L. *sambūcus* elder; cf. It. *sambucato* flavoured with elder flowers.] A kind of fritter flavoured with elder flowers.

?1390 *Forme of Cury* (1780) 77 Sambocade. Take and make a Crust..& take a cruddes..do þerto sugar..& somdel whyte of Ayrene, & shake þerin blomes of elren. c1420 in *Q. Eliz. Acad.* 90 Semaka fryez. c1430 *Two Cookery-bks.* 50 Samaca. *Ibid.* 62 Frutoure Samata. c1440 *Anc. Cookery* in *Househ. Ord.* (1790) 450 At the seconde course..a leche and samakade, and bake mete. c1467 *Noble Bk. Cookry* (ed. Mrs. Napier 1882) 45 To mak samartard tak wetted cruddes [etc.]. 1502 *Arnolde's Chron.* Q iiij b/2 Freature semeca.

Sambock, obs. form of SJAMBOK *sb.*

Samboo, variant of SAMBUR.

‖**Sambook** (sæ·mbŭk). Also 6 **sambuco**, 9 **sambucco, sambuk.** [Origin uncertain: in Arab written سنبوق *sanbūq*. Cf. Pg. *zambuco*, It. *sambuco*.] 'A kind of small vessel formerly used in Western India, and still on the Arabian coast' (Yule).

1582 N. LICHEFIELD tr. *Castanheda's Conq. E. Ind.* I. x.

26 b, They discouered two Sambucos (which are little Pinnaces). 1855 BURTON *Pilgr. El-Medinah & Meccah* I. 263 The Sambuk [is a vessel] from 15 to 50 [tons burden]. 1887 L. OLIPHANT *Episodes* (1888) 15 A sambook or craft such as are now used in those seas [about India].

‖**Sambouse.** *Obs.* Also 7 **samboyse.** [Persian سنبوسه *sanbūsaʰ* (phonetically *samb-*), whence Arab. *sanbūsaʰ, -saj, -sak, -saq* (Dozy).] A pasty of hashed meats.

1609 W. BIDDULPH in T. Lavender *Trav.* (1612) 36 Wee dined [near Aleppo] with Musmelons, Sambouses, and a Muclebite. 1630 CAPT. SMITH *Trav. & Adv.* xiii. 25 Samboyses and Muselbits are great dainties.

Sambre, variant of SAMBUR.

Sambu, variant of SAUMBUE *Obs.*

‖**Sambuca** (sæmbiū·kă). Also in anglicized forms: 4, 6 **sambuke**, 5 **-buce**, 6 **-buque**, 9 **sambuc**. [L. *sambūca*, ad. Gr. σαμβύκη, prob. of Eastern origin, cogn. with Aramaic סבכא *sabb'kā* which it renders in the Book of Daniel. See SACKBUT.]

1. *Ancient Music.* 'A triangular stringed-instrument of a very sharp shrill tone' (Lewis & Short).

1382 WYCLIF *Dan.* iii. 5 Harpe, sambuke, sautrie, symfonie. 1545 ASCHAM *Toxoph.* I. (Arb.) 39 This I am sure, yat lutes, harpes, all maner of pypes, barbitons, sambukes, ..be condemned of Aristotle. 1845 *Encycl. Metrop.* IX. 451 The sambuc was, it is believed, similar to the psaltery. 1902 W. L. NEWMAN *Politics of Aristotle* III. 550 The sambuca was high-pitched and piercing in tone.

2. *Roman Antiq.* A military engine for storming walls.

1489 CAXTON *Faytes of A.* II. xxxv. 154 Sambuce is an engyn whiche is made in manere of a harpe able to perce a walle. 1594 R. ASHLEY tr. *Loys le Roy* 117 The rest followed them by the Sambuque.

Sambucco, variant of SAMBOOK.

Sambucene (sæ·mbiusīn). *Chem.* [f. L. *sambūc-us* elder tree + -ENE.] (See quot. 1875.)

1872 J. H. GLADSTONE in *Jrnl. Chem. Soc.* Ser. II. X. 3, I would suggest the following:—..Hydrocarbon from Elder. Sambucene. 1875 WATTS *Dict. Chem.* 2nd Suppl. 1073 *Sambucene*, $C^{10}H^{16}$, the terpene from elder oil.

Sambuco, sambuk, variant ff. SAMBOOK.

Sambuke, sambuque, obs. ff. SAMBUCA.

Sambur (sæ·mbəɹ). Forms: 7 **sabre**, 9 **sabir, samboo, sambar, samber, sambhur, sambhar, sambre, sambur, saumer.** [a. Hindi *sābar, sāmbar*.] The Indian elk, *Rusa aristotelis*.

1698 FRYER *Acc. E. India & P.* 175 Our usual Diet was.. spotted Deer, Sabre, Wild Hogs, and sometimes Wild Cows. 1813 in J. Forbes *Oriental Mem.* (ed. 2) II. 400 (Y.) Four large sabirs or samboos, one considerably bigger than an ox. 1862 BEVERIDGE *Hist. India* I. Introd. 11 The saumer, or black rusa of Bengal. 1864 TREVELYAN *Compet. Wallah* (1866) 161 Sambhur, a gigantic deer of the elk species. 1883 MRS. BISHOP in *Leisure Ho.* 85/1 The palandok..and the sambre may not be far off.

attrib. 1829 E. T. BENNETT *Tower Menag.* 187 The Samboo Deer..belongs to the Rusa group. 1883 LD. SALTOUN *Scraps* II. 175 Long yellow sambur-skin boots. 1898 R. G. BURTON *Tropics & Snows* 261 He may find a sambhur stag.

†**Sa·m-cloth.** *Obs.* [app. repr. OE. **sǣmclāð* (see SEAM *sb.*[1] and CLOTH *sb.*). Huloet's explanation might suggest derivation from SAM-, though that prefix is not found with sbs.] (See quots.)

1552 HULOET, Samcloth or vesture from the bealye downward, *limus*. 1688 R. HOLME *Armoury* III. 98/2 A Samcloth, a cloth to sow on, a Canvice cloth. *Ibid.*, A Samcloth, vulgarly a Sampler.

Samdel, variant of SOMEDEAL.

Same (sēim), *a.* (*pron., adv.*). Forms: 4–7 **sam**, 5 **samme**, 6 **some**, 3– **same**. [ME. *same*, a. ON. *same* masc., *sama* fem., neut., rarely in str. form *sam-r* (Sw. *samma, samme*, Da. *samme*); a Com. Teut. word, but lost in OE. and OS. (which have only the derived adv., in OE. *swā same*, OS. *so sama, -o*, likewise) and in the mod. Teut. langs. retained only in Eng. and Scandinavian. Cf. OHG. *sama* same (rare, though the derived adv. *sama, -o*, likewise, similarly, is common), Goth. *sama* same:—Indogermanic **somo-*, whence Skr. *samá* level, equal, same, Gr. ὁμό-ς same (cf. ὁμαλός level), OIrish *som* same.

Ablaut-variants of this root are (1) **sem-* in Gr. εἷς (:-**sems*) one; (2) **sǝm-* in OTeut. **sumo-* SOME, Skr. *sama* any, every, Gr. ἅμα together, L. *similis* like, OIrish *samail* likeness, image, Welsh *hafal* like; also as prefix in Skr. *sakṛt* acting at once, Gr. ἁπλόος, L. *simplex* simple; (3) *sōm-* in Skr. *sāma* similarity, OSl. *samŭ* same, OE. *sōm* agreement (see SEEM *v.*).]

The ordinary adjectival and pronominal designation of identity, equivalent to the older ILK *a.*[1], to L. *idem*, Gr. ὁ αὐτός, Ger. *derselbe*. Normally preceded by *the*, exc. after a demonstrative; the omission of the article occurs only in dialectal or vulgar speech and in certain specially elliptical varieties of diction (e.g. in commercial correspondence). As the prefixed article is functionally a part of the word, it is often difficult to distinguish the simple predicative use (= 'identical') from the absolute and elliptical uses.

A. *adj.*

I. Not numerically different from an object indicated or implied; identical.

1. With forward reference: Identical with what is indicated in the following context.

It is remarkable that this use is all but entirely absent from the writings of Shakspere; the only clear instance appears to be quot. 1598 in 4 below.

a. Followed by a clause with relative pronoun (*that, who, which*) or relative adverb (*when, where*). Cf. VERY *a.*

In this construction *that* sometimes has not the strict pronominal syntax, but is equivalent in meaning to 'in (on, by, etc.) which', 'where', 'when'. Cf. the similar use of F. *que*.

c1200 ORMIN 9914 He mihhte makenn cwike menn þær off þa same staness, þat stodenn þær bi Sannt Johan. 1340 HAMPOLE *Pr. Consc.* 4511 Þan sal Iewes þe sam lawe halde, þat þai haf. *Ibid.* 5288 Þis taken..sal noght be þe sam cros, ne þe sam tre, On whilk God was nayled fot and hande. 1537 STARKEY *Let. to Pole* in *England* (1878) p. xlvij, Euen the same thyng wych you percas thynke hathe byn the chefe roote of thys motyon. 1633 EARL MANCH. *Al Mondo* (1636) 141 The old saying is a good one, Doe that every day, which thou wouldest doe the same day that thou dyest. 1702 ADDISON *Dial. Medals* I. Wks. 1766 III. 22 He would often show us the same face on an old Coin that we saw in the Statue. 1707 — *Pres. State War* ¶ 7 ibid. 246 The same causes which straiten the British commerce, will naturally enlarge the French. 1711 BUDGELL *Spect.* No. 77 ¶ 5 At the same time that I am endeavouring to expose this Weakness in others. 1809 J. ROLAND *Fencing* 89, I return to the same situation where I found your blade at the time I began my first motion. 1810 SOUTHEY *Let.* 5 Aug. in *Life* (1850) III. 290 As for my contempt of the received rules of poetry, I hold the same rules which Shakspeare, Spencer, and Milton held before me, and desire to be judged by those rules. 1849 MACAULAY *Hist. Eng.* v. I. 561 Care was taken that the prisoner should pass through the same gate and the same streets through which Montrose had been led to the same doom. 1876 J. DENNIS *Stud. Eng. Lit.* 422 He defends it on the same ground that he would defend the 'Lycidas' of Milton. 1904 *Blackw. Mag.* Oct. 578/2 They may recite his [Shakspere's] works with the same restraint of gesture..which interpreted his works in his own day.

b. With ellipsis of the relative pron. or adv. Also (in careless use) followed by a pa. pple with ellipsis of relative and copula.

1514 *Rec. St. Mary at Hill* 21 Vppon condicion that they shall kepe solemply, my seid Obett or Annuersary yerely for euermore þe same day of the Moneth my sowle shall depart from þe body, in þe parisshe church of Seint Mary at hill within london. 1647 CLARENDON *Hist. Reb.* v. § 449 The standard itself was blown down the same night it had been set up. 1710 SWIFT *Jrnl. to Stella* 29 Sept., Why do you trouble yourself, Mistress Stella, about my instrument? I have the same the Archbishop gave me; and it is as good now the Bishops are away. 1831 SCOTT *Ct. Rob.* v, So many princes..aim, it is pretended, at nothing else than the same extravagant purpose announced by the brute multitude who first appeared in these regions. 1855 *Orr's Circ. Sci., Org. Nat.* III. 307 It is regarded with the same interest accorded in Europe to its red-breasted relative.

†**c.** In the 16–17th c. often followed by *that* with ellipsis of the verb, so that *the same that* becomes equivalent to 'the same as' or 'the same with'. *Obs.*

1577 FULKE *Answ. True Christian* 64 The Pope chosen by the councell of Constance, was of the same iudgement that the councell. 1582 G. MARTIN *Manif. Corrupt. Script.* iii. 44 Here he citeth many authors and dictionaries idly, to prooue that *idolum* may signifie the same that Image. 1601 HOLLAND *Pliny* I. 88 The next marches of this higher prouince is the same that the tract of Tarracon. *Ibid.* 105 The Pisidians..whose chiefe colony is Cæsaria, the same that Antiochia. 1643 TRAPP *Comm. Gen.* xi. 30 Some say, that Iscah in Chaldee signifieth the same that Sarai in Hebrew. 1652 LOVEDAY tr. *Calprenede's Cassandra* II. 132 And having applyed unto them the same things that to my Master's, they laboured to recover him from the wound he was in. 1664 H. MORE *Exp. 7 Epist.* viii. (1669) 124 So that I understand by φιλαδελφία the same that ἀγάπη, universal Love. 1671 MILTON *P. R.* III. 413 Such was thy zeal To Israel then, the same that now to me.

d. Followed by *as*. Now the commonest construction.

Four varieties of use may be noted. (*a*) *As* may serve as a relative adv. or pron. introducing a clause (cf. 1 a); (*b*) it may precede the subject or object of a verb omitted by ellipsis; (*c*) by ellipsis of the copula, it may be followed by sb. or pronoun denoting that with which identity is stated; (*d*) it may elliptically precede an adv. or phrase.

(*a*) 1340 HAMPOLE *Pr. Consc.* 835 Þan sal he on þe same wys hethen wende..right als he cam þe first day fra his moder wam. c1400 *Rule St. Benet* (Verse) 2371 On þe sam wise sall iik soueraygn Do os þai wil take o-gayn. a1548 HALL *Chron., Edw. IV* 196 He was the same person and of the same good mynde towarde the kynge, as he was before the tyme of hys legacion. 1705 ADDISON *Italy, Rome* 350 The Horse and Man on the Medal are in the same Posture as they are on the Statue. 1827 HALLAM *Const. Hist.* (1842) II. 257 *note*, She was exactly in the same predicament as Philip had been during his marriage with Mary I. 1861 M. PATTISON *Ess.* (1889) I. 40 A patent of Henry II.., in which he..licenses the sale of Rhenish wine at the same price as French is sold at. 1894 SWINBURNE *Stud. in Prose & P.* 36 Entering college at the same age as Fletcher had entered six years earlier.

(*b*) 1691 *Emilianne's Frauds Romish Monks* 148 We follow'd this Troop of Pilgrims at a small distance, being Mounted in the same manner as they, tho' we could not joyn our selves in company with them. 1839 URE *Dict. Arts* 1086 7 Salt springs occur nearly in the same circumstances..as the salt rock. 1881 JOWETT *Thucyd.* I. 179 The sailors in the fleet all received the same pay as the soldiers. 1895 CHITTY in *Law Times Rep.* LXXII. 866/1 Other rules in Order XLV. point in the same direction as the first rule of the order.

(*c*) 1715 tr. *Gregory's Astron.* (1726) I. II. 351 The Ratio of *GH* to *IK*, which is the same as the given Ratio of the Sines of the Arcs *AB, CD*. 1807 ROBINSON *Archæol. Græca* III. xxi. 325 Olympia, a city of the Pisæans, or, as some say, the same as Pisa.

(*d*) 1662 BP. HOPKINS *Funeral Serm.* (1683) 39 They return again to the same glut of lusts and pleasures as before. 1702 ADDISON *Dial. Medals* II. Wks. 1766 III. 69 You see the metaphor is the same in the Verses as in the Medal. 1716 — *Freeholder* No. 42 ¶ 6 We receive the same profit from them, as if they were the Produce of our own Island. 1845 M. PATTISON *Ess.* (1889) I. 24, 'I again consulted your magnificence, and you gave the same answer as before.'

e. Const. *with*. The regimen of *with* may denote either (*a*) a participant in the possession, attribute, etc. qualified by *the same*, or (*b*) that with which the object mentioned is said to be identical.

(*a*) 1387 TREVISA *Higden* (Rolls) II. 259 Þerfore of þre þe firste kyngdoms, as it were of þe same age wiþ þe kyngdom of Assiries, firste we schal write. 1601 DOLMAN tr. *La Primaud. Fr. Acad.* (1618) III. 803 The blossomes have the same nature with the fruite. *Ibid.* 804 The seede and roote of this plant have the same operation with the leafe. 1609 HOLLAND *Amm. Marcell.* 42 The bishop, being of the same mind and opinion with the rest, was [etc.]. 1660 BARROW *Euclid* VI. xxvi, Then is that Parallelogram about the same diagonal with the whole. 1699 BENTLEY *Phal.* Pref. 69 He is of the same size for Learning with the late Editor. 1740 *Johnson's Debates* 2 Dec. (1787) I. 23 Debate relating to a seditious paper of the same kind with the considerations on the Embargo on provisions. 1753 CHAMBERS *Cycl. Supp.* s.v. *Bridge*, Rochester bridge is built in the same style with that of London. 1763 GOLDSM. *Misc. Wks.* (1837) II. 502 They are incapable of the same docility with terrestrial animals, and are less imitative of human perfections. 1803 SOUTHEY *Let.* 9 June in *Life* (1850) II. 212 Scott, it seems, adopts the same system of metre with me. 1837 LOCKHART *Scott* I. x. 325 [He] died..at the same age with Burns and Byron, in 1811. 1842 R. I. WILBERFORCE *Rutilius & Lucius* 111 Words of the same nature with those he had heard were chanted at intervals. 1858 H. SPENCER *Ess.* I. 254 This.. will be found to come under the same generalization with the others.

(*b*) c1380 WYCLIF *Serm.* Sel. Wks. I. 319 As þe spirit þat is mannis soule is þe same persone wiþ him, so the secounde persone of God is þe same persone wiþ þis man. 1607 TOPSELL *Four-f. Beasts* (1658) 225 The Chaonian Horses are the same with the Aprirolan Horses. 1618 HALES *Gold. Rem.* II. (1673) 62 He could not be ignorant that his quality was the same with theirs. a1641 BP. MOUNTAGU *Acts & Mon.* (1642) 179 She was native..of Phrygia and so peradventure was the same with Trojana. 1681 T. FLATMAN *Heraclitus Ridens* No. 30 (1713) I. 197 The third was a Paper of Directions, what, and how to plead, which was also denied him, being the same thing with allowing him Council. 1764 GOLDSM. *Introd. Gen. Hist. World* Misc. Wks. 1837 I. 531 The materials to which we have had recourse are the same with those which other historians for several ages have employed before us. 1829 JAS. MILL *Hum. Mind* (1869) II. 194 It rested with him to prove that the expectation of a pleasure, or of a pain, is the same thing with the desire, or aversion. 1873 FREEMAN *Hist. Ess.* Ser. II. 188 This was no difficulty to the Greeks and Macedonians, who looked on the Egyptian Ammon as the same god with their own Zeus.

†**f.** In certain rare constructions: (*a*) const. *of* (perh. a Gallicism); (*b*) const. *to*. *Obs.*

1692 DRYDEN *St. Euremont's Ess.* 5 'Tis an extraordinary thing to find a Successor endowed with the same Qualities of his Predecessor. 1721 BRADLEY *Philos. Acc. Wks. Nat.* 13 And the Nourishment and Difference of Colours given these Bodies..I suppose to be produced by a cause nearly the same of that which gives us the different Colours in the Leaves and Flowers of Vegetables. 1756 TOLDERVY *Hist. 2 Orphans* III. 33, I am of the same opinion to the gentleman, who spoke last. 1771–2 *Ess. fr. Batchelor* (1773) I. 96 They fancy themselves in the same situation of the Jews, when their being victors, or vanquish'd, solely depended on the raising or depressing of Moses's hands.

2. With backward reference: Identical with what has been indicated.

1340 HAMPOLE *Pr. Consc.* 25 Þe sam God sythyn was þe bygynnyng And þe first maker of alle thyng. 1340–70 *Alex. & Dind.* 896 Also ʒe sente vs to saie in þe same time Of oþur maneres mo miche for to lakke. 1362 LANGL. *P. Pl.* A. Prol. 106 Tauerners to hem tolde þe same tale Wiþ good wyn of Gaskoyne And wyn of Oseye. c1400 *Pety Job* 70 in 26 *Pol. Poems* 123 Into poudre must I crepe, ffor of that same kynde I am. c1400 *Rule St. Benet* (Verse) 1234 And sche ken þe perils of cursing, Sche salbe cursid for þat same þing. a1578 LINDESAY (Pitscottie) *Chron. Scot.* (S.T.S.) I. 147 About the same tyme rang money cuning men be quhose labouris & trawell goode letteris flurischit. 1685 BOYLE *Eng. Notion Nat.* 384 How great a Difference there may be between a Body consider'd absolutely, or by itself, and the same Body consider'd in such Circumstances, as it may be found in. 1886 LINDLEY in *Law Rep.* 32 Chanc. Div. 23 The same observations are true of all other contracts similarly circumstanced.

†**b.** = The aforesaid. *Obs.*

1338 R. BRUNNE *Chron.* (1810) 126 To Normondie ageyn suld turne þe duke Henry, & Ingland alle holy after Steuen þe kyng Suld turne to þe same Henry, withouten geynsaiyng. 1455 *Cal. Anc. Rec. Dublin* (1889) I. 286 And in case that the sam man or person in hys takyng, make recistens not to be take. 1480 *Coventry Leet Bk.* 429 We send yewe same bill herin enclosed. 1517 TORKINGTON *Pilgr.* (1884) 9 Thursday, the vij Day of May, we retornyed by the same watir of Brent to Venese ageyne. 1535 COVERDALE *Eccl.* xii. 9 The same preacher was not wyse alone, but taught the people knowlege also: he gaue good hede, sought out the grounde and set forth many parables.

†**c.** *The same day*: to-day. *Obs.*

c1475 *Rauf Coilȝear* 848 On loud said the Sarazine: 'I heir the now lie! Befoir the same day I saw the neuer with sicht'.

3. Expressing the identity of an object designated by different names, standing in different relations, or related to different subjects or objects. In this use the sb. qualified by *same* often denotes an

indeterminate or hypothetical object, so that *the* becomes (with a sing.) functionally equivalent to the indefinite article, or (with a plural) redundant; hence result occasional ambiguities.

Cf. the Fr. 'Deux mots qui signifient *une* même chose', '*De* mêmes causes doivent produire *de* mêmes effets' with the ambiguous English 'Two words which signify *the* same thing', '*The* same causes must produce the same effects'.

1621 BP. MOUNTAGU *Diatribæ* 553 Bacchus and Sabasius is the same god. 1662 STILLINGFL. *Orig. Sacræ* II. vi. § 14 Both these Prophets considered the same people under the same circumstances, and with the same conditions. 1670 *Moral State Eng.* 160 At this time a Germain and a Fleming were in the same Pension in the Town. 1690 LOCKE *Hum. Und.* II. i. § 9 Having Ideas, and Perception, being the same thing. 1713 STEELE *Englishman* No. 8. 55 The same Person is to be paid twice for the same thing. 1738 tr. *Guazzo's Art Conversation* 221 They cannot live peaceable together in the same House. 1765 A. DICKSON *Treat. Agric.* I. (ed. 2) 33 Some kinds of animals,..such as horses, cows, and sheep, are nourished by the same food. 1797 *Encycl. Brit.* (ed. 3) III. 457/2 The flowers are male and female upon the same or different roots. 1809–10 COLERIDGE *Friend* (1865) 142 Sooner or later the same causes, or their equivalents, will call forth the same opposition of opinion, and bring the same passions into play. 1828 SCOTT *F. M. Perth* xix, With whom I have so often sat at the same board, and drunken of the same cup. 1835 *Penny Cycl.* III. 437/2 The old barcarolle was sung in parts, at stem and stern of the same boat, by its own gondoliers. 1868 LOCKYER *Elem. Astron.* iii. § 10 (1879) 55 All the planets travel round the Sun in the same direction. 1879 HARLAN *Eyesight* ii. 16 Even in the same eye, half of the iris is sometimes brown, and the other half blue. 1884 BRETT in *Law Times Rep.* 10 May 315/2, I have come to the conclusion ..that the Legislature intended in this case to be verbose and tautologous, and to say the same thing twice over.

b. More explicitly, *one and the same*.

[After L. *unus et idem*, Gr. (ὁ) εἷς καὶ ὁ αὐτός.]

1551 T. WILSON *Logike* S iv b, Out of one and the same floure the Bee sucketh hony, and the spider draweth poison. 1584 ? SIDNEY *Disc. Def. Earl of Leicester* Misc. Wks. (1829) 272 In sum, in one the same man, all the faults that in all the most contrary-humoured men in the world can remain. c1650 LEIGHTON *Serm.* xviii. Wks. 1869 II. 227 Never think that one and the same soul can have much pride and much of Christ. 1659 H. MORE *Immort. Soul* II. i. 113 Perception being really one and the same thing with Reaction of Matter one part against another. a1806 HORSLEY *Serm.* (1816) II. xxvi. 304 A sameness of the terms..would be an argument for assigning one and the same meaning to the promises. 1862 LATHAM *Channel Isl.* III. xviii. (ed. 2) 411 They belong to one and the same class.

4. Coupled for emphasis with a synonymous adj.: †*that ilk* (*thilk*) *same*, †*the same self*, †*the same very*, *the very same*. See also SELFSAME.

The same self was exceedingly common in the 16th c.

13.. *Cursor M.* 1919 (Gött.) Þat ilk same day [*Cott.* þat ilk dai, *Fairf.* þat same day]. 1390 GOWER *Conf.* I. 95 Thilke same speche Which, as thou seist, thou schalt me teche. a1450 MYRC *Par. Priests* 668 Þenne schale he wyth hys owne hondes Brenne þat ylke same bondes. 1503 *Rolls of Parlt.* VI. 522/2 They..shall have..lyke auctorite..as the same selfe Bisshoppes shulde, ought or myght do. 1526 *Pilgr. Perf.* (W. de W. 1531) 24 And the same selfe mysteryes he afterwarde declared to his discyples. 1589–90 *Reg. Privy Council Scot.* IV. 465 Baith having the same selff freindis and commoun enemeyis. 1590 L. LLOYD *Diall of Daies* 169 Q. Metellus triumphed over Creet at the same verie day that Pompei the great triumphed over the Pyrats on sea. 1594 SHAKS. *Rich. III*, III. ii. 49 This same very day. 1598 — *Merry W.* IV. v. 37 Shee sayes, that the very same man that beguil'd Master Slender of his Chaine, cozon'd him of it. 1692 R. L'ESTRANGE *Fables* ix. 9 The Snake, after his Recovery, is the very same Snake still, that he was at first. *Ibid.* xviii. 19 Several of the very same Birds that she had foreward'd.

5. Appended redundantly to a demonstrative (*this, these, that, those, yon*). Common in 16–17th c.; usually expressing some degree of irritation or contempt, sometimes playful familiarity. (Cf. the vulgar *this here, that there*.) Now *arch.*

Out of the 95 instances of the word *same* in Shakspere, 55 occur in collocation with a demonstrative.

For examples in which *same* has its normal force when preceded by a demonstrative, see senses 1–3.

1340–70 *Alex. & Dind.* 107 In þis same wise. 1598 SHAKS. *Merry W.* v. i. 18 That same knaue (Ford hir husband). 1603 — *Meas. for M.* v. i. 270 Call that same Isabell here once againe. 1625 BACON *Ess., Truth* (Arb.) 499 This same Truth, is a Naked, and Open day light. 1628 MILTON *Vac. Exerc.* 16, I pray thee then deny me not thy aide For this same small neglect that I have made. 1634 — *Comus* 738 Be not cosen'd With that same vaunted name Virginity. 1726 SWIFT *On reading Young's Univ. Passion* Wks. 1751 X. 246 If that same *Universal Passion* With ev'ry Vice hath fill'd the Nation. 1808 SCOTT *Marm.* I. xxv, If this same Palmer will me lead From hence. 1816 J. WILSON *City of Plague* II. iii, What is the use of these same lamps? 1871 R. ELLIS *Catullus* x. 26 Just for courtesy lend me, dear Catullus, Those same nobodies.

6. Phrases. *At the same time*: see TIME *sb.* *By the same token*: see TOKEN *sb.*

II. In modified senses.

7. Applied to an object as having the same attributes with another or with itself at another time; exactly agreeing *in* (amount, quality, operation, etc.). Of a person: Unchanged in character, condition of health, etc. Chiefly *predicative* (cf. B. 1, 2). Constructions as in 1–3.

Phrase, *Much the same*, approximately the same (cf. MUCH *adv.* 3).

1667 MILTON *P. L.* I. 256 The mind is its own place, and in it self Can make a Heav'n of Hell, a Hell of Heav'n. What matter where, if I be still the same. 1669 STURMY *Mariner's Mag.* IV. 138 If the Course and Distance had been first agreed upon from the Place they were bound to, to be just the same, unto the..Land they first descried. 1718 *Free-thinker* No. 91 ¶ 5 Human Nature is perpetually the same, ever subject to the same Passions and Corruptions. 1758 R. PRICE *Rev. Quest. Morals* viii. (1769) 293 *note*, A distinction much the same with this may be found in the letters between Dr. Sharp and Mrs. Cockburn. 1836 J. GILBERT *Chr. Atonem.* ix. (1852) 284 God himself remains the same before and after the interposition of Christ. 1838 PRESCOTT *Ferd. & Is.* II. vi. II. 518 Bigotry is the same in every faith and every age. 1855 MACAULAY *Hist. Eng.* xv. III. 585 His salary was the same with that of the Lord Lieutenant. 1860 LD. LYTTON *Lucile* II. II. iii, Do not think that years leave us and find us the same! 1861 M. PATTISON *Ess.* (1889) I. 48 The Steelyard passed with the rest of the parish by the same easy gradations from the old to the new faith. 1893 *Bookman* June 86/1 Her ambitions superficially so different at different times, and yet substantially the same.

b. *predicatively*. Of a person: Unchanged in behaviour *to* another.

1850 DICKENS *Dav. Copp.* ix, But she was always the same to me. She never changed to her foolish Peggotty.

c. Corresponding in relative position.

1672 PETTY *Pol. Anat.* (1691) 18 About 504 M. of the Irish perished..between the 23 of October 1641 and the same day 1652. 1848 THACKERAY *Van. Fair* xxviii, He and I were both shot in the same leg at Talavera. 1856 SIR G. C. LEWIS *Lett.* (1870) 317 The Foreign Office..now holds the same place in our social economy as the Colonial Office used to hold. 1891 'J. S. WINTER' *Lumley* xii, The doctors..have decidedly better hopes than they had yesterday at the same time.

8. Predicatively: Equally acceptable or the contrary; indifferent. Also *all the same*, *just the same*.

1803 MARY CHARLTON *Wife & Mistress* I. 245 He don't vally what he says to young or old, man or woman—it's all the same to old gruffy! 1838 DICKENS *Nich. Nick.* vii, It's all the same to me. 1847 UPHAM *Mme. Guyon & Fénélon* II. iii. 31 (Funk) To Daniel the lion's den and the monarch's palace are the same.

9. Predicatively, without article: Characterized by sameness, monotonous. *rare.*

1891 *Pall Mall G.* 3 Feb. 6/2 The choruses in 'Judith' are numerous, and to the lay mind perhaps a little same.

III. 10. *Comb.*, as *same-kidneyed, -seeminess, -sized, -soundingness*; **same-ways** *adv.*, in the same direction.

1674 N. FAIRFAX *Bulk & Selv.* Ep. Ded., The *same-kidneyed men, who have..a sharp flowt at the end of their tongue. 1839–48 BAILEY *Festus* xx. 231 Lest long *sameseemingness should send me mad. 1764 *Museum Rust.* III. lii. 229 Let this be done deep, and still in the *same-sized ridges. 1839–48 BAILEY *Festus* iv. 33 The sea..In its sublime *samesoundingness laughed out. 1887 SIR W. THOMSON in *Nature* 3 Oct. 546/2 Every A is at the centre of an equal and similar, and *same-ways oriented, tetrahedron of O's.

B. *absol.* and as *pron.* (Constructions as in A.)

1. The same person or persons.

1340–70 *Alex. & Dind.* 780 ʒe ben soþli þe same of wham þei so tolde. c1366 CHAUCER *A.B.C.* 77 Now queen of comfort sithe þou art þat same To whom j seeche for my medicyne [etc.]. 1616 B. JONSON *Epigr.* xxxiii, On Sir Iohn Roe...To the same. 1817 JAS. MILL *Brit. India* II. v. ix. 707 An appeal from the King's Council, to the King in Council, was ridiculed, even by the opponents of the bill, as an appeal from the same to the same.

†**b.** Conjoined with a personal pronoun or with a designation of a person, to indicate identity with one who has been mentioned. *Obs.* [A latinism.]

1377 LANGL. *P. Pl.* B. III. 26 Thanne lauʒte þei leue, þis lordes, at Mede. With that comen clerkis to conforte hir þe same. 1548 UDALL, etc. *Erasm. Par. Acts* 1 With the aduise and consente of the moste prudent and the same his moste dere vncle. 1598 GRENEWEY *Tacitus, Ann.* II. xvii. (1622) 57 Shew the people of Rome Augustus neece, and the same my wife [L. *Augusti neptem eandemque conjugem meam*].

2. The same thing. (See A. 1, 2, 3.) †Formerly also *that same, this same*.

1340–70 *Alex. & Dind.* 1009 But þe same þat ʒe so by vs siff trowe Longeþ, ludus, to ʒou þat liuen so in ese. 1390 GOWER *Conf.* I. 19 Who that here wordes understode, It thenkth thei wolden do the same. c1400 *Destr. Troy* 9772 Þe sam to my-self, sothli, may happyn. c1400 *Rule St. Benet* (verse) 488 And also crist in his god-spell Of þis same makes minde o-mell. a1450 MYRC *Festial* 8 Anon he made to take hym, and constrayne hym forto haue done þe same. a1536 TINDALE *Pathw. Script.* Wks. (1573) 383/2 What soeuer is done to the lest of vs..it is done to Christ, and what soeuer is done to my brother (if I be a Christen man) that same is done to me. 1576 FLEMING *Panopl. Epist.* 242, I have commended S— unto you oftentimes: and do the same againe at this instant. 1677 GALE *Crt. Gentiles* II. IV. 489 Here that common Proverbe holds true, 'When two do the same it is not the same'. 1687 A. LOVELL tr. *Thevenot's Trav.* I. 112, I failed not to speak to our Vice-Consul of the Light I had seen in the Isle of Samos, and he told me all the same that the rest did. 1711 J. GREENWOOD *Eng. Gram.* Wallis's Pref. 2 So the French Words *guerre* [etc.].. signify the same with these English Words. 1812 SOUTHEY *Let. to Jas. White* 16 Feb. in *Life* (1850) III. 328 It is the same in our age that it was in our youth. 1848 KINGSLEY '*Bad Squire*' xiv, If your misses had slept, squire, where they slept, Your misses would do the same. 1864 NEWMAN *Apologia* v. (1904) 168/1 When I became a Catholic, nothing struck me more..than the English out-spoken manner of the Priests. It was the same at Oscott, at Old Hall Green, at Ushaw. 1896 A. E. HOUSMAN *Shropshire Lad* xliii, Bring the eternal seed to light, And morn is all the same as night.

†**b.** Phrases. *Of the same*: in the same way. *To the (this) same*: to the same effect. *With the same*: at the same moment. *Obs.*

1399 LANGL. *Rich. Redeles* Prol. 14 All þe londe..ros with him rapely to riȝtyn his wronge, For he shullde hem serue of þe same after. c1400 *Rule St. Benet* (verse) 373 Also we se ʒit to þe same. *Ibid.* 461 For hali writ sais on þis wise: 'Þe fole with word may non chastese.'..And to þis sam. als clerks may kun, Þe wise man sais: 'Chastise þi sun [etc.].' 1603 HOLLAND *Plutarch's Mor.* 1027 He spake the word, and with the same, Immediatly out came the name.

¶**c.** With omission of article. *rare*[−1].

1638 BRATHWAIT *Barnabees Jrnl.* II. (1818) 45 What I was once, same I am now.

†**3.** Pleonastically emphasizing a demonstrative, used absol. or with ellipsis of sb. *Obs.*

1588 SHAKS. *L. L. L.* II. i. 194 Sir, I pray you a word: What Lady is that same? 1591 — *Two Gent.* III. i. 138 What Letter is this same? 1592 — *Rom. & Jul.* IV. v. 147 What a pestilent knaue is this same. 1611 BIBLE *Acts* xxiv. 20 Let these same here [1881 *R. V.* these men themselves] say, if they haue found any euill doing in mee.

4. *The same*, †*that* (or *this*) *same*: the aforesaid person or thing. Often merely the equivalent of a personal pronoun; he, she, it, they. Now *rare* in literary use; still common in legal documents; also (with reference to things) in commercial language (where *the* is sometimes omitted). Cf. G. *der-, die-, dasselbe*.

1362 LANGL. *P. Pl.* A. III. 27 Þenne [lauʒten] þei leue þis lordynges, at Meede. Wiþ þat þer come Clerkes to Cumforte þe same. c1400 *Lansdowne Ritual* in *Rule St. Benet*, etc. 143 Þe nouyce sal..singe þare thrise: 'Suscipe me, domine' &c. Þe couent..sall reherce þe same again thrise. and 'Gloria patri'. c1400 MAUNDEV. (1839) viii. 97 Upon that same schalle he sytte,..righte as himself seyde. c1450 *Cov. Myst.* ii. (Shaks. Soc.) 25 Take this appyl and ete this ssame, This ffrute is best as I the telle. 1474 CAXTON *Chesse* Ded., That ye sawe gladly the Inhabitants of yᵉ same enformed in good, vertuous, prouffitable and honeste maners. 1484 — *Fables of Æsop* III. vii, [Men] ought to preyse and loue the chirche and the commaundements of the same. 1500–20 DUNBAR *Poems* lii. 11 Ʒour Hienes can nocht gett ane meter, To keip your wardrope, nor discreter, To rule ʒour robbis, and dress the sam. 1503 in Kerry *Hist. St. Lawrence, Reading* (1883) 111 Also ij staynyd clothis wᵗ ryddels to þe same. 1509 FISHER *Funeral Serm. C'tess Richmond* Wks. (1876) 290 Above all these same there is a foure maner of noblenes. 1535 COVERDALE *Lev.* xiii. 40 Whan the hayres fall out of the heade of a man or a woman, so that he is balde, the same shall be cleane. 1548–9 (Mar.) *Bk. Com. Prayer, Collect 1st Sunday after Epiphany*, Graunt that they maie both perceaue and knowe what thinges they ought to do, and also haue grace and power faithfully to fulfill the same. 1583 STUBBES *Anat. Abus.* II. (1882) 65 Watermen haunt the waters, and fishes swim in the same. 1590 SHAKS. *Com. Err.* IV. i. 11 In the instant that I met with you, He had of me a Chaine, at fiue a clocke I shall receiue the money for the same. 1596 SPENSER *F. Q.* IV. x. 5 That was a temple..faire renowmed ..Much more then that which was in Paphos built, Or that in Cyprus, both long since this same. 1611 BIBLE *Matt.* xxiv. 13 But he that shall endure vnto the end, the same shall be saued. 1621 in Owen & Blakeway *Hist. Shrewsb.* (1825) I. 574 Laid out in stocking up of the gorst in Kingsland, making the same into faggottes. 1667 PRIMATT *City & C. Build.* 8 An over-shot-mill, which is the water brought to the top of the wheel, in landers or troughs which cast the same into Buckets made in the wheel for the receipt of the same, the force and weight of which water drives the same. 1772–84 *Cook's Voy.* (1790) V. 1755 The natives thinking we were determined to pay not the least consideration, at length ceased to apply for the same. 1818 CRUISE *Digest* (ed. 2) III. 324 If such tenant for life die on the day on which the same was made payable, the whole [rent must be paid]. 1819 KEATS *Isabella* ii, Her lute-string gave an echo of his name, She spoiled her half-done broidery with the same.

b. †As an answer when addressed by name; = 'I am he'. *Obs.* Also *colloq.* in confirming a conjecture as to the identity of a person mentioned by the speaker.

1599 SHAKS. *Much Ado* II. i. 191 *Ben.* Count Claudio. *Clau.* Yea, the same. 1889 *Chatterbox* 24 Aug. 323/1 'Have you ever heard of Red Jim?' 'The bushranger, do you mean?' asked Allan. 'The same. Well, this man [etc.]'.

†**c.** (*The*) *same*; = DITTO. *Obs.*

1486 *Bk. St. Albans* b iij, Take the Juce of percelly Moris otherwise calde percelly Rootis, and thossame of Isop. 1615 R. COCKS *Diary* 18 June (Hakl. Soc.) I. 11 He gave me a present of 3 nestes gocas, with their trenchers and ladells of mother of perle, with 10 spoons same, and a peece of white Liquea cloth. 1663 GERBIER *Counsel* 72 Rafters ten and seven inches, Purloyns the same, Plates the same.

†**d.** Chiefly Her. *Of the same*: of the kind or description last mentioned. *Obs.*

a1548 HALL *Chron., Hen. VIII* 25 The Kyng was apparelled in almayne ryuet crested & his vambrace of the same. ?a1588 *Glover's Ordinary* 28 in *Edmondson's Her.* I, Ar. in fesse three pellets betw. two bars sa. in chief two goats heads erased gu. attired or.; in base one of the same. *Gethinge.* 1625 BACON *Ess., Building* (Arb.) 553 A Greene Court Plain, with a Wall about it: A Second Court of the same, but more Garnished.

5. quasi-*sb.* An identical thing. *nonce-uses.*

1690 DRYDEN *Amphitryon* v. i, *Tran.* Two drops of water cannot be more like. *Pol.* They are two very sames. 1700 — *Ovid's Met.* XV. Fables 515 Ev'n our own Bodies daily change receive,..Nor are to Day what Yesterday they were; Nor the whole same to Morrow will appear.

C. *adv.* and in adverbial phrases.

1. *The same*: **a.** in the same manner. Const. *as*. *To think the same of*: to have the same (good opinion of (a person). Similarly, *to feel the same to*.

Now rare in literary use; common *dial.*, often with omission of *the*.

1766 *Museum Rust.* III. 240 Sow the seed broad-cast, ..then barrow it in, the same as turnep seed. 1827 D.

JOHNSON *Ind. Field Sports* 154 There is a physical cause for this, which operates the same in India as in the holy land. 1861 GEO. ELIOT *Silas M.* xviii. 325 You'll never think the same of me again.

b. = 'all the same': see 2. *Obs.* exc. *poet.*

1782 MISS BURNEY *Cecilia* v. viii, Suppose I am a cabinet-maker? When I send in my chairs, do I ask who is to sit upon them? No; it's all one to me..; I must be paid for the chairs the same, use them who may. 1884 BROWNING *Ferishtah* (1885) 39 For as our liege the Shah's sublime estate Merely enhaloes, leaves him man the same, So [etc.].

2. *All the same*: in spite of what has been mentioned; even if circumstances had been otherwise; nevertheless, notwithstanding.

1803 MARY CHARLTON *Wife & Mistress* I. 121 But who would have thought of my Lady Countess having a maid sent with young Miss, whilst my Dolly have nothing to do, but to milk a cow or two, and dust and scrub a bit, and cook a bit; and could all the same wait upon she too! 1845 DISRAELI *Sybil* VI. iv, What you say is well worth attention; but all the same I feel we are on the eve of a regular crisis. 1852 CLOUGH *Poems*, etc. (1869) I. 187 This winter is extraordinarily mild: to day a little hoar frost, but bright sunshine all the same. 1856 F. E. PAGET *Owlet of Owlst.* 164 No, thank you. Obliged to you, Henry, all the same. 1861 J. PYCROFT *Agony Point* (1862) 340 Audrey remarked that the said allowance made little difference; the money would have gone all the same. 1868 SWINBURNE *Blake* 176 A man is locked up, with keys of gold indeed, yet is he a prisoner all the same. 1878 RUSKIN *Let. to Dr. J. Brown* 21 Oct., I was very sorry to come away. All the same, I'm glad to be at home again.

3. *Just the same*: **a.** Exactly in the same manner. Const. *as*. **b.** None the less.

1874 ALDRICH *Prudence Palfrey* xiv. 281 And in the meantime Dillingham will continue his visits here just the same? 1901 H. MCHUGH *John Henry* 59 'My mother was a lady', so She said, but just the same She ate boiled cabbage with a knife Except when company came.

Same, variant of SAM *adv.* and *v. Obs.*; obs. f. PSALM; var. SEAM, lard; obs. f. SHAME *sb.* and *v.*

†**Sa·med,** *adv. Obs.* Forms: 1 **samod, somed, somod**, 3 **somed, someð, somet.** [OE. *samod* = OS. *samod, samad*, Du. (17th c.) *samet*, OHG. *samet, samit, samant* (MHG., mod.G. *samt*), Goth. *samaþ*, f. OTeut. **samo-* SAME *a.*] Together.

Beowulf 1063 Þær wæs sang and sweg samod ætgædere for Healfdenes hildewisan. a900 CYNEWULF *Crist* 1236 Þær bið on eadʒum eðʒesyne Þreo tacen somod. a1000 *Cædmon's Gen.* 789 (Gr.) Þa hie fela spræcon sorhworda somed, siþhiwan twa. c1205 LAY. 20132 Ford we biliue þeies uhte alle someð [? somed] heom to. *Ibid.* 25747 Þat heo sculden somed faren. a1225 *Leg. Kath.* 532 Ha somet seiden, þæt [etc.].

Same(i)kle, etc.: Sc. ff. *so mickle*; see SO *adv.*

Samel (sæ·mĕl). Also 7 **sammell**, 7–8 **sammel**; *erron.* 8 **sandal, -el.** See also SAMMEN. [Of obscure origin; possibly repr. an OE. **samǣled* half-burnt, f. SAM- + pa. pple of *ǣlan* to burn.] Of a brick or tile: Imperfectly burnt.

1663 GERBIER *Counsel* 26 To suffer no Sammell Bricks to be made use of. *Ibid.* 28 See the Brick-layers take good sollid Bricks to hue, since if any thing Sammel the work will molder away. 1703 T. N. *City & C. Purchaser* 43 He had burnt several Kilns of Tiles and..not had above to waste, broken, and Sandal Tiles in all. 1716 *Lond. Gaz.* No. 5446/8 All that are samel, or under burnt, to be excluded. 1727–51 CHAMBERS *Cycl.* s.v. *Brick*, *Samel*, or *sandal bricks*, are such as lie outmost in a kiln or clamp, and consequently are soft and useless; as not being thoroughly burnt. 1745 *De Foe's Eng. Tradesman* iii. (1841) I. 23 The brick-maker's men..turned their hands from the grey, hard, well-burnt bricks, to the soft, sammel, half-burnt bricks. 1845 *Encycl. Metrop.* VIII. 443/2 The outside bricks are necessarily under-burned. These are called samel bricks.

Sa·meliness. [f. SAMELY *a.* + -NESS.]

†**1.** Identity. *Obs.*

1662 J. CHANDLER *Van Helmont's Oriat.* 22 An unexcusable disagreement of every Similitude, remote from identity or sameliness. *Ibid.* 338.

2. Want of variety, monotony.

1897 WEBSTER (citing Bayne). 1901 *Westm. Gaz.* 10 Oct. 4/2 The sameliness of Longfellow's trochaic metre in 'Hiawatha'.

Samely (sēⁱ·mli), *a.* [f. SAME *a.* + -LY[1].] Without variety; monotonous.

1799 *Trans. Soc. Arts* XVII. 122 To..separate parts [of the forest] that were in some places too heavy and samely. 1821 CLARE *Vill. Minstr.* I. 58 O samely naked leas, so bleak, so strange! 1844 KINGLAKE *Eöthen* xvii. (1864) 198 The earth is so samely, that your eyes turn towards heaven. 1902 *Monthly Mus. Record* 1 Jan. 16 Mr. Thomas F. Dunhill's Sixteen Variations on an original theme are too long and samely.

†**Sa·men,** *a. Sc. Obs.* Forms: 4 **saymne**, 4–6 **sammyn(e**, 4–7 **samyn**, 4–9 **samine**, 5–6 **samin, samyne**, 6 **sammin, samyng**, 7–8 **samen.** [A derivative of SAME *a.*; the formation is obscure; possibly due to the influence of next.] = SAME.

1375 BARBOUR *Bruce* I. 252 And in the samyn tym come him to His wyff. c1375 *Sc. Leg. Saints* v. (*Johannes*) 348 Sancte Iohne ʒet but abaysitnes Þe samyne drink tuk neuirþe-les. 1456 SIR G. HAYE *Law Arms* (S.T.S.) 25 Alssua in the samyn wys, did the Emperour Frederike. c1480 HENRYSON *Test Cres.* 58 For worthie Chauceir, in the samin buik, In gudelie termis, and in Ioly veirs, Compylit hes his cairis. 1513 DOUGLAS *Æneis* VII. v. 184 Geif that my mynd can ocht ymagine rycht, I wene that he suld be the samyn knycht. a1555 LYNDESAY *Tragedy* 331 Brether,..quhen ze were consecrat, ʒe oblyste ʒow all on the sammyn wyse. 1577–95 *Descr. Isles Scotl.* in Skene *Celtic Scotl.* III. App. 425 Yit thai keip the lawis and uses of the samine for the maist part. c1600 MONTGOMERIE *Cherrie & Slae* 1503 Lyk as befoir we did submit, Sae we repeit the samyn ʒit. 1638 CHAS. I in Spalding *Troub.* (Bannatyne Cl.) I. 62 Wee have taken notice therof and doe give you heartiely thanks for the samen. 1671 R. MACWARD *True Noncont.* VII. 398 The samine is there truely and more fully to be found. 1678 SIR G. MACKENZIE *Crim. Laws Scot.* II. xv. § 4 (1699) 214 He writes upon the Bill, soverty is found; & subscribes the samine. 1725 RAMSAY *Gentle Sheph.* III. iii, And had I fifty times as meikle mair Nane but my Jenny should the samen skair. 1815 FINLAYSON *Rhymes* 95 (E.D.D.) Thousands are o' the samen mind.

†**Sa·men,** *adv. Obs.* Forms: 1–3 **somen**, 3 *Orm.* **samenn**, 3–5 **samen**, 4 **saman, samine, sammin, sammyne, samun**, 4–5 **samin, sammyn**, 4–6 **samyn**, 4–7 **sammen**, 5 **samene, samne, sampnen, samyne, samynge, somun, somyn.** [OE. **samen, sǫmen* (with prep. *æt sǫmne*) = OFris. *samin, semin, to-semine, to saminen*, OS. *saman, at-samna, to samne* (MLG. *sam(m)ene, to samene*), MDu. *samen, te-samen* (Du. *tezamen*), OHG. *saman, zi samane* (MLG. *zesamene*, mod.G. *zusammen*), ON. *saman, til samans* (Sw. *samman, tilsamman(s*, Da. *sammen, tilsammen*), Goth. *samana*, f. root of SAME *a.* Cf. Skr. *samanā* together.] = SAM, together, mutually. For *in samen* see INSAME.

c975 *Rushw. Gosp.* John xxi. 2 Werun somen simon petrus & ðe ðeʒn seðe wæs cweden didimus. c1200 ORMIN 377 Þeʒʒ baþe samenn cwemmdenn Godd þurrh heore rihhtwisnesse. c1230 *Hali Meid.* (MS. Titus) 59 Ha ne muhen nawt somen [*MS. Bodl.* somet] earden in heuene. c1250 *Gen. & Ex.* 40 In firme biginning, of noght Was heuene and erðe samen wroght. a1300 *Cursor M.* 7151 Thre hundreth fox he samun knitt, (I wat noght hu he on þam hitte). *Ibid.* 11998 And iesus samen his handes smat, and said. 1340 HAMPOLE *Pr. Consc.* 1849 Bot þe body and þe saul..Lufes mare samen þan man and hys wyfe. c1375 *Sc. Leg. Saints* i. (*Petrus*) 111 Þan kissit þai [ilk] oþer sammyne, gretand faste with gastly gammyne. c1400 *Destr. Troy* 10118 Seyuyn dayes somyn sesit pai noght. c1400 MAUNDEV. (Roxb.) xxviii. 128 Þai ware all gadred sammen. c1420 *Sir Amadace* (Camden) lv, A fayre knaue child hade thay somun. 1435 MISYN *Fire of Love* 78 We suld schewe lufly songis, to we be..broght in-to þe inward dwellyngeplace, samne takand a seet emongis heuenly citesenes. c1450 *Mirour Saluacioun* 3217 In this ffasscicle of mirre ware bonden samen paynes alle. 1513 DOUGLAS *Æneis* V. vi. 16 On athir half, than gaderis hym about Of Troianis samyn and Sicilianis a rowt.

†**Sa·men,** *v. Obs.* ? Aphetic for EXAMINE *v.*

?1613 ROWLANDS *Paire Spy-knaves* (1872) 6 They samen him according to their skils.

Samen, obs. form of SAM *v.*

Samene, variant of SAMEN *adv.*, together.

Sameness (sēⁱ·mnès). [f. SAME + -NESS.]

1. The quality of being the same; = IDENTITY 1, 2.

1581 MULCASTER *Positions* xxxii. (1887) 118 They were ill sundred, whom the samenes of time so vniteth together. 1607 *Schol. Disc. agst. Antichr.* I. i. 28 They meane a samenesse for some proportion that is betweene them. 1678 CUDWORTH *Intell. Syst.* I. iv. 559 We worship, the Father of Truth, and the Son the Truth it self, being Two Things as to Hypostasis; but one in Agreement, Consent, and Sameness of Will. 1690 C. NESSE *O. & N. Test.* I. 119 If there be the sameness in sinning, the same shall be in suffering. 1690 LOCKE *Hum. Und.* I. iv. § 4 Our Idea of sameness, is not so setled and clear, as to deserve to be thought innate in us. 1736 BUTLER *Anal.* I. i. 17 Personal identity or the sameness of living agents. 1753 *Scots Mag.* XV. 17/2 The sameness of the electrical fire with that of lightning. 1759 CAPELL *Prolusions* Pref. (1760) 7 Sameness of rythmus, sameness of orthography, and a very near affinity of words and phrases. 1827 WHATELY *Logic* App. (ed. 2) 305 Sameness, in the primary sense, does not even necessarily imply Similarity. 1875 JOWETT *Plato* (ed. 2) IV. 139 Likeness is sameness of affections.

2. Absence of variety, uniformity, monotony; an instance of this.

1743 H. WALPOLE *Let. to Mann* 27 Jan., We are in such a state of sameness that I shall begin to wonder at the change of seasons and talk of the Spring as a strange accident. 1765 FORDYCE *Serm. Yng. Wm.* (1767) II. viii. 20 There will arise..a sameness and a flatness. 1880 J. W. CROKER in Smiles *Mem. J. Murray* (1891) II. xxiii. 86, I shall endeavour to enliven a little the sameness of my author. 1842 VIGNE *Trav. Kashmir* II. 404 The scenery is sameness itself. 1886 RUSKIN *Præterita* I. 238 The steady occupations, the beloved samenesses, and the sacred customs of home.

3. ? *nonce-use.* Agreement in character or style.

1790 in W. Wrighte *Grotesque Archit.* Frontisp., Each will require a sameness to the Spot, For this a Cell, a Cascade or a Grot.

†**Sa·menfere.** *Obs.* [f. SAMEN *adv.* + FERE *sb.*[1]] A fellow-traveller, an associate.

13.. *E. E. Allit. P.* B. 983 Þay slipped bi & syȝe hir not þat wern hir samen feres.

†**Sa·mening.** *Obs.* Forms: 1 **somnung**, 1–2 **samnung**, 3 **samening, somnunge, sompnunge**, 4 **samenyng, samnyng, sampninge.** [OE. *samnung*, vbl. sb. f. *samn-ian* SAM *v.*: see -ING[1].] **a.** A gathering, an assembly. **b.** Intercourse, communion.

c950 *Lindisf. Gosp.* Mark i. 23, & wæs in somnung [c1160 *Hatton* samnunge] hiora monn in gast unclæne. c1200 *Trin. Coll. Hom.* 215 Me is andsete þe samninge of þe hinderfulle. c1230 *Hali Meid.* 12 (Bodley MS.) Þet bestelich gederunge, þet scheomelese sompnunge [*Titus MS.* somnunge], þet ful of fulðe stinkinde & untohe dede. c1250 in *Rel. Ant.* I. 23 Hy troue hy þeli gast, and hely kirke, þe samninge of halghes. c1250 *Gen. & Ex.* 1442 He faʒnede hire wið milde mod, Here sameni[n]g was clene and god. c1330 R. BRUNNE *Chron. Wace* (Rolls) 2719 Gret noise at her samny[n]g was. *Ibid.* 6718 At Londone þey sette a Parlement;..And þus þey seyde at þer sampninge.

†**Sa·menly,** *adv. Obs.* Also 4 **sammenly.** [f. SAMEN *adv.* together + -LY[2].] Together.

a1300 *Cursor M.* 28391 Munk, nunne, or spused wijf, þat sammenly aght to lede þair liue. 1357 *Lay Folks Catech.* 91 The hali gast, That samenly comes of bothe the fadir and the son.

†**Sa·mentale,** *sb.* and *a. Obs.* Forms: α. 3 **somentale**, 4 **samentale, sammentale.** β. (as *adj.* only) 4 **samer-tale, samirtale, sammertale.** [App. f. SAMEN *a.* + TALE *sb.* Cf. SAMTALE *a.*

The β forms seem to represent a genitive phrase = 'of the same tale' (ON. **samrar*, unrecorded str. genit. sing. fem. of *sam-r* SAME *a.*; *tǫlu* genit. of *tala* TALE); the sb. may have arisen from the substitution of a phrase with prep. for the genitive phrase.]

A. *sb.* Concord, agreement.

a1225 *Ancr. R.* 426 Seihnesse & some [*MS. T.* sachtnesse & somentale]. a1375 *Cursor M.* 683 (Fairf.) Þe bestes weren in samen tale [cf. B].

B. *adj.* Concordant, agreeing.

a1300 *Cursor M.* 683 Þe bestes self war samer-tale. *Ibid.* 10169 Was suilk a cuple neuer nan, Sua sammertale [*Gött.* samirtale], wit-vten strijf. *Ibid.* 23521 Þai er sa selcut samen tale.

†**Sa·menward,** *adv. Obs.* [f. SAMEN *adv.* + -WARD.] Together.

a1375 *Cursor M.* 15117 (Fairf.) Þai geddered ham sammeward & mened ham of þaire care.

Sameria, variant of SAMARA.

†**Sa·meron,** *dial.* (Yorks.) *Obs.* Also 6 **samoron**, 6–7 **samron**, 7 **sameran**, 7 **sammaron.** See quot. 1684.

1556 *Knaresb. Wills* (Surtees) I. 73 Thre yerdes of sameron. 1564 *Ibid.* 96, xj paire of samoron and hardin sheetes, xiij s. iiij d. 1583 in *Ripon Charter Acts* (Surtees) 380, xl yeredes of sameron, 20 s. 1598 *Knaresb. Wills* (Surtees) I. 211 My best blankett, samron and a harden shete. 1617–18 *Ibid.* II. 50 One paire of sameran sheetes. 1638 *Ibid.* 162 One little paire of samron shetes. 1684 G. MERITON *Yorksh. Dial.* 45 Thy Sammaron web..Is stown. *Ibid.* 107 (Alphabetical Clavis), *Sammaron*, is a Cloath between Linnen and Hempen, not altogether so course as the one, nor fine as the other.

Samer-tale: see SAMENTALE.

Samerytane, obs. form of SAMARITAN.

Sameyel, Samfast, obs. ff. SAMIEL, SHAMEFAST.

Samfayl(e, -ffayl: see SANS FAIL.

Sam-hal: see SAM-.

Samian (sēⁱ·miăn), *a.* and *sb.* [f. L. *Sami-us*, Gr. Σάμιος (f. *Sam-us, -os*, Gr. Σάμος) + -AN.]

A. *adj.* Of or pertaining to Samos, an island in the Ægean Sea, the birthplace of Pythagoras. **Samian earth** (see quot. 1728). **Samian letter**, the letter Υ, used by Pythagoras as an emblem of the different roads of Virtue and Vice. **Samian stone** (see quot. 1728). **Samian ware**, originally, pottery made of Samian earth; hence the designation of a fine kind of pottery found extensively on Roman sites.

1580 NORTH *Plutarch, Pericles* (1595) 182 The Samian prisoners. 1601 HOLLAND *Pliny* II. Table, Samian earth of two kinds. *Ibid.*, Samian stone. 1693 DRYDEN *Persius* III. 109 Where the Samian Y directs thy Steps to run To Virtue's narrow Steep, and Broad-way Vice to shun. 1728 CHAMBERS *Cycl.*, *Samian Earth*, Earth brought from the Isle of Samos..esteemed very astringent, proper to dry, and draw Wounds...There is also a *Samian Stone*, taken out of the Mines in the same Island...'Tis astringent and cooling, and is also used by the Goldsmiths to burnish their Gold, and give it a greater Lustre. 1742 POPE *Dunc.* IV. 151 When Reason doubtful, like the Samian letter, Points him two ways, the narrower is the better. 1821 BYRON *Juan* III. *Isles of Greece* xiii, Fill high the bowl with Samian wine! 1859 LUARD in *Archæol. Cantiana* II. 7 The articles found consisted of Samian ware of various shapes. *Ibid.*, The vases, urns, and Samian vessels, were filled with bones.

B. *sb.* A native or inhabitant of Samos.

1580 NORTH *Plutarch, Pericles* (1595) 181 He..kept the Samians besieged within their owne citie. 1759 W. WILKIE *Epigon.* v. 138 Ulysses then, with thirst of glory fir'd, The Samian left, and to the prize aspir'd. 1886 *Encycl. Brit.* XXI. 249/2 The great battle of Mycale (480), which..freed the Samians from the Persian yoke.

Samie, obs. form of SHAME *v.*

Samiel (sēⁱ·miĕl). Also 8 **sameyel.** [a. Turkish سميل *samyel*, f. *sam* a. Arab. *samm* (see SIMOOM) + *yel* wind.] The Simoom.

(Sometimes confused with SHAMAL, north wind.)

1687 A. LOVELL tr. *Thevenot's Trav.* II. 54 Having spoken so much of the Samiel, it is but reasonable I should relate what I have been told of it. 1774 GOLDSM. *Nat. Hist.* (1824) I. 153 A very dangerous wind prevails, which the natives [of Persia] call the *sameyel*. 1815 J. SMITH *Panorama Sci. & Art* II. 49 The samiel or mortifying wind of the deserts near Bagdad. 1817 MOORE *Lalla R., Veiled Prophet* (ed. 2) 90 Burning and headlong as the Samiel wind.

Samin, obs. form of SAM *v.*[1]

Samin(e, var. ff. SAMEN *a.* and *adv. Obs.*

†**Sa·ming.** *Obs.* [f. SAM *v.* + -ING. Cf. SAMENING.] A meeting, assembly.

c1400 *Land Troy Bk.* 3823 Suche a peple was neuere y-sene..To-geder broght at o samyng.

Samiri, variant of SAIMIRI.

Samirtale: see SAMENTALE.

‖**Samisen** (sæ·misen). Also **samsien.** [Japanese form of Chinese *san-hsien* (*san* three, *hsien* string).]

SAMITE.

A Japanese guitar of three strings, played with a plectrum.

Samite (sæ·mᵻt), *sb.* Also **samit, samyt**. [a. OF. samit, samiz. Forms ...]

A rich silk fabric woven in the Middle Ages, sometimes interwoven with gold. Also, †a garment or a cushion of this material.

†jardarly. (Scarlet) plush.

Samlet (sæ·mlet). [Contracted f. SALMON + -LET. Cf. the earlier SALMONET.] A young salmon.

Sammy, variant of SIMOOM.

Samnite, obsolete variant of SAMITE.

Sam·ly, *adv.* Obs. [f. SAM *adv.* + -LY.] Agreeably.

Sammen obs. f. SAMEN. Also **salmon**. [Etymologizing alteration of SAMEL = SAMEL.

Sammel, sammens, sammel: see SAMENE.
Sammer: see SAMMLE.

Sammin, Sammit: see SAMMIN.

Sammy (sæ·mᵻ), *sb.* *Leather-dressing.*

Sample (sæ·mᵖl). [a. AF. *assample* = OF. essample EXAMPLE.]

Samoan (sæmōʹ·ən), *a.* and *sb.* [f. *Samoa*, an island kingdom of the Pacific, + -AN.]

A. *adj.* Pertaining to Samoa, or the Samoans.

B. *sb.* a. A native of Samoa.

†Samolus (sæ·mŏlŏs), *sb.* [a. L. *Samolus* (Pliny); said to be a Celtic word.] *Bot.*

Samp (sæmp), *sb.* *U.S.* Also †**sampe**. [a. Algonkin *nasamp* (Wood *Vocab.* 1634), Narragansett *nasaump*.]

Sampan (sæ·mpæn), *sb.* Also 7-8 **champan**, 8 **sampane, sampaan, 9 sampaan, sampang, sampan**. [a. Chinese *san-pan* (san three, *pan* board).]

Samphire (sæ·mfəɪə(r)). Forms: 6 **sampere, samphire, 6-8 sampier, 6-9 sampire**, 7 **samper, sampyr, 7- samphire**. [a. F. *(herbe de) Saint Pierre* ...]

1. The plant *Crithmum maritimum* (growing on rocks by the sea), the aromatic saline fleshy leaves of which are used in pickle. Also called *Rock samphire.*

Samothracian (sæmŏþrēʹʃǐˌæn), *sb.* and *a.* [f. L. *Samothracia*, Gr. *Σαμοθρᾴκη*, an inhabitant of Samothrace.]

Sample (sæ·mᵖl), *sb.* Forms: 4 **sampel, saumpel, -pul, -ple, saumpil, 4-7 sampill, 4-6 sampill, saumple, 5 sampill(e, sampulle, 6 ME. *asaumple, aphetic f. *essample*: see EXAMPLE *sb.*]

Sampel, obs. form of SAMPLE.

Sample (sæ·mᵖl), *v.* [f. SAMPLE *sb.*]

SAMPLER.

79 SANATIVE. SANATORIUM. 80 SANCTIFIED.

Sampler (sæ·mplə(r)). [ME. SAMPLER *sb.* + -ER¹.]

Sampling (sæ·mplɪŋ), *vbl. sb.* [f. SAMPLE *v.* + -ING¹.] The action of the vb. SAMPLE.

Sampsuchine (sæ·mᵖsjūkᵻn). [ad. mod.L. *sampsuchinum*, Gr. *σαμψύχινον* (oil of) marjoram.] Oil of marjoram.

Samshoo, Samshu (sæ·mʃū), *sb.* [Chinese.] Also **samsoo, samshaw, samshoo, samshu, san-shoo**.

Samson (sæ·msən). Also 6-8 **Sampson**. [a. L. (Vulgate) *Sam(p)son*, Gr. (LXX) *Σαμψών*, a Heb. proper name.]

Samsonistic (sæmsŏnistɪk), *a.* [f. SAMSON + -ISTIC.]

Samson's post. [a. SAMSON, SAMPSON.]

Samuel (sæ·mjuˌəl), *sb.* [a Heb. proper name.]

Sanable (sæ·nəbᵊl), *a.* Obs. [ad. L. *sānābilis*, f. *sān-āre* to heal: see SANE *v.*] That heals or is concerned with healing; curative, *rare*.

Sanative (sæ·nətɪv), *a.* [a. OF. *sanatif*, -*ive*, ad. med.L. *sānātīv-us*, f. *sānāt-*, ppl. stem of *sānāre* to heal, f. *sān-us* healthy.]

Sanatorium (sænətōˈrǐ·ŏm). Pl. **sanatoria**. Also *erron.* **sanatorium**. [a. mod.L. *sānātōrium*, f. late L. *sānātōri-us*, f. *sānāt-*, ppl. stem of *sānāre* to heal.]

Sanatory (sæ·nətəri). [As if ad. mod.L. *sānātōri-us*, f. *sānātor*, agent-n. of *sānāre*; see -ORY.]

Sanctificate, *v.* *rare*. [f. eccl. L. *sanctificāt-*, ppl. stem of *sanctificāre*; see SANCTIFY and -ATE³.]

Sanctification (sæŋktᵻfᵻkēʹʃən), *sb.* [a. eccl. L. *sanctificātiōn-em*, n. of action f. *sanctificāre*; see SANCTIFY.]

Sanctificator. *Obs. rare⁻¹.* [a. L. *sanctificātor*.]

Sanctified (sæ·ŋktᵻfəɪd), *ppl. a.* [f. SANCTIFY + -ED¹.]

SANCTUARY

2. Affecting holiness ; sanctimonious.

Sanctify, v. ...

Sanctifiedly, adv. ...

Sanctifier. One who sanctifies or makes holy ; spec. the Holy Spirit.

Sanctify, v. Forms : 4 seintefie, 5 seintifie, saytifie, -efy, (6 santifye, -yfy ;) 4 saynctyfy, 6 sanctifie, 5- sanctify. [ME. seintefie, -er, later (after Latin) sanctifie, a. OF. saintifier (12th c.), sanctifier, mod. F. sanctifier.]

† 1. Law. To set apart religiously for an office or function ; to consecrate (a king, etc.). Obs.

† 2. To consecrate, make a saint of. Obs.

† 3. To honour as holy ; to ascribe holiness to.

Sanctifying, ppl. a. [f. SANCTIFY v. + -ING².]

Sanctifying, vbl. sb. [f. SANCTIFY v. + -ING¹.] The action of the verb SANCTIFY.

† Sanctilege. Obs. rare. [After MARTILEGE : see RAT.]

Sanctilogy (sæŋktɪlɒdʒɪ). rare. [f. L. sancti- sanctus Saint, after martirologium MARTILOGE.] A catalogue of saints, or a collection of saints' lives. Cf. SANCTOLOGY.

Sanctiloquent (sæŋktɪˈlokwent), a. rare. [f. L. sancti-, sanctus holy + loquent- ; see LOQUENT.]

Sanctimonial (sæŋktɪˈmoʊnɪəl), a. rare. [ad. late L. sanctimonialis.]

Sanctimonious (sæŋktɪˈmoʊnɪəs), a. [f. L. sanctimonia sanctity + -OUS.]

Sanctimoniously, adv.

Sanctimoniousness.

Sanctimony (see sanctimonious).

Sanction (sæŋkʃən), sb. [a. F. sanction (16th c.) or ad. L. sanction-em action of ordaining as inviolable under a penalty, also a decree or ordinance, n. of action f. sancīre to render sacred or inviolable, ordain, decree, ratify.]

1. gen. A building or place set apart for the worship of God or of one or more divinities.

Sanctionable (sæŋkʃənəbl), a. rare. [f. SANCTION v. + -ABLE.] That may be sanctioned.

Sanctional (sæŋkʃənəl), a. rare. [f. SANCTION sb. + -AL.]

Sanctionary (sæŋkʃənərɪ), a. rare. [f. SANCTION sb.]

Sanctionative, a. rare. [f. SANCTION sb. + -ATIVE.]

Sanctioned, ppl. a. [f. SANCTION v. + -ED¹.]

Sanctioner (sæŋkʃənər). [f. SANCTION v.]

Sanctioning, ppl. a. [f. SANCTION v. + -ING².]

Sanctuaried (sæŋktʃuːərɪd), a. rare. [f. SANCTUARY sb. + -ED².] That is made, or contains, a sanctuary.

† Sanctuarium. rare. [L.] = SANCTUARY sb.

Sanctuarize (sæŋktʃuːəraɪz), v. rare. [f. SANCTUARY sb. + -IZE.] trans. To shelter by means of a sanctuary or sacred privileges.

Sanctuary (sæŋktʃuːərɪ), sb. Forms : 4-6 saint-, -uary, seint-, seyntuar(y)e, -uarie, (e)warie, -wary(e, (5 seyntiwarie, 5 ceynte-wary(e, seyntery)) ; 6 saintu-, -wary, (6 saintuary, sentory, cent-), 6 sanctuarie, -uary ; 4-7 santuary(e, (6 saintuaire, mod. F. sanctuaire (whence the form SAINTUAIRE), mod. L. sanctuarium.]

1. gen. A building or place set apart for the worship of God or of one or more divinities.

† Sanctorial, a. rare. [f. SANCTUARY sb. + -ORIAL.]

† Sanctorium. rare. [L.]

† Sanctum. Obs.

Sanctuary.

Sanctum (sæˑŋktǒm), sb. Also 9 pl. rare sancta. [L. sanctum, neut. of sanctus holy.]

Sanctus Bell.

Sand (sænd), sb. Forms: 1–2 sand, sond, 3–6 sond, 6 sand; 3 saand, sund, 5 saande, sonnd, sound (6 aonnde, sownde.), 5–6 saynd; 6 OE. sǫnd, sǫnd str. fem., f. OTeut. *samdi- = *samdo- in
1. The action of sending; that which is sent, a message, present; (God's) dispensation or ordinance.

Sanctus Bell. Forms: α 5–6 sanctus bell, β 5–6 sanctes, saunctes, (-ys,) 6 saunce, saunse, 6–7 (9 anrd.) sauns, saunce, sance, 6–7 (9 arch.) saints, 7–8 saint's, 6–7 saint- bell, 5 saunze, 6–7 saints, 7–8 saint's.

Sand. (continued)

8. *Anat.* and *Path.* Applied to various substances resembling sand, present either normally or as morbid products in certain animal organs or excretions.

9. General Combinations.

10. Special combinations:

Sand, v. [f. SAND sb.]

1. trans. To run (a ship) on a sandbank; also pass. of a person, to be aground.

2. To sprinkle with or as with sand.

3. To overlay with sand, to bury under a sand drift; also to sand up, over.

4. To intermix sand (with sugar, wool, etc.) for purposes of fraud.

5. To grind or polish with sand.

Sandal (sæˈndăl), sb.[1] Forms: 5 sandell, 6 sandall, apostel(e), 5– sandal; β. 6 (in Lat. form), 6 sandalia. [a. L. sandalium, a. Gr. σανδάλιον, dim. of σάνδαλον.]

1. A protective covering for the sole of the foot fastened by means of thongs.

2. A strap for fastening a low shoe or slipper.

3. A strip or band of some kind passed over the instep or round the ankle.

4. attrib., sandal shoon (arch.), sandals.

Sandal (sæˈndăl), sb.[2] Forms: 5 sandell, 6 sandall, apostel(e), dall, 7 sandall, 7– sandal. [ad. L. sandalium (cf. sandalia) as fem. sing. Sp., Pg. sandalia, F. sandal, etc.]

1. = SANDALWOOD, in its various applications.

2. Applied, usually with distinguishing epithet, to trees of other genera, which produce a wood often used as a substitute for the true sandalwood.

Sandalo: see SANDAL sb.[2]

†**Sandaphic** (sb. = [a. L. sandaphia.] ' A Coffin or Beere' (Cockeram 1623).

Sandanac (sæˈndănăk). Forms: 6 sandafache, 7–8 –arack, 7–9 –arach, 8 –arick, 9 –aric, 7 sanderick, 8 sandrick, 9 sandrake, 8–9 sandrac, 7– sandarac. [ad. L. sandarac-a, a. Gr. σανδαράκη.]

1. Red arsenic sulphide. = REALGAR.

2. A resin which comes in small tear-like or globular grains.

Sandarac: see SANDAL sb.[1]

Sand-bag, sandbag, sb. [SAND sb.[2] + BAG sb.]

1. gen. (See in proverbial simile.)

Sand-bank. [f. SAND sb.[2] + BANK sb. 1.]

1. A bank of sand formed in a river or sea by the action of tides and currents.

Sand-bath. [f. SAND sb.[2] + BATH sb.[1]]

1. A vessel of heated sand used as an equable heater for retorts, etc. in various chemical processes.

Sand-bed. [f. SAND sb.[2] + BED sb.]

1. A bed, layer or stratum of sand.

Sand-blast. [f. SAND sb.[2] + BLAST sb.]

1. A continuance for depolishing or grinding glass, stone, wood or metal by means of a jet of sand impelled by compressed air or steam.

Sand-blind, a. Now arch. and dial. [Prob. a comb., SAM- and SAND + BLIND a.]

Sanded (sæˈndĕd), ppl. a. [f. SAND v. + -ED.]

1. Of a sandy colour.

2. Sprinkled with sand.

Sand-eel. [f. SAND sb.[2] + EEL.]

A fish of the genus Ammodytes, having a slender, cylindrical, silvery body resembling that of an eel.

Sandeling, Sandelin wood, obs. forms of SANDLING, SANDALWOOD.

Sandell, obs. form of SANDAL sb.[1] and sb.[2]

Sandemanian (sændimeɪˈnɪăn) a. (+(2)at.) a. & b. a member of a religious sect developed by Robert Sandeman (1718–1771) from the Glassites. b. adj. Of or belonging to the Sandemanians.

Sander (sæˈndə), sb. [f. SAND v. + -ER[1].]

1. One who or something which sands or sprinkles with sand; one who collects sand.

Sanderling (sæˈndəlɪŋ), sb. [Possibly repr. OE. *sand-yrðling, 7, 9 sandling. A small wading bird, Calidris arenaria.

Sanders (sæˈndəz). Also saunders. (See quot. 1892.)

Sandever, -devoire : see SANDIVER.

Sand-eyed, a. Obs. rare–[1]. [f. SAND sb.[2] + -ED.]

Sand-fly. [f. SAND sb.[2] + FLY sb.[1]]

1. A small fly or midge, esp. one belonging to the genus Simulium.

Sand-glass. [f. SAND sb.[2] + GLASS sb.[1]]

A contrivance for measuring time, consisting of two glass vessels of approximately conical shape.

Sandhi (sæˈndhɪ), variant of SANJAK.

Sand-glass: variant of SANJAK.

Sandarine, variant of SANJAK.

Sand-hill. [SAND sb.[2]] A hill or bank of sand; esp. a dune on the sea-shore.

Sandiman, Obs. Forms: α. 1 sander man, β. 1 sondem sandermann, 3 sonder(e man, 3–4 sandirman. β. 3 sondes, 4 sondesmon, 4–5 sondes-, saundes-, saundus-, 5 saundis-man, 7 ME. sandes, gentil.

Sandia (sandɪɑ). Also saundra. [Sp.] A water-melon.

Sandiferous, a. Obs. rare–[1]. [f. SAND sb.[2] + -(I)FEROUS.] Producing sand.

Sandiness (sæˈndɪnes). [f. SANDY a. + -NESS.]

1. The quality or condition of being sandy.

Sanding (sæˈndɪŋ), vbl. sb. [f. SAND v. + -ING[1].]

The action of the vb. Sand in various senses.

Sandiver (sæˈndɪvə). Forms: 4 sanddyuer, 5 sandefer, 7 sandever, sandevoire, 6 sandivere, 7 sandiver, 6– sandiver. [App. a. F. suin de verre.]

A liquid saline matter found floating over the glass after vitrification; glass-gall.

Sandpaper, v. [f. next.] trans. To smooth with or as with sand-paper; also with down.

Hence **Sandpapering** vbl. sb.

Sandpaper, sb. [f. SAND sb.[2] + PAPER sb.]

Sandpiper. [f. SAND sb.[2] + PIPER[1].]

A common name for any limicoline bird which is not a plover or a snipe; esp. Tringoides or Actitis hypoleucus, the Common Sandpiper.

Sand lark, sand laverock. [f. SAND sb.[2] + LARK sb.[1], LAVEROCK.]

A name applied, chiefly locally, to some of the smaller limicoline birds.

Sandre, obs. form of SANDER, SANJAK.

Sand-ridge. [f. SAND sb.[2] + RIDGE sb.] A ridge of sand; a sandbank.

Sandstone. [f. SAND sb.[2] + STONE sb.] A rock consisting of consolidated sand.

Sandy, a. and sb. [f. SAND sb.[2] + -Y[1].]

Sandix, obs. form of SANDIVER.

Sandling (sæˈndlɪŋ). Also sandel, sawn-delyage. [f. SAND-EEL + -LING.]

Sandish, a. Obs. rare. [f. SAND sb.[2] + -ISH.]

Sandwich (sæˈndwɪtʃ), sb.[1] [Said to be named after John Montagu, 4th Earl of Sandwich (1718–

1792), who once spent twenty-four hours at the gaming-table without other refreshment than some slices of cold beef placed between slices of toast.

Sandwich, v. [f. prec.] trans. To smooth with or as with sandwich.

Sandwich, sb.[2] Obs. [? Name of the town of Sandwich, Kent.]

Sandwichman. [f. SANDWICH sb.[1]]

Sandwort (sæ'ndwɔɹt). [f. SAND sb.² + WORT sb.¹] A name given to the genus *Arenaria* and other plants growing in sandy localities.

Sandy (sæ·ndi), sb. Also 5 **Sande**, 6 **Sandie**. A shortened form of the name Alexander, chiefly as applied to a Scotchman. Hence used as a nickname for a Scotchman.

Sandy (sæ·ndi), a. Forms 1 sandig, 4 *sondi*, 4–5 *sondy*, 6, -*y*, *sandy*. [OE. *sandig* (= Sw., Da. *sandig*).]

1. Of the nature of sand; composed of or containing a large proportion of sand.

2. *fig.* Resembling sand as lacking the quality of cohesion or stability.

3. *Qualifying* the names of colours.

4. Of persons or their hair: Having yellowish or reddish hair.

5. *Special Comb.*, as **sandy blight** *Austral.*, a kind of ophthalmia in which the eye feels as if full of sand (*Morris*); **sandy carpet**, a moth (see quot.); **sandy laverock** = SAND LARK; **sandy mocking-bird** *U.S.*, the brown thrush, *Harporhynchus rufus*; **sandy pate**, a sandy-haired person; **sandy ray**, *Raia circularis*. Sandy-ray.

Sandyish (sæ·ndiiʃ), a. [f. SANDY a. + -ISH.] Somewhat sandy.

Sandyx (sæ·ndiks). *Hist.* Also sandix (Dicts.). [L. *sandyx*, *-dix*, a. Gr. *σάνδυξ*, -*δῐκ*.] A red pigment, mentioned by ancient writers.

Sane (sein), a. [ad. L. *sānus* healthy; cf. F. *sain*, Sp., It. *sano*, Pg. *são*.]

1. Of the body, its organs or functions: Healthy, sound, not diseased.

2. Of the mind: Sound; healthy. Bayward wrote a poem on preserving the body in a sane and sound state.

Sanguine (sæ·ŋgwin), a. and sb. [ad. L. *sanguineus*, f. *sanguin-*, *sanguis* blood.]

Sanguineous (sæŋgwi·niəs), a. [f. L. *sanguineus* (see prec.) + -OUS.]

Sanies (sei·niiiz). [L.] A thin fœtid pus mixed with serum or blood.

Saniferous — **Sanify** — **Sanified** — **Sanies** — **Sanitarian** — **Sanitarium** — **Sanitary** — **Sanitarize** — **Sanitaries** — **Sanitarist** — **Sanitate** — **Sanitation** — **Sanitationist** — **Saniterous** — **Saniti-ferous** — **Sanitist** — **Sanitude** — **Sanity**

Sanjak — **Sanjakate** — **Sanjak-bey** — **Sanjakdar** — **Sanjakship** — **Sankara** — **Sank dragoon** — **Sanke** — **Sanko** — **Sann**

Sannah — **Sannup** — **Sannyasi** — **Sanop** — **Sanpan** — **Sans** — **Sans fail** — **Sans bell** — **Sanscrite** — **Sansculotte** — **Sansculottic** — **Sansculottish** — **Sansculottism** — **Sansei** — **Sans fail** — **Sanserif** — **Sanskrit**

Sanskritic — **Sanskritist** — **Sanskritize** — **Sans nombre** — **Sans-peer** — **Sant** — **Santal** — **Santa Claus** — **Santalaceous** — **Santalate** — **Santalic** — **Santalin** — **Santa Maria** — **Santar** — **Sante** — **Santir**

Santrel — **Santon** — **Santonate** — **Santonic** — **Santonica** — **Santonin** — **Santoninic** — **Santonous** — **Santorini** — **Santour** — **Santy**

Santur — **Santus** — **Sap** — **Saouari** — **Saouari**

Sap

b. *fig.* To make way in a stealthy or insidious manner. Also *trans.* in to *sap one's way*.

Sap, *sb.* Anglicised form of Sapan.

Sape, *sb.*

Sap, *v.¹* *Obs.*

Sapadillo, dillo : see SAPODILLA.

Sapajou (sæˈpadʒū).

Sapan, sappan (sæˈpæn). Also 6-7 sappon, 7 sappon.

Saphena (saˈfīnă).

Sap-green, *sb.* (and *a.*). [f. SAP *sb.¹* + GREEN, prob. after Du. *sapgroen*.]

Sap-head.

Sap-headed, *a.* foolish, stupid.

Saphena (saˈfīnă). Anat. 7 saphen.

Sapid (sæˈpid), *a.* [ad. L. *sapidus* savoury, f. *sapĕre* to taste: see SAPIENT *a.*).] Cf. F. *sapide* ; the direct descendant is *sade* (obs.).]

Sapidity (sapiˈditi). [ad. L. *sapiditās*, f. *sapidus*: see prec. and -ITY.]

Sapidless, *a.* *nonce-wd.* [Badly f. SAPID + -LESS.] Flavourless.

Sapidness. *Obs.*

Sapience (seiˈpiəns).

Sapiency (seiˈpiənsi).

Sapient (seiˈpiənt), *a.* and *sb.*

Sapiential (sæpiˈenʃəl), *a.*

Sapiently (seiˈpiəntli), *adv.*

Sapin. *Obs.*

Sapindaceous (sæpindeiˈʃəs), *a.* *Bot.*

Sapin-tree.

Sapi-utan (Malay *sāpi ūtan* 'wild ox').

Sapless, *a.*

Sapling (sæˈpliŋ). Forms: 5 saplyng, 6 sapplyng, 7-9 saplin, 8 sappling, 6- sapling.

Sapo (seiˈpo).

Sapogenin (sæpˈodʒenin). *Chem.* [f. SAPO(NIN + -GEN + -IN.]

Saponaceous (sæponeiˈʃəs), *a.*

Saponaceousness.

Sapona-city. *rare (jocular).* [irreg. f. SAPONACEOUS + -ITY.] Soapiness.

Saponarin. *Chem.*

Saponary, *a.* and *sb.* *Obs. rare.* [ad. med.L.]

Saponifiable (sæponifaiˈəb'l), *a.*

Saponification (sæˌpɒnifikeiˈʃən). [a. F. *saponification*.]

Saponifier (sæˈpɒnifaiə(r)).

Saponify (sæˈpɒnifai), *v.* [a. F. *saponifier*.]

Saponin (sæˈponin). *Chem.* [a. F. *saponine*.]

Saponite (sæˈpɒnait). *Min.*

Sapodilla (sæpodiˈlă).

Saponule.

Sapor (seiˈpɒ(r)). [a. L. *sapor* taste.]

Saporal.

Saporate.

Saporific (sæporiˈfik), *a.*

Saporosity.

Saporous (sæˈpərəs), *a.*

Saporal (sæˈpərəl), *a.* *rare.*

Saponaria.

Saponarin.

Sapota (sapouˈtă).

Sapotaceous (sæpoteiˈʃəs), *a.* *Bot.*

Sapped (sæpt), *ppl. a.*

Sapper (sæˈpə(r)).

Sapphic (sæˈfik), *a.* and *sb.*

Sapphire (sæˈfaiə(r)). Forms: 2-6 saphir, 3-7 saphir, 4-5 safir(e, (saphire), safer 5.

Sarcodic, a. (De Candolle) [f. Gr. σαρκώδης Sarco- and ἔριμα Derma.] The fleshy layer in some seeds lying between the internal and external integuments.

Sarcode (sɑːkˈəʊd), sb. [f. Gr. σάρξ, σαρκ-.] pertaining to, or the nature of sarcode; protoplasmic.

Sarcoid (sɑːkɔɪd), a. and sb. [f. Gr. σάρξ, σαρκ- + -oid.] A. adj Resembling flesh; flesh-like: applied to sponges, polyps, etc. B. sb. A sponge particle.

Sarcolactic (sɑːkəʊlæktɪk), a. Chem. [f. Sarco- + Lactic.] Sarcolactic acid: an acid, isomeric with lactic acid, obtained from muscular tissue.

Sarcolite (sɑːkəlaɪt), Min. [f. Gr. σάρξ + λίθος stone.] A silicate of aluminium, sodium, and calcium found in flesh-coloured crystals.

Sarcology (sɑːˈkɒlədʒɪ), [f. Sarco- + -logy.] 1. That branch of anatomy which treats of the fleshy parts of the body. 2. The therapeutic method or theory which involves or advocates the internal administration of the extractives of the organs of animals for the purpose of affecting the corresponding organs of the human body.

Sarcoma (sɑːˈkəʊmə), [mod.L, a. Gr. σάρκωμα (Galen), f. σαρκοῦν to become fleshy, f. σάρξ, σαρκ- flesh.] 1. Path. A fleshy excrescence.

Sarcophagal (sɑːˈkɒfəɡəl), a. rare. [f. L. Sarcophag-us + -al.] 1. Flesh-devouring, flesh-consuming.

Sarcophage (sɑːkəfeɪdʒ), [ad. L. Sarcophagus.] 1. A grave, a sepulchre.

Sarcophagous (sɑːˈkɒfəɡəs), a. Zool. [f. mod.L. Sarcophag-us + -ous.] 1. Flesh-devouring, flesh-eating.

Sarcophagus (sɑːˈkɒfəɡəs), Pl. -phagi (-faɪdʒaɪ). Also 8 -fagus. [L., a. Gr. σαρκοφάγος, orig. adj., f. σάρξ, σαρκ- flesh + -φάγος eating.] 1. A kind of stone reputed among the Greeks to have the property of consuming the flesh of dead bodies deposited in it, and consequently used for coffins.

Sarculate, v. rare. [f. L. sarculāt-, f. sarculum hoe.] trans. To hoe.

Sard (sɑːd), sb.[1] Also 4 saarde. [ad. L. sarda, a synonym of sardius: see Sardius.] A variety of cornelian, varying in colour from pale golden yellow to reddish orange.

Sardachate (sɑːdəˈkeɪt), [f. Sard sb.[1] + Achate sb.[1]] A gem composed of layers of sard and agate.

Sardan, a. Obs. rare⁻¹. [ad. L. Sardanius (?with supposed correction of form after Gr. Σαρδόνιος).] = Sardoin.

Sardanapalian (sɑːdənəˈpeɪlɪən), a. [f. Sardanapal(us.] Of or characteristic of Sardanapalus.

Sardel (sɑːdɛl), Obs. Also 6-7 -dell, 8-9 -del. [ad. It. sardella, dim. of sarda = L. sarda.] A fish, Clupea sardina.

Sardine (sɑːdiːn, -dɪn), sb.[1] Forms: 5-6 sardyn, 5 sardeyn, 6 8 sardin (6 surdone), 7 sardina (-inas), 7-8 sardina (7 pl. sirdena's, -dinnasen), 7-8 sardine (7 pl. sirdena's), 9 sardine, sardina.

Sardine, sb.[2] [ad. L. Sardius, a. Gr. σάρδινος, σάρδιον, a precious stone mentioned by ancient writers.]

Sardius (sɑːdɪəs), Also 4, 6 sardis, 5-6 sardeos, -dos (-dus ; also 7 in anglicized form 6 sardye, 7 sardie.) [L. sardius (Vulg.), ad. Gr. σάρδιος, a precious stone mentioned by ancient writers.]

Sardin, sb. Obs. Forms: 3-5 sardine, 5 -dyne, 7 sardoine. [a. OF. sardine.]

Sardoin (sɑːdɔɪn), sb. Obs. rare⁻¹. [ad. L. Sardonius.] Epithet of the Sardonian herb.

Sardin, sb. Obs. rare⁻¹. [? influenced in form by prec.] Epithet of the Sardonian herb.

Sardonic (sɑːˈdɒnɪk), a. and sb. [ad. F. sardonique (16th c.), a. L. sardonicus, an alteration (by substitution of suffix -ic) of sardonius: see Sardonian.]

Sardonical (sɑːˈdɒnɪkəl), a. In a sardonic manner.

Sardonically (sɑːˈdɒnɪkəlɪ), adv. In a sardonic manner.

Sardonyx (sɑːdənɪks), [f. Sardoine + -onyx.] A variety of onyx or stratified chalcedony having white layers of sard or more strata of sard.

Sarge, variant of Cirge.

Sargent, obs. form of Sergeant.

Sargo (sɑːgəʊ), [Sp. sargo = L. sargus : see Sargus.] A fish, one of the family Sparidae.

Sargus (sɑːgəs), [L. — Gr. σάργος.] A fish of the genus Sargus, the type of the family Sparidae.

Sari, Sarie: see Saree, Serry v.

Sarif, obs. form of Sheriff.

Sark (sɑːk), sb. and north. Also 4-5 serk (6 seyrk), syrk, 5-6 serke, 4-7 sarke, 7 syrio, saric (7 sarc, 9 local), 9 serk, sark. [OE. serc masc. (also in extended form serce, weak fem.) = ON.]

Sarking (sɑːkɪŋ), vbl. sb. Sc. Also attrib. 1. sa-sking-board, fell, -roof.

Sarkinite (sɑːkɪnaɪt), Min. [Named (Sarkinit) in 1885 by A. Sjögren, f. Gr. σαρκινος fleshy, in allusion to its flesh-red colour and greasy lustre + -ite.] Arsenate of manganese, of flesh-red or rose-red colour.

Sarkless (sɑːkles), a. Sc. and north. [f. Sark sb. + -less.] Without a sark. Also transf.

Sarling (sɑːlɪŋ), Obs. Also sarlik, sarlyk. [Calmuck sarlik, cited by Gmelin in Novi Comm. Acad. Sci. Petrop. (1760) V. 342.] = Yak.

Sarmatian (sɑːˈmeɪʃɪən), a. and sb. [f. L. Sarmatia the land of the Sarmatae (Gr. Σαρμάται) + -an.] A. adj. Of or belonging to Sarmatia, a region anciently known as Sarmatia, now occupied approximately by the Russians and Poles. B. sb. = Sarmatic b.

Sarmatic (sɑːˈmætɪk), a. [ad. L. Sarmaticus, f. Gr. Σαρματικός.] Of or relating to Sarmatia or the Sarmatae.

Sarment (sɑːmənt), Bot. [ad. L. sarmentum.] Cf. OF. sarmentace. (See quot. 1863.)

Sarmentose (sɑːmɛnˈtəʊs), a. Bot. [ad. L. sarmentōs-us, f. sarmentum : see Sarment and -ose.] Cf. OF. sarmenteux.

Sarmentous (sɑːˈmɛntəs), a. [ad. L. sarmentōs-us: see Sarment and -ous.]

Sarmon, -oun, obs. forms of Sermon.

Sarn, Sarne, dial. forms of Soreness.

Sarole-man, sarole. (See quot. Cf. Sarosel.)

Sarong (sɑːˈrɒŋ), [Malay sārung, prob. from some mod. form of Skr. śāraṅga variegated.] 1. (See quot. 1895.)

Sarot, var. Sarrow.

Sarpe, obs. form of Sherpa.

Sarpler (sɑːplə(r)), [a. AF. sarpler(e), var. of sarplier(e), sarpliere: see Sarplar.]

Sarplar (sɑːplə(r)), Obs. exc. Hist. Forms: 4-5 sarpillere, sarpliere, 5-7 sarpler(e, 5 serpler, 6 sarpeler, 7 sarpler. [a. AF. sarpler, var. sarplier(e), OF. serpelliere.]

Sarplath (sɑːpləθ), Sc. Obs. Forms: 5-6 sarplaith, sarplath. [var. of prec.]

Sarpo[1], sb. Also 8 sapro, 9 sapo. [Sp. sapo, lit. 'toad'.]

Sarpo[2], sb. Obs. [f. Surplice.]

Sarpe-cloth, Obs. Also 6 serpe-cloth. [Shortened f. Sarpler + Cloth. Cf. Sc. forms sarplaith, sarplath.]

Sarra, obs. form of Sahara.

Sarrazin, Sarracin, obs. forms of Saracen.

Sarray (sɑːreɪ), Obs. rare. [Littel suggests that the word is a derivative (with suffix -aria) of OF. sarré, var. of serré; cf. Serry v.]

Sarrasin, var. Saracen (sb.) and a.

Sarray, v. Obs. [f. Ar-, As- + Ray v.] trans. To array, set in order.

Sarrasin, Sarre, obs. ff. SARACEN, SORE.
Sarreliche, -ly, var. ff. SARRALY adv. Obs.
Sarreverence: see SIR-REVERENCE.
Sarrie, Sarrilich: see SARRALY, SARRALY.

† Sarrition. Obs. [f. L. sarrītiōn-em, n. of action f. sarrīre to hoe, weed.] The action of hoeing or stirring the soil.

Sarrusophone (sărŭ·sŏfəun). [f. Sarrus + -PHONE.] A brass instrument of the oboe class, played with a double reed. Hence **Sarrusopho·nist**, a performer on the sarrusophone.

Sarry, obs. variant of SAVOURY a.

Sarsa (să·rsă). Also sarsa. [Short for next.]
= SARSAPARILLA 1. Also attrib.

Sarsaparilla (să"rsăpĕ·rĭlă). Forms: a. 6-8 sarsa parilla, (6-parilla), 7-8 sarsaparilla, 9-7 sarcaparilla, 6-parilla, -perilla, sarsagarilla, 7-perilla,8-parill, 7-sarsaparilla; β. 6-7 salsaperilla, 6-8 -parilla, 6-parigile, -partilla, 7-parilla, salooperilla, 9 salsaparilla; 7 3 sasaparilla. a. Sp. sarzaparilla, f. zarza (? a Basque sartzi 'bramble') + parilla, dim. of parra vine, the sarsaparilla being a climbing plant.

Sarse see SAUCE, SEARCE.

Sarsen (să·rsĕn). Also sarsden, -don, sarsen. [app. a corruption of SARACEN.] One of the numerous large boulders or blocks of sandstone found scattered on the surface of the chalk downs.

Sarsenet, sarcenet (să·rsĕnĕt). Forms: 5 sarsinett, -ynett, sarsanette, 6 sarsaynet, sarsenet(e, (sarsenet, sarsynet, sarsenete), sersenett, sarsnet(t, sarcenet(e), 6-9 sarsenet, &c. A. sb.² sarsinet (1373 in Arch. Acts. 397/16, Publ. Rec. Office: see N & Q. 8th Ser. I. 129), prob. a dim. of sarzin SARACEN (see 4?), suggested by OF. drap sarrasinoit, med.L. pannus sarracenicus, lit. 'Saracen cloth'.

A. A very fine and soft silk material made both plain and twilled, in various colours, now used chiefly for linings; a dress made of this.

† b. With following adj. (after Fr. use.)

Sartorial (sărtō·rĭăl), a. [f. L. sartor, -oris, a tailor or his art; characteristic of a tailor.

Sartorian (sărtō·rĭăn), a. Obs. [f. L sartor, a tailor + -AN.] Of or belonging to a tailor or his art.

Sartorite (să·rtŏrəit), a. Min. [Named by J. D. Dana in 1868 after Sartorius von Waltershausen, f. his name, + -ITE²] Sulph-arsenide of lead, found in dark, lead-grey, orthorhombic crystals.

† Sartorius. Obs. rare⁻¹. [mod.L. sartorius (musculus): see SARTORIAL a.

So called as being concerned in producing the cross-legged position in which a tailor sits at work.] A long narrow muscle which crosses the thigh obliquely from within.

† adj.: fg. Resembling sarsenet in softness. (Said of speech, manners, etc.) Obs.

† Sartry. Obs. rare⁻¹. [a. OF. sartrie, sartre: f. L. sartor: -ENY.] A tailor's workshop.

† Sartrin. Obs. rare⁻¹. [a. OF. *sartrin (recorded as sartraim), ad. med.L. sartrinus tailor's shop, related to SARTOR.] A tailor's shop.

† Sarum. Med.L. Sarum (indeclinable), app. evolved from a misunderstanding of the abbreviation Sar for Saresberie. The ecclesiastical name of Salisbury, used attrib. in

Sarus (sĕ·rŭs). Also sarrus. [Hindi sāras.] The Indian crane Grus antigone.

Sa, ss (să să), int. Obs. See also SESSA. The Fr. exclamation ça, çà, redupl. of çà [lit. here, hither], 'interjection familiere pour exciter, encourager' (Littré). Formerly used between persons delivering a thrust. Also used as a nickname for a fencing-master.

Sartage (să·rtĕdʒ), sb. a. OF. sartage, f. sartir to clear ground, f. sart: see prec.]

Sartle (sartl): see SAUCE, SEIRE.

Saso, obs. variant of SAUCE, SEIRE.

Saser, obs. form of SAUCER.

Sash (săʃ), sb.² Forms: 7 shash, 7 shase, 8 -nash, 7- sash. (Originally shash, a. Arab. shash muslin, turban-'sash') Obs.

† 1. A band of a fine material worn twisted round the head as a turban by Orientals. Obs.

2. A silken or other material worn wound about the waist or over one shoulder.

† b. fut for : One who wears a 'sash'. Obs.

2. A scarf, often with fringe at each end, worn by men, either over one shoulder or round the waist. esp. Mil. (see quot. 1876). Also, a similar article worn round the waist by women and children.

Sash (săʃ), sb.² Also 7 shash, shas.
1. A frame, usually of wood, enclosed and fitted with one or more panes of glass forming a window or part of a window : esp. a sliding frame or each of the two sliding frames of a SASH-WINDOW. Also (now only U.S.) applied to a casement.

In early use denoting a glazed frame of wood as distinguished from a leaded window, but now usually applied to a sliding frame in contradistinction to a casement.

b. attrib. and Comb., as sash ribbon ; sash-capped oil ; sashway, outer sash.

Sashoon. Obs. exc. U.S. Also 7 sashune, shashune, shasoon. [Comps a. F. chausson, stocking, f. chausse: see SASH.] A stuffed leather part formerly worn inside the leg of a boot; also, see quot. 1875.

Sash-window. [f. SASH sb.²] A window consisting of a SASH or glazed wooden frame; esp. one having a sash or a pair of sashes made to slide up and down, as distinguished from a casement.

Hence **Sash-windowed** ppl. a., furnished with sash-windows; **Sash-windowing** vbl. sb. (nonce-wd.), the action of furnishing with sash-windows.

Sashy, sas'shay (să·ʃe), v. U.S. vulgar. [Corruption of CHASSÉ v.] intr. To 'chassé' across; hence, to move to and fro, 'dance' round or around.

Sasin (să·sĭn). Also sassin. [Nepalese.] The common Indian antelope, Antilope bezoartica or cervicapra.

Sasine (sĕ·sĭn). Sc. Law. [Sc. var. of obsolete SEISIN.] after Law Latin sasina. The act of giving possession of feudal property. Also, colloquially, the instrument by which the fact of possession of feudal property is proved ('Infeft').

Sassafras (să·săfrăs). Forms: 6 sassafras, sassafras, saxa-, saxfra-; 7-8 sassafras, 8-9 sassafras. [a. Sp. sassafras (F. sassafras, Pg. saxafras), of unknown origin. An N.O. Lauri-nea), also called Sassafras Laurel and Ague-tree, with green aromatic flowers and deciduous three-lobed leaves, native in North America, where it is said to have been discovered by the Spaniards in 1528.

Sassanian (săsē·nĭăn), sb. and a. Also -ide. [ad. med.L. Sassanidæ pl., f. Sassan, Sassan : see prec + -IDE.] A. A descendant of Sassan (see quot.), a member of the dynasty which ruled ancient Persia from the early part of the 3rd century A.D. to the Arab conquest in the 7th.

Satan (sĕ·tăn). Forms: 1-3 satan, 4-7 sathan, 4-9 satan. [Late L. Satan, indeclinable (Gr. Σατᾶν (late Gr. Σατανᾶς : Heb. śāṭān adversary, one who plots against.

Satanic (sătæ·nĭk), a. [f. SATAN + -IC.] 1. Of or belonging to Satan; characteristic of, befitting Satan; infernal.

Satanism. [f. SATAN + -ISM.] 1. A satanic or diabolical disposition, conduct, spirit, or contrivance.

SATCHEL.

Satchel (sæˈtʃel), *sb.* 1 (coachael), sachel, 5-7 sachal, 6-7 sachelle, seechell, 5-7 sachell, 6 sechell, sachell, 5 satchell, 5-7 satchel. [a. OF. *sachel* ː·L. *saccellus*, dim. of *saccus* SACK 2 b.]

1. A small bag; *esp.* a bag for carrying school-books, with or without a strap to hang over the shoulders.

Satchel (sæˈtʃel), *sb.* 2 *rare*. [f. prec.] *trans.* To make a 'bag' (of game). b. To harbour (something) on one, as in a satchel.

Satcheled (sæˈtʃeld), *a.* [f. SATCHEL *sb.* + -ED 2.] Having or carrying a satchel.

Sate (seɪt), *v.* 1 Also 7 satt. [App. a pseudo-etymological alteration of SADE *v.*, after L *sat*, satis enough: cf. SATIATE *v.*]

1. *trans.* To fill or satisfy to the full (with food); to indulge or gratify to the full by the satisfaction of any appetite or desire.

SATIABLE.

Satiable (seɪˈʃiəb'l), *a.* Chiefly *poet.* [f. SATE *v.* + -ABLE.] That may be satiated.

Satiate (seɪˈʃieɪt), *ppl. a.* [L. *satiātus*, pa. pple. of *satiāre*: see SATIATE *v.*] Satiated.

Satelite: obs. form of SATELLITE.

Satellite (sæˈtelaɪt), *sb.* Also 6, 7-9 pl. -s, satellitian, satellitium.

Satellitian (sætelaɪˈtiːən), *a.* [f. prec.] Belonging to satellites.

Satellitic (sætelaɪˈtɪk), *a.* [f. SATELLITE + -IC.]

Satellitious (sætelaɪˈtɪʃəs), *a.* *Obs.* [L. *satellitius*.] Consisting of, having the character of, satellites.

Satellitium (sætelaɪˈtɪəm), *Astrol. Obs.* [L. = body-guard, retinue.] A retinue of companions.

Satyr ... The night before Saturday.

SATIATE.

Satiate (seɪˈʃieɪt), *v.* Forms: 5-6 saciat(e, -ate, socyat(e, -ate. [f. L. *satiāt-*, ppl. stem of *satiāre* to satisfy.]

1. *trans.* To fill, satisfy (with food). Hence *gen.*, to gratify to the full (a person or his desires), to satisfy the cravings of.

2 To gratify beyond one's natural desire; to weary or disgust by repletion; to glut, cloy, surfeit.

Satiation (seɪʃiˈeɪʃən). [ad. L *satiātiōn-em*, n. of action f. *satiāre* to SATIATE.] The action of satiating or fact of being satiated.

SATIN.

Satin (sæˈtin), *sb.* A silk fabric with a glossy surface on one side, produced by a method of weaving by which the threads of the warp are caught and looped by the weft only at certain intervals. [a. F. *satin* (14th c.).]

SATIRE.

Satine (sæˈtiːn). [Fr. (*bois*) *satiné* (Littré, *Hist. Pl.* (1869))] A kind of satin wood.

Satined (sæˈtind), *ppl. a.* [f. SATIN *sb.* + -ED 2, after L *satiné*.] Having a satin-like surface.

Satinet (sæˈtinɛt). Also satinette.

Sating ... form of SATIN.

Satire (sæˈtaɪə(r)), *sb.* Also 6-7 satyre, 7 satyr, 8 satire, -ir. [a. F. *satire* (14th c.), or ad. L. *satira*, *satura*.]

I. 1. A poem, or in modern use sometimes a prose composition, in which prevailing vices or follies are held up to ridicule.

Satiric (sæˈtɪrɪk), *a. Obs. rare.* [f. L. *satiricus*.] Satirical.

Satirical (səˈtɪrɪkəl), *a.* Forms: 6 satyrical, 6-8 satirical.

Satirically (səˈtɪrɪkəli), *adv.* In a satirical manner; by derisive comment.

SATIRIZER.

Satirist (sæˈtɪrɪst), *sb.* [f. SATIRE + -IST.] A writer of satires; a satirist.

Satirize (sæˈtɪraɪz), *v.* Also 7 satyrize, 7-8 satyrise, 8-9 satirise. [ad. F. *satiriser*.] *trans.* To assail with satire; to censure or describe or ridicule in a satire.

Satirizer (sæˈtɪraɪzə(r)). [f. SATIRIZE *v.* + -ER 1.] One who satirizes.

Sa·tirising, ppl. a. [f. SATIRIZE v. + -ING 2.]
That satirizes.

Satirus, satiry var. SATYR.

Satisization (sætisdi·zən). Civil Law. ? Obs. [f. L. satisdatio-n a giving of bail or security, n. of action f. satisdare to give bail, f. satis enough + dare to give. Cf. OF. satisdacion, -cion, -tion, 13th c. in Godefr.] Giving security.

Satisdiction, nonce-wd. [f. L. satis enough + diction-em saying (see DICTION), after satisfaction.] Saying enough.

Satisfaction (sætisfæ·kʃən). Forms: 4–8 satis-, 4–6 satys- 4 -facioun, 4–7 -facioun, 4–5 -fac(c)ioun, -facio(u)n, -facion, -facioune, (-facoun), 5–7 -faction, 6 -faceyon, -factyon; 5–7 satisfaction (13th c. satisfaccion, 13th c. satisfacion, facion) = Pr. satisfaccio, Sp. satisfaccion, Pg. satisfaçao, It. satisfazione, sodisfazione, soddisfazione, n. of action f. satisfacere to SATISFY.] The action of satisfying; the state or fact of being satisfied.

I. With reference to obligations.

1. The payment in full of a debt, or the fulfilment of an obligation or claim; the atoning for (rarely † of) an injury, offence, or fault by reparation, compensation, or the endurance of punishment. Also, *quasi-concr.*, the pecuniary or other gift or penalty, or the act, by which a debt or obligation is discharged or an offence atoned for. Phrases, *to make* (or † *do*) *satisfaction*; *in satisfaction* (*of*). Now chiefly in *Law*.

2. *Eccl.* (The earliest recorded use in Eng.) The performance by a penitent of the penal and meritorious acts enjoined by his confessor as payment of the temporal punishment due to his sin: the last of the constituent parts of the sacrament of penance. Cf. DEEDDOTE. (Phrases as in 1.)

3. *Theol.* The atonement made by Christ for sin, according to the view that His sufferings and merits are accepted by the Divine justice as an equivalent for the penalty due for the sins of the world. So *doctrine of satisfaction*. Occas. said of Christ himself as the victim by whose sacrifice the satisfaction was made.

4. The opportunity of satisfying one's honour by a duel; the acceptance of a challenge to a duel from the person who deems himself insulted or injured. Chiefly in phrases, *to give, demand satisfaction*.

b. In particularized use: An act of compensation or amends; an amount paid in compensation; a penalty. Now rare.

II. With reference to desires or feelings.

5. The action of gratifying (an appetite or desire) to the full, or of contenting (a person) by the complete fulfilment of a desire or supply of a want; the fact of having been gratified to the full or of having one's desire fulfilled. Phrases, *to the satisfaction of* ; *to give satisfaction*.

b. *To give oneself satisfaction* : to be assured of an illusion. Obs.

II. With reference to desires or feelings.

c. *Law. To enter* (*up*) *satisfaction* : to place on the record of a court a statement that the payment ordered by it has been duly made. So *entry of satisfaction*.

Satisfactional, a. + -NESS.] The state or character of being satisfactional.

Satisfactoriness (sætisfæ·ktərinəs). [f. SATISFACTORY a. + -NESS.] The state or character of being satisfactory.

Satisfactorious, a. *Obs. rare* -1 . [med.L. satisfactori-us, f. L. satisfactor-ius to SATISFY. Cf. satisfactory.] Satisfactory.

Satisfactoriously, adv. [f. prec. + -LY 2 .] Making satisfaction. Hence **Satisfacto·riously,** adv., satisfactorily.

Satisfactory (sætisfæ·ktəri), a. [ad. F. satisfactoire (14th c. in Hatz.-Darm.), ad. med.L. satisfactori-us, f. L. satisfactor-. Cf. satisfactorius to SATISFY. Cf. Sp., Pg. satisfactorio, It. satisfactorio.] **A** *adj.*

Satisfier (sæ·tisfəiˀəɹ). [f. SATISFY + -ER 1 .]

Satisfy (sæ·tisfəi), v. Forms: 5–6 satisfye, -fie, (6 -fey, -fay), 6– satisfy. [a. OF. satisfier, f. L. satisfacere to satisfy, f. satis enough + facere to make, do. Cf. Sp., Pg. satisfacer, It. satisfare, sodisfare.]

I. *trans.* To pay off or discharge fully; to liquidate (a debt); to fulfil completely (an obligation), comply with (a demand). Now somewhat rare.

2. To make amends or reparation for; to expiate.

Satrap (sæ·træp, sei·træp). Forms: 4–5 sa-trape, 4–5 -trap, (4 -trappe). [ad. L. satrapa, satrapes, a. Gr. σατράπης, ad. OPers. *khshathrapāvan* protector of the country (= Skr. *kshatra-pā*).]

1. The governor of a province in the ancient Persian monarchy. **2.** *transf.* A subordinate ruler; often suggesting an imputation of tyranny or ostentatious splendour.

Satrapal (sætrəpəl, sei-), a. [f. SATRAP + -AL.] Of or pertaining to a satrap.

Satrapate (sei·træpeit, sæ-), sb. [f. SATRAP + -ATE 1 .]

Satrapess. A female satrap.

Satrapian, a. *Obs. rare.* Of or pertaining to a satrap; satrapal.

Satrapic, a. [ad. Gr. σατραπικός, f. σατράπης.] Of or pertaining to a satrap.

Satrapical, a.

Satrapy (sæ·træpi, sei-). Forms: 4–5 sa-trapie, (6 satrapie). [ad. L. satrapīa, a. Gr. σατραπεία, f. σατράπης SATRAP.] A province ruled over by a satrap.

Sattar, Sattee, obs. ff. SATIN, SETTER (ship).

Satte, obs. form of SATURDAY.

Satti, Sattie, var. SUTTEE.

Satting, obs. f. SETTING.

Sattle, obs. form of SETTLE.

Satty, obs. f. SETTLE (ship).

Sature, obs. form of SATYR.

Saturable (sæ·tiurəb'l), a. [f. SATURATE + -ABLE.] Capable of being saturated.

Saturant (sæ·tiurănt), a. and sb. [ad. L. *saturant-em*, pr. pple. of *saturāre* to SATURATE.] **A** *adj.* Saturating; impregnating to the full. **B** *sb.* = ABSORBENT sb. 1.

Saturate (sæ·tiureit), v. [ad. L. *saturāt-*, ppl. stem of *saturāre* to fill, satisfy, saturate, f. *satur* full. Cf. F. *saturer*.]

1. To satisfy, satiate. *Obs.* **2.** To impregnate, soak thoroughly, imbue with.

SATURATED ... **SATURATE** ... **Saturating** ... **Saturation**

Saturday ... **Sature** ... **Saturity** ... **Saturn** ... **Saturnal** ... **Saturnalia** ... **Saturnally** ... **Saturnian** ... **Saturnine**

Saturninely ... **Saturnity** ... **Saturnious** ... **Saturnism** ... **Saturnist** ... **Saturnize** ... **Saturnly** ... **Saturnulike** ... **Satyr** ... **Satyra** ... **Satyras** ... **Satyress** ... **Satyriasis** ... **Satyric** ... **Satyrical** ... **Satyrion**

Satyrisk ... **Satyrize** ... **Sauba** ... **Sauce**

Top row page headers:

SAUCE-ALONE.	129	SAUCERY.	SAUCIATE.	130	SAUFEY.

Sauce-alone ... **Saucepan** ... **Sauced** ... **Saucedness** ... **Sauceless** ... **Saucely** ...

Saucer ... **Saucer-eyed** ... **Saucerful** ... **Sauceless** ... **Saucery** ...

Sauciate ... **Saucisse** ... **Sauciate** ... **Saucily** ... **Sauciness** ... **Saucing** ... **Saucisse** ...

Saucy ... **Sauder** ... **Saue** ... **Sauerkraut, sourcrout** ...

Bottom row page headers:

SAUGER.	131	SAULIE.	SAULT.	132	SAUNTERING.

Sauger ... **Saught** ... **Saughen, sauchen** ... **Saught** ... **Saughtel** ...

Saulie ... **Saulm, Saulmon** ... **Sault** ... **Saulte** ... **Saulie** ... **Saul-tree** ...

Sault ... **Saum, Saumon** ... **Saumur** ... **Saunce** ... **Sauncing bell** ...

Saunter ... **Saunder** ... **Saunders blue** ... **Saunter** ... **Sauntering** ...

| SAUNTERING. | 133 | SAUSAGE. | SAUSAGE. | 134 | SAVAGE. |

Sauntering ... **Saunter** ... **Saur** ... **Saurel** ... **Saurian** ... **Sauriostoma** ... **Saurocephalus** ... **Saurio-coprolite** ... **Saurian** ... **Sauroid** ... **Saurognathae** ... **Saurognathous** ... **Saurography** ... **Sauropsida** ... **Sauropod** ... **Sauropoda** ... **Saurops** ... **Saurornis** ... **Saury** ... **Sausage** ...

Sausage ... **Sauce** ... **Sauté** ... **Sauter** ... **Sauterel** ... **Sauterne** ... **Saussurite** ... **Savable** ...

| SAVAGE. | 135 | SAVAGE. | SAVAGED. | 136 | SAVE. |

Savage ... **Savaged** ... **Savagedom** ... **Savagely** ... **Savageness** ... **Savagery** ... **Savagess** ... **Savagine** ... **Savagious** ... **Savagism** ... **Savanna** ... **Savant** ... **Savate** ... **Savation** ... **Save** ...

Save (sēⁱv), *v.* Forms: α. 3–5 (6 *Sc.*) **salve**; *Sc.* 5–6 **sa(u)lf(f**, 6 **salfe, salffe**. β. 3–5 **sauve**; also (chiefly *north.* and *Sc.*) 3–6 **sauf(e**, 4–5 **sawf(e, sawff**, 4–6 **sauff**. γ. 4 *Kent.* **sove** (**sovi, sovy**). δ. 3– **save**; also (chiefly *north.* and *Sc.*) 4–6 **saw(e**, 4–5 **saf(e**, 4–6 **saff(e**; *Sc.* 5–6 **saif(f**, (6 **saaf**). [a. OF. *salver, sauver* (= Pr., Sp., Pg. *salvar*, It. *salvare*):—late L. *salvāre* to save, f. L. *salv-us* SAFE.]

I. To rescue or protect.

1. *trans.* To deliver or rescue from peril or hurt; to make safe, put in safety. Const. *from*, †*out of*.

a. a living being.

c 1250 *Kent. Serm.* in *O. E. Misc.* 32 Lord saue us for we perisset. 13.. *Guy Warw.* 7226 God..þat..heldest Daniel fram þe lyoun, Saue me fram þis foule dragoun. c 1375 *Sc. Leg. Saints* xxxiii. (*George*) 116 To saf his douchtir fra þat wrak. c 1470 *Gol. & Gaw.* 1009 Thus may thow saif me fra syte. a 1533 LD. BERNERS *Huon* xc. 284 He that alwayes hath saued me out of all perelles wyll not forsake me at this tyme. a 1578 LINDESAY (Pitscottie) *Chron. Scot.* (S. T. S.) II. 55 Gif ȝe..salve his servandis ffre the daith so far as ȝe may. 1591 SHAKS. *Two Gent.* IV. iv. 3 One that I sau'd from drowning. 1692 R. L'ESTRANGE *Fables* ix. 9 Save a Thiefe from the Gallows, and he'll Cut your Throat. 1719 DE FOE *Crusoe* I. (Globe) 63 Did not you come Eleven of you into the Boat, where are the Ten? Why were not they sav'd and you lost? 1848 THACKERAY *Van. Fair* xxxii, She fell on her knees, and thanked the Power which had saved her husband. 1852 MRS. STOWE *Uncle Tom's C.* vii, 'O Mr. Symmes!—save me—do save me—do hide me!' said Eliza.

b. one's life (similarly, one's body, carcass, head, neck, etc.). *To save one's skin*, to escape unhurt. *To save one's bacon*: see BACON 5 a.

1297 R. GLOUC. (Rolls) 9231 So þat to saui is lif þe castel vp hii ȝolde. 13.. *K. Alis.* 3811 He lefte his pray, and fleygh to hors, For to save his owne cors. 1470 HENRY *Wallace* II. 271 His fostyr modyr..Did mylk to warme, his liff giff scho mycht saiff. a 1533 LD. BERNERS *Huon* lxvii. 230 He besought our lorde god to saue his body fro mysfortune. c 1570 W. WAGER *The longer thou livest* 477 (Brandl), Neither mockes nor gaudes shall your skinne saue. 1611 SHAKS. *Cymb.* V. iii. 67 To day, how many would haue giuen their Honours To haue sau'd their Carkasses? 1685 [see NECK *sb.*¹ 3 d]. 1803 *Med. Jrnl.* IX. 458 A great many lives were saved by the salutary practice of inoculation. 1855 MACAULAY *Hist. Eng.* xxi. IV. 544 To have done all in his power to save both the head of Stafford and the head of Russell. 1896 A. E. HOUSMAN *Shropshire Lad* xlvii, See my neck and save your own.

c. a people, state, city.

c 1375 *Sc. Leg. Saints* xxxiii. (*George*) 106 His douchtir.. to þe dragone suld be gyffine, to sauff þe ton. 1474 CAXTON *Chesse* II. v. (1883) 59 He shuld empioye alle his entente to saue the comyn wele. 1533 BELLENDEN *Livy* I. v. (S. T. S.) I. 34 My citee was sauffit be þi helpe. 1607 SHAKS. *Cor.* V. iii. 133 If it were so, that our request did tend To saue the Romanes, thereby to destroy The Volces whom you serue. 1728 POPE *Dunc.* I. 197 Could Troy be sav'd by any single hand. 1852 TENNYSON *Ode on Wellington* 200 Yea, let all good things await Him who cares not to be great, But as he saves or serves the state. 1894 J. T. FOWLER *Adamnan* Introd. p. xxi, The Bards were saved, but reformed.

d. To rescue (property) from shipwreck, fire, etc.

1582 N. LICHEFIELD tr. *Castanheda's Conq. E. Ind.* I. xli. 95 There was kindled in the same [ship] a great fire, so that nothing was saued, but onely the men. 1591 SHAKS. *Two Gent.* I. i. 156 Go, go, be gone, to saue your Ship from wrack. 1615 R. COCKS *Diary* (Hakl. Soc.) I. 73 The fyre was so vehement that littell or nothing was saved. 1787 PARK *Mar. Insurances* 141 Whereas the circumstance of the lighters being saved, and the ship lost, was accidental. 1878 MRS. HUNGERFORD *Molly Bawn* xxxviii, I saved them [*sc.* diamonds] from the fire.., and have had them re-set.

e. *absol.*

1560 BIBLE (Geneva) *Isa.* lix. 1 The Lords hand is not shortened, that it can not saue. 1593 SHAKS. *Rich. II*, II. ii. 80 Your husband he is gone to saue farre off, Whilst others come to make him loose at home. 1732 POPE *Ess. Man* II. 201 The same ambition can destroy or save. 1781 COWPER *Charity* 226 Oh, 'tis a godlike privilege to save! 1860 W. WHITING *Hymn*, Eternal Father, strong to save.

2. *Theol.* To deliver (a person, the soul) from sin and its consequences; to admit to eternal bliss. [Gr. σῴζειν, L. (Vulg.) *salvum facere, salvare, salvificare*.]

a 1225 *Leg. Kath.* 1025 Monnes unmihte; þet he neodeles nom upon him seoluen, us for to saluin. 1340 *Ayenb.* 98 Godes zone þet com to þe wordle to zeche an to souy þet þet wes uorlore. 1362 LANGL. *P. Pl.* A. I. 82 Tech me.. Hou I may saue my soule. 1382 WYCLIF *Mark* xvi. 16 He that schal bileue, and schal be baptisid, schal be sauyd [*v.r.* saaf]; sothli he that schal bileue not, schal be dampned. [So 1535 COVERDALE, 1611.] — *James* i. 21 In myldenesse receyue ȝe the word insent, that mai saue ȝoure soules. [So in later versions.] c 1449 PECOCK *Repr.* II. xviii. 261 If it be seid..'The crosse of Crist saued the world..', the dewe vndirstonding ther of is this: 'Crist bi his crosse..saued the world'. a 1500–34 *Coventry Corpus Chr. Plays, Shearmen* 546 A seyd there schuld a babe be borne,..To sawe mankynd that wasse for-lorne. 1526 *Pilgr. Perf.* (W. de W. 1531) 20 b, I am passed my purgatory, and I am saued. 1549 LATIMER *6th Serm. bef. Edw. VI* (Arb.) 166 We can not be saued wythout fayeth, and fayth commeth by hearynge of the worde. 1601 SHAKS. *Twel. N.* III. ii. 75 For there is no christian that meanes to be saued by beleeuing rightly, can euer beleeue such impossible passages of grossenesse. 1666 BUNYAN *Grace Abound.* § 202, I was again much under this Question, Whether the Blood of Christ was sufficient to save my Soul? 1786 BURNS *For G. H. Esq.* 4 But with such as he, where'er he be, May I be sav'd or d——'d. c 1830 MOORE *Epitaph on Tuft Hunter* 20 He'd rather be Genteelly damn'd beside a Duke Than sav'd in vulgar company. 1840 CARLYLE *Heroes* iv, Luther learned now that a man was saved not by singing masses, but by the infinite grace of God. 1893 F. THOMPSON *Poems* 61 There is no expeditious road To pack and label men for God, And save them by the barrel-load.

absol. a 1340 HAMPOLE *Psalter* xiii. 1 Þat is, þare is na god þat dampnes or safes. 1858 ARNOT *Laws fr. Heaven* Ser. II. xiii. 101 It is grace accepted that saves.

b. in asseverative phrases, *as I hope to be saved*, †*so God* (or *Christ*) *save me*, etc.

c 1386 CHAUCER *Can. Yeom. Prol. & T.* 808 Ye shul paye fourty pound, so god me saue. c 1450 HOLLAND *Howlat* 120 So me Crist saif. c 1530 LD. BERNERS *Arth. Lyt. Bryt.* 300 As I be saved, ye be ful gentil and noble. 1710 SWIFT *Jrnl. to Stella* 23 Dec., Remember poor Presto, that wants you sadly, as hope saved. 1711 *Ibid.* 30 June. 1749 FIELDING *Tom Jones* VIII. xi, As I hope to be saved, I will never mention a word of it.

c. *transf.* To reclaim from moral laxity, or the like; to be the 'salvation' of.

1894 SIR E. SULLIVAN *Woman* 98 How often you hear it said that marriage has improved a man—that it has saved him!

3. Used in certain formulas of benediction, greeting, etc.; as *God save you!* †Also (in greetings) with omission of the subject.

(*God*) *save the mark*: see MARK *sb.*¹ 18.

c 1330 *Arth. & Merl.* 7034 (Kölbing) Wele yfounden, child Wawayn, Crist saue þi miȝt & þi mayn. c 1386 CHAUCER *Knt.'s T.* 2250 God saue al this faire compaignye. Amen. 1530 PALSGR. 698/1 God save you, whiche sayeng we use when we come firste to ones presence. 1591 SHAKS. *Two Gent.* I. i. 70 Sir Protheus: 'saue you: saw you my Master? 1632 MASSINGER *City Madam* IV. iv, *Luke*. Then, as I said ..you were tickl'd when the beggars cry'd, Heaven save your honour. 1706 FARQUHAR *Recruit. Officer* III. ii, Save ye, save ye, Gentlemen. 1888 LOWELL *Heartsease & Rue* 178, I have seen him some poor ancient thrashing Into something (God save us!) more dry.

b. *esp.* in *God save the king!* and the like.

c 1290 *Beket* 755 in *S. Eng. Leg.* I. 128 Sire king, he seide, god þe loke, and saui þi dignite! 1340–70 *Alex. & Dind.* 811 Þus dindimus þe dere king enditeþ his sonde, & god bysecheþ to saue þe soueraine prinse. 1350–70 in *Eulogium Hist.* (Rolls) III. 87 *Regem* [*Henricum II*] *Theutonica lingua sic affatur*: Godde saue the kyng. [In *Giraldus* (Rolls) VIII. 180 God houlde dhe, cuning.] 1535 COVERDALE 2 *Sam.* xvi. 16 He sayde vnto Absalom: God saue the kynge. 1540 PALSGR. *Acolastus* II. iii. M j b, *Aue rex*, or god saue your royall maiestie. 1558 *Procl.* in Strype *Ann. Ref.* (1709) I. II. App. i. 389 God save the quene. a 1627 SIR J. BEAUMONT *Bosw.-field* (1629) 9 Some with loud shouting, make the valleyes ring. But most with murmur sigh: God saue the King.

†4. To spare instead of killing, allow to live, give (one) his life. Often coupled with *slay*. *Obs.*

a 1300 *Cursor M.* 5549 Þis midwimmen..did noght als þe king þam badd, Bot sauued þai þar childer liues. c 1385 CHAUCER *L. G. W.* 1917 So that the site was al at his wille, To sauyn hem hym leste or ellis spille. 1470 HENRY *Wallace* IV. 256 Wallace commaundede thai suld na wermen saiff. 1474 CAXTON *Chesse* II. iv. (1883) 52 Whan he sauyth the lyf of them that he may slee. 1549 *Compl. Scot.* xii. 100, I ordand ȝou to slay doune al the romans, and nocht to saif ane of them. 1588 LAMBARDE *Eiren.* IV. xvi. 586 To saue or slay the Sparow that he holdeth closed in his hand. 1593 SHAKS. 2 *Hen. VI*, IV. vii. 124 And therefore yet relent, and saue my life. 1642 *Laws of War Army Earl Essex* 20 None shall save a man that hath his offensive Armes in his hands, upon paine of losing his prisoner.

absol. c 1386 CHAUCER *Prol.* 663 For curs wol slee, right as assoillyng sauith. 1390 GOWER *Conf.* III. 207 Where him hapneth the victoire, His lust and al his moste gloire Was forto sle and noght to save.

5. To deliver *from* some evil which is likely to befall one; to protect from something which would be unwelcome or untoward; to ensure (one) immunity from some hurt or annoyance.

a 1300 *Cursor M.* 2985 Fra toche of hir i saued þe, þat þou suld not sin in me. 1362 LANGL. *P. Pl.* A. I. 23 Þat on Clothing is from Chele ow to saue. c 1450 MYRC *Festial* 293 Þonkyng hym þat sauid hym wyth hys blessing from poysynnyng. 1530 PALSGR. 698/1, I save one from daunger, as harnesse doth ones persone, or as medecyne, or preservatyve dothe ones helth, *je contregarde*. a 1533 LD. BERNERS *Huon* lv. 186 The good harneys saued Huon fro all hurtes. a 1586 SIDNEY *Arcadia* II. (Sommer) 103 But Zelmanes comming saued Dorus from further chiding. 1827 O. W. ROBERTS *Voy. Centr. Amer.* 226 He saved me from much interruption and many annoying questions. 1860 TYNDALL *Glac.* I. xvi. 118 A sudden effort was necessary to save me from falling. 1886 C. E. PASCOE *Lond. of To-day* xviii. (ed. 3) 162 This route has the advantage, too, of saving one from the crowd.

b. used in invocation or aspiration: esp. with sarcastic emphasis.

1738 POPE *Univ. Prayer* 33 Save me alike from foolish Pride, Or impious Discontent. 1784 COWPER *Task* I. 499 But save me from the gaiety of those Whose head-aches nail them to a noon-day bed. 1798 CANNING *New Morality* 210 in *Anti-Jacobin* 9 July, Save, save, oh! save me from the candid friend!

c. To be a protection, defence, or means of deliverance to.

1412–20 LYDG. *Troy Bk.* III. 90 And some wil haue also no viser To saue his face, but only a naser. 1470 HENRY *Wallace* II. 71 Couert of treis sawit him full weille. 1543 GRAFTON *Contn. Harding* 489 A goodly glose, by the whiche that place that may defend a thefe, may not saue an innocent. 1771 *Junius Lett.* lxvii. 333 But it shall not save you. The very sunshine you live in is a prelude to your dissolution.

6. *refl.* (in senses 1 and 5). Often = to get away, escape (F. *se sauver*).

a 1225 *Ancr. R.* 98 O none wise ne muwe ȝe betere sauuen ou suluen. c 1320 *Sir Beues* 836 Him com strokes so gret plente þat fain he was to weren is hed And saue him self fro þe ded. c 1450 MYRC *Festial* 133 Wherfor, gentyll knyght, gos hens fast and saue þyselfe. 1593 SHAKS. 3 *Hen. VI*, V. ii. 48 Flye Lords, and saue your selues. a 1715 BURNET *Own Time* (1724) I. 585, I saved my self out of those difficulties by saying to all my friends, that I would not be involved in any such confidence. 1729 W. FUNNELL *Voy.* 144 He and his company got to his boat, and so saved themselves to the ship. 1817 *Ballad of Waterloo* 18 All panic struck, the legions fled, 'Twas *save himself who cou'd*. 1819 SCOTT *Ivanhoe* xl, The only course by which he could save himself from degradation and disgrace.

†b. *refl.* and *intr.* To avoid loss. *Obs.*

a 1548 HALL *Chron.*, *Hen. VI* 139 b, So both parties, rather myndyng to gain or save then to lose, departed for that tyme. *Ibid.* 141 b, Thenglishemen sometyme saved, and sometyme gained, but the moste losse lighted on the Frenchemen. 1696 PHILLIPS (ed. 5) s. v., A Tradesman is said to save himself that neither gets nor loses.

7. †a. To heal, cure, restore to health. *Obs.* b. Later only as a specific use of sense 1: To rescue from a sickness which threatens to prove mortal; = to save the life of.

1362 LANGL. *P. Pl.* A. VIII. 17 Hou heore schabbede schep schal heore wolle saue. 1387 TREVISA *Higden* (Rolls) VI. 367 He was hard i-holde with a strong sikenesse, and myȝte nouȝt be i-heled noþer i-saved wiþ no manere medecyne. 1390 GOWER *Conf.* III. 32 Bot as a man that wolde him save, Whan he is sek, be medicine. a 1400–50 *Alexander* 2558 My-self with a serop sall saue [*Dublin MS.* safe] ȝow belyue. 14.. *Officium Resurrect.* 7 in *Non-Cycle Myst. Plays* 3 Why suffred he so forto dy, Sithe he may all sekenes saue? 1615 R. COCKS *Diary* (Hakl. Soc.) I. 63 Soe our chirurgion was sent for to assist the Duch chirurgion to save the [wounded] man, yf it were possible. 1848 THACKERAY *Van. Fair* xli, Her own little boy was saved, actually saved, by calomel, freely administered, when all the physicians in Paris had given the dear child up.

8. To keep, protect or guard (a thing) from damage, loss, or destruction.

1387 TREVISA *Higden* (Rolls) IV. 429 And so þe strokes were i-lette, and þe walles i-saved. 1387 *Charters*, etc. *Edinb.* (1871) 35 To cast the watir owte and to save the werc fro the watir. c 1450 MYRC *Festial* 39 Hys hall was yche day of the ȝere new strawed..forto saue knyghtys cloþys þat setton on þe flore. 1553 WILSON *Rhet.* (1585) 117 Fond is his purpose, that being in the Raine, casteth his garment in a bush, and standeth naked himself, for sauing the glosse of his gay coate. 1669 STURMY *Mariner's Mag.* V. xii. 63 A Ferril of Brass may be put thereon to save the Head from cleaving. 1672 WISEMAN *Wounds* II. 90 If the Toes with part of the foot was shot off, cut off the lacerated parts smooth, but with care to save as much of the foot with the heel as you can. 1712–14 POPE *Rape Lock* II. 93 To save the powder from too rude a gale. 1735 — *Donne Sat.* ii. 72 His Office keeps your Parchment fates entire, He starves with cold to save them from the fire. 1907 HODGES *Elem. Photogr.* 97 Over-exposed prints may possibly be saved by further diluting the developer.

†b. To guard (property) from loss or from passing into other hands; to keep in safe possession (for oneself or another). *Obs.*

1389 in *Eng. Gilds* (1870) 81 Also, ye skyueyns of ye gylde yat hauen ye catel in hande, scholene fynden borwes to ye alderman, for to sauen ye catel, and for to bringe it forht at ye general morspeche, wyht-outen ani lettyng. 1393 LANGL. *P. Pl.* C. x. 272 When þy lord lokeþ to haue a-louaunce for hus bestes, And of þe monye þow haddist þer-myd hus meoble to saue. 1526 TINDALE 1 *Tim.* vi. 20 O Timothe save that which is geven the to kepe. 1533 BELLENDEN *Livy* I. ii. (S. T. S.) I. 15 The realme of latynis and troianis was sauffit to þis childe Ascanius be prudent tutorie of lavinia his moder.

†c. To have (a person) in safe keeping. *Obs.*

c 1386 CHAUCER *Doctor's T.* 200, I deeme anon this cherl his seruant haue; Thou shalt no lenger in thyn hous hir saue.

†d. To make (a place) secure. *Obs.*

1338 R. BRUNNE *Chron.* (1810) 294 Þe toun he suld so saue, þat he suld not ascape.

e. *To save one's pocket*: to avoid spending one's money.

1883 *Law Times Rep.* XLIX. 9/1 The tenant for life may have indirectly benefited himself or saved his own pocket.

f. *To save one's face*: to avoid being disgraced or humiliated. Similarly, *to save* (another's) *face*.

[Originally used by the English community in China, with reference to the continual devices among the Chinese to avoid incurring or inflicting disgrace. The exact phrase appears not to occur in Chinese, but 'to lose face' (*tiu lien*), and 'for the sake of his face', are common.]

1898 *Westm. Gaz.* 5 Apr. 5/1 Unquestionably the process of saving one's face leads to curious results in other countries than China. 1900 *Daily News* 25 June 4/5 The communiqué in the Russian 'Official Messenger' provides the necessary formula by the adoption of which the Chinese Government can save its face.

9. To keep intact or unhurt, preserve, maintain, safeguard (honour, credit, chastity, and the like).

a 1300 *Cursor M.* 11232 Right sua al plain,..he com and yede, Saufand his moder hir maidenhede. c 1350 *Will. Palerne* 527 My worschipe to saue. 1375 BARBOUR *Bruce* II. 338 Wyrk ȝhe then apon swylk wyss, That ȝour honour be sawyt ay. c 1386 CHAUCER *Sqr.'s T.* 523 Til that myn harte..Graunted hym loue, vpon this condicioun, That euermore myn honour and renoun Were saued. 1390 GOWER *Conf.* I. 19 Good is to save With penance and with abstinence Of chastite the continence. 1588 SHAKS. *L. L. L.* IV. i. 26 Thus will I saue my credit in the shoote. 1617 MORYSON *Itin.* I. 148 Who to save the reputation of the Virgin, confessed that he came to rob the house. 1665 BOYLE *Occas. Refl.* II. xi. (1848) 130 'Twould be much easier for the mistaken Physitian to save his Credit, than for the unprepar'd Sinner to save his Soul. 1733 POPE *Ep. Cobham* 125 Must then at once (the character to save) The plain rough Hero turn a crafty Knave? 1851 LYTTON *Not so Bad* II. i. 29 The loan saved my credit, and made my fortune.

b. To safeguard (a right, possession) *to* a person.

c 1460 FORTESCUE *Abs. & Lim. Mon.* xiv. (1885) 144 Whether the kynge mey gyve such rewarde..off his revenues, savynge to hym selff sufficiant ffor the sustenance off his estate. 1499 *Reg. Privy Seal Scotl.* I. 50/1 A precept of confirmation of the crownarschip of Carrik..Salffand to the kingis hienes service auch and wont. 1544 tr. *Littleton's Tenures* 41 b, Yf a man let lande to another for terme of lyfe sauynge the reuersyon to him. 1571 *Act* 13 *Eliz.* c. 29 § 6 Savinge to all and every person or persons..all such Rightes..wᶜʰ they..had, might or should have had, of, in or to any the Mannors Lordshippes [etc.]. 1642 tr. *Perkins' Prof. Bk.* x. § 648. 279 The Lord doth grant the rent unto a stranger saving unto him his seignory. 1863 H. COX *Instit.* I. v. 23 We find a clause..introduced saving the king's rights.

†c. ? To keep, observe (a duty, rule). *Obs.*

1390 GOWER *Conf.* I. 85 Wherof I can noght bothe save My speche and this obedience. c 1400 *Rule St. Benet* (verse) 538 And all þai aw be day & night To saue þis rewle in all þer myght.

†d. To preserve the credit of (one's word, oath).

c 1425 *Eng. Conq. Irel.* xxix. 72 A man stode þer besyde & herd, & wold, hys thankes, saue [*v.r.* Sawe] þe prophetes sawe. 1595 *2nd Pt. Contention* (1843) 125 He shew your grace the waie to saue your oath.

10. With adj. complement: To keep or preserve *whole, unhurt*, etc.

†*To save harmless*: see HARMLESS *a.* 2.

a 1300 *Cursor M.* 5037 Lauerd..sauue mi childir hale to me. c 1440 *Alphabet of Tales* 223 Ane angell..opynd þe dure and savid þe seale hale at Saynt Remigius sett on itt. 1535 COVERDALE *Ezek.* xviii. 27 When the wycked man turneth awaye from his wickednesse..he shal saue his soule alyue. 1595 SHAKS. *John* II. i. 225 To saue vnscratch'd your Citties threatned cheekes. 1611 BIBLE 2 *Kings* vii. 4 If they saue vs aliue, we shall liue. 1784 COWPER *Task* I. 566 Which, kindled with dry leaves, just saves unquench'd The spark of life. 1859 TENNYSON *Enid* 894 To Save her dear lord whole from any wound.

†11. To store, preserve, keep in sound condition.

1398 TREVISA *Barth. De P. R.* V. xxxvi. (Bodl. MS.), He [the heart] is holowȝ to fong blood, and he is þikke to saue it. 1601 HOLLAND *Pliny* II. 507 After that, it ought to be dried in the Sun, and saued in a brasen box. 1602 CAREW *Cornwall* (1723) 33 They [the Fish] are saued three maner of wayes: by fuming, pressing, or pickelling. 1728 POPE *Dunc.* I. 151 There sav'd by spice, like mummies, many a year, Dry Bodies of Divinity appear.

b. *intr.* To remain in good condition, to last without spoiling, to 'keep'. ? *U.S.*

1891 *Century Dict.*, *Save*..To be capable of preservation: said of fish: as, to *save* well.

12. *trans.* †a. Astr. *To save the appearances, the phenomena* [tr. Gr. σῴζειν τὰ φαινόμενα (e. g. in Proclus *Hypotyp.* v. § 10); cf. It. *salvar le apparenze*, F. *sauver les apparences*]: said of a hypothesis which satisfactorily explains the observed facts. See also SALVE *v.*² 1. *Obs.*

1625, 1643 [see PHENOMENON 1 c]. 1667 MILTON *P. L.* VIII. 82 When they come to model Heav'n And calculate the Starrs, how they will weild The mightie frame, how build, unbuild, contrive To save appeerances.

Hence (? orig. allusively) b. *To save appearances*: to contrive to keep up an appearance of propriety, solvency, or the like. (So in Fr. and It.) Cf. APPEARANCE 12 b.

1711, 1761 [see APPEARANCE 12 b]. 1844 THIRLWALL *Greece* VIII. lxiii. 222 Sparta sent only a handful of men to save appearances. 1876 'OUIDA' *Winter City* viii. 234, I suppose it 'saves society', at least it saves appearances.

13. To prevent the loss of (a game, match, wager, etc.). Also, in Racing slang, to 'hedge' so as to protect (oneself, one's 'book') from loss, or so as to recover (a certain sum) out of one's losses.

1611 SHAKS. *Cymb.* II. iv. 94 The description Of what is in her Chamber, nothing saues The wager you haue laid. 17.. in Lillywhite *Cricket Scores* (1863) I. Pref. 10 If a striker nips a Ball up just before him he may fall before his Wicket, or pop down his Batt before Shee comes to it to Save it. 1837 D. WALKER *Sports & Games* 217 The striker ..must never follow a ball so far that, in case of no runs being obtained, he cannot return to save his wicket. 1862 PYCROFT in *London Soc.* II. 114/1 As to his bowling, it might have saved the game. 1869 'WAT. BRADWOOD' *The O. V. H.* xx, And even his lordship began to grudge that he had not just saved his book upon him [a horse] in consonance with the Major's advice. 1885 *New Bk. Sports* 58 But in the Eton field..even in the sorest straits, by the feet, and by the feet alone, must the goal be saved.

†b. To make (a dangerous voyage) safely. *Obs.*

1698 FRYER *Acc. E. India & P.* 77 This holds with little intermission till..the first Full Moon in August; when our Europe Ships, if they save their Passage about the Cape, venture to make in here.

14. 'To take or embrace opportunely, so as not to lose' (J.); to be in time for, manage to catch.

1732–3 SWIFT *Reas. Rep. Sacram. Test.* Wks. 1751 IX. 245 The same Persons..were..faithful Subjects to Cromwell, yet being wise enough to foresee a Restoration, they seized the Forts and Castles here [in Ireland]..; just saving the Tide, and putting in a Stock of Merit sufficient to preserve [etc.]. 1802 CANNING in G. Rose *Diaries* (1860) I. 456, I have but a moment to save the post. 1833 I. TAYLOR *Fanat.* vi. 203 That they may save the hour of..appointment. 1849 THACKERAY 12 June in *Scribner's Mag.* I. 409/2 The note must go this instant to save the post. 1865 TROLLOPE *Belton Est.* vii. 73 There arises a question whether under such circumstances the train can be saved.

†b. *To save one's distance, time*: to manage to arrive at (a given point or time) after being delayed.

1790 R. CUMBERLAND *Observer* No. 142 § 3 (1791) V. 184 Whether Nicolas saved his distance..we shall not just now enquire. 1806 J. BERESFORD *Miseries Hum. Life* VI. iv, Riding out to dinner, many miles off, on a beast that will not quit his walk, while you know that nothing short of a full gallop will save your time.

II. To reserve, lay aside.

15. To keep for a particular purpose or as likely to prove useful; to set apart, lay by, reserve.

c 1400 *Rule of St. Benet* (verse) 1582 Þat euer-ilkon wil of hir laue þe third part til hir sopper saue. 1592 SHAKS. *Rom. & Jul.* I. v. 9 Good thou, saue mee a piece of Marchpane. 1719 DE FOE *Crusoe* I. (Globe) 136, I saved the Skins of all the Creatures that I kill'd. 1747 MRS. GLASSE *Cookery* (1796) xiv. 210 Take..a bunch of turnips, pare them, save three or four out, put the rest into the water. 1845 *Visit to Bury St. Edmunds* 90, I have one pair [of shoes]; they were almost worn out when father died, and as mother can't buy any more, I save them for Sundays.

16. *spec.* To collect and keep (seed) in stock for sowing.

1657 W. COLES *Adam in Eden* xxiii. 47 The Roots [of Clary]..perish after the Seed-time: it is most usuall to save it; for the Seed seldom riseth of its own shedding. 1763 MILLS *Syst. Pract. Husb.* IV. 128 The best way to save the seeds of this plant, is [etc.]. 1801 *Farmer's Mag.* Jan. 92 It is feared the bulk of the people will not be able to save seed for next crop.

b. To dry (corn, hay, peat) by exposure to the air; to harvest, stack. Cf. *win*.

1719 DE FOE *Crusoe* I. (Globe) 120 When it [the corn] was growing and grown, I have observ'd already, how many Things I wanted, to Fence it, Secure it, Mow or Reap it, Cure and Carry it Home, Thrash, Part it from the Chaff, and Save it. 1764 *Museum Rust.* I. lxxxiii. 361 The farmers pile them up in one of their offices, with an outside facing of bog turf well *saved*. 1824 MISS MITFORD in L'Estrange *Life* (1870) II. 183 The Northumberland people have an idiom of 'saving hay' for 'making hay'. 1892 JANE BARLOW *Irish Idylls* i. 8 A turf-stack..when newly 'saved'..looks like a solidified shadow of the little house.

c. To extract (gold) from quartz.

1877 RAYMOND *Statist. Mines & Mining* 69 The gold is easily saved, being clean, angular, and not very small; hence the proportion saved by the mill-process is notably greater than in any other locality in California.

d. *To save clean in Whaling* (see quot.).

1891 *Century Dict.* s. v., *To save clean*, to save all (the blubber) in cutting in: a whaling-term.

17. To store up or put by (money, goods, etc.) by dint of economy; to reserve instead of spending, consuming, or parting with.

1362 LANGL. *P. Pl.* A. VIII. 27 Treuþe..Bad hem Bugge Boldely what hem best lykede, And seþþen sullen hit a-ȝeyn And saue þe wynnynge. 14.. *How Good Wife taught Dau.* 170 in *Q. Eliz. Acad.* 49 Þei..þat wyll thryue, and þer gode saue. 1600 SHAKS. *A. Y. L.* II. iii. 39, I haue fiue hundred Crownes, The thriftie hire I saued vnder your Father. 1753 JOHNSON *Adventurer* No. 84 ⁋ 14 A nobleman's butler, who has furnished a shop with the money he has saved. 1842 TENNYSON *Dora* 50 But Dora stored what little she could save, And sent it them by stealth. 1856 FROUDE *Hist. Eng.* (1858) II. vi. 95 He was able to save money for his son's education.

b. *absol.*

1595 LODGE *Fig for Momus* H 1 b, Counsell, how to spend, and saue. 1776 ADAM SMITH *W. N.* II. iii. I. 410 Whatever industry might acquire, if parsimony did not save and store up, the capital would never be the greater. 1859 SMILES *Self-help* ix. 234 Add guinea to guinea; scrape and save; and the pile of gold will gradually rise. 1878 JEVONS *Pol. Econ.* ix. 86 It is idle to say that the better-paid working men cannot save.

c. with *up*. Also *absol.*

1834 [see SAVED *ppl. a.* 2]. 1850 SMEDLEY *Frank Fairlegh* iv, A parting gift from my little sister Fanny, who..had saved up her pocket-money during many previous months, in order to provide funds for this munificent present. 1884 BLACKLEY *Thrift & Indep.* 20 To try the system of saving up a little week by week. *Ibid.* 57 If, by an effort, he save up.. £30. *Ibid.* 91, I set myself to save up for my own old age.

18. To avoid spending, giving, or consuming (money, goods, etc.); to keep (a given amount) from being spent or consumed or lost and so retain it in one's possession. Also with indirect obj. (with or without *to*): To enable a person to avoid spending, giving, or losing.

a 1400 *Minor Poems fr. Vernon MS.* 545/345 *Ki sauuer veut soun doner, Cortois seit de soun manger*;..He may saue moneye and gete þat wol be curteys of his mete. 1539 in W. A. J. Archbold *Somerset Rel. Houses* (1892) 73 Ther will be a great soome of money that shalbe salved to the kinges highnes therbye. 1590 SIR J. SMYTH *Disc. Weapons* 6 b, And so consequentlie in their whole Armies to saue the pay of a great sort of Captaines..and other Officers. 1596 SHAKS. 1 *Hen. IV*, III. iii. 48 Thou hast saued me a thousand Markes in Linkes and Torches. *Ibid.* v. i. 99, I..will, to saue the blood on either side, Try fortune with him, in a Single Fight. 1617 MORYSON *Itin.* I. 207 The said Ianizare ..will easily save a man more then his wages. 1661 PEPYS *Diary* 20 Aug., When we came to look for our coach we found it gone, so we were fain to walk home afoot and saved our money. 1693 in C. R. Wilson *Old Fort William* (1906) I. 12 That old Maxim..That a Penny saved is two Pence gott. 1712 SWIFT *Let. Eng. Tongue* Wks. 1755 II. I. 197 You have already saved several millions to the publick. 1801 *Farmer's Mag.* Nov. 406 By carrying this plan into execution, the public..would save not less than four millions *per annum*. 1854 RONALDS & RICHARDSON *Chem. Technol.* (ed. 2) I. 257 With suitable flues, the saving of fuel is much greater when turf and wood are employed than is the case with coal;..⅓rd being saved in the case of wood, and ¼th only in that of coal. 1860 TROLLOPE *Framley P.* xxxii, Mr. Sowerby then got into another cab..Anyone else would have saved his shilling, as Mrs. Harold Smith's house was only just across Oxford Street.

†b. *absol.* Of a commodity: To effect a saving in use, 'to be cheap' (J.).

a 1626 BACON *Compounding of Metals* Baconiana (1679) 94 Brass Ordnance..saveth both in the quantity of the Material, and in the charge and commodity of mounting & carriage.

c. With immaterial obj., e. g. labour, time, distance to be travelled, etc.

1579 W. WILKINSON *Confut. Fam. Love* B ij, Therefore saue labour for making any further reply hereunto, least you doe but lose your trauaile herein. 1600 SHAKS. *A. Y. L.* II. vii. 8 He saues my labor by his owne approach. 1601 — *Twel. N.* II. ii. 6 You might haue saued mee my paines, to haue taken it away your selfe. 1612 BACON *Ess.*, *Despatch* (Arb.) 248 To chuse time, is to saue time. 1687 A. LOVELL tr. *Thevenot's Trav.* II. 3 Fair weather beginning with the New Moon, made the Captain repent that he had not passed through the Phare of Messina, which would have saved him fifty miles in his course. 1847 MARRYAT *Childr. N. Forest* iv, Edith..baked all the oatmeal cakes, which saved Alice a good deal of time. 1889 J. K. JEROME *Three Men in Boat* 149 We had dispensed with tea, so as to save time.

19. To be careful or economical in the use of; to use or consume sparingly.

1600 SHAKS. *A. Y. L.* II. vii. 160 His youthfull hose well sau'd, a world too wide For his shrunke shanke. 1719 DE FOE *Crusoe* I. (Globe) 62 For I eat sparingly; and sav'd my Provisions (my Bread especially) as much as possibly I could. 1729 SWIFT *Direct. Serv.*, *Butler* Wks. 1751 XIV. 21 To avoid burning Day-light, and to save your Master's Candles. 1816 SCOTT *Old Mort.* xl, Next she enlarged on the advantage of saving old clothes to be what she called 'beet-masters to the new'. 1847 C. BRONTË *Jane Eyre* xxix, Everything..including the carpet and curtains—looked at once well worn and well saved.

20. To treat carefully, so as to obviate or reduce fatigue, wear and tear, etc. *To save oneself*, to reduce the amount of one's exertions.

[1756 CHESTERF. *Let. to Son* 14 Dec., Adieu! I am going to the ball, to save my eyes from reading, and my mind from thinking.] 1785 G. A. BELLAMY *Apology* (ed. 3) III. 82 To make use of the theatrical phrase, I never saved myself, but often suffered my feelings to possess me so entirely, as that they deprived me of the power of voice. 1847 MARRYAT *Childr. N. Forest* xviii, My eyes are getting weak, and I wish to save them as much as possible. 1856 WHYTE MELVILLE *Kate Cov.* v. 52 White-Stockings, whom I had ridden down [to the races], to save Brilliant. 1859 GEO. ELIOT *Lifted Veil* ii, Supposing that he wished merely to save her nerves. 1907 SYMONS-JEUNE *Art of Punting* 17 Beginners..in order to save themselves and ease the strain on their arms..shove crooked and turn the punt round.

III. To avoid or prevent (something undesirable).

A development from sense 18; sense 21 arises naturally from the sense 'to avoid paying or losing'. Cf. also sense 5.

21. To avoid for one's own part or enable another to avoid (some burden or inconvenience): *occas.* to avoid or obviate the necessity for. *Const.* indirect obj. of the person (oneself or another) who is relieved.

1606 G. W[OODCOCKE] tr. *Justin* Epit. Emp. Hh 3 b, By meanes whereof, a little tract of time would saue him a great deal of wrath. 1615 R. COCKS *Diary* (Hakl. Soc.) I. 75 And about midnight [he] departed towards Crates; which saved the geveing a present of 2 damaskt fowling peeces, yf he had staid till morninge. 1654 GAYTON *Pleas. Notes* IV. xvii. 259 How might'st thou by this *effugium* have sav'd all thy misfortunes? 1681 DRYDEN *Span. Friar* IV. ii. 58 Will you not speak to save a Lady's Blush? 1699 — *Ep. J. Driden* 11 Without their cost you terminate the cause And save the expense of long litigious laws. 1780 *Mirror* No. 95 Take my advice, my dear Bell, and save yourself the trouble. 1790 SCOTT *Let.* in *Lockhart* (1837) I. vi. 163 My letters lie there for me, as it saves their being sent down to Rosebank. 1813 SOUTHEY *Nelson* II. 135 The hurt done by their splinters would have been saved also. 1815 SCOTT *Guy M.* xxiii, The best way's to let the blood barken upon the cut—that saves plasters. 1886 *Manch. Exam.* 13 Mar. 5/2 The only use of paper money is in saving the wear and tear of gold. 1899 *Allbutt's Syst. Med.* VIII. 77 A tendency to take quick steps, as if running forward to save a fall.

†b. *To save* (a woman's) *longing*, to anticipate and so prevent it. Also *transf.* *Obs.*

1593 *King Leir* I. ii. 133 (Malone Soc.), Madam, to saue your longing, this it is. 1607 SHAKS. *Timon* I. i. 261 Sir, you haue sau'd my longing, and I feed Most hungerly on your sight. 1614 B. JONSON *Barth. Fair* III. i. (1631) 48 Looke, Win, doe, looke a Gods name, and saue your longing. 1656 OSBORN *Adv. Son* II. xvi. 54 Our Beldame Eve, to save her longing, sold us all for an Apple. 1665 HEAD *Eng. Rogue* (1874) I. 88 Come hither Sirrah, I know what you would have, I'le save your longing.

c. *Games.* To prevent the opposing side from gaining (a run, goal, etc.). *To save two, three, four runs* (Cricket): to prevent the scoring of a second, third, or fourth run for a hit. Also (in football, hockey, etc.) *absol.* = to save a goal.

1816 LAMBERT in Box *Eng. Game Cricket* (1877) 34 Long Stop.—This man should stand a proper distance behind the wicket, to save a run, if the ball should not be stopped by the striker, or wicket keeper. 1850 'BAT' *Cricket. Manual* (1851) 49 Long Leg..usually stands to save four runs. 1867 SELKIRK *Guide to Cricket Ground* 35 *Saving the Run*.—Stopping and returning the ball so quickly that the batsmen dare not attempt a run for fear of being run out. 1889 *Field* 5 Jan. 29/3 For the losers, Jackson in goal saved well on several occasions [hockey]. *Ibid.* 12 Jan. 65/2 But his shot was saved by the goal-keeper [football].

d. *Well saved*: an applauding expression used when a rider has avoided a fall; also (in games) when a brilliant 'save' has been made.

1859 WHYTE MELVILLE *Digby Grand* I. i. 10 As he fell upon his head into the road, and recovered himself without unhorsing me,..'Well saved, my lad, and devilish well ridden too', said the jolly General.

†22. To afford protection from. *Obs.*

1583 *Leg. Bp. St Androis* Pref. 46 in *Satir. Poems Reform.* I. 348 The plesant plane-trie will the leavs vnfauld With fairest schaddow to save the sone in symmer.

†23. To meet or overcome (a doubt); = SALVE *v.*² 2. *Obs. rare*.

1591 SPENSER *M. Hubberd* 194 Right well, deere Gossip, ye advized haue, (Said then the Foxe) but I this doubt will save.

IV. Idiomatic uses of certain parts of the verb. (For those of the pr. pple. see SAVING *prep.*)

24. The infinitive *to save* has been used to mean: †a. On condition of not injuring. Cf. sense 9.

1297 R. GLOUC. (Rolls) 1260 Ac ich wolde to sauui lif & lime bringe him to ech lawe. [Cf. ante 1242: þat he vor is neueu wolde..Do hey amendement, sauue lume & lif.]

†b. Saving, having regard to (one's honour, 'presence'). See SAVING *prep.* 2.

1375 BARBOUR *Bruce* III. 173 'Schyr', said he,..'To sauff ȝour presence, it [is] nocht swa'. c 1470 *Gol. & Gaw.* 1008 And grant the frekis on fold farar to fall, Baith thair honouris to saif.

†c. Except, excepting; = SAVE *prep.*

c 1425 WYNTOUN *Orig. Cron.* IV. ix. 1170 Al þe cite þan fande þai Withe þar fais nere wptane, To sauff þe Capitalle allane. *Ibid.* IV. xvi. 1600 For nane þar gouernalle þar had, To sauff barnnys of ȝoutheide.

†25. The pa. pple. *saved* was used in absolute construction with a sb., with the sense: Preserving ..safe or intact, without detriment to, making reservation of. Cf. SAFE *a.* 5.

Sometimes placed before the sb.: cf. *except, considered*.

c 1400 *Apol. Loll.* 52 And þus he may lefuly, sauid his ordre. 1432–50 tr. *Higden* (Rolls) VIII. 79 That he wolde submitte hym to his grace, his honoure and crowne of his realme salvede. 1487 *Rolls of Parlt.* VI. 390/2 Saved alwey to your Grace..of the said Fee Ferme xviii li. vs. 1539 in W. A. J. Archbold *Somerset Rel. Houses* (1892) 71 We haue determyned (your lordeshippes pleasure savyd) to differ the same vnto our return. 1580 LYLY *Euphues* (Arb.) 335, I haue aunswered your custome, least you should argue me of coynes, no otherwise then I might mine honour saued, and your name vnknowen.

†V. 26. In combinations of verb-stem + object, used *attrib.* or *adj.*, as *save-soul, save-stake*.

1654 WHITLOCK *Zootomia* 178 Such A Spirit were of A Save stake, if not promoting Prudence, as they call it. 1799 E. DU BOIS *Piece Family Biog.* III. 129 Martha was gone on a save-soul pilgrimage to a neighbouring village.

Save (sēⁱv), *quasi-prep.* and *conj.* Forms: α. 3–5 **sauf**, 5–6 **saufe**, 5 **sawf, sauff, saauf**; 3–5 **saf**, 4–5 **safe, saaf**, 4–6 **saff(e**, 5 **sef**; 5–6 **salf**, 6 **salfe, saulfe**; 5–6 *Sc.* **saif(f**. β. 3–4 **sauve**, 4 **sawve**, 5 **sawe**, 4–6 **salve**, 4– **save**. [Developed from SAFE *a.* 5, in imitation of the similar development in the use of the equivalent F. *sauf*.

Already in OF. the adj. *sauf*, fem. *sauve*, prefixed to a sb. in the absolute construction (= L. *salvō, salvā*: see SAFE *a.* 5) had often the sense 'being excepted', so that it became (like the analogous *except* ppl. adj. in Eng.) functionally equivalent to a prep., and was eventually treated as such, the masc. form *sauf* being used even before a fem. sb. Cf. Sp. *salvo*, Pr. *salt*.

The β forms may partly represent the OF. *sauve* in collocation with a fem. sb., and partly the ME. form of the plural adj. But the later exclusive use of the form *save* is probably due to the identification of the word with the imperative of the vb.: cf. *except*, which appears to have been similarly apprehended as an imperative.

The use of a nominative after *save* (see 1 b) may perhaps be a trace of the originally adjectival character of the word; it is, however, to be noted that the same thing occurs with all the quasi-prepositional words of the same meaning, including even *saving* and *excepting*, which are in origin pr. pples. of transitive verbs.]

1. *quasi-prep.* Except, with the exception of, but. Often strengthened by the addition of *only* (*alone*, †*alonely*, †*anerly*, †*one*); also tautologically *save and except*, Sc. †*bot saiff*.

α. a 1300 *Cursor M.* 17288+438 Alle to-geder þai whore sauf thomas of ynde allone. 13.. *E. E. Allit. P.* B. 1749 Heȝest of alle oþer, saf onelych tweyne. c 1470 HENRY *Wallace* XI. 134 Sexte and vi xvi to ded has dycht, Bot saiff vii men at fled out of thair sycht. 1470–85 MALORY *Arthur* XX. vii. 808 Howe they were alle slayne sauf hym self al only. a 1533 LD. BERNERS *Gold. Bk. M. Aurel.* (1546) S v, Al thinges haue an ende at last by deth, saufe onely deathe. 1538 WRIOTHESLEY *Chron.* (1875) I. 86 All the lightes of waxe in every church to be taken downe, saffe onely the roode-loft light. 1579 in *10th Rep. Hist. MSS. Comm.* App. v. 430 No kynd of..tymber..salfe onely fuell of wood for fyre.

β. a 1300 *Cursor M.* 19485 Disciplis folud þai sa herd þat þai þam draf vte o þair ward, Sauue þe apostels þat þam ledd. 13.. *Gosp. Nicod.* 482 (Addit. MS.) Bedrede I lay fourty ȝhere fully sawe two. 1362 LANGL. *P. Pl.* A. II. 210 Saue Meede þe Mayden no mon dorste abyde. c 1380 WYCLIF *Last Age of the Church* (1840) 28 Euery lettre in þe abece may be souned wiþ opyn mouþ saue .m. lettre one. c 1425 *Eng. Conq. Irel.* vi. 18 Trew frendes fonde he non, sawe Robert, steuenes son. 1451 *Rolls of Parlt.* V. 220/1 The last day save oon of august. 1548 HALL *Chron.*, *Hen. IV* 21 No Chronicler save one, maketh mencion what was the very cause. 1617 MORYSON *Itin.* I. 77 The aforesaid boats are..covered all save the ends with black cloth. 1749 FIELDING *Tom Jones* VII. xi, We spent the next evening, save one, in London. 1808 G. ELLIS *Let.* in Lockhart *Scott* (1837) II. iv. 143 The most pleasing poem in our language—save and except one or two of Dryden's fables. 1850 TENNYSON *In Mem.* cv. 23 No dance, no motion, save alone What lightens in the lucid east. 1878 STUBBS *Const. Hist.* III. xviii. 140 All that remained to England in France, save Calais, was lost.

b. followed by the nominative of a pronoun. (App. the normal construction.)

α. c 1400 MAUNDEV. (1839) xxii. 245 Saf only thei that ben dwellynge with hym. a 1450 *Knt. de la Tour* 25 For ferde that ani other shulde haue the loue of her sauf he hym selff. c 1500 *Three Kings' Sons* 133 Then were they alle slayne, sauf y.

β. c 1386 CHAUCER *Can. Yeom. Prol. & T.* 802 Saue I and a frere, In Engelond ther kan no man it make. 1430–40 LYDG. *Bochas* IX. xxi[i]. (1494) F vj, There is a lyue left none of the blode Saue I alone of the royall lyne. 1528 TINDALE *Obed. Chr. Man* 79 b, Wilt thou so teach..that no man shall have knowlege..in Gods worde save thou only? 1601 SHAKS. *Jul. C.* III. ii. 66, I do intreat you, not a man depart, Saue I alone, till Antony haue spoke. *Ibid.* v. v. 69 All the Conspirators saue onely hee, Did that they did, in enuy of great Cæsar. 1667 MILTON *P. L.* II. 814 That mortal dint, Save he who reigns above, none can resist. 1821 BYRON *Juan* III. *Isles of Greece* xvi, Where nothing, save the waves and I, May hear our mutual murmurs sweep. 1866 DASENT *Gisli* 5 No one has ever challenged me before this day, save thou.

c. followed by the accusative of the pronoun.

1382 WYCLIF *Ecclus.* xxxvi. 5 For ther is noon other God, saue thee, Lord. 1607 SHAKS. *Timon* IV. iii. 507 But all saue thee I fell with Curses. 1893 F. THOMPSON *Hound of Heaven* 180 Whom wilt thou find to love ignoble thee, Save Me, save only Me?

†d. = but for. *Obs.*

1522 MORE *De quat. Noviss.* Wks. 83/1 Spiritual pride.. carieth with it a blindnes almost incurable saue gods gret mercye. 1820 KEATS *Eve of St. Agnes* xxv, She seem'd a splendid angel, newly drest, Save wings, for heaven.

2. *conj.* Introducing a sentence which states an exception; now only in the full form *save that*; = EXCEPT C. 1.

α. a 1300 *Fall & Passion* 23 in *E. E. P.* (1862) 13 God saf him..foules bestis an þe frute saf o tre he him forbede. 1387 TREVISA *Higden* (Rolls) VII. 339 In his tyme þe monkes of Caunterbury..were nouȝt onliche to seculer men, sauf þat þey lefte nouȝt [liȝt]liche her chastite. 1463 *Bury Wills* (Camden) 36 Lych to the tothir, saf they be not garnysshed. 1501 DOUGLAS *Pal. Hon.* II. vii, My curage grew, for quhat cause I nocht wait, Saif that I hald me payit of thair estait. a 1533 LD. BERNERS *Golden Bk. M. Aurel.* (1546) M j, His face was lyke a man, saufe it hadde but one eye.

β. c 1350 *Will. Palerne* 436 Min hert hol i haue now ..saue a fers feintise folwes me oft. c 1386 CHAUCER *Frankl. T.* 216 He was despeyred, no thyng dorste he seye, Saue in his songes somwhat wolde he wreye His wo. 1388 WYCLIF *Mark* vi. 5 And he myȝte not do there ony vertu, saue that he helide a fewe sijk men. 1547 *Test. Ebor.* (Surtees) VI. 265 Salve onlie that the said Thomas shall [etc.]. 1617 MURE *Misc. Poems* xx. 6 My muse, qᵗʰ noght doth challenge worthy fame, Saue from Montgomery sche hir birth doth clayme. 1634 SIR T. HERBERT *Trav.* 187 Naked from the waste vpwards, save that their heads are couered. 1750 GRAY *Elegy* 9 Save that from yonder ivy-mantled tow'r The moping owl does to the moon complain. 1842 R. I. WILBERFORCE *Rutilius & Lucius* 270 Then all was still, save that a vast gush of fire rose up for a moment. 1871 R. ELLIS *Catullus* xiv. 1 Calvus, save that as eyes thou art beloved, I could verily loathe thee for the morning's Gift.

¶ *confused use.*

1530 TINDALE *Answ. More* III. Wks. (1573) 305/2 M. More ..proueth nothing saue sheweth his ignoraunce.

b. = 'But that', 'were it not that'. Cf. 1 d. ? *Obs.*

c 1600 SHAKS. *Sonn.* lxvi. 14 From these would I be gone, Saue that to dye, I leaue my loue alone.

c. Introducing a hypothetical case of exception, = 'unless', 'if..not'; cf. EXCEPT C. 2.

1390 GOWER *Conf.* II. 119 And thus I mai you sothli telle, Save only that I crie and bidde, I am in Tristesce al amidde And fulfild of Desesperance. 1870 TENNYSON *Holy Grail* 80 Who wept and said, That save they could be pluck'd asunder, all My quest were but in vain. *Ibid.* 86 Save that he were the swine thou spakest of. 1897 F. THOMPSON *New Poems* 186 'Tis said there were no thought of hell, Save hell were taught.

†d. As an adversative, = 'but on the contrary'.

1362 LANGL. *P. Pl.* A. Prol. 77 Saue hit nis not bi þe Bischop þat þe Boye precheþ. c 1400 *Lanfranc's Cirurg.* II. v. 163 And if..þe herte be hurt, þere lijþ no cure þeron, saue he schal die anoon; for þe herte takiþ no lijf of no lyme of al þe bodi, saue þe herte ȝeueþ lyues to euery lyme of þe bodi. 1422 tr. *Secreta Secret.*, *Priv. Priv.* 188 Kynde vs hath grantid two eighen and two eeris, Saue but one tonge.

3. Followed by an adv. or advb. phrase or clause, expressing the manner, time, etc., in regard to which an exception is to be made; = EXCEPT C. 3.

α. c 1420 HOCCLEVE *Min. Poems* 154/405 Womman, with my swerd, slee wolde I thee heere, Sauf for awe of god. c 1450 *Merlin* I. 12 Be-fill yowe neuer this merveyle saf ones? 1540–1 ELYOT *Image Gov.* (1549) 113 Beyng not instructed in any occupacion or science, saulfe onely in feates perteynyng to warre.

β. c 1320 *Sir Beues* 2270 Al is pes þar ichaue went, Saue in þe loond of Dabilent. 1390 GOWER *Conf.* II. 172 And yit withoute experience Salve only of illusion. 1577 KENDALL *Flowers of Epigr.* 7 Thy garments all and some Do smell of Mirrhe, and saue of Mirrhe no sent doth from thee come. 1598 H. B. *Rdr. to Chaucer* in *Speght* a v b, Unknowne to vs, saue only by thy bookes. 1611 BIBLE 1 *Kings* xxii. 31 Fight neither with small nor great, saue only with the king of Israel. 1667 MILTON *P. L.* XII. 258 Over the Tent a Cloud Shall rest by Day, a fierie gleame by Night, Save when they journie. 1750 GRAY *Elegy* 7 Save where the beetle wheels his droning flight. 1864 M. J. HIGGINS *Ess.* (1875) 165 Save and except in a dead calm she is utterly unseaworthy. 1875 MANNING *Mission Holy Ghost* xiv. 397 For fifty years he never left Rome, save only when he went out of the walls to visit the Seven Churches. 1879 FROUDE *Cæsar* viii. 79 There was no longer, therefore, any excuse for its meeting, save on special occasions.

b. Followed by an inf. (with or without *to*).

c 1400 *Beryn* 660 He..had no thing to doon Saff shake a lite his eris, & trus, & be goon. c 1450 MYRC *Festial* 17 'What schall þat serues ben'. Þen sayde he: 'þe same, worde for worde, þat ys yn hor natyuyte, saue turne þe natyvyte ynto þe concepcyon'. 1534 TINDALE *John* xiii. 10 He that is wesshed, nedeth not save to wesshe his fete. 1819 SCOTT *Ivanhoe* xl, If thou hast aught to do, save to witness the misery thou hast caused.

c. *Save for*: exception being made for, but for.

1594 SHAKS. *Rich. III*, IV. iv. 303 Of all one paine, saue for a night of groanes Endur'd of her, for whom you bid like sorrow. 1610 — *Temp.* I. ii. 282 Then was this Island (Saue for the Son, that [s]he did littour heere..) not honour'd with A humane shape. 1879 ESCOTT *England* xxv. (1881) 403 The well-conducted soldier, save and except for a more or less constant *ennui*..may pass his days in comparative comfort. 1879 MᶜCARTHY *Own Times* II. 283 The Black Sea is, save for one little outlet.., a huge land-locked lake. 1894 HALL CAINE *Manxman* IV. xvi. 262 Saue for the slumbering fire, all was dark within the house.

¶ 4. Phrases like *save your grace, save your reverence* belong to SAFE *a.* 5. See also GRACE *sb.* 6 d, REVERENCE *sb.* 5; and cf. SAVING.

'Save your displeasure' (quot. c 1500) is perh. due to a confusion between this use and sense 1 above.

13.. *Seuyn Sag.* (W.) 687 Sauue your grace, wene ich hit nowt, Hit euere com in his thout. c 1500 *Three Kings' Sons* 139 It semeth, saufyour displeasir, that [etc.].

Save, obs. form of SAFE, SALVE *sb.*¹

Saveable: see SAVABLE.

†**Saveage.** *Obs. rare*⁻¹. [f. SAVE *v.* + -AGE. Cf. SALVAGE.] The action of saving.

1507 in Leadam *Sel. Cases Crt. Star Chamber* (Selden Soc.) 243 The seid ij gromes wer fyne for the sauege of their lyues to draw out their weppyns.

Save-all (sēⁱ·vǭl). [f. SAVE *v.* + ALL.]

1. A means for preventing loss or waste.

a 1655 SIR T. MAYERNE *Archimag. Anglo-Gall.* Pref. (1658) 2 This Book is a Save-all; It suffers nothing to be lost. 1776 ADAM SMITH *W. N.* I. xi. III. I. 281 [The poultry] as they are fed with what would otherwise be lost, are a meer save-all. 1870 *Echo* 28 Nov., Wretched shifts and saveralls of reserve and recruiting systems are enough to engage their attention, so far as their war administration is concerned.

2. A receptacle for collecting matter which would otherwise be lost and not utilized. Also *attrib.*

1797 *Monthly Mag.* III. 301 A refrigerator, from which proceeds an additional worm, to receive the spirit [in cooling and condensing], before it goes to the save-all. 1823 J. BADCOCK *Dom. Amusem.* 149 The fat of every kind collected in our kitchens, being rendered, or melted down from day to day, and cast into a 'save-all tub', will be found to produce very good soap. 1833 LOUDON *Encycl. Archit.* § 1443 There is, immediately beneath the fountain [for spirits], a saveall, or pierced plate of pewter, through which the drippings from the glasses percolate, and are collected in a shallow basin below. 1884 *Health Exhib. Catal.* 71/2 Front Damper acting as a 'Tidy Betty' with Cinder-sifter or Save-all attached.

3. A contrivance to hold a candle-end in a candlestick while burning so that it may burn to the end; a common form is a pan with a projecting pin in the centre on which the candle-end is fixed.

c 1645 HOWELL *Lett.* (1655) IV. xxi. 58 In som this light goes out with an ill-favor'd stench; But others have a saveall to preserve it from making any snuff at all. 1682 HARTMAN *True Preserv. Health* 348 Heat the pin of a save-all, and then thrust it into the bigger end [of a small candle], and so set it upon a candlestick. 1747 *Gentl. Mag.* XVII. 444/2 Death's a dark-lanthorn, life a candle's-end Stuck on a save-all, soon to end in stink. 1895 *Army & Navy Price List* 15 Sept. 1316/2 [Candle] Saveall, White..each 0/4½.

4. A money-box to receive small savings or contributions.. Also *dial.* (see quot. 1841).

1837 HOWITT *Rur. Life* (1842) 228 In this manner..enter your rooms..monks with their little saveralls in their hands, collecting for hospitals. 1841 HARTSHORNE *Salopia Ant.* 555 *Save-all*,..an earthen bottle with slits at the sides, destin'd to receive all the savings of children.

5. A niggardly, stingy, miserly person. Now *dial.*

1785 GROSE *Dict. Vulgar Tongue*, *Saveall*,..also a miser. 1820 KEATS in *Life* II. 63 There is old Lord Burleigh, the high-priest of economy, the political save-all.

6. *Naut.* A sail set under another sail or between two other sails. Also *attrib.*

1794 *Rigging & Seamanship* I. 83 Vessels with one mast ..have..above the cross-jack, a small sail, called a save-all top-sail. 1846 in YOUNG *Naut. Dict.* 1878 D. KEMP *Man. Yacht Sailing* 366 *Save-all*, a water sail; a sail set underneath booms in light weather.

7. A pinafore; overall. *dial.*

1864 MRS. LLOYD *Ladies of Polcarrow* 103 Ever since I was a boy in a save-all. 1888 JESSIE FOTHERGILL *Lasses of Leverhouse* iv. 34 The black alpaca monstrosity which I..denominated a save-all.

8. *attrib.* or *adj.* Parsimonious, stingy.

1812 SOUTHEY *Ess.* (1832) I. 141 The paltry proceedings of those save-all politicians, who boast of their economy in banishing newspapers from the public offices. 1856 R. W. PROCTER *Barber's Shop* xi. (1883) 65 Still pursuing his save-all theory of a pin a day is a groat a year.

Saved (sēⁱvd), *ppl. a.* [f. SAVE *v.* + -ED¹.]

1. Delivered from damnation. Also *absol.*

a 1300 *Cursor M.* 10867 His folk al saued þan sal he mak. 14.. *Less. of Dirige* 409 in 26 *Pol. Poems* 120 Þe sauyd excusyd, þe dampnyd accusyd, As thay deseruyd echon haue. 1509 H. WATSON *Ship of Fools* Prol. (1517) A ij b, That through theyr labour they may be of the nombre of yᵉ saued. 1688 BUNYAN *Jerus. Sinner Saved* (1886) 123 If thy desires be firm..to become the saved of Christ, and His servant. 1868 H. LAW *Beacons of Bible* 78 Every saved soul shines for ever a monument of..sanctifying grace.

2. a. Hoarded, laid by; also with *up*. b. Economized; not spent or wasted.

1732 POPE *Ep. Bathurst* 194 Benighted wanderers, the forest o'er, Curse the sav'd candle and unop'ning door. 1834 S. BAGSTER *Managem. Bees* Pref. 6 Often..have I spent the saved-up shilling to run into..the old menagerie in Exeter 'Change. 1875 SMILES *Thrift* vi. 93 Saved money, however little, will serve to dry up many a tear.

Saveine, obs. form of SAVIN.

Saveloy (sæ·vĕloi). [Corruption of F. *cervelas* (sɛrvəla): see CERVELAT.]

1. A highly seasoned cooked and dried sausage.

1837 DICKENS *Pickw.* lv, Mr. Solomon Pell..regaling himself..with a cold collation of an Abernethy biscuit and a saveloy. 1857 SMILES *Life & Labour* 333 Soyer, the gastronomist,..would stop at a stall in the Haymarket and luxuriate in eating a penny saveloy.

2. *Saveloy marble* (see quot.).

1839 *Civil Engin. & Arch. Jrnl.* II. 452 *Cervellata*. Saveloy marble, red ground, white and green, with very fine interlaced white veins.

†**Savement.** *Obs.* Also **sauvement.** [a. OF. *sauvement*, f. *sauver* SAVE *v.*: see -MENT. Cf. Pr. *salvamen*.] Safety, salvation.

13.. *Guy Warw.* 3840 Iesu,..Saue him fram cumberment, & him ogain bring in sauement. c 1315 SHOREHAM 7 *Sacram.* 406 Þorwe creymie anoynt strange he bi-combe His sauuement to winne. 13.. *E. E. Allit. P.* B. 940 Þer soȝt no mo to sauement of cities aþel fyue. a 1450 *Knt. de la Tour* cxi. (1906) 151 Symeon..saide with a high voys, 'Lo! here the clere light, and the sauement of the worlde'. 1485 CAXTON *Chas. Gt.* 236 By the is made the path of sauement.

Saven, obs. form of SAVIN.

Savenap(e, rare var. ff. SANAP *Obs.*

Saveo(u)r(e, obs. forms of SAVIOUR, SAVOUR.

Saver (sēⁱ·vəɹ). Also 4 **sauver**, 4–5 **savere**, 6 ? **sawar**. [f. SAVE *v.* + -ER¹. Cf. SAVIOUR.]

1. One who saves, preserves, or rescues from death, evil, or destruction; a saviour or preserver.

In early use said of Christ = SAVIOUR; now only used when *saviour* would seem inappropriate.

a 1300 *Cursor M.* 10541 Of hir sal cum þat man sauuer [*other MSS.* sauere]. c 1410 HOCCLEVE *Mother of God* 10 Modir of mercy..Saver of us by thy benevolence. 1538 BALE *Brefe Comedy Baptist* in *Harl. Misc.* (1744) I. 99 Your kynge, your sauer and redemer. *Ibid.*, For all men shall se their mercyfull sauer playne. 1608 B. JONSON *Masque at Ld. Haddington's*, Sauer of his King. 1700 C. NESS *Antid. Armin.* (1827) 58 Salvation is the work of the saved, not of the saver. 1833 M. SCOTT *Tom Cringle* xix, A statue erected to Lord Rodney the saver of the Island as he is always called from having crushed the fleet of Count de Grasse. 1872 TENNYSON *Gareth & Lynette* 858 For strong thou art and goodly therewithal, And saver of my life. 1891 *Longman's Mag.* Feb. 373 He hated his rescuer and saver.

†b. One who keeps or preserves a thing from destruction or waste. *Obs.*

1422 tr. *Secreta Secret.*, *Priv. Priv.* 213 And therfor the nedyth to haue a constabil that shal not bene a destruere of thy trees, but a Kepere and a Sauere. 1573 TUSSER *Husb.* (1878) 168 Where all thing is common, what needeth a hutch? where wanteth a sauer, there hauocke is mutch.

c. One who saves (property) from wreck or destruction; a salvor.

1629 in Boys *Sandwich* (1792) 749 And do further ill entreat the savers and finders thereof [wrecks]. 1820 W. SCORESBY *Acc. Arctic Reg.* II. 329 The propriety of appropriating all wrecked stores to the use of the savers.

†2. 'One who escapes loss, though without gain' (J.). (Primarily a gaming term.) *To make* (oneself or another person) *a saver*: to insure against or compensate for a loss. *Obs.*

1591 FLORIO *2nd Fruites* 71 *S.* What can I doe withall? I can not mend it. *A.* If I thought one hand would make me a sauer, I would play. c 1613 MIDDLETON *No Wit like a Womans* II. iii. (1657) 58 You'd need have a clear way, because y'are a bad pricker. *Mrs. Low.* Yet if my Bowl take bank, I shall go nigh To make my self a saver. 1668 HOWE *Bless. Righteous* xx. 388 Heaven were a poor Heaven, if it would not make us savers. 1676 LEE *Sophon.* IV. i. 45 Your Armies are the Cards which both must play; At least come off a saver if you may. 1687 DRYDEN *Hind & P.* III. 344 For laws of arms permit each injured man To make himself a saver where he can. 1691 — *Arthur* II. 18 He puts the gain of Britain in a Scale, Which weighing with the loss of Emmeline, He thinks he's scarce a Saver. a 1700 SEDLEY *Poems* Wks. 1722 I. 46 We'll Game and give off Savers too.

3. One who saves, economizes, or hoards up.

1548 FORREST *Pleas. Poesye* 56 Some muste bee Sauers, Store is no sore. 1601 F. GODWIN *Bps. of Eng.* 460 A good sauer makes a well doer. 1727 SWIFT *St. Irel.* Wks. 1755 V. II. 167 Hence alone comes the dearness of land, since the savers have no other way to lay out their money. 1755 JOHNSON, *Saver*. ..3. A good husband. 1830 CUNNINGHAM *Brit. Paint.* I. 319 A saver of bits of thread. 18.. COBDEN in Smiles *Self-help* (1859) 218 The accomplishment of all other great works.. has been done by the savers, the thrifty. 1869 *Daily News* 14 Dec., The small farmers are great savers.

4. A means of saving or economizing.

1664 EVELYN *Sylva* xxii. (1679) 111 We find it [*sc.* the Fir] an extraordinary saver of Oak. 1901 *Munsey's Mag.* XXV. 393/2 The railroad,..when it can be used, is a wonderful saver. 1903 *Westm. Gaz.* 26 Oct. 15/1 The invention is a great labour-saver.

5. *Racing slang.* A hedging bet.

1891 N. GOULD *Doub. Event* xvii. 123 Wells says Perfection will win,..but I've put a saver on Caloola.

Saver(e, Saveray, obs. ff. SAVOUR, SAVORY.

Save-reverence: see SIR-REVERENCE.

Saverey, -ie, obs. forms of SAVORY, SAVOURY.

†**Savernapron.** *rare.* [? corruption of AF. **save-naperon*, f. *saver* SAVE *v.* + *naperon*: see APRON. Cf. *savenappe* SANAP.] A table-napkin.

1422–3 *Abingdon Rolls* (Camden) 94 Item vij sauernaprons, Item x alie sauernaprons debiles.

Saverous, obs. form of SAVOROUS.

Savery(e, obs. forms of SAVORY, SAVOURY.

Savete(e, Saveure: see SAFETY, SAVOUR.

Savey, savvy (sæ·vi), *sb. slang.* Also 8 **scavey**, 9 (*Sc.* **savie**), **savvey, sabe.** [The Sc. *savie* is perh. a. F. *savez* (*-vous*) do you know? The later slang use is f. SAVEY *v.*] Practical sense, intelligence; 'nous', gumption.

1785 [see SAVEY *v.* below]. 1825–80 JAMIESON, *Savie*, knowledge, experience, sagacity, Loth. ? 185. B. HARTE *Chiquita* 9 Hedn't no savey—hed Briggs. 1884 E. INGERSOLL in *Harper's Mag.* Sept. 508/2 They don't need much savvey for that. 1890 'R. BOLDREWOOD' *Col. Reformer* (1891) 47 He could ride the best, but the black boy had twice as much savey. 1892 KIPLING & BALESTIER *Naulahka* 273 You have been romping around for six months after something you hadn't the sabe to hold when you'd got.

Savey, savvy (sæ·vi), *v. slang.* Also 8 **scavey**, 9 **sabe(e, savvey.** [Orig. Negro-Eng. and Pigeon-Eng., after Sp. *sabe usted* you know.] *trans.* To know.

1785 GROSE *Dict. Vulgar Tongue*, *Scavey*, sense, knowledge; 'massa me no scavey', master I don't know, (*negroe language*) perhaps from the French scavoir. 1828 *Life Planter Jamaica* 137 Dey hab not savey dat de storekeeper hab be deir broder Joseph. 1833 MRS. CARMICHAEL *West Indies* II. 131 As I went on, I paused and asked them if they 'savey' what I said, (comprehended me). *Ibid.* 135 Misses, you no peak lie, me savey dat well. 1865 NIXON *Peter Perfume* 58 The 'no sabee' dodge to try they'd fain. 1874 B. HARTE *Wan Lee*, I asked if the juggler was the father of the baby. 'No sabe!' said the imperturbable Hop Sing, taking refuge in that Spanish form of non-committalism so common in California. 1890 'R. BOLDREWOOD' *Col. Reformer* (1891) 51 Now do you savey?

Saveyne, Savico: see SAVIN, SABICU.

Savin, savine (sæ·vin). Forms: α. 1 **safene, -ine**, 1, 5– **savine**, 4–6 **savyne, saveine**, 5–6 **-eyne**, 7 **saven**; 4, 6– **savin**; β. 6–7, 9 **sabine**, 8 **sabin.** [a. OF. *savine* (in mod.F. replaced by the learned form *sabine*, whence the β forms above) = Sp., Pg. *sabina*, It. *savina*:—L. (*herba*) *Sabina*, lit. 'Sabine herb' (*Sabīna* fem. of *Sabīnus* SABINE).

Cf. G. *saben-, sevenbaum* (for the many corrupt forms see Grimm), Du. *zevenboom*.]

1. A small bushy evergreen shrub, *Juniperus sabina*, a native of Europe and Western Asia, with spreading branches completely covered with short imbricating leaves, and bearing a small, round, bluish-purple berry.

The name is also applied to certain trees or shrubs resembling *Juniperus sabina*, as the Sea Wormwood, *Artemisia maritima*; the dwarf Juniper, *Juniperus nana*; *Cæsalpinia pulcherrima* (Indian savin); in the U. S. to the Red Cedar, *Juniperus virginiana*, and to *Torreya taxifolia*, one of the stinking cedars; and in the W. Indies to *Cæsalpinia bijuga*, *Fagara lentiscifolia* and *Xanthoxylum Pterota*.

c 1000 *Sax. Leechd.* II. 312 Nim þas wyrte safenan & mersc mealwan. *Ibid.* III. 38 Wyll in buteran þas wyrta..sauinan & curmeallan & feferfugean. a 1387 *Sinon. Barthol.* (Anecd. Oxon.) 18 *Ebel*, *i.* savin. 1390 GOWER *Conf.* III. 130 Ther is an herbe which men calleth Saveine. a 1400 *Pistill of Susan* 69 Þe sauyne [*MS. Phillipps* saveyne] and sypres, selcouþ to sene. 1567 MAPLET *Gr. Forest* 61 Sauin, is one of those kindes which..beareth leafe all seasons of the yeare. 1590 SPENSER *F. Q.* III. ii. 49 But th' aged Nourse ..Had gathered Rew, and Savine. 1607 TOPSELL *Four-f. Beasts* 240 Agolethros and Sabine are poyson to Goates. 1707 MORTIMER *Husb.* (1721) II. 188 Sabin or Savin will make fine Hedges, and may be brought into any sort of Form by clipping. 1811 A. T. THOMSON *Lond. Disp.* (1818) 730 Ointment of Savine. Take of fresh leaves of savine, two parts; yellow wax, one part; lard, four parts. 1838 T. THOMSON *Chem. Org. Bodies* 464 Oil of sabine. It is obtained from the leaves of the *juniperus sabina*. Limpid. Has the odour and flavour of sabine. This plant furnishes a great deal of oil. 1861 MRS. STOWE *Pearl Orr's Isl.* i. 8 Only savins and mulleins, with their dark pyramids or white spires of velvet leaves, diversified the sandy wayside. 1884 SARGENT *Rep. Forests N. Amer.* 183 *Juniperus Virginiana*...Red Cedar. Savin. *Ibid.* 186 *Torreya taxifolia*...Stinking Cedar. Savin.

2. The dried tops of this shrub, used as a drug.

Savin is strongly poisonous; it possesses emmenagogic properties, and hence was a common means of procuring abortion. It is also an antheimintic, used chiefly in veterinary practice.

c 1000 *Sax. Leechd.* II. 100 Wiþ þon ilcan ȝenim safinan ȝnid to duste. 1573 TUSSER *Husb.* (1878) 97 Sauin, for the bots. 1590 BARROUGH *Meth. Physick* III. lvi. 193 Incessions made of the decoction of laurell berries, & leaues,..motherwort, horehound, saueine, althæa, cammomill [etc.]. 1614 MARKHAM *Cheap Husb.*, *Bull* xxix. 58 There is nothing killeth wormes in the bodies of cattell sooner then Sauen chopt small and beaten with sweet Butter. 1693 DRYDEN *Juvenal* vi. 775 Help her to make Manslaughter; let her bleed, And never want for Savin at her need. 1736 BAILEY *Housek. Dict.* 321 *Savin*, is of an incisive, penetrative and attenuating quality..; being powdered and mix'd with fresh butter, it is given to the quantity of a dram to persons troubled with the asthma. 1843 R. J. GRAVES *Syst. Clin. Med.* xxvi. 334 They were treated with lapis infernalis, Plenk's liniment, and powdered savine.

3. *attrib.* and *Comb.*, as *savine-berry, -bush, -cerate, -oil, -tops, -tree*; *savin-leaved* adj.

1681 GREW *Musæum* II. § ii. I. 219 *Savine-Berrys. About as big as those of the common Juniper, and of a blackish blew. 1672 JOSSELYN *New Eng. Rarities* 3 In these Gullies grow *Saven Bushes. 1826 S. COOPER *First Lines Surg.* (ed. 5) 448 A discharge should be kept up from the blistered surface by means of the *savine cerate. 1829 *Glover's Hist. Derby* I. 126 *Lycopodium alpinum*, mountain or *savin-leaved club-moss. 1858 SIMMONDS *Dict. Trade*, **Savine-oil*, an essential oil obtained by distilling the tops of the savine plant. 1695 BLACKMORE *Pr. Arth.* VII. 645 Henbane, Wormwood, Hemlock, *Savine Tops. 1611 TOURNEUR *Ath. Trag.* IV. i, There growes a *Sauin-tree next it forsooth. 1696 SLOANE *Catal. Plant. Jamaica* 128 Savine Trees. *Ibid.* 149 Indian Savin Tree. 1864 GRISEBACH *Flora W. Ind. Islands* 737 Savin tree: *Cæsalpinia bijuga* and *Fagara lentiscifolia*.

Saving (sēⁱ·viŋ), *vbl. sb.* [f. SAVE *v.* + -ING¹.]

1. The action of the verb SAVE; an instance of this. a. The action of rescuing or protecting; †a deliverance.

a 1300 *Cursor M.* 12775 Wijt we þan for quat resun For saueing of vr dampnacioun, Þat he now suilk baptizing mass? a 1340 HAMPOLE *Psalter* xi. 6 Safynge of rightwis and dampnynge of wickid. c 1460 FORTESCUE *Abs. & Lim. Mon.* vi. (1885) 123 For the repressynge off rovers, sauynge off owre marchauntes, owre fisshers, and the dwellers vppon owre costes. 1523 LD. BERNERS *Froiss.* I. xxxix. 53 Syr Henry wolde nat let his wepon go for sauyng of his honour. 1571 GOLDING *Calvin on Ps.* xviii. 50 This election was myghtely ratifyed by continewall successe of savinges. 1611 BIBLE *Heb.* xi. 7 Noah..prepared an Arke to the sauing of his house. 1676 MOLLOY *De Jure Marit.* II. v. (1688) 240 If the Ship perishes only, and the Goods are safe, in that case the Goods ought to pay a proportion of a fifth or tenth penny, according to the easie or difficult winning or saving of the said Goods. 1848 CLOUGH *Amours de Voy.* I. 21 All the foolish destructions, and all the sillier savings.

b. The action of saving or economizing in expenditure (of money, time, labour, etc.); an instance of this, a reduction in expenditure.

1551 *Cal. Anc. Rec. Dublin* (1889) 426 For the..sawing of expenssis to the citizens. 1640 G. HERBERT *Jacula Prud.* 110 No Alchymy to saving. 1731–8 SWIFT *Pol. Conversat.* ii. Wks. 1751 XII. 259 *Lord Smart*. Come, hang Saving: bring us up a Halfp'orth of Cheese. 1778 C. HUTTON *Bridges* 5 Fewer arches..will produce great savings in the expence. 1832 HT. MARTINEAU *Life in Wilds* vi. 77 A great saving of time and labour. 1848 MILL *Pol. Econ.* I. v. § 5 (1876) 45 Saving, in short, enriches, and spending impoverishes. 1854 RONALDS & RICHARDSON *Chem. Technol.* (ed. 2) I. 257 The saving of fuel is much greater when turf and wood are employed. 1883 *Law Rep.* 11 Q. B. Div. 569 The object of the society being the encouragement of saving.

c. In games: cf. SAVE *v.* 21 c.

1889 *Field* 26 Jan. 123/1 It was only the brilliant saving of Holmes, and the sound defence of the backs generally, that averted two or three scores.

2. *concr.* A sum of money saved; chiefly *pl.* sums of money saved from time to time (by the exercise of economy) and put by or hoarded up.

1737 *Gentl. Mag.* VII. 656/2 If he could save 500 or 1000*l.* a Year out of his Estate, he would certainly apply that Saving towards discharging his small Debts. 1786 MRS. A. M. BENNETT *Juvenile Indiscr.* I. 215 My hard savings and earnings. 1809 MALKIN *Gil Blas* v. i. ⁋ 62 More than half my savings were laid out on repairs. 1824 MISS MITFORD *Village* Ser. I. 239 She had three or four hundred pounds to bequeath, partly her own savings, and partly a legacy from a distant relative. 1888 BRYCE *Amer. Commw.* III. xliii. II. 132 The working man who puts his savings into the house he lives in.

b. In the navy: (see quot. 1815).

1815 *Falconer's Dict. Marine* (ed. Burney), *Savings of Provisions*, implies the bread, wine, spirits, beef, pork, butter and cheese, which have been saved by the different persons or messes in any of his Majesty's ships, from the established allowance of those species; and for which the purser pays them, at the expiration of one, two, or three months at furthest, agreeable to the credit prices stated in his instructions. 1901 *Westm. Gaz.* 28 Aug. 8/2 The Committee dwells upon the difficulty of framing an ideal ration so long as canteens and the 'savings' system exist.

3. A salvo, reservation, saving clause. Now only in *Law*.

1477 *Rolls of Parlt.* VI. 171/1 All Offices, Fees, Rents and Annuitees..other than Rents services, be in no wise comprised or conteyned in this saving. 1542–3 *Act* 34 & 35 *Hen. VIII*, c. 5 § 9 The sauinges reseruinges and prouisions ..of the saide former act. 1765 BLACKSTONE *Comm.* I. 367 Therein the tenant swore to bear faith to his sovereign lord, in opposition to all men, without any saving or exception. 1875 DIGBY *Real Prop.* viii. (1876) 343 The Statute of Uses contained a saving in favour of wills made before the first day of May, 1536. 1884 SELBORNE in *Law Times Rep.* L. 315/1 The savings from a repealing clause would not apply to any express antecedent provision of the Act inconsistent with them.

4. *attrib.* and *Comb.*: †**saving bank**: see SAVINGS BANK; †**saving-box**, a money-box for savings; †**saving('s institution** = SAVINGS BANK.

1691 *D'Emilianne's Frauds Rom. Monks* 151, I have since understood, that all Tradesmen in Italy do each of them keep a Saving-box, into which they put what Mony they can spare during the whole Year in order to their going in Pilgrimage. 1830 J. T. PRATT *Hist. Savings Banks* p. vij, The imperious necessity of Saving Institutions for the industrious Poor. 1832 *Encycl. Amer.* XI. 216/2 *Savings Institutions*, or, as they are often called *Savings Banks*.

Saving (sēⁱ·viŋ), *ppl. a.* [f. SAVE *v.* + -ING².]

1. That delivers, rescues or preserves from peril; that protects or guards from anything undesirable.

1535 COVERDALE *Ps.* xii[i]. 5 My hert is ioyfull in thy sauynge health. 1692 R. L'ESTRANGE *Fables* xxix. 29 There's No Living however without Law: and there's No Help for't in many Cases, if the Saving Equity be Over-rul'd by the Killing Letter of it. 1718 G. SEWELL *Proclam. Cupid* 15 Woman..A Guardian Angel, and a saving Saint. 1804

WORDSW. *Vaudracour & Julia* 194 The silver shower, whose reckless burthen weighs Too heavily upon the lily's head, Oft leaves a saving moisture at its root. 1885–94 R. BRIDGES *Eros & Psyche* June xvi, And with that lie the wounded man they slew, Hiding the saving truth which well they knew.

b. *Saving piece*: a piece of wood to prevent injury to the machine in the process of cutting.

1839 URE *Dict. Arts*, etc. 160 [Machine for cutting the edges of books, banknotes, &c.] Upon this latter board is placed the 'material to be cut', with a saving piece between it.

2. *Theol.* That delivers from sin and eternal death by the power of God's grace.

a 1300 *Cursor M.* 8097 Sceu vs þe sauuand tre, sir king. 1597 HOOKER *Eccl. Pol.* v. lx. § 2 That they..might..obteine as well that sauing grace of imputation which taketh away all former giltines. 1671 MILTON *P. R.* 474 But to guide Nations in the way of truth By saving Doctrine. *a* 1711 KEN *Hymns Festiv.* Poet. Wks. 1721 I. 3:9 May I from his own Writings learn His Love, and Saving-Truths discern. 1712 POPE *Messiah* 107 But fix'd his word, his saving pow'r remains. 1732 BERKELEY *Alciphr.* vii. § 11 That notion of a saving faith which is required in a Christian. 1809–10 COLERIDGE *Friend* (1865) 207 Good works may exist without saving principles..; but saving principles..never can exist without good works.

3. *gen.* That delivers from moral or intellectual error; also, of a quality, 'redeeming', exempting from unqualified condemnation or censure. Often as a direct transference from sense 2.

1599 SHAKS. *Hen. V*, v. ii. 217 If euer thou beest mine, Kate, as I haue a sauing Faith within me tells me thou shalt. 1735 POPE *Prol. Sat.* 40 And drop at last, but in unwilling ears, This saving counsel, 'Keep your piece nine years'. 1852 TENNYSON *Ode Dk. Wellington* iv, Foremost captain of his time, Rich in saving common-sense. 1865 M. ARNOLD *Ess. Crit.* ix. (1875) 373 The obedience demanded by theology and the knowledge demanded by philosophy are alike saving. 1902 ELIZ. BANKS *Newspaper Girl* 210, I am not, I believe, without a saving sense of humour.

4. Accustomed to save, hoard up, or economize; avoiding unnecessary expenses; tending to reduce expenses; parsimonious, economical.

1581 PETTIE *Guazzo's Civ. Conv.* II. (1586) 88 b, If you will haue riches to be a help to Gentrie, it shall behooue a man rather to bee sauing, that he may be able to keepe himselfe rich. 1606 CHAPMAN *Mons. D'Olive* I. i, Indeed that's the savingst way. 1625 BACON *Ess., Expense* (Arb.) 53 A Man had need, if he be Plentifull, in some kinde of Expence, to be as Sauing againe, in some other. As if he be Plentifull in Diet, to be Sauing in Apparell. 1712 ARBUTHNOT *John Bull* I. x, Not but that she lov'd Mony, for she was of a saving Temper. 1729 SWIFT *Direct. Serv., Butler* Wks. 1751 XIV. 26 Be saving of your Candles. 1771 LUCKOMBE *Hist. Print.* 225 A saving way, similar to this, was..from three sets of Punches..to cast six different Bodies of Letter. 1848 THACKERAY *Van. Fair* xi, Mrs. Crawley was a saving woman and knew the price of port wine.

†**5.** 'Not turning to loss, though not gainful' (J.); neither winning nor losing. *Obs.*

1614 ? BRETON *I would & would not* lxxiii, When weather-beaten Sailes, with winde, & raine, Scarce make a Sauing-Voyage home againe. 1632 in *10th Rep. Hist. MSS. Comm.* App. v. 478 The greate plentie of corne that remaines uppon their handes, and which they cannot utter at any saveing price. 1645 WITHER *Vox Pacif.* 94 A likely means, to get a saving-game. 1709 POPE *Let. Wycherley* 20 May *Lett.* (1735) I. 40, I can be content with a bare saving Game, without being thought an eminent Hand. 1713 ADDISON *Guard.* No. 97 ¶ 3 Silvio..was resolved to make a saving bargain of it. 1765 *Museum Rust.* IV. 174, I have no great expectations from this plantation, though, I fancy, it will be a saving crop. 1826 SCOTT *Mal. Malagr.* iii, A country, where industry and skill can but play a saving game, at best, against national disadvantages. 1828–32 WEBSTER (with example: 'the ship has made a saving voyage').

6. Making a reservation; furnishing a proviso.

1700 TYRRELL *Hist. Eng.* II. 853 With a Saving Clause, that it should not be drawn into Example. 1838 DICKENS *Nich. Nick.* l, 'Will you prevent me?' asked Sir Mulberry, with a laugh. 'Ye-es, if I can;' returned the other, promptly. 'A very proper saving clause, that last', said Sir Mulberry; 'and one you stand in need of'. 1835 BROWNING *Before* 32 Now, enough of your chicane of prudent pauses, Sage provisos, sub-intents, and saving-clauses.

Saving (sēⁱ·viŋ), *prep.* and *conj.* [absol. use of the pr. pple. of SAVE *v.* Cf. *excepting*.] **A.** *prep.*

1. Excepting, except; = SAVE *prep.* 1.

c 1386 CHAUCER *Knt.'s T.* 1980 No man myghte gladen Theseus Sauynge his olde fader Egeus. *c* 1440 *Alphabet of Tales* 139 His guidis wer all tane fro hym safeyng a mantill. 1513 DOUGLAS *Æneis* I. Prol. 155 The thre first bukis he hes ourhippit quyte, Salfand ane little twiching Polidorus, And the tempest sent furth be Eolus. 1569 *Reg. Privy Council Scot.* Ser. I. II. 4 Sauffing suche as ar attaynted. 1650 TRAPP *Comm. Exod.* v. 4 Anie thing seem's due work to a carnal minde saving God's service. 1808 SOUTHEY *Lett.* (1856) II. 115 Saving Joanna Baillie, we had no very interesting people this season. 1887 SAINTSBURY *Hist. Elizab. Lit.* viii. (1890) 302 There is no complete collection even of the poems, saving a privately printed one.

†**b.** *All saving but, ne saving but*: excepting only. *Obs.*

a 1400–50 *Alexander* 3707 A lande, as þe buke tellis, a large & a noble, All sauand bot serpentis & oþire sere bestis. *Ibid.* 4037 Sen at we loy nouthire gemmes, ne Iuwels in cofirs, Pelour, pirre, ne perle, ne na proude wedis, Ne sauand bot to sustene with oure awen sary craftis.

†**c.** With pers. pron. in the nominative. *Obs.*

1526 TINDALE *Rev.* ii. 17 And in the stone a newe name wrytten, which no man knoweth, savinge he that receaveth hit. [So 1611.] 1588 PARKE tr. *Mendoza's Hist. China* 254 Al their people [were] cast away, sauing they, who escaped by vsing great diligence. 1594 SPENSER *Amoretti* xxxv. 14 All this worlds glory seemeth vayne to me, And all their showes but shadowes, saving she.

†**d.** = but for; cf. SAVE *prep.* 1 d. *Obs.*

1540 *Aberd. Reg.* (1844) I. 173 And to deliuer thair schip agane, with her pertinentis, safand awentour of see, to the saidis Thomas and Robert.

2. Without prejudice or offence to. *Saving (one's) reverence*: see REVERENCE *sb.* 5 b.

c 1386 CHAUCER *Merch. T.* 522 And finally he dooth al his labour As he best myghte sauynge his honour To haste hem fro the mete in subtil wyse. 1387 TREVISA *Higden* (Rolls) VIII. 79 Savynge his owne worschippe [L. *salvo honore suo*]. *c* 1400 [see REVERENCE *sb.* 5 b]. *c* 1400 *Destr. Troy* 7587 Therfore, sothely me semeth, sauyng your wille, Hit is bettur þis bold kyng in the burgh hold. 1530 TINDALE *Answ. More's Dial.* Wks. (1573) 253/2 When we say..I beshrew him sauing my charitie, there we take it for patience. 1562 WINȜET *Cert. Tractates* I. (S.T.S.) I. 9 And ȝow (saifing ȝour dew honoris we speik). 1577 FULKE *Confut. Purg.* 382 But sauing his wisedome, he must geue vs leaue to aunswere for our selues. 1596 HARINGTON *Metam. Ajax* Answ. Let., Euen so I must write in this discourse, some time indeede as homely (sauing your worship) as you shall lightly see. 1596 SHAKS. *Tam. Shr.* II. i. 71 Sauing your tale Petruchio, I pray let vs that are poore petitioners speake too? 1607 NORDEN *Surv. Dial.* I. 15 Sauing your tale, Sir, we poore Country-men doe not thinke it good to haue our Lands plotted out. 1611 BEAUM. & FL. *Knt. Burn. Pestle* II. ii, You looke so grim, and, as I may say it, saving your presence, more like a Giant than a mortal man. 1837 HALLAM *Lit. Eur.* I. iii. § 96 His own opinions, saving the authority of the church, he was willing to defend. 1907 ELIZ. ROBINS *Convert* ii. 24 There's nothing I should quite so much hate talking about as politics—saving your presence.

b. *Saving correction* [= F. *sauf correction*]: subject to correction; if I am not mistaken. *rare.*

1830 A. W. FONBLANQUE *Eng. under 7 Administr.* (1837) II. 65 It seems to me, saving correction, that this does not concern us.

†**3.** With the reservation of. *Obs.*

1477 *Exch. Rolls Scotl.* VIII. 403 *note*, To be haldin..to the said Johne and Agnes..saulfing alanerly to ws and oure successouris the cariage of samekl of the saidis landis as the said Johne and Agnes occupiis [etc.]. 1609 SKENE *Reg. Maj.* 43 Saifeand alwise the service to the other over-lord, for the landis haldin of him.

†**4.** In default of, for lack of. *Obs. rare.*

c 1400 *Destr. Troy* 1126, I will say for myself, sauyng a bettur, As me thinkes full throly with-outyn threp more.

B. *conj.*

1. = EXCEPT, SAVE *conjs.* **a.** With clause introduced by *that*. Also, † with ellipsis of *that*.

1535 COVERDALE *Eccl.* v. 12 And what pleasure more hath he that possesseth them, sauynge that he maye loke vpon them with his eyes? 1578 LYTE *Dodoens* I. iii. 8 The wilde kinde of Buglosse is like to the small Buglosses..sauing the leaues be rougher, smaller, and narrower. 1600 J. PORY tr. *Leo's Africa* vi. 269 The flesh..tasteth not much vnlike to the flesh of a dunghill-cocke, sauing that it is more tough. 1720 MRS. MANLEY *Power of Love* I. 40 The Count of Briançon's Affairs seemed to keep the same Situations, saving his Love more and more increased, as his Hopes abated.

b. With advb. phrase. Also (rarely) *saving for* = but for, except as regards.

1473 *Rental Bk. Cupar-Angus* (1879) I. 168 Wilzam beand alegyt and fre of al aucht and wunt seruys, savand gyfe in tyme of harueyst we gader our tendis that he supple and help efter as we neyd. 1523 LD. BERNERS *Froiss.* I. cclxviii. 397 The duke of Lancastre..thought to haue gone and dyned in the frenchmens lodgynges (sauynge for the fyre and smoke that they had made wolde not suffre him). 1538 CRANMER in *St. Papers Hen. VIII*, I. 590 To graunte hensforth none other lycence to any other printer saving to theym, for the printyng of the said Bible. 1550 CROWLEY *Last Trump.* 1218 Delite in nothyng sauinge in doynge thy duty. 1611 BIBLE *Matt.* v. 32 Whosoeuer shall put away his wife, sauing for the cause of fornication, causeth her to commit adultery. *a* 1661 FULLER *Worthies, Suff.* (1662) III. 54 Though the general breadth be but twenty [miles], saving by the Sea-side. 1840 DICKENS *Old C. Shop* i, Saving in the country I seldom go out until after dark. 1877 SWINBURNE *Note C. Brontë* 54 Saving for her 'plentiful lack' of inborn baby-worship.

†**2.** Provided that. *Obs.*

1592–3 in Ellis *Orig. Lett.* Ser. III. IV. 111 The which Clergie government they would have to be exempted from the temporall government, saving they speake not agaynst the Prynces government towching the supremacye.

Savingly, *adv.* [f. SAVING *ppl. a.* + -LY [2].]

1. In saving, a sparing, or frugal manner.

1553 GRIMALDE *Cicero's Offices* I. (1558) 47 To leade our life sauinglie [L. *parce*], chastelie, sagelie, and soberlie. 1673 R. HEAD *Canting Acad.* 167 They begin to quaff at *Ut*, savingly. 1883 R. G. WHITE *Wash. Adams* 7 Having lived savingly in the past on fewer hundreds a year.

2. *Theol.* In a way that ensures salvation. Common in the 17th c.

1629 H. BURTON *Babel no Bethel* 31 If any..come to beleeue otherwise then that Church teacheth them, to wit, sauingly, whence haue they that beleefe? 1648 JENKYN *Blind Guide* iv. 120 The naturall man hath no power to know savingly the things of the Spirit of God. 1719 DE FOE *Crusoe* I. 260, I seriously pray'd to God, that he would enable me to instruct savingly this poor Savage. 1877 W. BRUCE *Comm. Rev.* 5 Practical love is the last link in the chain which connects man savingly with his Maker.

Savingness (sēⁱ·viŋnės). *rare.* [-NESS.]

1. 'Tendency to promote eternal salvation' (J.).

a 1658 DURHAM *Comm. Rev.* II. iii. (1660) 123 One in the search and trial of the sincerity and savingnesse of his Grace, is not only [etc.]. *a* 1677 MANTON *Christ's Eternal Exist.* vii. (1685) 193 Now if the fulness of the Godhead dwelt in him who gave this Covenant, we cannot deny either the certainty or the perfection, or the savingness of it.

2. The quality of being saving, sparing, frugal or parsimonious.

1727 BAILEY, vol. II, *Savingness*, Frugality. 1755 in JOHNSON. 1876 A. J. EVANS *Through Bosnia* i. 32 The savingness of the race was noticeable in their clothing, which was the same they had brought with them from Bulgaria.

Savings bank. Orig. **saving bank**, also **savings' bank**. [f. *savings* pl. (see SAVING *vbl. sb.* 2) + BANK *sb.*[3]] An institution for encouraging thrift, by receiving small deposits at interest.

In the United Kingdom there are four classes of these institutions: *trustee savings banks*, which are under the control of the National Debt Commissioners (with whom the whole of their funds must be invested), but are locally managed by bodies of trustees, who are prohibited from receiving remuneration for their services; savings banks for the army, navy, and merchant seamen, established respectively by the War Office, the Admiralty, and the Board of Trade; *post office savings banks* (see POST OFFICE); and *voluntary savings banks*, which are private establishments not under government control.

1817 *Act 57 Geo. III*, c. 105 Sched. A, The sum above stated is the exclusive Property of the Saving Bank specified in this our Order. 1819 *Ann. Biography* III. 215 In him [*sc.* G. Rose] the..system of saving banks found an active friend and patron. 1844 *Regul. & Ord. Army* 150 The Regimental Savings' Bank. 1886 C. E. PASCOE *London of To-day* xxvi. (ed. 3) 242 Investments in Consols have been placed within the reach of the poor through the medium of the Savings Bank. *Ibid.* xliii. (ed. 3) 382 Communications from the Savings Bank Department.

Saviour (sēⁱ·vyəɹ). Forms: 3–4 **sauveur**, 3–5 **sauveour**, 3–5 **saveour(e**, 4 **sauveor**, **saveor**, **-iur**, **-our**, **safeoure**, *Sc.* **safare**, **saweoure**, 4, 6 **sauvour**, **savioure**, 4–6 **savyour(e**, 5 **savyowur**, 5–6 **savyor**, 6 **salveour**, **-iour**, *Sc.* **salvior**, **salweour**, 4, 6–8 (9 chiefly *U.S.*) **savior**, 4– **saviour**. [a. OF. *sauveour* (mod.F. *sauveur*) = Pr., Sp., Pg. *salvador*, It. *salvatore*:—late L. *salvātōr-em*, agent-n. f. *salvāre* to SAVE.]

1. One who delivers or rescues from peril.

a 1300 *Cursor M.* 4666 His nam þai chaunged, fra þat our, And cald him 'warld sauueour'. *c* 1375 *Sc. Leg. Saints* i. (*Petrus*) 674 And petir till hym [Paul] þis can say:..far wele ay..lledar of heile and saweoure!' 1535 COVERDALE *Ecclus.* xlvi. 1 A greate sauioure vnto the electe of God. 1560 DAUS tr. *Sleidane's Comm.* 120 Saynct Genevefa is the saviour of Paris. 1611 BIBLE *Neh.* ix. 27 Thou gauest them sauiours, who saued them out of the hand of their enemies. 1711 POPE *Temp. Fame* 163 Bold Scipio, saviour of the Roman state; Great in his triumphs, in retirement great. 1774 WILKES *Corr.* (1805) IV. 185 Those who..now dare to persecute the saviour of India. 1871 BROWNING (*title*) Prince Hohenstiel-Schwangau: Saviour of Society. 1887 A. E. HOUSMAN *Shropshire Lad* i, To fields that bred them brave, The saviours come not home to-night.

b. *transf.* in nonce-uses.

c 1399 CHAUCER *Purse* 16 (Fairf.) Now purse that ben to me my lyves lyght And saveour as doun in this worlde here. 1552 LATIMER *Serm. 1st Sund. Epiph.* (1584) 297 Likewise shippes and boates..vpon the Seas are Sauiours, for they saue vs from the fury, rage, and tempest of the Sea. 1804 *Something Odd* III. 126 Thus died the means I had looked to as the saviour of myself and children.

2. He who saves mankind from sin and its consequences: as a title of God, and esp. of Christ (in the latter application often *Our Saviour*). Now always with capital S.

a 1300 *Cursor M.* 15015 Welcum sauuer! lang has þou ben, Al sal thoru þe be bett. 13.. *Coer de L.* 2087 He swore a ful grete othe, By Jesu Cryst our Saviour. 1362 LANGL. *P. Pl.* A. xi. 66 Whi wolde god vr saueour suffre such a worm In such a wrong wyse the wommon to bigyle? *a* 1450 MYRC *Instr. Par. Priests* 12 Ȝef þow plese thy sauyoure ȝef thow be not grete clerk Loke thow moste on thys werk. 1472 *Rec. St. Mary at Hill* 16 In the name of our lord Ihesu Criste our Savyour: Amen. *c* 1500 *Lancelot* 2096 This is the vyrgyne, this is the blessit flour That Ihesu bur that is our salweour. 1513 BRADSHAW *St. Werburge* II. 354 The yere of our saueour in his humanite viii hundreth complet .v. and seuentie. 1602 SHAKS. *Ham.* I. i. 159 That Season..Wherein our Sauiours Birth is celebrated. 1643 SIR T. BROWNE *Relig. Med.* I. § 3 At the sight of a Crosse or Crucifix I can dispense with my hat, but scarse with the thought or memory of my Saviour. 1667 MILTON *P. L.* XI. 412 Hail Son of God, Saviour of Men. *a* 1738 SWIFT *Serm. Mutual Subj.* (1744) 11 Our Saviour tells us that every Man is our Neighbour. 1753 HANWAY *Trav.* (1762) I. III. xxviii. 121 Who is the king, the lawgiver, the redeemer, and the savior. 1813 SHELLEY *Q. Mab* VII. 144 Millions shall live and die, Who ne'er shall call upon their Saviour's name. 1864 TENNYSON *En. Arden* 783 O God Almighty, blessed Saviour,..Uphold me, Father.

†**b.** *To receive one's Saviour*, *to give* (a person) *his Saviour*, etc.: common ME. phrases referring to the reception and administration of the Eucharist.

c 1400 *Rom. Rose* 6434 But thou yeve me my Saviour At Ester. *a* 1450 MYRC *Instr. Par. Priests* 1883 And ȝef he aske hys sauyour, Gyf hym hyt wyþ gret honour. 1470–85 MALORY *Arthur* XVII. xi. 706 Thenne asked she her saueour and as soone as she had receyued hit the soule departed from the body.

3. Saint Saviour. (See SAINT *a.* 3.) †**a.** Used in oaths. *Obs.* **b.** [= eccl. L. *ecclesia Sancti Salvatoris*], the title of the cathedral church of Rome, usually called St. John Lateran. **c.** The title of the monastic order founded by St. Bridget.

13.. *Guy Warw.* 5318 Þou wroche glotoun losaniour, þou schalt þe ȝeld, bi seyn Sauour. *c* 1330 *Arth. & Merl.* 2903 (Kölbing) Forth went anon sir Kay & ledde his fader, sir Antour, to þe chirche of seyn sauour. 1728 CHAMBERS *Cycl.* s.v., Order of St. Saviour, is a religious Order founded by St. Bridget. 1873 J. H. BLUNT *Myrr. our Ladye* p. xi. The Monastery of St Saviour and St Bridget of Syon of the Order of St Augustine.

4. *attrib.* (appositive), as in *saviour-ark*, *-arm*, *-god*, *-youth*; also *saviour-like* adj.

1836 GLADSTONE in *Good Words* (1871) 366 Is there..no *saviour ark That..bears the children, loved of God and blest, Unto the land of rest? 18.. SHELLEY *Assassins* ii. Prose Wks. 1888 II. 158 How many holy liars..would his *saviour arm drag from their luxurious couches. 1738 WESLEY *Ps.* xxiv. vi, This is the chosen Royal Race That seek their *Saviour-God to see. 1587 GOLDING *De Mornay* xxx. 568 There are two commings of Christ, the one in lowlynes.., Poore, Lowely, and *Sauiourlyke; and the other in maiestie. 1801 SOUTHEY *Thalaba* x. xxxv, Laila rush'd between To save the *saviour Youth.

Hence **Sa·viouress**, a female saviour; **Sa·viourhood**, **Sa·viourship**, the quality or fact of being a saviour.

c 1553 LATIMER in Foxe *A. & M.* (1563) 1309/2 When men can not be content that she [*sc.* our Lady] was a creature saued, but as it were a sauioresse, not neding saluation. 1649 JER. TAYLOR *Gt. Exemp.* III. Disc. xix. 143 Polycrita Naxia [expired] being saluted the Saviouresse of her countrey. 1650 FULLER *Pisgah* IV. v. 91 Finding an Egyptian wronging an Israelite he kils him; shewing therein some signes of that Saviour-ship, which God intended him for. 1864 P. BROOKS *Myst. Iniq.*, etc. xviii. (1893) 317 What if there had been for ever a Saviourhood in the Deity. 1893 *Athenæum* 30 Dec. 919/2 The Indian Buddhist Cult of Avalokita and his Consort Tārā the Saviouress. 1900 R. J. CAMPBELL in *Chr. World Pulpit* 31 Jan. 71 The Saviourhood of Christ. 1905 MARZIALS *Browning* 49 Unfolding the mysteries of his saviourship of society.

Saviour, savir, obs. forms of SAVOUR.

†**Savite.** *Obs.* [f. the name of Professor P. Savi + -ITE [1].] = NATROLITE.

1852 *Amer. Jrnl. Sci. & Arts* Ser. II. XIV. 64 Savite.

Savite, Saviur, obs. ff. SAFETY, SAVIOUR.

‖**Savoir faire** (savwar fɛ̄r). [Fr.; *savoir* (formerly often miswritten *sçavoir*) to know, know how (inf. used subst.) + *faire* to do.] Tact, address; the instinctive knowledge of the right course of action upon any given emergency.

1815 SCOTT *Guy M.* xxxv, He had great confidence in his own *savoir faire*. 1840 BARHAM *Ingol. Leg.* Ser. II. *Black Mousquetaire*, He..show'd so much of the true *sçavoir faire*. 1886 *Manch. Exam.* 15 Mar. 5/5 Sir Charles Warren has the versatility and *savoir-faire* which will enable him to do good work as Chief Commissioner of the London police.

‖**Savoir vivre** (savwar vīvr). [Fr.; *savoir* (see prec.) + *vivre* to live.] Ability in the conduct of life, knowledge of the world and of the usages customary in good society.

1755 MASON *Let. to Gray* (1853) 30 Though France is remarkable for its *savoir vivre* and Italy for its *virtù*, yet Germany is the reservoir of solid literature. 1806 J. PINKERTON *Recoll. Paris* II. 98 The use of red wine with oysters shews great want of *sçavoir vivre*. 1878 GEO. ELIOT *Dan. Der.* xlviii, People with any *savoir vivre* don't make a fuss about such things.

‖**Savonette** (sæ·vŏnet). Also 8 **savonet**. [Fr. (now written *savonnette*), dim. of *savon* soap: see -ET.] (See quots.)

1706 PHILLIPS (ed. Kersey), *Savonet*, (*Fr.*) a Wash-Ball or other Sort of Compound, to wash the Face or Hands with. 1866 COOLEY *Toilet* 438 Savonettes; Soap Balls; Wash Balls..are made of any of the mild toilet-soaps, scented at will, generally with the addition of powdered starch or farina, and sometimes, sand.

b. *Savonette-tree* [= F. *arbre à savonnettes*], a W. Indian tree, *Pithecolobium micradenium*, the bark of which is used as a substitute for soap.

1864 GRISEBACH *Flora W. Ind. Islands* 787.

Savor: see SAVOUR *sb.* and *v.*

Savorous (sēⁱ·vŏrəs), *a.* Also 4–7 **saverous**, 5 **savoruss**, *Sc.* **sawouris**, 5–7 **savourous**. [a. OF. *saverous*, *savorous* (mod.F. *savoureux*):—late L. *sapōrōsus*, f. *sapōr* SAPOR: see -OUS.]

1. Of good savour, pleasant to the taste.

c 1450 HOLLAND *Howlat* 705 Many sawouris salss with sewaris he send. 1580 NISBET *N. T., Mark* ix. 49 Salt is gude; gif salt be vnsauorous, in quhat thing sal ye mak it sauorous? 1604 E. G[RIMSTONE] tr. *Acosta's Hist. Indies* III. xvi. 170 There are two kindes of fishes breed in this Lake.., the one they call Suches, which is great and savorous. 1891 F. TENNYSON *Daphne*, etc. 274 Garden sweets.. And savorous herbs that lay together crush'd.

†**b.** *fig.* That is relished or enjoyed; delightful.

? *a* 1366 CHAUCER *Rom. Rose* 84 Than yonge folk entenden ay For to ben gay and amorous, The tyme is than so savorous. 1483 CAXTON *Gold. Leg.* 366/4 Though she were resplendysshaunt, wel sauerous and ryght ful of grete myracles. 1567 PAINTER *Pal. Pleas.* II. 157 b, To gather that soote and sauorous frute which louers so egerly sue for at maydens handes. 1657 tr. '*Idiota's*' *Div. Lover, Holy Exerc.*, But if it proue..that some other worke, or Exercise, is, or would be more sauourous or rellishinge to thy Spirit.

†**2.** Full of relish, greedy. *Obs.*

1491 CAXTON *Vitas Patr.* (W. de W. 1495) I. cxv. 138 b, Many notable lordes..somwhat to content his sauourous appetyte..sende oft tymes to hym grete sommes of money.

Hence **Sa·vorously** *adv.*

1480 CAXTON *Ovid's Met.* xv. iii, The tyme was somtyme that the peple lyvyd wᵗ out etyng of flesshe; & wer norysshyd saverously of the fruytes of the trees & of herbes.

Savory (sēⁱ·vŏri), *sb.* Forms: [1 **sæþerie**], 4–6 **saverey**, 5 **savereye**, **saferay**, **savry**, 5–6 **saveray**, 6–7 **savery(e**, **saverie**, **savorie**, 7 **savourie**, 7–9 **savoury**, 7– **savory**. [Ultimately from L. *saturēia*; the form-history is uncertain.

On the one hand the ME. *saverey* might descend (with substitution of v for ð) from OE. *sæðerie*, a. early OF. *saðereie (later *sarrie*, whence the dim. *sarriette* surviving in mod.Fr.) = Pr. *sadreia* (whence 16th c. Fr. dial. *sadriege*, Sp. *ajedrea*, and perh. by metathesis the synon. *sajerida*) :—L. *saturēiam*. On the other hand, Estienne (*De Re Rustica*, 1570) cites an It. *savoreggia* and F. *savorée*, and the latter appears in Cotgr. 1611 as *savorée*. The existence of these forms suggests that the ME. *saverey* may be an adoption of an unrecorded OF. form which had the v either as a phonetic development in hiatus (cf. F. *pouvoir* for early OF. *pooir*) or through the influence of *saveur* SAVOUR.

Independent adoption of the Latin word appears in OE. *saturege*, ME. SATUREIE, MHG. *saterje* (G. *saturei*), It. *satureja*, corruptly *santoreggia*, Pg. *saturagem*.]

1. Any plant of the genus *Satureia* (N. O. *Labiatæ*), esp. the annual herb *Satureia hortensis* (Garden, Summer Savory), or the perennial *S. montana* (Mountain or Winter Savory), natives of the south of Europe, cultivated for use as flavouring ingredients in cooking.

[*c* 1000 *Sax. Leechd.* II. 314 Feldmoran sæd, sæþerian sæd, petorsilian sæd.] *a* 1387 *Sinon. Barthol.* (Anecd. Oxon.) 37 *Satureia*, *tymbra idem*, saverey. *c* 1420 *Liber Cocorum* (1862) 32 Take sawge, persoly, ysope, saveray, Onyons gode. *c* 1430 *Two Cookery-bks.* 18 Take a Capoun ..& sethe hym in Water, percely, Sauereye & Salt. *c* 1440 *Pallad. on Husb.* Tabula 374 Coriaundir, popy, saury, senuy, oynet. 1483 *Cath. Angl.* 319/1 Saferay, s[a]tureia, *herba est*. 1502 ARNOLDE *Chron.* (1811) 171 And ete alle maner fishe wᵗ..vergews made with good erbis sawge & sauery. 1573 TUSSER *Husb.* (1878) 94 Summer sauerie. 1597 GERARDE *Herbal* II. clxv. 460 Winter Sauorie is a plant resembling Hyssope. 1697 DRYDEN *Virg. Georg.* IV. 43 Wild Thyme and Sav'ry set around their Cell. 1786 ABERCROMBIE *Gard. Assist.* 79 Savory—sow of the summer and winter kind. 1849 BALFOUR *Man. Bot.* § 967 Many Labiates, such as Thyme..Savoury,..&c., are used..to flavour sauces and dishes. 1881 *Encycl. Brit.* XII. 289 The Winter Savory, *Satureja montana*, a hardy evergreen undershrub.

2. *Dyer's Savory*, the Saw-wort, *Serratula tinctoria*. 1874 *Treas. Bot.* Suppl.

3. *attrib.* and *Comb.*: *savory-seed*; *savory-leaved* adj.; **savory oil** (see quot.); **savory thyme**, *Thymus virginicus*, an American herb.

1822 *Hortus Anglicus* II. 394 *Aster Linariifolius*. *Savory-leaved Star Wort. 1896 BRANNT *Anim. & Veg. Fats* II. 577 *Savory oil..both the summer savory, *Satureja hortensis*, L., and the winter savory, *S. montana*, yield by distillation..a volatile oil. *c* 1440 *Pallad. on Husb.* III. 580 Now *saury seed in faat vndunged londe Doth wel. 1822 *Hortus Anglicus* II. 105 Virginian or *Savory Thyme.

Savour, savor (sēⁱ·vəɹ), *sb.* Forms: 3–5 **savur**, 4 **safour**, **safer**, **sauvur**, **savoyre**, *Sc.* **sawure**, **-oure**, **-or**, **-eoure**, 4–5 **savore**, 4–6 **savoure**, **saver**, 5 **saveure**, **saveoure**, **savowre**, **savyr**, *Sc.* **sawour**, 5–6 **savir**, 6 **savre**, **savowr**, **savyour**, **savar**, **sawr-**, 7 **saviour**, 8 *Sc.* **sa'r**, 4– **savour**, **savor**. [a. OF. *savur*, *savour* (mod.F. *saveur*) = Pr., Sp., Pg. *sabor*, It. *savore*:—L. *sapōrem* taste, savour (see SAPOR), f. *sapĕre* to taste.]

1. Quality in relation to the sense of taste; a specific mode of this quality, as sweetness, bitterness, etc.; a taste. Also in fig. context.

Now *rare*, exc. as denoting a touch or admixture of some taste other than the proper or prevailing taste of a substance, a 'smack'.

a 1225 *Ancr. R.* 102 Þes cos, leoue sustren, is a swetnesse & a delit of heorte, so unimete swote & swete, þet euerich worldes sauur is bitter þer ajeines. *a* 1300 *Cursor M.* 13404 He dranc and feild gode sauur. 1303 R. BRUNNE *Handl. Synne* 9988 Hit semeþ brede, as is syȝt, And as brede, sauer haþ ryȝt. *c* 1315 SHOREHAM *Poems* I. 686 Ne lef non oþer, crysteman, For safour ne coloure. For þat colour, ne þat sauour Ne beþ nauȝt þer inne cryste. 13.. *E. E. Allit. P.* B. 995 For his make was myst, þat on þe mount lenged In a stonen statue þat salt sauor habbes. 1393 LANGL. *P. Pl.* C. xv. 187 Þe larke..is loueloker of lydene, And swettur of sauour. 1422 tr. *Secreta Secret., Priv. Priv.* 208 By the tonge we felen the dyuersite of Sauores, Swetnes and bittyrnesse, Saltnesse and egyrnesse, and other Saueoure. *a* 1510 DOUGLAS *K. Hart* I. 420 Servit thai war of mony dyuerss meis, Full sawris sweit. 1587 GOLDING *De Mornay* i. (1617) 7 Sounds, Sents, Savors, and Feelings. 1600 SURFLET *Country Farm* III. xlix. 533 Cyders differ one from another, especially in colour and sauour or relish. 1671 MILTON *P. R.* II. 342 Meats of noblest sort And savour. 1725 POPE *Odyss.* xv. 155 Viands of various kinds allure the taste Of choicest sort and savour; rich repast! 1774 tr. *Chesterf. Let. to Son* (8 June 1741), [The waters] are very heating, and disagreeable to the taste, having the savour of rotten eggs. 1841 ELPHINSTONE *Hist. Ind.* I. 233 Qualities of body; namely,—colour, savour, odour, feel [etc.].

b. The power of affecting the sense of taste, esp. agreeably; sapidity, tastiness.

c 1440 *Alphabet of Tales* 65 Ther wyne had nowder colour nor savor. 1483 CAXTON *G. de la Tour* m iv b, They ete black brede and metes of lytyll sauoure. 1816 SCOTT *Old Mort.* xiii, I see auld fruit has little savour—our suffering and our services have been of an ancient date. 1882 'OUIDA' *Maremma* I. 12 The lads felt that when no more tales could be told of the king of Maremma, savour would be gone out of the goatsflesh roasted in the charcoal in the woods.

†**c.** Flavouring, spice. *Obs.*

1422 tr. *Secreta Secret., Priv. Priv.* 187 Lette hungyre yeue the talent, and not Sause ne Saueure.

2. A smell, perfume, aroma. *poet.* and *arch.*

[So occas. L. *sapor* and the verb *sapĕre* (Pliny). Some traces of this use occur in OF., though it seems to have been rare; in mod.Fr. it is entirely unknown.]

a 1300 *Cursor M.* 1381 And cipres, be þe suete sauur, Bitakens ur suete saueeur. 1303 R. BRUNNE *Handl. Synne* 11567 She broȝt a smel of grete sauour. 1382 WYCLIF *John* xii. 3 The hous is fillid of the sauour of oygnement. *c* 1400 *Laud Troy Bk.* 6027 The boydies that ther ded lay, That hadde be sclayn In fight that day; Ther come of hem a foul sauour. *c* 1450 MYRC *Festial* 142 Þus as þe flesche rostyd, þe sauer þerof went out into þe strete. 1481 CAXTON *Myrrour* II. vi. 75 [The panther] gyueth oute of his mouth so swete a savour and smell, that anon the bestes that fele it seche hym. 1508 DUNBAR *Tua Mariit Wemen* 8 Throw the sauar sanatiue of the sueit flouris. *a* 1593 MARLOWE *Edw. II*, v. v, I was almost stifeled with the sauour. 1631 GOUGE *God's Arrows* III. § 88. 349 Plagues oft arise..from noisome savours. 1697 DRYDEN *Virg. Georg.* IV. 88 Then Melfoil beat, and Honey-suckles pound, With these alluring Savours strew the Ground. 1820 SHELLEY *Hymn Merc.* xxii, For the sweet savour of the roasted meat Tempted him though immortal. 1871 FARRAR *Days of my Youth* ii. (1876) 20 Like a sweet savour, like a precious heritage, it lingers here.

b. in figurative context.

a 1225 *St. Marher.* 4 He is leoflukest lif for to lokin uppon, and swotest to smeallen; ne his swote sauur, ne his almihte mihte..ne mei neauer littlin ne aliggen. *c* 1500 *Joseph Arim.* (E.E.T.S.) 51 Heyle, tresour of Glastenbury moost imperyall, In sauour smellynge swete as eglantyne.

c. In the translations of the Bible from Tindale (1526) onwards, *savour* occurs very freq. as rendering of Gr. ὀσμή, Heb. ריח *rēaḥ* smell; in the Old Testament *lit.* of the smell of sacrifices and incense regarded as pleasing to God, in the N. T. *fig.* chiefly with reference to spiritual sacrifices.

See, e.g., *Gen.* viii. 21, *Num.* xxviii. 13, *Ezek.* vi. 13, 2 *Cor.* ii. 15, *Eph.* v. 2.

d. Used *fig.* for: Repute, estimation; = ODOUR 4 b. Now only *poet.*

1535 COVERDALE *Exod.* v. 21 Ye have made the sauoure of us to stynke before Pharao. 1639 FULLER *Holy War* II. xv. (1640) 64 Since which time the bad sauour of his life came to the Popes nose, who sent a Legate to depose him. 1726 W. PENN in *Life* Wks. (1782) I. 53 These several Things agreed upon, being of good Savour and Report. 1872 TENNYSON *Gareth* 377 Then came in hall the messenger of Mark, A name of evil savour in the land, The Cornish king.

3. In various uses, originally *fig.* from sense 1.

†**a.** Attractive quality, merit. value. *Obs.*

a 1225 *Ancr. R.* 138 Salt bitocneð wisdom; vor salt ȝiueð mete wordnesse & wisdom ȝifð sauur. 13.. *K. Alis.* 2839 (Bodl. MS.) Tofore þe kyng com on harpoure And made a lay of gret sauoure. *c* 1330 *Cast. Love* 72 Þauh hit on Englisch be dim and derk, Ne nabbe no sauer bi-fore a clerk. 1483 CAXTON *Golden Leg.* 220 b, She had sotbly the bame of good odour and sauoure in conuersacion.

†**b.** Character, style, sort. *Obs.*

1605 SHAKS. *Lear* I. iv. 258 This admiration Sir, is much o' th' sauour Of other your new pranckes. 1639 ROUSE *Heav. Univ.* x. (1702) 153 Let the excellent and unmatchable ointments of Christ Jesus give an excellent savour to your works.

c. Essential virtue or property: with allusion to Matt. v. 13 (and Luke xiv. 34). Also, power to excite relish, interest.

1650 I. WEEKES *Truth's Conf.* i. 11 This is to put a nonsense upon the place, and to destroy the savor that is in it. 1850 MARSDEN *Early Purit.* (1853) 334 Principles which are permitted to lie barren soon lose their savour. 1885 PATTISON *Mem.* 298 All the savour of life is departed.

d. A 'smack', tinge, or admixture.

1795 BURNS '*O ay my wife*' 5 Some sa'r o' comfort still at last, When a' my days are done, man. 1867 MACFARREN *Harmony* ii. 66 Practised by modern musicians when they wish to give an antique savour to any particular passage.

†**4.** Relish or taste for something; delight, satisfaction. *To catch (a) savour*: to acquire a taste or liking. *Obs.*

a 1225 *Ancr. R.* 232 We ne iuindeð swetnesse in none þinge þet we wel doð, ne sauur of heorte. 13.. *Coer de L.* 3047 To mete hadde he no savour To wyn, ne watyr, ne no lycour. ? *c* 1400 LYDG. *Æsop's Fab.* Prol. 2 Wysdom is more of pris than gold in cofres To theym, that have savour in lettrure. *Ibid.* i. 65 Losengeours..Whiche have savour in slewth and sluggardy. *Ibid.* ii. 101 When a iorrour haþe caught sauour ones To be forsworn, custom makeþ hym strong. *c* 1412 HOCCLEVE *De Reg. Princ.* 393 Hast þou in me ony gretter sauour þan þat þou haddest first whan þou me sy. *c* 1430–40 *Abbey of Holy Ghost* in Horstm. *Hampole* I. 333 Plente of oyle, þat es for to hafe delyte and sauoyre in god. 1483 CAXTON *G. de la Tour* m iv, Good wynes, whereto the good heremyte tooke soo good a sauoure that he had..dranke soo moche, that he was dronke. 1555 WATREMAN *Fardle of Facions* II. iv. 140 When they had caughte a sauour in this holye daye loytering,..thei made a longe holy daye also of the whole seuenth yere.

†**5.** Perception, understanding. *Obs.*

1387–8 T. USK *Test. Love* III. iv. (Skeat) 79 Of this have I yet no savour, without better declaration. 1548 UDALL, etc. *Erasm. Par. Matt.* iii. 1–6 Christ..of whome they had a certayne sauour and vnderstandyng. 1633 G. HERBERT *Temple, Dialogue* iii, But as I can see no merit, Leading to this favour: So the way to fit me for it, Is beyond my savour.

Savour, savor (sēⁱ·vəɹ), *v.* Forms: 3 **savur(e**, 4 **savir**, **savyre**, **safer**, 4–5 **savere**, 4–6 **saver**, **savoure**, 5 **savre**, **savyr**, 4– **savor**, **savour**: *Sc.* 4 **sawer**, 5 **sawour**, 6 **sair-**, **sawr-**, 8 **sar**, **sa'r**. [a. OF. *savourer*, *savorer* (mod.F. *savourer*) = Pr. *saborar*, Sp., Pg. *saborear*, It. † *savorare* (now in learned form *saporare*):—late L. *sapōrāre*, f. *sapōr-* SAVOUR *sb.*]

I. To have a savour.

†**1.** *intr.* Of food or drink: To taste (well or ill); chiefly, to have an agreeable taste. Often with *dative*; hence *trans.* to be agreeable to the taste of. *Obs.*

a 1300 *Cursor M.* 3647, I sal þam dight til his be-houe, A mete als he was wonto loue: It sal him sauur al to will, Ete he sal þer-of his fill. 1362 LANGL. *P. Pl.* A. VII. 249 Ete not, Ich hote þe til hunger þe take. And sende þe sum of his sauce to sauer þe þe betere. *c* 1386 CHAUCER *Pars. T.* ¶ 48 For soothly, there is no thyng that sauoureth so wel to a child as the Milk of his Norice. 1432–50 tr. *Higden* (Rolls) VIII. 17 Þer was no licoure that savoured his mowthe or that he myȝhte discerne in that hit made his chekes colde. 1530 PALSGR. 698/2 This potage savoureth, whiche we use whan the meate is sodden to the pottes bottome. 1563 HYLL *Art Garden.* (1593) 129 In the fourth day, to sprinckle your seedes with water..for by that meanes (saith he) they will sauour much better. 1634 G. HERBERT tr. *Cornarus' Treat. Temperance* 8 That Proverb, wherewith Gluttons use to defend themselves, to wit, *That which savours, is good and nourisheth*. 1686 W. HARRIS tr. *Lemery's Course Chem.* 119 Water..that's heated or boil'd in a Copper vessel for a whole day together, savours not at all, or not so much, of the Copper.

†**b.** *fig.*

c 1450 tr. *De Imitatione* III. xxxix. 109 To whom þou sauorist, what shal not sauore him ariȝt? and to whom þou sauorist not, what þinge may turne him to mirþe? [L. *cui tu sapis*.. *Et cui tu non sapis*.] 1526 *Pilgr. Perf.* (W. de W. 1531) 8 Syth the mater is all spirituall, it shall but lytell sauour or please them that be carnall.

2. *intr.* To give forth a (specified) scent or odour; to smell *of* something. *arch.*

13.. *Cursor M.* 6368 (Gött.) Þa wandis..euer þai held lijf and flour, Sauirand wid a suete sauur. 1303 R. BRUNNE *Handl. Synne* 1396 As a medue hyt was grene,..And saueryd swete as spycerye. 13.. *E. E. Allit. P.* C. 275 Þer in saym & in sorȝe þat sauoured as helle, þer was bylded his bour. *c* 1450 MYRC *Festial* 50 For þer nys no brent sence þat sauereth so swete yn mannys nase, as doþe a deuote oreson yn Goddys nase. 1500–20 DUNBAR *Poems* xxxiv. 34 'Fy', quod the Feynd, 'Thow sairis of blek, Go clenge the clene and cum to me'. 1526 *Pilgr. Perf.* (W. de W. 1531) 154 Was dulcet & swete to yᵉ mouth..& sauoured wele to the nose. 1549 LATIMER *Ploughers* (Arb.) 18 As the saffrone bagge..doth euer after sauoure and smel of the swete saffron that it conteyned. 1601 HOLLAND *Pliny* II. 111 Parthenium ..bringeth forth a white floure, sauouring like an apple, and having a bitter tast. 1870 W. MORRIS *Earthly Parad.* III. IV. 218 The spilt blood savoured horribly.

†**b.** Without qualifying word: To smell offensively, stink. *Obs.*

1536 *Primer Eng. & Lat.* 121 b, Whan he [*sc.* Lazarus] in the same foure dayes had lyen So that hys body beganne to sauoure. *a* 1591 H. SMITH *Serm.* (1637) 348 Like the snuffe of a candle, which all men looked upon even now when it shined, and now it so savours, that they tread it under foot.

3. *fig.* †**a.** To be agreeable or pleasing. Const. *to* or *dative*. *Obs.* **b.** With qualification: To be *well* or *ill* pleasing. *arch.*

a 1300 *Cursor M.* 25883 'Man', he sais, 'quin cuth þow fele Hu pine o þis lijf sauure wele'. 1362 LANGL. *P. Pl.* A. IX. 102 But ȝit sauereþ me nat þi siggynge. 1450–1530 *Myrr. our Ladye* 4 That lyke it [the service] goyth dayle as throughe your mouthes so let yt synke & sauoure contynually in youre hartes. *a* 1609 SIR F. VERE *Comm.* (1657) 94 This advise could not savour to that young Nobleman. *a* 1660 *Contemp. Hist. Irel.* (Ir. Archæol. Soc.) I. 275 All the sermon of that daie..was of this and such other like stuffe, as not pleasinge or sauoringe unto Christian eares. 1668 HOWE *Bless. Righteous* (1825) 78 Nothing savours with me; I take comfort in nothing. 1842 TENNYSON *Vision of Sin* xxiv, What is loathsome to the young Savours well to thee and me.

4. a. *To savour of*: to show traces of the presence or influence of; to have some of the characteristics of; to have the appearance of proceeding from.

1548 CRANMER *Catech.* Ep. Ded., [We] sauer longest of that thynge that we fyrste receaue and taist of. 1577 HANMER *Anc. Eccles. Hist.* 110 The phrase of that epistle sauoreth very muche of the Greeke tongue. 1612 DRAYTON *Poly-olb.* To Rdr. A 1, The Idle Humerous world must heare of nothing that..sauors of Antiquity. 1647 N. BACON *Disc. Govt. Eng.* I. iii. 9 The matter of that Epistle savoureth of the purer times of the Church. 1700 DRYDEN *Fables* Pref. *A 2, I have written nothing which savours of Immorality or Profaneness. 1722 RAMSAY *Three Bonnets* I. 120 Your courtship sars sae rankly O' selfish interest. 1749 FIELDING *Tom Jones* I. x, Such solicitations from superiors too often savour strongly of commands. 1790 BURKE *Fr. Rev.* 234 But the institutions savour of superstition in their very principle. 1870 J. H. NEWMAN *Gram. Assent* II. viii. 332 Cromwell, whose actions savoured of the boldest logic, was a confused speaker. 1894 H. DRUMMOND *Ascent of Man* 47 A spectacular act..savours of the magician.

b. *trans.* in the same sense.

1574 WHITGIFT *Def. Answ.* ii. 109 For it neyther savoureth the spirite of God, neither yet any modest and good nature, but [etc.]. *a* 1634 RANDOLPH *Muses Looking-gl.* III. iii. (1638) 53 Would thou wert worth the killing. *Colax.* A good wish, Savouring as well discretion, as bold valour. 1667 MILTON *P. L.* x. 1043 Wilful barrenness, That..savours onely Rancor and pride. 1906 *Athenæum* 23 June 758/2 'One ail for thee and me', instead of 'wail'; 'went by her like their flames', instead of 'thin flames'—these savour the printer.

II. To give a savour to.

†**5.** *trans.* To flavour with salt or spice. *Obs.*

13.. *E. E. Allit. P.* B. 825 Þenne ho sauerez with salt her seuez vchone. 1387 TREVISA *Higden* (Rolls) IV. 243 Flessche i-savered i-not by what verrtu of herbes. *c* 1400 *Lanfranc's Cirurg.* 75 Kyddes & lambres, & kalffes isaveryde with agresta. *c* 1440 *Pallad. on Husb.* XII. 494 Yf hit be not sauered worth a flie, Olyues grene ygrounde in hit let stie. 1508 DUNBAR *Flyting* 192 Powderit with prymross, sawrand all with clowiss. 1693 LYDE *Retaking 'Friend's Adventure'* 9 Beef without any Salt to savour it.

†**6.** To impart a taste or flavour to. *Obs. rare*[−1].

1303 R. BRUNNE *Handl. Synne* 9986 Þarfore hys wysdom, hys owne rede, Sauerþ hyt [Christ's flesh] yn wyne and brede.

7. To season, flavour; to give tone or character to.

1579 LYLY *Euphues* (Arb.) 44 These old huddles, hauing ouercharged their gorges with fancie, accompt al honest recreation meere folly, and hauing taken a surfet of delight, seeme now to sauour it with despight. 1889 J. JACOBS *Æsop's Fables* I. 196 He..has left out..that pinch of humour that has savoured the fabulist.

8. To impart a savour or scent to.

1832 HT. MARTINEAU *Ireland* ii. 28 On many a petition, savoured with a scent of potheen, did he turn his back.

III. To perceive a savour.

9. *trans.* To taste, to perceive by the sense of taste. In mod. use, to taste with relish, to dwell on the taste of; also *fig.*, to give oneself to the enjoyment or appreciation of.

c 1430 *Pilgr. Lyf Manhode* II. cxxix. (1869) 125 And j shulde neuere be at ese if j sauowrede swete thing. *c* 1440 *Gesta Rom.* lvi. 373 (Add. MS.) When he sauours the soure barke with oute for bitternesse he leuyth the swete kyrnelle with in. 1865 *Pall Mall G.* 17 June 11/1 We savour at our leisure the delicate satire which we were too excited to appreciate duly. 1869 BROWNING *Ring & Bk.* XI. 1762 Deal each judge His dole of flattery and feigning,—why, He turns and tries and snuffs and savours it As an old fly the sugar-grain. 1883 'HOLME LEE' *Loving & Serving* I. iii. 42 He moved hither and thither about his silent house,.. savouring his strange pain. 1889 MAX O'RELL *Jacques Bonhomme* 70 Savoring in advance the long list of dainties for the day.

†**b.** To relish, enjoy (flavours). Also *absol.* *Obs.*

1387 TREVISA *Higden* (Rolls) VIII. 17 He wolde seie þat he savered nouȝt, for his kelede his mouþ and his jowes. 1426 LYDG. *De Guil. Pilgr.* 16990 For tyl I hadde gone to Scole with Trybulacion, I savoured fful lytil in the soote mylk of grace. 1566 *Pasquine in Traunce* 65 If a man giue them any deintier meate, they can not sauour it, and suche as they sauoure not, they vtterly dispise.

10. To be conscious, or sensible of (an odour). † Also *absol.* *Obs.* or *arch.*

1382 WYCLIF *Ecclus.* xxx. 19 What shal profiten sacrifice to the maumet? and forsothe he shal not eten, ne sauouren [Vulg. *nec odorabit*]. *c* 1450 MYRC *Festial* 191 And þerwyth he felde þe swetyst smell þat euer he saverde. *a* 1542 WYATT *That the Season of Enjoyment* 23 What vaileth the flower To stand still and wither; If no man it savour It serves only for sight. 1605 SHAKS. *Lear* IV. ii. 39 (1st Qo.) Filths sauor but themselues. 1864 *Daily Tel.* 8 Sept., You have the moor pretty much to yourself, can savour all its wild perfume, and listen to all its cries.

11. To relish, like, care for. *Obs.* or *arch.*

So *thou savourest* in all versions of Matt. xvi. 23 from Wyclif 1380 to 1611; Vulg. *sapis*, Gr. φρονεῖς, Revised Version 1881 *thou mindest*.

c 1340 HAMPOLE *Prose Tr.* 1, I sauyre noghte joye that with Jhesu es noghte mengede. *c* 1390 CHAUCER *Truth* 5 Savour no more than thee bihove shal. 1451 CAPGRAVE *Life St. Aug.* 1 To þese both þe holy apostell saide he was dettour, to paye ech of hem aftir þat he sauoured. 1526 *Pilgr. Perf.* (W. de W. 1531) 148 b, Some blynded with sensualite & carnall pleasure, sauouryng nothynge but yᵗ onely that is delectable to yᵉ body. 1584 LODGE *Alarum* (Shaks. Soc.) 77 Those that are earthly minded savor not the things that are of God. 1599 B. JONSON *Cynthia's Rev.* III. iv, Sauours himselfe alone, is onely kind And louing to himselfe. 1633 FORD *Broken H.* I. i, Beauteous Penthea wedded to this torture By an insulting brother,..he savours not humanity, Whose sorrow melts not into more than pity, In hearing but her name. 1678 BUNYAN *Pilgr.* I. (1900) 23 He [Worldly Wiseman] savoureth only the doctrine of this world. 1693 NORRIS *Pract. Disc.* (1698) IV. 223 Those false Relishes and depraved Tastes of the Soul which dispose it to Mind and Savour the Earth, and Earthly things. 1868 E. EDWARDS *Ralegh* I. xviii. 376 To give prominence to such rumours as they know will be savoured at their own Court.

†**12.** To perceive, apprehend; to discover traces of. Also, to experience. *Obs.*

a 1340 HAMPOLE *Psalter* xciii. 8 The vnwis, withouten kunynge, & fulis, withouten purnyaunce of the tother warld, that ere in noumbire of cristen men, vndirstandis and sauyrs this. *c* 1440 *Gesta Rom.* (Add. MS.) 110 But wolde god, that wrechid man.., sauered and vndirstode, and ordeyned for his laste Ende! 1509 BARCLAY *Shyp of Folys* (1874) I. 248 Such seldom savour fortune's happiness. 1567 *Gude & Godlie B.* (S. T. S.) 146 That we, in hartis, may sauour Thy mercy and thy fauour. 1602 WARNER *Alb. Eng.* XIII. lxxvii. (1612) 317 By now, perhaps, thou sauorests [*sic*] some Godhead. 1659 HEYLIN *Certamen Epist.* 8 In your writings I savour a spirit so very distant from my disposition, that I have small hopes that my words will escape your displeasure.

†**b.** *To savour out*: to scent out, get wind of. *Obs.*

1724 RAMSAY *Elegy John Cowper* i, There's none..Could sa'r sculdudry out like John.

†**c.** *intr.* To have a suspicion *of*. *Obs. rare*[−1].

1594 MARLOWE & NASHE *Dido* III. ii, Sister, I see you sauour of my wiles.

Savour, obs. form of SAVIOUR.

†**Sa·vourable**, *a.* *Obs. rare*[−1]. [a. OF. *savourable*, f. *savourer* to SAVOUR.] Pleasing to the taste.

1502 ATKYNSON tr. *De Imitatione* III. vi. 200 Loue..that maketh..bitter thynges swete & sauorable.

Savoured (sēⁱ·vəɹd), *ppl. a.* [f. SAVOUR *sb.* + -ED.] Having savour, with defining adv.

1590 SPENSER *F. Q.* II. vii. 51 Hearbs and fruits..Not.. sweet and well savored, But direfull deadly black. 1609 *Shaks. Tr. & Cr.* Ep. ¶ 2 (1st Qo.), So much and such sauored salt of witte is in his Commedies, that they seeme.. to be borne in that sea that brought forth Venus.

Savourer (sēⁱ·vərəɹ). [f. SAVOUR *v.* + -ER [1].] One who savours (in various senses).

1655 FULLER *Ch. Hist.* IV. ii. § 61. 172 She was..a great Savourer and Favourer of Wickliffe his Opinions. 1898 MONEY-COUTTS *Rev. St. Love* 3 Be all the blight of God's immediate ban on savourers of poison at the feast of Love.

Savourie, obs. form of SAVORY and SAVOURY.

Savourily (sēⁱ·vərili), *adv.* Also **savorily**. [f. SAVOURY *a.* + -LY [2].]

1. In a savoury manner, with a pleasing smell or taste, appetizingly. Also, † with relish or appetite.

1398 TREVISA *Barth. De P. R.* XVIII. ix. (Bodl. MS.), A serpent..eteþ more sauoryly [*ed.* 1495 sauvurly] þanne þaie dede bifore þe chaunginge of þe skynne. 1617 MORYSON *Itin.* III. II. iii. 81 Apples or peares first dried, then prepared with cinamon and butter very sauourily. 1670 NARBOROUGH *Jrnl.* in *Acc. Sev. Late Voy.* (1711) 49, I can eat Foxes and Kites as savourily as if it were Mutton. 1790 BLAKE in Gilchrist *Life* (1863) I. 86 Here and there I saw one savourily picking the flesh off of his own tail. 1823 LAMB *Elia* Ser. II. *Old China*, We would eat our plain food savorily. 1841 *Fraser's Mag.* XXIII. 679 Two small pullets were brought in,..smelling most savouryly. 1886 R. F. BURTON *Arab. Nts.* (abr. ed.) III. 103 Roasted meat, With basting oil so savourily replete!

†**2.** *fig.* Heartily, pleasurably; appreciatively. Also, in religious use (cf. SAVOURY *a.* 2 b).

1643 MILTON *Divorce* II. iii. (1644) 38 Yet that he commanded the allowance of adulterous and injurious divorses for hardnes of heart,..they can very savourily perswade themselves. 1662 J. CHANDLER *Van Helmont's Oriat.* 12 Which being seen, and savourily known, I admired my former ignorances. 1676 O. HEYWOOD *Diaries*, etc. (1883) III. 147 A blind man prayed pertinently and savourily.

Savouriness (sēⁱ·vərinės). [f. SAVOURY *a.* + -NESS.] The quality of being savoury, in various senses of the adj.

1398 TREVISA *Barth. De P. R.* XIII. i. (1495) 438 The.. lyghtenesse and sauerynesse therof [*sc.* of reyne water] shewyth the subtylnesse of her substaunce. 1576 GASCOIGNE *Steele Gl.* (Arb.) 72 These be my priests, the seasning of the earth Which will not leese their Savrinesse, I trowe. 1599 MINSHEU *Span. Gram.* 82 It is great saourines to dine or eate, and not to paie any shot. 1681 H. MORE *Exp. Dan.* Pref. 53 This was the tenour of the Testimony..which they witnessed with great savouriness and assurance. 1792 A. YOUNG *Trav. France* I. 277 All sorts of vegetables have a savouriness and flavour, from rich sauces, that are absolutely wanted to our greens boiled in water. 1801 *Sketch of Paris* I. xxxviii. 455 The savouriness of their cooking. 1859 GEO. ELIOT *Adam Bede* I. v, His mental palate..found a savouriness in a quotation from Sophocles or Theocritus that was quite absent from your text in Isaiah or Amos.

Savouring (sēⁱ·vəriŋ), *vbl. sb.* [f. SAVOUR *v.* + -ING [1].]

1. The action of the vb. SAVOUR, in various senses.

c 1386 CHAUCER *Pars. T.* ¶ 885 Thy fiue wittes, that been sighte, herynge, smellyng, tastynge or sauouringe, and feelynge. *c* 1430 *Pilgr. Lyf Manhode* I. lxxii. (1869) 42 Ne that shulde not meeue thee that at the taast, and at the sighte, at the smellinge, and at the sauouringe, bred and wyn it may seeme thee. *a* 1450 *Knt. de la Tour* (1868) 59 Touchinge, and cussinge and saweringe made of fals delite that Eue dede to ete the apille. 1574 tr. *Life 70 Archb. Canterb.* C v b, If they had been closed in lead, and well spiced,.. they might haue been kepte from sauoringe yet a while.

†**2.** *concr.* A perfume. *Obs.*

1382 WYCLIF *Rev.* v. 8 Golden fioles ful of saueringis, whiche ben the preyers of seyntis.

†**3.** Something that gives a faint notion. *Obs.*

1513 DOUGLAS *Æneis* I. Prol. 44 Ȝit with your leif, Virgill ..I wald..Write sum savoring of thi Eneados.

Sa·vouring, *ppl. a.* [f. SAVOUR *v.* + -ING [2].]

1. Having a (defined) smell or taste.

1578 LYTE *Dodoens* I. i. 2 The highe Almaignes do call it ..sweete smelling, or sauering Southrenwood. 1596 DALRYMPLE tr. *Leslie's Hist. Scot.* I. 44 Sueit sairing flouris. 1612 WOODALL *Surg. Mate* Wks. (1653) 39 Cynamon water ..helpeth a bad or evil savouring breath.

2. Pleasing, relishing.

1598 DANIEL *Civ. Wars* I. xciv, He who had no thought so hie to clime (With savouring comfort still allur'd along).

3. Imparting savour or relish.

1886 *Athenæum* 17 Apr. 517/2 The lotos there has its sweets sharpened with a savouring bitterness.

Savouringly (sēⁱ·vəriŋli), *adv.* [f. prec. + -LY [2].] In a relishing manner.

1647 TRAPP *Comm. Jas.* iv. 9 And mourn savouringly and soakingly, with a deep and down right sorrow. 1848 *Fraser's Mag.* XXXVIII. 311 You would..have done just what I did,—smilingly, gently, savouringly, peel, slice, and eat, three raw turnips.

Savourless (sēⁱ·vəɹlės), *a.* Also 6 **saverles**, *Sc.* **sairles**, 7, 9 **savorless**, 9 *Sc.* **sareless**, **saurless**. [f. SAVOUR *sb.* + -LESS.] Destitute of savour; tasteless or odourless; of immaterial things, void of interest or efficacy, insipid.

1398 TREVISA *Barth. De P. R.* III. xx. (1495) 67 The tongue is sauourles that he maye the better take all maner sauour of thynges. 1552 HULOET, Sauourles or wythoute sauoure, *inodorus*. 1607 DONNE *Serm.* xxii. (1640) I. 223 In my grave..I..shall be all insipid, tastlesse, savourlesse dust. 1633 BP. HALL *Occas. Medit.* § 128. 319 The rose-tree hath a sweet flowre, but a savour-lesse root. 1657 TRAPP *Comm. Ps.* xxxiv. 8 All flesh is savourles to him that hath tasted of the Spirit. 1886 BRUCE *Mirac. Elem. Gosp.* ii. 74 Cast out as savourless salt. 1907 *Outlook* 12 Oct. 451/2 Most of his jests when repeated seem almost savourless.

Hence **Sa·vourlessness**.

1841 H. F. CHORLEY *Music & Manners* III. 179 The intrinsic savourlessness of the Mass which it [the orchestra] was performing, a *fade* composition by Morlacchi.

†**Sa·vourly**, *a.* *Obs.* Also 4 **saverly**. [f. SAVOUR *sb.* + -LY [1].] = SAVOURY *a.*

13.. *E. E. Allit. P.* A. 226, I hope no tong moȝt endure No sauerly saghe say of þat syȝt. 1583 GOLDING *Calvin on Deut.* lxiii. 383/2 Manna..was a good & sauorly nourishment. 1608 WILLET *Hexapla Exod.* 669 The burning of flesh of it selfe is not so pleasant and sauourly.

†**Sa·vourly**, *adv.* *Obs.* Forms: 4–6 **saverly**, 5 **saverely**, 6 **savor-**, **saverlie**, 6–7 **savourely**, **savorly**, 5–7 **savourly**. [f. SAVOUR *sb.* + -LY [2].]

1. With enjoyment; with relish; pleasantly; agreeably; keenly.

13.. *Gaw. & Gr. Knt.* 1937 Þen acoles he (þe) knyȝt, & kysses hym þryes, As sauerly & sadly as he hem sette couþe. *c* 1440 *York Myst.* xxix. 80 Wherfore we counsaile you This cuppe sauerly for to kisse. 1495 [see SAVOURILY 1, quot. 1398]. 1560 PILKINGTON *Expos. Aggeus* H ij, The labouryng man..feedes sauerly on brown bread, thin drynke, and a poore supper. 1637 *Brief Relat. Passages Star Chamber* 25 A Bee came and pitched on the Nosegay, and began to suck the flowers very savourly. 1683 TRYON *Way to Health* 350 The Cannibals feed on Humane Flesh, and will most savourly gnaw a Shoulder of Man. 1690 DRYDEN *Amphitryon* I. i, He..snuffs up Incense so savourly, when 'tis offer'd him by a fair Hand.

b. Of weeping: Passionately, bitterly.

1662 H. MORE *Antid. Ath.* III. iv. § 4 Other sometimes bearing the Image of Christ in her arms, weeping savourly. 1722 DE FOE *Col. Jack* ii, Then I fell a-crying as savourly as I did before, when I thought I had lost it.

2. With understanding; with appreciation; wisely; effectively.

c 1450 tr. *De Imitatione* I. i. 2 For who euere wol understonde þe wordes of crist pleinly and sauerly, he must studie to conforme all his lif to his lyf. 1529 MORE *Supplic. Soulys* Wks. 301/1 But than he speaketh so sauorlie hereof, that it well appereth of hys wyse wordes he neyther canneth anye skill therof, nor neuer came in the house. 1619 FOTHERBY *Atheom.* II. vi. § 1 (1622) 246 Which folly that wise King derided very sauorly. 1663 BUNYAN *Chr. Behav.* Wks. 1692 I. 595/2 For Christians to commune savourly of God's Matters one with another, it is as if they opened to each others Nostrils Boxes of Perfume. 1664 H. MORE *Myst. Iniq.* vi. 119 Which life I conceive S. Paul describes very savourly, when he saith, That the Kingdom of Heaven is.. righteousness, and peace, and joy in the Holy Ghost.

Savoury (sēⁱ·vəri), *a.* and *sb.* Forms: *α.* 3 **savure**, *compar.* **savurure**; *β.* 4–5 **savery**, **savori**, 4–6 **saverey**, 5 **saveray**, **sauvury**, 6 **savrie**, **savourye**, *Sc.* **sau'rie**, 6–7 **savourie**, **savorie**, 7 **saverie**, 4–9 **savory**, 6– **savoury**; *γ.* *contracted* 5 **sarry**. [Early ME. *savure*, app. a. OF. *savouré* sapid, fragrant, pa. pple. of *savourer*: see SAVOUR *v.* In the 14th c. the ending was associated with the native *-y*, so that the adj. was apprehended as f. SAVOUR *sb.* + -Y.] **A.** *adj.*

1. Pleasing to the taste; appetizing; agreeable.

1382 WYCLIF *Mark* ix. 48 Forsoth euery man schal be saltid, or maad sauori, with fier. 1387 TREVISA *Higden* (Rolls) I. 365 At Glyndalkan aboute þe oratorie of Seint Keynewyn wilewys bereþ apples as it were appel treen, and beeþ more holsom þan sauory. 1393 LANGL. *P. Pl.* C. XIX. 65 Tho þat sitten in þe sonne-syde sonner aren rype, Swettour and saueriour. *c* 1400 MAUNDEV. (Roxb.) xxx. 136 Þai er riȝt sauoury in þe mouth. 1584 COGAN *Haven Health* cxcii. (1636) 172 Cookery..may make that savoury, which of it selfe is unsavoury. 1611 BIBLE *Gen.* xxvii. 31 And hee also had made sauoury meate, and brought it vnto his father. 1725 POPE *Odyss.* IV. 300 All..with keen gust the sav'ry viands share. 1837 M. DONOVAN *Dom. Econ.* II. 35 The natives of some part of Australia eat a kind of caterpillar..of which they compose a dish to them highly savoury. 1865 KINGSLEY *Herew.* v, Savoury was the smell of fried pilchard and hake; more savoury that of roast porpoise.

b. Gratifying to the sense of smell; fragrant.

Now rare exc. in negative context: cf. *unsavoury*.

1560 DAUS tr. *Sleidane's Comm.* 209 b, They..perfume the house with the graines of Juniper, and other savoury thinges [L. *aliisque rebus odoratis*]. 1859 DICKENS *T. Two Cities* II. i, Cruncher's apartments were not in a savoury neighbourhood. 1871 R. ELLIS *Catullus* xiii. 11 Perfume savoury.

2. *fig.* **a.** Pleasant; acceptable.

a 1225 *Leg. Kath.* 1527 Mi swete lif, se swoteliche he smecheð me & smealleð þat al me þuncheð sauure & softe þat he sent me. *c* 1230 *Hali Meid.* 39 Ah schal ifinden him ai swettere & sauurure. *c* 1374 CHAUCER *Troylus* I. 405 If it be wikke, a wonder thinketh me, Whenne every torment and adversitee That cometh of him, may to me savory thinke. 1545 *King's Primer, Graces* **iv, O Lord Jesu Christ without whom nothing is swete nor sauery,..blesse vs & our supper. 1602 SHAKS. *Ham.* II. ii. 463 One said there was no Sallets in the lines, to make the matter sauoury. *a* 1677 BARROW *Serm.* Wks. (1716) III. 57 The sense of having lived well..is a far more solid and savoury pleasure than the most ample revenue can afford. 1875 RUSKIN *Fors Clav.* xlix. 11 The delicious parable, savouriest of all Scripture to rogues. 1885 R. L. & F. STEVENSON *Dynamiter* 100 Something taking in the way of colour, a good, savoury choice of words.

†**b.** In religious phraseology. (*a*) Full of spiritual 'savour'; spiritually delightful or edifying. (*b*) Having the savour of holiness; of saintly repute or memory. *Obs.*

(*a*) *c* 1449 PECOCK *Repr.* I. xvi. 89 The maner of outring which is sauory in a sermonyng. 1450–1530 *Myrr. our Ladye* 49 An other [wyse] is to take hede to the letter only, after the lytterall understondynge. And thys ys sometyme sauory, sometyme bareyne, after that the letter ys. 1563 FOXE *A. & M.* 1354/2 Many such like answers and reasons, mery, but sauery..proceaded from that man. 1626 BP. HALL *Contempl. O. T.* XXI. i. 336 A forced discontinuance, makes deuotion more sauoury, more sweet to religious hearts. *a* 1720 SEWEL *Hist. Quakers* (1795) I. III. 230 Practised by the savouriest of people called Quakers. 1726 PENN in *Life* Wks. (1782) I. 98 Leaving the Man in a sensible and savoury Frame. 1855 MACAULAY *Hist. Eng.* xiii. III. 295 His letters and speeches are, to use his own phraseology, exceeding savoury..He had a text of the Old Testament ready for every occasion.

(*b*) 1642 D. ROGERS *Naaman* Ep. Ded. 4 Hath made your name sweet and savoury in the Church of God. 1731 WODROW *Corr.* (1843) III. 487 You need not be told what a great loss this Church will be at by this good and worthy gentleman's death, whose name will be for ever savoury in this Church.

3. Used, in contradistinction to *sweet*, as the epithet of articles of food having a stimulating taste or flavour.

1661 RABISHA *Cookery Dissected* 157 If you would have it baked savoury, season it with Pepper, Salt, Cloves [etc.]. 1769 MRS. RAFFALD *Eng. Housekpr.* (1778) 283 Pigeons in Savory Jelly. 1806 A. HUNTER *Culina* (ed. 3) 278 Omelette, a Savoury one.

B. *sb.* A savoury dish (see A. 3); *spec.* a cooked dish, flavoured with appetizing ingredients, served at the beginning or end of dinner as a stimulant to appetite and digestion.

1661 RABISHA *Cookery Dissected* 138 Another way for a savory. 1844 TUPPER *Heart* xvii. 168 The board was overloaded with solid sweets and savouries. 1896 ANTHONY HOPE *Phroso* i, 'Why, how early you two have dined!' cried Beatrice. 'You're at the savoury, aren't you? We've only just come.'

Savoury, Savowr(e: see SAVORY, SAVOUR.

Savoy (sǟvoi·). Also 6 **Savoie**, **Savoye**. [a. F. *Savoie*, the name of a region of S. E. France, south of the Lake of Geneva.]

1. In full, *Savoy cabbage* (†*cole*, †*colewort*, †*kail*, *sprouts*). A rough-leaved hardy variety of the common cabbage, much grown for winter use.

1578 LYTE *Dodoens* IV. vi. 552 Sauoye Colewurtes. 1597 GERARDE *Herball* II. xxxvi. 247 Sauoie Cole is also numbred among the headed Coleworts or Cabbages. 1657 W. COLES *Adam in Eden* lxxxvi, The Savoy Cole and the Cole-flory ..must be sowed in April. 1689 in *Thanes of Cawdor* (Spald. Club) 353, 1 unce Savoy kaell. 1699 EVELYN *Acetaria* § 11 The Broccoli from Naples..are very delicate, as are the Savoys. 1707 MORTIMER *Husb.* (1721) II. 132 The Savoy Cabbage, which is one of the best sort and very hardy. 1747 MRS. GLASSE *Cookery* 58 Savoys Forced and Stewed. 1764 ELIZA MOXON *Eng. Housew.* (ed. 9) 132 To boil Savoy Sprouts. 1855 DELAMER *Kitch. Gard.* (1861) 57 There is a vulgar idea..that Savoy cabbages are improved by exposure to frost. 1856 GLENNY *Gard. Every-d. Bk.* 17/1 Frosts, that will kill all other greens, will leave Savoy Sprouts.. untouched. 1881 *Encycl. Brit.* XII. 287/2 The savoys come into use in autumn, and continue until the spring.

2. In full, *Savoy biscuit*. A kind of sponge-biscuit, made of finger-shaped pieces of paste covered with sifted sugar which when baked are joined together in pairs; so also *Savoy drop*, *ring*. Similarly *Savoy cake*, a large sponge cake baked in a mould; also called a *Savoy mould*. **Savoy bag**, a bag with a narrow orifice through which the paste for making the biscuits is laid out.

1764 ELIZA MOXON *Eng. Housw.* (ed. 9) Suppl. 10 Slips of bread cut long like Savoy biskets. 1822 *Cook's Oracle* (ed. 4) 494 Savoy Cake, or Sponge Cake in a Mould. 1854 G. READ *Compl. Biscuit & Gingerbr. Baker's Assist.* (ed. 2) 76 Savoy Cakes...Almond Savoy Cakes. *Ibid.* 77 Savoy Biscuits and Drops. 1862 FRANCATELLI *Eng. & Foreign Confectioner* 96 These Savoy biscuits should present a smooth surface, and be of a light fawn colour. 1866 *Massey's Biscuit Bk.* 3 Savoy Drops...Savoy Rings. 1889 R. WELLS *Bread & Biscuit Baker* 47 The Savoy Biscuits must be laid out from a savoy bag on 'cap' paper one half round and one half long. The French Savoys must be laid out oval, and when baked two are to be put together. 1892 *Encycl. Pract. Cookery* (ed. Garrett) I. 138/2 A Biscuit-bag, sometimes called a 'savvy-bag' being used very much to prepare Savoy Biscuits.

†**Savoy·an**, *a.* and *sb.* *Obs.* = SAVOYARD.

1601 E. A. *True Disc. Queen's Voy.* title p., Herevnto is annexed, the first Sauoyan; wherein is set forth the right of the conquest of Sauoy by the French, and the importance of holding it. 1607 TOPSELL *Four-f. Beasts* 46 They are vsed by the Lotharingians and Sauoyens for meat. 1611 COTGR., *Rave de Savoye*, the Sauoyan Rape, the greatest kind of Turnep. 1653 A. WILSON *Jas. I* 94 The Savoyan Agents bringing more Gold in their hands than on their backs.

Savoyard (sǟvoi·aɹd), *sb.* and *a.* [a. F. *savoyard* (fem. *-arde*), f. *Savoie*: see SAVOY and -ARD.]

A. *sb.*

1. A native or inhabitant of Savoy.

Well known in other countries as musicians itinerating with hurdy-gurdy and monkey.

1756–7 tr. *Keysler's Trav.* (1760) I. 271 The steward of the houshold is the marquis de Coudray,..a Savoyard. 1770 [see HURDY-GURDY 1]. 1839 *Penny Cycl.* XV. 517/1 They [*sc.* marmots] are taken by the Savoyards and others principally that they may be exhibited by those itinerants. 1906 W. WALKER *Calvin* vii. 166 The Savoyards pressed Geneva and made travel unsafe on the roads.

2. An inhabitant of the precinct of the Savoy Palace in London, which formerly possessed the right of sanctuary.

a 1700 B. E. *Dict. Cant. Crew*, *Rum-dukes*, the boldest Fellows amongst the Alsatians, Minters, Savoyards, &c. 1855 MACAULAY *Hist. Eng.* xxii. IV. 775 At length, in 1697, a bill for abolishing the franchises of these places..received the royal assent. The Alsatians and Savoyards were furious.

B. *adj.* Belonging to Savoy.

1880 RANKEN *Hist. France* VII. i. VII. 238 The Savoyard army. 1841 JAMES *Brigand* ii, Why baron, who would have thought to meet you thus in a Savoyard inn?

Savoyre, savre, obs. forms of SAVOUR.

Savrie, Savry, Savte, Savur, obs. ff. SAVOURY, SAVORY, SAFETY, SAVOUR.

Savvey, savvy, variant forms of SAVEY.

Savyour, savyr(e, obs. forms of SAVOUR.

Savyte, obs. form of SAFETY.

Saw (sǭ), *sb.*[1] Forms: 1 **sagu**, **saga**, 4 **sagh**, 4–7 **sawe**, 5 **sae**, **saghe**, **saȝe**, 5– **saw**. [OE. *sagu* str. fem., in oblique cases *sage* (also *saga* wk. masc.) = OHG. *saga*, MLG., MDu. *sage* (Du. *zaag*), ON. *sǫg* (Sw. *såg*, Da. *sav*, † *saug*):—OTeut. *sagā str. fem.; the ablaut-var. *segā appears in OHG. *sega* (MHG. *sege*, mod.G. *säge*); cogn. w. OE. *seax* (:—*sahso-) knife, SAX, f. pre-Teut. root *sok-: *sek- to cut; cf. L. *secāre* to cut.]

1. A cutting tool consisting of a plate (or, in some forms, a band or a tube) of metal (usually steel), one edge of which is formed into a continuous series of teeth. (Some saws for cutting stone are without teeth.) In the original form of the tool, represented by the HAND-SAW, and in some varieties of more modern invention, e.g. the pit-saw (see PIT *sb.*[1] 14), the saw is moved backwards and forwards, each movement in one direction deepening the groove or 'kerf' made in the wood or other material to be cut. In other varieties, as the circular saw and the band-saw, a continuous movement in one direction is substituted for the reciprocating movement.

Ordinarily *saw* means the complete instrument including the handle, frame, or the like, necessary to fit it for use; but sometimes the word is applied to the 'saw-plate' or 'saw-blade' alone.

Also with defining words, indicating special varieties of form, structure, mode of operation, or purpose, as in *band saw*, *circular saw*, *compass saw*, *drag saw*, *endless saw*, *frame saw*, *fret saw*, *gate saw*, *hand saw*, *ice saw*, *joint saw*, *keyhole saw*, *lock saw*, *meat saw*, *mill saw*, *panel saw*, *pit saw*, *rabbet saw*, *rip saw*, *sash saw*, *tenon saw*, *web saw*. These terms, so far as they have been thought to require notice in this Dictionary, are treated either under their first element or as main words. A considerable number of kinds of saws used for surgical purposes are distinguished by the names of their inventors, as *Butcher's*, *Ferguson's*, *Gowan's*, *Hey's*, *Liston's saw*.

c 1000 ÆLFRIC *Gloss.* in Wr.-Wülcker 106/22 *Serrula*, saga, *vel* snide. *a* 1100 *Gerefa* in *Anglia* IX. 263/1 Hy sceal.. habban..æcse, adsan, sage. *a* 1300 *Cursor M.* 27376 Away to sagh þam ilk crote, wit þe sagh o penance treu þat þe frut spring efter neu. *c* 1340 *Nominale* (Skeat) 525 File sawe and spindelle. 1387 TREVISA *Higden* (Rolls) II. 363 Þis Perdix..took a plate of iren, and fyled it, and made it i-toþed as a rugge boon of a fische, and þanne it was a sawe. *a* 1400–50 *Alexander* 4096 A burly best with a bake as bedell as a saȝe. 1432–50 tr. *Higden* (Rolls) II. 75 After that Ysay was kytte with a sae of tree. 1533 *Ld. Treas. Acc. Scotl.* VI. 155 Ane saw send to the werkmen in Lochaber to cut the tymmer for the artailzerie. 1681 GREW *Musæum* IV. § i. 360 A Box of Anatomick Instruments; sc. Saws, Steel and Ivory Knives [etc.]. 1784 COWPER *Task* v. 145 No sound of hammer or of saw was there. 1826 J. SMITH *Panorama Sci. & Art* I. 16 Saws for cutting metals, are made very narrow,..and stretched by a screw at one end. 1886 *Encycl. Brit.* XXI. 343/2 The principal modern use of the saw is to divide wood.

transf. and *fig.* 1593 SHAKS. *Lucr.* 1672 Euen so his sighes, his sorrowes make a saw, To push griefe on, and back the same grief draw. 1621 BURTON *Anat. Mel.* I. ii. III. viii. 138 Faction, hatred, livor, emulation, which..are, *serræ animæ*, the sawes of the soule. 1871 KINGSLEY *At Last* iv, You..see aloft the saw of the mountain ridges against the black-blue sky.

†**b.** In obsolete phrases. *To draw the saw (of contention or controversy)*: to keep up a fruitless dispute. *To be under the saw of contention*: (of a question) to be the subject of profitless dispute. *To hand the saw*: to take turns, change parts, *with* another in some work or function. *To hold* (a person) *at the long saw*: to keep in suspense.

1654 JER. TAYLOR *Real Pres.* A 1, The Question of Transubstantiation, which hath already so many times passed by the Fire and under the Saw of Contention. 1659 BP. WALTON *Consid. Considered* 305 Yet if he think fit to draw this saw of contention further,..I [etc.]. 1674 N. FAIRFAX *Bulk & Selv.* 101 Now because ghost cannot hand the saw thus with body..Thence 'tis [etc.]. 1688 *Lond. Gaz.* No. 2329/3 It would be of little avail to draw the Saw any longer of Answers and Retorts. 1710 PRIDEAUX *Orig. Tithes* Pref. 12 Neither will I draw the saw of contention with any one in answering any of the Cavils. *a* 1733 NORTH *Life Ld. Kpr.* (1742) 79 So, between the one and the other, he was held at the Long Saw above a Month. 1768 WESLEY *Wks.* (1872) XIV. 343 Having neither leisure nor inclination to draw the saw of controversy.

2. *Zool.* A part or organ with teeth like those of a saw. Also Comb. *saw-bearing* adj.

1664 HUBERT *Catal. Rarities* (1665) 32 A very great Saw, or weapon of a Saw-fish, with the which he torments the Whale. 1747 GOULD *Eng. Ants* 4 The double Saw is a hard bony Substance. *Ibid.*, They [*sc.* Ants] have four or five Teeth in a Saw. 1754 FIELDING *Voy. Lisbon* Wks. 1882 VII. 64 The sting or saw of a wasp. 1854 A. ADAMS, etc. *Man. Nat. Hist.* 222 Saw-bearing Hymenoptera (*Securifera*). 1866 *Chamb. Encycl.* VIII. 508/2 Whales are said to be sometimes killed by sawfishes, and the saw has been sometimes driven into the hull of a ship. 1871 T. R. JONES *Anim. Kingd.* (ed. 4) 360 The saws of the various species of Tenthredo are as diversified as the habits of the insects to which they belong. 1885 G. S. FORBES *Wild Life Canara* 51 A great saw-fish, which measured about twenty-one feet from the end of the saw to the tail.

3. [Properly a distinct word, f. SAW *v.*] **a.** A sawing movement. (In recent Dicts.). **b.** *Whist.* = SEE-SAW.

Supplement, p. 3873; Corrigenda, p. 4092; Spurious words, p. 4093; Books quoted, p. 4094

Sawbill (sǭ·bil). *A name applied to various birds with serrated bills.*

Sawn (sǭn), *ppl. a.* Also **6 sawen, 7 sawne.**

Sawder, -dre, obs. forms of SOLDER.

Sawdust (sǭ·dʌst), *sb.* The small particles detached from a tree, plank, etc. in the process of sawing.

Sawed (sǭd), *ppl. a.* and *sb.*[-ED.] That has undergone the operation of sawing.

Saw-fly. An insect of the family *Tenthredinidæ*, distinguished by the saw-like construction of the ovipositor.

Sawflom, Sawfte: see SAUCEFLEME, SAFETY.

Saw-gate. The passage of a saw through the wood that is being sawn.

Sawing (sǭ·iɳ), *vbl. sb.* The action of the verb SAW.

Sawing (sǭ·iɳ), *ppl. a.*

Sawney (sǭ·ni), *sb.* A Scotchman; a fool.

Sawt, obs. form of SALT, SAULT, SAUT.

Sawter(e, obs. form of PSALTER, PSALTERY.

Sax (sæks), *sb.* A chopping-tool used for trimming slates.

Saxatile (sæ·kstil, -il), *a.* Also **2 saxatil.** Living among rocks.

Saxboard. Boat-building.

Sax-cornet: see under SAX-HORN.

Saxe (sæks), *sb.* Used attrib. to designate articles which come from Saxony.

Saxhorn, saxhorn (sæ·kshǫrn). The name given to a group of brass musical instruments of the trumpet kind, invented by a Belgian, Charles Joseph Sax.

Saxatile ... **Saxicava** (sæksi·kǎva). A genus of bivalve boring molluscs.

Saxicavous (sæksi·kǎvəs), *a.* Hollowing out rock or stone.

Saxicola (sæksi·kǒla). *Zool.* A genus of passerine birds, the stone-chats.

Saxicoline (sæksi·kǒlin). *Zool.* and *Bot.*

Saxicolous (sæksi·kǒləs), *a.* Growing on rocks.

Saxifragaceous (sæksifrægē·ʃəs), *a. Bot.*

Saxifragant (sæksi·frəgant), *a.* and *sb.*

Saxifrage (sæ·ksifrėdʒ), *sb. Bot.*

Saxon (sæ·ksən), *sb.* and *a.*

Saxon ... *Pyrochrænci* ... **Ent.** A kind of moth, *Hadena rectilinea*.

Saxondom ... The aggregate of Saxon people or communities.

Saxonial, *a.* *Obs.* [f. med.L. *Saxonia* Saxony + -AL.] *adj.* a. 3. b. *sb.* A Protestant of Saxony.

Saxonic, *a.* 1. Of or belonging to Saxony. 2. Belonging to the Anglo-Saxons or their language.

Saxonical, *a.* *Obs.* rare. [f. prec. + -AL.] In the Saxonic manner.

Saxonish, *a.* rare. [f. SAXON + -ISH.] Belonging to the Saxons; resembling what is Saxon.

Saxonism (sæˈksəniz'm). [f. SAXON + -ISM.] 1. An Anglo-Saxon idiom or expression; Anglo-Saxon characteristics in speech.

Saxonist (sæˈksənist). 1. A Saxon scholar; one learned in Anglo-Saxon.

Saxonite (sæˈksənəit). *Geol.* [f. SAXON + -ITE.] A name proposed for a group of peridotite rocks composed of olivine and enstatite.

Saxonise (sæˈksənaiz). [f. SAXON + -ISE.] 1. *trans.* To make Saxon or Anglo-Saxon.

Saxony (sæˈksəni). 1. The country of the Saxons, the country of Germany. 2. A kind of wool, and cloth made from it. 3. *attrib.*

Saxophone (sæˈksəfoun). [f. the name *Sax* (see SAX-HORN) + Gr. φωνή voice, sound.] A brass wind-instrument with a clarinet mouthpiece, invented about 1840 by Adolphe Sax.

Saxotromba (sæksotroˈmbə). [Formed as prec. + L. tromba trumpet.] Another brass wind-instrument.

Say (sei), *sb.¹* Forms: 5-6 saye, seeay, seye, see, see, 6-7 say, 6-7 saie. [a. OFr. *saie*, *seie*, soe, soye, 6 sayne, 6 saja. — L. *saga*, pl. of *sagum* military cloak.] 1. A cloth of fine texture resembling serge.

Say (sei), *sb.²* [f. SAY *v.*] 1. What a person says; words as compared with actions; also, a saying, dictum. *Obs. exc. poet.*

Say, *v.* Forms: *a.* 1 seccgan, seeggan, -eon, seogan, *smcg(g)ean, 1-2 secgean, secgen, seegen, 1-3 seggen, 3-4 segge, 3-4 seig(g)e, sugge, 2-3 sigge, seie, sei, (3-4 sei, sey, sai), seie, saie, 4-6 saie, 6-7 saie, says, 5 sayen, (*errm. 4-5, 6, 9 arch.*) sain, 6 sayen, (*errm.* sayan), 4-5, 6, 9 sayne, saine, 5-6 sayn; with various inflexions. [Common Teut. verb.]

B. Signification.

In Eng., as in other Teut. langs., *say* is an approximate synonym of *speak*, from which it differs in having normally as its object a particular word or series of words, or a sentence representing the meaning of a particular series of words. Cf. *speak* and its representatives in Romanic (which, however, have also retained the senses that are now expressed in Eng. by *tell*, &c.).

I. *trans.* To utter or pronounce (a specified word or words, or an articulate sound). Also, in wider sense, used of an author or a book, with quoted words as object.

2. To declare or state in words (a specified fact, thought, opinion, or intention). Said of a speaker, writer; also of a literary composition, a proverb, etc. Const. to († in OE. and ME. simple *dative*).

| SAY. | 153 | SAY. | SAY. | 154 | SAYING. |

Sayall, variant of SEYAL.

Saycrying, Saydly, obs. ff. SACRING, SADLY.

Sayer (sē‧ᵊɹ). One who says.

Sayette. A professional reciter. Cf. DISOUR. Obs.

Sayable (sē‧ab'l), a. Capable of being said.

Saying (sē‧iŋ), vbl. sb. 1. The action of SAY v.: utterance, enunciation, recitation. + Saying-again = ALARM haring, recitation.

| SAYING. | 155 | SCAB. | SCAB. | 156 | SCABBED. |

Saynite (sē‧nəit). Min. [a. G. Saynit (F. von Kobell 1853), after Sayn, Prussia, its locality.]

Saynure. Obs. Also in sayeur.

Sayon. Obs. rare⁻¹. [F.] A kind of sleeveless jacket.

Sayr (e), obs. forms of SEIZE.

Sayne, sayni, obs. forms of SEIZE.

Say-so (sē‧soʊ), sb. colloq. (chiefly U.S.) A person's mere word or assertion.

Say-well. Obs. exc. dial.

Sayyid (sī‧id). Also sayid, saiyid, seyyid, &c. [Arab. sáyyid, lit. 'lord', 'prince'. Cf. CID.]

Sbirro (zbɪr‧ro). Pl. sbirri. [It.] An Italian police officer.

Sbloha. An unmeaning oath: cf. prec. and Od's both.

Scab (skæb), sb. [a. ON. skabb; cf. MSw. skabb-or, skab.]

Sbody. Obs. rare⁻¹. Shortened form of God's body.

Sbores. Obs. rare⁻¹. [f. God's.] A euphemistic oath.

Scabbard (skæb‧ard), sb.¹ Forms: a. 3 scau-, 4-6 scauberc, 4-5 scaub-, 4 skauberk. [a. AF. escauberc (recorded only in pl. escaubers), OF. escalberc.]

Scabbed (skæbd), ppl. a. [f. SCAB sb. + -ED².] 1. Having the scab or a similar skin-disease; of the scalp, tinea capitis.

SCABBEDNESS.

Scabbedness. [f. SCABBED + -NESS.] The condition of being scabby, fit, and fig.

Scabbiness. [f. SCABBY + -NESS.] The condition or quality of being scabby.

Scabbing (skæ·biŋ), vbl. sb. [f. SCAB v. + -ING.]
1. The process of forming a scab.
2. *Iron-founding.*

Scabble (skæ·b'l), v.

Scaber.

Scabrid

Scaberulose

Scabia

Scabid

Scabies (skē·bii·z), sb.

Scabine

Scabious (skē·biəs), sb.

Scabious, a.

Scabiosity.

Scabiousness.

Scabredity.

Scabredness.

Scabrate

Scabreity.

Scabrid (skæ·brid), a.

Scabridity.

Scabridulous.

Scabrin.

Scabrities

Scabrid

SCABRIUSCULOUS.

Scabriusculous.

Scabrous (skē·brəs), a.

Scabrousness.

SCABRO-

Scabro- (skæ·brō-), used as combining form of L. *scaber* SCABROUS.

Scabrosely

Scabrosity.

Scabwort (skæ·bwŏɹt), sb.

Scad (skæd), sb.1

Scad, sb.2

Scad, sb.3

Scaddle, a. and adv.

Scaddle, v.

Scade.

Scaff (skæf), v.1

Scaff, sb.1

Scaff, sb.2

Scaffer

Scaffery.

SCAFFOLD.

Scaffle.

Scaffling

Scaffling, sb.

Scaffmaster.

Scaffolage.

Scaffold (skæ·fŏld), sb. Forms: 4 scaffot, 4-5 skaffald, 4-6 scaffold, etc.

SCAFFOLD.

B. Signification.
1. A temporary platform usually supported on poles or (sometimes) trestles, but occasionally suspended, and designed to hold the workmen and materials employed in the erection, repairing, or decoration of a building.

SCAFFOLDING.

Scaffoldage.

Scaffolder (skæ·fŏldəɹ). [f. SCAFFOLD sb. + -ER.]

Scaffoldize, v.

Scaffolding (skæ·fŏldiŋ), vbl. sb. Forms: 4 skaffaldyng, etc.

SCAFFOLDIZE.

Scaffoldize, v. Obs. [f. SCAFFOLD sb. + -IZE.] trans. To convert into scaffolding.

Scaffle, obs. var. SCAFFOLD v.

Scaffoldie, obs. var. SCAFFOLD sb.

Scag, sb.

Scaglia (skæ·ljə), sb.

Scagliola (skælyō·lə), sb.

Scaife (skēf), sb. local. Also scafe, skief, skife, skeef.

SCALD.

Scale, sb.

Scalage (skē·lėdʒ), sb.

Scald (skɔld), v.1

Scald, sb.

Scald, a.

Scalded

Scaldfish

Scalable (skē·ləb'l), a.

Scala (skē·lə), sb.

Scalar (skē·ləɹ), a. and sb.

Scalariform (skælæ·ɹifŏɹm), a.

Scalary

Scalawag

Scald (skɔld), sb.1

Scalade (skælē·d), sb.

Scaladize

Scalary, a.

Scalawag, sb.

a. 1682 GREW *Anat. Pl.* III. I. i. 105 A scalloped Parenchymous Ring, or a Ring of many short and slender white Arches. 1778 M. HARRIS *Aurelian* p. xvii, Inferior Wing scalloped. 1793 MARTYN *Lang. Bot.*, *Scalloped leaf*, this term may be applied to the *folium Repandum*. 1819 J. F. STEPHENS in *Shaw's Gen. Zool.* XI. 43 The feathers that cover the sides of the neck are scalloped in the centre. 1821 CLARE *Vill. Minstr.* II. 111 Scallop'd briony. 1869 [see *hook-tip*, HOOK *sb.* 18]. 1900 B. D. JACKSON *Gloss. Bot. Terms*, *Scalloped*, crenate.

β. 1768 PENNANT *Brit. Zool.* (1776) II. 414 The toes extremely singular, being edged with scolloped membranes like the coot. 1819 SAMOUELLE *Entomol. Compend.* 423 Geometra emarginata. The scolloped Double-line. 1872 COUES *N. Amer. Birds* 51 The lobation may be either scolloped, or cut out at the joints, as in the coot, or plain.

Comb. [cf. SCALLOP *sb.* 3]. 1832 J. RENNIE *Consp. Butterfl. & Moths* Index, Scolloped Winged Broad Bar.

b. Of articles of dress.

1687 *Lond. Gaz.* No. 2234/4 A brown colour close-bodied Coat, with scollop'd Pockets. 1716 GAY *Trivia* I. 32 The wooden Heel may raise the Dancer's Bound, And with the scallop'd Top his Step be crown'd. 1863 LONGF. *Wayside Inn, Sicilian's T.* 83 The King's Jester, thou Henceforth shalt wear the bells and scalloped cape. 1888 *Lady* 25 Oct. 378/1 Cloth hats and bonnets, with scalloped edges.

c. Of utensils, architectural features, etc.

1766 *Compl. Farmer* s.v. *Mole* 5 O 4/2 Scoop them out at once, with what Mr. Bradley calls a scolloped mole-hill plough. 1840 BUEL *Farmer's Comp.* 150 The concave, or scalloped roller, is adapted to the form of ridges. 1870 F. R. WILSON *Ch. Lindisf.* 176 The caps of the columns.. are scalloped. 1881 YOUNG *Every Man his own Mechanic* § 9/2 Leather edging with scalloped edges or strips of American leather cloth should be attached to the shelves.

2. *Cookery.* (See SCALLOP *v.* 2.)

1737 *Ochtertyre House Bk. Acc.* (1907) 3 Scollopt oysters. 1791 HUDDESFORD *Salmag.* 93 And shoals of bawling choristers He ate, like scallop'd oysters. 1827 HONE *Every-day Bk.* II. 58 Stewed oysters! I ordered scolloped!

3. Wearing a scallop-shell. *rare.*

1832 G. DOWNES *Lett. Cont. Countries* I. 324 A pilgrim regularly scalloped.

Scalloper (skǫ·ləpəɹ). [f. SCALLOP *v.* and *sb.* + -ER [1].] **a.** One who makes scalloped ornament, etc. **b.** One who gathers scallops.

1881 *Instr. Census Clerks* (1885) 70 Lace Finishing... Scolloper. *Ibid.* 83 Glass Scolloper. 1887 GOODE, etc. *Fisheries U. S.* v. II. 577 At Wickford, R. I., there live a few scallopers, and three boats are owned.

Sca·lloping, sco·lloping, *vbl. sb.* [f. SCALLOP *sb.* or *v.* + -ING [1].] The action of the vb. SCALLOP. Also *concr.*, scalloped ornament, edging, marking, or the like.

a 1800 *Peggy Irvine* iv. in Child *Ballads* V. 301/2 Her petticoats was of the silk so fine, set out with the silver and scolloping. 1889 A. R. WALLACE *Darwinism* 255 Minute examination detects differences in form and scalloping of the wings.

attrib. 1875 KNIGHT *Dict. Mech.*, *Scalloping-tool* (*Saddlery*), a tool for giving an ornamental edge to leather straps.

So **Sca·lloping** *ppl. a.*, forming 'scallops'.

18.. WHITTIER *Prose Wks.* (1889) II. 381 A long scalloping range of hills.

Sca·llop-shell. Cf. ESCALLOP-SHELL.

1. The shell of the scallop, or, more usually, one valve of it: freq. with reference to its being a pilgrim's badge. (Cf. note s. v. ESCALLOP-SHELL.)

1530 PALSGR. 265/2 Scaloppe shell, *quocquille de saint Jacques*. 1562 *Inv. St. Margaret's Westm.* in *Malcolm's Londinium* IV. 137 One Cope of crimson velvet with scallop shells of silver. *a* 1618 RALEIGH *Pilgrimage* 1 Give me my Scollap-Shell of Quiet, My Staff of Faith to lean upon. 1747 MRS. GLASSE *Cookery* ix. 95 Put your Oysters into Scollop-shells for that purpose. 1819 SCOTT *Ivanhoe* xxviii, By the scallop-shell of Compostella, I will make a martyr of him.

attrib. 1807 W. IRVING *Salmag.* (1811) II. 102 The outside of the boxes inlaid with scallop shell-work.

2. Collectors' name for the moth *Triphosa* (*Eucosmia*) *undulata*.

1829 J. F. STEPHENS *Catal. Brit. Insects* II. 140.

Sca·llum, *v.* *Basket-making.* [Of obscure origin.] *trans.* (See quot.)

1875 *Encycl. Brit.* III. 423/1 These [*sc.* the stout osiers that are to form the ribs of the basket] are forced or plaited, 'scallumed', between the rods of the bottom from the edge to the centre, and are turned up, 'upset', in the direction of the sides.

† **Sca·lly,** *a.* *Obs. rare.* [f. SCALL + -Y.] = SCALLED. Cf. SCALY *a.* 4.

1530 PALSGR. 323/1 Scally or scoursy, *roigneux*. 1699 DAMPIER *Voy.* II. II. 74 Over its [the Alligator's] Eyes there are two hard scally Knobs, as big as a Mans Fist.

Hence † **Sca·lliness.** (Cf. SCALINESS.)

1610 MARKHAM *Masterp.* I. xcv. 189 Any drynesse or scallynesse of the skinne.

Scallywag, scallawag (skæ·liwæg, -āwæg). *slang* or *colloq.* (orig. *U.S.*) Also 9 **scal(l)i-, scala-, scallo-, skalle-.** [Origin obscure.]

1. A disreputable fellow; a good-for-nothing; a scapegrace, blackguard; in *Trade Union slang*, a man who will not work.

1848 BARTLETT *Dict. Amer.*, *Scalawag*, a favorite epithet in western New York for a mean fellow; a scape-grace. 1855 HALIBURTON *Nature* I. 112 You good-for-nothing young scallowag. 1893 LELAND *Mem.* II. 178 There are so many scallawags from the East come here, that we are obliged to be a little particular. 1891 *Labour Commission Gloss.*, *Scallywags*, an opprobrious term, equal to scamp or villain, applied to men who will not work.

2. An impostor or intriguer, esp. in politics; in *U. S. Hist.*, a native white of the southern states who was willing to accept the reconstructionary measures.

1864 SALA in *Daily Tel.* 27 Sept., The councilmen too often belong to the comprehensive genus 'scallywag'. They have intrigued and speechified, and stumped their ward. 1879 TOURGEE *Fool's Err.* (1883) 111/25. 1885 *Times* (weekly ed.) 29 May 12 Our correspondent tells us that the new system [*i.e.* of Mental Healing] has not yet fallen into the hands of the 'Scalawags'. 1886 *Forum* Apr. 128 Then came the absurd process called Reconstruction, with its swarm of leeches, carpet-baggers and Scalawags.

3. *U. S.* A name for undersized or ill-conditioned cattle. Perhaps the original use of the word.

1854 *New York Tribune* (Cattle Rep.) 24 Oct. (Cent. Dict.), The number of miserable 'scallawags' is so great that.. they tend to drag down all above themselves to their own level. 1868 *Daily News* 18 Sept., Wade Hampton explained the origin of the term..by saying that 'scalawag' was the name applied by drovers to lean and ill-favoured kine.

Scalmuse, Scalop(e, Scalo(u)n, Scalour: see SHAWM, SCALLOP, SCALLION, SQUALOR.

Scalp (skælp), *sb.*[1] Also 4–7 **skalp,** 5–7 **scalpe,** 6 **skalpe;** (chiefly *Sc.*) 5, 8 **skap,** 6 **scawpe, skape,** 7 **scop,** 8–9 **scaup, scawp,** 9 **scap.** [Northern ME. *scalp*; presumably of Scandinavian origin, though the Eng. senses are not found in any Scandinavian or Teut. language. Cf. ON. *skálp-r* sheath, Da. dial. *skalp* shell, husk, MLG. *schulpe, scholpe*, MDu. *schelpe* (Du. *schelp*) shell; the sense of these words suggests derivation from OTeut. **skal-*, **skel-* (see SCALE *sb.*[1]), but a Teut. *p-* suffix is not known.

The It. *scalpo*, given by Oudin 1540 with the rendering *le test*, and by Florio 1611 with the rendering 'scalp', seems to be of doubtful genuineness. The Eng. word in sense 3 has passed into several European langs.: F. *scalpe*, G., Sw. *skalp*.]

1. The top or crown of the head; the skull, cranium. Now only *Sc.* and *north. dial.* (*scaup, scap*).

a 1300 *E. E. Psalter* vii. 17 His wiknes in his scalp doune falle. *c* 1400 MAUNDEV. (Roxb.) xxxiv. 153 Of þe scalpe [*v.r.* brayn panne] of þe heued he gers make him a coppe. *c* 1460 *Towneley Myst.* xvi. 353 Then thi skalp shall I clefe. *c* 1480 HENRYSON *Mor. Fab.*, *Trial of Fox* 1026 (Charteris MS.) With bludie skap, and cheikis bla and reid. 1508 DUNBAR *Test. Kennedy* 52 To hede of kyn, bot I wait nought Quis est ille, than I schrew my scawpe [*Bann. MS.* skape]. 1535 COVERDALE *Ps.* lxvii[i]. 21 The God that smyteth his enemies vpon the heades & vpon the hayrie scalpes. [Similarly 1611.] 1541 R. COPLAND *Guydon's Quest. Chirurg.* Diij b, What is the skull or scawpe of the heade? Answere. It is that parte of the heade that is full of heare, wherin the anymal membres are conteyned. 1590 SHAKS. *Mids. N.* IV. i. 69 Take this transformed scalpe, From off the head of this Athenian swaine. 1598 STOW *Surv.* 270 In digging the foundation of this newe woorke..there were founde more then an hundred scalpes of Oxen, or Kine. 1607 TOPSELL *Four-f. Beasts* 124 [Their] hornes..grow..not to their bones or skalps, but to their skin. 16.. *Robin Hood & Tanner* ix, If I get a knop upon the bare scop thou canst as well shite as shoote. 1650 G. P. *Comenius' Janua Ling.* xxiv. 297 If the skull [*marg.* scalp, brainpain] bee one entire bone. 1724 RAMSAY *Vision* iii, To..skonce my skap and shanks frae rain. 1899 J. LUMSDEN *Edin. Poems & Songs* 198, I wat for't sune his Scotch scap reissils.

fig. 1596 NASHE *Saffron Walden* F 2 Not content to haue the naked scalp of his credit new couered with a false periwig of commendations.

b. The head or skull of a whale exclusive of the lower jaw. In recent Dicts.

2. The integument of the upper part of the head, usually covered with hair and moving freely over the underlying bones.

Formerly often †*hairy scalp*; cf. quot. 1535 in sense 1. Possibly this Bible phrase (a literal rendering of the Heb.) may have caused the development of sense 2.

1616 BULLOKAR *Eng. Expos.*, *Scalpe*, the haire skinne of the head. 1651 BIGGS *New Disp.* ¶ 259 Those fained vapours ..stirre up the tempest of the diseases causation, before they can come to the hairy scalp. 1656 BLOUNT *Glossogr.*, *Scalp* (*pericranion*), the skin compassing and covering all the skull. 1676 WISEMAN *Chirurg. Treat.* v. ix. 374 The Hairy scalp. 1725 *Bradley's Fam. Dict.* s.v. *Turning-Evil*, Then take a long sharp Knife and a Hammer, and cut the Scaup two Inches square, and turn it up. 1800 *Med. Jrnl.* III. 443 Five or six small spiculæ of bone worked themselves through the scalp, (the wound being healed). 1872 DARWIN *Emotions* xiv. 352 The naked scalp of a very young infant reddens from passion. 1894 H. DRUMMOND *Ascent Man* 117 Every one has met persons who possess the power of moving the whole scalp to and fro.

Phrase. 1842 TENNYSON *St. Sim. Styl.* 2 From scalp to sole one slough and crust of sin. 1890 TALMAGE *From Manger to Throne* 78 Christian infidels..who are from scalp to heel surcharged with unbeliefs.

transf. 1658 SIR T. BROWNE *Gard. Cyrus* iii. 47 He that inquireth into the little bottom of the globe-thistle, may finde that gallant bush arise from a scalpe of like disposure.

b. *Her.* The skin of the head of an animal.

1688 HOLME *Armoury* II. 166/1 The Horns of a Bull fixed upon the curled Skalp..with two Ears. Sable. 1722 NISBET *Syst. Her.* II. iv. 337 The Attirings of a Stag fixed to the Scalp. 1828–40 BERRY *Encycl. Her.* II, *Dymock*... Crest..the scalp of a hare, the ears erect sa.

3. The scalp with the hair belonging to it cut or torn from a man's head: prized by American Indians as a battle trophy.

1601 HOLLAND *Pliny* VII. ii. I. 154 The former Anthropophagi..whom we have placed about the North pole,..use.. to weare the scalpes, haire and all, in steed of..stomachers before their breasts. 1677 W. HUBBARD *Narrative* I. 19 Two or three miles further they came up with some Heads, Scalps, and Hands cut off from the bodies of some of the English. 1748 WASHINGTON *Jrnl.* 23 Mar., Writ. 1889 I. 3 We were agreeably surprized at ye sight of thirty odd Indians coming from war with only one scalp. 1781 GIBBON *Decl. & F.* xxvi. II. 24 The scalps of their enemies formed the costly trappings of their horses. 1817 J. BRADBURY *Trav. Amer.* 42 The dance of the scalp. 1837 W. IRVING *Capt. Bonneville* I. iv. 76 The chief..had his scalps to show and his battles to recount. 1867 PARKMAN *Jesuits in N. Amer.* xix. (1875) 282 Eleven fresh scalps fluttered in the wind.

b. *fig.* as the symbol of a victory gained.

1870 M. D. CONWAY *Earthward Pilgr.* xxiii. 276 The savage creed that wears the scalp of Shelley at its belt. 1902 C. N. & A. M. WILLIAMSON *Lightning Conductor* 141 If I had been, that girl wouldn't have got back into the house without being proposed to, and having another 'scalp' to count, as they say American beauties do.

4. A wig made to cover a part of the scalp.

1801 *Chron.* in *Ann. Reg.* 458 [Patent] for a method of making perukes and scalps. 1843 THACKERAY *Ravenswing* i, Mr. Eglantine, the celebrated perruquier..whose..patent ventilating scalps are known throughout Europe.

5. A bare piece of rock or stone standing out of water or surrounding vegetation (thus resembling a hairless skull). *Sc.* and *north. dial.* (pronounced and often written *scaup*).

1721 RAMSAY *Prospect of Plenty* 215 (1877) I. 52 Plenty shall cultivate ilk scawp and moor. 1722 *Newcastle Courant* 1 Sept. Advt. (E. D. S. 71) The Ship called the John and Margaret,..now lying upon the Scalp against Mr. Jennison's Key, North Shields. 1865 G. TATE in *Hist. Berw. Nat. Club* (1868) V. 151 On the scalp of the rock where it dips into the hill, four figures are traceable. 1871 *Daily News* 21 Aug., There there is a bare 'scaup' of boulders and scanty turf. 1903 *Expositor* Jan. 11 The grey argillaceous soil is shallow, stony and constantly interrupted by scalps, ledges and knolls of naked limestone.

b. The cap of a mountain. Chiefly *poet.*

1810 SCOTT *Lady of L.* III. ix, Ben-an's grey scalp the accents knew. 1816 BYRON *Ch. Har.* III. lxii, The Alps,.. whose vast walls Have pinnacled in clouds their snowy scalps. 1848 CLOUGH *Bothie* I. 58 The frosty scalp of the Cairn-Gorm. 1875 J. GRANT *One of the 600* III. xxi. 290 When the snows of Christmas whiten the scalps of Largo and the Lomond Hills.

6. *attrib.* and *Comb.* **a.** (sense 1) **scalp-house** *dial.*, a charnel house.

1890 *Murray's Handbk. Lincolnshire* 113 Below is a groined undercroft, known as the 'scaup (skull-) house'.

b. (sense 2), as *scalp hair, length, muscle, wound.*

1805 SOUTHEY *Madoc* II. xvi, On the front it [the spear] met him, and plough'd up The whole scalp-length. 1851 H. MELVILLE *Whale* iii. 24 There was no hair on his head..nothing but a small scalp-knot. 1868 DARWIN in *Life & Lett.* (1887) III. 99, I believe all anatomists look at the scalp-muscles as a remnant of the *Panniculus carnosus*. 1879 *St. George's Hosp. Rep.* IX. 237 Forty cases of simple scalp-wounds. 1890 BILLINGS *Med. Dict.*, *Scalp-tumor*, caput succedaneum; cephalhæmatoma.

c. (sense 3), as *scalp-bearer, -dance, -hunter, -mark, -merchant, -trophy*, etc.; **scalp-knife** = *scalping-knife*; **scalp-lock,** a long lock of hair left on the head (the rest being shaved) by North American Indians as a challenge to their enemies; **scalp-money,** money paid as a reward for 'bringing in' scalps of men or animals.

1722 S. SEWALL *Diary* 13 June (1879) II. 351 Council would have had subsistence and £100 Scalp-money. 1795 COLERIDGE *Conciones ad Pop.* 46 In America the recent enormities of their Scalp-Merchants. 1807 J. BARLOW *Columb.* v. 52 Ax, quiver, scalpknife on the girdle hung. 1827 J. F. COOPER *Prairie* II. i. 5 His head was shaved to the crown, where a large and gallant scalp-lock seemed fearlessly to challenge the grasp of his enemies. 1851 MAYNE REID *Scalp Hunt.* xvii. 121, I became a scalp-hunter. 1866 WHITTIER *Snow-Bound* 261 How the Indian hordes came down...And how her own great-uncle bore His cruel scalp-mark to four-score. 1877 G. GIBBS *Tribes of W. Wash.* 222 A figure of a man, with a long queue, or scalp-lock, reaching to his heels. 1878 C. TUTTLE *Border Tales* 17 The weird music of the scalp-dance. *Ibid.* 18 One by one the squaws fell in behind the scalp-bearer.

Scalp (skælp), *sb.*[2] Chiefly *Sc.* and *north.* Forms: 6 **skap, scawip, skalp, scalfe, scalph,** 7 **scap,** 7, 9 **scaup,** 6– **scalp.** [Perh. a specific use of prec. (cf. sense 5), but the forms with *f, ph* point to the possibility of a different origin. Cf. SHELP.] A bank providing a bed for shellfish, *esp.* oysters and mussels; an oyster or mussel bed or colony. (Often *mussel-, oyster-scalp.*)

1521 *Aberdeen Reg.* (1844) I. 98 Nane of the mussillis ..now beginnin to gader one ane now skap at the northt watter, besyd the Cunningar hillis. ?15.. *Aberd. Reg.* (Jam.), The scawip of mussillis & kokilliss. 1552 HULOET, Muskleskalp. *Ibid.*, Oyster scalph, *ostrifer*. [Cf. ELYOT *Dict.*, *Ostrifer*, the place in the sea, whiche is apte to ingender oysters.] 1557 *Sel. Pleas Crt. Admiralty* (Selden Soc.) II. p. lxvi, Mussel scalfe. 1587 *Burgh Rec. Edin.* (1882) 488 To caus brek the swame of the mvssill scalp in the heavin of Leyth. 1593, 1879, 1896 [see MUSSEL *sb.* 4]. *a* 1672 WILLUGHBY *Ornith.* III. (1676) 279 Avis hæc *the Scaup-duck* dicta est, quoniam scalpam [RAY (1678) 365 *Scaup*] i.e. pisces testaceos fractos seu contritos esitat. 1793 *Statist. Acc. Scot.* VIII. 461 A *scalp* of a small kind of mussels. 1862 *Macm. Mag.* Oct. 503 There used to be great battles between the men of Newhaven and the men of Fisherrow, principally about their rights to certain oyster-scalps. 1882 *Standard* 26 Sept. 2/1 Boston Deep, which is admirably suited for mussel culture, returns, now that the 'scalps' are protected, over 500*l.* per annum.

† **Scalp,** *v.*[1] *Obs.* [ad. L. *scalpĕre*.] *trans.* To cut, carve, engrave; to scrape, scratch.

1552 [implied in SCALPING *vbl. sb.*[1]]. 1662 EVELYN *Chalcogr.* i. 9 With the..stile, we only cut the Vernish, razing, and Scalping as it were, the Superficies of the Plate. *a* 1764 R. LLOYD *Poet. Wks.* (1774) I. 95 Critics..Should..not, unskilful, yet with lordly air, Read Surgeon's lectures while they scalp and tear. 1802 M. MOORE *Lascelles* II. 23 The points of their swords scalped off their noses.

Scalp, *v.*[2] Also 7 **skulp** (?). [f. SCALP *sb.*[1] From Eng. are F. *scalper*, G. *skalpiren*, Du. *scalpeeren*, Sw. *skalpera*.]

1. *trans.* To cut off the scalp of (a person): chiefly said of the North American Indians.

1676 N. S. *Narrat. New-Eng.* 14 Laying him for dead, they flead (or skulp'd) his head of skin and hair. 1697 S. SEWALL *Diary* 13 Sept. (1878) I. 459 Indians shot and scalped him about noon. 1754 H. WALPOLE in *World* III. 285 The Chippoways and Orundaks are still very troublesome. Last week they scalped one of our Indians. 1867 PARKMAN *Jesuits in N. Amer.* xix. (1875) 281 They sought out the bodies, carefully scalped them, and set out in triumph on their return. 1877 G. GIBBS *Tribes of W. Wash.* 192 None of the western tribes within my observation have pursued the practice of scalping the slain.

absol. *c* 1778 *Conquerors* 61 Whose Indians scalp'd and carry'd desolation..to christian nation.

fig. 1849 N. HAWTHORNE *Let. to H. Mann* 8 Aug., I shall do my best to kill and scalp him in the public prints. 1856 FERRIER *Inst. Metaph.* XI. ix. (ed. 2) 298 Dr. Reid and his followers, instead of scalping a doctrine, have merely tomahawked a word.

b. *U. S. political slang.*

1891 *Century Dict.*, *Scalp*,..to destroy the political influence of, or punish for insubordination to party rule.

2. *transf.* **a.** *U. S.* (See quot. 1895.)

1895 *Funk's Stand. Dict.*, *Scalp*, to level by cutting off, as the tops of cradle-knolls and the knobs of logs laid in corduroy roads; as, to scalp a road.

b. *dial.* To strip off (the turf or upper soil).

1806 FORSYTH *Beauties Scot.* IV. 524 Unmerciful destroyers of all the grounds around them, scalping and tearing up every bit of better soil. 1866 EDMONDSTON *Shetland & Orkney Gloss.*, *Scalp*; 'To scalp the land'—to pare off the surface of the soil, S.

3. *Milling.* **a.** To separate the 'hair' or 'fuzz' from (wheat, etc.) by attrition and screening. **b.** To separate the different sizes of wheat, etc. from one another by means of sieves or screens.

1883 NEFTEL *Rep. Flour-Milling* (10th Census U.S.) 16 The wheat is scalped in four reels. 1884 [see SCALPING *vbl. sb.* 2, 3].

4. *Stock Exch.*, etc. To buy at very low rates so as to be able to sell at less than official rates.

1883 *Pall Mall G.* 15 Oct. 12/1 A professional speculator, who 'scalped' the market on a big scale for a small profit per bushel. 1891 *Century Dict.* s.v., To scalp railway-tickets.

Scalp, *v.*[3] *rare.* = SCAPPLE *v.*

1725 *J. Webb's Stone-Heng* 88 They were scalped [*ed.* 1665 scappled] at the Quarries. 1883 *Stonemason* Jan., It is then trimmed (or scalped) into shape by men called block-choppers.

Scalped (skælpt), *ppl. a.*[1] [f. SCALP *v.*[2] + -ED [1].] **a.** Having the scalp torn off. **b.** Of a mountain: Having a naked summit. Of land: Having the turf stripped off.

1754 SHEBBEARE *Matrimony* (1766) II. 275 A long list of ruined Virgins by means of this Act will undoubtedly be as acceptable to its Abettors as a Number of scalped Christians to an Indian Chief. 1855 BROWNING *Childe Roland* xxx, A tall scalped mountain. 1890 *St. Nicholas* May 556/2 Many a good in-field [for base-ball] has no turf on it, and is called a 'scalped' field.

Scalped, *ppl. a.*[2] *dial.* In quot. **scauped.** [f. SCALP *sb.*[2] + -ED [2].] Cultivated on a 'scalp'.

1894 *Standard* 10 Feb. 6/7 'Scauped', or cultivated mussels.

Scalpeen (skælpī·n). *Anglo-Irish.* [Of obscure origin: cf. SCALPIN.] (See quot.)

1834 LOVER *Leg. & Stories Irel.* Ser. II. 18 Peter..determined on a cargo of scalpeens. *Ibid.* 55 Scalpeens is pickled mackerel.

Scalpel (skæ·lpĕl), *sb.* [ad. L. *scalpell-um, -us*, dim. of *scalper, scalprum*. Cf. F. *scalpel* (in 16th c. *scalpelle*), G. *skalpel*.] A small light knife used in surgical and anatomical operations.

1742 SIMSON in *Edin. Med. Ess.* V. I. 445 The Scalpel is about an Inch in length, and a third in Breadth. 1879 T. BRYANT *Pract. Surg.* II. 5 Shaving the redundant mass off the cartilage with a scalpel. 1893 W. R. GOWERS *Man. Dis. Nerv. Syst.* (ed. 2) II. 333 If a scalpel be passed over the surface, it removes a little pyo-lymph.

attrib. 1742 SIMSON in *Edin. Med. Ess.* V. I. 447, I contrived the Scalpel-ring I have sent you the draught of, which may be used safely with the Uterus at any Distance.

b. *fig.*

1818 SCOTT *Rob Roy* xxi, Whoever should happen to overhear their character discussed in their own servants'-hall, must prepare to undergo the scalpel of some such anatomist. 1851 H. REED *Lect. Eng. Lit.* xi. (1855) 339 It demands, too, for this serious service the most acute intellectual scalpel which the metaphysician can handle.

Hence **Sca·lpel** *v. trans.*, to cut with a scalpel; **Scalpe·llic** *a.*, involving the use of the scalpel.

1748 tr. *Vegetius' Distempers of Horses* 53 Let the whole Circumference of the Soal of the Hoof be scalpelled or cut with a Lancet. 1877 RUSKIN *Wks.* IV. 155 *note*, Ocular and passionate study of nature [as opposed to] telescopic, scalpellic and dispassionate.

Scalpe·lliform, *a.* *Bot.* [ad. mod.L. *scalpelliformis*: see prec. and -FORM.] 'Having the form of a common penknife-blade, but planted vertically on a branch' (*Treas. Bot.* 1866).

Scalper [1], **scauper** (skæ·lpəɹ, skǭ·pəɹ). [Partly a. L. *scalper*, by-form of SCALPRUM, partly f. SCALP *v.*[1] + -ER [1].]

†**1.** *Surg.* = SCALPRUM 1. *Obs.*

1656 BLOUNT *Glossogr.*, *Scalper* or *Scalping Iron* (*scalprum*), a Surgeons Instrument, to scrape or take away corrupt flesh from the bones; a Lance to let blood with.

2. *Engraving.* A kind of graver used for hollowing out the bottom of sunken designs.

1688 HOLME *Armoury* III. 308/1 The Scalper, is a kind of Graver with a flat point; its use is to clear the bottoms of broad Letters or Escochions sunk into the Metal. 1821 CRAIG *Lect. Drawing*, etc. vii. 377 A large square tool, called a scawper. 1855 tr. *Labarte's Arts Mid. Ages* iv. 122 With scalpers he tooled or hollowed out all the spaces. 1869 *Eng. Mech.* 10 Dec. 298/3 Scaupers are used for cutting out the white parts of the block.

Scalper [2] (skæ·lpəɹ). [f. SCALP *v.*[2] + -ER [1].]

1. One (esp. an American Indian) who removes scalps.

1795 COLERIDGE *Conciones ad Pop.* 45 Did not this employment of merciless Scalpers rouse the indignation of Britons? 1807 J. BARLOW *Columb.* VI. 371 Scalpers and ax-men rush from Eerie's shore. 1884 E. P. ROE in *Harper's Mag.* Mar. 617/2 This treacherous scalper of birds.

fig. 1904 *Sat. Rev.* 29 Oct. 536 The scalpers of the yellow press had not time to put on their war-paint.

2. *U. S. slang.* **a.** One who buys and sells at a profit, but at a price lower than the official one, unused portions of long-distance railway tickets.

1882 *Nation* 5 Oct. 276 (Cent. Dict.) The eternal quarrel between railroads and scalpers. 1892 C. ROBERTS *Adrift Amer.* 51, I went round to all the railroad ticket agents, called scalpers, in the city, and at last decided to go down as far as Topeka in Kansas, as that was the cheapest journey I could pick out for the distance.

b. *Stock Exch.* One who sells stock at lower than the official rates.

1888 *Pall Mall G.* 15 Oct. 12/1 'Old Hutch,' by which title B. P. Hutchinson has been known on the Chicago Board of Trade for years as the champion scalper and speculator. 1891 *Times* 8 Oct. 11/1 Late trading was dull, but steady, on moderate covering by 'scalpers'.

3. A scalping-knife. *rare.*

1893 LELAND *Mem.* II. 297 A tussle *à la Choctaw*, with biting, gouging, tomahawk and scalper.

4. A 'scalping' machine: see SCALP *v.*[2] 3.

1886 W. A. HARRIS *Techn. Dict. Fire Insur.* 251 *Scalpers*, or *Scalping Reels*, the simple hexagon dressing-reels with iron shaft, iron arms, and iron rails clothed with tin or steel-wire cloth. *Ibid.* 252 Wheat is partially crushed by rollers, and afterwards passed through the scalpers and the silk dressing-machines.

Scalph, obs. form of SCALP *sb.*[2]

†**Sca·lpin.** *Obs.* Also 5–6 **scalpyn,** 6 **scalphyn,** 7 **scalpion.** [Of obscure origin: cf. SCALPEEN.] The whiting.

c 1400 *Little Red Bk. Bristol* (1900) II. 72 Toutz maners grociz pissouns, cestassauoir Samoundes, Congres, Melewels, Lenges, Hakes, Scalpyn et Harrynges venauntz au dite ville de Bristuyt hors del meer. 1548 (30 June) *Admiralty Court Oyer & Terminer* 35 Departyd therewithe [i. e. with a fishing boat] from Poole towards Wynchelsey on Scalpyn fare. 1549 in *Pat. & Close Rolls, Irel.* (1861) I. 196 [For every cwt. of] scalphyn [or other fish 1*d.*]. 1602 CAREW *Cornwall* 35 Whitings (in the East parts named Scalpions).

† **Sca·lping,** *sb.* *Obs.* [? f. SCALP *sb.*[1] + -ING [1].] (See quot.)

1746 CATESBY in *Phil. Trans.* XLIV. 126 Mr. Joice, in digging the Foundation of an House..found, at the Depth of 6 Feet, a Part of a Jaw-bone..; then one Foot of Scalping or Sand-bed; then eighteen Inches of Stone.

Sca·lping, *vbl. sb.*[1] [f. SCALP *v.*[1] + -ING [1].] In † **scalping iron** = SCALPER [1] 1.

1552 HULOET, Scalping yron for a surgeon, *scalpellum, scalprum*. [Also in later Dicts.]

Sca·lping, *vbl. sb.*[2] [f. SCALP *v.*[2] + -ING [1].]

1. a. *Surg.* The laying bare of the bone of the skull by cutting and raising the scalp.

1739 SHARP *Surg.* xxvii. 139 For it never happens that we inquire for a Fracture of the Scull by scalping, but that the Scalp itself is contus'd. 1787 *Med. Commun.* II. 153 Which he had experienced before the scalping and trepanning. 1897 *Syd. Soc. Lex.*

b. The tearing off of the scalp of an enemy.

1747 *Gentl. Mag.* 43 Scalping is cutting the skin from the eyebrows round the head and peeling it off. 1876 BANCROFT *Hist. U. S.* VI. xxiv. 3 He taunted Burgoyne with the murders and scalpings by the Indians in his employ.

2. In technical and slang uses (see the vb.).

1871 COWIE *Shetland* viii. 158 (E. D. D.) The ruinous process of 'scalping', or removing the turf of the commons for manuring the farms. 1882 *Nation* 5 Oct. 276 (Cent. Dict.) A corporation like the Pennsylvania Railroad must protect itself against loss through scalping. 1884 KNIGHT *Dict. Mech.* Suppl., *Scalping* (*Milling*), brushing the hair or fuzz from the ends of wheat grain to prevent its getting into the flour. 1894 *Standard* 3 May 7/1 (Farmer) A scalping of the Stock at the expense of the genuine investor. 1902 *Dundee Advertiser* 23 Apr. 4 Numbers of crofter grazings have been spoiled..by 'scalping', irregular peat cutting,.. and careless heather burning.

3. *attrib.* and *Comb.*, as *scalping act, party*; fig. in *scalping measure*; **scalping-machine** (see quot.); **scalping-tuft,** a scalp-lock.

1750 in Temple & Sheldon *Hist. Northfield* (1875) 381 Our Men will not venture out after the Enemy on any Scalping Act whatsoever. 1757 WASHINGTON *Lett.* Writ. 1889 I. 454 *note*, They have detached their principal force into many scalping parties. 1777 FOX in *Hansard's Parl. Hist.* (1814) XIX. 523 The most violent, scalping, tomahawk measures. 1826 J. F. COOPER *Mohicans* iii, The well-known and chivalrous scalping-tuft. 1883 NEFTEL *Rep. Flour-milling* (10th Census U. S.) 9 The resultant 'chop' is separated into..flour, middlings, and bran, by means of bolts technically called 'scalping-reels'. 1884 *Bath Herald* 27 Dec. 6/5 A 'scalping' machine..separates the 'middlings' from the larger pieces of wheat.

Sca·lping, *ppl. a.* [f. SCALP *v.*[2] + -ING [2].] That scalps (in various senses).

1762–71 H. WALPOLE *Vertue's Anecd. Paint.* (1786) V. 75 A scalping Indian. 1903 *Times* 3 Mar. 9/2 Chicago, March 2. Wheat...Scalping traders were moderate buyers.

Sca·lping-knife. [SCALPING *vbl. sb.*[2]] A knife such as is used by the North American Indians in scalping their enemies.

1759 JOHNSON *Idler* No. 40 ¶ 7 A..Mohawk Indian warrior,..with his scalping-knife, tom-ax and all other implements of war! 1825 MACAULAY *Ess.*, *Milton* (1843) I. 8 The Mohawk hardly feels the scalping-knife while he shouts his death-song. 1867 PARKMAN *Jesuits in N. Amer.* xxii. (1875) 328 They had no motive for exchanging the comforts of home..for..the scalping-knives of the Iroquois.

b. *fig.* and allusively.

1764 CHURCHILL *Gotham* I. 5 Whilst her brave rage, not satisfied with life, Rising in blood, adopts the Scalping-Knife. 1831 SCOTT *Ct. Robt.* Introd. Addr. ¶ 37 Peter Pattison's last labours shall now go down to posterity unscathed by the scalping-knife of alteration.

Scalpless (skæ·lplĕs), *a.* [f. SCALP *sb.*[1] + -LESS.] Without a scalp.

1756 J. CLUBBE *Misc. Tracts, Physiognomy* (1770) I. 17 The scalpless musty skull of the famous Helen. 1850 KINGSLEY *Alton Locke* I. vi. 90 A tall cast of Michael Angelo's well known skinless model—his pristine white defaced by a cap of soot upon the top of his scalpless skull.

Scalpriform (skæ·lprifǭɹm), *a.* [f. L. *scalprum* (see next) + -FORM.] Chisel-shaped: applied to the incisors of rodents.

1828 *Lancet* 3 May 130/2 These chisel or scalpriform teeth. 1839 *Penny Cycl.* XIV. 454 Rhizophaga. Two scalpriform incisors in both jaws. 1870 ROLLESTON *Anim. Life* 6.

‖ **Scalprum** (skæ·lprŏm). Also 7 *erron.* **scalpra.** [L., f. *scalpĕre* SCALP *v.*[1]]

1. *Surg.* A rasping instrument; a raspatory.

1688 HOLME *Armoury* III. xx. (Roxb.) 235/2 The Scalpra or Scraping Toole; it is to scrape or shave bones with all. 1767 GOOCH *Treat. Wounds* I. 303 With the knife appropriated to this use and the scalprum, a piece of the scalp is to be removed. 1858 MAYNE *Expos. Lex.*, *Scalprum*.. Name for a denticular raspatory used in trepanning.

2. *Anat.* The cutting edge of an incisor. Also, a scalpriform incisor.

1842 BRANDE *Dict. Sci.*, etc., *Scalprum*, in Mammalogy, the cutting edge of the incisor teeth.

† **Sca·lptize,** *v.* *burlesque nonce-wd.* [f. L. *scalpt-*, *scalpĕre* SCALP *v.*[1] + -IZE.] *trans.* To scratch.

1708 MOTTEUX *Rabelais* v. xx. 60 You have..scalptiz'd your Heads with frequent Applications of your Ungicules.

Sca·lpture. *rare.* [ad. L. *sculptūra*, f. *scalpt-*, *scalpĕre* SCALP *v.*[1]] Carving, graving.

1656 BLOUNT *Glossogr.*, *Scalpture*,..a graving in Mettal, a cutting or scratching. 1850 LEITCH tr. *C. O. Müller's Anc. Art* Introd. § 27 (ed. 2) 10 Scalpture (the art of cutting stones and dies).

Scalpy (skæ·lpi), *a. dial.* [f. SCALP *sb.*[1]] Having a thin covering of soil suggesting a scalp.

1621 BRATHWAIT *Omphale* in *Nat. Emb.* 222 Where scalpie hils and sandie vales imply, The ploughmans toile's requited slenderly. 1808 JAMIESON, *Scalpy* (pron. *Scaupy*), a term applied to ground, when the soil is thin. 1877 *N. W. Linc. Gloss.* s.v., Some's so near th'rock it's scalpy, and, in a way o' speakin', good to nowt.

Scalt: see SCALD *a.*[2] and SCALD *v.*

Scalter, scaltre, var. ff. SHALTREE *Obs.*

Scaly (skē[i]·li), *a.* Also 6–7 **skaly,** 6–7, 9 **scalie,** 7 **scaily,** *Sc.* **skailly,** 7–9 **scaley.** [f. SCALE *sb.*[2] + -Y.]

1. Abounding in, covered with, or consisting of scales; having a surface that peels off in thin plates or layers.

1538 ELYOT *Dict.*, *Squammosus*, skaly. 1594 PLAT *Jewell-ho.* III. 74 If your teeth be verie scalie, let som expert Barber first take off the scales. 1615 CROOKE *Body of Man* 442 The scalie Sutures of the Temple-bones. 1682 WHELER *Journ. to Greece* I. 14 The surface..is covered with a scaly rock. 1793 *Gentl. Mag.* May 422/1 An altar-tomb, or altar, of scaly stone. 1857 MILLER *Elem. Chem.*, *Org.* III. 82 A scaly, sweetish, gummy mass. 1892 E. LAWLESS *Grania* II. 7 The wind..tearing off fragments of scaly stone from the rocks.

2. Of fishes, serpents, and other animals; freq. in poetry = pertaining to or consisting of fish (*scaly flock, herd, nation, tribe*).

1528 PAYNELL *Salerne's Regim.* O ij b, The more skaly that fishe is, the better hit is. 1595 SPENSER *Epithal.* 57 The silver scaly trouts. *c* 1614 SIR W. MURE *Dido & Æneas* III. 127 The skailly squadrones of the liquid lakes. 1629 MILTON *Hymn Nativ.* xviii, The scaly Horrour of his foulded tail. 1666 DRYDEN *Ann. Mirab.* xv, So hear the scaly herd when Proteus blows. 1704 POPE *Windsor For.* 139 The patient fisher takes his silent stand,..With looks unmov'd, he hopes the scaly breed. 1741 *Compl. Fam.-Piece* I. ii. 108 Season the Scaley Side first. 1828 STARK *Elem. Nat. Hist.* I. 450 The body of these fishes is scaly. 1857 J. HAMILTON *Less. from Gt. Biogr.* (1859) 278 His own line quivered with a scaly captive. 1872 BAKER *Nile Trib.* viii. 115 A strip of the scaly hide of a crocodile.

b. In specific names, usu. repr. L. *squamosus, squamatus*, or *squameus*: see quots. *Scaly anteater, scaly lizard*, names for the pangolins.

1681 GREW *Musæum* I. iii. 46 The Scaly-Lizard..is a yard and ½ long. 1774 GOLDSM. *Nat. Hist.* (1862) I. VI. iii. 468 The Pangolin, which has been usually called the scaly lizard. 1802 SHAW *Gen. Zool.* III. 74 Scaly Tortoise. *Testudo Squamata*. 1812 *Ibid.* VIII. 463 Scaly Lory. *Psittacus squameus*. 1840 *Penny Cycl.* XVII. 186/1 Pangolins, a name in common use to designate the Scaly Ant-eaters. 1872 COUES *Key N. Amer. Birds* 227 Genus *Scardafella* Bonaparte. Scaly Dove.

c. *Scaly fish* (slang): see quot.

1796 GROSE *Dict. Vulgar T.* (ed. 3), *Scaly Fish*, an honest, rough, blunt sailor.

3. Of plants and their parts: Covered with scales or consisting of scale-like elements.

1597 GERARDE *Herbal* II. ccxxxviii. 588 Small scaly knops, like to the knops of Corne flower. 1688 HOLME *Armoury* II. 80/2 The Arbor Vitæ, or Tree of Life hath a small scaly leaf. 1786 ABERCROMBIE *Gard. Assist.* 242 The main bulbs of lilies, of the scaly tribe, will not keep good so long out of the ground as the solid bulbous kinds. 1839 LINDLEY *Introd. Bot.* III. (ed. 3) 470 *Scaly*.., covered with minute scales, fixed by one end; as the young shoots of the Pine tribe. 1857 A. GRAY *First Less. Bot.* (1866) 46 When the scales are narrow and separate, as in the Lily, the bulb is said to be scaly. 1884 BOWER & SCOTT *De Bary's Phaner.* 622 Rhizomes with scaly leaves.

b. **Scaly fern** or **spleenwort,** the ceterach. **Scaly water-moss,** *Fontinalis squamosa*.

1796 WITHERING *Brit. Plants* (ed. 3) III. 789 Scaly Water-moss. 1859 MISS PRATT *Brit. Grasses* 224 Common Ceterach, or Scaly Spleenwort.

4. Of skin diseases. *Scaly ringworm*, tinea imbricata. *Scaly tetter*, psoriasis.

1575 TURBERV. *Venerie* lxxix. (1908) 228 The skaly Mange, which..taketh off the skinne where it goeth. 1796 MORSE *Amer. Geog.* I. 112 Those who make a free use of it,..have a scaly appearance, not unlike the leprosy. 1799 *Med. Jrnl.* II. 112 Scaly Tetter. 1826 S. COOPER *First Lines Surg.* (ed. 5) 194 In the majority of cancerous diseases, the skin has a yellowish or lead-coloured tinge, and is dry and scaly. 1898 P. MANSON *Trop. Dis.* Introd. p. xiii, Tropical scaly ringworm.

b. *transf.* Of trees: Infested with the scale insect.

1894 *Times* 14 May 3/4 This [wash] is strained before being sprayed upon the scaly trees.

5. Of armour. Cf. *scale-armour* s. v. SCALE *sb.*[2] and SCALED. Chiefly *poet.*

1597 SHAKS. 2 *Hen. IV*, I. i. 146 A scalie Gauntlet now, with ioints of Steele, Must gloue this hand. 1747 GRAY *Cat* 16 Their scaly armour's Tyrian hue. 1781 GIBBON *Decl. & F.* xviii. II. 120 His cuirassiers..glittering with their scaly armour. 1791 COWPER *Iliad* xv. 641 His corslet thick With plates of scaly brass.

6. *Min.* (See quots.)

1796 KIRWAN *Elem. Min.* (ed. 2) II. 339 Brown Scaly Iron Ore. 1815 AIKIN *Man. Min.* (ed. 2) 200 *Scaly Talc*,..an aggregate of minute scales of a greenish colour. *Ibid.* 202 *Scaly Chlorite*,..composed of glimmering scaly particles. 1816 R. JAMESON *Min.* (ed. 2) III. 243 Red Ironstone. This species is divided into four subspecies, viz. Scaly Red Ironore [etc.].

7. *slang.* Poor, shabby, despicable; *esp.* (of persons) mean, stingy; occas., in poor health, 'seedy'.

1793 SOUTHEY *Lett.* (1856) I. 19 Poor Anax! he was quite scaly before his departure, but is now recovering apace. 1821 EGAN *Life in London* II. iii. (Farmer), If you are too scaly to tip for it, I'll shell out, and shame you. 1823 *Spirit Publ. Jrnls.* 233 They had proved themselves so very scaley, by forgetting to remember the waiter. 1844 DICKENS *Mart. Chuz.* xxviii, A reg'lar scaly old shop, warn't it? 1875 BESANT & RICE *Harp & Cr.* I. x. 206 If I were an author—they are a scaly lot, and thank Heaven I am not one.

8. *Comb.*, chiefly parasynthetic. **Scaly-bark (hickory),** the hickory or hickory nut.

1634 MILTON *Comus* (Facsimile MS. 1899, 13), The scalie-harnest dragon. *c* 1712 PETIVER *Gazophyl.* vii. 64 Scaly-like Fruit. 1781 LATHAM *Gen. Syn. Birds* I. 246 Scaly-breasted Parrakeet. 1803 SHAW *Gen. Zool.* IV. 400 Scaly-tailed scarus. 1816 R. JAMESON *Char. Min.* (ed. 2) 237 Scaly foliated, when the folia cover each other only partially. 1836 *Penny Cycl.* VI. 332/1 *Carya alba*, white-shell-bark, shag-bark, scaly-bark hickory (*Juglans squamosa*, Michaux). 1859 MISS PRATT *Brit. Grasses* 21 Scaly-stalked Club-rush. 1893 *Advance* (Chicago) 23 Mar., A pretty young woman rings your bell to ask, 'You all buy some scaly-barks?'

Scalyon, obs. form of SCALLION.

Scam, obs. form of SHAME; var. SCAUM *v.*, *Sc.*

Scamandee, variant of SCAMATO *Obs.*

Scamander (skămæ·ndəɹ), *v.* [app. f. the name of the river *Scamander* (Σκάμανδρος Homer), in imitation of MEANDER *v.*

Cf. Yorks. dial. '*skimaundering*, hanging or hovering about' (*Almondbury Glossary*).]

intr. To wander about, take a devious or winding course. Hence **Scama·nder** *sb.*, devious progress.

1864 *Hotten's Slang Dict.* (ed. 3) 220 *Scamander*, to wander about without a settled purpose. 1858 M. COLLINS *Sweet Anne Page* II. 193 Isola had given up 'scamandering'. 1873 — *Miranda* II. 247 When he got into an unknown town, it was his wont to sinuously scamander through it. 1873 *St. Paul's Mag.* Feb. 133 His two..doggish friends ..made miles of scamander for his every furlong.

† **Sca·mato.** *Obs.* Forms: 6 **scamato,** 7 **scammatie, scamoty, scamandee.** [app. repr. some mod. Gr. corruption of med. Gr. ἑξάμιτον SAMITE.

Cf. mod. Chios dialect σκαμάγκι and σκαμάνδρα, σκαμανδρον 'spun cotton' (Paspates Χιακὸν Γλωσσάριον, 1888; in a quot. there given the latter is associated with δίμιτον: cf. quots. below).]

Some kind of textile fabric.

1570 CAMPION in *Hakluyt's Voy.* (1599) II. I. 115 For we do vse to buy..of their Scamato and Dimite, that the poore people make in that towne [*sc.* Chio]. 1605 PURCHAS *Pilgrimes* II. 1812 The downie or woolly substance..of which the Ilanders doe make a certaine stuffe called Dimitie, and another called Scammatie. 1660 *Act 12 Chas. II*, c. 4 Scamoty the peece containing seven yardes & ½..vij s. vj d. 1687 A. LOVELL tr. *Thevenot's Trav.* I. 99 In most of these Villages are made the Stuffs, which they call Dimite, and Scamandee.

Sca·mble, *sb.*[1] *Sc.* and *north.* Forms: 5 **skamyll,** 9 **skemmel;** 6 *pl.* **skaymlis, scamles, scamells, scambills, skemlis,** 7 **skemmillis.** [Northern var. of SHAMBLE *sb.*; prob. due to Scandinavian influence; cf. ON. *skemill*, Da. *skammel* footstool.]

1. A bench; now, 'a kind of long form used in a farm-house kitchen' (E. D. D.).

c 1470 HENRY *Wallace* XI. 1352 Thai xxx[ty] dayis his band thai durst nocht slaik, Quhill he was bundyn on a skamyil off ayk. 1885 HALL CAINE *Shadow of a Crime* x, [He] had placed the benches called skemmels down each side.

† **2.** *pl.* (const. as *sing.*). A slaughter-house (also *fig.*); a meat or fish market; a shambles. *Obs.*

1549–50 *Stirling Burgh Rec.* (1887) I. 58 To brek fischis apon the skenlis of the foirgate. 1561 *Aberdeen Reg.* (1844) I. 334 For makking of ane skaymlis of tre at the fysche cors, for laying of the quhyt fysche tharupoune. 1570 BUCHANAN *Admonit.* Wks. (1892) 23 Sum convoyaris of him to ye scamles that slew his guidschir. 1572 *Satir. Poems Reform.* xxxv. 94 We sall avenge it on that clan, Ȝour freind that to the scambills sauld. 1582–8 *Hist. Jas. VI* (1804) 195 They marchit..to Edinburgh, and plantit a gairdhous at the comon scamells. 1607 *Stirling Burgh Rec.* (1887) I. 116 The fische skemmillis.

† **Sca·mble,** *sb.*[2] *Obs. rare.* [f. SCAMBLE *v.*] A scramble, confused struggle.

1609 J. DAVIES *Humours Heau'n on Earth* I. clxxxiii. (Grosart) 23/1 Here Bugs bestirre them, with a bellowing rore, As at a Scamble we see Boyes to sturre, Who for Soules scamble on a glowing flore; Biting and scratching, like the Cat and Curre. 1664 H. MORE *Myst. Iniq.* I. xvi. 320 This pretended Triumvirate is no Supreme Magistracy, but a Political Scuffle or Scamble or transient Shuffle betwixt these three men, Octavius, Antony and Lepidus.

Scamble (skæ·mb'l), *v.* Also 6 **skamble,** 9 *Sc.* and *dial.* **skammel, skemmel, -il, skemmle, skemble.** [Of obscure origin; app. related both to SHAMBLE and SCRAMBLE *vbs.*, which are not recorded until much later.]

†**1.** *intr.* To struggle with others for money, fruit, sweetmeats, etc. lying on the ground or thrown to a crowd; hence, to struggle in an indecorous and rapacious manner in order to obtain something. Const. *for, after*. *Obs.* (now superseded by SCRAMBLE).

1539 TAVERNER *Erasm. Prov.* (1545) 22 b, The apes.. skambled and went together by ye eares for the nuttes. 1553 *Respublica* I. iii. 176 *Avar*...Therefore catche that catche maye, hardely, & spare not,..the Devyll ys a knave an I catche not a flyce,..I doubte not to skamble and rake as well as one. 1589 PUTTENHAM *Eng. Poesie* I. xxvi. (Arb.) 66 Ladies and gentlewomen..with their handes wantonly scambling and catching after the nuttes. 1595 SHAKS. *John* IV. iii. 146 England now is left To tug and scamble, and to part by th' teeth The vn-owed interest of proud swelling State. 1600 HOLLAND *Livy* XLIV. xlv. 1199 The king,..laid out fiftie talents among them upon the river side to scamble for. 1609 [see SCAMBLE *sb.*]. 1621 BURTON *Anat. Mel.* I. ii. III. xv. 178 *margin*, I had no money, I wanted impudence, I could not scamble, temporise, dissemble. 1636 SIR T. WENTWORTH *Let.* in *Carte's Coll.* (1735) 6 Every man had his money at a day, not scambling one before another without so much as giving of thanks. 1668 J. OWEN *Expos. Ps.* CXXX. 68 This may consist with an obstinate resolution to scamble for something upon the account of self endeavours. 1687 WOOD *Life* 5 Sept. (O. H. S.) III. 237 After the king had don his breakfast, they began to scramble [MS. 19 D (3) fol. 90 scamble]. [In Wood's MS. drafts of this portion of the *Life* the word occurs several times, variously written *scramble* and *scamble*.]

† **b.** To struggle wildly. *Obs.*

1591 LYLY *Sapho & Phao* IV. iii, He [a stockdoue]..scambling to catch hold to harbor in the house hee had made,.. sodainely fell.

2. *trans.* To scatter (money, food) for a crowd to scramble for. *Obs.* exc. *dial.*

Also Sc. (Roxb.) '*Skemmel, skammel*, to throw things hither and thither in a slovenly and careless way' (Jam.).

1573–80 TUSSER *Husb.* (1878) 112 Keepe threshing..to haue to be suer fresh chaffe in the bin. And somwhat to scamble, for hog and for hen. 1600 HOLLAND *Livy* LXIX. 1246 C. Marius..had purchased a sixth Consulship by a largesse of money skambled amongst the tribes. 1894 *Northumbld. Gloss.* s. v., At weddings it is customary to scamble money after leaving the church.

† **3.** To seize in a scuffle; hence, to take in a rapacious or unscrupulous manner. Const. *away*. *Obs.*

1599 SANDYS *Europæ Spec.* (1629) 150 Hee will not be a raiser of new stirrs in Italy; as divers of them to scamble somewhat for theyr owne haue beene. 1638 FORD *Fancies* I. iii, Perhaps The scambling halfe a duccat now and then To rore and noyse it with the tatling hostesse. 1695 WOOD *Life* 9 Nov. (O. H. S.) III. 495 There were only some gentlemen and ordinary people..in the Area who [after the king's departure] rudely scamb[l]ed away all the banquet.

4. *intr.* To make one's way as best one can; to stumble along. *lit.* and *fig.* Now only *dial.*

Also Sc. 'to climb or walk over slight or loose obstacles, to climb over rocks or walls' (Jam. s. v. *Skemmel*).

1571 CAMPION *Hist. Irel.* To Rdr. (1633), From thence to Henry the Eight, because nothing is extant orderly written, ..I scamble forward with such records as could be sought up. 1579 GOSSON *Sch. Abuse* 23 b, I haue in my voyage suffred wrack with Vlisses, & wringing-wett scambled with life to the shore. 1621 BURTON *Anat. Mel.* I. ii. III. xv. 181 When they contemne Learning, & think themselues sufficiently qualified, if they can write & read, or scamble at a piece of Evidence. 1683 H. MORE *Cursory Refl. Baxter* 8 Having scambled through a multitude of Authors carelesly and superficially, he was [etc.]. 1706 PHILLIPS (ed. Kersey), *To Scamble*, to rove or wander up and down. 1901 MISS HAYDEN *Trav. round Village* ii. 42 You had best try an' scamble through the water afoor 'tis too late. *Ibid.* xv. 254 How do 'ee manage to scamble along wi'out Kizzy?

† **b.** To make shift, find means somehow. *Obs.*

1608 *Merry Devil Edmonton* D 4 b, Be ready but to take her at our hands, Leaue vs to scamble for her getting out.

† **c.** To make shift for a meal. *Obs. rare*[−1]. (Cf. SCAMBLING *vbl. sb.* b.)

1591 LYLY *Sapho & Phao* III. ii, *Molus*. I am in the depth of my learning driuen to a muse, how this lent I shall scamble in the court, that was woont to fast so oft in the Vniuersitie. *Criti*. Thy belly is thy God.

† **d.** quasi-*trans.* *To scamble out*: to get through (a period of time) in a haphazard way. *Obs.*

1571 CAMPION *Hist. Irel.* xi. (1633) 34 In this division they scambled out a few yeares, untill the malice of Carassus a Britaine forced a quietnesse betweene them.

5. To throw out the limbs in a loose and awkward manner in walking; to shamble. *Obs.* exc. *dial.*

1633–1852 [see SCAMBLING *ppl. a.*]. 1825 JAMIESON, *Skemmel, skemble, skammel.*

6. *trans.* To collect in a haphazard or irregular manner; to 'scrape' *together, up*. Now *dial.*

1577 HARRISON *England* Ep. Ded., It may be..that your Honour will take offence at my rashe and rechlesse behauiour vsed in the composition of this volume, and much more that being scambled vp after this maner, I dare presume [etc.]. *c* 1592 MARLOWE *Jew of Malta* I. i. (1633) B 3, They say we are a scatter'd Nation: I cannot tell, but we haue scambled vp More wealth by farre then those that brag of faith. 1603 KNOLLES *Hist. Turks* (1621) 541 Before the enemie should perceive the weaknesse of his power, which was not great, and scambled up upon the suddain. 1638 WOTTON *Let. to Bacon* 6 Nov. in *Reliq. W.* (1672) 471 With this dispatch I will intermingle no other vulgar subject, but hereafter I will entertain you with as jolly things as I can scamble together. 1834 *Tait's Mag.* I. 544/2 Each might, without much difficulty, 'scamble up some sort of husband' from among the corps.

7. To remove piecemeal; to cut *away*.

1707 MORTIMER *Husb.* 426 Finding my Wood cut in patches, and other parts of it scambled and cut before it was at its Growth. 1888 *Athenæum* 11 Feb. 186/2 This band..was left untouched when the sculptor scooped or scambled away the substance to give depth of space for the relief of the two figures.

Hence **Sca·mble-shamble** *v.* (*nonce-wd.*) *intr.*, to lounge or shamble.

1887 RUSKIN *Præterita* II. 332 He went scamble-shambling on, a plague to the end.

Scambler (skæ·mbləɹ). *Sc.* Also 6 **scamler, skam(e)lar.** [app. f. SCAMBLE *v.* + -ER [1].

The vb., however, is app. not recorded in Sc. before the 19th c., and derivation from SCAMBLE *sb.*[1], a bench, would not be inconsistent with the sense. Cf. Gael. *sgimilear*.]

A parasite, sponger.

1500–20 DUNBAR *Poems* lxiii. 45 On ȝour hienes follows eik ..Scaffaris, and scamleris in a nuke, And hall huntaris of draik and duik. 1508 KENNEDIE *Flyting w. Dunbar* 37 Skaldit skaitbird, and commoun skamelar. 1533 BELLENDEN *Livy* v. iii. (S. T. S.) II. 153 Þe maist parte of þe knichtis ..war passand like skamlars throw þe cuntre. 1721 J. KELLY *Sc. Prov.* 274 It is well ken'd your Father's Son was never a Scambler. [*Foot-note.* One that goes about among his Friends for Meat.] 1755 JOHNSON *Scambler* (Scottish), a bold intruder upon one's generosity or table.

Scambling (skæ·mbliŋ), *vbl. sb.* [-ING [1].] The action of the vb. SCAMBLE.

c 1538 R. COWLEY in Ellis *Orig. Lett.* Ser. II. II. 98 Such havok and skameling as they make was never seen, to the utter pilling and beggering of the land. 1584 *Leycesters Commonw.* 106 And how so euer thes two conioyned Earles, do seeme for the tyme to draw together, and to playe bootie: yet..Hastings for ought I see, when he commeth to the scambling, is like to haue no better luck by the Beare, then his auncestor had once by the Boare. 1599 SHAKS. *Hen. V*, v. ii. 218. 1659 GAUDEN *Serm.* etc. (1660) 9 Whatever scambling and confusion in Civil and Regular Magistracy mens ambition brought on the state of the Jews, yet [etc.]. 1878 GROSART *H. More's Poems*, Mem. Introd. 10/1 Those noble old folios, matterful and painstaking, and putting to shame the literary scambling of to-day.

b. † The action of making shift for a meal or for meals. *Scambling day*: see quot. (*obs.*). Also, a makeshift or informal meal. Now only *dial.*

c 1512 *Regul. Northumberld. Househ.* (1770) 80 This is the ordre of the Service of Meat and Drynk to be servyd upon the Scamlynge Days in Lent Yerely as to say Mondays and Setterdays thrughe out Lent and what they shall have att the said Scamlyngs. 1563 PILKINGTON, etc. *Burnynge Paules Ch.* I iiij, Some..eat more at that one dynner, than the poore man can get at three scamlinges on a day. 1606 MARSTON *Parasitaster* II. i, Come Sir, a stoole boy, the Court Feasts are to vs Seruitors Court Fasts, such scambling, such shift for to eate and where to eate. 1873 W. P. WILLIAMS & W. A. JONES *Somerset. Gloss.*, *Scamblin*, irregular meal.

Scambling (skæ·mbliŋ), *ppl. a.* [-ING [2].]

†**1.** Contentious, rapacious. *Obs.*

1599 SHAKS. *Much Ado* v. i. 94, I know them,..Scambling out-facing, fashion-monging boyes. 1599 — *Hen. V*, I. i. 4 The scambling and vnquiet time. *a* 1639 WOTTON *Life Buckingham* (1642) 29 He was no sooner entred into the Town, but a scambling Souldier clapt hold of his bridle. 1691 *New Disc. of Old Intreague* xvi. 28 Whose regular noise,..Some dreadful scambling combate did present.

2. Clumsily or carelessly executed; slipshod, slovenly; makeshift. Also of a person: Blundering, bungling.

1589 NASHE *Anat. Absurd.* C j, Who is it, that reading Beuis of Hampton, can forbeare laughing, if he marke what scambling shyft he makes to ende his verses a like. 1599 HARSNET *Discov. Fraud. Darrel* 275 It is not likelie that the Diuell coulde bee dispossessed, by such almost priuate, slender, interrupted, and scambling prayers. 1653 H. MORE *Antid. Ath.* II. vii. § 5 (1712) 61 Or if you will say, that there may some scambling shift be made without them [etc.]. 1856 P. THOMPSON *Hist. Boston* 721 [Provincialisms.] You've made a scambling dinner, I fear. 1884 ROGERS *Six Cent. Work & Wages* II. 412 The establishment of a rule that members of such unions would denounce and expose dishonest and scambling work.

3. Irregular, rambling, scattered.

1592 WYRLEY *Armorie* 67 The scambling chace eight leaes endurd right, Ending almost at the gate of Reans. 1657 OWEN *Review Nat. Schism* ix. 141 To declare the way of his exerting his Authority..is not a matter to be tossed up and down in this scambling chase. 1658 EVELYN *Diary* 27 Sept., To Bedington,..a fine old hall, but a scambling house. 1680 MORDEN *Geog. Rect.*, *Ganges Penins.* 404 Her Capital City, which is large but scambling. 1702 D. GRANVILLE *Rem.* (Surtees) 241 Letters..to my scatter'd, scambling, and sometimes scabby sheep. 1786 tr. *Sparrman's Voy.* 324 Being ..upon a plain under the shelter of a few scambling thorn-trees. 1891 *Reports Provinc. Dev.* (E.D.D.) There wad'n on'y two or dree scamlin ones [*sc.* pheasants] down thick way.

4. Straddling, shambling.

1633 FORD *Love's Sacr.* v. i, Can you imagine, Sir, the name of Duke Could make a crooked leg, a scambling foot, ..fit for a Ladies pleasure, no. 1658 ROWLAND tr. *Moufet's Theat. Ins.* 952 The Gnat..hath six long crooked scambling legs..growing from his prominent breast. 1852 R. S. SURTEES *Sponge's Sp. Tour* viii. 33 On horseback, Tom was a.. hard-bitten little fellow..., while on foot he was the most shambling, scambling, crooked-going crab that ever was seen.

Hence **Sca·mblingly** *adv.*

1611 COTGR. s.v. *Griffe*, *Griffe graffe*, by hooke or by crooke,..scamblingly, catch that catch may. 1755 in JOHNSON.

Scame, variant of SCAUM; obs. form of SHAME.

† **Sca·mel.** *Obs. rare*[−1]. Meaning uncertain: the statement in quot. 1866 is of doubtful value. Some have proposed to read *staniel*.

1610 SHAKS. *Temp.* II. ii. 176 And sometimes I'le get thee young Scamels from the Rocke. [1866 H. STEVENSON *Birds of Norfolk* II. 260 At Blakeney Mr. Dowell states that bar-tailed godwits are known to the local gunners by the singular appellation of 'Picks' and 'Scamells'...He believes by 'Scamells' are meant the females and those found singly in autumn.]

Scamely, obs. form of SCAMMONY.

Scamler, Scamles: see SCAMBLER, SCAMBLE *sb.*[1]

Scammatie, variant of SCAMATO *Obs.*

† **Sca·mmel,** *a.* *Obs. rare*[−1]. [Perh. connected with SCAMBLE *v.*: cf. Sc. *skemmel* 'a tall, thin, ungainly person' (Jam.); also dial. *scrammel* 'a lean, gaunt, ill-favoured person or animal' (E.D.D.).] Lean, scraggy.

1658 tr. *Porta's Nat. Magic* II. ix. 39 That [mule] which is begotten of the wilde Asse, cometh nothing behind the other, but only that it is unruly and stubborn, and somewhat scammel, like the Sire [L. *nisi, quod..strigosum patris proferet habitum*].

† **Scammo·nial,** *a.* *Obs. rare*[−1]. [f. L. *scammōni-um* + -AL.] = SCAMMONIATE *a.*

1657 TOMLINSON *Renou's Disp.* v. xiii. 167 Rhabarb or some scamoniall Medicine is often added to Cassia.

† **Scammo·niate,** *a.* and *sb.* *Obs.* [ad. mod.L. *scammōniātus* (neut. *-ātum* as used subst.), f. L. *scammōnium* SCAMMONY.] **A.** *adj.* Made with or containing scammony; hence, purgative. Also *fig.*

1620 BP. ANDREWES *Serm.*, *Holy Ghost* xiii. (1629) 740 Neither Scammoniate, tormenting the conscience; nor yet Opiate stupifying it. 1651 BIGGS *New Disp.* § 113 A Scammoniate medicine. 1725 *Phil. Trans.* XXXIII. 389 The hot, scammoniate, aloetic Purgers seem not so proper.

B. *sb.* A medicine containing scammony; a purgative medicine.

1665 M. N. *Med. Medicinæ* 389 Ill-corrected Scammoniates.

Scammonic (skămǫ·nik), *a.* *Chem.* [f. L. *scammōn-ium* SCAMMONY + -IC.] *Scammonic acid* = jalapic acid: see JALAPIN.

1864 WATTS tr. *Gmelin's Handbk. Chem.* XVI. 408.

Scammonin (skæ·mŏnin). *Chem.* [Formed as prec. + -IN.] = JALAPIN. 1863 WATTS *Dict. Chem.*

† **Scammonite,** *a.* *Obs. rare*[−1]. [ad. L. *scammōnites*, a. Gr. σκαμμωνίτης, f. σκαμμωνία SCAMMONY.] Medicated with scammony.

1601 HOLLAND *Pliny* XIV. xvi. I. 421 In like maner also is made the Scammonite wine.

Scammony (skæ·mŏni). Forms: 1 **scamonie,** (**-am,** Lat. *accus.*), 3 **scamoi(e)ne,** 5 **scamely,** 5–6 **scamonie, scammonye,** 5–7 **scamony,** 5 **skamonye,** 7 **-ony,** 6–7 **scammonie,** 6– **scammony.** [ad. L. *scammōnia, scammōnium* (also *scammōnea*), a. Gr. σκαμμωνία, -ώνιον. Cf. OF. *scamonee, escamonie* (mod.F. *scammonée*), Pr., Sp., Pg. *escamonea*, It. *scamonea*.]

1. A gum-resin obtained from the tuberous roots of *Convolvulus Scammonia* (see sense 2) used in medicine as a strong purgative; also, the dried tuberous root from which the drug is prepared.

Also with qualifying word indicating the place of export, esp. in *Aleppo, Smyrna scammony*.

c 1000 *Sax. Leechd.* II. 272 Nim scamoniam þæt peniȝ ȝewege & ȝegnid smæle. *Ibid.*, Wyrtdrenc scamonian ȝeceos þus. *c* 1205 LAY. 17740 Appas..dude þer to atter þa scamoiene [*c* 1275 scamoine] hatte. 1436 *Libel Eng. Policy* in *Pol. Poems* (Rolls) II. 173 That wee shulde have no nede to skamonye, Turbit, euforbe [etc.]. *c* 1475 *Non-Cycle Mystery Pl.* (E.E.T.S.) 73/506, I haue gyven hyr a drynke made..wyth scamely. 1526 *Grete Herball* cccciii. (1529) Cc iij b, Scamony is often contrefayted with mylke of y[e] herbe of catapucie. 1626 BACON *Sylva* § 19 You may make it as strong a Purging Medicine, as Scammony. 1875 H. C. WOOD *Therap.* (1879) 470 Scammony acts upon the system like jalap, but is somewhat more irritating.

fig. 1678 B. R. *Let. Pop. Friends* 4 What Protestant Scammony is strong enough to make a thorough-pac'd Catholick Disgorge Infallibility?

b. (See quot.)

1849 BALFOUR *Man. Bot.* § 956 A spurious kind of Scammony has been prepared from the root of *Convolvulus* (*Calystegia*) *sepium*; and several plants belonging to the order Asclepiadaceæ yield a purgative exudation which has been used under the names of Montpellier and Bourbon Scammony.

2. The plant *Convolvulus Scammonia*, native in Syria and Asia Minor, having a fleshy root which furnishes the scammony (sense 1) of commerce.

1567 MAPLET *Gr. Forest* 61 Scammony..hath a leafe like Iuie. 1597 GERARDE *Herbal* II. cccv. 716 Of Scammonie, or purging Bindweed. 1785 MARTYN *Rousseau's Bot.* xvi. 191 This genus contains several remarkable plants; as Scammony..and Jalap.

3. *attrib.*

1871 GARROD *Mat. Med.* (ed. 3) 282 Compound Scammony Powder...Scammony Mixture. *Ibid.* 283 Scammony resin also forms an important ingredient in extractum colocynthidis compositum. 1887 BENTLEY *Man. Bot.* (ed. 5) 627 This Scammony as also Scammony Root, and Scammony Resin, are official in the British Pharmacopœia.

Scamoniall: see SCAMMONIAL.

Scamoty, variant of SCAMATO *Obs.*

Scamp (skæmp), *sb.* Also 9 *Sc.* **skemp.** [f. SCAMP *v.*[1]]

1. A highway robber. *arch.*

1782 MESSINK *Choice of Harlequin* (Farmer), Ye scamps, ye pads, ye divers. 1785 GROSE *Dict. Vulgar Tongue*, *Scamp*, a highwayman; royal scamp, a highwayman who robs civilly; royal foot scamp, footpads who behave in like manner. 1809 G. ANDREWES *Dict. Slang*, *Scamp-foot*, a street robber, a foot pad, spicer. 1834 H. AINSWORTH *Rookwood* III. v, A rank scamp!

† **b.** Highway robbery. *Obs.*

1786 *Life Miss Davies* 11 He resolved to go upon the scamp. 1812 J. H. VAUX *Flash Dict.* s.v., The game of highway robbery is called *the scamp*...*Done for a scamp* signifies convicted of a highway robbery.

2. A good-for-nothing, worthless person, a ne'er-do-well, 'waster'; a rascal. Also *playfully* as a mild term of reproof.

α. 1808 JAMIESON, *Scamp*, a cheat, a swindler; often used as to one who contracts debt, and runs off without paying it, *Loth.*, *Perths.* 1825 BROCKETT *N. C. Gloss.*, *Scamp*, a mean rascal, a fellow devoid of honour and principle. 1833 MARRYAT *P. Simple* xxix, He was a sad scamp. 1837 DICKENS *Pickw.* xlvii, Those are the cleverest scamps I ever had any thing to do with. 1844 LOCKHART *Let.* 13 May in *Life & Lett.* (1897) II. 199 Ben Disraeli, the Jew scamp, has published a very blackguard novel. 1874 L. STEPHEN *Hours in Libr.* (1892) II. vi. 181 The prodigal who has been with scamps in gambling-houses. 1878 BROWNING *Poets Croisic* 133 This scamp Voltaire!

β. 1818 HOGG *Brownie of Bodsbeck* I. 110 Ye're surely some silly skemp of a fallow, to draw out your sword on a puir auld woman. 1824–7 MOIR *Mansie Wauch* xxii. (1828) 339 Skemps that had not wherewithal to pay lawful debts.

3. *U. S.* (See quots.)

1882 JORDAN & GILBERT *Synopsis Fishes N. Amer.* 538 *Trisotropis falcatus* Poey.—Scamp. 1884 G. B. GOODE, etc. *Nat. Hist. Aquatic Anim.* 413 Another fish..*Mycteroperca falcata*, is called at Pensacola by the name 'Scamp'.

Scamp (skæmp), *v.*[1] [app. cogn. with SCAMPER *v.*, which occurs earlier. An earlier evidence of the word may exist in the mock-heraldic SCAMPANT (*c* 1585).] *intr.* † **a.** *cant.* (See quot. 1753). **b.** *Sc.* With advs. *about, off.* (See quot. 1867).

1753 *Disc. John Poulter* (ed. 7) 39 I'll scamp on the Panney; [=] I'll go on the Highway. 1867 GREGOR *Banffsh. Gloss.*, *Scamp*, to go about in an idle manner; often with the idea of mischief; followed by *aboot* and *through*.

Scamp (skæmp), *v.*[2] [Prob. of dialectal origin; cf. SKIMP *v.*, used *dial.* in the same sense; the source may possibly be ON. *skemma* to shorten, f. *skamm-r* short: see SCANT *a.*]

1. *trans.* To do (work, a task, etc.) negligently or hurriedly. Also *to scamp off, over*. Cf. SKIMP *v.*

1837 WHITTOCK *Bk. Trades* (1842) 392 (*Printer*) The best work which cannot be 'scamped' over. 1861 SMILES *Engineers* I. 11 From the very earliest times the tendency to 'scamp' work seems to have existed. 1867 G. MUSGRAVE *Nooks in Old France* I. ii. 80 A perilous mode of scamping off their work. 1888 W. P. FRITH *Autobiog.* III. v. 112 A portrait, in which..the man's figure had been what we call 'scamped'.

absol. 1859 SMILES *Self-Help* viii. 211 There are tradesmen who adulterate, contractors who 'scamp' [etc.].

2. *U. S. intr.* (in quot. quasi-*trans.*) To be stingy or excessively economical. Cf. SKIMP *v.*

1894 C. MERIWETHER in *Nation* 16 Aug. 116/2 If three or four dollars more are added for rent, the tenant either scamps the life out of himself and family, or crops the land to death.

3. *Comb.*: **scamp-work,** scamped work.

1840 MARRYAT *Olla Podr.* xxviii, To use a joiner's phrase, everything abroad is comparatively scamp-work. 1884 E. H. PLUMPTRE in *Expositor* Apr. 275 What we call 'scamp-work' in building was as common..in Ezekiel's time, as it is with us.

Hence **Scamped** *ppl. a.*

1871 CARLYLE in *Mrs. Carlyle Lett.* III. 198 The house was..misbuilt..a despicable, cockney, scamped edifice. 1885 J. G. WOOD *My Garden Wall* in *Longm. Mag.* VI. 518 This one little bit of 'scamped' brickwork is almost the only part that is worth watching.

† **Sca·mpant.** *Obs.* *nonce-wd.* [quasi-*Her.* after RAMPANT; cf. SCAMP *v.*]

c 1585 in *Rel. Ant.* II. 122 [Burlesque coat of arms] A lyther lad scampant, a roge in his ragges.

‖ **Scampavia** (skampavī·a). Also 8 **scampavie.** [It., f. *scampare* to run off, decamp (see DISCAMP *v.*) + *via* way, away.] A swift sailing vessel used in the Mediterranean.

1723 *Pres. St. Russia* I. 35 Three Russian Scampavies full of Russian Soldiers. 1802 *Naval Chron.* VIII. 122 Quick sailing little vessels called scampavias. 1867 SMYTH *Sailor's Word-bk.*, *Scampavia*, a fast rowing war boat of Naples and Sicily.

Scamper (skæ·mpəɹ), *sb.*[1] [f. SCAMPER *v.*] The action of scampering, in the senses of the vb.; also, an instance of this. Also in the phrases *to be on* or *upon the scamper, to put to the scamper.*

1697 VANBRUGH *Æsop* Pref., The first day it [*sc.* this Play] appear'd, 'twas routed.., the fourth it gave a vigorous Attacque, and the fifth put all the Feathers in Town to the scamper. 1766 COLMAN & GARRICK *Clandestine Marr.* v. ii, If we had not watch'd them and call'd up the fammaly, they had been upon the scamper to Scotland by this time. 1809 MALKIN *Gil Blas* IV. xi. ¶ 4 Those who are always on the scamper see a great deal of the country. 1885 *Field* 7 Feb. 147/3 A fox..led hounds a short but merry scamper over a stiff country. 1888 BURGON 12 *Gd. Men* II. v. 4 He loved..a scamper round the garden.

Scamper (skæ·mpəɹ), *sb.*[2] [f. SCAMP *v.*[2] + -ER [1].] One who scamps work.

1851 MAYHEW *Lond. Labour* II. 199 To a notorious 'scamper', he one morning sent three cart-loads of 'mac' at 1*s.* a load, all to be used in the erection of..one..house. 1884 C. GIBBON *By Mead & Stream* II. xxxii. 144 Work was scamped: he detected it, and dismissed the scampers.

Scamper (skæ·mpəɹ), *v.* [Of uncertain origin.

In our quots. first recorded in 1667, but very common between that date and 1700. Not improbably the word was originally military slang, either from obs. Du. *schampen* 'to escape or flie, or to be gone' (Hexham 1660), which is a. OF. *escamper* to decamp, or from It. *scampare* to decamp, run away: see DISCAMP *v.* A less likely, though possible, supposition is that it represents a ME. derivative of the OF. word, preserved in some non-literary dialect.]

† **1.** *intr.* To run away, decamp, 'bolt'. *Obs.*

1687 T. BROWN *Saints in Uproar* Wks. 1720 I. 89 It rejoices me to consider, with what wonderful Alacrity you [*sc.* St. Ursula and her Virgins] scamper'd over the Alps, and without a Farthing of Money in your Pockets. 1688 in Ellis *Orig. Lett.* Ser. II. IV. 144 Upon beat of drum..[they] have scampered away, and by flight provided for their safety. 1693 DENNIS *Impartial Critick* iii. 18 *Beaum*...But whose are those Verses? If they are thine, I scamper immediately. 1697 DAMPIER *Voy.* I. 189 We were forc'd to cut our Cables in all haste, and scamper away as well as we could. *a* 1700 B. E. *Dict. Canting Crew*, *Scamper*, to run away, or Scowre off, either from Justice, as Thieves, Debtors, Criminals, that are pursued; or from ill fortune, as Soldiers that are repulsed or worsted. 1788 FRANKLIN *Autobiog.* Wks. 1840 I. 191 The wagoners took each a horse out of his team and scampered. 1822 BYRON *Juan* VIII. lxxv, The Turks at first pretended to have scamper'd. 1833 M. SCOTT *Tom Cringle* ix, The few of the Pirates who had escaped having scampered into the woods.

2. To run or caper about nimbly; to go or journey hastily from place to place. Also with advs. *about, away, off*, etc.

1691 [see SCAMPERING *vbl. sb.*]. 1697 DAMPIER *Voy.* I. 517 For which reason, I suppose, they represented so many Serpents scampering about in the printed Picture that was made of him. 1760–2 GOLDSM. *Cit. W.* Pref., I have been set up for half-pence, to fret and scamper at the end of my chain [like a dancing bear]. 1833 HT. MARTINEAU *Manch. Strike* i. 3 Barefooted children were scampering up and down these stairs at play. 1835 WILLIS *Pencillings* II. xlvi. 63 The current scampers through between the two castles. 1873 HOLLAND *A. Bonnic.* iii. 60 A black fox dashed across our way, and, giving us a scared look, scampered into cover. 1882 MISS BRADDON *Mt. Royal* II. i. 3 He is devoured by impatience to be scampering off again.

fig. 1870 MISS BRIDGMAN *R. Lynne* II. xiii. 285 She could just scamper through the scales.

Hence **Sca·mpered** *ppl. a.*

1894 MRS. DYAN *Man's Keeping* (1899) 249 After a scampered-through breakfast. 1906 *Daily News* 21 Mar. 6/5 The usual scampered mid-day meals.

Scamperer (skæ·mpərəɹ). [f. SCAMPER *v.* + -ER [1].] One who scampers; † ? a street ruffian.

1712 STEELE *Spect.* No. 276 ¶ 3 A very gay..old Man.. who has been, he tells me, a Scowrer, a Scamperer, a Breaker of Windows [etc.]. 1802 MISS EDGEWORTH *Manœuvring* vi. (1809) 149 This ever idle, ever busy scamperer. 1804 *Hull Advertiser* 4 Feb. 3/3 A gang of scamperers. 1871 TYNDALL *Forms of Water* § 14 ¶ 123 They were no idle scamperers on the mountains that made these wild recesses first known.

Scampering (skæ·mpəriŋ), *vbl. sb.* [f. SCAMPER *v.* + -ING [1].] In the senses of the verb.

1691 MOUNTFORT *Greenwich Park* II. iii. 22 *Sir Tho*... Let's have a Dance...*La. Haz.* I think we had better Dance at Home...*Sir Tho.* Agreed, then we'll first to Supper, and then for a Rubbers at scampring. 1765 TUCKER *Lt. Nat.* II. 677 Nobody else can know in what instances I have restrained its [*sc.* a horse's] scamperings. 1843 MACAULAY *Ess.*, *Mme. D'Arblay* ¶ 40 A cry of 'The King!' was set up. A general scampering followed. 1865 G. MACDONALD *A. Forbes* 25 A terrible noise of scrambling and scratching and scampering in the very room beside her.

Scampering (skæ·mpəriŋ), *ppl. a.* [f. SCAMPER v. + -ING[1].] In senses of the verb.

Scamphood (skæ·mphud). The quality of being a scamp.

Scamping (skæ·mpiŋ), *vbl. sb.* The action of SCAMP v.[2]

Scamping (skæ·mpiŋ), *ppl. a.* That behaves as a scamp; good-for-nothing.

Scamping (skæ·mpiŋ), *ppl. a.* [f. SCAMP v.[2] + -ING[2].] That behaves as a scamp.

Scampish (skæ·mpiʃ), *a.* [f. SCAMP sb. + -ISH.] Having the character or disposition of a scamp; characteristic of a scamp.

Scampsman (skæ·mpzmæn). *Obs.* [f. scamp's, Scamp sb. 1 b + Man sb.] A highwayman.

Scampy (skæ·mpi), *a.* [f. SCAMP sb. + -Y.] = SCAMPISH.

Scan (skæn), *sb.* [f. SCAN v.] The action of scanning; close investigation or scrutiny; perception, discernment; a scanning look.

Scan (skæn), *v.* Also *a.* 4-7 scanne, 6-7 scann, skan(ne. *β.* 5-6 sound. [a. L. *scandĕre*, lit. to climb, in late L. 'to scan' verses. (Cf. F. *scander* (perh. the source, but in F. it. dicts. first cited from the 16th c.), Sp. *escandir*, It. *scandere* (also to climb), Sp. *skandizen*, Du. *skanderen*.]

Scance (skæns), *sb.* Also 6-7, 9. [f. SCANCE v.] A glance; a glimpse. b. A gleam (of light).

Scance (skæns), *v.[1]* *Obs.* Chiefly *Sc.* Also 6-7, 9 skanze, 7-8 scanse. [app. f. L. *scans*-, ppl. stem of *scandĕre* to climb, to scan.]

Scance (skæns), *v.[2]* *Obs.* [Of obscure origin; cf. ASKANCE.]

Scandal (skæ·ndæl), *sb.* Forms: 1 *scandle*, *scandlu*, *scandl* 3-6 *scandal*, *scandale*, 7 *scandall*, 6- *scandal*. [Early ME. *scandle*, *scha(u)ndle*, a. OF. *escandle*, Central OF. *eschandle*, semi-popular ad. eccl. L. *scandalum* cause of offence or stumbling, ad. Gr. σκάνδαλον.]

Scandalizer (skæ·ndəlaizə·r). [f. SCANDALIZE v. + -ER[1].]

Scandaling (skæ·ndəliŋ), *ppl. a.* [f. SCANDAL v. + -ING[2].] The action of the verb SCANDALIZE in various senses.

Scandaling (skæ·ndəliŋ), *ppl. a.* 1. Causing offence.

Scan·dalled, *a.* *Obs.* Also *7* scandald. [f. SCANDAL v. + -ED[1].]

Scandalize (skæ·ndəlaiz), *v.* and *sb.* Also *8* scandalose, scandalous.

Scandalous (skæ·ndələs), *a.* [ad. L. *scandalosus*, f. *scandalum* SCANDAL *sb.*]

Scandalously (skæ·ndələsli), *adv.* In a scandalous manner.

Scandalousness. [f. SCANDALOUS *a.* + -NESS.] The quality of being scandalous.

Scandal magna·tum. [L. *scandalum magnatum*, pl. of *magnis magnate*.]

Scandalscope. *Obs.* [irreg. f. L. *scandere* to climb + -SCOPE (used unmeaningly).] A machine.

Scandia (skæ·ndiə). *Chem.* [f. *Scandia* (see prec.).]

Scan·dic, *a.* [f. *Scandia* (see prec.) + -IC.]

Scandinavian (skændinē·viən), *a.* and *sb.* [f. L. *Scandinavia* + -AN.]

Scanmag (skæ·nmæg). *colloq.* [Abbreviated form of SCANDALUM MAGNATUM.]

Scannable (skæ·næb'l), *a.* [f. SCAN v. + -ABLE.] That can be scanned.

Scanner (skæ·nə·r). [f. SCAN v. + -ER[1].] One who or that which scans.

Scanning (skæ·niŋ), *vbl. sb.* [f. SCAN v. + -ING[1].]

Scanning (skæ·niŋ), *ppl. a.* [f. SCAN v. + -ING[2].]

Scansion (skæ·nʃən). [ad. L. *scansion*-em, f. *scandĕre* to climb.]

Scansionist (skæ·nʃənist). [f. SCANSION + -IST.]

Scansorial (skænsō·riəl), *a.* and *sb.* [f. mod.L. *scansori-us* + -AL.]

Scansory (skæ·nsəri), *a.* *rare.* [ad. mod.L. *scansori-us*.]

Scant (skænt), *sb.* *Obs.* exc. *dial.* Also *4-7* skant, *5-6* skante, *6* skaunte. [a. ON. *skant* (neut. adj. used *absol.*: see SCANT *a.*)]

Scant (skænt), *a.* and *adv.* Forms: *4-8* skant, *5* skaunt, *6-7* scante, *6-9* skant, *6- scant*. [a. ON. *skamt*, neut. sing. of *skamm-r* short, brief.]

Supplement, p. 3873; Corrigenda, p. 4092; Spurious words, p. 4093; Books quoted, p. 4094.

Scaphocerite. ...proposes the term scaphocephalic to indicate the same boat-like head-form. 1888 *Amer. Naturalist* July 614 Scaphocephalism...occurs from defective parietal bone formation. *Mayne's Med. Voc.* (ed. 6) Scaphocephalous.

Scaphocephaly (skǽfŏsérəit). [f. Gr. σκάφη boat + κέρας horn + -ITE.] The third section of the antenna of an arthropod.

1877 HUXLEY *Anat. Inv. Anim.* vi. 374 Next, a basicerite, to the outer portion of which a flattened plate...here called the scaphocerite, is articulated. 1895 STEBBING *Crustacea* iv. 38 A thin plate, known as the antennal scale... while those who love long words are privileged to call it the scaphocerite.

Scaphoid (skǽ‑foid), *a.* and *sb.* [ad. mod.L. *scaphoīdēs,* a. Gr. σκαφοειδής, f. σκάφη boat: see -OID. Cf. F. *scaphoïde.*] **A.** *adj.* Shaped like a boat. Chiefly *Anat.* and *Zool. Scaphoid bone* = B. The fossa of the helix of the ear. *Scaphoid fracture:* the fossa of the helix of the ear.

1891 A. MOSSO *Anatomy* (ed. 3) 51 The Ligaments stretching from the Heel-bone to the Scaphoid Bone.

B. *sb.* [Short for *scaphoid bone*; in mod.L. *scaphoïdes.*] The first navicular carpal bone in Mammalia, or the corresponding bone in the foot. See NAVICULA A. 1.

Scaphoidal. *a. Obs. rare* -1. [Formed as SCAPHOID + -AL.] Boat-shaped, hollowed out.

Scapiform (ska‑pĭfṝm), *a.* [f. L. *scāp-us* SCAPE.] Having the form of a SCAPE (in various senses).

Scapigerous (ska‑pĭ‑dʒĕrəs), *a. Bot.* [f. L. *scāp-us* SCAPE + -GEROUS.] Bearing a scape; having a stalk devoid of leaves.

Scapling, *vbl. sb. Obs.* [f. SCAPPLE v. + -ING.] The action of the verb SCAPPLE; scappling.

Scapolite (skǽpŏləit), *sb. Min.* [f. Gr. σκᾶπ-ος SCAPE + -LITE.] One of a group of minerals (including dipyre, ekebergite, marialite, etc.) composed of silicates of aluminium, calcium, and sodium.

Scappe: see SCAB 1, SCAPE *v.*, SHAPE, SKEP.

Scappel, obs. form of SCAPPLE 1.

Scappelboll-ing, -*y.* *Obs.* ? Hotheaded.

Scapple (skǽp'l), *v.* [a. AF. *escapler*, escappler = OF. *escapler, eschapler* to cut off.] **1.** To reduce the faces of (a block of stone) with a tool; to dress a stone surface without making it smooth.

Scapplement (skǽp'lmęnt), *sb.* [f. prec. + -MENT.] The smaller chips removed in the process of scappling.

Scapula (skǽpiŭlă), *sb.* [a. L. *scapula* (usu. in *pl.*), fragments of stone chipped off in scappling.] **1.** The shoulder-blade. **Also** *concr.* in *pl.,* fragments of stone chipped off in scappling.

Scapular (skǽpiŭlăr), *a.* [ad. mod.L. *scapulāris,* f. L. *scapula*: see SCAPULA and -AR.]

Scapulary (skǽpiŭlări). [a. L. *scapulāre:* see SCAPULA.]

Scar (skār), *sb.*[1] Forms: 4-skeorre (skoerre), skarre, 5-7 scarre, 6-7 scar; also 5-6 skar, 6 skerre, skeer, 7 skair. Also SCAUR. [App. a. ON. *sker* neut. (Da. *skjær,* Sw. ...)]

Scarab (skǽrăb), *sb.* [ad. F. *scarabée,* 6-7 *scarabe,* 7 *scarab,* -*ubb.* [ad. F. *scarabée,* or L. *scarabaeus*]] A beetle, esp. the sacred beetle of the ancient Egyptians. **1.** In early use, a beetle of any kind (chiefly referred to as supposed to be bred in and to feed upon dung).

Scarabæan (skǽră‑bīăn), *a.* and *sb.* [f. SCARABAEUS + -AN.] Of, pertaining to, or characteristic of, a scarabæus or scarab.

Scarabæoid (skǽră‑bĭoid), *sb.* and *a.* [f. SCARABAEUS + -OID.] **A.** *adj.* Of or pertaining to the *Scarabæidæ,* a large family of lamellicorn beetles, including cockchafers, stag-beetles, dung-beetles, etc.

Scaraboid (skǽrăboid), *sb.* and *a.* [f. mod.L. *scarabaeus* (Leach 1817), f. L. *scarabaeus:* see SCARABAEUS and -OID.] A beetle of, or pertaining to the *Scarabæidæ.*

Scaramouch (skǽrămauʧ), *sb.* Also *scaramouche.* [a. F. *scaramouche,* ad. It. *Scaramuccia.*] A cowardly and foolish boaster of his own prowess, who is constantly being cudgelled by Harlequin.

Scarbage: see SCRABBAGE. **Scarborough** (skār‑bŏrǒ), **warning.** Very short notice, or no notice at all; a surprise.

Scarce (skĕəs), *a.* and *adv.* Forms: 3-7 scarce, skars(e), 4-5 scarse, (5 scarsse), skarce, 6 scarce, skars, scars, 6-7 scarse, skarse, scace, scaice... [ad. ONF. *escars, escharse* (central OF. *eschars, eschers*), mod.F. *échars,* It. *scarso.*]

Scarifier (skæ·rifəiəɹ). [f. Scarify v. + -er 1.] **1.** One who or something which scarifies. *lit.* and *fig.*

1566 Securis *Detection* D ij b, Playster makers, clyster geuers, scarifiers, letters out of bloud, &c. 1683 Salmon *Doron Med.* i. 79 Cicatrizers, or 'Scarrifyers'. 1855 Dickens *Lett.* (1880) I. 403, I have almost finished No. 3, in which I have relieved my indignant soul with a scarifier. 1862 Thackeray *Philip* xvi, There is an air of fashion in everything which Digges writes,..which makes me pretty certain that D. was my scarifier.

2. = Scarificator 1.

1611 in Cotgr.; and in later Dicts.

3. *Agric.* An implement for loosening the soil.

1797 Billingsley *View Agric. Somerset* 278, His [Rev. J. Cooke's] instruments called the scuffler, and scarifier, are the best contrivances I ever beheld, for the pulverization of the soil. 1880 J. W. Hill *Guide Agric. Implements* 472 Improved four-wheel wrought iron lever Scarifiers.

4. *Road-making.* A machine used for breaking up a road. Cf. Scarify v. 3 b.

1892 *Daily News* 21 Oct. 5/5 Our new acquaintance 'the scarifier', whose operations when the roadway of the Thames Embankment is remaking attract so much attention. 1901 *Athenæum* 1 June 697/2 Scarifiers..appear to have been first introduced in England in 1884; and these machines form very valuable adjuncts to steam rolling.

Scarify (skæ·rifəi), *v.* Also 6–8 **scarrify.** [a. F. *scarifier* (13–14th c. in Hatz.-Darm.), ad. late L. *scarīficāre*, altered form of *scarīfāre* to scarify, ad. Gr. σκαριφᾶσθαι, recorded in the senses 'to scratch an outline, sketch lightly, to do anything slightly or slovenly' (L. & Sc.), f. σκάριφ-ος pencil, stilus.]

1. *trans.* (chiefly *Surg.*) To make a number of scratches or slight incisions in (a portion of the body, a wound). Hence *gen.* to cover with scratches.

1541 R. Copland *Galyen's Terap.* F iv, Yf it appere pale, ..it must be scarified and made to blede. 1582 Stanyhurst *Æneis* ii. (Arb.) 43 You me byd, O Princesse, to scarrify a festered old soare. 1601 Holland *Pliny* xxxii. vii. II. 440 Divers..with foure..teeth of this serpent, scarifie the gums of the upper chaw, in case the teeth therein doe ake. 1604 R. Cawdrey *Table Alph.*, *Scarifie*, to launce, or open a sore. 1662 Evelyn *Chalcogr.* 19 By Insculping, Scarrifying, and making a kind of Incision into it. 1749 Fielding *Tom Jones* ii. ix, The captain..had his veins scarified. 1751 Smollett *Per. Pic.* xxxix. (1779) II. 28 Fixing her nails in his antagonist's face, she scarified all one side of his nose. 1788 Gibbon *Decl. & F.* lv. V. 552 They shaved their hair, and scarified their faces. 1855 Lubbock *Preh. Times* xiii. (1878) 459 The body was scarified in horizontal bands. 1875 *Trans. Clin. Soc.* IX. 169 These places were accordingly scarified under the ether spray. 1908 H. D. Rolleston *Dis. Liver* 118 The local pain..[should be] relieved by cold applications, poultices, scarifying the skin [etc.].

transf. 1861 Geo. Eliot *Silas M.* xi. 198 If I offend her, she's sure to scarify my throat with black pepper the next day.

b. *fig.* To make sore, wound. Also, in mod. use, to subject to merciless criticism.

1582 Stanyhurst *Æneis* ii. (Arb.) 55 Theese woords theyre valiant courradge dooe scarrifye deeply. 1714 *Spect.* No. 595 ¶ 6 You have Quartered all the foul Language upon me, that could be raked out of..Billingsgate, without knowing ..whether I deserve to be Cupped and Scarified at this rate. 1721 (*title*) Medicina Flagellata, or the Doctor scarify'd. 1844 Disraeli *Coningsby* i. ii, There..he..cut up a rising genius..or scarified some unhappy wretch. 1884 *West. Morn. News* 13 Sept. 4/4 Next week he will be heard at Northampton, whither he goes to scarify the Tories.

c. *transf.* (? Associated with Scar *sb.*) To cover with scars, to scar.

1687 *Lond. Gaz.* No. 2271/4 A Chesnut Gelding.., scarrified with the Farcie in both his hind Legs. 1697 *Ibid.* No. 3318/4 A Bay Nag with the near Flank a little Scarrified with some former hurt. 1862 Dana *Man. Geol.* 540 Mount Monadnock..is scarified from top to bottom on its northern and western sides.

¶ **d.** App. misused for: To anoint (a wound).

1595 Warner *Alb. Eng.* ix. xlix. (1612) 226 Which had scarrifide our wounds, if wounded, with the Balme Of her sweete Presence. 1607 Topsell *Four-f. Beasts* 78 Then scarifie the wound with that oyntment, till it be wrought in.

2. To make incisions in the bark of (a tree).

c 1440 *Pallad. on Husb.* iv. 601 The turgent trunk let scarifie, That humour effluent out of hit hie. 1658 tr. *Porta's Nat. Magic* iii. xvii. 98 Boring the stock, or scarrifying it round about. 1824 Loudon *Encycl. Garden.* § 7455 As the trees get old..or infected with canker,..or rottenness, they are scarified. 1856 Olmsted *Slave States* 326 Every tree..was scarified for turpentine. 1887 Lady Brassey *Last Voy.* xiii. (1889) 300 The vineyards [Australia]..were not in their best looks, having only just been scarified, as the process is called. It means cutting off the branches and reducing the vines to small and ugly bushes, destitute of leaves at this season.

3. a. *Agric.* To break up or loosen (ground) with a scarifier. **b.** *Road-making.* (Cf. quot. 1817 and Scarifier 4.)

1805 R. W. Dickson *Pract. Agric.* I. 21 Instruments..for scarifying and stirring the earth between the rows of drilled crops. *Ibid.* 468 Scarifying the corn, first operation. 1817 in *Repert. Arts*, etc. XXXII. 132 Secondly, a harrow, which is intended to scarify the uneven parts of any road, leaving it even after the operation, previous to the use of the great roller. 1893 *Jrnl. R. Agric. Soc.* Dec. 822 Scarify or cultivate the stubble as soon as possible.

absol. 1829 *Glover's Hist. Derby* I. 196 Skerrify [*sic*] and harrow two or three times over each field.

Hence **Sca·rifying** *vbl. sb.*

1533 Elyot *Cast. Helthe* (1541) 53 b, Letting of bloude, scarifieng callid cupping, sweating, &c. 1667 *Decay Chr. Piety* Pref. § 10 It being too probable that this is Gods last experiment upon us, like the causticks and scarifyings to a lethargic patient. 1783 Cullen *First Lines Physic* § ccxcv. Wks. 1827 II. 32 To draw blood..by cupping and scarifying. 1880 Jefferies *Hodge & M.* II. 74 He contracts to do their ploughing and scarifying at so much per acre.

attrib. 1599 A. M. tr. *Gabelhouer's Bk. Physicke* 363/2 Scarifye the skinne of the tumor with scarifyinge instrumentes. 1865 *Morn. Star* 15 Mar., To try whether the scarifying process may not do more to bring South Carolina back to the Union than [etc.].

Sca·rily, *adv.* [f. Scary *a.* + -ly 2.] Timidly.

1880 Howells *Undisc. Country* ix. 133 The light..was held scarily aloft above the head of an elderly woman.

Scaring (skē·riŋ), *vbl. sb.* [f. Scare *v.* + -ing 1.] The action of the vb. Scare.

1573–80 Tusser *Husb.* (1878) 32 No scaring with dog. 1580 *Reg. Privy Council Scot.* III. 295 Scarring and debarring of the salmound fischeis. 1611 Cotgr., *Espouventement*..a frighting, fraying, skaring. 1852 G. W. Johnson *Cottage Gard. Dict.* s.v. *Scares*, It is best to employ boys for the short time scaring is required.

Scaring (skē·riŋ), *ppl. a.* [f. Scare *v.* + -ing 2.] That scares; terrifying.

1641 Milton *Reform.* ii. Wks. 1851 III. 64 As a tender Mother takes her Child and holds it over the pit with scarring words that it may learne to feare, where danger is. 1764 Goldsm. *Trav.* 205 As a child, when scaring sounds molest, Clings close and closer to the mother's breast. 1813 Coleridge *Night-Scene* 37 A rude and scaring note, my friend! 1879 Baring-Gould *Germany* II. 207 Let not women be frightened by the scaring name.

† **Sca·riole.** *Obs.* Also 5 **skariole,** 6 **scaryole.** [ad. (through med.L.) It. *scariola* (whence F. *escarole, scarole.*] Broad-leaved endive.

c 1400 tr. *Secreta Secret., Gov. Lordsh.* 73 Wylde letus þat feldmen clepyn skarioles. 1422 *Ibid., Priv. Priv.* 244 Letus sauage, that is y-callid scariole. 1526 *Grete Herball* cl. (1529) I v, Endiuia is endyue...It is otherwyse called scaryole. 1597 Gerarde *Herbal* ii. xxvii. 222. 1658 Phillips, *Scariole*, a kind of herb otherwise called broad leaved endive. 1725 *Bradley's Fam. Dict.* s.v. *Syrup*, Two Leaves of Succory, Dandelion, Endive or Scariole.

Scariose (skē·riōᵘs), *a.* *Bot.* [ad. mod. L. *scariōsus*, of obscure origin.] = Scarious.

1785 Martyn *Rousseau's Bot.* xxvi. (1794) 383 The scales in the Artichoke are scariose or ragged. 1806 Galpine *Brit. Bot.* 21 Glumes scariose. 1881 Baker in *Jrnl. Linn. Soc.* XVIII. 279 Stipules large, brown, deltoid, scariose.

† **Scariot(h.** *Obs.* Aphetic forms of Iscariot.

c 1380 Wyclif *Wks.* (1880) 49 þei leden wiþ hem a scarioth stolen fro is eldris by þefte to robbe pore men bi beggynge. c 1550 R. Bieston *Bayte Fortune* B iij b, Great cause hath now the Scariot to wepe & to bewaile it.

Scarious (skē·riəs), *a.* [ad. F. *scarieux*, ad. mod.L. *scariōsus* Scariose *a.*]

1. *Bot.* Having a dry and shrivelled appearance.

1806 Turton tr. *Linn. Syst. Nat.* VII. Expl. Terms, *Scarious*, dry and rigid, as if dead. 1819 *Pantologia*, *Scarious leaf*, in botany. 1872 Oliver *Elem. Bot.* ii. 261 The scarious perianth by which the Order [*Juncaceæ*] is distinguished from Liliaceæ. 1882 G. Allen in *Nature* 17 Aug. 372 The corolla is thin and scarious.

2. *Zool.* Dry, not fleshy.

1861 Hulme tr. *Moquin-Tandon* i. 49 In some animals.. the tongue is scarious cartilaginous, or provided with a corneous investment. 1872 Coues *Key N. Amer. Birds* 47 When the harder sorts of either scutella or plates are roughened without obvious elevation, the leg is said to be scabrous or scarious.

Scaritid (skæ·ritid), *a.* [f. mod.L. *Scaritēs*: see below.] Pertaining to the *Scaritini*, a tribe of ground-beetles of the family *Carabidæ*, typified by the genus *Scarites*. So **Scari·tidan,** a beetle of this tribe.

1837 Kirby *Richardson's Fauna Bor.-Amer.* IV. 6 *Oxygnathus* De Jean, and some of the other Scaritidans. 1890 *Century Dict.* s.v. *Morio*, The genus pertains to the scaritid section of *Carabidæ*.

† **Sca·rkle,** *v.* *Obs. rare*⁻¹. [Cf. Disparple, Disparkle vbs.] *trans.* To scatter, disperse.

c 1450 *Roll* in *3rd Rep. Hist. MSS. Comm.* (1872) 280/1 For therby be the Frensshemenne riched, the Englishmenne povered; they mightly recured of men & peple, we distroied; they to gader, we assundred scarkeled.

Scarlad, scarlat, obs. ff. Scarlet *sb.* and *a.*

† **Scarla·tical,** *a.* *nonce-wd.* Having the prejudices characteristic of those who wear the 'scarlet' of a doctor of divinity or law.

1672 Wood *Life* (O. H. S.) II. 243 Dr. Clerk..lazy and idle, scarlaticall.

Scarlatina (skāɹlătī·nă). *Path.* Also 9 **scarlet(t)ina.** [a. mod.L. *scarlatina* (Sydenham 1676), a. It. *scarlattina* (used by Lancelotti in 1527), fem. of *scarlattino* adj., dim. of *scarlatto* Scarlet. Cf. F. *scarlatine*, Sp., Pg. *escarlatina.*] = Scarlet fever. (Popularly often misapprehended as denoting a milder form of the disease than that designated by the vernacular term.)

1803 *Med. Jrnl.* X. 455 Several children were..seized with the measles and scarlatina. 1813 Wilberforce *Let.* in *Life* (1838) IV. 131 One of our children having had the Scarlettina. 1845 G. E. Day tr. *Simon's Anim. Chem.* I. 300 Persons suffering from scarlatina. 1863 Miss Braddon *Eleanor's Victory* III. i. 16 She looks as if she were going to a ball; or going to have the scarlatina.

allusively 1823 Moore *Fables Holy Alliance* 49 Woe to Kings when Freedom's fever Once turns into a Scarletina!

Scarlatinal (skāɹlătī·năl), *a.* [f. prec. + -al.] Belonging to, or resulting from, scarlatina.

1861 Graham *Pract. Med.* 683 Hence, for want of caution at this time we may have the scarlatinal dropsy. 1878 L. Browne *Throat & Dis.* 137 In scarlatinal sore throat the local differences are not so well marked.

Scarlatiniform (skāɹlătī·nifǭɹm), *a.* [f. Scarlatin-a + -(i)form.] Resembling the rash or eruption of scarlatina.

1866 Flint *Princ. Med.* (1880) 1042 A scarlatiniform eruption. 1899 *Allbutt's Syst. Med.* VIII. 65 Eruptions of toxic character, erythematous, scarlatiniform [etc.].

Scarlatinine (skāɹlătī·nin). [f. Scarlatin-a + -ine.] The hypothetical infectious principle of scarlatina.

1864 Farr in *Rep. Reg. Gen.* Suppl. 34 When any zymotic matter such as varioline, scarlatinine or typhine finds its way into a village or street, it is more likely to pass from house to house. 1897 *Allbutt's Syst. Med.* II. 164 A toxine has been extracted from the urine, of which the chemical composition has been ascertained, and to which the name Scarlatinine has been given.

Scarlatinoid (skāɹlătī·noid), *a.* and *sb.* [-oid.] **a.** *adj.* Having the appearance of scarlatina. **b.** *sb.* One of a group of Erythemas which closely resemble scarlatina.

1886 Fagge *Princ. Med.* (1888) I. 172 A diffused scarlatinoid eruption. 1899 *Allbutt's Syst. Med.* VIII. 464 The first group which they call Puteoloids and Scarlatinoids comprises the erythemas which simulate the erythematous eruptive fevers in all their stages.

Scarlatinous (skāɹlătī·nəs), *a.* [f. Scarlatin-a + -ous.] Affected with scarlatina.

1878 T. Bryant *Pract. Surg.* I. 141 Scarlatinous tonsils.

Scarlatte, obs. form of Scarlet *sb.* and *a.*

† **Scarle.** *Obs.* Also 5 **skerel(e.** [Earlier *skerel*, f. *skerre* Scare *v.*: see -el.] A scarecrow.

c 1440 *Promp. Parv.* 457/2 Skerel, *larva* [c 1460 Winch., skerele]. 1483 *Cath. Angl.* 321/2 A scarle or visern, *larua*.

Scarless (skā·ɹlės), *a.* [f. Scar *sb.*1 + -less.]

1. Showing no scar; lacking blemish.

1630 Drumm. of Hawth. *Flowres of Sion* D 2, Amidst that Masse of Ruines they did make, Safe and all scarrelesse yet remaines my Minde. 1863 *Possib. Creation* 103 The living canvass..is..as scarless and unsullied, as if it had never been touched by the burning pencils of the sun. 1891 Meredith *One of our Conq.* I. xii. 226 His pride in appearing woundless and scarless.

2. Leaving no scar.

1823 Byron *Juan* xiii. lxxxii, Escaping with a few slight scarless sneers.

Scarlet (skā·ɹlėt), *sb.* and *a.* Forms: 3–7 **scarlat, skarlet,** 4 **scarleit, scharlette,** 4–6, 8 **scarlett,** 5 **scarlatte, scarlad, skarlot,** 5–6 **scarlot, skarlat,** 5, 8 **skarlett,** 6 **scarlette, skarlette, skarlote, skerlyt,** 3– **scarlet.** [Aphetic a. OF. *escarlate* sb. fem. (mod.F. *écarlate*) = Pr. *escarlat* masc., *-ata* fem. In Fr. and Pr. recorded from the 12th c.; the other Rom. forms are later: Sp., Pg. *escarlate, -ata*, It. *scarlatto*, med.L. *scarlat(t)um, -a, scarlettum* (1204 in *Excerpta Historica* 393). In Teut. the word appears as ON. *skarlat, skallat*, MHG. *scharlât*, early mod.Flem. *schaerlat*; also, with etymologizing alteration (cf. Lake *sb.*5), MHG. *scharlach(en*, MLG., Du. *scharlaken* (whence Da. *skarlagen*, Sw. *skarlakan*, Icel. *skarlak, skarlakan*). From It. are prob. mod. Gr. σκαρλάτον, Church Slav. *skrŭlato*, Serbian *skrlet*, Turk. *iskerlet*.

If the OHG. *scarlahhan*, in a gloss explained as 'shorn cloth' (*rasilis*) be identical with this word (the interpretation as well as the form being due to popular etymology), it is the earliest evidence of its existence. It is hardly possible that this OHG. word can be the source of the Rom. forms. The prevailing view is that OF. *escarlate* is an alteration of Pers. سقلات *saqalāt, siqalāt, suqlāt*, a kind of rich cloth, a derivative of which appears as Ciclatoun. (The form سقرلاط *saqirlāṭ*, given in some Arabic dictionaries, is modern and prob. adopted from some European language.)]

A. *sb.*

1. † **a.** In early use, some rich cloth, often of a bright red colour, but (according to Fr., MDu., and med.L. sources) also sometimes of other colours, as 'pers', blue, green, brown. *Obs.* **b.** In later use, cloth or clothing of the colour described in 2.

† *Scarlet in grain* (*s. engreyned, grayned s.*, etc.): cloth fast dyed of a scarlet colour (cf. Grain *sb.*1 10 and Ingrain *a.*). It is doubtful whether 'scarlet and grene', frequently occurring in ME. poetry in descriptions of splendid attire, originated in a misunderstanding of this phrase.

c 1250 *Death* 10 in *O. E. Misc.* 168 Ȝe þat sittet i-schrud wið skarlet and wið palle. 1297 R. Glouc. (Rolls) 6390 A robe he let him ssape uerst of blod red scarlet þere. 13.. *K. Alis.* 4987 Hy clothen hem with grys and ermyne With golde and siluer and skarlet pers fyne. 13.. *Reinbrun* v, Scarlet and grene wel y-wrouȝt. c 1375 *Cursor M.* 25463 (Fairf.) Nauþer aske I skarlet ne grene Ne purtraied stede. c 1380 *Sir Ferumb.* 4464 And we han her scarletes & grene, & cloþes of tarse. c 1386 Chaucer *Sir Thopas* 16 His rode is lyk scarlet in grayn. a 1400 *Morte Arth.* 3459 And one he henttis a hode of scharlette fulle riche. 14.. *Guy of Warw.* 8996 Hys lymmes were bare and euyll beseyn, That some tyme were clad in scarlet in greyne. a 1420 *Wyclif's N. T., Rev.* xviii. 16 Wo! wo! thilke greet citee, that was clothid with bijs and purpur, and reed scarlet. 1480 *Coventry Leet-bk.* 438 The seid Recordor answered & saide that they shuld not be relesed þerof for þe best pece of scarlet in Englond. a 1533 Ld. Berners *Huon* ix. 23 Huon toke hys cloke of skerlat & wrappyd it about hys arme. 1545 *Rates Custom ho.* d vj b, In primus a brode cloth payeth xii. A

scarlette xxiiii. a 1548 Hall *Chron., Hen. V*, 52 b, The Mayre of London..appareled in orient grayned Skarlet. 1588 Hickock tr. *Frederick's Voy.* 31 Ships bring cloth of Wooll, Scarlets, Veluets, Opium and Chickenes. 1649 J. Master *Daily Expense-bk.* 4 Aug., For 4 ya & half of right french scarlet at 45ˢ. 1662 *Comenius' Janua Ling. Triling.* 96 Sattins, damasks, scarlets, cobweb-lawns [etc.]. 1796 Burke *Regic. Peace* iv. Wks. IX. 123 An Ambassador, whose robes are lined with a scarlet dyed in the blood of Judges. 1859 Tennyson *Elaine* 501 Then the trumpets blew Proclaiming his the prize, who wore the sleeve Of scarlet, and the pearls.

2. A brilliant vivid red colour, inclining to orange.

c 1440 *Promp. Parv.* 442/2 Scarlet, colowre, *lutus.* 1530 Palsgr. 265/2 Scarlet a reed colour. 1648 Herrick *Hesper.*, *Weeping Cherry*, Which rubies, corals, scarlets, all For tincture, wonder at. 1690 Locke *Hum. Und.* iii. iv. § 11 His Friend demanding what Scarlet was? the blind Man answered, It was like the sound of a Trumpet. a 1734 R. North *Life John North* (1742) 237 Scarlet was commonly called the King's Colour. 1788 Cowper *Gratitude* 29 This moveable structure of shelves,..Where flaming in scarlet and gold My poems enchanted I view. 1856 Ruskin *Mod. Paint.* IV. v. iii. § 24. 53 In this chord the scarlet is the most powerful colour. 1894 K. Grahame *Pagan P.* 68 A riot of scarlet on gold, the red poppy of our native fields tosses heavy tresses with gipsy *abandon*.

b. A pigment or dye of this colour. In recent use also *spec.*, any one of a certain group of coal-tar colouring matters used in scarlet pigments and dyes.

1653 Jer. Taylor *Serm. for Year* (1678) 333 A ship laden with Persian Carpets, and the ingredients of the rich Scarlet. 1672 W. S. *Polygraphice* 178 For a Scarlet. Take Vermilion, and deepen it with Lake or Indian Red. 1859 Geo. Eliot *Adam Bede* xxi, He had already a high reputation in the district for his dyes, and he was bent on discovering some method by which he could reduce the expense of crimsons and scarlets. 1862 O'Neill *Dict. Calico Print. & Dyeing* 61 The best scarlets are still obtained from cochineal alone as colouring matter. 1886 tr. *Benedikt's Chem. Coal-tar Colours* 198 The scarlets have replaced cochineal to a considerable extent in wool-dyeing.

3. Official or ceremonial costume of scarlet, as the uniform of a soldier, the gown or robe of a doctor of divinity or law, a judge, a cardinal, etc.; also, the scarlet coat worn in the hunting field (= Pink *sb.* 6). Hence *occas.* the rank, dignity, or office signified by a scarlet robe.

1496 in *Rep. Hist. MSS. Comm. Var. Coll.* (1907) IV. 212 All they of the xxiiij that hath be maire shall ride in scarlett ayenste the Kynge. 1568 T. Howell *Arb. Amitie* (1879) 81 For Fortune may as then, make kings as pleaseth her: Since she the riche and noble men, to scarlets can prefer. 1610 B. Jonson *Alch.* i. iii, This Summer He will be of the Clothing of his company. And, next spring, call'd to the Scarlet. 1654 H. L'Estrange *Chas. I* (1655) 110 The Lord Maior with his confraternity of Aldermen also mounted and in their Scarlets. 1685 Rycaut *Contn. Lives Popes* 16 After this he made little account of his Scarlet, or degree of Cardinal. 1706 Hearne *Collect.* (O. H. S.) I. 311 White Kennett..sometimes waited on Dr. Wallis to Church with his skarlett. 1764 *Oxf. Sausage* 38 The splendid Fortunes and the beauteous Face..Too soon are caught by Scarlet and by Lace. 1885 *Field* 7 Feb. 147/3 A good man in scarlet is down at the first fence. 1891 Morris *Poems by the Way* (1896) 17 What mayor shall rule the hall we built? Whose scarlet sweep the floor?

4. † **a.** One who wears a scarlet uniform or insignia; e.g. a judge. *Obs.*

1628 Feltham *Resolves* i. viii. 18 Open Rebukes are for Magistrates, and Courts of Iustice: for Stelled Chambers, and for Scarlets, in the thronged Hall. c 1683 *Restoration* in *Villiers* (Dk. Buckhm.) *Wks.* (1775) 103 Do the Lords bow, and the regarded Scarlets, Kiss their gam'd goles, and cry we are your servants?

b. *occas.* Persons clothed in scarlet; men in the hunting field (cf. Pink *sb.* 6 b) or on the golf links; also soldiers in red uniform.

1827 *Sporting Mag.* XIX. 353 The whole field was fairly pounded: I was one among the number, and consider myself a good bit of scarlet too. 1842 G. F. Carnegie *Golfiana* in R. Clark *Golf* (1875) 150 He whirls his club to catch the proper swing, And freely bets round all the scarlet ring. 1896 A. E. Housman *Shropshire Lad* xxxv, Gay the files of scarlet follow.

† **5.** ? An aristocratic street ruffian, a Mohock.

1755 J. Shebbeare *Lydia* (1769) II. 437, I expected to have seen her..encouraging the young bloods, bucks and scarlets at a riot in Drury-lane.

6. Short for *scarlet strawberry* (see B. 4 c).

1815 Sir Jos. Banks in *Trans. Hort. Soc.* I. 55. 1824 J. Barnet *Ibid.* (1826) VI. 155 Princess Charlotte's Strawberry ..is perhaps the richest of all the Scarlets. 1828 *Trans. Hort. Soc.* (1830) VII. 345 Old Scarlet.

7. A small moth, *Erastria ostrina.*

1832 J. Rennie *Consp. Butterfl. & Moths* 97 The Scarlet (*E. ostrina*, Curtis) appears in June.

B. *adj.* (Originally the sb. used attrib.)

1. Having, or pertaining to, the colour scarlet (see A. 2).

c 1386 Chaucer *Wife's Prol.* 559 Therfore I made my visitacions,..And wered vpon my gaye scarlet gytes. 1436 in *E. E. Wills* (1882) 107 All-so I wol that Iohn Melbourne haue my scarlet goune furred with martrouns. 1479 in *Eng. Gilds* (1870) 415 He to come in..his Skarlat cloke furred. 1501 Douglas *Pal. Hon.* i. xlvi, Purpour colour, punik and skarlote hewis. a 1586 Sidney *Arcadia* iii. (Sommer) 248 Sixe maides, all in one liuerie of skarlette petticotes. a 1633 T. Taylor *God's Judgem.* ii. vii. (1642) 110 He kept two or three tall fellowes in Skarlet Liveries. 1677 Wood *Life* (O.H.S.) II. 386 The chancellour,..and the rest of his retinew, put on scarlet habits. 1717 Lady M. W. Montagu *Let. to Mrs. T.* 1 Apr., Mine [*sc.* a sofa] is of scarlet cloth, with a gold fringe. 1784 Cowper *Task* i. 320 The sycamore, capricious in attire, Now green, now tawny, and ere autumn yet Have chang'd the woods, in scarlet honours bright. 1816 Keats *To my Brother George* 130 The poppies show their scarlet coats. 1879 *St. George's Hosp. Rep.* IX. 722 She also now had a scarlet eruption.

b. Clothed in scarlet, wearing a scarlet uniform or distinguishing dress.

1591 Shaks. *1 Hen. VI*, i. iii. 56 Out Tawney-Coates, out Scarlet Hypocrite. 1642 Milton *Apol. Smect.* Wks. 1851 III. 280 The invincible warriour Zeale shaking loosely the slack reins drives over the heads of Scarlet Prelats and such as are insolent to maintaine traditions. 1902 *Words of Eyewitness* 3 There is no more universally beloved individual in the world than this same scarlet Atkins.

c. Red with shame or indignation. † Also *transf.* blushing, indignant.

1865 Baring-Gould *Werewolves* xii. 222 Several times his face had become scarlet, and his eyes had fallen. 1881 W. H. Mallock *Rom. 19th Cent.* II. 120 She flushed scarlet.

transf. 1593 Shaks. *Rich. II*, iii. iii. 99 But ere the Crowne he lookes for, liue in peace, Ten thousand bloody crownes of Mothers Sonnes Shall ill become the flower of Englands face, Change the complexion of her Maid-pale Peace To Scarlet Indignation.

2. *fig.* **a.** Of an offence (after Isa. i. 18), hence *occas.* of an offender: Heinous, deep-dyed.

[1613 Shaks. *K. Hen. VIII*, iii. ii. 255 (To Wolsey) Thou scarlet sinne.] 1641 J. Shute *Sarah & Hagar* (1649) 206 Who doth forgive..even foul sins, crimson, scarlet iniquities, upon humiliation. 1656 Sir G. Wharton *Hemerol.*, *Proeanaph.* 30 The Final cause [of earthquakes], is a sign of an Angry God, justly provoked by the Scarlet crimes of a sinful People. 1709 Mrs. Manley *Secret Mem.* (1720) IV. 97 How preach up, as thou dost, Vertue and Moderation, when thy self art Scarlet deep tinged with the highest Crimes?

b. in allusions to the glaring effect of the colour.

1820 Hazlitt *Lect. Dram. Lit.* 16 The deathblow which had been struck at scarlet vice and bloated hypocrisy.

3. General combinations: **a.** parasynthetic, as *scarlet-barred, -blossomed, -breasted, -circled, -coated, -coloured, -crested, -flowered, -haired, -moustached* adjs.; frequent in specific names of animals and plants.

1832 J. Rennie *Consp. Butterfl. & Moths* 227 The *Scarlet Barred Gold (*Lampronia sanguinella*, Stephens). 1845 *Florist's Jrnl.* 178 The well-known *scarlet-blossomed currant. 1822 Latham *Gen. Hist. Birds* II. 121 *Scarlet-breasted Parrot...Inhabits New-Holland. 1704 Pope *Windsor For.* 116 His purple crest, and *scarlet-circled eyes. 1693 R. Duke in *Dryden's Juvenal* iv. (1697) 78 So many Sesterces were swallow'd down, To stuff one *Scarlet-coated Court Buffoon. 1617 Hieron *Wks.* (1619) II. 317 The citie of Rome..may shew her selfe to bee indeed that *Scarlet-coloured Harlot, described by John in his Reuelation. 1753 Chambers *Cycl. Supp.* s.v. *Lychnis*, The lesser *scarlet flowered Constantinople lychnis. 1872 *Routledge's Ev. Boy's Ann.* 419/1 The *Scarlet-Haired Poppy. 1872 Coues *Key N. Amer. Birds* 192 Bill dark; *scarlet-crested, *scarlet-moustached.

b. qualifying the name of a colour, as *scarlet-crimson, -red, -vermilion.*

1882 *Garden* 7 Oct. 312/2 Of older self-flowers..Joseph Green, bright *scarlet-crimson. c 1386 Chaucer *Prol.* 456 Hir hosen weren of fyn *scarlet reed. 1590 Spenser *F. Q.* i. ii. 13 A goodly Lady clad in scarlot red. a 1711 Ken *Christophil* Poet. Wks. 1721 I. 510 She saw the Place where Jesus bled, And dy'd the Turff of Scarlet-red. 1882 *Garden* 29 July 104/2 It has flowers..of bright scarlet-red hue. *Ibid.* 25 Mar. 196/2 Many drooping flowers..of a brilliant *scarlet-vermilion hue.

4. Special collocations: **scarlet-day,** † **scarlet-gown day,** an occasion in university or civic life observed by the public wearing of state or official robes of scarlet; † **scarlet-grain,** = Alkermes 1, cf. Kermes; **scarlet lady, whore, woman,** abusive epithets applied to the Church of Rome in allusion to Rev. xvii. 1–5; **Scarlet Lancers,** nickname for the 16th Lancers, from their distinctive red tunic; **scarlet rash,** a scarlet eruption, symptomatic of certain diseases; **scarlet ward,** a part of a fever hospital reserved for patients suffering from scarlet fever.

1632–33 in *Publ. Colon. Soc. Mass.* VIII. 361 [That the lecturer should preach on all the] *scarlet days, as they name them. 1721 Amherst *Terræ-Fil.* No. 39 (1726) II. 51 He preached it upon a scarlet day, when the vice-chancellor and all the doctors go to church in red. 1888 *Daily News* 11 June 5/7 In University parlance it was a Scarlet Day. 1710 J. Chamberlayne *St. Gt. Brit.* ii. iii. (ed. 23) 663* The *Scarlet-Gown Days in the University of Oxford. 1597 Gerarde *Herbal* iii. xxx. 1158 The Oke which beareth the *scarlet graine is a small tree. 1601 Holland *Pliny* xxvii. ix. II. 280 The berrie Coccum Gnidium, in colour resembleth the Scarlet graine. 1807 Syd. Smith *Peter Plymley's Lett.* ii, I will not dispute with you whether the Pope be or be not the *Scarlet Lady of Babylon. 1873 *Punch* 23 Aug. 72/2 Let us be just even to the Scarlet Lady. 1885 'J. S. Winter' (*title*) Bootles' Baby: a story of the *Scarlet Lancers. 1822–29 *Good's Study Med.* (ed. 3) III. 16 The *angina gangrænosa* (sore throat with *scarlet-rash) usually commences in the winter or the spring. 1888 Honnor Morten *Sk. Hosp. Life* 51 The laconic order, 'To the *Scarlet Ward', is given. 1648 Winyard *Midsummer-Moon* 1 The *Scarlet-whore of Babylon spawn'd it with her menstruous profluviums. 1709 *Tatler* No. 190 ¶ 2 Nor yet did that Epistle at all come unto thee from the Mansion-House of the Scarlet Whore. 1816 Southey *Poet's Pilgr.* ii. iii. 10 *note*, I have seen her somewhere called the *Scarlet Woman. 1867 Lowell *Gt. Publ. Char.* Wks. 1890 II. 274 The latter old lady [*sc.* the Church of Rome] may be the Scarlet Woman, or the Beast with ten horns, if you will.

b. In names of birds, insects, etc.: **scarlet cantharis,** a beetle, *Cantharis cardinalis*; **scarlet finch,** *Fringilla coccinea* (Shaw); **scarlet grosbeak,** the Cardinal-bird; **scarlet ibis,** *Eudocimus ruber*, a bird congeneric with the typical Ibis, native in tropical America; **scarlet lory,** a name given to several birds of the Parrot-tribe; **scarlet macaw,** *Psittacus macao*, a parrot native in S. America and the West Indies; **scarlet mite,** *Trombidium holosericeum*; **scarlet mussel,** a shell-fish (see quot.); **scarlet snake,** a name applied to two colubriform snakes of tropical America (see quot.); **scarlet sparrow,** *Tanagra rubra*; **scarlet spoonbill,** *Platalea ajaja*; **scarlet tanager,** the Red bird, *Pyranga rubra*; **scarlet tiger** (moth), *Hypercampa dominula.*

1806 Shaw *Gen. Zool.* VI. 81 One of the most elegant insects of this genus is the *Scarlet Cantharis. 1783 Latham *Synopsis Birds* III. 270 *Scarlet Finch...Inhabits Sandwich Islands. 1837 Gould *Birds of Europe* III. Pl. 206 *Scarlet Grosbeak. 1785 Pennant *Arctic Zool.* II. 458 *Scarlet Ibis. 1751 G. Edwards *Nat. Hist. Birds* iv. 172 The *Scarlet Lory. 1811 Shaw *Gen. Zool.* VIII. 533 *Psittacus grandis*..Scarlet Lory. *Ibid.* 386 The *Scarlet Maccaw. 1826 Kirby & Sp. *Entomol.* III. 492 The little *scarlet mite..(*Trombidium holosericeum*). 1672 *Phil. Trans.* VII. 5022 The *Scarlet-Mustle, having a purple-vein, which being prickt with a needle yeilds a perfect Purple or Scarlet Juyce that will not be washt out of the Linnen died therewith. 1842 Holbrook *N. Amer. Herpet.* III. 127 *Rhinostoma coccinea*...The Scarlet Snake. *Ibid.*, The 'Couleuvre écarlate' (Scarlet Snake) of Bosc is quite another animal, doubtless the *Calamaria elapsoidea*. 1764 G. Edwards *Glean. Nat. Hist.* iii. 278 The *Scarlet Sparrow. 1829 Shaw *Gen. Zool.* XI. 642 *Scarlet Spoonbill. 1808–13 A. Wilson *Amer. Ornith.* (1831) II. 226 *Scarlet Tanager. 1832 J. Rennie *Consp. Butterfl. & Moths* 42 The *Scarlet Tiger (*Hypercampa Dominula*, Stephens) appears in June.

c. In names of plants and fruits: **scarlet banana,** *Musa coccinea*; **scarlet-bean** = *scarlet runner*; **scarlet cardinal-flower, scarlet lobelia,** *Lobelia cardinalis* (see Cardinal-flower); **scarlet convolvulus,** *Ipomæa coccinea*; **scarlet geranium,** a pelargonium with scarlet blossoms, largely used as a bedding-plant (see Geranium 2 and Pelargonium); **scarlet maple,** *Acer rubrum*; **scarlet oak,** *Quercus coccinea* (see Oak 1 b); also † the Holm Oak, *Quercus Ilex*; **scarlet painted-cup** (see Painted *ppl. a.* 4); **scarlet pea** (see quot.); **scarlet pimpernel,** *Anagallis arvensis* (see Pimpernel 3 and 3 b); **scarlet runner** (bean), *Phaseolus multiflorus* (cf. Bean 3); **scarlet sage,** *Salvia fulgens*, a native of Mexico (Miller *Plant-n.* 1884, 245); also *S. splendens*, a native of Brazil (*Cent. Dict.* 1891); **scarlet seed,** a name of two tropical trees (see quot. 1866); **scarlet strawberry,** any cultivated variety of the Virginian Strawberry, *Fragaria virginiana*, having scarlet 'fruit'; **scarlet thorn,** *Cratægus coccinea.*

1885 Lady Brassey *The Trades* 29 The *scarlet banana. 1731 Miller *Gard. Dict.* s.v. *Phaseolus*, The *Scarlet Bean. 1852 Mrs. Carlyle *Lett.* II. 168 Some scarlet beans that were growing in his own piece of garden. 1698 *Scarlet Cardinal-Flower [see Cardinal-flower]. 1856 O. W. Holmes *Aut. Breakf.-t.* x. (1895) 253 Dream of that winding shore Where scarlet cardinals bloom—for me no more. 1823 Crabb *Technol. Dict.* s.v. *Scarlet*, *Scarlet-Convolvulus. 1760 *Scarlet geranium [see Geranium 2]. 1870 Ruskin *Lect. Art* vi. 162 There are few flowers of which the impression on the eye is more definitely of flat colour, than the scarlet geranium. 1874 *Scarlet lobelia [see Lobelia]. 1833 *Penny Cycl.* I. 79/2 The nursery-men usually call this species the cut-leaved *scarlet maple. 1597 Gerarde *Herbal* iii. xxx. 1159 For want of a fit English name, we haue thought good to christen it by the name of *Scarlet Oke, or Scarlet Holme Oke: for Ilex is named of some in English Holme. 1712 J. James tr. *Le Blond's Gardening* 148 The Scarlet-Oak, or Holm. 1882 *Garden* 13 May 323/3 A specimen of the Scarlet Oak. 1753 Chambers *Cycl. Supp.* App. s.v. *Pea*, *Scarlet Pea,..the English name of a genus of plants, called by Linnæus *Glycine*. 1855 Miss Pratt *Flower. Pl.* IV. 238 *Scarlet Pimpernel. 1824 Loudon *Encycl. Gard.* (ed. 2) § 3634 The *scarlet runner ranks first for its prolific property and long continuance in fruit. 1756 P. Browne *Jamaica* 368 The *Scarlet-seed. 1866 *Treas. Bot.*, Scarlet-Seed. *Ternströmia obovalis*, and *Lætia Thamnia*. 1786 Abercrombie *Gard. Assist.* 256 The *scarlet strawberry. 1882 *Garden* 12 Aug. 145/3 The *scarlet Thorn.. is a bold, vigorous-growing American species.

Hence **Sca·rletness.** *rare.*

1611 Florio, *Scarletezza*, rednesse, scarletnesse.

† **Sca·rlet,** *v.* *Obs.* [f. Scarlet *sb.*] *trans.* To clothe in scarlet; to colour scarlet. Chiefly *passive*. Hence **Sca·rleted** *ppl. a.*, in quot. tinged with scarlet.

1553 Bale *Vocacyon* 10 The Idolatour, the tyraunt, and the whoremonger are no mete mynisters for hym, though they be neuer so..fynely forced, pylyoned, and scarletted. 1641 J. Jackson *True Evang. T.* i. 49 The whole earth is almost a purple Island, scarletted and redded with the bloud of Martyrs. 1685 Sir G. Mackenzie *Religious Stoic* ii. 23 At which we should scarlet our cheeks with blushes. 1688 R. Holme *Armoury* iv. ix. (Roxb.) 382/1 Fine scarletted murrey.

† **Scarletee·r.** *Obs.* [f. Scarlet *sb.* + -eer.] One clothed in scarlet, as a soldier in uniform, or a doctor in the gown of his degree.

1637 N. Whiting *Albino & Bellama* 142 Then say (faire Lady) truth I doe not jeere, Will you be wedded to a scarleteere? 1677 Wood *Life* (O. H. S.) II. 386 The chancellour, with the bedells before him and the scarleteers after him.

Sca·rlet fe·ver. A contagious febrile disease, distinguished by a scarlet efflorescence of the skin and of the mucous membrane of the mouth and pharynx. Also known as Scarlatina.

1676 Jas. Cooke *Marrow Chirurg.* vi. ii. (1685) 214 The first and last [*i.e.* Small-Pox and Rossalia] of these were in Warwick at the writing hereof; the last going under the name of Scarlet Fever. 1799 M. Underwood *Dis. Childhood* (ed. 4) I. 227 Whenever the Scarlet-fever becomes epidemic among adults, children rarely fail being attacked by it in great numbers. 1848 Thackeray *Van. Fair* i, Poor Miss Birch died of the scarlet fever. 1876 Bristowe *Theory & Pract. Med.* (1878) 156 Down to the sixteenth or seventeenth century scarlet fever was confounded with measles.

b. An instance or an attack of this disease. *rare.*

1775 Sheridan *St. Patr. Day* i. i, He had rather see his daughter in a scarlet fever than in the arms of a soldier. 1870–2 Liddon *Elem. Relig.* iv. § 1, [He] will be..as well as another who may have happily survived a scarlet fever.

† **Sca·rletite.** *nonce-wd.* [f. Scarlet *sb.* + -ite.] One who hunts in scarlet (see Scarlet *sb.* 3).

1829 *Sporting Mag.* XXIII. 426 The wagons..were..some of them occupied by scarletites from Melton.

Sca·rlety. *nonce-wd.* [f. Scarlet *sb.* + -y.] Having a tinge of scarlet.

1840 Ruskin *Diary* 23 Aug. in *Harrison* (1902) 53 Note the intense scarletty purple of the shattered larch stems.

Scarling, Scarlot: see Skirling, Scarlet.

Scarmesh, -mige, -moge, -m(o)uch(e, etc., obs. forms of Skirmish *sb.* and *v.*

Scarn, Scarnes(se, obs. ff. Scorn, Scarceness.

† **Sca·ro.** *Obs.* It. form of Scarus.

1722 Diaper tr. *Oppian's Halieut.* i. 215 Here Scaro's feed. *Ibid.* i. 219, ii. 1078, iv. 58, 61.

† **Scaro·tique.** *Obs. rare*⁻¹. = Escharotic.

1673 *Phil. Trans.* VIII. 6054 The touch of an hot Iron, the application of Vitriol or other Scarotiques.

Scarp (skāɹp), *sb.*1 *Her.* Also **scarpe.** [a. ONF. *escarpe* = Central OF. *escharpe* (mod.F. *écharpe*), lit. sash: see Scarf *sb.*] A diminutive of the bend sinister, one-half its width, crossing the shield diagonally from the sinister chief to the dexter base. (Cf. Scarf *sb.*1 5 a.)

1562 Legh *Armory* (1597) 64 b, Knowe that this [bende sinyster] conteineth as much in breadth as a dexter bende doth. The halfe whereof is called a Scarpe, and no bastard's mark, neither may it be charged with any thing. 1610 Guillim *Heraldry* ii. v. (1611) 52. 1780 Edmondson *Her.* II. Gloss. s.v. *Scarpe*, In blazon, it should be named Scarp, without mentioning the word sinister. The French call it a Bar. 1868 Cussans *Her.* (ed. 4) 58.

Scarp (skāɹp), *sb.*2 Also 6–7 **scarpe**; and see Scarf *sb.*3 [ad. It. *scarpa*, whence F. *escarpe* Escarp.]

1. *Fortif.* = Escarp *sb.* 1.

1589 Ive *Pract. Fortif.* 10 The scarpe that the Curtin will make may bee some 28. foote, or more or lesse. 1654 Cokaine *Dianea* iv. 280 On the top they [the walls] are made after the fashion of a scarpe. 1709 Luttrell *Brief Rel.* (1857) VI. 471 The enemy..lye 2 leagues off behind the scarp. 1876 Bancroft *Hist. U. S.* III. xiii. 199 The left extended to a scarp surmounted by an abattis.

† **b.** The total pitch or 'batter' of a bank. *Obs.*

1639 R. Norwood *Fortif.* 113 If the ditch be dry it must be the deeper, and have the lesse scarpe. 1669 Staynred *Fortif.* 7 The Inward Scarp of the Parapet...The outward Scarp of the Rampire...The Scarp of the Ditch.

2. The steep face of a hill; = Escarp *sb.* 2.

1802 Playfair *Illustr. Huttonian Theory* 410 The scarps of the hills face indiscriminately all points of the compass. 1901 H. Trench *Deirdre Wed* 32 Far up, where darkling copses over-grow Scarps of the gray cliff from his river'd base.

Scarp (skāɹp), *v.*1 [f. Scarp *sb.*2] *trans.* To cut to a steep face, to slope; also *to scarp away, down*; = Escarp *v.*

1803 Wellington *Let.* in Gurw. *Desp.* (1837) II. 584 The rock is scarped on each side. 1807 G. Chalmers *Caledonia* I. i. iv. 157 The top of the bank..was artfully scarped away, to augment the strength of the defences. 1829 Scott *Anne of G.* iii, The elevation of the site..was on this side a steep eminence, which had been scarped like a modern glacis, to render the building more secure. 1865 Geikie *Scen. & Geol. Scot.* iii. 66 The result has been..to scarp the coasts of the Shetlands into the most rugged and fantastic cliffs. 1894 Wolseley *Marlborough* II. 173 The rock on which this fort stands was scarped towards the city. 1905 R. Haggard in *Windsor Mag.* Jan. 244 The rock upon one side of it had often been scarped by the hand of man.

Hence **Scarped** *ppl. a.*, reduced to a steep face, laid bare, cut away, steep.

1823 *Treat. Field Fortif.* 26 When the earth scarped off is used to encrease the height, the original surface should be cut [etc.]. 1837 Carlyle *Fr. Rev.* III. v. vi, Redoubts are carried, and Passes and Heights of the most scarped description. 1850 Tennyson *In Mem.* lvi, 'So careful of the type?' but no. From scarped cliff and quarried stone She cries 'a thousand types are gone: I care for nothing, all shall go'. 1877 L. Morris *Epic of Hades* ii. 102 Once the waters Broke louder on the scarpèd reefs.

Scarp (skāɹp), *v.*2 *Agric.* [Of obscure origin; possibly the same word as prec.] *intr.* Of land: To be torn up irregularly.

1843 *Jrnl. R. Agric. Soc.* IV. ii. 563 The land is not liable to scarp, as after the common roller. 1866 Blackmore *Cradock Nowell* xi, His mighty forehead would scarp and chine like the headland when the plough turns.

Scarp-bolt (skā·ɹpbōᵘlt). *Shipbuilding.* Also *erron.* **scarf-.** [App. a. Da. *skarpbolt* lit. 'sharp bolt'.] (See quot. 1852.)

[1852 J. Fincham *Outl. Ship Build.* (ed. 3) 26 The long bolts, through the knee of the head, and the deadwood, are pointed bolts (Swedish, *skarpbultar*; Danish, *skarpbolte*; Dutch, *puntbout*; German, *scharf-bolzen*..).] 1867 Smyth *Sailor's Word-bk.* s.v. *Bolt*, Scarp-bolts and keel-bolts, pointed, not clinched, used for false keel or temporary purposes. 1875 Knight *Dict. Mech.* 2051 Scarf-bolt.

Scarph(e, obs. forms of Scarf *sb.* and *v.*

Scarpine (skā·ɹpīn). Also 6 *Sc.* **scarpene.** [ad. It. *scarpino* (dim. of *scarpa* shoe), whence F. *escarpin*, Sp. *escarpino.*]

† **1.** A light shoe. *Obs. rare*⁻¹.

a 1586 in Pinkerton *Anc. Sc. Poems* (1786) 184 Thair dry scarpenis..; Thair mullis glitteran on thair feit. 1611 Florio, *Scarpini*, Scarpines, Pumps, or Sockes.

2. *Hist.* An instrument of torture for the feet. (Cf. Boot *sb.*3 3.)

1855 Kingsley *Westw. Ho!* vii, I was put to the scarpines, whereof I am..somewhat lame of one leg to this day.

Scarping (skā·ɹpiŋ), *vbl. sb.* [f. Scarp *v.*1 + -ing 1.] A steep slope; the rocky face of a hill. † Also *pl.* the amount of slope or batter in an escarp.

1639 R. Norwood *Fortif.* 105 The scarpings thereof [*sc.* of the Rampire] within and without are [etc.]. 1909 *Contemp. Rev.* Apr. 478 The scarpings of an overhanging cliff.

Sca·rpment. *rare*⁻¹. [Aphetic for Escarpment, after Scarp *v.*1] = Escarpment 1.

1862 Lewin *Jerusalem* 223 The foundations of the Temple were..formed by scarping the sides of the rock and carrying up a wall upon the scarpment.

Scarpyn, obs. form of Scorpion.

Scarr(e, obs. forms of Scar, Scare.

Scarred (skāɹd), *ppl. a.* [f. Scar *v.* + -ed 1.]

1. Of a human or animal body or its parts: Bearing scars or traces of wounds or sores.

c 1440 *York Myst.* xxxiii. 35 Ȝaa, and with schath of skelpys yll scarred. 1872 L. P. Meredith *Teeth* 176, I have seen the scarred hero of many battles cry like a child when called upon to have a tooth extracted. 1899 *Allbutt's Syst. Med.* VI. 22 Especial attention was directed to the exclusion of cases of scarred kidneys, of which there were many.

2. *transf.* Of inanimate objects: Bearing traces of injury, weathering, or the like. Often of rocks, etc.: Broken as by a convulsion of nature.

1600 Marlowe *Lucan* i. C j, Headles darts, olde swords With vgly teeth of blacke rust fouly scarr'd. 1816 Shelley *Mont Blanc* 71 How hideously Its shapes are heaped around! rude, bare, and high, Ghastly, and scarred, and riven. 1877 Black *Green Past.* xxxvii, In the sheer precipices..scarred with ruddy rocks and sunless woods.

3. *Bot.* (See quot.)

1793 Martyn *Lang. Bot.*, *Cicatrisatus truncus s. caulis.* A scarred stem. Marked with the remains of leaves that have fallen off. 1839 Lindley *Introd. Bot.* iii. (ed. 3) 468.

Scarre-fire, obs. variant of Scare-fire.

Scarrify(e, obs. forms of Scarify.

Scarring (skā·riŋ), *vbl. sb.* [f. Scar *v.* + -ing 1.] The action of the vb. Scar in various senses; an example of this; *concr.* an assemblage of scars.

1816 J. Scott *Paris Revisited* (ed. 3) 221 The charges of the cavalry had trampled deep scarrings into the ground. 1898 *Allbutt's Syst. Med.* V. 327 [There was] slight scarring in the right bronchus. 1906 *Q. Rev.* Jan. 151 The results in regard to scarring were good.

Scarring (skā·riŋ), *ppl. a.* [f. Scar *v.* + -ing 2.] That scars, in various senses of the verb; causing a blemish; undergoing cicatrization.

1833 J. H. Newman '*Latest born of Jesse's race*' 28 Strange, that guileless face and form To lavish on the scarring storm! 1899 *Allbutt's Syst. Med.* VIII. 771 In scarring lesions the [hair] follicles are destroyed.

Scarrubb, obs. form of Scarab.

Scarry (skā·ri), *a.*1 [f. Scar *sb.*1 + -y.] Precipitous, rocky.

1382 Wiclif *Job* xxxix. 28 In heȝe sett scarri flintis [Vulg. *in præruptis silicibus*] he [*sc.* the eagle] bideth. 1577 Harrison *England* i. xi. [xv.] 31 b, in *Holinshed*, The Ure ..receyueth the Burne, by south west (as it dyd the Wile, from very deepe scarry rockes, before at Askaran). 1853 G. Johnston *Nat. Hist. E. Bord.* I. 80 A high, steep, scarry, and partially wooded bank. 1901 H. Trench *Deirdre Wed* 32 Many a mountain's scarry flank.

† **Sca·rry,** *a.*2 *Obs.* [f. Scar *sb.*2 + -y.] Of the nature of a scar; also, marked with scars.

1653 Urquhart *Rabelais* i. ii, If they might be reduc'd t'a scarry stuffe [F. *à cicatrice*]. 1695 *Lond. Gaz.* No. 3113/4 The Hair wanting on the Rump, a gall'd scarry back. 1894 *Monthly Packet* Christmas No. 193 Scarry indentations [in buns] made by small dried currants.

† **Sca·rry,** *a.*3 *Obs. rare*⁻¹. ? Thin, meagre.

1422 tr. *Secreta Secret., Priv. Priv.* 239 But thay men wych haue the body more scarry, and the ouertures streyte, shulde vse Sotille diet and in lytill quantite.

Scars(e, Scarsement, obs. ff. Scarce, -ment.

Scarsitee, obs. form of Scarcity.

Scart (skāɹt), *sb.*1 *Sc.* Forms: 5, 9 **scarth,** 6 **skarth,** 8–9 **skart,** 7– **scart,** 9 **scrath** (? error). [The forms *scarth, scart*, are successive corruptions of Scarf *sb.*] The Cormorant, *Phalocrocorax carbo*. Also applied to the Shag, *P. graculus.*

c 1450 Holland *Howlat* 181 The Scarth a fische fangar, And that a perfyte. 1513 Douglas *Æneis* v. iii. 49 A standand place quhar skarthis with ther beikis..glaidlie thaim pronȝe and bekis. 1720 Sibbald *Hist. Fife & Kinross* 45 The Fowls which most frequent the Bass are the.. Scarts [etc.]. 1816 Scott *Antiq.* viii, D'ye think ye'll help them wi' skirling that gate like an auld skart before a flaw o' weather? 1852 J. Wilson in *Blackw. Mag.* LXXII. 395 He sits a cormorant on the tree of life...A scarth—not an eagle—not a swan. 1892 Black *Three Feathers* 183 The black rocks basked in the sunlight, the big skarts standing on their ledges, not moving a feather.

Scart (skart), *sb.*2 *Sc.* [Metathesis of Scrat *sb.*]

1. A scratch.

a 1585 Polwart *Flyting w. Montgomerie* 555 With scartes and scores, athort his frozen front. 1718 Ramsay *Christ's Kirk Gr.* iii. xvii, Wi' her nails she rave his face, Made a' his black baird bloody Wi' scarts that day. 1871 C. Gibbon *Lack of Gold* xi, Folk never see a scart on their ain backs. 1897 Crockett *Lad's Love* xxvii. 266 It never does to mislippen the scart o' a pin on the thickest skull.

2. A mark made by a pen.

1824 Scott *St. Ronan's* iii, What signified, she said, a wheen bits of paper, wi' black and white scarts upon them, that he ca'd bushes, and trees, and craigs? 1861 Ramsay *Remin.* Ser. ii. 122 He has nayther comed himsel', nor had the ceevility tae sen' us the scart o' a pen.

Scart (skāɹt), *sb.*3 *rare.* [? var. of Scat *sb.*] A gust, puff (of wind); a strip (of cloud).

1860 G. H. Kingsley in F. Galton *Vac. Tour* 127 Donald, who assures me that some day a scart of wind will snatch the paper out of my hand. 1899 *Pall Mall Mag.* Apr. 568 The gusty wind blew thin wisps and scarts of cloud athwart the sharp hooks of the crescent moon.

Scart (skart), *v.* *Sc.* Also, 4, 6, 9 **skart.** [Metathesis of Scrat *v.*]

1. *trans.* To scratch, scrape. Also *absol.*

c 1375 *Sc. Leg. Saints* xxvii. (*Machor*) 249 With hyre handis [she] skartyt hir face. 1508 Dunbar *Tua Mariit Wemen* 93 To see him scart his awin skyn grit scunner I think. 1560 Rolland *Seven Sages* 36 With skarting [scho] causit hir face to bleid. 1821 Scott *Pirate* xv, Ye scart the land with a bit thing ye ca' a pleugh. 1893 Crockett *Stickit Minister* 75, I fand the hoose, by scartin a match an' readin' the plate on the gate.

† **2.** To gather together carefully. Also *absol.*

1629 Mure *True Crucifixe* 2573 If Loue of Money,.. Moue thee to scrape, to scart, to pinch, to spare. 1725 Ramsay *Gentle Sheph.* i. ii, And syne the fool-thing is obliged to fast, Or scart anither's leavings at the last.

† **3.** *trans.* To scribble. *Obs. rare*⁻¹.

1826 J. Wilson *Noct. Ambr.* Wks. 1855 I. 144 I've skarted some odds and ends wi' the keelivine on brown paper.

Hence **Sca·rted** *ppl. a.*, scribbled over.

1814 Scott *Wav.* lxv, And what use has my father for a whin bits o' scarted paper?

Scartch, obs. form of Scratch.

Scarth (skāɹþ), *sb.*1 Also 4–5 **skarth.** [a. ON. *skarð* neut., notch, cleft, mountain pass (MSw. *skardh* neut., notch, diminution, ruin, *skardher* masc., broken piece) = OE. *sceard* Shard, Sherd.]

† **1.** A fragment, sherd. *Obs.*

a 1340 Hampole *Psalter* xxi. 15 My vertu..is wex vile as a pot scarth. 13.. *Childh. Jesus* 340 in *Archiv Stud. neu. Spr.* LXXIV. 331 His pechere he brake..And Jhesu gadirde þe skarthes. c 1460 *Towneley Myst.* xii. 160 The mylk pycher was layde, The skarthis was the tokyn.

fig. 1482 Caxton *Trevisa's Higden* iii. xviii. 132 b, Both the wyues..chidden him alto scarthes by one assente.

2. A cliff, a bare rock. *dial.*

1863 Baring-Gould *Iceland* iii. 45 To our right was a bold scarth of dark rock thronged with ravens. 1869 *Lonsdale Gloss.*, *Scar, Scarth*, a line of rock bare of vegetation.

† **Scarth,** *sb.*2 *Obs.* [Altered form of Scrat *sb.*] An abortion, monster; a hermaphrodite.

1508 Dunbar *Flyting* 58 Revin, raggit ruke, and full of rebaldrie, Scarth fra scorpione, scaldit in scurrilitie. 1508 — *Tua Mariit Wemen* 92 Ane skabbit skarth, ane scorpioun. a 1578 Lindesay (Pitscottie) *Chron. Scot.* (S. T. S.) I. 145 Of the skartht [c 1603 scratche (MS. B.), c 1598 scarcht (MS. I.)] yat was born of baith the kyndis maile and female.

Scartling (skā·ɹtliŋ). *Sc.* [f. Scart *sb.*1 + -ling 1.] A young scart or cormorant.

1893 *Blackw. Mag.* Sept. 444 In several nests were found young scartlings—fluffy, dull-grey, ungainly creatures.

‖ **Scarus** (skē·rŭs). Pl. **scari** (skē·rəi). [L. *scarus*, a. Gr. σκάρος.] A fish described by ancient writers; in mod. use, the name of the typical genus of the family *Scaridæ*; a fish of this genus, a Parrot-fish. Cf. Scar *sb.*4, Scare *sb.*3, Scaro.

1601 Holland *Pliny* ix. xvii. I. 245 The fish called Scarus ..is said to chew cud. 1774 Goldsm. *Nat. Hist.* III. 6 The salmon also is said to be of this number [ruminants]: and, if we may believe Ovid, the scarus likewise. 1803 Shaw *Gen. Zool.* IV. ii. 394 Green Scarus [etc.]. 1848 Dickens *Dombey* xii, The sounds of the fish called scari. 1885 *Encycl. Brit.* XVIII. 324 Ever since the time of Aristotle it has been maintained that the Scarus ruminates.

Scarved (skāɹvd), *ppl. a.* = Scarfed.

1885 Pebbing *Hard Knots* 81 The noted beauty—she who was admired, courted, beautifully scarved and apparelled.

Scary (skē·ri), *a.*1 Also 6 (9 *vulgar*) **skeary,** 9 **scarey,** *vulgar* **skeery.** [f. Scare *sb.*2 + -y 1.]

1. Terrifying, frightful.

1582 Stanyhurst *Æneis* iv. (Arb.) 109 But toe the, poore Dido, this sight so skearye beholding, What feeling creepeth? 1827 J. F. Cooper *Prairie* II. v. 68 If any can pretend to know the world, or to have seen scary sights, it is myself! 1854 'Marion Harland' *Alone* xiii, A Giant Grim, who frequents places of amusement to corner children, and relate scary stories to them. 1894 D. C. Murray *Making Novelist* 29 Whatever the miners thought about it, it was rather a scarey business for me.

2. Frightened, timorous.

1827 J. F. Cooper *Prairie* II. vi. 92 A skeary comrade in the woods is apt to make a short path long. 1842 in *Coquet-Dale Fishing Songs* (1852) 104 The scary trout glides swiftly out. 1887 I. R. *Ranche Life Montana* 137 My mount was a young 'scarey' horse. 1873 Carleton *Farm Ball.* 8 Women are skeery critters. 1894 Fenn *Real Gold* 138, I want to talk. It keeps one from feeling a bit skeary.

Scas(e, obs. forms of Scarce.

† **Scat,** *sb.*1 *Obs.* (*rare* after OE.). Also 3 **sat.** [OE. *sceat* masc., = OFris. *sket*, OS. *skat* (MLG., Du. *schat*, whence next), OHG. *scaz* (MHG. *schaz*, mod.G. *schatz*), treasure, ON. *skatt-r* tribute (whence Scat *sb.*3; Da. *skat*, Sw. *skatt*), Goth. *skatt-s* piece of money, money:—OTeut. **skatto-z*. Cf. Sceat.

The *sc* stands for (ʃ); if the word had survived its form would be **shat*.]

Treasure, money; in ME. only in phr. *scat and s(c)rud.*

a 1122 *O. E. Chron.* (Laud MS.) an. 1070, Swa maneȝa ȝersumas on sceat & on scrud & on bokes swa nan man ne mæi oðer tællen. a 1200 *Moral Ode* 367 Ne sal þer ben naðer scat ne srud ne wereldes wele none. c 1250 *Gen. & Ex.* 795 God gaf him ðor siluer and gold, And hird, and orf, and srud and sat. *Ibid.* 3169 Quat-so he boden, srud or sat, Egipte folc hem lenen ðat.

† **Scat,** *sb.*2 *Obs. rare*⁻¹. In 5 **scatte.** [a. Du. *schat*: see prec.] Treasure.

1481 Caxton *Reynard* xvi. (Arb.) 35, I haue so grette scatte and good of syluer and of gold that seuen waynes shold not conne carye it away.

Scat (skæt), *sb.*3 Also 5 **skatte,** 5–6 **skait,** 6–9 **scatt, skat(t.** [a. ON. *skatt-r*: see Scat *sb.*1]

1. a. *gen.* A tax, tribute. Now only *Hist.* with reference to countries under Scandinavian rule.

1502 *Reg. Privy Seal Scot.* I. 116/1 The rasing of al unlawis, eschetis, proffittis, skattis and dewiteis according to the said regalite. 1506 *Exch. Rolls Scot.* XII. 703 That the fredome and privelege of halikirk be observit.. without ony scatt, stent, taxation, or extortion to be maid in tyme cuming. 1513 Douglas *Æneis* Prol. 24 Wrangys to redres suld weyr be vndertane, For na conquest, reif, skat nor pensioun. 1863 Longf. *Wayside Inn, K. Olaf* xvi. xii, Laying waste the kingdom, Seizing scatt and treasure. 1886 J. Corbett *Fall of Asgard* ii. 22 He will not be content with setting his men over us and taking scatt.

b. In Orkney and Shetland, the land-tax paid to the Crown by a udal tenant. † Also, in certain parts of Scotland and the north of England, the designation of various local imposts in the 15–17th c.

1577 in D. Balfour *Oppressions in Orkney & Zetld.* (1859) 18 Ane dewtie thai pay to the Kingis Majestie for thair scat and landmales zeirlie. 1598 *Aberdeen Reg.* (1848) II. 172 Ilk howsholder in Futtie..to pay the skait vsid and wont. 1612 *Sc. Acts Jas. VI* (1816) IV. 481/2 Toillis, anchorages..scattis, land maillis [etc.]. 1814 Shirreff *Agric. Orkney* 30 Subject only to the tax of scat and tithe. 1821 Scott *Pirate* xviii, We must pay scat and wattle. 1838 Bell *Dict. Law Scot.*, *Udal Right* is that right in land, which though dependent on the Crown as superior, for payment of a tribute called Skat, is completed [etc.]. 1859 in D. Balfour *Oppressions in Orkney & Zetld.* 128 *Skat*, the Tax upon all land occupied by Odal-red, for the support of the Crown, and expense of government.

2. *attrib.*, as *scat-field, scat tax*; † **scat gild,** the payment or tax of 'scat'; † **scat haver, malt,** oats, malt, taken in payment of 'scat'; **scat land,** land subject to 'scat'.

14.. *Customs of Malton* in *Surtees Misc.* (1890) 60 For sellyng of the same [heryng] thay schall gyffe to yᵉ *skattegyld iiij d. 1483 in R. Davies *York Records* (1843) 175 In esyng of the tolls, murage, bucher penys & skaitgyld. 1344–5 *Durham Acc. Rolls* (Surtees) 172 Decem boll avene que vocatur *Scathaver de bondis de Heworth. 1450–51 *Ibid.* 187 Et de va rec. pro xij bollez de Scathaver. 1502 in Peterkin *Rentals of Orkney* (1820) 12 Item wᵗ flawis j d terre *scatland anᵈ in butter scat vij d. 1438–9 *Durham Acc. Rolls* (Surtees) 63 Pro 7 bondis antedictis in precio 7 quar. de *Scatmaltez sic sibi vend. hoc anno. 1868 D. Gorrie *Summers & Winters in Orkneys* v. 158 Ruga who collected the King of Norway's corn, or the *Scatt-tax in Orkney. 1881 *Standard* 26 July 5 [Shetland] The sheep and ponies run on the 'Scatfield', or common; and the 'Scat tax' is not a popular impost.

Scat (skæt), *sb.*4 *dial.* (See E.D.D.) [Perh. onomatopœic; the identity of the word in the various senses is uncertain. Cf. Squat *sb.*]

1. A blow or buffet.

1872 Mrs. Lynn Linton *Joshua Davidson* 6 It was a laugh..that seemed to mean the same thing as 'scat',—our Cornish word for a blow. 1901 Mrs. E. L. Voynich *Jack Raymond* 173 The soft and pitying eyes seemed to shame him 'like a scat in the face'.

2. 'Anything burst or broken open; the sound of a rent; the sharp sound of a bullet' (E.D.D.). Cf. Scat *v.*3 and *adv.*

1895 Crockett *Bog-Myrtle* 294 A shot rang out, followed immediately by the 'scat' of a bullet against the rock.

3. A brief spell of weather; a short turn of work.

1880 *Cornwall Gloss.* s.v., A scat of fine weather. 1882 F. W. P. Jago *Anc. Lang. Cornwall* 256 A scat of frost. 1895 E. M. Stooke *Not Exactly* i. 24 An' cashionally 'e dooes a scat to gardenin'.

4. A sudden or passing shower of rain.

17.. *Prov.* in Brice *Gazetteer* (1759) s.v. *Haldon*, When Haldon hath a Hat, Kenton beware a Skat [Risdon (1714) 47 Squatt]. 1834 G. Roberts *Lyme Regis* 252 *Scatt*, a shower. 1897 E. Phillpotts *Lying Prophets* ii. vi. 187 Presently a scat of heavy rain on a squall of wind shut out the harbour for a time.

† **Scat,** *v.*1 *Obs.* In 5–6 **scatte.** [In Caxton, a. MDu. *schatten*, f. *schat* Scat *sb.*2; in the Sc. use perh. a. ON. *skatta*, f. *skatt-r* Scat *sb.*3] *trans.* To oppress by exactions.

1481 Caxton *Reynard* xlii. (Arb.) 114 Whan they be myghty and doubted thenne ben they extorcionners and scatte and pylle the peple. 1543 *Aberdeen Reg.* (1844) I. 191 The toune is hauely murmurit be the landmen, that the vittell hyaris of the merkat, scattis thame grytlie in taking of sampills, scheyt-schakkingis, and sic oder ewill vsit custum. a 1578 Lindesay (Pitscottie) *Chron. Scot.* (S. T. S.) I. 67 He conselled thame [to] exerceis skarting [*v.r.* scatting] and oppressioun wpoun the realme.

† **Scat,** *v.*2 *Obs.* In 6 **skatt,** 6–7 **scatt.** [Alteration of Scot *v.*, due to association with Scat *sb.*3] *intr.* In phrase *to scat and lot* (later *to scat or contribute*) = 'to scot and lot', i.e. to contribute equally to the defraying of some charge or cost.

1560 *Burgh Rec. Edin.* (1875) III. 87 Personis..quhilkis ..nother scattis lottis extentis walkis nor wardis nor yit beris na portable charges within this burgh. 1581 in *Rec. Convent. Roy. Burghs* (1870) I. 117 The acts of burrowes maid anent the scatting and lotting for pilleit and cassin guids. 1594 *Ibid.* 449 Nather skatt and lott with thame. 1612 *Ibid.* II. 340 That no monye sould scatt or contribute with onye goods castin or pilleyit.

Scat (skæt), *v.*3 *dial.* [Cf. Scat *sb.*4] *trans.* To break in pieces, shatter.

1837 J. F. Palmer *Dial. Devonsh. Dial.* 79 To *Scat*, to dash any fragile body on the ground. 1893 'Q.' (Quiller-Couch) *Delect. Duchy* 306 The van..scat itself to bits against the bridge.

Scat (skæt), *adv. dial.* Also **skat, scatt.** [Prob. onomatopœic: cf. Scat *sb.*4] *To go scat*: to fall down; to break in pieces; to become bankrupt.

1867 Rock *Jim an' Nell* xxix. (E. D. S. No. 76), I've trad upon a patch, I'm veared a shall go scat. 1887 'Q.' (Quiller-Couch) *Dead Man's Rock* 7 Finally my father's bank broke —or, as we say in the West 'went scat'. 1887 Baring-Gould *Gaverocks* xxxiii, Little Ruth wiped up the mess made by the broken eggs. Poor Ruth was sore distressed at their 'going scatt' on the floor.

Scat, *int. colloq.* [? identical with 'ss cat!' (i.e. a hiss followed by the word *cat*) used in driving away cats.] Begone! Hence jocularly used as verb (*intr.*).

1869 Mrs. Whitney *We Girls* x. (1874) 218 'Scat!' cried Stephen. And Ruth scatted. 1880 J. C. Harris *Uncle Remus* xxii. (1883) 110 W'en ole man Rabbit say 'scoot', dey scooted, en w'en ole Miss Rabbit say 'scat', dey scatted.

Scatald, obs. form of Scattald.

Scatch1 (skætʃ). Forms: 5–6 **scache,** 6 **skache,** 7 **skatch,** 6–8 **scatch,** 9 *dial.* **sketch.** [a. ONF. *escache* = Central OF. *eschasse* (mod.F. *échasse*), whence Du. *schaats* Skate *sb.*2]

1. A stilt; usually pl. *scatches*. *Obs.* exc. *dial.*

1545 Elyot *Dict.*, *Grallatores*, they which dooe goe on styltes or skaches. 1570 Levins *Manip.* 5/44 A Scache, *grallus*. 1653 Urquhart *Rabelais* ii. i, Others grew in the legs, and to see them, you would have said they had been ..men walking upon stilts or scatches. 1681 W. Robertson *Phraseol. Gen.* (1693) 915 Never,..till geese go on scatches. 1730 Bailey (fol.), *Scatches*, Stilts to put the Feet in to walk in dirty Places. 1893 Baring-Gould *Cheap Jack Zita* xii, Sketches?—does that word puzzle you..? They are what some folk call stilts.

2. ? A scaffold-pole. [So F. *échasse.*]

1420 *Searchers Verdicts* in *Surtees Misc.* (1890) 15 William of Alne..sall fynde the brygges, the scaches, nayles, and all the tymbre that sall ga un to the gutter.

† **Scatch**2. *Obs.* Also 5–6 **scache.** [ad. It. *scaccia* (ska·tʃa), whence F. *escache.*] An oval bridle-bit. Also *scatch-mouth.*

1565–80 Blundevil *Art Riding* iii. xxiii. 51 Some are called Canon bits, some scatches. 1598 Florio, *Scaccia*, the mouth of a bit called a scache. 1607 Markham *Caval.* ii. (1617) 56 The next bytt you shall vse after the Cannon, shall bee the plaine Scatch. 1611 Cotgr., *Scace*, a Scatch bit. 1704 *Dict. Rust.* (1726) s.v. *Bit*, The ends of a Scatch-mouth can never fail, by reason of their being over-lapped.

Scate, obs. form of Skate.

† **Sca·tebrous,** *a.* *Obs. rare*⁻⁰. [f. L. *scatebra* a gushing forth, f. *scatēre* to gush, spring forth: see -ous.] (See quots.) Hence † **Scatebro·sity.**

1721 Bailey, *Scatebrosity*, a flowing or bubbling out. *Scatebrous*, bubbling out like Water out of a Spring, abounding. 1755 Johnson, *Scatebrous*, abounding with springs.

Scater, obs. form of Scatter *v.*

Scathe (skēⁱð), *sb.* Now *arch.* and *dial.* (see E.D.D.). Forms: 3– **scathe, scath,** 3–4 **sckathe,** 3–7 **skathe,** 3–8 **skath,** (4 **skade,** 5 **scade**); *Sc.* and *north.* 4–9 **scaith, skaith,** 4–7 **skaithe,** 5 **scaythe,** 5–6 **skaitht,** 6 **skayth(t, scaithe, skeath.** Also 3–5, 7 **schath,** 3–6 **schathe,** 4 **schatht.** [The existing word is a. ON. *skaðe* wk. masc., harm, damage (Sw. *skada* fem., Da. *skade*) = OE. *sc(e)aða* masc., one who injures, malefactor, also (rarely) hurt, injury, OFris. *skatha, skada* injury, OS. *skaðo* masc., malefactor, MDu. *schade* masc. and fem. (Du. *schade* fem.), injury, OHG. *skado* masc. (MHG., mod.G. *schade*):—OTeut. **skaþon-*, f. root **skaþ-*, whence Goth. *skaþis* harm, *skaþjan* = Scathe *v.*; the ablaut-var. **skōþ-* is represented in ON. *skōð* neut., that which harms, *skǽð-r* harmful. On the other hand, Layamon's *scaðe* in sense 1 almost certainly had (ʃ), and represents the OE. *sceaða* (the mod. form of which would have been **shathe*). The ME. spelling with *sch-* is of doubtful phonetic interpretation: in most of the verse examples the word thus written alliterates with *sk-*, and must therefore be regarded as of Scandinavian etymology; but some of the other instances may possibly (though there is no definite evidence) represent the native word.

The Teut. root **skaþ-* is believed to represent an Indo-germanic **skath-*: *skēth-*; cf. Gr. ἀ-σκηθής unscathed.]

† **1.** One who works harm; a malefactor; a wretch, fiend, monster. *Obs.*

Beowulf 274 Sceaða ic nat hwylc, deogol dædhata. c 1000 *Ags. Gosp.* Matt. xxvii. 38 Ða wæron a-hangen mid hym twegen sceaþan. c 1205 Lay. 1923, & þus þe heȝe scaðe ferde to helle. *Ibid.* 14945 He wende þat hit weore soð þat þeo scaðe sæide. *Ibid.* 25877 For nu anan cumeð þe scaðe þe alle þine leomen wule to-draȝen.

2. Hurt, harm, damage.

Usually sing. and without article; but also occasionally with *a* (etc.) or in pl.

a 1000 *Cædmon's Gen.* 549 Cwæð, þæt sceaðena mæst eallum heora eaforum æfter siððan wurde on woruldе. c 1250 *Gen. & Ex.* 2314 Ðis sonde hem ouertakeð raðe, And bicalleð of narme and scaðe. a 1300 *Cursor M.* 6686 Þe smiter sal quite his lechyng And þe scath [*Gött.* skade] of his liging. c 1325 *Metr. Hom.* 4 Hou thai mai yem thaim fra schathe. 1377 Langl. *P. Pl.* B. iii. 57 Who may scape þe sklaundre þe skaþe is sone amended. c 1440 *York Myst.* xviii. 77, I praye þe lorde, kepe us fro skathe. *Ibid.* xxxiii. 35 With schath of skelpys yll scarred. 1450 in *Charters*, etc. *Edinb.* (1871) 71 We ar informit..þat þai dreid the evil and skath of oure enemeis of England. 1527 Andrew *Brunswyke's Distyll. Waters* K iv, For all that it muste be knowen for the great schathe that therof myght come. a 1578 Lindesay (Pitscottie) *Chron. Scot.* (S.T.S.) I. 22 It sall redound to his avantage and to our gret skaith and schame. 1606 Drayton *Ode written in the Peak* 30 Strong Ale and Noble Cheare, T'asswage breeme Winters scathes. a 1670 Spalding *Troub. Chas. I* (1829) 2 To the great hurt and skaith of the king's lieges. 17.. Ramsay *Falling of a Slate* v, Watching sylphs flew round, To guard dear Madie from all skaith. 1785 Burns *Death & Dr. Hornbook* ix, I red ye weel, tak care o' skaith, See, there's a gully! 1874 Symonds *Sk. Italy & Greece* (1898) I. xvi. 355 Round them [obstacles]..he passed nimbly, without scar or scathe. 1895 Huxley in *Life* (1900) II. xxiii. 401 It was cheering..to hear that you had got through winter and diphtheria without scathe.

b. Phr. *To do* (*work*, † *make*) *scathe*, to do harm. *Const.* indirect (dative) object, with or without *to*. † *To wait* (one) *scathe* [= Icel. *veita einhverjum skaða*], to inflict injury upon.

c 1205 Lay. 12026 Mælga wes inne Scise þer he scaðe makede. *Ibid.* 15784 Ne doð heo noht muchel scaðe. c 1250 *Gen. & Ex.* 850 An ðere he werken sckaðe and bale. c 1300 *Havelok* 1352 Dwelling haueth ofte scaþe wrouth. 1303 R. Brunne *Handl. Synne* 5987 Or ouþer skaþe he wyl hym weyte. c 1350 *Will. Palerne* 4051 Þat no burn nere so bold ..to wait þe werwolf no maner schaþe. c 1470 Henry *Wallace* i. 111 Is nayne in warld, at scaithis ma do mar, Than weile trastyt in borne familiar. c 1489 Caxton *Sonnes of Aymon* xiii. 308 Grete hurte & scathe was there made of bothe partes. 1588 Shaks. *Tit. A.* v. i. 7 And wherein Rome hath done you any scathe, Let him make treble satisfaction. 1595 *Locrine* v. ii. 33 Nor can I finde in heart to worke his scathe. 1632 T. Taylor *God's Judgem.* i. i. xvi. (1642) 57 His owne side came to the worse, doing more scath to themselves, than to their enemies. 1715 *Wodrow Corr.* (1843) II. 114, I cannot tell particularly what skaith they did. 1834 H. Miller *Scenes & Leg.* xxii. (1850) 316 They were doing great skaith, it was said, to victual and drink. 1865 J. M. Neale *Hymns on Paradise* 68 If manifold temptations Of the fiend should work thee scathe.

c. The corresponding passive notion is expressed by *to get, have, take scathe*. † Also, *to catch, find, hent, kep, thole*, etc., *scathe.*

1303 R. Brunne *Handl. Synne* 10648 Sey me þe soþe, and, as y am knyȝt, þou ne shalt haue for me skaþe ne plyȝt. 1362 Langl. *P. Pl.* A. iv. 65 Withouten gult, god wot gat I þis scaþe. 13.. *E. E. Allit. P.* B. 151 Lest he skaþe hent. 1375 Barbour *Bruce* viii. 358 Menand the scath that he had tane. c 1400 *Destr. Troy* 5103 Hit is skille for his skorne, þat he scathe thole. c 1420 *Avow. Arth.* xvi, He began to dotur and dote Os he hade keghet scathe. 1470–85 Malory *Arthur* x. xxx. 464 To redresse the harmes and the scathes that he had of them. 1513 Douglas *Æneis* iii. v. 116 How grete harme and skaith.. That childe hes caucht throw lossing of his modir! 1549 *Compl. Scot.* vi. 60 The fyir slaucht vil consume the vyne viht in ane pipe..& the pipe vil resaue na skaytht. 1572, 1721 [see Kep *v.* 2 b]. 1586 Warner *Alb. England* i. vi. (1589) 20 He tolde what skath the Centaures late..had found. 1642 in Row *Hist. Kirk* (Wodrow Soc.) p. xvii, Suche personis as had cum from Irland, and had gottin great skaithe thair. 1730 T. Boston *View this & other World* 263 He could not miss to catch skaith, if all the better care were not taken to prevent it. 1839 Harr. Campbell *Only Daughter* iii, The Laird of Kilmore..took no scaith from the..attractions of the Misses Sibellas, and Miss Anabels of the county, and at the age of forty he was still a bachelor.

d. Alliteratively coupled with *scorn*. Chiefly *Sc.*

a 1300 *Cursor M.* 23338 For þair misfair suld þai not murn, Ne ans for þair skathes skurn [*Gött.* schathes schurn]. c 1400 *Destr. Troy* 1874 For to wreke vs of wrathe, & the wegh harme Bothe of skathe & of skorne. 1508 Dunbar *Tua Mariit Wemen* 358 And thus the scorne and the scaith scapit he nothir. 1674 Ray *N. C. Words* 41 One doth the skath, and another hath the scorn. Prov. 1755 Johnson, *Scath* in Scotland denotes spoil or damage: as, he bears the scath and the scorn. A proverb. 1864 Carlyle *Fredk. Gt.* xv. iv. (1865) V. 308 Let us take the scathe and the scorn candidly home to us.

e. *quasi-concr.* A physical hurt or damage.

c 1440 *Pallad. on Husb.* i. 1116 Conuenyent hit is to knowe, of bathis Whil speche is mad, what malthis hote & colde Are able, ther as chynyng, clift, or skathe is, To make hit hool and watir wel to holde.

f. Something which works harm.

1579 Gosson *Sch. Abuse* (Arb.) 46 The Adders death is her own broode, the Fencers scath, his own knowledg. 1795 Macneill (*title*) Scotland's Skaith. 1883 Henley *Bk. Verses* 102 The pride I trampled is now my scathe, For it tramples me again.

Supplement, p. 3873; Corrigenda, p. 4092; Spurious words, p. 4093; Books quoted, p. 4094

g. *spec.* 'Injury supposed to proceed from witchcraft' (Jam.).

1795 *Statist. Acc. Scot.* XVI. 122 This is done with a view to prevent skaith, if it should happen that the person is not canny. 1899 J. Spence *Shetland Folk-Lore* 111 The person who attempted to cross a fisherman's path when on his way to the boat, intended to do him scathe.

3. Matter for sorrow or regret. In various phrases, as *It is scathe*, it is a pity. *It is (great) scathe of him*, he is a great loss. *To think (no) scathe of, think (it) no scathe*, (not) to regret, think (it) no harm. [Cf. G. *schade*.]

c1250 *Gen. & Ex.* 2298 In fulsum-hed he wurðen glaðe, Iosep ne ðoht ðor-of no scaðe. c1300 *Havelok* 2006 But it is of him mikel scaþe: I woth þat he bes ded ful raþe. 13.. *Guy Warw.* 1542 Sir, in þe sond he liþe, & þat is scaþe. 13.. *Gaw. & Gr. Knt.* 674 Bi Kryst, hit is scaþe, þat þou, leude, schal be lost. c1386 Chaucer *Prol.* 446 But she was som del deef, and þat was scathe. c1450 *Merlin* xxxiii. 678 And that was grete scade that thei sholde die so soone. 15.. *Christ's Kirk Gr.* viii, Grit skayth wes'd to haif skard him. 1787 W. Taylor *Scots Poems* 11 (E.D.D.) To cheat the rich some think nae skaith. 1870 Morris *Earthly Par.* III. iv. 57 They deemed it little scathe indeed That her coarse homespun ragged weed Fell off from her round arms.

†4. An injury, damage, or loss for which legal compensation is claimed. In pl. = damages; also, costs or expenses incurred by the claimant. Chiefly *Sc. Obs.*

1456 Sir G. Haye *Law Arms* (S.T.S.) 136 He may demaund his scathis at the lord, be way of accioun of dett. c1500 Arnolde *Chron.* (1811) 118, I promyse to make good all costis and scathes that may growe therby for defaute off payment. 1504 in Littlejohn *Aberd. Sheriff Crt.* (1904) 48 Thomas Leslie..protestit for thar costs skaithts and expenses. 1678 Sir G. Mackenzie *Crim. Laws Scot.* i. xix. § xv. (1699) 104 The Unlaw to be ten Pound, and mends to the Party, conform to the skaith.

5. *attrib.* and *Comb.*, as *scathe-deed, -work*; objective, as *scathe-causer, scathe-taking* vbl. sb.

c1205 Lay. 1547 Swa þe rimie wulf þane he wule on cheapen scaðe were wrchen. *Ibid.* 29578 Þa hine isend hafden mid heore scaðe deden. a1300 *Cursor M.* 28161 Quen i sagh oþer men mistad, of his fare wald i be gladd, for his ded and his vn-hele, for skath takyng of his catell. 1559 *Mirr. Mag., Hen. VI* xiii, If likewise such as say the welken fortune warkes, Take Fortune for our fate, and sterres therof the markes, Then destiny with fate, and Gods wyl all be one: But if they meane it otherwise, skath causers skyes be none.

Scathe (skēið), *v.* Forms: 2–5 **skathe**, 4–9 **scathe, scath**, (4 **sckathe**); chiefly *Sc.* 5–6 **skayth(e**, 6 **ska**, 5–9 **scaith**, 8–9 **skaith**. [a. ON. *skaða* impers., it hurts (Sw. *skada*, Da. *skade* to hurt, injure); corresponding to OE. *sc(e)aðian* to injure, rob, OFris. *skathia* to injure, OS. *scaðon* (Essen Gl.) to slander, Du. *schaden* to injure, OHG. *skadôn* (MHG., mod.G. *schaden*):—OTeut. **skaþōjan*, f. **skaþon-* Scathe *sb.*

ON. had also another verb from the same root, *skeðja* (pa. t. *skalde*), corresponding to OE. *sceððan* (orig. strong, pa. t. *scéd*, pa. pple. (*ge*)*sceaðen*, whence by analogy an inf. form *sceaðan*; commonly weak, pa. t. *sceðede*), Goth. *skaþjan* (pa. t. *skōþ*). There is no evidence, however, that the ON. *skeðja* was adopted in English, or that either of the OE. vbs. (with initial ʃ) survived into ME.]

1. *trans.* To injure, hurt, damage. Now *arch.* and *Sc.*

c1200 Ormin 4468–9 Forr ʒiff þu skaþesst aniʒ mann þu skaþesst firrst te sellfenn. c1380 *Sir Ferumb.* 759, Y schal scaþye hem niʒt & day þat bileueþ on Mahounde. a1400 *Relig. Pieces fr. Thornton MS.* 26 He þat will noghte sckathe his euencristyn, he sall noghte consente ne na conseille gyffe to do hym ill. c1460 *Towneley Myst.* xxii. 365 Syrs, I haue a greatt Iornay That must be done this same day, Or els it will me skathe. 1470–85 Malory *Arthur* ii. iii. 90 That wille I not, sayd the knyghte, for hit wylle scathe me gretely and now do yow none auaylle. 1566 *Reg. Privy Council Scot.* I. 468 Throw the quhilk [false coin].. this commoun weill hes bene greitlie hurt, and oure Soveranis and thair trew subjectis defraudit and skaythit. 1592 Shaks. *Rom. & Jul.* i. v. 86 This tricke may chance to scath you. 1728 Ramsay *Last Sp. Miser* xvi, But that ne'er skaith'd or troubled me, Gin I grew rich. 1784 Burns *Ep. J. Rankine* v, Think, wicked Sinner, wha ye're skaithing. 1829 H. Miller *Lett. on Herring Fish.*, I manna skaith the rape. 1840 Barham *Ingol. Leg.* Ser. i. *St. Nicholas*, Holy Church ..the wolves doth mock who would scathe her flock.

†b. *spec.* To subject to pecuniary loss. (The amount is expressed by a second object or introduced by *of*.) *Obs.*

1456 Sir G. Haye *Law Arms* (S.T.S.) 167 He aw to be payit of the baroune of all his soume of lenth that he war scathit of. ?1496 in *Lett. Rich. III & Hen. VII* (Rolls) II. 69 Ther entred neuer a straunger ship here sithins Midlent, and that hath skathed the Kinges grace c.li. 1600 Darrell *Detect. Harsnet's Lying Disc.* 202 The poore man..had as leue she had so kindly imbraced another as him, for the salutation..scathed him 4. nobles. 1602 *How Man may chuse Good Wife* C 1, Ile crosse thy name quite from my reckoning booke: For these accounts, faith it shall scathe thee somewhat.

†c. *absol.* To do harm. *Obs.*

1470 Henry *Wallace* viii. 1132 It ma nocht scaith, suppos do na waill.

2. To injure or destroy by fire, lightning, or similar agency; to blast, scorch, sear. *poet.* and *rhet.*

This, and the derived sense 3, appear to have been developed from the Milton passage (quot. 1667), perh. partly through sound-association with *scorch*.

[1667 Milton *P. L.* i. 613 As when Heavens Fire Hath scath'd the Forrest Oaks,..With singed top their stately growth though bare Stands on the blasted Heath.] 1810 Scott *Lady of L.* iii. x, The monk resumed his mutter'd spell:..The while he scathed the Cross with flame. 1813 — *Rokeby* iv. iii, The pine-tree scathed by lightning-fire. 1814 — *Ld. of Isles* iv. viii, Seek not the giddy crag to climb, To view the turret scathed by time. 1831 Carlyle *Sart. Res.* ii. viii, The fire-baptised soul, long so scathed and thunder-riven, here feels its own Freedom. 1844 Thirlwall *Greece* VIII. lxiii. 240 The flames that scathed Thermus. 1882 Farrar *Early Chr.* II. 213 The whole country had been scathed with fire and drowned in blood.

fig. 1842 Manning *Serm.* (1843) I. vi. 83 Familiar consent to evil..scathes and deadens the spiritual sense.

3. *fig.* To sear or 'wither' with fierce invective or satire. Cf. Scathing *ppl. a.*

1852 Robertson *Serm.* Ser. iii. (1857) 152 At the same time that He scathed with indignant invective the Pharisees. 1867 Froude *Short Stud.* Ser. i. I. 77 (*Erasmus & Luther* ii.) His satire flashed about,..scathing especially his old enemies the monks.

Hence **Scathed** *ppl. a.*

1791 Gilpin *Forest Scenery* ii. 71 Many of the oaks are scathed, and ragged. 1831 Scott *Ct. Robt.* xxix, The hulk of the Grecian Admiral, burnt to the water's edge, and still sending forth a black smoke from its scathed beams and planks. 1842 Borrow *Bible in Spain* vi, Its scathed and gigantic crags. 1873 Miss Broughton *Nancy* III. 152 Is that one withered scathed little stick to be our sole protection against the storm?

†Sca·thefire. *Obs.* Also 7 **scath-, skath-, schath-**, 8 *dial.* **scale-**. See also Scarefire. [f. Scathe *sb.* + Fire *sb.* Cf. G. *schadenfeuer*, Da. *skadeild*, Norw. *skadeverme*.] A destructive fire or conflagration.

1632 Heywood *2nd Pt. Iron Age* v. i. I 4, These horrid sights Lighted by scathe-fires. 1658 W. Burton *Itin. Anton.* 155 Her frequent Schathfires have rendred her not less magnificent, but more famous. a1663 Bramhall *Vind. fr. Popery* vi. (1672) 115 In a great Scathfire it is wisdom not only to suffer those Houses to burn down which are past quenching, but [etc.]. 1796 Pegge *Derbicisms* Ser. i. 60 (E.D.S.) *Scale-fire*, when a house or town is on fire.

Scatheful (skēi·ðfŭl), *a. arch.* Forms: see Scathe *sb.* [f. Scathe *sb.* + -ful. Cf. Ormin's *unnskaþefull*.] Hurtful, harmful, injurious.

c900 tr. *Gregory's Dial.* 209 Swa þonne ʒeweorðeð þæt we becumað þonne fram þam idlan wordum to þam sceaðfullum. 1375 Barbour *Bruce* v. 249 Gif the hapnys ony thing, That anoyus or scathfull be. 1513 Douglas *Æneis* ii. i. 34 And sum, wondring, the skaithfull gift beheld. 1527 Andrew *Brunswyke's Distyll. Waters* B j b, This water..withdryveth the scadefull swellyng in the bely. 1586 Warner *Alb. Eng.* i. v. (1589) 15 Hercules..with skathfull strokes bestird his Club so well,..that [etc.]. 1601 Shaks. *Twel. N.* v. i. 59 With which such scathfull grapple did he make With the most noble bottome of our Fleete. 1855 Singleton *Virg., Georg.* i. I. 80 That scathful rust should prey upon its stalks.

†Scathel, *a. Obs.* Forms: 4 **scathel, -ylle**, 5 **skethill, skathil(l, -ell**, 6 **skatell**. β. 5 **schatell, schathill**. See also Scaddle *a.* [a. ON. **skǫþull* = OHG. *scad(h)al, scadel, scatal, -el*, Goth. *skaþuls*:—OTeut. **skaþulo-*, f. **skaþ-*: see Scathe *sb.*] Injurious, harmful, dangerous. Also *absol.* as *sb.*

a1300 *Cursor M.* 28773 Almus askes to be wroght o rightwis aght,..for elles vnmedi sal it be, scathel and wrangwise als to þe. 13.. *E. E. Allit. P.* C. 155 Mony ladde þer forth-lep to laue & to Rest, Scopen out þe scaþel water, þat fayn scape wolde. a1400 *Morte Arth.* 32 Scathylle Scottlande by skylle he skyftys as hym lykys. *Ibid.* 1642 That no skathelle in the skrogges skorne vs here-aftyr. c1400 *Destr. Troy* 4067 Ascalaphus, a skathil duke & skant mon in wer. *Ibid.* 13442 There were sones vpposyde,..To Askathes full skete, skethill of hor hond. a1400–50 *Alexander* 2992 Þat skapid..skatheles fra all his schathill dukis [*Dubl.* scapett.. schatheles..schatell]. 1515 *Scot. Field* 342 in *Chetham Misc.* (1856) II, Those skatell Scotts, that all the skath diden.

Scatheless (skēi·ðlĕs), *a.* Forms: see Scathe *sb.* [f. Scathe *sb.* + -less. Cf. ON. *skaðlauss*.] Without scathe; unharmed. †Const. *of*.

c1200 Ormin 12038 ʒiff þatt he lupe dun All skaþelæs till eorþe. c1350 *Will. Palerne* 1855 To a-schape schaþles fram þat schamful best. a1366 Chaucer *Rom. Rose* 1550 That scathles, fulle sykerly, I myght unto the welle goo. a1400–50 [see Scathel]. 1563 *Reg. Privy Council Scot.* I. 241 To keip him skaithless of the samyn[penalty]. 1818 Scott *Hrt. Midl.* xv, 'I wad ware the best blood in my body to keep her skaithless,' said Jeanie. 1865 Trollope *Belton Est.* xxviii. 341 It is a game from which you will come out scatheless, but I have been scalded. 1884 *Law Times* LXXVIII. 57/1 The wife and the fortunate individual who shared her indictment escaped scatheless.

Hence **Sca·thelessly** *adv.*

1844 Tupper *Heart* xi. 121 In the hope..of ruining him, if not of getting scathelessly off themselves. 1858 J. H. Bennet *Nutrition* vi. 209 The soldier who..passes scathlessly through twenty campaigns.

†Sca·thely, *adv. Obs.* [f. Scathe *sb.* + -ly 2.] With damage or injury. Only in allit. phr. *to scape* (or *aschape*) *scathely*.

c1350 *Will. Palerne* 2794 Þat we so scaþli ar a-schaped god mowe [we] þonk. a1400–50 *Alexander* 642 If any scolere in þe scole his skorne at him makis, He skapis him full skathely bot if he skyp better.

Scathing (skēi·ðiŋ), *ppl. a.* [-ing 2.]

1. That scathes or blasts (see Scathe *v.* 2).

1794 Coleridge *Monody Death Chatterton* 51 The scathing lightning. 1813 Byron *Corsair* i. x, Mark how that lone and blighted bosom sears The scathing thought of execrated years! 1858 Gladstone *Homer* II. 180 He launches the scathing thunderbolt.

2. Of invective, etc.: Very sharp and damaging; searing, 'withering', cutting.

1865 Lecky *Ration.* (1878) I. 251 Week after week he launched from the pulpit the most scathing invectives. 1893 *Times* 28 Apr. 9/4 Mr. Goschen's speech was a scathing exposure of the contrast between promise and performance.

Hence **Sca·thingly** *adv.*

1847 *Tait's Mag.* XIV. 238 A feeling of his insignificance flashed scathingly on the quivering pride of Robert Anderson. 1868 E. Edwards *Ralegh* I. xxii. 497 That Duke of Savoy whom Milton has made scathingly famous.

Scatire, obs. form of Scatter *v.*

Scatol, variant of Skatol *Chem.*

Scatologic (skætǫlǫ·dʒik), *a.* [f. Scatolog-y + -ic.] Of or pertaining to scatology (sense 1).

1891 J. G. Bourke (*title*) Scatalogic [*sic*] Rites of all Nations. 1897 in *Syd. Soc. Lex.*

Scatology (skătǫ·lŏdʒi). [f. Gr. σκατ-, σκῶρ dung + -(o)logy.]

1. That branch of science which deals with diagnosis by means of the fæces. 1897 in *Syd. Soc. Lex.*

2. That branch of palæontology which treats of fossil excrement or coprolites. In recent Dicts.

3. Filthy literature. *rare.*

1876 *N. & Q.* Ser. v. V. 31 Mr. Swifte's suggestion that *scatology* may be derived from *scateo*. 1887 Saintsbury *Elizab. Lit.* x. 370 A large quantity of mere scatology and doggerel.

Scatomancy (skæ·tomænsi). [ad. mod.L. *scatomantia*: see prec. and -mancy.] Divination or diagnosis based on the examination of the fæces.

1569 J. Sanford tr. *Agrippa's Van. Artes* lxxxiii. 145 b, For this cause Scatomancie, Oromancie, Drymimancie, be called the diuinations or Prognostications of Phisitians, gathered by ordures and vrines. 1861 Reade *Cloister & H.* xxvi, I studied at Montpelier...There learned I Drimimancy, Scatomancy, Pathology [etc.]. 1897 in *Syd. Soc. Lex.*

†Scatomanter. *Obs. rare*—1. [irreg. ad. mod.L. *scatomantis*, f. Gr. σκατ(ο)- dung + μάντις prophet.] One who practises scatomancy.

1569 J. Sanford tr. *Agrippa's Van. Artes* lxxxiii. 145 b, [The name *Scatophagos*] afterwards was deriued to all Phisitions, in suche wise, that wee call them Scatophagians and Scatomanters, that is, ordure eaters, and lookers on ordure.

Scatophage (skæ·tofēidʒ). [ad. mod.L. *scatophag-us*, a. Gr. σκατοφάγος: see Scatophagous *a.* Cf. F. *scatophage* adj.] A scatophagous insect or animal; esp. a dung-fly. In recent Dicts.

†Scatopha·gian. *Obs. rare*—1. [f. mod.L. *scatophag-us* (see next) + -ian.] One who feeds on dung. 1569 [see Scatomanter].

Scatophagous (skătǫ·făgəs), *a.* [f. mod.L. *scatophag-us*, a. Gr. σκατοφάγος, f. σκατ(ο)-, σκῶρ dung: see -phagous.] Feeding upon dung.

1891 in *Century Dict.* 1896 *Nature* 16 July 247/2 In *Stomoxys*,..the larvæ are normally scatophagous.

Scatoscopy (skătǫ·skŏpi). *rare*—0. [Cf. prec. and -scopy.] Inspection of the fæces for the purpose of divination or diagnosis. In recent Dicts.

Scatses, obs. pl. form of Skate *sb.*2

Scattald (skæ·tăld). *Orkney and Shetl.* Also 7 **scat(t)ell**, 8 **scatald, scatteld, scat(t)hold, scattald, -old, scathald, skattald**. [ad. local Scandinavian **skatthald* (= ON. *skatt-r* Scat *sb.*3 + *hald* Hold *sb.*)] The common ground for pasture or furnishing fuel, etc. of a district. Hence **Sca·ttalder**, one who shares in the scattald. Also *in-scattalder* = 'scattalder'; *out-skattalder*, a resident in the district who has no share in the scattald.

1615 *Acts etc. Orkney & Shetl.* (Maitl. Cl. 1840) II. 174 Anent going throuch thair nychtbours scattell...It sall not be lesum to ony persone..to go throuch his nychtbouris scatell or comontie with ane scheip dog Except [etc.]. a1733 *Shetland Acts* 32 in *Proc. Soc. Ant. Scot.* (1892) XXVI. 201 That every scatald have a sufficient pund. *Ibid.* 35 ibid., All horses belonging either to outscattalders or inscattalders. *Ibid.* 39 ibid., That the Sheriff..ride the marches thereto by the parish..when required thereto by the scattalders. 1809 A. Edmonston *Pres. St. Zetland* I. 148 The uncultivated ground, outside of the enclosure [or town], is called the Scatthold, and is used for general pasture, and to furnish turf for firing. 1883 *Chamb. Jrnl.* 211 Beyond the turf dikes is the scattald or common.

Scatter (skæ·təɹ), *sb.* [f. Scatter *v.*]

1. The action or an act of scattering; wide or irregular distribution; dispersion. Now chiefly with reference to shot.

1642 J. W[eall] *Prepar. Fast* 4 We are exposed aswell to Forraigne and intestine mischiefes. This divide and scatter, if it be not prevented, will be no small curse. 1650 T. Vaughan *Anthroposophia* 68 Advt. to Rdr., Let Them [*sc.* the Galenists] not mangle, and discompose my Book with a scatter of Observations, but proceed Methodically to the Censure of each part. 1893 *Westm. Gaz.* 14 Dec. 5/1 Had there been no deflection from the hard skull the shot ..would have been smaller in scatter than it is.

2. A small quantity loosely distributed or interspersed; a scattering, sprinkling. *rare.*

1859 R. F. Burton *Centr. Afr.* in *Jrnl. Geog. Soc.* XXIX. 158 Its soile displays quartzose sand, with scatters of granite. 1888 *Daily News* 17 May 5/8 The bodice, too, had a scatter of diamonds and pearls.

Scatter (skæ·təɹ), *v.* Forms: 2 **scatere**, 3–6 **scater, skater**, 4 **schatre, scatir(e**, 4–5 **scatre**, 5 **skatre**, (**schatir**), 6 **scattre, skattir, sketer**, 7 **skatter**, 6– **scatter**. [Early ME. (12th c., Midland); of obscure origin; formed with iterative suffix (see -er 5).

This and Shatter *v.* (which appears much later) are commonly regarded as respectively northern and southern representatives of an OE. **sc(e)aterian*, which is referred to a supposed Teut. root **skat-* cogn. w. Gr. σκεδ-αννύναι to scatter. The etymological identity of the two vbs. seems, however, doubtful, although they have some affinity of sense. It is true that in ME. *scatter* occurs only in northern and midland texts, with one exception (quot. 1330, sense 3); and that in this sole southern instance the MS. spells it with *sch*, which should normally stand for (ʃ). But initial (sk) from OE. *sc* in a native word would be no less abnormal in northern and midland than in southern English. The alleged cognates in Du. and LG. are questionable. Two instances are cited of MDu. *schaderen*, with the senses 'to squander (money)', 'to shed (blood)'; but this does not agree in form. The sense 'to scatter' assigned to early mod.Du. *schetteren*, rests on the authority of Kilian, whose citation of the Eng. word renders his testimony suspicious. The Du. and MLG. *schateren* to resound, to laugh uproariously (MLG. once, to be shattered by an explosion) would seem to be onomatopoeic; at least their sense cannot easily be derived from that assigned to the alleged Teut. root. Cf. Scat *v.*2 and Squatter *v.*]

1. *trans.* To dissipate, squander (goods or possessions). *Obs.* or *arch.*

1154 *O. E. Chron.* an. 1137, He hadde ʒet his tresor ac he to deld it & scatered sotlice. c1380 Wyclif *Serm.* Sel. Wks. II. 78 For ʒif þes ordres geten nevere so myche good, þei seien þat al is þer ordris, and it were a deedli synne to scatire þes goodis in þe world. 1522 More *De quat. Noviss.* Wks. 94 They would..neuer be so mad, gredily to gather together that other men shal merely sone after scatter abrode. c1645 Howell *Lett.* vi. xvii. (1650) I. 204, I leave the rest of all my goods to my first-born Edward, to be consum'd or scatterd (for I never hoped better). a1716 South *Serm.* (1744) VIII. 326 And was it not worth the..seeing his substance scattered, his children struck dead [etc.].

absol. 1879 G. Campbell *White & Black* 243 Mr. J—— says the Germans are the only men who are saving; all the rest scatter.

2. To separate and drive in various directions (a body of men or animals, a collection of things); to disperse, dissipate (a quantity of matter); to dispel (clouds, mists).

a1300 *E. E. Psalter* xvii. 16 [xviii. 14] And he sent his arwes, and skatered þa. 1382 Wyclif *Matt.* xxvi. 31, I shal smyte the sheperde, and the sheep of the floc shulen be scatered. 1582 Stanyhurst *Æneis* i. (Arb.) 19 Duck downe theire fleete with a tempest, Or ships wyde scatter. 1594 Shaks. *Rich. III*, iv. iv. 513 Buckingham's Armie is dispers'd and scatter'd. 1596 — *Merch. V.* i. i. 33 Dangerous rocks, Which touching but my gentle Vessels side Would scatter all her spices on the streame. 1596 Dalrymple tr. *Leslie's Hist. Scot.* II. x. 453 Lyk a certane sone, new risen to skail and skattir the Cloudis of al tumulte. 1657 W. Coles *Adam in Eden* xxiii. 49 The Leaves of wild Clary.. put into Pottage..scatter congealed blood. c1788 Burns *Ep. to R. Graham* 26 Some spumy, fiery, *ignis fatuus* matter, Such as the slightest breath of air might scatter. 1860 Tyndall *Glac.* i. iii. 30 A breeze..keen and hostile, scattering the snow. 1871 Freeman *Norm. Conq.* IV. xviii. 117 The terrible name of Odo scattered them in all directions. 1879 Miss Braddon *Clov. Foot* xxviii, 'What has become of all the photographs?'..'Given to Tom, Dick and Harry —scattered to the four winds. I have not kept one of them.'

absol. 1594 T. B. *La Primaud. Fr. Acad.* ii. 283 It is the nature of this enemy of mankind [*sc.* the Devil] to scatter, to disioyne and separat.

fig. 1613 Purchas *Pilgrimage* (1614) 45 So doth God scatter the counsells of his enemies. [Cf. *Vulg. Ps.* xxxii[i]. 10 *Dominus dissipet consilia gentium*.] 1822 Shelley tr. *Calderon* iii. 145 So that Heaven May scatter thy delusions. 1869 Lecky *Europ. Mor.* I. iii. 430 No one did more to scatter the ancient superstitions than did Cicero.

b. *intr.* for *refl.* To separate and disperse; to go dispersedly or stragglingly. † Also of a hawk: To go to a distance.

c1430 *Syr Gener.* (Roxb.) 158 And kepe we vs to-gedre trew That we skater not a-sondre. 1486 *Bk. St. Albans* b iij b, When thay [a Couy of partrichys] be putt upp, and begynne to scatre, ye most haue markeris to marke some of thaym. 15.. *Scot. Field* 513 in *Chetham Misc.* II, When the Skottes..seen our men skelter They..came downwarde. 1593 Shaks. *2 Hen. VI*, iii. ii. 126 The Commons like an angry Hiue of Bees That want their Leader, scatter vp and downe. 1610 Guillim *Heraldry* ii. v. (1611) 46 The Fillet is shaped long and narrowe for the more commodious vse of women in..restraining of their haire from scattering about theire browes. 1626 Bacon *Sylva* § 138 Sound diffuseth it selfe in round..; But if the Sound, which would scatter in Open Aire, be made to goe all into a Canale; It must needs giue greater force to the Sound. 1771 *Encycl. Brit.* II. 541/2 She [the falcon] must also have two good bells, that she may be found when she scattereth. 1795 Southey *Joan of Arc* vi. 309 Aright, aleft, The affrighted foemen scatter from his spear. 1796 Withering *Brit. Plants* II. 74 The stems generally decline and scatter from each other, instead of being upright and close together. 1817 Shelley *Rev. Islam* vi. xix, When on my foes a sudden terror came, And they fled, scattering. 1909 *Blackw. Mag.* Aug. 230/2 The fugitives scattered for miles, bearing appalling tales of massacre.

c. *refl.* Now *rare* or *Obs.*

1535 Coverdale *1 Chron.* xv. [xiv.] 9 The Philistynes came, and scatered them selues beneth in ye valley of Rephaim. 1579 Tomson *Calvin's Serm. Tim.* 128/2 They be enimies to the Churche, and scatter themselues farre from vs. 1625 B. Jonson *Staple of N.* iv. ii. 175 *Shr.* He'll let you ha' your liberty—. *Alm.* Goe forth, Whither you please, and to what company—. *Mad.* Scatter your selfe amongst vs.

†d. *trans.* To separate, drive apart (one or more individuals *from* the main body). *Obs.*

1588 Earl of Leicester in *Defeat Sp. Armada* (Navy Rec. Soc.) II. 35 Two of the greatest carracks that the King of Spain had in his fleet, being scattered from the rest. a1661 Fuller *Worthies, Derbysh.* (1662) i. 234 Their ships with the violence of the wind were much shattered, and the Bonaventure, scattered from the other two ships.

†e. *fig.* To dissipate, distract (the mind, etc.).

1450–1530 *Myrr. Our Ladye* 122 A warnynge to take hede that yf the mynde were eny thynge scatered before, then to gather yt ageyne to gyther. 1625 B Jonson *Staple of N.* iv. ii, Look, look, how all their eyes Dance i' their heads (obserue) scatter'd with lust! 1715 tr. *T. à Kempis' Chr. Exerc.* iii. xv. 138 If thou art hereby scattered in thy Mind.

3. *trans.* To throw about in disorder in various places.

c1330 *Arth. & Merl.* (Kölbing) 553 Ac þo þai come þider eft, Her werk was al vp aleft & yschatred here & þere. c1386 Chaucer *Can. Yeom. Prol. & T.* 361 The pot tobreketh..And somme [of the metals] are scatered al the floor aboute. 1860 Tyndall *Glac.* i. xx. 142 The fragments of rock scattered about were..polar.

†b. To throw down (a thing) negligently; to drop. *Obs. rare*—1.

a1640 *Wizard* (MS.) (Nares), It is directed to you; some love-letter, on my life, that Luce hath scattered.

4. To distribute to various positions; to place here and there at irregular intervals. Chiefly in *pa. pple.*

c1380 Wyclif *Sel. Wks.* III. 445 Mykel more if newe religious be skaterud in Cristendome. 1549 Allen *Par. Leo Jude upon Rev.* 8 These are ye messengers of Antichrist, scattrid thoroweout the whole worlde. 1712 Swift *Let. Eng. Tongue* Wks. (1755) II. 184 William the Conqueror proceeded much further; bringing over with him vast numbers of that nation, scattering them in every monastery. 1837 Lockhart *Scott* I. x. 326 Many tributes to his memory are scattered over his friend's other works. 1858 Ruskin *Pol. Econ. Art* ii. 130 So long as works of art are scattered through the nation, no universal destruction of them is possible. 1882 P. G. Tait in *Encycl. Brit.* XIV. 583/1 If stars be scattered through infinite space, with average closeness.

†b. *intr.* in pres. pple. used with a vb. of rest (= 'scattered'). *Obs.*

1555 Watreman *Fardle Facions* Pref. 6 From Adam to the floud..when men liued skateryng on the earthe. 1716 Church *Philip's War* (1867) II. 149 He answered, there were several Families, but they liv'd scattering. 1726 Leoni *Alberti's Archit.* I. 66/2 Laying all the..earth into the furrow again inward, so that none might lie scattering outward.

5. *trans.* To throw or send forth so that the particles are distributed or spread about; to sow or throw (seed, money, etc.) broadcast; to sprinkle, strew; to diffuse (fragrance).

c1450 *St. Cuthbert* (Surtees) 4682 Molle on þair heueds þai scaterd. 1530 Palsgr. 699/1, I scatter small thynges abrode, as peasyn, or beanes. 1535 Coverdale *Ps.* cxlvii. 16 He..scatereth ye horefrost like ashes. 1606 Shaks. *Ant. & Cl.* ii. vii. 25 As it [*sc.* the Nile] ebbes, the Seedsman Vpon the slime and Ooze scatters his graine. 1644 Symonds *Diary* (Camden) 54 Some of our men by the King's command scattered some papers, that if any would come in.. they should be pardoned. 1698 Fryer *Acc. E. India & P.* 107 The Governor..bestows his Largess..liberally scattering Rupees. 1821 Shelley *Ginevra* 126 The matin winds from the expanded flowers Scatter their hoarded incense. 1861 Miss J. M. Campbell in Bere *Garland of Songs* 61 We plough the fields and scatter The good seed on the land.

absol. 1748 Gray *Alliance* 17 Scatter with a free, though frugal, Hand.

b. *transf.* and *fig.* Also, †to spread (reports, a prophecy).

1576 Fleming *Panopl. Epist.* 118 O ioyfull report, and most acceptable rumour, which was scatered abroade. 1601 Shaks. *All's Well* i. ii. 54 His plausiue words He scatter'd not in eares, but grafted them To grow there and to beare. a1662 Heylin *Laud* ii. (1671) 251 The Lady Davies.. scatters a Prophesie against him. a1771 Gray *Birds* 2 The Sibyl scatters his loose notes. 1858 Longf. *M. Standish* iv. 74 A hand-grenade, that scatters destruction around it.

c. *intr.* for *refl.*

1577 B. Googe *Heresbach's Husb.* i. (1586) 35 When it [Pulse] is rype it must be gathered..for it scattereth very soone. 1642 Jer. Taylor *Episc.* (1647) 233 The Bishop should separate the scabbed sheep from the sound, least their infection scatter. 1720 De Foe *Capt. Singleton* v. (1840) 93 The small shot..scattered among them. 1817 Shelley *Rev. Islam* vi. xlvi, A wood Whose bloom-inwoven leaves now scattering fed The hungry storm.

d. Of a gun, a cartridge: To distribute (the shot). Chiefly *absol.*

1741 *Compl. Fam.-Piece* i. ii. 320 You must also be well acquainted with the Condition of the Gun, whether it be apt to scatter, or carry the Shot round within Compass. 1823 J. F. Cooper *Pioneers* i, The gun scatters well. 1881 Greener *Gun* 439 Cartridge loaded to scatter the shot.

e. *Physics.* Of a surface, semi-opaque substance: To throw back (light) brokenly in all directions.

1833 Herschel *Astron.* § 45 (1839) 32 The sun..illuminates the atmosphere and clouds, and these again disperse and scatter a portion of its light in all directions. 1882 P. G. Tait in *Encycl. Brit.* XIV. 583/2 In order that a surface may be illuminated..it must be capable of scattering light.

6. To sprinkle or strew *with* something.

1590 Spenser *F. Q.* i. x. 35 A narrow way, Scattred with bushy thornes and ragged breares. 1667 Milton *P. L.* xi. 649 Now scatter'd lies With Carcasses and Arms th' ensanguind Field Deserted. 1720 De Foe *Capt. Singleton* vi. (1840) 106 The ground was scattered with elephant's teeth. 1902 E. Phillpotts *River* i, Where the desert spread, all scattered with great stones.

7. *Comb.*: **scatteraway** *rare*, dispersion; **scatter-charge, load**, a charge for a gun, made to distribute the shot when fired; † **scatter-story**, one who 'spreads' a report or story; **scatter-tuft**, the genus *Sporochnus*, one of the algals (*Cassell's Encycl. Dict.*, 1887); † **scatter-wise** *adv.*, in straggling order.

1851 Sir F. Palgrave *Norm. & Eng.* I. 325 So complete was the *scatteraway, that one of the brethren never stopped till he reached Saint-Gall. 1881 Greener *Gun* 439 The *scatter-charge has good penetration at 30 and 40 yards. 1901 *Ibid.* (ed. 8) Index, *Scatter loads. a1680 Hacket *Cent. Serm.* (1675) 734 Ælian, and some other such *scatter-stories as himself, do make more reports of..unreasonable creatures, than of reasonable men. 1875 Dasent *Vikings* III. xviii. 278 They sail very *scatter-wise in coming back, if, indeed, these few ships be part of the host.

Scatterable (skæ·tərăb'l), *a.* [f. Scatter *v.* + -able.] That may be scattered.

1800 Herschel in *Phil. Trans.* XC. 523 The rays of heat are..less refrangible than those of light; and may be, also, if I may introduce a convenient term, less scatterable.

Scatteration (skætərēi·ʃən). *rare.* [f. Scatter *v.* + -ation.] The action of scattering.

1776 Mrs. A. Grant *Lett. fr. Mountains* (1806) I. 212 After the dissolution and scatteration of last year's happy trio. 1865 *N. Y. Times* 25 Feb., The scatteration of Cobb's forces. 1900 *Engineering Mag.* XIX. 750/2 Scatteration of effort is dissipation of energy.

Scatteraway: see Scatter *v.* 7.

Sca·tter-brain. [f. Scatter *v.* + Brain *sb.* Cf. the earlier Shatterbrain.] One who is incapable of serious connected thought; a heedless, giddy person.

1790 Cowper *Let.* 31 July *Wks.* 1836 VI. 324 Though I have seen you but once,..I have found out that you are a scatter-brain. 1898 Baring-Gould *Old Eng. Home* xii. 284 The generality of these scapegraces are simply scatterbrains.

So **Sca·tter-brained** *a.*, that is a scatter-brain; characteristic of a scatter-brain.

[1747: cf. *scattered-brained*, Scattered *ppl. a.* 6.] 1804 Currie in *Creevey Papers* (1904) I. i. 30 A scatter-brained fellow. 1866 Carlyle *Remin.* I. 122 A cheerful scatter-brained creature.

Scattered (skæ·təɹd), *ppl. a.* [f. Scatter *v.* + -ed 1.] In senses of the verb.

1. Of a flock, tribe, company of persons, troops, etc.: Disunited and dispersed; disorganized; also, spread out in all directions.

1388 Wyclif *Jer.* l. 17 Israel is a scaterid flok. 1593 Shaks. *3 Hen. VI*, ii. vi. 93 And hauing France thy Friend, thou shalt not dread The scattred Foe, that hopes to rise againe. 1786 Burns '*The gloomy night*', The Hunter now has left the moor, The scatt'red coveys meet secure. 1855 Macaulay *Hist. Eng.* xx. IV. 412 From the field of battle he made his way..to the neighbourhood of Louvain, and there began to collect his scattered forces.

b. *fig.* Of feelings, thoughts, etc.: Distracted, discomposed; vagrant. Now *rare* or *Obs.*

1638 Junius *Paint. Ancients* 26 It doth require some labour to settle our wild scattered thoughts. 1667 Milton *P. L.* xi. 294 Adam..his scatterd spirits returnd, To Michael thus his humble words addressd. 1819 Scott *Ivanhoe* xiv, One word from Isaac..recalled her scattered feelings.

2. Widely separated one from another; placed here and there; spread over a wide area; straggling.

1595 *Polimanteia* in Brydges *Brit. Bibl.* I. 281 Mourne.. for the trulie Hon. Ferdinandos death: whom the scattered teares haue honoured in some few sonnets. 1617 Moryson *Itin.* i. 112 Having passed long space,..we found scattered houses we came within a Musket shot of the mountaine. 1715 Pope *Iliad* I. *Ess. on Homer* 4 Having got other scatter'd Stories of Homer. 1791 Burns *Lament for Earl Glencairn* iii, Ye scatter'd birds that faintly sing. 1828 Scott *F. M. Perth* xxvii, A few aged and scattered trees. 1845 Budd *Dis. Liver* 175 Ulceration of the gall-bladder.. may lead to scattered abscesses in the substance of the liver. 1897 *Westm. Gaz.* 11 Mar. 2/1 The Poor-law Conference.. showed a remarkable consensus of opinion in favour of the substitution of the boarding-out and scattered home system for the present barrack schools.

3. Cast or driven about loosely in all directions; thrown broadcast. †Of the hair: Disordered.

1667 Milton *P. L.* i. 304 His Legions..lay..Thick as scattered sedge Afloat, when with fierce Winds Orion arm'd Hath vext the Red-Sea Coast. 1785 Cowper *Task* vi. 221 Oh Winter, ruler of th' inverted year, Thy scatter'd hair with sleet like ashes fill'd..I love thee! *Ibid.* 317 The sparrows peep...Well they eye The scatter'd grain. 1875 J. Main *Abercrombie's Ev. Man his own Gard.* 40 Let the grass be rolled with a wooden roller, to which any scattered worm-cast earth will readily adhere.

†b. Of a single thing: Cast off; thrown negligently, let drop. *Obs.*

1596 Spenser *F. Q.* v. ii. 3 Whom having lost,..And finding in the way the scattred scarfe, The fortune of her life long time did feare. 1600 Shaks. *A. Y. L.* iii. v. 103 To glean now and then a scattred smile, and that Ile liue vpon. 1781 Cowper *Table-T.* 674 [He], like a scatter'd seed at random sown, Was left to spring by vigour of his own.

4. *spec.* **a.** *Bot.* Occurring at wide and irregular intervals (see quots.).

[1640: cf. Scatteredly.] 1796 Withering *Brit. Plants* I. 225 Cal. none, (except some scattered sheaths). *Ibid.* III. 176 Root-leaves on leaf-stalks, somewhat toothed, edged with scattered hairs. 1839 Lindley *Introd. Bot.* (ed. 3) III. 492 Scattered (*sparsus*); used in opposition to whorled, or opposite, or ternate, or other such terms. 1872 H. C. Wood *Fresh-w. Algæ* 54 Filament single, mostly scattered.

b. *Ent.* (See quot.)

1826 Kirby & Sp. *Entomol.* IV. 313 Scattered (*Sparsi*). When simple eyes are separate from each other and not arranged in a certain order.

c. *Physics.* Of light: Refracted and dispersed in all directions.

1808 Herschel in *Phil. Trans.* XCIX. 280 The [prismatic] bows are formed by scattered light. 1878 Abney *Treat. Photogr.* xii. 88 The blurring caused by the reflection of the scattered rays from the plate.

5. Covered with scatterings; strewn or littered with something. *rare.*

1798 Bloomfield *Farmer's Boy, Winter* 56 [He] Fills the tall racks [with hay] and leaves a scatter'd road.

6. *Comb.*: † **scattered-brained** = Scatter-brained.

1747 *Mem. Nutrebian Crt.* II. 14 [Expressions] such as easy fool, scattered-brained madman.

Scatteredly (skæ·təɹdli), *adv.* [f. Scattered *ppl. a.* + -ly 2.] In a scattered manner; disorderedly, irregularly; †intermittently.

1611 Speed *Theatre Gt. Brit.* i. § 3 All other Ilands and Ilets, which doe scatteredly inuiron it. 1640 Parkinson *Theat. Bot.* 283 Sometimes also growing scatteredly on the stalks. 1684 H. More *Answ. Remarks upon More's Expos.* 275 What is more scatteredly and interruptedly done as to time, and place,..is..represented as done at one time, and in one place. 1847 Hardy in *Proc. Berw. Nat. Club* II. No. 5. 252 Elytra..minutely and scatteredly punctulate. 1882 R. A. Proctor in *Knowledge* No. 41. 176 Meteors of the Perseid system may..be seen..in greater number, but with shorter paths near Perseus; more scatteredly, but with longer paths at a distance from that constellation.

Scatteredness (skæ·təɹdnĕs). *rare.* [Formed as prec. + -ness.] Scattered condition.

1667 H. More *Div. Dial.* v. iv. (1713) 408 The Defectuousness and Scatteredness of the Prophecies.

Scatterer (skæ·tərəɹ). [f. Scatter *v.* + -er 1.] One who scatters, in the senses of the verb.

1535 Coverdale *Nahum* ii. 1 The scaterer shal come vp agaynst the, & laye sege to the castell. 1555 Philpot *Apol. for Spitting upon Arrian* A 8 b, Least you might appeare to be scatterers wt heretiks, rather than gatherers together with Christ. 1616 T. Scot *Philomythie* i. (ed. 2) F 2, There beire be not a scatter-good, the third is commonly a lose-all. [*sic*] There be few scraping fathers, but their children prooue witty scatterers, or foolish retainers. 1738 Wesley *Hymns*, '*The Sun of Righteousness appears*' i, Adore the Scatterer of your Fears, Your Rising Sun adore! 1872 Spurgeon *Treas. Dav.* Ps. lix. 11 He who is the shield of his people is the scatterer of their enemies.

Scattergood (skæ·təɹgud). [f. Scatter *v.* + Good *sb.* (sense 7).] One who dissipates or squanders goods or possessions; a spendthrift.

1577 Kendall *Flowers of Epigr.* 56 A mery iest of a scattergood. 1659 W. Brough *Sacr. Princ.* 220 If the first heire be not a scatter-good, the third is commonly a lose-all. 1818 Scott *Br. Lamm.* v, That young scattergood, the Laird of Bucklaw. 1884 Blackmore *Tommy Upmore* II. 178 You have heard what careless scattergoods all honest sailors are.

Sca·tter-gun. *U.S. colloq.* [f. Scatter *v.* + Gun *sb.*] A shot-gun.

187. G. H. Kingsley *Sport & Travel* v. (1900) 142, I take up my scattergun and wander away. 1891 C. Roberts *Adrift Amer.* 237 A 'double-pronged scatter gun'.

Scatterheaded, *a. rare*—1. = Scatter-brained.

1867 E. FitzGerald *Lett.* (1889) I. 308 A scatterheaded Paddy like myself.

Scattering (skæ·təriŋ), *vbl. sb.* [-ing 1.]

1. The action of the verb Scatter, in various senses; also, an instance of this.

1382 Wyclif *Jas.* i. 1 James..to the twelue kynredis, that ben in scateringe abrood, helthe. a1425 *Cursor M.* 15541 (Trin.) Þis nyʒt shal ben a scateryng [*v.rr.* sculd, skaile, parting] bitwene ʒou and me. 1545 Joye *Exp. Dan.* xii. 121 There muste nedis folowe..skaterings and dissipacions of nacions. 1588 Sir J. Hawkins in *Defeat Sp. Armada* (Navy Rec. Soc.) I. 359 By the occasion of the scattering [*MS.* schateringe] of one of the great ships from the fleet. 1662 Stillingfl. *Orig. Sacræ* iii. i. § 1 By reason of the promiscuous scatterings of good and evil in this life. 1866 B. Stewart *Heat* § 189 (1876) 186 As in the case of light.., so also with regard to heat there is a diffuse reflection or scattering about of the rays.

attrib. 1833 Herschel *Astron.* § 45 (1839) 33 Were it not for the reflective and scattering power of the atmosphere, no objects would be visible to us out of direct sunshine... This scattering action of the atmosphere [etc.].

2. *concr.* That which is scattered.

a1340 Hampole *Psalter* cxlvi. 2 *Dispersiones israelis congregabit*...þe scatiryngis of israel he sall gadire. 1546 *Supplic. of Poore Commons* (E.E.T.S.) 71 They..must leue the latward fruit, with the scateryng of theyr corne, for the poor to gather. a1662 Heylin *Laud* i. (1671) 156 Which alone will be able to bind up the scatterings of divided affections into strength. 1692 South 12 *Serm.* (1697) II. 155 The former Instances of Temporal Prosperity, which are but (as it were) the promiscuous Scatterings of his Common Providence. 1747 W. Gould *Ants* 36 A white Substance, not altogether unlike the Scatterings of fine Sugar. 1908 *Betw. Trent & Axeholme* 107 On the grass.. lies a thick scattering of petals.

b. A sparse number or amount; a small proportion (of persons) interspersed.

1628 Earle *Microcosm.* xxxii. G, He has his sentences for Company, some scatterings of Seneca and Tacitus. 1690 C. Nesse *Hist. O. & N. T.* I. 180 The gentile world wherein God had some scatterings of holy ones. 1896 *Strand Mag.* XII. 348/1 There is a scattering of Europeans among the divers.

Scattering (skæ·təriŋ), *ppl. a.* [f. Scatter *v.* + -ing 2.]

1. In intransitive senses. **a.** That disperses in all directions; hence vagrant, roving, stray. †Of action: Erratic.

c1450 *Brut* i. 191 Thus staterand [*Tread* scaterand] Scottes, holde y for sottes, of wrecches vnwar. [Cf. Skiterende Scottes *v.r.* c1330 in Langtoft *Chron.* (Rolls) II. 252.] 1555 Eden *Decades* (Arb.) 121 The naked seely sowles were slayne for the most parte lyke scateryng sheepe. 1604 Shaks. *Oth.* iii. iii. 151 Nor build your selfe a trouble Out of his scattering, and vnsure obseruance. 1691 Ray *Creation* i. (1692) 36 The scattering Spirits remaining in the Heart may for a time being agitated by heat, cause these faint Pulsations. 1718 Rowe tr. *Lucan* iv. 190 The scatt'ring clouds disclos'd the piercing light. 1724 De Foe *Mem. Cavalier* (1840) 122 They sent about twenty scattering troopers.

b. Lying scattered or spread out over a comparatively wide area; occurring sparsely or irregularly; sporadic; of a composite thing, having its parts so spread out; straggling. Now chiefly *U.S.*

Of votes (*U.S.*): Miscellaneous, cast for candidates whose poll is too small to call for separate enumeration.

1610 Holland *Camden's Brit.* i. 439 A small village it is in these daies, inhabited in scattering wise. 1642 Fuller *Holy & Prof. St.* v. xiv. 414 Then first he sells..some stragling mannour..as counting the gathering of such scattering rents rather burdensome then profitable. 1677 Hubbard *Indian Wars* (1865) II. 256 Many of these scattering Plantations in our Borders..were contented to live without..Yoake of Government. 1697 Dryden *Virg. Georg.* iv. 192 Yet, lab'ring well his little Spot of Ground, Some scatt'ring Potherbs here and there he found. 1709 Strype *Ann. Ref.* xxxii. 325 Now to gather up a few more scattering passages that happened this year. c1710 Celia Fiennes *Diary* (1888) 164 They being scattering houses, here one, there another. 1828–32 Webster, *Scattering*, not united; divided among many; as, scattering votes. 1856 Olmsted *Slave States* 642 Washington is a mean, scattering village. 1875 Whitney *Life Lang.* xiii. 266 When the Etruscans were Latinized, but for the scattering words which they had written down, their speech passed out of all reach of knowledge. 1879 A. Johnston *Hist. Amer. Politics* (1884) 221 The Electoral votes..were found to be, for President, Grant, 286, T. A. Hendricks, of Indiana, 42, and 21 scattering. 1888 *Amer. Jrnl. Psychol.* I. 408 Letters appearing in the record less frequently than five per cent of these numbers have been regarded as scattering errors.

c. That scatters or falls here and there.

1761 Wesley *Jrnl.* 20 June (1827) III. 61 We had only some scattering drops [of rain]. 1794 Nelson 21 Jan. in Nicolas *Disp.* (1845) I. 364 They only got a few scattering shot at us.

2. That causes dispersion.

1808 Herschel *Col. Rings* in *Phil. Trans.* XCIX. 280 A scattering glass applied to the incident ray, had no other effect than to diminish the brightness of the [prismatic] bow.

Hence † **Sca·tteringness.** *Obs. rare*—1.

1747 in *Col. Rec. Pennsylv.* V. 102 The scatteringness of the Settlements..must ever render them liable to Depredations.

Scatteringly (skæ·təriŋli), *adv.* [f. Scattering *ppl. a.* + -ly 2.] In a scattering manner; so as to disperse in all directions; not compactly and in a body; irregularly; intermittently.

1570 Foxe *A. & M.* (ed. 2) 250/1, I thought here good to packe them all in one general heape together, as I finde them in Malmesbery, and in other sondry autors scateryngly recited. 1597 Gerarde *Herbal* i. ci. 163 The Humble Bee Orchis hath..leaues, which growe scatteringly about the stalke. 1652 Heylyn *Cosmogr.* iv. 127 The Houses scatteringly built amongst Hills and Gardens. c1680 Sir T. Browne *Tracts* 126 Some [Gradual Verses] are scatteringly to be found in Homer. 1746 S. Simpson *Agreeable Historian* I. 300 This town..consists of one Street, lying scatteringly almost a Mile in Length. 1880 W. G. T. Shedd *Homiletics* v. 118 Too many sermons are composed scatteringly all along through the week.

Scatterling (skæ·təɹliŋ). [f. Scatter *v.* + -ling 1.] A wandering or vagabond person; a vagrant. Also *transf.* Now *arch.*

1590 Spenser *F. Q.* ii. x. 63 Yet oft annoyd with sondry bordragings Of neighbour Scots, and forrein Scatterlings. 1611 Speed *Hist. Gt. Brit.* ix. ix. § 8. 510/2 But God was no better pleased with these, then with the other scatterlings at Lincolne. 1824 *Blackw. Mag.* XVI. 517 From mossy hillock, and tremulous stalk, We gather'd the lovely scatterlings.

attrib. 1880 Blackmore *Mary Anerley* II. iv. 62 The four ..had nothing to do with, and little to say to, any of the scatterling folk about them.

Scattermouch (skæ·təɹmautʃ). [Alteration of Scaramouch after Scatter *v.*] (See quot. 1892 and cf. Scaramouch 2.)

1892 Stevenson & L. Osbourne *Wrecker* 194 *note*, In sea lingo (Pacific) Dutchman includes all Teutons and folk from the basin of the Baltic; Scattermouch, all Latins and Levantines. 1894 Crockett *Raiders* (ed. 3) 360 Scattermouches and ruffians from the four seas.

Scattery (skæ·təri), *a.* [f. Scatter *v.* + -y.] Characterized by scattering; scattered; sparse; straggling.

1816 L. Hunt *Rimini* i. 4 And the far ships, lifting their sails of white Like joyful hands, come up with scattery light,..true to the wished-for day. 1847 Ld. Jeffrey *Let.* 20 Apr. in Ld. Cockburn *Life* (1852) II. 413 The village is very small and scattery, and all mixed up with trees. 1877 Blackmore *Erema* xvi. (1880) 96 Not to benefit the world in general, in a large and scattery way—but to right the wrong of my own house.

†Scatu·riency. *Obs. rare*—1. [f. next: see -ency.] The condition of being scaturient.

1667 H. More *Div. Dial.* iii. xlv. (1713) 544 Is it so difficult to determine, whether is more expedient,..Fruitfulness or Sterility, or if you had rather, Aridity or Scaturiency?

Scaturient (skătiū·riĕnt), *a.* [ad. L. *scatūrient-em*, pr. pple. of *scatūrīre*, f. *scatēre* to flow out.] That flows out or gushes forth.

1684 tr. *Bonet's Merc. Compit.* vi. 221 The glandulous substance of the Paps is a little contracted, so that they do not so readily receive the milky humour, that way scaturient. 1805 *Edin. Rev.* VII. 214 He wielded..a pen so scaturient and unretentive, that..he himself must have been often astonished..at the extent of his lucubrations. 1831 Lamb *Elia* Ser. ii. *Newspapers 35 yrs. ago*, We well remember.. sallying forth..to trace the current of the New River..to its scaturient source. a1876 M. Collins *Pen Sketches* (1879) I. 150 The drip and tinkle of its scaturient waters.

†Scaturi·ginous, *a. Obs. rare.* [f. L. *scatūrīgin-ōsus*, f. *scatūrīginēs* pl. gushing waters, f. *scatūrīre*: see Scaturient and -ous.] Full of or abounding in springs. In quots. *fig.*

1656 Blount *Glossogr.*, *Scaturiginous*,..that bursts out, or runs over, out of which water riseth. 1708 *Brit. Apollo* No. 36. 2/1 Our Querist..has exhausted his Scaturiginous Brains, to explore Epithets. 1709 *Ibid.* II. No. 64. 2/2 Thou..from whose Scaturiginous Inventive Faculty, such a Multiplicity of Horisonant Phrases arise.

Scaubard, -art, -erc, etc., obs. ff. Scabbard *sb.*1

Scaud, variant form of Scald *a.*1 and *v.*

Scauff, obs. Sc. form of Scaff *sb.*

Scaul, obs. f. Scall *sb.* and Sc. f. Scold.

Scaulde, var. f. Scald *a.*1; obs. f. Scald *v.*

Scaum (skǭm), *sb. Sc.* and *dial.* Also **scam, scame, skaum**. [Belongs to Scaum *v.*]

1. A burn or scorch; 'the act of singeing clothes by putting them too near the fire, or by means of a hot iron' (Jam.); also, a mark of burning.

1813 Picken *Poems* I. 132 (Jam.) But ay whan Satan blaws the coal, I find it's best the scaum to thole. 1874 G. Macdonald *Malcolm* II. xix. 260 To hide a scaum she had taen for a' her pride.

2. A thin haze or mist; a light, misty vapour.

1824 Mactaggart *Gallovid. Encycl.* 421 There is red scaum, white scaum, and many others. By the colour or hue of the scaum do Watherwiseakers guess about coming weather. 1825 Jamieson, *Scaum o' the sky*. 1877 J. Veitch *Hist. & Poet. Sc. Border* xii. 426 A wide-spreading web of greyish cloud, the skaum of the sky.

Scaum (skǭm), *v. Sc.* and *dial.* Also **scam(e, skaum**. [Of obscure origin.]

1. *trans.* To burn slightly, scorch, char. Also, 'to bespatter' (Brockett *N. C. Gloss.*, ed. 2, 1829).

a1670 Spalding *Troub. Chas. I* (Bannatyne Club) II. 247 Ane fyrie cros of tymber, quhairof everie point of the cros was scamit and brynt with fyre. 1808 Jamieson *App.*, *To Scam*, to scorch. 1825 — *To Scaum, Scame*, v.a. to burn slightly; to singe. 1841 W. Aitken *Poet. Wks.* 53 Some had their claes tied in a clout To keep them frae be'n scaumed. 1882 *Pall Mall G.* 26 July 4/2 Then comes a bitter March wind, with snow and sleet, which 'scam' the soft plants, and leave them withered as if they had been touched by fire.

2. 'To envelope in a mist or haze, to shade' (E.D.D.).

1871 P. H. Waddell *Ps.* lxxx. 10 The heights they were scaumed wi' her shadow.

Scaumpioun, obs. form of Champion.

†Scaunt, *a. Obs. rare*—1. [Aphetic form for *ascaunt*. See Askant *adv.*] Oblique.

1741 *Betterton's Eng. Stage* v. 66 The Contraction of the Lips and the Scaunt Look of the Eyes, expresses the Gesture of a deriding and malicious Person.

Scaup (skǭp). Short for Scaup-duck. Also *Comb.* *scaup-pochard* (rare) = scaup-duck.

1797 Latham in *Trans. Linnean Soc.* IV. 116 The trachea of the Pochard, at first sight, seems to be similar to that of the Scaup. 1824 J. F. Stephens in Shaw's *Gen. Zool.* XII. ii. 198 Scaup pochard (*Fuligula Marila*). *Ibid.* 200 The Scaup..inhabits Iceland, and the more northern parts of the continents of Europe and America. 1905 *Blackw. Mag.* June 768/2 A small party of scaup..next came into focus.

Scaup, variant form of Scalp *sb.*1 and *sb.*2

Scaup-duck (skǭ·p,dɒk). [?f. *scaup* Scalp *sb.*2: see quot. a1672.

The Icel. *skálphœna* (*hœna* = hen), occurring once as the nickname of a man, is prob. unconnected.]

A duck of the genus *Fuligula*, esp. *Fuligula marila*, inhabiting the seas of northern Europe, Asia, and America.

a1672 Willughby & Ray *Ornith.* iii. (1676) 279 Avis hæc *the Scaup-duck* dicta est, quoniam scalpam i.e. pisces testaceos fractos seu contritos esitat. 1785 Pennant *Arctic Zool.* II. 565 Scaup Duck. 1797 *Encycl. Brit.* (ed. 3) I. 661/1 The maula, or scaup-duck, is less than the common duck. 1886 Newton *ibid.* (ed. 9) XXI. 378/2 The female Scaup-Duck can be readily distinguished from the Dunbird or female Pochard by her broad white face.

Scauper, variant form of Scalper 1.

Scaur (skǭɹ). Chiefly *Sc.* [dial. var. of Scar *sb.*1] A precipitous bank; a cliff; the ridge of a hill.

1805 Scott *Last Minstr.* i. xii, Is it the roar of Teviot's tide, That chafes against the scaur's red side? 1834 H. Miller *Scenes & Leg.* iv. (1857) 45 Its place on the rock has ever since remained as undistinguishable as the scaurs and cliffs around it. 1859 Tennyson *Elaine* 54 Down the shingly scaur he plunged. 1871 M. Collins *Marq. & Merch.* II. i. 6 Hesper shone Like a beacon over the mountain scaurs. 1883 Stevenson *Silverado Sq.* 243 Dwarf pines..grew thinly among loose stone and gravel scaurs. 1897 Kipling *Capt. Cour.* ix. 193 Scaur and ravine changed and rolled back to jagged mountains.

Scaur, var. Scar *a.*; obs. Sc. f. Scare *v.*

Scaurie (skǭ·ri). *Orkney* and *Shetland*. Also **scorey, scourie, scowry, skoray, scorie, sko(r)rie, skory**. [Scandinavian: cf. Norw. *skaare* (Aasen), ON. *skáre*.] The young of any kind of gull.

1805 G. Barry *Orkney Isl.* 303 The Brown and White Gull..which the people here call the scorey, is much more rarely met with than most others. 1806 P. Neill *Tour Orkney & Shetland* 25 The Brough..is the resort and nursery of hundreds of scauries, or herring-gulls (*larus fuscus*). I believe the Orkney name scaurie is applied to this gull only while it is young and speckled; and it loses its speckled appearance after the first year. 1821 Scott *Pirate* v, For your harvest on the crag, I suppose you mean these scowries, or whatever you call them. 1844 W. H. Maxwell *Sports & Adv. Scot.* xxxviii. (1855) 300 A skoray, or young kittiwake. 1899 J. Spence *Shetland Folk-Lore* 14 The plee o' the skorie, the birr o' the snipe.

†Scaut, *v. Obs.*—0 [Origin obscure; connexion with mod. dial. *scaut*, to push with the feet, is unlikely.] *intr.* ?To dart. Hence **Scautand** *ppl. a.*

a1400–50 *Alexander* 4200 Þire Cocatricesse in creuessis þar kindiles þai brede, Scorpions many score scautand neddirs.

Scavage (skæ·vedʒ), *sb.* Also 5 **scawage**, 6 **skawage, skavag(e**, 7 **scavadge**. [a. AF. *scawage*, *schawage* (*Rolls of Parlt.* an. 1402), = North-Eastern OF. *escauwage*, f. *escauwer* to inspect, ad. Flemish *scauwen* = OE. *scéawian* Show *v.*

The OE. synonym was *scéawung* (see Showing *vbl. sb.*), the ME. form of which was adopted into AF. as *scewynge* (1419 in *Liber Albus* 223). In the 15th c. lawyers were aware of the etymological meaning, and invented the word Shewage as an explanatory synonym.]

1. A toll formerly levied by the mayor, sheriff, or corporation of London and other towns on merchant strangers, on goods offered for sale within their precincts. The toll was prohibited by Act 19 Hen. VII, c. 8. Also *attrib. Obs.* exc. *Hist.*

1474 Caxton *Chesse* iii. vii. (1481) h vij b, And by the purse been signefyed them that receyue the costumes, tolles, scawage, peages and duetees of the cytees and townes. a1500 Arnolde *Chron.* (1811) p. xiv, The marchaundyses wherof skauage ought to be taken in London, and how meche. 1502 in I. S. Leadam *Star Chamber Cases* (1903) 90 He was Skavage gatherer in London, both to the maire and Shreves there. *Ibid.* 92 There was skavage askyd by oone James skavage gatherer then of oone Skrevener Freman of Excestre for cloth bi him brought to London by water, and he refusid to pay it. a1513 Fabyan *Chron.* vii. 338 This yere [1252] the cytezyns [of London] had graunted of ye Kyng, yt no cytezyns shulde paye scauage or tolle for any bestis by them brought, as they before tymes had vsed. 1530–1 *Act 22 Hen. VIII*, c. 8 § 4 The tables so to be sette upp in the Cytie of London touchynge Scavage. 1583 *Rates Custom ho.* g iij, *heading*, Scauadge. 1641 W. Hakewill *Libertie of Subject* 123 There are other duties then Customes and Subsidies due upon the landing of wares; for example Wharfage, Cranage, Scavage and such like. 1676 Molloy *De Jure Marit.* ii. xiv. (1688) 325 Scavage is an ancient Toll or Custom exacted by Mayors, Sheriffs, &c. of Merchant-Strangers for Wares shewed or offered to sale within their Precincts. 1800 Colquhoun *Comm. Thames* xi. 332 Of Scavage (i.e. Shewage or Surveying) of certain Goods imported by Foreign Merchants.

†2. The fulfilment of the duties of a scavager.

1547 in E. B. Jupp *Carpenters' Co.* (1887) 386 Item payd to the skavynger for hys hole yeres skavag,..ijs.

†3. Refuse, etc. scavenged from the roads. *Obs.*

1706 in J. E. Cox *Ann. St. Helen's Bishopsgate* vii. (1876) 127 Mr. Chewter had leave to sink a place for laying in of dung or scavage.

Sca·vage, *v. rare.* [Back-formation from Scavager.] *trans.* = Scavenge *v.* Also *intr.* for *refl.* (*fig.*). Hence **Sca·vaging** *vbl. sb.*

1851 Mayhew *Lond. Labour* II. 222/1 The scavaging work, moreover, was 'scamped'. *Ibid.* 252/2 The depreciation of wages in the scavaging trade. *Ibid.* 259 The street-orderly system of scavaging the metropolitan thoroughfares. 1852 *Meanderings of Mem.* I. 56 The brain will scavage and the breast unstuff.

Sca·vager. Also **skavager**. [a. AF. *scawager*, f. *scawage* Scavage *sb.*: see -er 2.

1307 in R. R. Sharpe *Cal. Lett. Bk. C. City of London* (1901) 151 *note*, Pro curia de scawageriis. 1419 *Liber Albus* (Rolls) 333 Lez scawageours averont iiii deniers pur chescun tile nusance issint remoez ou debrusez.]

†1. An officer whose duty it was to take 'scavage', and who was afterwards also charged with the duty of keeping the streets clean. *Obs.*

1477–9 *Rec. St. Mary at Hill* (1905) 89 Item, paid to the Skauagers for the pament endited. viij d. 1536 *City of Lond. Rep.* ix. 183 b, in *Vicary's Anat.* (1888) App. iii. 171 Item, for by cawse compleynt was made by one of ye scavagers of ye Warde of Faryngdon, for kepyng of the stretes there vnclene. 1835 *App. Munic. Corpor. Rep.* ii. 845 Searchers for unwholesome Meat. Scavager to gather the Money. Gaoler.

2. Used for Scavenger 2. *rare.*

1851 Mayhew *Lond. Labour* II. 218 The nominal wages of the scavagers. *Ibid.* 221, 252.

Sca·vagery. *rare*—1. [f. Scavage *sb.* + -ery.] = Scavengery.

1851 Mayhew *Lond. Labour* II. 217/2 In scavagery, the average hours of daily work are twelve. *Ibid.* 259/2 When the sages of the city sewers did not consider any proposed improvement in scavagery worthy their attention.

Sçavan(t: see Savant.

Scavel (skæ·vĕl). *dial.* Also 5, 7 **scavell**, 6–7 **skavell**, 6 **skavel**, 7 ?**skeval**, 9 **skafell, skaffel, scaffle**. [?f. ON. *skafa* to scrape, Shave *v.*] A small spade (see quot. 1823).

c1440 *Jacob's Well* xxvii. 178 Now schal I telle ʒou, how ʒe schal caste out þe hard wose of ʒoure synne..wyth a scauel of confessioun. *Ibid.* 179 A scauel, in þe heued beforn, hath a scho of yren, scharp & myʒti, & an heued, hole & narow, & a long stele, an handyll. 1559 in Boys *Sandwich* (1792) 737 One workeman with a spade or skavell may digg in one howre C. foote. 1573 Tusser *Husb.* (1878) 38 With skuppat and skauel, that marsh men alow. c1613 Spelman *Relat. Virginea* 47 They digg many holes which before the English brought them scauels and spades they used to make with a crooked peece of woode. 1823 Moor *Suffolk Wds.* 352 *Skaffel*, a small spade or skuppet used in draining... It differs from a spade in not tapering toward the edge, and in having its sides slightly turned up.

b. *attrib.*, as *scavel work*; **scavel-man, scavel spitter** (see quots.).

1581 in C. Welch *Tower Bridge* (1894) 103 [A number of] showtmen, now called *scavelmen. 1584 *Faversham Parish Reg.* (MS.), John Price a scauelman or dicker. 1587 Fleming *Contn. Holinshed* III. 1544/2 A great manie marshmen were assigned to laie the fleech vpon the sides of the wals, and were called scauelmen. 1803 *Naval Chron.* XV. 58 The scavelmen are a description of labourers..who attend to clean and pump the docks, and in general assist the shipwrights. 1750 Blanckley *Nav. Expositor*, *Scavel Spitters, are a small Spade, only shod half way, and are used for digging Clay. 1642 *Burghmote Book B, Canterb.* (MS.), Which persons are appointed for the *Scavell work and are disired to digge Turf and earth for the fortification.

Scavenage (skæ·vĕnēdʒ). [Irreg. f. Scaven(ge) + -age.] The action or work of scavenging.

1878 *Lancet* 12 Jan. 64 The system of scavenage for the borough. 1885 *Scientific American* 9 May, The Jewish priests maintained a system of scavenage, themselves supervised the cleansing of cities and habitations.

Scavenge (skæ·vĕndʒ), *v.* [Back-formation from Scavenger.]

1. *trans.* To clean *out* (dirt, etc.).

a1644 Quarles *Sheph. Orac.* ii. (1646) 22 Should I but name The Tithe of that base dunghill trash, brought in By your Dominicans, scaveng'd out agin By worse Franciscans.

2. To scrape dirt from (the streets); also, to cleanse (the surface of a river).

1851 Mayhew *Lond. Labour* II. 197/2 In wet weather there is at least twenty times more 'mac' than dung scavenged. 1866 *Act* 28 & 30 *Vict.* c. 89 § 52 The Conservators shall cause the Surface of the Thames to be effectually scavenged, in order to the Removal therefrom of Substances liable to Putrefaction.

transf. 1858 Kingsley *Misc., Chalk-Stream* I. 182 They are Vorticellæ; and every one of those bells, by the ciliary current on its rim, is scavenging the water—till a tadpole comes by and scavenges it.

3. *absol.* or *intr.*

1883 *Harper's Mag.* Mar. 528/1 We saw fleeting glimpses of working-women scavenging, hanging out clothes, huckstering. 1894 *Daily News* 26 Apr. 2/4 Mr. Milvain.. objected to the Conservancy being released..of their power to scavenge eastward.

Scavenger (skæ·vĕndʒəɹ), *sb.* Also 6 **skavinger, -ynger, scavengere**, 6–8 **scavinger**, 7 **skavenger**. [Altered form of Scavager, with intrusive *n* as in *passenger, messenger*.]

1. = Scavager 1. Now only *Hist.*

1547 [see Scavage *sb.* 2]. 1598 Stow *Surv.* 328 In Sepulchers parish common Counsaile six, Constables foure, Scauengers foure [etc.]. 1638 *Tarlton's Jests* C 1 b, When Tarlton dwelt in Gracious street..he was chosen Scauenger, and often the Ward complained of his slacknesse, in keeping the streets cleane. 1677 Thoroton *Nottinghamsh.* 492 There is an Officer of the Town called the Scavenger, that looks to the Pavement and Streets of the Town, and attends upon the Majors wife. 1695 *Lond. Gaz.* No. 3053/2 An Act for Exempting Apothecaries from Serving the Offices of Constable, Scavenger, and other Parish and Ward-Offices. 1766 Entick *London* IV. 4 The government of this ward is in one alderman,..seven scavengers, and a beadle. 1835 *App. Munic. Corpor. Rep.* i. 172 (Aberystwith), The Scavengers are appointed in the same manner. The persons usually selected for this office are the churchwardens and overseers of the poor, and they employ the paupers in sweeping the streets.

†b. As the title of an official under the East India Company. *Obs.*

1702 *MS. list* in Yule s.v., John Butt, Scavenger and Cornmeeter, Tevenapatam, Merchant. 1760 *Fort William Cons.* in Long *Sel. Rec. Gov.* (1869) 245 (Yule) Mr. Handle, applying to the Board to have his allowance of Scavenger increased..we allow him Rs. 20 per month more than before.

2. A person whose employment is to clean streets, by scraping or sweeping together and removing dirt. † Also, a person employed to keep clean a church.

1530 Palsgr. 266/1 Scavenger that clenseth stretes, *boueur*. 1563–83 Foxe *A. & M.* 19/2 And as in the other vnder wardens cometh the order of Scauingers: so neither doth the Popes Monarchy lacke his kaynilrakers. 1598 Bp. Hall *Sat.* vi. ii. 99 To see..a cloked Frere Sweating in the channell like a Scauengere. 1642 *Laws of War Army Earl Essex* 21 The rest [shall] serve for Pioners and Scavengers, till a worthy exploit take off that Blot. 1690 C. Nesse *Hist. & Myst. O. & N. Test.* I. 101 The sorry scavengers who live honestly by emptying privies. 1696 *Act* 8 & 9 *Will. III*, c. 37 § 1 To the end the Dirt and Soyl may be heaped ready for the Scavenger to carry away. 1714 Mandeville *Fab. Bees* (1733) I. p. xi, Now would I ask if a good citizen..might not assert that dirty streets are a necessary evil inseparable from the felicity of London, ..without any prejudice either to the blackguard or the scavingers. 1725–6 in J. L. Chester *Westm. Abbey Reg.* (1876) 316 John Chittham, Scavenger to this Church: in the South Cloister. 1802 Mar. Edgeworth *Moral T.* (1816) I. xvi. 136 The scavenger, with his broom..was clearing away a heap of mud. 1865 Dickens *Mut. Fr.* iv. xiv, A scavenger's cart happening to stand unattended..Mr. S. found it impossible to resist the temptation of shooting Mr. Silas Wegg into the cart's contents.

b. *transf.* One who or something which removes dirt or putrid matter. Applied to various animals that feed on decaying matter, esp. the scavenger beetle.

1596 Nashe *Saffron Walden* 1 Chiefe scauinger of chins. 1614 Markham *Cheap Husb.* i. *Swine* i. 87 The Swine..is the Husbandmans best scauenger,..for his food and liuing is by that which would else rot in the yard. 1648 Winyard *Midsummer-Moon* 4 Thus sinkes and common shoares are the best scavengers. 1719 Baynard *Health* (ed. 2) 6 And Fasting's Nature's Scavenger. 1845 Darwin *Voy. Nat.* i. (1879) 10 Numerous spiders, which I suppose prey on these small attendants and scavengers of the waterfowl. 1854 Owen in *Orr's Circ. Sci., Org. Nat.* I. 164 The sturgeons may be called the scavengers of the great rivers which they frequent. 1858 Baird *Cycl. Nat. Sci.* 48/1 The argala..is extremely useful in removing noxious animals, and devouring all sorts of carrion. It is called the scavenger in Calcutta. 1868 *Rep. U. S. Commissioner Agric.* (1869) 307 The *Silphidæ* (burying or sexton beetles, scavengers, &c.). 1899 *Allbutt's Syst. Med.* VII. 719 The spider-cells..act as phagocytes or 'scavengers', multiplying upon and removing the degenerate nerve-elements.

c. *fig.* in various uses: One who collects filth; one who does 'dirty work'; a dishonourable person. Also, in favourable sense, one who labours for the removal of public evils.

1562 Pilkington, etc. *Burnynge Paules* A vij, In like maner where thys scauenger sweping the stretes with his bookes..hais spoken the truth, not trulye..I shal passe ouer it with silence. 1582 Stanyhurst *Æneis* Ded. (Arb.) 9 Are there not diuerse skauingers of draftye poetrye in this oure age, that bast theyre papers with smearie larde [etc.]. 1598 B. Jonson *Ev. Man in Hum.* ii. ii, The gentleman-citizen hath satisfied me, Ile talk to no scauenger. 1642 Milton *Apol. Smect.* Wks. 1851 III. 265 That Suburbe sinke, as this rude Scavinger calls it,..shall be in my account a more honourable place then his University. 1767 A. Campbell *Lexiph.* (1774) Pref. 30, I am no other than a literary scavenger. 1771 *Junius Lett.* lxvii. (1788) 340 *note*, In the senate, their abilities have confined them to those humble, sordid services, in which the scavengers of the ministry are usually employed.

3. A child employed in a spinning-mill to collect loose cotton lying about the floor or machinery. Also, a roller used to collect the loose fibres or fluff; also called *scavenger-roll*.

1833 Lytton *England & Engl.* (ed. 2) I. 201 My children shall never go into a factory, more especially as scavengers and piecers. 1835 Ure *Philos. Manuf.* 289 The masters paid the spinners the full allowance of wages for these piecers and scavengers, as they are called. 1853 — *Dict. Arts* (ed. 4) II. 831 In the mules we notice a peculiar arrangement of 'scavenger' is applied. The object of this apparatus is to clear particles of waste from the top of the carriage, and the operation is effected by means of a roller.

4. *attrib.* and *Comb.*, as *scavenger duck, shovel, work*; *scavenger-like* adj. and adv.; **scavenger-cell** = Phagocyte; **scavenger-roll** (see sense 3); † **scavenger-stuff** (see quot. 1787).

1899 *Allbutt's Syst. Med.* VIII. 324 In the lowest layer *'scavenger' cells and nuclei cover the spindle cells. 1884 *Good Words* Nov. 746/2 A band of *scavenger ducks picking up the garbage. 1611 Cotgr., *Voyer*, a Surueyer..of highwayes..who..*Scauinger-like, giues order that they be made cleane. 1890 *Spectator* 28 June, When such scavenger-like work is thus forced upon a man of letters, it is [etc.]. 1611 Cotgr., *Paelle à bourbe*, a *Scauingers shouell;..such a one as durt is vsually remoued, or taken vp, with. 1787 Winter *Syst. Husb.* 332 *Scavenger stuff, is a mixture of coal ashes and street dirt. 1835 Ure *Philos. Manuf.* 312 There is so little *scavenger work required in fine spinning, on account of the small quantity of waste from the long-stapled cotton.

b. In designations of certain animals (see 2 b): **scavenger-beetle**, a necrophagous beetle, especially one of the family *Scaphidiidæ*; **scavenger-crab**, any crab which feeds on dead animal matter; **scavenger-vulture** (see quot.).

1854 A. Adams, etc. *Man. Nat. Hist.* 182 *Scavenger-Beetles (*Scaphidiidæ*). 1857 A. White *Pop. Hist. Brit. Crust.* Index, *Scavenger-crab. 1894 *19th Cent.* XXXVI. 436 Scavenger crabs line this coast in myriads. 1885 Hornaday *2 Yrs. in Jungle* vi. 61 No wonder the builder of such a nest is called the *scavenger vulture [*Neophron percnopterus*].

Sca·venger, *v. rare.* [f. Scavenger *sb.*]

1. *trans.* To remove dirt from, chiefly *fig.*; also, to make dirty with scavenging.

a1644 Quarles *New Distemper* (1645) 3 All the Romish Rubbish and Trumpery was scavengerd out of this [the new Reformed] Church. 1806–7 J. Beresford *Miseries Hum. Life* (ed. 3) ii. x, After having scavengered your hands and gloves in slaving to drag up each [shoe out of the quagmire].

2. *intr.* To work at scavenging.

1843- [implied in Scavengering *vbl. sb.*]. 1894 *Season* X. 71/3 Scavengering with bent spine in the gutter.

Scavengering (skæ·vĕndʒəriŋ), *vbl. sb.* [f. Scavenger *v.* + -ing 1.] The action or work of removing filth, etc. from the streets. Also *attrib.*

1841 *Literary Gaz.* 11 Dec. 801/3 M. de Lucy..recommended that steam should be used for melting the snow.., in order to facilitate the process of scavengering. 1843 *Penny Cycl.* XXVI. 472/2 In Cairo these vultures are.. prized for their scavengering services. 1860 *All Year Round* No. 72. 510 The..management of a barrow, as applied to scavengering, is a matter of serious moment. 1885 *Daily News* 31 Jan. 5/1 The scavengering alone costs 1,300*l.* a year.

fig. 1869 *Echo* 26 Aug. 4 It is..a sort of moral scavengering to which the Commissioners are condemned.

Scavenger's daughter. Also **Skevington's, Skeffington's daughter.** [From a jocular perversion of the name *Skevington*. See Daughter 6 c.] An instrument of torture (invented in the reign of Hen. VIII by Leonard Skevington or Skeffington, Lieutenant of the Tower), which (bringing the head to the knees) so compressed

Scavengery. The municipal or state arrangements for cleaning and removing dirt, refuse, etc.; the action of collecting and removing dirt from the streets.

Scaw (skọ), obs. form of SCALP, SKAW. [Shetland dial. repr. ON. *skaga*.]

Scaw, obs. form of SCALE.

Scaw. obs. form of SCALE.

Scawage, obs. form of SCAVAGE.

Scawbard, -art, -ert, obs. ff. SCABBARD sb.[1]

Scawbe, obs. form of SCALD sb. and a.

Scawe, Obs. rare⁻¹.

Scawed, sb. So. [Ec. prec. + -ED.] Spotted.

Scawl, Sc. form of SCALL.

Scawl, Sc. form of SCOLD.

Scawp, obs. var. of SCALP sb.[1]

Scayne, variant of SQUAMOUS, squeamish.

Scayne, variant of SKEAN, obs. form of SKEIN.

Scayse, obs. Sc. form of SCARCE adv.

Scaum (skọ̄m), Sc. sb.

Scawlerous, Obs.

Scealc, Sealt-, obs. ff. SHAMBLE sb.[1]

Scealegia (skele'ldʒiǎ), Path.

Scelerate (se'lerāt), a. and sb. Also -6-9 scelerat, 8-Sc. scelerait.

Scelerous (se'lerəs), a. Obs.

Scelestious, a. rare⁻¹.

Scelet, obs. form of SKELETON.

Scelidate (se'lidǒt), a.

Scelides (se'lidēz), sb. pl.

Scelidosaur (se'lidǒsǒr), Palæont. [ad. mod. L. *Scelidosaurus*, f. Gr. σκελίς -ίδος rib of beef + σαυρος lizard.]

Scelidosaurus (se'lidǒsǒ'rəs), Palæont.

Scelidotherium (se'lidǒþī'riəm), Palæont.

Scellum (ske'ləm), Also **scelm, skellum**. [ad. Du. *schelm*.] Also anglicized form Scallum.

Scene (sīn), sb. Also 6-7 scheme, 6 scean, 8 scen.

1. a. A scene in an Italian opera; the words and music of the scene.

2. [= F. *scène*.] The stage or theatre taken as the point of view from which the dramatic art or the histrionic profession is viewed.

3. The action or representation of a piece upon the stage; a stage-performance; a play or drama in representation.

4. The place in which the action of a play, or part of a play, is supposed to occur.

5. A subdivision of an act of a play (or of a short play which is not divided into acts).

Scenario (sčīnā'rǒ), [It., f. *scena* Scene.] A sketch or outline of the plot of a play, giving particulars of the scenes, situations, etc.

Scenary, sb. [repr. L. *scenari-* : see -ARY[1] A.]

1. 'The disposition and consecution of the scenes of a play' (J.); = SCENARIO.

2. 'The representation of the place in which an action is performed' (J.).

3. = SCENERY 3.

Scene, obs. form of SKEIN.

Scene (sīn), sb.

10. An action, episode, complication of events, or situation, in real life.

11. An exhibition of excited or strong feeling between two or more persons; a stormy encounter or interview. To make a scene, to make a disturbance, 'kick up a row'.

III. 12. A canvas for the reception of images projected from a lens. Also *scene-plate*.

IV. 13. *attrib.* and *Comb.*, as (sense 1) **scene-making**; **scene-dock** [DOCK sb.[3]], the place in which scenes are stored in a theatre; **†scene-drawer** —SCENE-SHIFTER; **†scene-keeper**, one who has charge of the scenes in a theatre; **†scene-man**, a scene-painter; one who paints the scenery for the theatre; **scene-painting**, the art of painting scenes for the theatre; **scene-perspective**, *fig.* descriptive writing in a bold and vivid style; also *attrib.*; **scene-plate** (see sense 12); **scene-plot**, the list and description of the scenes in a play; **scene-room**, a room where scenes are stored (in quot. *fig.*); **†scene-work**, dramatic representation in scenes. Also SCENE-SHIFTER.

Scene, obs. form of SEINE.

Scene-ful, a. rare⁻¹. [-FUL.] Abounding in scenes or scenery.

Scenery (sī'nəri). [Alteration of SCENARY, as if f. SCENE + -ERY. The word is not in Johnson, who gives only SCENARY.]

1. Dramatic action; a moving exhibition of feeling. Obs.

2. Represented on the stage.

3. The decoration of a theatre-stage, consisting of painted hangings, slides, etc., representing the scenes of action; theatre-scenes collectively.

4. The general appearance of a place and its natural features, regarded from the picturesque point of view; the aggregate of picturesque features in a landscape.

5. In relation to painting or sculpture: Representing a 'scene' or incident in which several persons are grouped.

Scene-shifter. One who shifts and arranges the scenes during the performance of a play.

Scenic (sī'nik, se'nik), a. Also 7 **scenick**. [a. F. *scénique* (14th c.), = It. *scenico*, ad. L. *scēnicus*, a. Gr. σκηνικός belonging to the stage, theatrical, a. σκηνή SCENE.]

1. Of or belonging to the stage, dramatic, theatrical.

Scenical (se'nikăl), a. Also 5 **scenicall**, 6-7 **scenicall**, 7 **scenicall**, 6 **sceneocal**. [f. L. *scēnic-us* + -AL[1].]

1. Of or belonging to the stage; = SCENIC a. 1.

Scene-shifter. See prec.

Scenically (sī'n-, se'nikăli), adv. [f. prec. + -LY[1].] In a scenic or theatrical manner.

Sceni-fic, a. Obs. [= SCENE + -IFIC.] Scenic.

Scenite (sī'nǒit), a. and sb. [ad. late L. *scēnīta*.]

Scenograph (sī'nǒgraf). rare⁻¹. [ad. Gr. σκηνογραφ-, as next.]

Scenographic (sī'nǒgra'fik), a. [ad. F. *scénographique* or L. *scēnographic-us*.]

Scenographical, a. = SCENOGRAPHIC.

Scenography (sčīnǒ'grăfi). [ad. L. *scēnographia*, a. Gr. σκηνογραφία.]

Scenopegia (sī'nǒpī'dʒiǎ). Also anglicized **scenopegy**. [L. *scēnopēgia*, a. Gr. σκηνοπηγία.]

Scent (sent), sb. Forms: 4-7 (9 rare) **sent**, 5-6 **cent**, 6 **cente**, 7 **sente**. [ME. *sent*, f. SCENT v.]

1. The faculty or sense of smell. Chiefly, and now exclusively, with reference to animals (esp. dogs) which find their prey or recognize objects by this sense.

2. The odour of an animal or man as a means of pursuit by a hound; hence a track or trail so indicated by this odour.

3. An odour, smell; esp. a pleasant smell or perfume; simple *attrib.*, as *scent-bottle*, *-cask*, *-casket*, *-sachet*; instrumental, as *scent-laden* adj.; also *scent-sniffing* adj.; *scent-bag* (see quot.); **scent-box**, a box in which scents are kept; **scent-bottle**, a small bottle for holding scent; a bottle of scent; spec. an ornamental bottle containing scent; also *attrib.*; etc.

Scenograph. (See above.)

Scent, *sb.* Forms: 5–7 (9 *dial.*) *sent*, 6–7 *sente*, (7 *sent*) *scent*, 7 *scent*. [f. *sentir* to feel, perceive, spec. to smell : — Pr., Sp., Pg. *sentir*, It. *sentire* : — L. *sentīre* to feel, perceive.]

I. 1. *trans.* Of a hound or other animal : To follow or track (game, prey, etc.) by the smell; also, to *scent out.*

2. *intr.* Of a hound or other animal : †a. To perceive the smell of (a quarry). Obs. b. To hunt by the sense of smell; also, to 'smell about', sniff the air for a scent.

3. To exhale an odour, to smell. So F. *sentir*. Now *rare* or Obs.

Scented, *ppl. a.* [f. SCENT *v.* and *sb.*]

Scenter (se'ntər). [f. SCENT *v.* + -ER¹.] One that or which scents, in the senses of the vb.

Scentful (se'ntful), *a.* [f. SCENT *sb.* + -FUL.]

Scenting, *vbl. sb.* [f. SCENT *v.* + -ING¹.]

Scenting, *ppl. a.* [f. SCENT *v.* + -ING².]

Scentless (se'ntles), *a.* [f. SCENT *sb.* + -LESS.]

Scepsis (ske'psis), *sb.* [Gr. σκέψις inquiry, hesitation, doubt, f. σκέπ-τεσθαι: see SCEPTIC.]

Sceptic, sceptic (ske'ptik), *a.* and *sb.* [ad. F. *sceptique* adj. and sb., or its source late L. *scepticus*, Gr. σκεπτικός.]

Sceptical, skeptical (ske'ptikăl), *a.* [f. SCEPTIC + -AL¹.] In a sceptical manner; like a sceptic.

Sceptically, skeptically, *adv.* [f. prec. + -LY².]

Scepticalness, skepticalness. Obs. *rare*. [f. SCEPTICAL + -NESS.]

Scepticism, skepticism (ske'ptisiz'm). [ad. mod.L. *scepticismus*, f. late L. *scepticus*: see SCEPTIC and -ISM. Cf. F. *scepticisme*.]

Scepticity (skeptis'iti), *sb.* rare⁻¹. [f. SCEPTIC + -ITY.] The quality of being sceptical.

Scepticize (ske'ptisəiz), *v.* [f. SCEPTIC + -IZE.]

Sceptre (se'ptər), *sb.* Forms: 3–6 ceptre, ceptur, 5 septur, 5–6 septre, sceptur, 5–7 septer, 4–6 ceptir, 4–7 sceptre, 5 scepture, 5 sceptour, 6 sceptyr, 7 sceptar, 6 sceptre. [ME. *ceptre, septre,* a. OF. *sceptre, ceptre* (mod.F. *sceptre* = Sp. *cetro,* It. *scettro,* etc.), ad. L. *scēptrum,* a. Gr. σκῆπτρον staff, sceptre, f. σκήπτειν to prop oneself, lean on something.]

Sceptred (se'ptərd), *ppl. a.* [f. SCEPTRE *sb.* + -ED².] Bearing a sceptre; invested with regal authority.

Sceptreless, *a.* rare. [f. SCEPTRE *sb.* + -LESS.]

Sceptry, *a.* [? Contracted f. *sceptred*.]

Scerne, *v.* Obs. *rare⁻¹.* [Aphetic for DISCERN *v.*]

Scevity, var. SCEVITY. **Scew**, obs. f. SKEW.

Sch. This sequence of letters corresponds in present or past English spelling to the various sounds or combinations of sound *ʃ, tʃ, sk, s, sʃ.*

Schediasm (ske'diazm). [ad. Gr. σχεδίασμα, f. σχεδιάζειν to extemporize, f. σχέδιος offhand.]

Schediastic, *a.* Obs. rare⁻¹. [ad. Gr. σχεδιαστικ-ός.]

Schedium (skī'diəm), *sb.* Obs. rare⁻¹. [ad. L. *schedium*, Gr. σχέδιον.]

Schedula (ske'diulă). [mod.L.]

Schedule (ʃe'diul, U.S. ske'diul), *sb.* Forms: 5–6 cedule, scedule, 6–7 schedule, 6–7 cedull, 7 chedull.

Schedule, *v.* [f. prec.]

Schedulize (ske'diuləiz), *v.* [f. SCHEDULE + -IZE.] To make schedules.

Scheel see SHEAL.

Scheelin see SHILLING.

Scheelite (ʃī'ləit). *Min.* [Named after K. W. *Scheele*, discoverer of tungstic acid + -ITE.]

Scheelitine (ʃī'litin). *Min.* Also scheeletine.

Scheererite (ʃī'rərəit). *Min.* [Named after H. T. *Scheerer*, a Swedish chemist + -ITE.]

Schelchenes, *sb. pl.* Obs. *rare.* Also 3 -ine. [OE.]

Scheldrake, obs. f. SHELDRAKE.

Schelling (ʃe'liŋ, Du. xe'liŋ). *Obs. exc.* Hist. [Du. *schelling,* schilling, skilling.]

Schelm (ʃelm). *arch.* Also 6–7 shelm.

Schelochi, *sb.*

Schema (skī'mă). Pl. **schemata** (skī'mătă), -s. [mod.L., a. Gr. σχῆμα.]

Schematic (skīmæ'tik), *a.* [ad. Gr. σχηματικός.]

Schematical (skīmæ'tikăl), *a.* Obs. [formed as prec.]

Schematically, *adv.* [f. prec. + -LY².]

Schematism (ske'mătiz'm). [ad. Gr. σχηματισμός.]

Schematist (skī'mătist). [f. SCHEMA + -IST.]

Schematize (skī'mătəiz), *v.* [ad. Gr. σχηματίζειν.]

Schematology (skīmătɒ'lŏdʒi). *rare.* [f. Gr. σχῆμα + -LOGY.]

Schematomancy, *rare.* [f. Gr. σχῆμα + -MANCY.]

Scheme (skīm), *sb.¹* Forms: 7 sceme, sceame, 7– scheme. [ad. L. *schēma*.]

[The following is a best-effort reading of the principal headwords and entries on this densely-printed Oxford English Dictionary page; much of the microscopic quotation text is not legible at this resolution.]

†3. In wider sense: A diagram; a figure drawn to illustrate a mathematical proposition, or to elucidate descriptions of natural phenomena, machinery, etc.; a map or plan of a town; an architect's designs for a building; and the like. *Obs.*

†b. A plan, design; a programme of action; a preconceived design or plan of an undertaking or a literary work, etc. Phrases, *to † cast, lay a scheme.*

Schemeless (skī′mlĕs), *a.* [f. SCHEME + -LESS.] Destitute of plan; lacking a plot.

Schemer (skī′məɹ), *sb.* [f. SCHEME v. + -ER¹.] 1. One who devises or enters into schemes.

Schemery (skī′məɹi), *sb.* [f. SCHEME v. + -ERY.] Scheming practices.

Scheming (skī′miŋ), *vbl. sb.* [f. SCHEME v. + -ING¹.] The action of the vb. SCHEME; planning, contrivance.

Scheming (skī′miŋ), *ppl. a.* [f. SCHEME v. + -ING².] That schemes; contriving, plotting.

Schemist (skī′mĭst), *sb.* [f. SCHEME sb. + -IST.] 1. A framer of 'schemes' or horoscopes; an astrologer. **†2.** One who is concerned with intrigues; a plotter.

Schene, obs. form of CHAIN, SCENE.

Schenick, Schenp, obs. forms of SCHENE, CHEAP.

†Schepen (skī′pən, in Du. ʃχē′pən), *sb.* [Du.] An alderman or municipal magistrate.

†Schethe. *Obs.* [f. SCHEME sb.² + -ED².]

Schemed, *a. Obs.* [f. SCHEME sb.² + -ED².]

†Scherand. *Sc. Obs.* [Origin obscure.]

†Scherand, var. of ESCHEW v.

Scherm (ʃɛrm). *South Africa.* Also skarm, skerm, schirm. [f. Du. schirm screen.] A screen or barrier constructed of brushwood or the like, to serve as a protection for troops, as an ambuscade from which to shoot game, or to prevent cattle from straying.

Scherzando (skertsɑ′ndō), *adv.* [It.] *Mus.* Playfully, sportively; used to indicate that a movement or passage is to be rendered in a lively manner.

Scherzo (skɛ′rtso). *Mus.* [It., lit. sport, jest; of Teut. origin: cf. MHG., mod.G. *scherz* sport.] A movement of a lively character, occupying the second or third place in a symphony or sonata.

Scheveel. *Obs.*

Schiavone (skjɑvō′nā). [It.]

Schiedam (skī′dam). Also schiedamm, skī′dam. A variety of gin, so called from the town in Holland where it is distilled.

Schiller (ʃi′ləɹ). *Min.* [Ger., play of colours, glistening brightness.]

Schillerize (ʃi′ləɹaɪz), *v.* [f. SCHILLER + -IZE.]

Schillerization (ʃiləɹaɪzē′ʃən). [f. SCHILLER + -IZATION.]

Schilling (ʃi′liŋ). Also schelling. [Ger.] See SHILLING.

Schimmel (ʃi′məl). A grey or roan horse.

Schindylesis (skindilī′sis). *Anat.* [mod.L., a. Gr. σχινδύλησις.] An articulation formed by the reception of a thin plate of one bone into a fissure or groove in another.

Schine. *Obs. rare* ⁻¹. [ad. L. *Vulgate schinus*, a Gr. σχῖνος the mastic-tree.]

Schinkel, Schinkle. *Obs. rare* ⁻¹. [Du. *schinkel* knuckle.]

Schip, obs. form of SHIP, SHEEP.

Schipperke (ʃi′pərkē). [Du. dial., lit. 'little boatman'.] A kind of lapdog.

Schir, obs. form of SHEER, SIR.

†Schiras. [ad. Shiraz in Persia.]

Schirme, Schirmschule, Schirra, etc., see SCIRRHUS, SHERIFF, etc.

Schism (si′z'm). *sb.* Forms: 4–7 scisme, cisme, 4–6 sisme, cysme, scysme, etc. [ad. L. *schisma*, a. Gr. σχίσμα cleft, division.]

Schisma (ski′zmɑ). *Pl. schismata.* Also σχίσμα. [Boethius, quoting Philolaus, special use of Gr. σχίσμα division: see SCHISM.]

†Schism, *v. Obs. rare*. [f. SCHISM sb.]

†Schismal. *Obs. rare* ⁻¹. [f. SCHISM sb. + -AL.]

Schismarch (si′zmɑːk). [ad. med.L. *schismarcha*, f. *schisma* SCHISM + -arch.]

†Schismate. *Obs. rare* ⁻¹.

Schismatic (sizmæ′tik), *a.* and *sb.* Forms: 4–6 scismatike, cismatik, cysmatyk, 6–7 schismatic, 7– schismatick. [a. OF. *cismatique, scismatique* (mod.F. *schismatique*), ad. L. *schismaticus*, a. Gr. σχισματικός, f. σχίσμα: see SCHISM.]

Schismatical (sizmæ′tikal), *a.* [f. prec. + -AL.] Of the nature of schism; guilty of the offence of schism.

Schismatically (sizmæ′tikali), *adv.* In a schismatical manner.

†Schismaticalness. *Obs. rare* ⁻¹.

Schismaticate (sizmæ′tikeit), *v. Obs.* [f. med.L. *schismaticat-*, ppl. stem of *schismaticare*.]

Schismatize (si′zmætaɪz), *v.* [f. SCHISMAT-IC + -IZE.]

Schismic, *a.* [f. SCHISM sb. + -IC.]

Schist (ʃist). *Geol.* Also 16th c. scisth, in 18th c. *chist, schistus, schiste.* [a. F. *schiste* (16th c.), ad. L. *schistos, schistus* (lapis), a. Gr. σχιστός divided, cleft.]

Schista'ceous, a. Bot. [f. SCHIST + -ACEOUS.]
Having the colour of schist or slate, blue-grey.

Schi'stic, a. Obs. rare⁻¹. = SCHISTOUS.

Schi'stone. [ad. assumed Gr. *σχιστόνη*, f. *σχίζειν* to split: see SCHISM *sb.*] Dividing, analytical. (In quot. *humorously* pedantic.)

Schi'stoid, a. Geol. Obs. [f. SCHIST + -OID.]
Pertaining to, resembling a schist. = SCHISTOID.

Schistite (ski'stəit), *a.* Acoustics. [See quot.] Of a system of musical temperament.

Schi'stify, v. Obs. rare⁻¹. [ad. F. *schistifier*.]

Schistoid (ji'stoid), *a. i.* Geol. = SCHIST¹ + -OID.

Schistocœpus (ji.stoke'pəs), a.

Schistosity (ji.stɒ'siti), *a.* Geol.

Schiston (ji'stɒn), *a.* [f. SCHIST¹ + -OUS.]
1. Geol. = SCHISTOSE *a.* 2.
2. Formed of schist.

Schi'stus, a. Also 9 shistus. [f. SCHIST.]

Schive, v. Bot. rare⁻¹.

Schizo- (ski'zo, skɑip), irreg. representing Gr. *σχίζειν* to split; combining with other words of Greek origin in various scientific forms.

Schizocarp (ski'zokɑːp), Bot. [Gr. *καρπός* fruit], a term applied to dry fruits which break up into two or more one-seeded pericarps without dehiscing.

Schizocœ'rpic, Schizocœ'rpous adj., resembling or belonging to a schizocarp (*Cent. Dict.* 1891).

Schizocœle (-sīl) Zool.

Schi'zocoil, a. Zool.

Schi'zodon Zool.

Schizodont Zool.

Schi'zogamy Bot.

Schizogenesis Biol.

Schizogna'thous a.

Schizogony (-g'gɒni) Zool.

Schi'zoid a.

Schi'zolite (Haeckel)

Schizomycete (-mət'sīt) Bot.

Schizomycetous

Schizo'nt Zool.

Schi'zopod Zool.

Schizo'rhiza

Schi'stoma

the order Stomapoda.

Schi'zoma. Obs. Also skizoo; *pl.* schizoos, scizzi, scissis. [ad. SKETCH *sb.*] A sketch.

Schlafrock (ʃlɑ'frok) Obs., f. *schlaf* on to sleep + *rock* coat, gown.] A dressing-gown.

Schlöss (ʃləs). [Ger.] A (German) castle.

Schnapper (ʃnæ'pəs). Formerly also snapper.

Schnauze (ʃnaʊtsə).

Schnebelite (ʃnə'bəlait). [f. the name Schnebel.]

Schneiderian (ʃnəi'diriən) a. Anat.

Schnorrer (ʃnɔ'rəs). Jewish. [Yiddish var. of G. *schnurrer*, f. schnurren (slang) to go begging.] A Jewish beggar.

†Schœne. Obs. Also schene. [ad. L. *schœnus*, a. Gr. *σχοῖνος*, rope, etc.]

Schœnobatic (skīnobæ'tik), *a.*

Schœnobates (skīnɒ'bətīz).

Schoenanth (skī'nænθ). Obs. Also (erron.) schenanth.

Scholar (skɒ'lɑr). Forms: 1 sceolere, scolere, 3-7 scoler, 4-5 scolere, 4-6 scoler, 5 soolare, sholere, scolär; (*Caxton* scoolyer), 5-6 scoller, 5-7 scooller, 6 scolaer, -air, scollar, skolar, ler, 6,7 schooller,-ar, schooler, 7 schoolar,skool-ler, skolar, (scholar), 6-9 *vulgar* schollard, 9 scholard, 6- scholar. [OE. *scolere, scolere* (=OHG. *scuolari*, MHG. *schuolaere*, early mod.G. *schuler*, now *schüler*), ad. late L. *scholār-is* (f. *schola* SCHOOL), with substitution of the native ending -ER¹.]

1. One who is taught in a school; now *esp.* a boy or girl attending an elementary school.

b. *attrib.* and *Comb.*

2. One who has acquired learning in the 'Schools'; a learned or erudite person; *esp.* one who is learned in the classical (*i.e.* Greek and Latin) languages and their literature.

3. One who is receiving, or has received, his instruction or training from a particular master; a pupil (*of a master*). Now *arch.* or *rhetorical*.

4. A student who receives emoluments, during a fixed period, from the funds of a school, college, or university, towards defraying the cost of his education or studies, and as a reward of merit.

Scho'larless, a. rare⁻¹. [f. SCHOLAR + -LESS.] Without scholars or pupils.

Scho'larlike, a. and adv. [-LIKE] **A.** adj.

†Schola'ster. Obs. [a. med.L. scholaster, ad. OF. scolastre, escolastre (mod.F. écolâtre), altered form of scolaste, a. L. scholastes: see next.]

Schola'stic (skɒlæ'stik), a. and sb. [ad. L. scholasticus, a. Gr. σχολαστικός studious, learned, subst. a learned man, scholar, f. σχολάζειν to have leisure, f. σχολή leisure: see SCHOOL sb.]

Scholasti'cal, a. Now rare.

Scholasti'cally, adv. = SCHOLASTICAL + -LY 2.

Scholasti'cism (skɒlæ'stisiz'm). [f. SCHOLASTIC + -ISM.]

Schollio'grapher. [f. late Gr. σχολιογράφος, f. σχόλιον SCHOLIUM: see -GRAPHER.] A writer of scholia.

Scholion (skɒ'liɒn). *pl.* **-a.** Now rare. [Gr. σχόλιον.]

Scholiast (skɒ'liæst). [ad. late Gr. σχολιαστής, f. σχολιάζειν.]

Scholiastic, a.

Scho'liast, v.

Scholium (skɒ'liəm). Pl. scholia. [med.L. scholium, a. Gr. σχόλιον.]

Scho'ly, v. Obs. [f. SCHOLY sb.]

School (skūl), sb.¹ Forms: 1 scól (? scolu), 2-3 scole, 3-6 scoole, 5-7 schole, scole, (Sc. scole, scule), 4-6 scole &c. [OE. scōl fem., scōle, ad. L. schola, a. Gr. σχολή leisure, employment of leisure, a school.]

I. A place or establishment in which boys or girls, or both, receive instruction.

SCHOOL. 213

SCHOOL. 214

SCHOOL. 215

SCHOOL. 216

SCHOOLGIRLISH.

Hence **Schoolgirlishness**.

School-house.

1. A building appropriated for the use of a school; also, the dwelling-house provided by the school authorities for the use of the schoolmaster or schoolmistress, usually attached to or adjoining a school.

 d. The employment or profession of teaching in school; 'schoolmastering'. *rare.*

Schoo·ling, *vbl. sb.*¹ [f. SCHOOL *v.*¹ + -ING¹.]

1. The action of teaching, or the state or fact of being taught, in a school; scholastic education.

 b. *transf. and fig.*

Schoo·ling, *vbl. sb.*² [f. SCHOOL *sb.*² or *v.*² + -ING¹.]

 The action of swimming together in schools or shoals.

Schoo·ling, *ppl. a.*¹ [f. SCHOOL *v.*¹ + -ING².]

1. That schools, instructs or educates; also, †admonishing, reproving.

Schoo·ling, *ppl. a.*² [f. SCHOOL *sb.*² or *v.*² + -ING².] That swim together in 'schools'.

Schoo·lingly, *adv. nonce-wd.* [f. SCHOOLING *vbl. sb.*¹ + -LY².] So as to afford a lesson.

† School·ish, *a.* *Obs. rare*⁻¹. [f. SCHOOL *sb.*¹ + -ISH.] Savouring of the 'school'; scholastic.

School-keeper, **schoo·lkeeper.**

1. One who 'keeps school'; applied to a schoolmaster or mistress.

2. The caretaker of a school building.

Schoolless (skū·lles), *a.* [f. SCHOOL *sb.*¹ + -LESS.] Having no school, or attending no school; not belonging to or connected with a school.

Schoolman (skū·lmæn). *U.S.* Also *-marm.* A schoolmistress.

Schoolman (skū·lmæn). *U.S.* Also *-marm.* A schoolmistress.

 † 2. Disciplinary correction, chastisement; also, admonition, reproof, scolding. *Obs.*

Schoolman (skū·lmæn), *pl.* **-men** [SCHOOL *sb.*¹]

1. One of the succession of writers, from about the 9th to the 14th century, who treat of logic, metaphysics, and theology as taught in the 'schools' or universities of Italy, France, Germany, and England; a mediæval scholastic.

 b. *transf.* and *fig.*

 † 2. *To have in schooling:* to be engaged in tutoring or admonishing. *Obs.*

3. *a.* The training or exercising of horse and rider in the riding-school. *b.* The exercising of horses in the hunting field. Also *attrib.*, as *schooling-match.*

4. *slang.* (See quots.)

Schoo·ling, *vbl. sb.*² School, a low gambling party.

Schoolmaster (skū·lmastə), *sb.*¹ Forms: *se* SCHOOL *sb.*¹ and MASTER *sb.*¹ [f. SCHOOL *sb.*¹ + MASTER *sb.*¹ Cf. G. *schulmeister*, Sw. *skolmästare*, Da. *skolemester.*]

1. The master of a school, or one of the masters in a school.

 Schoolmaster of Grammar: a teacher of Latin in a school.

Schoo·lmaster, *v.* [f. SCHOOLMASTER *sb.*¹]

1. *trans.* To govern, regulate, or command in the manner of a schoolmaster. *rare.*

Schoo·lmastering, *vbl. sb.* [f. SCHOOLMASTER *sb.*¹ + -ING¹.] The occupation or profession of a schoolmaster; also, an education in school.

2. Accommodation for teaching.

Schoolt, variant of SKATE, shallow.

Schoolward (skū·lwərd), *adv.* and *a.* [f. SCHOOL *sb.*¹ + -WARD.] *A. adv.* Towards school; in the direction of school.

 B. *attrib.* or as *adj.* Directed or going toward school.

 So **Schoo·lwards** *adv.*

Schooly (skū·li). *U.S.* [Cf. SCHOOL *sb.*¹]

Schooner (skū·nər). Forms: 8 **scooner**, **skooner**, 8- **schooner**. [Of uncertain origin; recorded early in the 18th c. in *America*; the present spelling, which occurs only a few years later, may be due to form-association with *school*, or with Du. words having initial *sch*. The word has passed from English into most of the European langs.: Du. *schooner*, *schoener*, G. *schoner*, *schooner* (recorded 1786), F. *schooner*, *schoaner*, Da. *skonnert*, Sw. *skonare*, *skonert*.]

1. A small sea-going fore-and-aft rigged vessel, originally with only two masts, but now often with three or four masts and carrying one or more top-sails.

2. *transf.* A schooner-rigged vessel.

Schooner (skū·nər), *sb.*² [Of obscure origin; perh. a fanciful use of SCHOONER *sb.*¹ A tall glass, used for lager-beer and ale.

Schorl (ʃɔl). *Min.* Forms: 8 **schorl**, 8-9 **shirl**, **shorl**, **shorl**, *a.* G. *schorl*, in the 18th c. also *schörl*, *schirl*, *schorl*, *schörl*, *schörlich*, *schörlich*, in 16th c. *schrul*; of obscure origin. From Ger. are F. *schorl*, Du. *skörl*.] Tourmaline, esp. the black variety.

Schorlaceous (ʃɔrleɪʃəs), *a. Min.* Also 8 **sh-**. [f. SCHORL + -ACEOUS.] Of the nature of schorl.

Schorlous (ʃɔ·rləs), *a. Min.* Also 8 **sh-**. [f. SCHORL + -OUS.] Of the nature of schorl.

Schorl-rock (see quot. 1882); so **schorl-schist**.

† Schorlous, *a. Min. Obs. rare*⁻¹. [f. SCHORL + -OUS.] Resembling or having the nature of schorl.

Schorl-y, *a. Min. Obs.* [f. SCHORL + -Y¹.] Containing schorl; chiefly in *schorly granite*.

Schorn(e, **Schorte**, obs. ff. SCORN, SHIRT.

Schott (ʃot), *sb.* [Ger.] A crevasse.

Schottische (ʃɒtiʃ), *sb.* Forms: 8 **scotticé**, a lively dance resembling the Highland fling. *Military*

 b. *Highland* or *Balmoral Schottische:* a lively dance resembling the Highland fling.

Schottische (ʃtiʃ), *v. intr.* To dance a schottische.

Schout (skaut), *sb.* [Du. *schout.*]

Schraw, obs. ff. SHE, SHEW, SHREW.

Schrund, variant of SCOUT *sb.*²

Schreiberite (ʃraɪbərəit). *Min.* [Named after J. Schreiber.]

Schrund [†sb. Obs.] [Ger.] A crevasse.

Schynd, **skynd.** *Orkney* and *Shetland.*

Scia-, app. aphetic for Ischia.

Scian (saɪən), *a.* [f. *Scio*, mod. It. name of the anc. *Chios.*] Of or pertaining to Scio or Chios.

Sciagraphy (saɪæ·grəfi). *n.* 6 **scio-** [medL., app. aphetic for the *L. sciagraphia* (Gr. σκιαγραφία)].

Sciagraphical (saɪægræ·fikl), *a.* Also 7-8 **scio-** [Formed as prec. + -ICAL.] Of or pertaining to sciagraphy; of the nature of a sciagraph.

Sciagraphically *adv.* see SCIAGRAPHY.

Sciamachy, obs. form of SCIOMACHY.

Scian, obs. form of *L. Scia*, mod. It. name of the Greek island *Chios*; the Scian and the Teian muse...Have found the tune your shores refuse.

Scians, obs. form of SCIENCE.

Sciapod (saɪ·pɒd), *sb.* *n.* 6 errors. Bio-podes. [L., *a.* Gr. σκιάπους, pl. σκιά-ποδες + σκιά shade + πού-, πούς foot.] A fabulous people of Libya whose feet were said to be large enough... to serve as sunshades.

Sciatherical, obs. variant of SCIOMACHY.

Sciatheric (saɪəθe·rik), *a.* of a sun-dial. Also 7-8 **sciatherick**, sciatherical.

Sciatherical (saɪəθe·rikl), *a.* Forms: 7 **scio-**, 8 **sciatherical**, **sciatherick**.

Sciatic (saɪæ·tik), *sb.* and *a.* Forms: 6 **scyatyke**, **sci]atica**, **syatike**, 7 **sciatique**, (**sciatik**), 7-8 **sciatick**, 8- **sciatic**. [f. *sciatica*, corrupt form of L. *ischiadicus* (see ISCHIADIC). Cf. F. *sciatic*, Sp. *ciática*.] *A. adj.*

1. Affecting the hip or the sciatic nerves.

2. Of or belonging to the ischium or hip.

Sciatic, a.[2] Naut.[?] Obs.

Sciatica (sai̯ætika). Forms: 5 cyetica, sytyon, seyetyta, ciatica, 5-6 siatica, 6 seatica, schiatica, 6-7 syatica, 6 sciatica, sciatike, sciatticæ, 6 sciatica. [a. med.L. *sciatica* (*passio*), fem. of *sciaticus* SCIATIC a.]

b. An attack of this disease.

b. *Sciatica cress* (see quot. 1866).

Sciatical (sai̯ætikăl), a. [f. SCIATIC + -AL.]

Scibility. Obs. [f. L. *scibilis* knowable]

Scien, obs. form of SCION.

Science (sai̯əns). Forms: 4 siens, science, sciens, 4-5 syens, Forms: 4 siens, science.

Scientifically, adv.

Scientious, a. Obs. rare⁻¹.

Scientist (sai̯əntist), sb.

Scientistic, a.

Scientive, a. Sc. Obs.

Scienty, a. Sc. rare⁻¹.

Scil-, in Sci-.

Scilla (silă). [L.—Gr. σκίλλα.] Bot.

Scilli-tic, a. Pharmacy.

Scilli-tin. Pharmacy.

Scilliticus, a.

Scimitar (simităr). Forms: 1-6 simitarie, scimitar, -tar, simitar, -ter.

Scincoid (siŋkoid), a. and sb.

Scincoidian (siŋkoi̯diăn), a. and sb.

Scind, v. rare.

Scinth, sb. Obs. or arch.

Scintill, v. Obs.

Scintillate, v.

Scintillation (sintilēi̯ʃən).

Sciolism (sai̯olizm).

Sciolist (sai̯olist).

Sciolous, a.

Sciolus (sai̯olus). [L.]

Books vpon coniecture. 1658 Burton *Comment. Itin. Antonianus* 34 Yonders. aduises to exclude these words, ... as a presence found in by some learned writers.

Sciomancy, variant of SCIAMANCY.

Scioman̄cer (sɑiˈ·omansə₂). Also 7 *-mantle,* 8 *-mantic.* [ad. mod.L. *sciomantia*, f. Gr. σκιά, shadow + *-µαντία* : see -MANCY. Cf. F. *scíomance* (Cotgr. 1611).] Divination by communication with the shades of the dead.

1645 Cockeram, *Sciomancie,* diuination by shadowes. 1647 A. Ross *Mystag. Poet.* iii. (1675) 307 This ... was Sciomancy, or a sight of shadows only, not Necromancy.

Scion (sɑi·ən). Forms: *α.* 4-5 *cyoun*, 5-6 *cyon*, 4-7, 9 *sion*, 6-7 *sion*, 7 *scyon*. *β.* 5 *cyon*, 6-9 *cion*, 7-8 *ci-, cyen*, 9 *cy-*. *ence*, 6-7 *sciens, sient*, 7 *sience*, *cions, cyons,* mis. *science, cyence, scient.* *δ.* 4-9 *scyon*, 5 *scioun*, 7 *soi-, scyen, syion.* [a. OF. *cion, cyon, sion,* mod.F. *scion* (Picard *chion*), of obscure origin.

The early forms in OF are inconsistent with the commonly assumed derivation from *scie* to saw.]

1. *†a. gen.* A shoot or twig; also, a sucker. *Obs.*

exc. fig. 5. *spec.* A slip for grafting, a graft.

2. An heir, a descendant.

Scioptic (sɑiˈ·optik), *a.* and *sb.* [f. Gr. σκιά shadow + *ὀπτικός* pertaining to vision : see OPTIC *a.* Formed as prec. (*v.* examples), would appear to be a correction of the less regularly formed SCIOPTRIC.] = SCIOPTRIC.

Sciopticon (sɑiˈ·optikɒn), *sb.* rare. [f. prec., or obscurely after *catoptric, dioptric.* Cf. SCIOPTIC.] A. *adj.* Scioptic *bsld*: a kind of magic lantern.

Sciopticon (sɑiˈ·optikɒn), *sb.* and *sb.* rare. [f. SCIOPTIC + *-ON.*] = SCIOPTRIC.

Scioptricall, -ique: see SCIATHERICAL, -THERIC.

Scion (sɑiˈ·ɒn), *a.* [ad. mod.L. *scion.*] Having knowledge.

Scire facias (sɑi·əɹi feˈiʃiæs), *v.* [Subst. use of the Law Latin phrase *scire facias,* 'do (him) to wit', the characteristic words of the writ.]

Scirrhosity (sirɒ·siti), *sb.* Also 6 *scirrhosity,* 7 *scirrosity,* 7-8 *scirrhosity,* 8 *scyrrosity,* ... [ad. mod.L. *scirrhōsitās*, f. late L. *scirrhōsus* : see SCIRRHOUS.]

Scirrhosity (sirɒ·siti), *sb.* Also 6 *scirrhose,* 7 *scirrhous,* 8 *scirrhous.* [ad. F. *scirrheux* (16th c.; now *squirreux*), ...]

†Scirrhose, *a.* *Obs.*—¹ = SCIRRHOUS.

Scirrhosity, *sb.* Also 7 *scirrhose.* Also 6 *scirrhose,* 7 *scirrhus, scyrrhus.* [ad. med.L. *scirrhus.*]

†Scirrhus, *sb.* *Obs.* [mod.L. *scirrhus,* ...] A hard, firm, and almost painless swelling or tumour; now *spec.* a hard cancer.

Scisme, obs. form of SCHISM.

Scism/a, -e, -al, obs. forms of SCHISM, etc.

Scissel (si·sel). Also 7 *scisell,* 9 *sissel, scis·sile.* [a. F. *cisaille* 'the clipping of coyne presently after the stampe' (Cotgr. 1611), verbal noun from *cisailler* to clip with shears.]

Scisma: see SCISSIBLE *a.*, quot. 1626.

Scissible (si·sib'l), *a.* [ad. L. *scissilis*, f. *scindĕre* to cut or divided ; *spec.* in *Min.*, that splits into laminæ, *cleavable.*]

Scission (si·ʃən). [a. F. *scission* (14th c. in Hatz.-Darm.) or ad. L. *scissiōn-em,* n. of action of *scindĕre* to cut or cleave.]

Scissiparity (sisipæ·riti). *Biol.* [f. L. *scissi-* ppl. stem of *scindĕre* to cut or divide + *-par-ere* to produce, bring forth + *-ITY.* Cf. PARITY²] Reproduction by fission, fissiparity, schizogenesis.

Scissure (si·ʃɪə, si·ʃjʊə). [ad. L. *scissūra,* f. *sciss-, scindĕre* to cut, divide : see SCISSION.] A longitudinal cleft or opening made by cutting or separation of parts ; a rent, fissure.

†Scite, *Obs.*—¹ [ad. L. *scitum* (*plēbis*) a decree or ordinance (of the people), neut. pa. pple. of *scíscĕre* to accept, approve, have to appoint, decree, ordain.] [See quot.]

Scite, obs. form of CITE *v.* and CITY.

Scite, *v.,* obs. form of CITE *v.*

†Sciure, *Obs.*—¹ [f. L. *sciūrus* squirrel.]

Scivat/ing, *vbl. sb.* *rare.*

Sclaff (sklæf), *v.* *Golf.* [A use of Sc. *sclaff* to strike with the open hand or with anything having a flat surface , 'to walk in a clumsy way without properly lifting the feet, to shuffle along'.

Sclate, obs. form of SLATE *sb.*

Sclave, Sclavic, Sclavonian: see SLAV, etc.

Sclera (skliˈə·rə). *Anat.* [f. Gr. σκληρός hard.] The sclerotic coat of the eyeball.

Scleragogy (skle·ragodʒi). *Obs.* [ad. Gr. σκληραγωγία hardy training, f. σκληρός hard, harsh + ἀγωγή conducting, guiding.] Severe discipline or training ; hard treatment of the body ; mortification.

Scleral (skli·əral), *a.* *Anat.* [f. SCLERA + *-AL.*] Of or pertaining to the sclera or sclerotic coat of the eye.

Scleranth (skli·rænθ). *Bot.* [Shortened ad. mod.L. *Scleranthus* (see below).]

Sclerema (skliˈ·rēmă). *Path.* [mod. L. ...] A hard, localised induration of the skin.

Sclerenchyma (sklirɛ·ŋkimă). Also anglicized **sclerenchym.** [mod. L., f. Gr. σκληρός hard + ἐγχυμα an infusion, after *par-enchyma.*]

Sclerenchymatous (sklirɛŋki·matəs), *a.*

Sclerite (skliˈ·rəit). *Zool.* [f. Gr. σκληρός hard + *-ITE.*]

Sclero- (skli·ro), occurring in scientific terms.

Sclerodermic (sklirə·dɜ·mik), *a.* [f. SCLERO- DERM + *-IC.*]

Scleroderma (sklirə·dɜ·mă). *Path.* Also anglicized **scleroderm.** [mod.L., f. Gr. σκληρός hard + δέρμα skin.]

Sclerogenoid (skli·rodʒenoid), *a.* and *sb.* *Zool.*

Sclerotic (skliˈrɒ·tik), *a.* and *sb.* 1. *Anat.* [f. SCLEROTIC a.]

Sclerotic.
2. of medicines: Adapted to harden the tissues.
3. *Path.* or pertaining to sclerosis; affected with sclerosis.
4. *Bot.* Hardened, stony in texture.

Sclerotin.

Sclerotical, a. = Sclerotic. Also sclerotoid. Resembling a sclerotium.

Sclerotis. *Obs.*

Sclerotitis = Sclerotitis.

Sclerotitis. Inflammation of the sclerotica.

Sclerotium.

Sclerotoid, a.

Sclerotome.

Scleroty. [ad. L. *sclerotē*]

1. A sclerous element intervening between successive myotomes.

Sclerotomy.

Scleroty.

Sclerous.

Sclerectomy.

Sclopet.

Sclopette.

Scoad.

Scoal.

†Scob.

Scobby.

Scobiform, a. *Bot.* Like sawdust in form.

Scobina.

Scody.

Scoff, *sb.¹*

Scoff, *sb.²*

Scoff, *v.¹*

1. *intr.* To speak derisively; mock; jeer.
2. *trans.* To scoff at, deride, ridicule irreverently.

Scoff, *v.²*

1. *trans.* To eat voraciously; devour; also *gen.*

Scoffer.

Scoffery.

Scoffing, *vbl. sb.*

Scoffing, *ppl. a.*

Scoffingly, *adv.*

Scog.

Scoggan.

Scoge.

Scoffle.

Scoffer. One who scoffs.

Scoffingly.

Scogging.

Scog, *sb.*

Scoggin. *Obs.* The name of John Scoggin.

Scogginal.

Scogginism.

Scogginly.

Scoggin-ry.

Scoinson.

Scoobirt.

Scogh.

Scoinson. *Arch.*

Scoke. *Obs.*

Scold, *sb.*

Scold, *v.*

Scolding, *vbl. sb.*

Scolding, *ppl. a.*

Scoldingly, *adv.*

†Scoldster. *Obs.*

Scole.

Scoliosis. *Path.*

Scolion.

Scoleciform, a.

Scolecid.

Scolecite.

Scolecology.

Scoleciform.

Scolex.

Scoliosis.

Scoloc. *Hist.*

Scolopendra.

Scolopendrine.

Scolopendriform.

Scolopendrium.

Scolopendroid.

Scolophore.

Scolp.

Scolytid.

Scolytoid.

Scomber. A mackerel.

Scombre.

Sombre.

| SCOMBROID. | 233 | SCONCE. | SCONCE. | 234 | SCOOP. |

Scombroid (skṃˈbroid), *a.* and *sb.* Also (earlier) scomberoid. [f. Gr. σκόμβρος + -oid.] *A. adj.* Resembling the mackerel; belonging to the family Scombridæ.

Scome, Scomer, obs. ff. SCUM, SUMMER.

Scomfish (skṃˈfiʃ), *v. Sc.* and *north.* Also ǂ scomfice, 8-9 scumfish; *pa. pple.*, 4 scomfyste, 8 scumfist. ǂ*a.* = SCOMFIT *v.* Obs. *b.* To suffocate, stifle, choke (with heat, smoke, a bad smell). Also, to injure, 'do for'.

Scomfit, *sb. Obs.* Forms: 4 scoumfyt, sconfit, scoumfit, 5 -fite, 6 skumfite. †*a.* = SCOMFIT *v.*; cf. DISCOMFIT *sb.* Defeat, discomfiture.

Scomfit, *v. Obs.* Forms: 4 scoum-, scoom-, scounfit, 6 -fyt, -phit, 6-8 scum-, scom-, scoun-fit, -fite, 4-5 -fete, 5 -fyt, 4-5 scomfite, scomfite, 5 skomfit(e, -fyt, 4-5 scoumfyghte, scoum-, scomfite, 6 scomfyte; also regularly scomficed, etc. [Short-ened f. DISCOMFIT *v.*] *trans.* To defeat, vanquish, discomfit.

Sconce (skɒns), *sb.*[1] Forms: 4-6 sconse, 6 skonce, sconc(e, (5 sconsse, 7 skonse, 8 sconse), 6-7 skonce, *obs.* 4 sconce, sconce, (5 sconsse, 6 skonce); *8 dial.* skonce; (7 sconсе), *7-8* skonce, akonce, skance, scans. [a. Du. schans (in early mod.Du. also schantse, schientse), also schans, schancz. The word (of which the synonymous early mod. Du. schwanze, schoentze, seems to be a variant) is found also in late MHG. and mod.G. schanze fem.; in the 16th c. it had in Du. the sense "brushwood", 'bundle of sticks', 'earthwork made with gabions' (cf. the bundling gabions). The ultimate origin is obscure; the later Romance forms are prob. from the Germanic.]

†**1.** A lantern or candlestick with a screen to protect the light from the wind, and a handle to carry it by (as distinguished from a lantern carried suspended from a staff). *Obs.*

2. A flat candlestick with a handle for carrying.

2 b. A bracket-candlestick, usually of brass or iron, to fasten against a wall; *esp.* an ornamental bracket for holding one or more candles, often fitted with a mirror. Also, a candle-bracket for a piano, etc.

3. A street-lamp or lantern attached to a wall. Only in descriptions of Covent Garden.

4. *attrib.*, as *sconce candlestick, light, maker.*

Sconce (skɒns), *sb.*[2] *a.* 6-7 sconse, akonse. [Of obscure origin; possibly a slang use of SCONCE *sb.*[1] or of SCONCE *sb.*[3] (though in one quot. recorded earlier than the latter).] A jocular term for: The head; *esp.* the crown or top of the head; hence, 'head', ability, sense, wit.

Sconce (skɒns), *sb.*[3] Forms: 4-6 sconse, 6 skonce, sconse, (5 sconso, 7 konss, 8 *dial.* akance, *6-7* sconce, 6 sconce, 7 skonse. [a. Du. schans (in early mod.Du. also schantse, schientse), also schans, schancz.]

3. dial. A screen, partition.

4. (*b. sconce-piece*.) A low water-washed iceberg (*see quot. 1876*).

5. Comb.: sconce-battle, a particular mode of drawing up troops in the field; sconce-building, sconce-korf (Du. schans-korf), a gabion.

Sconce (skɒns), *sb.*[4] [f. SCONCE *v.*[2]]

1. At Oxford (formerly also at Cambridge): To fine, mulct; often with the penalty a second object. Formerly said of university and college officials, with reference to fines inflicted for breaches of discipline. Now only of undergraduates when dining in hall.

2. *intr.* [f. SCONCE *sb.*[4]] At Oxford (formerly also at Cambridge):

Sconce (skɒns), *v.*[2] *Obs.* [Of obscure origin. As a term of University slang, it may have arisen from some far-fetched reference to SCONCE *sb.*[2]]

1. *trans.* At Oxford ('formerly also at Cambridge') To fine, mulct.

†b. *To screen off*; to take off, rebate. *Obs.*

Sconce, *v.*[3] *Obs.* [f. SCONCE *sb.*[3] Cf. Du. (*schansen*).]

1. *trans.* To fortify, entrench; in later use, to shelter, protect. To sconce away &c., to ward off.

SCOOP. | 235 | SCOOPER. | SCOOPFUL. | 236 | SCOPE. |

Scoop (skūp), *sb.*[1] [f. SCOOP *v.*]

1. The action or an act of scooping.

d. Applied to a mechanical contrivance for drawing water.

2. A similar instrument for scooping.

†b. A grafer's knife. *Obs.*

3. An instrument with a spoon-shaped or gouge-shaped blade, used for cutting out a piece from some soft material, or for removing a core or an embedded substance. *a.* Applied to various small utensils in domestic use: chiefly short for *apple-scoop, cheese-scoop, potato-trap*, for which see the first element.

Scoop (skūp), *v.* Also 4-5 scoupe, 6 scoupe. [f. SCOOP *sb.*[1]]

1. *trans.* To lade or bail out (water) with or as with a scoop.

b. *intr.* To lade water (in a boat) with a scoop; *also fig.*

†c. *intr.* Of a bird: To swoop on.

Scooper (skūˈpəɹ), *sb.* [f. SCOOP *v.* + -ER[1]]

1. One who 'scoots' or goes hurriedly.

Scoopful (skūpˈful), *sb.* [f. SCOOP *sb.*[1] + -FUL.] A quantity that fills a scoop.

Scooping (skūˈpɪŋ), *ppl. a.* [-ING[2].] That scoops, in the sense of the verb.

Scoot (skūt), *v.* Also scout. [Echoic.]

1. *intr.* To make a hollow as with a scoop.

Scooter (skūˈtəɹ), *sb.* [f. SCOOT *v.* + -ER[1].]

Scopa (skōˈpa), *sb. Ent.* [L. *scopa*, in class. use only in pl. *scopæ*, a broom or brush.]

Scoparin (skōˈpərɪn), *sb.* [f. mod.L. *scoparius* + -IN[1].] A diuretic principle found in common broom.

Scoparious (skōˈpɛəriəs), *a.* [f. mod.L. *scoparius*.]

Scope (skōp), *sb.*[1] [ad. It. *scopo* aim, purpose, a mark or object to shoot or aim at.]

1. A mark for shooting or aiming at.

4. *Med.* A plan or method of treatment.

| SCOPE. | 237 | SCOPIFORM. | SCOPIOUS. | 238 | SCORCH. |

Scope ... (entry continues)

† Scopa ...

Scopal, a. Obs. rare.

† Scopeful ...

Scopeless ...

Scopelid, a.

Scopelin ...

Scopeloid ...

† Scopine ...

† Scope, v.¹ Obs. rare.

† Scope, v.² Obs. rare.

Scops ...

† Scopula ...

† Scopulous ...

† Scopiferous ...

Scopiform ...

† Scopious, a. Obs.

Scopol- (skōp·ŏl), comb. form.

Scopolamine ...

† Scopperil ...

Scoppet ...

Scoptic, a. and sb. rare.

† Scoptical, a. Obs.

Scopula ...

Scor ...

† Scorbuch, -buicke. Obs.

Scorbute ...

Scorbutic, a. and sb.

Scorbutical, a.

Scorbutically, adv.

Scorbuticism ...

Scorbutus ...

Scorce ...

Scorch, v.¹

| SCORCH. | 239 | SCORE. | SCORE. | 240 | SCORE. |

† Scorching, ppl. a.²

Scorchingly, adv.

† Scorcherasse. Obs. rare.

Scorched, ppl. a.

Scorcher ...

Scorching, ppl. a.¹

Scordatura ...

Scordium ...

Score (skōɹ), sb.

Scorchedarrow ...

Scorched ...

Supplement, p. 3873; Corrigenda, p. 4092; Spurious words, p. 4093; Books quoted, p. 4094

† Scorel, sko·rel. Obs. Loppings of trees.

Scoreless (skō·rles), a. [f. Score sb. + -less.]

1. Making no 'score' or tally.

2. In a game: having no score.

Scorer (skō·rəɹ). [f. Score v. + -er.]

1. One who marks trees for felling.

2. Any instrument used for scoring (see quots.).

3. In a game or contest: one whose duty it is to keep a record of the score.

Scoria (skō·riă). Pl. **scoriæ** (skō·rié), rarely **scorias**. [L. scoria, Gr. σκωρία, dross, a. var. σκωρ, dung. Cf. scoria.]

1. The slag or dross remaining after the smelting out of a metal from its ore. Also transf.

† 2. An item to one's score; to hazard.

3. To transf. To line, furrow, or groove.

Scoriaceous (skō·rié·ʃəs), a. [f. scoria + -aceous.] Having the nature of scoria.

† Scoriation. Obs. rare. [Aphetic form of Excoriation.] = Excoriation.

Scorification (skō·rifikē·ʃən). [ad. F. scorification.] The process of reducing to scoria; formation of scoria or slag.

Scorifier (skō·rifəɪəɹ). [f. Scorify + -er.]

Scorify (skō·rifəɪ), v. [f. Scoria + -fy.]

1. trans. To reduce to scoria or slag.

2. To convert (lava) into scoria.

Scoring (skō·riŋ), vbl. sb. [f. Score v. + -ing.]

Scoriation. 243

Scorious (skō·riəs), a. [f. Scoria + -ous.] Of the nature of scoria; abounding in scoria.

† Scorium. Obs. Erroneously formed sing. to Scoria, mistaken for a plural.

† Scorken, v. In 3 (Orrm) scorrkenn. To shrivel up, scorch.

† Scorkle, v. Obs. rare. Altered form of pret.

Scorn (skɔːn), sb. Forms: 1-2 skarn, 2 scorne, 4-7 scorne, 4-5 skorn, scorne, scorne, scorn. [Early ME. skarn, skerne, scharn, a. OF. escarn, escharn.]

1. Mockery, derision, contempt; in mod. use, indignant or passionate contempt.

Scorn (skɔːn), v. Forms: 1 scyrnan, 2-3 scarnen, scornien.

Scorned (skɔːnd), ppl. a. [f. Scorn v. + -ed.]

Scorning (skɔ·niŋ), vbl. sb. [f. Scorn v. + -ing.]

Scorn. 244

Scorner (skɔ·nəɹ). [f. Scorn v. + -er.]

† Scorning-stock. Obs.

† Scornful (skɔ·nfʊl), a. and adv. Obs.

Scornful (skɔ·nfʊl), a. [f. Scorn sb. + -ful.]

1. Full of scorn, contemptuous, derisive.

Scornfully (skɔ·nfʊli), adv. [f. prec. + -ly.]

Scornfulness (skɔ·nfʊlnes). [f. Scornful + -ness.]

Scorn-proof, a.

Scornless, a. Free from insult or contempt.

Scorn.liche, adv. Obs. rare.

Scorpæna (skɔːpī·nă). [L. scorpaena, Gr. σκόρπαινα.] A kind of fish.

Scorper (skɔ·pəɹ). [A misspelling of scauper.] A graving-tool for working in hollowing bowls, for cutting away ground; also used in removing the metal from engraved parts of carvings or chasings.

Scorpiac

Scorpiac, *Obs.*⁻¹ [a. late Gr. *skorpiakos* pertaining to a scorpion, f. *skorpios* SCORPION: see -AC.]

Scorpio (skɔˑɹpiəʊ). [L., *a.* Gr. *skorpios* SCORPION.]

1. A zodiacal constellation, the Scorpion.

Scorpioid (skɔˑɹpiɔid). *a.* and *sb.* [ad. Gr. *skorpioeidēs*, f. *skorpios* SCORPION: see -OID.]

Scorpioides (skɔːpiɔiˑdiːz). *sb.* *Bot.*

Scorpiolides

Scorpiolous-a, *L.* scorpi-ous (see SCORPION)

Scorpion (skɔˑɹpiən). Also 3 *scorpiun*, 4–6 *scorpioun*, 4–6 *scorpyon*, *scorpio̧n*.

Scorpion grass, a plant of the genus *Myosotis*.

Scorpionid (skɔɹpiɒˑnid). *sb.* *rare*. [f. SCORPION + -OID.]

Scorpionist, *Obs. rare*⁻¹. [f. SCORPION + -IST.]

Scorpionry, *Obs. rare*⁻¹ [f. SCORPION + -RY.]

Scorpius

Scorsoner, *Obs. rare*.

Scorse, *sb.* *Obs.*

Scorser, *Obs.*

Scorshelatin

Scortation (skɔːteiˑʃən). *rare*.

Scory, *sb.* [Anglicized form of SCORIA.]

Scot, *sb.*¹

Scot

Scorza (skɔˑɹza). *Min.* Also *skorza*.

Scot, *sb.*² [a. ANCIEN *Lunc.* with. Achar 12 We 'Scotchess now the meaning of a Pardon.]

Scot-**ale**, *scot*-**ale**. *Obs. exc. Hist.* Also 2 *scotta̧le*.

Scotal, *scotal*. *Obs.*

Scotch, *sb.*¹ In 5 *scoch*, 8 *scotch*, *dial.* *scotch*. [Cognate with SCOTCH *v.*¹]

Scotch, *v.*¹

Scotch, *sb.*²

Scotch, *sb.*³ Also 7 *skatch*, *g* Scot'sh. [Belongs to SCOTCH *v.*²]

Scotch (skɔtʃ). *a.* and *sb.*⁴ In 7 Scot'sh. [Contracted var. of SCOTTISH.]

Scotch, *a.* and *sb.*

Supplement, p. 3873; Corrigenda, p. 4092; Spurious words, p. 4093; Books quoted, p. 4094

or Pinaster, will grow on the North or East side. 1840 Loudon tr. *Köllar's Treat. Insects* 363 The Scotch Pine Bark-Beetle. *Hylesinus (Hylurgus) piniperda*, Fabr. 1863 Prior *Plant-n.* 184 *Scotch-Primrose. 1731 Miller *Gard. Dict.* s.v. *Rosa* 6, The strip'd *Scotch Rose...The sixth Sort is found wild in Scotland. 1820 J. Sabine in *Trans. Hort. Soc.* (1822) IV. 281 The Scotch Rose has been, and still is, sometimes called the Burnet Rose; it is the Rosa spinosissima of the English authors. 1787 Lightfoot *Flora Scot.* I. 140 Convolvulus foliis reniformibus pedunculis unifloris..Sea Bindweed. *Scotch Scurvy-Grass.

B. *sb.* (Elliptical uses of the adj.)

1. *The Scotch* (pl.): The inhabitants of Scotland or their immediate descendants in other countries.

1781 J. Ripley *Sel. Orig. Lett.* 41 Let the words English and Scotch be entirely obliterated and lost in that more ancient and significant word Britons. 1818 Scott *Rob Roy* iv, The Scotch of that period were guilty of similar injustice to the English. 1825 Loudon *Encycl. Agric.* § 4718 The fine powder which is produced by husking the corn,..forms the sowens of the Scotch. 1861 Pearson *Early & Mid. Ages Eng.* xxviii. 337 Meanwhile, the Scotch were divided by a quarrel as to who should lead the van.

b. *Scotch and English*: the English Border name for prisoner's base; cf. *French and English* (see French *sb.* 2 b).

1802 W. Hutton *Hist. Roman Wall* 105 The children of this day, upon the English border keep up the remembrance [of former scenes] by a common play, called *Scotch and English*, or, *The Raid* (inroad). 1825 Jamieson, *English and Scotch*, a common game among young people. 1869 Mrs. Somerville *Personal Recoll.* (1872) i. 22 In our play-hours [at school in 1790] we amused ourselves..at 'Scotch and English', a game which represented a raid on the debatable land, or Border between Scotland and England, in which each party tried to rob the other of their playthings.

2. The Scotch language: see A. 3.

a 1700 B. E. *Dict. Cant. Crew, Sawny*, a Fool. *He's a meer sawny*, he is very soft, tho' (in Scotch) it is only for Alexander. 1818 Scott *Hrt. Midl.* iv, Which is to say, in plain Scotch, the gallows. 1824 — *Redgauntlet* let. iii, I myself have since that time acquired Scotch in perfection, and many a Scotticism withal. 1878 *Encycl. Brit.* VIII. 400/2 The revival of [interest in] Lowland Scotch last century. 1896 Ashby-Sterry *Tale of Thames* viii, I can read French as well as I can English, but it is impossible for me to comprehend Scotch.

3. Often *elliptically* (the sb. being contextually known), e.g. for *Scotch whisky*; also = a glass of Scotch whisky. Also formerly for *Scotch snuff*.

1823 J. Badcock *Dom. Amusem.* 100 The finely levigated snuff, known as 'Scotch'. 1886–96 Marshall *He Slumbered* ('Pomes,' 118) (Farmer) In the early evening watches he had started well on Scotches. 1893 H. Crackanthorpe *Wreckage* 125 Two bitters and a small Scotch. 1894 Sir J. Astley *Fifty Yrs. Life* II. 124 And over a drop of Scotch and a cigar discuss the leading topics of the day. 1898 G. B. Shaw *Plays* II. *You never can tell* 307 *Waiter*..Scotch and syphon for you, sir?

Scotch (skɒtʃ), *v.*[1] Forms: 5 **scocche, skocche, schoche,** 5–6 **skoche,** 6 **scotche,** 6–7 **skotch,** 6– **scotch.** [Of obscure origin; identity with Scorch *v.*[3] (first in 16th c.) is hardly possible.]

1. *trans.* To make an incision or incisions in; to cut, score, gash. ? *Obs.*

c 1412 Hoccleve *De Reg. Princ.* 3727 With his nayles cracched he his face, And scocched [*Roxb.* skocched] it with knyues, and to-rente. c 1450 *Two Cookery-bks.* 101 Schoche him (the fish) by þe hede in þe backe,..And skoche him in two or iij. peces in þe bak, but noȝt thorgh. 15.. *Scot. Field* 218 *Chetham Soc. Misc.* II, Our Englishmen full egerly attilde them to shott; Skochen the cruell Scottes with their kene arrowes. 1562 Turner *Herbal* II. 46 b, If ye will haue the iuice, ye must scotche & pryck the rootes in many places. 1576 Turberv. *Venerie* xliii. 131 When they haue well skotched it (the deer-skin) with their wood-kniues, that the houndes may the more easily teare off the fleshe. 1596 Nashe *Saffron Walden* Ep. Ded. C 3 b, I..will deliuer him to thee to be scotcht and carbonadoed. 1601 Holland *Pliny* IV. v. I. 74 Thus many creekes doth scotch and cut Peloponnesus. 1651 T. Barker *Art of Angling* (1653) 17 Wash the Eele cleane...Scotch it all along both the sides. 1675 Han. Woolley *Gentlew. Comp.* 129 Scotch with your knife the back of the Carp. 1747 Mrs. Glasse *Cookery* 33 When you have clear'd the Pig of both [skin and hair], scotch him down to the Bones.

absol. 1573 Tusser *Husb.* (1878) 73 How euer ye scotch, saue pole and crotch.

†**b.** Phr. *To notch and scotch.* (? A term used in Tennis: cf. Scotch *sb.*[1] 3.) *Obs.*

1607 Shaks. *Cor.* IV. v. 198 He scotcht him, and notcht him like a Carbinado. 1797 Mme. D'Arblay *Lett.* Dec. (1891) IV. 49 They play all day at tennis, and learn with vast skill to notch and scotch and go one.

2. Theobald's generally accepted conjectural reading of *Macb.* III. ii. 13, 'We have scotch'd the snake, not kill'd it' (see Scorch *v.*[3]), has become a stock quotation, in which the verb *scotch* is taken to mean: To inflict such hurt upon (something regarded as dangerous) that it is rendered harmless for the time.

1798 Cooke in *Ld. Auckland's Corr.* (1862) III. 393, I fear relaxation and too much clemency: but the snake must be killed not scotched. 1820 Byron *Mar. Fal.* III. ii. 268 Would that the hour were come! We will not scotch, But kill. 1843 Le Fevre *Life Trav. Phys.* II. II. viii. 279 The malaria is scotched, not killed, and the intermittent returns at some future period. 1879 Merivale *Early Ch. Hist.* ii. 86 It was by Augustine most of all that the Arian heresy was scotched, if not actually killed. 1894 Baring-Gould *Deserts S. France* II. 113 From the time of St. Louis, the feudal power in France was scotched, though far from killed.

b. To crush, stamp upon, stamp out (something dangerous).

1825 *Q. Rev.* XXXII. 277 If we, in our own language, were to scotch the insidious forgetfulness, we might, perhaps, be accused of 'coarse and insulting abuse'; and shall therefore only cite the gentle remonstrance of Lord Byron. 1880 A. H. Huth *Buckle* I. iii. 189 Attempting to scotch the pestiferous germs of heresy. 1908 *Expositor* Dec. 527 Fanaticism which constitutes a danger to mankind should be scotched.

Hence **Scotched** *ppl. a.*, cut, scarred; also in *scotched collops*, an etymologizing perversion of *Scotch collops*; **Sco·tching** *vbl. sb.*

1559 Feckenham in Strype *Ann. Ref.* (1709) I. App. ix. 26 There was no scotchinge nor cuttinge of the Faces and Legs of the Crucifix and Image of Christ. 1625 Lisle *Du Bartas, Noe* 98 The Lombard left,..Unto the skotched [*balafrez*] Hunnes the divers furrowd marge Of Ister. 1708 W. King *Art Cookery* 21 A Cook perhaps has mighty things profest, Then sent up but two Dishes nicely drest, What signifie Scotcht-Collops to a Feast.

Scotch (skɒtʃ), *v.*[2] Also 8 **skatch.** [f. Scotch *sb.*[2]]

1. *trans.* To block or wedge (a wheel, log, gate, etc.) so as to keep from moving or slipping. Also with *up* (see quot. 1898). Also *fig.*

1642 Fuller *Holy & Prof. St.* II. xiii. § 4 Hedges and counterhedges..serve for barracadoes, and will stick as birdlime in the wings of the horse, and scotch the wheeling about of the foot. 1645 T. Hill *Olive Branch* (1648) 29 If now jealousies and misunderstandings should creep in, and scotch the wheel. 1663 Dryden *Wild Gallant* I. i. (1669) 2 Then will I first scotch the Wheeles of it, that it may not run. 1706 Phillips (ed. Kersey) To *Skatch a Wheel*. 1713 M. Henry *Conc. Meekness & Quietn. of Spirit* (1822) 141 Abigail prudently scotched the wheels of his passion. 1844 Emerson *New Eng. Reformers* Wks. (Bohn) I. 259 Stop, dear nature, these incessant advances of thine; let us scotch these ever-rolling wheels. 1859 F. A. Griffiths *Artil. Man.* (1862) 125, 2 has charge of the..skidding, scotches the wheels. 1866 *Cornh. Mag.* Sept. 323 It was..noticed that near most of the gates that would have had to be opened, a stone was lying, as if it had been used to 'scotch' it. 1887 *S. Chesh. Gloss.* s.v., To *scotch* a ladder is to 'foot' it, and thus prevent its slipping. 1895 Ld. Watson in *Law Times Rep.* LXXIII. 636/2 Hopper..insufficiently scotched the waggon which ran down the incline and killed the deceased. 1898 Ansted *Dict. Sea Terms* s.v., To be *scotched up* is to be supported, as a boat may be when propped or 'scotched up' against a quay by timber shores or legs.

b. *fig.* To render inoperative, cripple the action of; to frustrate (a plan).

1876 L. Stephen *Eng. Th. 18th C.* I. 33 The name of Spinozism was of course dreaded by them [*sc.* the Deists]; they take care both to avoid the imputation, and to make it undeserved by carefully scotching their logic. 1895 in *Funk's Stand. Dict.* 1897 'O. Rhoscomyl' *White Rose Arno* 163, I scotched the project of retreat for this council, at any rate.

†**2.** *intr.* (Chiefly with negative.) To hesitate, scruple, boggle, or stick *at*; to hesitate *to do* something. Also, to haggle *with* a person *for* something. *Obs.* exc. *dial.*

1601 Dent *Pathw. Heaven* 74 For when [men] come to giuing vnto holy and necessarie vses, then they will sticke at a pennie, and scotch at a groat, and euery thing is too much. 1627 J. Carter *Plain Expos.* 47 He will have vs value our humilitie, loyaltie, and pliablenesse to the higher powers..at so high a rate, as to scotch at no hardship, to give them, or their assignes, iust content. *Ibid.* 81 God hath giuen the greater,..wherefore out of question, hee will not scotch with vs for the lesse. a 1825 Forby *Voc. E. Anglia*, *Scotch v.* to spare; to refrain...So when we say 'I did not scotch to tell him my mind', we mean 'I did not at all mince the matter'. 1887 *S. Chesh. Gloss.*, *Scotch*, to hesitate, stick at. 'He scotches at nowt'.

3. *intr.* Of a horse: ? To boggle, shy.

1894 Sir J. Astley *Fifty Yrs. Life* II. 216 Soon after he [*sc.* a racehorse] started he began to scotch, and was on the point of stopping to kick.

Hence **Sco·tching** *vbl. sb.* Also **Sco·tcher** *nonce-wd.*, an implement for scotching or blocking.

1800 Mar. Edgeworth *Parents' Assist.* (1856) 460, 'I call this thing my scotcher,' said Paul, 'because I always scotch the wheels with it.' 1859 F. A. Griffiths *Artil. Man.* (1862) 110 This is called scotching, or chocking.

Scotch, variant of Scutch *sb.* and *v.*

Scotch bonnet.

1. (See Bonnet *sb.* 1.)

a 1803 J. Beattie (*title*), To the Right Honourable Lady Charlotte Gordon, Dressed in a Tartan Scotch Bonnet, with plumes. 1840 Dickens *Old C. Shop* xvii, Their Scotch bonnets, were ornamented with plumes of jet black feathers. 1876 A'Beckett *Holiday in Scot. Highlands* 29 The sentry..in spite of wearing a Scotch bonnet, had evidently been born in the sister island.

2. *pl.* **a.** The fairy-ring mushroom, *Marasmius oreades*. **b.** The bonnet-pepper, *Capsicum tetragonum*.

1696 Ray *Synopsis Stirp. Brit.* (ed. 2) 13 Fungus lamellatus,..Scotch-bonnets. 1858 Simmonds *Dict. Trade*, *Scotch-bonnets*, a name for the champignon; also for a variety of capsicum. 1861 H. Macmillan *Footn. Page Nat.* 256 Every one is familiar with the common campignon or Scotch bonnets, which form those sour ringlets in the grassy meadows popularly called fairy rings. 1866 in *Treas. Bot.*

Scotch cap.

1. A man's head-dress made of thick firm woollen cloth, without a brim, and decorated with two tails or streamers.

One form is the Glengarry which is elongated, with a depression in the middle. Another is the Balmoral, which is round and flat, the top projecting all round the head.

1591 Spenser *M. Hubberd* 209 Vpon his head an old Scotch cap he wore. 1595 *Locrine* IV. ii. 20 *Stage-Direction*, Enter Strumbo with a pitchforke and a scotch-cap. 1889 Clark Russell *Marooned* (1890) 274 Nothing was wanting to him but his Scotch cap.

2. *U.S.* **a.** The wild black raspberry, *Rubus occidentalis.* 1891 in *Century Dict.*

b. The salmon-berry, *Rubus parviflorus.*

1902 in Webster *Suppl.*

†**Scotch cloth.** *Obs.* A textile fabric resembling lawn, but cheaper; said to have been made of nettle fibre.

1675 Grew *Anat. Plants, Trunks* (1682) 139 Hemp, is nothing else but the Sap-Vessels of the Barque of the Plant so called. And Scotch-Cloath, is only the Housewifery of the same Parts of the Barque of Nettle. 1696 J. F. *Merch. Wareho. laid open* 37 Scotch Cloth..is a sort of white Sleasie Soft-Cloth,..and since Callico hath been dear, is much used for Linnens for Beds and for Window Curtains. a 1704 T. Brown *Dial. Dead, Reas. Oaths* Wks. 1711 IV. 76 A Physician turn'd a Zealous Expounder of the Bible; or a Sworn Friend of Scotch-Cloth, reconciled to Lawn-Sleeves. 1738 *Gentl. Mag.* VIII. 147/1 A high Altar..at which a brawny Priest officiated in a Habit of Scotch Cloth.

attrib. 1705 Hickeringill *Priest-cr.* (1721) I. 54 Because this is a Prying Age, and Scholarship and Craft is not now ..confin'd to a Cassock, or Scotch-cloth Sleeves.

Scotcheon, obs. form of Scutcheon.

Scotcher, variant of Scutcher.

Sco·tchery. *nonce-wd.* [f. Scotch *a.* + -ery.] Scotch characteristics.

1740 H. Walpole *Let. to Conway* 23 Apr., His solemn Scotchery is a little formidable.

Scotchify (skɒ·tʃifai), *v.* [f. Scotch *a.* + -(i)fy.] *trans.* To render or make Scotch. Hence **Sco·tchified** *ppl. a.*; also **Scotchifica·tion.**

1795 *Jemima* II. 94 That man..who sometimes talks scotchified. 1817 J. Evans *Excurs. Windsor*, etc. 487 The general character of the place [Ostend] was marked by the long windows and Scotchified gable ends of the houses. 1824 J. Gilchrist *Etym. Interpr.* 272 Even the English are perceived to be Scotchified in their speech after a short residence in the North. 1832 *Fraser's Mag.* VI. 501 [It] is only a Scotchification of a well-known Spanish proverb. 1850 T. McCrie *Mem. Agnew* 211 They begged him not to 'Scotchify' their Sunday. 1891 *Daily News* 19 Jan. 5/6 The 'Scotchification of Essex'—we use the local expression. ..It is all owing to Scotch agriculturists taking a fancy for Essex farms.

Scotchiness (skɒ·tʃinės). [f. Scotchy *a.* + -ness.] The state or condition of being Scotchy.

1815 Southey *Lett.* (1856) II. 411 [Murray's letters have] a certain cast of Scotchiness about them. 1876 J. Brown *Lett.* (1907) 247 Your mother would have rejoiced in Bogle —his sense, his homeliness,..his Scotchiness.

Scotchion, obs. form of Scutcheon.

Scotch-Irish, *a.* Belonging to that part of the population of northern Ireland which is descended from Scotch settlers. Also *absol.* in plural sense. So **Scotch-Irishman.**

1876 Bancroft *Hist. U.S.* IV. iii. 333 But its convenient proximity to the border counties of Pennsylvania and Virginia had been observed by Scotch-Irish Presbyterians and other bold and industrious men. 1883 *Harper's Mag.* Feb. 421/2 The so-called Scotch-Irish are the descendants of the Englishmen and Lowland Scotch who began to move over to Ulster in 1611. 1897 *Outing* (U.S.) XXX. 136/2 Late in the afternoon we got into the Scotch-Irish part of the valley.

†**Sco·tchism.** *Obs. rare*[−1]. [f. Scotch *a.* + -ism.] A Scotch peculiarity. (Cf. Scotticism.)

1737 Ozell *Rabelais* III. 231 *note*, This is not a Scotchism but an Irish-ism.

Scotchman (skɒ·tʃmæn). Also 6 **Scotcheman,** 7 *Sc.* **Scotsshman.** [f. Scotch *a.* + Man.] A man of Scottish nationality.

The usual English name; the prevalent form used now by Scotch people is Scotsman.

1570 Levins *Manip.* 21/3 Scotcheman, *Scotus*. 1597 P. Lowe *Chirurgerie* title, The Whole Covrse of Chirurgerie. ..Compiled by Peter Lowe Scotchman. 1632 Massinger *City Madam* II. ii, May the Great Fiend, booted & spurr'd With a Sithe at his girdle, as the Scotchman saies, Ride headlong down her throat. 1671 Fraser *Polichron.* (S. H. S.) 491 After the peace he went up to Pole with other Scotsshmen. 1706 Phillips (ed. Kersey), *Scots* or *Scotch-men*, the People of Scotland, a part of Great Britain. 1763 Johnson in *Boswell* (1791) I. 231 The noblest prospect which a Scotchman ever sees is the high-road that leads him to England! 1773 Macpherson *Ossian's Poems* (1806) I. *Dissert.* 37 A Scotchman, tolerably conversant in his own language, understands Irish composition. 1820 Scott *Monast.* Introd. Ep., 'Then,' said I, 'you are a native Scotchman..?' 'Not so, answered the monk; 'I am a Scotchman by extraction only.' 1821 Lamb *Elia* I. *Imperf. Sympathies*, I have been trying all my life to like Scotchmen and am obliged to desist from the experiment in despair.

Comb. 1833 L. Ritchie *Wand. by Loire* 26 Determining.. to be exceedingly prudent and Scotchman-like.

b. (Also *Flying Scotchman*.) A familiar name for the Scotch express (London to Edinburgh) on the Great Northern and on the London & North-Western Railway. Cf. Irishman b (*b*).

1874 R. C. Rapier *Signals Railw.* 56 On arriving at King's Cross, the Flying Scotchman had not yet departed. [1879 Flying Scotsman: see Scotsman.] 1881 Reynolds *Engine-driving Life* 59 The same express-men..were proceeding down a bank..at about 3 a.m. in summer with the 'Scotchman'. 1885 G. Dolby *Dickens as I knew him* 33 A railway carriage which was being dragged along at the rate of fifty miles an hour by the 'Flying Scotchman'. 1892 *Strand Mag.* Feb. 195 This Scotch Express (significantly named 'The Flying Scotchman') is believed to be the fastest train in the world.

c. A travelling draper or pedlar: see Scotch *a.* 1 b. *dial.* (See examples in *Eng. Dial. Dict.*)

1851 Mayhew *Lond. Labour* I. 381 Mother, here's the Tallyman, Mother, here's the Scotchman.

d. *Scotchman hugging a Creole*, a West Indian name for various species of *Clusia*.

1835 M. Scott *Tom Cringle* xiv, Do you see that Scotchman hugging the Creole? 1889 *Boston* (Mass.) *Jrnl.* 25 May 6/6 One more queer tree is the wild fig, familiarly called 'Scotchman hugging a Creole'.

e. A New Zealand name for a smaller kind of the prickly bushy grass called 'Spaniard' (*Aciphylla colensoi*).

1895 W. S. Roberts *Southland in* 1856, 39 (Morris) As we neared the hills speargrass of the smaller kind, known as 'Scotchmen', abounded, and although not so strong and sharp-pointed as the 'Spaniard', would not have made a comfortable seat.

2. *Naut.* A piece of hide, wood, or iron, etc. placed over a rope to prevent its being chafed.

1841 R. H. Dana *Seaman's Man.*, *Scotchman*, a large batten placed over the turnings-in of rigging. 1850 R. G. Cumming *Hunter's Life S. Afr.* (1902) 1/2 On the top of this are placed coarse Kaffir mats made of reeds, which act as a Scotchman (to use a seafaring phrase), to keep the waggon sail, which is of stout canvas, from chafing. c 1860 H. Stuart *Seaman's Catech.* 83 A Scotchman should be made of leather,..to allow the new skin to harden. 1882 Nares *Seamanship* (ed. 6) 68 How is the lower rigging protected from being cut by the futtock rigging? By lashing iron Scotchmen on the shrouds.

3. *S. African.* A florin. (See quot. 1879.)

1879 Atcherley *Trip Boërland* 55 In dealing with the Kafirs, I frequently heard the term 'Scotchman' applied to a two-shilling piece: and upon enquiry was informed that an enterprising gentleman of that nationality having once passed a large number of florins to the Kafirs as half-crown pieces, the latter had ever since christened the florin 'Scotchman'. 1887 Rider Haggard *Jess* x, Jantjé spat upon the 'Scotchman', as the natives in that part of Africa [Transvaal] call a two-shilling piece.

4. *U.S.* The 'Scotch duck', *Charitonetta* (or *Bucephala*) *albeola*. 1895 in *Funk's Stand. Dict.*

5. *colloq.* A Scotch fir.

1901 'Lucas Malet' *Sir R. Calmady* VI. vii, 'What shall we do with it [a piece of land]?' 'Oh, plant,' she said. 'With the ubiquitous Scotchman?' 'It wouldn't carry anything else, except along the boundaries.'

Scotchness (skɒ·tʃnės). [f. Scotch *a.* + -ness.] Scotch quality or character.

1865 G. Macdonald *A. Forbes* xxviii, Annie had a certain Scotchness in her which made her draw back from the offer. 1892 Stevenson *Let. to J. M. Barrie* (1899) II. 247 My own Scotchness tends to intermittency.

Sco·tchwo·man. [f. Scotch *a.* + Woman; orig. two words.] A woman who is a native of Scotland or of Scotch descent.

1818 Scott *Hrt. Midl.* xxxiii, The neat, clean, quiet-looking little Scotchwoman, who now stood before her. 1827 — *Chron. Canongate* v, Knowing her honesty,..and, although a Scotchwoman, her cleanliness and excellent temper.

Scotchy, *sb. colloq.* [f. Scotch *a.* + -y.] A nickname for a Scotchman.

1861 *Two Cosmos* II. 62 Will you come it now, Scotchy, and I don't mind if I forgive you if you can lick me?

Scotchy (skɒ·tʃi), *a.* [f. Scotch *a.* + -y.] Having the characteristics of what is Scotch.

1815 Southey *Lett.* (1856) II. 414 It is impossible that any compositions can be more booksellerish and more Scotchy. 1896 Ashby-Sterry *Tale of Thames* viii, I don't read them all [*i.e.* Scott's novels]. Some of the very Scotchiest ones I can*not* stand.

Comb. 1874 A. J. C. Hare *Story My Life* (1900) IV. xvii. 258 A great Scotchy-looking house.

†**Scote,** *sb.*[1] *Obs.* [Cf. Du. *schoot* 'sheet' (i.e. rope), whence OF. *escoute* (mod.F. *écoute*).] ? A kind of cable.

1394 *Issue Roll*, Easter 17 Rich. II, 5 Sept. (Devon) [Five cables, weighing 5941 lbs...two] scotes [weighing 348 lbs.].

†**Scote,** *sb.*[2] *Obs. rare.* [? a. MDu. *schote*, a definite quantity of some article.] = Beat *sb.*[3]

1633–4 *N. Riding Rec.* III. 365 A labourer for stealing 7 scotes of hemp. *Ibid.*, A labourer presented for stealing 7 beates or scotes of hemp.

Scote (skōut), *sb.*[3] *dial.* [Of obscure origin: cf. Norw. *skota* pole, bar, forked stick; also OF. *escot* (mod.F. *écot*) stump.] (See quot. 1890.)

1839 *Herefordsh. Gloss.*, *Scote*, a dragstaff (Glouc.). 1890 *Glouc. Gloss.* 132 *Scote*, an ironshod staff attached to the axle of the hind wheel of a waggon to prevent it running back down hill.

Scote (skōut), *v. Obs.* exc. *dial.* Also 7–8 **scoat,** 9 **scort.** [f. Scote *sb.*[3] Cf. Scotch *v.*[2]] *trans.* To set a drag upon (the wheel of a wagon).

1642 R. Harris *Serm.* 45 This is that that scoat's the businesse in publike. 1678 Phillips (ed. 4), To *Scoat*, to put a Stone or peece of Wood under a Cart to stop it from going forward. 1890 *Glouc. Gloss.* 132 *Scort* or *Scote*.

Scoteino·graphy. *nonce-wd.* [f. Gr. σκοτεινό-ς dark + -γραφία: see -graphy.] Illegible writing.

1779 Twining *Let.* 17 Sept., in *Parr's Wks.* (1828) VIII. 267, I thought myself a tolerable adept in this art of scoteinography, but I give you the wall.

†**Scoteo·graphy.** *Obs.* [irreg. f. Gr. σκότεο-ς gen. of σκότος darkness + -γραφία writing: see -graphy.] (See quot.)

1803 J. Gough in *Nicholson's Jrnl.* VII. 53 Scoteography or the Art of Writing in the Dark.

Scoter (skōu·təɹ). [Of obscure origin.] A duck of the genus *Œdemia*, esp. *Œdemia nigra*, a native of the Arctic regions and common in the seas of Northern Europe and America. Also *scoter-duck*.

1674 Ray *Collect., Catal. Birds* 96 The Scoter: *Anas niger*. 1768 Pennant *Brit. Zool.* (1776) II. 494 Scoter...This bird is allowed in the Romish church to be eaten in Lent. 1808–13 A. Wilson & Bonaparte *Amer. Ornith.* (1831) III. 212 Scoter duck. 1845 *Zoologist* III. 1077 The scoter..has occurred twice in winter at some water in Basing parish. 1870 Gillmore tr. *Figuier's Reptiles & Birds* 239 The writers of the Middle Ages and the Renaissance..had very vaguely described the Scoter Duck.

†**Sco·terlope,** *v. Obs.* [Metathesis of Scoperloit *v.*, after Lope *v.*] *intr.* ? To wander aimlessly.

1583 Golding *Calvin on Deut.* xix. 113 God mindeth to try our obedience, by restreining vs from..scoterloping ouer the fieldes (orig. F. *de courir à travers champs*) to raught at euerie thing that we like off.

Scotewache, obs. variant of Scoutwatch.

†**Scotewine.** *Obs. rare*[−1]. [Cf. Scot *sb.*[3] 2, Scotart.] An alleged name for the hare.

a 1325 *Names of Hare* in *Rel. Ant.* I. 133 The scotewine, the skikart.

Scot-free, *a.* Also *rarely* 6 **scotchfree,** 7 **scotts-free.** See also Shot-free. [f. Scot *sb.*[2] + Free *a.* Cf. MDu. *scholvrî* (the mod.Du. *schotvrij* 'shot-proof' is independently formed), OSw. *skutfri-r.*] Free from payment of 'scot', tavern score, fine, etc.; exempt from injury, punishment, etc.; scatheless. Almost exclusively *predicative*; esp. in the phrase *to go scot free*.

In the mod. use of the expression, 'scot' is probably often interpreted as a mere intensive.

? 12.. *Charter of* 1066 in Kemble *Cod. Diplom.* IV. 191 Scotfre and gauelfre, on schire and on hundrede. 1531 Tindale *Expos. 1 John* (1537) 22 The poore synner shulde go Skot fre without oughte at all. 1546 *St. Papers Hen. VIII*, XI. 129 What damages their cuntrey and peple had suffred by this warre, and that Your Majestie went not all scott free. a 1548 Hall *Chron., Edw. IV*, 233 They payed no money, but were set scot free. 1567 Maplet *Green Forest* 93 Daniell scaped scotchfree by Gods prouidence. 1579–80 North *Plutarch, Tiberius & Caius* (1595) 878 Caius..had charged the poore citizens with an annuall rent for the lands ..Liuius..did please them by..letting them haue the lands scotfree. 1622 Mabbe tr. *Aleman's Guzman d'Alf.* II. 231 The first speaker scapes scot-free. 1665–6 Wood *Life* (O. H. S.) II. 73 Oxford escaped scot fre of the plague. 1740 Richardson *Pamela* (1824) I. 117 She should not, for all the trouble she has cost you, go away scot-free. 1792 Wolcot (P. Pindar) *Odes of Condolence* Wks. 1794 III. 237 Scot-free the Poets drank and ate; They paid no taxes to the State! 1819 Scott *Ivanhoe* xii, Do as much for this fellow and thou shalt pass scot-free. 1858 R. S. Surtees *Ask Mamma* xiv. 45 The sporting inhabitants thereof preferred the money-griping propensities of a certain Baronet..to the scot-free sport with the frigid civilities of the noble Earl. 1875 Stubbs *Const. Hist.* xiv. I. 133 The people had not been heavily taxed, and the clergy had passed..scot-free. 1877 Black *Green Past.* xiii, When some notorious offender has got off scot free.

¶ **b.** ? Mis-used for: Without inflicting damage.

1652–66 in Gilbert *Contemp. Hist. Irel.* I. 25 [They] shooted at him with earnest leuell, and not scotts-free for presently he was tumbled to the earth deadly wounded.

‖ **Scotia** (skōu·ʃiă). *Arch.* [L. *scotia* (Vitruvius), a. Gr. σκοτία, f. σκότος darkness (so called from the dark shadow within the cavity); cf. F. *scotie*.] A hollow moulding. = Casement 1.

1563 Shute *Archit.* 11 The nethermost Trochilus or Scotia. 1664 Evelyn tr. *Freart's Archit.* 125 Our Workmen retain the antient Scotia..but more vulgarly they call it the Casement. 1789 Smyth tr. *Aldrich's Archit.* (1818) 90 Other particles of an order are hollow, the common name to which is scotia. a 1878 Sir G. Scott *Lect. Archit.* (1879) I. 152 In England another kind of base is frequent, in which a bead is substituted for the scotia.

†**Sco·tian,** *a. nonce-wd.* [f. med.L. *Scōtia* Scotland + -an.] Of or belonging to Scotland.

1803 Leyden *Scenes Infancy* I. 232 But long Their fame shall flourish in the Scotian song.

Scotic (skɒ·tik), *a.* Also 8–9 **Scottic.** [ad. late L. *Scōticus, Scotticus*, f. *Scōt-us, Scott-us*: see Scot *sb.*[1]]

†**1.** Used as a designation for the Scottish dialect.

c 1645 Howell *Lett.* (1655) II. 74 The English speech.. hath..divers subdialects..but her chiefest is the Scotic, which took footing beyond Tweed about the last conquest.

2. Pertaining to the ancient Scots.

1796 Morse *Amer. Geog.* II. 183 The uncorrupted native language of the Irish is the Gaedhloc, or Scottic. 1851 D. Wilson *Archæol. & Preh. Ann. Scot.* 470 Cairbre Riada, a celebrated Scottic warrior. *Ibid.* 479 The Scotic line of princes. 1873 *Contemp. Rev.* XXI. 253 Our method of colonization has failed with the children of the Scotic race. 1882–3 *Schaff's Encycl. Relig. Knowl.* II. 1232 Celestius, the companion of Pelagius, is supposed by some to have been of Scotic, i.e., Irish origin. 1900 Macbain in Skene *Highlanders Scot.* 400 Donald being likely a Scotic prince.

†**Sco·tical,** *a. Obs. rare*[−1]. [Formed as prec. + -ical.] Of or belonging to Scotland; Scottish.

a 1548 Hall *Chron., Hen. IV* (1550) 16 b, Wherof the occasion shall bee to you declared accordyng to the Scoticall histories.

Scotican (skɒ·tikăn), *a.* [f. late L. *Scōtic-us* (see Scotic), after Anglican.] Of or pertaining to the Scots ecclesiastically.

1635 [see Anglican *a.* 1]. 1830 Chambers *Jas. I*, II. ix. 257 Equalizing the Anglican and Scotican Churches. 1844 *Bp. Sage's Wks.* I. Mem. 23 They regarded the Scotican Church..as schismatical.

Scoticè, -icism see Scotticè, -icism.

Scoti·ety. *humorous nonce-wd.* [f. the name *Scōtus*, in imitation of scholastic terms.] The essential nature of John Duns Scotus.

1655 Fuller *Ch. Hist.* III. 97 The very Scotiety of Scotus belongeth to England as his Native Country.

Scotify: see Scottify.

†**Sco·tism**[1]. *Obs.*[−0] [f. late L. *Scōt-us* Scot + -ism.] = Scotticism.

1570 Levins *Manip.* 146 [Words that end in *isme*] be of three sortes...The second be taken of a countrey or language, as of..Scotte, *Scotisme, Scotismus*.

Scotism[2] (skōu·tiz'm). *Theol.* [ad. med.L. *Scōtismus*, f. *Scōt-us* (see Scotist) + -ism.]

1. The teaching of Scotus or the Scotists.

a 1871 G. S. Morris tr. *Ueberweg's Hist. Philos.* (1872) I. 454 Scotism is..like Thomism, one of the doctrines in which Scholasticism culminates. 1886 *Encycl. Brit.* XXI. 429/2 Hervæus Natalis (*ob.* 1323) and Thomas Bradwardine (*ob.* 1349) were determined opponents of Scotism. 1900 *Month* July 50 This would go to show that Scotism, for which England had been celebrated in the middle ages, had already lost its hold on English Catholic thought.

2. *pl.* (*nonce-use*.) Subtleties such as are characteristic of the Scotists.

1645 Milton *Tetrach.* 28 These ages wherin Canons, and Scotisms, and Lumbard Laws, have dull'd, and almost obliterated the lively Sculpture of ancient reason.

Scotist (skōu·tist), *sb.* and *a. Eccl.* [ad. med.L. *Scōtista*, f. *Scōtus*: see below.] **a.** *sb.* A follower or disciple of John Duns Scotus (known as 'The Subtle Doctor'), a scholastic philosopher and theologian of the 13th c., whose system in many respects was opposed to that of Thomas Aquinas. (See Dunce.) **b.** *adj.* Belonging to the Scotists.

1530 [see Dunce, etym. note]. 1562 tr. *Jewel's Apol.* 21 How happeneth it then that the Scotistes and the Thomistes do agree no better about merytes of conueniency, and merites of duety? 1661 tr. *Erasm. Life Colet* in *Colet's Serm.* 75 His Bishop..was a superstitious and stubborn Scotist. 1709 Pope *Ess. Crit.* 244 Scotists and Thomists now in peace remain Amidst their kindred cobwebs in Duck-lane. 1884 *Catholic Dict.* (1897) 826/2 Decrees were passed requiring the Scotist doctrine to be taught in all the Franciscan schools. 1886 *Encycl. Brit.* XXI. 429 This primacy of the undetermined will..was the central contention of Scotists against the Thomist doctrine.

†**Scoti·stical,** *a.*[1] *Obs.* [f. prec. + -ical.] Pertaining to or characteristic of the Scotists.

1600 tr. *Garzoni's Hosp. Incur. Fooles* A 4 b, Betweene them and Folly there is a iust Logicall equipollence..and a Scotisticall Identitie. 1716 M. Davies *Athen. Brit.* III. *Diss. Drama* 4 The Thomistical and Scotistical Schools and Preaching Orders of Dominicans, Franciscans [etc.].

†**Scoti·stical,** *a.*[2] *Obs.* [f. Scot *sb.*[1] + -istical (see -istic).] ? Favouring what is Scottish.

1650 A. B. *Mutat. Polemo* 14 Neither can they imagine whether these Scotisticall Pioneers will be Scots or no Scots.

†**Sco·tistry.** *Obs. rare*[−1]. [f. Scotist + -ry.] The habit of thought proper to a Scotist.

1651 Fuller *Abel Rediv.*, *Colet* 105 His own Bishop, of whose Sophisticall Scotistry the Deane made no great account, and the Bishop as little of his Ciceronian Divinity.

†**Sco·tize,** *v. Obs.* Also 6–7 **scottize.** [f. Scot *sb.*[1] + -ize.] *intr.* To imitate the Scots; to favour Scottish ways. Hence **Sco·tizing** *ppl. a.*

1593 Abp. Bancroft *Dangerous Positions* 41 *headline*, English Scottizing for Discipline. 1607 Sir J. Harington *Nugæ Ant.* (1804) II. 25 His Majestie had long since understanding of his wryting against the genevising and scotising ministers. 1623 W. Lisle *Ælfric on O. & N. Test.* To Rdr. 13 An Englishman Scottizing once to our King was roundly reproued for it. 1659 Gauden *Tears Ch.* III. xix. 323 A Scotizing zeal. a 1662 Heylin *Laud* IV. (1668) 328 The English had Scotized in all their Practises. *Ibid.* V. 460 Thereby drawing on himself the general hatred not only of the Scots, but Scotizing English.

†**Sco·tized,** *ppl. a. Obs.* [f. prec. + -ed[1].] Imbued with Scottish (ecclesiastical) principles.

1657 Sanderson *Serm.* Pref. § 24 The rigid Scotised, through-paced Presbyterian on the one side and the giddy Enthusiast on the other. 1711 G. Hickes *Two Treat. Chr. Priesth.* Pref. Disc. 220 The High-scotized Flyers..among the Presbyterians.

†**Sco·tnail.** *north. Obs.* Forms: 4 **scot-,** 4–5 **schot-,** 5 **shot-.** [Cf. Du. *schotspijker* (f. *schot* ? partition + *spijker* nail).] Some kind of nail. Cf. Scotsem-nail.

1349–50 in *Bp. Hatfield's Surv.* (Surtees) 202 In spykings ferri, lednaylls, schotnaylls et bordnaylls empt. pro aula cooperienda ut supra, 3s. 10d. 1349–50 *Durh. Acc. Rolls* (Surtees) 550 Spykyng', et Scotnayls pro fonte infra Abbathiam. 1374 *Ibid.* 211 Et in spikyngs, schetnaill' [? read schotnaill'], stanbrod..42s. 5d. 1449–50 *Ibid.* 239, 200[ma] del spikynger, 2.0[ma] del shotnaill. 1454 *Ibid.* 149 Item..ij wayneclowtez cum spikyng et shotnayll.

Scoto- (skɒ·to, skōu·to), combining form of late L. *Scōtus* Scot *sb.*[1], prefixed (with hyphen) to ethnic adjs. (rarely sbs.) either with the sense 'belonging to Scotland', as in *Scoto-Britannic, -Celtic, -English, -Gaelic, -Gallic, -Norwegian, -Scandinavian* adjs., *Scoto-Norman* sb., or with the sense 'partly Scottish and partly...', as in *Scoto-Irish* adj.

1650 B. *Discollimininum* 45 The good man is in such a wofull Scoto-Britannick pickle. 1824 G. Chalmers *Caledonia* III. III. vi. 253 This Scoto-Irish people. 1828–43 Tytler *Hist. Scot.* (1864) I. 249 The Saxons and the Scoto-Normans. 1837 Lockhart *Scott* II. 332 The clergy of the primitive Scoto-Celtic Church. 1846 C. Innes *Liber de Calchou* (Bannatyne Club) Pref. 30 The permanent incorporation of

the Scoto-Saxon lowlands with the kingdom of Scotland proper. 1851 D. Wilson *Archæol. & Preh. Ann. Scot.* 490 The subsequent history of the Scoto-Norwegian kingdoms. *Ibid.* 522 Scoto-Scandinavian relics. 1858–61 Ramsay *Remin.* vi. (1870) 245 Scoto-Gallic words were..differently situated. 1867 Burton *Hist. Scot.* I. vii. 261 The Scoto-Irish saints. 1876 Smiles *Sc. Natur.* viii. (ed. 4) 138 Their language is Gaelic, whereas that of the rest of the county [Banffs.] is Scoto-English. 1905 *Athenæum* 7 Oct. 466/1 Most purely Scoto-Gaelic words prefix the article.

Scotograph (skōu·tŏgraf). [f. Gr. σκότο-ς darkness + -γραφος: see -graph.] An instrument for writing in the dark, or without seeing.

1869 Nuttall *Dict. Sci. Terms*, *Scotograph*, an instrument with which a blind person may write.

Scotography (skotǫ·grăfi). *rare.* [f. Gr. σκότος darkness: see -graphy.] The exhibition of the effect of the Röntgen rays; the production of a picture by means of such rays; = Radiography. Hence **Scotogra·phic** *a.* = Radiographic *a.*

1896 Sir Alfred Wills in *Times* 10 Mar. 12/2 [The X rays] have very little in common with light. Would not 'scotography' be a better name for their work than 'photography'? 1895 *Westm. Gaz.* 18 Mar. 1/3 A correspondent who was present on Friday sends us some notes of that remarkable 'skotographic' séance.

‖ **Scotoma** (skotōu·mă). *Path.* Pl. **scotomata** (skotōu·mătă). [late L. *scotōma*, a. Gr. σκότωμα dizziness, f. σκοτοῦν to darken, make dim-sighted, f. σκότος darkness.]

†**1.** Dizziness accompanied by dimness of sight; = Scotomy. *Obs.*

1543 Traheron *Vigo's Chirurg.* Interpr. s.v. *Scotomia*, Some go about, to make a foolysh difference of scotoma, and vertigo. 1822–29 *Good's Study Med.* (ed. 3) IV. 534 Hence Linnæus..has even made scotoma, or dizziness with blindness and a tendency to swoon, a distinct genus also.

2. An obscuration of part of the visual field, due to lesion of the retina or of the ophthalmic centres in the brain.

1875 Walton *Dis. Eye* 645 Without limitation of the visual field or scotomata,..direct vision may be much diminished in the region of the yellow spot. 1897 *Allbutt's Syst. Med.* III. 219 Central scotoma, or loss of vision in the central part of the field, is common [in diabetes].

†**Scotoma·tical,** *a. Obs. rare.* [f. med.L. *scotōmatic-us* (f. *scotōma*: see prec.) + -al.] Suffering from or under the influence of scotoma.

1656 Blount *Glossogr.* a 1691 Baxter in *Reliq. B.* (1696) I. II. 199. I was then under great Weakness and Soporous or Scotomatical Ilness of my Head.

‖ **Scoto·mia.** *Path.* [med.L., irreg. f. *scotōma*, after names of diseases in *-ia*.] = Scotoma 1.

1543 Traheron *Vigo's Chirurg.* Interpr. s.v., *Scotomia*. They shoulde saye, Scotoma, and it is a disease, when [etc.]. 1728 Chambers *Cycl.*, *Scotomia*, or *Scotoma*, in medicine, a dizziness or swimming in the head. 1879 Khory *Digest Med.* 13 There may be flashes of light or muscæ volitantes or scotomia.

†**Sco·tomy.** *Path. Obs.* [Anglicized form of Scotomia.] = Scotoma 1.

c 1400 *Lanfranc's Cirurg.* 118, & if þat he hadde scotomie, þat is to seie a maner sijknes, whanne þat þer semeþ as flien or oþere smale gnattis fleen tofore his yȝen. a 1500 in James *West. MSS. Trin. Coll. Camb.* (1902) III. 494 Scotomye is such a sekenes of the Brayne that maketh a man to seme that he sethe flyes or blake thingis in þe eyre. 1533 Elyot *Cast. Helthe* II. xxxiv. (1541) 50 In swellyng of the body and legges..mygrimes, and scotomies, which is an imagination of darkenes. 1605 B. Jonson *Volpone* I. iv. (1607) C 2, How do's he, with the swimming of his head? *Mos.* O, Sir, tis past the Scotomy; he, now, Hath lost his feeling, and hath left to snort. a 1640 Massinger, etc. *Old Law* III. ii, I ha got the Scotony [*sic*] in my head already, The whimsy: you all turne round, do not you dance gallants? 1710 T. Fuller *Pharmacop.* 222 We employ it [i.e. the Infusion] with happy Success in..Scotomy, &c.

†**Sco·toscope.** *Obs.* [f. Gr. σκότο-ς darkness + -scope.] An instrument which enables the user to see in the dark.

1664 Pepys *Diary* 13 Aug., There comes also Mr. Reeve with a microscope and scotoscope..a curious curiosity it is to discover objects in a dark room with. c 1670 Collins in Rigaud *Corr. Sci. Men* (1841) II. 291 The perfection of telescopes, microscopes, scotoscopes, and burning glasses.

†**Sco·try.** *Obs. rare*[−1]. [f. Scot *sb.*[1] + -ry.] The Scots collectively.

c 1470 Harding *Chron.* CCXL. (1812) 420 *note*, Betuene the see of the West occion, And the hilles of Scotlonde occident, The wilde Scotrie have their propre mancion.

Scots (skɒts), *a.* (*sb.*) Orig. *Sc.* and *northern*. Forms: 4 **Skot(t)is,** 4–6 **Scottis,** 5–7 **Scottes,** 6 **Skottes, Scotes, Scotis,** 6–8 **Scotts,** 7– **Scots.** [Orig. *Scottis*, northern var. of Scottish. (Cf. *Inglis* English.)

For the relation in use between this form and the two others, see Scotch *a.*]

1. Of or belonging to Scotland or its inhabitants, Scottish, Scotch.

a 1352 Minot *Poems* (ed. Hall) i. 79 And þarfore many a Skottis brid With dole er dight þat þai most dwell. 1473 Warkw. *Chron.* (Camden) 2 The Scottes host. 1500–20 Dunbar *Poems* lxxxvii. 40 Fair gem of joy, Mergreit of the I meyne: Gladethe thoue Queyne of Scottis regioun. 1513 Douglas *Æneis* I. Prol. 103 This buik I dedicate, Writing in the language of Scottis natioun. 1622 Malynes *Anc. Law-Merch.* 80 Scots-coale, Wheat, Barley and all kind of graines in both Kingdomes. 1637 Monro *Exped.* II. 23 The other Scots Officers of the Regiment. 1797 Dr. Burney *Let. to Mme. D'Arblay* 28 Sept., A Scots lady. 1827 Hallam *Const. Hist.* xvii. (1857) III. 337 The Scots parliament took care to bring on the crisis by the act of security in 1704. 1902 Buchan *Watcher by Threshold* 125 He thought Scots games inferior to southern sports.

b. Qualifying the name of a coin or a money of account (in contradistinction to *sterling*), as *mark Scots, penny Scots, pound Scots, shilling Scots* (see the sbs.). Also in names of weights and measures denoting a particular variation from the English standard, *Scots acre, boll, mile, pint, stone, Troy weight* (see the sbs.). Now *arch.* or *Hist.*

1520 *Charges conc. Dk. Albany* in G. Douglas *Wks.* (1874) I. Introd. 109 Fourty thousand pund of Scottis money. *Ibid.*, Bettir than ten thousand pundis Scottis. 1632 [see Milk *sb.* 2]. 1641 in Cochran-Patrick *Rec. Coinage Scot.* (1876) I. Introd. 30 The king hes vpon the coinage of euerie Scots staine of silver bulyion 64 li. 1697 in A. I. Ritchie *Churches of St. Baldred* (1880) 39 Whoever shall desire the great bell to be rung to any burial, must pay for the same ten shillings Scots. 1765 *Museum Rust.* IV. 455 From eleven to twelve pecks, Linlithgow measure, of Dutch or Riga seed, is generally sufficient for one Scots acre. 1775 *Brit. Chronol.* an. 1719 II. 51/2 An act for laying a duty of two pennies *Scots*..upon every pint of ale or beer that shall be vended or sold within the town of Inverness. 1791 Burns *Tam o' Shanter* 7 We think na on the lang Scots miles.. That lie between us and our hame. c 1792 *Encycl. Brit.* (ed. 3) X. 718/1 It was enacted by..James VI that it [the pint] should contain 55 Scots Troy ounces of the clear water of Leith. 1801 *Farmer's Mag.* Jan. 72 In one instance, the produce is stated to be..92 Scots bolls per English statute acre. 1824 Scott *Redgauntlet* xx, What say ye to anither pint? or shall we cry in a blithe Scots pint at once? 1838 W. Bell *Dict. Law Scot.* s.v. *Schools*, The salaries of the schoolmasters were to be fixed at from 300 to 400 merks Scots. *Ibid.* s.v., Sterling money is twelve times the value of the same denomination of Scots money. 1883 *American* VI. 270 A legacy by word of mouth is good to the extent of £100 Scots, or £8 6s. 8d. sterling.

c. With reference to law. Cf. Scottish *a.* 1 e.

In this application recent literary usage favours the form *Scots* rather than *Scottish* or *Scotch*, but Scottish legal writers have apparently never followed this rule.

1766 Blackstone *Comm.* II. iv. 57 These inferior feudatories ..held what are called in the Scots law 'rere-fiefs'. 1773 (*title*) An Institute of the Law of Scotland..By John Erskine ..Sometime Professor of Scots Law in the University of Edinburgh. 1820 *Trials for High Treason Scot.* (1825) I. 15 The old Scots law of treason was by no means well defined.

d. In the names of trees and plants. More commonly Scotch.

c 1710 Celia Fiennes *Diary* (1888) 20 On ye right side of ye house is a large grove of firrs halfe scotts halfe norroway. 1728 Bradley *Dict. Bot.* II, *Scots Scurvy-Grass*, i.e. *Soldanella*. 1797 *Encycl. Brit.* (ed. 3) XIV. 761/2 The [*pinus*] *rubra*, commonly called the Scots fir, or pine. 1903 *Q. Jrnl. Forestry* Jan. 70 The whole enclosure was planted in the spring of 1905 with oak,..larch, and Scots pine.

†**e.** *Scots goose*: the barnacle goose. (So Norfolk dial. *Scotch goose*: see *E. D. D.*)

1668 Charleton *Onomast.* 98 *Anser Bernicla*, the Barnacle, or Scots-goose.

2. Of language: **a.** The distinguishing epithet of the dialect of English spoken by the inhabitants of the Lowlands of Scotland. Also *absol.* as *sb.*, the Scottish dialect.

1542 *Sc. Acts Mary* (1814) II. 415/1 It salbe lefull to all our souirane ladyis lieges to haif þe haly write baith þe new testament and þe auld in þe vulgar toung In Inglis or scottis of ane gude and trew translatioune. 1563 Winȝet *Cert. Tractates* Wks. (S. T. S.) I. 74 'By' in Scottis and in Inglis toung is nocht ane. 1596 Dalrymple tr. *Leslie's Hist. Scot.* II. 179 Translating the Æneids of Virgil in scotis; sa rycht..that ilk scotis verse concordet with the latin. 1788 in *Shirrefs' Poems* (1790) p. xxvi, For Scots is neither flat nor lame:..When we had kings and courts at hame, They spake nae ither. 1818 Scott *Rob Roy* xxvii, Kilted loons that dinna ken the name o' a single herb or flower in braid Scots, let abee in the Latin tongue. 1839 Hallam *Lit. Eur.* II. v. § 77 It would be a great omission to neglect..the Scots and English ballads. 1861 *Two Cosmos* I. 294 To use a good old-fashioned Scots phrase. 1902 Buchan *Watcher by Threshold* 281 She speaks broad Scots.

b. Used quasi-*Hist.* for: Scottish Gaelic. *rare*[−1].

1831 Scott *Cast. Dang.* v, An antique language,..being a species of Scots or Gaelic, which few would have comprehended.

3. Characteristic of or peculiar to Scotland or a Scotsman. Now *rare* or *Obs.*

1616 W. Haig in J. Russell *Haigs* (1881) 163 That Scots kindness (ever ready to a friend, but oft inconsiderate). 1812 *Sporting Mag.* XXXIX. 17 Captain Barclay..has reduced Crib from upwards of sixteen stone to the above weight, by Scots living.

4. *Mil.* **a.** In names of regiments in the British Army, as *Scots Fusiliers, Scots Greys* (see Grey *sb.* 8), *Scots Guards*. **b.** In names of bodies of mercenaries in foreign service, as *Scots Brigade, Scots Dutch* (see the equivalent forms under Scotch).

1637 Monro *Exped.* II. 25 Which..thereafter was still called the Scots Briggad commanded by Hepburne. 1646 *Sc. Acts Chas. I* (1870) VI. I. 597/2 Sr. Robert Murray Lieut: colonell to the Scotis Regiment of the guard in France. 1823 Scott *Quentin D.* vii. *note*, Such disputes between the Scots Guards, and the other constituted authorities of the ordinary military corps, often occurred. 1862 A. K. Murray *Scottish Regiments* 70 The Scots Fusilier Guards, with the Grenadiers and Coldstreams, were stationed in the chateau and grounds of Hougomont. 1867 Burton *Hist. Scot.* III. xxvii. 108 The celebrated Scots Guard was established—it is said to have begun in the few who survived the slaughter at Verneuil. 1883 *Macmillan's Mag.* XLVII. 443 Twenty-five mounted infantry of the 2nd Battalion Royal Scots Fusiliers. 1893 Stevenson *Catriona* xii. 132 Lieutenant-colonel in a regiment of the Scots-Dutch.

†**Sco·tsem-nail.** *Obs.* Also 4 **scotsem, scotsum-, scotsom-,** 5 **scotseme-, scotesem-, schotsem-.** [Presumably formed as Scotnail; the middle syllable may be Seam *sb.*, rivet.]

1336 in J. R. Boyle *Hedon* (1895) App. 17 In C. clavis de scotsem emptis..iij d. 1371 *Fabric Rolls York Minster* (Surtees) 7 In 10.m. de Scotsomnail emptis pro celura. 1408 *Durham Acct. Roll* in *Eng. Hist. Rev.* XIV. 518, ccclx schotsemnaylle, c ad viii d; c clavis parvis [etc.]. 1434 *Fabric Rolls York Minster* (Surtees) 53 In xij.m de stonebrodes, in v.m Scotesemnailes, 5s. 5d. In vij.m occc Scotsemnailes, 9s. 2d.

Scotsman (skɒ·tsmæn). Forms: 4 **Scottis man,** 5 **Scottys man, Scottes man, Scotesman,** 5–6 **Scottisman, Scottesman,** 6 **Scotisman,** 7 **Scotts man,** 7–8 **Scots-man,** 6– **Scotsman.** [f. Scots *a.* + Man (orig. two words).] = Scotchman.

c 1375 Barbour *Bruce* XI. 8 Quhen he herd schir Philip say, That Scottis men had set ane day To fecht [etc.]. c 1425 Wyntoun *Cron.* IX. xxi. 401 Þar Scottismen fel gret tynsaille. c 1490 *Paston Lett.* III. 366, I conceyve also that the same Thomas is noysed in Norffolk for a Scotesman borne. 1515 *Minute of Council* in G. Douglas *Wks.* (1874) I. Introd. 61 My Lord Gouernour traistit nocht that ony Scotisman in the realme wald sek help at Inglismen in his doingis. 1548 W. Patten *Exped. Scot.* D viij b, But what saynte so euer he bee, he is sure no Scottes mans frend. 1565 Stapleton tr. *Bede's Hist. Ch. Eng.* III. xxi. 97 These priestes were called Cedda, Adda, Betti, and Diuna, who was a scottesman borne, the other thre english. 1637–50 Row *Hist. Kirk* (Wodrow Soc.) 441 Books and Treatises published by Scotts men. 1780 *Mirror* No. 82 The Earl of Bute, who was both a Scotsman and a favourite. 1818 Scott *Hrt. Midl.* iv, Are not we, like them, Scotsmen and burghers of Edinburgh? 1879 *G.N.R. Tourist-guide* 1 The splendid express known as the 'Flying Scotsman'. 1902 Gairdner *Eng. Ch. 16th Cent.* xiii. 246 The Protector might..have reckoned on the devotion of a little band of Scotsmen in a Scottish stronghold by the sea to assist him.

Hence **Sco·tsmanship,** the nature or quality of a Scotsman.

1828 *Examiner* 56/2 If there is gallantry in Dudley, conceit in Ellenborough, Scotsmanship in Melville. 1894 R. Wallace in *Life & Last Leaves* (1903) 485 'Proud' of his Scotsmanship, he might [etc.].

Sco·tswoman. [Scots *a.*] = Scotchwoman.

1820 Scott *Abbot* iii, 'The slothful hinds!' exclaimed Mary, thinking and feeling like a Scotswoman of the period. 1822 — *Nigel* viii, The old Scotswoman.

Scott(e, variant forms of Scot.

Scottall, Scottel(l, obs. ff. Scotale, Scuttle.

Scottic, variant of Scotic.

‖ **Scotticè, Scoticè** (skǫ·tisi), *adv.* [med.L. *Scotticē, Scōticē*, f. late L. *Scottic-us, Scōtic-us* Scottish.] In Scotch.

1818 Scott *Hrt. Midl.*, *note* L, *Lockman*, so called from the small quantity of meal (Scotticè, *lock*) which he was entitled to take. 1861 *Two Cosmos* II. 129 An enormous pair of old worn-out shoes (Scotticè, bauchles).

Scotticism, Scoticism (skǫ·tisiz'm). [f. late L. *Scōtic-us* (*Scotticus*) + -ism. The spelling with *tt* has prevailed owing to the analogy of *Scottish*.]

1. An idiom or mode of expression characteristic of Scots; esp. as used by a writer of English.

1717 De Foe *Mem. Ch. Scot.* II. 137 This is a Scoticism in Speech. 1759 W. Robertson *Hist. Scot.* VIII. Wks. 1851 II. 323 Many of those vicious forms of speech, which are denominated *Scotticisms*, have been introduced by them [lawyers] into the language. 1772 Wesley *Jrnl.* 11 Dec. (1827) III. 470 The book is wrote with great accuracy of language, (allowing for a few Scotticisms). 1815 L. Hunt *Feast of Poets* Notes 62 His style in prose, setting aside it's Scotticisms, is very well where [etc.]. 1892 B. Matthews *Americanisms & Briticisms* 16 The Scotticisms of the North Briton.

2. Scottish sympathies.

1807 G. Chalmers *Caledonia* I. II. i. 230 His ardour of Scoticism hurries him headlong, from the paths of truth. 1862 Lowell *Lett.* I. 361 He seems to me a remarkably good critic, where his Scoticism doesn't come in his way.

Scotticize (skǫ·tisaiz), *v.* [f. late L. *Scotticus* (*Scōticus*, Scottish, Scotch (see Scotic) + -ize.]

1. *trans.* To imbue with Scottish ideas or characteristics.

1763 Wilkes *N. Briton* No. 34 None but Scots or Jacobites, or such English as are Scotticized, must expect favour or preferment under him. 1859 Masson *Brit. Novelists* iii. 204 He [Scott] has Scotticized European literature.

2. To give a Scottish form to (a foreign word); to turn (a work) into Scottish dialect.

1874 Small *Douglas' Wks.* I. Pref. 165 He accordingly, in his version of Virgil, does not scruple to Scotticise a Latin word. 1901 Law *N. T. in Scots* (S.T.S.) Introd. 13 A Scotticised transcript of it was added..at the end of the volume.

Scottified (skǫ·tifaid), *ppl. a.* Also 7 **scotified.** [f. next + -ed[1].] Having Scottish characteristics.

1644 Needham *Case of Commonw.* 67 The ambition of a few scotified English. 1763 Wilkes *N. Briton* No. 37 P 4 The chaste and scrupulous integrity of the knot of Tories, Scottish members, and Scottified English. 1814 Scott in *Lockhart* (1839) III. 315, I think you will like it [*The Lord of the Isles*]: it is Scottified up to the teeth.

Scottify (skǫ·tifai), *v.* Also **Scotify.** [f. Scott(ish) + -(i)fy.] *trans.* To render Scottish.

1869 F. J. Furnivall *Forewords Q. Eliz. Acad.* 17 The conclusion then forced on me was, that Adam Loutfut..had copied the poem from an original, and scottified it as he copied. 1881 *Athenæum* 8 Jan. 55/3 The chap-books sold by Scotch pedlars at the annual Lammas Fair of Kirkwall [Orkney] played an important part in Scottifying the ver-

nacular. 1902 G. G. Smith *Spec. Mid. Scots* p. xxxv, It may be a 'Scotifying' of S[outhern] *those*.

Hence **Scottifica·tion,** the process of 'Scottifying'; quasi-*concr.* a rendering into Scottish dialect.

1869 F. J. Furnivall *Forewords Q. Eliz. Acad.* 17 Which scottification I hope some day to print opposite Caxton's own text. 1894 A. J. Balfour in *Times* 21 July 3/2, I watch with satisfaction the gradual Scottification of England by this great golfing propaganda. 1900 *Westm. Gaz.* 11 May 2/2 Scotification is clearly Lord Rosebery's policy.

Scottish (skǫ·tiʃ), *a.* and *sb.* Forms: [1 **Scyttisc, Scyttysc, Scittisc**], 2 **Scottysc,** 3 **Scottisc,** 5 **Scottissh,** 6 **Scottys(s)he, Skottishe, Skottyshe,** 6–7 **Scottishe, Skottish,** 7–9 **Scotish,** 6– **Scottish.** [Late OE. (12th c.) *Scottisc*, a new formation on *Scotta* Scot *sb.* + *-isc*, -ish[1], replacing the older *Scyttisc* with umlaut. Cf. MDu., Du. *schotsch*, LG. *schottsch*, G. *schottisch* (earlier *schöttisch*), ON. *skotsk-r*.] **A.** *adj.*

1. Of or belonging to Scotland or to the people of Scotland; esp. of persons: of Scotch nationality, birth, or descent. †*Scottish cap* = Scotch cap.

[c 900 tr. *Bæda's Hist.* III. xxi. (1890) 222 Se nyhsta wæs Scyttisces cynnes; þa oðre wæron Englisce.] c 1205 Lay. 20355 Patric þe ricche mon þat wes a Scottisc þein scone an his londen. c 1450 *Merlin* xiii. 197 For thei were but two scottissh myle fro the town. 1507 in *Songs, Carols*, etc. (E.E.T.S.) 154 Þer was gret plente of Skottishe samon. 1548 W. Patten *Exped. Scot.* I. vij, The Skottish gouernor..caused the erle Bothwel to be let out of prison. 1553 in *Roy. Engin. Jrnl.* 3 Mar. (1910) 174 Euery souldiour to have Jackes covered wt fustian & Skullis with Scotishe cappes. 1596 Shaks. *1 Hen. IV*, I. iii. 259 Then once more to your Scottish Prisoners. Deliuer them vp without their ransome straight. 1618 J. Taylor (Water-P.) *Pennylesse Pilgr.* E 4, The olde Prouerbe of a Scottish Miste was verified, in wetting mee to the skinne. 1637 Monro *Exped.* I. 55 Here also our Scottish High-landmen are prayse-worthy. 179. Burke *Let. to W. Smith* Wks. IX. 407 A zealous Anglican or Scottish Church principle. 1827 Scott *Chron. Canongate* ii, A..broken-down Scottish laird. 1876 Bancroft *Hist. U.S.* II. xlii. 559 The settlement of the Scottish emigrants at Port Royal.

b. In the names of various trees and plants: cf. Scotch 4 b, Scots 1 d.

1855 Miss Pratt *Flower. Pl.* V. 279 *Scottish Asphodel. 1796 Withering *Brit. Plants* (ed. 3) II. 297 *Scottish lovage, or Sea Parsley. 1855 Miss Pratt *Flower. Pl.* IV. 232 *Scottish Primrose. 1597 Gerarde *Herbal* II. ccxciii. 690 *Soldanella*..in English Sea Withwinde,..of some..*Scottish Scuruie grasse.

†**c.** (See quot.)

1623 J. Taylor (Water-P.) *Praise Hemp-seed* 7 Many a Gallant..Hath got the Spanish pip,..or the Scottish fleas, or English Pox, for al's but one disease.

d. *Mil.* *Scottish Guard* = *Scots Guard*. *Scottish Rifles* (see quot 1888).

1823 Scott *Quentin D.* v, With these followers, and a corresponding equipage, an Archer of the Scottish Guard was a person of quality and importance. 1888 Lawrence-Archer *Brit. Army* 240 The King's Own Scottish Borderers. *Ibid.* 246 The Cameronians...This peculiar old corps..now forms the first battalion of the Scottish Rifles.

e. Used with reference to law. Cf. Scots *a.* 1 c.

1726 (*title*) Minor Practicks, or, a Treatise of the Scottish Law. Composed by..Sir Thomas Hope..Advocate to His Majesty King Charles I. 1826 Scott *Jrnl.* 9 June, The consequence of this will in time be, that the Scottish Supreme Court will be in effect situated in London. Then down fall—as national objects of respect and veneration—the Scottish Bench, the Scottish Bar, the Scottish Law herself. 1875 *Encycl. Brit.* II. 633/2 *Art and Part*, a term used in Scottish Law to denote the aiding or abetting [etc.].

†**2.** *Scottish earth Min.*, strontian. *Obs.*

1796 Kirwan *Elem. Min.* (ed. 2) I. 13 Scottish, or Stronthian Earth.

†**3.** *transf.* Marked by Scottish characteristics.

1532 More *Confut. Barnes* VIII. Wks. 739/2 The rude rimelesse runninge of a scottishe ieste. 1610 Marcelline *Triumphs Jas. I* To France B 4 b, My life is innocent, my heart Christian, my tongue to Scottish, and he is too good and wise a King, to bee flattered by any. c 1620 A. Hume *Brit. Tongue* I. vii. (1870) 18 The assumption is Scottish, and the conclusion Inglis.

4. Applied to the language (see Scots *a.* 2).

1780 *Mirror* No. 83 The Scottish dialect is our ordinary suit; the English is used only on solemn occasions. 1818 Scott *Rob Roy* iv, This was the first time I had heard the Scottish accent. 1862 *Chamb. Encycl.* IV. 66/1 Gavin Douglas (died 1522), whose best work is a translation of Virgil's Æneid into Scottish verse.

5. *Comb.*, as *Scottish-hearted*; **Scottish-French,** French spoken by Scots; **Scottish-Irish** = Scotch-Irish.

1823 Scott *Quentin D.* v, The well-known sound of the *Scottish-French was as familiar in the taverns near Plessis, as that of the Swiss-French in the modern *guinguettes* of Paris. 1818 — *Hrt. Midl.* xviii, Walking hand in hand with the real noble *Scottish-hearted barons. 1876 Bancroft *Hist. U.S.* IV. xviii. 443 Presbyterians of *Scottish-Irish descent.

B. *sb.* (absolute uses of the adj.)

1. The Scottish language.

1759 Robertson *Hist. Scot.* Wks. 1851 II. 368 The letters were very early translated into Scottish. 1818 Scott *Rob Roy* xxxv, Nor was there the least tincture of that vulgarity, which we naturally attach to the Lowland Scottish. 1886 *Encycl. Brit.* XXI. 541/2 Bellenden also translated the first five books of Livy into Scottish.

2. *The Scottish* (with pl. sense): the Scots. *rare.*

1632 *Swed. Intelligencer* II. 13 The Scottish have hitherto had the honour and the danger, to be the first men that are put upon such a businesse. 1814 Scott *Wav.* xviii, The large measure which the Scottish allowed of their land. 1831 — *Cast. Dang.* xx, The necessary conditions were speedily agreed on, which put the Scottish in possession of this stronghold.

†**Sco·ttish,** *v. Obs. rare*[−1]. In 7 **Scotish.** [f. the adj. (Cf. *to English*.)] *trans.* To render in the Scottish tongue.

1623 Lisle *Ælfric on O. & N. Test.* To Rdrs. c 4 b, At length I lighted on Virgil Scotished by the Reuerend Gawin Douglas.

†**Sco·ttishman.** *Obs.* [f. Scottish *a.* + Man.] = Scotsman.

[1387 Trevisa *Higden* (Rolls) VI. 389 Þe Scottyshe men ..took a carabum..and wente þerynne.] 1523 Surrey in Ellis *Orig. Lett.* Ser. I. I. 213 Bothe with thies contreymen and Scottishmen. 1530 Palsgr. 268/1 Scottyssheman, *Escoyssoys*. 1548 W. Patten *Exped. Scot.* G vij, The Scottishmens pykes wear as long or lenger then their staues. 1632 *Swed. Intelligencer* I. 86 One Scottish-man protested he had kill'd 18 men with his owne hand. 1748 Smollett *Rod. Rand.* xliii. Contents (1760) II. 41 We are accosted by a priest, who proves to be a Scottishman. 1808 Scott in *Lockhart* I. i. 3 Every Scottishman has a pedigree. 1831 — *Cast. Dang.* xix, It seems almost unnatural for Scottishmen and English to meet and part without a buffet.

Scottishness (skǫ·tiʃnės). [f. Scottish *a.* + -ness.] The quality of being Scottish.

1859 Ramsay *Remin.* 154 It is the Scottishness that gives the zest.

Scotty (skǫ·ti), *sb. colloq.* [f. Scot *sb.*[1] + -y.] A nickname for a Scotchman.

Scotty (skǫ·ti), *a.* [f. Scot *sb.*[1] + -y.] **a.** Having the characteristic temperament of a Scot. **b.** [Cf. Scot *sb.*[1] 4.] Angry, 'cross'.

1892 Stevenson *Let. to J. M. Barrie* (1899) II. 247 We are both Scots besides, and I suspect both rather Scotty Scots. 1901 *Blackw. Mag.* Feb. 220/2 It made me scotty with every one and every thing.

Scotylle, Scouce: see Scuttle, Scouse.

Scoug, Scouk: see Scug, Skulk.

Scoul, Scould, obs. forms of Scowl, Scold.

Scoulding: see Sculding *Orkney and Shetl.*

Scoule, obs. form of Scold, Scull.

Scoulerite (skū·ləɹait). *Min.* [Named after Dr. J. *Scouler*.] An impure variety of mesole; also, a pipe-stone from N. America, having a similar composition.

1840 R. D. Thomson in *Lond. & Edin. Phil. Mag.* Ser. III. XVII. 408 My son..distinguished it [this mineral] by the name of Scoulerite, in honour of Dr. Scouler. 1843 J. E. Portlock *Geol.* 215 The Scoulerite variety occurs, rarely, at Portrush in small spheres. 1890 Ansted *Elem. Geol., Min.* etc. § 422 Scoulerite, Pipestone.

Scoulion, Scoull(e, obs. ff. Scullion, School.

Scoult, obs. form of Scout *sb.*[4]

Scoulyon, Scoum, obs. ff. Scullion, Scum.

Scoumar, variant of Scummer, pirate.

Scoumfit(e, -phit, etc.: see Scomfit.

Scoundrel (skau·ndrĕl), *sb.* and *a.* Also 6 **skown-, skoundrell, scondrell,** 7 **skundrell, scoundril,** 8 **scoundrell.** [Of unknown origin.

Derivation from Sc. Scunner *sb.* and *v.* is inadmissible on phonological grounds; and although *scoundrel* is now vernacular in Scotland (pronounced skū·nrĕl or skū·ndrĕl), all the early examples of the word are English. The phonetic character of the word suggests a Fr. origin; it might conceivably represent an AF. derivative of *escondre* to abscond, but the late date of its first occurrence is against this supposition.]

A. *sb.* 'A mean rascal, a low petty villain' (J.). Now usually with stronger sense: An audacious rascal, one destitute of all moral scruple.

1589 Warner *Alb. Eng.* VI. xxxi. 137 Must I, thought I, giue aime to such a Skrub and such a Saint, That Skowndrell, and this Counterfeit. 1589 R. Harvey *Pl. Perc.* 22 You see my quarter staffe, is it not a blesse begger, thinke you? A washing blow of this is as good as a Laundresse,.. and must needs dry beate a skoundrell, if it be artificially managed. 1594 Lodge *Wounds Civ. War* IV. G 3, *Clown.* Haue I master thou scoundrell? I haue an Orator to my master. 1601 Shaks. *Twel. N.* I. iii. 36 By this hand they are scoundrels and substractors that say so of him. 1605 Chapman *All Fooles* V. i. I 3, Your Mother..a lustie stoute Woman, bore great Children, you were the verie skundrell of am all. 1623 Bingham *Xenophon* 119 If you take away my life, you shall put an honest man to death for a cowards and a scoundrels sake. 1711 Swift *Jrnl. to Stella* 17 Nov., I often advised the dissolution of that Parliament, although I did not think the scoundrels had so much courage. 1734 Pope *Ess. Man* IV 212 If your ancient, but ignoble blood Has crept thro' scoundrels ever since the flood. 1775 Johnson in *Boswell* 7 Apr. (1791) I. 478 Patriotism is the last refuge of a scoundrel. 1834 Southey *Doctor* liii. (1862) 121 When a woman is married for the sake of her fortune, the chances are five hundred to one that she marries a villain, or at best a scoundrel. 1837 Dickens *Pickw.* xxxi, 'They are great scoundrels,' said Mr. Pickwick. 1877 Tennyson *Harold* IV. i, My father, Who shook the Norman scoundrels off the throne. 1879 Froude *Cæsar* xv. 224 He saw these high-born scoundrels coming home loaded with treasure. 1886 Stevenson *Treasure Isl.* i, If you keep on drinking rum, the world will soon be quit of a very dirty scoundrel!

b. *attrib.* and *appositive*.

1837 Carlyle *Fr. Rev.* II. I. ii, Of a Jourdan Coupe-tête, who has skulked thitherward..and will raise whole scoundrel-regiments. 1850 — *Latter-d. Pamph.* II. 9 [Model Prisons.] The 'sympathy' of visitors..for his interesting scoundrel-subjects..was evidently no joy to this practical mind. Pity, yes:—but pity for the scoundrel-species? 1894 H. Nisbet *Bush Girl's Rom.* 120 This scoundrel-fool Shafton had been the cause of his misfortunes.

B. *adj.* Now *rare.*

1. Of a person: That is a scoundrel; having the characteristics of a scoundrel; scoundrelly. Of a company: Composed of scoundrels.

1643 Milton *Divorce* II. i. (1645) 33 We read, not that the scoundrel people, but the choicest, the wisest, the holiest of that nation have frequently us'd these lawes. a 1700 B. E. *Dict. Canting Crew*, *Scab*, a..Scoundril-Fellow. 1710 Swift *Jrnl. to Stella* 21 Dec., I met that beast Ferris,..and that scoundrel dog is as happy as an emperor. 1715 Hearne *Collect.* (O. H. S.) V. 53 The Printer is that scoundrel Rascal Curle. 1727–46 Thomson *Summer* 1640 The cruel wretch ..has squander'd vile, Upon his scoundrel train what might have cheered A drooping family of modest worth. 1807 Crabbe *Par. Reg.* III. 789 We'll vex those scoundrel-boys. 1833 L. Ritchie *Wand. by Loire* 187 The scoundrel governor ..was the Duke of Montpensier.

2. Pertaining to or characteristic of a scoundrel. Of conduct: Mean, unprincipled.

1681 Hickeringill *Dial. Philantus & Timoth.* iii. 5 Shouldest thou not in all justice and Conscience, instance something..that deserves..such scoundrel, Billings-gate Ribaldry? a 1704 T. Brown *Declam. in Def. Gaming* Wks. 1709 III. I. 134 What..is there more scoundrel? What more beastly, than a man depriv'd of his Manhood..by an Inundation of Claret? 1729 Mandeville *Bees* II. 101 An Italian No-man of Scoundrel Extraction. 1731 Medley *Kolben's Cape G. Hope* (1738) I. 227 He [*sc.* the Hottentot dog] makes such a Scoundrel-Figure, that all his good Qualities together, are hardly a Ballance for it. 1738 J. Hildrop *Let. Commandm.* (ed. 4) 17 Stealing we all know is the most pitiful, scoundrel Act of Injustice. 1748 Thomson *Cast. Indol.* I. l, 'A penny saved is a penny got'—Firm to this scoundrel maxim keepeth he. 1757 Warburton *Lett. to Hurd* xciii. (1809) 218 He..died..here in England; but of so scoundrel a temper, that he avoided ever coming into my sight. 1757 Mrs. Griffith *Lett. Henry & Frances* (1767) III. 84, I am shocked at the mean, scoundrel Behaviour of Mr. P——. 1850 Thackeray *Pendennis* lviii, Her parents..encouraged me, with all sorts of coarse artifices and scoundrel flatteries.

†**3.** Of a thing: Base, degraded in character or type. *Obs. rare.*

1700 Astry tr. *Saavedra's Royal Politician* II. 160 Trade was ruin'd by this troublesome, scoundrel Metal. 1727 A. Hamilton *New Acc. E. Ind.* II. xxxviii. 75 Their Religion is also a Sort of scoundrel Mahometism.

Hence **Scou·ndrel** *v. trans.*, ? to treat as a scoundrel, to vilify. **Scou·ndreldom,** the world of scoundrels, scoundrels collectively; also = Scoundrelism. †**Scou·ndrelish** *a.*, befitting a scoundrel. **Scou·ndrelship,** the behaviour of a scoundrel, scoundrelism. **Scou·ndrelry,** scoundrels collectively.

1701 W. Nicolson *Let.* 9 May in Evelyn *Diary & Corr.* (1906) 721 This being one of the matters wherein I am scoundreled by the late reply of Dr. Wake. 1705 Rowe *Biter* I. i, I being in somewhat scoundrelish, or, as your Honour calls it, scurvy Terms with him my self. 1837 Carlyle *Diamond Necklace* xvi, Let the eye of the mind ..astound itself with the magnificent extent of Scoundreldom; the deep, I may say unfathomable, significance of Scoundrelism. 1856 *Chamb. Jrnl.* VI. 361, I was dirty and grim-looking enough to represent any amount of scoundrelship. 1859 Sala *Tw. round Clock* (1861) 415 It is astonishing to find how much foreign riff-raff and alien scoundrelry will turn up at a masquerade. 1864 *Reader* 23 Jan. 101/1 With such consummate scoundrelship in the foreground, one may be pretty sure..that there is no lack of incident. 1864 Kingsley *Rom. & Teut.* iii. 68 All greedy villains and adventurers, the scoundreldom of the whole world. 1876 Froude *Hist. Eng.* lxix. XII. 111 Either as an effect of looseness of life, or from inherent scoundreldom of temperament.

Scoundrelism (skau·ndrĕliz'm). [f. Scoundrel *sb.* + -ism.] The character, conduct, or practices of a scoundrel; also, a piece of scoundrelism, a scoundrelly act or trait.

1611 Cotgr., *Villaquerie*, villanie, roguerie, rascalitie, skowndrellisme. 1773 Johnson in Boswell *Tour Hebrides* (1785) 111 Why, Sir,..There is generally a scoundrelism about a low man. 1837 Carlyle *Fr. Rev.* I. v. ix, Thus ..shall the Bastille be abolished from our Earth; and with it, Feudalism, Despotism; and one hopes, Scoundrelism generally. 1890 G. B. Shaw *Fabian Ess.*, *Socialism* 194 Hungry mobs, nuclei of all the socialism and scoundrelism of the city. 1902 F. E. Hulme *Proverb Lore* ii. 61 The epigrams [of John Davies] are, most of them, of a most offensive character...There are two hundred and ninety-two of these scoundrelisms.

Scoundrelly (skau·ndrĕli), *a.* [f. Scoundrel *sb.* + -ly[1].] Having the character of a scoundrel; of, belonging to, or characteristic of a scoundrel; characterized by scoundrelism.

1790 Burns *Let.* 2 Mar., Mankind are by nature benevolent creatures, except in a few scoundrelly instances. 1816 Scott *Antiq.* vi, I have directed the constables to take up that old scoundrelly beggar, Edie Ochiltree, for spreading disaffection. 1826 Cobbett *Rur. Rides* (1885) II. 266, I read on till I got to the base and scoundrelly part of the address. 1847 Thackeray in *Fraser's Mag.* Jan. 116/2 Tom Starlight, the poacher,..inveighing against the tyranny of a scoundrelly aristocracy. 1862 Carlyle *Fredk. Gt.* VIII. iv. III. 18 Money back! 'I will none of His scoundrelly money'. 1885 *L'pool Daily Post* 9 Feb. 4/8 A scoundrelly pasha..opened the gates of the city and let the Mahdi in.

†**Scou·ndrelously,** *adv. rare*[−1]. [f. Scoundrel + -ous + -ly[2].] In a scoundrelly manner.

1681 Hickeringill *Dial. Philantus & Timoth.* xiii. 28 Thou handlest the matter..so scoundrelously, and so far below the Rules of all Logick and Morality.

Scouner, obs. form of Scunner *v.*

Scoup (skaup), *v.* Chiefly *Sc.* Forms: 5–6 **scoupe,** 6 **skowp,** 8 **scowp,** 7– **scoup.** [Of

SCOURING. 257 SCOUT. SCOUT. 258 SCOUTY-AULIN.

SCOVAN. 259 SCOWLING. SCR-. 260 SCRAG.

SCRAPE. 265 SCRAPER SCRAPE-TRENCHER. 266 SCRAT

SCRAT. 267 SCRATCH SCRATCH-BRUSH.

Scratch-brush ... *trans.* To polish by means of a scratch-brush.

Hence **scratch-brusher**, a workman who operates a scratch-brush; **scra'tch-brushing** *vbl.*

Scratched ...

Scratcher ...

Scratching ...

Scratching-board ...

Scra'tchingly *adv.* ...

Scratchless ...

Scratchy *a.* ...

† **Scra'tchets** ...

Scratchification ...

+ **Scra'ttle** *v.* ...

Scraugh ...

+ **Scraw** *sb.¹* ...

Scraw *sb.²* (Anglo-Irish, Sc., Manx.)

Scrawl *(skrǫl), v.¹*

+ **Scraw** *v.* ...

+ **Scrawl** *sb.² Obs.* ...

+ **Scrawla'tion** *Obs. rare⁻¹* ...

Scrawl *(skrǫl), v.² Obs.*

Scrawled *(skrǫld), ppl. a.*

Scrawler ...

Scrawl-ing *ppl. a.¹*

Scrawling *(skrǫl.in), vbl. sb.*

Scrawly *(skrǫl.i), a.*

Scrawm ...

Scrawny *(skrǫ.ni), a. U.S.*

Scray *(skrē¹).*

Scray *v.*

Scray-fish ...

† **Scray'foot** *Obs.* ...

Scraze *(skrēz), v. dial.*

Screak *(skrīk), v.*

Screaky *(skrī.ki), a.*

+ **Screa'ling** ...

Scream *(skrīm), sb.*

Scream *(skrīm), v.*

Screamer ...

Screaming *(skrī.min), vbl. sb.*

Screaming *(skrī.min), ppl. a.*

Screamy *(skrī.mi), a.*

Scree *(skrī).*

Screech *(skrīʧ), sb.*

Screech *(skrīʧ), v.*

Screechy *(skrī.ʧi), a.*

Screeching *(skrī.ʧin), vbl. sb.*

Screeching *ppl. a.*

Screech-owl. Also ‖ **skreech-,** 8 **scriech-**

Screed *(skrīd), sb.*

Screed *(skrīd), v.*

Screeding *(skrī.din), vbl. sb.*

Screen *(skrīn), sb.¹*

SCREW

SCREEN.

2. Arch. A partition of wood or stone, pierced by one or more doors, dividing a room or building into two parts.

b. Eccl. (See CHANCEL-, ROOD-SCREEN.)

c. A wall thrown out in front of a building and masking the façade.

3. transf. Applied to any object, natural or artificial, that affords shelter from heat or wind.

4. Something interposed so as to conceal from view. Also *fig.*

c. Mil. A small body of men detached to cover the movements of an army.

d. A line or belt of trees planted to give protection from the wind.

5. fig. A means of securing from attack, punishment, or censure. Also, anything which intervenes obstructively.

SCREENED.

6. Mining. To apply to various portions of optical, electrical, and other instruments, serving to intercept light, heat, electricity, etc.

7. To shut off by something interposed. *rare.*

8. To hide from view with a screen; to shelter from observation or recognition.

9. An arrangement of bars at the end of an overflow pipe, to prevent the escape of fish from a pond.

10. To apply to various portions of optical, electrical, and other instruments.

SCREENER.

2. Sifted by means of a screen.

3. Posted upon a screen. (See SCREEN *sb.* 5.)

SCREENER.

Screener (skrī·nəɹ). [f. SCREEN v. + -ER.] (See quot. 1816.)

SCREENING.

Screening (skrī·niŋ), *ppl. a.* [f. SCREEN v. + -ING.] That screens; that hides or protects.

SCREW.

Screw (skrū), *sb.* [Forms: *screw*, *skrew*, *skrue*, *scrue*.]

1. The general name for that kind of mechanical appliance of which the operative portion is a helical groove or ridge (or two or more parallel helical grooves or ridges) cut either on the exterior surface of a cylinder (*male screw*) or on the interior surface of a cylindrical cavity (*female screw*).

2. Mech. One of the mechanical powers; treated as a modification of the inclined plane.

Scribbly (skri'bli), *a.* [f. SCRIBBLE *sb.* + -Y.] Characterized by scribbling; resembling a scribble. Scribbly gum, *Australian*, a variety of gum-tree (see quots.).

Scribe (skraib), *sb.* Also 4-6 **scrybe**. [ad. L. *scriba* writer, amanuensis, secretary, f. *scrībĕre* to write. Cf. F. *scribe* (14th c. in Hatz.-Darm.).]

1. *Jewish Hist.* A member of the class of professional interpreters of the Law after the return from the Captivity; in the Gospels often coupled with the Pharisees as upholders of ceremonial tradition.

2. *trans. Hist.* A general designation for an public official (whether of high or low rank) concerned with writing or the keeping of accounts; a secretary, clerk.

3. Used as the official designation of various public functionaries performing secretarial duties.

Scribe (skraib), *v.* Of obscure history; in sense 1 perh. aphetic for DESCRIBE *v.*; in sense 2 partly ad. L. *scrībĕre* to write, partly f. SCRIBE *sb.*

Scribing (skrai'biŋ), *vbl. sb.* [-ING¹.]

Scriber (skrai'bəɹ). [f. SCRIBE *v.* + -ER¹.]

Scribism (skrai'biz'm). [f. SCRIBE *sb.*¹ + -ISM.] The teaching and literature of the ancient Jewish scribes (SCRIBE *sb.*¹ 1); the qualities of the scribes.

Scribo-critical, *a.* *Obs. rare⁻¹.* [f. SCRIBE *sb.*¹ + -CRITICAL.] Characteristic of or relating to the scribes (SCRIBE *sb.*¹ 1).

Scrible, -el, obsolete forms of SCRIBBLE, SCRIBBLER.

Scrick-shoe, obs. form of SCRICK-SHOE.

Scridian (skri'diən). *Sc.* Also **scridan**. [a. Gael. *sgridan*.] (See quot. 1820.)

Scride (skraid), *v.* *Sc.* *Obs.* [f. SCRED *v.*¹]

Scrieve (skriv), *v.* *Sc.* and *north. dial.* Forms: 6 skrimishe, skrymishe, scrimishe, scromeys, scoramble 4-6 SCRIMISH *v.* Cf. the later form SCRIMMAGE *v.*

Scrike (skraik), *sb.* Now only *dial.*; see *Eng. Dial. Dict.* For forms see the vb. [f. SCRIKE *v.*]

Scrike (skraik), *v.* Now only *dial.* See *Eng. Dial. Dict.*

Scrim (skrim), *sb.* [Of obscure origin.] A kind of thin canvas used for lining in upholstery, and for other purposes.

Scrimer (skrai'məɹ). *Obs. rare⁻¹.* [ad. F. *escrimeur*, f. *escrimer* to fence.] A fencer.

Scrimmage (skri'medʒ), **scrummage** (skrʌ'medʒ). Forms: 5 skrimishe, skrymishe, scrimishe, scromeys, 6 SCRIMISH *sb.* Cf. the later form SCRIMMAGE *v.*

Scrimmage, scrummage, *v.* [f. SCRIMMAGE *sb.* + -ER¹.] One who takes part in a scrimmage.

Scrimmaging, scrummaging, *vbl. sb.* [f. SCRIMMAGE *v.* + -ING¹.] The action of the vb.

Scrimshank (skrim'ʃæŋk), *v.* *Mil. slang.* Also **skr-.** [Of obscure origin.] To shirk duty. Hence **Scrim'shanking** *vbl. sb.* and *ppl. a.*; also an act of 'scrimshanking'; **Scrim'shanker.**

Scrimshaw (skrim'ʃɔ), *sb.* *Naut.* [Of obscure origin; the surname *Scrimshaw*, if not actually the source, may have influenced the form of the word.]

Scrine, *sb.* Forms: *a.* 3, 5-6 scryne, 6 scrine, scrynne, skryne, 6-7 skrine; *β.* 3 scrane, 6 scrone. [a. OF. *escrin*, *scrin* (mod.F. *écrin*) = Pr. *escrin*.]

Scrip (skrip), *sb.*¹ *arch.* Forms: 3-7 scryppe, 4-5 scrippe, scrype, 4-6 scrip, 5 scripe, skryppe, 5-6 skryppe, 7 scripp. Prob. a. ON. *skreppa*.

Scrip (skrip), *sb.*² *Obs. exc. dial.*

Scrip (skrip), *sb.*³ [Short for *subscription receipt*.] Originally, a receipt for a portion of a loan subscribed.

Scripless (skri'ples), *a.* [f. SCRIP *sb.*³]

Scrippage (skri'pedʒ). [f. SCRIP *sb.*¹ + -AGE.]

Script (skript), *sb.* [In ME. an etymological spelling of SCROW = *sb.*; *escript*]

Script², *Obs.* [var. of SCRIP *sb.*³]

Scriptoir, -our, *Obs.* [Aphetic *a.* OF. *escriptoire*, -* secrétaire* = SCRITTOIRE.]

Scription (skri'pʃən). *Obs.* [ad. L. *scriptiōn-em*, n. of action f. *scrībĕre.*]

Scriptoir, -our, *Obs.*

Scriptor (skri'ptɔɹ). *Obs.* [a. L. *scriptor*.]

Scriptorial (skriptɔ'riəl), *a.*

Scriptorium (skriptɔ'riəm). Pl. scriptoria, -iums. [med. L., f. *scriptōri-us*]

Scriptory (skri'ptəri), *a.*

Scriptour: see SCRIPTOR, SCRIPTURE.

Scriptule, *Obs. rare.*

Scriptural (skri'ptiūral), *a.* [ad. L. type *scrīptūrāl-is*, f. *scrīptūra* SCRIPTURE.]

Scripturalism (skri'piŭrăli'z'm). [f. prec. + -ISM.] Close adherence to or dependence upon the letter of Holy Scripture.

Scripturalist, †f one well versed in Holy Scripture.

Scripturality (skriptiŭræ'litĭ). The quality or condition of being scriptural or based upon Holy Scripture.

Scripturalize (skri'piŭrălaiz), v. rare. [f. SCRIPTURAL + -IZE.] trans. To render bright, modify and scripturalize a little.

Scripturally (skri'piŭrăli), adv. [f. SCRIPTURAL + -LY.] In accordance with the Scriptures; by means of Scripture.

Scripturalness (skri'piŭrălnĕs). [f. -NESS.] = SCRIPTURALITY.

† Scripturarian. Obs. [f. mod. L. scrīptūrāri- (see next.)] One who makes Holy Scripture the sole authority for religious belief.

† Scripturary. Obs. [ad. mod. L. scrīptūrāri-us, f. scrīptūra SCRIPTURE : see -ARY.] = prec. Also as adj.

Scripture (skri'ptiŭ), sb. Forms: 4-6 scripture, scripture, 5 scrypture, skrypture, 5-6 scriptur, 5-7 scripture, 6 scriptur, scriptor, scriptur, scripture, scryture, 4-6 -ture, 5-6 -tur; also written scripture (mod.F. écriture), Sp., Pg. escritura, It. scrittura.]

1. (Usually with capital initial.) The sacred writings of the Old or New Testament, or (more usually) of both together; Holy Writ; the Bible. Often with holy prefixed.

2. The action or art of writing; handwriting.

3. An inscription or superscription; a motto, legend, or posy.

4. A written record or composition; pl. writings, &c.

Scripturing, vbl. sb. Obs. [f. SCRIPTURE sb.]

Scripturism (skri'piŭtri'z'm). [f. SCRIPTURE sb. + -ISM.]

1. Reliance upon the Scriptures alone; devotion to Scripture.

Scripturist (skri'piŭtrist). [f. SCRIPTURE sb.]

1. One who is versed in the Scriptures.

2. One who bases his religious belief or opinions upon Scripture alone.

† Scripture, obs. form of SCRIPTURE.

Scrive, v. Obs. Forms: 4 scrive, scryve, 5-6 scryve, scrive, 6 scrive. [a. OE. scrīfan = OS. scrīban OHG. scrīban (MHG. scrīben, G. schreiben), ON. skrīfa.]

1. intr. To go, pass; in OE. also, to glide, creep; to wander.

2. To fall or lapse (into error, sin).

Scritch, sb. and v. : see SCREECH.

Scrive-board (skrə̄i'vbōəd). Shipbuilding. [f. SCRIVE v.] A large drawing-board made of planks, on which the lines of a vessel are scribed.

Scriven (skri'v'n), v. Obs. [f. SCRIVEN- er.] trans. and intr. (with advb.) To write.

Scrivener (skri'vnər). Forms: 4 scriveyner, 4-6 skriveyner, 5 skri-, scryvenere, skerevener, 5-6 scryvenor, 5-7 scryvener, etc. [Extended form of ME. scrivein, scriveyn.]

Scrivenership (skri'vnərʃip). [f. prec.] The office or occupation of a scrivener; also, the writings of a scrivener.

Scrivening (skri'vnin), vbl. sb. [f. SCRIVEN v. + -ING².] Following the occupation of a scrivener.

† Scrivenish, a. In the manner of a scrivener.

Scrivenly, a.

Scriver, obs. form of SCRIVENER.

Scriving (skrəi'viŋ), vbl. sb. [f. SCRIVE v.] attrib. in scriving-board = SCRIVE-BOARD; scriving-iron = scribing-iron.

Scrobe (skrəub), sb. [L. scrob-is trench.]

Scrobicular, a.

Scrobiculate (skrəubi'kiŭléit), a. Bot. and Zool.

Scrofula (skrə̄'fiŭlă), a. Path. [mod. L., f. SCROFULA + -OSE.]

Scrofula (skrə̄'fiŭlă), sb. Path. and Zool. [mod. L.]

Scroll (skrəul), sb. Forms: 5-8 scrowle, 6 scrole, schrole, skrole, scroll, 6-7 scrowle, 5 scrowl, 7 scroul, scrowell, skroule, skroule, 5 scroll, scroull, scrol.

1. A roll of paper or parchment; usually one with writing upon it.

Archit., Roll-moulding...It is sometimes called the "scroll moulding, from its resemblance to a scroll of paper or parchment with the edge overlapping. **1866** GEO. ELIOT *F. Holt* xlv, As if she had to work out her deliverance from bondage by finishing a "scroll-paper chain. **1875** *Daily News* 1 Mar. 7/3 A large Louis XV. *ormolu* carriage clock, in a "scroll-shaped case. **1893** GROSE *Ouphaléss* viii. 139 Young leaves curled up "scroll-wise. **1775** ASH, *Scroll-wise (in se West to West to West, Sugar-leaves and minced-pies of yew*: "scroll-work of box). **1822** SCOTT *Nigel* III. xi The three doors full of oak, relieved by the quaint and beautiful runnled iron scroll-work as characteristic of this style of architecture.

b. objective; as *scroll-cutter, -cutting, -filer*; instrumental; as *scroll-cut* adj.

1875 *Cen. Engin. & Arch. Jrnl.* I. 74/1 Separated by "scroll-cut standards. **1892** *Daily Cmon.* 28 Apr. 3/1 Gun Engraving. Wanted at once good "scroll cutter. **1874** RICHARDS *Operator's Handbk.* 172 For "scroll cutting, slitting, and with narrow blades generally, the matter of teeth has not so much importance. **1880** *Instr. Census Clerks* (1885) 92 Whitesmith...'Scroll Filer.

c. Special combinations: **scroll-bone** (see quot.) ; **scroll chair**, a chair with a carved scroll ornament; **scroll-chuck**, a lathe-chuck with a spiral arrangement for operating the jaws; **scroll-copy**, a rough draft or copy; **scroll-creeper** *Arch.* (see quot.); **scroll-drum** *Mech.*, a drum of tapering form; **scroll-finis**, a scroll containing the word "finis"; **scroll-gait** *Rot.*, a malformation consisting in the curling over of a leaf caused by an insect; **scroll-gear** (see quot.) ; **scroll-guard**, (see quot. 1824) ; **scroll-head** = *wense* 4; **scroll-iron**, -lathe (see quots.) ; **scroll-saw**, a saw for cutting scrolls; so *scroll-sawing*; **scroll-wheel**, a wheel actuated by scroll-gear.

1891 *Century Dict., Scroll-bone*... "scroll-bones are the rhinocerobinals, maxilloturbinals, and spheno-turbinals. **1874** in *Archaologia* XLII. 294 One lage Chaire with a longe chaldm, two "scroble chaires, two hyghe stooles. **1875** KNIGHT *Dict. Mech., 'Scroll-chuck.* **1790** SOUTH *Let. in Luckhart* (1837) I. 65. **1742** he used "scroll copy of an essay on the origin of the feudal system. **1849** ──

object of scruple. Scrupling vbl. sb. and ppl. a.

Scrupleless, a. rare⁻¹. [f. SCRUPLE + -LESS.] Having no scruples, unscrupulous.

Scruple, s. 6 scruples. [irreg. f. SCRUPLE sb. + -NESS.]

Scrupler (skrū⁷pləz), [f. SCRUPLE v. + -ER¹.]

Scruplesome, a. rare⁻¹. [f. SCRUPLE sb. + -SOME.] Inclined to be scrupulous.

Scrupulant, a. Obs. rare⁻¹. [f. L. scrupulant-.]

Scrupular, a. Obs. rare. [ad. L. scrupulāris (scrip-), f. scripulus SCRUPLE sb.¹.] Of or amounting to a scruple in weight.

Scrupulist. Obs. [f. SCRUPLE sb. and v.]

Scrupulosity (skrūpiŭlǫ·sĭtĭ). [ad. F. scrupulosité (14th c. in Littré) or ad. L. scrupulositās-em, f. scrupulōsus: see -OSITY.]

Scrupulous (skrū⁷piŭlǝs), a. [ad. L. scrupulōsus, f. scrupulus SCRUPLE sb.¹: see -OUS.]

Scrupulously, adv. [f. prec. + -LY².]

Scrupulousness. [f. SCRUPULOUS + -NESS.]

Scrupulus. Obs. rare⁻¹. [L.]

Scrutable (skrū·tǎb'l), a. [f. L. scrūt-ārī to search + -ABLE.]

Scrutation (skrūtēⁱ·ʃǝn). [ad. L. scrūtātiōn-em, n. of action f. scrūtārī: see next.]

Scrutator (skrūtēⁱ·təɹ). [a. L. scrūtātor, agent-n. f. scrūtārī to search, examine.]

Scrutatory (skrū·tǎtǝɹĭ), a. [f. L. scrūtāt-, ppl. stem of scrūtārī + -ORY.]

Scrutatrix (skrūtēⁱ·trĭks). [L.]

Scrute. rare⁻¹. [ad. L. scrūtārī: see SCRUTATOR.]

Scrutin (Fr. skrütɛ̃). [Fr.]

Scrutineer (skrūtĭniə·ɹ). [f. SCRUTINY + -EER.]

Scrutinant, a. rare. [f. L. scrutinant-, stem of scrutinārī.]

Scrutinate, v. [f. L. scrutin-, + -ATE³.]

Scrutination (skrūtĭnēⁱ·ʃǝn). [n. of action f. prec.]

Scrutinator. [agent-n. f. SCRUTINATE.]

Scrutineer (skrūtĭniə·ɹ). [f. SCRUTINY + -EER.]

Scrutinize (skrū·tĭnǝɪz), v. [f. SCRUTINY + -IZE.]

Scrutinizer. [f. prec. + -ER¹.]

Scrutinous (skrū·tĭnǝs), a. [f. L. scrutin- + -OUS.]

Scrutiny (skrū·tĭnĭ), sb. [ad. L. scrūtinium, f. scrūtārī to search.]

Scrutoire, variant of SCRUTOIRE.

Scruze (skrūz), v. Now dial. and arch. [Of obscure origin.]

† Scry, sb.¹ Obs. Forms: 4–6 scry(e, 5–6 skry(e, 6 scrie, skrie. [Aphetic form of ASCRY or ESCRY: cf. SCRY v.]

Scry, sb.² Sc. exc. dial. [? f. SCRY v.]

Scry (skrəɪ), v.¹ [Aphetic of DESCRY v.¹]

Scry (skrəɪ), v.² Sc. and north. Also 8 skry. [Aphetic form of DESCRY v.]

Scryer (skrəɪ·əɹ). [f. SCRY v.¹ + -ER¹.]

Scu, obs. form of SHOE.

Scub, Obs. exc. dial. [repr. OE. scurua, scūa shadow.]

Scudard, Obs. [Aphetic form of ESCUAGE?]

Scubard. Obs. rare⁻¹. [a. OF. (en) escubard.]

Scud (skɒd), sb.¹ Also 7 scudde, 8 scudd. [f. SCUD v.]

Scud (skɒd), v. [Also 6 skud, 8 scudd.]

Scud, sb.² Sc. dial. [app. related to SCREEN sb.]

Scudd.

Scuddaler (skɒ·dǝlǝɹ). Shetl. Also explan. scudler, scudder. [Ultimate origin obscure.]

Scudder (skɒ·dǝɹ). [f. SCUD v.¹ + -ER¹.]

Scuddick, Obs. exc. dial. [f. SCUD v. + -ICK.]

Scuddle (skɒd'l), v.¹ Now dial. [Frequentative f. SCUD v.¹]

Scuddy (skɒ·dĭ), a.¹ Now dial. [f. SCUD + -Y.]

Scuddy, a.² Obs. [f. SCUD sb.² + -Y.]

Scudler, variant of SCUDDALER.

Scudo (skū·dō), sb. [It.]

Scuffle (skɒf'l), sb. [f. SCUFFLE v.¹]

Scuffle, sb.² [Du. schoffel.]

Scuffle

Scuffler (skɔ·fləʌ). Also 7 souflar. [f. Scuffle v.¹ + -er¹.]

Scuffler (skɔ·fləʌ). [f. Scuffle v.² + -er¹.]

Scuffy (skɔ·fi), a. Sc. [f. Scuff v. + -y.]

Scug, sb.¹ Sc. and north. Forms: 5–7 (9) scoug, 6 skug, 6– scug (Sw. skugga fem., Da. skygge).

Scug, sb.² Sc. and north. Forms: 5–7 scoug, 6 skug.

Scug (skɔg), v.¹ Sc. and north.

Scug (skɔg), v.² Sc. and north.

Sculch (skʌltʃ). dial. and U.S. Also sculsh, sculsht, skultch. [var. of Culch.]

Sculder. Obs. rare⁻¹. [Connected with ON. skilja to divide.]

Sculduddery, sculduddry, 8–9 sculduddery, 9 skulduddery, U.S. skuldudery. [Of obscure origin.]

Scull, sb.¹ Also 7 skull. Sc. skull, Sculker.

Scull, sb.² Also 7–9 skull, 7 scul.

Scull, sb.³ Also 5 scoul, 5–8 skull, 7 sculle, 9 skull. [Of obscure origin.]

Scull (skɔl), v. Also 7 skull.

Scullduddery. var. Sculduddery.

Sculler (skɔ·ləʌ). [f. Scull v. + -er¹.]

Scullery (skɔ·ləri). Forms: 4 squillerye, 4–5 squyllery, 5 sculrye, 6 skulry, 6– scullery. [a. ONF. escuelerie.]

Scullion (skɔ·lyən). Forms: 6 squylyon, 6– scullion.

Scullogue (skɔ·ləʌg). [ad. Irish scológ.]

Sculp, sb.¹ Obs. [f. Sculp v.¹]

Sculp (skʌlp), sb.² N. Amer. dial. [f. Sculp v.²]

Sculp (skʌlp), v.¹ Obs.

Sculp (skʌlp), v.² N. Amer. dial. [f. Sculp sb.²]

Sculpin (skɔ·lpin), sb. Also 8 scolping, sculpion, 9 sculpen, scolping. [Corruption of Scorpene?]

Sculptile (skɔ·lptil), a. and sb. Obs. [ad. L. sculptilis.]

Sculptitory, a. Obs.

Sculptor (skɔ·lptəʌ). [a. L. sculptor, agent-n. f. sculpere to carve, engrave, sculpture.]

Sculptress (skɔ·lptres). Also 7 sculpteress. [f. Sculptor + -ess.]

Sculptural (skɔ·lptiūral), a. [f. Sculpture sb. + -al.]

Sculpturally (skɔ·lptiūrali), adv. [f. Sculptural + -ly².]

Sculpture (skɔ·lptiūʌ), sb. Also 6 sculture. [ad. L. sculptūra.]

Sculptured (skɔ·lptiūʌd), ppl. a. [f. Sculpture v. + -ed¹.]

Sculpturer (skɔ·lptiūrəʌ).

Sculpturesque (skɔlptiūre·sk), a. [f. Sculpture sb. + -esque.]

Sculpturing (skɔ·lptiūriŋ), vbl. sb. [f. Sculpture v. + -ing¹.]

Sculpturist. Obs. rare⁻¹. [f. Sculpture sb. + -ist.]

Sculpy. Obs. rare⁻¹. [Alteration of Sculpture, after words such as pulpy.]

Scult. var. Scolt, Schout.

Scum (skʌm), sb. Forms: 4–5 scume, 4–6 skume, 6 schume, 5– scum. [prob. a. MLG. schūm.]

Scum (skʌm), v. Forms: 4 scume, 4–6 skume, 5– scum. [partly f. Scum sb.; partly a. OF. escumer.]

Scumber (skɔ·mbəʌ), sb. Obs. exc. dial. Also 7 skommer, skomber. [Aphetic f. Discumber.]

Scumber, v. Obs. exc. dial.

Supplement, p. 3873; Corrigenda, p. 4092; Spurious words, p. 4093; Books quoted, p. 4094.

Scumble, *trans.* To void (ordure) ; *fig.* to produce (something foul)...

Scumble (skɪʊ̆mb'l), *v.* [f. SCUMBLE *v.*] A thin coat (of colour) put on by scumbling ; a softened effect produced by scumbling (see SCUMBLE *v.* 1 and 2).

Scumble (skɪʊ̆mb'l), *v.* [f. SCUMBLE *v.*: f. SCUMMING *ppl.a.*]
1. *trans.* In *Oil Painting*. To soften or render less brilliant (the colours in a portion of a picture) by overlaying with a thin coat of opaque or semi-opaque colour ; to spread or 'drive' (a colour) thinly over a portion of a picture in order to soften hard lines or blend the tints ; to produce (an effect) by this process.

2. *intr.* To practise scumbling.

Hence **Scumbled** *ppl.a.*, **Scumbling** *vbl.sb.*

Scumbling *vbl.sb.*

Scumble ... (see quots.)

Scummer, *v.* Obs. rare. [f. SCUMMER *sb.*]

Scummer-hearse, Obs. rare. [f. SCUMMER *sb.*]

Scumming (skɪʊ̆mɪŋ), *vbl.sb.* [f. SCUM *v.* + -ING1.]
1. a. The action of removing scum from the surface of a liquid. Also *fig.*

2. *concr.* The scum or process of forming or throwing up.

Scummer (skɪʊ̆mə(r)), *sb.1* [f. SCUM *v.* + -ER1.]

Scummy (skɪʊ̆mɪ), *a.* [f. SCUM *sb.* + -Y1.]

Scummer (skɪʊ̆mə(r)), *sb.2* Forms...

Scummered *ppl.a.*

Scumless (skɪʊ̆mlɪs), *a.*

Scummed (skɪʊ̆md), *ppl.a.*

Scup (skɒp), *sb.1 U.S.* [See quot.]

Scuppaug (skəpɔ·g), *sb. U.S.* [Shortened *f.* Narragansett *mishcùppaûog*, cf. *mishquip*: see SCUP *sb.1*]

Scup, *sb.2 U.S. dial.* [a. Du. *schoppen*, cf. *schop*, SCOOP *v.*] A swing.

Scup, *sb.3 U.S.* [Shortened *f.* SCUPPAUG.]

Scuppaug variant of SCUP *sb.1*

Scupper (skɒpə(r)), *sb. Naut.* Chiefly *pl.*

Scupper (skɒpə(r)), *v. Mil. slang.* [perh. f. prec. *sb.*, but the connexion of meaning is not clear.] 1. *trans.* To surprise and massacre.

Scuppered *ppl.a.*

Scuppernong (skɒpə(r)nɒŋ), *U.S.* The name of a river in North Carolina.

Scup-paul, *sb.*

Scuppet, *sb. Obs. exc. dial.* Forms...

Scuppet, *v. Obs. exc. dial.* Also 7 *scoppet.*

Scur (skɜ(r)), *v. U.S.* [See quot.]

Scour, variant of SKIRR *v.*: obs. f. SHOWER.

Scourage, variant of SCOURAGE1, SCURVY *sb.*

Scurdge, obs. form of SCOURGE *v.*

Scurdy, *Sc. Obs.* A kind of rock, whinstone.

Scure, obs. form of SKEWER.

Scurrell, **Scuree**, obs. f. SQUIRREL, SCOURGE1.

Scurf (skɜf), *sb.1* Forms...

Scurf (skɜf), *sb.2* Also 5 *scurfe*, 7 *scorfe, skurfe*.

Scurf (skɜf), *sb.3* Also 5 *scurffe, scorfe*.

Scurf, *v.* [f. SCURF *sb.1*]

Scurfily (skɜfɪlɪ), *adv.* [f. SCURFY *a.*]

Scurfiness (skɜfɪnɪs), *sb.*

Scurfy (skɜfɪ), *a.* Forms...

2. *transf.* Covered as with scurf incrusted ; resembling scurf.

Scurrility (skʊ·rɪlɪtɪ), *sb.* Forms...

Scurn, *sb. Obs.* [ad. OF. *escorne* (mod.F. *écorne*).]

Scurn, *v.* [a. OF. *escurner*, *escorner*.]

Scurr, variant of SCUR *v.*, SKIRR *v.*

Scurrage, variant of SCOURAGE1.

Scurrier, obs. f. SCORRIER.

Scur-rier, *Obs.* Forms 1, 5, 6 *scourrour*, 6 *scurrer*, *scurrier*, *skyrrer*; β. 6 *scourreour*, *-iour*, *-yer*, *scurrier*, 7 DISCOVERER; cf. the 14th c. *skowrour* s. v. SCOURER1.

Scurril (skʊ·rɪl), *a.* Forms: 6–7 *scurrile*, 6 *scurril*, 7 *skurril*; β. 6 *scurrill*, *-ile*. [ad. L. *scurrīlis*, f. *scurra* buffoon.]

Scurrile (skʊ·rɪl, -aɪl), *a.* [ad. L. *scurrīlis*: see prec.]

Scurrility (skʊ·rɪlɪtɪ), *sb.*

Scurrilize (skʊ·rɪlaɪz), *v. rare.* [f. SCURRILE *a.* + -IZE.]

Scurrilous (skʊ·rɪləs), *a.* [f. L. *scurrīlis* + -OUS.]

Scurrilously (skʊ·rɪləslɪ), *adv.*

Scurrilousness (skʊ·rɪləsnɪs), *sb.*

Scurrit (skʊ·rɪt), *sb. dial.*

Scurry (skʊ·rɪ), *v.* [Shortened from HURRY-SCURRY.]
1. *intr.* To run rapidly...

Scurry (skʊ·rɪ), *sb.* [f. prec.] 1. The act of scurrying ; a hurried movement, a rush ; hurry, haste, bustle.

Scurs, variant of SCORSE *sb.* and *v.*

Scurval, obs. form of SCURVY *sb.*

Scurvied (skɜvɪd), *a.* Affected with scurvy.

Scurvily (skɜvɪlɪ), *adv.* [f. SCURVY *a.* + -LY2.]

Scurviness (skɜvɪnɪs), *sb.*

Scurvy (skɜvɪ), *sb.* [f. SCURVY *a.* + -Y1.]

Scurvy (skɜvɪ), *a.* Forms...
1. A disease characterized by general debility of the body, extreme tenderness of the gums, foul breath, subcutaneous eruptions and pains in the limbs...

Scurvy-grass (skɜvɪgrɑs), *sb.* Also SCURVY-GRASS.

Scusation (skɪʊzeɪ·ʃən), *sb. Obs.* Aphetic form of EXCUSATION.

Scuse (skɪʊz), *sb. Obs. exc. dial.* Aphetic form of EXCUSE *sb.*

Scuse (skɪʊz), *v. Obs. exc. in Illiterate use.* Aphetic form of EXCUSE *v.*

Scut (skʌt), *sb.1* [Perh. a. early mod. Du. *schut*, *schutte* enclosure, etc.]

Scut (skʌt), *sb.2*

Scut, *a. and sb.3*

Scuta, pl. of SCUTUM.

Scutage (skɪʊ·tɪdʒ), *sb. Hist.* Also 5–6 *scutagia*. [ad. med.L. *scūtāgium*, f. *scūtum* shield.]

Scutal (skɪʊ·tæl), *a.* [f. L. *scūtum* + -AL1.]

Scutate (skɪʊ·teɪt), *a.* [ad. L. *scūtātus* armed with a shield.]

Scutch (skʌtʃ), *sb.1*

Scutch (skʌtʃ), *v.* [ad. F. *escoucher*, *escousser*.]

2. 'One of the pieces of wood which in a thrashing mill beats out the grain' (Jam.). Cf. SCUTCHER.

Scutch (skŏtʃ), *sb.³ dial.* Var. of SCOTCH, altered form of QUOTCH *sb.¹*

Hence **Scutched** *ppl. a.*

† Scutchane'le *v. Obs.* [f. *scutchanele*, obs.]

Scutcheon, obs. form of SCUTCHEON.

Scutcheoned (skŏtʃənd), *ppl. a.* [f. SCUTCHEON *sb.* + -ED.]
1. Furnished or decorated with scutcheons.
2. *Zool.* Bearing scutcheons or scutes.

Scutcheonless (skŏtʃənlĕs), *a.* [f. SCUTCHEON *sb.* + -LESS.] Having no scutcheon.

† Scutcheonry *Obs. rare.* [f. SCUTCHEON *sb.* + -RY.] Emblazoned figures collectively.

† Scutcher¹. *Obs.* Also **scutcher, skutcher.** [f. SCUTCH *v.¹*] A stick, a whip.

Scutcher² (skŏtʃər). Also **scutcher, skutcher.** [f. SCUTCH *v.* + -ER.]
1. An implement or apparatus for scutching.
2. A person employed in scutching.

† Scutchery. *Obs.* Knavery. [Chiefly in Nashe.]

† Scutchin. *Obs.* f. Corruption of CUTCH.

Scutcheon. *v.²*

Scutch-grass.

Scutching (skŏtʃɪŋ), *vbl. sb.²* [f. SCUTCH *v.²*]
1. The action of SCUTCH *v.²* 1.

Scute (skiūt), *sb.* Also **scutte, skute.** [ad. *scūtum* shield, whence OF. *escut, escu.*]
1. An English name for the French coin called *écu*.
2. *Zool. & Ent.* Of an insect: 'Having a visible scutellum.'

Scutel, obs. form of SCUTTLE *sb.¹*

Scutella, pl. of SCUTELLUM.

Scutellar (skiūtĕlər), *a.* [ad. mod.L. *scutellāris.*] Pertaining to a scutellum.

Scutellarin (skiūtĕlārin). *Chem.* [f. SCUTELLARIA + -IN.]

Scutellate (skiūtĕlāt, -let), *a.* [ad. mod.L. *scutellātus.*]
1. *Bot.* (See quot.)
2. *Zool.* Covered with scutella.

Scutellated (skiūtĕlātĕd), *ppl. a.* [f. prec.]

Scutellation (skiūtĕlāʃən). *Zool.*

Scutelliform (skiūtĕlifōrm), *a.*

Scutellum (skiūtĕlŏm). Pl. **scutella.** [mod.L.]
1. *Bot.* (See quots.)
2. *Zool. & Ent.* The third of the four sclerites.

Scutibranchiate (skiūtibrăŋkiāt), *a.* and *sb.*
A member of this group.

Scutifer (skiūtifər), *a.* [L. *scūtifer.*]
Scutiferous (skiūtifĕrəs), *a.*

Scutiform (skiūtifōrm), *a.* [ad. late L. *scūtiformis.*] Shield-shaped.

Scutiger (skiūtidʒər), *a.* and *sb.*

Scutigera (skiūtidʒĕra), *sb.* [mod.L.]

Scutigerous (skiūtidʒĕrəs), *a.* [f. L. *scūtiger.*]

Scutiped (skiūtiped), *a.*

Scutter (skŏtər), *v.* intr. *colloq.* and *dial.*
Hence **Scuttering** *vbl. sb.*

Scuttle (skŏt'l), *sb.¹* Forms: 1 **scutel**, 4–5 **scutell**, 5 **scutelle** (scutylle, scutyll), **scottill**, (7 dial. **scotle**), 6 **scuttle.** [OE. *scutel* in sense 1 = L. *scutella* dish, platter.]

Scuttle (skŏt'l), *sb.²* [?]

Scuttle (skŏt'l), *sb.³* [Altered form of CUTTLE *sb.¹*]

Scuttle (skŏt'l), *v.¹* [f. SCUTTLE *sb.¹*]

Scuttle (skŏt'l), *v.²* [f. SCUTTLE *sb.²*]

Scuttle (skŏt'l), *v.³*

† Scuttle (skŏt'l). *Obs.* Also **scutill, scuttill.** [ad. Sp. *escotilla*, Pg. *escotilha*; the sense 'a scuttle' is expressed by the derivatives f. *escoutillon*, Sp. *escotillon*, F. *escoutille*.]

Scuttle (skŏt'l), *sb.⁴* Also **scutle, scuttel.** [f. SCUTTLE *v.¹*]

Scuttled (skŏt'ld), *ppl. a.*

Scuttleful (skŏt'lful). [f. SCUTTLE *sb.¹* + -FUL.]

Scuttler (skŏt'lər).
1. In *Manchester*: One who takes part in a 'scuttle' or street-fight. See SCUTTLE *v.³*

Scuttle (skŏt'l), *sb.⁵* Also *error.* **scutle.** [ad. mod.L. *scutella*, dim. of *scutum* shield.]

Scuttling (skŏt'lɪŋ), *vbl. sb.¹* [f. SCUTTLE *v.¹*]

Scuttling (skŏt'lɪŋ), *vbl. sb.²* [f. SCUTTLE *v.³*]

Scye (saɪ). *Tailors' cant.* [A use of a Sc. and Ulster dialect word (written also *scy, si, sie*, in glossaries) meaning 'the opening of a gown, etc., into which the sleeve is inserted'; the part of the dress between the armpit and the chest (E.D.D.); of obscure etymology.]

Scyelite (saɪĕlaɪt). *Min.* [f. the name of Loch *Scye* in Caithness + -LITE.]

Scylla (sɪla). [L.; a. Gr. Σκύλλα.]

Scymetar, Scymitar, obs. ff. SCIMITAR.

Scyphose (saɪfŏs), *a.* [f. SCYPHUS + -OSE.]

Scyphula (sɪfiūla). *Path.* Usually *pl.* **scyphulæ.** [mod.L. *scyphula*, dim. of *scyphus.*]

Scyphus (saɪfəs). Pl. **scyphi** (saɪfaɪ). [mod.L. *scyphus*, a. Gr. σκύφος, cup.]

Scytale (sɪtălɪ). *Antiq.* Also 6 in Latin form **scytala.** [L., a. Gr. σκυτάλη.]

and size. Hence, a secret dispatch conveyed by this method.

1580 North *Plutarch, Lysander* (1595) 487 To him selfe they sent immediately that which they call Scytala...The Scytala is in this sort. When the Ephori doe send a Generall, or an Admirall to the warres, they cause two litle round staues to be made [etc.]...These two litle staues they call Scytales. *Ibid.*, This little scrowle of parchment also is called as the rowle of wodde, Scytala. 1640 G. Watts tr. *Bacon's Adv. Learn.* vi. 268 A Spartan letter sent once in a Scytale or round cypher'd staffe. 1838 Thirlwall *Greece* xxxvii. V. 17 A scytalé would at all times be sufficient to procure whatever they wished.

Scyte, obs. f. Site *sb.*[1], Sheet *sb.*

Scyth (siþ). Now *rare*. Forms: 4 **Sithe (Schyte, Schite, 5 Scite, Shite, Scytte)**, 7 **Scythe**, 9 **Scyth**. [ad. L. *Scytha*, Gr. Σκύθης.] A Scythian.

1387 Trevisa *Higden* (Rolls) II. 257 Of Egipcians in þe souþ, and of Sithes [MS. a Schytes; Caxton, Shites] in the norþ. 1480 Caxton *Descr. Scot.* (1520) 1/1 Scottes ben called as it were scyttes for they came out of Scicia. 1557 North *Gueuara's Diall Pr.* (1619) 707/1 The Greekes the Romaines, ..the Scythes were alwayes temperat in eating and drinking. 1596 Spenser *State Irel.* Wks. (Globe) 632/2 The old English also which there remayneth have gotten up theyr cryes Scythian-like. ..And herein also lyeth open an other manifest proofe that the Irish be Scythes or Scotts. 1871 P. Smith *Anc. Hist. East* xxiii. § 12 (1881) 473 The *Sacæ* of Greek writers on Persian affairs are simply Asiatic Scyths.

Scythe (saið), *sb.* Forms: α. 1 **sigdi, siðe**, 3–6 **syþe**, 4–7 **sith**, 5 **cithe**, (**sythy**), 5–6 **cythe**, 6 **syith**, 6–7 **syth, sieth**, 7 **siethe, seith, sight, syeth**, 3–9 **sythe**, 4–9 **sithe**; β. 5 **seth**, 7 **saith**; γ. 7 **scith, scithe**, 7– **scythe**. [OE. *siðe* masc., earlier **sigði* (written *sigdi* in Epinal Gl.) = LG. *seged, seid, sicht*, ON. *sigð-r* (mod.Icel. *sigð* fem., Norw. *sigd, sigde, sidde* masc.) :—OTeut. **segiþjo-z*, f. root **seg-* to cut, whence the synonymous OS. *segisna* (MLG., MDu. *seisene*, Du. *zeisen, zeis*), OHG *segansa* (MHG. *segense, seinse*, G. *sense*).

The etymologically correct spelling *sithe* was preferred by Johnson, but his authority has not prevailed against the currency of the spelling with *sc*, due to erroneous association with L. *scindere* to cut. Cf. *scissors*.]

1. An agricultural implement for mowing grass or other crops, having a long thin curving blade fastened at an angle with the handle and wielded with both hands with a long sweeping stroke.

α. c 725 *Corpus Gloss.* 834 *Falcis*: wudubil, siðe, riftras. c 825 *Epinal Gloss.* 62 *Falces*, uudubil, sigdi, riftr. c 1000 Ælfric *Hom.* II. 162 Befeoll an siðe of ðam snæde into anum deopan seaðe. 13.. *Coer de L.* 6788 They slowen Sarezynes al soo swythe, As gres fallyth fro the sythe. 1382 Wyclif *Isa.* ii. 4 Thei shul bete togidere their swerdes in to shares and ther speres in to sithes. 1404 *Durham Acc. Rolls* (Surtees) 396 Item..1 fot ax, 1 cithe, 1 hamer. 1523 Fitzherb. *Husb.* § 23 Take hede that thy mower mow clene and holde downe the hynder hand of his sith. 1580–3 Greene *Mamillia* i. 12 The grasse looketh better being vncut, then that which withereth with the sieth. 1612 Drayton *Poly-olb.* xvi. 48 Thou sawest great-burthen'd Ships through these thy valleys pass, Where now the sharp-edg'd Sithe sheeres vp the spyring grasse. 1632 Milton *L'Allegro* 66 And the Mower whets his sithe. 1766 *Ann. Reg.* 62 Samples of home-made sithes. 1822 T. Taylor *Apuleius* vi. 120 There, likewise, were sithes, and all the instruments of harvest. 1828–32 Webster, *Sythe*.

β. 14.. *Nom.* in Wr.-Wülcker 728/40 *Hec falx*, a sykyl, or a seth. 1625 *Althorp MS.* p. lxi, To Gibson one daie waiting on my lo. of Southampton in the parke with the saith yor lop bid him call for 00 01 00.

γ. 1602 J. Bruen in Hinde *Life* (1641) 147 My son..took up a scith to see how he could mow, and the scith entered in at his stocking. 1716–8 Lady M. W. Montagu *Lett.* I. xxxviii. 151 He was..followed by..several reapers..with scythes in their hands, seeming to mow. 1863 Macdonald *D. Elginbrod* i. x. (1871) 47 The day arrived when the sickle must be put into the barley, soon to be followed by the scythe in the oats. 1875 J. Wilson in *Encycl. Brit.* I. 362/1 The common scythe ..is very extensively used for reaping grain in all parts of the kingdom.

2. *transf.* and *fig.*, esp. as the attribute of Time or Death.

1387–8 T. Usk *Test. Love* i. Prol. 99 Sithen al the grettest clerkes..with their sharpe sythes of conning al mowen and mad therof grete rekes and noble. 1506 *Kal. Sheph.* (Sommer) 90 They fyght and cose on eche other wonder with the sythe of deuyls dredabyll. c 1600 Shaks. *Sonn.* xii, And nothing gainst Times sieth can make defence Saue [etc.]. 1659 Pecke *Parnassi Puerp.* 112 Time devours Things; His Sithe our Legs will hit. a 1711 Ken *Hymnotheo* Poet. Wks. 1721 III. 185 See how Death preys on humane Race; Out with his Scythe the Tyrant goes, Great Multitudes at once he mows. 1809 Byron *Bards & Rev.* 632 Whet not your scythe, suppressors of our vice! Reforming saints! 1854 Brewster *More Worlds* i. 16 The swarm of human life.. has never been perceptibly reduced by the scythe of famine, of pestilence, or of war. 1883 O. W. Holmes *Loving-cup Song* 29 Old Time his rusty scythe may whet.

3. A weapon having a long curving blade resembling a reaping hook. *Obs.* exc. *Hist.* with reference to scythed chariots (see Scythed *a.*).

a. a 1300 *Havelok* 2553 Hand-ax, syþe, gisarm, or spere. a 1400–50 *Alexander* 3058 For-þi þe chariots in þe chace choppid þaim to deth, Þe cartis þat I carpid of with þe kene sithis [*v. r.* sythez]. c 1500 *Melusine* 302 But the geaunt stert vp lyghtly, in grete yre, & as geffray passed by, he smote hys hors behynd with hys sythe of fyn stele. 1610 Holland *Camden's Brit.* i. 30 They use axeltrees armed at both ends with hookes and sithes.

4. *attrib.* and *Comb.*: a. Simple attrib., as *scythe-blade, -handle, -smith, -stick, -sweep, -work*; *scythe-like* adj.

a 1400–50 *Alexander* 3023 Chariotis..sett aþire side full of *sythe-bladis, Kene keruand as knyfes. 1829 Scott *Rob Roy* Introd. and half, He supplied the want of guns and swords with scythe-blades set straight upon their handles. 1707 Mortimer *Husb.* (1721) II. 51 It is also good for Rake and *Scythe-handles. c 1835 *Encycl. Metrop.* (1845) XXIII. 464/2 Giving the edge of the fin a *scythe-like shape. 1633 J. Clarke *Two-fold Praxis* 24 In the street next above, bee shoemsmiths, *sythesmiths, bladesmiths, cutlers. 1890 Amphlett *Hist. Clent* 119 Philip Cix, also a scythesmith. 1831 Loudon *Encycl. Agric.* (1857) § 7799 *Scythe-sticks and stones for sharpening scythes, hay-knives. 1856 Allingham *Mowers* 7 A *scythe-sweep, and a scythe-sweep, We mow the grass together. 1598 Sylvester *Du Bartas* ii. ii. iii. *Colonies* 713 Their flowry Fleece Affords us *Sithe-work yearly twice or thrice. 1904 Edith Rickert *Reaper* 183 He was stiff with scythe-work.

b. objective, as *scythe-grinder, -maker, whetting*; *scythe-bearing* adj.

1633 Drumm. of Hawth. *Poems* (1656) 165 The old Lucadian *Syth-bearing Sire..for thee feeles flames of sweet desire. 1619 *Canterb. Marr. Licences* (MS.), Robert Brooke of Goudhurst, *sightgrinder. *Ibid.*, Edward Male of Goudhurst, *sightmaker. 1833 J. Holland *Manuf. Metal* II. 55 Hay and straw knives are manufactured by the scythe-makers. 1857 FitzGerald *Let. to Cowell* 27 June, One wakes to the tune of the Mower's *Scythe-whetting.

c. similative, as †*scythe-billed, -shaped*, †*-tusked* adjs.

1668 Charleton *Onomast.* 103 *Falcinellus*..the *Scyth-bill'd Heron. 1815 S. Brookes *Introd. Conchol.* 80 The animal of *Anomia tridentata* has two flat arms somewhat *scythe-shaped. 1612 *Two Noble K.* i. i. 79 Most dreaded Amazonian, that hast slain The *scythe-tusk'd boar.

d. instrumental, as *scythe-armed* adj.

1811 Scott *Don Roderick* ii. xxv, The scythe-arm'd Giant turn'd his fatal glass. 1838 Thirlwall *Greece* xxxiii. IV. 304 Scythe-armed chariots.

5. Special combinations, as †**scythe-bill**, a suggested name (after mod.L. *Falcinellus*) for the Glossy Ibis; **scythe-chariot** *Hist.* = *scythed chariot* (see Scythed *a.*); **scythe-cradle**, a framework of wood fastened to a scythe for carrying the mowings clean into the swath; **scythe-hook, -sickle**, a reaping-hook with a smooth cutting blade as contrasted with one in which the edge is cut into teeth; †**scythe-land** (see quot.); †**scythe-sand** (see quot.); **scythe-snathe, -sned** *dial.*, the curved handle to which the blade of the scythe is attached; **scythe-stone**, a whetstone for scythes; also in *Comb.*

1678 Ray *Willughby's Ornith.* 295 The Falcinellus of Gesner and Aldrovand, which we may English, The *Sithe-Bill. 1695 J. Edwards *Author. O. & N. Test.* III. 215 With these *sithe-chariots they mowed men down. 1695 Kennett *Par. Antiq.* s.v. *Carecta*, In Kent a *Sithe-cradle, or rack of wood fastened to a sithe for carrying the mow'd barley clean into the swath. 1884 *Century Mag.* Jan. 447/1 Grain was reaped with sickles, though *'scythe-cradles' were not unknown. 1844 H. Stephens *Bk. Farm* III. 1079 The smooth edged sickle, or *scythe-hook. 1597 Skene *De Verb. Sign.* s.v. *Husbandland*, Hvsbandland conteinis commonly 6. aikers of sok & *syith land: That is of sik land as may be tilled with ane pleuch, or may be mawed with ane syith. 1686 Plot *Staffordsh.* 154 An excellent sand to whet their Sithes, whence it has the denomination of *Sithe-Sand. 1844 H. Stephens *Bk. Farm* III. 1055 The *scythe sickle is so called, because of its being provided with a cutting edge. 1845 S. Judd *Margaret* ii. i. (1871) 184 His bare head pillowed on a *scythe-snath. 1907 'J. Halsham' *Lonewood Corner* xix. 212 Ne'er he nor his father afore him ever bought a *scythe-sned. 1688 *Lond. Gaz.* No. 2413/4 Who hath formerly been an Apprentice to a *Scythe-Stone Cutter near Darby. 1879 Rutley *Study of Rocks* xiv. 278 The Rotherham stone is worked for building purposes and for grindstones, and that at Hart Hill for scythe-stones.

Scythe (saið), *v.* [f. Scythe *sb.*]

†1. *intr.* To use a scythe. *Obs. rare*[−1].

1573–80 Baret *Alv.* M 541 He that sietheth with a bill, or he that vseth a sieth or hooke, a mower, *falcarius*. [After Elyot's (and Cooper's) rendering of *Falcarius*: 'He that fighteth with a bill'.]

2. *trans.* To cut or mow with a scythe.

1597 Shaks. *Lover's Compl.* 12 Time had not sithed all that youth begun. 1892 Henley *Song of Sword* 9 Where the tall grain is ripe Thrust in your sickles:..Scything and binding The full sheaves of sovranty.

3. *intr.* To move with a sweeping motion as of one mowing with a scythe. *nonce-use.*

1897 Kipling *Capt. Courageous* v. 111 The foresail scythed back and forth against the blue sky.

Scythed (saiðd), *ppl. a.* [f. Scythe *sb.* and *v.* + -ed.]

1. Furnished with a scythe; esp. *Hist.* (= Gr. δρεπανηφόρος, L. *falcatus*) of war-chariots provided with scythes fastened to a revolving shaft projecting from the axle-trees; attributed by classical writers to the Persians and the Britons.

a 1400–50 *Alexander* 3821 For with his florantis olifants him folowed a thousand, Of sithid chariotis. 1618 Bolton *Florus* (1636) 120 Three hundred thousand foot, and not a lesse number of Horse, and of seithed Chariots. 1750 Warton *Verses, Montaubon* 19 Galgacus' scythed, iron car. 1816 Scott *Bl. Dwarf* vi, Let Destiny drive forth her scythed car through the..trembling mass of humanity.

2. Cut down with a scythe.

1865 Swinburne *Poems & Ball.* Ser. i. 209 *Before Parting*, And yet who knows what end the scythed wheat Makes of its foolish poppies' mouths of red?

Scytheless (sai·ðlės), *a.* [f. Scythe *sb.* + -less.] Without a scythe.

1817 Coleridge *Limbo* 5 Scytheless Time with branny hands. 1857 Ruskin *Pol. Econ. Art* ii. (1868) 98, I tell you, Time is scytheless and toothless; it is we who [etc.].

Scytheman (sai·ðmæn). Also 8–9 **scythesman.** [f. Scythe *sb.* + Man *sb.*[1]]

1. One who uses a scythe.

1577 Peacham *Garl. Eloq.* P ij b, Reapers cutting downe Corne in euery fielde, Sithmen labouryng harde. 1605 *1st Pt. Jeronimo* iii. ii, As sithmen trim the long haird Ruffian fields, So fast they fall. 1797 Coleridge in J. Cottle *Early Recoll.* (1837) I. 215 When the scythes-man o'er his sheaf Caroll'd in the yellow vale. 1844 H. Stephens *Bk. Farm* III. 1050 The scytheman requires a person to follow him and carefully gather the corn he has mown into sheaves in bands. 1894 Crockett *Raiders* 297 Three kinds of sand he brought me to see, but not being a scytheman I could not tell the difference.

b. A member of an irregular body of troops armed with a scythe as a weapon.

1849 Macaulay *Hist. Eng.* vi. II. 23 Another said that he should be glad to know how the Devonshire trainbands, who had fled in confusion before Monmouth's scythemen, would have faced the household troops of Lewis. 1889 Doyle *Micah Clarke* 138 See that your scythesmen line the quickset hedge upon the right.

2. *fig.* Applied to Time and to Death.

1818 Scott *Rob Roy* x, 'The old scythe-man has moved so rapidly,' I answered, 'that I could not count his strides.' 1844 W. H. Maxwell *Scotland* xxxix. (1855) 305 Time, that villanous old scytheman. 1909 *Daily News* 1 Apr. 4 The stroke of the dread scythesman.

Scyther (sai·ðəɹ). [f. Scythe *v.* + -er[1].] A mower; *esp.* with allusion to Time. Cf. Scytheman.

1863 Macdonald *D. Elginbrod* i. x. (1871) 47 David..was the best scyther in the whole country side. 1901 Meredith *Reading of Life* 2 And unto the pallid Scyther Either points us.

†**Scy·thiac**, *a. Obs.* [See -ac.] = Scythian.

1794 Sullivan *View Nat.* II. 280 There is a strong similarity between the Hebrew and the Scythiac languages.

Scythian (si·þiăn), *a.* and *sb.* Also 6–7 **Sythian.** [f. L. *Scythia*, a. Gr. Σκυθία (f. Σκύθης Scyth) + -an.]

A. *adj.*

1. Pertaining to Scythia, an ancient region extending over a large part of European and Asiatic Russia, or to the nomadic people by whom it was inhabited.

1567 Golding *Ovid's Met.* xv. 312 Hypanis That springeth in the Scythian hilles. 1587–90 Marlowe *1st Pt. Tamburl.* i. i. 44 Tamburlaine, that sturdie Scythian thiefe. 1596 Spenser *State Irel.* Wks. (Globe) 630/1 For though it [Nomadism] be an old Scythian use, yet it is very behoofull in that countrey of Ireland. a 1625 Beaum. & Fl. *Four Plays in One, Tri. Death* vi, What Scythian snow so white? what crystal chaster? 1776 Mickle tr. *Camoens' Lusiad* Introd. 14 The irruptions of northern or Scythian barbarians. 1882 Ruskin *Bible of Amiens* iii. 100 The northern kingdoms are moated from the Scythian desert by the Vistula.

transf. 1814 Scott *Wav.* xxxii, All the domestic accommodations of milk, poultry, butter, &c., were out of the question in this Scythian camp.

2. Special collocations: **Scythian antelope** = Saiga; **Scythian disease** [for the reason for the name, cf. Herodotus I. cv], atrophy of the male organs of generation, accompanied by loss of masculine attributes (*Syd. Soc. Lex.* 1898); **Scythian insanity**, the mental perversion occurring in the Scythian disease, manifested in the assumption of female dress and habits (*ibid.*); †**Scythian lamb**, = Barometz; **Scythian stone**, some mineral.

1608 Topsell *Serpents* 147 The gall of this beast [*sc.* the Dart] mixed with the Sythian Stone, yealdeth a very good Eye-salue. 1659 R. Lovell *Herbal* 524 Scythian Lamb *Agnus Scyth.* 1781 Pennant *Quadrupeds* I. 86 Scythian Antelope. 1800 Shaw *Gen. Zool.* II. 339 The Saiga or Scythian Antelope, is an inhabitant..of all the deserts from the Danube and the Dnieper to the river Irtish.

†3. *Philol.* Used as a designation for the Ural-Altaic family of languages. *Obs.*

1885 Whitney *Philol.* in *Encycl. Brit.* XVIII. 779/1 Ural-Altaic (Scythian, Turanian) Family.

B. *sb.*

1. A person belonging to the race by which Scythia was inhabited; = Scyth.

1543 Becon *Invect. agst. Swearing, Cert. Lawes* Wks. 1560 I. 223 b, The law among the Scythyans was yt, if [etc.]. 1590 Marlowe *2nd Pt. Tamburl.* iii. v, Raile not proud Scythian. 1596 *Edward III*, ii. i. 72 That it may rayse drops in a Tarters eye, And make a flyntheart Sythian pytiful. 1781 Gibbon *Decl. & F.* xxvi. (1787) II. 563 *note*, In speaking of all, or any, of the northern shepherds of Europe, or Asia, I indifferently use the appellations of *Scythians*, or *Tartars*. 1883 Morfill *Slavonic Lit.* ii. 38, I shall not discuss the question here as to whether the Scythians were a Mongolian or Indo-European race.

2. The language of Scythia.

1668 Wilkins *Real Char.* i. i. § 3. 3 The European Tartar, or Scythian, from which some conceive our Irish to have had its original.

3. Comb. *Scythian-like* adj. and adv.

1596 Spenser *State Irel.* Wks. (Globe) 632/2 The old English also which there remayneth have gotten up theyr cryes Scythian-like, as the Geraldins Croum-abowe. *Ibid.* 633/1, I thought this manner of lewd crying and howling not impertinent to be noted as uncivill and Scythian-like.

Scythic (si·þik), *a.* [ad. L. *Scythicus*, a. Gr. Σκυθικός, f. Σκύθ-ης Scyth.] Scythian.

1623 Lisle *Ælfric on O. & N. Test.* Pref. 5 But we shall hence, some to the thirsty Moore, To swift Oront of Creet, to Scythicke shore. 1634 Sir T. Herbert *Trav.* (1638) 20 The Arimaspi..not seldome from their Scythic holes attempting the conquest of Mammon inclos'd in the Rhyphean hills. 1802 Pinkerton *Mod. Geog.*, *Turkey in Asia* II. 15 The original population of these regions consisted chiefly of Scythic nations. 1871 P. Smith *Anc. Hist. East* xxiii. § 12 (1881) 473 *note*, The Scythic element in the population of Western Asia.

†**Scy·thical**, *a. Obs.* [Formed as prec. + -al.] Befitting the Scythians, barbarous.

1559 Morwyng *Evonym.* Pref. A ij b, There is also..a heauenlye water..whiche boothe Democritus and Mercury Trimegistus knewe: callinge it sometimes a deuine water, sometimes a Scythicall liquor. 1602 F. Hering *Anat.* 20 Such Schythicall..torturing and massacring of Men.

Scything (sai·ðiŋ), *ppl. a.* [f. Scythe *v.* + -ing[2].] That cuts like a scythe.

1822 'B. Cornwall' *Flood of Thessaly* i. 448 Fierce as the North In March, when scything blasts strip all the bones.

†**Scy·thism.** *Obs.* [ad. late Gr. Σκυθισμός, f. Σκύθης Scyth: see -ism.] a. The type of paganism to which the religion of the Scythians belonged. b. (See quot. 1793.)

1609 Bible (Douay) *Gen.* Contin. Ch. 48 The second mother of al Sectes beginning after the flood..was Scythisme. 1793 Hely tr. *O'Flaherty's Ogygia* Pref. 59 The Scythians are looked upon to be the most ancient people. *Ibid.* 70 Wherefore that interval of time..between the deluge and the Babylonian monarchy ..is denominated a scythesm, as Epiphanius affirms. 1816 G. S. Faber *Orig. Pagan Idol.* I. 86 From their supposed founders..we may call the one Scythism, and the other Ionism.

Scy·thized, *a. rare.* [f. L. *Scyth-a* Scyth + -ize + -ed[1].] Assimilated to the Scythians.

1861 W. L. Bevan *Student's Man. Anc. Geog.* i. iii. § 7 (1864) 35 The inhabitants of this district were partly Scythized Greeks, but mainly Scythians.

Scytho- (sai·þo), combining form of L. *Scytha*, *Scythes* Scyth; prefixed (with hyphen) to ethnic sbs. or adjs. with the sense 'partly Scythian and partly . . .', as in *Scytho-Aryan, -Greek, -Median.*

1844 W. D. Cooley *Larcher's Notes on Herod.* iv. cv. II. 57 The Scytho-Greeks. 1871 P. Smith *Anc. Hist. East* xxiii. § 10 (1881) 472 *note*, Which is sometimes expressed by calling them Scytho-Aryans. *Ibid.* § 12. 473 The Persian and Scytho-Median columns [of the Achæmenid inscriptions].

'**Sdeath** (zdeþ), *int. Obs.* exc. *arch.* A euphemistic abbreviation of *God's death* (see God *sb.* 14 n) used in oaths and asseverations.

1606 *Sir G. Goosecappe* i. ii, S'death they put not all their virtues in their smockes..as our Ladies doe. 1607 Shaks. *Cor.* i. i. 221 Sdeath. 1616 B. Jonson *Ev. Man in Hum.* ii. i, 'Sdeath, he mads me. 1697 Cibber *Woman's Wit* iii. 31 S'Death, Sir, is that a Question to ask a Dying Man? 1735 Pope *Prol. Sat.* 61 'Sdeath I'll print it. 1821 Scott *Kenilw.* xl, 'Sdeath! to think on it is distraction! 1869 Browning *Ring & Bk.* xi. 1279 'Sdeath! Here's a coil raised.

†**Sdeign**, *sb. Obs. rare.* In 6 **sdeigne, sdaine.** [ad. It. *sdegno*, f. *sdegnare*: see next.] Disdain.

1594 Spenser *Amoretti* v, Scorn of base things, & sdeigne of foule dishonor. 1596 — *F. Q.* v. v. 51 So she departed, full of griefe and sdaine.

†**Sdeign**, *v. Obs.* Also 6 **s'dain, sdaine, sdayn, s'deigne**, 7 **sdain, sdein.** [ad. It. *sdegnare*, aphetic var. of *disdegnare* to Disdain. Sometimes used as an English shortening of *disdain*.]

1. *trans.* = Disdain *v.* in various senses.

1590 Spenser *F. Q.* iii. i. 40 They sdeigned such lasciuious disport. *Ibid.* 55. 1591 — *M. Hubberd* 679 As if he..sdeign'd the low degree. 1596 — *F. Q.* v. v. 44 Yet durst she not disclose her fancies wound,..for doubt of being sdayned. 1596 Fitz-Geffrey *Sir F. Drake* xxv. B 5, Sdaine nott that our harsh plaints should beate your eares. 1599 H. Buttes *Dyets Drie Dinner* A a 3, Come welcome Guest: s'deigne not..this shot-free entertainement. 1614 Drumm. of Hawth. *Tears Death Mœliades* A 3 b, The Shepheards left their Flocks with downe-cast Eyes, Sdaining to looke vp to the angrie Skies. 1667 Milton *P. L.* iv. 50 Lifted up so high I sdeind subjection.

2. *intr.* = Disdain *v.* 3.

1590 Marlowe *Edw. II*, v. ii. H 4 b, Why yongling, s'dainst thou so of Mortimer?

†**Sdei·gnful**, *a. Obs.* Also 6 **sdainfull**, 8 **'sdeignfull.** [f. Sdeign *sb.* + -ful.] Disdainful.

1596 Spenser *F. Q.* v. ii. 33 In sdeignfull wize he drew vnto him neare. 1598 Tofte *Alba* (1880) 22 A Sdainfull thought through Hatred doth arise. 1600 Fairfax *Tasso* vii. xlii. 125 The Prince (whose lookes his sdainfull anger show). *Ibid.* xx. cxxviii. 389 She shrikes, and twines away her sdeignfull eies. 1748 Shenstone *Schoolmistress* xxix. in Dodsley *Poems* I. 259 As he who now with 'sdeignfull fury thrill'd Surveys mine work; and levels many a sneer.

†'**Sdeynes**, *int. Obs.* Shortened form of *God's deynes*, *God's dines*: see Dines.

1616 B. Jonson *Ev. Man in Hum.* ii. i, 'Sdeynes, I know not what I should say to him, i' the whole world. [1601 *reads* Faith...] *Ibid.* ii. ii, 'Sdeynes, and I swallow this, Ile nere draw my sword..againe. [1601 *reads* S'blood and I...]

†'**Sdi·ggers**, *int.* = *God's diggers* (see God *sb.* 14).

1687 A. Lovell tr. *Bergerac's Com. Hist.* 25 S'diggers.

‖**Sdru·cciola**, *a. Obs. rare.* [It. *sdrucciola* (*sc. rima*), fem. of *sdrucciolo*), lit. 'slippery', whence Sp. *esdrújulo*, used similarly with reference to versification.] Epithet of that kind of rhyme in which the words ending the lines are accented on the antepenultimate; trisyllabic (rhyme).

English writers on verse have sometimes used *sdrucciolo*, or the phrase *versi sdruccioli*, as a foreign technical term, esp. in referring to Italian poetry.

a 1586 Sidney *Apol. Poetry* (Arb.) 71 Lastly, euen the very ryme it selfe, the Italian cannot put in the last silable, by the French named the Masculine ryme, but still in the next to the last, which the French call the Female; or the next before that, which the Italians terme *Sdrucciola*. The example ..of the *Sdrucciola* [is] *Femina, Semina.* 1605 Chapman *All Fools* ii. i. 176 In any Rime Masculine, Feminine, Or Sdrucciolla [*printed* Sdruciolla].

†**Se**, *pron.* (*def. art.*) OE. and early *ME.*: see The.

Se, obs. form of Say *sb.*[3]

1567 *Wills & Inv. N. C.* (Surtees 1835) I. 267, xxix milk bowells & skeles, one stand, one se, ij kyrnes.

Se, obs. form of So *adv.*, See *sb.* and *v.*, She.

Se-, *prefix*, occurring only in Latin derivatives, represents the L. *sē-*, identical with the OLatin *sē* (also *sēd*) prep. and adv., without, apart. With prepositional force the L. *sē-* occurs in one or two adjs., as *sēcūrus* secure (from **sē cūrā* without care); with advb. force (= apart) it is chiefly found in verbs, of which the following (as also their derivatives) have come into English in adapted forms: *sēcēdĕre, sēcernĕre, sēclūdĕre, sēdūcĕre, sēgregāre, sēparāre.* The form *sēd-* occurs in *sēditio* sedition (lit. 'going apart').

The L. *sē, sēd* is believed to be related to the pronoun *sē*, oneself. It is disputed whether the *d* of *sēd* is an ablative sign or represents a particle *-de.*

Sea (sī), *sb.* Forms: 1 **sǽ**, (1 **seo**), 2–3 **sæ**, 2–6 **se, see**, 4 (*Ayenb.*) **zo**, (**seo, sæo**), 4–5 **cee**, 4–6 *Sc.* **sey**, 6 *Sc.* **seye, sie**, 2– **sea.** *Pl.* 1 **sǽs, sǽas, sǽ**, 4 **sen**, 4–5 **sees**, 4–6 (chiefly *Sc.*) **seis**, 6 **seaes, sease**, (**saezes**), **seeis**, *Sc.* **seyis, seyes**, 6– **seas.** [Common Teut.: OE. *sǽ* str. masc. and fem. corresponds to OFris. *sē* masc., OS. *sēo, sēu*, dat. *sēwa* masc. (MLG. *sē*, MDu. *see* masc. and fem., Du. *zee* fem.), OHG. *sēo, sē*, dat. *sēwe* masc., sea, lake, pond (MHG. *sē* masc. and fem., sea, lake, mod.G. *see* masc., lake, *see* fem., sea), ON. *sǽ-r, sjá-r, sjó-r* masc. (Sw. *sjö*, Da. *sø*), Goth. *saiw-s* masc., sea, also marsh:—OTeut. **saiwi-z*.

The word has no certain affinities, and it is doubtful whether the *w* represents a pre-Teut. *w* or (by Verner's Law) a pre-Teut. *q*[w] (or *kw*). On the assumption of a guttural root, and of the priority of the sense 'marsh' (occurring in Gothic) it has been suggested that the word may be cogn. w. OHG. *gisig* (*gisic, gesik*), found in glosses as a collective for ponds or marshes (*stagna, paludes*), and with the OHG. *sīgan* to flow down, sink, OE. *sīgan* to descend: see Sye *v.*]

I. The simple word.

1. The continuous body of salt water that covers the greater part of the earth's surface. Often *poet.* with epithet as *broad, deep* (see Deep *a.* 1), †*large, salt* (see Salt *a.*[1] 1), †*side, wide, wild*, etc.

Since Early Middle English always with prefixed article, exc. in phrases with preps. (see esp. 1 c and 10–17).

Beowulf 2394 Ofer sǽ side. c 1205 Lay. 30496 On þare sæ brade. c 1275 *Moral Ode* 82 in *O. E. Misc.* 61 He makede fysses in þe sea. c 1385 Chaucer *L. G. W.* 2163 In an yle, amid the wilde see. c 1386 — *Knt.'s T.* 1098 Fletynge in the large see. c 1400 *Destr. Troy* 1982 Blouen to þe brode se. c 1430 *Syr Gener.* 6353 Toward the cee he rode a pase. 1593 Shaks. *Rich. II*, ii. i. 46 This precious stone, set in the siluer sea. 1647 H. More *Philos. Devot.* 32 As the thankfull Rivers pay What they borrowed of the Sea. 1779 Cowper *Olney Hymns* iii. xv. 3 God moves in a mysterious way, His wonders to perform; He plants his footsteps in the sea, And rides upon the storm. 1807 Wordsw. *Sonn. to Liberty* i. xii, Two Voices are there; one is of the sea, One of the mountains; each a mighty Voice. 1842 Tennyson *Farewell* i Flow down, cold rivulet, to the sea.

b. For *ocean sea, sea ocean, sea of ocean*, see Ocean *sb.* 1. Also *the great sea* (*of ocean*).

c 1290 *St. Michael* 632 in *S. Eng. Leg.* I. 317 The gret se of occean. *Ibid.* 654 Þe eorþe amidde þe grete se ase a luyte bal is round. 1500–20 Dunbar *Poems* lxvi. 67 Our all the grit se occeane. 1513 Douglas *Æneis* iv. ix. 14 Neir by the end of the gret occiane see, Thar as the son..gois doun.

c. Often coupled with *land*, to express the idea of the whole surface of the earth; similarly †*sea and earth, sea and sand.* Also with preps., as *by land and sea, on sea or land*, etc.

c 1000 *Ags. Gosp.* Matt. xxiii. 15 Ȝe befarað sæ & eorþan þæt ȝe don anne elþeodine. 1338 R. Brunne *Chron.* (1810) 281 At his wille to be, bi se & bi land. 1340 *Ayenb.* 37 Of zuichen þer byeþ uele maneres ine londe and ine ze. a 1352 Minot *Poems* (ed. Hall) iii. 1 God þat schope both se and sand. c 1366 Chaucer *A. B. C.* 50 Neither in erthe nor in see. c 1386 — *Man of Law's Prol.* 127 Ye seken lond and see for yowre wynnynges. a 1400 *Pistill of Susan* 254 Was neuer more sorweful segge bi see nor bi sand. 1475 *Bk. Noblesse* (Roxb.) 8 Batailes bothe by lond and see. 1530 Lyndesay *Test. Papyngo* 756 Quhat thow hes hard, be landis, or be seis, Off ws Kirkmen. 1805 Wordsw. *Eleg. Stanzas, Peele Castle* 15 The light that never was, on sea or land. 1849 Macaulay *Hist. Eng.* II. 300 Cimon and Lysander, Pompey and Agrippa, had fought battles by sea as well as by land.

d. *pl.* Different parts or tracts of the ocean. (Often merely *poet.* or *rhetorical*, like *waters*.)

c 825 *Vesp. Psalter* xxiii. 2 He ofer sæas [Vulg. *super maria*] ȝesteaðelade hie. c 1000 Ælfric *Gen.* i. 10 And God ȝeciȝde þa drixnisse eorðan and þæra wætera ȝegaderunga he het sæs [Vulg. *maria*]. c 1430 Lydg. *Lyke the Audience* 44 in *Pol. Rel. & L. Poems* (1903) 49 Shipmen..that haue experience In troubly seis. 1550 Br. Day in Ellis *Orig. Lett.* Ser. iii. III. 303 No lesse vnpleasaunt..than it is to the merchaunte to sayle againe in those seeis wherin he hathe suffered shipwrack before. 1600 *Will* in *Yorks. Archæol. Jrnl.* (1902) XVII. 121 In the name of Gode, the maker of heven and yerth, the saezes and all that therin ys. 1605 Shaks. *Macb.* ii. ii. 62 This my Hand will rather The multitudinous Seas incarnadine. 1820 Keats *Ode to Nightingale* vii, Magic casements, opening on the foam Of perilous seas. 1871 R. Ellis *Catullus* iv. 18 To carry thence a master o'er the surly seas.

e. In a more or less pregnant use, with reference to naval operations, the shipping trade, the profession or employment of a sailor, life on shipboard, etc. *To keep the sea*: to prevent the enemy from occupying it, to keep it clear for one's own ships and traffic.

1338 R. Brunne *Chron.* (1810) 161 Bernard of Bayoun, þat was kepand þe se [orig. *ke la mer gardait*]. c 1386 Chaucer *Prol.* 276 He wolde the see were kept for any thing Bitwixe Middelburgh and Orewelle. 1414 26 *Pol. Poems* xiii. 108 Whanne ȝe han made pes wiþynne,..Strengþe ȝoure marche, and kepe þe see. 15.. '*Doun by ane Rever*' 41 in *Dunbar's Poems* (1893) II. 306 Gif thow beis ane marchand man, And wynnis thy living be the see. 1556 *Chron. Grey Friars* (Camden) 18 Thys yere the lorde Tallbot..was made.. amyralle of the see. 1625 Bacon *Ess., Greatness Kingd.* (Arb.) 489 To be Master of the Sea, is an Abridgement of a Monarchy. *Ibid.* 491 The Command of the Seas. a 1674 Clarendon *Hist. Reb.* xi. § 64 Who did not think that the fleet could have been so soon ready for sea. 1707 Freind *Peterborow's Cond. Sp.* 178 Without the assistance of the sea, the best dispositions in Italy are useless. 1745 *Life Bampfylde-Moore Carew* 9 His Friends..put him on board a Man of War, but neither the Sea, nor any settled Employ agreeing with his wandering Inclinations, he soon forsook the King's Service. 1776 Adam Smith *W. N.* ii. v. I. 447 The antient Egyptians had a superstitious antipathy to the sea. 1849 Macaulay *Hist. Eng.* iii. I. 302 As soon as he came back from sea he was made Colonel of a regiment of foot. 1889 *Sat. Rev.* 16 Mar. 304/1 We are afraid that few Englishmen at present claim the sovereignty of the seas for their country.

f. Proverbs, proverbial phrases, and similitudes.

1591 Shaks. *Two Gent.* iv. iii. 33 A heart As full of sorrowes, as the Sea of sands. 1601 — *Twel. N.* ii. iv. 103 As hungry as the Sea. 1637–1894 [see Devil *sb.* 22 b]. 1614 T. Gentleman *England's Way to win Wealth* 45 *marg.*, The Sailors Prouerbe: The Sea and the Gallowes refuse none.

g. **High sea.** (Now usually *pl.*) The deep or open sea; the main sea or main. *spec.* in *Law* (*sing.* and *pl.*): (*a*) The main sea; the sea as far as it is regarded as being within the jurisdiction of the courts of admiralty; (*b*) The area of the sea not within the territorial jurisdiction of any nation, but the free highway of all nations.

Cf. F. *haute mer*, L. *altum* (*mare*), and the OE. compound *héahsǽ* quoted below.

[a 1000 *Boeth. Metr.* xi. 3 Se is eac wealdend woruldȝesceafta heofones & eorðan & heahsæ.] c 1300 *Havelok* 719 And sone did he leyn in [a ship] an ore, And drou him to þe heye se. a 1400–50 *Alexander* 61 He saȝe þam in þe hiȝe see sailand to-gedire. 1490 Caxton *Encydos* vi. 27 Whan they were well on the waye oute of the lande, in the hye see. c 1532 Ld. Berners *Huon* xlvi. 155 They came in to the hye see and had wynde at wyll. 1765 Blackstone *Comm.* i. Introd. iv. 107 The main or high seas are part of the realm of England. 1836 W. Irving *Astoria* III. xvii. 226 They had heard of the frigate Phœbe and the Isaac Todd being on the high seas. 1888 Bryce *Amer. Commw.* I. 580 Piracies and felonies committed on the high seas.

2. A part of the general body of salt water, having certain land-limits or washing a particular coast, and having a proper name, as *the Red, Black, Irish, Adriatic Sea.* †*The great sea*: the Mediterranean. *The Severn Sea* (arch.): the Bristol Channel. †Formerly sometimes in pl., as *the Red, Irish, Indian Seas*; cf. Narrow seas.

c 825 *Vesp. Psalter* cxxxv. 13 Se todaelde Ðone readan sae. c 1290 *St. Michael* 636 in *S. Eng. Leg.* I. 317 Ech oþur se among us here, ne beo heo so gret non, Nis bote a lime of þulke se. 1382 Wyclif *Numb.* xxxiv. 6 The west plage forsothe shal begynne fro the greet see. [So 1611 and 1884 (*Revised*).] 1390 Gower *Conf.* I. 362 To passe over the grete See To werre and sle the Sarazin. 1500–20 Dunbar *Poems* viii. 13 To the Turk sey all land did his name dreid. 1533 Bellenden *Cron. Scot.* i. (1541) A i, Pharo..quhais son..wes drownit..wt all his army in ye reid seis. 1563 Sackville *Induct. Mirr. Mag.* v, The Beare, that in the Iryshe seas had dipt His griesly feete. 1577–87 Holinshed *Chron.* I. 167/1 The Danes..comming into the Seuerne sea. 1614 T. Gentleman *England's Way to win Wealth* 20 When as they [*sc.* herrings] come into Yermouth Seas yearely about S. Luke, and sometimes before. 1634 Sir T. Herbert *Trav.* 43 The River Indus, which their ingulfes herselfe into the Indian Seas. 1635 Swan *Spec. Mundi* vi. § 2 (1643) 187 The sea, is a part of the ocean, to which we Cannot come but through some strait. 1641 Evelyn *Diary* 28 Sept., We sailed over a sea call'd the Plaet, which is an exceeding dangerous water. 1886 *Encycl. Brit.* XXI. 578/2 Any part of the ocean marked off from the general mass of water may be called a sea. In geography the name is loosely applied: for instance, the Arabian Sea is an open bay, Hudson's Bay is an enclosed sea.

b. *The four seas*: the seas bounding Great Britain on the four sides. Phr. *Within the four seas* = in Great Britain.

a 1325 *MS. Rawl.* B. 520 lf. 30 Þe chef lordes..þat beþ of plener age ant bi þinne þe four sen ant out of prisone. a 1400–50 *Alexander* 4406 Þe soile ne þe foure sees suffice ȝowe nouthire. 1642, 1886 [see Four *a.* 1].

c. *Astr.* The name of 'seas' is still given to those darker portions of the moon's surface which were formerly supposed to be covered with water.

1873 Proctor *Moon* 383 Index to the Map of the Moon. Table I. Grey Plains, usually called Seas.

3. A large lake or landlocked sheet of water,

whether salt or fresh. *Obs.* exc. in *inland sea* and in proper names, as the Sea of Galilee, the Dead Sea, the Caspian Sea, the Sea of Aral.

c 893 K. Ælfred *Oros.* i. i. § 9 Þeah sume men secgen þæt [the Nile] þær wyrcð micelne sæ [*vastissimo lacu exundare*]. c 1000 *Ags. Gosp.* John vi. 1 Æfter þyson for se hælend ofer þa galileiscan sæ, seo is tiberiadis. a 1225 *Ancr. R.* 230 And te swin anonriht urnen & adreinten ham suluen iðer see. c 1250 — [see Dead Sea]. 1375 Barbour *Bruce* xv. 275 A myle wes betuix the seis. 1590 [see Inland B. 1]. 1665 Sir T. Herbert *Trav.* (1677) 186 This [the Caspian], as other Seas, is a gathering together of perpetual Waters nourished with Springs. 1876 *Encycl. Brit.* V. 176/1 The Caspian Sea..is the largest of those salt lakes or closed inland seas which may be considered as 'survivals' of former oceanic areas.

4. The volume of water in the sea considered in regard to the ebb and flow of the tide. †*Full sea*, high tide (also *fig.*). †*The sea was in*, it was high water.

c 1000 *Sax. Leechd.* III. 176 Þonne þu wyte þæt sæ si ful. c 1205 Lay. 22019 Whænne þa sæ vleded. *Ibid.* 22025 Þenne þa sæ falleð in. 1390 Gower *Conf.* I. 35 The See now ebbeth, now it floweth. c 1391 Chaucer *Astrol.* ii. § 46 In which place of the firmament the mone being, maketh fulle see. 1470 Henry *Wallace* x. 419 The sey was in, at thai stoppyt and stud; On loud he cryt and bad thaim tak the flud. a 1500 *Brut* (Lamb. MS.) 583 Remembres how ye drowned at full see. 1536 in *Sel. Pleas Crt. Admiralty* (1894) I. 58 Goyng from the porte of London at a full see with a full wynde. 1621 Burton *Anat. Mel.* Democr. to Rdr. 27 A Satyrrical Roman in his time thought all vice, folly, and madness were at a full sea. 1677 W. Hubbard *Narrative* (1865) I. 181 But it was now full Sea with Philip his Affairs. 1805 Forsyth *Beauties Scot.* III. 512 During spring tides these sluices are opened, and at full sea they are shut.

5. With an epithet indicating the roughness or smoothness of the waves, the presence or absence of swell, etc. Hence without qualification = a heavy swell, rough water.

c 888 K. Ælfred *Boeth.* xiv. § 1 Ful oft we fageniað smyltre sæ. c 1205 Lay. 12005 Þe sæ wes wunder ane wod and ladliche iwraððed. 1390 Gower *Conf.* I. 282, I wode as doth the wylde Se. 1555 Towrson in *Hakluyt's Voy.* (1589) 103 We..found the entrance very ill, by reason that the sea goeth so high. 1641 Evelyn *Diary* 27 Sept., We..sailed again with a contrary and impetuous wind, and a terrible sea. c 1743 Woodroofe in *Hanway's Trav.* (1762) I. iv. lix. 275 When there is any sea, the breakers are visible. 1745 P. Thomas *Jrnl. Anson's Voy.* 114 We found a large under-rolling Sea. 1769–80 Falconer *Dict. Marine* s.v., A long sea implies an uniform and steady motion of long and extensive waves; on the contrary, a short sea is when they run irregularly, broken, and interrupted, so as frequently to burst over a vessel's side or quarter. 1834 Marryat *P. Simple* xxviii, We were now past Devil's Point, and the sea was very heavy. 1837 T. Hook *Jack Brag* xx, It was pitch-dark, a good deal of sea on. 1840 Longf. *Wreck of Hesperus* xi, Some ship in distress, that cannot live In such an angry sea! 1865 *Daily Tel.* 8 Dec. 5/6 During the passage..they had continued fine weather, and no sea.

b. The direction of the waves or swell.

1769–80 Falconer *Dict. Marine*, *Sea*..is..applied by sailors..to their [waves'] particular progress or direction. Thus they say,..the sea sets to the southward. Hence a ship is said to head the sea, when her course is opposed to the setting or direction of the surges. *Ibid.* ii, *Franchir la lame*, to head the sea; to sail against the setting of the sea.

c. A large heavy wave.

1582 Stanyhurst *Æneis* i. (Arb.) 21 Theire ships too larboord doo nod, seas monsterus haunt theym. 1632 Lithgow *Trav.* iii. 93 Two huge broken Seas, which twice couered the..boat. 1769–80 Falconer *Dict. Marine*, *Sea*..is.. applied by sailors, to a single wave...Thus they say, a heavy sea broke over our quarter, or we shipped a heavy sea. 1861 Lady Duff-Gordon in F. Galton *Vac. Tourists* (1864) 121 A sea struck us on the weather side. 1892 W. Pike *Barren Ground N. Canada* 26 The heavy fresh-water seas broke with great violence on the weather shore.

6. *Salt* or *bitter sea*: sea-water. *poet.*

1602 Marston *Antonio's Rev.* iv. ii. G 3 b, They'l..eat like salt sea in his siddowe ribs. 1697 Dryden *Virg. Georg.* iv. 622 His finny Flocks about their Shepherd play, And rowling round him, spirt the bitter Sea. 1840 Longf. *Wreck of Hesperus* xxi, The salt sea was frozen on her breast.

7. *fig.* With reference to metaphorical sailing, drowning, waves, etc.; also, a copious or overwhelming quantity or mass (*of* something). See also 4.

a 1200 *Vices & Virtues* 45 On ðessere michele sea of ðare bitere woreld. 1574 Higins *Mirr. Mag.* i. Induct. v, Sithe those on whom, for Fortunes giftes we stare, Ofte sooniste sinke in greatest seas of care. a 1586 Sidney *Apol. Poetrie* (Arb.) 59 A whole Sea of examples woulde present themselues. 1602 Shaks. *Ham.* iii. i. 59 To take Armes against a Sea of troubles. 1613 — *Hen. VIII*, iii. ii. 360, I haue ventur'd.. This many Summers in a Sea of Glory, But farre beyond my depth. 1632 Massinger *Emp. East* iii. ii, The peoples ioy In seas of acclamations flow in, To wait on yours. 1667 Milton *P. L.* x. 718 In a troubl'd Sea of passion tost. 1692 T. Watson *Body Divin.* 363 Men will for a drop of Pleasure drink a Sea of Wrath. 1816 Scott *Antiq.* i, The elder traveller..plunged, nothing loath, into a sea of discussion concerning urns, vases [etc.]. 1822 Lamb *Elia* Ser. ii. *Conf. Drunkard*, To waste whole seas of time upon those who pay it back in little inconsiderable drops of grudging applause. 1872 Bagehot *Physics & Pol.* (1876) 220 A complex sea of forces and passions trouble men in life and in action.

8. *transf.* a. A large level tract (*of* some material substance or aggregate of objects).

1585 T. Washington tr. *Nicholay's Voy.* iv. x, In al this sandy sea, is found no water. 1644 Evelyn *Diary* 2 Nov., We could perceive nothing but a sea of thick clouds. 1654 *Ibid.* 22 July, After dinner,..we passed over the goodly plaine, or rather sea of carpet. 1667 Milton *P. L.* iii. 440 So on this windie Sea of Land, the Fiend Walk'd up and down alone. 1770 Langhorne *Plutarch* (1851) II. 598/2 The billows of an immense sea of sand surrounding the whole army. 1849 Macaulay *Hist. Eng.* x. II. 655 All the space as far as Charing Cross was one sea of heads. 1862 Miss Braddon *Lady Audley* xxxvii, His uncle's wife, in a criminal dock, hemmed in on every side by a sea of eager faces. 1869 Tozer *Highl. Turkey* I. 340 The open country extends in a sea of green vegetation.

b. Hyperbolically, a great quantity of liquid, esp. (in figurative context) of blood. So, allusively, *Red Sea* (see 2), with reference to blood or wine.

1598 Chapman *Hero & Leander* iii. 323 And all this while the red sea of her blood Ebd with Leander. 1646 Quarles *Sheph. Oracles* vii. 83 Oyl-steep'd Anchovis, landed from his brine, Came freely swimming in red seas of wine. 1756 Burke *Nat. Soc.* Wks. I. 77 These wars, which have spilled such seas of blood. 1821 Scott *Kenilw.* i, We will have one of Friar Bacon's pupils..to conjure them [such troublesome thoughts] away.—Or, what say you to laying them in a glorious red sea of claret, my noble guest? 1864 Lowell *Fireside Trav.* 279 The ghost of a creed..may be laid, after all, only in a Red Sea of blood.

9. *Antiq.* The great brazen laver in the Jewish Temple. [Literally from Heb.]

1382 Wyclif 1 *Kings* vii. 23 He made forsothe the ȝoten see. c 1450 *Mirour Saluacioun* (Roxb.) 47 Thilk see of brasse Whilk in the entree of the Temple of Jerusalem sette was. 1899 Sayce *Early Israel* vi. 251 In the court of the temple was a 'sea' or 'deep', like that which was made by Solomon.

II. Phrases.

10. **At sea.** a. Out on the sea, on ship-board; (sailing, trafficking, fighting, etc.) on the sea; in employment as a sailor. Also †*at the seas*.

a 1300 *Cursor M.* 13284, At see sant Iohn and Iam he fand. 1585 T. Washington tr. *Nicholay's Voy.* i. v. 4 Wee discouered at the Seas [Fr. *en plaine mer*] two Foystes. 1596 Shaks. *Merch. V.* i. i. 177 Thou knowest that all my fortunes are at sea. 1601 Holland *Pliny* xxxiv. v. II. 491 The beake-heads..which were taken from them in a conflict at sea. 1672 C. Manners in *12th Rep. Hist. MSS. Comm.* App. v. 24 The Duke is at sea allready, to draw by his example others to the fleete. a 1687 Sir W. Petty *Polit. Arith.* iii. (1690) 55 To persuade the World..how considerable the King of France was..at Sea. 1793 [see At *prep.* 5]. 1836 Marryat *Midsh. Easy* xix, I have not been long at sea, and, of course, cannot know much about these things.

b. *fig.* In a state of mind resembling the condition of a ship which is out of sight of land and has lost her bearings; in a state of uncertainty or perplexity, at a loss. Also *all at sea.*

1768 Blackstone *Comm.* iii. xxvii. 440 If a court of equity were still at sea, and floated upon the occasional opinion which the judge who happened to preside might entertain of conscience in every particular case. 1818 Cruise *Digest* (ed. 2) I. 486 If there were not the same rules of property in all courts, all things would be as it were at sea; and under the greatest uncertainty. 1855 Dickens *Dorrit* ii. ix, Mrs. Tickit..was so plainly at sea on this part of the case..that Clennam was much disposed to regard the appearance as a dream. 1893 Selous *Trav. S. E. Africa* 219, I was rather surprised to find that he seemed all at sea, and had no one ready to go with me.

11. **Beyond (the) sea** or **seas.** Out of the country, in foreign parts, abroad. Cf. Beyond B. 1. For *beyond-sea* as adj. see Beyond D.

c 900 tr. *Bæda's Hist.* v. xix. (1890) 458 Mid þy he þa ȝena wæs beȝeondan sæ wuniende. a 1122 *O. E. Chron.* an. 1041 (MS. C.) Fram beȝeondan sæ. c 1205 Lay. 29149 Sum fleh bi-ȝeonden sæ in to Bruttaine. 1340 *Ayenb.* 165 Ine þe londe be-yende þe ze. 1485 *Rec. St. Mary at Hill* 28 A standyng bed, corven with estrich borde of beyond see makyng. 1536 in *Sel. Pleas Crt. Admiralty* (1894) I. 56 All my goods whersoever they may be found as well on this syde the see as beyende the see. 1555 *Burgh Rec. Edin.* (1871) II. 227 Sindry schippis cumin furth of Burdeaux, Scherand, and vtheris places beyond sey. 1590 J. Smyth in *Lett. Lit. Men* (Camden) 58 When her Majestie called me from beeyond the seas. 1640 May *Hist. Parl.* i. ii. 23 The Reformed Churches beyond the Seas. 1710 Swift *Jrnl. to Stella* 26 Oct., He is a very ingenious man, and a great scholar, and has been beyond sea. 1879 Miss Braddon *Cloven Foot* xxxii, The husband, or lover, may have been out of the way —beyond seas, perhaps.

12. **By sea.** †a. Close to the sea, at the seaside. (Now *by the sea*). b. By way of the sea, on or over the sea (as a mode of transit or conveyance). c. In the region of the sea, at sea. (See also sense 1 c.)

c 1205 Lay. 1485 Heo forð fusden toward sele Brutun þer he bi sæ wonede. 1375 Barbour *Bruce* xiii. 615 Send the Kyng by se Till Balmeburch in his awne cuntre. c 1470 Henry *Wallace* ix. 1131 Few fled with him, and gat away be see. 1625 Bacon *Ess., Greatness Kingd.* (Arb.) 489 We see the great Effects of Battailes by Sea. 1719 De Foe *Crusoe* i. (Globe) 6 One of my Companions being going by Sea to London. *Ibid.* 293, I had been very unfortunate by Sea. [1836 Longf. (*title*) The Castle by the Sea.] 1891 Ld. Hobhouse in *Law Times Rep.* LXV. 562/2 From the Melbourne factory they carried butterine by sea to Sydney.

†13. **By long sea.** Short for *by long sea passage*: see Long *a.*[1] 18. Also *by the long seas*.

1645 Evelyn *Diary* Aug., I made a collection of divers curiosities..which I sent for England by long sea. 1694 Luttrell *Brief Rel.* (1857) III. 290 Two dispatches are sent to our fleet at Cadiz, one by way of the Groyn, the other by long sea. 1721 Strype *Eccl. Mem.* ii. iii. II. 265 To pass into Ireland, either by the long Seas, or by Bristow.

14. **On** or **upon the sea.** (In early use *on* or *upon sea*.) a. On the sea's surface, afloat, at sea, on shipboard. In OE. also = in the sea. b. Of a dwelling, etc.: At the sea's edge, on the sea-coast.

c 900 tr. *Bæda's Hist.* i. xiii. (1890) 48 We..oððe sticode beoð oððe on sæ adruncene. a 1000 *Colloq. Ælfric* in Wr.-Wülcker 94 For hwi ne fixast þu on sæ. *O. E. Chron.* an. 877, Þa mette hie micel yst on sæ. c 1200 Ormin 13296 Þatt iss to farenn uppo sæ, To fisskenn affterr fisskess. c 1330 R. Brunne *Chron. Wace* (Rolls) 9795 Colgrin had a broþer on þe se. 1389 *Eng. Gilds* (1870) 48 Þorow losse on þe se. a 1400–50 *Alexander* 83 For he him-self is on þe se with siche a somme armed. c 1489 Caxton *Sonnes of Aymon* xiv. 327, I fled in to Spayn to Alaffre vpon the see. 1560 in *Sel. Pleas Crt. Admiralty* (1897) II. 25 The marrynors ..in eny ship or vessel laboring and travayling upon the seaes. 1558 Grafton *Chron.* II. 711 The Bastard.. made sayle with all haste, and roued on the Sea, as before he was accustomed. 1832 Tennyson *Pal. of Art* 97 In a clear-wall'd city on the sea. 1860 W. Whiting *Hymn*, '*Eternal Father, strong to save*' 6 O hear us when we cry to Thee For those in peril on the sea.

15. **Over (the) sea.** a. Of motion: Across the sea, to the other side of the sea. b. Of position: On the other side of the sea; abroad. Cf. Over-sea *a.* and *adv.*, Over-seas *adv.*

O. E. Chron. an. 894 (end) Ond þæt wæs ymb twelf monað þæs þe hie ær hider ofer sæ comon. c 1205 Lay. 3502 Ouer sea icomen, hauene sone anomen. 1338 R. Brunne *Chron.* (1810) 25 He..ferde ouer the se, & conquerd Normundie. 1377 Langl. *P. Pl.* B. xiii. 392 If I sent ouer see my seruauntz to Bruges. 1458 *Cal. Anc. Rec. Dublin* (1889) 300 Ther marchandys, the wyche they takyth ovre the se. 1583–1886 [see Over-seas *adv.*]. 1616–1895 [see Oversea *adv.*]. 1845 Browning *Time's Revenges* 1 I've a Friend, over the sea.

16. **To sea** (also †*to the sea*). Out on the water, on a voyage, or on ship-board. *To go to sea*, to go aboard ship, go on a voyage; to enter upon, or follow, the profession of a sailor; †also with ellipsis of the verb. *To put, put off, put out, to sea*: see Put *v.*[1] 7, 8, 45 n, 47 j. *To stand out to sea*: see Stand *v.*

c 900 tr. *Bæda's Hist.* i. xiii. (1890) 48 Us drifað þa ellreordan to sæ. c 1205 Lay. 19368 To þere sa heo wenden. c 1275 *Ibid.* 11968 Hii seileden [down the Thames] forte hii to see come. c 1375 *Sc. Leg. Saints* xviii. (*Egipciane*) 474 Til I percase a-pone a day saw men of luby & egipe hast þame to sey, for to schype. 1488 *Paston Lett.* III. 344 All suche capeteyns as wente to the see in Lente..makythe them redy to goo to the see ageyn as schortely as they can. 1584 Cogan *Haven Health* ccxvii. 216 Wherefore if any be desirous to vomit, let them rather go to the Sea. 1591–5 Spenser *Colin Clout* 209 Let him to sea. 1677 Yarranton *Eng. Improv.* 41, I waited upon the Lord Clarendon and some other Gentlemen to Sea. 1686 tr. *Chardin's Trav. Persia* 53 The Ottoman Fleet..putting to sea from Constantinople, Landed in Candy. 1726 Shelvocke *Voy. round World* 61 He knew I was not allowed an ounce of fresh provisions to sea with me. 1849 Macaulay *Hist. Eng.* v. I. 550 On the afternoon of the second of May he stood out to sea before a favourable breeze.

17. **To take the sea** (also †*to take sea, the seas*, ME. *to nim the sea*). To go on board ship, embark; to start on a sea-voyage, launch forth, put out to sea (said also of the ship). Cf. F. *prendre la mer*.

c 1205 Lay. 1281 Bi Ruscikadan heo nomen þa sæ. *Ibid.* 4966 Þer he þa sæ nom. c 1400 *Land Troy Bk.* 4099 And Achilles toke the see With his vitayles and his naue. c 1489 Caxton *Sonnes of Aymon* xxiv. 530 Reynawde dyde doo hale vp saylle, & toke the see. 1542 Udall *Erasm. Apoph.* 287 The marynners,..beeyng lothe to take ye seaes, Pompeius hymself first of al entreed into the shippe. a 1604 Hanmer *Chron. Irel.* (1809) 366 For want of skill they could not take the seas, but were tossed with winde and weather, along the Coast. 1641 Earl Monm. tr. *Biondi's Civil Warres* iv. 68 The 27. of April he tooke sea at Dover. 1867 Swinburne *Ess. & Stud.* (1875) 119 The first hymn of Orpheus as Argo takes the sea. 1890 S. Lane-Poole *Barbary Corsairs* vii. 83 He..was able to take the sea with a fleet of eighty-four vessels. 1903 *Daily Chron.* 30 July 3/1 All the ships ..are able to touch 24 knots, but their lines and the way they take the sea is cause of common complaint.

III. Attributive uses and combinations.

18. Simple attributive: a. Of or belonging to the sea or a sea, as *sea-arm, -basin, bed*, †*-bore, brim, -brink*, †*-flash, -floor, harbour, -haven, -marge, -pull, -spray, -tide, -wave.*

1637 Heywood *Descr. Royall Ship* (1638) 28 The Great Colosse..who bestrid The spacious Rhodian *Sea-arme. 1865 W. G. Palgrave *Arabia* II. 203 Between the islands runs a narrow sea-arm. 1884 Geikie *Phys. Geog.* xiv. (1886) 123 Most of the great *sea-basins. 1838 *Penny Cycl.* XI. 142/2 So as to stain the whole *sea-bed for 1000 feet or yards in depth. c 1325 *Metr. Hom.* (Small) 135 That betes thaim wit dede and word Als *se bare betes on schip bord. 1621 G. Sandys *Ovid's Met.* ix. (1626) 225 With blood the *sea-brimme blusht. 1879 F. W. Robinson *Coward Consc.* i. iii, A country full of life and animation even to its sea-brim. a 1300 *Horn* 151 (Camb. MS.), Bi þe *se brinke No water þe na drinke. c 1830 S. Rogers *Italy* (1839) 84 On the sea-brink, another train they met. 1634 Sir T. Herbert *Trav.* 7 Sometimes the surges or *Sea-flashes doe rebound top-gallant height. 1855 Kingsley *Glaucus* (1878) 60 The variety of its rocks, aspects, and *sea-floors. 1648 Hexham ii, *Een Zeehaven*, A *Sea-haven, or a *Sea-harbor. 1843 Carlyle *Past & Pr.* v. 89 No monstrous pitchy City, and Seahaven of the world! 1610 Shaks. *Temp.* iv. i. 69 Thy *Sea-marge stirrile. 1896 Kipling *Seven Seas* 68 The *sea-pull drew them side by side, gunnel to gunnel laid. 1812 Sir J. Sinclair *Syst. Husb. Scot.* i. 47 Withering mentions a thorny shrub..which stands the *sea-spray. 1601 Holland *Pliny* v. i. I. 90 It.. is only not overflowed by the *sea tides. 1727–46 Thomson *Summer* 1600 The loud *sea-wave. 1860 Tyndall *Glac.* i. xxv. 185 The sea-waves..sometimes reach the shore before the wind which produces them.

b. That is an attribute or quality of the sea, as *sea-blink, -calm, -murmur, -music, -roughness, -shine, -smell, -voice.*

1850 B. Taylor *Eldorado* xxxiii, Far away to the right I saw the *sea-blink along the edges of the sky. 1821 *Sea-calm [see *sea-roughness* below]. 1818 Shelley *Eugan. Hills* 347 A dell..Which the wild *sea-murmur fills. 1819 — *Prometh.* iii. iii. 27 And thou, Ione, shalt chant fragments of *sea-music. 1821 Lamb *Elia, Witches* (end), The billows gradually subsiding, fell from a *sea-roughness to a sea-calm, and thence to a river motion. 1867 Augusta Wilson *Vashti* xiv, The greenish *sea-shine breaking through the dense foliage. 1880 Swinburne *Studies in Song* 179 Streak on streak of glimmering seashine crosses All the land. 1833 Tennyson *Rosalind* ii, Fresh as the early *seasmell blown Through vineyards from an inland bay. 1859 — *Guinevere* 245 And strong man-breasted things stood from the sea, And sent a deep *sea-voice thro' all the land.

c. Consisting of sea, as *sea-frontier, -lane*, †*-limit, -path, pool*, †*-tract, -valley.*

1905 *Westm. Gaz.* 15 Aug. 3/1 The *sea-frontier of England. 1878 Tennyson *Revenge* v, And the little Revenge ran on thro' the long *sea-lane between. 1577 Dee *Memor. Navig.* 59 All, within the *Sea-limits of our Brytish Royalty. 1653 Milton *Ps.* viii. 22 Fowl of the Heavens, and Fish that through the wet *Sea-paths in shoals do slide. 1596 Spenser *State Irel.* 2, I heard it often wished also..that all that land were a *Sea poole. 1883 *Fisheries Exhib. Catal.* p. lxxxvii, A Seapool arranged as a grotto. 1600 R. Johnson *Kingd. & Commw.* 169 So huge a *sea-tract full of hauens. 1857 Emerson *Poems* 81 *Sea-valleys and the deep of skies Furnished several supplies.

d. (Phenomena) occurring at sea, as *sea-cloud, dew, -meteor, -storm, -sunset*, †*-tempest.*

1811 Scott *Don Roderick* xxxvi, That *sea-cloud, in size like human hand. 1888 F. Cowper *Captain of Wight* (1889) 306 The *sea-dew glittered on spar and mast and straining sail. a 1818 M. G. Lewis *Jrnl. W. Ind.* (1834) 39 The above-mentioned floating lights are a kind of *sea-meteors. 1610 Shaks. *Temp.* i. ii. 177 And now I pray you Sir..your reason For raysing this *Sea-Storme? 1839–52 Bailey *Festus* 428 Nor that it now sinks Like a *sea-sunset. 1871 Tennyson *Last Tourn.* 505 A low sea-sunset glorying round her hair. c 1400 *Sc. Trojan War* ii. 1011 And sene þat so þe *see-tempestes Lownyt not, nor yhet toke restes.

e. (*a*) Deposited by or in the sea, as *sea-clay*, †*-gravel, -mud, -ooze, -slob*, †*-slub, -slutch*, †*-turf, -warp*; (*b*) formed by the sea, as †*sea-concretion*; (*c*) proceeding from the sea, as *sea-blast, fog, fret, -gale, haze*, etc.

1798 Southey *Henry the Hermit* 25 And underneath a rock that shelter'd him From the *sea-blast, he built his hermitage. 1531 *Lett. & Pap. Hen. VIII*, V. 183 Longe cartes caryng of see turff and *see clay from the floo marke. 1695 J. Edwards *Author. O. & N. Test.* III. 282 Others would persuade us that it [Stone-henge] is a *sea-concretion. 1796 H. Hunter tr. *St.-Pierre's Stud. Nat.* (1799) I. 171 Long belts of land and *sea-fogs, which accompany the melting of all ices. 1846 Brockett *N. C. Words* (ed. 3), **Sea-fret*, a wet mist, or haze proceeding from the sea inland. 1882 W. B. Scott *Poet's Harvest Home* 33 But still she stared across the bar Through blinding locks and blind seafret. 1821 Scott *Pirate* i, A garden..produced such vegetables as..the *sea-gale would permit to grow. c 1440 *Jacob's Well* 304 Þin herte is lyche þe *see-grauel & sande, þat sokyth in, & drynketh in, all waterys, and ȝit þe see is neuere full. 1864 Tennyson *Enoch Arden* 673 Till anon drawn thro' either chasm,..Roll'd a *sea-haze and whelm'd the world in gray. 1726 Leoni *Alberti's Archit.* II. 125/2 If their holes were stopt up with *Sea-mud, or ashes, it wou'd destroy them. 1669 Worlidge *Syst. Agric.* (1681) 68 All manner of *Sea-Owse, Owsie-mud, or Sea-weeds,..are very good for the bettering of Land. 1823 E. Moor *Suffolk Words*, **Sea-roke*, a fog or mist suddenly approaching from the direction of the sea. 1869 *Zoologist* Ser. ii. IV. 1943 A gray sea-roke drifting in across the sand-dunes. 1883 *Chamb. Jrnl.* 20 It was no easy matter to distinguish between salt *seascud and driving rain. 1776 M. Murray in *A. Young's Tour Irel.* (1780) I. 279 Part [manured] with *sea-slob and lime mixed. 1610 W. Folkingham *Art of Survey* i. x. 30 They vse both Orewood, Sea-sand, and *Sea-slubbe for soylings. 1795 J. Holt *Agric. Lanc.* 126 *Sea slutch, from the Ribble and Wyre, is in some places adjacent, made use of as a substitute for marle. 1880 Tennyson *Sea Dreams* 52 A full tide Rose with ground-swell, which, on the foremost rocks Touching, upjetted in spirts of wild *sea-smoke. 1531 *Sea turf [see *sea-clay* above]. 1705 Addison *Italy, Pesaro* etc. 142 Expos'd to the Winds and Salt *Sea-Vapours. 1839 *Civ. Engin. & Arch. Jrnl.* II. 450/1 By introducing fascine jetty work, which greatly accelerated the deposit of the *sea warp.

f. Situated in or by the sea, as *sea-cape, -cave*, †*-city, crag, -down, -dune, -flat, -grove, -hall, -home, -marsh, -point, -quag, -scar, -terrace, -wold, -wood.*

a 1876 M. Collins *Th. in Garden* (1880) II. 251 *Seacapes divine which the merry winds whiten. 1805 Scott *Last Minstrel* vi. xxiii, But the *sea-caves rung, and the wild winds sung, The dirge of the lovely Rosabelle. 1849 M. Arnold *Forsaken Merman* 61 Come back to the kind sea-caves! 1600 J. Pory tr. *Leo's Africa* i. 29 All the *sea-cities and inland-cities of Barbarie. 1595 Duncan *App. Etym.* (E. D. S.), *Scopulus*,..a *sea-craig. 1865 Swinburne *Chastelard* i. ii. 30 Between the *sea-downs and the sea. 1885 Tennyson *Flight* xxiii, We shall light upon..Some lodge within the waste *sea-dunes, and hear the waters roar. 1823 Cobbett *Rur. Rides* (1885) I. 275 The wheat on..the *sea-flats at Havant. 1830 Tennyson *Merman* ii, Then we would wander away..To the pale-green *sea-groves. *Ibid.*, I would fill the *sea-halls with a voice of power. a 1746 Holdsworth *On Virg.* (1768) 400 There could be no fleet lying there, no *sea-marshes, no lines drawn across them to intercept communication. 1736 *Gentl. Mag.* VII. 357/2 To be built on the *sea-point of the same Island. 1882 Stevenson *New Arab. Nts.* II. ii. 15 The Graden Floe and the other *sea quags that fortified the shore against invaders. 1535 Stewart *Cron. Scot.* II. 415 Ane fair castell standand on the *se skar. 1868 Ld. Lytton *Chron. & Char., Siege Constant.*, The solemn obelisks And sombre cypress stripe with blackest shade *Sea terraces. 1884 Geikie *Phys. Geog.* xxiii. (1886) 217 Fig. 40 View of an old sea-terrace or raised beach, with sea-worn caves on its inner margin. 1830 Tennyson *Mermaid* iii, We would run to and fro, and hide and seek, On the broad *sea-wolds in the crimson shells. 1902 Buchan *Watcher by Threshold* 113 A *sea-wood of alders slipping from the hill's skirts to the water's edge.

g. Occasionally = 'at the sea-side', as *sea-place, -quarters, -sojourn*, †*-watering-place.*

1824 Coleridge *Let. to H. F. Cary* (1895) 733 Both Mrs. G. and myself have returned much benefited by our sea-sojourn. 1833 T. Hook *Parson's Dau.* ii. xiv, 'Where's St. Leonard's?' 'Oh, the sea watering-place, close to Hastings'. *Ibid.* ii. iii, The proposition of her removal to some sea-watering place. 1861 Mrs. Carlyle *Lett.* III. 81 East Cliff..would be perfect as sea-quarters if it weren't for the noise. 1877 P'cess Alice *Mem.* 25 July (1884) 356 The nicest sea-place I have been as yet.

h. Pertaining to the sea as a sphere of warlike operations, as *sea army, battle, campaign, conquest, dominion, empire*, etc.

1600 E. Blount tr. *Conestaggio* 181 The arriuall of his *sea-armie. 1835 *Partington's Brit. Cycl. Arts* s.v. *Signals*, The movements of a sea-army having a necessary dependence on the wind, they cannot [etc.]. 1598 Hakluyt *Voy.* I. 12 In the yeere 1156..there was a *Sea-battell fought. 1678 Marvell *Growth Popery* Wks. 1875 IV. 264 This fatal conclusion of all our *Sea-champaynes. 1627 May *Lucan* iii. Argt., Brutus maintaines The siege, and Cæsars first *Sea-conquest gaines. 1652 Needham tr. *Selden's Mare Cl.* 58 The *Sea-Dominion of the Lydians. 1696 B. Kennett *Rom. Antiq.* ii. i. iv. (1717) 46 The *Naumachiæ*, or Places for the Shows of *Sea-Engagements. 1712 Addison *Spect.* No. 299 ¶ 2 Such an one commanded in such a Sea Engagement. 1910 *Nation* 22 Jan. 671/2 They controlled a *Sea-empire over the Aegean. 1577 Dee *Memor. Navig.* 59 Our *Sea-forces preuayling. 1669 R. Montagu in *Buccleuch MSS.* (Hist. MSS. Comm.) I. 444 Four *sea regiments of three thousand men a-piece. 1681 C. Irvine *Hist. Sc. Nomencl.* Ded. *iv, By your careful Conduct, you made Britain triumph over her most powerful *Sea-Rival. 1577 Dee *Memor. Navig.* 21 Ap; propriat to her peculiar Iurisdiction and *Sea Royallty. *Ibid.* 5 That expert and hardy Crue of some Thousands of *Sea soldiers wold be to this Realme a Treasor incomparable. 1708 J. Chamberlayne *St. Gt. Brit.* i. ii. ii. (1710) 53 He can soon Man the same with the best Sea-Soldiers in the whole World. 1615 *Trade's Incr.* 33 This goodly engine of our *sea-state. a 1649 Drumm. of Hawth. *Jas. IV*, Wks. (1711) 64 A *sea-victory obtained by Sir Andrew Wood. 1727 Arbuthnot *Tables Anc. Coins*, etc. 241 This *Sea War cost the Carthaginians five hundred Quinquiremes.

i. Sea-going, as Sea-boat, *sea-coble, -ship.* Also in fanciful terms descriptive of various kinds of sea-going vessels, as *sea-car, -castle, -coffin*, †*-kennel, -terrier*, †*wasp.*

1851 C. L. Smith tr. *Tasso* xvii. liv, Over the self-same paths which the *sea-car Had traced in coming, backward hence it goes. 1655 Marq. Worcester *Cent. Invent.* § 16 How to make a *Sea-castle or Fortification Cannon-proof. 1841 Ld. J. Manners *England's Trust* 18 On furthest ocean's heaving breast meanwhile Ride the sea-castles of our merchant-isle. 1878 Tennyson *Revenge* iv, Till the Spaniard came in sight, With his huge sea-castles heaving upon the weather bow. 1505 *Berwick Reg.* in *Var. Collect.* (Hist. MSS. Comm.) I. 9 That all the *see cowbells commynge frome the se shall lande upon this syde of the water of Twede. 1565 [see Coble[1] 2]. 1899 *Pall Mall Mag.* Feb. 230 Many coasters were called *Sea-coffins after Mr. Plimsoll..denounced the ship-owner as the rapacious destroyer of his species. 1676 Wycherley *Pl. Dealer* iii. i, You shou'd be ty'd up again, in your *Sea-kennel, call'd a Ship. 1535 Coverdale 1 *Kings* x. 22 The kynges *Seeshippe yt sayled vpon the See with ye shippe of Hiram. 1838 Longf. *Beowulf* 20 He bade him a sea-ship..prepare. 1865 E. Burritt *Walk to Land's End* 275 The Fowey seamen made a remarkable reputation in their day with their little *sea-terriers. 1666 Dryden *Ann. Mirab.* cliii, She seems a *sea-wasp flying on the waves.

j. Pertaining to life at sea; used or worn at sea; as *sea-biscuit, -boot* (hence *sea-booted* adj.), *bread, cap*, †*-cates, coat*, †*compass*, etc. Also, characteristic of life at sea or of seamen, nautical, as *sea-bow, -gibberish, -hornpipe, -language, manners*, etc.

1680–90 Temple *Ess. Health & Long Life* Wks. 1731 I. 283 A Spoonful of Powder of *Sea-bisquet. 1851 H. Melville *Whale* ix, A low rumbling of heavy *sea-boots among the benches. 1897 Kipling *Capt. Cour.* v. 107 With his *sea-booted feet cocked up on the table. 1748 Smollett *Rod. Rand.* (1812) I. 11 My uncle after two or three *sea-bows expressed himself in this manner. 1876 Davis *Polaris Exp.* xi. 261 A hash made of dried salmon and *sea-bread. 1601 Shaks. *Twel. N.* iii. iv. 364 Now you haue no *sea-cap on your head. 1688 Jane Barker *Poet. Recreat.* i. 92 The best of *Sea-Cates we wish for thy Diet. c 1578 Frobisher in *Proc. Rec. Comm.* (1833) 562 At Bristo, wher his carde and his *se-clothes dyd ly to pawne. 1687 *Lond. Gaz.* No. 2290/4 A black Negro..having a *Sea-Coat lin'd with white Bays. 1570 J. Dee *Math. Pref.* a iv b, Certaine Landmarkes ..well hable to be skried, in what point of the *Seacumpase they appeare. 1712 J. James tr. *Le Blond's Gardening* 81 This Instrument is generally furnished with the Sea Compass. 1867 Smyth *Sailor's Word-bk.*, *Sea-pie*,..a favourite *sea-dish in rough weather. 1889 *Century Dict.*, *Furling-line*, a line wound spirally about a sail and its yard in furling. Also called '*sea-gasket*'. 1608 Sylvester *Du Bartas* ii. iv. iii. *Schisme* 929 Strike, strike our saile (the Master cryes) amain,..but hee cryes in vain; For, in his face the blasts so bluster ay, That his *Sea-gibb'rish is straight born away. 1602 Shaks. *Ham.* v. ii. 13 Vp from my Cabin My *sea-gowne scarft about me in the darke. 1699 Dampier *Voy.* II. i. 91 My Guide carried my Sea-gown, which was my covering in the night. 1745 *Life Bamfylde-Moore Carew* 58 He..furnishes himself with a tattered *Sea-Habit. 1687 *Lond. Gaz.* No. 2256/4 With a *Sea Hankerchief about his Neck. 1798 O'Keeffe *Wild Oats* i. i, *John.* You know, on our quitting harbour—. *Sir Geo.* Damn your *sea-jaw, you marvellous dolphin, give the contents of your log-book in plain English. 1855 Dickens *Dorrit* i. vi, The doctor was amazingly shabby, in a torn and darned rough-weather *sea-jacket [etc.]. 1884 Sir F. S. Roberts in *19th Cent.* June 1069 *Sea-kits should be issued gratis [to the army] as required. 1728 Chambers *Cycl.*, *Offing*, in the *Sea-language, that part of the Sea a good distance from Shore. 1838 *Civ. Engin. & Arch. Jrnl.* I. 358/1 A *sea lead is charged at its heavy end with a small iron tube. 1740 Johnson *Life Drake* Wks. 1816 XII. 99 Bred from his earliest years to the labour and hardships of a *sea life. 1853 Kane *Grinnell Exp.* v. (1856) 35 The recurring noonday, the meridian starting-point of sea-life. 1829 Marryat *F. Mildmay* iv, My *sea manners were not congenial to the drawing-room. 1668 *Lond. Gaz.* No. 262/4 A *sea Neckcloth about his neck. 1659 Torriano, *Avaria*, a *sea-phrase, viz. a..distribution of the losse made, when [etc.]. 1778 Miss Burney *Evelina* (1791) II. xxxvii. 248, I suppose it to be some sea-phrase. 1886 Stevenson *Kidnapped* x, Then there came a single call on the *sea-pipe, and that was the signal. c 1611 Chapman *Iliad* ii. 538 King Agamemnon, on these men, did well-built ships bestow To passe the gulfie purple sea, that did no *sea rites know. 1834 'H. Collingwood' *Under Meteor Flag* 172 He made an elaborate *sea-scrape with his right foot. 1857 Dufferin *Lett. High Lat.* (ed. 3) 400 [We] were nearly run into ourselves by a clumsy merchantman, whom we had the relief of being able to abuse in..the most racy *sea-slang. 1748 *Anson's Voy.* i. ix. 91 Some place..where ships might refresh and supply themselves with the necessary *sea stock for their voyage. 1840 F. D. Bennett *Whaling Voy.* II. 349 This fruit..is very eligible for sea-stock. 1659 Rushw. *Hist. Coll.* 415 All manner of Tackle, *Sea-stores, and Ammunition. 1834 Marryat *P. Simple* viii, We were ordered to the dockyard to draw sea-stores. 1603 Dekker *1st Pt. Honest Wh.* i. ii. *Stage-dir.*, Enter Fustigo in some fantastic *sea-suit. 1710 Pope *Let. to H. C.* (1735) I. 105, I agree with you in your Censure of the Use of *Sea-Terms in Mr. Dryden's Virgil. 1898 Ansted (*title*), A Dictionary of Sea Terms. 1747 Mrs. Glasse *Cookery* xi. 125 To make *Sea Venison.

k. Applied to pay received or 'due for actual service in a duly-commissioned ship' (Smyth *Sailor's Word-bk.* 1867).

In sea-pay, †*at sea-wages*: (of a sailor) in actual service on the sea; (of a ship) in commission.

1490 *Act 7 Hen. VII*, c. 1 § 2 If the Captain be at Sea-wages, he [shall] shewe the departing..of the said Soldier.. to the Admiral of the Navy. 1667 Pepys *Diary* 29 Aug., My Lord Crewe and his friends take it very ill of me that my Lord Sandwich's sea-fee should be retrenched. 1758 *M. P.'s. Let. on R. N.* 6 When such Ships shall have been eighteen Months in Sea-pay, the Wages of the first twelve Months shall be paid. 1889 *N. & Q.* 7th Ser. VII. 81/2 The fleet then left by Pepys in sea-pay comprised 76 vessels, and the men numbered 12,040.

l. Applied to works of art or literature, narratives, etc., representing the sea or life at sea, as *sea-eclogue, -sonnet, -story, -subject, -tale, -yarn*, etc. So also *sea-painter, -poet.*

1712 (*title*) Nereids: or *Sea-Eclogues. 1909 *Q. Rev.* July 140 Joseph Autran the *sea-poet of Marseilles. 1659 *Lady Alimony* iii. iii. F 4, Let us have a *Sea-sonnet before we lanch forth in our Adventure-Frigot. 1855 (*title*) *Sea Stories: tales of discovery, adventure, and escapes. 1885 *Academy* 21 Nov. 338/3 Mr. Russell undoubtedly 'struck oil' with his earlier sea-stories. 1850 Marg. F. Ossoli *Wom. in 19th Cent.* (1862) 267 Painters of *sea-subjects. 1888 F. M. Crawford *With Immortals* II. 129, I used to ..listen to the *sea-tales of the sailors. 1890 'R. Boldrewood' *Col. Reformer* (1891) 157 Spinning *sea-yarns all night.

m. Applied to nautical maps and charts, as †*sea-chart, -map, -plat*, etc. Also Sea-book, -card 1.

c 1635 N. Boteler *Dial. Sea Services* (1685) 266 This *Sea-cart is also called a Plot. 1745 Pococke *Descr. East* II. i. 210 The modern sea carts make it [Cyprus] only one hundred and thirty-five [miles] in length. 1669 Sturmy *Mariner's Mag.* iv. iii. 157 By the true *Sea-chart you are arrived at G. 1883 *Encycl. Brit.* XV. 520/2 By 1601 Mercator's projection was in use for all sea charts. 1632 Sherwood, A sea-card, or *Sea map, *Carte marine, Hydrographie.* 1839 *Penny Cycl.* XIV. 405/1 There are two kinds of terrestrial maps—geographic or land maps, and hydrographic or sea maps. 1697 Dampier *Voy.* I. 416 The Drafts or *Sea-plats being first consulted, it was [etc.].

n. By sea; also, pertaining to navigation or maritime or naval affairs; as *sea-business, -carriage*, †*-concernment, -passage, -passenger, -route, -trade, -traffic, -transport*, †*-wandering*, etc. Also Sea-voyaging.

1625 K. Long tr. *Barclay's Argenis* iv. xv. 289 The hurly-burly of such as were unskilfull in *sea-business, was like to bring no lesse danger than the storms violence. 1712 M. Henry *Daily Commun. with God* (1866) 45 Whatever your employment be, in country-business, city-business, or sea-business,..go about them in the fear of God. 1766 Smollett *Trav.* I. xx. 315 This wine is of a strong body,..and improves by *sea-carriage. 1868 Rogers *Pol. Econ.* iii. (1876) 20 The relative values of food, clothing, metals, and sea-carriage remain the same. a 1687 Petty *Pol. Arith.* i. (1691) 27 Wherefore he whom this latter Party doth affectionately own to be their Head, cannot probably be wronged in his *Sea-concernments by the other. 1615 *Trade's Incr.* 2 A man may runne a course this way [by fishing] to enrich himselfe..more easily..then any other *sea-course can persuade vs to. 1619 Hieron *Wks.* I. 643 It is an allusion to a sea-course: When he the admirall hangs out a lanterne, and all that come behind steere to that. a 1586 *Sea-discipline [see Land-service]. 1666 Marvell *Corr.* lviii. Wks. (Grosart) II. 197 The *sea-news is not good from severall places. 1634 Sir T. Herbert *Trav.* 2 The description of our *Sea passage. 1873 M. Arnold *Lit. & Dogma* (1876) 181 Because a man has frequently to make sea-passages, he is not gifted with an immunity from sea-sickness. 1592 Greene *2nd Pt. Conny-catching* Wks. (Grosart) X. 89 Syrens, who sitting with their watching eies vpon the rockes to allure *Sea-passengers to their extreame preiudice. 1858 Timbs *Curiosities of Sci.* Ser. i. 184 Ocean highways: how *sea-routes have been shortened. 1886 C. E. Pascoe *Lond. To-day* xliii. (ed. 3) 372 In communication with the Continent by the shortest sea route. 1664 Exton *Maritime Dicæol.* i. iii. 14 Other things..done—either on or at the sea, con-

Supplement, p. 3873; Corrigenda, p. 4092; Spurious words, p. 4093; Books quoted, p. 4094

SEA. 313 SEA. SEA. 314 SEA.

SEA. 315 SEA. SEA. 316 SEA.

Europe; **sea-spurge**, a maritime spurge, *Euphorbia Paralias*; **sea-spurrey**, *spurrey sandwort* (see quots.); **sea-starwort**, *Aster Tripolium*; **sea-stock** (also *great sea stock*), *Matthiola sinuata*; †**sea-stock-gillyflower** = prec.; **sea sulphur-weed**, -*wort*, *Peucedanum officinale*; **sea-thrift** – SEA-PINK 2; †**sea-trifoly**, *Astragalus Glaux*; †**sea wartwort**, a variety of spurge, *Euphorbia Peplis*; **sea-weed**, ~**wheatgrass**, the wheatgrass *Triticum junceum*, growing on sandy sea-shore; **sea-withwind**, *Convolvulus Soldanella*; †**sea-wormwood**, *Artemisia maritima*.

...

Sea-animal. [ANIMAL sb.]
1. An animal or creature living in the sea.

...

Sea-ape. [APE sb.]
1. The sea-urchin. *Obs.*

...

Sea-apple. [APPLE sb.]

Sea-bank. [BANK sb.]
1. † a. The sea-coast of sea-shore; *Obs.*

...

Sea-bass. *U.S.* [BASS sb².]

Sea-beach. [BEACH sb.] – BEACH sb.

Sea-bear. [BEAR sb¹.]
1. The sea-urchin. *Obs.*

Sea-beat, a. [BEAT ppl. a.] = next.

Sea-beaten, a. [BEATEN ppl. a.]

Sea-bat. [BAT sb.]
1. A flying-fish, esp. the flying gurnard, *Dactylopterus volitans*.

Sea-bath. [BATH sb¹.] A bath or bathe in the sea.

Sea-bathing. Bathing in the sea.

Seaboard (sī'bōₐd), sb. and a. Forms: see SEA sb. and BOARD sb. Also 9 -bord. [f. SEA sb. + BOARD sb.]

Sea-bordering, a. rare. Bordering on the sea.

Sea-born, a. Born in or of the sea. Of persons, etc., chiefly mythological, esp. of Venus.

Sea-borne, a. [BORNE ppl. a.]
1. Conveyed by sea.

2. Of a ship, etc.: Carried or floating on the sea. See also quot. 1867.

Sea-bottom.

Sea-bound, a. [BOUND ppl. a.²] Bound or confined by the sea.

Sea-bream. A name applied to several sparoid fishes, esp. *Pagellus centrodontus.*

Sea-breeze. [BREEZE sb².]
1. A breeze blowing from the sea.

Sea-bull. [BULL sb¹.]
1. The male of the sea-cow or seal.

Sea-cabbage.

Sea-calf. [CALF¹.] A common name for seal, esp. the common seal, *Phoca vitulina.*

Sea-captain. The captain or commander of a ship; usually applied to the captain of a merchant vessel.

Sea-card. [CARD sb².]
1. A chart of the sea (see CARD sb² 3 b and CHART sb. 1).

Sea-coal. [COAL sb.]
1. Old English. *Obs.*

Sea-coast.

Sea-cob.

Sea-cob²,

Sea-cock. [COCK sb¹.]

Sea-colewort.

Sea-conny.

Sea-conny², sea-cony, sea-connie = (App. a perversion of *sukkani*.)

Sea-cornet.

Sea-cow. [COW sb¹.]
1. The MANATEE; also applied to other sirenians, as the dugong.

Sea-cucumber. † a. [transl. of L. *cucumis*.]

Sea-daisy.

Sea-devil.
1. A devil supposed to inhabit the sea.

Sea-dike. [Cf. Du. *zeedijk*.]

Sea-crab. [CRAB sb¹.]
1. A marine crab, as distinguished from a river- or land-crab.

Sea-crow. [CROW sb¹.]
1. A local name for several birds.

Sea-cob, -crab, sea-crow.

Sea-dog. [Cf. Du. *zeehond*, G. *seehund*.]
1. The common or harbour seal, *Calocephalus vitulinus*; also (in California), one of the eared seals, *Zalophus californianus*.

Sea-dragon. [DRAGON¹.]

Sea-eagle.
1. An eagle of the genus *Haliaetus*, esp. the White-tailed Eagle, *H. albicilla* (see EAGLE sb. 1 b).

Sea-eel. [EEL sb¹.]
1. A univalve mollusc of the genus *Haliotis*.

SEA-EGG. 321 SEA-GATE. SEA-FOOD. SEA-GATE. SEA-GATE. 322 SEA-HORSE.

SEAL

Sea-egg.
1. An ECHINUS or sea-egg.
2. A kind of madrepore, *Madrepora Echinus*.

Sea-elephant. The elephant seal, *Macrorhinus elephantinus* or *proboscideus*. Formerly applied to the morse or walrus.

Sea-face. The face or side (of a cliff, etc.) exposed to the sea.

Sea-fan. [Fan sb.] An alcyonarian polyp of the sub-order *Gorgoniacea*, esp. *Rhipidogorgia (Gorgonia) flabellum*.

Sea-fardinger. [Alteration of Du. zeevaarder SEAFARER, after Du.] A seafarer.

Sea-fare. [Fare sb.]
1. **a.** Food obtained from the sea. **b.** Fare or food on board ship.
2. Travel by sea, a sea-voyage.

Seafarer. [f. SEA sb. + FARER.] A traveller by sea, esp. one whose life is spent in voyaging, a sailor.

Seafaring. Travelling by sea; the business or calling of a sailor.

Sea-faring, sb. [f. SEA sb. + FARING vbl. sb.] Travelling by sea; the business or calling of a sailor.

Sea-food. Obs. exc. arch. The sea, the tide.

Sea-fowler. One who fowls at sea.

Sea-fox. [tr. L. *vulpes marina* (Pliny).] The Thrasher-shark, *Alopias vulpes*; also SEA-APE.

Sea-front. That portion or side of a building, etc. which faces the sea.

Sea-frontage. An extent of sea-front.

Sea-froth.

Sea-garden.

Sea-gate. [Gate sb.]
1. A gate towards, or giving access to, the sea; or a convenient approach to the sea.
2. A place of access to the sea.
3. One of a pair of supplementary or outer gates opening outwards, placed seawards in entrance of an exposed dock or tidal basin, as a safeguard against a heavy sea.

Sea-girt. Girt or surrounded by the sea.

Seago, obs. form of SIEGE sb.

Sea-god. [Cf. OE. *sǽgod* occurring as a proper name in O.E. Chron.] A sea-bird.

Sea-going. Going or travelling by sea.

Sea-grape.
1. The glasswort, *Salicornia herbacea* and *Salsola Kali*.
2. The plant Ephedra.

Sea-grass. A grass which grows by the sea.

Sea-green. adj.
1. A sea-green colour.

Sea-gull.

Sea-hare. A mollusc, *Aplysia depilans*.

Sea-hawk.

Sea-hedgehog.

Sea-hog. A porpoise.

Sea-holly. The plant Eryngo.

Sea-holm.

Sea-horse.
1. A name for the pipe-gurnard, *Trigla lyra*, and the lump-fish, *Cyclopterus lumpus*.
2. Housewife.
3. A collector's name for a moth, the *Hadena thalassina*.
4. The walrus.

Sea-hound. [tr. L. *canis marinus* (Pliny).]
1. A dog-fish.

Sea-ish. a. Obs. rare. [f. SEA sb. + -ISH.] Of or pertaining to the sea.

Sea-island. a. The designation of a fine variety of cotton grown on the islands off the coast of Georgia and South Carolina.

Sea-kale. [f. SEA sb. + KALE sb.; cf. the southern form *sea-cole*, SEA sb. 23 f.]
1. A cruciferous plant, *Crambe maritima*, found wild on the shores of western Europe.

Sea-king.
1. One of the piratical Scandinavian chiefs, who in their raids and succeeding centuries ravaged the coasts of Europe.

Seal. (si'l). Forms: 1. 4 seolh, 4 zeel; 5. 5 selghe, 5-6 selcht, 5-7 seloche, 5-8 selch, 6 saylch, solk, 9 sealgh. β. 3 seil, 3-6 sele, 4-7 seal, 5 sael, 6 seale, 8 seele, etc. γ. 4 soole, 5-7 seale, 6 seall, seayle, seayll, 7 soale, seil, sayle, 7 seal 4-9 seal. Also SOILE.
1. A member of the family *Phocidæ*, sub-order Pinnipedia, of aquatic carnivorous mammals, with limbs developed into flippers and adapted for swimming.

Seal. (si'l) sb2. Forms: 1. 4 seel, 4-7 seel, 5 sele, 3-6 seil, 3-6 seel, 4 seale; 4-6 sele, seele; seall, seile, 6-7 seall. β. 3 seele, 4-7 seale, 5-8 seal; 6-8 seale.
1. A device (e.g. a heraldic or emblematic device, a word or sentence) impressed on a piece of wax or other plastic material adhering or attached to cords or parchment slips to a document as evidence of authenticity or attestation; also, the piece of wax, etc. bearing this impressed device.
2. A device for making such an impression.
3. That which "seals" a person's lips.

Great Seal. The seal (in sense 3) used for the authentication of documents of the highest importance, esp. the impression of this on wax.

Sixth Seal.

SEAL.

Seal, *sb.³*

Seal, *sb.⁴*

Seal, *v.¹*

Seal, *v.²*

Seal, *v.³* intr. To hunt for seals.

Sealable, *a.*

Sea-lark.

Sea-law.

Sea-lawyer.

Sealch, **-ie**, *sb.* Orkney and Shetland.

Sealed, *ppl. a.*

Sea legs, *pl.*

Sealer.

SEALER.

Sealery.

Sea-line, *sb.*

Sea-lights.

Sea-light.

Sealing, *vbl. sb.*

Sealing, *ppl. a.*

Sealing-wax.

Sea-lion.

Sea-lungs.

Sealskin.

Sea's.

Sealskin.

Seam, *sb.¹*

Seam, *sb.²*

Column 1 (SEAM)

with a definite quantity, varying according to the commodity and land.

Seam, v.¹ [f. SEAM sb.¹]

1. trans. To sew the seam or seams of; to fasten or join on, together, up with a seam or seams.

2. trans. and intr. To form a seam-stitch; to make a seam or seam-stitch in (a piece of knitting).

Seam, v.² [f. SEAM sb.²] trans. To dress (down) with grease.

Seam, obs. form of SEEM.

Seaman, n.² [f. SEAM sb.¹]

Seamanlike, a.

Seamanly, adv.

Seamanship.

Sea-maid.

Sea-mark.

Column 2 (SEA-MARK)

Seaman, sb. [SEA + MAN.] Pl. -men. [f. SEA sb. + MAW.]

Seamless (sīˑmlĕs), a.

Sea-maw. Now dial.

Seamed (sīmd), ppl. a.¹

Seamed, ppl. a.²

Seamer.

Seamew (sīˑmiū).

Seamless, a.

Seaming (sīˑmiŋ), vbl. sb.

Seamless.

Sea-mouse.

Column 3 (SEA-MAW)

Sea-maw.

Seam-rent.

Seamster, sempster (sĕmˑstə, seˑmˑstə).

Seamster, n.

Sea-monk.

Sea-mouse.

Seamstress, sempstress (seˑmstres, -trĕs).

Sea-moss.

Seamost.

Seamoth.

Sea-mouse.

Column 4 (SEAMSTRESSY)

Seamster, sempster.

Seamstress, sempstress.

Seamstressing, nonce-wd.

Seamstress-ship.

Seamstressy. Obs. rare⁻¹.

Column 1 (SEAMSTRY)

Seamstry, sempstry. Obs. [f. SEAMSTER + -Y.]

Seamy (sīˑmi), a. rare⁻¹. [f. SEAM sb.¹ + -Y.]

Seam, variant of SEME Obs.

Seam, obs. f. SCREE; variant of SENE Obs.; synod. of SEENAHILD, variant form of SENNACHIE.

Séance (se'āns). [Fr. séance a sitting, f. OF. seoir (:—L. sedēre) to sit.]

Sean, variant of SEINE sb.

Sea-nettle.

Seangroen, obs. form of SENGREEN Obs.

Seanachilde, variant form of SENNACHIE.

Sean, obs. form of SEEN.

Sea-nymph.

Column 2

Sea-onion.

Sea-orange.

Sea-otter.

Sea-officer.

Sea-owl.

1. The lump-fish, Cyclopterus lumpus.

2. The puffin.

Sea-ox.

Sea-pad.

1. The hippocampus, cf. SEA-COW.

2. The five-finger.

Sea-parrot.

Sea-pheasant.

Sea-pie¹. [PIE sb.¹]

Sea-pie². [PIE sb.²]

Sea-pink. [PINK sb.⁴]

Column 3 (SEA-PINK)

Sea-pink.

Sea-piece. [PIECE sb.]

Sea-pig.

Sea-pike¹. [PIKE sb.⁴]

Sea-plant.

Sea-poose, variant of SEA-PUSE (sense 4).

Sea-pork.

Seaport (sīˑpǫət). [PORT sb.³]

Sea-power (sense 4).

Sea-power.

Sea-purse.

Seapy, obs. form of SEPOY.

Sea-quake.

Column 4 (SEA-PLANT)

Sea-plant. [PLANT sb.]

Sea-plane.

Sea-pork.

Sear¹, v.

1. A portion of a gun-lock which engages with the notches of the tumbler in order to keep the hammer at full or half cock.

Sear² (sīə), a. Forms: 4-6, 7 sere, 5-8 sear.

Sear³, v.

Sear⁴ (sīə), v. Obs. Forms: 4-6, 7 sere, 5-8 sear.

Sea-raven.

Searce (sǫəs), sb. Obs. Forms: [? 4 sas], 5 sarse, sars, sarce, 5-6 serce, 6-8 sierce, 7-9 searce, 8 searce.

Supplement, p. 3873; Corrigenda, p. 4092; Spurious words, p. 4093; Books quoted, p. 4094.

2695

Searce (sɛəs), *sb.* ... A sieve or strainer.

Searcer (sɛəsəɹ). ... One who searces or sifts.

Search (sɜːtʃ), *sb.* Forms: 4–7 serche, serge, 5–6 searche, 5–7 serch, 6– search.

1. The action or an act of searching; examination or the purpose of finding a person or thing.

Search (sɜːtʃ), *v.* To go about (a country or place) in order to find, or to ascertain the presence or absence of, some person or thing; to explore in quest of some object.

Searchable (sɜːtʃəbl), *a.* Capable of being searched.

Searchant ... *nonce-wd.*

Searcher (sɜːtʃəɹ). Forms: a. 4–6 serchere, 5–7 sercher, etc. One who or that which searches.

Searchery. The office of a searcher.

Searchful, *a.* Full of anxious attention; diligent in search.

Searching, *vbl. sb.* The action of the verb SEARCH in its various senses.

Searching, *ppl. a.* 1. Of observation or examination: Minute, rigorous, penetrating, keenly observant.

Searchingly, *adv.* In a searching manner.

Searchingness. Searching quality or nature.

Searchless, *a.* Inscrutable, impenetrable, resisting investigation.

Search-light. An electric arc-lamp fitted with a reflector and suspended in a frame so that it may throw a beam of light in any desired direction.

Searge, obs. form of SERGE.

Seargeant, obs. form of SERGEANT.

Sea-rim. The horizon at sea.

Searing, *vbl. sb.* That withers or becomes parched.

Sea-robin. A gurnard or trigloid fish.

Sea-rod. A pennatulaceous polyp of the family *Virgularia*.

Sea-room. Space at sea free from obstruction in which a ship can be manoeuvred easily.

Sea-scape, seascape (siːskeɪp). A picture of the sea; a sea-piece.

Sea-scorpion. Any fish of the *Scorpaenidae*.

Sea-serpent. 1. Any ophidian inhabiting the sea.

Sea-shell. A marine shell, the shell of any salt-water mollusc.

Sea-shore. The coast of the sea, or the land lying adjacent to the sea.

Seaside, sea-side (siːsaɪd). The margin or brink of the sea.

Sea-slug. ...

Sea-snail. ...

Sea-snake. ...

Sea-snipe. ...

Season, sb. ...

Seasonable, a. ...

Seasonableness. ...

Seasonal, a. ...

Seasonally, adv. ...

Seasonedness. ...

Seasoner. ...

Seasoning, vbl. sb. ...

Sea-song. ...

Sea-spider. ...

Sea-spot. ...

Sea-spring. ...

Sea-star. ...

Sea-stream. ...

Seat, sb. ...

thairin. 1574 Ibid. II. 378 For the administratioun of justice upon offendouris,..in the north partis..far distant frome the ordinar sait of justice. 1818 Scott Hrt. Midl. iv, 'Is he a lord of state, or a lord of seat?'...'A lord of seat—a lord of session.—I fash mysell little wi' lords o' state.'

d. Sc. The court of Kirk-session. ? Obs.

1558 Reg. St. Andrews Kirk Session (1889) I. 313 The quhilk day Andro Alexander is admonisched be the Superintendent and Seat.

†4. 'Stool', evacuation of the bowels. (Cf. Siege sb. 3 b.) Obs.

1697 Phil. Trans. XIX. 367 The Juice of the leaves of Betonica, in Spring, will not Work by Vomit and Seat as well as the Roots.

5. The 'set' or 'sit' (of a garment). ? Obs.

1824 Miss Ferrier Inher. xxi, And only look at my ruff!..Colonel Delmour has spoil'd the seat of it.

II. Place or thing to sit upon.

6. The place on which a person is sitting, or is accustomed to sit; a place to seat one person at a table, in a public building, conveyance, etc.

c 1205 Lay. 30841 Þat folc hafden alle iʒeten and arisen from heore seten. a 1300 Cursor M. 15282 Quen þis super was all don, Iesus ras of his sette [other texts sete; rime lete]. c 1380 Wyclif Sel. Wks. II. 62 And þei loven first seetis at soperis. 1470–85 Malory Arthur x. vii. 424 Kynge Arthur..maade hym knyght of the table round and his seate was where the good Knyghtes sir Marhaus seate was. 1567 Gude & Godlie Ball. 102 Full slyddrie is the sait that thay on sit. 1575 Gascoigne Posies, Flowers (1907) 91 Me thought I was a loft, and yet my seate full sure: Thy heart dyd seeme to me a rock which ever might endure. 1600 Weakest goeth to Wall G 2, Sexton, I haue sought thee in euery seate in the Church. 1697 Dryden Virg. Georg. iv. 496 Starting at once from their green Seats, they rise; Fear in their Heart, Amazement in their Eyes. 1716 Lady M. W. Montagu Let. to C'tess of Mar 14 Sept., She ordered me a seat at her right hand. a 1763 W. King Polit. & Lit. Anecd. (1819) 244 He went every Sunday to St. James's church, and used to sit in Mr. Salt's seat. 1832 Tennyson Œnone 21 Till the mountain shade Sloped downward to her seat from the upper cliff. 1873 O. W. Holmes Addr. Opening Fifth Avenue Theatre 99 See where the hurrying crowd..Streams to the numbered seat each paste-board fits. 1908 R. Bagot A. Cuthbert iii. 22 Then she stalked out of the church. Fortunately we were in the free seats, near the door.

transf. and fig. 1399 Langl. Rich. Redeles iii. 49 Thanne cometh..Anoþer proud partriche..And sesith on hir sete [MS. alteration of cete] with hir softe plumes, And houeth þe eyren. 1590 Shaks. Mids. N. ii. ii. 81 When thou wak'st, let loue forbid Sleepe his seate on thy eye-lid. 1741–2 Gray Agrippina 51 If bright ambition from her craggy seat Display the radiant prize. 1784 Cowper Tiroc. 432 For Providence..In spite of all the wrigglers into place, Still keeps a seat or two for worth and grace.

b. Hence, the use of, or right to use, a seat (in a church, theatre, conveyance, etc.). Cf. Sitting.

1520 Churchw. Acc. St. Giles, Reading 9 Recd of Thoms Gyles for his wifes sete iiijd. c 1618 Moryson Itin. iv. (1903) 149 A Countesse..litle or nothing respected..in the Church, where she could hardly gett a seate. 1815 tr. Paris Chit-Chat (1816) III. 176 To-day it is discussed how much should be exacted for seats on the day when Monseigneur comes to confirm. 1844 O. W. Holmes Lines Berksh. Jubilee 51 We'll give you at least..a seat on the grass, And the best of old—water—at nothing a glass. 1879 J. Kerr Ess. Castism & Sectism 79 She paid a pound out of her scanty wages for a seat in the church.

c. A right to sit as a member, or the position of being a member, of a deliberative or administrative body, esp. of Parliament or other legislative assembly; a place (whether occupied or temporarily vacant) in the membership of the House of Commons, Congress, or the like.

Sometimes qualified by the designation of that one of the contending parties to which the holder of the (Parliamentary) seat belongs: e.g. 'The polls for three Liberal and three Conservative seats will be declared to-morrow'.

1774 Burke Sp. Amer. Tax. Wks. II. 399 In the year sixty-five..not having the honour of a seat in this house. 1787 J. Jay in Sparks Corr. Amer. Rev. (1853) IV. 153 Members who will find it convenient to make their seats subservient to partial and personal purposes. 1798 Tyrwhitt in Paget Papers (1896) I. 138 All those who purchased Seats are selling as well as they can. 1818 Scott Hrt. Midl. li, He was generally respected by those of his own profession, as well as by the laity who had seats in the Assembly. 1849 Macaulay Hist. Eng. iv. I. 453 Jeffreys..very soon after the death of Charles, obtained a seat in the cabinet. 1885 Manch. Exam. 10 July 5/4 A seat on the Committee will compel them to hear..the first principles of economical science. 1885 Encycl. Brit. XVIII. 309/2 By the English Reform Act of 1867..twenty-six seats were taken from boroughs...Seven other English boroughs were disfranchised by the Scottish Reform Act of 1868, these seats being given to Scotland.

7. Something adapted or used for sitting upon, as a chair, stool, sofa, etc. Also spec. a bench to seat one or more persons; a horizontal board or framework in a boat, vehicle, etc.; † a sedan chair.

c 1375 Cursor M. 14734 (Fairf.) Þaire setis [Cott. setles, Trin. seges] þer þai in con sete he kest ham doun vnder þaire fete. c 1440 Pallad. on Husb. i. 1094 Anend the setis [of a bath] sette bit so withoute The fourneys. 1584 Churchw. Acc. S. Andrew's, Canterb. (MS.), For a borde to make seates in the belfry & braggett's, vj. 1588 Hickock tr. Frederick's Voy. 40 b, The noble men neuer goe on foote, but are caried by men in a seat. 1667 Milton P. L. v. 392 Rais'd of grassie terf Thir Table was, and mossie seats had round. 1784 Cowper Task v. 162 But in order due Convivial table and commodious seat..were there. 1818 Shelley Rosalind 106 They came To a stone seat beside a spring. 1875 Jowett Plato (ed. 2) III. 700 A light chariot without a seat. 1879 Encycl. Brit. IX. 848/1 [The Romans'] chairs, couches, and seats were of similar shape to those of the Greeks.

b. in narrower sense: That part (of a chair, saddle, etc.) upon which its occupant sits.

1778 Miss Burney Evelina (1791) II. 251 Miss Mirvan and I jumped involuntarily upon the seats of our chairs. 1809 Malkin Gil Blas iv. xi. ¶ 5 Chairs without any seats. 1875 Knight Dict. Mech., Seat, the broad part of a saddle on which the rider sits; also, the top piece on a gig saddle. 1879 Encycl. Brit. IX. 850/1 The seats, backs, and ends are stuffed and upholstered with rich materials.

8. Contextually applied to the chair set apart for the holder of some position of authority or dignity, the throne of a king or a bishop, or the like, the throne of God or of an angel. Hence fig. the authority or dignity symbolized by sitting in a particular chair or throne. Regal or royal seat (arch.), † seat-royal, a royal throne.

a 1200 Vices & Virtues 105 Iusticia et iudicium preparatio sedis eius,..Rihtwisnesse and dom, hi makieð godes sate. c 1200 Ormin 11959 Þe deofell brohhte Jesu Crist Wiþþutenn o þe temmple Uppon an sæte uppo þe rof,..Forr þær wass greʒʒþedd sæte o lofft Till þa þatt shollden spellenn. 1390 Gower Conf. II. 155 King of Crete He hadde be; bot of his sete He was put doun. c 1400 Gamelyn 855 Gamelyn sette him doun in the Iustices seet. a 1533 Ld. Berners Huon xlii. 141 Thou art not worthy to sytt in a sete royall. 1533 Bellenden Livy iii. xxii. (1903) II. 36 He callit þe consullis to raise ane new contentioun to þare seittis. 1593 Shaks. 3 Hen. VI, i. i. 26 This is the Pallace of the fearefull King, And this the Regall Seat: possesse it Yorke. 1617 Purchas Pilgrimage (ed. 3) 595 The King comes forth in open audience, sitting in his Seat-royall. 1659 Hammond On Ps. xx. 6 Paraphr. 116 As if by his own right hand from heaven, his holy seat of mansion, he should reach out deliverance to him. 1667 Milton P. L. vi. 27 On to the sacred hill They led him high applauded, and present Before the seat supreme. 1676 Dryden Aurengz. v. i, I, for myself, th' Imperial Seat will gain. 1746 Francis tr. Horace, Epist. i. vi. 80 A third..Can give or take the Honours of the State, The Consul's Fasces, and the Prætor's Seat. 1820 Shelley Witch of Atlas 634 The king would dress an ape up in his crown And robes, and seat him on his glorious seat.

b. spec. The throne of a particular kingdom.

1599 Shaks. Hen. V, i. i. 88 Of his true Titles to some certaine Dukedomes, And generally, to the Crowne and Seat of France. Ibid. i. i. 269 We neuer valew'd this poore seate of England. 1896 A. Austin England's Darling i. i, And in the seat of Mercia Ceowulf rules.

† c. Apostolic seat [F. Siège apostolique], Holy seat [F. Saint-Siège], Peter's seat: the papal chair, its occupant or his office. (Cf. See sb.) Obs.

1560 Daus tr. Sleidane's Comm. 16 b, He that hathe the Seate and faith of Peter, was ever taken for his successour. 1563 Winʒet tr. Vincent. Lirin. viii. Wks. (S.T.S.) II. 25 Pape Steuin.., Prælat of the Apostolik Sait [apostolicæ sedis antistes]. 1588 Parke tr. Mendoza's Hist. China 405 The authoritie where with they do it, is not knowen,..the seat apostolicke did neuer giue it them. 1673–4 Clarendon Relig. & Policy (1811) I. 202 The reserving of the first-fruits of all vacant benefices to the holy seat.

† d. as the title of an order of angels; = Throne. (Used to render L. sedes.) Obs.

1398 Trevisa Barth. De P. R. ii. x. (1495) 37 The thyrde Ordre is the ordre of Thrones...Ysidore & therfore Denys calle theym þe hyghest setes [sedes altissimæ] for they ben hye as it were by auctoryte of god ordened for to deme... Sadde setes [Sedes compactæ] for they ben couenable & conuenyently Joyned towchynge the Joynture & conuenyentes of domes of god. 1577 tr. Bullinger's Decades iv. ix. 737/2 Truely the Apostle sayth, Whether seates, (thrones) whether lordships, whether principalities, whether powers.

9. The sitting part of the body; the posteriors. Also jocularly, seat of honour (and nonce-variations).

1607 Topsell Four-f. Beasts 189 A plaister thereof..cureth also all tumours in the priuy parts, and in the seate. 1727 Gay Fables xxiii. 80 They stick with pins my bleeding seat. 1782 Cowper Gilpin 84 The snorting beast began to trot, Which gall'd him in his seat. 1785 R. Cumberland Observer No. 24 ¶ 12 With one kick, pretty forcibly bestowed upon the seat of dishonour. 1792 Wolcot Pair of Lyric Ep. 18 Behold him seiz'd, his seat of honour bare; The bamboo sounds—alas! no voice of Fame. 1796 Burke Regic. Peace iii. (1892) 148 The Turk..gave him two or three lusty kicks on the seat of honour. 1809 Malkin Gil Blas v. i. ¶ 3 My seat of vengeance was firked most unmercifully. 1820 Combe Syntax, Wife ii. 289 While with his spade the conq'ror plied, Stroke after stroke, the seat of shame, Which blushing Muses never name. 1835 Hood Dead Robbery iii, The stiff 'un that he thought to meet Starts sudden up, like Jacky-in-a-box, Upon his seat! 1878 Athletic World 10 May 66/2 A well-ventilated [bicycle-] saddle is the best preventative for those blisters which favour the seat of honour.

b. That part (of a garment, esp. of a pair of trousers) which covers the posteriors.

1835 Marryat Jac. Faithf. ii, I had a pair of trowsers with no seat to them. a 1849 Hawthorne Twice-told T., Village Uncle, Another [fellow] has planted the tarry seat of his trousers on a heap of salt.

10. The 'form' of a hare. ? Obs.

[Cf. Gr. ἡ καθέδρα τοῦ λαγὼ Xen. Cyneg. iv. § 4]

1735 Somerville Chase ii. 25 So the wise Hares Oft quit their Seats, lest some more curious Eye Shou'd mark their Haunts. 1856 'Stonehenge' Brit. Sports i. ii. vi. 139 The Form of the Hare, or as it is sometimes called, her seat.

11. Boot-trade. An engagement to work at making boots of a specified kind. Const. of.

1791 J. Lackington Mem. xvii. 114, I could not bear the idea of returning to the leather-branch; I therefore attempted and obtained a seat of Stuff in Bristol. Ibid. xviii. 118, I left my seat of work at Bristol, and returned..to Taunton. 1896 Daily News 2 Mar. 10/6 Boot trade. Wanted, a Seat of Woman's Work.

III. Residence, abode, situation. [Cf. L. sedes.]

12. Applied spec. (after L. sedes) to: The abiding place or resting place (of departed souls); a position in this place. Now arch. or poet.

c 1275 Sinners Beware 52 in O. E. Misc. 73 Wikede beoþ þe sete [sc. Hell] And the wurmes eke þat doþ þe saule teone. a 1300 Cursor M. 25448 Reu me lauerd..and wiss me waies þare þare santes has þair seli sete. 1390 Gower Conf. III. 36 Thanne he preide Unto the Patriarch and seide: Send Lazar doun fro thilke Sete, And do that he his finger wete In water. c 1440 Alphabet of Tales 416 Behold! I se hevyn oppyn & a seatt ordand for me. 1561 Daus Bullinger on Apoc. (1573) 218 b, The soules passing out of the body before the end and last iudgement go right into the blessed seates. 1593 Shaks. Rich. II, v. v. 112 Mount, mount my soule, thy seate is vp on high. 1707–45 Watts Hymn, 'How bright these glorious Spirits', How came they to the happy Seats of everlasting Day? 1832 Tennyson Œnone 129 Gods, who have attain'd Rest in a happy place and quiet seats Above the thunder.

13. (Cf. 8.) A city in which a throne, court, government is established or set up; a capital.

c 1400 Destr. Troy 1630 Priam..a pales gert make Within the Cite full Solempne of a sete riall. 1585 T. Washington tr. Nicholay's Voy. ii. xiii. 49 Mehemet..resoluing to keep there the seat of his empire. 1595 T. Bedingfield tr. Machiavelli's Florent. Hist. i Rome, the antient Emperiall seate. 1678 Wanley Wond. Lit. World v. i. 467/2 Constantinople was taken by Mahomet, and made the chief Seat of the Turkish Empire. 1719 De Foe Crusoe ii. (Globe) 541 Peking, the Royal Seat of the Chinese Emperor. 1836 Thirlwall Greece xii. II. 85 This [Miletus] was the seat chosen by Neleus himself. 1851 Dixon W. Penn i (1872) 4 His seat of government was far away from the coast.

b. (Cf. 8 c.) = See sb. Now only seat of a bishop.

1387 Trevisa Higden (Rolls) II. 77 Þe chief moderchirche of al Wales, and þe chief sete [Caxton see]. c 1475 Harl. Contin. Higden (Rolls) VIII. 436 Maister John Barnette, bischop of Worcester, was translate to the seete of Bathe. a 1552 Leland Itin. IV. 16 The which was at that tyme nother of his Inheritaunce nor Purchace, but as a thing taken of the Sete of Wiccestre in Farme. 1582 Reg. Privy Council Scot. III. 474 The cheptoure of the seitt of Glasgow. 1888 Bryce Amer. Commw. II. iii. 296 In England a city is usually taken to be a place which is or has been the seat of a bishop.

14. The thing (esp. the organ or part of the body) in which a particular power, faculty, function or quality 'resides'; the locality of a disease, sensation, or the like.

1390 Gower Conf. III. 100 The dreie Colre..his propre sete [L. domus] Hath in the galle, wher he duelleth. 1398 Trevisa Barth. De P. R. v. ii. (1495) 102 The heede is pryncypall place and seete of wyttes. 1676 Grew Musæum, Anat. Stomach & Guts vi. 26 The said Three Ventricles..are the Seat of Tast. 1753 R. Russell Diss. Sea Water 182 The Patient..complained only of those Parts, which were the late Seat of the Disease. 1777 Priestley Matt. & Spir. I. iv. (1782) 47 We formed a judgment concerning the necessary seat of thought. 1842 J. H. Newman Par. Serm. VI. vii. 98 The heart may be considered as the seat of life. 1843 R. J. Graves Syst. Clin. Med. xxviii. 363 Mercurial ostitis of the head is a very common form of disease: its more usual seats are the frontal and parietal bones. 1860 Tyndall Glac. i. xxvii. 196 The air itself between the eye and the distant pines being the seat of the colour. 1862 H. Spencer First Princ. II. v. § 57 (1875) 185 The string is the seat of a tension generated by the motion of the ball. 1874 Carpenter Ment. Phys. i. ii. § 61 (1879) 63 The Sensorial centres whose seat is in the head. 1892 W. R. Gowers Man. Dis. Nerv. Syst. I. 333 The lesions of chronic myelitis resemble those of acute myelitis in seat and distribution.

b. Similarly, of the soul or its parts.

1579 Hake Newes out of Powles iv. (1872) D iij b, The stomack ouerchardgde..Doth make the minde and inwarde man vnfit for reasons seate. 1716–17 Bentley Serm. xi. 383 [His heart is] the Seat of selfishness. 1751 Jortin Serm. I. iii. (1771) 57 A mind tormented with furious passions, the seat of hopes which are disappointed. 1847 R. W. Hamilton Rewards & Punishm. viii. (1853) 365 Sin has its seat in the soul. 1850 McCosh Div. Govt. iii. i. (1874) 309 We regard the will as the seat of all virtue and vice.

15. A place where something takes place, or where some particular condition of things prevails. Seat of war [= L. sedes belli]: the region in which warfare is going on.

c 1560 A. Scott Poems xxxv. 4 Alwayis to fle iniquite And sait of syn and schame. 1565 Cooper Thesaurus s.v. Sedes luxuriæ. Cic. The seate or habitation of riot and sensualitie. 1593 Shaks. Rich. II, iv. i. 140 In this Seat of Peace. 1662 Stillingfl. Orig. Sacræ ii. i. § 2. 110 Those parts which were furthest remote from the seat of those grand transactions. 1673 Temple Observ. United Prov. i. 44 The other retires into Holland, and makes that the seat of the War. a 1687 Petty Pol. Arith. i. (1690) 9 A plain open Country..where the seat of War may be both Winter and Summer. 1736 Butler Anal. ii. vii. 259 Foretelling, at what Time Rome or Babylon or Greece..should be the most conspicuous Seat of..Tyranny and Dissoluteness. 1803 Wellington in Gurw. Desp. (1837) I. 432 Forage, for which every large body of troops must depend upon the country which is to be the seat of its operations. 1810 Crabbe Borough xii. 303 And who shall say where guided? to what seats Of starving villany? of thieves and cheats? 1876 A. J. Evans Through Bosnia iii. 87 Many Croats and Slovenes..were..leaving for the seat of war. 1878 Huxley Physiogr. xvii. 278 The region which has been the seat of these changes.

b. A city or locality in which (a branch of trade, learning, etc.) is established.

1585 T. Washington tr. Nicholay's Voy. ii. xiii. 49 Galata, being the seate of trade of the Geneuoises. 1610 Holland Camden's Brit. i. 488 Cambridge..was a seat of learning about the time of King Henry the First. 1788 Priestley Lect. Hist. v. xxxvi. 264 So little attention was given to matters of science in Europe, their former seat. 1849 Macaulay Hist. Eng. v. I. 585 Taunton..was a celebrated seat of the woollen manufacture. 1865 Dircks Life Marq. Worc. i. 1 Blackfriars was..the seat of fashion. 1868

Freeman Norm. Conq. (1876) II. vii. 153 It was in those days the chief seat of the Irish slave-trade.

16. A place of habitation or settlement (of a tribe, people, etc.). Also transf. (of birds).

1535 Stewart Cron. Scot. II. 217 Baith Scot and Pecht..war baneist all out of tha boundis, And Saxonis sone in thair saittis set doun. c 1611 Chapman Iliad xv. Comment., We often see with a clap of thunder doves or other fowles driven headlong from their seates. 1614 Raleigh Hist. World iv. vii. § iii. 301 These Gaules were the race of those, that issued out of their Countrie, to seeke new seates in that great expedition. a 1674 Clarendon Hist. Reb. xi. § 146 The seat of the old Irish..was the province of Ulster. 1697 Dryden Virg. Georg. i. 327 Betwixt the midst [the torrid zone] and these [the frigid zones], the Gods assign'd Two habitable Seats for Humane Kind. 1762 Hume Hist. Eng. I. i. 2 The convenience of feeding their Cattle was even a sufficient motive for removing their seats. 1835 Thirlwall Greece v. I. 149 Corinth, one of the principal seats of the Minyan race. 1853 J. H. Newman Hist. Sk. (1873) II. i. 13 Central Europe was not at that time the seat of civilized nations.

† b. Seat and soil [= L. sedes ac solum (Livy)]: a region of habitation. Obs.

a 1400–50 Wars Alex. 1749 All þe gracious godis..þat sauys sete & soile & sustaynes þe erth. 1614 Raleigh Hist. World i. iii. § 3. 38 [Certain places are said in Scripture to resemble Paradise:] being compared to a seat and soyle of farre exceeding excellencie. Ibid. § 5. 40 Or if the soile and seate had not remained, then would not Moses, who wrote of Paradise about 850 years after the floud, haue described it so particularly.

c. = Country-seat.

1607 Norden Surv. Dial. iii. 85 Let Princes haue their Palaces, and great men, their pleasant seates. 1610 Holland Camden's Brit. i. 481 Rising-castle..the seat in times past of the Albineys. 1796 Pegge Anonym. (1809) 325 Houses, better than farm-houses, but not sumptuous enough to be called seats or capital mansions. 1812 Crabbe Tales iii. 56 And guests politely call'd his house a seat. 1847 Tennyson Princess Prol. 98 And here we lit on..lady friends From neighbour seats. 1859 W. Collins Q. of Hearts i, No gentleman's seat is within an easy drive of us.

† 17. Local or geographical position or situation. Seat of living: habitat (of an animal). Obs.

1607 Topsell Four-f. Beasts 660 We shall manifest, that either the colour or seate of liuing, cannot agree with the Strepsiceros. 1614 Raleigh Hist. World i. iii. § i. 33 The Lord God planted a garden, Eastward, in Eden...Of this seate and place of Paradise, all ages haue held dispute. 1663 Butler Hud. i. i. 173 He knew the Seat of Paradise, Could tell in what Degree it lies. 1695 Woodward Nat. Hist. Earth i. 36 But the Sea..left these Shells there as marks of its ancient bounds and seat.

18. Position (of ground, a city, habitation) as regards surroundings, climate, etc.; situation, site; hence, the position of a person or living thing with regard to habitation or situation.

1549 Russell in Froude Hist. Eng. (1882) IV. 435 They found the rebels strongly encamped, as well by the seat of the ground as by the entrenching of the same. a 1566 R. Edwards Damon & Pithias (1908) C ij b, But mee thinkes, this is a pleasant Citie, The Seate is good, and yet not stronge. 1574 R. Scot Hop Garden (1578) 9 The Hoppe that lykes not..his seate, his grounde,..or the manner of his setting &c. commeth vp..smaill in stalke. 1591 Florio 2nd Fruites 29 You are lodged then in a verie good seate [In buon sito]. 1605 Shaks. Macb. i. vi. 1 This Castle hath a pleasant seat. 1615 G. Sandys Trav. 6 Although the seate of the Towne be excessive hot, yet it is happily qualified by a North-East gale. 1625 B. Jonson Staple of N. iii. Intermeane, In Siluer-streete, the Region of money, a good seat for a Vsurer. 1625 Bacon Ess., Building (Arb.) 547 Hee that builds a faire House, vpon an ill Seat, committeth Himselfe to Prison. 1673 Temple Observ. United Prov. i. 44 Holland..was strong by its nature and seat among the Waters that encompass and divide it. 1693 Dryden Persius vi. 1 Has Winter caus'd thee, friend, to change thy seat, And seek in Sabine air a warm retreat? a 1701 Sedley 4th Bk. Virg. Georg. Wks. 1778 I. 26 First, for your Bees a seat and station chuse Shelter'd from winds.

† 19. A definite place (on a surface, in a body or organ, in a series). Obs.

1574 H. Baker Well-spring Sci. (1617) 2 [In Numeration] a place is called a seat or roome that a figure standeth in. 1576 Fleming tr. Caius' Dogs (1880) 2 Of these three sortes ..so meane I to entreate, that the first in the first place, the last in the last roome, and the myddle sort in the middle seate, be handled. 1578 Banister Hist. Man i. 9 That Seame..rising from the hollowes of the temples, pearseth, through the middle seates of the eyes. 1653 Ld. Brouncker tr. Des Cartes' Compend. Mus. 40 Unlesse all the Tones of these be removed by a Fourth or Fifth, from their proper Seat. 1676 in Willis & Clark Cambridge (1886) II. 521 The Seates or places where the same Bookes are to be putt..shall have the name of the said Sr Thomas Sclater putt upon them. 1726 Leoni Alberti's Archit. I. 39 b, If..Buildings obstruct your Sight from discovering and fixing upon the exact Seat of every Angle. 1775 T. Sheridan Art of Reading 38 For many Contiguous letters [of the alphabet] as they now lie are performed in such different seats and with such different exertions of the organs.

† b. = Locus 2. Obs. (? nonce-use.)

1628 T. Spencer Logick 14 Aristotle assigneth ten places, or seates of arguments, in the fourth Chapter of his Categories.

† 20. A term of the game of Post and Pair. Obs.

1680 Cotton Compl. Gamester xxii. (ed. 2) 106 You must first stake at Post, then at Pair; after this deal two Cards apiece, then stake at the Seat.

IV. Basis, foundation, support.

† 21. A place prepared for something to be erected or set up upon it; a building site. Obs.

1615 Markham County Contentm. i. i. 14 Against the side of this hill would be cut or digged diuers large and broad seats one aboue an other,..which seats would bee..boorded ..on the sides..and also close boorded aloft,..the number of these seats would bee according to the number of your Hounds. a 1647 Hayward Edw. VI (1630) 85 A Church by Strand-bridge, and two Bishops houses, were pulled downe to make a seat for his new building. 1662 Gerbier Principles 14 But as for a Seate on Moorish Grounds.., in effect 'tis to Build perpetually.

† b. transf. in Perspective. (See quot.)

1815 R. Brown Princ. Pract. Perspective 3 Seat is the space that an object would occupy on the ground plane.

22. That part of a thing upon which it rests or appears to rest, usually the broadest part; the base.

1661 N. N. Drayning Fenns 7 Banks..9 foot high and 60 foot wide at seat or bottom. 1681 Grew Musæum i. § vi. i. 139 The first..is the Edible Button Fish. These have very great Prickles, with Seats or Bases proportionable. 1828 P. Nicholson Masonry 37 A horizontal section of a wall, through the base-line, is called the seat of the wall. 1830 Hedderwick Mar. Archit. 118 Seat, the bottom part of a timber; the seat of the floors is that part which rests on the keel. c 1850 Rudim. Navig. (Weale) 114 The eddy which the ship draws after her at her seat or line of flotation. 1855 Franke Beil's Technol. Dict. II. 452 Seat of wooden bellows (the lower or fixed chest or box), der Unterkasten, Gîte.

23. Mech. A part or surface upon which the base of something rests.

1805 Shipwright's Vade-m. 129 Seat, the scarph or part trimmed out for a chock, &c. to fay to. 1844 H. Stephens Bk. Farm I. 414 The beam being received into the seats formed on..the palms [of a plough]. 1858 R. Murray Marine Engines (ed. 3) 71 It more frequently happens that the valve fits its seat so badly as to allow of the escape of steam. 1875 T. Seaton Fret Cutting 103 Carvers leave a level place called a seat, where this extra thickness is required, and glue on a piece. 1875 Knight Dict. Mech., Seat, that part of the bore of a chambered piece of ordnance at which the shell rests when rammed home. 1884 F. J. Britten Watch & Clockm. 129 A hole is drilled so much less in size than the jewel as to allow of a firm seat for it. 1886 Encycl. Brit. XX. 583/1 To obtain the requisite convexity by rounding the formation surface or seat of the road.

24. Mining. a. The floor of a mine. b. The stratum (of clay, rock, etc.) upon which coal lies.

1860 Eng. & Foreign Mining Gloss. (ed. 2) 43 [Derbyshire terms.] Seat, or Sole, the floor or bottom of the mine. 1867 Smythe Coal 25 The floor, thill, or seat.., of the coal is an underclay.

25. Shoemaking. A piece of leather pegged or sewn to the boot as a foundation for the heel.

1832 Worc. Exhib. Catal. iii. 30 The nails..spread as they go in so as to nail the heel closely round the seat of the boot. 1895 Hasluck's Boot Making vii. 107 If a pegged seat is wanted, it must be arranged for before the boot is lasted, as it is necessary to skive the stiffener much thinner..than is wanted for a sewn seat.

† 26. Used to render L. sedes in technical senses. a. Anat. Seat of the heart: see quots. 1398. Seat of the skull: app. the cheek-bone. b. Surg. [after Gr. βέλεος ἕδρη, Hipp.] See quot. 1634. Obs.

1398 Trevisa Barth. De P. R. v. xxxvi. (1495) 149 And the herte hath in the brede therof two grystlewe bones, whyche ben callyd the setes therof. Ibid. v. lix. 175 In the mydyll of the herte of a beest is a grystyll bone sette in the brede therof and that is callyd the seet and subtylte of the herte. 1552 Udall tr. Geminus' Anat. B vij b/2 The seate of ye scull, whych we call the stonny seate [orig. sedes calvariæ, quam lapidosam dicimus]. Ibid., Thys seate together wyth hys felowe on the other syde, we call the cheake bones. 1634 T. Johnson tr. Parey's Chirurg. x. i. 337 Hippocrates ..in his Booke..seemes to have made 4. or 5. kinds of fractures of the Scull...The 4. is named Sedes, or a seat. Ibid. 338 Seate, when the marke of the weapon remaines imprinted in the wound, that the wound is of no more length, nor bredth than the weapon fell upon.

V. 27. Phrases. a. To hold, keep a or one's seat: to remain seated, to keep from falling; also, to retain one's position as a Member of Parliament. Similarly, to lose one's seat.

c 1400 Destr. Troy 7409 Than Achilles..Al to hurlet the helme of þe high prinse; But hym seluyn was safe, & his seate helde. 1599 Shaks. Hen. V, i. i. 36 Nor neuer Hidra-headed Wilfulnesse So soone did loose his Seat. 1602 — Ham. i. v. 96 While memory holds a seate In this distracted Globe. 1605 — Macb. iii. iv. 54 Sit worthy Friends:..Pray you keepe Seat. 1745 Life Bamfylde-Moore Carew 66 The Quack being no longer able to keep his Seat [on horseback] falls headlong. 1847 Tennyson Princess v. 485 Part [of the riders] reel'd but kept their seats. 1881 Gladstone Sp. at Leeds 7 Oct. in Times 8 Oct. 6/3, I never was called upon ..to exercise an option between Leeds and Mid Lothian. My seat for both was lost by my acceptance of office.

b. † To make one's seat (obs.), to take a seat: to sit down. To take one's seat: to take the sitting-place assigned to one; to assume one's official position, to be formally admitted to Parliament or Congress.

c 1400 Rule of St. Benet 1791 Of þam þat er not redi þair To say þe grace & take þer sete. c 1425 Cursor M. 8291 (Trin.) On a bowʒe he [sc. an angel] made his sete Of þat tre þat was so swete. 1593 Shaks. 3 Hen. VI, iii. iii. 10 On the ground, Where I must take like Seat vnto my fortune. 1769 Cowper Queen's Vis. London 2 When long sequester'd from his throne George took his seat again. 1802 Mar. Edgeworth Moral T. (1816) I. 222 The..judge having taken his seat. 1817 Shelley Rev. Islam ii. 997 Ere this power can make In human hearts its calm and holy seat. 1818 Cruise Digest (ed. 2) III. 238 A writ of summons was issued to him, and he took his seat accordingly. 1847 C. Brontë J. Eyre xxxiv, I took a seat: St. John stood near me. 1855 Macaulay Hist. Eng. xii. III. 203 About two hundred and fifty members took their seats. 1865 H. Phillips Amer. Paper Curr. II. 49 [He] took his seat in congress as one of the delegates from Pennsylvania.

c. To take a or the back seat, orig. U. S., fig. to take up the least prominent position, to occupy a subordinate place.

1868 in Farmer's Slang Dict. s.v. Back Seat, [Andrew Johnson's famous saying in 1868 that in the work of Reconstruction traitors should take back seats.] 1888 Bryce Amer. Commw. II. xlvi. 195 A leader came to care for his influence within his State chiefly as a means of gaining strength in the wider national field...The State, therefore, had, to use the transatlantic phrase, 'to take the back seat.'

VI. Combinations.

28. General relations: a. simple attrib., as seat cushion, frame, lug, pillar, rail, row, stitch; objective, as seat borer, maker, owner.

1875 Guide High Wycombe 56 [Chair-] *seat-borer. 1860 G. A. Spottiswoode Tac. Tour 82 We suddenly saw *seat-cushions, books, and plaids neatly lifted out by the wind. 1881 Young Every Man his Own Mech. § 781 The front and back of the *seat-frame are connected by short rails. 1875 Guide High Wycombe 56 [Chair-] *seat-maker. 1898 Cycling 34 The *seat pillar [of a bicycle] should never project more than two inches from the *seat lug. 1891 Century Dict., *Seat-rail,..one of the horizontal members of the frame which forms or supports the seat, as in a chair or sofa. 1837 Carlyle Fr. Rev. II. vi. iii, The Thirty *seat-rows of that famed Slope are again full. 1895 Hasluck's Boot Making ii. 47 One way to sew them [sc. upper and sole] together again is by loop-stitching...The *seat-stitch is another way.

29. Special comb.: seat-arch, an arched recess in a wall having a flat place to serve as a seat; seat-back, a piece of tapestry, leather or other material for covering the back of a seat (Cent. Dict. 1891); seat-board, (a) (see quot. 1884); (b) = seat-tree; (c) a board suspended from scaffolding to serve as a seat for a workman; seat-bone Anat., the innominate bone or hip-bone; more strictly the Ischium; seat-box (see quot.); seat-breaker, a shoemaker's tool (see quot.); seat-clay = next (Cent. Dict.); seat-earth, one of the various names applied to the bed underlying a coal-seam; seat-file, a shoemaker's file for smoothing the 'seat' of a boot; seat-holder, (a) one who occupies a particular seat; (b) one who rents or owns a seat or sitting (esp. in a church, theatre, etc.); seat-house dial., a dwelling-house, 'the manor on an estate' (Jam.); seat-iron, a shoemaker's tool (see quot.); seat-mate U. S., one who shares the same seat with another; seat-mongering, trading in parliamentary seats; seat-owner, one who owns a 'pocket-borough' or a county seat; seat-piece Shoemaking = sense 25 (above); seat-rent, the amount paid for a sitting in a church; seat-seller, one who sells parliamentary seats; hence seat-selling; seat-sock, a sock for the heel of a boot or shoe; seat-stone = seat-earth; seat-transom Naut. (see quot.); seat-tree, the seat of a hand-loom; seat wheel (see quot. 1895); seat-worm, a thread-worm, Oxyuris vermicularis, infesting the fundament.

1703 T. N. City & C. Purchaser 224 A pair of Stone-peers with *Seat-arches. 1884 F. J. Britten Watch & Clockm. 233 *Seat Board..in a long case clock [is] the shelf that supports the movement. 1891 H. Johnston Kilmallie I. i. 6 When the laddie's legs had grown almost sufficiently to warrant his elevation to the *seat-board'. 1901 J. Black's Carp. & Build., Scaffolding 68 The crack in the side of the stack was successfully repaired by the men working from seat boards suspended from the platform above. 1662 Comenius' Janua Ling. Triling. 48 The *seat-bone under the loins is called the flank-bone. 1895 Ramsbotham Obst. Med. & Surg. 4 The os ischium, os sedentarium, or seat-bone. 1801 Felton Carriages (ed. 2) I. 149 The *seat-box, a box made to slide under the seat...It is..convenient to carry linen, &c. 1895 Hasluck's Boot Making viii. 130 To make up the seat after the seat has been nicely pared up, damp the leather and use the *seat breaker, rubbing it evenly round the seat. 1877 Huxley Physiogr. 236 Each bed of coal is supported by a layer of shale known as under-clay or *seat-earth. 1891 in W. Andrews Bygone Northamptonshire 194 The implements of [the shoemaker's] craft,..the awl, clincher.., hammer, *seat-file. 1825 Hone Every-day Bk. I. 1184 A large space, which..greatly to the discomfiture of the lower *seat-holders, was nearly occupied by spectators. 1842 Card. Wiseman Ess. (1853) I. 378 The English seat-holder surrounded by all the luxury of worsted-worked cushions [etc.]. 1483 in Finchale Priory (Surtees) 96 And the sayd Sr Georg sall repare..the forsayd messuag' that is to say on *seyt house of v rowmys on terne of v rowmys. 1885 J. B. Leno Boot & Shoemaking xvii. 137 The *Seat Iron. This once popular piece of kit has been partially superseded by the seat wheel; but many of the best workmen still employ it to set the seat..before using the seat wheel. 1885 New York Times 26 Dec., The mother, tho' wholly unaware of her *seat-mate's identity, did her utmost to protect him. 1813 Examiner 12 Apr. 237/1 My Lord Castlereagh's *seat-mongering. 1818 Cobbett Pol. Reg. XXXIII. 355 On the absolute sway of the great *seat owners over King, Ministers, and People. 1885 J. B. Leno Boot & Shoemaking viii. 55 *Seat pieces for common work may be cut from almost any scraps of leather. 1865 Ch. Times 11 Mar. 76/4 The incumbent raised the *seat-rents to prevent the parishioners taking seats. 1821 Cobbett Rural Rides (1853) 14 Their blue arms and lips, would have made any heart ache, but that of a *seat-seller or a loan-jobber. 1817 — Pol. Reg. XXXII. 14, I did not believe that there could be any such thing as *seat-selling. 1895 Hasluck's Boot Making viii. 145 Gent's boots or shoes will only want a *seat-sock. 1876 Green Coal i. 25 *Seat-stones vary very much in their composition, the generality of them are clays. 1805 Shipwright's Vade-m. 129 *Seat transom,

that transom which is fayed and bolted to the counter-timbers, next above the deck transom, at the height of the port sills. 1790 A. Wilson Poems & Lit. Prose (1876) II. 242 'Groans fr. Loom', Go,..live o'er a *seat-tree—on nought! 1885 *Seat wheel [see seat iron above]. 1895 Hasluck's Boot Making viii. 130 Run the seat-wheel evenly round [the edge of the seat], so that it leaves..one straight line of regular indentations. 1893 R. H. Harte Local Therap. 158 Lime-water is used with advantage as an injection to destroy *Seat-worms.

Seat (sīt), v. [f. Seat sb.]

1. trans. To place on a seat or seats; to cause to sit down.

1613 Shaks. Hen. VIII, i. iv. 31 So now y'are fairely seated. 1662 J. Davies tr. Olearius' Voy. Ambass. 298 Their Poets and Historians are great frequenters of these places...These are seated in a high Chair, in the midst. 1669 Evelyn Diary 15 July, This ended, we were..seated by the Vice-Chancellor amongst the Doctors on his right hand. 1676 Wiseman Wounds ii. 91 Seat him [sc. the patient] so as it may be for your conveniency. 1725 Lond. Gaz. No. 6382/4 The Great Master..seated the Proxy down in the Stall. 1805 T. Lindley Voy. Brasil 150 The old man seated me. 1847 C. Brontë Jane Eyre xxiii, He seated me and himself. 1859 Geo. Eliot Adam Bede xlv, Dinah raised her gently from her knees, and seated her on the pallet again. fig. 1776 Toplady Hymn, 'Holy Ghost, dispel our Sadness', Seat us with Thy saints in glory. 1859 Tennyson Merlin & V. 727 Because of that high pleasure which I had To seat you sole upon my pedestal Of worship.

b. refl. To take one's seat, sit down. Const. at, in, upon, etc.

1589 Greene Menaphon (Arb.) 37 1st fit an Eagle seate him with a Flie! 1622 Mabbe tr. Aleman's Guzman d'Alf. ii. 100 To seate him-selfe sure in the Saddle. 1765 J. Brown Chr. Jrnl. 204 Yonder fly has seated himself upon the surface of a rough stone. 1779 Mirror No. 9 We went at an early hour, and seated ourselves in the middle of the pit. 1818 Scott Hrt. Midl. xx, 'Wha was it?'..said Effie, seating herself upright. 1833 T. Hook Parson's Dau. ii. xiv, Lady Catherine good-naturedly seated herself at the piano-forte. 1864 Lowell Fireside Trav. 245, I saw the landlady..seat herself amply before a row of baskets.

† c. intr. for refl. To sit down; also (of animals) to lie down. Of a hare: To sit in its form.

1596 Spenser F. Q. vi. ix. 4 The folds, where sheepe at night doe seat. 1609 W. M. Man in Moon (Percy Soc.) 7 Long had they not seated, but one knocked at the gate. 1610 Guillim Heraldry iii. xiv. (1660) 166 You shall say that a Hare Seateth or Formeth. 1686 Blome Gentl. Recr. ii. 76 A Hare Seateth or Formeth, a Coney Sitteth. 1760–72 H. Brooke Fool of Qual. (1809) IV. 146 There, seating,..I will now tell you, my uncle, says he.

d. trans. To cause or enable to sit in or on a throne, chair of state or office, or other seat of authority or dignity. Hence, to establish (a person) in a position of authority or dignity. Formerly without const., † to enthrone (a king).

1593 Shaks. 3 Hen. VI, i. i. 22 Before I see thee seated in that Throne, Which now the House of Lancaster vsurpes, I vow by Heauen, these eyes shall neuer close. 1600 E. Blount tr. Conestaggio 101 They doubted not to seate a King, at their pleasures. 1606 G. W[oodcocke] Hist. Justine ii. x. 13 Xerxes being thus mutually seated in the kingdome. 1667 Milton P. L. i. 720 To inshrine Belus or Serapis thir Gods, or seat Thir Kings. 1670 Cotton Espernon i. i. 22 By that means [she] seated her self absolute Mistress of that Court. 1715 Pope Iliad I. Ess. Homer 2 There is also in Mankind a Spirit of Envy or Opposition which makes them uneasy to see others of the same Species seated far above them in a sort of Perfection. a 1763 W. King Polit. & Lit. Anecd. (1819) 185 He [Burnet] was a better pastor than any man who is now seated on the bishops' bench. 1831 Scott Ct. Robt. xxiv, I could ill have kept my seat in the high place where Heaven has been pleased to seat me. 1847 Tennyson Princess iii. 143, I find you here but in the second place, Some say the third..We will seat you highest.

e. To put into a seat in a deliberative assembly.

1797 Burke Let. Affairs Ireland Wks. IX. 457 The new representative was at that time seated and installed by force and violence. 1818 Cruise Digest (ed. 2) III. 165 He was summoned to parliament..and was seated in the place of the ancient Barons of Berkeley. 1845 Disraeli Sybil iv. vii, Many of whom he has succeeded in seating in the parliament of his country. 1866 Pall Mall Gaz. No. 378. 1341/1 Mr. Kinglake has been seated for Bridgewater.

f. To find seats for; to accommodate with seats or sitting room; to assign seats to. Of a building, room, etc.: To afford sitting accommodation for.

1828–32 Webster, Seat,..to place in a church; to assign seats to. In New England..it is customary to seat families for a year or longer time; that is, assign and appropriate seats to their use. 1856 Merivale Rom. Emp. xli. (1871) V. 67 The first object..was to seat the greatest number of the people possible. 1887 Pall Mall Gaz. 9 Sept. 2/2 Each theatre should be registered and advertised as capable of seating a specified number.

2. Passive. To be sitting, to be in a sitting posture.

1608 Shaks. Per. ii. iv. 7 When he was seated in A Chariot of an inestimable value. 1703 Tate Hymn, 'While Shepherds watched', While Shepherds watched their flocks by night All seated on the ground. 1791 Cowper Yardley Oak 139 Seated here On thy distorted root. 1848 Thackeray Van. Fair xxiv, Osborne from his chair regarded Dobbin seated blank and silent opposite to him. 1875 W. S. Hayward Love agst. World i, Three young men are seated at breakfast.

3. trans. To place as a resident in a district or country; to settle or establish (a people, a body of colonists, etc.) in a particular locality. Now rare.

1589 Warner Alb. Eng. Prose Addit. 161 Seated wee must bee, and here wee would be. 1599 Shaks. Hen. V, i. ii. 62 Charles the Great Subdu'd the Saxons, and did seat the French Beyond the Riuer Sala. 1612 in Capt. Smith Map Virginia ii. 96 Mr West hauing seated his men at the Falles, presently returned...The President..followed him to the falles: where he found this company so inconsiderately seated, in a place not only subiect to the rivers invndation, but [etc.]. 1639 Fuller Holy War ii. xxvi. (1640) 77 The Carmelites..were first seated at Newenden in Kent. 1719 De Foe Crusoe i. (Globe) 197 Providence, which so happily had seated me at the Brasils, as a Planter. 1776 Gibbon Decl. & F. x. (1782) I. 295 In the age of the Antonines, the Goths were still seated in Prussia. 1797 Washington Let. Writ. 1892 XIII. 406 If..they could have been first seated as tenants. 1910 Hirth in Encycl. Brit. VI. 191/1 Whether the Chinese were seated in their later homes from time immemorial,—or whether [etc.].

† b. refl. To take up a permanent abode, to settle (in a place). Obs.

1601 R. Johnson Kingd. & Commw. (1603) 112 Whose tenants to injoy the liberties granted to Nepolitans, did forsake their owne..to seate themselves there. 1639 Fuller Holy War v. v. (1640) 236 They wonne the Island of Rhodes from the Turks..and there seated themselves. 1755 Acts Assembly Pennsylv. (1762) II. 54 Many Persons residing in this Province have seated themselves on certain large Tracts of Land, neither having Property therein, or paying Rent for the same. 1797 Encycl. Brit. (ed. 3) X. 693/1 At length, in 1638, the Dutch seated themselves here [Mauritius].

† c. intr. for refl. To settle down permanently, to establish a residence, to fix or take up abode. Obs.

1622 Relat. Eng. Plant. Plymouth, New Eng. 4 Some of our people..desired..to travaile by Land into the Countrey,..to see whether it might be fit for vs to seate in or no. 1683 Bingham Xenophon's Anab. iii. ii. 48 If he perceived, we prepared our selues to seat here. 1697 in W. S. Perry Hist. Coll. Amer. Col. Ch. I. 44 Abundance of People were desirous to seat there. 1709 J. Lawson New Voy. Carolina 141 [This] would doubtless be a great prejudice to the Planters that should seat there.

transf. 1612 T. Taylor Comm. Titus ii. 3 The knowledge of God seateth not in their hearts. 1655 Vaughan Silex Scint. i. 126 Thy root sucks but diseases; worms there seat And claim it for their meat.

d. passive. To have one's 'seat' or mansion in a specified place.

1683 Evelyn Diary 13 Oct., A..gentleman, seated neere Worcester, and very curious in gardening. a 1845 Barham Ingol. Leg. Ser. iii. Blasphemer's Warning (init.), In Kent we are told There was seated of old, A handsome young gentleman. 1859 Symonds' Diary (Camden) 75 note, Although the grandfather of Sir Richard became seated in Cornwall by his marriage with a coheiress of Trethurffe.

4. trans. With a thing as object: To place in a 'seat' or situation. (Rare exc. passive as in 5.) a. To set or secure in its proper place; to fix in proper position on a base or support. Now only Mech. † Also intr. for refl. to lie, rest upon.

1605 B. Jonson Volpone ii. i, In youth it perpetually preserues, in age restores the complexion; seat's your teeth, did they dance like Virginall iacks, firme as a wall. [Cf. 1667 s. v. Seated ppl. a. 1.] 1662 R. Mathew Unl. Alch. 153 Clap into thy Furnace an iron Kettle, and let the bottom thereof seat upon the iron Barr. 1688 Holme Armoury iii. 89/2 Seat the Shooe, fit it to the Foot [of a horse]. 1872 Spon's Dict. Engin. v. 1804 The slotted head of the common wood screw is frequently split when much force is required to seat it or to remove it.

b. To locate or establish in a specified place.

1603 Knolles Hist. Turks (1638) 143 He himselfe made choice of the city Neapolis..to seat his regall Palace in. 1650 Bulwer Anthropomet. xi. (1653) 183 Neither would she have seated the mouth in so eminent, open, and conspicuous a place. c 1750 Shenstone Elegy i. 30 In thy youthful soul Love's gentle tyrant seats his awful throne.

† c. To found (a city). Obs. rare.

1612 Heywood Apol. for Actors i. 23 Thebes, seated by Cadmus. a 1657 W. Bradford Plymouth Plantation (1856) 368 Their neigbours of ye Massachusets..had some years after seated a towne (called Hingam) on their lands.

5. In passive, to have its seat, be situated.

a. Of a country, town, house, etc.: To be situated in a certain position; to have a certain kind of situation (e. g. as regards salubrity or pleasantness).

1577 B. Googe Heresbach's Husb. iv. (1586) 172 Euery house is not so seated, as it hath erable ground about it. 1593 Shaks. Lucr. 1144 Some darke deepe desert seated from the way, That knowes not parching heat, nor freezing cold, Will wee find out. 1615 Brathwait Strappado 83 A pleasant Vale seated belowe Some steepy Mount. 1631 Weever Anc. Funeral Mon. 284 The Mannor of Shurland seated Eastward from hence. 1633 Heywood Eng. Trav. iii. F 3 b, [The house] 'tis well seated, Rough-cast without, but brauely lined within. 1655 Marq. Worcester Cent. Invent. § 100 To..furnish Cities with water though never so high seated. 1700 Dryden Sigism. & Guisc. 221 The Garden, seated on the level Floor. 1707 Mortimer Husb. (1721) I. 93 Lands seated on Marle are usually very rich. 1857 Zoologist XV. 5618 The house was seated in a pretty garden. 1872 Yeats Growth Comm. 52 Seated on the confines of Europe and Asia, it [Byzantium] links the two shores of the Bosphorus. 1877 Huxley Physiogr. 213 London..is seated on clay.

b. Hence of a person with reference to his dwelling. Also fig.

1596 Shaks. Merch. V. i. ii. 8 They are as sicke that surfet with too much, as they that starue with nothing; it is no smal happinesse therefore to be seated in the meane. 1598 Hakluyt Voy. I. 65 When we came vnto Bathy..we were seated a good league distant from his tabernacles. 1601 B. Jonson Poetaster ii. i. (init.), You are most delicately seated here, full of sweet delight and blandishment! an excellent ayre! 1624 Wotton Elem. Archit. i. 5 By no meanes to build too nere a great Neighbour, which were in truth to bee as vnfortunately seated on the earth, as Mercurie is in the Heauens. 1803 Wellington To Lieut.-Gen. Stuart in Gurw. Desp. (1835) II. 73 It appears..that we shall have a war immediately, or a protracted negotiation with Scindiah and the Rajah of Berar, seated upon the Nizam's frontier.

† c. Of a material object: To have a certain place (e. g. in the body, in a building). Obs.

c 1580 Sidney Ps. (1823) xxii. ix, Whose hart..Doth melt away, though it be inmost seated. 1632 G. Herbert Priest to Temple xiii. (1830) 35 A poor man's box conveniently seated, to receive the charity of well-minded people. 1728 Chambers Cycl. s.v. Eye, In Birds, and some other Creatures, the Eyes are so seated, as to take in near a whole Sphere.

d. Of a seed or fruit (with transferred notion of sense 2): To be fixed on something, or in a particular place.

1857 T. Moore Handbk. Brit. Ferns (ed. 3) 8 The part of the vein on which the sorus is seated is called the receptacle. 1882–4 Cooke Brit. Fresh-w. Algæ I. 175 Dwarf males seated upon or about the oogonia.

e. Of an immaterial thing, a quality, feeling, etc.: To have its seat or abode in a certain place.

1602 Shaks. Ham. iii. iv. 55 See what a grace was seated on his Brow. 1622 Fletcher Sea Voy. i. iii, The greatest plagues that humane nature suffers, Are seated here, wildnesse, and wants innumerable. 1691 Hartcliffe Virtues 263 Their Inclinations, which are seated in the Heart. 1748 Melmoth Fitzosborne Lett. lii. (1749) II. 61 The latter [i. e. generosity] is seated in the mind. 1820 Hazlitt Lect. Dram. Lit. 8 We there see..the same thoughts passing through the mind and seated on the lips.

f. Of a disease: To have its seat in a certain part of the body. Also To be deeply seated: lit. to be situated far below the surface; hence (often fig.) to be firmly established in the system, to be beyond the reach of superficial remedies.

a 1619 Fotherby Atheom. i. xiii. § 3 (1622) 140 His plague was seated into his bowells. 1647 N. Ward Simp. Cobler 6 Fiery diseases, seated in the spirit, embroile the whole frame of the body. 1843 R. J. Graves Syst. Clin. Med. xxvi. 330 Spongy chancres..were seated on the inner lamella of the prepuce. 1871 Smiles Charac. vii. 212 note, The disease had become too deeply seated for recovery. 1893 W. R. Gowers Man. Dis. Nerv. Syst. (ed. 2) IV. 333 [Miliary tubercles are] seated in the pia mater.

† 6. trans. To 'plant' with inhabitants, people, settle (a country). Obs. (App. N. American.)

1684 in Pennsylv. Arch. I. 85 Vpon. Lands not Seated before in ye Dukes Time. 1776 C. Carroll Jrnl. Vis. Canada in B. Mayer Mem. (1845) 78 The country on each side of the St. Lawrence is level, rich, and thickly seated; indeed, so thickly seated, that the houses form almost one continued row. 1784 Washington Writ. 1891 X. 366 To see these lands seated by particular societies.

7. To fix a seat on (a chair); to repair (trousers, a chair) by renewing or mending the seat.

1762 Foote Orators ii. (1780) 46 As I was sitting cross-legged on my shop-board, new seating a cloth pair of breeches. 1828–32 Webster, Seat,..to repair by making a seat new; as, to seat a garment. 1886 Pall Mall Gaz. 15 Apr. 14/1 Then the chair is handed over to the women to be 'seated'.

8. To furnish (a building, a room, etc.) with seats.

1818 Scott Rob Roy xx, A portion of which was seated with pews, and used as a church. 1870 F. R. Wilson Ch. Lindisf. 69 The nave is now seated with two rows of low-backed benches. 1899 Eclectic Mag. Feb. 201 A..carriage which was seated for fifteen.

b. (See quot.) Cf. 1 f.

1828–32 Webster, Seat,..to appropriate the pews in, to particular families; as, to seat a church.

Seatage (sī·tėdʒ). [f. Seat v. + -age.] Seating accommodation.

1889 Daily News 19 July 2/2 More than half the total seatage.

Seated (sī·tėd), ppl. a. [f. Seat sb. and v. + -ed.]

1. Fixed in position. Obs. or arch.

1605 Shaks. Macb. i. iii. 136 Whose horrid Image doth vnfixe my Heire, And make my seated Heart knock at my Ribbes. 1667 Milton P. L. vi. 644 From their foundations loosning to and fro They pluckt the seated Hills with all thir load, Rocks, Waters, Woods.

† 2. With adverb: (Well) situated; (well) provided with a 'seat' or mansion. Obs.

1621 in Kempe Losely MSS. (1836) 456 Bruxells..being a well seated and well watered towne as evr I sawe. 1663 Gerbier Counsel b 5 Your..well seated Pallace with a wood at its back. 1720 De Foe Capt. Singleton (1906) 278 Mr. Knox was so well seated, and could not be supposed to leave such an estate.

3. Sitting down; in a sitting posture or condition. The Seated Lady, the constellation Cassiopeia.

1818 Scott Rob Roy xx, The seated part of the congregation. 1870 Murray's Handbk. Essex, etc. 206 Seated figures of the Apostles serve as pinnacles of the buttresses. 1886 Proctor in Sci. Amer. 3 July 3/3 Low down, between north and north-east, we find the Seated Lady (Cassiopeia).

4. Of a room, etc.: Provided with seats.

1829 Bentham Justice & Cod. Petit., Abr. Petit. Justice 37 The appeal goes..from the four-seated court in Westminster Hall to the House of Lords.

5. Provided with a seat, as a chair, pair of trousers, etc. Only in parasynthetic formations, as double-, hard-, two-seated, etc.

1841 J. T. Hewlett Parish Clerk II. 163 Several hard-seated wooden chairs. 1898 Cycling 21 Cycling knickerbockers should all be double-seated outside. 1903 Westm. Gaz. 25 Sept. 8/2 Two-seated vehicles.

6. U.S. (See quot.) Obs. exc. Hist.

1877 W. H. Burroughs On Taxation 208 In Pennsylvania, prior to 1844, seated lands, that is, lands occupied by residence, or cultivation, could not be sold for taxes.

Seater (sī·təɹ). rare. [f. Seat sb. and v. + -er.]

† 1. N. American. ? One who apportions the sittings in a meeting-house. Obs.

1713 S. Sewall Diary 4 May (1879) II. 381 Mr. Pemberton declares a Necessity of adding to the number of the Seaters.

Ibid. 10 June II. 389 Mr. Pemberton..would not have me resign my Seaters place now.

2. Comb.: two-seater, a motor-car having two seats.

1906 Daily Chron. 15 Nov. 3/6 Two-cylinder, two-seater car.

† **Seath.** Obs. Also 7 seth (9 seeth). [OE. séað masc. = OFris. sâth (NFris. soath, suad, suas, EFris. sôth, sôd, WFris. saed), LG. sood draw-well, MHG. sôt:—OTeut. *sauþo-z.] A pit, hole, well, or pool.

c 950 Lindisf. Gosp. Mark xii. 1 Wingeard gesette monn & ymb-salde haga & dalf seað [L. lacum]. c 1205 Lay. 841 Heo nomen þæt þær & wel hit biburiede inne deope seaðen. 1656 Smith & Webb Vale-Royal i. 66 A Seth or pit of that Brine. 1877 E. Leigh Cheshire Gloss., Seath or Seeth, an old word, found in some legal documents, for a brine-pit.

Seath, var. Saithe; obs. f. Seethe v.

Sea·-thief. [Cf. G. seedieb.] A pirate, a sea-rover.

c 1050 Voc. in Wr.-Wülcker 317/26 Archipiratta, heah sædeof. 1387 Trevisa Higden (Rolls) I. 173 Sclauonia..haþ wylde men and see þeues. Ibid. VI. 415 Þe see þeves of Danes. 1576 Curteys Two Serm. C j b, Th'one be Sea theeues suche as lye in the straights and corners of the Sea, & take other mens goods from them by force. 1627 Drayton Elegies, Lady Aston's Dep. 50 Or if some proling Rouer shall but dare, To seize the ship..., Let the fell fishes of the Maine appeare, And tell those Sea-thiefes, that [etc.]. 1891 E. Peacock N. Brendon I. 59 The sea-thieves were taken by surprise.

transf. 1591 Sylvester Du Bartas i. v. 340 Those small white Fish..Combine themselves, that their joynt strength doth hold Against the greediest of the Sea-theeves' sallies.

Seathin, obs. form of Shittim.

Sea·-thistle.

1. The sea-holly, Eryngium maritimum. ? Obs.

In quot. c 1265 perh. the water-caltrops (Caltrop 3).

c 1265 [see Caltrop 3]. 1608 Topsell Serpents 43 The Sea-thistle called Eryngium marinum, which some call Sea-hull, or Huluer. 1626 Bacon Sylva § 568 Eryngium, (Sea-Thistle). 1805 Forsyth Beauties Scot. II. 365 The coast..produces scurvy-grass, colewort, and sea-thistle.

† 2. The echinus or sea-urchin. Obs.—[1]

1661 Lovell Hist. Anim. & Min. 230 They are so full of prickles, that they cannot be held, therefore some call them the Sea Thistles.

† 3. In full sea-thistle weed: ? gulf-weed. Obs.

1703 Dampier Voy. III. i. 14 We..saw Flying-fish, and a great deal of Sea-Thistle Weed floating. 1727 Dorrington Philip Quarll (1754) 66 We saw some Flying-fish, and a great deal of Sea-thistle swimming.

Seating (sī·tiŋ), vbl. sb. [f. Seat sb. and v. + -ing [1].]

† 1. The action of providing with a residence, or of settling in a country; quasi-concr. opportunity for settling, footing. Also (N. American) colonization, settlement (of a country). Obs.

1596 Spenser State Irel. Wks. (Globe) 666 Also doe I greatly mislike the lord Deputyes seating at Dublin. 1603 Knolles Hist. Turks (1638) 153 Promising also to giue them aid for the seating of them there [in Achaia and Bœotia]. 1611 Speed Hist Gt. Brit. v. vii. § 9 There are reported to haue come into Ireland..& finding no seating there to haue entered into Britaine. 1624 Wotton Elem. Archit. 6 In the seating of our selues..Builders should bee as circumspect as Wooers. 1699 Phil. Trans. XXI. 441 At the first Seating of Maryland there were several Nations of Indians in the Country.

2. The action of providing with seats; the manner in which a building, etc. is seated; concr. the seats with which a building, etc. is provided.

1880 Daily News 7 Oct. 2/5 The seating of the church is but little altered. 1895 Ibid. 11 Dec. 5/3 Additional seating has been provided.

3. Material for upholstering the seats of chairs, etc.

1833 J. Bennett Artificer's Lexicon 366 Seating. Horse-hair for sofas, chairs, &c. 1858 Simmonds Dict. Trade, Seating, horse-hair fabric, American leather, or other materials, made for covering the cushions of chairs, couches, &c. 1909 Athenæum 20 Mar. 340/1 Chair seating..most of this seating is now done with split canes instead of rushes.

4. Mech. A fitted support for a part of a structure or machine, usually pl. or collect. sing.

1844 Civil Eng. & Arch. Jrnl. VII. 191/1 An arrangement like that of the plunger pump, which permitted both valves to be fixed in seatings. 1868 Fairley Gloss. Coal-Mining Bristol, etc. 29 Seating, the place in the pumps where the clack is seated. 1889 Hasluck Model Eng. Handybk. (1900) 71 The seatings for the lugs of the cylinder.

5. That part of a structure, etc. which rests on some other part. Ship-building (see quot. 1805; and cf. Seat sb. 22).

1805 Shipwright's Vade-mecum 129 Seating, that part of the floor which fays on the deadwood; and of a transom which fays against the post. 1838 Civil Eng. & Arch. Jrnl. I. 178/2 The wedges were then struck, and the weight of the ribs thrown upon their seatings and head joints. 1889 in Anglin Design of Structures (1891) 488 All girders shall have seatings of the best hair felt, graduated in lengths so as to insure the pressure being on the centre of bearing when the greatest load is on the girder.

6. attrib. a. (of sense 4), as seating block, plate.

1838 Civ. Engin. & Arch. Jrnl. I. 178/1 The masonry at each end [of the bridge] was ready to receive the cast-iron seating plates of the wood arch. 1884 Health Exhib. Catal. 55/1 Boiler Seating Blocks.

b. (in the sense of providing seats or sitting room for), as seating accommodation, capacity.

1887 Pall Mall Gaz. 9 Sept. 2/2 In no case should the seating capacity [of a theatre] ever be exceeded. 1907 H. Wyndham Flare of Footlights i, The seating accommodation [of the theatre] embodied every new device for the comfort of its occupants that ingenuity could suggest.

Seatless (sī·tlės), a. [f. Seat sb. + -less.] Having no seat or seats (in any sense of the sb.).

1807 J. Barlow Columb. ii. 229 What a world their seatless nations led! 1826 The Ass i Apr. 1 A sleeveless coat and seatless breeches. 1859 All Year Round No. 30. 78 The third-class carriages..were..seatless and unsheltered cattle-trucks. 1871 Pall Mall Gaz. 19 Jan., Three seatless chairs.

Sea·-toad.

1. A name given to several fishes, as a. The fishing-frog or angler, Lophius piscatorius. b. U. S. The sculpin. c. 'The toadfish, Batrachus tau' (Cent. Dict. 1891).

1558 Rondelet Gesner's Hist. Anim. iv. 961 Seetode id est rubetam marinam Anglicè. c 1540 J. Smyth Hund. Berkeley (1885) 319 An haddocke, a Roucote, the sea tad. 1700 C. Leigh Nat. Hist. Lanc., etc. i. 186 The Rana Piscatrix or Sea-Toad found frequently in the River Wire in Lancashire. 1884 Goode, etc. Nat. Hist. Aquatic Anim. 258 On our Atlantic coast are found several species of this family [Cottidæ], generally known by the name 'Sculpin', and also by such titles as..'Sea-toad', and 'Pig-fish'.

† 2. ? Some kind of starfish. Obs.—[1]

1710 Sibbald Fife & Kinross 84 Stella Marina squamosa; the Fishers call it the Sea-Toad, for that in colour it resembles a Toad.

3. The great spider-crab (see quot.).

1857 A. White Brit. Crustacea 22 The Hyas...Mr. Gordon says that the fishermen there [sc. Moray Firth] call it 'sea-tead', that is sea-toad.

4. ? nonce-use. A turtle.

1754 Garrick Prol. to J. Brown's 'Barbarossa', He eat a great Sea-Toad! It came from Indies—'twas as big as me, He call'd it Belly-patch and Capapee.

Seaton, obs. form of Seton.

Sea-tortoise. A marine tortoise or turtle. Also Comb. sea-tortoise-shell.

[1398 Trevisa Barth. De P. R. xviii. cviii. (1495) 850 The see Tortuca etyth all thynge and his mouth is stronger than any other beestes mouth.] 1601 Holland Pliny xi. xxxvii. I. 339 The sea-Tortoise hath neither tongue nor teeth. 1681 Grew Musæum iii. § i. i. 260 The spaces betwixt which [rows], are cancellated much after the manner of the Sea-Tortoiseshell. 1698 Fryer Acc. E. Ind. & P. 122 A Sea-Tortoise was brought to the Fort, in length Six Feet. 1750 G. Edwards Nat. Hist. Birds IV. 206 The Sea-Tortoise is commonly call'd by our Sea-Captains Turtle. 1881 Freeman in W. R. W. Stephens Life & Lett. (1895) II. 237 A terrapin is..a small turtle or sea-tortoise.

Sea·-town. Now rare. (Common in 17th c.) A town situated on or near the sea, a sea-port town.

1578 J. Stockwood Serm. 24 Aug. 36 Cesarea was a Sea-town, not far from the Mount Carmel. 1622 Bacon Hen. VII, 61 A maritime Prouince, full of Sea-townes, and Hauens. 1796 Burke Regic. Peace Wks. VIII. 373 These two islands, with their extensive, and every where vulnerable coast, should be considered as a garrisoned sea-town. 1905 Westm. Gaz. 30 Jan. 2/3 The darkening roofs of the sea-town.

† **Sea-tree.** Obs.

1. A huge polyp [L. arbor marina].

1601 Holland Pliny xxxii. xi. II. 451 [The 'greatest monsters' of the sea are] The Sea-Trees, Whirlepooles [etc.]. 1611 Florio, Albero,..a monstrous sea-fish, called the Sea-tree.

2. Some tree-like seaweed.

1601 Holland Pliny xiii. xxv. I. 402 The branches and leaves of the sea trees, so long as they were under water looked greene, but when they be taken forth, presently dried with the heat of the Sunne. 1666 J. Davies Hist. Caribby Isles 127 Sea-Trees...Certain Trees which are immediately glaz'd with a salt-peter, which renders them extremely white. Some conceive them to be a kind of Coral. 1755 tr. Pontoppidan's Nat. Hist. Norway i. 152 The ocean here produces various species of large vegetables, which are known by the name of sea-trees. 1758 Phil. Trans. L. 634 This pivot..forms something like the knot of the sea-tree. 1823–4 in Encycl. Metrop. (1845) XV. 298/2 The sea-tree lines many parts of the coast [of St. Bartholomew], has its leaves platted together, and looks as if it was completely glazed.

Sea·-trout.

1. The Salmo trutta, = Salmon-trout 1; also the bull or grey trout, S. eriox.

1745 tr. Egede's Descr. Greenland 91 Small Salmon or Sea-Trout of different Kinds and Sizes. 1769–76 Pennant Brit. Zool. III. 259. 1875 F. Francis in Encycl. Brit. II. 41/1 Next to the salmon ranks in value for sport the sea-trout. Of these there are two kinds: 1st, The salmon-trout (Salmo trutta); and 2d, The bull or grey trout (Salmo eriox).

2. In U. S. and Australia applied to other fishes.

1859–62 Sir J. Richardson, etc. Mus. Nat. Hist. (1868) II. 126 The Sea-trouts of Australian seas belong to the genus Arripis. 1884 Goode, etc. Nat. Hist. Aquatic Anim. 267 (Hexagrammus decagrammus..)...From San Francisco southward, the names 'Rock Trout' and 'Sea Trout' are common. Ibid. 362 With the other members of the genus [the Squeteague] is spoken of under the name 'Sea Trout'. 1891 Century Dict., Sea trout, 1. Any catadromous trout or char, as the common brook-trout of the United States, Salvelinus fontinalis.

3. attrib.

1875 F. Francis in Encycl. Brit. II. 41/1 A day's sea-trout fishing. 1904 Gallichan Fishing & Shooting in Spain 28, I was soon trying to lure him with a sea-trout fly.

Sea-trumpet.

† 1. A trumpet-shell or triton-shell. Obs.

1668 Charleton Onomast. 177 Cancellus in Buccino degens, the bigger Souldier-Crab dwelling in the Sea-Trumpet.

2. A kind of trumpet used at sea.

1776 Burney Hist. Mus. I. 522 The Concha, Tromba Marina, or Sea-Trumpet.

3. A very large seaweed, Ecklonia buccinalis. So called because the hollow upper part of the stem when dried, is used as a trumpet at the Cape of Good Hope.

1829 Loudon Encycl. Plants (1836) 945 L[aminaria] buccinalis furnishes the singular vegetable production called the sea-trumpet. 1866 Treas. Bot. s.v. 1882 J. Smith Dict. Pop. Names Plants 419 Trumpet, Sea (Ecklonia buccinalis) a strong-growing seaweed of the Laminaria section of Algæ.

Seatsman (sī·tsmăn).

† 1. A shoemaker. Obs. rare. Cf. Seat sb.

1719 D'Urfey Pills V. 241 The Character of a Seat's-man; written by one of the Craft.

2. One who makes the seats of clogs.

1881 Instr. Census Clerks (1885) 76 Patten, Clog Maker ..Clog Clasper. Clog Seatsman.

Seattica, obs. form of Sciatica.

† **Sea·t-town.** Obs.

1. A town used as the head-quarters of an army.

1591 Savile Tacitus, Hist. iii. xxxii. 133 It was chosen ..for the seate-towne of the warre [L. belli sedes]. 1610 Holland Camden's Brit. i. 237 Robert Bishop of Constance..chose it for the Seat-towne of the whole warre.

2. A capital town, = Seat sb. 13.

1601 Holland Pliny vi. xxvii. I. 138 The auncient royall pallace and seat towne of the Persian K[ings].

Sea-turtle [1]. The black guillemot.

1678 Ray Willughby's Ornith. 326 The Greenland-Dove or Sea-Turtle: Columba Groenlandica dicta. 1752 J. Hill Hist. Anim. 446 The Colymbus with webbed feet, and three toes to each. The Sea-turtle. 1896 Newton Dict. Birds s. v. Turtle, Greenland Turtle and Sea-Turtle are sailors' names for the Black Guillemot.

Sea-turtle [2]. A turtle or sea-tortoise.

1764 Ann. Reg. 92 Lately taken..on the Devonshire coast ..a sea-turtle, about seven feet long. 1860 Gosse Rom. Nat. Hist. (1861) 357 Two pairs of paddles, very much like those of a sea-turtle.

Seatwell, obs. form of Setwall.

Seau, Seaul: see Sew, pottage; Seal sb.[2]

Sea-unicorn.

1. The Narwhal.

1646 Sir T. Browne Pseud. Ep. iii. xxiii. 167 The Sea-Unicornes,..are of that strength and bignesse, as able to penetrate the ribs of ships. a 1711 Ken Edmund Poet. Wks. 1721 II. 30 The Angel a Sea-Unicorn espy'd. 1853 Kane Grinnell Exp. xxxvii. (1856) 340 That monodontal process which gives them their name of sea-unicorn.

attrib. 1858 Simmonds Dict. Trade, Sea-unicorn Tooth, a name for the spiral horn or tusk of the narwhal

2. = Sea-bat 3.

1830 J. F. South in Encycl. Metrop. (1845) XXI. 722 Near the openings of the nostrils is a little, hard, horny appendage, terminating in a tubercle, and hence the fish [Malthe vespertilio] has sometimes been called the Sea Unicorn.

Sea·-urchin.

1. An animal of the genus Echinus (see Echinus 1) or the order Echinoidea.

1591 Sylvester Du Bartas i. v. 382 What stile can worthily declare (O! Galley-Fish,..and Sea-Urchin) your dexterity In Sailor's Art. 1681 Grew Musæum i. § vi. i. 139 The round Sea-Urchin or Button-Fish. Echinus orbicularis. Ibid., The Great Oval Sea-Urchin. Echinometra Aristotelis. 1704 Petiver Gazophyl. iv. 36 Mr. James Cuninghame found this elegant Sea Urchin on the Coast of China. 1895 tr. Boas' Text-bk. Zool. 134 In some Sea-urchins the body is almost spherical.

¶ 2. Humorously applied to a young sailor.

1824 W. Irving T. Trav. (1850) 414 The domineering spirit of this boisterous sea-urchin at length grew quite intolerable.

Seave (sīv). north. Forms: 5, 9 seve, 5 reyfe, 5, 9 seive, 8 seave, 8–9 sieve, 6– seave, 9 seeave (see also Eng. Dial. Dict.). [a. ON. sef (Sw. säf, Da. siv).] A rush; also, a rushlight.

14.. Nominale in Wr.-Wülcker 712/9 Hic papirus, a seue [printed sene]. c 1450 St. Cuthbert (Camden) 470 He began þe seiues graythe, And made a fournays for þe bell. 1483 Cath. Angl. 327/2 A Seyfe, iuncus. 1594 in Trans. Cumb. & Westm. Archæol. Soc. (1903) III. 152 None..shall mowe or sheare any seaves between Tailbothe and Sleddaile. 1684 Meriton Yorksh. Dial. 72 Then strike a Fire, and leet a Seave I Reed. 1777 Wallingfen Inclos. Act 21 Seaves, reeds, whinns, or sods.

b. attrib., as † seave-busk (= bush), -candle, -light; seave-cap, the black-headed bunting.

1483 Cath. Angl. 327/2 A *Seyfebuske, iuncetum. 1703 Thoresby Let. to Ray Philos. Lett. (1718) 336 Seaves, pill'd Rushes, of which they make *Seav Candles. 1866 Atkinson Prov. Names Birds, *Seave-cap..Black-headed Bunting Emberiza Schœniclus.

Seave, Seaven, obs. ff. Sieve sb., Seven.

Seaver, obs. form of Sever.

Sea-view.

1. A picture representing a scene at sea, a 'seascape'.

1781 Reynolds Journ. Flanders & Holl. Wks. 1797 II. 80 The picture..appears to be a sea-view. 1817 Lady Morgan France v. (1818) II. 37 Altering the position of the pictures ..and adding to their number the sea-views of Vernet.

2. A view or prospect of the sea, or at sea.

1864 A. McKay Hist. Kilmarnock (1880) 289 A fine sea-view from the hills of Dundonald. 1872 Calverley Fly Leaves (1903) 32 Those 'Lodgings with an ample sea-view', Which were..'To Let'. 1897 'A. Hope' Phroso ii. (1905) 25 About half-way up,..and commanding a splendid sea-view, stood an old grey battlemented house.

Sea-voyage. A voyage by sea.

1609 Field Woman a Weathercock i. (1612) C 2, Captain, what think'st thou of such a woman in a long Sea Voyage? a 1649 Drumm. of Hawth. Poems (1656) 204 Life a Sea-voyage is, Death is the Haven. 1726 Swift Gulliver ii. iv, Having been long used to sea voyages, those motions, although sometimes very violent, did not much discompose

Seavy. 1. A wall or embankment to prevent the encroachment of the sea, or to form a breakwater, etc.

Sea-wall.

Seaward, adv. and a.

Sea-washed, a. Washed by the sea; exposed to the 'wash' of the sea.

Sea-water. 1. The water of the sea, or water taken from the sea.

Sea-willow.

Sea-wind. A wind from the sea; a wind blowing from the sea.

Sea-wing.

Sea-way, sea way. 1. A way over the sea; the sea as a means of communication; the open sea.

Sea-weary, a.

Seaweed.

Sea-worm.

Seaworthiness.

Seaworthy.

Sea-worn, a. Worn or abraded by the sea; also worn out or wrecked by it.

Sea-wrack. Forms: see Wrack.

Se-baptism. Eccl. Hist.

Se-baptist.

Sebacic.

Sebaceous.

Sebat (se'bæt), Shebat. [Heb.] The eleventh month of the Jewish ecclesiastical year and fifth of the civil year.

Sebate. Chem.

Sebastian.

Sebate.

Sebific, a.

Seblet.

Sebolith. Path.

Seborrhœa. Path.

Sebow, variant of Sibbo.

Sebum (sī'bŏm).

Sebundy (sē'bŭndĭ). Also 8 sibbandy, -ondy, sybundee, 9 seboonde, sith'bundy, 9 silb'bundi, sib'bandi, sebundee, -y, sibi, sirbandi, sibondi.

Secability.

Secable.

Secale (sĕkē'lĭ). Bot.

Secancy.

Secant (sē'kănt).

Secede (sĕsī'd), v.

Seceder (sĕsī'dăr).

Secern (sĕsĕ'rn), v.

Secerned (sĕsĕ'rnd), ppl. a.

Secernent (sĕsĕ'rnĕnt).

Secerning.

Secernment (sĕsĕ'rnmĕnt).

Secesh (sĕsĕ'sh). U.S. Hist.

Secess.

Secession (sĕsĕ'shŏn).

Secessional.

Secessionism.

Secessionist.

Secessive, a.

Seck (sĕk), a.

Seckel (sĕk'ĕl). Also Seckle.

Secle.

Seclude (sĕklū'd), v.

Secondariness. [f. SECONDARY a. -NESS.] The quality of being secondary or subordinate.

Secondary, (sekǎrndări), a. and sb. Also 4-5 secondarye, secondaries, secundari, arye, 4-7 secundarie, 4-6 secondary, 5-7 secondari(e. [ad. L. secundāri-us of the second class or quality, f. secund-us: see SECOND a. and -ARY.]

Secondary, adv. Obs. rare. [f. SECONDARY a. -LY².] = SECONDARILY.

Second sight.

Second-handed, a. Now chiefly dial.

Secondly (sekǎndli), adv. [f. SECOND a. -LY².]

Secondment. rare. [f. SECOND v. + -MENT.]

Secondrate, a.

Secour, variant of SECUTOR Obs., executor.

† Secre, a. and sb. Obs. Also 4-5 secree, secre.

Secrecy (sī′krēsi). Forms: 4-5 secrenes, 6 secretie, 7(9) 6 secrecie 6 secretie ; 4 secreste, 6-9 secrecy- [f. SECRE a. + -CY.]

Secrement. Obs. rare-¹. [ad. L. secrement-um, f. secernere, secretum to secrete. Cf. EXCREMENT.]

Secrenes(s, obs. forms of SECRECY.

Secret (sī′krĕt), a. and sb. Also 4-5 secrete, 4-6 secrette, 5 secreet, 5 secrett, 5-6 secrete, secreate, (secri). [a. F. secret, ad. L. sēcrēt-um, pa. pple. of sēcernĕre to separate, divide off (se- apart + cernĕre to separate). Cf. F. secrète, Pr. secreto, Pg. secreto, It. secreto, segreto.]

Secret (continued)

stranger, being transported And kept in secret studies.

h. Of a committee, conclave, etc.: Conducted with secrecy; that keeps its deliberations unknown to the public.

i. Hidden from sight; not discernible or visible; unseen. Chiefly *poet.*

k. Of a place, drawer, passage, or mechanical contrivance: Designed to escape observation or detection. *Secret ink:* 'invisible' or 'sympathetic' ink.

l. Of a sound: Little audible. *Obs. rare.*

m. Of an agent: That works in secret. Of a person: That is secretly (what is expressed by the sb.).

†l. *Secret Flowers of Edgar.* 27 The Stockdoves secret parts make lumpifsh, dull, and deddie.

2. In various specific collocations.

a. *Secret Counsel.* Sc., the Scottish Privy Council.

b. *Secret service.* Services rendered to a government, the nature of which cannot be disclosed to the public, but which are paid for from a fund set apart for the purpose. Also *attrib.*, as *secret service fund, money; secret-service agent, man,* one employed on secret service by government. Also *transf.*

c. *Secret society,* an organization formed to promote some cause by secret methods, its members being sworn to observe secrecy.

d. *attrib.,* as *secret-natured, -tongued.*

B. sb.

1. Something kept secret.

b. Something unknown or unrevealed or that is known only by initiation or revelation; a mystery; chiefly *pl.,* the hidden affairs or workings (of God, Nature, Science, etc.).

2. Of a person: † Reserved or reticent in conduct or conversation (*obs.*); not given to indiscreet talking or the revelation of secrets; silent as to any matter, uncommunicative. Close.

†3. That is entrusted with a person's private or secret affairs; that is a confidant; intimate with.

†4. *fig.* of silence, night.

5. Some fact, affair, design, action, etc., the knowledge of which is kept to oneself or shared only with those whom it concerns or to whom it has been confided; something that cannot be divulged without violation of a command or breach of confidence. Frequently with an adj. prefixed, esp. as an intensive, as *a dead, entire, profound secret.*

b. In Liturgical use: A prayer or prayers said by the celebrant in a low voice after the Offertory and before the Preface. See SECRETA 1.

6. In the Biblical phrase, *the secrets of (one's) heart.*

7. (Chiefly in senses 3-4.) *To be in* (rarely † *on*) *the secret,* to be one of the participants in a secret; *† to be of secrets with,* to share the confidence or secret (of a person); *to be* (a person) *into the secret,* to confide (to him) the secret (of an affair, trade); hence *slang* (see quots. a 1700 [?, 1801]); *to make a secret of* (something), to make (it) a matter of concealment, to keep (it) unknown.

8. *An open secret :* something which is ostensibly a secret, but which requires little effort or penetration to discover.

9. *pl.* A private place; *retreat, privy.*

†10. *pl.* The external organs of sex.

11. *pl. Secreta,* a privy place, *retreat.*

II. Hence, an infallible prescription, a specific.

Secret, v. *rare.* [f. SECRET *sb.*]

In the induced form it is not easy to distinguish between *secret* and SECRETE v.

†Secretariate (-ekrĕ·ri·ăt, -ĭt). *Also* †secretoria. [ad. late L. *secretōria,* -us the office or a secretary.]

Secretariat(e (-ekrĕ·ri·ăt, -ĭt). Also F. *secretariat,* ad. med.L. *secrētāria*-us the office of official position of a secretary; the body or department of secretaries; the place where a secretary transacts business; preserves records, etc.

Secretaire (sěkrĕtē·r). *Also* 6 secretaire, 7 secretarie, etc. [a. F. *secrétaire.*]

Secretarial (-ekrĕtē·riăl), *a.* [f. SECRETARY + -AL] Of or pertaining to a secretary, secretaries, or to the business of a secretary.

Secretariate. See SECRETARIATE.

Secretary (sě·krĕtări). [ad. med.L. *secrētārius* one entrusted with private or secret matters; a confidant; f. *secrētum* SECRET *sb.*]

1. One who is entrusted with private or secret affairs.

2. One whose office it is to write for another, esp. one who is employed to conduct correspondence, keep records, and (usually) to transact various other business for another person or for a society, corporation, or public body.

Secretaryship (sě·krĕtărĭʃip). [f. prec. + -SHIP.] The office or position of a secretary.

Secrete, v. [ad. L. *secrēt-,* ppl. stem of *secernĕre* to separate: see SECERN, SECRETE.] *trans.* To keep secret, conceal, hide.

Secrete, v. Phys. [f. L. *secrēt-,* ppl.] To separate or elaborate from the blood or sap.

Secretion (sěkrī·ʃən). [a. F. *sécrétion,* ad. L. *secrētiōn-em* a separation.] The act of secreting; the product of secreting.

Secretional (-ekrī·ʃənăl), *a.* [f. prec. + -AL.] Of the nature of secretion.

Secretitious (-ekrĕtí·ʃəs), *a.* Produced by secretion.

Secretive (sě·krĕtiv), *a.* [f. SECRETE v. + -IVE.]

Secretiveness (sě·krĕtivnĕs). [f. prec. + -NESS.]

Secretly (sī·krĕtli), *adv.* [f. SECRET + -LY.] In a secret manner, in secret; not openly or publicly.

Secretness (sī·krĕtnĕs). Secrecy; privacy; reticence.

Sect (sekt), *sb.* [a. AF. and OF. *secte,* ad. L. *secta,* f. *sect-,* ppl. stem of *sequī* to follow.]

1. A class or kind (of persons).

2. In connexion with religion.

3. A religious order.

SECT. (continued)

†**1.** The (human) race. *Obs. rare.*

dex. Now only in illiterate use.

†**2.** Distinctive costume (of a class or order). Also *transf.* the 'garb' or guise (of humanity). *Obs.*

†**3.** Body of followers or adherents. *Obs.*

4. A religious following; adherence to a particular religious teacher or faith.

b. (*a*) A system of belief or observance distinctive of one of the parties or schools into which the adherents of a religion are divided; sometimes *spec.*, a system differing from what is deemed the orthodox tradition; a heresy. *Obs.*

†**Sect,** *v.* nonce-word. [f. SECT sb.] *a. trans.* To treat as a sect. *b.* To *set it*: to behave as a sect.

5. The systeme or body of adherents of a particular school of philosophy.

b. A religious sect.

Sectal (sĕktăl), *a.* [f. SECTARY (or its allied noun L. *sectārius*) + -AL.] Pertaining to or distinctive of sect. Chiefly used with reference to Indian religions.

†**Sect,** *v.²* *Obs.* [L. *sect-*, ppl. stem of *secāre* to cut.] *trans.* To cut or divide (into equal parts).

Sectarial (sĕktē˙riăl), *a.* and *sb.* [f. SECTARY + -AL.]

1. Pertaining to a sectary or sectaries; belonging to a schismatical sect' (Phillips, ed. Kersey, 1706). *Obs. exc. Hist.*

Sectarianise (sĕktē˙riănaiz), *v.* [Formed as prec. + -IZE.]

1. *intr.* To act in a sectarian manner.

2. *trans.* To render sectarian, to reduce to the level of a sect; to imbue with sectarian feelings or principles.

SECTARIAN.

†**b.** With pseudo-etymological reference: a 'section' of mankind. *Obs.*

†**7.** = SECT (mea. *b*).

†**8.** Law. Sect of court (med. L. *secta curiæ*): 'Suit and Service done by Tenants at the Court of their Lord' (J. Harris *Lex.* Techn. 1710, II).

6. In modern use, commonly applied to a separately organized religious body, having its distinctive name and its own places of worship; a 'denomination'. Also, in a narrower sense, one of the bodies separated from the Church. The *sects*: applied by Anglicans to the various bodies of Dissenters, by Roman Catholics to all forms of Protestantism.

Sectarian (sĕktē˙riăn), *a.* and *sb.* [f. SECTARY + -AN.] *A.* adj.

1. Of or pertaining to a sect; characteristic of sectaries; sectarian.

2. A variety of 'sectarism'; a sectarian body.

†**Sectarist.** *Obs.* [f. SECTAR-Y + -IST.]

SECTARIANISM. 362

1. Originally, an adherent of the 'sectarian party' (i.e. the Independents) as designated by the Presbyterians; subsequently, a member of a schismatic sect, a schismatic. Now chiefly *Hist.*

2. An adherent of a specified sect; a sectary of a particular teacher. Now *rare*.

3. A bigoted adherent of a sect; one whose views or sympathies are sectarian.

Sectarianism (sĕktē˙riănĭz'm). [f. prec. + -ISM.] The sectarian spirit; adherence or excessive attachment to a particular sect or party, esp. in religion; to resent too often, adherence or excessive attachment to, or undue favouring of, a particular 'denomination'.

Sectarianize (sĕktē˙riănaiz), *v.* [f. SECTARIAN + -IZE.]

1. *intr.* To act in a sectarian manner.

2. *trans.* To render sectarian, to reduce to the level of a sect; to imbue with sectarian feelings or principles.

3. A follower or disciple of a particular leader, teacher, party, or school. Now *rare* (with mixture of sense 1). Also, a votary of a particular study, pursuit, etc.

SECTION. 362

Hence **Secta·rianizing** *vbl. sb.* and *ppl. a.*

Sectarian·ity. [See -ITY.] In a sectarian manner.

Sectarism (sĕ˙ktăriz'm), *sb.* [f. SECTARY + -ISM.]

1. The principles, spirit, or practice characteristic of sectaries; sectarianism.

2. A variety of 'sectarism'; a sectarian body.

Sectary (sĕ˙ktări), *sb.* (and *a.*) [a. F. *sectaire*, ad. med. L. *sectārius*, freq. of *sectāri*, freq. of *sequī* to follow.]

1. A follower, one who follows a particular school, teacher, or leader; a partisan, sectary.

A. sb.

1. A member of a sect; one who is zealous in the cause of a sect.

2. An adherent of a schismatical or heretical sect. In the 17–18th c. commonly applied to the English Protestant Dissenters. Now chiefly *Hist.*

3. A follower or disciple of a particular leader, teacher, party, or school. Now *rare* (with mixture of sense 1). Also, a votary of a particular study, pursuit, etc.

Hence Sectar·ianity.

SECTION.

Section (sĕ˙kʃən), *sb.* Also 6 sectioun, 7 -tion. [ad. L. *sectiōn-em*, n. of action f. *secāre* to cut. Cf. F. *section*.]

2. A part cut off; a division.

3. A subdivision of a written or printed work, a statute, or the like. Often represented by the symbol § (representing a numeral figure); also abbreviated *sect.* (rarely *sec.*).

4. A part separated or divided off from the remainder; one of the portions into which a thing is cut or divided. *a. gen.*

b. Division into parts. *Obs.*

a. U.S. A portion of a sleeping-car containing two berths.

5. A subdivision of a military unit.

6. The act of cutting or division. *Obs.*

SECTION.

7. *Comb.* *a.* objective; as (sense 5) *section-cutter, -cutting, -smoother*; (sense 3) *section-commander, -leader*; (sense 3) *section-gang, -master*.

b. Special comb.: *section-beam* (see quot.); *section-house* (see quot. 1856); *section-line* (see quot.); *section-mark* (in sense 3 above); *section-liner* (see quot.); *section-plane* (see quot.).

Sectional (sĕ˙kʃənăl), *a.* (and *sb.*) [f. SECTION + -AL.]

1. Pertaining to a section or division of a larger part. *a.* Pertaining to a section or subdivision of a country, society, or population; sometimes (of interests) *local*, in this respect partial.

2. Pertaining to or relating to a section as a technical or scientific term.

3. Composed or made up of several sections or parts fitting into one another.

Sectionalism (sĕ˙kʃənălĭz'm). [f. SECTIONAL + -ISM.] Confinement of interest to a narrow sphere, narrowness of outlook, some restriction of minor local, political, or social distinctions.

Sectionalist (sĕ˙kʃənălĭst), *sb.* [f. SECTIONAL + -IST.]

Sectionalize (sĕ˙kʃənălaiz), *v.* [f. SECTIONAL + -IZE.] *trans.* To divide into sections or parts.

Sectionally (sĕ˙kʃənăli), *adv.* [f. SECTIONAL + -LY.]

Sectionary (sĕ˙kʃənări), *a.* and *sb.* [f. SECTION + -ARY.]

Sectionism.

SECTOR. 364

Sectiuncle, sectiuncule. [f. L. *secti-, section* + *-uncula*.] A small section.

Sector (sĕ˙ktəɹ), *sb.* Also 6–7 sectour, sectoure. [ad. late L. *sector* (Boethius), a special use of L. *sector* cutter, f. *sect-*, ppl. stem of *secāre* to cut; in sense 2 ad. F. *secteur*, ad. L. *sector*.]

1. *Geom.* A plane figure contained by two radii and the arc of a circle, ellipse, or other central curve intercepted by them.

2. *Geom.* A solid generated by the revolution of a plane sector about one of its radii.

3. A mathematical instrument consisting of two rulers connected by a joint, and divided into scales.

Sectoral (sĕ˙ktərăl), *a.*

Sector·ial, *a.* (and *sb.*)

able, so other fixed, making an angle, and of a circumferential limb...

Sector (se'ktǝr), *sb.* To divide into sectors; to provide with sectors.

Sector, *v.* To divide into sectors.

Sectoral (se'ktǝral), *a.* [f. Sector *sb.* + -al.] Pertaining to a sector.

Sectorial (sektō·riǎl), *a.* [f. Sector *sb.* + -ial.] Of or pertaining to a sector. *a.* Pertaining to the instrument called a sector.

Sectorial, *sb.*

Sectory, obs. form of Sectary.

Sectoure, var. *ff.* Sector *Obs.*, executor.

Sectroid (se·ktroid), [f. Sector + -oid.] The curved surface of two adjacent groins in a vault.

†Secutary. *Obs.* [Altered from of Sectary, after words like *textuary*.] = Sectary.

Secutre, var. *ff.* Sector *Obs.*, executor.

†Secure. *Obs.* rare. [ad. mod. L. type *sectūra*, f. L. *secāre* to cut: see -URE.] A retion, cutting, incision.

Secubate, *v. Obs.* [ad. L. *sĕcŭbāt-*, ppl.

stem of *sĕcubāre*, f. *sē- (see Se- *pref.) + *cubāre* to lie down. [See quot.]

Secular (se·kiŭlǝr), *a.* and *sb.* Forms: 3-6 secular, 4-5 seculere (4 seculere, secler, 4-5 seclere, 5 seculier, 5- secular), 4 of, secular (mod.F. *séculier*), ad. L. *sæculāris*, f. *sæculum* generation, age, in Christian Latin 'the world', esp. as opposed to the church: see Secular.

I. Of or pertaining to the world.

1. *Eccl.* Of members of the clergy: Living 'in the world' and not in monastic seclusion, as distinguished from 'regular' and 'religious'. *Secular canon*: see Canon *sb.*[2] *Secular abbot*: a person not a monk, who had the title and part of the revenues, but not the functions of an abbot.

b. Of or pertaining to secular clergy.

2. Belonging to the world and its affairs as distinguished from the church and religion; civil, lay, temporal. Chiefly used as a negative term, with the meaning non-ecclesiastical, non-religious, or non-sacred.

b. Of or belonging to an age or long period.

II. Of or belonging to an age or long period.

3. Occurring or celebrated once in an age, century, or very long period. *Secular games, plays, shows* [L. *ludi sæculares*]: in ancient Rome, games continuing three days and three nights celebrated once in an 'age' or period of 120 years. *Secular poem* [L. *carmen sæculare*], a hymn composed to be sung at the secular games.

4. *Astron.* Of or belonging to an 'age' or long period.

7. In scientific use, of processes of change: Slowing, a period of enormous length; continuing through long ages. *Astr.* Chiefly of changes in the orbits or the periods of revolution of the planets, in its *secular acceleration, inequality, equation, variation*. The terms *secular acceleration, secular variation* were formerly also used (with reference to the sense 'century' of *L. sæculum*) for the amount of change per 100 years; similarly *secular precession* [see quot. 1817].

Secularism (se·kiŭlǝriz'm). [f. Secular *a.* + -ISM.]

1. One of the secular clergy; a secular. *nonce*-use.

2. The doctrine that morality should be based solely on regard to the well-being of mankind in the present life, to the exclusion of all considerations drawn from belief in God or in a future state.

Secularist (se·kiŭlǝrist), *sb.* (and *a.*). [f. as prec.]

1. One who advocates secular *vs.* a secular.

2. One who believes in or advocates Secularism.

Secularistic (sekiŭlǝri·stik), *a.* [f. Secularist + -ic.] Of, pertaining to, or characterized by secularism.

Secularity (sekiŭlæ·riti). Forms: 4 secularite (1333 in Hatz.-Darm.; there may have been an *A.F. seculerté*, whence Wyclif's form), or directly ad. med.L. *sæculāritās*, f. L. *sæculāris*: see -ITY.

Secularization (sekiŭlǝraizē··ʃǝn). [f. Secularize: see -ATION.] cf. F. *sécularisation* (16-17 c. in Hatz.-Darm.).

1. The conversion of an ecclesiastical or religious institution or its property to secular possession and use; the conversion of an ecclesiastical state or sovereignty to a lay one; an instance of this.

2. The giving of a secular or non-sacred character or direction to (art, studies, etc.); the placing (of morals) on a secular basis; the restricting (of education) to secular subjects.

Secularize (se·kiŭlǝraiz), *v.* [f. Secular *a.* + -IZE.]

1. *trans.* To make secular; to convert from ecclesiastical to civil possession or use; esp. to place (church property) at the disposal of the secular power.

2. To render secular or non-sacred in tone, spirit, etc.

3. To dissociate or separate from religious or spiritual concerns, to convert to material and temporal purposes.

Secularly (se·kiŭlǎli), *adv.* [f. Secular *a.* + -LY[2].]

1. As a secular or lay person; in accordance with secular procedure; non-ecclesiastically.

2. In a worldly manner; in a manner characterized by the absence of religion.

Secularness (se·kiŭlǝrnes). *Obs.* [f. Secular *a.* + -NESS.] Secularity.

†Secularty, *a.* *Obs. rare-[1].* [f. Secular + -TY[2].] Secular.

Secund (se·kŭnd), *a.* *Bot.* and *Zool.* [ad. L. *secundus* following: see Second *a.*] Arranged on or directed towards one side only; esp. *Bot.* of the flowers, leaves, or other secondary parts.

†Secundan, *a.* *Obs.* [ad. L. *secundānus*, f. *secundus* Second *a.*: see -AN[1].] Pertaining to a second; secondary; second-class.

Secundate, *v.* *Obs. rare.* [f. ppl. stem of *secundāre* to direct favourably, f. *secund-us* favourable, f. *secundus*: see Second *a.*] *trans.* To direct favourably. (See quots.)

Secundation. *Obs. rare-[1].* [app. f. L. *secund-us*, *secundāre*: see prec.] the evil deity of the dualistic system of Secundus.

Secundian (sĕkŏ·ndiǎn), *sb. Obs. rare-[1].* [f. *Secundus* + -IAN.] A follower of Secundus, a Gnostic heresiarch of the second century.

Secundinal, *a.* (See quots.) pl.

stem of *secundāre* to direct favourably, f. *secund-us*.

Secundiflorous (-ĭflō·rǝs), *a.* *Bot.* [f. Secund + *-i-* + L. *flōr-em* flower + -ous[2].] Having flowers secundly disposed, or with the flowers of an inflorescence secund.

Secundine (se·kŭndĭn, -ain). Also 4-6 secondyne, (4-7, 6-7), *seconding*. [ad. late L. *secundīnæ pl.* (for which class. Latin had *secundæ*), f. *secundus* following: see Second *a.*, and -INE[1].]

1. *Obstetrics.* The placenta and other adjuncts of a fœtus extruded from the womb after the expulsion of the fœtus in parturition; the afterbirth.

2. *Bot.* The second or inner of the two coats or integuments of an ovule, originally the inner one, later applied to the outer covering: see Primine.

Secundo (sĕkŭ·ndo), *adv.* and *sb.* [ad. L. *secundō*, ablative of *secundus* Second *a.*] In the last sense: 'in the second place'; used both strings and secundine to note.

Secundogeniture (sĕkŏndojĕ·nitiŭr). Also *-ture*, form of *secundus* Second *a.*, after *primogeniture.* The right of succession or inheritance belonging to a second son; the possession so inherited.

Secundoprimary, *a.* *Bot.* (See quot.)

Secundus (sĕkŏ·ndǝs), *a.* Used in various med. Latin phrases, sometimes occurring in Eng. contexts. *Secundum artem* (or L. *arte*), 'according to art', in accordance with the rules of the art (chiefly of medicine); *Secundum magis et minus* (or L. *magis et minus*), 'according to more and less'; in a quantitative manner or respect; in various degrees. *Secundum naturam* (literary or L. *arte-m natura*), 'according to nature'; *Secundum quid* (L. *secundum quid*), in some particular respect only (opposed to *simpliciter*, L. de).

Secundare (sĕkŭndā·re), *a. rare.* [L. *secundus*.] Second.

Secure (sĭkiŭǝr), *a.* (and *adv.*). Forms: 6- secure (6-7 *sicure, seccure*, 6 *siccure*). [ad. L. *sēcūrus* free from care, f. *sē-* (see Se-) + *cūra* care: cf. Sicker, Sure, which is a doublet through OF.]

I. 1. Feeling no care or apprehension.

2. Confident in expectation; feeling certain of something in the future.

II. Having or affording ground for confidence; safe (objectively) certain.

3. Rightly free from apprehension; protected from or not exposed to danger; safe.

4. Of a place, of means of protection or guardianship: Affording safety.

5. Predictability; a certain custody; safely in one's possession or power.

6. Free from risk as to the continued or future possession of acquisition or desirable event.

B. quasi-*adv.* and *adv.* (Chiefly *poet.*)

II. 1. *trans.* To make secure; to free (a person) from care or apprehension.

2. To make (a person) sure of; to assure; to guarantee.

3. Of a place, etc.: To make safe or secure; to guard, protect.

4. Of a person: To make secure or safe.

Secure, *v.* [f. Secure *a.*]

SECURE. (continued)

their Mold'ring is upon them. ... To They carry much of their Carriages on sledges to secure their falling in the streetes.

†**f.** To render (an action) safe; to secure for transit. *Obs.*

g. *Mil.* To render secure from attack or molestation by the enemy; to take defensive means for the safe execution of (a movement, e.g. a retreat, the crossing of a river); to guard efficiently (a pass, a defile).

h. *Mil.* To secure arms: 'to hold a rifle or musket with the muzzle down, and lock well up under the arm, the object being to guard the weapon from the wet' (Ogilvie 1882).

†**t.** To secure off. *Obs.*

3. To make secure or certain.

†**a.** To make (a person) secure of a present or future possession, of any supporter, etc. Also *const.* to with infinitive. *Obs.*

b. To put in safety, 'get in' (a crop).

†**4.** To secure (something). *rare.* (In quot. *passive.*)

5. To seize and confine; to keep or hold in custody; to imprison. Now somewhat *rare.*

†**6.** To make fast or firm.

7. To make secure or certain (something); to ensure.

†**a.** To make fast.

b. To get possession of, make sure of.

†**c.** To establish (a person) securely *in* some position, privilege, etc.

d. To establish (a person) securely *in* some position, privilege, etc.

Secured ... *ppl. a.* [f. SECURE v. + -ED.] In senses of the verb: Assured; firmly

1653 HOLCROFT *Procopius, Goth. Wars* ...

Secureful, *a.* *Obs. rare⁻¹.* [f. SECURE *a.* + -FUL.] Protecting.

Securely, *adv.* [f. SECURE *a.* + -LY⁻².]
1. In a secure manner (in various senses).

Securing, *ppl. a. rare.* [f. SECURE *v.* + -ING⁻².]

Securiform. (*sikiū̆ri-fŏɹm.*) [f. SECURI-FORM.] Ax-shaped, having the form of an axe or hatchet.

Secure-ment (*sikiū̆ə-mĕnt*). *rare.* [f. SECURE *v.* + -MENT.] The action or an act of securing.

Securer (*sikiū̆rəɹ*). *rare.* [f. SECURE *v.*] One who or that which secures, in various senses of the verb.

Securi- (*sikiū̆ri-*, *sekiū̆ri*), combining form of L. *secūris* ax, † *secūre* to cut. Used in various scientific terms.

Security (*sikiū̆riti*). Forms: 5 **securytye**, **securite** *a.*, 6-7 **securitye**, **securitie**, 6- **security.** [ad. L. *sēcūritās*, L. *secūritē* (in Hatz.-Darm.), Sp. *seguridad*, Pg. *seguridade*.]

1. The condition of being secure.
1. The condition of being protected from or not exposed to danger; safety.
2. Freedom from care, anxiety or apprehension. Now chiefly, well-founded confidence, certainty.
3. Freedom from doubt; confidence, assurance. Now *rare.*

of my friend, that, and every thing that concerns him.

b. As securing the payment of a debt, etc.

4. The quality or state of being fixed or attached, stability, fixity.

5. A means of being secure.

6. Something which secures or makes safe; a protection, guard, defence.

II. As securing the payment of a debt, etc.

7. Property deposited or made over, or bonds, recognizances, or the like entered into, by or on behalf of a person in order to secure his fulfilment of an obligation, and forfeitable in the event of non-fulfilment; a pledge, caution.

8. *Law* security.

9. As securing a person's 'good behaviour', his appearance in court at a specified time, or his performance of some undertaking.

10. A document held by a creditor as guarantee of his right to payment.

11. *Mil.* security.

III. (II. *concr.* senses 8, 10) *security-bond, -writ*; also *security-box,* a device for securing a motor-tyre to the rim; *security-grinder, jocular,* an assiduous reviser of securities.

SECUTOR.

†**Secutor, secutour.** *Obs.* Forms: 4 **seketur, 4 sekatour, 4 seke-, -teke-, -secutour, 5 sekka-, secu-, -secoutour, secoutur, secutur, -or, sektour'e, 4 sectour, 5 sek-tour, sectour, 6-7 sectour, 5 sektare, sectore.** [Aphetic form of EXECUTOR.] = EXECUTOR.

†**Se·cutorship** *rare* = EXECUTORSHIP.

†**Sedany.** The name of a country-dance.

Sedan (*sidæ·n*). Forms: 7 **sedan,** (7 *errors.*) **se-dam.** [Of obscure etymology.

1. A covered chair or portable cabin, to seat one person, borne on two poles by two bearers, one in front and one behind.

2. *ellipt.* SEDAN-CHAIR.

Sedan chair. Now *Hist.* = SEDAN 1, 1 b.

Sedan chair, *attrib.*

†**Se·dant,** *a.* *Her.* *Obs. rare⁻¹.* [? quasi-Fr. spelling of SEDENT *a.* = SEIANT.]

Sedate (*sidē·t*), *a.* [ad. mod.L. *sēdāt-us,* f. *sēdāre* to settle, allay, make calm or quiet; f. root *sēd-* as in L. *sĕdēre:* see SIT *v.*]
1. Calm, quiet, composed (*only sober, collected*).

Se·date, *v.* [f. L. *sēdāt-,* stem of *sēdāre:* see 1-2.] *trans.* To make calm or quiet; to assuage, allay. Hence † *Se·dating vbl. sb.*

Sedately (*sidē·tli*), *adv.* [-LY⁻².] In a sedate manner; without passion or excitement.

Sede·cimarti·culate, *a.* *rare⁻¹.* Having sixteen joints.

†**Sede·ntiple** *Obs.⁻¹.* [f. L. *sēde·cim* sixteen, after DECUPLE.] A quantity sixteen times another.

SEDECUPLE.

Barn. Rudge i, John looked sedately and solemnly at his questioner.

Sedateness (*sidē·tnĕs*), *n.* [f. SEDATE *a.* + -NESS.] The quality or fact of being sedate (see the adj.).

Sedation (*sidē·ʃən*), *n.* [ad. L. *sēdātiōn-em,* n. of action from *sēdāre:* see SEDATE *v.*]
1. The action of allaying, assuaging, making calm or quiet.

Sedative (*se·dătiv*), *a.* and *sb.* [ad. med.L. *sēdātīv-us,* f. *sēdāt-,* pa. ppl. stem of *sēdāre:* see SEDATE *v.*]
A. *adj.* Having a soothing, assuaging, or soothing.

B. *sb.* A sedative medicine.

†**Se·date-ment.** *Obs.⁻¹.*

†**Sede,** *v.* [L. *sĕdē-re.*] *intr.* To sit.

†**Sede.** *Obs.* [L. *sēdēs* seat.]

1. = SEAT 18. **8.** *Sede celestial,* the throne of God.

2. = SEAT 26, 13.

SE DEFENDENDO.

†**Se defendendo** (*sī· dēfende·ndo*). *Law.* [Law Latin: *sī* himself, *defendendo* abl. gerund of *defendĕre* to defend.] In self-defence': a plea which if established is held to remove legal guilt from a homicide.

†**Sedeful,** *a.* *Obs.* Also 1-2 *sideful.* [OE. *sidful,* f. *side* more = OS. *sithu* (De. *sede* item), OHG. *sita* (G. *sitte* habit).]

Sedentarily (*se·dĕntarili*), *adv.* [f. SEDENTARY *a.* + -LY⁻².] In a sedentary manner.

Sedentariness (*se·dĕntarinĕs*). [f. SEDENTARY *a.* + -NESS.] The condition or quality of being sedentary.

Sedentary (*se·dĕntari*), *a.* and *sb.* [ad. F. *sédentaire,* ad. L. *sedentāri-us,* f. *sedent-,* pr. pple. of *sedēre* to sit.]
I. Of habit, occupation, etc.: Requiring continuance in a sitting posture.

Seder, sēdor, of CEDAR, SEDEN.

Sedered (*sedē·ɹd*). *Sc.* [L. *sēdērunt* there were sitting' (the following persons), 3rd pers. pl. of... to be put again.]

SEDGE.

lated in her lap in the course of a long morning's sederunt.

Sedentary (continued)

b. *Zool.* Of animals that sit or sit still.

Sedge (*sedʒ*), *sb.¹* Forms: **1 secg, secg** (sech, seic, seeg, segg, secge, 3 segge, 4-7 segge, 4-6 seg, segge, 7 seggge,) **5- sedge.** [OE. *secg* wk. masc. ... cogn. w. MLG. *segge, sagge, segher,* Du. *zegge.*]

1. Any of various coarse grassy, rush-like or flag-like plants growing in wet places; also (in different localities) variously applied *spec.* to plants of the cyperaceous genus *Carex* and *Cladium,* ...

Sedge. ... the Sweet Flag (*Acorus*) and the Wild Iris (*Iris Pseudacorus*).

Sedgy (se·dǧi), *a.* ...

Sedile (sēdəi·lē), *pl.* **Sedilia** (sēdi·liă).

Sediment (se·dimĕnt), *sb.*

Sedimental (sedime·ntăl), *a. and sb.*

Sedimentary (sedime·ntări), *a. and sb.*

Sedimentation (se·dimĕntē·ʃən).

Sedimentous, *a.*

Seditial, *a.*

Sedition (sēdi·ʃən), *sb.*

Seditionary (sēdi·ʃənări), *a. and sb.*

Seditioner, *a.*

Seditionist (sēdi·ʃənist).

Seditious (sēdi·ʃəs), *a.*

Seditiously (sēdi·ʃəsli), *adv.*

Seditiousness, *sb.*

Seduce (sĭdiū·s), *v.*

Seduced (sĭdiū·st), *ppl. a.*

Seducedly, *adv.*

Seducee, *sb.*

Seducement (sĭdiū·smĕnt), *sb.*

Seducer (sĭdiū·sɑ(r)), *sb.*

Seducible (sĭdiū·sĭb'l), **seduceable** (sĭdiū·sĕb'l), *a.*

Seducing (sĭdiū·siŋ), *ppl. a.*

Seducingly (sĭdiū·siŋli), *adv.*

Seduction (sĭdʌ·kʃən).

Seductionist (sĭdʌ·kʃənist).

Seductive (sĭdʌ·ktiv), *a.*

Seductively (sĭdʌ·ktivli), *adv.*

Seductiveness, *sb.*

Seductress (sĭdʌ·ktres).

Sedulity (sĭdiū·lĭti).

Sedulous (se·diŭləs), *a.*

Sedulously, *adv.*

Sedum (sī·dəm), *sb.*

Sedyl, *obs. form of* SCHEDULE, CIDER.

Sedyr, *obs. form of* CEDAR.

Supplement, p. 3873; Corrigenda, p. 4092; Spurious words, p. 4093; Books quoted, p. 4094

See (sīˈ), sb.[1] Forms: 3–4 ce, 3–5 see, see, 3–6 se, 4–5 sey, 6–7 sea, 4 see, 3–6 se, 4–5 sey, 6–7 sea, see. [a variant (influenced by the Latin) of *sit*, *sied*:—popular L. † *sēdem*, altered form (after *sedēre* to sit) of classical L. *sēdem* (*sēds*) a seat.]

1. A seat, place of sitting.

† **a.** *gen.* (Only in early poetical use.) *Obs.*

2. Ecclesiastical uses.

a. The seat, chair, or throne of a bishop in his church ; = CATHEDRA 1. Now *only arch.*

b. The office or position indicated by sitting in a particular episcopal chair ; the position of being bishop of a particular diocese.

See (sī), *sb.*[2] *rare.* [f. SEE v.] In nonce-uses : **a.** *To have a see*, to have a vision ; *(ad)* ; **b.** with cognate obj., *I have seen my see.*

See (sī), *v.* Forms and Inflexions : *see* Present and Infinitive.

A. Inflexional Forms.

I. *Infinitive* seon, *sēon*, *blīcе*, sēan, sēan, *Northumb.* seа, 2 syen, 2–3 seо(n, 2–5 seo(n, 3 se(о(n, 3–4 sеon, sеon, sеe, 4–6 sеe(n, etc.

SEE. 379 SEE. SEE. 380 SEE.

B. Signification and Uses.

A. The simple verb.

I. *trans.* To perceive (light, colour, external objects and their movements) with the eye, to have the sensation of sight.

4. *trans.* With mixed literal and figurative sense : To perceive by visual tokens. Also *absol.*

5. To direct the sight (literal or metaphorical) intentionally ; to look at, contemplate, examine, inspect, or scrutinize ; to visit (a place) ; to attend (a play, etc.) as a spectator.

Seeming, ppl. a. and sb. For Forms see the verb. [f. SEEM v.² + -ING¹.] The action of SEEM v.² in various senses.

1. The action or fact of appearing to be (to the mind or to bodily sense); appearance.

2. + By seeming, to seeming, in seeming, in all seeming, to all appearance.

2. The form in which a person or thing seems or appears; look, aspect.

3. External appearance considered as deceptive, or as distinguished from reality; an illusion, a semblance.

Seemingly (sī·miŋli), adv. Also 5 semenly, 6 semynaly. [f. SEEMING ppl. a. + -LY¹.]

1. Fittingly, becomingly. Now somewhat rare.

2. To external appearance, apparently. (Distinguished from but not necessarily opposed to really.)

Seemingness (sī·miŋnes). [f. SEEMING ppl. + -NESS.]

1. The quality or fact of seeming to be something; unreal pretence; plausibility.

2. Semblance, seeming existence or presence.

Seemless, a. Obt. exc. arch. Also 6-7 see(a)melesse, 7 seemer-less. Unseemly; shameful; unfitting.

4. Used adverbially with other adjectives to form hyphened compounds with the sense of 'having a (specified) appearance'.

Seemlihead, arch. (written -hed after Spenser). [f. SEEMLY a. + -HEAD.] The condition of being seemly; seemliness.

+**Seemlihood.** Obt. rare⁻¹. In 5 semely hode. [f. SEEMLY a. + -HOOD.] = SEEMLIHEAD.

Seemlily, adv. Obt. Forms: 4 semlily, 5 semely, 6 semelily, 6 semelily, 7 seemlily. [f. SEEMLY a. + -LY².] In a seemly manner; becomingly.

Seemliness (sī·mlines). Forms: see the adj. [f. SEEMLY a. + -NESS.]

+1. Pleasing appearance; elegance or handsomeness of form (of the body or its parts); gracefulness, attractiveness (of things, actions, etc.). Obt.

2. Of things: Pleasant (esp. to the sight); handsome in appearance; of fine or stately proportion.

3. Of conduct, speech, appearance: Conformable to propriety or good taste; becoming, decorous.

+b. A becoming degree, 'fairly'. Obt. rare.

2. A small spring; a jet or source of water.

+b. Apparently, seemingly. dial.

Seen (sīn), ppl. a. [pa. pple. of SEE v.]

Percolation or oozing of water or fluid; leakage; also that which oozes.

Seepy (sī·pi), a. U.S. [f. SEEP v. + -Y.] (See quot.)

Seer¹ (sī·ə, in sense 1 also sī·ə). Forms: 4 seere, 5 sere, 6-8 seear, 6 sear, 4 seer. [f. SEE v. + -ER¹. Cf. G. seher.]

1. gen. One who sees. Cf. SEE-ER.

2. spec. One who sees visions.

3. A magician; one who has the power of second sight. Also a crystal-gazer, a scryer.

Seeress. [f. SEER¹ + -ESS.] A female seer.

Seer-fish: see SEA-FISH.

Seerge, obs. form of SEARCH v., SERGE.

Seering, var. of CERING obt. sb.

+Seersaw (sī·əpī). Indian. Also 7 searapah, serpow, 7-8 serpaw. [Urdū sarápá, a Pers., sar head + á pá foot.] A complete suit.

Seership (sī·əʃip). [f. SEER¹ + -SHIP.]

1. Your seership: a mock title of address to a 'seer'.

2. The office or function of a seer.

Seersucker (sī·əsɔkər). Also 8 sirsakas, 9 seersucker. [East Indian corruption of Pers.]

See-saw (sī·sĭ), sb. and a. [A reduplicating formation symbolic of alternating movement; the particular form may be suggested by SAW v., to which the oldest example refers. Cf. SITHOT.]

See-saw, v. [f. SEE-SAW sb.]

1. intr. a. To move up and down, or backwards and forwards; to undergo a see-saw motion; also to play see-saw.

2. trans. To cause to move in a see-saw motion.

Seethe (sīð), v. Forms: inf. 1 séoþan, 2-3 sethen, 3-6 sethe, etc.; pa. t. 1 séaþ, etc.; pa. pple. 1 soden, etc.

1. trans. To boil; to make or keep boiling hot: to subject to the action of boiling liquid; esp. to cook (food) by boiling or stewing; to boil, seethe.

b. intr. To boil.

Seethe, var. of SAITHE.

+**Seethed,** ppl. a. [f. SEETHE v. + -ED¹.] Boiled.

Seether. Obt. [f. SEETHE v. + -ER¹.]

1. One that seethes or boils.

2. A utensil for boiling. nonce-use.

Seething (sī·ðiŋ), vbl. sb. [f. SEETHE v. + -ING¹.] The action of SEETHE v.

1. The state of being boiling hot.

2. Ebullition, intense inward commotion.

Seething, ppl. a. [f. SEETHE v. + -ING².]

1. Boiling; in a state of ebullition.

2. fig. In a state of inward agitation, turmoil, or 'ferment'.

Seethingly, adv.

Seg. obs. form of SEDGE.

Segge, obs. pres. pl. of SEE v.

Seege, obs. form of SIEGE.

Seethe, obs. form of SETH.

Seven, obs. var. of SEVEN.

Seventh, obs. form of SEVENTH.

tap. 1844 H. Stephens Bk. Farm. II. 129 An aged bull that is castrated is called a segg. 1856 Morton Cycl. Agric. II. 725 Seg. (Suff., Yorks., Norf.), any animal castrated when full grown.

Hence **Seg** v. dial. trans. (See quots.)

1886 Cheshire Gloss., Segged, castrated, but only applied when the operation is performed on full-grown animals. 1887 S. Chesh. Gloss., Seg, to castrate a full-grown animal.

Seg (seg), sb.² dial. (See Eng. Dial. Dict.) [a. ON. sigg neut., hard skin (Norw. sigg, Ross).] A callosity, esp. on the hand.

1865 B. Brierley Irkdale I. vii. 130 They startn o'feighten ..an' never gi'en o'er till they'n segs ole o'er 'em. 1900 Brit. Med. Jrnl. 15 Feb. 378 Callosities (called planker's 'segs') on the thenar and hypothenar eminences.

Seg, obs. or dial. form of Sedge.

‖**Segador.** Obs.⁻⁰ [Sp., agent-n. f. segar to reap.] 'A reaper, a Mower, a Harvest-man' (Blount Glossogr. 1656).

Segamore, obs. form of Sagamore.

Segan, variant of Sagan Jewish Antiq.

Segar: see Cigar.

†**Segara.** Obs. [quasi-Sp. form of segar, Cigar (Sp. cigarro).] A cigar.

1785 R. Cumberland Observer No. 88 ⁋ 1 Taking the segara from his mouth. Ibid. ⁋ 4 In his pockets he had..a small bundle of segaras.

Segathy, variant of Sagathy.

Sege, obs. form of Sedge, Segge, Siege.

Segement, obs. form of Segment.

Segeneration (sīdʒenərēⁱ·ʃən). rare⁻¹. [f. L. sē Se- + Generation.] (See quot.)

1888 Gulick in Linn. Soc. Jrnl. (Zool.) XX. 200 Many species are now divided into two or more intergenerants, between which there is little or no intercrossing. This state of freedom from crossing I call segeneration.

Segerstane, -ston(e, etc., obs. forms of Sexton.

Segg, obs. or dial. form of Sedge.

Seggar: see Saggar.

†**Seggard.** dial. Obs. = Safeguard sb. 8.

1746 Exmoor Scolding (E.D.S.) 34 Th'art olways a vustled up in an old Jump, or a Whittle, or an old Seggard. 1790 Grose Provinc. Gloss. (ed. 2) Suppl., Seggard, safeguard. A kind of riding surtout so called. West.

†**Segge**¹. poet. Obs. Forms: 1 secg, 3 sæg, 3–4 (6) seg, 3–6 segge, 4–6 sege, 4 segg, (seegge, 5 seege, seghe, seige), 6 sedge. [OE. secg = OS. segg, ON. segg-r:—OTeut. *sagjo-z.] A man. (In the 16th c. only contemptuous.)

Beowulf 208 (Gr.) Secg wisade, lagucræftiȝ mon, landȝemyrcu. Ibid. 633 Þa ic on holm ȝestah, sæbat ȝesæt mid minra secga ȝedriht. c 1205 Lay. 7991 Heo ledden in heore scipen..moni forhfulne sæg sare iwunded. Ibid. 5109 Þer weore segge songe [c 1275 gleomenne songe]. Ibid. 20854 Þene siȝeð him to segges vnder beorȝen. 1340–70 Alex. & Dind. 165 Of þe seggus þat he sai bi-ȝonde þe side stronde. 1377 Langl. P. Pl. B. xx. 333 'I am a surgien', seide þe segge 'and salues can make'. a 1400 Morte Arth. 1574, I had leuer see hym synke one the salte strandez, Than the seegge ware seke, that es so sore woundede. c 1470 Henry Wallace III. 53 Robert Boid, quhilk wald no langar bide Vndir thrillage of segis of Ingland. c 1475 Rauf Coilȝear 713 Thair was seruit in that saill Seigis semelie. 1508 Dunbar Flyting 13 For and I flyt sum sege for schame sould sink. 15.. Scot. Field 113 in Chetham Soc. Misc. II, Then sumoned he his sedges, in soondry places. 1557 Grimald Death Zoroas 98 in Tottel's Misc. (Arb.) 122 Wherwith a hole route came of souldiours stern, And all in peeces hewed the silly seg. 1567 Drant Horace, A.P. B vij, Through this and such the sillie segge lay plasde in puddle still. Ibid., Ep. I. ii. C iij, Duke Nestor, sillie carkinge segge.

†**Segge**². Obs. rare⁻¹. [? a. OF. seiche (:—L. sēpia).] ? A cuttle-fish.

c 1300 [see Lax sb.¹]

Segge, obs. form of Say v.¹, Sedge, Siege.

Segged (segd), a. dial. [f. seg, dial. var. of Sedge.] Seated with sedge or rushes; rush-bottomed. Also Comb. segged-seated adj.

1872 Mrs. H. Wood Within the Maze xii, The plain segged-seated chairs stood pretty thick. 1873 — Master of Greylands xvi, A small apartment looking to the kitchen-garden, with an old carpet on its floor, painted segged chairs, and a square piano against the wall.

†**Se·gger.** Obs. rare. [f. segge Say v. + -er¹.] One given to 'talking', a boaster, braggart.

c 1440 York Myst. xxviii. 201 Ȝone segger [sc. Christ] þat callis hym-selffe a sire.

Segger, Seggerson, obs. ff. Sayer¹, Sexton.

†**Segging.** Obs. rare. Used in echoes of the Du. proverb zeggen is goedkoop, 'saying is cheap.'

1546 J. Heywood Prov. K iij, The Ducheman saieth, that seggyng is good cope. 1613 F. Robartes Revenue Gosp. 104 Alasse, alasse, segging is no good coping.

†**Seggon.** Obs. rare⁻¹. [Of obscure origin; connexion with Segge seems unlikely.] A term of depreciation or pity (meaning uncertain).

1573–80 Tusser Husb. (1878) 174 Poore seggons halfe starued worke faintly and dull.

Seggrum (se·grəm), dial. Also 8 seagrim. The Common Ragwort, Senecio jacobæa.

1633 Johnson Gerarde's Herbal II. xxviii. 281 The first is called in Latine, Herba S. Iacobi..: in English, S. James his Wort...In Holdernesse in Yorke-shire they call it Seggrum. 1766 Museum Rust. VI. 450 Ragwort,..Seggrum, or Seagrim. 1788 W. H. Marshall Yorksh. II. 350 Seggrums; senecio jacobæa; ragwort.

Seggy, obs. or dial. form of Sedgy.

Segh(e, obs. forms of See v., Siege, Sigh v.

Segholate, variant of Segolate.

Segment (se·gmĕnt), sb. Also 6 seagment, 7 segement. [ad. L. segment-um, f. sec- (euphonically seg- before m), secāre to cut: see -ment.]

1. A piece cut or broken off; a fragment. rare.

1586 Ferne Blaz. Gentrie II. 98 Antichrist..deuiseth by councels and synods hat all signes, images, seagments or reliques of holy men..should be adored. c 1680 A. Hume Brit. Tongue II. v, This s ɜum haldes to be a segment of his, and therfoer now almost al wrytes his for it, as if it wer a corruption. 1704 Ray Creation I. (ed. 4) 58 The Segments and Cuttings of some Plants. 1832 Lytton Eugene A. I. i, He also quarrelled with him the oftenest and testified the least forbearance at the publican's segments of psalmody. 1837 Carlyle Fr. Rev. I. VII. xi, The truest segment of Chaos seen in these latter Ages!

2. Geom. A plane figure contained by a right line and a portion of the circumference of a circle. In full segment of a circle. Also, see quot. 1728.

In quot. 1626 loosely used for arc.

1570 Billingsley Euclid III. Def. v. 81 b, A section or segment of a circle, is a figure comprehended vnder a right line and a portion of the circumference of a circle. 1626 Donne Serm. lxvii. (1640) 677 The earth it selfe being round, euery step we make upon it, must necessarily bee a segment, an arch of a circle. 1728 Chambers Cycl. (ed. 2), Segment is sometimes also extended to the parts of ellipses, and other curvilinear figures. 1806 Hutton Course Math. (ed. 5) I. 42 To find the Area of any Elliptic Segment. Find the area of a corresponding circular segment.

b. Segment of a sphere: a solid figure bounded by a portion of the surface of a sphere and an intersecting plane.

1570 Billingsley Euclid XII. Prop. xvi. 376 Of segmentes, some are greater then the halfe sphere, some are lesse. 1704 J. Harris Lex. Techn. I, Segment of a Sphere, is a part of it cut off by a Plane;..therefore the Base of such a Segment must always be a Circle, and its Superficies a part of the Surface of the Sphere.

c. A segmental portion of anything having a circular or spherical form.

1646 Sir T. Browne Pseud. Ep. VII. iv. 346 Even unto.. such as live under the pole, for halfe a yeare some segments [of a rainbow] may appeare at any time and under any quarter. 1700 Dryden Ceyx & Alcyone 265 Indu'd with Robes of various Hew she flies, And flying draws an Arch (a segment of the Skies). 1837 Brewster Magnet. 326 A frame..contains the segment of a glass cylinder.

d. Her. A bearing representing a portion of a circular object.

1828–40 Berry Encycl. Her. I, Segment, one side only of a coronet, &c.

3. Geom. The finite part of a line between two points; a division of a line.

1617 Speidell Geom. Extract. 24 Let BA be the greater segement giuen, and the whole line is required. 1885 Leudesdorf Cremona's Proj. Geom. 53 Let us examine the relation which exists between the lengths of two corresponding segments AB, A'B' [of two straight lines].

b. Acoustics. Each of the portions into which the length of a vibrating string, wire, etc. is divided by the nodes.

1863 Atkinson Ganot's Physics 160 The part vibrating between two nodal points is called a ventral segment. 1870 Everett Deschanel's Nat. Philos. 832 The division into segments is often distinctly visible when the string of the sonometer is strongly bowed. 1879 [see Node sb. 6 a].

4. Each of the parts into which a thing is or may be divided; a division, section.

1762 Bp. Lowth Introd. Eng. Gram. 157 A sentence or Member is again subdivided into Commas, or Segments. 1847 Lewes Hist. Philos. (1867) I. 236 By the second segment of the intellectual world understand me to mean all [etc.]. 1847 L. Hunt Men, Women, & B. I. ii. 22 Being unable to divide the orange into its segments, he ventures upon a great liquid bite. 1886 Ruskin Præterita I. x. 307, I must ..cease talk of pictorial and rhythmic efforts..and go back to give account of another segment of my learning.

5. Bot. Each of the portions into which a leaf or other plant-organ is divided by long clefts or incisions.

1713 P. Blair Misc. Observ. (1718) 104 Flowers..divided into five Segments. 1723 — Pharmaco-Bot. I. 18 The Bottom Leaves generally consist of five Pair of Segments. 1796 Withering Brit. Plants (ed. 3) I. 80 Segment (lacinium), the small parts of a leaf, cup, or petal, included between the incisions. 1877 Hulme Wild Flowers I. Summary 6 Borage...Calyx of five segments, very deeply cleft. 1880 A. Gray Struct. Bot. iii. § 4. 98 When a leaf is divided or parted and these primary lobes again lobed or cleft, the lobes of first order are called Segments (sometimes divisions or partitions), and the parts of these, Lobes.

6. Biol. and Embryol. a. Each of the longitudinal divisions composing the body in some animals, esp. in the Articulata; a somite, metamere.

1826 Kirby & Sp. Entomol. IV. 297 Segment (Segmentum). The great inosculating joints of the body. 1828 Stark Elem. Nat. Hist. II. 127 Articulata. The third great division of the Animal Kingdom consists of animals which have their body or members composed of segments or articulated rings. 1872 H. A. Nicholson Palæont. xiv. 143 The body [in Arthropods] is composed of a series of segments or 'somites', arranged along a longitudinal axis.

b. A cell formed by segmentation.

1862 Darwin Orchids v. 207 The three proper ovule-bearing cords or segments. 1882 Vines Sachs' Bot. 139 The other daughter-cell..appears..like a piece cut off from the back or side of the apical cell,..and is hence called the Segment.

7. Anat. Each complete series of bones forming a vertebra of the spinal column; also, each of the three annular divisions of the cranium proper.

1844 Owen Anat. Vertebr. Anim. iii. 42, I define a vertebra, as one of those segments of the endo-skeleton which constitute the axis of the body [etc.]. 1880 Günther Fishes iv. 64 There is no trace of vertebral segments or ribs.

b. A division of the spinal cord and nerves.

1855 H. Spencer Psychol. (1872) I. I. ii. 16 We find the nervous system formed of a series of centres, each sending fibres to the different organs of its own segment. 1899 Allbutt's Syst. Med. VIII. 623 Zoster on the face tends to follow the distribution of the three main peripheral branches of the ganglion rather than to be distributed over the supply of 'root areas' or segments'.

8. = Segment (or Segmental) arch (see 9 b).

1836 Parker Gloss. Arch. (1850) s. v. Arch, The only forms used by the ancients were the semicircle, the segment, and ellipse, all of which continued prevalent till the pointed arch appeared. a 1878 Sir G. Scott Lect. Archit. (1879) I. 146 The pointed arch had obtained universal predominance, though without involving the rejection of the semicircular or the plain segment.

9. attrib. and Comb. a. simple attrib., as (sense 6) segment-boundary, (sense 5) segment-leaf; segment-shell (see quot. 1862).

1893 J. Tuckey Amphioxus 119 Thereby is introduced the later characteristic curvature of the *segment boundaries [of the mesoblastic somite]. 1731 Miller Gard. Dict., *Segment-leaves, are Leaves of Plants divided or cut into many Shreds. 1862 F. A. Griffiths Artil. Man. (ed. 9) 192 The *Segment Shell consists of thin cast iron cylinders, enclosing a series of segments of the same metal, cast separately, and built upon an iron disc.

b. In many combinations with the meaning Segmental (sense 1), esp. in the names of mechanical appliances, parts of machinery, etc., indicating the shape of the essential or working part, as segment-arch, -rack, -roof, vault (see quots); segment-gear, -saw, -valve, -wheel, -window (see Knight Dict. Mech. 1875 and Suppl. 1884).

1807 Archit. Publ. Soc. Dict., *Segment arch. 1835 Ure Philos. Manuf. 196 The..stretching-roller has its axle mounted in the *segment-racks. 1838 Civ. Engin. & Arch. Jrnl. I. 225/2 From these springs a *segment roof. 1776 G. Semple Building in Water 123 Erect a competent Number of Pillars..and thereon turn *segment Vaults and Arches.

Segment (se·gment), v. [f. Segment sb.]

1. trans. To subject to the process of segmentation or division and multiplication of cells; to produce (new cells) by this process.

1859 Todd's Cycl. Anat. V. 79/2 The whole yolk is segmented in mammalia. 1877 Huxley & Martin Elem. Biol. 50 The new cells which are successively segmented off from the terminal cell.

2. intr. Of a cell or ovum: To divide or split up and give origin to one or more new cells by the process of Segmentation.

1888 Rolleston & Jackson Anim. Life Introd. 24 In some Rotifera, Crustacea, and Insecta one polar body only is formed, and the ovum then proceeds to segment.

3. trans. To divide into segments.

1872 Humphry Myology 5 The caudal muscles therefore consist of a 'dorsal' and 'ventral' muscle on each side, ..transversely segmented by the membranous septa and the vertebral processes running into it. 1878 A. H. Green, etc., Coal iv. 121 The axis, prefiguring what in most vertebrates becomes segmented and ossified into the centra,..retains [etc.].

Segmental (segme·ntăl), a. [f. Segment sb. + -al.]

1. Having the form of a segment (or, loosely, of an arc) of a circle.

1837 Fraser's Mag. XVI. 151 Giving its point a segmental sweep from Penlee Point..to the Mew-stone. 1856 'Stonehenge' Brit. Sports II. I. viii. § 5. 346/1 This segmental form is better than the straight bit. 1869 Rankine Machine & Hand-tools Pl. N 1, A segmental bevel wheel.

b. Arch. Of an arch, a pediment, window-head, etc. Hence segmental-arched, -headed adjs.

1816 Rickman Archit. in J. Smith Panorama Sci. & Art I. 131 A segmental arch has its centre lower than the spring. 1849 Freeman Archit. 350 The segmental arch..is both more horizontal and less elegant than the four-centred. 1851 — Window Tracery 253 Of Segmental-Headed Windows. Ibid. 254 By a segmental head I of course understand one in which the centre (or centres) is very much below the line of the constructive impost. Ibid. 255 Segmental windows filled with Reticulated tracery. 1867 A. Barry Life Sir C. Barry iii. 84 Angular and segmental pediments. 1867 Church News 31 July 327/2 A small chamber with a segmental arched vault.

2. Of, pertaining to, or composed of segments or divisions. In various applications (Anat., Biol., Acoustics, etc.).

1854 Owen in Orr's Circ. Sci., Org. Nat. I. 172 Giving the first indication of the segmental character of the skeleton. 1856 T. Williams in Phil. Trans. (1859) CXLVIII. 93 Under the appellation of the 'segmental organ', accordingly, it is proposed to describe that viscus upon the basis of which..are always ingrafted the true generative structures [in Annelids]. 1870 Everett Deschanel's Nat. Philos. 1067 Index, Segmental vibration, 832. 1879 F. M. Balfour in Q. Jrnl. Microsc. Sci. XIX. 8 The first part of the urino-genital system to develop is the segmental duct (Vornieregang of Fürbringer), which is formed by a groove-like invagination of the peritoneal epithelium. 1888 Huxley & Martin Elem. Biol. i. 169 The pronenal (segmental) duct. 1888 [see Segmentally]. 1898 Syd. Soc. Lex., Segmental organ, an organ consisting of a primitive epithelium-lined tubule opening at one end on the body-surface, and at the other into the cœlom or body-cavity. It is the type of the primitive kidneys.

b. Path. Characterized by segmentation or division into segments.

1898 Allbutt's Syst. Med. I. 189 Segmental degeneration of the nerves.

Segmentally (segme·ntăli), adv. [f. Segmental a. + -ly².] In a segmental manner.

1888 Huxley & Martin Elem. Biol. iii. 244 These [excretory] organs, being thus segmentally arranged, are termed segmental organs or nephridia. 1900 Miall & Hammond Harlequin Fly ii. 84 Tracheal gills..may be ventral,..caudal, ..segmental (i. e. segmentally repeated).

Segmentary (segme·ntări), a. [f. Segment sb. + -ary. Cf. F. segmentaire.]

1. Of the nature of or resembling a segment or an arc of a circle; segmental.

1853 Kane Grinnell Exp. xxxv. (1856) 314 Clouds, assuming a segmentary or arch-like form. Ibid. 321 Attracting attention by..its well-defined segmentary character.

2. Pertaining to segments or divisions; composed of segments.

1898 Syd. Soc. Lex., Segmentary, made up of segments. 1899 Allbutt's Syst. Med. VIII. 99 Such a segmentary anæsthesia could not be produced by lesion of either the cord nerve-roots, or nerve-trunks.

Segmentate (se·gmĕnteⁱt), a. [f. Segment sb. + -ate². (L. had segmentātus ornamented with strips of cloth.)] Formed of segments, segmented.

1875 Encycl. Brit. II. 292/2 The abdomen [of an Araneid] is covered with a continuous integument neither annulate nor segmentate.

Segmentation (se·gmĕntēⁱ·ʃən). [f. Segment v. + -ation.]

†1. 'A cutting into small pieces, an embroidering' (Blount Glossogr. 1656). Obs.⁻⁰

2. The process of division into segments, chiefly in various biological applications; spec. in Embryology, the process by which, in the Metazoa, the germinal cell or protoplasmic mass is converted by division into a multitude of cells, which become metamorphosed into the tissues of the body.

1851 Carpenter Man. Phys. (ed. 2) 487 The first change.. in the Mammalian ovum, is the 'segmentation' of the yolk; the entire mass of which..resolves itself..into..segments. 1880 A. Gray Struct. Bot. iii. § 4. 98 Lobation or Segmentation. 1882 Vines Sachs' Bot. 293 The leaves undergo a segmentation similar to that of the stem. 1884 A. Sedgwick in Q. Jrnl. Microsc. Sci. XXIV. 43 On the Origin of Metameric Segmentation [etc.]. 1910 Spectator 30 July 173/1 This segmentation of the tribe into clans would lead us to the discussion of exogamy.

b. attrib., as segmentation cavity = Blastocele; segmentation sphere, see quot. 1898.

1888 Huxley & Martin Elem. Biol. i. 166 The cleavage cavity (segmentation cavity); small and central. 1898 Syd. Soc. Lex., Segmentation sphere, one of the cells of a fertilized ovum that has undergone segmentation. 1909 Contemp. Rev. Apr. 447 Each segmentation sphere contained all the characters necessary to produce the entire organism.

Segmented (se·gmĕntĕd), ppl. a. [f. Segment v. + -ed¹.]

1. a. Anat., Zool., etc. Consisting of segments or similar parts arranged in a longitudinal series.

1854 Owen in Orr's Circ. Sci., Org. Nat. I. 176 In the cod-fish..it forms no part of the segmented neuroskeleton. 1870 Rolleston Anim. Life Introd. 124 The segmented Vermes.

b. Bot. Of a leaf: Divided into segments or lobes.

1883 G. Allen in Nature 15 Mar. 466 The divided but more broadly segmented leaves of those tall open-field species, cow-parsnip..and Alexanders.

2. Embryol. Of an ovum, a cell: Divided or split up by segmentation into cells.

1875 Encycl. Brit. III. 682/2 [Biology.] In the segmented body, the segments may or may not give rise to symmetrically or asymmetrically disposed processes. 1877 Huxley & Martin Elem. Biol. 106 The segmented ovum: composed of a large number of small cells.

Segne, obs. form of Seine.

Segnior, -orie, -y: see Seignior, Seigniory.

Se·gnitude. rare⁻⁰. [ad. med.L. segnitūdo, f. L. segnis: see next and -tude.] = Segnity.

1818 in Todd; hence in later Dicts.

†**Se·gnity.** Obs.⁻⁰ [ad. L. segnitāt-em, f. segnis slow, sluggish: see -ity.] (See quots.)

1623 Cockeram II, Slothfulnes..Segnity. 1656 Blount Glossogr., Segnity, negligence, slowness, slothfulness; also barrenness.

[**Segnotic**, erron. form of Stegnotic a. and sb.]

Segnoury, -nurie, -nyorye: see Seigniory.

Sego (sīˑgo). U.S. [Said to be Ute Indian.] A showy-flowered plant, Calochortus Nuttallii, of the western United States, with an edible bulb.

1883 Harper's Mag. 709/2.

Segolate, segholate (se·gŏlĕt), a. and sb. Heb. Gram. [a. mod.L. seg(h)olātus, f. Heb. סְגוֹל sᵉgōl, the name of the vowel-point ֶ and of the sound (e, ę) which it represents.

The name sᵉgōl means lit. 'bunch of grapes', alluding to the shape of the character.]

a. adj. Originally, of a disyllabic noun: Having the vowel sᵉgōl in both syllables. Now commonly in extended sense, as the distinctive epithet of the class of disyllabic nouns having an unaccented short vowel (normally sᵉgōl) in the last syllable.

b. sb. A segolate noun.

1831 M. Stuart Gram. Hebr. § 100. 46 All Segholate forms, i.e. those which have a furtive vowel in their final syllable. Ibid. § 119. 56 Aleph penult, in words that would regularly be Segholates. 1837 G. Phillips Syriac Gram. 25 One of the old forms of segolate nouns in Hebrew. 1884 Cheyne Isaiah I. 291 The word is a so-called 'Segolate' in form.

Segoon (sĭgūˑn). Fencing. Obs. or arch. Also 8 seco(c)oon, sagoone. [a. F. seconde, pronounced (sǝgõnd).] = Seconde 2.

1721 D'Urfey Two Queens Brentf. II. i, Straight, in Seccoon, grim Death shall be his Lot. 1730 H. Blackwell Compl. Fencing Master 9 Which seven [thrusts] are these following: Carte, Tierce, Sagoone [etc.]. 1777 Sheridan Sch. Scand. v. ii, Sir Peter is dangerously wounded—By a thrust in segoon quite through his left side. 1903 Longm. Mag. Apr. 530 A thrust in segoon.

Segra (sīˑgrā.) [Perh. a native W. Indian name.] = Sequa.

1864 Grisebach Flora W. Ind. Islands 787 Segra-seed: Feuillea cordifolia. 1891 in Century Dict.

Segreant (se·grĭ,ănt), a. Her. Forms: 6–7 sergreant, 8 Dicts. sergreiant, 7– segreant. [Originally sergreant, of obscure etymology; probably corrupt; s'érigeant ('erecting itself') has been conjectured.] An epithet applied to a griffin (in quot. a 1695, perh. erroneously, to a falcon).

The real meaning of the term seems to be unknown. In some examples it is combined with passant; if this be not an error, the explanation in modern books, 'Rampant with wings expanded', cannot be correct.

? a 1550 in Baring-Gould & Twigge West. Armory (1898) 5 Bligh: Azur a griffon sergreant arg. 1562 Legh Armory 106 A Griffin sergreant Or.—Wherefore saye you Sergreante? —For that he is halfe byrd, half beast. 1610 Guillim Heraldry III. xxvi. 181 Hee beareth Argent, a Griffon Passant, hiswings displaied Sable...Leigh in his Blazon of this Beast, addeth this word Sergreant, in regard of his two-fold forme. c 1630 Risdon Surv. Devon § 95 (1810) 91 A Griffin, segreant, or. 1882 Gibbon Introd. Lat. Blasoniam 60 Segreant..is the proper term for a Griffon displaying his Wings, Segreant ses aisles, as ready to fly. a 1695 Wood Oxford (O.H.S.) III. 146 Armes are 'parted per chevron azure and argent, in chief two falcons sergreant or'. 1763 Brit. Mag. IV. 415 On a wreath, a gryphon passant, segreant, sable.

Segregable (se·grĭgăb'l), a. rare⁻¹. [f. L. sēgregā-re Segregate v.: see -able.] That may be segregated.

1907 Contemp. Rev. June 908 Where the parent types differ in more than one pair of segregable characters we have new combinations of the parental characters.

†**Se·gregant**, a. Obs. rare⁻¹. [ad. L. sēgregant-em, pres. pple. of segregāre to Segregate.] Separated, divided.

1647 Ward Simple Cobler 5 Tolerations of divers Religions, or of one Religion in segregant shapes.

Segregate (se·grĭgĕt), a. and sb. [ad. L. sēgregātus, pa. pple. of sēgregāre: see Segregate v.]

A. adj.

1. Separated, set apart, isolated. Now rare.

In early use often † as pa. pple.

1426 Lydg. De Guil. Pilgr. 9399 The Body..Whan yt ys fro the segregat, Dysseueryd & separat. c 1480 St. Ursula (Roxb.) A j, So were the nobles from Brytayne segregate. 1532 More Confut. Tindale Wks. 428/1 Those holye consecrate companyes, the tone segregate from paynims by the sacrament of baptysme, the tother segregate fro the laye peple by the sacrament of order. 1563 Foxe A. & M. (1596) 1004/2 He was segregatus a peccatoribus—clean segregate from all kind of uncleanness. 1670 G. H. Hist. Cardinals III. II. 279 Two or three Cardinals, segregate from the other Factions. 1685 Baxter Paraphr. N. T. 2 Cor. vi. 17–18 A holy people segregate to the Lord. 1865 Spectator 14 Jan. 32 It is true they have been celebrating their defeat..in a more morose and segregate manner than is here suggested.

2. spec. (Zool., Bot., etc.). Separated (wholly or partially) from the parent or from one another; not aggregated.

1793 T. Martyn Lang. Bot., Segregata Polygamia. Segregate Polygamy...When several florets comprehended within a common calyx are furnished also with their proper perianths. 1846 Dana Zooph. iv. (1848) 82 Segregate, when the buds are separate from the parent, except at base, each forming a distinct shoot or branch. 1882–4 Cooke Brit. Fresh-w. Algæ I. 29 Either single, segregate, or associated in families.

B. sb.

1. Math. One of a smallest select aggregate of products of irreducible covariants which suffices to provide by linear combination all covariants of every degree and order.

1878 Cayley Math. Papers X. 339 The effect of this was to enable me to establish for any given degree in the coefficients and order in the variables..a selected system of powers and products of the covariants, say a system of 'segregates'. Ibid. 345 The terms in the expansion of the R. G. F. [i. e. Real Generating Function] may be called 'segregates', and the terms not in the expansion 'congregates'.

2. Bot. (See quot. 1900.)

1871 Britten in Trans. Newbury Field Club I. 36 In this first enumeration aggregate species only..are entered; the segregates being noticed in the second..list. 1900 B. D. Jackson Gloss. Bot. Terms s.v., A Segregate is a species separated from a super-species.

Hence **Se·gregateness**.

1668 Wilkins Real Char. II. i. 34.

Segregate (se·grĭgeⁱt), v. Also 6–7 segregat. [f. L. sēgregāt-, ppl. stem of sēgregāre to separate from the flock, hence to set apart, isolate, divide, f. sē- (see Se-) + greg-, grex flock.]

1. trans. To separate (a person, a body or class of persons) from the general body, or from some particular class; to set apart, isolate, seclude.

In early use often with allusion to the Vulgate renderings of Heb. vii. 26, segregatus a peccatoribus, and of Jude 19, qui segregant semetipsos.

1542 Becon News out of Heaven G j, Your Bysshop shalbe godly, innocent, fautles, segregated from synners. 1552 Latimer 4th Serm. Lord's Pr. (1584) 145 b, This is the cause wherefore he will haue hys flocke segregated from the wicked. 1552 — Serm. 5th Sund. Epiph. ibid. 322 So the Anabaptistes in our time..segregated themselues from the companye of other men. 1582 N. T. (Rhem.) Jude 19 These are they which segregate them selves, sensual, having not the Spirit. 1602 T. Fitzherbert Def. 54 The Apostles.. were commanded by the holy ghost to segregat Paul and Barnabas. 1678 Cudworth Intell. Syst. 891 Nature absolutely Dissociates and Segregates men from one another, by reason of the Inconsistency of those Appetites of theirs. 1749 Fielding Tom Jones XIII. ii, He rambled about some time before he could even find his way to those happy mansions, where fortune segregates from the vulgar, those magnanimous heroes. 1799 Coleridge in Mrs. H. Sandford T. Poole & Fr. (1888) I. 299 But dear Wordsworth appears to me to have hurtfully segregated and isolated his being. 1852 Ld. Cockburn Jeffrey I. 200 Certain peculiarities, or habits, which segregated him from the whole human race. 1884 Law Rep. 14 Q. B. Div. 278 Mr. Newitt has..segregated himself from Mr. Saffery in the trust. 1904 Dor. P. Hughes Life H. P. Hughes xxiii. (1907) 632 That innate instinct which ever aimed at uniting, not segregating groups of Christians.

2. To separate or isolate (one thing from others or one portion from the remainder); to place in a group apart from the rest; esp. Chem., Geol., etc. (of natural agencies) to separate out and collect (certain particular constituents of a compound or mixture). In scientific classification: To remove (certain species) etc. from a group and place them apart.

1579 Fulke Conf. Sanders 662 Christe vouchsafed to segregate it from other wood, to make it the instrument of his passion. 1625 Jackson Creed v. xxxiv, The prototype is conspicuous in the image, it is not segregated from it. 1691 Taylor Behmen's Theos. Phil. 73 Like a Refiner's fire which segregates Metals. 1744 Bp. Berkeley Siris § 190 The pure fire is to be discerned by it's effects alone; such as..the segregating heterogeneous bodies, and congregating those that are homogeneous. 1831 D. E. Williams Sir T. Lawrence I. 167 Had these superb paintings been segregated in a national gallery. 1842 Grove Corr. Phys. Forces (ed. 6) 100 The energy of the rays having been used up in decomposing the carbonic acid. The carbon thus segregated by the sun's rays is ready to give out heat and light, whenever it may be recombined with oxygen. 1872 W. S. Symonds Rec. Rocks x. 360 The limestone must have been segregated in deeper and tranquil waters. 1872 C. King Sierra Nevada vii. 134 By an Act of Congress, the Yosemite Valley had been segregated from the public domain. 1911 Q. Rev. Jan. 290 In a true reference to the people the issue would be segregated.

b. Mining. (U. S.) See quot.

1881 Raymond Mining Gloss., Segregate, Pac. To separate the undivided joint owership of a mining claim into smaller individual 'segregated' claims.

3. intr. for refl. To separate from a main body or mass and collect in one place.

1863 Bates Nat. Amazon vii. (1864) 169 The Mauhés are considered..to be a branch of the great Mundurucú nation; having segregated from them at a remote period. 1870 Proctor Other Worlds xi. 261 Whether clusters of them will eventually segregate from their neighbours..it is as yet ..impossible to judge. 1877 Fraser's Mag. XVI. 401 Most of the provinces had segregated into independent principalities.

Hence **Se·gregated** ppl. a.; **Se·gregating** vbl. sb.

a 1628 Preston New Covt. (1629) 221 My Word is as fire; It is a segregating thing, that differenceth, and puts a separation betweene the scum, and the liquor. 1652 News fr. Low-Countr. 1 Those four segregated forms. 1844 Disraeli Coningsby IV. x, To the segregating genius of their great Lawgiver, Sidonia ascribes the fact that they had not been long ago absorbed among those mixed races. 1855 J. R. Leifchild Cornwall 127 By the segregating power of electric action. 1855 J. Phillips Man. Geol. 513 We may collect masses of true granite,..compact felspars, and many other segregated varieties. 1874 Raymond 6th Rep. Mines 518 That the extensions, bought by Raymond..were..on segregated ground far to the south.

Segregation (se·grĭgēⁱ·ʃən). [ad. late L. sēgregātiōn-em, n. of action f. L. sēgregāre: see prec.]

1. The action of segregating. a. The separation or isolation of a portion of a community or a body of persons from the rest.

1615 N. Byfield Coloss. i. 18 (1628) 122 The Church..is Holy by segregation from the sinnefull world. a 1677 Manton Serm. Ps. cxix, cxxx. (1725) 600 Mat. 25. 32, 33...There is a congregation and then a segregation. 1829 Southey Sir T. More (1831) I. 384 There would be that segregation from the community into particular societies. 1849 A. Bryson Med. Statist. in Man. Sci. Enq. 435 The utter impossibility of complete segregation [of fever patients], even in the most roomy vessel. 1859 Tennent Ceylon II. VII. iii. 138 The social segregation is carried to such an extreme, that members of the several classes..refuse to associate together. 1861 Beresf. Hope Eng. Cathedr. 19th C. vi. 215 The provision which the early Eastern Church made, with true Oriental feeling, for the segregation of women into galleries. 1904 Brit. Med. Jrnl. 17 Sept. 631 Manson has also declared segregation to be the first law of hygiene for the Europeans in the tropics.

b. Dispersion, break up (of a collective unity).

1604 Shaks. Oth. II. i. 10 What shall we heare of this [sc. a storm]? A Segregation of the Turkish Fleet.

c. The separation of a portion or portions of a collective or complex unity from the rest; the

isolation of particular constituents of a compound or mixture.

1612 Woodall Surg. Mate Wks. (1653) 273 Segregation is the solution of that which was whole and perfect into parts divided, which flow not together as colliquables dissolved. 1634 T. Johnson Parey's Chirurg. XXVII. viii. (1678) 668 Vinegar is made by the corruption of Wine, and the segregation of the fiery and airy parts. a 1734 North Exam. III. x. § 1 (1740) 658 Now I have but one Matter more to work up,..which is a Segregation of Libel from History, which this Author has blended together. 1798 W. Taylor in Monthly Mag. V. 190 These observations..tend to authorize the segregation of a very fine set of oracles from those of Isaiah, Jeremiah, and Ezekiel. 1836 Buckland Geol. & Min. xxi. (1837) I. 551 A fourth hypothesis considers veins to have been slowly filled by Segregation, or infiltration... Segregation of this kind may have taken place from electro-chemical agency, continued during long periods of time. 1878 Bell Gegenbaur's Comp. Anat. 43 Ontogenetic facts point to the primitive segregation of the nervous system from the ectoderm. 1886 Ld. Coleridge in Law Times LXXXI. 65/2 The general costs of the action, which remain after the segregation of these separate costs.

Comb. (Geol.). 1875 J. W. Dawson Dawn of Life ii. 28 Many of the veins are not true fissures but..segregation veins. 1888 Teall Brit. Petrogr. 447 Segregation vein, a vein which has been produced by the segregation of the component mineral matter of a rock along fissures.

†d. spec. Separation from a church or ecclesiastical organization: chiefly in reproachful sense, schism. Obs.

1555 Philpot in Coverdale Lett. Martyrs (1564) 219 If we behold through yᵉ iniquity of tyme, segregations to be made wyth counterfayt religion. 1662 H. Hibbert Body Divin. II. 56 Let the seperatist..through his sullen segregation..be a thief to himself. 1683 Corbet Nonconf. Plea 26 There is a great difference between inimical segregation, like sedition in a Commonwealth; and a going severally upon weighty reasons.

2. The condition of being segregated.

1668 Wilkins Real Char. IV. ii. 407 To which [companionship] the opposite..is being in a state of Segregation from others. 1728 Bp. T. Wilson in Keble Life xi. (1863) 386 Sooner than unite with her [the church of Rome]..I should rather choose to live in a state of segregation. 1841 L. Hunt Seer (1864) 81 To show the selectness and segregation of their accomplishments.

3. concr. Something segregated; in early use, † a schismatic body.

1563 Winȝet Bk. Quest. Wks. (S.T.S.) I. 98 Ȝe dissent fra the..haly Kirk vniuersall, and als fra the segregatioun of all heretikis afoir ȝow. 1605 in 10th Rep. Hist. MSS. Comm. App. v. 372 The schismatick uniting himselfe unto their congregations, or rather, as this Sainct sayeth, unto their segregations. 1859 Murchison Siluria xix. (ed. 3) 493 Veinstones or original segregations of gold. 1869 F. Galton Heredit. Genius 376 We must..consider each human or other personality..as a segregation of what already existed. 1877 Raymond Mines 146 Number of feet in claim is 600, being a segregation of the north end of the Ophir Mine.

Segregational (se:grĭgēⁱ·ʃənăl), a. [-al.] Of, pertaining to, or characterized by segregation.

1875 Ure's Dict. Arts (ed. 7) I. 812 Clays..from which the oxide of iron has been abstracted; partly by a segregational process, drawing together the iron into ferruginous nodules of hydrous sesquioxide.

Segregative (se·grĭgeⁱtiv), a. [ad. med.L. sēgregātīvus, f. L. sēgregāre: see Segregate v.]

1. Having the power or effect of separating. † a. Gram. and Logic. A general designation for adversative (or † discretive) and disjunctive conjunctions. Hence of a proposition, Consisting of members joined by a segregative conjunction.

1588 Fraunce Lawiers Log. II. vii. 95 b, The segregative axiome is that whose conjunction is segregative, and therefore is fittest to dispose disagreeable arguments which must be severed. The segregative is either disjunctive or discretive. 1626 A. Wotton Art Logick II. vii. 142 That word is a conjunction Segregatiue, which severeth or divideth the parts of speech each from other.

b. Having the property of separating the elements or constituent parts of matter.

1674 T. Flatman Belly God 95 The Vintner..With segregative things as Pigeons eggs Strait purifies, and takes away the dregs. 1858 Sat. Rev. 20 Nov. 502 Iron-stone nodules ..are..probably the result of a segregative power.

2. Of persons: Given to separation or disunion. Of an individual: Unsociable.

1685 H. More Refl. Baxter 24, I leave him..to consider what a pleasant thing it is to Flesh and Blood to be a Segregative Rabboni. 1875 Whitney Life Lang. ix. 158 The influences of barbarism, beyond narrow limits, are prevailingly segregative, a wild race..breaks up into mutually jealous and hostile divisions. 1888 Mrs. H. Sandford T. Poole & Fr. I. 157 Coleridge was as social as Wordsworth was segregative in his tendencies.

†**Se·gstar.** Sc. Obs. [Prob. repr. med.L. sacristārius, through some OF. form.] = Sexton.

1531 Aberdeen Reg. (1844) I. 143 And the segstar and his seruand to ansuer for the keiping of the kirk zard to the maisteris of kirk vark.

‖**Seguidilla** (segidī·lʸa). Also 8 sequedilla, 8–9 seguedilla; 9 (after Fr.) segua-, seguidille. [a. Sp. seguidilla (whence F. séguidille, séguedille), f. seguida following, sequence, f. seguir (:—L. sequī) to follow.] A Spanish dance in ¾ or ⅜ time; also the music for such a dance.

1763 Court & City Mag. Apr. 191/2 (Stanf.) He joined the others and danced a Sequedillas. 1775 R. Twiss Trav. Portugal & Sp. 167 A seguedilla is only a part of a tonadilla [sic]. 1780 Ann. Reg. II. 11 A monotonous drawling seguidilla that serves the nurses as a lullaby to put their children to rest. 1811 Scott Don Roderick II. xxxiv, And rung from village-green the merry seguidille. a 1852 Moore Oh! remember the time 5 When I taught you to warble the gay seguadille, And to dance to the light castanet. 1854 Thackeray Newcomes xxiii. I. 222 Percy sings a Spanish seguidella, or a German lied [etc.].

Segundo (sĕgʊ·ndo). [f. the name of Juan Segundo, the author of a book on bridle bits.

The British Museum has a copy in Spanish dated 1855, and one in French dated 1829. An English translation, 'from the original Spanish MS. which was dedicated to George IV. in 1832', was printed in Latchford's book cited below.]

A kind of bridle bit. Also attrib.

1860 Whyte Melville Mkt. Harb. xvii, An animal that may have the pace of a race-horse, but requires a segundo bridle, and a hundred-acre field to turn him in. 1871 B. Latchford The Loriner List of Engravings, Segundo Bit, No. 41. Buxton Segundo, No. 81.

Segur, obs. form of Saggar.

1752 Gentl. Mag. XXII. 348 Great kiln for segurs.

Seh(e, Sehel, obs. ff. See v., Seal sb.²

†**Se·helich**, a. Obs. rare. [? f. stem of See v. + -lich, -ly¹. Cf. the synonymous OE. gesewenlic, f. the pa. pple.] That may be seen, visible.

a 1225 Leg. Kath. 249, & hereð & hersumeð seheliche schaftes. a 1225 St. Marher. 11 Glistinde gimstan of all seheliche þing ant untsehelich baðe.

Sehen, -ene, obs. ff. See v., Sene a.

Sei, obs. f. Say v.¹, See v.; var. Sey sb.²

Seiannte, Seiant(e, obs. forms of Sejant.

Seicentist (sēitʃe·ntist). [ad. It. seicentisti pl., f. seicento: see next.] An Italian artist or man of letters of the seventeenth century.

1905 Athenæum 25 Mar. 376/3 The rest of the Italian School is of minor importance, though one or two of the Seicentists are here..well represented.

‖**Seicento** (sēitʃe·nto). [It.: short for mil seicento one thousand six hundred.] The seventeenth century considered as a period of Italian art.

1908 R. Bagot A. Cuthbert iv. 29 Beautiful specimens of Italian cabinets of the cinquecento and seicento.

Hence **Seice·ntoist** (rare) = Seicentist.

1830 Fraser's Mag. I. 146 The architect..has thought proper to have recourse to the 'seicentoists'.

Seich, obs. pa. t. of See v.

Seiche (sēⁱʃ). Physiogr. [a. Swiss Fr. seiche, perh. a graphic adoption of G. seiche, sinking (of water).

Not connected, as is usually stated, with F. seiche, sèche, 'a portion of the sea-bottom left uncovered at low tide'.]

(See quots.)

1839 G. Roberts Dict. Geol., Seiches (Swiss term): an occasional undulation of the water of lakes, like a tide wave, sometimes to the height of five feet, supposed to be caused by the unequal pressure of the atmosphere. 1852 Tr. Ross Humboldt's Trav. I. i. 24 M. Vaucher thinks that the tides in the lake of Geneva, known by the name of the seiches, arise from the same cause. 1898 G. H. Darwin Tides ii. 37 Although, then, it is possible to indicate causes competent to produce seiches, yet we cannot as yet point out the particular cause for any individual seiche.

Hence **Seicho·meter** [-meter] an instrument for measuring seiches.

1903 Nature 23 Apr. 599/2 Sir John Murray..exhibited a seichometer with which he hoped in the coming season to get a more definite and precise record of these oscillations.

Seicle, obs. Sc. form of Siecle.

Seid(e: see Sayyid, Said ppl. a., Seed.

Seidg(e, obs. forms of Siege.

Seidlitz (se·dlits). Also 8 seydlitz, 9 sedlitz. The name of a village in Bohemia, where there is a spring impregnated with magnesium sulphate and carbonic acid. Used attrib. in † Seidlitz salt, magnesium sulphate; † Seidlitz water, an artificial aperient water of the same composition as the water of the Seidlitz spring. Hence in Seidlitz powder (arbitrarily named, merely on account of its aperient property), a dose consisting of two powders, one of tartaric acid and the other of a mixture of potassium tartrate and sodium bicarbonate, which are to be dissolved separately, and the solutions mixed and drunk during effervescence.

1784 Cullen tr. Bergman's Phys. & Chem. Ess. I. 439 The Seydlitz, Seydschutz, or Epsom salts are got by evaporation from the water of fountains in the places from whence they borrow their names. 1802 Med. Jrnl. VIII. 491 The Sedlitz water is another sort of artificial mineral water introduced by Mr. Paul in this country...This water consists of vitriolated magnesia,..and is so powerfully impregnated with carbonic acid, as to render the bitterness of the salt scarcely discoverable. 1815 Specif. Savory's Patent No. 3954, The combination of a neutral salt or powder which possesses all the properties of the medicinal spring at Seidlitz, in Germany, under the name of the Seidlitz Powders. 1837 Dickens Pickw. xx, Another clerk..was mixing a Seidlitz powder, under cover of the lid of his desk. 1872 Baker Nile Tribut. viii. 122 The simple effect of mixing a seidlitz powder was a source of amusement.

Seie(n, obs. ff. Say v.¹, See v.

Seif, Seige: see Sief Obs., Siege.

Seigh(e, etc.: see Say v.¹, See v., Sigh v.

Seigne, variant of Senye Obs.

Seignette (sen'e·t). Also 8 Saignette. The name of a French chemist of the seventeenth century used attrib. in Seignette salt, (earlier † Seignette's salt, F. sel de Seignette), a name for potassium and sodium tartrate, Rochelle salt.

1753 Chambers' Cycl. Suppl., Seignette's salt, a name given in France to a kind of sal polycrestus [etc.]. 1758 Reid tr. Macquer's Chym. I. 126 This salt is another sort of soluble Tartar. It is called Saignette's Salt, from the inventor's name. 1863 Fownes Chem. (ed. 9) 566 Tartrate of potassa and soda; Rochelle or seignette salt.

‖**Seigneur** (seⁿ'ö·r). Also 8 erron. seignieur. [Fr.:—L. seniōr-em: see Senior, and cf. Seignior and Signor.] a. In French History, a feudal lord; a noble taking his designation from the name of his estate. b. In Canada, the holder of a Seigneury; one of the landed gentry.

1592 Surv. France To Rdr., William of Saluste Seigneur of Bartas. 1775 Jefferson Let. Writ. 1892 I. 489 This St. Luc is a great Seigneur amongst the Canadians and almost absolute with the Indians. 1776 C. Carroll Jrnl. (1845) 79 These are the rich men in Canada: the seigniors are in general poor. 1876 Lowell Ode 4th July II. i, The lands no serf or seigneur ever trod. 1883 R. W. Dixon Mano IV. vii. 155 They whom distress and poverty constrain Against the seigneurs and their heavy dues To meet in conjuration, and complain. 1888 Lighthall Young Seigneur 2 'Oh. the seigneurs have not yet altogether disappeared', said the Montrealer to the Ontarian. 1907 F. W. Raffety Burke's Wks. IV. Pref. 10 Every newspaper recalled the murder of a seigneur; but on the other side the sufferers were too ignoble to be known.

Comb. 1873 Browning Red Cott. Nt.-cap 139 To sit free and take tribute seigneur-like.

Seigneurage: see Seignorage.

Seigneuress (sēⁱ·niŭrĕs). [a. F. seigneuresse, fem. of Seigneur.] A woman who exercises feudal authority; also, the wife of a seigneur.

1849 [Mrs. Wilde] tr. Meinhold's Sidonia Sorc. II. 130 Your feudal lady and seigneuress, Sidonia Bork. 1888 Lighthall Young Seigneur 118 How is Monsieur the Seigneur? And how is Madame the Seigneuresse?

Seigneurial (sēⁱniūᵊ·riăl), a. Also erron. 7 signeural, 8–9 seigneural. [a. F. seigneurial, f. seigneur, influenced by seigneurie (Hatz.-Darm.). Cf. Seignoral.] Pertaining to a seigneur (in France or Canada). Also sometimes used in wider sense = Seignorial.

1656 Heylin Surv. France IV. ii. 174 So did the Vidames disclaim their relation to the Bishop, and became Signieural or honorary also. 1673 Temple Observ. United Prov. i. 7 Seigneurial Jurisdiction over the Inhabitants. 1757 Burke Abridgm. Eng. Hist. III. vi. Wks. 1812 V. 650 From them [the clergy] were often taken the bailiffs of the seigneurial courts. 1792 A. Young Trav. France I. 259, I was sorry to see, at the village, a carcan, or seigneural standard, erected, to which a chain and heavy iron collar are fastened, as a mark of the lordly arrogance of the nobility, and the slavery of the people. 1834 K. H. Digby Mores Cath. v. vi. 156 In the seigneural chapel of the church of Mery-sur-Oise. 1865 Q. Rev. July 17 There was a something repugnant to the just pride of the Highland gentleman in the very idea of parting with his seigneurial rights, even for a season. 1887 Spectator 5 Nov. 1514/2 Canada could never have made much real progress under the seigneurial system.

Seigneury (sēⁱ·niŭri), ‖**seigneurie** (seⁿyöri). Hist. Also 9 seignurie, -ury. [ad. F. seigneurie, later form of seignorie (see Seignory), assimilated to seigneur.

1. a. Fr. Hist. A territory under the government of a seigneur. b. In Canada, a landed estate held (until 1854) by feudal tenure.

1683 Apol. Prot. France ii. 22 They have turn'd out of all Jurisdictions and Seignuries (which are almost infinite in France) all Protestants who had been admitted Officers in those Jurisdictions. 1763 Ld. Holland in Jesse Selwyn & Contemp. (1843) I. 269 Here is a large and good house..in the midst of a most extensive seigneurie. 1825 J. Nicholson Oper. Mech. 453 The chatelleine or seigneurie of Lille alone makes annually between 30,000 and 40,000 barrels. 1872 Miss Yonge Cameos (1877) II. viii. 100 The seigneurie of Garre, which lay near his own castle of Blein. 1903 Times 12 Dec. 8/6 His father, from whom he inherited the seigneurie, was the most prominent French leader of the rising of 1837.

2. In Canada, the mansion of a seigneur.

1895 G. Parker When Valmond came vi. (1896) 115 The old sergeant went to the Seigneury, knocked, and was admitted to a room where were seated the young Seigneur, Medallion, and the avocat. 1895 Outing (U. S.) XXVI. 415/2 As he passed one of the cottages within half a mile of the seigneurie, the sound of a piano made him stop short.

Seignior (sēⁱ·niŏɹ). Forms: 4 segnour, seynour, seignoure, 4–5 seignour, seynowre, seyngnour, seynȝowre, senyour, -owr, seniour, sene-, senei-, senȝe-, senyeour, 5, 7 seniour, 6 senȝ-, seneȝe-, seinȝeour, senȝe-, senyor, senȝeoure, senior, 7 seignor, seigniour, 7–9 seignior. [a. AF. segnour, OF. seignor, -eur (mod.F. seigneur, a Com. Rom. word = Pr. senhor, Sp. señor, Pg. senhor, It. signore:—L. seniōrem, acc. of senior elder (see Senior). Cf. Seigneur, Señor, Signor, Sir, Sire, all ultimately of the same etymology.]

1. In early use, synonymous with Lord; a person high in rank or authority, a ruler, a feudal superior; the lord of a manor. Now rare, and chiefly as a more vernacular substitute for Seigneur in speaking of a French feudal noble.

13.. K. Alis. 1455 (Laud MS.), Þe keyes hij token in his honde Of her Cites of her honoure And maden hym her liege seignoure. 1393 Langl. P. Pl. C. XII. 269 Now beeþ

þese seintes, as men seyen, and souereynes [v.r. seynours] in heuene. c 1400 Destr. Troy 13056 Then the Seniour [i.e. Menelaus] full sone, with seasonable windes, Cairet fro Crete with his clene nauy. 1552 Lyndesay Monarche 5758 Thare sall our Senȝeouris of the cessioun Off all thare faltis mak cleir confessioun. 1648 Gage West Ind. 39 A hundred thousand men of Warre..were sent by the Seniours of Mexico and Tezcuco to encounter Cortez. 1656 Blount Glossogr. 1706 Phillips (ed. Kersey), Seignior or Signior,..Lord, Master. In a Law Sense, the Lord of the Fee, or of the Manour. 1809 A. Henry Trav. 9 Late in the evening, I reached Les Cèdres, and was carried to the house of M. Leduc, its seignior. 1834 K. H. Digby Mores Cath. v. vii. 218 In the year 1245, was buried..a pious seignior, de Romilly, who dwelt at Romilly-sur-Seine. 1876 Bancroft Hist. U. S. V. iii. 113 They denied the authority of the French nobility as magistrates, and resisted their claim of a right as seigniors to command their military services.

b. As a title of address. Obs. exc. arch.

c 1330 Arth. & Merl. 3607 (Kölbing) Merlin com þe king to & to hem seyd: Bieu segnours [MS. sengours], ȝe ben yswore to king Arthours. c 1440 York Myst. xxx. 73 [To Pilate] My seniour, will ye see now þe sonne in youre sight. c 1460 Towneley Myst. xx. 8 Seniours, seke to my sawes, ffor bryssyng of youre bonys. 1528 Roy Rede me (Arb.) 67 Worsshipful seniours we must theym call Requyrynge that we shulde to theym obeye. 1823 Scott Quentin D. xix, 'Surely not, good seignior', answered the burgher.

†2. Used to represent It. Signor or F. Seigneur in designations of Italians or Frenchmen. Obs.

a 1578 Lindesay (Pitscottie) Chron. Scot. (S.T.S.) II. 187 Seinȝeour Dauid the Italian secriter. 1588 Rot. Scacc. Reg. Scot. XXI. 410 For chalmer maill and ledding to Senyeour Du Barras, Francheman. 1718 Free-thinker No. 15. 101 Seignior Camillo and Seignior Alessandro..entered.

Seignior, obs. form of Senior.

Seigniorage, seignorage (sēⁱ·nyŏrĕdʒ). Also 6 s(e)ignowrage, 8 seignourage, 5, 9 seigneurage. [a. OF. seignorage, seigneurage (mod.F. has seigneuriage), f. seigneur: see Seigneur, Seignior, and -age. Cf. It. signoraggio.]

†1. Lordship, dominion. Obs.

1656 Blount Glossogr. 1798 W. Taylor in Monthly Mag. V. 353 Opinions of hereditary right..must either be allowed to establish their superstitions (the monarchy or seigniorage of certain families),..or must be coerced in the exercise of their claims. 1820 Wiffen Aonian Hours (ed. 2) 47 Her [Europe's] throne has been an armed seignorage.

2. A duty levied on the coining of money for the purpose of covering the expenses of minting, and as a source of revenue to the crown, claimed by the sovereign by virtue of his prerogative.

1444 Rolls of Parlt. V. 109/1 Wherof our Sovereign Lord to have and take for his Seigneurage vii d in nombre. 1543 tr. Act 9 Hen. V Stat. II. c. 2 Payeng yᵉ seignowrage & cunage of golde after the rate of .v.s. for the pounde of the tower. Ibid., With the signowrage and coynage as afore is sayde. 1658 Phillips. 1695 Locke Further Consid. Money 84 This at least they were not mistaken in, that they brought Work to the Mint, and a Part of the Money coined to the Crown for Seignorage. 1797 Monthly Mag. III. 352 Delivering out, without deduction for seignorage, duty, workmanship, or even waste, the full value of all bullion brought in to be coined. 1805 Earl Liverpool Treat. Coins 102 Augmentation of revenue was expected from the additional profits, which would in such case arise, from the right of Seigneurage. 1880 Del Mar Hist. Prec. Metals 125 The royalties, seignorages, convoy-duties, and other impositions..which the Portuguese monarchs levied upon the gold product of Brazil. 1885 Manch. Exam. 7 Apr. 4/5 The proposal often made of deducting a seigniorage from the intrinsic value of the coinage. 1891 Daily News 6 Nov. 3/5 Any profit which the State gets from note circulation, seigneurage, and the like.

3. A duty claimed by the over-lord upon the output of certain minerals, a royalty.

a 1859 Macaulay Hist. Eng. xxv. V. 265 With that domain they had as little to do as with the seignorage levied on tin in the Duchy of Cornwall.

¶4. Alleged to signify: 'Profit' (Webster 1847–54); 'The money paid on a copyright by a publisher to an author' (Webster 1864, marked 'Eng.'). Cf. Lordship sb. 6, Royalty 6 e.

†5. attrib. seigniorage fine, a royalty paid to the over-lord in return for the concession of a privilege. Obs.

1800 Asiat. Ann. Reg. 318/1 Perhaps a seigniorage fine to government for permission to sink a new well.

†**Sei·gnioresse.** Law. Obs. Also 7 segnioresse, seignoresse, signioresse. [a. OF. seignoresse, var. of seigneuresse.] = Seigneuress.

a 1604 Hanmer Chron. Irel. (1809) 386 If the eldest sister should take homage of the yonger, she should be as a segnioresse to them all. 1642 tr. Perkins' Prof. Bk. vi. § 459. 200 If a woman be seignoresse and a man be tenant. 1651 tr. Kitchin's Courts Leet (1653) 313 If a Woman Signioresse take her Tenant to Husband.

†**Seignio·rity, seigno·rity.** Obs. [a. OF. seignourité, f. Seigneur: see -ity.] Lordship, governance.

1525 Ld. Berners Froiss. II. ccxxiv. 291 They..founde a great nombre of Ladyes and damosels, who had the sygniorite of that isle. 1596 Lodge Marg. Amer. 10 Your couetous longing after riches, your ambitious hunting after seignioritie, haue occasioned this warre. 1598 Spenser Brief Note Irel. Wks. (Grosart) I. 540 Then was he..to loose that seignoritie wᶜʰ he claimed of that land.

Sei·gniorship. rare. [f. Seignior + -ship.] The rank or condition of a seignior. In quot. used as a form of address.

1823 Scott Quentin D. xiv, Your seigniorship.

Seigniory, seignory (sēⁱ·nyŏri), sb. Forms: 3–4 senurre, 4–5 senurie, senery, 5 senowrye; 4 Sc. senȝhory, senȝeroy, senȝhowry, 4–5 senyoury (Sc. senȝoury, senȝory), seniourie, 5–7 seniory, seniorie, (5 seniore), senȝowry, 6 senȝeory, -ie, 6–7 senyeory; 3 seynorye, 4 seynu(r)rye, 4 seynore, seinuri, 5 seynourye; 4 seinȝnery, 4–5 sengnurie, syngnory; 4 segnoury, 6 segnorie, segniory, 6–7 segniorie, 6 segeyorye; 3–6 seygnery, seignori(ȝ)e, seiȝnory, 4–5 seignurie, 4–6 seignorye, seygno(u)rye, seignourie, -y(e, seygnourie, 4–7 seigniorie, (7 seigniore, siegniory, seignieurie), 4– seignory, 6– seigniory. [a. OF. seignorie (mod.F. refashioned seigneurie), f. seigneur: see Seignior. Cf. Sp. señoria, Pg. senhoria, It. signoria. See also Seigneury, Signory.]

†1. Lordship, domination, sovereignty. Obs.

c 1290 S. Eng. Leg. 115/320 Ȝif he hadde of is owene flesche al-ovt þe seignorie. 1297 R. Glouc. (Rolls) 3858 He wolde wende Vor to winne seygnorie aboute in oþer ende. 13.. K. Alis. 597 (Laud MS.) He shal habbe seignorye Of þis rounde myddell erd. 1375 Barbour Bruce XII. 298 Covaitis of senȝhory. c 1400 Laud Troy Bk. 3159 Thei made lettres..To eche a lond and prouynce That Gregeys hadde in seygnorye. 1456 Sir G. Haye Law Arms (S.T.S.) 209/11 Mony has jurisdiccioun and seignoury be way of dede, and nocht be way of lawe. 1474 Caxton Chesse II. v. (1883) 66 Whan thou haste moste seignourye and lordships than shalt thou [etc.]. a 1547 Surrey Æneid II. 467 That many yeres did hold such seignorie. a 1548 Hall Chron., Hen. IV 1 The Turke..by the discord of christen princes hath amplified greatly his seigniory and dominion. 1638 Sir T. Herbert Trav. (ed. 2) 66 If hee would..do homage to him, he should re-accept his seniory. 1649 G. Daniel Trinarch., Hen. IV ccclxi, The more Politicke Molls, (who in fatter Soyles, have Seigneiorie). 1684 Contempl. St. Man I. ii. 20 What were..the Seignory of the World, but Vanity of Vanities?

b. quasi-arch. Your seignorie = 'your lordship': attributed to a foreign speaker.

1829 Scott Anne of G. xxix, 'It may be your seignorie is right', answered the guide. Ibid. xxx.

2. spec. Feudal lordship or dominion; the authority, rights, and privileges of a feudal lord.

1464 Rolls of Parlt. V. 524/1 Articles of Liberteez to Seignorie apperteynyng. 1567 in F. J. Baigent Crondal Rec. (1891) 171 With suche segnyorye and preferment of the said under tenauntes as the personne so atteyncted had before the said atteyndour. 1620 J. Wilkinson Coroners & Sherifes 3 Alwaies saving to the King and to other Lords their Seignories and Franchises. 1834 Pringle Afr. Sk. xiv. 473 Reserving to the chiefs certain rights of seigniory over the respective domains. 1851 Dixon W. Penn xxii. (1872) 188 James thought..the rights of seigniory too large.

b. A particular feudal lordship; in English Law chiefly, the relation of the lord to the tenants of a manor.

Seigniory appendant, seigniory in gross: see quot. 1886. By some writers seigniory has been used as equivalent to 'seigniory in gross'.

1466 Paston Lett. II. 283 Their ancestors had been possessed of a court and seniory in the town of Paston. 1482 Rolls of Parlt. VI. 204/2 Any Tenaunt holdyng..by Knyghts service, by reason of any Seignorie or Lordshipp. 1553 Act 1 Mary Stat. II. c. 5 Any person..having a Seignorie by reason of any Castells,..[etc.]..of him..holden by Knightes service. 1586 J. Hooker Hist. Irel. 113/1 in Holinshed, Matthew did..seeke to vsurpe the name of a segniorie of the Oneiles, and the dominions apperteining to that segniorie and surname. 1597 Shaks. 2 Hen. IV, IV. i. 111 Were you not restor'd To all the Duke of Norfolkes Seignories, Your Noble, and right well-remembred Fathers? 1607 J. Norden Surv. Dial. II. 43 He may haue thereby a kind of seignory, a Lordship or gouernement in grosse ouer his Tenants by contract or couenant, but no Mannor. c 1600 Bacon Elem. Com. Law ii. (1630) 7 If tenant in ancient demesne be disseised by the Lord, whereby the seigniory is suspended,..Francke fee is no plea. 1652 tr. Fitzherbert's New Nat. Brev. 6 If a man hold of a Lord, as of Seigniory in gross, which is not any Manor, for which Seigniory he cannot keep any Court. 1730 M. Wright Tenures 30 Neither could the Lord alien or transfer his Seigniory or Superiority to another, without the Consent of his Feudatary. 1844 J. Williams Real Prop. (1879) 322 By the grant of an estate in fee simple, he necessarily parted with the feudal possession...The grantee, however, became his tenant. ..This simply having a free tenant in fee simple was called a seignory. 1875 Digby Real Prop. i. § 3 (1876) 50 note, If the lord retained no lands in his own hands, but all the lands within the manor were held by free tenants, he was said to have a seignory, or a seignory in gross. 1886 Encycl. Brit. XXI. 623/2 They [seignories] are regarded as incorporeal hereditaments, and are either appendant or in gross. A seignory appendant passes with the grant of the manor; a seignory in gross—that is a seignory which has been severed from the demesne lands of the manor to which it was originally appendant—must be specially conveyed by deed of grant.

3. The territory under the dominion of a lord; esp. a feudal domain. Sometimes used for Seigneury with reference to France or Canada.

1338 R. Brunne Chron. (1810) 49 Whan Knoute had resceyued boþe þe seignories, He parted þe lond in foure parties. 1489 Caxton Faytes of A. I. i. 6 To recoure londes, seignoryes or ther thynges. 1532–3 Act 24 Hen. VIII, c. 7 Prouided alwayes, that euery lorde marcher haue the forfaytes..within their seignoryes, liberties, and [sic] frauncheses royall. 1601 Holland Pliny v. xxix. I. 107 A third Seignorie or Shire there is that goeth to Apamia. 1603 Knolles Hist. Turks (1638) 71 The Venetians; by whom it was holden as a part of their seignorie almost an hundred yeares. 1646 Bp. Maxwell Burd. Issach. 7 Crime..committed, within the Seignory of this pettie Principality. 1818 Cruise Digest (ed. 2) I. 3 The codes of the Germans..were superseded by these local customs: each seignory and province had its own. 1839 Stonehouse Axholme 144 The Lord of the Manor..could search for stolen goods within the extent of his seignory.

fig. 1579 Northbrooke Dicing Ep. Ded., I will poure out prayers vnto the Lord of heauen & earth to sende you.. after this life neuer ceassing, and endlesse ioyes in the heauenlie Seignorie. a 1586 Sidney Arcadia III. (Sommer) 268 In one place lay disinherited headers, dispossessed of their naturall seignories.

4. A body of 'seigniors' or lords. Often with reference to Italy, = Signoria, Signory 4.

1485 Caxton Chas. Gt. 88 Ye myght be blamed, seen that your seygnorye ne your lordes be not here now present. 1517 Torkington Pilgr. (1884) 12 The Duke..with all the Senyorye went in ther Archa triumphali. 1603 Knolles Hist. Turks (1638) 84 Ouer all which, the seignorie neuertheless had a generall care. 1872 Lowell Dante Wks. 1890 IV. 134 The new decree by which the seigniory of Florence recalled a portion of the exiles.

Seigniour, obs. form of Senior.

†**Sei·gnorable**, a. Obs. rare⁻¹. In 5 senȝeorabill. [a. OF. seignorable, f. seigneur: see Seigneur and -able.] Pertaining to or characteristic of a lord, lordly.

c 1475 Rauf Coilȝear 717 Thair was seruit in that saill Seigis semelie, Mony Senȝeorabill Syre on ilk syde seir.

Seignoral (sēⁱ·nyŏrăl), a. Hist. Also 7–9 seigniorал. [f. Seign(i)or + -al.] = Seignorial; cf. Seigneurial.

1627 in Rushw. Hist. Coll. (1659) I. 508 And yet it was by him thus said. That the Kings of England always have had a Monarchy Royal and not a Monarchy Seignoral. 1658 Cleveland Rustick Rampant 149 A Tyrannie after the Turkish mode, a Monarchy seigniorall. 1790 Burke Fr. Rev. (ed. 2) 219 The bishopricks and cures, under kingly and seignoral patronage,..are sometimes acquired by unworthy methods. 1809 Ann. Reg., St. Papers 733/2 All seignioral courts of justice are abolished in Spain. 1886 Pall Mall Gaz. 5 June 4/1 The history of Chantilly as a seigneural residence goes back to a very early period.

Seignorial (sēⁱnyōᵊ·riăl), a. Also seigniorial. [f. seignor, Seignior + -ial. Cf. F. seigneurial.] Pertaining to a seignior or seigniors.

1818 Hallam Mid. Ages (1872) I. 209 Several other small emoluments of himself and his successors,..were in that age rather seigniorial than royal. 1823 Southey Penins. War I. 721 Provincial custom-houses were abolished, and all seignorial courts of justice. 1877 Mrs. Oliphant Makers Flor. vi. 158 This liberal and almost splendid existence, with its seignorial amusements of hunting and hawking.

†**Sei·gnorize**, v. Obs. [f. seignor, Seignior + -ize (in early use after F. † signoriss-, signorir). See also Signorize v.] intr. To hold sway, act as lord. Const. in, over.

1634 W. Tirwhyt tr. Balzac's Lett. I. 26 Those Statesmen, who made accompt to Seignorize in all Assemblies. 1799 W. Taylor in Robberds Mem. (1843) I. 283 A woman may be..a Mrs. Arlberry in the art of Seignorizing over men.

†**Sei·gnorous**, a. Obs. [ad. OF. seignoureux: see Seigneur and -ous.] Lordly, noble. Hence † **Sei·gnorously** a., in the same sense.

c 1477 Caxton Jason 121 b, And in fauour of youre seignoureuse gentilnesse..I shal renewe you as sayd is. 1481 — Godfrey clxxxvii. 274 In to thynner part of the temple were fledde moche grete peple of the toun by cause it was the moost seynorously and rial place of the toun.

Seignory, sb.: see Seigniory.

†**Sei·gnory**, v. Obs. rare. [a. OF. seignorier, seigneurier, f. seigneur: see Seignior.]

1. intr. To exercise mastery.

1474 Caxton Chesse III. iv. g 2 b, Hit is sayd in prouerbe that a man ought to seignorie ouer the riches, and not to serue hit. 1483 — Gold. Leg. 306/1 Thordre of domynacion whiche seygnoryeth aboue other that ben lower.

2. trans. To govern.

c 1475 Partenay 5090 Terry seignoried A full large contre.

Seih, seihȝe, obs. ff. See v.

Seihtle, variant of Saughtel v. Obs.

c 1200 Vices & Virtues 3 Ga ærst and seihtle wið ðine broðer.

Seik: see Sack sb.¹, Sick a., Sikh.

Seil, obs. f. Ceil v., Sail sb.¹; Sc. var. of Sile v.²

Seilde(n, -in(e, -yn, obs. ff. Seld and Seldom.

Seile, obs. f. Ceil v., Sail v.¹, Seel v.²

†**Sei·ler.** Obs. rare. [f. seil var. Ceil v. + -er¹.] One who 'ceils' (Ceil v. 2); a house-painter or plasterer.

1672 in E. B. Jupp Carpenters' Co. (1887) 303 The Company of Joyners and Seilers London. 1688 Holme Armoury III. 148/2 Seiler or House Painter.

Seili(en, obs. forms of Sail v.¹

Seill: see Seele, canopy, Sele, happiness.

Seille, seily, obs. forms of Sail sb.¹, v.¹

Seilye, variant of Seely a. Obs.

Seim(e, Seiment, obs. ff. Seem v.², Cement.

†**Sein**, v. Obs. Also 6 seyn. [a. OF. seignier:—L. signāre to Sign.] trans. To sign, seal.

1258 Procl. Hen. III in Trans. Philol. Soc. 1868–9, 21 We senden ȝew þis writ open iseined wiþ ure seel. 1549 in R. G. Marsden Sel. Pleas Crt. Admir. (1897) II. 70, I have written and seynidde this presentt with myne owne proper handde. 1638 Hamilton Papers (Camden) 3 We command you expreslie..to publis the proclamatioun forthwith drauen up with your oune hand, which we have seined. a 1660 Contemp. Hist. Irel. (Ir. Archæol. Soc.) I. 136 He seined his fiat to the conformation of the said requeste.

Seine, obs. f. SAINT, SAY². | **Seind**, obs. f. SEND v.

Seine (sīn), v. Also *sean*, *sain*. [f. SEINE *sb*.¹] **a.** *intr.* To fish or catch fish with a seine. **b.** *trans.* To catch with a seine, also to use a seine in.

Seine, obs. f. SEE v., SENE v., SYNE.

Seiner (sī′nər). Also *seaner*. [f. SEINE *sb.*¹ + -ER¹.] A fisherman who uses a seine, or one employed to haul in a seine. Also a seine-boat.

Seine-boat. A boat adapted for carrying and throwing out a seine.

Seinie, variant of SENDLE *adv.*, seldom.

Seint(e = see SAINT, SEYNT *Obs.* (girdle).

Seintefie, -ifie, obs. ff. SANCTIFY v.

Seintewarte, -tinarie, etc. : see SANCTUARY.

Seintye, -atie, var. ff. SENE *sb.³*, SENYE *Obs.*

Seip, -age, -ing, var.ff. SEEP, SEEPAGE, SEEPING.

Seipter, obs. form of SCEPTER *sb.*

Seir, obs. Sc. forms of SEAR *a.*

Seiren, error, form of SIREN.

Seir-fish, seer-fish, etc.

Seise, obs. *Sc.* [The first element is a corruption of the F. name *serra* lit.]

Seize, *v. Law.* The usual spelling of SEIZE v.

Seis, obs. form of CEASE v., SYCE.

Seisant, error, form of SEIZANT.

Seise, obs. form of SEARCH v.

Seisin (sī′zin), *sb.* Forms: 3-4 seisin, 4-5 seizy(e, seisine, 3-7 seyng(e, 4-7 seisin, 4-5 sesun, seson, seson, seynne, 6 *Sc.* sessing, 7 seising : also sasine.

Seizin (sī′zin), *v. Obs.* [f. SEISIN *sb.*] To give seisin of (property).

Seisable, var. SEIZABLE *a.*

Seism (sīzm), *sb. rare.* [ad. Gr. σεισμ-ός.] An earthquake.

Seismal (sαi′zmăl), *a. rare.* [f. Gr. σεισμ-ός.]

Seismic (sαi′zmik), *a.* [f. Gr. σεισμ-ός earthquake + -IC.] Pertaining to, of the nature of, an earthquake.

Seismicity (sαizmi′siti), *n.* [f. SEISMIC + -ITY.]

Seismal

Seismism (sαi′zmiz'm), *n.* [f. SEISM + -ISM.]

Seismo- combining form f. Gr. σεισμ-ός.

Seismogram (sαi′zmogræm), *n.* [f. SEISMO- + -GRAM.] The record of a seismograph.

Seismograph (sαi′zmográf). Also *siesmo-*. [f. SEISMO- + -GRAPH.] An instrument for recording automatically the phenomena of earthquakes.

Seismographer (sαizmɒ′gráfər), *n.* [f. SEISMOGRAPH + -ER¹.]

Seismographic (sαizmográ′fik), *a.*

Seismography (sαizmɒ′gráfi), *n.*

Seismologic (sαizmolɒ′dʒik), *a.*

Seismological (sαizmolɒ′dʒikăl), *a.* Relating to seismology.

Seismologist (sαizmɒ′lodʒist), *n.*

Seismology (sαizmɒ′lodʒi), *n.* [f. SEISMO- + -LOGY.]

Seismometer (sαizmɒ′mitər), *n.* [f. SEISMO- + -METER.] An instrument for measuring the intensity, direction, and duration of earthquakes.

Seismometric (sαizmomε′trik), *a.*

Seismometry (sαizmɒ′mitri), *n.*

Seismoscope (sαi′zmoskōp), *n.*

Seize (sīz), *v.* Forms: 3-8 saize, 3-4 sayse, 3-5 seyse, 4-5 seyse, 4-6 seise, 6-7 cease, 6-7 ceaze, 6-7 ceize, ceese) 6-7 seize.

Seized (sīzd), *ppl. a.* [f. SEIZE v. + -ED.]

Seisement. *Obs.* [f. SEIZE v. + -MENT.]

Seisin, variant of SESEMENT *Obs.*

Seiser (sī′zər). Also 6 seiseur, 6 seysere, -our. [f. SEIZE v. + -ER¹.]

Seising (sī′ziŋ), *vbl. sb.* [f. SEIZE v. + -ING.]

Seisure (sī′ʒər), *n.* [f. SEIZE v. + -URE.]

Sejant (sī′dʒănt), *a. Her.* Forms: 6 seand, seiaunte, sejeaunte, 7 seiant, sejant.

Sejoin (sīdʒɔi′n), *v. Obs. rare.* [ad. L. sējungĕre.]

Sejunct (sīdʒʌŋ′kt), *ppl. a. Obs. rare.* [ad. L. sējunct-us.]

Sejunction (sīdʒʌŋ′kʃən), *n. rare.* [ad. L. sējunctiōn-em.]

Sejunctive (sīdʒʌŋ′ktiv), *a. Obs. rare.* [ad. L. sējunctīv-us.]

Sejungible (sīdʒʌ′ndʒib'l), *a. rare.* [ad. L. sējungĕre + -IBLE.] That may be separated or sejoined.

Selenyl (ˈseliˌnil). *Chem.* [f. Selen-ium + -yl.] A compound radical consisting of one atom of selenium and one of oxygen.

Soler, obs. var. Celure, Sealer, Seller², Soler; obs. f. Cellar, Sealer.

Selerer, obs. form of Cellarer.

Seleri, obs. form of Celery.

Selerite, -ite, Selestial, obs. f. Celerity, Celestial, Selette, obs. form of Sellette.

Seleucian (sĭˈlūsĭan), a. *and sb.* [f. L. Seleuc-us + -an.] = Seleucid a.

Seleucid (sĭˈlūsid), a. and sb. [f. L. Seleucid-æ, Gr. Σελευκίδαι: see below.] a. sb. One of the Seleucidæ, or members of the dynasty founded by Seleucus Nicator (one of the generals of Alexander the Great) which reigned over Syria from 312 to 65 B.C., and subjected a great part of Western Asia. b. adj. Pertaining to the Seleucid.

Self (self), pron., a., and sb. Forms: 1 self; 1-4 silf, 1-3 sylf, sæolf, 2 sulf, 3 sulf, 5-7 selfe, 6 silfe; 5-6 selph, 6 sealf, seylfe, sill); 1 selfa, silfe, etc.; 2 seolue, 3 seoluen, 3 sulfe, suluen; 5-6 selues, 6-selven [Com. Teut.: OE. self, silf, seolfa wk., corresponding to OFris. self siv, selva wk., OS. self silf, selbo wk. (MLG. sulf, selve) and your corsping al. (Du. self) wk. selva, selfe OHG. self, silf, selbo wk. (MHG. selp, selbe) ON. only str. sialf-r (Icel. sjálfr, Sw. sjelf, Norw. sjøl, Da. selv), Goth. silba wk. :—UTeut. *selƀo. The ultimate etymology is obscure; many scholars regard the word as a compound of the pronominal stem se- (cf. Goth. s-ik, G. s-ich) and -lƀo.]

Supplement, p. 3873; Corrigenda, p. 4092; Spurious words, p. 4093; Books quoted, p. 4094

1. With advs. related to actual or possible formations in a and f (above).

2. Compounds with as, pples. and ppl. adjs. in which *self-* denotes the agent or instrument (as the agent) ...

3. Compounds in which *self-* is adverbial: **a.** with abs., adjs., vbs., advs. ...

b. with adjs. and related sbs., vbs., pples. ...

5. Compounds in which *self-* is in the adjective relation ...

b. = inherent in, depending upon, or proceeding from oneself (itself), one's nature, etc. ...

c. with pples. = from or out of oneself or itself (as a source or point of origin) ...

4. In technical use, forming compounds to designate machines, appliances, or processes by or in which certain operations are performed without human or animal agency or special manipulation or adjustment for the purpose ...

Self-abnegating ppl. a. ...
Self-abuse. [SELF- 1.]
Self-accusation. [SELF- 1 a.]
Self-acted, ppl. pple. Obs. [SELF- 2.]
Self-acting, ppl. a. [SELF- 3 b, 4.]
Self-action. [SELF- 1 a.]
Self-active, ppl. a. [SELF- 3 b.]
Self-abasement, ppl. a. [SELF- 2.]
Self-abasing, ppl. a. [SELF- 2.]
Self-actor. [SELF- 4.]
Self-admiration. [SELF- 1 a.]
Self-abnegation. [SELF- 1 a.]

Self-admired ppl. a., **Self-admirer**, **Self-admiring** ppl. a.
Self-annihilation. [SELF- 1.]
Self-applauding. [SELF- 1 f.]
Self-applause.
Self-applausive = SELF-APPLAUDING.
Self-assertion. [SELF- 1 a.]
Self-assurance. [SELF- 1 d.]
Self-assured, self-assuring, self-assuringly...
Self-binder ppl. a.
Self-black. Chiefly northern. Also 6 selblake.
Self-blood. [SELF- 1.]
Self-boasting, vbl. sb. [SELF- 1 b.]
Self-born ppl. a. [SELF- 3 a.]
Self-bred ppl. a. [SELF- 3 b.]
Self-centered, self-centred ppl. a. [SELF- 3 a.]
Self-central a. [SELF- 3 a.]
Self-centre.
Self-centring, -assertive...
Self-colour, -coloured.
Self-command. [SELF- 1 a.]
Self-complacence, -complaisance.
Self-complacency. [SELF- 1 a.]
Self-complacent ppl. a.
Self-conceit. [SELF- 1 a.]
Self-confidence. [SELF- 1 a.]
Self-confident ppl. a. Now somewhat rare.
Self-congratulation. [SELF- 1 a.]
Self-congratulating, -congratulatory adjs.
Self-conjugate a. Math. [SELF- 3 a.]
Self-conscious a.
Self-contained ppl. a. [SELF- 2.]
Self-consistency. [SELF- 3 a.]
Self-consistent ppl. a. [SELF- 3 a.]
Self-contempt. [SELF- 1.]
Self-content ppl. a., sb. [SELF- 3 a.]
Self-contradiction. [SELF- 1.]

Self-contradiction. ... the imputation of Selfe Contradiction.

Self-contradictory adjs.

Self-control.
1. Control of oneself, one's desires, etc.

Self-conviction. Conviction of oneself (or one's work in conviction of).

Self-convicted, ppl. a. Convicted by one's own words or action.

Self-created, ppl. a. Created, brought into existence, or constituted by oneself.

Self-creation.

Self-creating, -creative adjs. capable of self-creation.

Self-culture. The cultivation or development by one's own efforts of one's mind, faculties, manners, etc.

Self-defeat.

Self-death.

Self-deceit.

Self-deceived, ppl. a. Deceived by oneself, marked by self-deception.

Self-deception. The action or fact of deceiving oneself; self-delusion.

Self-deceptious, -deceptive adjs.

Self-defence. The act of defending oneself, one's rights or position.

Self-defensive, a. Of, or pertaining to, or involving the principle of, self-defence.

Self-delight. Delight in oneself, one's being or existence.

Self-delivery. Automatic delivery.

Self-dependency.

Self-dependent, a. Possessing or characterised by self-dependence.

Self-deluded, ppl. a. Deluded by oneself, suffering from self-delusion.

Self-deluder, -deluding ppl. a.

Self-delusion. The act of deluding oneself; an instance of this.

Self-denial. [Self- 2.] Denial or abnegation of oneself; sacrifice of one's desires or interest.

Self-denier. One who practises self-denial.

Self-denying, vbl. sb. [Self- 1 e.] Self-denial.

Self-denyingly adv.

Self-dependently adv.

Self-despair. [Self- 1 d.] Despair of oneself.

Self-destroyed, ppl. a. [Self- 2.] Destroyed by oneself.

Self-destroyer.

Self-destruction. [Self- 2.] Destruction of oneself, one's life; esp. self-murder, suicide.

Self-destructive, a. [Self- 1 e.] Having the property of destroying or annulling itself (or each other).

Self-determination. [Self- 1.] Determination of one's mind or will by itself towards an object.

Self-determined, ppl. a.

Self-determining, vbl. sb.

Self-devoted, ppl. a. [Self- 2.] Characterized by self-devotion.

Self-devotedness.

Self-devotion. Devotion of oneself, one's life, etc.

Self-defence.

Self-diffidence.

Self-distrust. Distrust of oneself, one's powers, etc.

Self-effacement. [Self- 1.] The keeping of oneself out of sight or in the background.

Self-elect, a. [Self- 2.] Self-elected.

Self-elected, ppl. a.

Self-election.

Self-end. Obl. Chiefly pl.

Self-essence.

Self-essential, -essentiated adjs.

Self-estimate. [Self- 1.] Estimate or valuation of oneself.

Self-evidence. [Self- 1 d.] Evidence of its own truth.

Self-evident, a. [Self- 3 b.] Evident of itself without proof; axiomatic.

Self-evidently adv.

Self-evidencing ppl. a.

Self-evolution. Evolution of oneself.

Self-exaltation. Exaltation of oneself, one's proceedings or merits.

Self-examination. Examination of oneself with regard to one's conduct, motives, etc., esp. as a religious duty.

Self-exciting, ppl. a. Electr.

Self-exile.

Self-existence. Existence of a being by virtue of his inherent nature independently of any other being.

Self-existent, a.

Self-existing.

Self-existency.

Self-experience. Personal trial or experience.

Self-explained, ppl. a. Explained by itself, self-evident without specific explanation.

Self-faced, ppl. a.

Self-feeling.

Self-fertile, a. Bot. [Self- 3 b.] Of a flower.

Self-glorification. [Self- 1.] Glorification or exaltation of oneself.

Self-glorious, a. [Self- 2.] Marked by vain-glory or boasting.

Self-glory, Self-glorying vbl. sb. and ppl. a.

Self-flatterer [Self- 2.] Flatterer by oneself.

Self-flattering ppl. a.

Self-forgetful, a. [Self- 1 e.] Forgetful of oneself.

Self-formation. [Self- 1.] Formation or production without extraneous aid; self-development of the mind or character.

Self-formed ppl. a.

Self-good. [Self- 1 a.] Personal benefit or interest.

Self-governed, ppl. a. [Self- 2.]

Self-government. [Self- 1 a.]
1. Self-control, self-command.

Self-governing ppl. a.; autonomous.

Self-glorification.

Self-glorifier.

Self-glorifying ppl. a.

Self-gratulation. [Self- 1.] Self-congratulation.

Self-gratulating, -gratulatory adjs.

Self-guard. Obl. rare. In 6 -gard.

Self-ful, a. Obl. [Self- 3 b + -FUL.] Full of self, self-centred.

Self-fulness.

Self-hate.

Self-heal. [Self- 1 a.]

Self-feeling.

Self-identical, a. Philos.

Self-identity.

Self-idolater. One who idolizes or worships self.

Self-idolatry.

Self-idolizing ppl. a.

Self-indulgence.

Self-ill. a. Obl. rare. Harmful to oneself.

Self-importance. The sense of one's own value, etc.

Self-important, a.

Self-helping ppl. a.

Self-help. [Self- 1 a.]

Self-helpful, a.

Self-helpfulness.

Self-homicide. Now rare.

Selfhood. [-HOOD.]

Self-improvable, a. [Self- 2.] Capable of self-improvement.

Self-improvement.

Self-improved, ppl. a. [Self- 2.] Improved by oneself.

Self-improving ppl. a.

Self-inconsistency. [Self- 1.]

Self-induced, ppl. a. Electr.

Self-inductance. Electr.

Self-induction. Electr.

Self-indulgence. [Self- 1 c + INDULGENCE.] Indulgence of one's own desires, passions, etc.

Self-indulging, vbl. sb.

Self-inflicted, ppl. a.

Self-inflicting, vbl. sb.

Self-infliction.

Self-instructed, ppl. a.

Self-instruction.

Self-interested. [See INTERESSED.]

Self-interest.

Self-interested, ppl. a.

Self-interestedness.

Self-involution.

Self-involved, ppl. a.

Selfish, a.

Self-justifier.

Selfishly, adv.

Selfishness.

Self-kill, v.

Self-killing, vbl. sb.

Self-kindled, ppl. a.

Self-knowing, ppl. a.

Self-knowledge.

Self-known, ppl. a.

Self-law.

Self-lived, ppl. a.

Self-living, ppl. a.

Self-loss.

Selfless, a.

Selflessly, adv.

Selflessness.

Self-life.

Self-like.

Self-lost, ppl. a.

Self-lough, local.

Self-love.

Self-lover.

Self-loving, ppl. a.

Self-limited.

Self-limiting.

Self-limitation.

Self-mate, v.

Self-minded, a.

Self-motion.

Self-motive, a.

Self-moved, ppl. a.

Self-movable, a.

Self-movement.

Selfly, adv.

Self-murder.

Self-murderer.

Selfness.

Self-offence, rare.

Self-offerer.

Self-one, a.

Self-open, v.

Self-opened, ppl. a.

Self-opening.

Self-opinionate, ppl. a.

Self-opinionated, ppl. a.

Self-opinionative.

Self-opiniated, ppl. a.

Self-opinion.

Self-originate, ppl. a.

Self-originated, ppl. a.

Self-origination.

Self-originating, ppl. a.

Self-partial, a.

Self-partiality.

Self-pity.

Self-pleasing, vbl. sb.

Self-pleasing, ppl. a.

Self-complacency.

Self-pleasure.

Self-poise, sb.

Self-poised, ppl. a.

Self-possess, v.

Self-possessed, ppl. a.

Self-possession.

Self-praise.

Self-preservation.

Self-preservative.

Self-pride.

Self-raised, ppl. a.

Self-raising, ppl. a.

Self-realization.

Self-reflection.

Self-regard.

Self-regarding, ppl. a.

Self-regulating, ppl. a.

Self-regulation.

Self-regulative, a.

Self-reliance.

Self-reliant, a.

Self-reliantly, adv.

Self-renounced.

Self-renunciation.

Self-repellency.

Self-repelling, ppl. a.

Self-reproach.

So **Self-repro′ched** ppl. a. **Self-repro′chful**, **Self-repro′ching** (a., (hence-repro′chingly).

Self-repu′gnance. Now rare. [SELF- 1 d.] Self-contradictory quality or character. So **Self-repu′gnancy**; **Self-repu′gnant** a., self-contradictory.

Self-repu′lsion. Now rare. [SELF- 1 a.] The action of self-repellent molecules or substances. So **Self-repu′lsive** a., self-repellent.

Self-respe′ct. [In sense 1, SELF- 5 a.; in senses 2 and 3, SELF- 1 d.]

So **Self-respe′ctful** (hence -respe′ctfulness.), **Self-respe′cting** ppl. a.

Self-restrai′nt. [SELF- 1 a.] Restraint imposed by oneself upon one's actions, etc.

So **Self-restrai′ned**, **Self-restrai′ning** ppl. a./sb., marked by or involving self-restraint.

Self-revea′led. ppl. a. [SELF- 2.] Revealed by one's own action. So **Self-revea′ling** vbl. sb. and ppl. a., **Self-revea′lment**.

Self-re′velative, **Self-re′velatory** adj.

So **Self-re′velative**, **Self-re′velatory** adj.

Self-reve′lation. [SELF- 1 a.] Revelation of oneself.

Self-ri′ght. a. [Back-formation f. SELF-RIGHTING.] 1. To right itself. So **Self-ri′ghted**; **Self-ri′ghter**, a self-righting boat.

Self-ri′ghteous, a. [SELF- 3 b.] Righteous in one's own esteem.

So **Self-ri′ghteously** adv.; **Self-ri′ghteousness**, the condition of being self-righteous; righteousness for which one gives oneself credit.

Self-ri′ghting, vbl. sb. [SELF- 1 b.] Of a boat : The action of righting itself after being upset. So **Self-ri′ghting** ppl. a.

Self-sa′crifice. [SELF- 1 a.] Sacrifice of oneself; the giving up of one's own interests, happiness, and desires, for the sake of duty or the welfare of others.

So **Self-sa′crificed** ppl. a.; **Self-sa′crificer**, one who self-sacrifices; **Self-sa′crificial** a., **Self-sa′crificing** ppl. a., making a sacrifice of one's life, etc. (whence -sa′crificingly adv., -sa′crificingness).

Self-sa′tisfaction. [SELF- 3 a.] The condition or quality of being self-satisfied.

Self-sa′tisfied, ppl. a. [SELF- 1 f.] That satisfies oneself; affording self-satisfaction.

Self-sa′tisfying, ppl. a. [SELF- 1 f.] That satisfies oneself; affording self-satisfaction.

Self-secure, a. [SELF- 1 c.] Sure of oneself, one's position, etc.

Self-said., ppl. a. Obs. [SELF pron. c3 a. + SAID pple.] Selfsame.

Self-sa′me. (se′lfsem), a. (sb.) [f. SELF a. + SAME.] Now literary.

Self-reve′lation of oneself.

Self-see′king, vbl. sb. [SELF- 1 c., 7 c.] The seeking after one's own welfare before that of others; prosecution of selfish ends.

So **Self-see′king** ppl. a.

Self-sci′ence. [formed as next: cf. SCIENCE.]

Self-slain, ppl. a. rare. [SELF- 2.] Slain by one's own hand.

Self-slaughter. [SELF- 1 a.] = SELF-MURDER.

So **Self-slaying** ppl. a.

Self-slaughtered. ppl. a., self-murdered.

Self-sowed, ppl. a. — next.

So **Self-sown** ppl. a.

Self-subsistent a. [SELF- 3 b.; in sense 1 rendering Gr. αὐτάρκης.]

1. Sufficient in or for oneself(1) without aid or support from outside; able to supply one's needs oneself. Now rare or Obs.

Self-sub′stance. [SELF- 1 a.]

Self-sub′sistence, [SELF- 3.] The condition or quality of subsisting alone without dependence on or support of anything external.

So **Self-sub′sistency.**

Self-suffi′cient, a. [SELF- 3 b; in sense 1 rendering Gr. αὐτάρκης.]

Self-suffi′ciency. [next: see -ENCY; in sense 1.]

So **Self-suffi′ciently** adv.

Self-suggested, ppl. a. [SELF-.] Suggested by oneself; caused by self-suggestion.

Self-sugge′stion. [SELF- 3 b.]

Self-suppo′rted ppl. a. [SELF- 2.] Supported by oneself; without external aid, (of a physical object) without requiring the usual support (of an enterprise) paying its way; **Self-suppo′rting** a.

Self-support. [SELF- 1 d.] The act of supporting oneself (itself) without external assistance; the fact of being self-supporting.

Self-surrender. [SELF- 1 d.] The surrender or giving up of oneself to an influence, emotion, or the like.

So **Self-surre′ndering** ppl. a.

Self-sustained. ppl. a. [SELF- 2.] Sustained by one's own power or efforts; (rarely in a physical sense) held up without support.

Self-sustaining ppl. a., (hence-sustai′ningly adv.); **Self-sustai′nment**; **Self-su′stenance.**

Self-sustenta′tion.

Self-taught, ppl. a. [SELF- 2.] Taught by oneself without aid from others; self-educated.

b. Of that which is learnt : Acquired by one's own unaided efforts.

Self-tor′ment. [SELF- 1 a.] Tormenting of oneself. So **Self-torme′nted** ppl. a.

Self-torme′nter vbl. sb. and ppl. a.; **Self-torme′nting** (occas. used to render the title of Terence's play, *Heautontimorumenos*).

Self-trust. [SELF- 1 d.] = SELF-CONFIDENCE.

So **Self-tru′sting** vbl. sb. and ppl. a.

Self-united, ppl. a. [SELF- 2.] United in oneself alone with one's self.

Self-vi′olence. Obs. [SELF- 3 a.] The laying of violent hands upon oneself : a euphemistic term for SELF-MURDER.

So **Self-vi′olent** a.

Selfward (se′lfwəd), adv. and a. Chiefly E.U.S. [f. SELF + -WARD.] A. adv. Towards or in the direction of oneself.

B. adj. Tending or directed toward oneself.

Hence **Selfwardly.**

Selfwards, adv. [-WARDS.] = SELFWARD adv.

So **Self-wee′ning**, vbl. sb. Obs. [SELF- 1 b.] Self-opinion, self-conceit. So **Self-wee′ning** ppl. a., self-opinioned, self-conceited.

Selion (sī′ljən), Hist. and local. Forms: 5 selion, seylon, 6 seyllone, selyon, 7 selioun, 8-9 selion. Also Anglo-L. sellio, sellyon, sillyon.

Self-wi′lly, a. [f. SELF-WILL + -Y1. Cf. good-willy, ill-willy, and Selfwilly.] Self-willed.

Self-wi′ly, adv. Obs. Also 4 selwilli. [f. prec.] without aid.

Self-wi′sdom. [formed after next; cf. SELF- 3 b.] The condition of being self-wise.

Self-wi′tnessed, ppl. a.

So **Self-wi′tness.**

Self-wrought, ppl. a. [SELF- 2.] Produced or brought about by oneself.

Self-willed, a. Also 5-willyd, Sc. -willis, 6-wyld, 6-7 -wild, 7 wil'd; 5 selwillyd. [f. SELF-WILL sb. + -ED2.] Governed by one's own will or desires; obstinate.

Hence **Self-wi′lledly.** Obs. rare.

Self-wi′lledness, the quality or condition of being self-willed.

Selk, obs. form of SILK.

Selkouth, var. SELCOUTH a.

Selcra, obs. form of SILLABUB.

Sell (sel), sb.1 Obs. exc. dial. Forms: 1 sella, 6-7 sell, 7 sel. [OE. *sella*, *syl*- corresponds to OFris. *selle* to give, MLG. *selle*, OHG. *sella*, Goth. *salian* to give.] A saddle.

Sell (sel), v.1 Pa. t. and pa. pple. **sold** (sōld). Forms : 1 see below. [A Com. Teut. wk. vb.: OE. *sęllan*, pa. t. *sealde*, pa. pple. *seald*, corresponds to OFris. *sella* to give, sell, ON. *selja* to give up, hand over, OS. *sellian*, OHG. *sellen*.]

A. Illustration of Inflexional Forms.

1. Present stem.

2. To give up (a person) treacherously to his enemies; to betray (a person or cause) for money or other reward; (in early use) to hand over to punishment or destruction.

Sell *v.* (continued)

b. To dispose of (one's commission in the army) by sale under the purchase system. Now only *Hist.*

c. To hand over (a person, a people) into slavery or bondage for a sum of money. In Biblical use (after Heb.), often merely (without reference to a price received), To hand over to the dominion of another, to enslave. Hence *fig.*

d. *refl.* To make an offender (*pay for*) to inflict vengeance for (an injury). Chiefly qualified by *dear*, *dearly*, or an equivalent adverb. Phrase: *To sell* (another's act, an offence) *dear*, to exact a heavy penalty for. *To be dear or dearly sold*, to be attended with great cost.

11. **Sell off.** *trans.* To dispose of by sale: to sell the whole of (one's stock, possessions, etc.)

12. **Sell out.** *a. trans.* To distribute by sale.

b. To dispose of (stock, shares, etc.) by sale. Also *absol.*

c. *intr.* To dispose out of the army. Now only *Hist.*

d. *trans.* To dispose of the whole of (one's stock, property, etc.) by sale. Also *absol.*

13. **Sell over.** *trans.* †a. To sell again. *Obs.*

b. To transfer by sale. Also *absol.*

14. **Sell up.** *trans.* To dispose of the whole of (a person's stock, goods, etc.) by sale. *Obs.*

b. To dispose of the whole or a portion of the goods (of an insolvent or bankrupt person) for the benefit of his creditors. Also with the goods as obj.

‡**Se'ler**[2]. *Obs. rare*—. [ad. OF. *celier* (mod. F. *cellier*).] A storehouse, larder.

Se'lyon, obs. f. CHILDING, SEALING *vbl.*

Sem, obs. form of SEAM, SEEM.

Semantic (simæ'ntik), *a.* and *sb.* [ad. Gr. *σημαντικός* = *σημαίνειν* to show, signify. Cf. F. *sémantique.*] **A.** *adj.*

Semaphore (se'mafōr), *sb.* [ad. F. *sémaphore*, f. Gr. *σῆμα* sign + *-φορος* bearing.]

Semaphoric (semafo'rik), *a.* [f. SEMAPHORE *sb.* + -IC. Cf. F. *sémaphorique.*] Relating to, or of the nature of, a semaphore.

Semaphorist (semǽforist), *sb.* One who works a semaphore.

Semasiology (simēisiɒ'lŏdʒi). [f. Gr. *σημασία*, meaning + -LOGY.] That branch of philology which deals with the meanings of words, sense-development, and the like.

Sematography. [f. Gr. *σηματο-*, comb. form of *σῆμα* sign + *-γραφία* writing.] The use of signs or symbols (instead of letters) in writing. So **Sematographic**, *a.* of or pertaining to sematography.

Sematology (sēmatɒ'lŏdʒi). [f. Gr. *σηματ-*, *σῆμα* sign + -LOGY.]

1. Used by Smart for: The doctrine of the use of 'signs' (esp. words) in relation to thought and language.

2. = SEMASIOLOGY.

b. *attrib.*

Semblable (se'mblăb'l), *a.* (*sb.*) Also 4-6 *semblable*, -semblauble, (5-7 -blaby) 6-billabile, -blablye, 6-7 -blable, (7 -blable). [a. F. *semblable*, f. *sembler*: see SEMBLE.]

Semblance (se'mblăns). Also 4-6 *-aunce*, (4 -auns, -aunse), 5 semblans. [a. OF. *semblance*, f. *sembler*: see SEMBLE.]

SEMBLANT. 433	SEMBLE.	SEMBLE. 434	SEMEIOTICS.

Semblant ... (continued)

Semble, variant of SEMBLY *Obs.*

Sembling, *ppl. a. Obs.*

Semblative, *a. Obs. rare*

Semblablely, *adv. Obs.*

Semblance

Semeiotics ...

Semeiography (sīmaiˈgrăfi). In Dicts. also *semi-*.

Semeiologic ...

Semeiological, *a.*

Semeiologist ...

Semeiology (sīmaiˈɒlɒdʒi). Also 7 *erron.* semeology, 9 semeiology. ...

Semeiotic ...

Semeiotics (sīmaiˈɒtiks). Also 9 *semiotics.* ...

SEMEL. 435	SEMI-.	SEMI-. 436	SEMI-.

Semester, *obs.* form of SEMPSTER.

Semestral, semestral ...

Semi, *sb.*

Semilune ...

Semblable, -ness, -awry ...

Semold ...

Semedela, -ness, -awry ...

Semi, semblemed, semelmed ...

Semeli, semelich, obs. forms of SEEMLY *a.*

Semeline, semelin *Min.* ...

Semelfactive (semelˈfaktiv), *a. Gram.* ...

Semelicide, Semely: see SIMILITUDE, SEEMLY.

Semen (sīˈmɛn) ...

Sementation ...

Sementing ...

Semet, *Bot. Obs.* ...

Semi- (semi), *prefix.* Also 4-7 *semy*, 5-6 *semy-*.

spherical, as callai, astroitæ. 1664 POWER *Exp. Philos.* I. 37 You shall in the Microscope see those 2. black spots to be semi-spherical eyes. 1896 VIZETELLY tr. *Zola's Rome* 198 A spacious round chamber with semispherical ceiling.

Se·mispheˈroid. [SEMI- 6 a.] Half a spheroid.

1775 ASH, *Semispheroid*. 1798 HUTTON *Course Math.* II. 325 In the semisphere, or semispheroid; the distance from the centre is ⅜r, or ⅜ of the radius.

Hence **Semispheroi·dal** *a.*, of the form of a semispheroid.

1664 POWER *Exp. Philos.* I. 6 The Gray, or Horse-Fly. Her eye..'tis of a semisphæroidal figure. 1822 J. PARKINSON *Outl. Oryctol.* 48 Semi-sphæroidal masses. 1839 *Proc. Amer. Philos. Soc.* I. 71 Semi-spheroidal cavities.

‖**Semita** (se·mită). *Zool.* [mod.L. use of L. *sēmita* narrow way or path.] A band of minute close-set tubercles which bear ciliated clubbed spines, characteristic of the spatangoid sea-urchins.

1877 HUXLEY *Anat. Inv. Anim.* ix. 574 These bands of peculiarly modified spines are called *semitæ* or *fascioles*. 1888 ROLLESTON & JACKSON *Anim. Life* 558.

Hence **Se·mital** *a.* [cf. L. *sēmitālis* belonging to footpaths], of or pertaining to a semita.

1877 HUXLEY *Anat. Inv. Anim.* ix. 573 Fig., Semital tubercles...Semital spine.

Semitar(ie, obs. forms of SCIMITAR.

†**Se·mitate,** *v. Obs. rare*⁻⁰. [f. L. *sēmita* path + -ATE.] *intr.* 'To make pathes, to divide into pathes or ways' (Blount *Glossogr.* 1656).

†**Semitaur.** *Obs.* In 6 **-tawre.** [ad. L. **sēmitaurus*, f. *sēmi-* SEMI- 2 + *taurus* bull.] A creature shaped half like a bull.

1592 BRETON *Pilgr. Parad.* (Grosart) 8/2 Some Semitawres, and some, more halfe a Beare. 1614 SYLVESTER *Bethulian's Rescue* vi. 108 He sees Chimeras, Gorgons, Mino-Taures, Medusas, Haggs, Alectos, Semi-Taures.

Semite (se·məit). [ad. mod.L. *Sēmīta*, f. late Latin *Sēm*, Gr. Σήμ Shem: see -ITE. Cf. the earlier SHEMITE.] A person belonging to the race of mankind which includes most of the peoples mentioned in Gen. x. as descended from Shem son of Noah, as the Hebrews, Arabs, Assyrians, and Aramæans. Also, a person speaking a Semitic language as his native tongue.

1875 WHITNEY *Life & Growth Lang.* xii. 247 None but the Semites have, since the dawn of the historic period, seriously disputed with our family the headship of the human race. 1882 FARRAR *Early Chr.* II. 199 The mutual aversion of Semites and Aryans thus finds ample illustration in the literature of both. 1886 RAGOZIN *Chaldea* ii. v. (1891) 237 Nor did the Semites preserve a separate existence.

Semiter(e, -erie, obs. forms of SCIMITAR.

Semitertian (semitɜ̄·ɹʃăn), *a.* (*sb.*) *Old Path.* [ad. mod.L. *sēmitertiāna* (*febris*), rendering Gr. ἡμιτριταία HEMITRITÆAN; see SEMI- and TERTIAN.] Applied to an intermittent fever which combines the symptoms of a quotidian and a tertian fever, consisting of a paroxysm occurring every day with a second stronger one every other day.

1611 FLORIO, *Hemitritèa febbre*, a Semitertian feauer. 1696 RIDGLEY *Pract. Physick* 1.8. 1749 SHORT *Hist. Air*, etc. I. 223 In some Places few recovered who had it [*sc.* Peripneumony] accompanied with a violent Fever. Semitertians were next dangerous. 1888 FAGGE & PYE-SMITH *Princ. Med.* (ed. 2) II. 165 The 'hemitritæus', i. e. semitertian, a form of ague mentioned by Galen.

Semitic (sǐmi·tik), *a.* and *sb.* Also 9 **Semmetic.** [ad. mod.L. *Sēmīticus*, f. *Sēmīta* SEMITE. Cf. F. *sémitique*, Sp., Pg., It. *semitico*, G. *semitisch*. Cf. SHEMITIC.] **A.** *adj.* Of or pertaining to the Semites. (In recent use often *spec.* = Jewish.)

1826 PRITCHARD *Res. Phys. Hist. Mankind* II. 210 The Semitic nations. 1835 J. B. ROBERTSON tr. *Schlegel's Philos. Hist.* vi. (1846) 206 The people of the Semitic race. 1839 T. MITCHELL *Frogs of Aristoph.* Add. 411 *note*, The Semitic origin of this worship. 1885 FLOWER in *Jrnl. Anthrop. Inst.* XIV. 382 Hamitic and Semitic Melanochroi. 1886 [see SEMITISM 1 b].

b. In linguistic sense: The distinctive epithet of that family of languages of which Hebrew, Aramæan, Arabic, Ethiopic, and ancient Assyrian, are the principal members. Hence (in *Semitic scholar, studies, grammar, philology*, etc.) concerned with the Semitic languages.

1813 *Q. Rev.* X. 267 (Adelung's *Mithridates*) The Arabian family is called by our author Semitic. 1827 BUCKINGHAM *Trav. Mesopot.* II. 385 In any of the Semmetic languages. 1850 DONALDSON *New Cratylus* (ed. 2) § 100. 150 These arguments of the great Semitic scholar have been violently combated by one of his countrymen. 1877 *Smith & Wace's Dict. Chr. Biog.* I. 470/1 (*Chosroes*), There is a large Semitic element in the Pehlvi language.

B. *sb.* **a.** A Semite (*rare*). **b.** The Semitic family of languages; *occas.* the Semitic language of Babylon in opposition to Sumerian. **c.** *pl. U.S.* The scientific study of the language, literature, etc. of Semitic peoples.

1875 WHITNEY *Life & Growth Lang.* xii. 251 The scale of dialectic differences is much less in Semitic than in Indo-European. 1879 tr. *Brugsch's Hist. Egypt* II. 107 *note*, A very remarkable word which shows a full knowledge of Semitic in the writer. 1886 *Athenæum* 21 Aug. 238 [Pauli's] view that the Etruscans were neither Indo-Europeans nor Semitics. 1895 *Min. 9th Nat. Council Congr. Ch.* (U.S.A.) 239 With the growing interest in Semitics..it is not easy to get the time for study which these subjects demand. 1899 SIR H. HOWORTH in *Eng. Hist. Rev.* Oct. 626 Written in the primitive language of Babylonia and in Semitic.

Hence **Semi·ticism** = SEMITISM.

1907 *Expositor* Nov. 434 The number of real Semiticisms is therefore smaller than was supposed. 1908 *Spectator* 18 Apr. 625/1 Further, he discusses the 'semiticism' of the Greek Bible,—what it is, and what it is not.

Semiticize (sǐmi·tisəiz), *v. trans.* [f. SEMITIC *a.* + -IZE.] = SEMITIZE *v.*

1859 R. F. BURTON *Centr. Afr.* in *Jrnl. Geog. Soc.* XXXIX. 48 The..Sawahili races, mulattos, originally African, but semiticised like the Moplahs of Malabar by Yemeni or Omani blood [etc.]. 1881 *Athenæum* 9 July 48/1 The word became Semiticized by the Assyrians into Dumuzu.

Hence **Semi·ticised** *ppl. a.*; **Semi·ticizing** *vbl. sb.*

1863 R. F. BURTON *Wand. W. Africa* I. 188 With..faces like the Semiticized negroids generally. 1887 *Athenæum* 28 May 698/3 He informs us..that Anu was a Semitic god, whereas it is only a Semiticized form of the Accadian Anna. 1885 *Academy* 3 Jan. 15/1, I used to watch with much interest the Semiticising of foreign names in Syria.

†**Semi-tile.** *Obs.* In 5 **semy tyll.** ? Alteration of **samel tile* (see SAMEL) = half-baked tile, by association with SEMI-.

1448 *Cov. Leet Bk.* 232 That no tyler frohensfurth ley no semy [*MS.* seny] tyle ne crased tyle. 1454 *Ibid.* 279 Quod non vendant aliquam Semy tyll, nec illi qui tegulant ponant huiusmodi semytyll.

Semitism (se·mitiz'm). [f. SEMITE + -ISM.]

1. The attributes characteristic of the Semitic peoples. Also, the fact of being Semitic.

1851 LATHAM *Man & his Migrations* 146 The amount of Semitism in certain families. 1863 W. L. BEVAN in *Smith's Dict. Bible* II. s.v. *Philistines*, A period when the distinctive features of Hamitism and Semitism were yet in embryo.

b. In recent use, Jewish ideas or Jewish influence in politics and society.

1885 *Guardian* 6 May 697/3 The rivalry which exists with Catholicism and Semitism. 1886 W. J. TUCKER *E. Europe* 198 The Church of Rome will never countenance semitic innovations of any sort. The Catholic party must be propped up by staunch opponents to semitism.

2. A Semitic word or idiom; also (*nonce-use*) Semitic speech.

1869 FARRAR *Fam. Speech* iii. (1870) 114 The soberest conclusion seems to be..for the present to exclude Egyptian from the dignity of being a kind of ante-historic Semitism. 1886 HUXLEY in *19th Cent.* Apr. 498 The Egyptian language, during the period of the nineteenth dynasty, is said by Brugsch to be as full of Semitisms as German is of Gallicisms. 1898 SIR H. HOWORTH in *Eng. Hist. Rev.* Jan. 11 These Semitisms [in Egyptian], moreover, are partly popular, partly literary in origin.

Semitist (se·mitist). [f. SEMITE + -IST.] One versed in Semitic languages, literature, etc.; a Semitic scholar.

1885 *Athenæum* 10 Jan. 46/2 It will be for Semitists to decide if these words were borrowed from Hebrew. 1908 *Ibid.* 30 Aug. 282/2 The majority of Semitists consider the word to be connected with Sin, the Babylonian Moon-god.

Semitize (se·mitəiz), *v.* Also †**Semetize.** [f. SEMITE + -IZE.] *trans.* To render Semitic in character, language, or religion.

1869 BALDWIN *Preh. Nations* iv. (1877) 159 The language of Phoenicia is said to have been Semetized. 1880 CHEYNE *Isa.* xx. I. 118 The name is..therefore non-Semitic, but the Assyrians..Semitised it into Sarru-kinu. 1895 *Athenæum* 6 Apr. 447/3 We have a school who would roundly semitize the whole Greek civilization.

Hence **Se·mitized** *ppl. a.*; **Se·mitizing** *ppl. a.* Also **Semitiza·tion,** the action of the verb.

1885 W. R. SMITH in *Encycl. Brit.* XVIII. 756/1 [The Philistines] were a Semitic or at least a thoroughly Semitized people. 1886 *Encycl. Brit.* XXI. 656/1 The partial Semitization of the southern districts of Abyssinia. 1884 CHEYNE *Isa.* xix. (ed. 3) I. 119 The political history of Palestine assisted this Semitising process.

Semitonal (se·mitōnăl), *a.* [f. SEMITONE + -AL.] = SEMITONIC.

1863 OUSELEY in *Guardian* 18 Nov. 1082/1 It is..improbable that they would ever have abandoned a semitonal scale ..in order to adopt so very different a system as their present one. 1891 *Athenæum* 17 Oct. 524/3 Double-basses..maintaining a semitonal trill.

Hence **Se·mitonally** *adv.*, = SEMITONICALLY.

1876 STAINER & BARRETT *Dict. Mus. Terms* s.v. *Descant*, Notes altered semitonally by accidentals. 1885 *London & Prov. Mus. Trades Rev.* 15 Sept. 7 The trumpet calls are accompanied by the violins rising semitonally.

Semitone (se·mitōn). [f. SEMI- + TONE *sb.*; cf. late L. *sēmitonium*, OF. *semithon* and Gr. ἡμιτόνιον HEMITONE. Senses 2 and 3 (usually written *semi-tone*), are new formations distinct from 1.]

1. *Mus.* An interval approximately equal to half a tone, the smallest interval in the ordinary scales; a minor second.

Semitones are *chromatic* or *minor*, *diatonic* or *major*, and *enharmonic*: see these words.

1609 DOWLAND *Ornith. Microl.* 17 A Semitone..is a rising from one Voyce to another, (by an imperfect second) sounding flatly: and it is onely betwixt the Voyces *Mi, fa.* It is called a Semitone, not because it is halfe a Tone..but because it is an imperfect Tone. *a* 1680 CAMPION *Counterpoint* Wks. (1909) 192 A lesser Third consists of a Tone, and a Semi-tone. 1753 *Chambers' Cycl.* Suppl. s.v. *Interval*, The lesser flat seventh is equal to the sixth major and semitone major. 1811 BUSBY *Dict. Mus.* (ed. 3), The Semitone-Major is produced by rising a degree... The Semitone-Minor, by passing from a natural note to its sharp. 1848 RIMBAULT *Pianoforte* 33 A tone always includes both a Chromatic and a Diatonic semitone. 1876 tr. *Blaserna's Sound* vii. 133 Raising a note a semi-tone signifies raising that note to its sharp, as lowering it a semi-tone signifies lowering it to its flat.

2. *Art.* An intermediate tone or tint in a picture; = HALF-TONE 2. (Cf. *semi-tint* s.v. SEMI- 8.)

1782 *Mrs. Delany's Life & Corr.* III. 97 *note*, The greatest harmony of colouring from the various semi-tones of tint laid on. 1821 CRAIG *Lect. Drawing*, etc. iii. 155 The semitones, formed by the reflected lights in his pictures, appear scarcely distinguishable. 1906 *Daily Chron.* 5 Apr. 8/1 The soft tones and semi-tones seem to melt..into one another. *fig.* 1911 CHESTERTON *Crit. & Apprec. Dickens* 154 Anyone who thinks that Dickens could not describe the semi-tones and the abrupt instincts of real human nature.

3. A soft or gentle tone of voice; an undertone.

1837 DISRAELI *Venetia* I. vi, Speaking in a semi-tone. 1894 *Advance* (Chicago) 4 Oct., Preachers should pray less in semi-tones, and preach more in thunder tones.

Semitonic (semitǫ·nik), *a. Mus.* [f. SEMITONE + -IC.] Pertaining to or consisting of a semitone or semitones; (of a scale) chromatic.

1728 CHAMBERS *Cycl.* s.v. *Scale*, This, then, is the present Scale for Instruments, *viz.* Between the Extremes of every Tone of the natural Scale is put a Note, which divides it into two unequal Parts, called Semi-tones, whence the whole may be called the *Semitonic scale*. 1760 STILES in *Phil. Trans.* LI. 706 In the diatonic genus, the diapason consisting of five tonic and two semitonic intervals. 1833 RUSH *Philos. Human Voice* (ed. 2) 332 *note*, It is the diatonic shake, the semitonic not being found in his [*sc.* the mocking-bird's] song. 1838 G. F. GRAHAM *Mus. Comp.* 7/1 The chromatic scales formed from these consist of a semitonic (or so-called semitonic) series between the key-note and its octave.

Hence **Semito·nically** *adv.*, by a semitone or semitones.

1838 G. F. GRAHAM *Mus. Comp.* 25/1 The cadence is complete, from the third of dominant rising semitonically..to the tonic itself. 1867 MACFARREN *Harmony* iii. 113 Chromatic notes, which must always be quitted semitonically.

Semitor, -orie, obs. forms of SCIMITAR.

Se·mi-transpa·rency. [f. next: see -ENCY.] The quality or condition of being semi-transparent; partial transparency.

c 1793 *Encycl. Brit.* (1797) XI. 434/1 This ore is so called from its colour and semitransparency, by which it resembles horn or colophony. 1860 GOSSE *Rom. Nat. Hist.* 161 The obscure semi-transparency of the texture of the animal.

Se·mi-transpa·rent, *a.* Chiefly *scientific*. [SEMI- 7.] Partially or imperfectly transparent.

c 1793 *Encycl. Brit.* (1797) XI. 434/1 Corneous ore..is foliated and semitransparent. 1857 MILLER *Elem. Chem.*, *Org.* (1862) iv. § 1. 253 They possess the property of rendering paper semitransparent, producing what is well known as a greasy stain. 1870 DICKENS *E. Drood* iv, Her semi-transparent hands were clasped together. 1883 *Encycl. Brit.* XVI. 390/1 Common Opal: semitransparent, vitreous.

Semitte, obs. form of SEMMIT *Sc.*

†**Semitune.** *Obs.* Also 5 **-toyn.** [early f. SEMITONE: see TUNE *sb.*]. = SEMITONE 1.

1486 *Bk. St. Albans* d iij b, Of hawkys Bellys..Looke.. that thay be..not both of oon sowne: bot that oon be a semytoyn vnder a noder. 1607 HEYWOOD *Wom. Killed w. Kindn.* I. iii, Her Bels..had not both one waight, Nor was one semi-tune aboue the other.

Se·mi-u·ncial, *a.* (*sb.*) *Palæography*. [SEMI- 5 a.] Name of a style of writing intermediate between uncial and minuscule.

a 1734 NORTH *Life Ld. Kpr. North* (1742) 16 It is not well to write, as the Fashion now is, uncial or semiuncial Letters, to look like Pigs Ribs. 1815 SCOTT *Guy M.* xlix, The letters are uncial or semi-uncial, as somebody calls your large text-hand, and in size and perpendicularity resemble the ribs of a roasted pig. 1883 I. TAYLOR *Alph.* v. ii. 173 [Irish script] is usually called the Irish uncial or semi-uncial.

†**Semiu·stulate,** *pa. pple.* [ad. L. *sēmiustulātus*: see SEMI- 1 and USTULATE.] Half-burnt; also **Semiu·stulated**; so **Semiustula·tion,** a half burning.

1621 BURTON *Anat. Mel.* I. i. II. v. (1651) 21 Assation is a concoction of the inward moisture by heat, his opposite is a semiustulation. 1623 COCKERAM I, *Semiustulated*, halfe burnt. 1721 BAILEY, *Semiustulate*, (*semiustulatus* L.) half burnt or consumed by fire.

†**Semivif,** *a. Obs.* In 4–5 **semi-, semy-, seme-, -uyf, -uijf.** [ad. L. *sēmivīvus*, f. *sēmi-* SEMI- 1 + *vīvus* alive.] Half alive, half dead.

1377 LANGL. *P. Pl.* B. xvii. 55 Semiuyf he semed [C. xx. 55 *semiuiuus*, *v.rr.* semiuyf, semeuijf]. *a* 1400 *Beryn* 2202 He sat hym down softly on a stall, Semyvif for sorow.

Semi-vi·treous, *a.* [SEMI- 7 a.] Partially vitreous.

1782 WEDGWOOD in *Phil. Trans.* LXXII. 317 By a very strong fire, they are changed to a porcelain or semi-vitreous texture. 1807 T. THOMSON *Chem.* (ed. 3) II. 339 Semivitreous oxide of lead. 1813 BAKEWELL *Introd. Geol.* (1815) 421 Semivitreous lava. 1890 *Q. Jrnl. Geol. Soc.* XLVI. I. 74 Finely vesicular rhyolitic rock with compact semivitreous green-grey base.

So **Se·mi-vitrifica·tion, -vi·trified** *ppl. a.*

1753 *Chambers' Cycl.* Suppl., *Slacken*,..a term used by the miners to express a spungy and semivitrified substance. 1791 E. DARWIN *Bot. Gard.* I. Notes 52 The semivitrification, which constitutes porcelain. 1794 KIRWAN *Elem. Min.* (ed. 2) I. 396 That which produces enamels and semi-vitrifications. 1841 *Proc. Amer. Philos. Soc.* II. 4 The semivitrified quartz rock of the western part of the Hoosae mountain. 1889 C. T. DAVIS *Pract. Treat. Bricks*, etc. (ed. 2) 78 A degree of heat when semi-vitrification and shrinkage take place.

†**Semivocal,** *a.* and *sb. Obs.* [ad. L. *sēmivocālis* (in sense A. 2, B., transl. of Gr. ἡμίφωνος): see SEMI- and VOCAL *a.*] **A.** *adj.*

1. Applied to the sound of trumpets, drums, etc. (see quots.).

1614 ADAMS *Divell's Banket* 28 By vocall speeches, semivocall Drummes and Trumpets, mute Ensignes. 1688 HOLME *Armoury* III. xix. (Roxb.) 167/2 A Semivocall signe, is that which is distinguished by the Trumpet, or other warlike Instrument.

2. That is a semivowel.

1828–32 WEBSTER, *Semivocal*, pertaining to a semivowel; half-vocal; imperfectly sounding.

B. *sb.* A semivowel.

1530 PALSGR. Introd. p. xxiii, Theyr consonantes be devyded in to mutes and liquides or semivocalles.

Semivowel (se·mivauəl). [f. SEMI- 7 c + VOWEL, after L. *sēmivocālis*: see prec. Cf. F. *semi-voyelle*.] A vocal sound that partakes of the nature of a vowel and of a consonant; a letter representing such a sound.

The general literary use echoes that of the Roman grammarians, who applied the term to the spirants and liquids (including nasals), *f, l, m, n, r, s, x.* As a technical term the word now most commonly denotes only *w* and *y*, but sometimes it includes these together with the liquids and nasals, chiefly in their non-syllabic values.

1530 PALSGR. Introd. p. xxiii, The latines in soundyng of theyr liquides or semi vowelles begyn with *e*. 1552 HULOET s.v. *X*, X is a semiuowell, and hathe the voice of a double consonante for the which in olde writinges *cs* and *gs* was vsed. 1656 BLOUNT *Glossogr.*, *Semivowels*, certain Consonants so called, because they have the sound of Vowels, As *f, l, m, n, s.* 1668 WILKINS *Real Char.* III. xii. 369, (*S*) the correspondent mute (though it be commonly reckoned for a semivowel). 1726 BROOME *Notes Pope's Odyss.* XVII. 46 When Homer..paints a beautiful face, or an engaging object, he chuses the softest vowels, and most smooth and flowing semivowels. 1751 JOHNSON *Rambler* No. 88 ⁋ 3 By tempering the mute Consonants with Liquids and Semivowels. 1841 LATHAM *Eng. Lang.* II. ix. 165 The Semivowel *y*. 1876 BANCROFT *Hist. U. S.* II. xxxvi. 409 The whole Iroquois family never use the semivowel *m*.

attrib. 1860 O. W. HOLMES *Elsie V.* xix. (1891) 261 The foam-flowers dropping as the grass-flowers drop,—with sharp semivowel consonantal sounds,—*frsh.*

Semland(e, -ant(e, -aunt, var. ff. SEMBLANT.

Semlar, var. SOMLER *Sc. Obs.*, butler.

Semle, obs. f. SEEMLY *a.*; var. SEMBLE *v. Obs.*

Semli, -lich(e, -like, obs. forms of SEEMLY.

Semly, obs. f. SEEMLY; var. SEMBLE *sb.* and *v.*

Semmar, -er, var. forms of SEMAR *Obs.*

Semme, Semmetic: see SEEM *v.*², SEMITIC *a.*

Semmit (se·mit). *Sc.* Forms: 5 **semat,** 6 **semitte,** 9 **semmit, -et.** An under-shirt or vest.

1456 SIR G. HAYE *Law Arms* (S.T.S.) 64 Cesar brocht with him nouthir wapyn na armuris na othir defence bot in his semat. 1562–3 *Act 5 Eliz.* c. 22 § 1 Unles suche person ..doo make..therof tawed..Leather or Parchement or otherwise converte the same into Semittes Panelles [etc.]. 1888 *Glasgow Even. Times* 15 Oct. 3/5 Offering a petticoat and semmit in pledge. 1904 *C. T. C. Gaz.* Feb. 91 A tight-fitting woollen semmit next the skin (thin and light)...I also carry a semmit made of Welsh flannel, made wide and of full size...I wear this semmit during the evenings, and also sleep in it under my nightshirt.

†**Se·mnable** *a.*, †**Se·mnably** *adv.* Used by Fuller = SEMBLABLE *a.*, SEMBLABLY *adv.*

1651 FULLER *Abel Rediv.*, *Huss* 19 That semnably with rhetoricall flusculations I should endevour to adorne his memoriall. 1659 — *Appeal Injured Innoc.* III. 57 As Marriners..are fain to fetch a compass; Semnably, I..was faine to go about. *a* 1661 — *Worthies*, *Northumb.* (1662) II. 302 From Berwick to Dover three hundred miles over: That is from one end of the land to the other. Semnable the Scripture expression, From Dan to Ber-sheba.

‖**Semnopithecus** (semnǫpiþī·kǫs). [mod.L. *semnopithēcus*, f. Gr. σεμνός revered, holy + πίθηκος ape.] A genus of long-tailed, long-limbed Asiatic monkeys. Also, a monkey of this genus: often in anglicized form **Se·mnopithec** (-þek), or **-thece** (-þīs). Hence **Semnopithe·cine** *a.*, pertaining to the subfamily *Semnopithecinæ*, or to the genus *Semnopithecus*; *sb.*, a semnopithecine monkey. **Se·mnopithe·coid** *a.* and *sb.* = prec.

1824 HORSFIELD *Zool. Res. Java* 9 The comparisons which I have been enabled to make of the skulls of various Semnopitheci and of Gibbons. 1838 [? RENNIE] *Nat. Hist. Monkeys*, etc. (Libr. Entert. Knowl.) 216 The tails, likewise, are much longer in the semnopithecs than in any of the ordinary monkeys. 1891 *Century Dict.*, Semnopithece...Semnopithecine [*a.* and *sb.*]...Semnopithecoid [*a.* and *sb.*].

Semola (se·mǫlă). [a. It. *semola* bran.] A trade name for a special variety of semolina.

1853 [see SEMOLETTA]. 1858 SIMMONDS *Dict. Trade*, *Semola*, an Italian name for bran; but often erroneously applied by grocers, and other vendors, to semolino. 1882 in OGILVIE; and in later Dicts. 1895 *Stores' Price-list*, Gluten Preparations for Special Dietary...Semola.

‖**Semoletta** (semǫle·tă). *rare.* (In some Dicts. *erron.* **semolella.**) [It. *semoletta*, dim. of *semola*: see SEMOLA.] A variety of semolina.

1844 T. WEBSTER *Encycl. Dom. Econ.* 767 Semolina..is called also *soojee*: and a still smaller kind, called semoletta, is sifted out of the other. 1853 T. C. ARCHER *Pop. Econ. Bot.* 56 Semolina, Semoletta, Semola, Semola rarita, Soojee, and Urena, are names used to designate a product of wheat.

Semolina (semǫlī·nă). Also **semoulina,** ‖**semolino.** [Altered form of It. *semolino*, dim. of *semola* bran: see SEMOLA.] An article of food consisting of those hard portions of 'flinty' wheat which resist the action of the millstones, and are collected in the form of rounded grains. (See also quot. 1858.) Also *attrib.*, as *semolina pudding*.

1797 UNDERWOOD *Dis. Children* III. 82 To broth may be added light puddings, made of bread, semolina, tapioca, or rice. 1845 ELIZA ACTON *Mod. Cookery* (ed. 2) 395 A good Semoulina pudding. 1858 SIMMONDS *Dict. Trade*, *Semolino*. ..The commercial name for the fine hard parts of wheat rounded by attrition in the millstones, imported chiefly from Italy...In France the name semolino is given to the large hard grains of wheat retained in the bolting machine, after the fine parts have been pressed through its meshes. 1884 *Bath Herald* 27 Dec. 6/4 It is sought, while dividing the bran from the interior of the grain, to break up the latter, not into flour but into fragments known as 'semolina', or 'middlings'. 1904 'E. NESBIT' *Phœnix & Carpet* xii. 219 When lunch came it was just hashed mutton and semolina pudding.

Semond: see SEMEND *Obs.*, salmon.

Semonde, Semoom: see SIMMON *sb.*¹, SIMOOM.

†**Semoted,** *a. Obs. rare*⁻¹. [f. L. *sēmōt-us*, pa. pple. of *sēmovēre* to separate, f. *sē-*, apart, SE- + *movēre* to move: see -ED¹.] Separated, removed.

1542 BECON *Pathw. Prayer* vii. D iv, Is it ynough yf I pray with my mynde, the herte beynge semoted from mundane affayres?

Semoulina, obs. form of SEMOLINA.

†**Semo·vedly,** *adv. Obs.* [f. SE- + MOVED *ppl. a.* + -LY².] Cf. SEMOTED.] Separately.

1593 NASHE *Christ's T.* 38 b, None I will semouedly allude to, but onely attaint vice in generall. 1623 COCKERAM I, *Semouedly*, meaning one alone.

Sempect (se·mpekt). *Hist. rare*⁻¹. [ad. med.L. *sempecta, senpecta, sympecta*, ad. Gr. συμπαίκτης playfellow.] A term formerly used in the Benedictine Order, according to Pseudo-Ingulf applied to monks over fifty years old, who were allowed special privileges on account of age.

This seems to be a misapprehension. In the Benedictine Rule itself (cap. xxvii) *senpectæ* denotes the elder monks chosen by the abbot to visit (secretly) an excommunicated brother and to encourage him if likely to fall into despair.

1865 KINGSLEY *Hereω.* xx, Only the ancient sempects—some near upon a hundred and fifty years old—wandered where they would.

‖**Semper-** (se·mpəɹ), the L. adv. *semper* always, used in various nonce-combinations (in imitation of SEMPERVIRENT, etc.), as **semper-annual** *a.*, unceasing in annual succession; **semper-green,** an evergreen; **semper-identical** *a.* [after L. phrase *semper idem*, always the same]; **semper-juvenescent** *a.*, always growing younger; **semper-lenity,** unvarying gentleness.

1623 COCKERAM II, Accustomed Gentlenesse, *Semperlenity*. 1694 WESTMACOTT *Script. Herb.* 18 The common Bay-tree, which is a sempergreen, is now commonly found in most Gardens. 1880 ? WAINEWRIGHT *Ess. & Crit.* (1880) 98 That perfectly semperidentical display of idiosyncratic egotism which runs through..all his varieties. 1830 *Fraser's Mag.* I. 342 Blisses of an immortal and semperjuvenescent life. 1861 G. MEREDITH *Evan Harrington* xxviii, Supposing Lord Mayor's footmen to be plumed like estridges...What must Lord Mayors be and semperannual Lords?

Sempervirent (sempəɹvəi·rĕnt), *a.* [f. L. *semper* always + *virent-em*, pr. pple. of *virēre* to be green.] Evergreen.

1668 WILKINS *Real Char.* II. iv. § 6. 109 Bacciferous sempervirent shrubs. 1693 *Phil. Trans.* XVII. 762 It is sempervirent, and grows in sandy places. 1857 A. GRAY *First Less. Bot.* (1866) Gloss., *Sempervirent*, evergreen.

Sempervirid (sempəɹvi·rid), *a. Bot.* [Formed as prec. + L. *virid-is* green, VIRID *a.*] = prec.

1911 in WEBSTER. [*Obs.* or *rare*.]

†**Sempervive.** *Obs.* Also 8 (after Sp.) **sempre vive.** [Anglicized form of SEMPERVIVUM. Cf. F. †*sempervive* (Cotgr. 1611), Sp. *siempreviva*.] The houseleek.

1625 PURCHAS *Pilgrims* I. 27 An herbe (which for his forme is scarce to be discerned from a Semperuiue). 1626 BACON *Sylva* § 29 The greater Semperviue..will put out Branches, two or three yeares. 1764 GRAINGER *Sugar Cane* IV. 124 With sempre vive Unload their bowels.

attrib. *a* 1722 LISLE *Husb.* (1752) 257 Purge them with aloes, or sempervive leaves cleared of their outward skins.

‖**Se·mper-vi·vens.** *Obs. rare*⁻¹. [mod.L., f. L. *semper* always + *vivens*, pr. pple. of *vivĕre* to live.] The houseleek.

1672 W. HUGHES *Amer. Physit.* 98 Of Semper-Vivens.

‖**Sempervivum** (sempəɹvəi·vǫm). [L. *sempervivum* neut. of *sempervīvus* ever-living. The fem. *sempervīva* (sc. *herba*) was also used.] **a.** The houseleek. **b.** A genus (Linnæus 1737) of crassulaceous plants containing the houseleek, *S. tectorum* and about 50 other species; a plant of this genus.

1591 PERCYVALL *Span. Dict.*, *Yerva puntera*, semperuiuum, *Aizous*. 1655 FULLER *Hist. Cambr.* 134 Two Serpents, erected, azure,..having a branch of semper vivum proper betwixt their heads. 1666 J. DAVIES tr. *Rochefort's Caribby Isl.* 62 *Semper-vivum*. There are in these Islands several kinds of Herbs that never dye or wither. 1882 *Garden* 3 June 306/1 To see the pleasing tints and forms of the Sempervivums at the present season makes one wonder why these plants are not grown in every rock garden.

Sempill, obs. Sc. form of SIMPLE *a.*

Sempitan, obs. f. SUMPITAN, Malay blow-gun.

Sempitern (se·mpitɜ̄ɹn), *a. arch.* Forms: 4–7 **sempiterne,** 6 **sempyterne,** 6– **sempitern.** [a. OF. *sempiterne*, ad. L. *sempiternus*, f. *semp-er* always (cf. *æviternus*: see ETERNE *a.*).] = next.

1390 GOWER *Conf.* III. 88 That is the god, whos mageste Alle othre thinges schal governe, And his beinge is sempiterne. *c* 1440 CAPGRAVE *Life St. Kath.* IV. 1586 Than is oure feyth grounded on noo lye, But on swhiche thyng whiche is sempiterne. 1535 STEWART *Cron. Scot.* I. 505 In sempiterne rememberance to be Of Christis deith and Cristianitie. 1624 DARCIE *Birth of Heresies* Ded., Vnder whose Sacred Sempitern Defence Long liue, Chast Star. 1683 E. HOOKER *Pordage's Myst. Div.* Pref. Ep. 107 The only True, semper eadem, sempitern, ever-adorable and superbenedict Tri-une Deitie. 1866 BLACKMORE *Cradock Nowell* xxviii, That asylum is inviolable and sempitern, I hope. 1876 J. ELLIS *Caesar in Egypt* 66 Those unexampled Temples sempitern.

Sempiternal (sempitɜ̄·ɹnăl), *a.* Also **sempiternall, sempyternal, -el,** 5–7 **semipiternall,** 6 **sempyternall,** 6–7 **sempeternal.** [a. F. *sempiternel* (13th c. in Hatz.-Darm.), or ad. late L. *sempiternāl-is*, f. L. *sempitern-us*: see SEMPITERN *a.* and -AL.] Enduring constantly and continually; everlasting, eternal.

14.. *Pol. Rel. & L. Poems* (1903) 113 As thou art cyte of god, & sempiternal throne, Here now, blessyd lady, my wofulle mone. 1432–50 tr. *Higden* (Rolls) III. 183 Trawthe is immortalle, immutable, and sempiternalle. 1566 PAINTER *Pal. Pleas.* xxvii. (1569) 55 A miraculous acte, and worthie (in deede) of sempiternall remembraunce. 1579–80 NORTH *Plutarch*, *Camillus* (1595) 152 Some writers say, that they [*sc.* the Vestals] had nothing els in keeping but the sempiternall fire. 1632 LITHGOW *Trav.* x. 437 Queene Elizabeth of sempiternall renowne. *a* 1730 G. GUTHRIE *Monogr.* (1900) 66 Fearing it might be a sempiternal work to him. 1784 COWPER *Task* II. 499 All truth is from the sempiternal source Of Light Divine. 1831 J. JEKYLL *Corr.* 18 July (1894) 274 Dull dinners..with the sempiternal saddle of mutton. 1860 GEN. P. THOMPSON *Audi Alt.* III. cxxiv. 75 Two sources of war are sempiternal. 1884 *World* 20 Aug. 8/1 We have discovered the elixir of sempiternal juvenility.

Sempite·rnally, *adv.* [f. prec. + -LY².] Everlastingly, eternally.

1509 BARCLAY *Shyp of Folys* (1874) I. 27 God is aboue and regneth sempiternally [1570 sempeternally] Whiche shall vs deme at his last Jugement. 1635 PAGITT *Christianogr.* App. 22 The Word and his Spirit sempiternally proceed from God, and are sempiternally in him. *a* 1693 *Urquhart's Rabelais* III. v, That is to be done infinitely and sempiternally. 1879 ESCOTT *England* xi. (1881) 161 The filthy back-kitchen of the den, sempiternally reeking with the fumes of bad drink and vile tobacco. 1895 ZANGWILL *Master* II. x. 245 It wore a sempiternally festive air.

†**Sempite·rnity.** *Obs.* [ad. late L. *sempiternitās*, f. L. *sempitern-us*: see SEMPITERN *a.* and -ITY.] Duration without end; perpetuity.

1599 NASHE *Lenten Stuffe* 22 Or thou wilt commend thy muse to sempiternity, and haue images and statues erected to her after her vnstringed silent interment. *a* 1676 HALE *Prim. Orig. Man.* (1677) 227 A Supposition of a future Sempiternity would produce the same difficulty, without such interposition of the Divine Wisdom and Providence. 1802 in *Spirit Publ. Jrnls.* VI. 261 All concurred in the sempiternity of merit that they were determined to discover in him in all time forthcoming.

†**Sempiternize,** *v. Obs. rare*⁻¹. [f. SEMPITERN *a.* + -IZE.] *trans.* To perpetuate.

a 1693 *Urquhart's Rabelais* III. viii, The sempiternizing of Human Race.

†**Sempiternly,** *adv. Obs.* [f. SEMPITERN *a.* + -LY².] = SEMPITERNALLY *adv.*

c 1450 *Mirour Saluacioun* (1888) 140 The gude entre in the joye of thaire lord sempiternely.

Sempite·rnous, *a.* ? *Obs. rare.* [ad. OF. *sempiterneux*, f. L. *sempitern-us*: see SEMPITERN *a.* and -OUS.] Sempiternal.

1653 URQUHART *Rabelais* II. xv, A sempiternous Crone and old Hag. *Ibid.* II. xvii, Great old sempiternous trots [Fr. *grandes vieilles sempiterneuses*]. 1809 W. IRVING *Knickerb.* VI. iv. (1849) 335 A race of pestilent sempiternous beldames.

‖**Sempiternum** (sempitɜ̄·ɹnǫm). *Obs.* [L. *sempiternum*, neut. of *sempiternus* SEMPITERN.] A quality of woollen cloth made in the 17th c. and similar to PERPETUANA. Cf. EVERLASTING *sb.*

1633 in *Naworth Househ. Bks.* (Surtees) 295 For one yearde and a halfe of Sempiternum iiij. vjᵈ. *Ibid.* 300. 1665 BRATHWAIT *Comm. Two Tales* 65 She would have her Husband's Lining of any Stuff rather than *Perpetuano* or *Sempiternum*.

Semplar, obs. form of SAMPLER.

1685 BOYLE *Salubr. Air* Pref. 1 To give a Semplar or Specimen of what may be done upon the other Heads of the designed History.

Semple, obs. form of SIMPLE.

Sempre vive, variant of SEMPERVIVE *Obs.*

Sempster, Sempstress, etc.: see SEAMSTER, SEAMSTRESS.

‖**Semsem** (se·msem). [Arab. سمسم *simsim*, prob. ad. Gr. σήσαμον.] = SESAME. Also *attrib.*

1866 LIVINGSTONE *Jrnl.* I. (1873) I. 17 Some sorghum, semsem seed [etc.]..constitute the commerce of the port. 1896 *Daily News* 24 Nov. 11/2 The valleys..were covered with plantations of Indian corn,..tobacco, semsem oil, and banana. 1899 *19th Cent.* Aug. 273 An interminably long stretch of dhurra cultivation appears, varied by sem-sem plants.

Semster, -stress(e, obs. ff. SEAMSTER, -STRESS.

Semulacre, obs. variant of SIMULACRE.

‖**Semuncia** (simɒ·nʃiă). *Rom. Antiq.* Pl. **-iæ** (simɒ·nʃi,ī). [L. *sēmuncia*, f. *sēmi-* SEMI- + *uncia* OUNCE *sb.*¹] A half-ounce, the twenty-fourth part

of an *as*. Also anglicized †**Semunce** (*rare*⁻⁰). Hence **Semu·ncial** *a.* [ad. L. *sēmunciāl-is*].

1656 BLOUNT *Glossogr.*, *Semuncial*, of or belonging to half an ounce. 1658 PHILLIPS, *Semuncial*, belonging to a semunce, *i.* half an ounce. 1887 HEAD *Hist. Nummorum* 43 Bronze coins of Uncial and Semuncial weight, B.C. 217–89.

†**Semy,** *a. Obs.* Also **cemy.** [Of obscure origin; possibly an inference from some compound of SEMI-.] (See quot.) Hence †**Se·myly** *adv.*

c 1440 *Promp. Parv.* 66/1 Cemy, or sotelle.., *subtilis*. Cemely, or sotely, *subtiliter*. *Ibid.* 452/2 Semy.., *subtilis*. Semyly.., *subtiliter*.

Semy, Semyed, obs. ff. SEMÉE, SEMÉED.

Semylacre, -ylytude, obs. ff. SIMULACRE, SIMILITUDE. **Semyld,** pa. t. of SEMBLE *v.*¹ *Obs.*

†**Se·mys,** *a. Obs. rare*⁻¹. [App. = G. *sämisch* (15th c. also *semisz*) a kind of soft leather.] The distinctive epithet of some kind of leather.

1508 *Acc. Ld. High Treas. Scot.* (1902) IV. 25, iiij skinnis of blak semys leddir to be ane doublat to the King.

‖**Sen** (sen), *sb.* Also †**seni,** †**senni.** [Japanese.] A Japanese copper or bronze coin (see quot. 1897). Chiefly *collect.* as *plural*.

1802 PINKERTON *Mod. Geog.*, *Japan* iii. II. 166 The Seni, of copper or iron, are strung like the Chinese pieces of a similar value. 1839 *Penny Cycl.* XV. 326/1 Sennis, or Cashes, are small pieces of iron, copper, or brass, having a square hole in the middle, through which, as in China, they are strung on a wire or thread. 1875 BEDFORD *Sailor's Pocket Bk.* ix. (ed. 2) 316, 10 Rin = 1 Sen = ½d. 1895 C. HOLLAND *My Japanese Wife* 75 To be English spells generosity in Japanese eyes in the matter of sen for her own little pocket. 1897 *Daily News* 27 Sept. 5 The sen..is nominally equal to a halfpenny, though in fact only worth half that coin.

Sen (sen), *adv.*, *prep.*, and *conj.* Now *rare*. Chiefly *Sc.* and *north*. Also 5 **senne,** 6 **senn.** [Contracted form of *sethen*, SITHEN: cf. SENE, SIN, SYNE, and SINCE.]

A. *adv.* Then, afterwards; also ago. *rare*.

c 1460 *Towneley Myst.* xx. 259 She weshyd hym with hir terys weytt, and sen dryed hym with hir hare. 1867 J. P. MORRIS *Siege o' Brou'ton* 3 (Lanc. Gloss.) That's a conny lang time sen now.

B. *prep.* From, after; subsequent to.

c 1330 R. BRUNNE *Chron. Wace* (Rolls) 24 Sen þe tyme of sir Noe. *c* 1400 MAUNDEV. (Roxb.) xvi. 74 Þe kyng..had.. ay were, sen þat tyme. 1456 SIR G. HAYE *Law Arms* (S. T. S.) 30 Sen the passioun of Crist,..the haly kirk was never ȝit in pes. *c* 1460 *Towneley Myst.* xx. 714 It has bene told, sen many a day, sayngys of hym full sare. 1577 FULKE *Confut.* 7 There was neuer greater store in the church of Christ, sen Christ his time. 1593 (*title*), Actis of Parliament, past sen the Coronatiovn of the Kingis Maiestie.

C. *conj.* **1.** From or since the time that.

1338 R. BRUNNE *Chron.* (1810) 28 Þe tend ȝere of his regne sen he was crouned Kyng. 1375 BARBOUR *Bruce* III. 496 Sen the king discumfyt was At Meffan, he herd neuir thing [etc.]. *c* 1400 MAUNDEV. (Roxb.) i. 4 It es lang sen it fell oute of þe hand. *c* 1421 *Lessons of Dirige* 231 in 26 *Pol. Poems* 114 Trowest þou ouȝt þat y..Shal..ȝelde rekenyng sen y bygan? 1552 LYNDSAY *Monarche* 329 Sen I could ryde. 1599 ALEX. HUME *Hymns* ii. 219 Sa great a wonder was not heard, sen first the warld began. 1829 BROCKETT *N. C. Gloss.* (ed. 2) s.v., Its lang syne, sen he left us. 1871 J. RICHARDSON *Cummerland Talk* Ser. I. 18 (E. D. D.) Theer's been a deal o' ups an' doons sen I went to scheul.

2. Seeing or considering (*that*). [Cf. SEEN *conj.*, which may have been partly confused with this.]

13.. *Gosp. Nicod.* 53 Sen he to blind has gifen þe sight..., whi suld he vnto ded be dight? *a* 1340 HAMPOLE *Psalter* lxxxiv. 8 Sen þat he is turnyd away fra þe vnrest of þis life. 1423 JAS. I *Kingis Q.* cxliv, 'Now wele,' quod sche, 'and sen that It is so, That in vertew thy lufe is set with trueth [etc.].' *c* 1460 *Towneley Myst.* xxvi. 292 Sen I for luf, man, boght the dere,..I pray the hartely,..luf me agane. *a* 1500 *Lancelot* 1019 Bot, hart, sen at yow knawith she is here,.. Now is thi tyme. *a* 1533 LD. BERNERS *Huon* xviii. 49 Huon, sen thou woldest be agreed with me, Then [etc.]. 1588 A. KING tr. *Canisius' Catech.* 122 Sen we have sufficientlie according to our present purpose spokin hitherto. *a* 1756 PENNECUIK *Coll. Sc. Poems* 48 Sen your'e gotten out o's grips, Gi'e John a bucky.

Sen: see SAINT, SAY *v.*¹, SEE *v.*, SEND *v.*, SENE *a.*

Sena, obs. form of SENNA.

[**Senacion,** anglicized form of med.L. *senaciōnem*, for L. *seneciōn-em* groundsel, SENCHION.

1526 *Grete Herball* cccxviii. (1529) Y iij b, Whan receptes expresseth Senacions in the plurell nombre it is to wyte cresses. But yf senacion be wryten in the synguler nombre, it is an other herbe.]

†**Se·nage.** *Obs.* Also 4 **synage,** 6 **senagy.** [a. OF. *senage* (f. *sene* synod: see SENE and -AGE) or its med.L. form *senagium* (1292 in *Durh. Acc. Rolls*, Surtees Soc., p. 490).] Money paid for synodals, a tribute due to the bishop or archdeacon (or bursar) at Easter.

c 1380 WYCLIF *Wks.* (1880) 249 And whanne bischopis & here officeris comen & feynen to visite,..wrecchid curatis ben nedid to festen hem richely & ȝeue procuracie & synage. *Ibid.* 436 [is is a foul offis of a prest to robbe his puple to ȝyue to bischop or erchedekene godis þat god biddiþ not, as senage & procurasies. 1546 *Yorks. Chantry Surv.* (Surtees) 30 Paiable yerely to the archebysshope of Yorke for proxies and senagies. 1684 *Cowel's Interpr.* (ed. Manley), *Senage*, There goes out yearly in Proxege and Senege 33s. 6d.

Senarian (sĭnē·riăn). *Ancient Prosody. rare.* [f. L. *sēnār-ius*: see next + -IAN.] = next.

1803 PORSON *Let. to A. Dalzel* in *Mus. Crit.* (1826) I. 330 The fifth foot of a Senarian. 1895 *Q. Rev.* Oct. 34 The great Greek Iambic line is of course the Senarian, consisting of six Iambics or their equivalents.

‖**Senarius** (sĭnē·riŏs). *Prosody.* Pl. **senarii.** [L. *sēnārius* adj., consisting of six each, f. *sēni* adj. pl. six each, f. *sex* six; used subst. by ellipsis of *versus* verse.] (More fully, *iambic senarius*.) A (Greek or Latin) verse consisting of six feet, each of which is either an iambus or some foot which the law of the verse permits to be substituted; an iambic trimeter.

1540 PALSGR. *Acolastus* I. i. C iij b, All the versis of this scene be *Senarii*. 1811 ELMSLEY in *Edin. Rev.* XIX. 80 The fifth foot of a tragic senarius cannot be a spondee, except in three cases. 1832 [see PYTHIAMBIC]. 1869 H. SNOW *Theocritus*, *Epigr.* xvi. Notes (1873) 219 The lines are alternately iambic senarii and hendecasyllables.

Senarmontite (senā·ɹmǫntəit). *Min.* [Named after H. de *Senarmont*, who first described it + -ITE¹.] A native tri-oxide of antimony, crystallizing in colourless or greyish-white octahedrons.

1851 DANA in *Amer. Jrnl. Sci.* Ser. II. XII. 209.

†**Se·nary,** *sb. Obs.* [ad. L. *sēnārius* adj. (see next) used subst. by ellipsis.]

1. [= *senarius* (*numerus*).] The number six; a set or sequence of six things; in the 17th c. often, the six days of the Creation.

1570 BILLINGSLEY *Euclid* x. lxx. 280 b, Hetherto hath bene spoken of sixe Senaryes, of which the first Senary [*sc.* of propositions] contayneth the production of irrationall lines by composition. *Ibid.* lxxiii. 282 b, Here beginneth the Senaries by substraction. 1653 H. MORE *Conject. Cabbal.* (1713) 16 Wherefore God having thus compleated his work in the Senary, comprehending the whole Creation in Six orders of things, he ceased from ever creating any thing more. 1686 GOAD *Celest. Bodies* II. xiv. 339 They will bring you Cold and Heat, Calm and Storm,..in one Senary of Days. 1693 PASCHALL in *Phil. Trans.* XVII. 816, I divided the Νυχθήμερον into four Senaries of Hours.

2. *Prosody.* = SENARIUS.

1579 G. HARVEY *Two other Lett.* (1580) 64 This foote [*sc.* the trochee]..is..quite thrust out of doores in a pure and iust Senarie. 1828 *Classical Jrnl.* XXXVII. 127 'ΑΛΛ' ὅμως are words frequently employed by Euripides at the end of an Iambic senary.

Senary (sī·nări, se·nări), *a.* [ad. L. *sēnārius*: see SENARIUS.] Pertaining to the number six. *Senary scale*: the scale of arithmetical notation of which the radix is six. *Senary division*: division into six parts.

1661 BLOUNT *Glossogr.* (ed. 2), *Senarie*, that contains or belongs to the number six. 1721 BAILEY, *Senary*, that which consists of Six. 1755 JOHNSON, *Senary*, belonging to the number six; containing six. 1820 P. BARLOW in *Nicholson's Jrnl.* XXV. 183 Thus, in the binary scale only two characters are wanted, namely 1 and 0; in the senary, six; in the decimal, ten. *Ibid.* 186 Transform 11111 to the senary scale. 1830 LINDLEY *Nat. Syst. Bot.* 81 The Cephalotus of Labillardière, offers a remarkable exception to the usual characters..in the senary division of its flower [etc.]. 1881 BAUERMAN *Syst. Min.* ii. 11 The only other class of symmetry possible in crystals is senary or hexagonal, corresponding to a rotation of one-sixth of a revolution, such as that of a regular hexagonal prism about its axis.

Senassee, obs. var. SUNYASEE, Indian ascetic.

Senate (se·nĕt). Forms: 3 **senaht,** 4 **senas,** 4–7 **senat,** 6 **cenate,** *pl. Sc.* **senat(t)is,** 4– **senate.** [a. F. *senat*, *senaz* (mod. F. *sénat*), ad. L. *senātus* (*u*-stem), lit. council of old men, f. *sen-em* (nom. *senex*) old (see SENIOR *a.*), absol. old man: see -ATE¹. Cf. Pr. *senet*, Sp., Pg. *senado* It. *senato*, G. *senat*, Du. *senaat*.]

1. An assembly or council of citizens charged with the highest deliberative functions in the government of a state. **a.** In ancient Rome: A legislative and administrative body, consisting originally of representatives elected by the patricians, and in later times composed partly of appointed members and partly of the actual and former holders of certain high offices of state.

c 1205 LAY. 25388 Þis weoren þa sixe þe þat senaht al biwusten. 13.. *K. Alis.* 1477 His lettres come Into þe cite of grete Rome. Þe riche people, & þe senas, Spaken togedres of þis cas. *c* 1375 *Sc. Leg. Saints* xxix. (*Placidas*) 352 Al þe hale senat [of Rome]. *c* 1460 FORTESCUE *Abs. & Lim. Mon.* xvi. (1885) 149 The Romaynes, while thair counsell callid þe senate was gret, gate, through þe wysdome off that counsell, the lordschippe off gret partye of the world. 1531 ELYOT *Gov.* I. ii. (1880) I. 20 The Senate..which was fyrste ordayned by Romulus. 1614 GORGES *Lucan* v. 166 The Consuls both did then decree The Senate should assembled be. 1775 HARRIS *Philos. Arrangem.* Wks. (1841) 247 Cato..used to read philosophy in the senate-house, while the senate was assembling. 1879 FROUDE *Cæsar* viii. 79 The Senate was.. a body composed of men of any order who had secured the suffrages of the people.

b. Applied to bodies having more or less similar functions in other states of the ancient world, esp. as the equivalent of Gr. γερουσία (lit. 'body of elders') and βουλή (lit. 'council').

a 1586 SIDNEY *Arcadia* I. (Sommer) 21 b, By the king and Senat of Lacedæmon, Demagoras was..banished the countrie. 1607 SHAKS. *Timon* v. i. 132 Th' Athenians By two of their most reuerend Senate greet thee. 1656 HARRINGTON *Prerog. Pop. Govt.* I. xii. 108 The Senate of the Beane being the proposing-Assembly (for that of the Areopagites, called also a Senate, was a Judicatory) consisted of four hundred Citizens chosen by Lot, which was performed with beanes. 1738 GLOVER *Leonidas* I. 408 Lacedæmon's senate now approach'd. 1842 *Smith's Dict. Grk. & Rom. Antiq.* s.v. βουλή, This senate of 500 [at Athens] was divided into ten sections of fifty each, the members of which were called prytanes (πρυτάνεις), and were all of the same tribe.

c. In the Middle Ages, and subsequently, used as the official title of the governing body in various free cities of Europe.

c 1374 CHAUCER *Boeth.* I. pr. iv. (1868) 19 At þe citee of verone whan þat þe kyng gredy of comune slauȝter caste hym to transporten vpon al þe ordre of þe senat þe gilt of his real maieste. 1530 in Ellis *Orig. Lett.* Ser. III. II. 193 The day after our coming the Senate [at Nuremberg] sent gentilmen to shew us their provision of harneis, ordinance, and corne. 1838 *Murray's Hand-bk. N. Germany* 444/1 In the election chamber (Wahlzimmer), the Senate of Frankfort now holds its sittings. 1841 W. SPALDING *Italy & It. Isl.* III. 344 On the mainland there are four Supreme Tribunals, called Senates, placed at Turin, Chambery, Nice, and Genoa. 1880 H. A. WEBSTER in *Encycl. Brit.* XI. 404/1 According to the present constitution [of Hamburg].., the legislative power is in the hands of the senate [of 18 members] and the general body of citizens, and the executive is committed to the senate alone.

d. *gen.* The governing or legislative assembly of a nation. Often applied, more or less rhetorically, to the British parliament.

1560 DAUS tr. *Sleidane's Comm.* 15 b, That he appointe a Cenate or counsell within the empire. 1584 D. FENNER *Def. Ministers* (1587) 12 At the table of whose Hon. Senat [app. of Privy Council], our supplications were..read. 1659 MILTON *Let. Friend* Wks. 1738 I. 583 Being now in Anarchy, without a counselling and governing Power..the first thing to be found out with all speed, without which no Commonwealth can subsist, must be a Senate, or General Council of State. 1718 PRIOR *On Corrup. Man.* vi, And senates vote, as armies fight, for pay. 1742 *Johnson's Debates* (1787) II. 139 (Ld. Hervey) It declares, my Lords, that there is now an enquiry depending before the Senate. 1775 ABIGAIL ADAMS in *Fam. Lett.* (1876) 227 Whether you are in the American Senate [*i.e.* Congress] or on board the British fleet, is a matter of uncertainty. 1787 *J. Lewis's Mem. Dk. Glocester* 58 *note*, [The Duke of Buckingham] was..an eloquent orator in the British Senate. 1809–10 COLERIDGE *Friend* (1865) 22 The pernicious influence of this lax morality extends from the nursery and the school to the cabinet and senate. 1848 THACKERAY *Van. Fair* lviii, He says there is no place in the bar or the senate that Georgy may not aspire to.

†**e.** Applied (perh. in passages translated from Latin) to the Corporation of London. *Obs.*

a 1548 HALL *Chron.*, *Hen. V* 52 b, The Mayre of London and the Senate appareled in orient grayned Skarlet. 1568 GRAFTON *Chron.* II. 633 Continuall watch was kept by the Maior and senate of London,..for the preseruacion of the peace, and continuance of good order.

f. In the 18th and 19th c. adopted as the official name for the upper and smaller branch of the legislature in various countries, as the United States (and each of the separate states of the Union), France, Italy, etc.

1780 ABIGAIL ADAMS in *Fam. Lett.* (1876) 388 Hancock will be Governor, by a very great majority; the Senate [of Massachusetts] will have to choose the Lieutenant-governor. 1789 *Constit. U.S.* Art. I. § 3 The Senate of the United States shall be composed of two senators from each state. 1796 T. TWINING *Trav. Amer.* (1894) 52 From the hall of the Representatives, I went to that of the Senate, or Upper Chamber. *a* 1817 DWIGHT *Trav. New Eng.* (1823) IV. 159 New Hampshire... The legislature consists of a senate and house of representatives, chosen annually by ballot. 1887 W. C. FORD *Amer. Citizen's Man.* I. 11 In all the States the upper or smaller House is known as the Senate.

g. *transf.* and *fig.*

1540 PALSGR. *Acolastus* v. i. Y ij, Suerly the senate of my harte is sedicious. 1735 POPE *Prol. Sat.* 209 Like Cato give his little Senate laws And sit attentive to his own applause. 1880 COMBE *Syntax*, *Consol.* II. (Chandos) 152 Sometimes my bosom's senate sits In silent thought. 1821 SHELLEY *Hellas* Prol. 73 The senate of the Gods is met, Each in his rank and station set.

2. In the University of Cambridge, and in some other British universities, the official title of the governing body. Cf. SENATUS.

The Senate of the University of Cambridge corresponds to the Convocation of Oxford University, and consists of all Doctors, Masters of Arts, Law, and Surgery, and Bachelors of Divinity, who keep their names on the books. In the newer English universities, Durham, London, Liverpool, Birmingham, etc., the senate is a smaller body, its composition being different in different universities. In Scotland, the Latin form *Senatus* (*Academicus*) is commonly employed.

1736 *Charter* etc. *Coll. Will. & Mary, Virginia* 78 Concerning the College Senate. 1748 SALMON *Foreigner's Comp. Cambr.* 16 All Graces intended to be proposed to the Senate, must first pass the *Caput*. 1797 *Cambr. Univ. Cal.* 147 By the senate is meant all the doctors and masters of arts in the university, who have their names on the boards of their college. 1804 *Med. Jrnl.* XII. 286 Regulations enacted by the Senate of the University of Glasgow, respecting Degrees in Medicine. 1889 R. GILBERT *Liber Scholast.* 50 The Senate [of Cambridge], in 1818, decreed the foundation of three scholarships.

b. *U.S.* In some American colleges, a council composed of members of the faculty and elected students, having the control of the discipline, etc., of the students. 1891 in *Century Dict.*

†**3.** A senate-house. *Obs. rare.*

1616 BULLOKAR *Eng. Expos.*, *Senat*, the Counsell house, where the Magistrates of a citie assemble themselues. 1623 COCKERAM I. 1700 tr. *Danet's Dict. Grk. & Rom. Antiq.* s.v. *Senatus*, The Tribunes of the People at first stood at the Door of the Senate to know their Deliberations.

¶**4.** Misused for: A senator. *Obs. rare.*

157. SEMPILL *Compl. Fort.* 87 in *Satir. Poems Reform.* xliii, Of Julius Cesar..Slaine be his Senatis,..By his awin kinsmen Brutus and Cassus. *Ibid.* 210 To keip sic senattis it sall decore ȝour land. 1609 *Ev. Woman in Hum.* C 4 b, The olde Senate has put on his spectacles, and Lentulus and hee are turning the leaues of a dog-hay, leaues of a worme eaten Chronicle, and they want Tullies iudgement.

5. *attrib.* as *senate-chamber, -fight, -hall*, etc.

a 1700 EVELYN *Diary* June 1645, The Senate-hall [at Venice]. 1736 THOMSON *Liberty* v. 568 In the warm struggles of the senate-fight. 1737 SAVAGE *Of Public Spirit* 161 Bid Courts of Justice, Senate-chambers join, Till various All in one proud Work combine! 1855 DICKENS *Dorrit* II. vii, The rugged remains of temples and tombs and palaces and senate halls and theatres.

Se·nate-house. [HOUSE *sb.*¹]

1. A house or building in which a senate meets.

c 1550 N. SMYTH tr. *Herodian* II. 18 He wente too the Senate house. 1601 SHAKS. *Jul. C.* II. ii. 52 Wee'l send Mark Antony to the Senate house. 1634 MILTON *Comus* 389 Musing meditation most affects The pensive secrecy of desert cell,..And sits as safe as in a Senat house. *a* 1700 EVELYN *Diary* 4 Oct. 1641, The Senate-house of this city [Antwerp] is a very spacious and magnificent building. 1709 ADDISON *Tatler* No. 162 ⁋ 7 It was usual for them to expel a Senator who had been guilty of great Immoralities out of the Senate-House. 1886 *Encycl. Brit.* XX. 815 The Curia or senate-house.

transf. *a* 1586 SIDNEY *Arcadia* II. (Sommer) 129 b, The senate house of the planets was at no time so set, for the decreeing of perfection in a man, as at that time all folkes skilful therin did acknowledge. 1608 SHAKS. *Per.* I. i. 10. 1821 SHELLEY *Hellas* Prol. 2 It is the day when all the sons of God Wait in the roofless senate-house, whose floor Is Chaos.

2. *spec.* The building which serves for the meetings of the senate of a university, esp. of Cambridge.

1748 SALMON *Foreigner's Comp. Cambr.* 15 The Senate-House is a magnificent and elegant Building; the Length [etc.]. 1769 GRAY (*title*), Ode performed in the Senate-House at Cambridge. 1797 *Cambr. Univ. Cal.* 148 In the senate-house the elections of all the officers of the university take place, the appointments of the magistrates, the admissions to degrees, congregations, and consultations upon important matters by the senate, and by a statute of the university, no language is to be spoken therein but Latin. 1862 CALVERLEY *Verses & Transl.* (1894) 43 Past the Senate-house I saunter.

b. *attrib.* **Senate-house examination,** examination for degrees in Cambridge University; so **Senate-house examiner**; **Senate-house problem,** a mathematical problem proposed in a Senate-house examination.

1837 *Math. Probl. fr. Senate-House Exam. Papers* Pref. 7 Questions which have actually been set from time to time, at the Senate-House examinations. 1855 *Househ. Words* 8 Dec. 442/2 He harassed me with questions about the book as pertinaciously as any senate-house examiner. 1875 CAYLEY *Math. Papers* (1896) IX. 246 A Senate-house Problem.

†**Senatical,** *a. Obs. rare.* [f. SENATE + -ICAL.] Of or pertaining to a senate.

1651 *Animadv. Macdonnel's Answ. Eng. Ambass.* 48 Or incroach upon the Senaticall part and right of the people. 1652 PEYTON *Catastr. Ho. Stuarts* (1731) 49 That which overthrows Monarchy, the same overthrows a Senatical Government.

†**Senatoire.** *Obs. rare*⁻¹. [a. OF. *senatoire*, ad. med.L. *senātōrium*, f. L. *senātor*.] A senate-house.

1474 CAXTON *Chesse* II. ii, Whan he was comen home from the senatoire. [Cf. SENATORY *sb.*¹ 2.]

Senator (se·nătəɹ). Forms: 3–5 **senatur,** 3–7 **senatour,** 4–5 **cenatour, sinatour,** 4–6 **senatoure,** 5 **cenatoure, senatowre,** (6 **senatour**), 6– **senator.** [a. OF. *senateur* (mod.F. *sénateur*), ad. L. *senātor*, f. *sen-em*, *senex* old, old man; a parallel formation with *senātus* SENATE. Cf. Sp., Pg. *senador*, It. *senatore*.]

1. A member of a senate. **a.** A member of the ancient Roman senate.

In some of the early examples (*c* 1290, *c* 1386, 1390, and perhaps others) the writers evidently attribute to antiquity the usage of their own time, according to which 'the senator of Rome' was the title of a single high official. See sense 2.

c 1205 LAY. 25337 Þat was burh þa senaturs þa þet sinað heolden. *c* 1290 *St. John* 81 in *S. Eng. Leg.* 404 For þe senatour him a-slovȝ: þat was þo of rome, In contek þat heom was bi-twene. 13.. *Senyn Sag.* 1267 Amorewe aros that sinatour. *c* 1386 CHAUCER *Man of Law's T.* 863 For which this Emperour hath sent anon His senatour..And othere lordes..On Surryens to taken heigh vengeance. 1390 GOWER *Conf.* I. 199 This Lord, with whom sche scholde go, Of Rome was the Senatour. *c* 1400 *St. Alexius* 65 Perfore þe riche Emperoure Of þe Cite made hym Cenatoure. 1422 YONGE tr. *Secreta Secret.* xxxi. 178 The Sinatouris of the Cite [of Rome]. 1475 *Bk. Noblesse* 1 The noble cenatoure of Rome Kayus son. 1513 DOUGLAS *Æneis* Comm., Wks. II. 292 Quhen Cesar was slayn by the Sanatouris. 1540–1 ELYOT *Image Gov.* xxxix. (1544) 101 b, For thy pacience, wysedom and temperance, we deeme the worthy to be admitted into the college of Senatours. 1696 B. KENNETT *Romæ Antiquæ* II. III. ii. (1717) 101 The right of naming Senators belong'd at first to the Kings; afterwards the Consuls chose, and refer'd them to the People for their Approbation: But at last the Censors engross'd the whole Privilege of conferring this Honour. 1834 LYTTON *Pompeii* I. vii, 'The emperor has been giving a splendid supper to the senators,' answered Sallust.

b. A member of the senate or governing council in other states of antiquity.

1586 SIR E. HOBY *Pol. Disc. Truth* viii. 23 The Ephores, hauing chosen a Senator that was very true, commanded him [etc.]. 1607 SHAKS. *Timon* v. i. 139 The Senators of Athens, greet thee Timon. 1656 STANLEY *Hist. Philos.* v. *Plato* iii. (1687) 159/2 That he was a Senator, implies he was full thirty years old at that time, according to Solon's Law. 1790 COWPER *Odyss.* VIII. 56 He..led the way, whom follow'd all The sceptred senators. 1837 THIRLWALL *Greece* xxxv. IV. 379 The senators, ephors, and other magistrates [at Sparta].

c. A member of the senate or governing body in certain mediæval and modern cities of Europe. Cf. SENATE 1 c.

1560 DAUS tr. *Sleidane's Comm.* 79 b, The bishop of Strausborough writeth letters to divers of the senatours. 1604 SHAKS. *Oth.* IV. i. 230 The Duke, and the Senators of Venice greet you. 1682 *Lond. Gaz.* No. 1737/2 The Count d'Archinto has received his Patent from Spain, to be first Senator of Milan. 1741 LADY M. W. MONTAGU *Let. to Montagu* 25 Aug. (1893) II. 95 The senators [at Genoa] can converse with no strangers during the time of their magistracy. 1762 *New Biogr. Dict.* IX. 222 s.v. *Peiresc*, They..were sent to Aix to their uncle Claude Fabri, their father's elder brother, who was senator there. 1782 J. ADAMS in *Fam. Lett.* (1876) 404 [At the Hague] I am going to dine with..a number of Ambassadors and Senators. 1860 MOTLEY *Netherl.* I. (1868) I. 12 The Sage-Men chose annually a board of senators.

d. *gen.* A member of a governing body or parliament. Often applied (unofficially and sometimes rhetorically) to a member of either House of the British Parliament.

1387 TREVISA *Higden* (Rolls) VII. 35 Þerfore was i-made a counsaile of þe real strete of Calne..Þere seten in an hiȝe hous þe senatoures of Engelond. *a* 1513 FABYAN *Chron.* VI. ccxvi. (1811) 234 A nyce folysshe couenaunte ought nat to be holden,..without the hole assent of the senatours of the same lande. 1553 EDEN *Treat. New Ind.* (Arb.) 17 The Magistrates..are no lesse estemed then amonge vs Senatoures or Lord of the Counsayl. 1648 A. LEIGHTON *App. Parlt.* Ep. Ded., To the right Honourable & High Court of Parliament. Right Honorable and High Senators. Such hath beene the care [etc.]. 1660 TATHAM *Roy. Oak* 8 Holding..in the other [hand] a statute Book as a Senator and maintainer of laws. 1708 SWIFT *Predict. for* 1708, 6 At home, the Death of an old famous Senator will happen on the 15th. *a* 1763 W. KING *Lit. & Polit. Anecd.* (1819) 35 [The Duke of Wharton's] speech..was indeed not unworthy of the oldest and most accomplished senator..in either House of Parliament. 1776 J. ADAMS in *Fam. Lett.* (1876) 215, I had rather build stones upon Penn's hill, than to be the first Prince in Europe, or the first General or Senator in America. 1849 MACAULAY *Hist. Eng.* ii. I. 171 He had, during the first year of the Long Parliament, been honourably distinguished among the senators who laboured to redress the grievances of the nation. 1894 SIR J. ASTLEY *Fifty Yrs. Life* II. 123 How those forty senators [*sc.* the Irish M.P.'s] (or their successors) have been going on since, is notorious.

e. In vaguer sense: A counsellor, statesman; †a leader in State or Church. Also *fig.*

c 1400 *Rom. Rose* 4999 Peyne and Distresse, Syknesse and Ire, And Malencoly, that angry sire, Ben of hir paleys senatours. 1535 COVERDALE *Ps.* civ. [cv.] 22 That he might enfourme his prynces after his wil, and teach his Senatours wysdome. ?1548 tr. *Viret's Expos. XII Art. Chr. Faith* M vj b, Euen so hathe the churche hys spirituall policie.. and hys pastures, ministers, and senatoures. 1597 HOOKER *Eccl. Pol.* v. lxxvi. § 6 That which children might haue seene, their grauest Senators could not discerne. 1656 BLOUNT *Glossogr.*, *Muncerians*, a sort of Anabaptists, so called from Tho. Muncer, who was their Prophet, Senator and General, when they rose in Rebellion in Suevia and Franconia, &c. 1820 KEATS *Hyperion* I. 73 Those green-rob'd senators of mighty woods, Tall oaks.

f. The official title of a member of the senate or upper house of the legislature in the United States, in modern France, Italy, etc.

In the U.S., *Senator* prefixed to the surname denotes a member of the federal Senate, not of the Senate of a particular state.

1788 J. STOKES in *M. Cutler's Life*, etc. (1888) II. 275 The Constitution of the United States pleases me much, but you ought to allow the people to have the power of appointing Senators-extraordinary in cases of exigency, as of war, or national distresses. 1837 CARLYLE *Fr. Rev.* I. III. viii, The long-gowned Senators of France. 1863 BRIGHT *Sp.*, *Amer.* 30 June (1876) 139 He has been for many years a Senator from the State of Mississippi. 1877 *Encycl. Brit.* VII. 347/1 He [Dombrowski] was named in 1815 general of cavalry and senator palatine of the new kingdom of Poland. 1905 R. BAGOT *Passport* iii. 17 He was a well-known scientist,..and, in recognition of his work in the domain of physical science, had been created a senator of the Italian kingdom.

2. In Papal Rome: The title given at various periods from the 12th c. onwards to the civil head of the city government, appointed by the Pope.

[*c* 1290, *c* 1386, 1390: see sense 1 a, and the note.] 1832 G. DOWNES *Lett.* xxvi. I. 427 In this [Senatorial] palace are held the sittings of Rome's one senator, and of the Judges of the Tribunal. 1841 W. SPALDING *Italy & It. Isl.* II. 153 Anarchy of Rome..induced Innocent in 1354 to send him [Rienzi] back as a governor with the title of Senator.

3. *Senator of the College of Justice*: in Scotland, the official designation of a Lord of Session.

1540 *Sc. Acts Jas. V* (1814) II. 371/2 Þe president vicepresident and senatoures [of the College of Justice]. 1562 in *Acts of Sederunt* (1790) 4 The Senatours, ordinaris of our College of Justice, institute be our maist nobill fader of gude memorie. 1905 *Westm. Gaz.* 3 Jan. 8/2 One of the Senators of his Majesty's College of Justice in Scotland.

†**4.** *The Senators*: a convivial London club in the 18th c. *Obs.*

1761 *Ann. Reg.* IV. II. 51/1 He was a respectable member of The Killers of Care,..The Senators [etc.].

5. The Ivory Whale-gull.

[*a* 1713 RAY *Syn. Avium* 126 Raths-herr i.e. Senator *Friderici Martens*.] 1832 MACGILLIVRAY *Brit. Birds* V. 508 *Cetosparactes eburneus*. The Ivory Whale-Gull...Senator.

Senatorial (senătō·riăl), *a.* [f. L. *senātōri-us* (f. *senātōr-em* SENATOR) + -AL. Cf. F. *sénatorial* (1727 in Hatz.-Darm.).]

1. Of or pertaining to a senator or senators; characteristic of or befitting a senator; consisting of senators. **a.** With reference to ancient Rome, or to other states of antiquity.

Senatorial order: the highest of the three ranks of citizens in the later Roman republic.

1791 COWPER *Iliad* x. 490 Hector, with all the Senatorial Chiefs [x. 414 ὅσοι βουληφόροι εἰσί]. 1842 *Smith's Dict. Grk. & Rom. Antiq.* 831/1 It has been supposed by Niebuhr ..that a senatorial census existed at Rome at the commencement of the second Punic war. 1850 MERIVALE *Rom. Emp.* ii. (1865) I. 53 Whole cities and states placed themselves sometimes under the protection of a senatorial patron. *a* 1859 DE QUINCEY *Aelius Lamia* Wks. 1860 X. 306 A Roman noble, a man..of senatorial rank.

b. With reference to modern senates.

1740 *Johnson's Debates* (1789) I. 19 (Sir R. Walpole), The authority which can be conferred only by senatorial sanctions. 1765 BLACKSTONE *Comm.* I. ii. 175 Not as at Venice, and many other senatorial assemblies. 1796 COLERIDGE *Watchman* No. 1. 20 The attack on the Duke of Bedford, for enjoying the senatorial office by hereditary right. 1855 THACKERAY *Newcomes* ii, He eschewed honours senatorial. 1897 *Edin. Rev.* Jan. 145 The senatorial leader.

2. Of a Roman province under the Empire: Administered by the senate (not by the emperor).

1841 W. SPALDING *Italy & It. Isl.* I. 102 Into those provinces which were senatorial, the senate continued to send pro-consuls or prætors as Governors. 1879 FARRAR *St. Paul* (1883) 342 Bithynia [was] at that time a senatorial province.

3. *U.S.* 'Entitled to elect a Senator: as, a *Senatorial* district' (*Cent. Dict.* 1891).

Hence **Senato·rially** *adv.*, in a senatorial manner.

1754 A. DRUMMOND *Trav.* i. 17 The mother was chearful; the father senatorially grave. 1821 *Examiner* 83/1 Whatever may be thought senatorially of the modest assertion,.. the people at large may laugh at it.

Senatorian (senătō·riăn), *a.* (and *sb.*). [f. L. *senātōri-us* (see prec.) + -AN. Cf. OF. *senatorien* (Godef.), mod.F. *sénatorien* (1690 in Hatz.-Darm.).]

A. *adj.*

1. Of or pertaining to a senator; = SENATORIAL *a.* 1. Now chiefly as applied to the senatorial order of ancient Rome, its members, their privileges, etc.

1614 GORGES *Lucan* iv. 167 The Senatorian ordred state Is neuer chang'd by place or date. *Ibid.*, That great Senatorian traine. 1629 MAXWELL *Herodian* 74 Yet was he far exceeded in Birth by many of the Senatorian Order. 1665 MANLEY *Grotius' Low C. Wars* 940 Janinus, having setled himself into a Senatorian Gravity, began thus to speak. 1781 GIBBON *Decl. & F.* xxxi. III. 199 The dignity of the senatorian rank. 1830 J. H. MONK *Bentley* (1833) II. 327 This distinguished prelate had already displayed his senatorian talents in the discussion on the Pension Bill, and other occasions. 1880 R. OWEN *Sanctorale Cathol.* 12 Mar. 136 He was of a high senatorian family at Rome.

2. = SENATORIAL *a.* 2.

1842 G. LONG in *Smith's Dict. Grk. & Rom. Antiq.* 801/1 The Senatorian provinces.

B. *sb.* ? *nonce-use*. A partisan of the senate.

1869 SEELEY *Ess. & Lect.* (1870) 21 [Augustus] began as a professed Senatorian;..he became ultimately emperor.

†**Senato·rical,** *a. Obs.* [f. SENATOR + -ICAL.] = SENATORIAL *a.*; also ruled over by a senate.

a 1618 RALEIGH *Maxims of State* vi. Rem. (1664) 9 And so that State is Senatorical or Aristocratical. 1655 tr. *Com. Hist. Francion* v. 10 The Advocate marched in magnificent array, with a Senatorical countenance.

†**Senatorious,** *a. Obs. rare*⁻¹. [f. L. *senātōri-us* (see SENATORIAL *a.*) + -OUS.] = SENATORIAL *a.*

1664 H. MORE *Myst. Iniq.* 280 This Head of the Roman Hierarchy with his purple Cardinals are so Emperour-like and of such a Senatorious splendour.

Senatorship (se·nătəɹʃip). [f. SENATOR + -SHIP.] The office or dignity of a senator.

1602 CAREW *Cornw.* II. 120 From which step his courage and wisedome raysed him by degrees to..the Senatorship of Rome. 1837 CARLYLE *Fr. Rev.* III. III. ix, We have got to the last scene of all, that ends this history of the Girondin Senatorship. 1909 *Contemp. Rev.* Aug., *Lit. Suppl.* 12 The senatorship conferred on him by Napoleon.

†**Senatory,** *sb.*¹ *Obs.* [ad. med.L. *senātōrium*, f. L. *senātōr-ius* (see SENATORIAL *a.*): see -ORY¹.]

1. The senatorial order or body.

Chaucer's use is due to mistaking the adj. for a sb.

c 1374 CHAUCER *Boeth.* III. pr. iv. (1868) 74 Þe rente of þe senatorie [is noþing but] a gret charge [L. *et senatorii census gravis sarcina*]. 1528 ROY *Rede me* (Arb.) 40 As for the comens vniuersally And a greate parte of the senatory Were of the same intencion. 1614 RALEIGH *Hist. World* v. ii. § 6. 400 The Achaians..by a Senatorie and two Prætors, ordered all things in their Commonweale.

2. A senate-house. (Cf. SENATOIRE.)

1474 CAXTON *Chesse* II. ii, And thus hit happend anone after that alle the wyues of rome cam to the senatorye.

Senatory (se·nătǫri), *sb.*² Also **-orie.** *French Hist.* [ad. F. *sénatorerie*, f. L. *senātor* SENATOR: see -ERY.] The landed estate granted to a senator under the consulate and the first empire.

1804 *Revol. Plutarch* III. 164 Lucien was..afterwards ordered to visit his senatories on the Rhine. 1810 *Ann. Reg.* 503 A senatory shall be established in the departments of Rome and Trasimene. 1827 SCOTT *Napoleon* xxix. Wks. 1870 XI. 349 Monsieur Fargues, senator of the district of Bearn, whom these plots..interested as having his senatorie for their scene. 1898 J. B. RYE in *Eng. Hist. Rev.* July 490 You leave in twenty-four hours, to live in your senatory.

Supplement, p. 3873; Corrigenda, p. 4092; Spurious words, p. 4093; Books quoted, p. 4094

† **Senatory**, a. Obs. rare. [ad. L. senātōri-us (see SENATORIAL a.): see prec.] Of, pertaining to, a senate. = SENATORIAL a.

Senatress (se'nătrĕs), rare. [f. SENATOR + -ESS.] A female senator; a female of senatorial rank.

Senatus (sɛnēɪtəs). [L.: see SENATE.] The title given to the governing body in certain universities. More explicitly *senatus academicus*: see SENATE 2.

Sena tus consultum. Pl. *consulta*. Also anglicized *senātus consult* (†-cōnsult 1.). A decree of the ancient Roman senate.

Senau, var. of SENECH id. and v.

Senco, var. CENSE; obs. f. SENSE, SINCE.

Sencoal, Sencer: see SENESCHAL, CENSER.

† **Sench**, v. Obs. Also 3 *senche*, 4 *ysenche*, etc. (See also ASENCH 2.) [OE. *sęnčan* = OS. *senkian*, OHG. *senchan* (MHG., mod.G. *senken*), ON. *søkkva* (Sw. *sänka*, Da. *sænke*), Goth. *sagqjan*:—OTeut. *sankwjan*, causative of *sig̓kwan* SINK v.] 1. To sink, plunge.

Send (send), *sb.* 1 Naut. Also *scend*. [Belongs to SEND v.2 Cf. SEND sb.2 1 q.] 1. The carrying or driving impulse of a sea or wave; more fully *send of a sea* or *of the sea*.

2. A sudden plunge (of a boat) *aft*, forward, etc.

Send (send), *sb.*2 Pa. t. and pa. pple. sent (sent). Forms: *Infin.* 1 *sendan*, 2-3 *senden*, (3 *seind*, *sinde*, *sent*), 2-6 *sende*, 4 *Kent. zende*, 5 *sendy*, *cendyn*, 5c *sen*, 3 *send*, 3rd *sing. pres. ind.* 1-3 *sendeþ*, 1-5 *sent*, 3rd *pers. sing. pres.* and *pa. t. sende*, etc.

Send (send), *v.*1 Pa. t. and *pa. pple.* sent (sent). ... To send direct or to go to or to be conveyed.

* *with a person as object.*

I. *trans.* To commission, order, or request (a person) to go to or into a place or to a person. Chiefly, to dispatch as a messenger or on an errand.

Supplement, p. 3873; Corrigenda, p. 4092; Spurious words, p. 4093; Books quoted, p. 4094

Sensational, a. [f. SENSATION + -AL.]

1. Of or pertaining to or dependent upon sensation or the senses.

2. Of philosophical theories: Regarding sensation as the sole source of knowledge.

3. Of works of literature or art, hence of writers: Dealing in sensation (see SENSATION 3 a); aiming at violently exciting effects. Also of incidents in fiction or real life: Calculated to produce a startling impression.

Sensationalism (sensəˈfənālizm). [f. SENSATIONAL + -ISM.]

1. Philos. The theory that sensation is the only source of knowledge.

2. Addiction to what is sensational in literature or art.

Sensationalist (-ist). [f. SENSATIONAL + -IST.]

1. Philos. One who regards the senses as the ultimate source of all knowledge.

2. One who deals in or is given to sensationalism.

Sensationalistic, a. [f. prec.]

Sensationalize (sensəˈfənāləz), v. [f. SENSATIONAL + -IZE.]

Sensationism (sensəˈfənism). [= SENSATIONALISM 2.]

Sensationist (-ist). [f. SENSATION + -IST.]

Sensationmonger (-ˌmʌŋgər). [f. SENSATION + MONGER.]

Sensative: see SENSITIVE.

† **Sensator.** Obs. rare. [f. SENSATE v. + -OR.]

Sensatorial, a. [f. SENSATE v. + -ORIAL.] = SENSORIAL.

† **Sensatory**, a. [f. SENSATE v. + -ORY.] = SENSORY.

Senscer, obs. form of CENSER.

Senschops, obs. var. of SHENDSHIP.

Sense (sens), sb. Forms: 4 sens, 4–6 sence, 7 Sc. senss, 5– sense. [a. F. sens or L. sensus (in senses 1, 2, 8 sens, late L. sensus = judgement or meaning), f. sentire to feel. Cf. Fr. sens, sente, Sp. seso, Pg. siso, It. senso.]

I. Faculty of perception or sensation.

1. Each of the special faculties, connected with a bodily organ, by which man and other animals perceive external objects and changes in the condition of their own bodies. Usually reckoned as five—sight, hearing, smell, taste, touch. Also called outward or external sense (cf. 8).

2. pl. The faculties of corporeal sensation considered as channels for gratifying the desire for pleasure and the lusts of the flesh. Also sing.

† b. Used for: An organ of sense. Obs.

3. Applied to similar faculties of perception, not scientifically delimited, or only conjectured to exist.

4. collect. sing.

† 5. Capability of feeling, as a quality of the body and its parts; liability to feel pain, irritation, etc. To the sense, to the quick. Obs.

6. A general term for the faculties of perception (including the 'five senses': see 1), which are in abeyance when their owner is asleep or otherwise unconscious. Also sing., any one of these faculties. Cf. 10.

7. Applied to faculties of the mind or soul compared or contrasted with the bodily senses; usually with some defining word, as inner, interior, internal, inward sense. Moral sense: see MORAL 2. 1 d.

8. The perceptive faculty of a conscious animal or being.

9. collect. sing.

II. Faculty of feeling.

10. The mental faculties in their normal condition of sanity; one's 'reason' or 'wits'. (Cf. 6.) In one's (right) senses, in one's right mind. To bring (a person) to his senses: to cure of his folly (one who is behaving 'madly'). Out of one's senses, out of one's mind.

11. Natural understanding, intelligence, esp. as bearing on action or behaviour; practical soundness of judgement.

12. A feeling or perception of (something expressed) through the channels of touch, taste, etc.

† 13. A more or less vague perception or impression of (an outward object, as present or imagined).

14. A more or less indefinite consciousness or impression of (a fact, state of things, etc.).

III. Meaning, signification.

18. The meaning or signification of a word or phrase; also, any one of the different meanings of a word, or that which it bears in a particular collocation or context.

Sense (sens), v. [f. SENSE sb.]

1. trans. To perceive (an outward object) by the senses; also, to feel (pain). Obs.

2. To feel, be conscious of (an inward state, etc.).

3. To perceive, become aware of, 'feel' (something present, a fact, state of things, etc.) by direct perception but more or less vaguely or instinctively.

† b. Said of sleep, death, the grave, etc. Obs.

Sensed (senst), ppl. a. [f. SENSE sb. + -ED². Cf. F. sensé, L. sensatus: see SENSATE a.] Only with limiting word (adj. or adv.).

1. Having a specified sense of meaning.

2. Having wit or senses. Obs.

Senseful (ˈsensfʊl), a. [f. SENSE sb. + -FUL.]

1. Full of sense or meaning; significant.

2. Full of good sense; sensible. Obs. rare⁻¹.

b. quasi-adv. Unreasonably. Obs. rare⁻¹.

Senseless (ˈsenslɪs), a. Forms: see SENSE sb. Also superl. 6–7 senseles, senceless. [f. SENSE sb. + -LESS.]

1. Of persons, their bodies or organs: Destitute or deprived of sensation; physically insentient.

† 2. To expound the sense or meaning of; to ascribe a meaning to; to take or understand in a particular sense. Also, to explain (to be something). Obs.

3. Intelligent. Obs.

Senselessly (ˈsenslɪsli), adv. [-LY²] Also insensibly, foolishly, irrationally. Also, unconsciously, insensibly.

1. In a senseless manner, foolishly, irrationally. Also, without sense or meaning; unmeaning, purposeless.

2. Destitute of mental sensibility, incapable of feeling or perception; unconscious, insensible.

Senselessness (ˈsenslɪsnɪs), sb. [f. SENSELESS + -NESS.]

1. Absence of or incapacity for feeling (physical or mental); insensibility, impassibility. Also, unconsciousness or insensible condition, as in sleep, etc.

2. Foolishness, irrationality.

Sensement. *Obs.* Forms: sensement, sensyment, -iment, sensement, sens(i)-ment, sensement. [a. OF. *sensement*, pseudo-etymological spelling (as if ad. *sensement*, *censement*), f. *sens-er* to give a decision : see -MENT.] A decision, judgement.

Senser, obs. f. CENSER 2 b 2. var. CENSER 2 b 2.

Sensewalite, obs. form of SENSUALITY.

Senshalship, obs. form of SENESCHALSHIP.

[**Senshaw** (*se·nʃǫ*), [perh. repr. Chinese *sien-sha* (raw thread, and gauze).] A Chinese gauze-like silk fabric.

Sensibilitous, a. *nonce-wd.* [f. SENSIBILITY + -OUS.] Cultivating 'sensibility'.

Sensibility (*sensibi·liti*), [ad. L. *sensibilitās*, f. *sensibilis* : see SENSIBLE a. and -ITY.]

I.

1. *a.* *pl.* Sensible species ; the emanations from bodies, which were supposed to be the cause of sensation. *b.* Capability of being perceived by the senses. *Obs. rare.*

2. Power of sensation or perception ; the specific function of any of the organs of sense (*obs.*). Now often, the (greater or less) readiness of an organ or tissue to respond to sensory stimuli ; sensitiveness.

3. Mental perception, awareness of something.

4. Emotional consciousness ; glad or sorrowful, grateful or resentful recognition of a person's conduct, or of a fact or a condition of things.

Sensibilize (*se·nsibiləiz*), *v.* [f. late L. *sensibil-is* SENSIBLE + -IZE, after F. *sensibiliser*.] *trans.* To render sensitive. Hence **Se·nsibiliˌzer**. a. *Phys.* (see quot. 1900).

Sensible (*se·nsibl*), *a.* (*sb.*). Also 4–6 sencyble, senyble, 5 sensibill, -yll, censible, 6 sensybul, sensibil, 6–7 sencible, (sensable, 8 sencible), [a. F. *sensible*, or ad. L. *sensibilis*, f. *sens-*, ppl. stem of *sentire* to perceive : see -IBLE. Cf. Sp. *sensible*, Pg. *sensivel*, It. *sensibile*.]

I. That can be felt or perceived.

1. Perceptible by the senses. (In *Philos.*, opposed to INTELLIGIBLE 3 : in this use now *rare*.)

Sensile (*se·nsil, -əil*), *a.* [ad. L. *sensilis*, f. *sens-* : see prec.] Capable of sensation.

Sensibleness (*se·nsibl'nes*). [f. SENSIBLE a. + -NESS.]

1. The quality or state of being sensible or capable of sensation ; sensibility ; sensitiveness.

2. Of persons : Intelligibility, impressiveness.

3. Of speech : Intelligibility, impressiveness.

4. Tenderness of feeling, sensibility. *Obs.*

5. The state or fact of being sensible or emotionally (esp. gratefully) conscious of something. Const. *of* ; rarely with *clause*. *Obs.*

6. Perceptibility. *Obs.*

7. The quality or state of being sensible or having good sense ; intelligence, sound judgement.

Sensibly (*se·nsibli*), *adv.* Also 6 sencibly, sensible, sensibil, 6–7 sensibly ; (uncontracted form : 7 sensibely), [f. SENSIBLE a. + -LY.]

1. In a manner perceptible to the senses ; so far as can be perceived.

2. With inward sensation or feeling.

3. In an appreciable degree.

4. Intelligently, sensibly, with good sense ; so as to show good judgement.

Sensifi·c, *a. rare.* [f. L. *sensi-*, *sentire* to feel + -FIC.] Producing sensation.

Sensifica·tion. [as prec. + -ATION.]

Sensific, *a.* [ad. L. *sensific-us*, f. *sensi-*, *sentire* to feel + -FIC.] Producing sensation.

Sensation (*se·nseiʃən*), *sb.* [ad. med.L. *sensātiōn-em*, f. *sensāt-*.]

Sensifer·ous, *a. rare.* [f. L. *sensifer* + -OUS.] = SENSIFIC.

Sensigenous (*sensi·dʒinəs*), *a.* [f. L. *sensi-* + -GENOUS.] Producing sensation.

Sensile (*se·nsil, -əil*), *a.* [f. L. *sens-*, *sentire* to feel + -ILE.] Sensitive ; endowed with sensation, *esp.* SENTIENT to feel.

Sensism (*se·nsiz'm*). *rare.* [f. SENSE sb. + -ISM.] The devotion to the things of sense, sensuality.

Sensist (*se·nsist*). *rare.* [f. SENSE sb. + -IST.] = SENSATIONALIST 1.

Sensitie. *Obs. rare—¹.* [app. f. L. *sensi-*.]

Sensitive (*se·nsitiv*), *a.* and *sb.* Forms: a. 5 sensitife, sensitif, 6 sensytyve, sensitive, 7 sensitive. β. 6–8 sensative, 7 sensative, [a. OF. *sensitive* (14th c. in Hatz.-Darm.), pple. *sensitif*, -ive = Sp., Pg., It. *sensitivo*.]

1. Of sensation or the senses.

2. Of or pertaining to the senses.

3. Sensitive plant ; herb, shrub, tree.

Sensitive plant (Æ. *hispida*) ; American Sensitive plant (*Cassia nictitans*), also called *Wild Sensitive plant* and *Sensitive Pea* (see FEA 3).

Sensitively (*se·nsitivli*), *adv.* [f. SENSITIVE a. + -LY.]

1. Feelingly, tenderly ; with the emotions as distinguished from the intellect.

2. With reference to feeling : Acutely, intensely.

3. In a sensitive manner.

Sensitiveness (*se·nsitivnes*). [-NESS.]

1. The power or capacity of sensation.

2. Tenderness of feeling.

3. The quality of being sensitive.

Sensitivism.

Sensitometer.

Sensitometry.

Sensitory.

Sensive.

Sensize.

Sensor.

Sensory.

Sensorial.

Sensorium.

Sensual.

Sensualist.

Sensualization.

Sensualize.

Sensually.

Sensualness.

Sensuist.

Sensuosity.

Sensuous.

Sensuousness.

Sensyne.

Sent.

Sensy, Sensie.

Sensory.

Sentence.

SENTENCE. 469 SENTENTIOUS. SENTENTIOUSLY. 470 SENTIMENT.

Sentence (se'ntĕns), *sb.* Also 7 **sentense**. [a. F. *sentencer*, f. *sentence* SENTENCE *sb.* Cf. med.L. *sententiare*.]

† **1.** *intr.* To pass judgement. *Obs.*

† 2. *trans.* To judge, or apportion by legal decision. *Obs.*

† **3.** To decree or order judicially. *Obs.*

† **4.** *tr.* To decide judicially. *Obs.*

5. To declare judicially or authoritatively. Chiefly with complement. *Obs.*

6. To pass judgement on the person or his actions, the merit of anything). *Obs.*

7. To pronounce sentence upon ; to condemn to a punishment.

8. In various nonce-uses : *a.* To report sentences. Also *absol. intr.* To compose sentences.

b. To influence by axioms. Also *To sentence it* : to speak in aphorisms.

Hence **Sentenced**, *ppl. a.* **Sentencing**, *vbl. sb.*

Sentencell, *obs. form of* SENTINEL.

Sentener, *obs. form of* CENTENIER.

Sentenia, *obs. form of* SENTENTIA.

Sententia (sententiă). *pl.* Now *rare.* [ad. L. *sententiā* in the form of a sentence, f. *sententia* : see SENTENCE *sb.* and -IA.]

1. Containing, or of the nature of, 'sentences' or 'maxims'. *Obs.*

† Sentencioner. *Obs. rare*–¹. [f. *sententi-a* + -oner.] A commentator or lecturer on the Book of Sentences (see SENTENCE *sb.* 2 b.)

Sententious (sentē'nʃəs), *a.* [ad. L. *sententiōs-us*, f. *sententia* SENTENCE *sb.* : see -OUS. Cf. F. *sentencieux* (15th c. in Hatz.-Darm.).]

† 1. Full of meaning ; also, of persons, full of intelligence or wisdom. *Obs.*

2. Of the nature of a 'sentence' or aphoristic maxim. *Obs.*

3. Of discourse, style, etc. : Abounding in pointed maxims, aphoristic. In recent use sometimes in bad sense, affectedly or pompously formal.

4. Of persons : Given to the utterance of maxims or pointed sayings. Now often in bad sense, addicted to pompous moralizing.

Hence **Sente'ntiously**, *adv.* **Sente'ntiousness**, *sb.*

Sentiment (se'ntĭment), *sb.* Also 4-7 **sentement**. [a. OF. *sentement* (13th c.), ad. med.L. *sentimentum*, f. L. *sentīre* to feel ; cf. Sp. *sentimiento*, Pg. *sl. sentimento.*]

1. Personal experience, one's own feeling. *Obs.*

2. Sensation, physical feeling. In later use, a knowledge due to vague sensation. *Obs.*

3. Sensible quality ; in quot. = flavour. *Obs.*

4. Intellectual or emotional perception. *Obs.*

5. An epigrammatical expression of some striking or agreeable thought or wish, often of the nature of a proverb or in proverbial language.

6. *pl.* The sum of a person's sentiments.

7. a. What one feels with regard to something ; mental attitude (of approval or disapproval, etc.) ; an opinion or view as to what is right or agreeable.

8. a. Refined and tender emotion ; exercise or manifestation of 'sensibility' ; emotional reflection or meditation ; appeal to the tender emotions in literature or art.

SENTIMENTAL. 471 SENTINEL. SENTINEL. 472 SENTURE.

Sentimental (sentĭme'ntăl), *a.* [f. prec. + -AL. The word *sentimental*, according to *Littré* and Hatz.-Darm., is an adoption of the Eng. word as used by Sterne ; so also G. *sentimental*.]

1. Of persons, their dispositions or actions : Characterized by sentiment. Originally in favourable sense : Characterized by or exhibiting refined and elevated feeling. In later use : Addicted to indulgence in superficial emotion ; apt to be swayed by sentiment.

2. *absol.* (with *the*). † Also (*a nonce-use*) as a sentimental person.

Hence **Sentime'ntally**, *adv.*

Sentimentalism (sentĭme'ntăliz'm). [f. SENTIMENTAL *a.* + -ISM.]

1. The sentimental habit of mind ; the disposition to attribute undue importance to sentimental considerations, or to be governed by sentiment in opposition to reason.

Sentimentalist (sentĭme'ntălist). [f. SENTIMENTAL *a.* + -IST.]

Sentimentalize (sentĭme'ntălaiz), *v.* [f. SENTIMENTAL *a.* + -IZE.]

1. *intr.* To indulge in sentimental thoughts or expressions. Also *with about.* Cf. SENTIMENTIZE *v.*

2. *trans.* To make (a person, etc.) sentimental ; to imbue (a person, work of art, etc.) with sentiment.

Hence **Sentimentalized**, *ppl. a.* **Sentimentalizing**, *vbl. sb.*

Sentimentally, *adv.* (sentĭme'ntăli).

Sentinel (se'ntĭnel), *sb.* Forms : 6-7 **centinel**, 6 **sentinell**, 6 **centronel**, **centronell**, **cantonel**, **sentonell**, **sentinell**, 7 **centinell**, **sentonel**, 6– **sentinel**. [a. F. *sentinelle* (1546), ad. It. *sentinella*, Pg. *sentinella* = Fr.]

1. One who keeps guard ; one who watches over a person, a place, etc. ; a guard, watch.

2. *Mil.* A soldier placed on guard to prevent the passing of an unauthorized person.

Sentinel, *v.* [f. SENTINEL *sb.*]

1. *trans.* To stand guard over, to watch as a sentinel.

2. *intr.* To act as sentinel, stand sentinel, keep watch.

3. To furnish with or as with a sentinel or with sentinels.

Sentinelship, *sb.* (se'ntĭnelʃip). [f. SENTINEL *sb.* + -SHIP.] The office or duties of a sentinel.

† Senting, *ppl. a. Obs. rare*–¹. [As if f. *sent v.*]

Sention, *obs. form of* CENTION.

Sentisection (sentĭse'kʃən). [f. L. *sentīre* to feel + *section*-em SECTION.]

Sentition (sentĭʃən). *rare*–⁰. [Badly f. L. *sentīre.*]

Sentry (se'ntri), *sb.* Forms : 7 **sentrie**, (**centrie**, -**tree**, **sentery**), 7-9 **sentery**, 8– **sentry**. [Perh. a shortening or back-formation of *sentery* = SENTINEL *sb.*]

1. A sentinel, a guard.

2. A shelter-box for a sentinel.

Sentry-box. [f. SENTRY *sb.* + BOX *sb.*²] A box to shelter a sentry in bad weather.

Sentry-go. [Orig. a phrase of command = SENTRY, GO !] The duty of a sentry.

† Senture. *Obs. rare.* [a. F. *ceinture*.] A girdle.

Sentware, -y, obs. ff. SANCTUARY sb.¹

Senty, obs. form of SEVENTY.

†Sentynode, variant of CENTINODY.

Senvie, obs. form of SINFUL a.

Senvule, obs. form of SEIGNIORY.

†Senvy. Obs. Forms: 3 senel, 3–4, 6 senvey, 4–5 senvei, 4–5 senewye, 4, 6 senvy, synevey, 4–7 senvey, 5 senvyne, sensfee, synewey, 6 senvye, 4gyvy, sinvy, 6–7 sennie, senvy, 7 senvye, senvy. [a. OF. senvé, -vi, -vei (mod.F. sénevé)=pop. L. *sinápitium, f. sinápi-i mustard.]

Separable (se'pǎrǎb'l), a. Also 5–7 separable, l. *siparabilis*: see SEPARATE v. and -ABLE.]

1. Capable of being separated.

Separate (se'pǎret), pa. pple., a. and sb. Forms: 5–6 separat, 5–7 separat, 6–8 seperate, 5 separate. ad. L. *siparāt-us*, pa. pple. of *siparāre*: see SEPARATE v.]

†a. as past ppl. Separated.

Separate (se'pǎret), v. Also 6–8 seperate, [ad. L. *siparāt-*, ppl. stem of *siparāre*, f. se- + *parāre* to make ready, prepare.]

I. Transitive senses.

1. To put apart, set asunder (two or more persons or things, or one from another); to disunite, disconnect, make a division between.

Separately (se'pǎretli), adv. [-LY².] In a separate manner, singly, severally, apart.

Separateness. [-NESS.] The quality, state, or fact of being separate.

Separatical (sepǎrǎ'tikǎl), a. Pertaining to separation in religion.

Separating (se'pǎreitiŋ), ppl. a. [f. SEPARATE v. + -ING².]

Separation (sepǎrei'ʃǎn), sb. [a. F. *séparation*, ad. L. *siparātiōn-em*, n. of action f. *siparāre* to SEPARATE.]

1. The action of separating or parting, or setting or keeping apart; the state of being separated or parted.

Separationism (sepǎrei'ʃǎn-iz'm). [-ISM.] Advocacy of separation, or of a theory of separation.

Separatism (se'pǎrǎtiz'm). [f. SEPARATE + -ISM.] The disposition to separate or to a separate Church or State; the principles and practices of Separatists.

Separatist (se'pǎrǎtist). sb. and a. [f. SEPARATE + -IST.]

Separatistic (sepǎrǎti'stik), a. [f. SEPARATIST.]

Separator (se'pǎreitǎr). Also separater. [ad. late L. *siparātor*, agent-n. f. L. *siparāre*: see SEPARATE.]

1. One who or something which separates; spec.

†Separatory (se'pǎrǎtǎri), a. and sb. [ad. mod.L. *siparātōrius*, f. *siparāre* to separate: see -ORY.] Having the function of separating.

†Separe, v. Obs. Also 5–6 separ, 6 separe. [a. F. *séparer*, ad. L. *siparāre*: see SEPARATE v.]

Sepelible, a. Obs. [ad. L. *sepelibilis*, f. *sepelīre* to bury.]

Sepelition. Obs. [ad. L. *sepelitiōn-em*.] Burial.

Seperate, -ation, etc.: obs. ff. SEPARATE, etc.

Sephardi (sĕˈfaˑdi). *Plural.* **Sephardim** (-dim), -dîn (-dîn). [mod. Heb. ספרדי *Sĕphardī*, רד *Sĕphārad*, the name of a country mentioned only *Obad.* 20, and identified by the Rabbins with Spain.] A Spanish or Portuguese Jew, a Jew of Spanish or Portuguese descent. Also *attrib.* Hence **Sephaˑrdic** *a.*, pertaining to the Sephardim.

Sephen (seˑf̆n). Also **sephin**. [a. mod.L. *sephen* (specific name), a. Arab. سيفن *safan*, sha-green.] A kind of sting-ray. Also *attrib.*

Sephiroth (seˑfiˑrŏþ), *pl.* Rarely in *sing.* **sephira**. [late Heb. ספירות *sĕphīrōth*, *pl.*, ספירה *sĕphīrāh*, a number.] In the philosophy of the Cabbala, the ten hypostatized attributes or emanations by means of which the Infinite (אין סוף *ēn sōph*) enters into relation with the finite. Hence **Sephiˑrothic** *a.*; **Se(h)iˑroth** *adj.*, pertaining to the Sephiroth.

Sepia (sîˑpĭă), *sb.* Also 9 **sepaia**, 9 **sepha**, etc. [a. L. *sēpia*, a. Gr. σηπία.] The cuttle-fish; now *rare* exc. *Zool.*, a cuttle of the genus *Sepia* or family *Sepiadæ*; also, the genus itself.

2. In full **sepia bone**: Cuttle-bone, *esp.* as used in pharmacy, etc.

3. a. A brown pigment prepared from the "ink" or secretion of the cuttle-fish; the colour of this pigment. Also *attrib.* and *Comb.*

b. The inky secretion itself. *rare.*

4. *ellipt.* A sepia drawing.

Sepiacean (sîˑpĭăˑsĭan) *a.*, and *sb.* *Zool.* Pertaining to, or a member of, the group *Sepiacea* of cuttle-fishes. Also **Sepia'cea** *sb. pl.*

Sepiadan (sîˑpĭădan) *a.* *Zool.* Belonging to the mantle or the sac of the Sepiacea.

Sepian, *a.* *Obs.⁻¹* [f. L. *sēpia* + -AN.] Inky.

Sepic (sîˑpik) *a.* *rare⁻⁰.* [f. SEPIA + -IC.] Pertaining to sepia; done in sepia, as a drawing.

Sepiment (sepiment). Now *rare* or *Obs.* [ad. L. *sēpimentum*, f. *sēpīre* to hedge, f. *sēpes* hedge.] A hedge, fence.

b. *transf.* and *fig.* Something that encloses or guards.

Sepioid (sîˑpĭoid), *Zool.* [f. SEPIA + -OID.] A cuttle-fish of or related to the genus *Sepia.*

Sepiola (sîˑpĭoˑlă), *Zool.* Also anglicized **sepiole** (c.f. *sepiole*, Cuvier). [L., dim. of SEPIA.] The name of a genus of small cuttle-fishes.

Sepiolite (sîˑpĭŏlɒit). *Geol.* [ad. G. *sepiolith* (Glocker 1847), f. Gr. σηπίον SEPIUM : see -LITE.] Meerschaum.

Sepiostaire (sîˑpĭŏˑstɛ̄ə), *Zool.* Also in shortened form **sepiost**. [ad. F. *sépiostaire*, f. Gr. σηπίον + ὀστρέον bone + -aire (cf. -ARY).] f. CUTTLE-BONE.

Sepium (sîˑpĭŭm), *Zool.* [mod.L. use of Gr. σηπίον.] f. in various form **sepion**. [mod.L., a. Gr. σηπίον.] CUTTLE-BONE.

Sepiolite, etc.

Sepoy (sîˑpɔi), *sb.* (*a.*) Forms: 7 **seapoy**, 8 **sepoy**, **sipahi** (*nāipī*), **sipoy**, **sepoy**. B. 8 **sipahi**, 9 **sipoy**. [prob. through Pg. *sipai* = Urdu = Pers. *sipāhī* horseman, soldier, f. *sipāh* army. Cf. F. *cipaye*. See also SPAHI.] In the following quot. the word is used in its orig. sense of "horseman."

A native of India employed as a soldier under European, *esp.* British, discipline.

b. *attrib.*, as *sepoy band; sepoy Raj,* f. Baboolal's honorarius, consigned to a soldier under European, *esp.* British, discipline.

2. A division of a nation or tribe; a clan: orig. in reference to Ireland.

Sepone, *v.* [f. L. *sēpōnĕre* (see next; reduced by analogy of point n.¹ and its compounds.] **1.** *trans.* To set aside, dismiss from consideration.

2. To set apart or reserve.

Sepose (sîˑpōˑz), *v.* *Obs.⁻¹* [f. L. *sēpōsit-, ppl.* stem of *sēpōnĕre* SEPONE.] = prec. 1, 2.

Seposit, *v.* *Obs.* [ad. L. *sēpositum*, in action f. *sēpōnĕre* SEPONE.] Setting aside.

Sepoy: *v.* previous. See SEPOY.

Sepsine (seˑpsĭn). [f. L. *sēpsis* (see next): reduced by analogy of Point n.¹ and its compounds.] **1.** *trans.* To set aside, dismiss from consideration.

Sepsine (seˑpsĭn). A poisonous crystalline substance obtained from decomposing yeast.

Sepsis (seˑpsis). *pl.* **sepses** (-sēz). [mod.L., a. Gr. σῆψις, f. σήπειν to make rotten.] Putrefaction, putrescence.

Sept (sept), *sb.¹* [app. var. of SECT or SEPTUM.] **1.** An enclosure; an area marked off for a special purpose: a fold (*fig.*).

2. *Arch.* A dividing screen, railing, etc.

Sept (sept), *sb.²* [Also 6 **cepte**, 6–7 **sept**, 7 **cept**, **seapt**. [prob. a var. of *sect*, which is used in the 16th cent. (see SECT *sb.* 5).] A clan: orig. in reference to Ireland.

Septa, *pl.* of SEPTUM.

Septal (seˑptăl), *a.¹* [f. SEPT⁻¹ + -AL.] Pertaining to, consisting of, or forming a septum or septa.

Septal (seˑptăl), *a.²* [f. SEPT² + -AL.] Of or pertaining to a *sept*.

Septan (seˑptăn), *a.* [ad. mod.L. *septāna* (*febris*), tr. Gr. ἑβδομαῖος (Galen), f. L. *septem* seven.] Designating a fever of which the paroxysm recur every sixth (according to old reckoning, every seventh) day.

Septangle. *Obs.* [ad. late L. *septangulus*, f. *septem* seven + *angulus* ANGLE.] A heptagon.

Septangled, *a.* = next.

Septangular, *a.* [f. prec. + -AR.] Seven-angled, heptagonal.

Septaria: see SEPTARIUM.

Septarian (septɛ̄ˑrĭăn), *a.* [f. SEPTARI-UM + -AN.] Of the form or nature of septaria.

Septarium (septɛ̄ˑrĭŭm), *Geol.* [L. -aria (-ĕriă).] [mod.L., f. L. *septum* : see SEPTUM and -ARIUM.] A nodule or concretion of a limestone, ironstone, or the like, of which the parts near the centre are cracked, the spaces between being filled with some mineral.

Septemberish. Also **Septembrish**. [f. SEPTEMBER + -ISH.] Pertaining to, like that of, September.

Septembrian (septeˑmbrĭăn), *a.* and *sb.* *rare.* [f. SEPTEMBER + -AN.] Belonging to September.

Septemberism (septeˑmbĕriz'm), the action or policy of the Septembrists.

Septembrize (septeˑmbrŏiz), *v.* *orig.* *Fr. Hist.* Also **-brise**. [ad. F. *septembriser*, f. *septembre* SEPTEMBER; see -IZE.] *trans.* and *intr.* To assassinate like the Septembrists.

Septembrizer (septeˑmbrəizəɹ). Also **-ber**, **-bri**. [f. prec. + -ER.]

Septennial (septeˑnĭăl), *a.* (*sb.*). Also 7 **septyn-**, 8 **septen-**, 9 **septen-**. [f. L. *septennis* (f. *septem* seven + *annus* year) + -AL.] **1.** Pertaining to or lasting, seven years.

Septenary (seˑptĕnări), *a.* and *sb.* Also 7 **septye**, 8 **septin-**. [ad. L. *septēnārius,* f. *septēnī* seven each.] **A.** *adj.* **1.** Pertaining or relating to the number seven; forming a group of seven.

Septenate (seˑptĕnēt), *a.* *Bot.* [f. L. *septēni* seven each + -ATE³.] Growing in sevens, having seven divisions, heptamerous.

Septentrion (septeˑntrĭŏn), *sb.* and *a.* *Now arch.* Also 4–5 **septem-**, 6 **septen-**. [ad. L. *septentriō*, sing. of *septentriōnēs,* orig. the seven stars (*triōnēs*) of the constellation of the Great Bear, the Little Bear.] **1.** *pl.* orig. *Astr.* The constellation of the Great Bear near the North Pole.

Septentrional (septeˑntrĭŏnăl), *a.* and *sb.* *Now arch.* Also 4–5 **septem-**, 6 **septen-**. [ad. L. *septentriōnālis,* f. *septentriō* : see prec. and -AL.] **A.** *adj.* Belonging to the north, northern; specifically, the north.

Septentrionalize. *rare.* [f. prec. + -IZE.] *trans.* To make septentrional.

Septennium (septeˑnĭŭm). [L., f. *septem* seven + *annus* year.] A period of seven years.

Septer, -tre, -ier: see SCEPTER, etc.

Septfoil (seˑtfɔil). Also **6–7 set-**. [ad. late L. *septifolium*, f. *septem* seven + *folium* leaf; tr. seven-leaf.] **1.** The plant tormentil.

Septic (seˑptik), *a.* and *sb.* [ad. L. *sēpticus,* a. Gr. σηπτικός, f. σήπειν to make rotten.] **A.** *adj.* **1.** Causing or promoting putrefaction; putrefactive, putrescent.

Septically (seˑptikăli) *adv.*, in a septic manner.

Septicidal (septisŏiˑdăl) *a.* *Bot.* [f. SEPTUM + L. *caedĕre* to cut + -AL.] Applied to the form of dehiscence in which the pod splits through the dissepiments. Hence **Septiˑcidally** *adv.*

Septicity (septiˑsiti). [f. SEPTIC + -ITY, after F. *sépticité.*]

Septifoil: see SEPTFOIL.

Septiform (seˑptifɔɹm), *a.* [f. L. *septum* SEPTUM + -FORM.] Having the form of a septum.

Septennate (septeˑnēt). [f. L. *septem* seven + -ATE¹.] A period of seven years.

SEPTIESM. 481 **SEPTUAGINT.** **SEPTUAGINTAL.** 482 **SEPULCHRE.**

† **Septiesm.** *Cards. Obs.* [a. OF. *septiesme* (mod. F. *septième*), ordinal of *sept* seven.] A sequence of seven.

Septiferous (sept-ifĕrǒs), *a.* [f. SEPTI-² + -FEROUS.] Having a septum or septa.

Septiform (se'ptifǫǫrm), *a.²* [ad. mod.L. *septiformis* or f. *septum* + -FORM.] Sevenfold.

Septile, *a.* [ad. L. *septīlis*: see SEXTILE.] Pertaining to a septum or septa.

Septilion (septi-lyǫn). *Arith.* [ad. F. *septilion* (16th cent.), f. *septem* seven, after *million*.] The seventh power of a million, denoted by 1 followed by 42 cyphers.

† **Septimanarian.** *Obs.* [f. med.L. *septimānārius*, f. *septimāna* week.]

Septimestral (se'ptimestral), *a.* [f. L. *septimestris* of seven months.] Of seven months.

Septime (se'ptim). [ad. L. *septimus*, ordinal of *septem* seven.]

Septimole. *Mus.* = SEPTOLE.

† **Septimulary**, *a.* Obs.

† **Septimus**, *a.* late L. *septimus.*

Septin. *Mus.* = SEPTOLE.

Septolet. *Mus.* = SEPTOLE.

Septon (se'ptǫn). *Obs.* [mod.L., a. Gr.]

Septule (se'ptiūl), *a.* *Nat. Hist.*

† **Septum.** Pl. *septa* (se'ptă). [a. L. *septum*, *sēptum* seven *n.* or *adv.*, partition.]

Sequel (sī'kwĕl). Forms: 5-7 *sequele*, 5 *sequayl*, 6 *sequaile*, 6 *sequell*, 6-8 *sequell*, *north. sequel*, 7 *sequill*, 6- **sequel**. [a. OF. *sequel* (13th c. in Hatz.-Darm.), ad. L. *sequēla*, f. *sequī* to follow.]

SEPULCHRE. 483 **SEQ.** **SEQUA.** 484 **SEQUEL.**

Sequel, v. Obs. rare. [f. SEQUEL sb.] That followed after, subsequent.

Sequel, v. Obs. [ad. L. sequēlā.] trans. To follow. Hence **Sequelled** ppl. a.

Sequela (sĭ·kwī·lă). Pl. **sequelae** (sĭ·kwī·lī·). [a. L. sequēla.] Pl. sequelæ.

Sequence (sī·kwĕns). Also 4–6 sequens. [ad. late L. sequentia, L. sequent-em pres. pple. seguī to follow + -ENCE.]

I. Succession, following.
1. The fact of following after or succeeding.
2. A person's following (cf. SEQUEL sb. 1).

Sequelarly, adv. Obs. rare⁻¹. [f. L. sequēla.] Subsequently.

Sequence, v. Also 4–6 sequens.

II. 7. Eccl. A composition in rhythmical prose or accentual metre said or sung, in the Western Church, after the Alleluia and before the Gospel. Sometimes called a prose: see PROSE sb. 2.

Sequency (sī·kwĕnsĭ). Now Hist. [a. OF. sequencier (AF. sequencer), ad. L. sequentiārius.] A book containing sequences.

Sequencer, Hist. [ad. med.L. sequentiārius (sequentiārium) Old Servie-bks.] = SEQUENCER.

Sequeme. Surg. Obs. [L., ult. 'Follow me'.] The name of a flexible probe used in medieval surgery.

Sequent (sī·kwĕnt), a. and sb. [ad. L. sequent-em, L. sequent-em, pres. pple. of seguī to follow.]
1. That follows or comes after.
2. That succeeds or is subsequent in time or serial order.

Sequential (sĭkwĕ·nʃăl), a. [f. late L. sequentia SEQUENCE: see -AL.]
1. Following as a sequel to. Or to some things; forming a sequence.

Sequently (sī·kwĕntlĭ), adv. [f. SEQUENT a. + -LY.] In sequence.

Sequester (sĭkwĕ·stər), sb. Obs. Also 4 suquestre. [a. L. sequester, prob. f. sequī.]
1. A follower, attendant.

Sequester (sĭkwĕ·stər), v. [a. OF. sequestre-r.]

Sequester v.
1. To seclude (a person, thing, or place) from general access or intercourse; to keep apart from society.
2. To confiscate, appropriate, to take forcible possession of.

Sequestered (sĭkwĕ·stərd), ppl. a. Also 7 sequestred.
1. Separated; cut off from congenial surroundings.

Sequesterer (sĭkwĕ·stərər). Obs. rare. Also 6 sequesterer.

Sequestra, pl. of SEQUESTRUM.

Sequestral (sĭkwĕ·străl), a. nonce-wd. [f. L. sequester, sequestr- + -AL.]

Sequestrable (sĭkwĕ·străbl), a. [f. SEQUESTER v. + -ABLE.] Capable of being sequestered, liable to sequestration.

Sequestrate (sĭkwĕ·strēt), v. Also 6–7 sequestratt. [ad. late L. sequestrāt-us, L. pple. of sequestrāre: see SEQUESTER v. and -ATE³.]
1. Separated, cut off from.

Sequestrated (sĭkwĕ·strētĕd), ppl. a. Also 7 sequestrated. [f. SEQUESTRATE v. + -ED¹.]
1. Separated; cut off from congenial surroundings.

Sequestration (sĭkwĕstrē·ʃən). Forms: 4–5 sequestracioun, 5 sequestracyo(u)n, 5–6 sequestracion, 6 sequestration. [ad. late L. sequestrātiōn-em, f. L. sequestrāre: see prec.]
1. An act or the action of sequestering, banishment, exile; esp. Civ. Law, a cutting off from the privileges of Church-membership; excommunication.
2. Seizure, confiscation.
3. Separation, disjunction.
4. A state of being sequestered, separation, retirement.
5. Path. (See quot.)
6. (See quot.)

Sequestrator (sĭkwĕ·strētər). [a. late L. sequestrātor.]

Sequestratrix (sĭkwĕstrē·trĭks). Obs. rare⁻¹. [a. L. sequestrātrīx.] A female sequestrator.

Sequestre, obs. f. SEQUESTER.

Sequestrotomy (sĭkwĕstrŏ·tŏmĭ). Surg. [f. SEQUESTR-UM + Gr. -τομία a cutting.] The operation for the removal of a sequestrum.

Sequestrum (sĭkwĕ·strəm). Path. Pl. **sequestra**. [mod.L. use of L. sequestrum.]

Sequin (sī·kwĭn), sb. Now Hist. Also S sequin. Also 8 cequin, chequin, zechin. [a. F. sequin.]

Seraglio (sĕrā·ljō, sĕrǎ·lĭō). Also 6 serail. [ad. It. serraglio (orig. Venetian), worth about 9 shillings. Also used as a name for a former Turkish coin.]
1. An Italian gold coin (originally Venetian).
2. A Turkish palace, esp. the palace of the Sultan at Constantinople.

Serai (sĕrā·ĭ), var. of SERAGLIO, SERAI.

Serang (sĕrǎ·ŋ). [Pers. sarhang.] = SERANG.

Serapheim, var. SERAPHIM.

Serai, obs. form of SERAI.

Seraphic, a.

Seraphim, sb. pl.

Seraglio.—popular L. *serraiculum* enclosure, place of confinement (cf. med.L. *serraiculum* fastening of a door), f. *serrāre* (whence It. *serrare*, F. *serrer*, Sp. *cerrar*) to *serre* to lock up, close, f. *sera* lock or bolt. The It. word was, from similarity of sound, used to render the Turkish *serāi* lodging, palace [see SERAI].

1. Enclosure, place of confinement.

1. The part of a Mohammedan dwelling-house (esp. of the palace of a sovereign or great noble) in which the women are secluded; the apartments reserved for wives and concubines; a harem.

II. = SERAI 1.

3. A Turkish palace, *esp.* the palace of the Sultan at Constantinople.

4. A place of accommodation for travellers.

5. A warehouse.

III. 7. *attrib.* and *Comb.*: seraglio-guard, lady, window; seraglio cake, a name given to a kind of fancy bread.

Serai (sərai'). Forms: 7 sarray, sera, noraw(e, serray, suray, surroie, 7, 9 sarai, -ay, 8 serauee, 9 seraee, seray, -oy, 8- serai. [a. Pers. (orig. Persian) سراى serāi lodging, residence, palace. Cf SERAGLIO, BERM.]

1. In various Eastern countries, a building for the accommodation of travellers; a caravanserai.

2. A Turkish palace; esp. the palace of the Sultan at Constantinople.

†3. Misused for SERAGLIO 1: A harem.

†Serai 2 (sərai'). *Anglo-Ind.* in this sense.

‡Serai 3 (sərai'). [Anglo-Indian, repr. Urdu (orig. Arab.) سراہى *surāhi*.] 'A long-necked earthenware (or metal) flagon for water' (Yule).

†Seraï, var. SERRY *v.* Obs.

Serail (sərail'). Now rare. Forms: 6 serall, serell, 7 serrall, serraill, serray(e, 7- serail. f. ... cf. serraglio : see SERAGLIO. Cf. Sp. serallo.]

1. = SERAGLIO 1.

2. A barrack for Turkish soldiers: = SERAGLIO 6.

3. A barrack for Turkish soldiers: = SERAGLIO 6.

Seral(sə-rāl), *n.* Geol. [f. U.S. sī-rā-late -AL: see quot.] A *adj.* Used by H. D. Rogers to designate the Millstone Grit formation of the Pennsylvanian Coal-measures. Also *absol.* or *sb.* Used as a name for this formation.

†Seraph. Now rare. Forms: 6 serrall, serafil, 7 seraïl(l)e, serrall, serraye,7- serail. f. Arab. *sharīf* : see SHARIFF. Cf. IT.

[† taraffo.] A Turkish gold coin ; a sequin.

Seraphs, var. GIRAFFE.

Seraglio-window. *Ibid.* 523 The chief guardian of the "seraglio ladies. *Ibid.* 523 The Grand Signior was at the "seraglio window.

Seraphic. [Back-formation from the plural SERAPHIM, SERAPHIN (on the analogy of *cherubim, -in* and *cherub*). (Perh. first used by Milton.)]

Cf. F. *séraphique*, med. L. *seraphicus*.

1. = SERAPHIC A.

2. Resembling a seraph, either in beauty or in fervour of exalted devotion.

b. Of discourse, actions, appearance : Showing ecstasy of devout contemplation.

4. *Special collocations*: Seraphic doctor, a title given...to St. Bonaventura (in Spain also popularly to St. Teresa); seraphic Father, a title given to St. Francis; seraphic friar, a Franciscan, honour of the three honourable Post ; seraphic hymn, the Sanctus; seraphic person, an 'angel'.

b. *fig.* A seraphic person, an 'angel'.

3. *Coal.* A fossil shell. Cf SERAPHIN 4.

Seraphical (sĕrə-fikăl), *adv.* [f. SERAPHICAL + -LY 2.] In a seraphic manner.

Seraphicism, *n.* [f. SERAPHIC *a.* + -ISM.] Pretence of 'seraphic' raptures.

Seraphim (se-răfim). *sb. pl.* Forms: 1, 5-7, 9 *arch.* seraphin, 3 serafin, 4 serafyn, 5 ceraphin, secheraphym, 5 phyn, seraphyn, seraphyn. Also 6 serophim.

Also 6 *sing.* SERAPH.

Seraphic (sərăfik). *a.* (and *sb.*) Forms: 1 seraphic, 7- seraphic.

1. Pertaining to the seraphim : = SERAPHIC 1.

2. Resembling seraphim in the sense of zealot.

b. *fig.*

b. Of ideas, etc. : Lofty, sublime. Cf. SERA-PHIC *a.* 2 b. In quot. *ironical*). *Obs.*

4. A Swedish order of knighthood. (See quot.)

5. *Geol. sing.* and *collect.* A fossil crustacean of the genus *Pterygotus.*

6. A mouth of the genus *Zalophora.* Also *seraphim-moth.*

Seraphin (se-răfin). *sb.* Also *seraphine.* [f. SERAPH + -IN.]

Seraphine (se-răfin). Also *seraphina.* [f. SERAPH + -INE.]

Seraphism (se-răfiz'm). *n.* Ecstatic devotion.

†Seraphium. *Obs.* = SERAPHINE.

†Seraʹphin. *n.* Obs. = SERAPHINE.

Serapias. *n.* [L. *serapias*, f. the name of the Egyptian god *Serapis.*] Formerly, a book-name for various orchids, and for the dried roots of these as used in pharmacy.

Serapic (sĕrăpik), *a.* [f. L. *Serapis* + -IC.] Of or pertaining to the Egyptian god *Serapis.*

Serapion. *Obs.* [ad. L. *Serapium.*]

Serapis. *n.* [ad. L. *Serapis*.]

I. = SAGAPENUM.

Serasker. = SERASKIER.

Seraskier (sĕrăskī-ə'). *n.* Also seraskuer. [f. Turkish pronunciation of Pers. ... Arab. عسكر *askar* army.] The title of the Turkish Minister of War, who is also commander in chief of the army.

Serb (səʳb), *sb.* and *a.* Also *Syrbe.* [a. Servian *Srb*, Serb. Cf. F. *Serbe*.] 1 *a.* A native of Servia, a Servian.

2. The Servian language.

Serbian (səʳbi'ǎn), *a.* and *sb.* Also *Syrbe.* [f. prec. + -IAN.]

Serbonian (səʳbōni'ǎn), *a.* [f. L. *Serbōnis* + -IAN.]

Serbo-, combining form of SERB, as *Serbo-Croatian, -Italian.* Cf. SERVO-.

Sere, var. CERE *sb.* Obs.

Serch, obs. form of SEARCH *sb.* and *vb.*

Sercel, var. of CIRCLE.

Sercelé, obs. forms of CINGLET.

Serch. Obs. forms of SEARCH *sb.* and *vb.*

cellar. a. In Western Asia, a cellar or under-ground chamber. b. In Egypt, a secret passage or chamber in an ancient tomb.

Sere, *adv.* and *a.2* *Obs.* (exc. *dial.*) Forms: 3-5 ser, 3-6 seir, 4-6, 4 soyre, schere, 4-7 5 (*dial.*) seere, 5-6 seyr, 5-7 seere, 5-8 sere. [OE. *sēar*, dry, withered.]

Serens (se-rənz). *Obs. rare.* [It. (Neapolitan)]

1. Separate, distinct ; each in particular, single.

b. *fig.*

2. Divers, various, sundry.

Sere, *sear*, *v.1* and *sb.1* [L. *sēres* to mend bar for hair.] 1. Dry, withered. Now *poet.* or *rhetorical.*

Sere, *sb.* Obs. [f. Servian *sēre.*] 1. Separately, severally. *Sere twice*, on two separate occasions.

2. *Comb.*, as sere-coloured, parti-coloured; (so sere-wise adv., in divers ways.

Sere, var. CERE *sb.* and *v.*, SEAR *sb.* and *v.*

Sere, *v.* Obs. form of SIRRAH.

Sereau, *n.* and *sb.* [L. *Sēres* (see SERES) + -AN. Cl. SERIAN, SERIC.] *adj.* Of or pertaining to the Seres ; silken. *Sere*, *sear*, see SEAR *sb.*

Serein (sĕrẽ'). *Meteorology.* [F. ad. L. *serēnus.*] A fine rain falling from a cloudless sky after sunset.

Sere. 1. Dry, withered.

Serelepes, *adv.* seirelepes, -s. Also *3 serelepe,* -es, *4 serelepe, 4-5 serelepis,* ... [f. SERE *adv.* + -LEPES.]

Serene (sĕrī'n), *a.* (and *sb.*) Forms: 4 *sereen,* 6 *sereine,* 5- serene. [ad. L. *serēnus* clear, calm, (of weather, etc.). Cf. OF. *serī, serin, serein,* mod.F. *serein,* Sp., Pg., It. *sereno.*]

1. Of the weather, air, sky : Clear, fine, and calm (without cloud or rain or wind).

b. as *adj.* Separate, distinct ; sundry, various.

2. Other natural phenomena (e.g. the sea):

Serene.

b. *transf.* Restful to the eye, expressive or suggestive of repose.

All serene, a slang phr. for 'all's well', 'all right'.

4. An honorific epithet given to a reigning prince (esp. of Germany), formerly also to a member of a royal house, etc.: sometimes jocularly applied to anything appertaining to a prince or so designated. Also *most serene* = med.L. *serenissimus*, It. *serenissimo*. Cf. **Serenity** 4.

5. *Drop serene*: Milton's rendering of med.L. *gutta serena* amaurosis: see **Gutta** 1 b. Hence allusively (quot. 1843).

6. *quasi-adv.*

Serenely (sĭrī'nli), *adv.* [f. **Serene** *a.* + -**ly**2.] In a serene manner.

Sereneness (sĭrī'nnes). [f. **Serene** *a.* + -**ness**.] The quality of being serene; serenity.

Serenate [f. **Serenade** *sb.*]

Serenian. [f. L. *serēn-us* serene + -**ian**.]

Serenify, *v.* [f. **Serene** *a.* + -**fy**.] To become serene.

Serenissime, *a.* and *sb. rare.* [a. F. *sérénissime* (13th c.), ad. L. *serenissimus*, superl. of L. *serēnus*, serene.] A 'most serene'; an honorific epithet bestowed on certain princes. Also *sb.*, one so entitled.

Serenissimo, *a.* and *sb.* [It.] = prec.

Serenissimus. [L.] = prec. Also Pl. -i, also -es.

Serene (sĭrī'n), *v.* Now *rare* or *Obs.* [ad. L. *serēnāre*, f. *serēn-us* **Serene** *a.* Cf. 16th c. F. *serener* (Ronsard).] *trans.* To make serene.

1. To make (the sky, air) clear, bright, and tranquil. Also, to clear *from* (cloud).

+ b. To clarify, make clear and bright (a liquid).

2. To make (a person, his mind, etc.) calm and tranquil.

Serene, obs. form of **Siren**.

Serenity (sĭrē'nĭti). [a. F. *sérénité*, ad. L. *serēnitāt-em*, f. *serēn-us*: see **Serene** *a.* and -**ity**.]

1. Clear, fair and calm weather; clearness and stillness of air and sky.

2. Tranquillity, peacefulness (of conditions, etc.).

3. Cheerful tranquillity (of mind, temper, countenance, etc.).

4. A title of honour given to reigning princes, etc.

Serenize (se'rĕnaiz), *v. rare.* [f. L. *serēnus* + -**ize**.]

Sereno (serē'nō). [Sp.] A Spanish nightwatchman.

Sermount, obs. form of **Surmount**.

Serodin.

Seres (sīə·rēz), *pl.* [L. *Sērēs* (Gr. *Σῆρες*), pl.] The name of a people anciently inhabiting some part of Eastern Asia (prob. China), whose country was believed to be the original home of silk. Hence † *the Seres' wool*, silk.

†Seresith. [f. **Sere** *a.*2 + **Sith** *sb.*1] Several times.

†Serety. [f. **Sere** *a.*2] Variety.

Serou (h')f: ... forms of **Sorrowful.**

Se-reverence, variant of **Sir-reverence.**

Serf (sărf). [a. OF. *serf*:—L. *servum*, acc. of *servus* slave. Not in use in ME., the mod. Eng. word being a re-adoption, chiefly through Fr. translations of foreign histories, and finally (from the latter part of the 18th c.) from the political condition of the peasantry in certain European countries, esp. Russia.]

1. A slave, bondman. Also *fig.*

2. A person in a condition of servitude or modified slavery, distinguished from what is properly called 'slavery' in that the services due to the master, and his power of disposal of his 'serf', are more or less limited by law or custom.

Serf, obs. form of **Serve** *v.*1

Serfage (sɜ·rfedʒ). [f. **Serf** + -**age**; cf. **Serfdom**.]

1. = **Serfdom.**

2. The body of serfs collectively; the serf-class.

Serfdom (sɜ·rfdəm). [f. **Serf** + -**dom**.] The state or condition of a serf; bondage.

Serfhood (sɜ·rfhud). [f. **Serf** + -**hood**.] The collective body of serfs.

Serfish (sɜ·rfiʃ), *a.* [f. **Serf** + -**ish**1.] Having the (debasing) qualities of one in a servile condition; characteristic of a serf. Hence **Serfishness.**

Serfism (sɜ·rfizm). *rare.* [f. **Serf** + -**ism**.] The state of things characterized by the existence of serfs.

Serfship (sɜ·rfʃip). [f. **Serf** + -**ship**.] Serfdom.

Serge (sɜrdʒ), *sb.*1 [a. F. *serge*, earlier *sarge* (12th c.):—pop. L. *sarica*, for *serica* neut. pl. taken as fem., f. L. *sēricus* silken.] A woollen fabric.

Serge, *sb.*2 ... A wax candle.

Sergeancy, serjeancy (sɑ·rdʒǝnsi). [f. **Sergeant** + -**cy**.]

1. The office or rank of a sergeant.

2. The district or province held by or under the jurisdiction of a sergeant.

Sergeant, serjeant (sɑ·rdʒǝnt), *sb.* Forms: α. 3-4 *serganz*, 3-5 *sergant(e*, 4 *seriaunz*, 4 *sergaund*, 4-5 *sergeaunt*, 6 *sergeant*; β. 4-6 *sergeant*; γ. etc.

1. A servant; a man, attendant, servant. *Obs.*

2. An officer, ranking below a knight, who attended on his lord. *Obs.*

+ 4. An officer whose duty is to enforce the judgements of a tribunal or the commands of a person in authority; one who is charged with the arrest of offenders or the summoning of persons to appear before the court. *Obs.*

5. As a title borne by a lawyer. (Now always written *serjeant*.) A member of a superior order of barristers (abolished in 1880), from which, until 1873, the Common Law judges were always chosen (hence a serjeant was always called by a judge 'my brother So-and-so'). More explicitly, *serjeant(-)at(-)law*; formerly also *serjeant of the coif*: see **Coif** *sb.* 3 b.

b. **Common serjeant** (at Law). A judicial officer appointed by the Corporation of London as an assistant to the Recorder.

c. **Prime serjeant**: the title given until 1805 to the first in rank of the (Irish) serjeants-at-law in Ireland. [Now called *first serjeant.*]

6. In the titles of certain inferior officers employed by the Corporation of the City of London, and by other municipal bodies.

Sergeant, serjeant (sɑ·rdʒǝnt), *sb.* [Continued]

yearly unto him a bow, or a speare, or a dagger, or a launce, or a spurre of gold &c.

4. The office of a sergeant or a serjeant in various senses; e.g. an appointment by writ or patent of the crown as serjeant-at-law; also the commission of sergeant in the army.

+ b. *transf.* A servant (of God, of Satan). *Obs.*

+ c. *transf.* A servant of God, an instrument, agent, or minister.

† 3. A tenant by military service under the rank of a knight in the old class attending on a knight in the field.

7. *Mil.* (Now always written *sergeant.*) In modern use, a non-commissioned officer of the grade above that of corporal. In the 16th c. the title, most explicitly *† sergeant of a band* [= Fr. *sergent de bande*], appears, like many other military titles, to have indicated a much higher rank than in later times.

8. In the titles of certain inferior officers employed by the Corporation of the City of London, and by other municipal bodies.

9. Prefixed appositively to various designations of offices in which sergeants are employed, as *sergeant armourer, bugler, clerk, cook, drummer, farrier, instructor, master tailor, saddler, schoolmaster, tailor, trumpeter.*

10. *Comb.* **Sergeant Baker** *Australian*, a fish of New South Wales.

Sergeant-at-arms. See **Serjeant-at-arms.**

Sergeant-fish. A fish.

Sergeant-general. *Obs.* = **Serjeant-major** 1 b.

Sergeant-major. [f. **Sergeant** + **Major**.]

1. In the 16-17th c., a military title variously applied to officers widely different in rank and function. b. A field officer, one in each regiment, next in rank to the lieutenant-colonel.

2. *Mil.* The highest grade of non-commissioned officer.

Sergeantry, serjeantry (sā'dʒəntri). *Obs.* Also **5 sergantry, serientrie, -rye; serjanterye.** [f. SERGEANT + -RY.]

Sergeanty, serjeanty (sā'dʒənti). *Hist.* Forms: α. **5 serjauntie (5 sergeaunte), 6 ser-geauntie, sergantie, 7-serjeanty.** β. **4 ser-jaunte, 5 serjaunte, serjeauntie, 7 serjeauntie, 7 serianty, serjeauntis, 7-serjeanty.** [a. OF. *sergantie, -ie, serjanté, seryanté* (cf. SERGEANTRY); later *serjantie* and -TY.] The usual spelling is now **serjeanty.**]

1. A form of feudal tenure on condition of rendering some specified personal service to the king.

2. Distinguished as *grand* and *petit* (or *petty*) *serjeanty*.

Sergette (sādʒet). [a. F. *sergette*, dim. of *serge*.] See *quot.*

Sergreant, -lant, -launt(e, sergond, -ont(e, obs. ff. SERGEANT.

Sergre(t)ant: see SERGEANT *Her.*

Seri, variant of SIRIH.

Serial (sɪə'rɪəl), *a.* and *sb.* [ad. mod.L. *seriālis,* f. *seri-ēs* SERIES and -AL. Cf. F. *sérial* (1861), *sériel* (1874).] **A.** *adj.* Belonging to, forming part of, or consisting of a series ; taking place or occurring in a regular succession.

B. *sb.* **1.** A literary composition.

Seriality (sɪəriæ'lɪti). [f. SERIAL + -ITY.] Serial arrangement ; SERIALISM.

Serially (sɪə'rɪəlɪ), *adv.* [f. SERIAL *a.* + -LY.] In a *series,* in serial arrangement.

Seriate (sɪə'rɪeɪt), *a.* [ad. mod.L. *seriātus,* f. *seri-ēs* SERIES.] Arranged or occurring in one or more series or rows.

Seriatim (sɪərɪeɪ'tɪm), *adv.* [ad. med.L., f. *seri-ēs* after GRADATIM, LITERATIM.] One after another, one by one in succession.

Seriation (sɪərɪeɪ'ʃən). [ad. mod.L. *seriātiōn-(em,* f. *seri-ēs* SERIES and -ATION.] Succession in a series ; serial formation of or into a series.

Seriatly, *adv. Obs. rare⁻¹.* [f. SERIATE + -LY.]

Seric (serɪk), *a.* *rare.* [ad. L. *sēric-us,* Gr. σηρικός, f. Σῆρες (see SERES).] Of or belonging to the Seres.

Serican, variant of ZARERA.

Serica (se'rɪkə). [a. late L. *sērica,* neut. pl. of *sēricus* SERIC.]

Sericeous (sɪrɪ'ʃəs), *a.* [f. L. *sēric-eus,* (Chiefly *Zool.* and *Bot.*) Covered with silky hairs.]

Sericio (sɪrɪ'tʃɪoʊ). *Obs.*

Sericic (sɪrɪ'sɪk), *a. Chem.* Also *-ino.* [Formed as SERIC(E + -IC.)]

Sericin (se'rɪsɪn). *Chem.* [f. SERIC(EOUS + -IN.)]

Sericite (se'rɪsaɪt). *Min.* [ad. G. *sericit* (Glocker 1847), f. L. *sēric-um* silk : see SERIC and -ITE.]

Sericiculture (sɪrɪ'sɪkʌltʃə). [f. L. *sēricicum* silk + *cultura* CULTURE.]

Sericon (se'rɪkən). *Alch. Obs. rare.*

Sericterium (serɪk'tɪərɪəm). *Entom. Pl. -eria* (-ɪrɪə). [mod.L.]

Sericultural (serɪ'kʌltʃərəl), *a.* [f. next + -AL.] Pertaining to or engaged in sericulture.

Sericulture (se'rɪkʌltʃə), *sb.* [a. F. *sériciculture,* f. L. *sēric-um* silk + *culture*.] The production of raw silk and the rearing of silkworms for the purpose.

Sericulturist. [f. prec. + -IST.]

Seridolath, northern f. *cered cloth* : see CERED.

Séries (sɪə'riz, sɪə'rɪz). Pl. (8-) **series,** (7-8, *rare in 9*) **seríes, serieses,** (7-8, 9) **series's** [a. L. *series,* f. *ser-ĕre* to join, connect. Cf. F. *série,* Sp., Pg. *série.*]

1. General senses.

2. A continued state or supply. *Obs.*

3. The connected sequence (of discourse, writing, thought). *Obs.*

4. The connected sequence of events.

5. Order of succession ; sequence. *Obs.*

6. A number of magnitudes, degrees of some attribute, or the like, viewed as capable of being enumerated in a progressive order.

II. Technical senses.

7. *Arith.* A set of terms in succession.

8. A set of coins, medals, or the like, belonging to a particular epoch, locality, dynasty, or government.

9. A set of literary compositions having certain features in common, published successively or intended to be read in sequence.

Serif (se'rɪf). *Typog.* Also **serif** [formerly **ceriph, seripph, sceripph, surryph** : see SANSERIF.] One of the fine cross-strokes at the top and bottom of a letter.

Seriff, variant of SHEREEF.

Serific (sɪrɪ'fɪk), *a. rare.* [irreg. f. L. *sēric-um* silk (see SERIC) + -FIC.] Producing silk.

Seriform (sɪə'rɪfɔːm), *a. rare.* [f. SER-ES + -FORM.] Applied to a division of the Ugro-Finnish races comprising the Chinese, Siamese, etc., and to the group of languages spoken by these peoples.

Serigraph (se'rɪgrɑːf). [irreg. f. L. *sēric-um* silk (see SERIC) + -GRAPH.] An instrument for testing the uniformity of raw silk.

Serimeter (sɪrɪ'mɪtə), an instrument for testing the strength of silk thread.

Serimony, -y, obs. form of CEREMONY.

Serin (se'rɪn). Also **6 seryne, -one.** [a. F. *serin,* canary of uncertain origin.] In early examples perh. the canary (*Serinus canarius*) ; in modern ornithology, a bird of the genus *Serinus.*

Seriola (sɪrɪ'oʊlə), a genus of fishes.

Serious (sɪə'rɪəs), *a.* [ad. med.L. and F. *sérieux,* *-euse.* a. L. *sēriōsus,* f. *sēri-us.*] **1.** Of a person : grave, sedate, sober in demeanour ; earnest.

2. Of actions, etc. : having involved earnest purpose or thought.

3. Important, grave ; attended with danger.

Seriousness (sɪə'rɪəsnɪs). [f. SERIOUS + -NESS.] The quality or condition of being serious.

Seriously (sɪə'rɪəslɪ), *adv.* [f. SERIOUS *a.* + -LY.] In a serious manner.

Serjant, -jaunt, -jeant, obs. ff. SERGEANT.

Serjeant, etc. : see SERGEANT, etc.

Serjeanty, etc. : see SERGEANTY.

Serment, *Obs.* Also **5 sarment.** [a. OF. *serment, -ement, sairement* (mod.F. *serment*) :— L. *sacrāmentum* SACRAMENT.] An oath.

Sermocinate (sā'məsɪneɪt), *v.* [f. L. *sermōcināt-,* ppl. stem of *sermōcinārī,* f. *sermōn-* SERMON.] To talk.

Sermocination (sāməsɪneɪ'ʃən). *Obs.* Also **7 cerm-.** [ad. L. *sermōcinātiōn-(em.]*

Sermon (sā'mən), *sb.* Forms : α. **3-4 sermun, 3-5 sarmun, 4-5 sarmoun, 4-7 sar-moun, 5 sermoune, 4-6 sermond, 7-9 sear-mond, 8 var-gar sarment, sarmond, 7 sar-mond** [a. OF. *sermun, -on* (mod.F. *sermon,* Pr., Sp., It. *sermone,* Pg. *sermão*) :— L. *sermōn-em,* *sermo* talk, discourse, speech.]

1. Something that is said ; talk, discourse. *Obs.*

2. *spec.* A discourse delivered from the pulpit, founded upon a text of Scripture.

Sermonary, *a.* and *sb.*

Sermoncinate, etc. : see SERMOCINATE.

[Densely printed dictionary columns — Oxford English Dictionary entries for
SERMON, Sermoned, Sermoneer, Sermonee, Sermonet, Sermonette, Sermonic,
Sermonical, Sermoner, Sermonet, Sermoning, Sermonish, Sermonist,
Sermonize, Sermonizer, Sermonizing, Sermonoid, Sermon-ology, Sermonless,
Sero-, Serolin, Serological, Seron, Seroon, Serosity, Serotine, Serotinous,

[Dictionary columns continuing with SERPENT and related entries:
Serpent-bearer, Serpent-eater, Serpentaria, Serpentarius, Serpentiferous,
Serpentigenous, Serpentine, Serpentinian, Serpenticide, Serpentiform,

Serpentine verse, a metrical line beginning and ending with the same word.

Serpentine marble.

Serpentine powder. [See SERPENTINE *sb.*]

Serpentine stone, *med.L. lapis serpentinus*, rendering Gr. *λίθος ὀφίτης*; cf. OPHITE 1.]

Serpenting, *vbl. sb. Obs.*

Serpentine, *v. Obs.*

Serpentinely, *adv.* [f. SERPENTINE + -LY².] In a serpentine manner; in a serpentine path.

Serpentine-like, *a.* [-LIKE.] A *adj.*

Serpently, *adv.* [f. SERPENT *sb.* + -LY¹.]

Serpentic, *a.* [f. SERPENTINE + -IC.]

Serpentining, *ppl. a.* [f. SERPENTINE *v.* + -ING².] Winding or coiling like a serpent; winding, sinuous.

Serpentinian, *a.* [f. L. *serpentinus*.]

Serpentinic, *a.* [f. SERPENTINE + -IC.]

Serpentinize, *v.* [f. SERPENTINE *sb.* + -IZE.]

Serpentinoid, *a.* [f. SERPENTINE + -OID.]

Serpentinous, *a.* [f. SERPENTINE *sb.* + -OUS.]

Serpentization, *sb.* [f. as prec.]

Serpentine-stone.

Serpentry, *sb.* [f. SERPENT *sb.* + -RY¹.]

Serpet, *sb. Obs. rare*⁻¹. [error for Turkish *sepet* wicker basket.] A kind of basket.

Serpigo (sǝ(r)paigo), *sb.* Now *rare*. [med.L. *serpigo* (-*gin*-), a creeping serpent-like of mortal worms.]

Serpigo, *v. Obs. rare*⁻¹. [f. SERPIGO *sb.*]

Serpula (sə̄·rpiŭlǎ), *sb.* [L. = small serpent, dim. of SERPENS.]

Serpulan, *a.* and *sb.* [f. SERPULA.]

Serpulet, *sb.* rare⁻¹. [f. prec., or irreg. f. L. *serpyllum*.]

Serpuloid, *a.* (*sb.*) [f. SERPULA + -OID.]

Serpulæan, **Serpulian**, **Serpulida**, **Serpulidan**, **Serpulite**, **Serpulitic**.

Serra (se·rǎ), Pl. **serræ**, **serras**. [L. = saw, saw-fish.]

Serradilla (serǎdi·lǎ). Also -*illa*.

Serranid (se·rǎnid), *sb.* [f. mod.L. *Serranus* (see below).]

Serranoid (se·rǎnoid), *a.* and *sb.*

Serrate (se·rei·t), *a.* [ad. mod.L. *serrāt-us*.]

Serrated (se·rei·ted), *ppl. a.* [f. prec. + -ED².]

Serration (serēi·ʃən), *sb.* [ad. mod.L. *serrātio*.]

Serratiform, *a.* [f. L. *serrāti-* + -FORM.]

Serratirostral, *a.* [f. L. *serrāti-* + ROSTRAL.]

Serrature (se·rǎtiŭr), *sb.* [ad. L. *serrātūra*.]

Serratus (serēi·tŏs), *sb.* [mod.L., short for *serratus magnus*, which ...]

Serre, *sb.*, form of SERAIL.

Serre, *v.* [a. F. *serre*-, vbl. sb. f. *serrer*.]

Serre, obs. form of SEAR.

Serring, *vbl. sb.* [f. SERR *v.* + -ING¹.]

Serrulate (se·riŭleit), *v.* [f. mod.L.]

Serrulate, *a.* [f. mod.L. *serrulāt-us*.]

Serrated (se·rǎted), *a.* [Formed as prec. + -ED².]

Serrulation (seriŭlēi·ʃən), *sb.*

Serry (se·ri), *v.* Also *sarry*(e), **serrie**, **serree**.

Sert, obs. form of CERUSE.

Serviceable, *a.* Obs. Also **serveable**.

Servage (sə̄·rvedʒ), *sb.* [a. F. *servage*, f. *servir*.]

Servager, *sb. Obs. rare*⁻¹.

Servagery (sə̄·rvedʒəri), *sb. Obs.* [f. SERVAGE + -ERY.]

Serval (sə̄·rvǎl), *sb.* [a. F. *serval*, F. *serval*.]

Serval, obs. form of SERVILE.

Servaline, *a. Zool.* [ad. mod.L. *servalinus*.]

Servant (sə̄·rvǎnt), *sb.* Forms: *a.* 2-7 *servant*, 4 *servon*, *serfaunt*, 4-5 *servaunt*, *-aunte*, 4-6 *servawnt*, 4-5 *seruaunt*.

1. A personal or domestic attendant; one whose duty is to wait upon his master or mistress, or do certain work in his or her household.

2. One who is under the obligation to render certain services to, and to obey the orders of, a person or a body of persons, esp. in return for wages or salary.

3. A servant of God; esp. as a title of humility in the opening of prayers, etc.

4. In various transferred uses.

Supplement, p. 3873; Corrigenda, p. 4092; Spurious words, p. 4093; Books quoted, p. 4094

c. **collect.** *pl.* Friendly or professional assistance.

V. Waiting at table, supply of food ; hence, supply of commodities, etc.

VI. *Law.* **b.** The action or an act of serving (a writ, notice, etc.) upon a person.

33. *Law.* **b.** The action or an act of serving (a writ, notice, etc.) upon a person.

34. *Tennis.* The act of 'serving' the ball or starting it in play ; a particular player's manner of doing this ; the ball served.

35. *Naut.* Small cord, or the like, wound about a rope to protect it.

Service² (sɔ̄·ɹvīs). Forms : 4-6 servis(e, serves, servyse, 6 cervise, cervise, 6-8 servise ; 6 service, 8 servace. &c. [a. F. *sorbe*.]

Serviceability (sɔ̄ɹvisăbiliti). [f. next + -ITY.] Capability or readiness for service ; usefulness.

Serviceableness. [f. SERVICEABLE + -NESS.] The quality of being serviceable.

Serviceably, *adv.* [f. SERVICEABLE + -LY².] With a disposition to serve, obediently.

Servient (sɔ̄·ɹviĕnt), *a.* [ad. L. *servient-em*, pr. pple. of *servire* to serve.] † Also, performing service.

Servientes, Servities, Servitium.

Serviette (sɔ̄ɹvi·ĕt). Forms : *6 Sc. 5-7 serviot*, 6 servit, 6 Sc. 6-7 servit, 8 servite, 6, 9 servot; 7-8, 9 Sc. servet, 9 serviet. [a. F. *serviette*, f. *servir* SERVE v.]

Servile (sɔ̄·ɹvail), *a.* and *sb.* Forms : 4-6 servyle, (5 servylle, servil), 6-7 servill, (6 Sc. servall), 7 servell. [ad. L. *servil-is*, f. *servus* slave.]

Servilely (sɔ̄·ɹvail,li), *adv.* Also 6-7 servilly, (7-illye). [f. SERVILE a. + -LY².] In a servile manner.

Servileness (sɔ̄ɹvail,nĕs), *rare.* [f. SERVILE + -NESS.] Servility.

Servilism (sɔ̄·ɹviliz'm). [f. SERVILE a. + -ISM.] Servilism.

Servility (sɔ̄ɹvi·liti). [f. SERVILE a. + -ITY. Cf. F. *servilité* (18th c. in Hatz.-Darm.)]

Serving (sɔ̄·ɹviŋ), *vbl. sb.* [f. SERVE v.¹ + -ING¹.]

Serving (səˈvɪŋ), ppl. a. [SERVE v. + -ING[2].]

1. That serves, or does service to; another; that acts as a servant. Often hyphened to the qualified sb. as in *serving-maid*, SERVING-MAN, -WOMAN.

2. Of a soldier, etc.: That is in service.

3. Of things: Subsidiary. *Obs.*

4. Of things: That acts as a servant.

Serving-ma-n. Now arch. [SERVING ppl. a.]

1. A man who serves; a male servant or attendant. (Common in 16th and 17th centuries.)

2. *Serving-man's joy:* a name for Rue. *Obs.*

Serving-wo-man. Now arch. [SERVING ppl. a.] A female servant or attendant.

Servitary (səˈvɪtəri). *local.* – SERVITOR 5.

Servito (səˈvɪt), sb. and a. *Obs. med.l.*

Servitor (səˈvɪtər). Forms: 4–5 servytour, 4 servitur, 4–8 -servitour, 4–8 servitor, (servitor, servitour), 5–6 servytoure, -tir, (servytur), 5 servitore, 6 servitour, 6–8 servitore, -uir, (servytor), 7 servitor, servatore, 5–servitor. [a. OF. servitor (mod.F. serviteur), a. L. servitor, agent-n. f. servire.]

1. A (male) personal or domestic attendant (in early use chiefly, one who waits at table); a man-servant. Now arch.

2. One who serves in war; a soldier; spec. one of a class of persons to whom lands were assigned in Ulster in the reign of James I, as having served in a military or civil office in Ireland. *Hist. exc. Hist.* in the specific use.

3. One who serves in a subordinate office; an official; an officer; an attendant.

4. *Oxford University.* In certain colleges, one of a class of undergraduate members (no longer existing under that title: see quot. 1852) who received their lodging and most of their board free, and were excused lecture fees.

Servitorial (səˈvɪtoˈrɪəl), a. rare. [f. prec. + -AL.] Of or pertaining to a servitor (in any sense).

Servitorship (səˈvɪtərʃɪp). [f. SERVITOR + -SHIP.] a. The position, state, or duties of a servitor at an Oxford college. *Obs. exc. Hist.*

Servitress (səˈvɪtrɛs). [See SERVITOR and -TRESS.] A female servant or attendant.

Servitrice (səˈvɪtrɪs). *Obs.* [a. OF. servitrice, fem. of servitor: see SERVITOR.]

Servitry (səˈvɪtri). *Obs.* [f. med.L. servitor + -Y[3].]

Servitude (səˈvɪtjuːd). Also 5–6 servytude, 6 servitude. [a. F. servitude, ad. L. servitūdo, f. servus slave: see -TUDE.]

1. The condition of being a slave or a serf, or of being the property of another person; absence of personal freedom. Often, and now usually, with additional notion of subjection to the necessity of excessive labour. Also, a (more or less rigorous) state of slavery or serfdom.

2. A person's (period of) service (in the Navy).

3. Compulsory labour as a punishment for criminals. Chiefly penal servitude: see PENAL at 1 c.

b. With reference to animals: Subjection to mankind. Now rare.

Servitude, a state of degrading or burdensome subjection.

Servoice, var. CERVOICE. *Obs.*

Servo-motor (ˈsɜːvoʊˈmoʊtər). [ad. F. servo-moteur (1873 in Littré Suppl.), f. L. servus slave + F. moteur MOTOR.]

Servulate, v. *Obs. rare*–[1]. [f. L. servulus slave; + altar subulate, imit.] To enslave thoroughly.

Servward, obs. form of STEWARD.

Servo, obs. Sc. form of SERVE v., SORROW.

Seryauntre, variant of SERGEANTRY.

Seryf,f, obs. forms of SERVE v.?

Serythe, -yte, obs. forms of CEREMONY.

Seryn, obs. Sc. form of SIREN sb.

Ses: see CEASE, SAY sb.?, SEE, SEES.

Sesame (ˈsɛsəmi). Forms: 6 sesima, se'sam, si'sam, 7 sesami, 6–8 sesam, 6–9 sesamie, 7 sesame, (9, -6) seesam, also sesamum, and sisamus. – Gr. σήσαμον, σήσαμον, prob. of oriental origin, but the relation to the Semitic forms (Syriac shūshmā, Jewish Aramaic shūmshemā, Arab. simsim) is not clear.

Sesamine (ˈsɛsəmin), a. [f. L. sesamum sesame + -INE[1].]

Sesamoid (ˈsɛsəmɔɪd), a. and sb. [ad. L. sēsamoeidēs, a. Gr. σησαμοειδής.]

Sesamum (ˈsɛsəməm). *Obs.* [mod.L., ad. L. sēsamum.]

Sesban (ˈsɛsbæn). [ad. F. sesban, ultimately α. Arab. saisabān.] Any leguminous plant of the genus Sesbania.

Sescuple (ˈsɛskjuːp'l), a. Now rare. [ad. L. sescuplus or sescuplex, var. sesquiplus, -plex, f. sesqui- SESQUI- + -plus, -plex -FOLD.]

Sesel, variant of SESELI.

Se'sokyn. *Obs.* Also su'skyn. se-skyn, i. act six = siξ, sublx, -six -kyn = -kin. [a. MDu. sestkyn, f. set six slx: see SESSE.] A Dutch coin of the value of six sesterces.

Sesour, variant of SISER, cider.

Se'skyn, *Obs.* Also suskyn. [a. MDu. sestkyn, f. set six slx = six, slx = -kin.] A Dutch coin of the value of six.

Sesquialter (ˈsɛskwiˈæltər), a. [f. L. sesqui- SESQUI- + alter.] – SESQUIALTERA.

Sesquialteral (ˈsɛskwiˈæltərəl), a. [f. L. sesquialter: see prec.] – SESQUIALTERA 1.

Sesquialterous (ˈsɛskwiˈæltərəs), a. [f. L. sesqui- SESQUI- + alter.] – SESQUIALTERA 1.

Sesquiduplicate (ˈsɛskwiˈdjuːplɪkeɪt), a. [ad. mod.L.]

Sesquipedal (ˈsɛskwɪˈpiːd'l, sɛsˈkwɪpɪd'l), a. and sb. [ad. L. sesquipedal-is, f. SESQUI- + ped-, pes foot: see PEDAL.]

Sesquipedalian (ˌsɛskwɪpɪˈdeɪlɪən), a. and sb. [f. L. sesquipedalis SESQUIPEDAL and -IAN.]

Sesquiplicate (ˈsɛskwɪˈplɪkeɪt), a. [ad. mod.L. sesquiplicatus.]

Sesquisalt (ˈsɛskwɪˌsɔːlt). *Chem. Obs.*

Sesquitertian (ˌsɛskwɪˈtɜːʃən), a. and sb. [f. L. sesquitertius + -AN.]

Sesquitertianal. ... when any ... Quantity contains another once and one third.

Sesquitertianate (est·wit3ʃe), *a.* ...

Sess (ses), *sb.*[1] Also 7 *sesse.* ...

Sess, *sb.*[2] *Obs.* [perh. var. of SA-SA, or possibly a, F *cesses* 'cease'.]

Sess, *sb.*[3] *Obs.* *rare*[-1]

Sess, *sb.*[4] *Obs.* *Obs.*

Sessa, *int.* *Obs.*

Session (se·ʃən), *sb.* Forms: 4–6 sessioun, 5 sessiun, sessyoun, 5 cessioun, 5–6 cession, sessyon, session.

Sesuiline, *a.* *Obs.*

Sessile (se·sil, se·sil), *a.*

1. Having no footstalk.

2. *Zool.* Of limbs or organs : Immediately in contact with the structure to which they are attached.

Sessilifolious, *a.*

Sessile-eyed, *a.*

Sessility (se·si·liti), *n.*

Sessing, *vbl. sb.* *Obs.*

Sess, *int.* *Obs. exc. dial.*

Sessa, variant of CESS *sb.*

Session (se·ʃən), *sb.*

1. The action or an act of sitting ; the state or posture of being seated ; occupation of a seat or an assembly or the like ; also a manner of sitting.

2. *spec.* The 'sitting' of Christ at the right hand of God.

3. The sitting together of a number of persons (esp. of a court, a legislative, administrative, or deliberative body) for conference or the transaction of business.

4. A judicial sitting.

† a. *gen.* A sitting of a judge or judges to determine causes ; a judicial trial or investigation.

5. *Scots Law.* & *Hist.* The name given to a court of justice.

Sessional (se·ʃənăl), *a.*

Sessionally, *adv.*

Sessionary, *a.*

Sessioner (se·ʃənəɹ). *Sc. Obs.* Also 7 *-air.*

Sessions (se·ʃənz), *v.* *slang.* [f. *sessions*, pl. of SESSION *sb.*] *trans.* To commit (a person) to the sessions for trial.

Sessile, *v.* *dial.*

Sessment, *Obs.*

Sess, Also 6 *sesse*, 6–7 *sesse-*, *sease-*, *sess(e-*, 7 *sease*, *sessee.*

Sessons, *-oun*, *obs. Sc.* forms of SEASON.

Sessor (se·səɹ), *Obs.*

Sess-pool, *Sestain*, var. f. CESS-POOL, SEXTAIN.

Sest(e, obs. ff. pa. t. and pa. pple. of CEASE.

Sestet, *Sextet.*

Sesto, obs. form of SIXTH.

Sester (se·stəɹ). Now only *Hist.* Also 4 *ces-tre*, *sesstar*, 6 *cester*, *sester.* [OE. *sester* (also *sextar*) and AF., *sestre* = OF. *sester*, -*ier* = *med.L. sextārium* SEXTAR, SEXTARY.]

Sestern, *Sestertium.*

Sestertium, *sb.* pl. *-tia.*

Sestertius (sestəɹ·ʃi·ŭs), *sb.* Pl. *sestertii* (-ʃiəɪ) ; also 6 *sex-*, *-tia*, *-tias* 7 *-tias*. [L.]

Sestertce, obs. form of CISTERN.

Sestet (se·stet), *sb.* [ad. It. *sestetto.*]

Sestett, **sestetto** (sest·ʃt·o), *sb.* [ad. It.]

1. *Mus.* A composition for six voices or instruments.

Sestiad (se·stiad), *sb.* [f. L. *Sestos.*]

Sestina (sestī·nă), *sb.* [It. *sestina.*]

Sester, **sestern**, *Obs.* Also 5 *ceastron*, 6 *sestern*, *neystern*, 7 *sestorn*, *var.* SEXTER ; cf. *sestern*, *sextern*. — See also SEXTERN.]

Sestole, obs. var. ff. SEXTOLE, q.v.

Sesuncia (ses·un·ʃiă), *sb.* [L.]

Set, *sb.*[1] Also 4–5 *sette*, 6–7 *sett.* [In most senses, aphetic : cf. SEXTOLE.]

Set, *sb.*[2] Also 5 *sette*, 6–7 *sett.*

Set (set), *sb.*[3] Also 4–5 *sette*, 6 *sette*, 6 *sett*.

1. The action or setting or condition of being set.

2. *Scots Law.* The action of setting to sale or letting of land.

3. A mining lease. Chiefly *Cornwall.*

4. Of a woman : A determined attempt to gain a man's affections.

5. A determined stand, in argument or in movement.

6. The act of a dog in setting game.

II. The manner or position in which a thing is set.

11. The way in which something is set down in writing. *Obs.*

12. Tendency, inclination ; determination (of the mind, character, action, etc.) in a certain direction.

13. The direction in which a current flows or a wind blows ; also, the action of the water, etc. in taking a particular direction.

14. The build or make of a person. *Obs. exc. dial.*

15. *Weaving.* (Usually *sett.*) The adjustment of the reeds (of a loom) necessary for the making of a fabric of a particular texture.

III. Something which is set.

† **20.** An iron marked out for a harrow. *Obs.*

21. (Usually *sett.*) The area of ground worked by a particular mining company. Chiefly *Cornwall.*

22. (Usually *sett.*) A number of stones of a size.

23. 'Any thing not sown, but put in a state of growth with the ground' ...

SETTEE. | 553 | **SETTER.** | **SETTER.** | 554 | **SETTING.**

Settee, a vessel used in the mediterranean, rigged and navigated similar to xebecs or galleys, with settee-sails instead of lateen-sails. **1800** *Dominican Archbishop Seaman* (1802) 151 On the 11th [Nov. 1800] we captured a settee.

† Settee.² *sb. rare.* [Of unknown origin.] A double pinner for the head. **1688** RANDLE HOLME *Armoury* II. 482/1 A Coronet settee... over the Head, and by doubling it makes it stand as a great height both above and besides the Face.

Settee (se'tï̄), *sb.* [perh. a fanciful variation of SETTLE *sb.*: see -EE².] A seat (for indoors) holding two or more persons, with a back and (usually) arms; occasionally also with divisions (see quot. 1784). In America sometimes furnished with rockers.

Setter (se'tə̄ɹ), *sb.¹* Also § -6 *Sc.* **settar**, 6 *S.-arw.*, 7 *setter*. [f. SET v. + -ER¹.] I. The... **1. 1. gen.** One who or something which sets, in various senses of the vb.

b. With adverbial extension or complement. See also SETTER-FORTH, etc.

2. A workman employed to 'set' something.

b. *Woollen Manuf.* (See quot. 1787.)

c. A workman who sets jewels.

Setter, *sb.²* *dial.* [f. SETTER v.] A seton or issue produced by 'setting': see the vb.

Setter(e) (se'tə̄ɹ), *v.* Also 6 *sytor.* [f. SETTER in SETTERWORT.] *trans.* To insert a piece of setterwort under the skin (of an animal) in order to produce an issue.

Setter-day, obs. form of SATURDAY.

Setter-forth. [See SET v. 144.] One who sets forth (in various senses); one who promulgates an opinion, who equips an expedition, etc.

Settergrass, *sb.* *exc. dial. rare.* In 4 **saturgresse**, 5 **sotyr gryssse**, 6 **-grasse**; also, the fact of being set.

†Setter-on. *Obs.* [See SET v. 148.]

Setter-out. *rare.* [See SET v. 149.]

Setter-to. *Obs.* [See SET v. 152.]

Setter-up. [See SET v. 154.]

Setterwort. Also 6 *syter wurt.*

**[Perh. adopted from MLG.; Diefenbach s.v. *Elleborum* gives a great variety of synonymous forms in MHG. and MLG. such as *sitro*, *sitir-*, *sitti-*, *siter-*, *sutton*, *sutwort*, *-wort* [f. HG. *sitter-*, *siter-* etc.; ME. *siter-*, *sitti-* etc.]] The plant bear's-foot or Fetid Hellebore, *Helleborus fœtidus*; also the Green Hellebore, *H. viridis*.

Setting (se'tiŋ), *vbl. sb.* [f. SET v. + -ING¹.]

I. 1. The action of the verb SET in various transitive senses; putting, placing, planting, etc. Also, the fact of being set.

b. An ambush or snare.

c. *Sport.* (a) The action of a dog in indicating a particular game or scent.

II. *Smelting.* The manner of placing retorts in a furnace; *concr.* a group or set of retorts thus placed.

11. The process or fact of becoming set, hard, or stiff; coagulation.

12. The flowing of a current in a particular direction; the direction of flow. Also.

III. Combinations. 13. With various advbs., as *setting-down*, *-forth*, *-in*, *-off*, *-out*, *to:* see the corresponding combinations of SET v.

14. Attributive, in many senses of technical instruments and appliances, as *setting-chisel*, *-dibble*, *-hammer*, *-iron*, *-knife*, *-pin*, *-screw*, *-vessel*, etc.; *setting-board*, (a) a board used by glaziers in lead-work (see quot. 1703): (b) a board used by card-makers, pinmakers, etc.

†Setting dog. *Obs.* A dog trained to 'set' game: = SETTER *sb.¹* 11.

Setting-pole, a pole used by wildfowlers for propelling a boat or punt on mud-banks, securing wounded birds, etc.

Setting-stick. A stick used for making holes for 'setting' or planting.

II. *Printing.* The action of setting up type.

4. A ledge or platform.

b. (a) *setting-gang* (see quot. 1833). **c.** (See quot.)

5. *Firework Manuf.* A projection on the upper surface of the block used in filling tourbillon cases.

Settle (se't'l), *sb.¹* *Obs. exc. Sc. rare.* [= SETTLE *v.*] The action of the verb SETTLE; settling, settlement.

Settle (se't'l), *v.* Forms: 1 *setl*, *setel*, *setol*, *sætl*, *sotl*, *seatl*, *sitl* (-ol, -ul, -ut); 3 *settel*, *seotell*, *setle*, *6* *settle*, *6-7* *setel*, *6* *settel*, 6-7 *settle*, 7 *setle*; also *sattle*. [OE. *setl* neut., *pl. setlu* (also, in Northumb., *pl. setlas*, also *setla*) = LANG-SETTLE [OE. *self neut.*], *pl. setlu* (also, in Northumb., *pl. setlas*); allied to Goth. *sitls* masc.:—OTeut. *setlo-* pre-Teut. *sedlo-*, cogn. w. L. *sella* (:—*sedlā*), L. Independmanist root *sed-*, OTeut. *sat-, sit-* SIT v.]

† b. *fig.* in passive: To be 'seated', situated.

2. To place (material things) in order, or in a convenient or desired position; to adjust (a person's clothing).

3. To place (a person) in an attitude of repose, so as to be undisturbed for a time.

4. To fix or establish (a person's abode, residence, etc.).

5. To fix, implant (something) in (a person's heart, mind, etc.). Obs.

6. In passive: To be installed in a residence, to have completed one's arrangements for residing.

SEVEN SISTERS. 565 **SEVENTH.** **SEVENTH.** 566 **SEVEN YEARS.**

Seven sisters. [See also SISTER *sb.*]

† 1. The Pleiades. *Obs.*

2. *first.* Seven cannons, resembling each other in size and make, cast by Robert Borthwick and used at the battle of Flodden.

3. a. A name for two common appellations. *dial.*

b. *Seven sister-(s) rose:* a climbing rose producing densely clustered heads of white, cream, or pinkish flowers.

A popular name for *Melanocereus terricolor*, an Indian bird of gregarious habits.

† Sevensithe's, *adv. Obs.* Forms: see SEVEN and SITHE *sb.*[1] [OE. *seofon síþa, síþum*: cf. ON. *sjaunsinnum*.] Seven times.

Sevensome, *a.* + -SOME. Cf. Fris. *saunsóme.* Consisting of seven.

Hence **Se·venomeness,** the quality of being 'sevensome'.

† Seven stars. (Also ME. *sterres seuen*.) [OE. *seofon stéorran:* see SEVEN and STAR *sb.*, but also collect. neut. *sifore... stéorran*=WFris. *saunstjerre*, WFlem. *seven(ge)stjerre*, MLG. *sevensterne,* Du. *seven-sterne*, O11G. *sibunstirni*, -*sterri* (MHG. *sibenstern, G. siebichal*), OE. *septistéllum*.] **a.** The Pleiades. **b.** The plough. **c.** The seven planets.

The Great Bear.

SEVER.
 567

Sever (se·vər), *v.* Also 5 *soyvr, soyvre, Sc. sevvir,* 6 *sevour, seaver, Sc. niver, -ir, syver, sewer.* [a. AF. *severer, OF. sevrer, sovrer, severer,* mod.F. *sevrer* to wean—pop. L.*[1] siperdere,* L. *separare* to SEPARATE, *severare*.]

I. Transitive senses.

1. To part apart, as asunder (two or more persons or things; or one from another); to part or separate by putting in different places.

SEVERABLE.
 568

II. *intr.* (Cf. the reflexive uses in branch I.)

9. Of a person: To go away, part, be sundered or parted.

Severable (se·vərăb'l), *a.* [f. SEVER *v.* + -ABLE.] Capable of being severed or separated; ‖ distinct, separate. *Severable contract:* see *quot.* 1848.

Several (se·vĕrăl), *a., adv.,* and *sb.* Also 4–8 *all, (5 -ell, -ele, 6 -all, -alle, 6 -el, -il, -yll ...)*

Severians, ..a sort of Heretics that condemned marriage...

Severing, (ˈsɛvərɪŋ), *vbl. sb.* [-ING¹.] The action of the verb SEVER in various senses.

Severing, *ppl. a.* [-ING².] That severs.

† **Severing**, *ppl. a.* [-ISH.] Somewhat severe.

Severish, *a. rare.* [-ISH.] Somewhat severe.

† Severite¹. *Obs.* [... the name *Sevitrut* (see SEVERIAN) + -ITE¹.] — SEVERIAN 1 and 2.

Severite² (ˈsɛvəraɪt). *Min.* [Name† from Saint-Sever (Landes, France) + -ITE¹. Cf. *sévérite*.] A synonym of LÉVYNITE.

Severity (sɪˈvɛrɪtɪ). [a. F. *sévérité*, ad. L. *sevēritās*, f. *sevērus* severe: see -ITY. Cf. It. *severità*, Sp. *severidad*, Pg. *severidade*.]

1. Strictness or sternness in dealing with others; stern or rigorous disposition or behaviour; rigour in treatment, discipline, punishment, or the like.

2. Strictness or austerity of life, morals, etc.

3. Strictness in matters of thought or intellect; rigid accuracy or exactness; undeviating conformity to truth or fact. Also *pl.* instances of this.

4. Austere purity or simplicity of style, taste, etc.

5. Rigour in condition (of weather or climate); especially of cold.

6. An act or instance of severity.

Severy (sɛˈvɛrɪ). *Arch.* Forms: 5 severy-e, -oy; *pl.* 4 seweruus, 5 severeye, civerys, (civers, cyfres), 6 severey(e)s. [ad. OF. *civoerie*, *civoirie*, etc.] A bay or compartment of a vaulted roof. Also, a compartment or section of scaffolding.

† **Sévigné** (seːvɪˈɲeɪ). Forms: 8 sevigne, -née. [F. name *Sévigné*, that of Marie de Rabutin-Chantal, marquise de Sévigné (1627-96).] A kind of bandeau.

Sevile, Sevillioun, *obs. ff.* CIVIL, CIVILIAN.

Sevillan, var. SEVILLIAN.

Seville (sɛˈvɪl), *a.* [f. *Seville* (see next): see -IAN.]

Sevillian (sɛˈvɪljən), *a.* and *sb.* [f. *Seville* + -IAN.] *a. adj.* Of or pertaining to Seville. *b.* *sb.* A native or inhabitant of Seville.

Sevocation (sɛvəˈkeɪʃən), *rare—¹.* [ad. L. *sēvocāre*: see SEVOKE *v.* and -ATION.] The action of calling apart or aside.

† Sevoke, *v. Obs.* [ad. L. *sēvocāre*, f. *sē-* apart, aside + *vocāre* to call.]

† Sevous, *a. Obs. rare—¹.* [ad. L. *sēbōsus*, f. *sēvum* SUET.] Of the nature of suet or tallow.

Sèvres (ˈsɛvrə), *sb.* Forms: 8 Sève, Seve, 8–9 Sèvre, Sèvres. [The name of a town in France, near Paris.] The designation of a costly porcelain made at Sèvres.

Sew (sjuː), *v.¹* Pa. t. and pa. pple. **sewed**, **sewn**. Forms: 1 seowian, siwian, siowian, seowan, sēowan, sīwan, 2–3 seowen, seowin, 4 sewe, 5 suwen, 6–9 sew, (5 Sc. schew, 6–7 sow, 7–9 Sc. shew, 5–sewed, 7 sewd, etc.), 5– sew.

Sew (sjuː), *v.²* Forms: 1 sēawan, 4–5 sewe, 6–8 sew. [OE. *sēawan*, to drain, etc.]

Sewable (ˈsjuːəbl), *a.* [f. SEW *v.¹* + -ABLE.] Capable of being sewed.

Sewage (ˈsjuːɪdʒ), *sb.* [Formed after SEWER *sb.¹*.]

Sewage, *v.* [f. prec. *sb.*]

Sewaged (ˈsjuːɪdʒd), *ppl. a.* [f. SEWAGE *v.* or *sb.*]

Sewan, Sewant: see SUANT *sb.* and *a.*, SUANT.

Sewar, obs. form of SEWER, SOWAR.

Sewary, variant of SOWARRY.

Sewch, Sewcharie, obs. ff. SEUCH, SUDARY.

Sewe, obs. form of SEW, SIEVE, SOW *v.*, SURD.

Sewed (sjuːd), *ppl. a.* [f. SEW *v.¹* + -ED¹.]

Sewel (ˈsjuːəl), *sb.* [Of obscure origin.]

Sewen, obs. form of SEVEN.

Sewer (ˈsjuːər), *sb.¹* [An early ME. *asseour*, OF. *asseour*, etc.] An artificial channel or conduit, now usually covered and underground, for carrying off and discharging waste water and the refuse from houses and towns.

Sewer (ˈsjuːər), *sb.²* [An early ME. *asseour*.] *Obs.* An attendant at a meal who superintended the arrangement of the table, the seating of the guests, and the tasting and serving of the dishes.

Sewer (ˈsjuːər), *v.¹* [f. SEWER *sb.¹*] To provide with sewers; to drain by means of sewers; a method or system of draining by sewers.

Sewerage (ˈsjuːərɪdʒ), *sb.* [f. SEWER *sb.¹* + -AGE.] Drainage by means of sewers; a system of draining by sewers.

Sewery, obs. form of SURE.

Sewin (ˈsjuːɪn), *sb.* [Of obscure origin.] A kind of salmon-trout (*Salmo cambricus* or *eriox*), frequent in Welsh rivers.

Sewing (ˈsjuːɪŋ), *vbl. sb.* [f. SEW *v.¹* + -ING¹.] One who sews.

Sewing, *vbl. sb.* [f. SEW *v.²*] The action of the verb SEW *v.²*

Sevocation (duplicate)

Sew (sjuː), *v.³* *Obs.* [f. SEW *sb.*]

Sewel, var. SHEWEL.

Sewol, var. SHEWEL *Obs.*, scarecrow.

Sewster (ˈsjuːstər), *sb. Now dial.* [f. SEW *v.¹* + -STER.] A sewer; a seamstress.

sewinges i. d. 1769 Pennant *Brit. Zool.* III. 248 Taken in the river Wye, where it is known by the name of Sewin, or Shewin. 1805 Duncumb *Agric. Heref.* 17 The botcher resembles the suin taken in the Welsh rivers. 1834 *Proc. Berw. Nat. Club* I. ii. 52 The sewin will most likely prove our Scotch hirling or whiting. 1861 *Act* 24 & 25 *Vict.* c. 109 § 4. 1900 *Field* 28 July 153/1 There is not a better sea trout or sewin river in North Wales.

Sewin^2 (siū·in). Corrupt form of *sewel*, Shewel.

1886 Walsingham *Shooting* (Badm. Libr.) I. 201 A substitute for nets in covert shooting, where it is desirable to stop the winged game rather than the ground game, is commonly known as 'sewin'. 1898 *Encycl. Sport* II. 85/2 (Pheasant) The number of stops may be materially reduced by the use of the sewin.

Sewin(e, obs. Sc. forms of Seven.

Sewing (sōu·iŋ), *vbl. sb.*^{1} Forms: 3 **seuwingue, 4–5 sewinge, 4–6 sowinge, 5 sawyng, sowenge, soyng, 5–6 sewin, 5, 7, sowing,** 6 *Sc.* **schiuine, 7 soweing, soeing, 4– sewing.** [f. Sew *v.*^{1} + -ing^1.]

1. The action of Sew *v.*^{1}; the use of a needle and thread; the uniting of pieces of material (etc.) by this means. In *Bookbinding*: see Sew *v.*^{1} 1 c.

c 1290 *S. Eng. Leg.* 261/18 With spinningue and with seuwingue hire liflode heo wan. 1428–9 *Rec. St. Mary at Hill* 71 The lauendere for a hole ȝere wasshynge & sowenge ..ij s. 1484 Caxton *Fables of Alfonce* xiii, [A tayller] whiche surmounted alle the other in shapynge or sewynge. 1566 in Fleming *Mary Q. of Scots* (1897) 506 Item for schiuine and the fassoune and pontis. 1597 A. M. tr. *Guillemeau's Fr. Chirurg.* 13/3 Sowinge of a wounde is a vnitinge and coupling together of the dissevered partes with a threded needle. 1691 Ray *Creation* III. (1704) 322 To manage the Needle in Sowing and the Pen in Writing. 1872 Yeats *Techn. Hist. Comm.* 155 The rise of the tailor's art did not take the constant occupation of sewing out of the hands of women. 1874 Knight *Dict. Mech.* s.v. *Bookbinding*, A machine for folding sheets for gathering, sewing and binding.

b. with prefixed word denoting the kind.

1878 Jevons *Primer Pol. Econ.* 72 Those who were not.. wise enough to learn machine-sewing, receive better wages for hand-sewing than they would formerly have done.

2. *concr.* Work sewn; materials to be sewn; the stitches or seams of anything.

c 1400 *Lanfranc's Cirurg.* 143, & þanne bynde þe nose wiþ two bandis..þe toþir schal be leid aboue þat he mowe kepe þe plumaciols, poudre, & þe sowynge. 1565 in Fleming *Reform. Scot.* (1910) 610 Four coffarris with hir clayis and sewingis. 1706 Hearne *Collect.* (O.H.S.) I. 177 (Near to the Sewing), not at ye Top of ye Page. 1845 Mrs. M. J. Howell *Hand-bk. Dress-making* 47 No opportunity should be lost in making the sewing look well. 1865 Hatton *Bitter Sweets* iii, Mrs. Grey looked up from her sewing.

3. *pl.* Sewing thread or silk: see 4.

1844 G. Dodd *Textile Manuf.* vi. 184 Sewings are compound threads of silk, wound, cleaned, doubled and thrown, with especial reference to their ultimate use as sewing-silk. 1853 Perkins *Haberdashery* (ed. 8) 24 Cloth Sewings—coarse large skeins for tailors' use. 1862 *Catal. Internat. Exhib.*, Brit. II. No. 3656, Dyed and polished yarns and sewings.

4. *attrib.* and *Comb.*, as *sewing-work*; = employed in sewing or in teaching sewing, as *sewing-class, -maid, -mistress, -society, -woman*; of materials used for sewing, as *sewing cotton* (Cotton *sb.*^{1} 3), †*gold* (Gold *sb.* 4), *silk, silver* (Silver *sb.* 4), *thread, worsted*; of contrivances, etc. for holding materials to be sewn, as *sewing-bird, -frame* (Frame *sb.* 13 b), *-horse, -press* (Press *sb.*^{1} 10), *table*; **sewing-brod** *Sc.*, a tailor's board; **sewing-clerk**, in the glove trade, a district collector of sewing done by home-workers; † **sewing-rope**, ? some kind of rope used for scaffolding.

1875 Knight *Dict. Mech.*, *Sewing-bird,...a device for holding the work while sewing...It has assumed many forms, the bird being ornamental and holding the work in its beak. 1790 A. Wilson *Callamphitre's Elegy*, He at the *sewing-brod was bred, And wrought gude serge and tyken. 1864 Laycock *Lanc. Rhymes* 62 We couldn't have an easier job nor goin' to th' *sewin' class. 1884 *Pall Mall Gaz.* 16 May 4/1 The glove-making counties are mapped out into circuits, each of which has its *sewing clerk or commercial traveller. 1826 *Haberdasher's Guide* 13 Coloured *Sewing Cottons. 1828 *Art Book-binding* 1 *Sewing-frame, with brass or iron keys, to fasten the cords or bands. 1876 *Encycl. Brit.* IV. 43/1 When taken out of the sewing-frame the fly-leaves are pasted on. 1534 *Acc. Ld. High Treas. Scot.* VI. 191 Twa gret hankis..*sewing gold. 1566 in Fleming *Mary Q. of Scots* (1897) 505 Item of schiuine gold iiij doubil hankis. 1875 Knight *Dict. Mech.*, *Sewing-horse, a harness-maker's clamp for holding leather while being sewed. 1886 *York Herald* 23 Aug. 1/3 Useful *Sewing-maid. 1870 *Act* 33 & 34 *Vict.* c. 75 § 3 The term 'teacher' includes assistant teacher, pupil teacher, *sewing mistress. 1613 M. Ridley *Magn. Bodies* 6 Smaller wiers, *sowing-needles and such like small waights. 1779 *Phil. Trans.* LXIX. 540, I stuck the point of this sewing needle to the lower extremity of a steel magnet. 1860 Tyndall *Glac.* I. xx. 144 If a common steel sewing needle be substituted for the iron [etc.]. 1728 Chambers *Cycl.* s.v. *Bookbinding*, They are then sew'd in the *Sewing-Press. 1842 *Penny Mag.* 24 Sept. 380/2 When the book is taken from the sewing-press, an inch or two of each string is left hanging to it. 1336 *Acc. Exch. K. R.* 19/3 m. 4 *Sewenge rope [made of skin (*pelle*)]. a 1515 *Build. Louth Steeple* in *Archæologia* X. 74 Paid to Robert Beverley for 6 bunch sewing rope, o o 5. 1809 *Sporting Mag.* XXXIII. 281 The *sewing-school, the pastry-school, were then essential branches of female education. 1480 *Wardr. Acc. Edw. IV* (1830) 136 *Sowing sylk, j lb. ij unces and a quarter. 1621 in Kempe *Losely MSS.* (1836) 426 Stitching and soeing silke, 4s. 6d. 1826 Miss Mitford *Village* II. 190 Trimmings, ribands, sewing-silk, and lining. 1546 in *Extracts Edin. Burgh Rec.* (1871) II. 126 *Sewing sylver, to be sawld in punds. 1842 Dickens *Amer. Notes* (1850) 32 They have among themselves a *sewing Society to make clothes for the poor. 1875 Knight *Dict. Mech.*, *Sewing-table, a table or bench at which signatures of books are sewed to the cords or bands by which they are fastened together, and also secured in the cover. 1566 in Fleming *Mary Q. of Scots* (1897) 499 Four pound of fyne *suyng threide. 1850 Miss Pratt *Comm. Things Sea-side* iv. 247 Scarcely larger than a sewing thread. 1847 Mrs. Carlyle *Lett.* II. 15 All the *sewing women I knew of being unable to come. 1722 De Foe *Col. Jack* (1840) 343 She..took up her *sewing-work. 1612 *Sc. Bk. Rates* in *Halyburton's Ledger* (1867) 296 *Sewing worsett the dozen pound weght thairof.

† **Sewing**, *vbl. sb.*^{2} *Obs.* [f. Sew *v.*^{2} + -ing^1.] The action of a sewer; the arrangement of the guests and serving up of dishes or courses.

a 1483 *Liber Niger* in *Househ. Ord.* (1790) 37 The manner of sewing of dishes at the dressour. 1513 *Bk. Keruynge* in *Babees Bk.* 270 Here foloweth sewynge of flesshe. *Ibid.*, The borde of sewynge. *Ibid.* 286 Here endeth the boke of seruyce, & keruynge, and sewynge. 1607 Hakewill *Apol.* (1630) 430 Dinner and supper was served in with all accustomed ceremonies, as sewing, water, grace, carving, say taking, &c. 1660 R. May *Accompl. Cook* (1665) B 4 b, The Sewing of Fish...To go to the sewing of fish, muscalade, minews in sew [etc.]. [1812 Southey *Omniana* II. 71 The terms of carving and sewing.]

Sew·ing, *ppl. a.* [f. Sew *v.*^{1} + -ing^2.] That sews.

1837 Carlyle *Fr. Rev.* I. vii. iii, The fair sewing fingers.

Sewing, -ly, var. ff. Suing, Suingly.

Sew·ing-machi·ne. [Sewing *vbl. sb.*^{1}]

1. A machine designed to perform the operation of sewing.

1847 *Artizan* Mar. 65/1 Sewing Machine. A new machine for sewing has recently been invented [etc.]. 1858 Hogg *Shelley* II. 417, I thought very little of it [*sc.* Cleopatra's Needle] ..after having seen the sewing-machine in London. 1869 E. A. Parkes *Pract. Hygiene* (ed. 3) 411 Two pieces of waterproof cloth, sewn together by the sewing-machine. *attrib.* 1873 'Susan Coolidge' *What Katy Did at Sch.* ii. 37 The nice half-dozens of pretty underclothes came home from the sewing-machine woman's. 1875 Knight *Dict. Mech.* s.v. *Bobbin*, A bobbin for sewing-machine shuttles.

2. *Bookbinding.* (See quot.)

1880 Zaehnsdorf *Bookbinding* 176 *Sewing-machine*, a recent invention for the sewing of books with wire instead of thread.

Hence **Sew·ing-machi·nist.**

1881 *Instr. Census Clerks* (1885) 75 Sewing Machinist.

Sewinti, obs. form of Seventy.

Sewirer, obs. comparative of Sure.

Sewit, obs. f. Suit. **Sewl**, var. f. Sull. *dial.*

Sewn (sōun), *ppl. a.* [pa. pple. of Sew *v.*^{1}] Stitched, fastened by means of sewing. Chiefly with prefix, as *hand-sewn, machine-sewn.*

1866 *Chamb. Encycl.* VIII. 645 The operator, who keeps drawing the sewn cloth off at the eye-end of the needle. 1881 *Instr. Census Clerks* (1885) 73 Sewn Ornament Maker. 1895 *Hasluck's Boot Making* iii. 57 Shoemakers call all work sewn that is treated with a round awl; while stitching is only technically applied where the square awl is used.

Sewn(e, obs. forms of Seven.

Sewr(e, Sewrance, obs. ff. Sure, Surance.

Sewre, obs. form of Sewer *sb.*^{1}, *sb.*^{2}

Se·wster. *Obs.* exc. *Sc.* Forms: 4–5 **sewestre, -stare, sou-, sowe-, sywester(e, 4–9 sewster, 5 sew-, sowstare, 5–9 sowster, 6 seu-, sewe-, sewstar.** [f. Sew *v.*^{1} + -ster. Cf. Fris. dial. (Hinderloopen) *syster.*] A sempstress.

1391 *Earl Derby's Exped.* (Camden) 86/26 Edwyne Moreyn sewster pro filo ab ipsa empto. 1393 Langl. *P. Pl.* C. vii. 362 Sesse þe sywestere [*v. rr.* sowester, sewestare, sewestre, soustere; A. v. 158 souters, *v. r.* soustere; B. v. 315 souteresse, *v. r.* sowestere]. c 1440 *Promp. Parv.* 454/2 Sewstare, or sowstare (sowares) *sutrix.* c 1440 *Jacob's Well* 40 Taylourys, sowsterys. 1519 Horman *Vulg.* 238 Brotherers, sylkewomen, and all seusters craftis occupye redyls. 1550 Bale *Engl. Votaries* II. 29 A younge wenche..whych was a very connynge sowster. 1567–9 Jewel *Def. Apol.* (1611) 450 Labouring Women, and Sewsters, and Seruants, and Handmaids. 1590 *Maldon* (Essex) *Liber C.* 121 Le sewester sive silkewoman. a 1637 B. Jonson *Sad Shepherd* II. iii, At every twisted thrid my rock let flie Unto the sew'ster, who did sit me nigh. 1657 C. Beck *Universal Char.* K 7 b, A sewster. 1824 MacTaggart in Trotter *East Galloway Sk.* (1901) 370/1 When plowman Tam meets sewster Bess His dogg'rel rhymes he'll chime till her. 1825 Jamieson, *Sewster*, a sempstress. [ed. 1882 also *Sowster*.]

Sewte, obs. f. Suit *sb.* **Sewy**, obs. f. Sue.

Sewyn, obs. pa. pple. of See *v.*

Sewyr, obs. form of Sure *v.*

Sex (seks), *sb.* Also 6–7 **sexe**, (6 **seex**, 7 pl. **sexe**, 8 *poss.* **sexe's**). [ad. L. *sexus* (*u*-stem), whence also F. *sexe* (12th c.), Sp., Pg. *sexo*, It. *sesso*. Latin had also a form *secus* neut. (indeclinable).]

1. Either of the two divisions of organic beings distinguished as male and female respectively; the males or the females (of a species, etc., esp. of the human race) viewed collectively.

1382 Wyclif *Gen.* vi. 19 Of alle thingis hauynge sowle of ony fleħs, two thow shalt brynge into the ark, that maal sex and femaal lyuen with thee. 1532 More *Confut. Tindale* II. 152, I had as leue he bare them both a bare cheryte, as wyth the frayle feminyne sexe fall to far in loue. 1559 Aylmer *Harborowe* E 4 b, Neither of them debarred the heires female..as though it had ben..vnnatural for that sexe to gouern. 1576 Gascoigne *Philomene* xcviii, I speake against my sex. a 1586 Sidney *Arcadia* II. (1912) 158 The sexe of womankind of all other is most bound to have regardfull eie to mens judgements. 1600 Nashe *Summer's Last Will* F 3 b, A woman they imagine her to be, Because that sexe keepes nothing close they heare. 1615 Crooke *Body of Man* 274 If we respect the..conformation of both the Sexes, the Male is sooner perfected..in the wombe. 1634 Sir T. Herbert *Trav.* 19 Both sexe goe naked. 1667 Milton *P. L.* ix. 822 To add what wants In Femal Sex. 1671 — *Samson* 774 It was a weakness In me, but incident to all our sex. 1679 Dryden *Troilus & Cr.* I. ii, A strange dissembling sex we women are. 1711 Addison *Spect.* No. 10 ₱6 Their Amusements..are more adapted to the Sex than to the Species. 1730 Swift *Let. to Mrs. Whiteway* 28 Dec., You have neither the scrawl nor the spelling of your sex. 1742 Gray *Propertius* II. 73 She.. Condemns her fickle Sexe's fond Mistake. 1763 G. Williams in Jesse *Selwyn & Contemp.* (1843) I. 265 It would astonish you to see the mixture of sexes at this place. 1780 Bentham *Princ. Legisl.* vi. § 35 The sensibility of the female sex appears..to be greater than that of the male. 1814 Scott *Ld. of Isles* vi. iii, Her sex's dress regain'd. 1836 Thirlwall *Greece* xi. II. 51 Solon also made regulations for the government of the other sex. 1846 *Ecclesiologist* Feb. 41 The propriety and necessity of dividing the sexes during the publick offices of the Church. 1848 Thackeray *Van. Fair* xxv, She was by no means so far superior to her sex as to be above jealousy. 1865 Dickens *Mut. Fr.* II. i, It was a school for both sexes. 1886 Mabel Collins *Prettiest Woman* ii, Zadwiga had not yet given any serious attention to the other sex.

b. *collect.* followed by plural verb. *rare.*

1768 Goldsm. *Good-n. Man* iv. (Globe) 632/2 Our sex are like poor tradesmen. 1839 Malcom *Trav.* (1840) 40/1 Neither sex tattoo any part of their bodies.

c. *The fair(er), gentle(r), soft(er), weak(er) sex*; *the devout sex*; *the second sex*; † *the woman sex*: the female sex, women. *The* † *better, sterner sex*: the male sex, men.

[1583 Stubbes *Anat. Abus.* E vij b, Yᵉ magnificency & liberalitie of that gentle sex. 1613 Purchas *Pilgrimage* (1614) 38 Strong Sampson and wise Solomon are witnesses, that the strong men are slaine by this weaker sexe.] 1641 Brome *Jovial Crew* III. (1652) H 4, I am bound by a strong vow to kisse all of the woman sex I meet this morning. 1648 J. Beaumont *Psyche* xiv. l, The softer sex, attending Him And his still-growing woes. 1665 Sir T. Herbert *Trav.* (1677) 22 Whiles the better sex seek prey abroad, the women (therein like themselves) keep home and spin. 1665 Boyle *Occas. Refl.* v. ix. 176 Persons of the fairer Sex. a 1700 Evelyn *Diary* 12 Nov. an. 1644, The Pillar..at which the devout sex are always rubbing their chaplets. 1701 Stanhope *St. Aug. Medit.* I. xxxv. (1704) 82, I may.. not suffer my self to be outdone by the weaker Sex. 1732 [see Fair *a.* 1 b]. 1753 Hogarth *Anal. Beauty* x. 65 An elegant degree of plumpness peculiar to the skin of the softer sex. 1820 Byron *Juan* IV. cviii, Benign Ceruleans of the second sex! Who advertise new poems by your looks. 1838 *Murray's Hand-bk. N. Germ.* 430 It is much frequented by the fair sex. 1894 C. D. Tyler in *Geog. Jrnl.* III. 479 They are beardless, and usually wear a shock of unkempt hair, which is somewhat finer in the gentler sex.

¶ **d.** Used *occas.* with extended notion. *The third sex*: eunuchs. Also *sarcastically* (see quot. 1873).

1820 Byron *Juan* IV. lxxxvi, From all the Pope makes yearly, 'twould perplex To find three perfect pipes of the third sex. *Ibid.* v. xxvi, A black old neutral personage Of the third sex stept up. [1873 Ld. Houghton *Monogr.* 280 Sydney Smith..often spoke with much bitterness of the growing belief in three Sexes of Humanity—Men, Women, and Clergymen.]

e. *The sex*: the female sex. [F. *le sexe.*] Now *rare.*

1589 Puttenham *Eng. Poesie* III. xix. (Arb.) 235 As he that had tolde a long tale before certaine noble women, of a matter somewhat in honour touching the Sex. 1608 D. T[uvill] *Ess. Pol. & Mor.* 101 b, Not yet weighing with himselfe, the weaknesse and imbecillitie of the sex. 1631 Massinger *Emperor East* I. ii, I am called The Squire of Dames, or Servant of the Sex. 1697 Vanbrugh *Prov. Wife* II. ii, He has a strange penchant to grow fond of me, in spite of his aversion to the sex. 1760–2 Goldsm. *Cit. W.* xcix, The men of Asia behave with more deference to the sex than you seem to imagine. 1792 A. Young *Trav. France* I. 220 The sex of Venice are undoubtedly of a distinguished beauty. 1823 Byron *Juan* XIII. lxxix, We give the sex the *pas.* 1863 R. F. Burton *W. Africa* I. 27 Going 'up stairs', as the sex says, at 5 a.m. on the day after arrival, I cast the first glance at Funchal.

f. Without *the*, in predicative quasi-adj. use = feminine. *rare.*

a 1700 Dryden *Cymon & Iph.* 368 She hugg'd th' Offender, and forgave th' Offence, Sex to the last!

2. Quality in respect of being male or female.

a. With regard to persons or animals.

1526 *Pilgr. Perf.* (W. de W. 1531) 282 b, Yᵉ bee, whiche neuer gendreth with ony make of his kynde, nor yet hath ony distinct sex. 1577 T. Kendall *Flowers of Epigr.* 71 b, If by corps supposd may be her seex, then sure a virgin she. 1616 T. Scot *Philomythie* I. (ed. 2) A 3 Euen as Hares change shape and sex, some say Once euery yeare. 1658 Sir T. Browne *Hydriot.* iii. 18 A critical view of bones makes a good distinction of sexes. a 1665 Digby *Chym. Secrets* (1682) II. 225 Persons of all Ages and Sexes. 1667 Milton *P. L.* I. 424 For Spirits when they please can either Sex assume, or both. 1710–11 Swift *Jrnl. to Stella* 7 Mar., I find I was mistaken in the sex, 'tis a boy. 1757 Smollett *Reprisal* IV. v, As for me, my sex protects me. 1825 Scott *Betrothed* xiii, I am but a poor and neglected woman, feeble both from sex and age. 1841 Elphinstone *Hist. India* I. 349 When persons of different sexes walk together, the woman always follows the man. 1882 Tenison-Woods *Fish N. S. Wales* 116 Oysters are of distinct sexes.

b. with regard to plants (see Female *a.* 2, Male *a.* 2).

1567 Maplet *Gr. Forest* 28 Some seeme to haue both sexes and kindes: as the Oke, the Lawrell and such others. 1631 Widdowes *Nat. Philos.* (ed. 2) 49 There be sexes of hearbes..namely, the Male or Female. 1720 P. Blair *Bot. Ess.* iv. 237 These being very evident Proofs of a necessity of two Sexes in Plants as well as in Animals. 1790 Smellie *Philos. Nat. Hist.* I. 245 There is not a notion more generally adopted, than that vegetables have the distinction of sexes. 1848 Lindley *Introd. Bot.* (ed. 4) II. 80 Change of Sex under the influence of external causes.

3. The distinction between male and female in general. In recent use often with more explicit notion: The sum of those differences in the structure and function of the reproductive organs on the ground of which beings are distinguished as male and female, and of the other physiological differences consequent on these; the class of phenomena with which these differences are concerned.

Organs of sex: the reproductive organs in sexed animals or plants.

a 1631 Donne *Songs & Sonn.*, *The Primrose* Poems 1912 I. 61 Should she be more then woman, she would get above All thought of sexe, and think to move My heart to study her, and not to love. a 1643 Cartwright *Siedge* III. vi, My Soul's As Male as yours; there's no Sex in the mind. 1748 Melmoth *Fitzosborne Lett.* lxii. (1749) II. 119 There may be a kind of sex in the very soul. 1751 Harris *Hermes* Wks. (1841) 129 Besides number, another characteristic, visible in substances, is that of sex. 1878 Gladstone *Prim. Homer* 68 Athenè..has nothing of sex except the gender, nothing of the woman except the form. 1887 K. Pearson *Eth. Freethought* xv. (1888) 429 What is the true type of social (moral) action in matters of sex? 1895 Crackanthorpe in *19th Cent.* Apr. 607 (art.) Sex in modern literature. *Ibid.* 614 The writers and readers who have strenuously refused to allow to sex its place in creative art. 1912 H. G. Wells *Marriage* II. § 6. 72 The young need..to be told..all we know of three fundamental things; the first of which is God,..and the third Sex.

¶ **4.** Used, by confusion, in senses of Sect (q. v. 1, 4 b, 7, and cf. 1 d *note*).

1575–85 Abp. Sandys *Serm.* xx. 358 So are all sexes and sorts of people called vpon. 1583 Melbancke *Philotimus* L iij b, Whether thinkest thou better sporte & more absurd, to see an Asse play on an harpe contrary to his sex, or heare [etc.]. 1586 J. Hooker *Hist. Irel.* 180/2 in *Holinshed*, The whole sex of the Oconhours. 1586 T. B. *La Primaud. Fr. Acad.* I. 359 O detestable furie, not to be found in most cruell beasts, which spare the blood of their sexe. a 1704 T. Brown *Dial. Dead, Friendship* Wks. 1711 IV. 56 We have had enough of these Christians, and sure there can be no worse among the other Sex of Mankind [i. e. Jews and Turks]? 1707 Atterbury *Large Vind. Doctr.* 47 Much less can I imagine, why a Jewish Sex (whether of Pharisees or Saducees) should be represented, as [etc.].

5. *attrib.* and *Comb.*, as *sex-distinction, function*, etc.; *sex-abusing, transforming* adjs.; **sex-cell**, a reproductive cell, with either male or female function; a sperm-cell or an egg-cell.

1642 H. More *Song of Soul* I. III. lxxi, Mad-making waters, sex trans-forming springs. 1781 Cowper *Expost.* 415 Sin, that in old time Brought fire from heav'n, the sex-abusing crime. 1876 Hardy *Ethelberta* xxxvii, You cannot have celebrity and sex-privilege both. 1887 *Jrnl. Educ.* No. 210. 29 If this examination craze is to prevail, and the sex-abolitionists are to have their way. 1889 Geddes & Thomson *Evol. Sex* 91 Very commonly the sex-cells originate in the ectoderm and ripen there. 1894 H. Drummond *Ascent of Man* 317 The sex-distinction slowly gathers definition. 1897 J. Hutchinson in *Arch. Surg.* VIII. 230 Loss of Sex Function.

Sex (seks), *v.* [f. Sex *sb.*] *trans.* To determine the sex of, by anatomical examination; to label as male or female.

1884 Gurney *Diurnal Birds Prey* 173 The specimen is not sexed, neither is the sex noted on the drawing. 1888 A. Newton in *Zoologist* Ser. III. XII. 101 The..barbarous phrase of 'collecting a specimen' and then of 'sexing' it.

Sex, obs. form of Six.

Sex- (seks), repr. L. *sex* six in combination (as in *sexangulus* Sexangular, *sexennis* Sexennial), occurs in many mod. formations, chiefly scientific or technical. (In some of these Sexi- is also used.)

1. Forming parasynthetic compounds, as *sexannulate* (= six-ringed), *sexarticulate, sexcuspidate, sexlocular, sexradiate, sextubercular, -tuberculate* adjs. (see Annulate, etc.); **sexdi·gital, -di·gitate, -di·gitated** (also **sedigital**, etc. after L.) *adjs.*, having six digits (fingers or toes); **sexdi·gitism**, the condition of having six digits; **sexdi·gitist**, one who has six digits; **sexfa·rious** *a.* *Bot.* [mod.L. *sexfarius*], see quot.; **se·xfid** *a.* [mod.L. *sexfidus*], divided into six segments; **sexta·ctic** *a.* *Math.*, pertaining to or involving six coincident points of contact.

1856 W. Clark *Van der Hoeven's Zool.* I. 317 *Loxocera*,.. Abdomen elongate, *sexannulate. *Ibid.* 345 *Chironomus*, ..Antennæ filiform,..in females *sexarticulate. 1899 *Proc. Zool. Soc.* 560 In the molars..the derivation from the *sexcuspidate type is equally recognizable. 1898 *Syd. Soc. Lex.*, *Sexdigital, having six digits. 1868 Darwin *Anim. & Pl.* II. xii. 13 The child of the fifth generation would have only 1-32nd part of the blood of his *sedigitated ancestor. 1775 Ash *Suppl.*, *Sexdigitism. 1825 A. Clarke *Bible Comm.* II. 2 Sam. xxi. 20 Maupertius..says, that he met with two families near Berlin, where sexdigitism was equally transmitted on both sides of father and mother. 1880 Proctor *Rough Ways* 211 In a branch of a well-known Scotch family sex-digitism—after continuing for three or four generations—has apparently disappeared. 1775 Ash *Suppl.*, *Sexdigitist. 1900 B. D. Jackson *Gloss. Bot. Terms*, *Sexfarious, presenting six rows, extending longitudinally round an axis. 1760 J. Lee *Introd. Bot.* I. xi. (1776) 26 In respect to its Segments..it [a calyx] is.. *Sexfid, in six. 1785 Martyn *Rousseau's Bot.* xxiv. (1794) 341 The exterior calyx..in Alcea is sexfid. 1777 Robson *Brit. Flora* 34 *Sexlocular, divided into six cells, as in Asarum. 1853 Macdonald & Allan *Bot. Word-bk.* 29 *Sexlocular*, applied to a pericarpium which has six internal divisions or cells. 1874 J. E. Gray in *Ann. Nat. Hist.* Ser. IV. XIII. 288 Sponges with spicules of the *sexradiate type. 1859 Cayley *Math. Papers* (1891) IV. 228 The twenty-seven *sextactic points form nine groups of three each. 1893 *Ibid.* (1897) XIII. 387 Halphen assumes that $a^2d - 3abc + 2b^3$ is the sextactic reciprocant. 1890 *Nature* 20 Mar. 467/1 The addition of a postero-internal cusp in the bunodont series gives us the *sextubercular molar. 1899 *Proc. Zool. Soc.* 558 The unworn molars..are..*sextuberculate.

b. *Chem.* In the names of classes of compounds, denoting the presence of six atoms, molecules, or combining proportions of the substance indicated by the second part of the compound, as *sexalu·minate, sexbo·rate, sexde·cyl.* Also in other kinds of words: † **sexba·sic** *a.*, having six combining proportions of the base; **sexva·lent** *a.*, having an equivalence of six, combining with or replacing six hydrogen atoms.

1836 T. Thomson *Min., Geol.*, etc. I. 219 The mineral might be considered as composed of 2 atoms sexaluminate of magnesia 1 atom tersilicate of magnesia. 1841 Brande *Chem.* (ed. 5) 839 A hydrated sexbasic nitrate of lead is formed. 1849 Watts tr. *Gmelin's Handbk. Chem.* III. 89 Sexborate of soda. 1868 *Fownes' Chem.* (ed. 10) 632 Sexdecyl, or Cetyl Alcohol,..also called Ethal, is obtained from spermaceti. 1872 Watts *Dict. Chem.* VI. 243 Sulphur, regarded as sexvalent, may take with it into combination the quinquivalent group. 1877 — *Fownes' Chem.* I. 256 Sexvalent elements, or Hexads.

2. Combined with a numerical element: **sexde·cimal, se·xduode·cimal, sexo·ctonal** *adjs.* (see quots. 1816, 1822); **sexde·cimo** = Sextodecimo; **sexmillena·rian** *a.*, holding the doctrine of the 'sexmillenary duration' of the world: **sexmi·llenary, -mille·nnial** *adjs.*, of 6000 years.

1816 R. Jameson *Char. Min.* (ed. 2) 201 *Sex-decimal, when the planes that belong to the prism..and those which belong to the two summits, are the one six, and the other ten in number, or *vice versa*. In the same manner, we say, *octodecimal*, '*sex-duodecimal*' [etc.]. 1870 J. Power *Handy-bk.* 112 *Sex-decimo,—sixteenmo; contraction, 16mo, now called foolscap 8vo. 1851 A. P. Stanley in *Life & Lett.* (1893) I. 429 A conversation..going on between the Dean, Dr. Spry, and the *sexmillenarian C——. 1728 Earbery tr. *Burnet's St. Dead* II. 16 The Prophecy of the Jews..of the *Sexmillenary Duration thereof [*sc.* of the World]. 1684 T. Burnet *Th. Earth* II. 34 The prophecy..concerning the *sexmillennial duration of the world. 1822 P. Cleaveland *Min.* (ed. 2) I. 36 Quadridecimal, octodecimal,..octosexdecimal, *sexoctonal, &c. when..a prism or the middle part of a crystal, and the two summits have the number of faces, indicated by the several names respectively. Thus..plomb carbonaté (carbonate of lead) sexoctonal.

Sexa-, irreg. for Sex-, Sexi-.

1891 *Century Dict.*, *Sexadecimal.* 1905 Kamensky *Mendeléeff's Princ. Chem.* (ed. 3) I. 441 *note*, Sulphur is bivalent towards hydrogen, and sexavalent as regards oxygen.

Sexagecuple, *a.* *rare.* [f. L. *sexāgintā* sixty, after *decuple.*] Proceeding by sixties.

1728 Chambers *Cycl.* s.v. *Minute*, The Divisions of Degrees are Fractions, whose Denominators increase in a Sexagecuple Ratio.

Sexa·genal, *a.* [f. L. *sexāgēnī* 60 each + -al.] = Sexagenary *a.* In recent Dicts.

Sexagenarian (se:ksădʒĭnēə·riăn), *a.* and *sb.* [f. L. *sexāgēnāri-us*: see Sexagenary and -ian.]

A. *adj.* Of the age of sixty years. Also, characteristic of one sixty years old.

1862 T. A. Trollope *Marietta* I. ii. 27 A sexagenarian sire. 1889 Gunter *That Frenchman* iii. 28 He gives a sexagenarian nudge to his companion.

B. *sb.* A person sixty years old.

1738 Chambers *Cycl.* (ed. 2) s.v. *Sexagenary*, Some casuists dispense with sexagenarians for not fasting. 1826 Syd. Smith *Wks.* (1859) II. 88 The rouged cheek of the sexagenarian. 1870 Disraeli *Lothair* xxxv, Your enamoured sexagenarians.

Hence **Sexagena·rianism**, the state of being sixty years old.

1876 Hardy *Ethelberta* xlii, The sort of sexagenarianism beside which a young woman's happiness can sometimes contrive to keep itself alive in a quiet sleepy way.

Sexagenary (seksæ·dʒĭnări), *a.* and *sb.* [ad. L. *sexāgēnāri-us*, f. *sexāgēnī* sixty each, distributive of *sexāgintā* sixty.

In some dicts. of the 18th and 19th c. the word is accented *se·xagenary*, in some of the 18th *sexage·nary.*]

A. *adj.*

1. *Math.* Of or belonging to the number 60; composed of or proceeding by sixties; pertaining to a scale of numbers of which the modulus is 60.

Sexagenary arithmetic = Sexagesimal *arithmetic*. *Sexagenary table*, a table of proportional parts which shows at sight the product or quotient of any two sexagenary numbers to be multiplied or divided.

1594 Blundevil *Exerc.* I. (1597) 34 (*bis*), The Sexagenary progression is alwaies to be vsed, as well in Diuision as in Multiplycation. *Ibid.* 37 b, The description and vse of the Sexagenarie Table. 1669–70 Flamsteed in Rigaud *Corr. Sci. Men* (1841) II. 93 In the study of..Mr. Halton I once saw one [*sc.* a mathematical canon] of Vlaccus to every ten sexagenary seconds. 1721 Bailey, Sexagenary Arithmetick. 1785 Hutton *Math. Tables* 1 Ptolemy, who used the sexagenary arithmetic for this division of chords and arcs, and for astronomical purposes. 1795 T. Maurice *Hindostan* (1820) I. I. viii. 274 The emperor Yu,..who flourished.. about the middle of the third great sexagenary cycle. 1819 Jas. Wilson *Dict. Astrol.* 398 Leaving the left hand column for the seconds, but they may be made to answer to any sexagenary proportion.

2. = Sexagenarian *a.*

1638 Mayne *Lucian* (1664) 141 Though he was a Sexagenary Bridegroome. 1755 Chesterf. in *World* IV. 132 The sexagenary widow remembers that she was handsome, but forgets that it was thirty years ago. 1819 Byron *Wks.* (1846) 799/1 Having a sexagenary aunt of my own. 1821 *Blackw. Mag.* X. 88 Some will have this to be the due consequences of sexagenary decay. 1856 Mrs. Browning *Aur. Leigh* I. 1038, I count it strange..That nearly all young poets should write old, That Pope was sexagenary at sixteen.

B. *sb.*

†**1.** *Math.* and *Astr.* = Sexagesimal B. *sb.*

1668 Glanvill *Plus Ultra* 23 The Decimal Arithmetick, which avoids the tedious way of computing by Vulgar Fractions in..Sexagenaries in Astronomy. 1704 J. Harris *Lex. Techn.* I. s.v., Sexagesimal Fractions, or Sexagenaries, are such as have always 60 for their Denominator. 1728 Chambers *Cycl.*, *Sexagenary Tables*, are Tables of proportional Parts, shewing the Product of Two Sexagenaries, or Sexagena's that are to be multiplied; or the Quotient of Two, to be divided.

2. = Sexagenarian *sb.* Now *rare* or *Obs.*

1814 Scott *Wav.* xliii, The lad can sometimes be as dowff as a sexagenary like myself. 1841 Moore *Mem.* (1856) VII. 290, I..went down an English country dance of fifty couples on the stone floor, no trifling achievement for a sexagenary.

Se·xagene. *Math.* Also in L. form. [ad. mod. L. *sexāgēna* fem. sing. f. L. pl. *sexāgēnī, -æ, -a*: see prec.] A quantity or number multiplied by sixty or a power of sixty; an arc of sixty degrees. *First, second*, etc. *sexagene*: the first, second, etc. stage in ascending order of a sexagesimal scale of numeration or measurement.

1570 Dee *Math. Pref.* *ij, The Astronomers, for spede.. haue deuised a peculier maner of orderyng numbers, about theyr circular motions, by Sexagenes, and Sexagesmes. 1597 Blundevil *Exerc.* I. (ed. 2) 37 In those Tables are often vsed two kinds of denominations,..Sexagenæ and..Sexagesimæ,..the denomination Sexagenæ being set ouer any number doth signifie that the vnite of the Integrum is multiplyed by 60. But the denomination Sexagesimæ doth signifie that the vnite of the Integrum is diuided by 60. 1674 Jeake *Arith.* (1696) 233 Bring all the Circles and Signs, or Sexagenae thereof, into Degrees. 1694 tr. *Oughtred's Key Math.* 32, 53°. 09'. 34″. *i. e.* 53 second Sexagenes; 9 first Sexagenes; and 34 Unites. 1709 Manley *Syst. Math., Arith.* (1729) 77 Days also are accounted in Sexagenes, so that 60 Days make one Prime Sexagene: and sixty Prime Sexagenes, or 3600 Days makes one Second Sexagene, etc. 1728 [see Sexagenary B].

Sexagesima (seksădʒe·simă). *Eccl.* Also 4 **sexagesime**, 5 **-ym(e, -in, sexagesme**, 7 **sexagesm.** [Eccl. L., fem. (*sc. diēs*) of L. *sexāgēsimus* sixtieth, f. *sexāgintā* sixty. For the etymological meaning see Septuagesima.] In full *Sexagesima Sunday*: the second Sunday before Lent. (Also † *Sunday in S.*: cf. Septuagesima 2.) Hence *S. week.*

c 1380 Wyclif *Sel. Wks.* I. 102 Sexagesime Sonday Gospel. c 1400 *Table of Lessons*, etc. in *Wycl. Bible* IV. 685 The Sonday in Sexages. c 1450 *Godstow Reg.* 193 At the fest of Sexagesyme fyfty shillyngis. c 1450 *Mirk's Festial* 69 Þys day ys called yn holy chirch Sonday in Sexagesin. 1483 Caxton *Golden Leg.* (1892) I. 30 The sexagesme sygnefyeth the tyme of reuocacion. 1549 *Bk. Com. Prayer*, The Sunday called Sexagesima. 1658 in Morris *Troubles Cath. Foref.* (1872) I. vi. 314 Upon Sexagesima Sunday before Prime. 1710 Wheatley *Bk. Com. Prayer* v. § 9 The Gospel for Sexagesima-Sunday..admonishes us to be careful in the performance of our duty. 1883 *Cath. Dict.* (1897) 559/2 To fast three days in Sexagesima and three in Quinquagesima week. 1886 E. Miller *Text. Guide* 111 The Tuesday after Sexagesima.

Sexagesimal (seksădʒe·simăl), *a.* and *sb.* [ad. med.L. *sexāgēsimālis*, f. L. *sexāgēsimus* (see next).]

A. *adj.* Proceeding by sixties; *esp.* pertaining to, involving, or based upon division into sixty equal parts (as seconds and minutes).

Sexagesimal arithmetic, a method of computation based on the number 60. *Sexagesimal table* = Sexagenary *table*.

1685 Wallis *Alg.* vii. 20 Concerning this Process, by Sexagesimal Multiplication. *Ibid.*, The Sexagesimal Tables of Multiplication. *Ibid.* 21 The Arabs..have introduced.. their Table of Sines.., expressed in like manner by Sexagesimal Parts. 1694 tr. *Oughtred's Key Math.* 29 If there be several Sexagesimal Species joined to Integers, suppose 127. 32'. 00″. 09‴. 45⁗. 1728 Chambers *Cycl.*, *Sexagesimal*, or *Sexagenary Arithmetick*, a Method of Computation, proceeding by Sixties. 1780 M. Taylor (*title*) A Sexagesimal Table, exhibiting, at sight, the result of any proportion, where the terms do not exceed sixty minutes. 1785 Hutton *Math. Tables* 1 The sexagesimal division both of the radius and of the parts [of every circle]. 1826 *Encycl. Metrop.* (1845) I. 439/2 Stifelius ventured to simplify the sexagesimal notation. 1876 tr. *J. Verne's Adv. Engl. & Russ.* iv. 36 The length of the pendulum that beats the sexagesimal second. 1887 *Academy* 3 Sept. 144/2 The sexagesimal numeration which we employ for the division of the hour.

b. *Sexagesimal fraction*: a fraction whose denominator is 60 or a power of 60.

1685 Wallis *Alg.* vii. 19 Writers of Astronomical or Sexagesimal Fractions. 1749 S. Lowe *Arithm.* 72 Thus it is.. that Sexagesimal fractions..are reduc'd to decimal. 1858 *Catal. MSS. Univ. Libr. Camb.* III. 61 A table of the square roots of numbers from 1 to 100, calculated to three places of sexagesimal fractions.

B. *sb. pl.* Sexagesimal fractions; also, the system of sexagesimal fractions.

1685 Wallis *Alg.* vii. 20 By this way of Multiplication and Division in Sexagesimals. 1694 tr. *Oughtred's Key Math.* 29 The Conversion of Sexagesimals into Decimals. 1706 W. Jones *Syn. Palmar. Matheseos* 93 By this Proposition, Fractions are reduced..into Decimals, Sexagesimals &c. 1794 Cunn *Doctr. Fractions* 62 Sexagesimals are such places of Figures below Unity, that decrease in a 60th rate. 1873 *Rep. Brit. Assoc.* I. 25 The table is prepared as if for three places of sexagesimals. 1907 *Athenæum* 9 Nov. 589/1 The Elamites appear also to have used a decimal system of notation instead of the Babylonian sexagesimals.

Hence **Sexage·simally** *adv.*, into sixtieths.

1888 *Encycl. Brit.* XXIV. 489/1 The talent of the 80 grain system was sexagesimally divided. 1900 *N. & Q.* Ser. IX. V. 290/1 There is no utility, only needless complexity, in dividing 1° of arc sexagesimally.

† **Sexage·sime**, *a.* and *sb.* *Obs. rare.* [As next.] Sixtieth (part).

1632 W. Forster tr. *Oughtred's Circles of Proportion* 66 To reduce sexagesime parts into Decimals. Diuide the sexagesimes giuen by 60.

† **Se·xagesm.** *Math. Obs.* [ad. mod.L. *sexāgēsima* (sc. *pars*), fem. of L. *sexāgēsimus*, ordinal of *sexāgintā* sixty.] A sexagesimal fraction. Also, the sixtieth part of a degree, a minute.

1570 [see Sexagene]. 1635 Gellibrand *Variation Magn. Needle* 13 The differ. is 11^{min} MZB..which converted into sexagesmes is 11 gr. 0 min., 0 Sec. [1674 Jeake *Arith.* (1696) 233 To turn *Sexagenae* into Integers, or Decimals into *Sexagesimae*, multiply continually by 6, every time removing the *Separatrix* one place.] 1685 Wallis *Alg.* vii. 18 For 1/7, (because this cannot be exactly expressed in Sexagesms) they would put 8'. 1734 *Phil. Trans.* XXXVIII. 470 The Declination of all needles (especially if touched by different Magnets) is different a few Sexagesms.

Sexagon (se·ksăgǫn). [mod.L. *sexagōnum*, alteration of *hexagōnum* Hexagon by substitution of L. *sex* 'six' for the first syllable.] = Hexagon.

1616 Rathborne *Surveyor* IV. 114 To inscribe a Sexagon within a circle giuen. 1688 Holme *Armoury* III. ix. 377/2 A Sexagone, Hexagone, or Exagon. 1873 'Ouida' *Pascarèl* III. vi, The white sexagons of the stars of Bethlehem grew amongst the grasses. 1908 *Daily Chron.* 19 Feb. 9/6 Show-case,..sexagon shape.

Sexagonal (seksæ·gŏnăl), *a.* [f. mod.L. *sexagōn-us* (see prec.).] = Hexagonal.

1750 tr. *Leonardus' Mirr. Stones* 76 The beryl has a clear sexagonal form [orig. L. *sexagonam formam*]. 1802–3 tr. *Pallas's Trav.* (1812) I. 409 Sepulchral buildings of a sexagonal, heptagonal, or octagonal form. 1882 *Harper's Mag.* July 192 *note*, A reticulated sexagonal pattern, which gives the surface the appearance of being honey-combed.

† **Sexangle.** *Obs. rare.* [ad. L. *sexangulus*, f. *sex* six + *angulus* Angle *sb.*^{2} Cf. Sisangle (1551).] A hexagon.

1651 J. F[reake] *Agrippa's Occ. Philos.* II. xxiii. 253 Triangle, quadrangle, sexangle [orig. L. *hexagonum*], septangle, octangle, and the rest. 1788 T. Taylor *Proclus* I. Pref., As Barocius observes, why..should not πεντάγωνος and ἑξάγωνος be rendered quinquangle and sexangle. 1795 Hutton *Math. Dict.*, *Sexangle*, in Geometry, a figure having 6 angles, and consequently 6 sides also.

So † **Sexangled** *a. rare*$^{-1}$ [after late L. *sexangulātus*], = next.

1509 Hawes *Past. Pleas.* III. iv, The fayre tower..Was all about sexangled. 1730 Bailey (folio), *Sex-Angled* [with Geometricians] having six Angles, as in the Figure.

Sexangular (seksæ·ŋgiŭlăr), *a.* [ad. late L. *sexangulār-is*, f. *sexangulus*: see Sexangle.] Having six angles; hexagonal.

1608 Topsell *Serpents* 94 If you eye well their [*sc.* hornets'] nestes, you shall finde them all for the most part exactly sexangular or sixe cornered. 1637 Wotton *Will* in Walton *Life* (1670) 71 Item, A piece of Christal Sexangular, (as they grow all). 1701 Grew *Cosm. Sacra* I. iii. § 27. 15 The known Figure of Nitre, is a Sexangular Prisme. 1860 *Merc. Marine Mag.* VII. 25 The Beacon is sexangular. 1880 Günther *Fishes* 344 Teeth sexangular.

So † **Sexa·ngularly** *adv.*, in a sexangular form; † **Sexa·ngulary** *a.* = Sexangular *a.*

1658 R. White tr. *Digby's Disc. Cure Wounds* (ed. 2) 72 Armoniac salt (both form it self) in Hexagons of six points, as the snow doth, which is sexangulary. 1681 Grew *Musæum* I. iii. 35 Cancellated with little squares..on the top of the back, sexangularly. 1701 — *Cosm. Sacra* I. iii. § 21. 14 Diamonds are often sexangularly pointed.

Sexcentenary (seks,se·ntĭnări), *a.* and *sb.* [In A. 1, f. L. *sexcentēnī*, distributive of *sexcentī* 600; in A. 2 and B, f. Sex- + Centenary.]

A. *adj.*

1. Pertaining to the number 600: see quot.

1779 J. Bernoulli (*title*) A Sexcentenary Table: exhibiting, at sight, The Result of any Proportion, Where the Terms do not exceed 600 Seconds or 10 Minutes. 1842 *Penny Cycl.* XXI. 320/1. 1888 *Encycl. Brit.* XXIII. 9/1.

2. Relating to a period of 600 years.

1864 *Times* 15 June 11/3 The sexcentenary Festival of Merton College, Oxford.

B. *sb.* The six-hundredth anniversary (of an event).

1885 *Encycl. Brit.* XVIII. 98/1 Worcester College..has recently celebrated the sexcentenary of its first building in 1283 as Gloucester Hall. 1909 *Q. Rev.* Jan. 138 The sexcentenary of the birth of Dante.

† **Sexcuple**, *v.* *Obs. rare.* [irreg. f. L. *sex* six, after Decuple.] *trans.* To multiply by six.

1674 Jeake *Arith.* (1696) 200 The Square of 16, sexcupled and multiplyed by the square of 8, makes 98, 304.

Sexe, obs. form of Six.

Sexed (sekst), *a.* [f. Sex *sb.* + -ed^2.]

1. As the second element of a parasynthetic compound: Pertaining to one or both of the sexes (specified by the prefixed word).

1598, 1873 Double-sexed [see Double C. 1]. a 1616 Beaum. & Fl. *Four Plays in one* Wks. (1647) 27/2 Tie up my sight, let not soft nature so transformed be (and lose her gentler sex'd humanitie) to make me see my lord bleed. 1621 J. Taylor (Water P.) *Superbiæ Flagellum* C 6, Shamelesse double sex'd Hermophradites, Virago Roaring Girles. 1883 Meredith *Poems & Lyrics* 140 Alas, that I should have to say it! bad Is two-sexed upon earth.

2. Of an animal or plant: Having sex; not neuter or asexual.

1891 *Century Dict.*

† **Sexenary**, *a.* *Obs. rare.* [irreg. f. L. *sex* six, after Septenary.] = Senary *a.*

1815 Hutton *Math. Dict.*, *Sexenary* or *Sextuple Scale* of Notation. 1864 Webster.

Sexenna·rian. *rare*$^{-1}$. [f. L. *sexenn-is* (f. *sex* six + *annus* year) + -arian.] A six-year-old child. So **Sexe·nnuary** *a.*, sexennial; **Sexe·nnate** [after Septennate], a period of six years.

1753 W. Maitland *Hist. Edin.* II. 223 A Sexenary [*sic*, *for* sexennuary] Account of Burials in the City of Exeter. 1821 *Blackw. Mag.* X. 138 Scholars..mostly quinquennarians, or at most sexennarians. 1890 *Times* 7 Feb. 5/2 The Government contemplated the consolidation of the sexennary bonds. 1898 *Ibid.* 15 Dec. 5/1 A further increase in the navy beyond the limits of Admiral Tirpitz's sexennate.

Sexennial (seksĕ·niăl), *a.* [f. L. *sexennis* or *sexennium* (see prec.) + -al.] Continuing for a period of six years; occurring every six years.

1646 J. Temple *Irish Reb.* 81 That as in England there past an Act for a Trienniall Parliament, there may passe in Ireland another for a Sexenniall Parliament. 1676 in *Fasti Aberd.* (1854) 317 The sexennial residence of the regents and masters of philosophie in the colledges. 1790 Burke *Fr. Rev.* 300 Your new contrivance of sexennial elective judicatories. 1818 Colebrooke *Import Colonial Corn* 230 The recent sexennial period (1812–1817). 1890 *Daily News* 21 Feb. 4/6 The sexennial bonds will be consolidated in Perpetual Three per Cent. Rentes.

Hence **Sexe·nnially** *adv.* (1854 in Webster.)

Sexern, variant of Sixern.

1906 H. W. Smyth *Mast & Sail* 114 *note*, Very few 'sexerns' are now being built.

Sexfoil (se·ksfoil), *a.* and *sb.* [f. Sex-, after *trefoil, cinquefoil.*] **A.** *adj.* Having six foliations.

1848 *Rickman's Styles Archit.* Introd. 26 A small sexfoil gable window. 1906 *Proc. Soc. Antiq.* 6 Dec. 261 The chalice is 5^9/$_{16}$ inches high, with a sexfoil foot. 1907 E. A. Jones *Ch. Plate I. Man* Introd. 16 The sexfoil depression is superseded..by a single circular depression.

B. *sb. Arch.* and *Her.* = Sixfoil.

1688 Holme *Armoury* II. iv. 60 He beareth Argent, a Sexfoile, or a Sisefoile, Sable. 1828–40 Berry *Encycl. Her.* I, *Sexfoil*, or *Sisefoil*, is a grass, or flower, with six leaves, formed like the cinquefoil which has five. 1851 Pugin *Chancel Screens* 85 With images of angels in sexfoils.

Sexfoiled (se·ksfoild), *a.* [f. prec.] = prec. A.

1846 *Ecclesiologist* VI. 69 The clerestory is Middle-Pointed, of sexfoiled circles. 1851 Turner *Dom. Archit.* II. iv. 167 The highest part of which [window] is sex-foiled.

Sexhindman. *Hist.* [Altered form of OE. *siexhynde mon* (in Instituta Cnuti, c1110, *sexhende-, -hændeman*, also *sexhindus*) lit. six-hundred man.] A thane of the middle class, assessed at 600 shillings.

1729 Jacob *Law-Dict.* s.v. *Hindeni*, The middle Class [were] valued at Six hundred Shillings, and called Sexhindmen.

Sexhood (se·kshud). [f. Sex *sb.* + -hood.] The quality or condition of belonging to one or other sex; status with reference to sex.

1866 J. B. Rose *Ovid's Met.* 79 For seven long years to a changed sexhood bound. 1891 *Advance* (Chicago) 5 Mar., To lift women from mere sexhood up toward glorious womanhood.

attrib. 1869 Bushnell *Woman Suffrage* vii. 62 Their sexhood qualities of variation.

Sexi-, occas. used as combining form of L. *sex* six: **Se·xifid** = *sexfid* (see Sex- 1). **Se·xiped(e** [L. *ped-, pēs* foot] = Hexapod. **Sexipo·lar** *a.*, having or involving six magnetic poles. **Sexisylla·bic** *a.*, of six syllables; so **Sexisy·llable**. **Sexitube·rcular, Sexiva·lent** *adjs.* = *sextubercular, sexvalent* (see Sex- 1, 1 b).

1860 Worcester *Sexifid. 1847 *Blackw. Mag.* LXI. 756 The delicate monsters, the savoury *sexipedes, with whom Typee and his comrades had to wage incessant war. 1889 MacColl *Mr. Stranger's Sealed Packet* v, All the creatures ..were quadrupeds; there were no quintipeds, sexipeds, or anything of that sort among them. 1855 Ogilvie *Suppl.*, *Sexisyllable. 1854 Emerson *Lett. & Soc. Aims* (1883) 35 The decasyllabic quatrain, or the octosyllabic with alternate *sexisyllabic, or other rhythms. 1874 J. P. Cooke *New Chem.* 244 The four *sexivalent atoms of sulphur are the centres of subordinate groups connected with this nucleus.

Sexiferous (seksi·fĕrŏs), *a.* *Bot.* [f. L. *sex-us* Sex *sb.* + -ferous.] Bearing sexual organs.

1819 Lindley tr. *Richard's Obs. Fruits & Seeds* 15 There is then no such thing as a naked seed..proceeding from an ovulum with a covering that is simple, and consequently immediately sexiferous.

Sexi·llion. [f. L. *sex* six, after *million, billion*.] = Sextillion. 1850 in Ogilvie.

Se·xing, *vbl. sb. rare.* [f. Sex *v.* + -ing^1.] Attribution of sex.

1834 Gen. P. Thompson *Exerc.* III. 6 'That blind and unconscious matter cannot, by any of her combinations,' (Why *her*? This sexing is a stock receipt for mystification).

† **Sexious**, *a.* *nonce-wd.* [? for **sections*, f. Sect *sb.* + -ious.] ? Sectarian.

1592 Marlowe *Massacre Paris* 857 (Brooke), To ouerthrow those sexious Puritans.

† **Sexism.** *Obs. rare*$^{-1}$. [ad. OF. *sixiesme* (mod. *sixième*) sixth.] = Sixieme.

1688 Holme *Armoury* III. xvi. (Roxb.) 73/2 A Sexism, is a sequence of 6 cards.

Sexit, obs. Sc. form of Sixth.

Sexless (se·kslĕs), *a.* [f. Sex *sb.* + -less.] Without sex; lacking the characteristics of sex; asexual.

1598 [see Sireless]. 1714 Mandeville *Fab. Bees* (1733) II. 99, I perfectly lothe the sight of those sexless animals [*sc.* eunuchs.] 1853 Kingsley *Hypatia* II. ii. 40 Which..I must leave to be uttered only by the pure lips of sexless priests. 1865 Lecky *Ration.* I. 374 Sometimes the soul was pourtrayed as a sexless child, rising out of the mouth of a corpse. 1903 F. W. Maitland in *Camb. Mod. Hist.* II. xvi. 583 One reading of her character, and perhaps the best, makes her heartless and nearly sexless.

b. *Nat. Hist.* = Neuter *a.* 4.

1827 *Blackw. Mag.* XXII. 363 Like two sexless bees, from flower to flower, They wander'd unreproved. 1858 Lewes *Sea-Side Studies* 283 The insect which issues from the egg [of the aphis] is a wingless sexless insect. 1877 Darwin *Forms of Fl.* Introd. 6 Between the sexless, female and hermaphrodite states of these latter flowers, the finest gradations may be traced.

Hence **Se·xlessly** *adv.*, in a sexless manner; without reference to sex; **Se·xlessness**, absence of sexual power or characteristics.

1864 Jas. Manning *Possessive Argument* 56 In Wicliff's translation, 'And Mary..turnid again to *his* own house' Luke i. 56, the masculine possessive pronoun appears to be applied sexlessly. 1873 Pater *Renaissance* viii. 194 Here, there is a moral sexlessness, a kind of impotence. 1891 Eliz. R. Pennell in *Mary Wollstonecraft's Rights Wom.* Pref. 23 The new sham sexlessness of emancipation.

† **Se·xly**, *a.* *Obs. rare*$^{-1}$. [f. Sex *sb.* + -ly^1.] Characteristic of one's sex.

1601 Q. Eliz. *Sp. to last Parlt.* 30 Nov. A 3 b, Should I ascribe any of these things vnto my selfe or my sexly weakenesse, I were not worthy to liue.

Sexpartite (sekspā·ɹtəit), *a.* [ad. mod.L. *sexpartit-us*: see Sex- and Partite *a.*] Divided into or consisting of six parts.

1760 J. Lee *Introd. Bot.* I. xiv. (1776) 39 In respect to their Number the Stigma may be Sexpartite, divided into six Parts. 1775 J. Jenkinson *Brit. Plants* 234 The cup is monophyllous, sex-partite, campanulated. 1830 Whewell *Archit. Notes* 25 A roof consisting of six cells, which may be called, therefore, sexpartite. 1849 Freeman *Archit.* 367 The vaulting is usually quadripartite, but sometimes sexpartite.

Sexst, obs. 2nd sing. ind. pres. of See *v.*

Sex sum, obs. form of Sixsome.

Sext (sekst). Also 5 **sexte, syxt.** [In sense 1, ad. L. *sexta* (sc. *hōra* hour), fem. of *sextus*, ordinal of *sex* Six. In sense 2, ad. L. *sextus* (sc. *liber* book). In sense 3, ad. L. *sexta* (sc. *pars* part). Cf. F. *sexte*, G. *sexta, sexte*.]

1. *Eccl.* The third of the lesser canonical hours; so called because belonging orig. to the sixth hour of the day (midday). Also *pl.* (cf. Nones).

An early name was 'midday': see Midday 1 b.

c 1425 *St. Elis. of Spalbeck* in *Anglia* VIII. 118/7 Atte a dewe oure, and, as me menib, bytwix sexte & noon. 1446 Lydg. *Nightingale Poems* I. 342 Sygnyfinge all the tydes, ..Whech that haue be fro tierce vnto syxt. 1481 Caxton *Reynard* v. (Arb.) 10, I will now go forth, for I haue yete to saye my sexte, none, and myn euensonge. 1526 *Pilgr. Perf.* (W. de W. 1531) 164 b, All the seruyce of god & houres canonicall.., matyns, pryme, tierce, sext, none, euensonge & complyn. 1753 Challoner *Cath. Chr. Instr.* 212 Terce, Sext, and None, begin with *Pater, Ave* &c. 1805 Southey *Ballads & Metr. T.* Poet. Wks. VI. 118 'Tis the hour of noon..And the Sexts are begun. 1877 J. D. Chambers *Div. Worship* 195 On Ash Wednesday, after Sext there might be a Sermon. 1898 Chr. Wordsw. *Med. Services* 28 On Sundays and semi-doubles at Lincoln Terce was followed by High Mass; and Sext and None then were sung after the Mass.

2. *Eccl.* The sixth book added to the Decretals by Pope Boniface VIII.

1656 in Blount *Glossogr.* 1883 *Cath. Dict.* (1897) 115/1 Of these five collections—namely, the Decretals, the Sext, the Clementines, the Extravagants of John XXII., and the Extravagants Common—the 'Corpus Juris Ecclesiastici' is made up.

3. *Mus.* **a.** An interval of a sixth. **b.** An organ stop of two ranks of pipes having an interval of a sixth between them.

1876 Stainer & Barrett *Dict. Mus. Terms*, *Sext*, the name of an organ stop of two ranks, having the interval of a sixth between them, namely, a twelfth and tierce.

Sext, obs. form of Sixth.

Sextain (se·kstĕ́n). *rare.* Also 7 **sestain.** [? Alteration of obs. F. *sestine*, after *quatrain, sixain.*] = Sestina.

1639 Drumm. of Hawth. *Conv. w. B. Jonson* Wks. (1711) 226 Sextains, madrigals, and songs, echoes and equivoques.

1658 Phillips, *Sestain*, a stanza consisting of six verses. 1880 *Macm. Mag.* XLIII. 49/1 Dante..has paid him the practical compliment of imitating one of his favourite metres, viz. the sestina, or sextain.

Sextan (se·kstăn), *a.* [ad. mod.L. *sextāna* (sc. *febris* fever), f. L. *sext-us* sixth: see -an.] Designating a fever of which the paroxysms recur every fifth (according to old reckoning, every sixth) day.

1657 *Expert Physician* 123 The Quintan, Sextan, Septan, and Nonan Feavers. 1897 *Allbutt's Syst. Med.* II. 318 Further modifications have been recognised by nosologists as quintan, sextan, octan.

Sextant (se·kstănt). Also formerly in Latin form 6–7 **sextans** (7 **-ance**?). [ad. L. *sextant-*, *sextans*, sixth part (of an as, acre, etc.), f. *sextus* sixth: see -ant.]

† **1.** The sixth part of the Roman as. *Obs.*

1601 Holland *Pliny* XXXIII. x. II. 480 That purse..wherein every man put his sextant, *i.* the sixt part of an As. 1656 Blount *Glossogr.*, *Sextant*, a coin less then that called Quadrant, by the third part.

† **2.** The sixth part of a circle. *Obs.*

1596 Blagrave *Uran. Astrolabe* H 2, The Sextans of a circle. 1609 — *Dyalling* 141 Describe the Sextans, A.B.C. 1656 J. B. *Descr. Carpenters Rule*, etc. 137 The Dyal it self is in form of a Quadrant, Sextance, or Circle, according as you please. *Ibid.* 139. 1730 Bailey (folio), *Sextant*, with Mathematicians is the 6th Part of a Circle, or an Arch comprehending 60 Degrees.

3. An astronomical instrument resembling a quadrant, furnished with a graduated arc equal to a sixth part of a circle, used for measuring angular distances between objects, esp. for observing altitudes of celestial objects in ascertaining latitude at sea.

Tycho Brahe, *Astron. Instaur. Mech.* (1602) A 5, states that he gave the name *sextans* to this instrument.

1628 Burton *Anat. Mel.* II. ii. IV. (ed. 3) 264 To examine and calculate the motions of the Planets..by those curious helps of glasses, astrolabes, sextantes [1632, sextants], quadrants. 1726 Swift *Gulliver* III. iii, Stored with great variety of sextants, quadrants, telescopes [etc.]. 1774 M. Mackenzie *Marit. Surv.* 32 Hold the Sextant vertically, and direct the Sight to some Object in the Horizon, or between you and the Sky, under the Sun. 1828 Moore *Pract. Navig.* 156 Hadley's Sextant is constructed on the same principles as the Quadrant; but ..the Arch is extended to 120°..; it is also provided with some appendages not generally annexed to a Quadrant. 1860 Dickens *Lett.* (1880) II. 125 His sextant (which is about the size and shape of a cocked hat), on being applied to his eye, entirely concealed him. 1868 Lockyer *Elem. Astron.* § 520 If we require to measure simply the angular distance of one celestial body from another, we employ a sextant.

4. *Bot.* Each of a group of six segment-cells; also *attrib.*

1875 Bennett & Dyer tr. *Sachs' Bot.* 122, 123 The section of the stem now appears as if composed of six cells or sextants, whose walls are placed nearly radially, forming a six-rayed star... Hence the walls..are called sextant-walls... The sextant-cells are still further broken up. 1884 Bower & Scott *De Bary's Phaner.* 19 Then follows in each of these the division into alternately dissimilar sextants.

5. *Astr.* The constellation *Sextans*.

1795 Hutton *Math. Dict.*, *Sextans*, the Sextant, in Astronomy, a new constellation, placed across the equator, but on the south side of the ecliptic. 1875 *Encycl. Brit.* II. 817/1 The constellations added by Hevelius are the following:..—..10. Sextans, The Sextant.

Sextantal (sekstæ·ntăl), *a.* [f. L. *sextans* (see prec.) + -al.] Pertaining to or based on the ancient Roman *sextans* (see prec. 1).

1887 B. V. Head *Hist. Num.* 37 Bronze coins of the Roman sextantal and uncial systems.

† **Sextantary**, *a.* *Obs.*$^{-0}$ [ad. L. *sextantāri-us.*] (See quot.)

1656 Blount *Glossogr.*, *Sextantary*, of or belonging to the measure, quantity or weight of Sextant.

Sextar (se·kstăɹ). *rare.* [ad. L. *sextār-ius*: see next. Cf. Sester.] = Sextary.

1559 Morwyng *Evonym.* Pref., Sieth ij sextars of the juice of Roses. 1601 Holland *Pliny* XIV. xiii. I. 418 Among donatives..certaine sextars or quarts of milke have been many times given. 1656 Dugdale *Warwicksh.* 340/1 In the time of the said King Edward [the Confessor] the Shirivalty of this County..answered lxvli. in money and xxxvi. Sextars of honey. 1707 Fleetwood *Chron. Prec.* 68 In 1125, a Sextar or Quarter of Wheat, at 01l 00s 00d. *Ibid.* 73 Sir H. Spelman says, that at Paris, a *Modius Vini* holds 36 *Sextarios*, and that a *Sextar* is 8 Pints. 1774 T. West *Antiq. Furness* II. 33 [transl.], I also grant that they hall sell each sextar of ale dearer by one penny than is done at Appleby.

Sextary (se·kstări). Also in Latin form. [ad. L. *sextāri-us*, f. *sextus* sixth: see -ary. Cf. Sester, Septier.]

1. An ancient Roman liquid measure containing the sixth part of a Congius. Also used loosely = Sester 2, Septier.

1382 Wyclif *Lev.* xiv. 10 He shal take..bisides a sextarie of oyle. 1398 [see Congius 1]. a 1483 *Liber Niger* in *Househ. Ord.* (1790) 24 One sextarie of wyne; viii gallons of ale. 1559 Morwyng *Evonym.* Pref., It consisteth of v sextaries of water, ii sextaries of hony. 1607 Topsell *Four-f. Beasts* 256 Let the fasting patient..take three sextaries Warme of that milke. 1633 N. Hunt *Handmaid Arith.* 387 The Spanish Sextarius. 1679 Blount *Anc. Tenures* 76 A Sextary of July-Flower Wine. 1737 Whiston *Josephus, Antiq.* VIII. ii. § 9 The bath is able to contain seventy-two sextaries. 1809 Bawdwen *Domesday Bk. York*, etc. 291 Value in King Edward's time forty shillings and two sextaries of honey. 1833 *Penny Cycl.* I. 472 The Attic amphora contained.. seventy-two sextaries, equal to about two gallons, five pints and a half of English wine-measure.

2. A dry measure containing the sixth part of a Modius. (Cf. Sester 3.)

1382 Wyclif *Exod.* xxix. 40 The fourthe part of hyn, that is a sextarye, that is a mesure of two pownd. 1398 Trevisa *Barth. De P. R.* XIX. cxxviii. (1495) 932 Sextarius is the mesure of two pounde..and is Cenix in grewe. 1646 Sir T. Browne *Pseud. Ep.* VII. xviii. 380 If every man of the Army had had a chenix of Corne a day, that is a sextary and halfe, or about two pints and a quarter. 1674 Jeake *Arith.* (1696) 89 Whether by confounding the Attick and Roman Sextaries ..I know not. 1707 [see Sester 3]. 1737 Whiston *Josephus, Antiq.* IX. iv. § 4 The Hebrews bought a sextary of dove's dung, instead of salt. 1837 Wheelwright tr. *Aristoph. Clouds* II. i, I ask..what thou thinkest the most perfect measure, The trimeter or the tetrameter? *Str.* I think that nought beats the half sextary.

† **3.** Any of the six divisions of the city of Venice.

1617 Moryson *Itin.* I. 78 The City [of Venice]..is of old divided into six sextaries, or six parts vulgarly *sestieri*. 1651 Howell *Venice* 13 Six Councellors, whose peculiar priviledg is to be chosen out of the six Precincts or Sextaries of the Citty.

Sexte, Sexten, obs. forms of Sixth, Sixteen.

Sextend, obs. Sc. form of Sixteenth.

Sextene (sekstī·n). *Chem.* [f. L. *sext-us* sixth + -ene.] = Hexene.

1873 Watts *Fownes' Chem.* (ed. 11) 554.

Sextene, obs. form of Sixteen.

Sextennial (sekste·niăl), *a.* *rare*$^{-1}$. [irreg. f. L. *sext-us* sixth, after *sexennial.*] = Sexennial.

1814 J. Adams *Lett. J. Taylor* x. Wks. 1851 VI. 468 The legislatures of the several states are balanced against the senate by sextennial elections.

† **Sextern**^{1}. *Sc. Obs.* Variant of Sestern.

1425 *Sc. Acts Jas. I* (1814) II. 12/1 The ald boll first maid be king Dauid contenit a sexterne [orig. *sextarium*] þe sexterne contenit xij galonnis. 14.. *Assise of Measures* in *Sc. Acts* (1844) I. 310 Item þe boll sall contene a sexterne viz. xij gallonis of aile.

Sextern^2 (se·kstəɹn). [ad. med.L. *sexternum, -us*, f. L. *sex* six, after *quaternum, -us* (see Quire *sb.*^{1}), variants of *quaternio*, Quaternion.] A quire consisting of six sheets.

1885 E. Maunde Thompson in *Encycl. Brit.* XVIII. 144 Sexterns, or quires of six sheets (twelve leaves).

Sexters, rare obs. pl. of Sesterce.

1541 Paynell tr. *Felicius' Conspir. Catiline* xiv. 20 b, Who so euer wolde detect the conspiracie,..shoulde haue his freedome, and an hundred sexters.

Sextes, obs. pl. form of Sect *sb.*^{1}

Sextet (sekste·t). Also **-ett.** [Alteration of Sestet after L. *sex* six. (In sense 1, a. G. *sextett.*)]

1. = Sestet 1.

1841 tr. *Schindler's Beethoven* II. 380 Sextett in E flat, for two Violins, Alto, two Horns, and Violoncello. 1880 *Academy* 28 Feb. 168/1 A sextett in A major, op. 48, for two violins, two violas, and two violoncellos, by Anton Dvořák.

2. A stanza of six lines.

a 1850 Rossetti *Dante & Circle* I. (1874) 36 Two sextetts followed by two quattrains. 1877 Dowden *Shaks. Primer* vi. 86 Paris scatters his blossoms with one of those graceful love-speeches in the form of a rhymed sextet.

3. A group or set of six persons or things.

1873 W. Boyd (*title*) Sextet of Morse Alphabets. 1896 (*title*) A Sextet of Singers, or Songs of Six.

4. 'A bicycle for six riders' (*Cent. Dict.* Suppl. 1909). Cf. Sextuplet.

Sextetto. Alteration of Sestetto: cf. prec.

1876 Stainer & Barrett *Dict. Mus. Terms.*

† **Sexti-**, occas. combining form of L. *sextus* sixth, used in the sense of 'six': **Sextipartite** *a.*, drawn up in six copies; **Sextipartition**, division by six; **Sextise·ction**, division into six parts. *Obs.*

a 1548 Hall *Chron.*, *Hen. IV*, 12 The sedicious congregacion..made an indenture sextipartite..in the whiche eche bounde him selfe to other..for the destruccion of Kynge Henry. 1674 Jeake *Arith.* (1696) 34 Sextipartition, or to divide by 6. 1697 G. K. *Discov. Geom. Problems* 9, I shall begin with the Sextisection, and then proceed to the Quinquisection.

Sextic (se·kstik), *a.* and *sb.* *Math.* [f. L. *sext-us* sixth + -ic.] **A.** *adj.* Of the sixth degree or order.

1853 [see Quintic *a.*]. 1867 Cayley *Math. Papers* (1893) VI. 249 The discriminant of this sextic function contains the factor *c*. 1872 — in *Proc. Lond. Math. Soc.* IV. 105 On the Mechanical Description of Certain Sextic Curves.

B. *sb.* A quantic, or equation, of the sixth degree; a curve of the sixth order.

1872 Cayley in *Proc. Lond. Math. Soc.* IV. 110 The curve is consequently a unicursal sextic, or sextic with 10 dps. 1885 J. Hammond in *Amer. Jrnl. Math.* VII. 327 On the Syzygies of the Binary Sextic and their Relations.

Sextiene, obs. form of Sixteen.

† **Sextier**, variant of Sester.

c 1483 Caxton *Dialogues* 7/19 *Cannes dun sestier* Cannes of a sextier. *Ibid.* 21/8 By quarters or by sextiers, By poundes or by half poundes.

Sextile (se·kstəil, -il), *a.* and *sb.* Also 7 -ill. [ad. L. *sextilis* (in class. L. only with *mēnsis* or ellipt., as the earlier name of August), f. *sextus* sixth: see -ile.] **A.** *adj.*

1. Astrol. *Sextile aspect*, the aspect of two heavenly bodies which are 60° or one sixth part of the zodiac distant from each other.

1557 H. Baker *Rules Ute Almanacs* B vij b, ✱ Signifieth sextile aspecte: whiche is caused, by the distaunce of two sygnes betwene two planettes. 1614 Chapman *Androm. Lib.* C 4 b, Venus in aspect Sextile or Trine. 1638 Wilkins *New World* v. (1707) 40 When she [the Moon] is about a Sextile Aspect distant from the Sun. 1715 tr. *Gregory's Astron.* (1726) I. 204 If a Sixth Part of the Zodiac lies between them, they are said to have a Sextile Aspect. 1815 Scott *Guy M.* iii, Signs and planets, in aspects sextile, quartile, trine, conjoined or opposite. 1896 [see Quartile *a.*].

† **2.** (See quot.) *Obs. rare*$^{-0}$.

1656 Blount *Glossogr.*, *Sextile* or Sextilian moneth,..the moneth of August.

B. *sb.*

1. *Astrol.* A sextile aspect. Phr. *in* (*a*) *sextile*.

1592 *Greene's Vision* Wks. (Grosart) XII. 278 Canst thou ..tell the course of the Starres, setting downe their aspects, opposities, times, and sextiles? c 1650 Sir C. Heydon *Astrol. Disc.* (1650) 74 Six Sextiles equal to six aequilater Triangles, fill the whole space about a point, which is equal to four right Angles. a 1625 Fletcher *Bloody Brother* IV. ii, Mars being Lord of the Geniture in Capricorne, Is..now a Sextile here, With Venus Lady of the Horoscope. 1638 Wilkins *New World* I. (1684) 114 If you behold the Moon ..when she is in a Sextile with the Sun. 1667 Milton *P. L.* x. 659 Thir planetarie motions and aspects In Sextile, Square, and Trine, and Opposite. 1837 Whewell *Hist. Induct. Sci.* (1857) I. 176 By observation of the moon, when she was nearly in trine and in sextile with the sun. 1880 Shorthouse *J. Inglesant* xvi, Venus also casting a sextile to the cusp of the ascendant.

2. A sixth form boy at Eton.

1865 C. M. Westmacott *Eng. Spy* (1907) I. 33 He is our captain, a Sextile, a Roue. 1838 W. Cory *Lett. & Jrnls.* (1897) 3 Westmacott, Bullock, and Tarver, all sextiles.

† **Sexti·lian**, *a.* *Obs. rare*$^{-0}$. [f. L. *sextilis* Sextile: see -ian.] (See quot.)

1623 Cockeram I, *Sextilian moneth*, the moneth of August. 1656 [see Sextile 2].

Sextillion (seksti·lyən). *Arith.* [ad. F. *sextillion*, f. L. *sex* six, after *septillion, octillion.*] The sixth power of a million, denoted by 1 followed by 36 cyphers. In American (following the later Fr.) use, the seventh power of a thousand, denoted by 1 followed by 21 cyphers. Hence **Sexti·llionth** *a.* and *sb.* (in recent Dicts.).

1690 Locke *Hum. Und.* II. xvi. § 6 Sextilions. 1730 Malcolm *New Syst. Arith.* 8 Quintillions, (or a Million of Quadrillions;) Sextillions, (or a Million of Quintillions). 1861 T. L. Peacock *Gryll G.* xxi, He..adorned the surface of the ice with successions of 898, till they amounted to as many sextillions, with their homogeneous sequences. 1870 Phipson *Guillemin's Sun* 39 This sum of work is represented by 510 sextillions of kilogrammetres. 1881 Walt Whitman *Leaves of Grass, Song of Myself* xxxi, I believe ..a mouse is miracle enough to stagger sextillions of infidels.

Sextine (se·kstin). [ad. F. *sextine*, ad. Pg. *sextina* = It. Sestina.] = Sestine.

1598 Yong *Diana* 31 After she had plaied a while on it, she began to sing this Sextine following. 1884 R. F. Burton (*title*) Camoens. The Lyricks. Part I. (Sonnets, Canzons, Odes, and Sextines) Englished by Richard F. Burton.

attrib. 1823 Roscoe tr. *Sismondi's Lit. Eur.* IV. 438 Camoens also wrote some sextine pieces [orig. F. *sextines*].

Sextine, obs. form of Sixteen (*a.* 3).

1599 Nashe *Lenten Stuffe* 7 This sextine centurie.

Sextinva·riant. *Math.* [f. L. *sext-us* sixth + Invariant.] An invariant of the sixth degree.

1876 Sylvester in *Amer. Jrnl. Math.* I. 112 On the principal forms of the general sextinvariant to a quartic and quartinvariant to a sextic.

† **Se·xtiply**, *v.* *Obs. rare.* [ad. med.L. *sextiplicāre*, inferior form of *sextuplicāre* Sextuply *v.*] *trans.* To multiply by six.

1602 J. Davies (of Heref.) *Microcosmos* 86 So, some Affections our soules browes vnbend, And other some doe sextiply each dent. 1602 — *Mirum in Modum* xv. Wks. (Grosart) I. 6/2 And thus executes Their pow'res as one, though sextiplied in sutes.

Sexto (se·ksto). [a. L. *sextō*, ablative case of *sextus* sixth: cf. Quarto, etc.] The designation of the size of a book, or of the page of a book, in which each leaf is one-sixth of a sheet.

1847 De Morgan *Arithm. Bks.* Introd. 11 When he folds a sheet of paper into six leaves, making what ought to be a sexto book, he calls it a duodecimo printed in half sheets.

Sexto-decimo (seksto,de·simo). = Decimo-sexto, q.v. (Cf. Sixteenmo.)

[1626 S. Ward *Let.* in R. Parr *Life of Usher* (1686) 344 A Book of large 16°.] 1688 Holme *Armoury* III. xv. (Roxb.) 23/1 A sextodecimo booke, is of 16 leaues in a sheete. 1819 Dibdin *Typogr. Antiq.* IV. 282 Justification of Man, &c. 1548. Sextodecimo.

Sextole (se·kstoul). *Mus.* Also (Dicts.) **sestole.** [a. G. *sextole*, arbitrarily f. L. *sext-us* sixth: cf. Quintole.] A group of six notes to be played in the time of four. So **Se·xtolet.**

1854 J. Schuberth *Mus. Hand-bk.* (ed. 4) 233 *Sextole*, a group of 6 notes, having the value of 4 equal notes. 1876 Stainer & Barrett *Dict. Mus. Terms*, *Sextolet*, or *Sextuplet.* 1883 *Grove's Dict. Mus.* III. 478/1 Sextolet.

Sexton (se·kstən). Forms: α. 4–5 **segerstone**, 4–6 **-ane**, 6 **-en**, (**sequestern, segerson**), 6–7 **segerston**, 7 **seggerston**; 6 **sagar-, sacarston**, 6–7 **sagerston**. β. 5 **secristeyn**, 5 **-ane, -oun, sekyrsteyn**, 6 **secri-, secra-, secrestan**. γ. 4 **sekesteyn**, 4–6 **sexteyn(e, -eine**, (4 **-eyene, -ein**, 5 **-een, cexteyne**, 6 **cyxten, seixten**), 5–6 **sextayn(e, -one**, 5–7 **sexten**, (5 **sex(e)sten**, 6

SEXTON.

sextine, 7 -aine, -an, -in, equivalent. 6- **sexton**; 6 **saxton**, etc. [a. AF. *segrestaine* — OF. *segrestein*, *sacrestein*, -in, etc. (whence med.L. *segrestanus*), semi-popular ad. med.L. *sacristānus* SACRISTAN (of which this word is a doublet). The trisyllabic (*a* and *δ*) forms are almost entirely confined to northern texts; cf. the early quots. A 1. SACRISTAN.]

1. A church officer having the care of the fabric of a church and its contents, and the duties of ringing the bells and digging graves.

2. — SEXTONESS, SACRISTAN 2.

3. A sexton beetle.

SEXTON and subsequent entries.

SEXTUPLICATION.

Sextuor (se'kstiuɔ). *Mus.* [a. F. *sextuor*, f. L. *sex* six, after QUATUOR. Cf. *septuor*.] = SEXTET 1.

† Sextuple. *Mus. Obs.* [ad. F. *sextuple*, or ad. med.L. *sextuplus*: see next.] See quot. (= SEXTUPLE A 2.)

† Sextuary, *Obs. rare⁻¹.* [f. SEXTON + -ARY.] = SEXTONSHIP.

† Sextenary, *Obs. rare⁻¹.* [f. SEXTON + -RY.] The office or position of a sexton.

Sextry (se'kstri). Also 4 *sextri(e)*, 5 *cextrie*, 5-6 *sextry*, 6 *sextery*, 7 *sextary*. [Of obscure formation; perh. f. SEXTON after *vestry*, or an alteration of OF. *sacristie* (mod.F. *sacristie*), by metathesis of *r*.]

† 1. = SACRISTY.

† 2. The residence of a sacrist or sacristan.

† 3. *attrib.*: **sextry barn**, **land** (see quots.).

Sextuplex (se'kstiupleks), *a.* [ad. med.L. *sextuplex*, after *triplex*, f. L. *sex* six, after *quadruplex*, etc. Cf. SEXTUPLE a.] Sixfold.

Sextuplicate. *Obs. rare⁻¹.* [f. med.L. *sextuplicāt-*: see SEXTUPLICATION.] A group of six persons.

Sextuplica'tion. *rare.* [f. med.L. *sextuplicāt-*: see prec.] Multiplication by six.

SEXTUPLY.

† Sextuply, *v.* *Scots Law.* *Obs. rare⁻¹.* SEXTUPLY v. [ad. med.L. *sextuplicāre*, f. *sextuplic-*: see next.] Sextuplication.

Sextuply (se'kstiupli), *adv.* [f. SEXTUPLE a. + -LY 2.] In a sixfold manner.

Sexual (se'ksiuăl), *a.* [ad. late L. *sexuāl-is* (5th c.), f. L. *sexus*: see SEX.]

Sexualism (se'ksiuăliz'm). [f. SEXUAL a. + -ISM.] Sexuality as a principle of action or thought.

Sexualist (se'ksiuălist). *rare.* [ad. mod.L.; *sexualista* (Linnæus 1735).]

Sexuality (seksiuæ'liti). [ad. SEXUAL a. + -ITY.]

Sexualize (se'ksiuălaiz), *v.* [f. SEXUAL a. + -IZE.]

Sexualness (se'ksiuălnes). *rare⁻¹.* [f. SEXUAL a. + -NESS.]

Sexuparous (seksiu'părəs), *a.* *Biol.* [f. mod.L. *sexus* SEX + *-PAROUS.*]

Sexvirate (se'ksvaireit). [ad. late L. *sexvir-i*, after *triumviratus*: see -ATE 1.]

SEYNT.

Sey³ (sei). *Sc.* Also 8 *say*. [Of obscure origin.]

Seyle, *Sc.* variant of SEAL, young onion.

Seyn, var. SAYYID. **Seyde**, obs. f. SAID, SEED.

Seynt and subsequent entries.

SEYNTURE.

Seynt, obs. form of SAINT, SINGED *ppl. a.¹*

Seynt(e)ry, **-tuarie**, etc.: see SANCTUARY *sb.¹*

Seynt graal, obs. form of SANGRAAL.

† Seynture. *Obs. rare⁻¹.* [a. F. *ceinture*. Cf. CENTURE.] A waist-belt.

Seyny, obs. f. SENA.

SHABBIFY.

Sh, a consonantal digraph representing the simple sound (ʃ). In late OE. this sound was represented by the combination *sc*, which retained its original phonetic value (sk) only in words of foreign origin.

Sh-, sh', formerly used for *she* in certain elisions, as *sh'as* for *she has*.

Sh., abbreviation of *shilling*.

Sha (ʃɑ). † Shortened f. SHAPO.

Shab (ʃæb), *sb.* Forms: 1 *sceabb*, *sceb*, 3 *schabbe*, 4 *shabbe*, 4- *shab.* [OE. *sceabb* = ON. *skabbr*, etc.]

Shab (ʃæb), *v.* *Obs. exc. dial.* [Of obscure formation.]

† Shabbaroon. *Obs.* [f. SHABBAROON.]

Shabberoon. *Obs.* Also 7 *shabaroon.* [f. SHAB *sb.*]

Shabbily (ʃæ'bili), *adv.* [-LY 2.] In a shabby manner (see *shabby* 1).

Shabbiness (ʃæ'bines). [-NESS.] The quality or state of being shabby (in various senses).

Shabble (ʃæ'b'l). Also SHABLE.

Shabby (ʃæ'bi), *a.* [f. SHAB *sb.* + -Y. Cf. SCABBY.]

Shabble, shable (ʃæ'b'l). *Sc.* Also 7 *shabel*, *sable*. [ad. G. *schabel*, or ? Hungarian *csäbrág*.]

SHABBILY.

6. Comb. as **†shabby-looked**, **-looking** adjs.

Sha-bby-genteel'. [f. SHABBY a. + GENTEEL.]

Shabrack, shabrach (ʃæ'bræk). Also **†shabracque**, **shabraque**, **shabrag**, **schabracke**. [ad. G. *schabracke*, *schabrack*, f. Turkish *čaprak*, a saddle-cloth.]

Shabu, shabub, shawbube. *Obs.* [app. repr. G. *schabab*.]

Shack, *sb.¹* *dial.* [? Short for SHACK-RAG.]

Shack, *sb.²* *dial.* and *U.S.* [? Short for SHACK-RAG.]

Shack, *v.* [f. SHACK *sb.¹*]

Shacking, vbl. n.

Shack-rag, *sb.* and *a.* *dial.* [f. SHACK + RAG *sb.*]

Shack, a.² dial. [f. SHACK sb.¹]

Shackerell. Obs. Also a shaker(e)l.

Shackfork, dial. variant of SHAKEFORK.

Shack-haired, a. Also shack-. Shaggy.

Shackle (ʃæˈk'l), sb.¹ Forms: 1 sceonul, scacul, 3 schakil, 4 schackle, schakel, 4–5 schakle, 3 shakil, 4 schakyll, schakil, 5–6 shakyl, 5–7 schakel, 6–7 schackel, 7 schackell, 9 dial. shackle, (schackle), 9 dial. shackle. [OE. sceacul fetter, corresp. to LG. schakel, HG. dial. schakel link of a chain, ON. skǫkull.]

Shacklebone. Obs. rare.

Shackly (ʃæˈkli), a. dial.

Shackory. Obs. rare.

Shackle.¹, v.¹ [f. SHACKLE sb.¹]

Shack-bag. Also shack-back.

Shackback. dial.

Shackle-bone. Sc. and dial.

Shackle (ʃæˈk'l), sb.² Forms: 5 schaklyn, -ylle, 6 shakel, shakle, shakkle, 6–7 shackel, -shackle. [f. SHACKLE v.²]

Shackle-bolt. [f. SHACKLE sb.¹ + BOLT sb.¹]

Shackle, v.² (See Eng. Dial. Dict.)

Sha·ckle, v.³ dial. [f. SHACKLE sb.²]

Sha·ckle, sb.³ [f. SHACKLE v.³]

Shad (ʃæd), sb.¹ Forms: 1 sceadd, 6–7 shadd, (7 shad), 7, 9 ghad, 6– shad. [OE. sceadd.]

Shad, sb.² dial.

Shad-belly, U.S. [f. SHAD sb.¹ + BELLY sb.]

Shad, v. rare. [f. SHAD sb.¹]

Shadder. dial.

Shaddock (ʃæˈdək). Also 8 shattock, shad-dock, shaddoc, shad(d)ock. [Named after a Captain Shaddock: see quot. 1707.]

Shade (ʃeːd), sb. Forms: 1 sceadu, scead, scead, 3 sced, scead, 3 scade, 4 schade, 4–6 shade. [ME. schade, repr. OE. sceadu str. fem., sceadu str. neut.]

The ME. schade, mod.Eng. shade, descend regularly from the nom. sceadu of the fem., and from the dat. sceade, which is common to the fem. and the neut. sb.

I. Comparative darkness.

1. Partial or comparative darkness; absence of complete illumination.

2. Comparative obscurity.

II. Protection from light and heat.

III. Something that shades.

| SHADE. | 589 | SHADER. | SHADINE. | 590 | SHADOW. |

Shade (ʃeid), sb.¹ Also 4 schade, 8–9 dial. shad. [f. SHADE sb.]

... (dense dictionary text) ...

Shadely, obs. forms of SHADOW.

Shadow (e, obs. forms of SHADOW.

Shadine (ʃodīn). [f. SHAD sb., after SARDINE.] A trade name for the menhaden, preserved in oil like a sardine.

Shadiness. The quality or condition of being shady.

Shading (ʃeidiŋ), vbl. sb. [f. SHADE v.¹ + -ING¹] The action of SHADE v.¹ in various senses.

Shadoof, Shadouf, obs. and dial. forms of SHADDOCK.

Shadow (ʃædo), sb. Forms: 1 sceadu, 2 sceaduwe, 3 schadewe, sceadwe, sceadwe, scadewe, 3–5 schadewe, 3–6 schadwe, 4 shadewe, schadue, schadu, 4–5 schadow, schadwe, 6 schaddow, 7 schaddo, schaddoe, 6–7 schaddow, 7 schadow, shaddow, 4– shadow. [OE. sceadu.]

| SHADOW. | 591 | SHADOW. | SHADOW. | 592 | SHADOW. |

band², one of a series of parallel bands, alternately light and dark, seen passing over any light-coloured surface immediately before and after totality in a solar eclipse; **shadow-bird**, a popular name for Scopus umbretta, a bird of nocturnal habits native in Africa and Madagascar; **shadow-building** (see quot.); **shadow canoe** (cf. shadow-building); **shadow catcher** (a) one who grasps at retains trifles; (b) a photographer; **shadow-fish**, a sundial; **shadow-fight**, a fighting with shadows (i.e. imaginary foes), a fight between shadows, a sciamachy; **shadow-figure**, a shadow-fish—SCIÆNA; **shadow-grass**, (Lonnia sylvatica;) **shadow-half, -part**, 'that portion of land which lies towards the north, or is not exposed to the sun' (Jam.); **shadow-house**, a summer-house; **shadow-light**, a reflected light; **shadow-line**, (a)= line of shadows (sense 4 d); (b) a line cast by the shadow of an upright portion of the dial of a sun-dial; **shadow-photograph**, a picture taken by means of the Röntgen rays; hence **shadow-photography**; **shadow-picture**; **shadow-play**, a play in which the actors appear as shadows cast upon a screen placed between the stage and the auditorium; **shadow-plough**, **shadow-script** (? nonce-use), markings in shadow ; **shadow-stitch**, 'in lace-making, a mode of using the bobbins so as to produce delicate openwork borderings and the like' (Cent. Dict.

Supplement, p. 3873; Corrigenda, p. 4092; Spurious words, p. 4093; Books quoted, p. 4094

Shadowed (ˈʃædoud), ppl. a. [f. SHADOW v. + -ED.]

1. Protected from light and heat; furnished with shade.

2. Obscured or darkened by shadow or shadows. Also transf. and fig.

3. Represented in shadow; depicted by shadowgraphs.

Shadowgram (ˈʃædougræm), sb. + -GRAM.

Shadowgraph (ˈʃædougraf), sb. [f. SHADOW sb. + -GRAPH.]

1. A picture formed by a shadow (usually, of the operator's hand or hands) thrown upon a screen or other lighted surface; an exhibition of a series of such pictures as a form of entertainment.

2. A picture or photograph taken by means of X-rays, a radiograph.

Hence **Shadowgraph** v., intr. to produce shadowgraphs; trans. to depict by shadowgraphs, take shadowgraphs of. **Shadowgraphic** a., pertaining to shadowgraphs. **Shadowgraphist**, one who produces shadowgraphs. **Shadowgraphy**, the production of shadowgraphs.

Shadowily (ˈʃædouli), adv. [f. SHADOWY a. + -LY.] In a shadowy manner; like a shadow.

Shadowiness (ˈʃædouines). [-NESS.]

Shadowing (ˈʃædouiŋ), vbl. sb. [-ING¹.] The action of the vb SHADOW in various senses.

1. The action of affording shadow or protection from the sun; the state of being protected from the sun; protective overshadowing or shielding.

2. Something affording shade, a canopy, curtain. Obs. rare.

3. The act of casting a shadow upon something; obscuration of light; quasi-concr. shadows cast upon something. Also fig.

Shadowist (ˈʃædouist). [f. SHADOW sb. + -IST.]

1. A contractor of slabs. Obs.

Shadow-land. A place conceived as the abode of phantoms and ghosts, an imaginary land of spirits.

Shadowless (ˈʃædoules), a. [f. SHADOW sb. + -LESS.]

1. Casting no shadow.

2. Enveloped in shadow; obscured by shadows.

Shadowly (ˈʃædouli), adv. [f. SHADOW sb. + -LY¹.] In the manner of a shadow.

Shadowous, a. Obs. rare. [f. SHADOW + -OUS.] Shadowy, shady.

Shadowy (ˈʃædoui), a. Forms: 4 shadewy, schadewy, shadwye, 5 shadwy, schadowye, 6 shadowry, 7 shadowey, 4- shadowy. [f. SHADOW sb. + -Y¹.]

1. Resembling of the nature of a shadow. a. Unsubstantial, impalpable; transitory, fleeting; unreal, imaginary.

2. Of the nature of a shadow, as opposed to substance; figurative, typical. Obs.

Shady (ˈʃeidi), a. Also 7-8 shaddy. [f. SHADE sb.]

1. Affording shade.

2. b. fig. phr. On the shady side of; older than (a specified age).

3. slang. Of questionable merit or prospects; uncertain, unreliable.

Shaft (ʃaft). Obs. Forms: 1 sceaft (also 4—), 3—4 scheft, 4 shaft, etc. [Common Teut. wanting in Gothic: OE. sceaft masc.—OFris. skeft (Hettema), OS. skaft masc.), ON. skapt neut. (Sw., Da. skaft)—OTeut. *skaftu-, *skafti(z)—pre-Teut. *skabto-.]

1. Creation, origin (OE. only); make, constitution, nature or species.

Shaft (ʃaft). Forms: 1 sceaft, 3 scaeft, scæft, 3 scheft, 4 schaft, 4-5 schafft, schafte, 5 chaft(e, shafte, 4- shaft; also 5 schaffe, 6 schaff, 7 schaft, 5- shaft. [OE. sceaft masc.—OFris. skeft, MDu., Du., (also LG.) schacht, OHG. scaft (MHG., mod.G.) schaft.]

1. The long slender rod forming the body of a lance or spear, or of an arrow. Also of a staff, harpoon, etc.

2. An arrow. Cloth-yard shaft, see CLOTH-YARD.

3. b. In various Natural History uses.

4. b. A feud in the parish of St. Dunstan's, Canterbury, formed from a pole carried by the warden in procession.

5. a. Arch. A slender column, esp. one of the small columns which are clustered round pillars, or used in the jambs of doors or windows, in arcades and various other situations.

6. b. The body of a column or pillar between the base and the capital. Also the 'die' of a parapet.

7. a. One of the long bars, between a pair of which a horse is harnessed to a vehicle; a shaft.

8. The upright part of a cross; esp. the part between the arms and the base.

9. Arch. The body of a column or pillar between the base and the capital.

10. attrib. and Comb. in Sense 2 (arrow, etc.), as shaft-arm, -band, -head, -maker, shaft-armed, -like, -straight, -strong adjs.; shaft-wise adv., in cylindrical form.

Shaft (ʃaft), *sb.*[1] [L. SHAFT *sb.*[2]]

1. *trans.* To fit an (arrow-head, a weapon or tool) with a shaft.

Shaft *sb.*[2]

† Shafting.

Shaftless, *a.*

Shafted, *ppl. a.*

Shaft-eel. *Obs.*

Shafter (ʃaftə).

Shaftesburian (ʃaftsbēuriən), *a.* Also **Shaftesburean.**

† Shaftesbury.

† Sha-ftesbury. *Obs. dial. rare.*—

Shafting (ʃaftiŋ). [f. SHAFT *sb.*[2] + -ING[1].]

Shaftment (ʃaftmənt). *rare.* [f. SHAFT *sb.*[2] + -MENT.]

Shaftman (ʃaftman). *Mining.* [f. SHAFT *sb.*[2] + *man*, SHAFT *sb.*[2]] A man employed in sinking shafts.

Shafty (ʃaˑfti), *a.* [f. SHAFT *sb.*[2] (sense 9) + -Y[1]]

† Shafting. *Obs.*

Shaftless

† Shafting. *Obs.*

Shaftment, *Obs. exc. dial.* Forms :

Shaftman. *Mining.*

Shag, *sb.*[1] Forms : 1 *sceacga*, 6-7 *shagge*, 7-9 *shagg*, 7-9 *shag*, etc. [OE. *sceacga*]

b. *Westminster School slang.* (See quot. 1902.)

Shag, *sb.*[2] [A. tow, rascally fellow.

Shag, *sb.*[3], variant of SHACK *sb.*[3]

Shag (ʃæg), *sb.*[4] A. Now *rare* or *arch.* Also 6 **shagg**, 7 **shagge.** [From attrib. use of SHAG *sb.*[1]]

1. Having shaggy hair.

† Shag-barked.

Shagbot (ʃæˑgbɒt), *a.*, *bush*, **-but**, *obs. H. SACKBUT*[1].

Shagganette, *obs. form of* SAGAMITÉ.

Shagaamuffin, *obs. var. of* SHAGREEN, CHAGRIN *q.v.*

Shagged (ʃæˑgd), *ppl. a.* Now *rare.* Forms : 1 *sceaʒede* (*sceaʒode*), 6 **shagg'd**, 7 **shag'd**, 7 **shagg'd**, etc. [OE. *sceaʒede*, f. *sceacga* SHAG *sb.*[1] See -ED[2].]

1. Having or covered with shaggy hair ; rough with hair. Chiefly and of animals.

Shag (ʃæg), *v.*[1] [f. SHAG *sb.*[1]]

1. *trans.* To be shaggy ; to hang down in a shaggy manner. *Obs.*

Shag (ʃæg), *v.*[2]

† Shagamuffin, *Obs. rare*—[1]. [Alteration of RAGAMUFFIN, after SHAG *sb.*[4]] A term of abuse.

c. Jagged ; having a rough, uneven surface.

2. Of plants, etc. : Long and rough ; shaggy.

3. *transf.* Of plants, etc. : Long and rough ; shaggy.

Shaggily (ʃæˑgili), *adv.* [-LY[2]] In a shaggy manner ; so as to be shaggy.

Shagginess (ʃæˑginɛs). [f. SHAGGY *a.* + -NESS.] The quality of being shaggy.

Shagreen, Shaggrin, *see* SHAGREEN, CHAGRIN.

Shaggy (ʃæˑgi), *a.* Also 6-7 **shaggie**, 8 **shaggy.** [f. SHAG *sb.*[1] + -Y[1].]

1. Covered with or having long coarse or bushy hair. Of persons : Unkempt.

2. Consisting of or resembling rough shaggy hair.

3. Of textile material : Having a long, rough nap ; rough or coarse in texture.

4. *fig.*

5. Of persons or animals : Covered with coarse bushy hair.

6. Of a skin, or garment, etc. : Covered with coarse bushy hair.

c. Of a textile material : Having a long, rough nap ; rough or coarse in texture.

† Shag-hair, *a.* and *sb.* [f. SHAG *sb.*[1] + HAIR *sb.*] = next. *sb.* A 'shag-haired' person.

Shag-haired, *a.* arch. [f. SHAG *a.* + HAIRED *a.*]

† Shag-rag, *sb.* and *adj.*

† Bla-gling, *vbl. sb.*

Shag-rag (ʃæˑgræg), *sb.* and *a.* dial. [f. SHAG *sb.*[1] and RAG *sb.*] A. *sb.* A ragged, disreputable person ; a low rascal. B. *adj.* Ragged, rascally.

Shagreen (ʃægrīn). Also 7-8 **shagrin**, **shagreen**, 8 **shaggreen**, 7-9 CHAGRIN. [Var. CHAGRIN *sb.*]

1. A species of untanned leather with a rough granular surface, prepared from the skin of the horse, ass, etc., or of the shark, seal, etc., and frequently dyed green.

b. *attrib.* or as *adj.*

Shagreen (ʃægrīn), *v.* [f. prec., or ad. F. *chagriner*, f. *chagrin*.]

Shagreened (ʃægrīnd), *ppl. a.* [f. prec. + -ED[1].] Covered with or having the appearance like 'shagreen' or shark-skin.

Shah (ʃā). Forms : 6 **schaw**, 6-7 **shaugh**, 7 6-9 **shaw**, 7 **shabaw**, 7-8 **shaw**, 7-8 (*s*)**haoh**, **schah**, **sha**, 9 **shauh**, 7 **shaugh**, 7-8 **shaw**, 9 **shah.** [Pers.]

Shaik, variant of SHEIKH.

Shail (ʃeɪl), *v.* Obs. exc. *dial.* Forms : 4-5 **schayle**, 5 **schaile**, (6 **shayle**, **scaile**), 6 **shayle**, 7-9 **shail.** [Possibly a metathetic derivative of OE. *sceolh* oblique.]

Shaird, Shairn, *see* SHARD, SHERD.

Shak, *obs. f.* SHACK, SHAKE.

Shako (ʃæˑkoʊ). Forms : 8-9 **schako**, 8-9 **shako**, 9 **chaco**, **schako**, **shakos**, *pl.* **shakoes**. [a. F. *schako*, ad. Hungarian *csákó.*]

Shale (ʃeɪl), *sb.*[1] Also 7-8 **shaile**, **shayle**. [a. G. *schale* shell, husk, peel, rind.]

Shale (ʃeɪl), *sb.*[2] *rare.* [ad. G. *schale* bowl.]

Shale (ʃeɪl), *v.*[1] [f. SHALE *sb.*[1]]

Shale, *v.*[2] *obs. or dial. f.* SHEAL.

Shall (ʃæl, ʃəl), *v.* Pa. t. **should** (ʃʊd, ʃəd). Forms : see below. [A common Teut. verb.]

Shallop (ʃæˑləp), *sb.* Also 6-7 **shalop**, 7 **challop**, **shalup**, **shallope**. [a. F. *chaloupe.*]

Shallot (ʃəˈlɒt). [Aphetic f. ESCHALOT.]

Shake (ʃeɪk), *sb.*[1] [f. SHAKE *v.*]

1. The act of shaking ; an instance of this ; a shaking movement.

2. The shaking out of corn from the ear. Also in comb. *shake-time.* Cf. SHACK *sb.*[1]

3. A crack or fissure in timber, etc.

Shake (ʃeɪk), *v.* Pa. t. **shook** (ʃʊk) ; pa. pple. **shaken** (ʃeɪˑkn). Forms : see below. [A common Teut. verb.]

SHAKENLY.

2. Moved generally, with a blow or shock; hence, weakened in structure.

Shakenly, *adv. rare.* [-LY².] In a shaken manner.

Shaker (ʃeɪ·kər). Also ʒ schakare, -ere, 6 *Sc.* schakar, (var.), schaccare. [f. SHAKE v. + -ER¹.]

1. One who or something which shakes (in the transitive senses of the verb).

†3. A person of loose life. *Obs.*

†4. *a.* In the 17th c. applied to various sectaries whose devotional exercises were accompanied by 'shaking' or convulsions; often used as equivalent to QUAKER. *Obs.*

Shakeress, a female Shaker. **Sha·kerism**, the principles and practice of Shakerism.

Shakescene (ʃeɪ·kskiːn). *arch. rare.* [f. SHAKE v. + SCENE *sb.*] An allusion to the name Shakspere.

Sha·ke-rag, *sb.* and *attrib.* or *adj.*, beggarly.

Shakescene: *see* SHAKERISM, *etc.*

Shakily (ʃeɪ·kɪli), *adv.* [f. SHAKY *a.* + -LY².]

SHAKING.

Shakiness (ʃeɪ·kinɛs). [f. SHAKY *a.* + -NESS.] The condition of being shaky.

Shaking (ʃeɪ·kɪŋ), *vbl. sb.* [-ING¹.]

1. The action of the verb SHAKE, in any sense.

†b. The gathering, harvesting, falling or shedding (of fruit or grain). *lit.* and *fig. Obs.*

7. *pl. and Comb.* The QUAKING-GRASS, *Briza media*; also *shakshakers* and *Sc. silver shakers.*

†c. *pl.* Shaking of the sails.

Shako (ʃæ·koʊ). Also schakos, schako; and *vars.* [ad. F. *shako.*]

Shakudo (ʃæ·kudoʊ). [a. Japanese *shakd dō*, *ad.* an older form of Chinese *ch'ih t'ung* red copper.] A Japanese alloy of copper and gold.

Shaky (ʃeɪ·ki), *a.* Also shakey. [f. SHAKE v. *sb.*¹ + -Y¹.]

1. Of timber: Fissured = SHAKEN 2.

SHALE.

Shale (ʃeɪl), *sb.*¹ Also shail, shale. [OE.]

Shale, *sb.*² Also shail, 9 shail. [OE.]

Shalder, *sb.*¹ Also 9 shalder, schalder, shaalder. [Of obscure origin.]

SHALE.

Shale, *variant of* SHALE *sb.* and *v.*¹

Shaleman, obs. form of SPAWN.

†Shaler, *sb.*² rare⁻¹. [f. SHALE v. + -ER¹.] One who 'shales' or shells.

†Shaler *v.* rare⁻¹. [f. *prec.* or SHALE *sb.*²] To shell.

Shaling, *vbl. sb.* Obs. [f. SHALE v.¹ + -ING.] The action of removing the outer shell or husk; also *pl.* the shell or husks removed.

Shalk, obs. form of CHALK *sb.*

SHALL.

Shall (ʃæl), *v.*¹ [A common Teut. vb.: OE. *sceal*, *scal*, etc.]

A. Inflexional Forms.

I. Present tense.

B. Signification.

SHALL.

schald and *comb.*, simple *attrib.*, as *shale*
the gray alum rock of this place.

*** The past tense *should* with modal function.

Shalloon (ʃæˈluːn), *sb.* [a. F. *chalon*, *chalons*, f. *Chalons*, name of a town.] A closely woven woollen material chiefly used for linings.

Shallop (ʃæˈləp). [a. F. *chaloupe*.] 1. A light open boat.

Shallot, shalot (ʃæˈlɒt). Also 7 shelot, 9 shalott, scallotti. [a. F. *échalote*, OF. *eschalotte*, *escalongne*.] A small onion used for flavouring.

Shallow (ʃæˈloʊ), *a.* and *sb.* Forms: 4-5 schalowe, 5-7 shalowe, 6 Sc. scholow, 6-7 shallowe, 7-9 shallow, 8 shallow, shalloop, 8 shallow, shalloon. See also Shoal. [Of obscure origin.]

Shallowed, *ppl. a.* [f. SHALLOW v.]

Shallowing (ʃæˈloʊɪŋ), *vbl. sb.* [f. SHALLOW v.] The action of the vb.; a making or becoming shallow.

Shallowly (ʃæˈloʊlɪ), *adv.* [f. SHALLOW a. + -LY².] In a shallow manner.

Shallowness (ʃæˈloʊnɪs). [f. SHALLOW a.] The quality of being shallow.

Shallow, *v.* [f. SHALLOW a.]

Sha'ly, Anglicized var. of CHALLIS, *sb.*

Shalt (ʃælt, ʃɒlt), 2nd *Sc. dial.* Also q shault, shawlt. [See SHALL v.]

Shaly, *a.* [f. SHALE *sb.*² + Y¹.]

Sham (ʃæm), *sb.*¹ and *a.* Also 7 shamm. [Of obscure origin: the word first appears as slang in 1677.]

Sham, *v.* [See SHAM *sb.*]

Shama (ʃɑːmə). [Hindi *shāmā*.] A cereal cultivated in India, *Panicum frumentaceum* (colmanii).

Shamable, *a.* [f. SHAME *sb.* + -ABLE.]

Shamalo (Telugu *Shamā*lō). See SHAMA.

Shaman (ʃæˈmæn, ʃɑːmən). Also shamaan. [a. Ger. *Schamane*, Russ. *shamán*, f. Tungus *saman*.] A priest-doctor among various tribes of Asia.

Shameful. Forms: see SHAME sb. and -FUL. [f. SHAME sb. + -FUL.]

†1. Modest, shamefaced. Obs.

2. Full of shame; that brings shame; disgraceful.

3. That brings to shame; that causes or ought to cause shame; disgraceful, scandalous.

†4. Shameful parts: the secret parts, organs of sex.

†5. Applied to language: Casting shame, opprobrious, vituperative. Obs.

Shamefully, adv. [f. SHAMEFUL a. + -LY.]

1. In a manner that causes shame or disgrace; with indignity; disgracefully.

Shamefulness. [f. SHAMEFUL a. + -NESS.]

†1. Sense of shame or disgrace. Also, bashfulness, modesty. Obs.

Shameless, a. Forms: see SHAME sb. and -LESS. [OE. sc(e)amléas, sc(e)omléas: see SHAME sb. and -LESS.]

1. Lacking shame, destitute of feelings of modesty; impudent, audacious, immodest; insensible to disgrace.

2. Indicating or characterized by absence of shame or modesty. Of actions: Indicating absence of shame on the part of the agent, impudent.

Shamelessly, adv. [f. prec. + -LY.] In a shameless manner, without shame.

Shamelessness. [f. SHAMELESS a. + -NESS.]

1. The quality of being destitute of shame or modesty; impudence.

2. In a good or neutral sense: Freedom from shame, unashamedness.

Shamer. rare. [f. SHAME v. + -ER.] One who or something which shames.

Shametise, obs. form of CHAMETISE adv.

Sha'mevous, a. Obs. [f. SHAME sb. after beauteous, plenteous. Cf. SHAMEVOUS¹.] Shameful, disgraceful.

Shamew, Shamewe, obs. forms of CHAMOIS.

Shami, variant of SHAMMY sb.

Shamiana, Shamianah, variant of SHAMIANA.

Shamir. [Heb.] 'An awning or fat tent-roof without sides' (Yule); a flat awning or canopy.

Sha'moise, a. Obs. [f. SHAM sb.] Of the nature of a sham; hoax, or trued.

Shamly, obs. form of SHAMBLE sb.

Shaming, vbl. sb. [f. SHAME v. + -ING¹.] The action or fact of putting to shame.

Sha'ming, ppl. a. [f. SHAME v. + -ING¹.] That shames or puts to shame.

Shamle, Shamly, var. SHAMBLE sb.¹, SHAMELY.

† **Shammade,** var. CHAMADE. Obs.

Shammar, obs. form of SHAMMER.

Shammas, variant of SHAMMES.

Shamble, obs. form of SHAMBLE sb.¹

Shammar, obs. form of SHIMMER.

Shammatize, obs. form of SHAMMATIZE adv.

† **Sha'mmatize,** v. Obs. [ad. Heb. shammath excommunication, whence the denom. vb. shammith to excommunicate.] trans. To excommunicate.

Shammer. [f. SHAM sb. + -ER.] One who shams.

† **Sha'mmish,** a. Obs. [f. SHAM sb. + -ISH.] Of the nature of a sham.

Shammel, obs. form of SHAMBLE sb.¹

Shammy. Also 7 shammie, 8 shamy, shammoy. [f. CHAMOIS 2.] trans. To prepare (leather) by working oil or grease into the skin.

Shammy, sb. and a. Forms: 7 shamoy, chamois; also 8-9 shammy, chammy... Also 7 shammie, 8 shammee. [A later form of CHAMOIS.]

Shammock, sb. and v. dial. Also shammuck. trans. To walk with a shambling or unsteady gait; to slouch; to dawdle.

† **Shamo'is,** sb. Obs. var. of CHAMOIS.

Shamois, obs. form of CHAMOIS.

Shamoy, obs. forms of SHAMMY.

Shampoo, v. Also 8-9 shampo, champoo, champo, shampou, shampou. [Hind. châmpo, imper. of châmpnā to press.]

1. trans. To subject (a person, his limbs) to massage.

2. (The ordinary modern sense.) To subject (the scalp) to washing and rubbing with some cleansing agent, as soap and water, shampoo powder, etc.

Shampooing, vbl. sb.

Shampoo, sb. The action or operation of shampooing.

Shamrock, sb. Forms: 6 shamrote, 7 shamrock; also 6-7 shamroke, sham-rock. [Ir. seamróg, dim. of seamar trefoil, clover.]

1. A plant with trifoliate leaves, used (according to a late tradition) by St. Patrick to illustrate the doctrine of the Trinity, and hence adopted as the national emblem of Ireland; a spray or leaf of this.

This Plant is worn by the People...upon...St. Patrick's Day. It being a current Tradition, that by this Three-Leaded Grass, he endeavoured to set forth to them the Mystery of the Holy Trinity.

Shamsheer. Also 7 shemsheer, 9 shumsheer. [Pers. ...] shamshir. = SCIMITAR 1.

Shan, sb.³ of obscure origin. The name of one of the fighting factions into which the peasantry of the South of Ireland were formerly divided.

Shandry, variant of SHANDRYDAN.

Shandrydan, sb. Also shandry-dan, shandridan, -radan, shan-dradan; shandardan, -ery-dan, -eradan; shat-terydan, shatteradan. [Of obscure origin.]

Shandy, sb. North-country dial. Also shandree, shandry. Fresh, shortened from next, which however is later in our quots.

Shandy, a. Also shandee. [Of obscure origin; connexion with OE. scand masc.]

Shanghai, sb. [f. Shanghae, -hay. Cf. Shanghai or Shanghai, the name of one of the chief seaports of China.]

1. A long-legged, large breed of domestic fowls, with feathered shanks, reputed to have been introduced from Shanghai; now developed into the brahma and cochin.

Shanghai, v. trans. Naut. slang. (orig. U.S.) To drug or otherwise render insensible, and ship on board a vessel wanting hands.

Shangy, Shangie, sb. Sc. and north. Also shangie. A shackle; a... hook or tackle to which a cow is bound in the byre.

Shank, sb. Forms: 1 sconca, sceanca, scanca, 3 schanke, scanke, 4-6 shanke, 5-6 shank, schank, shanke, shancke, 6-7 shanke, 6- shank. [OE. sceanca masc., sconca masc., scanca masc.]

1. That part of the leg which extends from the knee to the ankle; the tibia or shin-bone. Also (now popularly) the leg as a whole; chiefly pl.

2. The part of the leg corresponding to this in other animals.

3. a. In various technical uses: The stem or straight part of anything.

b. The straight part of a nail or pin, between the head and the point.

c. The lower part of the foreleg of some animals, spec. of a horse, that part between the so-called knee and the fetlock, corresponding to the metacarpus.

d. Sc. A stocking; the part of this which covers the leg; esp. a stocking in process of being knitted.

e. Sc. The shaft of a gallows.

Shank-bone. The tibia of an animal.

Shanked (ʃæŋkt), a. [f. SHANK sb. and v. + -ED.]

Shanker, obs. form of CHANCRE.

Shanking, vbl. sb. [f. SHANK v. + -ING.]

Shannachie, variant of SENNACHIE.

Shannon, obs. form of CHANNEL.

Shanny (ʃæ·ni), sb. An artificial salmon fly used of the river Shannon in Ireland. In full Shannon fly.

Shanny, a. dial. Bashful, shy.

Shanny, variant of SHANNY a. dial.

Shant, variant of SHANT'A a. dial.

Shant (ʃænt). slang. [f. SHANTY sb.] A quart, a pot; a pot of drink.

Shank (ʃæŋk), sb. [f. SHANK sb.]

Shank, variant of CHANK.

Shantee, obs. form of SHANTY.

Shantihrews (intr.v.) Sc. Also q shawin-trewse, shantruse. ['Gael. seun-triubhas, old trousers.'] The name of a Highland tune and dance.

Shanting (ʃæntɪŋ). [f. the name of a province of North-east China where it is manufactured.] A soft undressed Chinese silk (formerly undyed, since 1907 dyed to any shade of colour).

Shanty (ʃæ·nti), sb. [prob. corruptly a. F. chantier (see CHANTIER) used in Canada in the sense: 'an establishment regularly organized in the forests in winter for the felling of trees; the head-quarters at which the woodcutters assemble after their day's work' (Clapin, Dict. Canad.-Fr., 1894).]

Shanty (ʃæ·nti), v. [f. SHANTY sb.] intr. To live in a shanty or temporary log hut.

Shap (ʃæp). [a. F. chape in the same sense (Littré Suppl.)] (See quot. 1924.)

Shapable, Shapeable, variant of SHAPABLE.

† **Sha·pand**, sb. rare⁻¹. Also a schaphand. obs.

Shape (ʃēp), sb. Forms: 1 æscæp, 3030 æp, scæap, 2-6 schap, 5 scaap, scape, schape, 3 (Orm.), 3 schape, 3-7, 9 dial. shap, 4-6 schapp(e, 4-7 shapp, 5 chap, 6 schaip, 6 schap, 7 schaip, 6 chape, 9 dial. shap; 4-5 schape, 4-6 schapp, 4-7 shape, 7 shape.

Shape (ʃēp), v. 1. 1 shaped (ʃēpt), ppl. shaped (ʃēpt), arch. shapen (ʃē·pən). Forms: Inf. and pres.-stem. 1 sceppan, scyppan, 4-6 schape, 7 schap, shape.

Shapeless (ʃē·plĕs), a. [f. SHAPE sb. + -LESS.] 1. Without shape or form; having no definite or regular shape.

Shapel (ʃē·pĕl), a. [f. SHAPE sb. + -FUL.] † 1. Having a (specified) shape.

Shapable, shapable (ʃē·pab'l), a. [f. SHAPE v. + -ABLE.] 1. Capable of being shaped, plastic.

Shapeau, obs. form of CHAPEAU.

Shapely (ʃē·pli), a. [f. SHAPE sb. + -LY.] 1. Having a pleasing shape or appearance.

Shapelessness. Destitute of beauty or elegance of form, unshapely.

Shapeliness (-prj'lines). [f. SHAPELY a. + -NESS.] The condition of being shapely.

Shapeling. Obs. rare⁻¹. [f. SHAPE sb. + -LING 2.] A small form or embryo.

Shapely (ʃēˈplɪ). a. Also 4-5 shaply, (4 schaplíche, sohaply(t), suhap(p)uly, comparatíve schapelokest), 4-6 schaply. [f. SHAPE sb. + -LY¹. (OE. had *gesceáplic adv., fitly).]

1. Fit, likely, suitable; also like (recommended, commendable). Obs.

2. One who or something destined (in the required shape; one who fashions (material).

Shaper (ʃēˈpəɹ). [f. SHAPE v. + -ER¹.] 1. The Creator or Maker (of the universe). Obs.

2. One who or something which fashions or makes (material).

b. spec. in various trades, the designation of an operative. Also shaper up.

3. A machine or tool for shaping material, etc. a shaping-machine (see SHAPING vbl. sb. 4).

4. attrib. and Comb.

Shaping (ʃēˈpɪŋ), vbl. sb. [f. SHAPE v. + -ING¹.] 1. The shaping, or the giving shape to.

Shaping (ʃēˈpɪŋ), ppl. a. [f. SHAPE v. + -ING².] That shapes, in the senses of the verb.

Shapio(u)n. Sc. Obs. In 6 sch-. [Of obscure formation; related to F. chapeau hat.] Some kind of head-dress.

Shapoo. Obs. f. CHAPOO Her. Obs.

Shapoo (ʃəˈpuː). Also shapu, shapur; shortened SHA. [Tibetan sha-pho 'wild sheep' (Jaeschke).] A kind of sheep (Ovis vignei) found in Ladák (Kashmir) and Tibet.

Shapournet, obs. f. CHAPOURNET Her. Obs.

Shapparcon, shapperoon, obs. f. CHAPERON.

Shappen, shappo, etc. B. CHEVEAU.

Shapster, -yster, variant SHEPSTER.

Shaps (ʃæps), sb. pl. U.S. Also chaps. [Shortened from Mexican Sp. chaparejos.] Leather riding breeches.

Shapy. obs. f. variant of SHEAR v.

Shar, obs. f. SHEAR v.

Sharan, dial. variant of SHARN.

Sharawaggi, -dzi. Also sharawadgi. [Of unknown origin.]

Shard, shard (ʃɑːd, ʃɑ̀d). sb.¹ Forms: 1 sceard, 4 shord, 4-5 schorde, 5 schorde. [OE. sceard.]

Shard (ʃɑːd), sb.² Variant of CHARD.²

Shard (ʃɑːd), v.¹ [f. SHARD sb.¹]

Shard-born, -borne, a.

Share (ʃɛəɹ), sb.¹ Forms: 1 scear, scear, scar, 4 schar, schaar, 4-6 share. [OE. scear, scaer, cutting, division (recorded in the senss ‘consure' and 'division or fork of the body'; SHEAR sb.).] 1. The part or portion (of something) which is allotted or belongs to an individual, when distribution is made among a number; also, the portion or quota which is contributed by an individual.

2. A part taken in (an action, experience, etc.).

3. The cause; a definite portion of a property owned by a number in common; spec. each of the equal parts into which the capital of a joint-stock company or corporation is divided.

Share (ʃɛəɹ), sb.² scear, share, 4-6 share. Also 4 SKAIR. [ME. share, schar:—OE. scearu str. fem., cutting, division.] 1. The part of (something) that is allotted or belongs to an individual.

Share (ʃɛəɹ), v. [f. SHARE sb.¹] 1. trans. To divide and apportion in shares between two or more recipients.

2. Of two or more persons: To share with (a person) in something.

Sharer (ʃɛəˈɹəɹ). [f. SHARE v. + -ER¹.] 1. One who shares (const. of or in the verb).

Supplement, p. 3873; Corrigenda, p. 4092; Spurious words, p. 4093; Books quoted, p. 4094

an effectual sharer in the virtue of his intercession.

¶ 2. A member of a company of players, who paid the expenses, and received the profits, and employed the 'journeymen' members of the company.

† b. A shareholder, one who owns a share in a joint concern.

Sharevort : see SHARE *sb.²* b.

Sharg (ʃarg). In 7 **sh̄arge**. [a. Gael. *searg.*] = next.

Shargar (ʃaˑrgaɹ). *Sc. Also* **sharger**. [Altered form of prec.] A lean, thin, stunted person or animal; a weakly child. *Also attrib.*

Sharing (ʃëˑrⁱŋ), *vbl. sb.¹* [f. SHARE *v.¹* + -ING¹.] The action of SHARE *v.¹*

Sharing (ʃëˑrⁱŋ), *ppl. a. Obs.* [f. SHARE *v.¹* + -ING².] That shares or shears.

Shark (ʃaɹk), *sb.¹* *Also* 6-7 **sharke.** Of obscure origin.

1. A selachian fish of the sub-order *Squali* of the order *Plagiostomi*, in popular language chiefly applied to the large voracious fishes of this suborder, as the genera *Carcharodon*, *Carcharias*, etc.

b. *Comb.* **Angel-shark,** an Angel-shark, the monk-fish, *Squatina angelus*; **Gangetic shark,** *Carcharias gangeticus*, inhabiting some rivers; **Greenland shark,** the North Atlantic shark *Læmargus borealis*; **Grey shark,** the small shark *Carcharinus americanus*; **Hammer-headed shark,** the *Zygæna malleus*; **†Long-tailed shark,** the Fox-shark; **Sea-shark,** a shark of the high seas, esp. 'a large shark of the family *Lamnidæ*'.

b. *Comb.* **Shark-gull,** one who is both knave and dupe.

†Shark, *sb.²* *U.S. local.* [f. SHARK *sb.¹*] *intr.* To fish for sharks.

Sharkish, *a.* Like a shark; on this account.

Sharking, *vbl. sb.*

Sharking, *ppl. a.*

Sharklet (ʃaɹklet). *rare.* [f. SHARK *sb.¹* + -LET.] A young shark.

Sharn (ʃaɹn). *dial. and Sc. Forms:* 1 **scearn,** 5 **scharne,** **schorn,** **shern, sharn.** Dung; cow-dung.

Sharn-bug. *Obs. exc. dial. Also sharn-.* [f. SHARN + BUG *sb.²* = prec.

†Sharn-penny. *Obs.* In 2 **scor-peni, scharn-penny.** [f. SHARN + PENNY.] A payment of a penny yearly for each cow, which was due from the burgesses of Bury St. Edmunds to the Abbey as lord of the manor.

Sharny (ʃaɹnⁱ), *a. dial. and Sc.* Also *sharny-faced* adj.; *sharny-peat* (see quot. 1808).

Sharoot, Sharout : variants of CHEROOT.

Sharp (ʃaɹp), *a. and sb.* Forms: 1-3 **scearp,** 2-3 **scarp,** 3-6 (7-9 *dial.*) **scharp, scharpe,** etc.

I. 1. Well adapted for cutting or piercing; having a keen edge or point: opposed to *blunt.* Having a keen cutting edge. Also said of the edge.

2. Having a tapering shape; brought to a fine point so as to be used for piercing. Said also of the point itself.

Saturday a tendency to sharp, which was at times unpleasantly noticeable.

8. With reference to form only (without implication of cutting or piercing).

9. Tapering to a (relatively) fine point.

b. Of a person: Eager.

6. Of feelings: Keen, ardent. *Obs.*

7. Of sound: Penetrating, shrill, high-pitched.

b. Of an accent: = ACUTE *a.* Also *sharp.*

B. *sb.*

1. A sharp weapon; *spec.* a small sword (in 18th cent. part of a civilian's attire); a rapier used for duelling as opposed to a 'blunt' or buttoned weapon. *Obs. or arch.*

SHARP

SHARPEN

SHARPENED

SHARPER

SHARPING

SHARPNESS

SHARP-NOSED

SHARPSHIP

SHARPSHOOTER

SHARP-SHOT

SHARP-WITTED

SHASTER

‖ Shastri (ʃæstri). Also 7 shastree, 9 shastree. [Hindī *śāstrī*, Skr. *çāstrin*, nom. sing. *çāstrī*, f. *çāstra* SHASTER.] One who is learned in, or teaches, the shastras.

Shastya, obs. form of CHASTISE.

† Shat 1. Obs. [Ir. *stad*, lit. jewel.] Used as a term of endearment in addressing an Irish person.

† Shat 2. Obs. *rare*−1. Mentioned as a colloq. or slang term for a tatler.

Shata, obs. var. t. of SHOOT.

Shathmont, var. SHANDRIDAN.

Shatter (ʃætə(r)), sb. [f. SHATTER v.]

Shattering (ʃætəriŋ), vbl. sb. [-ING1.] The action of the verb SHATTER; an instance of this.

Shatter-brain. Also SHATTER-BRAINS.

Shattered (ʃætəd), ppl. a. [f. SHATTER v. + -ED1.]

Shatterer (ʃætərə(r)). [-ER1.] One who shatters.

Shatter-headed, a. Obs. *rare.* = SHATTER-BRAINED.

Shattern, var. SHATTERN.

Shattery (ʃætəri), a.

Shattle, obs. form of SHUTTLE.

Shattock (ʃætək), obs. form of SHADDOCK.

Shau, obs. form of SHAW, SHOW.

Shanchle (ʃɔːxl), sb. Also 8 shoochel, also SHAUFFLE 2.

Shattuck, obs. form of SHADDOCK.

Shauchle, Sc. variant of SHUFFLE v.

Shauchled (ʃɔːxld), a.

Shanchly (ʃɔːxli), a. Sc. Also -ley. [f. SHAUCHLE v. + -Y1.]

Shanchling, a. [f. SHAUCHLE v. + -ING2.]

Shauder, obs. var. of SHODDER.

Shaul, var. SHOAL, SHOALING.

Shauld, Shauling: see SHOAL, SHOALING.

Shaulm, -me, obs. forms of SHAWM.

Shaul, obs. variant of SHOAL.

Shaum, variant of SHALY *Sc. dial.* (pony).

Shaume, -melle: see SHAWM, SHAMBLE sb.

Shauneen, variant of SHONEEN.

Shauntee, obs. form of SHANTY 2 (JAUNTY a.).

Shaup, sharp (ʃɔːp). Sc. [Prob. copse. w. ON. *skálp* = scabbard, Du. *schelp, schulp* shell.]

† Shaualdour. Obs. Also shavaldwre, shawaldoure, -dower(e, schawal, -dour, -dour, schall-dour.

SHAVE (ʃeɪv), sb.1 Forms: 1 sceafa, sceafan, scafan, sceafan, scafan (3rd pret. *scaf*), 4−5 schawe, 5 schaff, 5−7 schave, 6 schawe, 7 shawe, 4 schavyn, 8 Sc. *schaff*, 4−5 shawe, 7 schavie, 4− shave.

Shave (ʃeɪv), v. Forms: *Inf.* 1 sceafan, scafan, 2 (3rd pret.) scaaf, scof?, 4−5 schave, schaven, 6 schaff, 5−6 schawe, schavin, 4− shave.

‖ b. U.S. cant. (a) An exorbitant discount on a note.

Mil. slang. An unauthenticated report.

Shave (ʃeɪv), v. Forms: 1 scafan, 5−6 schave, etc.

SHAVING.

Shave (continued)

Shaveling (ʃeɪvliŋ), sb. and a. Forms: 7 shaveling.

Shaven (ʃeɪv'n), ppl. a. Forms: see the verb.

Shaver (ʃeɪvə(r)). [f. SHAVE v. + -ER1.] 1. One who shaves with a razor.

Shavery (ʃeɪvəri). *nonce-wd.* [jocularly formed f. SHAVE v.]

Shaving (ʃeɪviŋ), vbl. sb. [-ING1.] 1. The action of scraping or cutting off a thin layer from a surface; *spec.* the removal of the hair or beard with a razor.

† b. = TONSURE sb. 3. Obs. *nonce-use.*

Shave-grass. [f. SHAVE sb. + GRASS.]

Shave-hook. [f. SHAVE sb. + HOOK.]

Shave-rush. U.S. rare. [f. SHAVE + RUSH.] Cf. SHAVE-GRASS.

Shave-weed. Obs. = SHAVE-GRASS.

Shavewort. Obs. rare−1. [f. SHAVE sb. + WORT.]

Shavie (ʃeɪvi). Sc. [f. SHAVE v.] A trick.

shaving-iron, a razor.

shaving-linen.

Shaving (continued)

Supplement, p. 3873; Corrigenda, p. 4092; Spurious words, p. 4093; Books quoted, p. 4094

SHEAF. 649 SHEAR.

sheaves, **1797** T. HOLCROFT tr. *Stolberg's Trav.* III. lxxxi.

Sheaf (ʃiˑf), *sb.*[1] [OE. *scēaf* sb. = -y.] Consisting of or resembling a sheaf or sheaves.

Sheah, Sheak, var. ff. SHIAH, SHE-OAK.

Sheakin, dial. form of SHACKLE *sb.*[1]

Shealing: see SHEELING, SHIRLING, SHILLING.

Sheamoie, sheamie, obs. ff. SHAMMY.

Shea-oak, variant of SHEA.

Shear (ʃiˑr), *sb.*[1] Forms: *sing.* 1 scéar, 3–6 schere, 4 scheers, 4–6 shere, 6 shere, 6–7 sheir, 6 scheir, 7–9 sheer, 8 schear...

Sheaf (ʃiˑf), *v.* 1 Trans. To bind into a sheaf or sheaves; also with *up*. Also *absol.*

Sheafage (ʃiˑvidʒ), *sb.* [f. SHEAF *sb.* + -AGE.] Sheaves in the aggregate.

SHEAR. 650 SHEAR.

Shear (ʃiˑr), *sb.*[2]

SHEAR. 651 SHEAR.

shorne. *wk.* 4 schard, 4–5 schard, 6 chard, 7– sheared. A Com. Teut. verb...

SHEAR. 652 SHEARLING.

Shear-head. [f. SHEAR *sb.*[1] and *sb.*[2]]

Shear-hook. *Naut. Obs.* [f. SHEAR *sb.*[1] + HOOK *sb.*] A sickle-shaped hook intended to destroy the enemy's rigging.

Shear-hog. [SHEAR *v.*]

Shear-hulk: see SHEER-HULK.

Shear-legs. [SHEAR *sb.*[1]] A device consisting of two poles fastened...

Shearling (ʃiˑliŋ). Forms: 4 schorling, 5– shearling, 6 shereling, 9 *dial.* shirling. 1. A sheep that has been once shorn.

†2. The fleece of such a sheep. *Obs.*

Shearman (ʃiə·mæn). Forms: 3 sherman, 3–6 schere-, 4–7 sheere-, 5–6 s(c)her-, 5–7 shearman.

1. One who shears woollen cloth. Now *Hist.*

Shearmen, variant forms of SHARMEN.

Shears *pl.* = SHEAR sb. [1]

Shear-shole, variant of SEARCHERY sb.

Shear steel (1827-).

Shear Thursday = SHEER THURSDAY.

Shearwater (ʃiə·wɔːtə). 1. A bird of the genus *Puffinus*, esp. *P. anglorum*, the Manx Shearwater (= MANX a.), and *P. major*, the Greater Shearwater.

2. *U.S.* The Black Skimmer, *Rhynchops nigra.*

†Shearwort, a. *Obs. rare⁻¹.*

Sheat, sb. dial. Also 6 *pl.* shettee, 7–9 sheet, 8 scheat, 9 shet.

Sheat, Sheat(e, obs. ff. SHEATH [2], SHEET.

Sheath [1] (ʃiːþ). Forms: 1 sceáð, sceóð, 1–3 scéð, 3–6 schethe, scheþe, 4–7 sheth(e, 4–6 s(c)hethe, 4–7 (8–9 *dial.*) sheath, 5 scheithe, sheeth, 6–7 sheathe, 7 *micispr.* sheath, 8 sheath.

1. A case or covering into which a blade is thrust when not in use; usually close-fitting and conforming to the shape of the blade, as of a sword, dagger, knife, etc. Cf. SCABBARD.

†2. A limiting layer of surrounding cellular tissue (B. D. Jackson *Gloss. Bot. Terms*, 1900). Also [3] the lower, longer portion of the cell-wall in division in Oedogonium [4] (*ibid.* Add.). Bundle-sheath: see HERDLE [5].

3. *Anat.* The connective tissue covering which closely invests a part or elongated organ.

4. *Zool.* A tube-like case, covering, or protection, e.g. a hair-follicle, the covering of the sting, etc. of an insect.

†Sheath [2]. *Obs.* Forms: a. 4 scheathe, 9 sheth(e, 7 *misprint* skeath, 7–8 sheath, 9 *dial.* shet(t)e, scheyde.

Sheathe (ʃiːð), *v.* Forms: 5 schethe, 6–9 sheath, 7 sheath.

1. *trans.* To put or plunge (a sword, etc.) into a sheath.

Sheathery (ʃiːðəri). [f. SHEATH [1] + -ERY.] Sheaths and similar articles collectively.

Sheath-fish [1] (ʃiːþfiʃ). sheat-fish (Ph.). Also sheete. The catfish, *Silurus glanis.*

Sheath-fish [2]. [f. SHEATH [1] + FISH sb.] The razor-fish.

Sheath-fish [3].

Sheathing (ʃiːðiŋ), *vbl. sb.* [f. SHEATHE v. + -ING [1].]

1. a. The action of putting into a sheath.

b. The action of putting on a protective layer to a ship's bottom; also, the method or manner in which this is done.

Sheathless (ʃiːþles), a. [f. SHEATH [1] + -LESS.]

1. Of a sword, etc.: Not encased in a sheath.

Sheathy, a. *Obs. rare.* [f. SHEATH [1] + -Y.]

Sheave (ʃiːv), sb. [Variant of SHIVE sb. [2] (ʃiv), with vowel-lengthening: cf. prec.]

Sheave, v. [f. SHEAVE sb. [1] + -ED [2].]

Sheaved, a.

Sheaved (ʃiːvd), *ppl. a.* [f. SHEAVE [1] + -ED [1].]

Sheavy (ʃiːvi), a. [f. SHEAVE sb. + -Y.]

Sheaw, Sheabandar, obs. ff. SHOW, SHABUNDER.

Shebang (ʃibæŋ). *U.S. slang.* [Of obscure origin.]

1. A hut, shed; one's dwelling, quarters.

2. Applied to a vehicle.

Shebash, variant of SHABASH.

Shebeen (ʃibiːn). *Also* sheebean, shibbeen. [Orig. Anglo-Irish; of obscure origin.]

Shechanize, v. *Obs. rare.*

Shechinah, variant of SHEKINAH.

Sheck, obs. form of SHERIKH.

Shecklaton, variant of CICLATOUN *Obs.*

Sheckle = SHACKLE, SHEKEL, SHOCKLE.

Shed (ʃed), sb. [1]

Shed (ʃed), sb. [2]

Shed (ʃed), v. [1]

Shed (ʃed), v. [2]

b. In a telegraph-line insulator, a covering in the form of an inverted cup, a 'petticoat'.

1859 *Abridgm. Specif. Patents, Electr. & Magn.* 236 No sheds or bell coverings are applied, but the wire is varnished [etc.]. 1910 *N. Hawkins' Electr. Dict.*, *Shed of Insulator*, the petticoat of a line wire insulator.

4. *attrib.* and *Comb.*, as *shed-smithy*; *shed-fashion*, *-wise* advs.; *shed-like* adj.; in sense 'kept, employed, done in a shed', as *shed-cow*, *-feeding*, *-man*; **shed roof**, a roof with only one slope (as in a lean-to shed); hence *shed-roofed* adj.

1898 *Jrnl. R. Agric. Soc.* June 415 When an outbreak occurs among a herd of *shed-cows. 1807 P. Gass *Jrnl.* 61 The roofs were made *shed fashion, rising from the inner side. 1856 Morton *Cycl. Agric.* II. 841/1 In some trials of *shed-feeding. 1835 R. Willis *Archit. Mid. Ages* ix. 140 A long, low, *shed-like porch. 1899 Rider Haggard *Farmer's Yr.* 352 The kirk..is a very plain building, white-washed and shed-like in appearance. 1857 *Househ. Words* 27 June 605/1 At large stations they [the porters] form two distinct bodies, called technically yardmen and *shedmen. 1805 R. W. Dickson *Pract. Agric.* I. 61 It is probably the best and cheapest method to make them with *shed-roofs. 1907 M. C. F. Morris *Nunburnholme* 76 The chancel itself had a shed-roof of mean description. 1836 Parker *Gloss. Archit.* (1850) I. 432 The body of a church is span-roofed and its aisles *shed-roofed. 1837 Carlyle *Fr. Rev.* III. iv. vi, There, in their two-hundred and fifty *shed smithies,.. let them forge gun-barrels. 1650 in *Sussex Archæol. Collect.* XXIV. 280 The said cottage and stable is built *Shedwise against the Castle wall of Tymber and Mudd walles.

Shed (ʃed), *sb.*³ *rare.* [f. Shed *v.*¹] Something that is or has been shed: e.g. a silkworm's cocoon; a light fall of snow; the cast shell of a crab.

1648 Herrick *Hesper.*, *Fairie Temple* 137 And then he dons the Silk-worms shed (Like a Turks Turbant on his head). 1876 Blackmore *Cripps* vii, A little powdery shed of flakes had come at noon that very day. 1911 Webster, *Shed*..5. That which is or has been shed, as the molted shell of a crab or other crustacean. *Colloq.*

Shed (ʃed), *sb.*⁴ *local.* [Cf. Scad⁵ and *shad salmon* 'small salmon of from five pounds' to eight pounds' weight' (*Shropshire Word-bk.* 1879).] A young salmon from one to two years old.

1861 *Act 24 & 25 Vict.* c. 109 § 4 All migratory fish of the genus salmon, whether known by the names..gravelling, shed, scad,..or by any other local name. 1882 [see Skegger].

†**Shed**, *sb.*⁵ *Obs.* Also **shede**, **sheade**. Variants of Schede, a written paper.

1510 Stanbridge *Vocabula* (W. de W.) C ij b, *Scheda*, a shede. 1590 *Calepini Dict.* (1594) II. 531 *Scheda*..Angl. A sheet or shed of paper. *a* 1593 H. Barrow *Brief Discov.* To Rdr. p. iij, Where such was the rage of the enimie, as he [the author] might not keepe one sheade by him, whiles he was writinge of an other.

Shed, sched, Sc. forms of Shade *sb.*

c 1591 *Rob Stene's Dream* (Maitland Club) 3 A sched, but substance, and no moir. *c* 1730 Ramsay *Vision* xxviii, And all as saft and gay appeird As ane Elysion shed.

Shed (ʃed), *v.*¹ Pa. t. and pa. pple **shed**. Forms: 1 **sc(e)ádan, scédan**, 2–5 **shode(n, -scheode(n**, 3 **scheade(n**; 2–3 *Ormin* **shædenn**, 2–6 **shede(n**, 3 **ssede**, 3–5 **schede(n**, 4–7, 8–9 *dial.* **sheed(e, sched**, 5 **scheed**, 5–6 **schedde**, 6 *Sc.* **schad, scheid**, 6–7 **shedd(e**, 6–8, 9 *dial.* **shead**, 8 *dial.* **shade**, 4– **shed**; 3 *sing. pres. ind.* (occas. contracted forms) 1 **-scét, -scát, -sceát**, 2 **schet**, 2–3 **shat**. *Pa. t.* 1 **-scéd, -scéad**, 3 **sad**, 3–6 **sched**; 1 **sc(e)ádde** (? **scéadde**), 2–3 **scedde**, 2–5 **schedde, shadde**, 3 **scede, chadde**, 3–4 **ssedde**, 3–5 **shed(d)e, schadde**, 4 **scade**, 4–5 **schad, shad**, 5–6 **schede, shadd**, 6 *Sc.* **s(c)hedd, schaid**, 6–7 **shead**, 7 (9 *dial.*) **shodd, shod**, 4– **shed**; 1 **-sceádade**, 4 **schedide**, 4–5 **scheded**, 5 **schedded**, 5–6 **scheddit**, 9 *dial.* **shedded, sheaded**. *Pa. pple.* 1 **sceáden** (? **scéaden**), 2 **-sceden**, 3 **scheden, scede**, 4–5 **schede, shede**; 3 **sced(d, i-sced, sad(d**, 3 (*Ormin*), 5 **shadd**, 4–5 **shad** (4 **yshad**), 4 **i-schod, y-ssed**, 4–5 **schad, yshed, yschad**, 5 **xad**; 4–6 **sched** (3–5 **schedd, isched**, 4 **isedd, yssed**, 4–5 **shadde**, 5–6 **shedde**, 6 *Sc.* **scheid**, 4, 6 *Sc.* **schedde** (4 **yschedde**), 9 *dial.* **shod, shud**, 4– **shed**: 1 **ʒesceádad**, 5–6 **shedded, 6sheeded**. [A Com. Teut. verb (wanting in Scandinavian), originally str. (redupl.): OE. *sc(e)ádan, scéadan*, pa. t. *sc(e)ád, scéad*, pa. pple. *sc(e)áden* (?*scéaden*), corresponds, either directly or with consonant-ablaut, to OFris. *skêda, skêtha* wk. (mod.Fris. *skiede, schéde*, NFris. *skêr, skial, skias*), OS. *skêdan, skêthan*, pa. pple. *giskêthan*, MLG. *schêden, scheiden*, MDu. *schêden, scheiden, scheen, scheien* (mod.Du. *scheiden*, pa. t. *scheidde*, pa. pple. *geschieden*), OHG. *sceidan*, pa. t. *sciad, scied*, pa. pple. *gisceidan* (MHG. *scheiden*, pa. t. *schiet*, pa. pple. *gescheiden*; mod.G. *scheiden*, pa. t. *schied*, pa. pple. *geschieden*), Goth. *skaidan*, pa. pple. *skaidan-s*; the vb. in all these langs. has the sense to separate, divide; the forms represent two distinct types of the Teut. root, **skaiþ-* (: **skiþ-*) and **skaid-* (: **skid-*); for cognates in Teut. see Sheath *sb.*, Shide *sb.* The pre-Teut. **skeit-* : **skoit-* : **skit-*, from which both the Teut. types descend (with difference due to consonant-ablaut), is not directly represented outside Teut., but is prob. related to the widespread Indogermanic root **sk(h)eid-* : **sk(h)oid-* : **sk(h)id-*, occurring, e.g., in Skr. *chid-* to split, Lith. *skëdżu* I make thin, separate, divide, *skëda* chip of wood, Gr. σχίζειν to split, σχίζα billet of wood, L. *scindĕre* to cut, cleave.

The original OE. *sc(e)ádan* would normally yield (midland and southern) ME. and mod.E. *shode*, which is occas. found in writings from the 12th to the 15th c. It would appear that by the side of the original form OE. had (presumably in certain districts, but evidence is lacking for localization) an altered form *scéadan*, with change of rising into falling diphthong; from this the modern *shed* (ʃed) descends by a development parallel to that of *bread, dead*, from OE. *bréad, déad*.

The OE. verb retained its strong conjugation in WS., but in Northumbrian occurs only as weak (usually with forms *-scéadade, -scéadad* on the analogy of the *ô* stems; rarely contracted *scéadde*). In early ME. there were forms like *sched* pa. t., *schenen* pa. pple., representing the original strong conjugation; forms like *schedid*, representing the wk. forms of OE.; and forms like *schèdde, schèdd*, prob. not repr. ONorthumb. *scéadde*, but new formations due to the analogy of vbs. like *rede* (read), *lede* (lead), etc. The mod. pa. t. and pa. pple. *shed* are prob. to be regarded as representing the last type of conjugation, which was by far the most frequent in ME.]

1. *trans.* To separate, divide. Now only *dial.*, chiefly in farming uses: To separate (lambs) from the ewes, or (calves) from the cows; to separate (cattle, sheep) from the herd or flock. †*To shed the shanks* (Sc.): to set the legs apart.

c 1000 *Soul's Addr.* 148 (Gr.) Þonne sceadene beoþ þa synfullan & þa soðfæstan on þam mæran dæge. *c* 1200 Ormin 16865, & forrþi wass þatt name hemm [*sc.* the Pharisees] sett, Forr þatt teȝȝ wærenn shadde, Swa summ hemm þuhhte, fra þe folle þurrh haliȝ lif & lare. *c* 1200 *Trin. Coll. Hom.* 67 Ure louerd ihesu crist..shodeð þe gode fro þe iuele. Et statuet oues a dextris..and shodeð þe rihtwise an his rihthalue. *a* 1225 *Ancr. R.* 270 Þe ȝeteward..ouh forto winden hweate, & scheaden þe eilen & tet chef urom þe clene cornes. *c* 1250 *Gen. & Ex.* 266 Quan al man-kinde ..Sal ben fro dede to liue broȝt, And sell sad fro þe forwroȝt. *c* 1315 Shoreham III. 63 þat doþ þat manye yschoded [*altered to* y-schodred] ben Fram heuene-ryche festes. 1338 R. Brunne *Chron.* (1725) 174 He salle sched vs o sonder, fro Acres salle we go. *Ibid.* 305 Þer scheltron sone was shad [Langt. *severé*] with Inglis þat were gode. 1390 Gower *Conf.* III. 136 Logique hath eke in his degre Betwen the trouthe and the falshode The pleine wordes forto schode, So that nothing schal go biside. *a* 1400 *Relig. Pieces* (E.E.T.S.) 61 The sonne to schede þe day fra þe nyght. *c* 1470 Henry *Wallace* v. 77 Wallace mycht nocht a graith straik on him gett: Ȝhett schede he thaim, a full royd slope was maid. 1535 Stewart *Cron. Scot.* (Rolls) I. 15 Schulderis wer schorne and sched the bodie fra. 1550 Lyndesay *Sqr. Meldrum* 904 Iudge ȝe gif he hir schankis sned. *c* 1553 in Strype *Eccl. Mem.* (1721) III. App. xi. 28 God..myndeth now to..shede out the Gootes from the Shepe. *c* 1560 A. Scott *Poems*, *Ballad Want. Wemen* 30 For conȝie ȝe may chawcht hir To sched hir schankis in twane. 1584 B. R. tr. *Herodotus* I. 60 The mighty river Gyndes being in this sort shed and derived into..360. brookes. 1600 Holland *Livy* VI. xxv. 234 In the view and account taken of the captives there were some of them known to be Tusculanes, who were shed apart from the rest. 1677 W. Nicolson in *Trans. Roy. Soc. Lit.* (1870) 318 [Cumberl. and Westm.] *Shed*, to part asunder. 1791 Learmont *Poems* 276 I've lambs to shed, and sheep a clipping too. 1824 Mactaggart *Gallovid. Encycl.* 425 *Shed*, to separate; to separate the calves from the cows, we *shed* them. 1844 H. Stephens *Bk. Farm* II. 87 The sheep selected for market are the best conditioned at the time, and to ascertain this it is necessary to handle the whole lot and shed the fattest from the rest. *absol.* 1844 H. Stephens *Bk. Farm* II. 618 Those shepherds who dog, force, and shed much about a march, I consider them as bad herds for their masters as for the neighbouring farmer.

†b. To set apart, draft off *from* a community. *Obs.*

1584 B. R. tr. *Herodotus* I. 54 They ioyned fellowship with other their countreymen which before tyme were shed from the city to inhabite that place.

†c. *refl.* To separate oneself, part *from*; to come apart. Also (of troops) to scatter *asunder*.

c 1200 Ormin 3200 Forrþrihht anan he..shadde himm all þweorrt ut fra menn. *c* 1400 *Laud Troy Bk.* 7764 He schet aboute him fer & ner..The Gregeis offte In-sunder hem scheded. *a* 1578 Lindesay (Pitscottie) *Chron. Scot.* (S.T.S.) II. 90 The new wark zeid frome the auld and sched the self.

†d. *intr.* for *refl.* To separate, divide, come apart; to part company; to depart; to part *with* a possession. *Obs.*

c 1000 *Sax. Leechd.* II. 116 Þonne dæȝ & niht scade, drince þonne þone drenc. 1338 R. Brunne *Chron.* (Rolls) 991 Þe Gregeys schadden sone a-onder. 13.. *E. E. Allit. P.* A. 411 Þow wost wel when þy perle con schede, I was ful ȝong & tender of age. 1572 Mascall *Plant. & Graff.* 37 Ye shall binde it so, till the fruites or cliftes be couered.. with your sayde hempe, except the oylet and his tayle, the which ye must not couer, for that tayle will shed apart, if the shielde doe take. 1576 Gascoigne *Grief of Joy* IV. iii. Wks. 1910 II. 548 Thou showldest fore-see, that fagott sticks do hold, Together fast, and seldome list to shedd. 1585 Jas. I *Ess. Poesie* (Arb.) 45 Such was the loue, and reuerence they her bure, Ilk day whill euen, ay whill they shedd at night. 1603 *Philotus* lxxxix, Be Christ I sall thy nurture nip, Richt scharply or wee sched. 1659 W. Guthrie *Chr. Gt. Interest* II. (1724) 214 If thou hast a Desire after Jesus Christ,..and cannot think of parting with his blessed Company for ever, or, if thou must shed with him, yet dost wish well to him [etc.].

2. *trans.* **a.** To part, or divide (the hair; also the hair or wool of an animal). Also *refl.* of the person. Now *Sc.* and *dial.*

a 1300 *Cursor M.* 18848 Metli har was on his chin, And als his hefd was scheud [*Gött.* sched] in tuin. 1387 Trevisa *Higden* (Rolls) V. 369 Þey used to schere of þe heere of hir heed from þe molde to þe nolle, but to fore þey hadde lokkes i-schod [*β.* ysched; L. *discriminatam*] hongynge doun to þe mouth. 1388 Wyclif *Judith* x. 3 Sche schedide [1382 platte] the heer of hir heed. 1390 Gower *Conf.* I. 101 Bot with no craft of combes brode Thei myhte hire hore lockes schode. *c* 1430 *Pilgr. Lyf Manhode* II. lxxiv. (1869) 103, I loue better..to keembe myn hed, to shede me [Fr. *graner mon chef*]. 1523–34 Fitzherb. *Husb.* § 42 Than take hym, and shede the woll with thy fyngers, there as the scab is, and with thy fynger laye a lyttell terre therypon. 1530 Palsgr. 717/1 Shede your heare that hangeth so yvell favouredly aboute your eares. 1548 Patten *Exped. Scot.* C viij b, A fellowe lyke a man..red hedded, curld rounde about & shedded afore. 1607 Topsell *Four-f. Beasts* 411 Make a salue thereof, and with your finger annoint all the sore places, sheading the haire as you go. 1610 Guillim *Heraldry* IV. vii. (1632) 296 The Combe is.. of most vse with women for shedding and trimming their haire and head-tires. 1621 G. Sandys *Ovid's Met.* VI. (1626) 111 Her haire She forthwith sheds. 1822 A. Cunningham *Tradit. Tales*, *Mother's Dream* (1887) 123 He shed back his long and moistened locks from a burning and bewildered brow. 1832 Motherwell *Poems* 41 Let me shed by your hair. 1844 A. Rodger in *Songs for Nursery* 44 Let me shed your shining hair. 1888 Doughty *Trav. Arabia Deserta* I. 595 He was of goodly great stature, with.. hair shed..and hanging down from the midst in tresses. *intr.* for *refl.* 13.. *E. E. Allit. P.* B. 1690 Faxe fyltered ..Þat schad fro his schulderes to his schyre wykes.

b. *Weaving.* To divide (the warp-threads), to make a 'shed' in (a web). Cf. Shed *sb.*¹ 6.

1839 Ure *Dict. Arts* 1285 The weaver..thus sheds the warp, by lifting and depressing each alternate thread. 1863 J. Watson *Weaving* 196 It has been explained how a common Web is shedded, and a few words will show the difference for the shedding in this loom.

†3. To cleave, divide (something) with a knife, weapon, etc. *Obs.*

13.. *K. Alis.* 2772 Ac, ar the gate weore y-loke, Mony ponne was to-broke;..And mony brayn was y-schad. 13.. *Gaw. & Gr. Knt.* 425 Þe scharp of þe schalk..scade hit in twynne. *c* 1470 *Gol. & Gaw.* 604 Ane schene scheild and ane schaft, that scharply was sched.

†b. *transf.* Of birds, fishes: To 'cleave' (the air, the water) in flight or swimming. *Obs.*

c 1480 Henryson *Mor. Fab.*, *Preiching of Swallow* vii, The foullis..Scheddand the air with pennis greit and small. 1599 Alex. Hume *Hymn* ii. 184 The little friand fish in flude, and dentie volatil, Quhilks shedds the waters, & the winds, be traps them at his wil.

†4. To scatter, sprinkle; in later use only, to sow (seed). *Obs.*

c 1000 *Sax. Leechd.* II. 38 Wiþ wyrmum on eaȝum ȝenim beolonan sæd scead on gleda. *c* 1374 Chaucer *Boeth.* I. met. i. (1868) 4 Heeres hore ben schad [orig. *funduntur*] ouertymelyche vpon myne heued. 1382 Wyclif *Gen.* xxxviii. 9 He..shede the seed into the erthe. 1608 Willet *Hexapla Exod.* 535 The seede which was shed the former yeere. 1633 P. Fletcher *Pisc. Eclogues* v. ii, That primrose there Which 'mongst those violets sheds his golden hair, Seems the sunnes little sonne, fixt in his azure spheare. *c* 1770 Hunter in Winter *Syst. Husb.* (1797) 173 The drill plow.. which by..shedding the seed and covering it, leave[s] the land stocked with plants.

fig. 1414 26 *Pol. Poems* (1904) 58 Þan god wil..Drede and stryf among hem shede.

†b. To disperse, scatter; to rout, put to flight.

c 1250 *Gen. & Ex.* 672 Ðat folc is wide on londe sad. 1387 Trevisa *Higden* (Rolls) VII. 493 Þere sche bode here knyȝtes þat were al i-sched. *c* 1480 Henryson *Test. Cress.* (Charteris) 18 The Northin wind had purifyit the Air, And sched the mistie cloudis fra the sky. 1633 P. Fletcher *Purple Isl.* XII. lxv, His tail, whose folds were wont the starres to shed, Now stretcht at length, close to his belly clings.

c. *dial.* To rake out (a fire).

1873 Murdoch *Doric Lyre* 26 (E.D.D.), I had shed my fire An' hame was ettlin' to retire.

d. To throw off, repel (rain, sunlight, etc.). Now chiefly *dial.*

c 1400 *Anturs of Arth.* ii. (Douce MS.), Schurde in a short cloke, þat þe rayne shedes. 1616 Surflet & Markham *Country Farm* II. lxii. 318 Neither must they be made as some are flat at the top, and shallow, but ascending pyramid wise, smaller and smaller till it come to the top, for thereby it..sheddeth off the raine much better. 1778 [W. H. Marshall] *Minutes Agric.* 30 Aug. 1774, The elevation would shed off the rain, and prevent its lodging in the ears. 1818 Scott *Hrt. Midl.* xxviii, But it sheds the sun weel aff. 1885 *Harper's Mag.* Apr. 796/2 As a shaggy dog sheds water from his coat. 1886 C. Scott *Sheep-Farming* 99 The straw has finally to be raked down on the outside, so as to shed rain well.

†e. *refl.* and *intr.* To be dispersed, scatter. *Obs.*

1456 Sir G. Haye *Law Arms* (S.T.S.) 61 The bataill of Pompee began to sched and till irk, and toke the flicht. 1535 Stewart *Cron. Scot.* (Rolls) III. 429 Lyke ony scheip tha schud it all and sched, Quhair euir tha come befoir his face tha fled. 1579 Spenser *Sheph. Cal.* Oct. 35 Sike prayse is smoke, that sheddeth in the skye. 1589 *Pasquil's Ret.* A iiij, The great Empire of..Alexander, like a flame of fire in a heape of flaxe, when it was at the highest, did shed it selfe suddainlie in the ayre. 1650 Fuller *Pisgah* II. v. xviii. 173 That the Pillar of Smoak which ascended from the sacrifice, curled only upwards in direct wreaths to heaven, without any scattering, or shedding it self abroad.

5. To spill (liquids), let fall (crumbs, etc.). *Obs.* exc. *dial.*

a 1225 *Ancr. R.* 344 Of alle kudde & kuðe sunnen, ase of prude..of sum uals word..of schorn leihtre, of scheden crumen oðer ale, oðer leten þinges muwlen oðer rusten.

c 1380 *Sir Ferumb.* 2296 Schad was al þe wyn. 1526 *Pilgr. Perf.* (W. de W. 1531) 47 The vessell can not holde yᵉ wyne, but anone it breketh, & so shedeth the wyne. 1580 Lyly *Euphues* (Arb.) 455 By carrying water in a siue, not shedding one drop from Tiber to the Temple of Vesta. 16.. *Boy & Mantle* 181 in *Percy Fol. MS.* II. 311 He said, 'there was noe Cuckolde shall drinke of my horne, But he shold itt sheede, either behind or beforne.' 1622 Mabbe tr. *Aleman's Guzman d'Alf.* II. 315 In pulling forth my Handkerchiefe, I had shed all my money. 1785 Trusler *Mod. Times* II. 83 A bag of tea..was burst, and a good deal of the tea shed. 1839 Sterling *Alfred the Harper* xviii. Poems 136 Grim sat the chiefs;..His iron mace was grasped by one, By one his wine was shed. 1847 *Ockley's Hist. Saracens* (ed. 4) 216 *note*, The crafty Harmozanda shed the vase to the ground. 1866 Waugh *Ben an th' Bantam* iv. 73 His jackass..broke her pitcher, an' sheeded th' milk. *Ibid.* 74 Are yo noan beawn to pay for th' milk 'at wur shed, then?

absol. *c* 1430 *Stans Puer* 60 in *Babees Bk.*, Fille not þi spoon lest in þe cariage It scheede bi side.

†b. *intr.* Of a liquid: To spill *over*. *Obs.*

1601 Dolman *La Primaud. Fr. Acad.* III. (1618) 769 If one put neuer so little water into a vessell already brimme-full, the vppermost part thereof will shedde ouer.

6. *trans.* To pour, pour out. (The ordinary rendering of L. *fundere, effundere*, etc.)

†a. Of a personal agent: To pour (water, etc.). Also with *out*. *Obs.*

a 1225 *Ancr. R.* 320 'Effunde sicut aquam cor tuum'. 'Sched ut', he seið, Ieremie, 'ase water þine heorte'. 1382 Wyclif *Exod.* xxiv. 6 And so Moyses took the half parti of the blood, and putte it into chalices: and that other party he shedde [Vulg. *fudit*] vpon the auteer. 1398 Trevisa *Barth. De P. R.* XIX. xxxvi. (1495) 879 Cerusa is gendryd and comyth of vapour of stronge vynegre effusyd and shedde on thynne plates of leed. 1483 Caxton *Golden Leg.* 247/2 He shadde water on his hede and baptysed hym in the name of Jhesu Crist. 1530 Palsgr. 701/2, I shedde out lycoure out of a vessel. 1595 *Locrine* III. Prol. 11 A subtill Adder..Priuily shead his poison through his bones. 1614 Gorges *Lucan* I. 37 Then doth he take a faire large bull..And twixt his hornes pure wine he sheads. 1621 G. Sandys *Ovid's Met.* II. (1626) 42 Banefull poyson; which she sheads Into her bones, and through her liuer spreads.

b. Of a vessel, receptacle, a fountain, etc.: To pour forth (its contents).

1430–40 Lydg. *Bochas* VIII. xii[i]. (1494) D j, Which lyke a conducte vpon euery syde Shad out water as any cristall clere. 1668 Culpeper & Cole *Barthol. Anat.* I. xvii. 47 They are..Veins and Arteries..which end at the Heads of the Caruncles, into which they shed their wheyish humor. 1870 Bryant *Iliad* XVI. 4 As when a fountain sheds Dark waters streaming down a precipice.

†c. *refl.* Of a river, etc.: To discharge itself. Also, to overflow *over* its banks. *Obs.*

1555 Watreman *Fardle Facions* I. iii. 34 Gently sheadyng hymself ouer his bancques, he [Nilus] leaueth in the countrie a merueilous fertilitie. 1610 Holland *Camden's Brit.* I. 696 Coc making no long course sheadeth himselfe into Wherf. *c* 1630 Risdon *Surv. Devon* § 28 (1810) 34 The riveret Sid shedding itself into the sea.

†d. *fig.* To 'pour out' (one's heart, feelings, prayers, etc.). *Obs.*

c 1420 *Prymer* (1895) 67 [*Ps.* xlii. 4], I biþouzte of þese þingis, & y schedde out in me my soule. 1526 *Pilgr. Perf.* (W. de W. 1531) 137 Ronne to our lorde, & shede forth your herte before hym. 1596 Dalrymple tr. *Leslie's Hist. Scot.* I. 111 And throuch thair prayers, quhilkes ydenly wᵗ al diligence thay sched for thair cuntrey, appeir to mitigat the ire of God.

e. To emit, give forth, pour out (spawn, eggs, †seminal fluid, etc.).

c 1386 Chaucer *Pars. T.* 503 Vnkyndely synne by which man or womman shedeth hire nature in manere or place ther as [etc.]. 1398 Trevisa *Barth. De P. R.* XIII. xxvi. (1495) 458 Ryuer fysshe and fresshe of marreys sheden more theyr pesen and ofter than other fysshe. *a* 1450 Myrc 1046 Take also wel in mynde, Ȝef þou haue sched þyn owne kynde, Slepynge or wakynge nyȝt or day. 1538 Bale *Thre Lawes* II. B vj b, I was with Onan not vnacquaynted, Whan he on the grounde hys increase shed. 1584 B. R. tr. *Herodotus* II. 93 These male fishe as they passe still onwarde shed theyr seede by the way. 1617 Moryson *Itin.* I. 154 There is a Fountaine, or a statua of a woman..and this statua shed water from all the haires of the head. 1630 in Binnell *Descr. Thames* (1758) 66 Roaches do then shed their Spawn. 1697 Dryden *Virg. Georg.* III. 440 From their Groins they shed A slimy Juice, by false Conception bred. 1822–29 *Good's Study Med.* (ed. 3) I. 534 [Polypi] which, if they discharge any thing, shed blood. 1855 Browning *An Epistle* 24, I have shed sweat enough, left flesh and bone On many a flinty furlong of this land. 1864 *Rep. Sea Fisheries Comm.* (1865) II. 1189/1 This was fresh spawn just shed. 1880 *Times* 21 Dec. 6/4 The large number of salmon just ready to shed their eggs.

7. To cause (blood) to flow from the body by cutting or wounding; to let fall (a person's blood) on the ground, etc.

c 1205 Lay. 5187 Heo smiten to-gædere..redde blod scede; rinkas feollen. *a* 1225 *Ancr. R.* 402 Þis blod, for ou i-sched upo þe herde two treon, schal makien ou Sarepciens. *c* 1290 *Beket* 2185 in *S. Eng. Leg.* 169 Forto gaderi of þe blode þat i-sched was on þe grounde. *a* 1300 *Cursor M.* 1129 His blod on erth sced lijs. *Ibid.* 4151 Þat na blod o him be schedd. *c* 1300 *K. Horn* (Laud MS.) 920 Cubert hem broute al honder He schedde of here blode And makede hem al wode. *a* 1325 *MS. Rawl.* B. 520 lf. 50 *Blodwite*, þat is quite of amerciaments for blod isedde. *c* 1375 *Sc. Leg. Saints* i. (*Petrus*) 376 Ger wipe myn blud of ȝon stede, quhare I for þe gert it be schede! 1387 Trevisa *Higden* (Rolls) I. 429 Þe blood reed, Þat þe mayde Wynefrede Schadde at þat putte. *c* 1400 Maundev. (1839) xxxi. 307 In that Cytee is no man so hardy, to schede Blode of no man. *c* 1400 *Destr. Troy* 7929 My body hath þou brisit, & my blode shed. *c* 1450 *Cov. Myst.* (Shaks. Soc.) 275 Ȝe xal drynk myn blood with gret devocyon, Wheche xal be xad ffor mannys love.

1526 *Pilgr. Perf.* (W. de W. 1531) 256 b, After that all his blode was shed. 1705 Addison *Italy* 3 Ulysses here the Blood of Victims shed. 1847 Mrs. Kerr tr. *Ranke's Hist. Servia* 128 Their attendants had already come to blows, and did not separate until blood had been shed.

b. With pregnant sense. (*a*) *To shed the blood of* (another person or persons): to kill in a manner involving effusion of blood; often *loosely*, to kill by violent means (whether blood is literally shed or not). So *to shed blood*: to destroy human life by violent means. *To shed much, little blood*: to destroy many, few lives. (*b*) *To shed* (one's own) *blood*: to undergo wounds or violent death in battle, martyrdom, or the like (*for* some person or cause, one's country, etc.).

(*a*) ?*a* 1100 *Ags. Ps.* xiii. 6 (Spelman) Hrade fot beora to aȝeotenne [*Trin. Coll. MS.* to scedende] blod. *c* 1275 *Passion Our Lord* 346 in *O. E. Misc.* 47 Þe gywes were ful bysie to scheden his blod. *c* 1290 *S. Eng. Leg.* 73 He mid vnriȝhte hadde i-sched mani ane mannes blod. *a* 1300 *Cursor M.* 11805 Hu had he hert to sced þair blod þat neuer did til him bot godd? 1340 *Ayenb.* 239 Moche uolk weren ysslaȝe and moche blod þer y-ssed. 1382 Wyclif *Ps.* cv. 38 And thei shadden [1388 schedden] out the innocent blod. 1430–40 Lydg. *Bochas* VIII. x[i]v. (1494) D iij b, And where he rode cristen blode he shadde. 1471 Caxton *Recuyell* (Sommer) 156 Many ther were that her blood was shedde on the lande. 1500–20 Dunbar *Poems* lxii. 43 His saikles blude agane thai sched. *c* 1560 A. Scott *Ps.* li. 58 Lord God, deliuer me, and gyd Frome schedding blude, and homicyd. 1577 Grange *Golden Aphrod.* etc. Q ij, Bloud shall be shedde for bloud, and life shall pay for lyfe. 1596 Dalrymple tr. *Leslie's Hist. Scot.* II. 27 That day in that feild was sched mekle scotis blude. 1697 Dryden *Virg. Past.* VIII. 65 Relentless Love the cruel Mother led The Blood of her unhappy Babes to shed. 1719 De Foe *Crusoe* I. 235 The Thoughts of shedding humane Blood for my Deliverance, were very terrible to me. 1823 Scott *Quentin D.* xxxv, He is a man of holy church—we may not shed his blood. 1838 James *Robber* ii, I will shed no blood, except in our own defence. 1847 C. Bronte *Jane Eyre* vi, They shed blood they had no right to shed.

(*b*) 13.. *Song. Virg.* 15 in *O. E. Misc.* 194 Bi-sek him.. Þat for ous alle sad is blod. *a* 1250 *Owl & Night.* 1616 For heom ich chadde mi blod. *c* 1315 Shoreham I. 83 To wesschen ous cryst schedde his blod And water out of hys wonde. *c* 1375 *Sc. Leg. Saints* xxxvi. (*Baptista*) 1009 Þat haly nowmir to fulfil, Þat sched þare blud for cristis sak. 1471 Caxton *Recuyell* (Sommer) 624, I my self haue shedde moche of my blood. 1535 Fisher *Ways Perf. Relig.* Wks. (1876) 385 Men and women for his loue haue shead theyr blood. 1586 T. B. *La Primaud. Fr. Acad.* I. (1594) 203 This monarch [Alexander] sustaining infinite labor, and cheerefully sheading his blood. 1707 Freind *Peterborow's Cond. Sp.* 173 My Subjects are in a disposition to shed the last drop of their Blood for me. 1844 *Mem. Babylonian Princess* II. 63 This spot, where our Saviour shed his blood to save all mankind from everlasting death.

8. To emit and let fall in drops.

a. With *tears* as obj.

c 1175 *Lamb. Hom.* 157 Swiche teres scedde M. Magdalene þa heo wosch ure drihtenes fet. 1423 Jas. I. *Kingis Q.* cxvii, And of my cristall teris that bene schede, The hony flouris growen vp and sprede. 1575 Gascoigne *Kenelworth* Wks. 1910 II. 128 Marke what teares they shed. *c* 1610 *Lives of Women Saints* 102/9 Who can recounte what plentie of teares she shodd for her owne sinnes, and the necessities of gods church. 1705 Addison *Italy*, *Pavia* 37 A Tear that our Saviour shed over Lazarus. 1862 Miss Braddon *Lady Audley* xxxv, He could only shed childish tears of despair and terror. 1908 [Miss E. Fowler] *Betw. Trent & Ancholme* 45 One [child] was sobbing and shedding tears.

slang. 1864 *Hotten's Slang Dict.*, *Shed a tear*, to take a dram or glass of neat spirits..'Now then, old fellow, come and shed a tear!'

†b. *absol.* To shed tears. *Obs. rare*⁻¹.

16.. ? Webster & Rowley *Cure for Cuckold* II. iii. (1661) C 4 b, O Urse, give me leave to shed!

c. With obj. rain, dew, etc.

1590 Spenser *F. Q.* II. iii. 24 And, when she spake, Sweet words like dropping honny she did shed. 1697 Dryden *Virg. Georg.* III. 520 Rising Cynthia sheds her Silver Dews. *c* 1730 Ramsay *Masque* 106 And cease, black clouds, to shed, or wet, or snaw. 1812 J. Wilson *Isle of Palms* III. 293 When evening sheds her dew.

†d. *intr.* Of rain, snow, etc.: To fall. *Obs.*

13.. *Gaw. & Gr. Knt.* 506 Schyre schedez þe rayn in schowrez ful warme. *Ibid.* 956 Hir brest..Schon schyrer þen snawe, þat scheder [*read* schedez] on hillez. *c* 1386 Chaucer *Monk's T.* 843 But swich a reyn doun fro the welkne shadde That slow the fyr. 1616 Surflet & Markham *Country Farm* II. lxii. 319 If anie raine happen to fall thereupon, yet it may by no meanes sinke into the Hiue, but rather fall off, and shed vpon the earth.

9. *trans.* To send forth as an emanation.

a. To throw (light) *upon* something. *lit.* and *fig.*

In the figurative use of the phrase *shed* is in our quots. not found before the 19th c.; earlier *throw* or *cast* was used.

c 1200 *Trin. Coll. Hom.* 161 Þis edie maiden seinte marie of hire holie licame shedeð þat soðe liht þe lihteð alle brihte þinges on eorðe and ec on heuene. 13.. *Cursor M.* 17883 (Gött.) Þat light es nu apon vs schede Þar we sitte in þe schadu of dede. *c* 1400 Lydg. *Compl. Bl. Knt.* 3 And Phebus gan to shede his stremes shene Amid the Bole. 1599 Sir J. Davies *Nosce Teipsum* Ded. iv, In euery place as Cynthia sheds her beames. 1775 R. Chandler *Trav. Asia M.* viii. (1825) I. 30 The stars shone in a clear blue sky, shedding a calm serene light. 1805 Wordsw. *Prelude* XIV. 279 O capacious Soul! Placed on this earth to love and understand, And from thy presence shed the light of love. 1853 Robertson *Serm.* Ser. III. xxi. (1876) 272 He has been shedding a glory round human life. 1853 Kingsley *Hypatia* xix, A lamp of strange form hung from the ceiling, and shed a dim and lurid light. 1860 [see Light *sb.* 6 a]. 1865 Dickens *Mut. Fr.* III. vi, You come like I don't know what ..shedding a halo all around you. 1912 *Times* 19 Oct. 7/3 The statement..sheds little light upon a situation still enveloped in mystery.

†b. With inverted construction: To suffuse *with* light. *Obs.*

1412–20 Lydg. *Troy Bk.* I. 2771 Sche..sawe þat þe ferþe parte Of þe mone was schad with newe liȝt.

c. To give forth, diffuse (fragrance, sound, heat, etc.); to pour out, impart (influence, blessings, qualities, etc.). Also with advs., *abroad*, †*forth*, †*out*.

a 1325 *Prose Psalter* xliv. 3 Grace is shadde in þy lippes. 1412–20 Lydg. *Troy Bk.* I. 2612 And holsomm bawme is schad among þe grene. *c* 1500 *Melusine* iv. 22 This might not be perfightly knowen, yf thou shadd nat vpon the men somwhat of thy full & deuyne grace. 1525 Tindale *N. T.* Prol., Tyll Christ have..powred into him that selfe good thynge whych he shedeth forth afterwarde on other. 1526 — *Rom.* v. 5 For the love that god hath vnto vs is shed abrod [Gr. ἐκκέχυται] in oure hertes [so later versions] by the holy gost, which is geven vnto vs. 1535 Coverdale *Acts* x. 45 The gifte of yᵉ holy goost was shed out also vpon the Heythen. 1587 Golding *De Mornay* Pref. (ad fin.), Now God vouchsafe to shead out his blessing vpon this worke. *Ibid.* iv. 47 The heate which the Sunne sheadeth into vs from aboue. 1642–7 H. More *Song of Soul* III. i. v, Wakend by piercing trump, that farre doth shed Its searching sound. 1709 Steele *Tatler* No. 130 ¶ 11 All the Prosperity and Success which Heaven ever shed on a Mortal. 1716 Gay *Trivia* II. 443 Now, heaven-born Charity! thy blessings shed. 1760–72 H. Brooke *Fool of Qual.* (1808) I. 155 For him the stars shine and shed influences upon earth. 1769 Gray *Ode for Music* 73 Bid it round heaven's altars shed The fragrance of it's blushing head. 1807 Moore *Ir. Melodies*, '*Harp that once*' 2 The harp that once through Tara's halls, The soul of music shed. 1812 Cary *Dante, Parad.* IV. 115 Whose lively words Still shed new heat and vigour through My soul. 1837 Carlyle *Fr. Rev.* III. III. vi, The waving of it shed terror through the souls of men. 1852 Mrs. Stowe *Uncle Tom's C.* xvi, Your piety sheds respectability on us. 1877 R. H. Hutton *Ess.* (ed. 2) I. Pref. 19 An infinite power shed abroad in the world.

absol. 1525 Tindale *N. T.* Prol., Be faith we receave of god, and be love we shed oute agayne.

10. To cast off by natural process.

a. To cast off as exuviæ; to undergo the falling of (hair, etc.).

1510 Stanbridge *Vocabula* (W. de W.) C vj b, *Depennesco*, to multe, or to shede fethers. 1530 Palsgr. 701/2 I shede my heare, my heare falleth. 1594 Marlowe & Nashe *Dido* I. i. 36 Venus Swannes shall shed their siluer downe. 1721 Bradley *Philos. Acc. Wks. Nat.* 91 The Stag and some other sorts of Deer are subject to shedding and renewing their Hornsannually. 1732 A. Monro *Anatomy* (ed. 2) 170 Some more of those [teeth]..are shedded. 1818 Scott *Hrt. Midl.* xxxi, A broken and soiled white feather, intersected with one which had been shed from the train of a peacock. 1833 *Hunter's Catal. Physiol. Ser. Comp. Anat. Mus. Coll. Surg.* I. 100 [Elephants] do not shed their teeth as other animals do that have more than one. 1845 Judd *Margaret* II. xi. (1874) 346 When hens are shedding their feathers they don't lay eggs. 1899 *Allbutt's Syst. Med.* VIII. 537 It is very common for the whole of the nails to be shed in the attack. *Ibid.* 809 The epidermis becoming shed.

transf. and *fig.*

1776 Foote *Capuchin* II. (1778) 116 When the sun and summer of plenty returns, I shall shed my coat like a colt. 1853 Kane *Grinnell Exp.* xvi. (1856) 121 The floes..now shed off dusty wreaths of snow. 1865 Swinburne *Chastelard* v. i. 175 The day comes when a woman sheds her sin As a bird moults. 1910 *Spectator* 20 Aug. 269/1 He sheds his bad reputation as a snake its skin.

b. Of trees, plants: To lose, cast off (leaves, flowers, bark, etc.).

1598 Barnfield *Poems*, *Compl. Poetrie* xv, The Trees (for sorrowe) shead their fading Leaues. 1667 Milton *P. L.* IX. 893 From his slack hand the Garland wreath'd for Eve Down drop'd, and all the faded Roses shed. 1798 Sophia Lee *Canterb. T.*, *Yng. Lady's T.* II. 295 The myrtles.. [were] shedding their uncherished blossoms over the perishing works of man. 1819 Shelley *Ode to West Wind* 16 Thou on whose stream, mid the steep sky's commotion, Loose clouds like earth's decaying leaves are shed. 1857 Livingstone *Trav.* xxiii. 462 Some of the bushes and trees are green; others are shedding their leaves.

†c. To cause the shedding of (leaves). *Obs.*

1697 Dryden *Virg. Georg.* II. 558 When Storms have shed From Vines, the hairy Honours of their Head.

d. Of plants: To let fall, cast (seed) out of the receptacle.

1523–34 Fitzherb. *Husb.* § 35 In some countreys..they do fan theyr corne, the whiche is..a great saueguarde for shedynge of the corne. 1573 Tusser *Husb.* (1878) 128 Hops dried in loft, aske tendance oft, And shed their seedes, much more than needes. 1720 P. Blair *Bot. Ess.* Pref. 6 The Apices..are ready to shed the Dust when it [the Flower is expanded. 1815 J. Smith *Panorama Sci. & Art* II. 634 As it is apt to shed its seed when ripe, it is advisable to cut it with the dew upon it. 1862 Ansted *Channel Isl.* IV. xx. (ed. 2) 476 Owing to a bad habit of leaving the crops till over-ripe, large quantities are shed on the fields.

e. *colloq.* To drop, let go; to give away (something of no particular value).

1855 Dickens *Dorrit* I. xxi, Whether it had occurred to his good friend, that Society might not unreasonably hope that one so blest in his undertakings,..would shed a little money in the direction of a mission or so to Africa? 1897 Mary Kingsley *W. Africa* 391, I shed a box of lucifer matches on her,..knowing that one of the great charms of a white man to a black is this habit of shedding things.

11. *intr.* for *refl.*

†a. Of the hair: To fall off. *Obs.*

1523–34 Fitzherb. *Husb.* § 110 Myllettes..causeth the heare to sheede. 1530 Palsgr. 701/2 Your heares shede, you

wyll waxe balde. 1607 Topsell *Four-f. Beasts* 487 The same also being mingled with a certaine oyle and warmed together, and anointed vpon the head of any one, whose hair doth shed,..doth immediatly helpe and cure the same. 1611 Middleton & Dekker *Roaring Girl* I 4 b, His haire sheds off. 1644 Digby *Nat. Bodies* xxxvii. § 4. 326 We see the haire of women with childe, is apt to shedde. 1755 H. Baker in *Phil. Trans.* XLIX. I. 22 When I saw this man, in the month of September last, they [wart-like growths] were shedding off in several places.

b. Of grain: To fall from the ear. Also of leaves or flowers: To drop off.

1557 Tusser *100 Points Husb.* § 96 The corne, being ripe doe but shead as it stande. 1584 Cogan *Haven Health* xlix. 57 Artichokes..[are] thought to make euill iuice, especially when the flowers begin to shed. 1606 Shaks. *Tr. & Cr.* I. iii. 319 The seeded Pride That hath to this maturity blowne vp In ranke Achilles, must or now be cropt, Or shedding breed a Nursery of like euil To ouerbulke vs all. 1681 R. L'Estrange *Tully's Offices* 103 All Disguises pass away, and shed like Flowers. 1707 Mortimer *Husb.* 355 The broad leaved Lime..bears a very fine broad Leaf, only it is apt to shed too soon. 1760 R. Brown *Compl. Farmer* II. 81 White oats are apt to shed most as they lie, and black as they stand. 1790 W. H. Marshall *Midl. Counties* II. 442 To *Shade*, to shed, as corn. 1844 *Jrnl. R. Agric. Soc.* V. I. 284 The wheat..sheds very easily, that is, the corn or grain falls very readily out of the husk.

12. To slope. Now *dial.*

1530 Palsgr. 702/1, I shedde, as an hyll dothe slopewyse downwardes to the valley...It is a pleasaunt syght to se howe the hylles shedde on eache syde in to the medowes. 1688, 1747 [see Shedding *ppl. a.* 1 3]. 1826 Wilbraham *Chesh. Gloss.* (ed. 2), To *Shead* is also to slope down ground regularly.

13. The verb-stem in combination: †*shed-fork*, app. = pitchfork; †*shed-spade*, ? a dungfork or graip.

1559 *Richmond Wills* (Surtees) 134, ijᵒ shede forks, ijᵒ shed spaids. 1706 Mrs. Centlivre *Platonick Lady* IV. iv. (1707) 57 All my Rigging hangs as if 'twas zhaked on with a Zhed Vork, as the old Zaying is.

Shed (ʃed), *v.*² [f. Shed *sb.*² 1.] *trans.* †**a.** To roof over. *Obs.* **b.** To place in a shed.

1546 Wriothesley *Chron.* (1875) I. 175 The 15ᵗʰ daie of September the forreine buchers beganne to keepe their markett in Leeden Hall, which was sheded rounde aboute for them to stand dry. 1850 *Jrnl. R. Agric. Soc.* XI. II. 419, I have left off shedding my own sheep. 1887 *Pall Mall Gaz.* 21 Mar. 2/1 As to hay feeding and shedding during the winter, that is quite impracticable.

Shed (ʃed), *ppl. a.* [pa. pple. of Shed *v.*¹]

†1. Separated: ? in several ownership. *Obs.*

1425 in *Rep. MSS. Ld. Middleton* (1911) 107 No man with comyn herd ne with sched herd com on the wold after gresse be mowen to it [be] maked and led away. *Ibid.* 108 Nother comyn herd ne sched herd com' in the qwyte corn feld to the korn [be] lad awey.

2. Fallen; discarded, cast off.

c 1430 *Chev. Assigne* 119 Of sadde leues of þe wode wrowȝte he hem wedes. 1847 H. Miller *Test. Rocks* viii. (1857) 318 It is not credible that all the solid shed antlers of such a species of deer could be carried by the same cause to such a distance. 1893 E. Reeves *Homeward Bound* 43 The shed bark hanging over its branches and clinging to its trunk like a sheeted ghost.

3. Of blood, tears (see Shed *v.*¹ 7, 8). Also *dial.* of liquids: Spilt.

1824 Mrs. Cameron *Pink Tippet* III. 17 'There is no use in crying for shed milk,' answered Betty. 1899 *Allbutt's Syst. Med.* VI. 155 Clots formed in shed blood.

4. (See Shed *v.*¹ 2 b.)

1839 Ure *Dict. Arts* 1285 The weaver..drives the fly-shuttle swiftly from one side of the loom to the other, between the shed warp yarns.

†**Shed·dable**, *a.* *Obs. rare*⁻⁰. [f. Shed *v.*¹ + -able.] That can be shed or poured out.

1570 Levins *Manip.* 2/17 Shedable, *fusilis*.

Shedded (ʃe·ded), *ppl. a.*¹ [f. Shed *v.*¹ + -ed¹. Cf. Shed *ppl. a.*]

†1. Cleft, divided. *Obs. rare*⁻¹.

c 1550 Rolland *Crt. Venus* IV. 612 The scheddit scheilds.

2. Cast off, fallen. *rare*⁻¹.

1818 Keats *Endymion* IV. 769 Its hazle cirque of shedded leaves.

3. Of hair, wool: Parted, separated, divided.

1844 H. Stephens *Bk. Farm* III. 1111 The bath thus made is administered by means of a tin-flask..provided with a long spout, by which to pour it along the shedded wool of the sheep.

Shedded (ʃe·ded), *ppl. a.*² [f. Shed *v.*² + -ed².] Placed in a shed.

1850 *Jrnl. R. Agric. Soc.* XI. II. 419 The shedded lot [of sheep] did..best in January, and the folded lot in March.

Shedder (ʃe·dəɹ). [f. Shed *v.*¹ + -er¹.]

1. One who sheds, in various senses of the verb.

c 1388 in *Wyclif's Sel. Wks.* III. 474 Leste Crist dampne ȝowe for traytouris and monquellers and scheders of his blode. 1555 Eden *Decades* I. VII. (Arb.) 91 Cruel enemies and sheaders of the Spanyshe bludde. *a* 1625 Fletcher *Bloody Brother* IV. iii, But your parts in all dues to crying blood For vengeance in the shedder, are much greater. 1712 E. Cooke *Voy. S. Sea* 273 The seventh Inca, whose Name signifies, Shedder of bloody Tears. 1880 Miss Braddon *Just as I am* xiii, He was never a shedder of blood.

2. *spec.* **a.** A female fish of the *Salmonidæ* after spawning.

1588 Lambarde *Eiren.* IV. iv. 450 If any person..haue taken there any Salmons or Troutes, out of season, that is, being kippers, or shedders. 1848 [see Kipper *sb.* 1].

b. A name for a crab during the period when it is casting its covering integument or shell.

1872 Schele de Vere *Americanisms* 390.

3. *Comb.* (sense 2), as *shedder-crab*, *-salmon*, *trout*.

1860 Bartlett *Dict. Amer.* (ed. 3), *Shedder-crab*, a crab which has recently cast his shell, also called a Soft Crab. 1884 E. P. Roe *Nat. Ser. Story* v. in *Harper's Mag.* Apr. 733/2, I was still..fishing,..and fastened on my hook a peeled shedder crab. 1558 *Act 1 Eliz.* c. 17 § 1 That no person.. shall..take and kyll any..*shedder Salmons, or *shedder Trowtes. 1787 Best *Angling* (ed. 2) 139 Any kepper or shedder salmon.

Shedding (ʃe·diŋ), *sb.* [f. Shed *sb.*¹ + -ing¹.] Sheds collectively; a collection of sheds.

1883 *Times* 26 July 7/5 Shedding of large capacity will be provided. 1889 Skrine *Mem. E. Thring* 152 These were ..scheming new bonfires. Whose barns or sheddings were safe? 1898 *Field* 14 May 741/1 Long rows of shedding.

Shedding (ʃe·diŋ), *vbl. sb.* Also 7 **schiding**. [f. Shed *v.*¹ + -ing¹.] The action or an act of the verb Shed in various senses.

1. Separation, parting, division. Also *concr.* = Shed *sb.*¹ Now only *dial.* Cf. Sheading.

c 1200 Ormin 16863 Forr Farisew bitacneþþ uss Shædinng onn Ennglissh spæche. 1303 R. Brunne *Handl. Synne* 12418 'Dymynucyon'..ys to mene also anoþer þyng, Of þy synne to make shedyng. *c* 1440 Hylton *Scala Perf.* (W. de W. 1494) II. xxxvi, And this is the yefte of loue that makyth shedynge atwyx chosen soules & reproued. 1598 Florio, *Scriminatura*, the shedding or diuiding of a womans haires of a head. 1611 Cotgr. s.v. *Greve*, *La greve des cheveux* (&, *les cheveux departis en greve*), the shedding, or shading of the haire; the parting thereof on the forehead (after the old fashion). 1768 Ross *Helenore* 103 Gin he look'd blyth, the lassie looked mair, For shame was past the shedding o' her hair. 1872 Black *Adv. Phaeton* xxix, Then we got out to that 'shedding' of the roads, which marks the junction of the highways coming down from Glasgow and Edinburgh.

Comb. 1609 Bible (Douay) *Isa.* iii. 20 Our Lord shal take away..the sheading combes.

b. *dial.* (*concr.* in *pl.*). See quot.

1844 H. Stephens *Bk. Farm* II. 39 The lambs, dinmonts, or wethers, that are drafted out of the fat stock, are called the sheddings or tails.

c. *Weaving.* The division of the warp threads in such a manner as to permit of the passage between them of a shuttle containing the weft. Also *attrib.*

1863 J. Watson *Weaving* 84 The shedding being repeated two times over. 1876 Barlow *Weaving* 111 Shedding motions may be classed into about six varieties. 1888 *Encycl. Brit.* XXIV. 466/1 The three principal motions, shedding, picking and beating up, are of course the same in both [looms]. *Ibid.*, The treadles called the shedding tappets.

2. Effusion, pouring out; esp. of blood, tears, †secretions.

c 1200 *Trin. Coll. Hom.* 65 Ne bringð no synful man quemere loc þenne teares sheding. *a* 1225 *Ancr. R.* 262 Ȝet nabbe ȝe nout wiðstonden uorte þet þe schedunge of ower blode. 1560 Daus tr. *Sleidane's Comm.* 465 b, They could not kepe them from sheding of teares. 1657 W. Coles *Adam in Eden* ii. 5 It helpeth..the shedding of the gall. 1760–72 H. Brooke *Fool of Qual.* (1809) III. 38 Their persons were rendered sacred..by unction, or the shedding of hallowed oil upon them. 1874 O'Shaughnessy *Music & Moonlight* 200 Base sheddings of base blood.

†b. Infusion, diffusion. *Obs.*

1398 Trevisa *Barth. De P. R.* III. ix. (1495) 55 By vertue of spredynge and of shedynge of the spyryte of felynge in to all the synewes, all the makynge of the body is founde able to moeue. *c* 1430 *Pilgr. Lyf Manhode* III. xix. (1869) 185 In whiche we hadden putte fillinge of þe grete tresores of Paradys, þat was the sweete shedinge of oure grace.

†c. *Shedding of nature*: gonorrhœa. *Obs.*

1584 Cogan *Haven Health* xlii. 52 A verie good medicine for the shedding of nature.

3. Dropping, scattering or letting fall, or parting with something.

1362 Langl. *P. Pl.* A. VII. 9 Summe schul souwe sakkes for schedyng of Whete. 1523–34 Fitzherb. *Husb.* § 35 [Some] do fan theyr corne, the whiche is..a great saueguarde for shedynge of the corne. 1600 J. Pory tr. *Leo's Africa* I. 38 Unnaturall shedding of haire. 1732 A. Monro *Anatomy* (ed. 2) 170 This Shedding of the Teeth is of good Use. 1863 A. Ewing in A. J. Ross *Mem.* (1877) 356 Our life has far more in it than is suggested by the growing and shedding of leaves.

b. *concr.* in *pl.* Shed leaves, etc.

1803 Wordsw. *Poems Imag.*, *Yew-trees* 22 Upon whose grassless floor of red brown hue, By sheddings from the pining umbrage tinged Perennially. 1856 Aird *Poet. Wks.* 294 She trode the dun-brown sheddings of the pine.

c. The letting fall of seeds.

1721 Pope *Let. to E. Blount* 21 Oct., Old Fletcher of Saltoune said one day to me, '..I am like a Tree without a Prop, and without young Trees of my own shedding, to grow round me, for Company and Defence.'

Shedding (ʃe·diŋ), *ppl. a.* [f. Shed *v.*¹ + -ing².] That sheds, in various senses of the verb.

1. †a. Of liquids: Self-diffusing. *Obs.*

1587 Golding *De Mornay* xv. 272 The bodie is in the Soule, as..a sheading or liquid thing in a thing that is not liquid [orig. *comme..le coulant en ce qui ne coule point*].

b. Dropping or casting leaves or petals.

1687 Dryden *Hind & P.* III. 439 The shedding trees began the ground to strow With yellow leaves. 1782 J. Scott *Poet. Wks.* 261 And green slopes redden with the shedding rose.

c. (See quot.)

1796 Withering *Brit. Plants* (ed. 3) I. 81 Shedding (caducus) continuing but a short time. *Ibid.* 262 Cup 4 leaves, leafits egg-shaped, coloured, shedding.

d. *Shedding tooth*: any of the primary or milk teeth, which fall out and are replaced by the permanent teeth.

1799 Home in *Phil. Trans.* LXXXIX. 258 A view of the grinding surface of a shedding tooth. 1822–29 *Good's Study Med.* (ed. 3) I. 47 The permanent teeth have separate sockets of their own; and..do not lie immediately under the corresponding shedding teeth. 1833 *Hunter's Catal. Physiol. Ser. Comp. Anat. Mus. Coll. Surg.* I. 100 The shedding tooth falls some time before the succeeding tooth can supply its uses.

e. *fig.* Of divisions of time: Passing.

1816 L. Hunt *Rimini* III. 134 The glass that told the shedding hours.

†2. Dividing, parting, separating. *Obs. rare.*

a 1674 Bunyan *Reprob. Asserted* i. (1696) 2 These words were shedding words, they sever between Men and Men.

†3. Sloping. *Obs.*

1688 Holme *Armoury* III. 73/1 A Barn with a shedding Ridg. 1747 Hooson *Miner's Dict.* Q 1 b, If a Rock appears to the Day,..where it seems to cut off, and more especially on Sheeding ground.

Shedding, Shede, obs. ff. Sheading, Sheath.

Sheder (ʃī·dəɹ). *dial.* Forms: 6–7 **shidder**, 7 **shether**, 8 **sheeder**, 9 **sheder**. [f. She + ? Deer: cf. Heder.] A female sheep; spec. a lamb from eight or nine months old to her first shearing.

1579 Spenser *Sheph. Cal.* Sept. 211 For, had his wesand bene a little widder, He would haue deuoured both hidder and shidder [*Gloss* He and she. Male and Female]. 1680 T. Granger *Div. Logike* 169 As appeares by hether, and shether, *i.* male, and female. 1633 J. Fisher *Fuimus Troes* III. ix. Chorus, Hidder, eke and shidder. 1799 A. Young *Agric. Lincoln.* 325 They are forced to sell their heeders, and joist their sheeders in the spring. 1851 *Jrnl. R. Agric. Soc.* XII. II. 341 The 'heder' hogs being grazed on the seeds, and the 'sheders' on grass.

Shee, Sheeah, Sheed(e: see She, Shiah, Shed.

Sheeding, Sheef(fe: see Sheading, Sheaf *sb.*

Sheeite, Sheek: see Shiite, Sheikh.

Sheel (ʃīl), *v.* Now *dial.* Forms: α. 5 **schel**, 6 **scheill**, 7 **s(c)heele, scheil**, 7–9 **sheal**, 8–9 **shiel**, 9 **sheil**, 8– **sheel**; β. 5 **schylle**, 6 **shyll**, 6– **shill**. [Related to Shale *sb.*¹; the early history is obscure.

The α forms possibly repr. OE. **scielian* (in *āscylian* 'enucleare'), f. *scealu* Shale *sb.*¹ The β forms, exc. in the northern examples, perh. belong to a distinct though synonymous word, a derivative of Shell *sb.*]

trans. To shell; to take off the husk or outer covering of. Hence **Sheeled** *ppl. a.*

α. 1473 *Rental Bk. Cupar-Angus* (1879) I. 182 Payand.. ix chalder of vitale of the kyngis met, half beir half meil, the meil twise schelit. 1508, 1583–4 [implied in Sheeling *vbl. sb.*]. 1605 Shaks. *Lear* I. iv. 219 That's a sheal'd Pescod. 1615 G. Sandys *Trav.* II. (1637) 116 *Rosetta*..perhaps deriued of *Ros*, which signifieth *Rice*, and so named for the abundance that it vttereth; (they here shealing monethly three hundred quarters). 1612 in *Trans. Cumb. & Westm. Archæol. Soc.* (N. S.) III. (1893) 155 That the Milner..doe neither sheele nor grinde any Skillinge of any Mans dwelling in another Lordshipp. 1681 *Ibid.* 159 Noe Tennant or Farmer ..Shall grinde or Scheele any Wheate, Bigg, Barley, Pease ..att any other Mill. 1709 Lady G. Baillie *Househ. Bk.* (S.H.S.) 79, 10 stone twist shield meall. 1765 *Museum Rust.* IV. 457 After sheeling, the seed should be well cleansed from bad seeds. 1801 *Farmer's Mag.* Apr. 214 It was first shealed on the barley mill. 1816 Scott *Bl. Dwarf* xvii, We took their swords and pistols as easily as ye wad shiel peacods. *a* 1824 G. Beattie *John o' Arnha'* etc. (1826) 83 She mussels sheel'd, an' wan her bread. 1861 Smiles *Engineers* II. 105 Barley was shealed by pounding the grains with water in the hollow of a stone until by that means the husks were rubbed off. 1862 Hislop *Prov. Scot.* 101 He would need to be twice sheeled and ance grund that deals wi' you.

β. *c* 1440 *Promp. Parv.* 446/1 Schyllyn owte, of coddys, *exsil(l)iquo*. Schyllyn, or schylle notys, *enucleo*. *Ibid.* 446/2 Schyllyn oysterys, and thyngys closyd yn schellys, *excortico*. 1483 *Cath. Angl.* 336/1 Schylled pyse..., *pise exiliqué*. 1508 in *Reg. Mag. Sig. Scot.* 1510, 747/1, 4 bollas..albe et bone farrine vulgariter nuncupat. twise schillit mele. *c* 1522 Skelton *Why nat to Court?* 108 Or pescoddes they may shyll. 1702 Lady G. Baillie *Househ. Bk.* (S.H.S.) 66 For Shild pies..2 peck out of 5 p. 1703 Thoresby in Ray *Philos. Lett.* (1718) 336 To *Shill*, as Pease to take them out of the Swads. 1799 J. Robertson *Agric. Perth* 163 When the barley is twice shilled, i.e. put twice through the mill, on purpose to take off the rind more compleatly, and then grinded small. 1862 C. C. Robinson *Dial. Leeds Gloss.* s.v. *Shill*, 'Shillin' peis'; 'shillin' beins'—unshelling peas and beans.

Sheel(l, Sheeld(e: see Shiel, Shield.

Shee·ling, shi·lling, *vbl. sb.* Forms: α. see Sheel *v.* β. 6 **shillinge**, 6–7 **schilling**, 6, 8–9 **shilling**, 8–9 **shillen**, 9 **shillin**. [f. Sheel *v.* + -ing¹.]

1. The action of Sheel *v.*

α. 1583–4 *Burgh Rec. Edin.* (1882) IV. 320 That thai diligentlie awaitt vpoun the scheilling of the quheitt pertening to the said nichtbouris of the baxteris. 1606 in *Sel. Rec. Kirk Sess.* etc. *Aberd.* (1846) 198 The haill millers..to absteine from millinge, grindinge or scheilinge on the Sabboth day in tymes cumminge. 1801 *Farmer's Mag.* Apr. 214 It [common barley] produced nearly 21 pecks and a half..of common barley-flour,.. 4 lb. of husks from the shealing, and [etc.]. 1844 H. Stephens *Bk. Farm* II. 350 The protuberances of the rootlets and woolly ends should not have been rubbed off by any process, such as sheeling.

β. *c* 1440 *Promp. Parv.* 446/2 Schyllynge, of notys. 1906 Woodruffe-Peacock *Ideal Thoroughbred Stud* 14 'The dry shilling' so prevalent in the spring months, which is so serious a throw-back to both plant and animal growth.

2. The grain removed from the husk, also the husks of oats, wheat, etc.

α. 1597 in *Spalding Club Misc.* (1841) I. 173 And than the said mylne..grund efter hir auld forme, and made gude meill and scheiling. 1667 *Rec. Baron Crt. Stitchill* (S.H.S.) 46 It is..ordained that the owner of the corne mak their awn shelling in all tyme cuming. 1844 J. Ballantine *Miller of Deanhaugh* x. 177 Rank an' station! bran an' sheelings! exclaimed the miller. 1902 *Ardrossan Herald* 31 Jan. 2/3 The multure is a quantity of grain, sometimes in kind, as wheat, oats, pease, and sometimes manufactured as flour, meal, sheeling.

β. 1508 Dunbar *Flyting* 147 Thow and thy quene, as gredy gleddis, ȝe gang with polkis to mylne, and beggis baith meill and schilling. *Ibid.* 243 Chitterlilling, ruch rilling, lik schilling in the milhouse. 1546 *Reg. Mag. Sig. Scot.* 7/2 Cum una firlota de lie thirl beir et una firlota de lie ring schilling. 1690 J. Mackenzie *Siege London Derry* 39/1 There was Oats, Shilling, and Malt in Town, which could not be used for want of Mills. 1681 O. Heywood *Diaries* (1881) II. 286 A stroke of shilling standing on the table. 1729 P. Walkden *Diary* (1866) 85 Sent son Thomas towards Preston with a load of shilling to sell. 1795 *Statist. Acc. Scot.* XV. 117 *Shillen*, i.e. shealing, or hulter corn, is measured by the tacksman of the mill, and is paid, not in shealing, but in meal. 1910 G. Henderson *Norse Infl. Celtic Scot.* v. 117 In Lowland Scots *shillin*, unhusked grain.

3. *attrib.* and *Comb.*, as *sheeling cylinder, groats, machine, time*, etc.; **sheeling-hill**, a hill or eminence where grain was winnowed by the wind, so **sheeling-mound**; **sheeling-seeds**, the husks of corn, esp. oats, also the grain that has been freed from the husk; **sheeling-stone** (see quot. 1880).

1844 H. Stephens *Bk. Farm* II. 351 The first process which wheat undergoes in grinding is in being put through the *sheeling cylinder. 1585–6 *Shuttleworths Acc.* (Chetham Soc.) 91 A peke of *shillynge groates. 1597 in *Spalding Club Misc.* (1841) I. 174 The *schilling hill of the Mylne of Fedderet. 1816 Scott *Old Mort.* vii, Instead of..waiting patiently for whatever dispensation of wind Providence was pleased to send upon the sheeling-hill. 1840 J. Hodgson *Hist. Northumbld.* II. III. 118 *note*, A shilling-hill, as a place to deet or winnow the groats of oats from the husks that had been shilled off them, before machinery was invented for the purpose, was not an uncommon appendage to a mill. 1911 E. Beveridge *North Uist* i. 11 At a *shieling-mound close to the southern base of Marrival is Tobar Chuithairidh. 1715 Pennecuik *Wks.* (1815) 87 (E.D.D.) The husks or *shilling seeds are again separated by the farmers. *a* 1867 W. Anderson in *Mod. Sc. Poets* Ser. II. (1881) 238 A cushion stuff't wi' sheelin' seeds. 1563 in *Rates Exeter Canal* in *Archæologia* XXVIII. 18 For everye boate loadinge with beare, *shillingstones, lyme, wood, cole [etc.] iiij.*d.* 1880 *Antrim & Down Gloss.*, *Shilling stones*, the pair of stones in a corn mill which are used for taking the husks off oats. 1895 Sir H. Maxwell *Dk. of Britain* xix. 281 It is his custom to go frequently up during the *sheiling-time.

†**Shee·ling**, *ppl. a.* *Obs. rare*⁻¹. [f. Sheel *v.* + -ing².] That is in process of peeling off.

1708 tr. *Cowley's Plants* I. C.'s Wks. III. 288 All thy shealing Scabs rub off again.

Sheen (ʃīn), *sb.*¹ Forms: 6 *Sc.* **scheyne**, 6–7 **sheene**, 7– **sheen**. [f. Sheen *a.*, assumed to be connected with Shine *v.* (The sb. is virtually a verbal noun to *shine*.) Cf. Sheen *v.*]

1. Shining, brightness. In recent use chiefly, gleaming, lustre, radiance as of a body reflecting light; a gleam. *rare* before the 19th c.

1602 Shaks. *Ham.* III. ii. 167 And thirtie dozen Moones with borrowed sheene, About the World haue times twelue thirties been. 1614 Gorges *Lucan* VI. 240 And modest Cynthias siluer hue Vnto a pallid colour grew...As if the earth had bene betwene To barre her of her brothers sheene. 1629 Milton *Hymn Nativ.* xv, Thron'd in Celestiall sheen. 1634 — *Comus* 893 The azurn sheen Of Turkis blew. *Ibid.* 1003 Far above in spangled sheen Celestial Cupid her fam'd son advanc't. 1768 Beattie *Minstr.* I. xxii, The southern Sun diffus'd his dazzling shene. 1798 Coleridge *Anc. Mar.* I. xiv, And through the drifts the snowy clifts Did send a dismal sheen. 1815 Byron *Destr. Sennacherib* i, The sheen of their spears was like stars on the sea. 1830 Tennyson *Song*, '*The Lintwhite*' 28 Thy locks are all of sunny sheen. 1881 J. Hatton *New Ceylon* ii. 51 [A pearl] of a peculiarly brilliant sheen. 1879 Black *Macleod of D.* I. 178 The beautiful blue sheen on its scales. 1888 Annie S. Swan *Doris Cheyne* ii. 30 Her hair..had a sheen like gold upon it. 1906 Williamson *Lady Betty across Water* 288 The green of the waving trees seemed to be reflected in their complexions in little sheens and shimmers.

b. *transf.* and *fig.*

1828 Coleridge *Gard. Boccaccio* 47 And last, a matron now, of sober mien Yet radiant still and with no earthly sheen. 1831 Carlyle *Sartor Res.* III. iii, Ever in the dullest existence there is a sheen either of Inspiration or of Madness. 1863 W. Phillips *Sp.* vi. 114 No sheen of official position would ever lead us.

c. Gorgeous or bright attire.

[1631 Milton *Marchioness of Winchester* 73 With thee there clad in radiant sheen, No Marchioness, but now a Queen.] 1802 Mrs. Radcliffe *Gaston de Blondeville* Posth. Wks. (1826) II. 348 They saw plainly enough knights, esquires and pages..in all their splendour; and lady-aunts and lady-cousins in the galleries, in all their sheen and joyance. 1812 Byron *Ch. Har.* I. lxxiv, In costly sheen and gaudy cloak array'd. 1898 Newbolt *Isl. Race* 94 Stepped she not with a grace entrancing, Slenderly girt in silken sheen?

2. The pupil of the eye. *Sc.* (? *Obs.*)

c 1500 Kennedy *Passion of Christ* 581 For as I writtin into Doctouris fand. He wes mair tender [into] his body, Than is be scheyne into a mannis e. 1808 Jamieson, *Sheen of the eye*, the pupil of the eye.

Sheen (ʃīn), *sb.*² *slang.* [Of obscure origin: cf. Shan.] Base coin. Also *attrib.* or *adj.*

1864 *Hotten's Slang Dict.* 226 *Sheen*, bad money. 1888 Payne *Eavesdropper* II. ii. 80 'Can you smash a thick un

for me?' inquired one, handing his friend a sovereign. 'You're sure it ain't sheen?' returned the other, with a diabolical grin. 1890 Barrère & Leland *Dict. Slang*, *Sheen* (Scotch), bad money. Probably alluding to the 'glitter', or possibly from German *schein*, a bank-bill.

Sheen (ʃīn), *a.* Now *poet.* Forms: 1 **sciéne, scéne, scéone, sciene, scýne, scíne**, 2–4 **scene**, 3 **sceone, sschene**, 3–4 **scen**, (? **schine**), 3–6 **schene**, 3–6, (8–9) **shene**, 4 **schen**, (**sene**), 5 **schenne, sshene**, 6 **shen**, 4–7 **sheene**, 5 **scheene**; 3 **scone**, *Sc.* 4–6 **scheyne**, 5 **sheyn**, 6 **schein(e, schane**; 6– **sheen**. *compar.* 1 **sciénra**, 3 **schenre, schennure**, 4 **schenure**. [OE. *sciene* = OFris. *skêne* (mod.Fris. *skjin*), OS. *scôni* (MLG. *schône, schôn*; Sw. *skön*, Da. *skjøn*, prob. from LG.), MDu. *schôn(e* (mod.Du. *schoon*), OHG. *scôni*, earlier *scaoni* (MHG. *schœne, schœn*, mod.G. *schön*), Goth. *skaun-s*:—OTeut. **skauni-*, **skaunjo-* f. root **skau-* to behold: see Show *v.*

The Gothic *ibnaskauns* like-formed, *guþaskaunei* likeness of God, suggest that the word may originally have meant 'having (a certain) appearance'. For the development of the eulogistic sense, cf. *sightly, shapely*, L. *forma* form, beauty, *formosus* beautiful.

In English (and app. to some extent in OHG. and OS. where it glosses *lucidus, splendidus* etc.) the sense was influenced by association with the root of Shine *v.* In early examples it is often difficult to determine whether the sense is merely 'beautiful', or whether there is some added notion of 'shining, bright'.

The form *sceone* in Ormin, which implies the pronunciation (skøːnə), is unexplained. The identically written form in Layamon, however, seems to be merely an instance of the practice, common in 12–13th c. texts, of writing *eo* for *eo*.]

1. Beautiful. **a.** Of persons (esp. women), their appearance, features, etc.

Beowulf 3017 Mæȝð scyne. *a* 900 Cynewulf *Crist* 1387 Ic ðe swa scienne ȝesceapen hæfde. *c* 1000 *Genesis* 265 Cwæð, þæt his lic wære leohte & scene. *c* 1200 *Vices & Virtues* 95 Nis ðar non swo god leiȝe se teares: hie makieð scene ansiene. *c* 1205 Lay. 13331, & he haueð to quene mine dohter þa is scone. *a* 1225 *Ancr. R.* 398 And Absalones schene wlite. *a* 1300 *Cursor M.* 24080 His face þat forwit was sa scene [*v.rr.* schen, shene]. *Ibid.* 28505 Gernand i haf oft ben Desird o þire wymmen scen. *c* 1300 *Sir Orfeo* 356 Al þe utmast wal Was clere and schine [*v.rr.* schone, gan schyne] as cristal. *c* 1350 *Will. Palerne* 3296 So schene he was to se in his semli armes. *c* 1374 Chaucer *H. Fame* III. 446 Graunte vs, lady shene Eche of vs, of thy grace a bone. *c* 1400 *Destr. Troy* 3070 Shulders full shaply, shenest of hewe, Full plesaund & playn. *a* 1450 *Le Morte Arth.* 2612 The mayde was full shene to shewe. *a* 1536 *Songs, Carols*, etc. (1907) 10 Hayle be thou Mary, maydyn shen. *a* 1586 ? Montgomerie *Banks of Helicon* 6 Declair, ȝe bankis of Helicon,..Gif ony of ȝour Muses all, Or nymphes may be peregall Vnto my lady schein? 1589 Greene *Menaphon* (Arb.) 43, I saw a little one, A bonny prety one, As bright buxsome and as sheene As was shee. 1590 Spenser *F. Q.* II. i. 10 Her daintie corse so faire and sheene. 1747 Mason *Musæus* 104 Belinda far surpast my beauties sheen.

†b. (*The*) *sheen*: used after a woman's name.

c 1205 Lay. 3098 Þe duc of Cornwaile scal habbe Gornoille & þe Scottene king Regau þat scone [*c* 1275 þe scene]. *c* 1320 *Sir Tristr.* 756 Slawe was rouland þan And ded blaunche þe schene. *c* 1386 Chaucer *Knt.'s T.* 210 The fresshe Emelye the sheene.

c. Of animals, inanimate objects, places, etc.

c 1000 *Phœnix* 591 Him folgiað fuȝlas scyne. *c* 1000 *Panther* 19 (Gr.) Deor wundrum scyne. *c* 1205 Lay. 19767 Vt heo droȝen sone amppullen scone [*c* 1275 six ampulles] ifulled mid attere weten alre bitterest. 12.. *Moral Ode* 340 (Egerton MS.) in *Lamb. Hom.* 179 Go we þene narewe wei and þene wei grene þer forð-fareð lutel folc ac it is feir and scene. *c* 1275 *Ibid.* 337 (Jesus MS.) in *O. E. Misc.* 70 Go we þene narewe wey þen wey so schene. 13.. *Gosp. Nicod.* 125 (Cott. Galba MS.) Þaire armes set on schaftes schene [*Harl. MS.* sene]. *c* 1350 *Will. Palerne* 3411 Many a schene scheld scheuered al to peces. *a* 1352 Minot *Poems* (ed. Hall) xi. 2 In schawes ful schene. *c* 1400 *Sowdone Bab.* 118 Carrikes, Galeis and shippes shene, vij hundred were gadered al in fere. *c* 1400 *Rom. Rose* 3713 By hir atyre so bright and shene, Men might perceyve..She was not of religioun. *c* 1400 *Destr. Troy* 330 With shotes of shire wode shene to beholde. 1423 Jas. I *Kingis Q.* xcv, His long[e] ȝalow lokkis schene. *c* 1435 *Torr. Portugal* 487 Abowght a facon schene. *c* 1470 Henry *Wallace* IV. 370 Thar I was born amang the schawis scheyne. *c* 1470 Harding *Chron.* CCXLII. App. xxx. iv, Four and twentie myles to Lamarke so shene. 1513 Douglas *Æneis* I. vii. 63 Rowmyng about the large temple schene. 1596 Dalrymple tr. *Leslie's Hist. Scot.* I. 17 Amang fair forrests and schawis schene. 1785 Burns *Vision* I. 67 Down flow'd her robe, a tartan sheen, Till half a leg was scrimply seen. 1873 Symonds *Grk. Poets* xi. 374 Narcissus will I twine, and lilies sheen.

†d. *absol.* (quasi-*sb.*) A fair one; a beautiful woman. *Obs.*

13.. *E. E. Allit. P.* A. 965 Þat schene sayde, þat god wyl schylde, 'Þou may not enter with-inne hys tor'. *c* 1400 *Destr. Troy* 8144 Than the bysshop to his barne barely onswart, And shend to þat schene all in short wordes. *c* 1420 *Avow. Arth.* xl, Thay so a schene vndur schild, Come prekand fast aure the filde, On a fayre stede. 1540 Palsgr. *Acolastus* III. v. R iij, A kisse, my lyght .i. my hart of golde, or my bryght and sheene, this is sweter then honye. *a* 1568 *Bannatyne MS.* (Hunter. Club) 627 Besek that schene with hummill reuerence The to ressaif.

†e. In non-material senses: Beautiful, attractive; noble, illustrious; pure, clean (*from* sin). *Obs.*

c 1205 Lay. 24326 To þan..þer com þe king Angel king of Scotlonde mid sceone his folke. *a* 1300 *Cursor M.* 18535 Þis hight [*i.e.* promise] þat was sa scene [*v.rr.* shene, schene], Suld tid þam thoru a maiden clene. *c* 1400 *Destr. Troy* 600, I will shunt for no shame of my shene fader, Ne no hede to my heale, þat I thee helpe shall. *c* 1430 *Hymns Virg.* (1867) 18 Þi passioun make us briȝt & schene In wil, in worde, in dede & þouȝt! 1460 in *Pol. Rel. & L. Poems* (1866) 254 Fro seuene synnes þou make me schene.

2. Bright, shining, resplendent.

In early use this sense may have been merely contextual, the adj. being applied in the sense 'beautiful' to objects (e.g. heavenly bodies, jewels, metals) the beauty of which is dependent on their brightness. In later use, owing to association with Shine *v.*, Sheen *sb.*¹, the sense 'shining' is felt as primary.

900 Cynewulf *Crist* 695 Hwæt sindan þa ȝimmas swa scyne buton god sylfa? *c* 1200 Ormin 3431 He sette a steorrne upp o þe lifft Full brad, & brihht, & shene. *a* 1225 *Ancr. R.* 362 In þe ariste of domesdeie, hwon ure vlesches schal blikien schenre þen þe sunne. 13.. *E. E. Allit. P.* A. 1145, I loked among his meyny schene. ? *a* 1366 Chaucer *Rom. Rose* 1512 He thoughte of thilke water shene To drinke and fresshe him wel withalle. 1377 Langl. *P. Pl.* B. XVIII. 409 'After sharpe showres', quod pees 'moste shene is þe sonne'. *c* 1402 Lydg. *Compl. Bl. Knt.* 3 In May, whan..Phebus gan to schede his stremes shene Amid the Bole. 1412–20 — *Troy Bk.* I. 623 Þe schene sonne. 1513 Douglas *Æneis* XII. iv. 40 O thou brycht son, with thy schene bemis glaid. 1535 Stewart *Cron. Scot.* (Rolls) I. 105 And cled thame all..In silk and syper, and in siluer schene. *a* 1542 Wyatt *Compl. Absence His Love* 39 in *Tottel's Misc.* (Arb.) 74 Those shene lightes: that wonted for to clere My darked panges of cloudy thoughts. 1590 Shaks. *Mids. N.* II. i. 28 By fountaine cleere, or spangled star light sheene. 1591 Spenser *M. Hubberd* 1066 That he might be seene Of the wilde beasts in his new glory sheene. 1591 R. W[ilmot] *Tancred & Gism.* III. iii. (1592) D 3, But why doth he that sprung from Ioues high head? And Phœbus sister shene, despise thy power? 1607 Walkington *Optic Glass* 147 To see the Sunne and Moone..in their sheene glory. 1633 P. Fletcher *Purple Isl.* III. vi, Like rubies sheen. 1748 Thomson *Cast. Indol.* I. iii, Glittering Streamlets..hurled every-where their Waters sheen. 1798 Coleridge *Anc. Mar.* v. vi, The upper air burst into life! And a hundred fire-flags sheen, To and fro they were hurried about. 1808 Scott *Marm.* v. viii, His vest of changeful satin sheen. 1817 Shelley *Marianne's Dr.* 20 The veiny lids, whose fringe is thrown Over thine eyes so dark and sheen. 1838 Barham *Ingol. Leg.*, *Witches' Frolic*, And fairer, I ween, The ivy sheen That thy mouldering turret binds, Than the Alderman's house. 1839 Longf. *Voices of Night*, *Prelude* i. 5 Where, the long drooping boughs between Shadows dark and sunlight sheen Alternate come and go.

b. Of a day, the sky, etc.

1503 Hawes *Examp. Virt.* xiv. 296 A daye of gladnes bryght and shene. *a* 1510 Douglas *K. Hart* I. 95 Quhilk hes na craft to knaw the wynter weit, Suppois that sommer schane dois thame reskew. 1577–87 Holinshed *Hist. Eng.* II. ii. 8/2 Thou that maist passe aloft in airie skies so sheene. 1599 *Warn. Faire Wom.* II. 341 It is my love. O how the dusky night Is by her coming forth made sheen and bright! 1714 Gay *Sheph. Week*, *Monday* 3 No chirping lark the welkin sheen invokes. 1839 Mrs. Browning *Romaunt Page* xxx, 'Look up—there is a small bright cloud..' The page looked up—the cloud was sheen. 1891 F. Thompson *Sister-Songs* (1895) 16 There she sat amid her ladies, Where the shade is Sheen as Enna mead ere Hades' Gloom fell thwart Persephone.

†c. Bright-coloured. *Obs.*

13.. *Gaw. & Gr. Knt.* 2314 Þe schene blod ouer his schulderes schot to þe erþe. 1603 Florio *Montaigne* II. xxxiv. 425 Iulius Cæsar..In his Warres..was accustomed to weare a verie rich garment and of a sheene and garish colour. 1810 Scott *Lady of L.* IV. xii, If pall and vair no more I wear, Nor thou the crimson sheen.

†d. absol. *The sheen*: the bright weapon; also, the bright sun. *nonce-uses.*

13.. *Gaw. & Gr. Knt.* 2268 Þat oþer schalk wyth a schunt þe schene wyth-haldez. 13.. *E. E. Allit. P.* C. 440 For to schylde fro the schene, oþer any schade kest.

e. quasi-*adv.*

a 1225 *Ancr. R.* 246 A muchel wind alið mid a lutel rein & te sunne þer efter schineð þe schennure. *c* 1330 R. Brunne *Chron. Wace* (Rolls) 11251 Cloþes of golde þat schon so schene. *c* 1400 *Destr. Troy* 1649 The windowes..[were] shapyn full shene all of shyre stones. 1446 Lydg. *Nightingale Poems* ii. 194 My Ien blynde, that whylom shoone so sheene. 1835 Lytton *Rienzi* I. xi, The moonlight stole soft and sheen. 1872 Holland *Marble Prophecy* 31 They flash and shine among the flowers While dripping sheen in golden showers.

Sheen (ʃīn), *v.* Forms: 4 **schen**, 4–6 **s(c)hene**, 6 **schein**, *Sc.* **scheyne**, 6– **sheen**. [f. Sheen *a.*]

1. *intr.* **a.** = Shine *v.* *lit.* and *fig.* Now only *Sc.* and *dial.* (in Sc. the ordinary word.)

c 1375 *Sc. Leg. Saints* v. (*Johannes*) 256 Far palacis þat sal leste euirmare, schenand with gemmys oure-alquhare. *Ibid.* xxv. (*Julian*) 54 Fore he wae þane schenand in til halynes. *c* 1420 *Anturs of Arth.* 329 (Douce MS.) Þene vnclosed þe cloudes, þe sone con shene. *c* 1470 Henry *Wallace* III. 119 The sone was rysyne our landis schenand brycht. 1523 Skelton *Garl. Laurel* 1358 Luna that so bryght doth shene. *c* 1530 *Crt. of Love* 81 No saphir ind, no rube..There lakked than..That may the castell maken for to shene. *a* 1542 Wyatt *Ps.* xxxvii. 97, I have well seene the wycked sheene lyke goolde lustie and grene as Lawrell lasting aye. 1556 *Chron. Grey Friars* (Camden) 69 Abowte Ester was sene..three sonnes shenynge at one tyme in the eyer. 1562 in *Sel. Rec. Kirk Sess.* etc. *Aberd.* (1846) 4 That gud lyfe, conversatioun, and maneris may scheyne. *a* 1565 Sir T. Challoner tr. *Boeth.* I. met. iii. 15 All sodeynly the Sonne..sheens the worlde over. 1588 A. King tr. *Canisius' Catech.* 9 Our lord Iesus thairfor sittis one the rycht hand of the power of god,..scheinand brychtlie with maiestie altogither diuin. 1819 Gall *Poems* 126 Thy ee will wake nae mair, That sheened sae fu' o' glee.

b. *poet.* To cast a gleam, glisten.

1812 Byron *Ch. Har.* I. xvii, This town, That, sheening far, celestial seems to be. 1856 Meredith *Shav. Shagpat*

Sheening.

Sheenly, adv. rare.

Sheeny (ʃīˈnɪ), sb.¹ slang. Also **sheen**(e)y, **sheeny**, -ie. [Of obscure origin: cf. Russ. *жид*, Pol., Czech *žid* (pronounced žīd) a Jew.] A Jew.

Sheeny (ʃīˈnɪ), a. [f. SHEEN sb. + -Y.] Covered with sheen, full of sheen; having a bright, shiny surface.

Sheep (ʃīp). Forms: 1 sćéap, scép, scép, 2 scæp, sceap, 3 scep, 3–4 schep, 4 ssep, schepe ...

1. Any animal of the ruminant genus *Ovis*.

b. *transf.* and *fig.*

c. With qualifying word denoting the species.

d. *Similative* (often passing into figurative) uses.

e. *fig.* In biblical and religious language, applied to persons.

2. attrib. and **Comb.**

SHEEP-BITING.

Sheep-biter.

Sheep-biting, *ppl. a.* and *sb.*

Sheep, v.

Sheep-bite, v.

Sheep-hook. Now rare.

SHEEPCOT.

Sheepcot (ʃīpˈkɒt).

Sheepcote (ʃīpˈkəʊt).

Sheepfold.

664 SHEEP'S EYES.

Sheepish (ʃīˈpɪʃ), a. (adv.).

Sheepishly, adv.

Sheepishness.

Sheeplike, a.

Sheep-master.

Sheep-mark.

Sheep-pen.

Sheep's eye.

SHEEP'S-EYE ... **Sheepshank** (ʃī·pʃæŋk). *sb.*

1. The shank or leg of a sheep.

Sheep's-head. Also *Sc.* sheep-head.

1. The head of a sheep; the dish consisting of this.

2. *Naut.* In full †**sheepshank** *knot* ...

Sheep-phea-ser.

1. One who shears sheep.

Sheep-shearer.

1. The act or practice of shearing sheep.

Sheep-shearing, *vbl. sb.*

Sheep-shears, *pl.* [f. SHEEP + SHEAR.] Cf.

Sheep-tick, †**sheep's tick**. [See TICK.] A horny, bristly, wingless fly, *Melo-*

Sheepskin. Also *sheep's skin.* [Cf. NFris. *shāpskun.*]

1. The skin of a sheep; *esp.* one used as a garment or in the making of a garment.

2. The skin of sheep used for parchment, for the making of drumheads, in bookbinding, etc.

3. A preparation used in washing sheep; sheep-dip.

Sheep-walk. A tract of grass-land used for pasturing sheep.

Sheep-wash, *sb.*

1. The washing of sheep before shearing; the place where sheep are washed.

2. A preparation used in washing sheep; sheep-dip.

Sheepy (ʃī·pi), *a. rare.* [f. SHEEP + Y¹.]

Of, pertaining to, or resembling sheep.

Sheer (ʃīəɹ), *sb.¹* *Naut.* Also 8 **share**, 9 **shear**.

Sheer, *sb.²* *Naut.* 7, 9 **shear**, 8 **share**. [f. SHEER *v.*¹]

1. An abrupt divergence or deviation of a vessel from the line of her course; a swerve.

2. *attrib.* and *Comb.*, as **sheer-batten**, a batten ...

Sheer (ʃīəɹ), *v.*¹ *Naut.* Forms: 7–8 **share**, 7 **shear**, 7– **sheer**.

Sheer, *v.*² *rare.* [f. SHEER *sb.*³]

Sheered (ʃīəɹd), *a. Naut.* [f. SHEER *sb.*² + -ED¹.]

Sheer-hulk, **shear-hulk**. [f. SHEER, SHEAR ...

Sheerly (ʃīəɹli), *adv.* Also 5 *Sc.* **scheirly**, 6 **sheerely.** [f. SHEER *a.* + -LY².]

Sheerness (ʃīəɹnes), *sb.* [f. SHEER *a.* + -NESS.]

The quality of being sheer (see the adj.).

Sheerman, obs. form of SHEARMAN.

Sheer Thursday. Also *Sc.* **skeirly**, 6 **sheerely.**

Sheet (ʃīt), *sb.¹*

1. A broad piece of linen or cotton stuff, canvas, or the like, for covering, swathing, protecting from injury, etc.

Sheet, *sb.²* *Naut.*

Shell-out. Billiards. [f. phr. *shell out* : see SHELL v. 7.]

Shell-pad. *Obs.*

Shell-work.

1. Work consisting of an arrangement of shells in patterns for ornamentation; shells lining the walls of an artificial grotto.

†2. Shells adhering to a ship's bottom. *rare.*

Shelly, *a.* *nonce-wd.* [f. SHELL *sb.* + -Y.] A shell.

Shelly (ʃeˈli), *a.* [f. SHELL *sb.* + -Y.]

1. Abounding in (sea)shells; of a geological formation, containing wholly or mainly of shells.

2. Consisting of or the nature of a shell; forming a covering resembling a shell; shell-like.

†**Shelt**, variant of SHELT *v.*

Shelta (ʃeˈlta). Also *shelter*. [Of obscure origin : for the form of the name that are used in the 'language' itself, see quot. 1891.]

†**Sheltbeam.** *Obs.*

Shelter (ʃeˈltə). Also 6 *shealter*, 7 *shelture*. [Of obscure origin : possibly f. *sheld* SHIELD *v.* + -TURE in imitation of words like *jointure*.

1. A structure affording protection from rain, wind, or sun; in wider sense, anything serving as a screen or a place of refuge from the weather.

2. Something which affords a refuge from danger, attack, pursuit, or observation; a place of safety; *Mil.* a wall or bank behind which persons can obtain safety from gunshot.

3. The state of being sheltered; the state of being protected from the elements; security from attack.

4. To screen or protect from rain, wind, cold, the sun, etc. Chiefly of a thing, *rarely* of a personal agent.

b. To give protection to.

c. *refl.* To take shelter; to take refuge from pursuit or attack.

Shelterage (ʃeˈltərĕdʒ). Also 7 *sholtridge*.

Sheltered (ʃeˈltəd), *ppl. a.* [f. SHELTER *v.* + -ED.]

Shelterer (ʃeˈltərə). One who shelters.

Sheltering (ʃeˈltəriŋ), *vbl. sb.* [f. SHELTER *v.*]

Sheltering, *ppl. a.* [f. SHELTER *v.* + -ING.]

Shelteringly, *adv.* [-LY.]

Shelterless (ʃeˈltəlĕs), *a.* [f. SHELTER *sb.* + -LESS.]

Sheltery (ʃeˈltəri), *a.* *Obs.* [f. SHELTER *sb.* + -Y.]

Shelty. [Prob. some error : cf. *shanty*, *shieling*.] Used for : A hut, shed.

Shelty, **shelty** (ʃeˈlti). Also 7 *sheltie*. Also SHELTIE. [a. Russ. шотландскій (*šotlandskij*), related to *Shetland* (q.v. *pallatis*).]

Shelve (ʃelv), *sb.¹* [A new sing. evolved from *shelves* pl. of SHELF *sb.²*] = SHELF *sb.²* Also *Comb.*

Shelve (ʃelv), *sb.²* [f. SHELVE *v.³*]

Shelve (ʃelv), *v.¹* [f. SHELF *sb.* (sense 1).] A ledge or shelf of rock, or mountain.

†**Shelve**, *v.²* *Obs.* [perh. an arbitrary alteration of *shelde* SHIELD *v.*] = SHELVE *v.²*

1. *trans.* To project like a shelf, overhang.

2. *trans.* To provide with shelves, esp. to furnish a library, etc.; with bookshelves.

3. To place on a shelf or shelves; esp. to place or arrange (books) upon shelves.

4. *Ag.* To lay aside a on a shelf, to put away or up as done with. b. To remove (a person) from active service. Also *refl.*

Shelve (ʃelv), *v.³* [Of uncertain origin.]

1. *intr.* Of a surface : To slope gradually. Also *with assurg. to, off,* etc.

Shelvement. *Obs.* (see 1 above).

Shelver¹ (ʃeˈlvə). A workman employed to tilt carts.

Shelver² (ʃeˈlvə). *rare.* One who shelves or puts aside.

Shelving (ʃeˈlviŋ), *vbl. sb.¹* [f. SHELVE *v.¹*]

Shelving, *vbl. sb.²* Also *dial.* *shilven*, *shelven*, etc.; *Sc. Eng. Dial. Dict.*

1. The action of the verb SHELVE *v.²*

Shelvy, *a.* *Obs.* [f. SHELVE *v.³* + -Y.]

Shelving (ʃeˈlviŋ), *ppl. a.¹* [f. SHELVE *v.¹* + -ING¹.]

1. The tilting or tipping up of carts to deposit the load.

2. The fact or condition of sloping; the degree of sloping; a sloping surface; a shelve.

Shench, *sb.* Forms : 1, 3 *sceno*, 2-3 *senc*, *senche*. [OE. *scenc* = OFris. *skenk*, MDu. *schenc*, etc.]

Shench, *v.* *Obs.* Forms : 1 *scencan*, *scencgean*, 3 *senchen*, 3 *schenche*, *schenke*, etc. [OE. *scencan*, etc.]

Shend (ʃend), *v.¹* Now *dial.* and *arch.* Pa.t. and pa. pple. SHENT (ʃent). Forms : 1 (*ge-*) *scendan*, (*sceondan*, *-scyndan*), 2 *sceonden*, 3 *scenden*, *sconde*, *sconden*, *s(c)onde*, (*Ormin*) *shennd*, 3-5 *schende*, 4 *s(c)hende*, *ssende*, *schynde*, etc.

Shend, *v.²* *Obs.* [App. a corruption of SHIELD *v.*, arising from confusion with *fend*, or association with FEND *v.* or DEFEND *v.*]

†**Shend**, *sb.* *Obs.* Forms : 3-4 *schendful*, *a.* + *schendful*, *a.*

†**Shendful**, *a.* *Obs.* Forms : 3-4 *schendful*, *a.* schending; shameful, disgraceful. Also *schendful*, *a.*

†**Shendfully**, *adv.* *Obs.* [-LY².] Ignominiously, disgracefully, infamously.

Shending, *vbl. sb.* *Obs.* [-ING¹.] The action of SHEND *v.¹*; contusion, disgrace.

Shendlac. *Obs.* In 2 *schendlac*. [OE. *scendlác*.]

Shendnesse. *Obs.* In 3 *schendnesse*.

Shendship (ʃeˈndʃip). *Obs.* Forms : 4-5 *s(c)hend-*, (*e*)*hand-*, etc.

1. *trans.* To disgrace, put to shame, revile, scold.

2. To blame, reproach, reprove; to revile, abuse.

†b. To put to shame by superiority. *Obs.*

†5. *intr.* To bring to destruction. Also, *in* refl. sense, to injure oneself.

†6. In the *Destruction of Troy* the phrase *to shend* of is app. equivalent to the transitive uses, to destroy.

Shendshipful, a. *Obs. rare.* [f. SHEND-SHIP + -FUL.] Disgraceful, ignominious.

Shene, *Obs. rare.* Forms: 1 **scénan,** scenen, scenen, scenen; see also TO-SHENE v. [OE. scéanan = -préttan. *Táeguere.*]

Sheol (ʃiːˈɒl, ʃiˈəl). [Heb. שְׁאוֹל *shĕʾōl.*] The underworld; the abode of the dead or departed spirits, conceived by the Hebrews as a subterranean region clothed in thick darkness, return from which is impossible.

Shep, *Obs., etc. dial.* Also 4–5 **schep, chep.** [Short for SHEPHERD.]

Shepherd (ʃɛpərd), *sb.* Forms: 1 **scéap-hirde, scéap-, scéaphyrde,** 2–3 (Orrm) **schéap-hirde,** 1 **sceaphorde,** 2 **schephurde,** etc.

I. 1. A man who guards, tends, and herds a flock of sheep (grazing at large); usually one so employed for hire; or one of a pastoral people who herds (his own) sheep, goats, etc.

2. *fig.* A spiritual guardian or pastor of a 'flock'.

II. Combinations: **shepherd's calendar,** a calendar containing weather predictions and seasonable instructions for the use of shepherds.

Shepherd's club, shepherd's dial, shepherd's needle, shepherd's pouch, shepherd's purse, shepherd's rod, shepherd's weather-glass.

Hence **She·pherded** *ppl. a.,* protected, guarded.

Shepherdess (ʃɛpərdɛs). [f. SHEPHERD sb. + -ESS.] A woman or girl who tends sheep; also *fig.* Also in pastoral poetry (see SHEPHERD 1).

Shepherdism. *rare.* [f. SHEPHERD + -ISM.] The action of tending or guiding (sheep) as a shepherd; an instance of this.

Shepherdize (ʃɛpərdaɪz), v. *rare.* [f. SHEPHERD + -IZE.] To act the part of the shepherd (or shepherdess); to pretend to lead the pastoral life.

Shepherdling, *rare.* [f. SHEPHERD sb. + -LING.] A little shepherd.

Shepherdly, a. *Obs.* [f. SHEPHERD sb. + -LY.] Pertaining to or like shepherds; pastoral.

Shepherd's purse.

Shepherd king.

Sheraton (ʃɛrətn). [The name of Thomas Sheraton (1751–1806), a furniture maker and designer.] Designating a style of furniture developed in England towards the end of the 18th cent., chiefly by Thomas Sheraton. Also *absol.*

Sherbet (ʃɜːbət). Also 7 **zerbet, ser-serbet, serret, sherbec, shiriot's, sherbett, sherbeth, -beet, shrub, -bett,** etc. [Turkish and Persian *sharbat.*] 1. a. A cooling drink of the East, made of fruit juice and water sweetened, often cooled with snow.

Sherbertee. Also **sherbe, sherbeta.** [Arab. شربة *sharbat.*] The wife of a Moroccan Shereef.

Shereefian (ʃəˈriːfiən), a. [f. SHEREEF + -IAN.] Of or pertaining to the Shereef of Morocco.

Sherif: see SHEREEF, SHERIFF.

Sheriff (ʃɛrɪf). Forms: 1 **scírgeréfa,** 2 **scyrrevo, scir-reuen, scirreue, 3–5 schirreve,** etc. [OE. *scírgeréfa,* f. *scír* SHIRE + *geréfa* REEVE.] 1. a. The chief officer of the Crown in a county or shire.

Hence a judge or governor of Morocco; also, the ruler of any of the district of Arabia.

Sheriff.

Sheriffalty.

Sheriffdom.

Sheriffess. Obs. rare. [-ESS.] A woman who held the office of sheriff (when hereditary).

Sheriffhood. Obs. Forms: see SHERIFF.

Sheriffship.

Sheriffwick.

Sherris sb.

Sherris-sack.

Sherry, sb.[1]

Sherrivalleys, variant of SHERRYVALLIES.

Sherry (jeri).

Sherry, v.[1] dial. Also 9 shirry.

Sherry, v.[2] nonce-wd.

Sherry-cobbler.

Sherryvallies.

Sherris.

Sherve.

Sherwood.

Sheth.

Sheth-band.

Sheugh.

Sheva.

Shevel, v. Sc. and north.

Shevelled, ppl. a. rare and arch.

Sherbrevet.

Shiah (ʃiːə).

Shibboleth (ʃiˈbɒleθ).

Shibol.

Shibouk.

Shicer (ʃaɪzə).

Supplement, p. 3873; Corrigenda, p. 4092; Spurious words, p. 4093; Books quoted, p. 4094

†1. trans. To separate. Obs.

2. To curdle (milk). Also intr. to become curdled.

Shillal, Shillela, variant of SHILLET.

Shillalagh (ʃi'leːlə, -ɑː). Forms: (7 **Shelela**), 8 **shelaly, shillaley,** 8–9 **shillala,** 6 **shilala, shillala's,** 8–9 **-elagh, shillely, -aly, shillalah,** 8– **shillelagh.** [The name of a barony and village in Co. Wicklow.] An Irish cudgel of blackthorn or oak.

Shilliber (ʃi'libə·ɹ). [Named after George *Shilliber*, coach-proprietor (1797–1866).] **a.** A name given to the omnibus for some time after its introduction into London by Shilliber in 1829. **b.** A vehicle containing a mourning-carriage and hearse combined.

Shilling (ʃi'liŋ). Forms: 1 **scilling, scylling,** (**-inge**), 3 **schelling,** 4 **syllyng, 4–5 schillyng, 4–5 schylling,** 5 **shullyng, schullyng,** 6 **shylling, -ynge,** 6–8 **schilling,** 7 **shilling.** [Common Teut. OE. *scilling* masc. = OFris. *skilling,* OS. *scilling* (Du. *schelling*), OHG. *scilling* (MHG., G. *schilling*), ON. *skillingr* (clok also *skiðingr,* Sw., Da. *skilling*), Goth. *skilliggs* — Adopted in OSlav. as *skĭlǫ,* in Sp., Pr. It. as *scellino* (13th c.).]

Shillingless (ʃi'liŋles), a. [-LESS.] Not having a shilling ; being without (even) a shilling.

Shillingsworth (ʃi'liŋzwəɹθ). Formerly **-worth** (cf. *pennyworth*) is now rare. In the current form the *s* is the sign of the possessive (whether sing. or pl.).) An amount or quantity which is or may be bought for a shilling ; also, the amount of service a shilling-worth of gratitude is naturally paid.

Shilloo (ʃi'luː). Anglo-Irish. A loud shouting or outcry. Hence **Shilloo'ing** vb. sb.

Shilly (ʃi'li). north. Also **shillow, shilly, shelly, shullin,** etc. [Connected with SHILLET. Manx has *shillee* : man is uncertain.]

Shilly-shally (ʃi'liʃæli), adv. phr., a., sb. [At first written *shill I, shall I,* altered form of *shall I, shall I*: see SHALL v. B. 7 a (d). For the vowel-alteration cf. *dilly-dally, wishy-washy.*]

A. To stand *shill I, shall I*: to vacillate, to be irresolute or undecided. Also to go *shill-I-shall-I,* to stand at shilly-shally.

Shilly-shally, sb.

Shilly-sha·llyer. [f. prec. vb. + -ER¹.] One who shilly-shallies.

Shiment, -mont see SHELVEMENT.

Shilpit (ʃi'lpit). Sc. Also **shilpet, shelpit.** [Etymology unknown : cf. SKIRPIT.] Sc. dialect: Pale and sickly-looking ; weak, feeble, puny.

Shim (ʃim), sb.¹ Also 7 *shimm.* [? Repr. some prehistoric form, perh. related to OE. *scima, scinu.* Bright.]

Shim, sb.² An instrument used in hoeing.

Shim, v. To wedge up or fill out to a fair surface by inserting a thin wedge or piece of material.

Shimeena, variant of SHAMIANAH.

†Shimmand, ppl. a. Obs. 1 *scymmid.* [app. f. SHIM sb.¹ + -ED².] Dapple-grey.

Shimmer (ʃi'məɹ), v. [Common Teut.: OE. *scimerian* = MLG., MDu. *schemeren.*] To shine with a tremulous or flickering light ; to gleam faintly. In early use also, to shine brightly, glitter.

Shim (ʃim), sb.³ dial. Also 8 *sheim.* [Origin unascertained. It is doubtful whether all the following senses belong to one word.]

Shimmer, sb.

Shimmering, vbl. sb. [f. SHIMMER v.¹ + -ING¹.] Cf. (M)LG. *schemeringe,* MHG. *schemerunge* twilight, G. *schimmerung* coruscation.] The action of the vb. SHIMMER.

Shimmering, ppl. a. That shimmers.

Shimmery (ʃi'məri), a. [f. SHIMMER v.¹ + -Y¹.] Giving out a shimmering light.

Shimmy (ʃi'mi), sb. dial. Also *shimmey.* dial. and U.S. corruption of CHEMISE.

Shimozzle, variant of SHEMOZZLE.

Shimper, v. local. [app. corrupt f. SHIMMER v. with intrusive *p (shim¹er).*] = SHIMMER v.

Shim-sham, sb. exc. dial. Reduplication of SHAM sb. and a.

Shin (ʃin), sb. Forms: 1 *scinu, scina,* sb. *scyne,* 3 *schyne, scine, schine,* 7 *schin, shin.* [OE. *scinu* str. fem. = MDu. *schene* (Du. *scheen*), MLG. *schene,* OHG. *scina* (MHG. *schine,* G. *schiene*).]

Shin (ʃin), v. Forms: 7 *scinne,* 7 *shinne,* 8– *shin.* [f. SHIN sb.]

Shindig. U.S. [See quots.] A dance or party.

Shindle, sb. [local variant of SHINGLE.] A wooden roofing-tile.

Shindy (ʃi'ndi). local. [? Alteration of SHINTY.]

Shindle, v.

Shindy. U.S.

Shinbauwde. [Obs. In 5 **schynbawde.** -bawde, -baude.] (The first element is app. SHIN sb., the second is obscure.) A greave (leg-armour).

Shinbin (ʃi'nbin). Also *-been, -ban, -bane.* [Burmese *shin-byu,* f. *shin* to put together side by side + *pyu* white.]

Shin-bone (ʃi'nbəun). Forms: 1 *scin-ban,* also 3 *shine,* 4 *chine,* *shin-,* etc. [OE. *scinbán* = NFris. *skenbin, skenbüüsen* (Du. *scheenbeen*), MLG. *schēnebēn* (G. *schienbein*) etc.]

Shindle, Anglo-Irish form of SHINE.

Shind, obs. form of SHEND v.

†Shibber. Obs. In 4 *schyndre,* 5 *chyndre.* [? Echoic. Cf. FLINDERS.] trans. and intr. To shiver or shatter in pieces.

Shindig. U.S. [See quots. Shindy, SHY sb.

Shine (ʃain), sb.¹ [f. SHINE v. They all were taken out of mine, Big Dawn of the sunrise that was... from the shine of the dawn.]

Shine (ʃain), sb.² [OE. *scēon,* also 3 *schine,* 4 *schyne, schyn,* 4–6 *shyne,* 6– *shine.*]

Shine (ʃain), v. Forms: 1 *scīnan,* 2–6 *schine,* 3–6 *shyne,* 4–5 *schyne,* 5 *schene,* 5–6 *shyne,* 6– *shine.* [OE. *scīnan* str. vb. (pa. t. *scán, scinon,* pa. pple. *scinen*) = OFris. *skīna,* OS. *skīnan* (MDu. *schijnen,* Du. *schijnen*), OHG. *scīnan* (MHG., G. *scheinen*), ON. *skína,* Goth. *skeinan* — OTeut. *skīnan,* f. root *skī-* by means of the present-stem formative *-n,* which was carried through into the pret. stem and pple.]

al as schene as þe sunne. c 1230 *Hali Meid.* 11 Nis hit nower neh gold al þat ter schineð. a 1300 *Cursor M.* 8484 Stedfast stode þe marbel stan, On-ferr þe golden letters scan. 1338 R. Brunne *Chron.* (1725) I. 148 Of gold schone his coroun. 13.. *E. E. Allit. P.* A. 80 Wyth schymeryng schene ful schrylle þay schynde. c 1386 Chaucer *Prol.* 198 His heed was balled, þat shoon as any glas. c 1470 *Gol. & Gaw.* 20 Thair baneris schane with the sone, of siluer and sabill. 1526 Tindale *Luke* ix. 29 His garment was whyte, and shoone. 1577 T. Kendall *Flowers of Epigr.* 73 His tongue did lispe, his visage shinde. 1588 Shaks. *L. L. L.* iv. iii. 246 O 'tis the Sunne that maketh all things shine. 1667 Milton *P. L.* iii. 508 Thick with sparkling orient Gemmes The Portal shon. 1751 Lavington *Enthus. Meth. & Papists* iii. (1754) 78 The whole House shined. 1808 Scott *Marm.* vi. Introd. 53 The huge hall-table's oaken face, Scrubb'd till it shone. 1860 Tyndall *Glac.* ii. i. 237 A rook's feather may be made to shine with magnificent iridescences. 1888 Henley *Bk. Verses* 118 Clear shine the hills.

indirect passive. 1737 Whiston *Josephus, Hist.* iv. x. § 1 When they saw the riches of Rome..and found themselves shone round about..with silver and gold.

b. To be bright *with*.

1606 Shaks. *Ant. & Cl.* i. iii. 45 Our Italy, Shines o're with ciuill Swords. 1733 *Revol. Politicks* v. 37 The Streets in the Evening every where shined very gloriously with Bonefires. 1883 R. W. Dixon *Mano* ii. ii. 68 The altar shone With gold and silver.

3. To be radiant or brilliant with high colouring, rich array, or the like; to be effulgent with splendour or beauty; to make a brave show. Now *rare*.

971 *Blickl. Hom.* 7 Seo hwitnes þære lilian scineþ on þe. c 1375 *Cursor M.* 23696 (Fairf.) Mani flouris..neuer-mare þe colour tine bot as paradis salle þai shine. a 1400 *Pistill of Susan* 106 (MS. I.) Þe chaumpet, þe cheuerell, þat schon opon heyght. c 1450 *Mirk's Festial* 132 Þes two woymen þat schynen passyng all oþyr, wer two comyn woymen. 1513 Douglas *Æneis* i. vi. 163 Her nek schane like unto the roise in May. 1577 T. Kendall *Flowers of Epigr.* 84 b, In all thy body bewty shines, thy forhed shineth fair. a 1639 Carew *To A. L.* 64 When a fair lady's face is pined, And yellow spread where red once shined. 1781 Cowper *Truth* 70 [The pheasant] retreats..To the close copse..And shines without desiring to be seen. 1823 Scott *Quentin D.* xxxii, We are somewhat shorn of our train, .. but you, cousin, must shine out for us both. 1833 Tennyson *Œnone* 176 Her light foot Shone rosy-white. 1837 Carlyle *Fr. Rev.* I. i. ii, Some centennial Cactus-flower, which after a century of waiting shines out for hours! 1878 Susan Phillips *On Seaboard* 199 In the golden meadows, where the cowslip and crowsfoot shone.

4. In various fig. applications (cf. 5 and 6), with retention of literal phraseology.

c 1000 *Ags. Gosp.* Matt. xiii. 43 Þonne scinað ða rihtwisan swa swa sunne on hyra fæder rice. a 1225 *Ancr. R.* 246, & te soðe sunne, þet is Jesu Crist, schineð þerefter schennure to þe soule. a 1300 *Cursor M.* 12574 Þe clernes self o godds light Schan on him. 1382 Wyclif *Matt.* v. 16 So shyyne ȝoure liȝt before men, that thei see ȝoure good werkis. c 1400 *Rom. Rose* 5357 Whan Richesse shyneth bright, Love recovereth ageyn his light. c 1450 Capgrave *Life St. Gilbert* xv, Ther schone, or ellis schyned, in þe soule of þese women a fayr beute of precious perles, of swech goostly richesse. 1526 Tindale *2 Cor.* iv. 6 It is god.. which hath shyned in oure hertes, for to geve the light of knowledge off the glorious god. 1535 Coverdale *Isa.* ix. 2 As for them that dwel in the londe of the shadowe of death, vpon them shal the light shyne. 1594 Marlowe & Nashe *Dido* ii. i. 481 In whose stern faces shin'd the quenchles fire. 1611 Shaks. *Cymb.* v. v. 476 The Radiant Cymbeline, Which shines heere in the West. 1654–66 Earl Orrery *Parthen.* (1676) 212 A Virtue, greater than euer yet had shin'd on earth. 1700 Dryden *Fables* Pref. C 2, Chaucer ..is a rough Diamond, and must first be polish'd e'er he shines. 1773 R. Lowth *Serm. Rom.* xii. 11 p. 6 Their Learning..was such as could only have shined in dark times. 1837 Carlyle *Fr. Rev.* I. ii. viii, For we shall still find Hope shining..as a mild heavenly light it shone; as a red conflagration it shines. 1849 T. Woolner *My Beautiful Lady* xii, How beautiful she is! A glorious gem She shines above the summer diadem Of flowers!

5. Of persons: To be conspicuous or brilliant in ability, character, achievement, or position; to be eminent or distinguished, to excel.

c 900 tr. *Bæda's Hist.* i. xii. (1890) 44 Se nama ðære Romaniscan þeode, se ðe mid swa lange scean & bryhte. c 1375 *Sc. Leg. Saints* xxvii. (*Machor*) 318 A man that schane of halynes. c 1400 *Apol. Loll.* 43 If we schyn in þeis vertues. 1474 Caxton *Chesse* ii. v. (1883) 69 Hit was better and more noble thynge to shyne in good maners than in vayssell. 1560 Daus tr. *Sleidane's Comm.* 202 To shyne before theyr flock with honest examples of lyfe. 1647 Clarendon *Hist. Reb.* i. § 131 He shined in the House of Peers. 1710 Steele *Tatler* No. 244 ¶ 1 An Ambition to excel, or, as the Term is, to shine, in Company. 1747 H. Walpole *Let. to Mann* 3 July, We shine at sea; two-and-forty sail of the Domingo fleet have fallen into our hands. 1805 T. Harral *Scenes of Life* I. 113 That cause in which British valour had so often shined triumphant. 1818 Byron *Juan* i. xxiii, If there's anything in which I shine, 'Tis in arranging all my friends' affairs. 1836 Thirlwall *Greece* xvii. III. 2 He..never shone as an orator. 1859 *Habits of Gd. Society* xiv. 349 The people who were stupidest before, suddenly shine out quite brilliantly. 1889 *Harper's Mag.* Mar. 561/1 There was..a special reason which made me resolved to shine at this ball at whatever cost.

6. Of something immaterial: To appear with conspicuous clearness; to be brilliantly evident or visible; to stand out clearly.

c 1340 Hampole *Prose Treat.* 12 In þis gyfte schynes contemplacyone. 1387 Trevisa *Higden* (Rolls) IV. 449 A noble soule schoon by virtues in þat litel body. 1456 Sir G. Haye *Law Arms* (S.T.S.) 6 His grete beautee schynit sa before all otheris. 1471 Caxton *Recuyell* (Sommer) 247 Alle good manyeres began to growe and shyne in hym. a 1586 Sidney *Arcadia* ii. (Sommer) 127 b, Then shined foorth indeede all loue among them. 1594 Hooker *Eccl. Pol.* iii. xi. § 9 The wisedom of God, which shineth in the bewtifull varietie of all things. 1632 Massinger *Maid of Hon.* iv. iv, The reverence and Majesty of Iuno Shinde in her lookes. 1667 Milton *P. L.* ii. 304 Princely counsel in his face yet shon. 1725 Pope *Odyss.* xiv. 204 In all the youth his father's image shin'd. 1853 C. Bronte *Villette* xx, What fun shone in his eyes as he recalled some of her fine speeches! 1888 'J. S. Winter' *Bootle's Childr.* vi, How the aged look faded off her worn face, and the sweet prettiness of former days began to shine out again.

b. To be clearly evident *through* an outward appearance.

1590 Shaks. *Two Gent.* ii. i. 40 These follies are within you, and shine through you like the water in an Vrinall. 1605 — *Macb.* iii. i. 128 Your Spirits shine through you. 1628 Feltham *Resolves* ii. [i.] xlvii. 138 To see the Countenance, (through which perhaps there shin'd a louely Maiesty..). 1858 Hawthorne *Fr. & It. Note-bks.* II. 31 The babe Jesus in her arm, with his Father shining through him. 1859 Tennyson *Marr. Geraint* 545 Yniol's rusted arms Were on his princely person, but thro' these Princelike his bearing shone.

†**7.** *To shine through*: to be transparent. *Obs.*

1675 Alsop *Anti-Sozzo* iii. ii. 207 This [reasoning] is very thin Stuff; it shines through.

8. *trans.* To shed light upon, illuminate. *rare.*

1398 Trevisa *Barth. De P. R.* viii. xvii. (1495) 325 The mone is alway halfe shyned of the sonne. a 1700 Ken *Hymnotheo* Poet. Wks. III. 355 God shines his Son, the Son God's shine reflects.

9. To cause (light) to shine, emit (rays). Also *fig.*

1588 Greene *Perimedes* H 2 b, Her eyes shines fauour, courtesie, and grace. 1590 — *Never too late* (1600) E 3, Eyes that lighten and doe shine, Beames of loue that are diuine. 1647 Saltmarsh *Spark. Glory* 118 God..shines forth his wisdom..upon the world. 1661 Feltham *Resolves* ii. xvi. 211 If it be but by reflection only, the beams are reverberated bright, as is the Sun that shines them. 1852 Thackeray *Esmond* ii. vii, She approached, shining smiles upon Esmond.

b. To show the light of (a lantern).

1895 P. H. Emerson *Birds, etc. Norfolk Broadland* xxxvi. 103 The sparrow-catcher comes of a night and shines his bright lantern, and the foolish birds fly at it like moths at a candle.

10. a. *To shine down*: to surpass in brilliance.

1613 Shaks. *Hen. VIII*, i. i. 20 The French..like Heathen Gods Shone downe the English. 1866 'Annie Thomas' *Walter Goring* xxxvii, 'Take it, Walter', she continued, 'give it to her; tell her she shines me down.'

b. To drive *away* by shining.

1884 Tennyson *Becket* iii. i, Not The sun himself..Could shine away the darkness of that gap.

11. To cause to shine, put a polish on; *U.S.* (inflected *shined*) to black (boots).

1613 R. C. *Table Alph.* (ed. 3), *Varnish*, shine, set a glosse vpon. 1872 Calverley *Arab* 27 And thou hintest withal that thou fain would'st shine..these bulgy old boots of mine. 1872 O. W. Holmes *Poet Breakf.-t.* xii, I wonder if they would find the seven-branched golden candlestick. ..I should like to..shine it up (excuse my colloquialisms). 1872 B. Harte *Heiress of Red Dog* (1879) 188 Shine your boots, sir? 1892 Gunter *Miss Dividends* ix, While his large boots have been very brightly shined by the boot-black.

12. *U.S.* (*Hunting.*) To throw the light of a lantern, etc. on (the eyes of an animal); to locate the position of (an animal) in this way.

1845 [W. T. Thompson] *Chron. Pineville* 169 (Bartlett *Dict. Amer.* 1860) You see the way we does to shine the deer's eyes is this—we holds the pan of fire so, on the left shoulder, and carries the gun at a trail in the right hand. 1872 Schele de Vere *Americanisms* 541 Daniel Boone, while fire-hunting, shined a pair of mild blue eyes which struck him as not belonging to the game he was seeking. 1910 Roosevelt *Afr. Game Trails* x. 226 We had discovered that the way to get this..nocturnal animal was by 'shining' it with a lantern at night.

Shi·neless, *a.* [f. Shine *sb.*[1] + -less.] Without brightness.

1882 G. Macdonald *Princess & Curdie* iii, A dull, shineless twilight filled the place.

Shiner (ʃəi·nəɹ). [f. Shine *v.* + -er [1].]

1. An object that shines.

1398 Trevisa *Barth. De P. R.* viii. xvi. (1495) 322 The sonne is..shyner of heuen [L. *fulgor olympi*]. 1633 G. Herbert *Temple, Christmas* 29 Till I finde a sunne Shall stay, till we have done; A willing shiner. 1655 Vaughan *Silex Scint.* iii. *Thalia Rediv.* 239 O blessed shiner, tell me whither Thou wilt be gone when night comes hither! 1765 J. Brown *Chr. Jrnl.* 140 Where will yon glow-worms of carnal diversions,..yon shiners in the dark, be? 1844 Willis *Lady Jane* i. 326, I cannot shine—but I can see a star—Are there not worshippers as well as shiners? 1859 F. Mahony *Rel. Fr. Prout* 403 A small twinkling shiner ..in the wide canopy of heaven.

b. *pl.* Some Russian instrument of torture.

1630 [F. Constable] *Pathomachia* iii. iv. 29 Vnlesse thou confesse, the Russian Shiners, the Scottish Bootes,..and Peare of Confession shall torment thee.

c. *pl.* Coin, money, *esp.* sovereigns or guineas; occas. *sing.*, a silver or gold coin. *slang.*

1760 Foote *Minor* ii. Wks. 1799 I. 251 To let a lord of lands want shiners; 'tis a shame. 1806 Surr *Winter in Lond.* II. 63 So I shows him a shiner. 1838 Dickens *O. Twist* xix, Is it worth fifty shiners extra, if it's safely done from the outside? 1851 Mayne Reid *Scalp Hunters* ix, I will bring you a mule-load of Mexican shiners. 1887 Hayter *My Christmas Adv.* 9 Within my purse and pocket scarce a shiner.

d. A mirror; *spec.* one used by cheaters at cards. *slang.*

1812 J. H. Vaux *Flash Dict.*, *Shiner*, a looking-glass. 1819 *Sporting Mag.* (N. S.) IV. 230 He then asked me if I had bought shiners? which means glasses. 1909 *Tit-Bits* 14 Aug. 515/2 The 'shiner' is carried separately in the pocket until needed, while the gambler smokes the pipe.

e. *colloq.* A silk hat.

1867 F. Francis *Bk. Angling* vi. 154 A tall black hat, or one of the genus termed 'shiner'.

2. One who shines: **a.** One who excels or is eminent.

1810 *Splendid Follies* III. 106 He was never formed for a shiner through life. 1847 Halliwell, *Shiner*, a clever fellow. *North.*

b. *pl.* A nickname for the Northumberland Fusiliers, formerly the 5th Foot.

1891 *Dict. Nat. Biog.* XXV. 3/1 The 5th was..popularly known as the 'Shiners', from its smart appearance and attention to parade details.

c. A bootblack.

1912 *19th Cent.* Nov. 1018 An occasional white face may be seen even among the noisy shiner boys, and the little white shiner works continuously.

3. Applied to various small silvery fishes; the young of the mackerel; *U.S.* any of various small freshwater fishes, chiefly cyprinoids as the dace.

Golden shiner, a fish of the genus *Notemigonus*.

1836 Yarrell *Brit. Fishes* I. 124 The young Mackerel, which are called Shiners, are from four to six inches long by the end of August. 1836 J. Richardson *Fauna Bor.-Amer.* iii. 122 *Cyprinus* (*Leuciscus*) *chrysoleucas*...New York Shiner. 1839 Kirtland in *Bost. Jrnl. Nat. Hist.* III. 339 *Luxilus elongatus*...The Red-bellied Shiner. *Ibid.* 341 *L. dissimilis*...The Spotted Shiner. 1844 O. W. Holmes *Lines Berksh. Jubilee* 46 Oh, what are the prizes we perish to win To the first little 'shiner' we caught with a pin. 1888 Goode *Amer. Fishes* 99 The 'Sailor's Choice'..bears several other names..as the 'Porgy' and 'Shiner'. 1893 *Outing* XXII. 89/2 A golden shiner about five inches in length.

b. = Silver-fish 2. (In mod. Dicts.)

†**Shi·ness.** *Obs. north.* In 1 scinisse, 4 schinnes. [f. Shine *v.* + -ness.] Light, brightness.

c 950 *Lindisf. Gosp.* Mark xiii. 24 Ðe mona ne sele' scinisse his [*splendorem suum*]. a 1300 *Cursor M.* 23633 Ɉat scene schinnes [*Gött.* þe schene schining] o cristal.

Shiness, variant spelling of Shyness.

Shingle (ʃi·ŋg'l), *sb.*[1] Forms: 3 scincle, 3–6 shyngle, 4 schingel, schingle, schyngil, scingle, shyngel, -yl, singel, 4–6 schyngle, shingell, 5 chyngle, chyngyl, 5–6 schyngyl(l, shingil(l, shyngul(l, 6 s(c)hengle, shengyll, shyngyll(e, syngle, 6–7 single, 7 shingelle, 4– shingle. [ME. *scincle*, *shyngle*, app. representing (? through an AF. modification) L. *scindula*, later form of *scandula*, commonly held to be due to the influence of Gr. σχινδαλμός.

L. *scindula* is represented in Germanic by OHG. *scindala*, *scintila*, MHG. *schintel*, (also mod.) *schindel*, MLG. *schindele*, MDu. *schindel*: cf. Shindle. L. *scandula* passed into Romanic as F. *échandole*, It. *scandola*.]

1. A thin piece of wood having parallel sides and one end thicker than the other, used as a house-tile.

c 1200 *Vices & Virtues* 95 De faste hope..is rof and wrikð alle ðe hire bieð beneðen mid ðe scincles of holie bohtes. c 1305 *Land Cokaygne* 57 in *E. E. P.* (1862) 157 Þe scingles alle Of cherche cloister boure and halle. 1335–6 in Bayley *Tower Lond.* (1821) App. i. p. ij, Item in defectibus aulæ domini regis in coopertura, shyngles, coquinæ, pistrinæ. 1398 Trevisa *Barth. De P. R.* xvii. clxviii. (Bodl. MS.), The laþþe..is nailed þwarteouer to þe rafters and theron hongeþ sclattes, tile, and schingels. 14.. *Voc.* in Wr.-Wülcker 610/13 *Scindula*, a shyngul. 1510 Stanbridge *Vocabula* (W. de W.) B iv b, *Scandula*, a shyngylles [*sic*]. 1577 B. Googe *Heresbach's Husb.* ii. (1586) 106 Shingles.. are to be cutte betwixte midde Winter, and the beginning of the Westerne Windes. 1591 Percivall *Sp. Dict.*, *Ripia*, a lath, a single. 1669 Worlidge *Syst. Agric.* 214 Shingles are to be preferred before Thatch. 1785 *Gentl. Mag.* LV. ii. 49 The houses are almost all of wood, covered with the same; the roof with shingles. 1817–8 Cobbett *Year's Resid. Amer.* (1822) 317 Your house..covered with cedar shingles. 1886 Ruskin *Præterita* I. 299 The Jura cottage..is covered with thin slit fine shingles.

(*b*) *collect. sing.*

c 1330 *Arth. & Merl.* 5874 Arthour smot on hem, saunfaile, So on þe singel dope þe haile. c 1340 *Nominale* (Skeat) 481 Couert one tiel ou cene, Hilde with tile or with schyngle. c 1440 *Pallad. on Husb.* i. lxxv, Heled weel with shyngul, tile, or broom. 1552 in *Archæol. Cant.* (1872) VIII. 128 For makyng vj thowsen of schyngle & iiij honder xxix s. 1557 in *Shropsh. Par. Docum.* (1903) 58 Re'd of mr Vicar for olde Shengle vi[d]. 1575 *Ibid.* 65 For on thowsand of shyngle xviii[s]. 1872 Yeats *Techn. Hist. Comm.* 132 Their roofs of shingle or of thatch. 1899 Baring-Gould *Vicar of Morwenstow* ix, The roof was covered with oak shingle.

b. fig. phr. (orig. Australian colloq.). *A shingle short*: 'a tile loose': said of one who is mentally deficient.

1852 Mundy *Antipodes* III. i. 17 Let no man having, in colonian phrase, 'a shingle short' try this country. 1885 Mrs. C. Praed *Head Stat.* xviii. II. 6 I've been given to understand that poets are usually a shingle short.

c. *gen.* A piece of board. (Cf. *shingle-board*.)

1825 Scott *Betrothed* ii, A long low hall, built of rough wood lined with shingles. 1825 J. Neal *Bro. Jonathan* III. 150 A piece of shingle, which he was pretending to whittle, after the fashion of your 'nait'ral born' Yankee. 1844 *Cath. Weekly Instr.* 114 The hut was low, built of shingles. 1894 Miss E. L. Banks *Campaigns Curios.* 143, I had neglected to provide myself with a shingle, with small holes, in which to place my flowers, to make them stand upright.

d. *U.S.* A small sign-board.

1847 J. M. Field *Drama in Pokerville* (Bartlett 1860), The 'No Admittance!' which frowned from a shingle over the door. 1865 Holland *Plain Talk* iv. 131 When a boy changes his roundabout for a coat, he is ready to 'stick out his shingles'. 1879 Tourgee *Fool's Err.* i. 10 He studied law ..and hung out his shingle.

2. *attrib.* and *Comb.*, as *shingle-laden*, *-laying*, *-maker*, *-wise*; † **shingle-board** = sense 1, 1 c; **shingle-nail**, a nail used in fixing shingles in building; **shingle-oak**, (*a*) the laurel oak, *Quercus imbricaria*; (*b*) the she-oak; **shingle-weaver**, **-wood** (see quots.).

Several other compounds are given in Knight's *Dict. Mech.* and the recent U. S. dicts.

c 1300 in *Black Bk. Admiralty* (Rolls) II. 192 Menu bord qe lem appele baryl bord ou *shyngel-bord. 1589 Hakluyt *Voy.* 286 The roofes..are couered with shingle boordes. 1637 Heywood *Royall Ship* 13 Lined with shingle-boards, or wainscot-plankes. 1881 *Chicago Times* 14 May, The vessel is *shingle-laden. 1866 Rogers *Agric. & Prices* I. xv. 279 *Shingle-laying is sometimes paid by the thousand. 1792 in E. G. Ingham *Sierra Leone* iii. (1894) 46 Bakers, 4...*Shingle Maker, 1. 1836 Haliburton *Clockm.* Ser. i. iii, A shingle-maker's shed. 1303–4 *Acc. Chamberl. Chester* (1910) 42 Bordnail, *schingelneil, latnail. 1554 in *Shropsh. Par. Docum.* (1903) 55 Half a m of syngle nayle. 1867 Lowell *Fitz Adam's Story* 417 He had been known to cut a fig in two And change a board-nail for a shingle-nail. 1886 Morse *Jap. Homes* 79 Bamboo pins..are used as shingle-nails. 1818 T. Nuttall *Genera N. Amer. Plants* II. 214 *Quercus imbricaria* ;*Shingle Oak). 1889 Maiden *Native Plants Austral.* 15 *Casuarina stricta*,..'Shingle Oak', 'Coast She-oak'. 1860 Bartlett *Dict. Amer.* (ed. 3), *Shingle-weaver*, a workman who dresses shingles. 1872 Coues *N. Amer. Birds* 46 Scales..apt to be imbricated, or fixed *shingle-wise. 1864 Grisebach *Flora W. Ind. Islands* 787 *Shingle-wood: *Nectandra leucantha*.

b. passing into *adj.* = (*a*) consisting of, covered or built with, shingles, as *shingle house*, *roof*; (*b*) used in making shingles, as *shingle machine*.

1810 W. Irving *Life & Lett.* (1864) I. 245 More pleasing in the sight of Heaven..than building a dozen shingle church steeples. 1819–20 — *Leg. Sleepy Hollow* Sk.-Bk. (1821) 299 The money invested in..shingle palaces in the wilderness. 1848–54 Webster, *Shingle-roofed*, having a roof covered with shingles. a 1850 Mrs. Browning *Runaway Slave* xi, When the shingle-roof rang sharp with the rains. 1858 Simmonds *Dict. Trade*, *Shingle-machine*, an American machine for riving, shaving, and jointing shingles, which is capable of making 30,000 per day. *Ibid.*, *Shingle-mill*, a saw-mill for cutting planks or logs into shingles. 1868 *Rep. U. S. Comm. Agric.* (1869) 56 Board and shingle sugar-houses. 1899 Baring-Gould *Vicar of Morwenstow* ix, A shingle roof he would have or none at all.

Shingle (ʃi·ŋg'l), *sb.*[2] Forms: α. 6– chingle, 6–7 *Sc.* chyngill. β. 6– shingle. [Of obscure origin; the forms with *ch-*, which are somewhat the earlier and are mainly Sc. and East Anglian, suggest an echoic origin (cf. *chink*). The change of *ch-* to *sh-* is paralleled in the history of Shiver *v.*[2] The relation of this word to Norw. *singl* coarse sand, small stones, NFris. *singel* (large) gravel, is not clear.]

1. Small roundish stones; loose, waterworn pebbles such as are found collected upon the seashore. **a.** *collect. sing.*

α. 1598 Hakluyt *Voy.* I. 556 Chingle and great stones being skorched in that fiery gulfe. 1603 *Reg. Mag. Sig. Scot.* 517/2 Arenam et lie chyngill et lapides super ripas dicte aque. 1611 in *Extracts Rec. Convent. Burghs Scot.* (1870) II. 327 To caus the fyscher boits to be ballastet.. with chyngill onlie, and nocht with staynes. 1633 J. Done tr. *Aristeas' Hist. Septuagint* 51 In the Superficies..was represented..the Flood Meander, ..in the Channell of which, one might see a Splendor of Precious Stones, representing his rowling waues, which Chingle was of Carbuncles [etc.]. 1787 W. H. Marshall *Provinc. Norfolk* (E.D.S.), *Chingle*, gravel, free from dirt. 1798 *Statist. Acc. Scot.* XX. 27 The surface is not above a foot or 18 inches from the chingle. 1807 Headrick *Arran* 232 This stratum is not visible on the sea beach, being probably covered with chingle or stones.

β. 1676 *Phil. Trans.* XI. 627 The shores..are for the most part sandy, but only in some points there is some shingle cast up. 1717 S. Sewall *Diary* 28 Sept., Not to fetch any more Shingle from the point, to mend the Causey. 1778 *Eng. Gazetteer* (ed. 2), Ramsey, in the Isle of Man... standing upon a beach of loose sand, or shingle. 1833 Lyell *Princ. Geol.* III. 271 A violent and transient rush of waters which tore up the soil to a great depth, excavated valleys, gave rise to immense beds of shingle. 1867 'Ouida' *Cecil Castlemaine*, etc. 239 In dashed the bay through the park-gates, sending the shingle flying up in small simoons. 1882 Geikie *Text-bk. Geol.* ii. ii. § 6. 155 In shingle the stones are coarser, ranging up to blocks as big as a man's head or larger. 1894 Crockett *Raiders* 116 The swell broke upon a beach of shingle and sand.

b. *collect. pl.* (Locally the name of a pebbly beach or bank; cf. quot. 1577 in 2 β.)

1574 W. Bourne *Regim. Sea* xxii. 60 At the comming from Portland you shall haue .35. fadoms, and small shingles. a 1608 Dee *Relat. Spirits* i. (1659) 115 The shingles, through the which the Spring runs. 1706 Phillips (ed. Kersey), *Shingles*,..the Name of a Shelf, or Sand-bank in the Sea, about the Isle of Wight. 1803 Southey in *Ann. Rev.* I. 9 A neck of land chiefly composed of sand, shingles and drift wood. 1818 Scott *Rob Roy* xviii, The way..was a happy interchange of bog and shingles. 1842 Sedgwick in *Hudson's Guide Lakes* (1843) 188 The overlying..beds of limestone are..separated from the..beds of slate, by masses of conglomerate or cemented shingles. 1848 Thackeray *Van. Fair* xxv, Just as the nymph..stepped out of the little caravan on to the shingles. 1862 Ansted *Channel Isl.* i. iv. 79 The shingles here do not afford a landing-place.

2. A beach or other tract covered with loose roundish pebbles.

α. 1513 Douglas *Æneis* x. vi. 34 In the schald scho stoppis, and dyd stand Apon a dry chyngill or bed of sand. a 1825 Forby *Voc. E. Anglia*, *Chingly*, abounding in small stones, etc., commonly applied to a newly repaired road. The loose pebbly beach is called the chingle or shingle.

β. 1577 Harrison *England* i. ix. 22 b, in *Holinshed*, We meete with y[e] fal of a water neere to S. Catherins chapple as we sailed by y[e] Shingle. 1674 N. Fairfax *Bulk & Selv.* 200 A world of Sea-stones on the shingle. 1822 T. Mitchell *Com. Aristoph.* II. 182 He has robb'd the sea-shore, And has hived such a store As would give a large shingle its coating. 1856 Emerson *Eng. Traits, Ability* Wks. (Bohn) II. 34 The enchantments of barren shingle and rough weather.

3. *attrib.*, as *shingle-ballast*, *bank*, *beach*, *-bed*, *-stone*, *track*, *trap*; *shingle-covered*, *-formed* adjs.; **shingle-tramper** (see quot.).

1801 *Naval Chron.* V. 270 The many instances of injury arising from the use of *shingle ballast. 1888 F. Cowper *Cædwalla* i. 15 The scrub on the top of the *shingle bank. 1834 Marryat *Peter Simple* xxvi, Oh! with what joy did I first put my foot on the *shingle beach at Sallyport. 1881 *Rep. Geol. Explor. New Zealand* 123 The Dart flows along a wide *shingle-bed. 1875 W. McIlwraith *Guide Wigtownshire* 51 A narrow, *shingle-covered opening in the cliffs. 1897 Mary Kingsley *W. Africa* 116 Masses of *shingle-formed conglomerate. 1614 T. Gentleman *England's Way* 25 Their haven [viz. Southwold, Suffolk] is..stopped vp with Beach and *Chingle-stone. 1863 Lyell *Antiq. Man* 31 One of the round shingle stones. 1886 Kendall *Poems* 201 He camps by the side of a *shingle track. 1867 Smyth *Sailor's Word-bk.*, *Shingle-tramper*, a coast-guard man. 1839 *Civil Eng. & Arch. Jrnl.* II. 85/2 Shingle has a decided tendency to drive eastward, and convert harbours lying in its course into what have been designated '*shingle traps'.

Shingle, *sb.*[3] Erron. f. Single *sb.* 1 b.

1660 Howell *Parly of Beasts* 51 That lovely white Hinde (though she hath som black spots about her shingle)..she was once a Woman. 1661 Morgan *Sph. Gentry* i. vi. 81 [The tail] of the Hart is the Tail, and the Ro-buck or Deer the Shingle. 1688 Holme *Armoury* ii. vii. 132/1.

Shingle (ʃi·ŋg'l), *v.*[1] [f. Shingle *sb.*[1]]

1. *trans.* To cover, roof (a house, etc.) with shingles.

1562 Withals *Dict.* 42 b/2 *Scandulo*, to shyngle. 1577 V. Leigh *Surv.* I ij, Whether..slated, shingled, or thatched. 1638 Bp. Mountagu *Art. Enq. Visit.* A 2, Is your Church leaded, tiled, slated, shingled, thatched with straw or reede. 1796 J. Adams *Diary* 27 July, I rode up to the barn, which Mr. Pratt has almost shingled. 1833 [Seba Smith] *Lett. J. Downing* xxi. (1835) 124 He'll new shingle our old barn for nothin. 1865 'Artemus Ward' *Trav.* ii. xii, When the Lion House was ready to be shingled.

transf. 1885 *Harper's Mag.* Mar. 533/1 The..walls and ..roof are shingled with slate. 1891 *Century Mag.* Nov. 61 We constructed a low châlet.., shingling it with swamp grass.

2. *U.S.* **a.** To cut (hair), properly so as to give the effect of overlapping shingles, by exposing the ends of hair all over the head; also *absol.*

1857 Holland *Bay Path* 232 (Thornton *Amer. Gloss.*), I'm great on cutting hair. I don't suppose there's anybody in the settlement can shingle like me...By the way, don't you want your hair cut? I don't know how I'm going to get along, unless you do have it jest shingled. 1864 R. F. Burton in *Anthropol. Rev.* II. 51 To 'shingle off' their hair as closely as possible. 1909 Kate Wiggin *Susanna & Sue* xii, It's kind of pityish to have your hair shingled.

b. To cover like a shingled roof.

1858 O. W. Holmes *Aut. Breakf.-t.* 11 A somewhat more than middle-aged female, with a parchment forehead and a dry little 'frisette' shingling it.

c. (See quot.)

1860 Bartlett *Dict. Amer.* (ed. 3), *To shingle*, to chastise. A shingle applied *a posteriori* is a favorite New England mode of correcting a child.

Shingle, *v.*[2] *Iron-manuf.* [ad. F. *cingler*, ad. G. *zängeln*, f. *zange* tongs, pincers.] *trans.* To subject (the puddled ball) to pressure and blows from a hammer so as to expel impurities.

1674, etc. [see Shingling *vbl. sb.*[2]]. 1784 in *Abridgm. Specif., Iron & Steel* (1858) 13 Shingling, welding, and manufacturing iron and steel into barrs, plates, rods, and otherwise. *Ibid.* 365 The slabs, having been shingled..to the sizes of the grooves in my rollers. 1825 J. Nicholson *Oper. Mech.* 768 These loops are..brought to a white or welding heat, and then shingled into half-blooms or slabes. 1861 Fairbairn *Iron* 105 The old method of shingling the puddle balls..was to reduce them to shape by a heavy hammer called the forge-hammer or helve.

†**Shingle,** *v.*[3] [? f. Cingle, girdle, with assimilation to Shingles.] *trans.* To girdle *round*.

1621 T. Williamson tr. *Goulart's Wise Vieillard* 35 Till the gout is in their knees, or the dropsie doth painefully shingle them round.

Shingled (ʃi·ŋg'ld), *ppl. a.*[1] [f. Shingle *sb.*[1] or *v.*[1] + -ed.]

1. Covered or tiled with shingles; in first quot., ? having the outer timbers overlapping like tiles, clinker-built.

1362 Langl. *P. Pl.* A. x. 170 Eihte soules And of vche beest A Couple, Þat in þe schynglede schup schullen ben I-saued. 1577 V. Leigh *Surv.* I ij, Buildinges..whether.. Tyled, slated, shingled, or thatched. 1818 J. Hassell *Rides & Walks* II. 107 The church has a shingled tower. 1881 *19th Cent.* Aug. 306 The prevalence of shingled spires in the wooded districts. 1885 C. F. Holder *Marvels Anim. Life* 216 To capture the rain-water from the shingled roof.

2. Arranged tile-wise, imbricated.

1884 Coues *N. Amer. Birds* 94 Individual feathers of the notæum..smoothly shingled or imbricated.

Shi·ngled, *ppl. a.*[2] [f. Shingle *sb.*[2] + -ed [2].] Covered with or consisting of shingle or rounded pebbles.

1802 Bloomfield *Rural Tales* 53 May your days Glide on, as glides the Stream that never stays; Bright as whose shingled bed..May all your..Virtues shine! 1888 Henley *Bk. Verses* 156 The shingled shore.

Shi·ngled, *ppl. a.*[3] See Shingle *v.*[2]

1884 W. H. Greenwood *Steel & Iron* xvi. 305 The shingled blooms will not be uniformly homogeneous if they are produced from different-sized puddled balls.

Shi·ngler [1]. [f. Shingle *sb.*[1] or *v.*[1] + -er [1].] One who shingles houses, etc.; also *U.S.* 'one who or a machine which cuts and prepares shingles' (Ogilvie 1882).

1445 in *5th Rep. Hist. MSS. Comm.* 528/1 Paid 2 shyngelers and a boy, mending the old rofe of the church 20*d.* 1554 in *Shropsh. Par. Docum.* (1903) 55 Paid to the syngler & his man ii[s] vii[d]. 1562 *Act 5 Eliz.* c. 4 § 23 Any Persone using or exercising Tharte or Occupation of a..Thatcher or Shingler. 1688 Holme *Armoury* iii. ix. 394/2 There is four sorts of Trades, that formerly used to cover Houses,..viz. the Plumer, with Lead;..the Shingler with clift Wood [etc.]. 1865 P. B. St. John *Snow Ship* ix, Nothing is more necessary to a backwoods-man than to be a good shingler—that is to know how to select the right tree and how to cut it. 1886 Morse *Jap. Homes* 79 The shingler takes a mouthful of these pegs.

Shi·ngler [2]. *Iron-manuf.* [f. Shingle *v.*[2] + -er [1].] One who or a machine which shingles puddled iron.

1832 Ht. Martineau *Hill & Valley* iv, The shingler who hammers the balls of metals into an oblong form. 1864 Webster, *Shingler*,..a machine for shingling puddled iron, or making it into blooms. 1875 Knight *Dict. Mech.*, *Shingler*, an eccentric..roller revolving within a concave and pressing the dross out of the loop. 1881 Greener *Gun* 221 The puddler takes the bloom with a pair of tongs, runs with it to the tilt hammer and hands it over to the shingler.

Shingles (ʃi·ŋg'lz), *sb. pl.* Also 4 schingles, 5 cingules, sengles, 5–6 shyngles, 6 chingles. [Representing med.L. *cingulus* (MS. gloss in Du Cange), var. of *cingulum* girdle, used to render Gr. ζώνη or ζωστήρ in the medical sense.] An eruptive disease (*Herpes zoster*) often extending round the middle of the body like a girdle (whence the name); usually accompanied by violent neuralgic pain.

1398 Trevisa *Barth. De P. R.* xvii. xciii. (Tollem. MS.), Aȝens icchynge and scabbes wett and drye and aȝens schingles [*Bodley MS.* cingules, *ed.* 1495 shyngles]. c 1450 *M. E. Med. Bk.* (Heinrich) 78 Ther ys an euel, þat men callen þesengles. 1527 Andrew *Brunswyke's Distyll. Waters* G ij, The onnatural hete named shyngles on the bodye. 1546 Phaer *Bk. Childr.* Bb viij b, Our Englysshe women call it the fyre of Saynt Anthonye, or chingles. 1614 W. B. *Philos. Banquet* (ed. 2) 86 The oyle of Nuttes..helpes the shingles. 1712 Swift *Jrnl. to Stella* 10 May, The doctors said that they never saw anything so odd of the kind; they were not properly shingles, but *herpes miliaris*, and twenty other hard names. 1782 W. Heberden *Comm.* xxiii. (1806) 126 The herpes, or shingles..consists of a heap of watery bladders. 1899 *Allbutt's Syst. Med.* VIII. 618 On hearing that it is the 'shingles' and that it is not catching.

b. A similar disease in horses.

1639 T. de Gray *Compl. Horsem.* 74 This disease is also called by some the shingles in a horse. 1725 *Bradley's Fam. Dict.*, St. Anthony's Fire, a Disease Horses are subject to,.. call'd by some the Shingles.

Shi·ngling, *vbl. sb.*[1] [f. Shingle *v.*[1] + -ing [1].] Tiling with shingles or cutting shingles. Also *attrib.*, as *shingling-hatchet*, etc.

1703 T. N. *City & C. Purchaser* 243 *Shingling*, the laying on of Shingles. 1859 F. S. Cooper *Ironmongers' Catal.* 157 Shingling Hatchets. 1864 Lowell *Fireside Trav.* 32 An Indian tomahawk, which had too much the peaceful look of a shingling-hatchet. 1875 Knight *Dict. Mech.*, *Shingling-bracket*, a device to enable a carpenter to stand on a roof while nailing on shingles. *Ibid.*, *Shingling-gage*,..for adjusting shingles in the proper position for nailing. 1910 Lady D. Nevill *Under Five Reigns* iv, Shingling is a craft quite distinct from ordinary builder's or carpenter's work.

b. Arrangement in overlapping layers.

1903 *U. S. Geol. Surv.* Prof. Paper 13. 48 In numerous sections of these deposits the shingling of the gravels is well marked.

Shi·ngling, *vbl. sb.*[2] *Iron-manuf.* [f. Shingle *v.*[2] + -ing [1].] The action of Shingle *v.*[2]

1674 Ray *Coll. Words* 128 This Loop they take out with their shingling tongs, and beat it with Iron sledges..that so it may..be in a capacity to be carried under the hammer. Under which they then removing it,..beat it with the hammer very gently, which forces cinder and dross out of the matter, afterwards..they beat it thicker and stronger till they bring it to a Bloom...This operation they call shingling the Loop. 1840 *Civil Eng. & Arch. Jrnl.* III. 298/1 The roasting, smelting, refining, puddling, shingling, balling, and drawing-out. 1881 Greener *Gun* 222 The loss in the puddling is about 15 per cent., in the shingling and rolling about 14 per cent.

attrib. 1674 [see above]. 1839 Ure *Dict. Arts* 706 The shingling mill..consists of two sets of grooved cylinders. 1857 G. Wilkie *Iron Manuf.* 108 A 60-horse engine will drive a shingling-hammer [etc.]. 1873 *Iron* 5 Apr. 356/1 The shingling-forge fitted with a 5-ton wrought iron helve.

Shi·ngling, *ppl. a.* [f. Shingle *v.*[1] + -ing [2].] Used advb.: In a tile-wise arrangement.

1840 R. H. Dana *Bef. Mast* xxix, As to whether the hides should be stowed 'shingling' or 'back-to-back and flipper-to-flipper'.

Shingly (ʃi·ŋgli), *a.*[1] [f. Shingle *sb.*[1] + -y.] Covered with shingles or wooden tiles.

1857 Whittier *Last Walk in Autumn* xxi, The..shingly town-house, where The freeman's vote for Freedom falls.

Shingly (ʃi·ŋgli), *a.*[2] Also *Sc.* 8 chinlie, chingily, 9 chingly; 9 shingley. [f. Shingle *sb.*[2] + -y.] Consisting of or covered with shingle; of the nature of shingle.

α. 1775 L. Shaw *Hist. Moray* 78 The hard chinlie beach. 1797 *Statist. Acc. Scotl.* XIX. 5 In several parts it [*sc.* the soil] is gravellish or sandy, or chingily. 1807 Headrick *Arran* 281 For slight, sandy, or chingly soils.

β. 1789 *Phil. Trans.* LXXX. 91, I landed, within the sound, on a white shingly beach, the stones of which are all chert. 1802 W. Forsyth *Fruit Trees* xxiii. (1824) 343 Shingly and gravelly soils. 1810 Scott *Lady of L.* iii. vii, Benharrow's shingly side. 1843 *Chamb. Jrnl.* 45/3 As they stood upon the shingley beach to see him start. 1869 Tozer *Highl. Turkey* I. 291 The broad shingly bed of a river. 1870 Hawthorne *Engl. Note-bks.* (1879) I. 211 Covered with gray shingly stones.

Shinily (ʃəi·nili), *adv.* [f. Shiny + -ly [2].] With a shiny surface or appearance. So **Shi·niness**, shiny condition.

1872 Ruskin *Eagle's N.* § 154 What sort of shininess there is on the end of a terrier's nose. 1894 *Contemp. Rev.* Oct. 760 The utmost shininess that can be got out of it will not replace one-tenth part of the light. 1894 A. Morrison *Mean Streets* 138 His short hair clung shinily about his bullet head.

Shining (ʃəi·niŋ), *vbl. sb.* [f. Shine *v.* + -ing [1].] The action of the verb Shine; emission or shedding of light; gleaming, beaming.

a 1300 *E. E. Psalter* cix. 3 In schinenges of haliyhes bright [Vulg. *in splendoribus sanctorum*]. 13.. *K. Alis.* 641 (Bodl. MS.) Þe erþe shook, þe see bycom grene, Þe sonne wiþdrouȝ shynyng shene. 13.. *Cursor M.* 23688 (Gött.) Þe schene schining of cristal. 1398 Trevisa *Barth. De P. R.* viii. xli. (Tollem. MS.), Schinynge is out spryngynge and stremynge oute of þe substaunce of lyȝte. c 1400 *Destr. Troy* 919 For chynyng of the chene stone he shont with his hede. c 1460 *Towneley Myst.* xxvi. 117 The moyn and starnes of shynyng blan. a 1586 Sidney *Arcadia* iii. (Sommer) 265 b, He..might spie sometimes..the shining of armour, like flashing of lightning. 1613 Purchas *Pilgrimage* (1614) 560 Grashoppers doe..come in such quantitie that they intercept the shining of the Sunne like a Cloud. 1725 Ramsay *Gentle Sheph.* iii. iii, I've seen with shining fair the morning rise. 1852 Thackeray *Esmond* i. v, Harry could see the shining of a steel breastplate he had on. 1852 M. Arnold *Self-Depend.* vi, With joy the stars perform their shining. 1905 F. Young *Sands of Pleasure* ii. viii, The cold, alert shining of her eyes.

b. *transf.* and *fig.*

c 1374 Chaucer *Boeth.* iii. pr. ii. (1868) 67 Yif that dignitees lesen hir shyninge by chaunginge of tymes. 1430–40 Lydg. *Bochas* i. vii. (1544) 10 b, Whan his shining was waxt vp to y[e] ful After the chaunge of fortunes lawe His glorye gan discrecen. a 1586 Sidney *Arcadia* ii. (Sommer) 127 Men of vertue suppressed, lest their shining should discouer the others filthines. *Ibid.* iii. 249 Our trust is that you yet will not denie the shining of your eies vpon vs. 1656 *Artif. Handsom.* 129 All their Oratorious polishings and shinings are but false beames. 1715 De Foe *Fam. Instruct.* i. i. (1841) II. 5 We are but as dark as we were before; for we were none of us the better for all your hypocritical shining. a 1778 Toplady in *Bk. Praise* (1866) 446 The shinings of His grace Soften my passage through the wilderness.

attrib. 1748 Richardson *Clarissa* (1768) IV. 64 The time of Adversity is your Shining-time.

Shining (ʃəi·niŋ), *ppl. a.* [f. Shine *v.* + -ing [2].]

1. That shines; luminous, lustrous, gleaming, beaming; also, of bright or brilliant aspect or exterior; resplendent in dress or equipment.

a 900 *O. E. Martyrol.* 22 Nov. 208 Þa stod se engel biȝ hyre myd scynendum fyðerum. c 1050 *Voc.* in Wr.-Wülcker 431/23 *Limpidis*, scinendum. a 1225 *Ancr. R.* 224 'Demonium meridianum', þet is, briht schininde deouel. c 1275 *Serving Christ* 18 in *O. E. Misc.* 91 In schynynde wede. 1382 Wyclif *Lam.* iv. 7 Whitere is Nazareis than snoȝ, shynendere [1388 schynyngere] than mylc. c 1475 *Rauf Coilȝear* 559 Bot I the knew, that is sa schynand. 1533 Bellenden *Livy* ii. xxi. (S.T.S.) I. 215 Þai war iij[c] and vj knichtis in schynyng armoure. 1552 Abp. Hamilton *Catech.* (1884) 40 The cleir schenand sonne. 1565 J. Phillip *Patient Grissell* 702, I neither haue faire Helins shape, nor comly shininge hew. 1626 Bacon *Sylva* § 352 Shining woods, being laid in a Dry Roome,..lose their Shining. 1664 Sir R. Howard & Dryden *Ind. Queen* ii. i, Showres sometimes fall upon a shining day. 1667 Milton *P. L.* vii. 401 Fish ..with thir Finns & shining Scales. 1719 De Foe *Crusoe* ii. (Globe) 559 Tiles..of a deep shining Black. 1776 Gibbon *Decl. & F.* xiii. I. 377 A bag of shining leather filled with pearls. 1825 T. Hook *Sayings* Ser. ii. *Passion & Princ.* x. III. 183 A bright shining house-maid. 1845 Kitto *Cycl. Bibl. Lit.* s. v. *Egypt*, The climate is..exceedingly hot; the atmosphere clear and shining. 1852 Thackeray *Esmond* i. ix, On a shining chestnut horse. *Ibid.* ii. iii, That busy, shining scene of the Thames swarming with boats and barges. 1860 Tyndall *Glac.* i. ii. 21 All covered with shining snow.

b. as an epithet of coin. † *Shining clay*, gold.

1668 Hopkins *Van. World* Wks. (1710) 5 What are Gold and Silver, but diversified Earth, hard and shining Clay? 1677 Horneck *Gt. Law Consid.* v. (1704) 306 The tears I shed, for being deprived of a little shining clay. 1746 Francis tr. *Hor., Sat.* ii. iii. 203 From out his Bags he pours the shining Store.

c. *Nat. Hist.*, etc. (See quots.)

1792 Withering *Brit. Plants* (ed. 2) III. 399 Pileus brown, shining, glutinous. 1793 Martyn *Lang. Bot.*, *Lucidum folium*...Bright, shining. 1839 Lindley *Introd. Bot.* iii. (ed. 3) 471 Shining (*nitidus*); having a smooth, even, polished surface; as many leaves. 1850 Ansted *Elem. Geol., Min.* etc. § 310 The degrees of intensity [*sc.* of lustre] are denominated as follows:—. *Shining*, when an image is produced, but not a well-defined image. Ex., Calcareous spar, Celestine. 1871 W. A. Leighton *Lichen-flora* 109 Lobes ascending, glabrous and shining.

d. Hence as specific name of animals and plants (rendering L. *lucidus*, *lucens*, *splendidus*, etc.).

1626 Bacon *Sylva* § 475 The Shining Willow, which they call Swallow-Taile. 1771 J. R. Forster *Flora Amer. Septentr.* 7 Potamogeton lucens. Pondweed, shining. 1783 Latham *Gen. Synopsis Birds* III. 56 Shining Thrush, *Turdus nitens*. 1784 Cullum *Hist. Hawsted* App. 232 Shining Dove's-foot cranesbill (*Geranium lucidum*) in hedges. 1809 Shaw *Gen. Zool.* VII. 372 Coppery-green shining Crow. 1865 *Intell. Obs.* VII. 102 The male Satin or Shining Bower Bird.

2. Phr. **a.** *Shining light* (after John v. 35): a person conspicuous for some excellence.

1526 [see Light *sb.* 5 a]. 1563 Winȝet tr. *Vincent. Lirin.* ix. Wks. (S.T.S.) II. 27 That schyning licht of al the sanctis, ..maist blissit Cypriane. a 1796 Burns *Holy Willie's Prayer* ii, A burnin' an' a shinin' light To a' this place! 1869 Trollope *He knew*, etc. xviii. (1878) 100 Her aunt was regarded as a shining light by very many good people in the county. 1887 *Field* 19 Nov. 790/1 In the opening part of the game, Stadden, Robertshaw, and Brooke had been the shining lights.

b. *To improve the shining hour* (after Watts, see quot. 1720): to make good use of time.

1720 Watts *Div. Songs* xx, How doth the little busy bee improve each shining hour! 1866 'Annie Thomas' *Walter Goring* ii, Though he had been seeming to improve the shining hours very much to his own satisfaction.

3. With reference to intellectual or moral qualities: Eminent, distinguished, brilliant. Now *rare*.

c 900 tr. *Bæda's Hist.* iii. xix. (1890) 210 Se wæs in wordum & dædum beorht & scinende. c 1400 tr. *Secreta Secret., Gov. Lordsh.* xxxvii. 69 Þe vertu of þy shynynge lyf shal be..gladyd þerby. c 1420 Hoccleve *Mother of God* 101 Seint Ion Shynynge apostle & euangelist. 1513 *Life Hen. V* (1911) 7 The life and shyninge Acts of this most victorious Kinge. 1593 G. Harvey *Pierce's Super.* 173 The siluer streaming fountaines of flowingest witt, and shiningest Art. c 1665 Mrs. Hutchinson *Mem. Col. Hutchinson* (1846) 31 Nor was his soul less shining in honour than in loue. 1702 Addison *Dial. Medals* i. 11 One that endeavoured rather to be agreeable, than shining in conversation. 1711 — *Spect.* No. 73 ¶ 4 Men of the greatest and the most shining Parts. 1761 Hume *Hist. Eng.* II. xxix. 154 Charles duke of Bourbon..was a prince of the most shining merit. 1781 Cowper *Retirem.* 560 Anticipated rents, and bills unpaid, Force many a shining youth into the shade. 1818 Scott *Hrt. Midl.* xxxvii, [His] most shining quality was courage in the field of battle. 1881 M. Raleigh *Alex. Raleigh* i. 7 [He] was regarded as a boy of good but not shining ability.

4. Of looks: Radiant, beaming.

1821 Lamb *Elia* i. *My relations*, A..shining sanguine face. 1852 Thackeray *Esmond* i. xiii, Greeting him with one of her shining looks.

5. *Comb.*

1802 Shaw *Gen. Zool.* III. 464 Shining-black Snake. 1822 *Hortus Anglicus* II. 120 Shining-leaved Fig Wort. 1895 K. Meyer *Voy. Bran* I. 71 A red-eared shining-white cow.

Shi·ningly, *adv.* [f. prec. + -ly [2].] In a shining manner; with a shining appearance; brightly, brilliantly.

1382 Wyclif *Luke* xvi. 19 Sum man was rich,..and he eet ech day schynyngli [L. *splendide*]. c 1440 *Gesta Rom.* lxvi. 305 (Harl. MS.), Þe myȝty men and riche men of þis wordle, þat hath golde, and goodis shynyngly. 1556 J. Heywood *Spider & F.* xliii. 17 The show..Upon the ten flies parte showth more shininglie Then on the one spiders side. 1611 Speed *Hist. Gt. Brit.* ix. xx. § 5 Let vs now behold his vertues as they are shiningly deduced into action. 1612 R. Sheldon *Serm. St. Martin's* 15 A God, shiningly appearing in Christ. 1824 Galt *Rothelan* I. ii. iv. 181 His eye, which was ever shiningly intellectual. 1836 *Tait's Mag.* III. 447 The silver spoons and forks were laid shiningly side by side in a varnished press. 1859 Sala *Tw. round Clock* (1861) 163 Her ladyship's own private bank is in a shiningly aristocratic street. 1891 'L. Keith' *Lost Illus.* II. xix. 208 Shiningly, spotlessly, insolently new.

So **Shi·ningness**, brightness, brilliance.

1703 *Phil. Trans.* XXV. 1538 The shiningness being wholly occasioned by the reflexion of the Light from the polisht sides. 1752 Sir H. Beaumont *Crito* 41 *note*, The Epithets *marmoreus*, *eburnens*, and *candidus*, are all applied..to the Shiningness here spoken of. 1837 *New Monthly Mag.* XLIX. 24 Albeit swaying so our thoughts In shiningness and motion.

Shinlog (ʃi·nlǫg), *sb.*[1] *Brickmaking.* (See quot. 1703.) Hence **Shinlog** *v.*, to close (the mouth of a kiln) with shinlog.

1703 T. N. *City & C. Purchaser* 48 They damm up the Mouth of the Kiln..with their Shinlog, as they call it (which is pieces of Bricks piled upon each other, with wet Brick Earth, instead of Mortar). This Shinlog they make so high, that there is but just room above it to thrust in a Faggot. *Ibid.*, The Mouth being thus Shinlog'd, they proceed to put in Faggots. 1825 J. Nicholson *Oper. Mech.* 534.

†**Shi·nlog,** *sb.*[2] *Obs.* [app. f. *shin* in Shinbin (cf. the form *shinbeam*) + Log *sb.*[1]] = Shinbin.

1842 *Penny Cycl.* XXIV. 141/2 Pieces called 'shin-logs', and admirably adapted for ship-timbers.

Shinner (ʃi·nəɹ). [f. Shin *sb.* or *v.* + -er [1].]

†**1.** A stocking. *Obs. rare*[−1].

1585 Higins *Junius' Nomencl.* 167/1 *Caliga*,..an hose, a nether stocke, a shinner.

2. A blow or kick on the shin. *dial.*

1835 Marryat *Olla Podr., Moonshine*, I'll give you a shinner on your lower limb. 1869 *Lonsdale Gloss.*

3. *U.S.* 'One who borrows money by the practice of shinning' (Bartlett).

1840 in Schele de Vere *Americanisms* (1872) 305 Coxcombs and dandies, loafers and nibblers, Shavers and shinners.

4. *U.S.* One who 'shins round'; an active person.

1838 J. C. Neal in Schele de Vere *Americanisms* (1872) 305 'Shin it, good man!' ejaculated a good-natured urchin, 'shin it as well as you know how!' The qualification was a good one, Berry not being well calculated for a shinner of the first class.

Shi·nning, *vbl. sb.* [f. Shin *v.* + -ing [1].]

1. *Football.* The act of kicking an opponent on the shin.

1873 *Gentl. Mag.* Apr. 388 Mauling, hacking, kicking, shinning, collaring—such are among the terms and rules of the [Rugby] game. 1899 Shearman, etc. *Football* 70 All charging is fair, but no..shinning or back shinning either of the ball or players is allowed.

2. *U.S.* (See quot. 1864.)

1864 Webster, *Shinning*, a running about borrowing money temporarily to meet pressing demands. 1872 Schele de Vere *Americanisms* 306 This process of *shinning* is resorted to whenever the merchant or banker is *short*.

Shinny (ʃi·ni), *sb.* Also shinney, shinnie. [? f. the cry used in the game *shin ye*, *shin you* (also *shin your side*), of obscure origin; cf. *hummie*, a dial. name for shinty, and the cry *hun you*, *shin you* (Sheffield Gloss.); see also Shinty. Other dial. names of the game are *shinnins*, *shinnock*, *shinnup*; also *shinder* vb.] A (north-country and American) game similar to hockey, played with a ball and sticks curved at one end; also, the stick and the ball used in this game.

1672 in Maidment *Bk. Scotish Pasquils* (1868) 181 He..did transub Himself to ball, the Parliament to club, Which will him holl when right teased at ane blow, Or els Sir Patrick will be the shinnie goe. 1794 *Gentl. Mag.* Mar. 216 *Shinney*, a stick rounding at one end, to strike a small wooden ball with. 1810 *Ann. Reg.* 532 Contending parties, in the northern counties of England, exert themselves to drive the shinney to its goal. 1860 J. F. Campbell *Tales W. Highl.* (1890) I. 202 He..gets him to make an iron shinny. 1893 Leland *Mem.* I. 51 The nose of the [sturgeon] fish..being greatly coveted by us small boys wherewith to make a ball for 'shinny'.

attrib. 1794 *Gentl. Mag.* Mar. 216 *Shinney-hah*, a game so called. 1825 R. Chambers *Trad. Edin.* II. 78 A group of little pensioners, who regularly annoyed him for a shinny ball, or some such article. 1856 Kane *Arctic Expl.* II. xxi. 206 Each of them had a walrus-rib for a..shinny-stick.

Shinny (ʃi·ni), *v.* *U.S.* [f. Shin *sb.*] *intr.* To shin *up* a tree.

1888 T. Stevens *Around the World* 307 The trees..are.. swarming with monkeys...Shinnying up the toddy-palms.

Shinto (ʃi·nto). Also Sin-to, Sintu, -oo. [Japanese, f. Chinese *shin tao* way of the gods.]

1. The native religious system of Japan, the central belief of which is that the mikado is the direct descendant of the sun-goddess and that implicit obedience is due to him.

1727 tr. *Kæmpfer's Hist. Japan* I. 203 Sinto..is the Idol-worship, as of old established in the Country. 1829 *Encycl. Metrop.* (1845) XX. 474/2 The first..Faith of the Japanese, is that of the *Sin-to*. 1875 *N. Amer. Rev.* CXX. 282 The abolition of Buddhism and the establishment of pure Shinto. 1906 *Athenæum* 19 May 602/3 Of pure Shinto ancestor-worship was no part, while phallism in a very pronounced form was intimately associated with it.

b. *attrib.*

1727 tr. *Kæmpfer's Hist. Japan* I. 207 The whole System of the Sintos Divinity. *Ibid.*, The Sintosju or adherents of the Sintos Religion. 1829 *Encycl. Metrop.* (1845) XX. 475/2 The Sin-syu, or maintainers of the Sin-to creed. 1880 E. J. Reed *Japan* I. 47 The worship of the Shinto gods. 1888 L. Oliphant *Epis. in Adv.* 222 Two Buddhist or Sintoo shrines, perched upon pinnacles of rock.

c. *adj.* = Shintoistic.

1904 Sladen *Playing the Game* i. xii, The idea of the Kami..was Shinto rather than Buddhistic.

2. An adherent of Shinto beliefs.

1829 *Encycl. Metrop.* (1845) XX. 477/1 The Gods worshipped by the Sin-tos are principally..departed Spirits deified. 187. Ripley & Dana *Amer. Cycl.* IX. 537 (Cass.) The Shintos believe in a past life, and they live in fear and reverence of the spirits of the dead.

Hence **Shi·ntoism** = Shinto 1; **Shi·ntoist** = Shinto 2; **Shintoi·stic** *a.*, belonging to or characteristic of Shinto; **Shi·ntoize** *v.*, *trans.*, to render Shintoistic.

1727 tr. *Kæmpfer's Hist. Japan* I. 226 Orthodox Sintoists go in Pilgrimage to Isje once a year. 1857 R. Tomes *Amer. in Japan* xiv. 337 The prevailing religions of the Japanese are Buddhism and Sintooism. 1863 *Chamb. Encycl.* V. 686/1 The minor deities of Sintuism are very numerous. 1875 *N. Amer. Rev.* CXX. 296 Buddhism..and the bakufu were, in the eyes of a Shintoist, all one and the same. 1889 E. Arnold *Seas & Lands* xiv. (1895) 218 Pure Shintoism does not admit of any external decoration or images. 1893 in Barrows *World's Parl. Relig.* I. 453 A pilgrimage to various..Shintoistic and Buddhistic temples. 1895 Griffis *Relig. Japan* vii. 212 Is Japanese Buddhism really Shintoized Buddhism, or Buddhaized Shinto?

Shinty (ʃi·nti). Also shintie. [Formation obscure; ? for *shin t'ye*, cf. *shin ye* (see Shinny).]

1. = Shinny.

1771 Pennant *Tour Scot.* 167 The shinty, or the striking a ball of wood or of hair. 1793 *Statist. Acc. Scot.* V. 72 On holidays, all the males of a district..met to play at football, but oftener at shinty. 1808 Jamieson, *Shinty*, the club used in playing [shinty]. 1876 J. Grant *Burgh Sch. Scot.* ii. v. 180 The rough but manly old game of 'shinty' has not yet quite fallen into desuetude. 1882 *Jamieson's Sc. Dict.*, *Shinty*, the ball or knot of wood is called Shintie.

attrib. 1863 N. Macleod *Remin. Highl. Par.* iii, Few games..demand more physical exertion than a good shinty match. 1865 *Morning Star* 1 Feb., Past your ear whizzes a shinty ball.

2. = Shindy 3.

1848 Thackeray *Van. Fair* liv, There's a regular shinty in the house; and everything at sixes and sevens. The landlord's come in and took possession.

Shiny (ʃəi·ni), *a.* Also 6 shynie, 6, 9 shiney. [f. Shine *sb.*[1] + -y.] Full of light or brightness; luminous; having a bright or glistening surface.

1590 Spenser *F. Q.* iii. vi. 6 Vpon a Sommers shynie day. 1596 — *Hymn Heav. Beauty* 51 Affixe thine eye On that bright shynie round still moving Masse. 1606 Shaks. *Ant. & Cl.* iv. ix. 3 The night Is shiny. 1699 Pomfret *Dies Novis.* 50 Ere ruin blasted from the shiny sky. 1760–72 H. Brooke *Fool of Qual.* (1809) IV. 126 The evening being calm and shiny. 1846 Landor *Exam. Shaks.* Wks. 1853 II. 298/1 Sir Silas looked red and shiny as a ripe strawberry on a Snitterfield tile. 1868 Whyte Melville *White Rose* xlv, Umbrella, shiny boots, tall hat, go-to-meeting coat. 1874 Ruskin *Fors Clav.* xlvi. 229 The fattest, shiniest, spottiest trout I ever saw. 1881 C. Whitehead *Hops* 52 The lower sides of the leaves are whitish and shiny.

b. *fig.* Beaming, radiant.

1876 Geo. Eliot *Dan. Der.* xlvi, He looked round with shiny gladness.

c. *Comb.* (parasynthetic).

1882 *Daily News* 7 Jan. 5/4 The shiny-hatted and sealskin-clad rabble. 1898 R. Kearton *Wild Life at Home* 23 Slugs..thin little black shiny-skinned..ones.

d. *advb.*

1596 Spenser *F. Q.* iv. vi. 20 Goldsmithes cunning could not vnderstand To frame such subtile wire, so shinie cleare. 1903 Conrad & Hueffer *Romance* v. ii, His yellow jaws as shiny-shaven as of old.

B. *sb.* A shiny or bright object.

The shiny (slang), money.

1856 Reade *Never too Late* i, We'll soon fill both pockets with the shiney in California. 1889 Conan Doyle *Micah Clarke* 235 The silk and lace are done in these squares covered over with sacking—a thousand of Mechlin to a hundred of the shiny [i. e. the silk].

Ship (ʃip), *sb.*[1] Forms: 1–5 scip, (1, 4 scipp, 1–3 scyp, 3 sip), 3–4 schup, ssip, 3–7 schip, 4–5 s(c)hyp, shipp, schype, schippe, (4 schypp, shup, scippe, shyppe, schepe, 5 chip(pe, schyppe, shep), 4–6 schipp, 4–7 shippe, 5–6 shyppe, s(c)hipe, shype, shepe, 5–7 shipp, (6 sheppe, *Sc.* scheip(e), 4– ship. [Com.Teut.: OE. *scip* str. neut. = OFris. *skip*, *schip* (NFris. *skapp*, *shep*, WFris. *skip*), OS. *skip*, MLG. *schip*, *schēp* (LG. *schipp*), MDu. *sc(h)ip*, *sc(h)eep*, Du. *schip* (oblique *scheepe*, comb. *scheeps-* beside *schip-*), WFlem. *scheep*, OHG. *scif*, *skef* (MHG. *schif*, *schef*, G. *schiff*), ON. *skip* (Sw. *skepp*, Da. *skib*), Goth. *skip*; the ultimate etymology is uncertain. The Germanic word appears in Romanic as F. *esquif*, It. *schifo*, etc., see Skiff *sb.*[1]]

1. A large sea-going vessel (opposed to a *boat*); *spec.* (in modern times) a vessel having a bowsprit and three masts, each of which consists of a lower, top, and topgallant mast.

In OE. used also for small craft, as ON. *skip*.

c 725 *Corpus Gloss.* (Hessels) S 188 *Scaphum*, scip. c 888 Ælfred *Boeth.* xxxviii. § 1 Da se Aulixes..to þam ȝefohte for, þa hæfde he sume hundred scipa. c 1050 *O. E. Chron.* (MS. C) an. 1048, Eadward cining & þa eorlas foran æfter þam ut mid heora scypun. c 1200 *Vices & Virtues* 45 Hlested hwat ðe hlauerd seið, ðe ðat scip auh, to ðe stieresmannen. a 1225 *Juliana* (Royal MS.) 32/12 Þu leddest israeles folc purh þe reade sea buten schip druifot. c 1250 *Kent. Serm.* in *O. E. Misc.* 32 And so hi were in þo ssipe so a-ros a great tempeste of winde. a 1300 *Cursor M.* 13280 Petre and andreu..Wit a word þai leit þair scipps tuin [*Gött.* schippis]. 1362 Langl. *P. Pl.* A. x. 160 A schup of schides and Bordes. c 1374 Chaucer *Former Age* 21 No ship yit karf the wawes grene and blewe. c 1375 *Sc. Leg. Saints* vii. (*Jacobus Minor*) 370 Quhat schepe þat brokine ware a-pone þat coste. c 1400 *Three Kings Cologne* (1886) 84 Þat þey had suffrid hem priuelich to passe ouer þe see in her scheppys. c 1485 *Digby Myst.* (1882) iii. 1423 Master of þe shepe, a word with the. 1541 *Test. Ebor.* (Surtees) VI. 149, I give to Mathue Wilson my shipe called Marie Janies. a 1578 Lindesay (Pitscottie) *Chron. Scot.* (S.T.S.) I. 355 The skiper of the scheipe. 1596 Shaks. *Merch. V.* i. iii. 182 My Shippes come home a month before the daie. 1671 Milton *Samson* 714 A stately Ship Of Tarsus, bound for th' Isles Of Javan or Gadier. 1708 E. Ward *Wooden World Diss.* (1708) 84 There's near as much Stuff drops from his [a sea-cook's] Carcass every Day as would tallow the Ship's Bottom. 1707 *Lond. Gaz.* No. 4380/3 One of the Rocks not being a Ships length to Leeward of her. 1798 Coleridge *Anc. Mar.* i. vi, The ship was cheer'd, the harbour clear'd. 1873 Longf. *Wayside Inn* iii. *Elizabeth* iv, Ships that pass in the night, and speak each other in passing. 1889 Welch *Naval Archit.* viii. 102 The bottom and side plating of all ships is arranged in longitudinal layers or strakes. 1911 *Encycl. Brit.* XXIV. 876/2 Ships with four and five masts were employed by several countries during the 19th century.

¶ Ships are now personified as feminine, but usage has varied (see the following quots.).

The use of the masc. pron. in the 17th and 18th cent. was prob. suggested by the application of *man* to a ship in *Dutchman*, *merchantman*, *man-of-war*. In instances before c 1650 *his* may mean 'its'.

1375, etc. [see She 2]. c 1426 *Poem on Agincourt* in Hazl. *E. P. P.* (1866) II. 97 Euery shyp wayed his anker.., They hoysed theyr sayles sayled a lofte. 1588 Kyd *Househ. Phil.* Wks. (1901) 278 In a shyppe the Rudder ought to be no lesse then may suffise to direct hys course. 1611 Shaks. *Wint. T.* iii. iii. 93 The Shippe boaring the Moone with her maine Mast. [1622 *Recov. Exchange* in Arb. *Eng. Garner* IV. 595 'A sail!' 'a sail!': which, at last, was discovered to be another Man of War of Turks. For he made towards us. 1627 Capt. Smith *Sea Gram.* xiii. 59 A saile, how beares she or stands shee, to wind-ward or lee-ward, set him by the Compasse; he stands right ahead, or on the weather-Bow, or lee-Bow.] 1635 Hakewill *Apol.* (ed. 3) Argt., As a Ship which..cannot move beyond the length of his Cable. 1676 Streynsham Master *Diaries* (1911) II. 93 Wee mett a great Dutch ship neare Nassapore point. He wore a Flagg. 1784 *New Spect.* XIII. 2/1 The last [ship was] drowned and swallowed up, within sight of his own shore.

b. Without article, chiefly in dependence on a prep. Also *to take ship* (see Take *v.* 24 c).

c 900 tr. *Bæda's Hist.* iv. i. (1890) 256 Swa eode he in scip & ferde to Breotone. a 1122 *O.E. Chron.* (Laud MS.) an. 1046, Hi..wurpon hine on þone bat..& reowan to scipe. c 1205 Lay. 1098 Brutus nom Ignogen & into scipe [c 1275 to sipe] lædde. 1297 R. Glouc. (Rolls) 1464 Þe emperour bigan to fle mid is folc atte laste To scipes. c 1350 *Will. Palerne* 5088 Partenedon passed to schepe & his puple after. c 1386 Chaucer *Miller's T.* 354 Er þat he myghte brynge his wyf to shipe. 1474 Caxton *Chesse* ii. iv. (1883) 45 Guion fledd also in to affrique by shipp. 1568 Grafton *Chron.* II. 29 He..went to Ship, setting aside all perils. 1597 Hooker *Eccl. Pol.* v. lxvii. (1611) 358 Finding him againe as soone as themselues by shippe were arriued on the contrary side. 1888 [see Ex 2]. 1912 *Times* 19 Dec. 20/3 Oats..American white, ex ship, 18s. 4½d.

c. In legal enactments often with greatly extended application, as in the following quot.

1870 *Act 33 & 34 Vict.* c. 90 § 30 'Ship' shall include any description of boat, vessel, floating battery, or floating craft; also any description of boat, vessel, or other craft or battery, made to move either on the surface of or under water, or sometimes on the surface of and sometimes under water.

d. In rowing parlance, applied to the racing eight-oar boat; also used playfully of other craft.

1878 Stevenson *Inland Voy.* 14 The bargee is on shipboard —he is master in his own ship—he can land whenever he will. 1888 Woodgate *Boating* 147 She..was once specially borrowed by Corpus (Oxon) during the summer eights, and was said by that crew to be a vast improvement on their own ship. 1896 Ashby-Sterry *Tale of Thames* v, Here they leave their ship and quietly stroll up to the New Inn. 1901 *Daily News* 1 Apr. 5/7 The..steadiness of their ship.. helped the Oxford men very much.

e. *fig.* Applied to the state.

1675 *Machiavelli's Prince* ix. Wks. 212 But when times are tempestuous, and the ship of the State has need of the help..of the Subject. 1894 Gladstone *Odes of Horace* iii. viii. 26 Though the State-ship somewhat heave. 1913 *19th Cent.* Feb. 305 The Ship of the State of China is still labouring in a storm-swept ocean.

2. With qualifying word or phrase indicating the kind or use:

King's ship (now Hist.), one of the fleet of ships provided and maintained out of the royal revenue; a ship of the royal navy; later, a ship-of-war equipped at the public expense (opp. to *privateer*); so †**ship-royal**. †**Great ship**, a ship-of-war.

For *flagship*, *hospital-ship*, *ice-ship*, *line-of-battle ship*, *long ship*, *merchant ship*, *post-ship*, *private ship*, *slave-ship*, *steamship*, *store-ship*, *troop-ship*, *warship*, etc. see the first elements; for *ship of burden*, *of countenance*, *of the line*, *of post*, *of state*, see these sbs.; also Ship-of-war.

[1350 in Rymer *Fœdera* (1825) III. i. 195 Johannes Wille, magister navis regis vocatæ La Piente.]

a 1400–50 *Wars Alex.* 65 Gales & grete schipis full of grym wapens. 1450 Lomner *Let. to J. Paston* 5 May, Yn the syght of all his men he was drawyn ought of the grete shippe. 1485–7 *Naval Acc. Hen. VII* (1896) 36 The Kings ship cald the Grace dieu. 1495 *Ibid.* 161 The costes of Kepyng the Kynges Ship Ryall called the Soueraigne. 1512 in Rymer *Fœdera* (1712) XIII. 328/2 All Prisoners, beyng Chieftens ..and one Shippe Royall being of the Portage of Two Hundred Tonnes or above..Reserved to our said Soveraign Lord. 1568 Grafton *Chron.* II. 688 The Easterlynges.. approched the Englishe ship as nere as their great shippes could come at the lowe water. 1660 Fuller *Mixt Contempl.* ii. 31, I never did read..that ever Queen Elizabeth had any Ship-Royal, which..carried the Memorial of any particular Conquest she got. 1690 C. Nesse *Hist. & Myst. O. & N. Test.* I. 116 The Church here is a mighty Queen, a ship-royal. 1697 Dampier *Voy.* I. 50 There escaped but one Kings-ship, and one Privateer. *Ibid.* 357 Captain Swan had his men as much under command as if he had been in a Kings Ship. 1758 J. Blake *Mar. Syst.* 45 The commander of the king's ship is obliged to make up his loss by pressing hands from the merchant ships. 1804 Holt *Shipping & Navig. Laws* (ed. 2) Introd. 36 Foreign seamen, who shall have served in time of war three years on board a king's ship.

3. In fig. and allusive phrases, *esp.* where *ship* typifies the fortunes or affairs of a person, etc. or the person himself in regard to them.

To be in the same ship, cf. Boat *sb.* 1 d; *to give up the ship*, *to burn one's ships*, see Burn *v.* 9 c. *When one's ship comes home* (or *in*), when one comes into one's fortune.

1500–20 Dunbar *Poems* ix. 165 Thow mak my schip in blissit port to arryif, That sailis heir in stormis violent. a 1548 Hall *Chron., Hen. VII*, 27 Doubting not to bring his ship to the porte desired. 1643 Prynne *Sov. Power Parl.* App. 209 Those who are conversant in the same danger, are said to be in the same Ship. 1680 *Debates Parl.* (1681) 117 Is not all England in danger to be lost? Let us secure the Ship, before we dispose of the Cabbins. 1816 Jefferson *Writ.* (1899) X. 4 My exhortation would rather be 'not to give up the ship'. 1820 Shelley *Œd. Tyr.* i. i. 245, I drove her—afar!..From city to city, abandoned of pity, A ship without needle or star. 1851 Mayhew *Lond. Labour* I. 175 One [customer] always says he'll give me a ton of taties when his ship comes home. 1855 Thackeray *Newcomes* lxv, That Mr. Ratray who has just come out of the ship, and brought a hundred thousand pounds with him. 1880 Cable *Grandissimes* liii, Nobody ever gives up the ship in parlour or veranda debate. 1886 D. C. Murray *Cynic Fortune* xii, The wealthy relative..proposed to supply him with an income of a hundred pounds per annum until the major's next expected ship should come in. 1898 *Allbutt's Syst. Med.* V. 816 It is well in the case of a new patient at any rate to postpone a final diagnosis till the ship is in calmer waters. 1900 Mahan *War S. Africa* v, Not the courage that throws away the scabbard, much less that which burns its ships.

4. *transf.* Applied to various objects that are, or are conceived to be, navigated.

†**a.** Noah's ark. **b.** as in *airship* = dirigible balloon. **c.** *Ship of the desert*, *desert-ship*: the camel. **d.** *Ship of Guinea* = *Guinea ship* (b) s. v. Guinea 1.

[a 1300 *Cursor M.* 9674 Noe..in þat scip allan was in.] 1422 Yonge tr. *Secreta Secret.* xxxvii. 193 In Noe's ship he and his wif, har thre sonys and har wiffis sawid were. c 1485 *Digby Myst.* (1882) iii. 1351 In þe shep of noee. 1526 R. Whytford *Martiloge* 12 b, Saynt Noe that made the shyppe. 1579 T. Stevens in Hakluyt *Voy.* (1599) II. ii. 99 A thing swimming vpon the water like a cocks combe (which they call a ship of Guinea). [1615 G. Sandys *Trav.* 138 Camels. These are the ships of Arabia, their seas are the deserts.] 1823 [see Desert *sb.*[2] 1]. 1824 [see Desert *sb.*[2] 5]. 1878 Bosw. Smith *Carthage* xxi. 439 Those ships of the desert, the long line of his camels.

5. A vessel, utensil, ornament, etc. shaped like a ship. Also (in first quot.), the noble coined under Edward III, which bore the image of a ship.

c 1420 Hoccleve *Min. Poems* xvii. 29, vj[c] shippes grete, To yeue vs han yee grauntid & behight. 1490 Caxton *Eneydos* v. 22 Cymphes..ben in maner of lityl bokettis, or lytyl shippes, of a strange stone. 1525 in Ellis *Orig. Lett.* Ser. i. I. 271 A ship of silver for the almes disshe. 1575–6 *New Yrs. Gifts* in Nichols *Progr. Eliz.* (1823) II. 1 A juell of golde, being a shippe, set with a table dyamonde of fyve sparcks of dyamondes.

b. An incense boat. Now *Hist.*

1422 *Rec. St. Mary at Hill* (1904) 14 Also iij senseres of siluer & gilt Also ij sheppis of seluere. 1472 in Swayne *Churchw. Acc. Sarum* (1896) 5 A ship of silver in passel gilt without spone. 1546 S. Fish *Supplic. Poore Commons* 75 Torches, tapurs, shepe, sensoures. 1593 *Rites of Durham* (Surtees) 8 Two Shipps of silver, parcell gilt, for principall dayes. 1843 Pugin *Apol. Rev. Chr. Arch.* 51 b, Two thuribles, with a ship for incense. 1898 J. Wickham Legg in *Yorksh. Archæol. Jrnl.* XV. 132 *note*, A censer with coals, a ship with incense, and a spoon.

†**c.** The nave (see Nave *sb.*[2]) of a church. *rare.*

1613 tr. *Mexio's Treas. Anc. & Mod. T.* 713/1 One of his Prophets made a conuocation..of all the people, in the great Shippe of the great Church.

d. *Saltmaking.* The vessel into which the brine runs from the pits.

1669 *Phil. Trans.* IV. 1065 They fill their Panns again with new Brine out of the Ship, (so they call a great Cistern by their Panns sides, into which their Brine runs through the Wooden Gutters from the Pump, that stands in the Pitt). 1674 Ray *Coll. Words* 175. 1753 *Chambers' Cycl. Suppl.*

e. *Astron.* The Argo Navis, a southern constellation extending between Canis major and Centaurus from the equator nearly to the pole.

1599 T. Hill *Sch. Skil* 23 The image named the Ship, hath 45 stars. 1822 Barlow in *Encycl. Metrop.* (1845) III. 508/1 [The milky way] traverses the constellations Cassiopeia,..Canis Major, and the Ship. 1868 Lockyer *Guillemin's Heavens* (ed. 3) 334.

†**6.** A shipful, shipload. *Obs.*

1455–6 *Cal. Anc. Rec. Dublin* (1889) 290 A shype of iryn that come yn before Michalmas. c 1595 Carew *Excell. Eng. Tongue* in G. G. Smith *Eliz. Crit. Ess.* (1904) II. 292 When wee would be rid of one, wee vse to saye..by circumlocution ..another in your steede, a shipp of salte for you.

7. A ship's company or crew.

1338 R. Brunne *Chron.* (1810) 170 Do dight & mak ȝow bone, þe schip ere Sarazins alle. 1648 *Hamilton Papers* (Camden) 222 The twelue schipps that haue declared for the King doeth much startill ther former inclinations. 1748 *Anson's Voy.* ii. iv. 157 It was not the most eligible place for a ship to refresh at.

b. *Old ship*, a jocular address to a sailor.

1849 Cupples *Green Hand* i, 'Come, old ship, give us a yarn!' said the younger forecastle-men to an old one. *Ibid.* vi, 'What's the odds, Harry, old ship?' said Tom.

8. *attrib.* and *Comb.*

a. Simple attrib. = of or for, pertaining to, or concerning a ship or ships, used or fitted for use on board ship, as *ship-accounts*, *-beak*, *-bell*, *-canal*, *-captain*, †*-dock*, †*-gun*, *life*, etc. (Cf. the compounds with *ship's*, 9 c.)

1815 Scott *Guy M.* xliii, *Ship-accounts and other papers. 1613 T. Godwin *Rom. Antiq.* (1614) 9 Those *ship beakes called in Latine *Rostra*. 1871 Longf. *Wayside Inn* ii. *Musician's T.* iv. iv, When the dismal *ship-bell tolled. 1688 Holme *Armoury* iii. xv. (Roxb.) 35 The *ship bow or loofe. 1847 *Niles' Reg.* 13 Nov. 165/2 A *ship canal wide and deep enough to float a first-rate man-of-war. 1858 Simmonds *Dict. Trade*, *Ship-captain*, the master and commander of a merchant-vessel. 1865 W. G. Palgrave *Arabia* II. 195 We fell in with a ship-captain. 1887 J. Ball *Natur. S. Amer.* 356 The passengers..were resting in their *ship-chairs. 1847 *Niles' Reg.* 2 Oct. 70/2 To construct a *ship channel, so to speak, to the St. Lawrence. 1676 Marvell *Mr. Smirke* 15, I suspected..that the Animadverter had been some *Ship-Chaplain. 1699 Dampier *Voy.* II. iii. 68 The Planters..were certain of a Hurricane, and warned the *Ship-Commanders to provide for it. 1585 Higins *Junius' Nomencl.* 398/1 *Navale*, a *shipdocke, which is a place where ships are builded and repaired. 1659 Kilburne *Kent* 73 [Deptford] famous for the Shipdock, Storehouse and Corporation there for the Navy. 1552 Huloet, *Shyp drudge,..*Mixonauta*. c 1000 *Gl. Prud.* in *Germania* (N.S.) XI. 389/42 *Bellum classicum*, *scypgefeoht. 1647 Hexham i, A ship-fight, *een schip-vecht*. 1408 tr. *Vegetius' De Re Milit.* (MS. Digby 233) lf. 226/1 *Schipfiȝttynge asketh to haue a loft see & nouȝt rowe see. 1720 De Foe *Capt. Singleton* xvii. (1840) 289 The *ship firing is not at him. 1715 *Lond. Gaz.* No. 5374/2 They placed two *Ship-Guns on the Bridge. 1799 *Hull Advertiser* 7 Sept. 4/3 The thirty two pounder ship-gun. 1844 Manwaring *Seaman's*

Supplement, p. 3873; Corrigenda, p. 4092; Spurious words, p. 4093; Books quoted, p. 4094

705

SHIP. | SHIP. | SHIP. | 706 | SHIP.

SHIP. | 707 | SHIP-BOY. | SHIP-BREAKER. | 708 | SHIPMAN

Shipmast. **Ship-master.** **Shipmate.** **Shipment.** **Ship-money.** Now *Hist.* **Ship-owner.** **Shippable.** **Shippage.** **Shipper.** **Shippen**, variant of SHIPPON. **Shipping**, *vbl. sb.* **Ship-of-war.** **Ship-shape.** **Ship-shaped.** **Ship-timber.** **Shipwreck.**

Shipwrecked, *ppl. a.* **Shipwrecker.** **Shipwrecking**, *vbl. sb.* **Shipwrighting**, *vbl. sb.* **Shipwrightry.** **Shipwrighty**, *a. rare.* **Shipwright**, *sb.* **Shipyard.** **Shir**, obs. form of SIR, SHIRE *sb.* and *a.* **Shirai.** **Shire**, *sb.* **Shire.** **Shire-ground.** *Hist.* **Shire-horse.** **Shireless**, *a.* **Shireman.** **Shire-moot.** **Shireness.**

Shirewick, obs. form of SHERIFF.

† Shirewick, *sb.* [f. SHIRE *sb.* + -WICK.] = SHERIFFWICK.

Shirgian, Snirk *v.*

† Shirk, *sb.¹* Obs. Also *sherke, sherk, shurk.*

Shirk, *sb.²* [f. SHIRK *v.*]

† Shirk, *sb.³ Obs. rare.*¹ [Prob. a. Ger. dial. *schirk* (in Nemnich 1793).] The sturgeon.

Shirk (ʃɜːk), *v.* Also *shirke, shurk, shirke, sherk.*

Shirky (ʃɜːki), *a.* rare.¹

† Shirl, *sb.¹ Obs. rare.*¹

Shirl, *sb.²*

Shirl (ʃɜːl), *a.* and *adv.*

Shirl (ʃɜːl), *v.*

Shirl, *sb.* In 8 *shurl.*

Shirl, *v.*

Shirley. *Obs.* or *spurious.*

Shirlcock (ʃɜːlkɒk), *dial.* Also *shelcock, shircock, shirllcock.*

Shirley (ʃɜːli), *v.* intr.

Shirr (ʃɜː), *v.*

Shirra, *north.* form of SHERIFF.

Shirred (ʃɜːd), *ppl. a.*

Shirring (ʃɜːrɪŋ), *vbl. sb.*

Shirrot, variant of SHIRREL.

Shirrow, *north.* form of SHERROW (MOUSE).

Shirry (ʃɜːri), *v.*

Shirt (ʃɜːt), *sb.*

Shirt (ʃɜːt), *v.*

Shirted (ʃɜːtɪd), *ppl. a.*

Shirting (ʃɜːtɪŋ), *vbl. sb.*

Shirtee (ʃɜːtiː), *U.S.*

Shirty (ʃɜːti), *a. slang.*

Shish (ʃɪʃ), *int.* Also *shush.*

Shisham (ʃɪʃæm), *sb.*

Shism, obs. form of SCHISM.

Shist, Shistose, Shistus: see SCH-.

Shit (ʃɪt), *sb.* Also *shite.*

Shit (ʃɪt), *v.*

Shitbrow

Shite: see SHIT.

Shiten, Shitten (ʃɪtn), *a.*

Shittah (ʃɪtə), *sb.*

Shittim (ʃɪtɪm), *sb.*

Shittle, *a. Obs.*

Shittle, *sb.*

Shitten: see SHIT.

Shitepoke (ʃɪtpəʊk), *U.S.*

Shitterow (ʃɪtərəʊ), *sb.*

Shive (ʃaɪv), *sb.*

Shivareen

Shivaree (ʃɪvəriː), *U.S.* = CHARIVARI.

Shive (ʃaɪv), *sb.*

Shive (ʃaɪv), *v.*

Shivel

Shiver, variant of CHIVE *sb.² Obs.*

Shiver (ʃɪvə), *sb.¹*

Shiveless

Shivareen

Shivares (ʃɪvəz), *sb. pl.*

Shive (ʃaɪv), *sb.*

Shiver (ʃɪvə), *sb.²*

Shiver.

Shiver (ʃɪvəɹ), sb.¹ [f. SHIVER v.¹]

1. An act or a condition of shivering; a quivering or trembling; esp. of the body under the influence of cold, emotion, etc. Phrase, (all) in a shiver.

b. transf. and fig.

2. (The) shivers: an attack of shivering; often spec. the ague.

Shiver (ʃɪvəɹ), sb.² [f. SHIVER v.²]

1. A fragment, small piece; a splinter.

b. fig.

Shiver (ʃɪvəɹ), v.¹ Forms: α. 3 shivre, 4 achivre(e, 4–5 schyver, 5 shifer, 4–6 shyver, shiever, 6– shiver; β. 4–5 schever, 5 schevere, schei[z]r, (shivere) 4–6 shever, 7 shevre, shaver. Cf. MDu. scheveren (G. schäpfern).]

1. trans. To break or split into small fragments or splinters.

2. intr. To fly in pieces; to split.

Shiver (ʃɪvəɹ), v.² [f. SHIVER sb.¹]

1. intr. To tremble, shake, quiver; esp. to tremble with cold or fear.

2. trans. (causative.) To give a sensation of chill to, to cause (a person or object) to shiver.

b. To cause (a jaw), to tremble (obs.); to pour out or give forth with a trembling motion.

2. Naut. a. intr. (of a sail): To flutter or shake (in the wind).

b. trans. To cause (a sail) to flutter in the wind, to bring a sail edge-on to the wind.

3. Trembling with a shrinking movement.

4. To quiver; to tremble with a shaking movement.

Shivered, ppl. a.¹ [f. SHIVER sb.² + -ED².]

Shivered, ppl. a.² [f. SHIVER v.¹]

Shiverer¹ (ʃɪvəɹəɹ). [f. SHIVER v.¹ + -ER¹.]

One who breaks (something) into small pieces.

Shiverer² (ʃɪvəɹəɹ). [f. SHIVER v.² + -ER¹.]

One who trembles or shakes.

Shiverine. Sc. Obs. Also 6 shiverrine, shivering, 6–7 schivereen. [? Some kind of derivative of F. chèvre goat.] 7 A goat-skin.

Shivering, vbl. sb.¹ [f. SHIVER v.¹ + -ING¹.]

1. The action or an act of SHIVER v.¹

2. concr. A fragment, splinter.

Shivering, vbl. sb.² [f. SHIVER v.² + -ING¹.]

1. The action or an act of SHIVER v.²

2. Causing a shivering feeling, chilly.

3. Inclined to shiver.

Shivering, ppl. a.¹ [f. SHIVER v.¹ + -ING².]

1. That causes to shiver with cold, chilly.

b. intr. To cause to flutter or shake.

Shivering, ppl. a.² [f. SHIVER v.² + -ING².]

1. That causes to shiver with cold, chilly.

2. Trembling with cold, fear, etc.

3. Causing a shivering feeling.

Shiveringly, adv.¹ rare⁻¹.

Shiveringly, adv.² [f. prec. + -LY².]

Shiverish, a. dial.

Shivers. pl. of SHIVER.

Shivery¹ (ʃɪvəɹɪ), a.¹ [f. SHIVER sb.² + -Y¹.] Apt to split into flakes, brittle, flaky.

Shivery² (ʃɪvəɹɪ), a.² [f. SHIVER sb.¹ or v.² + -Y¹.]

1. Characterized by a shaking, quivering motion, or appearance of motion.

2. Inclined to shiver.

3. Causing a shivering feeling, chilly.

Shivey (ʃɪvɪ), a. dial. Also shivvy (ʃɪvɪ), and SHEAVY.

Shoad, shode (ʃəʊd). local. Forms: 7–9 shoad, (8 shodd), 7– shode, shoad(e, 9 shadd, 7–8 shade. [Prob. a derivative of OE. scéadan to divide, separate; see SHED v.¹] Mining. Loose fragments of tin, lead, or copper ore mixed with earth, lying on or near the surface and indicating the proximity of a lode.

Shoal, sb.¹ [OE. scol, sceol.] A multitude or large number (of fish, etc.) swimming together; a crowd.

Shoal, sb.² [var. of SHOLE sb.²]

Shoal, a. [var. of SHOLD, SHOAL sb.²]

Shoal, sb.³

Shoal, v.¹

Shoal, v.²

Shoaler.

Shoaliness.

Shoaling, ppl. a.

Shoaly (ʃəʊlɪ), a.¹

Shoaly, a.²

Shoaly, adv.

Shoat, sb.¹ Also 7 shote, shoat.

Shoat, sb.² dial. and U.S. Forms: 7 shote, 8–9 shoat(e, shoote, shoyte, 7 shoat, shote, 5 shute, 8–9 shot. [Cf. W.Flem. schote, schoteling.]

Shoch.

Shock, sb.¹ [cf. shock sb.² or MDu. schok.]

Shock, sb.² Obs. exc. dial. Forms: 6 shocke, shouke, 6–7 shoack(e, 7 shock.

1. A group of sheaves of grain placed upright and supporting each other in order to permit the drying and ripening of the grain before carrying. Phrase, In shock.

2. transf. A crowd of persons; a heap, bunch, bundle (of things).

3. Comb. [? shock-head.]

Shock, sb.³ Comm. Now only Hist.

1. A lot of sixty pieces. (Used with reference to certain articles of merchandise originally imported from abroad.)

2. A German money of account = 60 groschen.

Shock, sb.⁴ [G. (L.G., M.L.G.) schok, schocke.]

Shock, sb.⁵ [Derivation obscure.] A dog with long shaggy hair.

Shock, sb.⁶

1. Mil. The encounter of an armed force with the enemy in charge or onset; the collision of two mounted warriors or jousters charging one another.

2. A sudden and violent blow, impact, or collision.

3. A sudden agitation or disturbance of the mind or feelings; usually, the mental agitation produced by a sudden and disagreeable surprise.

4. Med. A sudden debilitating effect produced by over-stimulation of nerves, intense pain, violent emotion, etc.

5. Med. A sudden debilitating effect produced by over-stimulation of nerves, intense pain, violent emotion, etc.; the condition of nervous exhaustion resulting from this.

6. A momentary stimulation of a nerve.

Shock, v.¹

Shock, v.²

Shock, v.³

Shock, a. [? Formed as next adj.] A thick mass (of hair).

Shock, a. [? Back-formation from SHOCK-DOG.]

SHOCK. 721 SHOCKING. SHOCKINGLY. 722 SHOE. SHOE. 723 SHOE. SHOE. 724 SHOE.

SHOE

SHOE

shoode, showed, shoyd, 7 shoad, shoud, 7–9 shoed, (7, 9 *erron.* shodden), 4– shod. [OE. *scógan*, corresp. to MLG. *schoigen, schoien, schoen*, Du. *schoeien*, OHG. *scuohôn, scuohan* (MHG. *schuohen, schuon*, mod.G. *schuhen*), ON. *skúa* (MSw. *skoa*, Sw., Da. *sko*):—OTeut. **skôhôjan*, f. **skôho-* SHOE *sb.*

The doubling of the *d* and the consequent shortening of the vowel in ME. *schodde* pa. t., *schodd* pa. pple. (whence the mod. *shod* pa. t. and pa. pple.) are anomalous. (An OE. example occurs in Wulfstan *Hom.* p. 173, Unsceoddum fotum.) Cf. MSw. *skodde* pa. t., and Sw. *skodd* pa. pple. The case is parallel to that of *fledde, fledd* from FLEE *v.* (where Sw. also has the corresponding gemination).

1. *trans.* To put shoes on (one's feet); to put on (one's) shoes; to clothe or protect the feet with shoes; to provide (a person, oneself) with boots or shoes.

c897 ÆLFRED *Gregory's Past. C.* v. 44 Sceoȝeað eowre fett. c1000 ÆLFRIC *Gram.* xxvi. (Z.) 158 *Calceo* vel *calcio* ic scoȝe me. c1000 — *Hom.* (Th.) II. 382 Se engel cwæð, Begyrd þe, and sceo þe, and fyliȝ me. a1225 *Ancr. R.* 16 Þer efter scheoinde ou & cloðinde, siggeð Pater Noster & Credo. a1300 *Havelok* 1138, I ne may hire fede, ne cloþe, ne sho. c1366 CHAUCER *Rom. Rose* 842 And shod he was.. With shoon decoped, and with laas. 1387 TREVISA *Higden* (Rolls) I. 411 They..gooþ i-hosed and i-schod. 1398 — *Barth. De P. R.* XVIII. xcvi. (1495) 842 Ofte apes shoo them-self wyth shoon that hunters leue in certen places slyly. 1530 PALSGR. 704/1, I shoo one, I put shoes upon his fete. 1599 THYNNE *Animadv.* 13 [Chaucer's name] signyfyinge one who shueth or hooseth a manne. 1794 C. PIGOT *Female Jockey Club* 195 Government..cannot spare wherewithall to keep the poor fellows feet properly shoed. 1846 MRS. KIRKLAND *West. Clearings* 10 The shoemaker..travels from house to house, shoeing the family. 1855 LONGF. *Hiawatha* XV. 24 Shod with snow-shoes..Forth to hunt ..went Chibiabos. 1910 *Nation* 30 July 644/1 Women never learned to shoe themselves till they took to playing outdoor games with men.

Proverbial. 1546 J. HEYWOOD *Prov.* I. xi. (1867) 32 But who is wurs shod, than the shoemakers wyfe. 1581 PETTIE tr. *Guazzo's Civ. Conv.* I. (1586) 20 He ought to stop his eares..and to walke amongst them (as the saying is) shood amongest the thornes.

2. To provide (a horse, etc.) with a shoe or shoes. †Also with *up*. *Shod all round*: completely shod.

c1205 LAY. 22291 Heo wipeden hors leoue..heo sceren heo scoiden [c1275 and soide hire stedes]. 1387 TREVISA *Higden* (Rolls) IV. 395 He..schodde his mules wiþ silver. 1435 *Coventry Leet-bk.* 185 The smythes..shall..show straungers horsies as-well on Sondais as on othur weke-days,..apon the payn of xld. 1523–34 FITZHERB. *Husb.* § 142 Gyue thy horse meate, se he be showed well. 1605 SHAKS. *Lear* IV. vi. 188 It were a delicate stratagem to shoo A Troope of Horse with Felt. 1639 T. DE GRAY *Compl. Horsem.* 290 You may shooe him up, but drive no naile at that place. a1648 LD. HERBERT *Autobiog.* (1886) 205 He staid in the highway..until my horse was shoed. 1776 *Pennsylvania Even. Post* 27 June 320/2 A Bay Mare,..a natural trotter, shod all round, remarkably bad to shoe behind. 1870 THORNBURY *Tour rd. Eng.* II. xxiii. 139 The forge of the blacksmith who shoed Tyrrell's horse. 1889 F. E. GRETTON *Memory's Harkback* 149 He shod her all round, and she never kicked once.

fig. 1731–8 SWIFT *Pol. Convers.* I. 95 *Lady Smart.* This is his Fourth Wife; then he has been shod round. 1788 GROSE *Dict. Vulg. T.* (ed. 2) s.v. *Shod*, A parson who attends a funeral is said to be shod all round, when he receives a hat-band, gloves, and scarf.

b. Phrases. *To shoe the goose, gosling*: see those words; similarly *to shoe the gander*, †*the daw*. Also, †*To shoe the goose* (slang): to get drunk. *To shoe the wild mare*: see MARE¹ 2 b.

1566 DRANT *Horace, Sat.* I. ix. E iij, All the reaste mighte blow their nayles, or go to shough the dawe. 1594 NASHE *Unfort. Trav.* C 2 b, Galen might goe shooe the Gander for any good he could doo. 1611 COTGR. s.v. *Bertrand*, *Deschausser Bertrand*, to be drunke,..to whip the cat, shoo the goose.

3. To protect (the point, edge or face of a thing, esp. something made of timber) with a plate, rim, ferrule or sheath of metal, etc.

c1205 LAY. 7831, & þa Bruttes..nomen longen ræftres.. mid stronge irene heo weoren i-scod. 1496 *Acc. Ld. High Treas. Scot.* I. 290 Item, for..irne to Johne Lam, to scho the quhelis..xxvjs. 1531 *Lett. & Papers Hen. VIII*, V. 183 To John Locker for sewing mouldes with ireon for the brykmakers. 1565 COOPER *Thesaurus*, *Aries*,..a great peece of timber shodde with brasse, in facion like a rammes heade. 1585 T. WASHINGTON tr. *Nicholay's Voy.* IV. xiii. 126 b, Bootes..shodde vnderneath with yron. 1601 *Shuttleworths' Acc.* (Chetham Soc.) 134, ij speades shoud with iren, ijs. 1618 in Charnock *Mar. Archit.* (1801) II. 205 Shovells steele shodden. 1789 BURNS *Capt. Grose's Peregr.* vii, A broom-stick o' the Witch of Endor, Weel shod wi' brass. 1823 P. NICHOLSON *Pract. Build.* 303 The ends of the piles are cased or shoed with pointed iron. 1829 *Chapters Phys. Sci.* 138 In the processes of hooping barrels, and shoeing wheels. 1869 RANKINE *Machine & Hand-tools* Pl. P 21 These bars ..are shod at their lower cutting ends with serrated or notched steel faces for chipping the stone. 1911 *Act 1 & 2 Geo. V*, c. 45 § 2 (4) The driving wheels of a locomotive.. shod with diagonal crossbars of not less than three inches in width.

b. Naut. *To shoe the anchor*: (see quot. 1644).

1644 MANWAYRING *Sea-mans Dict.* 3 The ground may be soft and ozie; In such places we use to shooe the Anchor, that is, to put boords to the flooke..and make it much broader. 1769 FALCONER *Dict. Marine* (1789). 1867 in SMYTH *Sailor's Word-bk.*

4. *transf.* To cover or protect as with a shoe or shoes.

1639 FULLER *Holy War* IV. xiii. (1640) 191 The shores there being not shod against the sea with huge high rocks. 1807 *Prize Ess. & Trans. Highl. Soc.* III. 448 The surface turfs are carefully laid aside, and after the peats are taken out, these turfs are brought back..and placed upon the part that was made bare. This operation is called shoeing the moss. 1837 LONGF. *Frithiof's Homestead* 24 On a bear skin (the skin it was coal-black, Scarlet red was the throat, but the paws were shodden with silver), Thorsten sat.

Shoe, obs. form of SHOW *sb.* and *v.*, SOW *v.*

Shoeblack (ʃū·blæk). [f. SHOE *sb.* + BLACK *v.*] One who cleans boots and shoes for a livelihood.

1778 FOOTE *Trip to Calais* I. (1778) 21 As I live, a couple of shoe-blacks. 1831 CARLYLE *Sart. Res.* II. ix, Will the whole Finance Ministers..of modern Europe undertake to make one Shoeblack happy?

attrib. 1862 G. H. TOWNSEND *Man. of Dates* s.v. *Shoe-blacks*, The existing ragged school shoeblack brigade was founded in 1851.

b. *Shoe-black Plant* = *shoe-flower* (SHOE *sb.* 6 c).

1858 SIMMONDS *Dict. Trade*, *Shoe-black*,..a name in Jamaica for the *Hibiscus rosa sinensis*. 1866 *Treas. Bot.* I. 583/1 *Hibiscus Rosa sinensis*...These flowers..are used ..in Java for blacking shoes, whence the plant is frequently called the Shoe-black Plant.

So †**Shoe-blacker**, a shoeblack. **Shoe-blacking**, (*a*) = BLACKING *vbl. sb.* 3 b; (*b*) the blacking and polishing of shoes.

1755 JOHNSON *Dict.*, *Japanner*..2. A shoeblacker. 1843 M. A. RICHARDSON *Local Hist. Table Bk., Hist.* II. Index, Shoe blacker. 1890 L. C. D'OYLE *Notches* 13 They were.. the only persons possessed of shoe-blacking. 1908 ALICE TERTON *Lights & Shadows in Hosp.* x. 166 His interest in the shoe-blacking soon waned.

Shoed (ʃūd), *ppl. a.* [f. SHOE *sb.* or *v.* + -ED.] Furnished or protected with a shoe or shoes; shod.

See also SLIP-SHOED *a.* and *high-shoed* var. of HIGH-SHOD.

1601 *Will of W. Snawdon of Winterton, Lincs.*, One shoed waine with the furniture belonging to it. 1612 *Inv.* in *Antiquary* (1906) Jan. 28 A shoed shovel, a shoed spade. 1908 *Edin. Evening News* 14 July 2 [He] kicked her with his shoed feet.

Shoef, obs. pa. t. of SHAVE *v.*

Shoe-goose: see STAGUSH.

Shoe-horn (ʃū·hǭɹn), *sb.* In 5, 6 *Sc.* schone-, shone-, ?-schune.

1. A curved instrument of horn, metal, etc. used to facilitate the slipping of one's heel into a shoe by placing it between shoe and heel; a shoeing-horn.

1589 *Burgh Rec. Edin.* (1882) IV. 540 Ane schone horne 30d. 1612 *Sc. Bk. Rates* in *Halyburton's Ledger* (1867) 315 Shone hornes the dozen vis. 1874 BURNAND *My time* xxiv. 213 Giving his back the graceful outward bend of a shoe-horn.

2. *fig.* = SHOEING-HORN 2.

1630 BP. G. GRÆME *Let.* in *Miscellany S. H. S.* (1904) II. 255 Sone, cum not in such termis, for..I fear that if more be offered it will be takin, be warie, ye be no schurehorne [? *read* schunehorne]. 1869 *Lonsdale Gloss.*, *Shoe-horn*, a puffer at an auction. 1894 *Northumberld. Gloss.*, *Shoe-horn*, a helper on. One employed to bid for the sellers at sales.

3. = SHOEING-HORN 3.

1864 ATKINSON *Prov. Names Birds*, *Shoe-horn.* Avocet —*Recurvirostra avocetta*. 1895 P. H. EMERSON *Birds Norfolk Broadland* lxxxvi. 281 And you know 'tis an avocet, or 'shoe-horn', as the old Broadsmen call him.

Shoe·-horn, *v.*

†1. *trans.* To cuckold. (Cf. HORN *v.* 2) *Obs.*—1

c1650 BRAITHWAIT *Barnabees Jrnl.* II. xvi. H 6, Venus swore it, She'd shoe-horn her Vulcans forehead.

2. To put or thrust (a thing) *upon* (a person) or (a person) *into* (a position) by means of an 'instrument' or 'tool' for the purpose.

1859 W. CHADWICK *Life De Foe* v. 292 A penny trash, shoe-horned upon the public for buyers, by the addition of the Shortest Way with Daniel De Foe. 1901 *North Western Daily Mail* (Barrow) 6 Mar., A non-expert..who is shoehorned into a position like that of the War Secretary.

3. *intr.* To act as a 'shoe-horn' at a sale. *dial.* (Cf. SHOE-HORN *sb.* 2.) 1904 *Eng. Dial. Dict.*

Shoeing (ʃū·iŋ), *vbl. sb.* Forms: 4–6 shoyng(e, (4 ssoinge), 4–7 shoing, 5 schoynge, schoing, 5–6 scho(w)yng, 6 showing, showyng(e, shouing, (schevyng, 7 schewing), 6–8 shooing, 7– shoeing. [f. SHOE *v.* + -ING¹.]

1. The action of SHOE *v.*; the action of putting shoes on a person or animal, or of furnishing a pile, wheel, etc. with a shoe.

c1440 *Promp. Parv.* 447/2 Schoynge, of menn, *calceacio*. Schoynge, of hors, *ferracio*. 1458 *Nottingham Rec.* II. 366 For vj. powls schoyng and þe powls ijs. 1515 *Acc. Ld. High Treas. Scot.* V. 32 Item..for..the schoyng of gun cartis..iij li. x s. 1523–34 FITZHERB. *Husb.* § 109 Enterfyre is a sorance, and cometh of yll shoynge. 1657 W. COLES *Adam in Eden* cxii, Laid or bound to a Horses foot that is grievously pricked with shooing. 1707 FLEETWOOD *Chron. Prec.* v. 149 For Hay, Oats, Litter and Shooing. 1840 THACKERAY *Catherine* vii, My horse wants shoeing. 1883 'ANNIE THOMAS' *Mod. Housewife* 67 The only broad rule that can be laid down for the successful shoeing of children is [etc.].

2. *concr.* a. Shoes collectively.

a1340 HAMPOLE *Psalter* cvii. 10 In til ydumy I sall streke my shoynge. 1382 WYCLIF *Exod.* iii. 5 But lowse thow thi shoyng [*v.r.* schone] fro thi feyt. c1450 *Godstow Reg.* 394 And..the forsaid hugh shold fynde the forsaid Anneys..in vitaile clothyng and shoyng. 1480 CAXTON *Chron. Eng.* ccxxvi. 233 They were more lyche to tormentours and deuels in hir clothyng and shoyng. 1483 *Cath. Angl.* 337/2 A schoynge, *ferramentum*. *Ibid.*, Schoynge of a byschope (*v.r.* schon of a bischoppe), *sandalia*. 1530 PALSGR. 267/1 Schowyng of an horse, *ferrure*.

b. The protective casing or covering with which a thing is shod.

1805 R. W. DICKSON *Pract. Agric.* I. 378 A strong lever, shod with iron, and having the iron shoeing bent a little upwards. 1806 MORISON *Decis.* XXXIII. 14296 The shoeing or causewaying in the river..must be taken away. 1870 *2nd Rep. Dep. Kpr. Irel.* 20 The sides of the tray are fitted with a light shoeing of wood. 1892 R. C. LESLIE *Sea-Boat* 162 *Shoeing*, an iron band to protect the keel.

3. *attrib.* and *Comb.*, as *shoeing forge, -hammer, -shed, -stool, -trade*; **shoeing smith**, a smith who shoes horses.

1889 *Harper's Mag.* June 13/2 Outside the town you find the *shoeing forges. 1753 *Chambers' Cycl.* Suppl., **Shoeing-hammer*. 1833 LOUDON *Encycl. Archit.* § 418 The *shoeing-shed ought to have rings in the walls for the..halters of the horses being shod, to be fastened to. 1809 *Sporting Mag.* XXXIII. 41 Mr. Goodwin, *shoeing-smith. 1851 DICKENS *Gt. Expect.* I. ix. 146 'Should you, Pip?' said Joe, drawing his *shoeing-stool near the forge. 1865 H. KINGSLEY *Hillyars* I. ii. 11 His business was..what we call a good *shoeing trade, principally with the omnibus horses.

Shoe·ing-horn. [SHOEING *vbl. sb.*]

1. = SHOE-HORN *sb.* 1.

c1440 *Promp. Parv.* 447/2 Schoynge horne, *parcopollex*. 1523–34 FITZHERB. *Husb.* § 142 Shoyng horne, boget, and shoes. 1614 B. JONSON *Barth. Fair* I. ii, Oyly as the Kings constables Lampe and shining as his Shooing-horne. 1713 SWIFT *Elegy Death Partridge* Misc. (1727) 100 The Horned Moon, which heretofore Upon their Shoes the Romans wore..And whence we claim our Shoeing-Horns. 1825 T. HOOK *Sayings* Ser. II. *Man of Many Fr.* I. 250 A pair of pumps into which, with the assistance of..a shoeing-horn, the old gentleman had compressed his proper proportions. 1855 DICKENS *Dorrit* xxii, A little instrument like a shoeing horn for serving it [snuff] out.

attrib. 1623 FLETCHER *Rule a Wife* IV. i, Here's a shooing-horn Chain gilt over.

Proverbial. 1508 STANBRIDGE *Vulgaria* (W. de W.) B v, His nose is lyke a shoynge horne. 1659 HOWELL *Lex.*, *Prov.* 4/1 Every one cannot have a nose like a shooing-horn.

2. *fig.* a. An appetizer for food or drink.

1536 *Remedy for Sedition* 19 b, We haue to many sawces, to many showying hornes to drawe in meate. 1575 *Gammer Gurton* I. i, I..caught a slyp of bacon..Which..Shall serue for a shoinghorne to draw on two pots of ale. 1622 MABBE tr. *Aleman's Guzman d'Alf.* II. 275 The hungry sauour of our porrige was a shooing-horne to draw downe the hardnesse of our bread. 1737 OZELL *Rabelais* I. 152 *note*, Thus we say, a Red Herring is a shoing-horn to a Pot of Ale. 1815 SCOTT *Guy M.* xxiv, This [conversation] served as a 'shoeing-horn' to draw on another cup of ale.

b. Something serving to facilitate a transaction, to bring on a condition, or to procure acceptance for something else.

1584 D. FENNER *Def. Ministers* (1587) 71 This was nothing but a shoing-horne, to pull on a page or two more. 1621 BURTON *Anat. Mel.* I. ii. II. vi. 115 Voluntary solitarinesse ..gently brings on as a Siren, a shoeing-horne, or some Sphinx to this irrevocable gulfe [Melancholy]. 1759 FRANKLIN *Ess.* Wks. 1840 III. 198 It appeared..that a treaty and a purchase went on together, that the former was a shoeing-horn for the latter. 1819 SCOTT *Leg. Montrose* v, A long story, my lord,..is..the best shoeing-horn for drawing on a sound sleep. 1864 SIR T. SEATON *From Cadet to Colonel* xvii. 358 An occupation that was a certain shoeing horn for cholera.

attrib. a1704 T. BROWN *Walk round London*, *Tavern* Wks. 1709 III. III. 6 As soon as that [his money] begins to fail, then her Shooing-horn Looks and Freedoms, are turn'd into moody Pouts.

c. A person used as a tool by another; esp. one who is employed as a decoy.

1602 *Narcissus* 441 O, that same youthe's the scummer of all skorne, Of surquedry the very shooing horne. 1606 SHAKS. *Tr. & Cr.* v. i. 61. 1692 WOOD *Ath. Oxon.* II. 494 Oliver had made him..his shooing horn, merely to serve his turn. 1712 ADDISON *Spect.* No. 536 ¶ 5 Most of our fine young Ladies..retain in their Service..supernumerary and insignificant Fellows, which they..commonly call *Shoeing-Horns*. These are..designed..when a good Offer comes, to whet and spur him up to the Point. 1864 CARLYLE *Fredk. Gt.* XVI. vii. IV. 335 D'Arnaud—once Friedrich's shoeing-horn and 'rising-sun' for Voltaire's behoof.

†3. The Avocet: = SHOE-HORN *sb.* 3. *Obs.*

1668 SIR T. BROWNE *Let.* Wks. 1836 I. 400 A shoeing-horn or barker, from the figure of the bill and barking note.

†4. A cuckold's horn: see HORN *sb.* 7. In quot. *attrib.* (Cf. SHOE-HORN *v.* 1.)

1663 KILLIGREW *Pars. Wedding* v. iv, Fine y' faith, none but the small Levites brow to plant your shooing-horn-seed in? How now?

Hence †**Shoe·ing-horn** *v.* = SHOE-HORN *v.* 2.

1658–9 *Burton's Diary* (1828) IV. 77 This House does not intend to trepan, or shoeing-horn, any body.

Shoe·kin. *nonce-wd.* [-KIN.] A small shoe.

1844 THACKERAY *Contrib. Punch*, *Wand. Fat Contrib.* ii. Wks. 1898 VI. 60 A Belgic child..in little wooden shoekins.

Shoel, obs. form of SHOAL *sb.*¹

Shoe-leather. Leather for the making of shoes; the leather of which (one's) shoes are made.

1660 BOYLE *Spring of Air* 13 A sucker,..upon which is nail'd a good thick piece of tan'd shoe Leather. 1818 LADY MORGAN *Autobiog.* (1859) 119 As good a lad as ever stepped in shoe-leather. 1828–32 WEBSTER, *Shoe-leather*, leather for shoes. 1889 JESSOPP *Coming of Friars* ii. 89 The poor man's loaf was..as tough as his shoe-leather.

b. put for the wear of shoes in walking.

1576 FLEMING *Panopl. Epist.* 319 He counteth me..such a one as is altogether unworthy of a litle shoe leather, when he is sent for. 1675 V. ALSOP *Anti-sozzo* iii. 114 No need to look out, if they had sufficient at Home, they might save Shooe leather. 1874 RUSKIN *Fors Clav.* IV. xliv. 166 He walked to Ulverstone; spent nothing but shoe-leather on the road.

Shoeless (ʃū·lès), *a.* [f. SHOE *sb.* + -LESS.] Without shoes.

1627 DRAYTON *Agincourt* 59 A shoolesse Souldier there a man might meete. 1825 LAMB *Elia* Ser. II. *Barbara S—*, And then came staring upon her the figures of her little stockingless and shoeless sisters. 1875 JOWETT *Plato* (ed. 2) I. 134 He found that the other animals were suitably furnished, but that man alone was naked and shoeless.

Hence **Shoe·lessness.**

1843 [G. P. R. JAMES] *Commissioner* xxxvi. 220 She had found her shoelessness not very pleasant.

Shoemack, -make, obs. forms of SUMACH.

Shoemaker (ʃū·mēˈkəɹ). Forms: see SHOE *sb.* and MAKER; also 6 *north.* shounemaker (from the *plural*).

1. One whose trade it is to make shoes.

1381 *Rolls of Parlt.* III. 112/2 Johannes Stotesbury, Childe-shomakere. c1440 *Alphabet of Tales* 164 A philosophur.. þat boght a payr of shone on a tyme of a sho-maker. 1519 *Presentm. Juries* in *Surtees Misc.* (1890) 32 That the shounemaker sewe well thayre shown. 1621 in Kempe *Losely MSS.* (1836) 430 To ye shoo maker for boots and shoes..4li. 3s. 1824 MISS MITFORD *Village* Ser. I. 5 Our shoemaker..employs three journeymen. 1865 DICKENS *Mut. Fr.* I. vii, His expression and stoop are like those of a shoemaker.

b. in Latin proverb (cf. LAST *sb.*¹ 2 c.).

1587 GOLDING *De Mornay* (1592) 155 The Shoomaker ought not to presume aboue the Pantople. 1768–74 TUCKER *Lt. Nat.* (1834) II. 173 Carrying the shoe-maker beyond his last, and encroaching upon the province of divines.

2. a. In the names of various fishes.

[1688 HOLME *Armoury* II. 377/2 Table, Shoomaker fish 15 16. *Ibid.* II. xv. 350 The Hollanders call it [the Tench] a Schoemaker]. 1836 J. RICHARDSON *Fauna Bor.-Amer.* III. 120 *Cyprinus* (*Catastomus*) *nigricans.* (Le Sueur.)..This species is..an inhabitant of Lake Erie, where it is known to the fishermen by the names of 'Shoemaker', and 'Black Sucker'. 1884 GOODE *Nat. Hist. Aquatic Anim.* 326 The Threadfish, *Blepharis crinitus*.., also known as the 'Shoemaker-fish'. *Ibid.* 332 The Runner, *Elagatis pinnulatus*.., known..at Pensacola as..'Shoemaker', is ..abundant on the..coasts of Florida. 1891 *Century Dict.* s.v. *Coral*, Coral shoemaker, a fish of the family *Teuthididæ* and genus *Teuthis* or *Acanthurus*, living in the coral reefs of the Seychelles. 1904 *Eng. Dial. Dict.*, *Shoemaker*, the lesser weever, *Trachinus vipera*; also in comb. *Master shoemaker*.

b. A name for the bird *Skua antarcticus*.

1867 SMYTH *Sailor's Word-bk.*, *Egmont*, or *Port Egmont Fowls*, the large Antarctic gulls with dark-brown plumage, called *shoemakers*.

3. *Comb.* †**shoemaker-loo** *U.S.*, some game at cards.

1813 R. B. THOMAS *Farmer's Alm.* (Boston, U. S.) Dec. in Kittredge *Old Farmer & Almanack* (1904) 95 Tom Teazer, well known at the grog shops for a dabster at shoemaker loo.

b. Combinations of possessive, as *shoemaker's craft*, but chiefly in the names of tools and appliances, as *shoemaker's awl, black* (BLACK *sb.* 1 b), *end* (END *sb.* 6 c), *hammer, knife, nippers, paste, rasp, thread, wax*; also **shoemaker's bark-tree** (see quot.); **shoemaker's holiday**, †(*a*) see quot. 1607; also applied to Monday (see Dekker *Shoemaker's Holiday* III. i); (*b*) used jocularly (after the title of Dekker's play, a 1600) for a day's holiday or 'outing' in the country; **shoemaker's spasm**, a synonym given to tetany because of the liability of shoemakers to be affected by it; †**shoe-maker's stocks** *slang*, shoes which pinch the feet.

1647 HEXHAM I, A *shoe-makers aule. 1874 *Treas. Bot.* Suppl., *Shoemaker's bark-tree, a Montserrat name for *Byrsonima spicata*. 1563 HYLL *Art Garden.* (1593) 91 The seedes..being mixed with *shomakers blacke, doth take away warts. 1530 PALSGR. 267/1 *Shoomakers crafte, *cordovanerie*. 1540 *Maldon* (Essex) *Liber B.* 158 Idem Andreas in arte sive occupacione de shomakerscrafte bene et fideliter servivit dictum Cornelium. 1598– *Shoemaker's end [see END *sb.* 6 c]. 1895 P. N. HASLUCK *Boot Making* 18 A *shoemaker's hammer, knife, nippers, glazing iron, and rasp. *Ibid.* 27 *Shoemaker's Rasp. 1607 *Christmas Prince* III. (1816) 47 *Tuesday* [loq.]..Bouzer I am not, but mild, sober Tuesday..if I light not on St. Hewsday. *Footnote.* The *Shoemakers holy-day. 1768 GOLDSM. in *European Mag.* (1793) Sept. 172/1 And now my dear boy, if you are not better engaged, I should be glad to enjoy a Shoe-maker's holiday with you. 1822 SCOTT *Let.* 23 June in *Lockhart* (1837) V. 189 Castle Street is bad enough, even with the privilege of a hop-step-and-jump to Abbotsford, by way of shoemakers' holiday. 1647 HEXHAM I, A *shoe-makers knife. 1842 DICKENS *Amer. Notes* vii, [He] would have gladly stabbed me with his shoemaker's knife. 1688 HOLME *Armoury* III. 349/2 These..Shoomakers Nippers..having a sharp point in the end of one [shank]; and a slit in the other, to strain up a Tack. 1866 *Athenæum* Feb. 243/3 The paste to be used for all prints..should be *shoemakers' paste. 1899 *Allbutt's Syst. Med.* (1910) VIII. 578 Of 399 cases [of Tetany]..174 occurred in shoemakers (*'shoemaker's spasm'). a1700 B. E. *Dict. Cant. Crew*, **Shoemakers-stocks*, pincht with strait Shoes. 1607 TOPSELL *Four-f. Beasts* 420 Fasten on each side of the hole, two ends of *Shoomakers thread. 1603 DEKKER *Wonderf. Yr.* Wks. (Grosart) I. 132 *Shooemakers waxe being laide to a byle. 1885 LENO *Boot & Shoemaking* 221 Shoemakers' Wax..is composed generally of..pitch and resin, with 10 per cent. of tallow.

Hence **Shoe·makeress**, a female shoemaker. **Shoe·makerish** *a.*, resembling that of a shoemaker.

1860 *All Year Round* Sept. 523/2 They all bought their shoes of a woman who was called Mother Rousselle...The shoemakeress [etc.]. 1866 HOWELLS *Venetian Life* xiv. 204 With bead-black eyes and of a shoemakerish presence.

Shoemaking (ʃū·mēˈkiŋ), *vbl. sb.* [f. SHOE *sb.* + MAKING *vbl. sb.*] The making of shoes.

1611 COTGR., *Cordouannerie*, Shoo-making. 1859 DICKENS *T. Two Cities* I. vi, The white head that bent low over the shoemaking. 1910 MRS. H. M. TIRARD *Bk. of Dead* i. 18 All the trades are also represented, shoe-making, boat-building, pottery-making [etc.].

Shoer (ʃū·əɹ). Forms: 1 scóere, scóehere, 5 schoer, 6 shooer, 9– shoer. [OE. *scóere*: see SHOE *v.* and -ER¹.] One who shoes. In OE. a shoemaker; later usually, one who shoes horses, etc.

c725 *Corpus Gloss.* (Hessels) S 696, *Sutrinator*, scoere. a900 *Leiden Gloss.* 122 in *O. E. Texts* 115 *Sutrinator*, scoehere. 1483 *Cath. Angl.* 337/2 A Schoer, *ferrarius*. 1562 J. HEYWOOD *Prov. & Epigr.* (1867) 159 We should haue as many goose shooers as geese. 1861 OLMSTED *Journ. Cotton Kingdom* I. 111 He tells Prior that if he can find a first rate shoer..not to lose him. 1902 *19th Cent.* Aug. 313 The mystic shoer Wayland Smith.

Shoerl, variant of SCHORL.

1789 *Phil. Trans.* LXXX. 81 Indurated clay and shoerl.

Shofar, variant of SHOPHAR.

Shof(e, shoff(e, obs. forms of SHOVE *v.*

Shoffle, Shofful, obs. ff. SHUFFLE, SHOVEL.

Shoful (ʃōu·ful). *slang.* Also showfull, shouful, schofell, shofle, schoful. [a. G. *schofel* worthless stuff, rubbish (primarily Yiddish, and thence adopted in London slang, though it has long been in ordinary German use), subst. use of G. *schofel* base, mean, worthless, repr. the German-Jewish pronunciation of Heb. שפל *shāphēl* low.]

1. Counterfeit money. Also *attrib.* or *adj.*, counterfeit. *Comb.* **shoful-man, -pitcher**, one who passes counterfeit coin; so *shoful-pitching*.

1851 MAYHEW *Lond. Labour* I. 24/1 [Costermonger's slang] Showfulls, Bad money. 1856 — *Gt. World London* 47 The 'shoful-men', or those who plunder by counterfeits; as coiners and forgers of checks, and notes, and wills. 1859 *Hotten's Slang Dict.*, **Showfull-pitcher*, a passer of counterfeit money. 1860 *Ibid.* (ed. 2), **Showfull-pullet*, a 'gay' woman. 1863 W. B. JERROLD *Signals of Distress* 106 The passers of base coin, shofulmen,..will be sensibly strengthened. 1891 CAREW *Autobiog. Gypsy* 417 Got down and heaved the sack-ful o' shoful into the water.

2. A hansom cab. Also (rarely) *shoful-cab*.

[Possibly a distinct word; the explanation in quot. 1851 does not seem altogether certain.]

1851–61 MAYHEW *Lond. Labour* II. 488/2, I don't think those 'shofuls' (Hansoms) should be allowed. *Ibid.* III. 351/1 Hansom's..are always called 'showfulls' by the cab-men. 'Showfull', in slang, means counterfeit, and the 'showfull' cabs are an infringement on Hansom's patent. 1854 *Househ. Words* VIII. 76 A hackney cab is a shoful. 1862 *Offic. Catal. Internat. Exhib.* I. No. 1444 Original builders of the shofle or gentleman's Hansom. *Ibid.* No. 1367 New brougham 'shofle'. 1869 *St. James' Mag.* III. 285 There ought to be other conveyances beyond the 'Growler and Shofle'.

3. A low-class tavern. ? *rare.*

1851 MAYHEW *Lond. Labour* I. 259/1 'A rackety place, sir,..one of the showfuls; a dicky one; a free-and-easy'.

Shog (ʃǫg), *sb.* Now only *dial.* and *arch.* Forms: 6 schogg, 7–8 shogg, 7– shog. [f. SHOG *v.*]

†1. A shaking condition. *Obs. rare.*

1596 DALRYMPLE tr. *Leslie's Hist. Scot.* II. 141 Gif thir tua landis he ma vanquis, Scotland, he thinkis, will be in a schogg. 1689 N. LEE *Princess of Cleve* IV. iii, I feel a gorgeing pain..A shog of Blood and Spirits.

2. A shake, jerk.

1611 COTGR., *Bransle*,..a shake, shog, or shocke. 1669 STURMY *Mariner's Mag.* v. xii. 68 Thrust in the Ladle, being full, give it a shog, then strike off the heaped Powder. 1709 STEELE *Tatler* No. 39 ¶ 2 My learned friend assured me further, that the earth had lately received a shogg from a comet. 1724 HEARNE *Collect.* (O.H.S.) VIII. 280 He warned her to hold by the ropes..that so she might not fall, if there happened any greater shog than ordinary.

transf. 1728 RAMSAY *Fox & Rat* 20 Thus thou, great King, hast by thy conqu'ring Paw, Gi'en Earth a Shog, and made thy Will a Law. 1785 BURNS *Address to Deil* xvi, Ye cam to Paradise incog.,..An' gied the infant world a shog. 1888 STEVENSON *Black Arrow* Prol. 11 This will be a rare shog to poor Sir Oliver; he will turn paper-colour.

3. A shogging gait. Cf. SHOG *v.* 3.

1885 DODGE *Patroclus & Penelope* 25 In early days, horses were mainly ridden on a canter or a gallop. If perchance a trot, it was a mere shog.

Shog (ʃǫg), *v.* Now chiefly *dial.* Forms: 4–7 shogge, (5 shogke), 5–6 schog(ge, 6 shugge, (shougge), 7–8 shogg, 8 shogue, (shug), 5– shog. [ME. *shogge*, prob. related to OHG. *scoc* (pl. *scogga*) oscillation, swinging, a swing, MHG. *schock*, *schocke* swing, see-saw, MDu., Du. *schok* shake, jolt, MLG., MDu., MHG. *schocker* to swing, oscillate, shake. The word was doubtless felt as phonetically symbolic of the character of the movement denoted; cf. JOG *v.* See also SHOCK *v.*¹]

1. *trans.* To shake or roll (something heavy) from side to side; to rock (a cradle); to shake, agitate (a liquid or the vessel containing it); to jolt or jar (some one or something).

1388 WYCLIF *Matt.* xiv. 24 The boot..was schoggid with wawis [Vulg. *jactabatur fluctibus*]. c1420 *Chron. Vilod.* 3015 Þey houe, þey drawe, þey shogkeden hit [*sc.* the shrine] also. c1440 *Pallad. on Husb.* XI. 322 Of wynys soure is taught to make swete Wit barly floure...And oon doth dregge of swete wyn therto; Of gliricide [*read* glicci-ride] a part he hath infuse Al drie, & longe yshogged it wol vse [L. *utuntur, cum diu vasorum commotione miscuerint*]. c1550 *Droichis Part of Play* 38 in *Dunbar's Poems* 315 He, quhen he dansit, the warld wald schog. 1663 PURCHAS *Pilgrims* II. 1659 Now their [children's] Couch hangs in the Aire, within little Beds of coard, or little Chaires, where they shogge and rocke them. 1665 HOOKE *Microgr.* 31 If care be taken that the tube in erecting be not shogged. 1787 W. H. MARSHALL *Norfolk* (1795) II. 388 To *Shug*, to shake; as hay, &c.

†b. To shake (a person) in order to cause pain or annoyance, or to rouse from sleep; to jog (a person) in order to attract attention. Also rarely *to shog upon* in the same sense. *Obs.*

c1440 *York Myst.* xl. 100 They schogged hym, they shogged hym his lymes all in sondir. c1495 *Epitaffe*, *Skelton's Wks.* (1843) II. 389. I shogged him, I s... 1530 PALSGR. 705/1 Shougge nat so upon him to wake him out of his slepe. *Ibid.* 706/1 Shugge. 1534 MORE *Comf. agst. Trib.* II. Wks. 1189/2 Rudely and boystuously shogge hym & wake him. c1613 MIDDLETON *No Wit like Woman's* II. ii. 107 *Philip.* May I crave one word, madam? [*stage-direction.*] Shogs his Mother. 1651 H. MORE *Enthus. Tri.* (1656) M 2, You onely mutter against the present..as one shogged while he dreams upon his pillow.

†c. *fig.* To 'shake' mentally; to upset, discompose; to irritate, annoy. *Obs.*

1639 CADE *Serm.* 50 The deadly arrow sticks in the flesh, and shogs and galls him. 1688 PENTON *Guardian's Instruct.* (1897) 47 His Brains have become so shogged, he cannot think in a fortnight. 1701 STEELE *Chr. Hero* ..Cæsar..a little shogg'd with reiterated ill Omens.

2. †a. *refl.* (obs.) and b. *intr.* To jerk; to shake to and fro, to rock; †to be shaken, to be insecurely fixed, to get shaken *out*.

a. a1400–50 *Wars Alex.* 5018 Þan schogs him þe tree & schoke hire schire leues.

b. c1450 *Mirk's Festial* 174 As he hyet on his way, þe box schuget out of his bosome. 15.. in Ritson *Anc. Songs* (1792) 365 For amendyng of a chalys foote yt schogged. 1609 HOLLAND *Amm. Marcell.* XVI. x. 63 Neither was he seene so much as to give a nod with his head..or his wheele shogged. 1658 ROWLAND tr. *Moufet's Theat. Insects* 900 Let there be two handfuls distance between every Hive, that one shogging or shaking, the next may stand unmoved. 1841 R. CHAMBERS *Pop. Rhymes Scot.* Big it [the castle] in a bog Where 'twill neither shake nor shog.

†c. *intr.* Of troops: To waver, become unsteady.

1642–4 VICARS *God in Mount* 147 All the enemies Horse began to shogge a little.

3. To walk, ride or move with a succession of bumps or jerks; to jog along. Now usually, to advance at a steady easy pace, to travel steadily on.

c1400 *Destr. Troy* 11089 Restorit full stithly..wise, Shot into sheltrons shoggond full þicke. 1513 *Scot. Field* 94 in *Chetham Soc. Misc.* II, Shott into Scotland..and shoggeth over the water, Into Scotland. 1530 PALSGR. 704/1 The carte shogged so faste that I went it wolde have fallen downe. 1719 RAMSAY *Ep. Hamilton* iii, 20 Be blythe, and let the Warld e'en shog, as it thinks fit. 1857 KINGSLEY *Two Y. Ago* xxviii, They shog from side to side. 1893 J. A. BARRY *Steve Brown's Bunyip* 115 Shogging steadily on..I at length reached the creek.

b. To go away, begone. Also with *off*. *Obs.* exc. *dial.* (see *Eng. Dial. Dict.*).

1599 SHAKS. *Hen. V*, II. i. 47 Will you shogg off? *Ibid.* II. iii. 48 Shall wee shogg? a1625 FLETCHER *Coxcomb* II. ii, Come, prethee let's shogg off, and browze an hour or two.

†4. Of troops: To move gradually to one side. Also *trans.* of a commander, to cause (troops) to move gradually to one side. *Obs.*

1650 CROMWELL *Let.* 4 Sept. in *Carlyle* (1845) II. 55 The Enemy drew down to the right wing..; shogging also their foot and train much to the right. 1654–66 EARL ORRERY *Parthen.* (1676) 691, I gave strict order to all my Army to shog still toward the right hand.

Hence **Sho·gged** *ppl. a.*

1594 R. CAREW *Tasso* (1881) 73 Nor shogged earth so euer bideth throwes, When bigge in wombe she doth the vapours close.

Shogging (ʃǫ·giŋ), *vbl. sb.* [-ING¹.] The action of SHOG *v.*; a shaking, jolting, jerking, etc.

c1440 *Promp. Parv.* 447/2 Schoggynge,..*agitacio*. 1563–83 FOXE *A. & M.* 1492/1 Rogers..being found asleepe, scarse with much shogging could be awaked. 1600 HOLLAND *Livy* XXVII. xxix. 650 Scarce able to endure the shogging and shaking of the horselitter. 1725 *Bradley's Fam. Dict.* s.v. *Shoeing*, So as the Heads of the Nails may enter into the same, appearing somewhat above the Shoe, that they will stand sure without shogging, and endure Danger.

b. *spec.* in *Lace manuf.* (See quots.)

1839 URE *Dict. Arts* 732 One of these two combs, in the double bolt machine, has an occasional lateral motion, called shogging. 1878 A. BARLOW *Hist. Weaving* 336 This motion of the comb-bar is technically called 'shogging', and by its means the diagonal arrangement is given to the threads. *Ibid.* 362 The 'shogging' motion of the comb-bar.

Sho·gging, *ppl. a.* [-ING².] That shogs.

1581 STUDLEY tr. *Seneca's Hippol.* 61 The shogging axel made crake with swagging sway. a1800 PEGGE *Suppl. Grose* s.v. *Shog*, A shogging horse. a1881 J. CAIRD in *Mod. Scott. Poets* Ser. II. 123 The mavis will sing..Aff the shoggin' boughs o' the sauchen tree. 1897 'O. RHOSCOMYL' *White Rose Arno* 272 A sort of shogging trot.

Shoggle (ʃǫ·g'l), *v.* Chiefly *dial.* Also 8 schogle, 9 shoogle, shogle, shuggle. [Frequentative f. SHOG *v.*: see -LE. Cf. G. *schuckeln* to shake, jostle, walk unsteadily.]

1. *trans.* To shake, to cause to move; to shake (something or somebody) *off*.

1577 GOOGE *Heresbach's Husb.* IV. 159 b, You must in no wise shake them, or shoggle them..: by shaking of the egges, the Chickins haue been hatched lame. 1822 GALT *Sir A. Wylie* xxxiv, If, by ony mischance, she had been shooggled aff [the coach] whar would I hae been then! a1844 W. MILLER in Whitelaw *Bk. Scott. Song* 6/2 Stravagin' wuns begin To shoggle and shake the window-brods. 1855 ROBINSON *Whitby Gloss.*, To *Shoggle*, to joggle.

2. *intr.* To shake; to swing about, to dangle; to shake or settle *down*.

c1730 RAMSAY *Vision* v, A braid-sword schogled at his thee. 1896 CROCKETT *Cleg Kelly* xxix, I'll juist lock them in and they'll [soon] hae shuggled doon as quaite as a session.

3. To walk unsteadily.

1884 *Reports Provinc.* (E.D.D.), The old cat was shuggling about in the hole. 1896 B. MITFORD *Sign of Spider* xxvii. 268 It stood for a moment in rigid immobility, then..it shoggled over the ridge. *Ibid.* 274 The fearful Thing.. shoggled away in the direction whence it had come.

Sho·ggy, *a.* [f. SHOG *sb.* + -Y.] Shaky, insecure.

1866 D. MITCHELL *Hist. Montrose* 22 Sandy Fullerton.. ascended to the narrow shoggy scaffold at the top of the spire.

‖**Shogun** (ʃōu·gun). Forms: 7 shongo, 8–9 seogun, (9 djogoun), s(h)iogoon, sjogun, 9 ziogoon, 9– shogun. [Jap. *shōgun*, short for *sei-i-tai shōgun*, 'barbarian-subduing great general', bestowed on the first holder of the office in 1192. *Shōgun* is a Japanese sound-substitution for Chinese *chiang chün* (*chiang* to lead, *chün* army).] The hereditary commander-in-chief of the Japanese army, until 1867 the virtual ruler of Japan. Also called TYCOON.

By successive usurpations of power, the Shogun or Tycoon had become the real ruler of Japan, though nominally the subject of the Mikado, and acting in his name. This state of things was misunderstood by Europeans, and it was erroneously supposed that there were two emperors in Japan, the Mikado (who was the object of a loyalty of the nature of religious devotion) being called 'the spiritual emperor', and the Shogun 'the temporal emperor'. In 1867, with the abolition of the feudal system, the Mikado assumed the actual sovereignty, and the reign of the Shoguns came to an end.

1615 R. COCKS *Diary* (Hakl. Soc.) I. 5 His wife is sent back to her father Shongo Samme, King of Edo and to succeed in the Empire. 1727 SCHEUCHZER tr. *Kæmpfer's Japan* App. I. 65 It was thought expedient, that the Seogun, or Crown-General, should be sent against them at the head of the imperial army. 1863 ALCOCK *Capital of Tycoon* II. 233 The Seogun, or Dai-Seogun. 1875 *N. Amer. Rev.* CXX. 281 The fall of the shogun's (tycoon's) government. 1879 AUDSLEY & BOWES *Keramic Art Japan* I. Pref., The difficulty which modern writers have found in deciding upon the correct mode of spelling the single word Shôgun; in the Japanese Government Reports we find it written Shogun; Mr. F. Ottwell Adams..writes it..Shôgun; Mr. Dickson, Shiogoon; Mr. Mossman, Siogoon; Mr. Mitford, Shogun; Dr. Siebold, Sjôgun; and Mr. Satow..Shôgun.

b. *attrib.* as designating fashions or art belonging to the Japanese feudal period.

1889 SIR E. ARNOLD *Seas & Lands* xiv. (1895) 226 A seated figure, which might have been taken at first for the chief triumph of the Shogun carvers' work. 1904 D. SLADEN *Playing the Game* I. vi, Tied in the elegant and fantastic Shogun knots which are the formal way of fastening up presents in Dai Nippon.

Hence **Sho·gunal** *a.*, pertaining to a shogun, the shoguns, or the shogunate; **Sho·gunate**, the office or dignity of a shogun or the shoguns; **Sho·gunite** (*rare*), a partisan of the shogunate; **Sho·gunship** = *Shogunate*.

1841 *Mann. & Cust. Japanese* 357 The Annals begin to tell..of rival heirs contending for the siogoonship. 1873 MOSSMAN *New Japan* 333 The despotic rule of the Mikados before the Siogoonate was established. 1883 E. M. THOMPSON *R. Cocks' Diary* (Hakl. Soc.) I. 5 *note*, Iyéyasu held the Shogunate only two years. 1890 SIR E. ARNOLD *Seas & Lands* xxii. (1895) 364 The rebels, or Shogunites, were defeated. 1899 C. J. HOLMES *Hokusai* 14 His artistic reputation had even spread to the Shogunal court.

Shoir, obs. form of SHORE *sb.* and *v.*

Shoit(e, shoitte, obs. forms of SHOAT.²

Shok, obs. f. SHOCK *sb.*; obs. pa. t. of SHAKE *v.*

Shoke, obs. f. SHOCK; obs. pa. t. of SHAKE *v.*

Shokinge, obs. pres. pple. of SUCK *v.*

Shokk(e, obs. forms of SHOCK *sb.*

‖**Shola**¹ (ʃōu·lä). [Hindī *sholā* (*çolā*) = Bengali *solā*.] = SOLA¹.

1836 FANNY PARKS *Wand. Pilgr.* (1850) II. 100 Each float was formed of eight pieces of sholā..When this light and spongy pith is wetted, it can be cut into thin layers, which, pasted together, are formed into hats. 1884 *Sunday at Home* June 373/2, I cannot but grieve to see the graceful shola disappearing fast before the planter's axe.

attrib. 1876 J. H. BALFOUR in *Encycl. Brit.* IV. 100/2 Æschynomene aspera (Shola plant, the Rice-paper plant of India). 1887 BENTLEY *Man. Bot.* (ed. 5) 726 They are not so durable as the Sola or Shola hats of Calcutta.

‖**Shola**² (ʃōu·lä). Also sholah. [Tamil *çolāi*.] A thicket or jungle, in Southern India.

1862 MARKHAM *Trav. Peru & India* xxiii. 38 A wooded ravine or *shola*. *Ibid.* 383 There are many *sholas* which will be found equally well adapted for the growth of the hardier chinchonas. 1863 SIR V. BROOKE in O. L. Stephen *Mem.* (1894) 109 She [the tigress] got weaker and weaker, let go the boar, and slunk off to the *sholah*.

Sholdarry, variant of SHOOLDARRY.

Shold(e, obs. forms of SHOAL.

Sholder(e, sholdre, obs. forms of SHOULDER.

Shole (ʃōul). *Naut.* [Of obscure origin. Cf. SHOE *sb.* 5 j.] (See quots.)

1711 W. SUTHERLAND *Shipbuild. Assist.* 26 The Transoms ought to be level, but especially the Wing Transom, securing all very well with Shores, which ought to be plac'd on Timber Foundations, called Sholes. 1805 *Shipwright's Vade-M.* 131 *Sholes*, pieces of oak or plank, placed under the soles of the standards; or under the heels of the shores, in docks or slips where there are no groundways, to enable them to sustain the weight required without sinking.

Shole, obs. form of SHOAL, SHOVEL.

Sholt. *Obs.* exc. *dial.* Also 6 shault, 9 shoult (*E. Angl. Gloss.*, 1895). A cur.

1587 HARRISON *England* III. vii. 231/2 in *Holinshed*, Besides these also we haue sholts or curs dailie brought out of Iseland. 1592 GREENE *Conny-catch.* Wks. (Grosart) XI. 65 The Boy..neuer saw a Dog nor Bitch, but a little prickeard Shault, that kept the Mil doore. a1825 FORBY *Voc. E. Anglia*, *Sholt*, a cur.

Sholve, obs. var. SHOVEL *sb.*

Shomach, -acke, obs. forms of SUMACH.

Shomaker(e, obs. forms of SHOEMAKER.

†**Shome.** *Obs. rare.* In 4 schome. ?Some kind of adornment for horses. Hence (?) **Schom** *v. trans.*, to adorn with this.

a1310 in Wright *Pol. Songs* (Camden) 239 Nou beth capelclaweres With shome to-shrude; Hue boskeþ huem with botouns, Ase hit were a brude. 1500–20 DUNBAR *Poems* lxi. 3 Quhy sould not palfrayis thane be prowd, Quhen gillettis wilbe schomd and schroud.

Shome, obs. form of SHAME *sb.*

Shon, obs. form of SHUN.

†**Shond**, *sb.*¹ *Obs.* Forms: 1 sceand, sceond, scond, 1–3 scand, 2–3 *Ormin* shande, 3 scond(e, sond(e, ssonde, 3–5 schonde, 4 schounde, schond, 4–5 shonde, (5 shont). [Com. Teut.: OE. *scand, scond* fem. corresponds to OFris. *skonde*, (M)Du., (M)LG. *schande*, OHG. *scanta* (MHG., mod.G. *schande*), Goth. *skanda*:—OTeut. **skandō*, f. **skando-* ashamed (OHG. *scant*, OE. as subst. masc. *scand*: see next):—**skamdo-* pa. pple. of **skam-*: see SHAME *sb.*] Shame, disgrace, infamy, ignominy; scandal. *To do* (some one) *shond*, to treat with indignity; *to bring, make to shond*, to disgrace, ruin.

a900 CYNEWULF *Crist* 1274 Þonne is him oþer earfeþu swa some scyldȝuin to sconde. c1100 *O. E. Chron.* (MS. D.) an. 1076, Sume ȝe tawod to scande. c1200 ORMIN 11956 Forr þatt wass..Hiss aȝhenn shame & shande. c1205 LAY. 7032 Þe ȝunge wifmen & þe ælde he makeden to sconde. c1250 *Gen. & Ex.* 2714 Ðat ðhuȝte moyses michel sond. 1297 R. GLOUC. (Rolls) 1493 To spousy þe emperours doȝter hit nere him no ssonde. c1315 SHOREHAM 7 *Deadly Sins* 45 Wyth schame and eke wyth schounde. c1384 CHAUCER *H. Fame* 88 And shelde hem fro pouerte and shonde. c1400 *St. Alexius* 80 (Laud 463) Þou most þole shame & shonde, al for my sake. c1450 LOVELICH *Grail* xiv. 28 With his Ax he wrowhte hem Mochel schonde.

†**Shond**, *sb.*² *Obs.* Forms: 1 sceand, sceond, 3 sconde. [OE. *scand, scond*: see prec.] An infamous person, a deceiver, charlatan, recreant.

c725 *Corpus Gloss.* (Hessels) S 165 *Scurra*, scond. c1000 ÆLFRIC *Saints* xvii. 159 Ac þyllice sceandas sceolan siðian to helle. c1205 LAY. 23668 Beon he in ælche londe iqueðe for ane sconde.

†**Shond**, *v.* *Obs. rare.* [f. SHOND *sb.*¹ Cf. SHEND *v.*] *trans.* To harm, injure.

1338 R. BRUNNE *Chron.* (1725) 226 Þe Sarazins do grete wreche, þe Cristen for to schond. c1450 LOVELICH *Grail* xiii. 886 For Erthly Man was non leveng In londe That so moche he hated, ne wolde schonde.

†**Sho·ndful**, *a.* *Obs.* [OE. *sceandfull*, f. OE. *sceand* SHOND *sb.*¹ + -FUL.] Shameful, disgraceful; infamous. Hence †**Sho·ndfully** *adv.*

a900 *O. E. Martyrol.* 29 Aug. 156 He [John Baptist] wæs heafde becorfen for scandfulra wifa bene, and for..scondfulles gebeorscypes hleahtre. c1175 *Lamb. Hom.* 31 Þis him wule þunche swiðe strong and swiðe scondful þet he [etc.]. c1330 *Arth. & Merl.* 9198 Better is to sterue worþschipliche þan long to liuen schandfulliche.

†**Sho·ndly**, *a.* *Obs.* Forms: see SHOND *sb.*¹ Also 2 sandlice. [OE. *sceandlic*: see SHOND *sb.*¹ and -LY¹.] Shameful, disgraceful, vile.

888 ÆLFRED *Boeth.* xiv. § 3 Ȝif hit ær scandlic wæs, ne bið hit no ðy fæȝerre. a1175 *Cott. Hom.* 239 Wat sceol se wrecce don þe bufon iseȝð his hlaford..him selfe bi sandlice senne beswapen. c1205 LAY. 2274 Ne scal þe nan man scilden wið scondliche deaðe. c1330 *Arth. & Merl.* 4276 We no haue pouer Arthour oȝen..No for Merlin,..Þat can so michel schandliche werk.

Shone, pa. t. and pa. pple. of SHINE *v.*

Shone, obs. pl. of SHOE; obs. f. SHUN *v.*

Shoneen (ʃōunī·n). *Anglo-Irish.* Also shauneen. [f. mod. Irish *Seón*, ad. Eng. *John* + *-in* diminutive suffix.] (See quot. 1910.)

c1840 KEEGAN *Leg. & Poems* (1907) 67 The likes of him, a bandy-legged shoneen. 1889 *Times* 30 Jan. 6/5, I hope to bear of ye shooting Hubert Davis..the shauneen of a landlord. 1909 *Ibid.* 21 Jan. 6/6 What difference did it make whether a man got a 'shoneen' education in Belfast or in Oxford so long as he was not educated an Irishman. 1910 P. W. JOYCE *English as we Speak it in Irel.* 321 *Shoneen*, a *gentleman* in a small way: a would-be gentleman who puts on superior airs. Always used contemptuously.

†**Shongable.** *Obs. rare.* [f. *shon* pl. of SHOE *sb.* + *-gable* in imitation of older compounds: see GAVEL *sb.*] A tax on the making of (a particular kind of) shoes.

a1400 in *Eng. Gilds* 339 Euerych sowtere þt makeþ shon of newe roþes leþer, shal bote..twey pans, in name of shongable.

Shonie, obs. form of SHUN *v.*

†**Shonk**, *v.* *Sc.* *Obs. rare.* In 5 schonk. [Of obscure origin.] a. *trans.* To shatter. b. *intr.* To burst forth. Hence †**Sho·nkand** *ppl. a.* (*Sc.*)

c1470 *Gol. & Gaw.* 619 Thair speris in splendris sprent, On scheldis schonkit and schent. c1470 HENRY *Wallace* III. 147 The schafft to schonkit off the fruschand tre. *Ibid.* 156 Vpon the flouris schot the schonkan blude.

Shonke, Shonne, obs. ff. SHANK, SHUN.

Shont(t, obs. forms of SHUNT *v.*

Shoo (ʃū), *v.* Forms: 7 shough, 8–9 shue, 9 schue, sheugh, 8– shoo. [f. SHOO *int.*¹ Cf. It. *scioiare* (Florio).]

1. *trans.* To scare or drive away (fowls, etc.) by calling out 'shoo'. Also with *away, from, off, out* (*of*).

1622 BRETON *Strange News* (Grosart) 12/2 With that the Cock-master came in..and shought away the Hen. c1798 T. BROWN *Auld Daisy* 40 Ah waved my hat an' shoo'd 'em all away. 1819 W. TENNANT *Papistry Storm'd* iii. (1827) 106 Think alswa How to rebut and schue awa Thir damnit faes. 1872 'SUSAN COOLIDGE' *What Katy did* viii, 'Shue'-ing away the other children. 1912 CHESTERTON *Manalive* 161 'Get inside! get inside!' cried Moon hilariously, with the air of one shooing a company of cats.

2. *intr.* To cry out 'shoo' in order to frighten or drive away fowls, etc. Const. *at*.

c1746 J. COLLIER (Tim Bobbin) *View Lanc. Dial.* (1806) 22 Still they kept shuing. 1881 MRS. MOLESWORTH *Adv. Herr Baby* 120 It was very funny to see the way the little footman went 'shoo-ing' at the poor cat.

3. To hasten away, as after being 'shooed at'.

1851 STERNBERG *Northampt. Gloss.* 95 Lady lock, lady lock! shoo all the way home. a1869 C. SPENCE *Fr. Braes of Carse* (1898) 192 The fairies..beat the beldames blank and hollow, And sent them sheughing down the Ballo'. 1882 P. ROBINSON *Under the Sun* III. v. 213 If the domestic says *shoo* to her [the cat] she shoos at once.

Hence **Shoo·er**, in comb. *bird-shooer*.

1849 HALLIWELL *Pop. Rhymes* 179 This is the universal bird-shooer's song in the midland counties.

Shoo (ʃū), *int.*¹ Forms: 5 schowe, ssou, 7 shooe, shooh, shue, shcogh, 7–8 shough, 9 shu(h, shue, sho (etc.: see Eng. Dial. Dict.), 9– shoo. [An instinctive exclamation; cf. LG. *schu*, MHG. *schu, schuo* (mod.G. *schu*), F. *shou*, It. *scioia*.] An exclamation used to frighten or drive away poultry, birds, or other intruders. Also *shoohoo*. Also as *sb.*

1483 *Cath. Angl.* 338/1 Schowe ssou, *jntericccio est*. 1611 FLORIO, *Scioiare*, to cry shooe shooe, as women do to their hens. 1623 FLETCHER & ROWLEY *Maid in Mill* v. i, Shough, shough, up to your coop, Pen-Hen. 1639 J. CLARKE *Paræmiologia* 145 He cannot say shooh to a goose. 1675 HOBBES *Odyss.* xv. 139 An eagle..seis'd a great white tame goose grazing near: The standers-by shouted and cri'd, Shue! shue! But yet away the eagle bore him clear. 1681 OTWAY *Soldier's Fort.* IV. (1683) 49 Shoogh, shoogh, get you into a corner when I bid you, shoogh, shoogh, shoogh, what there already? 1822 T. MITCHELL *Aristoph.*, *Wasps* I. ii. II. 191 Shuh! shuh! foolish bird, must I stone 'ee? 1829 J. HUNTER *Hallamsh. Gloss.*, *Shoo*, the interjection used in frighting away birds from their prey. 1852 DICKENS *Bleak Ho.* xxxix, Shoohoo! Get out, you goblin! 1891 J. L. KIPLING *Beast & Man India* ii. 44 The servant shows the master a fowl standing on one leg. The master crows sho! and the fowl runs away with two. 1894 CROCKETT *Raiders* xxxvii. 311 An owl flew by..and I heard him say, 'Shoo, you beast!' 1896 JANE BARLOW *Mrs. Martin's Comp.* 41 A..burly man, who says 'shoo-shoo' to a..cluster of tiny yellow ducks.

Shoo (ʃū, ʃu), **sho** (ʃō), *int.*² *dial.* and *U.S.* Also shuh, shah. [Instinctive: cf. prec.] An exclamation indicating impatient or contemptuous rejection of a statement. Cf. PSHAW.

1845 S. JUDD *Margaret* I. xi, 'Sho! it's humans you are speaking of', replied Nimrod. 1856 P. THOMPSON *Hist. Boston* 722 *Shoo* or *Shah.* Pshaw! a peevish reply. 1883 J. C. HARRIS in *Century Mag.* May 139/2 Shoo! won't my ole 'oman holler! 1900 WEYMAN *Sophia* xiv, 'Sho!' Lady Betty cried contemptuously.

Shoo, obs. form of SHE, SHOE, SHOW *v.*

Shooba, shoobe, variant forms of SHUBA.

Shooch, dial. variant of SHEUGH *sb.*

Shood, shude (ʃūd). *dial.* Also 7 shud, 9 shewd. [Prob. cogn. w. MLG. *schode*, MHG. *schôte*, mod.G. *schote* husk, pod of peas or beans, f. **skeu-* to cover; the OE. form may have been **scéod* (*sceód*) corresponding formally to ON. *skjóð* fem., skin bag.] The husk of oats after threshing. Usually in *pl.* Also † = SHIVE *sb.*²

1601 HOLLAND *Pliny* XIX. i. II. 4 But what shall bee done with all the hard refuse [from the flax],..the short shuds or shives that are either driven from the rest in the knocking, or parted in the hetchelling. 1691 RAY *N. C. Words* (ed. 2) 62 *Shoods*, Oat-hulls; *Darbish*. 1829 J. HUNTER *Hallamsh. Gloss.*, *Shewds*, the outer coat of oats, sometimes called *shiffs*. 1879 MISS JACKSON *Shropsh. Word-bk.*, *Shoods*, husks of oats,—'this wutmil's full o' shoods'. 1886 *Cheshire Gloss.*, *Shudes*, husks of oats, sifted from the meal. Bacon is often stowed away in a chest amongst shoods.

Shood, Shooe, obs. ff. SHOD *a.*, SHOE.

Shoof(e, obs. pa. t. of SHAVE *v.*, SHOVE *v.*

Shooffell, shoof(f)le, obs. ff. SHUFFLE *v.*

Shook (ʃuk), *sb.* Now chiefly *U.S.* [? f. SHOOK *ppl. a.* Cf. SHAKEN *cask*.] 'A set of staves and headings sufficient for one hogshead, barrel, or the like, prepared for use and bound up in a compact form for convenience of transport. Boards for boxes prepared or fitted for use and packed in the same way bear the same name' (*Cent. Dict.* 1891).

[1768, 1794: see SHOOK *ppl. a.*] 1796 MORSE *Amer. Geog.* (ed. 3) I. 250 [Exports of U.S.] Shooks. 1860 *Merc. Mar. Mag.* VII. 120 Shooks are free of duty. 1894 *Times* 16 Aug. 6/3 Casks and barrels, empty, sugar-box shooks and packing boxes and packing box shooks, of wood.

b. 'Furniture made in parts and not set up, but shipped in packs' (Knight *Dict. Mech.* 1875).

Hence **Shook** *v. trans.*, to pack in shooks.

1847 in WEBSTER; and in later Dicts.

Shook (ʃuk), *ppl. a.* In educated use only *arch.* [pa. pple. of SHAKE *v.*] = SHAKEN *ppl. a.*

1695 BLACKMORE *Pr. Arthur* III. (1696) 68 And the shook Sphears, with loud Hosannahs ring. 1768 *Massach. Gaz.* in Thornton *Amer. Gloss.* s.v., A few large shook hogsheads. 1794 MORSE *Amer. Geog.* (ed. 2) 256 [Exports of U.S.] Wood..Shingles, Shook Casks, Casks, Laths. 1897 F. THOMPSON *New Poems* 25 Reversing the shook banners of their song.

Shool (ʃūl), *v.* *dial.* and *slang*. Also 8–9 shule, 9 shoal. [Of obscure origin; hardly identical with *shool* var. of SHOVEL *v.* In Ireland it seems to have been associated with Irish *siubhail* to go, travel; *shooler* (see below) seems to correspond to Irish *siubhlach* vagrant.] *intr.* To go about begging; to sponge, to acquire some advantage by insidious means; also to skulk.

1736 J. LEWIS *Isle of Tenet* (ed. 2) 38 *Shooling*, begging, to go a Shooling. 1748 SMOLLETT *Rod. Random* xli, When they found my hold unstowed, they went all hands to shooling and begging. 1785 GROSE *Dict. Vulgar T.*, *Shoole*, to go skulking about. 1842 LOVER *Handy Andy* xxxiv, 'Throth, you do me wrong', said the beggar, 'if you think I came shooling'. a1876 M. & FR. COLLINS *Village Comedy* (1878) I. xxii. 297 As we watch these daring damsels starting to 'shool', we cannot help wishing them some lively adventures. 1899 'MARTELLO TOWER' *At School & Sea* 73 Hullo, Dil, at it again, shooling (that is, getting things) on the youngsters.

b. *trans.* To impose on (a person).

1745 *Life Bampfylde-Moore Carew* 138 One Day he met with an English Doctor, whom he shuled as a cast-away Seaman.

c. To carry as a pretence.

1880 CLARE *Rural Life* (ed. 3) 125 Who takes delight To shool her knitting out at night.

Hence **Shoo·ler**, one who 'shools'.

1830 CARLETON *Traits Irish Peas.* (1843) I. 62 What tribes of beggars and shulers. 1856 P. THOMPSON *Hist. Boston* 722 *Shooler*, one who intrudes upon his neighbour, and forces an invitation to dinner, &c.

Shool, obs. and dial. form of SHOVEL.

‖**Shooldarry** (ʃūldæ·ri). *Ind.* Also shoaldarree, sholdarry. [Urdū چھولداری *chholdārī*, of obscure origin.] 'A small tent with steep sloping roof, two poles and a ridge-piece, and with very low side walls' (Yule).

1808 ELPHINSTONE in Colebrooke *Life* (1884) I. 182, I have now a shoaldarree for myself, and a long paul for my people. 1902 T. W. WEBBER *Forests Upper India* v. 46 The baggage consisted of a small sholdarry tent, 6 feet square.

Shoole, obs. form of SHOAL *sb.*

Shoomack, -ak(e, obs. forms of SUMACH.

Shoon, pl. f. SHOE; obs. pa. t. of SHINE *v.*

Shoone, obs. f. pa. t. of SHINE *v.*

Shoop (ʃūp). *north.* Forms: 5 schowpe, 8–9 shoup, showp, 9– shoop. See also CHOOP. [The forms *shoop, choop* perh. represent aberrant pronunciations of ON. **hjúpa* (MSw. *hiupa*, Norw. dial. *hjupa*, Da. *hybe*) = OE. *héope* HIP *sb.*²]

The fruit of the rose; = HIP *sb.*²

1483 *Cath. Angl.* 338/1 A schowpe, *cornum*. A schowpe tre, *cornus*. 1721 *MS. Cook Book* in *Girl's Own Paper* (1886) VII. 729 How to Candy Shoups. 1781 J. HUTTON *Tour to Caves* (ed. 2) 95 *Shoup*, an hep. 1804 *Europ. Mag.* XLV. 326/2 [Shaped] like a hip or a shoup on a rose-tree. 1878 *Cumberld. Gloss.*, *Choop, Shoop*, the fruit of the wild rose.

Shoop, obs. pa. t. of SHAPE *v.*

Shoope, Shoore, obs. ff. SHOP *sb.*, SHORE.

Shoot (ʃūt), *sb.*¹ Forms: 6 s(c)hute, 6 schote, 5 schoyt, 6 shote, 6 showt, 6–7 shoote, 7 shout, 5– shoot. [f. SHOOT *v.*

In early examples it is sometimes difficult to distinguish this word from certain other derivatives of the same root. In the early 16th c. the spellings *shote* and *shoote* are both ambiguous, so that only the shade of meaning can determine whether the word is *shoot* (rhyming with *root*) f. the pres.-stem of the vb., or the older SHOTE (rhyming with *throat*). The 16th c. examples of the spelling *s(c)hute* belong to the present word, but down to the 14th c. this spelling (with *u* = *ü*) represents the OE. *scyte*: see SHUTE *sb.*]

1. An act of shooting (with fire-arms, a bow, etc.); a discharge of arrows, bullets, etc.: = SHOT *sb.* Now only *arch.*

1534 MORE *Comf. agst. Trib.* I. Wks. 1157/2 This marke ..we shal nowe meate for the shoote and consider..bow farre of your arrowes are from the prik. 1545 ASCHAM *Toxoph.* I. (Arb.) 89 The strongest men, do not drawe alwayes the strongest shoote. *Ibid.* II. 107 For in a rayne and at no marke, a man may shote a faire shoote. 1546 *Plumpton Corr.* (Camden) 250 Tomorrow..I must..ride to Tankersley.. & mete my Lord of Shrewsburry, who will be thear tomorrow by ij of the clock, & se a showt at a stage [= stag]. 1565 COOPER *Thesaurus* s.v. *Conficere*, He killed twelue at xii. shootes. 1583 MELBANCKE *Philotimus* R iv b, O that I mighte haue a shoote at one of the Deares in his Parke. 1629 WADSWORTH *Pilgr.* iv. 35 In 12 shootes more they strooke downe our maine Mast. 1676 SHOTTEREL & DURFEY *Archerie reviv'd* 78 If in measuring a Shoot, the Mark be stirred out of its place, he loseth the Shoot that removed it. 1692 R. L'ESTRANGE *Fables* lxvi. 65 As a Country Fellow was making a Shoot at a Pigeon. 1775 *Pennsylvania Even. Post* 30 Nov. 551/1 The riflemen..declare that they can hit a man every shoot if within two hundred and fifty yards. 1801 T. ROBERTS *Engl. Bowman* 293 A *Shoot*, an arrow shot. 1888 STEVENSON *Black Arrow* Prol. 8 How many a rogue would give his two crop ears to have a shoot at either of us! *Ibid.* v. vi. 306, I have two score men at my whistle, and with one shoot of arrows I could answer for you all.

fig. 1590 *Cobler of Canterb.* 2 All men..saide, that he [Chaucer] shot a shoote which many haue aimed at but neuer reacht to. 1682 DRYDEN & LEE *Dk. Guise* I. i, *Pol.* But one prime Article of our holy League, Is to preserve the King, his Power and Person. *Cur.* That must be said, you know, for Decency; A pretty Blind to make the Shoot secure.

†b. Range, distance or reach of a shot; shooting distance. *Obs.*

1530 SIR D. LYNDESAY *Test. Papyngo* 941 They haue ane Boumbard..Within quhose schote there dar no Enimeis Approche thare place. 1545 ASCHAM *Toxoph.* I. (Arb.) 33 There was nothing within his retche and shote. 1613 BEAUM. & FL. *Hon. Man's Fort.* IV. ii, Hence, and take the wings of thy black Infamy, to carry thee beyond the shoot of looks, Or sound of curses. 1641 EARL MONM. tr. *Biondi's Civil Warres* IV. 64 Chartier brings the two Armies face to face within the shoote of a Culverin. 1676 *Acc. Exam. Joan Perry* 3 He went again with him about a Bows shoot into the Fields. a1700 EVELYN *Diary* Apr. 1646, Nor could we any where see above a pistol shoote before us. 1719 DE FOE *Crusoe* I. (Globe) 236 So that I might come within shoot of them before I should be discover'd.

†c. Weapons for shooting, firearms. *Obs.*

1469 *Paston Lett.* III. 372 That, with ther gret multitude of gannes [sic], with other shoot and ordynaunce, ther shall no man dar appere in the place.

†d. A charge (of powder). *Obs.*

1645 SYMONDS *Diary* (Camden) 276 Their ammunition was so spent that the enemy gave the soldjer many shootes of powder to make the conditions good.

e. A game-shooting expedition; the result of such an expedition.

1852 VISCOUNTESS CANNING in Hare *Story Two Noble Lives* (1893) I. 360 The Prince is much pleased with his shoot this year. One day he killed five stags. 1877 'WILDFOWLER' *Shooting Trips* Ser. II. II. 99 We should arrive at Ford in time for a stroll and a 'shoot' along the river Arun. 1895 SIR W. W. HUNTER *Old Missionary* iii. 59 Their return ..was celebrated by a big shoot in the jungle.

f. A shooting party.

1885 *Field* 4 Apr. 446/1 At a big shoot in Warwickshire. 1894 'J. S. WINTER' *Red Coats* 69 Miss Dawson..gave big dinners and big shoots.

g. The right to shoot game in a given area; also the area itself.

1861 MRS. JENKIN *Who Breaks Pays* II. 93, I hear Sir Frederick a taken the shoot hisself, and bought Bill Fordham's black hunter. 1892 GREENER *Breech-Loader* 221 The sportsman whose shoot is small and the game..scarce and wild, will be unable to practise driving to any advantage. 1900 *Field* 29 Sept. Advt. p. vi/2 Wanted, a good rough shoot, commencing season 1901–1902, on Lease; plenty of rabbits essential; 2000 to 5000 acres.

h. A shooting match or contest; a round of shots in such a contest.

1892 GREENER *Breech-Loader* 102 Some men who attend second-rate pigeon shoots and do not take their own guns. 1892 *Times* 23 July 6/1 Volunteer Aggregate...One shoot at 200, one at 500, and three at 600 yards. Seven shots at each. 1894 *Daily News* 12 June 8/6 The full scores of the first 'shoot' for places in the 'English Twenty' at Bisley.

2. The action of shooting, sprouting, or growing; the amount of growth (also *concr.* the new wood, etc. produced) in a certain period. Also †the mounting or rising (of the sap).

1572 MASCALL *Plant. & Graff.* (1592) 9 For to set the Pine tree, ye must set or plant them of Nuts, in March, or about the shoote of the sappe. 1661 BOYLE *Certain Physiol. Ess.* (1669) 91 Others content themselves to chuse a hazel rod (which some will have to be all of the same years shoot). 1664 EVELYN *Kal. Hort.* Jan. (1679) 8 Cut off all the shoot of August, unless the nakedness of the place incline you to spare it. 1733 W. ELLIS *Chiltern & Vale Farm.* 266 The Clover makes a quick Shoot, and will get a large second Head. 1832 *Boston Herald* 8 May 3/5 The shoot of Spring grass is also unusually late, and slow in vegetation. 1896 *Daily News* 19 Sept. 2/5 The crops presented at harvest what to agriculturists is known as 'two shoots', i.e., a crop composed of ripe and also unripe grain.

b. A young branch which shoots out from the main stock of a tree, plant, etc.

a1450 *Fysshynge w. Angle* (1883) 8 Take a feyr schoyt of blake thorne. 1578 LYTE *Dodoens* I. liv. 80 This plante [*Linaria*] hath diuers small shutes or scourges bearing small narrow leaues. 1634 MILTON *Comus* 296, I saw them under a green mantling vine..Plucking ripe clusters from the tender shoots. 1780 P. BLAIR *Bot. Ess.* i. 10 If it be put into a Pot, and all its Stolones or Shoots be taken off. 1796 WITHERING *Brit. Plants* (ed. 3) I. 81 Shoot (*surculus*) the branch of a Moss. 1812 *New Bot. Gard.* I. 6 The French in Canada eat the tender shoots in spring as Asparagus. 1842 LOUDON *Suburban Hort.* 497 Cut smooth the lower end of the shoot or cutting, and stick it into fine leaf or other rich mould about an inch deep. 1863 GEO. ELIOT *Romola* viii, The fresh shoots among the darker green of the oak. 1909 J. G. FRAZER *Psyche's Task* iv. 38 The shoots of the sweet potato had flowered and withered long ago.

c. *fig.* An offshoot; a growth or sprout from a main stock.

c1610 *Women Saints* 71 Kinesburge and Kineswide were daughters to Penda, a Pagan thoughe king of Mercia, both shootes of a dead stocke or truncke. 1749 SMOLLETT *Gil Blas* XII. v. (1782) IV. 237 His excellency..immediately..for his equivocal heir, and new shoot from the stock of the Guzmans. 1833 LONGF. *Outre-Mer*, *Sexagenarian*, Monsieur d'Argentville was a shoot from a wealthy family of Nantes. 1882 CHILD *Eng. & Sc. Pop. Ball.* I. The ballad we are dealing with is a wild shoot from the story of Judith and Holofernes. 1899 J. MATHEW *Eaglehawk & Crow* ii. 9 Upon the aboriginal Australian stock was grafted a strong Malayo-Dravidian shoot.

d. *transf.*

1611 SHAKS. *Wint. T.* I. ii. 128 Thou want'st a rough pash & the shoots that I haue To be full, like me. 1671 GREW *Anat. Pl.* I. iv. (1682) 28 Those Fibrous Shoots which run from the Pith in the Root. 1822–29 *Good's Study Med.* (ed. 3) It is better..to distinguish by the phrase polypous excrescences, caruncles, or shoots, such adscititious productions as may have a resemblance to them [i.e. to nasal polypi] in other organs. 1847 PRESCOTT *Peru* III. i. (1862) II. 11 Ridges of barren land, that seemed like shoots of the adjacent Andes. 1851 S. P. WOODWARD *Mollusca* I. 18 The oyster..enlarging his shell by annual 'shoots' for four years. 1861 *The Oyster* 35 These [overlapping plates of the oyster-shell] are technically termed 'shoots', each of them marks a year's growth.

e. Applied to the forms of crystals ?likened to those of a plant. Cf. SHOOT *v.*

a1728 WOODWARD *Nat. Hist. Fossils* I. (1729) I. 158 Spar of a yellow Hue, shot into numerous trigonal pointed Shoots of various Sizes. *Ibid.*, Hexangular Sprigs or Shoots of Crystal of various Sizes. 1748 *Phil. Trans.* XLV. 264 I tried Alum, which fully answered everything I wanted; for it restored the Salt to its natural cubical Shoots.

3. A motion or movement (of a thing) as in shooting or being shot in a particular direction; also the space or distance covered by such a shoot or by a push. *spec.* (see quot. 1903).

c1596 *Sir T. More* IV. iii. 20 Thence some shoot..Being carried by the waues, our boate stood still Just opposite the Tower. a1658 LOVELACE *The Falcon* x, At two charges at first view With her brigade of Talons; through Whose Shoots, the wary Heron beat, With a well counterwheel'd retreat. 1863 HAWTHORNE *Old Home*, *Up Thames* II. 130 [The journey by river is] far preferable to the..yet tiresome shoot along the railway track. 1865 'A. BRADWOOD' *The O. V. H.* xxx, They have nearly..made the shoot to the Middlesex shore [in the University boat-race]. 1881 MACDONALD *Mary Marston* II. xiii. 233 Into her eyes she would call up her soul and there make it shine in light, in gleams and sparkles, shoots and coruscations. 1898 *Times* 25 June 7/2 Both [yachts] had a long shoot into the eye of the wind. 1903 EDWARDS-MOSS in Lehmann & Watson *Eng. Sport* 178 In order then to give a better shoot (*i.e.* pace between the strokes) when the boat is coming forward for the next stroke, there must be an increased power put into each stroke.

b. Of an immaterial thing: A sudden advance.

1752 JOHNSON *Rambler* No. 200 ¶ 4, I felt at first a sudden shoot of success an honest and disinterested joy. 1777 HUME *Ess. & Treat.* (1777) I. 125 The sciences..are enabled to make..considerable shoots. 1837 CARLYLE *Fr. Rev.* I. VII. i, Many things too, especially all growing things, grow by shoots and fits. 1839 HALLAM *Hist. Lit.* II. iv. § 16 We find it near the end of Elizabeth's reign, when our literature made its first strong shoot.

c. A sharp short twinge (of pain).

1756 FOOTE *Engl. fr. Paris* II. Wks. 1799 I. 122, I burn—Ah, there's a shoot. 1822–29 *Good's Study Med.* (ed. 3) IV. 320 The lancinating shoots darted both downward ..and upward. 1892 SWINBURNE *Sisters* II. i. 36 Between the shoots and swoonings, off and on, it was. 1899 J. HUTCHINSON in *Arch. Surg.* X. 76 The shoots of pain were like those of an electric discharge.

†d. = THRUST *sb.* 3 (*a*). *Obs.*

1772 C. HUTTON *Bridges* 58 The weight of the pier ought ..to..exceed in effect the shoot of the arch. 1823 P. NICHOLSON *Pract. Build.* 340.

e. A detachment and falling away or tumbling down (as of part of a cliff); a landslip.

1820 SCORESBY *Acc. Arctic Reg.* I. 104 Vast quantities of broken ice denoted recent shoots of the seaward edge [of an iceberg]. 1889 W. RYE *Cromer* 68 In 1832, there was so heavy a shoot of the cliff..that [etc.].

4. *Weaving.* One movement or throw of the shuttle between the threads of the warp; the length of thread thus placed; also, the weft.

1717 PARNELL *Homer's Battle of Frogs & Mice* II. Along the Loom the purple Warp I spread, Cast the light Shoot, and crost the silver Thread. 1731 MORTIMER in *Phil. Trans.* XXXVII. 107 Wherefore they fasten a Sort of *Potlart* to as many of these simple Chords as there are Threads of the Warp to be pull'd up at every Shoot or every Throw of the Shuttle; by which means the Figure shews itself on the right Side, where the Warp is... 1736 *Act 9 Geo. II*, c. 37 § 7 The Shoot Yarn..shall be close struck with four Shoots of treble Thread in the Distance of every two Feet. 1810 J. T. in *Risdon's Surv. Devon* Introd. p. xxv, The other yarn, of a softer twist, is called the abb or shoot. 1831 G. R. PORTER *Silk Manuf.* 231 The commoner sorts of ribands, are composed..with both warp and shoot, of Bengal silk. 1840 *Civil Engin. & Arch. Jrnl.* III. 139/2 An improved method of throwing the shoot or weft to be used in weaving woollen cloth. 1844 G. DODD *Textile Manuf.* vi. 201 Plain silks, as well as other woven fabrics, consist of threads crossing each other at right angles; the 'long-threads' being technically called the warp, and the 'cross-threads' the shoot or weft. 1888 J. PATON in *Encycl. Brit.* XXIV. 464/1 A new shed is formed, the last made pick or shoot being enclosed between the intersecting warp sheds.

5. A heavy and sudden rush of water down a steep channel; a place in a river where there occurs a rapid. (Confused with CHUTE 1; cf. SHUTE.)

SHOOT. 733 SHOOT.

SHOOT. 734 SHOOTER.

SHOOTING. 735 SHOOTING.

SHOOTING STAR. 736 SHOP.

SHOP.

Shop, *sb.*

Shop-board.

Shopful.

Shophar.

Shopkeeper. [f. SHOP *sb.* + KEEPER.] One who carries on business in a shop.

Shopocracy. Shopkeepers as a class aspiring to social importance; a wealthy or influential body of shopkeepers.

SHOPPER.

Shopper (ʃǫpəɹ). [f. SHOP *v.* + -ER[1].] One who frequents a shop or shops for the purpose of inspecting or buying goods.

Shoppiness.

Shopping (ʃǫpiŋ), *vbl. sb.* [f. SHOP *v.* + -ING.] The action of visiting a shop or shops for the purpose of making purchases or of examining the goods exposed for sale.

Hence **Sho·pkeeperess** *nonce-wd.*, a female shopkeeper. **Sho·pkeeperism.** **Sho·pkeeperism**, as a class. **Sho·pkeepery.**

Shopkeeping, *vbl. sb.* The keeping of a shop, the business of a shopkeeper.

Shoppish (ʃǫpiʃ), *a.* [SHOP *sb.* + -ISH[1].] Characteristic of persons connected with a shop; also = SHOPPY *a.*

Shoppy (ʃǫpi), *a.* 1. Of the nature of 'shop' or professional concerns or conversation.

Shop-window.

Shorage, *Obs.* [f. SHORE *sb.*[1] + -AGE. (Perh. formed by Cotgrave as a rendering of *rivage*.)] (See quot. 1611.)

SHORE.

Shorde, obs. form of SWORD.

Shore (ʃǫə), *sb.*[1] Forms: 4–7 schore, 5 sohor, 5–7 *Sc.* schoir, 6 shawre, 6–7 shoare, *Sc.* shoir, 6–8 shoar, (7 shoore), 5– shore. [ME. *schore*, *sc.* shore, corresp. to MLG. *schore*, *schare* shore, ...] 1. The land bordering on the sea or a large lake or river.

Shore (ʃǫə), *sb.*[2] Also 7 schore, 5, 6 schoyr, 5–7 *Sc.* schoir, 6–7 schore, 7 shoar, shoare. [MLG. *schore*, *schare* shore.]

Shore (ʃǫə), *sb.*[3] Also 4 score, schore, 6 schoir. [Possibly repr. OE. *scorn* ...]

SHORE.

Shore (ʃǫə), *sb.*[4] Also 4 ssore, schore, 7 shoare. [f. SHORE *v.*]

Shore, *sb.*[5] *Sc. Obs.* Forms: 4–5 schor, schoyr(e, schore, 6, 7 schowr(e.) [Related to SHORE *v.*[3]] Menace, threatening.

†Shore, *a.* Chiefly *Sc. Obs.* Also 4, 5 schore, 6 schoir.

Shore (ʃǫə), *sb.*[6] Also 4 ssore, schore, 7 shoar. [f. SHORE *v.*[1]]

Shore, *sb.*[7] *Obs.* pa. t. of SHEAR *v.*

Shored, [f. SHORE *sb.*[1]]

Shoreless, *a.* Without a shore or boundary; also *fig.* Boundless.

Shore-lark.

Shoreling. *Obs.*

SHORE-GOING.

Shore-going, *a.* Going, living, etc., on shore.

Shoreless (ʃǫəles), *a.* [f. SHORE *sb.*[1] + -LESS.] Having no shore. a. Of a sea, or what is compared to a sea: Boundless.

Shoreman (ʃǫəmən). Also *Sc.* (sense 2) **shoresman**. [f. SHORE *sb.*[1] + MAN *sb.*] 1. A dweller by the seashore.

Shore, *v.*[1] *Sc. Obs.* Also 4 schore, 5 schoore, 6– shore. [Belongs to SHORE *a.*]

Shore, *v.*[2] *Obs.* Also 4 ssore, schore, 5–6 schore, 6–7 shoare. Of obscure origin; perh. cogn. w. SHORE *a.*]

Shore, *v.*[3] *Obs.* Also a variant of SCOUR *v.*[2]

Shore, *v.*[4] [f. SHORE *sb.*[4]]

Shore, *v.*[5] *Obs.* Also 4 ssore, schore, 7 shoar(e. [f. SHORE *sb.*[4]]

SHORE-GOING.

Shore-going, *vbl. sb.* Going ashore (from the sea); living on shore. (Cf. SEA-GOING.)

Shoreward (ʃǫəwəɹd), *adv.* and *a.* [f. SHORE *sb.*[1] + -WARD.]
A. *adv.* Towards the shore.

SHORT.

Shoring (ʃǫəɹiŋ), *vbl. sb.*[1] [f. SHORE *v.*[4] + -ING.] Propping, supporting.

Shoring (ʃǫəɹiŋ), *vbl. sb.*[2] *Obs.* [f. SHORE *v.*[1] + -ING.] Threatening.

Shoring, *ppl. a.*[2] *Obs.* Threatening.

†Shorling. *Obs.* Forms: 5–6 shorlyng, *Sc.* schorlyng, 6 shorling.

Shorn, *pa. pple.* and *a.* [f. SHEAR *v.*] Forms: see the verb.

Short (ʃǫət), *a.*, *sb.*, and *adv.* Forms: *a.* 1 sceort, scort, 2–7 schort, (3 ssort, 4–5 schorte, scort), 4–7 shorte, 1, 4– short. [OE. *sceort*, *scort* = OHG. *scurz* short.] A. *adj.* I. With reference to spatial measurement. 1. Having small longitudinal extent; of limited length.

Shortly

Shortly (ʃɒˈtli), adv. [f. SHORT a. + -LY [2].]

1. Briefly, concisely, in few words.

2. In a short time; not long after the present or the point reached in a narrative; soon.

3. Abruptly, curtly, sharply.

Shortness

Shortness (ʃɔːtnɛs). [f. SHORT a. + -NESS.]

1. The quality or fact of being short in duration, linear magnitude, serial extent, etc.; absence of length, brevity.

| SHOULDERING. | 757 | SHOUT | SHOUTER | 758 | SHOVE. |

2. concr. Something which projects or supports as a shoulder. †Also = EPAULEMENT.

Shouldering (ʃǝˑuldǝrɪŋ), vbl. sb.¹ [f. SHOULDER v. + -ING¹.] The shouldering.

Shoulder-joint. The joint of the shoulder; the articulation by which the arm or foreleg is connected with the trunk.

Shou·lderwise, adv. [See -WISE.] So as to form a shoulder.

Shoulder-, ord: see SHOVELER, SHOVELARD.

Shoulder-knot. A knot of ribbon or lace, sometimes enriched with jewels, worn on the shoulder by men of fashion in the 17th and 18th c.; also a knot, formerly of ribbons of the family colours, now of lace, worn on the shoulder by some livery servants.

Shou·piltin, shoopiltee, -ie. [Derivative of ON.]

Shoulder-piece.

1. a. Antiq. A piece of armour covering the shoulder.

b. A piece or each of the pieces of material composing the shoulder of a garment.

2. = BURY sb.¹ 1, th. †conr.

3. The piece forming the shoulder (of a tool, etc.).

4. Each of the two short straps which go over the shoulders, connecting and supporting the fore and back parts of a garment.

Shout (ʃaʊt), sb.¹ Forms: 4 schoute, 4-6 schowt, schoute, showte, 4-8 schout, 5 (schout), schowte, 6-7 showt, 4-9 shout, 7-9 (dial.) shoot. [See SHOUT sb.²]

1. intr. To utter a loud call, to make a loud outcry expressive of joy, exultation, etc. or to raise an alarm, to incite to action, etc.

† Shou·ter¹. The master of a 'shoot' for flat boats. Obs.

Shou·ter² (ʃaʊˑtǝɹ). [f. SHOUT v. + -ER¹.]

1. One who shouts or cries out loudly; one who acclaims or applauds.

Shou·ther, variant of SHOUDER.

Shouting (ʃaʊˑtɪŋ), vbl. sb. [f. SHOUT v. + -ING¹.]

Shout (ʃaʊt), sb.² Obs. exc. dial. (Sc.) : see Eng. Dial. Dict. Forms: 4 schowte, 4-5 schoute, 4-5 showte, 4-7 showt, 5 scoute, shoute, prob. a. MDu. schûte : see SCHUIT, SCOUT sb.³] A flat-bottomed boat.

Shout (ʃaʊt), sb.³ Forms: 4 schoute, 4-6 shoute, schowte, 4-7 showt(e, schout, 6 shout, 7 Sc. shout. [This and the related SHOUT v. first appear in the 14th c. The sb. corresponds formally to ON. skúta, skúte, a small boat.]

1. A loud, vehement cry expressing joy, grief or pain, fear, triumph, warning, encouragement, etc.; a loud cry to attract attention at a distance; a tumultuous uproar by a large body of people.

† b. Said of other loud sounds.

† 2. To insult with a clamorous outcry; = to shout at (see 1 b). b. To welcome with shouts.

† 3. Said of other loud sounds.

a. transf. Applied to any loud noise or cry forcing itself upon the attention.

Shovel (ʃʌˑv'l), sb. Forms: 1 scofl, -scobl, 3 sceofle, 3-4 sceovele, 4-5 schovyll, schovylle, 4-5 schovele, schovel, schouvel, schowvel, 4-6 schovelle, -olle, 5-6 schovell, schowel, shovell, 5-7 shovyl, 5-9 shovell, shovel, shoull. [OE. scoflu, sceofl, scufle.]

1. A spade-like implement, consisting of a broad blade of metal or other material (more or less hollow and often with upturned sides), attached to a handle and used for raising and removing quantities of earth, grain, coal or other loose material.

b. Special comb.: shovel-bill = SHOVELER²; shovel-cultivator U.S. = shovel-plough; †shovel-groat = SHOVEL-GROAT; †shovel-hat, a hat of the genus Scaphirhynchus; †shovel-man, a labourer who uses a shovel; shovel-nose, a name having the shape of and fulfilling the functions of a shovel; also attrib.

† Shove-board. Obs. rare. [f. SHOVE (after next) + BOARD sb.] = SHOVEL-BOARD.

Shove-groat. Obs. exc. dial. [f. SHOVE v. + GROAT sb.] = SHOVEL-BOARD. (Cf. SLIDEGROAT, Slip-groat.]

Shovel, v.¹

† Shove-board. Obs. rare. [f. SHOVE (after next) + BOARD sb.] = SHOVEL-BOARD.

| SHOVE. | 759 | SHOVEL | SHOVEL. | 760 | SHOVEL-BOARD. |

...to shove the gangway on the vessel.

b. To force (a person, etc.) onwards by pushing. Also, to cause to fall over (a cliff, etc.) or out of (a place) by a push.

To throw down with a push.

2. intr. To push, to apply force against (an object) in order to displace or overthrow; †fig. to apply one's energies to (a task); also, to make an attack on, try to overthrow (a person), as in indirect passive).

3. spec. To propel (a boat or other vessel) either by pushing at the stern or with a pole worked from the inside. Also absol.

With out, off, or loose, from. (a) trans. To launch (a boat) by means of a steady push applied just at or near the shore. (b) To push one's vessel away from the shore. Also transf. of the boat.

4. Without the notion of difficulty. To push (something) so as to make it slide along a surface or in a groove or channel; also to move up or down by pushing.

a. To put surreptitiously or improperly: const. in, on, under, out of, etc.

or hastily) into a place or receptacle; also to thrust aside, away.

c. To push out of a position, away, by gradual encroachment.

d. To push off, to move along, move away.

† b. To bring into prominence. Also, to impel, urge forward in a course of action. Obs.

c. To move (anything) with a push.

† d. Of wind or water: to drive, propel, impel. Obs.

† e. To assist, help forward. Obs.

To urge (a horse) to a faster pace.

c. (Chiefly colloq.) To put or thrust (carelessly)

Shovel (ʃʌˑv'l), v.² Now rare. [app. a frequentative f. SHOVE v. Cf. SHUFFLE v.] to make movements with the feet; esp. to shuffle in dancing.

Shovel-board. Forms: 6 schovel-bord, schoveborde, 6(s)chovelarde, 6 (s)hovel-bord; 7 shovelborde, shovelboard, shovel-bord, shoveled, shovel-board, 8- shovel-board; 7 shoffle-, 8 shuffle-. [The earliest alteration of SHOVE-BOARD, q.v. an unexplained alteration of SHOVE-BOARD.]

1. A game in which a coin or other disk is driven by a blow with the hand along a highly polished board, floor, or table marked with transverse lines. The game is also played in a larger form on the open deck of a ship.

2. The board, floor, or table on which the game is played.

Shovel-groat. = SHOVE-GROAT, SHOVEL-BOARD.

Supplement, p. 3873; Corrigenda, p. 4092; Spurious words, p. 4093; Books quoted, p. 4094

Shovel-board, Shoveller, Shoveling, Shovel hat, Shovelful, Shoveller, Shove-net, Shover, Shovin, Shoving

Show, sb.¹

Show, v.

Show-board, Show-bread, Show-folk, Show-window, Showing, Shown

Show, sb.²

Show, v.

** Uses in which the being seen is an unintended or incidental result.

9. To show (a part of the body) to be seen.

a. To show one's head, face, etc.: to allow self to be seen, make an appearance.

b. To display (a countenance, looks, etc.) of to blush. To show tears†: to weep.

c. To show (a person) one's heels, a clean or fair pair of heels: to flee (from him). (Cf. F. montrer les talons.) Also reversed of a ship. Similarly †to show (a person) the back, etc.

d. Of a thing: To be or become visible.

11. Of plants, the seasons, etc.: To bring forth to view, display (fruit, flower, etc.).

e. Of animals or plants: To display (their colours, beauties, etc.).

f. Of a luminous body: To display (its light).

12. Of a thing: To be the means of displaying, revealing to sight, or allowing to be seen; to serve to exhibit or indicate.

13. To have visibly (some external feature or mark); to have (a part of himself) in a position exposed to view.

14. To enable a person to discover or identify (a visible object) by pointing to it, or by conducting him to a place where it can be seen. Also, to direct a person's observation to the various parts or features of (a country, town, building, or any complex object). † To show with one's finger†: to point to.

15. To guide (a person, etc.) along or in; to lead (him) through.

16. To exhibit or manifest (by outward signs).

17. To exhibit, allow to be seen (some inward quality, feeling, condition, etc.) by one's outward appearance; occas. said of the appearance. Also with clause. Also to show a sign or signs (of, that ...).

18. To display (a quality, condition, feeling, etc.) by one's action or behaviour; to give proof of possessing. Also to show a sign or signs (of).

† d. To set or offer (an example) in one's own person. Also of a thing.

19. To inflict (shame, a judgement).

† **21.** To put forth, exert (one's power, strength). Also of things. Const. on, against. Obs.

22. To exhibit, announce, declare, narrate, state, tell (a fact, story, news, etc.); to describe, give an account of. † Also with forth. Now arch.

† b. With that and clause, or absol. Obs.

23. To communicate, reveal, make known to one; to make evident or clear, explain, expound. In ME. to confess (one's sins). Also with forth, obs.

† b. With that or as and clause, or with complementary obj.: To reveal, make evident. Also said of a book, writing, deed, etc. Obs.

24. To decree, award, assign (to a person) in a legal or formal manner; to fix or appoint authoritatively; to declare, make an award (that). In later use Sc. Obs.

25. To prove, demonstrate (a fact, statement) by argument, reasoning, allegation of evidence or instances, experiment, etc.

b. With that clause (or as...).

26. To set forth, represent (a thing as being) by statement or argument.

27. To point out, reveal, make known; to make evident or clear, explain, expound. In ME. to confess (one's sins).

28. To prove, make out (a person or thing) to be (something). Also with accus. and inf.

† b. With complementary obj.: To prove, make out (a person or thing) to be (something). Also said of a book, writing, etc. Obs.

†36. Show-away a. (Cf. 32.) Given to display, ostentatious.

37. Show-down. In Card-playing, the act of laying down one's cards with their faces up; also, the revealing of hands.

29. To appear in public, make a display in public. In mod. use chiefly colloq. (cf. b.): To appear in company or society; to make an appearance in an assembly, among guests, etc.

30. With complement (adj. or †sb.): To look, seem, appear, arch.

b. To disappear or discredit by a showman; to exhibit as an impostor or an imposture; to expose (a person's faults, ignorance, misdeeds, etc.).

VI. intr. To be seen, be visible.

28. To be or become visible; to make an appearance. Said of persons and things.

b. With adv. or advb. phrase: To present an appearance (specified by the adv.); to make a (good, bad, etc.) show or display.

c. With adv. or advb. phrase: To have an appearance (specified by the adv.); to make a (good, bad, etc.) show or display.

27. Show up. a. In school language: To hand up (a scholar) for punishment.

b. To disappear or discredit by a showman.

c. To exhibit oneself for money.

d. Comm. Of a commodity: To appear or be prominent in the market.

30. With complement (adj. or †sb.): To look, seem, appear, arch.

b. With adv. or advb. phrase.

33. Show out. To become visible, emerge from obscurity or concealment. colloq.

34. Show out. a. ? To become visible, emerge from obscurity or concealment. colloq.

b. To become prominent, to catch the eye.

35. Show up. To appear conspicuously or in relief.

Showable (Jo·ăb'l), a. Also show-. [f. SHOW sb. + -ABLE.]

1. Demonstrative, able to prove. Obs. rare—¹.

2. Capable of being shown or exhibited.

Showance (Jo·ɑns). rare. [f. SHOW sb. + -ANCE.]

1. Demonstration, proof. Obs.

2. Appearance, look. Obs.

Show-bread. [SHOW sb. 33.] A Box in which objects of curiosity are exhibited; esp. a box containing a peep-show.

Showd, Showed, obs. forms of SHOE, SHOVE.

Showel(l, obs. forms of SHOVEL.

Shower (Jau·ər), sb.¹ Forms: 1 scúr, scéor, seryr, 3 scur, shur, 3–5 schour, 3–7 showre, 4 shour, 4–6 schour, 4–7 schowre, 5 showr, 5–6 schowyr, showyr, 6 schouer, schowre, 6–7 showre, (OE. scúr str. masc. (also once scíron wk. f.) (mod.G. schauer) = OFris. skúr fem. (WFris. schoer, NFris. schúr), MDu. scuer (mod.Du. schoer), OHG. scúr (MHG. schûr, mod.G. schauer), ON. skúr fem. (Sw. skur, Da. skur), Goth. skúra fem. storm.] 1. A fall of rain, of short duration and (usually) comparatively light. Also, a similar fall of sleet or hail, rarely of snow. See also HAIL-shower, RAIN-shower, SNOW-shower.

b. In various dialects the word may be applied to a continuous fall of rain lasting for hours.

c. transf. A copious fall or flight of solid objects, esp. of missiles. Also of blows.

2. With a qualification of kind, a hail, rain-, etc., shower.

3. fig. A copious or liberal supply bestowed.

b. attrib. and Comb.: shower-cloak, -like, -producing, -proof, †-raised, -shedding, †-swelled adjs.; shower-bouquet, 'a large bouquet from which many small bouquets depend by ribbons of various lengths' (Webster 1911); shower-cloud, a cumulo-nimbus cloud (see quot. 1910).

c. In mod use: A copious downfall of anything coming or supposed to come from the clouds or sky; in recent use often of meteors.

Shower (Jau·ər), sb.² 1. odsewere, (edware) ; 2 seawere, (seawere), 3–4 schewere, 4–5 schewer, 4 schowere, 5 showere, agent noun from SHOW v.; cf. OHG. scauwári (MHG. schouwære, mod.G. schauer) looker, spectator, watchman, etc. In later times formed from SHOW v.+-ER.]

1. One who looks out, observes, or inspects; a watchman.

†2. A mirror. Obs.

3. spec. One who shows, points out, or exhibits.

SHOWER-BATH. — SHOWING. (col. 769–770)

Showerful, *a.* [f. Shower *v.* + -ful.] Abounding in showers.

Showeriness (ʃauˈə·rɪnes). [f. Showery + -ness.] The state of being showery.

Showering (ʃauˈə·rɪŋ), *vbl. sb.* [f. Shower *v.* + -ing¹.] The action of Shower *v.*; also *concr.*, that which is showered.

Showerless, *a.* [f. Shower *sb.* + -less.] Without a shower.

Showery (ʃauˈə·rɪ), *a.* [f. Shower *sb.* + -y.]

Show-glass. [Show *sb.*¹] A glass case for exhibiting valuable or delicate goods.

Show-house. [Show *sb.*¹]

Showily (ʃouˈɪlɪ), *adv.* [f. Showy + -ly².] In a showy manner; with display.

Showiness (ʃouˈɪnes). [f. Showy + -ness.] The quality of being showy.

Showing (ʃouˈɪŋ), *vbl. sb.* [f. Show *v.* + -ing¹.]

Show-ish, *a.* [f. Show *sb.*¹ + -ish¹.] = Showy *a.*

Showl, obs. form of Shoal, Shovel.

Showler. [Of obscure origin.] A local name for the Dace.

Showll, obs. form of Shovel.

Showman (ʃouˈmæn). [Show *sb.*¹]

Show-place. [Cf. *G.* schauplatz = theatre.] A place for public shows or spectacles; a theatre.

Showrde, obs. form of Sword.

Showroom (ʃouˈrūm). [Show *sb.*¹] A room used for the display of goods or merchandise.

Showy (ʃouˈɪ), *a.* [f. Show *sb.*¹ + -y.] Characterized by show.

Shoya, shoyhoy (foi,hoi). [Imitative of the cry used for scaring birds.]

Shoya, obs. form of Soy.

SHRAPE. — SHREW. (col. 771–772)

Shrape, *v.* Obs. Forms: 1 scrapian, 3 schrape, 4–6 shrape. [OE. scrapian; see Scrape *sb.* and *v.*] To scratch, scrape (*lit.* and *fig.*).

Shrapnel (ʃræ·pnel), *sb.* Also *erron.* -ell. [f. the name of Gen. H. Shrapnel, who invented this shell during the Peninsular War.]

Shrave, obs. variant of Shroff.

Shravey. *local.* (See quots.) Hence **shrav(e)y** *a.*

Shrav'ial. *local.* Small refuse wood or faggots.

Shread, obs. form of Shred.

Shread-head. *local.* (Cf. next.)

Shreadings, *sb. pl.* Building. ? Obs.

Shreak, obs. variant of Shriek.

Shream, *v.* Obs. rare.

Shrave, *v.* Obs. rare.

Shred (ʃred), *sb.* Forms: 1 screáde, scréade, 3 shrede, 4 schrede, 5 shrede, 6–7 shrede, *pa. pple.* shred. [OE. scréade str. fem.]

Shred (ʃred), *v.* Forms: 1 screádian, scréadian, 4–6 shrede. [OE. scréadian; see Shred *sb.*]

Shredder (ʃre·dər).

Shredding (ʃre·dɪŋ), *vbl. sb.* [f. Shred *v.* + -ing¹.]

Shredding (ʃre·dɪŋ), *ppl. a.*

Shred (ʃred), *ppl. a.* [pa. pple. of prec.]

Shreddings, variant of Shreadings.

Shreddy (ʃre·dɪ), *a.* [f. Shred *sb.* + -y¹.] Consisting of or resembling shreds; hanging in shreds, ragged.

Shredded (ʃre·ded), *ppl. a.* [-less.]

Shredless (ʃre·dles), *a.* [-less.]

Shredlet (ʃre·dlet). [-let.] A small shred.

Shredling. Obs. rare⁻¹. In 7 shread-ling. A minute portion.

Shrew (ʃrū), *sb.*¹ Also shrewe. Forms: 1 screáwa, 6 shrewe, etc. [OE. screáwa, screawa.]

Shrewd (ʃrūd), *a.* [f. Shrew *sb.*¹]

Shrewdly (ʃrū·dlɪ), *adv.*

Shrewdness (ʃrū·dnes). [-ness.]

Shrewe, obs. form of Shrew.

Shrew, obs. form of Shrewd.

Shrew, *v.* [f. Shrew *sb.*¹]

Shrew, variant of Shrow *v.* Obs.

Shrewdie, obs. form of Shroud.

SHREW

be some mixture of the (†synonymous OE. *scírfmús*); cf. the dial. *sarrow* = SERVE 9.

The absence of evidence for the word between the OE. period and the 16th century is remarkable; its place may have been supplied locally in M.E. by *erdshrew* (q.v. earth-shrew), though this, with its apparent meaning *harvestman, harvest-louse, mouse*, summary (with prefixed *V 3*), is not recorded before the 13th century.]

1. Any of the small insectivorous mammals, belonging to the genus *Sorex* or the family *Soricidæ*, much resembling mice but having a long sharp snout: a SHREW-MOUSE.

...

Shrew (ʃrū), *sb*[2]... **Forms:** α. 4-5 **schrewe**, **shrewe**, 5 **schrew**, 4-6 **shrewe**, **shrewe**, 4-6 **shrewen**, 6 **shrew**, 6 **shrewe**, 7 **shrew**...

2. *attrib.* and *Comb.*, as *shrew-bitten, -like*; *shrew-afflicted* = *shrew-struck*; *shrew-ash* (see quot. 1776); *shrew-mole*, a mole of either of the genera *Scalops* and *Scapanus*; *shrew-run, para-lysed* (as supposed) as the result of being overrun by a shrew-mouse; so *† shrew-running* (see quot.); *shrew-stroke*, the fact or condition of being shrew-struck; *shrew-struck* = *shrew-run*.

SHREWDHEAD. 775 SHREWLY.
SHREWMOUSE. 776 SHRIEVALTY.

Shrewdish (ʃrū´diʃ), *a.* [f. SHREWD + -ISH.] Somewhat or fairly shrewd.

Shrewdly (ʃrū´dlī), *adv.* **Forms:** *see* SHREWD *a.*; also 6 *scrodely*, 6-7 *shrodly*. [f. SHREWD *a.* + -LY[2].]

†1. Evilly, ill; wickedly; maliciously. *Obs.*

Shrewd|ness (ʃrū´dnes). **Forms:** *see* SHREWD *a.*; also 5 *schredenes*. [f. SHREWD *a.* + -NESS.]

Shrew|dom. *Obs.* [f. SHREW *sb*[2] + -DOM.] Wickedness.

†Shrewdship. *Obs.* [f. SHREWD *a.* + -SHIP.]

†Shrewhead. *Obs.* *rare.* [f. SHREW *sb*[2] + -HEAD.]

Shrewing. *vbl. sb.* [f. SHREW *v.*] In 4 *shrewenge.*

Shrew|ing, *ppl. a.* [f. SHREW *v.*] Scolding.

Shrewmouse (ʃrū´maus), *sb.* form of SHREW.

Shriche, variant of SHRITCH.

Shride, *obs. form* of SHRED.

Shride, *v.*[1] *Obs.* **Forms:** 1 *scrýdan, scrídan*, 2-3 *scruden*, 3 *shriden*, 3-4 *schride*, 3-5 *shrid(e, 4-5 *shride*, *shryde*; 3rd *sing. pres. ind.* (contracted) *scrýt*, 1 *scred*, 3 *shrut*. [OE. *scrýdan* = ...]

1. *trans.* To clothe, provide with clothes.

Shride, *v.*[2] *Obs.* Also 4-5 *schride*. *dial.* [var. of SHRED *v.*]

Shrideled...

Shrieking (ʃrī´kiŋ), *vbl. sb.* [f. SHRIEK *v.* + -ING[1].] The action of the verb SHRIEK.

Shrieking, *ppl. a.* [f. SHRIEK *v.* + -ING[1].]

Shrieky, *a.* *colloq.* [f. SHRIEK *sb.* + -Y[1].]

Shrieval (ʃrī´val), *a.* Of or belonging to a sheriff.

Shrievalty: see SHERIFF, SHRIVE.

Shrife, obs. form of SHRIVE v.

Shrift (ʃrift), sb. Now arch. or Hist. Forms: [...] [OE. scrift sb., corresp. to OFris. skrift, and f., MHG., G. schrift, etc.]

1. Penance imposed by the priest after confession; chiefly in phr. as to take, win shrift; to do shrift; to give shrift; [...]

2. The imposition of penance implying absolution, shrift came to be apprehended in certain contexts as = absolution. [...]

3. A confession.

4. To go, come to shrift: to resort to confession, penance. Also = to seek to shrift. [...]

5. Confession to a priest; auricular confession; also, the sacrament of penance. [...]

Shrift, v. rare. [f. prec.] trans. = to shrive.

Shrift-father, = shriver. Also 4 schryvefader, 5 schryffader. [f. SHRIFT sb. + FATHER sb.: cf. ON. skriptafaðer.]

†Shriftness. Obs. rare. [...] Confession.

family Laniidæ, characterized by a strong hooked and toothed beak; the majority of them are insectivorous, but several species, as the (Great or European) Grey Shrike, Lanius excubitor, prey upon mice and small birds; = BUTCHER-BIRD.

Shrike, v. Obs. exc. dial. Also 4-5 schrike, schryke, 4-6 shryke. [Parallel to SCRIKE v. (see SCK-); later representing an OE. *scrīcan (cf. SHRIKE sb.²) = Norw. skrīka, Da. skrige.] SHRIEK v. [...]

Shrike-fisher, [...]

†Shriftness, [...]

Shrill (ʃril), a. Forms: [...] [ME. shrille, related to LG. schrell of sharp tone or taste, G. schrill (late 18th cent.).] A. adj.

Shrill (ʃril), v. [f. SHRILL a.] 1. intr. Of a voice, cry: To sound shrilly. [...]

Shrilly (ʃri·li), a. Chiefly poet. [-Y.] Shrill. [...]

Shrim (ʃrim), v. Now dial. [OE. scrimman] 1. trans. To shrink, contract.

Shrimp (ʃrimp). Forms: 4-5 schrympe, 4-6 schrimpe, 5-7 shrimpe, 5 schrymp, 6 scrympe, 6 shrympe, shrymppe, 6 schrimp, 7- shrimp. [Prob. cogn. w. MHG. (MG.) schrimpen, schrimpf.] sb.

Shrimp, v. [f. SHRIMP sb.] 1. Catching shrimps. **Shrimping**, vbl. sb. [...]

Shrimpish (ʃri·mpiʃ), a. [f. SHRIMP + -ISH.] Diminutive, puny, insignificant.

Shrimplet. [-LET.] A little shrimp.

Shrimpy (ʃri·mpi), a. [f. SHRIMP + -Y.] Abounding in shrimps. [...]

Shrinal (ʃrai·nəl), a. [f. next + -AL.] Containing or forming a shrine.

Shrine (ʃrain), sb. Forms: 1-2 scrin, scryn, 3 scrine, 3-6 schrine, 4-7 shryne, 5-6 schryne, 4-7 shryne, 4-6 shrine. [...]

Shrine (ʃrain), v. [f. prec.] 1. trans. To enclose (relics) in a shrine; to enshrine. [...]

Shrined (ʃraind), ppl. a. [f. SHRINE v. + -ED².] 1. Enshrined. [...]

Shrineless, a. [-LESS.] Having no shrine.

Shri·n-let, [f. SHRINE + -LET.] A little shrine.

Shrining, vbl. and vbl. sb. [f. SHRINE v.]

Shrink (ʃriŋk), sb. [f. SHRINK v.] An act of shrinking, shivering, cowering, etc.; a shrug. [...]

Shrink (ʃriŋk), v. Pa. t. shrank (ʃræŋk), pa. pple. shrunk (ʃrʌŋk). Forms: 3 schrinke, 4-6 schrynke, 4-6 shrynke, 4 schrenke, 4-6 schrinke, 6-7 shrinke, 6- shrink. [OE. scrincan.] [...]

I. Intransitive senses. 1. To wither or shrivel through withdrawal of vital fluid or failure of strength. Obs. [...]

2. To cover with rich ornament. Obs. [...]

II. 4. To become reduced in size, volume, or extent, esp. to contract through heat, cold, or moisture. [...]

Shroud (ʃraud), sb.[1] Forms: 1 scrūd...

Shroud (ʃraud), sb.[2]

Shroud, sb.[3] Now dial.

Shroud, v.[1]

Shroud, v.[2]

Shroud (ʃraud), v.[3]

Shroudage (ʃraudedʒ), poet.

Shrouded, ppl. a.

Shroudedly, adv.

Shroudless, a.

Shrouding, vbl. sb.[1]

Shrouding, vbl. sb.[2]

Shrouding, vbl. sb.[3]

Shrouding, ppl. a.

Shroud- plate.

Shrouds.

Shroud-laid, ppl. a.

Shroud-line.

† Shrove sb. Obs. exc. dial.

Shrove-cake.

Shrove-penny.

† Shrove Sunday. Obs.

† Shrove Thursday. Obs.

Shrove Tuesday.

Shrove-tide.

† Shrove Monday. Obs.

Shroving, vbl. sb. Obs. exc. dial.

Shrowardly.

Shrowardly, adv.

Shrowd(e, obs. forms of SHREWD, SHROUD.

Shrub (ʃrʌb), sb.[1]

Shrub (ʃrʌb), sb.[2]

Shrub, sb.[3]

Shrub, v.[1]

Shrub, v.[2]

Shrubbed (ʃrʌbd), a.

Shrubbery (ʃrʌbəri), sb.

Shrubbiness.

Shrub-bish, a.

Shrubble.

Shrubby, a.

Shrubling.

Shrubbing, vbl. sb.

Shrubbed.

Shrubless.

† Shruff[1] Obs. exc. dial.

† Shruff[2] Obs.

Shrug (ʃrʌg), v.

Shrug, sb.

Shrugging, vbl. sb.

Shrugging, ppl. a.

Shruggish, a.

Shthabbah.

Shub, Shubo.

Shuck (ʃʌk), sb.

Shruff.

Shrunk (ʃrʌŋk), ppl. a.

Shrunken (ʃrʌŋkn), ppl. a.

Shuck: see SHEUGH, SUCH.

Shuck, *sb.* [app. by-form of CHUCKLE *v.*] *intr.* To chuckle; also, to knock.

Shuck, *sb.* form of SHUCK *sb.*[1]

Shuck, *sb.*[1] [cogn. form of SHOCK.]

1. A husk, pod, or shell; *esp.* the outer covering or strippings of Indian corn, chestnuts, hickory nuts, etc. See CORN-SHUCK.

2. *pl.* As of little or no value.

3. As a type of something valueless.

4. *pl.* in negative phr., *esp.* in *not worth shucks* = good for nothing.

Shudder, *sb.* [f. SHUDDER *v.*]

1. An act of shuddering; a convulsive tremor of the body occasioned by fear, repugnance, or chill.

2. A tremulous or vibratory movement; a quiver.

Shudder, *v.* Forms: 4 shodder, 5 shodur, shuder, shoter, shadyr [?], 5-6 shoder, 6-shudder [ME. *shuddren*, *schuddren*.]

1. *intr.* To have a convulsive tremor of the body caused by fear, abhorrence, or cold; hence, to tremble with horror or dread.

2. Charact. of or accompanied by shuddering.

3. To cause, produce, or cause by shuddering.

Shudderingly, *adv.* In a shuddering manner; with a shudder or shudders.

Shuddersome, *a.* [f. SHUDDER + -SOME.] Causing a shudder.

Shuddery, *a.* [f. SHUDDER + -Y.] Characterized by or causing shuddering; 'creepy'.

Shue, *shoo*, *v. Sc.* [See SHOVE *v.*, etym. note.]

Shuff, *a., dial.* [see Eng. Dial. Dict.] [dial. var. of SHY *a.*] Shy.

Shuff, obs. form of SHOVE *v.*

Shuffle (ʃʌf'l), *v.* [f. SHUFFLE *v.*]

1. A shifting from one place to another; an interchange of positions. *Obs.*

2. *trans.* To cause to shudder. *nonce-use.*

3. *intr.* To move tremulously, vibrate, quiver.

4. *trans.* To shake off with a shudder.

5. *intr.* and *trans.* To chuck.

Shuffle (ʃʌf'l), *sb.* [f. SHUFFLE *v.*]

1. A shifting from one place to another; an interchange of positions. *Obs.*

2. To manipulate (the cards in a pack) so as to change their relative position.

3. A trickly exchange or alternation (of arguments, expedients, etc.).

4. Movement of the feet along the ground without lifting them; a gait characterized by such movement.

5. An evasive trick, evasion, subterfuge.

Shuffle (ʃʌf'l), *v.* Forms: 6 shoofle, shooffell, shuffli, -ull, whofle, 6-7 shuffel, 6-8 shuttle, 7 shofle, 6-shuffle.

1. *trans.* To produce or put in (a card or certain succession of cards) in shuffling.

2. *trans.* To move the feet along the ground without lifting them, so as to make a scraping noise.

3. *intr.* To move the feet along the ground without lifting them.

Shuffle (ʃʌf'l), *sb.*

1. One who mixes up or jumbles. *Obs.*

2. One who acts in a shifty or evasive manner; a slippery, shifty person.

Shuffle-board: see SHOVEL-BOARD.

Shuffled, *ppl. a.* [-ED.]

Shuffler (ʃʌf'lər), *sb.* [SHUFFLE *v.* + -ER.]

1. One who mixes up or jumbles.

2. One who acts in a shifty or evasive manner; a slippery, shifty person.

Shufflingly, *adv.* [prec. + -LY.] With a shuffling gait; in a shuffling or evasive manner.

Shuffly (ʃʌf'li), *a.* [f. SHUFFLE *v.* + -Y.] Of bricks: Friable from being badly burnt.

Shuffling, *vbl. sb.* [SHUFFLE *v.* + -ING.]

1. The action of moving the feet along the ground without lifting them; the dragging and scraping of the feet.

2. The re-arrangement of the cards in a pack.

3. The shifting of a thing from or from one place to another; change of the position (of things) with reference to each other; mixing or jumbling together.

Shug, variant of SHOG *v.*

Shuggie-shue, *sb. Sc., Ir.* and *north.* Also ? 9 shoggie-shou, -show, 9 shuggy shou, -shew, -show, -shaw. [Cf. SHOG and SHUE *sb.*] The pastime of swinging; a swing (esp. at a fair), hence *jocularly* the gallows.

Shuggle, Shugh, *var.* ff. SHOGGLE, SHEOGH.

Shug, *sb. Sc.* form of SHOG *sb.*

Shulwar (ʃʊlwɑːr). Also shulwaur. [Pers. شلوار *shalwār*. Cf. SHERRYVALLY, SHERWAL] *pl.* Persian loose trousers.

Shumac, Shuman: see SUMACH, SHAMAN.

Shumbrawul: see SHEMSHEER.

Shumefour, variant of SHAMEFACE.

Shun (ʃʌn), *sb.* [f. SHUN *v.*]

Shun (ʃʌn), *v.* Forms: 1 scunian, 3 scunien, ssonien, sonen, sunen, 3-4 shonien, shunien, 3-5 schon(e, 4-5 shonen, schon(e, 4-6 shonne, schone, shone, schonne, 4-7 schune, shonne, 5 schunne, shone, 6-7 shoon, shun, 6-shun.

1. *trans.* To avoid; to keep away from, keep clear of, eschew.

2. To seek safety by concealment or flight from (an enemy, his pursuit, etc.).

3. To avoid (a person, his company, etc.).

Shunning, *vbl. sb.* [SHUN *v.* + -ING.] The action of avoiding.

Shunning, *ppl. a.* [-ING.] That avoids.

Shunt (ʃʌnt), *sb.*[1] [f. SHUNT *v.*]

Shunt (ʃʌnt), *v.* Forms: 4 schunt, 5 schont, 6-shunt.

1. *trans.* To shift from one position to another.

SHUNT.

798 SHUT. SHUT. 794 SHUT.

Shunt (ʃɒnt), v. Forms: 5 shunt, 4 shont, 5 ʒohund, shount, 5– shunt. Pa. t. 4 schunt, 5 shount, schounte; schontid, 6– shunted. [Of obscure origin.

Shunted, ppl. a. [f. SHUNT v. and sb. + -ED.]

Shunter (ʃɒntə). [f. SHUNT v. + -ER¹.]

Shunting (ʃɒntiŋ), vbl. sb. [f. SHUNT v. + -ING¹.]

Shurrel, **Shurral**, var. ff. SHARN, SHIRREL.

Shurn, v. Obs. rare. In 2 schurn, 5 schorne, 6 shurne, 7 sherne. [Altered form of SCURN v.] trans.

Shurry, v. Obs. [f. SCURRY? v.—OE. scorf.]

Shut (ʃɒt), sb. Forms: a. 7–8 shutt, 8 shoot, 7– shut; β. 5 schott. [f. SHUT v.]

Shut (ʃɒt), v. Pa. t. and pa. pple. shut. Forms: Pres. stem a. 1 scyttan, 3–4 schutte, 4–5 schytte, 4–6 shutte, 5–6 shytte, shot, 7 shutt, 6– shut. β. 4 sette, 5 (3 sing. pres. ind. 4 saet, imper. 3 scete, 4 sette), 4–5 schette, 4–5 schette, (5 scheet), 5–6, 9 dial. shet; 4 –scytte, 5–6 shett, 5 shet, 8 shet. γ. 4 schitte, 4 shytte, 4 (3 sing.) schiteth, 5 dial. shit.

Shut, ppl. a.

Shut-down. [f. SHUT v. 13.] A shutting down; the closing of a factory, etc. Also attrib.

Shut-off. [Cf. SHUT v. 16.] Something which shuts off.

Shut-purse. Obs. rare⁻¹. In 4 sette, purse. [f. SHUT v. + PURSE sb.] The shutter of the purse; one who is close-fisted.

Shuttable, a. rare⁻¹. [f. SHUT v. + -ABLE.] Capable of being shut.

Shut-to. [f. SHUT v. (sense 11) + -ABLE.] Riddance.

Shutter (ʃɒtə). sb. [f. SHUT v. + -ER¹.]

SHUTTER.

negative of *secure*. **1890** *Bailey Photogr. Ann.* II. Advt. 2, 9 Leica, Plate-changing and 'shutter-setting is effected by simply drawing out and pushing back the rod shown in Lect. The 'shutter-speed is, of course, the 'shutter speed was slower in comparison with the moving wheels of a hgaes repeated 'shutter work ... the best plan is to use a medium quantity of alkali.

Shutter (ʃʌ'təɹ), *v.* [f. SHUTTER *sb.*]

1. *trans.* To close with a shutter. Also *with advb. adv.* **1826** R. HALL in Lockhart *Scott* (1837) VIII. 361 I found the windows shuttered up. **1845** LYTTON *Martins of Cro'M.* xxii. 309 The doors were closed, the windows shuttered. **1863** DICKENS *Uncomm. Trav.* xii. Here in Garraway's, bolted and shuttered and barred. **1890** HALL CAINE *Bondman* (1906) 5, 1 am who had seized and shuttered her lantern, coming late.

b. *transf. and fig.*

1855 SMEDLEY *H. Coverdale* xxxix. The grinning opening and shutting jaws.

2. *refl.* (with advb. complement). To close oneself in, shut oneself up.

1855 STEVENSON *Inland Voy.* 60 A workman or a pedlar cannot shutter himself off from his few comfortable neighbours. **1880** *Athenæum* 14 Aug. 207 The farmers...would shutter themselves in and drink strong beer and gin for days and days on end.

Shuttered (ʃʌ'təd), *ppl. a.* [f. SHUTTER *v.* and *sb.* + -ED.] Closed with shutters; provided with shutters.

1890 TALFOURD *Facadius Rambler* I. 133 Green-shuttered white 'Pensions'. **1885** E. J. STEVENSON *Dynamiter* ii. 9 Shop after shop displayed its shuttered front. **1895** P. H. JOHNSTON in *Arkansaic Trial.* 68 It must have had its grated and shuttered opening.

Shuttering, *vbl. sb.* [f. SHUTTER *v.* + -ING.] **1.** The action of the vb. SHUTTER *sb.* Material for making shutters.

1885 W. COBY *Lett. & Synch.* (1897) 213 This is a detestable practice, shuttering; I rebel against it. **1892** *Manch. Spcif. Detail* 321 Movable sheet-iron shuttering.

b. *concr.* Shutters collectively (= SHUTTER *sb.* + -LESS.) Without a shutter.

1884 LYTTON *F. Clifford* i. A high, narrow, shutterless casement. **1885** R. BUCHANAN *Annan Water's,* The wind ...rattled the shutterless windows.

Shutterwise, *adv.* [f. SHUTTER *sb.* + -WISE.] After the manner of or like a shutter.

1880 Mrs. R. O'REILLY *Sussex Stor.* I. 315 He swept the drawers out and his paraphernalia off the board, and fastened it shutterwise.

Shutting (ʃʌ'tɪŋ), *vbl. sb.* [f. SHUT *v.* + -ING.]

1. In *trans.* senses of the verb: closing, fastening up, drawing together, etc.

c1386 CHAUCER *Rom. Rose* 1398 For ther is noon so litel thing So hid, no closed with shutting. That it ne is seen. **1440** *Promp. Parv.* 447/2 Schetynge, or lokynge wythe lokkys, *sera* etc. **1382** WYCLIF *Marriage* 126 The shuttings of windows. **1895** O. H. *HIST. Cardinals's* III. 74 The small shutting of their mouths. **a1774** Jos. J. STRANGE *Rep.* (1782) I. 653 The day of the shutting of the Exchequer. **1779** R. WATSON *Philip. Sph.* 36 For schetyng of the...bell clasper viij d. **1441** *Naval Acc. Hen. VII* (1896) 130 Shutyng & Amesyng of v boltes. **1583** *Leic. Corr. Churchw. Acc.* (1889) 71 For the ssytynge of the dore boltes. **1779** G. H. *Hist. Cardinal's* 11. 70 Shutting and amesyng of the...

2. Welding, splicing.

1490 in *Archæol. Jrnl.* XVI. 149 For schetyng of the...bell clasper viij d. **1393** Shutyng & Amesyng of v boltes. **1599** *Churchw. Acc. Canterbury* For the setyng of the xij belles. **1571** *Stranger Aeth* 130 The schetyng of iiij belles. **a1744** Jos. J. STRANGE *Rep.* (1782) 1. 653 L. Street. The joining or welding one piece of iron to another.

3. Something which closes fast, a bar, shutter. Usually *pl.* Also, a junction, a place where two things come together.

c1440 *Promp. Parv.* 447/2 Schetynge, or schetynge, *corruge*, *clausura*. **1450-80** tr. *Secreta Secret.* xxxv. 12 Than toste with thyn heed, for the inclosed shutting of windows. **1895** G. H. *Hist. Cardinal's* II. 70 You must...fasten opening glasses to the shutting of the joynts. **a1693** J. TRAPP *Comm. Wks.* (1865) III. 74 The Bar or Shutting (of the door of a bee-hive) is to be made four square, of some heavy Matter, as Lead.

3. In intransitive senses of the verb: The close of a day, evening, etc. ; nightfall.

1596 SPENSER *Faeries, Ann.* 1. v. (1840) 8 In the night, or in the shutting of the evening. *1705 Flisk. Sir J. Morgan's Papyr.* 13 The Major-General blamed the Excellency, that he would give orders to them...to keep themselves in readiness. At the shutting of the Night he would fall on.

4. In *comb.* with various advs.

c1440 *Promp. Parv.* 445/2 Schettynge in, *inclusio*... Schettynge owte, *exclusio*. **1575** LANEHAM *Let. 2.* 86 In the shuttings vppe and down of the Sun, shutting in of nights, belong to Zephyr. **1640** Ld. F. VANE *God in Mount* 93 A little before shutting in of day-light. **1602** De Fox *Pilgrim* (Ridg.) 94. I mention'd shutting of houses vp. **1798** in Nicolas *Disp. Nelson* (1846) VII. 36 civ, The thickness of the smoke at the shutting in of the evening. **1836** TOOKES O. *Found* xxvii. The ship was not closed, although it was the usual hour of shutting up. **1793** SCRIVENER *Lect. Ordi.* Text. 14 The deliberate shutting out of a large...portion of mankind. **1798** *Daily News* 3 Mar. 1/4 The shutting down of the mines in America. **1897** *Allbutt's Syst. Med.* VI. 749 The sudden shutting off of the blood-supply to a limited area of the brain.

b. *Specific* uses: shutting off (see quot.); shutting up (*a*) see quot. 1852 ; (*b*) welding ; (*c*)

shutting-up time: the hour for closing the shop, etc. ; shutting together = *shutting up (b.)*

1891 J. F. SMITH *Watch & Clothm.* 240 'Shutting Off. A term used to describe the operation of throwing the whole wing wheels of a hgaes watch) out of action. **1890** G. W. JOHNSON *Cottage Gard. Dict.* 84 'Shutting-up is closing the lights of frames, pits, greenhouses, etc., when they have been opened for the admission of air. **1885** CANON *Smiley's Forge* 43 Joining two pieces of bar or rod together which the smith usually denominates 'shutting up' or 'shutting together'. **1894** *R. BOLDREWOOD' Robbery under Arms* xxv, It was late. All the shutting-up shops in the street were closed.

Shutting, *ppl. a.* [-210 ²] That shuts.

1393 *Archæologia* XXXV. 431 Pluggis...half-drops bathe each shutting bell [of a flower]. **1890** T. F. LYNCH *Templ. Trixal* v. 67 A shutting gate...we hear. **1891** ELWORTHY *Horns of Honour* ii. 143 The grinning opening and shutting jaws.

Shuttle (ʃʌ'tᵊl), *sb.* ¹ Forms : 1 *scútel,* 4-9 (now *dial.*) *shittle,* 5 *shotil, shetil, schytle,* 4-9 *scuttle, schut, s* (*schutytle,* 6 *sheytl, shuytl(l), shyttle), shittell, shottle, 7 shuttle, shuttel,6 shuttle.* CT. ON. *skutull* harpoon ; also Sw., Da. *skyttel* (of obscure history) and Du. *skytte,* Norw. *skyt, skjot* = sense 2 below.]

1. OE. A dart, missile, arrow. *Obs.*

1777 *Jacusum,* scitotil. **c1000** *Ags. Ps. Thorpe* lxiii. 7 Syndon hyre wit scytelum cilda agiwen cadicar.

2. An instrument used in weaving for passing the thread of the weft to and fro from one edge of the cloth to the other between the threads of the warp. *Fly shuttle* (see FLY *sb.* ² 8).

The normal form of the shuttle resembles that of a boat, whence its name in various langs. (L. *navicula, F. navette,* G. *weberschiff*). Along the middle is an axis or 'spindle', on which revolves the 'quill' or 'bobbin', a cylinder carrying the thread of the weft.

1380 in Dugdale *Monasticon* (1817) II. 163a From yr wyllowe coppes eft. Item pro iiij skittles pro eodem opere iij vjd. **c1440** *York Memorandum Bk.* (Surtees) I. 83 Cum instrumenta dicti artificii vocata shott...shuttles. **1440** *Promp. Parv.* 447/2 Schuytyle (or *shytylle, navicula, panus*). **1420** STANBRIDGE *Vocabula* (W. de W.) C j b, *Pecten,* the shuttyll. **1572** LEVINS *Manip.* 179/37 A weavers shittell. **1589** WITHER *A BC for Laymen* 131 The sliding to and fro of the shettle in weaving. **1683** G. R. PORTER *Silk Manuf.* 211 The shuttle is formed from a piece of boxwood. **1796** F. [G. FOWLER] *Fairm. Treaty* § 4 *Enclosure* 24 John's loom and shuttle could be heard.

b. *fig.* and in imitative use.

1599 MARS. *Mercy* IV. v. 24, Nak't nor Gollah with a Weauers beame, because I know alas, life is a Shuttle, *1340* YONGE *Alt.* xxv. 89. How swift the shuttle flies, that weaves thy shroud. **1844** *Tennyson's Life, Young Amer.* Wks. (Bohn) II. 35g The locomotive and the steamboat like enormous shuttles shoot every day across the thousand threads of national looms. **1895** KIPLING *Seven Seas* § Swift shuttles of an Empire's loom that weave us, main to main. **1896** A. AUSTIN *England & Darling* ii. iv. When war's loud shuttle shall have woven peace, etc.

b. *fig.* A thread-carrying device in the form of a weaver's shuttle, used for knotting, tatting and embroidery.

1811 Mrs. DELANY *Lett.* 4 Jan. Ser. 11 (1861) I. 37 Mrs. Jeffreys has bought me a very cheap shuttle. **1771** RAVAUD *Let. to Mrs. Delany* 8 Nov. 1772, I want to know if the inclosed knotting is what you would have it...In merit...is entirely owing to the instrument with which it is fabricated, the manageable shuttle of singular service. **1882** CAULFEILD & SAWARD *Dict. Needlework* 476 [Recent improvements in Tatting.] The use of a second thread, or Shuttle...enables straight lines and scallops to be worked, as well as the original ovals.

b. A reciprocating thread-holder in a sewing-machine, which carries the lower thread through the loop of the upper one to make a lock-stitch.

1860 tr. *Abridgm. Specif. Patents, Sewing* (1871) 76 The application of a muffle, in combination with a needle. **1860** *Chrs Dict. Arts* III. 647 A small shuttle, which has a horizontal motion beneath the cloth, how caused to pass through this loop, carrying with it its own thread. **1875** *Knight Dict. Mech.* 2116/2 The [Singer sewing-] machine makes a lock-stitch by means of a straight eye-pointed needle and a longitudinally reciprocating shuttle.

b. In a telephone (see quot.).

1879 PRESCOTT *Sp. Telephone* 388 One of its coils is connected to a V-shaped piece of metal, termed the shuttle, which, in its normal position, rests with one end against an adjustable screw.

4. A carved type-bar (in some typewriters) guided into position by a race. **1901** in Frone.

4. A shuttlecock. Also the game. *Obs. exc. in Badminton.*

c1440 *Promp. Parv.* 447/1 Schytle, chyldyn game, *sagittella.* **1398** H. SWIFT *Descr.* (1801) 252 Or into a shittle, which filtereth from the hand of a child. **1895** *Officials Loan Barbanidos* 11.
— M. RAIDEN 1 C. *Obs. Game.* rare⁻¹.

Perh. only a mistranslation of L. *radius,* one sense of which is 'weaver's shuttle'.

1560 *Cooemur' Tannu Ling. Trilling.* 48 One arm loure which is mayd to 'shuttle'.

2. ? A shutter or a partition.

6. † a. A trochoid shell (see quot. 1750). *Obs.*

b. In full *weaver's shuttle,* a shuttle-shell, esp.

1881 P. J. SMITH *Watch & Clothm.* 240 'Shuttling Off. A term used to describe the operation of throwing the whole wing wheels of a hgaes watch) out of action. **1799** BURROW *Elem. Conch.* 109 Bulla Volva. **1815** SOWERBY *Geneva* Shell. **1884** CANON *Smiley's Forge* 43 Joining two pieces of bar or rod together which the smith usually denominates 'shutting up' or 'shutting together'.

† a. The instrument or the mechanism carrying the thread of the weft.

8. A *shuttle-tile* (see 9 b.)

8. *attrib.* and *Comb.* Obvious combs. (senses 2 and 3) as *shuttle-driver, -maker, -quill* ; also *shuttle-shaped* adj., *shuttlewise* adv. ; (sense 6) a *shuttle-trough.*

1860 *Encycl. Brit.* Suppl. II. 796/1 From its lower end there go two small cords to the 'shuttle-eye. **1341** in Riley *Mem. Lond.* (1868) 384 [William Blakeney] 'Salter, of the cavity of the 'shuttle-eye. **1576** PETTY in *Birch Hist. Roy. Soc.* (1756) I. 50 To which purpose there is somewhat considerable in the winding the yarn upon these 'shuttle-quills. **1899** BINGLEY *Anim. Biog.* (1813) II. 194 The eyes are lodged in a 'shuttle-shaped band of black. **1864** E. J. THOMSON *Seit. Mech.* 307 Porcuberment None of the 'shuttle to hire open speculation. **1879** HOWELLS *Lady of Aroostook* iii. 38 The ferryboats plying 'shuttlewise back and forth between other shores made a refreshing sound.

2. A *special* combs. : *shuttle-bearer,* the lay or batten of a loom ; *shuttle-bone,* †(a) each of the bones of the forearm ; (b) the navicular bone in the foot of a horse ; *shuttle-box,* ((a) the cavity in the side of a shuttle to hold the spindle (*obs.*) ; (b)) a tray or case at the end of the shuttle-race to receive the shuttle (Knight *Dict. Mech.* 1875) ; *shuttle-carrier,* the arm or other device which reciprocates the shuttle in a sewing-machine ; *shuttle-crab,* a paddle-crab, *Callinectes hastatus* (*Cent. Dict.* 1891) ; *shuttle-feather* (see quot.) ; †*shuttle-prick,* the spindle of a shuttle ; *shuttle-race,* the ledge or track along which the shuttle passes ; *shuttle-service,* a service of shuttle-trains ; *shuttle-shell,* a gastropod of the family *Radius* ; †*shuttle-spire,* the *shuttle-prick* ; *shuttle-train,* a train running a short distance to and fro, as on a short branch line ; *shuttle-trough* = *shuttle-box (c).*

1883 *Cass. Philos. Manuf.* 230 Exercising their arms and shoulders...by resting their hands on the lay or 'shuttle-bearer. **1868** *House Anatomy* n. xvii. 236 The Cubitus ... doth consist of two Bones; the 'Shuttle Bone. **1825** P. NICHOLSON *Operat. Mech.* 107 A 'shuttle box, or box to receive the shuttle at the end of the lay. **1881** *Uri's Dict. Arts* III. 649 (*Weaving*) A ledge...which forms the 'shuttle race' for carrying the shuttle in 'picking' from and to the shuttle boxes at each end of the lay. **1820** *Uri's Dict. Arts* III. 649 (Weaving-machine), At the commencement of the return of the shuttle, an inclined piece upon the 'shuttle carrier bears against a lateral stud upon one end of a short rocking or oscillatory shaft. **1896** *Bath Daily Chron.* 20 Apr. 1/7 The practice known as 'shuttle-kissing'—sucking the weft through the eye of the Shuttle. **1883** *Man. Fox & A shuttle* prick below. **1851** G. R. PORTER *Silk Manuf.* 216 A shell, called the 'shuttle spire...being formed by making the bottom bar broader than the side rails. **1888** *Nottm. Earthly Jour.* 1. 328 (Cripti 8 *Psyche*). As 1 drove the 'very shuttle through the shuttle-race. **1875** *Abridgm. Specif. Patents, Sewing* 14 Sewing by means of a vibrating needle and a shuttle travelling in a circular 'shuttle-race. **1809** P. F. CARPENTER in *Rep. Smithsonian Instit.* 1860, 199 Family 'Ovulidae. Egg and 'Shuttle Shells. **1744** SHAW *Pract.* (1756) I. 214 [Anat.] The wrist...consists of eight bones; the first is called...the 'shuttle-bone (*Os naviculare*). **1754** *Lond. Mag.* XXIII. 94 The Part of a Shuttle are, the 'Shuttle Tongue, or bit is put a piece [of wood], and fits round the Pin of Shuttle Prick in the shuttle.

† Shuttle, *sb.* ² *Obs.* Forms : 1 *scytel,* *scotel,* 4 *sscettel,* 5 *schettel,* *schyt(y)l* ; β. 1 *scytells, scytrylls, scrytols, soctelis,* 4 *sketles.* [OE. *scytel, scyt(e)l(-)* prehistoric *'skutil, -(o)l,* *'skel-* in *scytan* to shut ; the two OE. words have different authors, but that is here treated in ME. : see *ME. sketel,* *F.* *shite! shittel.*

The mod. dial. *shuttle (shittle, shettle, shettle)* horizontal bar of a gate (see *Eng. Dial.*) is a later development of sense 1.

1. A bolt or bar, as of a door.

c1000 *Ags. Ps.* Thorpe vi. Evil-door ... Cf. OE. *scytel* and *scytan* to shut ; the two OE. words have different authors, but that is here treated in ME. in the same word.] **1275** *Lay* 327, Beside a chest. And ther with 'shuttel' open'd it up. Cf. WFris. *skoattel, EFris. schüttel, Whis. schötel.*

† Shuttle, *adv.* *Obs.* Forms : *1 scytell,* *scotel, scytely,* [f. prec.], unsteadily, shakily.

1660 PEPYS *Diary* 14 Feb. 1/2 to which purpose the quill to coil there for the axis whereas it rowis, and moves as shortley upon it as may be.

Shuttle (ʃʌ'tᵊl), *v.* *Obs. exc. dial.* In 6 *shuttle.* [Partly or perh. wholly f. SHUTTLE *sb.* ¹ ; possibly in part a frequentative f. SHOOT *v.* : see -LE.]

1. *intr.* To move to and fro like a shuttle. Also, to throw swiftly.

1550 COVERDALE *Spir. Perle* xxii. 160 His 3ᵗ hath an heavy burthen vpon hys back, yᵗ more he shuttle'd and mouch yᵗ same, y' more doth it grease hym...**1893** *Speed Eutail* Ioix. He would but grippid me by the cuff o' their neck, and the back of the breeks and shuttled me through the door [*Shetland* dial. (1687) ed. (Halliw.). Nor can you deeme them shuttle-headed fellows, Who for the Lord are so exceeding zealous. **1880** *Kenny* Sings 1. † is it not strange, that in that Shuttle-head Three Kingdoms rumen should be buried I 1685 J. Corbon *Making Salt in Aug.* 19 A mixture of harsh shuttle things. † The 'shuttle prick 'Shuttle-Virgin Staxyll, 'Iscut Le. applied to any dryess or easily slipping matter; as grain, seeds, sand, &c. **1888** STEVENSON *Black Arrow* i. ii. [See there now shuttle-witted and thin-skinned.

2. *intr.* To move or go backwards and forwards.

Also a shuttle ; to travel quickly to and fro.

1847 *English Illustr.* lxxxii. In the clear line the trouts shuttled from stone and crevice. **1892** CARLYLE *Fr. Rev.* II. v. 1, Their corn-go in marching and shuttling, in the interior of the country. **1860** CHARLES *Maid* n. iv. 4-3 though a section of roadway shuttled to and fro between the shores. **1900** *Spectator* 22 Sep. Faster ships shuttle to and fro weaving the political web more and more rapidly.

3. *tr.* To ply the shuttle, weave. (See *Eng. Dial. Dict.*)

Hence **Shu'ttling** *ppl. a.*

1880 *All Year Round* No. 41 244 That began in a whirling, shuttling movement.

Shuttlecock (ʃʌ'tᵊlkɒk), *sb.* [f. SHUTTLE *sb.* ¹ *q. v.* for forms) + COCK *sb.* ¹ Cf. SHUTTLE-cork.]

1. A small piece of cork, or similar light mate-

1614 T. GODWIN *Rom. Antiq.* xvii. **154** 15 By the drawing aside of some wainscot shuttles...a newe partition might seem to be put up.

1. A flood-gate which opens to allow the flow and regulate the supply of water in a mill-stream. Also a similar gate in a shutter-dam or the cut-off sections of a shutter-dam (*Cent. Dict.* 1891).

1822 Shutter *Wny not to* (*see* quot.). **1861** SKELTON *Why not to* (*see* quot.). **1895** BENNEN *St. Hol. Jory* Second wayes he them could entertaine. With dice, with cards... With shittlecocks. **1604** *Nomis London Stuffs* 79 This playing with a shittlecocke, or tossing empty bladders in the aire. **1594** MIDDLETON *Ant & Nightingale* 6 C 3 b, His head was clene vp to white Feathers like a Shuttle-Cock. **1625** BURTON *Anatomy* Oct. C 5 b, The shuttle-Cocke with the Battel-doore is in pretty house exercise. **1606** BUSVAH *Water of Life* 116 (ed.), Your idle Vanities about as the Play-thing a Shittle-cock in the aire. **1737** STATESMAN *Trip to Scarb.* Prol. Made up, like shittlecocks, of cork and feather. **1807** C. K. SHARPE *Let.* 13 Jan. *Corr.* 288 1, 239 With long stiff feathers they crowned their heads that the shuttlecocks on the battledores of empty tongues. **1892** Tennyson *Foresters,* In *Battledore* and Shuttlecock, the missile employed, which consists of a cork crowned with feathers, from 3 to 5 inches in length.

2. A small dart or stop through which metal is allowed to pass from the trough to the mould.

1846 SIMMONDS *Dict. Trade,* **1875** KNIGHT *Dict. Mech.* 2116/2 The shuttle...a plug of wood or iron which enters and closes the opening for the discharge of metal. **1847** *Proc. R. Agric. Soc. VI.* 11. 620 The shuttlecock or 'shuttle'...the 'shuttle' or flood-gate.

3. *fig.* Something that is thrown or tossed to and fro ; hence *fig.* anything unstable, shifting, or changing ; a person or thing liable to move or change.

1609 *W. M. Man of Nonsuch* iii (ed.) D3 A perfect shuttlecock, To and fro, hither and thither. **a1627** MIDDLETON *No Wit* v. i. 79 A shittlecock...to bandie here and there. **1679** DRYDEN *Troilus* v. i. 69, I thought I had ben a shittlecock. **1852** *Tennyson Tourn.* V. 11. 34 A shuttlecock of Gawaine and Geraint. **1850** R. HUNTER *Life & Letters* 154 A set of disclosed papers, tost up with wind and ribs, and deposited in shuttle fifteen...**1849** CARLYLE *Let.* 3 Feb. Old Franc's Love's dance 4 A sort of shuttlecock to be thrown from pole to pole as they pleased.

Hence **Shuttle-cock** *v. trans.*, to throw, send backwards or to toss like a shuttlecock.

1654 L'ESTRANGE *Brief Hist. Times* 1. 4 Translation, and Industry, the Bug-bear of the Times, has not been more Shittle-Cockt, then this Argument. **1824** MISS MITFORD *Village* II. 75 A piece of news shuttlecocked. **1825** *Examiner Making* Salt in Aug. 19. a mixture of harsh shuttle things. **1852** THACKERAY *Virgin.* Ixvii, Well, we must be shuttlecocked about a little till we are married. **1884** HARTE *Washington in N. Jersey* in *Middleton,* etc. 24 I'd like to get a shuttlecock on to G. W. some day.

b. A trial, an experiment ; a 'shot'. *dial.*

1824 R. WALPOLE *Let. to Tindasel* J 398 Just a shuttle-cock or to. **1893** MRS. DYAS *Scarlet Let.* ii. 34 If I could be at a shuttlecock.

2. *intr.* To move or go backwards and forwards.

1851 LILLYWHITE'S *Cricket Ann.* 103 A good field and dry field, in Lillywhite's Cricket Ann. 1869 by a stroke of bad field play, shy.

Shy (ʃaɪ), *sb.* ¹ Forms : 1 *scéoh* (? *inflected scéos*), 3 *scheoh, scheowe, 5 schey, 6 shey,* -7 shie, shy. [OE. *scéoh* = OHG. *sciuh, scieh* (MHG. *schiech,* mod.G. *scheu*) :-- WGer. *skeuhaz.*]

Shy'-cock. *Obs.* [f. SHUTTLECOCK *sb.* ¹ + -ing¹.] The action of using a shuttle (also *fig.*) ; the action of fixing the cup in the shuttle ; *conv.r.* that which serves the purpose of a shuttle.

1611 H. H. COLE *Castiel* Ind. 2716 E. *Scaria.* 'shuttling'. **1861** *All Year Round* No. 41 244 That began in a whirling, shuttling movement.

Shuttle-pin. *Obs.* [SHUTTLE *sb.* ²] Some part of a shuttle.

1683 MAXWELL *Cattle, Horses* (1696) 119 Harnesses...and all things belonging thereunto, as...belly wanters with back, or shoottle pin, tells to carry loomes with.

† Shuttler (ʃʌ'tᵊləɹ), *sb.* *Obs.* [f. SHUTTLE *v.* (sense 3) + -ER¹.] A weaver.

1847 *English Illustr.* lxxxii. He was the prettiest shuttler I ever saw in my life.

SHY.

...

Shy (ʃaɪ), *v.* ¹

[Of obscure origin.]

The earliest use suggests that it may have arisen in some way from the expression SHY COCK.]

1. *intr.* To throw a missile, esp. at anything ; to aim at a jerk. Const. *at.*

1789 BENTHAM *Def. Usury* xiii. 164 He looks upon it as a sort of cock for him, to shie at ... they have shied ... **c1800** *Glouc. Songs,* 11 He shied. **1875** To shy at a cock, to shy at a cock, to throw a cock with a stick. Kent. **1852** J. H. REYNOLDS *Fancy* (1906) 74 The fancy will stick, to win a hit The lucky-box of brown pipes. One stubborn shy Throws wit'd by 100 wizard'd wit. **1874** BRETHAL 213 A fragile stay of a public room. **1838** *Blackw. Mag.* Feb. 229/2 Gambling hells and shy at wit.

2. *trans.* To fling, throw, jerk, toss ; with *at.*

1820 KEAN *Boxiana* IV. 179 The Birmingham Youth ... also shied his castor with a roundabout air. **1848** THACKERAY *Adu. Younger Son* 284 He then shyed his pebble-cocked hat. **1857** MARRYAT *Yacob Faithful* xxiii, I went down a-shying at ...**1857** C. BEDE *Verdant Green* ii. viii, When you come to any empty bottles...he couldn't stand that sort of game. **1877** MRS. LYNN *Too Late a ...* **1875** *Ptbms.* II. 164 [Anat.] He looked upon it as a sort of cock ...

b. *transf. and fig.*

1854 SCOTT *Jrnl.* 10 Mar., I cannot keep up the well without shying a bone' comm.ter. **1861** *Sat. Rev.* 12 Oct. 479/3 Ardennanians put for many years Peoples come together in a mass, and a few palaces shied down upon a rubbishy heads. 1866

HELPS *Realmah* (1876) 245 He would merely shy barbarous words, half-Latin, half-Greek at us. **1861** C. M. SERVAILE ...**1807** *Truth* 4 Sept. 374/1 The term paid for accommodation were a chance that the bargain had been a Shylockian one. **1899** GUNTER *King's Stockbroker* 13 A 'Let it kill your hordes!' With this Shylock slain in his mind,—

2. *Diss illusiontmue* as Why [do] they shys so strangely at this new Inggament! **1778** S. CASE 8 Dec. in *Mem. D'Arblay's Diary* (1832) I. 135. I mean such freedoms as this new Inggament! **1778** S. CASE 8 Dec. in Mem. D'Arblay's Diary (1832) 1. 135 I mean such freedoms as many ladies of the strictest character,...perhaps would shy at being intimate with. **1785** Mas. D'AMLAV *Diary* 19 June, He was too well-bred to force himself upon, and finding I shied, he left me alone. **1804** *Word of Honor* 11. ii. 600 Mrs. CROMWELL R. Brook *V. Virginia* 11. xv. 248 She is shying from the thought. **1841** publicity is given to this arrangement, the more difficult for Evelyn to shy at the man. **1842** *LLOYD'S LIVE Weekly ...* **1842** *Span. Maid* Rev'r & Wendy v. 12 The only thing he at the shy I was the night at the man's blood. **1842** *LLOYD'S LIVE Weekly ...* **2.** Of a horse : To shrink or start back or aside through sudden fear. Const. *at, rarely from.*

1798 J. LAWRENCE *Treat. Horses* 1. 168 Thoroughbred hacks are...the least liable to shy of all others. **1847** *Mary Quentin De Iu,* The horse strayed from the horse. **1865** Gen. T. THOMPSON *Audi Alt.* III. 117 There is no use in being ill-humoured because a horse shies. **1868** *Atlantic Patagonian* ...**1889** D. C. MURRAY *Old Blazer's Hero* vi. 79 Every now and then...a horse stumbled or, occasionally shying wildly at the glimmering whiteness of some heap of bleached guanaco bones. **1840** *Encycl. Sport.* 5. 347/1 (*Driving*) *Shy,* to spring suddenly either sideways or backwards from fear, or from excess of spirits.

b. *fig.*

1762 *Sporting Mag.* XXXIX. 22 It struck me that the Black shyed his adversary. **1864** *Ibid.* N. S. IV. 236 *fg.* He had too much of the Teddy Tay spirit about him to wince or shy it.

3. To render timid or shy ; to frighten *off.*

1825 YOUATT *Dog* III. 84 A rate given at an improper time...disgusts the honest hound. It shies and prevents from hunting the timid one. **1893** KANE *Grinnell Exp.* 8 xvi. 1873 213 birds prepared to thrust back to windward shied them off.

Hence **Shy'ing** *vbl. sb.* and *ppl. a.*

1809 LAWRENCE *Treat. Horses* 1. 8 This was not the effect of starting or shying, to which she [the mare] was at no time addicted. **1869** J. H. NEWMAN in W. Ward *Life* (1912) I. 215, I hope my shying, as I do, will not keep you from speaking out. A spae De. ANGEL *Aubridge.* (1906) II. 80 They seemed to go suddenly mad, like shying horses or stamped mare.

Shy, *adj.* ¹ Chiefly *collog.* Also 8 *shie.* [Of obscure origin.]

1. *intr.* To throw a missile, esp. at anything ; to aim at a jerk. Const. *at.*

...

of a malicious...have often suspected or the surest the dearest friends. **1843** KANE *Grinnell Exp.* xxviii. (1856) 124 Dec 1873/1 There came previous shynesses that were becoming.

Shyful, variant of SHERIFFUL *a.* *Obs.*

Shype ac, variant of CHIP-AX.

c1390 *Det. Carpenters Tools* in *Hazl. E. P. P.* (1864) 1. 78 With schyp ac.

Shyppe, obs. form of SHIP.

Shyrrywyke, obs. form of SHERIFFWICK.

Shyryff (*e,* etc. obs. forms of SHERIFF.

Shyst, obs. form of SCHIST.

Shyster (ʃaɪ'stəɹ), *U.S. slang.* Also *shyster.* [Of obscure origin.

It might be f. *Say a* (sense 3, disreputable) + *-ster* ; but this sense of the adj. is app. not current.]

A lawyer who practises in an unprofessional or tricky manner ; especially, one who haunts the prisons and lower courts to prey on petty criminals ; hence, any one who conducts his business in a tricky manner (*Funk's Stand. Dict.* 1895).

1856 *Knickerb. Mag.* Apr. XLVII. 434 (Thornton *Amer. Glass.*) If they abuse the right of lawyers to humanity. **1856** *Thornton Amer. Gloss.* ...

Shyne, obs. form of SHINE.

Shynde, variant of SHEND *a.* [f. SHY *v.* ¹]

Shyness (ʃaɪ'nᵊs), *sb.* Also 8 *shiness.* [f. SHY *a.* ¹] The condition or quality of being shy.

...

Si.—St.

Si (sī). Mus. [Cf. quots. 1850 and 1875. For various accounts as to the originator, see Grove Dict. Music and Littré.] In solmization, the seventh note of the scale.

Siamese (sɑiămīz), a. and sb. [f. the name of the country Siam + -ESE. Cf. F. Siamois.]

Siatica, obs. form of SCIATICA.

Sib (sib), sb.[1] Now rare. Also 1 sibb, 4 syb; [various forms]. [Common Teut.: OE. sib(b) = OFris. sibbe, OS. sibbia, sibbea (MLG. sibbe), OHG. sippia, sippa (MHG. and G. sippe), ON. *sif (pl. sifjar), Goth. sibja, related to next.]

1. Kinship, relationship

Sib (sib), a.[2] Forms: 1 sib, 1-4, 6, 9 sibb, 4-6 syb (5 sybb), 8 Sc. sub; [1-]. [OE. sib(b), a. sibbe, 4, 6 sibbe, 5-6 syb(be.]

1. Related by blood or descent; akin.

Sib (sib), v. Obs. [f. SIB sb.]

Sibbed, a. dial. [Sin a.²] Akin.

Si bbens (also -ans, -ins), var. of SIVVENS.

Sibbered, -ridge: see SIB.

Sibber-sauce. Obs. exc. dial.

Sibilous (sibiləs), a. [f. L. sibil-us sb.]

Sibilus (sibiləs), a. [= L. sibil-us sb.]

Sibilant (sibilănt), a. and sb. [a. L. sibilant-, pres. pple. of sibilāre to hiss, whistle.]

Sibilate (sibilēt), v. Also 9 sibillate.

Sibilation (sibilēˑʃən).

Sibilator (sibilētər), rare.

Sibilatory (sibilātəri), a. Also sibilli-.

Sibilous (sibiləs).

Sibling (sibliŋ). Obs. [f. SIB + -LING.¹]

Sib-man. Obs. [f. SIB a. + MAN.]

Sibness (sibnes). In later use only Sc. Also 7 sibbness.

Sibrit, **Sibred**. Obs. exc. dial.

Sibyl (sibil). Forms: 1 sybl (4 sibil), 5-7 sibill (7 sibyll), 4-5, 7 sibilla.

Sibylist (sibilist).

Sibylla (sibiˑlă). Also 4 sibla, 6-7 sibylla; 4 sybilla, 6-7 sybylla.

Sibylline (sibilain), a. and sb. [ad. late L. sibullīn-us, f. sibylla: see -INE.]

Sibyllism (sibiˑliz'm), n.

Sibyllist (sibilist). Also 7 SIBYLIST.

Sibyllize, v.

Sic (sik), a. Sc. and north. (Chiefly Sc.) Forms: 1-10 swilc, 5-7 syk (5 sylk 6 sylk).

Sic (sik), adv. [L. sic so, thus.]

Sic, Sc. and north. var. of SICK a.

Sicamore, obs. var. of SYCAMORE.

Sican, obs. form of SICKEN.

Siccan, a. Sc. and north. var. SICCAN.

Siccate (siˑkēt), v. Obs. rare. [ad. L. siccāt-, ppl. stem of L. siccāre. To make dry.]

Siccation (sikēˑʃən). Obs. rare.

Siccative (siˑkativ), a. and sb. [ad. late L. siccātīv-us.]

Sicca (siˑkă). Anglo-Indian. Also 7 sicca, 8 sikka. [Arab. sikkah.]

Siccant.

Siccific, a. Obs. rare.

Siccity (siˑkiti). Obs. [ad. L. siccitās.]

Siccor, obs. form of SICKER.

Siche, sb. Obs. Forms: 4 siser, cisar, 5 sichere, 6-7 sicher, sighe. [OE. sīc.]

Sichet, obs. form of SIGHT.

Sicilian (sisi'liăn), a. and sb. [f. L. *Sicilia* Sicily + -AN.]

A. adj. 1. Of or pertaining to Sicily or its inhabitants; characteristic of Sicily or the Sicilians.

2. **a.** In special collocations, as *Sicilian embroidery* (see quot. 1882); *Sicilian opening* (in chess); *Sicilian Vespers* (see quot. 1728).

b. In names of plants, products, etc., as *Sicilian hart-wound*, *radish*, *toad-flax*; *Sicilian earth*, *saffron*; *Sicilian sumach-plant*.

B. *sb.* 1. A native of Sicily.

2. = SICILIANE.

3. = SICILIENNE.

Sicilia'na. Also *sb.* *-ane*. [It., fem. of *Siciliano* Sicilian.] A dance of the Sicilian peasantry, resembling a jig; the music for this.

Sicilienne, obs. form of SYCAMORE.

Sioht, Sc. form of SIGHT.

Sicilian (sisi'liăn), a. and sb. [L. *Sicilia* Sicily + -AN.]

Sick (sik), a. and sb. Forms: α. 1-3 *seoc* (1 *seoch*, *sioc*), 2-3 *soc*(*k*)*e*; 3 *seoc*, *seec*, *soek* (3 *dint*.), 3, 6 *seoke* (3-*soke*); 4-5 *sike*, *syke*, 4 *sike* (4 *dial.*), 5 *sike* (5 *dial.*); 4, *soik*, *sike* (4, 9 *dial.*) *seok*, 5 *sayk*, 5-6 Sc. *soik*. β. 3 *suc*, *sic*, 3-6 *sik* (4 *sik*), 6-9 *syk*(*e*), 6- *sick*. γ. 4-9 *dial.* (5 *sikk*, 5-7 *sike*, *sicke*; *siik*, 5 *sike*, 6 *syke*; 7-9 *sik*).

I. 1. Suffering from illness of any kind; ill, unwell, ailing. Now chiefly literary and U.S.

2. Having an inclination to vomit, or being actually in the condition of vomiting.

3. In the condition of. Now *rare*.

II. †3. Mentally affected or weak. Now *rare*.

II. + 3. Wrongfully or morally ailing; corrupt through sin or wrong-doing.

4. Deeply affected by some strong feeling, as (*a*) sorrow, (*b*) longing, (*c*) envy, (*d*) repugnance or loathing, producing effects similar or comparable to those of physical ailments.

b. Of fish: in the spawning stage.

c. *Naut.* Requiring repairs.

5. *transf.* Disgusted, mortified, chagrined.

B. *absol.* or as *sb.* 1. *absol.* as *pl.* Those who, such as, are suffering from illness.

2. A person suffering from illness.

Sicken (si'k'n), v. 1. *intr.* To become affected with illness, to fall ill or sick. Also *const.* *of* or *with*.

2. To feel faint with horror or nausea; to revolt or experience revulsion at something.

b. To grow weary or tired of a thing.

3. *trans.* To affect with illness; to make sick.

4. *Chem.* Of mercury: to become 'sick'.

5. *trans.* To affect with illness; to make sick.

b. To affect with nausea, loathing, or disgust.

c. To render faint with fear or horror.

Sickener (si'k'nəə). 1. Something which nauseates or disgusts; an overdose or excess of anything; a sickening experience.

b. Used of a shot or blow.

Sickening (si'k'niŋ), *ppl. a.* [f. prec. + -ING.] 1. Falling or turning sick.

2. That disgusts, nauseates, or faints; repulsive, loathsome.

Sickeningly, *adv.* In a sickening manner.

Sicker (si'kəə), a. and adv. Now Sc. and north. dial.

Sicker (si'kəə), v. Now Sc. and north. dial.

Sicker-head, *a.* Cf. G. *sicherheit*; OHG. *sihhurheit*).

Sickerlaik, *sb.* Obs. exc. Sc. [f. SICKER + -laik.]

Sickerly, *adv.* Now Sc. and north. dial.

Sickerness, Obs. exc. Sc. [f. SICKER + -NESS.] Certain prospect or possession of something.

Sickerty. *Obs.*

Sicket, variant of SIKER.

Sick-house. Now rare.

Sickish, a.

Sickle (sik'l), *sb.*

Sickle, *v.* *Obs.*

Sickle-bill, *Ornith.*

Sickle-ham, -hough

Sickled (sik'ld), *a.* [f. SICKLE *sb.*] Rendered sickly or mawkish.

Sicklied, *a.*

Sicklify, *v. rare.* [f. SICKLE † + -FY.] *trans.* To make sick or sickly.

Sicklike, *obs. f.* SICK-LIKE.

Sickly, adv. [f. SICKLY *a.*] In a sickly manner.

Sickliness (sik'lines). [f.] The state or fact of being sickly; delicacy of constitution, ill-health.

Sickling [1]. [f. SICKLE *sb.*] The action of cutting with a sickle. Also *attrib.*

Sickling [2]. [f. SICKLE *sb.*] A sickly or delicate person.

Sick-list. [SICK *a.* 2 b.] An official list of sick persons, esp. soldiers or sailors.

Sickly (sik'li), *a.* Forms: 1 sēoc-, seoclic, 3–6 sekeli, 5 seckle, sekely, 5 syck-ly, 6–7 sicklie, 6 sycke(ly, 6 sickly.

Sickly, adv. *Obs.* rare. [f. SICK *a.* + -LY [2].] In a sick manner; with sickness.

Sickly, *v.* [f. SICKLY *a.*] To cover over (or o'er) with a sickly hue. Chiefly *fig.*

Sickman. *Obs.*

Sickness (sik'nes). Forms: 1 sēoc-, sēocnes, 3–6 siknes, etc. Also 3 sekenesse (Kilian).

Side. [SIDE *sb.*]

Sick-nurse, *sb.* [SICK *a.* 10.] A nurse who tends upon the sick.

Sick-nurse, *v.* to act as a sick-nurse.

Sick-nursish, *a.*

Sickel. *Cant. Obs.*

Sick-room. [SICK *a.* 10.] A room occupied by, or set apart for, the sick. Also *attrib.*

Siclatoun. *Obs.*

Sicle. Forms: α. 5 sikle, sicle, etc. – sickle. β. 4–6 cicle, 6 cycle. [a. OF.]

Sicle, *v.*

Siclo- (si-klo), used as combining form of L. *Siculus* Sicilian, as in *Siculo-Arabian*, *-Moresque*, *-Phœnician*, *-Punic*.

Sid. *Sc.* [app. a var. of SEED *sb.*, but the pron. (sid) is not used in *Sc.* in the usual senses of that word.]

Sida. [mod.L. (Linnæus).]

Sidcup, -duck.

Sidar, obs. variant of CIDER.

Sidder, *v. Sc. Obs.*[1] (Meaning obscure.)

Sidder, variant of SIDDOW.

Siddle, *sb.* [Of obscure origin.]

Siddow, sidder, *a.* Now *dial.* Forms: 6–7 sydowe, siddowe, 8– siddow (o swodow), 8–9 siddo, 8 sidden (older).

Side (said), *sb.*[1] Forms: 1 sīde, 3 sīde, 3 side (syde, syd), etc.

Side (said), *a.*[1] and *adv.*

Side, *v.*[1]

Supplement, p. 3873; Corrigenda, p. 4092; Spurious words, p. 4093; Books quoted, p. 4094.

Side-dish. [SIDE sb.] A dish which is accessory or additional to the principal one in a course; a dish of the kind commonly used for this purpose.

Side-door. [SIDE sb.] Cf. Fris. syddoar, MDu. zijdsdore (Du. zijdeur), G. seitentür.] A door in the side of a building, garden, or the like; a door on one side of, or subsidiary to, the main door.

Side-face. [SIDE sb.] The human face in profile; a view or representation of this.

Side-fly. ? Obs. [SIDE sb.] A species of horse-fly.

Side-glance. [SIDE sb.] A glance directed sideways.

Side-hill. Now U.S. [SIDE sb.] A hill-side, an acclivity.

Side-light. Also side light, sidelight. [SIDE sb.] Cf. Fris. sydljacht, -ljocht (in sense 2).]

Side-line, sb. [SIDE sb.]

Sideling, sb. [f. SIDE + -LING.]

Sideling, a. and adv.

Sideling, adv. and a.

Sidelings (sai'dliŋz), adv. Now dial.

Sidelong, adv. and a. Also side-long. [f. SIDE sb. + -LONG. Cf. MDu. sidelinges, MSw. sidholinges adv.]

Side-look. [SIDE sb.]

Sideman. Obs.

Side-rail. [SIDE sb.] A rail placed or fixed at the side of something.

Sideral (si'dĕräl). [ad. L. sideralis.]

Si-en, adv. [OE. sidan, f. sid SIDE a.]

Sideness. Obs. [f. SIDE a.]

Sidera. Obs.

Sideration. [ad. L. siderātiōn-.]

Siderate, v. Obs.

Side-pocket. [SIDE sb.]

Side-post. [SIDE sb.]

Siderism [1]. [f. L. sider-, sidus star.]

Siderism [2]. [f. Gr. σίδηρος iron.]

Siderite (si'dĕröit). Min.

Sideral (si'dĕräl). [ad. L. sideralis.]

Siderean, a. rare.

Sidereous, a. rare.

Sidereal (säi'dĕräl). Also 7–9 siderial (7 syd-).

Siderium.

Sideron, a. rare. [ad. L. sider-, sidus star.]

Siderograph (si'dĕrŏgraf).

Siderography.

Siderolite (si'dĕrŏlöit).

Sideromancy.

Side-rope. Also 6 sithe-.

Siderose, a.

Siderurgy (sidĕrŏ'rdʒi).

Sides, sb. pl.

Side-saddle. [SIDE sb.]

Side-saddle flower (or plant).

Side-shoot. [SIDE sb.] A shoot growing out from the side of a stem.

Side-slip. [SIDE sb.]

Side-show. [SIDE sb.]

Side-stick. Printing. [SIDE sb.]

Side-table. [SIDE sb.] A table placed beside the wall of a room.

Side-track. Orig. U.S. [SIDE sb.]

Side-track, v. Orig. U.S.

Sidesman.

Side-view. [SIDE sb.]

Sidewalk. Also side-walk, side walk.

Side-wall. [SIDE sb.¹]

Sideward, adv. and a. [f. SIDE sb.]

Sideward, a. Towards one side or the other.

B. adj. 1. Directed, moving, or tending towards one side.

Sideway, adv. and a. [SIDE sb.¹]

A. adv. =SIDEWAYS adv.

B. adj. Directed or moving towards or from one side; indirect; sidelong.

Sideways (sərdwēz), adv. and a. [f. SIDE sb.¹ + -WAYS.]

1. From one side.

2. Presenting the side instead of the front, or end; with the side foremost; in the direction of the side; facing to the side, etc.

B. adj. 1. Directed sideways; sidelong.

Side-waver, dial. Also ?-wiver, 9-wafer, -wefer. [Cf. NW.E. weaver, WAVER sb.²]

Side-way, sb. Also side-way. [OE. sīde-weg.]

1. A path or way diverging from, or lying to the side of, a main road; a byway: also fig.

Side-wind. Also side wind, sidewind. [SIDE sb.¹]

1. A wind blowing from one side, or on the side of a vessel, etc.

b. In figurative contexts.

2. fig. An indirect means, method, or manner. Chiefly in phr. by a side-wind.

Side-winded, a. —sense 3; also as adv., by a side-wind; indirectly.

Side-winder, U.S. and dial. [SIDE sb.¹ + winder a blow.]

Side-winder², U.S. [f. SIDE sb.¹ + WIND v.] A species of rattlesnake, Crotalus cerastes.

Side-wipe, sb. and U.S. [f. SIDE sb.¹ + WIPE v.] An indirect rebuke, censure, or hint. dial.

Side-wiper, sb.

Sidewise (saɪdwaɪz), adv. and a. [SIDE sb.¹ + -WISE.]

1. In a lateral direction; to one side; sidewards.

7. As adj. =SIDEWAY a.

Sidi (sī'dī). Forms: 7 seedi, syddy, 7-8 siddy, 8 siddee, 9 siddhee, seddai, sidi, sidi, seedy. [ad. Urdū sīdī, Marāthī sīddhī, at. Arab. saiyidī 'my lord': see SAYYID.]

Siding (sa'idiŋ), sb. [f. SIDE v.² + -ING.]

Siding (sa'idiŋ), ppl. a. [f. SIDE v. + -ING².]

Siding (sai'diŋ), vbl. sb. [f. SIDE v.¹ + -ING.] The action of the vb.

Sidling (sai'dliŋ), ppl. a. [f. SIDLE v. + -ING².]

Sidonian (saɪdōˈniǎn), sb. and a. Also 7 Syd-, Zid-. [f. L. Sīdōn-ius, a. Gr. Σιδώνιος, f. Sidon.] A native or inhabitant of Sidon.

Sidon (sai'don). [L. Sīdōn-ia, Gr. Σιδωνία.] The name of a city.

Sidra, obs. form of CIDER.

Sidth, dial. var. Also sith. [f. SIDE a. + -TH.] Length; depth.

Sief. Obs. rare. Also sieff, seif. [ad. Arab. شياف (see quot.)]

Siege (sīdʒ), sb. Forms: 3-7 sege (5 cege, seche), 4-5 seege, 4-5 seage, 6-7 seadge, 6 saige, 4-5 siege, 5-6 syege, 5 sedche, 6 sedge, ayedge, 7 sied(g)e, sie(d)ge, 6 seege. [a. OF. sege, siege, sige (mod.F. siège) :—pop. L. *sedium, L. *sēdes (class. sēdia, seige, siege). Hence also M.Du. siege, siegy, siedte seat, siege.]

Siege (sīdʒ), v. Forms: 4-5 (6 Sc.) sege, seche), 4-5 seege, 6-7 siege, 6 saige, 4-6 sedge, 6-7 siege. [f. prec., or aphetic f. BESIEGE.]

1. trans. To besiege, belenguer, lay siege to.

Sieger (sī'dʒər). Now rare. Also 6 Sc. segear. [f. SIEGE v.]

Sieging (sī'dʒiŋ), vbl. sb. [f. SIEGE v.] The action of besieging; a siege.

Siege-piece. [SIEGE sb. 6.]

Sienite, Sienitic: see SYENITE, SYENITIC.

Sienna (siēnnǎ). Also 8 siena. [Elliptic for terra di Sienna: see SIENNESE.] A ferruginous earth used as a pigment in oil and water-colour painting (called burnt sienna when it has been exposed to a red heat).

Sienese (siēnē'z), sb. and a. Also Siennese (Sienna (sena) + -ESE).

Sienite, Sienitic: see SYENITE.

Sierra (siē'ră). Also 7 sierr(o). [Sp., range of mountains, lit. 'saw'.] In Spain and parts of America now or formerly Spanish: A range of hills or mountains, rising in peaks which suggest the teeth of a saw.

Siesta (siē'stǎ). Also 7 siest. [Sp. siesta, med.L. sexta (sc. hora), the sixth hour; i.e. noon, the hottest part of the day.] An afternoon rest or nap.

Sieve (siv), sb. Forms: 1 sife, 1-2 sibe, 1-2, 5-6 syve (syfe), 4 syfe, 6 seve, 6 seyve, 7 syve, 6 sive, 4-6 seve, 4 seeve, 4-6 seve, 6 seve, 6 seave, 7 seive, 6-7 seaue, 5 seeue, seve, seveu, 7 sive; also 6 syef, syve, sefen, sefe), and MLG. seve, zeve. sijften.]

Sieve (siv), v. Cf. MDu. and MLG. seven, siften. [f. SIEVE sb.]

1. trans. To pass through a sieve; to sift or strain.

Sieveful. [See -FUL 2.] The fill of a sieve.

Sievel, *obs. form of* CIVIL.

Sieve-like, *a.* [See SIEVE *sb.*] Resembling a sieve; perforated like a sieve.

Sieve-maker. [SIEVE *sb.*] One who makes sieves.

Sieve-plate. [SIEVE *sb.*]

Siever. *Now rare or Obs.* Also 5 cyver, 7 seaver. [f. SIEVE *sb.*]

Sievier, *obs. form of* SAVIOUR.

Sievy. [f. SIEVE *sb.* + -Y.] Like a sieve.

Siew, **Slex**, *obs. forms of* SUE *v.*, SIX.

Siff, *obs. form of* SIEVE *v.*, SIFT *v.*

Si-filate, *v. rare⁻¹.* [irreg. f. L. *sīfilāre*: see next.] *trans.* To whisper.

Sifle (sifˊl), *v.* Also 4–5 syfle, 5 sifle. [ad. F. *siffler*, † *sifler* = sp. *silbare*, var. of *sibilāre*: see SIBILATE *v.*] *intr.* To blow with a sibilant sound; to whistle, hiss.

Si-flement, *Obs.⁻¹* [a. F. *sifflement*, f. *siffler*: see prec.] A whistling noise.

Sift (sift), *sb.* [f. SIFT *v.*]

† 1. A sieve. *Obs.*

2. The act of sifting (in quot. *fig.*); the fact of falling as from a sieve.

3. Something that falls or passes as if from the meshes of a sieve; sifting or sifted material (*Cent. Dict.* 1891).

Sift (sift), *v.* Forms: 1 siftan, 4 syften (5–7n), 6 siffte, 7 siff, sift (7 sift).

Sifted (siftˋed), *ppl. a.* [f. SIFT *v.*]

Sifter (siftˑaɪ). [f. as prec. + -ER¹.]

Sifting (siftˋiŋ), *vbl. sb.* [f. as prec. + -ING¹.]

Sifting, *ppl. a.* [f. as prec. + -ING².]

Sig, *sb.¹* [Cf. prec.] *trans.* To steep in, or sprinkle with, urine.

Sig, *obs. form of* SIGNATURE.

Sigaldre, *v.* *Obs.* *rare.* [? OF. *sige victory* + GALDER.]

Sigaldry, *Obs. rare.* Also 3 rie, 4 sygaldry. [f. prec. + -Y.] Enchantment, sorcery.

Sigh (saɪ), *sb.¹* Forms: 4 sihe(n, 4–5 syhe(n, 5 sygh(e)n; *also* 4–5 sik(e, sick(e, sigh.

Sigher (saɪˑaɪ). [f. SIGH *v.* + -ER¹.] One who sighs.

Sigheful (saɪˑful), *a.* [f. SIGH *sb.* + -FUL.] Sorrowful; *sighing*.

Sighing (saɪˋiŋ), *vbl. sb.* [f. SIGH *v.*]

Sighing, *ppl. a.* [-LY².] In a sighing manner; with or accompanied by sighing.

Sighinglyt, *adv.* [prec. + -LY².]

† Sighings, *Obs.⁻¹* [f. as prec. + -NESS.] The condition of uttering sighs.

Sight (saɪt), *sb.¹* Forms: 1 sihð, 2–3 sihðe (3 sihh-), 4 siht, 4–5 sight, syhte (–yt), 5 syȝt, 6 syȝth, sihte, 7 sight.

reserve them only for his first sight. 1655 in Picton *L'pool Munic. Rec.* (1883) I. 188 Repaired and amended..at yᵉ sight and discression of Mr. Maior. 1660 *Order Ho. Comm. as to Customs* (1663) 1 For a Bill of sight, Bill of Sufferance, or any other imperfect Warrant. 1821 J. SMYTH *Pract. of Customs* 327 A Merchant,..ignorant of the real quantities and qualities of his Goods,..may apply to the Collector and Comptroller for a Bill of Sight or View, in order that they may be brought on shore and examined. 1833 *Act 3 & 4 Will. IV*, c. 52 § 24 An entry by Bill of Sight.

c. *Line of sight*: (cf. LINE *sb.*² 11).

1589 [see LINE *sb.*² 11]. 1893 BALL *Story of Sun* 184 The amount of their movements along the line of sight.

12. a. Opinion, estimate, judgement; respect, regard, view. Now *rare*.

a 1300 *Cursor M.* 11853 'Godd men,' he said, 'quat es your sight O mi fader þat þus es dight?' 1362 LANGL. *P. Pl.* A. Prol. 32 Summe chosen Chaffare to cheeuen þe bettre, As hit semeþ to vre siht þat suche men scholden. ? *a* 1400 *Morte Arth.* 3289 The secunde sir .. þat sewede thame aftyre Was sekerare to my sighte, and saddare in armes. 1536 BELLENDEN *Cron. Scot.* IX. xix. (1541) B b iv, He had nothir reuerence to god, nor sicht to the commoun weil. *a* 1572 KNOX *Hist. Ref.* Wks. 1846 I. 419 At youre awin sychtis sche will sett fordwart that caus at hir power. 1607 in *Antiquary* XXXII. 242 To be disposed at the sight of [supervisors of will]. 1674 *Playford's Skill Mus.* III. 2, I assume that the true sight and judgment of the upper three must proceed from the lowest. 1851 WESTCOTT *Introd. Study Gospels* viii. (ed. 5) 396 The first step to a right understanding of the Gospels must be the abandonment of this point of sight.

†b. Knowledge, skill, insight. Const. *in*. *Obs.* (Very common in the 16th cent.)

1530 PALSGR. 270/1 Sight, knowledge, *perspicasité*. 1535 CRANMER *Misc. Writ.* (Parker Soc.) II. 303 Surely I do much marvel of them both..having such sight in scriptures and doctors. 1581 in *Confer.* II. (1584) M iij, His sight in Greke was very litle or none at all. 1600 *Dr. Dodypoll* I. ii. in Bullen *O. Pl.* IV. 108 His sweete discourse, His sight in Musick and in heavenlie Arts.

IV. 13. a. The pupil of the eye. Now *dial.*

c 1400 *Lanfranc's Cirurg.* 247 Macula is a wem in a mannys iȝe, & summe be white þerof & sittiþ vpon þe siȝt of þe iȝe, & summe bisidis þe siȝt. 1530 PALSGR. 270/1 Sight of the eye, *le noyre de loyil*. 1601 HOLLAND *Pliny* I. 155 In either eie they haue two sights or apples. 1683 SNAPE *Anat. Horse* III. viii. (1686) 123 The horney Tunicle or Coat of the Eye, with the pupilla or sight. 1736 BRACKEN *Farriery Impr.* (1757) II. 14 What they mean by the Ground of the Eye, is the Pupil or Hole thro' the Iris and Uvea, which the common People call the Sight of the Eye. 1751 R. PALTOCK *P. Wilkins* xiv. (1883) 43/1 His eyes were small and blue, with a large black sight in the middle. 1808 JAMIESON, *Sicht* of the ee. 1889 in *Eng. Dial. Dict.* (Yorksh.).

†b. A visor. *Obs.*

1508 *Acc. Ld. High Treas. Scot.* IV. 122 For the grathing of the gilt ermyt [*sic*] my Lord of Owbigne gaif the King and for making of ane new sicht to it. *a* 1548 HALL *Chron., Edw. IV*, 197 b, The point of the axe of the lord Scales happened to enter into the sight of the bealme of the bastard. 1597 SHAKS. *2 Hen. IV*, IV. i. 121 Their eyes of fire, sparkling through sights of Steele. 1654–66 EARL ORRERY *Parthen.* (1676) 647 He pull'd down the sight of his Helmet.

c. *pl.* Spectacles. Now *dial.*

1619 H. HUTTON *Follies Anat.* (Percy Soc.) 39 An aged man, which spectacles did use Having them filcht.., Fearing the thiefe would not his sights restore [etc.]. 1667 PEPYS *Diary* 18 Oct., I bought me two new pair of spectacles of Purlington..; and his daughter..do advise me two very young sights. 1823 E. MOOR *Suffolk Words* 350 *Sights*, spectacles, glasses. 1899 in *Eng. Dial. Dict.*

†d. (See quot.) *Obs.*⁻¹

1640 in Entick *London* (1766) II. 165 Glass-plates, or sights for looking-glasses.

14. An appendage to a surveying or observing instrument, serving to guide the eye.

1559 W. CUNNINGHAM *Cosmogr. Glasse* 137 A ruler with two sightes, which we moue to and fro. 1571 DIGGES *Pantom.* I. vii. D j b, Forget not to haue two equall fine plates of brasse persed in the middes (for your sightes). 1669 STURMY *Mariner's Mag.* II. xvi. 93 Take the Quadrant and look through the Sight at E. 1676 PHILLIPS *Purch. Pattern* 131 If a man have but a Ruler with sights..he may draw the foresaid lines to the several angles of the field. 1715 tr. *Gregory's Astron.* (1726) I. 282 A Quadrant..and an Index moving upon its Center, furnished with Telescopic Sights. 1790 BURKE *Fr. Revol.* Wks. V. 312 An accurate land-surveyor, with his chain, sight, and theodolite. 1833 HERSCHEL *Astron.* ii. 83 The tube or sight, fastened on the circle, works in the solid metallic centring. 1879 *Cassell's Techn. Educ.* IV. 93/1 This prism..has, when so placed, a notched 'sight' on its upper surface.

b. A device, of the nature of a projection or notch, on a fire-arm or piece of ordnance, etc., to assist in taking aim.

In fire-arms and ordnance the sights are usually two in number, one at or near the muzzle and the other near the breech, the latter being adjustable so as to vary with the distance. In large guns the forms are often very complex.

1588 LUCAR tr. *Tartaglia's Colloq. Shooting* 18 When the levell sight which is set uppon the mouth of the peece is precisely so high as the levell sight which is set uppon the taile of the peece. 1591 SIR J. SMYTH *Instr. Milit.* 191 All their mosquets should be of one heigth or caliver of bullets with open sights. 1647 HEXHAM I, The sight of a crosse-bow, *het gesight*. 1681 W. ROBERTSON *Phraseol. Gen.* (1693) 1128 The sight in a gun or cross-bow, *scutula*. 1847 *Infantry Man.* (1854) 34 The foresight is aligned through the back sight with the object. 1890 *Times* 6 Dec. 15/3 Thousands of rounds were fired so rapidly..that in some cases the sights were actually melted.

15. The opening in a picture-frame; that part of the picture which shows in this.

1850 [see *sight-measure* in 17].

V. 16. *attrib.* and *Comb.* (chiefly objective), as *sight-aching, -fitting, -hungry, -hunter*, etc.

1593 NASHE *Christ's Tears* Wks. (Grosart) IV. 224 The..*sight-aching botches of theyr vnsatiate intemperance, they will vnblushingly lay foorth. 1611 COTGR., *Advenant*, handsome,..well beseeming,..*sight-fitting. 1880 L. WALLACE *Ben-Hur* v. xii. 349 There the close of the exercises found them, patient and *sight-hungry as at the beginning. 1848 *Blackw. Mag.* Aug. 185 That professional *sight-hunters should go *sight-hunting. 1743 BLAIR *Grave* 288 The Star-surveying Sage close to his Eye Applies the *Sight-invigorating Tube. 1593 NASHE *Christ's Tears* Wks. (Grosart) IV. 194 *Sight-killingly with his..frownes, he shall teache him, both that he is, and what he is. 1605 SYLVESTER *Du Bartas* II. iii. I. *Vocation* 1008 What can the Sight of the *Sight-maker dim? 1610 SHAKS. *Temp.* I. ii. 203 Ioues Lightning, the precursers O'th dreadfull Thunder-claps more momentarie And *sight out-running were not. 1870 LOWELL *Study Wind.* I. 12 Their enemies were hidden in their own *sight-proof bush. 1784 COWPER *Task* IV. 759 That *sight-refreshing green Is still the liv'ry she [Nature] delights to wear. 1844 ALB. SMITH *Adv. Mr. Ledbury* vi, The majority of *sight-seekers..know..little about the venerable edifice. 1895 E. OWEN in *Wks. G. Edwards* p. ix, There were then no fashionable inns to give accommodation to sight-seekers. 1896 *Cath. Mag.* June 350 It would be happiness to add its name to our list of *sight-seen countries. 1596 FITZ-GEFFREY *Sir F. Drake* (1881) 31 Monsters of nature, Nile-bred Crocodiles, *Sight-slaying Basilisks. 1676 MARVELL *Mr. Smirke* 44 The King of Virginia, that had two Squires..to lift up his Eye-lids...I am not bound to be any of his *Sight-supporters. 1899 *Allbutt's Syst. Med.* VI. 613 There was a slight attack of left hemiplegia with headache, vertigo, and *sight-troubles.

b. In terms relating to the taking of surveys or observations, or denoting appliances used for this purpose, as *sight-alidade, -aligner, -angle, -beam*, etc.

1900 H. M. WILSON *Topogr. Surveying* vii. 161 A small *sight-alidade was devised by the author both for sighting directions, and for determining elevations by vertical angulation. 1892 GREENER *Breech-Loader* 97 The *sight-aligner and adjustable gun, invented in 1882. 1571 DIGGES *Pantom.* I. xxxiv. K iij b, From the Centre thereof, extend right lines.., wryting as before vppon euery of them the names of their places or markes, whereof they are the *sight Angles. *a* 1400 in Halliw. *Rara Mathem.* (1841) 63 Go toward it and froward it til þi *sight beme passe by þe heght of þe ȝerde and of þat thyng. 1669 STURMY *Mariner's Mag.* II. xiii. 82 The Sight-beams over the ends of the Crosses. 1859 RUSKIN *Perspective* Introd. 9 Through the Sight-point, S, draw a horizontal line GH, right across your paper from side to side, and call this line the *Sight-line. *Ibid.* i. 99 The *Sight-magnitude of a line is the magnitude which bears, to the real line, the same proportion that the distance of the picture bears to the distance of the object. 1874 J. W. LONG *Amer. Wild-fowl* i. 24 *Sight-piece small and close to the muzzle. 1859 RUSKIN *Perspective* Introd. 9 The point S is to represent the point opposite which you wish the observer of your picture to place his eye in looking at it. Call this point the *Sight-point. 1883 K. G. WHITE *W. Adams* 121 He threw up his left arm, and took a *sight rest on it [with his revolver]. 1731 W. HALFPENNY *Perspective* p. iv, The Groove E, wherein the *Sight-Staff slides to and fro. 1669 STURMY *Mariner's Mag.* II. xiv. 85 If you see all Skie and no Water, then draw your *Sight-Vane a little lower. 1863 A. YOUNG *Naut. Dict.* (ed. 2) 297 The sight vanes are pieces of brass standing perpendicularly to the plane of the instrument.

17. Special combs.: **sight-chase**, a chase in which the dogs hunt by sight; **†sight-court**, a place for public shows; **†sight-glasses**, spectacles; **sight-measure** (see sense 15); **sight-reader**, one who is able to read music at sight; so *sight-reading*; **†sight-shot**, the range of vision; **sight-singing**, the practice or art of singing at sight.

1897 *Outing* XXX. 127/1 Just in time to witness a short but pretty '*sight chase'. The dogs have seen the fox. 1553 GRIMALDE *Cicero's Offices* (1556) 87 *Sightcourts, galereywalkes, and new churches, the more reuerentlie I fynde fault with for Pompeyus sake. 1605 tr. *P. de Loyer's Treat. Spect.* 59 It is well knowne that ordinarily the spectacles or *sight-glasses do make letters to seeme more great than they are indeede. 1850 *Jrnl. of Design* IV. 58 *Sight measure 4¼ × 3½. 1866 *Athenæum* No. 2000. 277/2 The best *sight-readers in Europe. 1874 OUSELEY *Mus. Form* 5 A man may be a thoroughly accomplished musician,..a perfect sight-reader [etc.]. 1864 *Reader* 30 Apr. 551/2 The singer's power of independent '*sight-reading'. 1663 COWLEY *Ess., Obscurity*, It only makes me run faster from the place, till I get, as it were, out of *sight-shot. 1801 BUSBY *Dict. Mus.* s.v. *Solmization*, This preparatory exercise, so necessary to *sight-singing. 1898 *Westm. Gaz.* 29 Oct. 5/2 Sight-singing in elementary schools.

†Sight, *sb.*² *Obs.* Forms: 4 siȝt(e, 4–6 sight, 6 syght. [Cf. SIGHT *v.*² Not related to Du. *zucht*, which is for earlier **suft*.] A sigh.

a 1300 *Cursor M.* 15169 Mani sari sight [*v.r.* sigh, sikyng] ..þar sanc vn-til his hert. *c* 1350 *Will. Palerne* 924 My seknes wiþ my siȝtes sumtime slakes. 1584 LODGE *Forbonius & Prisceria* 30 Not waying of her many louing sightes, Her watrie eyes, her secret moane by nights. 1584 *Pleas. Com. Two Ital. Gentl.* D j, By the smoake of loouers scalding sightes [*rime* flightes].

†Sight, *sb.*³ *Obs. rare.* [? ad. LG. *sichte*: see SIFT *sb.*] A sieve or strainer.

1559 MORWYNG *Evonym.* 376 Pres it out strongly and put the decoction prest out through a wullen sight, and pres it out, that the substance may remaine in the sight.

Sight (səit), *v.*¹ Also 6 *Sc.* sycht, sicht. [f. SIGHT *sb.*¹ Cf. MDu. *sichten*, *zichten* (rare), G. *sichten* (naut.), Da. *sigte*, Sw. *sigta*.]

1. *trans.* **†a.** *Sc.* To look at, view, inspect, examine, scrutinize. *Obs.*

1596 *Peebles Burgh Rec.* (1872) 134 To..pas done with ane of the baillies to sycht the saidis stanis. 1598 *Supplication General Assembly* in *Misc. Wodrow Soc.* (1844) 402 Quhen as zour Grace hes sichtit thir our laboris. 1632 LITHGOW *Trav.* VII. 303 None of us all knowing what was in the Clogbags till they were sighted. 1678 SIR G. MACKENZIE *Crim. Laws Scot.* I. viii. § 1 The Body must in this case be sighted by Physitians. 1706 in J. Watson *Jedburgh Abbey* (1894) 42 That necessar it is workmen be imployed to sight and repair the samyn.

b. To examine by taking a sight.

1884 *Truth* 13 Mar. 372/1 He reports..that the rails, sighted crosswise, are not as true as they should be.

2. To get or catch sight of, to see, to get or go within sight of (anything).

1602 WARNER *Alb. Eng.* XIII. lxxvi. 315 Nor doth our Eiesight see it selfe, nor Soule that sighteth it. 1632 LITHGOW *Trav.* VIII. 375 Wilde beasts, whose hollow cryes, as we heard in the night, so we too often sighted their bodies in the day. 1819 O'MEARA *Trans. St. Helena* 36 The remarks which he asserts to have been made relative to sighting Napoleon. 1853 KANE *Grinnell Exped.* iv. (1856) 33 On the same day..we sighted the mountainous coast of Greenland. 1887 BESANT *World Went* vii, We sighted her one morning at daybreak.

b. *spec.* Of bills: (see quot.).

1866 CRUMP *Banking* v. 103 A bill drawn at so many days' sight, must be computed exclusively of the day on which it is sighted, and inclusively of the day it falls due.

3. *intr.* To take a sight, *esp.* in shooting.

1842 J. F. COOPER *Jack o' Lantern* xxviii, Together they sighted, and together they fired. 1883 *Harper's Mag.* Jan. 201/1 Then stooping and sighting along it, he moves the outer end of the lath. 1896 *Daily News* 27 July 9/3 He took matters very coolly, and sighted several times before he was satisfied.

†Sight, *v.*² *Obs.* Also 5 *Sc.* sicht-, 6 syght. [? f. *sight(e*, pa. t. of SICHE *v.*] *intr.* To sigh.

c 1375 *Sc. Leg. Saints* xxvi. (*Nicholas*) 1138 In his hart he mad mayne & sichtit sare. *c* 1450 *Abce* in *Q. Eliz. Acad.* 67 Be not to sadde, to sorry, ne sight not to deep. *c* 1475 in *Rel. Antiq.* I. 71 Whan other men doyth sleype, Thene do I syght and weype.

Si·ghtable, *a.* [f. SIGHT *v.*¹] Comparatively clear.

1888 *Times* 18 Aug. 5/1 At 3 o'clock the chief officer reported that the weather was 'sightable', with occasional rain.

Sighted (səi·ted), *ppl. a.* [f. SIGHT *sb.*¹ + -ED.]

1. Having sight of a specified kind.

See also *dim-, far-, long-, sharp-, short-, weak-sighted*.

1552– [see QUICK-SIGHTED]. 1586– [see CLEAR-SIGHTED]. 1594 NASHE *Unfort. Trav.* Wks. (Grosart) V. 159 Of an ill tree I hope you are not so ill sighted in graffing to expect good frute. 1596 SPENSER *Hymn Beauty* 235 Louers eyes more sharply sighted bee Then other mens. 1615 CHAPMAN *Odyss.* VI. 162 That he might see this lovely-sighted maid. *a* 1680 BUTLER *Rem.* (1759) II. 6 By which both senses being united Does render them much better sighted. 1791–3 in *Spirit Publ. Jrnls.* (1799) I. 17 Who guide the helm of Britain half-seas over, Yet double-sighted keep an eye on Port. 1846 RUSKIN *Mod. Paint.* II. III. xii. § 1 Any of us whose heart is rightly tuned, or whose mind is clearly and surely sighted. 1866 S. B. JAMES *Duty & Doctr.* (1871) 133 Uncivilized, imperfect-sighted heathen men.

b. Having sight *like* something specified.

1602 DOLMAN *La Primaud. Fr. Acad.* (1618) III. 643 Those are sighted like the bat, who see not the things most manifest in nature. 1611 SHAKS. *Wint. T.* I. ii. 388 Make me not sighted like the Basilisque.

2. Endowed with sight; able to see. Also *absol.*

1836 LANDOR *Minor Prose Pieces* Wks. 1853 II. 467 2 Above all others, blind or sighted, he is so ready to take advantage of the slightest word, that [etc.]. 1860 *Macm. Mag.* III. 56 If the sighted would help the blind. 1888 *Pall Mall G.* 31 July 2/2 Two pretty boats manned each by six blind little lads and one sighted person.

transf. 1887 *Athenæum* 17 Dec. 818/3 Without sighted supervision the industrial competition [of the blind] with seeing workmen is too unequal to be maintained.

3. Furnished or fitted with a sight or sights.

1859 *Musketry Instr.* 28 It may sometimes occur that the rifle is not accurately sighted as to elevation. 1879 *Man. Artill. Exerc.* 142 The gun is sighted centrally. 1893 SELOUS *Trav. S. E. Africa* 432 One's rifle ought to be carefully sighted up to at least four hundred yards.

4. (See quot.)

1873 MAXWELL *Electr. & Magn.* I. 306 If the hair as seen through the lens appears straight and bisects the interval between the black dots it is said to be in its sighted position.

Si·ghtening. [f. SIGHT *sb.*¹] In calico-printing, a fugitive colour used to test the quality of the work.

1875 KNIGHT *Dict. Mech.* 2176/2.

Sighter (səi·təɹ). [f. SIGHT *v.*¹]

†1. *Sc.* An inspector. *Obs.*

1708 in *Hist. Regality of Musselburgh* (1857) 22 The two present magistrates and sighters to be present at the cutting and selling.

2. In card-sharping: (see quot.).

1894 MASKELYNE *Sharps & Flats* 196 'Sighters'..are simply minute dots upon the faces of the cards.

3. A sighting shot in rifle or artillery shooting.

1897 *Times* 23 July 8/1 Black, a sighter for tie shots, made 11 [bulls] in succession. 1899 *Westm. Gaz.* 24 July 4/3 They had..to fire three tie-shots off with a sighter allowed.

†Si·ghtful, *a.* *Obs.* [f. SIGHT *sb.*¹]

1. Visible.

c 1375 *Sc. Leg. Saints* l. (*Catherine*) 369 [He] is a god,.. wnsichtfull and sichtfull bedene. 1387–8 T. USK *Test. Love* Prol. (Skeat) l. 58 The unsene privitees of god, made to us sightful..in our contemplacion and understonding. *Ibid.* III. ix. 98 How was it, that sightful manna in deserte to children of Israel was spirituel mete? 1545 RAYNOLD *Byrth Mankynde* Hh vij, These vaynes appering .. immediatly vnder the skyn, very conspicuous and syghtful.

2. Endowed with sight; seeing. Also *fig.*

1594 CAREW *Huarte's Exam. Wits* (1596) 59 The vnderstanding groweth more sharpe and sightfull. *Ibid.* 97, I cannot forgoe to thinke, that the reasonable soule seuered from the body..hath a power sightfull. 1613 CHAPMAN *Masque Inns of Crt.* Plays 1873 III. 106 Tis passing miraculous that your dul and blind worship should so sodainly turne both sightful and witful.

3. Sightly, pleasant to the eye.

1565 STAPLETON tr. *Bede's Hist. Ch. Eng.* 180 His priest.. set forth the buildinges with divers comely and sightfull workes. 1571 GOLDING *Calvin on Ps.* xvi. 11 The fulnesse of joye is matched ageinste the syghtfull entycements of the worlde.

Hence **†Si·ghtfulness**, the power of seeing. *Obs.*

a 1586 SIDNEY *Arcadia* II. (1605) 149 Let vs not winke though void of purest sightfullness. *Ibid.* 219 My praier is Thou maist loue her, that I may see thy sightfullnesse.

Sighth, obs. form of SITHE, to sigh.

Si·ght-hole. [SIGHT *sb.*¹] A hole to see through, *esp.* in a surveying or other instrument.

1559 W. CUNNINGHAM *Cosmogr. Glasse* 29 Then rayse up and downe the ruler (having two sight holes made in it) unto the sonne. 1596 SHAKS. *1 Hen. IV*, IV. i. 71 Wee of the offring side Must .. stop all sight-holes. 1646 EARL MONM. tr. *Biondi's Civil Wars* VI. 72 Slain by the splinter of a Lance which wounded him thorow the sight-hole of his Helmet. 1692 *Capt. Smith's Seaman's Gram.* II. xxiv. 130 Which will shew at what height the Sight-hole standeth. 1769 *Phil. Trans.* LIX. 296 A small sight-hole, made through a piece of brass. 1823 J. BADCOCK *Dom. Amusem.* 50 The sight-hole..is still unfurnished with a glass of any sort. 1898 *Engineering Mag.* XVI. 110/2 The sight-holes provided in the smoke-boxes of certain stationary boilers of the locomotive type.

†b. The pupil of the eye. *Obs.*

1670 *Phil. Trans.* V. 1027 They contract much their pupilla or sight-hole of the Eye.

Sighting (səi·tiŋ), *vbl. sb.*¹ [f. SIGHT *v.*¹]

†1. A method of cheating at dice. *Obs.*

c 1752 *Art & Myst. Gaming* Title-p., The Art and Manner of working with a Great-Box; Eclipsing, Sighting, Waxing and Popping, &c.

2. The action of looking, catching sight *of*, inspecting or examining, etc.

1853 KANE *Grinnell Exp.* xxv. (1856) 203 The mere sighting of a distant coast. 1896 *Daily News* 21 Dec. 2/1 Thus enabling the docking, sighting, cleaning, painting, and undocking of vessels to be accomplished in one tide.

3. The action of giving to a gun the proper elevation and direction to hit the object aimed at.

1884 *Times* (weekly ed.) 8 Feb. 1/3 The gunners were ignorant of the process of sighting. 1893 F. ADAMS *New Egypt* 235 The British Admiral bore ungrudging witness.. to the excellent sighting of the guns.

4. *attrib.*, esp. *sighting-shot*, a preliminary shot allowed to each competitor in a shooting-match.

1861 *Times* 12 July, They had sold..8,000 tickets for the sighting targets. 1872 *Daily News* 15 July, He..fired his two sighting-shot bull's-eyes straight from the shoulder. 1895 *Outing* XXVI. 397/2 The disk of the sighting rod is turned up to coincide with the sight. 1897 *Westm. Gaz.* 30 Nov. 5/1 The sighting-room of the Royal Gun Factories.

†Si·ghting, *vbl. sb.*² [f. SIGHT *v.*²] Sighing.

13.. *Cursor M.* 10496 (Gött.), To-quilys scho mened þus hir care, wid weping and wid sihting sare. 1520 *Calisto & Melib.* A iij, Craft in them renewyng that neuer decays, Theyre seyenges, sightynges, prouokynges, theyr plays.

†Si·ghting, *vbl. sb.*³ [? ad. LG. *sichting* (G. *sichtung*), vbl. sb. f. *sichten* to sift: cf. SIGHT *sb.*³] The result of straining; strained matter.

1559 MORWYNG *Evonym.* 376 Sieth this sighting to the thicknes of hony.

Sightless (səi·tlės), *a.* [f. SIGHT *sb.*¹ + -LESS.]

1. Unable to see; destitute of the power of sight; blind.

c 1250 *Gen. & Ex.* 1528 Ysaac Wurðede sighteles and elde swac. 1387–8 T. USK *Test. Love* I. i. (Skeat) 15 Thus witless thoughtful, sightles lokinge, I endure my penaunce in this derke prison. 1435 MISYN *Fire of Love* 54 And for he þis vtward Ioys onely desiris, in-wardly & vnsene blyndyd als wer sytheles to fyre gois. *a* 1585 MONTGOMERIE *Cherrie & Slae* 305 Baith sichtles, and michtles, I grew almaist at ainis. *c* 1600 SHAKS. *Sonn.* xliii, When in dead night thy faire imperfect shade..on sightlesse eyes doth stay. 1674 N. FAIRFAX *Bulk & Selv.* 47 Were all seeing things sightless, there would be no colours. 1725 POPE *Odyss.* VIII. 221 He who sightless wants his visual ray. 1791 COWPER *Iliad* v. 824 Sightless, of all thought bereft, He sank. 1842 LONGF. *Warning* ii, A cruel mockery of his [Samson's] sightless woe. 1879 G. ALLEN *Colour-Sense* iii. 27 The eye of the bee, of the cuttlefish, and of the eagle, have each apparently been separately developed from unlike remote sightless ancestors.

fig. 1781 COWPER *Charity* 416 The truth she loves a sightless world blaspheme. 1881 H. JAMES *Portr. Lady* liii, She performed this journey with sightless eyes, and took little pleasure in the countries she traversed.

b. Deprived of the sight *of* something. *rare*⁻¹.

1632 LITHGOW *Trav.* x. 470 Being sightlesse of company, and humane faces.

2. Invisible, unseen, dark; impenetrable by vision.

1589 WARNER *Alb. Eng.* II. xi. 44 The scouring windes that sightlesse in the sounding aire doe flie. 1603 HARINGTON in *Nugæ Ant.* (1804) I. 343, I have been well nighe driven heretofore into narrowe straits, amongste state rockes and sightless dangers. 1613 HEYWOOD *Braz. Age* Wks. 1874 III. 249 Hath any sightlesse and infernall fire Laid hold vpon my flesh? 1740 [S. BOYSE] *Deity* (1749) 11 He shuns the view of Sense, Lost in the blaze of sightless excellence. 1789 MRS. PIOZZI *Journ. France* I. 45 Following a soaring falcon through the half-sightless regions of the air. 1812 J. HENRY *Camp. agst. Quebec* 115 They were even sightless to us, we could see nothing but the blaze from the muzzles of their muskets. 1850 TENNYSON *In Mem.* cxv, Drown'd in yonder living blue The lark becomes a sightless song. 1888 B. W. RICHARDSON *Son of a Star* I. xii. 184 Touchless with human hands, Sightless with human eyes.

†3. Unsightly. *Obs.*

1595 SHAKS. *John* III. i. 45 Full of vnpleasing blots, and sightlesse staines. 1632 LITHGOW *Trav.* VIII. 375 Ah! sightlesse desarts! fil'd with barren Sands!

4. Out of sight.

1632 LITHGOW *Trav.* IX. 381 Tvnneis beene sightlesse left, I sought the Ile Of little Malta. 1816 SCOTT *Antiq.* xxxi. (motto), Their tears..as they fall, sink sightless.

Hence **Si·ghtlessly** *adv.*, without having the faculty of sight.

1847 in WEBSTER. 1883 E. ARNOLD *Indian Idylls* 241 He lay,..with fierce eyes Roving the wood, and seeing sightlessly. 1892 ZANGWILL *Bow Myst.* 159 His eyes ranged sightlessly after the boy.

Si·ghtlessness. [f. prec.] Lack of sight.

1847 in WEBSTER. 1853 RUSKIN *Stones Ven.* III. iv. § 13 It is one instance only out of the myriads which might be given of sightlessness in modern art. 1854 GREENWOOD *Haps & Mishaps* 90 There was a full assortment of the halt ..and the crippled—all degrees of sightlessness and unsightliness. 1893 R. JEFFREY *Visits to Calvary* 227 Your sightlessness is a sad deprivation.

Sightliness (səi·tlinės). [f. next.] Comeliness, handsomeness, beauty.

1561 T. HOBY tr. *Castiglione's Courtyer* I. A 2 b, A Citye in fourme of a palaice, and that not onelye with ordinarie matters,..but also for sightlynesse. 1598 BARCKLEY *Felic. Man* (1631) 658 The delectible shew and sightliness of the tree. 1642 FULLER *Holy & Prof. St.* IV. 303 Thus glasse-eyes may be used, though not for seeing but for sightlinesse. 1740–1 RICHARDSON *Pamela* (1824) I. xv. 25, I, a poor girl, who..had only a kind of imputed sightliness of person. 1767 T. BOSTON *Crook in Lot* (1805) 11 Faith will discover a hidden sightliness in it, under a very unsightly outward appearance. 1846 TRENCH *Mirac.* xviii. (1862) 313 Much that for its little sightliness was nothing accounted of, shall prove true metal. *a* 1878 SIR G. SCOTT *Lect. Archit.* (1879) II. 170 Another mode of giving sightliness to the squared dome.

Sightly (səi·tli), *a.* and *adv.* [f. SIGHT *sb.*¹ Cf. MDu. *sichtelijc* (Du. dial. *sichtelijk*), MHG. *sihtlich* (G. *sichtlich*), visible, etc.]

†1. Visible; conspicuous. *Obs.*

1532 MORE *Confut. Barnes* VIII. Wks. 775/1 The wel knowen church [is] so builded..that it shal alway be syghtlye, and can not be hyd. 1571 GOLDING *Calvin on Ps.* lxxiv. 12 Many manifest deliverances had bin exhibited too the elect people as it were uppon a syghtly stage. 1579 TOMSON *Calvin's Serm. Tim.* 7/1 [God] doeth not come downe from heauen, in sightly shape to speake vnto vs.

b. *U.S.* Of places: Open to the view; that may be seen from a distance; commanding a wide prospect.

1828–32 WEBSTER, We say, a house stands in a sightly place. 1892 ALICE M. EARLE *Sabbath in New Engl.* i. 5 Our Puritan ancestors dearly loved a 'sightly location'; and were willing to climb uphill cheerfully..for the sake of having a meeting-house which showed off well.

2. Pleasing to the sight; fair to look at; handsome, beautiful.

1562 J. HEYWOOD *Prov. & Epigr.* (1867) 148 In a Iuggler, that lightnes is sightly. 1592 GREENE *Conny Catch.* III. 11 In such sightlie roumes it may easily bee thought, Citizens vse not to haue anie thing meane. 1611 BIBLE *Transl. Pref.* ¶ 12 They did not..proportion the houses in such comely fashion, as had bene most sightly and conuenient. *a* 1652 BROME *Covent Garden* I. i, Here's Architecture exprest indeed! It is a most sightly scituation, and fit for Gentry and Nobility. 1748 *Anson's Voy.* II. xii. 264 They were mounted on very sightly horses. 1790 BURKE *Fr. Rev.* (ed. 2) 265 If their schemes were perfectly consistent in all their parts, it would make only a more fair and sightly vision. 1850 W. SCORESBY *Cheever's Whalem. Adv.* viii. (1858) 107 The sightly constellation of the southern cross. 1887 BALL *Nat. S. Amer.* 322 The absence of sightly buildings is not felt.

b. As *adv.* Handsomely, finely.

1591 HORSEY *Trav.* (Hakluyt Soc.) 224 This ambassador was..sightly enterteyned. 1592 WYRLEY *Armorie, Ld. Chandos* 42 They forward came bedect right sightly. 1610 HOLLAND *Camden's Brit.* I. 290 Nor Rhodes, with Alcal and Elba, regard the robes with crosse Sightly beset. 1784 COWPER *Task* III. 649 He, therefore, who would see his flow'rs dispos'd Sightly and in just order,..Forecasts the future whole.

Si·ghtman. *Sc.* [f. SIGHT *sb.*¹] One who is stationed to watch the movements of salmon.

1794 *Statist. Acc. Scot.* XI. 93 They are..called sightmen, because..they become wonderfully quick-sighted in discerning the motion and approach of..salmon.

Si·ght-see, *v.* [Back-formation from *sight-seeing* (cf. first quot.), f. SIGHT *sb.*¹ 1 c.] *intr.* To see sights, visit objects or places of interest.

1835 *Court Mag.* VI. 146 The ruins of Tintern,..Alas! now profaned by a sight-seeing crew. 1843 LADY GRANVILLE *Lett.* (1894) II. 345 She sight-sees from the dawn of day. 1887 *World* 23 Feb. 15 Who..sight-see all day, and return to their gilded cars to dine and sleep.

Si·ght-seeing, *vbl. sb.* [f. SIGHT *sb.*¹ 1 c.] The action or occupation of seeing sights.

1847 FR. A. KEMBLE *Later Life* III. 250 It involves what I have no taste for—i.e., sightseeing. 1883 F. M. PEARD *Contrad.* xiv, The duke escaped the sight-seeing which bored him.

attrib. 1863 J. C. JEAFFRESON *Sir Everard's Dau.* 87 Amongst the country folk..who paid Sharsted a sight-seeing visit. 1892 GUNTER *Miss Dividends* (1893) 109 Mrs. Livingston proposes a sight-seeing drive about the city.

Si·ght-seer. [f. as prec.] One who goes about to see the sights of a place or places.

1849 CURZON *Monast. Levant* xv. 204 Nothing better or worse than Englishmen and sightseers. 1860 THACKERAY *Round. Papers, Week's Holiday*, Humour and grotesqueness, which gives the sight-seer the most singular zest and pleasure. 1884 SALA *Journ. South* I. xx, The..society-loving patrons of the Roman season are a very different class from the sightseer.

Sightsman (səi·tsmǣn). [f. SIGHT *sb.*¹ Cf. SIGHTMAN.]

1. One who points out sights or objects of interest; a local guide, a cicerone.

a 1700 EVELYN *Diary* 6 Nov. 1644 Our Sights-man (for so they name certain persons here who get their living by leading strangers about to see the City).

2. One who reads or performs music at sight.

1776 BURNEY *Hist. Music* (1789) IV. vi. 263 This musician, who was..of considerable eminence..both as a sights-man and voluntary player. 1801 BUSBY *Dict. Mus.*, *Sightsman*, the appellation given to him who reads, or sings, music readily at first sight: hence we say, 'such a one is a good Sightsman'.

3. ? One who takes sight with a pistol.

1790 *Bystander* 169 How serious a thing it is to call all the duellists that ever lived, from the Roman Gladiators to the sightsmen of the present day, rascals.

Sight-worthy (səi·twɜ̄ɹði), *a.* [f. SIGHT *sb.*¹ + WORTHY *a.*] Worth seeing or visiting.

1605 DANIEL *Queen's Arcadia* Ded., For maiesty, and power, can nothing see Without it selfe, that can sight-worthy be. 1642 FULLER *Holy & Prof. St.* III. iv. 159 Cambridge...and Oxford,..where the worst Colledge is more sight-worthy then the best Dutch Gymnasium. 1791 BENTHAM *Mem. & Corr.* Wks. 1843 X. 263 For sight-worthy persons at Plymouth, More mentioned Mudge, whom you know of old. 1894 C. H. COOK *Thames Rights* 111 Objects not so sight-worthy as broadcloth.

Hence **Si·ght-worthiness.**

1849 J. FORBES *Physician's Holiday* ii. (1850) 13 A temporary halt may be called, according to the nature or sight-worthiness of the locality.

Si·ghty, *a.* *Obs.* exc. *dial.* [f. SIGHT *sb.*¹ + -Y. Cf. obs. Flem. *sightigh* (Kilian), MLG. *sichtich*, OHG. (*ge*)*sihtig*, MHG. *sihtig* (older G. *sichtig*), visible (in G. also 'seeing').]

†1. Sightly, fair, handsome. *Obs.*

1387 TREVISA *Higden* (Rolls) V. 269 A wonder faire mayde,..and wonder siȝty for men to byholde. 1533 BELLENDEN *Livy* I. iv. (S.T.S.) I. 28 The romanis dressit furth þis play In the maist solempne maner þai culd or mycht, to mak It þe more sichty and glorius to the pepill.

†2. Visible, conspicuous. (See also quot. *c* 1440.)

1398 TREVISA *Barth. De P. R.* XIX. i. (Bodl. MS.), The reson of siȝty þinge is roted and ischape in liȝt. *c* 1440 *Promp. Parv.* 455 Syghty, *visibilis*. *Ibid.*, Syghty, or glarynge,..*rutilans*. *c* 1475 *Partenay* 1229 Antony..in hys4 faw bare A hurt ful of pain Off a lyon, which al hys life bare ful sighty. 1533 BELLENDEN *Livy* v. xvi. (S.T.S.) II. 203 Þare souerane manhede & vertew was sa notabill and sichty. 1536 — *Cron. Scot., Cosmogr.* v. Biij, The peple thairof ar..maist sychty in craft of cheualrie. 1570 LEVINS *Manip.* 111 Sighty, *visibilis*.

3. Keen-sighted; clever. Now *dial.*

a 1425 *Cursor M.* 13448 (Trin.), Is noon so siȝty foule of eȝe [as the eagle], Ny so fer to fle may dreȝe. 1579 TOMSON *Calvin's Serm. Tim.* 453/1 We are sighty inough to our owne profite. 1869 *Lonsdale Gloss.*, *Sighty*, quick at seeing how a thing ought to be done.

Sigil (si·dʒil). Also 7 sigill. [ad. late L. *sigillum* (in class. L. *sigilla* neut. pl.), dim. of *signum*: see SIGN *sb.*]

1. A seal or signet. Also *attrib.*, as *sigil-mark*.

a 1610 PARSONS *Leicester's Ghost* (1641) 14 Giges went invisible By turning of the sigill of his Ring Toward his palme. 1657 TOMLINSON *Renou's Disp.* 132 Another figure ..imprinted by some sigil. 1814 CARY *Dante, Par.* XXVII. 48 Sigil-mark Set upon sold and lying privileges. 1880 WEBB *Goethe's Faust* I. i. 41 A book with sevenfold sigil is the Past! 1883 A. DOBSON *Old World Idylls* 243 Touched by the awful sigil of his right.

2. *Astrol.* An occult sign or device supposed to have mysterious powers.

1659 T. PECKE *Parnassi Puerp.* 153 Love scorns, that any Remora should be: That's the true Sigil, moving Gallantrie. 1672 SIR T. BROWNE *Let. Friend* § 13 Amulets, spells, sigils, and incantations, practised in other diseases, are seldom pretended in this. 1711 POPE *Temple of Fame* 105 Of Talismans and Sigils [they] knew the pow'r, And careful watch'd the Planetary hour. 1813 SCOTT *Trierm.* I. vi, Sign and sigil well doth he know. 1842 BARHAM *Ingold. Leg.* Ser. II. *Raising the Devil*, He drew the mystic circle's bound,..He traced full many a sigil there.

3. *Rom. Antiq.* A small image.

1738 CHAMBERS *Cycl.* s.v. *Sigillaria*, Some derive the origin of sigils and figures, in this solemnity, from the argei [etc.].

Sigilism (si·dʒiliz'm). [ad. mod.L. *sigilism-us*, f. Sp. *sigilo* seal (of confession).] (See quot.)

1865 *Englishman's Mag.* Feb. 114 The following appear to be the principal crimes against which the edicts of the Inquisition were fulminated..: immorality in the confessional, sigilism (or revealing the secrets of the confessional).

Sigilla, pl. of SIGILLUM.

†Si·gillar, *a.* *Obs.*⁻⁰ = SIGILLARY *a.* 1.

1656 BLOUNT *Glossogr.*, *Sigillar*, of or belonging to a Seal or Mark. 1658 PHILLIPS, *Sigillar*, belonging to a seal or sealing.

‖Sigillaria (sidʒilē·riă). *Geol.* [mod.L., f. *sigillum* seal: see SIGIL. Named by Brongniart (1822).] A fossil tree, the leaf-scars of which resemble the impressions of a seal, found chiefly in coal deposits.

1831–3 LINDLEY & HUTTON *Fossil Flora* I. 155 It is extremely probable..that Sigillaria was a Dicotyledonous plant. 1836 BUCKLAND *Geol. & Min.* I. 473 The longitudinal flutings of the trunks of Sigillariæ. 1849 J. H. BALFOUR *Man. Bot.* § 1183 Some suppose Sigillarias to be allied to Tree-ferns, others to Coniferæ. 1876 PAGE *Adv. Text-bk. Geol.* xiv. 255 We may notice the sigillaria, so called from the seal-like impressions on its fluted trunk.

Hence **Sigilla·rian** *a.* and *sb.*; **Sigilla·rid**; **Sigilla·r(i)oid** *a.*

1870 *Geol. Mag.* VII. 293 The fossil *sigillarian forests of Nova Scotia. 1883 *Science* I. 523/2 A number of animals entombed in stumps of sigillarians in the coal-measures of Nova Scotia. 1877 LE CONTE *Elem. Geol.* (1879) 316 The Lycopods [were represented] by gigantic Lepidodendrids and *Sigillarids. 1870 *Geol. Mag.* VII. 293 These specimens ..probably represented other types of *Sigillarioid trees. 1872 NICHOLSON *Palæont.* 474 The Sigillarioid plants, regarded by different authorities as being Coniferous, or Lycopodiaceous. 1879 GEIKIE in *Encycl. Brit.* X. 345/2 Lepidodendroid and *sigillaroid plants abound, as well as calamites.

Si·gillarist. *rare*⁻¹. [irreg. f. L. *sigill-um* SIGIL: cf. next.] A sigillographer.

1898 *Berks., Bucks., & Oxon Archæol. Jrnl.* Jan. 110 Mr. A. P. Ready, the well known sigillarist.

Sigillary (si·dʒilări), *a.* [f. (late) L. *sigill-um* SIGIL: see -ARY. Cf. F. *sigillaire* and med.L. *sigillarius, -aris* sb.]

1. Of or pertaining to a seal or signet; connected with the use or making of seals, etc.

1652 EVELYN *Corr.* (1827) IV. 4 All those sigillary formalities of a perfect instrument. 1895 *Athenæum* 13 July 57/2 Several of their seals are given, which are striking examples of the sigillary art.

2. Subject to, or characterized by, the influence of a sigil or charm.

a 1834 SURTEES in G. Taylor *Mem.* (Surtees) 233 That maiden kiss hath holy power O'er planet and sigillary hour.

Sigillate (si·dʒilėt), *ppl. a.* [ad. late L. *sigillāt-us*, pa. pple. of *sigillāre*: see next.]

1. *Bot.* Marked with impressions resembling those made by a seal.

[1866 HENSLOW *Dict. Bot. Terms* 173 *Sigillatus*, when a rhizoma is marked by scars left by the fall of branches successively developed upon it.] 1858 in MAYNE.

2. Of pottery: Decorated with impressed patterns.

1891 in *Cent. Dict.*

Sigillate (si·dʒileᶦt), *v.* Also 5 *pa. pple.* sygylate. [f. *sigillāt-*, ppl. stem of late L. *sigillāre* to seal, f. *sigillum* SIGIL.] *trans.* To seal; to seal up. Also *transf.*

1471 RIPLEY *Comp. Alch.* x. vii. in Ashm. (1652) 180 And in one Glas do all thys surely sygylate. 1612 WOODALL *Surg. Mate* Wks. (1653) 229 Mercurie..To sigillate thou do'st not fail. 1620 VENNER *Via Recta* vii. 111 By sigillating the mouth of the stomacke..they represse..the hot fumes that vaporate to the head. 1652 S. S. *Secretaries Studie* 200 To fasten, and, as it were, to sigillate, and affix to us the unmercifulness of men. 1833 *Fraser's Mag.* VII. 269 In one moment the passport was sigillated.

Si·gillated, *ppl. a.* [f. prec. + -ED¹.]

1. Impressed with a seal; esp. *sigillated earth*, Lemnian earth, sphragide (after med.L. *terra sigillata*).

Cf. Lithgow *Trav.* (1632) III. 97, 'The latter [name] is in force, because the earth being made up in little pellets, is sealed with a Turkish signet.'

1657 TOMLINSON *Renou's Disp.* 396* The best of medicinal earths..is that the shop-men call Lemnian Earth, and sometimes Sigillated Earth. 1697 EVELYN *Numismata* i. 11 Baked and sigillated Earth..used for money. 1852 TH. ROSS tr. *Humboldt's Trav.* II. xxiv. 502 It is known that great use is still made in the East of the bolar and sigillated earths of Lemnos, which are clay mingled with oxide of iron.

2. = SIGILLATE *ppl. a.* 2. (*Cent. Dict.*)

Sigillation (sidʒilēᶦ·ʃən). [See SIGILLATE *v.* and -ATION.] The action of sealing; the fact of being sealed; the impression of a seal.

1642 R. C. *Union Christ & Ch.* 4 That which..receiveth the Sigillation here below is like to the Shape and Forme of those things above. 1657 TOMLINSON *Renou's Disp.* 132 This..impressed form or sigillation is of little moment. 1802–12 BENTHAM *Ration. Judic. Evid.* (1827) II. 462 Since the art of writing has become comparatively common, sigillation, in the character of a source of real evidence, has gone completely out of use. 1840 G. S. FABER *Prim. Doctr. Regen.* 70 Its outward sigillation or official ratification is the ordinance of Baptism.

†Si·gillative, *a.* and *sb.* *Med.* *Obs.* [ad. med.L. *sigillātīv-us*: see SIGILLATE *v.* and -IVE. So obs. F. *sigillatif*.] **a.** *adj.* Serving to seal or close up. **b.** *sb.* An application serving to close a wound.

c 1400 *Lanfranc's Cirurg.* 342 Sigillatiuis, & cicatrizatiuis, & consolidatiuis ben al oon. 1541 COPLAND *Guydon's Form.* T ij b, The helpes conglutynatyues, consolydatyues, and sigillatyues be of .xvj. fourmes. 1612 WOODALL *Surg. Mate* Wks. (1653) 171 Quicksilver..is..so incarnative and so sigillative or siccatrizing. *a* 1693 *Urquhart's Rabelais* III. xxvi. 215 Sigillative cod.

Sigilled (si·dʒil'd), *a.* [f. SIGIL + -ED².] Wearing a seal or signet-ring.

1864 R. S. HAWKER *Quest Sangraal* 17 Beneath, came up a gloved and sigill'd Hand.

Sigillistic (sidʒili·stik), *a.* [See SIGIL and -ISTIC.] Pertaining to seals.

1867 *Herald & Genealogist* IV. 14 The study of our sigillistic antiquities.

Sigillographer (sidʒilǫ·grăfəɹ). [f. L. *sigillum* SIGIL: see -GRAPHER.] One who pursues, or is skilled in, the study of seals.

1882 *Proc. Soc. Antiq.* IX. 53 Of the foreign heraldic seals ..I have little to say..; their importance for the English sigillographer is but slight. *Ibid.* 181 This eminent palæographer and sigillographer.

Sigillography (sidʒilǫ·grăfi). [f. as prec.: see -GRAPHY.] The science or study of seals.

1879 *Athenæum* 27 Dec. 827 The splendid volume devoted by M. Demay to sigillography. 1886 *Ibid.* 11 Sept. 341/3 It is only of late years that much attention has been paid to Byzantine sigillography.

‖Sigi·llum. *rare*⁻¹. [See SIGIL.] A small figure of a person.

1637 B. JONSON *Sad Shepherd* II. ii, Binding characters, through which she wounds Her puppets, the sigilla of her witchcraft.

‖Si·gla. [L. *sigla* neut. pl., perh. a contracted form of *sigilla*, pl. of *sigillum* SIGIL.] Letters (esp. initials) or other characters used to denote words; abbreviations or marks of abbreviation.

1706 in PHILLIPS (ed. Kersey). 1801 *Gentl. Mag.* LXXI. II. 1097 The characters..belong not to any alphabet, but are probably *Sigla*. 1832 GELL *Pompeiana* II. 122 The sigla which are supposed to be the private marks of the scribes. 1869 TOZER *Highl. Turkey* II. 358 The small mark after the T is one of the sigla which it was customary in inscriptions ..to put..before and after numeral letters.

Hence **Sigla·rian** *a.*, pertaining to sigla.

1818 BURNEY in *Parr's Wks.* (1828) VIII. 643 Garrard is the only book on the Siglarian subject which I possess.

†Si·gle. *Obs. rare.* [ad. L. *sigla*.] (See quots. and SIGLA.)

1614 SELDEN *Titles Honor* 21 Their supposed Coat also, of later time, being foure *Betaes*...The *Betaes* are interpreted as the sigles of Βασιλεὺς Βασιλέων, Βασιλεύων Βασιλεῦσι. *Ibid.* 162 About those times χ alone was a known sigle for our Sauiour. 1656 BLOUNT *Glossogr.*, *Sigles*, notes, breviatures, initial Letters set for words.

Sigleton, late variant of CICLATOUN *Obs.*

Sigma (si·gmă). [L. *sigma*, Gr. σίγμα, the 18th letter of the Greek alphabet.]

1. The name of the Greek letter Σ, σ, ς, the equivalent of the English S, s, in its uncial form having the shape of C.

1607 TOPSELL *Four-f. Beasts* 290 Written with *Iota* and simple *Sigma*. 1736 AINSWORTH *Lat. Dict.* s.v. S, Which opinion is made more probable by the small form of the Greek *sigma*. 1833 *Penny Cycl.* I. 385/2 The difference between the *shin*..., and the Greek *sigma*..depends solely upon the altered position. 1859 MILLARD tr. *Kühner's Gr. Gram.* 4 The Sigma (σ), at the end of a word, takes the form ς. 1876 S. BIRCH *Rede Lect. on Egypt* 32 The final sigma of the Greeks is represented by the Egyptian sibilant.

2. Something having the form of S or C.

1788 GIBBON *Decl. & F.* liii. V. 481 The square before the sigma [= semicircular portico] was decorated with a fountain. 1877 COUES & ALLEN *N. Amer. Rod.* 32 The loops of enamel..do form a sort of sigma [etc.; see SIGMODONT].

Hence **Si·gmaspire** (see quot.). **Si·gmate** *a.*, having the form of a sigma. **Si·gmate** *v. trans.*, to add a sigma or *s* to (a word, stem, etc.); hence *sigmated* ppl. a. **Sigmatic** (sigmæ·tik) *a.*, characterized by the addition of sigma or *s* to the stem. **Sigma·tion**, the addition of *s* to a word, etc. **Si·gmatism**, **‖Sigmati·smus**, the marked use or repetition of *s*; an instance of this. **Si·gmatize** [cf. late Gr. σιγματίζειν] *v. trans.*, to mark with the letter *s*.

1887 *Encycl. Brit.* XXII. 417/2 (Sponges), One of the simplest forms [of microscleres] is the *sigmaspire..; it looks like the letter C or S, according to the direction in which it is viewed, its actual form being that of a single turn of a cylindrical spiral. 1887 *Amer. Naturalist* XXI. 937 [Sponges] with *sigmate flesh-spicules. 1849 T. K. ARNOLD *First Gr. Bk.* 5 The root of the future is got from the root of the present (or infinitive) by *sigmating it. *Ibid.* 22 The first Aorist of the Active is formed by adding a to the *sigmated root..and prefixing the augment. 1889 *N. & Q.* 7th Ser. VIII. 216/2 The question of the plural treatment, or otherwise, of some sigmated words is fair matter for discussion. 1888 KING & COOKSON *Sounds & Infl. Gr. & Lat.* xv. 444 The inflexions of the *sigmatic aorist. 1897 *Trans. Philol. Soc.* 233 We have also a subjunctive of the sigmatic aorist. 1889 *N. & Q.* 7th Ser. VII. 142/1 This fondness for pluralizing..is constantly showing itself both in a purely senseless *sigmation and in a duplication of the plural ending. 1889 *Classical Rev.* III. 270 The *sigmatism is quite Ovidian. 1891 *Athenæum* 21 Feb. 246/2 Sophocles, 'O.T.' 425, should have been quoted as the most remarkable, and at the same time effective, example of sigmatism in Greek tragedy. 1887 *Q. Rev.* Oct. 369 There are three inseparable necessities which may be remembered by a *sigmatismus —site, soil, and sympathy. 1654 H. L'ESTRANGE *Chas. I* (1655) 145 Mr. Prynne..was..to be stigmatized, or if you will *sigmatized, on both Cheeks with the letter S for a Schismatick.

Sigmodont (si·gmǫdǫnt), *a.* and *sb.* *Zool.* [f. Gr. σίγμα SIGMA + ὀδοντ-, ὀδούς tooth.] **a.** *adj.* Belonging to the *Sigmodontes*, a class of murine animals in which the molars exhibit sigmoid patterns. **b.** *sb.* An animal belonging to this class.

1877 COUES & ALLEN *N. Amer. Rod.* 32 The loops of enamel..do form a sort of sigma, but it is usually a broken and always a distorted one, never more evident than in some other sigmodont forms. 1884 *Encycl. Brit.* XVII. 5/1 A represents the upper molars of a Mus, and B the corresponding teeth of a Sigmodont. – *Ibid.* 6/2 Other groups,..probably descendants of Sigmodont Muridæ.

Si·gmoid, *a.* and *sb.* Chiefly *Anat.* [ad. Gr. σιγμοειδής: see SIGMA and -OID.]

A. *adj.* **1.** Having the shape of the uncial sigma C; crescent-shaped, semicircular.

Chiefly in *sigmoid cavity, notch, valve*.

1670 *Phil. Trans.* V. 2097 We did also observe two Ventricles with the tricuspid or sigmoid-valves. 1741 A. MONRO *Anat. Nerves* (ed. 3) 252 A large semicircular or sigmoid Concavity is left. 1798 HINDERWELL *Hist. Scarborough* II. I. 213 Nautilites, or Ammonites,..with sigmoid or curved ridges. 1831 KNOX *Cloquet's Anat.* 74 The condyle is separated from the coronoid process by the sigmoid notch. *Ibid.* 206 It is the inner side..of the head of the radius that is received into the small sigmoid cavity of the ulna. 1898 *Allbutt's Syst. Med.* V. 922 Relative insufficiency of the sigmoid valves due to dilatation of the aortic ring.

2. Having a double curve like the letter S.

Esp. *sigmoid flexure*, the last curving portion of the colon before terminating in the rectum.

1786 *Phil. Trans.* LXXVI. 306 The sigmoid flexure of the colon immediately presented itself to view. 1797 M. BAILLIE *Morbid Anat.* (1807) 174 The gut..is narrower at the sigmoid flexure than at any other part. 1848 *Proc. Berw. Nat. Club* II. 267 The flower stalk is..round,..gracefully bent in a sigmoid flexure. 1873 MIVART *Elem. Anat.* ii. 61 The beautiful sigmoid curvature of the vertebral column.

B. *sb.* **a.** The sigmoid flexure of the colon.

1891 in *Cent. Dict.* 1897 *Allbutt's Syst. Med.* III. 967 The sigmoid may be so distended as to reach quite over to the right side of the abdomen.

b. A sigmoid curve (*Cent. Dict.*).

Hence **Si·gmoidscope** (see quot.).

1904 *Brit. Med. Jrnl.* 3 Dec. 1503 By means of the electric sigmoidscope..a clear view of every portion of the inside of the bowel may be obtained, even as high as the top of the sigmoid flexure.

Sigmoidal (sigmoi·dăl), *a.* [See prec. and -AL.] = SIGMOID *a.*

1666 J. SMITH *Solomon's Portrait. Old Age* 233 The sigmoidal Portals hindering its return, it [the blood] must pass through the Streiner of the Lungs. 1753 *Chambers's Cycl. Suppl.* s.v. *Sigmoides*, The semicircular cavity of the cubit.. is sometimes also called the sigmoidal-cavity. 1826 KIRBY & SP. *Entomol.* IV. xxxviii. 55 The pupa..has likewise a pair of long sigmoidal ones [respiratory organs] on the back of the trunk. 1833–4 *Encycl. Metrop.* (1845) VI. 598/2 The beds of coal and accompanying strata are bent into a sigmoidal flexure. 1879 RUTLEY *Study of Rocks* xi. 187 At times they have a somewhat sigmoidal flexure.

Hence **Sigmoi·dally** *adv.*, in a sigmoidal manner.

1854 *Orr's Circ. Sci., Org. Nat.* I. 218 The femur..is sigmoidally bent. 1886 *Geol. Mag.* (N.S.) III. 150 The sigmoidally curved folds of the ganoine.

Sign (səin), *sb.* Forms: α. 3–6 sygne, 3–7 signe (4 sigine?), 5–6 sygn (5 sygyn?), 4– sign; 4–5 singne, 4–5 syngne (5 synn-); 4, 6–7 *Sc.* sing(e, 5–6 *Sc.* syng(e, 5 senge). β. 4–7 sine, 4–6 syne (4 synne, 5 syn, cyne, scien, 6 *Sc.* synd). [a. F. *signe*, † *sine*, ad. L. *signum* mark, token, etc.]

I. 1. A gesture or motion of the hand, head, etc., serving to convey an intimation or to communicate some idea. Freq. in the phrases *to make a sign* or *signs*, and *by signs*.

a 1225 *Ancr. R.* 70 Heo schal habben leaue to..makien signes touward hire of one glede chere. *c* 1350 *Will. Palerne* 2740 To þe hert & þe hinde he turned him a-ȝeine, & bi certeyn signes sone he hem tauȝt. *c* 1385 CHAUCER *L. G. W.* 2367 *Philomene*, She..preyede hym with signys to gon Vn-to the queen..And be signys swor hym manye an oth [etc.]. *c* 1400 MAUNDEV. (Roxb.) xxii. 100 Þai speke noȝt, bot ..makez signes as monkes duse. 1508 DUNBAR *Tua Mariit Wemen* 467, I have ane secrete serwand,..That me supportis of sic nedis, quhen I a syne mak. 1530 PALSGR. 702/2 I spake nothyng to him, but I shewed hym of it by signe otherwise. 1595 SHAKS. *John* IV. ii. 237 Thou didst vnderstand me by my signes, And didst in signes againe parley with sinne. 1626 BACON *New Atl.* 4 Warning us off by signes that they made. 1664 BUTLER *Hud.* II. ii. 758 Then Hudibras, with face and hand, Made signs for Silence. 1712 STEELE *Spect.* No. 454 ¶ 4 The Coachmen make Signs with their Fingers..to intimate how much they have got that Day. 1791 MRS. RADCLIFFE *Rom. Forest* x, The moment Peter saw her he made a sign of silence. 1839 FR. A. KEMBLE *Resid. in Georgia* (1863) 37 More by signs and dumb show than words. 1873 DIXON *Two Queens* XVI. ii. III. 193 Scores of starving men were ready on a sign to hunt him down.

†b. A show or pretence *of* something. *Obs.*

c 1400 MAUNDEV. (Roxb.) iii. 10 He made signe of etyng and feyned as he had etyn. 1485 CAXTON *Chas. Gt.* 230 The whyche..made to hym synge of loue and of subgectyon ..vnder the shadowe of decepcyon. *a* 1548 HALL *Chron., Hen. VI*, 91 b, Then he and all his companye made a signe of retraite.

c. A signal.

1601 SHAKS. *Jul. C.* v. i. 23 Mark Antony, shall we giue signe of Battaile?..No Cæsar. 1615 G. SANDYS *Trav.* 298 The Charioteers started their horses upon a signe given. 1678 *Life Black Prince* in *Harleian Misc.* (1809) III. 144 The sign of battle, being given by King Philip, was entertained with clamours and shouts. 1708 CHAMBERLAYNE *Pres. St. Gt. Brit.* (1710) 349 From the top..they made a Sign by Fire, when they apprehended any imminent Danger. 1817 SHELLEY *Rev. Islam* x. vii, With secret signs from many a mountain-tower, With smoke by day, and fire by night.

2. A mark or device having some special meaning or import attached to it, or serving to distinguish the thing on which it is put.

Freq. in *sign of the Cross* (cf. CROSS *sb.* 3 b).

c 1290 *S. Eng. Leg.* I. 84 Heo made þe signe of þe croiz. 13.. *Cursor M.* 6078 (Gött.), On ilk a post..A sine of tau T, make ȝe þer. 1393 LANGL. *P. Pl.* C. XV. 40 Crist cam and confermede and holy kirke made, And in sond a sygne wrot. *c* 1420 LYDG. *Assembly of Gods* 1040 Vertew commaundyd euery wyght To pauyse hym vndyr the sygne of the roode. *c* 1440 *Pallad. on Husb.* XI. 22 Now nede is sette a signe on euery vyne That fertile is, sciouns of hit to take For settyng. 1526 *Pilgr. Perf.* (W. de W. 1531) 26 b, Marked..not onely with the sygne of the crosse in our garmentis,..but also (I trust) with the sygne of tau in our soules. 1560 DAUS tr. *Sleidane's Comm.* 334 With his crosiers staffe [he] maketh the signe of the crosse upon the highest walles. 1653 H. MORE *Antid. Ath.* II. vi, Observing that several Herbs are marked with some Mark or Sign that intimates their virtue. 1733 BERKELEY *Th. Vision Vind.* § 40 A great number of arbitrary signs, various and opposite, do constitute a Language. 1769 ROBERTSON *Chas. V, State Europe* Note x, It was usual for persons who could not write, to make the sign of the cross in confirmation of a charter. 1833 N. ARNOTT *Physics* (ed. 5) II. 236 The common visual signs on the retina..are of all signs the most readily learned or understood. 1884 *Cath. Dict.* (1897) 258/1 The Church, accustomed to bless everything with the sign of the cross.

†b. A bookmark; = REGISTER *sb.*¹ 7 a. *Obs.*⁻⁰

1483 *Cath. Angl.* 340/1 A Syne of a buke, *registrum*.

c. A conventional mark, device, or symbol, used technically (as in music, algebra, botany, etc.) in place of words or names written in ordinary letters.

1557 RECORDE *Whetst.* S j b, Nombers Cossike, are soche as bee contracte vnto a denomination of some Cossike signe. *Ibid.* S ij b, There be other .2. signes in often vse, of whiche the firste is made thus + and betokeneth more: the other is made – and betokeneth lesse. 1597 MORLEY *Introd. Mus.* 104 The note whereupon the following part must begin, is marked with this signe .⁝. 1609 DOWLAND *Ornith. Microl.* 87 A signe is the successiue distribution of one and the same Close, in..a Song. 1662 PLAYFORD *Skill Mus.* I. x. (1674) 32 The Perfect of the Less..; its Sign or Mark is made thus. 1728 CHAMBERS *Cycl.* s.v. *Character*, Ordinarily..in Algebra, the Sign [of multiplication] is omitted, and the two Quantities put together. 1832 LINDLEY *Introd. Bot.* 422 In botany a variety of marks, or signs, are employed to express particular qualities or properties of plants. 1875 JOWETT *Plato* (ed. 2) IV. 150 Two minus signs in arithmetic or algebra make a plus.

†d. *Math.* A point. *Obs. rare.*

1570 BILLINGSLEY *Euclid* I. def. 1, A signe or point is that which hath no part. *Ibid.*, Vnity..is lesse materiall then a signe or poynt.

†3. A mark of attestation (or ownership), written or stamped upon a document, seal, etc. *Obs.*

1362 LANGL. *P. Pl.* A. II. 82 Þe Deede was a-selet, Be siht of sir Symoni and Notaries signes. 1377 *Ibid.* B. XX. 270, I wolde..þat ȝe were in þe Registre, And ȝowre noumbre vndre notaries sygne. *c* 1460 *Oseney Reg.* 133 The forsaide x. acris..lien in the Northefelde of the foresaide towne with owre syne woonyd i-seeled. 1474 CAXTON *Chesse* II. i. (1883) 22 Not only her promises but their othes her sealis and wrytynges & signes of their propre handes. 1558 in *10th Rep. Hist. MSS. Comm.* App. V. 388 In wittnes hereof we have..set hereunto our signes and common sealle. 1609 BIBLE (Douay) *Jer.* xxxii. 44 The fieldes..shal be written in a booke, and the signe shal be stamped on, and a witnes shal be taken.

†4. A figure or image; a statue or effigy; an imprint. *Obs.*

1362 LANGL. *P. Pl.* A. IV. 112 Bere no seluer ouer see þat bereþ signe of þe kyng. 1387 TREVISA *Higden* (Rolls) I. 229 Þere is anoþere signe and tokene to fore þe popes paleys; an hors of bras and a man sittynge þeron. *c* 1440 *Pol., Rel., & L. Poems* (1903) 152 Ther ys ȝette a syne of his fote On a marbull stone þer as he stode. 1589 WARNER *Alb. Eng.* VI. xxix. (1602) 143 For often Vprores did ensue for him, as vndeceast, Howbeit solemnely inter'd, himselfe, or Signe at least.

†5. a. A device borne on a banner, shield, etc.; a cognizance or badge. *Obs.*

c 1290 *S. Eng. Leg.* I. 153 Ane Croiz, þat Man fer isaiȝ,.. Þat was signe of is baner. *c* 1350 *Will. Palerne* 3213 Swete sire, ȝe me saye what signe is þe leuest to haue schape in þi scheld to schene armes? 1399 *Rolls of Parlt.* III. 452 That thei..gyf no Liverees of Sygnes, no make no Retenue of men. *c* 1420 LYDG. *Assembly of Gods* 355 A garland of yuy he [Bacchus] chase for hys sygne. 1461 *Coventry Leet-bk.* II. 319 [That they] neyther were ne vse oure most honnorable signe, nor any other lordes or gentilles signe, tokyn or lyuere. 1562 LEGH *Armorie* 47, I will therfore shewe you of signes yᵗ are borne, and do occupie the same Escocheon.

†b. Something displayed as an emblem or token; *esp.* an ensign, banner, standard. *Obs.*

c 1400 *Song Roland* 503 An C thousand of good men.. with proud synes of silk lifte on loft. *c* 1440 *York Myst.* xvii. 222 Vn-to þat Prince I rede we praye, That till vs sente his syngne [*sc.* the star] vnsoght. 1483 CAXTON *Gold. Leg.* 305/1 He is had among the companye of Angels as banerer and berynge the signe of oure lord. 1500–20 DUNBAR *Poems* xxxviii. 4 The signe trivmphall rasit is of the croce. 1596 DALRYMPLE tr. *Leslie's Hist. Scotl.* II. 300 Monie standarts and syngis..left be the Jnglismen, be the Scotis ar tane. 1667 MILTON *P. L.* VI. 776 The great Ensign of Messiah blaz'd Aloft by Angels born, his Sign in Heav'n.

†c. *spec.* A pilgrim's token. *Obs.*

1362 LANGL. *P. Pl.* A. VI. 12 An hundred of ampolles on his hat seeten, Signes of Synay and Schelles of Galys. *c* 1400 *Beryn* 171 Then, as manere & custom is, signes þere þey bouȝte. *Ibid.* 175, 191.

†d. *pl.* Insignia. *Obs. rare.*

1591 SPENSER *M. Hubberd* 1016 Yet at the last..He all those royall signes had stolne away.

6. A characteristic device attached to, or placed in front of, an inn (†house) or shop, as a means of distinguishing it from others or directing attention to it; in later use commonly a board bearing a name or other inscription, with or without some ornament or picture.

1467 in *Eng. Gilds* (1870) 405 That no person sille none ale out of his place, but be haue a signe at his dorre. *c* 1470 *Promp. Parv.* (K.) 456/1 Syne of an in. 1539 TAVERNER *Erasm. Prov.* (1552) 42 The Englysh prouerbe is this. Good wyne nedeth no signe. 1593 SHAKS. *2 Hen. VI*, v. ii. 67 Vnderneath an Ale-house paltry signe, The Castle in S. Albons. 1617 MORYSON *Itin.* III. 156, I did never see nor heare that they have any publike Innes with signes hanging out. 1667 PRIMATT *City & C. Build.* 69 Note, That they weigh with the Balconie, the Bars that are to fasten the sign thereunto. 1727 SWIFT *Imit. Horace* II. vi. 72 To read the Lines Writ underneath the Country Signs. 1780 *Mirror* No. 82 Putting up their pictures as signs for their taverns and ale-houses. 1816 J. SCOTT *Vis. Paris* (ed. 5) 91 The signs of the shops are very elegant;—that is to say, they are elegant for signs. 1859 JEPHSON *Brittany* ix. 134 The first thing that met my eye..was a sign over a public-house.

fig. 1642 FULLER *Holy & Prof. St.* I. viii. 20 Fools! who to perswade men that Angels lodged in their hearts, hung out a devil for a signe in their faces. *a* 1684 LEIGHTON *Wks.* (1816) 429 Fantastic garb in apparel, which is the very bush or sign hanging out, that tells a vain mind lodges within. 1885 SCOTT *Talism.* iv, I am but the vile and despised sign, which points out to the wearied traveller a harbour of rest and security, but must itself remain for ever without doors.

b. In phr. *at the sign of* (*the Bell, Sun*, etc.).

1501 *Alcock's Mons Perfect.* Colophon, Enprynted at London in flete strete at the sygne of yᵉ sonne by Wynkin de worde. 1542–3 *Act* 34 & 35 *Hen. VIII*, c. 12 One little lane stretching from the said way, to the signe of the bell at Drewry lane ende. 1672 *Heath's Flagellum* Title-p., Sold at his Shop at the Signe of the Crown. 1722 DE FOE *Col. Jack* (1840) 94 We baited at an inn, at the sign of the Falcon. 1749 FIELDING *Tom Jones* VIII. viii, Chose for their house of entertainment the sign of the Bell. 1828 SCOTT *F. M. Perth* xx, An appointment to meet with the others of his company at the sign of the Griffin.

†c. *At the sign of the moon*, in the open air by night. (After Fr. *à l'enseigne de la lune*.) *Obs.*

1613 PURCHAS *Pilgrimage* III. x. (1614) 294 They often lodge (saith Willamont) at the signe of the Moone; and the like moderation they vse in diet and apparel. 1679 G. R. tr. *Boaistuau's Theat. World* II. 107 The Souldier is for the most part always waking, having his Quarters at the Sign of the Moon.

II. 7. A token or indication (visible or otherwise) *of* some fact, quality, etc.

1297 R. GLOUC. (Rolls) 3744 Þer nas nour aboute kniȝt.. bot hii of sute were Of king arthures hous, oþer som signe þer of bere, Of robes oþer of armes. 13.. *E. E. Allit. P.* B. 489 Þat was þe syngne of sauyte þat sende hem oure lorde. *c* 1386 CHAUCER *Melib.* § 53 It is signe of gentil herte whan a man..desireth to han a good name. *c* 1400 *Lanfranc's Cirurg.* 181 If þe place be whijt & neische..it is a signe of fleume. 1484 CAXTON *Fables of Avian* viii, [He] hath shewed to the grete sygne or token of loue. *a* 1533 LD. BERNERS *Gold. Bk. M. Aurel.* (1546) C iii b, He bare in his hande the signe or token of the office, wherby he lyued. 1594 in *Cath. Rec. Soc. Publ.* V. 285 All with black hoods, which with us is a signe of gentlewomen. 1638 JUNIUS *Paint. Ancients* 228 Though it be no signe of a more polished, yet is it a marke of a greater wit. 1697 DRYDEN *Virg. Georg.* III. 670 The Causes and the Signs.. Of ev'ry Sickness that infects the Fold. 1750 GRAY *Long Story* 89 [It was] no sign of grace, For folks in fear are apt to pray. 1829 T. L. PEACOCK *Misfort. Elphin* x, They here found..materials of spinning and embroidering, and other signs of female inhabitancy. 1863 GEO. ELIOT *Romola* xxii, Working people..bearing on their dress or persons the signs of their daily labour. 1874 GREEN *Short Hist.* iv. § 5. 202 The exile of Gaveston was the sign of the Barons' triumph.

b. Used without const., or with clause following.

c 1380 WYCLIF *Sel. Wks.* II. 258 Signes of þe olde lawe weren toknes of oure signes now, as þei ben tokenes of þe blisse of hevene. 1422 tr. *Secreta Secret., Priv. Priv.* 232 They haue many tokenys or syngnes by wych a man may deme the Physnomye. 1483 CAXTON *Cato* 5 Of the foure Sygnes or tokens by whiche is knowen trewe loue. 1560 DAUS tr. *Sleidane's Comm.* 55 b, To axe of God a sygne wherby he maye testifie, that he careth for us. *a* 1656 BP. HALL *Rem. Wks.* (1660) 192 The thing signed is usually put for the sign itself. 1690 LOCKE *Hum. Und.* III. x. (1695) 277 The using of Words, without clear and distinct Ideas; or, which is worse, signs without any thing signified. 1766 GRAY *Impromptus* 12 A sign you have eat just enough and no more. 1833 TENNYSON *Two Voices* 270 Know I not Death? the outward signs? 1885 S. O. JEWETT *Marsh Island* xii, She never had given a single sign that she loved or meant to marry him.

c. Without article, in phr. *in sign of* (or *that*).

1297 R. GLOUC. (Rolls) 3986 Branches hii bere Of oliue, as in signe þat hii aȝen pays nere. *a* 1300 *Cursor M.* 5121 He kist þam all in signe o saght. 1362 LANGL. *P. Pl.* A. XI. 98 In signe þat I schulde bi-sechen hire of grace. 1474 CAXTON *Chesse* II. iv. (1883) 44 The kynge..gyrdeth a boute them a swerde in signe that they sholde abyde and kepe hym. 1546 *Reg. Privy Council Scot.* I. 30 In signe and takin herof my Lord Governour hes takyn baith thair handis. 1593 SHAKS. *3 Hen. VI*, IV. viii. 26 In signe of truth, I kisse your Highnesse Hand. 1611 SIR W. MURE *Mis Amours* 39 Receaue, in sing that thou hes won the field, The bow. 1718 POPE *Iliad* x. 321 In sign she favour'd their intent, A long-wing'd heron great Minerva sent. 1865 MILL *Exam. Hamilton* 381 An animal is called a bull, in sign of its possessing certain attributes.

d. *U.S.* The trail or trace of wild animals, etc.

Sometimes in pl., but the sing. is the technical use.

1847 RUXTON *Mexico & Rocky Mts.* xxi. 170 On the banks of the river I saw some fresh beaver 'sign'. *Ibid.*, We saw Indian sign on the banks of the river. 1851 MAYNE REID *Scalp Hunt.* xxxii. 243 Buffalo 'signs' appeared as we rode into them. 1890 L. C. D'OYLE *Notches* 68 We had noticed bear 'sign' in a thick patch of rose-bushes. *Ibid.*, Lots of fresh 'sign', but no bear.

8. A trace or indication *of* something; a vestige. Chiefly in negative phrases.

13.. *Seuyn Sag.* 2934 (W.), So he traueld monethes thre, And no signe of hyr kowth he se. 1390 GOWER *Conf.* III. 315 With the craftes whiche he couthe, He soghte and fond a signe of lif. *c* 1440 *York Myst.* xi. 100, I se ȝondyr a ful selcouth syght, Wher-of be-for no synge was seene. 1567 ALLEN *Def. Priesthood* 228 Wherof yet in most Churches ther remaineth a smal signe, by disciplin geuen [etc.]. *c* 1586 C'TESS PEMBROKE *Ps.* CXV. iii, [No] signe of sound their throates can show. 1715 LEONI *Palladio's Archit.* (1742) II. 66 The Aqueducts..whose Ruins and Signs are to be seen on the Road. 1726 SWIFT *Gulliver* I. i, I..could not discover any Sign of Houses or Inhabitants. 1795 *Ann. Reg., Hist.* 109 No signs of such an intention were perceivable. 1872 BLACK *Adv. Phaeton* xxx. 407 There is no sign of life in this wild place.

†b. A mere semblance *of* something. *Obs.*

1607 BRETON *A Murmurer* Wks. (Grosart) II. 8/2 Oh fine foole, how thou wouldest haue the signe of a man stand for a man? 1673 DRYDEN *Marr. à-la-Mode* II. i, If it be but to punish that sign of a Husband there; that lazy Matrimony. 1693 CONGREVE *Old Bach.* III. iii, I would not have you draw yourself into a premunire, by trusting to that sign of a man there.

9. An indication of some coming event; *spec.* an omen or portent.

13.. *Cursor M.* 22430 (Gött.), Forn domes-dai þai sal be sene, wid sorful sines ful fiȝf-tene. 1387 TREVISA *Higden* (Rolls) II. 165 Soche þey declareþ certeynliche by schewynge of tokenes and of synnes [*v.r.* synes] þat beeþ in suche a schulder boon. 1513 DOUGLAS *Æneid* IV. viii, How Dido send hir sistir Enee to pray, And of the grisly singis did hir affray. 1542 BOORDE *Dyetary* xl. (1870) 302 That there is lykle [*sic*] hope of amendment, but sygnes of deth. 1593 SHAKS. *3 Hen. VI*, v. vi. 44 The Owle shriek'd at thy birth, an euill signe. 1621 T. WILLIAMSON tr. *Goulart's Wise Vieillard* 94 The auncient Iewes had this saying, that it is *bonum omen*, a good signe to see an old man in a house. 1725 *Fam. Dict.* s.v. *Clouds*, When..waterish Clouds appear on the Tops of Hills, it is a Sign of Rain to follow. 1793 COWPER *Tale* 61 Seamen much believe in signs. 1817 SHELLEY *Rev. Islam* x. xvi, These signs the coming mischief did foretell. 1833 TENNYSON *May Queen* III. x, If it come three times, I thought, I take it for a sign.

10. An act of a miraculous nature, serving to demonstrate divine power or authority.

In Biblical use, after L. *signum*, Gr. σημεῖον.

a 1300 *Cursor M.* 13420 Þis was þe formast sign he did. *Ibid.* 13438 Sli signe did crist at þis bridall. 1382 WYCLIF *Acts* iv. 22 The man was more than of fourty ȝeeris, in the which this sygne of heelthe was maad. 1611 BIBLE *Acts* ii. 43 Many wonders and signes were done by the Apostles. 1665 J. SPENCER *Vulg. Proph.* 59 But every Sign is not (if we speak accurately) a Miracle. 1787 DE FOE *Syst. Magic* I. iii. (1840) 73 Pharaoh, in contempt of Moses and Aaron, and the sign or miracle they had shown. 1876 MELLOR *Priesth.* iv. 179 His hearers no sooner caught the word 'faith', than they demanded a sign which might warrant it.

†b. A marvel or wonder. *Obs.*⁻¹

a 1400–50 *Alexander* 4934 Sire, þou sall see with þi siȝt slike signes, or þou passe, As neuire segge vndire son saȝe bot þine ane.

11. *Astr.* One or other of the twelve equal divisions of the Zodiac, each distinguished by the name of a constellation and frequently denoted by a special symbol.

c 1340 HAMPOLE *Pr. Consc.* 4803 Þe twelfte day aftir, þe sternes alle And þe signes fra þe heven sal falle. 1390 GOWER *Conf.* III. 108 Ther ben signes tuelve, Whiche have her cercles be hemselve Compassed in the zodiaque. *c* 1430 LYDG. *Min. Poems* (Percy Soc.) 2 Whan Phebus was.. yronne Out of the signe, wiche callyd is aquary. 1483 CAXTON *Cato* e v b, The man whych is borne in a good planette or sygne. 1509 HAWES *Past. Pleas.* XXII. (Percy Soc.) 105 He sette..The bodies above to have their moving, In the xii. signes them selfe to domify. 1555 EDEN *Decades* (Arb.) 279 At that tyme the soonne was in the north signes. 1610 HOLLAND *Camden's Brit.* (1637) 182 Vnder what Signe in heaven Britaine lieth. *a* 1646 J. GREGORY *Posthuma* (1650) 299 Now look what Sign of the twelv shall bee found to rise up in the Horoscope or Angle of the East, that is the Sign-Regent of that Hous or Citie. 1709 STEELE *Tatler* No. 100 § 3, I was looking..on that Sign in the Heavens which is called by the Name of the Ballance. 1812 WOODHOUSE *Astron.* xxix. 289 The motions of Jupiter's satellites are according to the order of the signs. 1868 LOCKYER *Elem. Astron.* § 37 These are called the zodiacal constellations (very carefully to be distinguished.. from the signs of the zodiac bearing the same name).

†b. A constellation. *Obs. rare.*

1398 TREVISA *Barth. De P. R.* VIII. xxiii. (Bodl. MS.), Arcturus is a signe ymade of vij. sterres. *Ibid.*, Orioun is a signe that ariseth in wintere. 1490 CAXTON *Eneydos* xii. 46 The sygne of Oryon. 1565 COOPER *Thesaurus*, *Orion*.. was..translated among the sterres, & there is the signe called in latine *Jugula*. 1611 COTGR. s.v. *Orion*.

III. 12. *attrib.* and *Comb.*, as (sense 1) *sign-language, -maker, -speech, -talk*; (sense 2 c) *sign-symbol*; (sense 5) *sign-mark*; (sense 6) *sign-iron, -painter*; (sense 7) *sign-word*; (sense 11) † *sign-carrier*.

1653 R. SANDERS *Physiogn.* 1 A Zodiack..; the Latins call it *Signifer*, that is to say, *Sign-carrier. 1778 *Phil. Trans.* LXIX. 44 On passing through the streets of London in his walks, before the *sign-irons were taken down. 1836 in *Hist. Chesterfield* (1839) 45 Having a sign, sign-iron, sign-post, or shew-board suspended from or in front of such house. 1865 TYLOR *Early Hist. Man.* ii. 25 The teacher remarked that I did not seem to be quite a beginner in the *sign-language. 1889 MIVART *Orig. Hum. Reason* 66 Such a movement is a true 'sign', being a movement made depicting a fact with the intention of conveying to other minds the ideas of the *sign-maker. 1840 BROWNING *Sordello* IV. 387 The Kaiser's ominous *sign-mark had first place, The crowned grim twy-necked eagle. 1776 BURNEY *Hist. Mus.* I. 221 The painter should have had about the same degree of merit with a good *sign-painter in Europe. 1814 SIR R.

Supplement, p. 3873; Corrigenda, p. 4092; Spurious words, p. 4093; Books quoted, p. 4094

Sign ...

†Signacle ...

Signal ...

Signalize ...

Signalman ...

Signator ...

Signatory ...

Signature ...

Signet ...

Signifiance ...

Significance (signĭfĭkăns), *sb.* [a. OF. *significance*, or ad. L. *significantia*, f. L. *significare* to SIGNIFY: cf. SIGNIFICANCE. Not frequent before the 19th cent., but cf. next.]

1. The meaning or import of something.

2. Importance.

Significancy (signĭfĭkănsĭ). [See prec. and -ANCY.]

1. The quality of being highly significant or expressive; expressiveness.

2. Having or conveying a meaning; signifying something.

3. *significant figure*, in ordinary notation and decimal fractions, any one of the figures from 1 to 9, in contrast to the cipher.

Significantly (signĭfĭkăntlĭ), *adv.* [f. prec. + -LY².] In a significant manner; so as to convey some meaning; expressively, meaningly.

Significate, *sb.* OF. [ad. L. *significat-um*, pa. pple. neut. of *significare* to SIGNIFY.] That which is signified or prognosticated.

Signification (signĭfĭkēīˈʃən). Forms: 4- signific-, 5 signyf-, 5 signifyo-, 4-5 significacion. [a. OF. *signification*, or ad. L. *significatiōn-em*.]

1. The fact or property of being significant or expressive of something.

2. *significant figure*.

3. That which is signified by something; meaning, import, implication. Freq. const. *of*.

4. A sign, gesture, etc., serving to indicate desire or feeling. *Obs.*

Significatist. *Obs. rare.* [Cf. next and -IST.] One who...

Significative (signĭfĭkātĭv), *a.* and *sb.* [a. OF. *significatif*, -ive, ad. L. *significatīv-us*.]

1. Serving to signify something; having a signification or meaning.

2. Of, pertaining to, or of the nature of a sign.

Significatively, *adv.* [f. prec. + -LY².] In a significative manner; by adequate representation; expressively.

Significator (sĭgnĭfĭkātɔɹ). [a. med.L. *significator*, agent-noun f. L. *significare* to SIGNIFY. Cf. F. *significateur*.]

1. *Astrol.* The planet by which the querent or the quesited is specially signified.

Significatrix, *sb. rare.* [app. a. OF. *significatrice*, f. as prec.]

Signify (sĭgnĭfăɪ), *v.* Also 3-5 signe- (3, 5 -nie), 4-6 signy-, 4-6 signyf- (5 syni-), 5-6 signi-, Pr. 3 sing. *significat*, etc.; pa. t. and pa. pple. 4-6 -fied, -fyed. [a. F. *signifier* (12th c.), = Pr. *significar*, *-far*, Sp. and Pg. *significar*, It. *significare*, *significa*, L. *significare* to SIGNIFY.]

1. *trans.* To be a sign or symbol of; to represent, betoken, mean.

2. Of persons: To make known, indicate, declare.

3. To be significant or important; to matter, be of consequence or moment. (Usu. *negative* or *interrog.*)

Signifying, *ppl. a.* [-ING².] That signifies or denotes; significant. † *Signifying figure*, numeral (see SIGNIFICANT *a.* 3).

Signifying, *vbl. sb.* [f. SIGN *v.* + -ING¹.]

Signing (săɪnɪŋ), *vbl. sb.* [f. SIGN *v.* + -ING¹.]

1. The action of making or appending one's signature; confirmation by signature.

2. *Eccl.* The action of making the sign of the cross.

Signing (săɪnɪŋ). [-ING²] That signifies or denotes; a signing officer (see quot. 1867).

Signior, etc. *see* SIGNOR.

Signioresse, variant of SEIGNORESS.

Signless (săɪnlɛs), *a.* [f. SIGN *sb.* + -LESS.]

Sign-manual (săɪnˈmænjʊal). [SIGN *sb.* + MANUAL *a.*]

1. An autograph signature of the sovereign serving to authenticate a document.

2. *gen.* An autograph signature.

Signor (sīˈnjɔɹ). Also 6-9 *signior* (7 -iour, -ier); It. *signore*, *signor* (7 -ior, -iour, etc.), Sp., Pg. *señor*, f. *seignor* (12th c.), = L. *senior* SENIOR.]

Signora (sīˈnjōrə). [It., fem. of SIGNOR.]

Signorina (sīˌnjɔrīˈnə). [It., dim. of *signora*.] The Italian term of respect applicable to a young unmarried lady.

Signory (sīˈnjɔrɪ). [a. OF. *seignorie* (Godel.), med.L. *senioria*. See also SEIGNIORY.] Lordship, government.

1. *intr.* To rule, reign, have or exercise dominion.

2. *trans.* To govern, control, exercise dominion or rule over (anything).

Sign-post (săɪnpəʊst). [SIGN *sb.*]

1. A post supporting a sign, usually that of an inn.

2. A stretch of meadow; a field. *Obs.*

Signory (sīˈnjɔrɪ). Forms: *see* SIGNORY.

Sike (săɪk), *sb.* [Northern form of SITCH *sb.*] A small stream of water, a rill or streamlet, flowing through a flat or marshy ground.

Sike (săɪk), *a.* and *pron.* Sc., north. and dial. [var. of SICHE *a.*] Such.

Sike (săɪk), *v.* Now *dial.* Forms: 3-4 *siken*, 3-5 *syke*, 3-6 *sike*, *syk*, 9 *dial.* *soik* (var. of SICHE *v.*). [OE. *sīcan*, a var. of *sūgan* to sigh, whence later ME. *sike*, *syke* to draw breath.]

Siket. *Now dial.* Forms: 3-9 *siket*, 6 *syket*, 9 *sicket*, 7 *siquet*. [a. ONF. *siket* = OF. *siquet*.] Recorded chiefly in the Latinized forms *siketus*, *sicket*. A small watercourse or dike, a drain.

Silicide (silᵢˈsaɪd). Chem. [f. Silica + -ide.] A compound of silicon with one other element.

Silicification. = Silicification.

Siliciferous (silisˈifərəs), a. [f. L. silici-, silex Silex + -ferous. So F. silicifère.] Yielding or producing silex or silica.

Silicify (silᵢˈsɪfaɪ), v. [Cf. prec. and -fy.]

Silicious, a. variant of Siliceous.

Silicium (silᵢˈsɪəm). Now rare. = Silicon.

Silicle (ˈsɪlɪk'l). Bot. [ad. F. silicule or L. silicula.] A small short seed-pod.

Silico-, combining form of Silica or Silicon.

Silicon (ˈsɪlɪkən). Chem. [f. Silic(a + -on.] A non-metallic element.

Silicosis (silᵢˈkoʊsɪs). Path. [f. silic- Silex + -osis.] A lung disease induced by inhaling flinty or siliceous particles.

Silicula (silᵢˈkjuːlə). Bot. [L., dim. of Siliqua.] A short pod containing seed; a silicle.

Silicule (ˈsɪlɪkjuːl). Bot. [ad. L. silicula.]

Siliculose, a. Bot. [f. L. silicula + -ose.]

Siliqua (silᵢˈkwə). Pl. -quae. Bot. [L., = pod.]

Siliquose, Siliquous (silᵢˈkwoʊs, -kwəs), a. [ad. mod.L. siliquosus.]

Silk (silk), sb. and a.

Products of the silk-ribbon loom.

Silken (ˈsɪlk(ə)n), a.

Silk-throwster. [f. Silk sb. + Throwster.]

Silkworm. [f. Silk sb. + Worm.]

Silky (silˑki). ...
1. Silken; made or consisting of silk. ...
2. Having the delicate softness of silk. ...
b. Of liquor: Having a soft delicate taste. ...
3. Of speech, manners, etc.: Smooth, pleasing, ingratiating, insinuating. ...
4. Having the gloss or silk; resembling silk in lustre. ...
b. Having a texture like that of silk. ...

Sill (sil), sb.1 Forms: 6 a, 1 syl, 1, 5–6 syll, 6, 4 sulle, 4, 7 sille; 6 Sc. schyll, 7, 9 sil, 7–sill, 9 sull, 8, 9 sille, 9, 7 sile, 6 sell. [OE. syll and sylle, = MDu. sulle, sille, sul (LG. sull), related to MDu. sille (Fris. sille), MLG. sille (LG. zill), and to ON. and Norw. syll, syll (mod.Icel. syllo, MSw. and Sw. syll (dial. sill), Da. syld, also OHG. swelli, swelli (MHG. swelle, G. schwelle). The precise relationship of these types to each other, and to Goth. gasuljan to found, or to L. solea threshold of a wattled wall (Cassiod. is not clear.] ...

Silladar (silˑädar). Anglo-Ind. Also silledar, sillahdar. [a. Urdū (Pers.) silahdār, f. Arab. silāh arms, armour.] ...

Sill, sb.2 Dial. var. of THILL. ...

Sill, v. var. of SILE v. ...

Sillery (silˑeri). Also 7 Cel(l)ery. [f. Sillery near Rheims in the department of Marne, Champagne.] A high-class wine produced in and around the village of Sillery in Champagne. ...

Si·liograph. rare. [f. L. sillograph-us, ad. Gr. σιλλογράφος.] A writer of satires or lampoons; esp. applied to Timon of Phlius (c 268 B.C.). ...

Si·llograph-ist, rare. [f. L. sillograph-us, ad. ...] ...

Si·llogism, the form of SYLLOGISM. ...

Sillabub, dial. form of SYLLABUB. ...

Sill-bread, -board, var. forms of SILL. ...

Silli (silˑi). [f. SILLY a. + -Y.] ...

Sillily (silˑili), adv. [f. SILLY a. + -LY.] In a silly or foolish manner. ...

Silliman·ite (silˑimănait). Min. [f. the name of Benjamin Silliman, an American chemist (1779–1864); named by G. T. Bowen in 1824.] A silicate of alumina, occurring in slender rhombic prisms or in fibrous masses. ...

Silliness (silˑines). [f. SILLY a. + -NESS.] The quality of being silly; foolishness, senselessness. ...

Sillock (silˑŏk). Sc. Forms: 7 sellak, 8 -ok, 9 ook; 8 silak, 9 sillock, -ag; 8–9 sillik, -ock (9 sik), 8–sillock, and six gun. [app. f. SILL sb.] ...

Sillyhow, etc. forms of SILLY-HOW. ...

Silly (silˑi), a. and adv. Forms: ... [OE. sǣlig, gesǣlig, etc.] ...
1. Happy, blissful, blessed; fortunate, lucky. Obs. ...
b. Spiritually blessed; ... Obs. ...
2. ... pious, holy, good. ...
3. Helpless, defenceless;
b. Of inanimate things. Now Sc. ...
c. Weakly, feeble, sickly. ...
d. Scanty, poor, mean. ...
4. Lacking in judgement or common sense; foolish, senseless, empty-headed. ...

Si·lyish, a. rare. [f. SILLY a. + -ISH.] ...

Si·lyism. [f. SILLY a. + -ISM.] ...

Sillybob, Sillybub, obs. ff. SILLABUB. ...

Silly-how. Now Sc. and north. Forms: 6, 8–9 Sc. sely how, 9 -how; sealihood; 7 sylliss-how, 7–silly-how (7 sillie), 9 Sc. selly how, sillyhoo, north. Also how Hooye. ...

Silo (sailˑo). [a. Sp. silo (hence also F. silo), pied up to keep corn in.] ...

Silphium [f. L. silphium, a. Gr.] ...

Silt (silt), sb. Also 5 cylt(e, 6 sylt, 9 silth. [Of obscure origin, but app. denoting a salty deposit: cf. Da. and Norw. sylt, brine; ...] ...

Si·lting, vbl. sb. [f. SILT v.] ...

Silt, v. ...

Silt-up (silˑt·ŏp). ...

Silty, a. [f. SILT sb. + -Y.] ...

Silure (siliūˑr). Ichth. [a. F. silure, ad. L. silūrus SILURUS.] A siluroid fish, esp. the sheat-fish (Silurus glanis). ...

Silurian (siliūˑriăn), a. and sb. [f. L. Silur-es ... + -AN.] ...

Silu·rian, a. and sb.2 Geol. [ad. L. Silur- ... + -IAN.] ...

Silurid (siliūˑrid), a. and sb. Ichth. [f. mod.L. Silur-us ...] ...

Siluroid (siliūˑroid), a. and sb. Ichth. [f. SILUR-US + -OID.] ...

Silu·rus. Ichth. [L., a. Gr. σίλουρος.] A genus of fish typical of the family Siluridæ; a fish belonging to this genus. ...

Silva, silvan, etc.: see SYLVA, SYLVAN. ...

Silver (silˑvǝr), sb. and a. Forms: 1 seolfor (siolofr-, siolufr-), seolfer (-ur, -or), syolofr, 2–5 selver, -uer (seolver, 2–silfer, 2–4 selver, etc. ...] ...
I. One of the precious metals (in general use ranking next to gold), characterized in a pure state by its lustrous white colour and great malleability and ductility. Chemical symbol Ag. ...
2. The metal regarded as a valuable possession or medium of exchange; money, coin (chiefly Sc.), money in general. ...

SILVER.

7. †b. The price in silver of something. *Obs.*⁻¹

3. Articles made of silver; silverware, silver-plate.

4. The metal as used for the ornamentation of textile fabrics; silver thread. *Cloth of silver*: see CLOTH sb. 8 b.

5. As a tincture in heraldry, more commonly called ARGENT, but not *cit.* 1868.

7. a. A variety of insect, fish, bird, etc., having silvery colouring or markings.

8. A silvery colour of tint.

b. In logic, context.

9. Producing or yielding silver.

b. *U.S.* (See quot.)

10. Of or pertaining to, connected with, characteristic of, silver.

b. Denoting compounds of which silver forms a part.

c. Of or pertaining to silver articles or silverware.

d. Advocating, relating to, etc., the adoption of silver as a currency or standard.

11. a. Used for holding (silver) money.

b. Of payments, etc.: Made or levied in (silver) money.

c. With vbl. sbs. or nouns of action, as *silver-mining*, *-plating*, *-reduction*.

12. Having the whiteness or lustre of silver; silvery. Chiefly *poet.*

b. Of the hair, beard, or head, white with age. Also in fig. context.

c. With reference to the colour or lustre of silver.

d. In specific names of animals, birds, fishes, plants, etc.

15. With pres. pples., in the sense of 'like, or with, silver', as *silver-edying*, *-flashing*, *-flowing*, etc.

16. With pres. pples., in the sense of 'silver-bearing, *-producing*, *-shining*, *-shedding*.

17. Parasynthetic and instrumental, of the types *silvered*, *scaled*, *banded*, *browed*; *silver-bound*, *-mounted*, etc.

IV. 21. Special combs.: silver-ball, bar (see quots.); silver bath, a solution, esp. of silver nitrate, used for sensitizing photographic plates and printing paper; a dish to contain this; silver-beggar, a Japan (see quots.); silver bronze, silver marriage; silver bronze, an attrib.; silver aquatic, lunar caustic; silver-eyed a., wall-eyed; silver-foam, silver-foot, silver-fork attrib., designate a school of novelists depicting fashionable life; silver-gilt; silver-pill, the quotation for silver (see); silver-point, the process of making a drawing with a silver-pill; silver-powder, a preparation of bismuth, tin, and mercury, used for silvering; silver print, a photograph produced by silver-printing; silver-printing, (a) the process of producing a photograph on paper sensitized with a silver salt; (b) printing in which the letters, etc., appear of a silvery colour; silver quinsy, silver sickness; silver rain, silver sand, a fine white sand used in horticulture, etc.; silver-sick a., poverty-sick; silver-smith, a worker in silver; silver solder, a solder partly composed of silver; hence a. and vbl. sb.; silver-spat, a silver-bearing rock; silver-spoon (see quot.); silver-stick, an officer's staff; silver streak, a variety of granite; silver streak, the English Channel; also *attrib.*; silver-tail, -tailed a. (see quots.); silver thaw, the phenomenon of rain freezing as it falls.

weed, fern, -head, herb, knapweed, oak, pine (tree), poplar, thistle, wattle (see quots. and the various sbs.).

Silver age.
1. The second age of the world, according to the Greek and Roman poets, inferior in simplicity and happiness to the first or golden.

Silver-eye(s): see SILVER sb. 21 c, d.

Silver fir.
1. A tall species of fir (*Abies* or *Picea pectinata*), native to southern and central Europe and some parts of Asia, introduced into Britain in the 17th century and extensively used for planting.

Silver bush. Also *silver bush.*
1. The plant Jupiter's beard.

Silver (silˈvəɹ), v. Forms: 5 cilueryn, sylueryn, 6 sylver, 7-silver; also 9 sc. siller. [f. the sb. Cf. G. silbern, Du. verzilveren.]
1. *trans.* To cover or plate with silver; to coat with silver. Freq. with over.

2. To invest or suffuse with a silvery hue or lustre.

b. *Photogr.* Treated with a silver compound.

3. Suffused with silver lustre; silver-coloured; whitened with age. Chiefly *poet.*

Silverer. [f. SILVER v. + -ER¹.] One who silvers, esp. one who practises silvering or silver-plating as a trade.

Silverette. [f. SILVER sb. + -ETTE.] A fancy breed of domestic pigeon; a bird belonging to this breed.

Silver-fish.
1. One of various silver-coloured fishes found in different parts of the world.

Silver-foil. [SILVER sb. 2.] Also silver foil. Silver beaten out thin; silver-leaf.

Silver-footed, *poet.* [SILVER sb. 17, after the Homeric epithet for Thetis.]

Silver-glance. Also silver glance. [ad. G. silberglanz; see GLANCE sb.] A variety of silver = argentite.

Silver grain. Also silver-grain. [SILVER sb. 19.] Planting a tree or forests...

Silver grass. Also silver-grass. [cf. G. silbergras.]

Silver-grey, a. and sb. [SILVER sb. 19.]

Silvering, vbl. sb. [f. SILVER v. + -ING¹.]

Silverish, a. [f. SILVER sb. + -ISH.] Silvery in quality or character.

Silverize, v. [f. SILVER sb. + -IZE.]

Silver lead. Also silver-lead. *Obs.*

Silver-leaf. [SILVER sb.]
1. Silver beaten out thin; silver-foil.

Silver-leaved, a. Also -leafed.

Silverling. Now arch.

Silver-like, a. Also &-y.

Silverly, adv.

Silver (si'lvan), a. Now poet. and arch.

Silver-ore. Also silver-ore.

Silver paper. Also silver-paper.

Silver plate. Also silver-plate.

Silver-scaled, a.

Silver-smith (si'lvəsmiþ).

Silver-tongued, a.

Silver-tree. Also silver tree.

Silverware [Silver sb.]

Silverweed. Also silver-weed, silverwood.

Silver-white, a. and sb. [Silver sb.]

Silver wire. Also silver-wire. [Silver sb.]

Silver-wood. [Silver sb.]

Silver-work. [Silver sb. Cf. MDu. silver-, silverwerc (Du. zilverwerk), MLG. silver-werk, MHG. and G. silberwerk.]

Silverwort. Obs.—

Silvery, a.

Simagre. Obs. rare.

Simar. Forms: 7-simarre, simar (7-arr); 8-symar (9 seymar). Also cymar.

Simarouba (simă'rŭ̄bă). Bot. and Med. Also 8-9 simarouba.

Simarubaceous, a.

Simia (si'miă). Pl. simiæ (si'mi,ī).

Simian (si'miăn), a. and sb.

Similable, a. Obs. rare.

Similation. obs. form of SIMULATION.

Similacre, variant of SIMULACRE Obs.

Similar (si'milă), a. and sb. Also 7 similaire.

Similarity (similă'rĭtĭ). [f. SIMILAR a. + -ITY.]

Similarly (si'milălĭ), adv.

Similary (si'milărĭ), a. Obs.

Simile (si'milī), sb. Also 8, 7 simily.

Similitude (simi'litiŭd). Also 4-5 symyli-, 5 simyli-, 6-6 symylytu-, 5 symyli-, symelitude; 6 similitudo.

+ Similitudinarily, adv. Obs.

+ Similitu dinary, a., adv. Obs.

+ Simili tude, a. med.l.

Simility. Obs. rare.

+ Similitude. Obs. rare.

Similly (si'milli), adv. Obs.

+ Similancy. Obs. rare.

Similor (si'milŏ).

Simious (si'miăs), a.

Simitar, obs. form of SCIMITAR.

Simity. Obs. rare.

Simmer (si'mă), v.[1]

Simmering, vbl. sb.

Simnel (si'mnĕl), sb.

Simonial, a.

Simoniac (simŏ'ni,ăk).

Simoniacal, a.

Simonious, a.

Simonist (si'mŏnist).

Simony (si'mŏni, sĭ-).

Simoom (simū'm).

Simous (si'măs), a.

Simper (si'mpă), v.

Simpering, vbl. sb.

Simmian. Obs. rare.

Simmon (si'mən).

Simmon, *sb.* Sc. (chiefly *Shetland*). Also 7 simmin, sin, symmon; simmond, -ind. [f. ON. *síma* Síme. Cf. Gael. *simon*.] A rope or band made of straw or heath, esp. used in thatching; rope of this material. Also *attrib.*

Simnel (si'mnel). Now *arch.* or *local*. Forms: 3-4 simenel(l, 3-7 -nelle, symnel; 5-6 symnelle (5-ynel), 5-7 -nel, 5-9 -nel; 6-simnel(l, 6- simnel, 7 -nell, 7-8 simnell [a. OF. *simenel*, *seminel*, etc. (mod.F. dial. *simnel*), app. related in some way to L. *simila* or Gr. *semídalis* fine flour.

Simon (sai·mən). [Name of various persons, real and legendary.]

Simony...

Simoniacle, *Obs.* [a. OF. *simoniacle*, var. of *simoniacal*: cf. next.] A simoniac.

† Simoner, *Obs.* [var. of Simonier.] A simonist, simoniac.

Simoniac (simə·niæk), *sb.* and *a.*
A. *sb.*

Simonial, *a. Obs.* Simoniacal.

Simonian [ad. med.L. *Simōniānus*, f. *Simon* (see def.).]
A. *sb.* A member of an early Christian sect named after Simon Magus and regarded as heretical. (Cf. SIMONIST[1].)

Simoniacal, *a.* Also 7 simoniacall. [f. prec. + -AL.]
I. Of the nature of, pertaining to, or involving simony.

† Simonical, *a. Obs.* Also simoniacal. [f. SIMONY + -ICAL] = SIMONIACAL.

Simonier ...

† Simonious, *a. Obs. rare.* [f. SIMONY + -OUS.] = SIMONIACAL 1 and 3.

Simonist [f. SIMON-Y + -IST.] One who practises or upholds simony.

Simon Pure, *sb.* (*adj.*). [The name of a Quaker in Mrs. Centlivre's comedy *A bold stroke for a wife* (1717).]

Simony (si·mōni). Forms: 3-6 symonye, -ie (4-1), 4-9 symony; 3-7 simonie (4-9 e), 6 simoni, 6- simony.

Simoom (simū·m). Also *sam-*, *semoom*, *simūm*; *simoon*, *-oun*. [a. Arab. *samūm*, f. the root *samm* to poison.

Simoon (simū·n), *sb.* = prec.

Simorgh (si·mȯrg). Also *simurgh*.

Simosaur (sai·mŏsǭr). [f. next.] An animal belonging to the fossil genus *Simosaurus*. So **Simosau·rian**.

Simosaurus (saimŏsǭ·rəs). *Palæont.* [mod.L.]

Simous (sai·məs), *a. rare.* [ad. L. *simus*, Gr. *σιμός*.]

Simp, *sb.* U.S. *slang.* [Shortening of SIMPLETON.]

Simpai (Malay.) [See quot.]

Simper-de-cocket, *Obs.* Forms: (see quots.). [app. a fanciful formation from SIMPER

Simperer ... An affected coquettish air; a woman characterized by this; a flirt.

Simper, *v.* [f. SIMPER *sb.* + -ER[1].]

Simpering, *vbl. sb.* [f. SIMPER *v.*[1] + -ING[1].]
The action of the verb; an instance of this.

Simpering, *ppl. a.* [f. SIMPER *v.*[1] + -ING[2].]
1. That simpers or smiles affectedly. Said of a person or their features.

Simperingly, *adv.* [f. SIMPERING *ppl. a.* + -LY[2].]

† Simperingness, *sb.* Obs.—[1] [f. simpering *ppl. a.* + -NESS.]

Simpingly, *adv.* Obs.—[1] When you see the milk begin to boil simpingly.

Simpingly, *adv.* [f. SIMPERING *ppl. a.* + -LY[2].] With a simper; in a simpering manner.

Simpleness, *see* SIMPLENESS.

Simple, *a.* (*sb.*), *adv.* Forms: 3 simpel, -ul, 5 simpel, -ill, -ulle; 4-5 symple, 5-6 simpill, 5 sympyll (5 -yl), 5-7 symple, simple, sympull (5 -ull), 4-6, 6-sympil, 7-8 symple. Also 4-6, 6 simpel, 5-6 seempill (6 -yll), 7-8, 9 dial. simpel. [a. F. *simple*, ad. L. *simplus*, *simplicem*, etc.]

Simplehead. *Obs.*⁻¹

Simple-hearted, *a.*

Simple-minded, *a.*

Simpleness.

Simple, *sb.*¹

Simpleton.

Simplicity.

Simpler.

Simpless.

Simpless.

Simpless.

Simplesse.

Simple, *a.*

Simplician.

Simplicist.

Simplicitarian.

Simplicize.

Simpling, *vbl. sb.*

Simplingly, *adv.*

Simplism.

Simplist.

Simplistic, *a.*

Simplicitly.

Simplification.

Simplificator.

Simplifier.

Simplify.

Simply, *adv.*

Simplum.

Simpson.

Simson.

Simul-.

Simulacre.

Simulacrum.

Simular.

Simulate, *v.*

Simulate, *ppl. a.*

Simulately, *adv.*

Simulation.

Simulative, *a.*

Simulator.

Simulate, v. Cf. F. *simulateur*, Sp. and Pg. *simulador*, It. *simulatore*.

Simulation. ... (entries)

Simultaneousness.

Simulacrity.

Simule, v. ... to simulate or feign.

Simuler, feigner.

Simultal.

Simultaneity.

Simultaneous, a.

Simultaneously, adv.

Simurgh ... Also *simurg*, *simorg*.

Sin, sb.

Sin, v.

Sinapine.

Sinapinic.

Sinapis.

Sinapism.

Sinapisine.

Sinapoline.

Sinapt-line.

Sincaline.

Sin-born.

Since, adv., prep., and conj.

Sincere, a.

Sincerely, adv.

Sincereness.

Sincerity. [ad. L. *sincerita(t-)*, Sp. *sinceridad*, Pg. *sinceridade*, It. *sincerità*.] The character, quality, or state of being sincere.

1. Freedom from falsification, adulteration, or alloy; purity, correctness. *Obs.*

+b. Genuineness (of a passage). *Obs.*

2. Freedom from dissimulation or duplicity; honesty, straightforwardness.

Sincope: see **Syncope**.

Sinoh, variant of **Cinch** sb. and v.

Sinciput. [ad. L. *sinciput*.] *Anat.* The fore part (of the head), called **Sinciput**, or **Bregma**.

Sincopace, obs. form of **Syncopace**.

Sind (saind), sb. 8 **synd**, 9 **synde**, 9 **zyne**. A rinsing; a draught, a portion.

Sind (saind), v. *north.* and *Sc.* Also 5 **synde**, 8–**synd**; 9 **zyne, zine**.

Sindaw, *Obs. rare.* Also 6 **syndow**, -**daw**. The plant *Alchemilla vulgaris*, common Lady's mantle.

Sindal, Sindar, obs. forms of **Cendal**, **Cinder**.

Sindal, obs. forms of **Sendal**.

Sindel, obs. form of **Sendal**. **Sinder**, obs. f.

Sindle, Sindly, var. of **Sendle** adv. seldom.

Sine (sain). Also 6–7 **sign(e**. [ad. L. *sinus* a bend, bay, etc.; also, the hanging fold of the upper part of a toga, the bosom of a garment, and hence used to render the synonymous Arab.]

1. *A gulf or bay.* *Obs. rare.*

2. *Trig.* One of the three fundamental trigonometrical functions.

3. *attrib.* and *as adj.* Of the nature of a sine-curve; involving no radius or vector.

Sine (sain), prep. = **Syne**.

Sine, obs. form of **Sin** v.

Sine qua non (sain'i kwæ' nǫn). [L.] 'Relating to a single person or thing.'

Sinecubal, *obs.*

Sinecural (sai'n*ē*kiū*ə*rǎl), a. [f. next + -AL.] 'Relating to a sinecure.'

Sinecure (sai'n*ē*kiūə*r), sb. and a. Also 7 **zine**. [ad. L. *sine cūrā* without care.]

Sinecurism (sai'n*ē*kiūə*rism). The holding or enjoying a sinecure.

Sinecurist (sai'n*ē*kiūə*rist).

Sineth, adv., prep., and conj. *Obs.*

Sinetic (sin*ē*ti'k), a. = **Sinitic**.

Sinew (si'n*ē*ū), sb. Forms: 1 pl. seonuwa, seon(o)we, 2 seonewe, 3 sen(e)we, 3–4 senewe, 4–5 senewe, 5 senowe, 6 sinewe, etc.

1. A strong fibrous cord serving to connect a muscle with a bone or other part; a tendon.

2. *pl.* Breeches. *Obs.*

Sinew (si'n*ē*ū), v. [f. prec.]

1. *trans.* To furnish, strengthen, or knit with, as with sinews.

2. *fig.* To be the sinews of; to strengthen, invigorate.

Sinewed (si'n*ē*ūd), *ppl. a.* Also 8 **sinnewed**.

Sinewiness (si'n*ē*ū*ines). The character, state, or quality of being sinewy.

+Sinewish, a. *Obs.*

Sinewless (si'n*ē*ū*les), a. Also 6 **sinewe-** , 7 **sin(n)ewles**.

Sinewous, a.

Sinewy (si'n*ē*ū*i), a. Also 4–5 **senewy**; 5 **synowy**, etc. [f. **Sinew** sb. + -Y.]

1. Made of sinew; consisting of sinews.

Sinewy-bark, *Obs.*

Siney, obs. form of **Senvy**.

Sinful (si'nfūl), a. and sb. Forms: 1 **synfull**, etc.

Sinfully (si'nfūl*i), adv.

Sinfulness (si'nfūlnes).

Sing (siŋ), v. [OE. *singan*, pa. t. *sang*, *song*, pa. pple. *sungen*.]

1. To utter musically or in verse.

Hence **Singing** vbl. sb. and ppl. a.

Sing, v.² Sc. (and north.) Also **6 signe**. Pa. t. singed, singt, -it; also sang, sung. [Northern form of SINGE v., perh. based on the early pa. t. and pp. pple. singed, senged. Frequently conjugated after SING v.¹] trans. To singe.

Singe (sindʒ), v. Forms: 1 sæn(e)gan, sen(e)gan, 4 seng, 4-6 senge (5 seenge), 5-6 synge, 6 syndge, 6 singe, 7 sindge. [OE. sen(e)gan = OFris. senge, sengia, (WFris. singe, dial. zinge), MDu. and Du. sengen, MLG. and MHG. sengen (G. sengen, 7 zengen), related to Icel. sangr (singed) taste, Norw. sang singed appearance of burning. The stem *sang- may be related to SING v.¹ and have reference to the sound produced by violent singing.]

SINGING.

Single (sĩ'ŋg'l), a. Forms: 4-5 sengle, single, sengull, 5 syngle, syngil, syngyll, sengyll, 6 singil, sengle, syngle, 6 syngell, 7 single.

Single, obs. or dial. f. Cingle, cincture, etc.

Single (sĩ'ŋg'l), v. Also 5 syngle, 6 syngyll, 7 singel. [f. SINGLE a.]

SINGLE. | 81 | **SINGLE.** | 82 | **SINGLE-MINDED.**

(Dictionary entries, columns continued from preceding page)

Single-handed
a. [f. SINGLE a. 19.]
1 a. Of actions: Carried on or performed by one person; single, alone or unaided, or by one person on each side.
b. Adapted for using with one hand.
2. Working alone or unassisted; without the aid, help, or support of others; by one's self; unaided, unsupported.
Hence **Si·ngle** *ppl. a.*, selected.

Single-foot, sb.
U.S. [f. SINGLE a. + FOOT sb.] A single-footing gait.
So **Single-foot** *v. intr.*, **Single-footed** *a.*, **Single-footing** *vbl. sb.*

Single-acting, ppl. a.
[f. SINGLE a. 19.] Acting in one direction or by one method, spec. of a steam-engine (see quot. 1875). Opposed to DOUBLE-ACTING.

Single-breasted, ppl. a.
[f. SINGLE a. 19.] Of garments: Having only one thickness over the breast; not double-breasted.
Opposed to DOUBLE-BREASTED.

Single-eyed, a.
1. fig. Having the eye single or sound; sincere, honest, straightforward. (see quot. 1526.)
2. lit. Having one eye or eye-like mark; one-eyed, monoculous.

Single-hand, sb.
[f. SINGLE a. 18 + HAND sb.]
1. Performed, worked, managed, played, by one hand or person. Single-hand WICKET.
2. The single-hold doctrine of simple-stick, broad-sword, and foil.

Single-horse, sb.
[f. SINGLE a. 18.]
1. Of vehicles: Made to be drawn by a single horse; one-horse.
2. Used with or for one horse.

Single-line, a.
[f. SINGLE a. 18.]
1. Consisting of or having only a single line of plants, rails, etc.
2. Taking up, or making, one line in writing or printing.

Single-minded, a.
[f. SINGLE a. 19.]
1. Sincere in mind or spirit; honest, straightforward; simple-minded, ingenuous; single-hearted.

| 83 | **SINGLO.** | **SINGLURE.** | 84 | **SINGULAR.**

Singleness
[f. SINGLE a. + -NESS.]
1. Sincerity, straightforwardness, honesty, integrity; freedom from deceit, duplicity, or guile.

Single money
[f. SINGLE a. 3.] Small money, small change.

Singlet, sb.
local. An unlined woollen garment (knitted or woven), now usually close-fitting and worn as an undershirt or jersey. Also attrib.

Singleton
[f. SINGLE a. Cf. SIMPLETON.]
1. Card-playing. In whist or bridge: The only card of a suit in a hand. Also attrib.

Single-tree
U.S. and Austr. = SWINGLE-TREE.

Single-wicket
[f. SINGLE a. 19.] A form of cricket in which there is only one wicket and consequently only one batsman at a time.

Singling, vbl. sb.
[f. SINGLE v. + -ING 1.]
1. The action of the verb; selection from a number; separation from others. Also with out.

Singling, ppl. a.
rare. [f. SINGLE v. + -ING 2.]
That renders single or separates.

Singlo
[a. Chinese si 9 sunglo. (See def.)] A kind of green China tea.

Singlure
[f. SINGLE a. 1.] Singleness, uniqueness.

Singly, adv.
[f. SINGLE a. + -LY 2.]
1. One by one; one at a time; separately.

Sing-song, sb.
[f. SING v. + SONG sb.]
1. An informal concert of the convivial kind.

Singsong, a.
[f. prec.] Having a monotonous rise and fall in rhythm or tone.

Sing-song, v.
1. trans. To force by means of singing.
2. intr. To utter or express in a monotonous chant.

Singster
[f. SING v. + -STER.] A singer.

Singular, a.
[a. OF. singuler, -ier, and L. singularis, f. singuli single.]

SINGULAR.

this case said to be a singular point in regard to the differential equation.

4. Of persons: **†a.** Holding no office; having no special position: private. *Obs.*

b. *Singular successor*, in Scots Law, one who acquires real property by a single title (usually that of purchase) as distinguished from an heir, who succeeds by a general or universal title.

†5. Of the one: chiefly in Sc. use.

b. *sing.* Single.

6. Singular in form or dimensions. *Obs.*

II. **†7.** Separate, individual, singular. *Obs.*

b. *Esp.* in *singular sum or person. Obs.*

c. Specially; peculiar to one. *Obs., rare.*

†8. Of accounts: Eminent, distinguished, notable.

†b. Of persons: Eminent, distinguished, notable.

†c. Used in forms of address, esp. to a person of title. *Obs.* (Common in the 16th c.)

9. Separate from others by reason of superiority or pre-eminence.

†10. Above the ordinary in amount, extent, worth, or value; especially good or great; special, particular. *Obs.*

a. Of immaterial things, qualities, etc.

b. Of material things.

b. *esp.* Of profit, advantage, gain, etc. *Obs.*

†11. Remarkable; extraordinary, unusual, uncommon. Hence, rare, precious.

†12. Differing from others in opinion; standing alone; peculiar in this respect. *Obs.*

13. Different from or not complying with that which is customary, usual, or general; strange, odd, peculiar.

2. *Eccl.* One who holds a single benefice, as contrasted with a PLURALIST. *rare.*

†Singularitas. *Obs. rare.*

Singularity (singiulǣr'itĭ). Also **4 singularyte**, **5–6 -ite**, **5 -itee**.

†1. Singleness of aim or purpose; singleness of heart; wholeness of intention. *Obs.*

†1 b. *Quasi-adv.* Singularly, especially, particularly. *Obs.* (Cf. 9.)

2. The fact or condition of being alone or apart from others; solitariness. *Obs., rare.*

3. The quality or fact of being one in number or kind; singleness, oneness.

4. The singular number; a word in its singular form.

5. Distinction that is, of involving, some superior quality; special excellence or goodness. *Obs.*

6. *Eccl.* The fact or condition of being alone or apart from others; solitariness. *Obs., rare.*

7. The fact or quality of differing or dissenting from others or from what is generally accepted; esp. in thought or religion; personal, individual, or independent action, judgement, etc., esp. in order to render one's self conspicuous or to attract attention.

8. Individual character or property; individuality; distinctiveness.

†2. A single or separate thing or entity; a unit.

b. A distinctive, noteworthy, or curious thing; esp. *pl.*, notable features or objects; the sights (of a place).

b. a solitary instance.

†5. Private or personal profit or gain. *Obs.*

†6. Distinction due to, or involving, some superior quality; special excellence or goodness. *Obs.*

Hence **Si'ngularing**, **Si'ngularizing** *ppl. adjs.* Also **Singularization**.

Singularly (singiulǣrli), *adv.* Forms: **4 syngulerliche**, **5 singuleerliche**; **4–6 syng-**,

SINGULARNESS.

singularly (4–6 -lie, -lye). **B. 5–6 syngularly**, **6– singularly** (4–6 -LY²)

I. Singly; apart from, unaccompanied or unaided by, any or all others; by oneself or itself; one by one, separately, individually. *Now rare.*

b. With especial application or reference to one person or thing.

†2. Singularity; singular character. *Obs.*

†Singulous. *a. Obs.*

Singule, **Singult**, etc.: see these words.

Singultus, **Singult**, **Sob**, etc.

†Singulture. *Obs.*

Sinicism (sī'nisiz'm). [f. SINIC *a.* + -ISM.] Chinese manners, customs, or principles; affectation or adoption of what is Chinese.

Sinication (sinisaĭ'shŏn). [f. next + -ATION.] The action or process of Sinicizing.

Sinicize (sī'nisaiz), *v.* [f. SINIC *a.* + -IZE.] *trans.* To invest with a Chinese character.

Sinify (sī'nifai), *v.* [f. L. Sin(æ + -FY.] *trans.* To Sinicize.

Sinigrin. Chem. Also **sinnigrine.** [irreg. f. L. sinapi mustard + nigra black + -IN¹ or -INE².] Myronate of potassium.

Sinister (si'nistæ(r)), *a.* (and *sb.*) Forms: **4 senestre**, **sinistre**; **5–6 synyster**, **5–7 sinyster**; **5–7 sinister**, **6 syn-**, **sinister**.

1. Of or belonging to the left side or hand; left. Now chiefly *Her.* and *Archaic*.

b. *Her.* On, toward, or situated on, the left half of a shield (regarded from the bearer's point of view; cf. DEXTER).

2. Forboding or portending ill or misfortune or disaster; full of dark or gloomy suggestiveness; inauspicious, unfavourable.

b. Similar of suggestions, advice, etc. *Obs.*

c. Of actions, practices, etc.: Dishonest, unfair; dark, corrupt, labours, *means, ways.*

4. With evil intent or purpose; maliciously, malevolently.

Sinisterly, *adv. rare.*

Sinisterness, *rare.*

Sinistral, *a.* [f. L. *sinister* + -AL.] **1.** Of or pertaining to, or on the left side.

Sinistrad, *adv.* Anat. Towards the left side.

SINISTRALITY. 89 SINK. SINK. 90 SINK.

Sinistrorse (si'nistrōrs), *a.*

Sinistrous, *a.*

Sinitic (sini'tik), *a.*

Sinistration. *rare.*

Sinistrine, *a.*

Sinistro-, combining form of SINISTER.

Sinistrous (sinistrə'l), *a.*

Sinistrously *adv.*

Sink, *sb.*

SINK. 91 SINK. SINK. 92 SINK.

SINKABLE.

b. To drop or lower (the voice) in speaking; to render less audible.

25. a. To abandon or cease to use; to give up; to allow to be merged in something else.

b. To suppress in pronouncing.

c. To deduct (an amount) as not reckoning to the weight of a carcase.

27. To pay up or wipe out (a debt, etc.).

28. = Invest v.

29. To invest or spend unprofitably; to lose (money) in unfortunate investment, war, etc.

Sinkable (si·ŋkăb'l), a. [f. Sink v. + -able.]

Sinkage (si·ŋkėdʒ). [f. Sink v. + -age.] The

Sinkanter, var. Sincanter Obs. Sinkapace.
var. Cinquepace Obs. **Sinke**, obs. f. Cinquefoil.
Sinkefoile, -foyle, obs. ff. Cinquefoil.
Sinker (si·ŋkạr). Also 6 synker, 7 syn-.

I. 1. One who engraves figures or designs on dies.

2. a. A heavy weight attached to a net, fishing-line, etc.

3. One who causes (something) to sink.

II. 4. † a. A weight for pressing cheese. Obs.

b. In a stocking-frame or knitting-machine, a jack-sinker or a lead-sinker.

c. A weight attached to the chain or rope of a horse's stall-collar.

5. A weight of lead, stone, or other material for sinking a fishing-line or -net in the water. Cf. Sink-stone 2.

6. A lead, stone, or other metal for sinking; a base coin; also Cf. a dollar.

7. attrib., as sinker-bar, -wheel (in a knitting-machine), -sinker-bar, -net (in boring apparatus).

Sinkfield, -foil e, obs. ff. Cinquefoil.
Sink-hole (si·ŋkhō¹l). [f. Sink sb. + Hole sb.]

1. A hole or hollow into which foul matter runs

SINKING.

or is thrown; a sink, or a hole by which a sink is emptied.

2. A hole, cavern, or funnel-shaped cavity made in the earth by the action of water on the soil, rock, or underlying strata, and frequently forming the course of an underground stream; a swallow-hole. Chiefly U.S.

Sinking (si·ŋkiŋ), vbl. sb. [f. Sink v. + -ing¹.] Cf. Fin. sinking, Du. zinking, G. sinkung.]

1. The action of the vb. in intransitive senses:

b. In various fig. contexts.

c. Of the heart, spirits, health, etc.: Drooping, flagging.

3. Special uses: sinking-chain, part of the apparatus of a jolt boring-rod; sinking-fire, heart-burn, -jar (see quots.); †sinking-lead, a sounding-lead; sinking stage (see quot.).

Sinking fund. [See Sink v. 27 and Fund sb. 4 a.] A fund formed by periodically setting aside revenue to accumulate at interest, usually for the purpose of reducing the principal of a national, etc., debt.

Sink pors: see Cinque Ports.
Sink-stone. [f. Sink sb. + Stone sb.]

1. dial. A stone basin or sink, having a pipe attached for the escape of water; a hollowed stone with an opening leading to a drain.

2. a stone sinker for submerging a fishing-line or -net in water.

Sinky (si·ŋki), a. [f. Sink v. + -y¹.] Of sand or soil: Yielding. = Sinking ppl. a.

Sinless (si·nlės), a. Forms: 1-2 synleas, -nles, 7- sinless. [f. Sin sb. + -less.]

Free from, devoid of, without sin. Also const. of.

Hence **Si·nner** v. (with it), to act as a sinner.

† **Sinlessness**. Obs. rare. [f. prec. + -ness.]

Sinna, Sc. = Shall not.

Sinnep, Sc. variant of Sennet.

Sinnet. [Of obscure origin.]

Sinning (si·niŋ), vbl. sb. Forms: α 1 syng-, 3 singinge, singing (4 -yng), sunng-, -ynge, -ynge, 4 synynge, 7- sinning. [f. Sin v. + -ing¹.] The action of the verb in various senses:

Sinner (si·nạr), sb. Forms: 1 synnere, syngere, 3-5 sunnere, synner. [OE. synnere = OFris. sondere, MDu. sonder (Du. zondaar), OHG. suntāri (MHG. sünder, G. sünder).]

SINNINGLY.

Hence **Si·nningly** adv., **Si·nningness**.

Sinnop, -er: see Sinoper.

Sinny, Sc. variant of Sunny.

Sino-, combining form of Gr. Σῖνα, L. Sinæ (see Sinæan a.) the Chinese, as in Sino-gram, a Chinese written character; Sino-loger, = Sinologue; Sino·logical, a. relating to the Chinese language or literature (Webster Suppl. 1879); Sino·logist, Sino·logus, one versed in the Chinese language, or in the customs and history of China; Sino·logy, the study of things Chinese (Imp. Dict. 1882); Si·nophil a., fond of the Chinese.

Sinod(e, obs. form of Synod.
Sinod(e, -al, **Synode**, obs. ff. Synod(al, Sin-odoches, obs. f. Synecdoche. **Sinody**, var. Synody Obs.
Sin-o·ffering. [f. Sin sb. 6, prob. after Ger. sündopfer, used by Luther to render Heb. ḥattāth, f. ḥātā 'to sin.'] The portion of a Jewish religion, an offering (of an animal for sacrifice) made as an atonement for sin. Also transf.

Sinon (sai·nŏn). Also 6-7 Synon. [The name of the Greek who induced the Trojans to bring the wooden horse into Troy (Virgil Æneid II. 57 sqq.).] One who misleads by false tales; a perfidious person; a deceiver or betrayer.

Sinoper (si·nŏpạr). Obs. Forms: 5 sinopre, 5-6 synoper, synapour (Sc. -per, -6-7, -7 -per), 6-8 sinoper (6 seno-), 6 cinaper, 7-8 -per, var. of sinople Sinope. **Si·nople**, sinopre.

SINUATE.

synopar, 1530 Lyndesay Test. Papyngo 1112 Sc. ...sail knaw The nocion betuuit betwix hewin—Gold, Asure, Gowles, Purpour, and Synopill.

Sin-soiled (si·nsoild), a. [Sin sb. 6.] Blemished, stained, or soiled by sin.

Sinsyne, variant of Synsine.
Sinter (si·ntạr), sb. Also sintre. [ad. G. sinter; Min., combining form of Sinus sb.]

Sinto, **Sintu**, etc.: see Shinto, etc.
† **Sintze**, obs. f. Since.

Sinuate (si·niueit), a. [ad. L. sinuātus, pa. pple. of sinuāre: see Sinuate v.]

1. Bot. Of leaves: Having a margin made wavy or uneven by alternate rounded and larger sinuses and lobes; sinuous. Also similarly in Ent. of wing-cases, etc.

2. Conch. Having a sinus.

Sinuate (si·niueit), v. [f. ppl. stem of L. sinuāre: see prec.] intr. To creep or crawl in a winding course.

SINUATED.

Sinuated (si·niuei·tėd), ppl. a. [f. as Sinuate a. + -ed¹.]

† 1. Having a sinus or hollow. Obs. rare⁻¹.

2. Bot. Of leaves: = Sinuate a. 1.

Sinuation (siniuei·ʃən). [ad. late L. sinuātio, f. sinuāre to curve, etc.]

1. The act or fact of winding about, or pursuing a winding course.

2. A winding or bending in and out; a sinuosity.

Sinuose (si·niuōs), a. rare. [ad. L. sinuōsus: see next.] = Sinuous.

Sinuosity (siniɒ·sĭti), a. Forms: 7 sinuositee, 7- sinuosity. [ad. F. sinuosité (16th c.), or ad. med. or mod.L. sinuōsitās.]

1. The quality or state of being sinuous; sinuousness.

2. concr. A sinuous curve or bend; a winding.

Sinuous (si·niuəs), a. Also 7 sinewous (?). [ad. L. sinuōsus, f. sinus Sinus + -ōsus, or ad. F. sinueux.]

1. Characterized by or abounding in turns, curves, or sinuosities; winding, curving.

Sinupalliate (siniupæ·lieit), a. Conch. [f. sinus-stem of Sinus + Palliate a., or Palliatea.]

Sinus (sai·nŏs). Pl. sinuses (7 sinus, 7-9 sinusses). [L. sinus a curve, bend, fold, etc.]

1. Path. An imposture, abscess, or sore, forming a narrow suppurating tract and having a small orifice or opening leading from it.

2. a. A curvature, flexure, or bend; spec. in Zool.

3. Of animals: A cavity or hollow.

4. A hollow; a hollow place; spec. a channel or receptacle of blood.

b. A natural hole, cell, or cavity in the substance of a bone or other tissue, and either closed or having a relatively small opening.

phlebitis, pyæmia, thrombosis; sinus-like adj. Also **sinus probe** (see quot. 1884).

1883 Encycl. Brit. XVI. 678/1 Sinus-like spaces surrounding the viscera. 1884 Knight Dict. Mech. Suppl. 816/2 Sinus Probe, a vermicular pointed uterine curved probe, used in its peculiar branch of surgical operations. 1898 Allbutt's Syst. Med. V. 940 The presence or absence of sinus aneurysm. 1899 Ibid. VII. 575 The tissue intermediate between the original inflammation and the sinus wall.

Sinusoid (səi·nŏsoid). [a. F. sinusoïde, f. L. sinus Sinus + -oid.]

1. Math. A curve of sines (Curve sb. 1).

1823 Lardner Algebraic Geom. I. 200 A curve, represented by the equation y = sin. x, related to rectangular co-ordinates, is called the curve of sines, or the sinusoid. 1876 Proc. Lond. Math. Soc. VII. 213 Prof. Cayley described a surface, depending upon the sinusoid, which was being constructed for him. 1884 tr. Glaser de Cew's Magn. & Dynamo-electric Machines 254 If the magnetic field in which the armature rotated were uniform, this curve would be a true 'sinusoid', or curve of sines.

2. (See quot.)

1900 Minot in Proc. Boston Nat. Hist. Soc. 185 The [blood-] vessels of the first type are true capillaries... The vessels of the second type I propose to name 'sinusoids', on account of their resemblance to true sinus and also to separate them clearly from genuine capillaries.

Sinusoidal (səinŏsoi·dăl), a. [f. prec. + -al; cf. F. sinusoïdal.] Resembling, pursuing, flowing in, the wave-like course of a sinusoid.

1878 Mayer Sound 64 Hold the glass up to the light, and you will see a delicate wavy line, a sinusoidal trace. 1879 G. Prescott Sp. Telephone 54 The curve expressive of a simple pendulous vibration—that is a sinusoidal curve. 1900 Lancet 1 Dec. 1580/1 These patients have all been treated with the electrical bath and the sinusoidal current.

Hence **Sinusoi·dally** adv.

1888 Philos. Mag. Ser. v. XXVI. 373 Let f vary sinusoidally with the time.

Sinward (si·nwǭɹd), adv. [f. Sin sb. + -ward.] Toward or in the direction of sin. †Also to sinward.

1377 Langl. P. Pl. B. xiii. 346 Vche a mayde þat he mette he made hir a signe Semynge to-synne-ward. c 1440 Jacob's Well 111 Feendys noumbre þe steppys of man & womman to synne warde. 1642 Rogers Naaman 45 The thoughts that were roving helward, worldward, and sinward. 1644 T. Case Quarrel of Covenant 74 A people..may enter Covenant with God, with their hearts, Rome-ward, and Earth-ward, and Sin-ward. 1820 Mrs. Grant of Laggan Mem. & Corresp. (1844) II. 268 An infirmity always verging sinward.

‖ **Sion.** rare. [L. sion water-parsley, a. Gr. σίον some kind of marsh plant.] = Laver sb.[1] 1.

c 1000 Sax. Leechd. I. 254 Deos wyrt þe man sion & oðrum naman laber nemneþ byð cenned on wætum stowum. 1562 Turner Herbal II. (1568) 138 Sion is so muche hote as it is well smelling, when it is tasted. 1861 Reade Cloister & H. xciv, His remedies were 'womanish and weak'. Sage and wormwood, sion, hyssop,..and Faith, and all in small quantities except the last.

Sion, Sioun, obs. forms of Scion.

Sion(er, etc.: see Zion, er, etc.

Sip, sb. Also 7 sippe. [f. the vb.] A single act of sipping; a small quantity of some liquid taken in this way.

It is possible that sype in Caxton's text of Chaucer's Anel. & Arc. 193 may have been intended for sip, but the correct reading is schipe reward.

1633 P. Fletcher Poet. Misc. 131 The wine..did appeare no common grape: my haste could not forbeare a second sippe. 1665 Pepys Diary 19 Aug., A bottle of strong water, whereof, now and then, a sip did me good. 1687 A. Lovell tr. Thevenot's Trav. I. 33 They..bring it to you scalding hot, and so you must drink it, but at several sips, else it is not good. 1715 Chapfelow Right Way Rich (1717) 169 A sip of some comforting syrup. 1768–74 A. Tucker Lt. Nat. (1834) II. 234 A sip of Daffy's Elixir, in the morning rising, has proved a powerful means of grace. 1828 Scott F. M. Perth xvi, However Oliver might have relished a moderate sip of the same good wine. 1856 Longf. Gold. Leg. iv. Poet. Wks. (1910) 495/1 Between this cask and the Abbot's lips Many have been the sips and slips. 1887 Jefferies Amaryllis iii, If it was to be had, a sip of port wine.

b. fig. A mere taste of something.

1728 Young Love Fame vi. 442 Will the great Author us poor worms destroy, For now and then a sip of transient joy? 1852 De Quincey Sir W. Hamilton Wks. 1890 V. 307 A sip is all that the public collectively ever care to take from reservoirs of abstract philosophy. 1871 N. Sheppard Shut up in Paris 246 They take a little sip of a stroll, a little sip of sleep, and a little sip of manual labour.

Sip, v. Forms: 5 syppy(n, cyppyn, 6 syppe; 5, 7 sippe (5 scippe), 6– sip. [Of obscure origin; possibly a modification of sup intended to express a slighter action.

Kilian's 'Sippen, pitissare, sorbillare' is not otherwise certified, and is rendered suspicious by his citing 'Ang. sippe'; but a LG. sippen in the same sense is given in the Bremisches Wörterbuch, and appears to be genuine.]

1. intr. To take up liquid in small quantities with the lips; to drink by a sip or sips; freq. with of (a specified liquid, etc.). Also in fig. contexts.

c 1386 Chaucer Wife of Bath's Prol. 176 Than maystow chese, whether thou wolt sippe Of that tonne that I shal abroche. 14.. Lat.-Eng. Voc. in Wr.-Wülcker 604 Potisso, to syppy. c 1440 Promp. Parv. 456/2 Syppyn, nowȝt fully drynke, potisso, subbibo. 1530 Palsgr. 719/1 Syppe on, Cysse, and tell me what it is. 1584–7 Greene Carde Fancie Wks. (Grosart) IV. 162 Yea, let thy Concubine Castania..to sippe of the same sorrow. 1602 Shaks. Ham. iv. vii. 161 He haue prepar'd him A Challice..; whereon but sipping, ..Our purpose may hold there. a 1628 Preston Breastpl. Love (1631) 182 Yee doe here but sippe of this cuppe, but then ye shall drinke up the dreggs of it for ever. 1687 A. Lovell tr. Thevenot's Trav. I. 33 They all drink it sipping for fear of scalding themselves. 1733 Pope Hor. Sat. II. i. 47 Ridotta sips and dances, till she see The doubling Lustres dance as fast as she. 1780 Cowper Progr. Err. 581 With caution taste the sweet Circean cup; He that sips often, at last drinks it up. 1789 — Annus Mem. 18 As the bee.. Assiduous sips at ev'ry flow'r. 1810 Southey Kehama xxiv. v, As a man in social hour Sips of the grateful cup. 1859 Dickens T. Two Cities I. v, Who bent over their shoulders, to sip, before the wine had all run out.

transf. 1601 B. Jonson Poetaster III. i, As many as haue but the..audacitie to—sip of their lips. 1871 Athenæum 26 Aug. 273 The whole French nation..sip in drinking, they sip in reading, and they sip their work.

2. trans. To drink (liquid, etc.) in very small draughts; to imbibe, or partake of, by sipping. Said also of bees, etc.

1611 Cotgr., Humé, supped, sipped, or sucked vp [etc.]. a 1650 Crashaw Carmen Deo Nostro, Mary Magd. v, Every morn from hence A brisk Cherub somthing sippes. 1662 R. Mathew Unl. Alch. 191 Drink one quarter of a pint as hot as you can sip it. 1697 Dryden Virg. Georg. III. 505 Let 'em sip from Herbs the pearly tears Of Morning Dews. 1746 Hervey Medit. (1818) 187 Bees, industrious workmen! that..sip the mellifluous dews. 1784 Cowper Task III. 391 He enjoys..Sweet converse, sipping calm the fragrant lymph Which neatly she prepares. 1825 Lamb Elia II. Wedding, None told his tale. None sipt her glass. 1848 Thackeray Van. Fair lxii, The knowing way in which he sipped, or rather sucked, the Johannisberger. 1886 Pascoe Lond. of To-day xl. (ed. 3) 350 The places where ladies go to eat creams..and sip coffee.

b. fig. and transf.

1602 Marston Ant. & Mel. v. Wks. 1856 I. 67 Weele drinke a health, while they two sip a kisse. c 1614 Sir W. Mure Dido & Æneas I. 274 The shippe..sinking sippes the seas, by weight downe borne. 1632 Milton Penseroso 172 And every Herb that sips the dew. 1769 Sir W. Jones Palace Fortune Poems (1777) 13 The maid attentive sips Each word that flows, like nectar, from her lips. 1871 [see sense 1 transf.].

c. With advs., as off, up.

1656 Earl Monm. tr. Boccalini's Advts. fr. Parnass. I. (1674) 50 The Macedonians..thought to have sipt up every mans State in less than a moneths time. a 1763 W. King Polit. & Lit. Anecd. (1819) 13 Pope had sipped up all the brandy. 1863 W. C. Baldwin Afr. Hunting vii. 278 A large spoonful of mustard in a pint of warm water, which he sipped off like coffee!

d. fig. To take a mere taste of (something).

1618 Bolton Florus 105 That he might not seeme to have once sipt or skimd the honour of their Chastity. 1639 Fuller Holy War III. xiv. (1840) 139 Pleasures he rather sipped than drank off.

3. To take honey from (a flower) by sipping.

1697 Dryden Virg. Georg. IV. 76 The winged Nation.. skim the Floods, and sip the purple Flow'rs. 1727 Gay Beggar's Opera I. i, My heart..roved like the bee,..I sipt each flower. 1878 J. Miller Songs of Italy 81, I should sip but one, this one Sweet flower underneath the sun.

4. refl. To bring (oneself) into a certain state by sipping.

1823 Scott Quentin D. Introd., I gradually sipped and smoked myself into a certain degree of acquaintance with un homme comme il faut.

Hence **Si·pping** ppl. a.

1670 Eachard Cont. Clergy 31 That would much better fit some old soker..than his sipping..bibbership. 1871 N. Sheppard Shut up in Paris 246 This sip, sip, sipping race have been devoured by a race which does nothing by sips. 1898 Allbutt's Syst. Med. V. 993 Then peptonized milk.. may be swallowed in sipping fashion.

Sipage (səi·pedʒ). Sc. and U.S. [f. Sipe v. + -age. Cf. Seepage.] Leakage or oozing of water.

1825 in Jamieson Suppl. 1892 Trans. Amer. Soc. Civil Engin. XXVI. 572 The new levees..and..the land behind them [were]..very much affected by sipage.

Sipahee, sipahi, variants of Sepoy.

Sipars, obs. form of Cypress 3.

Sipe (səip), sb. Chiefly Sc. and U.S. Also sype. [Related to Sipe v. Cf. MDu. sijp, zijp (Du. dial. zijp), MLG. sīp, sipe, Fris. syp, sipe a ditch, channel, etc.]

1. The act of percolating or soaking through, on the part of water or other liquid; the water, etc., which percolates. (Cf. Seep sb.)

c 888 K. Ælfred Boeth. xxxiii. § 5 Seo eorðe hit helt & be sumum dæle swilgð, & for þam sype heo bið geleht. a 1583 in Sir J. Balfour Minor Pract. (1754) 588 Gif thair be ony persounis that settis furth under the yeird the sype of thair bark cobill,..or ony sype of kitching, to the King's water or well. 1777 in Cramond Ann. Banff (1893) II. 97 By the general sipe of the slating there is no mending of the slating without terring the sclates. 1839 Stonehouse Hist. Isle of Axholme 23 The water obtained from the wells sunk in the warp..is what is termed ground sype, i.e. water filtering through from the surface. 1894 Naturalist 23 There is no inflow or spring here apparently, so the water is only sipe.

attrib. 1892 Trans. Amer. Soc. Civil Engin. XXVI. 568 The water which thus transpires through the soil is called.. by the Americans of the Mississippi Valley 'sipe-water' (pronounced seep).

2. A small spring or pool of water.

1825 Jamieson Suppl., Sipe, Sype,..a slight spring of water; Perths. 1897 Butler Brit. Birds iv. 65 Here and there, many small ponds or 'sypes', and birch trees.

Sipe (səip), v. Chiefly Sc. and north. dial. Also sype. [OE. sipian wk. vb., = Fris. sypje, MLG. sipen (pp. gesypet); cf. MDu. sīpen, sypen (Du. dial. sijpen), MLG. sīpen, MHG. sīfen str. vb. Sw. dial. sipa, Da. sive are prob. from LG.

The length of the vowel in OE. sipian, and the relation between this vb. and the OE. sb. sype, are not clear. If the vowel was short, the modern representative would normally be Seep v., and the form sipe may really correspond to the continental strong vb.]

intr. Of water or other liquid: To percolate or ooze through; to drip or trickle slowly; to soak.

For various dialect modifications of sense, and transitive uses, see the Eng. Dial. Dict.

c 1000 Sax. Leechd. II. 252 Asete þonne on hate sunnan,.. þæt hit sipiȝe & sociȝe .iiii. daȝas oþþe ma. 1398, 1503 (see the vbl. sb. and ppl. a.). 1559 Morwyng Evonym. 2 Plinie ..writes of the wode that is called Smilax, how it will let sype through water mixt with wyne, and kiep the wyne still. 1781 J. Hutton Tour to Caves (ed. 2) Gloss. 97. 1825 Brockett N. C. Gloss., Sipe, to leak, to ooze or drain out slowly through a small crevice. 1891 Atkinson Moorland Par. 446 In this way a considerable amount of water was permitted to ooze and 'sipe' out and away.

Sipee·ra. Bot. Also sip(e)ira, -(i)era, sipiri. [Native name in Guiana.] a. Sipeera-tree, the greenheart tree (Nectandra Rodiæi) of Guiana; = Bebeeru. b. The bark of this tree.

1769 E. Bancroft Nat. Hist. Guiana 333 They contentedly recur to the use of Sipera, or Green-Hart-tree Apples. 1829 Encycl. Metrop. (1845) XX. 6/2 The timber of the Green Hart, or Sipiera tree, is very valuable. 1863 Chambers's Encycl. V. 92/2 The timber is commonly called Greenheart; the bark is better known as Bebeeru .. and Sipiri or Sipeira.

Hence **Sipee·rine.** Chem. [Named by Maclagan in 1843.] (See quot.)

1868 Watts Dict. Chem., Sipeerine, Sipirine, Sepeerine, an alkaloid existing, together with bebirine, in the..greenheart-tree... It was discovered by Rodie in 1834.

Siper (səi·pəɹ). north. dial. Also s(e)yper. [f. Sipe v.] An immoderate drinker; a toper.

1803 R. Anderson Cumbld. Ball. (c 1850) 66 The Hiverby lads at fair drinkin are seypers. 1885 Hall Caine Shadow of a Crime xxv, You're worse than he is, you old sypers.

Sipers, obs. form of Cypress 3.

† **Siphac.** Anat. Obs. Also α. 5 syphac, 6 cyphac, sifac, 7 siphack. β. 6-7 siphach. [a. med.L. siphac, syphac (whence also obs. F. siphach, Pg. sifac), a. Arab. صفاق çifāq, from the root صفق çafaqa to cover.] The peritoneum.

α. 1398 Trevisa Barth. De P. R. vii. lv. (Bodl. MS.), Hernia is a skynne in þe wombe and hatte Siphac also and brekeþ somtyme. c 1400 Lanfranc's Cirurg. 169 For to holde alle þese þingis, þe stomak & þe guttis is ordeyned a skyn, þat is clepid þe siphac. 1541 R. Copland Guydon's Quest. Chirurg. B j, The voyde places that are betwene the cyphac and the myrac. 1548 Vicary Anat. (1888) 64 That [part] which appeareth next vnder the Sifac is Omentum.

β. 1552 Udall tr. Geminus' Anat. C vj, Nexte within thys Abdomen or Mirach is contayned Siphach. 1587 T. Thomas Lat.-Eng. Dict. (1615), Peritonæum,..the inner rim of the bellie..; the Anatomists call it Siphach. [Hence in later Eng. Dicts.]

† **Siphany.** Obs. rare. Also sy-. [Of obscure origin.] The name of some flower.

1509 Invent. Plate, etc. (St. John's Coll., Camb.), Item ij copes of blew satyn..embrodride with Rede rosis and white syphanyes orfreide with rede satyn..embrodrid with portculis and white and blew syphanyes. Ibid., A vestment ard ij tunycles..garnyshed with siphanyes and margaretes with my ladies pose.

Sipher, obs. form of Cipher sb.

† **Si·pher**, obs. form of Cipher v. 8.

15.. in Grose Antiq. Rep. (1809) IV. 407 To myche wyndinge of the pipis is not the best, Whiche may cause them to sypher wher armoney shulde rest. Ibid., Wronge handlynge of the stoppis may cause them sipher fro the kynde.

Siphilitic, obs. form of Syphilitic.

‖ **Sipho** (səi·fou). Zool. [L. sīpho Siphon sb.] = Siphuncle 1.

1888 Rolleston & Jackson Anim. Life 458 The chambers are traversed by a tube—the sipho or siphuncle. Ibid. 464 The sipho is formed by two free folds.

Siphon (səi·fən), sb. Also 7-8 cyphon, 7- syphon. [ad. L. sīphōn-, sīpho (cf. prec.), ad. Gr. σίφων pipe, tube. Cf. F. siphon (1611), Sp. sifon, Pg. sifão, It. sifone.]

1. A pipe or tube of glass, metal, or other material, bent so that one leg is longer than the other, and used for drawing off liquids by means of atmospheric pressure, which forces the liquid up the shorter leg and over the bend in the pipe.

α. 1659 Leak Waterworks 6 A Syphon..hath that end which is without the vessell longer then the other. 1698 Fryer Acc. E. India & P. 306 The Water..forces it self in nature of a Syphon up to the highest Clifts. 1710 J. Clarke tr. Rohault's Nat. Philos. (1729) I. 75 If the Water in the Vessel be made to rise up into the Syphon. 1794 Sullivan View Nat. I. 283 The ebb and flow of springs..are likewise to be accounted for on the simple principle of the syphon. 1827 Faraday Chem. Manip. xxiv. 634 Bend a piece of glass tube into a syphon. 1907 Hodges Elem. Photogr. 28 A syphon to carry off the contaminated water.

β. 1660 Boyle New Exp. Phys. Mech. xxxv. 263 We resolved, instead of a List of Cotton, or the like Filtre, to make use of a Siphon of Glass. 1661 — Examen vi. (1682) 72 The passage of water through Siphons. 1745 Franklin Lett. Wks. 1887 II. 11, I applied the siphon..to the pipe of a water-engine. 1815 J. Smith Panorama Sci. & Art II. 125 Water will not therefore rise in a siphon, any more than in a pump, beyond the height of 33 feet. 1887 Encycl. Brit.

XXII. 95/2 The siphon has practically a certain minimum diameter for each liquid.

b. transf. A channel or tube through which water passes on the principle of the siphon.

1744 Thomson Autumn 829 Beneath th' incessant weeping of these Drains, I see the rocky Siphons stretch'd immense. 1756–7 tr. Keysler's Trav. (1760) IV. 139 A communication betwixt the caverns that lie one over another, by a kind of natural syphons. 1837 Whittock Bk. Trades (1842) 200 A vertical 'syphon' in the embankment of the reservoir composed of well wrought masonry or brick-work. 1878 Stevenson Inland Voy. 148 We had to take to the canal..; because, where it crossed the river, there was, not a bridge, but a siphon. 1889 Welch Text Bk. Naval Archit. xi. 129 The pump then becomes a syphon, the flow of water continues without further pumping.

c. ellipt. A siphon-bottle, esp. one containing aerated water.

1875 Knight Dict. Mech. 2189/2. 1898 G. B. Shaw Plays II. You never can tell 307 Waiter... Scotch and syphon for you, sir? 1905 Vachell The Hill iii, Upon the table were some siphons.

2. †a. A fire-bucket. Obs.—[0]

1688 Holme Armoury III. 296/2 A Fire Bucket, (or a Leather Bucket)... This is also called a Syphon, which is a kind of Vessel made of Tanned Hydes to carry Water in, to quench Fire that is raging amongst Dwelling Houses.

†b. (See quot.) Obs.—[1]

1724 Mason in Abridg. Patent Spec., Shipbuilding (1862) 10 A new machine called a siphon or an attracting engine,.. composed of two tubes one within the other.

c. A form of tube for milking cows.

1844 Stephens Bk. Farm II. 468 He..introduces the small tube of the siphon an inch or more into the teat. 1881 Shelden Dairy Farming 58/1 A silver 'syphon' or 'milking tube'.

3. Zool. a. = Siphuncle 1.

1822 J. Parkinson Outl. Oryctol. 174 The partitions, siphon, &c., of this fossil are those which are to be found in every species of Belemnite. 1858 Geikie Hist. Boulder vi. 107 The inner tube that traverses the centre of the chambers from end to end of the shell is called the syphon.

b. A tube-like organ serving as a canal for the passage of water or other fluid; also, a breathing-tube or suctorial organ.

1826 Phil. Trans. 353 The Buccinum, when completely buried, is enabled to communicate with the water by its respiratory syphon. 1840 Cuvier's Anim. Kingd. 445 A sucker, or siphon,..occupies the place of the mouth. 1872 H. A. Nicholson Palæont. 217 The margins or lips of these orifices are usually drawn out..into longer or shorter muscular tubes,..termed the siphons. 1888 Rolleston & Jackson Anim. Life 449 The mid-foot..forms two lobes which usually fuse together, and constitute the siphon.

c. (See quots.)

1888 Rolleston & Jackson Anim. Life 561 In the Desmosticha and Petalosticha a tube—the siphon—arises from the posterior extremity of the oesophagus and lies closely applied to the inner margin of the intestine into which it opens again at or near the end of the inferior coil. 1896 tr. Boas' Text Bk. Zool. 137 The so-called siphon, or accessory intestine, is a very peculiar structure occurring in most Echinoids.

4. Bot. One or other of a number of elongated cells which surround the large monosiphonous cell in the frond of certain florideous red algæ.

1889 Cent. Dict. s.v. Monosiphonous, Certain of the higher algæ..in which the siphons or pericentral tubes are wanting. 1902 Encycl. Brit. XXV. 269/1 The species of Polysiphonia, the 'siphons' of which may be regarded as one-celled branches.

5. attrib. In names of apparatus, etc., of which a siphon forms a part, or which involve the principle or use of the siphon, as siphon barometer, bottle, can (sense 2 c), condenser, cup, fountain, gauge, pump, recorder, trap, etc. Also siphon pipe, tube, = sense 1; **siphon-shell**, a gasteropod having a siphon (3 b); **siphon-worm** (see quot.).

Descriptions of most of these are given by Knight Dict. Mech. (1875) 2189–90 and Suppl. (1884) 817–8.

1835 Penny Cycl. III. 482/2 The *siphon barometer..was early adopted as more convenient than that of Torricelli. 1856 Orr's Circ. Sciences, Pract. Chem. 244, I employ a *siphon bottle such as is here represented. 1875 Knight Dict. Mech. 2189/2 An apparatus for filling *siphon-bottles with aerated liquids. 1844 Stephens Bk. Farm II. 468 The milker sits down as in the common method, fixing the *siphon can (pail) firmly between his knees. 1851 Official Catal. Exhib. I. 419 *Syphon douche. 1819–24 Encycl. Metrop. (1845) III. 388/1 Of the *siphon-fountain. 1842 Penny Cycl. XXII. 47/2 Such are Tantalus's Cup and the siphon fountain. 1819–24 Encycl. Metrop. (1845) III. 372/2 The *siphon-gage..differs from the short barometer-gage merely in this circumstance, that [etc.]. 1831 Lardner Pneumatics v. 294 The siphon gauge must be regarded as a more direct measure of the elastic force of the air in the receiver than the barometer gauge. 1838 Civil Eng. & Arch. Jrnl. I. 237/2 The whole circle of pipes..is supplied with water..by means of the *syphon pipe. 1873 F. Jenkin Electr. & Magn. xxiii. § 5 Sir William Thomson's *syphon recorder actually draws on paper the curves which we have learnt to construct theoretically. 1884 Knight Dict. Mech. Suppl. 788/1 The common *siphon trap as used in most sinks and water-closets. 1688 J. Smith The Baroscope § 74, I shall endeavour to demonstrate it in a *Cyphon-Tube... Take then a Glass Tube [etc.]. 1880 Bastian Brain iv. 75 Other bivalves possessing prolongations of the mantle known as siphon tubes. 1856 Eng. Cycl., Nat. Hist. IV. 802 The Sipunculidæ (*Syphon-Worms) have a retractile proboscis, at the base of which is placed the vent.

6. Comb., as siphon-bearing, cleaning, -filling; siphon-like adj. and adv.; siphon-mouthed, -shaped.

1688 J. Smith Baroscope § 74 Let about a Foot of the other End be turned up, Cyphon-like, in the Form of a Fish Hook. 1842 Brande Dict. Sci., etc. 1120 A family of Crustaceans, comprehending those which have a siphon-shaped mouth. 1858 Mayne Expos. Lex., Siphonostomus, having a siphon-like mouth. 1875 Knight Dict. Mech. 2189/2 Siphon-filling Apparatus, an apparatus for filling siphon-bottles with aerated liquids.

Siphon (səi·fən), v. Also syphon. [f. Siphon sb. Cf. mod.F. siphonner.]

1. trans. To draw off or bring up (liquid, etc.) by means of a siphon. Const. with advs., as off, out, or with preps., as from, into.

1859 Jrnl. R. Agric. Soc. XX. I. 135 The tolerably clear liquid was syphoned off. 1877 Raymond Statist. Mines & Mining 394 It is..siphoned off and a fresh charge put in. 1897 Allbutt's Syst. Med. III. 558 The contents [of the stomach] may be syphoned out.

2. To empty after the manner of a siphon.

1892 Pall Mall G. 15 Feb. 3/1 During this time many gullies and traps have been syphoned, giving free egress for sewer gas.

Hence **Si·phoning** vbl. sb.

1895 Parkes Health 53 The discharge of one closet may cause the siphoning of the trap of the other.

Siphon-, combining form of Gr. σίφων before vowels (cf. Siphono-), occurring in a few terms of Zool. and Bot., of doubtful currency in English, as siphonanth, -anthous, -apter, -apteran, -apterous.

1842 Brande Dict. Sci., etc. 1120 (Siphonapterans). 1858 Mayne Expos. Lex. (Siphonanthous, Siphonapterous). 1895 Funk's Stand. Dict.

Siphonage (səi·fŏnedʒ). Also sy-. [f. Siphon sb. + -age. Cf. F. siphonage.] The action of drawing off liquid by means of a siphon; also spec., the accidental emptying of a siphon-trap.

1855 Orr's Circ. Sci., Elem. Chem. 353 A heavy yellow liquor..sinks to the bottom, and may be withdrawn by syphonage. 1884 Century Mag. Dec. 260/1 Siphonage is due to the rapid movement through the trap of air. 1897 Allbutt's Syst. Med. III. 437 The stomach-pump or a free syphonage of the stomach may be promptly used.

Siphonal (səi·fŏnăl), a. Also sy-. [f. Siphon sb. + -al.] Having the form or character of a siphon; of or pertaining to a siphon. Chiefly Zool.

(a) 1826 Phil. Trans. 353 The syphonal, or posterior extremity of the valves [of Pholas candida]. 1851 Woodward Mollusca I. 85 The siphonal lappets of Paludina. 1880 Günther Introd. Study Fishes 130 The siphonal [stomach of Teleosteans]..presents the form of a bent tube or canal. (b) 1853 Phillips Rivers Yorks. iii. 112 Variable pressure on the water, derived from a curved or siphonal passage underground.

‖ **Siphonaria** (səifŏnē·riă). [mod.L. Siphonaria (Sowerby, 1824), f. L. sīphōn- Siphon.] A pulmonate gasteropod of the genus Siphonaria, distinguished by a siphon passing from the apex to the margin.

1861 P. P. Carpenter Lect. Mollusca 82 (Cent. Dict.), The Siphonarias have solid, conical shells, often overgrown with sea-weeds and millepores... They are found on almost all tropical shores.

Siphonate (səi·fŏnĕt), a. and sb. Zool. [f. Siphon sb. + -ate[2] 2.]

A. adj. Of molluscs: Furnished with, or characterized by having, a siphon.

1870 Rolleston Anim. Life 61 Representing the inhalant siphon of the siphonate orders. 1883 Encycl. Brit. XVI. 686/2 In this way the notches..are in the Siphonate forms converted into two separate holes.

B. sb. A mollusc furnished with a siphon.

1877 Le Conte Elem. Geol. (1879) 304 Lamellibranchs are divided into siphonates and Asiphonates, i.e. those with and those without breathing siphons behind. The Siphonates are the higher. Ibid., At present the Siphonates are the more abundant.

Si·phonated, a. Zool. [f. prec. + -ed[1] 2.] = Siphonate a.

1851 Woodward Mollusca I. 13 Most of the siphonated univalves are animal-feeders. 1863 Lyell Antiq. Man xxii. 442 A greater number in the lower division, that of entire-mouthed univalves, than in that of the siphonated.

Siphoned (səi·fənd), a. Also syphoned. [f. Siphon sb. + -ed[1].]

1. Zool. Siphonate.

1889 Hyatt Genesis Arietidae 13 The smaller siphoned species of the genera Endoceras and Sannionites.

2. Operated on by means of a siphon.

1897 Allbutt's Syst. Med. III. 512 My first syphoned patient..was admitted into the Leeds Infirmary with benignant pyloric stenosis.

Siphoneous (səifōu·niəs), a. Bot. Also sy-. [f. Siphon sb. + -eous.] Of the fronds of algæ: Composed of tubes; having a tubular structure.

1858 Mayne Expos. Lex. s.v. Siphoneus. 1892 Athenæum 14 May 636/2 Spirit specimens of Ascothamnion intricatum, an organism described as a siphoneous alga.

Si·phonet. Ent. [f. Siphon sb. + -et.] A small siphon or tube by which an aphis emits a sweet, honey-like fluid; a honey-tube.

1826 Kirby & Sp. Entomol. III. xxxiii. 393 Siphonuli (the Siphonets). Ibid. IV. xl. 120 The Aphides all secrete a fluid excrement.., which is ejected not only at the anal passage, but, in many, by two little siphonets also above it.

† **Sipho·nia.** Obs. [Of obscure origin.] A light kind of overcoat.

1853 Household Words VIII. 76 Not less can I set down as slang the verbiage by which coats are transformed into bis-uniques, alpacas,..and siphonias. 1859 Sala Gaslight & D. xxxiv. 391 Incongruously picturesque garments such as ponchos, togas, vicunas, siphonias, Inverness wrappers, &c. 1863 Morning Star 21 May, The Derby Days, when blue veils and siphonias..have been the main characteristics of the journey by road.

Siphonic (səifǫ·nik), a. Also sy-. [f. Siphon sb. + -ic.]

1. Zool. Of or pertaining to a siphon; siphonal.

1832 Owen Mem. Pearly Nautilus 63 The siphonic artery. 1836 Buckland Geol. & Min. (1837) I. 322 note, The siphonic apertures of the transverse plates.

2. Of or pertaining to, working by means of, on the principle of, a siphon.

1884 Century Mag. XXIX. 237 The siphonic action, or suction. 1884 Health Exhib. Catal. 59/2 Syphonic Water Closets, Urinal and Cistern. Ibid. 74/1 Automatic Syphonic System of Ventilation.

Siphoni·ferous, a. Zool. [f. Siphon sb. + -(i)ferous.] Having a siphon; siphonate.

Brande Dict. Sci., etc. (1842) 1120 gives Siphonifers as a rendering of mod.L. Siphonifera.

1835–6 Todd's Cycl. Anat. I. 519/1 All the other genera.. are provided..with an internal siphoniferous polythalamous shell. Ibid. 700/1 In the siphoniferous acephala having the foot short and rudimentary. 1837 Penny Cycl. VII. 432/1 In the siphoniferous branch of the family [Conchifera]. 1858 in Mayne Expos. Lex.

Sipho·niform, a. [f. as prec. + -(i)form.] Having the form or shape of a siphon.

1891 in Cent. Dict.

Si·phonless, a. rare—[1]. [f. Siphon sb.] Destitute of a siphon.

1862 Dana Man. Geol. 258 In both groups the species are mostly siphonless.

Siphono- (səi·fŏno), a. Gr. σιφωνο-, combining form of σίφων Siphon, used in various terms of Zool. and Bot., as **si:phonobra·nchiate** sb. and a.; **sipho·nogam**; **si:phonoga·mic** a.; **siphono·gamous** a.; **siphono·gamy**; **sipho·noglyph** (-glif); **si:phonogly·phe** (-gləi·fī); **siphono·phoran** sb. and a.; **si·phonophore** (-fōəɹ) sb. and a.; **siphono·phorous** a.; **sipho·nopod**; **siphono·podous** a.; **si:phonosto·matous** a.; **si·phonostome**; **siphono·stomous** a.; **si:phonozo·oid**: (see quots.).

Various other combs. of doubtful currency, such as siphonocladaceous, -clamydate, -gnathoid, etc., are given in recent Dictionaries.

1842 Brande Dict. Sci., etc. 1120 *Siphonobranchiates,..an order of Gastropods, including those in which the branchial cavity terminates in a tube or siphon more or less prolonged, by which the respiratory current of water is received and expelled. 1849 Craig, *Siphonobranchiate a. 1898 tr. Strasburger's Text-Bk. Bot. 431 The pollen-tubes..conduct the two generative cells to the egg-cell. The Phanerogams have accordingly been termed by Engler, *Siphonogams. 1900 B. D. Jackson Gloss. Bot. Terms 242/1 *Siphonogamic. 1891 Nature 17 Sept. 484 From another point of view karyogamy is..*Siphonogamous: karyogamy is effected by a tubular outgrowth from one or both of the gametes. 1900 B. D. Jackson Gloss. Bot. Terms 242/1 *Siphonogamy. 1894 Jrnl. Marine Zool. I. 78 The single *siphonoglyph giving attachment to the ventral pair of directive mesenteries. 1883 Phil. Trans. CLXXIV. 693 On the Ciliated Groove (*Siphonoglyphe) in the Stomodæum of the Alcyonarians. Ibid. 694, I propose to call this groove 'the siphonoglyphe'. 1888 Rolleston & Jackson Anim. Life 725 [One end of the mouth] leading into well marked grooves strongly ciliated known as gonidial grooves or siphonoglyphes. Ibid. 775 A *Siphonophoran has been variously regarded (1) as an assemblage of organs, or (2) as a colony of polymorphic zooids. Ibid. 775 note, The *Siphonophoran tentacle..is sometimes attached directly to the coenosarc. 1842 Brande Dict. Sci., etc. 1120 *Siphonophores,..a name given by Escholtz to an order of Acalephes, to which he refers those species which have no central digestive cavity, but simply isolated tubes. 1883 Century Mag. Sept. 733/2 The vapory, translucent siphonophores..lived contentedly in their glass prison. 1884 Riverside Nat. Hist. I. 106 The *Siphonophore fauna of the Mediterranean Sea. a 1843 Encycl. Metrop. VII. 267/1 The *Siphonophorous Order are..distinguished by the absence of any stomach. 1881 Encycl. Brit. XII. 555/1 The variously modified units of the siphonophorous colony. Ibid. XVI. 684/1 In embryo *Siphonopods..the sucker-bearing lobes of the fore-foot are truly podial structures. Ibid. 669/1 *Siphonopodous Cephalopods in which the inflected lateral margins of the mid-foot are fused so as to form a complete tubular siphon. 1872 H. A. Nicholson Palæont. 244 In a second group the aperture of the shell is notched in front; and the shell is said to be '*siphonostomatous'. 1837 Penny Cycl. IX. 460/1 Latreille..admitted into the class Crustacea 12 orders,.. the Ostrapods, the Xyphosures, and the *Siphonostomes. 1842 Brande Dict. Sci., etc. 1120 Siphonostomes,..a family of Crustaceans, comprehending those which have a siphon-shaped mouth for suction. Ibid., Siphonostomes... By M. de Blainville the term is applied to those gastropods which have the opening of the shell prolonged into a siphon. a 1843 Encycl. Metrop. VII. 278/1 All the pieces of the mouth can be accounted for in the *Siphonostomous Order. 1855 Ogilvie Suppl., Siphonostomous, a designation of animals with a siphon-shaped mouth for suction. 1881 H. N. Moseley Corals in Rep. Sci. Results Voy. Challenger 1873–76 II. 118, I propose to term in the case of Alcyonarians, in which there are two kinds of zooids,..the aborted polyps (zooids of Kölliker) '*siphonozooids'. Ibid. 119 The siphonozooid cavities are only about one-fifth the length of the autozooid cavities. 1896 tr. Boas' Text Bk. Zool. 114 The constant presence, in various Alcyonarians, of arrested individuals (siphonozooids).

Si·phosome. Zool. [f. Gr. σίφων siphon + σῶμα body.] The lower part of a siphonophore stem, bearing the reproductive and nutrient organs.

1891 in Cent. Dict. 1898 Sedgwick Textbk. Zool. I. 139 Two parts may be distinguished in it [the coenosome]—an upper part, the nectosome.., and a lower part, the siphosome, bearing the nutritive and reproductive organs.

Siphre, -yre, obs. forms of Cipher sb.

Siphuncle (səi·fɒŋk'l). [ad. L. sīphunculus, dim. of sīpho Siphon.]

1. Zool. A small canal or tube traversing and connecting the shell-chambers in certain cephalopods; = Siphunculus, and Siphon sb. 3 a.

1822 J. Parkinson Outl. Oryctol. 161 The most important part of this organ, the continuous siphuncle. 1862 Kaapley Links in Chain v. 103 A membranous tube termed the Siphuncle, which originating in the body of the nautilus in the outer chamber passes through all the partitions in succession. 1870 H. A. Nicholson Man. Zool. ii. (1875) 368 The function of the siphuncle is unknown, except in so far as it doubtless serves to maintain the vitality of the shell.

transf. 1866 Blackmore Cradock Nowell xxxv. (1883) 213 This flint has traversing it from pole to pole a thread, a spindle, a siphuncle of the richest golden hue.

2. Ent. A small siphon or suctorial organ.

1826 Kirby & Sp. Entomol. III. xxxiii. 363 Replaced by an exarticulate retractile tube, which exerts a retractile siphuncle. Ibid. xxxiv. 472 The siphuncle, which is the suctorious part, being first retracted within the tubulet.

Si·phuncled, a. Zool. [f. prec. + -ed[1].] Possessing or furnished with a siphuncle.

1847 in Webster (citing Buckland). 1851 Woodward Mollusca I. 77 Shell, mucro (only known) chambered and siphuncled.

Siphu·ncular, a. Zool. [f. L. sīphuncul-us + -ar.] Of or pertaining to, acting or serving as, a siphuncle.

1832 Owen Mem. Pearly Nautilus 46 The siphuncular apertures of the septa. 1851 Richardson Geol. viii. (1855) 250 An external, many-chambered shell, with a siphuncular tube passing through the chambers. 1888 Rolleston & Jackson Anim. Life 464 Siphuncular collars generally directed backwards.

Siphu·nculate, a. Zool. [f. as prec. + -ate.] = next.

1875 Blake Zool. 244 A shell which is external, many-chambered, and siphunculate. 1877 Encycl. Brit. VI. 738/2 The spiral-chambered and siphunculate shell of Spirula.

Siphu·nculated, a. Zool. [Cf. prec.] Possessing or furnished with a siphuncle.

1828–32 in Webster (citing Say). 1851 Mantell Petrifactions v. § 5. 459 The Phragmocone, or chambered, siphunculated, internal shell. 1877 Huxley Anat. Inv. Anim. viii. 532 The Tetrabranchiata possess an external chambered siphunculated shell.

‖ **Siphu·nculus.** Zool. Pl. -culi. [L. sīphunculus a little pipe, dim. of sīpho Siphon.] = Siphuncle 1.

Anglicized as siphuncule by Mayne Expos. Lex. (1858).

1752 J. Hill Hist. Anim. 121 A siphunculus carried the whole length of the shell [of the nautilus]. 1764 Phil. Trans. LIV. 48 The siphunculus of the Belemnite is always upon the verge of the chamber, or cell. 1822 J. Parkinson Outl. Oryctol. 164 The chambers divided by winding septa, pierced by a siphunculus always placed at the outer side. 1836 Buckland Geol. & Min. xv. § 3 (1837) I. 332 Families of fossil chambered shells, that possessed siphunculi.

Sipid (si·pid), a. rare. Also 7 sippid. [Back-formation from Insipid a.]

1. Savoury; = Sapid a. 1.

1623 Cockeram I, Sippid, sauorie. 1660 F. Brooke tr. Le Blanc's Trav. 237 The flesh of Crocodile..was wholesome, white, and sipid.

2. fig. = Sapid a. 3.

1908 A. Symons in Sat. Rev. 17 Oct. 480/2 The music was ..gay, rattling, sipid, voluptuously melodious.

Hence **Sipi·dity**, savour, flavour. rare—[1].

1880 Miss Bird Japan I. 233 It is..used everywhere.. to give sipidity to their otherwise tasteless food.

Siping (səi·piŋ), vbl. sb. Now dial. [f. Sipe v.] The action of percolating, oozing, etc.; the result of this; also pl., water or other liquid that has oozed or leaked.

1503 Eng. Misc. (Surtees) 30 So that no fylth..discend from the same swynstye..excepte yt it be by sipyuge, or casualtie. 1621 Granger On Eccl. 316 The siping through of waters into the house. 1808 in Jamieson. 1825– in dialect glossaries, etc. (Northumb., Yks.). c 1880 in Heslop Northumbld. Gloss. (1894) 644 Sandy gravel, with a small siping of water.

So **Si·ping** ppl. a. Also as adv.

1398 Trevisa Barth. De P. R. vii. lix. (Bodl. MS.), Whanne þe posteme is in state men schal vse temperinge þinges and scheding and naisshing and cypingg. 1642 H. More Song of Soul I. iii. 24 Here fifty Sisters in a sieve do draw Thorough-siping water. 1862 C. C. Robinson Dial. Leeds 408 A siping wet neet.

Sipirs, obs. form of Cypress 3.

Sipling (si·pliŋ), north. and obs. Sc. Forms: 6 suppline, syplin, syeppaling, 8 sippleing; 7, 9– sipling, 9 siplin', -lin. [perh. ad. OF. souplin a shoot of a tree (Godef.); as a mere var. of Sapling the change of vowel would be difficult to account for.] A sapling.

1513 Douglas Æneid III. i. 47 Quhar hepthorne buskis.. grew bye, And evin syplinnis of myrthus. Ibid. vii. xiv. 87 And a haill suppline of a gret myrtre. 1610 North Riding Rec. (1884) I. 186 To cutt upp young siplings of asshe & hassells. 1708 J. C. Compl. Collier (1845) 35 Young Plants or Sippleings, as we here call them, of Oak, Ash or Aller. 1807 R. Anderson Cumbld. Ball. (1881) 108 Wid a spur on my heel, a yek [= oak] siplin in ban. 1849– in dialect glossaries (Northumb., Durh., Cumb.).

Sipman, obs. form of Shipman.

Sipper (si·pəɹ). [f. Sip v. + -er[1].] One who sips; hence, a drinker or toper.

1611 Cotgr., Piailleur, a bibber, sipper, wine-swiller. 1614 B. Jonson Barth. Fair III. i, They are all sippers, sippers o' the city; they look as they would not drink off two pen'orth of bottle-ale amongst 'em. 1702 Baynard Cold Baths II. (1709) 381 Sippers of Brandy and spirituous distill'd Liquors. 1806 Surr Winter in London II. 233 Only look..at the difference of beef steak breakfasters, and the sippers of souchong! 1866 Meredith Vittoria viii. (1889) 62, I promised my Rosellina, my poppy-headed sipper, a red-wine evening. 1891 Leeds Mercury 27 May 5/2 Half a dozen gentlemen..sipping tea..; each sipper wears a tall hat.

fig. 1850 McCosh Div. Govt. (1852) 206 He is probably an idle dreamer, or a sipper of the sweets of literature.

Sipper-sauce, dial.: see Sibber-sauce.

† **Si·ppet**, sb.[1] Obs. rare. Also 6 syppet. [Cf. Sip sb. and -et.] A little sip.

a 1529 Skelton E. Rummyng 367 Here is an olde typpet, And ye wyll gyue me a syppet Of your stale ale. 1574 Hellowes Gueuara's Fam. Ep. (1577) 98 Shee drinketh.. but water mixed with wine: in such wise, that with her sippets none may..kill his thirst.

Sippet (si·pĕt), sb.[2] Also 6–7 syppet, 7 sippit, -ett, cippet. [app. intended as a diminutive of Sop sb. Cf. supett in the earlier Wycl. version 2 Sam. xiii. 8.]

1. A small piece of toasted or fried bread, usually served in soup or broth, or with meat, or used for dipping into gravy, etc.; a small sop.

1530 Palsgr. 270/2 Syppet a lytell soppe, tatin. 1600 Surflet Countrie Farme v. xxi. 720 Some do make sippets or small slices (as they call them) of bread dried vpon the coales. a 1655 Sir T. Mayerne Archimag. Anglo-Gall. No. 47 (1658) 41 Serve it up with brown bread, and sippets fryed with butter. 1693 Crowne Country Wit III. iii, See that the mutton broath have white bread sippets in it. 1747–96 Mrs. Glasse Cookery v. 42 Lay round them stewed spinage pressed and cut like little sippets. 1764 Eliz. Moxon Eng. Housew. (ed. 9) 71 When you dish it up take off the lid, and..cut the lid in sippets. 1826 Polwhele Trad. & Recoll. I. 139 The fresh boiled round of beef, with onions and sippets, welcomed my arrival. 1843 Tait's Mag. X. 142 Having leisurely buttered his sippets of crisp dry toast. 1887 Fenn Master Cerem. iii, She threw some of the sippets in, and began tasting the broth in an unpleasant way.

b. transf. A small piece of something; a mere fragment.

1613 Beaum. & Fl. Captain IV. iii, Come pre'thee leave this sadness,..This mumps, this Lachrymæ, this love in sippets. 1647 J. C[leveland] Char. Lond. Diurn. 1 It is an History in Sippets; the English Iliads in a Nut-shell. 1751 Ld. Cobham in Walpole Geo. II (1822) I. v. 117 He did not like cutting the government out into sippets. 1761 Colman Prose on Sev. Occas. (1787) I. 83 A vast variety of thin volumes, containing certain sippets of philosophy, morality, and the arts. 1888 Athenæum 30 June 822/2 Those fragments are portions of a whole.., not [to be] doled out in literary sippets.

2. attrib. and Comb., as sippet-brewis, -pudding, -shaped.

1653 Urquhart Rabelais I. xxi, Store of good minced meat, and a great deal of sippet-brewis. 1830 Dolby Cook's Dict. 452/2 Sippet Pudding.—Cut a small loaf into extremely thin slices [etc.]. 1837 Barham Ingol. Leg. Ser. I. Leech of Folkestone (1905) 74 The occasional presentation of a sippet-shaped billet-doux.

Hence **Si·ppet** v., to cut into sippets. rare.

1681 Chetham Angler's Vade-m. xxxix. § 6 (1689) 257 Sippet it and garnish the dish.

Sipping (si·piŋ), vbl. sb. [f. Sip v. + -ing[1].]

1. The action of the vb.; drinking by sips; also, a single act of this; a quantity taken at a sip.

c 1440 Promp. Parv. 78 Cyppynge of drynke, subbibitura. 1483 Vulgaria 15 b, See now wyth their syppynge what wyne thei haue dronken. 1534 More Comf. agst. Trib. III. xxvi. (1847) 306 The little sipping that our hearts should have here now. 1597 J. Payne Royal Exch. 6 O praye for a fore taste and sum sippinge of this greate supper. 1611 Cotgr., Piaison, a bibbing, sipping, tipling. 1617 Moryson Itin. III. 89 The Weomen of Germany have a custome to helpe their..Friends, by sipping of the cup. 1822–7 Good Study Med. (1829) I. 187 A little toast and water alone, taken in small sippings. 1826 F. Reynolds Life & Times I. 34 The sipping and gurgling of tea.

transf. 1886 F. Harrison Ess. 211 How different this from the critic's sipping of new books! 1891 Miss Dowie Girl in Karp. 219 Her aprons were darker than in the other villages of my sipping.

b. attrib. and Comb., as sipping-drink, etc.

1589 Nashe Anat. Absurd. Wks. (Grosart) I. 61 May not a man as soone surfet by eating a whole sheepe..as by the sipping taste of sundry dainties? 1648 Hexham II, Een.. Zuyp-dranck,..a Sipping-drinke. 1821 Scott Kenilw. i, If you call on your host for help for such a sipping matter as a quart of sack. 1871 Athenæum 26 Aug. 273 Perhaps their sipping disposition has something to do with their fall.

† 2. = Sippet sb.[2] 1. Obs. rare.

1535 Coverdale 2 Sam. xiii. 6 Let my sister..make me a syppynge or two, and that I maye eate it of hir hande. Ibid. 8 She toke floure,..and made him a syppynge.

Si·ppingly, adv. [f. Sipping ppl. a. + -ly[2].] By or in sips. Also transf.

1814 W. Taylor in Monthly Rev. LXXIV. 275 Theology is sippingly tasted. 1858 Chamb. Jrnl. IX. 201 He takes it, not sippingly and with gusto,..but..in large quantities.

Sipple (si·p'l), v. Also 6 syp-, 7 scipple. [f. Sip v. + -le 3.]

1. trans. To drink (liquor, etc.) slowly or by small sips; to sip up.

1566 Drant Horace, Sat. I. iii. B v, The man doth sipple up the brothe. 1570 Levins Manip. 141 To sypple, sorbillare. 1683 G. M[eriton] Yorkshire Ale (1685) 7 At the first they did but sipple up This rare Ambrosia. 1748 Smollett R. Random xlvi. (1817) II. 96 Improperly applied to the taking of coffee, inasmuch as people did not drink, but sip or sipple that liquor. 1832–53 Whistle-Binkie Ser. I. 14, I had not learn'd to sipple tea.

2. intr. To sip liquor or the like leisurely.

1607 Markham Caval. vii. (1617) 19 Distempered with heate.., which you shall plainely perceiue by his continuall desire to drinke and scipple. 1816 Scott Antiq. ix, The body had got sic a trick of sippling and tippling wi' the bailies and deacons when they met. 1819 — in Lockhart (1837) IV. ix. 294 You had better drink a bottle of wine on any particular occasion, than sit..and sipple at an English pint every day.

Hence **Si·ppling** vbl. sb. Also attrib.

1601 Holland Pliny xx. xxi. II. 72 The seed of Mallows ..sodden in milk and taken after a sippling sort. 1681 W. Robertson Phraseol. Gen. (1693) 1159 To spend all the day in sipling. 1687 A. Lovell tr. Thevenot's Trav. I. 33 They all drink it sipping..; so that being in a Coffee-hane..one hears a pretty pleasant kind of sippling musick.

† **Sippo.** Obs.—[1] [ad. Pg. sipo.] A liana.

1657 S. Purchas Pol. Flying-Ins. 207 They run among some Sippoes or Withes that run into the tree.

Sipress, -is, -ous, obs. ff. Cypress 3.

Sipu·ncular, a. Zool. [f. Sipuncul-us + -ar.] Of or belonging to the genus Sipunculus of gephyrean worms.

1841 Forbes Hist. Brit. Starfishes 254 Pallas, in his Miscellanea Zoologica,..has figured two English Sipuncular worms.

Sipu·nculid. Zool. [f. as prec. + -id[3].] A gephyrean worm of the family Sipunculidæ.

1888 Rolleston & Jackson Anim. Life 619 A caecum is sometimes present at the commencement of the rectum in Sipunculids. 1893 Proc. Zool. Soc. 328 The papillæ..characteristic of the skin of Sipunculids.

Sipu·nculiform, a. Zool. rare. [f. as prec. + -(i)form.] Having the form of a small pipe or of a sipunculus.

1838 Penny Cycl. XII. 270/2 The Sipunculiform Holothuriæ. Body more or less suddenly attenuated backwards.

Sipu·nculoid, sb. and a. Zool. [-oid.]

A. sb. Any member of the group Sipunculoidea of gephyrean worms.

1857 Agassiz Contrib. Nat. Hist. U.S. I. 78 The Sipunculoids appear to be more closely related to the Annulata than to the Holothurioids. 1885 Encycl. Brit. XIX 430 Forming with the Brachiopoda and Sipunculoids an isolated group.

B. adj. Of or belonging to the group Sipunculoidea.

1881 Nation 1 Dec. 435/1 The report on the Gephyrea, or Sipunculoid worms. 1885 Encycl. Brit. XIX. 431/1 The Sipunculoid Gephyræans..possessing identically this arrangement.

‖ **Sipunculus** (səipɒ·ŋkiŭlŏs). Zool. Pl. -culi. [L. sīpunculus, var. of sīphunculus Siphunculus.] A gephyrean annelid with a retractile proboscis, belonging to the typical genus of the family Sipunculidæ.

1841 Forbes Hist. Brit. Starfishes 252, I have represented the Sipunculus alive in a Periwinkle shell. Ibid. 255 It is very probable that several other minute Sipunculi inhabit the British seas. 1877 Huxley Anat. Inv. Anim. v. 247 A larval Sipunculus about 1/12 of an inch long.

Sipylite (si·piləit). Min. [f. Sipyl-us, one of the children of Niobe + -ite[1] 2 b.] (See quots.)

1877 Mallet in Amer. Jrnl. Sci. 3rd Ser. XIV. 397 On Sipylite, a new Niobate, from Amherst County, Virginia. 1881 Watts 3rd Suppl., Sipylite, a niobate,..associated with albanite and magnetite, and occasionally with a few large crystals of hydrous zircon.

† **Siquare.** Obs. Also 4 siquar, sequar; 5 Sc. sith(t)-, syth(t)ar, -ware. [Origin and precise form doubtful.] Period or point of time; moment. Chiefly in phr. in that siquare.

Very common in the Cotton MS. of the Cursor M., but usually altered in the other MSS. Otherwise recorded only in the Sc. Leg. Saints, where the forms should perhaps be written with sich-, as in Horstmann's edition.

a 1300 Cursor M. 5656 He sagh an egypcien ful sare Smit a juu in þat si-quare. Ibid. 12301 Þe barn frendes fra þat siquar Held iesum in wirscip mar þan ar. a 1400 Sc. Leg. Saints i. (Peter) 631 He saw cryst in þat sythware pas in hewine. Ibid. ii. (Paul) 306 In þat sithar.

‖ **Si quis** (səi kwis), sb. Also si-quis, siquis. [L. sī if, quis any one (sc. invēnerit, etc.), the opening words of the notice or bill (see def.) when written in Latin.]

1. A public intimation, notice, or bill, freq. one exhibited on a post, door, etc., requesting information, advertising something lost, or the like; in later use only Eccl., a notice, required in certain cases, intimating that a candidate seeks ordination, and asking if any one knows of any impediment.

1597 Bp. Hall Sat. II. v, Saw'st thou ever Siquis patch'd on Paul's church dore, To seek some vacant Vicarage before? 1599 Jonson Ev. Man out of Hum. III. i, Enter Caualier Shift, with two Siquisses in his hand. Ibid., The aduancement of a Siquis or two. 1601 Weever Mirr. Martyrs A 3 b, Set vp a Siquis, giue intelligence, That such a day shall be my Tragedie. 1611 Cotgr., Plaquard,..a Bill, Siquis, or Libell stucke vpon a post, &c. 1646 H. Moseley in Beaum. & Fl.'s Plays I. (1905) p. xiii, Therefore now I put up this Si quis, that whosoever hereafter happily meetes with it [etc.]. 1674 Marvell Reh. Transp. II. 48, I understood that he had sent out a general Siquis thorow his own Province. 1817 C. Hodgson Instr. Candidates Holy Orders 3 Form of notice or 'Si quis', and of the certificate of the same having been published in the church of the parish where the candidate usually resides. 1843 Hook Ch. Dict. 523 In the case of a Bishop, the Si quis is affixed..on the door of Bow Church. 1904 Wright & Neil Protestant Dict. s.v. Ordination, If the candidate had left the university and is living elsewhere, a notice must be published... This notice is known as a si quis.

attrib. 1609 Dekker Gull's Horn Bk. Wks. (Grosart) II. 235 The first time that you venture into Powles.., presume not..to cast an eye to Si quis doore.

2. slang. (See quot.)

1864 Slang Dict. 231 Si Quis, a candidate for orders.

Hence ‖ **Si quis** v. trans., to advertise for.

1713 Gentleman Instructed II. x. 186, I must excuse my Depart.., otherwise he may send Hue and Cry after me, and Si quis me in the next Gazette.

Sir (sɜ̈ɹ), sb. [Reduced form of sire Sire sb., the shortening being due to the absence of stress before the following name or appellation. The forms sore, sur(e may represent OF. sor or sieur, the oblique case of sire.]

A. Illustration of forms.

a. 4– sir (6 sirr, 6–7 S[r]), 5–7 syr.

1297– (see examples in B).

β. 3–6 ser, 4–5 sere.

a 1300 Cursor M. 27450 Sere biscop, ta god kepe. c 1386 Chaucer Sir Thopas 6 (Cambr.), His name was sere Thopas. a 1400–50 Alexander 182 Seses, seris, of ȝour syte. c 1444 Capgrave Life St. Kath. IV. v. 441 This grete noyse, seres, what may it bee? 1451 — Life St. Gilbert 112 The fayre tour..whech þou say, Ser Pope, is þe grete excellens of þi dignite. 1509 in Scott. Jrnl. Topogr. (1848) II. 120/2 Ser Wilȝeam Synclair of Wairseytt, Kny[ch]t.

γ. 5 sur, sure, sore.

? a 1400 Arthur 285 Hys worthynesse, sur Emperour, Passeþ Muche alle ȝowre. a 1400 Sir Degrev. 289 The doughty knyght sure Degrevaunt. c 1410 Sir Cleges 443 Sore, for thy corteci, Smyghte me no more! c 1425 Abraham's Sacr. 435 in Non-Cycle Myst. Plays, Lo! sovereyns and sorys, now haue we schowyd [etc.].

δ. Sc. 4–5 scher(e, 5 schyr, 5–6 schir (5 shir).

In later Sc. also Stir (cf. Stirrah).

1375 Barbour Bruce XVII. 494 Till schir Robert the douchty king. 1396 in Scott. Antiq. XIV. 217 Scher Henry Synclar, Erle of Orkynnay. c 1425 Wyntoun Cron. IX. xviii. 125 Schirris, I thank God and al ȝow. c 1459 Regist. de Aberbrothoc (Bann.) II. 103 Honorabile and wirschypful schyris. 1473 Acc. Ld. High Treas. Scotl. I. 43 A lettre to Schire James Ogilvy of Erly. 1550 Reg. Privy Council Scot. I. 84 Schir George Douglas of Pettindreicht Knycht. 1574 Satir. Poems Reform. xlii. 6 Schirs, is thair ony heir Quhais lornay lyes unto Dundie?

B. Signification.

I. 1. The distinctive title of honour of a knight or a baronet, placed before the Christian name († rarely the surname).

1297 R. Glouc. (Rolls) 10822 Sir hubert de boru & oþere þat in prison were ido. 13.. Gaw. & Gr. Knt. 387 Sir Gawan, so mot I þryue,..Þis dint þat þou schal dryue. c 1386 Chaucer Sir Thopas 6 (Lansd.), A knyht was faire and gent.., His name was sir Thopas. c 1440 Contin. Brut (1908) 437 Sir Henry Beauford, Cardynall, and Bisshop of Winchestre. 1488–94 Ld. Fitzwalter in Paston Lett. III. 343 Zowir lofyng cosyn, J. Sir Fytz Wauter. 1556 Chron. Grey Friars (Camden) 41 The lady Margarete Bowmer wyffe unto sir John Bowmer,..but she was the wyffe of one Cheyny, for he solde hare unto sir Bowmer. 1596 Spenser State Irel. (Globe) 667/2 [A grant] of New-castell to Sir Henry Harrington, and of..Fearnes to Sir Thomas Masterson. 1627 Hakewill Apol. (1630) 272 Sir Drake whom well the worlds end knew. 1645 Symonds Diary (Camden) 217 Sir Nich. Kemys was governour when Gerard came. 1711 Addison Spect. No. 112 ¶ 2 My Friend Sir Roger, being a good Churchman [etc.]. 1819 Shelley Peter Bell 3rd VI. xv, He never read them;—with amaze I found Sir William Drummond had. 1899 Fitzpatrick Transvaal fr. within (1900) 286 Sir Alfred Milner..commanded the entire confidence of the Uitlanders.

b. In transf. uses, as Sir Harry, John, Sydney, Timothy (see quots.).

See also Barleycorn 1 b and Roger de Coverley.

a 1700 B. E. Dict. Cant. Crew, Sir Timothy, one that Treats every Body, and Pays the Reckonings every where. 1808 Jamieson, Sir John, a close stool. 1812 J. H. Vaux Flash Dict., Sir Sydney, a clasp knife. a 1825 Forby Voc. E. Anglia, Sir Harry, a close-stool.

2. Applied retrospectively to notable personages of ancient, esp. sacred or classical, history. Now only arch.

a 1300 Cursor M. 4249 Sir putifar wel vndirstod þat ioseph was o gentil blod. c 1330 R. Brunne Chron. Wace 24 Sen þe tyme of sir Noe. c 1400 Sc. Trojan War (Horstm.) I. 215 Jasone, the gentile, With hys falow, schyr Hercules. c 1440 York Myst. xxx. 208 We will prese to Sir Pilate. c 1475 Henryson Orpheus & Eurydice 116 At þe last schir orpheus couth heir. 1513 Douglas Æneid vii. v. 110 Schir Dardanus, born of this cuntre eik. 1582 Stanyhurst Æneis III. (Arb.) 71 Woorthye syr Æneas, why..teare you A caytiefe forlorne?..I am named syr Polydor. 1598 Shaks. Merry W. I. iii. 83 Shall I Sir Pandarus of Troy become? Ibid. II. i. 122 Goe thou like Sir Acteon. 1821 Scott Kenilw. xxxii, The valiant Sir Pandarus of Troy. 1881 R. F. Burton tr. Camoens' Lusiad IV. 23 The Oriental hordes..Wherewith Sir Xerxes crost the Hellespont.

3. Used fancifully, or as a mock title.

1362 Langl. P. Pl. A. II. 82 Þe Deede was a-selet, Be siht of sir Symoni. a 1500 Bernard. de cura rei fam. (E.E.T.S.) 13 Schir drunkyiness þat syre doys no thing rycht. 1567 Jewel Def. Apol. v. 561 Here, yee saie, 'Sir Defender is pretily seene in humanitie'. 1581 T. Howell Devises (1879) 185 Tyll syr Phebus beames shall lose their light. 1592 Greene Disput. Wks. (Grosart) X. 254 Though the other youth beare the charges and was made sir pay for all. 1600 Shaks. Merch. V. I. i. 93 (Qq.), I am sir Oracle, And when I ope my lips, let no dog barke. 1610 — Temp. II. i. 286 This Sir Prudence, who Should not vpbraid our course. 1781 Cowper Hope 416 Lowest at the board..sat Sir Smug. 1822 Shelley Faust ii. 114 Does not Sir Mammon gloriously illuminate His palace for this festival? Ibid. 150 Sir Urian is sitting aloft in the air. 1879 Farrar in Expositor IX. 214 He suddenly confounds the highly self-satisfied Sir-oracle.

b. Sir Rag (see quots.).

1764 in N. & Q. 7th Ser. XII. 29/1 Thomas Hunt, from Leicester (a Sir-Rag to a Waggoner), died at y[e] George. 1891 Ibid. 132/2 A dusty set of tatterdemalions..constantly attended fairs and race-courses, and these poor scarecrows used to be called in my young days 'Sir-Rags'. Ibid., In the Midland Counties..the chief of a band of servants or workers, a foreman or overseer,..is the 'sir-rag'. Ibid. 133/1 Sometimes he or she is the 'head sir-rag', or, as some put it, 'head sir-rag, chief cork and bottle-washer'. 1901 J. Prior Forest Folk ii. 18 He looks at a body as if he were head Sir Rag.

†4. Placed before the Christian name of ordinary priests (also that of a pope). Obs. (Cf. Sire sb. 1 b, and Dan[1] a.)

It has been supposed that this use arose out of sense 5, but there appears to be no evidence for this, although the title (at least in later times) was clearly used in contrast to Master, and denoted that the priest had not graduated in a university. For the generalized use of Sir John see John 3.

c 1385 [see John 3]. c 1425 Wyntoun Cron. VII. vii. 207 Kynge Henry..wrat richt reuerendly Til þe pape Schir Adryane. 1450 Paston Lett. I. 170 Sir John Bukk, Parson of Stratford, physshed my stankys at Dedham. 1511–2 Rec. St. Mary at Hill (1905) 277 To sir Robert for Candell to sey his matens in the mornynges. 1550 Bale Image Both Ch. II. f vj, The most ragged ronnagate, and idle idiote among theym, is no lesse then a syr, whiche is a Lord in the Latin, as syr John, syr Thomas, syr Wylliam. 1554 Hilarie Resurr. Masse A viij, My smered Chaplens..I make them to be called Syrs euery one. 1573 Tyrie (title), The Refutation of ane Ansver made be schir Johne Knox. 1595 ?Greene George a Greene 1191 Well preacht sir Iacke, downe with your staffe. 1635 [see John 3].

†5. Used (as a rendering of L. dominus), with the surname of the person, to designate a Bachelor of Arts in some Universities. Obs.

1557 in Lamb Collect. Hist. Univ. Camb. (1838) 229 M[r] Turner, Father, Syr Whytgyfte the bachelor, Syr Bryges the eldest son. 1575 in Fowler Hist. C. C. C. (O.H.S.) 150 Too S[r] huker of Corpus christie college in Oxforde. 1614 Selden Titles Honor 54 How Dominus..is now familiar for Sir to euery Batchelor of Art in the Schools, all men know. 1655 Fuller Ch. Hist. IX. 71 Hall and his Popish faction (whereof M[r]. Potto, M[r]. Binnion, and S[r]. Appleby the Leaders) opposed his admission. 1690 S. Sewall Diary 2 July, Sir Mather in England yet had a Degree conferred on him. 1714 in Aubrey Lett. (1814) I. 294 Pray, Sir, will you do so much as send to Sir Wilkinson of Queen's? 1763 in Pierce Hist. Harvard Univ. 234 (Cent. Dict.), That Sir Sewall, B.A., be the Instructor in the Hebrew and other learned languages for three years. 1822 Nares s.v. Sir, At the Universities..a bachelor, who in the books stood Dominus Brown, was in conversation called Sir Brown. This was in use in some colleges even in my memory.

II. 6. Placed before a common noun, and forming with it a term of address, as Sir clerk, king, knight, etc. Now arch.

1297 R. Glouc. (Rolls) 10282 Sir king,..we beþ icome fram verre londe iwis. Ibid. 10309 Nou sir clerc, quaþ be king, ȝe mowe þretni ynou. c 1330 Amis & Amil. 757 Sir knight,..Whi seystow euer nay? c 1400 Rom. Rose 6390 Sir Preest, in shrift I telle it thee, That he..Hath me assoiled. 14.. Chaucer's Doctor's Prol. 10 Sir Doctour of Phisyke... Telle us a tale. c 1440 York Myst. xxx. 211 Sir Knyghtis [sc. Roman soldiers], þat are curtayse and kynde. 1591 Spenser M. Hubberd 589 Ah! sir Mule, now blessed be the day [etc.]. Ibid. 1033 Nay (said the Foxe) Sir Ape, you are astray. 1601 Shaks. Twel. N. III. iv. 298, I am one, that had rather go with sir Priest, then sir knight. 1611 — Wint. T. I. ii. 135 Come (Sir Page) Looke on me with your Welkin eye. 1794 Mrs. Radcliffe Myst. Udolpho xliv, 'Sir knight,' replied the baron, 'how is it possible that' [etc.]? 1820 Scott Monast. xxxiii, Saint Mary! what call you yon, Sir Monk? 1842 Tennyson Morte d'Arth. 152 Sir King, I closed mine eyelids, lest the gems Should blind my purpose. 1865 Kingsley Herew. iv, Now, then, sir priest,..go on with your story.

transf. 1826 Scott Jrnl. 14 May, Look where you will, Sir Sun, you look upon sorrow and suffering.

b. With contemptuous, ironic, or irate force.

c 1386 Chaucer Wife's Prol. 242 (Harl.), Sir [v.r. Sire] olde lecchour, let thi japes be. a 1529 Skelton Against Scottes 101 Syr skyrgalyard, ye were so skyt [etc.]. 1591 Troublesome Raigne of King John (1611) 27 Lim. Good words sir sauce, your betters are in place. Phil. Not you sir doughtie, with your Lyons case. 1599 Shaks. Much Ado v. i. 83 Come sir boy, come follow me Sir boy, ile whip you from your foyning fence. 1759 Sterne Tr. Shandy II. ii, So, Sir Critic, I could have replied; but I scorn it. 1825 Scott Betrothed xxix, 'How, sir knave!' said the King, angrily, 'is it for such as thou to dictate to our judgment?'

7. Used as a respectful term of address to a superior or, in later use, an equal (sometimes with additions as dear, †fair, †gentle, good); also formally in addressing the Speaker of a legislative assembly.

1320–30 Horn Ch. 721 Sir, miȝtestow hold him to þi nede,..Batayle miȝt þou bide. c 1375 Sc. Leg. Saints xli. (Agnes) 102 Certis, gud sir, maryt ame I. c 1460 Towneley Myst. iv. 228 Hir answere bese belife—'nay, sir!' 1509 Fisher Fun. Serm. C'tess Richmond Wks. (1876) 307 But ye wyll say vnto me, Syr yf we were sure of this we wolde not be sory. 1535 Coverdale Ruth ii. 13 She sayde: let me fynde fauoure (syr) before thyne eyes. 1590 Shaks. Com. Err. I. ii. 57 The Sadler had it Sir, I kept it not. 1638 Chillingw. Relig. Prot. I. ii. 97 For Gods sake, S[r], tell me plainly. 1662 Stillingfl. Orig. Sacræ Ded. 11 You see, Sir, to what an unexpected length my desire to vindicate [etc.]. 1709 Steele Tatler No. 45 ¶ 1, I heard a Voice cry, Sir, Sir!—This raised my Curiosity. 1794 Mrs. Radcliffe Myst. Udolpho xliv, 'Dear sir!' said Henri, 'here is an armchair..massy with gilding'. 1849 Thackeray Pendennis x, 'Sir to you,' said Mr. Foker politely. 1867 Smyth Sailor's Word-bk. 627 'Aye, aye, sir,' is the well-known answer from seamen. 1873 in Hansard Parl. Deb. 31 July 1389/1, I rise, Sir,..to make the Indian Financial Statement.

b. In pl., used in addressing two or more persons. In Scottish use passing into a mere exclamation (see the later quots.).

c 1400 Destr. Troy 4907 Þerfore, sirs,..Let make vs a message. 1459 Rolls Parlt. V. 369/2 Sirres, be mery, for yet we have moo frendis. c 1500 Adam Bel cxiv. in Child Ballads III. 27/2 Good syrs, of whens be ye? 1615 Ruggle Ignoramus IV. (1736) 50 Goodly, Sirs,..I shou'd have sworn it had been my Master Antonio. 1766 Fordyce Serm. Young Wom. (1767) I. vii. 304 Have you forgotten, Sirs, that what they see you admire,..they will be induced to think..worthy of admiration? 1816 Scott Old Mort. xxxix, 'But eh, sirs,' she continued,..'Eh, sirs! ye're sair altered, hinny'. 1825 Jamieson Suppl., Sirs, Sirse, Serse, interj., a common mode of address to a number of persons, although of both sexes; often pron. q. Sirce. 1894 Crockett Raiders (ed. 3) 96 Eh, sirce, but there's mony wonderfu' things in the warld.

c. Used in commencing or subscribing letters.

1425 Paston Lett. I. 19 Right worthy and worshepefull Sir. a 1448 Ibid. 71 Syr, I recummawnd me to zow. 1535 Starkey England (1878) p. xiii, Syr, I most hertely commend me vn to you. 1568 Peebles Burgh Rec. (1872) 73 His supplicatioun..:—Schirris, baillies, counsale, and communite of the burgh. 1628 Ussher in Lett. Emin. Lit. Men (Camden) 138 Deare Sir, I know not who should beginne first [etc.]. 1655 in Nicholas P. (Camden) 300 Which I shall desire you to keepe for y[e] use of, Sir, Your..humble seruant, Robert Phelipps. 1745 J. Elton in Hanway Trav. (1762) I. v. lxvii. 304 Sirs, I have been acquainted with your resolutions of August last. 1789 Burns Let. to Cunningham 4 May, My dear Sir, Your duty-free favour..I received two days ago. 1822 Lamb To J. Taylor 7 Dec., Dear Sir, I should like the enclosed Dedication to be printed. 1861 Brewster in Mrs. Gordon Home Life xix. (1869) 345 Sir,—I have only this moment seen..an advertisement of your picture [etc.].

8. Used with scornful, contemptuous, indignant, or defiant force. (Cf. Sirrah.)

1592 Greene Conny Catch. Wks. (Grosart) XI. 84, I.. account thee no honest man: For sir know I haue learned your pettegree. 1600 Shaks. A. Y. L. I. i. 80 Well sir, get you in: I will not long be troubled with you. 1632 Massinger City Madam II. ii, Lacy. By the city custom, madam? Lady. Yes, my young sir. 1675 Baxter Cath. Theol. II. xiii. 283 Sir, the City ringeth of you as one that greatly wrongeth the cause of God. 1782 in Brit. Tourist (1809) IV. 119 Sir! in a surly tone, [signifies] a box on the ear at your service!—to a dog it means a good beating. 1824 Scott St. Ronan's xxx, Sir, this is either a very great mistake or wilful impertinence...I am Captain Jekyl, sir. 1855 J. D. Burn Autobiogr. Beggar Boy (1859) 44 His uniform manner of addressing me was, by the withering and degrading title of 'sir!' 1861 Geo. Eliot Silas M. ix, I've been too good a father to you all... But I shall pull up, sir.

b. My dear sir, in remonstrance or expostulation.

1825 R. P. Ward Tremaine II. xxvi. 238 'And, indeed, my dear Sir—' 'I won't be Sir'd,' cried the Doctor.

9. Applied to women. Now dial.

1578 Whetstone Promos & Cassandra I. iv. vii, [To Dalia.] Ah syr, you would, be like, let my Cocke Sparrow goe. 1611 Beaum. & Fl. King & No K. II. i, Pan. [to waiting-women]. Sirs, leave me all. (Exeunt Women.) 1621 Fletcher Pilgr. II. i, Juletta. Would you know o' me, Sir? Alphonso. O' thee, Sir? ay, o' thee, sir; What art thou, Sir? 1688 Crowne Darius II. Dram. Wks. 1874 III. 411 Barsana [to her confidante, Oronte]. How ill you dress me, sir? 1818 Miss Ferrier Marriage ii, 'And ye tu bonny sir,' addressing Lady Juliana.

10. A person of rank or importance; a lord, a gentleman; one who might be addressed as 'sir'.

In early use equivalent to sire; in later examples usually by direct transference from sense 7.

13.. Coer de L. 3567 Whos hed it was my seres aske? c 1500 Young Children's Bk. 88 in Babees Bk., Wer-euer þou commys, speke honestly To ser or dame. 1585 T. Washington tr. Nicholay's Voy. I. xvii. 20 Taking with him to accompanie him the sir of S. Veran. 1601 Shaks. Twel. N. III. iv. 81 A sad face, a reuerend carriage,..in the habite of some Sir of note. 1611 — Cymb. I. vi. 160 A Lady to the worthiest Sir, that euer Country call'd his. 1698 Fryer Acc. E. India & P. 45 In one of their open Pagods..stands a Venerable Sir at the upper end. 1703 Rowe Fair Penit. II. ii, A talking Sir that brawls for him in Taverns. 1740–1 Richardson Pamela II. 354 On Tuesday Morning, my dear Sir rode out, attended by Abraham. 1847 Tennyson Princ. Concl. 102 Why should not these great Sirs Give up their parks some dozen times a year? 1854 Emerson Lett. & Soc. Aims, Poet. & Imag., Our little sir, from his first tottering steps,..does not like to be practised upon.

11. A parson or priest. Now dial. (Cf. 4.)

1591 Spenser M. Hubberd 390 But this good Sir did follow the plaine word. 1869 Lonsdale Gloss. 74/2 'Here's t' sir cumman' = Here's the clergyman coming.

Sir (sɜ̈ɹ), v. [f. prec.]

1. trans. To address (a person) as 'sir'. Also with up.

1576 R. Peterson Galateo (1892) 47 He that is wont to be (Sird) and likewise (Sirreth) other. 1600 1st Pt. Sir J. Oldcastle II. i, Sum. Sir, I brought it not my lord to eate. Harp. O, do you sir me now? 1722 De Foe Relig. Courtsh. I. ii. (1840) 68 Don't worship me and sir me now. 1748 Richardson Clarissa (1768) I. viii. 43 My Brother and Sister..Sirr'd him up, at every word. 1806–7 Poet. Reg. 179 Learn..To frown importance while they cap and sir ye.

1. Of or characteristic of a siren; alluring, seductive.

Sircar, var. **circlet** Circle.

Sirdar (sɪˈdɑɹ, sɑˈdɑɹ). Forms: a. 7, 9 serdar, 7 serrdaar. β. 8 sardar, surdâr, 9 sardar. γ. 8 sírdâr, 9 sirdar. [Urdu (Pers.) sar-dâr, f. Pers. *sar* head + AR possessor.]

In India and other Eastern countries, a military chief, a leader or general of a force or army; also _spec._ in recent use, the British commander-in-chief of the Egyptian army.

Sire (saɪə). Forms: a. 3–7 sire, 4–5 sir, 6 sier; 4 scire, 7 shire. β. 3–8 syre, cyrr, syrr, syer, 5–6 syer, 5–6 cyre, cyr; earlier 'vi_sire_-comp. L. _senior_, for OF, was _siesir_:-- '_siebe_-em for _seniōrem_...

Siren (saɪˈən), _sb._ 4 soreyn, ays, 5 syren, 6 siryn, syrene. β. 4-7 sirenes (5 syrenes); 6-8 syrens, 7 syreney (syriney). 7- 5- siren. 6- 5 syren-, 8 syriney.

SIRIASIS. | 103 | SIROCCO. | SIROCCOISH. | 104 | SISERARY.

Siriasis (sɪˈraɪəsɪs). _Path._ [a. L. _sīrīasis_, a. Gr. σειρίασις, f. σειριᾶν to be hot and scorching.] A disease affecting children...

Siroc (sɪˈɒk), _sb._ Now _rare_. Forms: 8- siroc (9 siroch), 8, 9 syroc. [ad. It. _sirocco_ ...]

Sirocco (sɪˈɾəʊkəʊ). Forms: 7 sirocho, 8 syrocco, 7, 9 siroco, 9 siroco, 9 siroco ...

Sirvente (sɪˈvɛnt), _sb._ Also _rare_ **sir-venta**, sir-venté.

Siserary (sɪˈsɛɾərɪ). Now _dial._ Forms: 5 serary, 7 sesarary, 8 sisarara, 7 sisserara, 8-9 -ary, 9 -ara; 7 sissara, 8-9 sisserara, 8-9 ara; [Popular corruption of CERTIORARI.]

4. A loud clanging noise.

Siskin (si'skin). [...]

1. A small song-bird, in some respects closely allied to the goldfinch [...]

2. Applied with defining words to various small birds related to or resembling the siskin.

3. *attrib.*, as *siskin finch*, *group*; *siskin-green*, a light green inclining to yellow; *siskin-parrot*, a small parrot of the genus *Nasiterna* (*Cent. Dict.*).

Siskow, Siskowet, variant of Siscowet.

Sismograph, -meter, variants of Seismograph, -meter.

Sisoure, obs. f. Scissors.

† Sispar (si'spa:r). *pos.* f. *side-spar*.

Siss, sb.[1] **Siss**, sb.[2]

Siss (sis), v. Also *sizz*, *noise-*, *syss-*.

Sissars, -ers, obs. forms of Scissors.

Sissonine, *rare*. [f. Sisonne, *sissone*: see Littré and Hatzfeld.] A certain step in dancing.

Sisso (si'sə). Also **sisoo**, **sseau**, **sisau**. [Urdū (Hindi) *sisā*.] A valuable Indian timber-tree, *Dalbergia Sissoo*.

Sist, sb. *in Sc. Law.* [f. the vb.] A stay or suspension of some proceeding [...]

Sist, v. *Sc. Law.* [L. *sistĕre* to cause to stand, etc., a reduplicated form corresponding to *stāre* to stand.]

1. *a. trans.* To stop, stay, or suspend (some proceeding, etc.), *esp.* by judicial decree.

b. To cause or order (one) to appear *before* a court; to summon or cite.

c. To place (oneself) *before* a court.

2. *intr.* To stop, cease, desist, stop. *Obs.*

Sistance, *Obs. rare*. **† Sistence**.

† Sistent, *Obs. rare*.

Sister (si'stə:r), sb. Forms: [...]

1. A female in relationship to another person or persons having the same parents. (Also applicable to female animals.)

2. A female member of a religious order, society, or gild; *spec.* a nun.

3. *a.* A female fellow-member of the Christian Church as a whole, or of some body or association within this.

b. A female fellow-member of the Christian Church as a whole, or of some body or association within this.

4. *a.* Used to designate qualities, conditions, etc., in relation to each other or to some kindred thing.

5. *attrib.*, in *sister-band*, *-love*, *-train*, *-triad*, etc.

Sister-in-law. Also **†** *sistir elawe*, etc.

2. To call (one) sister; to address as a sister.

3. To treat in a sisterly manner.

Sister-german. [f. Sister sb. + German a.[1]]

Si'sterhood (si'stəhud). Also **†** *sisterhode*.

1. The state or condition of being a sister; sisterly status or relationship.

2. A society of sisters; *esp.* a society of women who have taken certain vows and live together under conventual rule, or who are otherwise devoted to religious, or to charitable work as a vocation.

3. Of or pertaining to a sisterhood.

4. Used loosely to denote a number of females having some common aim, characteristic, or calling. Often in a bad sense.

Si'stering, *vbl. sb.* [f. Sister v.]

Si'sterless, *a.* [f. Sister sb. + -less.]

Si'sterlike, *a.* Also [...]

Si'sterliness. [f. next + -ness.]

Si'sterly, *a.* [f. Sister sb. + -ly[1].]

Si'sterly, *adv.* [f. Sister sb. + -ly[2].]

Si'sterling. [...]

Si'stership. [...]

Sistrum (si'strəm). Pl. **sistra** (sistrums).

† Sistern. *Obs.*

Sisymbrium (sisi'mbriəm). [...]

Sisyphean (sisifi'ən), *a.* Also [...]

Sisyphian (sisi'fiən), *a.*

Sisyrinchium (sisiri'nkiəm). [...]

Sit (sit), *v.* Forms: [...]

A. Illustration of Forms.

B. Signification.

Sit, sb.

8. 6- mate.

B. Signification.

I. *intr.* **1.** Of persons: To be or remain in that posture in which the weight of the body rests upon the posteriors; to be seated.

2. With prepositional phrases denoting the occupation of the person while seated : **a.** With *at* (table, meat, supper, etc.).

b. With *in*.

3. With complement denoting the manner (or place) of sitting (on a seat, etc., or on horseback) :

b. With adj. or advb. complement in figurative phrases (see quots. and the complementary words).

c. In other figurative phrases (see quots. and the various uses).

d. To occupy an episcopal, or the papal, see.

b. ellipt. To sit (see 25 b).

4. *a.* Of persons seated (usually at a table) for the purpose of, or while engaged in, eating, drinking, gaming, etc. (Cf. 2 a.)

5. To sit, a throne, saddle, etc.

6. *a.* To place oneself in a position for having one's portrait painted or for being photographed. Also *const. for* (one's portrait), *to* (a painter, etc.).

b. To serve as a model *for* a painting or a character in a novel. Also *fig.*

c. To present oneself for examination; to be a candidate for a fellowship.

7. To be, to continue or remain, in a certain state. Now *rare* and *Obs.*

b. With adjectival or other complement denoting the condition.

8. *a.* Of a court or other assembly : To hold a session; to be engaged in the transaction of business.

b. Of a member of a council or legislative assembly. Also *const. for* (a constituency).

9. *+ a.* To lie in wait or in ambush. *Obs.*

b. To remain at a siege. Cf. 21 c (*b*).

10. Of birds : To roost; also, to rest the body on the ground or other surface.

b. To take up, or continue in the posture necessary for the hatching of eggs. *Obs. const.*

11. Of things : To have place or location ; to be situated.

12. To rest the body *on* the knees ; to be in a kneeling posture. Cf. 19. *Obs. exc. dial.*

13. Of things : To have place or location ; to be situated.

14. In *fig.* phrases : To sit *nigh*, *near*, *close*, *at*, etc. : To affect one deeply.

15. *refl.* and *trans.*

16. Of clothes : **a.** With dative : To fit or suit (a person, etc.). *rare.*

17. 18.

IV. *With adverbs.*

21. Sit down. **a.** To seat oneself ; to take a seat. Cf. 18.

b. To go down on one's knees. Cf. 19. *Obs.*

c. To sit down accidentally; to the ground in a sitting posture.

d. *fig.* Of persons or things : To settle down in some way.

e. To settle or take up one's abode.

22. Sit in. To have a place as a player or (at the temperate game); see 11 dial.

23. Sit on. **a.** Also with *to*. (See quots.) Now *dial.*

24. Sit out. **a.** To sit apart from others, or to remain seated, so as take no part in a game, dance, etc.

25. Sit up. **a.** To raise the body from a recumbent to a sitting posture.

26. Sit on or **upon.** **a.** To sit in judgement or council, to deliberate, on (a matter or person).

27. To be occupied with (a matter, etc.) while sitting ; to pore over (a book).

28. Sit under. To listen to, be a hearer of, attend the church of (a minister or preacher).

+ 33. To set or place. *Obs. rare.*

+ 34. *Sc.* (and *north*.). To disregard, neglect, pay no heed or attention to (a command, call, etc.).

29. Sit with. **a.** *To* To put up with or tolerate; to stand (a wrong, etc.). Cf. 21 d.

35. To sit against, resist ; to endure, bear ; to put up with, go on with. Now *rare.*

36. To hold (a meeting).

30. *refl.* To seat (oneself.)

31. *trans.* To sit upon, to ride (a horse).

37. *intr.* **a.** To remain seated and take no part in (a game or dance). Cf. 24.

b. To remain sitting, so as to be present during the course of (something). Also *with it* (quot. 1530), implying endurance of something disagreeable.

Sit, the verbal stem in combs., as *+ sit-horse*, a riding-horse ; *+ sit-house*, &c. a residence.

b. Of a hen or hen-bird : To sit upon, to hatch (eggs). Also *transf.* (quot. 1828.)

Sitar (si'tär). *Ent.* [mod.L. (Latreille, 1802).] A coleopterous insect, of genus *Sitaris*.

Sitaris (si'tāris). *Ent.* [mod.L. (Latreille, 1802).]

Site, *sb.*[1] Forms : 3–5 *cyte*, 6 *syte*, 5–7 *sight*, 7 *site*. [ad. L. *situs* site, position.] **1.** The situation or position of a place, town, building, etc.

2. The ground or area upon which a building, town, etc., is, was, or is to be erected.

Site, *v.*[1] [f. prec.] **1.** *trans.* To locate, to place.

2. *Sc.* To cite, summon.

SITH. | 113 | SITH. | SITH. | 114 | SITH.

SITHE. | 115 | SITHENCE. | SITHRE. | 116 | SITTING.

Six-foot. [See SIX C. 1.]

1. Measuring six feet in length, breadth, or height.

2. Containing six (metrical) feet.

Six-footer (six-fut·əɹ). [f. SIX.]

‖ Sixiesme, Obs. rare. Also **sixiesm**. [F. *sixième* (*= sixiesme*, etc.), f. *six* six.] A sequence of six cards at piquet. *Sixieme major*, one consisting of ace, king, queen, knave, ten, and nine.

Sixpence (si·kspens). [f. SIX a. + PENCE.]

A sum of money equal in value to six pennies.

Sixpennyworth (sikspe·niwəɹþ). Also six-pen·n'orth (si·kspənaɹþ). [f. SIX a. + PENNY + WORTH sb.] Such as is worth sixpence; an amount which is or may be bought for sixpence.

Six-pounder (si·kspaundəɹ). [f. SIX a. + POUNDER sb.]

1. A cannon throwing about six pounds weight.

b. A shot weighing six pounds.

2. (See quot.)

Six-shooter, sb. Now arch. [f. SIX a. + SHOOTER sb.] Six times twenty, one hundred and twenty.

Six-shooter, sb. [f. SIX C. 1. + SHOOTER sb.] A repeating pistol or revolver capable of firing six shots without reloading; a six-chambered revolver. Also attrib.

Hence **six-shooting** vbl. sb. and ppl. a.

Six-sided, a. [f. SIX a. + SIDE sb.] Having six sides; hexagonal.

Sixpenny (si·kspəni). [f. SIX a. + PENNY.]

1. Of the value or price of sixpence.

2. Costing, or priced at, sixpence.

3. Bringing in pecuniary; having a subscription of sixpence; selling articles at sixpence.

Sixscore, sb. and a. Now arch. [f. SIX a. + SCORE sb.]

Sixteen (siksti·n, si·kstiːn), a. and sb.
Forms: 1 **sextóne**, **siex**-, **syxtóene**, 3 **siex-teon**, 3–4 **sixtene** (7 -tein). β. 1–6 **sextene** (5 cen-), 4–6 **sexten**, 4 **sextene,** 5–6 **sext-ene,** -eyne (5 -ine), 6 **sixtene.** γ. 4–6 **-OFtin,** 6 -**tyn.** δ. 4–7 **sexten,** etc.

Sixteenmo. [English reading of the symbol 16mo: cf. DUODECIMO, etc.]

Sixteenth (siksti·nþ), a. and sb.
Forms: a. 1 **sextéoþe,** 3 **-teoþe**, etc.

Sixteener (siksti·nəɹ). [f. prec. + -ER 1.]

1. One of a body of persons sixteen in number.

2. A youth of sixteen.

Sixter Obs.⁻¹ In 5 **syxter.**

Sixth (siksþ), a. and sb. Forms: a. 1 **sexta** (sesta, eesta), 2–5 **sexte** (2–4 **sexte**), etc.

Sixthly, adv. [f. prec.] In the sixth place.

Sixtieth (si·kstiːiþ), a. and sb. [OED. **sixtigóða,** etc.]

Sixty (si·ksti), a. and sb. Forms: a. 1 **siextig, syxtig,** 2 **sixti, sexti,** etc.

Sixty (si·ksti). 1. The abstract number sixty.

2. Followed immediately by a lesser numeral, as *sixty-one,* etc.

3. Forming part of an ordinal number.

b. With *aut,* or used absol. in this sense, esp. *sixty-fourth;* hence *sixty-fourther,* one who owns a sixty-fourth part of a vessel.

B. sb. 1. The abstract number sixty.

b. *Like sixty,* with great force or vigour; at a great rate. *colloq.* or *slang.* (Cf. FORTY A. b.)

2. *Sixty-four,* a cipher.

3. Sixty years of age.

Sixtyfold (si·kstifōld), a. (and sb.). [L. SIXTY + -FOLD.]

Sizar (səi·zəɹ). Also 6–9 **sizer** (7 **ciser**). [f. SIZE sb.] In the University of Cambridge, and at Trinity College, Dublin, an undergraduate member admitted under this designation and receiving an allowance from the college to enable him to study.

Size (səiz), sb.¹ Forms: 4 **syse,** 4–6 **sise,** 5 **syce, cyse, syys,** etc.

Sizable, a. Also 6–9 **sizeable.**

Sizarship (səi·zəɹʃip). Also 8 **sizership.** [f. SIZAR + -SHIP.]

Size (səiz), sb.² Forms: 5 **syse,** 5–8 **sise,** 6 **cyse,** 6–7 **syze, syse,** 7 **sice,** 6– **size.** [Possibly the same word as SIZE sb.¹]

Size (səiz), sb.³ Forms: 5 **syse,** 6–7 **syze, syse,** 7– **size.** [Of obscure origin.]

Size (səiz), v.¹ Forms: 5 **syse,** 5–8 **sise,** 6– **size.** [f. SIZE sb.¹]

1. *trans.* To regulate or control, *esp.* in relation to a fixed standard. *Obs.*

Size (səiz), v.² [f. SIZE sb.²]

Size (səiz), v.³ [f. SIZE sb.³]

SKENE

Skewso, obs. f. Scuse v. Skewt, var. Scoot v.

†Skey, obs. rare. A kind of boat.

†Skey (ski), sb. S. African. also Ski. The schei (schier). One of a pair of wooden bars passing through each end of an ox-yoke, to which the neckstraps are fixed.

†Skey, v., Obs.¹ [var. of Skeigh a.] Skittish.

†Skey, v., Obs.²
1. intr. To get clear, to sheer off.
2. trans. † To startle, come upon suddenly.

Skey, obs. f. Skay. var. Skeymishe, -mowe(e, obs. ff. Squeamish. Skeyn(e, obs. ff. Skein, Skene. Skeyr, obs. Sc. f. Skere. Skey3ren, var. Skair s. Obs.

†Ski (ʃi, ski), sb. Pl. **ski** (also skis). Also **she, skee**. [a. Norw. ski (ʃiː, ʃiː), also written skid) neut.—ON. skíð snow-shoe, billet of cleft wood,—OE. scíd billet of wood, dialects also skida (skjía, skjíe) fem.—Sw. skida (pl. skidor)—ON. skíða. The sb. before palatal vowels has the value of (ʃ).] The form skid, and Sw. pl. skidor, have occasionally been used in English context, but have not obtained general currency.

1. One of a pair of long slender pieces of wood fastened to the foot and used as a snow-shoe, enabling the wearer to slide down hill with great speed.

2. attrib. and Comb., as **ski-gathering, ski-excursion, jumping, -running; ski staff**, etc.

Skice, v.¹ Now dial. Also 6–7 **skiso**, 9 **skeyse**. [Of obscure origin.]
1. intr. To move quickly; to skip or frisk about; to run, etc.

†Skice, v.² Obs. rare. Alteration of slice Slice v.] trans. To slice, cut.

†Skick, v. Obs. rare. Also 4 **skyke**, 5 **skikke**. [var. of Skecke v.] trans. To skin; to smooth.

†Skiddaw, v. Obs. rare. Also 4–5 **skidaw**.

Skie, obs. form of Sky sb. v.

Skied, Skier, Skies: see Sky.

Skieve, var. Skeeve. Obs.; Skiff, var. Skew.

Skiagram (skáiˑ-græm), sb. Also **skiogram**. [f. Gr. σκιά shadow + -gram.]
An outline of the shadow of an object filled in with black (see quot. 1801); a picture painted or produced in this style.

Skiagraph (skáiˑə-grɑːf), sb. Also **skiogram**. [See Sciagraphy.] A photograph obtained by means of the Röntgen rays; a radiograph. —Sciagraph b. Hence **Ski-agraph** v. trans., to photograph by means of the Röntgen rays. **Skia-grapher**, a radiographer. **Skia-graphic**, of or pertaining to skiagraphy; radiographic. **Ski-agraphically** adv., after the manner of skiagraphy.

Skiagraphy (skáiˑə-grăfi). Also **skiography**. [See Sciagraphy.]
1. (See first quot.)
2. Radiography.

Skian, var. Skene. **Skiatic**, obs. var. Sciatic a.

Ski-bob. Now dial. Forms: 4–5 **skybot, skibet, 5 skibbit, 9 skibbes, skifret**. [Of obscure origin: cf. Skippet¹.] A small box; a small compartment in a chest, etc. Also transf.

Skice, v.¹ Now dial. Also 6–7 **skiso**, 9 **skeyse**. [Of obscure origin.]

Skick, v. Now dial. Also 6 **skyck**, **skikke**. [Of doubtful origin: both form and sense suggest some connexion with ON. skíð (see Ski) and Scd Shide, but skíð does not phonetically represent either of these.]
1. b. beam, plank, or piece of timber, esp. one of a number upon which something rests or is supported, or by which a thing is held in position.

Skid, sb. (snow-shoe): see Ski.

Skid (skid), sb.¹
1. trans. To apply or fasten a skid or brake to (a wheel) in order to retard its motion; to lock (a wheel) in this way.

b. To push or drag (a person) along.
2. Lumbering. To haul (logs) on or along skids; to pile or place on a skid way. Also absol.

Skid (skid), v.² rare. [variant of Scud v.]
intr. To go or quickly, to scud.

Skidding (See quot.)

2. A device for locking the wheel of a vehicle or for retarding its motion in descending a hill or slope; esp. an iron shoe chained to the vehicle and placed in front of the wheel so as to be caught between it and the ground.

Skid-dy, Ski dy-cock, dial. Forms, of skiddy-cock, or skiddy-cock, a water-rail.

Skied (skaid), ppl. a. [f. Sky sb. or v.]

Skie, obs. form of Sky v.

Skier, variant of Skyer.

Skiff (skif), sb.¹ Forms: 4–7 **skiph, skiffe**, 6 **skyfe, skyffe**, 6– skiff. 8 **sciffe**, 7 sciph. [a. F. esquif (1549), Sp. and Pg. esquife, It. schifo; ad. OHG. scif ship, boat.]
1. A small sea-going boat, adapted for rowing and sailing; esp. one attached to a ship and used for purposes of communication, transport, towing, etc. Hence, a small light boat of any kind.

Skier, variant of Skyer.

Skiff (skif), v. Forms: 4–6 skyph. [f. prec.]
1. intr. To move lightly and quickly, esp. so as barely to touch a surface; to glide, run, etc.; to skim.

†Skifskart. Obs. [f. Skick v.] An old name

Skilful (skiˑlfŭl), a. and adv. Forms: 4 **scolsol, skilful**; 4–6 **skylful, 5–6 skyllful, full; 4–7 -full, 4– skilful (6 skilful, 9 dial. -ful).**
1. Endowed with reason; rational; also, following reason, doing right. Obs.

2. attrib. and Comb., as **skill-maker, pan, tool**.

†Skilful, a. and adv. Obs.

Skilfulness. Also 5–6 skilful-, 7 **skilfulnesse**, 8 **skill-** [f. prec. + -ness.]
1. The quality of being reasonable. Obs.
2. The quality of being skilful; dexterity.

Skilless (skiˑlˌles), a. Also 3 skilless, 9 skill-less; 6 skilles, 6–7 skillesse, 9 skyllasse; skill-, sk.¹ + -less.]
1. Devoid of (or connected with) knowledge; ignorant.
2. Lacking skill; unskilled, unskilful.

Skill (skil), sb.¹ Forms: 3 skile, (4 skile), 4 skyl, skyll, skille, 5– skill; also 6 skyle, 5 skele, skeyle, sk.¹ [ad. ON. skil (neut.) distinction, difference, etc.; cf. Skill v.]

Skill (skil), v. Forms: 2–7 **skil, 3–7 skyl(l, skille, 4– skill** [ad. ON. skila to divide, separate, distinguish.]
1. trans. To separate, part form. Obs.

†Skill, sb.² Obs. rare. ? A skillet.

Skill, obs. variant of Skull¹, basket.

Skilled (skild), ppl. a. Also 6 skild. [f. Skill v.]
1. Of persons: Possessed of skill or knowledge; experienced or experienced.

Ski-llok, var. of Skellat, bell.

Skilless: see Skilless.

Skilligalee (skiˑligəliˑ) slang. Also **skilla-gelee**, and **-golee, -gloo**. [prob. a purely fanciful formation.]
1. A thin gruel or broth served out to prisoners, etc.

2. A thick flat piece of silver or other precious material.

Skilling

1. = Skilly sb.

2. With negative : A single coin of the smallest value.

attrib. Worthless, trifling.

Skilling (ski'liŋ). Forms : 4–5 skelyng, 7–9 skeeling, 9 skeling ; 8– skilling, etc. See also Skilling sb.

1. A shed or outhouse, esp. a lean-to, a penthouse. Current in the south of England, from Surrey to Dorset.

2. A small copper coin and money of account formerly in use in Scandinavia.

Skilling (void quot.), obs. var. Skeeling Sc.

Ski'lling, vbl. sb. rare⁻¹. [Skill v.¹]
† The operation of reasoning.

† **Skillwise**, a. Obs. rare⁻¹. [Skill sb.¹]

Skillion, sb.² Austr. [Alteration of skilling Skilling sb.¹]

Skim, sb. Also 6 skyme, 6–7 skimme.

† 1. = Scum sb. 1. Obs.

2. In earlier use taking the place of Scum sb.¹

1. † a. Scum sb. 1. Obs.

Skilless, a.

Skillet (ski'let).

Skilly (ski'li), a. Also 9 skilley. [Abbreviation of Skilligalee.] A kind of thin, watery porridge, gruel, or soup, commonly made from oatmeal, and used especially in prisons and workhouses.

Skilly-pot, Skilpot. U.S. [ad. Du. schildpad turtle.] The slider or red-bellied terrapin.

Skill, v. Also 6 skem(e, skym(e, 7 skeam-, 6–7 skimme. [prob. ad. ON.: *skima*.]

1. I. trans. To clear (a liquid or a liquid mass) from matter floating upon the surface, usually by means of a special utensil.

Skim-coulter. Agric. [f. Skim v.] A coulter fitted with a plate of iron or steel which shaves off the top-layer of the ground and turns it into the furrow.

Skime, v. north. dial. Also 8–9 skyme. [perh. a. ON. *skima* to peer, look about one.]

Skimback. U.S. local. [f. Skim v. + Back sb.¹] A North American river-fish.

Skimble-skimble, a., sb., and adv. [f. Scamble v., with varied reduplication in the first element : cf. *clitter-clatter*, *tittle-tattle*, etc.]

Skimmed (skimd), ppl. a. [f. Skim v.]

Skimmer (ski'məz).

Skimmer (ski'maz), sb. Forms : 4 skemour, 5 skemore, 4–5 skymour(e, 5 skymere, 5–6 skymer, 7 skymer ; 4 skemmer (6 schimer-), 7– (in other senses : 4 skymmar, 6 scemour, 8 scummer (sequamer) ; see Scummer sb. In later use also f. Skim v. + -er¹.]

† **Skimmer**, obs. Sc. form of Scumber v.

SKIMMIA. 143 SKIN. SKIN. 144 SKIN.

Skimmia. Bot. [mod.L. (Thunberg, 1784), f. Jap. (*miyama-) shikimi*, the name of the plant.]

Skim-milk, sb.
1. Milk with the cream skimmed off or otherwise removed. Also in fig. context.

Skim-milk, a.

Skim-pot, Skilpot. U.S.

Skimming, vbl. sb. [f. Skim v.]

Skimming-dish. [Skimming vbl. sb.]
1. A dish suitable for skimming with ; esp. one used in skimming milk or in cheese-making.

Skimmingly, adv.

Skimmington (ski'miŋtən).

Skimming-ness. Resemblance to skim-milk.

Skimp, v. [Of obscure origin : not in general use until very recently.] Scanty ; Scrimp a.

Skimp, a. [Cf. prec.] Scanty ; Scrimp a.

Skimped (skimt), ppl. a. Also 9 scimpit. [f. prec.] = Scrimped ppl. a.

Skimpily, adv.

Skimpiness.

Skimping, ppl. a. [f. Skimp v. + -ing²]

Skimpingly, Mining. [alteration of skimpings : (see quots.)]

Skimp-money.

Skimpy, a. [f. Skimp a. + -y¹.] Of a scrimp, scanty, meagre, or spare character ; lacking the proper fulness or size.

Skimshander = Scrimshaw.

Skin, sb. Forms : 3– skin (3, 4 skinn, 4 skyn, 4–6 skyne, 4–7 skyn(n)e), 3–5 skinn(e, 4–7 skinne ; 4–6 skin, 4–6 skyn, 5 scinne, 6 skine, 6 scine, etc.

Skin, sb.
I. 1. The integument of an animal stripped from the body, and usually dressed or tanned ; with or without the hair, or intended for this purpose ; a hide, pelt, or fur ; also occas., an article made of this.

Skin, v.
I. 1. trans. To strip or deprive of the skin ; to flay.

action of salt water and its combined air. 1869 Rankine *Machine & Hand-tools* App. 54 It is used to form a hard and impenetrable *skin* to a piece of grey cast iron by the process called *chilling*.

e. *Arch.* The facing of a wall, in contrast to the material in the heart of it.

1884 *Mil. Engin.* I. ii. 84 To have only a thin skin on the outside which could readily be knocked out by a crowbar. 1897 *Daily News* 23 Nov. 6/5 The disintegrated condition of the inner masonry..rendered impossible the project..of replacing the inside masonry without disturbing the 'skin'.

8. *Naut.* a. The planking, or iron plating, covering the ribs or frame of a vessel.

(a) 1769 Falconer *Dict. Marine* (1780), *Planking* is sometimes called 'laying on the skin', by the artificers. 1814 *Phil. Trans.* CIV. ii. 287 The ribs are covered by a skin of greater or less substance from the extreme ends of them to the keel or back bone. 1856 Kane *Arct. Expl.* I. xxxii. 444 The entire bulkhead was in a blaze, as well as the dry timbers and skin of the brig. 1867 Smyth *Sailor's Word-bk.* 629 *Skin*, this term is frequently used for the inside planking of a vessel, the outside being the *case*. 1886 *Pall Mall G.* 26 Aug. 4/1 The boat is most substantially constructed;..the skin being of mahogany three-eighths of an inch thick.

(b) 1862 *Times* 7 Mar., The 18 inches of wood between the armour and iron skin. 1883 Nares *Constr. Ironclad* 5 The plates forming the outer and inner bottoms or *skins* are rivetted on.

b. (See first quot.)

1841 Totten *Naval Text Bk.* 394 *Skin*, that part of a sail, when furled, which remains outside and covers the whole. c 1860 H. Stuart *Seaman's Catech.* 49 What cloth will you take for furling the spanker in a skin? The third from the leech. 1882 Nares *Seamanship* (ed. 6) 134 Gather up the skin, shaking the slack sail well down into it.

9. Used as a term of contempt.

1825 Jamieson *Suppl.*, *Skin*, a term applied to a person, as expressive of the greatest contempt; as 'Ye're naething but a nasty skin'. 1889 *Century Mag.* Dec. 277 Occasionally he would refer to the president of the Off-shore Wrecking Company, his former employer, as 'that skin'.

III. *attrib.* and *Comb.*

10. Attrib. a. In sense 'of, in, connected with, the skin', as *skin-disease*, *-furrow*, *-tint*, etc.

This type is very common in recent medical works.

1615 H. Crooke *Body of Man* 349 Betwixt the fleshy membrane and the skinne runne certaine vessels called *Skin-veines*. 1676 Marvell *Mr. Smirke* Wks (Grosart) IV. 16 'Tis a pitiful giddy..insect, ingendered..in every marish, can but run a pore thorow and give but a skinne-wound. 1769 Mrs. Raffald *Eng. Housekpr.* (1778) 57 Lay the feet over them the skin side up. 1864 W. T. Fox *Skin Dis.* 15 The unchangeable elements, in the teaching of skin pathology. 1865 *Chambers's Encycl.* VII. 363/1 Pellagra, at one time, the name of a loathsome skin-disease. 1880 *Nature* 28 Oct. 605 On the Skin-furrows of the Hand. 1896 *Peterson's Mag.* VI. 231/2 The skin-tints are less clear and warm than the same painter's 'Bubbles'.

b. In sense 'made, or consisting, of skin', as *skin-boat*, *-bottle*, *-canoe*, *-case*, etc

1593 Nashe *Christ's T.* Wks. (Grosart) IV. 214 Our costly skinne-cases could keepe vs from consuming to dust. 1647 J. Trapp *Comm. Luke* i. 59 A skin-bottle hanging in the smoke of filthy desires. 1761 *Ann. Reg.* 128 This plate is to be moved round,..rubbing it with a small skin cushion. 1808 Pike *Sources Mississ.* (1810) ii. 155 We..nearly compleated the frame of a skin Canoe. 1827 J. Holmes *Hist. United Brethren* i. (ed. 2) 7 The skin-boat is..from forty to fifty feet long, and proportionally broad and deep. 1871 W. Morris in Mackail *Life* (1899) I. 246 Skin shoes tied about the ankle with neat thongs. 1895 Scully *Kafir Stories* 123 He carried a small skin wallet slung to his waist.

11. Objective. a. With pres. pples., as *skin-breaking*, *-clipping*, *-piercing*, *-plastering*, etc.

1593 Nashe *Christ's T.* Wks. (Grosart) IV. 226 Those skin-playstring Painters. 1599 — *Lenten Stuff* ibid. V. 229 The curtaild skinclipping pagans. 1611 Cotgr., *Ratoire*,..a skinne-breaking oyntment. 1784 Cowper *Task* v. 141 Arrowy sleet, Skin-piercing volley, blossom-bruising hail. 1889 J. J. Thomas *Froudacity* 40 The skin-discriminating policy induced..since the abolition of slavery. 1891 Miss Dowie *Girl Karp.* 244, I listened open-eyed to the herd's bear statistics, literally skin-clamming as these were.

b. With verbal sbs., as *skin-cutting*, *-grafting*, *-healing*, etc.

1829 Scott *Anne of G.* xxvii, The other three are picked men, who will not fear their skin-cutting. 1860 Tomlinson *Arts & Manuf.* Ser. ii. *Leather* 25 When they are in the state of pelt, they are split...This is effected by means of a..machine called the 'skin-splitting machine'. 1876 *Clinical Soc. Trans.* IX. 30 During this period skin grafting was practised continuously. 1896 *Allbutt's Syst. Med.* I. 380 Manipulations cannot be begun upon wounded surfaces until skin-healing is complete.

c. With agent-nouns, as *skin-dealer*, *-dresser*, *-hunter*, *-preserver*.

1858 Simmonds *Dict. Trade*, *Skin-dealer*. *Ibid.*, *Skin-dresser*, a currier, or furrier. 1890 *Daily News* 9 Sept. 7/1 A brother..who carried on business as a furrier and skin-dresser. 1893 *Scribner's Mag.* June 794/1 Wholesale slaughter by skin-hunters has nearly destroyed the Platypus in some districts. 1893 *Daily News* 16 Feb. 5/5 No fewer than three taxidermists or skin preservers.

12. a. With past pples., as *skin-built*, *-clad*, *-peeled*, *-spread*.

a 1661 Holyday *Persius* (1673) 294 Who without heed.. praise thee so, That (skin-peel'd a-se!) thy self dost first cry, Hoe! 1823 Joanna Baillie *Poems* 260 Whilst travellers from their skin-spread couches rise. 1846 H. G. Robinson *Odes of Horace* ii. vi, Galesus' tide, Sweet to the skin-clad flocks. 1883 *Boats of World* 27 Two examples of skin-built canoes. 1886 *Encycl. Brit.* XXI. 113/2 Stilicho.. planted the cruel Goths, his 'skin-clad' minions, in the very sanctuary of the empire.

b. Misc., as *skin-like* adj., (*to the*) *skinward* adv.

1699 R. L'Estrange *Erasm. Colloq.* (1711) 302 That wears Linen above, and woollen to the Skinward. 1796 Withering *Brit. Plants* (ed. 3) I. 82 *Skinny*, or *Skin-like* ..,tough, thin, and semi-transparent, like gold beater's skin. 1847–9 *Todd's Cycl. Anat.* IV. i. 9 Gelatinous skin-like integument of the compound body.

13. Special combs.: **skin-bone**, an ossification in or of the skin; **skin-book**, a book made of parchment or vellum; **skin-bound** *a.*, having the skin tensely drawn; hide-bound; **skin-eater**, a moth or beetle which infests and destroys prepared skins or furs; **skin-faro**, *U.S.* (see quot. and *skin game*); **skin-finish**, a particular style of chasing in bronze; **skin-food**, a preparation for improving the skin; **skin friction**, the friction developed between a solid and a fluid or gaseous body; **skin game** (see quots.); **skin-graft** *v.*, to subject to the process of skin-grafting; **skinman**, a skin-dresser or skin-dealer; **skin-mark**, a merchant's mark; **skin-merchant**, a skin-dealer (see also quot.); **skin-plating**, metal plating forming the skin of a vessel; **†skin-prints**, tattoo-marks; **skin-scraper**, a strigil; **skin-sensory** *a.*, of or pertaining to the skin together with the sensory apparatus; **skin-vision**, the power of perceiving distinctions of light by means of the skin; **skin-wool**, wool taken from the skin of a dead sheep; **skin-worm**, the Guinea worm; **skin-yard**, a yard used for the working of skins.

1862 Cockayne *St. Marherete* Title-p., Now First Edited from the Skin Books. 1883 G. Stephens *Bugge's Stud. North. Myth. Examined* 33 The oldest known Swedish skin-book dates after 1250. 1799 Underwood *Dis. Childhood* (ed. 4) I. 130 Of which [tightness of the skin] further notice will be taken under the article of *Skin-bound. 1803 Beddoes *Hygëia* ix. 136 Except in a very close room, I feel as if skin-bound for days together. 1882 McCabe *New York* xxxix. 545 *Skin-faro..offers no chance whatever to the player. 1884 C. G. W. Lock *Workshop Rec.* Ser. iii. 19/2 This mode of chasing, called..in English '*skin-finish', is..only found on work of the best class. 1881 *Encycl. Brit.* XII. 518/2 The two principal causes of the resistance to the motion of a ship are the *skin friction and the production of waves. 1882 McCabe *New York* xxxix. 545 The '*skin game' is used, with the majority of the visitors, for the proprietor is determined from the outset to fleece them without mercy. 1897 R. F. Foster *Compl. Hoyle* 623 *Skin Games*, those in which a player cannot possibly win. 1900 *Brit. Med. Jrnl.* 12 May, Epit. Med. Lit. 74 The wound should be allowed to granulate and subsequently be *skin grafted. 1788 Biddle *Autobiogr.* (1883) 227 *Skinmen, breechesmakers and glovers. 1736 H. Bourne *Hist. Newcastle* 89 There are higher up this Isle..other Three Characters, which are the Merchants *Skin-mark. 1789 Brand *Hist. Newcastle* I. 278 *note*, Skin marks were not used instead of arms, but rather as distinct insignia appropriated to the profession of merchandise. a 1792 Burgoyne *Lord of Manor* iii. ii. (D.), I am..vulgarly called a recruiting dealer, or more vulgarly still, a *skin-merchant. 1869 Sir E. Reed *Shipbuild.* ix. 174 The fastenings of the stringer angle-irons connecting it with the *skin-plating. 1650 Bulwer *Anthropomet.* 237 The chief men and women have *skin-prints, as a brave kind of Gallantry. 1875 *Encycl. Brit.* II. 555/1 Blunted strigils or *skin-scrapers. 1879 tr. *Haeckel's Evol. of Man* I. ix. 270 The first of the secondary germ-layers, the *skin-sensory-layer. 1883 *Nature* XXVII. 399 Experiments with regard to the '*skin-vision' of animals. 1805 Luccock *Nature of Wool* 340 The *skin-wool is not usually found most plentiful where the stock of sheep is most heavy. 1884 W. S. B. McLaren *Spinning* (ed. 2) 71 With short wool, especially if it be skin wool, the rollers should be closed up. 1857 tr. *Küchenmeister's Anim. & Veg. Parasites* I. 398 Amongst the Germans it is known as ..the *skin worm,..leg-worm,..and Pharaoh's-worm. 1879 E. R. Lankester *Advancem. Sci.* (1890) 40 The skin-worm (*Demodex folliculorum*). 1885 *Manch. Exam.* 7 Apr. 4/7 A fire occurred..in Mr. Pryce Parry's *skinyard and wool warehouse.

Skin, variant of Skeen.

Skin, *v.* Also 6–7 **skyn**, **skinne** (6 **scinne**). [f. Skin *sb.* Cf. Norw. *skinna* to cover with skin.]

I. 1. *trans.* To furnish or cover with skin; to cause skin to form or grow on; to heal by the formation of skin. Also with *over*.

1547 Boorde *Brev. Health* cix. 41 b, After that incarnat the place and so skyn it. 1597 A. M. tr. *Guillemeau's Fr. Chirurg.* 39/2 We must..with an exsiccating plaster cure them, and soe skinne them. 1614 W. B. *Philosopher's Banquet* (ed. 2) 55 Fresh Butter skinnes the rawnesse of the throate. 1697 Dryden *Ded. Æneid* Ess. (Ker) II. 210 The wound was skinned; but the strength of his thigh was not restored. 1872 Geo. Eliot *Middlem.* i. x, He looks like a death's head skinned over for the occasion.

absol. 1601 Holland *Pliny* II. 272 It [aloe] is..a great healer, and that which vniteth & skinneth quickly.

b. In fig. contexts. † Also with *up*.

1602 Shaks. *Ham.* iii. iv. 147 It will but skin and filme the Vlcerous place. a 1659 Br. Brownrig *Serm.* (1674) II. xx. 253 They had skin'd up the sore, and yet, it breaks out in their Soul again. c 1750 Warburton *Serm.* ii. Wks. 1811 IX. 47 The wounds, our own earth hath formerly received, ..which though skinned over by time and human culture, are seen. 1796 Coleridge *The Destiny of Nations* 410 Short Peace shall skin the wounds of causeless War. 1880 McCarthy *Own Times* lx. IV. 337 He does not seem to have considered the difference between skinning over a wound and healing it.

c. *fig.* To cover (*over*) in some slight or superficial manner.

1603 Shaks. *Meas. for M.* ii. ii. 136 Authoritie..Hath yet a kinde of medicine in it selfe That skins the vice o' th top.

1650 *Nicholas Papers* (Camden) 191 It is to be feared your Amsterdam affaires are rather skinned than cured. 1658–9 Sir A. Haslerigge in *Burton's Diary* (1828) III. 104 It may be skinned over for a time, but will break out. The people are not pleased. 1796 Burke *Regic. Peace* Wks. 1842 II. 289 It is only their assured and confident expectation..that skins over their mischievous dispositions with a momentary quiet. 1833 T. Hook *Parson's Dau.* i. x, The objects of which (so thinly were they skinned over) were just as evident to Emma as to Lady Frances. 1850 Merivale *Rom. Emp.* ix. (1865) I. 372 This open rupture was with difficulty skinned over at the last moment.

2. a. *fig.* To clothe, attire. *rare.*

1599 B. Jonson *Cynthia's Rev.* ii. iv, You never skin'd a new [? = anew] beautie more prosperously in your life. 1610 Beaum. & Fl. *Scornf. Lady* ii. ii, Off with your husks; I'le skin you all in Sattin.

b. To cover with a skin or skins. *rare*⁻¹.

1618 in Foster *Eng. Factories India* (1906) I. 10 The jarres are all fild, stoped close, skyned, and marked with the distinction of the fruits.

c. *absol.* To put a good skin on cattle. *rare*⁻¹.

1765 *Museum Rust.* IV. 190 The largest pasture..will neither *skin* nor *tallow*, or, in other words, is fit for nothing but young stock.

d. *Naut.* (See quots.)

1815 Burney *Falconer's Dict. Marine* s.v., *To Skin up a Sail in the Bunt*, is to make that part of the canvas which covers the sail when furled, smooth and neat, by turning the sail well up on the yard. 1841 Totten *Naval Text Bk.* 394 To skin the sail up smooth is to turn it well up, and so as to cover the sail neatly and smoothly.

e. *Shipbuilding.* (See quot.)

c 1850 *Rudim. Nav.* (Weale) 141, Planking is often termed *skinning* the ship.

3. *intr.* To form skin; to become covered with skin; to grow a new skin; to heal *over* in this way. Also *fig.*

1579 Lyly *Euphues* (Arb.) 181 The sooner it skinneth, the sorer it festereth. 1654 H. L'Estrange *Chas. I* (1655) 124 Her excoriated carkasse began to skin again. 1763 Mills *Pract. Husb.* IV. 345 All suckers must be cut away from the root, and the place..smoothed with a knife; for then it will soon skin over. 1820 Southey *Lett.* (1856) IV. 129 If the ulcer skins over in that way, the quacks will exult in having wrought a cure. 1843 R. J. Graves *Syst. Clin. Med.* xxix. 392 The centre [of the ulcer] granulated and skinned naturally. 1891 Rider Haggard *Nada* xxxv, The hole in his skull skinned over.

II. 4. *trans.* To strip or deprive of the skin; to flay; to peel.

1591 Percivall *Span. Dict.*, *Desollar*..., to skin, to pul off the skin. 1687 A. Lovell tr. *Thevenot's Trav.* i. 246 The Crocodile is very strong, and one day as I caused one of them..to be skinned [etc.]. 1725 *Fam. Dict.* s.v. *Pears*, When they are off the Fire, stir, skin them, and squeeze about half a Lemon upon them. 1791 Boswell *Johnson* 3 Apr. 1779, A fishmonger who was skinning an eel alive. 1853 Soyer *Pantropheon* 167 It was necessary to skin the bird very carefully. 1875 Jowett *Plato* (ed. 2) I. 210 They may skin me alive, if they please.

b. To rub or scrape the skin off; to bark. Also *transf.*

1855 Jarves *Art Hints* 383 Almost every one of his pictures have been more or less skinned, to use an expressive term, by the carelessness of cleaners. 1856 Kane *Arct. Expl.* I. xiii. 167 It is the same hummock you skinned your shins upon. 1891 C. Roberts *Adrift Amer.* 97 My feet were already skinned in several places.

c. In phrases denoting excessive meanness or desire for gain, esp. *to skin a flint*.

1694 Motteux *Rabelais* v. vii, May I be broil'd like a Red-herring, if I don't think they are wise enough to skin a Flint. 1834 Marryat *P. Simple* (1863) 195 Report says, that she would skin a flint if she could. 1851 Mayhew *Lond. Labour* I. 134 They'd skin a flea for his hide and tallow. 1859 Lever *D. Dunn* iv, I was..brought up amongst fellows would skin a cat. 1884 [see Flint *sb.* 4].

5. To strip or pull *off* (a skin, etc.); to remove by drawing off inside out.

1658–9 in *Burton's Diary* (1828) IV. 228 They skin off your skin. 1683 Moxon *Mech. Exerc.*, *Printing* xxiv. ¶11 Having carefully skinned off the Film with the edge of the Slice. 1759 Martin *Nat. Hist.* I. 28 Turf of the Ground, skinned off, and burnt to Ashes. 1861 Dickens *Gt. Expect.* xxxi, Skin the stockings off,..or you'll bust 'em.

transf. 1896 Lillard *Poker Stories* ii. 59 Many a time I've seen a game player just skin off his watch and ring.. and play them in.

6. *intr.* To shed or cast the skin; to lose the skin by rubbing.

1772 *Ann. Reg.* 96/2 It skins every year; and its skin is said to be a remedy against the cramp. 1908 Gilbert Murray tr. *Aristoph., Frogs* i. ii, When all my shoulder's skinning, simply skinning.

7. *slang.* a. *trans.* To clean out (a person) at play.

1812 J. H. Vaux *Flash Dict.* s.v., To strip a man of all his money at play, is termed *skinning* him. 1864 *Daily Teleg.* 19 Oct., The gamblers did their best to give us fits; but in less than half an hour, sir, the little squaw she skinned the crowd. 1889 H. O'Reilly *Fifty Yrs. on Trail* 343 In less than two or three hours [to] be skinned out of every cent.

b. To strip (*of* clothing or money); to fleece by exactions or swindling.

1851 Mayhew *Lond. Labour* II. 71 Perhaps he gets 'skinned' (stripped of his clothes and money from being hocussed, or tempted to helpless drunkenness). 1892 *Spectator* 12 Mar. 364/2 Suppose the Emigration Trusts skin the emigrants until they stop emigration. 1898 *Eclectic Mag.* LXVII. 607 Some new device is invented for enmeshing and skinning the investor.

c. *Skin the lamb* (see quots.).

1864 *Slang Dict.* 232 *Skin the Lamb*, a game at cards, a

very expressive corruption of the term lansquenet...When a non favourite wins a race 'bookmakers' are said to skin the lamb. 1883 *Graphic* 21 Apr. 410/2 The Ring are enormous winners on the race, the majority having 'skinned the lamb'.

8. To exhaust or impoverish by excessive fishing, cropping, etc.

1867 F. Francis *Angling* vii. (1880) 274 He does not want to skin the stream. 1895 *Forum* (N.Y.) Sept. 8 To renovate the soil which had been 'skinned' in the days of slavery.

9. *U.S. slang.* a. *trans.* and *intr.* To copy or crib.

1849 *Yale Lit. Mag.* XV. 81 Never skin a lesson which it requires any ability to learn. 1851 Bristed *Five Yrs. Eng. Univ.* (1852) 381 Classical men were continually tempted to 'skin' (copy) the solutions of these examples. 1851 B. H. Hall *College Words & Customs* 430 'At Yale College,.. in our examinations,' says a correspondent, 'many of the fellows cover the palms of their hands with dates, and when called upon for a given date, they read it off directly from their hands. Such persons *skin*'.

b. *trans.* To abscond, make off, slip away. Also with *out*, to depart hastily.

1876 Besant & Rice *Gold. Butterfly* (1877) 254 You jest gether up your traps and skin out of this. 1894 *Outing* XXIV. 442/1 The hero..would never have been one could he have skinned for cover in time.

c. With *out*: To produce, display.

c 1895 *Thompson St. Poker Cl.* 42 Mr. Williams proudly skinned out three jacks and a pair of kings.

d. To glance over, examine.

1895 *Cornh. Mag.* Aug. 174 Each man skinned his cards and tried his hardest to look disappointed.

10. In phrases used as adjs.

1869 W. Morris in Mackail *Life* (1899) I. 203 If you had passed a week at this skin-'em-alive place. 1891 Miss MacEwen *Three Women in One Boat* 87 A good old skin-your-nose encounter.

Skin-coat. Also 6 **skyn coit**, **skincote**, **-coate**. [f. Skin *sb.* + Coat *sb.*]

1. A coat made of skin.

1533 *Acc. Lord High Treas. Scotl.* VI. 181 To begary the samyne doublet, and to begary ane skyn coit, v ½ quarteris veluot. 1589 Greene *Menaphon* (Arb.) 76 Am not I a Gentleman, though tirde in a shepheardes skincote.

†2. *transf.* A person's skin. *Obs.*

1589 *Hay any Work* (1844) 9, I will lay on load on your skincoat for this geare anon. a 1592 Greene *Jas. IV*, i. Proh., Ay engraued the memory of Boughon on the skin-coate of some of them. 1611 Cotgr., *Escailler*,..to beat, bethwacke, belabor the skin-coat of. 1653 Urquhart *Rabelais* ii. xvii, I will have their skin-coat shaken once yet before they die.

† **Skind**, *v.* *Obs.*⁻¹ [a. ON. *skynda* (so mod. Icel., Norw., and Sw.; Da. *skynde*), = OE. *scyndan*, OS. *skundian*, etc.] *trans.* To hasten.

c 1250 *Gen. & Ex.* 1989 Ðe chapmen skinden here fare, In to egipte ledden ðat ware.

Skin-deep, *a.* and *adv.* [f. Skin *sb.* 4 + Deep *a.* and *adv.*]

A. *adj.* Penetrating no deeper than the skin; superficial, shallow, slight: a. As a proverbial limitation of beauty, or in similar connexions.

a 1613 Overbury *A Wife*, etc. Wks. (1856) 37 All the carnall beauty of my wife, Is but skin-deep. 1687 Boyle *Martyrd. Theodora* iv. (1703) 49 Nor any of our sex ought to think skin-deep beauty as great a blessing, as 'tis an applauded one. 1725 Ramsay *Gentle Sheph.* iv. ii, Beauty that's only skin deep Must fade like the gowans of May. 1740–1 Richardson *Pamela* (1824) I. xcix. 484 Beauty is but a specious..recommendation, a mere skin-deep perfection. 1854 Spencer *Personal Beauty* Ess. (1891) II. 394 The saying that beauty is but skin-deep, is but a skin-deep saying. 1869 McLaren *Serm.* Ser. ii. v. 79 Moses' face shone, but the lustre was but skin deep.

b. Of wounds, incisions, etc. Also *transf.*

a 1613 Overbury *Charac.*, *Ordinary Fencer* Wks. (1856) 112 His wounds are seldome above skin-deep. 1805 Jefferson *Writ.* (1830) IV. 30 The skin-deep scratches, which we can make or find on the surface of the earth. 1841 Emerson *Method of Nat.* Wks. (Bohn) II. 222 But the thunder is a surface phenomenon, makes a skin-deep cut. 1877 A. B. Edwards *Up Nile* xix. 566 As for his wounds, they were literally skin-deep.

c. *fig.* in various contexts.

1657 Trapp *Comm., Ps.* xvi. 9 Their joy is but skin-deep. 1677 Horneck *Gt. Law Consid.* vii. (1704) 399 A few slight and skin-deep reflexions. 1730 T. Boston *Mem.* xii. 434 Denoting the skin-deep joy of ungodly men. 1766 Fordyce *Serm. Yng. Women* (1767) II. x. 130 Skin-deep and short-lived allurements. 1825 Lady Granville *Lett.* (1894) I. 362 The little faults are all skin-deep, and she is excellent. 1889 Gretton *Memory's Harkback* 251 The effect upon the hearers was, after all, but skin-deep.

B. *adv.* To the depth of the skin; in a superficial manner; superficially, slightly.

1633 P. Fletcher *Purple Isl.* vii. xiv, Caro, cursed damme of sinne,..Yet seems (skin-deep) most fair. 1660 F. Brooke tr. *Le Blanc's Trav.* 218 They have little horns which grow but skin-deep, mooving them as their ears. 1702 Steele *Funeral* ii, When I know her further than Skin-deep, I'll tell you more of my mind. 1796 Burke *Regic. Peace* Wks. 1842 II. 288 Stings that have penetrated more than skin-deep into my mind. 1864 Kingsley *Rom. & Teut.* iv. (1875) 100 He was but a wild man of the woods..polished over skin-deep with Roman civilization.

Ski·nflint. Also 7–9 **skin-flint**. [f. Skin *v.* 4 c + Flint *sb.*] One who would skin a flint to save or gain something; an avaricious, penurious, mean or niggardly person; a miser.

a 1700 B. E. *Dict. Cant. Crew*, *Skin-flint*, a griping,.. close-fisted Fellow. 1761 A. Murphy *Citizen* ii. i. An old miserly good for nothing skin-flint. 1791 A. Wilson *Laurel Disputed* Poet. Wks. (1846) 125 How skin-flint graned his pocks o' goud to loss. 1816 Scott *Antiquary* xi, It would have been long..ere my womankind could have made such a reasonable bargain with that old skinflint. 1840 Thackeray *Catherine* x, It is a pity that old skinflint should be in the way of both your fortunes. 1891 C. Roberts *Adrift Amer.* 226 Which sum the captain, who was a regular skinflint, said was far too much.

b. *attrib.* or as *adj.* Miserly, mean.

1789 Parker *Life's Painter* xiv. 114 The miser, that skin-flint old elf. 1854 H. Miller *Sch. & Schm.* v. (1857) 86 The skin-flint wife of a 'paper minister'. 1895 Zangwill *Master* ii. vii, By persuading some small skinflint dealer to cheat him.

Hence **Ski·nflinty** *a.*, niggardly; **Ski·nflintily** *adv.*, in a niggardly manner; **Ski·nflintiness**, **Ski·nflintism**, niggardliness, parsimony.

1861 *Lond. Rev.* 16 Feb. 170 Love of approbation,..for the time, conquers her native skinflintiness. 1893 *Columbus* (Ohio) *Disp.* 10 July, The rewards of 'skinflintism' are not great in the long run. 1899 *Daily News* 19 Sept. 6/1 He behaved skin-flintily to Max Müller. 1901 *Munsey's Mag.* XXV. 431/2 The man with the skinflinty heart.

Ski·nful. Also 9 **-full**. [f. Skin *sb.* + -ful.]

1. The quantity contained within the skin.

1650 Howell *Lett.* III. 4, I could willingly..return this small skinfull of Bones to my common Mother.

2. A quantity that fills a skin vessel.

1802 Southey *King Ramiro* xii, So he gave him..a skinful of wine to quench his thirst. 1863 Kinglake *Crimea* II. 195 That simple skinful of water which..is the life of men passing a desert. 1885 *Century Mag.* XXIX. 652/1 Well do I remember how at each well the first skinful [of water] was tasted all around.

3. As much as the skin can hold: a. As much as any one can drink.

1824 W. Irving *T. Trav.* II. 234 When he has no liquor at all, or when he has a skinfull. 1839 Thackeray *Fatal Boots* (1869) 348 On this night I had my little skinful,—for there was no stinting. 1886 W. Graham *Social Problem* 203 Why should I work, when I..can get my skinful?

b. *transf.* A full allowance; as much as one wants or cares for.

a 1779 D. Graham *Leper the Taylor* i. Writ. 1883 II. 116 Poor Sandy went home with a skinful of terror. 1869 W. S. Gilbert *Bab Ball.*, *Sir Macklin* v, He wept to think each thoughtless youth Contained of wickedness a skinful. 1897 *Pall Mall Mag.* Dec. 501 His men had had a skinful of fighting and short commons just before.

Skink (skiŋk), *sb.*¹ *Zool.* Forms: α. 6, 9 **scinc**, 7, 9 **scinck**, 7–9 **scink**. β. 7 **skinke**, 8 **skinc(k**, 6– **skink**. [a. older F. *scinc* (now *scinque*), or ad. L. *scincus*, ad. Gr. σκίγκος.] A small lizard (*Scincus officinalis*) common in northern Africa and Arabia, formerly regarded as of great value in medicine for its stimulative qualities; also, any lizard belonging to the same family (the *Scincidæ*).

α. 1590 Barrough *Meth. Physick* 182 Also the parts of scinces which embrace the reines. 1608 Topsell *Serpents* (1658) 693 There have been some that have reckoned Scinks and Lizards among worms. 1681 Grew *Musæum* i. iii. 48 The Scink..hath..short Legs, a flat and broad Foot like a Hand, with very short Toes. 1775 *Phil. Trans.* LXV. 246 Gulls, the scink, the leech,..&c. are all said to feel.. approaching changes of weather. 1802 Shaw *Gen. Zool.* III. i. 281 The Scink is one of the middle-sized or smaller lizards. 1854 *Orr's Circ. Sci., Org. Nat.* I. 275 Herbivorous..scinks, called, on account of the shape of the teeth, *cyclodus*. 1872 Humphry *Myology* 37 In the Scinc this portion..is quite separate in its whole length.

β. 1591 Sylvester *Du Bartas* i. vi. 200 Th' horned Cerastes, th' Alexandrian Skink. 1601 Holland *Pliny* II. 316 Much like to this kind is the Skink (whom some haue named the land Crocodile). 1718 Quincy *Compl. Disp.* 171 Skincks.—Some Authors have ascribed much to these as Alexipharmicks. 1831 Griffith tr. *Cuvier* IX. 237 The skink of pharmacopolists..does not exceed the length of six or eight inches. 1880 *Cassell's Nat. Hist.* IV. 296 The Skink inhabits the western and northern parts of Africa.

attrib. and *Comb.* 1790 J. White *Jrnl. Voy. N. S. Wales* 242 The Scincoid, or Skinc-formed Lizard. 1896 Lydekker *Roy. Nat. Hist.* V. 166 The skink tribe..are a very numerous family.

Skink, *sb.*² Now *rare*. Also 7 **skinck**, **skinke**. [In sense 1 ad. early mod. Du. or LG. *schenke*, repr. MDu., MLG., and MHG. *schenke* (rarely *schinke*), OS. *skenkio*, OHG. *scenko*, *scencho*, etc. In sense 2 from Skink *v.*]

1. A skinker; a tapster or waiter. In later use only *spec.* (see quot. 1847).

1603 J. Davies (Heref.) *Microcosmos* Wks. (Grosart) I. 21/1 O Skinck, how blest wert thou in his Loue That drue thee on. 1786 *Francis the Philanthropist* I. 172 Mr. Francis and his companion had friends of every rank, from the humble skink to the dignified..doctor. 1847 Halliw. s.v., In a family the person latest at breakfast is called the *skink*, or the *skinker*, and some domestic office is imposed or threatened for the day, such as ringing the bell, putting coal on the fire, or, in other cases, drawing the beer for the family.

2. a. *Sc.* Drink, liquor. (In contemptuous use.)

1824 Scott *St. Ronan's* xxxii, The wine!..puir, thin, fushionless skink it was. 1844 Ballantine *Miller Deanhaugh* xvi. 247 Jail beer was poor, thin skink for gentlemen who had drank claret after dinner every day for twenty years.

b. *pl.* (See quot.)

1888 Jacobi *Printers' Vocab.* 126 *Skinks*, an old term applied to drink—or drinking around the imposing stone in order to celebrate some auspicious occasion.

Skink, *sb.*³ *Sc.* Now *Obs.* exc. *Hist.* Also 7 **skinck**. [prob. ad. MLG. *schinke* (see next), either with ellipse of some word for 'broth', or with simple transference from the meat to the liquid.] A kind of soup made from shin of beef. Also *attrib.*

c 1575 Balfour *Practicks* (1754) 235 The air sall haue..ane butter-plait, ane skink-plait, ane beif plait, ane luggit disch. 1602 in Henderson *Old World Scotl.* (1893) 14 Ane dische of bruise, and ane uther of skink or kaill. 1626 Bacon *Sylva* § 45 Wee finde also that Scotch Skinck (which is a Pottage of strong Nourishment,) is made with the Knees, and Sinewes of Beefe, but long boiled. a 1682 Sempill *Blythsome Wedding* 72 There will be meal-kail and castocks, And skink to sup till you rive. 1790 Shirrefs *Poems* 210 Guid barley broth and *skink* came next. 1844 H. Stephens *Bk. Farm* II. 169 It was of this piece that the old favourite soup of Scotland, called *skink*, was made. 1893 Henderson *Old World Scotl.* 57 Its quality was very similar to that of the strong Lowland soup called skink.

† **Skink**, *sb.*⁴ *Obs.*⁻¹ [ad. LG. *schinke* (G. *schinken*), OHG. *scinca*, *scinco*.] Ham.

1630 J. Taylor (Water P.) *Gt. Eater Kent* 12 He cares not for..the sawsedge of Bolognia, the skink of Westphalia.

† **Skink**, *sb.*⁵, obs. variant of Skunk *sb.*

1774 Goldsm. *Nat. Hist.* III. ix. 381 The skink..resembles a polecat in shape and size. 1809 *Spirit Public Jrnls.* XIII. 2 Where'er the skink-ey'd Gallic pest Flings taint and uproar o'er the ball. 1824 Coleridge *Aids Refl.* (1848) I. 90 As..the skink and squash are treated by American woodmen, who turn their backs upon the fetid intruder.

Skink, *v.* Now *dial.* or *arch.* Forms: 4 **skynke**, 6–7 **skinke** (6 **skincke**, 7 **scinke**); 6 (9) **skynk**, **skinck**, 6– **skink**. [ad. MDu. or MLG. *schenken* (cf. OFris. *skenka*; ON. *skenkja*, Sw. *skänka*, Da. *skænke*), corresp. to OE. *scencan* Shench *v.*]

1. *trans.* To pour out or draw (liquor); to offer, present, serve (drink, etc.).

c 1386 Chaucer *Merch. T.* 478 Bacus the wyn hem skynketh al aboute. 1513 Douglas *Æneid* vii. iii. 90 In flacon and in skull Thai skynk the wyne. 1607 W. Barksted *Mirrha* (1876) 45 The Queen of Ioue..forc'd her to skinke so much, the iuice ran ore. 1635 Shirley *Lady of Pleas.* iv. ii, A drawer is my Ganymede: he shall skink Brisk nectar to us. 1667 Davenant & Dryden *Tempest* iv. iii, Hem! skink about his grace's health again. 1728 Ramsay *Last Sp. Miser* xxvii, And like dub-water skink the wine. 1806 R. Jamieson *Pop. Ballads* I. 221 They skinked the mead, and they skinked the wine. 1899 Lumsden *Edin. Poems & Sangs* 130 Stout Scots drink to me skynk.

†2. To fill with liquor; to pour liquor into. *Obs.*

1513 Douglas *Æneid* vii. iii. 62 Now skynk, and offer Jupiter, coupis full. 1558 Phaer *Æneid* vii. S iv b, Now skinke your cups to Ioue, and great Anchises cheerely cal. 1594 Greene & Lodge *Looking Gl.* H, Ile haue them skincke my standing bowles with wine.

3. *absol.* To draw, pour out, or serve drink; to wait on a company (see quot. 1785).

1591 Fletcher *Russe Commonw.* (Hakl. Soc.) 17 For that cause [they] called this newe citie by the name of Naloi, that is skinck or poure in. 1594 Greene & Lodge *Looking Gl.* Wks. (Grosart) XIV. 93 Villaines, why skinck you not vnto this fellow? 1630 J. Taylor (Water P.) *Penniless Pilgr.* Wks. i. 123/2 And No-body did drinke, and winke, and scinke. 1676 Hobbes *Iliad* i. 562 And then the Gods laught..outright, To see the lame and sooty Vulcan skink. 1755 Smollett *Don Quixote* iv. xiv. II. 425 Truce with your compliments and skink away, honest Tosilos. 1785 Grose *Dict. Vulgar T.*, To *skink*, is to wait on the company, ring the bell, stir the fire, and snuff the candles; the duty of the youngest officer in a military mess. a 1825 Forby *Voc. E. Anglia* 304 *Skink*, to serve at table; particularly to serve the guests with drink. 1845 S. Judd *Margaret* ii. vi. (1871) 260 Come crush a glass with..all this nice company. You have skinked quite long enough.

†4. *Sc.* To make a present of; to make *over* to another. *Obs. rare.*

1508 *Burgh Rec. Edin.* (1882) I. 117 Vpoun his gude warkmaneschip and gyding thai skynk him the tymmer of the auld ruf. 1637 Rutherford *Lett.* (1848) lxxxv. 156 If this had not been, I would have skinked over and foregone my part of paradise and salvation, for a breakfast of dead, moth-eaten earth. *Ibid.* lxxxviii. 163 Do we not sit far in our own light, to make it a matter of bairn's play, to skink and drink over paradise.

Hence **Ski·nked** *ppl. a.*

1598 Florio, *Mesciuto*, skinkt, powred or filde wine.

† **Ski·nkard.** *Obs. rare.* Also 7 **skinkird**. [f. Skink *v.* + -ard.] A tapster.

1615 Brathwait *Strappado* (1878) 11 To be a drudge.. Vnto the base-borne Skinkird bred in Hell. 1632 Marmion *Holland's Leaguer* ii. iii, Thou hast a noble wit and spirit, wench, That never was ordained for any skinkard T'engender with.

Skinker (ski·ŋkəɹ). Now *arch.* or *dial.* Also 6 **scincker**, **skincker**, **skynker**. [ad. MDu. or MLG. *schencker* (*schincker*), or f. Skink *v.* + -er ¹.]

1. One who draws, pours out, or serves liquor; a tapster; (see also quot. 1847 s.v. Skink *sb.*² 1).

1586 *Praise of Musicke* 51 That banquet of the gods where Vulcan plaid the skinker. 1603 Holland *Plutarch's Mor.* 444 The butler or skinker asked him how much he should poure out for everie one. 1647 C. Harvey *Schola Cordis* vi. 3 See how the hellish skinker plies his bowle. 1681 T. Flatman *Heraclitus Ridens* No. 15 (1713) I. 98 From rebellious Taps, and Tapsters and Skinkers, *Libera nos*. 1702 S. Parker tr. *Cicero's De Finibus* ii. 63 My Skinker perceives himself..agreably affected in filling me out a Glass when he has no Inclination to drink. 1813 J. Hogg *Queen's Wake* 24 Thrice did they drain th' allotted store And wondering skinkers dun for more. 1830 Lamb *Let. to W. Wordsworth* Wks. 1900 XII. 128 [Vulcan] the two-handed skinker. 1852 Hawthorne *Blithedale Rom.* II. xi. 206 Some old-fashioned skinkers and drawers..were

spreading a banquet. 1887 Browning *Parleyings* Wks. 1896 II. 733/2 The skinker fast brimmed Their glass with rare tipple's enticement.

† b. The constellation Aquarius. *Obs.*

1591 Sylvester *Du Bartas* i. iv. 278 Mean-while the Skinker, from his starry spout, After the Goat, a silver stream pours out. *Ibid.* ii. ii. iv. *Columnes* 418 On th' Azure steep Our Parents plac't a Skinker: and by him, Two silver Fishes in his flouds to swim.

†2. A jug or similar vessel used for skinking with. Also *attrib.* *Obs.*

1594 *Wills & Invent. N. C.* (Surtees, 1860) 245 The buttrye..ij hodg-heads,..j quarte potte, j skinker. 1600 *Will of Sir R. Bedingfeild* (Somerset Ho.), Silver wine pot called a Skynker. 1639 *12th Rep. Hist. MSS. Comm.* App. IX. 7 Four great flagons...10 Skinker potts. 7 Tankards. 1646 *Will of Estcourt* (Somerset Ho.), A deepe silver bason with a silver skinker.

Ski·nking, *vbl. sb.* [f. Skink *v.*] The action of pouring out or serving liquor. Also *attrib.*

1592 R. D. *Hypnerotomachia* 57 The skinking pottes.. were all of pure fine Gold. 1598 Florio, *Versatione*,..a skinking. 1611 *Ibid.*, A powring or skinking forth. 1631 Mabbe *Celestina* ix. 105, I know no better office at boord, then to fall a skinking. 1819 W. Tennant *Papistry Storm'd* (1827) 102 Had Bacchus sell been there,..for skinkin', He couldna weil hae blam'd the drinkin'.

Ski·nking, *ppl. a.* [f. Skink *v.*]

1. That skinks; wine-giving.

1582 Stanyhurst *Æneis* iii. (Arb.) 74 With nauye we passed By mounts of Nazon too skincking Bacchus alotted.

2. *Sc.* Thin, watery. (Cf. Skink *sb.*² 2.)

1786 Burns *To a Haggis* viii, Auld Scotland wants nae skinking ware That jaups in luggies. a 1894 Stevenson *St. Ives* xxvii, A pint of skinking claret.

Skinkle (ski·ŋk'l), *v.* *Sc.* [perh. a frequentative f. ON. *skína* to shine.] *intr.* To glitter, glisten, sparkle; to have a showy appearance.

17.. *Lord Thomas* xix. in Percy *Reliques*, It skinkled in their een. 1791 A. Wilson *Laurel Disputed* Poet. Wks. (1846) 127 Ae night the lift was skinkling a' wi' starns. 1888 *Glasgow Evening Times* 15 Oct. 2/6 A handful of flame which..merely skinkles on the window-panes.

Hence **Ski·nkling** *ppl. a.*

1790 A. Wilson *Poems* 205 Row't in a skinklan plaid. c 1795 ? Burns *Poem on Pastoral Poetry* iv, Squire Pope but busks his skinklin patches, O' heathen tatters! 1819 W. Tennant *Papistry Storm'd* (1827) 30 Or flee about on skinklin' wing, Like butterflies. 1849 Symington *Harebell Chimes* 104 Death lurks in its skinkling fire.

Skinless (ski·nlés), *a.* Forms: 5 **skin-**, **skynles**, 6 **skinne-**, 6–7 **skinlesse**, 8- **skinless**. [f. Skin *sb.* + -less.] Destitute or deprived of skin; having only a very thin skin.

c 1340 Hampole *Med. Pass.* in Horstman (1895) I. 98 Þe fleisch þere þe cros sittith is skinles & ouer-runne wiþ blood-rowis. 1484 Caxton *Fables of Æsop* v. ix, The wulf ranne aweye skynles. 1594 T. B. *La Primaud. Fr. Acad.* ii. 59 The head woulde bee very deformed if it were skinnelesse, where it is couered with haire. 1600 *Hosp. Incurable Fooles* A iv, Those skinlesse Snailes that lift vp their hornes for nothing. 1611 Cotgr., *Fricandeaux*, short, skinlesse, and daintie puddings. 1706 London & Wise *Retir'd Gard.* I. vii. 25 The..skinless Pear is a kind of Russelet in Shape and Taste. 1738 *Gentl. Mag.* VIII. 310/1 What is it that's born Skinless, flies Wingless, and goes roaring to Death? 1850 Kingsley *A. Locke* xxi, He was looking..at the skinless cast on the chimney-piece. *Ibid.*, He looked round again at the skinless man. 1891 Atkinson *Last of Giant-Killers* 78 He [the raven] pranced about on his [the wolf's] scraggy skinless carcase.

fig. 1859 *Sat. Rev.* 19 Mar. 331/2 There was nothing in it to make the most skinless man in existence wince.

Hence **Ski·nlessly** *adv.*

1859 Boyd *Recreat. Country Parson* (1862) 86 Not only are they themselves skinlessly sensitive [etc.].

Ski·nlet. *rare.* [f. Skin *sb.* + -let.] A thin skin; a membrane.

1598 Florio, *Cuticula*, a filme, a skin or skinlet, a thin rinde or pill. *Ibid.*, *Milza*,..a filme or skinlet.

Skinned (skind), *ppl. a.* [f. Skin *sb.* and *v.*]

I. 1. Having a skin, *esp.* of a specified kind.

c 1400 Maundev. (1839) xix. 206 In another Yle ben folk, that gon upon hire Hondes and hire Feet, as Bestes: and thei ben alle skynned and fedred. 1611 Cotgr., *Marmotte*, ..a little muddie fish, headed, skinned, and finned, like an Eele. 1641 Brome *Joviall Crew* iii, Oh here they come. They are delicately skin'd and limb'd. 1655 Moufet & Bennet *Health's Improv.* (1746) 260 Skate is skin'd like a File. 1727 *Philip Quarll* (1754) 3 These Fish are..skinned like a Mackerel.

b. With defining term prefixed, as *clean-*, *dark-*, *fox-*, *hard-*, *loose-*, etc.

See also Thick- and Thin-skinned.

1450–80 tr. *Secreta Secret.* 32 Kepe the fro fische þat is hard skynned. 1523 Fitzherb. *Husb.* § 56 Se that he [an ox] haue a brode ryb, and a thycke hyde, and to be lose-skinned. 1598– [see Rough-skinned *a.*]. 1611 Cotgr., *Poire d'amiot*, a yellow, and hard-skind Peare. 1665 Brathwait *Comment. Two Tales* (1901) 45 What Sir Raynard, ye fox-skin'd Chuffe. 1827 [see Fair *a.* 18]. 1893 F. Adams *New Egypt* 58 An English official,..having a lean, clean-skinned body. 1897 Watts-Dunton *Aylwin* iii. vi, A bright-eyed, dark-skinned little girl.

2. Of wounds, etc.: Covered with skin. Also with *over*.

1640 Br. Reynolds *Passions* xxvii. 288 Which like a skinn'd wound doth wrankle inwardly. 1739 S. Sharp *Surg.* p. xxx, The Edges of it in process of time, tuck in, and growing skinn'd and hard, give it the Name of a callous Ulcer. 1760–72 H. Brooke *Fool of Qual.* (1809) IV. 90 My wounds, though not skinned, were healing apace. 1809 Malkin *Gil Blas* xi. ix. ¶6 A wound imperfectly skinned over.

3. Covered with a layer (of something).

1684 T. Burnet *Theory Earth* i. 145 When the earth grows discolour'd and skin'd over. 1837 Wordsw. *Musings near Aquapendente* 193 From pavement skinned with moss.

II. 4. Stripped of the skin.

1673 Ray *Journ. Low C.* 404 Their [frogs'] flesh shows white and lovely as they lie in the markets skin'd and ready prepared. 1826 Scott *Woodstock* xxxii, The boy, whose appearance [was] not much dissimilar to that of a skinned rabbit in a livery. 1861 *Macm. Mag.* June 131 Birds and their eggs, skinned animals, and insects.

b. *colloq.* In phr. *to keep one's eye skinned*, etc., to keep a sharp look-out.

a 1859 *Traits Amer. Humor* (Bartlett), Keep your eye skinned for sign. 1887 Farrell *How He Died* 22 The reverend josser..kept his eye skinned. 1898 Kipling *Fleet in Being* iii, We kept a skinned eye on her.

Skinner (ski·nəɹ). Forms: 5 **scynner(e**, **schynnere**, **skynnar(e**, 6 **skynar**, 5–7 **skynner**, 6– **skinner**. [f. Skin *sb.* or *v.* + -er ¹. Cf. ON. *skinnari*, MSw. *skinnare*, Norw. *skinnar*.]

1. One whose work or business is concerned with the preparation of skins for commercial purposes.

1398 Trevisa *Barth. De P. R.* xviii. lxxv. (Bodl. MS.), [The cat] is ofte for his faire skynne itake of þe skynner and islayne & ihuylded. 1418 *Nottingham Rec.* II. 116 Johanne Crophyll, skynner. 1484 Caxton *Fables of Æsop* v. xvii, Theyr skynnes were good for to make mantels with, yf skynners myght haue them. 1542 Boorde *Dyetary* (1870) 249 Let your skynner cut both the sortes of the skynnes in smale peces tryangle wyse. 1592 Greene *Upst. Courtier* Wks. (Grosart) XI. 268 He began to tell me that by his art he was a Skinner. 1600 Surflet *Countrie Farme* 873 The skinners are woont to make stomachers to lay ouer the stomacke. 1675 Ogilby *Britannia* Introd., The Principal Companies..are the Mercers,..Skinners. 1859 C. Barker *Assoc. Principle* ii. 45 One Hinde, a citizen and skinner of London, lent to Henry IV. the sum of £2000. 1882 *Encycl. Brit.* XIV. 852/2 Seven of the livery companies of London .., the Mercers',..the Salters',..and the Skinners'.

attrib. 1794 R. Gray in Scott *Stat. Acc. Perth* (1796) 38 This corporation has a very convenient skinner-work.

2. One who removes the skin; a flayer.

1699 Dampier *Voy.* II. ii. iii. 98 Then the Hockser immediately Mounts, and Rides after more Game, leaving the other to the Skinners, who are at hand, and ready to take off his Hide. 1884 *Good Words* June 391/1 In districts where the game is abundant more skinners were enlisted.

3. *U.S.* One of a number of marauders who committed depredations on the neutral ground between the British and American lines during the War of Independence.

1775–83 [see Cow-boy 2]. 1821 J. F. Cooper *Spy* i, This poor opinion of the Skinners was not confined to Mr. Cæsar Thompson. 1825 J. Neal *Bro. Jonathan* III. 290 Who knows but you are one o' the tories yourself..or one o' the skinners? 1857 [see Cow-boy 2]. 1882 Lecky *Engl. in 18th Cent.* IV. 129 The loyalist banditti called the Skinners.

4. a. (See quot.)

1856 Mayhew *Gt. World London* 46 'Skinners,' or women and boys who strip children of their clothes.

b. A fleecer; also in racing slang (see quot. 1874 and cf. Skin *v.* 7 c).

1855 Doran *Knights & their Days* ix. 142 They are constituted the legal skinners of all sojourners among them. 1874 *Slang Dict.* 293 *Skinner*, a term among bookmakers. 'May we have a skinner,' i.e., may we skin the lamb. 1893 *Westm. Gaz.* 13 Apr. 5/2 Yesterday's race..resulted in what the sporting public, high and low, graphically describe as a 'skinner'. The bookmakers..do the skinning.

5. One who makes skin to grow. In quot. *fig.*

1660 Gauden *Slight Healers Publick Hurts* 43 Pretenders to heal, superficial skinners.

6. (See quots.)

1881 Day *Fishes Gt. Brit.* I. 278 Poullach..In the Channel those the size of a whiting are termed codlings and skinners. 1881 *Cassell's Nat. Hist.* V. 59 When Cod are of the size of Whiting they are termed Codlings and 'Skinners'.

Skinnery (ski·nəri). Also 5 **skynnery**. [f. Skin *sb.* + -ery.]

†1. Skins or furs collectively. *Obs.*

c 1460 J. Russell *Bk. Nurture* 946 To drapery & skynnery euer haue ye a sight.

2. A place where skins are dealt with for commercial or other purposes; the working premises of a skinner.

1480 *Wardr. Acc. Edw. IV* (1830) 131 Canvas in the Skynnery j. *Ibid.* 146 A lb' of threde delivered into the Skynnery for skynners to wirk with. 1483 *Cath. Angl.* 342/1 A Skynnery, *pelliparium*. 1827 Mackenzie *Hist. Newcastle* II. 716 There are some extensive tan-yards and skinneries in Newcastle. 1883 J. Martin *Reminis. Old Haddington* 84 There was long ago a tannery and skinnery at its termination.

Ski·nniness. [f. Skinny *a.*] The quality of being skinny; leanness, emaciation.

1727 Bailey, vol. II. [Hence in later Dicts.]

Skinning (ski·niŋ), *vbl. sb.* [f. Skin *v.*]

1. a. The action or process of covering with skin, or of forming a new skin; cicatrization, healing. Also with *over*, and *fig.*

1547 Boorde *Brev. Health* 49 For skynnynge of a place there is nothing shal skyn so sone as it wyl. 1633 Wotton *Lett.* (1907) II. 341 But whether these be the perfect cures or but skinnings over..will appear hereafter. 1638 A. Read *Chirurg.* ix. 66 We are not to goe about the skinning of the wound before the flesh bee somewhat higher than the naturall skin. 1739 S. Sharp *Surg.* Introd. 2 The first Stage of Healing..is by Surgeons call'd Digestion;..and the last, or skinning-over, Cicatrization. 1793 J. Hunter *Treat. Blood*, etc. Wks. 1837 III. 496 Therefore contracting and skinning are probably effects of one cause. 1813 J. Thomson *Lect. Inflam.* 455 The parts towards the centre may be so long kept from skinning, that the granulations may become weak.

b. *Naut.* (See quots.)

1846 A. Young *Naut. Dict.* 284 *Skinning*, a term used for planking a vessel. c 1850 *Rudim. Nav.* (Weale) 138 *Planking*, covering the outside of the timbers with plank; sometimes..called 'skinning'.

2. The removal, or stripping off, of skin; the fact of having the skin removed or rubbed off. Also *fig.*

1775 in Ash. 1837 W. Irving *Capt. Bonneville* I. 141 These..are bound to exert themselves..in taking beavers, which, without skinning, they render in at the trader's lodge. 1878 Spurgeon *Serm.* XXIV. 693 The skinning of flints and the driving of screws are practised by many people as if they were positively meritorious. 1891 C. Roberts *Adrift Amer.* 105 My feet were not yet quite well, after the skinning they had got coming over the trail from Wallace.

† b. Fleecing, plundering. *Obs. rare*⁻¹.

1686 tr. *Chardin's Trav. Persia* 347 Places for the skinning of strangers, who are reputed to be rich.

c. Impoverishing, exhausting.

1888 *Harper's Mag.* Mar. 559 The skinning of the land by sending away its substance in hard wheat is an improvidence of natural resources.

3. *attrib.*, as *skinning-apparatus*, *knife*, *process*, *table*.

1835–6 *Todd's Cycl. Anat.* I. 602/2 The skinning process takes place in this stage. 1864 Wheelwright *Spring Lapl.* 296 Hoping soon to see it lying on his skinning table! 1875 Knight *Dict. Mech.* 2196/1 *Skinning-apparatus*, a mechanical appliance for removing the hides from animals. 1884 *Good Words* June 391/1 The skinning knives did duty as table knives.

Skinnis, var. of ME. *kinnes*: see Kin *sb.*¹ 6 b.

Ski·nnum. [See quot. 1854.] A variety of domestic pigeon.

1854 Meall *Moubray's Poultry* 277 It is perhaps owing to the loose *skinny* eyes and bill..that they are vulgarly called 'Skinnums'. 1867 Tegetmeier *Pigeons* ix. 100 My skinnum was in his hand. Hurrah! the prize was mine.

Skinny (ski·ni), *a.* [f. Skin *sb.* + -y ¹.]

1. Consisting or formed of skin; resembling skin or film; cutaneous, membranous.

1573 Baret *Alv.* s.v. *Flie*, To flie with skinny winges. 1601 Holland *Pliny* xxiii. Proem, The bones charged with purulent and skinnie matter. 1615 Crooke *Body of Man* 236 Heere is also to be obserued a skinny Ligament. 1657 S. Purchas *Pol. Flying-Ins.* 6 The Bee hath four dry pellucid skinny wings. 1753 N. Torriano *Gangr. Sore Throat* 94 Those loosened Pieces of skinny Membranes. 1796 Withering *Brit. Plants* (ed. 3) III. 734 The middle row of scales the largest, all more or less membranaceous and skinny. 1805 *Med. Jrnl.* XIV. 71 Whirls..surrounded by a skinny sheath. 1875 Jowett *Plato* (ed. 2) III. 660 So the hair sprang up in the skin, being of a skinny and stringy nature.

fig. 1641 Milton *Ch. Govt.* i. Wks. 1851 III. 11 Settling in a skinny congealment of ease and sloth at the top.

Comb. 1822 *Hortus Anglicus* II. 351 *L. Scariosa*, Skinny cupped Liatris.

2. Of, pertaining to, or affecting, the skin. *rare.*

1611 Cotgr., *Peaucier*, skinnie; of, in, or belonging to, the skinne. 1737 Bracken *Farriery Impr.* (1756) I. 186 In cutaneous or skinny Distempers. *Ibid.* 246 An excellent Medicine in Skinny Disorders.

b. Lying next the skin.

1675 Han. Woolley *Gentlew. Comp.* 114 Take the rump-end of the Back-bone, and lay it with the skinny side upward.

3. Having the skin prominently shown; lacking flesh; thin, lean, emaciated.

1605 Shaks. *Macb.* i. iii. 45 Each at once her choppie finger laying Vpon her skinnie Lips. 1784 Ramsay *Health* 118 With skinny cheek, pale lips, and blood-run eyes. 1781 Sir J. Reynolds *Journ. Flanders* Wks. 1797 II. 29 The daughter of Herod..is rather beautiful, but too skinny and lean. 1812 Sir J. Sinclair *Syst. Husb. Scot.* ii. 127 Skinny shrivelled grain produces food weak and unsubstantial. 1857 Hughes *Tom Brown* ii. iii, His long skinny arms all covered with anchors and arrows and letters. 1879 *Sat. Rev.* 4 Oct. 415 A chicken..sometimes skinny and often ill-kept.

4. Mean, miserly, niggardly, stingy.

1833 Hood *Public Dinner* 152 The subscription still skinny. 1838 Holloway *Prov. Dict.*, *Skinny*, mean; inhospitable. 1890 *Lancet* 2 Aug. 246/2 As a rule, the whole of the men in a factory would contribute, and 'skinny' ones were not let off easily.

† **Ski·nster.** *Obs.* In 3 **skinnestere**. [f. Skin *v.* + -ster.] A female skinner.

1270 *Close Roll* 2 *Edw. I*, memb. 7 d, [Agnes] the skinnestere.

Skin-tight (ski·n₁təit), *a.* and *sb.* [Skin *sb.*]

A. *adj.* Fitting tightly to the skin; close-fitting.

1885 *Pall Mall G.* 14 Apr. 4/2 The skin-tight bodice which forbids all graceful, easy movements. a 1891 T. C. Crawford *English Life* 91 (Cent.), Pink skin-tight breeches met his high patent-leather boots at the knee. 1895 *Outing* Dec. 202/1 When these boots are on they are skin-tight everywhere.

B. *sb. pl.* Close-fitting nether garments.

1899 *Daily News* 6 Apr. 7/4, I should have to admit some who go along the Portsmouth road in skin tights.

Skintle (ski·nt'l), *a.* and *sb.* [? f. Skintle *v.*] (See quots.)

1889 C. T. Davis *Bricks, Tiles*, etc. (ed. 2) 135 The straight courses, pillar, hangers, and skintle bricks. *Ibid.* 136 The 'skintles' are the bricks set diagonally in order to tie the over-hangers together.

Skintle (ski·nt'l), *v.* Also **scintle**. [perh. for *squintle*, f. Squint *a.*] *trans.* To separate and

reset (half-dried bricks) at angles to each other, so as to complete the drying.

1876 *Encycl. Brit.* IV. 280/2 When half dry the bricks are separated somewhat (*scintled*), to allow free access of the air. 1904 A. Griffiths *Fifty Yrs. Public Serv.* 236 They dried slowly, and were regularly 'skintled', or rearranged so that the air might get all round them.

So **Ski·ntling** *vbl. sb.*; also as *adv.*

1836 *Penny Cycl.* V. 408/2 After the bricks are partially dried, another operation takes place, called 'skintling'. 1841 *Civil Eng. & Arch. Jrnl.* IV. 341/1 *note*, When the bricks have stood a few days, they are reset with a greater space between them, which operation is called *scintling*. 1889 *Science* XIII. 335/2 When dry, they [the bricks]..are carried in wheel-barrows and set 'skintling', or at angles across each other.

Skio: see Skeo. **Skiogram, -graph**, etc.: see Skiagram, -graph, etc.

Skip (skip), *sb.*¹ Also 5 **skyp(pe**, 5–7 **skippe** (6 **szkippe**). [f. Skip *v.*¹]

1. An act of skipping; a slight bound or spring. *Hop, skip, and jump* (see Hop *sb.*² 3).

c 1440 *Promp. Parv.* 290/2 Lawnche, or skyppe, *saltus*. c 1450 *Mir. Saluac.* (Roxb.) 165 The ydicus [*sic*] made a skippe fro heven to the anone. 1508 Dunbar *Gold. Targe* 19 For mirth of May, wyth skippis and wyth hoppis, The birdis sang vpon the tender croppis. 1647 Trapp *Marrow Gd. Authors* in *Comm. Ep.* 655 Father Latimer..suddenly gave a skip in the floor for joy. 1768 Sterne *Sent. Journ.*, *The Address*, Nor did I mount them [the steps] with a skip and a couple of strides. 1807–8 Irving *Salmag.* (1824) 80 She was a young lady of most voluminous proportions, that quivered at every skip. 1886 Stevenson *Kidnapped* ii, The woman..turned with a skip, and was gone.

fig. 1650 Bulwer *Anthropomet.* Pref., Whether by Art's rude force, or Natures skip I know not. 1667 Pepys *Diary* 26 Apr., And hath come into his place..with a great skip over the heads of a great many. 1817 Scott in *Lockhart* (1837) IV. iii. 84, I..had hoped..to have indulged myself with a skip over the Border.

b. = Leap *sb.*¹ 3.

1844 H. Stephens *Bk. Farm* II. 478 Two or three thorough skips are quite sufficient for the purposes of conception.

2. An act of passing from one thing or point to another with omission or disregard of what intervenes.

1656 Earl Monm. tr. *Boccalini's Advts. fr. Parnass.* i. v. (1674) 8 Not conferring places upon her Nobility by skips and leaps, but by degrees and gradation. 1665 Hooke *Microgr.* 127 Nor do I imagine that the skips from the one to another will be found very great. 1853 Kane *Grinnell Exped.* v. (1856) 36 To avert the disastrous consequences of a twelve hours' skip in their polar reckonings. 1883 S. C. Hall *Retrospect* I. 197 It is a long skip between 1789 and 1807.

b. *Mus.* A passing from one note to another at a greater interval than one degree.

1730 *Treat. Harmony* 29 It is only in the foresaid Skips that we can make use of Discords upon the accented Part of the Bar. 1869 Ouseley *Counterp. Canon & Fugue* vii, In three-part counterpoint skips are always to be avoided. 1873 H. C. Banister *Music* 53 Two successive wide skips in the same direction being generally undesirable.

c. Matter in a book which may be skipped in reading.

1833 Macaulay *Ess.*, *Walpole* (1897) 275 In his books there are scarcely any of those passages which, in our school days, we used to call *skip*. 1889 Hannay *Capt. Marryat* viii. 122 The scenes in which his heroines are on the stage are skip. Amine's appearances, however, are not skip.

3. [prob. short for Skip-kennel.] A footman, lackey, or manservant. In later use *spec.* at Trinity College, Dublin, a college-servant, a scout.

1698–1700 Ward *London Spy* vii. Wks. 1706 I. 157 As a Courtiers Footman when he meets his Brother Skip. 1716–20 *Lett. fr. Mist's Jrnl.* (1722) I. 142, I was surprized to see a Skip transformed so speedily into a Trumpeter. 1732 Dodsley *The Footman* 91 Then to the hall I guide my steps, Amongst a crowd of brother skips. 1839 Lever *H. Lorrequer* xiii, Call your own skip,..damn me if I'll be your skip any longer. 1884 *Punch* 22 Mar. 141/2 A good man once, now, so his skip informs me,..smokes six or seven pipes of strong tobacco..every night.

Skip, *sb.*² Also **skipp**. [var. of Skep *sb.* (q.v. for *skip* in other senses).] In mining or quarrying, a bucket, box, basket, cage, or wagon, in which materials or men are drawn up or let down.

1815 *Ann. Reg., Chron.* 86 Some colliers were descending into a coal pit,..five in one skip and four in the other. 1841 in Hartshorne *Salop. Ant.* Gloss. 1884 *Building News* 15 Aug. 283/3 The mortar and other rubbish was also lowered in skips.

attrib. 1875 J. H. Collins *Met. Mining* 75 A plan of a shaft with double skip-road adapted for wheels. 1875 Knight *Dict. Mech.* 2196/2 *Skip-shaft* (Mining), one boxed off by itself for the skip to ascend and descend in.

Skip, *sb.*³ *Sc.* [abbrev. of Skipper *sb.*²] The director or captain of a curling or bowling team or side.

1830 *Memorab. Curl. Maben.* 29 The other skips having arranged among themselves, the boards were selected [etc.]. 1862 *Chambers's Encycl.* III. 368/1 Sides are made up, usually consisting of four against four, with a director styled *skip* for each. 1881 *Sat. Rev.* No. 1318. 138 A great moorland farmer having to figure as skip on the one side.

Skip, *sb.*⁴ [f. Skip *v.*²] (See quots.)

1858 Simmonds *Dict. Trade*, *Skip*, in sugar-making in the West Indies, a charge or strike of syrup from the coppers. 1885 C. G. W. Lock *Workshop Rec.* Ser. iv. 163/2 The difficulty is determining the exact moment when the boiling of the 'sling' in the striking-teach must cease, i.e. when to make a 'skip'.

† **Skip**, *sb.*⁵ *Obs.*⁻⁰ (See quot.)

1688 Holme *Armoury* iii. 260/2 Goat skins are reckoned by the skip, which is 50 Skins.

Skip, *sb.*⁶ Abbrev. of Schipperke.

1895 *Our Dogs* I. 128/2 The best class of Skips ever seen in England.

Skip, *v.*¹ Forms: 4–6 **skippe** (4 **schippe**), 4–7 **skyppe** (5 **sckyppe**), 6 **skype**; 4- **skip** (4 **schip**, ? **scep**, 4–6 **scip**), 5 **skyp(p**, 6–7 **skipp**. [app. related to MSw. *skuppa*, *skoppa* in the same sense (cf. also Scope *v.*¹), but the history of the vowel is not clear.]

I. *intr.* 1. To raise oneself off the ground by a light and graceful movement; to spring or leap lightly and easily, *spec.* in the exercise of skipping with a rope.

a 1300 *Cursor M.* 23569 For to skip and for to rin, Quen it war better for to blin. 1390 Gower *Conf.* II. 95 With such gladnesse I daunce and skippe, Me thenkth I touche noght the flor. 1406 Hoccleve *La Male Regle* 120 Seeknesse.. paieth me my wage, So þat me neithir daunce list, ne skippe. c 1460 *Wisdom* in *Macro Plays* 54 For ioy, I sprynge, I sckyppe. 1530 Palsgr. 719 Are you nat ashamed to skyppe thus in your daunsynge, lyke a gyrle of the countray? 1576 Fleming *Panopl. Epist.* 227 The grasshopper.. skipped, leapt and chirpte, in her kinde. 1632 Lithgow *Trav.* i. 27 [These nymphs] would oft run races, skipping like wanton Lambes. 1706 E. Ward *Wooden World Diss.* (1708) 54 Up he skips upon his legs, as manfully as a Taylor upon a Shop-Board. 1792 Mme. D'Arblay *Diary* 24 Sept., Sophia skipped with joy, and Cecilia was all smiles. 1844 Hood *Skipping* i, Little Children skip, The rope so gaily gripping. 1877 A. B. Edwards *Up Nile* x. 259 He skips, and screams, and grins like an ubiquitous goblin.

fig. 1647 N. Bacon *Disc. Govt. Eng.* i. Concl. (1739) 201 If at any time he skipped higher, he afterwards fell lower.

b. With cognate accusative. *rare.*

1602 Marston *Antonio's Rev.* v. iv, Force the plump lipt god, Skip light lavoltaes in your full sapt vaines.

2. To spring or leap lightly in a certain direction or to a certain point; to move or advance by a skip or skips. Const. with advs. and preps.

a 1300 *K. Horn* 1361 (Ritson), The knyht to Horn gan skippe, And in his armes clippe. 13.. *K. Alis.* (Laud MS.) 1108 Hym to awreke, kyng Philipp Ouer þe table gan to skipp. 1382 Wyclif *Acts* xiv. 13 Barnabas and Poul.. scipten out into the cumpanyes. c 1450 *Merlin* xxvii. 552 Gaheries toke the horse..to Gueheret his brother, and made hym skippe in to the sadell. 1548 Udall, etc. *Erasm. Par. Mark* Pref. 4 Hou uncomely a thing it were if a Philosophier would..scip about the stage. 1582 Stanyhurst *Æneis* i. (Arb.) 23 On sands from vessels dooth skippe thee coompanye cheereful. 1634 Sir T. Herbert *Trav.* 158 Thus burthened, [he] shal trauell till hee come where he can skip into Paradice. 1676 Hobbes *Iliad* (1677) 266 Let none from hence again retire..Nor any man before the rest skip out. 1726 Cavallier *Mem.* i. 58 He was very much surprised to see Eighteen young Men skipping one after another into his House. 1786 tr. *Beckford's Vathek* (1883) 110 She skipped along with the alertness of an antelope. 1842 B. Hall *Patchwork* III. 146 Our walker skipped from rock to rock at a great rate. 1898 *Allbutt's Syst. Med.* V. 955 They skip up stairs two at a time.

fig. 1388 Wyclif *Ecclus.* xxxviii. 37 And thei schulen not skippe ouer in to the chirche. 1583 Greene *Mamillia* ii. Wks. (Grosart) II. 282 Insomuch that they say when the gods made beautie, they skipt beyond their skill. 1692 S. Patrick *Answ. Touchstone* 58 The Faith of the Gospel (unto which he now skips).

b. To hasten, hurry, move lightly and rapidly; to make off, abscond. Now *U.S. colloq.*

1338 R. Brunne *Chron.* (1810) 255 To Paris gan he skip, & held his parlement. c 1400 *Laud Troy Bk.* 2920 Eche man.. with his god schippes And alle here good thedur skippes. 1479 *Paston Lett.* III. 257 Ye had ned to be ware that th' Exchetor skyppe not from you, when he comyth to London. 1586 J. Hooker *Hist. Irel.* in *Holinshed* II. 142/2 The foresaid rebels, who skipped to and fro in such sort, that in no case could he find them at any aduantage. 1590 Greene *Orl. Fur.* (1599) 8 What is Orlando, but a stragling mate,.. Skipt from his countreye. 1830 Marryat *King's Own* xix, By Jove, you'd better skip for it, or you'll have what Captain M— says. 1890 L. C. D'Oyle *Notches* 107 So, to throw her father off the scent, on the appointed night we 'skipped' and went by way of Fort James.

3. To pass from one point, matter, etc., to another with omission of what intervenes; in mod. use *spec.* to do this in reading.

c 1385 Chaucer *L. G. W.* 622 *Cleopatra*, The weddynge & the feste to deuyse..It were to longe,..And for thy to thefeect thanne wele I skyppe. 1559 in Strype *Ann. Ref.* (1824) I. App. xi. 35 He that woulde challenge kyndred of Constantyne the Great, and woulde from his father skippe upp streight to Constantyne. 1611 Shaks. *Cymb.* iv. ii. 199, I had rather Haue skipt from sixteene yeares of Age to sixty. 1864 Burton *Scot Abroad* II. ii. 150, I must really spare the reader two thirds of this portentous list, and skip for him to the conclusion. 1873 Hamerton *Intell. Life* iv. iv. 163 The art of reading is to skip judiciously.

b. Similarly with *over*. Also sometimes, to pass *over* with very slight or superficial treatment.

1412–20 Lydg. *Chron. Troy* iii. 4417 Late him be with sorwe, And skippeth ouer wher 3e list nat rede. 1548 Elyot, *Praeterreo*,..to make no mencion of, to skippe ouer, to leaue out a thyng, that shulde be spoken of. 1654 Whitlock *Zootomia* 454 The nimble Perfunctorinesse of some Commentators (that skip over hard Places). 1725 Watts *Logic* 344 They skip over, and but lightly touch the drier part of their theme. 1843 Maitland *Dark Ages* xv. (1890) 274 As I am not writing history,..let us skip over rather more than a century. 1871 L. Stephen *Playgr. Eur.* (1894) x. 248, I might have skipped over these difficulties like the proverbial chamois.

4. Of things, in literal or fig. senses.

c 1386 Chaucer *Pars. T.* ¶ 361 In this wise skippeth venial in-to deedly synne. 1500–20 Dunbar *Poems* liv. 8 Quhou hir schort catt noiss vp skippis. 1568 *Like Will to Like* in Hazl. *Dodsley* III. 331 The barrel was turned to a ship, Which me-thought the wind made nicely to skip. 1610 G. Fletcher *Christ's Vict.* i. lxxxv, Bright Palestine, Whose woods drop honie, and her rivers skip with wine. 1663 S. Patrick *Parab. Pilgr.* (1667) 330 Just as the Loadstone draws Iron to it, and makes it skip into its Bosome. 1728 Pope *Dunc.* ii. 212 Quick sensations skip from vein to vein. 1840 Dickens *Old C. Shop* xviii, The landlord stirred the fire, sending the flame skipping and leaping up.

b. *Mus.* To pass from one note to another at an interval of more than one degree.

1868 Ouseley *Harmony* iii. (1875) 52 The seventh may skip sometimes to the fifth on the same bass.

II. *trans.* 5. To pass over in reading, or in going through a book, etc. Also with *over*, and in fig. context.

1526 *Pilgr. Perf.* (W. de W. 1531) 158 Not sparing your voyces, not clipping the syllables, nor skyppyng ony worde. 1597 Middleton *Wisd. Solomon* i. 7 Christ skips thy faults, only thy virtue reads. 1604 — *Father Hubbard's T.* Wks. 1885 VIII. 54 To skip it over and say that line were naught. 1660 Boyle *New Exp. Phys. Mech.* Preface p. iv, Those that are well versed in the New Philosophy..may skip what was design'd. 1753 Richardson *Grandison* (1781) IV. ii. 21 The Doctor looked so earnestly at me, when he skipped two sides of it. 1823 Lamb *Let. to Barton* 17 Feb., I do not think that I skipped a word of it [*sc.* a book]. 1875 R. F. Burton *Ultima Thule* I. xii, Let the reader 'skip' such photos if he likes.

b. To pass over without mentioning, dealing with, taking into account, etc.; to omit.

1531 Elyot *Governor* ii. xiv. (1557) 141 Oftentimes a.. loker on espieth a default, that the doer forgetteth or skyppeth ouer. 1593 Bilson *Govt. Christ's Ch.* 232 How childish an oversight was it for Paul to skip the whole bench of them. 1669 Br. Hopkins *Serm. 1 Peter* ii. (1685) 66 A day it was, that..we might well wish that the Year would skip it over. 1684 T. Burnet *Theory Earth* ii. 180 In reckoning up the chief patrons of it, he always skips Justin Martyr. 1787 Mme. D'Arblay *Diary* Apr., I shall skip useless recollections upon unpleasant subjects. 1875 Jowett *Plato* (ed. 2) III. 52 Two virtues remain; shall we skip one and go to the other? 1893 W. Forbes-Mitchell *Rem. Mutiny* 2, I intend to skip much that has already been recorded in the pages of history.

c. To pass over, pass by, without touching or affecting in any way. Also with *over*.

1599 B. Jonson *Ev. Man out of Hum.* iv. v, He, making a reverse blow,..enters the linings [of a doublet] and skips the flesh. 1607 Shaks. *Timon* iv. iii. 110 Let not thy sword skip one: Pitty not honour'd Age for his white Beard. 1625 Middleton *Women Beware W.* ii. ii, All means to come by riches or advancement Miss me, and skip me over! 1778 Br. Lowth *Transl. Isaiah* Notes xxxi. 162 He passed over, or skipped, those houses, and forbore to smite them. 1886 G. Allen *Darwin* ii. 25 It is fashionable to say..that the mental energy skips a generation. 1898 Manson *Trop. Dis.* viii. 155 Sometimes it [the plague] skips a house, a village, or a district.

d. To miss, escape from. *rare*⁻¹.

1630 J. Taylor (Water P.) *Wks.* ii. 132/2 Ther's nothing of him that doth hanging skip Except his eares.

6. a. To jump or leap lightly over (something); to go off, leave (rails).

a 1732 Swift *Tom Mullinex & Dick* vii, Tom could move with lordly grace, Dick nimbly skip the gutter. 1821 Clare *Vill. Minstr.* I. 121 Nelly lightly skipt the stile. 1903 *Daily Chron.* 18 May 6/5 A little later another car skipped the rails.

b. To absent oneself from, stay away from.

1824 Southey in *Life & Corr.* (1849) I. 141 Having one day skipped school to attend a concert.

c. *U.S. colloq.* To flee (the country).

1884 *Milnor* (Dakota) *Teller* 12 Sept., The granger school master..skipped the country this week.

7. To cause to skip, bound, or jump.

1683 Moxon *Mech. Exerc.*, *Printing* xxiv. ¶13 He skips his Balls both at once from the first and third Row to the second and fourth Row. 1841 Catlin *N. Amer. Ind.* (1844) II. lv. 194 The usual friendly invitation however was given ..by skipping several rifle bullets across the river. 1894 H. Gardener *Unoff. Pat.* 26 He had skipped pebbles on it and waded across it at low tide.

fig. 1867 F. H. Ludlow *Little Briggs & I* 217 Retired merchants, who had a passion for skipping away their hard dollars on the bottomless pond of fancy cattle-breeding.

III. 8. The verbal stem in comb., as **skip-bone**, = Skipjack 3; **skip-brain** *a.*, flighty, hare-brained; † **skip-frog**, the game of leap-frog; **skip-louse**, a tailor; **skip mackerel** *U.S.*, the blue-fish or skipjack; **skip-rope**, a skipping-rope (*Cent. Dict.*); **skip-tail**, a spring-tail; **skip-tooth** (see quot. 1875).

1603 J. Davies (Heref.) *Microcosmos* Wks. (Grosart) I. 30/1 This skipp-braine Fancy moves these easie Movers To loue what ere hath but a glimpse of good. 1727 Boyer *Fr. Dict.* ii, Skip-Frog, (a sort of Play, amongst Boys), *La Poste*. 1807 J. Beresford *Miseries Hum. Life* xx. (ed. 3) 271 We laugh that win, Since we pay but for one, tho' nine Skip-lice get in. 1839 *Penny Cycl.* XV. 188/1 The small insect called *Podura Plumbea*, the common Skiptail. 1875 Knight *Dict. Mech.* 2196/2 *Skip-tooth Saw*, a saw in which alternate teeth are cut out. 1884 Goode *Nat. Hist. Aquat. Anim.* 433 About New York they are called 'Skip Mackerel'. 1901 E. L. Arnold *Lepidus* 33 As he finished a drum-stick, or pitched a clean-picked skip-bone into the ferns.

Skip, *v.*² [ad. Du. *scheppen* (G. *schöpfen*) to ladle, bale, dip, draw (water), etc.] *trans.* To transfer (sugar) from one vessel to another in the process of manufacture.

Skip, v.³ [f. SKIP v.¹] trans. To command or direct (a teɛm in curling or bowling) as skip.

Skiph, obs. form of SKIFF sb.

Skip-jack (skiˈp·dʒak), sb. and a. Also 6 scip-jacke, -jake, 6–7 skipjacke, 7 -jacke. [f. SKIP v.¹ + JACK sb.¹]

†Skip-kennel. Obs. [f. SKIP v.¹ + KENNEL sb.²]

Skippable (skiˈpa·b'l). a. Also skipable. [f. SKIP v.¹ + -ABLE.]

Skippare (skiˈpaɪ), 6 skyppare, 6 skyppar. [f. SKIP v.¹ + -ARE.]

Skipper, sb.¹ Cant. [f. SKIP v.¹]

Skipper, sb.² [ad. MDu. or MLG. schipper, skipper, esquipar to EQUIP.]

Skipper, sb.³ rare⁻¹. [freq. of SKIP v.¹] In to skip or hop.

Skipper, a. dial. and Sc. Full of maggots.

†Skippesoon. Obs. rare. [ad. OFr. eskip(e)son, f. eskiper, esquiper to EQUIP.]

Skip't. [cf. SKIRRET.] A small round wooden box, used for the preservation of documents or seals.

Skippet. sb.² Obs. rare. In 5 skyppeto. [dim. of skip SKEP sb.]

†Skippet, v. rare. Also 5 skeppette. [dim. of SKEP sb.]

Skipping, vbl. sb.¹ [f. SKIP v.¹]
1. The action of the verb skip, in literal senses.
2. The action of skipping, in transferred senses.
3. Gun-making. (See quot.)

Skip'ping, vbl. sb.² [f. SKIPPER sb.²] In sugar-making: (see quots.). Also attrib.

Skip-ping, ppl. a. [f. SKIP v.¹]
1. That skips. Also spec. in skipping stickleback.
2. Characterized by skips.

Skippingly, adv. [f. prec. + -LY².] In a skipping manner; by skips.

Skippingrope. [f. SKIPPING vbl. sb.¹] A piece of rope, sometimes with a wooden handle at each end, used in the game of skipping.

†Skippon. Obs. rare. [cf. Skipper sb.²]

†Skippound. [ad. Du. schippond, or LG. schippund.]

Skippy (skiˈpi). a. [f. SKIP v.¹ + -Y¹.] Inclined to skip; characterized by skipping.

Skipple (skiˈp'l). U.S. Also 7 skepel. [ad. Du. schepel.]

Skire. a. Obs. [See SKIRE a.]

Skire Thursday. Sc. and north. dial. [See SKIRRET.]

Skiri-ing, ppl. a. [f. SKIRL v.¹]

Ski-rling, vbl. sb. local. Also scar-, scur-, sker-ling. [f. obscure origin.]

Skirl, v.¹ Sc. and north. dial. Forms: 4 skyrle, 5 skirle, 5 skyrl, 6 skyrille. [a. ON. skirla]

Skirl, v.² [Of obscure origin; also onomatopoeic.]

†Skirl, sb.¹ [f. SKIRL v.¹] Shrill cry.

Skirl, sb.² Sc. and north. dial.

Ski-rling, ppl. a. [f. SKIRL v.¹] Crying or sounding shrilly, screaming, etc.

Skirm, v. Obs. Forms: 4 skyrme, 4 skyrmen. [ad. OFr. eskermir, escremir.]

†Skirmery. Obs. rare. [ad. OF. *eskirmerie]

Skirmish, sb. Forms: 4–6 skarmuch, 4–6 -moch, 5 -moche, -masche, 6 -muisch(e, -muoch ; 4 skarmouche, -mouch ; 5 scaremouche, -mushe, -musshe, 6 -muss, 5 scarmishe, 6–7 -moche.

Skirmish, v. Forms: α. 4 scarmuche, -muysshe, -mushe, 5 -musshe, 6 -moosh; 4–6 scrymyssh(e, 5 skrymmysshe, 6 skyrmysshe.

Skirmishing, vbl. sb. [f. SKIRMISH v.] The action of the vb.

Skirmisher. One of a number of soldiers taking part in a skirmish or acting in loose order apart from the main body of an army or battalion.

Skirr, v. Obs. Also scaur, scurr. [Of obscure origin.]
I. intr. To engage in a skirmish or irregular encounter; to fight in small parties.

Skirl, sb. Obs. Also scaur, scurr. A sound of a grating, rasping, or whirring character.

Skirl, v. Sc. Forms: 4–6 skyrle, 6–7, 9 skirl, 5 scurle, 9 scurl. [Of doubtful origin; the form scur- may represent, if not due to Scand., ON. skyr-.]

†Skirl, v. Obs. To behave with contempt. b. trans. To mock, deride.

Skirr, v. Also scaur, scurr.

Skirret (skiˈret). Forms: α. 4 skyrwate, 5–6 skyrwyt (5 -wytte, skerwyrt), 6 schirewyt, 6 skyrwit or -whit, 7 -wicke. [Of doubtful origin.]

Skirret, sb.² [var. of SQUIRT sb.]

Skirret. Freemasonry. (See quots.)

Skirt (skə̄rt), sb. Forms: 4 skyrte, 4 skyrt, 4 schirt, 5 skirte, 6 skyrt.
1. The lower part of a woman's dress or gown.
2. The lower part of a man's gown or robe.
3. b. A rim or border; an edging.
4. The border, rim, outer portion, extremity, or tail-end of anything.

SKIRT. (continued)

8. The edge, margin, border, outer edge or lower slopes of a mountain or hill.

sing. ... *pl.* ...

b. *fig.* The beginning or end of a period of time. Chiefly *pl.*

10. A tract or piece of land forming a border, edge, or side of a river, country, etc. *Obs.*

b. A number of trees, etc., surrounding or bordering a place.

11. *attrib.* and *Comb.*, as *skirt-dancer*, *skirt-dance* sb., etc.

Skirt, v.

I. *trans.* 1. Chiefly *with reference to* natural features, scenery, or surroundings: a. To form the skirt or edge of; to lie alongside of; to bound or border.

b. *transf.* and *fig.*

II. *intr.* 5. a. Of persons: To travel, move, hang about, etc., on the outskirts or confines of something, or in a casual manner.

b. Of hunting-dogs: To leave the pack when following the scent of a place.

6. a. Of roads, rivers, etc.: To lie or run *along* or *round* the edge or border of a place, etc.

b. Of strata: To crop out.

7. a. Wearing a skirt or skirts. Freq. in recent use in *skirted rider*.

b. Of garments: Having a skirt.

Skirted, *ppl. a.*

Skirting, *vbl. sb.*

1. The action or fact of treating lightly or superficially. *Obs.*

2. *Devon dial.* (See quot. 1790.)

3. A border, edge, edging, or margin.

4. *Carp.* The narrow boarding, edging of slate or cement, etc., placed vertically along the base of the wall of a room, or other place in a building, next to the floor. Also *collect.*, material suitable for this. Cf. SKIRTING-BOARD.

5. *Austr.* The trimmings or inferior portions of a fleece.

Skirting, *ppl. a.* That skirts, in senses of the vb.

Skirting-board. The narrow board placed round the wall of a room, etc., close to the floor.

Skirter (skɜː˞tə˞). [f. SKIRT v. + -ER [1].]

Skirtle

Skirtless (skɜː˞tles), a. [f. SKIRT sb. + -LESS.]

Skirty, a.

Skirwire

Skirwingle, *Obs.* [Of obscure origin.]

Skis Thursday. Obs. var. of SHROVE Thursday.

Skit, *sb.*

Skit, *v.*

Skite (skəit), *sb.* *Sc.* and *north. dial.* [Related to SKITE v.]

Skite (skəit), *v.* *Sc.* and *dial.*

Skiter

Skitter (skɪ˞tə˞), *v.* intr.

Skittish (skɪ˞tɪʃ), a. [f. SKIT v. + -ISH.]

Skittishly, *adv.* In a skittish manner.

Skittishness. The quality of being skittish, in various senses.

Skittle (skɪ˞t'l), *sb.*

1. *pl.* A game played with nine pins set in a square upon a wooden frame, at one end of which is directed towards the players, who endeavour to bowl down the pins in as few throws as possible. Cf. NINE-PINS [1].

b. *attrib.* and *Comb.*, as *skittle-maker*, *-player*, etc.

Skittle, *v.*

1. *intr.* To play the game of skittles.

2. *trans.* To make skittle of.

Skittle-ball, **Skittle-dog**, **Skittler**, **Skittling**.

Skive (skəiv), *sb.*

Skive (skəiv), *v.* [ad. De. *skiif* (= ON. *skifa*).]

Skiver (skəi˞və˞).

Skiving (skəi˞vɪŋ), *vbl. sb.*

Skleir, **Sklent**, **Skleff**, etc.

Skulker (skə‧lkəɹ). Also 6 soulkery, scolo‧urya, scolkery, skoulkery. [f. SKULK v. + -ER¹.] The practice of skulking.

Skulking (skə‧lkiŋ), vbl. sb. [f. SKULK v. + -ING¹.]

Skulk, v. [as prec. + -ING².]

Skull (skʌl). Forms: α. 3 scolle, 4-6 scoll, 5 scolle; 3 skulle, 4-6 skull. β. 4-7 sculle, 6-7 scull. γ. 4-7 scole; 7-9 skole.

Skull, sb.² var. SCULL sb., oar.

Skulled (skʌld), a. [f. SKULL¹ + -ED².]

Skullery, var. SCOWBANKER slang.

Skull-cap sb. [f. SKULL + CAP sb.]

Skunk (skʌŋk). sb. U.S. slang. [f. prec.]

1. A North American animal of the weasel kind,

Skunk-cabbage, N. Amer.

Sku‧nkdom.

Sku‧nk-weed, U.S., = SKUNK-CABBAGE.

Skurie, obs. f. SCORN sb., SKIRT, var. SQUIRT.

Skurtile, -uy, obs. f. SCURVY sb. and a.

Skya, obs. f. SKEW sb.

Skwe, var. SKEW sb. Obs. Skwff, obs. f. SCOFF v.

Sky (skai). sb.¹ Forms: 3-4 (6 scki, schi); 3 skei, 4 skey; 3 skije, 4-7 skie, skye (5 scki, 4 schye, 7-9 skye) (4c6 -ski); 7 sky, sci, cloud.

†1. A cloud.

2. The skies, the clouds (obs.); the upper region of the air; the heavens. Chiefly poet.

Skybald, Sc. and north. dial. Forms: 6, skey-bald, 6-9 scybald, 9 skybal, -bel, scybel, -ble, etc. [Of obscure origin.] A low, rascally, or contemptible fellow; a lean or worn-out person or animal, a miserable article, etc.

Skye (skai). [f. SKY sb.¹ + -ER¹. Cf. SKIER.] A lofty hit at cricket.

Skyey, obs. form of SQUIRE sb.

Sky, v. [f. SKY sb.¹] slang. [see quots.]

Sky-coloured, a. Of the (blue) colour of the sky.

Sky-farmer [SKY sb.¹]

Sky-ful. [SKY sb.¹] As much, or as many, as the sky can hold.

Sky-high, adv. and a. [SKY sb.¹]

Skyish (skai‧iʃ), a. [SKY sb.¹ + -ISH.]

Skylark (skai‧lɑːk), sb. [f. SKY sb.¹]

Sky-like, a. [SKY sb.¹] Resembling the sky.

Sky-line. [SKY sb.¹] The line where earth and sky meet; the horizon.

Sky-parlour [SKY sb.¹]

SKYR — 161 — **SLAB** | **SLAB** — 162 — **SLABBY**

Skyr (skīˑɹ), [Icel.] A dish prepared from curdled milk; a kind of curd.

Skyˑre, varr. SKIRE *a.* and *adv.*, SKIRE *v.*

Skyˑrey, obs. form of SCURVY *a.*

Skyˑre, *etc.* in SKIRE.

Skyre (skīˑɹ), *v. intr.* To be bright or glaring; to flaunt. Hence conspicuous.

Sky-pilot: see SKY *sb.* 9.

Sky-scraping, *a.* [SKY *sb.*¹] High enough to appear to touch the sky; hence, remarkably high or lofty.

Skyward (skaiˑwəd), *adv.* and *adj.* Also 6 **skiew ward**. [SKY *sb.*¹]

Slab (slæb), *sb.*¹ Also 3 **sclabbe**, 4-6 **slabbe**, 7 **slabb**. [Of obscure origin.] A flat, broad, and comparatively thick piece or mass of anything solid.

Slab (slæb), *sb.*² Also 7 **slabbe**. [Related to SLAB *sb.*¹?] Semi-solid; viscid.

Slab (slæb), *sb.*³ *Naut.* [Cf. SLAB-LINE.]

Slab (slæb), *a.* Now chiefly *dial.* Also 6 **slabour**, 7 **slabbe**. Thick, viscid, slimy.

Slabber (slæˑbəɹ), *v.*¹ A saw or machine for removing the outside slabs from timber.

Slabber (slæˑbəɹ), *v.*² Now chiefly *dial.* Also **slobber**, **slubber**. To let fall saliva.

Slabbering, *ppl. a.* Characterized by slabbering.

Slabbery (slæˑbəri), *a.* Also **slabbry**. Slimy, sloppy.

Slabby (slæˑbi), *a.* Also **slabbie**. Viscid, slimy; muddy, sloppy.

SLABBY — 163 — **SLACK** | **SLACK** — 164 — **SLACK**

Slack (slæk), *sb.*¹ [Of doubtful origin: cf. older Flem. *siecke*, Du. *slak*.] Small refuse coal.

Slabby (slæˑbi), *a.* [f. SLAB *sb.*¹]

Slabbiness, *sb.*

Slab-line. *Naut.*

Slab reef. *Naut.*

Slab-sided, *a.* *U.S.*

Slab-stone. Also **slabstone**.

Slack (slæk), *sb.*² north. and *Sc.* Forms: 5 **slac**, **slakke**, **slake**, 5-6 **slak**, 6- **slack**.

Slack (slæk), *a.* and *adv.* Forms: 1 **sleac**, **slæc**, 3-4 **slac**, 4-6 **slak**, 4-7 **slacke**, 4- **slack**.

Slack (slæk), *sb.*³ [f. prec.]

Slack (slæk), *v.* Also 6-7 **slacke**, 6 *Sc.* **slak**.

must slacke, Wanting his mannage. **1831** R. SHENHAM *Tales* 37 When business had begun to slack.

12. To become less tense, rigid, or firm.

13. To become disintegrated under the action of moisture.

Slack-baked, *a.* [SLACK *adv.*] Of bread : Imperfectly or insufficiently baked.

Slacked, *ppl. a.* [f. SLACK *v.*]
1. Retarded; rendered slower.
2. Of lime : Slaked.

Slacken, *sb.* *= schlacke* dross of metal, etc. ; Slag.

Slacken (slæ'k'n), *v.* [f. SLACK *a.* Cf. the rarer SLAKEN *v.*, and Icel., Norw., and Sw. *slakna* (older Da. *slagne*)]
I. *trans.* To cause to become slower; to delay or retard.
2. To render less vigorous or eager ; to fall off or decline.

Slackened, *ppl. a.* [f. prec.]
1. Rendered less tense or firm.
2. Abated, mitigated; relaxed.

Slackening, *vbl. sb.* [f. prec.] One who, or that which, slackens or slakes.

Slack-jaw, *sb.* *slang.* Impertinent or insolent talk.

Slacker. [f. SLACK *v.*] = SLAKER 2.

Slacking, *vbl. sb.* [f. SLACK *v.*] The action of the *vb.*, in various senses.

Slacking, *ppl. a.* [as prec.] Making or becoming slack.

Slackly (slæ'kli), *adv.* Forms : 1 *sleaclice*, 4 *slacli*, 5-6 *slakly*, 6 *slacklie*, *-ly 6-7 slackly*; *slacklich*, 5-7 -*ly*. [f. SLACK *a.* + -LY [2].]
1. In a remiss or negligent manner; without due diligence or energy.
2. Without vigour or force ; slowly.

Slack-lime. [?f. SLACK *v.*] Lime in the state of being slacked.

Slackness (slæ'knes). Forms : 1 *sleacnes*, *-nys*, *slæcnys*, 4 *slacnesse*, *slaknes* []-*nese*, 5 *slaknesse*, 6 *slakes-*, 6-7 *slacknesse*, 6- *slackness*. [f. SLACK *a.* + -NESS.]
1. Lack of diligence or energy ; tendency to idleness or sluggishness; remissness.
2. Laxity; want of strictness.
3. Slowness ; tardiness.
4. Lack of vigour or strength ; sense of tension or tightness.

Slacky. *Sc. rare.* Also *slackie.* [Of obscure origin.]

Slade (slād), *sb. [1]* A slope, hollow; cf. also Da. dial. *slade* a piece of level ground (16th cent. in Kalkar), G. dial. (Westph.) *slade* dell; ravine.

Slade (slād), *sb. [2]* [Of obscure origin: perh. related to SLIDE *v.*] The sole of a plough.

Slade, *v.* [app. related to SLIDE *v.*] *trans.* To carry on a sledge.

Slade, *obs.* or *Sc. pa. t.* of SLIDE *v.*, Slaе.

Slaff. *Sc. dial.* (Meaning doubtful.)

Slag (slæg), *sb.* Also 6 slagge, 6-9 slagg. [a. MLG. *slagge* (whence also Sw. *slagg*) = G. *schlacke* (also *schlack*), of obscure etymology.]

Slaggy (slæ'gi), *a.* Also 8 slaggey. [f. SLAG *sb.* + -Y [1].] Of the nature of slag ; pertaining to or resembling slag.

Slag-hearth, *sb.* A furnace for treating the slag-products of lead-smelting.

Slaght, variant of SLAUGHT *Obs.*

Slaght-boome *var.* of SLAUGHTER-BOOM *Obs.*

Slag-lead. [SLAG *sb.*] Lead obtained by re-smelting grey slag.

Slaid, *var.* of SLAYED *Obs.*, *pa. t.* SLITE *v.*

Slaie, *var.* of SLAY *sb. [3]* ; also 4 slae, *var.* of SLAE.

Slaigh, dial. *var.* of SLOE.

Slaight, var. of SLEIGHT *Obs.*

Slain (slē'in), *ppl. a.* Also slaine, slayn. [See SLAY *v. [1]*.]

Slain, *var.* of SLAUGHT *sb.* Obs.

Slair, *Sc. variant of SLEER.* [See SLAY *v.*]

Slaister (slē'istar), *Sc.* and *north. dial.* [Cf. the *vb.*] A dirty or disgusting mess or compound; the act of working at or making this.

Slaister, variant of SKLEIN, *a.* verb.

Slait *sb.* and *v.* [See also SLATE *v. [2]*.]

Slake (slāk), *sb. [1]* *Sc.* and *north. dial.* Also slaik, 7-9 slaick. [Obscurely related to the synonymous SLACK and SLOKE.] A name given to several species of algae, including marine and edible kinds as *Ulva* and *Porphyra*, and also the freshwater sorts, as *Enteromorpha* and *Conferva.*

Slake (slāk), *sb. [2]* *Sc.* and *north. dial.* Also slaik, 7-9 slaik. [Obscurely related to the synonymous SLACK and SLOKE.]

Slake (slāk), *v.* [OE. *slacian* and *sleacian*, f. *slæc*, *sleac* SLACK *a.*]
I. *intr.* Of persons : To diminish the intensity of one's efforts; to become less energetic or eager ; also, to undergo or manifest a weakening or decrease in some specified respect. *Obs.*
2. *intr.* Of things : To diminish in tensity or force ; to become slack ; to slacken.

Slake, *sb. [3]* *Obs.* [Of obscure origin.] A splashy daub; a smear; a lick, wipe, soft stroke, etc.

Slaked, *ppl. a.*

Slakeless, *a.* Incapable of being slaked, quenched, or mitigated; insatiable.

Slake-trough. = SLACK-TROUGH.

Slakin: see SLACKEN *sb.*

Slaking, *vbl. sb.*

Slaky (slē'ki), *a.* Muddy.

Slam (slæm), *sb.* Also 7 *slamm.*

Slam, *sb.* rare.

Slaky (slē'ki), *a.*

Slam (slæm), *sb.*

Slam, *sb.* Also *slamm.*

Slam (slæm), *v.*

Slam, *v.*

Slander (slæ·ndə*l*), *sb.* Also 3–6 *sclaundre*, 4–6 *-dre*, 5 *-dir*; 4 *sclawndre*, 5 *dre*, *dur*, *dyr*); 5 *sklawander* (5–6

Slam-bang, *a.* and *adv.*

Slammakin, Slammerkin, *sb.* and *a.*

Slammer (slæ·məɪ), *sb.*

Slammerkin: var. SLAMMAKIN.

Slammerkin, *sb.*

Slamp, *a.*

Slampamp, *Obs.*[superfluous]

Slampant, *sb.*

Slander (slā·ndəɪ), *sb.* Also 3–6 *sclaundre*, 4–6 *-dre*, 5 *-dir*; 4 *sclawndre*, *-dur*, *-dyre*; 5 *sklawander* (5–6

**-dyr); 5 (*Sc.* 6–7) *sklander* (-dyr, 6 *Sc.* -dir, -dyr, 6 *sclaundre* (4–5 -dre, 5 -dere, 4, 6 slaundir, *OF.* esclandre, OF. esclandre, an alteration of *escandle*, ad. L. *scandalum* : see SCANDAL *sb.*]

Slander, *v.* Forms: 4 *sclaundre*, *sclaunder*, 4–5 *sclaundre*, *sclandre*,

Slanderer (slā·ndərəɪ). Also 4–6 *sclaund-*, 6–7 *sclander*, 7 *slaunderer*.
SLANDERER *v.*: see -ER[1].

Slanderful, *a.* *Obs.* rare. Also 5 *sclaund-*.

Slanderfully, *Obs.* rare. Also 5 *-fyl*.

Slandering, *vbl. sb.*

Slandering, *ppl. a.* **Sla·nderingly** *adv.*

Slanderous (slā·ndərəs), *a.* Forms: α. 5–7 *sclaundrous* (5–6 *-dr(o)us*), 6 *skla(u)nderous* (*Sc.* *sklanderus*), 7 *slandrous*; β. 6 *slaunderous* (4, 7 *-drous*), *OF.* *sclaundrous*.

Slanderously, *adv.*

Slanderousness, *sb.*

Slang, *sb.[1]* Chiefly *Sc. Obs.* Also SLOE. [a. MLor MLG. *slange*, Du. *slang*, G. *schlange*]

Slang, *sb.[2]* Now *dial.*

Slang, *sb.[3]* [Of obscure origin.]

Slang, *sb.[4]* *Anglo-Irish.* [a. *slanghan*.]

Slang, *sb.[5]* [A word of cant origin, the ultimate source of which is not apparent.]

Slang (slæŋ), *v.[1]* colloq. or slang. [f. SLANG *sb.[5]*]

Slang, *v.[2]* [f. SLANG *sb.[3]*]

Slanginess (slæ·ŋinēs), *sb.* [f. as prec. + -NESS.]

Slangish, *a.*

Slangily (slæ·ŋili), *adv.*

Slanginess, *sb.*

Slang-whang (slæŋ·hwæŋ), *v.* Chiefly *U.S.* [f. SLANG *sb.[5]* + WHANG *v.*]

Slang-whanger (slæ·ŋ·hwæŋəɪ), *sb.*

Slangy (slæ·ŋi), *a.*

Slank (slæŋk), *a.* Now *Sc.* and *north. dial.*

Slank, *sb.*

Slant (slant), *sb.[1]* Naut. [Later form of SLENT *sb.[1]*]

Slant, *sb.[2]*

Slant (slant), *a.*

that used at school, or to roof houses, or what is found among coals.

†**b.** Slate, or some slaty substance, used in the form of powder, esp. as a medicine; *Irish slat*, alum-slate. (Cf. SLATE *sb.*1 4 b.) *Obs.*

1639 T. DE GRAY *Expert Farrier* 265 Take of black or blew slat, and make it into fine powder. 1643 SIR B. GRENVILE *MS. Letter*, I am something sore, and did spitt bloud two daies..I had no slatt, neither do I now need it. 1665 SIR R. HOWARD *Committee* III, Go in and take some Irish slat by way of Prevention, and keep your self warm. 1684 in *Phil. Trans.* XX. 271 Irish Slat Pulveriz'd, and infus'd in Water.., would impart its Vitriolick Quality.

†**c.** Slate as a variety of stone or rock. *Obs.*

1591 SYLVESTER *Du Bartas* I. iii. 896 Slat, Jet, and Marble shall escape my pen, I over-pass the Salt-mount Oromene. 1681 GREW *Musæum* III. II. ii. 329 A Metalline Slat from the Tin-Mines. 1697 in *Phil. Trans.* XXVII. 467 The Slat above this Coal afforded only Stalks of Plants.

4. A long narrow strip of wood or metal, used for various purposes.

1764 *Museum Rust.* II. 189 Nailing of slats, old hoops, or laths, on the two sides and fore end of the cart. 1828–32 WEBSTER s.v., The slats of a cart or a chair. 1866 *Harvard Mem. Biogr., R. Ware* I. 242 The bulk of those now in bed must have lain on the slats of the bedstead. 1885 C. F. HOLDER *Marvels Anim. Life* 28 Arranged in transverse rows, like slats on a blind. 1890 HALLETT *1000 Miles* 277 When the floors are of split bamboo..the interstices between the slats are many and often large.

b. In vehicles: (see quots.).

1794 W. FELTON *Carriages* (1801) I. 31 The side pieces are called Slats, which are..hung on a centre pin or bolt to the elbow-rails. 1854 MISS BAKER *Northampt. Gloss.*, *Slats*, the sleepers or rails to support the bed of a cart. 1875 KNIGHT *Dict. Mech.* 2199/1 *Slat*,..a bent strip which bows over the seat and forms one of the ribs of the canopy.

5. a. *Basket-making.* (See quots.)

1837 HEBERT *Engin. & Mech. Encycl.* I. 153 The larger ones [*sc.* osiers] forming the slat and skeleton of the basket. 1851–4 *Tomlinson's Cycl. Useful Arts* (1867) I. 109/1 In this way the foundation of the basket, called the *slat* or *slate*, is formed. 1875 *Encycl. Brit.* III. 423/1 The whole now forms what is technically called the slath [*sic*], which is the foundation of the basket.

b. *dial.* A hurdle.

1883 C. R. SMITH *Retrosp.* I. 4 Some open hurdles, or slats as they are called in Kent.

6. *attrib.* and *Comb.* **a.** In senses 1–3, as *slat-coal*, *-pen*, *-pin*, *-stone*.

1412–3 *Abingdon Rolls* (Camden) 76 In sclatpynnes emptis xxd. 1436–7 *Ibid.* 114 Et in sclatpynnes et tyȝlpynnes emptis iiij s. c 1440 [see 1]. 1669 STURMY *Mariner's Mag.* IV. xii. 195 If you make it upon a Slat Stone,..you may wipe the Arch, that is lightly drawn by a Slat Pen.., off at pleasure. 1713 *Phil. Trans.* XXVIII. 222 This resembles a Slat-Coal of a Lead colour.

b. In sense 4, as *slat-awning*, *-bar*, *-bottom*, *-matting*.

Various other combs. are given by Knight *Dict. Mech.*

1875 KNIGHT *Dict. Mech.* 2199/1 A corrugated iron slat-awning. *Ibid.* 2202/1 *Slat-matting*, a floor covering of wooden slats or veneers on a flexible fabric, which may be rolled like a carpet. 1876 VOYLE & STEVENSON *Milit. Dict.* 358/2 *Slat Bar*, the bar of a siege howitzer limber between the splinter bar and bolster. 1883 *Cent. Mag.* Oct. 819/2 The olives are first dried in trays with slat bottoms.

Slat (slæt), *sb.*2 [f. SLAT *v.*2]

1. A slap; a slapping blow. Now *dial.*

1611 COTGR., *Truellée*, a trowell-full; or, a clap, slat, or slamp with a Trowell. 1746 *Exmoor Scolding* (E. D. S.) 101 Ad! chell gi' tha..a slat in the chups. 1837– in Devon and Somerset use (see *Eng. Dial. Dict.*). 1898 T. HARDY *Wessex Poems* 47 Such snocks and slats since war began Never saw recruit or veteran.

2. A sudden gust or blast *of* wind.

1840 R. H. DANA *Bef. Mast* xxv, The sail..by a slat of the wind blew in under the yard with a fearful jerk.

Slat, *sb.*3 *rare*⁻¹. In 8 **slatt**. [a. Irish *slat* rod, measuring stick.] (See quot.)

1780 YOUNG *Tour Irel.* I. 348 Frize..at a slatt or measure, four feet two inches long, and 20 to 23 inches wide.

Slat (slæt), *sb.*4 [? Irish.] A salmon out of season; a spent salmon.

1870 *Daily News* 16 Feb., An unclean and unseasonable salmon of the species called 'kelts' in Scotland and 'slats' in Ireland. 1882 DAY *Fishes Gt. Brit.* II. 69 After spawning this fish [salmon] is a kelt or slat. 1886 *Field* 27 Feb. 261/1 These 'slats' would then escape, and the cause of a great injury to the fishing be prevented.

Slat (*Cant*): see SLATE *sb.*2

Slat (slæt), *v.*1 Also 7 **slatt**. [f. SLAT *sb.*1]

1. *trans.* To cover with slates. Now *dial.*

c 1475 *Crabhouse Reg.* (1889) 61 Sche made the cloystir..and slattyd it. 1615 SIR R. BOYLE in *Lismore Papers* Ser. I. (1886) I. 79, I compounded with John Lambert to slatt my new stable in yoghall. 1667 in Earwaker *E. Cheshire* (1877) I. 114 Paid for slatting the Lych porch. 1881 in EVANS *Leic. Gloss.*

2. To furnish, or make, with slats.

1886 C. SCOTT *Sheep-Farming* 66 The hay-rack is slatted so closely that the sheep cannot put their heads through the bars.

Slat (slæt), *v.*2 Also 3 **sclatte**, 9 *dial.* **sclat**. [Of doubtful origin. Some of the senses resemble those of ON. *sletta* to slap, splash, etc., but this would not readily account for the currency of the word in south-western dialects. In sense 4 perh. partly imitative: cf. SLATTER *v.*2]

1. *trans.* To flap, cast, dash, impel quickly and with some force. Const. *down*, *against*, *on*, etc.

a 1225 *Ancr. R.* 212 Hwon heo ihereð þet god, heo sleateð [*v.r.* sclattes] adun boa two hore earen. 1611 COTGR. s.v. *Flacquer*, He squasht, slat, or squat her downe there. 1787 GROSE *Prov. Gloss.*, *To slat on*, to dash against, or cast on any thing. 1850 SCORESBY *Cheever's Whaleman's Adv.* xiii. (1858) 186 The danger from a whale's flukes and fins, as the monster slues and slats them round. c 1866 STATON *Rays fr. Loominary* 37 If he comes this way ogen ..aw'll slat some watter on him. 1897 HOWELLS *Landlord at Lion's Head* 95 She'll slat the letters down every which way, and you've got to hunt 'em out for yourself.

b. To knock *off* by impact or pulling.

1871 DE VERE *Americanisms* 545 Fishermen on the Eastern coast, who disengaged mackerel and other delicate-gilled fish by slatting them off the hook.

2. To strike, beat; to knock *out*.

1577–87 HOLINSHED *Chron.* III. 1034/2 A butcherlie knaue named Fulks..slat him in the head with a club. 1604 MARSTON *Malcontent* IV. iii, *Men.* How did you kill him? *Mal.* Slatted his braines out. 1837– in south-western dialect (see *Eng. Dial. Dict.*).

3. *intr.* (See quots.) *dial.*

1838 HOLLOWAY *Prov. Dict.*, *To slat* or *sclat*, to beat with violence against any thing, as rain against a window. 1854 MISS BAKER *Northampt. Gloss.* s.v., Why the water's slatting off your hat on to your coat.

4. *Naut.* Of sails: To flap violently.

1840 R. H. DANA *Bef. Mast* v, The great jib flying off to leeward and *slatting* so as almost to throw us off the boom. 1865 MRS. WHITNEY *Gayworthys* xxvi, The canvas slatting out and in, in great bights. 1881 CLARK RUSSELL *A Sailor's Sweetheart* III. vi. 256 The sail slatted so violently that it was as much as we could do..to get the canvas up to leeward.

b. In other contexts: To flap or slap.

1889 'MARK TWAIN' *Yankee at Court of K. Arthur* I. 120, I couldn't seem to stand that shield slatting and banging..about my breast. 1897 — *Man that corrupted Hadleyb.*, etc. (1900) 333 The removable desk-boards had been taken away, and nothing left for disorderly members to slat with.

Hence **Sla·tting** *vbl. sb.* and *ppl. a.*

1883 *Cent. Mag.* Oct. 942/1 All hands..jumping aloft like monkeys to roll up the slatting canvas. 1888 CLARK RUSSELL *Death Ship* I. 46 Every moment this terrible slatting threatened her other spars.

Slat (slæt), *v.*3 Now *dial.* [prob. ad. OF. *esclater* to break in pieces: cf. SLAT *sb.*1] *intr.* and *trans.* To split.

1607 TOPSELL *Four-f. Beasts* 415 It [the nail] slatteth and shiuereth in the driuing into two parts. 1609 HOLLAND *Amm. Marcell.* 424 Both head-peeces and habergeons were slat and dashed a peeces. 1708 *Burlesque of R. L'Estrange's Vis. Quevedo* 72 If his Horns had not been Flatted Perhaps my Head he might ha' Slatted. 1825– in dialect glossaries (chiefly south-western).

†**Slat**, *ppl. a.* *Obs.*⁻¹ [f. SLEAT *v.*1] Baited.

c 1300 *Pol. Songs* (Camden) 154 He sitteth ase a slat swyn that hongeth is eren.

Slatch (slætʃ). ? *Obs.* [A derivative of OE. *slæc* SLACK *a.*, with normal palatalization.]

1. = SLASH *sb.*4 *rare.*

1603 OWEN *Pembrokeshire* (1892) 91 A slatch they call a peece of coal by itselfe found in the erthe and is quicklie digged about and no more to be found of that peece.

2. *Naut.* † **a.** The slack of a rope. *Obs.*

a 1625 *Nomencl. Navalis* (Harl. MS. 2301) 126 When..parte of a Cabell or Roape doth hang slack,..then they said hale the Slatch of the Roape or Cabell. [Hence in Boteler, Holme, Harris, etc.] 1627 CAPT. SMITH *Seaman's Gram.* ix. 39 Hale vp the slatch of the Lee-boling. By Slatch is meant the middle part of any rope hangs ouer boord.

b. A brief respite or interval; a short period or spell (*of* some kind of weather, etc.).

a 1625 *Nomencl. Navalis* (Harl. MS. 2301), When it hath beene a sett of foule weather and that there comes an Interim..of faire weather,..they call it a little Slatch of faire weather. [Hence in Boteler, Holme, Harris, etc.] 1633 T. JAMES *Voy.* 79 Wee could neuer haue a cleere slatch from Ice, to haue it vp. 1703 SIR H. SHERE *Medit. Sea* in *Ld. Halifax's Misc.* 9 At certain times in the Winter Season, they take their Slatches of Flood and Ebb according to their Occasions. 1730 WRIGLESWORTH *Jrnl. of the Lyell* 7 Apr., This morning it blowing Hard,..so [we] must wait for a slatch of fair Weather. 1769 FALCONER *Dict. Marine* (1780), *Slatch*, is generally applied to the period of a transitory breeze of wind, or the length of it's duration. [Hence in later Dicts.]

Slate (slēⁱt), *sb.*1 Also (chiefly *north.* and *Sc.*) 4– **sclate** (5 **sclathe**), **sklate** (9 **sklet**); 5–9 **sclait** (6 **sclayt**), 5 **sklaytt**, 6 **sklaitt**, 6–9 **sklait**. [ad. OF. *esclate* fem., in the same sense as *esclat* masc., whence SLAT *sb.*1 After c 1630 the forms with *scl-*, *skl-* are exclusively northern and Scottish.

The earliest example of the form occurs in sense 3, but the development of the senses must have been the same as in SLAT *sb.*1]

1. A thin, usually rectangular, piece of certain varieties of stone which split readily into laminæ (see 4), used especially for the purpose of covering the roofs of buildings.

Also freq. called a *roofing-slate*, and with distinguishing terms as *blue*, *green*, *grey*, *white slate(s)*. For the older Sc. use of the word see SKAILLIE.

a. 1455 *Anc. Cal. Rec. Dublin* (1889) 284 Sclatys, bordes, gottorys, schall ly upon the key be the space of xx. dayes. 1456 SIR G. HAYE *Law Arms* (S.T.S.) 228 As a sclate fell of a hous and slewe a man. c 1540 BOORDE *The Boke for to Lerne* B ij, Many tyles or sklates. 1584 *Reg. Privy Council Scot.* III. 678 Becaus thair is sklaittis, lyme, sand and tymmer to be transportit..to his said palice. 1832 CARRICK in *Whistle-Binkie* (1890) I. 213 Some o' them gaed ower the sklates As weel's your dainty dow.

β. 1530 PALSGR. 706/1, I sclate a house with stone slates. 1570 LEVINS *Manip.* 39/12 A Slate, tyle, *tegula*, *later*. 1600 J. PORY tr. *Leo's Africa* III. 202 The roofe is couered with certaine blacke stones or slates. 1662 GERBIER *Principles* 36 The Roof..should be covered either with Lead or blew Slates. 1745 *Season. Advice Protestants* 17 The Houses, that were formerly in good Repair, and cover'd with Slates, decay. 1758 J. S. *Le Dran's Obs. Surg.* (1771) 65 A Slate fell upon her Head from the Top of an House. 1811 FAREY *Derbyshire* I. 428 At Sheffield these white and grey Slates are exclusively used. 1841 JAMES *Brigand* xix, The house was built of cold grey stone, with a roof of slates. 1889 H. C. SEDDON *Builder's Work* (ed. 2) 231 Ordinary roofing slates are sold by the number...Some of the largest sized slates are..sold by the ton, and hence are called ton slates or weight slates.

b. A slab of slate, † or other stony substance; a laminated rock.

1601 HOLLAND *Pliny* XVII. viii. I. 506 It [the Columbine marl] will resolve and cleave into most thin slates or flakes. 1601 R. JOHNSON *Kingd. & Commw.* 27 The Irish Ocean, a sea so shallow, and so full of rocks and slates [etc.]. 1876 *Encycl. Brit.* IV. 500 He [the slater] supplies sawn slates for shelving in larders and dairies.

c. In phr. *To have a slate loose* or *off*, to be weak in intellect. (Cf. TILE *sb.*)

[1857 W. COLLINS *Dead Secret* III. i, The college tutor.. facetiously likened his head to a roof, and said there was a slate loosened in it.] 1860 *Slang Dict.* 218 He has a slate loose. 1862 *Athenæum* 27 Sept. 397 On too good terms with himself to think that..there is a 'loose slate', in his intellectual covering. 1867 MISS BROUGHTON *Cometh up as a Flower* xxxv, You must have a slate off this morning, Nell!

d. A flat piece or plate of some other material used for the same purpose as a roofing-slate.

1887 *Archit. Soc. Dict.* VII. 87 'Glass slates' in roofing to lofts are sometimes used to admit light. *Ibid.* 89 Slating with very strong zinc slates. 1893 SPON *Mechanic's Own Book* (ed. 4) 617 Shingles, or wooden slates, are made from hard wood.

2. A tablet of slate, usually framed in wood, used for writing on.

c 1391 CHAUCER *Astrol.* II. § 44 Consider thy rote furst,.. & entere hit in-to thy slate. *Ibid.* § 45 Take alle the signes, ..& wryte hem in þy slate. 1571 DIGGES *Pantom.* I. xxviii, Ye must search Angles of position agayne, and marke them in the table or slate. 1635–56 COWLEY *Davideis* I. Wks. 1710 I. 315 Letters..painfully engrav'd in thin wrought Plates, Some cut in Wood, some lightlier trac'd on Slates. 1698 FRYER *Acc. E. India & P.* 112 A Board plastered over, which with Cotton they wipe out, when full, as we do from Slates or Table-Books. 1752 FOOTE *Taste* I, I can't remember her name, but 'tis upon the slate. 1768 TUCKER *Lt. Nat.* II. I. iii. 39 We proceed in the same manner a person would who should undertake to draw any plan assigned him upon a slate. 1826 *Art Brewing* (ed. 2) 53 We will now work a brewing according to the example in the instructions, on a slate. 1874 JEVONS *Princ. Sci.* (1900) 96, I have used a slate of this kind, which I call a Logical Slate, for more than twelve years. *transf.* 1897 *Army & Navy Stores List* 750 Opal Slates in Leather Frame. *Ibid.* 757 Porcelain Menu Slate.

b. *fig.* A record of any kind concerning or against a person; esp. in phr. *a clean slate*.

1868 E. YATES *Rocks Ahead* II. ii, He had passed the wet sponge over the slate containing any records of his early life. 1888 *Pall Mall G.* 27 Sept. 9/1, I can conceive nothing more desirable in the interests of these embarrassed tenants than that they should have a clean slate.

c. *U.S.* (See quot. 1888.)

1877 *N. York Tribune* 1 Mar. (Farmer), The facts about the latest Cabinet slate..are interesting as showing..the course of President Hayes in choosing his advisers. 1884 *American* VIII. 232 In dictated nominations, in the making of 'slates' for obedient party acceptance. 1888 BRYCE *Amer. Commw.* III. lxiii. II. 457 Some leading man.. sketches out an allotment of places; and when this allotment has been worked out fully, it results in a Slate, *i.e.* a complete draft list of candidates to be proposed for the various offices.

3. Roofing-slates collectively, or the material from which these are made.

a. a 1340 HAMPOLE *Psalter* civ. 23 Þai..did treson [to the Israelites] forto less þaim in werke of mortere and sclate. 1392 *Mem. Ripon* (Surtees) III. 116 In sal. Simonis Sklater cooperantis et ponentis lapides de sklate. a 1513 FABYAN *Chron.* v. (1811) 113 He buylded a royall mynstre of lyme and stoone, and coueryd it with platis of syluer in stede of sclate or leade. 1571 *Mem. Ripon* (Surtees) I. 309 Ten lode of sclait.

β. 1530 PALSGR. 720/2, I slate a house, I cover it with slate. 1555 EDEN *Decades* (Arb.) 194 Many also [are covered] with slate or other stone. 1582 N. LICHEFIELD tr. *Castanheda's Conq. Ind.* I. xl. 94 A greate citie, consisting of houses made of Earth, and couered ouer with broade stone or slate. c 1630 RISDON *Surv. Devon* (1810) 8 Of late days quarries of slate are found out, wherewith they cover houses. 1667 PRIMATT *City & C. Builder* 72 A Penthouse..covered with Tyles, Lead or Slate. 1725 *Fam. Dict.* s.v. *Slating*, Roofs cover'd with Slate, must be first Boarded over. 1841 *Penny Cycl.* XXI. 181/2 Houses of respectable appearance, roofed with slate.

4. An argillaceous rock of sedimentary origin, the different varieties of which have the common property of splitting readily into thin plates.

Many varieties are distinguished, esp. in *Geol.*, by special terms, as *clay*, *hornblende*, *mica*, *talc slate*.

1653 COGAN tr. *Pinto's Trav.* (1663) 254 The extream trouble his people were at in planting their ladders against the walls by reason of their bad scituation which was all of Slate. 1676 *Phil. Trans.* XI. 764 There is also a sort of Mineral we call a Slate, which is partly Coal, partly Alum-stone, partly Marcasite, which being laid up in heaps and burnt, are used for hardening the Coal-ways. 1738 CHAMBERS *Cycl.* s.v., The same impressions are also frequently found on other substances, as on the black slate that lies over veins of coals. 1796 KIRWAN *Elem. Min.* (ed. 2) II. 19 This [slaty

alum] is the stone called Black Slate, celebrated among the vulgar for its medicinal properties. 1811 A. T. THOMSON *Lond. Disp.* (1818) 24 The ore is first calcined with a low heat, so as to destroy the bituminous matter of the slate. 1852 LYELL *Elem. Geol.* (ed. 4) 266 The slate of Stonesfield ..is a slightly oolitic shelly limestone. 1872 RAYMOND *Statist. Mines & Mining* 254 The quartz is divided by a horse of slate into two parts.

†**b.** *Irish slate*, alum-slate, formerly used medicinally in the form of powder. *Obs.*

a 1704 T. BROWN *Wks.* (1720) III. 99 You must give him Irish Slate *quantum sufficit*. 1741 *Compl. Family-Piece* I. i. 22 Take of Irish Slate, *Sperma Ceti*, of each half a Dram.

c. With *a* and pl. A kind or variety of slaty rock.

1704 *Dict. Rust.* (1726) s.v. Some Directions..whereby the ..lasting Goodness of any Slate may be Experimented. 1728 CHAMBERS *Cycl.* s.v., Besides the Blue Slate, we have in England a Greyish Slate, call'd also Horsham Stone. 1841 *Penny Cycl.* XXI. 171/2 Undulations on slates and sandstones of every geological age. 1860 TYNDALL *Glac.* II. App. 430 The cleavage of slates is therefore not a question of stratification. 1903 MARR *Agric. Geol.* 234 Mudstones which, owing to the subsequent impress of cleavage, usually occur as slates.

5. A bluish-grey colour like that of slate.

1882 SIR W. CROOKES *Dyeing & Tissue-Printing* 141 Light Slate. *Ibid.* 145 Slate on Cotton Wool. 1897 *Westm. Gaz.* 12 Nov. 1/3 Far to the south, where the slate of the sea and the grey of the sky wove together.

6. *attrib.* and *Comb.* **a.** Attrib. in the senses 'made or consisting of slate', 'having the character of slate', as *slate-band*, *-bed*, *-belt*, *-book*, etc., *slate-clay*, *-coal*, *-marl*, *-spar* (see quots.).

1810 S. SMITH *Agricultural Survey of Galloway* 20 *note*, The proper schistus,..called by English miners shiver, and in Galloway *slate-band. *Ibid.* 21 Strata of a soft shivering argillaceous stone, which..is called in the country slate-band. 1839 DE LA BECHE *Rep. Geol. Cornw.* vi. 183 The *slate-beds in the valley between Milton and Maristow. 1858 SIMMONDS *Dict. Trade* s.v., A billiard-table with a slate-bed. 1882 *U.S. Rep. Prec. Met.* 458 On the eastern or *slate belt great activity is manifested. Most of the mines are situated near the contact of the slate and the granite. 1858 SIMMONDS *Dict. Trade*, **Slate-book*, two or more slabs of framed slate bound together for writing on. 1804 R. JAMESON *Min.* I. 312 *Slate clay, shale. 1839 URE *Dict. Arts* 962 The strata of this section contain numerous varieties of..slate-clay. 1805 R. JAMESON *Min.* II. 72 *Slate-Coal...Colour intermediate between velvet-black and dark greyish-black. 1883 GRESLEY *Gloss. Coal-m.* 225 *Slate Coal*, a hard, dull variety of coal, not unlike Cannel. 1803 A. HUNTER *Georgical Ess.* I. 233 A drachm of a friable *slate-marl afforded a residuum of eighteen grains of yellow sand. 1805 R. W. DICKSON *Pract. Agric.* I. 238 Where this sort of marle has a thin laminated structure.., it is frequently denominated *slate marle*. 1796 KIRWAN *Elem. Min.* (ed. 2) I. 344 The aggregate of quartz and mica..is, when it is slaty, called *slate mica, or shistose mica, or slaty mica. 1793 W. H. MARSHALL *W. Eng.* (1796) II. 344 The *slate-rock waters of this District are superior to those of any others. 1813 COLERIDGE *Remorse* II. i, There where the smooth high wall of slate-rock glitters. 1860 TYNDALL *Glac.* II. App. 432 Fossil shells are found in these slate-rocks. 1578–9 *Reg. Privy Council Scot.* III. 99 [They] enterit in the said hous,..and thairefter tuke doun the *sklait ruife. 1875 KNIGHT *Dict. Mech.* 2200/1 The pitch of a slate roof should not be less than 1 in h[eight] to 4 of length. 1821 SCOTT *Kenilw.* xx, A devil's ally, that can change *slate-shivers into Spanish dollars. 1858 SIMMONDS *Dict. Trade*, **Slate slab*, a sheet or plate of slate. 1804 R. JAMESON *Min.* I. 508 *Slate Spar...Its colour is milk, greenish and reddish white. 1858 J. NICOL *Elem. Mineral.* 203 *Slate spar*, thin, lamellar,..with a shining white pearly lustre and greasy feel. 1877 RAYMOND *Statist. Mines & Mining* 65 The character and features of this *slate-stratum. 1855 J. R. LEIFCHILD *Cornwall* 81 The *slate-system [of rocks] has obtained its full share of such attention. 1531 *Lett. & Papers Hen. VIII* (1880) V. 183 Payment to John Cornelis of Handwarp, for..making of *slate tyle. 1778 *England's Gaz.* (ed. 2) s.v. *Padstow*, The trade in slate-tiles. 1867 MUSGRAVE *Nooks & Corners Old France* II. 6 A lofty domicile..exhibiting laths, timbering and *slatework.

b. Instrumental, as *slate-formed*, *-spired*, *-strewn*; *slate-thatcher*.

1648 HEXHAM II, *Een Schalie-decker*, a Slate-thatcher, or Coverer. 1789 J. WILLIAMS *Min. Kingd.* I. 235 The thin slate-formed argillaceous strata of the coal metals. 1862 H. MARRYAT *Year in Sweden* I. 238 Lecko Slott with her grand slate-spired towers. 1890 'R. BOLDREWOOD' *Miner's Right* xxv. (1899) 116, I had crossed more than one crest of the slate-strewn ranges.

c. Objective, as *slate-cutter*, *-maker*, *-picker*, etc.; *slate-cutting*, *-dressing*, etc.

(*a*) 1780 *Westm. Mag.* Suppl. 730/1 Slate-mak[er]. 1833–4 J. PHILLIPS *Geol.* in *Encycl. Metrop.* (1845) VI. 703/1 The slate-workers of Stonesfield. 1875 KNIGHT *Dict. Mech.* 2200/2 *Slate-cutter*, a machine for cutting the edges of roofing or other slates.
(*b*) 1839 URE *Dict. Arts* 329 The stone slag, or copper cinder, resulting from the slate-smelting. 1875 KNIGHT *Dict. Mech.* 2200/2 Slate-beveling, -cutting, -making, -trimming, Machine. 1894 *Daily News* 13 June 5/2 Collecting data as to the methods of slate-dressing.

d. With names of colours, as *slate-blue*, *-brown*, *-grey*. Also *attrib.*, of a slate colour.

(*a*) 1796 KIRWAN *Elem. Min.* (ed. 2) I. 152 Leek green, or slate blue. 1839 URE *Dict. Arts* 619 For several other shades as..slate-gray. 1871 KINGSLEY *At Last* vii, A slate-blue heron rose lazily off a dead bough. 1883 *Cent. Mag.* Sept. 729 Latticed porticoes, and slate-brown paint.
(*b*) 1872 COUES *N. Amer. Birds* 233 Tail..entirely black, or with only a slight slate tipping. 1889 SAUNDERS *Brit. Birds* 646 The adult in summer has a slate or greyish-black hood.

7. Misc. and special combs., as *slate-like* adj., *slate-merchant*, *-mine*, *-pit*, *-quarry*, etc.; **slate-axe** (see quots.); **slate-board**, **-boarding** (see quot. –1833); **slate club**, a sharing-out club, whose accounts are nominally kept on a slate; **slate-frame** (see quot.); **slate-galiot**, a vessel carrying slates; **slate house** *Sc.*, a house with a slated roof; †**slate-incense**, ? (cf. note to SLAT *sb.*1); **slate-knife**, a knife used for splitting slates; **slate-land** (see quot.); **slate-nail**, **-peg**, **-pin**, a nail, peg, or pin used to fix a slate on a roof; **slate-saw** (see quot.).

1828–32 WEBSTER, **Slate-ax*, a mattock..used in slating. 1858 SIMMONDS *Dict. Trade*, *Slate-axe*, a mattock for shaping slates for roofing, and making holes in them to fasten them to the roof. 1842 *Civil Eng. & Arch. Jrnl.* V. 242/2 The *slate-boards are supported by five purlins 4 ft. apart. 1833 LOUDON *Encycl. Archit.* Gloss., **Slate-boarding*, boards placed on the roof, on which to nail the slates. 1888 *Daily News* 27 Dec. 7/5 He would pay her in the evening, as he was in a *slate club. 1891 J. F. WILKINSON *Mutual Thrift* 60 Taking London, we have a large number of old dividing clubs located in the East End, and known as 'Birmingham societies' or 'Slate clubs'. 1858 SIMMONDS *Dict. Trade*, **Slate-frame*, the narrow wood border for a writing-slate or slate-book. 1887 DOWDEN *Shelley* I. v. 235 When at length they set sail in a *slate-galiot, a storm whirled them quite up to the north of Ireland. 1554 *Reg. Mag. Sig. Scot.* 198 De domo tegulata, vulgo ane *sklait hous. 1815 in *Pennecuik's Wks.* 243 *note*, A wild and solitary site for a slate house, yet proper for a hunting seat. 1470–1 *Mem. Ripon* (Surtees) III. 217 In incenso vocato *Sclate-incense empto ad deserviendum in choro festis duplicibus principalibus, nil hoc anno. 1484–5 *Ibid.* 222. 1825 J. NICHOLSON *Operat. Mechanic* 622 The instruments used in splitting and cleaning slates are, *slate-knives, axes, bars, and wedges. 1733 TULL *Horse-Hoeing Husb.* xiv. 196 (Dublin ed.), Poor *Slate Land [*note*, lying upon Slate or Stone]. 1898 *Pop. Sci. Monthly* 523 Impressions..have been left upon *slate-like rocks. 1858 SIMMONDS *Dict. Trade*, **Slate-merchant*, an importer or wholesale dealer in slates. 1648 HEXHAM II, *Een Schalie-myne*,..a *Slate-mine. 1880 A. M'KAY *Hist. Kilmarnock* (ed. 4) 300 He now, with the forefinger of his left hand, got hold of a *slate-nail. 1875 KNIGHT *Dict. Mech.* 2201/1 **Slate-peg*, a kind of nail used in securing slates on a roof. 1579 in Willis & Clark *Cambridge* (1886) I. 312 Lathe,..*slatepyne, and nayles. 1736 DRAKE *Eboracum* I. ii. 64 At the end of each tile is a hole that would receive a common slate pin. 1611 COTGR., *Ardoisiere*, a *slate-pit, *slate quarrey. 1829 SCOTT *Bl. Dwarf* Introd., He was the son of a labourer in the slate-quarries of Stobo. 1846 TENNYSON *Golden Year* 75, I heard them blast The steep slate-quarry. 1875 KNIGHT *Dict. Mech.* 2201/2 **Slate-saw*, a machine for trimming the edges of roofing-slabs to shape. 1858 SIMMONDS *Dict. Trade*, **Slate-works*, a yard, etc. where slate is sawn or shaped. 1860 TYNDALL *Glac.* I. I. 6, I.. visited *slate-yards and quarries.

†**Slate**, *sb.*2 *Cant. Obs.* (See quots.)

a. 1567 HARMAN *Caveat* (1869) 61 Some of these goe with slates at their backes, which is a sheete to lye in a nightes. *Ibid.* 76 Their mothers carries them at their backes in their slates, whiche is theirshetes. [Hence in later works; in the *Dict. Cant. Crew* (a 1700) given as *slat*.] 1622 FLETCHER *Beggar's Bush* III. iii, To Mill from the Ruffmans, commission and slates.

b. a 1700 B. E. *Dict. Cant. Crew*, *Slate*, a half Crown.

Slate (slēⁱt), *sb.*3 [f. SLATE *v.*3] A severe criticism; a slating.

1887 LANG *Books & Bookmen* 19 'Slate' is a professional term for a severe criticism. 1889 HANNAY *Marryat* 157 Carlyle's savage 'slate' of him [Marryat] is unjust.

Slate, *sb.*4 *Sc. rare.* [Of obscure origin.] A slovenly, dirty person.

1725 RAMSAY *Christ's Kirk Gr.* II. vi, Had aff [= hold off], quoth she, ye filthy slate. 1806 JOHN HOGG *Poems* 74 (Jam.), The blether-lipped drunken slate!

Slate (slēⁱt), *v.*1 Also 6 **sclate**, **slaytt**, 7 *Sc.* **skleat**. [f. SLATE *sb.*1]

1. *trans.* To cover or roof with slates.

1530 PALSGR. 706/1 It is better to sclate a house with stone than to tyle it. 1554 in Willis & Clark *Cambridge* (1886) II. 470 Covenauntted wyth Odam to slaytt the new Buylding. 1605 *Ibid.* 491 Thomas Yates to slate yᵉ Hall. 1624 CAPT. SMITH *Virginia* IV. 108 Houses..built..warme and defensiue..as if they were tiled and slated. 1637–50 ROW *Hist. Kirk* (Wodrow Soc.) 471 Walls were not repaired nor the roofe skleated till three yeares after. 1708 S. SEWALL *Diary* 23 Aug., I pleaded that Mr. Dudley had been at great Charge to Slate his House. 1833 LOUDON *Encycl. Archit.* § 947 The gables are to be slated over. 1883 *Law Times Rep.* XLIX. 138/2 The defendant..had on several occasions employed S. to slate houses for him.
absol. 1727 SWIFT *Vanbrugh's House* Wks. 1755 III. II. 64 A lyrick ode wou'd slate; a catch Wou'd tile; an epigram wou'd thatch.

2. To put down (a name, etc.) on a writing-slate; to set down, book, *for* something.

1883 *Daily News* 18 Sept. 6/2 He had been 'slated' for a month—that is, his name was entered upon a slate in the porter's lodge, which indicated that he was dangerously ill. 1896 *Harper's Mag.* XCIII. 25/1 So the Professor was unconsciously slated for the office of hero.

Slate (slēⁱt), *v.*2 *slang* and *colloq.* [app. f. SLATE *sb.*1 Sense 2 appears to have originated in Ireland.]

1. *trans.* (See quot. 1865.) ? *Obs.*

1825 C. WESTMACOTT *English Spy* II. 158 Another point of amusement is *flying a tile* or *slating* a man as the phrases of the Stock Exchange describe it. 1865 *Slang Dict.* 234 *Slate*, to knock the hat over one's eyes, to bonnet.

2. To beat or thrash severely.

1825 KNAPP & BALDW. *Newgate Cal.* IV. 149/1 Slate him, the Dublin word for an unmerciful beating. 1857 KINGSLEY *Two Y. Ago* III. 159 Putting his head in cautiously for fear of drunken Irishmen, who might be seized with the national impulse to 'slate' him.

b. *Mil.* To punish (an enemy) severely.

1854 CHAMPION in Kinglake *Crimea* (1877) V. 375 'Slate 'em, slate 'em, my boys!' was his exulting..adjuration. 1885 WILSON *From Korti to Khartum* (1886) 163 Now we shall get 'slated', I thought..; a few good shots might have picked off every one on deck. 1902 'LINESMAN' *Words Eyewitness* 107 Their smaller guns..kept it up far into the night, slating the reverse slopes of the Krantz with wonderful accuracy.
transf. 1883 *Harper's Mag.* Apr. 688/1 A billiard table in an overcrowded hotel, even with a railway rug around one, is apt to 'slate' the sleeper before morning.

3. To assail with reproof or abuse; to rate or reprimand; to scold severely.

1840 *Blackw. Mag.* XLVIII. 210, I weep over the realm's decay, and have some notion of *slating*—excuse me for borrowing a word from the vocabulary of the new ministerial and courtly party of Ribandism—Lord Palmerston. 1860 *Slang Dict.* 218 *Slate*, to pelt with abuse. 1866 BROGDEN *Prov. Lincs.*, *Slate*, to scold. 1881 MRS. LYNN LINTON *My Love* II. 306 Val slated me hard enough. So we may cry quits over that.

b. To criticize (a book or author) severely; to castigate, cut up.

1848 A. WATTS in *Life* (1884) II. 258 And, when they'd been by critics slated, Had always the review to show 'em. 1870 'OUIDA' *Puck* xvi, That wretched Mouse, when he wants to slate a very good novel. 1890 SAINTSBURY *Ess. Eng. Lit.* p. xxv, You slated this [book], and it has gone through twenty editions.

Slate (slēⁱt), *v.*3 *north.* and *Sc.* Also 4–5 **slayt**, 6–7 *Sc.* **slait**. [ad. ON. **sleita*, corresponding to OE. *slǣtan*: see SLEAT *v.*1]

1. *trans.* To incite or set on (a dog). Also const. *on*, *at*, *against* (a person, etc.).

13.. *Metrical Hom.* (Vernon MS.) in Herrig *Archiv* LVII. 266 Þei sayh beestes..and þei hem bayted Wiþ houndes þat þei on hem slayted. c 1375 *Sc. Leg. Saints* xxx. (*Theodora*) 657 Þat feynd..slaytyt þaim full fellonly, & bad þai suld þat hure wery. 1501 DOUGLAS *Pal. Hon.* I. xxii, Diane..him in forme hes of ane hart translatit. I saw (allace) his houndis at him slatit. a 1568 BALNEVIS in *Bannatyne MS.* 393 Thairfoir had bound thocht scho be found, Or dreid thy doggis be slaittit. 1787 GROSE *Prov. Gloss.* s.v., To slate the dog at any one. 1796 in Pegge *Derbicisms* (E.D.S.) 63. 1828 CARR *Craven Gloss.*, *Slate*, to set on, to incite. 1876 *Mid-Yorksh. Gloss.* 126 I'll slate my dog against thine.

2. To bait, assail, or drive, with dogs. Also *fig.* Hence **Sla·ting** *vbl. sb.*

13.. *K. Alis.* 200 (Laud MS.), Þer was..Of lyons chace, of bere baityng, A-bay of bore, of bole slatyng. 1684 *Yorkshire Dial.* (ed. 2) 43, I did Slate him back than with our Dog. *Ibid.* 106 *To slate a Beast*, is to hound a Dog at him. 1755 *Guthrie's Trial* 143 (Jam.), It is much to be lamented, that people professing his name, should be so slaited and enslaved by transgression as many are.

Sla·te-colour. [SLATE *sb.*1] The bluish-grey colour of slate.

1826 KIRBY & SP. *Entomol.* III. xxxii. 303 The abdomen of the male is usually slate-colour. 1835 *Ladies' Cabinet* Nov. 338 Fashionable colours,..slate-colour and myrtle green. 1889 SAUNDERS *Brit. Birds* 642 The mantle is slate-colour.

Sla·te-coloured, *a.* [SLATE *sb.*1 Cf. prec.] Of the colour of slate, usually bluish-grey.

1801 SHAW *Gen. Zool.* II. II. 319 Slate-coloured Antelope. 1811 *Ibid.* VIII. I. 261 Slate-coloured Creeper. 1812 A. WILSON *Amer. Ornith.* VI. 13 Slate-colored Hawk, *Falco Pennsylvanicus*. 1836–7 DICKENS *Sk. Boz* (1850) 135/2 Grandmamma in a high cap, and slate-coloured silk gown. 1871 DARWIN *Desc. Man* II. xvi. (1890) 481 Young swans are slate-coloured. 1874 COUES *Birds N. W.* 162 *Passerella Townsendii*,..Slate-colored Sparrow.

Slated (slēⁱ·tĕd), *ppl. a.*1 Also *Sc.* **sclated**, **sklaitit**. [f. SLATE *v.*1 + -ED 1.] Covered with slate or slates. Used *pred.* and *attrib.*

pred. 1611 COTGR., *Ardoisé*, slated, couered with slates. 1634 BRERETON *Trav.* (Chetham Soc.) 50 Here..a brave fish-market, the stalls curiously slated. 1719 DE FOE *Crusoe* II. (Globe) 411 His House was as dry as if it had been til'd or slated. 1806 *Gaz. Scotl.* 600 There were 72 houses, of which 35 were slated. 1834 *Brit. Husb.* (L.U.K.) I. 104 The house and buildings are brick, and slated.
attrib. 1798 HUTTON *Course Math.* II. 90 The content of a slated roof. 1843 THACKERAY *Irish Sk.-bk.* xi, A dismal, rickety building, with a slated face. 1886 RUSKIN *Præterita* I. v. 168 The houses..with high and steep slated roof.

Slated (slēⁱ·tĕd), *ppl. a.*2 [f. SLATE *v.*2] Reproved, scolded; severely criticized or attacked.

1872 E. PEACOCK *Mabel Heron* I. 80 Think how he went away like a slated dog—rated I should have said. 1897 *Daily News* 13 Jan. 6/4 One of the consolations of the 'slated' author. 1899 *Westm. Gaz.* 18 Apr. 2/3 The athletic friends of the 'slated' authoress.

Sla·teful. [f. SLATE *sb.*1 2.] As much or as many as can be written on a slate.

1836 E. HOWARD *R. Reefer* xxvi, A slatefull of..*x*, *y*, *z*'s. 1866 E. B. ELLIOTT *Mem. Ld. Haddo* xviii. (1868) 350 A slateful of names had been gone through.

Sla·te-pencil. [SLATE *sb.*1]

1. A pencil, made of soft slate or other material, used for writing on a slate.

1759 *Phil. Trans.* LI. 483 Some wear, at their nostrils, slate pencils, about four inches long. 1810 *Risdon's Surv. Devon* p. xv, A manufactory of slate pencils has of late been established. 1875 KNIGHT *Dict. Mech.* 2201/1 The common irregularly shaped black slate-pencils..are made in Germany.

2. The material of which slate-pencils are made.

1801 *Phil. Trans.* XCI. 436 Children..often introduce.. pieces of slate-pencil, and even pins into their ears. 1838 DICKENS *Nickleby* i, Putting out at good interest a small capital of slate-pencil and marbles.
attrib. and *Comb.* 1882 BRET HARTE *Flip* ii, A greyish slate-pencil pallor. 1894 *Proc. Geol. Assoc.* XIII. 364 Slate-pencil-coloured strings of clay.

Slater1 (slēⁱ·təɹ). Also 5, *Sc.* 7–9 **sclater**, 5 *Sc.* **sclatar(e**; 6, *Sc.* 9 **sklater**, 6 *Sc.* **sklaittar**, **skleattar**; 6 **slaiter**. [f. SLATE *sb.*1 or *v.*1]

1. One whose work consists in laying slates.

a. 1408 *Mem. Ripon* (Surtees) III. 137 In sal. Will. Fyscher sclater operantis et emendantis. 1488 *Acc. Ld. High Treas. Scot.* I. 89 To a sclatar for the poyntin of al the place off Stirling. 1561 *Dunfermline Reg.* (Bann. Cl.) 434 To ye sklaittar and his servandis. c 1600 *Chester Pl.*, *Banes* 92 You wrightes and sklaters, with good players in showe. 1808 JAMIESON Addit., *Sclater*. 1823 GALT *Entail* xlix, His sklater that pointed the skews o' the house.

β. 1562–3 *Act 5 Eliz.* c. 4. § xxiii, Tharte or Occupation of a ..Tyler, Slater, Healyer, Tilemaker. 1591 *Wills & Inv. N. C.* (Surtees, 1860) 200 Thre slaiters and a boye. 1663 GERBIER *Counsel* 50 When some of the slates are broke, the Slater mends them with little charge. 1723 *Lond. Gaz.* No. 6222/9 Thomas Hookam,..Slater and Plasterer. 1823 P. NICHOLSON *Pract. Builder* 399 All quarry slates require this preparation from the slater. 1893 EARL DUNMORE *Pamirs* I. 46 Silvery roofs..deftly fitted by some cunning slater.
attrib. 1813 J. THOMSON *Lect. Inflam.* 241 A slater boy, dwelling in the village of Hamegecourt. 1844 H. STEPHENS *Bk. Farm* I. 196 The slater-work is then executed.

2. A wood-louse. Chiefly *Sc.* and *north. dial.*

a. 1684 SIBBALD *Scot. Illustr.* II. III. vii. 33 *Millepes Asellus, nostratibus* the Sclater. 1824 MACTAGGART *Gallovid. Encycl.* 361 He is also fond of eating sclaters. c 1873 G. JOHNSTON in *Hist. Berwick. Nat. Club* (1876) VII. 32 'Sclaters' were crawling on the paved floor.

β. 1802 *Eng. Encycl.* V. 627/2 *Millepedæ*,..Wood-lice, hog-lice, or slaters. 1873 DAWSON *Earth & Man* iii. 44 Modern slaters or wood-lice, which are not very distant relatives of these old crustaceans. 1876 SMILES *Sc. Nat.* vi. 97 Hosts of night-wandering insects,..slaters, centipedes and snails.

†**Sla·ter**2. *Obs.*⁻¹ [f. SLATE *v.*3] (See quot.)

1774 GOLDSM. *Nat. Hist.* IV. ii. (1862) I. 394 There are two varieties of this kind [the land-spaniel]; namely the slater, used in hawking to spring the game; and the setter, that crouches down when it scents the birds, till the net be drawn over them.

Sla·te-stone. Also 4, *Sc.* 8–9 **sklate**, 5 **sklaytt**, **sclathe**, 6–7 (9 *Sc.*) **sclate**. [SLATE *sb.*1]

1. A single piece of slate, or of thin stone serving the same purpose.

c 1440 *Alph. Tales* 307 He tuke þe knyght be þe nekk & threw hym oute þurgh þe thakk of þe howse..& his bowels fleuyd on þe sclathe stonys. 1493 *Mem. Ripon* (Surtees) III. 164 Pro xxiiij sklaytt stonys pro prædictis cameris. 1530 PALSGR. 271/1 Slate stone, *ardoyse*. 1610 HOLLAND *Camden's Brit.* 514 The neighbour inhabitants use to digge great plenty of sclate stones for their buildings. a 1618 RALEIGH *Invent. Shipping* 7 All that have Corne beate it in Morters, and make Cakes, baking them upon Slatestones. 1720 RAMSAY *Rise & Fall of Stocks* 156 'Tis a' sklate-stanes instead of money. 1778 W. PRYCE *Min. Cornub.* 74 The famous Delabole Slate-stones. 1818 SCOTT *Hrt. Midl.* viii, Then folk might see men deliver up their silver to the state's use, as if it had been as muckle sclate stanes. 1842 BORROW *Bible in Spain* xxiv, The huts were built of slate stones.

2. Stone of the nature of slate.

1392 *Mem. Ripon* (Surtees) III. 116 Pro coopertura cujusdam domus..cum sklatestane. 1748 J. HILL *Hist. Fossils* 446 Blueish glittering slate Stone. 1764 *Phil. Trans.* LIV. 51 In the slate-stone, they are generally crushed. 1796 W. H. MARSHALL *Econ. W. Eng.* II. 320 The material of building being a coarse schistus, or slate stone. 1871 TYNDALL *Fragm. Sci.* (1879) I. xii. 360 These flags are employed for roofing purposes..and receive the name of 'slatestone'.
attrib. 1796 W. H. MARSHALL *Econ. W. Eng.* II. 65 The materials of these hills appear to be chiefly rotten slate, or rusty slate-stone rubble.

Slather (slæ·ðəɹ), *v.* Chiefly *dial.* [Of obscure origin.] *intr.* To slip or slide; to move in a sliding or trailing manner.

1818 WILBRAHAM *Chesh. Gloss.*, *Slather*,..to slip or slide. 1890 *Glouc. Gloss.* s.v., The plank slathered away. 1909 KIPLING *Actions & Reactions* 115, I hate slathering through stuff.

Slath sword: see SLAUGH-SWORD.

Sla·tiness. *rare*⁻⁰. [f. SLATY *a.*] 'The quality of being slaty; slaty character.'

1882 in *Imperial Dict.* (Annandale).

Slating (slēⁱ·tiŋ), *vbl. sb.*1 [f. SLATE *v.*1]

1. The fixing of slates (on a roof or elsewhere); the business of fixing slates.

1579 in Willis & Clark *Cambridge* (1886) I. 312 They..shall perfectlye and workmanlye finishe the slateinge off the yd rouffe. 1583 *Shuttleworths' Acc.* (Chetham Soc.) 18 Wylliam Broune for slatynge seven dayes ijˢ iiijᵈ. 1663 GERBIER *Counsel* 63 Slating with blew Slates the workmen finding all, will cost seven pence per foot. 1825 J. NICHOLSON *Operat. Mechanic* 626 Slating is performed in several other ways. 1889 H. C. SEDDON *Builder's Work* (ed. 2) 231 The slating of roofs is paid for by the square of 100 feet super.
attrib. 1572–3 in Willis & Clark *Cambridge* (1886) II. 120 hundreth sclaiting latthes. 1863 SMILES *Indust. Biogr.* 297 As the slating trade did not keep him in regular employment.

2. *collect.* The slates covering a roof.

1816 J. SCOTT *Vis. Paris* (ed. 5) 24 The ancient slating reposes in venerable grey amongst moss and grass. 1838 Col. Hawker *Diary* (1893) II. 142 The shot rattled on the slating of my house. 1867 MUSGRAVE *Nooks & Corners Old France* II. 6 The slating here and there imitating scales.

3. The action of covering with a composition imitating slate; a kind of wash for blackboards.

1884 KNIGHT *Dict. Mech.* Suppl. 822/1 Black-board Slating may be accomplished with the following mixture. 1885 SPON *Mechanic's Own Book* 435 Black-board wash, or 'liquid slating'. *Ibid.*, To apply the slating, have the surface smooth.

Slating (slēⁱ·tiŋ), *vbl. sb.*2 [f. SLATE *v.*2]

1. A severe punishment; a beating.

1872 *Echo* 4 Sept., The Kilkenny Militia..really did..get a fearful slating to-day.

2. A severe reprimand or scolding.

1881 MRS. LYNN LINTON *My Love* II. 307 After that first 'slating', as the vulgar little creature called it, Valentine said no more. 1894 *Tablet* 24 Aug. 304, I hear the good nuns got a bit of a 'slating' from the Chaplain as a reward for their anxiety.

3. A severe criticism or literary castigation.

1870 'OUIDA' *Puck* xix, Extinguished by means of journalistic slating. 1890 *Literary World* 22 Aug. 143 It must be admitted that the slating was well deserved.

†**Slating**, *vbl. sb.*3 *Obs.*⁻⁰ [f. OF. *esclater*: see F. *éclater* (sense 7) in Littré.] (See quot.)

1688 HOLME *Armoury* III. 91/1 Slat-ing of Inamell, is taking Inamell off a Ring, and Inamelling it with another colour.

Slating (slēⁱ·tiŋ), *ppl. a.* [f. SLATE *v.*2] Severely critical or condemnatory.

1885 *Longm. Mag.* V. 499 A 'slating' article was in type for publication. 1900 *Daily News* 7 Dec. 7/1 A question whether 'booing' was more damaging than a 'slating' notice.

Slatish (slēⁱ·tiʃ), *a.* [f. SLATE *sb.*1 + -ISH.] Somewhat resembling the colour of slate.

1860 WRAXALL *Life in Sea* i. 11 The colour of the back is slatish grey with white spots. 1884 *Chambers's Jrnl.* Nov. 703/2 The musk-rat is..of a slatish-blue colour. 1887 CLARK RUSSELL *Frozen Pirate* I. ix. 134 The clouds..had taken a slatish tinge.

†**Sla·t-stone.** *Obs.* Also 4 **skalt-**, 6 **slatte-**. [f. SLAT *sb.*1] = SLATE-STONE.

1391 *Mem. Ripon* (Surtees) III. 108 In cc skaltstanes [*sic*] emp. pro emendacione j cameræ. c 1440 *Promp. Parv.* 458/1 Slat stone,..*ymbrex*. 1516 in *Wilts. N. & Q.* July (1905) 90 Too lodes of slattestone fro the Quarre of Cotteswolde. 1648 B. PLANTAGENET *Descr. New Albion* 6 Building and Slatstone. 1669 STURMY *Mariner's Mag.* v. xii. 46 In a Morter covered with a Slat-stone.

Slatter, *sb.* Also 4–5 **sclatter**, 5–6 **sklatter**, 6 **sklattar**. [f. SLAT *sb.*1 or *v.*1]

1. = SLATER1 1. Now *dial.*

1379 in *Yorks. Archæol. Jrnl.* V. 43 Henricus Sclatter & vxor, Sclatter, vjᵈ. c 1400 *Laud Troy Bk.* 1793 Sklatteres, Masons, and Carpenter, And other Men of alle mister. 1444 *Act 23 Hen. VI*, c. 12, Les gages ascun..maistre Tiler ou Sclatter. 1539 in W. H. Turner *Select. Rec. Oxford* (1880) 160 William Bybe, sklatter. Waltar Cuddesdon, sklattar. 1621 BURTON *Anat. Mel.* III. ii. VI. v. (1651) 575 As slatters sort their slattes, do they degrees and families. 1669 *Phil. Trans.* IV. 1009 The Sects (the hewing instrument of the Slatters). 1881 *Leic. Gloss.*, *Slatter*, one who 'slats' generally, but more particularly a slater.

†**2.** A wood-louse. = SLATER1 2.

1739 DR. CLARKE in Graham *Soc. Life Scotl. in 18th c.* (1899) I. i. 50 Give him twice a day the juice of twenty slatters squeezed through a muslin bag.

†**Sla·tter**, *v.*1 In 5 **slat(e)re**. [Cf. SLAT *v.*3]

1. *trans.* To slash or slit (clothes).

a 1400 *Hymns Virgin* (1867) 62 Slatre þi clothis boþe schorte & side. 1480 CAXTON *Cron. Eng.* ccxxvi. 233 Short clothes and streyte..on euery syde slatered [*Brut* 297 desslatered] and botened with sleues and tapytes of surcotes.

2. To split, to shiver.

c 1400 *Turnament Tottenham* 159 Ther were flaykes al to slatred [*v.r.* flatred],..Bollys and dysches al to schatred.

Slatter (slæ·təɹ), *v.*2 [Imitative: cf. SLAT *v.*2 4.] *intr.* To clatter. Also **Sla·ttering** *vbl. sb.*

1661 K. W. *Conf. Charac.* (1860) 20 The slattering of a cadent brickbat. 1830 *Blackw. Mag.* XXVII. 588 At first a low muttering is heard,..then a sort of sliding slattering noise, and finally a reverberating thundering crash. 1870 *Daily News* 1 Oct., The Prince might ride by with his escort slattering over the paved street.

Sla·ttering, *ppl. a. rare.* [f. the dialect verb *slatter* to spill or splash awkwardly, to slop, to waste, etc., of obscure origin.] Careless, slovenly.

1674 RAY *N. C. Words*, *A Dawgos* or *Dawkin*, a dirty, slattering woman. a 1677 BARROW *Serm.* I. vii. 79 All persons who would not lead a loose and slattering life, but design..to prosecute an orderly course of action. 1889 in *N. W. Linc. Gloss.* (ed. 2).

Slattern (slæ·təɹn), *sb.* and *a.* Also 7 **slaterne**, 7–8 **slatern**. [Related to prec.]

A. *sb.* A woman or girl untidy and slovenly in person, habits, or surroundings; a slut. (See also quot. 1639.)

1639 J. SMYTH in *Glouc. Gloss.* (1890) 199 A slaterne, i. e. a rude ill bred woman. a 1668 DAVENANT *Play-Ho. to be Let* Wks. (1673) 118 Good Housewife in House, not sauntering young slatern. 1669 DRYDEN *Royal Martyr* Epil., Here Nelly lies, who, though she liv'd a Slattern, Yet dy'd a Princess, acting in St. Cathar'n. 1710 ADDISON *Tatler* No. 243 ¶ 3 That Species of Women which we call a Slattern. 1766 FORDYCE *Serm. Yng. Women* (1767) I. ii. 76 Butterflies one day, and slatterns the next. 1845 MRS. NORTON *Child of Islands* (1846) 110 His wife a shrew and slattern. 1883 S. C. HALL *Retrospect* II. 314 The young girls were tawdry slatterns.

b. Applied to a man. *rare*⁻¹.

1849 THACKERAY *Pendennis* v, He was now..as great a dandy as he before had been a slattern.

B. *adj.* Slovenly, untidy, slatternly. Said of appearance, etc., or of persons.

(*a*) 1716 GAY *Trivia* III. 270 Beneath the Lamp her tawdry Ribbons glare, The new-scower'd Manteau, and the slattern Air. 1784 J. BARRY *Lect. Art* vi. (1848) 208 Works formed out of trite, vulgar, slattern matter. 1822 W. IRVING *Braceb. Hall* xvii. 146, I could not but admire a certain degree of slattern elegance about the baggage. 1861 D. COOK *Paul Foster's Daughter* ii, At the best his room has a slattern air.
(*b*) 1824 W. IRVING *T. Trav.* I. 340, I recognised..in his slattern spouse, the once trim and dimpling columbine. 1846 J. BAXTER *Libr. Pract. Agric.* (ed. 4) II. p. xlix, He plods his way to a fireless hut, where a slattern wife and ragged children receive him.
transf. 1896 *Westm. Gaz.* 16 Dec. 4/3 The slipshod writer and the slattern thinker.

Slattern (slæ·təɹn), *v.* [f. prec.]

1. *trans.* To fritter or throw *away* (time, opportunity, etc.) by carelessness or slovenliness.

1747 CHESTERF. *Lett.* (1774) I. ci. 242 Every fool, who slatterns away his whole time in nothings. 1755 — in *World* No. 148, I have known many a passion..(if I may use the expression) wholly slatterned away, by an unguarded and illiberal familiarity. 1785 *Town & Co. Mag.* Nov. 594 This class..frequently slattern away a reputation for the sake of idolatry. 1878 *N. Amer. Rev.* CXXVII. 103 The mournful folly with which they slatterned away the noblest opportunity.

2. To work *over* in a slovenly manner.

1807 E. S. BARRETT *Rising Sun* II. 4 Many of our great men in office..generally slattern over what they are obliged to do, by proxy.

3. *intr.* To play the slattern.

1856 MASSON *Ess.* vi. 246 [They] and the niece are slatterning about the house.

Sla·tternish, *a.* [f. SLATTERN *a.* + -ISH.] Somewhat slatternly.

1833 LYTTON *Godolphin* 10 Then, came a gentleman's wife, a pretty, slatternish woman, much painted.

Sla·tternliness. [f. next + -NESS.] The quality or fact of being slatternly.

1811 MISS L. M. HAWKINS *C'tess & Gertrude* II. 172 She ..was shocked to see the effect of domestic slatternliness. 1847 L. HUNT *Men, Women, & B.* I. vii. 126 Evidences that the esteem of a life is preferred to the slatternliness of the moment. 1869 TROLLOPE *He Knew* xlviii, [She] put down the deficiency to the charge of domestic slatternliness.

Slatternly (slæ·təɹnli), *a.* [f. SLATTERN *sb.*]

1. Of persons: Having the condition or habits of a slattern; slovenly; untidy.

c 1680 COTTON *Ep. to Sir C. Clifton* 49 One that had since bin ber Maid;..a slatternly ill-favour'd toad. 1753–4 RICHARDSON *Sir C. Grandison* (1781) VI. vi. 21 She...looked so shy! so silly! so slatternly! 1847 C. BRONTË *J. Eyre* vi, I am..slatternly; I seldom put, and never keep things in order; I am careless. 1865 E. C. CLAYTON *Cruel Fortune* I. 143 The tatterdemalion, slatternly, slipshod women who lounge..against the door-posts.
Comb. 1847 H. MELVILLE *Omoo* i, She turned out to be a small, slatternly-looking craft.

b. *transf.* Of artists or authors in respect of their work.

1762–71 H. WALPOLE *Vertue's Anecd. Paint.* (1786) IV. 70 The time he wasted on his works, in which at least he was the reverse of his slatternly cotemporaries. 1822 SCOTT *Let.* in *Lockhart* (1837) III. i. 21 When you have twenty things to tell, it is better to be slatternly than tedious.

2. Of appearance, etc.: Appropriate to, characteristic of, a slattern.

1776 MME. D'ARBLAY *Early Diary* 5 Apr., We saw the young and handsome Duchess..walking in such an undressed and slaternly manner. 1801 MAR. EDGEWORTH *Angelina* iv, The slatternly, dirty appearance of Araminta's dress. a 1853 ROBERTSON *Lect.* i. (1858) 33 A home made wretched by a wife's slatternly conduct. 1877 A. B. EDWARDS *Up Nile* xxii. 702 The rooms were untidy; the general aspect of the place was slatternly and neglected.

Slatternly (slæ·təɹnli), *adv.* [f. SLATTERN *a.* + -LY 2.] In a slovenly way.

1750 CHESTERF. *Lett.* (1792) III. ccxxxiv. 68 A fine suit, ill-made and slatternly or stifly worn,..only exposes the aukwardness of the wearer. 1841 TUPPER *Twins* iii, [She] lay slatternly abed, to nurse a head-ache till noon.

Slatternness (slæ·təɹn,nĕs). Also **slatterness**. [f. SLATTERN *a.* + -NESS.] Slatternliness.

1745 ELIZA HEYWOOD *Female Spect.* No. 16 (1748) III. 166 To give the artful stepmother an opportunity of accusing her of ill housewifry and slatterness. 1886 *New York Herald* IX. 196 You cannot expect neatness and order in any house where the daughters see nothing but slatterness.

†**Sla·tter-pouch.** Also **slatter de pouch**. *Obs. rare.* Some kind of dance or game.

c 1600 *Grobiana's Nuptialls* I. iii. (MS. Bodl. 30), Noe daunceinge unlesse it be the old slatter de pouch or yᵉ beares masque. 1654 GAYTON *Fest. Notes* III. iv. 86 Much did they suffer, but what did they? much When they were boyes at Trap, or slatter-pouch; They'd sweat untill they stank.

Sla·ttery, *a.* *rare*⁻¹. [Cf. SLATTER *v.*1] Of a brittle or shivery character.

1829 GLOVER *Hist. Derby* I. 58 This last mentioned coal is slattery and often sulphureous.

Sla·tting, *vbl. sb.* *rare.* Also 6 **sclattynge**. [f. SLAT *v.*1] = SLATING *vbl. sb.*1

1532 in W. H. Turner *Select. Rec. Oxford* (1880) 109 Excepte sclattynge and tymber owerhedde. 1583 in Hutton *St. John's Coll.* (1898) 62 Item for slatting of yᵉ lofer. 1757 *Phil. Trans.* L. 504 The slatting of the house cracked.

†**Sla·tty**, *a.* *Obs.* [f. SLAT *sb.*1 + -Y.] Slaty.

1661 J. CHILDREY *Brit. Baconica* 74 In a Clayie and slatty Countrey. 1686 PLOT *Staffordsh.* 120 They have harder, stony, slatty sorts of Marles. 1758 BORLASE *Nat. Hist. Cornw.* 59 The black and gritty, the shelfy slatty Soil, and the stiff reddish Soil.

Slaty (slēⁱ·ti), *a.* Also 7 **slatie**, 8 **slatey**. [f. SLATE *sb.*1 + -Y.]

1. Composed of slate; resembling slate; having the nature or properties of slate. Also of land: Lying upon slate (quot. 1733).

In the earliest quots. the sense is perhaps 'stony, rocky'.

a 1529 SKELTON *E. Rummyng* 258 Some go streyght thyder, Be it slaty or slyder; They holde the hye waye [etc.]. 1538 LELAND *Itin.* (1768) I. 62 An exceding..strong Castelle on a stepe Rok, having but one way by the stepe slaty crag to cum to it. 1611 COTGR., *Ardoisin*,..slatie, or, of slate. 1670 W. SIMPSON *Hydrol. Ess.* 65 Blew slate.. and other slaty stone mixed therewith. 1708 J. C. *Compl. Collier* (1845) 19 [The stone-coal] is subject to be a little Slaty. 1733 TULL *Horse-Hoeing Husb.* xiv. 199 These Estates consisted of Thin Slatey Land. 1796 KIRWAN *Elem. Min.* (ed. 2) II. 153 Slaty Copper ore, or Cupriferous Marlite. 1820 KEATS *Hyperion* II. 16 Hard flint they sat upon, Couches of rugged stone, and slaty ridge. 1865 J. T. F. TURNER *Slate Quarries* 5 From Newquay to above Boscastle the rocks..are of a slaty character.

2. Characteristic or typical of slate.

1796 KIRWAN *Elem. Min.* (ed. 2) I. 83 Of a slaty fracture. 1837 WHEWELL *Hist. Induct. Sci.* (1857) III. 445 The slaty cleavage never coincides with the direction of the strata. 1854 RONALDS & RICHARDSON *Chem. Techn.* (ed. 2) I. 45 The principal fracture is straight, slaty.

3. Slate-coloured.

1822–7 GOOD *Study Med.* (1829) II. 176 The slaty or purplish and granular saburra thrown up from the stomach. 1868 G. MACDONALD *Seaboard Parish* II. v. 77 The sun had disappeared under a cloud, and the sea had turned a little slaty. 1893 LYDEKKER *Horns & Hoofs* 202 A slaty patch extending from the shoulder and hip to the legs.

b. *Slaty Gum*: (see quots.).

1889 MAIDEN *Useful Pl.* 470 *Eucalyptus largiflorens*... Also called 'Slaty Gum', from the grey and white patches on the bark. *Ibid.* 524 *Eucalyptus tereticornis*...Called.. 'Slaty Gum' in New South Wales and Queensland.

4. Smacking of slate.

1824 HENDERSON *Anc. & Mod. Wines* 226 The better sorts [of Moselle wines]..sometimes contract a slaty taste from the strata on which they grow.

5. *Comb.* **a.** With names of colours, as *slaty-black*, *-blue*, *-green*, *-grey*.

1818 SCOTT *Rob Roy* xxx, A broken track along the precipitous face of a slaty grey rock. 1826 STEPHENS in Shaw *Gen. Zool.* XIII. II. 164 Slaty-black Graucalus with the head and neck..black. 1859 DARWIN *Orig. Species* i. (1860) 25 The rock-pigeon is of a slaty-blue, with white loins. 1874 T. HARDY *Far fr. Mad. Crowd* v, A coat.. approximating in colour to white and slaty grey.

b. Misc., as *slaty-headed*, *-like*, *-looking*, etc.

a 1866 R. DICK in Smiles *Life* (1878) 91 The cliffs—now yellowish, then reddish—now thin and slaty-like. 1876 *Nature* XIV. 580/1 A Slaty-headed Parrakeet. 1882 *Cent. Mag.* XXV. 241 Gray, slaty-looking little towns.

Slauchter, **-ir**, obs. Sc. forms of SLAUGHTER.

Slaue, obs. form of SLAVE *sb.* and *v.*

Slauen, **-eyn**, variants of SLAVIN *Obs.*

†**Slaugh**, obs. variant of SLAWK.

1743 BULKELEY & CUMMINS *Voy. S. Seas* 44 Most Part of our People eat a Weed that grows on the Rocks; it is a thin Weed of a dark green Colour, and called by the Seamen, *Slaugh*. *Ibid.* 62 Eat Slaugh and Sea-weed fry'd with Tallow-Candles.

†**Slaughmess.** *Obs.*⁻¹ [ad. older Flem. *slachmes*, f. *slach* (*slag*) blow, stroke + *mes* knife: cf. next.] A large knife used as a weapon; a dagger.

a 1548 HALL *Chron.*, *Hen. V*, 47 b, The fierce Brabanders and strong Almaines with long pykes and cuttyng slaughmesses.

†**Slaugh-sword.** *Obs.* Also 6 **slawght-**, **slath-**, 7 **slaug-**. [ad. older Flem. *slachsweerd* (Du. *slagzwaard*; Da. *slagsværd*, Sw. *-svärd*), or G. *schlachtschwert*.] A large two-handed sword.

a 1548 HALL *Chron.*, *Hen. VIII*, 235 b, Euery man hauing a iauelyn or slaughsword to keepe the people in aray. a 1575 tr. *Pol. Verg. Eng. Hist.* (Camden, No. 36) 11 A broode slawght swerde, and a dager sharpe onelie on the one side. 1590 SIR J. SMYTH *Disc. Weapons* 6 b, A fewe slath swords for the gard of their Ensignes. 1614 GORGES *Lucan* VI. 226 Those rough Tewtons..That vse long slaug-swords [*printed* slang-] in their mart.

†**Slaught**, *sb.* *Obs.* Forms: 3 **slaht**, 3–4 **slaȝt** (4 **slaȝte**, **slaȝþe**, **sclaȝt**), 4–5 **slaght** (5 -**te**, **slagh**); 4 **slawȝt**, **slawhte**, 5 **slawþe**, 6 **slawght**; 4 **slauht**, 5 **slauȝt**, 4–5 **slauȝte** (4 -**tte**), 4–7 **slaughte**. [Early ME. *slaht*, *slaȝt*, app. repr. OE. **sleaht* (cf. gen. pl. *wælsleahta*), var. of *slæht*, *sleht*, *sliht*, etc.: see SLEIGHT *sb.*2 The unmutated vowel corresponds to that of OFris. *slachte* (Fris. *slacht*), MDu. and Du. *slacht*, OS. *-slahta*, OHG. *slaht* (G. *schlacht*) and *slahta* (MHG. *slahte*), ON. and Icel. *slátr* masc. and *slátta* fem.]

1. Slaying; slaughter.

c 1205 LAY. 4263 Alken farinde mon, ȝef slaht oþer hæfde beoðe idon [etc.]. a 1225 *Leg. Kath.* 198 Þe keiser stod bimong þat sunful slaht. 13.. *E. E. Allit. P.* A. 801 As a schep to þe slaȝt þer lad was he. 1390 GOWER *Conf.* I. 362 Be wel avised..Of slawhte er that thou be coupable. 1422 tr. *Secreta Secret.*, *Priv. Priv.* 142 Yf the slaght be vnryghtfull, god shal answere, 'Who-So sleyth, he shal be slayne'. 1469 in 10*th Rep. Hist. MSS. Comm.* App. V. 307 All suche slaghts and kyllyng done in defennce. a 1586 SIDNEY *Arcadia* (1622) 298 Where shee had made a scaffold,..and there caused them to be kept, as ready for the slaughte. 1610 HEALEY *St. Aug. Citie of God* II. xi, Bad [spirits] are delighted with slaughtes and tragicall invocations.

2. *fig.* A stroke (of sorrow), spell (of sleep). *rare.*

13.. *E. E. Allit. P.* A. 59, I slode vpon a slepyng slaȝte. *Ibid.* C. 192 [They] Arayned hym..what raysoun he hade In such slaȝtes of sorȝe to slepe so faste.

3. A flash (of lightning). Cf. FIRE-SLAUGHT.

a 1300 *Cursor M.* 17372 His cher lik was slaght o fire. *Ibid.* 22680 All þe stanes..Sal smitt togedir wit sli maght Als thoner dos wit firen slaght.

†**Slaught**, *v.* *Obs. rare.* [f. prec., or ad. Du. (and LG.) *slachten* or G. *schlachten*.] *trans.* To kill, slaughter. Hence †**Slau·ghting** *vbl. sb.*

1535 COVERDALE *Prov.* ix. 2 Wysdome..hath slaughted, ..and prepared hir table. — *Jer.* xii. 3 Take them awaye, ..and apoynte them for the daye off slaughtinge. 1647 HEXHAM I. s.v., The time of slaughting beasts, *den slagh-tijdt*.

‖**Slaught-boom.** *Obs.* In 7 **slaught bome**, **slaght-boome**. [ad. Du. or LG. *slagboom* (hence Da. and Sw. *slagbom*), = G. *schlagbaum*, f. *slagen* to strike, fall, and *boom* beam, tree.] A beam used as a barrier.

1637 MONRO *Exped.* 7 The Castell..with Moates, Drawbridges, and slaught bomes without all. 1642 *Relat. Action before Cirencester* 4 Each end of the high street..was secured against Horse with strong slaght-boomes which our men call Turne-pikes.

Slaughter (slǭ·təɹ), *sb.* Forms: **a.** 4 **slahter**, **-tir**, 4–5 **slaȝter** (4 -**tter**), **slaghter** (5 -**tre**, **-tur**); 4 **slauh-**, **slauȝter**, 5– **slaughter** (5 **slawghtir**, 6 -**ter**); 4 **sclawtur**, **sclauter**, 6 **sklaut(t)er**; 5 **slawter**, **-tyr**, **slauther**, 6 **slauter**. **β.** *Sc.* 5–6 **slachtir** (5 -**tyr**, -**ter**), **slawchtir** (5 -**tyr**, 6 -**ter**), **slauchtir** (5 -**tyr**), 5–7 **slauchter** (6 -**tre**). [**a.** early ON. **slahtr* neut. (ON. and Icel. *slátr* butcher-meat, Norw. dial. *slaater* cattle for killing), f. the stem **slah-*: see SLAY *v.*1]

1. The killing of cattle, sheep, or other animals for food. (See also 4.)

a 1300 *E. E. Psalter* xliii. 24 Als schepe of slaghter wend er we. 1398 TREVISA *Barth. De P. R.* XVIII. i. (1495) 741 Fysshe fleeth..the place of wasshyng and of slaughter of other fysshe. c 1440 *Promp. Parv.* 458/2 Slawtyr, of beestys, *mactacio*. 1487 *Act 4 Hen. VII*, c. 3 The Slaughter of Beasts..had and done in the Butchery. 1697 DRYDEN *Virg. Georg.* IV. 794 From his Herd he culls, For Slaughter, four the fairest of his Bulls. a 1704 T. BROWN *Dial. Dead* Wks. 1711 IV. 77 A Son of Slaughter at White-Chapel converted to the observation of Fish-days. 1868 *Standard* 15 Dec. 6 The laws..that have traditionally been handed down with respect to the slaughter of cattle.

b. The skins of killed beasts. *rare*⁻¹.

1789 BRAND *Hist. Newcastle* II. 317 The ordinary of the tanners..enjoined..That each brother should have but one butcher to buy slaughter of.

2. The killing or slaying of a person; murder, homicide, esp. of a brutal kind.

a. a 1300 *Cursor M.* 6752 If þe son be risen þan, It sal be slaghter telld o man. c 1325 *Metr. Hom.* 38, I wille you telle Hou it of his slahter felle. c 1422 HOCCLEVE *Jereslaus's Wife* 882 No wight but shee Mighte of this slaghtre and murdre gilty be. c 1450 *Mirour Saluacioun* (Roxb.) 4 Dauid after the slaghter of Golie. 1587 *Mirr. Mag.*, *Porrex* vii, I procur'd hir wrath by slaughter of hir sonne. 1592 *Arden of Feversham* II. ii, The villaine hath sworne the slaughter of his maister. 1652 BURROUGHES *Exp. Hosea* vii. 142 It is a fruit, I say, of the slaughter of Christ and of his blood. a 1722 SIR J. LAUDER *Decis.* (1759) I. 13 Our law concludes all it finds with cold steel..guilty of the slaughter. 1820 SCOTT *Monast.* xxvii, He felt..indignant at the supposed slaughter of young Glendinning. 1825 — *Betrothed* xxxi, So singular were the tidings of the Constable's slaughter.

β. c 1375 *Sc. Leg. Saints* ii. (*Paulus*) 457 And þai..throw browthir slawchtir can þe file. c 1470 HENRY *Wallace* VI. 215 The saklace slauchter off hir. 1570 BUCHANAN *Admonit.* Wks. (S. T. S.) 23 Sum of þame ar counsalouris of þe kingis slauchter. 1596 DALRYMPLE tr. *Leslie's Hist. Scot.* I. 288 Throw counsell of his wyf he inuented the kings slauchtre.

3. The killing of large numbers of persons in war, battle, etc.; massacre, carnage.

a. 1338 R. BRUNNE *Chron.* (1810) 91 Sen þis greuance hard, þe slauhter & þe drede,..sone afterward þe kyng to ȝork ȝede. 1387 TREVISA *Higden* (Rolls) V. 307 Þat ȝere was þe grete slauȝter of Saxons. 1420–22 LYDG. *Thebes* III. (MS. Laud 557), He made of hem..So grete slaughter and occisioun, That as þe deth fro his swerd þey fled. c 1489 CAXTON *Blanchardyn* xxiv. 92 The grete damage and grete slawghtir that he had don of his folke. a 1533 LD. BERNERS *Huon* cxliii. 637 There was on both partyes such slauter that it was meruayle to behold it. 1597 J. KING *On Jonas* (1618) 199 What slaughter and hauocke it caused, what profusion of blood between the nobles and the commons. 1665 DRYDEN *Ind. Emp.* v. ii, Slaughter grows murder when it goes too far, And makes a Massacre what was a War. 1713 ADDISON *Cato* I. i, The field Strow'd with Rome's citizens, and drench'd in slaughter. 1750 GRAY *Elegy* 67 To wade through slaughter to a throne. 1835 W. IRVING *Tour Prairies* 122 The chief.. cut his way through the enemy with great slaughter. 1849 GROTE *Greece* II. lxix. (1862) VI. 224 These Greeks repelled the Persian assailants with considerable slaughter.
fig. 1526 *Pilgr. Perf.* (W. de W. 1531) 37 b, In oppression & slaughter of all true soules that resisteth hym. 1621 BURTON *Anat. Mel.* III. iv. I. iii, They make a slaughter of Scriptures.
transf. 1748 *Anson's Voy.* II. iv. 160 The slaughter [by scurvy] would have been..terrible.

β. 1375 BARBOUR *Bruce* XIX. 567 A felloun slauchtir maid thai thair. c 1470 HENRY *Wallace* V. 930 On Sotheron men full gret slauchter thai maid. 1513 DOUGLAS *Æneid* V. xiii. 98 Sic multitude Of slauchter he maid. 1596 DALRYMPLE tr. *Leslie's Hist. Scot.* I. 193 This, in the secunde ȝeir of his regne, maid gret slachter amang the Pechtes.

b. Personified.

1595 SHAKS. *John* III. i. 237 They were besmear'd and ouerstaind With slaughters pencill. 1735 SOMERVILLE *Chase* II. 496 Grim Slaughter strides along, Glutting her greedy Jaws. 1840 WHITTIER '*Maiden, with the fair brown tresses*' 129 When the red right-hand of slaughter Moulders with the steel it swung.

c. Persons slain in battle, etc. *rare.*

1757 W. WILKIE *Epigoniad* v. 122 Some, 'midst the heaps of slaughter sought their dead. 1764 GOLDSM. *Hist. Eng. in Lett.* (1772) I. 210 His body being found amidst a heap of slaughter.

4. In the phrases *to* or *for the slaughter*.

a 1400 N. T. (Paues) *Acts* viii. 32 As a schepe vnto þo slawghter was he ledde. 1535 COVERDALE *Ezek.* ix. 2 Euery man [had] a weapen in his honde to the slaughter. 1611 BIBLE *Ps.* xliv. 22 Wee are counted as sheepe for the slaughter. 1650 TRAPP *Comm. Num.* xxxv. 21 Wilful murtherers..should..be taken from the altar to the slaughter. 1719 DE FOE *Crusoe* I. 238 Two miserable Wretches..were now brought out for the Slaughter. 1784 COWPER *Task* VI. 421 Witness the patient ox,..Driv'n to the slaughter.

5. A particular instance or occurrence of slaying or massacre.

1483 *Cath. Angl.* 342/2 A Slaghter, *cedes*. 1535 COVERDALE *Numb.* xxxv. 6 Ye shall geue them sixe fre cities, that he which committeth a slaughter, maie flye thither. 1630 *R. Johnson's Kingd. & Commw.* 33 The slaughters made by the gunne. 1665 MANLEY *Grotius' Low C. Wars* 131 There was a horrible slaughter, for..those that fled could not escape their pursuers. 1722 DE FOE *Col. Jack* (1840) 229 We made a..terrible slaughter. 1836 THIRLWALL *Greece* III. xxii. 215 Of those who escaped this slaughter most met with death in some other form. 1855 MACAULAY *Hist. Eng.* xxi. IV. 575 They next resolved..that the slaughter was a murder.

†**6.** *Mil.* (See quots.) *Obs. rare.*

1581 STYWARD *Mart. Discipl.* I. 45 These..be placed in the heart of the battaile, vsuallie called the slaughter of the field, or execution of the same, who commonlie doe not fight but in verie great extremitie. 1598 BARRET *Theor. Warres* III. ii. 47 Halberdes or billes..we call..the gard of the ensignes, and slaughter of the field.

†**7.** A cut or slash; a wound. *Obs. rare.*

1592 GREENE *Upst. Courtier* Wks. (Grosart) XI. 274, I pray you how many slaughters do you make in a poore Calues skin? 1606 G. W[OODCOCK] *Hist. Ivstine* II. 12 This man, after innumerable slaughters receiued in the Battayle, as also hauing pursued the Enemy [etc.].

8. *fig.* **a.** An excessive cutting down *of* trees.

1657 W. COLES *Adam in Eden* cxv. 167 There hath been of late dayes, Such a Slaughter of Oaks, and other Trees, all over this Land.

b. A sweeping reduction in the price of goods in order to effect a clearance.

1891 in *Cent. Dict.*

9. *attrib.* and *Comb.* **a.** Attrib., in sense of 'intended or set aside to be killed for food', as *slaughter cattle*, *cow*, *lamb*, *ox*, *sheep*, *stock*.

1535 COVERDALE *Zech.* xi. 7, I myself fedde yᵉ slaughter shepe. 1607 TOPSELL *Four-f. Beasts* (1658) 496 Such as are killed they call the skins of slaughter-lambs. 1612 *Extr. Burgh Rec. Stirling* I. 132 Ilk slauchter kow passing langis the brig,..tua pennies. 1645 RUTHERFORD *Tryal & Tri. Faith* (1845) 43 It should be but the logic of a beast, if the slaughter ox should say [etc.]. 1863 W. C. BALDWIN *Afr. Hunting* vii. 301 Slaughter oxen or cows, and milch cows, are not to be had for money.

b. Attrib., with words denoting a place used for slaughtering, as *slaughter-pit*, *-place*, *-room*, *-shop*, *-yard*.

1688 BUNYAN *Jerusalem Sinner Saved* (1886) 13 Jerusalem was now become the shambles, the very slaughter-shop for saints. 1819 SCOTT *Leg. Montrose* vi, Ere we reach yon fatal slaughter-place. 1833 *Penny Cycl.* I. 8/2 Slaughter-rooms, built of stone. 1890 'R. BOLDREWOOD' *Col. Reformer* (1891) 218 All that's a turn too good for making slaughter-yard bacon, does for the Chinamen. 1897 *Daily News* 24 Feb. 5/2 The troops who have just entered the city found many of these slaughter pits.

c. Objective, as *slaughter-breathing*, *-dealing*, *-threatening* adjs.

1777 POTTER *Æschylus, Supplicants* 131 Pursuit's alarms, And slaughter-threat'ning arms. 1814 *Sporting Mag.* XLIII. 259 The slaughter-breathing lad in the blue coat. 1870 BRYANT *Iliad* II. XVIII. 214 His slaughter-dealing hands.

10. Misc. and special combs., as *slaughter-feast*, *-market*, *-stack*, *-weapon*, *-work*; **slaughter-master**, = SLAUGHTERER 3; **slaughter price** (see quot. and cf. 8 b); **slaughter shop**, = SLAUGHTER-HOUSE 4 b; **slaughter-skin** (see quot.) ? *Obs.*; †**slaughter-slave**, a vile executioner; †**slaughter sword** (see SLAUGH-SWORD); **slaughter-year** (see quot.).

1606 SYLVESTER *Du Bartas* II. iv. I. *Trophees* 201 This savage Beast, Which in his Fold would make a *Slaughter-feast. 1847 W. C. L. MARTIN *The Ox* 59/1 The cottier or small farmer, who could not pretend to rear beasts for the *slaughter market. 1841 GREENER *Sci. Gunnery* 181 The *slaughter-master..is a cormorant, who swallows the food of the weak. 1893 *Daily News* 27 Jan. 7/4 The bank premises had been written down to what was called in the north '*slaughter prices'—that was to say, not what they would fetch in the market, but as mere bricks and mortar. 1841 GREENER *Sci. Gunnery* 180 Tradesmen.. whose establishment bears the euphonious titles of the '*slaughter shop' and 'blood house'. 1753 *Chambers' Cycl.* Suppl., **Slaughter-skins*, a term used by our curriers ..for the skins of oxen, or other beasts, when fresh, and

Slaughter ...

Slaughterer ...

Slaughter-house ...

Slaughterman ...

Slaughterage ...

Slaughterdom ...

Slaughtered ...

Slaughtering ...

Slaunke ...

Slaughtering ...

Slauth ...

Slav. ...

Slave ...

Slaughterous ...

Slaughtery ...

Slaughter (Obs.) ...

Slaunke ...

Slavedom ...

Slave-driver ...

Slaveless ...

Slavelike ...

Slaveling ...

Slave-merchant ...

Slavery ...

Slaveocrat ...

Slaver ...

Slave-born ...

Slaved ...

Slaver ...

Slavering ...

Slavery ...

Slaving ...

Slave-trade ...

Slave-trader ...

Slavish ...

Slavian ...

Slavic ...

Slavonian ...

Slavonic ...

Slavonize ...

Slavification ...

Slavism ...

Slavonism ...

Slavonize ...

Slavishly ...

Slavishness, *sb.* Also **7 slavishnes**, **slavischnes**, *Sc.* **slaivischnes**. [f. SLAVISH *a*.]

1. Slavish quality or characteristics; servility.

2. A state of slavery; bondage. *Obs.*

3. Oppression, tyranny. *Obs.*

Slavism (slā'vi·z'm, slæ·viz'm). [f. SLAV *sb.* + -ISM.] The collective qualities or characteristics of the Slav peoples.

Slavist (slā'vist). [f. SLAVE *sb.* + -IST.] One who favours or upholds slavery; a member of the former pro-slavery party in the United States.

Slavistic (slā·vī'stik). [f. prec. + -IC.]

Slavo-, combining form (on Greek analogies) of SLAV: a. Used parasynthetically with terms denoting other peoples or countries, as *Slavo-Germanic*, *-Hungarian*, *-Lettic*, *-Lithuanian*, *-Phœnician*, etc.

b. Objective, or as denoting tendency to admire or favour the Slavs, Slavonic ideals, etc., as **Slavophil**, **Slavophilism**; or morbid dread of these, as **Slavophobe**, **Slavophobia**.

Slavocracy (slăvŏ'krasi). Also **slavocracy**. [f. SLAVE *sb.* + -CRACY, but with erroneous application.] The domination of slave-holders; slave-holders collectively as a dominant or powerful class.

Slavon, *obs.* form of SLAVONIAN.

Slavonian (slăvō'nĭăn). *sb.* and *a.* Also **6-7 Sclavonian**, **7-9 Sclavonian**. [f. med.L. *Sc(l)avonia* the country of the Slavs, f. *Sc(l)avus* SLAV.]

A. *sb.* 1. The language of the Slavs; Slavonic.

2. The Slavonic language. *rare⁻¹*.

3. The Slavonic race. Also *Comb.*

4. A native of Slavonia. Also *Sclavonian*.

B. *adj.* 1. Of or pertaining to the Slavs; Slavic.

2. Of or pertaining to Slavonic countries. In the bird-names *Slavonian falcon*, *grebe*.

3. Of or pertaining to the Austrian Slavonia. Also *Sclavonian*.

Slavonic (slăvŏ'nik). *a.* and *sb.* Also **6-7 Sclavonic**, **7-9 Sc-**. [ad. med.L. *Sc(l)avonicus*; cf. *Slavonian a.*] **A.** *adj.* 1. Of or pertaining to the Slavs or their language; Slavic; Slavonian.

B. *sb.* 1. The Slavonic language.

2. The language of the Slavs.

Slavonical, *a.* = prec.

Slavonicism, *sb.* The resemblance of Sclavonian to Latin and the other element of Greek.

Slavonise, *v.* Also *Slavonize*. To render Slavonic in language, character, political feeling, etc.

Slavonism [f. next.] The process of Slavonizing or of becoming Slavonised.

Slavonization [f. next.] The process of Slavonising or of becoming Slavonised.

Slavonize, *v.* Also **9 Sel-**. [f. SLAVON(IC) + -IZE.] 1. To render Slavonic in language, character, etc.

Slavonvoism, *rare.* Also **9 Scl-** + **-ISM.**]

Slawn, *obs.* form of SLOWN.

Slay (slei), *sb.¹* Also **slai**. Forms: 1 *slæ*, *sleá*, 5 *slae*, *sley*, etc. Also in comb. *slay-stick*. [Common Teut.: OE. *slǽa*, north. *slán*; cf. (4 *slág*), MDu. *slách* (*slaen*, *sla*), etc.] A weaving implement.

Slay (slei), *sb.²* *Obs.* Some kind of fabric.

Slay, *obs.* form of SLEIGH *sb.*

Slay (slei), *v.* Pa. t. *slew* (sliū), pa. pple. *slain* (slein). Forms: *see below.* [Common Teut.: OE. *sléan*, north. *sláa*; cf. (4 *slá*, OHG. *slahan*, etc.)]

A. *Illustration of forms.*

1. *Infin.* α. 1-3 **slean**, 3 **slean**, **sclein**, 4-5 **sleen**, 3 **slen**, 3-5 **slen**, § **slene**.

2. *Pres. Indic.* α. 1st *pers. sing.* (also *Subj.*) 1 **sleá**, 1, 3 **slea**, 4-6 **sley** (*e, slaye*).

2. *Pret.* *Indic.* α. 1st *pers. sing.* (also *Subj.*) 1 **slóh**, 2-3 **slouh**, 4-5 **slow**, 5-6 **slew**.

3. *Pa. pple.* α. 1 **slægen**, 4 **slayn**, **slain**, **slayne**; etc.

B. *Signification.*

I. 1. *trans.* To strike, smite, beat. *Obs.*

2. To strike (a spark, fire) from flint or other hard substance. *Obs.*

3. To throw or cast; to bring down heavily. *Obs.*

4. To strike or smite so as to kill; to put to death by means of a weapon.

5. To put to death on a crucifix. *Obs.*

6. To destroy (vermin, etc.) by some means. Also in *fig.* context. *Obs.*

II. 1. To be occupied in slaughter.

III. 1. To bring to spiritual death; to destroy with sin. *Obs.*

IV. To slay inhabitants of (a country). *Obs.*

V. To commit slaughter or murder. *Obs.*

6. To overcome with affliction or distress. *Obs.*

7. To destroy, extinguish, put an end to; to bring completely (*esp.* something bad). Cf. KILL *v.* 4.

Slayd, *obs. Sc.* form of SLED.

Slayer (slei·ǝɹ). Forms: α. 4 *slaer*, etc. [f. SLAY *v.* + -ER.]

Slaying (slei·ĭŋ), *vbl. sb.* [f. SLAY *v.* + -ING¹.] The action of the vb. To SLAY; killing, slaughter.

Slaying, *ppl. a.* Also **5 sleeing(e, sleing(e**. [f. SLAY *v.* + -ING².] That slays or kills.

Slayd, *obs.* form of SLED.

Sleabank, *obs.* form of SLEIGHT-BANK.

Sleak, *var.* of SLEEK *a.* and *v.*

Sleave (slīv), *sb.* Now *dial.* Forms: 4-6 *sleeve*, 6 *slave*, 6-7 *sleave*, 6-9 *sleave* (7 *sleeve*). [Of obscure origin.]

1. A slender filament of silk obtained by separating a thicker thread; silk in the form of such filaments.

2. *slang.* *Obs.* rare⁻¹.

Sleaved, *ppl. a.* = SLEAVE-SILK.

Slead, *var.* of SLED.

Sleak, *var.* of SLEEK *a.* and *v.*

Sleave-silk. *Obs.* material skeine of sleyd silke.

†Sleave-. [f. SLEAVE v.] Silk thread capable of being separated into smaller filaments for use in embroidery, etc.

Sleaving, *vbl. sb.* Now *dial.*

Sleazy, *sb.* [f. SLEAZY a.] The act or quality of being sleazy.

Sleazy, *a. Obs. rare.* [ad. L. *exsolutus*.]

Sleaziness, *rare.* [f. SLEAZY a.] The fact or quality of being sleazy.

Sleazy, *a.* Forms: 8 *sleazie*, *sleasie*, 8–9 *sleazy*, 7 *sleso-*, 8 *sleesy*, etc.

Sleck-trough. Now *dial.* [SLECK v.]

Sleck. *Obs.* [var. of SLEEK v.] *trans.* To make smooth.

Sleck-en, v. Now *dial.* Forms: 4–6 sleken, 4–5 slekyn, slekun, 9 slecken.

Sled (sled), *sb.1* [L. SLED sb.1]

Sledder. [f. SLED sb.1 or v.] One who conveys heavy articles by means of a sled.

†Sled-dier. [f. SLED v.] A horse that draws a sled.

Sled-ding, *vbl. sb.* [f. SLED v.]

Sledge (sledʒ), *sb.1* Forms: 1 sleog, slego, 2 slegge, 5 sleage, 8–6 sleedge, 4 sledg, 5 sledge, 6– sledge.

Sledge (sledʒ), *sb.2* Also 7 sledg. [a. MDu. *sleedse*.]

Sledge (sledʒ), *v.* [f. SLEDGE sb.1]

Sledge-hammer, *sb.* A large heavy hammer used by blacksmiths.

Sledging, *vbl. sb.* [f. SLEDGE v.]

Sledger. [f. SLEDGE sb.1 or v.2] One who drives or draws a sledge.

Sleech. *dial.* [Of obscure origin.] (See quot.)

Sleck (slek), *v. Cheshire dial.* [Of obscure origin.] (See quot.)

Sleck (slek), *sb.2* Also *slick*, **sleck**. [prob. f. prec.]

Sleech, *sb.2* *Naut.* [L. SLEECH sb.1] (See quot.)

Sleek (slīk), *a.* and *adv.* Forms: 6 sleke, slike, sloke, 6–7 sleik, sleike, slicke. [Later variant form of SLICK a.]

Sleek (slīk), *v.* [f. SLEEK a.] trans. To make sleek or smooth by rubbing or polishing.

Sleeked, *ppl. a.* [f. SLEEK v.]
1. Smoothed; having a glossy skin, etc.
2. Specious, flattering; artful; plausible.

Sleeken (slī'k'n), *v.* [f. SLEEK a. + -EN⁵.] *trans.* To make smooth and glossy.

Sleeker. [f. SLEEK v. + -ER¹.] One who sleeks; an implement used for sleeking leather, cloth, etc.

Sleekish (slī'kiʃ), *a.* [f. SLEEK a. + -ISH¹.]

Sleekly (slī'kli), *adv.* [f. SLEEK a. + -LY².] In a sleek manner. Also *fig.*, smoothly.

Sleekness (slī'knes). [f. SLEEK a.] The quality of being sleek.

Sleekstone (slī'kstoun). *Obs. exc. dial.* Also 5 sliek-, 7 sleeke-. [f. SLEEKSTONE.] A smooth stone used for smoothing and polishing.

Sleeky (slī'ki), *a.* [f. SLEEK a. + -Y¹.]
1. Marked by sleek condition.

Sleep (slīp), *sb.* Forms: 1 slǽp, 1–4 (9 *Sc.*) slep, 3 slep, 3–4 sleep (5 slepe, sclep), 3–6 sleep, 3–4 slape. [Com. WGer.]

Sleep (slīp), *v.* Pa. t. and pa. pple. **slept** (slept). Forms: *see* below. [Com. WGer.]

SLEEP.

B. Signification.

1. intr. 1. To take repose by the natural suspension of consciousness; to be in the state of sleep; to slumber. Also *occas.*, to fall asleep.

(dense dictionary text, illustrative quotations)

b. Implying sexual intimacy or cohabitation.

2. With *upon* or *on* (a matter), denoting the postponement of a decision till the following day.

3. to sleep like a top (cf. 3 c).

4. With *it*: To spend one's time in sleep. Also *with out*.

5. With *in*: To sleep in the house, or on the premises, where one is employed (contrasted with 'to sleep out'); also *Naut.*, to remain in one's berth all night; *Sc.* to oversleep.

b. With *in*, in passive, of a bed.

6. fig. To lie in death; to be at rest in the grave.

7. trans. a. Of limbs: To be numb, to be devoid of sensation, esp. as the result of pressure.

b. Of plants: To be in a quiescent or drooping condition.

c. To sleep away: To pass or spend (a certain time) in sleep.

SLEEPER.

SLEEPING

SLEEVE.

Sleeve (slīv), *sb.* Forms: *a.* 1 slefe, 4-5 sleue, sleve... [OE. *slēfe*, *slīefe*...]

1. That part of a coat, shirt, or other garment which covers the arm. In early use *freq.* a separate article of dress made to be worn at will with any body-garment.

Sleeved (slīvd), *ppl. a.* Also 5 slevid, 6 allewed, alowed, *Sc.* slewit. [f. SLEEVE *sb.* or *vb.*]

Sleeve-button. [SLEEVE *sb.*] A button for fastening the loose cuffs of a wristband or cuff, esp. the cuff of a shirt-sleeve; a sleeve-link.

Sleeve-fish. [Cf. SLEEVE *sb.* 5.] A fish of the family *Loligo*; esp. the common calamary or squid, *Loligo vulgaris*.

Sleeve-hand. †

Sleeveful. *rare.* [f. SLEEVE *sb.* + -FUL.]

Sleeveless (slī'vles), *a.* [f. SLEEVE *sb.* + -LESS.]

Sleeving (slī'viŋ), *vbl. sb.* [f. SLEEVE *vb.*]

Sleezy: see SLEAZY.

Sleft, *obs. pa. t.* of SLEEP.

Slegh, *obs. f.* SLY.

Sleigh (slā), *sb.* Also 8 slay. [f. the *vb.*] *intr.* To travel or ride in a sleigh. Also with *it*.

Sleigh-bell. [SLEIGH *sb.*] One of a number of small bells (see quot. 1859) attached to a sleigh or to the harness of a horse drawing it.

Sleight (slāit), *sb.* Forms: 3 sleighte, 4 slighte, 4–5 sleghte, sleighe, 5 sleyghte, 6 slighte, slight, etc. [a. ON. *slœgð* cunning, f. *slœgr* SLY.]

1. A sled or sledge used as a vehicle for passengers, usually drawn by one or more horses.

2. A sleigh or sled employed for the transport of goods over ice or snow.

Sleight (slāit), *sb.* Obs. Forms: 5 sleyghte, 6 slyrghti, alygh, 6–7 sleight. [f. SLEIGH *sb.*]

Sleight of hand. Also *sleight-of-hand.*

Sleighter, obs. f. SLAUGHTER.

†**Sleighter.** Obs. rare–1. [f. 4 sleiater, 6 slayter.] [f. SLAUGHTER *sb.*]

Sleightful, *a.* Obs. rare–1. [f. SLEIGHT *sb.*] 5–6 *Sc.* slichtfull, etc. Full of sleight or cunning; crafty.

Sleightily, *adv.* Obs. rare. [f. SLEIGHTY.]

Sleighty, *a.* *Sc.* Now rare. Forms: 5 *Sc.* slichtie, slechty, 6 slychti, etc. Crafty, cunning, subtle.

Slem. *rare.* Now *dial.* [Cf. Sw. *slem* (MSw. *slem*), etc.]

Slench (slentʃ), *v.* Now *dial.* Also 9 slinch, slinch.

†**Slene.** Obs. rare.

†**Slend.** *v.* trans. To slice or cut; to split.

Slender (slendər), *a.* (and *adv.*). Forms: 4–6 slendre, slendir, 5 -ar, slindir, 8, 4, 6 slendere, 5, 7 sclender, 5 sklendire, 6 sol-, sklender, [Of obscure origin.]

SLENDER.

† Slender, v. Obs. rare⁻¹. [f. prec.] trans. To attenuate.

Slender-beaked, a. [SLENDER a. 12.] Having a slender beak.

Slender-billed, a. [SLENDER a. 12.] Having a slender bill; tenuirostral.

Slender-bodied, a. [SLENDER a. 12.] Having a slender body.

Slenderish, a. Also 5-6 slenderly. Somewhat slender.

Slenderly, (sle·ndəli), adv. Also 5-6 sklendorly, 6-lye, -lie, -urly, sclenderly; 6 slendorlye, 6-7 -lie.

Slendish, a. [f. SLENDER a. + -ISH¹.] Rather slender.

Slenderness, (sle·ndənes). Also 6 slendrenesse, sclendernes; 7 slendernesse.

SLEUTH.

Slent, v. ... [Of obscure origin.]

Slent, n. Now dial. [Of obscure origin.]

Slent, v.¹ trans. To split or cleave; to break.

Slent, v.² ... To dangle, swing.

Slent, sb.¹ ... half. G. schlenkern

Slent, sb.² Now dial. Also **4 slinte,** s side-slip, pas slent

Slent, v.³ Now dial. Also **4 slinte,** 5 slente, dial. slent; cf. MSw. and Sw. dial. slent, slip.

Slenk, Obs. ⁻¹ A side-blow.

Slanter, sb.

Slester, variant of SLAISTER v.

Sletch, (sletʃ), v. rare. Now dial. 5 sletch, pa. t. slethte.

Slet, sb. ... = SLATE sb.¹

Slent, sb. ... = SLATE sb.¹

Sleuth (slūþ). Forms: 3-4 sloþ, 4-5 sloth, slog(e), slog(þ); 5 Sc. sloith, slouth, aluth(e), 5 Sc., 9 sleuth. [In sense 1 a. ON. sloð track, trail. In sense 2 ellipt. for SLEUTH-HOUND.]

Sleuth-hound (slū·þ·hound). Forms 4-5 slowth-, slewth-, sleuth-, 5-6 sluth(e)-, 7 slwth-hund; 5 slwthound, 6 slouthound 7 slugh-, 7 (9)

SLIBBER-SAUCED.

Sleuthless, a. [f. SLEUTH sb.¹] Slothful.

Sleu, (slū), v. Obs. Also **6 Sc. sleithe.** [f. SLEUTH-HOUND.]

Sleve, v. Obs. rare. Also **4 slefe,** Sc. slawve-.

Sleuth, a.² ... [Inferred from SLEUTH-HOUND.] Persistent, dogged.

Slew (slū), v.¹ Also slue, slieu. [f. SLEW v.²]

Slew (slū), sb.¹ Also slue, slieu.

Slew (slū), sb.² Also alue, slieu, sluy. U.S. and Canada. A marshy or reedy pool, pond, small lake, backwater, or inlet.

Slew-rope. Naut. Also slue-. [f. SLEW v.²]

† Sleul (slū), sb. rare. Also **sleawl, sleanuol, sleawol.** [app. f. SLED(TH) + -FUL.] Slothful.

Slibber, v. Obs. rare. Also **7 slibbir.** [= MDu.]

Slibber-sauce. Obs.

Slibber-sauced, ppl. a. Obs.

SLIBBER-SLABBER.

† Slibber-slabber, sb. Obs. Also **7 -slobber.** [Cf. prec. and SLABBER n.]

Slibber-slabber, a. Obs. attrib.

Slibbery, a. Obs. rare. Also **3 slibbri**; LG. (also Du. and MDu. slibberich). Slippery and slimy; lubric.

Slice (slais), sb. Forms a. 4 scly(c)e, sclice; 5 sclise, 5 sclyce, 6 Sc. sclyce; sclyse, 7 sclyce (6 slycee), 5-6 slyce, 6 slise, slyse, 5-7 slyce (6 slyce), 5-6 slice, 5-7 slice, excl (excluse) (mod.F. éclisse) splinter, shiver, small piece (of wood, etc.), wh. ad. L. See SLICE v.]

Slice, v. Forms: a. 4 sclyce, 5 sclice; -y, -i; 6 slise, 6 sclyce, 6 Sc. sclyce; 6-7 sclyse, 6 slyce, 7 slyse, -ice, etc. [ad. OF. esclicier, esclicier, etc.

Slicer (slai·səz). [f. SLICE v.] One who or that which slices.

SLICING.

Slice (slais), sb. continued.

† Sliced, ppl. a. [f. SLICE v.] 1. Cut into slices | cut through with a sharp instrument.

Slich, Slick, Sc. forms of SLEIGHT sb., SLIGHT a.

Slicing (slai·siŋ), vbl. sb. [f. SLICE v.] Muting. The action of the verb in various senses.

Slicing (slai·siŋ), ppl. a. [f. SLICE v.] Cutting, or that cleanly or cleanly.

Slick (slik), a. and adv. Orig. U.S. [f. SLICK v.]

Slick, sb. Now chiefly dial. and U.S. Forms: a. 4-6 slyke (5 slyk), slike, 6 slyke, Sc. slyke, 6-7 slick.

Slick (slik), v. Now chiefly dial. and U.S. Forms: 5-6 slyke, slike, 6 slick.

SLICKENSIDE.

Slicken, v. rare. [f. SLICK a. + -EN⁵.] trans. To make smooth or polished.

Slicken, a. rare. [f. SLICK a. + -EN.]

Slickens (slik·ens). U.S. [f. SLICK a.]

Slickenside (slik·n-said). Geol. [f. SLICKEN a. + SIDE sb.]

Slickensided ppl. a. and pa. pple.

Slickensiding vbl. sb.

Slicker (sli·kəɹ). [f. SLICK a. or v.]

1. a. A tool used for scraping or smoothing leather. (Cf. SLEEK v.)

2. U.S. A waterproof overcoat.

Slicking (sli·kiŋ), vbl. sb. [f. SLICK v.]

1. The action of making sleek or smooth, etc.

2. Smoothness.

3. Smartness.

4. Dexterity, cleverness.

Slickstone. Now rare. Also 4 slike-, 5 slyk-, 6 slyke-. [f. SLICK n. CF. ON. *slíkisteinn* (Norw. *sliksteinn*.) = SLEEKSTONE.

Slick-worm. Sc. (See quot. and cf. SLECK sb.)

Slid, sb. Now rare. Also 6 slidde, slydd-, slydd°.

Slicken (sli·k'n), adj. sb. [f. SLICK a. + -EN.]

1. Smoothly.

2. Cleverly, deftly.

Slickness (sli·knes). [f. SLICK a. + -NESS.]

Slid, a. Sc. Also 6 slide, slyd(e. [Related to SLIDE v.]

Slidder (sli·dəɹ), v. Now dial. Forms: 1 slid(e)rian, 5 slideren, slyder(yn), slydre, slidre; 3 sliddren, 7- slidder, 9 Sc. wd-, skliter. [OE. *slid(e)rian*, = MDu. *slid(d)eren*, *slidderen*, LG. *slidderen*, G. *schlittern*, a frequentative from OE. *slid-*.]

Slidderness. Obs. [f. SLIDDER a.] Slipperiness, smoothness. Also *fig.*

Slidage, ppl. a. rare. [See SLIDE v. A, 3 b.]

Slidden (sli·d'n), ppl. a. rare. [f. SLIDE v.]

Slid·der, sb. dial. [Cf. SLIDDER a. and v.] A trench or hollow running down a hill; a slope.

Sliddery, a. Now arch. and dial. Also 1 slidrig, 4 slydyr-, 6 slyd(d)rye, 7 -ery, sliddery, sled- (6 Sc.-erie), 5, 7-9 sliddery. [OE. *sliderig*, f. stem of SLIDDER v.]

A. adj. 1. Slippery; on which one readily slips.

† Slid·der, a. and adv. Obs. Forms: 1, 1-2 slidor, 5-6 slidar (4 -our, 5-yn), 5-6 slidir, 5-6 slydar (4-yr, 7-yr, -era); 4 sledyr, 4-5 sleder; 1 sliddor, 3-5 slider, -ir, 6 sclidere, 5 slidery, slyder. [OE. *slidor*, I. stem with initial SLIDE v.]

A. adj. 1. Slippery; on which one may readily slip.

B. adv. 1. Slidingly; in a sliding manner.

Slidderly, adv. Also 6 slike, 5 slidderly.

Slide (slaid), sb. Now dial. Forms: 1 slid, slide, 4-5 slyde, 5- slide.

1. a. The act or fact of sliding; an instance of this; also, the manner in which a thing slides.

Slidder (sli·dəɹ), v. Now dial. Forms: 1 alid(e)rian, 5 slideren, slyder(yn), slydre, slidre; 3 sliddren, 7- slidder, 9 Sc. wd-, skliter.

Slide (slaid), v. Pa. t. slid, pple. slid (slidden, slidden). Forms: 1 slidan, 3-5 slide, slyde, 5- slide.

1. *intr.* To move smoothly along a surface.

2. An earth-slip, a landslip, an avalanche; a place on a hill-side, etc., where this has happened.

3. A sliding mass or stretch of water.

4. *Mining.* A fracture in a lode resulting in the dislocation or displacement of a portion of it; a vein of clay, etc., marking such dislocation.

5. A ramp, or inclined sledge. (Cf. SLED v.)

6. a. A kind of sledge.

7. A sliding scale.

Slide (slaid), v. Pa. t. slid, pple. slid (slidden, slidden).

2. Of streams, etc.: To glide. Now rare.

3. Of reptiles, etc.: To glide, crawl. Now rare.

4. To move, go, proceed unperceived, quietly, or stealthily; to steal, creep, slink, or slip away; to get *out* of a place, etc.

5. To pass away, pass by, as to do.

6. With *let* (or *allow*). In later use *freq.*, to let (something) take its own course.

II. 5. To pass away, pass by, as to do.

b. *colloq.* To make off. Orig. U.S.

III. To slip; to lose one's foothold.

IV. *trans.* To cause to move with a smooth, uninterrupted motion.

b. Of speech or money, with reference to these; *spec.* (see quot. 1875).

c. Of the eye or teeth: To pass quickly from one object to another.

Slide-, the verbal stem or the sb. in combs. (sometimes *mod.* legitimate). A. With names of apparatus, implements, parts of machines, etc., characterized by a sliding action, as *slide-bar*, *-block*, *-bolt*, *-car*, etc.

Sli·deable, a. rare. [f. SLIDE v.] Liable to slide or alter.

Sli·deableness. [Cf. prec.] Fitness for sliding.

† Sli·de-groat. Obs. [f. SLIDE v. + GROAT.] Shove-groat, shovel-board.

Slider (slai·dəɹ). [f. SLIDE v. + -ER [1].]

1. One who slides; a skater.

Sli·de-rest. Also slide rest. [f. SLIDE v.] An appliance for holding tools in turning, enabling the tools to be variously held in relation to the material worked on.

Sli·de-rule. [f. SLIDE v.] A sliding rule.

Slide-thrift. Obs. [f. SLIDE v., after SLIDE-GROAT.]

Sli·de-valve. [f. SLIDE v.] A valve having a sliding plate for opening and closing an orifice; *spec.* one which does this alternately.

Sliding (slai·diŋ), vbl. sb. [f. SLIDE v.]

1. Shovelboard, slide-groat.

2. A sliding part of some mechanism.

Sliding (slai·diŋ), ppl. a. [f. SLIDE v.]

1. That slides or moves with a sliding motion.

2. Slippery, steeply sloping.

SLIMSKIN

The slimness of their bodies, and great length of tail. 1826 KEATS *Ep. to C. Cowden Clarke* 87 To see...meeting shadows streaking into slimness Across the tawny fields.

Slimsily, *adv.* Also **slimsy**. [f. SLIM a.] In a slim manner.

2. Artfulness, cunning.
1899 *Westm. Gaz.* 27 Dec. 1/2 Courage is no good unless it is backed up by what the Boers themselves call 'slimness'. 1900 *Daily Telegr.* 1 Oct. 6/1 A double dose of original slimness.

Slimskin, *U.S.* [f. SLIM a. + SKIN sb.] A set-elephant in an emaciated state.

Slimslack, *Obs.* [f. SLIM a. + SLACK sb.] A person mentally or physically defective.

Slimsy (sli'mzi), *a. U.S.* Also **slimpsy**. [app. f. SLIM a.] Flimsy, frail.

Slimy (slai'mi), *a.* Forms: 4-, 6, 8 **slimy** (5 slymy), 6-7 **slymie**; 6 slimie, 6-7 **slimie**, 6-7 **slymie**, 7 slimey. [f. SLIME sb. + -Y.]

1. Of the nature or consistency of slime; viscous.

2. Characterized by the presence of slime; covered with slime.

SLING

Sling, *sb.*[1] Forms: 4-, 4- sling (4 slenge), 4-6 slinge, 4-6 slynge (5 slynge); 4 slenge. *a. B. Sc.* 5 sloung, 6 sloung, 5-6, 9 slung. [app. of Continental origin, but the precise etymology is uncertain.]

Sling (slin), *sb.*[2] Also 5-6 slynge, slyng (5 slyngge). [f. SLING v.1]

Sling (slin), *sb.*[3] *Coal-mining.* Also **slyne** [Of obscure origin.]

Sling, *sb.*[4] Forms: 4 slenge, slynge, 4-5 slyng, 4-6 slynge, 7- sling. [Perhaps ultimately the same root as that of LG. *sling(e)*, G. *schlinge*, Sw. *slinga*, etc.]

SLING (p.214)

Sling (slin), *sb.*[5] Also 6 slynge. [f. SLING v.1]

SLING (p.215)

Sling (slin), *sb.*[6] Forms: 4 slynge, 4-5 slyng, 4-6 slynger, 7- sling. [f. SLING v.]

Sling (slin), *sb.*[7] Forms: 4 slynge, 4-5 slyng, 4-6 slynger, 7- sling.

Sling-stone. Also **slingstone**, **sling stone**; *Sc.* 5 slong, 8 sling stane.

Slinger (sli'ŋər), *sb.*[1] Also 5-6 slynger.

Slinger (sli'ŋər), *sb.*[2] One who is given to drinking slings.

Slinger, *v. Sc. Obs.* [ad. Du. slingeren (Fris. *slingerje*) or LG. *slingern* (Da. *slingre*)]

Slinging (sli'ŋiŋ), *vbl. sb.*[1] [f. SLING v.]

Slinging, *vbl. sb.*[2] The action of the vb. in various senses.

SLINK (p.215)

Slink (slink), *sb.* Also 7 slinke, slincke, 8 slynk. [f. SLINK v.]

Slink, *v.* Pa. t. and pa. pple. **slunk** (6-7 slunck). Forms: 1 slincan, 4 slynke, 5 slynck-, 7 slinke, slincke; 5 slink, 8 slinck, slenk. [OE. *slincan* to creep, crawl.]

Slink, *a.* Also 7 slinke, slinko, 8 slink. [f. SLINK sb.]

SLINKER (p.216)

Slinker (sli'ŋkər), *sb.* [f. SLINK v. + -ER[1].]

Slink-skins, *sb. pl.*

Slinking, *vbl. sb.* [f. SLINK v.]

Slinking, *ppl. a.* [f. SLINK v. + -ING[2].]

SLIP

Slip (slip), *sb.*[1] Forms: 5-7 slippe, 6-7 slyppe, 6-9 *dial.* slipp, etc.

Slip (slip), *sb.*[2] Forms: 5-7 slippe, 6-7 slyppe, etc.

SLIP. 217 SLIP. SLIP. 218 SLIP.

SLIP. 219 SLIP. SLIP. 220 SLIP-

Slip-cloth, *-cord.* see Slip sb.

Slip-coat. [Cf. sb.³ 2 b.] A kind of soft cream-cheese. Chiefly in *slip-coat cheese*.

Slipe (slaip), *sb.¹ Sc.* and *north.* Also 6 *Sc.* **slype**, 6 **stype**, [app. a. LG. *slīpe* (cf. MHG. *sleife* (G. *schleife*) sledge, train, loop, knot, etc., related to LG. *slīpen* to whet, and *slīpen* to drag (see *Grimm*) *Wb*. s.v. *schleifen*.]

Slip-knot (sli'pˌnɒt). Also *slip knot.* [f. Slip v.¹] A knot which has readily the slipped or untied.

Slippage (sli'pedʒ). [f. Slip v.¹ + -age.]

Slipped (slipt), *ppl. a.¹* [f. Slip v.¹]

Slipper (sli'pə), *sb.* Forms: see Slip sb.¹

Slipper (sli'pə), *a.* Obs. exc. dial. [OE. *slipor* = MDu., MLG. *slipper*, OHG. *slipfar* (MHG. *slipfer*), G. *schlipfer*.]

Slipper (sli'pə), *v.* [f. Slipper sb.]

Slipperish, *a. rare.* [f. Slipper a.] Somewhat slippery.

Slipperiness. Obs.⁻¹ Slipperiness.

Slipperly, *adv.* [f. Slipper.] Insecurely.

Slipperness. Obs. rare. [f. Slipper a. + -ness.] Slipperiness.

Slippery (sli'pərɪ), *a.* Also 6 *Sc.* **slipery**, 6-7 *slippery*, 7 **slipperie**; [Alteration of Slipper a., possibly after LG. *slipperig* (G. dial. *schlipperig*), ~ MHG. *slipferig* (G. dial. *schlipferig*).]

Slippy (sli'pɪ), *a.* Also 6 **slyppie**, 6-7 **slippie.** [f. MHG. *slipfic*, *-ig*. Obs. G.]

Slipping, *vbl. sb.* [f. Slip v.¹]

Slipping, *ppl. a.* [f. Slip v.¹] That slips, in senses of the intransitive vb.

Slippingly, *adv.* [f. prec.]

Slip-shoe. Obs. exc. dial. Also 6 CF. Obs.

Slip-rail. Austr. [Slip⁻ 1 b.] A fence-rail.

Slip-slap, *sb.* and *adv.*

Slip-slop (sli'pslɒp), *sb.* Also 7 (8 Sc.) **-slap**, **-slipslop.** [f. Slop sb.², with variation of vowel.]

Slip-string. Now dial. Also 6 **slypstryng**, 7 **slipp-string**; 6-7 **slipsttring.**

Slip-top(ped) *sb.* [Slip⁻.]

Slip-way. 1. A sloping way leading down into the water.

Sloe-tree ... ; also 9 *Sc.* and *north. slae.* [f. SLOE *sb.* + TREE *sb.*]

Slog-dollager, *obs.* variants of SLUGGARD.

Slogger (slɒgǝl), *sb.* [See quots.] *Obs.*

Sloe-worm, pl. obs. forms of SLOW-WORM.

Sloff, *v.* Now *dial.* [Imitative.] *intr.*

Slog (slɒg), *sb.* collog. [f. the vb.]

Slogger (slɒgǝr), *v. dial.* [Of obscure origin: cf. SLOGGER.]

Slogan (slōˈgǎn). Forms ... 6 slogorne, 7-slogrone, sluggorn(e, 8 slugorn, slogurn; 6 sloghorne, 6, 8 slughorne, 7, 9 slughorn. 8 slughorn, 7 slogan, 7 sluggan, 7 slughan; 8 slogan.

Sloka (slōˈkǎ). Also 8 sloca. [Skr. *śloka*.]

Sloid, obs. var. of SLOYD.

Sloka. = SLOKE.

Slaip, obs. form of SLEEP.

Slonk, *v. dial.* [Of obscure origin: cf. Du.]

Slook, *dial.* form of SLOUGH *sb.¹*

Sloom (slūm), *sb.¹* Now *north. dial.* [OE. *slúma* slumber, doze.]

Sloom, *v.¹ local.* Also *sb.* [Of obscure origin: the variant forms indicate an original *slum-.*]

Sloop (slūp), *sb.¹* [ad. Du. *sloep*, LG. *slūp(e)*, whence G. *schaluppe*.]

Sloop, *sb.²* Canada. [Of obscure origin.]

Sloor, obs. form of SLUR.

Slop (slɒp), *sb.¹* Also 6-8 sloppe, 7 slopp.

Slop (slɒp), *sb.²* Also 7 slappe, stoope. 4-5 slop, 6-7 sloppe.

Sloom (slūm), *v.²* [app. f. SLOOM *sb.¹*]

Slop (slɒp), *v.* [f. SLOP *sb.¹*]

Slop-basin. = SLOP-BOWL.

Slope (slōp), *sb.²* Also 7 sloap, 8 sloop.

Slope (slōp), *sb.³* [Aphetically f. ASLOPE *adv.*]

Slope (slōp), *v.* [f. SLOPE *sb.¹*]

Sloped (slōpt), *ppl. a.¹* [f. SLOPE *v.* + -ED.]

Sloper, *sb.* [f. SLOPE *v.* + -ER.]

Slopeways, *adv.* [f. SLOPE *sb.¹*]

Slopewise, *adv.* Now *rare* or *Obs.* — *prec.*

Slopiness, *rare.* [f. as prec.]

Sloping (slōˈpiŋ), *ppl. a.* [f. SLOPE *v.* + -ING¹.]

Slopingly (slōˈpiŋli), *adv.* [f. prec.]

Slopped, *ppl. a.¹* In 7 slopt. [f. SLOP *v.*]

Slopper, *sb.* [f. SLOP *v.*]

Slopper (slɒpǝr), *sb.²* [f. SLOP *sb.¹*]

Slopper (slǫ·pəɹ), sb.¹ [f. SLOP sb.¹ + -ER¹.] A dealer in slop-clothing.

†Slopper (also -APO), obs. variant of SLAPPER sb.

Slopper-work. The making of slop-garments; the articles thus made.

Slop-work. [f. SLOP sb.¹]

So Slop-worker, one who does slop-work.

Slopy (slǫ·pi), a. [f. SLOP sb.¹ + -Y¹.]

Slorp (slǫ·ɹp), v. dial. and Sc. [Cf. Du. and MLG. *slorpen* in the same sense. See also SLUBP v.]

Slorry, slory, dial. and colloq. R. SLUBBY.

Slosh (slǫʃ), sb. [Cf. next and SLUSH sb.]

Slosh (slǫʃ), v. [f. prec. or imitative.]

Slosh-wheel. (See quot.)

Sloshy (slǫ·ʃi), a. [f. SLOSH sb.] Slushy.

Slot (slǫt), sb.¹ Also 5-6 slote, 5, 8-9 slott.

Slot, sb.² Also 5-6 slote, 5, 8-9 slot.

Slot, sb.³ Obs. 6 slotte. [ad. AF. and OF. *esclot*]

Slot, sb.⁴ Forms: 4 slote, etc.

Slot, sb.⁵ Obs.⁻¹ Now dial. [ad. Du. or LG. *slot* (G. *schloss*)]

Slot (slǫt), v.¹ [f. SLOT sb.¹]

Slot, v.² trans. To pierce through the 'slot'.

Slot, v.³ trans. To trace by the slot; to follow the track (of a stag, etc.).

Sloth (sloʊθ, slǫθ), sb. Forms: α. 5 slawth, 8-5 slowth (5 slowþ), 4-6 slouthe, 7- sloth. β. 4 SLEUTH sb.¹

Sloth, v. [f. prec. sb.]

Slothful (sloʊ·θfʊl), a. Forms: 4-5 slouthful, etc.

Slothfully, adv.

Slothfulness.

Sloth-head. Obs.⁻¹

Slothy (sloʊ·θi), a. Sluggishly, lazily.

Slotted (slǫ·ted), ppl. a. Having a slot or slots.

Slotter, sb. [f. SLOT v.¹]

Slotting (slǫ·tiŋ), vbl. sb. [f. SLOT v.¹]

Slouch (slautʃ), sb. Forms: 6 sloutch, 7 slouch.

Slouch (slautʃ), v. [f. prec.]

Slouch-eared, a.

Slouched (slautʃt), ppl. a.

Sloucher (slau·tʃəɹ).

Slouchily, adv.

Slouchiness.

Slouching (slau·tʃiŋ), ppl. a.

Slouchingly, adv.

Slouchy (slau·tʃi), a.

Slough (slau), sb.¹ Forms: 4 slogh, etc.

Slough (slʌf), sb.² Forms: 4 slough, etc.

Slough (slʌf), v.

Slough (slʌf), sb.¹

b. The skin of a caterpillar, locust, etc. cast in the course of transformation; as from the nymphal to the imago stage.

c. Apparel, clothing.

d. A skin, caul, or membrane, enclosing or covering the body or some part of it.

Slough (slʌf), sb.²

Slough (slaʊ), sb.³

Slough (slʌf), v.¹

Slough (slaʊ), v.²

Slough-dog, -hound. Sc. and north.

Sloughful (slʌf-), a.

Sloughiness, rare⁻¹.

Sloughing (slʌf-), vbl. sb.

Sloughing (slaʊ-), vbl. sb.

Sloughy (slʌf-), a.¹

Sloughy (slaʊ-), a.²

Slovan, obs. form of SLUGGISH a.

Slouk, dial. and rare.

Slounge, v.

Slour, v.

Slouse, v.

Slough, obs. form of SLUGGISH a.

Slovak (slɒ-væk, slōvāk), sb. and a.

a sb. 1. A person belonging to a Slavonic race dwelling in the north-western part of Hungary.

2. The language or dialect spoken by this people.

b. adj. Of or belonging to the Slovaks, their language; Slovakish.

Slovakian (slōvæ-kiən), a. and sb.; Slovakish (slō-vækiʃ), a. and sb.

Slovan (slō-væn), sb.

Slove, obs. or dial. pa. t. of SLIVE v.

Sloven (slʌv-'n), sb. and a. Forms: 5 slovayn, 6 slovayne, slovyne, sloveyn; 6 slovyn, -in, slovyn, slooven, 6-7 slouen, 6- sloven.

1. A. +1. A person of low character or manners; a knave, rascal. Obs.

b. Slovenian; Slovenish.

A.2. sb. Belonging or pertaining to the Slovenes.

3. A. sb. The language of the Slovenes.

Slovene (slō-vīn, slōvī-n), sb. and a.

Slovenian (slōvī-niən), a. and sb.

Slovenish, a.

Slovenlily, adv. Also 7 slovingly.

Slovenliness, sb. Also 6 slovenlynes.

Slovenly (slʌv-'nli), a. Also 6 slouenly.

Slovenly (slʌv-'nli), adv. Also 6 sloovenry, 6–7 slovenlie, 7 slovenly.

Slovenry (slʌv-'nri), sb.

Slow (slō), sb.¹ Also 4 slaws, 4–5 slowe.

Sloven (slō-vn), sb.²

Slove (slōv), sb.³

Slow, obs. variant of SLOUGH sb.¹

Slow (slō), a. Forms: a. (Chiefly north. and Sc.) 1, 3– slaw, 1, 4–6 slawe, 5 slau, 9 sla. β. 2– slow (2 slow), 4–6 slowe, 3–4, 7 slo, slo, sloo. γ. 3 slovʒ, 3–4 slou, 4 slouʒe, 5 slowʒ, slouʒe. δ. 4–6 slowh, 5 selowh; 4 slothe. ε. —O'Neal, slaones, —MDu. and Du. sleeuw, slee, OS. sleu (MLG. and LG.), OHG. slêo (MHG. slê...Du.-...slō. γ...

1. 1. Not quick or clever in apprehending or understanding a thing; obtuse, dull; of persons. Also with in or of.

b. Of the mind, etc.

2. Naturally disinclined to be active or to exert oneself; constitutionally inert or sluggish; lacking in promptness or energy.

3. Not quick, ready, prompt, or willing to do something.

4. Tardy or dilatory in action; displaying a lack of promptitude or energy under particular circumstances; operating a comparatively long time in the performance of some act; doing something in a slow or deliberate manner.

b. Without intent, or with in.

5. Not readily stirred or moved to something (esp. anger, revenge, etc.); not too ready, willing, or susceptible. Also with into.

6. Of things, actions, etc.: Marked or characterized by slowness or tardiness.

b. Of fever, etc.: Not rapidly developing into a serious form; not acute.

c. Of persons: Having no briskness or animation; dull, lifeless, insipid; humdrum.

7. Of time, etc.: Passing slowly or heavily. Also rarely.

8. Taking or requiring a comparatively long time; lasting in progress, growth, etc.; very gradual.

9. Not in operation or effect.

b. With various complements implied, as (slow) in growing, coming in, rising, going off, etc.

10. a. Of fevers, etc.: Not rapidly developing into a serious form; not acute.

b. Characterized by slowness of motion, progress, etc. (In later quots. after Trope.)

c. Of pace, movement, etc.: Leisurely; not quick, fast, or hurried.

11. Of time, etc.: Passing slowly or heavily. Also sluggish manner; taking a long time to go.

Slow (slō), adv. Also 6 slawe, slaw.

1. In a slow or tardy manner; slowly.

b. To suffer delay; to be delayed. Obs.⁻¹

2. Comb. With pres. pples. and ppl. adjs., as slow-burning, -circling, -creeping, etc.

b. With pa. pples., as slow-breathed, -developed, etc.

Slow (slō), v. Also 6 slawe, slaw.

I. 1. trans. +1. To lose (time) by delay; to put off. Obs.⁻¹

2. To be tardy or slow in performing (business). Obs.⁻¹

3. To delay, check, retard; to make slower in some respect.

II. intr. 4. To slacken in pace; to move or travel more slowly.

Slowback, sb. arch. [f. SLOW a. + BACK sb.]

Slow-bellied, a.

Slow-belly, a. [f. SLOW a. + BELLY sb.]

Slow-coach, slow coach.

Slow-footed, a.

Slow-ful, *a. Obs.* Also **slowful(l**, **slou-ful**, 5–6 **slowful**, 6 **slowghful**, aloughful, *Sc.* **solawful**. [f. SLOW *a.*, perh. after SLOTHFUL *a.* (cf. SLEWFUL *a.*)]

1. Slack, slow, sluggish.

Slow-fulness, *Obs.* [f. prec. + -NESS.]
1. Sloth; slowness.
2. Ingratitude; thanklessness.

Slow-going, *a.* [Slow *adv.*]

Slow-hound, first element assimilated to SLOW *a.*] A sleuth-hound.

Slowing, *vbl. sb.* [Slow *v.*] The action of becoming or making slow(er); an instance of this. Also with *advs.*

Slowish, *a.* [Slow *a.* + -ISH.] Somewhat slow or dull.

Slowly (slō'li), *adv.* Forms: *a.* (latterly *north.* and *Sc.*) 1 slawlice, slaulice, -leoe, 2 slaw-liche; 4–5 slawly, 6 slawlie, slaulie. *β.* 8–4–5 slowliche, 5 sloel-, 4–5 slouely, 5 slowlye, 6 slowly, [f. SLOW *a.* + -LY.]
1 ¶ In writen regular manner; sluggishly; slackly. *Obs.*

Slowness (slō'nes), *sb.* [f. SLOW *a.* + -NESS.]

Slow-paced, *a.* [Slow *a.*]

Slow-worm, *-wyrm*, 5 *-worme*, 9 *north. dial.* slaa-slea(s), -worm; *Sc.* slaw-worm. *β.* 5 slawerm, -wyrm, 5 *-worme*, 6–9 -worm; 6 slooworme; 6 sloowoorme, 7 -worme, 7 9 -worm. [OE.]

Sloy, *Obs.* [? var. SLAY *sb.*]

Slub (slŏb), *sb.*1 *dial.* Mire; mud; ooze, mire.

Slubber (slŏ'bǎr), *sb.*1
1. One who manipulates a slubbing-machine.
2. A slubbing-machine.

Slubber (slŏ'bǎr), *v.* Now chiefly *dial.* Also 6 **sloubber**. [Probably of Du. or LG. origin]

Slubbered, *ppl. a.*

Slubberdegullion (slŏ'bǎrdigʌ'ljǎn), [f. SLUBBER + DEGULLION.] A slovenly or dirty fellow; a worthless person.

Slubbing, *vbl. sb.* [See *8* slobbing. [Of obscure origin.]

Slubby (slŏ'bi), *a.* *dial.* [f. SLUB *sb.*1 + -Y.] Muddy; sticky or slippery with mud.

Slud, *obs. rare.* [ad. Russ. слюда *slyúda* (locally *slída*, *slud*; Czech *slída*) mica.] Russian mica in thin transparent plates.

Sludge (slŏdj), *sb.* [? var. of SLUTCH *sb.*]

Sludge (slŏdj), *v.* [f. the sb.]

Sludged (slŏdjd), *ppl. a.*

Sludger (slŏ'dʒǎr), *sb.* An appliance for removing the sludge from a bore-hole, or for boring in quicksand.

Sludgy (slŏ'dʒi), *a.* 1. Muddy, miry, oozy.

Slue, obs. form of SLEW *v.*, SLOE, SLOO.

Sluff, obs. or dial. form of SLOUGH *sb.*2

Slug (slŏg), *sb.*1 Also 5–7 **slugge**, 7 **slougge**.

Slug (slŏg), *sb.*2 Also 7–8 **slugge**; 7 *aluge*. [Perhaps to SLUG *a.*]

Slug (slŏg), *sb.*3 *north.* and *U.S.* [See SLUG *v.*3]

Slug (slŏg), *sb.*4 [f. SLUG *v.*4]

Slug (slŏg), *a.* Obs. Now somewhat rare.

Slug (slŏg), *v.*1 [f. SLUG *sb.*1] trans. To shed (also, to drive, throw, -shot; *slug-loaded adj.*]

Slug (slŏg), *v.*2 Chiefly *north.* and U.S.

Slug (slŏg), *v.*3 U.S. To strike (also, to drive, throw, etc.)

Slug (slŏg), *v.*4 [f. SLUG *sb.*4 and *v.*3.] trans. To lay, slow, or inert; to lie idly or lazily. Also with *it.*

Slug-a-bed (slŏ'gǎbed), *sb.* Also 7 **slug-abed**, 9 **sluggabed**. One who lies long in bed through laziness.

Sluggard (slŏ'gǎrd), *sb.* and *a.* Forms: 4 **sloggard**, 5–6 **slogarde**, 6 **sloggard**; 5–6 **slugard**, 5– **sluggard**. [f. SLUG *v.*1 + -ARD.]

Sluggardize (slŏ'gǎrdǎiz), *v.* [f. SLUGGARD + -IZE.]

Sluggardness (slŏ'gǎrdnes). [f. as prec. + -NESS.]

Sluggardy (slŏ'gǎrdi), *Obs.*1 [f. as prec. + -Y.]

Sluggardy, *Obs.* Forms: *a.* 5 slog-ardye, 5– sluggardie, 7 slougardie. *β.* 5 slugardie, 5– sluggardy. [f. SLUGGARD *sb.* + -Y.]

Slugged, ppl. a. [f. SLUG v.[1] or sb.[1]] Sluggish.

Slugger[1]. [f. SLUG v.[1] + -ER[1].] A sluggard.

Slugger[2] (slʌrgəᵊ), U.S. [f. SLUG v.[3].]
1. = SLOGGER sb.[2]
2. A flat-surfaced boss, knob, or projection on a roll for crushing ore.

Slugger[3]. [f. SLUG sb.[3]] [See quot.]

+Sluggeress. [f. SLUG sb.[1]] Sluggishness, slothfulness.

Slugging (slʌrgiŋ), vbl. sb.[1] [f. SLUG v.[1]] Slogging; hard hitting; a beating.

Slugging (slʌrgiŋ), vbl. sb.[2] north. and U.S. [f. SLUG v.[2]] Slogging; hard hitting; a beating.

Slugging (slʌrgiŋ), ppl. a. [f. SLUG v.[1]] Slothful, sluggish.

Sluggish (slʌrgiʃ), a. Forms: 5 slugis(sh, -yss(e)h, sluggysssh, -us(c)h, -isshe, 6 -yashe, -ysh(e, -ysch, -ische (5 -esch, 6 -eash), 6- sluggish; 6 slougish, also (5) sluggyssshe, slougishe, 7 slouggish. [f. SLUG sb.[1] + -ISH[1].]
1. Of persons: Indisposed to action or exertion; inclined to be slow or slothful; not easily moved to activity.
b. Of animals; also (see quot. 1884.)
c. Of things: Inert.

Sluggishly, adv. In a sluggish or torpid manner; lazily, slowly.

Sluggishness. The character or quality of being sluggish, torpid, or slow. a. Of persons (or animals).
b. Of things.

Sluggy, a. [f. SLUG sb.[1]] = SLUGGISH a.

SLUICY

Metals 105 The Fox Creek and Boulder Creek sluicing claims have uniformly done well.

Sluicy (slū′si), a. Chiefly *poet.* Also 7 *sluicy.* [f. SLUICE sb. + -Y[1].]
1. Of rain, etc.: Falling or pouring copiously or in streams, as if from a sluice; streaming, drenching.
b. Resembling a sluice; acting like a sluice. *rare.*

Sluit (slūt). S. African. Also 9 sloot (local), (Cape) Du. *sloot* ditch. = LG. *sloot*, OFris. *slôt* [WFris. *sleat*.] A channel, ditch, or gully, usually one formed by heavy rain and drying during the greater part of the year.

Slum (slʌm), sb.[1] Also 8 slam. [Of cant origin, and in all senses except 2 = only in canting use.]
I. 1. A room. *Obs.*
2. A street; alley, court, etc., situated in a crowded district of a town or city inhabited by people of a low class or by the very poor; a number of these streets or courts forming a thickly populated neighbourhood or district where the houses and the conditions of life are of a squalid and wretched character. Chiefly *sl.*, and *freq.* in the phrase *back slum* (*q.v.*).
3. = Slang *Dict.*
II. = 5. Nonsensical talk or writing; gammon, blarney; also, gipsy jargon of cant. *Obs.*

SLUMBER.

Ibid. 311 Of these documents there are two sorts, 'slums' (letters) and 'fakements' (petitions).
7. 'A cheat or imposture.' (*Slang Dict.* 1859.)

Slum (slʌm), sb.[2] U.S. [? ad. G. *schlamm* in the same sense.] = SLUDGE sb.[1]

Slum, variant of SLOOM sb.[1] and sb.[2]

Slum (slʌm), v. [f. SLUM sb.[1]]
1. *trans.* Cant. [See quots.]
2. To do (work) hurriedly and carelessly.
3. *intr.* a. To go into, or frequent, slums for discreditable purposes; to saunter about, with a suspicion, perhaps, of immoral practice.
b. *To* keep to back streets to avoid observation.
c. To visit slums for charitable or philanthropic purposes, or out of curiosity, esp. as a fashionable pursuit. *Freq.* in phr. *to go slumming* (see SLUMMING *vbl. sb.*)

Slumber (slʌm′bəᵊ), sb. Forms: 4 *slomer*, *slumbre*; 5 *slumbir*, *slumbur*, *slommer*, *slombere*; 5-6 *slumbyr*; 6 *slombre*; 7 *slumber*. [f. SLUMBER v.]
1. Sleep.
2. A period or occasion of sleep or repose; freq., a light or short sleep.
3. Of things, faculties, etc.: To be dormant, inoperative, or quiescent.

SLUMBER.

20 *Aug.* 217 We are half way to Sunderland.
II. Intr. 1. To be at rest or asleep; to sleep.
2. *fig.* To lie at rest in death or the grave.
b. *fig.* To be inactive; to remain quiet or dormant.

Slumber (slʌm′bəᵊ), v. Forms: 4 *slom(b)er*, *slomyr*, 5 *slumbyr*, -*yre*, -*ur*, 5-6 *slomber*, 6 Sc. *slummer*, 8-9 *slombre*, 7 *slumbred*; also MHG. *slummer* (Du. *slummeren*, *slommeren*), etc.

Slumberer. One who slumbers; a sleeper.

Slumberful, a. [f. SLUMBER sb. + -FUL.]

Slumbering, vbl. sb. [f. SLUMBER v. + -ING[1].]

Slumbering, ppl. a. [f. as prec.]

Slumberingly, adv. In a slumbering manner; drowsily.

Slumberous, a. [f. SLUMBER sb. + -OUS.]

Slumberously, adv. [f. prec.] In a slumberous, drowsy, or sleepy manner; quietly, tranquilly, indolently, etc.

Slumberousness. [f. as prec.] Sleepiness, drowsiness.

SLUMMOCK.

Slumberless (slʌm′bəᵊles), a. [f. SLUMBER sb. + -LESS.] Obtaining or yielding no slumber; sleepless.

+Slumberness. *Obs.* [f. SLUMBER sb.] Sleepiness, somnolence; sloth, indolence.

Slumbersome (slʌm′bəᵊsəm), a. [f. SLUMBER sb. + -SOME.] Slumberous, sleepy.

Slumbery (slʌm′bəri), a. Now *rare* or *Obs.*

Slumbrous (slʌm′brəs), a. Also 8 *slumbrious*, 8-9 *slumb'rous*. [f. SLUMBER sb. + -OUS.]

Slumgullion (slʌmgʌ′ljən). *slang.* [Probably a fanciful formation.]

Slumming (slʌm′iŋ), vbl. sb. [f. SLUM v.]
1. *slang.* (See quot.)
2. The visitation of slums, esp. for charitable or philanthropic purposes.
b. *attrib.*, as *slumming expedition*, *party*.

Slummock, v. Also 9 *slommock*. [var. of Eng. *Dial. slammock*, *slammack*: see the *Eng. Dial. Dict.*]
1. *trans.* To eat greedily.
2. *intr.* To go untidily.
3. To move about awkwardly or clumsily. Also *transf.* of work.

Slummock, sb. [One of many recently acquired slumming friends.]
3. An inhabitant of the slums.

Slummy, a. [f. SLUM sb.[1]] Of, pertaining to, or characteristic of a slum or slums; resembling a slum.

Slumminess. The state of being slummy.

Slummocky, a. Also slummocky. [Cf. prec., and see the *Eng. Dial. Dict.* s.v. *Slummocky*.] Slovenly, untidy.

Slummy, a. [f. SLUM sb.1 + -Y.]
1. Given to frequenting the slums.
2. Of the nature of a slum; abounding in or possessing slums. Also *absol.*

Slump, sb.1 [Cf. a. LG. *slump* heap, mass, quantity (im *slump kôpen* to buy in the lump), — Du. *slomp*, Fris. *slompe.*]
1. A large quantity or number; chiefly in phrases *by* or *in (the) slump*, rarely *in a slump*, collectively or individually, collectively; in the lump.

Slump, v.1 [f. SLUMP sb.1]
1. *intr.* To fall or sink in or *into* a bog, swamp, muddy place, etc.; to fall in water with a dull splashing sound.

Slump, sb.2 [f. SLUMP v.1]

Slumper (*slœmpəx*), v. Also *slumpers*.

Slumpy (slœm'pi), a.2 Also *slumpey*. [f. SLUMP sb.1]

Slumpy, v. [f. SLUMP sb.1] Taking things in the lump; rough, general.

Slumwand (-), *adv.* [f. SLUM sb.1 + -.] In the direction of the slums.

Slunchin, obs. variant of LUNCHEON I.

Slung (slœŋ), v.1

Slung-shot, U.S. [f. *slung*, pa. pple. of SLING v.1] A shot, piece of metal, stone, etc., fastened to a strap or thong, and used as a weapon.

Slunk (slœŋk), v.

Slunk (slœŋk), ppl. a. [f. SLINK v.3] Of calves (cast prematurely).

Slunker, U.S. (*see quot.*)

Slup, v. Obs.-1 [Cf. SLOP v.]

Slur (slœx), sb.1 Now *dial.* Also 5 *sloor*, 5, 9 *slure*. [Of obscure origin. Cf. MDu. *slore* (Du. *sloor, sloerie*) a sluttish woman.]

Slur, sb.2 Obs. Also 7 *slurr.* [f. SLUR v.1]

Slur, sb.3 Now *dial.* Also 7 *slurr(e.* [f. SLUR v.1]

Slur (slœx), v.1

Slur (slœx), v. Also 5-8 *slurre*, 9 *dial.* [Related to SLUR sb.1 Also 3 *slurr* (schlurren, schlorren).]

Slur (slœx), v.2 [f. SLUR sb.1] 1. *trans.* To smear, stain, smirch, sully. Also *fig.*

Slurf, Obs. rare.-1 [Error for SCURF sb.1]

Slurg, v. Obs. rare. [Cf. G. dial. *schlurgen* to go about in a slovenly manner.] 1. *intr.* To slip sleepily or draggingly.

Slurp, v. *intr.* To suck up, take place.

Slurred (slœxd), ppl. a.

Slurring (slœx'riŋ), vbl. sb.1 [f. SLUR v.1] The action of SLUR v. in various senses.

Slurring, vbl. sb.2 [f. SLUR v.2]

Slurry (slœ'ri), sb. Now *dial.* Also 5 *slory*, 9 *slorry*. 1. Thin sloppy mud or cement.

Slurry (slœ'ri), v. Now *dial.* Also 5-6 *slory*. [Related to SLUR v.2]

Slush (slœʃ), sb.1 Also 8-9 *dial. slusa.* [Of doubtful origin: cf. SLUDGE and SLUTCH (both from the 17th cent.), and the more recent SLOSH.]

Slush (slœʃ), v. [f. SLUSH sb.1]

Slusher (slœ'ʃəx), U.S.

Slushiness, [f. SLUSHY a.] The quality of being slushy.

Slushy (slœ'ʃi), a. [f. SLUSH sb.1 + -Y.]

Slushy, sb. A ship's cook. = SLUSHER.

Slut (slœt), sb. Also 4-7 *slutte*, 5-6 *slutt*, *sklutt(e*, *schlutt*, *schlute*, *schluts*, in sense 1. [From having some resemblance in sound and sense also occur in the Scand. languages, as Da. *slaske*, *slöske* (from LG.), Norw. *slott*, *slota*, but connexion is very doubtful.]

Slut, v. Obs. rare. Also 6 Sc. *slute*, *slutt*. [f. SLUT sb.]

Slutch (slœtʃ), sb. [Of uncertain origin: cf. SLUDGE sb., and SLUSH sb.1]

Slutchy, a. [f. SLUTCH sb. + -Y.] Muddy, slushy.

Slutish, *see* SLEUTH sb.2 and v.1

Slutter, v. Now *dial.* Also 4 *sluthche*. [f. SLUTHER v. + -ER.]

Sluther (slœ'ðəx), v. *dial.* [var. of SLITHER v.1]

Slutly, *adv.* Obs.-1 [f. SLUT sb. + -LY.]

Sluttered, adv. Obs. rare. [f. next.] Befouled, dirtied.

Slutter, v. Obs. rare. Absurd. [f. prec.]

Sluttery (slœ'təri). Now *rare.* [f. SLUT sb.]

Sluttikin, a. (or sb.) dial.

Sluttily (slœ'tili), *adv.* [f. SLUTTY a.] Also *sluttishly*.

Sluttiness (slœ'tinəs), [f. SLUTTY a. + -NESS.]

Sluttishly (slœ'tiʃli), *adv.*

Sluttishness (slœ'tiʃnəs), [f. prec. + -NESS.]

Slutty (slœ'ti), a. Now *dial.* + -Y.] Dirty, foul; slovenly.

Sly (slai), a., *adv.*, and sb. Forms: a. 3 *slah*, 4 *sleʒ*, 4 *slaʒ*, *sleʒe*, *sleghe* (5 *scleʒ*, *slegh*); 3-4 *sley*, 4 *sleyʒ*, 3 *sleiʒ*, 3-4 *sleigh*, 3 *sleih*, 5 *sley(e*; 4 *sleyʒe*, *sleye*, 5 *slei(e*, 5-6 *slye*, 5- *sly*.

'Hence +**Slu'ttily** *adv.*; **Slu'ttiness.**

Supplement, p. 3873; Corrigenda, p. 4092; Spurious words, p. 4093; Books quoted, p. 4094

SMALLUM.

†Smallum, *adv.* *Obs.* [f. SMALL *a.* Cf. LITLUM *adv.*] In small pieces or quantities.

Smallums, 'small quantities'; small wares, in modern north. dial. use.

Small-wares, [SMALL *a.* 3.] (See quot. 1839.) Chiefly in *pl.*

†Small·y, *adv.* *Obs.* Forms: 4 smalliche, 4 -LY. 4 very common use *1525-1630.*]
1. In or into small or minute pieces, fragments, etc.; finely, minutely.
2. By a small number; sparsely, scantily.
3. In only a slight or small degree; to a small or limited extent; not much, very little. Freq. preceded by *but.*

Smaltine (smȯlt·ain). *Min.* [f. SMALT *sb.* + -INE[2].] Tin-white cobalt.

Sma·ltite. *Min.* [SMALT+-ITE[2]b.] = prec.

†Smal·to. Also *pl.* smalti (8 smalts). [It. *smalto*, from 9th cent.]

Smaltz (smȯlts). [app. the plural of SMALT taken as a sing.] = SMALT *sb.* 1.

Smalts (smȯlts), *sb.* *dial.* Also sma(l)m, amawm, smaum. [Of obscure origin.] *trans.* To smear, bedaub.

SMART.

Smalt (smȯlt), *sb.* (and *a.*) Also 6, 8 smalte, 7 smaut(e, (9, 1 F. *smalt* (cf. Du. *smalt*, G. *schmalte*), ad. It. *smalto* SMALTO.]
1. A species of glass, usually coloured a deep blue by oxide of cobalt, etc., and after cooling finely pulverized for use as a pigment or colouring matters.
2. A deep blue colour like that of smalt.
3. A piece of coloured glass. Cf. SMALTO.
4. *attrib.* and *Comb.*, as *smalt-blue*, *-furnace*, *-glass*, etc.; smalt-blue, powder blue.
B. *adj.* 1. Of or belonging to, consisting of, a smalgel; resembling that of a smaragel; of an emerald green.

Smaragdian, *a. rare.* [f. SMARAGD + -IAN.]

Smaragdine (smara·gdin, -din), *a.* Also 4 smaragdyn, -yn(e, -en, -an, -one, 6 smaragdina. [ad. L. *smaragdino-us* of emerald, a, Gr. *σμαραγδίνος*, f. *σμάραγδος* SMARAGDUS. Cf. OF. *smaragdine* sb., mod.F. *smaragdin*, -ine.]

Smaragdite (smara·gdəit). *Min.* [a. F. *smaragdite* (Saussure, 1796), f. Gr. *σμάραγδος* SMARAGD + -ITE[2] b. Cf. Ger. *σμαραγδῖτις* lithos).]

Smaragdus (smara·gdɵs). *Min.* Now *rare.* [L., a. Gr. *σμάραγδος*, first recorded in Herodotus.]

†Smaragd. *Obs.* [var. of SMARAGD, after Fr. forms in -*alde.*] = SMARAGD; an emerald.

Smarm: see SMALM *v.*

Smart (smart), *sb.*[1] Forms: 3 smi(s)rte, 3-5 smerte (4 -tte) 4-6, 9 *Sc.* smairt; 5-6 smarpt, 5 *Sc.* smayrt. [OE. *smeorte* wk. fem. (MDu. and MLG. *smerte*, *smarte* (Du. and LG. *smart*, Da. *smerte*, Sw. *smärta*), MHG. *smerze*, *smerz* (G. *schmerz* masc.), related to *smeortan* SMART *v.*]
1. Sharp physical pain, esp. as caused by a stroke, sting, or wound. Also with *a* and *pl.*
2. *transf.* Sharp mental pain, suffering, or distress; sometimes, suffering of the nature of punishment or retribution.
3. *adj.* 1. Of a whip, rod, etc.: Inflicting or causing pain; sharp, biting, stinging. *Obs.*
 b. Sharp, severe; inflicting severe punishment, etc. *Obs.*
 c. Of encounters, attacks, etc.
2. Of blows, strokes, etc.: Sufficiently hard or vigorous to cause pain. (In later use approximating to sense 5.) Also in *fig.* contexts.
3. *a.* Of the weather, etc.: Sharp, keen; painful, severe. *Obs.*
4. Quick, active; prompt.
5. Of persons: Quick, active; prompt.
6. Brisk or vigorous; having a certain degree of intensity, force, strength, or quickness.
7. Sharp in criticism or comment upon one.

SMART.

Smartful, *a.* *Obs.* [f. SMART *sb.*[1] + -FUL.] Painful, distressing.

†Smarthead. (the *a.* [f. SMART. Severity.

†Smarthole. *Obs.*[1] [f. SMART *v.* + HOLE *sb.*] Painful.

Smart-hoop. [perh. f. SMART *sb.*[1] or *a.*; but cf. also older Da. *smerte*, *smaert*, Sw. *smärt* slender, slim.] (See quot.)

Smarting, *vbl. sb.* [f. SMART *v.*] The fact or sensation of feeling a sharp pain, as caused by a wound, sore, burn, or the like.

Smarting, *ppl. a.* [f. as prec.]
1. Causing to smart; painful; sharp, acute.
2. Feeling sharp pain. Also *fig.*

Smartingly, *adv.* [f. prec. + -LY[2].] Painfully.

Smartish, (sma·rtiʃ), *a.* colloq. the form *smart* is also employed.]
1. *trans.* To make smart or spruce.
2. *intr.* To become smart.

Smart, (smart), *adv.* Forms: 3 smeorte, 3 smerte, 4-5 smert, *Sc.* smart. [f. SMART *a.*]
1. Of actions, etc.: Hard and fast overhand volley.

Smartly (sma·rtli), *adv.* Also 3-4 smert(e)·liche (4 *comp.* -loker), 4 smartliche, 4-5 smertli, 4-6 smeert(e)·ly. [f. SMART *a.* + -LY[2].]
1. Vigorously, forcibly; sharply (in respect of physical action).
2. Sharply (in respect of treatment, language, etc.); severely; curtly.
 b. Sharply (in respect of feeling); keenly; also, heavily, largely.
3. Promptly, quickly, briskly (and timely).
4. Handsomely, elegantly, fashionably.
5. Extreme cleverness or sharpness, esp. for one's own advantage. Chiefly *U.S.*

Smart-money, *sb.* [SMART *sb.*[1]]
1. A sum of money paid to soldiers, workmen, etc., as compensation for disablement or injuries received while on duty or at work.
2. Money paid to obtain the discharge of a recruit who has enlisted in the army.

Smartweed. Chiefly *dial.* and *U.S.* [f. SMART *a.* + WEED.] A name given to various species of *Polygonum*, esp. the acrid *Polygonum Hydropiper*.

Smart·y. [f. SMART *a.* + -Y[1].] A would-be-smart or witty person.

Smash (smaʃ), *v.* [Of doubtful origin: not clearly connected with prec.]
1. Counterfeit coin. Also in comb. *smash-feeder* (see quot. 1860).

Smash, *sb.*[1] [Cant. (Of doubtful origin) not clearly connected with prec.]
1. *dial.* or *colloq.* A hard or heavy blow. (In earliest quots. *pl.*)
2. To break (anything) in pieces violently; to dash to pieces; to crush, shatter, or shiver.

Smasher (smæˑʃəɹ). Orig. *Cant.*

Smashing (smæˑʃɪŋ), *vbl. sb.*

Smash, *sb.* *Cant.*

Smash¹, *v.* [f. Smash *sb.*]

Smashable (smæˑʃ·ab'l), *a.* [f. Smash *v.* + -able.]

Smashdom (smæˑʃdɔm). [f. Smash *sb.* + -dom.]

Smashed (smæʃt), *ppl. a.* [f. Smash *v.*]

Smasher¹ (smæˑʃəɹ).

Smashing (smæˑʃɪŋ), *ppl. a.* [f. Smash *v.*]

Smashing, *vbl. sb.*

Smashing-up.

Smatch (smætʃ), *sb.* [Of obscure origin.]

Smatch, *v.* *Obs.*

Smatch-up.

Smatcher.

†Smatchcock. *Obs.* rare. [Of obscure origin.]

Smatter (smæˑtəɹ), *sb.*

†Sma·tchless, *a.* *Obs.*

Smatter (smæˑtəɹ), *v.*

Sma·tterer.

Smattering (smæˑtərɪŋ), *vbl. sb.*

Sma·ttering, *ppl. a.*

Sma·tteringly, *adv.*

Smatter (smæˑtəɹ), *v.* [f. Smatter *v.*]

Smatterer (smæˑtərəɹ).

Smattery, *sb.* [f. Smatter *sb.*]

Smattery, *a.*

Smay (smē). *Now dial.* [Aphetic for Dismay *v.*]

Smeach (smītʃ), *sb.* 1 smeoru, -o, -a.

Sma·tering, *vbl. sb.*

Smear (smīəɹ), *sb.* 1 ameoru, -o, smeru, 7 smeer.

Smear (smīəɹ), *v.* Forms: α 1 smirian (smiran), 3 smirien, 4 smyrie.

Smeared (smīəɹd), *ppl. a.* [f. Smear *v.*]

Smearer.

Smeariness.

Smearing (smīˑərɪŋ), *vbl. sb.*

†Smearwort. *Obs.* Forms: 1 smeoru-, smeoruwyrt, 4 smerewort (Du. smeerwortel), MHG. smerwurz (G. schmeerwurz), MHG. schmeerwurz.

Smeary (smīˑərɪ), *a.* Also 6 smeary, smearye, 6-7 smeorie, smearie.

Smear-dab. [f. Smear *sb.* + Dab *sb.*]

Smeath (smīþ). *dial.* Also 7 smieth, 7/9 smethe. [Obscurely related to Smee.]

Smeddum (smeˑdəm). Forms: 1 smeodoma, smedma, 5 smeddum, 9 smeddum (9 -am). [OE., of obscure origin.]

Smee (smī). *dial.* and *U.S.* [Prob. a later form of Smeath.]

Smeeth (smīþ), *v.* 1 *Obs.* exc. *dial.* Forms: 1 smeocan, 1-3 smeoke, 3-4 smeke, 5-8 smeek, 7-9 smeik, 5-8 smeech. [OE., = MDu. smiecken, smuicken (Du. smieken).]

Smeech, *dial.* variant of Smitch *sb.*

Smeechy, *a.* *Sc.* Also 9 smoikie, 9 smeekie.

Smeek (smīk), *sb.* and *v.* *north.*

Smeeth (smīþ), *dial.* (Now rare.) *Obs.* exc. *dial.* Forms: 1 smeþe, 1-3 smeðe, 2-4 smeþe, 4-5 smethe, (5 smytthe), related to smooth Smooth *a.*

Smeeth (smīþ), *v.* variant of Smooth *v.*

Hence **Smi·lelessly** adv.; **Smi·lelessness**.

Smile·t, rare. Also 6 smylet. A little or slight smile.

Smiling, (smaɪ·liŋ), vbl. sb. [f. SMILE v.]

1. The action of the verb; an instance of this, a smile. Also transf. and fig.

b. transf. Pleasantly, agreeably, cheerfully.

Smi·lingness. The condition or expression.

Smilingly, adv. [f. prec.] In a smiling manner; with a smile or smiles.

Smilt, a. Obs.—¹ In 4 smylt. ? Fine.

Smilt, v. Obs.—¹ [? Cf. dial. smilt the milt of a fish.] intr. To melt slightly.

Smirch (smɜːtʃ), v. Also 6–7 smurch.

1. trans. To make dirty, soil, sully, or discolour (something) by contact or touch.

2. fig. A moral stain or flaw; a blot or blemish; a fault or defect.

Smirch, sb. Also 6–8 smorch, 7 smurch, smerch, smyrch. [f. SMIRCH v.]

1. A dirty mark or smear; a smudge; also, that which smirches or dirties.

2. Characterized by wearing a smile or smiles.

Smirched (smɜːtʃt), ppl. a. [f. prec.] Marked, soiled, made dirty, etc.; with a stain or smirch.

Smirchless, a. [f. SMIRCH sb.] Without leaving a smirch or stain.

Smirk (smɜːk), sb. [f. next.] Also 6 smyrke. An affected, conscious, or silly, conceited, smiling look.

Smirk (smɜːk), v. [OE. smearcian, smercian.]

1. An affected or simpering smile; a silly, conceited, smiling look.

2. To smile in a conceited, affected, silly, or offensively familiar manner.

Smirking, ppl. a. [f. SMIRK v.]

1. That smirks or smiles affectedly; simpering.

Smirkingly, adv. [f. prec.] In a smirking manner; with a smile.

Smirky (smɜː·ki), a. Also 6 smyrke. [f. SMIRK sb.] Smiling; inclined to smirk or simper.

Smirtle, v. Sc. [next.] intr. To smirk or smile. Also transf.

Smish. Cant. [App. a later form of MISH q.v.] (See quots.)

Smit (smɪt), pa. pple. and ppl. a. Forms: see SMITE. Arch. and dial. = SMITTEN.

Smit (smɪt), sb. [f. SMIT v.]

1. A stain or blemish.

2. Infection; contagion.

Smit, v. Obs. exc. dial. Forms: 1 smitta, smittia, 3 smit, 4–8 smitt(e, smyt. [OE. smitta v.]

1. trans. To mark or stain in some way; to colour or tinge; to smut. Also in fig. context.

2. To infect, taint, or infect with sin, guilt, etc.

Smit, Obs. var. of SMITE, SMITH.

Smitable, a. Now dial. Forms: 1 smite. A particle, bit.

Smitch (smɪtʃ), sb. Now dial. Forms: 1–2 smita, smyo, 3 smycho, 3, 9 smitche, 9 smitch.

Smitchel, sb. Now dial.

Smite (smaɪt), v. Forms: see below. [OE. smītan.]

A. Illustration of Forms.

B. Signification.

I. trans. 1. To strike, blemish. Obs.—¹

Smite ...

Smiter (sməitəɹ). Also 3 smittere, 4 smyttere. [f. SMITE v. + -ER.] One who smites.

Smith (smiþ). Forms: 1 smiþ, 4 smiþe, 3–smith, 5 (7) smithe ...

Smitham ...

Smither ...

Smithers ...

Smithery ...

Smithcraft ...

Smithfield (smiþfīld). [The name of a locality in London (orig. Smethefeld, i.e. smooth field), long celebrated as a market for cattle and horses, and as the central meat-market.]

Smithian (smiþ·iăn), a. [f. the surname Smith (see defs.).]

Smithite ...

Smithsonite (smiþ·sənəit). Min. [Named by Beudant (1832), after James Smithson (1765–1829), who had distinguished it from calamine (see quot.).]

Smith-work ...

Smithy (smiþ·i), sb. Forms: 1–4 smiþþe, 5 smyþþy ...

Smithy, v. ...

Smiting ...

Smitten (smit·ən), ppl. a. [See SMITE v. Also attrib.]

Smittle ...

Smitting ...

Smock (smǫk), sb. Forms: 1, 3 smoc, 3–5 smoke, 4–7 smok ...

Smocker (smǫk·əɹ) ...

Smock-face ...

Smock-faced, a. Now rare. [f. prec.]

Smock-frock ...

Smocking, vbl. sb. [f. SMOCK v. 4.]

Smock-mill ...

Smock-race ...

Smockster ...

Smoke (smōk), sb. Forms: 1 smoca, 6 Sc. smoik, 6–8 smoak, 6– smoke ...

Smokable (smōk·ăb'l), a. Also smoakable. [f. SMOKE v. + -ABLE.]

Smoke-face. Now rare. [f. SMOKE sb.]

Smoke-faced, a. ...

Smokeless, a. ...

Smoke-mill ...

Smogue: see SMUG.

Hearths. 1792 Stat. Acc. Scotl. IV. 316 For 6 miles in a well inhabited extent,..there was not a *smoke* remaining. 1883 Good Words XXIV. 717 There are [on Minglay] in all thirty houses, or 'smokes', as they are called.

3. Fume or vapour caused by the action of heat on moisture.

1398 TREVISA Barth. De P. R. v. xxxiii. (Bodl. MS.), Þat þe lunges mowe open and close þe hoote smoke of þe herte. 1422 tr. Secreta Secret., Priv. Priv. 218 Dronknesse makyth for-yetynge..by reyson that the grete smokkes gone vp to the brayn. 1562 TURNER Baths 9 They that woulde use the smooke or vaperouse ayer of this water. 1584 LYLY Alex. & Camp. II. i, Steeds..whose breathes dimmed the sun with smoake. 1621 BURTON Anat. Mel. II. ii. II. (1651) 239 To purge the heart and brain from ill smoakes and vapours that offend them. a 1693 Urquhart's Rabelais III. xxxvii. 311 Demanding payment for the Smoak of his Roast-meat. 1888 'R. BOLDREWOOD' Robbery under Arms xi. 136 You ought to have sense enough not to knock smoke out of fresh horses before we begin.

b. A mist, fog, or miasma (see later quots.).

1648 HEXHAM II, Een Roock der aerden, a Smoake, a Mist, or Dampe, rising out of the earth. 1788 FALCONBRIDGE African Slave T. 51 Together with what they call *the smokes* (a noxious vapour, arising from the swamps about the latter end of autumn). 1867 SMYTH Sailor's Word-bk. 635 *Smokes*, dense exhalations, mixed with the finer particles of sand, on the Calabar shores and borders of the Great Zahara desert, which prevail in autumn. 1897 MISS KINGSLEY W. Africa 94 Those thick wool-like mists called smokes, which hang about the whole Bight from November till May.

4. In proverbial, figurative, or allusive uses:

a. In miscellaneous applications or phrases.

1390 GOWER Conf. I. 211 When every thing was fulli spoke, Of sorwe and queint was al the smoke. 1526 State Papers Hen. VIII, VI. 542 Of whom..I have lernyd many strange thinges, wherof I smelt a smoke at Calays. 1580 LYLY Euphues (Arb.) 287, I perceiue..where the least smoake is, there to be the greatest fire. 1602 MARSTON Ant. & Mel. I. Wks. 1856 I. 13 His eyes looke as if they had bene hung In the smoake of his nose. 1670 G. H. tr. Hist. Cardinals I. I. 20, I..took my leave, as perceiving him fuller of smoak than of meat. 17.. in N. & Q. 3rd Ser. XII. 163/2 Never out of the smoke of your own chimney. 1774 Westm. Mag. II. 109 Their *summum bonum* lies in drinking themselves dead drunk,..playing smoak with the girls. 1854 MISS BAKER Northampt. Gloss. s.v., If a lent horse has been over-ridden, it is commonly remarked, 'He played smoke with that horse, he has been good for nothing since'. 1870 LOWELL Study Wind. 228 The first lesson of literature, no less than of life, is the learning how to burn your own smoke.

b. In the proverbs *There is no fire without smoke*, and *no smoke without fire*, or variants of these: (see FIRE sb. 1 h).

c 1450 MS. Douce 52 lf. 20 Where no fyre is no smoke. 1546- [see FIRE sb. 1 h]. 1650 HUBBERT Pill to purge Formality 133 There is no fire but there will be some smoak. 1654 GATAKER Disc. Apol. 11 There is seldom anie smoak, but where there is some fire. 1705 WYCHERLEY in Pope's Lett. (1735) I. 14 You must allow there is no Smoak but there is some Fire. 1820 COLERIDGE Lett., Conv., etc. I. 118 They..then exclaim: There is no smoke without some fire.

†**c.** *Out of the smoke into the fire*, etc., out of a small danger into a great one. *Obs.* (Cf. L. *de fumo in flammam*, Ammianus.)

1547 J. HARRISON Exhort. Scottes f iv b, Leaste by fleynge the smoke, we fall into the fyre. 1600 SHAKS. A. Y. L. I. ii. 299 Thus must I from the smoake into the smother. 1609 HOLLAND Amm. Marcell. xiv. ii. 25 Hee..went just as the old proverbe saith, out of the smoke into the light fire.

d. Used to designate anything having no real value or substance, or a mere shadow *of* something.

1548 tr. Papius' Conc. Apothecaries in Recorde Urinal Phys. (1651) 243 That the selfe-conceited..may learne to..brag and vaunt forth their vanities and smokes. 1559 Mirr. Mag. (1563) I v, Our kyngdomes are but cares,..our power a smouldring smoke. 1601-3 DANIEL C'tess Cumberland 35 The all-guiding Prouidence..mocks this smoake of wit. 1621 J. TAYLOR (Water P.) Superbiæ Flagellum D 3 Their Pride is..A smoake, a bubble. 1705 WYCHERLEY in Pope's Lett. (1735) I. 14 If Compliment be the Smoak only of Friendship. 1749 SMOLLETT Gil Blas x. i, Preferring the smoke of public applause to the real advantages which my friendship prepared for him. 1806 Sporting Mag. XXVIII. 279 In his opinion it was all smoke. 1875 JOWETT Plato (ed. 2) III. 122 The ambitious man will think knowledge which is without honour all smoke and nonsense.

e. Denoting a clouding or obscuring medium or influence.

1565 COOPER Thesaurus s.v. Fuligo, To speake obscurely: to cast a darke smoke or miste before their eies. 1581 J. BELL Haddon's Answ. Osorius 273 b, Why shamed he not to blind the eyes of the people with such smoakes? 1594 T. B. tr. De la Primaud. Fr. Acad. II. 333 Their eies dimmed with some smoake of honours. 1603 J. DAVIES (Heref.) Microcosmos Wks. (Grosart) I. 78/1 The Eyes that ..smoke of praise Doe dimme, are feeble-sighted. a 1677 BARROW Serm. Wks. 1716 I. 167 Truth will not be discerned through the smoak of wrathful expressions. 1864 TENNYSON Aylmer's F. 672 Thro' the smoke, The blight of low desires. 1873 FARRAR Silence & V. Ser. I. 22 Reading them..through the lurid smoke of sectarian hate.

f. Denoting fraudulent dealing in the fulfilment of bargains or promises; esp. *to sell smoke* (after L. *fumum vendere*), to act dishonestly, to swindle.

1589 GREENE Menaphon Wks. (Grosart) VI. 106 You get but a handfull of smoake to the bargaine. 1599 NASHE Lenten Stuff Wks. (Grosart) V. 306 That for your selling smoake you may be courtiers. 1655 tr. Sorel's Com. Hist. Francion IV. 24, I abandoned their conversation, because I found they were but sellers of smoak. 1692 WASHINGTON tr. Milton's Def. People Pref., To relieve the necessities of Nature..by selling of Smoke, as thou dost.

g. *To come to, end in, vanish into, smoke*, to come to nothing, be unrealized, be without result.

1604 E. GRIMSTONE Siege Ostend 184 Their subtill deuises are come to smoake. 1617 MORYSON Itin. II. 44 The ill successe of the Queenes affaires (whose..Royall Army they had seene vanish into smoke). 1683 TEMPLE Mem. Wks. 1720 I. 470 Thus ended in Smoke the whole Negotiation. 1704 Collect. Voy. & Trav. III. 699/2 His Designs vanished into Smoke. 1771 SMOLLETT Humph. Cl. (1815) 168, I take it for granted, this whole affair will end in smoke. 1853 MRS. CARLYLE in New Lett. & Mem. II. 68 One might let him scheme and talk, hoping it might all end in smoke.

h. *Like smoke*, very quickly, rapidly.

1833 M. SCOTT Tom Cringle x, Sail was made, and..she began to snore through it like smoke. 1840 MARRYAT Poor Jack vi, Away we all went like smoke. 1853 DICKENS Bleak Ho. xi, His brandy-balls go off like smoke. 1860 WHYTE MELVILLE Market Harb. 86 The hounds are running like smoke!

5. a. Tobacco. Now *rare* or *Obs.*

1612 WOODALL Surg. Mate Wks. (1653) 20* A small Gallon of Sack, and a pipe of the best smoake. 1616 R. C. Times' Whistle (1871) 71 Every skull And skip-iacke now will have his pipe of smoke And whiff it. 1649 J. TAYLOR (Water P.) Wand. West 19 They gave me smoake and drinke in Plimouth. 1853 'C. BEDE' Verdant Green I. vii, That if Mr. Larkyns was no smoker himself, he at least kept a bountiful supply of 'smoke' for his friends.

b. A cigar or cigarette. Also *fig.*

1882 BESANT All Sorts 112 The twopenny smoke, to which we cling, though it is made of medicated cabbage. 1893 C. G. LELAND Mem. I. 158 She was,..as we used to say at college of certain unpopular people, a 'bad smoke'.

6. [f. the vb.] A spell of smoking tobacco, etc.

1837 W. IRVING Adv. Capt. Bonneville II. 286 A crowd of visiters awaited their appearance, all eager for a smoke and a talk. 1890 'R. BOLDREWOOD' Col. Reformer (1891) 241 It was considered reasonable to devote half an hour to rest..and a smoke for the stockmen.

7. *Cape smoke*, a cheap kind of brandy drunk in South Africa.

1849 E. E. NAPIER Exc. S. Afr. II. 9 A young Hottentot, ..as fond of 'Cape Smoke'..as any of his tribe. 1880 GILLMORE On Duty 366 He produced a bottle of smoke (Cape brandy). 1893 Edin. Rev. Apr. 297 'Cape Smoke' is the most poisonous of all alcoholic drinks.

8. A Persian cat of a deep cinder-colour, with a white under-coat.

Also in combs., as *smoke-breeder, -fancier*, etc.

1893 Westm. Gaz. 17 Oct. 4/3 Miss Brigden's cat should not be overlooked among the 'smokes'.

II. *attrib.* and *Comb.* **9.** Attrib., in the sense of 'consisting of smoke', as *smoke-atmosphere, -burst, -cloud, -drift*, etc.

1837 CARLYLE Fr. Rev. I. IV. iv, It will burn..its whole *smoke-atmosphere too. 1852 M. ARNOLD Empedocles II. 417 Through the black, rushing *smoke-bursts, Thick breaks the red flame. 1837 CARLYLE Fr. Rev. II. I. iii, From yonder White Haven rise his *smoke-clouds. 1884 Athenæum 6 Dec. 739/1 Bars of light and shade belonging to the mist and *smoke-drift of London. 1864 LOWELL Fireside Trav. 8 Nor did the *smoke-palm of Vesuvius stand more erect and fair. 1890 SIR R. S. BALL Star-Land 235 We can make many experiments with *smoke-rings. 1813 HOGG Queen's Wake II. Wks. (1876) 19 His stature, on the mighty plan Of *smoke-tower o'er the burning pile. 1837 CARLYLE Fr. Rev. I. I. ii, Thou seest the *Smoke-vapour. 1598 MARSTON Sco. Villanie III. ix. 219 Belch impious blasphemies,..Snuffe vp *smoak-whiffs. 1808 SCOTT Marm. IV. xxx, The *smoke-wreaths..That round her sable turrets flow.

b. Used for, or promoting, the escape of smoke, as *smoke-flue, -funnel, -pipe*, etc.

1840 Cottager's Manual 7 in Husb. III. (L. U. K.), Vertical strata of gravel..alternating with *smoke-flues. 1799 G. SMITH Laboratory 143 A sort of funnel, like a *smoke funnel to an oven. 1853 URE Dict. Arts (ed. 4) II. 105 The *smoke-pipe of a subsidiary fire. 1856 KANE Arctic Explor. I. xxxi. 424 The *smoke-tubes of the stove.

c. Due to, or caused by, smoke, as *smoke-blackness, -nuisance, -smell*, etc.

1841 Civil Eng. & Arch. Jrnl. IV. 386 Smoke nuisance in large towns. 1874 RUSKIN Fors Clav. xxxix. 56 Golden light and song..are better than smoke-blackness. 1876 T. HARDY Ethelberta (1890) 81 Sniffing extraordinary smoke-smells which she discovered in all nooks and crannies of the rooms.

d. With names of colours, as *smoke-blue, -brown, -grey*, etc. (used as sbs. or adjs.).

London smoke: see LONDON.

1807 AIKIN Dict. Chem. & Min. II. 98/1 Its colour is ash or smoak-grey. 1839 URE Dict. Arts 388 Their ordinary tint verges upon yellow, or smoke-yellow. a 1847 ELIZA COOK Birds iii, There the smoke-brown Sparrow sits. 1901 CLIVE HOLLAND Mousmé 284 Overhung with smoke-blue mosquito curtains.

e. Having the colour of smoke; of a brownish or bluish grey colour. *Smoke quartz*, smoky quartz.

1872 E. HULL Build. & Ornament. Stones 175 *Smoke quartz*. This is a clouded variety [of rock crystal], with a brownish tint. 1884 Western Daily Press 11 Apr. 7/6 There are jackets of the finest cloth, geranium-red, electric-blue, smoke,..and brown. 1899 Westm. Gaz. 21 Sept. 3/2 The smoke fox, a blue-grey colouring which is really dyed. 1903 F. SIMPSON Bk. Cat xiv. 185 Perfect smoke cats..should be black, shading to smoke grey.

10. *Comb.* **a.** Objective, with pres. pples., adjs., agent-nouns, or nouns of action, as *smoke-burner, -burning, -consumer, -consuming, -consumption, -consumptive*, etc.

Many of these have been in common use from c 1840.

(*a*) 1596 FITZ-GEFFREY Sir F. Drake (1881) 96 O let our smoake-exhalinge breaths enfold A mightie cloud of sighes. 1612 SELDEN Illustr. Drayton's Poly-olb. xi. I. 139 Those foggie mists of error, and smoake-selling imposture. 1842 Civil Eng. & Arch. Jrnl. V. 42 This..furnace operates not upon the smoke-preventive, but upon the smoke-consumptive principle. Ibid. 131 The..furnace is in reality a smoke-burning and not a smoke-preventing. Ibid., Some new smoke-consuming theory. 1891 MORRIS News Nowhere 7 The soap-works with their smoke-vomiting chimneys were gone.

(*b*) 1604 JAS. I Counterbl. to Tobacco (Arb.) 111 Of so many smoke-buyers, as are at this present in this kingdome, I neuer read nor heard. 1838 Civil Eng. & Arch. Jrnl. I. 168 The adaptation of the patent smoke-consumer to a locomotive engine. Ibid. 344 The only effectual smoke-burner I have ever seen. 1851 Catal. Grt. Exhib. I. 328/1 Smoke condenser. 1891 Cent. Dict., *Smoke-washer*, a device for purifying smoke by washing as it passes through a chimney-flue.

(*c*) 1842 Civil Eng. & Arch. Jrnl. V. 42/1 An incarnation (so to speak) of the principles of smoke-prevention. 1851 Catal. Grt. Exhib. I. p. xcix, Apparatus for effecting Smoke-consumption. 1882 (title), Official Report of the Smoke-Abatement Committee.

b. Instrumental, with past pples., as *smoke-begotten, -bleared*, etc.

1872 C. W. KING Antique Gems & Rings 148 *Smoke-begotten theories of modern German sciolists. 1837 CARLYLE Fr. Rev. I. V. vi, A..dwarfish individual, of *smoke-bleared aspect. 1720 Mem. W. Stukeley (Surtees) I. 157 Their painted or rather *smoak-bound hides. 1822 LAMB Elia I. Distant Correspondents, Elms,..[with] *smoke-dyed barks, the theme of jesting ruralists. 1748 THOMSON Cast. Indol. I. lxx, Then *smoke enrolled Their oracles break forth. 1856 FROUDE Hist. Eng. (1862) I. 463 Those streets..so black and *smoke-grimed. 1818 SCOTT Hrt. Midl. xlii, The daily passage of so many *smoke-pennoned steam-boats. 1879 19th Cent. No. 31. 401 The swarming bustle of our *smoke-smothered towns. 1833 TENNYSON in Life (1897) I. 130 They are so *smoke-sodden. 1602 CAREW Cornw. 72 Hanging me thus vp, to be *smoke-starued ouer your chimnies. 1632 LITHGOW Trav. x. 429 There Fabrickes are..of *smoke-torne straw..and Raine-dropping watles.

c. With adjs., as *smoke-like, -proof, -tight*.

1840 R. H. DANA Bef. Mast xxviii. 98 We calked and pasted, and, so far as we could, made the ship smoke-tight. 1849 THOREAU Week Concord Riv. (1894) 4 Skirted..with alder-swamps and smoke-like maples. 1901 Westm. Gaz. 24 Dec. 7/2 One of the firemen donned a smoke-proof suit and helmet.

11. Special combs.: **smoke-arch** *U.S.*, the smoke-box of a locomotive (Webster, 1864); **smoke-bell, -board** (see quots.); **smoke-glass**, an eyepiece or spectacle of smoked glass; **smoke helmet**, a helmet used by firemen, enabling the wearer to see and breathe freely in the midst of smoke; †**smoke-hen**, a hen accustomed to perch in the smoke; **smoke-loft**, a loft in which the smoking of bacon, etc., is done; **smoke-mantle**, part of a furnace for roasting tin-ores; †**smoke-merchant**, a tobacconist; †**smoke-money**, money paid by householders as a due or tax (see quots. and cf. *smoke-penny*); **smoke night**, an evening meeting accompanied by smoking; **smoke-pence, -penny** (see quots. and *smoke-money*); **smoke-plant**, the Venetian sumach, *Rhus cotinus*, which has a feathery inflorescence suggestive of smoke; **smoke-proof**, an impression taken from a smoked type-punch, etc.; **smoke respirator** (see quots.); **smoke-sail** (see quot. 1846); †**smoke-seller** (see SMOKE sb. 4 f); also, a tobacconist; †**smoke-shop**, a tobacconist's shop in which accommodation for smoking was provided; †**smoke-silver**, silver paid as smoke-money; **smoke-talk** *U.S.*, a social meeting accompanied by smoking; **smoke test**, a method of testing the state of drains and pipes by means of smoke; **smoke-tree**, = *smoke-plant*; (also the American species *Rhus cotinoides*); **smoke-wood** (see quot.).

1875 KNIGHT Dict. Mech. 2223/2 **Smoke-bell*, a glass bell suspended over a gas-light, to intercept the smoke. 1850 OGILVIE, **Smoke-board*, a board hung in front of a fire-place, to keep the smoke from emerging into the apartment. 1769 Phil. Trans. LIX. 334 These two observers looked directly at the Sun, having their instruments armed with *smoke-glasses. 1889 Anthony's Photogr. Bulletin II. 373 A pair of light-tinted smoke glasses will afford great relief. 1900 Daily Mail 24 Apr. 3/2 An officer of the brigade donned a *smoke helmet. 1577 B. GOOGE Heresbach's Husb. IV. (1586) 162 b, The cause that the old people made choise in their quitrentes of *smoke Hennes, as of the best. 1657 H. CROWCH Welsh Trav. 11 Unto the *smoake-loft clim'd he than, and to the bacon crept. 1839 URE Dict. Arts 1246 The *smoke-mantle or chimney-hood, at the end of the furnace. a 1618 *Smoke-merchant [see *smoke-seller*]. 1662 PETTY Taxes 86 Of all the accumulative excises, that of hearth-money or *smoak-money seems the best. 1778 England's Gaz. (ed. 2) s.v. Brighthelmstone, The vicar here..claims the old episcopal custom of a penny per head (commonly called Smoak-Money, or the Garden-Penny). 1850 N. & Q. 1st Ser. II. 120/2 Smoke Money.. under this name is collected every year at Battle in Sussex. 1891 Melbourne Punch 2 June 378/3 The Mutual Store '*Smoke night' was held at the Vienna Cafe on Thursday evening. 1584 R. WILSON Three Ladies London I, For here were *smoke-pence, Peter-pence, and Paul-pence to be paid. 1631 WEEVER Anc. Funeral Mon. 176 Parsons, and Impropriators of Churches, at this day in many places of England, are payed this pennie vnder the name of a *Smoke pennie. 1652 Answ. Petit. Poor Husbandmen 19 The Parishioners do commonly blow away all the tithes due for firewood with a smoak penny. 1850 N. & Q. 1st Ser. II. 174/2 Smoke pennies are also yearly levied from most

of the inhabitants of the New Forest. 1856 A. GRAY Man. Bot. (1860) 76 Sumach...Leaves (simple in R. Cotinus, the **Smoke-Plant* of gardens). 1888 Encycl. Brit. XXIII. 699 The flame..blackens the letter, and thus enables an impression, called a '**smoke proof*', to be stamped on paper. 1902 DE VINNE Title-pages 79 Pleasing as a new ornament in this style might appear in the smoke-proof, it was sure to be a blotch in the print. 1866 C. F. T. YOUNG Fires, Fire-Engines, etc. 44 About the year 1824 one John Roberts..invented a '*smoke-respirator' or hood, by means of which a fireman could enter a burning building or room. 1884 Health Exhib. Catal. 60/1 Tyndale's Smoke Respirators are to enable the wearer to enter into most dense and pungent smoke with perfect safety. 1805 Naval Chron. XIII. 379, 90 yards of canvass were purchased to make her *smoke-sail. 1846 A. YOUNG Naut. Dict. 288 *Smoke-sail*, a small sail put up for the purpose of preventing the smoke of the galley from going aft to the quarter-deck, when the ship is riding head-to-wind. a 1618 SYLVESTER Tobacco Battered 812 Wks. (Grosart) II. 274 'Let the *Smoak-seller suffocate with Smoak': Which our Smoak-Merchants would no lesse befit. 1649 W. M. Wandering Jew (1857) 25 And when the miserable smoke-sellers die, how are they buried? 1798 Sporting Mag. XII. 194 The chit-chat of a Birmingham *smoke shop. 1802 BEDDOES Hygëia VIII. 31 Among..the artisans that croud the smoke-shops. 1664 SPELMAN Gloss. s.v., By the payment of *Smoke Silver to the Sheriff yearlie. 1698 in Ho. of Lords MSS. (1905) III. 257 The duty commonly called Smoak Silver, Peter Pence or Common Fine. 1893 Boston (Mass.) Jrnl. 25 Mar. 2/2 The Association of Railroad and Steamboat Agents..held a *smoke-talk..last evening. 1886 Encycl. Brit. XXI. 716 The '*smoke test' ..consists of filling the house-drain, soil-pipes, and waste-pipes with a dense and pungent smoke. 1860 WORCESTER, **Smoke-tree*. 1887 G. W. COX Cycl. Common Things (ed. 6) 573 The Venetian Sumach of Southern Europe is the common smoke tree or fringe tree of the gardens. 1863 PRIOR Plant-n., *Smoke-wood*, from children smoking its porous stalks, *Clematis vitalba*.

Smoke (smōᵘk), *v.* Forms: 1 smocian, smokian, 3 smokien, 3-4 smoken (5 smokyn), 4- smoke; 6-7 smoake, 6-9 smoak. [OE. *smocian*, f. *smoca* SMOKE sb. Cf., with different ablaut-grade, MDu. and Du., MLG. and LG., *smoken* (WFris. *smoke*), G. *schmauchen*; also the trans. LG. *smöken* (whence Da. *smøge*), G. *schmäuchen* (†*schmeuchen*):—**smaukjan*. See also SMEEK v.]

I. 1. *intr.* To produce or give forth smoke.

c 1000 ÆLFRIC Gen. xv. 17 Þa sloh þær micel mist and ferde swilce an ofen eall smociende. c 1000 Lambeth Ps. ciii. 32 Se þe æthrinð muntas & hiȝ smociað. c 1205 LAY. 25734 Þa iseȝen heo..a muchel fur smokien uppen ane hulle. c 1290 S. Eng. Leg. I. 233/490 Al þe se þare aboute barnde and smokede faste. 1388 WYCLIF Gen. xv. 17 A furneis smokynge apperide, and a laumpe of fier. c 1440 Promp. Parv. 460/2 Smekyn, or smokyn, *fumo, fumigo*. 1530 PALSGR. 723/1 This woode smoketh to moche, it is nat drye ynoughe. 1591 SAVILE tr. Tacitus, Agricola 261 The houses fired and smoking farre of. 1647 COWLEY Mistr., Discovery, The Gods may give their Altars o're; They'll smoak but seldom any more. 1700 DRYDEN Ovid's Met., Baucis & Philemon 52 With Leaves and Barks she feeds her Infant-fire: It smoaks. 1743 DAVIDSON Æneid VII. 203 The torch smoaking with grim horrid light. 1815 SCOTT Guy M. x, They perceived that she [the ship] grounded, smoked, and, finally, took fire. 1905 F. YOUNG Sands of Pleasure II. iii, The cigarette smoked unheeded in her fingers.

b. In fig. uses or contexts.

1535 COVERDALE Deut. xxix. 20 His wrath and gelousy shall smoke ouer soch a man. a 1548 HALL Chron., Hen. IV, 29 b, Where hertes still burne and malice continually smoketh. 1575 GASCOIGNE Glasse Govt. III. i, These young gallants are caught without a net..; no man gladder then I, for as long as that chimney smoketh, I..shall not go hungrie to bed. 1639 S. DU VERGER tr. Camus' Admir. Events 80 Glory is a perfume fit to smoake no where but before the Altar of vertue. 1677 HUBBARD Narr. 48 To cause his jealousie to smoak against those of his own heritage. 1834 DE QUINCEY in Tait's Mag. I. 196/1 Ireland was still smoking with the embers of rebellion.

c. Of a room, chimney, lamp, etc.: To be smoky, to emit smoke, as the result of imperfect draught or improper burning.

1663 PEPYS Diary 13 Jan., The dining-room smokes unless I keep a good charcoal fire. 1715 DESAGULIERS Fires Impr. 31 Every little cranny may be stopp'd up close without fear of the Room smoaking. c 1725 POPE Upon Dk. Marlborough's House at Woodstock 8 The chimneys..never smoke in any wind. 1807 GASS Jrnl. 176 We found our huts smoked; there being no chimnies in them except in the officers' rooms. 1826 SCOTT Woodst. xxi, It is best sitting near the fire when the chimney smokes. 1906 H. WALES Mr. & Mrs. Villiers xxiii, The lamp had been smoking in his room.

2. To give off or send up vapour, dust, spray, etc.; *esp.* to steam.

With quot. 1869 cf. SMOKE sb. 1 e.

13.. E. E. Allit. P. B. 226 As smylt mele vnder smal siue smokes for-þikke. 1533 J. HEYWOOD Mery Play 21 (Brandl), Whan I haue beten her tyll she smoke. 1577 B. GOOGE Heresbach's Husb. IV. (1586) 176 Their labour smokes and all of time [= thyme] doth smell, The Hony sweete that in their Coames they lay. 1617 MORYSON Itin. III. 97 These often heated meats, which smoaked on the outside, yet were cold on the inside. 1697 DRYDEN Virg. Georg. III. 274 The lab'ring Yoke and shining Shares, that make the Furrow smoak. 1732 POPE Ep. Bathurst 360 Two puddings smok'd upon the board. 1782 COWPER J. Gilpin 127 Which made his horse's flanks to smoke. 1802 PINKERTON Mod. Geogr. (1811) 329 The water smokes continually. 1863 W. C. BALDWIN Afr. Hunting ii. 57 It rained incessantly the whole night, and we..lay smoking and steaming. 1869 TENNYSON Holy Grail 18, I have seen this yew-tree smoke, Spring after spring, for half a hundred years.

b. To rise, spread, or move, like smoke.

In later quots. with suggestion of next sense.

1595 SHAKS. John V. iv. 34 This night whose blacke contagious breath Already smoakes [etc.]. 1726-46 THOMSON Spring 194 A yellow mist, Far smoking o'er th' interminable plain. 1781 COWPER Truth 238 See where it smokes along the sounding plain, Blown all aslant, a driving, dashing rain. 1821 CLARE Vill. Minstr. II. 106 Where the thin clouds smoke along the sky. 1904 J. CONRAD Nostromo I, They [clouds]..smoke in stormy trails across the snows of Higuerota.

c. To ride, drive, sail, etc., at a rapid pace or great speed. Const. *along* (prep. or adv.).

1697 DRYDEN Æneid VII. 909 Proud of his Steeds he smoaks along the Field. 1725 POPE Odyss. III. 615 The coursers.. held Their equal pace, and smoak'd along the field. 1735 SOMERVILLE Chase II. 232 Then like a foaming Torrent, pouring down Precipitant, we smoke along the Vale. 1827 SCOTT Chron. Canongate iii, Smoking along in his travelling chaise-and-four. 1894 Times 6 Aug. 5/2 The Vigilant came smoking along in style past Ryde.

d. *Austr. slang.* = SLOPE v.² 1.

1893 in Morris Austral Eng. s.v., 'Do not say we were here. Let us smoke.' 'Smoke'..is the slang for the 'push' to get away as fast as possible.

3. *fig.* †**a.** To fume, be angry. *Obs.*

a 1548 HALL Chron., Edw. IV, 212 The Duke..so fumed and smoked at the matter. a 1562 G. CAVENDISH Wolsey (1893) 47 Evyn so was she commaundyd to avoyde the court..; whereat she smoked.

b. *School slang.* To blush.

1862 FARRAR St. Winifred's iv, 'Why, you're smoking now,' said Henderson, as Walter..began to blush a little.

†**4.** To smart, to suffer severely. *Obs.*

In early use with allusion to actual burning; quot. 1773 partly belongs to sense 2.

a 1548 HALL Chron., Hen. VIII, 64 b, For feare to bee called heretike, and then they would make hym smoke or beare a faggot. 1595 in Cath. Rec. Soc. Publ. V. 352 The farewell was he would make hym smoake for yt before he departed the towne. 1679 DRYDEN Limberham V. i, Now I am resolv'd I will go see 'em, or some-body shall smoak for't. 1773 GOLDSM. Stoops to Conq. V, No such bad driving; the poor beasts have smoked for it.

II. 5. *trans.* To expose (a person, place, etc.) to the smoke of some curative, purifying, or aromatic substance; to fumigate, esp. as a means of disinfecting.

c 1000 Saxon Leechd. I. 116 Ȝenim þu þas ylcan wyrte, & smoca hit [sc. the child] mid. c 1400 tr. Secreta Secret., Gov. Lordsh. 83 [Let him] after smoke him with ensens couenable to þe tyme. 1530 PALSGR. 723/1, I wyll medyll me with no garmentes that were his tyll they be well smoked. 1546 BALE Eng. Votaries I. (1560) 92 b, They are..Censed, Smoked, Perfumed and Worshypped. 1599 SHAKS. Much Ado I. iii. 60 As I was smoaking a musty roome. 1665 in Ellis Orig. Lett. Ser. II. IV. 32, I smoke your house twice a week. 1772-84 Cook's Voy. (1790) IV. 1215 The ship was smoaked between decks with gunpowder. 1796 C. MARSHALL Gardening (1813) 398 Orchards, dung, dress, prune, or smoak them. 1840 R. H. DANA Bef. Mast xxix, The next day was Sunday, and a good day for smoking ship.

b. To expose or subject to smoke, so as to suffocate, stupefy, or make uncomfortable.

It is doubtful whether quots. 1824 and 1825 are based on real knowledge of the phrase they illustrate.

a 1154 O. E. Chron. an. 1137, Me henged up bi the fet & smoked heom mid ful smoke. 1617 BRATHWAIT Smoaking Age 87 That Alexander Severus would have smoaked such sellers of smoake. 1641 J. JACKSON True Evang. Temper I. 44 Others inverted..were so smoaked and suffocated to death. 1686 W. HARRIS tr. Lemery's Course Chym. (ed. 2) 483 Tabaco kills serpents..if you should smoke them with it. 1712 STEELE Spect. No. 358 ¶ 1 After which they have gone in a Body and smoaked a Cobler. [1824 SCOTT Redgauntlet let. i, Who taught me to smoke a cobbler? 1825 BROCKETT N. C. Gloss., Smoke-the-Cobbler, a mischievous pastime among children.] 1900 POLLOK & THOM Sports Burma vi. 202 They then smoke the bees until they are stupid.

fig. 1595 SHAKS. John II. i. 139 Ile smoake your skin-coat and I catch you right. 1601 B. JONSON Every Man in Hum. IV. ii, It vanished away like the smoke of tobacco; but I was smoked soundly first. 1680 V. ALSOP Mischief Imposit. xii. 98 They formed themselves into separate bodies for Government, and were soundly smok'd for it in the high Commission.

c. To fill with, expose to, smoke, esp. so as to blacken, discolour, or render obscure. Also const. *through* (quot. 1846).

1611 SHAKS. Cymb. V. v. 398 Let's quit this ground, And smoake the Temple with our Sacrifices. 1631 A. WILSON The Swisser II. i, With some quaint oath in 's mouth, smoaking his nostrills. a 1704 T. BROWN Walk r. Lond. Wks. 1709 III. III. 64 Others..sat smoaking their Noses, and drinking Burnt-Brandy. 1748 JOHNSON Van. Human Wishes 85 The painted face..Smoak'd in kitchens, or in auctions sold. 1800 Phil. Trans. XC. 274, I now took two green glasses; but found that they did not intercept light enough. I therefore smoked one of them. 1846 HOLTZAPFFEL Turning II. 730 The new piece is laid upon the original, the interstices of which are smoked through with a lamp. 1883 Cent. Mag. XXV. 849/1, I copy pictures and he smokes them and sells them as old masters.

d. To cure or preserve (bacon, fish, etc.) by exposure to smoke; to smoke-dry.

1757 WASHINGTON Lett. Writ. 1889 I. 413, I have directed the provision..to be smoked, if there are conveniences for doing it. 1767 Phil. Trans. LVII. 284 The herring..when salted and smoked. 1836 W. IRVING Astoria III. 251 Having no other food, she killed the two horses, and smoked their flesh. 1846 J. BAXTER Libr. Pract. Agric. (ed. 4) II. 311 Smoking the bacon is much better than merely drying it.

6. †**a.** With *out* or *away*: To convert into smoke. *Obs. rare.*

1382 WYCLIF 2 Chron. ii. 4 To brennen encense beforn hym, and to swote thingis to ben out smokid. 1686 tr. Chardin's Trav. Persia 154 The three Grains of Incense.. were strew'd upon a few Embers, and smoak'd away.

b. To drive *out* or *away* by means of smoke. Also *fig.*

1593 NASHE Christ's T. Wks. (Grosart) IV. 230 In smoaking this..trade out of his starting-holes. 1644 SANDERSON Serm. I. 115 The magistrate..that would speedily smoke away these gnats that swarm about the courts of justice. 1720 DE FOE Capt. Singleton xv. (1840) 259 William..proposed, that they should..smoke them out. 1829 SCOTT Anne of G. xxv, Till we smoke out of his earths the old fox Louis. 1870 MISS BRIDGMAN R. Lynne I. iv. 57 He drew out a second cigar, with the..view..of 'smoking her out'.

†**7.** To cause to smoke; to urge at a high speed. *Obs.*⁻¹

a 1658 CLEVELAND May Day ii, Whiles Phœbus..Smoaks his bright Teem along on the Grand Paw.

8. To get an inkling of, to smell or suspect (a plot, design, etc.). Now *arch.* (in common use c 1600-1850).

1608 CHAPMAN Byron's Consp. Wks. 1873 II. 201 Least so he might haue smokt our practises. 1667 DRYDEN & DK. NEWCASTLE Sir M. Mar-all I, Sir John, I fear, smokes your design. 1733 FIELDING Quix. in Eng. I. viii, Let me tell you,..I begin to smoke a plot. I begin to apprehend no opposition, and then we're sold, neighbour. 1770 DIBDIN Deserter II. i, Oh, Oh, I smoke this business.— Comrade, I'm off, I'm off. 1812 COMBE Syntax, Picturesque x. 214 An honest 'Squire, who smok'd the trick, Appear'd well-arm'd with oaken stick. 1837 BARHAM Ingol. Leg. Ser. I. Monstre Balloon vi, Such a trumpery tale every one of us smokes. 1886 BURTON Arab. Nts. (abr. ed.) I. 48 The man, not..smoking the plot, waxed exceeding wroth.

b. *absol.* To have an inkling or idea; to understand. Now *arch.*

1676 ETHEREDGE Man of Mode III. iii, Peace, they smoak. 1688 SHADWELL Sq. Alsatia IV, I am sharp, sharp as a needle; I can smoak now, as soon as another. 1757 FOOTE Author II, Oh, now I begin to understand..; ecod, I begin to smoke. 1842 BARHAM Ingol. Leg. Ser. II. Lay of St. Medard xxix, St. Medard paused,—he began to 'smoke'.

9. To make fun of, to jest at; to ridicule, banter, or quiz (a person). Now *arch.*

a 1700 B. E. Dict. Cant. Crew, *Smoke him, Smoke him again*, to affront a Stranger at his coming in. 1755 Connoisseur No. 54 ¶ 4 The Bucks..sat in another box, to smoke their rusty wigs and brown cassocks. 1778 MME. D'ARBLAY Early Diary (1889) I. 159 He..suffered us to laugh at his affectation.., even joining in our mirth and seeming happy to be smoaked. 1818 KEATS Lett. (1895) 245 We hated her and smoked her and baited her and I think drove her away. 1859 THACKERAY Virginians lxxxix, Our young men were accustomed to smoke her, as the phrase then was.

10. To observe, take note of, 'twig'. Now *arch.*

1715 ADDISON Drummer III. i, Thou'rt very smart, my Dear. But see! smoak the Doctor. 1762 FOOTE Orator II, Smoke the justice, he is as fast as a church. c 1826 J. WILSON Noct. Ambr. Wks. 1855 I. 199 Kit, smoke his eyes, how they glare. 1856 'T. GWYNNE' Young Singleton viii, 'Smoke the big-wig Lund!' whispered Fotheringay.

III. 11. *intr.* To inhale (and expel again) the fumes of tobacco, or other suitable substance, from a pipe, cigar, or cigarette. † Also with *it*.

1617 BRATHWAIT Smoaking Age 174 The sleeping Dormouse..sleepes but all Winter, but this Man i' th' Mist smoakes it all the yeare long: hee proportions his nose [etc.]. 1687 MONTAGUE & PRIOR Hind & Panth. Transv. 17 Your Pipe's so foul, that I disdain to smoak. 1722 HEARNE Collect. (O.H.S.) VII. 208 Even children were oblig'd to smoak. 1777 DALRYMPLE Trav. Sp. & Port. xvii, I declined the favour, but the others smoaked about. 1827 CARLYLE Germ. Rom. I. 7 Smoking vehemently on his black stump of a pipe. 1852 THACKERAY Esmond II. xi, Mr. Addison was..smoking out of his long pipe, and smiling very placidly. 1900 POLLOK & THOM Sports Burma v. 171 He was..never better pleased than when smoking away at a long Shan pipe.

12. *trans.* To use (tobacco, etc.) as material for smoking. Also *fig.* (quot. 1840).

1687 A. LOVELL tr. Thevenot's Trav. I. 259 Some..have in the mean while smoaked Tobacco, when it was given them. 1716 CHURCH Philip's War (1865) I. 28 Capt. Fullers party being troubled with the..lust after Tobacco, must needs strike fire to Smoke it. 1796 MORSE Amer. Geogr. II. 85 They also smoke tobacco to excess. 1811 [see HASHISH]. 1840 BARHAM Ingol. Leg. Ser. I. St. Odille xiv, So put that in your pipe..and smoke it. 1878 STANLEY Dark Cont. xviii. (1889) 324 The bandits' custom of smoking banghi (wild hemp).

b. To use (a pipe, cigar, etc.) in the act of smoking; to take (so many whiffs).

1706-7 FARQUHAR Beaux' Strat. I. i, He..smoaks his Pipe Eight and forty Hours together sometimes. 1762 STERNE Tr. Shandy VI. vi, My uncle Toby..lighted his pipe, and smoak'd about a dozen whiffs. 1820 W. IRVING Sketch Bk. II. 338, I found him..smoking his pipe in the..evening sunshine. 1837 DICKENS Pickw. xl, Send down word that he's to spend the change in cigars...I'll smoke 'em. 1902 ELIZ. BANKS Newspaper Girl 179, I never saw a woman smoke a cigarette till I came to London.

c. With *out* (= to the end, completely).

1705 tr. Bosman's Guinea 306 Which Pipe thus filled they without ceasing can easily smoak out. 1842 BORROW Bible in Spain xl, See, I have smoked out your cigar. 1871 M. COLLINS Marq. & Merch. II. vii. 216 She smoked one [cigarette] out right seldom.

13. To wear *out*, waste (*away*), bring *into* a certain state, etc., by smoking tobacco or some similar substance.

1604 JAS. I Counterbl. to Tobacco (Arb.) 106 If a man smoke himselfe to death with it (and many haue done).

1616 R. C. Times' Whistle (1871) 72 He..smokd out all his living at his nose. 1617 BRATHWAIT Smoaking Age 195 Sweet Youth, Smoake not thy time; Too precious to abuse. 1688 HOLME Armoury III. 294/2 He who smoaks away the chief of his time. 1823 SCOTT Quentin D. Introd., I gradually ..smoked myself into a certain degree of acquaintance with [him]. 1844 N. Brit. Rev. II. 81 Newton smoked himself into a state of absolute etiolation. 1893 C. G. LELAND Mem. I. 131 To go to their rooms..and smoke them sick or into retreating.

14. *intr.* Of a pipe: To draw.

1883 Harper's Mag. July 174/2 These 'church-wardens' smoke freely and softly.

Smo·ke-ball. [SMOKE sb. 1.]

1. *Mil.* A paper shell filled with a preparation which, when ignited, sends out clouds of smoke.

The ball is fired from a mortar, and the smoke serves to drive men out of mines, conceal manœuvres, etc.

1753 Chambers' Cycl. Suppl. s.v. Ball, *Smoak..Balls*, those which..darken a place, to prevent discoveries. 1760 Ann. Reg., Chron. 146/1 A smoke-ball burst in General Desaguiler's hand, and shattered his arm. 1802 JAMES Milit. Dict. s.v. Ball, Smoke-balls..continue to smoke from 25 to 30 minutes. 1828 SPEARMAN Brit. Gunner (ed. 2) 52 Balls..are of three descriptions, viz.—lead, light, and smoke-balls. 1859 F. A. GRIFFITHS Artill. Man. (1862) 86 The 8 in. Smoke ball burns about 4 minutes.

fig. 1796 Gentl. Mag. LXVI. II. 1011 When Christianity is assaulted..by the smoke-balls and stink-pots of English vagabonds.

attrib. 1809 Naval Chron. XXII. 286 Every rocket contains smoak-ball composition.

2. A ball used in trap-shooting, which, when struck by a shot, emits a puff of smoke.

1881 GREENER Gun 504 The latest improvement is the American smoke-ball, consisting of two hemispheres of paper placed upon a wooden ball.

3. A ball emitting smoke when ignited, used by thieves.

1899 Daily News 21 Mar. 7/2 Raising an alarm of fire by means of smoke balls ignited on the various floors. The smoke balls went beyond their commission and kindled a flame.

Smo·ke-black, *sb.* [SMOKE sb. 1.] A form of lamp-black obtained by the combustion of resinous materials.

1712 tr. Pomet's Hist. Drugs I. 204 The black sealing Wax is ting'd or colour'd with Smoak Black. 1841 LANE Arab. Nts. I. 130 An inferior kind is the smoke-black produced by burning the shells of almonds. 1858 SIMMONDS Dict. Trade, *Smoke-black*, a substance prepared by the combustion of different resinous bodies. 1896 DE VINNE Moxon's Printing 412 The crude smoke-black of commerce.

Smo·ke-black, *v.* [SMOKE sb. 1.] *trans.* To blacken with smoke.

1809-10 COLERIDGE Friend (Bohn) II. 302 The counterfeit frankincense which smoke-blacks the favourite idol of a Catholic village.

Smo·ke-box. [SMOKE sb.]

1. A receptacle for smoke. *rare*⁻¹.

1614 W. BARCLAY Nepenthes A 8, Not as the English abusers [of tobacco] do, which make a smoke-boxe of their skull.

2. *techn.* A chamber in a steam boiler between the flues and the chimney stack; in a locomotive placed at the base of the funnel.

1846 Penny Cycl. Suppl. II. 670/1 That construction of engine in which the cylinders are placed at the bottom of the smoke-box. 1855 LARDNER Mus. Sci. & Art VI. 127 The tubes..through which the hot gases..and smoke pass from the fire-box to the smoke-box. 1897 Pall Mall Mag. Mar. 354 The exceptional height of the Smoke-box..rendered it necessary to adopt a dwarfed funnel.

attrib. 1855 LARDNER Mus. Sci. & Art VI. 128 The smoke-box door, opening on hinges at the top. 1878 F. S. WILLIAMS Midl. Railw. 652 The smoke-box door did not fit tight.

Smoked (smōᵘkt), *ppl. a.* Also 7 smoakt, smoak'd, 8 smoaked. [f. SMOKE v. + -ED¹.]

1. Dried or cured by exposure to smoke; impregnated with smoke.

1603 DEKKER Wonderf. Yeare B ij b, For..some smoakt gallant, who at wit repines, To dry Tobacco with my holesome lines. 1648 HEXHAM II, Een Sore, a smoakt red Heering. 1700 T. BROWN tr. Fresny's Amusem. 117 The best smoak'd Beef in Christendom. 1747 WESLEY Prim. Physick (1762) p. xix, Pickled or smoaked or salted Food. 1830 M. DONOVAN Domest. Econ. II. 233 Smoked provisions are..apt to disagree with some persons. 1883 Fisheries Exhib. Catal. 370 Smoked Eels,..Smoked Plaice,..Smoked Herrings.

2. Obscured, made dark, by smoke.

1755 B. MARTIN Mag. Arts & Sci. 37 This small Telescope, in which I have put a smoaked Glass. 1819 SHELLEY Œdipus I. 400 I'll wager you will see them..With pieces of smoked glass. 1885 GOODALL Physiol. Bot. (1892) 383 A slowly revolving cylinder covered with smoked paper.

3. Tainted or spoiled in taste through contact with smoke.

1761 COLMAN Prose on Sev. Occas. (1787) I. 123 The water is smoaked, the butter rank, the bread heavy. 1857 ELTON Below Surface ix, A cup of smoked coffee and a dubious egg.

4. Of a smoke-colour. (Cf. SMOKE sb. 9 e.)

1827 GRIFFITH tr. Cuvier II. 75 *note*, The Smoked Kangaroo, the gray of which is somewhat deeper. 1885 Encycl. Brit. XVIII. 447 The shells usually present a dark colour about the edges, like that of 'smoked pearl'. 1898 Westm. Gaz. 18 Nov. 3/2 Dark brown fox fur, that which is called 'smoked fox'.

5. With *-down* or *-out*: Exhausted or consumed by being smoked.

1859 DICKENS Tale Two Cities II. xvi, He put down his smoked-out pipe. 1904 BENSON Challoners (1906) 76/2 Martin lit a cigarette from a smoked-down stump.

Smo·ke-dried, *ppl. a.* [SMOKE sb. 1.] Dried or cured by exposure to smoke.

1653 H. COGAN tr. Pinto's Trav. lxiv. (1663) 256 Onyons and some smoak-dried flesh. 1654 H. L'ESTRANGE Chas. I (1655) 118 Such a swarthy metamorphosis as neer resembled smoke-dryed Bacon. a 1704 T. BROWN Walk r. London Wks. 1709 III. III. 3, I made my Smoak-dry'd Infidel shew his Ivory Teeth. 1856 KANE Arctic Expl. II. x. 106 Our smoke-dried cabin is a scene worth looking at. 1882 DE WINDT Equator 72 The bunch of smoke-dried human heads.

transf. 1857 Chamb. Jrnl. 17 Jan. 47/1 The smoke-dried trees of our parks.

Smo·ke-dry, *v.* [SMOKE sb. 1: cf. prec.]

1. *trans.* To dry or cure (meat, fish, etc.) by exposure to smoke.

1704 Dict. Rust. s.v. Chesnut, It is best to beat the Fruit down from the Tree,..or if you don't, you must Smoke-dry 'em. 1796 STEDMAN Surinam II. xx. 111 They even took out the jaw-bones, which they smoke-dried. 1843 BETHUNE Sc. Fireside Stor. 62 He even spoke of having an old woman..hung up in the chimney, and smoke-drying her for three weeks. 1886 Encycl. Brit. XX. 174/2 Boiled, smoke-dried, and packed in bags.

2. *intr.* To become dried by the action of smoke. In quot. *transf.*

1855 SMEDLEY H. Coverdale ii, You've been smoke-drying in London..till you're out of condition.

Hence **Smo·ke-drying** *vbl. sb.*

1812 MISS L. M. HAWKINS C'tess & Gertr. I. 265 The discipline of a smoke-drying in one of the closest streets of the city.

Smo·ke-farthing. *Hist.* [SMOKE sb. 2 b.] An offering made at Whitsuntide by the householders of a diocese to the cathedral church; also, a hearth-tax (see quot. 1765).

1444 [see LINCOLN 1]. 1524 Churchw. Acc. St. Giles, Reading (ed. Nash) 22 To the Official for smoke farthyngs, iiijˢ jᵈ. 1575 in North St. Martin's, Leicester 144 For peterpence or smoke farthynges sometyme due to the Anthecriste of roome, xd. 1609 in W. Money Hist. of Newbury (1887) 529 P[ai]d for Pentecostalles, otherwise called smoke farthings. 1710 J. HARRIS Lex. Techn. II, *Smoke-farthings*, the Pentecostals, or Customary Oblations offered by the Inhabitants within any Diocess, when they made their Processione to the Mother or Cathedral Church. 1765 BLACKSTONE Comm. I. 323 As early as the conquest mention is made in domesday book of fumage or fuage, vulgarly called smoke farthings; which were paid by custom to the king for every chimney in the house. 1857 TOULMIN SMITH Parish 503 An 'Ale' held at the time of paying the 'Smoke-farthing' or Wax-silver. 1876 [see FUMAGE¹].

Smoke-ho, -oh. *colloq.* Also **smoko.** [f. SMOKE sb. 6.] A stoppage of work in order to rest and smoke. Also *attrib.*

1897 F. T. BULLEN Cruise 'Cachalot' viii, This done, it was 'Smoke-oh!' The luxury of that rest and refreshment was something to be grateful for. 1898 DAVITT Life & Progr. Austral. lxxvi. 424 There is a 'smoke-ho' time allowed in a few of the prisons. 1900 H. LAWSON On Track 133 We go through the day..in runs of about an hour and 20 minutes between smoke-ho's.

Smo·ke-hole. [SMOKE sb. 1.]

1. The vent or external orifice of a flue; a hole in the roof of a hut through which the smoke of the fire escapes.

c 1340 Nominale (Skeat) 479 For smoke a smoke-hole. 1493-4 Rec. St. Mary at Hill 201 In expences whane sartayne of þe paryshe yede to Awew þe smoke holys. 1663 GERBIER Counsel 22 Cover the top of Chimneyes..; the smoake holes can be..made on the sides. 1825 LOCKHART in Scott's Fam. Lett. (1894) II. 298 The smoke-hole..in the roof. 1856 KANE Arctic Expl. I. xxx. 406 A smoke-hole passed through the roof. 1891 RIDER HAGGARD Nada the Lily xxix. 240 Zinita..had climbed the hut, and now lay there in the dark, her ear upon the smoke-hole, listening to every word.

b. = FUMAROLE.

1899 Daily News 18 Nov. 7/2 No lava is flowing, and even the fumarole, or smoke-holes, give forth no sign.

†**2.** *transf.* or *fig.* **a.** An imposture, trick. **b.** A smoking-room. **c.** The mouth of a smoker. *Obs.*

1580 HOLLYBAND Treas. Fr. Tong s.v. Fourbe, We may easily judge of this stuffe, or smokehole, or guile. 1673 Charac. Coffee Ho. in Harl. Misc. (1810) VI. 468 The arch devil, wherewith this smoke-hole is haunted, is the town-wit. a 1704 T. BROWN Walk r. Lond. Wks. 1709 III. III. 59 Which unsavory Compliment was thus retorted.., viz. Stop your Smoak-hole Nincompoop.

Smo·ke-house. [SMOKE sb.]

†**1.** A dwelling-house. *Obs.*⁻¹

1672 PETTY Pol. Surv. Irel. (1719) 9 The simple Smoak-houses are..184,000.

2. A room in a tannery, heated by smouldering spent tan, where hides are unhaired.

1797 Encycl. Brit. (ed. 3) XVIII. 306/2 The stoutest and heaviest ox hides..are then hung on poles, in a close room called a smoke-house, in which is kept a smouldering fire of wet tan. [So in Ure Dict. Arts (1839) 764, Penny Cycl. (1842) XXIV. 37.] 1837 HEBERT Eng. & Mech. Encycl. II. 60 In some places, the hides were formerly piled wet one upon another..(or otherwise kept warm in what was called a smoke-house).

3. A house or room used for curing meat, fish, etc., by means of smoke.

1860 MAYNE REID Hunter's Feast xiv, A part of the bacon furnishes the 'smoke-house' for home consumption during the winter. 1894 Outing XXIV. 201/1 A rusty key that probably belonged to some smoke-house of long ago.

attrib. 1901 CABLE Cavalier liii, The servants were loading the smoke-house meat into a wagon.

Smo·ke-jack. [SMOKE sb.]

1. An apparatus for turning a roasting-spit, fixed in a chimney and set in motion by the current of air passing up this.

1675 EVELYN Let. in Aubrey Nat. Hist. Surrey (1719), The Smoke-Jack in my Brother's Kitchen-Chimney; which has been there, I have heard, near a hundred Years. 1754 MRS. DELANY Life & Corr. (1861) 301, I think I will have a smoke-jack; the man says he will..keep it in order for nothing. 1777 in Crts. Europe at Close of Last Cent. (1841) I. 180 Did you never see a smoke-jack, with a little man in red working away, and seemingly turning the wheel? 1832 BABBAGE Econ. Manuf. iv. (ed. 3) 36 The common smoke-jack is an instrument in which the velocity communicated is too great for the purpose required. 1884 JEFFERIES Red Deer ix. 172 In how few, even of the most ancient houses, are smoke-jacks still at work!

attrib. 1758 FRANKLIN Lett. Wks. 1840 VI. 536 This property of chimneys might, by means of smokejack vanes, be applied to some mechanical purposes.

†**b.** *transf.* The head, as the seat of confused ideas. *Obs.*

1761 STERNE Tr. Shandy III. xx, As for my uncle Toby, his smoak-jack had not made a dozen revolutions, before he fell asleep also. 1808 E. S. BARRETT Miss-led General 54 That part of the human frame which, in rational mortals, is denominated the Seat of reason; in others, a Smoke-jack.

2. *U.S.* A cowl or hood for the end of a railway-carriage stove-pipe (*Cent. Dict.* 1891).

3. A cargo-steamer.

1892 Daily News 3 Feb. 5/5 It may do for a 'smoke-jack' to lay off and wait for the fog, but not for a passenger ship with mails.

4. A smoke-nuisance inspector.

1898 Daily News 21 Nov. 8/6 The officer who carried out this duty was called a Smoke Jack.

Smokeless (smōᵘ·klės), *a.* [f. SMOKE sb. + -LESS.]

1. Emitting or producing no smoke.

1582 T. WATSON Poems (Arb.) 134 A Shipwracke of mans life; a Smoaklesse fire. 1732 POPE Ep. Bathurst 191 Tenants with sighs the smoakless tow'rs survey. 1795-1814 WORDSW. Excurs. VII 54 The smokeless chimney-top. 1856 KANE Arctic Expl. I. xxx. 405 The lamps were cheerful and smokeless. 1868 Daily News 2 Sept., It was found that the coals of the Aberdare collieries were comparatively smokeless. 1890 Nature 4 Sept., One of the important attributes of a smokeless powder.

2. Free from, clear of, smoke.

1631 BRATHWAIT Whimzies 53 To leave his smoakelesse house in the country..to riot in the citie. 1802 WORDSW. Westminster Bridge 8 All bright and glittering in the smokeless air. 1837 CARLYLE Fr. Rev. III. I. ii, The Sun shines; serenely westering, in smokeless mackerel-sky.

Hence **Smo·kelessly** *adv.*; **Smo·kelessness.**

1877 Echo 18 July 1/1 Its Smokelessness, Cleanliness, and Great Economy over all other descriptions [of coal]. a 1891 Engineer LXIX. 357 (Cent.), The appliances for..consuming coal smokelessly are already at work.

Smoke-oh: see SMOKE-HO.

Smoker (smōᵘ·kəɹ). [f. SMOKE v. + -ER¹. Cf. Du., Fris., MLG. *smoker*, LG. *smöker* (Da. *smøger*), G. dial. *schmaucher, schmöcher, schmeucher*.]

1. a. One who cures fish, bacon, etc., by means of smoke.

1599 NASHE Lenten Stuff Wks. (Grosart) V. 278 Our Herring smoker hauing worn his monsters stale throughout England. 1688 Lond. Gaz. No. 2331/4 A Smoaker in Philpot-lane, London. 1699 LUTTRELL Brief Rel. (1857) IV. 530 Jeffery Jefferyes, esq. the smoaker. 1831 JANE PORTER Sir E. Seaward's Narr. III. 29 Another had been a sausage-maker, or a beef and ham smoker. 1883 F. A. SMITH Swedish Fisheries 6 Scotch curers and smokers have, by private enterprise, been sent to Bohuslän.

b. One who jests at, or ridicules, others.

1812 COLMAN Broad Grins, Two Parsons lxxxv, These wooden wits, these quizzers, queerers, Smokers.

2. Something which emits smoke: †**a.** A war-vessel employed to conceal or assist hostile operations by discharging volumes of smoke. *Obs.*

a 1700 B. E. Dict. Cant. Crew, *Smoker*, a Vessel to Blind the Enemies, to make way for the Machine to Play. 1726 SHELVOCKE Voy. r. World 321 To bring me away in case I should have occasion to make use of mine as a Fire-ship, or a Smoaker. 1821 Self Instructor 587 Vessels of war are.. a machine-vessel, a smoaker.

†**b.** *colloq.* A steamer. *Obs.*⁻¹

1825 Sporting Mag. XVI. 211 We walked four miles early in the morning to the smoker.

c. A smoky chimney, locomotive, etc.

1883 J. MARTIN Reminisc. Old Haddington 29 Dr. Welsh's kitchen chimney was an inveterate smoker. 1897 Pall Mall Mag. Sept. 77 Strangers might suppose that American locomotives are inveterate smokers.

d. A contrivance for smoking bees.

1875 J. HUNTER Man. Bee-keeping (1884) 150 The simplest smoker of all is a roll of cotton rags.

3. One who smokes tobacco, opium, or the like.

1617 BRATHWAIT Smoaking Age 171 Yet of all these, none to me so profest enemies as these smokers of our Age. 1686 PLOT Staffordsh. 302 A great smoker, &c., that never spit in his life. 1727 DE FOE Protestant Monast. 10 He had been from his Youth a great Smoaker. 1796 MORSE Amer. Geogr. II. 86 Both sexes are great smoakers. 1820 BYRON Juan III. xxxiv, Afar, a dwarf buffoon stood telling tales To a sedate grey circle of old smokers. 1882 SALA Amer. Revis. (1885) 389 The deficient accommodation provided for smokers.

b. *Smoker's heart, throat*, a diseased condition of the heart or throat caused by excessive smoking. *Smoker's patch*, a smooth, bare white patch on the tongue due to the effects of smoking.

1889 Buck's Handbk. Med. Sci. VII. 110 Smoker's Patch. Ibid. VIII. 553 Catarrh and hoarseness are so frequent as to give rise to the name 'smoker's throat'. 1906 Daily Chron. 16 June 4/4 Nicotine..causing irregular action, and producing the condition known as smoker's heart.

c. *U.S.* A grade of tobacco for smoking.

1880 U.S. Census, Rep. Culture Tobacco 15 Class 1. Domestic Cigar Tobacco and Smokers.

4. a. A railway carriage or compartment assigned for the use of those travellers who wish to smoke.

1882 SALA Amer. Revis. II. 140 The car known as the 'smoker' is usually relegated to the least eligible part of the train. 1894 Outing XXIV. 116/1 We threw our bundles upon the platform of the smoker and climbed up after them.

b. A concert at which smoking is permitted.

1891 Wheeling 25 Feb. 401 The Upperthorpe C.C. held a very enjoyable smoker on Thursday evening last.

5. *School slang.* One who blushes.

1866 Routledge's Every Boy's Ann. 217 If you happen to blush, he whispers in your ear 'smoker'.

Smo·ke-room. [SMOKE sb. or v.] A room in a club-house, hotel, or the like, set apart for the accommodation of those who wish to smoke.

1883 Daily News 29 Sept. 3/2 A young man..in the smoke-room on the night of sailing from Queenstown. 1891 E. ROPER By Track & Trail ix. 125 We smokers left them and took up our quarters in our proper place, the smoke-room.

Smokery (smōᵘ·kəri). [f. SMOKE sb. or v. Cf. Fris. *smokerij* smoking.]

1. In contemptuous use (see quot.).

1657 J. WATTS Dipper Sprinkled 97 From the publick Ministery or Steeple-houses, (be it so) to private mysteries or smokeries, rather of their Chimney-houses.

2. Articles or materials used in smoking.

1837 New Monthly Mag. L. 86 Pipes of all sorts...—all nations and all people were represented in this vast arsenal of smokery.

3. A place used for smoking; a smoking-room, an opium-den, etc.

1901 Daily Chron. 29 May 5/6 The immorality of the 'smokeries' will probably suffice to close them as disorderly.

Smo·ke-stack. [SMOKE sb.]

1. *U.S.* **a.** The funnel of a steam-boat.

1862 RUSSELL Diary North & S. I. 166 The funnel, Yankeeicé smoke stack. 1864 Daily Telegr. 30 Aug., The Tennessee..surrendered, her rudder disabled, her smokestack carried away.

b. The chimney of a locomotive.

1875 KNIGHT Dict. Mech. 2227/1. 1890 Daily News 22 Sept. 5/5 The locomotive's smokestack was just out of the water.

2. The chimney of a stove; a chimney-stack.

1871 Daily News 9 Feb., Carrying the smoke-stack of a stove through the aperture. 1903 Westm. Gaz. 27 Jan. 7/1 The brick smoke-stack of the stoke-house.

Smo·kified, *ppl. a.* [f. as from *smokify*.] Discoloured or blackened by smoke. Also *transf.*

1819 Blackw. Mag. V. 732 Scrawlings of chalk spread each smokified wall. 1863 B. SAVILE Man ii. 75 Have you heard of the smokified Essays?

Smokily (smōᵘ·kili), *adv.* [f. SMOKY a. + -LY².] In a smoky manner; hazily.

1611 COTGR., *Fumeusement*, smoakily, fumingly, reekingly. 1755 JOHNSON, *Smuttily*, blackly; smokily. 1847 WEBSTER, *Smokily*, so as to be full of smoke. 1897 Westm. Gaz. 19 May 2/1 Obfuscations that move smokily across the face of truth.

Smokiness (smōᵘ·kinės). [f. as prec. + -NESS.] The character or quality of being smoky.

1587 GOLDING De Mornay xiv. (1592) 222 Our minde..is after a sort troubled..by the smoakiness of the imaginations. 1611 COTGR., *Fuligine*, soot, sootinesse; smoakinesse. 1656 BLOUNT Glossogr., *Fumidity*, smoakiness. 1727 BAILEY (vol. II), *Smokiness*, a being smoky, or infected with Smoke. 1881 Daily News 14 Dec. 5/3 The marked characteristic of last night's fog was its smokiness.

Smoking (smōᵘ·kiŋ), *vbl. sb.* [f. SMOKE v.]

1. The action or fact of emitting smoke, giving off steam or vapour, etc.

1530 PALSGR. 271/2 Smokyng, *fumiere*. 1611 COTGR., *Fumement*,..a smoaking. 1663 GERBIER Counsel 6 To prevent the smoaking of Chimneyes. 1715 Lond. Gaz. No. 5392/4 Any smoaking of Chimneys. 1852 DICKENS Bleak Ho. vi, The smoking and steaming of the heated horses.

2. The action of inhaling and exhaling smoke from a pipe, cigar, or the like.

1691 WOOD Ath. Oxon. II. 709 Given more to bibbing and smoaking than the duty of his Office. 1762 GOLDSM. Beau Nash 24 Smoaking in the rooms was permitted. 1849 MACAULAY Hist. Eng. iii. I. 369 Nowhere was the smoking more constant than at Will's.

†**3.** A bantering or quizzing. *Obs.*

1781 MME. D'ARBLAY Diary June, What a smoking did Miss Burney give Mr. Crutchley. Ibid. Aug., Whether he ..took the opportunity to give us all a smoking.

4. The curing of meat, etc., by exposure to smoke.

1819 in Pantologia s.v. 1872 YEATS Techn. Hist. Comm. 224 The efficacy of smoking depends on certain chemical products. 1901 BLACK Carp. & Build. vi. 65 The barrel..is covered over at the top, and the smoking proceeds.

5. *School slang.* Blushing.

1862 FARRAR St. Winifred's iv, Smoking is the name fellows give to blushing.

6. *attrib.* **a.** In combs. relating to the curing of provisions by smoke, or the production of smoke for some special purpose, as *smoking-house, knife, loft, pot, vessel, works*.

1648 HEXHAM II, Een roock-vat, a Censoir, or smoking vessell. 1706 PHILLIPS (ed. Kersey), *Thuribulum*, a Censer, or Smoaking-Pot, to burn Incence in. 1736 N. BAILEY Household Dict. Ll 2 A Smoking Closet for drying Tongues. 1759 R. BROWN Compl. Farmer 61 Curing bacon..by smoking lofts or closets, adjoining to the funnels of their chimneys. 1791 Trans. Soc. Arts IX. 136 The smoking works being erected at the foot, and the tar-funnel higher up the hill. 1805 LINDLEY Voy. Brasil (1808) 260 Flesh.. which they salt, and dry in the sun and smoking-houses. 1839 Mag. Dom. Econ. IV. 118 The hams..are smoked in smoking-houses. 1883 Fisheries Exhib. Catal. 62 New and Improved Smoking Knives for Fishermen.

b. In terms denoting things or places used for, or in connexion with, the smoking of tobacco, etc., as *smoking apparatus, -cap, -carriage*, etc.; **smoking-bean** *U.S.*, the catalpa bean, the pods of which are smoked by boys.

1771 MACKENZIE Man Feeling xxi, He took from his pocket a particular *smoaking apparatus. 1872 CALVERLEY Charades III. ii, Nor work *smoking-caps for cousins. 1871 M. COLLINS Marq. & Merch. III. ii. 67 The..gentlemen were..ensconced in a *smoking-carriage. 1891 PEACOCK N. Brendon I. 138 He put on a *smoking coat. 1878 H. SMART Play or Pay i, Appearing in a radiant *smoking-jacket that matched the cigar-case. 1843 HOLTZAPFFEL Turning I. 161 Meerschaum, Amber...are principally used for *smoking-pipes. 1897 Allbutt's Syst. Med. II. 885 In competition with the *smoking-shops, there are now shops where injections are to be had at so much the syringeful. 1884 Health Exhib. Catal. 57/2 The *Smoking Temple in the Classic style, with niches and divans in colour. 1796 MORSE Amer. Geogr. I. 259 Snuff, chewing and *smoaking tobacco. 1880 U. S. Census, Rep. Culture Tobacco 15 Other cigar and smoking tobacco.

c. In the sense of 'at which smoking takes place or is allowed', as *smoking-concert*, etc.

1809 A. HENRY Trav. 299 In smoking-feasts, or feasts of the pipe, or calumet, held in honour of the spirits. 1886 C. E. PASCOE London of To-day vi. (ed. 3) 78 The smoking concert..with its genial Bohemianism. 1895 Daily News 4 Feb. 5/3 The annual meeting of the club would be held.. as a smoking 'At Home'.

Smoking (smōᵘ·kiŋ), *ppl. a.* [f. SMOKE v.]

1. Emitting or giving out smoke.

c 1374 CHAUCER Boeth. I. metr. iv. (1868) 12 Þe vnstable mountaigne þat hyȝt veseuus, þat wircheþ oute..smokyng fires. 1382 WYCLIF Matt. xii. 20 He shal nat quenche smokynge flax. c 1400 Pilgr. Sowle III. vii. (Caxton, 1483) 55 The forneis was al enflammed with smokyng fyre. 1592 KYD Sp. Trag. I. i, Ere Sol had..slakte his smoaking charriot in her floud. 1611 COTGR., *Fumeau*, a brand, or smoaking sticke. a 1700 EVELYN Diary 7 Sept. 1666, Clambering over heaps of yet smoking rubbish. 1781 GIBBON Decl. & F. xxx. (1787) III. 171 The prospect of the smoking ruins. 1815 SCOTT Guy M. viii, This day have ye quenched seven smoking hearths. 1894 DOYLE S. Holmes 93 The chaplain stood with a smoking pistol in his hand.

fig. 1387 TREVISA Higden (Rolls) VII. 331 Lanfrank.. despisede þe smokynge..speche of mysbyleved men. 1587 GREENE Euphues Wks. (Grosart) VI. 176 Hir heart offred smoking thoughtes to Venus. 1677 W. ROW Suppl. Life R. Blair (1848) x. 171 Our smoking desires for a more strict union..did break forth into a vehement flame.

b. Of a chimney: = SMOKY a. 1 b.

1667 COLLINS in Rigaud Corr. Sci. Men (1841) II. 482, I have been troubled with smoking chimneys. 1693 EVELYN De la Quint. Compl. Gard. 77 A House with Smoaking Chimneys. 1728 CHAMBERS Cycl. s.v. Smoak, There are various Inventions for preventing and curing Smoaking Chimneys.

2. Giving out steam or vapour, sending up fine dust or spray, etc.

1593 SHAKS. 3 Hen. VI, II. iii. 21 Their Steeds, That stain'd their Fetlockes in his smoaking blood. 1607 — Cor. I. iv. 11 That we with smoaking swords may march from hence. 1697 DRYDEN Virg. Georg. II. 794 'Tis Time to set at Ease the smoaking Horse. 1716 POPE Iliad VII. 382 The victim falls; they strip the smoaking hide. 1784 COWPER Task III. 517 The smoking manure. 1848 DICKENS Dombey li, They have hot suppers every night,..with smoking drinks upon the board. 1888 STEVENSON Black Arrow 184 The Good Hope continued to tear through the smoking waves.

b. quasi-*adv.* in *smoking-hot*.

1816 KEATINGE Trav. (1817) I. 219 The paunch of a goat.. cut out, and applied..smoking hot, to the part. 1842 LOVER Handy Andy xxi, Where tea and coffee, toast and muffins,.. were all smoking-hot together.

3. Characterized by, addicted to, the smoking of tobacco. Also *transf.* and *absol.*

1617 BRATHWAIT (title), The Smoaking Age, or The man in the mist: with The life and death of Tobacco. Ibid. 174 More guerdon doe I receive of my love from the sleeping Dormouse, than the smoaking Gallants. 1888 G. TRUMBULL Birds 21 [The Widgeon is] known to voyageurs throughout the Fur Countries as Smoking-Duck. [Note.] Probably because its note was thought to resemble the puffing sound made while smoking. 1890 Pall Mall G. 29 Sept. 3/3 The lazy, the drunken, the smoking, the thriftless.

Hence **Smo·kingly** *adv.*, smokily.

1824 LADY GRANVILLE Lett. (1894) I. 334, I told you she was uncomfortably, smokingly lodged.

Smo·king-room. [SMOKING vbl. sb.] A room in a house, hotel, club, etc., set apart as a place for smoking in.

1689 SHADWELL Bury Fair III. i, We'll into my Smoaking-room and sport about a Brimmer. 1754 Connoisseur No. 48 ¶ 3, The Squire gets drunk..in the smoking-room. 1840 MARRYAT Poor Jack xiii, Most of those who prefer smoking collect in..the smoking room. 1890 'R. BOLDREWOOD' Col. Reformer (1891) 147 The same deserted library, the same populous smoking-room.

attrib. 1885 Pall Mall G. 20 Oct. 4/3 Jotting down short smoking-room stories.

Smokish (smōᵘ·kiʃ), *a.* [f. SMOKE sb. + -ISH.] Resembling smoke; somewhat smoky.

1477 NORTON Ordin. Alch. v. in Ashm. (1652) 69 Odor is a smokish vapour resolved with heate. 1530 PALSGR. 324/2 Smokysshe, *fumeux*. 1630 R. Johnson's Kingd. & Commw. 202 Their Water brackish, their Aire foggie and their Fire smokish. 1648 HEXHAM II, *Roockachtigh*, Smoakish, or Fumie. 1807 W. IRVING Salmag. (1824) 47 A yellowish, whitish, smokish, dirty-coloured shawl.

Hence **Smo·kishness.** *rare*⁻⁰.

1530 PALSGR. 271/2 Smokysshnesse, *fumevsete*.

Smoko: see SMOKE-HO.

Smoky (smōᵘ·ki), *a.* and *sb.* Also 4, 6-7 smokie, 7, 9 smokey; 6-7 smoakie, 6-9 smoaky. [f. SMOKE sb. + -Y.]

A. *adj.* **1.** Emitting smoke in considerable volume.

1310 St. Brendan (Bälz) 472 Þo seie hi..a lond derk inouȝ Smokie as it smyþes were. c 1407 LYDG. Reson & Sens. 4122 Than is the fire..Of smoky Ethna the mounteyn. c 1440 Promp. Parv. 461/1 Smoky, *fumosus*. 1576 GASCOIGNE Philomene Wks. 1910 II. 198 A Swallowe..builds in smoky chimney toppes. 1577 tr. Bullinger's Decades (1592) 127 To set up a percher, a taper, or a smoakie torch. 1613 PURCHAS Pilgrimage (1614) 775 They vse smokie fires in their rooms. c 1663 COWLEY To Light xv, In Sympathizing Night he rowls his smoaky Fires. 1726 GAY Fables I. xxiii. 11 A wrinkled Hag..Beside a little smoaky flame Sat hov'ring. 1818 BYRON Beppo xliii, Where reeking London's smoky caldron simmers. 1884 St. James' Gaz. 25 July 4/2 Letting off a quantity of the noisiest and smokiest fireworks procurable.

b. Of a chimney: Inclined to send out smoke into the room.

1639 J. SMYTH in Glouc. Gloss. (1890) 201 If many gossips sit against a smokey chimney the smoke will bend to the fairest. 1785 FRANKLIN (title), Observations on Smoky Chimneys. 1844 EMERSON Ess. II. Nature, It..cured the smoky chimney, silenced the creaking door. 1869 E. A. PARKES Pract. Hygiene (ed. 3) 141 The down current coming in puffs is one cause of smoky chimneys.

2. Of vapour, mist, etc.: Having the character or appearance of smoke; resembling smoke; smoke-like.

c 1374 CHAUCER Troylus III. 628 Every maner womman that was there, Hadde of that smoky reyn a verray fere. 1398 TREVISA Barth. De P. R. v. xxxvi. (Bodl. MS.), Þe breeste ..putteþ oute smoky vapour þat is ibred in þe hert. 1426 LYDG. De Guil. Pilgr. 11034 Two ful vnkouth skyes..off smoky mystes & vapours. a 1542 WYATT Ps. li. 20 There had owt off the sowth A lewk warme wynd browght forth a smoky rayne. 1662 H. HIBBERT Body of Divinity I. 205 By breathing..the gross and more smoky spirits are exhaled out of the breast. 1743 DAVIDSON Æneid VII. 203 The Smoaky Fluid in Foam overflows. 1784 COWPER Task V. 105 The light and smoky mist. 1817 J. BRADBURY Trav. Amer. 259 The atmosphere..becomes hazy, or what they term smoky. 1853 KANE Grinnell Exped. xxix. (1856) 246 The frost-smoke was in smoky banks to the north-west.

3. Full of, or charged with, smoke; rendered offensive or disagreeable by the presence of smoke.

1398 TREVISA Barth. De P. R. XII. iii. (Bodl. MS.), Þerefore here mewes moste be ferre fro smoky places. c 1407 LYDG. Reson & Sens. 6638 Anoon as he his torche hath queynt, The smoky air..Ran..in lengthe and brede. 1596 SHAKS. 1 Hen. IV, III. i. 161 O, he is..Worse then a smoakie House. 1608 D. T. Ess. Pol. & Mor. 39 To lodge within the inclosure of a smokie roofe. 1700 T. BROWN tr. Fresny's Amusements 116 At the Bar..a charming Phillis or two, invite you..into their smoaky Territories. 1749 BERKELEY Word to the Wise Wks. III. 440 It takes the peasant from his smoky cabin into the fresh air. 1806 Med. Jrnl. XV. 366 Ozanne received them in a smoky hut. 1869 E. A. PARKES Pract. Hygiene (ed. 3) 107 The effect of smoky town atmospheres in producing lung affections. 1891 C. JAMES Rom. Rigmarole 18 All through a smoky evening I spent in that inn parlour.

b. Blackened or begrimed by smoke.

1552 ELYOT Dict., *Fumosæ imagines*, olde smoky images. 1588 GREENE Metamorphosis Wks. (Grosart) IX. 50 Wilt thou..seeke with the smoky Cyclops to kisse Venus hand? 1634 MILTON Comus 324 In lowly sheds With smoky rafters. 1848 DICKENS Dombey xxiii, The two trees with the smoky trunks were blighted high up.

4. *fig.* Having the obscuring, objectionable, or unsubstantial qualities of smoke. *Obs.*

1533 MORE Answ. Poysoned Bk. Wks. 1035/1 The pestilent contagion of al such smoky communicacion. 1581 J. BELL Haddon's Answ. Osorius 277 b, Besides vayne crakes of smoky speeches, ye shewe no demonstration of sounde proofe. 1624 SKINNER in Parr Life Usher (1686) 358 Other points these devilish Spirits of the Jesuits..by their smoaky Doctrine do resist. 1633 HART Diet of Diseased II. xiv. 193 Their smoakie promises not being seconded by answerable events.

5. Having the flavour or odour of smoke; tasting or smelling of smoke.

1542 BECON Potation for Lent Wks. 1564 I. I. 45 From a smokie peece of Bacon. 1707 FLOYER Physic. Pulse-Watch 332 The smoaky Bitters, Cichory, Carduus. 1892 WALSH Tea 93 The 'smoky' and 'tarry' flavors possessed by many of them.

6. Of the colour of smoke; dark, dusky; *spec.* of a brownish or bluish shade of grey.

1555 EDEN Decades (Arb.) 280 Halfe an houre after the rysynge it appeareth troubeled dymme and smoky. 1598 B. JONSON Ev. Man in Hum. I. iii, To conceale such reall ornaments..as a Millaners wife do's her wrought stomacher, with a smokie lawne, or a black cypresse. 1647 HEXHAM I. (Colours), A Smokie colour, *een roock verwe*. 1750 tr. Leonardus' Mirr. Stones 38 Blackness is occasion'd by a smoaky and adust terrene. 1796 H. HUNTER tr. St.-Pierre's Stud. Nat. (1799) II. 106 The red and smoky colour of ... 1855 BREWSTER Life Newton I. vii. 171 A

Smolet, **Smolt**, etc.

large crystal of quartz of a smoky colour. 1897 *Allbutt's Syst. Med.* V. 81 It is present in small quantities only, the urine will be smoky.

b. In names of stones, etc. *smoky quartz.*

9. *attrib.* and *Comb.*, as *smoke-* (in sense 8).

10. Quite to suspect or take note; shrewd, sharp, suspicious. *Obs.*

Smolt (smōlt), *sb.* ... Also **smolte**. [OE.]

+1. Of weather: Fair, fine, calm. *Obs.*

+2. Pleasant, agreeable, affable. *Obs.*

3. Bright, shining; smooth, polished.

Smolt (smōlt), *a.* north. dial. Forms: 7 smought, smoute, 9 smout, 8 smoute, 1 smyrthe; 9 smuolth, 9 smooth. [OE. *smolt*...]

Smoot, obs. form of SMUT *sb.* and *v.*

Smooth (smūð), *a.* Also 3–6 smothe. [f.]

+1. † a. A level space. = SMEETH. *Obs.*

Smooth (smūð), *a.* Forms: 1 smoð, 4 smoþe, 4–6 smothe, 6 smoth; 4 smuthð, 4 smyrthe; 1 smǿð, 5 smouðe, 6 smoothe. [OE. *smoð*...]

1. Having a surface free from projections, irregularities, or inequalities; presenting no roughness or unevenness to the touch or sight.

Smoother (smō·ðər). [f. SMOOTH *v.*]

1. One who uses smooth or flattering language; a flatterer. *Obs.*

Smooth-faced, *a.* [f. SMOOTH *a.* 14.]

1. Of persons: Having a face free from hair, wrinkles, etc.; clean-shaven, beardless.

Smooth-headed, *a.* [f. SMOOTH *a.*]

Smoothing (smō·ðiŋ), *vbl. sb.* [f. SMOOTH *v.*]

Smoothing, *ppl. a.* [f. as prec.]

Smooth-leaved, *a.* [SMOOTH *a.* 14.]

Smoothing-plane.

Smoothness.

Smoothly (smūˈðli), *adv.*

Smore, *v.* Now *Sc.* Also 4 *smorre*.

Smother, *sb.*

Smorando.

Smot, *sb.* *Sc.* and *dial.*

Smot, *v.*

Smorther, etc., obs. ff. SMOTHER *sb.* and *v.*

Smother, *v.*

Smotherable, *a.*

Smotheration.

Smother-fire.

Smother-fly, *sb.*

Smotheriness.

Smothering, *vbl. sb.*

Smothering, *ppl. a.* [f. SMOTHER *v.*]

Smothered, *ppl. a.* [f. SMOTHER *v.*]

Smotherer.

Smother-kiln.

Smotherly, *adv.*

Smothery, *a.*

Smouch, *sb.* [var. of SMUTCH *sb.*]

Smouch (smautʃ), *v.*

Smoucher.

Smouldering, *vbl. sb.*

Smouldering, *ppl. a.* [f. SMOULDER *v.*]

Smoulder (smōuˈldai), *v.*

Smouldry, *a.* Obs. Also *smouldry.*

Smould, *v.* rare.

Smous, *sb.* [f. Du. *smous*]

Smouse, *v.*

Smudge, *sb.*

Smudge, *v.*

Smudge, *a.* Smart, trim.

Smudge, *sb.* Now *dial.* and *U.S.* [Of obscure origin.]

Smudge, *v.*[2] Now *dial.* and *U.S.* [Of obscure origin.]

Smudge, *v.*[3] *Obs. rare.* [Of obscure origin.] To make smart or trim; to deck or trick up.

Smudge, *sb.*[4] *Sc.* and *north.* [cf. Smudge *v.*] A blacksmith.

Smug, *a.* [a. LG. *smuk* pretty, neat.]

Smug, *v.* Also 7 smugge. [f. prec.]

Smugged, *ppl. a.* [f. Smug *v.*]

Smugger, *sb.*[1] One who smudges.

Smuggle, *v.*[1] Also 7 smukle. [ad. LG. *smuggelen*, Du. *smokkelen*, Sw. *smuggla*: see Smuggle *v.*]

Smuggle, *v.*[2] *Obs.* [Of obscure origin.]

Smuggleable, *a.* [f. Smuggle *v.*[1]] Capable of being smuggled.

Smuggled, *ppl. a.* [f. Smuggle *v.*[1]]

Smuggler, *sb.* Also 7 smuckellor, smuckler. [ad. LG. *smuggeler*, Du. *smuggelar*; Sw. *smuggler*: see Smuggle *v.*]

Smuggling, *vbl. sb.* [f. Smuggle *v.*[1]] Clandestine importation of goods, etc.

Smut, *sb.*[1] Also 5–7 smutt, 6–9 smoot. [Related to Smut *v.*; cf. LG. *smutt*.]

Smut, *v.* Also 6 smote, 7 smutt, smoot. [cf. EFris. *smutten*, LG. *smutten.*]

Smutch, *sb.* Also 7 smutch, smootch. [Of obscure origin: cf. Smudge *v.*]

Smur, *sb.* *dial.* and *Sc.* Also smurr, smir(r. [Of obscure origin.]

Smurry, *a.* Drizzly.

Smush, *a.* *Sc. Obs.* (Meaning uncertain.)

Smut-ball, *sb.* [Smut *sb.* 1.] A single grain of wheat or other cereal affected by smut or dust; a cohesive body of dust.

Smutch, *v.* Also 6 smutche, 7 smouch. [Of uncertain origin; related in some way to Smudge, which is recorded earlier as a vb.]

Smutter, *sb.* [f. Smut *v.*] One who smuts; a blotter, spotter, smutter.

Smutter, *v.* [f. Smut *v.*]

Smuttily, *adv.* [f. Smutty.]

Smuttiness, *sb.* [f. Smutty.]

Smutty, *a.* [f. Smut *sb.* + -Y.]

Smutch'd, *ppl. a.*

Smutting, *ppl. a.* [f. Smut *v.*] Making black or gloomy.

Smutty, *a.* Also 6–7 smootie, 7–8 smooty, 7 smuttie. [f. Smut *sb.* + -Y. Cf. G. *schmutzig.*]

Smyrna (smə˙na). A place-name (see def.)

Smyrnæan, *sb.* and *a.* Also 6 Smir-. [f. Smyrna + -ÆAN.]

Smyrnian, *sb.* and *a.* rare. Also 6 Smir-. [f. Smyrna + -IAN.]

Snaffle, *sb.* [Related to Snaffle *v.*; cf. MDu. and Flem. *snavel* beak, bill.]

Snaffle, *v.*[1] *dial.* Now *Sc.* [f. Snaffle *sb.*]

Snaffle, *v.*[2] *slang.* To rifle, to strip, to appropriate dishonestly. [Of obscure origin.]

Snack, *sb.*[1] Also 4 snak, 5 snacke. [f. Snack *v.*]

Snack, *v.* Also 7 snak. [prob. a var. of *snatch.*]

Snackle, *v.* *Sc.* [Of obscure origin.]

Snag, *sb.*[1] Also 6 snagg. [Of obscure origin.]

Snade, *Cornish dial.* [? Related to SNED *v.*] A piece cut from the tail of a mackerel for use as bait.

Snade, northern form of SNODE *Obs.*, sward.

Snaffle, error for *snaffle.*

Snag, *sb.*[2] *dial.* A small quantity of liquor.

Snack, *sb.*[3] *Obs.* A snatch, a small quantity.

SNAFFLE. | 297 | **SNAGGLE-TOOTHED.**

Snaffle (snæˈf'l). [f. SNAFFLE v.[1]]

Snaffle-bit, -bridle, -rein.

Snaffle (snæˈf'l), v.[1]

Snaffle (snæˈf'l), v.[2] dial. or slang. [Of obscure origin; cf. SNAFFLE sb.[2]]

Snaffle-headlay. Cant. Obs. [f. SNAFFLE v.[2]]

Snag, sb.[1]

Snag, sb.[2]

Snag, v.[1]

Snag, v.[2]

Snagged, ppl. a.

Snag-greet. | 298 | **SNAIL.**

†Snag-greet, sb.[1]

Snaggy, a.[1]

Snaggy, a.[2] Sc. and dial.

Snag-tooth. Cf. SNAGGLE-TOOTH.

Snail (snēl).

Snagger (snæˈgə(r)).

Snag-tooth. Cf. next and SNAG-TOOTH.

Snaggle-tooth. Cf. SNAG-TOOTH.

Snaggle-toothed, a. rare. [app. f. SNAG sb.[1]]

SNAIL. | 299 | **SNAKE.**

Snail (snēl), v.

Snailing, ppl. a.

Snailish (snēˈliʃ), a.

Snail-like, a. and adv.

Snailery (snēˈləri).

Snail-horn. Now dial. [SNAIL sb.[1]]

Snail stone (see quot.).

Snail-slow, a.

Snake (snēk), sb.

SNAKE. | 300 | **SNAKE.**

Snake (snēk), v.

Snap, etc.

SNAKE.

Snake (snēk), *sb.* ...

6. *U.S. slang.* To beat, thrash.

7. *U.S.* To take out surreptitiously.

Snake, *v.* ... Also **snake.** [prob. a. ON. *snaka* (Norw. *snake*, MDa. *snage*), to go snuffing or searching about; cf. G. dial. *schnaken* (*schnacken*) to creep.]

1. *intr.* To skulk or sneak.

2. *trans.* To get or obtain (a thing) furtively or surreptitiously; to steal or pilfer; to cheat (a person) out of something.

Snake-bird. Also **snakebird, snake bird.**

Snake-fence. *U.S.*

Snake-fish. [SNAKE *sb.*] One or other of certain fishes ...

Snake-head. Also **snakehead.** [SNAKE *sb.*]

Snakeless, *a.* [f. SNAKE *sb.*] Free from, not infested by, snakes.

Snakelet. *rare.* [-LET.] A small snake.

Snake-like. [f. SNAKE *sb.*] Like or resembling a snake or that of a snake; having the characteristic form of a snake; long and slender.

Snakeling. [f. SNAKE *sb.* + -LING.]

Snakeology. [f. SNAKE + -OLOGY.] The study of snakes.

† Snaker. *Obs.* [Cf. SNAKE *v.* and -ER.] One who approaches stealthily; a sneak.

Snake-root. Also **snake root, snakeroot.** [f. SNAKE *sb.*]

1. The root or rhizome of one or other of several American plants reputed to possess properties antidotal to snake-poison ...

2. One or other of these plants.

Snake-stone. Also **snakestone, snake stone.**

1. An ammonite. Now *dial.*

2. A porous or absorbent substance (as chalk) ...

Snakery (snē'kəri). [f. SNAKE *sb.* + -ERY [2].] A snake-house.

Snake's-head. [See SNAKE *sb.* 13.]

1. *attrib.* A snake's-head iris ...

2. = SNAKE'S-HEAD 2.

Snakeship (snē'kʃip). [f. SNAKE *sb.* + -SHIP.] The personality of a snake.

Snakeskin (snē'kskin). [f. SNAKE *sb.* + SKIN.]

† Snaksman. *Cant. Obs.* (See quot.)

Snake-weed.

Snakewise, *adv.* [f. SNAKE *sb.*]

Snake-wood. Also **snakewood.** [SNAKE *sb.*]

Snakily (snē'kili), *adv.* [f. SNAKY + -LY [2].]

Snakiness (snē'kinis). [f. SNAKY + -NESS.]

Snaking (snē'kiŋ), *vbl. sb.* [f. SNAKE *v.*]

Snaky (snē'ki), *a.* [f. SNAKE *sb.* + -Y [1].]

1. Formed or composed of snakes.

SNAP.

7. A brief and sudden spell of cold, winter, etc. Orig. *U.S.*

Snap, *sb.*

I. 1. A quick sharp sound or report.

2. A sudden snatch or catch at something; a quick movement or effort.

Snap, *v.* ...

IV. 15. *intr.* To break suddenly and (usually) ...

Snap-, in combination, as **snap action** gun (see quot. 1884); so **snapactional** adj.; **snap-apple** (see quot. 1833); **†snap-bag**, a SNAPSACK; **snap-bean** U.S. (see SNAP sb.[1]); **Click** sb.[1]); **snap-block** Naut. (see quot. 1875); **snap-dog**, Sc.a, a lurcher; **snap-dyke** Sc. (see quots.); **†snap-flag** = BECCAFICO; **snap-flask** (see quot. 1875); **†snap-haunce**, ? the stitchwort; **snap-plough**, local (see quot.); **†snap-rod** (see quot.); **snap-sound** Path., a snapping sound heard in auscultation; **snap-thought** attrib., used for noting ideas as they occur; **snap-tree**, weed (see quots.); **snap-willow**, local, the brittle or crack willow, Salix fragilis; **snapwood** (see quot.).

Snapdragon.

1. A popular name for one or other of the plants belonging to the genus Antirrhinum, esp. A. majus, a hardy plant bearing showy flowers, freq. grown in gardens.

Snape, sb.[3] Obs.—[1] (Meaning uncertain.)

Snape (snēp), v.[1] Now dial. Forms: 4 (9) snaip (4 snaipe), 4–5 snayp (5 snaype), 5 snape, 6 snepe, 9 dial. sneap. [ad. ON. sneypa to outrage, dishonour, disgrace (Icel. sneypa to chide, snub, Norw. snøypa to wither, draw in, pinch, etc., MSw. and Sw. snöpa to castrate).]

†1. trans. To be hard upon; to harass, pinch, or injure in some way. Obs.

2. To rebuke or snub (a person, etc.) sharply or severely; to check, restrain, or curb (a child); to call off (a dog). Now dial.

Snape (snēp), v.[2] Obs. rare.

Snaphaunce, snaphaunce (snæ·phɔns).
Now Hist. Forms: α. 6–7 snaphaunce, 6–7 snaphance (6 snaphan), 7 snaphaunch, 6, 8–9 snaphaunce; 7 snap-haunce, 8, 9 snaphaunces [Of Continental origin, repr. Du. and Flem. snaphaan a firelock, lit. a snapping cock, f. snappen SNAP + haan cock.]

Snap head. Also snap-head. [f. SNAP sb.]

1. A round head to a rivet, bolt, etc.

Snap-hook. [f. SNAP-.]

Snapper.

6. a. One or other of various fishes, esp. the West Indian Lutjanus Blackfordii or L. caxis; or other fish of this group, the N. American cone-fish, Sebastes marinus, and the Australian Pagrus unicolor (see quots. and b).

b. A snapping insect or animal.

Snapper, sb.[2] Sc. [f. SNAPPER v.[1]]
A stumble or trip. Freq. fig.; a slip in conduct; a fault or error; a scrape or difficulty.

Snapper (snæ·pəz), v.[1] Chiefly (and now only) north and Sc. Forms: 4 snaper, 6 snapper, 6–9, esp. 6–7 snapper (Sc. 9), 7 = snapper. [app. a frequentative from a stem *snap, corresponding to older and dial. G. schnappen to stumble, to limp, related to MHG. snaben, MLG. snaven, whence MDa. snaven, MSw. snava to totter, to reel, to fall.]

Snappern, ppl. a. [f. as prec.]

Snappily (snæ·pili), adv. [f. SNAPPY a.]

Snappiness (snæ·pinės). [f. SNAPPY a.]

Snapping (snæ·piŋ), vbl. sb. [f. SNAP v.]

1. The action of the vb. in various senses.

Snapping, ppl. a. [f. as prec.]

1. Sharp, curt, snappish; peevish, petulant.

Snappish (snæ·piʃ), a. [f. SNAP v. + -ISH.]

Snappishly (snæ·piʃli), adv. [f. prec.]

Snappishness (snæ·piʃnės). [f. prec.]

Snappy (snæ·pi), a. [f. SNAP v. + -Y.]

Snap-shot, sb. Also snap shot, snapshot. [f. SNAP-.]

Snap-shooter, snap-shooting.

Snap-shotter, -shottist, one who takes snap-shot photographs.

Snapsnorum (see quot.).

Snap-work. Also snapwork. [f. SNAP-.]

Snapy, a. Now rare. [Cf. sense to SNAPE sb.[3]]

Snare (snēəz), sb.[1] Forms: 1 sneare, 4–6 snayr, snare, Norw. snara, snore, snøre, snøre, 5 snore; also 7–9 snara, and f. snøra, snare (MLG. snare, snar); OHG. snaraha snare, and f. related to OHG. and MHG. snar (MLG. and LG. snare, snar), MDu. snare, snaer. [A word common to the Teut. langs.]

Snare (snēəz), v.[1] Forms: 1 sneare, 4– snare. [f. SNARE sb.[1]]

1. trans. To capture (small wild animals, birds, etc.) in a snare; to catch by entangling.

Snare, variant of SNATH v. *dial.*

†Snareful, *a.* Obs.⁻¹ [f. SNARE *sb.*] Full of snares; intangling.

Snareless, *a.* [f. SNARE *sb.*] Free from snares.

Snarer (snēˑ·rəz). [f. SNARE *v.*] One who sets snares or traps.

Snark (snāˑk), *sb.* [Corresponds to MLG. and LG. *snarken* (NFris. *snarke*, Sw. and Norw. *snarke*), MHG. *snarchen* (G. *schnarchen*, † *scharchen*) of imitative origin: cf. SNORK *v.*]

Snark (snāˑk), *sb.*² [Invented by 'Lewis Carroll' (C. L. Dodgson) in *The Hunting of the Snark* (1876).] An imaginary animal.

Snarl (snāˑl), *sb.*¹ Also 4–7 snarle, 9 *dial.* snarel. [f. SNARE *sb.* or *v.*: see -LE 1.]

Snarl (snāˑl), *sb.*² Also 4 snarlyn, 5–7 snarle. [f. SNARL *v.*²]

Snarl (snāˑl), *v.*¹ Also 4–7 snarle, 9 *dial.* snarl. [f. SNARE *sb.*]

Snarl (snāˑl), *v.*² Also techn. [f. SNARL *v.*⁴]

Snarled (snāˑld), *ppl. a.* [f. SNARL *v.*]

Snarler¹ (snāˑlɚz). [f. SNARL *v.*²]

Snarler² (snāˑlɚz). [f. SNARL *v.*¹]

Snarl-iron.

Snarley-yow. *Naut.* [After the name of the dog in Marryat's novel *Snarleyyow, or the Dog-Fiend* (1837).]

Snarling (snāˑlɪŋ), *vbl. sb.*¹ [f. SNARL *v.*¹]

Snarling (snāˑlɪŋ), *vbl. sb.*² [f. SNARL *v.*²]

Snarling (snāˑlɪŋ), *ppl. a.* [f. SNARL *v.*¹]

Snarlish, *a.* [f. SNARL *v.*¹]

Snarly, *a.*¹ [f. SNARL *sb.*¹ or *v.*¹]

Snarly, *a.*² [f. SNARL *sb.*² or *v.*²]

Snar-noise, *nonce-word.* [f. SNAR *v.*]

Snary (snēˑ·rɪ), *a.* [f. SNARE *sb.* + -Y.]

Snash (snæʃ), *sb.* Sc. [f. SNASH *v.*]

Snash (snæʃ), *v.* Sc. (and north. *dial.*)

Snaste (snēst), *sb.* [var. of SNOT *sb.*]

†Snaste, *v.* Obs. rare. [Cf. prec.]

Snatch (snætʃ), *sb.* Also 4–5 snecche, 4–6 snacche, snache. [Of obscure origin: perhaps related to SNACK *sb.*²]

Snatch (snætʃ), *v.* Also 2 snecchen, 4–5 snacche, snache. [Of obscure origin: cf. prec.]

Snatch-, the verb-stem used in combs.

Snatchable, *adj.* [f. SNATCH *v.* + -ABLE.] That may be snatched or seized.

Snatch-block, one block having a notch in one side to receive the bight of a rope.

Snatched (snætʃt), *ppl. a.* [f. SNATCH *v.*] Hurriedly or hastily obtained or taken.

Snatcher (snæˑtʃɚz). [f. SNATCH *v.*]

Snatchery, *nonce-wd.* Snatching.

Snatchily (snæˑtʃɪlɪ), *adv.* [f. SNATCHY *a.*] By or in snatches.

Snatchingly, *adv.* [f. *snatching*, pres. pple. of SNATCH *v.*] In a snatching manner; hurriedly.

Snatchy (snæˑtʃɪ), *a.* [f. SNATCH *sb.* or *v.*] Consisting of, characterized by, snatches; irregular.

8. = snath.

Snathe, Snaithe, obs. and *dial.* ff. SNEATH *v.*

Snead (snīd), *sb.* = SNATH.

Sneak (snīk), *sb.* Also 7 sneake. [app. f. SNEAK *v.*]

Sneak (snīk), *v.* Also 7 sneake.

This is a densely printed dictionary (Oxford English Dictionary) page containing entries for the following headwords arranged across six columns:

Columns (upper half): Sneak (cont.), Sneak-cup, Sneaker, Sneaker-snee, Sneakiness, Sneaking, Sneakingly, Sneak-, Sneaksbill, Sneaksby, Sneaksman, Sneak-up, Sneakily, Sneaky, Sneakingly, Sneap, Sneaping, Sneap-nose, Sneb, Sneck, Sneck-drawer, Sne-sne-draw, Snecked, Snecket, Sned.

Columns (lower half): Snedded, Sneeze, Snee, Sneed, Snee, Sneer, Sneerer, Sneerful, Sneeze, Sneezing, Sneezeweed, Sneezewort, Sneezy, Sneezing, Snell.

Snell, *v.* U.S. [f. SNELL *sb.*] *trans.* To tie or fasten (a hook) to a line.

Snelly (sne'li), *adv.* Also 2 snellioe, 4 snellioh, -lik. [f. SNELL *a.*] 1. Sharply, severely.

Snerte: see SNARCHE *v.*

† Mees, *v.* Obs. *rare.* [OE. (d)*snēosan*, f. *snūs* spit.] *intr.* Cf. ON. *sneisa* to spit.] *trans.* To run through with a weapon.

Snet, error in Phillips (1658) and some later Dicts.

† Snetched, *a.* Obs. [? Related to SNECK *v.*] Slaughtered.

Snetel, -ill, etc., obs. forms of SNIVEL.

† Sneve, *v.* Obs. [f. Icel. *snefja* to scent out; Norw. *snev* (also *snevi*, Icel. *snefil*) scent, hint, suspicion.] *trans.* To smell or smell at. Hence **Sne'ving** *vbl. sb.*

Snevel(l, etc., obs. forms of SNIVEL.

Snew, *v.* *dial.* [repr. OE. *snāw* (stem *snīw*, MSw. *snafi-*), f. *snāwan* to snow; MSw. *snāfva-*, Sw. *snāf*, Norw. *snøw*, *snøv*) narrow, tight.] Narrow; slender; slight; neat.

Snew, *v.* Obs. *rare.* Forms of SNIVEL.

5. Grievous, heavy, stinging; rigorous; painful.

† Snew, *v.* Obs. [OE. *snīwan*, = Du. *snuwen*, G. *schneien*.] *intr.* To snow.

2. To check by some hindrance or obstacle.

Snib, *v.* Sc. [Cf. SNIB *sb.*]

1. *trans.* To fasten (a door, etc.) by means of a snib or catch; to shut in its slot.

2. *trans.* To strike or hit sharply.

Snib, obs. form of SNIP, SNUB.

Snib-bing, *vbl. sb.* [f. SNIB *v.*] The action of rebuking, reprimanding, or checking.

Snick (snik), *sb.* [f. SNICK *v.*]

1. A small cut; a nick, a notch.

Snick, *sb.* slang *dial.* [Cf. SNICKING *vbl. sb.*]

2. Cricket. A light, glancing blow given to the ball by the batsman, sending it in the direction of the slips or to leg; a ball so hit.

Snick-a-snee: see SNICK OR SNEE.

Snick and snee. *Obs.* Also 7 snic (snik) and snee, snick and meer. [f. SNICK-A-SNEE 1.]

Snick (snik), *sb.* [f. SNICK *v.*]

Snick (snik), *sb.* Also 8 sneak. [prob. suggested by SNICK AND SNEE, etc. Connexion with SNEG *v.* or with Norw. and Icel. *snīkr*, Sw. dial. *snicka*, to carve, whittle, is very doubtful.]

Snicker (snik-az), *v.* Also 9 Sc. snicher. [imitative: cf. NICKER *v.* and SNIGGER *v.*]

1. *intr.* To laugh in a half-suppressed manner; to snigger.

2. *trans.* To cause to click or sound sharply.

Snicker, *sb.*

† Snickersnee, *v.* Obs. Also 8 snigger-, sneaker-, sneekar-. [f. as prec.] *intr.* To fight with knives; to use a knife as a weapon.

† Snickeraoeing *vbl. sb.* and *ppl. a.*

Snick and snee. *Obs.* Also 7 snio (snik) and snee, snick and meer.

Snick-a-snee, *sb.* *Obs.* Also 7 -ane. [f. prec.]

Snickle (snik'l), *sb.* *dial.*

Snickle, *v.* *dial.* [f. prec.]

† Snicket, *sb.* Obs. rare.

† Snicket, *v.* Obs.

Snico'ker, *sb.*

† Snick or snee, snick-and-snee, etc. *Obs.* Also 7-8 snicke or snee, etc.

Snickersnee (sni'kəzni), *sb.* Also snicker-, snigger-snee.

Snick-snarl. Now *dial.* [f. SNARL *sb.*] A tangle, knot, twist. Also *fig.* *snock-snarl.*

† Snick-up, *v.* Obs. *rare.* [? f. SNICK *sb.*] A hangman's rope; a halter.

Snick-up, *v.* Now *dial.* Also *snick-snarl.*

Snid, slang. *Obs.* A sixpence.

† Snidle, *v. dial.* 5 snythill. [prob. f. the stem of OE. *snīdan* to cut: see SNITHE *v.* With hiss *snyd* (knot) *snīle* in the same sense.]

Snider, (sna'dai). [See *decl.*] Snider rifle, a form of breech-loading rifle invented by Jacob Snider (1862). Also *ellipt.* for this.

Snidge. Now *Lanc. dial.* Also 6 snydge.

Sniff (snif), *sb.* [f. SNIFF *v.*]

Sniff (snif), *v.* Forms: 4-5 snyf, 6 sniffe, 8-sniff. [Imitative: cf. SNIVEL *v.* and SNUFF *v.*]

Snig, *sb.1* *dial.* Also 5-6 snygge, 6, 8-9 snigg. [Of obscure origin.]

† Snig, *sb.2* Obs. rare. [Dim. of SNAG *sb.2*]

Snig, *v.1* *dial.* Also 8-9 snigg.

Snig, *v.2* *Sc.* and *north. dial.* [Cf. SNIG *v.1*, and NIG *sb.2*]

Snigger (snig'az), *v.* Also *sniggle.* [imitative: cf. NICKER *v.* and SNICKER *v.*]

1. *intr.* To laugh in a half-suppressed manner; to snicker.

Sniggerer, *sb.*

Sniggering, *vbl. sb.* and *ppl. a.*

Snigging. [See SNIGGLE *v.*]

Snift (snift), *sb.* [f. SNIFT *v.*]

Snift (snift), *v.* Now *chiefly dial.* [imitative: cf. SNIFTER *v.*, and older Du. *snuften*, *snyften* (Da. *snøfte*), Sw. *snyfta* (MSw. *snypta*, *snöpta*.)]

Snifter (sni'ftaz), *sb.*

Snifting, *vbl. sb.* and *ppl. a.*

Snifter, *v.*

Sniffy (sni'fi), *a.* [f. SNIFF *sb.*] Cf. SNIFF *v.*

Snifting, *vbl. sb.*

Snift, *sb.* *techn.* [See *quot.* and SNIFTING *vbl. sb.*]

Snig-gle (snig'l), *v.* [See SNIGGING *vbl. sb.*]

1. *intr.* To fish for eels by the method known as sniggling.

2. *trans.* To catch (eels) by means of striking a hook into them.

Sniggle, *sb.* *dial.* [Dim. of SNIG *sb.1*] A snig or small eel.

Hence **Sni·ggled** *ppl. a.*

1844 TUPPER *Crock of G.* xlvi. 294 He wriggled like a sniggled eel.

Sniggle (sni·g'l), *v.*[2] [Imitative.] *intr.* To snigger or snicker.

1815 SCOTT *Guy M.* lii, As for the Dominie,..he looked at Lucy—he whimpered—he sniggled—he grinned. 1840 C. BRONTË in Mrs. Gaskell *Life* (1857) I. 215 [The preacher] did not whine; he did not sniggle. 1889 GUNTER *That Frenchman* vi, At which flattery the other sniggles and calls him a wit.

Hence **Sni·ggling** *ppl. a.*

1826 SCOTT *Woodst.* xii, Wildrake laughed without ceremony,..and was joined by a sniggling response from behind the cupboard.

Sni·ggle, *v.*[3] *dial.* or *colloq.* [Of doubtful origin. Cf. Norw. *snygla* to sponge, beg.]

1. *intr.* **a.** (See quot. 1837). **b.** To wriggle, crawl, creep stealthily.

1837 J. F. PALMER *Gloss. Devon Dialogue, To Sniggle*, (at taw) to shuffle the hand forwards in an unfair manner; *Unde* Sniggler. 1881 *Leicestersh. Gloss.* 247 *Sniggle*,..to wriggle away. 1900 FLORA A. STEEL *Hosts of the Lord* xxiii, There's a brute trying to sniggle along the wall.

2. *trans.* To get (a thing) *in* surreptitiously.

1881 *Oxfordsh. Gloss.* 98 *Sniggle in*, to get anything in an underhand manner. 1900 POLLOK & THOM *Sports Burma* vi. 190, I calculated that if I were successful in my application I could sniggle in those two days as well.

Sniggler[1] (sni·glər). [f. SNIGGLE *v.*[1]] One who fishes for or catches eels or salmon by sniggling.

1840 J. T. HEWLETT *P. Priggins* i, Like an eel in a wall, politely declining a sniggler's offer of a lobworm. 1864 *Q. Rev.* CXV. 186 Towards evening the juvenile sniggler knows that he has the best chance of success. 1890 *Daily News* 6 Nov. 5/1 The truth is that the apparent sportsmen are snigglers, not anglers.

Sni·ggler[2]. [f. SNIGGLE *v.*[2]] A sniggerer.

1876 ROBINSON *Whitby Gloss.*, *Sniggler*, a derider. 1886 in ELWORTHY *W. Somerset Wordbk.*

Sni·ggler[3]. [f. SNIGGLE *v.*[3]] One who plays in a manner not quite fair or correct.

1837 [see SNIGGLE *v.*[3] 1]. 1887 BLACK *Sabina Zembra* i, It has been affirmed..that the pool-players..break out into mild revelry; that derisive cheers overwhelm the 'sniggler'.

Sniggling (sni·gliŋ), *vbl. sb.* [? Related to SNIG *sb.*[1]]

1. The action or practice of fishing for eels by means of a baited hook or needle thrust into their holes or haunts.

1661 WALTON *Angler* xiii. (ed. 3) 193 Because you..know not what *snigling* is, I will now teach it to you..: take a strong small hook tied to a strong line.., and then into one of these holes,..or any place where you think an Eele may hide or shelter her self, there with the help of a short stick put in your Bait. 1669 WORLIDGE *Syst. Agric.* (1681) 260 Eels commonly abscond themselves under stones.., and under Timber, Planks, or such-like.., where you may take them by this way of Snigling. 1740 R. BROOKES *Art of Angling* I. xl. 85 Snigling or Brogling for Eels is another remarkable Method of taking them. 1787 BEST *Angling* (ed. 2) 55 There are two ways to take them in the day time called sniggling and bobbing. 1856 'STONEHENGE' *Brit. Rural Sports* 258 Sniggling is another mode of taking eels..and the apparatus consists in a strong needle [etc.]. 1885 *Sat. Rev.* 21 Nov. 673/1 'Sniggling'..is one of the most favourite ways of catching eels.

attrib. 1688 HOLME *Armoury* III. 103/1 A Snigleing, or Prokeing Stick, is a forked stick, and a short long Line with a Needle Bated with a Lob Worm. It is only for Eels in their holes. 1867 F. FRANCIS *Angling* iii. (1880) 91 A sniggling stick or rod.

2. In salmon-fishing (see quots.).

1890 *Scottish Leader* 20 Nov. 5 'Sniggling,' means fishing with rod and line and artificial fly, but the hook is made to sink in the water where fish are supposed to be, and the rod so jerked that they are hooked and quickly landed. 1891 *Ibid.* 13 Nov. 4 'Sniggling'..is a mode of fishing by which the hook takes the fish, and not the fish the hook.

Snight, obs. f. SNITE (the snipe).

†**'Snigs,** *int. Obs.* An abbrev. of *God's nigs* (see GOD *sb.* 14 b and cf. NIGS), used as a minced oath. Cf. 'SNIGGERS.

a 1643 CARTWRIGHT *Ordinary* III. ii, 'Snigs, another! *Ibid.* IV. i, 'Snigs, I would fain now hear some fighting news. 1675 COTTON *Burlesque upon B.* 72 S'nigs, well remembred! I'le be gone.

†**Snigsnarl,** obs. var. SNICK-SNARL.

1688 HOLME *Armoury* III. 288/2 The Yarn..is..tied up with a Lay Band, to keep it from ravalling or running into Snigsnarles or Knotted up.

Snik-a-snee, variant of SNICK-A-SNEE.

†**Snike,** *v. Obs.* [OE. *snícan*, prob. related to ON. *snikja* (Da. *snige*) to sneak.] *intr.* Of reptiles: To creep, crawl.

c 897 K. ÆLFRED tr. *Gregory's Past.* 311 On ðinre wambe & on ðinum breostum ðu scealt snican. *c* 1000 *Sax. Leechd.* III. 34 Wyrm com snican. *a* 1240 *Sawles Warde* in *O. E. Hom.* I. 251 þe laðe helle wurmes, tadden ant froggen, þe..snike**3** in ant ut.

Snikker-snee, obs. form of SNICKERSNEE.

†**Snilch,** *v. Cant. Obs.* (See quots.)

1676 COLES, *Snilches*, sees or eyes you. *a* 1700 B. E. *Dict. Cant. Crew*, *Snilch*, to Eye or See any Body.

Snip (snip), *sb.* Also 6–8 **snippe,** 6 **snypp,** 7 **snipp.** [Related to SNIP *v.*, and in some senses perh. directly of LG. origin: cf. LG. *snip* (G. dial. *schnipf, schnipp*) and *snippe* a small piece, etc., Du. and Fris. *snip* a snappish girl or woman.]

I. 1. A small piece or slip, esp. of cloth, cut off or out; a shred.

1558 in Feuillerat *Revels Q. Eliz.* (1908) 27 In to Iagges and Snippes for defacinge of torche bearers. 1606 SYLVESTER *Du Bartas* II. iv. I. *Tropheis* 1103 Her lips two snips of crimsin Sattin are. *c* 1620 MORYSON *Itin.* IV. 489 To weare a litle snipp of yellowe lace vpon the left syde of their Clokes. 1691 T. H[ALE] *Acc. New Invent.* 95 Cut a snip from the thickest and thinnest part. 1756 *Connoisseur* No. 115 ⁋ 7 A snip of hair, or the portrait of a cherry-cheeked gentleman,..are the only remaining proofs of those beauties. 1787 COWPER *Let.* 10 Dec., I thank you for your snip of cloth commonly called a pattern. 1837 CARLYLE *Fr. Rev.* II. VI. viii, Patriotism has torn their red coats into snips. 1849 ALB. SMITH *Pottleton Legacy* (1854) 24 Snips of the metal used in packing tea. 1864 CARLYLE *Fredk. Gt.* IV. 542 A snip of paper.

b. *transf.* or *fig.* (Freq. in Fuller.)

1650 FULLER *Pisgah* 370 No snip, or shred of empty space cut off from the squareness of the Oracle. *a* 1661 — *Worthies* (1840) III. 391 Yorkshire hath..Lancashire and a snip of Cheshire on the west. 1682 WHELER *Journ. Greece* III. 280 There might be some Mediterranean Snip of Land, running down between Ionia and Lydia.

†**c.** *spec.* Of glass: (see quot.). *Obs.*

1688 HOLME *Armoury* III. 385/2 A Snip, is the upper halfe, and sometymes a quarter or lesse of a Quarry, Three Snips goes for a quarry.

2. A white or light mark, patch, or spot on a horse, esp. on the nose or lip.

Cf. G. dial. *schnippe* a horse with a mark on the nose, *schnipp* a horse or cow with a narrow blaze.

1562 *Wills & Inv. N. C.* (Surtees, 1835) 202 A younge baye geldinge with a whyte snypp off [= on] ye nose. 1607 MARKHAM *Cavel.* II. (1617) 3 Your redde Sorrell, and your darke Chesnutte, are much graced, if..they be accompanied with any white markes, as..white snippes on the nose. 1679 *Poor Robin's Intelligence* in *Sporting Mag.* XXXIX. 61 Her colour was now coal black, with a star, snip, and one white foot. 1726 *Brice's Weekly Jrnl.* 25 Mar. 3 A Brown Bay Nag, with..a white Snip in one of the hinder Feet. 1799 *Hull Advertiser* 10 Aug. 2/2 A stout handsome chesnut gelding,..a white snip on his nose. 1820– in Sc. and north. dial. use (Jam. and *Eng. Dial. Dict.*). 1891 E. KINGLAKE *Australian* 118 That brown horse over there with a snip. 1893 M. H. HAYES *Points of Horse* xx. (1897) 222 A white or pink patch on either lip is called a 'snip'.

3. A small amount, piece, or portion, a little bit (*of* something). *Every snip*, every bit.

(*a*) 1588 SHAKS. *L. L. L.* III. i. 22 Keepe not too long in one tune, but a snip and away. *a* 1641 BP. MOUNTAGU *New Gagg* iii. 42, I like not that the ancient Fathers should be ..sent away like school boys with snips. 1749 SMOLLETT *Gil Blas* VII. xii. (1782) III. 89 Let me know what is the business, and I promise you shall get some snips out of the minister. 1833 CARLYLE *Misc.* (1857) III. 185 Picking up a few residuary snips.

(*b*) 1624 J. GEE *New Shreds* Pref. p. ii, Some snips of.. their legerdemaine trickes..here I display. *a* 1668 DAVENANT *Man's the Master* II. i, May not a man see a snip of her face? 1700 DRYDEN *Epilogue Dryden's Benefit* 14 The Poets..Tainted the Stage for some small Snip of Gain. 1831 CARLYLE in *Froude* (1882) II. 179 Sunday morning had a snip of a note from Empson. 1894 BLACKMORE *Perlycross* 50 My hair is such a trouble, I have half a mind sometimes to cut off every snip of it.

b. Applied to persons in depreciation or contempt. In later use: A young, slight, or diminutive person.

1625 MASSINGER *New Way* II. ii, This term-driver, Marrall, This snip of an attorney. 1838 [MISS MAITLAND] *Lett. fr. Madras* (1843) 221 Half the experienced men are kept in subordinate situations, and young raw snips placed over their heads. 1902 *Daily Chron.* 11 Feb. 5/1 Why, this snip is no better than anybody else when he lands here.

†**4.** A share or portion; a snack. *Obs.*

1655 tr. *Sorel's Com. Hist. Francion* I. 13 The Justice of the place..not willing to lose his Snip [etc.]. 1672 WYCHERLEY *Love in a Wood* I. ii, He watches them like a younger brother that is afraid to be mumped of his snip. 1698 FRYER *Acc. E. India & P.* 140 The Governor distributing to the Officers, and they to the Soldiers, every one having their Snips. 1702 STEELE *Funeral* III. ii, Take care of their Young Ladyships; you shall..have a Snip in the Sale of 'em.

b. *To go snips* (†or *snip*), to go shares (*with* some one, or *in* something), to share or participate in the profits. Now *dial.*

In very common use *c* 1680–1690, esp. by Hickeringill.

(*a*) 1668 DRYDEN *Even. Love* v. i, Pray, Sir, let me go snip with you in this Lie. 1687 R. L'ESTRANGE *Fairfax' Tasso* Pref. A 2, I recommend it to the Bookseller, for the common benefit, and..I go no snip with the Stationer.

(*b*) 1677 THORESBY *Corr.*, etc. (1830) II. 408 Some of our company went snips with them. 1682 TOPHAM *Rome's Tradit.* 209 The Subtil Old Gentleman..offered him (if he would promote the Trade) to go Snips. 1706 BAYNARD *Cold Baths* II. 202 Those that go Snips with their Apothecaries, are Villains of the first Magnitude. 1725 BAILEY *Erasm. Colloq.* (1733) 322 The Gamester..promises I shall go Snips with him in what he shall win. *a* 1800 PEGGE *Suppl. Grose* s.v. *Snaps*. 1861– in Sc. and north. dial. use (*Eng. Dial. Dict.*).

II. 5. A small cut or incision made by, or such as that made by, a pair of scissors; a wound of this nature. Also *dial.*, a small hole or crack.

1596 SHAKS. *Tam. Shr.* IV. iii. 89 What's this? a sleeue? ..Heers snip, and nip, and cut, and slish and slash. 1600 SURFLET *Countrie Farme* I. xxv. 159 If there be any snips in their skins, you shall apply vnto them melted waxe. 1682 WHELER *Journ. Greece* III. 219 Long sharp leaves.. without snips at the Edges. 1698 J. CRULL *Muscovy* 136 Bonnets, with a little snip open before and behind. 1775 ASH, *Snick*, a small snip or cut as in the hair of a beast. 1867 WAUGH *Tattlin' Matty* II. 24 Squirtin' wayter into my ear through a snip i' th corner o' th window. 1836 C. SCOTT *Sheep Farm.* 149 The snip and hole are used alternately, to designate..the exact part of the ear intended to be marked.

b. *Pottery.* A small projection on the lip of a vessel, the place for which is prepared by cutting a notch.

1834–6 BARLOW in *Encycl. Metrop.* (1845) VIII. 455 These manipulations fix on the clay vessels their handles, snips, spouts [etc.]. *Ibid.*, For snips of jugs, &c., a piece is cut out of the upper edge of proper size and shape.

6. An act of snipping; a single cut or clip *of* scissors, etc.

1676 WISEMAN *Surg. Treat.* 256, I laid it open by a snip of a pair of Scissors. *c* 1765 FLLOYD *Tartarian T.* (1785) 103/2 Four snips of a pair of scissars will initiate you. 1831 CARLYLE *Sartor Res.* I. v, Every snip of the Scissors has been regulated..by ever-active Influences. 1886 *Daily Telegr.* 14 Jan. (Cassell), A few snips of the scissors..and last year's robe will do duty for this.

b. A nip, pinch, bite, etc.

1767 S. PATERSON *Another Trav.* II. 41 He has a snip, or a flip, or a sting, or a fling, at almost every body! 1840 HOOD *Miss Kilmansegg*, *Education* 509 He got..Scratches, and pinches, snips, and snaps, As if from a Tigress or Bearess. 1880 BLACKMORE *Mary Anerley* xxxix, The bruising snip a hungry cow makes.

7. *slang* or *colloq.* A tailor. Also employed as an allusive personal name for a tailor.

(*a*) 1599 B. JONSON *Ev. Man out of Hum.* IV. v [iv], Well, now, master Snip, let mee see your bill. *a* 1634 RANDOLPH *Muses' Looking Gl.* IV. iii, Sir, here's Snip the Taylor Charg'd with a riot. 1694 MOTTEUX *Rabelais* IV. lii, At Paris..Snip Groignet the Taylor had turn'd an old Clementinæ into Patterns and Measures. 1824 W. E. ANDREWS *Rev. Fox's Bk. Martyrs* I. 252 Both Snip and Snob were burned for their pains. *a* 1849 H. COLERIDGE *Ess.* (1851) I. 206 Snip can do more—he can make you an impeccable pair of inexpressibles by simply taking the girth of your thumb. 1858 TROLLOPE *Dr. Thorne* II. iii. 56 Well done, Snip; go it again with the wax and thread.

(*b*) 1630 B. JONSON *New Inn* v. i. Hang him, poor snip, a secular shop-wit! He hath nought but his sheers to claim by, and his measures. *a* 1634 RANDOLPH *Muses' Looking Gl.* IV. ii, *Lup.* Where's my wife? *Colax.* Shee's gone with a young Snip, and an old baud. 1785 GROSE *Dict. Vulgar T.*, *Snip*, a taylor. 1808 J. MAYNE *Siller Gun* III. xxi, 'A ring, a ring!' the sutors cried; 'A ring, a ring!' the snips replied. 1853 R. S. SURTEES *Sponge's Sp. Tour* (1893) 26 'Very neat, sir; would look remarkably well on you, sir,' replies the obsequious snip. 1871 MISS BRADDON *R. Godwin* II. i. 6 Shall I give you a line to my snip?

8. *pl.* (See quot.)

1846 HOLTZAPFFEL *Turning* II. 915 Hand shears..are often called snips, to distinguish them from bench shears.

9. *pl.* Handcuffs. *slang.*

1891 *Newcastle Even. Chron.* 21 Feb. 3/2 Accused did not offer to go quietly till the police had the 'snips' on him. 1895 A. PATTERSON *Man & Nat.* 141 In a moment the slop..had the snips (handcuffs) on me.

10. *slang.* Something easily obtained or won; a sure thing, a certainty.

1894 ASTLEY *50 Yrs. Life* II. 181 The event looked a dead snip. 1899 *Westm. Gaz.* 24 July 5/3 The half-mile was described by the supporters of the Americans as a 'snip' for their men.

III. 11. *attrib.* and *Comb.*, as *snip-like*, *snip-nosed* adjs.; **snip-bag,** a bag for holding snips of cloth, etc.; †**snip-cabbage,** a tailor; **snip-faced** *a.* (of a horse), marked with a snip; **snip-jack,** a person of little account or worth (cf. quot.); **snip-nose** (see quot. 1753); †**snip-work,** *Glazing* (cf. 1 c above).

1703 [R. NEVE] *City & C. Purchaser* 154 Ordinary Houses ..are Glazed with Quarries, which is Bevel Work, so likewise is a great deal of Fret, and all Snip-work. 1708 E. WARD *Terræfil.* v. 35 The Gentleman and yonder Snip-Cabbage, his Taylor, [were] Commended for their Ingenuity. 1753 HANWAY *Trav.* (1762) II. XV. iv. 420 This man was from that time called *binnie buride*, or snip-nose. 1814 MOORE *New Cost. Ministers* v, While Y—m—th, with snip-like and brisk expedition, Cuts up..a large Cath'lic Petition. 1846 MARRYAT *Privateer's-man* xiv, 'I can do without such snip-jacks as you are.' 'Snip-jacks!'..replied I, 'if I must say it, we are better born and better bred than you or any of your connections'. 1878 DICKINSON *Cumbld. Gloss.*, *Snip feasst*. 1880 *Plain Hints Needlewk.* 35 Take one yard of 'cheese cloth'..out of the snip bag. 1880 DAY *Fishes Gt. Brit.* I. 130 *Trachinotus Cumberlandi*, the fisherman's name is Snip-nosed-mullet.

Snip (snip), *v.* Also 6 **snyppe.** [prob. of Du. or LG. origin: cf. Du., Flem., and LG. *snippen*, G. dial. *schnippen, schnipfen, schniffen*, to snip, snatch, etc.]

†**1.** *trans.* To take (something) quickly or suddenly; to snap or snatch. *Obs.*

1586 J. HOOKER *Hist. Irel.* in *Holinshed* II. 83/1 One of your horssemen promised me a choise horsse, if I snip one haire from your beard. Well, quoth the earle,..if thou plucke anie more than one [etc.]. 1633 ROWLEY *Match at Midnight* II. i, Well, and she be snipped by threescore and ten, may she live six-score and eleven. 1720 DE FOE *Capt. Singleton* i. (1840) 7 The captain seldom ordered anything.. but I snipt some of it for my own share.

absol. 1592 GREENE *Def. Conny Catch.* Wks. (Grosart) XI. 96 They will to snip and snap, that al the reuersion goes into hel. 1674 N. FAIRFAX *Bulk & Selv.* To Rdr., While we..snip here and snatch there from some of them.

2. To cut, to cut up or off, by or as by scissors or some similar cutting instrument.

1593 NORDEN *Spec. Brit.* (Camden) Pref. p. xiv, They have snippers wherwith they snyppe and pare their plates. 1649 G. DANIEL *Trinarch.*, *Rich. II*, xlii, Hee takes the Measure of his Maister's stuffe, And Snips it to a Size ..Convenient for his Fashion. *a* 1687 H. MORE *Cont.* *Remark. Stories* 420 They would be snipt and slasht full of holes. 1796 *Phil. Trans.* LXXXVI. 445 It was snipt a good deal, and several holes were worn in the middle. 1848 THACKERAY *Van. Fair* xl, He found Becky and her companion..busy cutting, ripping, snipping, and tearing all sorts of black stuffs. 1871 T. R. JONES *Anim. Kingd.* (ed. 4) 599 If one of these muscular capsules be snipped by means of a pair of very fine scissors.

fig. 1628 JACKSON *Creed* VI. Wks. VI. 83 For snipping this secret hypocrisy..this exercise of the civil sword hath no force or dint. 1674 J. B[RIAN] *Harvest-Home* ii. 5 Th' impartial Fates..With keenest Scissars snip lifes thread asunder. 1893 *Advance* (Chicago) 11 May, While the 'Higher Criticism' is laboriously snipping the book of Genesis into 'Elohistic' and 'Jehovistic' fragments.

b. *absol.* To make a cut or cuts with or as with scissors, etc. Also, of scissors: To cut.

a 1680 BUTLER *Rem.* (1759) II. 138 Like a Barber's Scissars, which are always snipping, as well when they do not cut, as when they do. 1827 SCOTT *Jrnl.* 7 Dec., I wish I have not made that article too long, and Lockhart will not snip away. 1848 DICKENS *Dombey* xxix, Miss Tox, ..arming herself with her scissors, began to snip and clip among the leaves. 1871 PROCTOR *Ess. Astron.* xxiv. 312 One can snip round the borders of a region until its size has been reduced.

c. To injure by chipping or taking small pieces out of.

1822– in north. dial. use (*Eng. Dial. Dict.*). 1884 *L'pool Mercury* 22 Oct. 5/5 The granite pedestal may be snipped; or a thousand other disasters may occur.

d. *Cricket.* To hit (the ball) lightly; to snick.

1890 *Pall Mall G.* 21 Aug. 6/3 Maclaren soon opens his account.., but gently snipping a ball from Streatfeild he is easily caught by Abel in the slips.

3. To cut *off* by means of scissors or other sharp instrument. Also *fig.*

1611 COTGR., *Mordiller*, to nibble, gnaw, fret, snip off. 1624 GATAKER *Transubst.* 214 Hee should have done well ..to have snipt off or concealed at least, the last clause. *a* 1625 FLETCHER *Fair Maid Inn* IV. i, Because I will not afflict you with any large bill Of circumstances, I'll snip off particulars. 1697 DAMPIER *Voy.* (1699) 339 He takes hold of the fore-skin with two sticks and with a pair of Scissors snips it off. 1742 H. BAKER *Microsc.* II. x. 122 A piece of the..Membrane..snipped off with a Pair of sharp Scissars. 1826 S. COOPER *First Lines Surgery* (ed. 5) 349 The new opening..is then to be enlarged by snipping off the flap of the iris. 1845 LANDOR *Imag. Conv.* I. 79 He has snipt off as much as he could pinch from every author of reputation. 1888 FREEMAN in Stephens *Life* (1895) II. x. 380, I simply had my uvula snipped off.

b. With *away, from, out of*, etc.

1768–74 TUCKER *Lt. Nat.* (1834) I. 101 By snipping away the superfluities of the paper from her figure. 1858 DICKENS *Lett.* (1880) II. 60 He is perpetually snipping pieces out of newspapers. 1896 *Pall Mall Mag.* May 16 A bullet snipped a corner from my hat.

c. To cut *out* by snipping. Also *fig.*

1800 *Asiatic Ann. Reg.* II. 113/2 He next proceeded very accurately to snip out their suspicions into four and twenty parts. 1855 O. W. HOLMES *Poems* 137 Boys..Who, for a very trifling sum, Will snip one's picture out.

4. To snub, check, repress. Now *dial.*

1601–14 [see SNIPPING *vbl. sb.* 3]. 1647 FULLER *Good Th. Worse T.* 24 If I were curb'd and Snip't in my younger yeares by feare of my parents, from those vicious excrescencies. 1823– in dial. use (Suffolk, Somerset, Devon).

5. Used adverbially to denote either sound or action.

a 1661 HOLYDAY *Juvenal* (1673) 189 How many towns he owns, who went snip, snip; As his quick sizzers my young beard did clip!

Snipe (snəip), *sb.* Forms: 4–6 **snype,** 4, 6 **snyppe** (7 **snippe**), 6 **sknipe,** 7– **snipe.** [Of doubtful origin: the ME. type *snipe* corresponds to a Scand. *snipa* recorded in Icel. *mýrisnipa*, Norw. *myr-, strandsnipa*. It is not clear how this is related to MDu. *snippe* (Du. and WFris. *snip*), MLG. and LG. (also older Da.) *snippe*, G. dial. *schnippe*, and MDu. *sneppe* (Du. *snep*), MLG. and LG. *sneppe* (hence Da. *sneppe*, Sw. *snäppa*), OHG. *snepha* (*snepfa*) and *snepho* (G. *schnepfe*, obs. or dial. *schneppe*).]

1. One or other of the limicoline birds of the genus *Gallinago* (formerly included in the Linnæan genus *Scolopax*), characterized by having a long straight bill, and by frequenting marshy places; esp. *G. cælestis* or *media*, the common English species.

c 1325 *Gloss. W. de Bibbesw.* in Wright *Voc.* 166 *Un oysel ke est dist becaz*, a snype (snyte). *c* 1350 *Wynnere & Wastoure* 349 Barnakes and buturs and many billed snyppes. *c* 1420 *Liber Cocorum* (1862) 35 To wodcok, snype, curlue also, The betore in fere with hom schalle goo. *c* 1440 *Promp. Parv.* 461/2 Snype, or snyte, byrde, *ibex.* 1530 PALSGR. 272/1 Snyppe, a byrde, *cigoigne*. 1551 *Sc. Acts, Mary* (1814) II. 484/1 Item the snype and qualyie,..ij d. 1565 COOPER, *Gallinago*, a wodcocke or a snype. *Ibid.*, *Rusticula minor*, a sknipe. 1611 COTGR., *Becassine*,..a Snite, or Snipe. 1655 MOUFET & BENNET *Health's Improv.* (1746) 179 Where they perceive a Worm's Hole, as I have seen Snipes to do, there they thrust in their Bill. 1758 JOHNSON *Idler* No. 33 ⁋ 16 Went to the common-room, and supped on the snipes with Dr. Dry. 1794 GISBORNE *Walks in Forest* vi. (1796) 104 The snipe flies screaming from the marshy verge. 1827 D. JOHNSON *Ind. Field Sports* 36 The Calcutta market is well supplied with..snipes. 1865 TENNYSON *On a Mourner* ii, Nature..greens The swamp, where humm'd the dropping snipe.

b. With adjs., denoting species of this bird.

See also *double snipe*, GUTTER-, HALF-, JACK-, MIRE-, WOOD-SNIPE.

a 1705 RAY *Syn.* (1713) 193 *Gallinago Maderspatana*,.. the Partridge-Snipe. 1785 PENNANT *Arct. Zool.* II. 471 Finmark Snipe, *Scolopax Gallinaria*. 1833 BINGLEY *Anim. Biogr.* (ed. 4) II. 302 It is stated, that the Common Snipes never frequent woods. 1839 AUDUBON *Ornith. Biogr.* V. 583 Common American Snipe, *Scolopax Wilsoni*. 1843 YARRELL *Brit. Birds* II. 611 *Scolopax grisea*, Brown Snipe. 1866 *Chambers's Encycl.* VIII. 788/1 The Great Snipe, or Solitary Snipe (*Scolopax* or *Gallinago major*),..abounds in the extensive marshes of continental Europe.

c. Applied to various species of birds resembling the snipe. Chiefly with distinguishing epithets.

See also *duck-snipe*, JACK-SNIPE, *painted, red-breasted, robin snipe*, SEA-SNIPE, *stone-, summer-snipe*.

1785 LATHAM *Gen. Synop. Birds* III. I. 154 *Brown Snipe. ..The head, neck, and scapulars, of a fine uniform cinereous brown. 1866 *Chambers's Encycl.* VIII. 788/1 The Red-breasted Snipe, or Brown Snipe (*Macrorhamphus griseus*) of North America has been occasionally seen in Britain. 1785 LATHAM *Gen. Synop. Birds* III. I. 155 *Dusky snipe. 1829 GRIFFITH tr. *Cuvier* VIII. 387 Red-shank, or *Gambet Snipe, *Tringa Gambetta*. 1887 *Encycl. Brit.* XXII. 200 The so-called *Pin-tailed Snipe *Gallinago stenura*. 1785 PENNANT *Arct. Zool.* II. 469 *Semi-palmated snipe, with a bill two inches long. 1839 AUDUBON *Ornith. Biogr.* V. 585 Semipalmated Snipe or Willet, *Totanus semipalmatus*. 1785 LATHAM *Gen. Synop. Birds* III. I. 148 *Spotted Snipe.

d. Without article, in collective sense.

1842 LOVER *Handy Andy* i, The delighted pointer would ..dash forward to the well-known 'bottoms' in eager expectancy of ducks and snipe. 1845 J. COULTER *Adv. in Pacific* iii. 29, I have often seen flocks of snipe crossing the bay. 1872 COUES *N. Amer. Birds* 249 In woodcock and true snipe the ear appears below and not behind the eye.

2. †**a.** The Egyptian ibis. *Obs.*

1432–50 tr. *Higden* (Rolls) II. 323 Bryddes callede snypes, odious to serpentes and amiable to men.

b. As a moth-name (see quot.).

1832 J. RENNIE *Butterfl. & Moths* 66 The Snipe (*Xylophasia scolopacina*, Haworth) appears in June.

3. As an opprobrious or abusive term.

1604 SHAKS. *Oth.* I. iii. 391 For I mine owne gain'd knowledge should prophane, If I would time expend with such [a] Snipe. 1730 SWIFT *Panegyric on the Dean* Misc. 1735 V. 133 Sir A—r, since you set the Pattern, No longer calls me Snipe and Slattern. 1896 CROCKETT *Grey Man* xii. 84 The Earl had set a little snipe of a raggetty loon to stir her up.

4. *slang.* **a.** *pl.* A pair of scissors.

1812 J. H. VAUX *Flash Dict.*, *Snipes*, scissors. 1834 AINSWORTH *Rookwood* III. v. (1878) 200 No slour'd hoxter my snipes could stay.

b. (See quot.)

1864 *Slang Dict.* 238 *Snipe*, a long bill or account; also a term for attorneys—a race remarkable for their propensity to long bills.

5. *ellipt.* = SNIPE-BILL 1.

1873 *Iron* 1 Feb. 78/2 Planes...Side snipe, per pair, 7/-.

6. *attrib.* and *Comb.*, as *snipe-bog, -dust, -shooter, -shooting, -shot*, etc.; also **snipe-eel,** (*a*) a species of fish belonging to the deep-sea family *Nemichthyidæ*; (*b*) the sea-pike or garfish, *Belone vulgaris*; **snipe-fly** (see quot.); **snipe's-head** (see quots.); †**snipe-knave,** a half-snipe, jack-snipe; **snipe-shell** (see quot. and cf. SNIPE-BILL 2).

1844 J. T. HEWLETT *Parsons & W.* xi, The road across the marshes and *snipe-bogs. 1851 KINGSLEY *Yeast* viii, Those five miles of heather and snipe-bog. 1861 *Times* 12 July, A creature who carries a smaller charge of *snipe dust in his head. 1882 JORDAN & GILBERT *Syn. Fishes N. Amer.* 363 *Nemichthyidæ*. (The *Snipe-Eels.) 1887 'J. BICKERDYKE' *Angling in Salt Water* 99 The Garfish,..Snipe Eel, or Sea Needle, is a long, slender fish [etc.]. 1890 *Science-Gossip* XXVI. 6 One of the larger *snipe-flies, the *Empis tesselata*. Notwithstanding the long snipe-like tongue or proboscis of the highly predatory Empis [etc.]. 1887 W. RYE *Norfolk Broads* 13 The finest *snipe ground in England. 1842 *Penny Cycl.* XXII. 51/2 Species with a very long tube and without spines... Example, *Murex Haustellum* ('Snipe's or Woodcock's head of collectors'). [Cf. SNIPE-BILL 2.] 1889 *Cent. Dict.*, *Caput gallinaginis*, the snipe's head; the crista urethræ. 1590 *Shuttleworths' Acc.* (Chetham Soc.) 60 Fourtene snypes and five *snype kneves xj[d]. *Ibid.* 61 Seventene snype kneves and foure snypes ix[d]. 1611 COTGR., *Deux pour vn*, a Snipe-knaue; so called, because two of them are worth but one Snipe. 1839 *Loudon's Nat. Hist.* 532 The *Snipe Shell (*Murex haustellus*, or *cornutus*), so called on account of the length of the prominency coming out of the shell. 1833 W. H. MAXWELL *Field Book* 494/2 When these birds are very plenty, the *snipe-shooters never make use of a dog. 1850 *All Year Round* No. 53. 66 The Analogist had the opportunity of studying the snipe-shooter of Albion. 1829 CARLYLE *Misc.* (1857) II. 7 Are not such lies themselves..equal to *snipe-shooting? 1848 THACKERAY *Van. Fair* iii, A fine, lonely, marshy, jungly district, famous for snipe-shooting. 1822 *Sporting Mag.* IX. 174 The best *snipe-shot complained that he had not killed more than sixty of these birds. 1832 BABBAGE *Econ. Manuf.* ii. (ed. 3) 23 A gun loaded with a quantity of sand, equal in weight to a charge of snipe-shot, kicks still more. 1854 BAKER *Rifle & Hound in Ceylon* vi. I had been firing snipe shot at him. 1805 BINGLEY *Anim. Biogr.* (ed. 3) II. 471 The *Snipe Tribe.

b. Forming adjs., as *snipe-beaked, -faced, -nosed*; *snipe-like* (also as adv.).

1812 *Pennant's Brit. Zool.* III. 190 Trumpet Fish..[*marg.*] Snipe nosed. 1850 JAMES *Old Oak Chest* III. 145 A little snipe-faced man. 1857 J. MILLER *Alcohol* (1858) 55 He who lives thus snipelike by suction. 1872 COUES *N. Amer. Birds* 252 A very snipe-like bird. 1895 LYDEKKER *Roy. Nat. Hist.* IV. 494 Snipe-beaked sandpipers.

Snipe (snəip), *v.* [f. SNIPE *sb.* 1.]

1. *trans.* To shoot or fire at (men, etc.), one at a time, usu. from cover and at long range; to pick off (a person) in this manner. Also *fig.*

1782 G. SELWYN *Let.* in *15th Rep. Hist. MSS. Comm.* VI. 621 Now people have been shot by platoons and in corps, the individual will be popped at or sniped, as they call it, from time to time. 1895 *Edin. Rev.* Jan. 14 The Indian soldier has been called on to be 'sniped' by fugitive dacoits. 1900 *Daily News* 30 Apr. 5/4 The other positions were sniped.

2. *intr.* To fire as in snipe-shooting; to shoot at an enemy in this manner (cf. prec.). Also with *at* and *away*.

1832 *Oriental Sporting Mag.* May (1882) II. 291/2 They were all found among high cliffs, and we generally sniped at them from a considerable height. 1844 tr. *Mir Hussain Ali's Life Tipu* xiv. 179 The Kuzzaks..remained all night attacking, or sniping and throwing rockets into the English camp. 1897 *Daily News* 4 Sept. 5/4 The enemy sniped away all day without effect. 1901 *Scotsman* 6 Apr. 9/5 Three hundred Boers hung on the rearguard, sniping but refusing battle.

Sni·pe-bill. Also **snipe's bill.** [SNIPE *sb.* 1.]

1. A kind of narrow moulding-plane with a sharp arris, for forming or cutting quirks. Also *attrib.*

1678 MOXON *Mech. Exerc.* IV. 70 Plains in use among Joyners, called Molding-plains; as, the Round,..the Snipes-Bill. 1728 CHAMBERS *Cycl.* s.v. *Plane*, Moulding-Planes,.. as the Round Plane, the Hollow, the OG, the Snipe's Bill, &c. 1842 GWILT *Archit.* Gloss., *Snipe's Bill Plane*, one with a sharp arris for getting out the quirks of mouldings. 1873 *Iron* 1 Feb. 78/2 Planes..Snipe bills, per pair, 5/.

2. *Conch.* The snipe-shell or snipe's head.

1713 PETIVER *Aquat. Anim. Amboinæ* iv, *Haustellum*,.. Snipes-bill.

†**3.** *Naut.* (See quot.) *Obs.*

1750 BLANCKLEY *Naval Expos.* 154 Snipe Bills are a Sort of Hooks used for fastening the Axle-trees of the Chain Pumps to the Bitts.

4. *U.S.* (See quots. Also written *snibel*.)

1860 WORCESTER, *Snipe-bill*, the bolt which connects the body of a cart with the axle. (Local, U.S.) 1902 *Webster's Suppl.*, *Snipe-bill*, a hinge beneath the body of a dumping cart, consisting of two interlinked eyebolts.

5. *attrib.* Resembling the bill of the snipe.

1795 J. WOLCOT (P. Pindar) *Pindariana* Wks. 1812 IV. 186 Her nose of snipe-bill race Which took a deal of stuff.

Sni·pe-fish. [SNIPE *sb.*]

1. Any fish of the genus *Centriscus*; esp. the trumpet-fish, bellows-fish, or sea-snipe, *C. scolopax*.

1668 CHARLETON *Onomast.* 123 *Scolopax*,..the Snipe-fish. 1681 GREW *Musæum* I. v. i. 101 The figure of his Bill, which is an entire Pipe, shaped almost like that of the Snipe-Fish. 1836 YARRELL *Brit. Fishes* I. 302 *Centriscus scolopax*, Snipe-fish. 1867 *Chambers's Encycl.* IX. 568/1 Trumpet-fish, or Snipe-fish (*Centriscus*), a genus of fishes..remarkable for the elongated and tubular snout. 1881 DAY *Fishes Gt. Brit.* I. 250 The trumpet, bellows-fish, woodcock or snipe-fish.

2. The snipe-eel (*Cent. Dict.* 1891).

Sniper (snəi·pəɹ). [f. SNIPE *v.*]

1. One who snipes, or shoots from concealment, etc.; a sharp-shooter.

1824 *E. India Mil. Cal.* II. 541 Several sepoys were killed and wounded by the enemy's snipers. 1897 *Daily News* 30 July 5/2 It is impossible to see the snipers, who generally stalk the sentries from behind stones. 1900 *Daily Telegr.* 27 Feb. 9/3 The artillery keep the Boer snipers down.

2. A snipe-shooter.

1840 E. NAPIER *Scenes & Sp. Foreign Lands* II. v. 140 With his brandy flask by his side, and his well filled bag, the sniper still wanders through his old haunts.

3. *U.S.* A prospector for gold or the like.

1902 *U. S. Geol. Surv., Prof. Paper* 10, 51 Some unsystematic work [searching for gold] was done during the fall of 1901 by snipers, usually working with rockers.

Snipey, freq. variant of SNIPY *a.*

Sniping (snəi·piŋ), *vbl. sb.* [f. SNIPE *v.*]

1. The action of the verb.

1773 *Let. fr. India* in J. W. Fortescue *Hist. Brit. Army* III. 141 [The soldiers..put their hats on the parapet for the enemy to shoot at, and] humorously called it sniping. 1891 *Daily News* 29 Dec. 2/1 The sniping of the outposts against each other. 1898 B. BURLEIGH *Sirdar & Khalifa* x. 162 Our camps upon the right bank of the Atbara were exceptionally open to sniping by night.

2. Snipe-shooting.

1875 *Ibis* 15 The doctor..was not accustomed to sniping, and our bag was not so full at the end of the day as it might have been. 1877 HALLOCK *Sportsman's Gaz.* 174 The pleasures of Bay bird shooting should not be spoken of in the same sentence with cocking or sniping.

b. *attrib.* Engaged in snipe-shooting.

1840 E. NAPIER *Scenes & Sp. Foreign Lands* II. v. 142 Frequently the slaughter committed by a sniping party is so great, that..nothing but the brains and trail are eaten, the rest being cast away.

Sniping (snəi·piŋ), *ppl. a.* [f. SNIPE *v.*] That snipes, or shoots from cover. *Sniping fire*, individual and irregular shooting from a concealed position.

1821 V. BLACKER *Mahratta War* II. i. 179 But even this advantage was greatly reduced, by their being exposed to a sniping fire from neighbouring walls. 1899 *Daily News* 24 Oct. 5/5, I was..able to help him out of range of this sniping fire.

Sni·pish, *a. rare.* [f. SNIPE *sb.* + -ISH.] Somewhat resembling the beak of the snipe.

1834 BECKFORD *Italy* II. 297 A priest or two with enormous spectacles on their thin snipish noses.

Snipo·cracy. [f. SNIP *sb.* 7 + -(O)CRACY.] The tailoring profession or its leading members.

1861 G. MEREDITH *Evan Harr.* xiv, By Jove! this comes it strong. Fancy the snipocracy here! 1912 *Nation* 20 Apr. 84/1 The glorified tailor,..the Marquis of Snipocracy.

Snipped (snipt), *ppl. a.* Also 6 **snipte,** 7– **snipt.** [f. SNIP *v.*]

1. *Bot.* Irregularly notched or serrated; incised.

1578 LYTE *Dodoens* 15 The lesser Clote Burre hath grayish leaues,..iagged or snipte round about the edges. 1601 HOLLAND *Pliny* XXV. vi. II. 220 The leaves..snipped and cut about the edges ordinarily in five parts. 1682 WHELER *Journ. Greece* I. 67 A fair leaf,..snipped about the edges with sharp-pointed teeth, like a great saw. 1796 WITHERING *Brit. Pl.* (ed. 3) III. 575 Stem-leaves snipt.

2. That has been subjected to snipping; jagged or irregularly cut.

1601 SHAKS. *All's W.* IV. v. 2 Your sonne was misled with a snipt taffata fellow there. 1611 COTGR., *Passe-poil*, a snipped, or iagged welt of Taffata, &c. in a garment. 1796 *Phil. Trans.* LXXXVI. 446 The snipt edges were hard. 1847 ALB. SMITH *Chr. Tadpole* lviii. (1879) 491 There were no cheerless grates filled up with snipped silver paper.

3. Of style: Clipped, disjointed.

1806 COLERIDGE *Lett.* (1895) 506 Persons who write in a hurry are very liable to contract a sort of snipt, convulsive style.

Snipper (sni·pəɹ). [f. SNIP *v.*]

1. *pl.* A machine or instrument for snipping or clipping; scissors.

1593 J. NORDEN *Spec. Brit.* (Camden) Pref. p. xiv, They have snippers wherewith they snyppe and pare their plates, which snippers..are so artificially placed, ..that by the mocion of the water also the snippers open and shut. 1603 FLORIO *Montaigne* II. ii. (1632) 192 When in Josephus we heare a childe all to rent with biting snippers. 1647 HEXHAM I, A pair of snippers, *een snip-schaerken*.

2. One who snips or clips; *spec.* a tailor.

1611 COTGR., *Tondeur*, a sheerer,..barber, vermine-snipper. 1648 HEXHAM II, *Een Knipper*,..a Snipper. *Ibid.*, *Een snipperaer*, a Snipper or a Cutter off. 1684 DRYDEN tr. *Maimbourg's Hist. League* Postscr. 35 As our Snippers go over once a year into France, to bring back the newest Mode, and to learn to cut and shape it. 1827 *Lancet* 10 Nov. 223/2 For the snippers of broad cloth and calf-skin I had little compassion. 1865 S. EVANS *Brother Fabian's MS.* 156 You'd be delighted to murder the snipper Who measures my waist for a skirt.

3. A cattle-dealer on a small scale.

1869 *Pall Mall G.* 9 Sept. 12 The snippers and provincial jobbers..furnish the raw material to the Aberdeen dealers and butchers.

†**Sni·ppering,** *vbl. sb. Obs. rare.* [Cf. LG. *snippern* (G. *schnippern*) to snip, cut small.] *pl.* Parings.

1599 A. M. tr. *Gabelhouer's Bk. Physicke* 143/1 The poulder of combured cobblers snipperinges of ould shoes. [1604 R. CAWDREY *Table Alph.*, *Snipperings*, payrings.]

Snipper-snapper. Now *dial.* [Of fanciful formation: cf. WHIPPER-SNAPPER.] A young insignificant or conceited fellow.

c 1590 MARLOWE *Dr. Faustus* xi. 1161 Ile seeke out my Doctor..: O yonder is his snipper snapper. 1600 DEKKER *Shoemaker's Holiday* iv, Quick snipper-snapper, away Firke, Scour thy throat. 1638 FORD *Fancies* I. ii, Thou'rt a prick-ear'd foist,..a knack, a snipper-snapper! 1677 *Poor Robin's Vision* 12 Having ended his discourse, this seeming gentile snipper-snapper vanisht. 1835 MOORE *Mem.* (1856) VII. 108 Far better worth listening to than many of the young snipper-snappers of his profession. 1854 MISS BAKER *Northampt. Gloss.*, *Snipper-snapper*, a small, insignificant, effeminate, self-conceited young man.

†**Sni·ppery.** *nonce-wd.* [f. SNIP *v.*] Snipping.

1639 [see SNAPPERY].

Snippet (sni·pėt). [f. SNIP *v.* + -ET.] A small piece cut off; a small fragment or portion.

1664 BUTLER *Hud.* II. iii. 824 Witches Simpling, and on Gibbets Cutting from Malefactors snippets. 1862 SALA *Seven Sons* III. 272 [She] used to cut her dress into snippets with a pair of scissors. 1885 LADY BRASSEY *In the Trades* 120 The droll little heaps, and dabs, and snippets in which everything was sold. 1897 F. THOMPSON *New Poems* 135 Snippets and waste From old ancestral wearings.

attrib. 1909 *Nation* 30 Oct. 191/1 One of them bears the tell-tale snippet-mark of a leaf-cutter bee.

b. In *transf.* or *fig.* uses.

1880 *Sat. Rev.* 2 Oct. 438/1 The mere sticking on to his dialogue of snippets from Elizabethan phraseology is a vain thing. 1882 F. HARRISON *Choice of Books* (1886) 296 The love of beauty is nothing of dilettantism to be cut into snippets and shreds. 1886 STEVENSON *Prince Otto* II. iv, That is a poor snippet of malicious gossip.

c. *spec.* A short passage taken from a literary work; a short scrap of literary matter of any kind.

1864 *Spectator* 12 Mar., These paragraphs and snippets from the Saturday Review. 1884 *Ibid.* 4 Oct. 1309/2 It is the latest stamp of the true 'classic' to be cut up into snippets for a birthday-book. 1897 *Month* Oct. 435 The text is in fact largely made up of a kind of patchwork of snippets which often amalgamate ill.

attrib. 1899 *Daily News* 5 July 8/2 He..reads nothing but sporting papers and 'snippet weeklies'.

Sni·ppetiness. [f. next.]. The state or condition of being snippety; scrappiness.

1878 *Spectator* 16 Feb. 220/2 The defect of Fraser's Magazine..is snippetiness, a habit of publishing so many articles that they are none of them exhaustive. 1890 *Athenæum* 7 June 730/1 A certain snippetiness of style and arrangement, which is too suggestive of paste and scissors.

Sni·ppety, *a.* Also -etty, -ity. [f. SNIPPET.] Of the nature of, suggestive of, a snippet or snippets; composed of snippets or scraps.

1864 *Spectator* 1406 The snippety style of American reporting. 1865 *Ibid.* 25 Nov. 1307/2 A..very clever, but somewhat snippety magazine. 1888 *Pall Mall G.* 25 June 1/1 More or less snippetty instalments of our Special Commissioner's Report.

Snipping (sni·piŋ), *vbl. sb.* [f. SNIP *v.*]

1. The action of the verb; cutting, clipping. Also with *off*.

1583 STUBBES *Anat. Abus.* II. (1882) 50 When they come to the cutting of the haire, what snipping and snapping of the cycers is there. 1611 COTGR., *Retaillement*, a shredding, clipping, snipping. 1648 HEXHAM II, *Een snipperinge*,..a Snipping off, or a Snip. 1867 MISS BRADDON *Doctor's Wife* xxxvii, She heard the horrible snipping of crape and bombazine going on all day.

attrib. 1648 HEXHAM II, *Knip-schaerken*, Snipping Cicers.

2. A part or piece snipped or cut off; a clipping, cutting. Usu. in *pl.*

1611 COTGR., *Retailleures*, shreds, clippings, snippings, parings. 1846 LANDOR *Imag. Conv.*, *Lucian & Timotheus* (1891) I. 321 Give me all the shreds and snippings you can spare me. They will feel like clothes. 1870 PEACOCK *Ralf Skirl.* II. 41 These little snippings of bright coloured raiment.

fig. and *transf.* 1862 *Sat. Rev.* 5 July 23 The remaining snippings from our author's book of ethical commonplaces. 1884 *Athenæum* 5 Jan. 21/2 By complete essays or sections, and not by mere snippings here and there.

†**3.** A snibbing, snubbing, or reproving. *Obs.*

1601 BRETON (*title*), No Whippinge, nor Trippinge: but a kinde friendly Snippinge. 1614 J. TAYLOR (*title*), The Nipping or Snipping of Abvses.

†**Sni·pping,** *ppl. a. Obs. rare.* In 5 **snypp-,** 6 **snypand.** [Of doubtful origin; the verb *snip* is not recorded till much later.] Nipping, biting with cold.

a 1400–50 *Alexander* 1360 As blast..As any snyppand [*v.r.* snappand] snawe þat in þe snape litis. 1513 DOUGLAS *Æneid* VII. Prol. 50 Scharp soppis of sleit, and of the snypand snawe.

Snippy (sni·pi), *a.* [f. SNIP *v.* Cf. Du. *snippig* (Fris. *snippich*), snappish.]

1. *dial.* Parsimonious, mean; covetous.

1727 BAILEY (vol. II), *Snippy*, parcimonious, niggardly. 1825– in dial. glossaries, etc. (*Eng. Dial. Dict.*).

2. *dial.* and *colloq.* Fault-finding, snappish, sharp.

1848 BARTLETT *Dict. Amer.* 318 *Snippy*, finical; and substantively, a finical person. A woman's word. 1887 GUNTER *Mr. Barnes* xx, So dictatorial!..And so snippy! 1896 *Harper's Mag.* June 23/2 She's too snippy for me.

3. Scrappy, fragmentary, snippety.

1886 *Pall Mall G.* 20 May 2/1 Paragraphs and very short articles which may fairly be regarded as 'snippy' bits.

Snip-snap (snip,snæp), *sb.* [f. SNIP *sb.* + SNAP *sb.*, used with imitative effect.]

In Bale *Thre Lawes* (1538) 1474 Hypocrisy addresses Infidelity as 'brother snyp snap'.

†**1.** The action of snipping or clipping with a pair of scissors or the like; an instance of this. Also *fig.*

1597 G. HARVEY *Trimming T. Nashe* Wks. (Grosart) III. 72 If heere I haue been too prodigall in snip snaps, tell me of it. 1638 FORD *Fancies* V. ii, The fashion of gentry, which is never complete till the snip snap of dexterity hath mowed off the excrements of slovenry.

2. Smart remark or reply; sharp repartee.

1727 POPE, etc. *Art of Sinking* 109 It is by virtue of this style that..Marcus Aurelius is excellent at snip-snap. 1781 C. JOHNSTON *Hist. J. Juniper* II. 246, I have amused myself with..playing a game at snip-snap, with Beatrice in Benedick. 1811 MISS MITFORD in L'Estrange *Life* (1870) I. 149 Letters should assimilate to the higher style of conversation, without the snip-snap of fashionable dialogue. 1872 TENNYSON in *Life* (1897) II. iv. 113 *note*, To print the names of the speakers..over the short snip-snap of their talk.

†**3.** = SNAPPER *sb.*[1] 2 b. *Obs.*[—0]

1736 AINSWORTH I, A snip snap, or snappers, *crotalum*.

Snip-snap (snip,snæp), *a.* [Cf. prec.]

†**1.** Making a snipping sound; working or acting by snipping or clipping. *Obs.*

1600 J. LANE *Tom Tel-troth* 120 These snip-snap sheers. 1643 *Mercurius Brit.* No. 28. 211 Barbers and every Snip-snap Jack which can tell the King a faire tale in his eare.

2. Of the nature of snip-snap; characterized by snip-snap or smart repartee.

1673 R. LEIGH *Transp. Reh.* 139 His snip-snap wit, hit for hit, and dash for dash. 1702 MOTTEUX *Prol. to Farquhar's Twin-Rivals*, With volleys of small shot, or snip-snap wit. 1752 A. MURPHY *Gray's Inn Jrnl.* No. 5, Run off from the Point, in a snip-snap Stile, with pert Question and Answer. 1830 H. LEE *Mem. Manager* I. iv. 152 A snip-snap mode of expression. 1861 S. BROOKS *Silver Cord* viii. (1865) 45 It is not a bit of snip-snap impertinence..that will frighten me. 1884 *Fortn. Rev.* Dec. 785 The snip-snap dialogue about prodigies.

b. Of persons: Given to snip-snap. *rare*[—1].

1785 [R. GRAVES] *Eugenius* II. xix. 126 He found she.. was not that pert, snip-snap formidable Beatrice, which he at first had some reason to think her.

3. Snappish, quarrelsome, irritable. *rare*[—1].

1770 C. JENNER *Placid Man* IV. iii. II. 23 In this kind of snip-snap disposition the family arrived in town.

Snip-snap (snip,snæp), *v.* [Cf. SNIP-SNAP *sb.*]

1. *intr.* To indulge in snip-snap or smart repartee; to speak in a snappy manner.

1593 G. HARVEY *Pierce's Super.* Wks. (Grosart) II. 313 If any whosoeuer will needes be offering abuse in fact, or snip-snapping in termes. 1826 MISS MITFORD *Village* Ser. II. (1863) 367, 'I believe..that you think I have nothing better to do than to read novels.' And so she snip-snaps to the end of the visit. 1845 JUDD *Margaret* I. xvii, Pluck snip-snaps with his wife, cracks on Hash, shows his white teeth to Margaret.

2. To snip; to clip with a snipping sound. Hence **Snip-snapping** *vbl. sb.*

1906 *Westm. Gaz.* 14 July 2/2 Scissors join in, with their snip-snapping, as a third bodice is cut out.

Snip-snap, *adv.* (and *int.*). ? *Obs.* [Cf. prec.] With snip and snap; with a snipping, snapping sound.

1588 SHAKS. *L. L. L.* v. i. 63 A sweet tutch, a quicke venewe of wit, snip snap, quick & home. 1596 NASHE *Saffron Walden* Ep. Ded., To torment him, and deal as snip snap snappishly with him, as euer he was delt withall. 1602 MIDDLETON *Blurt, Master-Constable* II. i, My sister shoots him off, snip-snap, at her pleasure. 1672 VILLIERS (Dk. Buckhm.) *Rehearsal* III. i. (Arb.) 67 For you shall see 'em come in upon one another snip snap..as fast as can be. 1793 L. WILLIAMS *Children's Friend* I. 16, I will..come with my bill-hook, and snip-snap, cut all those briars down to the ground.

Snip-snapper. *rare*[—1]. [Cf. SNIP-SNAP *v.*] A tailor.

1626 MIDDLETON *Anything for Quiet Life* II. ii, Not a word more, goodman snipsnapper, for your ears.

Snip-snap-sno·rum. [a. LG. *snipp-snapp-snorum* (also *-snurr*), = G. *schnipp-schnapp-schnorum* (or *-schnurr*), on which see the article in Grimm's Dict.] A round game of cards, played (esp. by the young) in various ways, in which the players on turning up the requisite cards respectively call 'snip', 'snap', and 'snorum'.

In R. Hardie *Hoyle made familiar* (1830) 80 the game is called 'Snip, Snap, Snore 'em', and in describing it the words *snip, snap*, and *snore* are employed.

1755 *Connoisseur* No. 52 ⁋ 6, I saw these strange women place themselves at a huge round table..to play..at Pope Joan and Snip-snap-snorum! 1784 *Laura & Augustus* I. 98 The..enlivening snip-snap snorum; which game they were then playing. 1820 MRS. TRENCH *Rem.* 439 His wife, his children, his garden,..fill up his day; as snip-snap-snorum does his evening. 1834 SOUTHEY *Doctor* (1837) IV. 72 It had been found convenient to set down the children.. to Pope-Joan, or snip-snap-snorum, which was to them a more amusing because a noisier game. 1887 BESANT *The World Went* xxiv, Bess..could play All-fours, Put, Snip-snap-snorum.

Snipy (snəi·pi), *a.* Also **snipey,** *Sc.* **snipie.** [f. SNIPE *sb.*]

1. Characterized by having a long pointed nose or muzzle suggestive of a snipe's bill. Also *Comb.*

1825 JAMIESON *Suppl.*, *Snipie-nebbit*, having a nose resembling a snipe's neb or bill. 1884 G. STABLES *Our Friend the Dog* vii, *Snipey*—Applied to the muzzle when peaked like a fox's. 1902 *Fur & Feather* 19 Sept. 232/3 Brindle [cavy] with white blaze,..rather snipy. 1904 H. COMPTON *20th Century Dog* II. 341 The long-legged, snipey-faced,..flat-sided specimens.

2. Resembling a snipe; snipe-like.

1888 LEES & CLUTTERBUCK *B. C. 1887* xvii. (1892) 183 In flight they [dowitchers] were not so snipey as the genuine article.

3. Frequented by snipe.

1903 *Blackw. Mag.* Sept. 368/1 The chief characteristics of this essentially snipey tract.

Snirt (snɔ̈ɹt), *sb.* Chiefly *north. dial.* and *Sc.* Also 8–9 **snert.** [f. next.] A suppressed laugh; a snicker.

1781 J. HUTTON *Tour to Caves* (ed. 2) Gloss. 96 *Snert*, an ineffectual effort to stifle a laugh. 1825 in JAMIESON *Suppl.* 1828– in north. dial. glossaries, etc. (see also *Eng. Dial. Dict.*). 1899 HALL CAINE *Shadow of Crime* xxiv, 'Saucer een,' said Mrs. Garth with a snirt.

Snirt (snɔ̈ɹt), *v. north. dial.* and *Sc.* Also 8–9 **snert.** [Imitative: cf. SNURT *v.*] *intr.* To laugh in a suppressed manner; to snicker.

1724 RAMSAY in *Evergreen* (1761) II. 15 Now let him snirt, and fyk her fill. 1791 J. LEARMONT *Poems* 2 They gang by ye wi' sic a huff, An' pridfu' caper, snirt, an' snuff, As gif Death ne'er meant them a cuff. 1829– in north. dial. glossaries. 1871 BLACK *Daughter of Heth* (1872) 34 The Whaup grew very red in the face and 'snirted' with laughter.

Sni·rtle, *v. Sc.* and *north. dial.* [f. prec. + -LE 3.] *intr.* To laugh in a quiet, suppressed, or restrained manner; to snigger.

1785 BURNS *Jolly Beggars* xlii, But though his little heart did grieve.., He feigned to snirtle in his sleeve. 1824 MACTAGGART *Gallovid. Encycl.* 112 The Dominie..fain wad fa' a laughing; He snirtles wi' his neb and snirks. 1887 J. SERVICE *Life Dr. Duguid* iv. 26 Her aul' worl' cracks and stories often mak me snirtle and laugh.

Snish, snishing: see SNEESH, SNEESHING.

†**Snit.** *Obs.*[—1] In 5 **snytte.** [Related to SNITE *v.*] The glowing part of the wick of a candle when blown out.

c 1430 *Chron. Vilod.* 1277 Þis mayde..blewe ouȝt þe leyȝt anone sodanly—Bot þe weke hulte stylle þe snytte.

Snitch, *sb. slang.* [Of obscure origin.]

†**1.** A fillip (on the nose). *Obs.*

1676 COLES, *Snitch*,..a fillip. *a* 1700 B. E. *Dict. Cant. Crew*, *Snitch*,..a Filip on the Nose.

2. The nose.

a 1700 B. E. *Dict. Cant. Crew*, *Snite his Snitch*, Wipe his Nose, or give him a good Flap on the Face. 1895 RYE *E. Angl. Gloss.* 204 Pull her snitch for her. 1902 *Westm. Gaz.* 3 July 2/1 As the..egg..broke on the 'snitch' of the Socialist candidate.

3. An informer; one who turns King's evidence. In the phr. *to turn snitch*.

1785 in GROSE *Dict. Vulgar T.* *c* 1800 in Byron *Juan* XI. xix. Note 14, She'll surely turn snitch for the forty—That her Jack may be regular weight.

Snitch (snitʃ), *v.* [Of obscure origin: cf. prec.]

1. *intr.* To inform *upon* a person; to peach, turn informer.

1801 *Sporting Mag.* XIX. 88 A man who is now in Chester Gaol and has been snitching about me. 1812 J. H. VAUX *Flash Dict.* s.v., To impeach or betray your accomplices, is termed *snitching upon* them. 1839 A. SOMERVILLE *Hist. Brit. Leg.* v. 105 How one of these had frequently threatened to *snitch*—or tell who stole the bridle. 1867 *Crim. Chronol. York Castle* 189 Wright,..finding that Norburn had been snitching, also made a confession.

b. *trans.* To inform or give evidence against (a person or accomplice). *rare*[—1].

1801 *Sporting Mag.* XIX. 88 Nadin asked him, how he knew the man had snitched him?

2. To catch by means of a noose or loop.

1900 *Daily News* 13 Oct. 8/2 The pike..is killed anyhow, 'shot at sight', or snitched with a wire loop, or netted.

Hence **Sni·tching** *ppl. a.*

1812 J. H. VAUX *Flash Dict.* s.v. *Snitch*, An informer, or tale-bearer in general, is called a *snitching* rascal.

†**Sni·tchel,** *sb. slang. Obs.* [Cf. SNITCH *sb.*] A fillip (on the nose).

1676 COLES, *Snitchel*, a fillip. *a* 1700 B. E. *Dict. Cant. Crew*, *Snitchel*, a Filip on the Nose.

Hence †**Sni·tchel** *v. Obs.*

a 1700 B. E. *Dict. Cant. Crew.* s.v. *Gig*, *Snichel the Gig*, Fillip the Fellow on the Nose.

†**Snitch'ems.** *Obs.*[—1] A card-game.

1798 *Sporting Mag.* XI. 150 The game of snitch'em's. This game may be ranked among the fairest games on the cards. [Description follows.]

Snitcher (sni·tʃəɹ). *slang.* [f. SNITCH *v.*]

†**1.** (See quot.) *Obs.*[—1]

1761 *Ann. Reg.* II. 51/1 He was a respectable member of ..the Bucks,—Bloods,—Snitchers,—Choice Spirits.

2. An informer, peacher; = SNITCH *sb.* 3.

1827 *Examiner* 796/2 He had committed hundreds of robberies, but would not confess them, as it might implicate other parties, and he scorned to be a snitcher. 1859 in *Slang Dict.* 97. 1862 C. C. ROBINSON *Dial. Leeds* 415 Ah niver wor a snitcher.

3. *pl.* Strings used by policemen in place of handcuffs. *Sc.*

1864 *Slang Dict.* 238 In Scotland Snitchers mean handcuffs. 1887 SERVICE *Life Dr. Duguid* xxvi. 168 The polisman never had the snitchers in his pooch.

Snite (snəit), *sb.*[1] Now *dial.* Forms: 1, 6– **snite,** 4–7 (8) **snyte,** 5 **snyghte, snyhte, snyȝt,** 6–7 **snight.** [OE. *snite* (also in comb. *wudusnite*), apparently not represented in any of the cognate languages.]

1. = SNIPE *sb.* 1.

Some distinction between *snite* and *snipe* is implied in the following entries in MS. Cott. Nero A. vi. (early 15th cent.):—fol. 165 *v*, Plouer, snytes, snypys, larkys; fol. 177 *r*, Ploueres, snytes, quaylys, snypys.

c 725 *Corpus Gloss.* A 138 *Acegia*, snite. *c* 1000 ÆLFRIC *Voc.* in Wr.-Wülcker 132 *Aceta*, snite, *uel* wudecocc. *c* 1325 [see SNIPE *sb.* 1]. 1363 in Riley *Memorials London* (1868) 312 A snyte, 1½d. 1382 WYCLIF *Isaiah* xxxiv. 11 The snyte [L. *ibis*] and the crowe dwelle shul in it. *a* 1400 *Sqr. lowe Degre* 323 With deynty meates that were dere;..Both storkes and snytes ther were also. *c* 1400 LYDG. *Churl & Bird* in *Minor P.* (Percy Soc.) 192 A downghille doke [is to thee] as deynte as a snyghte. 1515 BARCLAY *Egloges* iv. (1570) C v b/2 A shamfull rable..presumeth to indite, Though they have scantly the cunning of a snite. 1581 J. BELL *Haddon's Answ. Osorius* 374 Ill may the Snight the Woodcock twight for his long bill. 1604 DRAYTON *Owle* 947 The witlesse Wood-cocke, and his Neighbour Snite. 1688 *Phil. Trans.* XVII. 713 These passages are also in the Heads of Snites. 1694 MOTTEUX *Rabelais* IV. lix. (1737) 244 Snytes..Thistle-Finches. 1837– in Devon and Cornwall glossaries, etc. 1893 BARING-GOULD *Mrs. Curgenven* xlix, Widgeon, nor wild goose, hearn, and snite.

†**b.** Applied to species of birds resembling the snipe. *Obs.*

1694 *Martens' Voy. Spitzbergen* in *Acc. Sev. Late Voy.* II. 72 This Snite, which is also called the Strand-runner.., is no bigger than a Lark.

†**2.** As a term of abuse. *Obs.* Cf. SNIPE *sb.* 3.

1653 URQUHART *Rabelais* I. liv, Here enter not vile bigots, hypocrites, Externally devoted Apes, base snites.

3. *attrib.*, as †**snyte-knave,** a jack-snipe (cf. *snipe-knave* s.v. SNIPE *sb.* 6).

1611 COTGR. s.v. *Un*, *Deux pour vn*, the Snyte-knaue; tearmed so, because two of them are worth but one good Snyte.

†**Snite,** *sb.*[2] *Obs.*[—1] Also **snyt.** [Cf. WFris. *snjit, snitte* a spit or sprinkling of rain.] (See quot.)

a 1548 HALL *Chron.*, *Hen. VI*, 186 b, Their fell a small snyt [*Grafton* snite] or snow, which by violence of the wynd was driven into the faces of them.

Snite (snəit), *v.* Now *dial.* and *Sc.* Forms: 1 **snytan,** 5 **snytyn,** 5–7, *dial.* and *Sc.* 9 **snyte** (5 **snyth-**), 5– **snite** (5 **snete**); 6 **snytte,** 7 **snit, snett.** *Pa. t.* 4 **snytte.** *Pa. pple.* 4 **y-snyt,** 7 **snit.** [OE. *snýtan*, = ON. and Icel. *snýta* (Norw. and Sw. *snyta*, Da. *snyde*), OHG. *snûzan* (MHG. *snûtzen, sniuzen*, G. *schneuzen, schnäuzen*), MLG. *snûtten* (LG. *snüten*), Du. *snuiten* (WFris. *snute*): the stem *snût-* is prob. the same as that of SNOUT *sb.* Cf. also SNOT *sb.*]

1. a. *intr.* To clean or wipe the nose; to cast away mucus. **b.** *trans.* To remove by wiping, etc.

a 1100 in Napier *Contrib. O. E. Lexicog.* 58 Hræce & snyte bæftan him oððe adun be his sidan. *Ibid.*, Swa hwæt swa man him fram hræce oððe snyte, fortrede hit mid his fotum. *a* 1586 in *Maitland MS.* (Pinkerton, 1786) 185 They snyte, thoch thair na mister be, That ye may thair trim napkyne see. 1598 BP. HALL *Sat.* VI. i, So looks be like a marble toward rain, And wrings and snites, and weeps, and wipes again. 1632 HOLLAND *Cyrupædia* VIII. ii. 181 Hee inured them to this, neither to spit nor snit openly in sight. *a* 1779 GRAHAM *Writ.* (1883) II. 154 A weel blooded hissie..that snites the snotter frae their nose.

2. *trans.* To clean or clear (the nose) from mucus, esp. by means of the thumb and finger only; to blow. Also *fig.*, to tweak or pull.

c 1305 *St. Dunstan* 85 in *E. E. P.* (1862) 36 Mid his tonge he snytte hire nose, and tuengde hire sore. *Ibid.* 91 As god þe schrewe hadde ibeo atom ysnyt his nose. 1422 tr. *Secreta Secret., Priv. Priv.* 189 Therfor sayth Salamon, whoso ouer-harde Snythyth the noos, he draueth blode. *c* 1460 J. RUSSELL *Bk. Nurture* 284 in *Babees Bk.*, Pike not youre nose.., Snyff nor snitynge hyt to lowd. 1530 PALSGR. 724/1 Snytte thy nose, or thou shalte eate no buttered fysshe with me. 1601 HOLLAND *Pliny* XXXV. xi. II. 550 Theodorus drew one snetting his nose. 1632 — *Cyrupædia* 6 Even yet among the Persians it is held a shamefull thing..to snit the nose. *a* 1700 B. E. *Dict. Cant. Crew*, *Snite his Snitch*, Wipe his Nose, or give him a good Flap on the Face. 1701 GREW *Cosmol. Sacra* I. v. 26 Nor would any one be able to snite his Nose, or to Sneeze. 1785 GROSE *Dict. Vulgar T.*, *Snite*, to wipe, or slap. 1804 COUPER *Poetry* II. 61 (E.D.D.), Tibb snyted Madge's muckle nizz Till out the purple sprang. 1828– in many dial. glossaries, etc. (Cumb., Westm., Lancs., Chesh., Yks., Derby, Linc., Leic., Heref., Glos.).

†**b.** *Falconry.* Of a hawk, etc.: To wipe (the beak or bill) after feeding. *Obs.*

1486 *Bk. St. Albans, Hawking* a vj, An hawke snytith or sewith hir beke and not wipith hir beke. 1575 TURBERV. *Faulconrie* 289 Let hir tire against the Sunne, snyting and sewing hir beake a little at your discretion.

3. To snuff (a candle). ? *Obs.*

Cf. next for evidence of this use in OE.

c 1440 *Promp. Parv.* 461/2 Snytyn..a candyl, *emungo, mungo*. 1483 *Cath. Angl.* 347/1 To Snyte..a candelle, *mvngere*. ? *a* 1800 in Gordon *Bk. Chron. Keith* (1880) 65 [He could not] snite [the candles and attend to his Psalm Book at the same time.] 1808 in JAMIESON s.v.

†**Sni·tel(s.** *Obs. rare.* In 1, 4 **snytels,** 5 **-ele.** [OE. *snytels*, f. *snýtan* SNITE *v.*] = next 1.

c 1000 ÆLFRIC *Voc.* in Wr.-Wülcker 126 *Emunctorium*, candelsnyteis. 1388 WYCLIF *Numb.* iv. 9 The candilstike, with hise lanternes, and tongis, and snytels. *c* 1460 *Promp. Parv.* (Winch.), Snytele of a candel, *munctorium*.

Sni·ter. Also 5, 7 **snyter.** [f. SNITE *v.*]

1. *pl.* A pair of candle-snuffers.

1382 WYCLIF *Numb.* iv. 9 The candelstik, with the lanterns, and her toonges, and snyters. 1881 *Leicester Gloss.* 247.

2. One who wipes or snuffs.

1611 COTGR., *Moucheur*, a snyter, wiper, snuffer.

Snithe, *a. north. dial.* Also 9 **snyde.** [Related to next.] = SNITHING *ppl. a.*

1671 SKINNER *Etymol. Ling. Angl.*, *A Snithe-wind*, vox elegantissima agro Linc. usitatissima. Significat autem Ventum valde Frigidum & Penetrabilem,..ut nos dicimus, *a Cutting wind*. [Hence in Ray.] 1683 *Yorkshire Dialogue* 39 It is varra Snithe, And Ise flaid, Wife, it will be Frost Belive. 1828– in north. dial. use (*Eng. Dial. Dict.*). 1884 STREATFEILD *Linc. & Danes* 265 At the fore-end of the year the winds are often hask and snyde.

Snithe, *v. Obs.* exc. *dial.* [Common Teutonic: OE. *sníðan*, = OFris. *snítha* (*snída, snia*, WFris. *snije*), MDu. *sníden* (Du. *snijden*), OS. *snîðan* (LG. *sniden*), OHG. *snîdan* (MHG. *sniden*, G. *schneiden*), ON. *sníða* (Norw. and Sw. *snida*), Goth. *sneiþan*. The mod. dial. use may be from ON.] *trans.* To cut; †to kill by cutting.

c 725 *Corpus Gl.* (Hessels) D 342 *Dolatum*, ȝesniden. *c* 897 K. ÆLFRED *Gregory's Past. C.* 377 Ȝif hwelc god læce bið, ðe wel cann wunda sniðan. *c* 1000 ÆLFRIC *Hom.* II. 40 God..het niman anes geares lamb æt ælcum hiwisce, and sniðan on Easter-tide. *c* 1200 ORMIN 1338 Þe preost..toc & snaþ þatt oþerr bucc. *Ibid.* 14666 Tacc Ysaac þin wennchell, & sniþ itt, alls itt wære an shep. 1888 ADDY *Sheffield Gloss.* 226 Snithe a piece off with thy knife.

Snithe, dial. var. SNATH, scythe-pole; obs. f. SNY *v.* to swarm.

Sni·thing, *ppl. a.* Now *dial.* [f. SNITHE *v.*] Of wind, etc.: Nipping, cutting; piercing, sharp. (Cf. SNITHE *a.*)

a 1350 *St. Martin* 24 in Horstm. *Altengl. Leg.* (1881) 152 It was cald with weders wete, Snythand frost with snaw and slete. 1851 STERNBERG *Dial. Northampton* s.v., A snithing wind. 1881 *Leicester Gloss.* 247 *Snithing*,..applied to weather. 'A bloshing and snithing day.'

Sni·ting, *vbl. sb.* [f. SNITE *v.*]

1. The action of the verb; a blowing or wiping of the nose or beak; the snuffing of a candle.

c 1000 ÆLFRIC *Voc.* in Wr.-Wülcker 162 *Sternutatio*,.. snytingc, *uel* fneosung. *c* 1440 *Promp. Parv.* 461 Snytynge, of a nose or candyl, *munctura*. *c* 1460 *Vrbanitatis* 19 in *Babees Bk.*, Fro spettyng & snetyng kepe þe also. 1575 TURBERV. *Faulconrie* 306 And ye may perceive this disease by your hawkes often sniting & by making a noyze twice or thryse in hir snyting. 1611 COTGR., *Mouchement*, a snyting, or wiping of the nose. 1656 W. DU GARD tr. *Comenius' Gate Lat. Unl.* 57 The snivel..is detained by the hairs in the nostrils, that it may not flow down before sniting.

†**2.** The snuff of a candle. *Obs.*

c 1440 *Promp. Parv.* 461/2 Snytynge, of a candel, *munctorium, emunctorium*. 1483 *Cath. Angl.* 347/1 A Snytynge of a candelle, *licinus, licinum*.

3. *Comb.*, as †*sniting hole*; †**sniting instrument,** †**iron,** †**tongs,** candle-snuffers.

1388 WYCLIF *Exod.* xxxvii. 23 He made also seuene lanternes, with her snytyng tongis. 1398 TREVISA *Barth. De P. R.* v. ii. (Tollemache MS.), Þat þe open fumositeis and boystous filþe may be voyded and clensid by open and snytynge holes. *c* 1475 *Promp. Parv.* 461/2 (K.), Snytinge instrument, *munctorium, emunctorium*. 1483 *Cath. Angl.* 347/1 A Snytynge yren, *emunctorium*.

†**Sni·tling,** *ppl. a. Obs.*[—1] ? Trifling.

1682 H. MORE *Annot. Glanvill's Lux O.* 80 And now for that snitling Dilemma of the eager Opposer of Pre-existence.

Snitter, *v. Obs.* exc. *dial.* Also 4 **sniter-,** 5 **snyter-, sneter-.** [Of obscure origin: cf. SNITE *sb.*[2]] *intr.* Of snow: To fall. Hence **Sni·ttering** *ppl. a.*

13.. *Gaw. & Gr. Knt.* 2003 Þe snawe snitered ful snart, Þat snayped þe wylde. *c* 1400 *Anturs of Arth.* vii, Thay ran to the roches,..For the snyterand [*Douce* sneterand] snaue, that snaypely hom snellus. 1888 ADDY *Sheffield Gloss.* 227 *Snitter*, to snow.

†**Sni·tting,** *vbl. sb. Obs.*[—1] (Meaning doubtful.)

1387 TREVISA *Higden* (Rolls) II. 147 Þei beeþ i-cleped Pictes by cause of peyntynge and snittynge of woundes þat beeþ i-sene on hire bodies.

Sni·ttle, *sb.* Now *dial.* Also 7 **snitle.** [Of obscure origin.] A loop with a running knot; a noose, snare; a slip-knot.

1611 COTGR., *Lags courant*, a noose, grinne, snitle, running knot. 1642 *Proceedings at Banbury* 7 Till they had all their necks in a snittle. 1862 in C. C. ROBINSON *Dial. Leeds* 415. 1895 RYE *E. Angl. Gloss.* 203 *Snickle*, *Snittle*, a slip-knot.

Snive, variant of SNY *v.* to swarm.

Snivel (sni·v'l), *sb.* Forms: α. 5 **snevel, -yl,** 6 **-yll,** 6–7 **-il,** 7 **-ill;** 6 **sneuyll, -il,** 6–7 **-ill;** 6 **sneeuel, -ill,** 9 *Sc.* **sneevel, -il.** β. 6 **snyuell, sniuil, -yll,** 6–7 **-ell;** 7 **snivell, -ill,** 7– **snivel.** [f. SNIVEL *v.*]

1. Mucus collected in, or issuing from, the nose.

α. 14.. *Parts Body* in Wr.-Wülcker 631 *Pus nasi*, snevel of þe nose. *c* 1440 *Jacob's Well* 247 Wype wyth þi tunge oute of my nase þe snevyl þat hangyth þer-inne. 1530 PALSGR. 272/1 Snevyll whan it hangeth at ones nose, *roupie, boe*. 1540 — *Acolastus* I j, He wolde throwe the sneuyll of his nose into it. 1626 BRETON *Pasquil's Madcappe* xi, As sower, As beldam's milke that turned with her sneuill. 1671 W. SALMON *Syn. Med.* I. liv. 136 Without avoiding any thing, except bloody or filthy Matter, like Snevil.

β. 1519 HORMAN *Vulg.* 28 b, Thy nose is full of snyuell. 1548 ELYOT, *Mucosus*, snattye,..fulle of sniuyll. 1593 G. HARVEY *Pierce's Super.* Wks. (Grosart) II. 238, I will..squise thy braine to sniuell, whereof it was curdled. 1621 BURTON *Anat. Mel.* III. ii. VI. iii. (1651) 562 Snot and snivell in her nostrils, spittle in her mouth. 1682 *Eng. Elect. Sheriffs* 46, I will sooner worship the Sun, than..the Snot and Snivel of Loyala's Nose. 1739 R. BULL tr. *Dedekindus' Grobianus* 11 If with your Elbow you wipe off the Snivel, No Man alive shall be esteem'd more civil. 1871 R. ELLIS *Catullus* xxiii. 17 Thee sweat frets not,..Frets not snivel or oozy rheumy nostril.

b. A condition of the nose marked by the accumulation of mucus. Also *the snivels*.

1600 SURFLET *Countrey Farme* I. xxviii. 188 For the sniuell, take orpin and brimstone [etc.]. 1844 LOWSON *Mod. Farrier* 209 This affection is termed the snores or snivels. 1877 *Holderness Gloss.* 132/1 *Snivels*, a cold, accompanied by a difficulty of breathing, and a running at the nose.

†**2.** Saliva. *Obs.*[—1]

1697 *Phil. Trans.* XX. 50 The Snivel or Drivel that comes from the Mouth of a Dog..when mad.

†**3.** (See quot.) *Obs.*

1693 EVELYN *De la Quint. Compl. Gard.* II. 195 Grounds ..that being colder and stronger or heavier, easily infect them [lettuces] with slimy Snivel [= 'a sort of rotting moisture, hanging about some plants'].

4. A slight sniff indicating, or intended to suggest, suppressed emotion.

1848 DICKENS *Dombey* xxxix, Rob..took up the pieces one by one with a sob and a snivel for each. 1866 GILPIN *Songs Cumbld.* 280 Sae wi' snuffs an' sneevils [he] Rair't out. 1890 *Daily News* 18 Feb. 5/2 A carefully arranged and expressive 'snivel' is regarded as their most valuable acquirement.

b. A show or pretence of emotion; hypocritical expression of feeling.

1878 E. JENKINS *Haverholme* 194 Lords and ladies.. penned elegiacs to his praise in tears and snivel. 1886 *St. James's Gaz.* 9 Feb. (Cassell), The cant and snivel of which we have seen so much of late.

5. *attrib.* and *Comb.*, as *snivel-bottle, -guts, -monger, -nose*.

1690 DRYDEN *Amphitryon* III. i, A received opinion, snivel-guts. 1778 *Exmoor Scolding* Gloss., *Snibble-nose*, or rather *Snivel-nose*, one who snuffs up the Snot. 1792 WOLCOT (P. Pindar) *Ep. Sir W. Hamilton* Wks. 1812 III. 185 More snivel-bottles, jordens, and old jugs. 1896 A. MORRISON *Child Jago* 149 He preferred the frank rogue before the calculating snivel-monger.

Snivel (sni·v'l), *v.* Forms: α. 4 **snevele,** 5–6 **sneuel,** 6 **-il, snevel(l, -ill, -yll;** 9 *dial.* **sneavel,** *Sc.* **sneevil.** β. 4 **snyvele,** 5 **-elle,** 6 **snyuel,** 7 **sniuel,** 7– **snivel** (9 *dial.* **snivvel**). [OE. **snyflan* (implied in *snyflung* SNIVELLING *vbl. sb.*), f. *snofl* mucus. Cf. Da. *snøvle* (older *snevle*) to snuffle.]

1. *intr.* To run at the nose; to emit mucus from the nose; also, to draw up mucus audibly.

c 1325 *Gloss. W. de Bibbesw.* in Wright *Voc.* 173 Ely autre ne pout parler Une parole sanz nasyer, [*glossed*] snevelet, snyvele. *a* 1450 *Langland's P. Pl.* B. v. 135 (MS. Bodl. 814), Now awakiþ wratthe, wiþ two white eiȝen, And sneuelyng wiþ his nose. 1483 *Cath. Angl.* 347/1 To Snyvelle, *naricare*. 1508 KENNEDIE *Flyting w. Dunbar* 550 Out! out! I schout, apon that snowt that snevillis. 1526 SKELTON *Magnyf.* 1865 The snyte snyueled in the snowte and smyled at the game. 1614 B. JONSON *Barth. Fair* II. v, Do's so, snotty nose? Good Lord! are you sniueling? 1649

QUARLES *Virgin Widow* II, Must I be still yawling, and calling,..whilst y'are..potting, and piping, and driveling and sniveling! *a* 1722 LISLE *Husb.* (1757) 319 When they are sheared they catch cold, and will be glandered, and snivel very much.

b. *trans.* (See quot.) *rare.*

1530 PALSGR. 723/2, I snevell, I beraye any thynge with snyvell, *je amorue.* Se howe this boye snyvelleth his cote.

c. To clear (the nose) by snuffling.

1835 *Politeness & Gd.-breeding* 104 Never..snivel and snort a wet nose.

2. *intr.* To make a sniffing or snuffling sound expressive of real or assumed emotion; to be in, or affect, a tearful state.

1690 DRYDEN *Prol. to 'Mistakes'*, I left our young Poet sniveling and sobbing behind the Scenes, and cursing somebody that has deceiv'd him. 1712 STEELE *Spect.* No. 364 ¶ 4 To take a Lad from Grammar and..send him crying and snivelling into foreign Countries. 1791 COWPER *Iliad* II. 329 And whip thee hence Home to thy galley, sniveling like a boy. 1818 SCOTT *Hrt. Midl.* xxiii, What signified his bringing a woman here to snotter and snivel, and bather their Lordships? 1848 THACKERAY *Van. Fair* lxii, Every woman in the house was snivelling at the time. 1882 MISS BRADDON *Mt.-Royal* III. i. 22 Why do you stand there snivelling about him?

3. *trans.* **a.** To affect in some way by snivelling; to address in a snivelling manner. *rare.*

1668 R. L'ESTRANGE *Vis. Quev.* (1702) 268 To snivel and sneeze himself into another World. 1700 CONGREVE *Way of World* I. ix, Let 'em snivel and cry their Hearts out. 1717 *Entertainer* No. 25. 168 Thus they Whine and Snivel the Multitude, to enrich themselves and help forward the Faction.

b. To utter with a snivelling or sniffing sound; to shed (tears) snufflingly. Also with *out.*

1780 COWPER *Progr. Error* 310 Ye novelists, who mar what ye would mend, Sniv'ling and driv'ling folly without end. 1818 SCOTT *Rob Roy* xxx, I heard the former snivel out, in a very subdued tone, 'And ye'll ask her' [etc.]. 1851 THACKERAY *Eng. Hum.* vi. (1876) 328 That fine flower of love..over which Sterne snivelled so many tears. 1865 ALEX. SMITH *Summer in Skye* I. 237 The doctor saluted Flora and snivelled his compliments.

†**Snivelard.** *Obs. rare.* In 4–5 **sneuel-**, 5 **snyvelard.** [f. SNIVEL *v.*] A sniveller.

1398 TREVISA *Barth. De P. R.* v. xiii. (Tollemache MS.), The nose is sum tyme let..by bredynge of superfluite..in þe holis of the nose, as it fareþ in sneuelardis. 14.. *Lat.-Eng. Voc.* in Wr.-Wülcker 606 *Pusio*, a sneuelard. *c* 1440 *Promp. Parv.* 461/2 Snyvelard, or he þat spekythe yn the nose, *nasitus.*

Sni·veldom. *nonce-wd.* [f. SNIVEL *sb.* or *v.*] A slight cold causing one to snivel.

1767 C'TESS COWPER in *Mrs. Delany's Life & Corr.* Ser. II. I. 91, I caught the first cold I have had this year..; but it was only a 'sniveldom' and is gone off.

Sni·velled, *ppl. a.* [f. SNIVEL *sb.* or *v.*] Soiled or foul with snivel.

1530 TINDALE *Answ. More* (Parker Soc.) 124 That men should shrine his snivelled napkin, and not to believe his preaching. 1576 R. PETERSON *Galateo* (1852) 13 They spare not to snot their snivueld noses vppon them. 1581 G. PETTIE tr. *Guazzo's Civ. Conv.* I. (1586) 43 He woulde through negligence suffer his nose alwaies to be sneueled, and tooke no care to wipe it. 1619 R. WEST *Bk. Demeanor* 46 in *Babees Bk.* 292 To wipe thy snivelled nose Vpon thy cap. 1738 tr. *Guazzo's Art Convers.* 78 He was so negligent, as always to go with a snivell'd nose.

Sniveller (sni·v'ləɹ). Also 5 **sneveler.** [f. SNIVEL *v.*]

1. One who snivels or whines. Also in fig. context.

c 1450 *Cov. Myst.* (Shaks. Soc.) 396, I schal snarle tho sneveleris wyth rith scharp schouris. 1731 SWIFT *On his Death* Wks. 1755 III. II. 244 [He would] more lament, when I was dead, Than all the sniv'lers round my bed. 1791 WOLCOT (P. Pindar) *Ep. to Ld. Lonsdale* Wks. 1812 III. 13 Despise that thing call'd Meekness; 'tis a sniveller. 1905 *Speaker* 25 Feb. 512/2 Savonarola and his Piagnoni or snivellers..had a fatal influence on art.

2. A cold breeze (causing one to snivel).

1834 COL. HAWKER *Diary* (1893) II. 69 The pinching 'sniveller' was changed to a tempest. 1846 *Ibid.* 271 A chill that I took in a deadly cold 'sniveller'.

†**Sni·velliness.** *Obs.*[−1] [f. SNIVELLY *a.*] A soft glutinous state.

1662 CHANDLER *Van Helmont's Oriat.* 147 The Eggs of Fishes are at first more hard, and straightway..wax tender into a snivelliness.

Snivelling (sni·v'liŋ), *vbl. sb.* Also 2 **snyflung**, 5 **-ynge**; 5 **sneuelyng**, 6 **-ing**, etc. [See SNIVEL *v.*] The action of the vb. in various senses.

a 1100 in Napier *Contrib. O.E. Lexicog.* 58 Ȝif heora ænegum for unhæle hraca of breoste oððe snyflung of nosa derige. *c* 1430 *Freemasonry* (Halliw. 1840) 711 From spyttynge and snyflynge kepe the also. 1587 MASCALL *Govt. Cattle, Sheepe* (1627) 220 Sheep oftentimes wil haue the glaunders, and a sneuelling at their noses. 1655 MOUFET & BENNET *Health's Improv.* (1746) 380 Spitting, Sniveling and Yawning, are only the Fruits of Fulness or Idleness. 1693 *Apol. Clergy Scot.* 15 They never thought Sniveling necessary to make a great Saint. 1748 SMOLLETT *Rod. Rand.* lxi. (1804) 436 After a good deal of snivelling and sobbing. 1782 COWPER *To the Rev. Mr. Newton* 11 There is nothing but sniv'ling and blowing of noses. 1815 *Hist. J. Decastro* I. 44 Come, John,..let us have no more sniv'ling. 1875 EMERSON *Lett. & Social Aims* x. 256 Meantime we hate snivelling.

attrib. 1782 ELIZ. BLOWER *G. Bateman* II. 115, I war'nt there was fine sniveling work when ye parted. 1816 GILCHRIST *Philos. Etym.* 52 They only require a gentle grunt through the snivelling organs, to soothe dainty ears with much sweet melody.

Snivelling (sni·v'liŋ), *ppl. a.* Also 3 **snuvelinde**, 5 **snyvelande**; 4 **snyvelinge**, 5 **sneuelyng**, **snevyllynge**, etc. [f. SNIVEL *v.*]

1. Of the nose, etc.: Discharging, or full of, snivel. Also of persons, given to snivelling or snuffling.

c 1290 *S. Eng. Leg.* I. 319 Snvuelinde nose and wet mouth. 1483 *Cath. Angl.* 347/1 Snyvelande (*A.* Snevyllynge), *naricans, naricus.* 1608 SYLVESTER *Du Bartas* II. iv. IV. *Decay* 175 Stooping as she goes, With driveling mouth, and with a sniveling nose. 1615 *Baud, Ruffs, & Cuffe* (Halliw.) 16 He is a most filthy snivelling fellow..; he will wipe your nose of all, if you put the case to him. 1813 H. & J. SMITH *Rej. Addr.* 72 A snivelling fellow he's call'd by his foes, For he can't raise his paw up to blow his red nose. 1862 *Macm. Mag.* Sept. 380 Another, whom he remembers a little snivelling boy. 1902 *Times* 16 July 13/6 The wonderful picture of leering, chuckling, snivelling senility.

transf. 1858 R. S. SURTEES *Ask Mamma* xxiii, The landlady brought a snivelling mould candle into the cheerless.. little inn-parlour.

b. Of a cold: Accompanied by snivelling.

1687 MIÈGE *Gt. Fr. Dict.* II, A snivelling Cold, *un Rhûme.*

2. Sounding through the nose. *rare.*

1447 BOKENHAM *Seyntys* (Roxb.) 21 At the laste he thus owt abrayde Wyth a sneuelyng vooys & to hyr sayde. 1816 GILCHRIST *Philos. Etym.* xvii, To see this good, plain dialect superseded by snivelling, flippant, senseless French.

3. Displaying emotion or the semblance of it; mean-spirited, weak: **a.** Of persons.

1647 J. C[LEVELAND] *Char. Lond.-Diurn.* 8 Two of Mars his Petty-toes, such snivelling Cowards, that it is a favour to call them so. 1691 WOOD *Ath. Oxon.* II. 84 The snivling Presbyterians..did not stick to report that he died no better than a Brewers Clerk. 1732 FIELDING *Covent Gard. Trag.* I. vii, Without wine all human kind wou'd be One stupid, sniveling, sneaking, sober fellow. 1790 WOLCOT (P. Pindar) *Advice to Future Laureat* Wks. 1812 II. 343 The little snivelling spirit. 1805 DIBDIN in *Naval Chron.* XIII. 394 The snivlingest scoundrel that ever was seen. 1838 DICKENS *O. Twist* xxvi, Why not have kept him here among the rest, and made a sneaking, snivelling pickpocket of him at once? 1860 EMERSON *Conduct of Life* ii. Wks. (Bohn) II. 335 These Hoosiers and Suckers are really better than the snivelling opposition.

b. Of discourse, writings, etc.

1673 HICKERINGILL *Gregory F. Greybeard* 276 Pickt the peoples pockets with canting long snivelling sermons. 1707 HEARNE *Collect.* (O.H.S.) II. 19 A poor, sniveling discourse. 1767 STERNE *Tristram Shandy* IX. xii, That snivelling virtue of Meekness. 1771 SMOLLETT *Humph. Cl.* (1815) 4, I have received a snivelling letter from Griffin, offering to make a public submission, and pay costs.

†**Sni·vellish,** *a. Obs.*[−0] [f. SNIVEL *sb.*]

1530 PALSGR. 324/2 Snevylysshe, full of snevyll, *morueux.*

†**Sni·velly,** *a. Obs.* Also 6 **snevelly, sniuely, -elie**, 6–7 **sniuelly** (7 **-ie**). [f. SNIVEL *sb.*]

1. Of the nature of snivel or mucus.

1576 T. NEWTON tr. *Lemnie's Complex.* (1633) 175 A thicke, filthy, and snevelly Phlegme. 1608 TOPSELL *Serpents* (1658) 620 A foul, stinking, glutinous, and snivelly matter. 1658 ROWLAND tr. *Moufet's Theat. Ins.* 1109 Nothing else but snotty matter..or snivelly flegm.

2. Foul with snivel or mucus.

1580 HOLLYBAND *Treas. Fr. Tong*, *Morveux*, snotty, sniuelly. 1598 FLORIO, *Moccicoso*, snottie, sniuelie. 1600 SURFLET *Countrie Farme* I. xiii. 89 [The cow's] wide nostrels and sniuely.

Snoach (snōᵘtʃ), *v. dial.* Also 4, 9 **snoche**, 9 **snötch.** [Imitative.] *intr.* To snuffle; to breathe or speak through the nose, etc. Hence **Snoa·ching** *vbl. sb.*

1387 TREVISA *Higden* (Rolls) I. 11, I..schamede and dradde after so noble spekers..to putte forþ my bareyn speche, hosnes and snochynge. 1844 W. BARNES *Poems* Gloss. 350 *Snötch*, to speak or breathe hardly through the nose. 1881 *Isle of Wight Gloss.* 33 *Snoche*, to speak with a nasal twang. 1886 *W. Somerset Word-bk.* s.v. *Snoachy.*

Snoak, variant of SNOKE *v.*

Snoar, obs. form of SNORE *v.*

Snob (snɒb), *sb.*[1] Also 9 *Sc.* **snab.** [Orig. slang, of obscure origin.]

1. *dial.* or *colloq.* A shoemaker or cobbler; a cobbler's apprentice.

α. 1781 in Hone *Every-day Bk.* II. 837 Sir William Blase, a snob by trade. 1785 GROSE *Dict. Vulgar T.*, *Snob*, a nick name for a shoemaker. 1819 *Sporting Mag.* IV. 249 Tom Jenkins was known as a cobbler or snob. 1824 W. E. ANDREWS *Rev. Fox's Bk. Mart.* I. 252 Both Snip and Snob were burned for their pains. 1880 *Fraser's Mag.* Nov. 643 Even among the snobs the custom of the trade is against giving credit.

β. 1808 JAMIESON, *Snab*, a cant term for a..cobler's boy. 1813 PICKEN *Poems* II. 132 To flame as an author our Snab was sae bent. 1828 MOIR *Mansie Wauch* xiv, Rory Skirl, the snab, and Geordie Thump, the dyer. 1896 W. HARVEY *Kenneth-crook* 38 (E.D.D.), He had entered the craft in the usual way by being what the villagers called a 'snab'.

†**2.** *Cambridge slang.* Any one not a gownsman; a townsman. *Obs.* (Cf. CAD[2] 4.)

c 1796 in Whibley *In Cap & Gown* (1889) 87 Snobs call him Nicholson! Plebeian name. 1868 *Sporting Mag.* XXI. 428 A capital front rank of 'tassells',..all eager for a 'slap at a snob'. 1865 *Sat. Rev.* Sept. 298/2 Happily the annals of Oxford present no instance of a 'snob' murdered in the streets.

3. A person belonging to the ordinary or lower classes of society; one having no pretensions to rank or gentility.

1831 *Lincoln Herald* 22 July 3/6 The nobs have lost their dirty seats—the honest snobs have got 'em. 1834 W. H. BROOKFIELD in F. M. Brookfield *Cambridge 'Apostles'* (1906) iv. 66 *Snobs* go early [to the Grand Opera, Paris], buy pit tickets.., and beset comers at a quarter past seven to give them 5½ francs for their tickets. 1841 J. T. HEWLETT *Parish Clerk* III. 165 In the presence of a tail of snobs who accompanied him on his way. 1852 EARP *Gold Col. Austr.* 9 The majority of the colonists are essentially snobs, and they are justly proud of the distinction.

b. One who has little or no breeding or good taste; a vulgar or ostentatious person.

1838 MRS. SHERWOOD *Henry Milner* III. ix. 175 He is a genteel young man—no snob—quite the gentleman. 1843 THACKERAY *Irish Sk. Bk.* Wks. 1879 XVIII. 111 A vulgar man in England..chiefly displays his character of snob by ..swaggering and showing off in his coarse dull stupid way. 1859 *Slang Dict.* 97 *Snob*, a low, vulgar..person.

c. One who meanly or vulgarly admires and seeks to imitate, or associate with, those of superior rank or wealth; one who wishes to be regarded as a person of social importance.

1848 THACKERAY *Bk. Snobs* i, I mean by positive [Snobs] such persons as are Snobs everywhere..being by nature endowed with Snobbishness. 1860 H. MAYHEW *Upper Rhine* iv. i. 183 So necessary..are the professional titles considered by the supreme Snob of an authority from whom we quote. 1863 MISS BRADDON *J. Marchmont's Legacy* I. ii. 42 'What a snob I am,' he thought; 'always bragging of home'. 1882 MRS. RIDDELL *Pr. of Wales's Garden-Party* 127 He was..such a snob, he felt pleased his clerks should hear a butler ask for a situation.

4. = BLACK-LEG 3.

a 1859 DE QUINCEY (Webster), Those who work for lower wages during a strike are called snobs, the men who stand out being 'nobs'.

5. *attrib.*, as *snob ambition, -land, nature, ore*; **snob-stick,** = sense 4 (cf. KNOBSTICK 2).

Other examples occur in Thackeray's *Book of Snobs.*

1848 THACKERAY *Bk. Snobs* Pref., It is Beautiful..to sink shafts in society and come upon rich veins of Snob-ore. *Ibid.* xxxii, O you pride of all Snobland! O you crawling, truckling..lacqueys and parasites! 1860 *Slang Dict.* 221 *Snob-stick*, a workman who refuses to join in strikes, or trade unions. 1866 CARLYLE *Remin.* (1881) II. 189 What of snob ambition there might be in me. 1883 *Congregationalist* May 377 The snob nature comes out in strange ways.

Snob (snɒb), *sb.*[2] [Of obscure origin.] A game of cricket played with a soft ball and a thick stick in lieu of a bat.

1892 *Daily News* 6 May 5/2 They are subject to very dangerous accidents at cricket, and might well confine themselves to 'snob'. 1894 *Ibid.* 10 May 6/1 Snob, or stump cricket, is indeed an excellent game.

Snob, *v.*[1] Now *dial.* Also 3–5 **snobbe.** [Imitative.] *intr.* To sob. Hence **Sno·bbing** *vbl. sb.*

c 1300 *Old Age* vii. in *E. E. P.* (1862) 149, I snurpe, i snobbe, i sneipe on snovte. *a* 1380 *St. Ambrose* 940 in Horstm. *Altengl. Leg.* (1878) 23 He wept and snobbed and ofte abreid. 1388 WYCLIF *Lam.* iii. 56 Turne thou not awei thin eere fro my sobbyng [*v.r.* snobbyng] and cries. *c* 1420 *Chron. Vilod.* 1865 He with sore sykyng & snobbyng bothe Vnswered þe monke. *Ibid.* 1986 Þus ladyes alle.. snobbedone & sykedone fulle sore. 1608 MIDDLETON *Mad World* III. ii, She cannot hear me for snobbing. 1668 L'ESTRANGE *Vis. Quev.* (1708) 124 There was such Blowing, Snobbing, Sniveling,..that there was no enduring the House. 18.. in *Eng. Dial. Dict.* s.v., She neither sighed, nor snobbed, nor spoke, nor nothing. 1884– in dial. glossaries (Worc., Glouc.).

†**Snob,** *v.*[2] *Obs.*[−1] [? var. of SNUB *v.* Cf. SNOBBERLY *adv.*] *intr.* To gird *at* something.

1654 GAYTON *Pleas. Notes* III. vi. 107 A few words being spoken to Sancho, snobbing at his Insensiblenesse.

Snobber (snɒ·bəɹ). *colloq.* [f. SNOB *sb.*[1] 1.] A shoemaker, cobbler.

1900 *Daily News* 15 Aug. 6/4 She takes up with a worthy 'snobber' (shoemaker).

†**Sno·bberly,** *adv. Obs. rare.* [app. related to SNOB *v.*[2]] Snubbingly.

a 1300 *Cursor M.* 24024 Vn-reufulli þai can him raipe, Ful snoberli [*Edinb.* snubnerlik] him for to snaipe.

Snobbery (snɒ·bəri). [f. SNOB *sb.*[1] 3.]

1. The class of snobs.

1833 *Lincoln Herald* 15 Jan. 3/6 In 'talking conversation' with some of the Snobbery of Brummagem. 1887 *Twin Soul* II. xvi. 198 The admiration of all the 'snobbery' of London.

2. The character or quality of being a snob; snobbishness; vulgar ostentation.

1843 *Blackw. Mag.* LIII. 232 Snobbery, like murder, will out; and, if you do not happen to be a gentleman born [etc.]. 1853 GEO. ELIOT in Cross *Life* I. 315 They are two capital people, without any snobbery. 1891 *Speaker* 11 July 36/1 A type of snobbery which regards the established religion as a stepping-stone to respectability.

b. An instance of this; a snobbish trait.

1866 *Cornh. Mag.* Nov. 632 Arms sometimes indispensable in mixed societies against the pushing snobberies of vulgar wealth. 1880 *Cope's Tobacco Plant.* Oct. 536/1 Hence youth rivals with youth..in varying vulgarest snobberies with maddest absurdities.

Sno·bbess. Also **snobess.** [f. SNOB *sb.*[1] 3.] A female snob.

1869 *Punch* 14 Aug. 62/2 Reporters in front, snob and snobess behind! 1887 *Truth* 16 June 979 The crowd of snobs and snobesses.

Sno·bbiness. *rare.* [f. SNOBBY *a.*] Snobbishness.

1851 MILLAIS in J. G. Millais *Life* (1899) I. iv. 142 Revelling in snobbiness at having such distinguished persons at the farm.

Sno·bbing, *vbl. sb.*[1] [f. SNOB *sb.*[1] 1.] The cobbling, or partial making, of boots.

1880 *Fraser's Mag.* Nov. 643 It has become a custom to endeavour to get the necessary 'snobbing' done between Friday evening and Monday morning. 1900 ANNIE WAKEMAN *Autobiog. Charwoman* viii. 111, I could see meself a-learnin' the easy parts of shoe-makin'—sech as doin' the uppers, called snobbin'.

Sno·bbing, *vbl. sb.*[2]: see SNOB *v.*[1]

Snobbish (snɒ·biʃ), *a.* [f. SNOB *sb.*[1] 3.]

1. Of, pertaining to, or characteristic of a snob.

1840 DICKENS *Old C. Shop* lvi, This form of inquiry he held to be of disrespectful and snobbish tendency. 1846 THACKERAY *Snob Papers* Wks. 1886 XXIV. 332, I can conceive nothing more dangerous, insolent—Snobbish, in a word—than such an opposition. 1854 *Illustr. Lond. News* 8 July 7/2 The snobbish display of plush breeches. 1873 HAMERTON *Intell. Life* VII. iii. 242 You will not suspect me of a snobbish desire to pay compliments to royalty.

absol. 1848 THACKERAY *Bk. Snobs* Pref., It is Beautiful to study even the Snobbish; to track Snobs through history.

Comb. 1892 E. KINGLAKE *Australian* 144 It is doubtless not pleasant for the snobbish-minded man..to remember an origin of the kind.

2. Having the character of a snob.

1849 SAXE *Poems, Proud Miss M'Bride* xv, Depend upon it, my snobbish friend, Your family thread you can't ascend. 1863 W. PHILLIPS *Speeches* xv. 325 Snobbish sons of fathers lately rich. 1885 *Spectator* 30 May 714/2 Julian is..vain, cowardly, snobbish, and untrustworthy.

Hence **Sno·bbishly** *adv.*

1848 THACKERAY *Bk. Snobs* iii, It encourages the commoner to be snobbishly mean. 1892 ZANGWILL *Bow Myst.* iv. 51 One whom he seems snobbishly anxious to claim as a friend.

Sno·bbishness. [f. prec.] The character or quality of being snobbish.

1846 THACKERAY *Snob Papers* Wks. 1886 XXIV. 318 This ..shameful caricature of a man which Snobbishness has set up to worship it. 1859 JEPHSON *Brittany* xvi. 274 So the insolent young sham-aristocrat was punished for his snobbishness. 1881 HUXLEY *Hume* v. 106 One of the most curious peculiarities of the dog mind is its inherent snobbishness.

Sno·bbism. [f. SNOB *sb.*[1] 3.] The characteristic qualities of a snob; snobbishness.

1856 GEO. ELIOT *Ess.* (1884) 267 As long as snobbism runs in the blood, why should it not run in our speech? 1869 *Daily News* 2 Sept., All that has been said latterly about the snobbism of our countrymen..on their travels. 1884 *Contemp. Rev.* Oct. 545 Is there any society..where such a piece of snobbism could be represented as possible.

Sno·bbite. *rare*[−1]. In 8 **snobite.** [f. SNOB *sb.*[1] 2.] A townsman.

c 1796 in Whibley *In Cap & Gown* (1889) 87 Plebeian name Which ne'er would hand a Snobite down to fame.

Sno·bby, *a.* [f. SNOB *sb.*[1] 3.] Snobbish.

1846 MRS. GORE *Eng. Char.* (1852) 128 Thither comes the snobby gig, conveying red-faced individuals. 1858 RAMSAY *Remin. Sc. Life & Char.* 60 If we can't get in with the nobs,..we will never take up with any society that is decidedly snobby. 1888 *Temple Bar* Aug. 539 Perhaps he was snobby enough to object to my earning money.

Sno·bdom. [f. SNOB *sb.*[1] 3.] The aggregate of snobs; snobs collectively.

1846 *New Monthly Mag.* Sept. 31 The congress of *mauvais sujets* from all parts of Snobdom, who infest Wiesbaden. 1851 MAYNE REID *Scalp Hunters* xxvi. 196 In savage as in civilized life there is a 'snobdom'. 1873 W. S. MAYO *Never Again* iv. 48 We must go..to England,..where a more rigid tabooism gives a wonderful exaltation to the idols of snobdom.

Sno·blet. *rare*[−1]. [f. SNOB *sb.*[1] 3.] = next.

1847 ALB. SMITH *Chr. Tadpole* li. (1879) 439 He looked as good a type of the party snoblet, as could be imagined.

Sno·bling. [f. SNOB *sb.*[1] 3.] A little, young, or petty snob. Also *attrib.*

1848 THACKERAY *Bk. Snobs* xii, You see, dear Snobling, that..he might have been excused from interfering. 1876 *World* V. 13 Every brainless bank-clerk and snobling subinspector of constabulary. 1881 CLARK RUSSELL *Ocean Free Lance* II. iii. 149 The contemptuous usage every little snobling..thinks himself privileged to give us.

Snobocracy (snɒbɒ·krăsi). [f. SNOB *sb.*[1] 3 + -OCRACY.] The class of snobs, as having some power or exerting some influence.

1854 LEVER *Dodd Family Abr.* lxvii, The fun derived from watching the 'snobocracy' I have mentioned. 1858 KINGSLEY *Misc.* (1859) I. 138 Soliciting the votes, not of the people, but of the Snobocracy. 1885 *Manch. Exam.* 7 Apr. 4/4 The Orange flag..would be floating over the houses of the Dublin snobocracy.

Snobo·grapher. [f. as prec. + -(O)GRAPHER.] A writer on, a describer of, snobs. So **Snobo·graphy,** the description or delineation of snobs; **Snobo·logist, Snobo·nomer,** a student of, a specialist in, snobs.

1848 THACKERAY *Bk. Snobs* xxxv, Up that long avenue the *Snobographer walked in solitude. 1868 *Imperial Rev.* Mar. 272, I may mention..that Thackeray, the great Snobographer, hated a Cad much more than he hated a Snob. 1848 THACKERAY *Bk. Snobs* xxxviii, In the Country *Snobography my poor friend Ponto has been held up almost exclusively for the public gaze. 1884 *Sat. Rev.* 19 Jan. 76/1 The safer and wiser way in this infancy of the science of snobography is to refrain from the attempt at absolute aphorism. 1888 E. A. PARRY *Lett. Dorothy Osborne* Introd. 158 Both the circumstance and the doggerel should be very instructive to the *snobologist. 1848 THACKERAY *Bk. Snobs* xxiii, Some telescopic philosopher will arise one day, some great *Snobonomer [etc.].

Snochynge: see SNOACH *v.*

Snock. *dial.* [prob. imitative.] A knock; a smart blow.

1825 in JENNINGS *Obs. Dial. West Eng.* 71. 1898 T. HARDY *Wessex Poems* 46 Such snocks and slats since war began Never saw raw recruit or veteran.

Snod (snɒd), *a. Sc.* and *north. dial.* Also 7 snoode (?). [Of obscure origin: the stem may be the same as that of ON. *snoðinn* bald (Norw. *snoden* bare).]

1. Smooth, sleek; even. Also *absol.*

c 1480 HENRYSON *Fables, Wolf & Sheep* viii, He wald chais thame baith throw rouch and snod. 1513 DOUGLAS *Æneid* v. xiii. 24 His awin heid warpit with a snod olive, Heich in a schippis forcastell [he] did stand. *a* 1585 POLWART *Flyting w. Montgomerie* 562 Foot-foundied beasts.. Hes not their hair sa snod as other good. 1641 BEST *Farm. Bks.* (Surtees) 4 Howe to choose a good Tuppe. Lett him bee ..of a snoode and goode stapple. 1692 A. SYMSON in *Macfarlane's Geogr. Coll.* (S.H.S.) II. 102 The long beards and awnds are separated from the corne; and the corne made, as they terme it, more snod and easie to pass through the mill. 1695 KENNETT *Par. Antiq.* Gloss. s.v. *Snodde*, Wheat ears are said to be *snod* when they have no beard or awns. And a tree is *snod* when the top is cut smooth off. 1781 J. HUTTON *Tour to Caves* (ed. 2) Gloss. 96 *Snod*, smooth. 1790 MRS. WHEELER *Westm. Dial.* (1821) 18 A lile stiff fello, wie a varra snod feace. 1862 C. C. ROBINSON *Dial. Leeds* 416 A snod piece o' cloath—as snod as a bit o' silk!

Comb. 1855 WAUGH *Life & Local.* 201 Rough and free as so many snod-backed young modiwarps. 1898 A. OLLIVANT *Owd Bob* xiii. 117 Ye ox-limbed, snod-faced profleegit!

2. Of persons: Neat, tidy, trim, smart, spruce.

1691 RAY *N. C. Words* 66 *Snod*,..neat, handsome. 1719 RAMSAY *To Arbuckle* 71 A black-a-vic'd snod dapper fallow. 1756 MRS. CALDERWOOD *Jrnl.* (1884) 194 The niece was a little, snod, fair lass. 1822 GALT *Provost* xxvi, A tight and snod serving lassie. 1889 BARRIE *Window in Thrums* 14 Here comes the minister himsel', an' very snod he is.

b. Of things: Neat, trim, in good order.

1717 RAMSAY *Elegy Lucky Wood* iv, She..kept her housie snod and bein. 1785 HUTTON *Bran New Wark* 3 The gentleman that treads in black snod pumps. 1819 W. TENNANT *Papistry Storm'd* (1827) 41 His velvet breeks,..The snoddest pair o' his attire. 1837 R. P. GILLIES *Recoll. Scott* III. ix. 199, I see ye're admiring how *snod* the library looks there. 1894 CROCKETT *Raiders* xxii. (ed. 3) 195 My clothes were clean brushed and exceedingly neat and snod.

3. Comfortable, snug, cosy. Also as quasi-*adv.*

1695 KENNETT *Par. Antiq.* Gloss. s.v. *Snodde*, To lie snod and snug. 1888 BARRIE *When a Man's Single* (1900) 91/2 'Ay,' be said, with a chuckle, 'but I've a snod bit cornery up there for mysel''.

Snod (snɒd), *v.* [f. prec.] *trans.* To make smooth, trim, or neat; to tidy, put in order. Also with *down, off, up.*

1584 HUDSON *Judith* IV. 269 On stake and ryce, hee knits the crooked vines, And snoddes their bowes. *a* 1774 FERGUSSON *Poems* (1789) II. 7 Ye saw yoursel how weel his mailin' thrave, Ay better faugh'd an' snodit than the lave. 1791 J. LEARMONT *Poems* 85 The ploughman cultivates the field, The mower snods the common. 1819 SCOTT *Let.* in Lockhart (1837) IV. viii. 251, I have planted a number of shrubs, and am snodding up the drive of the old farm house. 1865 G. MACDONALD *A. Forbes* xxvi. 115 The.. tallow candles..had..to be *snodded* laboriously.

†**Snode.** *Obs.* Also 4 *north.* **snade.** [app. repr. OE. *snǽd, unrecorded variant of *snǽd* SNEDE, related to *sniðan* SNITHE *v.*] A piece or bit (of bread or other food); a morsel.

α. *c* 1150 *Voc.* in Wr.-Wülcker 548 *Offa*, snode. *c* 1275 *Passion our Lord* 108 in *O. E. Misc.*, [Judas ate the bread] And þe veond him on bi-com myd þerylke snode. *a* 1300 *E. E. Psalter* cxlvii. 17 He sendes als snodes [L. *frusta panis*, or *buccellas*] his cristal. 1340 *Ayenb.* 111 Þe lecherous ..þet..uorzuelþ þane guode snode wyþ-oute chewynge. *Ibid.* 218 Hy..eteþ þe blodi snoden.

β. 13.. *Cursor M.* 15387 (Gött.), Þe morsel laght iudas, wid þat ilk snade..croupe in him sathanas. 13.. *Metr. Hom.* (Vernon MS.) in Herrig *Archiv* LVII. 313 Was neuere Beggere þat þer bade At his hous gete bite or snade.

Snodly (snɒ·dli), *adv. Sc.* [f. SNOD *a.* + -LY[2].] Neatly, tidily, trimly.

1721 RAMSAY *Scribblers Lashed* 75 'Till by degrees it creeps right snodly, On hips and head-dress of the godly. 1791 J. LEARMONT *Poems* 304 Here's something here..will mak life's road to me fu' snodly sleekit. 1823 GALT *R. Gilhaize* lxxii, A clean cambric handkerchief very snodly prined over her breast. 1890 W. HOWSON *Cur. Craven* 118 Shadows flicker On the snodly whitewesh'd wa'. 1904 *Dundee Advertiser* 19 Aug. 6 We took the short road by Burns' Monument and the snodly theekit hoosie at the wayside.

‖**Snoek** (snūk). Also **snook.** [Du. *snoek* pike: cf. SNOOK[2].] At the Cape of Good Hope, the common name of the fish *Thyrsites Atun.* Also *attrib.* and *Comb.*

1853 PAPPE *Edible Fishes C. Good Hope* 24 *Thyrsites Atun.* Cuv. and Val. (Snoek; Snoek). 1872 HUTTON & HECTOR *Fishes N. Zealand* s.v. *Thyrsites Atun*, This is, I believe, the fish called snook in Cape Colony. 1889 *Science-Gossip* XXV. 50 The unhappy snoek-eaters wander about like so many grown children afflicted with mumps. 1896 BADEN-POWELL *Matabele Campaign* i, Old Cape Town just the same as ever...Malays and snoek fish everywhere.

Snoff. *Cornish mining.* [A survival of the early form of SNUFF *sb.*[1]] (See quots.)

1860 *Eng. & For. Mining Gloss.* (ed. 2) 23 *Snoff, or Match*, ..brown paper, or other slowly combustible substance, which is ignited at one end, the other being in contact with the rush or train in blasting. 1881 RAYMOND *Mining Gloss.*, *Snoff*, a short candle-end, put under a fuse to light it. 1891 J. H. PEARCE *Esther Pentreath* I. i, Dick having charged the hole with powder, set fire to the train with a 'snoff' from his candle.

Snoffe, obs. form of SNUFF *sb.*[1] and *v.*

Snog (snɒg), *a. north. dial.* and †*Sc.* [app. a. ON. *snøgg-r* smooth, short-haired, etc. (cf. the etym. note to SNUG *a.*[1]).] Smooth, sleek; neat, tidy. Hence **Sno·gly** *adv.*

1513 DOUGLAS *Æneid* XII. Prol. 186 All snog and slekyt worth thir bestis skynnis. 1615 CROOKE *Body of Man* 1111 Thin they are and conuex, that they might lye more snogly vpon the fingers. 1691 RAY *N. C. Words* 66 *Snog*, neat, handsome: as *snogly gear'd*, handsomely drest. *Ibid.*, *Snog* Malt, smooth with few Combs. 1818 SCOTT *Hrt. Midl.* xxxii, Thou wouldst be a mettle lass enow, an thou wert snog and snod a bit better. 1855 [ROBINSON] *Whitby Gloss.*, *Snod and Snog*, smooth and compact.

†**Snog,** *v. Obs.*[−0] [Cf. next.] *intr.* To bristle.

1530 PALSGR. 724/1, I snogge, *je herisonne.*

†**Sno·ggy,** variant of (or error for) SNAGGY *a.*

1670 COVEL in *Early Voy. Levant* (Hakl. Soc.) 141 They were all short, snoggy trees, much loaded with boughs.

Snogly, *adv.*: see SNOG *a.*

Snoif, obs. form of SNOOVE *v. Sc.*

Snoir(e, obs. Sc. forms of SNORE *sb.*

Snoke (snōᵘk), *v.* Chiefly *north.* and *Sc.* Forms: α. 4–5, 9 **snoke** (5 **snokyn**), 6 *Sc.* **snokk-**, 9 **snoak.** β. 6 **snooke,** 7– **snook** (8 *dial.* **snooac**). γ. 7– **snouk,** 8– **snowk.** [prob. of Scand. origin: cf. Norw. dial. *snōka* to snuff, smell.] *intr.* and *trans.* To snuff or smell; to go snuffing or smelling (at); to poke about with the nose. Also *fig.*, to sneak about, to keep watch *over*, etc.

α. *c* 1380 WYCLIF *Sel. Wks.* II. 83 Disciplis of Crist wenten into þe citee to bie hem mete; for þei snokiden not fro hous to hous and beggiden mete, as freris doon. *c* 1475 *Promp. Parv.* 462/1 (MS. K.), Snokyn, or smellyn, *nicto.* 1500 *Ortus Vocab.* BB vij, *Nicto*,..to snoke as a honde dos. 1513 DOUGLAS *Æneid* v. ii. 99 The drink, and eik the offerandis gret and small, [the snake] Snokkis [*v.r.* snokis] and likkit. 1831 J. WILSON *Noct. Ambr.* Wks. 1855 III. 98 After smellin an' snokin an' snortin at it for a while. 1834 M. SCOTT *Cruise Midge* xxi, He lay still, with the beast..poking down its head, and snorting and snoking at him.

β. 1570 LEVINS *Manip.* 159/35 To Snooke, *olfacere.* 1608 HIERON *Defence* II. 8 Whether he snooketh not as right into Rheames and Rome as maie be [etc.]. 1641 BEST *Farm. Bks.* (Surtees) 74 The hogges went snuffinge and snookinge from heape to heape. *a* 1652 BROME *New Acad.* II. i, I must not lose my harmlesse recreations Abroad, to snook over my wife at home. 1687 MIÈGE *Gt. Fr. Dict.* II, To Snook, or ly lurking for a thing. 1722 WODROW *Hist. Suff. Ch. Scot.* III. viii. II. 449 The Dogs would snook and smell about the Stones under which they were hid, and yet they remained undiscovered. 1788 W. H. MARSHALL *Yorksh.* II. 354 To *Snooac*, to smell in a snuffing manner. 1834 [SEBA SMITH] *Lett. J. Downing* (1835) 106 All we've got to do is to open that, and snook among old papers. 1891 R. FORD *Thistledown* ix. 163 That we do not gang..snookin' amang the snaw like mowdiewarts.

γ. 1624 SANDERSON *Serm.* I. 241 Like swine under the oaks, we grouze up the acorns, and snouk about for more. 1786 BURNS *Twa Dogs* 39 Wi' social nose [the dogs] whyles snuff'd an' snowket. 1861 QUIN *Heather Lintie* (1863) 76, I snouk aboot For 'tatty peels and banes o' herrin'. 1894 CROCKETT *Raiders* xlv. 384 Gin ony o' Agnew's men were gaun snowkin' roond, it micht cause misunderstandings.

Hence **Sno·king** *vbl. sb.*

c 1440 *Promp. Parv.* 462/1 Snokynge, *olfactus.*

†**Snoke-horn.** *Obs.*[−1] ? A sneaking fellow.

c 1460 *Towneley Myst.* ix. 80 Then were my worshyp lorne, If sych a swayn, a snoke borne, Shuld thus be my suffrane.

Sno·key, *a. rare*[−1]. [f. SNOKE *v.*] Adapted for snuffing or poking.

1828 *Blackw. Mag.* XXIII. 865 Nuzzling with that snokey nose of his.

Snood (snūd), *sb.* Forms: 1 **snod,** 6– (*Sc.* and *north.*) **snude** (9 **sneud**), 7– **snood** (9 **snoud**); *north.* 8 **snead,** 9 **sneiad;** *Sc.* 9 **snid, sneed,** etc. [OE. *snōd*, of obscure origin.]

1. A fillet, band, or ribbon, for confining the hair; latterly, in Scotland (and the north of England), the distinctive hair-band worn by young unmarried women.

c 725 *Corpus Gloss.* (Hessels) C 137 *Cappa*, snod. *a* 1000 in Wr.-Wülcker 204 *Cinthium, mitra*, snod. *c* 1000 ÆLFRIC *Hom.* II. 28 Þa lærde hi sum iudeisc man, þæt heo name ænne wernægel..and becnytte to anum bringe mid hire snode. *c* 1150 in Wr.-Wülcker 540 *Uitta*, snod.

1535 STEWART *Cron. Scot.* I. 377 Ȝone ma nocht saif thair bodie with ane snude. 1643 *Orkney Witch Trial* in *Abbotsford Club Misc.* I. 177 Ȝe said vnto hir that ȝe haid Vrsulla Alexanderis snood, quhilk ȝe haid keipit since ȝe put hir in hir winding sheit. 1677 NICHOLSON in *Trans. R. Soc. Lit.* (1870) IX. 319 *Snude*, a fillet, or hair lace. 1725 RAMSAY *Gentle Sheph.* II. iv, The rashes green..Of which..For thee I plet the flow'ry belt and snood. 1771 PENNANT *Tour in Scotl.* (1794) 213 The single women wear only a ribband round their head, which they call a snood. 1810 SCOTT *Lady of L.* III. v, No hunter's hand her snood untied, Yet ne'er again to braid her hair The virgin snood did Alice wear. 1840 BARHAM *Ingol. Leg.* Ser. II. *Blondie Jacke of Shrewsberie* (1905) 322 While her tresses are bound with a snood. 1889 R. BUCHANAN *Heir of Linne* vii, Her hair was bound up in a simple snood.

†**b.** ? A skein. *Obs.*[−1]

1425 in Kennett *Par. Antiq.* (1695) Gloss. s.v. *Snodde*, In viii snoden de Pakthred.

2. a. In sea-fishing: One of a number of short lines, each carrying a baited hook, attached at regular distances along the main line.

c 1682 J. COLLINS *Salt & Fishery* 112 To each of these are fastned 20 Snoods, *alias* Nossels, which are small Lines, with Hooks and Baits at them. 1769 PENNANT *Brit. Zool.* (1776) III. 205 The hooks are fastened to the lines upon sneads of twisted horse hair 27 inches in length. 1793 *Statist. Acc. Scotl.* VII. 204 The quantity of line..contains ..720 hooks,..one yard distant from each other, on snoods of horse hair. 1848 *Chambers's Information for People* I. 699 These are long lines, with hooks fastened at regular distances..by shorter and smaller cords called *snoods.* 1883 *Fisheries Exhib. Catal.* 7 Simple Machine, for making Norsels or Snoods of any length.

b. *Angling.* A hair or catgut line attaching the hook to the rod line.

1823 E. MOOR *Suffolk Words*, *Snood*, that part of an angler's line to which the hook is affixed. 1832 W. H. MAXWELL *Wild Sp. West* I. 263, I..lost time, hooks, and snoods. 1873 W. GRAHAM in *Harp of Perthshire* (1893) 149 My licht thrown snood scarce touched the flood When doun it flew like lichtnin'.

Snood (snūd), *v.* [f. prec.]

1. *trans.* To bind *up*, fasten *back*, or secure (the hair) with a snood.

1725 RAMSAY *Gentle Sheph.* I. i, Her cockernony snooded up fou sleek. 1793 *Statist. Acc. Scotl.* IX. 325 At home they went bareheaded, with their hair snooded back on the crown of their head, with a woollen string in the form of a garter. 1818 SCOTT *Hrt. Midl.* xiv, Her hands trembled as she snooded her fair hair beneath the riband. 1837 CARLYLE *Fr. Rev.* III. VII. ii, Her sweeping tresses snooded by glittering antique fillet. 1890 *Pall Mall G.* 29 Jan. 6/3 The new fashion of wearing the hair snooded low on the nape of the neck.

transf. 1856 S. DOBELL *Eng. in Time of War, Home, Wounded* 27 Where The larch is snooding her flowery hair With wreaths of morning shadow.

2. *Angling.* To attach (a hook) to a snood.

1840 MARRYAT *Poor Jack* vi, He was snooding a hook.

Snooded (snū·dėd), *ppl. a.* [f. SNOOD *sb.* or *v.*] Wearing a snood; bound by a snood.

1810 SCOTT *Lady of L.* III. xx, And plaided youth, with jest and jeer, Which snooded maiden would not hear. 1847 WHITTIER *Barclay of Ury* 81 The snooded daughter.. Smiled on him who bore renown. 1898 R. BUCHANAN *Father Anthony* xvii, Her hand stole up to her head and touched the snooded folds of the locks.

Snooding (snū·diŋ). [f. SNOOD *sb.* 2.] The material used for fishing-snoods.

1815 *Sporting Mag.* XLV. 153 Hempen snooding I always have sold, That will ne'er lose the fish, while the hook have her hold. 1873 G. C. DAVIES *Mount. & Mere* xix. 176 At short intervals were hooks attached to lengths of snooding. 1884 *Sat. Rev.* 603/1 The amateur, provided with his..Manchester snooding, his gut trace, and his artificial spinner.

†**Snook,** *sb.*[1] *north.* and *Sc. Obs.* Forms: 3 **snoc, snoke,** 4–5 **snuk(e, snwk,** 7 **snewke.** [Of obscure origin: cf. NOOK *sb.*] A projecting point or piece of land; a promontory.

c 1236 *Newminster Cartul.* (Surtees) 55 In illa parte agri quæ vocatur le Snoc. ? 1297 *Documents Illustr. Hist. Scotl.* (1870) II. 160 In factura pontis castri Berwyci, muri lapidei juxta mare subtus le Snoke. 1375 BARBOUR *Bruce* I. 188 Fra Weik anent Orknay To Mullyr-snwk in Gallaway. *Ibid.* IV. 556 On Turnberyis nwk [*v.r.* snuke] he may Mak a fyre. *c* 1470 HENRY *Wallace* VII. 1044 Furth thai fle Till Dwnottar, a snuk within the se. 1648 BLAEU *Atlas Engl., Map of Insula Sacra*, The Snewke or Conny warren.

Snook (snūk), *sb.*[2] [ad. Du. *snoek* pike: cf. SNOEK.] A name given to various fishes, esp. the sergeant-fish, *Elacate canada*, and the robalo, *Centropomus undecimalis.*

1697 DAMPIER *Voy.* (1699) 243 The Fish I observed here mostly, were what we call Snooks, neither a Sea fish nor fresh Water fish, but very numerous in these salt Lakes. 1725 SLOANE *Jamaica* II. 288 Snook. It was taken at Passage fort. 1827 O. W. ROBERTS *Voy. Centr. Amer.* 156 It [Caratasca Lagoon] abounds in various sorts of fish of the finest description, particularly mullet, calapaner, snoak, cavallee, and also manatee. 1858 SIMMONDS *Dict. Trade*, *Snook*, a common fish, both of the sea and the rivers of the West Indies, the *Centropomus undecimalis.* 1883 *Fisheries Exhib. Catal.* (ed. 4) 170 Model of Fresh-water Fishpot, for taking mullet, snook, &c.

Snook, variant of SNOKE *v.* and SNOOKS.

Snooker (snū·kəɹ), *sb.*[1] *Woolwich slang.* A newly joined cadet.

1872 *Routledge's Ev. Boy's Ann.* 148/1 These embryo generals..were called by the somewhat sneering terms of 'snookers' or 'last-joined'.

Snooker (snū·kəɹ), *sb.*[2] [Of obscure origin.] A game, played with balls on a billiard table, combining pool and pyramids. Also *snooker('s) pool.*

1889 DRAYSON *Pract. Billiards* 110 The game of snooker. 1896 W. BROADFOOT *Billiards* xiii. 424 Snooker—or to give it its full title, Snooker's Pool—is a hybrid game, half pool and half pyramids. 1905 GLASFURD *Rifle in Ind. Jungle* 70 The old Doctor and we two, after several games of 'Snookers', had passed into the ante-room.

Hence **Snoo·ker** *v.* (See quots.)

1889 DRAYSON *Pract. Billiards* 111 If each pool ball is covered by a pyramid ball, the player is said to be 'snookered'. 1896 W. BROADFOOT *Billiards* xiii. 426 If the striker is by law obliged to play on a red ball or on a coloured ball, but..is unable to do so directly, he is said to be snookered.

Snooks (snūks). Also **snook.** [Of obscure origin.] A derisive gesture, = SIGHT *sb.*[1] 7 c.

1879 A. J. C. HARE *Story Life* (1900) V. 218 If I put my hands so..(cutting a snooks), they might reproach me very much indeed. 1904 *Times* 24 Sept. 8/3 The young monkey puts his tongue in his cheek and cocks a snook at you. 1906 DAURY *Men at Arms* 36 Her Majesty's ship..cocked her jibboom snooks-fashion at her late enemy the sea.

Snool (snūl), *sb. Sc.* and *north. dial.* Also 8– *Sc.* **snule, snuil,** 9 *north.* **snuol.** [Of obscure origin.] A tame, abject, or mean-spirited person.

1718 RAMSAY *Christ's Kirk Gr.* III. xvi, Ye silly snool, Wae worth ye'r drunken saul. 1791 J. LEARMONT *Poems* 4 [They] lead ye on like arrant snools, 'Lang error's road. 1815 G. BEATTIE *John o' Arnha'* (1826) 13 Your snools in love, and cowards in war, Frae maiden grace are banish'd far. 1822 CARLYLE *Early Lett.* II. 51 You or any one of us will never be a snool; we have not the blood of snools in our bodies. 1882 J. WALKER *Jaunt to Auld Reekie* 87 Crouching snools are kin to gangrel bodies.

Snool (snūl), *v.* [f. prec.]

1. *trans.* To keep in subjection; to snub.

17.. RAMSAY *Address of Thanks* iv. Wks. 1877 I. 258 Our dotard dads, snool'd wi' their wives. *a* 1796 BURNS '*An' O for ane-and-twenty, Tam!*' ii, They snool me sair, and haud me down. 1830 GALT *Lawrie T.* IX. i. (1849) 406 The arrogance and high hand with which Mr. Bell was attempting to snool us all.

2. *intr.* To submit tamely; to cringe; to crawl meekly or humbly.

1786 BURNS *Bard's Epitaph* i, Owre blate to seek, owre proud to snool. 1810 TANNAHILL *Poems* (1846) 141 Never snool beneath the frown Of any selfish roggie. 1833 CHALMERS in Hanna *Mem.* (1851) III. 391 We had to snool back to London the way we came. 1895 'G. SETOUN' *Sunshine* ix. 198 Sandy 'snooled' through life with bovine equanimity.

Snoop (snūp), *v. U.S.* [ad. Du. *snoepen* (LG. *snōpen*) in sense 1.]

1. *intr.* To appropriate and consume dainties in a clandestine manner.

1848 BARTLETT *Dict. Amer.* 318 A servant who goes slyly into a dairy-room and drinks milk from a pan, would be said to be snooping.

2. To go *around* in a sly or prying manner.

1864 KIMBALL *Was he successful?* 178 Don't come snooping around to find out whether you sometimes go to the theatre. 1876 BESANT & RICE *Gold. Butterfly* xx, I see the gells snoopin' around with their eyes as soft as velvet. 1883 *Cent. Mag.* Sept. 744 He had no right to come snoopin' around where I was at work.

Hence **Snoo·per,** one who pries or peeps.

Snoop is also used as a sb. in the same sense.

1896 *Westm. Gaz.* 18 Mar. 3/1 Artists sketching whenever they can get a chance, and surrounded by 'snoopers'.

Snoore, obs. variant of SNORE *v.*

Snoove (snūv), *v. Sc.* Also 6 **snoif,** 9 **snuive, snuve.** [a. OScand. (east) **snōa* (MSw. *snoa*, Sw. *sno*, Da. *snoe*), = ON. and Icel. *snúa* (Fær. *snúgva*, Norw. *snu*). For the development of the *v*, cf. the etym. note to RO *sb.*]

1. a. *trans.* To twirl, cause to turn. **b.** *intr.* (See quot. 1808.)

1513 DOUGLAS *Æneid* VIII. vii. 100 To werk the lyne, To snoif the spyndill, and lang thredis twyne. 1722 RAMSAY *Three Bonnets* III. 80 A wife that snooves a spindle. 1808 JAMIESON s.v., A boy's top is said to *snuve*, when it whirls round with great velocity, preserving at the same time an equal motion.

2. *intr.* To move or advance steadily, or with a steady pace; to glide. Also *fig.*

1719 W. HAMILTON *Ep. to Ramsay* III. ii, The pleasure counterpois'd the cumber..And snoovt away like three-hand Ombre. 1786 BURNS *To Auld Mare* xiv, But just thy step a wee thing hastet, Thou snoov't awa. 1830 *Memorabilia Curliana* 106 Come snooving down white ice. 1881 R. BUCHANAN *God & the Man* III. 212 Many a sharp rap did the old ship get [from the ice] as she snooved along.

Snooze (snūz), *sb.* Also **snoose.** [Cf. next.]

1. *colloq.* A sleep; a nap, a doze.

α. 1793 W. ROBERTS *Looker-on* II. 315 That Shuter's self might heave his head From drunken snoozes. 1813 SIR G. JACKSON *Diaries & Lett.* (1873) II. 177, I..had not had my snooze half out, when a courier arrived. 1845 W. H. MAXWELL *Hints Soldier* I. 51, I question whether I could manage to obtain a snooze. 1886 J. R. REES *Pleas. Bk.-Worm* v. 178 With a warm ejaculation on his tongue, the interrupted sleeper returns to his snooze.

β. 1812 H. & J. SMITH *Rej. Addr., Talk Drury Lane* 51 Starting from short and broken snoose, Each sought his pond'rous hobnail'd shoes. 1869 *Daily News* 8 Oct., Seals like nothing better than a snoose on the sand.

2. *slang.* (See quots.)

1812 J. H. VAUX *Flash Dict.* s.v., A snooze sometimes means a lodging; as, where can I get a snooze for this darky, instead of saying a bed. 1839 *Slang Dict.* 34 *Snooze*, a bed. 1865 *Ibid.* (Hotten) 239 *Snooze-case*, a pillow-slip.

Snooze (snūz), *v. colloq.* [app. a cant or slang word of obscure origin.] *intr.* To sleep; to slumber, to doze.

1789 G. PARKER *Life's Painter* (*c* 1800) 138 The cull with whom she snooz'd. 1795 POTTER *Dict. Cant* (ed. 2), *Snooze*, to sleep. 1813 MOORE *Diary* VIII. 136 If..I had nothing to do but put on my nightcap and snooze quietly by their side. 1842 MRS. GORE *Fascination* 37 She withdrew, leaving him to snooze beside the fire. 1887 *Pall Mall G.* 20 Sept. 2/3 A swarm of literary drones, who go there to lounge, snooze, and gossip.

Hence **Snoo·zer,** one who snoozes.

1878 P. ROBINSON *In Ind. Garden* 32 A bird—perhaps the middle one of a long row of closely-packed snoozers. 1887 *Pall Mall G.* 20 Sept. 2/3 The non-workers..may be divided into two classes—the snoozers and the talkers. The snoozer, if he reads at all, is an aimless reader.

Snoo·ziness. [f. SNOOZY *a.*] The state of being snoozy or sleepy.

1887 *Temple Bar* Oct. 199, I was just beginning to realise a sense of comfort, and (if I may say so) downy snooziness.

Snoo·zing, *vbl. sb.* [f. SNOOZE *v.*] The fact of dozing or sleeping. Also *attrib.*

1811 *Lexicon Balatronicum*, *Snoozing ken*, a brothel. 1851 MELVILLE *Whale* I. xxxix. 274 Grand snoozing to-night, maty. 1867 BRIERLEY *Marlocks* 39 Old Makapenny had made several journeys from his 'snoozing crib' to the door.

Snoo·zing, *ppl. a.* [f. SNOOZE *v.*] Dozing, sleeping, slumbering.

1836 HOR. SMITH *Tin Trumpet* (1876) 183 What snoozing hum Ascends to thee?—what pæans, what adorings? 1883 STEVENSON *Merry Men, Treas. Franchard* v, The same snoozing, countryfied existence.

Snoozle (snū·z'l), *v. colloq.* or *dial.* [Cf. SNOOZE *v.* and NUZZLE *v.*[1]]

1. *intr.* To nestle and sleep or doze; to nuzzle.

1831 *Westm. Rev.* XV. 196 Comfortably snoozling like other birds deep in the fertilizing warmth of their downy boxes. 1862 SALA *Seven Sons* I. vii. 177 The little dog, snoozling on the hearthrug, lifted up his blinking eyes. 1881 G. D. LESLIE *Our River* 12 There were a lot of black Berkshire pigs snoozling in the straw.

2. *trans.* To thrust affectionately.

1847 E. BRONTË *Wuthering Heights* iii, A dog..that snoozled its nose over-forwardly into her face. 1894 'G. EGERTON' *Discord* 187 The dog..snoozles her snout into the palm of his hand.

Hence **Snoo·zledom,** the state of nestling and dozing in bed.

1865 D'ARCY THOMPSON *Odds & Ends* iii. ⊕ How precious are the last five minutes of snoozledom!

Snoo·zy, *sb. slang.* (See quot.)

1823 EGAN *Grose's Dict. Vulg. T.*, *Snoozy*, a night-constable.

Snoozy (snū·zi), *a.* [f. SNOOZE *v.*] Drowsy, sleepy, slumberous.

1877 C. KEENE in Layard *Life* (1892) ix. 255 This sea air.. makes me snoozy sometimes in the day. 1886 J. R. REES *Pleas. Bk.-Worm* v. 178 [He] sits in a stupid snoozy state.

Snop, *sb. dial.* [Imitative: cf. next.] A sharp blow or impact; the sound made by this.

1849 *Boy's Own Bk.* 12 Spans and snops. This is a very simple game; one player first shoots his marble, the second then endeavours to strike or *snop* it, or otherwise to shoot his own within a span of it. 1871– in south-western dial. glossaries. 1881 JEFFERIES *Wood Magic* II. iv. 110 His body.. rebounded with a snop, and he fell disabled and insensible to the earth.

Snop, *v. dial.* [Imitative.] *trans.* To strike sharply and smartly; to break in this way. Also *absol.*

1849 [see SNOP *sb.*]. 1882 JEFFERIES *Bevis* x, I see a man do that once...A' had a gate-hinge snopping um. *a* 1887 — *Field & Hedgerow* (1889) 141 To stand there swinging that heavy bit of wood all day meant meat and drink..for themselves and families..: but only a few of them could get barns to snop away in.

Snore (snōᵊɹ), *sb.* Also 6 *Sc.* **snor, snoir(e.** [f. the vb.]

†**1.** A snort; snorting. *Obs. rare.*

c 1330 R. BRUNNE *Chron. Wace* (Rolls) 1821 Þeyr teþ gnaisted wiþ nose snore, Hurtlede hedes set ful sore; Ilk oþer pulled, ilk oþer schok. 1513 DOUGLAS *Æneid* x. x. 72 For feir thai [*sc.* horses] start abak..And brak away with the cart to the schor, With stendis feyll and mony bray and snor.

2. A disease or affection which causes snuffling; the snivels.

a 1585 MONTGOMERIE *Flyting w. Polwart* 302 (Tullib.), The snuf, þe snoir, þe scheippisch, the schanker. 1844 W. JAMIE *Muse* 157 (E.D.D.), May he ne'er be subject unto snors. 1844 LOWSON *Mod. Farrier* 209 This affection is termed the snores or snivels.

3. An act of snoring; a harsh or noisy respiration through the mouth, or through the mouth and nose, during sleep.

1605 SHAKS. *Macb.* II. ii. 6 The surfeted Groomes doe mock their charge with Snores. I haue drugg'd their Possets. 1610 — *Temp.* II. i. 218 Thou do'st snore distinctly, There's meaning in thy snores. 1622 MABBE tr. *Aleman's Guzman d'Alf.* I. 133 The snores and snorts that came from them [a man and his wife]. 1826 F. REYNOLDS *Life & Times* II. 213 Then with a loud snore, he again sank into sleep. 1860 TYNDALL *Glac.* I. ii. 21 The sound rose and fell for several minutes, like a kind of intermittent snore. 1897 MARY KINGSLEY *W. Africa* 384 One of them has an abominable quavering, hysterical, falsetto snore.

b. *All of a snore*, filled with the sound of snoring. *rare.*

1834 BECKFORD *Italy* II. 244 Dark vestibules and guard-chambers (all of a snore with jaded equerries).

4. *transf.* A sound resembling that of a snore; a loud roaring or droning noise.

1709 *Brit. Apollo* No. 41. 3/1 She wak'd from Bag-pipe snore. 1832 DENNISTON *Craiguilder* 60 Now dark December's wintry snore Rang through the leafless wood.

5. *Mining.* A snore-piece.

1875 J. H. COLLINS *Met. Mining* 89 The suction pipe *a*, now called the 'wind-bore' or 'snore'.

Snore (snōᵊɹ), *v.* Also 7 **snoar,** 7–8 **snoore.** [prob. imitative: cf. SNORK *v.* and SNORT *v.*]

1. *intr.* Of animals, *esp.* horses: To snort. Now *dial.*

c 1400 *Laud Troy Bk.* 7738 The horses snored as it hadde thondred. 1530 PALSGR. 724/1, I snore..as a horse dothe. 1648 HEXHAM II, *Ruchelen*, to Grunt, or to Snoore like Hoggs. 1778 G. WHITE *Selborne* lxxxv, They [owls]..can snore and hiss when they mean to menace. 1786 BURNS *To Auld Mare* viii, How thou wad prance, an' snore, an' scriegh, An' tak the road! 1898 C. SPENCE *Poems* 57 He [a bull]..roared and bored and sniffed and snored.

b. *Sc.* and *north. dial.* Of things, wind, etc.: To make or give out a roaring or droning noise.

1823 GALT *R. Gilhaize* xiv, I never hear my ain bellows snoring at a gaud o' iron in the fire, but [etc.]. 1842 VEDDER *Poems* 75 A score of rival steamers..Hiss, flap, and snore, like river monsters. 1886 W. ALEXANDER *S. Augustine's Holiday* 135 The wind..Humming and snoring thro' rigging and spar.

c. Of a ship, etc.: To move or cut *through* the water with a roaring sound; to sail or travel quickly. Chiefly *Sc.*

1830 WILSON in *Blackw. Mag.* XXVII. 540 Our cut-water snores through the swell. 1834 M. SCOTT *Tom Cringle* x, She began to *snore* through it like smoke. 1849 CUPPLES *Green Hand* iii. (1856) 36 The pilot-boat snoring off close-hauled to windward.

2. To make harsh or noisy sounds in sleep by breathing through the open mouth or through the mouth and nose; to breathe in this manner during sleep. Also *poet.* or *rhet.*, to sleep heavily.

c 1440 *Promp. Parv.* 462/1 Snoryn, yn sleep, *sterto.* 1530 PALSGR. 724/1, I wylle nat lye with hym, he snoreth so in his slepe. 1576 FLEMING *Panopl. Epist.* 284 Nature hath not giuen unto men their essence & being..to slugge and snore in the couche of carelessnesse. 1609 HOLLAND *Amm. Marcell.* XXVII. xii. 323 Whiles the centinels by reason of securitie were found asleepe that they snored againe, the citie gate was set open. 1658 A. FOX *Würtz' Surg.* III. ii. 222 Sound peoples sleep is not alike, some snoar in their sleep, others without a noise. 1695 PRIOR *Prol. Dryden's 'Cleomenes'* 20 Most of you snor'd whilst Cleomenes read. 1725 POPE *Odyss.* IX. 440 Then nodding with the fumes of wine, [he] Dropt his huge head, and snoring lay supine. 1784 COWPER *Task* I. 90 The nurse sleeps sweetly, hir'd to watch the sick, Whom snoring she disturbs. 1818 SCOTT *Rob Roy* xxx, [He] tumbled himself into one of the cribs.. and soon was heard to snore soundly. 1860 TYNDALL *Glac.* I. xvi. 107 He assured me..that he did not snore, and we lay down side by side. 1900 POLLOK & THOM *Sports Burma* 286 A solitary tusker elephant sound asleep and snoring loudly.

fig. 1660 N. INGELO *Bentivolio & Urania* II. (1682) 89 The Soul, having snor'd many hundreds or thousands of years.

b. *I snore*, used as a mild expletive. *U.S.*

1790 *Mass. Spy* 30 Dec. (Thornton), In one village you will hear the phrase 'I snore',—in another, 'I swowgar'. 1836 HALIBURTON *Clockm.* Ser. I. xii, Now its fairly run out, that's a fact, I snore. *Ibid.* xxxvi, You will, I snore.

3. *trans.* With *out* or *away*: To spend or pass (time) in snoring.

1597 SHAKS. *2 Hen. IV*, IV. v. 28 Sleepe with it now, Yet not so sound..As hee whose Brow..Snores out the Watch of Night. *a* 1704 T. BROWN *Walk r. Lond., Tavern* Wks. 1709 III. III. 9 Where she Surfeits upon Sack,..and Snoars away the Remainder of her Life. 1746 FRANCIS tr. *Hor., Sat.* I. iii. 24 He drank the Night away Till rising Dawn, then snor'd out all the Day. 1781 COWPER *Hope* 510 The fullgorg'd savage at his nauseous feast Spent half the darkness, and snor'd out the rest. 1829 SCOTT *Anne of G.* xix, Some ..snored away the interval between their own arrival and that of the expected repast.

4. To bring into a certain state by snoring (cf. quots.).

1784 COWPER *Task* I. 97 Sleep Of lazy nurse, who snores the sick man dead. *a* 1793 J. PEARSON *Polit. Dict.* 10 If the House are too sleepy to cough him down, they'll soon snore him down.

5. To utter with a snore or with a sound resembling this. Also with cognate object.

1790 COLERIDGE *Inside the Coach* 22 Till ere the splendid visions close We snore quartettes in ecstasy of nose. 1889 GUNTER *That Frenchman* ii, Maurice..is already asleep and snoring the snores of an exhausted manhood. 1891 *Daily News* 9 Feb. 6/2 Some good people seemed to snore prayer; they were so sleepy.

Snore-, the stem of the vb. in comb., as *snore-hole, -piece* (see quots.).

1860 *Eng. & For. Mining Gloss.* (ed. 2) 63 **Snore-holes*, the holes in the windbore to admit the water. 1862 SMILES *Engineers* III. 45 The pumps frequently got choked by the sand drawn in at the bottom of the well through the snore-holes, or apertures through which the water to be raised is admitted. 1883 GRESLEY *Gloss. Coal-m.* 229. 1867 W. W. SMYTH *Coal & Coal-mining* 180 The lowermost portion [of the pump] is the so-called wind-bore, or *snore-piece, where the holes in the bottom..are of such size as to prevent the entry of chips or stones. 1883 GRESLEY *Gloss. Coal-m.* 229 *Snore-piece*, the lowest end of a pump sett through which the water passes.

Sno·reless, *a.* [f. SNORE *sb.*] Of sleep: Unaccompanied by, free from, snoring.

1830 *Blackw. Mag.* XXVII. 423 The snoreless sleep of the last upper-earth journey. 1845 *Ibid.* LVII. 391 The printer's devil..indulged in snoreless sleep.

Snorer (snōᵊ·rəɹ). [f. SNORE *v.*]

1. One who snores.

c 1440 *Promp. Parv.* 462/1 Snorare, *stertor.* 1611 COTGR., *Ronfleur*, a snorer, a snorter. 1694 MOTTEUX *Rabelais* xliii. (1737) 174 Old Goodman Æolus, the Snorer. 1751 SMOLLETT *Per. Pickle* (1779) II. lvii. 155 The face of the gaping snorer. 1864 DASENT *Jest & Earnest* (1873) I. 49 Our friend..is not the Club snorer whose feats he recalls so painfully. 1875 EMERSON *Lett. & Social Aims* I. 40 This unwritten play.., composed by the dullest snorer on the floor of the watch-house.

2. A stiff breeze or wind.

1871 *Daily News* 6 Nov., We lay our course famously, running..before a regular snorer—a strong sea on [etc.].

Snoring (snōᵊ·riŋ), *vbl. sb.* [f. SNORE *v.*] The action of the vb.

c 1440 *Promp. Parv.* 462/1 Snorynge, *stertura.* 1532 DU WES *Introd. Fr.* in *Palsgr.* 906 The snowring, *le ronfler.* *a* 1616 BEAUMONT *Charme* v. Poems (1640) H iv b, Sable Midnight makes all dumbe, But thy jealous husbands snoring. 1710 STEELE *Tatler* No. 208 ¶ 6 We have a Member of our Club, that when Sir Jeffery falls asleep, wakens him with Snoring. 1781 R. BURKE in *Burke's Corr.* (1844) II. 404 The meditations of the judge, the snoring of jurors. 1842 LOVER *Handy Andy* xxiv, The dormitory, where.. a concert of snoring began to be executed. 1897 WATTS-DUNTON *Aylwin* II. v, It was the snoring of Wynne in a drunken sleep: it filled the entire cottage.

b. *spec.* in *Path.* (see quots.).

1822–7 GOOD *Study Med.* (1829) I. 537 *Rhonchus Stertor.* Snoring. 1834 J. FORBES *Laennec's Dis. Chest* (ed. 4) 49 We can distinguish five principal kinds of rhonchi:..3. the dry sonorous rhonchus, or snoring.

Sno·ring, *ppl. a.* [f. as prec.]

1. That snores. Also *fig.*

1687 MIÈGE *Gt. Fr. Dict.* I, *Ronfleur*,..a snoring Man. 1714 GAY *Sheph. Week* vi. 36 Cic'ly, brisk maid, steps forth..., And kiss'd with smacking lip the snoring lout. 1809 PINKNEY *Trav. France* 131, I was lying at one end of a dirty room, the other being occupied by the snoring landlord. 1868 GEO. ELIOT *Sp. Gypsy* I. 118 He is of those Who steal the keys from snoring Destiny. 1894 *Outing* XXIV. 119/2 Great rocks which resemble the snouts of snoring humans.

2. Of a breeze: Strong, stiff.

1822 A. CUNNINGHAM *Mariner's Song* ii, But give to me the snoring breeze, And white waves heaving high. 1885 J. RUNCIMAN *Skippers & Shellbacks* 78 A snoring breeze came away from the southward.

3. Having the characteristic sound of a snore; loud and harsh.

1837 CARLYLE *Fr. Rev.* II. IV. iii, Sleeping Paris is now.. silent except for some snoring hum. 1879 *St. George's Hosp. Rep.* IX. 610 On the left side the respiration was loud and 'snoring'...Posteriorly the 'snoring' breathing was audible everywhere. 1898 *Allbutt's Syst. Med.* V. 1018 Most frequently it [a presystolic murmur] is snoring or rolling.

Hence **Sno·ringly** *adv.*

1824 *Blackw. Mag.* XV. 593 A set of prosy lines slumber along snoringly.

Snork (snɒ̄ɹk), *sb. dial.* [f. the vb.]

1. A snort or grunt; a noisy sniff or inhalation.

1814 in Hone *Every-day Bk.* II. 1115 The pig..gave a snork. 1824 MACTAGGART *Gallovid. Encycl.* 430 *Snork*, the snort of an affrighted horse. 1876–99 in Mid-Yks. and Cumbld. glossaries.

2. A young pig; a pigling.

1891 'SON OF MARSHES' in *Blackw. Mag.* Nov. 651 The farm lad who leads a family of snorks from one part of a wood..to another. 1895 — in *Month* Oct. 248 The little nose-twisting,..curly-tailed, winking, and blinking snorks.

Snork (snɒ̄ɹk), *v.* Now *dial.* [prob. ad. MDu. or MLG. *snorken* (still Du. and LG.; hence Da. *snorke*), variant of *snarken* SNARK *v.*]

1. *intr.* To snore.

1531 TINDALE *Exp. 1 John* (1537) 98 We..lye snorkyng lyke sloggardes. 1565 T. STAPLETON *Fortr. Faith* 121 b, Thou shalt not heare there the seruauntes snorke.

2. To snort or grunt; to breathe noisily. Said esp. of horses and pigs. Hence **Sno·rking** *vbl. sb.*

Other dial. senses are recorded in the *Eng. Dial. Dict.*

1807 HOGG *Pedlar* xxiv. Poems (1865) 66 The horses they snorkit for miles around. 1814 in Hone *Every-day Bk.* II. 1113 The pig ran snorking and grunting after her. 1868– in Sc. and north. glossaries and texts (*Eng. Dial. Dict.*). 1896 CROCKETT *Grey Man* xii, The old grouting wretch kept up such a snorking.

Hence **Sno·rker,** = SNORK *sb.* 2.

1891 'SON OF MARSHES' *On Surrey Hills* iii. 96 He reckoned it was one o' his young snorkers hed got out.

†**Sno·rkle.** *Obs.*[−1] [Cf. G. *schnörkel* curve, flourish.] ? A wrinkle, crease.

a 1340 HAMPOLE *Psalter* cxlvii. 5 Of þaim..cristis kirtil sall be made, wiþouten spot and snorkil.

†**Snorl,** *v. Obs.*[−1] (Meaning uncertain: perh. a misprint for *snarl.*)

1633 B. JONSON *Tale Tub* II. ii, Doe you mutter: Sir, snorle this way; That I may heare.

Snort (snɒ̄ɹt), *sb.* [f. the vb.]

†**1.** A snore. *Obs. rare.*

1619 H. HUTTON *Follies Anat.* (Percy Soc.) 22 At noon-tide to concoct he takes a snort, His drowsie sences hudwinkt in a cap, Leaning upon his chaire do take a nap. 1622 [see SNORE *sb.* 3].

2. An act of snorting; a loud sound made by a horse or other animal in driving breath through the nostrils with some force. Also *transf.*

1808 JAMIESON, *Snocker*, a snort. 1823 SCOTT *Quentin D.* xxxvi, Wishing..good-night in a tone resembling the snort of a shy horse. 1828 — *F. M. Perth* xvii, Inarticulate groans and snorts, like those of a dying boar. 1852 MRS. STOWE *Uncle Tom's C.* vi, He overturned Sam, and, giving two or three contemptuous snorts,..was soon prancing away. 1884 W. C. SMITH *Kildrostan* I. i. 77 Now and then the snort of steam Sounds from the headland far away.

b. A similar sound made by persons in order to express contempt, disdain, or other feeling.

1865 DICKENS *Mut. Fr.* I. x, Medusa..follows every lively remark made by that dear creature, with an audible snort. 1885 R. BUCHANAN *Annan Water* vii, The old man uttered a low snort of defiance. 1887 HALL CAINE *Son of Hagar* II. xvi, The lawyer gave a contemptuous snort and turned on his heel.

Snort (snɒ̄ɹt), *v.* Also 6–7 **snorte.** [prob. imitative: cf. SNORE *v.* and SNORK *v.*]

†**1.** *intr.* Of the nose: To turn *up*, as in sniffing.

a 1366 CHAUCER *Rom. Rose* 157 Hir nose snorted vp for tene, Ful hidous was she forto sene.

†**2.** To snore; to sleep heavily or sluggishly. *Obs.* Common from *c* 1590–1650 in this and the next group.

c 1386 CHAUCER *Reeve's T.* 243 This Millere hath so wisely bibbed Ale That as an hors he snorteth in his sleepe. — *Man of Law's T.* 692 He slepeth and he snorteth in his gyse. 1535 COVERDALE *Isaiah* lvi. 10 They are slepery: slogish are they, & lie snortinge. 1567 MAPLET *Gr. Forest* 96 All winter long he snorteth, and is as he were deade. 1591 SYLVESTER *Du Bartas* I. i. 809 Their Watch within their Corps de Garde About the fire securely snorted hard. 1602 MARSTON *Antonio's Rev.* I. i, Strotzo, to bed: snort in securest sleepe. 1648 GAGE *West Ind.* 141 Thus do they soundly sleep, and loudly snort after a dayes work. *a* 1680 CHARNOCK *Attrib. God* (1834) II. 534 Some rise out of their ..beds..at the first,..others lie snorting longer.

fig. 1653 JER. TAYLOR *Serm. for Year* 208 The spark of Divinity that dwels within is quenched, and the mind snorts, dead with sleep.

†**b.** In various fig. contexts. *Obs.*

1581 J. BELL *Haddon's Answ. Osorius* 25 Truly you sleape so soundly, that you snorte agayne. 1583 STUBBES *Anat. Abus.* (1882) II. 20 Many a one snorteth in palpable ignorance all daies of their life. 1597 J. KING *On Jonas* (1618) 14 Haue we not read..that although themselues slept and snorted in pleasure, yet their damnation slept not? 1630 DYKE *Myst. Self Deceiving* 353 Dauid lay snorting in his owne sin. 1642 *Vind. of the King* 2 The same malignant party..hath been supinely snorting.

†**c.** *refl.* To convert (oneself) *into* something by idleness. *Obs.*

1650 J. HALL *Parad.* 25 The King employed the people that way, who else might have sunke into Luxury, or snorted themselves into implacable enemies.

3. Of a horse: To make a characteristic loud or harsh sound by violently driving the breath through the nostrils, esp. when excited or frightened. Also said of other animals.

c 1386 [see 2 above]. 1530 PALSGR. 724/1 This jade snorteth as were a courser of ten pounde. 1577 B. GOOGE *Heresbach's Husb.* III. (1586) 116 If farr away There happen a noise,..he snuffes, and snortes at the same. 1600 FAIRFAX *Tasso* XX. xxix, He fomes, snorts, neies, and fire and smoake breaths out. 1601 HAKLUYT *Galvano's Disc. World* 85 Certaine fishes which make a noyse like vnto hogs, and will snort. 1697 DRYDEN *Virg. Georg.* III. 392 The Stallion ..snorts and trembles for the distant Mare. 1735 SOMERVILLE *Chase* II. 162 Snorting they breathe, their shining Hoofs scarce print The grass unbruis'd. 1786 tr. *Beckford's Vathek* (1883) 70 The horses snorted, stamped the ground, ..and plunged about without mercy. 1818 SCOTT *Br. Lamm.* xxiii, His horse..suddenly interrupted its steady and composed pace, snorted, reared, and..refused to proceed. 1825 T. HOOK *Sayings* Ser. II. *Man of Many Fr.* II. 41 The fat poodle snorting and wagging his little lionized tail. 1871 C. GIBBON *Lack of Gold* xxi, The horses were steaming and snorting with exertion.

fig. 1891 BARING-GOULD *In Troubadour Land* xviii. 252 The Crusaders were snorting for plunder and murder.

b. To rush *past* with snorts.

1899 F. V. KIRBY *Sport E.C. Africa* xi. 122, I obtained a glimpse of his dark grey hide as he [a rhinoceros] snorted past.

4. *transf.* Of things, esp. in later use of a railway engine: To make or emit a sound resembling or suggestive of a snort.

1582 STANYHURST *Æneis* II. (Arb.) 59 The riuer..Through the breach owt spurging...It brayeth in snorting. 1822 SHELLEY *Faust* II. 50 The giant-snouted crags,..How they snort, and how they blow! 1879 SALA *Paris herself Again* (1880) II. xxi. 320 The little circular railway puffed and screamed and snorted. 1902 'LINESMAN' *Words Eyewitness* 196 The lyddite shells, snorting slowly through the air like a goods train up a gradient.

5. Of persons: **a.** To express contempt or indignation by a snorting sound.

1818 SCOTT *Hrt. Midl.* xlvi, Duncan..snorted thrice, and prepared himself to be in a passion. 1827 — *Two Drovers* i, Ye needna snort, none of you Highlanders. 1889 GRETTON *Memory's Harkback* 300 Upon this conclusion, his reverence snorted, and turned upon his heel in dudgeon.

b. *dial.* and *U.S.* To laugh loudly or roughly.

1825 BROCKETT *N. C. Gloss.*, *Snort*, to laugh outright. 1834 [SEBA SMITH] *Lett. J. Downing* (1835) 27 We all snorted and snicker'd. 1835 HALIBURTON *Clockm.* Ser. I. xix, I thought I should have snorted right out two or three times.

6. *trans.* **a.** To utter with a snort; to give *out*, drive *away*, etc., by snorting († or snoring).

a 1634 RANDOLPH *Muses Looking-gl.* IV. iii, Your pittifull Worship snorting out pardons To the despairing sinner. 1796 BURKE *Reg. Peace* i. (1892) 27 The..tyrant Carnot shall have snorted away the fumes of the indigested blood of his Sovereign. 1840 THACKERAY *Barber Cox* Apr., 'Dat is gut! haw! haw!' snorted the Baron. 1900 POLLOK & THOM *Sports Burma* 376 He snorted defiance, challenging us, as it were, to approach nearer.

b. To eject or discharge through the nostrils with a snort; to spout *out* in this way.

1818 KEATS *Endymion* II. 885 Fish-semblances, of green and azure hue, Ready to snort their streams. 1853 KANE *Grinnell Exped.* iii. (1856) 28 Great..wallowing sea-hogs, snorting out fountains of white spray. 1868 BROWNING *Ring & Bk.* I. 901 The old Triton..A spray of sparkles snorted from his conch High over the caritellas.

c. To clear (the nose) with a snort.

1835 *Politeness & Gd.-breeding* 104 Never..snivel and snort a wet nose.

Snorter[1] (snɒ̄·ɹtəɹ). [f. SNORT *v.*]

1. One who or that which snorts († or snores); a person who utters a snort in scorn, indignation, etc.; also, a pig.

1601 HAKLUYT *Galvano's Disc. World* 85 Besides these there be certaine fishes which make a noyse like vnto hogs, and will snort, for which cause they be named snorters. 1611 COTGR., *Ronfleur*, a snorer, a snorter. 1662 J. CHANDLER *Van Helmont's Oriat.* 213 Surely that thing..renders the Snorters of the Schooles unexcusable. 1827 in Evans *Leic. Gloss.* s.v., To labourer Tom I give the swine: Snorters collected with great pains. 1894 *Westm. Gaz.* 25 Aug. 1/3

Supplement, p. 3873; Corrigenda, p. 4092; Spurious words, p. 4093; Books quoted, p. 4094

Snow — xii. 146 A remarkable bird, the snow pheasant or snow cock ... And in names of plants or fruits, as **snow-apple**, a variety of apple (Ash, 1775); **snow-bush**, one or other of various shrubs bearing a profusion of white flowers; **snow-gem** ... **snow-grass** ... **snow-pea** ... a variety of pear; **snow-plant**, a plant of the Sierra Nevada in California; **snow-rose**, a species of rhododendron.

Snow (snō), v. Pa. t. and ppl. **snowed**; **snaw'd**; Forms: α. Sc. and north. 4–5 **snaw**, 5 **snau**, 4 **snow**. β. 6–8 **snawed**, 9 **snaa'd**, **snaa's**; 6–9 **snowed**. γ. Pa. t. 4 **snew** ...

1. intr. It snows, snow falls. Also occas. with it.

2. To fall, descend, etc., in the manner of snow.

3. trans. To let fall as snow; to cause to descend in the manner of snow; to shower down.

4. To strew or cover with or as with snow. Also transf.

5. To cause (the hair, etc.) to turn white like snow.

6. With inf. To clunk, obstruct, incommode, imprison, etc., with snow. Usu. in pa. pple.

Snowball (snō'bōl), sb. Also 5 **snowballe**, 5–9 Sc. **snawbaw**; 5–7 **snow-ball**; 5 north. **snaball**, etc. Cf. WFris. snieball, MDu. snee(w)-, sneubal, Du. sneebol, Norw. snjo-, sno-snøga, snee, Da. snee-.

1. A ball of snow, esp. one made of a size convenient for throwing by hand.

2. trans. To throw a snowball at (a person); to pelt with snowballs. Also fig.

Snow-blind, a. Also **mowblind.** Blinded or having the vision affected by exposure to the glare of snow.

Snow-blindness. Also **snowblindness.** Blindness or defective vision caused by exposure of the eyes to the glare of snow.

Snowberry (snō'beri). A name given to various plants or shrubs bearing white berries, or to the fruit of these.

Snow-bird. Also **snow bird, snowbird.**

Snow-bunting. A fringilline bird, Plectrophanes nivalis, widely distributed in Arctic regions.

Snow-clad, a.

Snow-cold, a.

Snow dog tree.

+Snowdon.

Snowdon (snō'dn). Forms: [See note]

Snowdonian (snōdō'niən), a.

Snowed (snōd), ppl. a.

Snowfall (snō'fōl). **1.** One of the small masses in which snow commonly falls. **2.** The amount of snow falling at a particular place.

Snow-field. Also **snowfield.**

Snowflake. Also **snow-flake.** **1.** One of the small masses in which snow commonly falls.

Snow-goose. Also **snow goose.**

Snow-finch. Also **snow finch.** A species of mountain-finch.

Snowily, adv.

Snowing, vbl. sb.

Snowish, a.

Snowless, a.

Snow-like, a. and adv.

Snowman. Also **snow-man, snowman.**

Snowmanship.

Snow-plough. Also **snow plough.**

Snow-shoe. **1 a.** A kind of foot-gear enabling the wearer to walk on the surface of snow.

Snow-storm. Also **snowstorm.**

Snow-water. Also **snow water.**

Snow-white, a. Forms: **1 a.** White as snow; pure white.

Snow-wreath. **1.** A heap of snow blown together by the wind; a snowdrift.

Snowy (snō'i), a. and sb. Forms: **1.** Abounding in snow.

Snub (snʌb), sb. **1.** An act or instance of snubbing; a remark or action intended to repress or rebuke a person.

Snub, v.

+Snub, sb.

Snub-nose.

Snub-nosed, a.

Snuff-mill. *Sc.* [See prec. 1, and MULL *sb.*[6].] A snuff-box.

Snuffy (snŭ'fi), *a.*[1] 1 Annoyed, displeased; ready to take offence.

Snuffy, *sb.* [f. SNUFF *sb.*[3].]

Snuft. [See quot. 1611.) *Obs.* The snuff of a candle or the like.

Snufter, *sb. Obs.* [Cf. SNUFT *sb.*]

Snuftkin, variant of SNUFKIN.

Snug (snŭg), *sb.*[1] [f. SNUG *a.*]

Snug (snŭg), *a.*[1] and *adv.* Also 6-7 snugg.

Snug (snŭg), *v.* [Of obscure origin: cf. SNUG *a.*]

Snugger (snŭ'gəɹ). [f. prec. + -ER.]

Snuggery (snŭ'gəri). Also 9 -erie. [f. SNUG *a.*[1] + -ERY.]

Snug-gle (snŭ'g'l), *v.* [f. next.] An act of snuggling. Also with *down.*

Snuggle (snŭ'g'l), *v.* [f. SNUG *v.* + -LE.]

Snuggish (snŭ'giʃ). [f. SNUG *a.*] Somewhat snug; rather comfortable.

Snuggle (snŭ'g'l), *v.*[1] [f. SNUG *v.*[1] + -LE.]

Snugify (snŭ'gifai), *v.* [f. SNUG *a.*[1] + -IFY.]

Snugly (snŭ'gli), *adv.* [f. SNUG *a.*[1] + -LY.] In a snug or comfortable manner.

Snugging (snŭ'giŋ), *vbl. sb.*[1] [f. SNUG *v.*]

Snugging, *ppl. a.* *rare*[-1]. [f. as prec.] Snug, comfortable.

Snurl, *v.* *Obs.*[-1] [f. preceding.] To snuffle or snort.

Snurl, *sb. dial.* Also 9 snirl, snerl, etc. [Cf. WFlem. *snorrelen* to snuffle or snort.

Snuzzle, *v. Now dial.* Also 8 snuzle. [variant of NUZZLE *v.* Cf. SNOOZLE *v.*]

Snush, *sb. Obs.* [perh. imitative of a sneezing sound, but cf. Du. and Da. *snus*.]

Snush, *v. Obs.* [f. prec.]

Snust, *sb. Obs.* [Cf. prec.]

Snute, *Obs.* In 7 snewto, snut(e), snuyt. [ad. Du. *snuit* or Flem. *snuite, snute*: cf. SNOUT.]

Snut-nose. *Obs.* [= SNOT-NOSED *a.*]

Sny (snai), *sb. Shipbuilding.* [Cf. SNYING *vbl. sb.*]

Sny, *v.*[1] [f. prec.]

Sny (snai), *v.*[2] *Now dial.* Forms: 7 snithe, 9 snive; 7, 9 snie, 8-9 sny, 9 snye; 7 snie. [Of obscure origin.] *intr.* To abound, swarm, teem, be infested, with something.

Snying (snai'iŋ), *vbl. sb. Shipbuilding.* [Of obscure origin: cf. SNY *sb.*, and *sny, sny* abound.]

Snythe, *vars.* of SNATH, scythe-pole.

Snyth-hilt: see SNIDDLE.

So (sǭ), *adv.* and *conj.* Forms: (see below).

A. Illustration of Forms.

B. Signification.

I. 1. In the way or manner described, indicated, or suggested; in that style or fashion.

Supplement, p. 3873; Corrigenda, p. 4092; Spurious words, p. 4093; Books quoted, p. 4094

Soar (continued)

Soar, obs. form of Sore.

Soar, v.¹ Also 7 soare. [f. Soar sb., perh. partly after F. essor.]

Soare, obs. form of Sware, Sore.

Soarer (sōə·rəɹ). One who or that which soars, in various senses.

Soaring (sōə·riŋ), vbl. sb. [f. Soar v.¹]

Soaringly, adv.

Soarant, a. Her. = Soaring ppl. a. 2.

Soard, **Soare**, obs. forms of Sward, Sore.

Sob (sǫb), v.¹ Forms: 2 sobben (5 sobbyn), 4-6 sobbe (4 sobbe), 4-7 sobbe, 6-sob (7 sobb); 8-9 sob. [app. of imitative origin: cf. WFris. sobje, sobbe, Du. dial. zabbe to suck.]

Sobbing (sǫ·biŋ), vbl. sb. [-ing¹.]

Sobbingly (sǫ·biŋli), adv.

Sobby (sǫ·bi), a. Now dial. and U.S. [f. Sob v.²] Soaked; saturated with moisture; soppy.

So boing; Chiefly U.S. [f. So adv. + a bean, 9 saebein, 8 saebeins, 8-9 -biens, 9 -bins. [Elliptic for it so being that : So adv. 3 d.]

Sob, v.² Now dial. and U.S. [Of obscure origin.] trans. To soak, saturate, sop.

Sob (sǫb), sb.¹ [f. Sob v.¹]

Sob, sb.² = Sop sb.¹

Sober (sōə·bəɹ), a. Forms: 4-6 sobre, sobur (6 St. sobyr), 5 sobyre, -ire, 5-6 sobor, 6 (St. sobir, 7-9 dial.) sober, 7 sobre. [a. AF. sobre, OF. (and mod.F.) sobre = Pr., Sp. sobrio, It. sobrio, ad. L. sōbrius.]

Sobeit, conj. and sb.

Sobole (sǫ·bōl). Bot. [ad. L. sobolēs.]

Soboles (sǫ·bōlīz). Bot.

Soboliferous, a. Bot. [f. prec.]

Sobralite, Min. [f. the name of the Spanish physician and botanist, F. M. Sobral.]

Sobriety (sǫbrəi·ti). Also 5-7 sobrietie, 6 sobrietie, sobrietye. [ad. L. sōbrietās, or a. F. sobriété.]

Sober-minded, a. [f. Sober a. 14.]

Sober-mindedness. In a sober manner, in various senses of the adj.

Sobersides (sōə·bəɹsəidz). [f. Sober a. + Side sb.]

Sobriquet (sǫ·brikē). Also 8 soubriquet. [F., of uncertain origin.]

Socage (sǫ·kēdʒ). Forms: see Socage. Also 6-socage (7-scage, 7 sockage). [a. AF. socage, f. soc Soke sb. + -age.]

1. A right of local jurisdiction.

2. A creeping underground stem.

Socager (sǭ·kedʒə·r). Now *Hist.* Also 7- **soceager**, 8 **sockager**. [f. prec.] One holding land by socage tenure.

So-called, *ppl. a.* Also so called. **1.** In predicative use (properly without hyphen): Called or designated by that name.

Sociability (sǭʃiăbi·liti). Also 5 ? **socibbilite**. [f. next + -ITY. Cf. F. *sociabilité*, Sp. *sociabilidad*, Pg. *-idade*.] The character or quality of being sociable; friendly disposition or intercourse.

Sociable (sǭ·ʃăb'l), *a.* and *sb.* [a. F. *sociable* (= Sp. *sociable*, It. *sociabile*, 5, 6 **sociblle**), f. *sociâre* to unite, associate : see -ABLE.]

A. *adj.* **1.** Naturally inclined or disposed to be in company with others of the same species.

In birds (seequots. and cf. SOCIAL 6 c.)

5. In names of birds.

B. *sb.* **1.** One who likes and seeks the company of others ; disposed to be friendly or affable in company ; willing to converse in a pleasant manner.

Sociableness (sǭ·ʃăb'lnes). [f. prec. + -NESS.] The character or quality of being sociable, in the various senses of the word ; sociability.

Sociably (sǭ·ʃăbli), *adv.* [f. as prec. : see -LY.] In a sociable manner ; with sociability.

Social (sǭ·ʃăl), *a.* and *sb.* Also 6 *Sc.* **sociale**, **sociall**. [a. F. *social*, *-ale* (14th cent. in Godef.), = Sp., Pg. *social*, It. *sociale*, ad. L. *sociâlis*, f. *socius* friend, companion, associate.]

A. *adj.* †**1.** Capable of being associated or united in others. *Obs.*

B. *sb.* **1.** A social gathering or party, esp. one held by members of a club or society.

Socialism (sǭ·ʃăl,iz'm). [f. SOCIAL *a.* + -ISM. See also next.]

1. A theory or policy of social organization which aims at or advocates the ownership and control of the means of production, capital, land, property, etc., by the community as a whole, and their administration or distribution in the interests of all.

Socialist (sǭ·ʃăl,ist). [f. SOCIAL *a.* + -IST.]

1. One who advocates or believes in the theory of socialism ; an adherent or supporter of socialism.

Socialistic (sǭʃăli·stik), *a.* [f. prec. + -IC.]

Sociality (sǭʃiæ·liti). [ad. L. *sociâlitas* (It. *socialità*), f. *sociâlis* : see SOCIAL *a.* and -ITY.]

Socialization (sǭʃăl,aizēiʃən). [f. next.]

Socialize (sǭ·ʃăl,aiz), *v.* [f. SOCIAL *a.* + -IZE.]

1. *trans.* To render social ; to make fit for living in society.

Socially (sǭ·ʃăli), *adv.* [f. SOCIAL *a.* + -LY.]

Socialness. [f. SOCIAL *a.* + -NESS.] Social quality or character ; = SOCIALITY.

Sociate (sǭ·ʃiēit), *sb.* rare⁻¹. [ad. L. *sociâtus*.] An associate or colleague ; a companion or comrade. Also *transf.*

Sociate (sǭ·ʃiēit), *v.* Obs. [ad. L. *sociât-*, *sociâre* to associate.]

Sociation (sǭʃiēiʃən). [ad. L. *sociâtiôn-em.*] Association, conjunction, union.

Sociative (sǭ·ʃiătiv), *a.* Gram. [ad. F. *sociatif*, -*ive* SOCIATE *v.* and -IVE.] Denoting or expressing association.

Societal (sǫsai·etăl), *a.* [f. SOCIETY + -AL.] Societary ; socialistic.

Societarian (sǫsaietēə·riăn), *a.* and *sb.* [f. SOCIETY + -ARIAN.]

Societary (sǫsai·etări), *a.* [f. SOCIETY + -ARY.] Of, pertaining to, concerned or dealing with, the nature of, society.

Societism (sǫsai·etiz'm). [f. SOCIETY + -ISM.] Combination in a society or societies.

Society (sǫsai·eti). Forms : 6 **societie**, **societye**, 6-7 **socyetye**, **society**. [ad. F. *société* (mod.F. *société*), = It. *società*, Sp. *sociedad*, Pg. *sociedade*, ad. L. *societâs*, *-âtem*, f. *socius*.]

I. Association with one's fellow men, esp. in a friendly or intimate manner ; companionship or fellowship. Also rarely of animals (1774).

Socinian, *a.* and *sb.* ... Latinized form of the Italian surname *Sozzini.* ...

Socinianism. ... The doctrines or special views of the Socinians.

Socinianize, *v.* ...

Socinize, *v.* ...

Socio-, combining form (from Greek analogies) ...

Sociologic, *a.* ... [ad. F. *sociologique* (Comte): see SOCIO- 2 and -LOGIC.]

Sociology ... [ad. F. *sociologie* (Comte): ad. SOCIO- 2 and -LOGY.] The science or study of the origin, history, and constitution of human society.

Socius (*sōuʃiəs*). [L.] An associate or colleague.

Sock, *sb.*[1] ...

Sock, *sb.*[2] ...

Sock, *sb.*[3] [? ellipt. for SOCK-LAMB.] A pet child or young animal.

Sock, *sb.*[4] slang. [Of obscure origin] ...

Sock, *sb.*[5] *rare*[-1]. Abbrev. of SOCKET.

Sock, *v.*[1] slang. [Of obscure origin.] ...

Sock, *v.*[2] *south-w. dial.* [Imitative.] ...

Socked, *ppl. a.* [SOCK *sb.*[1]] Wearing socks.

Socker. = SOCCER.

Socket, *sb.* ...

Socket, *v.* ...

Sockless, *a.* ...

Sockdolager (*spkdʒ'lādʒə*). *U.S. slang.* ...

Sockeye (*sp'kʌɪ*). Also **sock-eye**, **suck-eye**, etc. *Zool.* ... The blueback salmon or nerka.

Sock-lamb [f. SOCK *sb.*[3]] A lamb brought up by hand; a pet-lamb. Also *transf.*

Sockle, *v.* ...

Sockless, *a.* Without socks.

Socky (*sp'kɪ*), *a.* dial. [SOCK *sb.*[2]] Wet, moist, spongy.

Socle (*sōu'kl*, *sɒkl*). Also **6 socle**, **soccle**. ...

Socman (*sp'kmæn*). Also **6 sok-**, **7–9 sock-**. ...

Socome, **socoot** ...

Socratian, *a.*

Socratic, *a.* and *sb.* ...

Socratical, *a.* ...

Socratism. ...

Socratist (*sp'krætist*), *v.* ...

Socratize (*sp'krætʌɪz*), *v.* ...

Socome ...

Socotrine (*sp'kotrin*), *a.* and *sb.* ...

Sod, *sb.*[1] ...

Sod, *sb.*[2] ...

Sod, *ppl. a.* and *sb.* [pa. pple. of SEETHE *v.*] ...

Sod, *v.*[1] ...

Sod, *v.*[2] ...

Soda (*sōu'də*). ...

Soda-water. ...

Sodaic (*sōudeɪ'ik*), *a.* ...

Sodality (*sōudæ'lɪti*). ...
1. Association or confederation *with* others; brotherhood, companionship, fellowship.
2. An established society ... a Roman Catholic sodality or religious fraternity.

Sodamide (sō'dămaid), *Chem.* [f. SOD-a + AMIDE.] A substance, usually of a crystalline colour, formed by treating sodium with gaseous ammonia (cf. quots.).

Sodamite, obs. form of SODOMITE. **Sodan**, obs. f. SOUDAN. **Sodan**(ie, -ly, etc., obs. ff. SUDDEN(LY. **Sodar**, obs. f. SOLDER *sb.*[?] **Sodary**, obs. f. SODARY.

Soda-water. Also *soda water.* [SODA + WATER *sb.*]

1. Water containing a solution of sodium bicarbonate, or more generally, charged under pressure with carbon dioxide (carbonic acid gas), strongly effervescent, and used as a beverage or stimulant.

2. *attrib.*, as *soda-water apparatus*, *-bottle*, *-fountain*, etc.

Sodded, ppl. a. Covered with sod.

Sodden (sō'd'n), ppl. a. [See note below.] Boiled ; cooked or prepared by boiling.

1. Boiled ; cooked or prepared by boiling. Now *rare* or *Obs.*

2. Of persons, their features, etc. : Having the appearance of, or resembling, that which has been soaked or steeped in water.

b. Characterized by leavinness, dullness, or want of vivacity.

Sodden (sō'd'n), v. [f. prec.]

1. *trans.* To make sodden ; to soak, to saturate with water.

b. To render (the faculties) dull or stupid ; to deprive of vivacity or freshness.

Soddenness (sō'd'nnes), [f. SODDEN ppl. a.] Sodden state, quality, or condition.

Sodding, vbl. sb. [f. SOD v.[?]]

Soddy (sō'di), a. [f. SOD sb.[?] + -Y.]

Sode, obs. and dial. form of SEETHE.

Sodeless, obs. f. SODLESS.

Sodelich, obs. f. SUDDENLY.

Soder, obs. form of SOLDER.

Sodger, var. of SOLDIER.

Sodic (sō'dik), a. *Chem.* Of, containing, or composed of sodium.

Sodiate, obs. f. SODIATE.

Sodio- (sō'diō-), comb. form of SODIUM, denoting the presence of that substance or its salts, as *sodio-ammonic*, *-aurous*, *-hydric*, *-platinic* salts, *sodio-salicylate*.

Sodium (sō'diŏm). *Chem.* [mod.L., f. SODA.]

1. An elementary alkaline metal (isolated by Davy in 1807), forming the basis of SODA, closely resembling potassium in its appearance and properties, and occurring most commonly in the chloride (common salt). Symbol Na (for Natrium).

2. *attrib.* To become soaked or saturated with water or moisture ; to grow soft or rotten in this way.

b. Of a liquor : To soak *into* something.

Hence **So·dened** *ppl. a.*

Sodless (sō'dles), a. [f. SOD sb.[?] + -LESS.] Devoid of, not covered by, sods.

Sodom (sō'dom). [The name of the city beside the Dead Sea, the wickedness and destruction of which are recorded in Gen. xviii-xix.] The Hebrew form of the name is *Sĕdōm* ; the Sept. has *Sodoma*, the Vulg. *Sodoma*, neut. pl. and fem.

1. An extremely wicked or corrupt place.

b. A variety of cider-apple. *Obs.*

Sodomical (sōdom'ikăl), a. [f. SODOMY + -AL.]

Sodomist (sō'dŏmist). [f. SODOMY + -IST.]

So·domite (sō'dŏmaɪt). Forms : 4-6 sodomite, 4-6 sodomyt(e, 5 sodomit, -ighte, sodam-, sodamyte, 6-7 sodomite, -ite ; also 5 Sodomitte, 6-7 sodomit. [a. OF. *sodomite*, ad. L. *Sodomīta*, Gr. Σοδομίτης, f. Σόδομα SODOM.]

1. An inhabitant of Sodom.

2. One who practices or commits sodomy.

Sodomitic (sŏdŏmɪt'ik), a. [f. SODOMITE + -IC.]

Sodomitical (sŏdŏmɪt'ikăl), a. [f. prec. + -AL.]

Sodomy (sō'dŏmi). Forms : 3-5 sodomy, 4. 6-7 [etc.]. [a. OF. *sodomie*, f. *Sodome* SODOM.] An unnatural form of sexual intercourse, esp. that of one male with another.

Sofa (sō'fă). Also 7 *soph*, 7-9 sopha ; 8 sophee, sophy, 9 *vulg.* *softy*. [- F. *sofa*, *sopha*, It., Sp., and Pg. *sofa*, ad. Arab. [...]]

1. A long, stuffed seat with a back and ends or end, used for reclining ; a form of lounge or couch.

Sofaed (sō'făd), a. [f. prec. + -ED.]

Sofane, *v.* pertaining to a sofa (*mœce-tœl.*).

Sofee, variant of SUFI.

Sofi, var. of SOUFRISM.

Sofit, var. of SOFFIT.

Soffit (sō'fit). *Arch.* Forms : 8, 7-8 soffita, 8 soffito, 8 sophita, 8 soffite, 7-8 soffit, sofite, 8-9 softe, soffit, 8 sofit, S-softh (5 -softe), 8 sophi, 8 softie, masc., f. *soft-* (L. *sub*) under + *pa. pple. of* *figere* to fix. The later forms are prob. after F. *soffite*.] The horizontal face of an architrave or overhanging cornice ; the under surface of a lintel, vault, or arch ; a ceiling.

SOFAED. | 367 | **SOFT.**

1. In Eastern countries, a part of the floor raised a foot or two, covered with rich carpets and cushions, and used for sitting upon.

Soft (sŏft), a. [etc.]

1. That which is agreeable, pleasant, or easy ; comfort, ease, *rare*.

Soft (sŏft), a. Also 7 Sc., 8-9 softe, 8-9 Sc. and *north.* saft. [f. the adj.]

1. That which is agreeable, pleasant, or easy ; comfort, ease, *rare*.

2. That which is soft or yielding ; the soft part of something ; softness.

3. Pleasing to the eye ; free from ruggedness or asperity. Also of colour, or with reference to this : Not crude or glaring ; quiet, subdued.

4. Causing or involving little or no discomfort, hardship, or suffering ; easily endured or borne.

5. Phonetics, a soft or voiced consonant.

SOFT. | 368 | **SOFT.**

10. Of words, language, etc. : **a.** Ingratiating, soothing, bland ; complimentary.

b. *esp. in Phonetics.* (Opposed to HARD *a.* 16.)

c. Not crude or glaring ; quiet, subdued.

13. *advb.* Softly, gently ; quietly.

Supplement, p. 3873 ; Corrigenda, p. 4092 ; Spurious words, p. 4093 ; Books quoted, p. 4094

SOFTNESS.

c. Fair and softly: see FAIR adv. 7, and sense 10 below. (Cf. SOFT adv. 7.)

4. Quietly, silently, noiselessly; lightly.

5. In ease or comfort; so as to be soft or comfortable; luxuriously.

6. In a subdued manner.

7. In small quantity. *Obs. rare.*

8. Gradually, gently.

9. Mildly, gently.

10. Used interjectionally — See SOFT *adv.* 8.

11. *Comb.* with *ppl. adjs.*, as *softly-hinted*, *-shadowed*, *-sprighted*, etc.

b. With or in soft surroundings.

+ δ. With quiet resignation. *Obs.*

† 7. In small quantity. *Obs. rare.*

Softness.

I. 1. Ease, comfort; delicacy, luxury; easy or voluptuous living.

2. Mildness, gentleness; tenderness of character or disposition.

3. A display or instance of gentleness or tenderness; a soft word or speech.

4. Weakness of character or disposition, effeminacy; lack of firmness; timidity, pusillanimity.

II. 4. The state, quality, or property of being soft to the touch, of yielding to pressure, of lacking hardness, firmness, etc.

b. Smoothness, calmness. *Obs.*[-1]

c. Softness of the pulse, the state when the blood-tension is low, so that the artery feels soft and easily compressible.

d. The property or quality (in water, etc.) of being soft.

e. Gentleness, mildness (of air, weather, etc.); warmth.

5. Freedom from harshness; mellowness.

6. Mildness, faintness.

7. Absence of hard or sharp outlines.

Soft-sawder.

Soft-shell.

1. *attrib.* In the specific names of animals: Provided with a soft shell: = SOFT-SHELLED 1.

b. A soft-shelled lobster. *U.S.*

Soft-shelled, *a.* [SOFT *a.* 29.]

1. Having a soft shell. Chiefly in specific names of animals.

Soft soap, *vbl. sb.* soft-soap. [SOFT *a.*]

1. A smeary, semi-liquid soap, made with potash.

2. *transf.* (U.S. Soft-SHELL 2.)

Soft-soap, *v.* Also soft-soap. [f. prec.]

1. *trans.* To flatter; 'soft-sawder.' *slang.*

2. *intr.* To use soft soap.

Soft-soaping, *vbl. sb.*; *ppl. a.*

Soft-solder, *v.* [f. solder *sb.*]

To unite, mend, etc., with soft solder.

Hence **Soft-soldered** *ppl. a.*

Soft-sawder, *a.* Also *9 S. saft.* [f. *soft* + *sawder.*]

1. Of persons: Having, or speaking with, a soft or gentle voice; plausible, affable.

2. Of words: Spoken softly, gently, or affably; persuasive.

SOFT WOOD.

Soft-wood, soft-wood. [SOFT *a.*]

1. Wood which is relatively soft or easily cut.

b. Sap-wood, alburnum.

Soft-wooded, *a.* [Cf. prec.] Having relatively soft wood.

Softy (sŏˑfti), *a.* or *collog.* Also softie, *Sc.* safty, saftie. [f. SOFT *a.*] A weak-minded or silly person; a simpleton, noodle, gull.

† Soft-jern, *a.* *Obs.* [f. SOFT *a.* + YEARN *a.*] Desirous of ease or luxury. Also **† soft-jerne,** love of ease. *Obs.*

Sofyme, Sofyr, Sofyster, -try, Sofwyn, obs. variants SOPHIME, SUFFER *v.*, SOPHISTER, -TRY, SUFFICE *v.*

Sog (sŏg), *sb.*[1] Now *loc.* Also 6 sogge, *9 sog.* (Related to Soo *v.*) A soft or marshy piece of ground; a swamp, bog, quagmire.

Sog (sŏg), *sb.*[2] *dial. U.S.* Also 6 sogg. [Of obscure origin.] A drowsy or lethargic state; a sleep, doze, stupor.

Sog (sŏg), *v.* *dial.* and *U.S.* Also 6 sogge. [Of obscure origin: cf. SOO *sb.*] A soft or marshy piece of ground; a swamp, bog, quagmire.

b. Resulting from, caused by, moisture or wetness.

2. *trans.* To announce the discovery or starting of (a hare) by this shout.

Soi-disant (swadizǟ), *a.* [F., f. *soi* one-self + *disant,* pres. ppl. of *dire* to say.] Self-styled; would-be. (Usually with implication of pretence or deception.)

Soil (soil), *sb.*[1] Forms: 4 soyle (5 soyile), 5-7 soyl, 6 soile, 5-7 soile, 6 (Sc.) soyll, 5-7 soile, 6 soile. [a. AF. *soil, soyl* in sense 2 b (1292-1305), app. representing L. *solium* (whence also Cf. *solum* (F. *sol*) ground. For *Sc.* forms see also SULYIE.]

I. 1. The earth or ground; the face or surface of the earth.

b. The lower ground, the plain. *Obs.*[-1]

2. A place or stretch of ground; a place or site.

b. With pron. poss. or genitive. *Obs.*

4. The state of property. *Obs.*

3. A land or country; a region, province, or district. Now *Obs.* or *arch.*

4. One's land of nativity; one's (native) land or country.

Soil (soil), *sb.*[2] Forms: 3 sullen, 5 suyle, sule; 3-4 sullen, 4-7 soyle, 5-7 soile (5 sole); 6-7 soyl, 7- soil. [ad. OF. *suilller,* *souiller* etc. (mod.F. *souiller*).]

1. A miry or muddy place used by a wild boar for wallowing in. *Obs.*

2. A pool or stretch of water, used as a refuge by a hunted deer or other animal. Freq. in the phr. to go, or come, to soil; to take († the) soil.

b. (See quots.)

Soil (soil), *sb.*[3] Also 7 soyle, 6 soyl. 5-7 soile (Parly *a.* OF. *souille, souile* (mod. F. *souille*) fem., or *soil, souil, sueil.* (mod. dial. *sueil, sueuy),* vertical, *f. souiller* SOIL *v.*[1] in part directly from the vb.]

† 1. A miry or muddy place used by a wild boar for wallowing in. *Obs.*

2. A lintel of a door or window.

Soil (soil), *v.*[1] Forms: 4-7 soyle, 6 soyl(e, 4-7 soile, 5-6 soile, 4- soil. [ad. OF. *souiller,* *suiller* etc.]

1. *trans.* To defile or pollute with sin or other moral stain. Also *absol.*

2. *reflexive.* To defile oneself.

† 3. *refl.* To degrade oneself.

3. To resolve, clear up, expound, or explain; to answer (a question).

4. To refute (an argument or objection); to overcome by argument; to answer.

5. To make foul or dirty, esp. on the surface; to begrime, stain, tarnish.

6. *fig.* To sully or tarnish; to bring disgrace or discredit upon (a person or thing).

7. Filth and other matter usually carried off by drains; sewage.

8. Ordure, excrement; the dung of animals used as a compost; manure. Cf. also NIGHT-SOIL.

9. *attrib.* and *Comb.,* as *soil-carrier, -cab, -man; soil-pipe,* a sewage or waste-water pipe; *soil-tank* (see quot. 1851).

Soil (soil), *v.*[2] [f. SOIL *sb.*[3]] *trans.* To feed or fatten (cattle, etc.) on fresh-cut green fodder, originally for the purpose of purging; to feed up or fatten (fowls).

Soil, *v.*[3] rare. [f. SOIL *sb.*[2]] *trans.* To supply or treat (land) with dung or other fertilizing matter; to manure.

b. *fig.* To sully or tarnish; to bring disgrace or discredit.

Soign, Soigne (swāˑnyē), *a.* Now *local.* Also 7 soyl(e. [f. SOIL *sb.*[1]]

Soile (soil), *Cornish dial.* Also 7-9 soil, 6 soyle, 6 soyl(e. [An irregular local variation of SILE *sb.*[1] or *v.*] A kind of net.

34 The Soile or Sea Calf, a Creature that brings forth her young ones upon dry land. 1674 Ray Coll. Words, Fishes 107 On the Rocks near the Lands end they often find the Phocæ (which they call Soils) sleeping. Ibid., They distinguish between Soils and Sieles: the Siele they affirm to be a Fish..much less then the soile, and not taken upon our Coasts. 1758 Borlase Nat. Hist. Cornw. 284 Among the quadruped reptiles we may reckon the seal or sea-calf, vulgarly called in Cornwall the Soyle. a 1863 Tregellas Cornish Tales (1868) 61 Haling the soils up from the say. 1880 W. Cornwall Gloss. 53/1.

Soile, obs. Sc. form of Sole sb.1

Soiled (soild), ppl. a.1 Forms: 3 suiled, 6–7 soyled, 7 soild, 6– soiled. [f. Soil v.1] Defiled; stained, dirtied. Also fig.

a 1225 Ancr. R. 158 Ich am a man mid suilede lippen. 1530 Palsgr. 324/2 Soyled, ord. 1588 Kyd Househ. Phil. Wks. (1901) 272 In the Kitchin, or other soyled places which may spoile or ray her garments. 1590 Spenser F. Q. II. i. 41 Vpon the soiled gras The dead corse of an armed knight was spred. 1671 Milton Samson 123 In slavish habit, ill-fitted weeds O're worn and soild. 1693 Dryden, etc. Juvenal xv. (1697) 373 One..Licks the soil'd Earth,..While reeking with a mangled Ombite's Blood. 1815 J. Smith Panorama Sci. & Art II. 425 It may be conveniently used for whitening soiled books and prints. 1883 Thomas Mod. Housewife 22 That cracked mirror, spoiled carpet, and soiled sofa.

Comb. 1905 M. Barnes-Grundy Vacill. Hazel 59 A soiled-looking man turned the corner of the lane.

Soiled, ppl. a.2 rare. [f. Soil v.4] Fed with fresh-cut green fodder.

1605 Shaks. Lear iv. vi. 124 The Fitchew, nor the soyled Horse goes too't with a more riotous appetite. 1811 Monthly Mag. XXXIV. 393/1 The condition of the soiled cattle and milch cows, surprized even those most convinced of the advantage of the system.

Soiled, a. [f. Soil sb.1] Having a particular or specified kind of soil.

c 1645 Howell Lett. I. ii. xv. (1655) 89 The Province..is far greater, more populous, better soyld, and more stor'd with Gentry. 1799 [A. Young] Agric. Linc. 9 This sinks again into another part of the various soiled vale to the Wolds. 1815 M. Birkbeck Journ. thro' France 68 A surface..as fruitful as a well-soiled plain.

Soiler: see Free-soiler.

Soilie, variant of Sc. Sultie Obs.

Soi·liness. rare. [f. Soily a.1] The state or condition of being soiled; soiled or dirty matter.

a 1626 Bacon Physiol. Rem. in Baconiana (1679) 98 To make proof of the Incorporation of Silver and Tin,..and to observe..whether it yield no soiliness more than Silver? 1650 Fuller Pisgah ii. iv. iv. 70 Whether the Priests..made use thereof [sc. a laver] to discover all soiliness in them before they washed.

† **Soiling**, sb. Obs.—0 [app. for siling, f. Sile v.1 2.] (See quot.)

1573–80 Baret Alv., A Soiling, a great opening, or gaping of the earth, as it were a deepnesse without bottome.

Soiling (soi·liŋ), vbl. sb.1 [f. Soil v.1]

1. The action of making or becoming dirty, tarnished, or stained. Also fig.

1580 Hollyband Treas. Fr. Tong, Salissure, fouling, soyling. 1612 Brinsley Lud. Lit. iv. (1627) 29 To keepe their bookes from soyling, or marring under their hands. 1635–56 Cowley Davideis i. 871 Thus Souls live cleanly, and no Soiling fear. 1643 Milton Divorce ii. xix, Which ..is rather a soiling then a fulfilling of mariage-rites. 1809 Naval Chron. XXII. 277 To remove any soiling it might have received. 1892 Photogr. Ann. II. 530 Thus avoiding soiling of the glass.

2. spec. (See Soil v.1 5 and 6.) Also attrib.

1549 Coverdale, etc. Erasm. Par. 2 Peter II. 19 The sowe hath washed..in vayne, if she by and by after she is washen, returne to the soylinges that she had gone from. 1856 'Stonehenge' Brit. Rur. Sports 82/2 The deer's haunt is called his lair;..where he rolls, his soiling-pool. 1884 Jefferies Red Deer vi. 102 They have their regular 'soiling-pits'—watery places or shallow ponds. 1899 Westm. Gaz. 18 Aug. 3/1 'Soiling,' or taking water, less frequently results in throwing hounds off the scent.

† **Soi·ling**, vbl. sb.2 Obs. [f. Soil v.2]

1. Assoilment, absolution.

a 1300 Cursor M. 29535 Gain cursing gode all es be-warr, And if þou wat þou ert þair-in His soilling seke wit-vten blin. c 1380 Wyclif Wks. (1880) 481 Whanne þer soyling & þer bynding acordide wiþ god in heuene. c 1400 Apol. Loll. 67 Þerfor þe causis are to be peysid, and þan power of byndiug and soiling is to be vsid. 1529 More Suppl. Souls Wks. 290 Blessing and cursing, cytıng, suspending and soyling.

2. Solution, explanation, answering.

c 1380 Wyclif Sel. Wks. I. 386 Þanne he putte in dede soilyng of þis questioun. 1388 — Dan. iv. 3 Thei schulden schewe to me the soilyng of the dreem. c 1500 Three Priests Peblis in Pinkerton Sc. Poems (1792) I. 11 Desyrand for to wit the solyeing Of this questioun, this probleme, and this dout. c 1530 L. Cox Rhet. (1899) 64 Confutacion is the soilynge of suche argumentes as maye be induced agaynste our purpose. 1548 Geste Priv. Masse 113 The soylyng of these two last recited scryptures.

Soi·ling, vbl. sb.3 ? Obs. [f. Soil v.3]

1. The action of treating land with manure or compost; manuring, dunging.

1607 Norden Surv. Dial. iii. 112 Any Tin-mines,..Marle, or Chalke-pits, slimie or moorish earth, fit for soyling of land. 1665 Voy. E. India 362 Which..doth so enrich their Land, which they never force..by Soyling of it. 1696 J. Cary Ess. Coyn 28 Well manured Lands, whose plentiful Crops do soon repay the Charge of Soiling laid out on them.

2. Manure; droppings of animals.

1610 Folkingham Art Surv. i. x. 26 Plinie reports that Ashes are in such request for soylings neere vnto Po, that they burne their Horse-dung to make them. 1626 Bacon Natural Hist. § 666 That Powdring [sc. dust], when a Shower commeth, maketh a kinde of Soyling to the Tree. 1789 Trans. Soc. Arts I. 148 All of these, together with the subsequent soilings of the sheep, left the land in admirable condition.

Soi·ling, vbl. sb.4 [f. Soil v.4]

1. The action or practice of feeding horses, cows, etc., on fresh-cut green fodder, originally in order to cause purgation.

1607 Topsell Four-f. Beasts 330 For this purgation is most necessary for Horsses, which is called soyling, and ought to continue ten daies together, without any other meat. 1770 Pennant Brit. Zool. IV. 48 They [sc. Persian horses] are fed with chopped straw,..and instead of soiling, are fed with new-eared or green barley. 1799 Washington Writ. (1893) XIV. 225 For spring, summer, and autumn, it is expected, that soiling or them on green food..will enable them to perform their work. 1832 Scoresby Farm Rep. 27 in Husb. (L. U. K.) III, By the practice of soiling, an arable farm may be made to support as much live stock as a grazing one. 1893 Times 11 July 4/1 Oats put in [among rye] promptly would give food for soiling or cutting in the autumn.

attrib. 1840 Penny Cycl. XXII. 193/1 Those countries where the soiling system is most universally adopted.

2. dial. (See quot.)

a 1825 Forby Voc. E. Anglia, Soiling, the last fattening food given to fowls when they are taken up from the stack or barn-door, and cooped for a few days.

Soi·ling, vbl. sb.5 [f. Soil sb.1] The action of covering with soil. Also techn. (quot. 1876).

1794 Wedge View Agric. Cheshire 21 Soiling with the plough is thus performed:..the ground..is split, or turned both ways upon the young plants. 1876 Encycl. Brit. IV. 280/2 A thin layer of ashes..is spread over the surface [of the hardened malm in brick-making] (this process being technically called soiling).

Soiling (soi·liŋ), ppl. a.1 [f. Soil v.1] That stains or soils; polluting, defiling.

1812 Cary Dante, Purg. xxx. 52 To save My undew'd cheeks from blur of soiling tears. 1880 Clare Poems Rural Life (ed. 3) 120 From soiling dew the butter-cup Shuts his golden jewels up. 1876 Geo. Eliot Dan. Der. lxvii, Dreading the soiling inferences of his mind.

† **Soiling**, ppl. a.2 Obs.—1 [f. Soil v.2] Of the nature of a refutation; confuting.

c 1449 Pecock Repr. ii. xviii. 255 To make a cleer soiling answere to the xiijᵉ argument.

Soill, obs. Sc. variant of Sole v.1

† **Soillart.** Obs.—1 [f. Soil v.1] A name given to the hare.

13.. MS. Digby 86 fol. 168 b, He shal saien on oreisoun In þe worshipe of þe hare.., þe go-bi-dich, þe soillart.

Soille, obs. Sc. form of Sole sb.1

Soilless (soi·l,lės), a.1 [f. Soil sb.1] Destitute or devoid of soil or mould.

1828–32 in Webster (citing Bigsby). 1853 Jrnl. R. Agric. Soc. XIV. i. 19 The steep, rugged, and nearly soilless sides and crags of the limestone. 1865 Spratt Crete I. 20 A bared and almost soilless part of the mountain-face.

Soi·lless, a.2 [f. Soil sb.3] Free from soil or stain.

1868 Geo. Eliot Spanish Gypsy i. 61 As innocent as opening flowers,..soilless, beautiful.

† **Soi·lness**, var. of (or error for) Soiliness.

a 1626 Bacon Physiol. Rem. in Baconiana (1679) 95 It will be sweeter and cleaner than Brass alone, which yieldeth a smell or soilness.

Soil-pipe: see Soil sb.1 10 and Soil sb.3 9.

† **Soilth.** Obs.—1 [f. Soil v.1 + -th 1.] An act or instance of soiling or staining.

1581 Mulcaster Posit. xl. (1887) 225 At home spoiles, soilthes, twentie things, are nothing in the parentes..eye.

Soilure (soi·liŭı). Also 4, 7 soylure. [a. OF. soilleure (mod.F. souillure), f. soillier Soil v.1]

The currency of the word in the 19th cent. is prob. altogether due to the instance in Shakspere.

1. Soiling, sullying, staining.

1297 R. Glouc. (Rolls) 8501 Þe bodies hii gaderede & vorbarnde hom echon,..so þat hii were Wiþoute soylure in clannesse al out maisters þere. 1859 Tennyson Elaine 7 Elaine..Guarded the sacred shield.., Then fearing rust or soilure fashion'd for it A case of silk. 1893 J. K. Ingram De Imitatione Pref. p. viii, The writing has..suffered from friction or soilure.

b. fig. (Common in recent literary use.)

1606 Shaks. Tr. & Cr. iv. i. 56 He merits well to haue her, that doth seeke her, Not making any scruple of her soylure, With such a hell of paine. 1873 Alice Cary Last Poems 114 Soilure of sin..Cannot harm thy hand so pure. 1888 G. Gissing Life's Morning I. iii. 110 With minds disengaged from anxiety of casual soilure. 1890 W. Watson Poems (1906) I. 29 From soilure of ignoble touch Too grandly free.

2. A stain, blot, or blemish.

1829 Landor Imag. Conv. Wks. 1846 II. 235 He did not conduct him amid flowers and herbage, where a fall would have only been a soilure to our frail human nature. 1895 Zangwill The Master iii. viii, Why had people besmirched the Creation with soilures of cynicism.

Soily (soi·li), a.1 Also 6 soilly, 7 soylie. [f. Soil sb.3 or v.1]

† 1. Apt to soil or stain. Obs.

1575 Laneham Lett. (1871) 40 A substauns..nether so.. brittl to manure az stone, nor yet so soily in vse. Ibid. 50 Fayr alleyz..with sand, not light or to soft, or soilly by dust, but..pleasaunt too walk on. 1605 Willet Hexapla in Gen. 215 The goodly outward rine or skinne onely doeth keepe in the filthie soylie embers.

2. Of the nature or character of soil or tarnish.

1631 Fuller Joseph's Coat, David's Sin xxxii, So spots of sinne the writer's soule did staine, Whose soylie tincture did therein remaine. Ibid., David's Repentance iv, I desire His soylie sinnes with deluges to scoure.

3. Soiled, stained, dirty.

1631 W. B. Touchstone Gold & Silver Wares 36 When your Touch-stone is..foul or soily, it may be taken off, by wetting it. 1748 Richardson Clarissa VI. 151 Methinks ..you are a little soily, to what we have seen you. 1771 T. Hull Sir W. Harrington (1797) III. 214 White sprigg'd muslin,..now so soily, and hung in such a manner,..as made her indeed a strange figure. 1890 Pall Mall G. 13 Feb. 2/1 A case..in which are packed..three or four damp, hot, and soily figures.

Soily, a.2 Also 8 soiley. [f. Soil sb.1] Of the nature of soil; like that of soil or mould.

1747 Hooson Miner's Dict. Q 3, Veins Strick into this Rachill..in a confused manner, being throne into Joynts, but they are Soiley. 1878 Scribner's Mag. XVI. 684/2 Away they went, mare and man,..with a decided soily aroma following them.

Soilyie, variant of Sc. Sultie Obs.

† **Soind**, obs. variant of Schynd.

1774 G. Gifford in Low Orkney (1879) 143 Property transmitted by a Deed called a Soind bill. Ibid. 144 The disponer delivered the Soind bill to the purchaser.

Soiour, obs. f. Soldier. **Soiour(e, Soiowryn**, varr. Sojour sb. and v. Obs.

Soir, obs. Sc. f. Soar v., Sore a. and adv.

‖ **Soirée** (sware), sb. [F. soirée evening, evening party, f. soir evening:—L. sērum late hour, neut. of sērus late.] An evening party, gathering, or social meeting. (See also Swarry.)

1820 Lady Granville Lett. (1894) I. 190, I had a soirée last night. 1836 in Col. Hawker Diary (1893) II. 107 We had a regular merry soirée on board, and did not leave till past nine. 1856 Mrs. Browning Aur. Leigh iii. 391 For exhibition in my drawing-rooms On zoologic soirées. 1892 Photogr. Ann. II. 621 Friends' Photographic Society...A soirée is held each winter.

Hence **Soirée** v. trans., to entertain at an evening party or parties. Also **Soiréean** a., **Soiréety** (nonce-words).

1826 Lady Granville Lett. (1894) I. 397 It has been hard work to dine and soirée all the people. 1834 Jekyll Corr. (1894) 328 This bustle and the eternity of parliamentary sittings keep London in a state of interest and soiréety. 1853 Jerdan Autobiogr. IV. 71 To be in readiness for the reception of the soiréean guests.

Soirn, Soit, obs. Sc. ff. Sorn v., Suit sb.

‖ **Soixantine.** rare—1. [ad. F. soixantaine, f. soixante sixty.] A period of sixty days.

1722 De Foe Hist. Plague (1756) 235 Then a body may be capable to continue infected..not a Quarentine of Days only, but a Soixantine, not only 40 Days but 60 Days or longer.

'**Soize**, dial. form of Size sb.1

Sojar, obs. Sc. variant of Soldier sb.

Sojer, dial. or colloq. form of Soldier sb. and v.

Sojett, variant of Suget (subject) Obs.

† **Sojour**, sb. Obs. Also 4 soiur, 4–5 soiour(e; 5 suriourе. [a. OF. sojur, sujur, etc. (later sejor, sejour, mod.F. séjour Séjour), shortened form of sujurn Sojourn sb.] Sojourn.

13.. Sir Beues 3435 Þanne anon, wiþ oute soiur, A wente to þat emperur. 1338 R. Brunne Chron. (1810) 274 Þe Scottis þat were with inne..Þe Baliol suld þam wynne out of þat soioure. c 1375 Sc. Leg. Saints xxix. (Placidas) 721 In þe sammyne tyme, quhare his wif mad surioure. c 1400 Rom. Rose 4282 The which is shette there in the tour, Fulle longe to holde there sojour. c 1430 Lydg. Min. Poems (Percy Soc.) 246 Skarsly thre monethys he holdith heer sojour. c 1450 Merlin xxii. 398 The kynge Ban and the kynge Bohors were nothinge at soiour.

† **Sojour**, v. Obs. Also 4 soioure, -en, 5 soi(o)wryn. [ad. OF. sojur-, shortened stem of sojurner Sojourn v.] intr. To sojourn.

c 1330 Arth. & Merl. 7269 (Kölbing), Lete we hem here soiouringe & speke of þe oþer kinge. c 1380 Wyclif Wks. (1880) 129 But lordis, & ladies namely, schullen soiouren amongis hem many ȝeris. a 1400 R. Brunne's Chron. Wace (Rolls) 4183 (Petyt MS.), Long ne wald he soioure ne rest. 1593 Bilson Govt. Christ's Ch. 7 Isaac and Jacob sojoured as strangers and peregrines in the land of Canaan.

† **Sojourant.** Obs.—0 = Sojournant.

1499 Promp. Parv. (Pynson) P ij b, Soioraunt.

Sojourn (sɒ·-, sɒ·-, sɒᵘ·dʒəɪn), sb. Forms: α. 3 surgerun, suriurn, 3–4 suriuren. β. 4 soiorn(e, 4, 7 soiourn(e, 5 soiurne, sojorne, 7– sojourn. γ. Sc. 5 su(d)ierne, 6 su(d)georne. [a. OF. surjurn, sujurn, sojorn, etc. (= It. soggiorno, Pg. and obs. Sp. sojorno), vbl. sb. from surjurner, etc.: see Sojourn v.

The stressing sojou·rn occasionally appears in poetry.]

1. A temporary stay at a place.

α. c 1250 Gen. & Ex. 2696 Ðoȝ was him ðat surgerun ful loð. Ibid. 3308 He maden siðen, fro elim, Mani suriuren in ðe desert sin.

β. 13.. Guy Warw. (A.) 2770 Anon after þe tende day Of her soiourn..Gij is to þe douke y-go. 1375 Barbour Bruce vii. 385 That he to Carleill than wald ga, And a quhill thar-in soiorn ma. c 1410 Master of Game (MS. Digby 182) xii, In longe soiourne þei leseth hir clees and hir feet. 1459 Rolls of Parlt. V. 363/1 The seid Prince shuld be in sojorne with the Kyng. 1605 Shaks. Lear i. i. 48 The Princes, France & Burgundy,..Long in our Court haue made their amorous soiourne. 1671 Milton P. R. iii. 235 Scarce view'd the Gallilean Towns, And once a year Jerusalem, few days Short sojourn. 1814 Wordsw. Laodamia 78 Meekly mourn When I depart, for brief is my sojourn. 1839 Thirlwall Greece VI. lii. 276 Here..he made a sojourn of sixty days.

1867 Freeman Norm. Conq. (1877) I. 215 The Normans were tired of Lewis's prolonged sojourn.

fig. 1804 H. K. White in Rem. (1825) 270 Your friend, and fellow-traveller in the Tearful sojourn of life.

γ. 1375 Barbour Bruce xx. 356 A weill gret sudiorne thair he mad. c 1375 Sc. Leg. Saints l. (Katherine) 4 He..to þe cite was cumyne,..& suiorne mad. 1528 Lyndesay Dreme 359 In tyll ane volt, abone that place of paine, Vnto the quhilk, but sudgeorne, we ascendit.

† b. A delay; a digression. Obs.

c 1330 Arth. & Merl. 6977 (Kölbing), Lete we now be þis soiourne & speke we of Oriens wroþ. 1508 Dunbar Tua Mariit Wemen 176 Wes neuer sugeorne wer [= worse] set na on that snaill tyrit.

2. A place of temporary stay. Also fig.

c 1350 Will. Palerne 3155 He..wasteþ al my londes, saue onliche in þis cite where soiourne wot i neuer. a 1400 Minor Poems fr. Vernon MS. xxviii. 23 Heil soiourne þat Godus sone to sent. 1423 Jas. I Kingis Q. cxiii, There as hir duelling is and hir soiurne. 1667 Milton P. L. iii. 15 Thee I re-visit now.., Escap't the Stygian Pool, though long detain'd In that obscure sojourn. 1768 Beattie Minstr. i. xxvi, Let those deplore their doom, Whose hope still grovels in this dark sojourn. 1810 Southey Kehama xxii. iv, This gloomy bourne, The dread sojourn Of Guilt and twin-born Punishment and Woe. 1858 Rawlinson tr. Herodotus ii. cxxxiii. II. 210 Visiting all the places that he had heard were agreeable sojourns.

Sojourn (sɒ·-, sɒ·-, sɒᵘ·dʒəɪn), v. Forms: α. 3 soriourni, 6 sourgorne. β. 3–4 soiorni, 4–6 soi-, sojorne (6 -eorne), sui-, sujorn(e; 3 soiourny, 3–7 soi-, sojourne (5 souj-), 4–5 soiurne, 4– sojourn. γ. 4 suggeorne, 5 -eourne, 5–6 sogeourn(e; 5 suggourne, sugiorne; 4 sugerne, 6 suggerne. δ. 5–6 sudiorn(e, 6 sudjourne, sudgeorne; 5–6 sudgern(e. [ad. OF. surjurner, sorjorner, and sujurner, sojorner, -journer (also sejorner, -journer, mod.F. séjourner) in the same sense. The forms in su-, so-, like It. soggiornare, represent a pop. L. *subdiurnāre (cf. med.L. subjornare, subjurnare), f. diurnum daily, day; those in sur-, sor- either represent a form with super- (cf. med.L. superdiurnare) or have been assimilated to other words with this prefix.]

1. intr. To make a temporary stay in a place; to remain or reside for a time.

α. c 1290 S. Eng. Leg. I. 147 To þe grete Abbeie to pountenie forto soriourni þere, he sende þis holi Man. 1513 Fabyan Chron. vi. cciv. (1811) 214 Whanne kynge Edmunde hadde a season sourgoyned [sic] at London, he than made towarde the Danys.

β. c 1290 S. Eng. Leg. I. 114 Þe king wende in-to Normandie for-to soiorni þere. a 1300 Cursor M. 3771 Sco send him son in-til aran,..Þar-to suiorn for hir sake. c 1340 Hampole Pr. Consc. 1374 For als gestes we here soiourne Awhile, til we sal hethen tourne. c 1430 Lydg. Min. Poems (Percy Soc.) 156 Whan watry Phebus had his purpoos take For a sesoun to sojourne in Aquarye. 1470–85 Malory Arthur iv. xix. 143 They soiourned there a vij nyghte. 1555 Eden Decades (Arb.) 133 Valladoleto where we nowe suiorne. 1582 Stanyhurst Æneis iii. (Arb.) 81 There we dyd al soiourne two dayes. 1641 J. Jackson True Evang. T. iii. 201 All the Papists which inhabited, or sojourned within the said limits. 1732 Lediard Sethos II. vii. 122 He desir'd leave to sojourn a month. 1781 Cowper Conversat. 530 The night, they said, is near, We must not now be parted, sojourn here. 1834 Lytton Pompeii i. ii, Several months ago I was sojourning at Neapolis. 1865 Trollope Belton Est. xiv, He was sojourning at an hotel in Bond Street.

refl. 1338 R. Brunne Chron. (1810) 3 The Englis kynges turned, þei mot do nomore, Bot soiorned þam a while in rest at Bangore.

γ. c 1325 Orfeo 47 Orpheo sugerneth in Crassens, That is a cyte of noble defens. c 1400 Maundev. (Roxb.) xxx. 136 Þare he suggeournes when him list. c 1440 Generydes 572 Lenger ther he thought not to sogeourne. 1530 Rastell Bk. Purgat. ii. xx. 4, I was in dyvers cytees..longe tyme abydyng and suggernyng. 1535 Coverdale Ezek. xiv. 7 A straunger, that sogeourneth in Israel.

δ. 1375 Barbour Bruce xvi. 47 Thai sudiornyt thair dayis thre In gret myrth and in rialte. 1470–85 Malory Arthur v. xii. 182 He..sudgerned there a tyme. 1513 Douglas Æneid xiii. xi. 80 Indigites, quhilk is als mekill to say As God induellar at thar sudiornis ay.

b. transf. or fig. of things.

c 1366 Chaucer A. B. C. 160 Vn-to þat court þou me aioune,..þer as þat merci euere shal soiourne. 1587 Turberv. Trag. Tales (1837) 26 Thus divers thoughts did sojourne in his brest. 1593 Drayton Ecl. vi. 13 Mirth is farre away, Nor may it soiourne with sad discontent. 1796 Kirwan Elem. Min. (ed. 2) I. 206 Iron in its metallic state, sojourning with water always extricates inflammable air.

† c. To be a lodger in another's house. Obs.

1573 Tusser Husb. (1878) 19 Once charged with children, or likelie to bee, giue ouer to sudgerne, that thinkest to thee.

† 2. To make stay; to tarry, delay. Obs.

1377 Langl. P. Pl. B. xvii. 83 Whan I seyȝ þis, I soiourned nouȝte but shope me to renne. 1412–20 Lydg. Chron. Troy i. 89, I wil no longer make digressioun, Nor in fables no more as now soiourne. c 1477 Caxton Jason 36 b, Hit behoueth no lenger to soiourne, for ye muste go or sende unto him with alle diligence. 1594 Dr. Faustus in Thoms E. Eng. Prose Rom. (1858) III. 403 Because the matter was as strange as true I have sojourned a little too long in it.

† 3. trans. To lodge; to rest or quarter (horses); to have as a lodger. Also transf. Obs.

1390 Gower Conf. III. 41 Whan thei weren thus sojorned,..Nero..The men let come in his presence. Ibid. 94 And ek it [i.e. rain] may be so sojorned In sondri places up alofte, That into hail it torneth ofte. ? a 1400 Morte Arth. 153 For-thi salle thow lenge here,..This seuenyghte in solace, to suggourne ȝour horses. 1424 Sc. Acts, Jas. I (1814) II. 4/1 Þe kyng forbiddis þat ony cumpanyis..thig or soiorne hors..on kirkmen. 1631 Archdeaconry of Essex Minute-bk. fol. 199 b, Enterteyninge and soiourninge in his howse..a fellowe verie negligent in cominge to divine service. 1690 Wood Life 30 April, [They] are sojourned there by one Thomson for 10s. a week each.

† 4. intr. To travel, journey. Obs.—1

1608 Sir J. Harrington in Nugæ Ant. (1804) I. 381, I did once relate to your Highnesse after what sorte his tacklinge was, wherewithe he did sojourn from my house at the Bathe to Greenwiche Palace.

Hence **So·journing** ppl. a.

1645 J. Bond Occasus Occid. 19 Sarah..the Patriarchesse, who willingly followed her sojourning husband up and downe in strange Countries. a 1684 Leighton Comm. 1 Peter Wks. (1868) 50 It continues all the time of this sojourning life.

† **Sojournant**, sb. and a. Obs. Forms: 5 sojournaunt(e, -nante, soiur-, sojornaunt, 6 sudjournente. [a. OF. sojournant, etc., pres. pple. of sojourner Sojourn v.]

A. sb. A sojourner; a visitor or guest.

c 1400 Plowman's Tale in Pol. Poems (Rolls) I. 327 Alas! the devill hath cleane hem blent, Soche one is Sathanas sojournaunt. 1477 Rolls of Parlt. VI. 186/2 The abiders and sojournantes of the same [town]. 1478 Paston Lett. III. 219 Your doughter of Sweynsthorpp and hyr sojournant E. Paston recomandyth hem to yow. 1536 in Lett. Suppress. Monasteries (Camden) 140 The gentlemens children and sudjournentes that ther doo lif.

B. adj. Sojourning; residing for a time.

1439 in Dugdale Monasticon (1823) IV. 553/2 Admitte noone sojournauntes wymment with owte lycence of us. 1546 Bale Eng. Votaries i. 63 The Chronycles all agre..that she was no nonne but a wenche soiornaunt in the nondrye.

Sojourner (sɒ·-, sɒ·-, sɒᵘ·dʒəɪnəɪ). Forms: 5 sogorner, 5–6 soiorner, 6–7 soiourner, 6– sojourner, 7 sojourno(u)r. [f. Sojourn v. + -er 1.]

1. One who sojourns; a temporary resident.

14.. Nom. in Wr.-Wülcker 689 Hic perhendinator, a sogorner. 1483 Cath. Angl. 348/2 A soiorner, perhendinator. 1535 Coverdale Lev. xxv. 40 As an hyred seruaunte and as a soiourner shal he be with the. 1539 Bible (Great) 1 Chron. xxix. 15 We be but straungers before the, and sogeourners, as were all oure fathers. 1605 Bacon Adv. Learn. ii. To King § 1 Queene Elizabeth was a soiourner in the world in respect of her vnmarried life. 1662 Act 14 Chas. II, c. xii. § 1 A native Householder, Sojourner, Apprentice, or Servant. 1756–7 tr. Keysler's Trav. (1760) III. 113 Whoe'er thou art, a native, foreigner, or sojourner. 1836 Lane Mod. Egypt. I. vi. 193, I replied that, being merely a sojourner in Egypt, I did not like..to take a wife. 1870 R. Anderson Missions Amer. Board III. 422 They were residents and not sojourners.

transf. 1803 Med. Jrnl. IX. 157 The Scarlet Fever and Sore Throat, which has for some time been an unwelcome sojourner in our neighbourhood.

2. A guest or lodger; a visitor.

1608 Shaks. Per. iv. ii. 149 Report what a sojourner we have. 1623 Middleton Women beware Women ii. ii. 176 We've no strangers, woman, None but my sojourners and I. 1660 Blount Boscobel i. 25 Mr. John Huddleston (a sojourner at Mr. Thomas Whitgreaves).

† b. A boarder living in a house, school, or college, for the purpose of receiving instruction.

a 1629 Hinde J. Bruen xxxvi. (1641) 114 [He] was very desirous to place them both as sojourners for a season in this gentlemans house. c 1672 Wood Life (O. H. S.) I. 108 Having..obtained a comfortable estate by the great pains he took in pedagogie, and by the many sojournours that he alwaies kept in his house. 1691 — Ath. Oxon. I. 13 He [Grocyn] became a Sojournor in Exeter Coll. 1765 Gentl. Mag. LV. i. 13 From thence to Oxford, where he [F. Nicholls] was admitted a commoner (or sojourner) of Exeter College [in 1714].

† **Sojourness.** Obs. rare. In 6 sojornesse. [f. as prec. + -ess 1.] A female sojourner.

1587 Turberv. Trag. Tales (1837) 120 That through three months, this Ladie hath been sojornesse with me.

† **Sojourney**, v. Obs. rare. [Alteration of Sojourn v., after journey.] intr. To sojourn.

1657 W. Rand tr. Gassendi's Life Peiresc ii. 170 Both of us sojourneyed with him at that very time. 1674 Marsden in W. Wilson Hist. Dissent. Ch. (1808) II. 466 O my soul, what a sojourneying state hath thy life been.

Sojourning (sɒ·-, sɒ·-, sɒᵘ·dʒəɪniŋ), vbl. sb. [f. Sojourn v. + -ing 1.]

1. The action or fact of staying temporarily in a place.

c 1290 S. Eng. Leg. I. 151 Þare he bi-lefde in soiourninge al þe ȝwile þat he wolde. 1375 Barbour Bruce iii. 386 He thocht he to Kyntyr wald ga, And swa lang soiowrnyng thar ma, Till wyntir weddir war away. c 1477 Caxton Jason 9 b, Peleus on the morne callid Jason and sayd that their long sojournyng displaisid him. 1528 Lyndesay Dreme 470 This Iupiter, withouttin sudgeornyng, Passis throw all the twelf planetis, full ewin, In ȝeris twelf. 1571 Golding Calvin on Ps. lxix. 35 Quiete continewance is matched ageinste soieorninge for a tyme. 1611 Bible Gen. xxviii. 4 The lande wherein thou art a stranger [marg. of thy soiournings]. 1701 Stanhope St. Augustine's Medit. iii. iv. 251 Let my present sojourning tend ever to thee.

† b. A place of temporary stay. Obs.—1

13.. K. Alis. 5209 (Laud MS.), Þennes hij wenten wiþouten duellyng, And souȝtten better soiournyng.

c. The time of temporary stay.

1611 Bible Exod. xii. 40 Now the soiourning of the children of Israel, who dwelt in Egypt, was foure hundred and thirtie yeeres. 1782 V. Knox Ess. cxliv. (1819) III. 131 Unfortunate boy [Chatterton]! poorly wast thou accommodated during thy short sojourning among us. 1825 Horne Introd. Script. (ed. 5) III. ii. i. 80 During the sojourning of the Israelites in the wilderness, Moses established [etc.].

† 2. Delay, respite. Obs. rare.

1375 Barbour Bruce i. 96 Haid ȝe tane keip how at that king Alwayis, for-owtyn soiournyng, Trawayllyt for to wyn senȝhory. c 1400 Laud Troy Bk. 6022 Gregeis were fayn of that grauntyng [of truce], For thei hadde nede of soiornyng.

Sojournment (sɒ·-, sɒ·-, sɒᵘ·dʒəɪnmĕnt). [ad. F. séjournement (OF. sojorne-, sujurnement), after Sojourn v.] The action of sojourning; a temporary stay.

a 1700 Evelyn Diary 2 May 1644, Tours, where we were design'd for the rest of the time I had resolv'd to stay in France, the sojournment being so agreeable. 1756 Amory Buncle (1770) I. 73 Was it possible for Abraham, during his temporary sojournments among them,..to persuade so many tribes to quit their dialect. 1819 Metropolis II. 239 After a sojournment of two months, she continued her route towards Paris. 1853 J. H. Newman Hist. Sk. Ser. ii. i. i. (1873) 7 A constant motive for them to seek out..places of sojournment elsewhere.

transf. 1756 C. Lucas Ess. Waters III. 178 Mercury.. makes a longer sojournment in the body than is generally judged. 1794 R. J. Sulivan View Nat. II. 169 The sea announces every where, its different sojournments.

Sokare, obs. form of Sucker.

Soke 1 (sōᵘk). Now chiefly Hist. Also 4 sok, 6–7 soake, 7–9 soak. [ad. med.L. soca, ad. OE. sócn Soken.]

1. A right of local jurisdiction; = Soc 1, Soken 3.

[a 1086 Domesday Bk. I. 225 b/2 Gitda tenuit cum saca & soca. Ibid. VI. 275/2 Abbas clamat socam huius ville. 1114–8 Laws Hen. I, ix. 11 (Liebermann), Soca..alia pertinet baronibus socam et sacam habentibus.]

1598 Stow Surv. 36, I..will and command, that they shall inioy the same well and quietly and honourably with sake and soke [etc.]. 1720 Strype Stow's Surv. ii. 12 My [i. e. King Stephen's] Demains with Sake, and Soke, and Toll, and Theam. 1809 Bawden tr. Domesday Bk. 460 Half a carucate of land..with sac and soke. 1859 C. Barker Associative Principle i. 27 Manorial privileges, such as soke, stallage, or tolls of markets and fairs.

2. A district under a particular jurisdiction; a local division of a minor character.

[a 1086 Domesday Bk. I. 324 Ad hoc manerium pertinet soca haec. 1147–50 Reg. de Dunfermelyn (Bann. Cl.) 8 Donauit..eidem capelle decimas dominiorum suorum in soca de Striuelin. 1200 Rot. Chart. (1837) 38/1 Do..decem libratis terre in soka nostra de Eyllesham.]

α. c 1350 in Eng. Gilds (1870) 350 To don here Offys al-so wel in þe sok as in þe Citee a-fore y-seyd. 1442 Rolls of Parlt. V. 58/2 The Maner of Snayth, and the Soke of Snayth, in the Schire of Yorke. 1482 Ibid. VI. 200/2 Within the said Cite, the Soke of the same, and the Shere of such or any of them. 1540 Act 32 Hen. VIII, c. 15 Dioceses..ben deuided into seuerall riddinges, wapentakes, and sokes. 1627 Speed England xxviii. § 7 It [Somersham] is the head of those fiue Townes, of which the Soke is composed. 1679 Blount Anc. Tenures 9 Coningsburg in Yorkshire..had twenty eight Towns and hamlets within its soke. 1766 Entick London IV. 305 Certain burgesses.. gave to the..church..all the lands and soke, called.. Knighten Guild. 1799 [A. Young] Agric. Lincoln. 231 A difference in the rights between the Soke of Bolingbroke and Holland Town, have hitherto protracted the proceeding. 1833 Rep. Comm. Municipal Corporations 333 Is it the practice to charge the Soke of Grantham with the maintenance of prisoners? 1873 J. Lewis Census 1871, 174 Lincolnshire..comprises 31 wapentakes, hundreds, liberties and sokes. 1884 Encycl. Brit. XVII. 556/2 The liberty or soke of Peterborough.

β. 1591 Fletcher Russe Commw. (Hakl. Soc.) 50 An ordinarie rent of money imposed upon everie soake or hundred within the whole realme. 1613 in Scott. Hist. Rev. Oct. (1910) 12 Being about to take a lease of the soake of Horncastle. 1704 Lond. Gaz. No. 4067/2 Your Majesty's ancient Borough and Soak of Doncaster.

3. (See quot. 1788 and Soken 2 b.)

1609 in Act 5 Geo. III, c. 26 Preamble, Suits, sokes, multures, and also all and singular profits. 1638 Slingsby Diary (1836) 22 Yᵉ Mills were worth a great deal more if they had had yᵉ same soak, which..they had, but now yᵉ soak is bought and sold. 1788 W. H. Marshall Yorksh. II. 354 Soke (vulg. sooac), an exclusive privilege claimed by a mill, for grinding all the corn which is used within the manor or township it stands in.

4. attrib., as soke-fee, -land, -mill, -reeve.

c 1290 Fleta ii. lv. (1647) 119 Quod fieri potest per Sokereves eorum in bustengo. 1741 T. Robinson Gavelkind v. 85 A Man seised of Land in Soke-Fee. 1858 Hogg Shelley II. x. 345 The proprietor of a large soke-mill. 1882 Elton Orig. Eng. Hist. 192 In some places..there are two kinds of copyhold land, the one called 'Bond-land' and the other 'Soke-land'. 1893 Baring-Gould Cheap Jack Zita II. 46 You send a sack of corn to the soak-mill, and you get back half a sack of flour.

† **Soke** 2. Obs.—1 = Sock sb.2 1.

The passage is translated from Littleton (ii. v. § 119), who says above 'soca idem est quod caruca, s. vn soke ou vn charue': cf. the note on Socage.

1661 J. Stephens Procurations 47 A great part of those Tenants which held of their Lords by Socage, did come with their Sokes (their Ploughs) certain dayes in the year to plough and sow the Demesnes of the Lord.

Soke, obs. form of Soak v., Suck v.

Sokel, obs. form of Suckle.

Sokelyng(e, obs. forms of Suckling.

Sokeman (sōᵘ·kmăn). Now Hist. Also 6–7 erron. -mayn. -main. [a. AF. sokeman or ad. Anglo-Lat. sokemannus (also sok-, socke-, sochemannus), f. the OE. word represented by Soke 1 and Soken + Man sb.1] A tenant holding land in socage; a socman.

[a 1066 Laws Edw. Confess. xii. (Thorpe), Manbote in Danelaxa, de vilano et socheman xii oras. a 1086 Domesday Bk. I. 273/2 Ibi apposuit Rex W. sex sochemanos pertinentes at Rapendune. 1235–59 Bracton ii. xxxv. (Rolls) I. 614 Tenentes, qui tenent sockagio, sockemanni dici poterunt. Ibid. iv. xxviii. III. 378 Et hujusmodi villani sokmanni, proprie dicuntur glebæ ascriptitii. c 1290 Britton (1865) II. 13 Ceux sount proprement nos sokemans et privelegez en ceste manere. 1367 in Vinogradoff Villainage in Eng. (1892) 116 note, Teux services comme gents de petits sokemans fierent en auncien temps. a 1399 Ibid. 91 note, Item sokemanni predicti filias suas non possunt maritare sine licencia domini. 1413 14 Hen. IV, f 34 in Year Book (1605) Hhh vj, Et auxy il ad diuersitie parenter sokeman de franktenure, et sokeman de base tenure. 1567 Fitzherbert Nat. Brev. 14 Quar les tenantz en auncien demesne sont appelles Sokemans, s. tenants del carue, anglice, le plough. 1581 Kitchin Court Leet 87 b, Mes est diuersitie enter Sokemaynes de franke tenure, et sokemaines de base tenure.]

1603 Stow Surv. vii. 64 The said Robert [Fitzwalter] ought to haue a sokeman. 1607 Norden Surv. Dial. iii. 100 There is also a copy-hold estate, called ancient demeisne, and the tenants, Sokemains. 1614 Selden Titles Honor 334 Sokemans were but Tenants in socage. 1749 Pote Hist. Windsor Castle 2 Together with fourteen sokemen and their lands. 1766 Blackstone Comm. II. 87 The statute 28 Edw. I. c. 1. declares, that a free sokeman shall give no relief. 1839 Penny Cycl. XIII. 245/2 No one was to be distrained..on account of land which he held in manors of the antient demesne of the crown as a sokeman. 1897 Maitland Domesday Bk. 142 The sokeman's hide or virgate..is composed of many scattered strips.

b. attrib. in † sokeman-mote.

13.. Rotuli Hundredorum (1818) II. 143/1 Item dicunt quod Ermoldus de Boys..solebat facere sectam ad Boxford ad sockemanemot pro terra Ricardi Serle.

Sokemanry (sōᵘ·kmănri). Now Hist. [ad. AF. sokemanerie or Anglo-Lat. sokemanria: see prec. and -ry.] The tenure of land by a sokeman; also, the sokemen collectively.

[c 1290 Britton (1865) II. 11 Sokemaneries sount terres et tenementz, qe ne sount mie tenuz par fee de chevaler, ne par graunt serjaunties, ne par petites, mes par simples services. a 1399 in Vinogradoff Villainage in Eng. (1892) 116 note, Quidam tenentes eiusdem manerii tenent terras et tenementa sua in sokemanria.] 1603 Stow Surv. vii. 64 What sokeman he will, so he be of the sokemanrie. 1679 Blount Anc. Tenures 119 If any of the Sokemanry shall be impleaded. 1766 Blackstone Comm. II. vi. 100 Britton also, from such their freedom, calls..their tenure sokemanries. 1865 Nichols Britton II. 5 note, Burgages and sokemanries are changed for such villenages into free tenure. 1896 Pearman Manor of Bensington 38 There were about forty four sokemanries.

Soken (sōᵘ·k'n). Now Hist. Forms: 1 (9) socn, 3 socne, sockne, 6 socon(e; 4 so(o)kne, sokene, 5 sokyn, 5– soken. [OE. sócn, = ON. and Icel. sókn (Norw. sokn; Sw. socken, Da. sogn parish), Goth. sôkns search, enquiry (cf. OHG. sôhni), f. sôk- stem of OE. sécan, ON. sœkja, etc., to Seek. See also the comb. Church-soken.]

† 1. An attack or assault. Obs. rare.

Beowulf 1777 Ic þære socne singales wæg modceare micle.

† 2. Resort to, or visiting of, a place; habitual going or haunting. Obs.

c 1000 Ælfric Hom. II. 508 Ða towende se biscop þæt weofod, and þa dwollican socne mid-ealle adwæscte. a 1023 Wulfstan Hom. (1883) 134 We..ure synna..georne betan mid..ælmessan & mid ciriclicere socne. c 1205 Lay. 2365 Þat inne swiðe feire stude from socne þes folkes. c 1290 S. Eng. Leg. I. 261 Heo þouȝte, for heo was so i-knowe,.. Þe lasse sockne heo hadde [= would have] of hire folie. c 1440 Promp. Parv. 463/2 Sookne, or custome of hauntynge.., frequentacio, concursus.

† b. spec. Resort of tenants or others to a particular mill to have their corn ground; the right of the mill to such custom. (Cf. Soke 1 3.) Obs.

c 1386 Chaucer Reeve's T. 67 Gret soken hath this meller, out of doute, With whete and malt, of al the lond aboute. 1523 Fitzherb. Surv. 9 b, That maner of gryndyng is called loue Socone, and the lordes tenauntes be called bonde socon. 1591 Knaresborough Wills (Surtees) I. 175 Dareley myIne, with the soken and suite there to belonginge.

† 3. Right of prosecution, legal investigation, or jurisdiction. Cf. Soke 1 1. Obs.

a 1023 Laws of Æthelred iii. xi, Nan man naȝe nane socne ofer cynges þegen buton cyng sylf. a 1066 in Kemble Codex Dipl. IV. 200 Swa ðæt nan scyrgerefe oððe motgerefe ðar habban æni socne oððe gemot buton ðes abbudes agen hæse. [1114–8 Laws Hen. I, xix. 2 (Liebermann), Omnium terrarum, quas rex in dominio suo habet, socnam pariter habet.] 1155 in Anglia VII. 220 Þæt ic hæbbe heom ȝeunnon..saca & socne..ofer heore aȝene men.

† b. (See quot.) Obs.—1

1387 Trevisa Higden (Rolls) II. 95 Soka, sute of court, and þerof comeþ Sokene, but Sokene oþerwhile is forto aske lawe in þe gretter court.

4. = Soke 1 2.

c 1030 in Eng. Hist. Rev. (1912) Jan. 15 Ðis is seo socn into Scyre-burna, mid folc-rihte. [c 1133–54 Libertas Lond. 4 Donec custos illius socne, in qua manserit, de recto tenendo uicecomiti defecerit.] 1362 Langl. P. Pl. A. ii. 78 Rondulf þe Reue of Rotelondes sokene. 1393 Ibid. C. iii. 111 Bette þe budele of banneburies sokne. 1465 Paston Lett. II. 204 Yt ys told me that ȝong Heydon reysyth mych pepyl in the sokyn. 1485 Rolls of Parlt. VI. 284/1 The Castell, Mannor and Lordshipp of Kimbalton, with the Sokyn of the same. 1601 Holland Pliny I. 535 About Venice and all that tract, the Willowes serue the turne and none else, by reason that the whole soken standeth so much vpon water. a 1670 in Blount Law Dict. s.v. Rime, In the Countrey hard was we That in our Soken shrews should be. 1861 Hook Lives Abps. I. v. 245 By his right of lord of the socn he could try and execute thieves found upon any of his estates. 1874 Stubbs Const. Hist. (1875) I. v. 80 The lord of a soken and patron of hundreds of servants and followers.

Soken, obs. f. pa. pple. Soak v.; var. Soaken v. Obs. **Soker**, obs. form of Soaker. **Sokere, Sokerel**, obs. ff. Sucker, Suckerel. **Soket**, obs. f. Socket sb.; var. Sucket Obs. **Sokey**: see Water sokey. **Sokil blome**: see Suckle-bloom. **Sokkat**, obs. f. Socket sb. **Sokket**, var. Sucket Obs.

‖ **Soko** (sōᵘ·kōᵘ). [Native African name.] A species of anthropoid ape discovered by Livingstone near Lake Tanganyika.

1870 Livingstone Last Jrnl. 24 Aug., The soko, if large, would do well to stand for a picture of the Devil. 1875 Zoologist X. 4359 The soko is so cunning, and has such sharp eyes, that no one can stalk him in front without being seen. 1898 E. P. Evans Evol. Ethics ix. 343 Some species of monkeys, like the chimpanzees and sokos, get up concerts of their own.

Sokour(e, obs. forms of Succour sb. and v.

Sol (sɒl), sb.1 [L. sōl (for earlier *sāol, *sāwol), = Gr. ἥλιος (Homeric ἠέλιος, Cretan ἀβέλιος), Skr. suvar, Lith. sáule, Goth. sauil, ON. and Icel. sól (Norw., Sw., Da. sol), Welsh haul.]

1. The sun (personified).

Used without article and written with capital S.

c 1450 Treat. Astrol. (MS. Ashm. 337) 2 Sol is hote & dry but not as mars is. 1592 Kyd Span. Trag. i. i. 23 Ere Sol had slept three nights in Thetis lap. 1593 Peele Poems Wks. (Rtldg.) 601 More beautiful..Than Sol himself amid the Planets seven. 1609 Ev. Woman in Hum. ii. in Bullen O. Pl. IV, His smile is like the Meridian Sol Discern'd a dauncing in the burbling brook. 1670 D. Denton Brief Desc. New York (1845) 19 The Vines..doth shelter them from the scorching beams of Sols fiery influence. 1712–4 Pope Rape Lock i. 13 Sol thro' white curtains shot a tim'rous ray. 1791 Cowper Retired Cat 62 Till Sol, declining in the west, Shall call to supper. 1820 Combe Syntax, Consol. v. (Chandos) 203 In bright Sol's diurnal round, No such delightful place was found. 1837 P. Keith Bot. Lex. 277 Clytie, inconsolable for the loss of the affections of Sol,..is represented as brooding over her griefs in silence and in solitude.

† 2. a. Alch. Gold. Obs.

a 1386 Chaucer Can. Yeom. Prol. & T. 273 Sol gold is, and Luna silver we threpe. [1460–70 Bk. Quintessence i. (1866) 3 Good gold naturel..is clepid of philosophoris sol in latyn.] 1477 Norton Ordin. Alch. iii. in Ashm. (1652) 41 Sol by it selfe, or Mercury alone, Or Sulphur with them. 1591 Sylvester Du Bartas i. iv. 400 Pure goldy-locks, Sol, States'-friend, Honor-giver. 1599 T. M[oufet] Silkwormes 45 Zeuxis his painted dogge shal barke and whine When loue they turne to Sol or Luna fine. 1606 J. Davies (Heref.) Select Husband Wks. (Grosart) II. 7/1 Though Beauty then seem Sol, at least as rich, It will be found but Lune, on Tryalls touch. 1610 B. Jonson Alch. ii. iii, Bright Sol is in his robe. 1651 [see Solary a. 2]. 1758 [see Jupiter 2 b].

† b. Her. (In blazoning by planets instead of metals) = Or sb. Obs.

1610 Guillim Heraldry 83 Hee beareth Luna, on a Chiefe Iupiter, a Cherub displaied, Sol. a 1646 J. Gregory Posthuma, Assyrian Monarchie (1650) 235 Emperors and Kings ought to bear Gold in their Arms, and then it might bee thus; The Field is Sol a Dove volant proper. 1706 Phillips (ed. Kersey), Sol..is taken..in Heraldry for the Gold Colour, in the Coats of Soveraign Princes. 1709 Hearne Collect. 6 Nov., Canterbury bears a Staff in Pale Sol. [1880 Encycl. Brit. XI. 691/2 Or, Yellow, Topaz, Sol.]

† c. ? The topaz. Obs.

1567 Maplet Greene Forest 21 Sol the Precious stone, is in colour like to the Sunne, and is called Sol, for that it giueth reflexions of Sunne beames.

Sol (sɒl, sōᵘl), sb.2 Mus. Also 6 soule, 7 soll. [The first syllable of L. solve: see Gamut.] The fifth note of Guido's hexachords, and of the octave in modern solmization; the note G in the natural scale of C major.

c 1325 in Rel. Ant. I. 292 Sol and ut and la, And that froward file that men clepis fa. a 1529 Skelton Bouge of Court 258 Wolde to God, it wolde please you some daye.. to..lerne me to synge, Re, my, fa, sol! 1565 Kyng Daryus 739 (Brandl), La, soule, soule, fa, my. 1596 Shaks. Tam. Shr. iii. i. 77 D sol re, one Cliffe, two notes haue I. 1626 Middleton Anything for Quiet Life v. ii, You shall never talk your voice above the key sol, sol, sol. 1662 Playford Skill Music (1674) 1 Ut and Re are now changed into Sol and La. 1728 Chambers Cycl. s.v. Sol-fa-ing, From fa to sol is a Tone; also from sol to la. 1797 Encycl. Brit. (ed. 3) XII. 547/2 From the adjuncts of the mode, that is to say, the modes of its two fifths, which for ut are fa and sol, and re and mi for la. 1842 Penny Cycl. XXII. 194/1. 1873 H. C. Banister Music 32 The lowest note, Sol, or G.

Hence **Sol** v. (in nonce-use).

1592 Shaks. Rom. & Jul. iv. v. 121 (Q.1), Ile re you, Ile fa you, Ile sol you.

‖ **Sol** (sɒl), sb.3 Now Hist. Also 6 soul. [Older F. sol (now sou Sou), = Prov. sol, Pg. and It. soldo, Sp. sueldo:—L. solidum, acc. of solidus (sc. nummus) a gold coin.] A former coin and money of account in France and some other countries, equal to the twentieth part of a livre, but varying in actual value at different times and places.

1583 Stocker Civ. Warres Lowe C. iii. 87 A pot of sweete mylke, a great and a halfe, and a pounde of butter two souls. 1605 B. Jonson Volpone iv. ii, This fellow, For six sols more, would plead against his Maker. 1611 Coryat Crudities 250 Every Chiquinie containing eleven Livers and twelve Sols: the Liver is nine pence, the Sol an halfe-penny. 1639 S. Du Verger tr. Camus' Admir. Events 352 He put his hand into his pocket, and thinking to draw out a Sol, which is little more than an English penny,..gave it him. 1748 Smollett R. Random xliv, My pay..amounted to five sols a day. 1789 Burke Corr. (1844) III. 122 A new paper-currency..which is to bear an interest of one sol in the livre. 1809 A. Henry Trav. 54 In this exchange, a pound of beaver-skin is reckoned at sixty sols. [1873 Hale In His Name i. 2 He would relax his hold on the odd sols and deniers as if he had never clung to them.]

† **Sol**, sb.4 Obs. [Abbreviation of solution: see Ob sb.1] The solution of a scholastic problem.

1588–1678 [see Ob sb.1].

‖ **Sol** (sōᵘl), sb.5 Pl. soles. [Sp. sol sun: see Sol sb.1] A Spanish-American (now Peruvian) silver coin worth about two shillings.

1884 Bedford Sailor's Handbk. 126 Peruvian Gold: 20 Sol Piece, £3 18 6. Ibid., Peruvian: Soles, £0 3 6. 1894 Daily News 20 Dec. 5/2 The United States dollar being substituted for the Central American silver dollar or sol as the standard of value. The value of the sol is about 50 cents. (U.S. currency).

† **Sol**, a. Obs. Also sole. [Related to Sole v.3 Cf. Solwy a.] Soiled, dirty.

c 1200 Trin. Hom. 57 Sume bereð sole cloð to þe watere forto wasshen it clene. Ibid. 163 His alter cloð [is] great and sole, and hire chemise smal & hwit, & te albe sol, & hire smoc hwit. a 1225 Ancr. R. 324 Wule a weob beon..mid one watere wel ibleched, oðer a sol cloð hwit iwaschen?

‖ **Sola** (sōᵘ·lă), sb. Also solah, and erron. Solar. [Urdū and Bengālī solā = Hindī sholā: see Shola.] A tall leguminous swamp-plant (Æschynomena aspera or paludosa) of India; the pith of this employed in making light hats. Used attrib. with hat, helmet, topee.

(a) 1848 tr. Hoffmeister's Trav. Ceylon, etc. vii. 248 With only a shirt and a 'solah' hat. 1857 Lady Canning in Hare Two Noble Lives (1893) II. 255 [The mounted volunteers] with sola helmets on their heads. 1901 Daily Chron. 27 May 4/5 Instead of the uncomfortable regulation helmet they are provided with Sola hats.

(b) 1845 Stocqueler Handbk. Brit. India (1854) 92 It will be prudent to wear a sola topee, or hat composed of the soft pulp of a tree. 1872 E. Braddon Life India ii. 20 [Where the trees] pour down richly-scented blossoms upon his sola topee. 1900 Blackw. Mag. Apr. 516/1 A solah topi with a green-lined rim.

‖ **Sola** (sōᵘ·lă), a. [L. sōla, fem. of sōlus Solus, and It. sola, fem. of solo Solo.]

1. Of females: Sole, solitary, alone.

1753 Richardson Grandison (1811) V. xxi. 137 Aunt Nell would not have descended sola into her greys, nor Cicely Badger neither, if they might have obtained the men of their choice. 1768 Miss Burney Early Diary (1889) I. 10, I should be content to love Sola—and let Dueto be reserved for those who have a proper sense of their superiority. 1825 T. Hook Sayings Ser. ii. Sutherl. I. 39 James..found the matron sola, and evidently prepared for a solemn discussion of the weighty affair.

2. techn. Of bills: (see quot.).

1866 Crump Banking v. 101 A 'sola' bill of exchange is a single bill, as distinguished from bills drawn in 'sets'.

† **Sola**, int. Obs. Also sowla. [Cf. Soho int. and hola Holla.] A call or cry to attract attention or notice.

1588 Shaks. L. L. L. iv. i. 151 Ah heauens, it is most patheticall nit. Sowla, sowla. 1596 — Merch. V. v. i. 43 Loren. Who calls? Clo. Sola, did you see M. Lorenzo?

† **So·lable**, a. Obs.—0 [f. L. sōlārī to comfort.]

1623 Cockeram i, Solelable [sic], which may be comforted.

Solace (sɒ·lės), sb.1 Forms: α. 3–6 solas, 5–6 solasse, 6 Sc. solaes, soles. β. 4– solace, 4–6 sollace. (See also Solance sb.) [a. OF. solas, later soulas (now dial.), = Prov. solats, Sp. solaz, It. sollazzo:—L. sōlācium, sōlātium, f. the stem of sōlārī to comfort, console. Cf. MDu. and MLG. solaes.]

1. Comfort, consolation; alleviation of sorrow, distress, or discomfort.

α. c 1290 S. Eng. Leg. I. 220 Hidere þou come for ovre solas, and nouȝt suych deol to make. c 1300 Life of Beket, etc. (Percy Soc.) 138 Vourty dawes he was, In a chaumbre al one withoute eni Solas. c 1400 Rom. Rose 2789, I shalle yeve thee..Three other thingis, that gret solas Doith to hem that be in my las. c 1440 Gesta Rom. v. 13 (Harl. MS.), I pray þe, wepe not, but make me solas and comfort, and chere me. 1530 Palsgr. 272 Solasse, comforte, solas, recomfort, solace.

β. 1338 R. Brunne Chron. (1810) 252 His solace was alle reft, þat scho fro him was gon, Ne no sonne him left. 1382 Wyclif Heb. xiii. 22 Forsothe, britheren, I preie ȝou, that ȝe suffre a word of solace. c 1400 Maundev. (Roxb.) Pref. 2 Þeroff þai hafe grete solace and comforthe. 1483 Caxton Gold. Leg. 203/2, I am with the and shalle gyue to the the solace of my seruaunt paule. 1575 Mirr. Mag., Hen. VI, xvii, The solace of my soule my chiefest pleasure was. 1593 Shaks. 2 Hen. VI, ii. iii. 21 Sorrow would [have] sollace, and mine Age would ease. 1611 Heywood Gold. Age i. i, I'le warre with comfort, be at odds with solace. 1677 Marvell Corr. Wks. (Grosart) II. 560 You will..have the usual solace of those who goe to law, that your adversary hath been at no lesse charges. 1768–74 Tucker Lt. Nat. (1834) II. 653, I want to lay in a stock of solace which shall not fail me in time of need. 1791 Mrs. Radcliffe Rom. Forest iv, She wept also that she could no longer seek solace in the friendship of Adeline. 1839 James Louis XIV, III. 143 Though the relief of reading was allowed as some solace to his overloaded heart. 1879 W. H. Dixon Royal Windsor II. xvii. 182 Time brought no solace to her widowed heart.

† 2. Pleasure, enjoyment, delight; entertainment, recreation, amusement. Obs.

α. 1297 R. Glouc. (Rolls) 370 To honti & to winne is mete & to abbe solas & game. a 1320 Sir Tristrem 2856 Þer was miche solas Of alle maner soun And gle. c 1386 Chaucer Frankl. T. 74 He goth to his cuntre,..Wher as he lyveth in

blisse and in solas. c 1430 Lydg. Minor Poems (Percy Soc.) 80 Thus thay songe..This melodious ympne withe grete solas. 1484 Caxton Fables of Poge iv. [Hunting and hawking] ought not to be done ful ofte, but somtyme for to take disporte and solas. 1525 Ld. Berners Froiss. II. clx. 178 b, For he kepte reuyll, daunsyng, and solas: and euery daye it was newe to begyn. 1551 R. Robinson tr. More's Utopia i. (1895) p. xciv, An yle..Ful fraight with worldly welth, with pleasure and solas.

β. a 1340 Hampole Psalter lxxvi. 3 He amonestis vs to pass fra erthly solace and ȝern anly delit of heuen. 1377 Langl. P. Pl. B. xviii. 217 God of his goodnesse..Sette hym in solace & in souereigne myrthe. c 1400 Pilgr. Sowle iv. i. (Caxton, 1483) 58 Hym nedeth of solace and disport wher with to appesen his herte. 1480 Caxton Myrr. ii. iii. 67 This is a place whiche is ful of solace, of playsances and of delices. 1519 Interlude Four Elements (Percy Soc.) 45 Let us go to the taverne agayn, And make some mery solace. 1590 Spenser F. Q. ii. vi. 3 And therein sate a Ladie fresh and faire, Making sweet solace to her selfe alone. 1615 G. Sandys Trav. 176 Sundry smal turrets are dispersed about, which serue for solace as well as for safe-guard. a 1629 Hinde J. Bruen xxix. (1641) 90 O how great was his rejoycing, and solace, when..he might rejoyce the soules of Gods people. 1667 Milton P. L. ix. 844 Great joy he promis'd to his thoughts, and new Solace in her return.

3. That which gives comfort or consolation, † brings pleasure or enjoyment, etc.

c 1290 Beket 178 in S. Eng. Leg. I. 111 For he scholde hire solas beo, and speke to hire with mouþe. a 1340 Hampole Psalter xxxvii. 11 In þere twa solaces man ioyes. c 1400 Maundev. (Roxb.) xix. 88 He hase forsaken..all þe ricches and solacez of þe werld. c 1450 tr. De Imitatione ii. v. 45 God allone..is be solace of mannys soule & very gladnes of herte. 1597 Hooker Eccl. Pol. v. lxxvi. § 8 All which solaces and comforts of this our vnquiet life it pleaseth God oftentimes to bestow. 1597 Bacon Ess., Of Honour & Reputation (Arb.) 74 Favorites, such as exceede not this scantling to bee sollace to the Soueraigne. 1667 Milton P. L. iv. 486 To have thee by my side Henceforth an individual solace dear. 1794 Mrs. Radcliffe Myst. Udolpho xxxiv, Tell your lady..that this [picture] has been my companion and only solace in all my misfortunes. 1849 Robertson Serm. Ser. i. viii. 125 He had cut himself off from the solaces of life.

4. Printing. (See quot. 1683.)

1683 Moxon Mech. Exerc., Printing 357 The Penalty for the breach of..these Laws and Customs is in Printers Language called a Solace. 1683 [see Solace v. 4]. 1888 Jacobi Printers' Vocab. 128 Solace, a penalty imposed by the chapel for the infringement of any of its rules.

† 5. Rose of solace, = Rosa solis 2. Obs.—1

1604 Meet. of Gallants at Ordinary C j b, To the comforting of his poore heart, he powrde downe a leauen shillings in Rose of Solace.

† **Solace**, sb.2 Obs. Also 6 sollace. [Of obscure origin.] Some substance used for dressing cloth.

1552 Act 5 & 6 Edw. VI, c. 6 § xiv, Whether the same Clothe or Clothes be well and sufficiently dressed and pressed withe the colde presse, without puttinge therto flox, solace, chalke, flower, or any other deceiptfull thinge. c 1560 Maldon Liber B. fol. 56 (MS.), Without puttinge therto flocks, sollace, chalke, flower, heare, or any yearne made of lambes wooll. 1613 May Decl. Est. Clothing v. 29 Flox of the same coulour ..which they can sheare as small as dust, which mixt with solace, they spread vpon the muster.., and where the cloth may bee seene.

Solace (sɒ·lės), v. Forms: 3–4 solaci, -cy, 3– solace, 4–5 solas(e, 5 solais, 6 solles, 8 solless. (See also Solance v.) [ad. OF. solacier, solasier, etc., later soulacier (now arch.), f. solas Solace sb.1 Cf. Sp. solazar, It. sollazzare, med.L. solatiari, -are; MDu. solasen, -acen.]

1. trans. To cheer, comfort, console; † to entertain or recreate.

1297 R. Glouc. (Rolls) 11511 Sir simon de Mountfort out of warde nom Sir edward him to solaci. 13.. Sir Beues 711 So him solaste þat mai, þat al is care wente awai. c 1380 Wyclif Sel. Wks. II. 226 Crist tauȝte men to suffre..and putte hem in hope þerfore to be solasid of God. c 1400 Destr. Troy 1620 Mony gaumes were begonnen þe grete for to solas. Ibid. 13984 Myche solast hir the sight of hir sone þan, To se the lede vppon lyue, þat ho louet most. c 1475 Harl. Contin. Higden (Rolls) VIII. 456 Thei destroyede a newe maner made..by that prior..for to solace hym and his breþer þer. 1588 Shaks. L. L. L. iv. iii. 377 We will with some strange pastime solace them. 1706 Phillips (ed. Kersey), To Solace, to afford Solace or Comfort. 1790 Cowper On My Mother's Picture 4 Thy own sweet smiles I see, The same that oft in childhood solaced me. 1812 J. Wilson Isle of Palms i. 506 And it may be such dreams are given..To solace them that mourn. 1868 Freeman Norm. Conq. (1877) II. 86 They were often solaced by the company of wives and children.

absol. 1820 Shelley Prometh. Unb. iii. iv. 32 Thy simple talk once solaced, now delights.

b. To make (a place) cheerful or pleasant.

1667 Milton P. L. vii. 434 From Branch to Branch the smaller Birds with song Solac'd the Woods. 1746 J. Hervey Medit. (1818) 186 Ye Birds..who wake the morn, and solace the groves with your artless lays. 1875 Grindon Life i. 8 The walls of old castles and abbeys, which..ivy and the faithful wallflower alone have solaced.

c. To allay, alleviate, assuage, soothe.

1667 Milton P. L. viii. 419 The cause of his desire By conversation with his like to help, Or solace his defects. 1712 Blackmore Creation v. 60 A Cause Supream,..Who, when implor'd, might timely Succour give, Solace our Anguish, and our Wants relieve. 1797 Mrs. Radcliffe Italian xvii, Paulo was contented to solace his conscience. 1819 Shelley Cenci iii. i. 311 We sate sad together Solacing our despondency with tears. 1833 Tennyson Two Voices 433 A little hint to solace woe.

2. refl. To give (oneself) comfort or consolation, † entertainment or amusement.

1340 Ayenb. 213 Þer-huile þet ich me solaci an playe, iche ne þenche none manne kuead. c 1400 Destr. Troy 1752 Siker were to sit and solas vs here. c 1470 Gol. & Gaw. 217 Thus thay solaist thame selvin, suthly to say. 1568 Grafton Chron. II. 107 Solacyng him-selfe with Musicall instrumentes & songes. 1583 Babington Commandm. (1590) 314 We dare solace our selues in soft beddes too long for our constitutions. 1639 Fuller Holy War iii. xv, Henry king of Jerusalem, as he was walking in his palace to solace himself, fell down..and brake his neck. 1691 Ray Creation ii. (1704) 464 With the Thoughts and Expectation whereof he solaces himself. 1746 J. Hervey Medit. (1818) 21 He solaced himself with the prospect of a long, long series of earthly satisfactions. 1860 Motley Netherl. (1868) I. v. 283 Duplessis-Mornay often solaced himself by distant communion with that kindred and sympathizing spirit. 1887 Ruskin Præterita II. 231 He solaced himself by making a careful collection of all the Florentine wild-flowers for me.

† 3. intr. To take comfort or consolation, recreation or enjoyment. Obs.

1340 Ayenb. 213 Huet kuead is hit yef ich guo playe and solaci. c 1475 Harl. Contin. Higden (Rolls) VIII. 447 Thei brente þeire faces with yrne that thei scholde not be knowen, and þat Ynglische men scholde not solace of þeire dethe. 1530 Palsgr. 724/2, I am werye of studyenge, I wyll go solace a lytell. 1592 Timme Ten Eng. Lepers 63 Friends do solace and joy together in honest and godly mirth. 1618 Bolton Florus (1636) 313 He,..surprised with the love of Queen Cleopatra, solaced on her bosome. 1673 Lady's Calling i. iii. § 6 Let him stand naked and hungry, whilst they are solacing with that which would relieve him. 1728 Vanbr. & Cibber Prov. Husb. i, She herself is solacing in one continual round of cards and good company.

4. trans. Of printers: To punish (one) corporally for non-payment of a 'solace'. Also transf.

1583 Moxon Mech. Exerc., Printing 357 If the Delinquent ..would not pay his Solace..they Solac'd him. 1784 B. Franklin in Ann. Reg., Chron. (1817) 385 This foolish letter is mere chit-chat between ourselves... If, therefore, you show it to any body,..I will positively solless you.

Hence **So·laced** ppl. a., comforted, consoled.

1836 Mrs. Browning Poet's Vow ii. ii, The solaced friends.

Solaceful (sɒ·lėsfŭl), a. rare. [f. Solace sb.1 + -ful 1.] Full of solace; pleasant, agreeable.

a 1618 Sylvester Job Triumphant iv. 687 The Lord accepted Job, and staid His Thrall-full State,..And turned it to Solace-full, from sad. 1884 J. Payne Tales fr. Arabic I. 225 How joyous and how solaceful was life in them whilere!

Solacement (sɒ·lėsmĕnt). [f. Solace sb.1 + -ment. So OF. sollace-, soulacement.] Solace, solacing, consolation.

1721 R. Keith tr. T. à Kempis, Solil. Soul xviii. 253 Being disappointed in thy outward Solacement. 1768–74 Tucker Lt. Nat. (1834) II. 545 Discovering daily new sources of solacement we had not discerned before. 1824 Scott Redgauntlet (1830) II. xix. 214 That..was a solacement of his feelings which was not at the moment to be thought of. 1871 Carlyle in Mrs. Carlyle's Lett. I. 370 Rather as in duty bound than with much hope of solacement.

Solacer (sɒ·lėsəɪ). [f. Solace v. + -er 1.] One who, or that which, solaces.

1611 Cotgr., Consolateur, a consolator, solacer, comforter. 1803 Lamb Let. to Coleridge in Final Mem. iv. 225 A pipe and some generous Port, and King Lear..had their effect as solacers. 1873 Miss Braddon Lucius Davoren I. Prol. i. 7 Tobacco, that sweet solacer of weary hours.

Solacing (sɒ·lėsiŋ), vbl. sb. [f. Solace v.] The action of the verb in various senses; † the fact of taking enjoyment or recreation.

13.. K. Alis. 6746 (W.), Now rideth Alisaunder,..with muche syngyng, In gret delit and solasyng. 1382 Wyclif 1 Cor. xiv. 3 He..spekith to men, to edificacioun,..and comfortynge, or solasynge. 1540–1 Elyot Image Gov. (1549) 81 In this solacyng he hunted the harte. c 1560 A. Scott Poems (S.T.S.) xviii. 43 Adew,..My mirth and sollesing Of erdly gloir. 1631 N. Hunt (title), New Recreations, or the Mindes release and solacing. 1683 Moxon Mech. Exerc., Printing 357 The manner of Solacing, thus.

So·lacing, ppl. a. [f. Solace v.] Conveying solace; consoling.

1721 R. Keith tr. T. à Kempis, Solil. Soul x. 179 The solacing Joy of the Spirit. 1837 Carlyle Fr. Rev. i. vii. vii, For wrath is contagious, and to pent Bodyguards is so solacing. 1862 H. Spencer First Princ. i. v. § 32 (1875) 115 The beliefs..were highly solacing ones. 1890 Pall Mall G. 20 Jan. 6/3 Miss Fowler received these solacing remarks with quiet serenity.

† **Sola·cious**, a. Obs. Forms: 5–6 solacius, 5–7 solacious; 5 solacyose, 5–6 -ous, 6 -ouse, Sc. -us; 6–7 solatious. [a. OF. solacieus (soulaceus, etc.), f. solas Solace sb.1 So Sp. solazoso.] Affording or giving solace, in various senses of the sb. (Common c 1500–1650.)

1375 Barbour Bruce x. 290 In company solacius He wes, and thar-with amorus. c 1450 tr. De Imitatione iii. xxiii. 92 Þou allone art hiest,..þou allone most swete & most solacious. 1451 Capgr. Life St. Gilbert 70 He talked mor þan ete, and with solacious countenauns wold he glade his gestis. a 1470 H. Parker Dives & Pauper (W. de W. 1496) iii. xvii. 153/1 The holy daye hath ben solacyous..both for soule and bodye. 1503 Hawes Examp. Virt. ii. xxvii, For they be so fayre and wounderous That theym to se it is solacyous. 1546 Bale English Votaries i. 18 b, Women greuouse and solacyouse. 1581 Marbeck Bk. Notes 1164 Delicious it is in aduersitie, & solatious in all weaknes. 1611 J. Davies (Heref.) Sco. Folly xliv, Fountaine of Conceits acute and solacious. 1641 Symonds Serm. Ho. Comm. P 3 What can be more solatious to a Christian Spirit? 1675 Cocker Morals 41 Old Friends to trust, old Gold to keep, old Wine To drink; are a solacious good old Trine. [1826 Galt Lairds xiii, Such solacious participation in the influences of the season, as he called it.]

Hence † **Sola·ciously** adv. Obs.

1526 Skelton Magnyf. 2395 Prosperyte to hym is gyuen solacyusly to man.

† **Solacy.** Obs.—1 [ad. L. solaci-um: see Solace sb.1] Solace.

1533 tr. Erasm. Comm. Crede 13 That laboure..the spyryte doth make dulcete and swete with so many solacyes and coumfortes.

† **Solagement.** Obs.—1 [ad. F. soulagement, † sollagement, f. soulager to relieve.] Relief.

1609 J. Davies (Heref.) Holy Rood F b, That in the Lab'rinth of his Languishment We may..find solagement.

Solah, variant of Sola sb.

† **Solaire**, var. (after OF. solaire) of salaire, obs. f. Salary sb.

1491 Caxton Vitas Patr. (W. de W. 1495) i. xxxvii. 48 b/2 He wold haue gyuen to the Maronner for his solaire a boke of the gospellis.

‖ **Solak.** rare. Also 6 sola (?), 7 solach, solaque. [a. Turkish صولاق ṣōlāq. So F. solak.] (See quots.)

The identity of the word in the first quot. is doubtful.

1520 Caxton's Chron. Eng. vii. 141 b/1 In yᵉ iiij yeare of kynge Henryes reygne came yᵉ Emperour of Constantynople with many greate solaes [Brut and Caxton lordes] & knyghtes. [1615 G. Sandys Trav. i. 75 The Pretorian footmen called the Solacchi, whereof there be in number three hundred.] 1678 Phillips, Solachs, those of the Grand Seigniors Foot-guard, who are about three hundred, attending upon him with Bows and Arrows. 1687 A. Lovell tr. Thevenot's Trav. i. 69 The Solaques are also of the Infantry, and are the Grand Signior's..Life-guard, for they attend the Grand Signior when he goes abroad in the city. 1802 James Milit. Dict., Solaks, bowmen or archers belonging to the personal guard of the grand signor.

Solan (sōᵘ·lăn). Forms: α. 5– soland (7 sorland), 6 solande, -end, 7–8 solund. β. 6 solane, 7– solan; 8 sollen. [f. ON. and Icel. súla (also Icel. hafsúla, Norw. havsula) gannet; the second element may be ON. ǫnd, and- (Norw., Sw., Da. and) duck. Originally Sc., but known to English writers from the middle of the 17th cent.]

1. The gannet (Sula bassana), a large sea-fowl resembling a goose, which frequents a few rocks and small islands of Britain, the Færöes, Iceland, and Canada.

c 1450 Holland Howlat 700 The Soland [as] stewart was sent; For he couth fro the firmament Fang the fische deid. 1749 Collins On Popular Superstit. x, Along the Atlantic rock, undreading climb, And of its eggs despoil the solan's nest. 1808 Scott Marm. iii. iii, The rafters..Bore wealth of winter cheer; Of sea-fowl dried, and solands store. a 1851 Moir The Bass Rock ii, At times the solan's wing..Brushed near us. 1873 Black Pr. Thule III. ix. 285 A white solan ..struck the water as he dived.

2. attrib. with goose, = sense 1.

α. 1536 Bellenden Chron. Scot. ix. (1541) B vj b, In it [the Bass Rock] ar incredible noumer of soland geis; ..And ar sene in na part of Albion, bot in this crag and Ailsay. 1596 Dalrymple tr. Leslie's Hist. Scot. (S.T.S.) I. 55 The neist Ile named Elsa..abundes in Solend geis, and monie vthiris sey foulis. 1651 Cleveland Poems 37 A Scot, when from the Gallow-Tree got loose, Drops into Styx, and turns a Solund-Goose. 1678 Butler Hud. iii. ii. 655 As Barnacles turn Soland-Geese In th' Islands of the Orcades. 1694 Falle Jersey ii. 73 Here are to be seen the famous Sorland Geese, whose Equivocal Generation..is received by many amongst Us for Truth. 1710 Sibbald Hist. Fife ii. 45 The Fowls which most frequent the Bass, are the Anseres Bassani or Soland-Geese. 1768 Pennant Brit. Zool. I. Pref. p. v, The clouds of Soland geese which breed on the Bass island. 1821 Sporting Mag. VII. 191 A Soland goose or gannet was shot by a fisherman of Southampton. 1843 Yarrell Brit. Birds III. 381 The Gannet, or Soland Goose.

β. 1583 Reg. Privy Council Scot. III. 624 To draw and alluir the auld solane geise to the boittis. 1668 Charleton Onomast. 95 Anser Bassanus,..the Solan Goose. 1698 M. Martin Voy. St. Kilda (1749) 4 A prodigious number of Solan Geese hatching in their Nests. 1725 Portland Papers (Hist. MSS. Comm.) VI. 111 The Bass..I think has no inhabitants but the Solan geese which breed there. 1816 Scott Antiq. vi, There was the relishing Solan goose, whose smell is so powerful that he is never cooked within doors. 1863 Intellect. Obs. Sept. 118 The Solan Goose is not so numerous upon Ailsa as the puffin.

Solanaceous (sɒlănēᵋ·ʃəs), a. Bot. [f. mod.L. Solanace-æ, f. L. sōlānum nightshade.] Belonging to the Solanaceæ, an order of gamopetalous plants which includes the genera Solanum, Capsicum, Atropa, Hyoscyamus, etc.

1804 Med. Jrnl. XII. 519 The fruits of several solanaceous plants, as the pseudocapsicum, and the common capsicum. 1822–7 Good Study Med. (1829) III. 309 The remark will apply to most of the narcotics, whether of the umbellate or solanaceous order. 1875 Athenæum 24 July 123/3 The influence of poisonous solanaceous plants,—especially belladonna,—on certain rodents and marsupials.

Solanal (sōᵘ·lănal), a. and sb. Bot. [f. L. sōlān-um.] a. adj. Of or pertaining to, related to, Solanum and other genera according to Lindley's classification. b. sb. A genus or plant related to Solanum.

1846 Lindley Veg. Kingd. 615 The Solanal Alliance... Natural Orders of Solanals. Ibid. 616 Solanal Exogens.

† **Solance**, sb. Obs. [Alteration of Solace sb.1, after forms in -ance.] Solace.

c 1375 Sc. Leg. Saints xxix. (Placidas) 728 As ȝung men wil do for solance, & als to mak þar acquintance. c 1400 Melayne 357 Ne hope ȝe noghte..Þat ne we sall solance see. Ibid. 831 Thay crownnede þe Sowdane.., Þat Solance was to seene.

So †Solance, *sb.* *Obs.*

Solander (sŏlæ·ndaɹ). [From the name of the Swedish botanist D. C. Solander (1736–1782).] A box made in the form of a book, for holding botanical specimens, papers, maps, etc.

Solander, obs. form of SALLENDER.

Solandra (sŏlæ·ndra). [mod.L.: see SOLANDER.] A genus of tropical American shrubs belonging to the *Solanaceæ* (sub-order *Atropeæ*); also, a plant belonging to this genus.

Solania (sŏlæ·nia). [f. SOLAN- + -IA.] An alkaloid found in the woody nightshade.

Solanicine (sŏlæ·nĭsin). *Chem.* [f. as prec. + -ICINE.]

Solanidine (sŏlæ·nĭdin). *Chem.* [Cf. prec.] (See quot.)

Solanine (sŏlæ·nĭn). *Chem.* Also **solanina, solanin.** [a. F. *solanine* (Desfosses, 1821), f. L. *solanum* SOLANUM.] A compound containing an alkaloid, found in various plants of the genus *Solanum*.

¶ **Solano** (sŏlā·no). [Sp.—L. *solanus,* f. *sol* sun.] In Spain, a hot south-easterly wind.

¶ **Solano** (sŏlā·no). *Obs.*

†Solanum (sŏlē·nŏm). [L. *sōlānum* nightshade.] A plant of the nightshade family, or the genus of gamopetalous plants of which this is the type; some amount or preparation of the plant used for medical purposes. Also *fig.*

Solar (sŏ·laɹ), *a.* and *sb.*[1] [ad. L. *sōlār-is,* f. *sōl* sun. Cf. F. *solaire,* Sp. *solar,* Pg. *solar,* It. *solare.*]

A. *adj.* 1. Of or pertaining to the sun, the course, light, heat, etc.

2. *Astrol.* Subject to the influence of the sun; having a nature or character determined by the sun.

3. sacred to the sun; connected or associated with the worship of the sun.

4. Representing or symbolizing the sun.

5. Sprung or descended from the sun.

6. *Solar* *metal, gold.* (Cf. Sol *sb.*[1])

b. *Solar metal,* a coloured metal. *Obs.*

c. Of light, heat, etc.: Proceeding or emanating from the sun.

Solar, *sb.*[2] *Photogr.* A solar print.

Solar (sŏ·laɹ), *sb.*[3] [a. OF. *solier,* etc.]

Solar(e, variant of SOLER *sb.*[1]

Solari, *a.* (*sb.*) *rare.* [f. L. *sōlāri-* diluvian Noah.]

Solarism (sŏ·lăriz'm). [f. SOLAR *a.* + -ISM.] The theory of solar myths; excessive use of, or adherence to, this theory.

Solarist (sŏ·lărist). [f. SOLAR *a.* + -IST.] One who holds the theory of solar myths, *esp.* to an excessive degree.

Solarium (sŏlē·riŏm). Pl. **solaria.** [L. *sōlārium,* f. *sōl* sun. Cf. SOLAR *sb.*[3]]

1. A sun-dial.

2. A terrace, balcony, or room exposed to the rays of the sun.

Solarization (sŏ‖lăraizē·ʃ'n). [f. SOLARIZE + -ATION.]

Solarize (sŏ·lăraiz), *v.* [f. SOLAR *a.* + -IZE. So F. *solariser.*]

1. To affect or modify by the influence of the sun or the action of its rays; *spec.* in *Photogr.,* to injure by over-exposure to light.

Solaris'm (sŏ·lăriz'm). [f. SOLAR *a.* + -ISM.]

†Solary, *a.* *Obs.*[-1] [ad. L. *solari-* : see SOLACE *sb.*]

Solaster (sŏlæ·staɹ). *Zool.* [mod.L., f. *sōl* sun + *aster,* Gr. ἀστήρ star.] A genus of starfishes, typical of those having more than five rays; a member of this genus, a sun-star.

Solation (sŏlē·ʃ'n). [f. *sol* SOL *sb.*[3] + -ATION; cf. L. type *sōlātio,* L. *solutio* to console.]

Solatium (sŏlē·ʃiŏm). [L. *sōlātium,* solace, related to *solāri* to console : cf. SOLACE *sb.*]

Sold, *v.*[1] *Obs.* Forms: 4–5 *soud,* 4–6 *sowd.* β. 5–6 *sould(e,* 6 *sowld.*[d], *sold.* [ad. OF. *soud-,* *sould-,* *sold-,* ...]

†Sold, *v.*[2] *Obs.* Forms: 4 *soud,* 4–6 *sowd-, sawd-.* β. 5–6 *sould(e,* 6 *sowald-, sold-.*

Sold, *pa. t.* and *pa. pple.* of SELL *v.*[1]

†Solde, *sb.* *Obs.* [a. F. *solde*; see SOLD *sb.*[3]]

†Soldado (sŏldā·do). *Obs.* [Sp. and Pg., f. *soldado,* pa. pple. of *soldar,* f. *soldo* pay. Cf. SOLDIER *sb.*]

Soldan (sŏ·ldan). Now *arch.* or *Hist.* Forms: 4 *soudan,* 4–6 *soldan,* etc. [a. OF. and AF. *soldan,* *souldan.*]

So·ldanine. [ad. It. *soldanella* of obscure origin; hence also Pg. *soldanella,* F. *soldanelle* (16th cent.). Cf. prec.]

Soldanelle. [F. *soldanelle.*]

†Soldanrie. [f. SOLDAN + -RIE.]

†Soldat. [F. *soldat*; see SOLDADO.]

†Soldatesque, *a.* *Obs.*[-1] [a. F. *soldatesque.*]

Solde (small coin): see SOLD *sb.*[3]

Soldear, obs. form of SOLDIER *sb.*

Solder (sŏ·ldaɹ, so·daɹ), *sb.* Forms: 4–5 *soudur,* 5 *sawe,* 5–7 *soder,* etc. [a. OF. *soudure,* *souldure,* etc.]

1. *trans.* To unite or fasten by means of a metallic solder. Also with *in,* *on,* *together,* etc.

Solder (sŏ·ldaɹ, so·daɹ), *v.* Forms: α. 4–5 *souder,* etc. [a. OF. *souder,* *souldur,* etc.]

So·lderable, *a.* [f. SOLDER *v.* + -ABLE.]

Solderer (sŏ·ldaraɹ). Also 6 *souderer.* [f. SOLDER *v.* + -ER.]

So·ldering, *vbl. sb.* [f. SOLDER *v.* + -ING.]

The action of joining or mending with solder.

Soldering, *ppl. a.* [f. SOLDER *v.* + -ING.]

So·ldery. *Obs.*[-1] [f. *souldiery.*]

Soldier (sŏ·uldʒaɹ), *sb.* Forms: 4 *soud-, sowd-,* etc. [a. OF. *soudier,* *soldier,* etc.]

Soldier (with differ-ent ending *soldier*, *-ier*, etc.), *-iour* (with, etc.) *sb.*

1. One who serves in an army for pay; one who takes part in military service or warfare; *spec.* one of the ordinary rank and file; a private.

2. *fig.*

3. *transf.* Used as a name for various animals, fishes, etc.

4. *attrib.*, as *soldier-caste*, *-city*, *-class*, *-craft*, etc.

5. Special combs., as *soldier-ant*, *-sense* 3 *c*; *soldier-beetle*, *-sense* 3 *b*; (old) *soldier bird*, an Australian bird, *Myiozetta sanguinolenta*, with bright red plumage; *soldier-bush*, *-soldier-wood*; *soldier disease*, *-sense* 5; *soldier-line* (see quot. *sense* 6); *soldier money*; *soldier-palmer*, an artificial fly used in angling; *soldier-pink dial.*, a minnow; *soldier plant*, *thighed* *a.*, *-wood* (see quot.).

6. *Zoologist* IV. 1900 The Red Gurnard, *Trigla cuculus*.

Soldier-crab. [Cf. SOLDIER *sb.* 3 *b*.] The hermit-crab.

7. *attrib.* and *comb.* Appositive, as *soldier-colonist*, *-hero*, *-laddie*, *-man*, etc.

Soldierdom. [f. SOLDIER *sb.* + -DOM.] The quality or nature of a soldier.

Soldieress. [f. SOLDIER *sb.* + -ESS.] A female soldier.

Soldierhood. [f. SOLDIER *sb.* + -HOOD.] The essential qualities of a soldier or soldiery; the condition of being a soldier.

Soldiering, *vbl. sb.* [f. the vb.]
1. The action of serving as, or being in the state of being a soldier; military service.

2. *attrib.*

Soldierize, *v.* [-IZE.]
1. *intr.* To serve as a soldier. Also with *it*.
2. *trans.* To make into a soldier.

Soldierlike, *a.* and *adv.* Also 6 *souldiour-*, 7 *souldierlike*, 9 *Sc. sodgerlike*. [f. SOLDIER *sb.* + -LIKE.]

Soldierliness. [f. next.] The quality of being soldierly.

Soldierly, *a.* and *adv.* Also 6-7 *souldier-*, 7 *soldiour-*, 8 *Sc. sogerly*. [f. SOLDIER *sb.* + -LY.]

Soldiership. [f. SOLDIER *sb.* + -SHIP.] The state or condition of being a soldier; the qualities of a soldier; military experience or skill. Also *fig.* (quot. 1561).

Soldierwood. [f. SOLDIER *sb.* + -WOOD.]

Soldiery. Forms: 6 *souldiary*, 6-7 *-iarie* (7 *-iourie*) 7 *sourry*, *-iorie*, *-iery* (7 *soulgery*); *soldierie*, *-iarie*, etc. [f. SOLDIER *sb.* + -Y, *or* ad. OF.]

Soldo. Pl. *soldi* (*sq̇ 7 souldyes*). [It. *-soldo*: see SOL *sb.*]

Soldure, obs. form of SOLDER *sb.*[1]

Sole, *sb.*[1] Forms: 4-5 *sool*, 4-6 *soule* (6 *sowle*), 6-7 *Sc. soille*, *soile*, 4 *sowle*, 6-7 *soule*; 6-7 *sole*, 7-8, 9 *dial. soal*. [a. OF. *sole* (mod.F. *sole* in special senses)...]

1. The lower part, bottom, or under surface of anything. Chiefly in more or less specific uses (cf. next).

Sole, *sb.*[2] Forms: 4-... *sole* (5 *sool*). [a. OF. (also mod.F.) *sole*, or *ad. L. solea*...]

1. A common British and European flat-fish (*Solea vulgaris* or *-olea*), highly esteemed as food.

Sole, *sb.*[3] [= F. *sole* = Sp. *suela*, It. *suola*...]

Sole, *a.* (and *adv.*) Forms: 4-... *sole*, *sool*, 5-6 *soole*, 5 *soule*, 6 *soul* (*fem. soule*), (6 *Sc. saul*), of the same origin as prec.; *agreeing* in sense with L. *solus* (whence F. *seul*, *sole*), also *ad. L. sola, -um*, *sole*, *-um*: cf. Sp. and It. *solo*; *Pr. sol*, *Sp. solo*, It. *sola*...

Sole, *v.*[1] [f. SOLE *sb.*[1]]

Sole, *v.*[2] [f. SOLE *sb.*[2]]

Sole, *v.*[3]

Soledad.

Solein, obs. form of SULLEN.

Sole, *v.*

Solecism. [*ad.* late L. *soloecismus*.]

Solecist (ˈsɒlēsist).

Solecistic, Solecistical, *a.*

Solecize (ˈsɒlēsaiz), *v.*

Soled (səʊld), *ppl. a.*

Sole-fish.

Sole-fluke.

Soleil.

Solein, *a. and sb. Obs.*

Soleiess, *a.*

Solely (ˈsəʊlli), *adv.*

Solemness.

Solemniation. *Obs.*

Solemnific, *a.*

Solemnity (sɒˈlemnɪti).

Solemnization.

Solemnize (ˈsɒlemnaiz), *v.*

Solemnizer.

Solemnizing, *ppl. a.*

† So·lemnly, a. Obs.⁻¹ [f. SOLEMN a. + -LY¹.] Of a solemn or sacred character.

Solemnly (sǫ·lemli), adv. Forms 1-4 solemplike, -liche; 4 solemlich, -ly, -lych; 4-6 solempnelich; 4-6 solempnely, -lie, 5 -li; solempnely (6-lie); 5-6 solemply. 7. 6 solemnelle, 6-7-ly. [CI. SOLEMN adv.] MDu. solem(p)nelic, -elijc.] In a solemn manner, in various senses of the adj.: ceremoniously, formally; gravely, seriously, etc.

Solemness.

Solempne (-ple), a. Obs. Forms 1-4 solemplike, etc.

Solemnize.

So·lemnly, variant of SOLEMNLY.

† Solemnty, Obs. In 4-5 solempte. [prob. a reduced form of ME. solempneté.] Solemnity.

† So·lemny, a. and adv. Obs. In 5 solempny. [f. SOLEMN a.] A. adj. Solemn.

Solemness (sǫ·lemnes).

Solemn.

† Solen, sb.¹ Obs. Also 5 solenne, 6 solennes, var. of solennes of Solenne a.]

A. adj. Solemn, in various senses.

Solen (sǫ·lĕn), sb.² [mod.L. Solen, Gr.] 1. Zool. The razor-fish, Solen ensis or siliqua.

2. Surg. (See quot.)

† So·lenander, Obs.

Solenette.

So·lenite.

† Solenium.

So·lenly, adv. Obs.

Solen.

Soleprop.

Soler, var. of SURPLICE.

Soler¹ (sǫ·lɛ̄).

† Soler², Obs.

Soler³.

Solert.

† Soleret, Obs.

Soleret(te, variants of SOLLERET.

† Solert, a. Obs. [ad. L. solert-, stem of sollers, f. sollus whole, entire + ars art.] Clever, wise; characterized by cleverness.

† So·lertiousness, Obs.

† So·lerty, Obs.

Solen (-lóˈn).

Soleship.

Sol-fa.

Sole-tree.

Solenoid (sǫ·lĕnoid, soˈ-lĕnoid).

Solenoidal.

So·lenly, adv.

† So·lent, adv.

Solepran.

Solewid.

Soleyn.

† Solf, v.

Solfatara.

Sol-fa (sǫˈl·fâ).

So·lfaing.

Sol·faist.

Soli.

Solert.

Solfeggio.

Solferino.

Soli (sóˈ·li).

† Solicit, sb. rare. Obs.

Solicit (sǫli·sit), v.

Solicitant.

† Solicitate, a. Obs. Also 6-7 sollicitate.

† Solicitate, v. Obs. Also 6-7 sol·, sollicitate.

Solicitation.

Solicitous.

Solicitude.

Solicitor.

Solicit (sǫli·sit), v. Forms: 5 solicyte, 6 sollicit, etc.

I. 1. To tempt, entice, allure; to attract or draw by enticement, etc. (Cf. 4.)

2. To entreat or petition (a person) for, or to do, something; to urge, importune; to ask earnestly or persistently.

† 6. To endeavour to draw out (a person); to exercise the mind.

7. Med. To seek to draw, to induce or bring on; to bring about.

II. 8. To conduct, manage, or attend to (business, affairs, etc.); to push forward or prosecute. Obs.

III. intr. 12. To make request or petition; to beg or entreat.

Solicitant (sǫli·sitant), sb. and a.

Solicitate.

Solicitation (sǫˌlisitēiˈʃən).

Solicitor (sǫli·sitəɹ).

Solicitorship. [f. prec. + -SHIP.]
The office, duty, or calling of a solicitor.

Solicitous (sŏliˈsitəs), a. Also 6–8 sollicitous.
[f. L. sollicit-us, var. sollicit-us (see SOLICIT a.) + -OUS. Cf. OF. sol(l)iciteux, -euse.]

Solicitously, adv. [f. prec.] In a solicitous manner, in various senses of the adj.

Solicitousness. [f. SOLICITOUS a.] The state or quality of being solicitous; care, concern; anxiety, solicitude.

Solicitrix (sŏliˈsitriks). Also 7 sollicitrix. [Solicitor, after forms in -trix.]

Solicitude (sŏliˈsitiūd). Also 7 sollicitude, 8 -ess. [ad. F. sollicitude (14th c.).]

Solid (sŏlid), a. and sb. [ad. L. solidus, var. sollidus. Cf. F. solide.]

Solid, sb.

Solidago (sŏlideigo). [med.L. Golden-Rod.]

Solidare. [Pr. Plants 396, Solidago, Golden-Rod.]

Solidarian, a.

Solidaric, a. [f. SOLIDAR-ITY + -IC.]

Solidarily, adv. [f. SOLIDARY a. + -LY.]

Solidarity (sŏliˈdæriti). [ad. F. solidarité.]

Solidarize, v. rare. [f. SOLIDAR-ITY + -IZE.]

Solidary, a. [L. solidar-e.]

Solidate, v. Now rare. [ad. med.L. solidat-, ppl. stem of solidare to make solid or firm.]

Solidify (sŏliˈdifai), v. [ad. F. solidifier: see SOLID a. and -(I)FY.]

Solidism (sŏliˈdizm). Med. [f. SOLID a. + -ISM.]

Solidist (sŏliˈdist). Med. [f. prec. and -IST.]

Solidity (sŏliˈditi). Also 6 solidytie, 6–7 solidite, -itie. [ad. F. solidité, or L. soliditāt-em.]

Solidly, adv. In a solid manner.

1. So as to be fixed or firm; firmly, securely.

2. The quality or condition of being materially solid; compactness and firmness of texture, structure, etc. Also fig.

3. a. Geom. The amount of space occupied by a solid body; volume, cubic or solid content.

b. Relative density or mass.

4. fig. Extension in the three dimensions of space.

5. A solid thing or body. Also fig.

6. b. Extension of the three dimensions.

Solidungular, a. rare.

Solidungulate, a. and sb.

Solidungulous (soli-ˈdʌngiūlǝs), a.

† Solidus. Obs. [L., a substantial use of solidus (sc. nummus).] The form solidus is the L. acc. pl.]

1. a. A gold coin of the Roman empire, originally worth about 25 denarii. †b. A shilling.

† So·lidus, a. Obs. [ad. L. solidus (sol) a curve showing the temperatures at which a series of alloys are completely solid.

Solien, a. Obs. rare.

Soligenous, a. rare.

Soligenite. rare—1.

† Soligene, a. Obs.

So·liloquent, a. rare.

So·liloquize, v. intr.

Soliloquizer. [f. prec. + -ER 1.]

Soliloquy (sǝliˈlǝkwi). [ad. L. soliloquium.]

1. An instance of talking to or conversing with oneself, or of uttering one's thoughts aloud without addressing any person.

2. trans. To utter in soliloquy.

Hence **Soli·loquizing** vbl. sb. and ppl. a.

So·liloquy, sb. Obs. or arch.

† Soli·lo·quium. Obs. Also 6 pl. soliloquias.

Solifidian (soliˈfidiǝn), sb. and a. Theol.

A. sb. One who holds that faith alone without works, is sufficient for justification.

B. adj. Consisting of, pertaining to, the doctrine of justification by faith alone.

Solifidianism. [f. prec. + -ISM.]

The doctrine or tenet of justification by faith alone.

Soliform (sǝuˈlifǝːm), a. Also 7 soli·forme.

Solifuge (sǝuˈlifjuːdʒ). [ad. L. solifuga, var. of solpuga.]

Solify, v.

Soligenous, a. Obs.

Solipedal, a. [f. L. solipes, solipedis.]

Solipede (sǝuˈlipiːd).

Solipsism (sǝuˈlipsiz'm). Metaph.

Solipsist (sǝuˈlipsist).

Solisequious, a. Obs. or arch. Also solisi·quous.

Soli-lunar, a.

Solist. Astrol. Obs.

Soling, vbl. sb.

Solino·mial, a. Obs.

Soliped (sǝuˈliped), sb. and a.

Solitaire (soliˈtɛǝr). [a. F. solitaire, ad. L. solitarius.]

1. A person who lives in seclusion, solitude, or retirement; a recluse.

Solitaire (continued).

2. A Jamaican bird (Myiodectes solitarius).

3. An extinct flightless bird (Pezophaps solitarius) formerly existing in the island of Rodriguez.

† Solitaire-, -are, a. Obs.

† Solitaire, sb.

Solitariness (sǝuˈlitǝrinǝs). Forms: 6 solyt-, solytary-, 6-7 -nes, solitariness, - nesse, 6- -ness.

1. The state of being solitary or alone; the fact of being or dwelling apart from society.

Solitarian (soliˈtɛǝriǝn), a. and sb. rare.

Solitarily (sǝuˈlitǝrili), adv.

Solitary (sǝuˈlitǝri), a. Also 5 solitari(e, 6 solytarie.

1. a. One who retires, or lives in solitude from religious motives; a hermit or recluse.

2. A solitude, lonely place. Obs.

Solitary (sǝuˈlitǝri), sb. Also 4-6 solytarie.

1. One who lives by himself in seclusion or retirement; one who avoids, or is deprived of, the society of others.

2. Zool. One of various insects, birds, etc. which live alone or in pairs only, as a solitary bee, cuckoo, dodo, etc.

3. A lonely, unfrequented, or uninhabited place.

Soliter, variants of SOLITAIRE a. Obs.

† Solitous, a. Obs.

Solitude (sǝuˈlitjuːd). Forms 6 soli-, 5-6 solytude. [ad. L. solitūdo, -dinem, f. solus alone.]

1. The state of being or living alone; loneliness, seclusion; absence of company.

2. loneliness (of places); remoteness from habitation; absence of life or stir.

Solivagant, a. and sb. [f. L. solivagant-, solivagans, pr. pple. of solivagari.]

Soll, variant of SOLE, SOWL.

Sollage, obs. form of SULLAGE.

Sollar (sǝuˈlǝr), sb.¹ Also 1 solor, soler,

1. An upper room or apartment in a house or other dwelling; esp. in later use esp. a loft, attic, or garret (sometimes used as a granary or store-room). Now arch. or dial.

2. Coal-mining. A platform in a mine, esp. one supporting a ladder.

Hence **So·llar** v. trans. to furnish with a sollar or flooring.

Sollar.

Sollar, v. Obs. rare.

Sollaret (sŏ'larĕt). *Archæol.* Also soleret, solerette. [a. F. soll-, soleret, dim. of soll-, soler, souler (mod.F. soulier) shoe.] A shoe composed of steel plates or scales, forming part of a knight's armour in the 14th and 15th centuries.

† Sollevate, v. Obs. rare. [f. L. sollevare]

† Sollevation. [ad.It. sollevazione]

Sol-lunar, a. *Med.* [f. Sol a1 + Lunar a.] Due to the conjunction of sun and moon.

Sollicker, **Sollicking**: see Solid, Solidify, etc.

Sollid, obs. form of Solid.

Sollie, obs. form of Soul.

Sollme, obs. form of Soam.

So·lmizate, v. *Mus.* Also sol-. **b.** *intr.* To employ solmization.

Solmization (sɒlmiˈzeɪʃən). *Mus.* Also sol-misation, -zation. **b.** *solmisation*, l. *salmiser*, i. Sol Sol.[+ ori Mi.] The action or practice of solmizing.

† Solo (sōˈlo), *sb.* and *a.* Also *pl.* solos (also soli). [It. *solo*—L. *sōlum*, *sōlus* alone.]

A. *sb.* **1.** A musical air, song, melody, or other piece of music being rendered or performed by one singer or player; a piece of vocal or instrumental music performed, or intended for performance, by a single person.

2. Made to accommodate one person. (Cf. A. 5.)

3. Of musical instruments, or the players of these: Playing or taking the solo part.

So·lograph, *rare —¹*. [f. Sol *sb.*¹, after *photograph*.]

Soloist (sōˈloist). *Mus.* Also *sb.* + -ist.] One who sings or performs a solo or solos.

Soloman (sɒˈloman). Also 6–7 Salomon. [The name of the Jewish king (Solomon in older English usage *Salomon*), L. *Salomon*, *Salomo*, Gr. Σαλωμών, Σολωμών, ad. Heb. שׁלֹמֹה] One who resembles, or is comparable to, Solomon, esp. in respect of wisdom or justice ;

profoundly wise person, a sage; also ironically, a wiseacre.

Solonian, a. [See Solon.] Of, pertaining to, connected with, Solon.

Solonchak (sɒlənˈtʃak). (also *solontchak*). [Russ.] A type of soil.

Solonetz (sɒˈlonets), also *solonetse*, *solonez*. [Russ.] A type of soil.

Solonette, variant of Solonette.

Solow, obs. form of Sullow, plough.

Solp, variant of Sowp *v.*, Self *v.* Obs.

Solpuga (sɒlˈpjuːɡə). Also 8 Sal-. [f. L. *solpūga*, *salpūga*.] **1.** A venomous ant or spider mentioned by classical authors.

2. *Ent.* A genus of tropical or semi-tropical spiders (belonging to the group *Solpugidæ* or *Sulifugæ*); a weasel-spider.

Solpugid (sɒlˈpjuːɡid), a. Also 8-ick. [f. as prec. + -ic.]

1. Ascribed to, originating with, Solomon.

2. Of the Solpugidæ (see prec. 2).

† Sols. Obs. Also solz. [older F. *sols*, var. of *sol* *Sol sb.*²]

† Solsclce, Elder Brother n. 1. They shall not share a Solz of mine between them.

† Solsecle. Obs. [ad. OF. *solsecle*, -sicle, etc.], ad. L. *solsequium*: see prec.] The marigold.

Solstice (sɒˈlstis). Also mod.F. *sol-*, *sol-*, solst., solsticial. [a. F. *solstice* (12th c.)]

1. One or other of the two times in the year, midway between the two equinoxes, when the sun, having reached the tropical point farthest from the equator and appears to stand still, i.e. about 21st June (the summer solstice) and 22nd December (the winter solstice).

4. Of plants: Coming up at the summer solstice; growing or fading rapidly.

5. Of insects, etc.: Appearing about the time of the summer solstice.

So long: see Long *adv.* 1 c.

Solonian. [See Solon.]

Solstitium (sɒlˈstiʃəm). Pl. *solstitia*. Also 6 solsticium. [L.]

† Solstice, v. Obs. rare.

Solstitial (sɒlˈstiʃəl), a. Also 6-7 -tiall, -stiall, 7-9 -tial; [a. F. *solstitial*, or ad. L. *solstitiālis*, f. *solstitium*: see prec.]

A. *adj.* **1.** Of or belonging to, connected with, a solstice or the solstices.

Solubility (sɒljuˈbɪlɪti). [f. next + -ity. Cf. F. *solubilité*.]

1. The quality or property of being soluble.

Soluble (sɒˈljubˈl), a. Also 5-6 solyble, so-luble, 6 solubil. [a. OF. (also mod.F.) *soluble*, -Sp. *soluble*, Fg. *solūvel*, It. *solubile*, ad. L. *solūbilis*, f. *solvĕre* to loosen, dissolve, etc.]

1. *Med.* a. Of the bowels, etc.: Free from constipation or costiveness; relaxed.

2. Capable of being melted or dissolved.

3. Capable of being solved or explained; solvable.

SOLUBLENESS. 407 SOLUTION. SOLUTION. 408 SOLVENT.

Solubleness (sɒˈljubˈlnes).

† Solute, v. Obs. [f. L. *solūt-*, ppl. stem of *solvĕre* to solve.]

1. *trans.* To solve, explain, clear up.

2. To dissolve; *refl.* –¹.

Solute (sɒˈljuːt), *sb.* Also *sulut-us*, or Gr. *sōlout-us*; see Solecism.] Provincially incorrect.

Solution (sɒˈljuːʃən). Also 4 *solu-cioun*, -ioun, 4-6 *solucion*, 6 *solucyon*, *solyacion*, 6- *solution*. [a. OF. *solucion*, -*tion* (mod.F. *solution*), ad. L. *solūtiōn-em*, or ad. L. *solutio*, *solūtio*, f. *solvĕre* to solve, loosen, etc.]

1. The action or process of solving; the state, condition, or fact of being solved.

2. A particular instance or method of solving or settling; an explanation, answer, or decision.

3. *Math.* The action, process, or means of solving a problem.

4. The action of dissolving or discharging.

Solvend. ?Obs. [L. *solvend-um*, neut. gerundive of *solvĕre* to solve.] Something to be dissolved.

Solvent (sɒˈlvent), a. and *sb.* [ad. L. *solvent-*, ppl. stem of *solvĕre* to loosen, etc.]

A. *adj.* **1.** Having the power of dissolving or of forming a solution.

2. Able to pay all one's debts or liabilities.

B. *sb.* **1.** That which dissolves.

louse as a solvent and aperient. 1823 LAMB *Elia* Ser. II. Pref., He took it [tobacco], he would say, as a solvent of speech.

4. A person able to pay all his debts.
1825 COBBETT *Rur. Rides* (1853) 354 Every insolvent blames a solvent, that will not lend him money.

Hence **So·lventlyl** *adv.*
1872 H. BUSHNELL *Serm. Living Subj.* 437 That personal life-giving spirit that will touch as it were solvently, all the secret bonds and propagative chains of causes.

Solver (sǫ·lvəɹ). [f. SOLVE *v.* + -ER [1].] One who solves.
1719 DE FOE *Crusoe* I. (Globe) 222 A Casuist, or a Solver of Difficulties. 1854 *Athenæum* No. 1920. 217/2 Solver of problems. 1876 *Academy* 30 Sept. 331/1 The lynx-eyed public solvers often detect some simple second solution. 1898 *Month* Nov. 550 The solver of their doubts and difficulties.

† **Solwe,** *v. Obs.* Forms: *pa. pple.* (and *pa. t.*) 4 solwid (sulwed), soluid, solewid, 4–5 solwyd, solowed; 5 *inf.* sol(o)wyn. [Related to older Flem. *soluwen, seulewen,* MHG. *sulwen,* or to OHG. *sologôn, sologōn* (MHG. *solgen,* also *sulgen*): cf. SOL *a.* and SOLE *v.*[3]]
1. *trans.* To defile, soil, sully.
a 1300 *Cursor M.* 10637 Vr lauerd wil him neuer bede To bul þat solewid es wit sinn. *Ibid.* 22491 Lauerd! how mai we þan þis thole, þat es sua sulwed in vr sin. c 1425 *Cast. Persev.* 3421 in *Macro Plays* 179 Man hathe..solwyd hes sowle with synnys seuene. c 1440 *Promp. Parv.* 464/1 Solwyn, or fowiyn (*P.* solowyn), *maculo, deturpo. Ibid.,* Solwynge (*P.* solowynge), *deturpacio, sordidacio.*
2. *intr.* To become soiled or dirty.
1303 R. BRUNNE *Handl. Synne* 9152 Heere ne nayles neuer grewe, Ne solowed cloþes, ne turned hewe.

† **Solwy,** *a. Obs. rare.* [Related to prec.] Dirty.
c 1320 *Sir Tristr.* 1777 Smockes hadde sche and y, And was solwy to sen. *Ibid.* 1788. c 1325 *Gloss. W. de Bibbesw.* in Wright *Voc.* 171 [E si la nape seit trop soyle;] [*gloss*] solwy.
Hence † **So·lwiness,** pollution. *Obs.*
a 1300 *Cursor M.* 10887 Wit-vten sin or sulwines Sal þou be maiden als þou es. *Ibid.* 29037.

Soly(e, obs. ff. SOLELY *adv.* **Solybubbe,** obs. f. SILLABUB. **Solycit(e, Solycytude,** obs. ff. SOLICIT *v.*, SOLICITUDE.

Solydyne, obs. var. CELANDINE.
1425 *Eng. Voc.* in Wr.-Wülcker 644 *Hec selidonia,* solydyne.

Solymæ·an, *a. rare.* [f. L. *Solyma* for *Hierosolyma* Jerusalem.] Of or belonging to Jerusalem.
1681 DRYDEN *Abs. & Achit.* 513 The Solymæan Rout.. Saw with Disdain an Ethnick Plot begun.

Solys(se)t, Solys(se)tacion, Solyster, obs. ff. SOLICIT *v.* and *a.*, SOLICITATION, SOLICITER.

‖ **Soma** [1] (sōᵘ·mă). [Skr. *sōma,* = Zend *haōma,* Pers. *hōm*: see HOM.]
1. An intoxicating drink holding a prominent place in Vedic ritual and religion.
The soma was prepared from the juice of a plant which is commonly supposed to have been *Asclepias acida* or *Sarcostemma viminale* (or *acidum*).
1827 [see sense 2]. 1843 *Penny Cycl.* XXVI. 174/2 The soma, when properly prepared, is a powerful spirit. 1869 T. C. BARKER *Aryan Civiliz.* i. (1871) 3 From the Hindoo he [the fire-god] has the fermented drink called soma. 1872 WHITTIER *Brewing of Soma* iv, From tent to tent The Soma's sacred madness went, A storm of drunken joy. 1876 *Encycl. Brit.* IV. 205/2 The soma..must have played an important part in the ancient worship, at least as early as the Indo-Persian period.
attrib. 1843 *Penny Cycl.* XXVI. 175/1 What else is this act of drinking the soma-juice but a kind of sacrament? 1874 L. J. TROTTER *Hist. India* I. i. 4 He [Indra] delights in drinking the sacred soma juice. 1876 *Encycl. Brit.* IV. 205 Among the Vaidik rites the soma-sacrifices are the most solemn and complicated. 1895 A. NUTT *Voy. Bran* I. 321 The immortality claimed by the soma devotee.
2. *Soma plant,* the plant yielding the soma-juice. Also *ellipt.*
1827 COLEBROOKE in *Trans. Royal Asiatic Soc.* I. 455 The presenting of expressed juice of the *soma* plant. 1866 *Treas. Bot.* s.v. *Asclepias,* The bruised stem and leaves of the Soma plant yield a juice [etc.]. 1882 *Cornh. Mag.* June 720 The soma plant, by which Indra conquers Vritra.

Soma [2] (sōᵘ·mă). *Phys.* [a. Gr. σῶμα body.] The body of an organism in contrast to the germ-cells. Also *attrib.* in *soma-plasm.*
1889 tr. *Weismann's Ess. Heredity,* etc. 122 It is necessary to distinguish between..the body in its narrower sense (*soma*) and the germ-cells. *Ibid.* 154 The perishable and vulnerable nature of the *soma.* 1902 *Encycl. Brit.* XXIX. 25/2 With Weismann, we suppose the germ-plasm to be different in kind from the general soma-plasm. 1904 *Brit. Med. Jrnl.* 15 Oct. 966 If the mother be addicted to drink, additional damage may be done to the soma during intra-uterine life.

Somal (sōᵘ·măl), *a.* [f. Gr. σῶμα body, SOMA [2].] Of or pertaining to the body.
1900 *Proc. Zool. Soc. Lond.* 20 Feb. 134 The slight difference in size between the dermal and somal chiasters.

† **Soma·ndric,** *a. Obs.*[−1] [f. Gr. σῶμα body + ἀνδρ-, ἀνήρ man.] Relating to the human body.
1716 M. DAVIES *Athen. Brit.* III. *Diss. Physick* 21 The Cause, why Providence..also has absconded the great Psyc[h]andrick as well as Somandrick Secret of the Chymical Grand Elixir.

Somaschian (somæ·skiăn), *sb.* and *a.* [f. It. *Somaschi,* pl. of *Somasco* (cf. next), f. *Somasca,* a place lying north-west from Bergamo in Italy.]
a. *sb.* A member of a religious order, chiefly engaged in charitable instruction, founded at Somasca by Gerolamo Emiliani about 1530. b. *adj.* Of or pertaining to this order.
1882–3 SCHAFF *Encycl. Rel. Knowl.* III. 2214 The order of the Somaschians..in the Roman-Catholic Church.

† **Somasque.** *Obs.* Also 7 **Somask.** [a. F. *Somasque,* ad. It. *Somasco,* f. *Somasca* (see prec.).] = SOMASCHIAN *sb.*
1686 tr. *Bouhours' St. Ignatius* v. 284 He had made the same Answer some Years before, in reference to the Somasques, and the Theatines. 1693 tr. *Emiliane's Monast. Orders* xviii. 188 The Fathers of the Christian Doctrin..petition'd to be united to the Somasks. 1706 tr. *Dupin's Eccl. Hist.* II. IV. xi. 450 Jerome Emiliani, a noble Venetian, in the year 1530 founded some Regular Clerks, called Somasques, from the name of the place where they lived.

Somatal (sōᵘ·mătăl), *a. Zool.* [f. Gr. σῶμα, σωματ- body.] Of or pertaining to the body.
1875 BLAKE *Zool.* 243 The animal is chiefly divided into a somatal and a pallial portion.

Somata·lgia. *rare.* [f. as prec. + Gr. -αλγία, f. ἄλγος pain.] Bodily pain or suffering.
1607 WALKINGTON *Opt. Glass* B j, *Somatalgia* and *Psychalgia,* the one the dyscrasie of the body, the other the malady and distemperature of the soule. 1908 G. S. HALL *Adolescence* I. 480 The readiness with which psychalgia passes to somatalgia.

Somatic (somæ·tik), *a.* and *sb.* [ad. Gr. σωματικός, f. σῶμα, σωματ- body. So F. *somatique.*]
A. *adj.* 1. Of or pertaining to the (or a) body; bodily, corporeal, physical.
1775 ASH, *Somatic,* corporeal, belonging to a body. 1816 BENTHAM *Chrestomathia* Wks. 1843 VIII. 187 Somatic, or Somatological fictitious entities. 1859 *Sat. Rev.* 10 Dec 709/1 Those in which somatic and psychical coefficients are manifestly intermingled. 1884 BLACKMORE *Tommy Upmore* I. iii. 23 Variant motions and emotions, both somatic and psychical.
b. *Anat.* and *Phys.* of parts of the body.
1859 HUXLEY *Oceanic Hydrozoa* 26 The diverticulum of the somatic cavity becomes pyriform. 1861 J. R. GREENE *Man. Anim. Kingd., Cœlent.* 6 The nutritive, or somatic, fluid occupying the general cavity of the body. 1881 *Jrnl. Microsc. Sci.* Jan. 73 The two layers of the mesoblast, somatic and splanchnic. 1899 *Allbutt's Syst. Med.* VI. 371 The termination of the somatic nerves derived from the segment of the cord.
c. *spec.* Pertaining to the soma in contrast to the germ.
1888 *Nature* 14 June 156/2 In the Metazoa, the germ-cells, instead of remaining single, give rise to the vast number of somatic cells which compose the adult structure. 1896 MRS. ROMANES *Life & Lett. Romanes* 35 It is demonstrated that the somatic tissues of the scion have exercised an effect on the germinal elements of the stock.
2. Affecting the body.
1835–6 J. A. SYMONDS in *Todd's Cycl. Anat.* I. 791 *note,* The writer is indebted to..Dr. Prichard for the suggestion of *somatic* [instead of *systemic*],..but he has not had the courage to introduce it into the text. 1839–47 CARPENTER *Ibid.* III. 757/2 Molecular death is not always an immediate consequence of somatic death. 1899 *Allbutt's Syst. Med.* VIII. 425 Hypnotism could do nothing in somatic affections.
B. *sb. pl.* Somatology.
1816 BENTHAM *Chrestomathia* Wks. 1843 VIII. 87 This branch of Art and Science is entitled to the appellation of Coenoscopic Anthropurgics, or Somatics. 1861 *Sat. Rev.* 15 June 621 The Germans retort by accusing their adversaries..of 'mechanical, soulless somatics (*somatik*)'.
So **Soma·tical** *a.*, 'corporeal, bodily, substantial' (Bailey, 1727); **Soma·tically** *adv.*
1847 tr. *Feuchtersleben's Med. Psychol.* 219 Somatically they [i.e. certain excitements] act at the expense of the brain. 1902 *Pop. Sci. Monthly* Mar. 421 But while the Seri Indians are so well developed somatically,..they have been no less notorious..for unparalleled laziness.

Soma·tico-, combining form of Gr. σωματικός SOMATIC *a.*, in *somatico-hedonistics* (see quot.).
1816 BENTHAM *Chrestomathia* Wks. 1843 VIII. 90 Under the name of Somatico-Hedonistics might be collected and comprehended those branches of art and science which, as above, have for their objects those modifications of pleasure, which have the body for their seat.

† **So·matism.** *Obs.*[−1] [f. as next + -ISM.] Materialism.
? c 1720 ? DE FOE *Apparition* D.'s Wks. 1841 XIX. 267 To the prevailing of Somatism and the Hobbean principle in these times.

Somatist (sōᵘ·mătist). [f. Gr. σῶμα, σωματ- body, SOMA [2] + -IST.]
† 1. A materialist. *Obs.*
1676 GLANVILL *Ess. Philos. & Relig.* IV. 33 The name and notion of such Somatists, as are for meer Matter and Motion, and exclude immaterial Beings. 1694 BURTHOGGE *Reason* 201 What will..[a] meer Somatist say to the Corps-Candles, or Dead Mens Lights, in Wales?
2. *attrib.* Pertaining to, connected with, the soma.
1908 *Outlook* 5 Sept. 298/1 The issue between the somatist or 'mnemic' theory, as presented by Mr. Darwin and the doctrines of Weismann.

Somato- (sōᵘ·mato), a. Gr. σωματο-, combining form of σῶμα, σωματ- body (see SOMA [2]), used in a number of scientific terms, as **so·matocyst,** a sac forming the proximal end of the hydrosoma in oceanic hydrozoa; **somatogene·tic** *a.*, **somato·genic** *a.* (see quots.); † **somato·gnosy,** somatology; **so·matoplasm,** soma-plasm; **so·matopleure** (see quot. 1874); **somatopleu·ric** *a.*, of or belonging to the somatopleure; **somato·tomy,** anatomy.
Many similar compounds occur in special works or are recorded in recent dictionaries, as *somatoblast, -chrome, -derm, -graphy, -phyte, -phytic,* etc.
1859 HUXLEY *Oceanic Hydrozoa* 31 The *somatocyst is narrow and subcylindrical. 1870 H. A. NICHOLSON *Man. Zool.* 79 The proximal end of the hydrosoma is modified into a peculiar cavity called the somato-cyst. 1905 G. A. REID *Princip. Heredity* i. 6 Acquired characters take origin (as a rule) in the cell-descendants of the germ-cell; that is, they are *somatogenetic in origin. 1889 in *Rep. Brit. Assoc.* 767 He [Weismann] uses the term *somatogenic to express those characters which first appear in the body itself. 1811–31 BENTHAM *Logic* App. Wks. 1843 VIII. 284 Somatology, *somatognosy, or somatics. 1889 tr. *Weismann's Ess. Heredity,* etc. 104 If the germ-plasm and the substance of the body, the *somatoplasm, have always occupied different spheres. 1890 WEISMANN in *Nature* 6 Feb. 320/2 My germ-plasm or idioplasm of the first ontogenetic grade is not modified into the somatoplasm of Prof. Vines. 1874 FOSTER & BALFOUR *Elem. Embryol.* 38 The upper (or outer) leaf of the blastoderm, from its giving rise to the body-walls, is called the *somatopleure. 1888 *Q. Jrnl. Microscopic Sci.* XXVIII. 111 The lower end lies outside the angle.., between the somatopleure and splanchnopleure. 1874 FOSTER & BALFOUR *Elem. Embryol.* 39 The *somatopleuric investment of the yolk sac. 1900 *Nature* 12 Apr. 560/2 Prior to the formation of the somatopleuric system represented by the cardinal veins, &c. 1851 DUNGLISON *Dict. Med. Sci.* 797/1 *Somatotomy.

Somatological (sōᵘmătolǫ·dʒikăl), *a.* [f. SOMATO- + -LOGICAL. Cf. F. *somatologique.*] Of or pertaining to somatology.
1816 BENTHAM *Chrestomathia* Wks. 1843 VIII. 149 Linnæus, the father, as he may be termed, of Somatological tactics. 1820 L. HUNT *Indicator* No. 54 (1822) II. 15 *Kubla Khan*..he calls 'a psychological curiosity'. It is so; but it is also and still more a somatological or bodily one. 1898 HADDON *Study of Man* 438 Instructions for making certain somatological observations.
Hence **So·matolo·gically** *adv.*
1888 *Science* 9 Nov. 227/2 Equal to denying that the Basques and the Fins belong somatologically to the white race. *Ibid.* 228/1.

Somato·logist. [See next and -LOGIST.] One who studies, or is skilled in, somatology.
1893 D. G. BRINTON in *Smithsonian Rep.* 594 The constant blending of extreme physical types which the somatologist discovers in the remains from the oldest cemeteries around that great interior sea.

Somatology (sōᵘmătǫ·lŏdʒi). [f. SOMATO- + -LOGY, or ad. mod.L. *somatologia* (O. Casmann, 1596). Cf. F. *somatologie* (1762).]
1. A treatise or science dealing with the properties of bodies.
1736 BAILEY (fol.) Pref., *Somatology,*..a Discourse of Matter or Substance in the General, the Natures and inseparable Properties of Bodies. 1813–21 BENTHAM *Ontology* Wks. 1843 VIII. 195/1 Somatology, the only branch of physics that comes under the cognisance of sense.
2. A treatise or science dealing with the human body in some respect.
1851 DUNGLISON *Dict. Med. Sci.*, *Somatology,* a treatise on the human body. Anatomy. 1868 PORTER *Human Intellect* (1870) § 3. 7 Somatology signifies the science of the body only, and is subdivided into anatomy and physiology. 1898 D. G. BRINTON in Haddon *Study of Man* 491 Somatology.—Physical and Experimental Anthropology.

Somatome (sōᵘ·mătōᵘm). [f. SOMA(TO)- + -TOME.] A section or segment of the body.
1856 GOODSIR in *Edinb. New Philos. Jrnl.* V. 121 To the constituent segment, with its diverging appendages, I apply the term Somatome... The constituent somatomes are invariably arranged in groups.
Hence **Somato·mic** *a.*
1882 *Trans. Linn. Soc.* II. III. 166 Only where the notochord lingers can any trace of somatomic division be seen.

Sombre (sǫ·mbəɹ), *a.* and *sb.* [a. F. *sombre,* of uncertain origin: cf. Sp. and Pg. *sombrio,* f. *sombra* shade. See also SOMBROUS *a.*]
A. *adj.* 1. Of inanimate natural objects and their attributes: Characterized by the presence of gloom or shadow; depressingly dark, dusky, or obscure.
1760 H. WALPOLE *Lett.* (1845) IV. 85 Painted ceilings, inlaid floors, and unpainted wainscots make every room sombre. 1777 W. DALRYMPLE *Trav. Sp. & Port.* cxxxii, This city.. had a sombre and poor appearance. 1792 A. YOUNG *Trav. France* 184 This coast..dark, gloomy, and silent;—a savage sombre air spread over the whole. 1816 SCOTT *Old Mort.* xliii, The first shoot..of the yet unbroken stream, and the deep and sombre abyss into which it was emptied. 1860 MAURY *Phys. Geog.* xv. § 674 The sombre skies and changeable weather of our latitudes. 1882 MISS BRADDON *Mt. Royal* vi, The dining-room was sombre and substantial.
2. Of persons, their appearance, etc.: Gloomy, lowering, dark and sullen or dejected.
a 1767 GRAINGER *Ode Solitude* 52 Late in Hagley you were seen, With blood-shed eyes, and sombre mien. 1813 BYRON *Island* III. vi, Till lifting up again his sombre eye, It glanced on Torquil. 1865 BARING-GOULD *Werewolves* vi. 75 The man..was a sombre ill-looking fellow.
b. Of thoughts, feelings, etc.: Melancholy, dismal, darksome.
1821 JOANNA BAILLIE *Met. Leg., Ghost Fadon* xxii, All Remain'd in sombre mood. 1832 DOWNES *Lett Contin. Countr.* I. 390 The entire shore is lined with dilapidated edifices, which would, under other circumstances, have awakened sombre reflections. 1877 MRS. OLIPHANT *Makers Florence* xii. (1877) 297 No doubt it cast a gleam of sombre hope upon his confinement.

3. Conveying gloomy ideas or suggestions.
1768 STERNE *Sent. Journ., Hotel at Paris,* Beshrew the sombre pencil! said I vauntingly. a 1854 H. REED *Lect. Eng. Lit.* x. (1878) 334 Sombre as the poem at first appears, it works its way on to happy hopes. 1874 L. STEPHEN *Hours Libr.* (1892) II. ii. 56 Such sketches are a pleasant relief to his more sombre portraiture.
4. Of colours or colouring: Of a dark shade or tinge; dark, dull.
1805 WILKES *Mem.* II. 175 The olive-tree..is a sombre brown, when one expects a green. 1835 J. DUNCAN *Beetles* (Nat. Lib.) 186 Those [insects] that derive their nourishment from decomposed vegetables are usually of a sombre hue. 1866 ROGERS *Agric. & Prices* I. xxii. 577 Ecclesiastics and persons of gravity affected sombre colours.
b. Of things in respect of colour. (Cf. 1.)
1829 GRIFFITH tr. *Cuvier* VIII. 315 Sombre Plover, *Charadrius Fuscus.* 1839 G. BIRD *Nat. Philos.* 333 The chloride of silver..becomes of a deep slate colour in the violet, and in the sombre space beyond it. 1851 BRIMLEY *Ess.* 158 He had originally a fine sombre complexion. 1872 YEATS *Techn. Hist. Comm.* 152 A sombre garb was worn by the nuns, and coarse cowls by the friars.
5. *Comb.*, as *sombre-clad, -coloured, -minded, sombre-looking* adjs.
1850 LYNCH *Theoph. Trinal* v. 83 Dissatisfied, querulous, sombre-minded persons. 1872 JENKINSON *Guide English Lakes* (1879) 337 A wild and sombre-looking mass of rocks and precipices. 1889 S. J. HICKSON *Naturalist in N. Celebes* 214 The pious and sombre-clad Christian natives. 1899 MACKAIL *W. Morris* II. 191 The vast sombre-coloured crowd.
B. *sb.* Sombre character; sombreness. *rare.*
1795 H. M. WILLIAMS *Lett. France* I. 164 Fonfrede and Ducos relieved the sombre of the piece by the habitual liveliness of their characters. 1811 *Henry & Isabella* I. 285 A deep sombre spread itself over every thing.

Sombre (sǫ·mbəɹ), *v.* [f. SOMBRE *a.*]
1. *trans.* To make sombre.
1787 HILDITCH *Rosa* II. 52 Life, like..the iris bow, is beheld glowing in vivid charms, or sombred by gloom. 1807 SIR R. WILSON in *Life* (1862) II. vii. 208 Our entertainment was somewhat sombred by the intelligence. 1825 *Blackw. Mag.* XVII. 44 The midnight moon Looks sombred o'er the forests. 1873 MORLEY *Rousseau* I. 315 One..whose imagination, already sombred by the triumphant cruelty and superstition which raged around him, was suddenly struck with horror.
2. *intr.* To become or grow sombre.
1848 *Tait's Mag.* XV. 422 The picture sombred. 1893 *Temple Bar* XCIX. 43 Day again had sombred into night.
Hence **So·mbred, So·mbring** *ppl. adjs.*
1849 WHITTIER *Lakeside* 28 This lake..Walled round with sombering pines. 1873 MASSON *Drumm. of Hawth.* xx. 453 The russet and the yellow coming in patches amid the doubly sombred green.

So·mbreish, *a. rare*[−1]. Somewhat sombre.
a 1845 BARHAM *Ingol. Leg.* Ser. III. *Knt. & the Lady* (1905) 471 Her thoughts having taken a sombre-ish train.

Sombrely (sǫ·mbəɹli), *adv.* [f. SOMBRE *a.* + -LY [2].] In a sombre manner.
1860 LD. LYTTON *Lucile* II. vi. § 4. 11 The brass-fronted,.. audible *avroc* gone sombrely forth. 1868 GEO. ELIOT *Sp. Gipsy* 351 The boats Went sombrely upon the sombre waves. 1876 — *Dan. Der.* xxx, The place was sombrely in keeping with the black roads.

Sombreness (sǫ·mbəɹnès). [f. SOMBRE *a.* + -NESS.] The state of being sombre; gloominess; gloom; dullness.
1847 in WEBSTER. 1866 *Times* 13 June, Mourning so deep ..that not even a speck of white relieved its sombreness. 1866 GEO. ELIOT *F. Holt* (1868) 53 The general air of sombreness and privation. 1887 *Scribner's Mag.* II. 167/1 The sombreness of the bordering houses.

Sombrerite (sǫmbrī·ərəit). *Min.* [f. *Sombrero,* one of the Antilles islands + -ITE [1] 2 b.] A compound of phosphate of lime and phosphate of alumina, found on the island of Sombrero and other small islands in the West Indies.
1862 T. L. PHIPSON in *Jrnl. Chem. Soc.* XV. 277 Its composition and properties prove it to be a new species, to which I have given the name sombrerite.

‖ **Sombrero** (sǫmbrēᵊ·ro). Also 7 sumbrero, -briero, 8 somerera (?). [Sp. *sombrero* (= Pg. *sombreiro*), f. *sombra* shade.]
† 1. An Oriental umbrella or parasol. *Obs.*
Purchas and Herbert also use the fuller expression *sombrero de sol.*
1598 HAKLUYT *Voy.* II. 258 With a great Sombrero or shadow ouer their heads..as broad as a great cart wheele. 1638 SIR T. HERBERT *Trav.* (ed. 2) 316 Some..hold a Sumbrero or Umbrella in their hands to lenefie the flaming Sun. 1698 FRYER *Acc. E. India & P.* 51 We saw two Sumbrero's (a Mark for some of Quality) held up in the Boat-stern. 1727 A. HAMILTON *New Acc. E. Ind.* I. xxvii. 338 Some lusty Dutch Men to carry their Palenqueens and Somereras or Umbrellas.
2. A broad-brimmed hat, usually of felt or some soft material, of a type common in Spain and Spanish America.
1770 *Gentl. Mag.* XL. 530 A brown cap or silk net, with a large flatted hat called a *sombrero* over it. 1823 SCOTT *Quent. D.* xiv, A slouched overspreading hat, which resembled the sombrero of a Spanish peasant. 1855 THACKERAY *Newcomes* I. 280 In a velvet coat with a sombrero slouched over his face. 1885 LADY BRASSEY *The Trades* 177 It is sometimes called..the hat-palm, the young shoots making excellent sombreros or panamas.
attrib. 1891 E. ROPER *By Track & Trail* ix. 134 Their hats were of the sombrero order. 1900 *Times* 29 Jan. 10/3 Graceful Khaki-coloured sombrero hats.

Sombrous (sǫ·mbrəs), *a.* [f. F. *sombre* SOMBRE *a.* + -OUS. Cf. obs. F. *sombreux,* Sp. and Pg. *sombroso.*] Sombre; of a sombre character or aspect.
1. Of inanimate natural objects and their attributes. Cf. SOMBRE *a.* 1.
c 1730 BURT *Lett. N. Scotl.* (1822) I. 286 Their..horrid gloom, made yet more sombrous by the shades..they communicate one to another. 1787–9 WORDSW. *Evening Walk* 156 Where..the sombrous pine And yew-tree o'er the silver rocks recline. 1803 *Forest of Hohenelbe* I. 50 The long sombrous avenue that led to the front of the Castle. 1833 M. SCOTT *Tom Cringle* xiv, The fast falling shades of evening were deepened by the sombrous shadow of the immense tree overhead. 1889 P. H. EMERSON *Eng. Idyls* 47 Ghostly loomed the baleful wreck and sombrous beacons of the channel.
absol. 1862 D. G. F. MACDONALD *Brit. Columbia* 332 The whole territory..is endowed with savage beauty.., and extremely interesting to the lover of the sombrous.
2. a. Of persons, etc. Cf. SOMBRE *a.* 2.
1792 *Childr. Thespis* 49 When once in a moon Sombrous John condescends..to glad all his friends. 1799 MRS. J. WEST *Tale of Times* II. 36 Smothered discontent often made him meet..inquiries..with the sombrous brow of sorrow. 1802 — *Infidel Father* I. 136 Though the sombrous air of melancholy never after left his face. 1834 CAMPBELL *Mrs. Siddons* II. viii. 200 Kemble, [acting] on this occasion, was uncommonly sombrous.
b. Of thoughts, feelings, etc. Cf. SOMBRE *a.* 2 b.
1751 WARBURTON *Pope's Wks.* III. 190 A poor despicable superstition, a low sombrous passion. 1771–2 *Ess. fr. Batchelor* (1773) I. 239 His dull sombrous imagination rendered him incapable of varying his ideas on any subject. 1817 J. EVANS *Excurs. Windsor,* etc. 373 Under these sombrous feelings, even at this early period of life [etc.]. 1834 CAMPBELL *Mrs. Siddons* II. iii. 78 A serious temper, somewhat inclined to be sombrous.
3. Of abstract ideas, conditions, etc.
1750 WARBURTON *Doct. Grace* I. Wks. 1811 VIII. 293 A sparkling luxuriancy of thought, and a sombrous rankness of expression. 1778 WARTON *Hist. Eng. Poetry* III. xxvii. 150 A certain uniform strain of sombrous gravity. 1795 SOUTHEY *To Lycon,* The venom'd juice will..Lull reason's powers to sombrous sleep. 1820 *Ann. Reg.* II. 724 The future for Spain appears again under a sombrous and disturbed aspect.
4. Of colours or colouring. Also *transf.* Cf. SOMBRE *a.* 4.
1792 S. ROGERS *Pleasures of Mem.* II. 167 Time's sombrous touches soon correct the piece. 1797 T. PARK *Sonn.* 95 Let him in sombrous colours paint her lot. 1802 MRS. J. WEST *Infidel Father* I. p. iii, The episodical characters have a use besides relieving the sombrous hue of the principal personages.
b. = SOMBRE *a.* 4 b.
1799 MRS. J. WEST *Tale of Times* I. 212 The messenger.. found the castle attired in the most sombrous weeds of woe.
5. *Comb.*, as *sombrous-looking* adj.
1802 MRS. J. WEST *Infidel Father* II. 302 The Hymeneal Vulcan sometimes sees as sombrous looking suppliants approach his altar.
Hence **So·mbrously** *adv.*; **So·mbrousness.**
1796 *Mod. Gulliver's Trav.* 129 He looked very sombrously. 1847 WEBSTER, *Sombrously,* gloomily. *Sombrousness,* state of being sombrous.

Some (sɒm), *indef. pron.*, *a.*[1], *adv.*, and *sb.*[1] Forms: 1–6, 9 *dial.* sum (9 *dial.* zum), 3–4 summ, 4–5, 6 *Sc.* sume, summe; 4 soumme, 5 soume, 5 (9 *dial.*) soom; 3–5, 7, 9 *dial.* som (4 zom, 7 *dial.* z'om), 5 somm, somp; 3–6 somme, 3– some (4, 9 *dial.* zome). [Common Teut.: OE. *sum,* = OFris. *sum* (NFris. *som*), MDu. *som, zom* (WFlem. *som, zom*), OS. *sum* (MLG. *sum, som*), OHG. and MHG. *sum* (G. dial. *sum, som, söm*), ON. *sumr* (Icel. *sumur,* Norw. *sum*; MSw. *sum, som,* Sw. *somt* neut., Da. *somme* pl.), Goth. *sums*; the stem is also found in Gr. ἀμο- (as ἀμόθεν from some place) and Skr. *sama* any, every. The word has had greater currency in English than in the other Teutonic languages, in some of which it is now restricted to dialect use, or represented only by derivatives or compounds, as WFris. *sommige, somlike,* Du. *sommige* (also *somtiids, somwijlen* sometimes), LG. *sömige* (G. dial. *summige*).]
A. *indef. pron.*
For *all and some, whole and some,* see ALL *a.* 12, WHOLE *a.*
I. In singular uses.
† 1. One or other of a number of persons; someone, somebody. In later use also in phr. *some or other. Obs.*
(*a*) *Beowulf* 1432 Sumne Geata leod of flanbogan feores getwæfde. a 1000 *Riddles* xv. 15 (Gr.), Þonne ic winde sceal sincfag swelgan of summes bosme. a 1225 *Ancr. R.* 70 Summes kurteisie is noðeleas iturnd hire to vuele. c 1290 *S. Eng. Leg.* I. 131 In þis place sum is þat wolde telle þe kinge fore, and maken him mi fo. 1484 CAXTON *Fables of Æsop* v. x, Whan somme good cometh to somme, it ought not to be reffused. 1509 HAWES *Past. Pleas.* XXIII. (Percy Soc.) 107 Upon one hande some hath thombes twayne; And other also somtyme armes thre. c 1581 LODGE *Reply Gosson's Sch. Abuse* (Shaks. Soc.) 23, I feare me some will blushe that readeth this, if he be bitten. 1729 G. ADAMS tr. *Sophocl., Antig.* III. i. II. 39 Therefore..despise he [Antigone], and suffer the Girl to marry some among the Dead.
(*b*) 1631 HEYLIN *Hist. St. George* 113, I wonder some or other hath not resolu'd the doubt. 1664 D. FLEMING in *Extr. St. Papers rel. Friends* (1912) III. 213, I am halfe of opinion, that some or other hath abused him in this Letter. 1682 BUNYAN *Holy War* (1905) 208 Word, by some or other, could not but be carried to the good King Shaddai.
† b. Const. *of* (or gen. pl.). Also of things. *Obs.*
c 888 K. ÆLFRED *Boeth.* xviii. § 2 He cyðde on sumre his boca ðætte þa get Romana nama ne come ofer þa muntas. c 1000 *Ags. Gosp.* Matt. xiii. 25 Þa com his feonda sum & ofer-seow hit mid coccele. *Ibid.* Mark viii. 28 Sume [secgað] sumne of þam witegum. c 1200 *Twelfth Cent. Hom.* 134 Ȝif nu eower sum,..smeað hwæt god beo. 1340 *Ayenb.* 15 Vor onneaþe yualþ þet me ne ualþ in-to þe þrote of zome of þe zeue heauedes. 1638 SIR T. HERBERT *Trav.* (ed. 2) 46 The Cutteries..have six and thirty Casts among themselves, from some of which none of them but is descended. 1656 SANDERSON *Serm.* (1689) 405 All such sins being easily reducible to some of the former three.
c. In the phr. *some of these* (..) *days,* some day soon; before very long.
1831 in Knapp *Life G. Borrow* (1899) I. 142 Young Simpson will be wanting an able assistant some of these days. 1848 NEWMAN *Loss & Gain* I. xiv, 'We shall have you a papist some of these fine days,' said he. 1851 BORROW *Lavengro* lxxiii, I should not be surprised if he were to come back some of these days.
† 2. *Some..., some, one...,* another. (Cf. 7.)
c 888 K. ÆLFRED *Boeth.* xxxiii. § 2 Þonne lufað sum ðæt, sum elles hwæt. c 1000 *Ags. Gosp.* Matt. xxv. 15 He sealde.. sumum twa [pund], sumum an. a 1225 *Ancr. R.* 6 Vor sum is strong, sum is unstrong. c 1250 *Gen. & Ex.* 834 Sum was king, and sum kumeling. c 1386 CHAUCER *Knt.'s T.* 2173 He mot ben deed,..Som in his bed, som in the depe see. 1390 GOWER *Conf.* III. 14 For som schal singe and som schal syke.
† 3. With ordinal numbers: One of (or with) a specified number. *Obs.*
For the use of the ordinal cf. G. *selbdritte, -vierte,* etc. In OE. the gen. plur. of the cardinal was employed, as *syxa, eahta, twelfa sum*: for the later history of this see -SOME [2].
a 1225 *Juliana* 79 And te sea sencte him on his þrituðe sum ant þer to þet fowre. 13.. *Sir Beues* 203 Him self was boute þe ferþe some Toward þat ferd. c 1320 *Sir Tristrem* 817 He busked and made him ȝare Hi[m] fiftend som of kniȝt. c 1425 [see THIRDSOME].
4. A certain indeterminate part of something; a portion. († In early use freq. following a noun or pronoun, or predicative.) Also *some..., some.*
c 900 *O. E. Chron.* (Parker MS.) an. 877, Þa..ȝefor se here on Miercna lond, & hit gedældon sum, & sum Ceolwulfe saldon. c 1000 *Ags. Gosp.* Luke viii. 5 Þa he þæt seow, sum feoll wið þæne weȝ.. And sum feoll ofer þæne stan. c 1275 *Prov. Hendyng* 98 Ȝef thou hauest bred & ale,..Þou del hit sum aboute. 1297 R. GLOUC. (Rolls) 98 He hadde þer to Scropssire som & aluendel of warewik ssire. 1387 TREVISA *Higden* (Rolls) I. 151 Amazonia..is som in Asia, and som in Europa. c 1440 *Promp. Parv.* 484/1 Sum, or sumwhat, or a part of a nowmyr or a noþer thynge. 1572 in Feuillerat *Revels Q. Eliz.* (1908) 162 Sum in Bowltes and sum by lb. 1588 KYD *Househ. Phil.* Wks. (1901) 245 Some was roste, some was backt. 1597 SHAKS. *2 Hen. IV,* Epil., Bate me some, and I will pay you some. 1611 BIBLE *Luke* viii. 6 And some fell vpon a rocke, and.. it withered away. 1796 C. MARSHALL *Gardening* xix. (1813) 371 As it is a small flower, pot some.
b. Const. *of* (the thing specified).
c 1175 *Lamb. Hom.* 133 Sum of þe sede feol an uppe þe stane. 1297 R. GLOUC. (Rolls) 101 Som of gloucestressire & of warewikssire al so. 1560 BIBLE (Geneva) *Lev.* iv. 7 The Priest also shal put some of the blood..vpon the hornes of yͤ altar. 1600 SHAKS. *A. Y. L.* IV. iii. 96 Some of my shame, if you will know of me What man I am. 1639 J. SMYTH in *Glouc. Gloss.* (1890) 200 Ga'as zo'm of thuck bread. 1694 CONGREVE *Double Dealer* v. v, Snuff some of my spirit of hartshorn. 1834–6 *Encycl. Metrop.* (1845) VIII. 762/1 In the act of drying, some of the lac is generally brought to the surface. 1872 MORLEY *Voltaire* (1886) 6 Some of it, much of it, has ceased to be alive for us now.
† c. (*By*) *some and some,* by little and little; by degrees; gradually. *Obs.* (Cf. 8 b.)
1398 TREVISA *Barth. De P. R.* XI. i. (Tollem. MS.), Vapoures, þat beþ gaderid sum and sum in þe erþe. *Ibid.* XVII. cxliii. (Bodl. MS.), Whan þe weþye is swiþe olde, þan he faileþ & roteþ somme and somme. 1602 J. RHODES *Answ. Romish Rhyme* 8 Your doctrine.., which did creepe Into the Church, by some and some.
† d. *Some and some,* something in return for something. *Obs.*
1573 GASCOIGNE *Herbes* Wks. 1907 I. 353 Recompence the lyke agayne: For some and some is honest playe. 1583 MELBANCKE *Philotimus* T j, Thinke some and some is honest play.
II. In plural senses.
5. An indefinite or unspecified (but not large) number of persons (or animals); certain persons not named or enumerated. Also *some or other.*
Beowulf 400 Sume þær bidon, heaðoreaf heoldon. c 888 K. ÆLFRED *Boeth.* xi. § 1 Sume beoð swiðe æþele & widcuðe on heora ȝebyrdum. c 950 *Lindisf. Gosp.* John vii. 44 Sumo..uilnadon ȝegrioppa hine. 1154 *O. E. Chron.* (Laud MS.) an. 1137, Sume hi diden in crucethus. c 1175 *Lamb. Hom.* 3 Heo urnen on-ȝein him..and summe mid ufele þeonke. c 1205 LAY. 27376 Heo sculleð beon islaȝene and summe quic iulaȝene. a 1250 *Owl & Night.* 1648 Summe of þe scheules makeþ. a 1300 *Cursor M.* 14739 Amang þir men..War sume þat duues boght and sald. 1375 BARBOUR *Bruce* vi. 440 Thai ourtuk sum at the last, And thame forout mercy can sla. c 1440 *Pallad. on Husb.* II. 283 Summe hem kepe Thre nyght in molten donge. 1450 *Paston Lett.* I. 125 Soom sey he wrotte moche [thing]. 1579 SPENSER *Sheph. Cal.* Sept. 152 Neuer was Woolfe seene, many nor some. 1601 HOLLAND *Pliny* I. 117 Some there be that think how it was first founded by Amphitus. 1675 H. MORE in R. Ward *Life* (1710) 361, I do not wonder that some or other are now and then so strangely assaulted. 1747 MRS. GLASSE *Cookery* ix. 88 Some love scalded Gooseberries with them. 1816 J. WILSON *City of Plague* II. i, Some, my son, Would bid thee trust in time. 1842 LOUDON *Suburban Hort.* 121 It feeds on worms..and

according to some, on roots. 1878 T. HARDY *Ret. Native* I. iii. (1890) 21, I shouldn't have cared about the man, though some may say he's good-looking.
b. Similarly of things.
c 975 *Rushw. Gosp.* Matt. xiii. 4 And þa he seow, sume gefeollun bi wæge & cuomun fuȝlas heofun & frætun. a 1225 *Ancr. R.* 28 Uor þe ten hesten þet ich ibroken habbe, summe oðer alle. 1382 WYCLIF *Matt.* xiii. 4 And the while he soweth, sum felden byside the weye. a 1400–50 *Alexander* 568 It..raynes doune stanys,..And some as hoge as þi hede fra þe heuyn fallis. c 1449 PECOCK *Repr.* III. xiv. 371 And so forth of manye othere staryng gouernauncis, semyng summe wijlde woode. 1547 BOORDE *Brev. Health* Pref., Many obscure termes,..some & fewe beynge Araby wordes. 1588 LAMBARDE *Eirenarcha* IV. xix. 595 There be also certain matters..appropriated, some to any, and others to some one, of the generall Sessions. 1607 SIR J. HARINGTON in *Nugæ Ant.* (1804) I. 47 Manie bowlts were roved after him, and some spitefullie feather'd.
† c. With pronoun or sb. in apposition. (Cf. B. 7 b.) *Obs.*
c 900 tr. *Baeda's Hist.* IV. vii[i]. 282 Þa sumu [*v.r.* sume] woe nu ȝemdon ȝeþeodan in þis user ciriclice stær. c 1000 *Ags. Gosp.* John vi. 64 Ac sume ȝe ne ȝelyfað. a 1122 *O. E. Chron.* (Laud MS.) an. 1101, Se cyng syððan scipa ut on sæ sende.., ac hi sume æft æt þære neode abruðon. c 1275 *Passion Our Lord* 43 in *O. E. Misc.* 38 Summe hi weren wyse, and duden al bi his rede. 1597 SHAKS. *Lover's Compl.* 148 Yet did I not, as some my equals did, Demaund of him. 1606 — *Tr. & Cr.* IV. v. 190 (Q.¹), That I haue said to some my standers by.
d. In possessive form. Now *rare.*
1565 COOPER *Thesaurus* s.v. *Capio,* Sommes consciences beganne to pricke them. 1597 BEARD *Theatre God's Judgem.* (1612) 44 Somes lot it was to be torn in pieces. 1653 BP. WEBBE *Pract. Quiet.* 253 Nor may I condemn all..for somes unquietness. 1675 E. WILSON *Spadacr. Dunelm.* 67, I fear I have spoken Ænigmatically..to somes understanding. 1823 BYRON *Juan* XIII. xxx, Howsoe'er it shocks some's Self-love, there's safety in a crowd of coxcombs.
6. With *of* (persons or things).
c 875 in *O. E. Texts* 178 Ðæt he spræc to his liornæra sumum. c 950 *Lindisf. Gosp.* Matt. xxviii. 11 Summe of ðæm haldendum cwomun in ða ceastra. c 1175 *Lamb. Hom.* 43 Summe of þan monne sare wepeð. c 1200 ORMIN 6574 Sume off ure little flocc þatt lefeþþ uppo Criste. c 1275 LAY. 12001 Somme of þaie sipes wonde mid þan wedere. 1303 R. BRUNNE *Handl. Synne* 9997 Lo here a tale for of ȝou sum. c 1386 CHAUCER *Can. Yeom. Prol.* 193 Somme of hem synke in to the ground. c 1449 PECOCK *Repr.* II. viii. 185 God wrouȝte tho myraclis in summe of tho placis more and ofter than in othere placis like. 1470–85 MALORY *Arthur* VIII. xxxiii. 323 Somme of them were sore hurte. 1537 *Thersytes* 99 in Pollard *Mir. Plays* (1890) 129 Some of the giauntes before Noes floud. 1588 KYD *Househ. Phil.* Wks. (1901) 267 A youth who..doth seme to write and mannedge some of their affaires. 1611 BIBLE *Rom.* xi. 17 If some of the branches bee broken off. 1664 PEPYS *Diary* 19 Mar., I spent the afternoon in paying some of the charges of the burial. 1748 HARTLEY *Observ. Man* I. i. 63 Some or other of those vibrations which are excited in it. 1779 *Mirror* No. 31, Some of our most celebrated historians have committed errors of the first sort. 1823 SCOTT *Quentin D.* xxxiii, Bring that rascal forward, some of you. 1855 MACAULAY *Hist. Eng.* xvi. III. 715 Some of those who opposed the bill. 1891 E. ROPER *By Track & Trail* xv. 217 Higher up..there are some of the most sublime scenes I have looked on anywhere.
7. *Some..., some,* = Some..., others. (Cf. 2.) † Formerly also in *some...than some, some and some.*
(*a*) c 888 K. ÆLFRED *Boeth.* xxxiii. § 5 Sume beorhtor sume unbyrhtor, swa swa steorran. c 1000 *Ags. Gosp.* Mark xii. 5 Sume hi beoton, sume hi of-sloȝon. 1154 *O. E. Chron.* (Laud MS.) an. 1140, Sume helden mid te king & sume mid þemperice. c 1200 *Trin. Coll. Hom.* 101 Sume sitteð and sume ligeð and sume we stondeð. a 1225 *Leg. Kath.* 37 Summe þurh muchele ȝeouen.., summe þurh fearlac. 13.. *K. Alis.* 2517 (W.), To divers castles he heom sent:..Some to Libye, some to Rome. c 1380 *Sir Ferumb.* 948 Of summe þay smyte of legges & armes, & of sum þe heuedes þay gerde. a 1400–50 *Alexander* 1330 All at he slayn fyndez, He makes to grave, some in grete, some in gray marbyll. c 1450 HOLLAND *Howlat* 64 Sum will me dulfully dicht, Sum dyng me to deid. 1523 SKELTON *Garl. Laurel* 250 Some whispred, some rownyd, some spake, and some cryde. 1568 GRAFTON *Chron.* II. 8 Some [fled] into Norway, and some into Denmarke, and some into one Countrie, and some into another. 1611 BIBLE *Psalms* xx. 7 Some trust in charets, and some in horses. 1685 TEMPLE *Misc.* II. *Gardens* (1690) 11 Like Rover Shots, some nearer an I some further off, but all at great Distance from the Mark. 1750 tr. *Leonardus' Mirr. Stones* 130 For some are gold, some silver, others copper, and others iron. 1837 P. KEITH *Bot. Lex.* 122 Some are annular, some are reticulated, some are dotted, and some akin to spirals. 1855 KINGSLEY *Westw. Ho!* xxv, Some ran; some did not run.
(*b*) c 1491 *Chast. Goddes Chyld.* ii. 7 Our lorde withdraweth him fro some more than fro some. 1526 *Inv. Goods Dk. Richmond* in *Camden Misc.* (1855) 19 Item, Counterpoints of all sortes, some bygger than some. 1547 *Bk. of Marchauntes* c vj b, My marchants, of whome truely some be wilier than some. 1821 SCOTT *Kenilw.* xli, Some are wiser than some,..and some are worse than some.
(*c*) 1522 SKELTON *Why not to Court?* 385 But there is some trauarse Bytwene some and some.
b. So *Some..., others* († *other*).
c 950 *Lindisf. Gosp.* Mark xii. 5 Sume ðurscun, oðero æc ofslogon. 1382 WYCLIF *Mark* xii. 5 Betynge summe, but sleynge othere. 1588 KYD *Househ. Phil.* Wks. (1901) 262 Some are naturally borne to commande, and others to obey. 1634 SIR T. HERBERT *Trav.* 189 Some have a smacke of Christ, others of Mahomet. 1696 in 13th *Rep. Hist. MSS. Comm.* App. VI. 41 By impowering some, and neglecting others. 1746 P. FRANCIS tr. *Horace, Art Poet.* 491 Some Charm when nigh, Others at Distance more delight your Eye. 1852 MISS YONGE *Cameos* (1877) III. iii. 21 The burghers hurried out, some with the straight cross of France, others with the saltire of Burgundy.
† c. Also *Some..., other some. Obs.*
1375 BARBOUR *Bruce* I. 32 For sum wald haiff þe Balleoll king;..And oþir sum nyt all þat cas. 1532 HERVET *Xenophon's Treat. Househ.* (1768) 74 For some haue gret plenty..and other some haue scantly so moche as they nede. 1585 T. WASHINGTON tr. *Nicholay's Voy.* II. xvi. 50 b, Cesternes.., supported some by vaultes, and othersom by.. pillars. 1611 [see OTHER SOME]. 1634 SIR T. HERBERT *Trav.* 141 Some place it in the circle of the Moone,..other some vnder the Circle of the Moone. 1700 S. L. tr. *Frykes' Voy. E. Ind.* 121 Some of 'em are far better than other some.
† 8. a. *Some after some,* = next. *Obs.*[−1]
1598 GRENEWEY *Tacitus, Ann.* IV. xvi. (1622) 115 Comming some after some, and dropping in by companies.
† b. *Some and some,* a few at a time, gradually. *Obs.* (Cf. 4 c.)
1686 tr. *Chardin's Trav. Persia* 63 He put my Goods aboard, some and some, as he saw his Opportunity. 1719 DE FOE *Crusoe* II. (Globe) 501 They came dropping in, some and some, not in two Bodies, and in Form.., but all in Heaps. 1769 G. WHITE *Selborne* xxiii, Persons who assert that the swallow kind disappear some and some, gradually, as they come.
B. *adj.*
I. With singular nouns. (See also 9 c.)
† 1. a. Of persons or places: A certain. *Obs.*
c 888 K. ÆLFRED *Boeth.* i, Þa wæs sum consul,..Boetius wæs ȝehaten. 971 *Blickl. Hom.* 15 Þa sæt þær sum blind þearfa be ðon weȝe. c 1000 *Ags. Gosp.* John xi. 1 Sum seoc man wæs ȝenemned lazarus of bethania. 1382 WYCLIF *Luke* i. 5 Ther was sum prest, Zacharie by name, in the dayes of Eroude. *Ibid.* xviii. 2–3 Sum iuge was in sum citee... Forsothe sum widowe was in that citee. a 1578 LINDESAY (Pitscottie) *Chron. Scot.* (S.T.S.) II. 87 Sum godlie man [*sc.* John Knox] was in the castell.
† b. = ONE *pron.* 2 b. *Obs.*
1382 WYCLIF *Acts* xxv. 19 Thei hadden aȝens hym summe questiouns..of sum Jhesu deed, whom Poul affermyde for to lyue. 1760 T. HUTCHINSON *Hist. Mass.* i. 86 A *quo warranto* had been brought by some Sir John Banks, attorney-general [etc.].
2. One or other; an undetermined or unspecified.
c 888 K. ÆLFRED *Boeth.* xxxvii. § 2 Þæt mon hæbbe ænne heafodbeaȝ gyldenne æt sumes ærneweȝes ende. c 1000 ÆLFRIC *Saints' Lives* xxxi. 651 Martinus..wolde for sumere neode wiþ hine spræcan. c 1200 ORMIN 228 Þeȝȝ wisstenn þatt himm wass þatt daȝȝ Summ unncuþ sihhþe shæwedd. a 1225 *Leg. Kath.* 811 Scheoteð forð sum word, & let us onswerien. c 1250 *Owl & Night.* 1265 Naueþ mon no sikerhede þat he ne may..adrede þat sum vnhap neih him beo. a 1300 *Vox & Wolf* 125 in Hazl. *E. P. P.* I. 62 For he thoute, mid soumme ginne, Him self houp [= up] bringe. 1387 TREVISA *Higden* (Rolls) I 101 Þat hul is ful hiȝe, so þat snowe lyeth all wey in som side of þat hille. c 1470 HENRY *Wallace* II. 391 Thow Scot, abide, I trow thow be sum spy. 1528 TINDALE *Obed. Chr. Man* 89 This worde..representeth allwaye some promise of God. 1581 J. BELL *Haddon's Answ. Osorius* 360 b, They rest their handes upon some staffe shaking and tremblyng. 1634 MILTON *Comus* 485 Som neighbour Wood-man, or at worst, Som roaving Robber. 1663 S. PATRICK *Parab. Pilgr.* (1687) 171, I believe you are desirous to have some list of these Enemies. 1725 POPE *Odyss.* VIII. 180 Some mean sea-farer in pursuit of gain. 1780 *Mirror* No. 94, Miss Sophia R. therefore keeps me right..or covers my deviations with some apology. 1825 SCOTT *Talism.* ii, They had even their knights, or some rank analogous. 1867 TROLLOPE *Chron. Barset* I. xxi. 177, I am going to ask him to put his case into some lawyer's hands. 1876 'OUIDA' *Winter City* vi. 128 A triptych of some old fogey of a painter.
b. In adverbial expressions of time and place, with or without a preposition.
See also SOMETIME, -WHERE, -WHILE.
(*a*) c 893 K. ÆLFRED *Oros.* I. i. 17 He sæde þæt he æt sumum cirre wolde fandian [etc.]. c 1000 ÆLFRIC *Hom.* I. 62 Þa becom se apostol æt sumum sæle to þære byriȝ Pergamum. c 1200 *Trin. Coll. Hom.* 185 Ðos seawe word seide ure drihten..at sume sele. a 1225 *Ancr. R.* 48 David..seide et sume time þat heo was etstert him. c 1250 *Owl & Night.* 293 At sum syþe herde i telle hw Alured seyde on his spelle. a 1300 *Cursor M.* 20081 In sum stanid on sum dai, Vneths he bar lif a-way. 1382 WYCLIF *Heb.* ii. 6 Sum man witnesside in sum place. a 1400–50 *Alexander* 204 Supposand þaim in sum tyme for sothe to be knawen. *Ibid.* (MS. D.) 755* He..stighillys hym in som stede a stable by hym one. 1616 B. JONSON *Forest* xiii, No lady, but at some time loves her glass.
(*b*) a 900 *O. E. Chron.* (Parker MS.) an. 896, Þa sume dæȝe rad se cyng up be þære eæ. a 1300 *Cursor M.* 13185 Men mai yeitt se sum sted in france [etc.]. 13.. *Seuyn Sag.* (W.) 2936 Bot wele in hert he hoped ay That he sold hir se sum day. a 1425 *Cursor M.* 956 (Trin.), I hete to sende hit ȝou sum tide. 1550 *Reg. Privy Council Scot.* I. 88 He hopis sum day to se his sone [etc.]. 1822 SHELLEY *Chas. 1st* II. 451 His Grace..expects to enter the New Jerusalem some Palm Sunday in triumph. 1845 BROWNING *Home Thoughts fr. Abroad* 4 And whoever wakes in England Sees, some morning, unaware [etc.]. 1865 RUSKIN *Sesame* i. § 13, I see it is true; or if I do not now, I hope I shall, some day.
c. With the indefiniteness emphasized by the addition of *or other* (cf. OTHER B. 5 a), *or another.*
1590 SHAKS. *Com. Err.* I. ii. 95 By some deuise or other, The villaine is ore-wrought of all my monie. 1615 W. BEDWELL *Arab. Trudg.* K iiij, How oft..shal you not meet with some exoticke and strange terme or other? 1697 DRYDEN *Dedic. Æneis* a iij b, Yet all this while I have been Sailing with some side-wind or other toward the Point I propos'd in the beginning. 1736 *Swift's Lett.* (1768) IV. 171, I received yours some day or other this week. a 1774 GOLDSM. *Surv. Exp. Philos.* (1776) II. 14 Certain it is that air is impregnated with salts of some kind or another. 1845 PATTISON *Ess.* (1889) I. 9 An impulse which will vent itself in some form or other. 1881 MRS. L. B. WALFORD *Dick Netherby* xii. 144 He must write some day or other.
d. With adjs. used absolutely. *rare.*
1579 SPENSER *Sheph. Cal.* Mar. 74 [I] Might see the mouing of some quicke, Whose shape appeared not. 1725 RAMSAY *Gentl. Sheph.* III. ii, The man's..possest With some nae good.
e. In suggestive or euphemistic use.
1725 RAMSAY *Gentl. Sheph.* v. iii, She's baith a slee and a revengfu' bitch, And that my some-place [= posteriors] finds.
† 3. Used with an indefinite or generalizing force similar to that of the plural (sense 7). *Obs.*
c 888 K. ÆLFRED *Boeth.* xxxiv. § 10 Sumes wuda eard bið on dunum. c 1000 ÆLFRIC *Hom.* I. 322 Sumum men he forgifð wisdom and spræce, sumum god inȝehyd, sumum micelne ȝeleafan. 13.. *Cursor M.* 10226 (Gött.), For þan was sum man god dredand. 1375 BARBOUR *Bruce* II. 295 Sum man for eryness will trymbill, Quhen he assayit is sodanly. 1481 CAXTON *Reynard* xxviii. (Arb.) 68 The ape ..is wyser in clergie than somme preest. 1535 COVERDALE *Ecclus.* vi. 9 And there is some frende that turneth to enemyte, and taketh parte agaynst the. *Ibid.* xx. 5 Some man kepeth sylence, and is founde wyse. 1565 COOPER *Thesaurus, Alburnum,* the fatte that is in some tree. 1638 JUNIUS *Paint. Ancients* 103 In some regard they tooke speciall notice of the difference of wits.
4. A certain (unspecified) amount, part, degree, or extent of (something), freq. implying 'not little, considerable'. † In OE. also with *the, his,* etc.
c 888 K. ÆLFRED *Boeth.* xxiv. § 4 Nis nan man þætte sumes eacan ne ðyrfe. c 893 — *Oros.* III. x. 140 He beæftan ȝebad mid sumum þæm fultume. c 980 *O. E. Chron.* an. 913, Sum his fultum worhte þa burȝ. a 1200 *Moral Ode* 25 in *O. E. Hom.* I. 161 Sendeð sum god bi-foren eow, þe hwile þet ȝe muȝen, to houene. c 1275 *XI Pains of Hell* 290 in *O. E. Misc.* 220 Poul kneld adowne..And prayd..Fore þe soulis in hel sum ryst haue þer. 1375 in Horstmann *Altengl. Leg.* (1878) 125/1 Bote rys, & go we eft wiþ mod For to seken vs sum fod. 1393 LANGL. *P. Pl.* C. III. 128 Þat god wolde were ydo with-oute som deceite. ? c 1440 *Pol., Rel., & L. Poems* (1903) 246 Lord! sende me sum 'amor' sede. 1478 *Paston Lett.* III. 237 He prayth yow to sende hym sum mony. 1562 *Child Marriages* 189 He came thither to get somme threde. 1590 SHAKS. *Mids. N.* I. i. 244 When this Haile some heat from Hermia felt. 1650 EARL MONM. tr. *Senault's Man bec. Guilty* 345 These wise men..mought have some cognizance of the truth. 1677 MARVELL *Season. Argum.*, etc. Wks. (1776) II. 562 Where he feathered his nest to some purpose. 1711 STEELE *Spect.* No. 100 ¶ 1 He immediately calls for some Posset-drink for him. *Ibid.* No. 106 ¶ 5 A Person of good Sense and some Learning. 1761–2 HUME *Hist. Eng.* (1806) IV. lxi. 589 Some state was upheld, but with little expense. 1831 SCOTT *Cast. Dang.* v, His master..had been a man of some reading. 1855 MACAULAY *Hist. Eng.* xviii. IV. 191 In the neighbourhood ..was some copsewood and some pasture land. 1890 *Law Times Rep.* LXIII. 767/1 There is some variation in the mode in which the custom is stated.
b. With partitive terms, as *part, degree,* etc.
See also SOMEDEAL, -PART, -WHAT.
c 1400 *Destr. Troy* 13553 Iff ye haue ferkit any fode to þis frith now,..ges me som part. c 1470 *Rauf Coilȝear* 56 For I trow..sum part salbe thyne. 1567 ALLEN *Def. Priesthood* 306 To geue pardon..is to release some parte, or all the enioyned penaunce. 1648 *Hamilton Papers* (Camden) 226 It is beliued that som parte of the caus is from Scotland. 1780 *Mirror* No. 82, But I can venture to assert, with some degree of confidence, that [etc.]. 1826 *Art of Brewing* (ed. 2) 2, I admit this to be correct advice, in some measure. 1870 J. E. T. ROGERS *Hist. Glean.* Ser. II. 7 Some part of its authority was due to its prestige.
c. With terms of time or space.
(*a*) c 900 tr. *Baeda's Hist.* v. xii. (1890) 432 Þa ic sume tid fram ðe ȝewat [etc.]. c 1060 *O. E. Chron.* (MS. C) an. 1055, Hiȝ..wendan..ut on Wealas, & þær laȝon sume hwile. a 1200 *Moral Ode* 147 in *O. E. Hom.* I. 169 Hefð he ifonded [it] summe stunde, he wolde al seggen oðer. a 1225 *Leg. Kath.* 8 Constantin ferde..in to Froncionde, & wunede summe hwile þear. c 1275 in *O. E. Misc.* 89 Þo heo stod ful vaste, and seoþþe sume stunde. c 1400 *Pilgr. Sowle* (Caxton, 1483) III. viii. 55 Al be hit that for somtyme theyr lewd lyf displesid to them seluen. c 1643 LD. HERBERT *Autobiog.* (1824) 33 He that can forbear speaking for some while, will remit much of his passion. 1658 J. WEBB *Cleopatra* VIII. i. 147 [He] continued sometime in the designe. 1710 ADDISON *Spect.* No. 12 ¶ 1 It was some time before I could settle my self in a House to my likeing. 1747 in E. H. Burton *Life Bp. Challoner* (1909) I. xiv. 223, I sent the lessons some time ago to Paris. 1838 *Proc. Berw. Nat. Club* I. 173 After lying some time among weedy rocks. 1845–6 TRENCH *Huls. Lect.* Ser. I. i. 13 No doubt for some while the Church did exist with a canon not full formed. 1891 E. PEACOCK *N. Brendon* I. 315 Basil hesitated for some time.
(*b*) 1594 PLAT *Jewell-ho.* 4 An earthern vessel of some receipte. 1610 SHAKS. *Temp.* II. i. 257 'Twixt which Regions There is some space. 1794 MRS. RADCLIFFE *Myst. Udolpho* xxxvi, At some distance among these woods stood a pavilion. 1820 MILNER *Suppl. Mem. Eng. Cath.* 313 These authors answered the challenge, each of them in a work of some length. 1867 FREEMAN *Norm. Conq.* (1877) I. App. 765 The old frontier lies some way to the north. 1869 TOZER *Highl. Turkey* I. 10 The town..is a place of some size.
d. With adjs., as *little, small, considerable,* etc.
1382 WYCLIF *Acts* xv. 33 Sothli sum litil tyme maad there, thei weren dismittid..with pees of bretheren. 1592 *Soliman & Pers.* II. i, I haue some little replie, if neede require. 1602 SHAKS. *Ham.* II. ii. 14 That you vouchsafe your rest heere in our Court Some little time. 1626 in *Rep. Hist. MSS. Comm.* Var. Coll. (1907) IV. 171 The necessitie of useing some small quantitie of bay salt therein. 1716 CHURCH *Philip's War* (1867) II. 53 Several of his men..was gone some considerable time. 1792 *Gentl. Mag.* 13/2 The bridge..is some little distance from the main street of Duffield. 1825 SCOTT *Betrothed* xxviii, Suppose him returning some brief time hence. a 1834 COLERIDGE in *Lit. Rem.* (1836) II. 198 Perhaps, the influence of a princess..may be some little excuse for Albany's weakness. 1902 *Encycl. Brit.* XXVIII. 407/1 Fishes..which swim some little distance above the actual sea-bed.

e. *U.S.* In predicative use: Of some account; deserving of consideration.
With quot. 1848 cf. the U.S. colloq. phrase *some pumpkins* s.v. PUMPKIN 2 b.
1848 RUXTON *Life Far West* (1849) 60 She's 'some' now, that is a fact, and the biggest kind of punkin' at that. 1849 in Bartlett *Dict. Amer.* (1859) s.v., Which was admitted by the oldest inhabitant to be 'some' in the way of cold winters.
5. *Some other* (see OTHER *a.* 5 b).
c 950 *Lindisf. Gosp.* Luke xvii. 12 Mið-ðy innfoerde sum oðer werc. c 1000 ÆLFRIC *Saints' Lives* xxxi. 691 Se ylca sulpicius and sum oðer broðor. c 1200 ORMIN 7476 Þatt teȝȝ.. shollden..farenn ham till here land All wiþþ summ oþerr weȝȝe. 1303 R. BRUNNE *Handl. Synne* 3470 As yn cherche to synge or rede, Or of sum oþer holy dede. 1362 LANGL. *P. Pl.* A. VIII. 34 Sette scolers to scole or to sum oþer craft. c 1449 PECOCK *Repr.* III. iv. 302 He which is ouerer..schulde louȝe him silf in sum other maner. 1560 WHITEHORNE *Ord. Souldiours* (1588) 6 The residue of the men..may be placed some other where. 1596 *Edw. III,* IV. vii, O, that I were some other countryman! 1611 [see OTHER *a.* 5 b]. 1640 tr. *Verdere's Rom. of Rom.* II. 193, I will take the power to love some otherwhere. 1699 R. L'ESTRANGE *Erasm. Colloq.* (1725) 200 He concluded to take some other Priest with him. 1732 [see OTHER *a.* 5 b]. a 1845 [see OTHERWHERE c]. 1858 HAWTHORNE *Ancestral Footstep* (1883) 514 The old Hospitaller must die in his bed, or some other how.
6. Followed by *certain* or *one* with limiting force (cf. ONE B. 7).
1561, 1591 [see CERTAIN *a.* 7 b]. 1565 COOPER *Thesaurus, Unus aliquis,* some one man. 1655 STANLEY *Hist. Philos.* (1687) 62/1 Respiring Flames at some certain part. 1746 FRANCIS tr. *Horace, Epist.* II. i. 53 Some certain Point should finish the Debate. *Ibid.* 76 In some one Excellence their Merit lies. 1865 RUSKIN *Sesame* ii. § 72 She should..follow at least some one path of scientific attainment.
II. With plural nouns.
7. Certain (taken individually).
Also with limiting terms as *certain, other*: cf. 5 and 6.
c 888 K. ÆLFRED *Boeth.* xxv, Þæt ælc ȝesceaft bið healdon hiren wið hire ȝecynde,..buton monnum & sumum englum. a 1122 *O. E. Chron.* (Laud MS.) an. 1119, Wæs mycel eorðbifung on suman steodan her on lande. c 1200 ORMIN 11214 Afftерr þatt sume wise menn O lare itt unnderrstanndenn. c 1250 *Owl & Night.* 879 Þeyh summe men beon þurhut gode. a 1300 *Cursor M.* 19550 Þof summen mai baptise Mai naman..Conferming giue, bot bi-scop hand. 1340 *Ayenb.* 196 Zom uolk byeþ þet onworþeþ þe poure. 1422 tr. *Secreta Secret., Priv. Priv.* 132 Sum Pryncis ther bene, that..takyn atte har talent trew men goodis. c 1491 *Chast. Goddes Chyld* 53 In somm outwarde signes the prophecye of the deuyll may be knowen. 1526 *Pilgr. Perf.* (W. de W. 1531) 6 Some persones..wyll muse or meruayle. 1562 WINȜET *Wks.* (S.T.S.) I. 23 The durris..wes calket also with sum notes of dishonour. 1596 SHAKS. *Rich. III,* I. iv. 125 Some certaine dregges of conscience are yet within mee. 1651 HOBBES *Leviath.* IV. xlvi. 374 Some..bodies sink naturally downwards. 1696 [C. LESLIE] *Snake in Grass* 88, I wou'd advise some Friends to go to the Dancing-School, and learn a more Gentle and Graceful Mien. 1723 DK. WHARTON *True Briton* No. 24. I. 208, I have heard some People very large in their Exclamations against Creeds and Forms of Faith. 1776 *Trial of Nundocomar* 23/1 Some days he has violent purgings, at other times he gets better. 1826 *Art of Brewing* (ed. 2) 15 Some gentlemen, however,..have studied the subject more particularly. 1855 J. PHILLIPS *Man. Geol.* 498 Oligoclase occurs in some granites. 1857 RUSKIN *Time & Tide* i. § 3 Every nation is fitted..for some particular employments or manufactures.
† b. With article or pronoun accompanying the noun. (Cf. A. 5 c.) *Obs.*
c 893 K. ÆLFRED *Oros.* I. i. 18 Þa teð hie brohton sume þæm cyninge. c 1000 ÆLFRIC *Hom.* II. 448 Ȝe maȝon ȝehyran sume his ðeawes. c 1000 *Ags. Gosp.* Matt. ix. 3 Ða cwædon hiȝ sume þa boceras him betwynan. c 1120 *O. E. Chron.* an. 1119, Sume þa castelas he mid strengðe genam. c 1205 LAY. 12001 Summe þe scipen wunden forð mid þan wederen. 1297 R. GLOUC. (Rolls) 2718 So þat some þe messagers to kermerdin come.
c. *Some...* (*other*) *some,* some... other(s). † Also with *than,* and ellipt. for *sometimes.*
c 888 K. ÆLFRED *Boeth.* xxxiv. § 10 Sumra wyrta.. eard bið on dunum,..sumra on merscum, sumra on morum. c 1000 ÆLFRIC *Hom.* II. 48 Sume lareowas sindon beteran ðonne sume. 1377 LANGL. *P. Pl.* B. xv. 95 Þere somme bowes ben leued and somme bereth none. 1430–40 LYDG. *Bochas* IX. xxxviii. L'Envoi, Some folke appayre, some dothe amende. 1551 [see OTHER SOME]. 1611 SHAKS. *Wint. T.* III. iii. 20 Sometimes her head on one side, some another. 1651–1875 [see OTHER SOME].
8. A certain number of; a few at least.
a 1122 *O. E. Chron.* (Laud MS.) an. 1048, Ða he wæs sume mila oððe mare beheonan Dofran, þa dyde he on his byrnan.
1589 PUTTENHAM *Eng. Poesie* (Arb.) 235, I know..Your some sweete smiles, your some, but louely lowrs. 1610 SHAKS. *Tempest* I. ii. 145 They hurried vs a-boord a Barke, Bore vs some Leagues to Sea. 1617 MORYSON *Itin.* I. 208 Some flaggons of rich wine, some very white bisket, some pruines and raisins. 1726 SHELVOCKE *Voy. r. World* 30 To dig a small garden to sow some Lettices, and other sort of sallading. 1785 [MRS. GRANT OF LAGGAN] *Lett.* (1807) II. 96 The house has no other inhabitant at present than an old Sybil..and some legions of rooks and daws. 1822 SCOTT *Nigel* x, It costs but..the journey of some brief days. 1842 LOUDON *Suburban Hort.* 95 The middle and hinder ones die after some weeks' struggle for existence. 1887 *Field* 12 Nov. 734/2 Displaying his science by some beautiful casts.
b. In adverbial expressions of time.
1382 WYCLIF *Acts* x. 48 Thanne thei preieden him, that he schulde dwelle with hem summe dayes.
1602 in Morris *Troubles Cath. Foref.* (1872) I. iv. 192 My abode..hath been for some years..in London. 1661 12th *Rep. Hist. MSS. Comm.* App. V. 6 Gervise Lucas served ..as gentleman of his horse some years. 1709 MANLEY *Secr. Mem.* (1736) I. 175 A comical Adventure happened to her some Nights ago. 1712 STEELE *Spect.* No. 322 ¶ 2 Some Years ago it happened that [etc.]. 1821 MOORE *Mem.* (1853) III. 273 Have not been very well these some days past. 1859 GEO. ELIOT *A. Bede* xxix, We shall meet with better feelings some months hence. 1891 E. PEACOCK *N. Brendon* I. 119 He has been here some years.
c. With addition of *few.*
1582 ALLEN *Martyrdom Campion* (1908) 36 This blessed man,..of whose life I thought good to set downe some few lines also. 1626 BACON *Sylva* § 470 If some few Pertusions be made in the Pot. 1665 BOYLE *Occas. Refl.* IV. xiv. (1848) 251 We..caught more in some few Minutes than we had taken in a whole hour before. 1820 KEATS *Isabella* xxxiv, For some few gasping moments. 1847 GROTE *Hist. Greece* (1862) III. xxv. 7 They had some few towns.
9. Used with numbers to indicate an approximate amount or estimate, and passing into an adv. with the sense 'about, nearly, approximately'.
c 888 K. ÆLFRED *Boeth.* xxxviii. § 1 Ða wæron hi sume ten gear on þam ȝewinne. c 900 *O. E. Chron.* (Parker MS.) an. 896, Þær wurdon..sume feower cyninges þegnas ofslæȝene. c 1205 LAY. 28983 Þa wunede bi-ȝeonde þere Humbre ..drenches sume sixe. 1567 MAPLET *Gr. Forest* 84 b, The floud Ganges hath Eles some 30 Foote long. 1582 in W. H. Turner *Select. Rec. Oxford* (1880) 424 Some three or fower acres of woode. 1632 MASSINGER *Fatal Dowry* II. ii, They skip into my lord's cast skins some twice a year. 1668 DRYDEN *Even. Love* II. i, I have some three hundred pistoles by me. 1787 BURNS *Auld Farmer's Salut.* iv, It's now some nine-an'-twenty year. 1836 MRS. CARLYLE *Lett.* I. 56 We expect John Carlyle in some ten days. 1865 RUSKIN *Sesame* I. § 33 This collection..would probably have been some thousand or twelve hundred pounds. 1892 *Photogr. Ann.* II. 648 The club consists of some 40 members.
b. With numerals denoting the time of day.
1596 SHAKS. *Tam. Shr.* IV. iii. 189, I thinke 'tis now some seuen a clocke. 1848 THACKERAY *Van. Fair* xxxii, At some ten o'clock the clinking of a sabre might have been heard.
c. Hence with singular nouns expressing time, distance, amount, etc.
(*a*) 1592 SHAKS. *Rom. & Jul.* v. iii. 257 When I came (some Minute ere the time Of her awaking). 1596 — *Merch. V.* III. ii. 9, I would detaine you here some month or two. 1822 SOUTHEY *Lett.* (1856) III. 348 A note from Murray some fortnight ago let me know [etc.]. 1875 B. MEADOWS *Clin. Obs.* 20 Face..not so free as some week or two back.
(*b*) 1595 *Drake's Voy.* (Hakl. Soc.) 7 We came to anchor some saker shott from a forte. 1601 R. JOHNSON *Kingd. & Commw.* (1603) 86 Distant from the towne some halfe mile. 1617 MORYSON *Itin.* I. 191 Some halfe musket shot distance. 1857 HUGHES *Tom Brown* I. iii, Which was distant some mile or so from the school. 1883 C. J. WILLS *Mod. Persia* 203 Some mile and a half through the deserted streets.
(*c*) 1846 S. WILBERFORCE *Sp. Missions* (1874) 98 In order that the English people might buy that luxury some penny a pound cheaper.
III. 10. With *other, one, few,* etc., used absolutely in sing. or plur.
(*a*) c 950 *Lindisf. Gosp.* Matt. xiii. 4 Sum oðer ȝefeollon neh woeg. *Ibid.* Luke ix. 27 Sint sume oðera her stondað ðaðe [etc.]. 1484 CAXTON *Fables of Auian* v, The leche whiche wylle hele somme other, ought fyrste to hele hym self. 1513 DOUGLAS *Æneid* VI. xv. 7 Sum wtheris better can thair causis pleid. 1592 *Soliman & Pers.* IV. ii, I would my maister had left some other to be his agent here. 1603 KNOLLES *Hist. Turks* (1621) 53 Some other in the meane time playing with his nose, and bobbing him in the face. 1760–2 GOLDSM. *Cit. W.* xiv. ¶ 3 There is Seneca, and Bolingbroke, and some others.
(*b*) 1546 *Supplic. Poore Commons* (E.E.T.S.) 85 Perhappes some one of vs hathe hylded C.shepe. 1598–9 HAKLUYT *Voy.* II. I. 56 Most rich & precious stones, some one of which is of more value then a whole kingdome. 1836 C. E. PASCOE *Lond. of To-day* xiii. (ed. 3) 366 To admire and covet, if not to buy, some one of its treasures.
(*c*) 1582 ALLEN *Martyrdom Campion* (1908) 16 Meaning by the state..the welfare of some few..upholden by this new religion. 1621 BP. MOUNTAGU *Diatribæ* 526 Vnlesse *some few,* & *Many* in your language be all one. a 1648 LD. HERBERT *Hen. VIII* (1683) 426 The use that may be made of some few, as two or three in euery Shire. 1735 *Gentl. Mag.* Feb. 106/1 Some few were well dress'd. 1875 HELPS *Soc. Press.* ix. 124 We think—at least, some few of us do—that [etc.].
(*d*) 1601 SHAKS. *Jul. C.* I. iii. 122 Some certaine of the Noblest minded Romans. 1607 — *Cor.* II. iii. 59 Some certaine of your Brethren.
C. *adv.* (See also B. 9.)
1. With comparatives: A little; slightly; somewhat. Chiefly *Sc.* and *north.*
a 1560 ROLLAND *Crt. Venus* I. 662 Quhill time this corps be sum better applyit. 1636 RUTHERFORD *Lett.* (1862) I. 172 My Well-beloved is some kinder..than ordinary. 1667 O. HEYWOOD *Heart-Treas.* xvi. (1825) II. 219, I am rich still, as rich as ever I was, and some richer. 1741 A. MONRO *Anat.* (ed. 3) 207 The superior bulbous Part of this Bone forms some less than the inferior Half of that..Cavity. 1785 BURNS *To W. Simpson* Postscr. xiii, I hope we..ken some better. 1807 P. GASS *Jrnl.* 219 Yesterday we gave him an Indian sweat, and he is some better to day. 1892 HESLOP *Northumbld. Gloss.* 669 She's some better thi day.
2. With verbs: a. A certain amount; a little.
1699 O. HEYWOOD *Diaries* (1885) IV. 162 She bled some still. 1821 *Joseph the Book-Man* 17 Joe in his day had travell'd some. 1822 HOGG *Tales & Sk.* (1837) VI. 272 He spoke some to himself likewise, but it was only one short sentence. 1834 J. HALL *Kentucky* II. 40, I hunt some, and snake a little. 1842 DICKENS in Foster *Life* III. iv. He may walk some, perhaps—not much. 1909 *Lady's Realm* Feb. 468/2 He hunted some, and fished some.
b. *U.S.* To some extent; in some degree; somewhat.
The variations of American usage are very fully illustrated in Thornton's *Amer. Gloss.* (1912) 827–9.
1825 in Thornton *Amer. Gloss.* s.v., [You are] on the huffy order, some, to night. 1843 J. G. WHITTIER in Pickard *Life* (1894) I. 281, I think some of attending the great anti-slavery convention. 1863 DICEY *Federal St.* I. 225 It used to amuse me some..to find that the slaveholders wanted more territory [etc.]. 1889 *Anthony's Photogr. Bulletin* II. 206 Having been troubled some of late to get clear results.
c. *U.S.* In emphatic use: Very much, very well, etc.
1866 LOWELL *Biglow P.* Ser. II. *The Courtin'* xiii, Thet night, I tell ye, she looked *some!* 1894 'G. EGERTON' *Keynote* 9 'How you love young things!' she says. 'Some.'
3. *dial.* and *U.S.* With adjs. (rarely with advs.): Somewhat.
1817 in Thornton *Amer. Gloss.* s.v., His clothes were some bloody. 1839 MARRYAT *Diary Amer.* Ser. I. II. 226 'Are you cold, miss?' said I to a young lady... 'Some,' was the reply. 1851 STERNBERG *Northampt. Dial.* s.v., It war some wet. 1858–61 E. B. RAMSAY *Remin.* (1870) p. xxi, The heat has made your skin some tender.
D. *sb.*[1] An unspecified amount, person, thing, etc. *rare.*
1830 GALT *Lawrie Todd* II. v, I have myself obstinacious objections—a considerable some—against 'em here parley voos. 1850 L. HUNT *Autobiogr.* xxiv. 381 Some whim, some enjoyment,..with a thousand other somes and probabilities.

† **Some,** *sb.*[2] *Obs.* [OE. *sóm,* ablaut-variant of the stem *sam-*: see SAME *a.*] Agreement, concord, peace. Usu. coupled with *saught*(*ness*) or *sib.* (Cf. SOME *a.*[2])
c 1000 ÆLFRIC *Hom.* II. 198 Ðam dom-bocum þe se Heofenlica Wealdend his folce ȝesette to some, and to sehtnysse. a 1011 *Laws Ethelred* vi. 25 (Liebermann), Beo eallum Cristenum mannum sibb and som ȝemæne, and ælc sacu totwæmed. c 1205 LAY. 4099 Heo speken þer to sæhte, to sibbe and to some. c 1225 *Ancr. R.* 426 Þis is o þing,.. þet is God leouest—seihnesse & some. c 1275 *Holy Church* 15 in *O. E. Misc.*, For hi heolden cristes men myd sib and myd some.

† **Some,** *sb.*[3] *Obs. rare.* [a. OF. *some* (mod. F. *somme*) horse-load.] The number of twelve thousand (nails or needles).
The use survives in mod.F. (Littré s.v. *Somme*).
1539–40 in *Archaeol. Cant.* (1893) XX. 243, 2 'some' of 'sprygg' 10s. 1545 *Rates of Customs* b viij b, Nidels, the some conteinynge xii M., xs. *Ibid.* c iij, Patten nayles the some, iis.

Some, obs. form of SOAM, SUM *sb.*

† **Some,** *a.*[2] *Obs.* [Reduced form of I-SOME *a.*]
1. United, reconciled; at peace, friendly. Chiefly in phr. *saught and some.* (Cf. SOME *sb.*[2])
c 1205 LAY. 9883 Þus heo weoren sahte & þus heo weoren some. c 1320 *Cast. Love* 520, I chul fleon and neuere come. Bote my sustren ben sauȝt and some. *Ibid.* 552 Maken Ichulle..Pees and Riht cussen and be sauȝt and some. a 1400 *Chron. R. Glouc.* (Rolls) 52 Of þe folc of denemarch þat ȝuyt ne buþ nouȝt some.
2. Characterized by peacefulness or quiet.
c 1400 *Beryn* 3233 And eke of thy condicioune both sofft & some.

Some, obs. form of SAME *a.*
a 1400–50 *Alexander* (D.) 2063 Þe some [*v.r.* selfe] sendesman he in þe sale fyndez.

-some, *suffix*[1], representing OE. *-sum,* = OFris. *-sum,* related by ablaut to OS. and OHG. *-sam* (G. *-sam,* Du. *-zaam*), ON. *-samr* (Sw. *-sam,* Da. *-som*), Goth. *-sams,* used in OE. to form adjs. from nouns and adjs., as *friðsum* peaceful, *genyhtsum* abundant, *ánsum* whole, *langsum* lasting, rarely from verbs, as *hýrsum, hearsum* obedient. A few of the OE. formations survived in early ME., but only two or three are now in use, as *longsome, lovesome, winsome.* In ME. a number of new examples appear, some of which soon became obsolete, as *beisome, folȝsome, friendsome, lustsome, wlatsome,* while others (chiefly dating from the 14th century) have remained current, as *cumbersome, fulsome, gamesome, gladsome, handsome, lightsome, loathsome, noisome, wholesome.* The early ME. *buhsum, buxum* is now represented by *buxom,* in which the suffix is disguised. In the 16th century appear *awesome, brightsome, darksome, healthsome, heartsome, quarrelsome,* and the unusual formation *timorsome.* Of later date are *adventuresome, bothersome, fearsome, frightsome, lonesome, plaguesome,* etc., and various nonce-formations as *clipsome, cuddlesome, dabblesome, divertsome,* some of which have a passive, others an active, sense.

-some, *suffix*[2], representing OE. *sum* after numerals in the genitive plural: see SOME *indef. pron.* 3. In ME. the inflexion disappeared, and the pronoun was finally treated as a suffix to the numeral, chiefly with the simple numbers from two to ten; for the history of these see TWOSOME, THREESOME, etc. Other examples are rare, and the *some* may be written as a separate word.
In OS. and OFris. *sum* was similarly used with the gen. pl., as OS. *fahora sum* (one of a few), OFris. *twira-, thrira-, fiuwerasum,* etc.; the latter are still represented by WFris. *tware-, trijere-, fjouwerеsom,* etc.
a 1300 *Cursor M.* 5233 Quen þai war gedir al to-gedir, Sex and sexti sum o liues þai war. c 1400 *Brut* 236 And also he commandede..þat þai shulde bene put in tuentysome and in hundredsome. c 1470 HENRY *Wallace* IX. 440 Off Scottis men thai semblyt hastely Nyne hundyr sum off worthi chewalry.

-some, suffix [3], later var. of -SUM suffix, occurring in a few words, as WHATSOME, WHERESOME, WHOSOME. Cf. SUMMER.

Somebody (sʌ·mbǫdi), sb. Also 6–8 some-body. [f. SOME a.[2] + BODY sb. 13.]

1. a. person unknown, indeterminate, or unnamed; someone, some person.

b. Somebody else, some other person.

c. With article of pron.

2. person of some note, consequence, or importance. Freq. with depreciatory or sarcastic force.

3. person whose name is intentionally suppressed; occas., the Devil.

+ Somachore, sb. Obs. In a sumewhere. Cf. SOME a.[1] + CHARE [1b].[1] On one occasion; some time.

Somed, variant of SAMED adv. Obs.; obs. var. SUMMED ppl. a.

+ Somedeal (sʌ·mdīl), sb., adv., and a. Now arch. or dial. Forms: 1 sum dæl, 2 summ dol, 4 sum del; 5, 6–sum deill, deyll; 1 (adv.) sume daeli, dele, 3 sume dale, 4–5 some dele (5 som dele, somme dele), 6 some-dele; 1 sumdale, delo, 3 somdel (4 sum-dell), 5, 6 (-) somdele, 6 sum-dele, 7 somedele; 6–7 somedeale, somedeal (6 somedale), 7 somedeale (6-deall). [f. SOME a.[1] + dei DEAL sb.[1] In advb. use partly representing the OE. instrumental forms sume dæle.]

A. sb. Some part or portion of some thing or things; some amount.

Somegate, adv. Sc. and north. dial. Also [f. SOME a.[2] + GATE sb.[3]]

1. In some place; somewhere.

2. In some way or manner; somehow.

Somehow (sʌ·mhau), adv. Also 8 some how, some-how. [f. SOME a.[1] + How adv.]

1. In some manner or by some means understood or defined; one way or another; someway.

2. In the phr. Somehow or other, or another.

Someone, var. of SOME ONE: see ONE.

Somer, obs. form of SUMMER sb. and v.

Somer castel: see SUMMER CASTLE.

Somersault (sʌ·mẹrsȱlt), sb. Forms: 6–somersault (7 -somer-), 6–7 -sault, 6–8 -saut, 7 -salt, 7 sommer-salt, simber salt. [ad. OF. sombresault, -saut, alteration of sobresault: see SOMERSET.]

Somerset (sʌ·mẹrset), sb. Also sommerset [f. the name of Lord Fitzroy Somerset, Baron Raglan]

Somerset, v.

Somersetian, sb. and a. [f. the name of the south-western counties of England.]

Somervillite. Min. [f. Mrs. Somerville.] A variety of melilite from Vesuvius.

+Some-say. Obs.[1] [f. SOME pron. + SAY sb.[1]] A reported saying or statement.

Something (sʌ·mþiŋ), sb., (adj.,) and adv. Forms: 1 sumþing, sum þing, 3–5 -þing, 4 sum þing, 5 -thyng, 5–6 -thing, 6– something; 6–thyng (6 e.m.), 7 somthing. [OE. sum þing, f. SUM a.[1] + þing THING.]

Somethingness. [f. as prec. + -NESS.] The fact or state of being something; real or material existence, entity.

Sometime (sʌ·mtain), adv., (adj.,) and a. Forms: see below.

Sometimes (sʌ·mtaimz), adv. Forms: 6 sometymes, 6–7 -times, 7 sum tymes, 8 -tymes; 6 somtymes, 6–sometimes. [f. SOME a.[2] + TYMES adv.]

Someway (sʌ·mwē), adv. Also SOME exc. dial. [f. SOME a.[2] + WAY sb.[1]]

1. In some way or manner; by some means; somehow.

Someways (sʌ·mwēz), adv. Now chiefly dial. Also 9 someways.

Somewhat (sʌ·mhwǫt), sb. and adv. Forms: α. 3 sumhwæt, -hwet (7 -hwot), 4 sumwhat (5-whate), 6-whatt (6-what); 4 sumwat, 4-whatt, 5 sumwhat, 5-wat, 6 somwhat; 5 sumquhat, 5 summat, 6 sommat.

(1901) 267 It is thought there is somewhat of theyr dooings in his works. 1658 W. Sanderson *Graphice* 33 Observe to hit the virtues of the Piece, and to refuse the Vices; for all Masters have somewhat of them both. *a* 1677 Barrow *Serm.* Wks. 1716 II. 71 Doth she not every where present spectacles of delight (somewhat of lively picture, somewhat of gay embroidery, somewhat of elegant symmetry). 1761 Hume *Hist. Eng.* III. liii. 147 By quitting somewhat of his royal prerogative. 1779 *Mirror* No. 10, By that too great niceness..they may mingle somewhat of disgust and uneasiness even in the highest and finest pleasures. 1848 Thackeray *Van. Fair* lxvi, A conversation of which he could not help hearing somewhat. 1876 Stedman *Vict. Poets* vi. 231 It must be acknowledged that somewhat of this applies to Tennyson's variations upon Theocritus.

b. Const. *of*, with a positive adj. Now *rare*.

1650 Earl Monm. tr. *Senault's Man bec. Guilty* 36 Tis the desire of seeing some what of new which draws us forth. 1669 Dryden *Tyrannic Love* i. i, Somewhat of mournful, sure, my ears does wound. 1751 Eliza Heywood *Betsy Thoughtless* I. 12 These words, as it proved, had somewhat of prophetic in them. 1870 N. Hawthorne *Eng. Note-bks.* (1879) I. 273 With somewhat of fantastic in the shape of the clock-tower.

c. = Something *sb.* 2 c.

1842 Helps *Ess., Treatment of Suitors* (1842) 110 You will naturally endeavour to give somewhat of a detailed explanation. 1863 Mary Howitt tr. *F. Bremer's Greece & Greeks* II. 3 It was somewhat of a surprise to me. 1868 Freeman *Norm. Conq.* (1877) II. 88 He was also somewhat of a time-server.

3. With limiting word or particle, as *somewhat else, more, over*, etc.

(*a*) 1390 Gower *Conf.* II. 96 As thogh I hadde lost a Ring Or somwhat elles. ?1580 Lodge *Reply Gosson's Sch. Abuse* Wks. (Grosart) I. 29 These things are not the chiefest poynts you shote at; thers somewhat els sticketh in your stomak. 1665 J. North in *Extr. State P. rel. Friends* (1912) III. 235, I haue some what els to ymparte vnto you. 1735 Ainsworth I. s.v. *Some*, I must talk of somewhat else.

(*b*) 1398 Trevisa *Barth. De P. R.* xix. cxxv. (1495) 925 The Suparticularis nombre conteyneth in comparison alle the lesse nombre and somwhat ouer. 1626 B. Jonson *Staple of N.* III. ii, You are a Courtier, Sir, or somewhat more. *c* 1643 Ld. Herbert *Autobiog.* (1824) 16, I shall therefore only say somewhat more of my mother.

b. *Somewhat between*, = Something *sb.* 1 d.

1823 Scott *Quentin D.* xxii, His gesture..was noble, and at the same time resigned, somewhat between the bearing of a feudal noble and of a Christian martyr.

4. A thing, quality, etc., worth considering or regarding; a person of note or importance.

1382 Wyclif *Gal.* ii. 6 Forsoth thei that weren seen for to be sumwhat, no thing to me ȝauen to gidere. 1526 Tindale *Gal.* vi. 3 Iff a man seme to hym silfe that he is somwhat when in dede he is nothynge. 1663 Dryden *Wild Gallant* iv. ii, Nay, the fool is a handsome fool, that's somewhat. 1838 Lowell *Lett.* (1894) I. 32 It were a strange thing indeed if there were not somewhat in such men as Milton, Sidney [etc.]. 1842 Tennyson *St. Simeon Stylites* 124 They think that I am somewhat...The silly people take me for a saint. 1859 Masson *Milton* I. 721 The living society of a place is also somewhat.

†**b.** *Of somewhat*, for some purpose. *Obs.*$^{-1}$

a 1400 *Sir Perc.* 854 It servede hym of somwhatt The wylde fyre that he gatt.

5. With *a*, *the*, etc., and pl. A certain undefined or unknown thing, quality, amount, etc.

1598 R. Bernard tr. *Terence* (1607) 30 'In the meane season I hope some-what may be done.'..'That some-what will prove just nothing.' 1654 Whitlock *Zootomia* 210 Pretty Somewhats they would meane, but sure They understand not themselves any more than I do. 1685 *Gracian's Courtier's Orac.* 220 Several men would be great, if they wanted not a somewhat, without which they never attain to the height of perfection. 1795 *Jemima* I. 218 He has a somewhat in his voice..so pleasant. 1806 H. Siddons *Maid, Wife, & Widow* II. 247 A habit of delivering his sentiments with a somewhat of more than dictatorial petulance. 1857 J. Raine *Mem. J. Hodgson* I. 126 Sending to Hodgson a somewhat which he had left behind him.

b. With preceding adj.

1685 *Gracian's Courtier's Orac.* 117 The secret charm, or the unexpressible somewhat; which the French call *Le Je-ne-sai-quoi*. 1710 Berkeley *Princ. Hum. Knowl.* § 80 Matter is an unknown somewhat—neither substance nor accident. 1785 M. Cutler in *Life*, etc. (1888) II. 229, I now believe, at least, that there is a certain somewhat, which produced a rotary motion in a sword. 1827 Coleridge *Table-t.* 30 Aug., Painting is the intermediate somewhat between a thought and a thing. 1855 Browning *One Word More* ix, Thus achievement lacks a gracious somewhat.

c. Const. *of* or with adj. following.

1817 Keatinge *Trav.* I. 272 Still here attaches..a somewhat of disgraceful to the idea of intoxication. 1825 Scott *Fam. Lett.* II. 354 They require the atmosphere of a cigar and the amalgam of a *summat* comfortable. *a* 1858 R. A. Vaughan *Ess. & Rem.* (1858) I. 50 A somewhat of their spirit of love..he found ever afterwards indispensable to his heart.

B. *adv.* In a certain degree or measure; to some (slight or small) extent; slightly, a little; rather.

1. a. Qualifying a verb.

c 1200 Ormin 16882 Þærþurrh wass sene þatt he þa Summwhatt bigunnenn haffde To lefenn o þe Laferrd Crist. *c* 1385 Chaucer *L. G. W.* Prol. 71 (Fairf.), Ye be diligent To forthren me somwhat in my labour. *c* 1410 *Sir Cleges* 147 Jn with hyr he gan goo, And sumwatt mendyd hys chere. *c* 1440 *Partonope* 4915 To her suster dyd she spek And somwhat her hert to her breke. 1526 Tindale *Acts* xxvi. 28 Sumwhatt thou bryngest me in mynde for to be come christen. 1577–82 Breton *Flourish upon Fancie* Wks. (Grosart) I. 17/2 These Drugges,..though they sumwhat please the tast, yet make the bosom stinke. 1646 Gaule *Sel. Cas.* 56 Hereupon it hath been somwhat dissented. 1688 Holme *Armoury* III. 308/1 The short Graver, which turneth up somewhat at the end. 1780 *Mirror* No. 82, Sir George Rodney's success has somewhat lessened their force. 1812 Cary *Dante, Parad.* II. 53 She somewhat smiled. 1877 J. D. Chambers *Divine Worship* 389 The Forms of these ejaculations varied somewhat.

b. Qualifying a preposition.

1492 Hen. VII *Let.* in G. Griffiths *Hist. Tong* (1894) 224 Desiring you that somwhat bifor the said tyme ye wol addresse you unto us. 1600 in Ingleby *Shaks. Cent. Praise* (Shaks. Soc.) 35 Somwhat before the play began. 1735 Johnson *Lobo's Abyssinia, Descr.* viii. 91 To drink somewhat beyond the bounds of exact Temperance. 1756 C. Lucas *Ess. Waters* I. 10 Spirit of nitre consists of somewhat above one fourth of pure acid. 1819 Byron *Juan* I. i, Sent to the devil somewhat ere his time.

c. *Somewhat as*, in much the same way, to some extent, as.

1872 Morley *Voltaire* (1886) 1 We may think of Voltairism in France, somewhat as we think of Catholicism. 1894 Crockett *Stickit Minister* 16 It ran or rather hirpled somewhat as follows.

2. Qualifying an adjective, adverb, or clause.

(*a*) *a* 1300 *Cursor M.* 11054 Þat mensking þam bi-tuin, Was sum-quat diuers, als i wene. *c* 1384 Chaucer *H. Fame* 1097 But for the ryme ys lyght and lewed Yit make hyt sumwhat agreable. *c* 1400 *Lanfranc's Cirurg.* 48 If þat ilke mater be not hard but sumwhat neische. 1466 *Mann. & Househ. Exp.* (Roxb.) 324 For a sadelle sumwhat worne, ij.s. viij.d. *a* 1533 Ld. Berners *Huon* xliii. 144 His coloure was sum what pale. 1595 in *Cath. Rec. Soc. Publ.* V. 335 His vtterance was somwhat vnready. 1667 Dryden & Dk. Newcastle *Sir M. Mar-all* v. ii, Would I were hanged if it be not somewhat probable. 1750 tr. *Leonardus' Mirr. Stones* 92 [It] is a stone of a crystal colour, and somewhat obscure. 1780 *Mirror* No. 105, Somewhat a-kin to the lovers of detraction are the offence-takers. 1826 *Art of Brewing* (ed. 2) 15 Their practice is governed by principles somewhat different. 1885 *Manch. Exam.* 12 May 5/2 It would seem..that the struggle was somewhat indecisive.

(*b*) 1542 Boorde *Dyetary* iv. (1870) 238 The seller vnder the pantry, sette somwhat abase. 1592 Kyd *Murther. J. Brewen* Wks. (1901) 290 When it grew some what late. 1637 Milton *Lycidas* 17 Begin, and somwhat loudly sweep the string. 1797–1805 S. & Ht. Lee *Cant. T.* I. 195 One, who, having somewhat unexpectedly succeeded to the family title. 1851 Mrs. Browning *Casa Guidi Wind.* II. 478 If..we Are counted somewhat deeply in their debt. 1869 Ruskin *Q. of Air* i. § 32 Somewhat saucily.

(*c*) 1578 *Reg. Privy Council Scot.* III. 35 Mony injurious wordis, sumquhat in contempt of our Soverane Lord. 1608 E. Grimstone *Hist. France* (1611) 457 A cunning woman, and some-what of her fathers humor. 1678 Bunyan *Pilgr.* I. 27 Now was Christian somwhat in a muse. 1818 Scott *Br. Lamm.* ix, The hounds and huntsmen seemed somewhat at a stand. 1828 Lytton *Pelham* liii, Somewhat of a lugubrious nature. 1833 Ht. Martineau *Berkeley* I. iii. 49 Martin looked somewhat at a loss for an answer, till his wife supplied him with one.

b. With a comparative adj. or adv.

c 1400 Maundev. (Roxb.) xi. 46 It es sumwhat hyer þan oþer placez of þe citee. 1484 Caxton *Fables of Auian* xxii, I blowe in hit for to haue it somwhat more cold than hit is. 1514 Barclay *Cyt. & Uplondyshman* (Percy Soc.) 6 And somwhat wyser be they also than we. 1597 Hooker *Eccl. Pol.* v. lv. § 5 Somewhat more plainly, to shew a true immediate reason..we acknowledge [etc.]. 1600 Pory tr. *Leo's Africa* vi. 275 The men of this place are black, but the women are somewhat fairer. 1696 Whiston *Th. Earth* iv. (1722) 317 The Lower Earthy Strata would be settling somewhat closer together. 1768 *Woman of Honor* III. 233 A range of thirteen chests rather somewhat larger than the common size. 1815 J. Smith *Panorama Sci. & Art* II. 173 The pan being brought to somewhat more than a red heat. 1866 Carlyle in *Mrs. C.'s Lett.* III. 255 She..went home somewhat better. 1875 Jowett *Plato* (ed. 2) I. 359 Tell me.., in somewhat plainer terms, what you mean!

c. With *of the* and a superlative adj. or adv.

1561 T. Hoby tr. *Castiglione's Courtyer* iv. (1577) Y vij b, Not to make wise to abhorre companie and talke, though somewhat of the wantonest. 1622 Mabbe tr. *Aleman's Guzman d'Alf.* I. 30, I got mee (though somewhat of the latest) hungry. 1656 Heylin *Surv. France* 218 The revenues of this Archbishoprick are somewhat of the meanest. 1818 Scott *Br. Lamm.* xvi, Your morning-draught has been somewhat of the strongest.

d. With *a* or *an* inserted before the adj. (or sb.) qualified.

1588 J. Read *Compend. Method.* 69 b, Barriga..receaued a wounde in his brest, with somewhat a long sword. *a* 1646 Gregory *Posthuma* (1650) 198 This was somwhat a tolerable impietie, for such great Astronomers to adore the Host of Heaven. 1680 R. L'Estrange *Erasm. Colloq.* 79 [He] may vouchsafe his Assistance also unto us, who are somewhat a larger Congregation. 1779 Johnson *Drake* Wks. 1787 IV. 417 Being obliged by this accident to somewhat a longer residence among the Moors. 1817 Whewell in Mrs. S. Douglas *Life* (1881) 25, I must acknowledge myself somewhat an idle correspondent so far as writing goes. 1891 Anne Mozley *Lett. J. H. Newman* I. iii. 103 There were certainly..definite points about him which made him somewhat a difficulty.

e. Preceded by an article or pron.

1779 *Mirror* No. 61, The contempt in which, to a somewhat unreasonable degree, he holds modern refinement. 1820 Scott *Monast.* xxi, The cooling my somewhat too much inflamed visage. 1849 Macaulay *Hist. Eng.* ii. I. 180 Her admonitions were given in a somewhat perfunctory manner.

f. Used as *adj.*

1819 T. Moore in *Mem.* (1853) II. 250 Lady Frances W. was to have come with them, but, to my somewhat disappointment, she had been called away.

†**3.** *Somewhat . . . somewhat*, partly . . . partly.

1390 Gower *Conf.* I. 2, I wolde..wryte a bok betwen the tweie, Somewhat of lust, somewhat of lore. *c* 1400 *Pilgr. Sowle* (Caxton) I. xxx. (1859) 34 He is lettid by the wey somwhat by foly of hym self, somwhat by other. *a* 1425 tr. *Arderne's Treat. Fistula*, etc. 38 Þai may ete and drynk and go, and somwhat sitte and somwhat slepe. 1552 Latimer *Serm.* (1607) 301 A king.., which was not their lawfull nor naturall king, but somewhat with craft and subtilty, and somewhat with power had gotten the Crowne.

†**4.** Followed by *with the* and a superlative, = Something *adv.* 2 f. *Obs. rare.*

1542 Udall *Erasm. Apoph.* 252 b, [She] begoonne somewhat with the soonest to have whyte heares in hir hedde. 1583 Golding *Calvin on Deut.* Pref. Ep. 2 Such discourse which might peradventure be somewhat with the longest. 1610 Holland *Camden's Brit.* 215 A small towne this is, standing somewhat with the lowest.

5. *Somewhat like*, in various senses (see Like *a.* 2 e, f).

1593 G. Harvey *Pierce's Super.* Wks. (Grosart) II. 229 Though she were a lustie bounsing rampe somewhat like Gallamilla. 1611 Cotgr., *Bellastre*,..passable, so so, somewhat like. *a* 1620 Dyke *Serm.* (1640) 379 If a man will sell a commodity, hee will sell it somewhat like, or hee will keepe it. 1662 J. Davies tr. *Olearius' Voy. Amb.* 165 It was somewhat like a Sturgeon, but was much whiter. 1748 Richardson *Clarissa* (1811) VI. 241 Why this is talking somewhat like. 1859 Geo. Eliot *A. Bede* viii, It's summat-like to see such a man as that i' the desk of a Sunday! 1890 *Science-Gossip* XXVI. 194 This is somewhat like the one examined by Schrötter.

†**Somewhatly**, *adv.* *Obs. rare.* Also 5 **sumwhatly, svmqwatly.** [f. as prec. + -ly^2.] Somewhat; to some (slight) extent.

c 1425 *St. Elizabeth of Spalbeck* in *Anglia* VIII. 108 A whyte lynnen garnemente sumwhatly trailynge on þe erthe. *Ibid.* 115 Sumwhatly streight vp towarde the auter. 1483 *Cath. Angl.* 371 Svmqwatly, *aliqualiter, vtrumque.* [*a* 1711 H. Lamp *Autobiog.* iii. (1895) 26, I staid there about six months, learning the English tongue somewhatly.]

Somewhen (sʊ·mhwen), *adv.* Also 4 **somwanne, sumwhan(ne.** [f. Some *a.*^{1} + When *adv.*] At some (indefinite or unknown) time; sometime or other. Common in recent use, esp. coupled with *somewhere*.

1297 R. Glouc. (Rolls) 5212 Of þe batayles of denemarch þat abbeþ ybe in þis londe... Worst hii were, vor oþere somwanne adde ydo [etc.]. 1863 Kingsley *Water-Bab.* 349 Some folks can't help hoping..that they may have another chance, to make things fair and even, somewhere, somewhen, somehow. 1875 Whitney *Life Lang.* ix. 174 Spoken somewhere and somewhen in the past. 1876 Freeman in W. R. W. Stephens *Life & Lett.* II. 134 To tarry with James Allen..till somewhen about next Wednesday.

So·mewhence, *adv.* *rare.* [f. Some *a.*^{1} + Whence *adv.*] From some (indefinite) place; from somewhere or other.

1564 Mrs. A. Bacon tr. *Jewel's Apol.* L iiij, Fearing that the people shoulde..somwhence els seeke a surer meane of their saluation. 1905 *Daily Chron.* 11 Aug. 4/7 That little boy seems to live on his imaginary trudge—somewhence—somewhither!

Somewhere (sʊ·mhwēəɹ), *adv.* and *sb.* Forms: 3 (*Orm.*) **summhwær**, 4 **sumwhare, -whore, -wher(e**, 6 **-whear**; 4 **sumquar(e, -quer**, 5 **-qwhare**; 4 **sum-, somwar**; 4 **some-**, 5 **somwhare**; 4 **sommewhere**, 5–7 **somwhere**, 5– **somewhere.** [f. Some *a.*^{1} + Where *adv.* Down to the end of the 16th c. freq. written as two words.]

A. *adv.* **1.** In or at some place unspecified, indeterminate, or unknown.

c 1200 Ormin 6929 Forr þatt he wass forrdredd tatt teȝȝ Himm shollden summwhær hidenn. 1297 R. Glouc. (Rolls) 4344 King arþure was þer of ywar, & þoȝte.. Wiþ al is poer bi þe wey somwar him kepe. *a* 1310 in Wright *Spec. Lyric P.* xxxix. 110 He hath hewe sum wher a burthen of brere. 1483 *Cath. Angl.* 371/2 Sumqwhare, *alicubi*. 1526 *Pilgr. Perf.* (W. de W. 1531) 106 An holy saynt..serued in many chirches, and some where here in Englande. 1638 Junius *Paint. Ancients* 14 Others..wander up and downe to meet somewhere with a refreshing shade. 1667 Milton *P. L.* ix. 256 What malicious Foe..somwhere nigh at hand Watches. 1796 Mme. D'Arblay *Camilla* IV. 390 A paper in her hand-writing, which she had somewhere lost. 1827 Scott *Chron. Canongate* Introd., As it was suspected that he was lurking somewhere on the property, his family were closely watched. 1859 Geo. Eliot *A. Bede* xxii, Arthur must be somewhere in the back rooms. 1878 G. Macdonald *Ann. Q. Neighb.* xxvi. 448 There's something wrong somewhere.

b. With correlative *somewhere* or *otherwhere*.

1398 Trevisa *Barth. De P. R.* xiii. iv. (Bodl. MS.), In coloure..somewhare he [a river] is clere and somewhare he is dymme. 1630 *R. Johnson's Kingd. & Commw.* 423 Many places lying waste, somewhere for want of water, somewhere for want of manurance, somewhere for abundance of light sand. 1632 Lithgow *Trav.* x. 493 A Regall Commission..beeing some-where obeyed, and other-where suspended.

c. *Somewhere else*, in some other place, elsewhere.

c 1500 *Communycacyon* (W. de W.) C ij, Man thou must alwaye suffre payne Here for thy synnes or somwhere elles. 1530 Palsgr. 823/1 Some where els, *quelque aultre part*. 1588 Shaks. *Tit. A.* iv. iii. 40 She is so imploy'd,..with Ioue in heauen, or some where else: So that [etc.]. 1611 Cotgr., *Ailleurs*, elsewhere, somewhere else. 1737 *Gentl. Mag.* VII. 603/2 We must therefore look some where else for the Cause of our present Uneasiness.

d. *Somewhere or another* or *other*.

1791 Charlotte Smith *Celestina* (ed. 2) I. 129 Here Daniel, prythee take and stow it somewhere or another. 1799 E. Du Bois *Piece Family Biog.* I. 59, 'I have heard somewhere or another,' said he, 'that' [etc.]. 1852 C. W-

Hoskyns *Talpa* i. (1854) 2 Somewhere or other in England there is a flat bleak high-lying district, which [etc.].

2. To some (unspecified or unknown) place. Usually with the verb *go*.

c 1403 Clanvowe *Cuckoo & Night.* 112 Now, gode Cukkow! go som-where away. *a* 1548 Hall *Chron., Edw. V*, 9 Is it not likely that she wyll send him somwhere out of the realme? 1590 Shaks. *Com. Err.* II. i. 5 Perhaps..from the Mart he's somewhere gone to dinner. 1592 Kyd *Sp. Trag.* III. x, To..carry you obscurely some where els. 1720 De Foe *Capt. Singleton* (1906) 37 We were upon a voyage and no voyage, we were bound somewhere and nowhere. 1780 Warner in Jesse *Selwyn & Contemp.* (1844) IV. 359 Charles is gone out of town somewhere to-day.

†**3.** In some places; here and there. *Obs. rare.*

1563 Nowell in *Lett. Lit. Men* (Camden) 20 The coopie ..was interlined and sumwhear blotted. 1578 Lyte *Dodoens* v. xxxiii. 593 The Turnep loueth an open place, it is sowen somwhere in vineyardes, as at Huygarden and the Countrie thereaboutes.

4. In some part or passage of a book, etc.; in some work or other.

1634 Sir T. Herbert *Trav.* 74 The Bashaw, in this Itenerary somewhere spoken of. 1732 Berkeley *Alciphr.* II. § 23 A fable, I somewhere met with in the writings of a Swiss philosopher. 1780 *Mirror* No. 102, Lord Chesterfield says somewhere, that, to..act with spirit, is to..act foolishly. 1820 Byron *Juan* iv. cx, As some one somewhere sings about the sky.

5. a. At some time *about* or *in* (a certain specified year, date, etc.).

1839 *Penny Cycl.* XIII. 168/1 He is said to have been born somewhere about A.D. 40. 1859 Ruskin *Two Paths* iii. § 91 An old English cottage,..perhaps built somewhere in the Charleses' times. 1891 C. James *Rom. Rigmarole* iv. 32, I woke up out of my nap somewhere about five o'clock.

b. *Somewhere about*, approximately.

1846 Ryland in *Life & Corr. Foster* II. 343 He kept his room somewhere about two months. 1876 Tait *Rec. Adv. Phys. Sci.* vi. 157 The sun's radiation is..somewhere about thirty-fold that of the same area of the furnace of a locomotive.

B. *sb.* Some unspecified or indefinite place.

1647 Cowley *Mistr.* (1669) 22 Then down I laid my Head; and for a while was Dead, And my freed Soul to a strange Somewhere fled. 1718 D'Urfey *Grecian Heroine* v. i, I would fain think now, But that my Spirits, with my Blood, are posting To their new some-where. 1786 Mrs. A. M. Bennett *Juvenile Indiscr.* I. 54 It was a somewhere, a home.

So **So·mewheres** *adv.* (*dial.* or *vulg.*)

1859 Bartlett *Dict. Amer.* (ed. 2) 428 A hundred dollars, or somewheres there along. 1883 Stevenson *Treas. Isl.* xxviii, I know you've got that ship safe somewheres.

Somewhile (sʊ·mhwəil), *adv.* Now *rare*. Forms: 2–3 **sum wile**, 3 **sum(e) hwile**, 4 **sumwhyle**, 4–6 **-while**; 4–5 **sumquile, -quyle**, 5 **-qwile**; 5 **somwhyle**, 7 **-while**; 5 **some wile, somewhyle**, 5–7, 9 **somewhile.** [f. Some *a.*^{1} + While *sb.*; cf. WFlem. *somwijl*. In early use freq. written as two words.]

1. †**a.** At or in some former time; erewhile; formerly. *Obs.*

1154 *O.E. Chron.* (Laud MS.) an. 1137, Sume ieden on ælmes þe waren sum wile rice-men. *c* 1230 *Hali Meid.* 5 Syon was sum hwile icleped þe hehe tur of Ierusalem. 13.. *K. Alis.* 1527 (W.), Ther was sum while, over us, A kyng that hette Neptanabus. 13.. *Gaw. & Gr. Knt.* 625 Hit is a syngne þat Salamon set sum-quyle. *a* 1400–50 *Alexander* 2994 Þan was an ymage within..Of Sexeres þat sum-quyle þat cite had to welde. 1591 Spenser *Ruins of Rome* 242 These.. Pallaces.. were shepheards cottages somewhile. 1654 H. L'Estrange *Chas. I* (1655) 65 That shell which was some-while the continent of so vast treasures of knowledge.

†**b.** *Somewhile since*, some time ago. *Obs.*

1652 Needham tr. *Selden's Mare Cl.* 115 Nor must wee let it pass, that somwhile since, there were two Constitutions pretended to in France.

c. *attrib.*, passing into *adj.* Former, sometime.

1860 Ainsworth *Ovingdean Grange* 11 Highly dangerous to the spiritual welfare of his somewhile flock. 1888 *N. & Q.* 7th Ser. VI. 19/1 Richard Doyle, somewhile illustrator of *Punch*.

†**2.** On a certain occasion in the past; once; at one time. *Obs. rare.*

c 1200 *Trin. Coll. Hom.* 43 We findeð on þe holie boc, þat ure helende..ferde sumwile mid mede ouere water. *a* 1300 *Cursor M.* 4751 Þe caf he cast o corn sumquile In þe flum þat hait þe nile. *c* 1585 C'tess Pembroke *Ps.* xcix. viii, For sinne they somewhile smarted. 1631 Gouge *God's Arrows* III. § 88. 349 The souldiers that came from Newhaven that was somwhile besieged, and after taken by the enemy.

3. At some (unspecified) time; at one time or other; at times, sometimes. Also †*at somewhile*.

c 1250 *Owl & Night.* 6 Þat playd wes..starc & strong, Sum hwile softe & lud among. 1390 Gower *Conf.* I. 367, I have herd sein..That thei som while here cause ladden Be merci. 1426 Lydg. *De Guil. Pilgr.* 11427 What ys the cause..That a swerd burnysshed cler, Somwhyle rusteth? *c* 1456 Pecock *Bk. of Faith* (1909) 252 Peraventure he schal have nede at sumwhile. 1559 *Mirr. Mag.* (1563) A iv, To serue kings in al pointes men must sum while breke rules. 1560 Whitehorne *Arte Warre* 9 b, Some while it hapned, that in one self time there were manie Emperours. 1579 Spenser *Sheph. Cal.* May 126 Tho vnder colour of shepeheards, somewhile There crept in Wolues, ful of fraude and guile. 1628 Gaule *Pract. The.* (1629) 109 An vniuersall King does not onely some-while fore-goe, but some-what resemble the King Eternall. 1629 in Bradford *Plymouth Plant.* (1856) 246 These now sente..must, some while, be chargable to you & us. 1855 J. Nichol in *Mem.* (1896) iii. 130 The 'beautiful vision' with which all lives worth living have been somewhile brightened.

b. With correlative *somewhile* or †*other whiles*.

a 1240 *Lofsong* in *O. E. Hom.* I. 205 Sumehwile to pleiful, to drupi oðer hwiles. 13.. *Cursor M.* 7433 (Gött.), Sumquile [*v.r.* oþerwhile] wid harpe, sumquile wid sang. *c* 1400 *Pilgr. Sowle* (Caxton) I. xx. (1859) 26 How ofte haue I warned the byfore, Som whyle aperte, som whyle pryuely. 1575 Vautrollier *Luther on Ep. Galat.* 161 In whom is found continually, somewhile the time of the law, and somewhile the time of grace. 1607 Hieron *Wks.* I. 399 It is tearmed some while, a blessing themselues; some while an encouraging themselues in a wicked purpose.

4. For some time.

1864 Pusey *Daniel* (1876) 302 His grandfather himself must have been somewhile dead.

So·mewhiles, *adv.* Now *dial.* or *arch.* Forms: 3 **sumehwules**, 6 **sumwhiles, somwhyles, somwhiles, somewhyles**, 6–7, 9 **somewhiles.** [f. as prec. with genitive or plural *-s*. Cf. WFlem. *somwijls*, Du. *somwijlen*.]

†**1.** At some former time; formerly. *Obs.*$^{-1}$

a 1225 *Ancr. R.* 276 Bihold, holie men þet weren sumehwules, hwu heo uesten, & hwu heo wakeden.

2. On some occasion(s); sometimes.

Freq. in the latter half of the 16th c.

1528 Tindale *Obed. Chr. Man* 150 b, The very Gods them selves which sell their pardone so good chepe or some whiles geve them frely for glory sake. 1559 *Mirr. Mag.* (1563) A iij, We let hang the true man somwhyles to saue a thefe. 1594 Carew *Huarte's Exam. Wits* x. (1596) 144 The profession of which they haue made choice (though somwhiles vnworthy). 1626 Fenner *Hidden Manna* (1652) B iij, For the Understanding and Will are somewhiles like Simeon and Levi. 1681 R. L'Estrange *Tully's Offices* 131 Without need some whiles of any other Company. *c* 1863 S. S. Jones *Northumbld.*, etc. 129 There was yen o' them it [= that] somewhiles did nae make things sae smooth as they might have been. 1890 D. G. Mitchell *English Lands* II. iii. 107 Among other writers..who went somewhiles to these suppers..was James Howell. 1901 A. J. Davies *Athirt Downs* II. iv. 72 Takes a deal of following somewhiles, that it do.

b. With correlatives, esp. *somewhiles . . ., somewhiles*, = Sometimes 1 b.

(*a*) 1547 J. Harrison *Exhort. Scottes* c vj b, Britayne was not always..vnder one Kyng.., but was gouerned somwhiles by one, and somwhiles by mo. 1606 G. W[oodcocke] *Hist. Iustine* iv. 21 The wind..sendeth foorth in many places, some-whiles flashes of fyre, other some-whiles againe most..dangerous vapors. 1612 Davies *Why Ireland*, etc. (1747) 16 Some whiles one prevailing,..somewhiles the other.

(*b*) *a* 1553 Udall *Royster D.* I. i, Sometime Lewis Loytrer biddeth me come neere; Somewhyles Watkin Waster maketh vs good cheere. 1560 Whitehorne *Arte Warre* 42 b, Some whiles thei fought with the enemies horses, an other while, thei rescued the fotmen. 1565 Allen *Defence Purg.* xv. 272 One while by the praysies of the doctors and antiquitye, and sumwhiles by thabasing of theime ageine.

†**3.** At some time *before*. *Obs.*$^{-1}$

1657 W. Rand tr. *Gassendi's Life Peiresc* II. 254 Having some whiles before procured [an]..Edition of his Divine Poems.

Somewhither (sʊ·mhwiðəɹ), *adv.* Forms: 5–6 **somwhether**, 6 **-whyther**, 7– **somewhither.** [f. Some *a.*^{1} + Whither *adv.*]

1. In some direction.

1398 Trevisa *Barth. De P. R.* III. xvii. (W. de W.) 61 The syghte is made by lynes that passyth not awaye forth ryght, but blenchyth somwhether asyde of the strayte waye. 1858 Carlyle *Fredk. Gt.* x. i. (1872) II. 575 Twilight, with here and there a transient spark falling somewhither in it. 1905 *Daily News* 2 May 6 But the time comes when the fashion must change somewhither.

2. To some place, = Somewhere *adv.* 2.

1530 Palsgr. 823/1 Somwhyther, *quelque part*. ?*c* 1560 *Trag. Rich. II* (1870) 40 Prethee sweete king letts ride somwhether and it be but to showe ourselues. 1588 Shaks. *Tit. A.* IV. i. 11 Some whether would she haue thee goe with her. *c* 1645 Tullie *Siege of Carlisle* (1840) 13 Bidding her convey the money somewhither. 1779 Forrest *Voy. N. Guinea* 290, I found several persons who..seemed to imagine me bound some whither. 1845 Carlyle *Cromwell* (1857) II. 71 The poor young King is much at a loss;—must go somewhither. 1877 W. Black *Green Past.* xxxiv, Like ghosts waiting for Charon to take them somewhither.

†**b.** *Somewhither else*, to some other place; elsewhere. *Obs.*

1623 in Ellis *Orig. Lett.* Ser. I. III. 125 [They] would faine hope that he was gone somewhither else then to Spaine. 1658 Earl Monm. tr. *Paruta's Wars Cyprus* 24 The latter ..endeavoured, that the Fleet might go some-whither else. 1700 Bp. Lloyd in Aubrey *Brief Lives* (1813) I. 102 We must think of removing you some whither else where you may have a subsistence.

†**So·mewho.** *Obs.*$^{-1}$ In 4 **somwho.** [f. Some *a.*^{1} + Who *pron.*] Some one; somebody.

1390 Gower *Conf.* I. 15 Ofte is sen that mochel slowthe ..Doth mochel harm, whan fyr is uppe, Bot if somwho the flamme stanche.

Somewhy (sʊ·mhwəi), *adv.* *rare.* [f. Some *a.*^{1} + Why *adv.*] For some reason or reasons.

1858 *Athenæum* 1 May 555 A buxom, shrill, mean, troublesome woman; yet somehow and some*why* not utterly detestable. 1864 Browning *Dram. Pers.* Wks. 1896 I. 610/1 You learn What some one was somewhere, somewhen, somewhy.

Somewise (sʊ·mwəiz), *adv.* Now *arch.* Also 5 **somwyse**, 6 **sumwise.** [f. Some *a.*^{1}: see -wise.] In some way or manner; to some extent. In recent use with *in*.

c 1440 *Alph. Tales* 293 Becauce he wold somwyse be occupyed ilka day. 1596 Dalrymple tr. *Leslie's Hist. Scot.* II. 105 To cause his subiectis lyue in peace with him, or sumwise slokne that hett hatred and Inuie betuene thame. *a* 1677 Barrow *Serm. Upright Walking* Wks. 1687 I. 60 That nothing can be really profitable..to us, which..doth not somewise conduce to our spiritual interest. 1848 D. G. Rossetti *Last Confession* Poems (1870) 67 The father's, brother's love—was changed, I think, in somewise. 1865 Swinburne *Chastelard* II. i, I thought I was..lying by my lord, and knew In somewise he was well awake.

Somir, obs. form of Summer.

Somital (sōu·mităl), *a.* *Zool.* [f. next.] Of or pertaining to a somite; somitic.

1890 in *Cent. Dict.* s.v. *Metameric*.

Somite (sōu·məit). *Zool.* [f. Gr. σῶμα body, Soma^2 + -ite.] One or other of the more or less distinct segments into which the bodies of many animals are divided.

1869 Huxley *Introd. Classif. Anim.* 77 The head of a Crustacean, an Arachnid, a Myriapod, or an Insect is composed of six somites. 1875 C. C. Blake *Zool.* 281 The number of segments or somites in the body of insects never exceeds twenty. 1888 Rolleston & Jackson *Anim. Life* 542 The abdomen..is made up of a number of distinct segments or *somites*.

Somitic (somi·tik), *a.* *Zool.* [f. prec. + -ic.] Of or pertaining to, having the form or character of, a somite.

1888 Huxley & Martin *Pract. Biol.* 243 These septa are metamerically arranged, one for each somitic constriction. *Ibid.* 244 A series of somitic compartments.

†**So·mler.** *Obs.* Chiefly *Sc.* Also 6 **summeleir, symleir, somme-, somlier, sommler, somlar, semlar.** [a. F. *sommelier*, f. *somme* pack.] A butler.

1543 *St. Papers Hen. VIII*, IX. 325 To gyve commaundement that your sommelier at Bordeaulx might be suffred to departe with such wynes as he had provided for Your Majestie. 1566 *Reg. Privy Council Scot.* I. 451 Leonard Baillie, summeleir to oure Soveranis. 1583 *Excheq. Rolls Scot.* XXI. 563 Threttie tunnis of full Burdehous wyne..at the cheis and contentment of his hienes somleris.

Somlich: see Seemly *a.*

†**Sommage.** *Obs. rare.* [a. OF. *sommage* (med. L. *summ-, sumagium*), f. *somme* pack.] Baggage; baggage-animals.

c 1500 *Melusine* 143 And he made to abyde in the valey all the sommage. *Ibid.* 277 The next day..desloged the vanward, and after the grete batayll, & the sommage & syn the ryergarde. 1502 tr. *Charter Forest* in Arnolde *Chron.* 80 b, For an horse beryng sommage [L. *sumagium*].

Somme, obs. f. Soam, Sum *sb.* and *v.* **Sommed**, obs. var. Summed *ppl. a.* **Sommer**, var. Somer *Obs.*; obs. f. Summer *sb.* and *v.*

†**Somme·rse**, *v.* *Obs.* [f. It. *sommerso*, pa. pple. of *sommergere* Submerge *v.*] *trans.* To submerge, overflow.

1632 Lithgow *Trav.* I. 14 This second Sodome should be sommerssed by water. *Ibid.* vi. 255 Many Citties, Mansions, and Stations, haue beene sommerssed with water.

†**Sommier**^{1}. *Obs. rare.* In 5 **sommyer.** [a. F. *sommier*.] A pack-horse; = Somer 1.

1485 Caxton *Chas. Gt.* 128 They sawe passe by the castel xx sommyers laden wyth vytayl. *Ibid.* 159 That euery man trusse hys gheer vpon the sommyers.

†**Sommier**^{2}. *Obs.* Also **summier.** [a. F. *sommier*, or alteration of *sommer* Summer *sb.*^{2} after this.] A bearing-beam in a building.

1623 T. Goad *Dolef. Euen Song* 11 By the breaking asunder of a maine Sommier or Dormer of that floare. 1625 Lisle *Du Bartas, Noe* 181 Mounting here and there ..Into the esparsed pipes o' th' Sommier thorow-bored. 1631 Gouge *God's Arrows* IV. § 15. 399 The maine Summier which crossed the garret was ten inches square.

†**So·mmite.** *Min.* *Obs.* [f. Mt. *Somma* near Naples + -ite^1 2 b.] Nephelite.

1805 R. Jameson *Min.* II. 565 Sommite...Its colour is greyish-white. 1823 W. Phillips *Min.* (ed. 3) 125 The Sommite usually occurs in grains, or in small regular hexahedral prisms. 1837 Dana *Min.* 291 Nepheline, *Spatum hexagonum*...Sommite.

Sommitie, obs. form of Summity.

Sommon, obs. form of Summon *v.*

Sommonce, Sommon(e)s, obs. ff. Summons *sb.*

Sommonicion, var. of Summonition.

Somn-, combining form of L. *somnus*, used in words based on L. *ambulāre* to walk; the oldest of these in English use are *somnambulation, somnambulism*, and *somnambulist*. (For variant, and in some cases earlier, terms see Noct-.) **Somna·mbulance**, sleep-walking, somnambulism. **Somna·mbulant** *a.*, walking in sleep, somnambulic; *sb.*, a somnambulist. **Somna·mbular** *a.*, of or pertaining to sleep-walking; also *erron.*, connected with, of the nature of, sleep. **Somna·mbulary** *a.*, = prec. **Somna·mbulate** *v. intr.*, to walk during sleep; *trans.*, to walk along (a place) while asleep; hence *somna·mbulating* ppl. a. **Somna:mbula·tion** [mod.L. *somnambulatio*], the action or fact of walking in sleep. **Somna·mbulator**, = next. **Somna·mbule** [a. F. *somnambule* (1690), Sp. and Pg. *somn-*, Sp. *sonámbulo*, mod.L. *somnambulus, -ambulo*], a somnambulist. **Somna·mbulency**, sleep-walking, or a fit of this; also *fig.* **Somna·mbulic** *a.*, of the nature of, pertaining to, etc., somnambulism; walking during sleep; hence **Somna·mbulically** *adv.* **Somna·mbulism** [F. *somnambulisme*, Sp. *-ismo*, mod.

L. *somnambulismus*], the fact or habit of walking about and performing other actions while asleep; sleep-walking. **Somna·mbulist**, one who walks, etc., while asleep; also *attrib.* **Somna:mbuli·stic** *a.*, somnambulic; hence **Somna:mbuli·stically** *adv.* **Somna·mbulize** *v. intr.*, to walk in sleep; *trans.*, to imagine during sleep-walking; also, to put into a sleep-walking state. **Somna·mbulous** *a.*, somnambulic (Dunglison, 1873).

1885 *Science* VI. 78 Committees were appointed on.. hypnotism, clairvoyance, and *somnambulance. 1905 *Daily News* 21 Jan. 6 His old habit or infirmity of somnambulance came back to him. 1843 Mrs. Carlyle *Lett. & Mem.* (1883) I. 231 Four such nights might have made a *somnambulant of a much stronger woman than me. 1866 Blackmore *Cradock Nowell* xlix, He was listless, passive, somnolent,—somnambulant. 1887 *Sat. Rev.* 15 Jan. 80 To walk in her sleep and to poison herself while in a somnambulant condition. 1830 Lytton *Paul Clifford* xvi. (1874) 193 The pair..mounted the stairs, arm-in-arm, in search of *somnambular accommodations. 1860 Mrs. Browning *Napoleon III in Italy* v, While the palpitating peaks break out Ecstatic from somnambular repose. 1862 Lytton *Str. Story* 14 An ardent believer of the reality of somnambular clairvoyance. 1827 Sutherland *Tales Pilgr.* 369, I had become a sleep-walker; but whither my *somnambulary adventures had conducted me, was a riddle I had yet to solve. 1833 Carlyle *Misc.* (1872) V. 127 This inarticulate age which slumbers and *somnambulates. 1840 — *Diamond Necklace* xiv, His Eminence again somnambulates the Promenade de la Rose. 1873 M. Collins *Squire Silchester* II. xiv. 178 The latter, sometimes overeating themselves, somnambulate. 1876 *Contemp. Rev.* June 126 A *somnambulating philosophy. 1794–6 E. Darwin *Zoon.* (1801) I. 325 Though in its greatest degree it has been called *somnambulation or sleep-walking, it is totally different from that sleep. 1803 Beddoes *Hygeia* ix. 130 The lady, whose reverie or somnambulation is described. 1862 G. Macdonald *D. Elginbrod* III. xvii, The next day she had a bad head-ache. This with her always followed somnambulation. 1822 Prichard *Dis. Nervous Syst.* I. 404 Hoffmann cites the case of a *somnambulator, which [etc.]. 1837 J. F. Cooper *Europe* II. 288 A woman, who was subject to the magnetic influence, or who was what is commonly called a '*somnambule*.' 1850 J. Braid *Observ. Trance* 30 The same discretion ought also to be extended to the modes of testing somnambules. 1877 Symonds *Renaiss. It.* iii. 147 Walking..like a somnambule sustained by an internal dream. 1829 I. Taylor *Enthusiasm* i. (1850) 10 The enthusiast passes through life in a sort of happy *somnambulency. 1865 Carlyle *Fredk. Gt.* xviii. iii. (1872) VII. 138 For nations have their somnambulencies. 1841 C. Mackay *Pop. Delusions* III. 366 The patient was thrown into the *somnambulic state. 1862 G. Macdonald *D. Elginbrod* II. xxxi, A reproduction of some previous somnambulic experience. 1880 Huth *Life & Writ. Buckle* I. 34 He..woke the landlady whose somnambulic figure.. had just frightened him. 1887 *Sat. Rev.* 11 June 848 When he wakes, he finds that he has *somnambulically made a pen-and-ink sketch. 1797 *Encycl. Brit.* (ed. 3) XVII. 534/2 Subject to that singular affection or disease called '*Somnambulism* or sleep-walking. 1820 Shelley *Witch Atl.* lxxv, The soldiers..Walked out of quarters in somnambulism. 1899 *Allbutt's Syst. Med.* VIII. 93 In somnambulism ..the secondary consciousness takes control of the whole individual. 1794 Mary Wollstonecr. *Hist. View Fr. Rev.* I. 275 It was dangerous to awaken a *somnambulist on the brink of a precipice. 1837 Barham *Ingol. Leg.* Ser. I. *Spectre of Tappington* (1905) 23 Never again was Lieutenant Seaforth known to act the part of a somnambulist. 1856 Froude *Hist. Eng.* I. 308 A revolution had been effected in Europe by a somnambulist peasant girl. 1887 *Encycl. Brit.* XXII. 158/1 Somnambulists have been observed to write letters or reports,..and play upon musical instruments. 1840 Dickens *Old C. Shop* (1867) 304 A *somnambulistic leave-taking and walking in her sleep. 1845 E. Warburton *Crescent & Cross* I. 216 A black little naked urchin sits on the splinter-bar, continually goading his somnambulistic team. 1899 *Allbutt's Syst. Med.* VIII. 167 Very rarely the patient may be also somnambulistic. 1845 E. Warburton *Crescent & Cross* II. 289 The slaves glided about silently and *somnambulistically, or stood with folded arms watching for a sign. *a* 1893 Symonds in H. F. Brown *Life* (1895) I. 71, I did not doubt that my spirit could somnambulistically travel from the place. 1832 *Figaro in London* 3 March 52/1 When he *somnambulizes upon the stage. *c* 1850 Whittier *Tales & Sk., Mag. & Witch Folk* Prose Wks. 1889 I. 400 A 'wise woman' dreamed, or somnambulized, that a large sum of money..lay buried in the centre of the great swamp.

†**Somna·ical**, *a.* *Obs.*$^{-1}$ [irreg. f. L. *somnus* or *somnium*.] Pertaining to sleep or dreams.

1655 Emmot *Northern Blast* 2 Many were the raptures which I dreamed to have, but all was but a Fancy or Somnaical.

†**Somne**, *v.*^{1} *Obs.* Forms: 1 **somnizean, somnian**, 3 **somnien (somni), somnen, sompnen, some(n).** [OE. *somnian*, var. of *samnian*: see Sam *v.*^{1} and cf. Sumne *v.*] *trans.* To assemble, gather, collect, unite.

a. *c* 825 *Vesp. Psalter* cxxviii. 7 Of ðæm ne ȝefylleð.. his sceat se ðe reopan somnað. *a* 1000 *Phœnix* 193 Þa swetestan [he] somnað & gædrað wyrta wynsume. *c* 1175 *Lamb. Hom.* 135 In halie chirche þer alle cristene men aȝen to beon isomned to gedere. *c* 1205 Lay. 4152 He somenede færd. *Ibid.* 30628 Þer heo gunnen somnien scipen uniuoȝen. *a* 1225 *Ancr. R.* 186 Wult tu to-dealen þet God haueð isompned? *a* 1250 *Prov. Ælfred* 34 in *O. E. Misc.*, He ou wolde wyssye..hw ye myhte..eure saule somnen to criste.

β. *c* 1205 Lay. 5122 Þa weoren al þas leoden at Lundene isomed. *c* 1275 *Ibid.* 18631 Þo hii to-gadere weren alle hi-somed.

†**Somne**, *v.*^{2} *Obs.* Forms: *α.* 3 **someni**, 3–4 **someny**, 4–5 **somene**, 5–6 **somen.** *β.* 4 **somne.** [Variant of *somony*, etc., Summon *v.*, with weakening and subsequent elision of the second vowel. See also Sompne *v.* and Sumne *v.*] *trans.* To summon.

α. 1297 R. Glouc. (Rolls) 3764 Is poer he let someny þat ysprad was wel wyde. *Ibid.* 10379 Þe pope..alle þe bissops of engelond let someni to rome. *c* 1380 Wyclif *Wks.* (1880) 357 If þei somene symple men for þis accusing. 1393 Langl. *P. Pl.* C. xxii. 214 Grace..consailede hym and conscience the comune to someny. 1401 *Pol. Poems* (Rolls) II. 89 Ȝe..somen men and threten hem, bot if thai ȝif ȝou gode.

β. *c* 1300 *Leg. Rood* (1871) 38 Þo þe giwes i-somned were, hi hadde schortliche gret fere. *c* 1380 Wyclif *Wks.* (1880) 250 Þei ben hurlid & somnyd fro day to day, fro fer place to ferþere. 1387 Trevisa *Higden* (Rolls) III. 201 Pictagoras..somnede hym to fore iuges.

Hence †**So·mning** *vbl. sb.* *Obs.*

1480 Caxton *Chron. Eng.* ccxii. 108 b, To warne the parties defendauntz thurgh somnyng ayene. 1529–30 *Rec. St. Mary at Hill* 349 Paid to a Somoner for Somenyng of Mr hiltons, preist, ij d.

†**So·mner.** *Obs.* Forms: *α.* 4 **som(e)nour**, 5 **somenor**, 6 **sommenor.** *β.* 4 **somenere**, 4, 6–7 **somner.** [f. *somene* Somne *v.*^{2}, or a. AF. *somnour*.] An official summoner. Also *transf.*

α. *c* 1320 *Pol. Songs* (Camden) 155 Ȝet ther sitteth somenours syexe other sevene. 1377 Langl. *P. Pl.* B. xv. 128 Sectoures and sudenes, somnoures and her lemmannes. 1474 *Cal. Anc. Rec. Dublin* (1889) 350 Walter Wotlon somenor. 1570 *Wills & Inv. N. C.* (Surtees 1838) 342 John Roddh'm the sommenr.

β. 1393 Langl. *P. Pl.* C. III. 59 Sysours and somners, shereyues and here clerkes. *Ibid.* x. 263 Hure salue ys of *supersedeas* in someneres boxes. 1521 *Coventry Leet-Bk.* 672 At suche tymes as they shal-be Reasonably warnyd by the somner. 1563 *Homilies* II. *Of Repentance* III, When the hyghest somner of all, whiche is death, shall come. 1585 T. Washington tr. *Nicholay's Voy.* III. xviii. 105 [They] haue like vnto Somners, as many brybes as they can carry away. 1608 Middleton *Trick to catch Old One* II. i, They may do anything there, and fear neither beadle nor somner.

Somni-, combining form of L. *somnus* sleep, occurring in a number of Latin compounds and English adaptations or imitations of these, as *somnifer* somniferous, *somnificus* somnific, etc. (see below).

Somnial (sǫ·mniăl), *a.* *rare.* [a. older F. *somnial*, or ad. L. *somniāl-is*, f. *somni-um* dream.] Of or relating to dreams.

a 1693 *Urquhart's Rabelais* III. xiv. 120 To presage or foretell an evil..in matter of Somnial Divinations. 1833 Coleridge in *Lit. Rem.* (1838) III. 397 The Somnial magic superinduced on..the active powers of the mind.

†**So·mniate**, *v.* *Obs.*$^{-1}$ [f. ppl. stem of L. *somniāre*, f. *somnium* dream.]

1. *trans.* To dream (something).

1657 Tomlinson *Renou's Disp.* 344 Who being too credulous have committed to presse what the imperite somniated.

2. To stupefy, make drowsy.

1719 De Foe *Vision of Angelic World* 23 More or less doz'd or somniated with the oppression of Vapours..which occasion sleep.

†**Somnia·tion.** *Obs. rare.* [See prec. and -ation.] A sleep; a dream.

1597 A. M. tr. *Guillemeau's Fr. Chirurg.* † iij, Beinge resuscitated..out of a profounde..somniation. 1599 — tr. *Gabelhouer's Bk. Physicke* 40/2 That expelleth all phantasticalle somniationes.

So·mniative, *a.* *rare*$^{-1}$. [See Somniate *v.* and -ative.] Relating to, or producing, dreams.

1827 Coleridge in *Lit. Rem.* (1839) IV. 422 A very rare ..conjunction of the somniative faculty..with the voluntary and other powers of the waking state.

†**So·mniatory**, *a.* *Obs. rare.* [See Somniate *v.* and -ory.] Of or pertaining to dreams or dreaming.

a 1693 *Urquhart's Rabelais* III. xiii, For the..unfolding of these somniatory [F. *somniales*] Vaticinations. *Ibid.*, I will to-morrow break my fast betimes after my somniatory exercitations [F. *songeailles*].

Somniculo·sity. *rare*$^{-0}$. [Cf. next and -ity.] 'Sleepiness, drowsiness' (Bailey, 1721).

Somni·culous, *a.* *rare.* [ad. L. *somniculōsus*, f. *somnus* sleep. Cf. obs. F. *somniculeux*.] **a.** Drowsy, sleepy. **b.** Inducing sleep.

1656 Blount *Glossogr.*, *Somniculous*, negligent, sleepy, drowzy, sluggish; also that makes drowzy or sleepy. 1819 L. Hunt *Indicator* No. 11 (1822) I. 84 Leaving the somniculous squire propped up in the saddle. 1820 *Ibid.* No. 54 (1822) II. 11 The plain is also full of all sorts of somniculous plants.

Somnifa·cient, *a.* and *sb.* [f. Somni- + pres. pple. of *facĕre* to make.] **a.** *adj.* Somnific. **b.** *sb.* A soporific. (*Cent. Dict.* 1891.)

†**Somni·feric.** *Obs.*$^{-1}$ [Cf. next and -ic.] A soporific.

1694 Salmon *Bate's Dispens.* (1713) 262/2 It is a most certain Somniferick and Sudorifick.

Somniferous (sǫmni·fĕrəs), *a.* [f. L. *somnifer* (f. *somni-* Somni- + *-ferre* to bring) + -ous. Cf. F. *somnifère*, Sp. and Pg. *somnifero*, It. *sonnifero*.]

1. Inducing sleep; soporific.

1602 Dekker *Satirom.* Wks. 1873 I. 255 Twas I that ministred to her chaste bloud, A true somniferous potion, which did steale Her thoughts to sleepe. 1633 Brome *Antipodes* II. iv, You slept most part o' th' journey hitherward, The aire was so somniferous. 1663 Boyle *Usef. Exp. Nat. Philos.* II. App. 345 A safe and moderately somniferous medicine in feavers. 1754 Dodsley *Agric.* III. 215 The scarlet poppy..Bows his somniferous head, inviting soon To peaceful slumber the disorder'd mind. 1799 Underwood *Dis. Childr.* (ed. 4) I. 360 If it follow any somniferous disease. 1837 Dickens *Pickw.* ii, The wine had exerted its somniferous influence. 1876 Harley *Royle's Mat. Med.* 764 The effects..of the other somniferous constituents of opium.

2. Somnolent, sleepy.

1798 in *Spirit Public Jrnls.* (1799) II. 400 A most somniferous Earl gave violent symptoms of animation. 1809 Irving *Knickerb.* (1861) 153 Those fat, somniferous, respectable burghers.

Hence **Somni·ferously** *adv.*

1836 *New Monthly Mag.* XLVI. 13 His translations..were somniferously dull. *a* 1852 Moore *Corn & Catholics* ix. Poet. Wks. (1872) 392 A row Of Poppies..Stand forth, somniferously flaming! 1865 E. C. Clayton *Cruel Fortune* II. 110 By degrees the heat, and the silence,..operated somniferously on Val.

†**Somni·fery.** *Obs.*$^{-1}$ [f. as prec. + -y.] A place of sleep.

1600 Tourneur *Transf. Metam.* (1878) 202 Unlock the rustie latch That leades into the cave's somniferie.

Somnific (sǫmni·fik), *a.* [ad. L. *somnificus*: see Somni- and -fic.] Causing sleep; somniferous.

1721 Bailey, *Somnifick*, causing sleep. 1727 A. Hamilton *New Acc. E. Indies* I. xxiii. 278 Others again take somnifick Medicines, and stand by the Pile till they fall on it while asleep. 1775 S. J. Pratt *Liberal Opin.* cxxxvi. (1783) IV. 254 A somnific fit again overtook him,..and, in the next instant, he was snoring in his chair. 1819 Moore *Diary* VIII. 189, I agree with you that a great part of 'Lara' is very prosy and somnific. 1834 Southey *Doctor* (1848) 3 The voice, the manner, the matter,..were all alike somnific.

Somnificator. *rare*$^{-1}$. [Cf. prec. and -ator.] One who induces sleep.

1806 Southey *Let.* in *Life* (1850) III. 33 The rector, a humdrum somnificator.

So·mnifuge. *rare*$^{-1}$. [See Somni- and -fuge.] A means of driving away sleep.

1890 Lowell *Lett.* (1894) II. x. 460 He [the nightingale] has a bad character among you as a *somnifuge*.

Somni·fugous, *a.* *rare*$^{-0}$. [Cf. prec.] 'Driving away sleep' (Bailey, 1721).

†**So·mnifying**, *ppl. a.* *Obs. rare.* [See Somni- and -fy.] Inducing sleep.

1634 Brereton *Trav.* (Chetham Soc.) 40 He also discoursed of..hemlock, which he said was of a most venomous, somnifying, stupifying, and intoxicating quality. 1770 Chatterton in Masson *Life* II. iii. (1874) 163 This somnifying liquor had made her voice so like the sweet echo of Miss Hill's that..I should absolutely have imagined it hers.

Somniloqua·cious, *a.* *rare*$^{-0}$. [See Somni- and Loquacious *a.*] 'Talking or apt to talk in sleep' (Bailey, vol. II, 1731). Also **Somni·loquence**, = *somniloquy*. **Somni·loquent** *a.*, talking in sleep. **Somni·loquism**, = *somniloquy*. **Somni·loquist**, one who speaks or talks while asleep. **Somni·loquize** *v. intr.*, to talk in (or as in) sleep. **Somni·loquous** *a.*, 'apt to talk in sleep' (Webster, 1847). **Somni·loquy**, the act or habit of speaking during sleep.

1841 W. C. Dendy *Philos. Mystery* 306 True *somniloquence is often preceded by a cataleptic state. *Ibid.* 304. 1804 Coleridge in *Blackw. Mag.* (1882) CXXXI. 123 The Ideatæ are but *somniloquent Ideotæ. 1821 — *Ibid.* X. 244 The *somniloquism of the prophetesses under the coercion of the Scandinavian enchanters. 1833 — in *Lit. Rem.* (1838) III. 397 How often the pen becomes the tongue of a systematic dream,—a *somniloquist! 1866 *Cornh. Mag.* Aug. 231 We may even be prompted to the action of the somnambulist, or somniloquist, without waking. *a* 1901 Myers *Human Personality* (1903) II. 6 The somnambulist, or rather the somniloquist. 1827 Coleridge *Blackw. Mag.* (1882) CXXXI. 119 Is it not melancholy to hear a man like Steffens *somniloquise in such a mystifying cant? 1847 Webster, **Somniloquy*, the talking of one in a state of somnipathy. 1899 *Allbutt's Syst. Med.* VII. 757 Sleep-talking or somniloquy, and sleep-walking or somnambulism, are states in which the whole brain is not asleep.

Somni·pathy. [See Somni- and -pathy.] 'Sleep from sympathy, or by the process of mesmerism' (Webster, 1847). Also **Somni·pathist**, 'a person in a state of somnipathy' (*Ibid.*).

Somnite, obs. form of Sunnite.

Somni·volency. *rare*$^{-1}$. [f. Somni- + *-volency*, ad. L. *-volentia* will, desire.] An intended soporific. Also **Somni·volent**, one who desires to sleep.

1748 Richardson *Clarissa* (1811) V. 345 If these somnivolencies (I hate the word opiates on this occasion) have turned her head. 1885 G. Meredith *Diana* xvi, The irrational repetition ploughed the minds of those unhappy somnivolents.

Somnolence (sǫ·mnŏlĕns). Also 4–6 **sompnolence.** [a. OF. *sompnolence* (mod.F. *somnolence*, = Sp. *somnolencia*, Pg. *so(m)nolencia*, It. *sonnolenza*), or ad. L. *somnolentia* (med.L. *sompnolencia*), f. *somnolentus*: see Somnolent *a.*] Inclination to sleep; sleepiness, drowsiness.

c 1386 Chaucer *Pars. T.* ⁋ 705 Than comth Sompnolence, þat is sluggy slombryng. 1390 Gower *Conf.* II. 94 That I no Sompnolence have used. *c* 1425 *Orolog. Sapient.* iii. in *Anglia* X. 349/32 Wolte þou be ouerlayde with sompnolence and ydelnesse. *c* 1475 *Partenay* 4616 Ho-so do slepe ..in sompnolence there, Alway perpetuall there abide shall he. 1542 Boorde *Dyetary* xix. (1870) 279 Onyons doth prouoke a man..to sompnolence.

1721 in Bailey. 1841 W. C. Dendy *Philos. Mystery* 367 Somnolence.—Trance.—Catalepsy. 1862 Merivale *Rom. Emp.* lxvi. (1865) VIII. 237 The dignified somnolence of an old-fashioned city like Athens. 1866 G. Macdonald *Ann. Q. Neighb.* ii. The people had dined and the usual somnolence had followed.

personif. 1390 Gower *Conf.* II. 92 Ther is yit on of compaignie, And he is cleped Sompnolence.

So·mnolency. [See prec. and -ency.] = prec.

1623 Cockeram I, *Somnolencie*, sleepinesse. 1727 in Bailey. 1810 Bentham *Packing* (1821) 141 Symptoms of somnolency begin to discover themselves. 1859 R. F. Burton *Centr. Afr.* in *Jrnl. Geogr. Soc.* XXIX. 283 It affects the head, prevents somnolency. 1875 H. C. Wood *Therap.* (1879) 218 Prolonged nausea, and retching, interrupted only by intervals of dreamy delirious somnolency.

Somnolent (sǫ·mnŏlĕnt), *a.* and *sb.* Also 5–6 **sompnolent.** [a. OF. *sompnolent* (mod.F. *somnolent*), or ad. L. *somnolentus* (med.L. *sompno-*), f. *somnus* sleep.]

1. Tending to cause sleepiness or drowsiness; inclining to sleep.

c 1475 *Partenay* 5376 Where it behouith to wacche nightes thre Without any sompnolent slepe to be. 1615 G. Sandys *Trav.* 292 Takes age in ease and sleepe content? Then Baiæ what more somnolent? 1824 Dibdin *Libr. Comp.* 531 An effect which we seek in vain in the somnolent pages of Lediard. 1855 Dickens *Dorrit* xix, He was again painfully aware of a somnolent tendency in Frederick. 1882 De Windt *Equator* 75 The noise made by the stream..had a very pleasant and somnolent effect.

b. Marked by sleepiness or slowness.

1812 *Q. Rev.* VIII. 64 The translator restricts his somnolent interrogation to Codrus. 1877 Wallace *Russia* v. 76 And I must do Anton the justice to say that he served me well in his own somnolent fashion.

2. Of persons: Inclined to sleep; heavy with sleep; drowsy. Also *transf.*

1547 Boorde *Brev. Health* xiii. (1557) B iij b, If the sycke person do vomit & be sompnouent [*sic*] or sleping. 1623 Cockeram I, *Somnolent*, sleepie. 1625 Jackson *Creed* v. xvi. Wks. IV. 118 Deriding the somnolent and sluggish gods of the Epicures. 1721 in Bailey. 1819 Scott *Leg. Montrose* v, I am no whit somnolent; I always hear best with my eyes shut. 1837 Barham *Ingol. Leg.* Ser. I. *Grey Dolphin* (1905) 45 Fasting and watching had made him more than usually somnolent. 1891 Hardy *Tess* (1900) 15/2 When they had passed the little town of Stourcastle, dumbly somnolent under its thick brown thatch.

b. *sb.* A somnolent or sleepy person; one affected with somnolence.

1841 W. C. Dendy *Philos. Mystery* 373 Like many other somnolents, she was morose and irritable, especially previous to the sleeping-fit.

Hence **So·mnolently** *adv.*, in a somnolent manner; sleepily.

1615 Jackson *Creed* IV. II. ix. Wks. III. 378, I know none but may have hope to escape so they will not..somnolently put off the evil day. 1827 *Blackw. Mag.* XXII. 384 Alciphron could not possibly have been more somnolently inclined. 1875 M. Collins *Sweet & Twenty* II. vi, An inquisitive investigative youth was Charles, who never threw away his time somnolently.

Somnole·scence. [See next and -ence.] The state or condition of being sleepy; inclination to sleep.

1831 *Fraser's Mag.* III. 102 The power of inducing the pleasurable sensation of somnolescence. 1898 E. Young *Kingdom of Yellow Robe* vi. 116 Mosquitoes whose buzzing and stinging are effective preventatives of somnolescence.

Somnolescent (sǫmnŏle·sĕnt), *a.* [f. Somnolent *a.*: see -escent.] Drowsy, sleepy; inert.

1845 Ford *Handbk. Spain* II. 725 Somnolescent over business and awake only to intrigue. 1886 *Encycl. Brit.* XX. 201/1 The animal..lies there in a somnolescent state for perhaps hours.

So·mnolism. *rare.* [f. Somnol-ent *a.* + -ism.] The state of being in a mesmeric sleep.

1849 Haddock *Somnolism & Psycheism* 19 Other persons of greater susceptibility..proceed quickly into a state of profound sleep,—or, as I propose to call it, Somnolism.

So·mnolize, *v.* *rare*$^{-1}$. [f. as prec. + -ize.] *trans.* To make drowsy or sleepy.

1831 *Fraser's Mag.* III. 451 The same sort of palaver with which the universities have thought fit to somnolize us.

Somno·pathy. *rare*$^{-0}$. = Somnipathy.

1851 Dunglison *Dict. Med. Sci.*, *Somnopathy*, somnambulism, magnetic.

†**Somnori·ferous**, *a.* *Obs.* [Erroneous form of Somniferous, after *soporiferous*.] Soporific.

1590 Barrough *Meth. Physick* I. xv. (1639) 24 Water wherein..poppy seed hath been sodden, or some somnoriferous compound. *Ibid.* II. x. 88 Sirupes of Poppy, and other somnoriferous medicines.

So **Somnori·fic** *a.*

1865 'Annie Thomas' *On Guard* ii, The first scene opened on a somnorific, sultry summer afternoon in London. 1880 G. A. Townsend *Tales Chesapeake* 196 The somnorific air of the Springs.

†**So·mnorine**, *a.* *Obs.*$^{-1}$ [irreg. f. L. *somnus*.] Seen during sleep.

1637 Venner *Treat. of Tobacco* in *Via Recta* 347 By reason of the somnorine visions which this fume doth greatly occasion.

Somnour, variant of Somner *Obs.*

Somnunge, variant of Samening *Obs.*

‖**So·mnus.** [L. *somnus* sleep, also personified as a divinity.] The god of sleep.

a 1599 Peele *Sir Clyomon* xxi. Wks. (Rtldg.) 522/2, I creep out of my drowsy den when Somnus hath suppress The head of every valiant heart. 1710 tr. *Quilletus' Callipædia* III. 144 But as she mourn'd, kind *Somnus* gently stole To her soft Eyes, and lull'd her sinking Soul.

Somod, var. Samed *adv.* *Obs.* **Somonce**, obs. f. Summons *sb.* **Somonde, Somone, Somoni, -ony**, obs. varr. Summon *v.* **Somoniter**, obs. var. Summonitor. **Somoron**, obs. f. Summer *v.* **Somoun, -own**, obs. ff. Summon *sb.* and *v.* **Somounce**, obs. f. Summons *sb.* **Sompe**, obs. f. Sump.

†**Sompnary.** *Obs.*$^{-1}$ [ad. med.L. *sompniaria* (sc. *ars*), f. *sompnium*, L. *somnium* dream.] Divination by dreams; oneiromancy.

a 1470 H. Parker *Dives & Pauper* (W. de W.) I. xxxiv. 73/1 To make ony dyuynynge..by songuary or sompnarye.

†**Sompne**, *v.* *Obs.* Also 5 **sompny.** [Variant of Somne *v.*^{2}, with insertion of *p* as in *nempne* Nemn *v.*] *trans.* To summon.

1362 Langl. *P. Pl.* A. II. 142 Þus sysoures ben sompned to be false to serue. *c* 1380 Wyclif *Wks.* (1880) 151 He schal be sompned, ponyschid & cursed. *c* 1386 Chaucer *Friar's T.* 49 (Harl.), Withoute maundement, a lewed man He couthe sompne. 14.. *Lat.-Eng. Voc.* in Wr.-Wülcker 573 *Cito*, to sompny. 1472 in *10th Rep. Hist. MSS. Comm.* App. V. 309 The seriaunt shal sompne ony suche att his house.

Hence †**So·mpning** *vbl. sb.* *Obs.*

c 1400 *Plowman's Tale* in *Pol. Poems* (Rolls) I. 330 To speake they shull not be so bold, For sompning to the consistorye. *c* 1400 *Brut* Prol. 1 Dioclician anon lete make a sompnyng. 1490–1 [see Sompnour].

†**Sompnour.** *Obs.* Also 5–6 **sompner(e.** [Variant of *somnour* Somner: cf. prec.] An official summoner.

a. 1377 Langl. *P. Pl.* B. III. 33 Sisoures and sompnoures, suche men hir preiseth. *c* 1386 Chaucer *Prol.* 543 Ther was ..A sompnour and a pardoner also. *c* 1400 *Plowman's Tale* in *Pol. Poems* (Rolls) I. 313 They taken to ferme her sompnours. 1490–1 *Rec. St. Mary at Hill* 164 Paide to William Iames, Sompnour, for sompnyng of iij tenauntes that owed monye to the chyrch, x d. 1555 W. Watreman *Fardle of Facions* II. xi. 256 Thei haue also certaine spiefaultes ordinarilye appoincted (muche like to our Sompnours).

β. 14.. *Lat.-Eng. Voc.* in Wr.-Wülcker 573 *Citator*, a Sompnere. *c* 1500 *God Speed the Plough* (Skt.) 65 Than cometh the Sompner to haue som rente. *a* 1535 *Frere & Boy* 478 in Hazl. *E. P. P.* III. 80 Thus they departed in that tyde, The offycyall and the sompnere.

Sompter, obs. form of Sumpter.

Somptious, obs. form of Sumptuous.

†**Somredness.** *Obs.*$^{-1}$ [Related to OE. *samrǣd* harmonious, united.] Concord, unity.

a 1225 *Ancr. R.* 254 Nimeð nu uorbisne hu god is onnesse of heorte, & somrednesse of luue þet halt þe gode somed.

†**Somrune.** *Obs.*$^{-1}$ [f. OE. *sǫm-, sam-* together + *rūn* Roun.] Council, consultation.

c 1205 Lay. 5479 Belin & Brenne beie to-sone nomen heom to ræde & to som rune.

Somun, Somyn, variants of Samen *adv.* *Obs.*

Somundare, obs. form of Summoner.

Somyr(e, obs. forms of Summer.

Son (sʊn), *sb.* Forms: *α.* 1 **sunu**, 1–2 **suna**, 2–5 **sune**, 4 **sunn(e**, 4–5 **sun**, 8 *Sc.* **sin.** *β.* 3–8 **sone** (4 **zone**), 4–5 **soone**, 4, 6 **soon**, 6 **soonne**; 5 **soun(e**; 4–7 **sonne**, 4– **son** (6 *dial.* **zon**, *Sc.* **schon**, 7 **sonn**). [Common Teut.: OE. *sunu* (gen. *suna*), = OFris. *sunu, sune, sone* (EFris. *sūnū*, WFris. *soan*, NFris. *sen, sên*, etc.), MDu. *sone, zone* (Du. *zoon*), OS. *sunu* (MLG. *sone*, LG. *sone, sön, sän*, etc.), OHG. *sunu, sun* (MHG. *sune, sun, son*, G. *sohn*), ON. *sunr, sonr* (Icel. *sonur*, Norw. and Sw. *son*, Da. *søn*), Goth. *sunus*. Outside of the Teutonic languages similar forms appear in Lith. *sūnus*, OSlav. *synŭ* (Russ. сынъ), Skr. *sūnu* (Zend. *hunu*). The root *su-* is also that of Gr. υἱός.

The declension in OE. is variable through confusion of the different cases and the introduction of new forms, as gen. sing. *sunes*, nom. pl. *sunan*, gen. pl. *sunena*. From early ME. the usual possessive and plural forms are those in *-es* or *-s*.

Senses 2–7 represent for the most part Biblical uses of the word, examples of which occur freely in all the English versions of the Scriptures.]

1. A male child or person in relation to either or to both of his parents. Sometimes said of animals.

See also Mother's son.

a. *Beowulf* 645 Oþ þæt..sunu Healfdenes secean wolde æfenræste. *c* 888 K. Ælfred *Boeth.* xxxviii. § 1 Þa wæs þær Apollines dohtor Iobes suna. 971 *Blickl. Hom.* 7 Ðu cennest sunu þone þu nemnest Hælend. *c* 1100 *O. E. Chron.* an. 1052 (MS. D), His sunan wæron eorlas & þæs cynges dyrlingas. *c* 1122 *Ibid.* an. 1121 (Laud MS.), Seo wæs Willelme þes cynges sune..to wife forȝyfan. *c* 1200 Ormin 488 And ta twa prestess wærenn Aaroness suness baþe. *c* 1250 *Gen. & Ex.* 2175 Alle we ben on faderes sunen. *a* 1300 *Cursor M.* 796 Of þat ilk appel bitt þair suns tethe ar eggeid yitt. 13.. *E. E. Allit. P.* B. 298 He had þre þryuen sunez & þay þre wyuez. *c* 1400 *Destr. Troy* 6567 Se ye not the sun of youre sure kyng..turnyt away? 1559 *Mirr. Mag., O. Glendour* vi, How would we mocke the burden bearing mule If he would brag he wer an horses sunne. 1786 Burns *Halloween* xvi, Our Stibble-rig was Rab M'Graen...His Sin gat Eppie Sim wi' wean.

β. *a* 1275 *Prov. Ælfred* 574 in *O. E. Misc.* 134 Sone min swo leue, site me nu bisides. *c* 1290 *S. Eng. Leg.* I. 21 Edwyne, is sone, was king i-maud. 1340 *Ayenb.* 48 Ne uorzakeþ nenne ne uader ne broþer ne zone. 1387 Trevisa *Higden* (Rolls) II. 385 Dedalus wiþ his sone Icarus. *c* 1412 Hoccleve *De Reg. Princ.* 2736 A man þat sone was To a conseil, was take in þis trespas. 1473 *Rental Bk. Cupar-Angus* (1879) I. 191 Thome Sowtar forsaid and his thre sonys. 1529 Cromwell in Merriman *Life & Lett.* (1902) I. 57, I gyue and bequethe to my saide Soon Gregorye A Bason. 1596 Bacon *Max. & Use Com. Law* II. (1635) 48 During the minority of his eldest sonn. 1681 Dryden *Abs. & Achit.* I. 32 Indulgent David view'd His Youthful Image in his Son renew'd. 1741–2 Gray *Agrip.* 67 If the son reign, the mother perishes. 1764 Goldsm. *Hist. Eng. in Lett.* (1772) IV. 39 Lord Colchester, son to the earl of Rivers. 1812 Southey *Let.* in *Life* (1850) III. 325 His name is Shelley, son to the member for Shoreham. 1857 Borrow *Rom. Rye* xxxix, Soliman..after his death befriended his young son. 1871 Smiles *Charac.* ii. (1876) 46 To inspire her sons' minds with elevating thoughts.

fig. 1781 Cowper *Heroism* 59 Famine, and pestilence, her first-born son.

b. In the phrase *son and heir*. Also *fig.*

1297 R. Glouc. (Rolls) 9607 In is warde he let do Henri is eldoste sone & is eir al so. 1338 R. Brunne *Chron.* (1810) 5 Sorow & site he made..For his sonne & heyre. 13.. *E. E. Allit. P.* B. 666, I schal..sothely sende to sare a son & an hayre. 1430–40 Lydg. *Bochas* I. viii, Of Phœbus..Poetes write that he was sonne and heire. 1481 *Cov. Leet Bk.* 475 The son & heir of hym that nowe pretendeth to be kyng. 1576 in *Excheq. Rolls Scotl.* XX. 372 Jhone Dromond,..quhe is schon and air to his fader Jhone Dromond. 1604 Dekker *Honest Wh.* I. v, As clean as your sons-and-heirs when they ha' spent all. 1833 Tennyson *Death Old Year* 31 To see him die..His son and heir doth ride post-haste.

c. = Son-in-law.

1533 *Test. Ebor.* (Surtees) VI. 38 My said sone Briane Tunstall. 1596 Shaks. *Tam. Shr.* v. ii. 78 *Bap.* Sonne, Ile be your halfe, Bianca comes.

2. *Theol.* The second person of the Trinity. (Cf. 4 a.)

c 825 *Vesp. Hymns* viii. 21 Bledsien we feder & sunu & ðone halȝan gast. *a* 900 *Halsunege* in *Durh. Rit.* (Surtees) 114 Ic eow halsiȝe on fæder naman, and on suna naman. *c* 1175 *Lamb. Hom.* 85 Þe feder and þe sune and þe halie gast. 1340 *Ayenb.* 12 Þe oþer article belongeþ to þe zone aȝe to his godhede. 1382 Wyclif *1 John* ii. 24 Ȝe shulen dwelle in the sone and the fadir. *c* 1420 [see God 5 d]. 1500–20 Dunbar *Poems* xliv. 29 That Sone is Lord, that Sone is King of kingis. 1548 *Bk. Com. Prayer, Athanas. Creed*, The Father is God, the Son is God. *a* 1628 F. Grevil in Farr *S. P. Eliz.* (1845) I. 108 We seeme more inwardly to knowe the Sonne. 1671 Milton *P. R.* II. 260 It was the hour of night, when thus the Son Commun'd in silent walk. 1728 Chambers *Cycl.* s.v. *Trinity*, Father, Son, and Holy Spirit. 1817 Shelley *Satan broke Loose* 5 The Father and the Son Knew that strife was now begun. 1858 Whittier *Trinitas* 56 Father, and Son, and Holy Call; This day thou hast denied them all!

3. One who is regarded as, or takes the place of, a son. †Also *spec.* at Cambridge, one presented for a degree by the 'father' of his college. †*White son*: see White *a.*

c 825 *Vesp. Psalter* ii. 7 Dryhten cwæð to me: Sunu min ðu earð; to deȝe ic cende ðec. *c* 1000 Ælfric *Exod.* ii. 10 And heo hine lufode, & hæfde for sunu hyre. *c* 1000 *Ags. Gosp.* John xix. 26 Þa cwæþ he to his meder: Wif, her ys þin sunu. *c* 1200 *Trin. Coll. Hom.* 19 Alle men ben godes children, for þat he hem alle shop, and ches hem to sunes and to dohtres. *a* 1400 *Relig. Pieces fr. Thornton MS.* 87 His mercy..That..me, a wreche, his sun walde make. 1567 *Gude & Godlie B.* (S.T.S.) 33 Quhome God ressaifis to his sone and air, Him will he scurge. 1574 M. Stokys in Peacock *Stat. Cambr.* (1841) App. A. p. x, The Father..shall call fourthe his eldest sone, & animate hym to dispute. 1665 in Wordsworth *Univ. Life 18th C.* (1874) 412 Then the Father calleth up the Answerer, and showeth him his sons. 1718 Prior *Solomon* III. 889 Let Thy command Restore, great Father, Thy instructed son. 1799 Wordsw. *The Fountain* 62 And, Matthew, for thy children dead I'll be a son to thee! 1877 Baring-Gould *Lives Saints* Oct. 305 The child afterwards lived and died in God's service at Ripon, and was called the bishop's son.

b. Used as a term of affectionate address to a man or boy by an older person or by one in a superior (esp. ecclesiastical) relation.

c 950 *Lindisf. Gosp.* Matt. ix. 2 La sunu forgefen biðon.. ðe synno ðina. 1390 Gower *Conf.* I. 108 Mi Sone, in alle maner wise, Surquiderie is to despise. *c* 1400 tr. *Secreta Secret., Gov. Lordsh.* 49 Soune most glorious, most rightful Emperour. *c* 1440 *Alph. Tales* 196 Þe bisshop sayd; 'Nay, son,..here hase bene a noder emperour of long tyme'. 1534 More *Comf. agst. Trib.* II. Wks. 1183/2 The Foxe..charged hym to..lye styll and sleepe lyke a good sonne. 1603 Shaks. *Meas. for M.* III. i. 161 *Duke.* Son, I haue ouer-heard what hath past between you & your sister. 1820 Scott *Monast.* xxv, 'Prove thy strength, my son, in the name of God!' said the preacher. *Ibid.* xxxii, 'Even now, if thou wilt,' said the Sub-Prior,..'come hither, my son, and kneel down'.

4. *Son of God*: **a.** Jesus Christ. (Cf. 2.) Also †*God's son*. Hence *Son-of-godship*.

c 950 *Lindisf. Gosp.* Luke xxii. 70 Cuoedon ða alle, ðu.. arð sunu godes. *c* 1200 Ormin 267 Till þatt Godess Sune Crist Himm shollde onn eorþe shæwenn. *c* 1250 *Gen. & Ex.* 403 And ȝet sal godes dere sune In ȝure kin in werlde wunen. *c* 1340 Hampole *Pr. Consc.* 5044 In..archaungel steven, And in þe son of Goddes awen beme. *c* 1400 *Rule St. Benet* (Prose) vii. 12 Als tapostil saide of godis sune. *a* 1529 Skelton *Prayer to Second Person* 2 O benygne Jesu,..The only Sonne of God by filiacion. 1588 Kyd *Housh. Phil.* 449 Wks. (1901) 250 For our worlde was dignified with the presence of the true Sonne of God. 1667 Milton *P. L.* III. 138 Beyond compare the Son of God was seen Most glorious. 1728 Chambers *Cycl.* s.v., The Son of God Created the World; the Son of God was Incarnate. 1817 W. Taylor in *Monthly Mag.* XLIV. 315 This claim to the son-of-godship renders the facts irrefragably certain. 1884 Addis & Arnold *Cath. Dict.* (1897) 900/1 The ideas..are applied to Christ, and

SON.

united to the doctrine of his generation as the Son of God before the world was made.

b. A divine being; an angel.

c. One spiritually attached to God.

4. Son of man: a mortal.

6. A male descendant of some person or representative of some race.

c. One who is characterized by the presence, possession, influence, use, etc., of some quality or thing.

7. A member or adherent of a religious body or order, or a follower of the founder of one.

b. *pec.* Jesus Christ.

Son (sʌn). *v.* rare⁻¹.

Sonance (sōu·năns). [f. L. *sonāns*.]

Sonancy (sōu·nănsi). [f. as prec. + -ANCY.] The quality of being sonant.

Sonant (sōu·nănt), *a.* and *sb.*

Sonata (sǒnā·tă). [It., fem. pa. pple. of *sonāre* to sound.]

Sonation (sǒnē·ʃən). rare⁻¹.

Son, *v.* rare⁻¹.

Sonde-cloud, *a.*

†Bonage. *sb.⁻¹* rare.

Bonance. *sb.*

Sonance (sō·năns), variants of **Sorse, Sonst.**

Sonce, Sonsy, variants of **Sorse, Sonst.**

Sonde, -day, etc. obs. forms of **Sunday.**

Sonder, obs. f. **Sunder, Sonne, Sonder.**

Sonder-cloud. *Obs.*

Sondre man: see **Sunder.**

Sondery. obs. form of **Sundry.**

Sondrey, -rie, -ry, obs. forms of **Sunder.**

†Sone. *Obs.⁻¹*

Sone, var. forms of **Soon, Soon,** Sb.

Soneri (sǒnē·rĭ). *Obs.* rare.

Song (sǫŋ), *sb.* Forms: 1. sang 1.-(latterly 2. song), OE. song, sb.

SONG.

1. The act or art of singing; the result or effect of this, vocal music; that which is sung (in general or collective sense).

2. Without article: The class of music represented by songs.

3. *attrib.*, as *sonata face, sonata kind.*

8. *Son-before-the-father,* a name given to various plants, as the willow-herb, meadow-saffron, coltsfoot, etc., on account of the flowers appearing before the leaves or because of some other peculiarity.

Hence **Bona·tioal** *v.* rare⁻¹.

Sonata, a short, simple form of composition.

Sonata, a metrical composition adapted for singing, esp. one in time and having a regular verse-form; occas., a poem.

So-ba·ntes. [f. L. *sonantia.*]

Song, obs. form of **Sound** sb., **Sun** sb.

2. With article: An individual song.

b. A ballad or lay; a lyric poem.

So-ba·ntes.

Song-bird, a songster.

Song·ful, a.

Song-book, the syrinx of a bird.

Song-smith, a composer or maker of songs.

Song-sparrow [Song sb.] A common North American song-bird of the genus *Melospiza.*

Songster (sǫŋ·stə). Forms: 1 sangestre, etc.

Songstress (sǫŋ·strĕs). A female singer; a poetess.

Son-in-law (sǫn·inlǭ). [Sox sb. and Law sb.]

Sonant, *a.* and *sb.* Uttered with voice or vocal sound; voiced.

Sonata (sǒnā·tă). [It., fem. pa. pple. of *sonāre.*]

†† A musical composition for instruments as opposed to one for voices (a *cantata*). *Obs.*

SONGFUL. 423 SONLESS. SONLIKE. 424 SONORESCENCE.

Songful (sǫŋ·ful), *a.* [f. Song sb. + -ful.] Abounding in song; musical, melodious.

Hence **So·ngfully** *adv.*; **So·ngfulness** *sb.*

Song-school. Now *Hist.* [Sox sb. C. MLG. *sanchschole*, Sw. *sångskola.*]

Songish, *a.* nonce-wd. [f. Song sb. + -ish.]

Songle (sǫŋ·gl). *dial.* [Var. of 7-9 songal, -all, 9 songow, -o, etc. (Current only in the counties on the Welsh border, but app. corresponding to obs. or dial. G. *sangel*, *sängel*, dim. of OHG. *sanga* (MHG., MLG., and G. *sange*), M.Fhem. *sange*, *sangke*, W.Flem. *sange* (De Bo), in the same sense.

Songless (sǫŋ·lĕs), *a.* [f. Song sb. + -less.]

Songlet (sǫŋ·let). A little song.

†Songly, *a.* *Obs.*

Songman (sǫŋ·man). 1. A man accustomed to sing songs.

2. A man who sings in a church choir.

Songow, *v.* dial.

Songy (sǫŋ·i), *a.* [f. Song sb.] Having the qualities of a song.

Sonhood (sǫn·hud). [Sox sb.] The condition or relation of being a son.

†Sonica, *int.* and *adv.* rare⁻¹. [? of obscure origin.]

Sonification (sǒnifikē·ʃən). *Zool.* [L. *soni-* (see next) + -FICATION.] The production of sound, on the part of insects, by other means than the vocal organs.

Soniferous (sǒni·fərəs), *a.* [f. L. *soni-*, combining form of *sonus* sound + -FEROUS.] Sound-bearing; conveying or producing sound.

Son-in-law (sǫn·inlǭ). [Sox sb. and Law sb.]

1. A daughter's husband.

Son-law. *Obs.* = Son-in-law 1.

Sonkish, obs. form of **Sunken** ppl. *a.*

Sonless (sǫn·lĕs), *a.* Also 3 sonelaes, 6 sonnes. Having no son.

Sonly (sǫn·li), *a.* Also 3-6 sonely.

Son-mother. *rare⁻¹.*

Song-thrush [Song sb. C. G. *sangdrossel*, *singdrossel.*] The common thrush (*Turdus musicus*).

†Songuary, *Obs.* rare.

Sonlike (sǫn·lǎik), *a.* Also 6-7 sonnelike. [f. Sox sb. + LIKE.] Resembling that of a son; filial.

Sonlike, *a.* Also 6-7 sonnelike. Filial.

Sonnet (sǫ·nĕt), *sb.* [ad. It. *sonetto*, Pr. *sonet*, dim. of *son* song, f. L. *sonus* sound.]

1. A short poem or piece of verse; in early use esp. one of a lyrical and amatory character. Now rare or *Obs.*

2. A short poem of fourteen lines, of five feet each, with rhymes arranged according to one or other of certain definite schemes.

Sonnet, *v.* [f. prec.]

1. To compose sonnets; *intr.* and *trans.*

Sonnetary, *a.* [f. Sonnet sb.]

Sonneteer (sǫnĕtīə·r), *sb.* [f. Sonnet sb. + -EER.]

1. A composer of sonnets; *usu.* in disparaging sense.

Sonneteer, *v.* [f. prec.]

Sonnetic (sǒne·tik), *a.* rare. [Sonnet sb.]

Sonneting, *vbl. sb.* [f. Sonnet v.]

Sonnetise, -ize (sǫ·nĕtǎiz), *v.* [f. Sonnet sb. + -ISE.]

Sonnetry (sǫ·nĕtri). *colleg.* Also *nonce.*

Sonnette, obs. form of **Sunset.**

Sonnetteer, var. **Sonneteer.**

Sonny (sʌ·ni). colloq.

Sonny, form of **Sunny** *a.*

Sonomanie. nonce-wd.

Sonometer (sǒno·mĕtə). [f. L. *sonus* sound + -METER.]

Sonorescence (sǒnŏre·sĕns). [f. L. *sonor-* and SONOROUS.]

Sonorescent, *a.* rare⁻¹. [Sonrot sb.]

Sonority (sǒnǫ·riti). [Cf. *sonore.* An adj., *sonore*, F. *sonore*, appears from 1620.]

Sonore, *a.* *Obs.* Also 6 sonowre, 6 sonour.

Sonore·scence. [L. *sonōr-* as SONOROUS + -ESCENCE.]

Sonorescent — Sonorous

Hence Sonoréscent a. 1882 E. H. Cook in *Philos. Mag.* May 378 A body such as hard rubber...would be called a *sonorescent* body, just as sulphate of quinine is a fluorescent body.

Sonoriety. rare⁻¹. 1879 W. Stokes *Trems. Dis. Chest* (1882) 278 The lung rapidly regains its sonoriety.

†Sonoríferous, a. Obs.⁻¹ [f. L. *sonor, sonōris* sound + -(I)FEROUS.] Conveying sound; soniferous. Also **†sonoriferously** adv., soundingly.

Sonorific, a. rare. [f. L. *sonor* sound + -(I)FIC.] Producing sound; now *spec.* of insects, producing other than vocal sounds (*Cent. Dict.*).

Sonórity. [a. F. *sonorité* or ad. L. *sonōritā-s, sonoritas*: see -ITY.] The quality of being sonorous.

Sonorous, a. [f. L. *sonōrus*, f. *sonor, sonōris* sound: see -OUS.]
1. Of things: Giving out, or capable of giving out, a sound, esp. of a deep or ringing character.
b. Of places, etc.: Resounding, roaring, noisy.
2. Of sounds: Having a loud, deep, or resonant character.
c. *fig.* Of language, diction, etc.

Soodle — Sooly

Soodle, v. dial. [Of obscure origin.] intr. To walk in a slow or leisurely manner; to saunter.

Soodly a., leisurely, slow. dial.

†Soofee, [Hindī *sūfī*.] A flour obtained by grinding Indian wheat; a nutritious food prepared from this.

Soom, north. and Sc. var. SWIM. **Soome,** obs. var. SUM. **Soon,** north. and Sc. var. SOON. **Sooned, -ed, -en,** obs. ff. SWOON. **Sooly,** a. Obs.⁻¹ ? Close, sultry.

Soon

Soon (sūn), a. [OE. *sōna* adv.]

A. Forms.
1. sing. 2–6 (7 Sc.) sone (4 sone), 2-5 suen, soene, sonne.
2. north. and Sc. a. 4-5 soyn, 4-5 soyne.
β. 4 sun, 4-5 suin, 5 sun, 5 soyn, 6 suin.

B. Signification.
I. 1. Within a short time (after a particular point of time specified or implied), before long, shortly; in a (comparatively) short space of time; at once, without delay, forthwith, straightway.
2. Readily, willingly; gladly.
3. Early, betimes; before the time specified or referred to.

Soot

Soot (sut), sb. [OE. *sōt*.]
1. The black substance consisting of fine particles carried up in the smoke of coal, wood, or other fuel.
2. attrib. and Comb.

Soot, v. To cover or treat with soot.

Soote, obs. f. SWEET.

Soot ... **Soote** ... **Sooted** ... **Booth** (sb.) ... **Sooth**

Soothe

Soother ... **Soothfast** ... **Soothfastness** ... **Soothful** ... **Soothing** ... **Soothingly** ... **Soothly** ... **Soothing** ... **Soothness** ... **Soothsay** ... **Soothsaying** ... **Soothsayer**

Soot-less, a.

Soot-ly, adv.

Soot-ness.

Sooty, a.

Soot-man.

Sooty-ly, adv.

Sootiness.

Soot-ish, a.

Sootily.

Soo-thsaying ppl. a.

Soothsayeress, a female soothsayer.

Sop (sɒp), sb.

Sop (sɒp), v.

Soper, **Soper'e**, obs. forms of SUPPER.

Soph (sɒf), colloq.

Sophism (sɒ'fizm).

Sophist (sɒ'fist), sb.

Sophister (sɒ'fistəɹ), sb.

Sophic (sɒ'fik), a.

Sophistic (sɒfi'stik), a. and sb.

Sophistical (sɒfi'stikăl), a.

Sophistically, adv.

Sophisticate (sɒfi'stikeit), v.

Sophisticated ppl. a.

Sophistication (sɒfistike'ʃən).

Sophisticator.

Sophistress.

Sophistry (sɒ'fistri).

Sophistry. Specious but fallacious reasoning; employment of arguments which are intentionally deceptive.

Sophomoric (Chiefly *U.S.*). Of or pertaining to, befitting or resembling, characteristic of a sophomore; hence, pretentious, bombastic, inflated in style or manner; immature, crude, superficial.

Sophorical, *a. U.S.*

Sophora (*Bot.*) A genus of leguminous trees, shrubs, or plants.

Sophorine, **Sophorine** *Chem.*

Sophy. A wise or learned man; a sage.

Sopit, *Obs.* Rendered dull or sluggish.

Sopite (*sō̆pəi·t*) *v.* Now *rare.*

Soporate, *v. Obs.*

Soporation, noun of action.

Soporative, *a.* and *sb.*

Soporiferous (*sō̆pori·fĕrəs*) *a.* and *sb.*

Soporific (*sō̆pori·fik*) *a.* and *sb.*

Soporose, Soporous, *a.*

Soppiness. The quality or condition of being soppy; wetness.

Sopping, *vbl. sb.* The action of the vb. in various senses; a thorough soaking or wetting.

Sopping, *ppl. a.* Soaking; drenched, saturated with water or rain.

Soppy, *a.*

Sopra (*sō·prā̆*) Chiefly *Mus.*

Sopragnard, *Obs. rare.*

Sopranist (*sop·rānist*) A soprano singer.

Soprano (*sŏprā·no̱*) *sb.* and *a. Mus.*

Sorage. *Obs. exc. arch.*

Soral (*sō̆·rǎl*) *a. Bot.* Of or pertaining to the sori of ferns.

Sorance. *Obs.*

Sorb (*sōrb*) *sb.*[1] The fruit of the service-tree (*Pyrus domestica*); a service-berry.

Sorbate.

Sorbet (*sō·rbĕt*) A cooling drink of the East.

Sorbefacient (*sōrbīfē·ĕnt*) *a.* and *sb.*

Sorbian (*sō·rbiǎn*) *a.* and *sb.*

Sorbic (*sō·rbik*) *a. Chem.*

Sorbin, Sorbine.

Sorbish (*sō·rbiʃ*) *a.* and *sb.*

Sorbite (*sō·rbəit*) *Chem.*

Sorbitol.

Sorbole.

Sorbonical (*sō·rboni·kǎl*) *a.*

Sorbonist.

Sorbonne (*sōrbon*) Also 6-7 Sorbone.

Sorcerer (*sō·rsĕrǎr*) *sb.*

Sorceress (*sō·rsĕrĕs*) A female sorcerer; a witch.

Sorcering, *vbl. sb.*

Sorcery (*sō·rsĕri*) The use of magic or enchantment; the practice of magic arts; witchcraft.

Sordid (sǫ'did), *a.* Also 6–7 sordide, 7 sorded. [a. F. *sordide* (16th c. in Godefroy; = Sp., Pg., It. *sordido*), or ad. L. *sordid-us* dirty, foul, base, mean, etc., f. *sord-* to be dirty: see *Sordes*.]

1. *Path.* a. Of suppurations, etc.: Corrupt, foul, repulsive; of the nature of sordes.

Sordidity. [f. Sordid *a.* + -ity.] Sordidness.

Sordidly (sǫ'didli), *adv.* [f. Sordid *a.* + -ly.] In a sordid manner; basely, meanly; mercenarily.

Sordidness (sǫ'didnǝs), [f. Sordid *a.* + -ness.] The state or quality of being sordid.

Sordine (sǫ'rdīn), *a.* and *sb.* Also 6 sordina. [ad. It. *sordina*, *sordino*.]

Sordidous (sǫ'rdidǝs), *a.* Obs. [f. L. *sordid-us* + -ous.] Sordid, in various senses.

So-rditude. Obs. rare. [ad. L. *sorditūdo*, f. *sordes*.] Sordidness.

Sore (sōǝ*r*), *sb.*[1] Forms: a. 1–3 sar (2–3 sær), north. and Sc. 4 sar, 4–5 sor (5 sare), 3 sor (3 soor), 4, 4–6 soore, 4–6 sore. [OE. sār neut., = OFris. sēr (WFris. sear, NFris. siar, sir), MDu., seer, zeer (Du. zeer), OHG., MHG. sēr (mod.G. sehr)...]

Sore (sōǝ*r*), *a.* Also north. sar, 4–6 sair, 5–6 saire, 6 sayre. [OE. sār]

Sore (sōǝ*r*), *adv.* Also sowre, 4–6 sowre, 6 soor, 5–7 soare, 9 sore.

Sore, *sb.*[2] Obs. exc. Hist. Also 5 soar, soore, 6 sore.

Sore, *obs.* variant of Soar *v.*

Sore, obs. variant of Soar sb.

Sore-head, -headed.

he the wordes..ne biereth. 1426 Lydg. *De Guil. Pilgr.* 8797 Sche kepeth hem..Sore shet wyth lok & keye. *a* 1483 *Liber Niger* in *Househ. Ord.* (1790) 69 Not to bouit it soe sore vpon the gurgeones. 1526 *Pilgr. Perf.* (W. de W. 1531) 29 b, It shetteth it self so sore..that..it is not so opened agayne. 1545 Ascham *Toxoph.* (Arb.) 111 The string..beynge sore twined must nedes knap in sunder.

10. To a great extent; greatly, very much.

Chiefly in contexts suggestive of sense 6, but sometimes merely intensive.

c 1440 *Pallad. on Husb.* I. 90 Ne picche hit not to[o] soore into the vale. 1470–85 Malory *Arthur* IV. vi. 126 And anone they felle on slepe, and slepte merueillously sore all the nyght. *a* 1533 Ld. Berners *Gold. Bk. M. Aurel.* (1546) C ij b, There was a lawe soore vsed and accustomed, and well kepte in the Romayne polycie. 1561 Hollybush *Hom. Apoth.* 34 Seth the Turtel wyth water, salt her not to sore. 1606 G. Woodcock *Hist. Iustine* xxxv. 113 So sore hated was Demetrius among all men. 1611 Shaks. *Cymb.* IV. ii. 225 Oh bill sore shaming Those rich-left-heyres. 1784 Cowper *Task* IV. 343 The wain goes heavily, impeded sore By..loads adhering close To the clogg'd wheels. 1812 Byron *Ch. Har.* I. ii, A shameless wight, Sore given to revel and ungodly glee.

11. With adjs. and advs.: Very, extremely, exceedingly. *Obs.* exc. *dial.*

1474 Caxton *Chesse* III. vii. (1883) 141 The kynge denys had a broder whom he louyd sore well. *c* 1489 — *Sonnes of Aymon* iii. 112 That I assaylled theym, it hath cost me sore dere. 1530 *Comp. Old Treat.* in Roy *Rede me* (Arb.) 171 The new testament..set forthe by Master William Tyndale, which they falsely pretende to be sore corrupte. 1596 Dalrymple tr. *Leslie's Hist. Scot.* I. 98 Scheiphouses ..of quhais burning thay ar nocht sair solist. 1638 Brathwait *Barnabee's Jrnl.* II. (1818) 61 Where growne surfoot and sore weary, I repos'd. 1860 Geo. Eliot *Mill on Fl.* III. ix, She was sore fond of us children.

12. *Comb.*, as *sore-holding*; *sore-dreaded*, *-meant*, *-pressed*, *-wearied*, *-won*, *-worn* adjs.

c 1450 *Merlin* xiv. 222 The haubrekes, that were stronge and sore-holdynge. 1567 *Satir. Poems Reform.* iv. 66 My langsum lyfe and sair tormentit Spirite. 1616 J. Lane *Contn. Sqr.'s T.* x. 330 Ann apparition, which seemd at first to bee some sore ment vision. 1638 Brathwait *Barnabee's Jrnl.* III. 121 Thence to Ferrybrig, sore-wearied Surfoot, but in spirit cheer'd. 1785 Burns *Cotter's Sat. Nt.* iv, To..deposite her sair-won penny-fee. 1787 *Minor* 28 That bedlam,..bedizened in sore-worn flounces. 1843 Bethune *Scottish Fireside Stor.* 279 It was that day.. Which brings to sair worn toil a time Of needful peace. 1866 G. Macdonald *Ann. Q. Neighb.* xxviii. (1878) 479 The sore-pressed garrison which had retreated to its last defence. 1870 J. Bruce *Life of Gideon* xviii. 335 Nigh to the spot on which those harnessed and sore-dreaded dreamers lay.

Sored, *a.* Chiefly *north.* Also 5 **sorede**, 5–6 **sorde**, 6 **sowerde**, 9 *Sc.* **sorit**. [f. Sore *a.*[2]]

1. Of horses, etc.: = Sorrel *a.* a. ? *Obs.*

1420 *E. E. Wills* (1882) 53 A sorede horse þat was bought off Henuden. *Ibid.*, Þe sorde hors. 1545 *Richmond Wills* (Surtees) 57 Item a sored horse, price xiij s. iiij d. 1587 *Knaresb. Wills* (Surtees) I. 158 A sowerde mare and a fole. 1825 Jamieson *Suppl.*, *Sorit*, of a sorrel colour; as, 'a sorit horse', Clydes[dale].

†**2.** Of colour: = Sorrel *a.* c. *Obs.*

1587 *Wills & Inv. N. C.* (Surtees, 1860) 288 One stud mare, of colour bawson sored.

Sored, *ppl. a. rare.* [f. Sore *v.*[1]] Pained; troubled.

a 1542 Wyatt in *Tottel's Misc.* (Arb.) 73 One onely hope hath stayed my life, apart: Which doth perswade such wordes vnto my sored minde.

Soredi- (sŏrī·di), comb. form of Soredi-um, used in a few terms, as **Sore·dial** *a.*, of the nature of, pertaining to, a soredium; **Sore·diate** *a.*, bearing or characterized by the prevalence of soredia; **Soredi(i)·ferous** *a.*, bearing soredia; caused by producing soredia; **Sore·diform** *a.*, = next; **Sore·dioid** *a.*, having the appearance, form, or character of a soredium or soredia.

1882 Vines tr. *Sachs' Bot.* 328 *Soredial branches, as they are termed, are thus produced. 1881 *Jrnl. Bot.* X. 115 The *sorediate form of *Pertusaria velata*. 1829 Loudon *Encycl. Plants* (1836) 949 *Ramalina*. Plant cartilaginous,.. somewhat shrubby, mostly *sorediferous. 1856 Lindsay *Pop. Hist. Brit. Lichens* 42 The disc of an apothecium is sometimes rendered abortive by sorediiferous degradation. 1859 Mayne *Expos. Lex.* 1174/2 *Sorediformis*, having the appearance of *soredia*..: *herediform. 1857 Berkeley *Cryptog. Botany* § 459. 418 Many other forms are assumed by the crusts of Lichens;..the *soredioid from the protrusion of groups of gonidia.

‖**Soredium** (sŏrī·diŏm). *Bot.* Pl. **soredia**. [mod.L., f. Gr. σωρός a heap. Cf. F. *sorédion*.] A thallus-bud or cell in lichens. Usu. in pl.

1829 Loudon *Encycl. Plants* (1836) 949 *Soredia* are little heaps of free, pulverulent bodies, mostly of a whitish color, placed on various parts of the frond. 1866 *Treas. Bot.* 867/2 The soredia predominating over the crust it assumes the name of *Lepraria*. 1882 Vines tr. *Sachs' Bot.* 327, *A* a simple soredium, consisting of a gonidium covered with a web of hyphæ;..*C* a group of simple soredia.

Sorefull, obs. variant of Sorrowful.

So·re-head, *a.* and *sb.* [See Sore *a.*[1] 9.]

A. *adj.* Irritable or out of temper 'like a bear with a sore head'; discontented, dissatisfied.

1862 *Major Jack Downing* vii. (1867) 61 [He] sed it done very well for some sore-hed Dimmycrat. 1902 *Academy* 22 Mar. 291/1 This is sore-head philosophy.

B. *sb. U.S. political slang.* A dissatisfied or disappointed politician.

1862 *Rocky Mountain News* (Denver) 16 Oct. (Thornton), What will the 'sore-heads' say now? 1878 *N. Amer. Rev.* CXXVI. 402 Each led by a little faction of sore-heads, desperate and reckless. 1888 Bryce *Amer. Commw.* III. lxiii. II. 458 Some discontented magnate objects and threatens to withdraw...If such a 'sore-head' persists, a schism may follow.

So **Sore-headed** *a.*, = Sore-head *a.*; hence **Sorehea·dedly** *adv.*, **Sorehea·dedness**.

1844 Hood *Tale of Temper* 53 No bear, *sore-headed, could be more cantankerous. 1888 *Pall Mall G.* 19 Dec. 2/1 The men are dissatisfied and 'sore-headed'. 1883 *Ibid.* 8 Jan. 3 *Soreheadedly punctilious about the proper respect paid them. 1885 W. Cory *Lett. & Jrnls.* (1897) 515 The gossip and the pecking and the *sore-headedness of country towns.

†**Sorely**, *a. Obs.* In 1, 3 **sarlic**, 3 **sorlich**. [OE. *sárlíc* (f. *sár* Sore *a.*[1]), = obs. Flem. *seerlick* (Kilian), OHG. *sêrlîh*; cf. ON. *sárlig-r*, MSw. *sârligh*.] Painful, sorrowful; sad.

Beowulf 842 No his lifgedal sarlic þuhte secga ænegum. *c* 888 K. Ælfred *Boeth.* xi. § 2 Manegra sarlicra wita hi gewilnodon wið þæm ecan life. 971 *Blickl. Hom.* 225 Þa wæron his sarlica cwide..þe ure Drihten..to þæm ærestan men cwæþ. *c* 1000 Ælfric *Saints' Lives* II. 140 He..cwæð him to sona mid sarlicre stemne. *c* 1205 Lay. 28457 Þa quene læi inne Eouwerwic, næs heo næuere swa sarlic [*v.r.* sorlich].

Sorely (sōᵊ·ɹli), *adv.* Forms: α. 1 **sarlice**, 3 **særliche**, 5 **sarely**; *Sc.* 6 **sairlye**, **-lie**, 6– **sairly**. β. 4 **sorly**, 5 **soreli(e**, 5– **sorely**. [OE. *sárlíce* (f. *sár* Sore *a.*[1]), = OFris. *sêrlîke*, MSw. *sârlika* (*-liga*): cf. ON. *sárliga*.]

In most senses tending to become a mere intensive.

1. In a manner expressive of great pain, grief, or distress.

c 888 K. Ælfred *Boeth.* xxvi. § 2 Ða onsac se Wisdom sarlice & cwæð [etc.]. 971 *Blickl. Hom.* 225 Þa wæron his ealle sona unrote, & sarlice gebærdon. *c* 1000 Ælfric *Gen.* xxi. 16 Heo..sæt hire feorran sarlice wepende. *c* 1055 *Byrhtferth's Handboc* in *Anglia* VIII. 309 Oft seo brodige henn, þeah heo sarlice cloccige, heo..þa briddas gewyrmð. 1748 Thomson *Cast. Indol.* I. xxi, They cannot fly, But often each way look, and often sorely sigh. 1841 Longf. *Childr. Lord's Supper* 348 Each bowed him, weeping full sorely.

2. In such a manner as to cause great pain or bodily injury; severely. Also *fig.*

a 900 Cynewulf *Juliana* 571 [He] sohte..hu he sarlicast þurh þa wyrrestan witu meahte feorhcwale findan. *a* 1000 *Soul & Body* 73 Þe sculon her..slitan sarlice swearte wihta. 1553 *Douglas' Æneid* II. (1710) 52/36 Baith hir tendir handes War strenzeit sairly boundin hard with bandes. 1590 Spenser *F. Q.* III. ix. 29 The wicked engine..secretly did glyde Into his hart, which it did sorely gryde. 1611 Shaks. *Wint. T.* v. i. 18, I did so: but thou strik'st me Sorely, to say I did. 1650 B. *Discolliminium* 32 Had it once left sucking the Mothers breasts so sorely. 1695 Ld. Preston *Boeth.* III. 119 Like that angry Insect..they sorely wound th' Enjoyer too. 1870 Bryant *Iliad* v. I. 173 Wilt thou be angry with me if I drive Mars, sorely wounded, from the battle-field? *Ibid.* xiv. II. 68 These Bore him to Ilium sorely suffering.

b. In a manner involving mental pain, distress, or dissatisfaction.

In OE. the sense 'regrettably, lamentably', occurs.

c 1450 *Godstow Reg.* 633 Hit is vn-semeli..þat contrauersi ..lawfully endid sholde be soreli I-meuid ageine. 1567 *Gude & Godlie B.* (S.T.S.) 61 Rycht sorelie musing in my mynde. 1567 *Satir. Poems Reform.* iv. 157, I speik not but pruife, quhilk I may sairlie rew. 1722 De Foe *Plague* 75 Sorely I repented of my rashness. 1828 Scott *F. M. Perth* xxix, I know my failing, and..so sorely dread that I cannot conquer it. 1865 Trollope *Belton Est.* xxxi. 376 She sorrowed to think that he should want such a thing so sorely. 1870 J. E. T. Rogers *Hist. Glean.* Ser. II. 134 Sorely against his will, Walpole was at last driven into war.

3. In such a manner as to press hardly or severely upon a person or thing.

c 1205 Lay. 6825 Særliche heo feohte, & fælden heore cnihtes. *c* 1400 *Melayne* 265 Þe Sarazene semblede so Sarely Þat þay felde faste of oure chevalrye. *c* 1400 *Destr. Troy* 3692 Sodenly þo sailes were sorely bestad. 1606 Shaks. *Ant. & Cl.* IV. vi. 19, I haue done ill, Of which I do accuse my selfe so sorely, That I will ioy no more. 1613 — *Hen. VIII*, IV. ii. 14 [He] brought him forward As a man sorely tainted, to his Answer. 1665 Manley *Grotius' Low C. Warr* 750 They begirt the Castle, and the sixth day after recovered it, being sorely assaulted and withall wanting of provision. 1725 De Foe *Voy. round World* (1840) 253, I would be sorely put to it for lodging. 1779 Warner in Jesse *Selwyn & Contemp.* (1844) IV. 259, I called upon the old duchess, who is 'sorely badly', as they say in Lincolnshire, with her old complaint. 1820 Scott *Monast.* xxxvi, Of these most were mounted on steeds which had been sorely jaded. 1846 Browning *Soul's Trag.* Wks. 1863 II. 460 The very measures of precaution, which pressed soreliest on himself. 1853 Kane *Grinnell Exp.* xlix. (1856) 465 It is an amorphous mass, so worn that it must have been sorely wrought before its release from the glacier.

4. To a great extent; in a high degree.

1562 Winȝet *Wks.* (S.T.S.) I. 5 Hes not mony..in thair perfite beleif..sairlye stummerit? 1605 Shaks. *Lear* II. iv. 304 Alacke the night comes on, and the high windes Do sorely ruffle. 1704 Swift *Batt. Bks.* Misc. (1711) 239 Who had tore off his Title-Page, sorely defac'd one half his Leaves [etc.]. 1786 Burns *To a Louse* i, Your impudence protects you sairly. 1831 Scott *Ct. Rob.* vii, 'Thou objectest sorely to my complexion,' said the negro. 1855 Dickens *Lett.* (1880) I. 399 The Association is sorely in want of able men. 1891 Farrar *Darkn. & Dawn* lv, To stay among them meant death, and his life was sorely needed by the Church of God.

5. *Comb.*, as *sorely-tempted*, *-worn* adjs.

1870 C. J. Vaughan *Earnest Words* (1878) 154 The sorely-tempted soul. 1891 Kipling *Light that Failed* ii. (1900) 16 A pair of sorely-worn riding-breeches.

†**Sorement**, variant of Serment 'oath' *Obs.*

a 1400–50 *Alexander* 1464 (MS. A.), When he..soyned him be his sorement þat sare him forthinkis.

Soreness (sōᵊ·ɹnĕs). Forms: α. 1 **sarnys**, **-nis**, 3 **særnes**, 4–5 **sarnes**, 4 **sarenes**, 6, 8– *Sc.* **sairness**. β. 4, 6 **sorenes**, 6 **sornes**, **soare-**, 6–7 **sorenesse**, 7– **soreness**. [OE. *sárnys* (f. *sár* Sore *a.*[1]), = OFris. *sêrnesse*, MHG. *sêrnisse*.]

1. The condition of being physically sore, in pain, or painful; pain, painfulness.

c 1000 Ælfric *Gen.* iii. 16 On sarnysse þu acenst cild. *c* 1000 — *Hom.* I. 122 Ure sarnyssa he sylf abær. 13.. in *Leg. Rood* (1871) 85 All for noght þou feynes þe, All þi sarenes will we se. *c* 1450 *St. Cuthbert* (Surtees) 4236 Þe sarnes sone it was astaynt. *c* 1480 Henryson *Sum Pract. Med.* 19 Nowdir fevir,..Seiknes nor sairnes. 1495 *Trevisa's Barth. De P. R.* (W. de W.) v. lviii. 175 The marowe heelyth..the sorenes of the throte and of the breestes. 1562 (*title*), Bulleïn's Bulwarke of defence againste all Sicknes, Sornes, and woundes. 1660 Blount *Boscobel* 42 Which.. serv'd to encrease rather then asswage the sorenesse of his feet. 1722–7 Boyer *Dict. Royal* II. s.v., Soreness of the Eyes, *Mal des yeux*. 1808 *Med. Jrnl.* XIX. 21 He complained of soreness in his mouth. 1876 Bristowe *Th. & Pract. Med.* (1878) 159 The soreness and inflammation of the throat subside.

2. Mental pain, distress, or irritation; irritability, touchiness.

c 1000 Ælfric *Gen.* vi. 6 He..wæs ȝehrepod mid heortan sarnisse wið innan. *a* 1300 *Cursor M.* 26377 Teres falland on þin ei Þe sarnes o þin hert to wrei. 1667 *Decay Chr. Piety* vii. 153 Whilest the soreness of his late pangs of conscience remains. 1721 Ramsay *Keitha* 8 His face speaks out the sairness of his heart. 1796 Nelson 15 July in Nicolas *Disp.* (1845) II. 211, I congratulate you on the soreness which the French feel for your strict blockade of the Port of Toulon. 1832 Lytton *Eugene A.* I. x, I leave you with more soreness at my late haste than I will acknowledge. 1889 *Law Times* LXXXII. 243/1 The soreness incident to separation has disappeared.

†**3.** Distress, trouble, misfortune. *Obs.*

c 1205 Lay. 13639 Ich eow wulle telle..of muche særnesse þe isiȝen is to londe.

4. Severe or serious character.

a 1586 Sidney *Arcadia* IV. (1598) 392 For with the sorenesse of the fall, if she had not had breath giuen her, she had deliuered a foolish soule to Pluto.

‖**Sorex.** *rare.* Also *pl.* **sorices**. [L. *sōrex* (*sōricis*) and *sorex*, related to Gr. ὕραξ.] A shrew-mouse, a shrew. Also *transf.*

1607 Topsell *Four-f. Beasts* (1658) 424 Lycinius the Emperor..called them..moths and sorices of the court. 1802 Shaw *Gen. Zool.* II. I. 65 Soricine Mouse..has the general appearance of a Sorex or Shrew.

Sorfait, obs. form of Surfeit *sb.* **Sorfeten**, obs. form of Surfeit *v.* **Sorfol**, **-ful**, obs. varr. Sorrowful *a.* **Sorgeon**, obs. f. Surgeon.

Sorgho (sǭ·ɹgo). Also 8 **sorgo**. [a. F. *sorgho* or It. *sorgo*, also *surgo*, med.L. *surgum*, *surcum*, *suricum* (12–13th cent.), of unknown origin.] = Sorghum (esp. 1 b).

1760 J. Lee *Introd. Bot.* App. 327 Sorgo, *Holcus*. 1862 Ansted *Channel Isl.* IV. xx. 476 It may be worth stating that the sugar grass, or sorgho, has been cultivated with success as an experimental crop. 1866 Watts s.v., The glumes..and stems of sorgho contain red colouring-matters. 1893 Watt *Dict. Econ. Prod. Ind.* VI. III. 277 The Sorgho, which is mainly cultivated on account of sugar.

attrib. 1862 Miller *Elem. Chem.*, *Org.* (ed. 2) ii. § 1. 74 Cane Sugar..is also contained in..the ripe sorgho grass.

b. *Sweet sorgho*, = Sorghum 1 b.

1861 Bentley *Man. Bot.* 697 *Holcus saccharatus*.. is called the North China Sugar-cane or Sweet Sorgho.

Sorghum (sǭ·ɹgŏm). Also 8 **sorgum**. [mod. L., f. It. *sorgo*: see prec.]

1. a. The cereal plant known as Indian millet, Guinea-corn, durra, etc. (*Andropogon sorghum*, also called *Holcus sorghum* and *Sorghum vulgare*).

1597 Gerarde *Herbal* I. v. 7 At the top..groweth a tuft or eare..like Sorghum. 1673 Ray *Journ. Low C.* 147 We had little other bread than what was made of Sorghum. 1706 Phillips (ed. Kersey), *Sorgum*, a sort of Millet-grain. 1780 *Encycl. Brit.* (ed. 2) V. 3694/2 The most remarkable of the foreign species [of *Holcus*] is the sorghum, or Guinea-corn. 1866 Livingstone *Last Jrnls.* i. (1874) I. 17 Some sorghum, sem-sem seed, gum-copal, and orchilla weed, constitute the commerce of the port. 1879 Lubbock *Addr. Pol. & Educ.* x. 193 Maize and sorghum, a fine tall cereal, which in the distance looks very like maize. 1883 R. Haldane *Workshop Rec.* Ser. II. 11/1 Rice, maize, wheat, sorghum, and rye are most largely used [for obtaining grain alcohol].

b. The Chinese sugar-cane (*Andropogon saccharatus*, also called *Holcus saccharatus* and *Sorghum saccharatum*). Usually *Sweet sorghum*.

1859 *All Year Round* No. 32. 126 The extensive cultivation of the sorghum, or Chinese sugar-cane, would give a fortune to the cultivator. 1867 A. Gray *Man. Bot.* (1874) 652 The Sweet Sorghum, and other cultivated races. 1884 tr. *De Candolle's Orig. Cultivated Pl.* 382 Sweet Sorghum ..taller than the common sorghum and with a loose panicle.

c. With distinctive names denoting other plants belonging to this genus (see quots.).

1860 *Darlington's Amer. Weeds*, etc. 411 *Sorghum nutans*. ..Nodding Sorghum. Wood Grass. *Ibid.* 412 *S. cernuum*, ..Drooping Sorghum. Guinea Corn.

2. A genus or group of grasses belonging to the tribe *Andropogoneæ* and including the species mentioned above; also, with *a* and pl., a species or variety belonging to this genus.

1842 *Penny Cycl.* XXII. 266 *Sorghum*, a genus of grasses.. The species form tall grasses with succulent stems. 1884 tr. *De Candolle's Orig. Cultivated Pl.* 380 Botanists are not agreed as to the distinction of several of the species of sorghum. *Ibid.*, A good monograph on the sorghums is needed. 1895–6 *Cal. Univ. Nebraska* 186 New crops, particularly forage crops, and the non-saccharine sorghums.

3. *U.S.* A kind of molasses made from sorghum-juice.

1883 *Chamb. Jrnl.* Apr. 269/1 Maple-sugar and sorghum are unequal to the demand. 1892 *Atlantic Monthly* May 664/2 Jars of lard and jugs of the inevitable 'sorghum' (home-made molasses) were securely tied up and buried in the woods.

4. *attrib.* and *Comb.*, as *sorghum-crop*, *-head*, *-seed*, *sugar*, etc.

Also *sorghum-pulling*, *-tugging* (De Vere *Americanisms* 287), *sorghum-evaporator*, *-knife*, *-mill*, *-stripper* (Knight *Dict. Mech.* 2246), *sorghum-blight*, *-midge*, *-smut*, etc.

1753 *Chambers' Cycl.* Suppl. s.v. *Juncus*, The sharp or pointed Rush, with sorghum heads. 1875 Knight *Dict. Mech.* 443/2 The necessities of the sorghum culture in the United States. 1883 *Times* 30 May 13 A sorghum crop.. which yielded over 2,200 gallons. 1883 *Science* I. 234/1 Others bearing, in all but size, a most striking resemblance to sorghum-seed. 1887 *Encycl. Brit.* XXII. 628/1 The cultivation of sorghum sugar.

b. In the sense 'made of or obtained from sorghum', as *sorghum beer*, *flour*, *molasses*, *syrup*.

1864 T. D. Wells *Our Burden* 38 Sorghum molasses, which was not known to this country in 1850. 1865 *Home News* 19 Dec. 5/1 A sample of sorghum flour made of Chinese cane. 1868 *Rep. U. S. Commissioner Agric.* (1869) 401 Strong vinegar can be made from sorghum sirup.

Sorgien, **-gon**, obs. ff. Surgeon. **Sorh(ful**, obs. varr. Sorrow(ful. **Sori**, pl. of Sorus.

Soricine (sǫ·risin), *a.* [ad. L. *sōricīn-us*, f. *sōrex* Sorex.] Resembling a shrew-mouse. Freq. in specific names of animals.

1781 Pennant *Hist. Quadrup.* II. 453 The Soricine Rat ..inhabits the neighborhood of Strasbourg. 1802 Shaw *Gen. Zool.* II. I. 65 Soricine Mouse. *Mus Soricinus*...This is an extremely small species. 1827 Griffith tr. *Cuvier* V. 72 *Vampyrus Soricinus* (Soricine Vampyre of Spix). *c* 1878 *Cassell's Nat. Hist.* I. 333 The Soricine Bat,..*Glossophaga soricina*...[It] is a small bat.

Sorie, obs. form of Sorry.

Sori·ferous, *a. Bot. rare.* [f. Sor-us + -(i)ferous.] Bearing sori.

1859 T. Moore *Brit. Ferns* (1864) 20 Ferns, the margin of whose frond is soriferous.

†**Soring**, *a. Obs.* In 5 **sowring**. [irreg. f. *sowre* Sore *a.*[2]] = Sore *a.*[2]

c 1450 *Godstow Reg.* 256 Yeldyng therof euery yere to hym..a spere-hawke sowryng [L. *unum spernarium sorum*] at lammas. *Ibid.* 257 And to the heires of ser Alisaundir of Swereford..a sowring sperehawke at lammasse.

†**Sorite**, Anglicized f. next. *Obs.*[—1]

1656 Hobbes *Liberty, Necess. & Chance* xxiv. 259 To pass by all the other great imperfections, which are to be found in this Sorite [etc.].

‖**Sorites** (sŏrəi·tīz). [L. *sōrītēs*, ad. Gr. σωρείτης, f. σωρ-ός a heap.]

1. *Logic.* 'A series of propositions, in which the predicate of each is the subject of the next, the conclusion being formed of the first subject and the last predicate' (Mansel).

In the Goclenian form, 'the subject of each proposition is the predicate of the next, the conclusion being formed of the last subject and the first predicate'.

1551 T. Wilson *Logike* H iij, We ioyne many causes, and many effectes together, wherof is made an argument, called *Sorites*. 1588 Fraunce *Lawiers Log.* II. ix. 99 As of many graynes is made a heape of corne, so of many degrees an argument called Sorites by this enthymematicall progression. 1654 Z. Coke *Logick* 148 Sorites is an imperfect Syllogism [etc.]. 1693 Dryden *Persius* VI. (1697) 296 *note*, Chrysippus the Stoick invented a kind of Argument, consisting of more than three Propositions; which is call'd *Sorites*, or a Heap. 1838 Sir W. Hamilton *Logic* xix. (1866) I. 369 The Sorites can be resolved into as many simple syllogisms as there are middle terms between the subject and predicate of the conclusion. 1870 Jevons *Elem. Logic* xviii. 156 The chain of syllogisms commonly called the Sorites.

b. An instance of this type of syllogism. Also as *pl.* (quot. 1798).

1581 J. Bell *Haddon's Answ. Osor.* 223 b, The Logicians that have described the fourme of a Sorites. 1588 Fraunce *Lawiers Log.* II. ix. 99 A sorites [is] but enthymematicall progression by certain degrees. 1620 T. Granger *Div. Logike* 285 A Syllogisme many wayes cryptike, is a Dilemma, and a Sorites. 1643 Sir T. Browne *Relig. Med.* I. § 18 An easie Logick may..with lesse than a Sorites resolve all things into God. 1725 Watts *Logic* III. ii. § 6 A Sorites is when several middle terms are chosen to connect one another successively [etc.]. 1798 Edgeworth *Pract. Educ.* (1811) II. 361 We have seen syllogisms, crocodiles, enthimemas, sorites, &c. explained and tried upon a boy of nine. 1860 H. Rogers *Ess.* III. 277 An ingenious sorites, by which we may at any time dispense with the positive testimony of an historian. 1870 K. H. Digby *Halcyon Hours* 261 No horn'd sorites here would I employ, No captious argument that would annoy.

c. In allusive use.

1711 Addison *Spect.* No. 239 ¶ 10 These Disputants convince their Adversaries with a *Sorites*, commonly called a Pile of Faggots.

2. *transf.* A series, chain, or accumulation *of* some thing or things.

1664 Power *Exp. Philos.* III. 191 Though Democritus his pit be never so deep, yet by a long Sorites of Observations, and chain of Deductions, we may at last fathom it. *a* 1670 Hacket *Abp. Williams* I. xiii. (1693) 11 Such a long Sorites of Sciences and Tongues. 1875 M. Collins in F. Collins *Lett. & Friendsh.* (1877) II. 24 Note this significant fact or sorites of facts.

b. *Math.* (See quots.)

1880 J. J. Sylvester in *Coll. Math. Papers* (1909) III. 440 Any such determinate representation of a fractional quantity I shall term a sorites. *Ibid.*, The elements of a sorites are analogous to the partial quotients of a regular continued fraction.

3. A sophistical argument turning on the definition of a 'heap'.

1768–74 Tucker *Lt. Nat.* (1834) II. 140 The like attack as was made of old by the Academics and Sceptics against the judgment of the senses, with their sophism of the *sorites*, or argument of the 'heap'.

4. A heap, pile.

1871 M. Collins *Marq. & Merch.* III. ix. 230 Such sorites of flaming anthracite may possibly cause cephalalgia.

Hence **Sori·tic** *a.* [cf. Gr. σωρειτικός], **Sori·tical**.

1656 Blount *Glossogr.*, *Soritical*, pertaining to such an Argument [*sc.* Sorites]. *a* 1693 *Urquhart's Rabelais* III. xxxviii. 320 Soritick fool. 1877 Blackmore *Cripps* II. v. 73 Nebules of logic, dialectic fogs, and..the pelting of soritic hail.

†**Sorlaque**, obs. variant of *solaque*, Solak.

1696 tr. *Du Mont's Voy. Levant* xiv. 175 After 'em came the Sorlaques, or Foot-Guards of the Body.

Sorn (sǭɹn), *v. Sc.* Also 6 **soirn**. [f. Sorren.]

†**1.** *trans.* To trouble or harass by exacting free quarters and maintenance; to live upon. *Obs.*

1563 *Reg. Privy Council Scot.* I. 248 The Clangregour.. birnis and slayis the pouer liegis of this realme,..takis thair gudis, sornis and oppressis thame. 1563–4 *Ibid.* 271 That ..nane of thame sould sorne or oppres our Soverane Ladiis liegis dwelland within the boundis of Stratherne. 1588–9 *Ibid.* IV. 342 Eftir thay had soirned, wracked, and spoilled the saidis baill Illis, thay..rased fyre.

2. *intr.* To take up free quarters or exact maintenance unjustifiably; to sponge *upon* others for food or lodging.

c 1575 *Balfour's Practicks* (1754) 24 That na persounis heirefter ludge nor sorne in housis or granges pertening to religious or ecclesiasticall men. 1638 H. Adamson *Muses Threnodie* (1774) I. 96 The Baliol proud, With English forces.., arrived at Kinghorne, And through the country mightily did sorne. 1725 Ramsay *Gentle Sheph.* III. iv, He gangs about sornan frae place to place. 1799 J. Robertson *Agric. Perth* 385 Why send the person..to corrupt, to pilfer and sorn upon your neighbours? 1816 Scott *Old Mort.* vi, You pretend to gie entertainments, that canna come by a dinner except by sorning on a carefu' man like me? 1876 Eadie *Thessalonians* 314 The idlers..had no right to 'sorn' on their friends or burden the funds of the church.

Sorname, obs. form of Surname.

Sorne, obs. f. *sworn*, pa. pple. of Swear *v.*

Sornee. *nonce-wd.* [f. Sorn *v.*] One who is sorned upon; a victim of sorning.

1797 Scott *Lett.* (1894) I. 10 As from being a sorner I am becoming a sornee [etc.].

Sorner (sǭ·ɹnəɹ). *Sc.* Also 5 **sornour**, 6 (9) **sornar**, 7 **soroner**. [f. Sorn *v.*] One who sorns; one who quarters himself upon others; a sponger.

1449 *Sc. Acts, Jas. II* (1814) II. 36/1 The away putting of sorneris, ourlyaris, & masterful beggaris. 1455 *Ibid.* 43/1 Item quhar euer sornoures be ourtane in tyme to cum, þat þai be delieryt to þe kingis schereffis. 1506 *Exch. Rolls Scotl.* XII. 704 The names of all thevis, pikaris, and sornars that oppress the cuntre. 1575 *Reg. Privy Council Scot.* II. 450 Certane sornaris, vagaboundis and utheris oppressouris of the cuntre. 1609 in Burt *Lett. N. Scotl.* (1818) II. 243 Eating up by sorners (*sturdy beggars*) and idle bellies. 1699 *Records of Elgin* (1903) I. 361 The counsell ordains notorious soroners, wagabonds and strangers to be instantly banished the burgh. 1797 [see Sornee]. 1821 Scott *Pirate* v, This is the house of his Lordship's factor, and no place of reset for thiggers or sorners. 1881 Masson *De Quincey* ix. 104 The prince of almoners for sorners and beggars.

So·rning, *vbl. sb. Sc.* [f. Sorn *v.*] The action or practice of exacting free quarters and maintenance, or of living at the expense of others.

1506 *Exch. Rolls Scotl.* XII. 704 That ye hald courtis ..for stanching of slauchtir, sornyng and oppression. 1563–4 *Reg. Privy Council Scot.* I. 271 Colin Campbell.. sall ansuer him self for the samyn crymes, sornyngis, oppressionis, and offencis. 1669 in *Macfarlane's Geneal. Coll.* (S.H.S.) I. 63 The Outragious Sornings of Glengairrie's Followers. 1678 Sir G. Mackenzie *Crim. Laws Scot.* I. xxxiv. § iii. (1699) 161 An habitual, and constant trade of Robbing, and sorning, is libelled. 1753 *Scots Mag.* Sept. 468/2 John Gun, for theft and sorning, was sentenced to be hanged. 1754 Erskine *Princ. Sc. Law* (1809) 514 Under which class may be included sorning, or the taking of meat and drink by force, without paying for it. 1829 Scott *Antiq.* Advert., All laws against sorning, masterful beggary, and every other species of mendicity, being suspended in favour of this privileged class. 1900 R. J. Drummond *Relat. Apost. Teaching* i. 15 Faith was made a plea for indolence and sorning.

So **So·rning** *ppl. a.*

1824 Scott *St. Ronan's* viii, A poaching, sorning sort of fallow. 1893 Agnew *Hered. Sheriffs Galloway* II. xxxi. 65 This sorning band, who had lived for days at free quarters.

Soro, obs. form of Sorrow.

Sororal (sŏrōᵊ·răl), *a.* [f. L. *soror* sister + -al. Cf. F. *sororal*.]

1. By one's sister; on a sister's side. *rare*[—1].

1654 Vilvain *Theorem. Theol.* viii. 212 Master John Down a..sororal Nephew to Bishop Juel.

2. That is a sister. *rare.*

1819 Lamb *Lett.* (1837) II. 55 How do you all do, amanuenses both—marital and sororal?

3. Of or pertaining to, characteristic of, a sister or sisters; sisterly.

1858 *Chambers's Jrnl.* IX. 239 Independent of either mother or sister—bound by no authority to either, except ..filial and sororal affection. 1869 Miss Mulock *Woman's Kingd.* III. 146 To see into what the sororal bond can degenerate, under given circumstances. 1836 Sir W. R. Hamilton in R. P. Graves *Life* (1885) II. 270 And Ladies, ..With love maternal, or sororal, view Thy gentleness.

Sororial (sŏrōᵊ·riăl), *a.* [f. L. *sorōri-us* sisterly + -al. Cf. F. *sororial*.] = prec. 3.

1836 T. Hook *G. Gurney* (1850) III. iii. 352 'Her brother' ..permitted his approbation of her sororial affection to produce a sort of fraternal acknowledgment. 1877 *World* VII. 7 The gauntlet of sororial criticism which he finds himself compelled to run.

Hence **Soro·rially** *adv.*, in a sisterly manner.

1825 T. Hook *Sayings* Ser. II. I. 23 Taking her *sororially* by the hand, she led her forth from the oak parlour.

†**Soro·riant**, *a. Obs.*[—0] [f. L. *sorōriant-*, *sorōrians*, app. f. *soror* sister.] (See quot.)

1656 Blount *Glossogr.*, *Sororiant Virgin*, a yong maid, whose Brests began to be embossed and round, or set out for shew.

So **Sororia·tion**. *rare.* (See quots.)

1658 Phillips, *Sororiation*, a swelling, or becoming round, and embossed like a young Virgin's breasts. 1859 Mayne *Expos. Lex.* 1175/1 *Sororiatio*,..the equally progressing development of the *mammæ* in the young female: sororiation.

Sororicide[1] (sŏrōᵊ·risəid). [ad. L. *sorōricīda*, f. *soror* sister + *-cīdĕre*: see -cide 1. Cf. F. *sororicide*.] One who kills his (or her) sister.

1656 Blount *Glossogr.*, *Sororicide*, a murderer of his own sister. 1721 in Bailey; and in later Dicts. 1881 *Philadel. Record* No. 3411. 2 Intending sororicides will do well to get this formula fastened in their memories. 1892 Besant *Ivory Gate* (1893) 195 If the envious man..denounces a man of reputation as a patricide, a sororicide, amicocide.

Sororicide[2] (sŏrōᵊ·risəid). [ad. late L. *sorōricīdium*, f. *soror* + *-cīdĕre*: see -cide 2. Cf. F. *sororicide*.] The action of killing one's sister.

1727 Bailey (vol. II), *Sororicide*, the Killing of a Sister. 1875 J. Hunter *Man. Bee-keeping* (1876) 115 The Workers prevent this sororicide by setting a guard over the unhatched Queens. 1889 *East. Morn. News* 10 Apr. 3/2 Supposed shocking sororicide.

Hence **Sororici·dal** *a.*

1878 Fr. A. Kemble *Rec. Girlhood* I. iii. 70 A quite unpremeditated inspiration..—to run away—probably alarmed my parents more than my sororicidal projects.

Sorority (sǫrǫ·riti). [ad. med.L. *sororitas*, or f. L. *soror* sister + -ity, after *fraternity*. Cf. obs. F. *sororité* (Cotgr. 1611).]

1. A body or company of women united for some common object, esp. for devotional purposes, † *U.S.*, the female section of a church congregation.

1532 More *Confut. Barnes* VIII. Wks. 761/1 This would he say for the comfort of yᵉ whole fraternitie and sororiti in general. 1645 Pagitt *Heresiogr.* (1647) 86 The Synod of New-England maketh not only the fraternity but (as they speak) the sorority to be the subject of the..power of the keyes. 1657 J. Watts *Dipper Sprinkled* 101 [The care] of the fraternity and sorority within their limits.

2. *U.S.* A women's society in a college or university. Also *attrib.*

1900 *Harper's Mag.* Sept. 450 One saw many of those neat little sorority pins the American girl proudly brings home from boarding-school or college. 1908 G. E. Cody (*title*), Jacquette: a Sorority Girl. 1909 C. W. Eliot *Univ. Administr.* 223 Sororities have, in general, the same merits and advantages as fraternities.

So·rorize, *v.* Somewhat *rare.* [f. L. *soror* sister + -ize, after *fraternize*.] *intr.* To associate *with* a person or persons as a sister or sisters; to form a sisterly friendship.

1875 *Temple Bar* Mar. 533 If there be a baby attached to either party, a general sororising is as inevitable as death. *a* 1876 M. Collins *Th. in Garden* (1880) II. i. 3 The beautiful girls..sororising with the rustic maidenhood of their parishes.

†**So·rory.** *Obs.*[—1] [f. L. *soror* sister + -y.] A sisterhood; a sorority.

1600 Tourneur *Transf. Metam.* lxviii, The ninefold Sorory themselves exiled, Euen from their natiue home to art's annoy.

Sorose, *a. Bot.* = Soriferous *a.*

1891 in *Cent. Dict.*

‖**Sorosis** (sŏrōᵊ·sis). [mod.L., f. Gr. σωρός a heap.]

1. *Bot.* (See quot. 1831.)

1831 Lindley *Introd. Bot.* I. ii. 180 *Sorosis*,..a spike or raceme converted into a fleshy fruit by the cohesion in a single mass of the ovaria and floral envelopes. 1845 *Encycl. Metrop.* VI. 122*/1 The fruit [*sc.* mulberry], called a sorosis by botanists, has a peculiar aromatic flavour. 1849 Balfour *Man. Bot.* § 557 Other instances of a sorosis are the Bread-fruit and Jack-fruit.

2. *U.S.* A women's society or club.

An arbitrary use of the botanical term, adopted as the name of the first club of the kind, founded in 1868.

1879 in Webster *Suppl.*

Soro·trochous, *a. Zool.* [f. Gr. σωρός heap: cf. Monotrochous *a.*] Of rotifers: (see quot.).

a 1843 *Encycl. Metrop.* (1845) VII. 266/1 The Wheel Organs are either *Monotrochous*,..or the ring is divided or manifold, as in the *Sorotrochous* Infusories. *Ibid.*, Two subdivisions of the Sorotrochous are also observed.

†**Sorous**, *a. Obs. rare.* Also 4 **sorus**. [f. Sore *a.*[1] + -ous.] **a.** Sorrowful, sad. **b.** Grievous, distressing.

a 1300 *Cursor M.* 16762 + 105 Al creatures for his ded made doil & pite, And þou þat he deed fore cannot sorus be. 1502 Arnolde *Chron.* (1811) 129 The most greuous sorous losses, imprisonment, and troubles.

‖**Sorpego**, obs. variant of Serpigo.

1631 T. Powell *Tom of All Trades* 49 Some of your Clarkly men complaine the moysture of their palmes. Others the Sorpego in their wrists.

Sorplers, obs. variant of Surplice *sb.*

†**Sorporr**, *v. Obs.*[—0] [f. *sor-* Sur- + Porr *v.* 3.] *trans.* To surfeit. Hence **Sorporring** *vbl. sb.*

c 1440 *Promp. Parv.* 8/2 Agrotonyd, or sorporryd wyth mete or drynke, *ingurgitatus*. *Ibid.*, Agrotonynge, or sorporrynge, *ingurgitacio*.

Sorra, dial. or colloq. f. Sorrow *sb.*

Sorrance, variant of Sorance.

†**Sorré.** *Cookery. Obs.* Also **sore**, **sorry**, **surre**. [app. a. OF. *soré*, pa. pple. of *sorer* to redden, f. *sore* Sore *a.*[2]] A dish made with chopped eels (or other fish, etc.) spiced and coloured. *White sorré* = *blanch-de-sore* (see Blaundsore).

c 1430 *Two Cookery-bks.* 25 Sore Sengle.—Take Elys or Gurnard,..take Safroun, & caste þer-to,..take poudere Gyngere, Canelle [etc.]. *c* 1440 *Anc. Cookery* in *Househ. Ord.* (1790) 446 Eles in Sorry. Take eles and cut hom on culpons, ..colour hit withe saunders. *Ibid.* 467 Eles in Surre. *a* 1450 *Tourn. Tottenham* The Feest vii. (Hazlitt *E. P. P.* III. 95), Blobsterdis in white sorre, Was of a nobull curry.

Sorrel (sǫ·rĕl), *sb.*[1] *Bot.* Forms: 4, 6–7 **sorell**, 5–6 **sorel**, 6–7 **sorrell** (6 **sowrell**), 6– **sorrel**. [a. OF. *surele* (12th cent.), *sorele*, *surelle* (mod.F. *surelle*), f. OF. *sur* adj., an adoption of the Germanic *sūr* Sour *a.*]

1. One or other of certain small perennial plants belonging to the genus *Rumex*, characterized by a sour taste, and to some extent cultivated for culinary purposes; esp. the common wild species, *R. acetosa*.

Earlier botanical names are *Acedula* (also *Acidula*), *Acetosa*, and *Oxalis*.

c 1440 *Promp. Parv.* 465/1 Sorel, herbe, *surella*. 1530 Palsgr. 272/2 Sorell an herbe, *ozeille*. 1548 Turner *Names Herbes* (E.D.S.) 69 Oxalis, in barbarus latin Acetosa or Acidula, in englishe Sorel or sourdocke. 1578 Lyte *Dodoens* 558 Sorrel is commonly sowen in gardens, and is to be found also growing wylde. 1600 Surflet *Countrie Farme* II. xv. 275 Sorrell & burnet..may be sowen in fine ground, and well manured, in the spring time, especially the sorrell. 1653 H. Cogan *Pinto's Trav.* xlvi. 180 Going into the woods we sustained ourselves with a certain herb like unto Sorrell. 1732 Arbuthnot *Rules of Diet* in *Aliments*, etc. I. 259 Several Plants known by their Taste, as Sorrel. 1763 Mills *Pract. Husb.* IV. 131 The seeds of the annual sorts of sorrel should be sown about the latter end of March. 1816 Keats '*I stood tip-toe*' 98 Her nimble toes Patting against the sorrel as she goes. 1868 *Rep. U.S. Commissioner Agric.* (1869) 394 'Acid' soils,..indicated by the growth of sorrel..and other sour plants. 1889 A. R. Wallace *Darwinism* (1890) 29 The sorrel..covers hundreds of acres with a sheet of red.

b. With distinguishing epithets, denoting various species of the genus *Rumex*.

For *Sheep's*, *Tree*, *Welsh sorrel* see these words.

1611 Cotgr., *Ozeille petite*,..*barren Sorrell. 1731 Miller *Gard. Dict.* s.v. *Acetosa*, The Northern barren Sorrel. 1797 *Encycl. Brit.* (ed. 3) XVII. 610/1 By means of the common *broad-leaved sorrel an excellent black colour is..given to woollen stuffs. 1855 Delamer *Kitchen Garden* (1861) 93 The best..is the Broad-leaved sorrel, of which a marked sub-variety, the Golden Sorrel, is almost exclusively cultivated in the environs of Dunkirk. *c* 1710 Petiver *Cat. Ray's Eng. Herbal* Tab. iii, *Common Sorrel. 1763 Mills *Pract. Husb.* IV. 130 The common sorrel, which grows naturally in pasture lands in most parts of England. 1785 Martyn *Rousseau's Bot.* xviii. (1794) 253 Common..Sorrel,..growing in meadows and pastures. 1597 Gerarde *Herbal* II. lxxx. 320 *Oxalis Crispa*, *Curled Sorrell. 1898 A. Irvine *Handbk. Brit. Plants* 379 *Rumex*,..*Dock Sorrel. 1886 [see Dock *sb.*[1] 4]. 1846–50 A. Wood *Class-bk. Bot.* 477 *Rumex acetosella*. *Field Sorrel. 1681 in *Thanes of Cawdor* (Spald. Club) 352 *French sorrell. 1731 Miller *Gard. Dict.* s.v. *Acetosa*, The Round-leav'd or French Sorrel. 1819 *Pantologia* s.v. *Rumex*, *R. scutatus*, French sorrel. 1829 [see French *a.* 5]. 1601 Chester *Love's Mart.* lviii, Sage, Scorpiades, and the *garden sorrell. 1855 *Golden sorrel [see *Broad-leaved sorrel* above]. 1578 Lyte *Dodoens* IV. 559 The fifth kind, which groweth in ditches, is called..in Englishe, *Great Sorrel, Water Sorrel, and *Horse Sorrel. 1597 Gerarde *Herbal* II. lxxx. 319 *Oxalis tuberosa*, *Knobbed Sorrell. 1731 Miller *Gard. Dict.* s.v. *Acetosa*, The Common or *Meadow Sorrel. 1753 *Chambers' Cycl.* Suppl. s.v., The great *mountain-sorrel. 1611 Cotgr., *Petite salette*, *Pettie Sorrell, sallet Sorrell. 1578 Lyte *Dodoens* V. ix. 558 *Oxalis Romana*, Tours Sorrel or *Romayne Sorrel. 1764 Mills *Pract. Husb.* IV. 130 The round-leafed garden, or Roman sorrel. 1796 [see Roman *a.* 14 b]. 1597 Gerarde *Herbal* II. lxxx. 320 *Oxalis Franca seu Romana*, *Round Sorrell. 1712 tr. *Pomet's Hist. Drugs* I. 25 Others will have the Leaf like round Sorrel. 1731 Miller *Gard. Dict.* s.v. *Acetosa*, The *Round-leav'd (or French) Sorrel. 1753 *Chambers' Cycl.* Suppl. s.v., The round-leaved garden-sorrel. 1855 Delamer *Kitchen Garden* (1861) 93 The Round-leaved sorrel..is not the kind to cultivate, except for variety. 1611 *Salad sorrel [see *Petty sorrel* above]. 1597 Gerarde *Herbal* II. lxxx. 321 *Oxalis minor*, *Small Sorrell. 1611 Cotgr., *Ozeille sauvage*,..*sowre Sorrell, the sowre Docke. 1578 *Tours sorrel, *Water sorrel [see *Roman sorrel* and *Great sorrel* above]. 1565 Cooper *Thesaurus*, *Cantherinum lapathum*, *wilde sorell. 1580 Hollyband *Treas. Fr. Tong*, *Ozeille sauvage*, wild sorrell.

2. The leaves of species of *Rumex* (see sense 1) used in cookery or medicine, or as a salad; a decoction or drink made from one or other of these plants.

a 1400 in *Rel. Ant.* I. 51 Drynk sorell, plantayne, and chekyn-mete. *c* 1420 *Liber Cocorum* (1862) 54 With gynger þo pigge eton shalle be, And sorel with þo moton. 1539 Elyot *Cast. Helthe* 24 Sorell. Being sodden, it louseth the bealy. 1575 Gascoigne *Posies* Ep. Yng. Gent., Wks. 1907 I. 12 If the Chirurgian which should seeke Sorrell to rypen an Ulcer, will take Rewe [etc.]. 1620 Venner *Via Recta* vii. 145 Sorell is good in hot seasons..for the cholericke. 1696 Floyer *On the Humours* vi. 68 Cyder, French and Rhenish Wines, Vinegar, Sorrel, Verjuice, Limons. 1746 Francis tr. *Horace*, *Sat.* II. iv. 37 Sorrel and White-Wine, if you costive prove, And Muscles, all Obstructions shall remove.. 1747–96 Mrs. Glasse *Cookery* v. 78 Take two handfuls of sorrel, pound it in a mortar.

3. †**a.** *Sorrel de boys*, = Wood-sorrel. *Obs.*

a 1400 *Stockholm Med. MS.* fol. 95 Alla .i. sorell de boye. 1548 Elyot, *Acidula*,..an herbe called sorrell de boys. 1552 Huloet, *Alleluya* herbe, otherwise called *Sorrell de Boys*. 1647 Hexham I. (Herbs), Sorell de boyes, or Cuckoes Sorell, *Kockocks Suyringh*.

b. With distinguishing epithets, denoting various species of *Oxalis* (wood-sorrel).

1647 [see prec.]. 1706 Phillips (ed. Kersey), *Alleluja*,.. an Herb otherwise call'd Wood-sorrel, or French Sorrel. *Ibid.*, *Oxalis*, wild Sorrel or Wood-Sorrel, an Herb. 1889 Maiden *Usef. Plants* 50 *Oxalis corniculata*,..'Clover Sorrel', or 'Sour Grass'. 1909 *Cent. Dict.* Suppl. s.v., Ladies' sorrel, *Oxalis stricta*.

4. With distinguishing epithet: One or other of various plants of other genera in some way resembling sorrel (see quots.).

1864 Grisebach *Flora Brit. W. Ind.* 787/2 *Climbing Sorrel, *Begonia scandens*. 1697 *Phil. Trans.* XIX. 375 *Acetosa* (a Plant of the Family with Rhubarb, which will be called The *Indian Sorrel, or Sower Docken). 1753 *Chambers' Cycl.* Suppl. *App.* s.v., *Indian Sorrel*, a name sometimes given to *ketmia*. 1760 J. Lee *Introd. Bot.* App. 327 Sorrel, Indian Red, *Hibiscus*. *Ibid.*, Sorrel, Indian White, *Hibiscus*. 1864 Grisebach *Flora Brit. W. Ind.* 787/2 Sorrel, Indian or red, *Hibiscus Sabdarifa*. 1843 Babington *Brit. Bot.* (1847) 273 *Oxyria reniformis*,..*Mountain Sorrel. 1889 Maiden *Usef. Plants* 35 *Hibiscus heterophyllus*,.. *'Queensland Sorrel'. 1829 Loudon *Encycl. Plants* 586 *note*, H[ibiscus] Sabdariffa..in the West Indies is called *Red Sorrel. 1864 Grisebach *Flora Brit. W. Ind.* 787/2 *Switch Sorrel, *Dodonæa viscosa*. 1887 Moloney *Forestry W. Africa* 303 Switch Sorrel of Jamaica..Shrub or small tree.

5. *pl.* Species of sorrel; sorrel plants.

1596 in *Analecta Scotica* II. 13 The seid of..sorrelis or sourochis. 1725 *Fam. Dict.* s.v., Alleluya..has all the same Qualities and the same Taste as the other Sorrels. 1841 *Penny Cycl.* XX. 221/2 Well known as troublesome weeds to the agriculturist, under the name of docks and sorrels. 1866 *Treas. Bot.* 998/2 The Sorrels are considered of great importance in French cookery.

6. *Salt of sorrel*, binoxalate of potash.

1800 tr. *Lagrange's Chem.* II. 209 Oxalic Acidulum, the Salt of Sorrel of the Shops. 1839 Ure *Dict. Arts* 192 Two drams of sal-ammoniac and half a dram of salt of sorrel. 1887 Bentley *Man. Bot.* (ed. 5) 654 A potassium salt of oxalic acid, commonly termed salt of sorrel.

7. *attrib.*, as *sorrel-flower*, *genus*, *leaf*, *seed*.

1753 *Chambers' Cycl.* Suppl. s.v., Sorrel seeds..are esteemed astringent. 1811 A. T. Thomson *Lond. Disp.* (1818) 350 Sorrel leaves are inodorous, and have a grateful ..acidulous taste. 1845 S. Judd *Margaret* I. xvii, The snowfields seemed to bloom with glowing sorrel-flowers. 1857 Henfrey *Bot.* 359 *Polygonaceæ*. The Sorrel Order. 1866 *Treas. Bot.* 998/1 *Rumex*, the Dock and Sorrel genus.

b. In the sense 'made from sorrel', as *sorrel drink*, *jam*, *sauce*, *sops*, *soup*, *water*.

1558 Warde tr. *Alexis' Secr.* 40 b, Thre vnces of endiue water, or sorell water. 1589 in H. Hall *Soc. Eliz. Age* (1887) 213 For rostinge the mutton and chickens and sorell soppes for the chickens. 1611 Cotgr., *Vinaigrette*, sorrell sawce. 1634 Heywood & Brome *Lanc. Witches* III. H.'s Wks. 1874 IV. 214 Here comes the payre of boyld Lovers in Sorrell sops. 1772 Mrs. Haywood *New Present for Maid* 155 Lay it in a dish with some sorrel sauce. 1855 Delamer *Kitchen Garden* (1861) 93 It is used..principally for sorrel-soup. 1862 in Veness *El Dorado* (1866) App. 122 Sorrel jelly,..sorrel jam, preserved papaws [etc.]. 1863 *Chambers's Encycl.* V. 359/1 *Hibiscus Sabdariffa*..affords a refreshing beverage, well known in the West Indies as Sorrel Cool Drink.

c. In the names of various plants, etc., as **sorrel-thorn**, **-vine**, **-wood** (see quots.). Also Sorrel-tree.

1799 *Med. Jrnl.* II. 80 The irritability inherent in the stamina of the flowers of the sorrel-thorn (*l'épine-vinette*). 1864 Grisebach *Flora Brit. W. Ind.* 787/2 Sorrel-vine, *Cissus acida*. 1874 *Treas. Bot.* Suppl. 1343/2 Sorrelwood (N[ew] Zea[land]), *Oxalis magellanica*.

Sorrel (sǫ·rĕl), *a.* and *sb.*[2] Forms: 5–8 (9 *arch.*) **sorel**, 5 **sorelle**, **sowrell**, 5–8 **sorell**, 6–7 **soril**; 6–7 **sorrell**, 7 **-ill**, 6– **sorrel**. [a. OF. *sorel* (*soreal*, *-eaul*, *-iel*), f. *sore* Sore *a.*[2] Hence also med.L. *sorellus*.]

A. *adj.* Of a bright chestnut colour; reddish brown: **a.** Of horses (or other animals).

1469 in *Somerset Med. Wills* (1901) 216, I will that my seruant William Wilson have a sorelle hackney of mine. 1543 *Test. Ebor.* (Surtees) VI. 175 A sorell geldinge. 1570 *Bury Wills* (Camden) 156 My sorrell meare coult. 1634–5 Brereton *Trav.* (Chetham Soc.) 39 Here, in their stable, four dainty sorrel pied horses. 1680 *Lond. Gaz.* No. 1520/4 A Sorrel, or Bright Chesnut Mare, about 14 Hands and a half high. 1704 Swift *Batt. Bks.* Misc. (1711) 252 A sorrel Gelding of a monstrous Size. 1706 *Lond. Gaz.* No. 4190/4 A sorrel chesnut Nag, a little crack winded. 1823 E. Moor *Suffolk Words*, *Sorrel*, chestnut-coloured, as applied to a horse. 1852 Mrs. Stowe *Uncle Tom's C.* iv. 23 How Mas'r Shelby was thinking of buying a new sorrel colt. 1884 Bible *Zech.* i. 8 Behind him there were horses, red, sorrel, and white.

b. Of hair or persons.

1600 Breton *Pasquils Fooles-cap* xxv, Shee, in a glasse, that sees her Sorrell haire, And straight will put it to the Painters die [etc.]. 1608 — *Mother's Blessing* lxxv, A sorrell foretop, and a sowish feature. 1634 Massinger *Very Woman* III. i, My sorrel slaves are of a lower price, Because the colour's faint. 1664 Butler *Hud.* II. i. 696 A Roan-Gelding.., a Lock on's hoof, A sorrel-mane. *a* 1700 B. E. *Dict. Cant. Crew*, *Sorrel-pate*, red Hair'd. 1708 *Brit. Apollo* No. 36. 2/2 Red Hair'd People, or Carrotty, Sandy, Sorrel, or what you will call them.

c. Of colour or hue.

1534 in *Wells Wills* (1890) 41 Oon mayre of sorell color. 1599 T. M[oufet] *Silkwormes* 72 How they color change, From blacke to browne, from browne to sorrel bay. 1611 Cotgr., *Saurir*, to..turne into a Sorrell colour. *Ibid.*, Vntill they [*sc.* herrings] haue gotten their Sorrell hue.

B. *sb.* **1.** A horse of a bright chestnut or reddish brown colour; also as the name of a horse. (So OF. *Sorel*.)

c 1430 Lydg. *Min. Poems* (Percy Soc.) 202 But on them she wyl have a bonde, As weel of bayard as of brende, And yit for sorelle she wyl stonde. 1482 in *Cely Papers* (Camden) 109 Grett sorell ys in good plyght. 1599 Hall *Sat.* VI. i. 223 Saint Georges Sorrell, or his crosse of blood. 1600 J. M. *New Metamorphosis* (Nares, 1859), Noe holla Jacke, nor Sorrell, hola boye, Will make them stay. 1708 *Brit. Apollo* No. 90. 3/1 O'er Hill and Dale on Sorrel, Noble Steed. 1748 Smollett *R. Random* ix, Sure my Lord's Sorrel is not resty. *Ibid.*, Sorrel, disdaining the rein, sprung forward. 1783–9 T. Day *Sandford & Merton* (1851) 442, I can assure you they are the true Suffolk sorrels, the first breed of working horses in the kingdom. 1842 Borrow *Bible in Spain* lvi, The horse was small but beautiful, a sorrel with long mane and tail. 1894 *Outing* XXIV. 383/2 At the easy, comfortable pace with which old sorrel jogs him to town on court days.

transf. 1803 J. Davis *Trav. Amer.* 378, I am no half-and-half breed; no chesnut-sorrel of a mulatto.

b. In allusive use: (see quot. 1710).

1705 Hickeringill *Priest-cr.* II. viii. 82 Those that (Profanely if not Traiterously) Drink a Health to Sorrel. 1710 *Answ. to Sacheverell's Serm.* 15 The King [William III] having..a fall from his Horse (called Sorrell),..which was thought to be the cause of his Death, they rejoyced at it, and did usually drink a Health to Sorrel.

2. A buck in its third year. Now *Obs.* or *arch.*

1486 *Bk. St. Albans*, *Hunting* e iv, And ye speke of the Bucke, the fyrst yere he is A fawne,..The secunde yere a preket, the iii. yere a sowrell. 1530 Palsgr. 272/2 Sorell, a yonge bucke. 1588 Shaks. *L. L. L.* IV. ii. 60 The Dogges did yell,..then Sorell iumps from thicket. 1616 *N. Riding Rec.* II. 122 John Turner presented for breaking the chase of the Rt Hon. Lord Burghley and shooting a sorell there. *a* 1700 Evelyn *Diary* 27 July 1654, I went to the hunting of a sorel deere. 1741 *Compl. Fam.-Piece* II. i. 310 If any Deer come out that is not weighty, or a Deer of Antlier, which is Buck, Sore, or Sorel. 1865 G. F. Berkeley *Life & Recoll.* II. 256 Doe or buck, pricket, sor or sorel, my orders from the Crown were that every one should be destroyed.

transf. 1612 *Christian turned Turk* (T.), I am but a mere sorell; my head's not hardened yet!

3. A sorrel or reddish-brown colour. Freq. with reference to horses.

1530 Palsgr. 272/2 Sorrell, colour of an horse, *sorrel*. *a* 1586 Sidney *Arcadia* (1622) 273 His horse was of a fiery sorrell, with blacke feete. 1611 Cotgr., *Alezan toustade*, a darke reddish colour, as of mettall burnt in the fire; a burnt sorrell. 1688 Holme *Armoury* II. 155/1 *Sorrel*, is more lighter than a light Bay, inclining to a Yellow. 1706 Stevens *Span. Dict.* I, *Alazán dorado*, betwixt Roan and Sorrel. 1787 Best *Angling* (ed. 2) 11 The best colours for lines are sorell, white, and grey. 1828 Carr *Craven Gloss.*, *Sorrel*, a colour between a chestnut and a red. 1860 O. W. Holmes *Elsie V.* (1887) 111 She was of the shade we call sorrel, or, as an Englishman would perhaps say, chestnut.

†**So·rrelled**, *a. Obs.* Forms: 5 **sorelt**, 5–6 **soreld**, 6 **sorelyd**, **sorellyd**, **-ed**, 7 **sorreld**. [f. Sorrel *a.* + -ed. Cf. Sored *a.*] Of horses: = Sorrel *a.* a.

1403 *Nottingham Rec.* II. 22 Item, j. equum sorelt, xij s. 1465 in *Mann. & Housek. Exp. Eng.* (Roxb.) 180 A man that browte the Kynge a fole soreld cowser. 1526 *Paston Lett.* III. 404 My Lord Harry of Stafforth..rydyng apon a sorellyd courser. 1553 *N. Country Wills* (Surtees) 231 To my cosyn..my soreld bald geldinge. 1613 *Liber Deposit. Archid. Colcest.* fol. 24, One sorreld mare with a white face.

So·rrel-tree. [Sorrel *sb.*[1]] The sourwood or elk-tree of North America, *Oxydendrum arboreum* (*Andromeda arborea*).

1687 *Phil. Trans.* XLI. 152 The Sorrel-tree bears a Leaf something like a Laurel. 1717 *Petiveriana* III. 247 Sorrel or Sowre-tree. Because its Leaves have that Taste; some are a Foot diameter. 1760 J. Lee *Introd. Bot.* App. 327 Sorrel-tree, *Andromeda*. 1821 W. P. C. Barton *Flora N. Amer.* I. 107 The sorrel tree itself, however, degenerates into a shrub. 1866 *Treas. Bot.* 472/1 The leaves of *Eubotrys arborea* have an acid flavour, whence the name of Sorrel-tree.

So·rren. *Sc.* and *Ir.* Now *Hist.* Forms: 3–4 **sorthyn**, **sorchyn**, 4 **sorryn**, **sorem**, 6 **sorehim**, **sorehon**, **soren**, 7 **sorehin**, **soreine**, 9 **sorren**. [ad. obs. Irish *sorthan*, explained as synonymous with *coinneamh*, *coinmheadh* (see Coynye), 'free quarters, living at free expense'. The Latinized form *sornagium* occurs in the 15th cent. Cf. Sorn *v.*] A service formerly required of vassals in Scotland and Ireland, consisting in giving hospitality to the superior or his men; a sum of money or other contribution given in lieu of this.

1289–1308 *Charter* in *Adv. Lib. MS.* 34. 3. 25, p. 194 Volo ..quod dictus dominus Adam, heredes sui vel assignati,.. sint quieti de Sorthyn et Tascal. *Ibid.*, Et volo etiam quod..habeant sorchyn fascal. *c* 1320 *Reg. Mag. Sig. Scot.* (1912) 533 *note*, Concessimus eidem quod dictas terras habeat..quiete de Sorem et Freelache. 1364 *Ibid.* 57, 1 Quod dicta baronia est libera de sorryn et fathalos.

1596 Spenser *State Irel.* (1633) 25 Cuddy, Coshery, Bonnaght, Shrah, Sorehin, and such others; the which (I thinke) were customes at first brought in by the English upon the Irish. *Ibid.* 204 They..exact upon them..all those kinde of services, yea and the very wilde exactions, Coignie, Livery, Sorehon[etc.]. 1600 Dymmok *Ireland* (1843) 8 Soren is a kind of allowance over and above the bonaght, which the Galloglass exact upon the poor people,..viz. 2s. 3d. for a day and a night. 1621 R. Bolton *Statutes Ireland* 429 If any person or persons..doe give any Scot or Scots..being men of warre, any wages, bonaghts, soreine, or any other intertainment. 1856 *Ulster Arch. Jrnl.* IV. 243 He rendered the chief-rents..in victual, called *sorren*, to McCarthy More. *Ibid.* 246 The first usage, that of giving *sorren*, grew in course of time into the formal payment of rent.

attrib. 1856 *Ulster Arch. Jrnl.* IV. 243 Land modernly held by *sorren* tenure. *Ibid.* 246 'Sorren land,' probably for most part arable.

Sorre·nto. The name of an Italian town in the province of Naples, used attrib. in *Sorrento edge*, *edging*, *lace*, *orange*, *work* (see quots.).

1856 Mrs. Pullan *Lady's Dict. Needlework* 25 Sorrento Edge [in Point Lace]. *Ibid.* 28 Sorrento Lace. 1875 Knight *Dict. Mech.* 2246/2 *Sorrento-work*, fret carving, done by a jig-saw. 1882 Caulfeild & Saward *Dict. Needlework* 453/1 Sorrento edging, used in modern Point Lace. 1896 *Daily News* 24 Dec. 3/2 The Neapolitan, or Sorrento orange,..is not smooth, but rather rough and unprepossessing, and its skin thick.

†**So·rrily**, *a. Obs.*[—1] In 3 **sorilich**. [f. Sorry *a.* + -ly[1].] Sorrowful, sad.

c 1200 *Trin. Coll. Hom.* 185 Sorehful is ure hider cume, and sorilich ure henen sið.

Sorrily (sǫ·rili), *adv.* Forms: α. 2–3 **sari-**, 3 **særiliche**, 4 **sarili**, 4–5 **-ly**. β. 2, 4 **soriliche**, 5 **soryly**, 5–7 **sorily**, 7– **sorrily**. [f. Sorry *a.* + -ly[2]. Cf. MHG. *sêrichliken*.]

†**1.** In a sorrowful manner; sadly, sorrowfully.

α. *c* 1175 *Lamb. Hom.* 39 Þu scalt bi-wepen þine sunne.. and ȝeoten þine teres swiðe sariliche. *c* 1205 Lay. 13626 Swiðe he gon to wepen & særiliche siken. *c* 1230 *Hali Meid.* 5 Nis ha þenne sariliche..akast, & in-to þewdom idrahen. *a* 1300 *Cursor M.* 14252 To fete sco fele him sarili. *c* 1400 *Ywaine & Gaw.* 1791 He luked up ful sarily.

β. *c* 1175 in *Fragm. Ælfric's Gloss.*, etc. (1838) 6 Ȝet sæiþ þeo sowle soriliche to þen licame [etc.]. 1387–8 T. Usk *Test. Love* II. iii. (Skeat) I. 60 [To] blobere and wepe til hem list stint, and sorily her mishap complayne. *c* 1400 *Rowland & O.* 459 And all þe lethirs þat þare ware Þay assembled soryly. *c* 1450 Lovelich *Merlin* 2460 Goth forth,.. and axeth the modyr the cause why, why that hire husbond wepeth so soryly. 1606 J. Carpenter *Solomon's Solace* i. 6 He..mingled his drinke with his teares,..sighed sorily, and lamented wofully.

†**2.** So as to cause sorrow; grievously; lamentably, pitiably. *Obs.*

a 1225 *Ancr. R.* 224 Swuðe ofte þer biuoren he hefde iseid him euer soð, uorte biswiken him soriliche on ende. *c* 1330 *Arth. & Merl.* 4810 (Kölbing), What Sarrazin so he mett, Wel soriliche he hem grett. *c* 1400 *Destr. Troy* 754 Þai solast hom samyn..With wevous werkes..Þat sorily dessauis, & men to sorow bringes. *c* 1440 *Jacob's Well* 116 Ȝe be soryly deed wyth þe poysoun of þe feend.

3. In a poor, wretched, or deplorable manner; miserably, wretchedly.

a 1586 Sidney *Arcadia* (1622) 73 Thy pipe, O Pan, shall helpe, though I sing sorily. 1586 T. B. *La Primaud. Fr. Acad.* I. (1594) 335 All his possession was but a little farme in the countrie sorily built. *a* 1625 Fletcher *Nice Valour* II. i, Yet goodness, whose inclosure is but flesh, Holds out oft times but sorrily. 1688 Bunyan *Jerus. Sinner Saved* (1886) 46 Churches would do but sorrily, If Christ Jesus did not put such converts among them. 1709 J. Johnson *Clergym. Vade M.* II. p. xlvi, 'Tis so sorrily related, and by one who lived so many hundred years after. 1768 Johnson *Lett.* (1788) I. 10 You serve me very sorrily. 1815 Scott *Let.* in *Lockhart* (1837) III. xi. 360 The Brunswickers and Hanoverians behaved very well; the Belgians but sorrily enough. 1856 Doran *Knights & their Days* xvi. 243 Rough games, that suited but sorrily with their calling. 1875 Kinglake *Crimea* (1877) VI. xi. 445 Thus sorrily lagged the males in their undesigned trial of speed.

Comb. 1824 Dibdin *Libr. Comp.* 607 In the sorrily-printed pages of the original London Post.

So·rriness. Now *rare.* Forms: α. 1 **sarignys**, 2 **-nesse**, 1–3 **sarinesse**, 4–5 **sarynes**; 3 **særinesse**, **-næsse**. β. 3–4 **sorinisse**, 3–6 **sori-**, **sorynesse**, 4 **sorinyshe**, 6 **-nes**; 6, 8– **sorriness**, 7–8 **sorryness**. [f. Sorry *a.* + -ness.]

†**1.** The state of being sorry; sorrow, grief, sadness; = Sorrowfulness. *Obs.*

α. *c* 1000 Ælfric *Saints' Lives* xxiii. 102 Hwæt mæg beon wop oððe sariȝnys, ȝyf þæt næs se mæsta æȝðres? *c* 1100 *O. E. Chron.* (MS. F) an. 616, Far þare sarinesse ðe he hæfde far þes cinges unȝeleauon. *c* 1175 *Lamb. Hom.* 103 Þe fifte sunne is *Tristicia*, þet is þissere worlde sarinesse. *c* 1205 Lay. 27560 Þer wes sarinesse, sorreȝen inoȝe. *a* 1340 Hampole *Psalter* iv. 1 Fra anguys and sarynes þou has broght me. 1483 *Cath. Angl.* 318/2 A Sarynes, *tristicia*.

β. *c* 1200 *Trin. Coll. Hom.* 35 Hwile mid sorinesse, hwile mid werinesse. *c* 1275 Lay. 13639 Ich ȝou telle rouþliche spelles of mochele sorinesse. 13.. *Guy Warw.* (A.) 372 Þe heuinisse, þe sorwe, and þe sorinisse, Þat me is on. 1387–8 T. Usk *Test. Love* II. xiv. (Skeat) I. 57 Trewly, this is the sorinesse of fayned love. *c* 1440 *Promp. Parv.* 465 1 Sorynesse, or hevynesse, *tristicia*. 1548 R. Hutten *Sum Divin.* G ij b, It is feare and sorines of conscience which perceiveth yᵗ god is angry with syn. 1571 Golding *Calvin on Ps.* li. 11 So as the sorynesse may settle itself deep in our harts. 1683 Crowne *City Politiques* II. i, Sorry? what does your sorryness signifie?

†**b.** With *a* and pl. An instance of being sorry.

c 1175 *Lamb. Hom.* 105 Þet þe mon on god blissie bitwuxe þa sorinessen þissere sterke worlde. *c* 1200 *Trin. Coll. Hom.* 71 Alse fele sorinesses swo ich haue on min herte for mine sinnes. *c* 1275 *Sinners Beware* 125 in *O. E. Misc.*, In eche sorinesse His saule he may brynge. 1587 Golding *De Mornay* xxix. 464 For the verie repentance of the best men, is but a sorinesse that they cannot be sorie enough.

2. The state or quality of being mean, poor, or paltry; poorness, meanness.

1668 Wilkins *Real Char.* II. i. 32 Indifferency,..Excellency,..Sorriness. 1727 Bailey (vol. II), *Sorryness*,..Paltriness, Meanness, Lowness of Value. 1891 T. Hardy *Tess* xxxix, The figure near at hand suffers..because it shows up its sorriness without shade.

Sorrip, obs. form of Syrup.

Sorrow (sǫ·roᵘ), *sb.* Forms: α. 1 **sorh**, **sorhȝ**, 2–3 **sorhe** (2 **sorhȝe**, 3 **seorhe**); 1 **sorȝ**, 2–4 **sorȝe** (3 **sorge**, **seorȝe**, 4 **sorȝe**, **sorghe**); 3 **soreȝe** (**-ege**), 5 **soroȝe**, **sorugh(e**. β. 3 **serrȝhe**, **sareȝe**; 3–4 **serewe**, 4–5 **serwe**, **sarow(e**; 9 *dial.* **sarrow**, **sarra(h**. γ. 3 **sorw**, **sorwȝe**, **seor(u)we**, 3–5 **sorwe**, **sorewe**. δ. 4–5 **soru**, **sorou** (4 **sorouu**), 5 **soro**, 6 **sourou**; 3–6 **sorow(e**, 5– **sorrow**, 6–7 **sorrowe**; 8–9 *Sc.* **sorro'**, 9 **sorra**. [Common Teut.: OE. *sorh*, *sorȝ*, = OFris. **sorge* (WFris. *soarch*, EFris. *sōargh*, *sūrghe*, NFris. *sörrig*, *surreg*, etc.), OLFrank. *sorga* (MDu. *sorghe*, Du. *zorg*), OS. *sorga*, *soraga*, *soroga* (MLG. *sorge*, *sorch-*, LG. *sorge*, *sörge*), OHG. *sorga* (MHG. and G. *sorge*), ON. (Icel., Norw., Sw., Da.) *sorg*, Goth. *saurga* (= **sorga*). Relationship to forms outside of Teutonic is uncertain.]

1. Distress of mind caused by loss, suffering, disappointment, etc.; grief, deep sadness or regret; also, that which causes grief or melancholy; affliction, trouble.

In OE. freq. in weaker sense, 'care, anxiety'.

α. *Beowulf* 1322 Ne frin þu æfter sælum; sorh is ȝeniwod Deniȝea leodum. *c* 888 K. Ælfred *Boeth.* vii. § 2 Ða ilcan [ðing]..ðe næfre nanne mon buton sorȝe ne forlætað. 971 *Blickl. Hom.* 103 Ne biþ þær sar ne ȝewinn,..ne sorȝ ne wop. *c* 1100 *O. E. Chron.* (MS. F) an. 870, Ealne his timan was ȝewinn & sorhȝe ofer England. *c* 1175 *Lamb. Hom.* 63 Þe saule of him is forloren and þe sorȝe is him biforen. *c* 1230 *Hali Meid.* 27 Weorldes uanite, þat wurðeð al to sorhe & to care. *c* 1250 *Orison of our Lady* 22 in *O. E. Misc.* 160 Al þis world schal ago Wið seorhe and wið sore. 1340 *Ayenb.* 71 Oþer in oþer zorȝe oþer ine blisse wyþoute endynge. 1390 Gower *Conf.* II. 144 His echedaies fantasie Of sorghe is evere aliche grene. *a* 1400–50 *Alexander* 249 Wheþire it be sele or soroȝe. *c* 1450 *Knt. de la Tour* (1868) 1 Fulle of soroghe and gladnesse, as mani lovers ben.

β. *c* 1200 *Moral Ode* 378 (Trin. Coll. MS.), Nis þar sareȝe ne sor non. *c* 1200 Ormin 4852 Þiss..drifeþþ fra þin herrte, All flæshliȝ care & serrȝhe & sit. *a* 1225 *Ancr. R.* 354 Ine sor & ine seoruw. *a* 1250 *Owl & Night.* 884 Hi ne seoþ her nowiht bute serewe. *a* 1300 *Body & Soul* in *Map's Poems* (Camden) 344 To synne and serwe was thi drauȝt. *a* 1400 *Pist. Susan* 145, I am with serwe biset on eueriche side. *c* 1400 *Apol. Loll.* 108 His trauel schal be-gynne in sarow.

γ. *a* 1200 *Vices & Virtues* 19 Ðar is sorwȝe and sarinesse for ðare muchele ortrewnesse. *a* 1250 *Owl & Night.* 431 Hwanne snouh liþ þikke & wide, & alle wihtes habbeþ sorewe. 1297 R. Glouc. (Rolls) 5044 Þe king him let ek in sorwe & in siknesse lede. *c* 1320 *Sir Tristr.* 578 Ouer londes he gan fare Wiþ sorwe and reweful chere. *c* 1440 *Jacob's Well* 66 Þou muste haue..full sorwe in þin herte for þi synne. 1473 Warkw. *Chron.* (Camden) 26 Suche goodes as were gaderide with synne, were loste with sorwe.

δ. *a* 1300 *Cursor M.* 24635 Seke i was and sar for soruu. *a* 1340 Hampole *Psalter* cxxvi. 3 Ȝe þat ete þe bred of sorow, þat is, ȝe þat make sorow in ȝoure pilgrimage. *c* 1375 *Cursor M.* 754 (Fairf.), To saue þaire self..or ellis in sorou for to lende. *c* 1400 Maundev. (Roxb.) iv. 13 Scho began to crie, as a thing þat had mykill sorowe. *c* 1420 *Chron. Vilod.* 1437 [They] weron in soro & penaunce alle þat nyȝt. 1508 Dunbar *Flyting* 21 Incres of sorrow, sklander, and evill name. 1559 *Mirr. Mag.*, *Hen. VI*, iv, A silly soule with woe and sorowe souste. 1590 Spenser *F. Q.* I. vii. 23 For earthly sight can nought but sorrow breed. 1602 Shaks. *Ham.* I. ii. 232 *Ham.* What, lookt he frowningly? *Hor.* A countenance more in sorrow then in anger. 1690 Locke *Hum. Und.* II. xx. (1695) 122 Sorrow is uneasiness in the Mind, upon the thought of a Good lost,..or the Sense of a present Evil. 1742 Gray *Adversity* 15 What sorrow was, thou bad'st her know. 1784 Cowper *Task* VI. 46 Sorrow has..subdu'd and tam'd The playful humour. 1841 Helps *Ess.*, *Aids Contentm.* (1842) 17 And we may remember that sorrow is at once, the lot, the trial, and the privilege of man. 1891 Farrar *Darkn. & Dawn* xlii, His face wore a look of sorrow and alarm.

b. In more or less personified use.

13.. *E. E. Allit. P.* B. 1080 Þer was solace & songe wher sorȝ has ay cryed. *c* 1400 *Rom. Rose* 4995 Labour and Travaile Logged ben with Sorwe and Woo, That never out of hir court goo. 1554–9 *Songs & Ball. Philip & Mary* (Roxb.) 1 Sorrowe hath caught me in her sner. 1621 Burton *Anat. Mel.* I. ii. III. iv, Sorrow,..the mother and daughter of melancholy. 1757 Gray *Bard* 62 And sorrow's faded form, and solitude behind. 1812 Byron *Ch. Har.* I. xcvi, How selfish Sorrow ponders on the past. 1850 Tennyson *In Mem.* lix, O Sorrow, wilt thou live with me?

c. In proverbs and phrases.

c 1420 *Sir Amadace* (Camden) iii, Bettur sayd soro thenne sene! 1788 *Grose's Dict. Vulg. T.* (ed. 2), Sorrow shall be his sops, he shall repent this. *Ibid.*, Sorrow go by me; a common expletive used by the presbyterians in Ireland.

2. With *a* and pl. An instance or cause of grief or sadness; an affliction or trouble.

α. *Beowulf* 149 Torn ȝeþolode wine Scyldinga, weana ȝehwelcne, sidra sorȝa. *a* 900 Cynewulf *Crist* 86 Swa eal manna bearn sorȝum sawað, swa eft ripeð. 971 *Blickl. Hom.* 5 Þæt æghwylc man sceolde..her on sorhȝum beon. *c* 1175 *Lamb. Hom.* 71 Þet lif and saule beon iborȝen and baðe ilesed ut of sorȝen. *c* 1205 Lay. 12332 Ah sone þer æfter sorȝen heom weoren ȝiueðen. *c* 1250 *Gen. & Ex.* 68 Pride..made ilc sorge, and euerilc bale. 13.. *E. E. Allit. P.* B. 563 Quen þe swemande sorȝe soȝt to his hert.

β. *a* 1300 *Harrow. Hell* (Digby) 28 Harde gates haui gon, Serewes suffred moni hon. *a* 1310 in Wright *Lyric P.* xxx. 89 Nis ther no leche so fyn, oure serewes to bete. *a* 1400 *Minor Poems fr. Vernon MS.* liv. 96 Ȝif eny serwe beo lyk to myn.

γ. *c* 1250 *Gen. & Ex.* 3742 Moyses told hem al ðis answere, And he ben smiten in sorwes dere. 1297 R. Glouc. (Rolls) 5923 Þe þridde ȝer..of aildredes kinedom, þe biginning of þis sorwe to engelonde verst com. *c* 1320 *Sir Tristr.* 368 Her sorwen and her care Þai witt þat frely fode. 1382 Wyclif *Eccius.* xxxviii. 7 In these thingus he..shal swage sorewen. *c* 1400 *Secreta Secret.*, *Gov. Lordsh.* 60 [It] brynges ynward sorwys to mannys bertys.

δ. *a* 1300 *Cursor M.* 9641 Sua þou wald his sorus slak. 1338 R. Brunne *Chron.* (1810) 7 Now of fiue sorowes.. Henry in his writyng telles what þei ware. *c* 1440 *York Myst.* xii. 7 And sithen what sorouse sor warre sene. 1477 Earl Rivers (Caxton) *Dictes* 8 The wiese men bere their greues & sorowes as they were swete vnto them. 1557 North *Gueuara's Diall Pr.* (1568) 300 There is great difference from the cares and sorrowes of weomen to that of men. 1602 Shaks. *Ham.* IV. v. 78 When sorrowes come, they come not single spies, But in Battaliaes. 1697 Dryden *Æneid* I. 307 The day, but not their sorrows, ended thus. 1713 Johnson *Guardian* No. 1 ¶ 5 All sorrows which can arrive at me are comprehended in the sense of guilt and pain. 1746 Francis tr. *Horace*, *Epist.* I. ii. 68 Nor House, nor Lands,..Can..drive one Sorrow from his anxious Breast. 1827 Pollok *Course T.* I. (1860) 17 Sorrows remembered sweeten present joy. 1890 Westcott *Gospel of Life* 270 Every sorrow and pain is an element of discipline.

b. *The Man of Sorrows*, Jesus Christ. (After Isaiah liii. 3.)

a 1853 F. W. Robertson *Serm.* Ser. v. (1890) i. 1 The Human Race typified by the Man of Sorrows. 1857 J. Hamilton *Less. fr. Gt. Biogr.* 170 The Man of Sorrows was not the man who would upbraid a breaking heart.

c. Applied to persons.

1637 Milton *Lycidas* 166 Weep no more, For Lycidas your sorrow is not dead. 1821 Shelley *Adonais* x, Our love, our hope, our sorrow, is not dead; See, on the silken fringe of his faint eyes [etc.].

3. Used as a term of imprecation, or of mere emphasis, in various phrases and constructions. In later use *Sc.* and *Ir.*, and freq. with *the* = the mischief, the devil.

a. In the phrase *Sorrow on* (a person or thing).

1325 *Poem Times Edw. II*, 178 in *Pol. Songs* (Camden) 331 Sorwe on that o frere that kepeth come there. 13.. *Minor Poems fr. Vernon MS.* xxxvii. 931 Serwe on heore hedes, but þei wel do! *c* 1440 *York Myst.* xxxii. 362 Now sorowe on such socoure as I haue soght. 1596 Shaks. *Tam. Shr.* IV. iii. 33 Sorrow on thee, and all the packe of you. 1823 Scott *Quentin D.* xvi, To deal with William de la Marck, on whose name be sorrow! 1862 Carlyle *Fredk. Gt.* XIII. ix. (1872) V. 96 The Duchess Dowager of Würtemburg also came, sorrow on her; a foolish talking woman.

b. In other phrases of imprecation.

13.. *Gaw. & Gr. Knt.* 2383 Of trecherye & vn-trawþe boþe bityde sorȝe & care! *c* 1386 Chaucer *Wife's Prol.* 308 But tel me wherfor hydestow with sorwe The keyes of thy chist away fro me? *c* 1400 *Gamelyn* 881 Sorwe have that rekke! 1526 *Pilgr. Perf.* (W. de W. 1531) 140 b, Yf than the porter wold come..& bydde vs walke forth vnthryftes with sorowe. *c* 1560 T. Ingelend *Disobedient Child* C j, God guye the sorow. 1776 Burns '*O Tibbie, I hae seen the day*' iii, But sorrow tak him that's sae mean. 1831 Miss Ferrier *Destiny* II. xxvi. 352 Aye, that you will, or sorrow take me! 1855 Tennyson *Maud* I. IV. ii, But sorrow seize me if ever that light be my leading star! 1896 P. A. Graham *Red Scaur* xvii. 258 Sorrow take the chance brought me among you!

c. As an emphatic negative. Chiefly with *a*.

1573 *Satir. Poems Reform.* xxxix. 87 Persauing that, sorrow mair thay socht it. 1583 *Leg. Bp. St. Androis* 791 But sorrow mair the men mycht gett. 17.. Ramsay *Wyfe of Auchtermuchty* xi, The sorrow crap of butter he gat. 1738 *Scotch Presbyt. Eloquence* 111 The Sorrow a Bit of your Dog will I be. 1818 Scott *Br. Lamm.* xxiv, Sorra a bit, if I were him. 1825 Croker *Fairy Leg. Irel.* I. 152 'Sorrow a know I know,' said Leary. 1865 Lever *Luttrell of Arran* xviii, The sorrow a word ever crossed your lips.

d. Inserted after *what*, *where*, etc., in impatient questions.

a 1631 Bruce *Upon Affair of Gowrie* in *Serm.* (1843) 193 The Earl..said—'What sorrow means all this haste?' *a* 1779 D. Graham *Yng. Coalman's Courtsh.* III. (1787) 22 What a sorrow ails you? 1796 *Two Cuckolds & Tint Quey* 16 What the sorro' way? D'ye think that I can watch her aye? 1861 R. Leighton *Rhymes & Poems* (ed. 2) 89 'Guidwife,' quoth John, 'did ye see that moose? Whar sorra was the cat?'

e. In miscellaneous uses with *the*.

1756 Mrs. Calderwood in *Coltness Collect.* (Maitl. Club) 178 The holydays play the sorrow with the poor people. 1819 Thomson *Poems* 131 (E.D.D.), The sorry's i' the cutty. 1839 Carleton *Fardorougha* iii, Her people's as proud as the very sarra. *Ibid.* v, Tut! go to the sarra. 1887 Service *Life Dr. Duguid* II. viii. 219 She should been brunt, the auld limb o' the sorrow!

Supplement, p. 3873; Corrigenda, p. 4092; Spurious words, p. 4093; Books quoted, p. 4094

4. The outward expression of grief; lamentation, mourning; *poet.*, tears. †In early use esp. *to make sorrow.*

†5. a. Physical pain or suffering. *Obs.*

†b. Mischief; harm, hurt, damage. *Obs.*

6. As a term of abuse, reproof, or depreciation applied to persons. Chiefly *north.* and *Sc.*

†7. Used in place of SORRY *a.* (Obs.)

8. *attrib.*, as *sorrow-cloud*, *-mate*, *-tithe*, *-smart*. A number of attributive compounds occur in OE.

b. *Comb.* Instrumental, with *pples.*, as *sorrow-beaten*, *-bowed*, *-hound*, *-closed*, etc.

c. *Comb.* Objective, with *pples.* and *vbl. sbs.*, as *sorrow-breathing*, *bringing*, *-ceasing*, *-making*, etc.

Sorrow (sρ'rou), *v.* Forms: *a.* 1 *sorȝian*, *sorhȝian*, 2-3 *sorȝen* (3 *sorȝen*, *sorhen*, -in), 4 *sorȝe*, 5 *sorȝe*.

I. *intr.* To feel sorrow or sadness; to regret or grieve; also, to exhibit signs of grief, to mourn.

2. *trans.* To feel care or anxiety; to be anxious.

b. To grieve for, mourn.

Sorrower (sρ'rouə(r)). [f. SORROW v. + -ER.] One who sorrows; a mourner.

Sorrowful (sρ'roful), *a.* Forms: *a.* 1-3 *sorhfull*, 3 *sorewf-*, *neor(u)hful*, *sorƿfolle*; 1 *sorȝ-*, 3 *sorȝ-*, 4 *sorhfull*, etc.

4. *quasi-adv.* = SORROWFULLY.

Sorrowfully (sρ'rofuli), *adv.* Forms: [see quots. and prec.]. [ME. *sorh-*, *sorȝfulliche*: see prec. and -LY².] In a sorrowful manner; to a distressing extent; sadly, pitifully, etc.

Sorrowfulness (sρ'rofulnes). Forms: [see quots. and the adj.]. [f. SORROWFUL + -NESS.] The state of being sorrowful; grief, sadness, melancholy.

Sorrowing (sρ'rouiŋ), *vbl. sb.* [f. SORROW v.] The action of the vb.; mourning, lamentation.

Sorrowing (sρ'rouiŋ), *ppl. a.* [f. SORROW v. + -ING².] That sorrows or mourns; mournful.

Hence **Sorrowingly** *adv.*

Sorrowless (sρ'roules), *a.* Also 1 *sorh-*, *sorȝ* SORROW *sb.* + -LESS¹.] Free from sorrow.

Sorrowy (sρ'roui), *a.* Also 4 *sorwy*, -y. [f. SORROW *sb.* + -Y¹.] Sorrowful.

Sorry (sρ'ri), *a.* Forms: *a.* 1 *sariȝ*, *sari*, 1-3 *sari*, 3 *sorȝ-*, *sori*, *seri*; *north.* and *Sc.* 4-5 *sari*, 4-6 *sorie*, 4-7 *sory*, 5-9 *sairie*. β. 3-6 *sori*, 3-7 *sory*, 6 *sorye*, *sorye*; 1 sorry, 6-7 sorrie.

I. With infinitive.

2. In later use (weakened sense, and often employed in the phrase 'I'm sorry') to express mere sympathy or apology.

3. Painful or distressed; sad; (of grief or sorrow).

4. Causing distress or sorrow; painful, grievous, dismal. *Obs.*

5. Vile, wretched, worthless, mean, poor; of little account or value: *a.* Of persons, (in general character or) in some special respect.

b. Of things.

Sorry (sρ'ri), *v.* Also 4 *sorwe*, -y. [f. SORRY *a.*] Sorrowful.

Sorry (sρ'ri), *adv.* [f. prec. Cf. OE. *sáriȝian.*] *intr.* To grieve, be sad; to complain, be sorry.

Sorrily (sρ'rili), *adv.* [f. SORRY *a.*] Somewhat sorry; rather sorrily.

Sorryish *a.* [f. SORRY *a.*] Somewhat sorry.

†Sorry-mood. *a. Obs.* [OE. *sáriȝmód* = OS. *stragmód*: see Mood *sb.*] Sorrowful.

†Sort, *sb.¹ Obs.* Also 4-5 *soort*, 5-6 *sorte*. [a. OF. *sort*, *sorte.*]

1. Destiny, fate, lot.

2. Lot or share.

Sort (sρrt), *sb.²* Also 4-6 *soort*, 5 *soorte*, 5 *sorte*, 6 sort. [a. OF. *sorte*, ad. med.L. *sorta*, *sorte*, alteration of L. *sort-*, *sort-* see prec. Cf. MLG. and G. *sorte*, WFris. *sarte*, *sorte*, Du. *soort*, Da. and Sw. *sort.*]

I. A kind, species, variety, or description of persons or things.
Preceded by 'of'.

1. *Of* a (certain) sort, of a certain kind, etc.

c. The choice resulting from such a casting of lots.

2. That which is allotted or assigned; a share or portion. *rare.*

3. That which is allotted or assigned; a share or portion.

4. A particular kind, class, or (of things) or persons(s).

5. *Of* (certain parts), etc.

6. *Of* (various parts), etc.

7. *All sorts* (of things or persons), = 'things or persons of all kinds or descriptions'. [Cf. 7 c.]

8. *All sorts of* (things or persons).

9. *Of* (various parts) etc.

10. *That of this sort of thing*, used to denote in a general way a thing, quality, etc., of a like or similar nature to that specified.

11. A particular class, order, or rank of persons.

b. *In'* or *into that sort* or within certain kinds of articles or goods. *In transf.*

12. *Of sorts*: a. Not in the usual or normal condition of good health or spirits; in a low-spirited, irritable, or peevish state, esp. through physical discomfort; slightly ill.

13. *+ sb.* Spices. *Obs.*

d. *Typog.* One or other of the characters or letters in a fount of type. Usu. in *pl.*

14. *Of sorts*: a. (Not in the usual or normal condition of good health or spirits; in a low-spirited, irritable, or peevish state, esp. through physical discomfort; slightly ill.)

16. *That's your sort* (also dial. *prov.*), as a term of approval. *slang.*

17. *A* number of persons associated together in some way; a band, company, group, crew, etc.

II. In phrases with *in.*

18. Manner, method, or way.

III. In phrases with *in.*

II. Qualified by demonstratives or similar words, as *in that*, *(the) like*, *what*, etc., *sort.*

19. In the same sense as prec. without qualifying adjective. *Now dial.*

†20. A (great, etc.) number or lot or portion of a number of persons or things. *Obs.*

movit þe faderis & commouns in diuers maner and sortis. 1560 DAUS tr. *Sleidane's Comm.* 350 b, They can fynde none that wyll go in that sorte. 1577 B. GOOGE *Heresbach's Husb.* I. (1586) 10, I thought in the like sort the wheele of a mill myght be turned. 1601 J. WHEELER *Treat. Comm.* 75 In what sort can her Maiesty..tolerate or suffer that [etc.]? 1670 DRYDEN *Conq. Granada* I. I. i, If we treat gallant strangers in this sort, Mankind will shun the inhospitable court. 1713 *Guardian* No. 1 ¶ 1 Not without some hope of having my Vanity..indulged in the sort abovementioned. 1782 COWPER *Gilpin* 93 His horse, who never in that sort Had handled been before. 1800 WORDSW. *Michael* 207 While in this sort the simple household lived From day to day. 1866 NEALE *Sequences & Hymns* 11 But in other sort, that midnight round their watch-fires' blaze they feast. 1871 FREEMAN *Norm. Conq.* IV. xviii. 287 Stores of corn..men brought together and destroyed in the like sort.

b. With distinguishing adj., as *in good, honest,* etc., *sort*. Now *rare*. † Sometimes with *a, any, some, this,* etc.

(*a*) 1548 GESTE *Pr. Masse* 81 Yf the signe be counterfayt and fayned, then nedes must the thing be in semblable sorte whyche is betokened. 1585 T. WASHINGTON tr. *Nickolay's Voy.* II. v. 35, I haue not seen..a nation..which studieth more in all honest sorte to obtayne the fauour of straungers. 1600 HAKLUYT *Voy.* (1810) III. 568 Wherein is showed in what good sort we liued with our masters. 1634 SIR T. HERBERT *Trav.* 79 Hee speedily affronted the Georgians, who receiued him in warlike sort. 1657 SPARROW *Bk. Com. Prayer* (1661) 42 He which prays in due sort, is..made the more attentive. 1713 SWIFT *Faggot* Wks. 1755 IV. I. 8 Stewards..who in solemn sort Appear with slender wands at court. 1784 COWPER *Task* VI. 377 Each animal..growl'd defiance in such angry sort, As taught him, too, to tremble in his turn. 1813 SCOTT *Trierm.* II. xviii, The champions, arm'd in martial sort. 1863 PATMORE *Angel in Ho.* II. I. x, According to such nuptial sort As may subsist in the holy court.

(*b*) 1592 KYD *Sp. Trag.* II. i. 100 Giue me notice in some secret sort. 1594 MARLOWE & NASHE *Dido* I. i, To wear Their bow and quiver in this modest sort. 1642 D. ROGERS *Naaman* 29 Jehoram,..who sent a cursed messenger before him..(met in a holy sort before God in the judgement of famine). *a* 1704 T. BROWN *Two Oxford Scholars* (1730) I. 9 He did not know how to maintain himself and his family in any tolerable sort.

c. *In some sort*, in a certain undefined or unknown way; to some extent or degree. Freq. in parenthetic use.

1556 *Aurelio & Isab.* (1608) H iij, The ladies leaste experimentede and wittey be in some sorte the chasteste. 1597 MORLEY *Introd. Mus.* Ded., To notifie vnto your selfe in some sort the entire loue..which I beare vnto you. 1615 W. LAWSON *Country Housew. Gard.* (1626) 7 The Sunne (in some sort) is the life of the world. 1653 H. MORE *Antid. Ath.* Pref., For it is the same Numen in us that moves all things in some sort or other. 1711 STEELE *Spect.* No. 52 ¶ 3 Our personal Deformities in some sort by you recorded to all Posterity. 1780 *Mirror* No. 97, Having seen Paris,..she thinks that she is authorised, and, in some sort, obliged to speak French. 1865 DICKENS *Mut. Fr.* I. vi, She was named after, or in some sort related to, the Abbey at Westminster. 1894 J. T. FOWLER *Adamnan* Introd. 17 The Christian hierarchy..in some sort succeeded to the Druids and the Brehons.

d. *In a sort*, in some sort or manner (see prec.); occas. with implication of inefficiency or inadequacy. † Also *in sort*.

1585 in *Eng. Hist. Rev.* Jan. (1913) 55 *note*, So many reasons..did in a sort work in me a confirmation [etc.]. 1592 KYD *Sp. Trag.* III. v. 17, I am in a sorte sorie for thee. *a* 1619 FOTHERBY *Atheom.* II. xi. § 5 (1622) 319 Which carried him vp, in a sorte, into Heauen. *c* 1643 LD. HERBERT *Autobiog.* (1824) 62 In Law also the Judge is in a sort superior to his King. 1710 STEELE *Tatler* No. 14 ¶ 2 The Criminal..was always sure he stood before his Country, and in a Sort before a Parent of it. 1788 *Pict. Tour thro' Pts. Europe* 3 A garden..wherein the enchantments of that of Armida seem in sort to be realized. 1825 SCOTT *Jrnl.* 6 Dec., H.M...shoots and fishes in a sort even to this day. 1874 BLACKIE *Self-Cult.* 72 Our only chance of becoming great in a sort is by participation in the greatness of the universe.

† **e.** *In no sort*, in no way, to no extent, not at all. *Obs.*

1570–6 LAMBARDE *Peramb. Kent* (1826) 215 They are in no sorte to be hearde, seeing that by no means they may iustly claime any manner of right in that lande. *a* 1625 JAS. I *Ps.* xxiii. 4 Yea, though I through death's shadow walke, Yet feare I in no sort. 1676 HALE *Contempl.* I. 5 The consideration of our latter end doth in no sort make our lives the shorter. 1708 SWIFT *Sacram. Test* Wks. 1755 II. I. 131 These are, in no sort, a number to carry any point. 1756 C. LUCAS *Ess. Waters* III. 70 They will in no sort mix.

† **f.** *In sort*, followed by *as* or *that*. *Obs.*

1548 GESTE *Pr. Masse* 83 Gelasius..impugneth the sayd transubstanciation as..uncredyble in sorte as followeth. 1594 CAREW *Huarte's Exam. Wits* vi. (1596) 84 To remaine ..affixed, in sort as the sparrowes are attached to birdlime. 1605 BACON *Adv. Learn.* II. 91 In all causes the first tale possesseth much, in sorte, that the preiudice thereby wrought will bee hardly remooued.

† **g.** *In all sorts*, altogether, completely. *Obs.*[−1]

1559 in Tytler *Hist. Scot.* (1864) III. 395 Your good mind, ..which as it is in all sorts undeserved on my side, so am I the more affected unto you therefor. 1611 COTGR., *Totalement*, totally,..throughly, in all sorts, altogether.

22. *After this, what,* etc., *sort, after a* (..) *sort*, in the preceding senses.

(*a*) 1551 ROBINSON tr. *More's Utopia* I. (1895) 61. After what sorte hooredome..maye be lawfull. 1569 J. SANFORD tr. *Agrippa's Van. Artes* 15 b, After this sorte the Greeke Historiographers..would attribute al thinges to themselves. 1577 B. GOOGE *Heresbach's Husb.* II. (1586) 57 b, The ordering of them is after one sort. 1604 E. G[RIMSTONE] *D'Acosta's Hist. Indies* IV. iv. 212 They drawe golde in those partes, after three sorts.

(*b*) 1551 ROBINSON tr. *More's Utopia* II. (1895) 132 But nowe the houses be curiously builded, after a gorgiouse and gallaunt sort. 1577 HANMER *Anc. Eccl. Hist., Euseb.* I. vi. (1663) 7 It remaineth that we begin after a compendious sort from the coming of our Saviour Christ in the Flesh. 1592 TIMME *Ten Eng. Lepers* A iij, The generall good.. hath moved me, though after a plaine and rude sort, to publish the same. 1857 SUSANNA WINKWORTH tr. *Life, Tauler* 67 The Master..received him after a most friendly sort. *a* 1894 CHRISTINA ROSSETTI *Venus' Looking-glass* Poems (1904) 289 Around whose head white doves rose.. and cooed after their tender sort.

(*c*) 1557 N. T. (Geneva) *Heb.* xi. 19 Death: from whence he receaued him also after a sort. 1581 E. CAMPION in *Conf.* III. (1584) Z, Man is also the offerer, after a sort. 1610 HOLLAND *Camden's Brit.* (1637) 631 After a sort he surrendered up his Crowne unto him. 1671 H. M. tr. *Erasm. Colloq.* 7 Not so well as I desire; truly I am well after a sort. 1724 A. COLLINS *Gr. Chr. Relig.* 153 The first place of Jeremiah was quoted,..and is still extant after a sort. 1837 CARLYLE *Fr. Rev.* II. II. ii, Captain Dampmartin,..who loves the Reign of Liberty, after a sort. 1879 S. C. BARTLETT *Egypt to Pal.* xii. 267 Into which the hand, with shut fingers, will fit after a sort.

† **23. a.** *Of this sort*, in this way or manner. *Sc. Obs. rare.*

1549 *Compl. Scot.* vi. 38 Of this sort i did spaceir vp ande doune but sleipe. *Ibid.* ix. 79 Of this sort god turnit the hazard of fortoune.

† **b.** So *On such* (*a*) *sort, on this sort*. *Obs.*

1557 *Tottel's Misc.* (Arb.) 136 Happy is be, that liues on such a sort: That nedes not feare such tonges of false report. 1585–6 *Reg. Privy Council Scot.* Ser. I. IV. 50 The saidis personis..on sic sorte persewis the saidis complenaris as thay dar not remane at thair awne duelling houssis. 1597 BEARD *Theatre God's Judgem.* (1612) 191 Permitting him to plague him on this sort, for his amendment. *a* 1632 T. TAYLOR *God's Judgem.* I. II. iv. (1642) 270 But to come to the fact, it was on this sort.

† **c.** *At all sorts*, at all points. *Obs.*[−1]

1612 W. SHUTE tr. *Fougasses' Venice* IV. vii. II. 13 A thousand Archers from Candy, and another thousand armed at all sortes from the Country of Albania.

† **Sort**, *sb.*[3] *Obs. rare.* Also **sortt, soortt**. [Perh. identical with prec.] Some measure or weight of figs and raisins.

By Rogers (*Agric. & Prices* IV. 668–9) considered to be equivalent to three frails.

1438–9 *Durham Acc. Rolls* (Surtees) 70 It. in ij Sortez ficuum et racemorum. *Ibid.* 77 Summa rec., ij Sortez et xx lb. 1453–4 *Ibid.* 289 In j soortt ficuum. 1481–90 *Howard Househ. Bks.* (Roxb.) 351 Item, for a sort of fygges, xij. s.

Sort (sǭɹt), *v.*[1] Also 5 **soortyn**, 5–7 **sorte**, 6 **sourt**, 9 *dial.* **soort**, etc. [Partly ad. L. *sortīrī* to divide or obtain by lot, or OF. *sortir* (mod. F. *sortir*, = It. *sortire*, Pg. *sortir*; cf. Pg. and Sp. *sortear*):—pop. L. **sortīre*, f. L. *sors, sort-* lot: see SORT *sb.*[1] In most senses, however, closely related to SORT *sb.*[2], and perh. partly repr. F. *assortir* ASSORT *v.*]

I. † **1.** *trans.* To allot, apportion, or assign. Usu. const. *to, for,* or with dat. of person. *Obs.*

c 1374 CHAUCER *Troylus* v. 1827 And forth he wente, shortly for to telle, Ther as Mercurie sorted him to dwelle. 1412–20 LYDG. *Chron. Troy* III. 440 Of our expleit þe trouþe to reporte, For whiche part Mars list þe feld to sorte. 1561 NORTON & SACKV. *Gorboduc* IV. ii, What cruell destenie, What frowarde fate hath sorted vs this chaunce? 1583 MELBANCKE *Philotimus* K j, How many sporting houres were sorted to the Astronomer C. Gallus. 1599 B. JONSON *Cynthia's Rev.* v. iii. [xi], How well Diana can distinguish times? And sort her censures? keeping to herself The doom of gods, leaving the rest to us!

† **b.** To dispose, ordain, order (events). Also *absol. Obs. rare.*

1592 WYRLEY *Armorie* 108 Thus coy fortune sourts, Some now aloft and then cast downe we see. 1594 SHAKS. *Rich. III*, II. iii. 36 All may be well; but if God sort it so, 'Tis more then we deserue or I expect. 1596 — *Merch. V.* v. 132 But God sort all.

† **2.** *intr.* To exercise or perform divination. *Obs.*[−1]

c 1450 *Merlin* ii. 39 Bringe hethir thy counsell, and the clerkes that sorted of this toure.

† **3.** *trans.* To distribute by lot. *Obs. rare.*

1513 DOUGLAS *Æneid* III. viii. 7 We sort our airis, and chasis rowaris ilk deill. 1582 STANYHURST *Æneis* I. (Arb.) 34 Shee..toyls too pioners by drawcut lotterye sorteth.

† **4.** To obtain as one's lot; to share in, partake of. *Obs. rare.*

1474 CAXTON *Chesse* IV. ii, Thus as in going out first into four poyntes he sorteth the nature of knyghtes. 1483 — *Gold. Leg.* 209/2 He hath ronne thrououte alle the world and with his prechyng hath purged it and yet he hath not sorted [L. *sortitus est*] heuen.

† **5.** To arrive at, attain to, result in, or reach (an effect, end, etc.). Cf. sense 7 a. *Obs.*

a 1548 HALL *Chron., Edw. IV*, 214 It was almost incredible to se what effect this new imaginacion..sorted and toke. 1593 PEELE *Edw. I*, VI. vi, When the war of rebels sorts an end, None might be prince..But such a one as was their countryman. 1612 SHELTON *Quix.* I. III. xiii. (1620) I. 255 Bidding her to hope firmly, that our good just Desires would sort a wish'd and happy End. 1656 W. COLES *Art Simpl.* 4 Their Medicines oft-times sort not their wished, but sometimes contrary effects.

† **6.** *intr.* Of events, etc.: To come about, to fall or turn out, in a certain way or with a certain result. *Obs.*

c 1477 CAXTON *Jason* 113 Sorceries..and..enchantements, wherof thaventure of the shippe sorted as sayd is. 1589 GREENE *Tullies Love* Wks. (Grosart) VII. 193 Promising all shoulde sort according vnto Lentulus minde. 1598 GRENEWEY *Tacitus, Ann.* xv. vi. (1622) 230 That the Romans many things had sorted luckily, and some to the Parthians. 1609 DEKKER *Ravens Almanack* Wks. (Grosart) IV. 241 Which sorted according to their expectations. 1626 BACON *Sylva* § 317 The Experiment sorted in this Manner. 1653 H. COGAN tr. *Pinto's Trav.* xxvii. 106 We had recourse to Mercy, which sorted well for us.

† **b.** Similarly with *out*. *Obs.*

1581 RICH *Farew.* (1846) 130 Seyng the matter sorted out as she looked for. 1593 MARLOWE *Edw. II*, II. i, [...] things sort out, as I hope they will. *a* 1637 N. FERRAR tr. *Valdes' 110 Consid.* (1638) 15 Having seen that..my determinations sorted out contrary to that which I determined. *a* 1656 USSHER *Ann.* (1658) 158 If things sorted out in the war, as he hoped they would.

† **c.** To come to effect; to be successful. *Obs.*

1613 PURCHAS *Pilgrimage* II. x. I. 137 Intending a plague to the men,..if their working had sorted. 1626 BACON *Sylva* § 351 It was tried in a Blowne Bladder..and it sorted not. *Ibid.* § 380 Which is a thing of great profit, if it will sort: But vpon Triall..there followed no Effect.

† **7. a.** To come or attain *to* an end, conclusion, effect, etc. *Obs.* (Common *c* 1575–1650.)

1543–4 *Act 35 Hen. VIII*, c. 10 Whiche good and profitable purpose can not sorte to conclusion, nor take good effect, without the ayde..of parliament. *a* 1548 HALL *Chron., Hen. VII* (1809) 498 The third request..never sorted to any effect or conclusion. 1582 N. LICHEFIELD tr. *Castanheda's Conq. E. Ind.* I. 16 b, Their mischeuous enterprise, which had been likely to haue..sorted to a sorrowfull hap and euent. 1606 *Weakest goeth to Wall* I iij, I will forbeare my knowledge 'till I see To what effect this cause will sort unto. 1652 H. THORNDIKE *Wks.* (1846) II. 540 If there were nothing to help the tenor of such instruments, things contrary would hardly sort to effect.

† **b.** To end in coming or leading *to* a specified result. *Obs.*

1586 A. DAY *Eng. Secretary* II. (1625) 91 Here is head, wit, mind and discretion, all sorting to one thing. 1598 FLORIO To Rdr. b ij, Let..the reapers of the fruites iudge betweene vs whose paines hath sorted to best perfection. 1656 BLOUNT *Hor? Subs.* 216 Euery mans own Method commonly sorteth best to his owne profit. 1624 BP. MOUNTAGU *Immed. Addr.* 51 Were our desires granted vs,..it would sort vnto our hurt and vtter vndoing.

† **c.** To turn out so as to answer or be agreeable *to* one's wish, desire, etc. *Obs.*

1592 *Soliman & Pers.* II. i. 238 Gentlemen, each thing hath sorted to our wish. 1606 G. WOODCOCK *Hist. Iustine* I. 5 Thinking that..the thing would so come to passe, as..afterward sorted to their desired wish. 1650 VAUGHAN *Anthroposophia* 2 These Indeavours sorting not to my purpose, I quitted this Booke-businesse.

† **d.** To fall *to* a person as a right or duty. *Obs.*

1622 DRAYTON *Poly-olb.* xxii. 634 To Salsbury it sorts the palm away to bear. *a* 1677 BARROW *Serm.* (1687) I. 142 The duties which upon that occasion are signified to concern people then, do no less now sort to us.

8. *trans.* To answer or correspond to, to fit or suit. Now *rare*.

1587 GOLDING *De Mornay* Ep. Ded., Well sorting your place and dignitie. 1603 KNOLLES *Hist. Turks* (1621) 380 Which not sorting his desire, the matter was again brought to parle. 1615 BRATHWAIT *Strappado* (1878) 126 To imitate all formes, shapes, habits, tyres Suting the Court, and sorting his desires. 1882 H. S. HOLLAND *Logic & Life* (1885) 22 Certain phenomena..which no other name suits or sorts.

II. 9. *trans.* To arrange (things, etc.) according to kind or quality, or after some settled order or system; to separate and put into different sorts or classes; to classify; to assort.

c 1358 [see SORTING *vbl. sb.*]. *c* 1440 *Promp. Parv.* 465/2 Soortyn, or settyn yn a soorte, *sortior*. 1482 *Rolls of Parlt.* VI. 221/2 That the Samon should be wele and truly packed and sorted in the same vessells. 1483 *Act 1 Rich. III*, c. 8 Preamble, Greate quantite of Wolles..which ben sorted the better from the worse, barbed and clakked. 1523 FITZHERB. *Husb.* § 134 Than sorte the trees, the polles by them-selfe, the myddel sorte by them-selfe. 1581 MULCASTER *Positions* xxxvii. (1887) 155 The maister..is no absolute potentate, to sorte mens children, as he liketh best. 1605 HEYWOOD *If you Know not me* Wks. 1874 I. 283 Past eight a clocke and neither ware sorted, Nor shop swept. 1684 in 3rd *Rep. Hist. MSS. Comm.* 427/1 Wee have sorted what papers we could at present find. 1718 *Free-thinker* No. 11. 71 Letters of every Kind come..which I sort according to their different Complexions. 1765 *Phil. Trans.* LV. 206 Mr. Rouse..invented a machine for sorting woollen thread upon the same principle with this. 1840 MARRYAT *Poor Jack* xiv, I found her..busy sorting a lot of old bottles. 1888 F. HUME *Mme. Midas* I. ii, When the office was empty, Slivers would go on sorting the scrip on his table.

absol. 1625 B. JONSON *Staple of N.* I. ii, They manage all at home, and sort, and file, And seale the newes, and issue them. 1847 *Jrnl. R. Agric. Soc.* VIII. I. 7 The breed..was left to chance or the management of shepherds, with whom it could not be a matter of interest to sort or improve.

b. Const. with advs. or preps., as *asunder, in* or *into* (sets or classes, etc.), etc.

1530 PALSGR. 725, I sorte a sonder the good from the badde, *je esplusche*. 1533 MORE *Answ. Poysoned Bk.* Wks. 1097/1 Al whych thinges I wil sort into theyr places. 1608 WILLET *Hexapla Exod.* 604 The other two curtains were sorted fiue and sixe together. 1644 MILTON *Areop.* (Arb.) 45 Those confused seeds which were impos'd on Psyche as an incessant labour to cull out, and sort asunder. 1688 *Lett. conc. Present State Italy* 99 The People are sorted in several Fraternities. 1885 *Manch. Exam.* 16 Mar. 5/2 A power of analysis..which would equip a mathematician is requisite to sort the material into order.

† **c.** To separate or distinguish (*from* something else). *Obs. rare.*

1551 T. WILSON *Logike* (1580) 61 b, We open the doubtfulnesse..of some woorde or sentence, by makyng a distinction ..and seuerally sortyng suche thynges, as then were thought to be euill set together. 1587 FLEMING *Contn. Holinshed* III. 1349/2, I meane so as physicke is now taken separatelie from surgerie, and that part which onelie vseth the band as it is sorted from the apothecarie. 1599 SHAKS. *Hen. V*, IV. vii. 77 That we may wander ore this bloody field,..To sort our Nobles from our common men.

10. To place in a class or sort; to give a place to; to classify. Also const. *after, among, as, together.*

1486 *Bk. St. Albans, Hawking* d iij, Thay [bells] be passing goode, for thay be wele sortid, well sownded. 1523 SKELTON *Garl. Laurel* 1280 Why shulde she take shame That her goodly name..Shulde be set and sortyd, To be matriculate With ladyes of astate? 1581 MULCASTER *Positions* xxxvi. (1887) 135 That wittes well sorted be most ciuill. 1595 *Locrine* I. i. 136 If thou follow sacred virtue's lore Thou shalt be..Sorted among the glorious happy ones. 1613 CHAPMAN *Maske Inns Crt.* Plays 1873 III. 92 After them were sorted two Cars Triumphall. 1626 BACON *Sylva* § 340 Mosse..may be better sorted as a Rudiment of Germination. 1687 TILLOTSON *Barrow's Wks.* I. Pref., The eight following Sermons are likewise sorted together. 1768–74 TUCKER *Lt. Nat.* (1834) I. 124 Sorting them together in a manner not done before.

b. Const. *with*.

1599 DAVIES *Immort. Soul* I. iii. (1714) 20 When she sorts Things present with Things past. 1607 *Scholast. Disc. agst. Antichrist* I. i. 50 The Crosse sorteth vs with the Papists, as much as the Garland sorted the Christians with the Pagans. 1669 STURMY *Mariner's Mag.* VII. iv. 8 This Dial..should be sorted rather with the Æquinoctial Dials, than with the Horizontal. *a* 1703 BURKITT *On N. T.* Mark xv. 37 It had been a sufficient disparagement to our Blessed Saviour to have been sorted with the best of men. 1876 GEO. ELIOT *Dan. Der.* i, A bony, yellow, crab-like hand.., a hand easy to sort with the square gaunt face.

11. With *out*. To take *out*, remove, or separate (certain sorts from others).

1534 MORE *Comf. agst. Trib.* II. Wks. 1177/2 The tother kynde is thys whych I rehersed second, and sorttyng out the tother twayne, haue kepte it for the last. 1601 DENT *Pathw. Heaven* 259 Thirdly, let there be sorted out all Hypocrites ..and cold Christians. 1728 CHAMBERS *Cycl.* s.v. *Herring*, These..are carefully sorted out. 1790 BURKE *Fr. Rev.* 187 They will sort out the good from the evil. 1868 LOCKYER *Guillemin's Heavens* (ed. 3) 393 There has not yet been time to sort out the real from the apparent nebulæ.

b. To choose or select in this way. Now *rare* or *Obs.*

1553 BALE *Vocacyon* in *Harl. Misc.* (Malh.) I. 330 God sorted me out, and appointed me from my mothers wombe. 1576 FLEMING *Panopl. Epist.* 441 You shall viewe..comely shapes,..suche as be chosen, picked, and sorted out for the nonce. 1606 DAY *Ile Gulls* I. iii, Sort out but fit time and opportunity. 1818 SCOTT *Hrt. Midl.* xxi, Few folk but mysell could hae sorted ye out a seat like this.

c. To divide or separate *into* smaller parts, etc. *Obs. rare.*

1546 BALE *Eng. Votaries* I. (1560) 12 For of [= by] them.. were the Iles of the Gentiles sorted out into regions. *c* 1580 T. DIGGES in *Archæol.* XI. 230 That waste vnder the castle, which beinge sorted out into convenient streetes [etc.].

d. To arrange according to sort.

1713 *Guardian* No. 120 (1756) II. 143 Her faculties are employed in shuffling, cutting, dealing, and sorting out a pack of cards. 1852 MRS. STOWE *Uncle Tom's C.* xii. 103 The other lady, sorting out some worsteds on her lap. 1862 SPENCER *First Princ.* II. xxi. § 165 (1875) 468 The waves are ever sorting-out and separating the mixed materials against which they break.

12. *refl.* **a.** To form sets or groups by some process of combination or separation.

1570–6 LAMBARDE *Peramb. Kent* (1826) 338 A Torneament ..in which the English men, of a set purpose,..sorted themselves against the strangers. 1601 HOLLAND *Pliny* II. 238 For the most part they sort themselues by couples like man and wife. 1692 R. L'ESTRANGE *Josephus, Antiq.* II. v. (1733) 34 They had their times of talking, and sorting themselves together. 1726 DE FOE *Hist. Devil* I. x. (1840) 132 The people necessarily sorted themselves into families and tribes after the confusion of languages. 1760–72 H. BROOKE *Fool of Qual.* (1809) IV. 55 The crowd had sorted themselves, the principals..into one groupe, the young men into another, and the fair maidens into another.

b. To associate or consort *with* another or others. (Cf. 19.) Also with *among*(*st*). Now *dial.* (freq. in 17th cent.).

1579 TOMSON *Calvin's Serm. Tim.* 1051/1 We see that S. Pauls meaning was by this word Common faith, to sort himself quietly with the rest. 1592 *Conspir. for Pretended Reform.* 1 They..willingly sorted themselues in familiaritie with such. 1642 D. ROGERS *Naaman* 36 Shall I..sort myselfe with such as are enemies? 1691 WOOD *Ath. Oxon.* I. 23 He found out Will. Tyndale in Germany, with whom for a time he sorted himself. *a* 1713 ELLWOOD *Autobiog.* (1714) 7, I always sorted myself with Persons of Ingenuity, Temperance, and Sobriety. 1877 in PEACOCK *Manley Gloss.*

13. To adapt, to fit, to make conformable *to* or *with* some thing or person. Now *rare* or *Obs.*

(*a*) 1561 in Tytler *Hist. Scot.* (1864) III. 147 In sorting your entertainment to every person. 1595 GOODWINE *Contin. Blanchardyn* (1890) 216 It hath pleased God to sorte our haps to our harts contentments. 1629 W. SCLATER *Exp. 1 Thess.* (1629) 509 Gods precepts..must be sorted to their seasons. 1822 AINSLIE *Land of Burns* 135 My auld crazy voice is better sorted to hammeart lilts than sic fine springs.

(*b*) 1591 SHAKS. *Two Gent.* I. iii. 63 My will is something sorted with his wish. 1607 DEKKER & WEBSTER *Sir T. Wyatt* D ij b, My lookes (my loue) is sorted with my heart. 1640 tr. *Verdere's Rom. of Rom.* II. 167 If I were at any time to bow unto the affection of a mortall wight, I should never chuse any other to sort my greatnesse withall.

† **b.** To bring *to* an end, effect, etc. *Obs.*

1591 *Troub. Raigne K. John* (1611) 38 Now euery thing is sorted to this end, Let's in. 1597 *Certain Prayers* in *Liturg. Serv. Eliz.* (1847) 677 Lord,..who by thy mighty power sortest to what effect thou wilt the counsels and actions of all men. 1632 LITHGOW *Trav.* III. 117 The diuine Maiestie doth swey the moments of things, and sorteth them in peremptory manner to..vnlooked for effects.

† **14.** To choose or select (time, opportunity, etc.) as fitting or suitable. *Obs.*

Freq. passing into the sense of 'to arrange, contrive, find, etc.'

1591 SHAKS. *1 Hen. VI*, II. iii. 27 I'll sort some other time to visit you. 1592 KYD *Sp. Trag.* IV. iv. 103 They had sorted leasure, To take aduantage..Upon my Sonne. 1624 HEYWOOD *Gunaik.* IV. 193 The young man's father, who sorted opportunitie to talke with his sonne. 1634 — & BROME *Lanc. Witches* II. H.'s Wks. 1874 IV. 192 What times hath she sorted for these journeyes?

† **b.** To choose (a thing or person) from others.

1591 SHAKS. *Two Gent.* III. ii. 92 Let vs into the City presently To sort some Gentlemen, well skil'd in Musicke. 1592 — *Rom. & Jul.* IV. ii. 34 To helpe me sort such needfull ornaments, As you thinke fit to furnish me. 1638 FORD *Lady's Trial* I. i, Ere now You might haue sorted me in your resolves, Companion of your fortunes.

15. To furnish, provide, or supply (a person, etc.) *with* (or *of*) something. In later use only *Sc.*

1598 BARRETT *Theor. Warres* I. i. 4 The strength of the Battaile is the armed Pike, so they be equally sorted with Harquebuze and Musket. *Ibid.* II. i. 26 How would you haue a Companie sorted with weapons? 1600 DYMMOK *Ireland* (1843) 14 It is well sorted with woodes and playnes. 1774 KEITH *Farmer's Ha'* xxvii, He tells them he's weel sorted now Of a' thing gude, and cheap, and new. 1825 JAMIESON *Suppl.* s.v., I can sort ye wi' a knife. 1898 LD. E. HAMILTON *Mawkin* xv. 200, I warrant we'll sort you with another, and as good a yin too.

16. *Sc.* and *north.* **a.** (Also with *up*.) To arrange or put in order; to put to rights in some respect.

The leading variations of sense are more fully illustrated in the *Eng. Dial. Dict.*

(*a*) 1827 CARLYLE *Germ. Rom.* IV. 45 Mine host has already in my presence begun sorting the apartment as if I were gone. 1833 LOUDON *Encycl. Archit.* § 81 The whole [roofing] to be laid with a sufficient lap, and to be carefully sorted in courses (laid so as that the joints may form regular lines). 1876 ROBINSON *Whitby Gloss.* s.v., 'Get all your things sorted up,' collected together.

absol. 1892 N. DICKSON *Kirk Beadle* 109 The preacher returned to the church and found the beadle busy 'sorting up'.

(*b*) 1816 SCOTT *Antiq.* xliii, The provost's gar'd the beacon light on the Halket-head be sorted up (that suld hae been sorted half a year syne). 1876 WHITEHEAD *Daft Davie*, etc. 121 The wick needed sorting, and the oil was low. 1877 FRASER *Wigtown* 62 Belsher..was once engaged sorting the lock of a cell in the Prison.

(*c*) 1816 SCOTT *Antiq.* xv, The powny hasna gane abune thirty mile the day;—Jock was sorting him up as I came ower by. 1816 — *Old Mort.* xxxvii, 'Ye may rely on your naig being weel sorted,' said Cuddie; 'I ken weel what belangs to suppering a horse'. 1868 VERNEY *Stone Edge* vii, Lydia was out in the farmyard 'sorting' the cows herself.

(*d*) 1817 *Lintoun Green* 166 Nor he is here tae sort me right. 1866 MISS MULOCK *Noble Life* iv. 61 She lifted up the poor child, tenderly and carefully—shook his pillows and 'sorted' him. 1890 NISBET *Bail up!* xxviii, Let me sort you up a little.

b. To deal effectively with (a person) by way of punishment, repression, etc.

1815 SCOTT *Guy M.* xxxiii, Bid them bring up the prisoner —I trow I'll sort him. 1825– in Sc. and north dial. glossaries and texts. 1878 A. R. HOPE *My Schoolboy Fr.* 265 'I will sort this Ghost,' said Kennedy.

17. In commercial use: To bring *up* to the usual stock or quantity.

1880 *Daily News* 15 Nov. 3/5 The orders..are merely to enable them to sort up sizes.

III. 18. *intr.* To suit, fit, or agree; to be in harmony or conformity. Const. *with*, † *to*, or † *together*. Now *arch.*

(*a*) 1590 SHAKS. *Mids. N.* v. i. 55 That is some Satire keene and criticall, Not sorting with a nuptiall ceremonie. 1599 — *Hen. V*, IV. i. 63 My name is Pistol call'd. *King.* It sorts well with your fiercenesse. 1610 W. FOLKINGHAM *Art of Survey* I. x. 33 Dry Marle sortes with moist Soiles. *a* 1652 BROME *Queenes Exch.* I. i. Wks. 1873 III. 460 Their Petulances sort not with this place. 1699 PEPYS in *Diary & Corr.* (1879) VI. 215 Of which book it would greatly sort with my Collection that I had a copy. 1709 POPE *Ess. Crit.* 322 For diff'rent styles with diff'rent subjects sort. 1780 COWPER *Progr. Error* 446 The text that sorts not with his darling whim, Though plain to others, is obscure to him. 1827 HARE *Guesses* (1859) 4 The vastness and awfulness of a mere sea-view would ill sort with the other parts of the..prospect. 1858 H. BUSHNELL *Nature & Supernat.* xi. (1864) 333 The miracles sort with the person of Christ and his mission. 1891 R. W. CHURCH *Oxford Movem.* xi. 178 However ill it might sort with the current language of Protestant controversy.

(*b*) 1590 GREENE *Orl. Fur.* Wks. (Rtldg.) 92 Mine emblem sorteth to another sense. 1604 BP. W. BARLOW *Sum Conf. Hampton Crt.* 27 They appeared before his Maiestie, in Turky gownes, not in their Scholastical habites, sorting to their degrees. 1651 *Sir W. Rawleigh's Ghost* Pref., A careless and pleasurable life, best sorting to our own desires and sen-suality. 1709 MRS. MANLEY *Secret Mem.* (1720) II. 248 Yet sorting to his Humour, we will not ask thee to give him too diffusive a Brightness.

(*c*) 1600 HOLLAND *Livy* XLIV. xxiv. 1185 A free citie and a King were,..by nature, enemies that possibly could not sort together. 1641 MILTON *Reform.* II. Wks. 1851 III. 58 Wee see that our Ecclesiall and Politicall choyses may consent and sort as well together..as Christians, and Freeholders.

† **b.** Without const. To be fitting; to accord; to be in place, to exist. *Obs.*

1593 SHAKS. *3 Hen. VI*, II. i. 209 The Queene is comming with a puissant Hoast... *War.* Why then it sorts, braue Warriors, let's away. 1606 — *Tr. & Cr.* I. i. 110 *Æneas.* Wherefore not a field? *Troy.* Because not there; this womans answer sorts. For womanish it is to be from thence. 1633 FORD *Broken H.* I. i, Some one, he is assur'd, may now and then (If opportunity but sort) preuaile. 1667 MILTON *P. L.* VIII. 384 Among unequals what societie Can sort, what harmonie or true delight?

c. *Sc.* To come to an agreement or settlement; to come to terms (*on* something).

1685 PEDEN in Walker *Life* (1827) 95 If ye be pleased with the Wares,..he and ye will soon sort on the Price. 1814 SCOTT *Wav.* xviii, I cannot tell you precisely how they sorted; but they agreed sae right that [etc.].

19. To associate, consort, go in company *with* others or *together*. (Cf. 12 b.) Also with *among* and without const. Now *rare* or *dial.*

(*a*) 1592 SHAKS. *Ven. & Ad.* 689 Sometime he runs among a flock of sheep.., And sometime sorteth with a herd of deer. 1612 BACON *Ess., Par. & Childr.* (Arb.) 274 The illiberality of Parents..towards their children..makes them..sort with meane companie. 1685 BURNET tr. *More's Utop.* 105 They should sort with another kind of Ministers. 1720 DE FOE *Capt. Singleton* xiii. (1840) 228 He went over to Captain Avery, and sorted with his people. 1784 COWPER *Tiroc.* 114 Too careless often as our years proceed, What friends we sort with, or what books we read. 1805–6 CARY *Dante, Inf.* xv. 120 A company, with whom I may not sort. 1886 ELWORTHY *W. Somerset Word-bk.* 695, I never don't try vor to sort wi' my betters.

transf. 1695 WOODWARD *Nat. Hist. Earth* IV. (1723) 193 Nor do Metalls only sort and herd with Metalls in the Earth.

(*b*) 1601 HOLLAND *Pliny* I. 233 That willingly these little creatures will not sort together vnlesse they be counter-trimen as it were. *Ibid.* 278 What fowles soeuer have crooked clawes sort not together in flocks. 1651 HOBBES *Leviath.* ... *State Nat.* 40 Men are apt to sort, to herd. 1709 MRS. MANLEY *Secret Mem.* (1720) II. 253 Thus could I imagine what genteel..Company would suffer him to sort with them? 1819 W. TENNANT *Papistry Storm'd* (1827) 77 He did dislike baith Pape and Deil; (Thir twa they sortit weil).

† **Sort**, *v.*[2] *Sc. Obs.* [ad. F. *sortir*, of doubtful origin.] *intr.* To sally out; to make a sortie.

1571 BANNATYNE *Jrnl.* (1806) 248 They of Edinburgh cvme furth hors and fute..; and they of Leyth..sortit. 1584 HUDSON *Du Bartas' Judith* VI. (1608) 93 The warriours strong, That kept the towne, now sorted furth in throng. *a* 1600 *Hist. Jas. Sext* (Bannatyne Club) 74 The regent sortit from Hammilton upon the 13 day of May [...] towart Dumbartan. *Ibid.* 98 The same was seen by the people of Edinburgh, that thair horsemen sortit [...].

Sortable, *a.* *Obs.* exc. *dial.* Also 6 **sortible**, 9 *dial.* **soortable**. [a. F. *sortable* (15th cent.), or f. SORT *v.*[1] + -ABLE.]

† **1.** Suitable, appropriate; fit or befitting. Usu. const. *to* (or *unto*). *Obs.*

1586 FERNE *Blaz. Gentrie* 339 To serue him in any seruice or office,..suche as be sortible to his degree. 1603 HOLLAND *Plutarch's Mor.* 1329 The Moone: which they seeing to be so subject to growing and decreasing..thought ..to be sortable unto the mutability of the Dæmons kinde. 1621 SANDERSON *Serm.* I. 196 There are generous and ingenuous and liberal employments, sortable to the greatest births and educations. *a* 1663 SIR K. DIGBY *Priv. Mem.* (1827) 17 Recreations..sortable to their age. 1818 SCOTT *Rob Roy* xxxiv, It's a pity his Excellency is a thought.. The like o' yoursell, or my son Hamish, wad be mair sortable in point of years.

2. *north. dial.* Capable of going together.

1641 BEST *Farm. Bks.* (Surtees) 110 In the choice of good deales,..that they bee sortable, i.e. all of one length, all of one breadth, and all of one thicknesse. 1876 ROBINSON *Whitby Gloss.* 180/1 *Soortable*, accordant or comformable.

† **3.** Of a cargo: Properly assorted; composed of suitable sorts. *Obs.*

1727 DE FOE *Tour Gt. Brit., Scotl.* 90 The Scots Merchants are at no Loss how to make up sortable Cargoes to send with their Ships to the Plantations. 1727 — *Eng. Tradesm.* viii. (1732) I. 84 When merchants send adventures to the colonies, 'tis usual with them to make up to each factor what they call a *sortable cargo*. 1818 SCOTT *Rob Roy* xxvi, The facilities which Glasgow possessed of making up sortable cargoes for that market.

Hence † **So·rtably** *adv. Obs.*

1607 in Plomer *Abstr. fr. Wills Eng. Printers* (1903) 42 If..Nicholas Bourne shall..take so manie bookes of mine thorough out all my warehouses as they shall sortably [...]. HIERON *Defence* III. 7 Shall not he who is a Christ at his table cary himselfe sortably to the [...] of coheir? 1611 COTGR., *Sortablement*, sortably, fitly.

† **Sortal**, *a. Obs.*[−1] [f. SORT *sb.*[2] + -AL.] Of or belonging to a particular sort or kind.

1690 LOCKE *Hum. Und.* III. iii. (1695) 231 That abstract Idea, which the General, or *Sortal* (if I may have leave so to call it from *Sort*, as I do *General* from *Genus*) Name stands for.

† **Sortance**. *Obs.*[−1] [f. SORT *v.*[1] + -ANCE.] Agreement, correspondence.

1597 SHAKS. *2 Hen. IV*, IV. i. 11 Here doth hee wish his Person, with such Powers As might hold sortance with his Qualitie, The which hee could not leuie.

‖ **Sortant**, *a.* *rare*[−0]. [F., pr. pple. of *sortir* SORT *v.*[2]] Of an angle: = SALIENT *a.*, the same as SALIENT ANGLE.

1842 GWILT *Archit.* Gloss., *Sortant Angle*, the same as *Salient Angle*.

Sortation (sǭɹtēⁱ·ʃən). [f. SORT *v.*[1]: see -ATION.] The action or process of arranging or sorting; arrangement, classification.

1844 *5th Rep. Dep. Kpr. Rec.* 6 The sortation [...] has been begun. 1885 J. W. HYDE *Royal Mail* xi. 164 Thus it will be seen that the sortation of letters is no mere mechanical process.

attrib. 1899 J. A. HARVIE-BROWN (*title*), On a Correct Colour Code or Sortation Code in Colours.

Sorte, obs. form of SHORT *a.*

Sortebrand, obs. form of SURTURBRAND.

Sorted (sǭ·ɹtéd), *ppl. a.* [f. SORT *v.*[1] Cf. ILL-SORTED *a.*]

1. Picked, chosen, selected.

1547 *Cal. Pat. Rolls Irel.* I. (1861) 154 A convenient number of sorted men for the relief of the Lord Deputy. 1632 HEYWOOD *2nd Pt. Iron Age* Ded., If you persist in the same opinion, when you shall spare some sorted houres to heare it read. 1839 URE *Dict. Arts* 812 The pure ore, or at least the very rich portion, called the *sorted mine*. 1844 MRS. BROWNING *Vis. Poets* cxcv, A company came up the aisle With measured step and sorted smile.

2. Assorted; arranged, classified.

1697 DRYDEN *Virg. Past.* Pref. (1721) I. 93 A curious Parterre of sorted Flowers. 1722 DE FOE *Col. Jack* (1840) 167 A sorted cargo of goods. 1784 COWPER *Task* III. 634 Grateful mixture of well-match'd And sorted hues. 1891 *Daily News* 2 Mar. 2/2 The sorted papers are thrown into different hoppers.

Sortely, obs. form of SHORTLY *adv.*

Sorter (sǭ·ɹtəɹ). [f. SORT *v.*[1] + -ER.]

1. One who sorts, arranges, selects, or classifies; *esp.* a wool-sorter. Also *transf.*

1554 *Act 1 Mary* c. 7 § 1 Forcers of Wolles..and Sorters of Wolles. 1562 J. HEYWOOD *Prov. & Epigr.* (1867) 201 The tounge is assinde, of woordes to be sorter. 1758 JORTIN *Life Erasmus* I. 488 It is plain More wrote it not—and.. he says he was a sorter of that book. 1776 ADAM SMITH *W. N.* I. i. (1869) I. 11 The shepherd, the sorter of the wool, the wool-comber, or carder. 1844 G. DODD *Textile Manuf.* iii. 96 The fingers of the sorter acquire by practice an extraordinary degree of sensitiveness. 1879 *Cassell's Techn. Educ.* IV. 339/2 Wool..is..divided into 'sorts' or qualities by experienced sorters or staplers.

b. *spec.* A letter-sorter.

a 1700 B. E. *Dict. Cant. Crew*, *Sorter*, (at the Post Office) that puts or Digests the Letters into Order or Method. 1737 J. CHAMBERLAYNE *St. Gt. Brit.* II. *List Offices* [in G.P.O.] 690 Sorters 16, of which 14 have 50l. per An. and the two last 40l. 1861 WYNTER *Soc. Bees* 3 Others again..carry the letters for the general delivery to the tables of the sorters. 1895 *Forum* (U.S.) Oct. 196 A sorter at the post-office..may accidentally sort one letter of his own out of a million.

2. With advs., as *out*.

1599 *Life More* in C. Wordsworth *Eccl. Biog.* (1817) II. 169, I was onlie a sorter out and placer of principall matters in the same [book] contained. 1881 *Instr. Census Clerks* (1885) 65/3 Worsted Manufacture: Sorter out, Spinner.

Hence **So·rtership**, the office or position of a letter-sorter.

1886 *Guide Civil Service* 293 Competitive Examination for Female Sorterships in the General Post Office, London.

Sorter, dial. or vulgar f. *sort of*: SORT *sb.*[2] 8 c.

† **Sortfully**, *adv. Obs.*[−1] [f. SORT *sb.*[2]] In a suitable or appropriate manner.

1606 CHAPMAN *Gent. Usher* Plays 1873 I. 281 Euery thing About your house so sortfully disposde That..One vice assists another.

† **Sortiary**. *Obs. rare.* [ad. med.L. *sortiarius, -a*, f. L. *sors, sort-* SORT *sb.*[1]]

1. One who practises sortilege.

1652 GAULE *Magastrom.* 333 Numa Pompilius, a Magician or Sortiary not inferior to any. *Ibid.* 342 In France, the magicians, astrologers, sortiaries, sorcerers, wizzards, and witches were so numerous [etc.].

2. = SORTILEGE[1] 1.

1653 GATAKER *Vind. Annot. Jer.* 3 No more then it is requisite for one to be over-much seen in geomancie, palmistrie, sortiarie, auspicie, or aruspicie.

‖ **Sortie** (sǭ·ɹtī), *sb.* Also 7 **sorti**. [F. *sortie* a going out, etc., f. *sortir* SORT *v.*[2]]

† **1.** (See quot. 1690.) *Obs.*

1690 ? EVELYN *Mundus Muliebris* 20 *Sorti*, a little Knot of small Ribbon, peeping out between the Pinner and Bonnet. *c* 1690 *Songs & Poems Costume* (Percy Soc.) 200 Her shabbarons next I'll show, Her sortie, and patches of black.

2. A dash or sally by a besieged garrison upon an investing force. Freq. in phr. *to make a sortie*.

1795 SEWARD *Anecd.* II. 217 If the enemy..thought fit to make any sortie from the town. 1811 WELLINGTON in Gurw. *Desp.* (1837) VII. 285 In case your *sortie* should succeed (which will place the war on its legs again in the best manner). 1843 PRESCOTT *Mexico* VI. vi. (1864) 386 To repel the sorties, made..by the militia of the capital. 1874 GREEN *Short Hist.* viii. § 9 A sortie from Dublin had already broken up Ormond's siege of the capital.

transf. 1827 SCOTT *Jrnl.* 2 Jan., The rheumatism, exasperated by my sortie of yesterday, has seized on my..knee. 1831 GREVILLE *Mem.* (1875) II. xiii. 119 She was mighty glorious about her *sortie* upon Lambton. 1859 *Once a Week* I. 455 He made a sortie from the box like a lion rushing into the circus.

b. Without article.

1845 D. COSTELLO *Tour Valley Meuse* 156 Subterraneous passages..used for sortie and retreat by the garrison of the castle.

c. *attrib.*, as *sortie corvette, party*.

1887 *Pall Mall G.* 11 Jan. 2/1, I am not..aware that Germany..proposes to employ 'sortie corvettes' in the absence of guns or submarine mines. 1896 MORRISON *Child Jago* iv, The defeated sortie-party from Jago Court.

3. a. A sally-port. **b.** An outlet (of a river).

1848 LYTTON *Harold* XII. vii, Three sorties, whence the defenders might sally. 1879 *19th Cent.* 1121 The Kalamas has its sortie opposite Corfu.

‖ **Sortie**, *v.* Also **sorty-**. [f. prec.] *intr.* To make a sortie; to sally. Hence **Sortieing** *ppl. a.*

1871 *Standard* 27 Jan., Pressing on, the sortying party advanced up the heights. 1899 *Westm. Gaz.* 23 Nov. 7/2 Unsuccessful attempts to sortie are supposed to have been made. 1904 *Daily Chron.* 23 May 5/1 To cover the movements of the sortieing force.

Sortilege[1] (sǭ·ɹtiledʒ). Also 5 **sortylege**. [a. OF. *sortilege* (mod.F. *sortilège*, = It., Sp., Pg. *sortilegio*), or ad. med.L. *sortilegium*, f. L. *sortilegus*: see next.]

1. The practice of casting lots in order to decide something or to forecast the future; divination based on this procedure or performed in some other way; † sorcery, magic, witchcraft.

1387 TREVISA *Higden* (Rolls) II. 43 In þat ilond is sortilege and wicchecraft i-vsed. For wommen þere selliþ schipmen wynde. 1430–40 LYDG. *Bochas* VI. iv. (1554) 142 He delited most..In sortilege and in sorcerye. 1483 CAXTON *Cato* F ij, This cursyd synne of sortylege haboundeth more in wymmen than in men. 1546 BALE *Eng. Votaries* I. 35 b, He sett vp a great scole at Caunterburye..and taught them..the art Magyck, Sortilege, Physnomye. 1584 R. SCOT *Discov. Witchcr.* XI. x. (1886) 159 The cousening art of sortilege or lotarie. 1730 BAILEY (fol.), *Sortilege*, a Soothsaying or Divination by Lots; also an Electing by casting of Lots. 1830 SCOTT *Demonol.* ii. 66 They endeavoured by sortilege..to find as it were a byroad to the secrets of futurity. 1850 MERIVALE *Rom. Emp.* vi. (1865) I. 275 Three times, he related, had lots been drawn;..each time he had owed his life to the chance of sortilege. 1881 STANLEY *Christ. Instit.* v. 87 Signs of what most Christians now would regard as mere remnants of sortilege and sorcery.

2. An act or instance of divining, choosing, or deciding by the drawing or casting of lots.

1600 HOLLAND *Livy* XLIV. xxii. 1183 As the gods in favour have directed this sortilege, so they will been present and propitious unto mee. 1795 WYTHE *Decis.* 104 Another lottery, according to which the destiny of every ticket ought to have been decided by a single sortilege. 1819 SCOTT *Ivanhoe* xxxvii, A woman infamous for sortileges and for witcheries. 1842 *Blackw. Mag.* LI. 282 All treasonable assumptions..commenced in the hopes inspired by auguries, prophecies, or sortileges. 1868 MILMAN *St. Paul's* ii. 20 All sortileges, auspices, divinations, and other works of the devil, were forbidden.

Sortilege[2]. *rare.* [ad. L. *sortileg-us* diviner, fortune-teller, f. *sort-, sors* lot + *legĕre* to choose. Cf. obs. F. *sortilegue*, It., Sp., Pg. *sortilego*.] One who practises divination or sorcery.

1483 CAXTON *Cato* Contents iv b, Ageynst them that ben sortileges of herbes and of wrytynges for to hele men or horses. *Ibid.* F j b, To the ende that none sette feythe to sortyleges ne to deuyners. 1855 MILMAN *Lat. Chr.* V. XI. ix. 253 He is a sortilege, and consults diviners and fortunetellers.

Sortileger. Now *rare.* Also 5 **sortyloger**, **-leger**. [See prec. and -ER. The form in *-loger* is based upon the med.L. *sortilogus* for *sortilegus*.] One who divines, chooses, or settles by drawing lots or otherwise; a diviner, fortune-teller.

c 1400 *Apol. Loll.* 54 Fraudars, misdoars, sortylogers. *Ibid.* 97 Sortilegeris, and oþer þat are put in þe general sentens and cursing of þe kirk. 1483 CAXTON *Cato* F ij, Often God permytteth and suffreth that, that the sortylegers and devynours maken to come. 1635 HEYWOOD *Hierarchy* I. Comm. 47 We read of three sorts of these Sortilegers or Fortune-tellers. *Ibid.* VII. Comm. 473 Now to speake of those Sortilegers and the effects of their Art. 1864 A. LEIGHTON *Myst. Leg. Edinb.* (1886) 224 All which signs seemed only the opportunity of the devout sortileger, who put her hand upon the Bible.

Sortile·gic, *a. rare.* [f. SORTILEGE[1] + -IC.] Dependent upon divination or sortilege.

1896 *17th Ann. Rep. Bureau Amer. Ethnol.* I. 259 The warfare of the Seri is largely sortilegic.

Sortile·gious, *a.* ? *Obs.* [f. SORTILEGE[1] or SORTILEGY.] Of the nature of, relating to or connected with, sortilege.

1603 SIR C. HEYDON *Jud. Astrol.* i. 12 Diuinations that were meerely superstitious, sortilegious, and diuellish. 1652 GAULE *Magastrom.* 29 But were all they of Babylon solely and wholly trained up to this sortilegious trade? *a* 1717 DAUBREZ *Rev.* (Lancaster, 1730) 46 Horace..makes their [*sc.* frogs] Blood an Ingredient in sortilegious Charms.

Sortilegist. *rare*[−1]. [f. SORTILEGE[1] + -IST.] One who arranges the drawing of lots.

1865 *Reader* 25 Nov. 598/1 This college sortilegist pretended to be much annoyed at the result he had taken such pains to procure.

‖ **Sortile·gium**. *rare.* = SORTILEGY 2.

1858 BAILEY *Age* 65 Suppose we try a sortilegium, eh?

Sortilegy (sǭɹti·lėdʒi, sǭ·ɹtiledʒi). Also 4–5 **sortelegye, -legie** (**-logie**), 6 **sortilegie**, 7 **-ligie**. [ad. med.L. *sortilegi-um*: see SORTILEGE[1].]

1. Divination by the casting or drawing of lots or otherwise; = SORTILEGE[1] 1.

1387 TREVISA *Higden* (Rolls) I. 411 Oft gyled was this brood,..For Merlyns prophecie, And ofte for sortelogie [*v.r.* sortelegie]. 1584 R. SCOT *Discov. Witchcr.* XIII. xxix. (1886) 278 The Aegyptians juggling witchcraft or Sortilegie. 1680 C. NESSE *Ch. Hist.* 269 He had by his sortilegy, or rather sorcery, found out his lucky day. 1839 DE QUINCEY *Mod. Superst.* Wks. 1853 III. 307 That mode of sortilegy which is conducted by throwing open priviledged books at random. 1883 J. PAYN *Thicker than Water* xxviii, Miss Blithers the elder, who believed in sortilegy, presented her with a tract, drawn at random from a whole sheaf of them.

2. An act or instance of this; = SORTILEGE[1] 2.

1643 SIR T. BROWNE *Relig. Med.* I. § 18. 39 Even in sortilegies and matters of greatest uncertainty, there is a setled and preordered course of effects. 1656 S. HOLLAND *Zara* (1719) 28 When that venerable Quack sold his Brethrens lives (by a Sortiligie) to save his own.

Sorting (sǭ·ɹtiŋ), *vbl. sb.* Also 4–5 **sortyng**, 5 *Sc.* **-en**, 6 **soorting**. [f. SORT *v.*[1] + -ING[1].]

1. The action of the vb., in various senses; arrangement, classification.

c 1358 *Durham Acc. Rolls* (Surtees) 561 Will'o Randman pro pylyng et sortyng lane. 1485 *Act 1 Hen. VII*, c. 10 § 7 The same Wolle shuld be..clene wounde, withoute any sortyng, barbyng or clakkyng. 1494 *Acc. Ld. High Treas. Scot.* I. 248 Giffyne for sorten of the tymmyr in the 3ard, iij s. iij d. 1554 *Act 1 Mary* c. 7 § 1 The..principall grounde of Clothmaking ys the true sorting of Wolles. 1599 B. JONSON *Cynthia's Rev.* v. iv, It is the sorting, and the dividing,..and the decocting, that makes the fumigation. 1625 MARKHAM *Souldier's Accid.* 1 For the Sorting of Armes, it is a good proportion to haue a Companie equally compounded of Armed men and Shot. 1690 LOCKE *Hum. Und.* III. iii. (1695) 230 The Essences of the sorts of Things, and consequently the sorting of Things, is the Workmanship of the Understanding. 1711 ADDISON *Spect.* No. 10 ¶ 6 The sorting of a Suit of Ribbons. 1765 *Phil. Trans.* LV. 205 In sorting, the skain to be examined is put upon the hook. 1856 DE QUINCEY in 'H. A. Page' *Life* (1877) II. xvii. 51 The separation and sorting of such innumerable papers. 1892 *Athenæum* 23 Apr. 530/1 We have..a little too much mere sorting of the varied intellectual material.

2. With *a* and pl. An instance of this.

1611 COTGR., *Assortissement*,..a sorting, or suiting of things together. 1764 *Museum Rust.* II. 38, I divide my fruit into three several sorts..; from these three sortings I have ..six several kinds of cyder. 1839 URE *Dict. Arts* 812 The substances..undergo another *sorting*, with greater or less care. 1871 CARLYLE in *Mrs. C.'s Lett.* (1883) II. 362 He did for me all manner of..summaries, copyings, sortings.

b. *Sc.* An assortment, supply, stock.

a 1779 D. GRAHAM *Leper the Taylor* I. Writ. 1883 II. 116 Poor Sandy went home with a skinful of terror, and a sorting of sore bones.

3. With advs., as *out, up*.

1890 W. J. GORDON *Foundry* 76 Then came a sorting out of the juniors from the seniors. 1890 *Daily News* 16 Dec. 6/4 The higher prices..have caused a little more sorting up.

4. *attrib.*, as *sorting-action*; *sorting-boom*, † *-cloth*, † *kersey*, *-machine* (see quots.).

Also, in recent use, with advs., as *sorting-out influence, sorting-up business, order, trade*, etc.

1897 *Geogr. Jrnl.* IX. 278 One of the most remarkable phenomena attending the distribution of earthy materials by wind (or water) is the *sorting action exercised by the fluid. 1887 *Lumberman's Gaz.* 8 Dec. 362 There is a system of '*sorting booms' by which the logs, each bearing a distinguishing mark, are distributed to their several ownerships. 1593 *3rd Rep. Hist. MSS. Comm.* 7/1 Woollen cloths..called vesses,..park cloths, or *sorting cloths made in Somersetshire. 1674 JEAKE *Arith.* (1696) 68 One Sack of Wooll..is accompted to make 4. Standard Clothes of clean Wooll called sorting Clothes. 1847 HALLIW., *Sorting-cloths*, a kind of short cloths, with a blue selvage on both sides of the lists, made in the Eastern counties. 1706 PHILLIPS (ed. Kersey), **Sorting-Kersies*, a sort of Cloth so call'd. 1875 KNIGHT *Dict. Mech.* 2246/2 *Sorting-machine ..for gaging leather strips as they are cut from the hide to certain regulated sizes.

b. In the sense 'in, at, or on which sorting is done', as *sorting-board, house, office, siding*, etc.

1766 ENTICK *London* IV. 191 In which is one of the sorting houses, under the comptrolment of the general penny-post. 1851 J. MILNE *Autobiog.* iv. 100 Aberdeen has become what is termed a sorting office. 1885 BOWMAN *Struct. Wool Fibre* 358 Sorting-board, the table on which wool is sorted. 1899 *Daily News* 4 Mar. 3/2 At Woodford there are extensive sorting sidings.

Sorting, *ppl. a.* [f. SORT *v.*[1] + -ING[2].]

1. That corresponds, agrees, or suits (with others of the same class or kind).

1535 *Wardr. Kath. Arragon* 24 in *Camden Misc.* III, Item, fyve pecis of hangynges of tapistrye soorting. 1547 *Harl. MS.* 1419 *A.* lf. 38 Nyne peces sorting.., every of theym lyned with Canvas.

2. That sorts, arranges, or classifies.

1912 *Civil Service Year Bk.* 61 The..pay of a Sorting Clerk and Telegraphist.

† **Sortise**, *v. Obs.*[−1] [f. OF. *sortiss-*, lengthened stem of *sortir* SORT *v.*[1]] *trans.* To acquire, obtain.

1474 CAXTON *Chesse* IV. ii, But whan he is ones meuyd fro his propre place,..than he sortiseth the nature of the comyn peple, and thus by good right he hath in hym self the nature of al.

Sortition (sǭɹti·ʃən). [ad. L. *sortitio*, f. *sortiri* to cast or draw lots.]

1. The casting or drawing of lots; selection, choice, or determination by lot.

1597 J. KING *On Jonas* (1618) 120 For so doth Tully define Sortition, that it is nothing else but hap-hazard. 1608 — *Serm.* 24 Mar. 11 Some reigne by vsurpation,..some by acquisition,..some by sortition or augurie. 1659 HAMMOND *On Ps.* xvi. 5 The old way of sortition was by staves or rods. 1790 BURKE *Fr. Rev.* 74 No mode of election operating in the spirit of sortition or rotation. 1849 GROTE *Greece* II. xliv. V. 371 The principle of sortition or choice by lot was never applied..to all offices at Athens. 1886 *Q. Rev.* July 12 In a certain Arcadian state sortition superseded election.

2. With *a* and pl. An act or instance of determining by lot.

1634 BP. HALL *Contempl., N. T.* IV. 273 The souldiers have ..cast lots upon thy seamlesse coat (those poore spoiles cannot so much inrich them, as glorifie thee; whose Scriptures are fulfilled by their barbarous sortitions). 1634 in *4th Rep. Hist. MSS. Comm.* 127 Whether the advowsons of benefices..be not passed by balls or sortitions to private residentiaryes. 1830 W. TAYLOR *Hist. Surv. Germ. Poetry* I. 275 The scourging, the crowning with thorns, and the sortition of the garments. 1887 MISS BETHAM-EDWARDS *Next of Kin Wanted* I. xiv. 190 The transfer of the property, by a distribution, sortition, or otherwise.

† **3.** An allotted share or portion. *Obs.*

1671 [R. MACWARD] *True Noncons.* 90 The Lords People .., whether..termed..lots, in order to their respective Pastors, whose sortitions, and divisions they are, or as being Gods heritage.

Sortli, obs. form of SHORTLY *adv.*

† **Sortly**, *a. Obs. rare.* [f. SORT *sb.*[2] + -LY[1].]

1. Of articles: That correspond or form a set.

1459 *Paston Lett.* I. 474, iiij. platers, parcell of ix. platers not sortely. *Ibid.*, v. platers, not sortely.

2. Appropriate; suitable.

1570 *Wit & Science* (1848) 46 Whereby I trust by my good Endever To that good Ladye, so sweete and so sortlye, A maryage betwene them ye shall see shortlye.

† **Sortly**, *adv. Obs. rare.* [f. SORT *sb.*[2] + -LY[2].] So as to agree or correspond; correspondingly, equally.

c 1557 ABP. PARKER *Ps.* cxix. Pref., Here letters all so sortely bound do shew in mysterie Eternall health may sure be found in scripture totally. 1566 — *Corr.* (Parker Soc.) 278 They be counted sortly learned with the best of them.

† **Sortment**. *Obs.* [f. SORT *v.*[1] + -MENT. Cf. It. *sortimento*.]

1. The action or process of sorting, separating, or arranging; sortation, classification.

1598 BARRET *Theor. Warres* 69 The due sortement and matching of these weapons to offend, and defend. 1622 F. MARKHAM *Bk. War* v. iii. 170 The iust number of the Army, together with the true sortment and division of euery weapon. 1755 in JOHNSON. 1778 PRYCE *Min. Cornub.* 233 When it comes to grass they make a sortment of the larger stones from the smaller.

2. A collection of assorted goods or articles; a sorted set or lot; an assortment.

1621 in Foster *Eng. Factories Ind.* (1906) I. 326 To write the bymarke of the sortement of every chest. 1657 in *Thurloe's St. Papers* (1742) VI. 56 In March we expected most of our chiefe merchants to come out for their easter sortment, against which tyme I desired you would be pleased to give orders at Freshford. 1719 W. WOOD *Survey Trade* 246 Manufacturing and making up proper Sortments of Goods. 1766 T. BROOKS *Coins E. Indies* 67 The finest Hysons, and all other Sortments of the Green-Teas.

b. *transf.* A set or number of persons.

1710 MILBOURNE *Meas. Resist.* 4 When a sortment of priests, as he with a peculiar elegance, expresses it, endeavour to bully us into slavery. 1760–72 H. BROOKE *Fool of Qual.* (1809) II. 39 A hundred and fifty visits,..and through such a sortment too, as your mercers say.

c. A kind or class of things.

1718 QUINCY *Compl. Disp.* 8 The Lightness of this Sortment of Matter. 1720 — in *Phil. Trans.* XXXI. 76 Thus for all cutaneous Foulnesses..the Cinnabar, the Æthiops, and all of that Sortment are in readiness.

Sorty (sǭ·ɹti), *a. colloq.* [f. SORT *sb.*[2] + -Y. Cf. WFris. *soartich* of a good sort.]

1. Of one kind or sort; similar, alike.

1885 *Field* 12 Dec. 845/1 Mr. W. Wheeler's cup pigs were ..not quite sorty as to hair, but otherwise a good lot.

2. Consisting of various sorts; mixed.

1899 *Daily News* 3 July 9/7 Phipps,..usually driving blacks, has got together a very 'sorty' team composed of a skewbald, a chestnut, and bays. *a* 1904 in *Eng. Dial. Dict.* s.v., The water is very sorty this morning—it is much colder at the bottom than on the top.

‖ **Sorus**[1] (sǭ·rǝs). Pl. **sori** (sǭ·rai). [mod.L., ad. Gr. σωρός heap.]

1. *Bot.* A cluster of capsules or spore-cases on the under surface of fern-leaves.

1832 LINDLEY *Introd. Bot.* I. iii. 196 In a third tribe the sori occupy the whole of the under surface of the frond. 1857 T. MOORE *Handbk. Brit. Ferns* (ed. 3) 8 The part of the vein on which the sorus is seated. 1876 HARLEY *Royle's Mat. Med.* 360 Sori elliptical, imbedded in the substance of the thallus, concave on one side.

2. A similar formation in algæ, lichens, or fungi.

1842 *Penny Cycl.* XXII. 266/2 The term sorus is sometimes applied to mere collections of spores or granules, as seen in many Algæ, of which *Delesseria alata* and *D. sinuosa* are examples. 1874 COOKE *Fungi* 38 The pustules, or sori, break through the cuticle in a similar manner.

† **Sorus**[2], obs. variant of SORA.

1775 A. BURNABY *Trav.* 25 They went out into an adjoining marsh to catch soruses...The sorus is not known to be in Virginia, except for about six weeks from the latter end of September.

‖ **Sory**, *sb. Obs.* [L. *sōry*, ad. Gr. σῶρυ. Cf. Sp. and It. *sori*.] A kind of mineral ore yielding vitriol; one or other kind of vitriol.

1601 HOLLAND *Pliny* II. 510 As for Sory, that which is brought out of Ægypt is counted best, and farre better than the Cyprian, Spanish, or African. 1657 TOMLINSON *Renou's Disp.* xiii. 27 Many efficacious Poysons also are drawn from Minerals,..as Quick-silver, red Lead, Parget, Vitriol, Sory, Sandarach [etc.]. [1728 BAILEY, *Sory*, a kind of Mineral, a sort of Vitriol made of Chalcitis or Cadmia. 1828–32 in WEBSTER. Hence in later Dicts.]

† **Sory**, *a. Obs. rare.* Also **soory, sowry**. [f. SORE *sb.*[3] + -Y, or ad. ON. *saurigr* (MSw. *sörogh*).] Filthy, dirty.

c 1440 *Promp. Parv.* 465/1 Soory, or defowlyd yn sowr or fylthe.., *cenosus, cenulentus*. *Ibid.* 466/2 Sowry, or defowlyd wythe fylthe.

† **Soryful**, obs. var. SORROWFUL *a.*

Prob. due to confusion with *sory* SORRY *a.*

c 1550 H. LLOYD *Treas. Health* c ij, Soryful syghes in sharpe agewes be to be fearyd. 1596 DALRYMPLE tr. *Leslie's Hist. Scot.* (S.T.S.) II. 239 Quhilke maid the king sa soryfull..that [etc.].

Soryp, obs. form of SYRUP.

Sose, obs. form of SOSS *sb.*

† **Sosh**. *Obs.*[−1] [Imitative. Cf. SOSS *sb.*[2]] A dull, heavy sound; a thud; = SOSS *sb.*[2]

1687 A. LOVELL tr. *Bergerac's Com. Hist.* 8, I fell with a sosh in the Valley below.

Soskin, variant of SUSKIN.

So so, so-so (sō·,sō·), *adv.* and *a.* (*sb.*). Also 6 **soo soo, soso**, 6–9 **so, so**, 9 *Sc.* **saesae**. [So *adv.* Cf. G. *so so*, Du. *zoo zoo*, WFris. *sa sa*, in similar use.]

For *so, so*, as a mere exclamation, see SO *adv.* 5 c.

A. *adv.* In an indifferent, mediocre, or passable manner or degree; indifferently, not quite satisfactorily: **a.** With verbs.

1530 PALSGR. 842/1 So so, *tellement quellement*. 1548 UDALL, etc. *Erasm. Par. Luke* vi. 73 b, This thyng, the pharisees could soso awaie withall, because it was a thyng.. of the common vsage. 1553 *Respublica* 647 My ladie, howe doe youe? *Respub.* Even so so, people. 1598 GRENEWEY *Tacitus, Ann.* XII. x. (1622) 171 His wife..endured the first flight so so, for feare of the enemy and loue of her husband. 1675 WOOD *Life* (O.H.S.) II. 318 Villerius Bathurst of Coll. Trin. [spoke] well, Philippus Clarke e Coll. Magd. so so. 1872 *Routledge's Ev. Boy's Ann.* 579 'And you have succeeded fairly?' 'So-so,' he answered. 1877 H. JAMES *American* vii. 120 'And are you enjoying it?'..'Oh, so-so,' he answered.

b. With pa. pples., ppl. adjs., and adjs.

1532 *St. Papers Hen. VIII*, VII. 396 The said old Abbot of Ferfa, reconcyled soo soo to the Pope, hath been of late at Rome. 1548 UDALL, etc. *Erasm. Par. Luke* v. 65 Seeyng the place to be so-so commodious for one to preache the ghospel in. 1600 SHAKS. *A. Y. L.* v. i. 29 *Clo.* Art rich? *Will.* Faith sir, so, so. 1828 SCOTT *Jrnl.* 30 Jan., Am I satisfied with my exertions? So so. 1861 WHYTE MELVILLE *Market Harb.* 41 'I suppose you are very well mounted yourself?' 'So-so,' was the reply.

c. With *but*.

1578 TIMME *Calvin on Gen.* 276 Seeing the Canaanites maintained their life but so so. *a* 1656 USSHER *Ann.* (1658) 151 To see the stipend duly paid.., which yet was but so so performed by him. 1720 C. SHADWELL *Sham Prince* v. i, And so we stitch up one another, and do but so so at the best. 1762 *Crazy Tales* 110 They pass their summers but so so, Drinking as long as they are able. 1820 HOGG *Bridal of Polmood* xvi, The king asked..how he had passed the night—he thanked his majesty, and said he had been but so so.

B. *adj.* Indifferent, mediocre, of middling quality; neither very good nor very bad, but usu. inclining towards bad. Freq. with *but*.

1. Of things: **a.** In predicative use.

(*a*) 1542 UDALL *Erasm. Apoph.* 313 b, The maister of the feaste had sette upon the table wyne that was but easie and soso. 1576 FLEMING *Panopl. Epist.* 120 If our fortune bee but so so, indifferent (I meane). 1616 R. C. *Times' Whistle* (1871) 63 Your white or Clarret Is but so so; he cares not greatly for it. 1682 D'URFEY *Butler's Ghost* 135 Doubting their luck would be but so-so, And that it would disgrace them all [etc.]. 1827 DE QUINCEY *Murder* Wks. 1854 IV. 9 It is no disparagement to say, that his performance was but so-so.

(*b*) 1591 SPARRY tr. *Cattan's Geomancie* 128 It is so-so for the ayre, for it will raine often times. 1611 COTGR., *Bellastre*,..fairish, reasonably faire, passable, so so. 1654 WHITLOCK *Zootomia* 260 These Elements to Books Compose go, Some good, some bad, and some So, So. 1712 SWIFT *Jrnl. to Stella* 18 Nov., I dined there t'other day, .. and our meat and drink was very so so. 1771 GOLDSM. *Haunch of Venison* 9 As in some Irish houses, where things are so so, One gammon of bacon hangs up for a show. 1820 BYRON *Blues* II. 77 The taste of the actors at best is so so. 1862 THACKERAY *Philip* xvi, Her pianoforte playing is very so-so indeed. 1871 B. TAYLOR *Faust* (1875) I. v. 90 My wish is great, my power is only so-so.

b. Used attributively.

1767 *Woman of Fashion* II. 48 You will, I fear, make but a so so Figure, as that domestic Animal, a Husband. 1788 WOLCOT (P. Pindar) *Peter's Pension* Wks. 1812 II. 18 Your man-traps..have had but so-so luck. 1837 BARHAM *Ingol. Leg.* Ser. I. *Grey Dolphin*, After leading but a so-so life. 1861 BURGON *Letters from Rome* 260 Acres of so-so statues, and nameless busts. 1899 A. WERNER *Capt. Locusts* 279 Having got together some very so-so writing materials. *Comb.* 1824 MISS FERRIER *Inher.* xviii, Very so-so looking strawberries.

2. Of persons: **a.** In respect of ability, character, position, appearance, etc.

1608 BP. ANDREWES *Serm.* (1841) II. 224 They that have not greatly gone astray, are but even so so. 1663 KILLIGREW *Parson's Wedding* I. ii, Ay marry,..this is a husband,.. and none of your so-so husbands. 1675 COTTON *Burlesque upon B.* 110 They pretty passable are though (Thank Jove) the Children are so so. 1775 MME. D'ARBLAY *Early Diary* (1889) II. 57 Mrs. Harris—a so-so sort of woman. 1823 BYRON *Juan* XIII. lxxxii, I've seen..a so-so matron boldly fight Her way back to the world. 1864 *Realm* 22 June 2 No one can deny that among the clergy there is more than a fair percentage of very so-so people.

b. In respect of health or physical condition.

a 1592 GREENE *Jas. IV*, Wks. (Rtldg.) 194 Our king is well, our queen so-so. 1662 J. WILSON *Cheats* I. v, *M. D.* I am afraid you are not well Sir. *Sc.* Yes—I am so, so. 1731 *Gentl. Mag.* I. 349 Howe'er it is, I scarcely know, I find myself but just so so. ?1800 W. B. RHODES *Bomb. Fur.* i. (1830) 7 We are but middling—that is but so so. 1838 DICKENS *O. Twist* xvii, 'Hoping you find yourself well, sir!' 'So-so, Mrs. Mann,' replied the beadle. 1857 HUGHES *Tom Brown* II. v, 'How's he?'..'So, so; rather done, I think, since his last fall.'

c. In respect of soberness.

1809 MALKIN *Gil Blas* II. iv. ¶ 4 We drank hard, and returned..in a pretty pickle, that is to say, so-so in the Gil Blas story. 1818 KEATS *Lett.* Wks. 1889 III. 158 Rice..had no occasion to crow, for he got a little so-so at a party of his, and was none the worse for it the next morning.

3. Marked by the excessive use of 'so' in writings or speech.

a 1800 PEGGE *Anecd. Eng. Lang.* (1814) 217 Our Cockney, however, may be supported in this his *so-so* language by respectable Historians.

Hence **So-so-so** *a.* (*nonce-use*.)

1768 MME. D'ARBLAY *Early Diary* (1889) I. 21 We had a large party to the Assembly on Monday, which was so-so-so.

So-soish, *a.* Also **so-so-ish**. [f. So-so.] Somewhat so-so; rather indifferent.

1835 *Tait's Mag.* II. 475 An imitation of..an old Scotch ballad—very so-so-ish. 1847 *Illustr. Lond. News* 4 Sept. 158/2 The jumping was only so-so-ish. 1888 FARJEON *Miser Farebrother* xiii, I like him, just a little, in a so-soish way.

Hence **So-soishly** *adv.*

1842 *Civil Eng. & Arch. Jrnl.* V. 236/2 Many..views being uninteresting in subject,..and but very so-soishly engraved.

† **Sospire**. *Obs.*[−1] [prob. ad. It. *sospiro*: see SUSPIRE *sb.*] A sigh.

1575 LANEHAM *Lett.* (1871) 60 With my spanish sospire, my french heighes.

† **Sospital**, *a. Obs.*[−0] [ad. L. *sospitalis*, f. *sospit-, sospes* safe, unhurt.] (See quot.) Also † **Sospitation** (cf. next).

1656 BLOUNT *Glossogr.*, *Sospital*,..that is cause of health; medicinable, wholsom, safe, free from danger. 1658 PHILLIPS, *Sospitation*, a keeping safe, and in health, preserving from danger.

† **Sospitator**. *Obs.*[−1] [a. L. *sospitator*, f. *sospitāre* to save: see prec.] A saviour.

1643 TRAPP *Comm. Gen.* xl. 20 In honour of God, our Sospitator, for his mercy in our creation.

Soss, *sb.*[1] Now *dial.* Also 5 **sos**, **soce**, 6 **sose**, 6–7 **sosse**. [? Imitative of the sound of lapping.]

1. † **a.** (See quots.) *Obs. rare.*

In many English dialects *soss* is used as a call to dogs and pigs at feeding-time.

c 1440 *Promp. Parv.* 465 Sos, howndysmete,.. *cantabrum*. 1530 PALSGR. 273/1 Sosse or a rewarde for houndes whan they have taken their game, *hvuee*.

b. *Sc.* and *dial.* A sloppy mess or mixture; a dish of food having this character.

1691 RAY *N. Co. Words* (ed. 2) 66 A *Soss*, a mucky Puddle. *a* 1728 *Kennett MSS.* (Halliw.), Of any one that makes several slops, or makes any place wet and dirty, we say in Kent, he makes a soss. 1802 SIBBALD *Chron. S. P.* IV. Gloss., *Soss*, a large dish of flummery. 1826 J. AITON *Domest. Econ.* (1857) 128 Tea sosses ought not to be introduced in the manse kitchen..: porridge is infinitely preferable. 1847 CHAMBERS *Tradit. Edinb.* 164 Lucky could furnish forth a soss—that is stew. 1886 *S. W. Linc. Gloss.* 137 You mak such sosses, for all the world like a pig.

2. A sloven, slut, or slattern.

1611 COTGR., *Halebreda*,..a luske, a slouch; a sosse. 1901 in *Eng. Dial. Dict.* s.v., A bonny soss you are, as Nancy Taylor 'ud mak'!

Soss (sǫs), *sb.*[2] Chiefly *dial.* [Imitative: cf. SOSS *v.*[2] and SOSH.]

1. The sound made by a heavy, soft body falling upon or otherwise coming in contact with a surface; a heavy, awkward fall. Chiefly in the phr. *with a soss*.

1718 RAMSAY *Christ's Kirk Gr.* III. iii, And wi' a soss aboon the claiths, Ilk ane their gifts down flang. 1796 W. H. MARSHALL *Yorksh.* (ed. 2) II. 346 'To fall with a soss', to fall plumb. 1802 SIBBALD *Chron. S. P.* IV. Gloss., *Soss*, the noise made by the fall of something heavy and soft..common in northern glossaries, etc. 1901 A. TROTTER *East Galloway Sk.* 59/2 Sandy came and sat down with a 'soss' on a chest by her bedside.

2. The sound made by impact upon water.

1885 *Pall Mall G.* 5 May 4/1 The soss, soss of her bows as she 'punches' the waves asunder.

Soss, variant of SASSE *Obs.*

Soss, *v.*[1] Now *north. dial.* and *Sc.* [f. SOSS *sb.*[1]]

1. *trans.* To make foul or dirty.

1557 TUSSER *100 Points Husb.* lxxii, Their milke slapt in corners, their creame al to sost. 1573 — *Husb.* (1878) 106 Her milke pan and creame pot, so slabbered and sost.

b. ? To drench, soak.

1587 *Mirr. Mag., Brennus* ix, The cause why Neptune did me tosse; Why boyling Seas with surges so me sosse.

2. *intr.* To splash in mud or dirt.

Also *Sc.*, to make or use sloppy food or other messes. 1575 *Gamm. Gurton* I. iv. 26 Cham faine a-bedde to dyg and delue, in water, myre and claye, Sossing and possing in the durte. 1876 C. C. ROBINSON *Mid-Yks. Gloss.* 131/2 *Soss*, to..tread heavily—implying a forceful impact or pressure, as when..the feet plash through it [*sc.* mud].

3. *trans.* To lap or lick up. Also with *up*.

1598 R. BERNARD tr. *Terence, Eunuch* v. iv, They will slabber & sosse up browne bread in pottage. 1703 THORESBY *Let. to Ray*, *Sosse*, v., [a word] proper to dogs..: also in northern dial. glossaries. 1892 M. C. F. MORRIS *Yorksh. Folk-Talk* 375 'T' dog 's sossin all t' cat milk.

Hence **So·ssing** *vbl. sb.*

1824 SCOTT *St. Ronan's* xxxii, A wheen cork-headed, barmy-brained gowks! that wunna let puir folk die in quiet, as die in quiet, wi' their sossings and their soopings.

Soss, *v.*[2] Now *dial.* and *Sc.* [Cf. SOSS *sb.*[2]]

† **1.** *trans.* To put *up* so as to rest softly. *Obs.*

1711 SWIFT *Jrnl. to Stella* 10 March, I went to-day into the City, but in a coach and sossed up my leg on the seat.

†**2.** *intr.* To move gently; to lounge lazily. *Obs.*
1711 Swift *Jrnl. to Stella* 7 June, Yes, yes, I remember Berested's bridge; the coach sosses up and down as one goes that way. 1723 — *Stella at Wood Park* Misc. 1735 V. 209 Poor Stella must pack off to Town:..From wholesome Exercise and Air, To sossing in an easy Chair.

3. To fall with a thud or heavy impact. Also *spec.* in *Mining.*
1789 Davidson *Seasons* 100 Providence oft gets into one scale, To keep the proper poise, when easfu' bliss, Into the other, sosses, overpond'rous. 1825 Jamieson *Suppl.*, *To Soss*, to fall down as a dead weight, to come to the ground as it were all in a piece. 1883 Gresley *Gloss. Coal-m.* 230 *Sos*, to sink into the floor under great pressure from overlying strata. 1898 C. Hyne *Capt. Kettle* 294 Looks like as if they were going to soss down slap on top of us.

b. To sit *down* heavily.
c 1790 A. Wilson in *Poems & Lit. Prose* (1876) II. 100 We'll hotch awa'..And soss down on yon sinny stane. 1879 Miss Jackson *Shropsh. Word-Bk.* 399 'Er sossed down i' the cheer all at wunst.

4. *trans.* To cast or throw heavily.
1855- in dialect glossaries, etc.

Soss, *adv.* Now *dial.* [Cf. Soss *sb.*[2] and *v.*[2]] With a heavy fall or dull thud.
1760 Sterne *Tr. Shandy* III. xxiv, Mrs. Bridget..fell backwards soss against the bridge. 1862- in northern glossaries.

Soss-, the stem of Soss *sb.*[1] used attributively in a few combs., with the sense 'fat, dirty, slatternly, etc.', as †*soss-bangle*, †*-belly* (see quots.).
1554 Bale *Declar. Bonner's Articles* xxix. 113 b, What is thy idolatrous mas and lowsye Latine seruice, thou sosbelly swilbol, but the very draf of Antichriste. 1691 Ray *S. & E. Co. Words* 115 A *Sosse-bangle*, a sluttish, slattering, lazy Wench; a Rustic word, only used by the vulgar. [Hence *soss-brangle* in Grose (1788).]

Sossage, -ige: see Sausage.

Sossel, -le, *dial.*: see Sozzle *v.*

So·ssle, *v. rare.* [?f. Soss *sb.*[1]] *intr.* To go *about* in an aimless idle manner.
1837 Miss Sedgwick *Live & Let Live* iii. 31 Your children get such shocking habits sosling about, and doing nothing, and living all in a clutter.

Sosteine, Sostenaunse, obs. ff. Sustain *v.*, Sustenance.

‖**Sostenente.** Also **sostinente.** [It., pres. pple. of *sostenere* Sustain *v.*] A device or contrivance attached to a pianoforte for the purpose of producing sustained notes like an organ. Also *attrib.*
1840 *Penny Cycl.* XVIII. 142/2 Mr. Mott's *sostinente* was an application of a cylinder and silk loops to an upright piano-forte. The..tones came forth somewhat like the tones of the seraphine. 1881 *Morning Post* 2 June, Messrs. Brinsmead have patented..the sostenente sounding board, capable of sustaining sound for 60 seconds. 1885 *Encycl. Brit.* XIX. 76/1 *note*, Mott..attracted much attention by a piano with sostenente effect..in 1817. *Ibid.*, But a sostenente piano..is no longer a true piano.

‖**Sostenuto** (sǫstėnū·to), *a.* and *sb.* Abbrev. **sost.** Also 8 **sustinuto.** [It., pa. pple. of *sostenere* Sustain *v.*]
A. *adj.* **1.** Of music: To be sung or played in a sustained manner. (Cf. quot. 1801.)
1724 *Short Explic. For. Wds. in Mus. Bks.* 1801 Busby *Dict. Mus.*, *Sostenuto*, a word implying that the notes of the movement, or passage against which it is placed, are to be sustained or held on to the extremity of their lengths. 1875 in Stainer & Barrett *Dict. Mus. Terms.*

2. Marked or characterized by being sustained or held on.
1835 *Court Mag.* VI. 220/2 A kind of Sostenuto or bow effect. 1887 Miss R. H. Busk *Folksongs Italy* 20 There is probably a sostenuto note in its air.

B. *sb.* A sustained sound or note. *rare*⁻¹.
1757 Foote *Author* Epil., Wks. 1799 I. 129 Divine Mingotti! what a swell has she! O! such a sustinuto upon B!

Soster(hode, obs. variants of Sister(hood.

So-styled, *ppl. a.* [So *adv.* 6 a.] Styled or designated by this term or name, but not properly entitled to or correctly described by it; so-called, so-termed.
1844 tr. *M. T. Asmar's Mem. Babylonian Princ.* II. 92 The so-styled civilized daughters of Europe. 1852 Thackeray *Esmond* II. x, The (so-styled) legitimate representatives of the Viscount Castlewood. 1888 Child *Eng. & Sc. Ballads* III. 104/1 *note*, The so-styled Robber Songs of the Russians.

Sot (sǫt), *sb.*[1] and *a.* Forms: 1- **sot,** 1-2, 6-7 **sott,** 2-7 **sotte,** 3, 5 **sote,** 6 **soote.** [a. OF. *sot* masc., *sote* fem. (mod.F. *sot*, *sotte*), of unknown origin; the med.L. *sottus* is recorded from c 800. Hence also MDu. *sot* (*sod*), *zot* (*zod*; Du. *zot*), MLG. and LG. *sot*, *sott*, MHG. *sot*.]
A. *sb.* †**1.** A foolish or stupid person; a fool, blockhead, dolt. *Obs.*
c 1000 Ælfric *Saints' Lives* xiii. 132 Ne bið se na wita þe unwislice leofað, ac bið open sott [*v.r.* sot]. c 1055 *Byrhtferth's Handboc* in *Anglia* VIII. 313 Seðe his agene spræce awyrt he wyrcð *barbarismus*. Swylce he cweðe þu sot, þær he sceolde cweðan þu sott. c 1175 *Lamb. Hom.* 29 Þa iuguleres and þa oðer sottes..habbeð an þonc. a 1250 *Prov. of Alfred* 412 Ne gabbe þu,..ne chid þu wyþ none sotte. a 1300 *Cursor M.* 2457 Þan said abram, þat was na sot, formast til his neueu loth. 1377 Langl. *P. Pl.* B. x. 8 She..badde hym be stylle, With suche wise wordes to wissen any sottes. 1422 tr. *Secreta Secret., Priv. Priv.* 157 Who-so nothynge thynkyth of thyngis y-passet. a sote and a fole he shall be callid. a 1500 *Flower & Leaf* 101 (Skeat), So sodainly, that, as it were a sot, I stood astonied. 1509 Barclay *Shyp of Folys* (1570) 85 Into the Church then comes another sotte. 1546 J. Heywood *Dial. Wit & Folly* (Percy Soc.) 14 No more dysernythe the sott, at yeres three score, Then th' ynosent borne within yeres thre before. 1602 J. Davies (Heref.) *Mirum in Modum* Wks. (Grosart) I. 25/2 Why hath a wise man, to his Sonne a Sotte? 1641 Milton *Animadv.* Wks. 1851 III. 235 The one is ever..a sot, an ideot for any use that mankind can make of him. 1712 Steele *Spect.* No. 492 ¶ 1 The Men are such unthinking Sots, that they do not prefer her who restrains all her Passions and Affections [etc.]. c 1745 Fielding *Lucy in Town* Wks. 1784 III. 438 That I should be such a sot as to suffer you!
Prov. a 1250 *Prov. Alfred* 421 Sottes bolt is sone i-scohte. c 1300 *Prov. Hendyng* in *Rel. Ant.* I. 111 Sottes bolt is sone shote.
Comb. 1610 Healey *St. Aug. Citie of God* xx. xxx. 833 Their..apparelling him [i.e. Christ] with sot-like habites, crowning him with thorne, striking him on the head, with reedes,..was nothing but a continuate insultation.

2. One who dulls or stupefies himself with drinking; one who commonly or habitually drinks to excess; a soaker.
1592 Nashe *Pierce Penilesse* Wks. (Grosart) II. 43 The Danes are bursten-bellied sots, that are to be confuted with nothing but Tankards or quart pots. 1626 R. C. *Times' Whistle* (1871) 63, I graunt you then a drunken sot may goe For one that is innocuous. 1654 Whitlock *Zootomia* 3 He that..drinketh not all his Wine before the Salt is taken away, and only for Digestion: Such a one is a Drunkard, a Sot, &c. 1693 Prideaux *Lett.* (1875) 160 We are here at a miserable passe with this horrid sot we have got for our Dean. He cannot sleep at night till dosed with drink. 1711 Shaftesb. *Charac.* (1737) II. 127 One, who abuses himself in this way, is often call'd a sot, but never a debauchee. 1750 Berkeley *Patriotism* § 10 Wks. 1871 III. 455 A sot, a beast, benumbed and stupefied by excess. 1818 Scott *Rob Roy* vi, They form a happy compound of sot, gamekeeper, bully, horse-jockey, and fool. 1856 Emerson *Eng. Traits, Ability* Wks. (Bohn) II. 34 Even the pleasure-hunters and sots of England are of a tougher texture. 1870 Thornbury *Tour rd. Eng.* II. xxii. 112 A poor, clever, worn-out sot.

3. *attrib.*, or in genitive combs., as †**sot-bay, sot's-hof, -hole,** a resort of drinkers; †**sot's cap,** a variety of sea-shell; †**sot-weed,** tobacco.
(*a*) 1532 More *Confut. Tindale* Wks. 711/1 A very cold consent of my goffe, that he found and tooke vp at sottes hoffe. 1706 E. Ward *Wooden World Diss.* (1708) 87 His Cruise is over, and he comes to an Anchor in Sot-Bay. 1755 *Gentl. Mag.* XXV. 208 It would not have cost me above four-pence half-penny to have spent my evening at Sots Hole. 1827 Hone *Every-day Bk.* 21 Dec. II. 1626 Some 'good fellow', who is good no where but in 'sot's-hole'.
(*b*) 1702 T. Brown, etc. *Lett. fr. Dead* II. Wks. 1707 II. 81 We had every one ramm'd a full charge of Sot-weed into our infernal Guns. 1747 *Scheme Equip. Men of War* 35 To add a small Composition of high-flavoured Sot-Weed. 1785 in Grose *Dict. Vulgar T.*
(*c*) 1713 Petiver *Aquat. Anim. Amboinæ* Tab. 16/28 *Pectunculus rostratus*,..Sots-cap.

†**B.** *adj.* Foolish, stupid. *Obs.*
c 1050 *Suppl. Ælfric's Gloss.* in Wr.-Wülcker 171/32 *Hebes*, dwæs, *uel* sott. a 1100 *Voc.* Ibid. 316/7 *Stultus*, stunt. *Sottus*, sot. c 1200 *Vices & Virtues* 67 'Ʒif ʒeure ani,' he seið, 'is ihealden for wis on ðare woreld, become sott, and swa he mai bien wis'. a 1225 *Leg. Kath.* 107 Luuede heo nane libte ploben ne nane sotte songes. c 1250 *Orison our Lady* 37 in *O. E. Misc.*, And alle mine sot dede Ich bidde hire to me bi-seo. 1648 Hexham II, *De Aldersotste*, the Most foolish, or the Sottest.

†**Sot,** *sb.*[2] *Obs.*⁻¹ [ad. Sp. *azote.*] A scourge.
1588 Parke tr. *Mendoza's Hist. China* 261 They began to whippe them vpon the calues of their legges with a sot made of canes.

Sot (sǫt), *v.* Also 5-6 **sott,** 6 **sotte.** [f. Sot *sb.*[1] (cf. MDu. *sotten*, *zotten* to be foolish), or aphetic for Assot *v.*]
1. *trans.* †**a.** To render foolish or doltish; to stupefy, to besot. *Obs.*
a 1400-50 *Wars Alex.* 4364 Ne foloȝe we na ficesyens ne philisophour scolis, As sophistri & slik thing to sott with þe pepill. 1554 Philpot *Exam. & Writ.* (Parker Soc.) 322 The cup of the Whore of Babylon, wherewith she hath sotted and made drunk the most part of Christendom. 1571 Golding *Calvin on Ps.* v. 11 He sotteth them with the spirit of drowsynesse and giddynesse. 1600 F. Thynne *Epig.* (1876) 53 Crisopeia,..whoe sotts him soe with her bewitchinge sight. 1626 Breton *Fantasticks* Wks. (Grosart) II. 5/2 Lone..crosseth wisdome, serueth Beautie, and sotteth folly. a 1700 Ken *Edmund* Poet. Wks. 1721 II. 297 Of Wine and Spirits..They..should Cellars drain, Which..should sot the Dane.
†**b.** To blurt *out* stupidly. *Obs.*⁻¹
1608 H. Clapham *Errour Right Hand* 44 He beginnes to puffe,..and then sotted out this question.
c. With *away.* To waste or squander by sottish conduct.
1746 Chesterf. *Lett.* cxii. (1792) I. 304, I must..have destroyed my health and faculties by sotting away the evenings. 1782 *Encycl. Brit.* (ed. 2) IX. 6908/1 Brandy-shops, in which the inhabitants used to sot away their time in drinking strong liquors and smoking tobacco. 1850 *Blackw. Mag.* Nov. 510 The elder son of the forementioned squire had muddled and sotted away much of his share in the Leslie property.
2. *intr.* To play the sot; to drink to excess; to soak. Also with *it.*
1633 Marmion *Antiq.* II. i. (1875) 217 You have been sotting on't all night with wine. 1711 E. Ward *Vulgus Brit.* ix. 99 Where day by day they us'd to sot, At All-fours, Cribidge, or at Put. a 1716 South *Twelve Serm.* (1717) VI. 397 Those, who should have been watching the Motion of the Enemy, were sotting it at their Cups. 1815 W. H. Ireland *Scribbleomania* 9 Periodical Writers that sot over beer. 1837 Dickens *Pickw.* vi, Beyond the few..reckless vagabonds with whom he..sotted in the alehouse, he had not a single friend.

Sot, obs. and dial. pa. t. and pa. pple. of Set *v.*; obs. f. Soot *sb.*; var. Swote (sweat) *Obs.*

Sotadean (sǫtădī·ăn), *a.* and *sb.* [f. L. *Sōtadē-us*, f. *Sōtadēs*: see next.] = Sotadic *a.*
1774 J. Patsall tr. *Quintilian's Inst.* IX. iv. II. 144 *note*, Sotadean verses consisted sometimes of iambics, sometimes of trochaics, sometimes of dactyls, and sometimes of anapæstics, which being read backwards made another kind of verse. 1830 Seager tr. *Hermann's Elem. Doctr. Metres* 96 Among the verses adduced by Hephaestion there are, besides the Sotadean, only two which appear to be really Ionic *à majori*.

Sotadic (sotæ·dik), *a.* and *sb.* Also 8 **Sotadick.** [ad. L. *Sōtadic-us*, f. *Sōtadēs*, Gr. Σωτάδης: see def.]
A. *sb.* **1.** A satire after the manner of Sotades, an ancient Greek poet noted for the coarseness and scurrility of his writings.
1645 Milton *Colast.* Wks. 1851 IV. 378 Perhaps, as the provocation may bee, I may bee driv'n to curle up this gliding prose into a rough *Sotadic*. 1836 *Fraser's Mag.* XIII. 742 Neither would the keenest bit of satire be a legitimate 'sotadic', without that dash of turbulence in it, and sweeping denunciation.
2. *Pros.* A catalectic tetrameter composed of Ionics *a majore.*
1830 Seager tr. *Hermann's Elem. Doctr. Metres* 97 [Plautus] has Sotadics in Aul. ii, 1, 30. sq. iii, 2. Amph. i, 1, 14. sq.
B. *adj.* **1.** Characterized by a coarseness or scurrility like that of Sotades.
1716 M. Davies *Athen. Brit.* II. To Rdr. p. xlv, Which favour was..deservedly refus'd to most Necromantick Sotadick and Arian Libels, by the common consent of all Christians.
2. Capable of being read in reverse order; palindromic.
? a 1814 T. Brown in Welsh *Life* vii. (1825) 350 The second syllable is..the sound reversed, like the reading of a Sotadic line. 1862 Wheatley *Anagrams* 9 Palindromic verses are also sometimes called Sotadic verses.
3. *Pros.* (See quot. and A. 2.)
1830 Seager tr. *Hermann's Elem. Doctr. Metres* 96 The most noted of Ionic verses *à majori* is the Sotadic, constructed for recitation only.
So **Sota·dical** *a. rare.*
1610 Healey *St. Aug. Citie of God* 642 Sotadicall verses: that is verses backward and forwards.

‖**Sota·na.** [Sp. *sotana.*] A gown or cassock.
1622 Mabbe tr. *Aleman's Guzman d'Alf.* II. II. vii. 161, I had furnished my selfe in Milan, with as much rich silke Grogram, as would serue to make mee a cloake, and a Sotana. a 1678 Marvell *Misc. Poems* (1681) 56 Thus armed underneath, he over all Does make a primitive Sotana fall.

†**Sotane.** *Obs.*⁻¹ [ad. It. *sottana.*] = Soutane.
1652 Howell *Giraffi's Rev. Naples* II. 70 A company of Priests appeared, who went with their Sotanes raised up.

Sote, obs. f. Soot *sb.*; var. Soot *a.* (sweet), Swote (sweat). **Sotel(e, -ell(e, Sotelnes, -te(e, -y(che,** obs. ff. Subtle *a.*, Subtleness, etc.

Soterial (sotī·riăl), *a. Theol.* [f. Gr. σωτηρία salvation.] Pertaining to salvation.
1879 H. Crosby *Christian Preacher* ii, The soterial pith of the Gospel is simple and soon exhibited.

†**Soteria·logy.** *Obs. rare.* = Soteriology.
1768-74 Tucker *Lt. Nat.* (1834) II. 421 He established a plan of soterialogy for the restoration and perfection of human nature. *Ibid.* 466, I would call this soterialogy or the plan of salvation.

†**Sote·rian,** *a. Obs.*⁻⁰ [f. as prec. or f. Gr. σωτήρ saviour.] (See quot.)
1623 Cockeram I, *Soterian day*, Good-friday.

Soteriological (sotīᵊriolǫ·dʒikăl), *a. Theol.* [ad. G. *soteriologisch*: see next.] Of or pertaining to soteriology or salvation. Also *Comb.*
1879 Farrar *St. Paul* II. 412 *note*, Lange classes the Epistles as 1. Eschatological. 2. Soteriological [etc.]. 1882-3 Schaff *Encycl. Relig. Knowl.* III. 2396/1 Whenever they undertook to remodel..a doctrine, they attached themselves to its anthropological or soteriological bearings. 1890 *Athenæum* 5 July 34/1 The tendency which..may be called the soteriological-Biblical.

Soteriology (sotīᵊriǫ·lŏdʒi). [f. Gr. σωτηρία preservation, salvation, or ad. G. *soteriologie*, F. *sotériologie.* Cf. Soterialogy.]
1. (See quot.) *rare*⁻⁰.
1847 Webster, *Soteriology*, a discourse on health, or the science of promoting and preserving health. [Hence in later Dicts.]
2. *Theol.* The doctrine of salvation.
1864 Shedd *Hist. Chr. Doctr.* II. 204 It was reserved for the Protestant church..to bring the doctrines of Soteriology to a correspondent degree of expansion. a 1880 W. L. McFarlan in *Scotch Serm.* 237 The whole of the eschatology of the schoolmen,..like their soteriology and their ontology, seems to the modern theologian..untenable.

So-termed, *a.* [So *adv.* 6 a.] So-called.
1843 R. J. Graves *Syst. Clin. Med.* xxvii. 344 They all get well under the (so-termed) antiphlogistic regimen. 1894 H. Nisbet *Bush Girl's Rom.* 118 It is only the so-termed freeman who is valueless.

Soterology (sǭtəˌrǫ·lŏdʒi). *Theol.* [ad. G. *soterologie*, f. Gr. σωτήρ saviour, f. σω-, stem of σώζειν to save.] (See quot.)
1882-3 *Schaff's Encycl. Relig. Knowl.* III. 2216 [Soteriology] is to be carefully distinguished from soterology, or christology, which treats solely of the person of the Redeemer.

Soth(e, obs. ff. Soot *sb.*[1], Sooth *sb.*, *a.*, Soothe *v.*

Sothe, obs. pa. t. and pa. pple. Seethe *v.*

†**So·thead.** *Obs.* Forms: 3 **sothade,** 3-4 **-hede,** 4 **-hed,** 7 **-head**; 4 **sotthede, -hed(d, soithede** (**soþede,** 5 **soþhede**). [f. Sot *a.* + -head. Cf. LG. *sottheit*, Du. *zotheid.*] Folly, foolishness, stupidity; a foolish act.
a 1200 *Vices & Virtues* 67 Ðe wise woreld-mann, he halt michel sothade ðat mann forlate..hus and ham. a 1250 *Owl & Night.* 1375 Þah heo beo god, me hine may mysfonge, & drawe hine to sothede. a 1300 *Cursor M.* 18235 Bot nu þi sothed wel es kydd. *Ibid.* 19194 And sua yee sceu all yur sotthedis. 14.. *Lat.-Eng. Voc.* in Wr.-Wülcker 567 *Baburra*, Sothede. 1690 *Andros Tracts* II. 35 A charge which their most Violent accusers had never yet sothead enough to alledge against them.

Sother, obs. f. Solder *sb.*[1] **Sothern,** obs. f. Southern *a.* **Sothero(u)n,** obs. ff. Southron.

†**So·thery,** *a. Obs.*⁻¹ (Meaning uncertain.) Perh. the old form of *Surrey* (Skeat).
1540 J. Heywood *Four PP.* 879 Theyr taylles well kempt, and..With sothery butter theyr bodyes anoynted.

Sothfast(nes, obs. ff. Soothfast(ness.

Sothiac (sōᵘ·þiǎk), *a.* [ad. F. *sothiaque*: see Sothic *a.* and -ac.]
1. = Sothic *a.* 1.
1834 Mrs. Somerville *Connex. Phys. Sci.* xiii. 100 The Egyptians..lost one year in every 1460 [*sic*],—their Sothiac period. 1842 *Penny Cycl.* XXII. 267/1 It is obvious that 1461 years of 365 days each, make 1460 years of 365¼ days. This period of 1460 Julian years was the Sothiac period. 1870 Emerson *Soc. & Solit.* vii. (1883) 151 The..scholar..who can unearth for me the buried dynasties of Sesostris and Ptolemy, the Sothiac era [etc.].
2. = Sothic *a.* 2.
1877 R. S. Poole in *Encycl. Brit.* VII. 729/2 Consisting of 1460 Sothiac and 1461 vague years. 1887 Mahaffy & Gilman *Alexander's Empire* xv. (1890) 158 *note*, This attempted reform of the calendar, by introducing the Sothiac year of 365 days and a quarter, is very interesting.
So **Sothi·acal** *a.* [F. *sothiacal.*]
1795 T. Maurice *Hindostan* (1820) I. I. iii. 101 This cycle of 1461 was called in Egypt the great Canicular year, or Sothiacal period. 1813 Pritchard *Phys. Hist. Man* viii. § 5. 451 *note*, The cycle of Nabonassar or the Sothiacal year. *Ibid.*, More than the whole Sothiacal period.

Sothic (sǫ·þik, sōᵘ·þik), *a.* [f. Gr. Σῶθις, an Egyptian name of Sirius, the dog-star.]
1. *Sothic cycle* or *period*, a period of 1460 full years, containing 1461 of the ancient Egyptian ordinary years.
1828 Wilkinson *Materia Hierog.* App. I. p. ii, This period is called 'the Sothic period'. 1860 R. S. Poole in W. Smith *Dict. Bible* I. 506/1 *Egypt*, The Egyptians are known to have used two great cycles, the Sothic Cycle and the Tropical Cycle. 1892 S. Laing *Human Origins* (1893) 117 They had invented a sothic cycle for the odd quarter of a day.
2. *Sothic year*, a year of 365¼ days, in contrast to the ordinary Egyptian year of 365 days.
1828 Wilkinson *Materia Hierog.* App. I. p. i, As the Egyptian Solar year, in every four years, loses a day of the Sothic. 1860 R. S. Poole in W. Smith *Dict. Bible* I. 505/2 *Egypt*, There appear to have been at least three years in use with the Egyptians.., the Vague Year, the Tropical Year, and the Sothic Year.

Sothly, -ness, -saw, obs. ff. Soothly, etc.

Sothrenwood, obs. f. Southernwood.

Sothro(u)n, obs. ff. Southron.

‖**Sotie**[1] (soti). Also 4 **sotye,** 5 **sottye,** 9 **sottie.** [OF. *sotie*, *sottie* (mod.F. *sotie* in sense 2), f. *sot* Sot *a.*]
†**1.** Foolishness, folly. *Obs.*
1390 Gower *Conf.* I. 60 Than haddest thou the gates stoke Fro such Sotie as comth to winne Thin hertes wit. *Ibid.* II. 209 The grete covoitise Of sotie and of fol emprise. 1483 Caxton *Gold. Leg.* 360/1 Whan he was yonge he was full of many sottyes and folyes.
2. A species of broad satirical farce, current in France in the 15th and 16th centuries.
1791-1823 D'Israeli *Cur. Lit.* (1866) 133 The sotties were more farcical than farce. 1837 *Penny Cycl.* IX. 417/2 Their most celebrated sotie, entitled 'The Abuse of the World',..is attributed to the historian Bouchet. 1879 *Encycl. Brit.* IX. 645/1 These performances..were soon rivalled by the more profane performances of the moralities, the farces, and the soties.

†**Sotie**[2]. *Obs.*⁻¹ [ad. Sp. *azotea*, Pg. *açotea.*] A terrace or flat roof.
1648 Gage *West Ind.* 47 Cortez desired Montezuma to goe up into the Sotie of his house..and to command his subjects to cease from their heat and fury.

Sotil(e, -ill(e, obs. ff. Subtle *a.* and *v.* **Sotile,** var. Citole *Obs.* **Sotilliche, -ly, -nes, -te(e,** obs. ff. Subtly, etc.

†**So·tly,** *adv.* and *a.* In 2 **sotlice,** 3 **-liche.** [f. Sot *sb.*[1] or *a.* Cf. MDu. *sotte-*, *zottelike* (Du. *zottelijk*).] **a.** *adv.* Foolishly. **b.** *adj.* Foolish.
1154 *O. E. Chron.* (Laud MS.) an. 1137, He todeld it & scatered sotlice. c 1205 Lay. 1970 Heo clepeden hit Cornwaile þurh heora sotliche cure. a 1225 *Leg. Kath.* 359 Alle ich iseo þine sahen sotliche isette.

‖**Sotnia** (sǫ·tniă). [Russ. сотня *sotnya* hundred, f. *sot-*, related to Skr. *çatam*, L. *centum*, etc.] A squadron of Cossack cavalry.
1863 Kinglake *Crimea* II. 212 He had..a brigade of regular cavalry, and nine sotnias of Cossacks. 1878 *N. Amer. Rev.* CXXVI. 150 On the 11th a party of Cossacks reached Pescherna..; one sotnia turned northward.

‖**Sotnik.** Also **Ssotnik, Sodnick.** [Russ. сотникъ *sotnik'*, f. *sotnya*: see prec.] A local official among the Cossacks; also, a commander of a sotnia.
1799 W. Tooke *View Russian Emp.* I. 426 Every stanitza..has..officers, the atamans, its sotnik [etc.]. 1814 tr. *Klaproth's Trav. Cauc.* 73 In the hundred-towns the Ssotniks..transacted the business. 1854 R. G. Latham *Native Races Russian Emp.* 56 Instead of the..Sodnick or head of a certain number of villages—these would have been the native nobles.

Sotraccion, obs. form of Subtraction.

†**So·tship.** *Obs.* Forms: 1-3 **sotscipe,** 3 **sothscipe, sotschipe,** 4 **shotshipe.** [f. Sot *sb.*[1]] Foolishness, folly.
c 1050 *Suppl. Ælfric's Gloss.* in Wr.-Wülcker 171/33 *Hebetudo*, dwæsnys, *uel* sotscipe. c 1131 *O. E. Chron.* (Laud MS.) an. 1131, Þet hi heafdon forloron S' Iohannes mynstre..þurh his mycele sotscipe. c 1205 Lay. 3024 Þa ȝet nolde þe leod-king his sothscipe bi-leuen. a 1225 *Leg. Kath.* 1961 Swa þet Katerine..swike hire sotschipes, & ure wil wurche. c 1300 *Havelok* 2079 Hweþer he sitten nou, and wesseylen, Or of ani shotshipe to-deyle.

†**So·ttage.** *Obs. rare.* [f. Sot *sb.*[1]] Foolishness, folly, stupidity.
1569 Newton *Cicero's De Senectute* ib, Suche is the..foolishe sottage and peruerse ouerthwartnes of waywarde people. 1596 Fitz-Geffrey *Sir F. Drake* (1881) 29 Hard yron-ages death-declining sottage.

Sotted (sǫ·tėd), *ppl. a.* [f. Sot *v.*, or aphetic form of *assotted.*] Rendered sottish or stupid; besotted.
c 1386 Chaucer *Can. Yeom. Prol. & T.* 788 This sotted prest, who was gladder þan he? 1387-8 T. Usk *Test. Love* I. x. (Skeat) l. 18 He..is holde for a foole, and sayd, his wit is but sotted. 1426 Lydg. *De Guil. Pilgr.* 3650 For ouht that I kan se, Ye be sottyd..Off newe. 1574 tr. *Marlorat's Apocalips* 49 The vngodly, being sotted in prosperitie, sleepe a dead sleepe. c 1585 [R. Browne] *Answ. Cartwright* 71 It is not a sotted not wilfull ignorance. 1612 *Two Noble K.* IV. ii. 45, I am sotted, Vtterly lost: My Virgins faith has fled me. a 1637 T. Carew *Poems, To B. Jonson* (1870) 84 Thy just chastizing hand Hath fixt upon the sotted age a brand. 1693 Dryden *Juvenal* vi. 798 The potion..turns his brains..The sotted moon-calf gapes. 1826 W. Elliott *The Nun* 101 The dark confines of each sotted breast. 1898 *Daily News* 21 Feb. 3/4 It tried the sotted drunkard to reclaim.
b. Const. *with* (or †*of*).
c 1460 Sir R. Ros *La Belle Dame* 326 So dulle of wyte, so sotyd of folye. 1563 Blundeston *Pref.* in *Googe's Eglogs* (Arb.) 29 Yf the Muse Be sotted so with this graue Study. 1588 Greene *Pandosto* (1843) 18 Having her sences so sotted with care. 1609 Bible (Douay) *Ecclus.* xxiii. 19 Lest..being sotted with thy daily custom, thou suffer reproch. 1681 Dryden *Span. Friar* IV. ii, Had I not been sotted with my zeal, I might have found it sooner.
†**c.** Const. *of*, *on*, or *upon.* *Obs.*
1470-85 Malory *Arthur* x. lvi. 508, I merueylle..what eyleth them to be soo mad and soo soted vpon wymmen. 1551 Warwick in Froude *Hist. Eng.* (1860) V. 354 *note*, These men..be so sotted of their wives and children. 1591 Lyly *Endym.* I. i, I hope you be not sotted upon the man in the Moone. 1691 J. Wilson *Belphegor* III. iv, So sotted on her, he's not himself.

Sottely, obs. form of Subtly.

Sotter, *v. Sc.* and *north. dial.* [Cf. G. dial. *sottern* (also *suttern*) in the same sense.] *intr.* To boil slowly, or with a dull sound.
1781 J. Hutton *Tour to Caves* (ed. 2) Gloss. 96 *Sotter*, to make a noise in boiling as any thick substance does. 1808 in Jamieson. 1819 W. Tennant *Papistry Storm'd* (1827) 39 The broo boils up wi' sotterin' sound.

†**So·tteran,** *a. Obs.*⁻¹ [ad. It. *sotterrano*, f. *sot-* under + *terra* earth.] Subterranean.
1648 J. Raymond *Il Merc. Ital.* 152 The old Poets cald it Aerius, because of the many Sotteran Caves in it.

†**So·ttery.** *Obs.* [ad. older (now dial.) F. *sotterie*, *soterie*, f. *sot* Sot *sb.*[1] Hence also MDu. *sotterie* (usually *sotternie*).] A piece of foolishness or folly.
1598 Florio, *Mattarie*, fooleries, madde tricks, sotteries. a 1603 T. Cartwright *Confut. Rhem. N.T.* (1618) 564 The reason..is a palpable sottery. 1663 S. Patrick *Parab. Pilgrim* (1687) 437 To accuse the fraud of the first beginners of these Stories, and the folly of them that follow their Sotteries. 1731 Medley *Kolben's Cape G. Hope* II. 46 The Governour..took an infinite pleasure in imposing all the fictions and sotteries he could upon every one.

Sotting (sǫ·tiŋ), *vbl. sb.* [f. Sot *v.* + -ing[1].] The fact or practice of playing the sot, or of indulging in sottish conduct.
1583 Babington *Commandm.* (1590) 176 An example of vnmeasurable sotting in bed. 1603 Breton *Packet Mad Lett.* I. xxviii, Now for sotting and slauery and for courting in knauery, be perswaded that time will imploy my purse to better purpose. 1707 Hearne *Collect.* (O.H.S.) II. 49 Which Faculty..he..lost by his Idleness and Sotting. 1760 *Cautions & Advices to Officers of Army* 88 Perpetual Sotting cannot fail of blunting your Faculties. 1820 Hazlitt *Table-T.* Ser. II. xvii. (1869) 358 Nothing could overcome this propensity to low society and sotting. 1869 H. Kingsley *Stretton* II. 206 She was a perfect and absolute mistress of the art of sotting.

‖**Sottise** (sotīz). [F., f. *sot* Sot *a.*] A silly remark or saying; a foolish action.
1673 Dryden *Marr. à la Mode* III. i, That's an excellent word to begin withal; as, for example, he or she said a thousand sottises to me. a 1734 North *Examen* I. iii. § 14 (1740) 131 Which is a Sottise past all Belief. *Ibid.* § 23. 136 A Sottise of the lowest Form of Secretaryship.

Sottish (sǫ·tiʃ), *a.* Also 6 **shottishe.** [f. Sot *sb.*[1] + -ish.]
†**1.** Foolish, doltish, stupid: **a.** Of persons, or their faculties. *Obs.*
1566 Drant *Horace, Sat.* II. iii. F viij, Ye shottishe, dotishe, doultishe dawes. 1583 Greene *Mamillia* Wks. (Grosart) II. 292, I meane not to be so..sottish as with free consent to crosse my selfe with perpetuall calamitie. 1621 Burton *Anat. Mel.* I. ii. III. xiv. (1651) 126 Such are many sottish Princes, brought into a fools Paradise by their parasites. 1678 R. L'Estrange *Seneca's Mor.* I. xi. (1696) 47 The sottish Extract of an ancient Nobility may be preferr'd before a better Man. 1708 Swift *Predict. for 1708* Wks. 1755 II. I. 150 How ignorant those sottish pretenders to astrology are in their own concerns. 1737 Whiston *Josephus, Antiq.* IX. xii. § 3 This king was so sottish and thoughtless of what was for his own good, that he would not leave off worshipping the Syrian gods when he was beaten by them.
†**b.** Of things or actions. *Obs.*
1586 A. Day *Eng. Secretary* II. (1625) 87 What is it that this blinde and sottish love draweth not a man headlong into? 1614 Raleigh *Hist. World* I. 181 It were sottish to conceive, that he would permit the Divell..to raise a Prophet from the dead in Saul's respect. 1641 Milton *Ch. Govt.* II. ii. Wks. 1851 III. 155 O but..the sottish absurdity of this excuse! 1692 Bentley *Boyle Lect.* ii. 62 It's altogether as reasonable as this sottish opinion of the Atheists. 1755 B. Martin *Mag. Arts & Sci.* 169 'Tis sottish to imagine that they were made to answer no End, but Man's Luxury, Diversion, or Use. 1796 Bp. Watson *Apol. Bible* 207 A style of extreme arrogance, and sottish self-sufficiency.
2. Given or addicted to, characterized or affected by, excessive drinking or coarse self-indulgence. Also *absol.*
1632 Lithgow *Trav.* III. 92 A right name for so sottish a fellow, for..I neuer saw him..truely sober. 1642 D. Rogers *Naaman* 4 Implunged into a life of sence and sottish sensuality. a 1721 Sheffield (Dk. Buckhm.) *Wks.* (1753) II. 160 What else are..the sottish debauches..of Alexander the Great? 1785 Paley *Mor. Philos.* III. iii. ix, I would make choice of..a town-life, for the mercenary and sottish. 1811 A. T. Thomson *Lond. Disp.* (1818) 292 The effects of opium..are..loss of appetite and a sottish appearance. 1849 Macaulay *Hist. Eng.* iv. I. 453 People who saw him only over his bottle would have supposed him to be a man gross indeed, sottish, and addicted to low company. 1871 C. Gibbon *Lack of Gold* xii, His face was sallow and sottish.
Comb. 1856 R. A. Vaughan *Mystics* (1860) I. 150 A slip-shod, sottish-looking tailor.

Sottishly (sǫ·tiʃli), *adv.* [f. prec. + -ly[2].] In a sottish manner.
1566 Drant *Horace, Sat.* II. i. E viij, They say that I am subiecte vnto drinke, And shotishely vppon excesse, laye out what so I thynke. 1589 G. Harvey *Pierce's Super.* I. Wks. (Grosart) II. 7, I am none of those, that..sottishly hugge theire owne babyes. 1629 Massinger *Picture* III. v, I am not So sottishly credulous to believe the devil Hath that way power. 1691 Hartcliffe *Virtues* p. xviii, He breaths short Sighs often, sleeps seldom, till he dyes as sottishly, as he lived. 1702 *Eng. Theophrastus* 274 A man of parts may love indiscreetly but not sottishly. 1828-32 Webster, *Stupidly*, with extreme dullness;..sottishly.

Sottishness (sǫ·tiʃnės). [f. as prec. + -ness.]
†**1.** Foolishness, folly, stupidity. *Obs.*
Very common in the 17th century.
1589 Fleming *Virg. Georg.* IV. 74 When as a sudden sottishnesse or follie had surprizd And caught th' unwary loner fast. 1604 T. Wright *Passions* IV. i. 108 Silence may proceed sometimes of sottishnesse, because a man knowes not how to reason. 1653 Holcroft *Procopius, Goth. Wars* I. 27 He laughed at their sottishnesse, in hoping to bring their Oxen to their Enemies walls so unadvisedly. 1691 T. H[ale] *Acc. New Invent.* p. xxiii, The idle conceit of the Fish Remora, which mens sottishness hath made a vulgar one. a 1758 J. Edwards in Spurgeon *Treas. David* IV. 301 The sottishness of their being insensible of God's all-seeing eye.
2. Condition or conduct typical of a sot: *esp.* indulgence in drinking to excess.
1648 G. Daniel *Eclog* iii. 315 In time depart [thou] From the bewitching Sottishnes of Sin. 1660 Ingelo *Bentiv. & Ur.* II. (1682) 161 They naturally sink themselves into an unspeakable Sottishness. 1706 Stanhope *Paraphr.* III. 222 The Sottishness of a debauched Understanding. 1785 Paley *Mor. Philos.* IV. ii. (1841) 180 That solitary sottishness which waits neither for company nor invitation. 1855 Maurice *Learning & Working* 322, I cannot conceive how a people, fallen..into feebleness, strife and sottishness, could have escaped the severest punishments. 1860 Pusey *Min. Proph.* 29 The stupid sottishness of the confirmed voluptuary.

Sottle, obs. form of Subtle *a.*

‖**Sotto voce** (sǫ·to vōᵘ·tʃe), *adv.*, *a.*, and *sb.* [It. *sotto* under + *voce* voice.]
1. In a subdued or low voice: **a.** Of speech.
1737 Chesterf. in *Common Sense* 10 Sept. (1738) 226 And in a half Voice, or *Sotto voce*, discusses her solid Trifles in his Ear. 1828 Lytton *Pelham* II. iii, A whole host of hangers-on, who were disputing, by no means *sotto voce*, whether Lady Gander was mad or not? 1853 'C. Bede' *Verdant Green* II. vi, 'As though they were bursting with envy—not to say with laughter,' added Mr. Bouncer, *sotto voce.* 1891 Farrar *Darkn. & Dawn* xii, 'Even proverbs warn me against him.' He quoted two, *sotto voce*, to Titus.
b. Of singing (or playing).
1775 *Ann. Reg.* II. 65 Gabrieli..sung all her airs in what they call *sotto voce*, that is, so low, that they can scarcely be heard. 1780 *Mirror* No. 89, That sort of singing below the full powers of the performer's voice, which the Italians call singing *sotto-voce*. 1801 Busby *Dict. Mus.*, *Sotto Voce*, an expression implying that the movement, or the passage,

over which it is written is to be played or sung moderately loud. 1872 C. King *Sierra Nevada* x. 218 Then *sotto voce*, for we were very near, he sang again.
2. *fig.* Quietly, privately.
1819 Scott *Let.* in *Lockhart* (1837) IV. vii. 226 Will you make these enquiries for me *sotto voce*?
3. As *adj.* Uttered, etc., in an undertone.
1809 Malkin *Gil Blas* IV. viii. ¶ 6 There was not a *sotto voce* passage during the whole visit. 1818 Scott *Rob Roy* viii, 'God forbid!' said the Justice, in a tone of *sotto-voce* deprecation. 1859 Geo. Eliot *A. Bede* liii, David's *sotto voce* performance of 'My love's a rose without a thorn'. 1885 *L'pool Daily Post* 7 May 5/3 There was a suggestion of..joviality in his *sotto voce* sallies.
4. As *sb.* A remark made in an undertone.
1868 H. A. Stern *Captive Missionary* viii. 185, I only heard from two an ironical *sotto voce*, 'Well, will you walk again?'

Sotule, Sotyl(e, Sotyly, etc., obs. ff. Subtle *a.*, Subtly *adv.*

‖**Sou** (sū). [F., earlier *soul*, *sol* Sol *sb.*[3] For earlier examples of the pl. *sous*, see Souse *sb.*[4]] A French coin, formerly the twentieth part of a livre, now used to designate the five-centime piece.
1814 *Sporting Mag.* XLIV. 60 We gave the postillions ten sous per post extra, to stimulate them to speed. 1823 Byron *Juan* XI. lxxv, They are young, but know not youth,..rich without a sou. 1866 *Cornh. Mag.* Nov. 532 Imagine..that I have been paying thirty-eight sous a pound. 1882 'Ouida' *Under Two Flags* (1890) 272 He had scarcely a sou in his pocket.

Sou, obs. form of Sew *v.*, Show *v.*, Sow *sb.*[1]

Souant, variant of Suant *a. Obs.*

Souari, variant of Saouari.
1849 Balfour *Man. Bot.* § 808 *Rhizobolaceæ*, the Souari-nut Family. 1866 *Treas. Bot.* 1074/2 *Souari-wood*, a durable timber of Demerara. 1885 Lady Brassey *The Trades* 112 The souari or butter-nuts..contain even more oleaginous matter.

Soubadaree, -y, obs. varr. of Subahdarry.

Soubah, -dar, -ship: see Subah, etc.

Soubget, -git, obs. forms of Subject.

‖**Soubise** (subīz). [From the name of the French general and courtier Charles de Rohan Soubise (1715-1787).]
†**1.** A kind of cravat. *Obs.*
1776 Anstey *Election Ball* (1808) 229 With a shoe like a sauce boat and steeple-clock'd hose And a silken soubise that bob'd up to his nose.
2. A kind of onion-sauce.
Usually *Soubise sauce*, or in F. form *Sauce Soubise*.
1822 Ude *French Cook* (ed. 7) 18 Purée of Onion, or Soubise. 1846 Soyer *Syst. Cookery* 22 Sauce Soubise. Peel six large onions [etc.]. 1861 Eliza Acton *Mod. Cookery* 126 Soubise. (English Receipt.)..Soubise. (French Receipt.) 1880 *B'ham Weekly Post* 6 Nov. 1/7 Mutton cutlets, dressed with Soubise sauce, are quite a different thing from mutton cutlets plainly fried.

‖**Soubresaut** (subrəso). [F.: see Somersault *sb.*] (See quot. 1849.)
1849 R. V. Dixon *Heat* 147 The phenomenon called 'soubresaut', or jumping motion, sometimes observed in liquids when in a state of ebullition. 1863 Grove *Contrib. to Sci.* 420 Boiling like sulphuric acid with soubresauts.

‖**Soubrette** (subret). [F., ad. Prov. *soubreto*, fem. of *soubret* coy, reserved, f. *soubra* to set aside.]
1. *Theat.* A maid-servant or lady's maid as a character in a play or opera, usually one of a pert, coquettish, or intriguing character; an actress or singer taking such a part.
1753 H. Walpole *Lett.* (1840) III. 33 There is a soubrette, called the Niccolina. 1774 *Ibid.* V. 391 A fat woman, rather elderly, who sometimes acted the *soubrette*. c 1820 S. Rogers *Italy* (1839) 57 He prompts the young Soubrette, conning her part. 1839 Hallam *Hist. Lit.* IV. vi. § 52 Congreve has made more use of the all-important soubrette, on whom so much depends in French comedy. 1871 *All Year Round* 24 June 91/1 Tragedy queens and comic soubrettes were alike to her, and she did not present them very differently to her audience.
attrib. 1887 *The Lady* 20 Jan. 38/2 Miss Sergisson played the small part of Maid with ease and grace, and wore a very becoming *soubrette* toilette of pink and grey cotton.
2. A lady's maid; a maid-servant.
1824 Miss Mitford *Village* Ser. I. (1863) 131 She united the pleasant and amusing qualities of a French soubrette, with the solid excellence of an Englishwoman of the old school. 1848 M. W. Savage *Bachelor of the Albany* (1854) 65 The Soubrette leading the way by stating the name of her mistress. 1880 Ruskin *Bible of Amiens* I. (1884) 4 The little white-capped Amienoise soubrette.
Hence **Soubre·ttish** *a.*
1891 E. Field *Bk. Western Verse* 198 Soubrettish ways these latter days Invite my praise, but never get it.

‖**Soubriquet** (sū·brikē, ‖ subrikę), *sb.* [a. older F. *soubriquet.*] = Sobriquet.
1818 Lady Morgan *Autobiog.* (1859) 95 That *soubriquet* was given me long after by Mirabeau. 1835 T. Mitchell *Acharn. of Aristoph.* 121 *note*, The soubriquet of *gapers* appears to have been attached to the citizens of Athens. 1867 Trollope *Chron. Barset* II. xlix. 57 Her name was Susan, but he had always called her Posy, having himself invented for her that soubriquet.
Hence **Sou·briquet** *v. trans.*, to nickname.
1880 Gordon *Bk. Chron. Keith* 110 James Henry, soubriqueted the Grammarian from his pedantry.

Soubtilite, obs. variant of Subtility.

‖**Soucar** (sau·kā̆r). Also 8 **saucar,** 9 **sahoukar, soukar, sowcar.** [ad. Urdū (Hindī) ساهوکار *sāhūkār* great merchant, etc.] A Hindoo banker or money-lender.
1785 Burke *Sp. on Nabob of Arcot's Debts* Wks. VI. 289 When a *saucar*, that is a money dealer, becomes security for any native prince [etc.]. 1799 Wellington *Suppl. Desp.* (1858) I. 378 A debt due by him to a soucar, by name of Rugobah. 1858 J. B. Norton *Topics* 180 When these new tenants are wealthy soucars..they will not cultivate the soil themselves. 1875 J. Wilson in G. Smith *Life* App. (1878) 633 Money which he had borrowed from Soukars and bankers. 1883 *Madras Mail* 5 Dec. 22/2 The Indian Sowcar has come to possess a notoriety hardly surpassed by that of the European Jew.
attrib. 1785 Burke *Sp. on Nabob of Arcot's Debts* Wks. VI. 237 The right honourable gentleman's favourite soucar cavalry.
Hence **Sou·caring,** money-lending.
1785 Burke *Sp. on Nabob of Arcot's Debts* Wks. VI. 237 The whole art and mystery..of the profession of soucaring.

Souccour, obs. f. Succour *sb.*

†**Souce**[1]. *Obs.*⁻¹ (Meaning uncertain.)
a 1450 *Fysshynge w. Angle* (1883) 3 With mysfedyng þen schall sche [*sc.* the hawk] haue the frounce, þe Rey, þe Cray, and mony oþer seknes þat bryngет hur to þe souce [1496 sowse].

†**Souce**[2]. *Obs.*⁻⁰ (See quot.)
1688 Holme *Armoury* III. 271/2 A kind of a Drinking Cup..is by some Gentlemens Buttlers termed a Souce, Goglet, or Goblet.

Souce, obs. f. Souse *sb.* and *v.* **Souch,** var. Sough *sb.* and *v.*; obs. form of Such *a.*

†**Souche,** *v. Obs.* In 4 **souchy, souche(n), scouche, schoche,** 4-5 **sowche.** [ad. OF. *souchier* (also *sos-*, *suscher*):—L. *suspicāri* to suspect.]
1. *trans.* To suspect, have suspicion of (a thing).
c 1325 *Lay le Freine* 69 Vif ich com hir to More than ichaue y-do, The abbesse wil souchy gile. c 1340 Hampole *Pr. Consc.* 788 He souches and trowes sone a thyng, Bot ful late he turnes fra þat trowyng. 1390 Gower *Conf.* I. 225 If so be myn herte soucheth That oght unto my ladi toucheth [etc.].
2. *intr.* To be suspicious (*of* something). *Obs.*
13.. *Seuyn Sag.* (W.) 1438 He saide nowt... But euer he souchede him of gile. 1338 R. Brunne *Chron.* (1810) 259 Werfore our kyng Edward in þouht fulle wele has souched. c 1400 *Land Troy Bk.* 12596 With foule venym—alle men souched—His bowe was bent.

Souchet: see Water-souchet.

Souchong (sūʃǫ·ŋ). [ad. Chinese *siao-chung* (Cantonese *siu chung*) small sort.] One of the finer varieties of black tea. Also *attrib.*
1760 *Ann. Reg.* 132 The East-India ships..have brought..62,900 [lb.] of souchong. 1777 Abigail Adams in *Fam. Lett.* (1876) 313, I feel as contented when I have breakfasted upon milk as ever I did with Hyson or Souchong. 1803 *Phil. Trans.* XCIII. 268 An ounce of Souchong tea produced 48 grains of tannin. 1850 E. FitzGerald *Lett.* (1889) I. 208 Now, animated by some very inferior Souchong from the village shop, I continue my letter. 1870 Dickens *E. Drood* vi, He finished his breakfast as if the flavour of the Superior Family Souchong..were a little on the wane.

Soucht, obs. Sc. pa. t. of Seek *v.*

Soucie: see Sussy *sb.*

†**Soucy.** *Obs.*⁻¹ [a. older F. *soucie* (mod.F. *souci*), ultimately repr. L. *solsequium.*] = Solsecle.
1549 *Compl. Scot.* vi. 57 Ther is ane eirb callit helytropium, the quhilk the vulgaris callis soucye.

Soucy: see Sussy *v.* **Soud(e,** varr. of Sold *sb.*[1], *v.*[1], *v.*[2]; Sc. varr. *should*, Shall *v.* **Soudainly,** obs. f. Suddenly.

Soudan (sūdā·n). Also **Sudan.** [Arab. سودان *sūdān*, pl. of *sūdā* black.] The part of Africa lying between the Sahara and the Equator. Hence **Soudane·se** *sb.*, an inhabitant of the Soudan (also as *pl.*); *adj.*, of or pertaining to the Soudan. **Sou·danize** *v. trans.* (see quot. 1884).
1875 Gordon in *G. in Central Africa* (1881) 77 Cowardly, lying, effeminate brutes these Arabs and Soudanese! 1884 *Pall Mall G.* 5 May 11/2 Let it be supposed that the Soudan..is tranquillized, its administration 'Soudanized', native Mudirs appointed [etc.]. 1887 *Encycl. Brit.* XXII. 277/2 The well-watered and arable Soudanese lands.

Soudan(e, obs. ff. Soldan. **Soudanly,** obs. f. Suddenly. **Soude,** var. Sold *sb.*[1], etc.; obs. pa. pple. Sew *v.*[1]

†**Soudee.** *Obs.*⁻¹ [a. OF. *soudee*, *soldee*:—med.L. *solidāta.*] A solidate.
c 1450 *Godstow Reg.* 158, ij. soudees of rent.

Souden, obs. f. Soldan. **Souder,** obs. f. Solder, Soldier. **Soudeo(u)r, Soudgour, Soudiar, -dior, -dioure,** obs. ff. Soldier. **Soudly:** see Suddly *a.* **Soudon,** obs. form of Soldan. **Soudour,** obs. f. Solder. **Soudra,** var. Sudra. **Soudre, Soudur(e,** obs. ff. Solder. **Soudyer, -your(e, -yre,** obs. f. Soldier.

Soue(n), obs. ff. Seven. **Souel,** obs. f. Sowl. **Souenyht,** obs. f. Seven-night. **Soueran(e,** etc., obs. ff. Sovereign, etc. **Souepe,** obs. f. Seventh. **Soufee,** obs. f. Sufi. **Souff,** var. Sowff *Sc.* **Souffis(s)ance, -ant,** varr. Sufficance, -ant *Obs.*

‖**Souffle** (sufl'). *Path.* [F.] A murmuring or breathing sound.
1879 Webster *Suppl.* s.v., The uterine *souffle*, a sound heard over the pregnant uterus. 1897 *Allbutt's Syst. Med.* IV. 274 On auscultation, a systolic souffle transmitted from the adjacent aorta is sometimes heard. 1900 *Lancet* 20 Jan. 164/1 The absence of the fœtal heart-sounds and of the uterine souffle is very important.

‖**Soufflé** (sū·flē, ‖ sufle), *sb.* and *a.* Also 9 **souflet, soufflée.** [F., pa. pple. of *souffler*:—L. *sufflāre*, f. *sub* under + *flāre* to blow.
The use of the fem. form *soufflée* is prob. due to its occurrence in *omelette soufflée.*]
A. *sb.* A light dish, either sweet or savoury, made by mixing materials with white of egg beaten up to a froth, and heating the mixture in an oven until it puffs up.
α. 1813 Ude *French Cook* 195 Soufflé of young Partridges. 1846 Soyer *Cookery* 575 Soufflés when well-made are excellent removes for the winter season. 1847 Disraeli *Tancred* I. i, I entrusted the soufflées to him. 1883 'Annie Thomas' *Mod. Housewife* 14 Ducklings and roast pigeons followed, then some pastry and a well-made *soufflé*.
fig. 1891 Meredith *One of our Conq.* xx, Our soufflé of sentiment will be seen subsiding under a breath.
β. 1831 *Society* I. 84 Take my plate..for some of the sweets near Miss Bradford. Not the souflet. 1836 B. Hall *Schloss Hainfeld* vii. 104 Last of all, a souflet worthy of Very's or Beauvilliers'.
b. *attrib.*, as *soufflé-case*, *-dish*, etc.
1846 Soyer *Cookery* 329 In a common pie-dish or silver soufflée-dish. *Ibid.* 564 A cover large enough for the soufflée-case. 1888 *Athenæum* 22 Sept. 377/3 Mere whipped-egg *soufflé* work of the most artistic kind.
B. *adj.* Of ceramic ware: Having liquid colour applied by means of blowing.
1878 Miss J. J. Young *Ceramic Art* 152 The soufflé decoration is characteristic.

†**Sou·fflement.** *Obs.*⁻¹ [a. F. *soufflement*, f. *souffler*: see prec.] Breathing, blowing.
1483 Caxton *Cato* c ij, Platon perceyued..that the pestylence came by the wnystelyng and soufflement of the sayd dragons.

†**Souffler.** *Obs.*⁻¹ [ad. F. *souffleur*, f. *souffler* to blow.] (See quot. and cf. Blower[1] 2.)
1674 J. Josselyn *Two Voy.* 4 Two mighty Whales we now saw, the one..making a great noise with puffing and blowing; the Seamen called her a Soufler.

Souffraunce, obs. f. Sufferance. **Soufre,** obs. form of Sulphur. **Soufrecan,** obs. form of Suffragan. **Sougan,** variant of Suggan.

Sough (sʊf, sau, *Sc.* sʊχ), *sb.*[1] Forms: 4-5 **swogh(e, swough(e,** 6 **swouch,** 6- **souch,** 7- **sough** (8 **zough**), 8- **sugh** (9 **seugh, soogh, sooch,** etc.); 4 **swowh,** 4-5 **swow(e,** 5 **sow,** 9 **soo.** [ME. type **swōh*, *swōȝ*, from the verb *swōȝen*: see Sough *v.*[1] From the 16th cent. almost exclusively Sc. and north. dial. until adopted in general literary use in the 19th.
The pron. (sʊf) is given by Smart (1836) and Ogilvie (1850).]
1. A rushing or murmuring sound as of wind, water, or the like, esp. one of a gentle or soothing nature.
c 1381 Chaucer *Parl. Foules* 247 Of sykys hoote as fuyr I herde a swow that gan a-boute renne. c 1384 — *H. Fame* 1031 Herestow not the grete swogh? ? a 1400 *Morte Arth.* 759 With þe swoghe of þe see in swefnynge he felle. 1508 Dunbar *Tua Mariit Wemen* 519 The soft souch of the swyr.. Myght confort ony creatur of the kyn of Adam. 1513 Douglas *Æneid* II. xi. 81 Ilk swouch of wynd, and every quhisper..affrayit [me]. 1785 Burns *Cotter's Sat. Nt.* ii, November chill blaws loud wi' angry sugh. 1792 Wordsw. *Descript. Sketches* 359 Faint wail of eagle.., and pine-wood's steady sugh. 1816 Scott *Old Mort.* xxxiii, It is the sough of the wind among the bracken. 1847 C. Bronte *J. Eyre* xii, That evening calm betrayed alike the tinkle of the nearest streams, the sough of the most remote. 1862 Carlyle *Fredk. Gt.* XIII. vi. (1872) 73 Whereupon solemn waving of hats; indistinct sough of loyal murmur. 1879 Miss Bird *Rocky Mount.* 101 The strange sough of gusts moving among the pine tops.
b. *Sc.* A canting or whining manner of speaking, especially in preaching or praying.
1723 Meston *Knight* Poems (1767) 15 Give them the sough, they can dispense, With either scant or want of sense. c 1730 Burt *Lett. N. Scotl.* (1818) I. 171 The prayers are often more like narrations to the Almighty than petitions..; and the sough as it is called (the whine) is unmanly. 1816 Scott *Old Mort.* xiv, Never stir, if my auld mither is na at the preaching again! I ken the sough o' her texts. 1894 'Ian Maclaren' *Brier Bush* ii. 60 He's a speeritually minded man, Maister Cosh, and has the richt sough.
2. A deep sigh or breath. Also *transf.*
c 1386 Chaucer *Miller's T.* 433 He siketh, with ful many a sory swough. a 1400 *Isumbras* 89 His hirde-mene mett he everylkone With a fulle drery swoghe. 14.. *Chaucer's Troylus* IV. 375 (Cambr. MS.), Among his sobbis & his sowis sore. 1616 B. Jonson *Epigrams* cxxxiii, The well-greas'd wherry now had got betweene, And bad her fare-well sough, vnto the lurden. 1788 *Voc. Bargie* in *Trans. R. Irish Acad.* II. 35 *Zough*, a sigh. 1790 Burns *Battle of Sherra-Moor* ii, My heart, for fear, gae sough for sough. 1885 *Field* 12 Dec. 832/1 From the loch would come the sough of a porpoise or the wild cry of a loon. 1901 G. Douglas *House with Green Shutters* 298 It was hours ere he slept, but at last a heavy sough told her he had found oblivion.
3. A rumour; a report.
1716 Wodrow *Corr.* (1843) II. 172 By the souch of members I imagine the Duke of Argyle will be named. 1816 Scott *Antiq.* xxix, There was a sough in the country about it, but it was hushed up. 1821 Galt *Annals of Parish* xii, I found..a sough of something extraordinar going on. 1900 Strain *Elmslie's Drag-net* 35, I had heard some sough o' a byre at Kelso that had been smitten.

4. *To keep a calm* (or *quiet*) *sough*, to keep quiet, to say little or nothing. *Sc.*
1808 Jamieson, *Keep a calm souch*, be silent. 1816 Scott *Old Mort.* xx, I'se aye keep a calm sough. 1863 Mrs. Gaskell *Sylvia's Lovers* (1874) 232 Not that I iver let on to them.., so keep a calm sough, my lad. 1880 Mrs. Lynn Linton *Rebel Family* xiii, So that, on the whole, keeping a calm sough was the best wisdom.
Hence **Sou·ghfully** *adv.*, with a soughing sound; **Sou·ghless** *a.*, silent, noiseless.
1851 W. Hay *Lintie o' Moray* 41 Gentle stream, Wi' soughless waters onward stealin'. 1890 Mrs. Barr *Friend Olivia* xx, The trees..talked soughfully among themselves.

Sough (sʊf), *sb.*[2] Forms: 4 **sogh, sohw,** 5 **swowȝe, swoughe,** 5- **sough** (6 **soughe,** *Sc.* **souch**), 7 **sowgh, saugh,** 9 *dial.* **sugh**; 8- **suff,** 9 **surf,** *dial.* **souffe, soof.** See also Sheugh. [Of obscure origin. Cf. Antwerp dial. *zoeg* a small ditch in a meadow.]
1. A boggy or swampy place; a small pool.
a 1300 *Cursor M.* 2501 Þai fled and fell vntill a sogh [*Gött.* sohw], And þar þair faas þam foluand slogh. a 1450 *Le Morte Arth.* 875 (Roxb.), In a foreste by a swoughe. 1515 *Scottish Field* 440 in *Chetham Misc.* (1856), On a soughe us beside, there seene we our enemies, Were moving over the mountains. 1612 Drayton *Poly-olb.* iv. 168 Then Dulas and Cledaugh, By Morgany doe drive her through her wat'ry saugh. 1869 'Ouida' *Puck* vii, The road..went through a shallow 'sough' of water. 1876- in dial. glossaries (Cumb., Yks., Heref.).
2. A small gutter for draining off water; a drain, a sewer, a trench.
c 1440 *Pallad. on Husb.* I. 515 The length [of the ox-stall is] as from the horn into the sough. 1523 Fitzherb. *Surv.* xxxv. 49 If this maner of dichynge wyll nat make the marres grounde drie, than must you make a sough vnderneth therthe as men do to gette cole. c 1570 *Diurn. Occurr.* (Bann. Cl.) 100 The said erle slipit ower ane souch, and tomblit doun the same. 1667 Primatt *City & C. Builder* 5 The charge of driving such Soughs or Trenches. 1681 *Rec. Burg. Sheffield* (1897) 217 For making a sough to the pinfold. 1763 *Ann. Reg.* II. 100/1 At proper distances, soughs are formed near the top of the canal, which prevents it from overflowing during immoderate rains. 1780 *Phil. Trans.* LXX. 316, I shall lay a sough of brick, which will convey it from the pump to the boiler. 1805 R. W. Dickson *Pract. Agric.* I. 301 The most difficult part of the business consists in laying the sough when in running sands. 1833 *Act 3 & 4 Will. IV*, c. 46 § 116 Any water pipe, sough, or watercourse already laid down..in..any of the streets. 1885 *Law Times' Rep.* LII. 356/2 Various old stone soughs, which ..received the sewage of a number of houses.
attrib. 1892 Eminson *Epid. Pneumonia at Scotter* 18 The out-door premises..drained off through some common sough pipes.
3. A subterranean drain to carry off the water in a mine; an adit of a mine.
1619 Atkinson *Gold Mynes Scotl.* (Bann. Cl.) 15 To frame or make a long sowgh, or scowring place, into which they bringe the streame water. 1653 Manlove *Customes Lead Mines* 260 (E.D.S.), Main Rakes, Cross Rakes, Brownhenns, Budles and Soughs. 1686 Plot *Staffordsh.* 137 This sort of damp..is that they commonly meet with in long Soughs for conveyance of water from the coale. 1747 Hooson *Miner's Dict.* T ij b, These Addits or Soughs if they prove soft, destroy a great deal of Timber, especially in Sand. 1778 W. Pryce *Min. Cornub.* 81 The Sough or Adit being one hundred fathoms below the surface. 1851 *Act 14 & 15 Vict.* c. 94 § 26 If any Person shall, by virtue of any Sough Engine or other Means, unwater or give Relief to any Mine or Vein which may be under Water. 1882 R. L. Galloway *Coal Mining* 25 The drainage of the mines was effected by means of the horizontal tunnels.., which were variously termed adits, watergates, soughs, surfs.

†**Sough,** *sb.*[3] *Obs. rare.* Also 5 **sugh.** [repr. OE. *sulh* plough: see Sull *sb.*] A ploughshare.
1432-50 tr. *Higden* (Rolls) VII. 265 Sche..passede by fulle stappes the ix. cultres or sughes with owte eny hurte. 1598 Florio, *Vōmere*,..the sough or ploughshare or culter. 1688 Holme *Armoury* III. 333/2 The Sough..[of a plough] is that as Plows into the Ground.

Sough, obs. f. pa. t. See *v.*; obs. f. Sow *sb.*[1]

Sough (sʊf, sau, *Sc.* sʊχ), *v.*[1] Forms: 1 **swōgan,** 5 **swoghe** (**squoe**), 6 *Sc.* **swouch, suowch, swoch**; 4 **souȝe,** 6 (9) **sowgh, sogh,** 6- **sugh,** 8- **sough** (9 *dial.* **suff**); *Sc.* 6 **sowch,** 6, 8- **souch,** 9 **sooch**; 5 **swowe,** 8 **swoo,** 9 *dial.* **sow, sou(e, soo.** [OE. *swōgan*, = OS. *swōgan* to move with a rushing sound; related to Goth. *ufswōgjan* (cf. OE. *swēgan* to sound, etc.; Norw. dial. *søgja* to murmur, rustle) and *swōgatjan* to sigh. Cf. also WFris. *swoegje* to pant.]
1. *intr.* To make a rushing, rustling, or murmuring sound.
a 900 Cynewulf *Crist* 950 On seofon healfa swoȝað windas. a 1000 *Genesis* 1375 Drihten..let..egorstreamas swearte swoȝan. 13.. *E. E. Allit. P.* C. 140 Þe see souȝed ful sore, gret selly to here. c 1400 *Anturs of Arth.* 55 By þe stremys so strange, þat swyftly swoghes [*v.r.* squytherly squoes]. c 1450 Holland *Howlat* 171 Swannis swowchand full swyth, swetest of swar. 1513 Douglas *Æneid* I. vi. 155 Ther wyngis swochand jolely. *Ibid.* v. iii. 76 The fludis ..souchand quhair thai fair, In sondir slydis. 1724 Ramsay *Royal Archers Shooting* iv, The feather'd arrows drive All soughing thro' the sky. 1728 — *Robt., Richy, & Sandy* 56 Torn frae its roots before it souchan fell. 1815 G. Beattie *John o' Arnha'* (1826) 25 The wind sough'd mournfu' throw the trees. 1857 Thoreau *Maine W.* i. (1864) 3 The white-pine tree..—its branches soughing with the four winds. 1884 Mrs. C. Praed *Zéro* iv, The wind soughed through the budding branches overhead in long monotonous swell.
b. *trans.* To utter in this manner.
1821 Clare *Vill. Minstr.* I. 29 Each rude-risen tempest ..Sughing its vengeance through the yellow trees.
2. *intr.* To draw the breath heavily or noisily; to sigh deeply.
c 1475 *Partenay* 1944 There gan he to sigh and sowghid for wo. *Ibid.* 2890 He sighed, soghed, wepte with teres many. 1806 R. Jamieson *Pop. Ballads* II. 338, I hear your mither souch and snore. 1847 H. Bushnell *Chr. Nurture* II. iii. (1861) 273 Dosing, all together, and sughing in dull dreams.
b. With *away*: To breathe one's last; to die.
1816 Scott *Old Mort.* xxxix, His uncle, poor gentleman, just sough'd awa wi' it in his mouth. 1886 Willock *Rosetty Ends* vi. (1887) 46 He muttered 'Puir Gyp', an' then he soughed awa.
3. *trans.* **a.** To hum (a tune). Also *fig.*
1711 Ramsay *On Maggy Johnstoun* x, I took a nap, And soucht a' night balillilow, As sound's a tap. 1721 — *Elegy on Patie Birnie* iv, His face could mak' you fain, When he did sough, 'O wiltu, wiltu do 't again!' 1805 J. Nicol *Poems* II. 133 (Jam.), I, 'mang many merry fouk, Can..sough a tune, an' crack a jock.
b. To utter in a sighing or whining tone.
1816 Scott *Antiq.* xxvii, He hears ane o' the king's Presbyterian chaplains sough out a sermon. 1818 — *Br. Lamm.* xviii, I hae soughed thae dark words ower to mysell.

Sough (sʊf), *v.*[2] [f. Sough *sb.*[2]]
1. *trans.* **a.** To face or build up (a ditch) *with* stone, etc. **b.** To make drains in (land); to drain by constructing proper channels. Also *absol.*
1688 *Norris Papers* (Chetham Soc.) 175 That all ditches which convey the water crosse the highway be soughed with wall stone, and well covered throughout. 1797 *Trans. Soc. Arts* XV. 209 This lot of land, considered as enclosed, but not soughed. 1836 *Hull & Selby Rlwy. Act* 6 To bore, dig, cut, embank and sough. 1868 C. W. Hatfield *Hist. Notices Doncaster* II. 285 Silver-street and French-gate were soughed in 1837-8.
2. *intr.* To reach, or get into, a sough.
1898 *Daily News* 19 Feb. 9/2 Lang Syne again raced by, and was a meritorious winner as the hare soughed.

Sou·ghing, *vbl. sb.*[1] [f. Sough *v.*[1]] The action of the verb; a rushing or murmuring sound.
? a 1400 *Morte Arth.* 931 Swowynge of watyr, and syngynge of byrdez. c 1400 *Destr. Troy* 1061 Swoghyng of swete ayre, Swalyng of briddes. 1582 Stanyhurst *Æneis* II. (Arb.) 63 The tre..with sowghing yt grunts, as wounded in hacking. 1713 Derham *Phys.-Theol.* IV. iii. 119 Which causeth a confusion in the Hearing, with a certain Murmur or Swooing like the fall of Waters. 1817 *Blackw. Mag.* I. 57 Carefully noticing the formation of the clouds..and the *soughing* of the winds. 1859 Miss Mulock *Romantic T.* 74 In the soughing of the solemn trees. 1879 Sala *Paris Herself Again* xvii, Then come the distant wailing and soughing of a sea of martial music.

Sou·ghing, *vbl. sb.*[2] [f. Sough *v.*[2]] The operation of draining or making drains. Also *attrib.*, as *soughing-tile*, *tool*.
1807 Vancouver *Agric. Devon* (1813) 133 Tunnelling, or soughing under the gateways, will be in proportion to..the facility of procuring soughing-tiles. 1840 *Civil Eng. & Arch. Jrnl.* III. 140/1 Improvements in the manufacture of cofered spades and shovels, soughing and grafting tools. 1868 Lady Verney *Stone Edge* xxi, I can't afford to lose back-rent, and present rent, and arrears for soughing.

Sou·ghing, *ppl. a.* [f. Sough *v.*[1]] Rushing, rustling, murmuring, etc.
Beowulf 3145 Wudurec astah.., swogende leȝ. 1513 Douglas *Æneid* VI. xi. 51 A wod with sowchand bewis schene. *Ibid.* VII. Prol. 74 Every lynde Quhyslyt and brayt of the swouchand wynde. 1806 J. Grahame *Birds of Scot.* 18 The dismal soughing wing, the doleful cry. 1859 Mrs. Gaskell *Round the Sofa* II. 111 The soughing November wind came with long sweeps over the fells. 1880 *Daily Tel.* 29 Oct., The nearly naked branches crackle and moan with the soughing, storm-presaging wind.

Sought (saut), *sb. north. dial.* Forms: 4 **soght,** 5 **souȝt,** 7 **sought,** 9 **sowt, soot.** [a. ON. **soht* (later *sótt*, Icel. and Fær. *sótt*, Norw. *sott*, Sw. and Da. *sot*), = Goth. *sauhts*, OS. *suht* (hence once in OE.), OHG. and MHG. *suht* (G. *sucht*), Du. *zucht*: cf. also OEFris. *secht*, OWFris. *siochte*. The stem *suh-*, *suk-* is an ablaut-variant of *seuk-*: see Sick *a.*] Sickness, illness, disease. In later use *spec.* a disease of sheep or other animals.
See also the combs. Gulesought and Lungsought.
a 1300 *Cursor M.* 14157 Wel þai trud þat he moght þair broþer sauue of al his soght. 14.. *MS. Sloane* 7, fol. 73 (H.), For the ȝalow souȝt, that men callin the jaundys. 1621 Brathwait *Nat. Embassie* (1877) 242 Scab, sought, the rot or any kind of murren. 1847 Halliwell, *Sowt*, the rot in sheep. *Westm.* 1876 Richardson *Cumbld. Talk* Ser. II. 150 Ye'r sheep dee i' t' seekness or t' sowt. 1878 *Cumbld. Gloss.* 91 *Sowt*, the joint-ill in lambs and calves.

Sought (sǫt), *ppl. a.* [pa. pple. of Seek *v.*] That is, or has been, searched for, desired, etc.
See also *long-sought* s.v. Long *adv.* 9 a.
a 1300 *Cursor M.* 3254 To mesopotany suith come he, And son he fand þe soght cite. 1382 Wyclif *Isaiah* lxii. 12 Thou..shalt be clepid a soȝt cite, and not forsaken. 1632 Lithgow *Trav.* III. 77 Now Creta comes..To my sought view. 1710 Berkeley *Princ. Hum. Knowl.* § 121 Having found the sought figures. 1725 W. Halfpenny *Sound Building* 21 Then..you will describe the sought Arches *v z t* and *w t.* *Ibid.* 22. 1883 'Annie Thomas' *Mod. Housewife* 149 The cleverness which makes her a sought woman in every *coterie*.
b. With *-after* or *-for.*
1605 B. Jonson *Volpone* IV. ii, When he mist His sought-for father. 1776 *The Refutation* 13 The sought-for bribe I doubt you'll never see. 1829 Bentham *Justice & Cod. Petit.* 12 Such supposed facts as..may be styled unknown or sought-for facts. 1881 *Trans. Obstet. Soc. Lond.* XXII. 66 He was the fashionable and most sought-after accoucheur.

Soughthistle, obs. f. Sow-thistle. **Soujour,** obs. f. Soldier *sb.* **Souk(e,** obs. varr. Suck. **Soukar,** obs. Sc. f. Sugar; variant of Soucar. **Souker,** obs. var. Sucker.

Soul (sōᵘl), *sb.* Forms: α. 1 **sawol, -al,** 1-2 **sawul,** 1, 4 **sawel** (1 **sauwel,** 4 **saw-, sauwil**), 1, 4-6 **sawl** (5-6 **sawll,** 9 *dial.* **sawl, seawl, zawl,** etc.), 2-6 **sawle**; 1, 4 **sauel** (4 **-il**), 3-7 (9 *dial.*) **saule** (3 **sæule,** 4 **zaule,** 5 **savle**); 1, 4-5, 6-9 *Sc.* and *north.* **saul,** 5-7 *Sc.* and *north.* **saull**; 5 **sal, saal,** 5-6 **sale,** 5-6 (9 *dial.*) **sall** (6 **salle**). β. 2-7 **sowle,** 5 **sowel,** 5-6 **sowylle,** 6 **sowll,** 8 *Ir.* **showl,** 9 *dial.* **sowl**; 3-7 **soule** (6 **zoule, soulle**), 5- **soul** (8 *dial.* **saoul**); 5 **sool** (6 **sooll**), 5-6 **solle,** 6-8 (9 *dial.*) **sole,** 7 **sol.** [Common Teut.: OE. *sáwol*, *sáwel*, *sáwl*, etc., = Goth. *saiwala*; the forms in the other languages show various degrees of contraction, as OHG. *sêula*, *sêla* (MHG. *sêle*, G. *seele*), OS. *sêola* (*siola*; MLG. *sêle*, LG. *seele*, *seel*), OLFrank. *sêla*, *sîla* (MDu. *siel-e*, *ziel-e*, Du. *ziel*), OFris. *sêle* (*siele*; WFris. *siel*, NFris. *seel*, *sial*, etc.); ON. *sála*, *sál* (Icel. *sál*, Norw. dial. *saal*), MSw. *sial*, *siäl*, *siel* (Sw. *själ*, Da. *sjæl*), whence Finn. *sielu*, Lapp. *siello*, etc. The ultimate etymology is uncertain.
For examples of the older genitive form without *-s*, see 18.]
I. †**1.** The principle of life in man or animals; animate existence. *Obs.* (freq. in OE. in Scriptural passages).
Beowulf 2820 Him of hreðre ȝewat sawol secean soðfæstra dom. c 825 *Vesp. Psalter* lxxvii. 50 [He ne] spearede from deaðe sawlum heara. c 1000 *Ags. Ps.* (Thorpe) xxxii. 16 Forþam þæt he ȝefriðe heora sawla fram deaðe, and hi fede on hungres tide. 1382 Wyclif *Jonah* i. 14 Lord, we bisechen, that we perishe not in the soule of this man. a 1450 tr. *De Imitatione* I. xviii. 20 For þei hated her soules, þat is to say, her bodely lyues, þat þei miȝt kepe hem in to lif euerlasting. 1535 Coverdale *Judg.* xii. 3 Whan I sawe yᵗ there was no helper, I put my soule in my honde, and wente agaynst the children of Ammon. 1611 Bible *Gen.* xxxv. 18 As her soule was in departing, (for she died). [1651 Hobbes *Leviath.* III. xxxviii. 241 Soule and Life in the Scripture, do usually signifie the same thing.] 1697 Dryden *Virg. Georg.* III. 744 The thriven Calves..render their sweet Souls before the plenteous Rack.
2. The principle of thought and action in man, commonly regarded as an entity distinct from the body; the spiritual part of man in contrast to the purely physical. Also occas., the corresponding or analogous principle in animals. Freq. in connexion with, or in contrast to, *body.*
Sometimes personified, as in the common mediæval dialogues between the soul and the body.
α. c 888 K. Ælfred *Boeth.* xxxiv. § 6 To þære saule & to þæm lichoman, belimpað ealle þas þæs monnes good ȝe gastlicu ȝe lichomlicu. 971 *Blickl. Hom.* 21 Eal swa hwæt swa se ȝesenelica lichama deþ oþþe wyrceþ, eal þæt deþ seo unȝesynelice sawl þurh þone lichoman. c 1000 Ælfric *Hom.* I. 16 Se man is ece on anum dæle, þæt is on ðære sawle. c 1200 Ormin 11498 Swa þatt te manness bodiȝ beo Buhsumm forþ wiþþ þe sawle. a 1300 *Cursor M.* 21757 (Edin.), Þe Sawil it hauis of strenþis þrin. 1340 *Ayenb.* 105 Þri þinges þet byeþ ine þe zaule, beþenchinge, onderstondynge, and wyl. a 1400-50 *Alexander* 4429 All þe sauour of ȝoure sauls is sattild in ȝour mouthis. 1483 *Cath. Angl.* 319 A Savle, *anima.* 1599 Alex. Hume *Hymns* i. 21 My sensis, and my saull I saw, Debait a deadly strife. 1737 *Gentl. Mag.* VII. 50 The coward lurks in Jockey's saul.
β. c 1175 in *Fragm. Ælfric's Gloss.*, etc. (1838) 6 Ȝet sæiþ þeo sowle soriliche to þen licame [etc.]. 12.. *Moral Ode* 394 To þere blisse us bringe god..þenne he vre soule vn-bint of licames bende. c 1386 Chaucer *Prol.* 656 But if [=unless] a mannes soule were in his purs. 1422 tr. *Secreta Secret., Priv. Priv.* 218 Here is i-prowid that the Sowle sueth the condycionys of the bodyes. c 1440 *Jacob's Well* 258 As þi soule is lyif of þi body, so is god lyif of þi soule. a 1547 Surrey *Eccl.* iii. Poems (1810) 355 Who can tell yf that the sowle of man ascende, Or with the body of it dye? 1596 Shaks. *Merch. V.* IV. i. 132 To hold opinion ..That soules of Animals infuse themselues Into the trunkes of men. 1621 Hakewill *David's Vow* 120 It is..vanity, to thinke that all passions either may be or should be utterly rooted out of the soule. 1681 Flavel *Meth. Grace* v. 111 If there be spiritual sense in your souls, there is spiritual life in them. 1716-8 Lady M. W. Montagu *Lett.* I. xxxix. 159 Our vulgar notion that they do not own women to have any souls, is a mistake. 1774 Goldsm. *Nat. Hist.* (1776) II. 207 It must be dreadful,..since it is sufficient to separate the soul from the body. 1841 Dickens *Barn. Rudge* iii, The absence of the soul is far more terrible in a living man than in a dead one. 1868 Helps *Realmah* ix. (1876) 247, I mean that there should be a double soul, taking the word 'soul' to include all powers, both of thought and feeling. 1897 Mary Kingsley *W. Africa* 441, I know many people have doubts as to the existence of souls in small boys of this class.
fig. 1829 Carlyle *Misc.* (1857) II. 106 Thus is the Body-politic, more than ever worshipped and tendered; but the Soul-politic less than ever.
b. Without article.
c 1000 Ælfric *Hom.* I. 276 Fixas and fuȝelas he ȝesceop on flæsce butan sawle. 13.. *E. E. Allit. P.* B. 290 Al schal doun & be ded & dryuen out of erþe, þat euer I sette saule inne. c 1374 Chaucer *Troilus* II. 1734, I coniure..On his half, which that sowle us alle sende. c 1430 *Hymns Virgin*

3. a. The seat of the emotions, feelings, or sentiments; the emotional part of man's nature.

4. In various phrases (see quots.).

5. *Metaph.* The vital, sensitive, or rational principle in plants, animals, or human beings. Freq. with *a, the,* and in pl.

II. 8. The spiritual part of man considered in its moral aspect or in relation to God and His precepts.

II. 9. The spiritual part of man regarded as surviving after death and as susceptible of happiness or misery in a future state.

III. 11. The disembodied spirit of a (deceased) person, regarded as a separate entity, and as invested with some amount of form and personality.

12. A person, an individual; †a living thing.

IV. In various special or technical uses.

15. (See later quots.)

16. The bore of a cannon (see quot. 1571).

17. The sound-post of a violin.

18. Used (with defining *a, the*) to denote a person of a particular character or in respect of some quality; freq. with a touch of contempt, compassion, or familiarity.

V. *attrib.* and *Comb.*

18. Genitive combs. + *a.* With forms representing the OE. gen. sing. *sáwle,* as *soul-host, -food, -leech,* etc. See also SOUL-HEAL, -HEALTH.

19. Simple attrib., as *soul-affair, -blood,* + *-case, concern'ment,* etc.

20. With the names of persons, etc. (chiefly agent-nouns), as *soul-crafter, -carver,* etc.

21. With vbl. sbs., as *soul-craving, -feasting, -humbling,* etc.

23. With *a, the,* pples., as *soul-benumbed, -blinded, -born, -felt,* etc.

24. With *a, the,* pples. forming objective combs., as *soul-adorning, -amazing, -hailing,* etc., adjs.

25. Special combs., as †*soul-ale,* an alehouse; drinking at the funeral of a person; a dirge ale; †*soul-mass,* a specially prepared cake or bun distributed in various northern or north-midland counties on All Souls' Day, esp. to parties of children who go 'souling'; †*soul-candle,* ? one of several candles placed about the coffin at a funeral 'service'; †*soul-case slang,* the body; †*soul chaplain,* a *soul-priest;* †*soul-charm,* an incantation; †*soul-friend* (see quot.); †*soul-groat,* a soul-penny; †*soul-house,* a model or representation of a house placed by the ancient Egyptians in a tomb to receive the soul of a dead person; *soul-paten,* -pennies, money subscribed by the members of a guild to pay for soul-masses; †*soul-priest,* a priest having the special function of praying for the souls of the dead; *soul-sleeper,* = SOUL-SORY; †*soul-sleeper,* one who holds the doctrine of psychopannychism; a psychopannychist.

Soul, soul-bell (S... SOUL *sb.*) The passing-bell. *Also*

Soul-heal, soul-bell *Obs.*

Soul-heal, *soul-heale* (S... SOUL *sb.* + HEAL *sb.*) *Obs.*

Soul-hatch *Obs.* [f. SOUL *sb.* + HATCH.]

Soulable, *a.* [f. SOUL *sb.*]

Soulament, *adv., adj.* = SOLELY.

Soulcan *sb.*

Soulcar *sb.* [f. SOUL *sb.* + CAR *sb.*]

Souled (S...) *a.* [f. SOUL *sb.* + -ED.]

†**Souled,** *ppl. a.* Obs.

Souless var. SOULLESS *a.*

Soul, *sb.* Also 5, 9 *dial.* sowl. [f. the sb.]

1. *trans.* To endow or endue with a soul.

2. *intr.* To go about collecting doles, properly on the eve of All Souls' Day.

3. To capture or catch souls. *rare*[-1]

Soul, obs. or dial. form of SOLE.

†**Soulack,** var. SOULAK *Obs.*

Soular, *a.* var. of SOLAR.

†**Soulament,** *sb.* Obs.

Souldan, etc., obs. forms of SULTAN.

Soulder, obs. form of SOLDER, SHOULDER.

†**Souldie,** *Obs. rare.* Also 5 *souldy.* [a. OF. *soudie, soldie,* f. *sold, soud* wages: see SOLD *sb.*[1], SOUD.] Pay, salary, wages.

†**Souldie** var. of SAULDIE *Obs.*

Soule, obs. form of SOLE, SOUL.

†**Souled,** *var.* of SULD *v.* Obs.

Soulet, *sb.* var. of SOULET.

†**Souleamer,** *adv.* Obs.

Souled (sauld), *ppl. a.* [f. SOUL *sb.* or *v.*]

†**1.** Endowed with a soul.

2. Endowed with a soul.

3. With qualifying terms: Endowed with a soul of a specified kind.

+**Soulet.** *Obs. rare.* Also *sowlet.* [app. f. SOUL *sb.* + -ET.]

1. A little soul.

2. *intr.* To go about collecting doles, properly on the eve of All Souls' Day. Chiefly in the phr. *a-souleting.*

Soulful (sau-lful), *a.* Also *soul-full.* [f. SOUL *sb.* + -FUL.]

1. Full of soul or feeling; of a highly emotional, spiritual, or æsthetic nature or character, or marked by this.

2. Expressive or indicative of deep feeling or emotion.

Soulfully, *adv.* In a soulful manner; with expression of deep feeling.

Soulfulness. The quality or state of being soulful.

+**Soul-heal, soul-heale.** *Obs.* [f. SOUL *sb.* + HEAL *sb.*]

a. The health of the soul; moral or spiritual well-being; salvation.

b. In general sense.

Soul-knell. [f. SOUL *sb.* + KNELL *sb.*] The knell rung or tolled at or after the death of a person. *Also fig.*

Soulless (sau-les), *a.* [f. SOUL *sb.* + -LESS.]

1. Having no soul; from whom or which the soul has departed. *Also fig.*

2. Of persons: Destitute of or wanting in the noble qualities of the soul; lacking spirit, courage, or elevation of mind or feeling.

Soullessly, *adv.* In a soulless manner.

Soullessness. The quality or state of being soulless.

Soul-scot, also *Hist.* Forms: 7 *sawl-scott,* 7- *soul-scot.* [f. SOUL *sb.* + SCOT *sb.*]

Soul-searching, ppl. a. [f. SOUL sb.2]
That searches, examines vigorously or severely, penetrates, etc., the soul.

Soul-shot, sb.: see SAWL-SHOT.

Soul-sick, a.: Also 4 sawlshot. [f. SOUL sb.2 + SHOT sb.1] = SOUL-SHOT.

Soul-sick a. [f. SOUL sb. 24.]
1. Of persons: a. Suffering from spiritual indisposition or dejection.

Soul-sickening, ppl. a. [f. SOUL sb.2]
Extremely depressing or dejecting.

Soul-silver : see SOUL sb. 25 and SOWL sb.

Soul-sleeper : see SOUL sb. 25.

Soulter, **Boultring**, **Soultry**, obs. ff. SULTER

Soultering app. a., SULTRY a.

Soulx, **souls**, Obs. Also 7 zoulxe. [f. souls, souls, pl. of soul, sol SOUL sb.3: see also SOUSE sb. 1 and 2.]

Soum (saum), sb.1 Sc. Now chiefly *Hist.* Forms:
6, 8-9 soume, 6-8 sowme, 6-7 summe, 8 soom, 8-9 soum. [app. the same as SUM sb. Hence Gael. suim in sense 2.]

Soum, v. Sc. Law. Also 7-8 sowm. [f. prec.] *trans.* To estimate the amount of (pasture) in terms of the 'soums' it can support.

Soum (saum), v. Sc. Law. Also 7-8 sowm.

Soumer, Obs. rare. [var. of SOMER.]

Soun, obs. form of SON, SOON, SOUND, SUN.

Sound (saund), sb.1 Forms: a. 1, 3-4 sund, 4 sound, 5-7 sownde, 6 sounde, 4- sound. 8, 5-7 sown, 6-7 sowne, 7 8- soon. [Partly OE. *sund* swimming, water, sea, and partly a. ON. *sund* swimming, strait (Norw. *sund* swimming, saddle, strait, ferry; Sw. and Da. *sund* strait; Gr. *sund* is a late adoption). The stem *sunda-* represents an early *sumda-*, pre-Teutonic *swm-tó-*, f. the stem of SWIM v.]
I.†1. The action or power of swimming. Obs.

Soum, sb.2 Sc. Obs. In 5 sowme, 5-6 soume. [a. OF. *sou(l)me*. Cf. sum, sum, somme : see SEAM sb.4 and SOMME sb.3] A horse-load; a pack. Also *attrib.* in *soum saddle*.
2. The swimming bladder of certain fish, esp. of cod or sturgeon.

Soun, sb.2 Sc. Now chiefly *Hist.* Forms:
6, 8-9 soune, 6-8 sowne, 4-7 summe, 8 soom. 5- soum. [app. the same as SUM sb. Hence Gael. suim in sense 2.]
1. The amount of pasturage which will support one cow or a proportional number of sheep or other stock.

Sound (saund), sb.2 Forms: a. 4 sune, 4-5 son(e, 4-5, 6 Sc. soun(e, 4-6 soun(e, sowun(e, 5-6 sownd(e, 6 Sc. soundt, 5 sownd, 6 sownde, 6- sound. 8. AF. soun, OF. son, mod.F. son, Latin or early OF. *sonus*, MDu. *son, soen,* from Latin or early OF.

Tennyson *Godiva* (1842) 37 sent a herald forth.

Sound (saund), sb.2
I. The sensation produced in the organs of hearing when the surrounding air is set in vibration in such a way as to affect these.

b. in the phr. *soun's* (or *souns*) *grass*.

Sound (saum), v.1 Sc. Law. Also 7-8 sowm.
II. A relatively narrow channel or stretch of water, esp. one between the mainland and an island, or connecting two large bodies of water.

d. the distance or range over which the sound of something is heard.

Sound, sb.3
3. A particular cause of auditory effect.

Soum, v.
b. in the cases of particular straits or inlets.

Sound (saund), v.3 Forms: 2 sunde, 4-5 sound(e, 5 sonde. [f. *sund* SOUND a. Cf. MLG. *sunt* (also *gesunt*, G. *gesund*), MSw. *sund.*] Health or soundness; safety or security. In prep. phr. *in or on, mid or with sound.*

†**Sound**, v.3
b. similarly with omission of *the*.

Sound, sb.3
6. A musical tone. Obs.

Sound (saund), a. Now dial. Forms: a. 5-7 sown(e, 7 sown, soon. 8. 6 sownde, soonde, 6-7 sownd, 8-9- sound. [The *round* of SOON sb. and ? adj.]

Sound, sb.
1. Of or pertaining to the soul.

Sound (saund), adv. [f. SOUND a.]
1. Without harm or injury; in safety or security.
2. To sleep sound, to enjoy deep, unbroken, or undisturbed sleep.
3. In a sound manner; heartily, soundly.

Soundness

Soundness (sū'ndnės). [f. SOUND a.]

1. The quality or state of being sound or free from disease; sound or healthy condition; healthiness.

Sound-post. [SOUND sb.² + POST sb.¹] A small peg of wood fixed beneath the bridge of a violin or similar instrument, serving as a support for the belly and as a connecting part between this and the back.

Soundrie, obs. var. of SUNDRY.

Soune, obs. var. SON, NOON, SOUND sb. and v.

Soup (sūp), sb.¹

Soup, sb.²

† Soupcon (sūpsõ·). [F.]

Souper

Soupify, v.

Soupiere

Soupling, Souparism

Soupy, a.

Soup maigre (sūp,mε·gr). [ad. F. soupe maigre: see SOUP sb. and MAIGRE a.] Thin soup, made chiefly from vegetables or fish.

Soupçon (sūp'sõ). [F.]

Soupy (sū'pi), a.

Sour (saur), a. and sb.¹ Forms: 1-4 sur (5 sur), 3-4 sure, 4-8 soure (4 soure), 4-sour; 4-8 sowr(e, 5 soure, 6 sewer.

Soup, obs. variant of SUP v., SWOOP v.

† Soupçon (sepsõ). [F., repr. OF. sospeçon, sospeçun—pop.L. *suspectiō, -ōne for L. suspiciō, -ōnem SUSPICION sb.]

Souper, obs. form of SUP v.¹ and v.² SOUPER.

Souple, a., and sb., var. SUPPLE. **Souplet** (obs. Sc.):

Soupling, Souparism

Sour (saur), v.

Sour crout, sour-crout. Also 7 sower crawt, 9 sourcrout; 8 sourcraut, 9-sour krout, 9 sour kraut. [Anglicized form of SAUERKRAUT.]

Sour dock, sour-dock. Now dial. [SOUR a. and DOCK sb.¹]

Source (sōrs). [a. F. source.]

Sourceless (sō'rslĕs), a.

Sourdine (suərdī·n), sb. and a. rare. [a. F. sourdine.]

Sour-dough. Now dial. and rare.

Sovereignly (*ˈsɒvrənlɪ*), *adv.* [f. SOVEREIGN *a.* + -LY².]

Sovereignty (*ˈsɒvrəntɪ*). Forms: (see SOVEREIGN *sb.* and *a.*). [a. AF. *sovereyneté*, *sovereinté*, OF. *souveraineté* (mod. F. *souveraineté*) : see SOVEREIGN and -TY.] The quality or condition of being sovereign.

Sovran (*ˈsɒvrən*), *a.* and *sb.* Chiefly *poet.* [Milton's spelling of SOVEREIGN, after *sovrano*.]

Sovrantee. *Obs.⁻¹* [f. SOVRAN.]

Sovranly (*ˈsɒvrənlɪ*). Chiefly *poet.* [f. SOVRAN *a.* + -TY.]

Sovranty (*ˈsɒvrəntɪ*). Chiefly *poet.* [f. SOVRAN + -TY.]

Sow (sou), *sb.¹* Forms: *a.* 1 suʒu, suʒa, suʒe-, 2 sugʒe, 3 soghe, rowʒe, 3, 5-7 sowe, sowghe, 6-9 sowe, *Sc.* sou, soo, soow, 6, 9 *Sc.* soo. *a.* *north.* dial. 5-7, 9 sew, 7 swine. [OE. *sugu* fem., also *sú* (:—OTeut. *sū-*, *suwō-*) = MLG., MDu. *sūge*, MHG. *sūge* fem., ON. *sýr* (acc. *sú*; MSw., Sw., and Da. *so*), also 1 *sú*, *sú* fem. *Sc.* *soo*, *sow* fem. The stem *su-* of doubtful origin, also appears in SWINE.]

Sow (sou), *sb.²* [prob. a use of SOW *sb.¹*]

Sow (sou), *v.¹* Pa. t. **sowed**. Pa. pple. **sowed**, **sown**. Forms: (see below). [Common Teut.: OE. *sáwan* strong vb.]

Sow (sou), *v.²* rare. [f. SOW *sb.¹*]

Sow (sou), *v.³* Obs. exc. *dial.* Also 4 **sowe**. [Of obscure origin.] A blow or stroke.

Sow-back. Chiefly *Sc.* Also **sowback**. [f. SOW *sb.¹* + BACK *sb.¹*]

Sow-bread. [tr. med.L. *panis porcinus*, or L. *panis* and *porcinus*; cf. also Flem. *verkensbrood* (Kilian), F. *pain de pourceau* (Cotgr.), Gr. *κυκλάμῑνος*.]

Sow-bug. Now *dial.*

Sowar (*saˈwɑː*), *Anglo-Indian.* Forms: *a.* **sowaar**, **suwar**, **suwarree**, etc. *b.* **sowar**. [Urdū (Pers.) *sawār* horseman.] A native horseman or mounted orderly; policeman, etc.; a native trooper.

Sowary (*saˈwɑːrɪ*), *Anglo-Indian.* Also 8 **sowarry** (*saˈwɑːrɪ*), **suwarry**, **suwaree**, **sowarree**. [Urdū (Pers.) *sawārī*.]

Sowce, obs. form of SOUSE.

Sowdel, var. of SOLDAN.

Sowdian, **-ane**, **-ane**, etc., obs. forms of SOLDAN.

Sowdle, etc. Obs. **Sowdear**, **-eour**, etc., obs. ff. SOLDIER *sb.*

Sowdy (sou'di). *Sc.* Also 7 **soudy**, 9 **souddie**, **soodie**, **souddy**. [Of uncertain origin. Cf. Fr. *soude*, *soudie*.]

Sowdyoure, variant of SOFTWOOD. Obs.

Sowel. Now *dial.* Forms : 1 **sazol**, **sahel**, 3 **suwel**, 4, 6, 9 **sole**, **sozel**. [OE. *sáhl*, *sáhel* = MHG. (now Swiss dial.) *seigel* rung of a ladder. Cf. SAIL *sb.*²] A stout stick or staff; a pole, cudgel, etc.

Sowens, obs. form of SOVTAN. Also **Sowans** (*sou'ənz*), *sb. pl.* *Sc.* (and Ir.). Forms: *a.* 6 **sowanis**, 7 **sowins**, 7 **sowans**, 8 **souans**, **sowins**, **sowens**, etc. 1. An article of food formerly in common use in Scotland (and some parts of Ireland), consisting of the farina remaining in the husks of oats by steeping, allowed to ferment slightly, and prepared by boiling.

Sower

Sowf

Sow-gelder

Sowing, vbl. sb.

Sowl, Now dial.

Sowl-metal

Sowmir, Sc.

Sowl, v.

Sowth (south), v.

Sowth, v.

Sowthe, obs.

Sow-thistle (sou'θis'l)

Soy (soi)

Soya (soi'ă)

Soygear, obs.

Soygne, var. of SOIGNE.

Soz-, combining form

Sozzle (sɒ'z'l), v.

Sozzle (sɒ'z'l), n.

Spa (spā)

Space (spēs), sb.

SPACE.

15. An interior or blank between words, in printed or written matter.

b. *Typog.* One or other of certain small pieces of cast-metal, of various thicknesses and shorter than a type, used to separate words (or letters in a word), and also to justify the line.

III. *attrib.* and *Comb.*

17. Simple attrib. **a.** In the sense of 'used for spacing (in printing, etc.)', as *space-key*, *-line*, *-rule*; also 'used for holding spaces', as *space-barge*, *-bar*, *-paper*.

b. *dial.* To measure (ground, etc.) by pacing.

18. In specific uses (see prec.).

III. *attrib.* and *Comb.*

Space-lattice … ; **space-nerve** … ; **space-telegrapher** … ; **space-telegraphy** … ; **space-weather** …

†Space. *sb.* Obs. rare. [ad. F. *espèce*: see SPECE.]

Space (spēs), *v.* Also 6 space. [f. SPACE *sb.* or ad. F. *espacer* (*† espacier, espacier*) to space, etc.]

†1. *trans.* ? To pave or lay. Obs.

2. To limit or bound in respect of space; to make of a certain extent.

Spaceable, *a. nonce-wd.* [f. SPACE + -ABLE.]

Spaceless (spē·slès), *a.* [f. SPACE + -LESS.] 1. That is not subject to or limited by space; infinite, boundless. Freq. coupled with *timeless*.

Spacer (spē·səɹ). [f. SPACE *v.* + -ER.]

Spacial, *-ly*, var. of SPATIAL(ITY, -LY.

†Spacier, *v.* *Sc.* Obs. [ad. OF. *espacier*: see SPACE *v.*]

Spacing (spē·sin̄), *vbl. sb.* [f. SPACE *v.* + -ING.] 1. The action of the verb, in various senses, or the result of this action. Also *with out.*

†Space. *v.* Obs. rare. [ad. F. *espace*: see SPACE *sb.*]

Spaceful (spē·sfŭl), *a.* rare. [f. SPACE *sb.* + -FUL.] Spacious, commodious, wide, extensive.

Spacelate, obs. form of SPHACELATE *v.*

†Spaciosity (spēsiǫ·siti). Obs. [ad. med.L. *spaciositas*, -sitatem, f. *spacios-us* SPACIOUS.]

Spacious (spē·fǝs), *a.* Also 4-5 **spacyous**, 5-7 **spacyous.** [ad. (med. L. *spaciosus*), f. *spatium* SPACE *sb.*]

1. Of lands, etc.: of vast, large, or indefinite superficial extent or area; wide, widely extended, extensive.

b. Covering a considerable distance.

3. Similarly of roads, streets, courts, etc.

Spaciously (spē·fǝsli), *adv.* Also 7 **spatiously.** [f. prec. + -LY.]

1. In a spacious house or place.

Spaciousness (spē·fǝsnès). [f. as prec. + -NESS.]

1. The state or quality of being wide, spacious, or roomy.

Spack, *a.* and *dial.* Obs. [ad. ON. *spak-* (*M.Sw. spaker*, Norw. and Sw. *spak*), quiet, gentle.]

Spacky, *adv.* Obs. Forms: *spackli, -ly, a.* **spakly** = SPAKLY *adv.*

SPADE.

below the staff. **b.** *dial.* To measure (ground, etc.) by pacing.

Spade (spēd), *sb.* Also 4, 7 **spad**; *Sc.* 6-7 **sped**, 6-7 **spaid.** [OE. *spadu, spadu* fem., and *spade, -an* masc. (MLG. *spade*, (M)Du. *spade*, *spa*), f. Aryan root *spē-*.]

1. A tool for digging, paring, or cutting ground, etc., usually consisting of a flattish rectangular iron blade socketed on a wooden handle which has a grip or cross-piece at the upper end, the whole being adapted for grasping with both hands while the blade is pressed into the ground with the foot.

b. *Sc. and north.* A spall spade.

c. The depth of a spade-blade.

2. Gentle, quiet, tame. Obs. rare.

†B. *adv.* Quickly, promptly, speedily. Obs.

2. Pr. To call a spade a spade, to call things by their real names, without any euphemism or mincing of matters.

Spade, obs. form of SPADO.

SPADE.

but altogether grosse, clubbye, and rusticall, as they whiche had not the witte to calle a spade by any other name then a spade.

b. In allusions to the above phrase.

An implement resembling a spade in form or use: **a.** One or other of various spade-like knives used by whalers, esp. one employed in flensing a whale; a blubber-spade.

3. *U.S.* The spade-bone.

Spade-bone.

by which one of the four suits in a pack of playing-cards is distinguished; hence *pl.*, the cards belonging to or forming this suit.

5. Special combs. **a.** *spade-arm*, the arm used in holding the hand-grip of a spade; *spade-bayonet* (see quot.); *spade-bit* …

Spade (spēd), *v.* Now *dial.* [f. SPADE *sb.*]

1. *trans.* To cut in the form of a spade. *rare*⁻¹.

2. To dig up, to remove, with a spade.

Spadeful (spē·dfŭl). Also *-full.* [f. SPADE *sb.* + -FUL.] A quantity that fills a spade; as much as a spade can hold or take up at one time.

Spade-graft. [SPADE *sb.* + GRAFT *sb.*] A spade's depth; as *spit*.

Spade-iron. Now *rare.* [f. SPADE *sb.*] The iron part, the blade or shoeing, of a spade.

Spadeless, *a.* [f. SPADE *sb.* + -LESS.] Without a spade.

Spader (spē·dǝɹ). [f. SPADE *v.*¹ + -ER.] One who works with a spade; an implement which digs, etc., by means of spades; also *dial.* a breast-plough.

†Spade, *v.*² *trans.*, associated with *spayd, spayed*, pa. pple. See SPADE *sb.*⁴]

Spadger (spæ·dgǝɹ). *dial.* or *colloq.* [Fanciful alteration of SPARROW.] A sparrow.

†Spadiard. [f. SPADE *sb.* + -ARD.] A labourer in the Cornish tin-mines.

Spadiceous (spǝdi·ʃǝs), *a.* Now *Bot.* [ad. mod.L. *spadiceus*, f. L. *spadix, -dicis* SPADIX.]

1. Of a reddish or brownish colour.

SPAEMAN.

spadices (*sic*) or light-red colour.

Spade (spēd), *sb.*⁴ Obs. [ad. L. *spado, -ōnem* eunuch.] An eunuch; a castrated person.

†Spadille. Obs. Also 8 **spadill.** [f. F. *spadille*, ad. Sp. *espadilla* (Pg. *espadilha*, It. *spadiglia*).] The ace of spades in ombre and quadrille.

Spading (spē·din̄), *vbl. sb.* [f. SPADE *v.*¹] The action of digging, working, striking, etc., with a spade.

Spademan (spē·dmǝn). Also **spadesman.** [SPADE *sb.*] One who uses a spade; a labourer accustomed to work with a spade.

Spadix (spē·diks). *Bot. and Zool.* [L. *spadix* a palm-branch broken off with its fruit.]

Spadroon *sb.* Obs. *rare.* Hist. [ad. Genevan dial. *espadron*, F. *espadon* ESPADON.] 'A sword much lighter than a broadsword, and made both to cut and thrust' (Grose).

Spadix.

Spae (spē), *v. Sc.* Also 6 **spay.** [a. ON. *spá* (Sw. *spå*), related to OE. *spōwan*.] *trans.* To foretell, prophesy.

Spaeman. *Sc.* Also 6 *-spay*, **spaeman.** [f. SPAE *v.* + MAN *sb.*; cf. Sw. *spåman*, Da. *spaamand.*] A prophet, soothsayer, fortune-teller.

Spae-wife. Sc. [f. SPAE + WIFE sb. Cf. ON. and Icel. *spádóma*, Da. *spaakone*, NFris. *spékewiif*.] A female fortune-teller; a witch.

†Spagnolet, *obs.* form of SPANIEL.

Spagyric, a. (sb.) [ad. SPANIOLIZE *v*.]

Spagyrical, a. Also 6-7 spagirical.

Spagyrically, adv. Also spagyricqually.

Spagyrist. Also 7-8 spagirist. [ad. mod.L. *spagirista* (cf. SPAGYRIC a)]

†Spahi. Also spahee. Forms: 6-7 spaoghi, 7-9 spahen, 7- spahi. [ad. Turkish (Persian) *sipáhí* : see SEPOY.]

Spail, Spaile, Spails, variants of SPALE.

Spain, variant of SPANE *v.*, to wean.

†Spalard. *Obs.* [? Related to SPALT.]

Spald, var. SPALD *Obs.* [f. SPALWED *ppl. a*]

†Spale, sb.[1] [OE. *spala* substitute : see SPELE *v*.] Sparing; respite or rest.

Spale, sb.[2] Sc. and north. Forms: 5-6, 9 spale, 5-6, 9 spaill, spaill.

Spale, sb.[3] Sc. and north. [Related to SPALL *sb*.]

Spall, sb.[1] [a. OF. *espaule, espalle*, = It. *spalla*]

Spall, sb.[2] [Related to SPALL *v*.]

Spall, v.[1] [Related to SPALL *sb*.]

Spaller (spô'ləʳ). [f. SPALL *v*.]

Spallier. [f. SPALL *v*.]

Spalling (spô'liŋ), *vbl. sb.* Also *attrib.*

Spallard, dial. form of ESPALIER.

Spalpeen (spælpī·n). *Irish.* [a. Ir. *spailpín*]

†Spalt, sb.[1] [Related to SPALL *v*.]

Span, sb.[1] Forms: 1 span(n), spon(n), 3-6, 4-6 sponne, 4-6 spanne, 4- span.

Span, sb.[2] Also 5-9 spanne. [a. Du. and LG. *span* (also MDu. and MLG.; G. *spann*, OHG. *spanna*)]

Span, sb.[3] Forms: 1 spon(n), 4- span. [ON. *spǫnn* (MDu., MLG. and LG. *spaan*)]

Span, v.[1] Forms: 1 spannan, 3-7 spanne, 4- span. [OE. *spannan*]

Span, sb.[4] Also 7 spanne. [app. related to SPAN *v*.]

Spancel (spæ·nsel). Also 9 dial. *spancill*, 8 *spancel*, 7-9 *spancell*, *spansell*. [a. Flem., Du. or LG. *spansel*]

Spancel, v. [f. SPANCEL *sb*.]

Spander-new, a. phr. Now *dial.* Also *spander-new*.

Spandrel (spæ·ndrel). *Arch.* Forms: 1-4 *spaundrel*, 6 *spandrell*, 7-9 *spandril*, 8-9 *spandril*. [a. AF. *spaundre*]

Spandy, a. *U.S.* rare. [var. of *spander* SPANDER-NEW.] Very good or fine; smart.

SPANED. 505 SPANGLE. SPANGLE. 506 SPANIEL.

SPANIEL. 507 SPANISH. SPANISH. 508 SPANISH.

Spanished, ppl. a.

Spanishly, adv.

Spanishly, adv.

Spank, sb.

Spank, v.

Spanker.

Spanking, vbl. sb.

Spanking, ppl. a.

Spankingly, adv.

Spankily, adv.

Spanless, a.

Spanner.

Spanning, vbl. sb.

Spannew, a.

Span-new.

Spar, sb.

Spar, v.

Spar, sb.

Spar, v.

Sparable.

Sparadrap.

Sparage.

Sparagus.

Sparaxis.

Sparble, v.

Sparch, sb.

Spar-deck.

Spare, v.

I. 1. Not in actual or regular use at the time spoken of, but carried, held, or kept in reserve for future use or to supply an emergency; esp. *Naut.* (see quot. 1769); additional, extra.

a. In attributive use.

The various types of context are illustrated by the different groups of quotations.

(*a*) 13.. *E. E. Allit. P.* C. 104 Cables þay fasten,..weȝen her ankres, Sprude spak to þe sprete þe spare bawe-lyne. *c* 1450 *Bk. Curtasye* 792 in *Babees Bk.*, The keruer anon.. Into þe couertoure wyn he powres owt, Or in-to a spare pece, with-outen doute. 1497 *Naval Acc. Hen. VII* (1896) 110 Spare extrees for faucons,..v. 1573 *Richmond Wills* (Surtees) 242, v. ireon teames,..ij spare crooks. 1590 SHAKS. *Com. Err.* I. i. 80 A small spare Mast, Such as sea-faring men prouide for stormes. 1600 MARSTON *Ant. & Mel.* II. Wks. 1856 I. 23 If you have any spare paire of silver spurs. 1691 T. H[ALE] *Acc. New Invent.* 43 A spare Set thereof [i.e. rudder-irons] sent to Sea with every Lead-sheathed Ship. 1709 *Lond. Gaz.* No. 4521/2 One of the Flukes of the Spare-Anchor [was]..shot off. 1769 FALCONER *Dict. Marine* (1780), *Spare*, an epithet applied to any part of a ship's..furniture, that lies in reserve, to supply the place of such as may be lost, or rendered incapable of service. Hence we say, spare top-masts, spare sails, spare rigging, &c. 1811 *Regul. & Orders Army* 276 All Spare Ammunition is given in to the nearest Ordnance Depôt. 1856 KANE *Arct. Expl.* II. xvi. 173 We carried spare tins, in case the others should burn out. 1893 KIPLING *Many Invent.* 2 We've just sent our regular engine to London, and this spare one's not..so accurate.

(*b*) *a* 1548 HALL *Chron., Hen. VIII*, 29 The master of hys horse folowed him with a spare horse. 1613 PURCHAS *Pilgrimage* (1614) 420 They bring with them three moneths victuall,..and a spare Horse for food, besides a better for seruice. 1708 J. C. *Compl. Collier* (1845) 33 The Charge of maintaining a spare Shift of Horses. 1781 GIBBON *Decl. & F.* xviii. II. 90 The custom of their warriors, to lead in their hand one or two spare horses, enabled them to advance and to retreat with a rapid diligence. 1822–56 DE QUINCEY *Confess.* (1862) 76 Here's a spare dromedary. 1850 R. G. CUMMING *Hunter's Life S. Afr.* I. 105 A horseman..accompanied by an after-rider leading a spare horse.

(*c*) *a* 1667 PETTY *Pol. Arith.* (1690) 107 There are spare Hands among the King's Subjects, to earn two Millions more than they do. 1897 *Daily News* 27 May 8/5 Driver R. Wilcockson, a spare driver,..gave evidence in regard to the irregular hours of the 'spare' men.

(*d*) 1700 *Guide for Constables* 12 He shall keep one or more spare beds for lodging of strangers. 1811 SCOTT *Let.* in *Lockhart* (1837) II. xi. 301 My present intention is to have only two spare bed-rooms. 1827 — *Surg. Dau.* i, A spare apartment, in which Doctor Gray occasionally accommodated..patients. 1881 YOUNG *Every Man his own Mechanic* § 806. 371 A spare bed which may be put up anywhere in a few minutes.

b. In predicative use. Now *rare*.

1497 *Naval Acc. Hen. VII* (1896) 87, ij pair wheles & a pair of hynder wheles spare. 1600 DYMMOK *Ireland* (1843) 7 His horse of service is alwaies led spare. 1621 LADY M. WROTH *Urania* 460 They onely riding in one Coach, two other went spare. *a* 1642 SIR W. MONSON *Naval Tracts* III. (1704) 324/1 Anchors lying spare at the River side. 1899 *Westm. Gaz.* 7 Dec. 5/2 Their ponies were running about spare all over the place.

†**c.** Of land, ground, etc.: Uncultivated, unoccupied, vacant. *Obs.* (exc. in sense 1 a or 2).

c 1470 *Gol. & Gaw.* 112 Sped hym on spedely on the spare mure. 1577 B. GOOGE *Heresbach's Husb.* I. (1586) 24 The ground that is yeerely sowen, and that hath lyne spare, is to be plowed thryse. 1665 SIR T. HERBERT *Trav.* (1677) 221 The number of Gardens, Cemeteries [etc.],..take up much more spare place than London doth. 1669 WORLIDGE *Syst. Agric.* 93 You may raise these Pollards in Hedgerows, and spare places.

†**d.** Of a leaf: Blank. *Obs.*[−1]

1705 HEARNE *Collect.* 13 July (O.H.S.) I. 5 A spare leafe, before a 4[to] Book of tracts.

2. That can be spared, dispensed with, or given away, as being in excess of actual requirements; superfluous. † Rarely as predicate.

a 1553 UDALL *Royster D.* (Arb.) 18 She shall haue the first day a whole pecke of argent...A pecke? *Nomine patris*, haue ye so much spare? 1613 BEAUM. & FL. *Captain* I. iii, When I..have enough spare gold To boil away, you shall be welcome to me. 1783 BURKE *Rep. Aff. India* Wks. 1842 II. 49 The supply destined for the London market is proportioned to the spare tonnage. 1818 TUCKEY *Narr. Exped. R. Zaire* iv. (1818) 141 The very little spare provisions the natives seem to have at this season. 1849 SIR F. B. HEAD *Stokers & Pokers* v. (1851) 53 A few of the.. men who had spare cash purchased the greater portion of these articles. 1855 KANE *Arct. Expl.* I. xiii. 149 All the spare morsels, the cast-off delicacies of the mess.

b. Of time: Not employed or taken up by one's ordinary or usual duties or occupations; leisure.

a 1610 HEALEY *Epictetus* (1636) 63 If thou hast any spare time, go. *c* 1643 LD. HERBERT *Autobiog.* (1824) 240 All the spare hours which I could get from my visits and negotiations. 1711 ADDISON *Spect.* (J.), The female world..have more spare time upon their hands, and lead a more sedentary life. 1885 G. ALLEN *Babylon* xvi, Minna was working hard in all her spare hours. 1885 'MRS. ALEXANDER' *At Bay* iv, The earliest spare moment he could find was devoted to Lady Gethin.

transf. 1633 G. HERBERT *Temple, Sunday* iv, The other dayes fill up the spare And hollow room with vanities.

II. †**3.** Of speech: Sparing; marked by reticence or reserve. *Obs. rare.*

13.. *Gaw. & Gr. Knt.* 901 Þenne was spyed & spured vpon spare wyse, Bi preue poyntez of þat prynce [etc.]. *c* 1460 *Towneley Myst.* xx. 294 This spekyng must be spar, and neuen it neuer..; let no man wyt where that we war.

4. Of persons, their limbs, etc.: Having little flesh; not fat or plump; lean, thin.

a 1548 HALL *Chron., Hen. VII*, 60 b, He was a man of body but leane and spare. 1597 SHAKS. *2 Hen. IV*, III. ii. 287 O, giue me the spare men, and spare me the great ones. 1614 ROWLANDS *Fooles Bolt* (Hunterian Cl.) 34 Thou worthy leane spare Gentleman. 1667 MILTON *P. L.* x. 511 His Visage drawn he felt to sharp and spare. 1709 *Tatler* No. 93 ⁋ 4 As I am spare, I am also very tall. 1716 SWIFT *Progr. Poetry* Wks. 1755 III. II. 162 Hard exercise and harder fare Soon make my dame grow lank and spare. 1808 SCOTT *Marm.* II. iv, Her cheek was pale, her form was spare. 1844 W. IRVING *Goldsmith* xiv. (1850) 172 He was upwards of six feet high, and very spare. 1885 *Spectator* 25 July 971/2 A man of spare figure, with a shrewd, humorous face.

transf. 1848 DICKENS *Dombey* lvii, Mrs. Miff assents with a spare nod of her mortified bonnet. 1865 — *Mut. Fr.* I. xv, The staircase, balustrades, and rails, had a spare look.

b. Const. *in* or *of* (flesh).

1632 SHERWOOD, Spare (of flesh), *desnué de chair*. 1842 TENNYSON *Talk. Oak* 92, I hold them [fairies] exquisitely knit, But far too spare of flesh. 1871 NAPHEYS *Prev. & Cure Dis.* I. i. 45 Spare in flesh.

c. Lacking body or substance; flimsy, thin.

1602 WARNER *Alb. Eng.* XIII. lxxix. (1612) 325 But all effects, and names to God his Essence come more short Than Sun-shine to the Suns-selfe, than to action spare report. 1858 LOWELL *Vis. Sir Launfal* II. iii, Sir Launfal's raiment thin and spare Was idle mail 'gainst barbed air.

d. *poet.* Growing thinly or sparsely.

1815 SHELLEY *Alastor* 527 Grey rocks did peep from the spare moss.

†**5.** Of persons: Sparing, temperate, or moderate *of* or *in* something, esp. diet or speech. *Obs.*

(*a*) 1563 FOXE *A. & M.* 1050/1 He [Hooper] was..spare of dyet, sparer of wordes, and sparest of tyme. 1615 BRATHWAIT *Strappado* (1878) 153 Another may we see, though spare of speech, And temporate in discourse, yet he may teach By his effectual words the rasher sort. 1658–9 in *Burton's Diary* (1828) III. 341, I am very spare of speaking. 1697 DRYDEN *Virgil, Life* (1721) I. 61 He was..spare of Dyet, and hardly drank any Wine.

(*b*) 1581 PETTIE tr. *Guazzo's Civ. Conv.* II. (1586) 71 b, We must be spare in speaking of things which are not easily beleeued. 1589 PUTTENHAM *Eng. Poesie* III. (Arb.) 298 A man to be in giuing free, in asking spare. 1599 SHAKS. *Hen. V*, II. ii. 131 Are they spare in diet, Free from grosse passion.

†**b.** Not lavish, liberal, or profuse, esp. in expenditure or living; frugal, niggardly, parsimonious; abstemious. *Obs.*

1577 HANMER *Anc. Eccles. Hist.* VII. xxxi. (1619) 143 Pierius was proved a spare man of life, and singular in Philosophy. 1583 STUBBES *Anat. Abus.* I ij b, But as some be ouer largeous, so other some are spare enough. 1633 P. FLETCHER *Poet. Misc.* 58 Oh happy pair, where nothing wants to either,..Fortune and nature being spare to neither!

c. *dial.* Displaying little exertion or energy; slow, dilatory.

1746– in south-western dial. glossaries, etc.

6. Characterized by meanness, bareness, economy, or frugality, esp. in regard to food.

1560 ABP. PARKER *Corr.* (Parker Soc.) 133 The unclean or negligent order and spare-keeping of the house of prayer. 1600 SHAKS. *A. Y. L.* III. ii. 20 As it is a spare life.., it fits my humor well: but as there is no more plentie in it, it goes much against my stomacke. 1634 MILTON *Comus* 767 She..Means her provision onely to the good, That live according to her sober laws, And holy dictate of spare Temperance. 1876 GEO. ELIOT *Dan. Der.* xxiv, To order the whole establishment on the sparest footing possible.

b. Of diet, fare, meals, etc.: Consisting of a comparatively small amount of food, esp. of a plain kind; not abundant or plentiful.

1570 JEWEL *View of Seditious Bull* (1582) 29 So that the quantitie be smal, and fit for sober and spare diet. 1607 ROWLANDS *Earl of Warwick* (Hunterian Cl.) 66 His diet of the meanest, hard and spare. *c* 1665 MRS. HUTCHINSON *Mem. Col. Hutchinson* (1846) 24 He was not talkative, yet free of discourse; of a very spare diet. *a* 1721 PRIOR *Wand. Pilgr.* 13 Spare diet, and spring-water clear, Physicians hold are good. 1784 COWPER *Task* IV. 173 When her patriots..Enjoy'd—spare feast!—a radish and an egg! 1841 BARHAM *Ingol. Leg.* Ser. II. *Nell Cook*, The Priory fare was scant and spare. 1842 COMBE *Digestion* 203 He was unable for study till five or six hours after even a very spare dinner.

transf. 1893 STEVENSON *Catriona* xxv. (1902) 306, I drink nothing else but spare, cold water.

c. *poet.* Scanty, meagre, rare.

1813 SHELLEY *Q. Mab* v. 202 Some servile souls, Whom cowardice itself might safely chain, Or the spare mite of avarice could bribe. 1842 TENNYSON *St. S. Styl.* 77 Eating not, Except the spare chance-gift of those that came To touch my body. 1888 *Cent. Mag.* May 26 Even now the reaper-beams appear, And gather in the clouds' spare aftermath.

7. As *adv.* Sparely; with spare diet. *rare.*

1813 SCOTT *Trierm.* III. iv, Yet still his watch the warrior keeps, Feeds hard and spare, and seldom sleeps.

III. **8.** *Comb.*, chiefly parasynthetic, as *spare-bodied*, *-built*, *-fed* adjs.; † **spare-handed** *adj.*, having a sparing hand.

1626 J. YATES *Ibis ad Cæsarem* I. 2 God is ample in Predestination unto life, but in the death of sinners spare-handed. 1742 JARVIS *Don Quix.* i, He was of a robust constitution, spare-bodied, of a meagre visage. 1813 SCOTT *Rokeby* II. xxii, His stately form, spare-built and tall. 1837 LOCKHART *Scott* IV. v. 157 For 'early to rise', unless in the case of spare-fed anchorites, takes for granted 'early to bed'. 1895 SCULLY *Kafir Stories* 133 Whitson was a sallow-faced, spare-built man of short stature.

Spare (spēəɹ), *v.*[1] Forms: 1 sparian, spear-, speorian, 3 sparien, spearien, 3–4 sparie (4 -ye), 3–5 spary; 4–5 sparen, 4– spare, 5–8 *Sc.* spair (6 spaare, spaer, 7 spayer, 9 *dial.* spaar). [Common Teutonic: OE. *sparian* (also *a-*, *ge-sparian*), = OFris. *sparia* (WFris. *sparje*, †*spearje*, NFris. *spari*, *spāri*), OS. and OHG. *sparōn* (MLG. and LG., MDu. and Du., MHG. and G. *sparen*), ON. *spara* (Icel., Norw., Sw. *spara*, Da. *spare*), f. a stem *spar-* (see SPARE *a.*) of uncertain relationship. The Teutonic word is the base of OF. *espargner* (mod.F. *épargner*), It. *sparagnare* and *sparmiare*.]

I. 1. *trans.* To leave (a person) unhurt, unharmed, or uninjured; to refrain from inflicting injury or punishment upon; to allow to escape, go free, or live. Usually with personal subject.

c 825 *Vesp. Psalter* lxxi. 13 God.. spearað dearfan & wedlan. *c* 897 K. ÆLFRED *Gregory's Past. C.* xlvi. 352 Hie ne sparodon ða synnfullan, ac slogon. *c* 1100 in Cockayne *Shrine* 17 Ne spared nu se fæder þan sune ne nan mann oðren; Ac ælc man winð ongean oðren. *a* 1122 *O. E. Chron.* (Laud MS.) an. 1086, He sætte..þeȝnas on cweartern, & æt nextan he ne sparode his aȝenne broðor. *c* 1175 *Lamb. Hom.* 121 Þa he ne sparede na ihesu crist his aȝene sune. *c* 1205 LAY. 27487 Nuste nan kempe whæm he sculde slæn on, and wham he sculde sparien. 1297 R. GLOUC. (Rolls) 8830 Sparie he wolde Mildemen & harde chasty þe proute. 1375 BARBOUR *Bruce* IX. 297 He..gert his men burn all Bouchane ..and sparit nane. *c* 1400 MAUNDEV. (Roxb.) xxxi. 142 Þare es nane spared þat es taken with a trespas. 1474 CAXTON *Chesse* II. iv. (1883) 53 To spare them & gyue hem her lyf. 1589? LYLY *Pappe w. Hatchet* (1844) 19, I am like death, Ile spare none. 1596 SHAKS. *Tam. Shr.* IV. iii. 153 Take thou the bill, giue me thy meat-yard, and spare not me. *a* 1628 PRESTON *New Covt.* (1634) 364 If men could have entered into Covenant and kept the Law, Christ had beene spared. 1697 DRYDEN *Virg. Georg.* IV. 758 Whom ev'n the savage Beasts had spar'd, they kill'd. 1780 COWPER *Fable* 34 An earthquake may be bid to spare The man that's strangled by a hair. 1825 SCOTT *Talism.* iii, Saladin had issued particular orders that he should be spared and protected. 1891 FARRAR *Darkn. & Dawn* xlii, They..demanded that there should be a trial, and that the innocent should be spared.

refl. 1297 R. GLOUC. (Rolls) 1609 Vor woch dede a man ssolde..Lese is on eye, & he him sulf ne sparde him sulue noȝt, Ac let pulte out is owe eye. *a* 1300 *Cursor M.* 26718 Þis man will we spare, For noght he spard him-self are.

b. With impersonal object (but implying or suggesting a person or persons). (Cf. 4.)

c 825 *Vesp. Psalter* lxxvii. 50 [He] ne spearede from deaðe sawlum heara. 1362 LANGL. *P. Pl.* A. VII. 21 Spynneth it spedily, spareþ noght ȝour fyngres. 1605 SHAKS. *Lear* II. ii. 72 Spare my gray-beard, you wagtaile? 1725 POPE *Odyss.* XV. 303 Receive the suppliant! spare my destin'd blood. 1757 GRAY *Bard* 107 Visions of glory, spare my aching sight. 1817 SHELLEY *Rev. Islam* x. xxiv. 1 Famine had spared the palace of the king.

c. To allow to be free or exempt *from* (or †*of*) some task, etc. Also *refl.* without const.

1375 BARBOUR *Bruce* v. 362 He him sparit na kyn thing, Bot prufit swa his fors..That throu his vorschip [etc.]. 1398 TREVISA *Barth. De P. R.* XVIII. cix. (Bodl. MS.), The more scheo [i.e. a cow] is forbore and spared fro [1495 of] trauaile, þe more slowe [s]he is. 1596 BACON *Max. & Use Com. Law* II. (1635) 7 By which the Earles were spared of their toyles and labours, and that was laid upon the Sheriffes. 1794 MRS. RADCLIFFE *Myst. Udolpho* xxxv, [The] housekeeper, now spared from further attendance by the entrance of the count.

d. To refrain from denouncing or exposing in strong terms; to deal gently or leniently with.

1535 COVERDALE *Job* xxxii. 21, I wil open my lyppes, and make answere. I will regarde no maner of personne, no man wil I spare. 1607 SHAKS. *Cor.* II. iii. 243 Sic[inus]. Lay the fault on vs. Brut[us]. I, spare vs not. 1649 MILTON *Eikon.* B 2, As he hath not spar'd his Adversaries, so to him will be us'd no more Courtship then he uses. 1728 T. SHERIDAN tr. *Persius* (1739) Ded. p. iv, I never did once either distinguish or spare you. 1771 *Junius Lett.* liv. (1788) 295 What public question have I declined? What villain have I spared? 1821 SCOTT *Kenilw.* xli, As Varney ..had been studious to spare the character of his patron. 1852 THACKERAY *Esmond* I. iv, My lady used not to spare Colonel Esmond in talking of him. 1891 FARRAR *Darkn. & Dawn* lii. 295 He shrank from eliciting a keenness of wit which had not spared the bloodstained Sylla.

e. To refrain from afflicting or distressing.

1794 MRS. RADCLIFFE *Myst. Udolpho* xxxviii, Emily.. was followed by the Lady Blanche,..whom she entreated to spare her on the subject of her distress. 1819 SHELLEY *Cenci* v. ii. 108 Oh, spare me! Speak to me no more!..Those solemn tones Wound worse than torture. 1856 CAPERN *Poems* (ed. 2) 143 Spare, oh, spare thy tender feelings.

2. *absol.* To exercise or show mercy, forbearance, or leniency.

a 1225 *Juliana* (Royal MS.) 70 A stalewurðe men ne sparie ȝe nawiht; ha haueð us alle scheome idon. *a* 1300 *Cursor M.* 3974 Esau ai he dred ful sare, For he was fel and wald noght spare. 1382 WYCLIF *Job* xxvii. 22 He shal senden out vp on hym, and not sparen. *c* 1420 *Prymer* 78 God, to whom it is proprid to haue merci & to spare euer more. 1422 tr. *Secreta Secret., Priv. Priv.* 181 He that is a gouernoure in tymes he shall Spare, and in tymes vengeaunse take. 1535 COVERDALE *Job* vi. 10, I wolde desyre him in my payne, that he shulde not spare. 1611 BIBLE *Prov.* vi. 34 He will not spare in the day of vengeance. 1736 *Gentl. Mag.* VI. 678 Spare, charmer spare! in prudence do! 1761 GRAY *Fatal Sisters* 34 Ours to kill, and ours to spare. 1825 SCOTT *Talism.* xxii, The lion Richard will spare when he has conquered. 1871 GROSART *H. Vaughan's Wks.* I. Ded. p. iv, Available and destined for the same august post (God sparing).

†**b.** Const. *to*. (After L. *parcere*.) *Obs.*

c 1340 HAMPOLE *Psalter* xviii. 13 Of myn hid [trespasses] make me clene, and of oþer spare til þi seruaunte. 1382 WYCLIF *Wisd.* xii. 16 To alle thou makest thee to sparen. *c* 1420 *Prymer* 47 Spare, lord, spare to þe puple.

3. *trans.* †**a.** To refrain from violating, infringing, or breaking. *Obs.*

1303 R. BRUNNE *Handl. Synne* 806 Of al þe festys þat yn holy chyrche are Holy sunday men oght to spare. 1387 TREVISA *Higden* (Rolls) VIII. 129 No privelege of persoun wheþer of holy cherche noþer fredom was i-spared.

b. To abstain from visiting (a sin, etc.) with due punishment; to forgive or pardon.

1388 WYCLIF *Job* xiv. 16 Sotheli thou hast noumbrid my steppis; but spare thou my synnes. *a* 1450 tr. *De Imitatione* III. lv. 132, I þonke þe þat þou hast not spared myn eueles. 1500–20 DUNBAR *Poems* lxx. 27 Thow, that on rude ws ransomit,..Spair our trespas. 1782 COWPER *Mut. Forbearance* 44 If infirmities..Are crimes so little to be spar'd.

c. To preserve or save (life) in place of destroying; to allow to continue or last.

1594 KYD *Cornelia* v. 445 To spare Thy worthles life that yet must one day perish. 1605 SHAKS. *Lear* II. ii. 66 This ancient Ruffian Sir, whose life I haue spar'd at sute of his gray-beard. 1781 COWPER *Expost.* 623 Those holy men..could not..spare a life too short to reach the skies. 1823 SCOTT *Quentin D.* xix, With what face darest thou ask any guerdon beyond my sparing thy worthless life? 1865 TROLLOPE *Belton Est.* i. 8 He hoped that the squire's life would be long spared. 1890 *Science-Gossip* XXVI. 167 Poor pussy began to purr, and that decided the verdict in favour of her life being spared.

4. To abstain from destroying, removing, damaging, or injuring (a thing).

c 897 K. ÆLFRED *Gregory's Past. C.* xviii. 140 Swæ sindon ða loccas to sparianne ðæm sacerde ðæt hie ða hyd behelizen. *c* 900 tr. *Baeda's Hist.* IV. xxvii, Cyricum ne mynstrum seo herehand sparode ne ne arode. 1338 R. BRUNNE *Chron.* (1810) 248 Holy who salle spare,..Whan þo þat hedes are do þer to no gode. 1382 WYCLIF *Rom.* xi. 21 Forsothe if God sparide not the kyndely braunchis, lest perauenture he spare not thee. *c* 1400 *Brut* li. 45 [They] destroyede al þing þat þai fonde; and no þing þai ne sparede. 1480 *Cov. Leet Bk.* 446 In their shotyng called rovyng,..[they] nother sparen corn ne grasse, but distroyen & defowlen hem. *a* 1586 SIDNEY *Arcadia* (1622) 368 Shee..was now about to put out his eyes, which all this while were spared. 1643 DENHAM *Cooper's H.* 155 What does he think our Sacriledge would spare, When such th' effects of our Devotion are? 1648 MILTON *Sonn.* viii. 10 The great Emathian Conqueror bid spare The house of Pindarus. 1759 JOHNSON *Rasselas* xxix, From the wonders which time has spared we may conjecture..what it has destroyed. 1794 MRS. RADCLIFFE *Myst. Udolpho* xlv, The beauty..of its delicate carvings, determined the count to spare this door. 1839 THIRLWALL *Greece* VI. 165 It was believed that Alexander ..was induced to spare it by the hope that it would soon surrender. 1879 S. C. BARTLETT *Egypt to Pal.* x. 225 Usually a large part of their branches had been cut off, even when the tree itself had been spared.

b. To save or protect (a thing) from damage, wear, or undue strain in some way.

1817 LADY MORGAN *France* I. (1818) I. 63, I remember our having alighted from our carriage to spare its springs in a sort of 'crack-scull-common' road.

II. **5.** To refrain from using or consuming; to use in a frugal or economical manner. Now *rare*.

c 1000 ÆLFRIC *Hom.* (Thorpe) II. 70 He sparode þæt gode win oð his aȝenum to-cyme. *a* 1300 *Cursor M.* 7927 For to spar his aun aght þis pouer mans scep he laght. 1398 TREVISA *Barth. De P. R.* VI. xiv. (Bodl. MS.), [A father] spareþ his owne mete to fede his chyld with. *c* 1440 *Jacob's Well* 143 Þou myȝt so spare þi purse, þat þou myȝt forfare þi-self. 1477 EARL RIVERS (Caxton) *Dictes* 14 It satisfieth not to spare metes and do euill dedis. *c* 1550 N. SMYTH tr. *Herodian* II. 19 He..also teacheth others to be frugall, and spare that them selues gette. 1589 GREENE *Menaphon* (Arb.) 34 She sparde no cuening milke, but went amongst the cream bowles, and made him a posset. 1635–56 COWLEY *Davideis* I. 869 Free Natures bounty thriftily they spent, And spared the Stock. 1651 HOBBES *Leviath.* II. xxx. 181 He which laboureth much, and sparing the fruits of his labour, consumeth little [etc.]. 1726 SWIFT *Gulliver* III. i, Being resolved to spare my provisions as much as I could. 1743 FRANCIS tr. *Hor., Odes* II. vii. 26 Thy Limbs from Toils of Warfare free, Nor spare the Casks reserv'd for Thee.

†**b.** To save, hoard, or store up. *Obs.*

c 1400 *Gamelyn* 320 My brother is a niggoun.., And we wil spende largely that he hath spared yore. 1483 CAXTON *Cato* F iij b, For men hath dyspended..in lytel tyme that whiche men hath acquyred and spared wyth grete labour. 1500–20 DUNBAR *Poems* xxxvi. 25 Sum grit gud gadderis and ay it spairis. 1579 SPENSER *Sheph. Cal.* May 84 The sonne of his loines why should he regard To leaue enriched with that he hath spard? 1648 GAGE *West Ind.* 160 What monies they have spared, after their own and their servants lawful maintenance. 1683 D. A. *Art Converse* 116 They can inform you of Twenty Arts how to gain and spare a Peny.

c. *absol.* To use or practise economy or frugality; to be parsimonious or niggardly; to live or act sparingly.

1377 LANGL. *P. Pl.* B. XII. 53 And riche renkes riȝt so gaderen and sparen. *c* 1420 *Sir Amadace* (Camden) ii, I myȝte lung spare, Or alle these godus qwitte ware, And haue noȝte to spend. *c* 1475 *Rauf Coilȝear* 202 Thairfoir sic [good fare] as thow seis, spend on, and not spair. *a* 1513 FABYAN *Chron.* VI. (1811) 234 He..gaue parte vnto suche knyghtes as he fauoured, and spared to theym that hadde wele deserued. 1573 TUSSER *Husb.* (1878) 204 For lordlie bent Must learne to spare. 1621 T. WILLIAMSON tr. *Goulart's Wise Vieillard* 73 It is a pleasing..excuse among men..to alledge that they spare for their children. 1667 MILTON *P. L.* v. 320 Where Nature..by disburd'ning grows More fruitful, which instructs us not to spare. 1737 POPE tr. *Hor., Epist.* II. ii. 290, I, who at some times spend, at others spare. 1792 BURNS *Country Lassie* iv, But some will spend, and some will spare. 1866 HOWELLS *Venetian Life* 325 Those people who attempt to maintain a certain appearance upon insufficient means,..and who spare in every possible way. 1889 — *Hazard New Fortunes* 94 They must spare in carriage hire at any rate.

prov. 1562 J. HEYWOOD *Prov. & Epigr.* (1867) 54 Euer spare and euer bare. 1573 TUSSER *Husb.* (1878) 23 Some spareth too late,..the foole at the bottom, the wise at the brim. 1677 MIÈGE *Fr. Dict.* II. s.v., To spare at the spiggot, and let it run out at the bung-hole. 1681 W. ROBERTSON *Phraseol. Gen.* s.v., Better spare at the brim, than at the bottom, *sera est in fundo parsimonia* [Seneca *Ep.* I. 5]. 1736 AINSWORTH I. s.v., It is too late to spare, when all is spent.

d. In passive: To be left over or unused.

1577 GOOGE *Heresbach's Husb.* § 149 You must feede them often by hand, when meate fayles abroade,..and not so much as Barly spared. 1793 SMEATON *Edystone L.* § 237 The mason took the mortar out of the bucket; and if any was spared, he still kept on beating. 1799 [A. YOUNG] *Agric. Linc.* 25 All that may be spared at night, should be thrown to the common mortar heap, and fresh stucco made in the morning. 1868 ATKINSON *Cleveland Gloss.* 481 Eat what thee likes, an' what's spared tak' awa' yamm fur t' bairns.

6. To abstain or refrain from using, employing, exercising, etc.; to forbear, omit, or avoid the use or occasion of; also, to use, or deal in, with moderation, economy, or restraint: **a.** In various special contexts.

(*a*) *c* 1000 ÆLFRIC *Hom.* II. 324 Se ðe sparað his ȝyrde, he hatað his cild. *a* 1250 *Prov. Ælfred* 451 in *O. E. Misc.*, Þe mon þe spareþ yeorde.., þat him schal on ealde sore reowe. 1393 LANGL. *P. Pl.* C. VI. 139 Ho so spareþ þe spring spilleþ hus children. *c* 1430 *Stans Puer ad Mensam* 91 (Lamb. MS.), Who þat spariþ þe rodde [*v.r.* the yerd] al vertues settiþ a-side. 1526 SKELTON *Magnyf.* 1955 There is nothynge that more dyspleaseth God Than from theyr chyldren to spare the rod Of correccyon. 1535 COVERDALE *Prov.* xiii. 24 He that spareth the rodde, hateth his sonne. 1664 BUTLER *Hud.* II. i. 844 Love is a Boy, by Poets styl'd, Then Spare the Rod, and spill the Child. 1841 LYTTON *Nt. & Morn.* II. iii, Spare the rod and spoil the child. 1855 THACKERAY *Newcomes* iii, I have a brother to whom my poor mother spared the rod, and who..has turned out but a spoilt child.

(*b*) *a* 1225 *Leg. Kath.* 807 Lure ow is to leosen ower swinkes lan, ȝe leoteð se lutel of, & spareð ower speche. *a* 1300 *Cursor M.* 16110 Sai me iesus, qui dos þou þus? to me na soth þou spare. *c* 1386 CHAUCER *Sompn. T.* 55 Tel forth thy tale, and spare it not at al. *c* 1400 *Pilgr. Sowle* (Caxton, 1483) IV. xxx. 78 Flaterers and forgeours that sparen the soothe ben nothynge profitable. 1481 CAXTON *Reynard* xxxiv. (Arb.) 100 Yf ye wyl spare the trouth and lye grete lesynges. 1508 DUNBAR *Tua mariit wemen* 40 Syne thai spak more spedelie, and sparit no materis. 1617 MORYSON *Itin.* II. 72 He might doe well to spare the rest of his speech. 1663 S. PATRICK *Parab. Pilgr.* xii. (1687) 79 Your blushes bid me spare this language. 1731 SWIFT *Death Dr. Swift* Wks. 1841 I. 657/2 Had he but spared his tongue and pen, He might have rose like other men. 1753 RICHARDSON *Grandison* V. iv. 27, I am put upon a task that grieves me, Ease my heart, by sparing my speech. 1820 SCOTT *Monast.* xxxvii, 'Spare your threats,' said Murray. 1848 THACKERAY *Van. Fair* xxix, Much painful and unavailing talk between them was spared. 1864–8 BROWNING *J. Lee's Wife* II. iii, Spare the curse!

(*c*) *a* 1440 *Found. St. Bartholomew's* (E.E.T.S.) 19 Whane thou cummyste yn to the Iewes strete, spare thy sporys, lose thy brydyll, lette thyn hors to my gouernaunce. *c* 1470 *Gol. & Gaw.* 305 Thayr wes na spurris to spair, spedely thai spring. 1575 GASCOIGNE *Glasse of Govt.* Wks. 1910 II. 26 But yet where youth is prone to follow ill, There spare the spurre, and use the brydell still. 1735 SOMERVILLE *Chase* III. 85 Flourish the Whip, nor spare the galling Spur. 1782 MISS BURNEY *Cecilia* VIII. i, Why, Sir, you have not spared the spur! 1831 SCOTT *Ct. Rob.* xvi, Come along.. like a good fellow, and for once I shall spare the whip.

b. In miscellaneous (partly *obs.*) uses.

a 1300 *Cursor M.* 5867 Dathait qua werkes on þam spar! Þan held þai þam harder þan ar. 1388 WYCLIF *Jer.* l. 14 Ouercome ȝe it [*sc.* Babyloun], spare ȝe not arowis, for it synnede to the Lord. 1515 *Plumpton Corr.* (Camden) 212, [I] entreated them to spare distreyning, till such tyme as I had sent unto you [etc.]. 1553 *Reg. Privy Council Scot.* I. 141 It is maist convenient and best to spair puneisment for the said cryme. 1573 TUSSER *Husb.* (1878) 97 Spare meadow at Gregorie, marshes at Pask, for feare of drie Sommer. 1687 A. LOVELL tr. *Thevenot's Trav.* I. 59 They spare not now and then a blow with a Cudgel by the by. 1831 SCOTT *Ct. Rob.* xxiii, Count Robert spared putting forth some part of the military skill for which he was celebrated. 1884 F. TEMPLE *Relat. Relig. & Sci.* v. (1885) 142 We recognise that we are bound to spare pain to all creatures that can feel.

c. Const. *to* and infinitive.

Freq. from the 14th to the 17th century; now *rare*.

a 1225 *Juliana* 26 Aut..wa wurðe him wurst þat te mest sparie wondreðe to donne. 13.. *Sir Beues* 4482 Sire Miles ..Lep vpon a dromedary, To prike wolde he nouȝt spary. 1377 LANGL. *P. Pl.* B. III. 51 Wist I that..I wolde nouȝt spare For to be ȝowre frende. *c* 1385 CHAUCER *Merch. T.* 1065, I schal not spare for no curtesye To speke him harm, that wold us vilonye. *c* 1440 *Partonope* 1707 Ye spared not in-to my bedde Homely to gonne. 1479 *Cov. Leet Bk.* 423 Not sparyng to do therin as lawe will for eny persone.. what-so-euer. 1526 *Pilgr. Perf.* (W. de W. 1531) 18 Some spare not to make insurrecyon and rebell agaynst theyr prelates and heddes. 1575 GASCOIGNE *Glasse of Govt.* Wks. 1910 II. 16 Spare not to commaund my service. 1637 BP. REYNOLDS *Serm.* (1638) 34, I shall spare to bee so injurious to your patience, and to the businesse wee attend upon. 1686 tr. *Chardin's Coronat. Solyman* 75 The Controller.. would not spare to inform the worst he could against him. 1808 SCOTT *Marm.* I. iv, And, from the platform, spare ye not To fire a noble salvo-shot. 1893 STEVENSON *Catriona* xxix. (1902) 346 Using travellers' freedom, we spared to wait for James More.

prov. 14.. *Lat. & Eng. Prov.* (MS. Douce 52) fol. 16 b, Who so sparyth to speke sparyth to spede. 1509 HAWES *Past. Pleas.* XVI. (Percy Soc.) 91 Who spareth to speke he to spede doth spare. 1546 HEYWOOD *Prov. & Epigr.* (1867) 31 Spare to speake spare to speede. 1567 TURBERV. *Epit.*, etc. (1837) 308 My Spencer, spare to speake, and euer spare to speed. 1748 SMOLLETT *R. Random* xxxiv, Remembering the old proverb, 'Spare to speak, spare to speed', [he] resolved to solicit the new captain's interest immediately. 1789 BURNS *Blue-eyed Lassie* ii. 1887 in *Eng. Dial. Dict.* s.v., He that spares to speyk, spares to speed.

d. In elliptical use: To refrain from doing something. Now *rare* or *Obs.*

c 1386 CHAUCER *Friar's T.* 39 Now telleth forth,.. Ne spareth nought, myn owne maister deere. *c* 1400 *Destr. Troy* 12736 Sho spilt hade hir spousaile, sparit ho noght. 1530 TINDALE *Wks.* (Parker Soc.) 343, I could more deeply have entered into the practice of our cardinal, but I spare for divers considerations. 1557 TUSSER *100 Points Husb.* lxxxi, In June washe thy shepe,..and kepe them from dust. ..Then share them and spare not. 1610 SHAKS. *Temp.* II. i. 24 *Alon.* I pre-thee spare. *Gon.* Well, I haue done. *a* 1680 J. DYKE *Right Receiv. Christ* (1640) 161 Talke and spare not.

†**e.** *absol.* To refrain from or forbear the use or exercise *of* something. *Obs. rare.*

c 1470 *Gol. & Gaw.* 274 A! lord, sparis of sic speche, quhill ye speir more. 1481 *Cov. Leet Bk.* 489 To commaunde vs to respite & spare for a season of callyng furth oure seid retynue.

7. To avoid incurring or being involved in, to save (expense or labour).

(*a*) *a* 1325 [see (*b*) below]. *c* 1400 *Cursor M.* 29060 (Cott. Galba), If þou fast þi spens to spare, thrise for to ete better þe ware. *c* 1420 *Avow. Arth.* xlviii, Ther was no spense for to spare, Burdes thay were neuyr bare. 1491 *Act 7 Hen. VII*, c. 22 Preamble, Put to your hand and spare no cost. 1548 ELYOT, *Parcere impensæ*, to spare coste. 1617 MORYSON *Itin.* I. 9 This fortification, wherein he hath spared no cost. 1621 in W. H. Hale *Prec. Causes of Office* (1841) 50 He said they haue no nede of popish reliques and that the parishe may spare their money for such thinges. 1693 in Willis & Clark *Cambridge* (1886) II. 376 It being necessary to retrench the expences, it was thought proper to spare the charge of the Organist. 1819 SCOTT *Ivanhoe* xxxiv, The gold thou shalt spare in her cause. 1848 THACKERAY *Van. Fair* lvi, A famous tailor..was summoned to ornament little George's person, and was told to spare no expense in so doing.

(*b*) *a* 1325 *MS. Rawl. B. 520* lf. 30 b, Þe king hath igraunted for te sparen trauail and despense of his men. 1526 *Pilgr. Perf.* (W. de W. 1531) 2 b, They..spared no labours neyther by see ne yet by lande. 1560 DAUS tr. *Sleidane's Comm.* 126 They wil spare neyther paynes nor peryl. 1603 KNOLLES *Hist. Turks* (1621) 1154 Meaning..by this means to spare their pouder, shot, and paines, and to reserue them to their better vses. 1675 J. OWEN *Indwelling Sin* xvi. (1732) 216 To spare the trouble in the Education of their Children. 1780 *Mirror* No. 101, These I spared no pains to cultivate and improve. 1827 FARADAY *Chem. Manip.* ix. (1842) 238 He should not spare pains to procure the best possible [filtering-paper]. 1832 HT. MARTINEAU *Life in Wilds* vi. 80 We must spare labour to the utmost till we can get a stock of labourers. 1892 *Photogr. Ann.* II. 601 No time, trouble, or expense has been spared in the matter.

b. To avoid, shun, keep clear of. Now *rare*.

c 1380 *Sir Ferumb.* 1553 Faste þay passede ouer al þe weys..; Ne sparede þay hulles, noþer valeys, bote prikede forþ with bost. 1387 TREVISA *Higden* (Rolls) VI. 37 He hated wyn dronkenes, ribaudye, and harlottrie; uppon caas forhete of þe contray he wolde have it i-spared. 1483 CAXTON *Gold. Leg.* 121 b/2 Haue pyte on thy self..that ye mayst.. wynne to spare the tormentes that ben yet to come. 1523 LD. BERNERS *Froiss.* I. ccx. 252 They spared nat the dangerous maresses, but went through them. 1590 SHAKS. *Mids. N.* II. i. 142 Shun me and I will spare your haunts. 1821 SHELLEY *Epipsych.* 183 And we know not How much..Of pleasure may be gained, of sorrow spared.

8. To dispense with from one's stock or supply, or from a number, quantity, etc.; to part with, to give or grant, lend, etc., to another or others, esp. without inconvenience or loss to oneself; to do without.

Also const. *to* (a person or persons), *from* or *out of* (a stock or store, etc.).

a 1225 *Ancr. R.* 416 Ȝif heo mei sparien eni poure schreaden, sende ham al derneliche ut of hire woanes. *a* 1300 *Cursor M.* 29057 Þe mete þat þou þi-self suld ete..þou sal it to þe pouer spare. *a* 1400 *Minor Poems fr. Vernon MS.* lv. i. 67 Ȝit of þi good wolde-tou not spare. 1481 *Cov. Leet Bk.* 454 To knowe..what able persones & howe many the Towne myght spare ouer þe seid iij[xx] men. *a* 1548 HALL *Chron., Edw. IV*, 31 b, The lord Beauchampe toke from her rereward, more ordinance then she might haue wel spared. 1560 DAUS tr. *Sleidane's Comm.* 398 b, No parte of that wheate, whiche is in the citie, can be spared. 1601 in Moryson *Itin.* (1617) II. 145 At this time he cannot well be spared from hence. 1613 PURCHAS *Pilgrimage* (1614) 516 He is Collector or Treasurer to the King of Ternate in those parts, and sends him what he can spare. 1651 HOBBES *Leviath.* II. xxiv. 129 It is necessary, that men distribute that which they can spare. 1769 JOHNSON *Lett.* (1788) I. 20, I..can easily spare the pine-apple. 1769 FALCONER *Dict. Marine* (1780), *Donner un grand hunier*, to spare a main top-sail to some other ship in company. 1827 FARADAY *Chem. Manip.* xvii. (1842) 463 When a drop only of the fluid can be spared, a glass plate..will support it. 1855 MACAULAY *Hist. Eng.* xii. III. 241 Kirke could spare no soldiers; but he had sent..some experienced officers. 1879 FROUDE *Cæsar* xx. 337 Cæsar and Pompey must each spare a legion for the East.

b. To reserve, retain, set aside or store up *for* some particular use or purpose; to keep in reserve.

a 1300 *Cursor M.* 5394 Þai had noþer worth ne ware þat þai moght for þair mete spare. [*Trin. MS.* Þei hadde no þing ȝare þat þei myȝte to her lyuelode spare.] *c* 1400 *Destr. Troy* 6502 The tother speire þat he sparit, [he] spent vpon hym. 1573 TUSSER *Husb.* (1878) 90 Land meadow that yeerly is spared for hay, now fence it and spare it. 1610 GUILLIM *Heraldry* I. iii. (1660) 19 It is taken up and spared for necessary purposes. 1795 *Gentl. Mag.* 542/2, I request you will spare room for one tribute more to his memory.

1886 G. E. PASCOE *Lond. of To-day* xxvii. (ed. 3) 251 The proper description of which would require more space than we can conveniently spare for the purpose.

c. To set apart, save, or give (time) from one's usual or ordinary duties or avocations; to have free, unoccupied, or unemployed.

a 1548 HALL *Chron., Hen. VI*, 82 b, This..politique Capitayne lost not one houre, nor spared one mynet, till he came before the citie of Burdeaux. 1565 COOPER s.v. *Succisivus*, Time spared from other businesse. *c* 1643 LD. HERBERT *Autobiog.* (1824) 71 That Exercise taking up more time than can be spared from a studious man to get Knowledge. 1742–3 WESLEY *Extr. Jrnl.* (1749) 59, I take such a proportion of time as I can spare every night, to discourse with each child apart. 1788 G. KEATE *Pelew Isl.* xxiii. 237 The portion of time which they could spare from providing for their natural wants. 1833 HT. MARTINEAU *Tale of Tyne* vii. 126 Can you spare a minute, just to look out of this window? 1875 JOWETT *Plato* (ed. 2) V. 423 Let all the citizens who can spare time hear..such causes.

d. In prec. senses as complement to the verbs *have* or *be*, or with ellipse of these.

1390 GOWER *Conf.* II. 396 Whan Somer hath lost al his grene And is with Wynter wast and bare, That him is left nothing to spare. 1530 PALSGR. 726/1 Sownde, mariner, let us se what water we have to spare. 1550 CROWLEY *Last Trumpet* 1198 Thou haste no tyme to spare, and spende in bankettyng. 1633 G. HERBERT *Temple, Ch. Porch* xii, For we have wit to mark them, and to spare. 1654 BRAMHALL *Just Vind.* v. (1661) 102 These [bishops] were few enough for their own province, and none to spare for Britain. 1705 DE FOE in *Lett. Lit. Men* (Camden) 322, I know your Lordship has but few minutes to spare. 1771 FRANKLIN *Autobiog.* Wks. 1840 I. 94 She brought me word she had no such sum to spare. 1836 MARRYAT *Japhet* xlvi, I had an hour to spare, before the coach started. 1863 W. C. BALDWIN *Afr. Hunting* v. 133, I won both events.., with three bullets to spare. 1878 *Masque Poets* 13 If we had only time to spare To taste the glories of the Spring.

9. With direct and indirect object: **a.** To give or grant; to supply (a person) with (something) out of a stock, quantity, etc.

1593 SHAKS. *3 Hen. VI*, II. vi. 78 Then the world go's hard When Clifford cannot spare his Friends an oath. *a* 1616 BEAUM. & FL. *Wit without M.* I. ii, She may spare me her misen, and her bonnets, strike her main Petticoat, and yet outsail me. *c* 1643 LD. HERBERT *Autobiog.* (1824) 138, I was without any meat but what my Footman spared me out of his pocket. 1711 *Lond. Gaz.* No. 4887/3 They outrunning us so very much, that they spared us half their Sails. 1784 COWPER *Task* I. 262 He spares me yet These chesnuts rang'd in corresponding lines. 1821 SCOTT *Kenilw.* xvii, Your nobleness will willingly spare your old servitor his crib and his mess. 1847 TENNYSON *Princ.* vi. 242 And now A word, but one,..Not one to spare her: out upon you, flint!

†**b.** To allow (one) to utter (a word). Also *ellipt.* *Obs.*

1560 *Trial Regic.* 24 Spare me but one Word. 1710 PALMER *Proverbs* 189 Out comes two or three 'If you'll give me leave s', as many 'Spare me's', 'with submission's', and 'I humbly conceive's'.

c. To save or relieve (a person, one's feelings, etc.) from (something).

1681 DRYDEN *Span. Friar* v. i, Spare my sight the pain Of seeing what a world of Tears it cost you. 1794 MRS. RADCLIFFE *Myst. Udolpho* xxxix, Spare me the necessity of mentioning those circumstances. *Ibid.* xlvi, Adding that he would spare her any difficulties that might occur. 1802 MAR. EDGEWORTH *Moral T.* (1816) I. 216, I shall spare you ..the reflections I have made on this occasion. 1856 KANE *Arct. Expl.* II. xxix. 287, I had a set of signals..which spared us the noise of the voice. 1893 SLOANE-STANLEY *Remin. Midshipm. Life* vi. 82, I was, however, spared this infliction.

refl. 1717 LADY M. W. MONTAGU *Let. to Pope* 1 Apr., I might spare myself the trouble. 1781 COWPER *Charity* 626, I might spare myself the pains to show What few can learn. 1841 W. SPALDING *Italy & It. Isl.* II. 102 We may spare ourselves the labour of looking for its essence. 1848 THACKERAY *Van. Fair* ii, Minerva thought wisely she could spare herself the expense of a master. 1884 *Manch. Exam.* 11 Oct. 5/1 They wrench off cupboard doors to spare themselves the trouble of closing them.

III. *intr.* **10.** *To spare for*: **a.** To desist or refrain from some action because or on account of (difficulty, opposition, loss, etc.).

Freq. *c* 1400; usually with a negative. Now *arch.*

a 1300 *Beket* (Percy Soc.) 61 Heo wende alone..And ne sparede for no sorewe that miȝte come hire to. *c* 1330 *King of Tars* 905 Bid him com hider with his ost,..For no thyng that he ne spare. *c* 1400 *Pilgr. Sowle* (Caxton) v. xiv. (1859) 81 For blandyssyng, for manace, ne for drede They spared not, but stoden by the trouthe. *c* 1430 *How Good Wife taught Dau.* 12 in *Babees Bk.*, Go to chirche whanne þou may, Loke þou spare for no reyn. *a* 1585 MONTGOMERIE *Cherrie & Slae* 370, He is bot daft that hes ado, And spairis for euery speiche. 1810 SCOTT *Lady of L.* v. xxxii, Spare not for spoiling of thy steed. 1823 — *Quentin D.* x, Throw down the screen—spare not for cup or goblet.

b. With negative: To refrain from action in order to avoid or save (expense, trouble, etc.); to be sparing of or in (something).

c 1400 *Destr. Troy* 233, I shall spare for no spence & bu spede wele. 14.. *Sir Beues* (E.) 3310 Þey sparyd neyber for syluyr ne golde. 1535 LYNDESAY *Satyre* 52 And sie the burgessis spair not for expence, Bot speid thame heir. 1593 MARLOWE *Edw. II*, I. iv, Spare for no cost. 1599 SHAKS. *Much Ado* III. v. 66 And we must doe it wisely. *Dogb.* Wee will spare for no witte I warrant you. 1657 EARL MONM. tr. *Paruta's Pol. Disc.* 55 Cesar never spared for any labour by which he might hope to purchase renown and glory. 1681 HICKERINGILL *Sin Man-Catching* Wks. 1716 I. 178 They plot their Work,..spare for no pains, no cost, not daunted with any ill success. 1723 *Briton* No. 12 (1724) 54 Crassus..spared for no Expence to purchase Voices. 1726 LEONI *Alberti's Archit.* II. 53 No Columns or Pilasters were spared for. 1793 SMEATON *Edystone L.* § 305 They did not spare for cold water to throw in my face and upon me.

IV. **11.** Combs. with the verbal stem, as *spare-good*, *-penny*, *-thrift*; also † **spare-chest**, a chest for spare money, a reserve fund.

1611 COTGR. s.v. *Manger*, *Il est à table, & n'ose manger*; (Applyable to a miserable spare-good). 1707 J. STEVENS tr. *Quevedo's Com. Wks.* (1709) 298 The Retentive Knight: containing much wholesome Advice for saving the Ready, and being free of good Words. Dedicated to the Society of Spare-Pennies. 1768 *Ann. Reg.* I. 117 The extraordinary expences occasioned by his Sicilian majesty's marriage.. will not be levied upon the state, but defrayed out of the savings of the spare-chest. 1803 *Ann. Rev.* I. 423 The manufacturer has to deal..with the spendthrift and the sparethrift.

Spare, *v.*[2] *north.* and †*Sc.* Also 5 spayr, 6 spair. [var. of SPAR *v.*[1] Cf. SPEAR *v.*[2]

Spareð, given as a variant in the *Ancr. R.* 70, is perh. an error for *sperreð*.]

1. *trans.* To bar, bolt, or secure (a door or gate).

1375 BARBOUR *Bruce* v. 389 The ȝettis than he gert thame spare, And sat and ete at all lasare. *c* 1375 *Sc. Leg. Saints* xxvi. (*Nicholas*) 363 Þocht þe ȝet wes before sparyt, with strinth he enterit In. *c* 1450 *St. Cuthbert* (Surtees) 5067 He fande þe mynster ȝatis spared; As a wodeman he fared. 1583 *Durham Dep.* (Surtees) 314 The said Edward doore was spaired all the tyme the said geis was in eatyng. 1677 NICOLSON in *Trans. R. Soc. Lit.* (1870) IX. 319 *Spare the durre*, shut to the door. 1825 BROCKETT *N. C. Gloss.*, *Spare*, to shut, to close. 1894 HESLOP *Northumbld. Gloss.* 674 'Spare the yett,' 'Spare the door,' are still in common use.

†**2.** To close (the lips or eyes) firmly. *Obs.*

c 1400 *Rule St. Benet* (Verse) 107 And spayr þi lipes, & hald þam still, So þat þay opyn noght with ill! *c* 1450 *St. Cuthbert* (Surtees) 3847 He spared his eghen and lay still.

†**3.** To shut up; to keep *out*. *Obs.*

c 1450 *St. Cuthbert* (Surtees) 4123 As a man in prisoun sparde. 1482 *Monk of Evesham* lv. (Arb.) 107 The crosse ..was lettyn done ageyne, and so sparyd other oute that wuld haue commyn in.

Spareable (spēə·răb'l), *a.* [f. SPARE *v.*[1]] That can be spared, in various senses of the verb.

1658–9 in Cobbett *Parl. Hist. Eng.* (1809) V. 173 You cannot doubt but the spareable part will be treasured up for the good of the subject. 1821 *Blackw. Mag.* X. 89 We intend shipping a cargo of our worst and most spareable puns on board the next whaler. 1887 BLACKMORE *Springhaven* (ed. 4) III. xix. 270 His great desire..was never to destroy his enemies, by the number of one man spareable.

Spared (spēəɹd), *ppl. a.* [f. as prec.] Saved up, reserved; not wasted or destroyed, etc.

1580 G. HARVEY *Three Lett.* 40 And my poore Muse hath spent hir spared store, Yet little good hath got. 1623 WODROEPHE (*title*), The spared houres of a Souldier in his travels. 1657 S. PURCHAS *Pol. Flying-Ins.* 189 They breed ..most commonly in Meadows, and spared layes, or else in a hole in the ground. 1874 W. BRUCE *Hebrew Odes* 41 The spared remnant of His host. 1894 H. NISBET *Bush Girl's Rom.* 104 The only spared man of that camp darted towards the bush.

†**Spare-dry**: see SPAR *sb.*[1] 6.

†**Spareful**, *a.* *Obs.* [f. SPARE *sb.*[1] or *v.*[1]] Sparing, frugal.

1565 STAPLETON tr. *Bede's Hist. Ch. Eng.* 107 How spareful personnes he and his predecessours were,..euen the place, where he bare rule, did witnesse. 1599 *Life More* in C. Wordsw. *Eccl. Biog.* (1853) II. 112 She was also spareful, and somewhat given to niggardliness. 1600 FAIRFAX *Tasso* IV. xxx, Her sparefull eie to spread his beames denaies.

Hence † **Sparefully** *adv.*; † **Sparefulness**.

1570 JEWEL *View Seditious Bull* (1582) 53 They labour truely, they liue sparefully. *a* 1586 SIDNEY *Arcadia* (1622) 214 Large-se his hands could neuer skill of sparefulnesse. 1618 RYVES in *Camden's Lett.* (1691) 236 We know how sparefully S. Augustine speaketh of them in his books De civitate Dei.

Spareless (spēə·rlės), *a.* and *adv.* [f. as prec.]

†**1.** Unstinted, unlimited. *Obs.*

a 1400–50 *Alexander* 5467 Sum spends on him of sponges a spareles noumbre.

2. Unsparing, merciless.

1589 *Rare Triumphes Loue & Fortune* I. in J. P. Collier *Five O. Pl.* (Roxb.) 87 What I have promist doubt not to be perfourmed; The sparelesse destinies my will affoorde: Let this defend thee, like a trusty swoord. 1605 SYLVESTER *Du Bartas* II. iii. II. *Fathers* 140 Alas! I could not but even dye for griefe, Should I but yeeld mine Age's sweet reliefe..Into the hands of hang-men's spare-lesse spight. 1826 R. S. HAWKER *Cornish Ball.*, etc. (1904) 220 Thy spareless foe Bears the fell shaft and fatal blow. *a* 1851 MOIR *Unknown Grave* vi. Poet. Wks. II. 346 When all the friends..Were vanish'd..; Pluck'd one by one by spareless Time.

3. As *adv.* Without stint.

1567 PAINTER *Pal. Pleas.* II. 427 With a fashion of attire to garnish their inward parts, so well as (sparelesse) they imploy vpon the vanishing pompe.

Sparely (spēə·ɹli), *adv.* [f. SPARE *a.* Cf. OE. *sparlīce*, MDu. *spare-*, *spaerlike*, MLG. *sparlike*, OHG. *sparalīhho* (MHG. *sperliche*, G. *spärlich*), ON. *sparliga* (MSw. *sparlika*).]

1. In a sparing, frugal, or stinted manner; not fully, amply, or copiously.

1559 *Decl. Doctr.* in Strype *Ann. Ref.* (1709) I. viii. 118 Indeed we do think that discreet ministers will speak sparely and circumspectly of them. 1571 GOLDING *Calvin on Ps.* xxxvii. 25 By their lyving sparely, they have alwais enough. 1601 HOLLAND *Pliny* I. 93 It is drunke vp, and therefore floweth more sparely. 1637 MILTON *Lycidas* 138 Ye valleys low..On whose fresh lap the swart Star sparely looks. 1784 COWPER *Task* IV. 379 They..find at eve, Ill clad and fed but sparely, time to cool. 1840 HOOD *Kilmansegg, Honeymoon* xxx, He drank—the reverse of sparely. 1867 A. BARRY *Sir C. Barry* iv. 101 Ornament is sparely applied.

2. Thinly; sparsely.

1836 [JAS. GRANT] *Recoll. Ho. of Lords* viii. 153 He is thin and sparely made, with a sallow complexion. 1841 C. MACKAY *Longbeard* ii, His hair..hung sparely over his temples.

Spareness (spēə·ɹnės). [f. SPARE *a.* Cf. OE. *spærnes* frugality, etc.] The quality of being spare, in various senses of the adj.

1648 HEXHAM II, *Magerheydt*, Leanenesse, or Sparenesse. 1649 HAMMOND *Chr. Obligations* 36 Returning the grosse habit of sin to a sparenesse and slendernesse of stature. 1822 GALT *Provost* viii. 55 He was, notwithstanding the spareness of his abilities, a prideful creature. 1826 HOOD *Recipe for Civilization* 142 She saw the spareness of her habits. 1897 *Allbutt's Syst. Med.* IV. 608 After the age of forty years persons either diverge into spareness or become more or less obese.

Sparer (spēə·rəɹ). Also 5 sparare. [f. SPARE *v.*[1] Cf. MLG. and G. *sparer*.]

1. A sparing, frugal, or thrifty person; one who spares in using anything.

c 1440 *Promp. Parv.* 467/1 Sparare, or he þat sparythe, *parcus*, *parca*. 1542 UDALL *Erasm. Apoph.* 73 b, Plato was a frugall man and a great sparer or housband. 1555 W. WATREMAN *Fardle Facions* II. i. 118 The Nabatheens of all other arabiens are the beste husbandes, and thriftiest sparers. 1601 HOLLAND *Pliny* XI. xix. 321 For otherwise they [bees] are very thriftie and overgreat sparers. 1635 J. GORE *Way to Well-doing* 25 A good sparer makes a good spender. 1816 SCOTT *Old Mort.* i, I am in general a sparer of the rod. 1882 *Pall Mall G.* 14 June 4/2 The Turk has slaves in plenty, and is no sparer of their labour.

b. A thing or substance which aids in sparing or saving.

a 1613 OVERBURY *A Wife*, etc. (1616) K vj b, Hee cannot away with Tobacco; for hee is perswaded (and not much amisse) that tis a sparer of bread-corne. 19.. *Buck's Handbk. Med. Sci.* V. 564 (*Cent. Dict. Suppl.*), The great power as proteid sparers which the carbohydrates exercise.

2. One who refrains from injuring or destroying.

1572 BOSSEWELL *Armorie* II. 78 b, He is the auenger, he is also the sparer. 1607 LLOYD *Pilgr. Princes* 37 b, His sodaine chaunge..from a spoyler of all places, to be a sparer now of his subjects. 1853 *Zoologist* II. 4011 The humane sparer of the poor hedgehog in the midst of his many foes.

Spare-rib. Also 8 spear-rib. β. 7 sparrib, 8 sparib, 8–9 spar-rib. [prob. ad. MLG. *ribbe-spēr* (see RIBSPARE) with transposition of the two elements, and subsequent association with SPARE *a.*] A cut of meat, esp. of pork, consisting of part of the ribs somewhat closely trimmed. Also *fig.*

α. 1596 NASHE *Saffron Walden* 48 Let's haue halfe a dozen spare ribs of his rethorique, with tart sauce of taunts correspondent. 1709 W. KING *Cookery* ix, Spear-ribs, surloins, chines, and barons. 1749 FIELDING *Tom Jones* (1775) III. 113, I have bespoke a shoulder of mutton..and a spare-rib of pork. 1834 MARRYAT *P. Simple* xxvii, There was plenty of pork,..a roast sparerib with the crackling on,..and pig's pettitoes. 1844 H. STEPHENS *Bk. Farm* II. 99 The ribs [of the sheep] are here left exposed at the part from which the shoulder has been removed, and constitute what are called the *spare-ribs*. 1887 JEFFERIES *Amaryllis* xii, Pigmeat—such as spare-rib, griskin, blade-bone, and that mysterious morsel, the 'mouse'.

β. 1607 BREWER *Lingua* II. i, Traile no speares, but sparribs of Porke. 1611 COTGR., *Cotis*, the sparribs of a porke. 1706 S. SEWALL *Diary* 24 Dec. (1879) II. 175 Din'd on Salt Fish and a Spar-Rib. 1748 *Anson's Voy.* III. v. (ed. 4) 449 There was a great quantity of provisions, particularly salted sparibs of pork. 1867 WAUGH *Tattlin' Matty* i. 11 They'n bin killin' a pig; an' hoo's brought me a bit o' spar-rib.

b. *attrib.*, as *spare-rib feast*, etc.

1737 *Ochtertyre Ho. Bks.* (S.H.S.) 90 The sparrib rost peices. 1867 G. EASTON *Autobiog.* i. (ed. 2) 18 The Sparerib Feast..took place immediately after the fatted ox had been killed.

Spare royal: see SPUR-ROYAL.

Spa·resome, *a.* [ad. G. *sparsam*.] Economical.

1864 MAYHEW *German Life* I. 285 We must be sparesome now, the feast days are near at hand.

Sparewe, obs. form of SPARROW.

†**Sparewort**, obs. variant of SPEARWORT.

1579 W. LANGHAM *Garden of Health* 614 Sparewort, stampe it and apply it..to the sciatica, to reare a blister.

Spa·rfle, *v.* *Sc. rare.* In 6 sparfal, 9 sperfle. [Alteration of SPARPLE *v.*] *trans.* To scatter or disperse; to squander.

Sparfeled in Greene's *Orpharion* (1599) 48 is prob. an error for *sparpeled*.

c 1575 *Diurn. Occurr.* (Bann. Cl.) 194 Bot or this tyme, the said men of weare hade sparfallit the best of thame. 1808–25 in JAMIESON (in form *sperfle*).

‖ **Sparganosis.** *Path.* [a. Gr. σπαργάνωσις (Dioscorides 2. 129 in old editions; but in 3. 41 σπάργωσις SPARGOSIS), for σπάργησις, f. σπαργᾶν to swell.]

†**1.** (See quot.) *Obs.*[−0]

1693 tr. *Blancard's Phys. Dict.* (ed. 2), *Sparganosis*, a Distention of the Breasts, occasioned by too much Milk. [Also in Phillips (1706), Bailey, Chambers (1753), etc.]

2. Puerperal swelling of the legs.

1822–7 GOOD *Study Med.* (1829) II. 633 This..was an instance of erratic or metastatic rheumatism rather than sparganosis. *Ibid.* V. 612 In a singular enlargement of the lower extremity produced by a puerperal sparganosis.

Sparge (spāɹdʒ), *sb.* Also *Sc.* spairge. [f. next.]

1. The act of sprinkling or splashing; a sprinkle or slight dash (of liquor, etc.).

1808 in JAMIESON. 1819 W. TENNANT *Papistry Storm'd* (1827) 56 Chariots and horse-hoofs round did scatter Scamander's sand wi' spairge and splatter. 1867 G. W. DONALD *Poems* (1879) 72/2 A spairge may put us in repair When coughs an' caulds our stammacks pester.

2. *Brewing.* A spray of warm water sprinkled over the malt.

1839 URE *Dict. Arts* 107 The malt is exhausted by eight or ten successive sprinklings of liquor.., which are termed in the vernacular tongue, *sparges*. 1859 W. MOLYNEUX *Burton-on-Trent* 244 The 'sparge' is set to run on the malt an additional quantity of water.

Sparge (spāɹdʒ), *v.* Also 8–9 *Sc.* spairge. [app. ad. OF. *espargier* or L. *spargĕre* to sprinkle; but in sense 1 answering to PARGET *v.* and having the earlier variants SPARGEN and SPARGET.]

1. *trans.* To plaster; to rough-cast.

1560 *Edinb. Burgh Recs.* 62 To reparrall the kirk, to lay the throwchis thairof of new and sparge the samyn. 1597 *Rec. Elgin* (1908) II. 48 The baill eldaris hes promeist a boll lyme ilk ane of thame to sparge the kirk withall. *a* 1670 J. LAMONT *Diary* (1810) 156 Att this time also, the forepairt of the house was sparged, with the tower-head. 1883 *Almondbury Gloss.* 125 *Sparge*, to point or plaster the inside of a chimney.

2. To bespatter, besprinkle. Also *fig.*

1786 BURNS *A Dream* vii, An' Will's a true guid fallow's get, A Name not Envy spairges. 1821 LIDDLE *Poems* 127 Auld Cloot at last may spairge ye lightly.

3. To dash, splash, or sprinkle (water, etc.) about. Also *fig.*

1785–6 BURNS *Address to Deil* i, O thou!..Wha..Spairges about the brunstane cootie To scaud poor wretches! 1808 JAMIESON, *Spairge*, to dash; as, to spairge water. 1875 G. MACDONALD *Malcolm* I. i. 5 Nobody..'at wad gang and spairge sic havers aboot her.

4. *Brewing.* To sprinkle (malt) with hot water. Also *absol.*

1839 URE *Dict. Arts* 107 It would keep up an uniform temperature in the goods, without requiring them to be sparged with very hot liquor. 1885 *Civilian* 3 Jan. 133/1 He, too, sparges for small beer with hot liquor.

Hence **Sparging** *vbl. sb.* Also *attrib.*

1590 in Pitcairn *Crim. Trials* (Bann. Cl.) I. III. 210 Quha had offendit him in nocht spargeing of his chalmer. 1836 *Penny Cycl.* V. 401/2 If sparging or sprinkling the water over the goods should be adopted..instead of mashing. 1839 URE *Dict. Arts* 107 The only serious objection to the sparging system is the loss of time by the successive drainages. 1859 W. MOLYNEUX *Burton-on-Trent* 245 The malt has had its regulated series of spargings. 1875 *Encycl. Brit.* IV. 274/2 The heat of the sparging water.. must be modified by circumstances.

Spargefa·ction. *rare*[−1]. [f. L. *spargĕre* to sprinkle: see -FACTION.] = next.

1704 SWIFT *T. Tub* Wks. 1768 I. 86 The operation was performed by Spargefaction in a proper time of the Moon.

Spargefica·tion. Also -ification. [f. as prec.: see -FICATION.] The action of sprinkling or scattering.

1835 MARRYAT *J. Faithful* ii, Wiping off his share of my liberal spargefication from his coat and waistcoat. 1836 E. HOWARD *R. Reefer* xiii, There was much spargefication of powder. 1892 *Sat. Rev.* 27 Aug. 257/1 There is a liberal spargification of melted butter over divers of the author's contemporaries.

Spa·rgelstone. *rare*[−1]. [ad. G. *spargelstein*, f. *spargel* asparagus.] Asparagus-stone.

1804 R. JAMESON *Min.* I. 540 Asparagus, or Spargel Stone.

†**Spargen**, *v.* *Sc.* *Obs.* In 6 spargein, -eon. [Cf. PARGEN *v.* and SPARGE *v.* 1.] *trans.* To parget.

1511 *Acc. Ld. High Treas. Scot.* IV. 284 For xvj puncheonis plaister,..send to Dingwall to spargein the wallis tharof. 1562 WINȜET *Wks.* (S.T.S.) I. 14 The prophetis of it, spargeonit thaim with vntemperit morter.

Hence † **Spa·rgener**, a pargeter. *Obs.*

1600 *Rec. Convent. Roy. Burghs* II. 89 Masouns, sklateris, painteris, sprugeneris. 1641 *Acts Parl. Scot.*, *Chas. I* (1870) V. 562/2 The haill Friemen of Masones,..spargineres, painteres.

Sparger (spā·ɹdʒəɹ). [f. SPARGE *v.*] An appliance for sprinkling water, esp. in brewing.

1858 SIMMONDS *Dict. Trade*, *Sparger*, a copper cylinder, used by brewers for dashing or sprinkling. 1875 KNIGHT *Dict. Mech.* 2254/1 *Sparger*, a sprinkler; usually a cup with a perforated lid, or a pipe with a perforated nozzle. 1888 *Wine, Sp. & Beer* 8 Mar. 141/2 The rake mash machine is driven from underneath, so that nothing impedes the action of the rotary sparger.

†**Sparget**, *v.* *Obs.*[−0] [var. of PARGET *v.* Cf. SPARGE *v.* 1 and SPARGEN *v.*] *trans.* To parget.

Two MSS. have *sparchyn*, which may belong to SPARGE *v.*

c 1440 *Promp. Parv.* 467 Spargettyn, or pargette wallys.., *gipso, limo*. *Ibid.*, Spargettynge, or pargettynge.

Spargification: see SPARGEFICATION.

‖ **Spargosis.** *Path.* [Gr. σπάργωσις: see SPARGANOSIS.] (See quot.)

1867 [W. J.] E. WILSON *Dis. Skin* (ed. 6) 914 *Spargosis*,.. a substantive term applicable to elephantiasis Arabum, and boucnemia...We prefer spargosis to sparganosis.

Sparhawk (spā·ɹhǭk). Now *arch.* or *dial.* Forms: α. 1 spearhabuc, spearhafoc, 4–7 sparhauk(e, 5–6 *Sc.*-halk, 5–7 -hawke, 6– sparhawk. β. 4–6 sperhauk(e, 5–7 -hawk(e. γ. 4, 6 sparehauk(e, 5 -hawk, 7 -haucke. δ. 4, 6 sperehauke, 5 -hawk(e. [OE. *spearhafoc*, f. the stem of *spearwa* SPARROW + *hafoc* HAWK: so ON. *sparrhaukr*.] A sparrowhawk.

α. *c* 725 *Corpus Gloss.* A 432 *Alictum*, spaerhabuc. *c* 1000 ÆLFRIC *Gloss.* in Wr.-Wülcker 132 *Accipiter*, *vel raptor*, spearhafoc. *a* 1300 *Cursor M.* 1789 Þe sparhauk flough be þe sterling. *c* 1374 CHAUCER *Troylus* III. 1192 What might or may the sely larke seie, Whanne that this sparhauk hath it in his foote? 1438 *Bk. Alexander Grt.* (Bann.) 12 It semis thay sparhalkis war & we lawrokis that durst bot dar. 1483 CAXTON *Cato* h vj b, It is sayd in a comyn prouerbe that crafte is better than the Sparhawke. 1560 ROLLAND *Seven Sages* 28 The Sparhalk is als swyft of flicht As the Griffoun. 1598 BP. HALL *Sat.* IV. iv. 88 Gallio may..tend his spar-hauke mantling in her mew. 1639 MASSINGER *Unnatural Combat* v. i, How her heart beats! Much like a partridge in a sparhawk's foot. 1661 J. CHILDREY *Brit. Bacon.* 13 Sparhawks, the most useless of Hawks. 1700 TYRRELL *Hist. Eng.* II. 820 The Ayries of Hawks, of Spar-Hawks. 1842 TENNYSON *Sir Lanc. & Q. Guinevere* ii, Sometimes the sparhawk wheel'd along. 1865 KINGSLEY *Herew.* iv, In the first [copse] there built an eagle, in the second there built a sparhawk. 1891 'SON OF MARSHES' *Surrey Hills* (1894) 44 Spar'hawk, the woodmen call him.

β. 1377 LANGL. *P. Pl.* B. VI. 199 What pieres preyed hem to do as prest as a sperhauke. 1387 TREVISA *Higden* (Rolls) I. 335 Þere is grete plente of..sperhaukes. 1456 SIR G. HAYE *Law Arms* (S.T.S.) 299 That he be lord of his subjectis, as to the quaile the sper-hauk. *c* 1489 CAXTON *Sonnes of Aymon* vi. 152 The kyng gaaf to hym a sperhawke. 1539 FITZHERB. *Survey.* xl. 26 Except it be an entiere rent, as a sperhauke or a horse. 1555 EDEN *Decades* (Arb.) 300 Haukes, as faulcons, gerfalcons, lanners, and sperhaukes. 1604 L. LLOYD *Briefe Conf. Divers Lawes* 32 The feather of a sperhawke in their caps.

γ. *a* 1400 MAUNDEV. (1839) xxii. 238 Gerfacouns, Sparehaukes, Faukons gentyls. 1486 *Bk. St. Albans* c viij b, She may be also callid a spare hawke for .ij. Resones, oon is she spariith goshawkys and tercellys both. 1550 J. COKE *Eng. & Fr. Heralds* § 8 (1877) 63 Also we have hawkes of the towre,..lykewyse goshawkes, and sparehawkes for ladyes. 1587 GOLDING *De Mornay* xxvi. (1592) 416 The Woolfe, the Foxe,..the Sparehauke, the Kyte & so foorth. 1612 *Shuttleworths' Acc.* (Chetham Soc.) 201 Foure sparehaucke boodes, xij[d]. 1890 J. WATSON *Nat. & Woodcraft* viii, The Gamekeeper..will record a black and bloody list of depredations against the 'spare'-hawk.

δ. 1398 TREVISA *Barth. De P. R.* XII. iv. (Bodl. MS.), Hereby it semeþ þ[t] *alietus* and a litel sperehauke is all one. *c* 1440 *Promp. Parv.* 468/2 Sperehawke.., *nisus*. *c* 1500 *Melusine* xxiv. 175 His enemyes fled byfore hym as the partrych doth byfore the sperehauke.

†**Sparily**, *adv.* *Obs.* [f. SPARY *a.*] Sparingly; moderately; with restraint.

1603 HOLLAND *Plutarch's Mor.* 1289 Otherwise the priests drinke thereof but sparily. 1605 — *Sueton.* 56 He granted the freedom of the City of Rome, most sparily. 1633 D. R[OGERS] *Treat. Sacr.* ii. 51 Using liberty sparily. 1642 — *Naaman* 36, I will more sparily touch forraine nations and Churches.

Sparing (spē·riŋ), *vbl. sb.* [f. SPARE *v.*[1]]

1. The action of saving, economizing, or using with frugality.

c 1386 CHAUCER *Pars. T.* ⁋ 835 Sparyng also þat restreyneth þe delicate ease to sitte long at his mete. *c* 1440 *Promp. Parv.* 467/2 Sparynge, *parcimonia*. 1565 COOPER *Thesaurus* s.v. *Circumscribo*, To limite riote within the boundes of thriftie sparyng. 1588 KYD *Househ. Phil.* Wks. (1901) 252 With industrie, sparing, and good husbandry [I] did much augment it. 1621 T. WILLIAMSON tr. *Goulart's Wise Vieillard* 72 Couetousnes..knowes no meane in sparing or spending. 1640 BP. HALL *Chr. Moder.* (Ward) 5 1 As too much bounty is prodigality, so too much sparing is niggardliness.

attrib. 1560 ROLLAND *Seven Sages* 96 Put spairing dayis and thame togidder, And sa small sall ȝe tyne. 1579–80 NORTH *Plutarch* (1895) III. 336 There was such store of gold and silver in the sparing cofers of their treasurie.

b. Const. *of* (the thing spared).

1377 LANGL. *P. Pl.* B. v. 442 In speche and in sparynge of speche. 1390 GOWER *Conf.* II. 287 For sparinge of a litel cost Fulofte time a man hath lost The large cote for the hod. 1573 TUSSER *Husb.* (1878) 38 A Jack for to saw vpon fewell for fier, for sparing of firewood. 1607 DOD & CLEAVER *Expos. Prov. xi–xii.* 177 This sparing of speech, when men reserue themselues for fit occasions. 1617 MORYSON *Itin.* II. 238 We haue vsed a great kind of sparing of the victuals in the store.

c. *pl.* That which is saved by economy; savings.

1628 GAULE *Pract. The.* (1629) Ep. Ded., The Sparings of want haue euer beene held more acceptable, then the Fallings of abundance. 1647 R. STAPYLTON *Juvenal* xiv. 141 First Poor little sparings, then th' insatiate thirst Of Getting. 1760 *Cautions & Adv. to Officers of Army* 124 Here is another Deduction to be made out of your Sparings. 1866 HOWELLS *Venetian Life* 66 The sparings for the whole week..are spent for this evening's amusement.

2. The action of leaving unhurt or uninjured, of showing mercy or forbearance, etc.

1375 BARBOUR *Bruce* VIII. 483 Thai..strak on thame forout sparing. 1422 tr. *Secreta Secret., Priv. Priv.* 181 The vertue of mekenesse kepyth the mene betwene Sparynge and vengeaunce. 1490 CAXTON *Eneydos* lxii. 162 They.. drewe out theyre sharpe swerdes. Theme was there noo sparynge. *c* 1526 *Plumpton Corr.* (Camden) 226, I pray you be contented to give sparing to the next head Cort at Spoforth. 1585 T. WASHINGTON tr. *Nicholay's Voy.* III. 110 b, [They] cast vpon the head of euery one of them three small buckets full, without sparing of their clothes. *c* 1611 CHAPMAN *Iliad* v. 205 The Reason I laid down Was but the sparing of my horse. 1910 *Daily Chron.* 22 Jan. 3/2 They appear to kill all they can, leaving the sparing to some other time.

†**b.** Respite, delay. *Obs. rare.*

a 1513 FABYAN *Chron.* VII. (1811) 344 The mayre and the cytezyns..desyred a sparynge of y[e] lordys tyll they myght speke w[t] the Kynge. 1532 *Dial. on Laws Eng.* II. xiv. 37, I pray the gyue a lytle sparynge & procede now for this tyme to som othe[r] questyon.

Sparing (spēə·riŋ), *ppl. a.* and *adv.* [f. as prec.]

1. Inclined to save; exercising economy or frugality in using or spending; niggard.

pred. *c* 1386 CHAUCER *Melib.* ⁋ 633 Ye schul use the richesses..in such a maner, that men holde yow nat skarce ne to sparynge. *c* 1400 *Rom. Rose* 5363 The riche men are loved ay, And namely tho that sparand bene. *c* 1440 *Alph. Tales* 66 Sho was so sparand, at sho wolde giff nothyng..vnto pure folke. 1568 GRAFTON *Chron.* II. 11 He was so couetous and sparing, that he woulde spende nothing more than he needes must. 1592 SHAKS. *Ven. & Ad.* 1147 It [*sc.* love] shall be sparing and too full of riot. 1807 CRABBE *Par. Reg.* I. 447 The wise frugality, that..saves to live; Sparing, not pinching, mindful though not mean.

attrib. *c* 1440 *Alph. Tales* 245 When he was a monke, he was a passand hard man, & a sparand. 1590 SHAKS. *Com. Err.* III. i. 27 A niggardly Host, and more sparing guest. 1601 F. GODWIN *Bps. Eng.* 91 He was a very frugal and sparing man, neuer esteeming pompe or outward brauery. 1639 J. CLARKE *Paræmiologia* 261 A sparing father, and a spending son. 1759 FRANKLIN *Ess.* Wks. 1840 III. 256, I most earnestly entreat you will not delay the supplies, nor deal them out with a sparing hand.

transf. 1766 JOHNSON *Let.* 14 Jan. in *Boswell*, The reasons, good or bad, which have made me such a sparing and ungrateful correspondent.

b. Observing economy or moderation, avoiding excess, in some specified respect. Const. *in*, *of*, †*for*, or †*to* (with inf.).

(*a*) 1604 E. G[RIMSTONE] *D'Acosta's Hist. Indies* IV. v. 217 Nature seemes more sparing in bringing it foorth. 1665 MANLEY *Grotius' Low-C. Warrs* 131 The People..are very sparing in imposing and granting Subsidies. *a* 1682 SIR T. BROWNE *Tracts* (1683) 98 The Books of Scripture..are often silent, or very sparing, in the particular Names of Fishes. 1756 C. LUCAS *Ess. Waters* I. 154 The ancient Romans were very sparing in the use of wine. 1797–1805 S. & HT. LEE *Canterb. T.* II. 447 [She was] sparing in all she provided for herself. 1849 MACAULAY *Hist. Eng.* iii. I. 389 It was no longer necessary for the King to be sparing in the use of..his undoubted prerogative. *a* 1862 BUCKLE *Civiliz.* (1873) III. ii. 71 And they, who had the power, were not sparing in the use of it.

(*b*) 1615 DAY *Festivals* v. 120 Giue me one that is greedy, and Covetous & to to sparing of expences. 1683 D. A. *Art Converse* 55 Be sparing of your complements before his rivals. 1735 BERKELEY *Free-think. in Mathem.* § 34 Wks. 1871 III. 320, I advise you to be more sparing of hard words. 1758 JOHNSON *Idler* No. 1 ⁋ 7 He is now grown sparing of communication. 1824 MISS L. M. HAWKINS *Annaline* I. 33 He is as sparing of his letters as a brewer of his malt. 1880 RUSKIN *Bible Amiens* i. (1884) 4 [One] neither wasteful of his time nor sparing of it.

(*c*) 1656 EARL MONM. tr. *Boccalini's Advts. fr. Parnass.* I. lxxv. (1674) 92 [He] was not sparing for any pains, in procuring that the Sentence might be favourable. 1690 LOCKE *Hum. Und.* I. iii. § 14 Those who talk so confidently of them are so sparing to tell us which they are.

2. a. Characterized by reticence or restraint in discourse or statement.

1568 E. DERING (*title*), A sparing Restraint of many lauishe Vntruthes. 1594 SHAKS. *Rich. III*, III. vii. 194 For reuerence to some aliue I giue a sparing limit to my Tongue. 1601 W. W[ATSON] (*title*), A Sparing Discoverie of our English Jesuits. 1701 NORRIS *Ideal World* I. vi. 364 A very sparing and reserved allegation of a great authority. 1901 *Harper's Mag.* CII. 805/2 A certain sparing touch, with which he presents situation and character by mere statement of fact.

b. Marked by economy or frugality.

1611 COTGR., *Taillé d'espargne*, cut with sparing worke. 1748 *Anson's Voy.* III. iii. (ed. 4) 438 To make the most of their jerked beef, by a very sparing distribution of it.

3. Small in amount, quantity, or extent; not lavish, liberal, or profuse; scanty, limited.

1602 BRETON *Mother's Blessing* xxiii, The sparing diet is the spirits feast. 1634 SIR T. HERBERT *Trav.* 147 Mouthes rather large then sparing. 1672 GREW *Anat. Pl., Idea* 10 The supplies from the Root being yet but slow and sparing. 1730–46 THOMSON *Autumn* 355 Be mindful of that sparing board, Which covers yours with luxury profuse. 1815 J. SMITH *Panorama Sci. & Art* II. 595 Where only the sparing use of lime is admissible, it should be used to the coping. 1857 MILLER *Elem. Chem., Org.* iii. § 5. 287 The sparing solubility of chloroform in water.

b. With agent-nouns: Slight, very moderate.

1860 SMILES *Self-Help* x. 273 Many of our most energetic and useful workers have been but sparing readers. 1883 V. STUART *Egypt* 230 He was a wonderfully sparing sleeper.

4. Forbearing; merciful, considerate.

c 1375 *Sc. Leg. Saints* xviii. (*Egiptian*) 733 To god ay lowynge be, þat..sparand Is to wrak of synful. 1605 SHAKS. *Lucr.* 1687 Let the traitor die; For sparing justice feeds iniquity. *a* 1626 BACON (J.), Their king..was sparing and compassionate towards his subjects. 1658–9 in *Burton's Diary* (1828) III. 329 It is easy to misconstrue the debates of this House if we be not sparing one with the other. 1786 BURNS *Holy Fair* xxi, Black Russell is na spairan: His piercin words like Highlan swords Divide the joints an' marrow.

5. As *adv.* Sparingly.

1623 PENKETHMAN *Handf. Hon.* II. xvii, Thy gaines vse sparing. 1627 FELTHAM *Resolves* II. xxiii. Wks. (1677) 42, I will never censure any man,..but sparing, and with modesty. 1742 YOUNG *Nt. Th.* II. 49 Part with it as with money, sparing.

Sparingly (spēə·riŋli), *adv.* [f. prec. + -LY[2].]

1. In a sparing or saving manner; frugally, economically.

c 1440 *Jacob's Well* 206 Þi wyif & chyld muste sparyngly as hem nedyth spendyn of þi euyl getyn good. 1571 GOLDING *Calvin on Ps.* xxxvii. 19 He teacheth us thriftynesse, by dealing out sparingly. 1598 R. BERNARD tr.

Sparingness (spä·riŋnes). [f. SPARING *ppl. a.*] The quality of being sparing; **a.** in respect of diet, living, expenditure, etc.

Spark (spärk), *sb.*[1] Forms: α. 1 *spearca*, *spearca*, 3–7 *sparke* (4 *spaerke*), 6 *sparcke*, 3 *sparke*, 3–4 *spark*, 4– *spark* (6 *Sc. sperke*). [OE. *spearca*, *spearc*, = MDu. *sparke*, (WFlem. *sparke*, *sperke*), MLG. and LG. *sparke*, of obscure origin: not represented in the other Teutonic languages. With most of the senses compare those of SPARKLE *sb.*]

Spark (spärk), *sb.*[2] [prob. a figurative use of prec.: cf. 1 q. quot. 1599.]

Spark (spärk), *sb.*[3] *v.rw. dial.* [Back-formation from SPARKED *ppl. a.* dial. 'A spotted or parti-coloured bullock.']

Spark (spärk), *sb.*[6] *Sc. sperk.* [Related to SPARK *sb.*[1], and agreeing in form with MDu. *sparke*, *sparken*.]

Sparked (spärkt), *ppl. a. dial.* (and U.S.) Also 6 *sparkyd*, 8–9 *-it*. [app. f. SPARK *sb.*[3]; cf. sense 3 SPARK *sb.*[3].]

Sparker. [f. SPARK *sb.*[1] + -ER[1].]

Spark·et·ting, *vbl. sb.* = SPERKETTING.

Spark·ish, *a.* rare. [f. SPARK *sb.*[2] + -ISH[1].] A small spark-like thing.

Spark·ily, *adv.* [f. next + -LY[2].]

Spark·iness.

Sparking (spä·rkiŋ), *vbl. sb.* [f. SPARK *v.*[1]] The action of emitting sparks; *spec.* in *Electr.*

Sparking, *ppl. a.* [f. SPARK *v.*[1]]

Sparkish (spä·rkiʃ), *a.* [f. SPARK *sb.*[2] + -ISH[1].]
1. Of persons: Having the character, airs, or manners of a spark or gallant.
2. Of things or dress: Smart, gay, elegant.
3. Of persons: Characteristic of, or appropriate to, a spark; of a smart or elegant make.

Sparkishly (spä·rkiʃli), *adv.* [f. prec. + -LY[2].] Like a spark or gallant; in a sparkish manner.

Sparkle (spä·rk'l), *sb.* Forms: α. 4 *sparkle*, 4–7 *sparkil*, 4–7 *y-okel*; 5 *sparkyl*, 5–6 *sparkel*, 5 *sparkil*, 6–9 *sperkel*; 6 *sperkle*, 7 *sparkle*, 7 *sperkle*, 8–9 *spirkil*. [f. SPARK *sb.*[1] + -LE.]

Sparkle (spä·rk'l), *v.*[1] Forms: α. 4–6 *sparkle*, 5–6 *sparkyl*, 5–6 *sparkel*, 6 *sparkill*, 6–9 *spirkle*; β. 4 *sperclen* (Dn. and Flem. *sparkelen*, WFlem. also *sperkelen*); WFris. *sperklje.*

Sparkle (spä·rk'l), *v.*[2] Obs. [f. SPARKLE *sb.* Cf. DISPARKLE *v.*]
1. *intr.* Of persons: To separate, scatter, or disperse.
2. *trans.* To cause to scatter or disperse; to drive in different directions. Also *sparkle away* (quot. 1703).
3. To cast abroad; to scatter, sprinkle, or strew.

Sparkler (spä·rklǝr), *sb.* [f. SPARKLE *v.*[1] + -ER[1].]
1. A small spark or sparkle.
2. A small sparkling ornament for a dress.
3. Reflecting or emitting rays of light; flashing, glittering, brilliant, resplendent.

Sparkless (spä·rkles), *a.* [f. SPARK *sb.*[1] + -LESS.] Free or devoid of sparks; sparkless.

Sparklet (spä·rklet), *sb.* [f. SPARKLE *sb.* + -ET.] A small sparkle or sparklet.

Sparkle-like, *a.* and *adv.* [f. SPARKLE *sb.* + -LIKE.]

Sparkless, *a.* Also *sparkleless*.

Sparkling (spä·rkliŋ), *vbl. sb.* [f. SPARKLE *v.*[1]] The action of emitting or reflecting sparks; glittering.

Sparkling (spä·rkliŋ), *ppl. a.* Also 4 *sparklinge*, 5–6 *sparkelynge*, 5 *sparkelynge*.
1. That emits sparks or sparkles.
2. Of wine, etc.: Effervescing with bubbles of gas; emitting gas in small bubbles.
3. Brilliant, glittering, lustrous.

Sparkling, *ppl. a.*

Sparklingly, *adv.*

Sparlire.

Sparky (späˈki), *a.*

Sparling (späˈliŋ).

Sparple, *v.*

Sparred (spärd), *ppl. a.*

Sparrest.

Sparring, *vbl. sb.*

Sparrow (spæˈroʊ).

Sparrow-bill.

Sparrow-blasted, *a. Obs.*

Sparrow-blasting.

Sparrow-grass, **sparrowgrass.**

Sparry (späˈri), *a.*

Sparry, *v.*

Sparrow-hawk. Also **sparhawk.**

Sparse (späːs), *a.*

Sparse, *v. Obs.*

Sparse-like, *a.*

Sparrow-mouth.

Sparrow-mouthed, *a.*

Sparsedly, *adv.*

Sparsed (späst), *ppl. adj.*

Sparsely (späːsli), *adv.*

Sparseness (späːsnes).

Sparsile, *a. rare.*

Sparsim (späˈsim), *adv.*

Sparsity (späːsiti).

Spar-stone, *Obs. exc. dial.*

Spart.

Spartacle.

Spartialite (spätˈiːəlait).

Spartle (späˈt'l), *sb. and a.*

Spartiate (spätˈiːeit).

Spartle, sb. Now dial. Also ? spartel. [Alteration of SPARTLE sb.² Cf. SPURTLE sb.²] A spatula.

Spartle, v.¹ Obs. Also ? spartel. [Alteration of SPARTLE v.¹ Cf. SPARKLE v.²] trans. To scatter, disperse. Hence ? Spartling vbl. sb.

Spartle, v.² S. [ad. (M)Du. or (M)LG. spartelen (also spertelen, in the same sense).] intr. To move the body or limbs in a sprawling or struggling manner.

Sparto, sb. Obs. [a. Sp. esparto.] Esparto.

Sparto station, sb. mod.L. spartostatica Stevinus, 1605), cf. Gr. σπάρτον rope: see STATICS.] The science or study of the strength of ropes.

Sparu, obs. form of SPARROW.

Sparus (spēʹrǎs). Pl. **spari** (spēʹrai). [L. ad. Gr. σπάρος. For Anglicized forms see SPAR sb.³ and SPARE sb.²] A sea-bream or gilt-head.

Sparver, sb. Obs. Forms: a. 5 sperwyr, spervir, 5-7 (9) sparver, 6 sparviour, 5-7 (9) sparvir, 6 7 sparviar. [ad. OF. espervier (espreiver) 'l'ensemble des pièces qui composent le crochet' (1380 in Godefroy).] Various senses.

Spasm (spæz'm), sb. Also 5-7 spasme. [ad. OF. spasme (F. spasme, Sp. and Pg. espasmo, It. spasmo), ad. L. spasma, macc., spasmus neut., a. Gr. σπασμός, σπασμα.]

1. Sudden and violent muscular contraction or a convulsive or painful character.

Spasmic (spæʹmik), a. [f. SPASM + -IC.] Spasmodic; convulsive.

Spasmodic (spæzmǫʹdik), a. and sb. [ad. med. or mod.L. spasmodicus, a. Gr. σπασμώδης, -ώδ-εος. See SPASM. So F. spasmodique, Sp. espasmodico, Pg. espasmodico.]

A. adj. 1. Of the nature of a spasm; characterized by spasms or convulsive twitches; marked by jerkiness or suddenness of muscular movement.

Spasmodical, a. Now rare or Obs.

Spasmodically, adv. 1. In a jerky or sudden manner.

Spasmodism (spæʹzmǫdiz'm). [f. SPASM + -ISM.] Spasmodic feeling or emotion.

Spasmolysis (spæzmǫʹlisis). [mod.L. SPASMO- + Gr. λύσις.]

Spasmology, sb. Obs. [ad. mod.L. spasmo-logia. So F. spasmologie.]

Spasmophilia, a. Affected with spasms.

Spasmous, a. [f. SPASM + -OUS. Cf. OF. spasmeux.] Characterized by spasms.

Spasmus (spæʹzmǫs). Obs. [L. spasmi. a. Gr. σπασμός.] = SPASM.

Spasmy (spæʹzmi), a. [f. SPASM + -Y¹.] Affected by spasms.

Spastic (spæʹstik), a. [ad. L. spasticus (Pliny), a. Gr. σπαστικός.] Of the nature of a spasm or sudden contraction; characterized by or affected by spasmodic symptoms or movements.

Spasticity (spæstiʹsĭti). [f. SPASTIC a. + -ITY.]

Spat (spæt). sb.¹ [Of obscure origin.] 1. The spawn of oysters or other shell-fish.

Spat (spæt), sb.² Short for SPATTERDASH.

Spat (spæt), sb.³ [app. an abbreviation of SPATULE.]

Spat (spæt), sb.⁴ Chiefly dial. or colloq. [Probably imitative: cf. SPAT v.¹] A tiff or dispute; a quarrel.

Spatch, v. Obs.⁻¹

Spatchcock, spatchcock (spæʹtʃkǫk). [See quot. 1785 and DISPATCH sb.¹]

Spate (spēt), sb. Orig. Sc. and north. Forms: a. 5-appt, 5-7 spait, 6-7, 9 dial. spaitt, 6-7 spat, 7 spaite, 9 spaight, 8, 6-7 speate, 9 spate.

Spathe (spēϸ), sb. [ad. L. spatha a spathe, broad flat piece of wood, etc.]

Spathaceous (spǎϸǣʹʃǒs), a.¹ Bot. A mod. L. *spathaceous: see SPATHE and -ACEOUS.]

Spathe-bill, rare⁻¹. [f. SPATHE sb.]

Spatheful, a. [f. SPATHE sb.]

Spathic (spæʹϸik), a. [f. SPATH- + -IC.]

Spathose, a.² Bot. rare. [f. SPATHE + -OSE¹.]

Spathulate, a. Bot.

Spathose, a.¹ Min. [f. SPATH- + -OSE¹.]

Spatial (spēʹʃǎl), a. Also **spacial**. [f. L. spatium SPACE + -AL¹.]

1. Having extension in space; occupying or taking up space; consisting of or characterized by space.

Spatiality (spēʃiæʹlĭti). [f. SPATIAL + -ITY.]

Spatially (spēʹʃǎli), adv. Also **spacially**. [f. SPATIAL + -LY².]

Spatiate (spēʹʃĭeit), v. [f. ppl. stem of L. spatiari.] intr. To walk about, wander, range, or roam.

Spatium (spēʹʃĭǒm). Obs. [L.] = SPACE.

Spatter (spæʹtǎr), v. [f. SPAT sb.¹ So WFlem. spatteren; cf. LG. spatten to splash.]

1. trans. To scatter or splash about.

Spatterdash (spæʹtǎrdæʃ). [app. a frequentative of the stem found in Du. and LG. spatten to burst, spout, etc.: cf. WFris. spatterje, Helgoland spatter to splatter.]

Spatterdashed (spæʹtǎrdæʃt), a.

Spatterdasher, sb. exc. dial. = SPATTERDASH.

Spattering, vbl. sb.

Supplement, p. 3873; Corrigenda, p. 4092; Spurious words, p. 4093; Books quoted, p. 4094.

Spattering, ppl. a. [f. as prec.] That spatters, in senses of the vb.

†Spatter-lash, -plash, var. SPATTERDASH.

Spatter-work: see SPATTER v. 7.

Spatting (spæ'tiŋ), vbl. sb. [f. SPAT v.[1]] Of shell-fish: The action or process of depositing spawn. Also attrib.

Spattle (spæ't'l), sb.[1] Obs. exc. dial. Forms: a. 1 spætl (spadl), 3 spattel, 5 -ell, -ill, -ylle, 6 -els, -yyl, spatteyl (Sc.-ild), 6 spatle, 6–7, 9 dial, spattle. β, 2–4 spotel, 4–5 -il, 5 -ill, 7 -yl, spottle, 4 spotel (spdl, shod Spold), f, *spdl, stem of spêtan 'to spit.' Cf. MLG. spittle, Spittle.]

1. A spatula. Now rare or dial.

†Spattle, sb.[2]

Spattle, sb.[3] dial. [Alteration of PATTLE sb., perh. after prec.] A plough-spade or other small spade. Also spattle-hoe.

†Spattle, v.[1] [f. SPATTLE sb.[1]]

†Spattle, v.[2]

Spattling, vbl. sb.[1] Obs.

Spattling, vbl. sb.[2] [f. SPATTLE v.[2]] Spattering; mottling.

Spattling, ppl. a. Also 6 -spatling. [f. SPATTLE v.[2]] Spattling poppy (or campion), bladder campion. Obs. exc. dial.

Spatular (spæ'tiŭlǎr), a. [f. SPATULA.] Having the form of a spatula. Also Comb.

†Spatulary, a. Obs.[1] [f. med.L. spatula shoulder-blade, SPATULA.]

Spatulate (spæ'tiŭleit), a. [ad. mod.L. spatulāt-us, f. spatula SPATULA. Cf. SPATHULATE a.] Having a broadened and rounded end like that of a common form of spatula.

Spatulated, a. = prec.

Spatulation, rare.[1] [f. SPATULATE a.] The fact or condition of being spatulate; a spatulate formation.

Spatule (spæ'tiūl), sb.[1] Also 6 spatell. [a. OF. spatule (also mod.F.), ad. L. spatula SPATULA. Cf. MDu. spatule, spatel.]

Spatule, sb.[2]

†Spatule, v. Obs.

Spatuliform, a. rare. [f. Spatula + -(I)FORM.] Spatula-shaped.

Spatulo-, a. [See next and stem.]

Spatulose (spæ'tiŭlǒus), a. [f. SPATULA + -OSE.] Resembling a spatula in form; spatulate.

†Spature. Obs. rare. Also 5 spatour. [f. spatuate or L. spatula, with change of suffix. Cf. SPATTER sb.[1]]

Spatulamancy [ad. med. or mod.L. spatulamancia, f. spatula SPATULA + -MANCY.]

Spaud, -e, obs. form of SPUD.

Spauld, -e, Sc. variant of SPALD, SPAULD, Spaune, SPAWN.

Spaul, variant of SPALD v., Spaune, Obs.

Spatly, varr. SPATTLE sb.[1], Spau, obs. f. SPA sb.

†Spandeler. Obs. rare. In a spandeler, 5 spaudelere. [f. OF. espalde SPAULD + -ER.]

Spaught, Obs. rare. Also 7 spaut, spowte. [Of obscure origin.] A youth, lad, or stripling.

Spavie, Sc. varr. SPAVIN sb.

†Spaul, v. Obs. rare. [In sense 1, ad. OF. espauler (mod.F. épauler); in sense 2, ad. OF. espauл'/ier, spatulate, rough at the apex.]

Spain, obs. form of SPAVIN.

Spavie, Sc. varr. SPAVIN sb.

Spavin (spæ'vin), sb.[1] Farriery. Forms: 3 spauayne, -eyne, spaueyne, 4 spavain. β. 6 spaven, spreven, 6-7 spavon, -ing, spavin, 7-9 Sc. spaivin). [ad. OF. esparvain, espavin (mod.F. éparvin), vb. of obscure origin.]

Spavin, sb.[2] Coal mining. [Of obscure origin.]

Spavined (spæ'vind), a. Also 7 -ane(d, 7 spavend, 7 spavin sb.[3]] Affected with spavin.

Spavin, v. trans., to affect with the spavin. rare.[1]

Spavie, v. Obs. rare.[1]

Spawl, var. SPALL sb., SPAULD.

Spawl (spǫl), v. Obs. exc. arch. Forms: 6 spal, 7, 9 spall, 7 spaul, 7–9 spawl; 7 spawle. [Of obscure origin; both date and form are against direct connexion with OE. spĕde SPOLD.]

1. intr. To spit copiously or coarsely; to expectorate.

2. trans. To enter in a coarse manner.

Hence **Spawler,** a spitter; **Spawling** ppl. a.

Spawling, vbl. sb. Now arch. [f. SPAWL v.]

Spawn (spǫn), sb. Forms: 6 spawne, 6 spaune, spaune, 7 spaen, 7– spawn. [f. SPAWN v.]

†1. The milt of a fish.

2. The animate eggs of fishes and various other oviparous animals.

Spawn (spǫn), v. Forms: 6 spaune, spawn, 7 spawne, spawne. [f. AF. espaundre, =OF. espandre (mod. ...]

Spawner (spǫ'nǎr). [f. SPAWN v. + -ER.]

1. A female fish, esp. at spawning time.

Spawning, vbl. sb. [f. SPAWN v.]

Spawning, ppl. a. [f. as prec.]

Spawned, ppl. a. [f. SPAWN v.]

Spay (spei), v. Forms: 4–5 spaye, 6–7 spaye, 7 spayen; pa. pple. spayed. [a. AF. espeier, cut with a sword, f. espee (F. épée) sword.]

Spay, sb. Obs. [f. SPAY v.]

Spaying, vbl. sb. [f. SPAY v.]

Spayad, Obs. Also 6 spaiad, 7 spade. [a. AF. *espeyad.]

Spayd, sb.[1] and a. Now only arch. Forms: 4–7 spayde, spade; also 6 spade, 7–8 spaid.

Spayd, v.

†Spayer. Obs. [f. SPAY v. + -ER.] A sluice.

Spayer, Obs. [var. of SPAY v.]

Spaying, vbl. sb. [f. SPAY v.]

Spayned, ppl. a.

Spay. [f. SPAY sb.]

Spaynol, -ol, var. SPANIEL Obs.

Spayre, var. SPARE sb. and v.

Speach(e, obs. forms of SPEECH sb.

Spead, obs. form of SPEED.

Speak (spīk), v. Chiefly Sc. and north. Forms: 3–5 speke (2 sb.), 4 speak (2 sb.), 5 speke (9 speik), 6–7 speake (3 sb.). [Partly for the northern form of ME. speke (OE. sprecan), partly ...]

Speak (spīk), v. Chiefly Sc. and north. Forms: α. 1 sprecan, 2–4 sprek, 2 sprec; 3 sprece, speke; 3 speke, speake, etc.

A. Illustration of Forms.

Spea·kership. [f. SPEAKER + -SHIP.]

Speak-house. Obs. [f. SPEAK v. + HOUSE sb.]

Speaking, vbl. sb. [f. SPEAK v.]

Speaking, ppl. a.

Spea·kingly, adv.

Speaking-trumpet.

Speaking-tube.

Spea·kless, a. Obs.

Spea·ky, a. Obs.

Speal-bone. Sc. and north.

Spean, v.

Spear, sb.

Speared, a.

Spear-grass.

Spear, v.

6. One or other of several Asiatic grasses or plants.

Spear-head. Also **spearhead.** [f. SPEAR sb.]

1. The sharp-pointed head or blade forming the striking or piercing end of a spear.

2. *fig.* and *transf.*

Spear-man (spɪəˈmæn). Forms: *see* SPEAR *sb.* and MAN. [f. SPEAR *sb.* + MAN sb.]

1. A soldier or warrior armed with a spear; one who carries a spear as a weapon.

2. Comb.

Spear-shaped, a. [f. SPEAR *sb.*] Resembling a spear in shape; pointed like a spear.

Spearman. [f. SPEAR *sb.*] = SPEARMAN.

Spear-staff, The staff or shaft of a spear; = SPEAR-SHAFT. Also *transf.*

Spearwort (spɪəˈwɜːt). Forms: **1** spere-wyrt, **3** -wurt, **5** -wourt, **6** -wort; **4-5** sperwort, **6** sperworte; **7** swort, **6-wurte**; **6** sperwort (7 spearwort), **6-** spearwort. [f. SPEAR *sb.* + WORT.]

Spearwort (spɪəˈmɪnt). [f. SPEAR *sb.*] The common garden mint, *Mentha viridis*, much used in cookery.

Spear-point. [f. SPEAR *sb.*]

1. The point of a spear.

2. *transf.* Something resembling the point of a spear.

Spear-rib, obs. form of SPARE-RIB.

Spearo, variant of SPEROE *v.*

Spear-shaft. [f. SPEAR + SHAFT sb.]

Spearing, ppl. a. *Obs.*[-¹] **a.** *spear*, var. of SPIRE *v.* 1. Rising in a point form.

Speariness, rare -¹. [f. SPEARY *a.*] The character of being speary or sharp-pointed.

Spearing (spɪəˈrɪŋ), *sb.* Chiefly *U.S.* [*ad.* Du. and G. *spiering* *smelt* (see SPARLING).] *a.* U.S.

Spear-like (spɪəˈlaɪk), a. [f. SPEAR *sb.*] Resembling a spear in shape or in sharpness.

Speary (spɪəˈrɪ), *a.*¹ [f. SPEAR + -Y¹.] Having the form of or ending in a point.

Speary, *a.*² [perh. f. SPEAR *sb.*², but cf. OF. *espeure*, var. of *espieure*] Spicery.

Speak, variant of SPEKE *v.*

Speary, *a.*² Slender, spindly.

Spec (spek), *sb.* colloq. and slang. [Short for SPECULATION] orig. American, but in English use from 1825.

Spec, var. of SPECK.

Special (speʃəl), *a.*, *adv.*, and *sb.* Forms: **3-6** specyal (4 -ell), **4-5**, **6-8** speciall, **5** specialle, **4-6** speciall, **6** spetiall, **4-** special.

b. In predicative use: Limited or restricted.

c. additional to the usual or ordinary.

4. Of persons: **a.** Appointed or employed for a particular purpose or occasion.

Spece. *Obs.* Forms: **4-7** spece (5 speche), **5-6** speece.

Spece, variant of SPICE *sb.*

† Specary. *Sc.* *Obs.*[-¹] [ad. med.L. *spicaria* (usually *spicatus*), L. *spica* spike.] *Nardus spicata*; spikenard.

† Specery. *Obs.* Also **-ari, -erie.** [ad. OF. *especerie* var. of *espicerie*.] Spicery.

Specialize (speʃəlaɪz), *v.* [f. as prec.] One who specializes.

Speciality (speʃɪˈælɪtɪ). Forms: **5** specialite, **5-6** -tye, **6** -tie, **6-7** -tye; **5-** speciality. [ad. OF. *especialité*, *speciality* (later *spécialité*) med.l.; *specialitat* (later med.L.).]

1. A special, particular, or individual point, matter, or item; *esp.* a particular, details.

2. A particular quality or characteristic; a special feature.

Specialism (speʃəˈlɪz'm). [f. SPECIAL + -ISM.] **1.** Restriction or devotion to a special branch of study or research; limitation to one department or aspect of a subject.

Specialist (speʃəˈlɪst), *sb.* (and *a.*). [f. prec. + -IST.] Of or pertaining to specialism or specialists.

Specialist, *a.* **1.** Of or pertaining to a specialist.

Specialization (speʃəlaɪˈzeɪʃən). [f. SPECIALIZE + -ATION.] The action or process of specializing or of becoming specialized.

Specialize (speʃəlaɪz), *v.* [ad. F. *spécialiser*.]

1. *trans.* To mention or indicate specially.

2. To render special or specific; to invest with a special character or function.

Specialized (speʃəˈlaɪzd), *ppl. a.* [f. prec.] Specially adapted, modified, or developed.

Specializing, *ppl. a.* [f. as prec.] That specializes.

Specially (speʃəlɪ), *adv.* [f. SPECIAL *a.* + -LY².]

Specialness. [f. SPECIAL *a.* + -NESS.] The quality of being special.

Special pleader [See PLEADER].

1. *Law.* A member of an inn of Court who devotes himself mainly to the drawing of pleadings, and to attending at Judges' chambers (Wharton).

Special pleader [See PLEADER.] A special plea; a piece of one-sided pleading.

Special pleading. [See PLEADING *sbl.* 1b.]

1. A pleading drawn with particular reference to the circumstances of a case, as opposed to general pleading.

2. The putting forward of special pleading; the art or science of drawing pleadings.

Specialty [ad. F. *specialité*... Chiefly in pl. and *specialties*]

Specie (spīʃi, spīʃəi̯), *orig.* adopted in the phr. *in specie* (see SPECIE). So MDu. and Du., MHG., Da. and Sw. *specie.*]

1. In the phrase **in specie.**

Species (spīʃīz, spīʃɪz), *sb.* [a. L. *species,* abl. sing. of *species* SPECIES, orig. adopted in the phr. *in specie* (see SPECIE). So MDu. and Du., MHG., Da. and Sw. *specie.*]

Specific (spīˈfik), *a.* and *sb.*

Specifical (spīˈfikal), *a.* Obs.

Specifically (spīˈfikali), *adv.* [as prec.]

Specification (spesifikēˈʃən). [ad. med.L. *specificātiōn-em,* n. of action f. *specificāre* SPECIFY; cf. F. *spécification* (17 cent.).]

b. Without const.

Specify (spe'sifai), v. Forms: 4–6 speoyfe (5–6 specyfy), 4–7 specefie, 4– specify (5–6 speoxyf.), 4 specefie, 5–6 spey. 6–7 speoxyf.) ...

Specificate, v. Obs. [f. SPECIFICATE v. -IVE. Cf. F. spécificatif, -ive (14th c. in Godef.).] That serves to specify or define specifically.

Specificatively, adv. Obs. [See prec.] Specifically.

Specificity (speisifi'siti). Chiefly Med. and Path. [ad. F. spécificité, or f. SPECIFIC a. + -ITY.] 1. The quality or fact of being specific in operation or effect.

2. The fact of being specific in character.

Speci·ficize, v. rare. [f. SPECIFIC a. + -IZE.] trans. To make specific.

Speci·ficly, adv. Obs. [f. In 7 -fquely. [f. SPECIFIC a. Cf. specificement.] Specifically.

Speci·ficness, n. rare. [f. as prec. + -NESS.] Specific character or quality.

Speci·fic·ous, a. Obs. [See prec.]

Specimen (spe'simen). Also 7, 9 dial. specimint. [L. specimen, f. specĕre to look, look at. Cf. F. spécimen, Sp. especimen.]

1. A means of discovering or finding out; an experiment. Obs.

2. A pattern or model.

3. An example, instance, or illustration of something, from which the character of the whole may be inferred.

4. A single thing selected or regarded as typical of its class; a part of anything taken as representative of the whole.

5. spec. An animal, plant, or mineral, a part or portion of some substance or organism, etc., serving as an example of the thing in question for purposes of investigation or scientific study.

Speci·minal, a. Obs. [f. L. specimin-, stem of specimen (see prec.) + -AL.] Of the nature of a specimen, example, or type.

Specio-, comb. form of L. species, employed in a few scientific terms of recent introduction, as speciography, -graphy, -logic, -logy. (Cf. SPECIE.)

Specious (spī'ʃəs), a. [ad. L. speciōsus beautiful, lovely, f. species appearance, form.]

1. Fair or pleasing to the eye or sight; beautiful, handsome, lovely; resplendent with beauty. Obs.

2. Fair in appearance; plausible, but wanting in genuineness or sincerity.

3. Of language, statements, etc.: Fair, attractive, but wanting in genuineness or sincerity.

Speciously (spī'ʃəsli), adv.[f. prec.] 1. So as to present a fair or respectable appearance. Obs.

Speciousness (spī'ʃəsnes). [f. SPECIOUS a.] 1. The quality of being speciously attractive, plausible, etc.

Speck (spek), sb.[1] Forms: 4–5 speck, 5 speo(e)ke, spoke; 4, 7–9 speck, 5 spekk, 6 spek. [OE. specca, not found in the cognate languages, but cf. SPECKLE sb.[2]]

1. A small spot of a different colour or substance to that of the material or surface upon which it appears; a minute mark or stain; a blemish. Occas. const. of (cf. 2).

Speck, sb.[2] Also 5 specke, 5–7 specke, 5 spe(e)ke, spoke; 4, 7–9 speck, 5 spekk. [OE. specc, 8 spec. Prob. related to SPECKLE sb.]

1. A small quantity or particle of something.

Speck, sb.[3] [a. Du. spek, or G. speck (+ speck, MDu. spec) or G. speck (MHG. spec, OHG. spac, spec), LG. speck; MLG. speck, whence MSw. sjäk, Sw. späck, Da. spæk), related to OE. spic.]

1 a. Fat meat, esp. bacon or pork. b. The fat blubber of a whale. c. The fat of a hippopotamus.

Speck (spek), v.[1] Now U.S. and S. African. Also 7 speke, 9 speck. [f. SPECK sb.[1] (+ speck, MDu. spec) or G. speck (MHG. spec, OHG. spac, spec); MLG. speck, whence MSw. sjäk, Sw. späck, Da. spæk), related to OE. spic.]

1. trans. To mark with specks; to dot after the manner of specks.

Speckle (spe'k'l), sb. Also 5 spakle, spakyl, spakkyl, specle, 6 speckle, spekle; 6–7 speckel, speckle, speckled; 7 spackled; 6 spekle. [f. Sp. speckle + -LE.]

Speckled (spe'k'ld), ppl. a. and sb. [f. SPECKLE v. + -ED.]

1. Covered, dotted, or marked with (numerous) speckles or spots; variegated or flecked with spots of a different colour from that of the main body; spotted.

Specklehood, rare. [f. SPECKLE + -HOOD.] The state of being speckled or spotty.

Speckliness, rare. [f. SPECKLY a.] The state of being speckly or spotted.

Speckless, a. [f. SPECK sb.[1] + -LESS.] Having no speck or that which precedes.

1788 WOLCOT (P. Pindar) *Peter's Proph.* 41 The beautiful deformities of nature! Birds without heads, and tails, and wings, and legs,..speckless eggs [etc.]. *a* 1827 WORDSW. *Misc. Sonn.* II. xix, If his thought stand clear,..Bright, speckless, as a softly-moulded tear. 1833 M. SCOTT *Tom Cringle* xviii, The second sun set—still the horizon was speckless. 1889 C. EDWARDES *Sardinia* 120 The speckless blue of the sky.

b. Free from specks of dirt, dust, etc.; scrupulously or spotlessly clean. Also in fig. context.

1827 PUSEY in Liddon *Life* (1893) I. vii. 137 Viewing their minds in the almost speckless mirror of his own. 1859 GEO. ELIOT *A. Bede* i, The leaded windows were bright and speckless. 1879 MACQUOID *Berksh. Lady* 159 Afraid of soiling his speckless shoes.

Hence **Spe·cklessly** *adv.*, **Spe·cklessness.**

1862 T. A. TROLLOPE *Marietta* I. x. 187 Signor Giusseppe Palli..equally rigid and bolt upright in his chair, equally specklessly black. 1876 MRS. WHITNEY *Sights & Ins.* xiii. 130 The whole turn-out is specklessly brilliant in finish. 1882 'F. ANSTEY' *Vice Versa* iv. 64 His dress..having all the uncreased trimness and specklessness [etc.].

Spe·ckling, *vbl. sb.* [f. SPECKLE *v.*] The action of the vb.; speckled marking or marks.

1611 COTGR., *Tacheture*,..a spotting, speckling, marking. 1648 HEXHAM II, *Een spickelinge*, a Speckling, or a Spotting. 1872 COUES *N. Amer. Birds* 254 More or less dusky speckling on the throat, breast and sides.

So **Spe·ckling** *ppl. a.*, producing speckles or blemishes. In quot. *fig.*

1602 MARSTON *Ant. & Mel.* IV. Wks. 1856 I. 45 O, this is naught but speckling melancholie.

Spe·ckly, *a.* [f. SPECKLE *sb.* Cf. MDu. *speckelich* (Du. *spikkelig*) speckled.] Full of or covered with speckles; speckled, spotted; freckled.

1704 *Phil. Trans.* XXV. 1758 Through which the Spot appeared distinct,..with an Eliptical Speckly mist about it. 1886 G. ALLEN *Kalee's Shrine* i. 17 The speckly dress and impossible bonnet. 1899 E. PHILLPOTTS *Human Boy* 95 A thick-necked, speckly, stumpy chap like Bray.

Specknell, obs. form of SPIGNEL.

Specksioneer (spekʃəniə·ɹ). *Whale-fishing.* Also **specktion(e)er, spectioneer, speckshioner.** [ad. Du. *speksnijer*, colloquial form of *speksnijder*, f. *spek* SPECK *sb.*[4] + *snijden* to cut. The Du. *ij* was formerly, and is still locally, pronounced as (ī).] A harpooner, usually the chief harpooner, of a whaler, who directs the operation of flensing the whale or cutting up the blubber.

α. 1820 SCORESBY *Acc. Arctic Reg.* II. 40 The office of specksioneer, as it is called by the English. The specksioneer is now considered the principal harpooner. *Ibid.* 299 The harpooners, directed by the specksioneer, divide the fat into oblong pieces or 'slips'. 1858 SIMMONDS *Dict. Trade, Spectioneer*, a whaling name for the first harpooner. 1863 MRS. GASKELL *Sylvia's Lovers* II. 89 They spoke of the specksioneer, with admiration enough for his powers as a harpooner and sailor. 1867 SMYTH *Sailor's Word-bk.* 641 *Specktioneer*, the chief harpooner in a Greenland ship.

β. 1836 *Uncle Philip's Convers. Whale Fishery* 87 There is among the harpooners one man called the specktioner, and as he commands, the harpooners cut the fat into long pieces. 1896 KIPLING *Seven Seas* 24 Up spake the soul of a gray Gothavn 'speckshioner.

†**Speckstone.** *Min. Obs.* [ad. G. *speckstein*, f. *speck* SPECK *sb.*[4] + *stein* STONE *sb.*] Soapstone, or the Chinese variety of this; figure-stone.

1794 SCHMEISSER *Syst. Min.* I. 194 To the harder kinds belong..the Chinese smectis, or speckstone, which takes a fine polish.

Speckt, error for *specht* SPEIGHT.

Specky (spe·ki), *a.* Also 7 **speckie,** 8 **speckey.** [f. SPECK *sb.*[1] + -Y.] Covered or marked with specks; speckled, spotted; having specks or spots of disease, discoloration, etc.

1382 WYCLIF *Gen.* xxx. 33 Alle that weren not dyuerse, and speckid [*v.rr.* specky, specke]. 1587 MASCALL *Gov. Cattle, Sheepe* (1596) 206 Although the skinne be specky and spotted of diuers colours. 1763 W. LEWIS *Phil. Comm. Arts* 65 In some parts it appeared specky or full of small holes. 1793 *Trans. Soc. Enc. Arts*, etc. XI. 17 For where the leaves curl, the fruit is always specky. 1856 MORTON *Cycl. Agric.* I. 48/1 When ground with wheat, they render the flour 'specky'. 1865 *Intell. Observ.* No. 37. 18 A turbid or specky appearance. 1884 F. J. BRITTEN *Watch & Clockm.* 34 Pieces [of steel] that have been cleaned in dirty benzine..will become specky in blueing.

transf. 1858 *Dublin Univ. Mag.* LII. 264 A style which might technically be termed specky and disfigured by some affectations which honest criticism must deplore.

Speckle(d, obs. ff. SPECKLE *sb.*, SPECKLED *ppl. a.*

Specs. Also **specks.** [Dial. or colloq. abbreviation of *spectacles* SPECTACLE *sb.*[1]] Spectacles for the eyes.

α. 1807 HOGG *Mountain Bard* Poet. Wks. 1838 II. 202 The miller.., wi' specks on his nose, To hae an' to view it was wondrous fain. 1815 G. BEATTIE *John o' Arnha'* (1826) 40 Wi' specks on nose,..The wary fiend loom'd bluff and big. 1882 BLACKMORE *Christowell* xxvii, Must have my thick specks.

β. 1826 J. WILSON *Noct. Ambr.* Wks. 1855 I. 125 Few o' them..that canna read big prent wi' powerfu' specs. 1853 CARLYLE in Froude *Life C. in Lond.* (1884) II. 127 She reads now with specs in the candlelight, as well as I; uses her mother's specs I perceive. 1873 CARLETON *Farm Ball.* 19 She got her specs from off the mantel-shelf.

†**Spect,** *v. Obs. rare.* [ad. L. *spect-āre* to look.] *intr.* To look or face in a specified direction.

1585 T. WASHINGTON tr. *Nicholay's Voy.* I. xvi. 17 b, Ther is another port which specteth towards the North. *Ibid.* II. vi. 35 The yle of Chio..lyeth in the sea Ionique specting Eastwardes.

†**Spectabi·lity.** *Obs.*[−1] [f. next, or ad. L. *spectābilitās*.] Display, show.

1637 GILLESPIE *Eng. Pop. Cerem.* II. iv. 20 Musculus reprehends Bishops, for..adding Ceremonies unto Ceremonies in a worldly splendor and spectability.

†**Spectable,** *sb. Obs. rare.* [Substituted for SPECTACLE *sb.*[1], after next or OF. *spectable* sb.] A spectacle.

1535 *Goodly Primer, Prayer Lord* C j b, For an effectual example, & spectable of all vertues. 1550 COVERDALE *Spir. Perle* xxviii. (1588) 269 Job, the spectable of patience.

†**Spectable,** *a. Obs.* [ad. L. *spectābilis* (f. *spectāre* to look) or a. OF. (also mod.F.) *spectable* (It. *spettabile*, Sp. *espectable*).]

1. Presentable to the sight; worthy of being seen or contemplated.

1432-50 tr. *Higden* (Rolls) I. 5 For in this tyme presente artes and lawes scholde falle vtterly, the exemplares of acciones spectable scholde not be patent. 1489-99 *Inscript. Holloway Chapel, Widcome* in Wood *Life* (O.H.S.) II. 409 Thys chapill floryschyd with formosyte spectabyll In honour of Mary Magdalen prior Cantlow hath edyfyd. 1611 T. HIGGONS *Serm. at Pauls Crosse* 42 My function and office.. was very spectable, yea honourable also. 1635 HEYWOOD *Hierarchy* III. Comm. 150 That by which a woman is made more faire and Spectable. 1665 J. SERGEANT *Sure Footing* 63 Experience of them.., by the venerable Sacraments, by the spectable Majesty of outward Ceremonies.

2. Capable of being seen; visible.

c 1440 *Pallad. on Husb.* IV. 692 Ther are in hem certeyn signys spectable Which is teschewe, and whiche is profitable. 1604 T. WRIGHT *Passions* V. § 4. 220 Divers times both proportion, comelinesse, or..other perfection be more spectable in the reiected, then in the accepted. 1622 *Tom Tell-Troath* in *Harl. Misc.* (1744) II. 405/1 The blasing Starr was not more spectable in our Horizon, nor gave People more Occasion of Talke. *a* 1655 T. ADAMS *Serm.* ix. Wks. 1861 I. 104 Their prayers were at the corners of streets;..and so more spectable to many passengers.

†**Spectabundal,** *a. Obs.*[−1] [f. L. *spect-āre* to look, after adjs. in *-bundus*.] Eager to see.

1652 URQUHART *Jewel* Wks. (1834) 230 By the inchanted transportation of the eyes and ears of its spectabundal auditorie.

Spectacle (spe·ktăk'l), *sb.*[1] Forms: 4- **spectacle** (5 **-acul**); 4 **spectakil,** 5 **-akele, -akyl(le,** 6 **-akle, -akill(e;** 7 **specktacle, -ikill.** [a. OF. *spectacle* (also mod.F.: see next), = It. *spettacolo*, Sp. and Pg. *espectaculo*, or ad. L. *spectāculum* (poet. *-āclum*), f. *spectāre* to look. Hence also G., Da., Sw. *spektakel*.]

I. 1. A specially prepared or arranged display of a more or less public nature (esp. one on a large scale), forming an impressive or interesting show or entertainment for those viewing it.

a 1340 HAMPOLE *Psalter* xxxix. 6 Hoppynge & daunceynge of tumblers and herlotis, and oþer spectakils. 1382 WYCLIF 2 *Macc.* v. 26 He stranglide togidre alle that camen forth to the spectacle, or biholdyng. 1542 BECON *Pathw. Prayer* A iij b, What an extreme enemy is the worlde... Howe doth it deiyghte vs with the beholdyng of the vayne spectacles therof! 1553 EDEN *Treat. New Ind.* (Arb.) 16 The Romaynes..were wont to put them [*sc.* the elephant and rhinoceros] together vpon the theater or stage, for a spectacle. 1607 TOPSELL *Four-f. Beasts* 315 The noblest horses..were ioyned together in chariots for races, courses, spectacles, games, and combats. 1617 MORYSON *Itin.* IV. 476 To which and to many musterings and other frequent spectacles, the people flocke in great numbers. 1641 J. JACKSON *True Evang. T.* II. 126 They abhorred Theaters, and publique spectacles, especially of blood. 1763 J. BROWN *Poetry & Music* iv. 43 The gentle Passions, and less affecting Actions, which might fill the Spectacles of a mild and peaceful Nation. 1782 J. WARTON *Ess. Pope* II. viii. 87 What solid reason can we give why the Romans..could yet never excel in tragedy, though so fond of theatrical spectacles? 1806 J. BERESFORD *Miseries Hum. Life* II. xii, Violent rain coming on, and continuing..during the whole of the spectacle. *c* 1854 H. REED *Lect. Eng. Lit.* ix. (1855) 290 It was a very fine spectacle, but it was nothing more than a spectacle. 1865 LECKY *Ration.* (1878) I. 324 He had written a treatise dissuading the Christians of his day from frequenting the public spectacles.

b. Without article.

1387 TREVISA *Higden* (Rolls) V. 375 In comyn spectacle þere me stood to beholde playes and som newe þinges. 1607 TOPSELL *Four-f. Beasts* (1658) 374 Cæsar when he was Dictator, presented in spectacle four hundred Lions. 1740 CIBBER *Apol.* 57 Sir William Davenant, therefore,..to make Head against their Success, was forc'd to add Spectacle and Musick to Action. 1809 PINKNEY *Trav. France* 98 The French..infinitely excell every other nation in all things connected with spectacle. 1835 LYTTON *Rienzi* x. vi, Gorgeous imagination rather than vanity..had led the Tribune into spectacle and pomp. 1866 CARLYLE in Froude *Remin.* (1881) II. 215 She was constantly in spectacle there, to herself and to the sympathetic adorers.

attrib. and *Comb.* 1834 *Edinb. Rev.* LX. 7 The spectacle-loving public of the seventeenth century. 1908 *Stage Year Bk.* 21 An ingeniously conceived..spectacle play.

2. A person or thing exhibited to, or set before, the public gaze as an object either (*a*) of curiosity or contempt, or (*b*) of marvel or admiration.

In 2 *Sam.* xxiii. 21 the later Wycliffite version has the literal rendering 'worthi of spectacle'.

(*a*) *a* 1380 *S. Paula* 97 in Horstm. *Altengl. Leg.* (1878) 4 To gode angeles and to men Spectacle mad forsoþe we ben. 1382 WYCLIF 1 *Cor.* iv. 9. 1382 — *Hebrews* x. 33 In that other ȝe [were] maad a spectacle bi schenschips and tribulaciouns. 1582 N. T. (Rhem.) 1 *Cor.* iv. 9 We are made a spectacle to the world, and to Angels and men. 1724 GAY *Captives* v, Let her be led a public spectacle. 1818 SCOTT *Hrt. Midl.* xii, How proud I was o' being made a spectacle to men and angels, having stood on their pillory at the Canongate.

(*b*) 1609 BIBLE (Douay) 2 *Sam.* xxiii. 21 He also stroke the Ægyptian, a man worthie to be a spectacle. 1794 GODWIN *Caleb Williams* 110 A man who..must stand alone the spectacle and admiration of all ages of the world. 1805-6 CARY *Dante, Inf.* XXIX. 130 And his rare wisdom Abbagliato show'd A spectacle for all. 1837 CARLYLE *Fr. Rev.* II. v. xii, There he stands, with unimpeachable passivity,..a spectacle to men.

3. A thing seen or capable of being seen; something presented to the view, esp. of a striking or unusual character; a sight. Also *fig.*

1434 MISYN *Mending Life* 127 Odyr says þat contemplacion is free sight in þe spectakyls of wysdom. 1509 HAWES *Past. Pleas.* xx. (Percy Soc.) 97 Alas! thought I, this is no spectacle To fede myn eyne, whiche ar now all blynde. *a* 1540 BARNES *Wks.* (1573) 346/2 S. Augustine sayth, Let vs not loue any visible spectakilles lest..by louing shadowes we be brought in to darknes. 1600 SHAKS. *A. Y. L.* II. i. 44 But what said Iaques? Did he not moralize this spectacle? 1648 WILKINS *Math. Magic* I. x. 66 Either of them might joyntly behold the same spectacles. 1784 COWPER *Task* I. 476 The paralytic..sits, Spectatress both and spectacle, a sad And silent cypher. 1794 R. J. SULIVAN *View Nat.* II. 15 The spectacle has in it something almost supernatural. 1829 *Chapters Phys. Sci.* 315 To observe this spectacle the back of the spectator must be turned towards the sun. 1839 FR. A. KEMBLE *Resid. in Georgia* (1863) 32 How shall I describe to you the spectacle which was presented to me. 1849 MACAULAY *Hist. Eng.* v. I. 645 Lord Stawell..was punished by having a corpse suspended in chains at his park gate. In such spectacles originated many tales of terror.

b. The sight or view *of* something.

1625 in Foster *Eng. Factories Ind.* (1909) III. 56 Whole rabbles of people, whose revengefull eyes never glutted themselves to behould the spectacle of our mizeries. 1658 in *Verney Mem.* (1907) II. 138 Trobled with the specktikill of a discontented sister. 1780 BENTHAM *Princ. Legisl.* xiv. § 1 The spectacle of your suffering gives me at least for a time a feeling of pleasure. 1816 SCOTT *Old Mort.* xxxii, The spectacle of their hurried and harassed retreat. 1852 H. ROGERS *Ecl. Faith* (1853) 3 The spectacle of the interminable controversies..occupied the mind of Germany. 1874 L. STEPHEN *Hours in Library* (1892) I. v. 185 The spectacle of a man tortured by a life-long repentance.

4. A sight, show, or exhibition *of* a specified character or description.

1484 CAXTON *Curiall* 5 They only that ben hyest enhaunsed ben after theyr despoyntement as a spectacle of enuye, of detraction, or of hate. 1665 MANLEY *Grotius' Low C. Wars* 681 Both near at hand, and far off, nothing [was seen] but terrible spectacles of horrour and dying. 1671 MILTON *P. R.* I. 415 A poor miserable captive thrall,..A spectacle of ruin or of scorn. 1746 HERVEY *Medit.* (1818) 50 How many dismal hours did that illustrious Sufferer hang, a spectacle of woe to God, to angels, and to men! 1791 BURKE *Corr.* (1844) III. 219 A spectacle of suffering royalty. 1839 FR. A. KEMBLE *Resid. in Georgia* (1863) 65 Such another spectacle of filthy disorder I never beheld.

b. With descriptive adjs. denoting the impression (agreeable, imposing, or otherwise) conveyed by the thing seen.

(*a*) 1560 DAUS tr. *Sleidane's Comm.* 115 b, The same woulde be a moste pleasaunt syght, and spectacle for the Lutherians. 1580 LYLY *Euphues* (Arb.) 433 Your eyes being too olde to iudge of so rare a spectacle. 1664 POWER *Exp. Philos.* I. 6 The Gray, or Horse-Fly: Her eye is an incomparable pleasant spectacle. 1698 FRYER *Acc. E. India & P.* 76 In the mean while Nature affords us a pleasant Spectacle for this Season. 1718 LADY M. W. MONTAGU *Let. to Lady Rich* 10 Oct., The shops being all set in rows so regularly well lighted, they made up a very agreeable spectacle. 1845 DARWIN *Voy. Nat.* viii. (1879) 162 The sea presented a wonderful and most beautiful spectacle. 1873 HAMERTON *Intell. Life* I. vi. (1876) 31 The magnificent spectacle of the universe.

(*b*) 1590 SPENSER *F. Q.* II. i. 40 Pitifull spectacle, as euer eye did view. 1602 MARSTON *Antonio's Rev.* V. vi, Whose hand presents this gory spectacle? 1653 H. COGAN tr. *Pinto's Trav.* ix. 30 Which was so dreadful a spectacle to us, as we had not the power to cry out. 1726 SWIFT *Gulliver* II. iv, The beggars..gave me the most horrid spectacles.. a European eye beheld. 1740 RICHARDSON *Pamela* (1824) I. 77, I shan't be able to stir out this day or two, for I am a frightful spectacle! 1837 DISRAELI *Venetia* I. ix, Mrs. Cadurcis indeed offered a most ridiculous spectacle. 1863 BRIGHT *Sp., Amer.* 26 Mar. (1876) 125 Privilege has beheld an afflicting spectacle for many years past.

II. †5. A means of seeing; something made of glass; a window or mirror. *Obs.*

c 1430 LYDG. *Lyfe of our Ladye* (MS. Bodl. 75) fol. 19 Riȝt as þe son percyd þorouȝ glas, Thorouȝ crystal beryl or spectacle, Wiþ oute harme. *c* 1430 — *Min. Poems* (Percy Soc.) 140 By his labour was cristened al this lond, Feith of our lord wex moor cleer than spectacle. 1439 in Sir W. Dugdale *Monast. Angl.* (1823) IV. 553/2 We ordeyne.. that ye..have no lokyng nor spectacles owte warde, thorght the wiche ye mythe falle in worldly dilectacyone. 1548 ELYOT, *Specularius*, he that maketh glasse windowes or spectacles, a glasiar. 1576 FLEMING *Panopl. Epist.* 49 Should I set before your eyes, as it were a spectacle or looking glasse, men of great noblenesse and passing fame? 1630 *R. Johnson's Kingd. & Commw.* 130 The first is Temperance, with a Diall and Spectacle.

†**b.** *fig.* A mirror, model, pattern, or standard.

c 1430 LYDG. *Min. Poems* (E.E.T.S.) 52 To all virgines merour and spectacle, Off hire merites of hevene crowned queene. 1483 CAXTON *G. de la Tour* e iij b, Here is a fair spectacle to euery woman to see in, and conceyue the tyme comynge. 1523 LD. BERNERS *Froiss.* I. cccc. 695 This harde and peryllous aduenture myght well be to hym a spectacle all his lyfe after, and an ensample to all other. *a* 1548 HALL *Chron., Hen. VI*, 101 The erles..determined first to ryde to London, as the chefe key, and common spectacle to the whole Realme. *a* 1575 tr. *Pol. Verg. Eng. Hist.* (Camden, No. 36) 217 Knowing the owld sayde sawe, that preestes weare the spectacle and looking glasse of the whole worlde.

†**c.** An illustrative instance or example. *Obs.*

1579 W. WILKINSON *Confut. Fam. Love* 65 b, Hee [Judas] should be a notable spectacle of God's vengeance. 1632 LITHGOW *Trav.* x. 489 When the Starres of great states decline.., and [are] made the deplored-for spectacles of the inconstancy of fortune. 1656 EARL MONM. tr. *Boccalini's Advts. fr. Parnass.* I. viii. (1674) 10 Through their Masters ingratitude and cruelty..they became the spectacle of all brutish usage.

6. A device for assisting defective eyesight, or for protecting the eyes from dust, light, etc., consisting of two glass lenses set in a frame which is supported on the nose, and kept in place by wires passing over the ears. Usually in *pl.*

sing. *c* 1386 [see c]. 1415 HOCCLEVE *To Sir J. Oldcastle* 417 Right as a spectacle helpith feeble sighte, Whan a man on the book redith or writ. 1447 BOKENHAM *Seyntys* (Roxb.) 27 Myn eyne bleynte Shuld be, ner helpe of a spectacle. 1589 PUTTENHAM *Eng. Poesie* III. xxv. (Arb.) 311 There be artes and methodes..by which the naturall is in some sorte relieued, as th'eye by his spectacle. 1628 DONNE *Sermons* 289, I thank him..that assists me with a Spectacle when my sight grows old. *c* 1640 J. SMYTH *Lives of Berkeleys* (1883) II. 408 Reading much, yet never used spectacle or other help. 1728 CHAMBERS *Cycl.* s.v. *Eye*, This Membrane, like a Kind of Spectacle, covers the Eye.

pl. *c* 1430 LYDG. *London Lackpenny* Min. Poems (Percy Soc.) 105 What will you copen or by? Fyne felt hattes, or spectacles to reede? *c* 1500 *Blowbol's Test.* 101 in Hazl. *E. P. P.* I. 96 No man may his letters know nor se, Allethough he looke trughe spectacles thre. 1561 T. NORTON *Calvin's Inst.* I. 11 b, Being holpen with spectacles,..they begin to read distinctlie. 1617 MORYSON *Itin.* III. 56 And because they cast up sand upon the passengers, some curious men use spectacles of glasse to preserve their eyes. 1656 RIDGLEY *Pract. Physick* 129 Use of Spectacles weakneth the sight, unless you wear them for need. 1728 PEMBERTON *Newton's Philos.* 383 Hence may be understood why spectacles made with convex glasses help the sight in old age. 1761 *Phil. Trans.* LII. 124 Plain spectacles..do not appear to have been known till a hundred years after. 1831 BREWSTER *Optics* xxxviii. 320 Spectacles and reading glasses are among the simplest and most useful of optical instruments. 1859 *Habits of Gd. Society* iii. 154, I am one of those people who wear spectacles for fear of seeing anything with the naked eye. 1887 RUSKIN *Præterita* II. 231 Tourists who pass their time mostly in looking at black rocks through blue spectacles.

transf. 1593 SHAKS. 2 *Hen. VI*, III. ii. 112, I..bid mine eyes be packing.., And call'd them blinde and duskie Spectacles.

b. In phr. *a pair of spectacles.* † Also without *of*.

1423 *Test. Ebor.* (Surtees) III. 75 De xxs receptis pro pare de spectakeles de argento et deaurato. 1463 *Bury Wills* (Camden) 15 A peyre spectaclys of syluir and ouyr gylt. 1529 MORE *Dyaloge* I. Wks. 147/1 And so should the scripture stand them in as good stede, as a paire of spectacles shold stand a blinde freer. 1589 PUTTENHAM *Eng. Poesie* III. xxv. (Arb.) 311 No lesse to be laughed at, then for one that can see well inough, to vse a paire of spectacles. 1666 PEPYS *Diary* 24 Dec., I this evening did buy me a pair of green spectacles, to see whether they will help my eyes or no. 1726 SWIFT *Gulliver* I. ii, A pair of spectacles (which I sometimes use for the weakness of mine eyes). 1756-7 tr. *Keysler's Trav.* (1760) III. 374 On the other side is another cardinal with a large pair of spectacles on his nose. 1827 FARADAY *Chem. Manip.* xxiii. (1842) 590 A pair of spectacles, with side as well as front glasses.

c. *fig.* A means or medium through which anything is viewed or regarded; a point of view, prepossession, prejudice, etc.

c 1386 CHAUCER *Wife's T.* 347 Povert a spectacle is, as thinkith me, Thurgh which he may his verray frendes se. 1579 W. WILKINSON *Confut. Fam. Love* 16 He that putteth on the Christall spectacles of Gods word. 1598 BARCKLEY *Felic. Man* (1631) 648 We behold our owne faults with spectacles that make things shew lesse. 1606 *Proc. agst. Late Traitors* 356 False informations, which are rightly called the spectacles of error. 1644 JESSOP *Angel Ephesus* 62 One of late looking on his words with an Episcopall paire of spectacles, blesseth himselfe at the reading of them. 1676 HOBBES *Iliad* Pref., They that..look upon it with the oldest spectacles of a Critick, may approve it. 1711 *Country-Man's Lett. Curat* 29 All the World hitherto had thought, these Horses and Chariots of Fire had been the Prophets Guard not his Danger; But they have wanted the Doctor's Spectacles. 1861 [see ROSE-COLOURED *a.* 3]. 1869 J. MARTINEAU *Ess.* II. 5 They offer you the spectacles they did not use. 1889 *Spectator* 28 Dec., He early recognised that it is a scholar's duty to interpret what he sees simply, without the spectacles of prepossession.

†**d.** A device for restricting the view of horses.

In both passages a rendering of It. *occhiali*.

1632 J. HAYWARD tr. *Biondi's Eromena* 3 The horse with his spectacles and covering. 1656 EARL MONM. tr. *Boccalini's Pol. Touchstone* in *Advts. fr. Parnass.* 305 The jealous Spaniards keep..a caveson upon his nose, a bit in his mouth, a spectacle on his eyes, as if they were afraid of him.

7. a. *ellipt.* A species of moth.

1819 SAMOUELLE *Entomol. Compend.* 422 *Noctua triplasia.* The dark Spectacle. *Noctua asclepiades.* The light Spectacle. 1832 J. RENNIE *Consp. Butterfl. & M.* 92 The Dark Spectacle (*Abrostola triplasia*) appears in July. *Ibid.*, The Spectacle (*Abrostola Asclepiadis*) appears the end of July.

b. *Zool.* A marking resembling a pair of spectacles.

1884 COUES *Key N. Amer. Birds* 815 Spectacled Guillemot...A pair of white spectacles on the eyes, and whitish about base of bill. 1908 E. M. GORDON *Indian Folk Tales* viii. (1909) 76 Two varieties of *cobra*, one with the spectacles and the other without them.

c. *pl.* A batsman's score of two zeros or 'duck's eggs' in a cricket match of two innings. Freq. in *a pair of spectacles*.

1892 in W. A. Bettesworth *Chats Cricket Field* (1910) 455. 1893 *Whitaker's Alm.* 613 Unlucky enough to make spectacles for his side against Middlesex. 1898 *Globe* 1 Sept. 5/5 Yesterday in a match..he made a pair of spectacles.

8. a. *pl.* The glazed openings in the cab-screen of a locomotive.

1878 F. S. WILLIAMS *Midl. Railw.* 503 We..see through the 'spectacles' of the powerful little engine..that [etc.]. 1896 *B'ham Weekly Post* 15 Feb. 8/7 The lid of the sandbox was blown off, and, rising in the air, was shot through the spectacles of the engine.

b. The device consisting of two frames containing respectively red and green glass worked at night in connexion with a railway semaphore.

1881 *Standard* 17 Dec. 2/5 When we got to the up-distant signal I called..attention to the fact that the arm and spectacle were thickly covered with snow. 1889 G. FINDLAY *Eng. Railway* 68 With the arm is a frame containing coloured glasses, and termed 'spectacles'.

c. A mechanical device attached to a phonograph (see quot.).

1889 *Pall Mall G.* 11 Mar. 1/1, I have just finished some improvements in the spectacle (a term given to the mechanical device holding the receiver and transmitter).

9. *attrib.* and *Comb.* (in sense 6), as *spectacle-frame, lens, -mark, years*; *spectacle-seller, -user, -wiper*; *spectacle-bestrid, -less, -like, -shaped* adjs.

1784 COWPER *Task* II. 439 At conventicle, where worthy men..strain celestial themes Through the prest nostril, *spectacle-bestrid. 1879 *Cassell's Techn. Educ.* II. 179/1 In the manufacture of blue steel *spectacle-frames. 1898 WATTS-DUNTON *Aylwin* XV. iii, A strongly marked indented line ..made by long-continued pressure of the spectacle frame. 1862 *Catal. Internat. Exhib., Brit.* II. No. 2899 Concave, convex, and meniscus *spectacle lenses. 1889 *Longman's Mag.* Oct. 619 Her brother's helplessness in his *spectacleless condition. 1663 GERBIER *Counsel* 13 Those *Spectacle-like cant Windows, which are of Glasse on all sides. 1796 P. RUSSELL *Indian Serpents Coromandel* 8 The spectacle-like mark on the hood. 1895 *Oracle Encycl.* II. 93 Specimens [of the Cobra] destitute of the *spectacle-mark come from the E. Indies. 1648 HEXHAM II, *Een bril-verkooper*, a *Spectacle..Seller. 1847 A. SMEE *Vision* 50 The knowledge possessed by even the better order of spectacle-sellers. 1802 SHAW *Gen. Zool.* III. I. 409 The neck marked above by a large black and white *spectacle-shaped spot. 1838 WELLINGTON *Lett. to Miss J.* (1890) 102, I return ..the *Spectacle Wipers which you was so good as to send me. 1657 R. AUSTEN *Fruit-trees* ii. 10 What a shame is it for a man to begin to learne his letters and to spell at *spectacle yeares!

b. In names of animals or birds having markings round the eyes, or elsewhere, suggestive of a pair of spectacles, as **spectacle bat, owl, snake, thrush, warbler.** (Cf. SPECTACLED *a.* 2.)

1827 GRIFFITH tr. *Cuvier* V. 69 *Phyllostoma Perspicillatum* (*Spectacle Bat). 1787 LATHAM *Suppl. Gen. Syn. Birds* I. 50 *Spectacle Owl..is less stout than the Cinereous Owl. 1829 GRIFFITH tr. *Cuvier* VI. 83 The Spectacle Owl,..*Strix perspicillata*. 1802 SHAW *Gen. Zool.* III. II. 409 *Spectacle Snake...The Coluber Naja, or Cobra de Capello, is a native of India. 1840 *Penny Cycl.* XVI. 60/2 The Asiatic species.., Spectacle-snake of the English,..may be considered as the type of the genus. 1783 LATHAM *Gen. Synop. Birds* II. I. 61 *Spectacle Thrush. *Ibid.* 452 *Spectacle Warbler..[has] a naked yellowish wrinkled skin, which encircles the eye all round, giving the appearance of wearing spectacles.

10. Special combs.: **spectacle-case,** a case of leather or other material in which spectacles are kept when not in use; **spectacle clew,** a form of double clew for a sail; **spectacle eye,** a spectacle glass; **spectacle furnace** (see quot.); **spectacle plate,** = sense 8 a; **spectacles-seat,** *slang*, the nose; † **spectacle telescope,** a binocular telescope or field-glass.

1597 *Shuttleworths' Acc.* (Chetham Soc.) 108 A *specta[c]le cace, vjd. 1690 *Lond. Gaz.* No. 2079/4 Lost.., a Black Shagreen Spectacle-Case. 1866 J. MARTINEAU *Ess.* I. 47 The spectacle-case may well be empty, if the glasses are already on the nose. 1863 *Appleby's Handbk. Mach. & Iron Work* 92 *Spectacle Clues, all sizes—Black, 35/0 per cwt. 1884 KNIGHT *Dict. Mech.* Suppl. 200/1 Ear-ring clew...Spectacle clew. 1862 *Catal. Internat. Exhib., Brit.* No. 2887 Lump of Brazilian pebble, from which slabs are cut and ground into *spectacle eyes. 1875 KNIGHT *Dict. Mech.* 2257 *Spectacle-furnace,..a furnace with two tap-holes, one above the other. 1900 *Daily Express* 19 June 5/7 Alongside the driver is a fireman,..frowning..through the *spectacle plate. 1895 MEREDITH *Amazing Marriage* xvi, Ben received a second spanking cracker on the *spectacles-seat. 1728 CHAMBERS *Cycl.* s.v., F. Cherubin, a Capuchin, describes a kind of *Spectacle-Telescopes, for the viewing of remote Objects with both Eyes; hence called Binoculi.

‖**Spectacle** (spektakl'), *sb.*[2] [F.: see prec.]

1. = SPECTACLE *sb.*[1] 1.

1749 CHESTERF. *Lett.* ccviii. (1792) 294 Go to whatever assemblies or *spectacles* people of fashion go to. 1768 EARL CARLISLE in Jesse *Selwyn & Contemp.* (1843) II. 336, I shall go to Fontainbleau on Saturday next. It is to be extremely dull; no *spectacle* at court. 1792 A. YOUNG *Trav. France* 217 If cheapness of living, *spectacles*, and pretty women, are a man's objects.., let him live at Venice. 1801 HELEN M. WILLIAMS *Fr. Rep.* I. xi. 110 The love of a *spectacle* is, you know, the ruling passion of the Parisians. 1837 LOCKHART *Scott* III. xi. 370 So mounted,..he witnessed the great closing *spectacle* on the *Champ de Mars*.

2. *spec.* A piece of stage-display or pageantry, as contrasted with real drama.

1752 T. SCROPE in Jesse *Selwyn & Contemp.* (1843) I. 149 Their *spectacles* were very grand, and their stage far surpasses ours; but their plays, in my opinion, fall as far short.

1835 T. MITCHELL *Acharn. of Aristoph.* 1059 *note*, The progress of the piece evidently requires here some little pageant or *spectacle*. 1860 *Once a Week* 14 July 70/1 The young Thespians..had to appear as Peace and Plenty, amidst a great display of red-light, at the end of a grand *spectacle*, which was drawing uncommonly well.

Spe·ctacle, *v. rare.* [f. SPECTACLE *sb.*[1]]

1. *trans.* To scrutinize through spectacles.

a 1734 NORTH *Lives* (1826) III. 131 The barons, each one after another, spectacled it over and over, and scarce believed their own eyes. 1888 MURDOCH *Readings* Ser. II. 47 Oh, ye may spectacle me as much as ye like, my fine man.

2. To provide with spectacles.

1880 *Sat. Rev.* No. 1295. 235 Of late years the practice of putting children into spectacles has increased with alarming rapidity...Spectacling them may be a wholesome preventive.

Spectacled (spe·ktăk'ld), *a.* [f. as prec.]

1. Provided with or wearing spectacles.

1607 SHAKS. *Cor.* II. i. 221 All tongues speake of him, and the bleared sights Are spectacled to see him. 1624 MIDDLETON *Game at Chess* II. i, When the Inquisitors came all spectacled To pick out syllables. 1779 *Mirror* No. 8, Those grave personages, whom you may observe daily..rising in a coffee-house in the full dignity of a spectacled nose. 1818 SCOTT *Hrt. Midl.* vi, Half-scared by the..spectacled old lady, by whom these tempting stores are watched. 1852 R. S. SURTEES *Sponge's Sp. Tour* xxix. 175, 'I think it will be a fine day,' he said,..turning his spectacled face up to the clouds. 1886 W. J. TUCKER *E. Europe* 215 A couple of spectacled professional gentlemen.

b. With distinguishing adjs.

1884 G. ALLEN *Philistia* I. 12 There was honesty..in those hazy blue-spectacled eyes. 1896 *Idler* Mar. 247/2 This innocent looking little gold-spectacled bald-headed gentleman.

2. In names of birds, animals, etc., having spectacle-shaped markings or the appearance of wearing spectacles (see quots. and SPECTACLE *sb.*[1] 9 b).

1831 GRIFFITH tr. *Cuvier* IX. Syn. 21 *Spectacled Alligator, *Crocodilus (Alligator) Sclerops*. 1835 *Penny Cycl.* IV. 87 The *Spectacled Bear, *Ursus Ornatus* of F. Cuvier, inhabits the Cordilleras of the Andes in Chili. 1894 LYDEKKER *Roy. Nat. Hist.* II. 23 The spectacled bear of the Peruvian Andes..is a small-sized black species. 1830 GRIFFITH tr. *Cuvier* XI. 188 The *Spectacled Cayman (*Crocodilus Sclerops*) is the most common in Cayenne. 1854 OWEN in *Orr's Circ. Sci., Org. Nat.* I. 197 They sustain a fold of integument, peculiarly coloured in some species—*e.g.*, the *spectacled cobra. *c* 1880 *Cassell's Nat. Hist.* IV. 304 The natives say that the Spectacled Cobra is a Snake of the city or town. 1872 COUES *N. Amer. Birds* 292 *Spectacled Eider,..a whitish space round eye, bounded by black. 1884 *Ibid.* 815 *Uria carbo*,..*Spectacled Guillemot. 1896 LYDEKKER *Roy. Nat. Hist.* V. 298 The little *spectacled salamander (*Salamandrina perspicillata*) of Italy. 1831 GRIFFITH tr. *Cuvier* IX. 274 Named *Spectacled Serpent, from a black line drawn on the widened part of its disk in the form of spectacles. 1861 HULME tr. *Moquin-Tandon* II. v. i. 259 The Naia or Spectacled Serpents—called also the Hooded Snakes. 1834 *Encycl. Metrop.* (1845) XXII. 397/1 The Snakemen [of India]..never use in their shows any other poisonous Snake than the *Spectacled Snake. 1871 *Cassell's Nat. Hist.* I. 262 Leaf-like organs, often of the most extraordinary forms (see the Head of the *Spectacled Vampire). 1829 GRIFFITH tr. *Cuvier* VI. 446 *Spectacled Warbler, *Sylvia Conspicillata*. 1894-5 LYDEKKER *Roy. Nat. Hist.* III. 493 The spectacled warbler builds its nest in a small bush about a foot from the ground.

Spectacle-glass. [SPECTACLE *sb.*[1]]

1. A lens of a pair of spectacles.

a 1583 in Halliwell *Rara Mathem.* (1841) 40 For makinge of the smallest sorte of them, commonly called spectacle glasses. 1697 *C'tess D'Aunoy's Trav.* (1706) 146 Proportionably as a Man's Fortune rises, he increases in the largeness of his Spectacle-Glasses and wears them higher upon his Nose. 1761-9 tr. *Voltaire's Works* XXVI. 196 (Jod.), A lentular spectacle-glass. 1852 MRS. STOWE *Uncle Tom's C.* ix, He..seemed particularly busy in clearing his throat and wiping his spectacle-glasses. 1879 *Cassell's Techn. Educ.* II. 177/1 Preference is usually given to bi-convex and bi-concave spectacle glasses.

†**2.** A lens used as, or in, a microscope or telescope. *Obs.*

1671 GREW *Anat. Pl.* I. i. (1682) 2 Magnified with a good Spectacle-Glass. *Ibid.* 20 A lesser sort, which by the help only of a good Spectacle Glass may be observ'd. *a* 1697 AUBREY *Lives* (1898) I. 283 Anno 1678, he [Halley] added a spectacle-glasse to the shadowe-vane of the lesser arch of the sea-quadrant (or back-staffe).

Spectacle-maker. [SPECTACLE *sb.*[1] 6, 7 c.]

1. One who makes spectacles.

1530 PALSGR. 274/1 Spectacle maker, *lunettier*. 1611 COTGR., *Besiclier*, a Spectacle-maker. 1674 BOYLE *Excell. Theol.* I. iv. 168 Des-Cartes does acknowledge with other writers, that perspective-glasses were..first found out.. casually by one Metius, a Dutch spectacle-maker. 1728 CHAMBERS *Cycl.* s.v. *Telescope*, Fifty Years afterwards, a Telescope..was made..by a Spectacle-maker of Middlebourg. 1839 *Penny Cycl.* XIV. 119/1 [List of City Companies] Spectacle-makers. 1883 *Encycl. Brit.* XVI. 258/1 Not only were spectacle-makers the first to produce glass magnifiers (or simple microscopes), but [etc.].

2. One who makes no score in either innings in a game of cricket.

1893 *Star* 8 July 4/2 The compiler has been cruel enough to set out a full..list of spectacle makers during the whole term of years.

Spectacular (spektæ·kiŭlăɹ), *a.* and *sb.* [f. L. *spectacul-um* SPECTACLE *sb.*[1]]

1. Of the nature of a spectacle or show; striking or imposing as a display.

1682 G. HICKES *Serm. bef. Ld. Mayor 30 Jan.* 4 The Spectacular sports were concluded. 1865 *Daily Tel.* 20 Nov. 5/1 The true interests of the drama may in the end be advanced by its separation from merely spectacular entertainments. 1876 BLACK *Madcap Violet* xliv. 382 That was all very well as a spectacular exhibition. 1884 *Nonconf. & Indep.* 13 Nov. 1094/1 The Lord Mayor's Show was a more ambitious and spectacular pageant than ever.

b. *absol.* That which appeals to the eye.

1876 J. PARKER *Paracl.* I. xvi. 257 The carnal mind loves the spectacular, the marvellous. 1896 J. M. MANLY *Introd. Macbeth* p. xxiii, The list of plays and masques indicates a growing tendency to the spectacular during the 2nd decade of the 17th century.

2. Pertaining to, characteristic of, spectacles or shows.

1864 *Daily Tel.* 16 Aug., They are fond of spectacular magnificence. 1876 MELLOR *Priesthood* vi. 293 It is easy.. to surround any ceremony..with a spectacular splendour which captivates the imagination. 1883 E. H. ROLLINS *New Eng. Bygones* 240 That climate..spread over the landscape a great spectacular glory.

3. Addicted to, fond of, spectacles.

1894 *Daily Tel.* 2 July 7/2 All the glory of uniform and the glow of colour beloved by the most spectacular nation in the world.

4. As *sb.* A spectacular display.

1890 *Pall Mall G.* 8 Apr. 7/2 An amphitheatre..in which spectaculars on a grand scale might be produced before a half-million spectators.

Hence **Specta:cula·rity,** spectacular quality or character.

1883 HOWELLS *Woman's Reason* xii, The bare spectacularity of the keeping..must all be eloquent of a boarding-house. 1891 — *Imperative Duty* 6 A certain civic grandiosity, a sort of lion-and-unicorn spectacularity.

Specta·cularly, *adv.* [f. the adj.] In a spectacular fashion; after the manner of a spectacle.

1859 DICKENS *T. Two Cities* II. i, He was permitted to be seen, spectacularly poring over large books. 1897 *Advance* (Chicago) 14 Jan. 43 The '7,000 free Christmas dinners', spectacularly served in barracks. 1901 *Munsey's Mag.* XXIV. 838/2 They moved slowly and spectacularly up the avenue.

†**Specta·culous,** *a. Obs.*[−1] [f. L. *spectacul-um* SPECTACLE *sb.*[1]] Spectacular.

1632 LITHGOW *Trav.* VI. 271 Setting them on their Altars, O spectaculous Images! adoring them for gods.

Spe·ctant, *a. Her.* [a. L. *spectant-*, stem of *spectans*, pres. pple. of *spectāre* to look.] (See quot.)

1825-7 W. BERRY *Encycl. Her.* I, *Spectant*, at gaze, or looking forward, sometimes termed *in full aspect*. The term is, likewise, applied to any animal looking upwards, with the nose bendwise.

Spectate (spektē·t), *v.* [f. L. *spectāt-*, ppl. stem of *spectāre* to look.] *intr.* and *trans.* To look or gaze (at). Hence **Specta·ting** *ppl. a.*

1709 in Ashton *Social Life Reign Q. Anne* (1882) I. 287 A Gentleman sitting on the Coach, civilly salutes the Spectating Company. 1854 DE QUINCEY in 'H. A. Page' *Life* (1877) II. xviii. 88 The thing to be spectated, or in base vulgar, the spectacle. 1858 — *Wks.* VII. App. 329 To the poor spectator (unless paid for spectating) [it] is sympathetically painful.

†**Specta·tion.** *Obs. rare.* [ad. L. *spectātio*, noun of action f. *spectāre* to look.] The action of beholding, observing, or inspecting.

1638 *Briefe Relat.* 16 The Execution of the Lords Censure in Starre-Chamber,..at the spectation whereof the number of people was so great [etc.]

†**Specta·tive,** *a. Obs.*[−0] [ad. L. *spectātīv-us*.] (See quot.)

1656 BLOUNT *Glossogr.*, *Spectative*, that belongs to speculation; speculative, contemplative.

Spectator (spektē·təɹ). Also 6–7 **spectatour.** [a. L. *spectātor*, agent-noun f. *spectāre* to look, whence also F. *spectateur* (1540), It. *spettatore*, Sp. and Pg. *espectador*.]

1. One who sees, or looks on at, some scene or occurrence; a beholder, onlooker, observer.

a 1586 SIDNEY *Arcadia* II. x. (1912) 211 [He] thought no eyes of sufficient credite in such a matter, but his owne; and therefore came him selfe to be actor, and spectator. *c* 1645 HOWELL *Lett.* (1650) II. 27 There is a true saying, 'That the spectator oft times sees more than the gamester'. 1651 HOBBES *Leviath.* II. xxxi. 189 A signe is not a signe to him that giveth it, but to him to whom it is made; that is, to the spectator. 1677 HUBBARD *Narrative* (1865) I. 16 In such Passages as were variously reported by the Actors, or Spectators, that which seemed most probable is only inserted. 1774 GOLDSM. *Nat. Hist.* (1776) II. 205 Even the agonies of the former rather terrify the spectators, than torment the patient. 1794 MRS. RADCLIFFE *Myst. Udolpho* xxxviii, Henri was a silent and astonished spectator of the scene. 1828 LYTTON *Pelham* xvi, There is some trick afloat to which we may as well be spectators. 1841 JAMES *Brigand* xxxii, The hall was totally void of spectators.

†**b.** *spec.* A scientific observer. *Obs. rare.*

1646 SIR T. BROWNE *Pseud. Ep.* I. iv. (1686) 10 They were conceived by the first Spectators to be but one Animal. 1787 *Families of Plants* I. 259 Jacquin, Brown, and other Spectators consider it as a distinct Genus.

2. *spec.* One who is present at, and has a view or sight of, anything in the nature of a show or spectacle.

1590 SPENSER *F. Q.* II. iv. 27 The treachour..Me leading, in a secret corner layd, The sad spectatour of my Tragedie. 1611 SHAKS. *Wint. T.* IV. i. 20 Imagine me (Gentle Spectators) that I now may be In faire Bohemia. 1690 T. BURNET *Theory Earth* II. 214 This being the last act and close of all humane affairs, it ought to..satisfie the spectators, and end in a general applause. 1716 LADY M. W. MONTAGU *Let. C'tess Mar* 14 Sept., All the men of quality at Vienna were spectators. 1784 COWPER *Task* V. 878 Gods.. that sit Amus'd spectators of this bustling stage. 1814 JANE AUSTEN *Mansf. Park* (1851) 103 Fanny began to be their only audience, and sometimes as prompter, sometimes as spectator, was often very useful. 1855 KINGSLEY *Westw. Ho!* xxvi, He had been a pitying spectator of the tragedy. 1897 'SARAH TYTLER' *Lady Jean's Son* x. 178 The opposite houses, crowded from top to bottom with spectators.

attrib. 1639 COKAINE *Masque* Dram. Wks. (1874) 13 When they have danced all they intended, the Lar, or one of the Masquers, invites the spectator-ladies with this song to join with them. 1891 *Daily News* 12 Oct. 3/5 The spectator portion of the baths was crowded to its utmost capacity.

3. Used as the title of various periodical publications. Also *Comb.*

Freq. with distinguishing epithets, as *The Catholic, Country, Modern, Monthly, Provincial, Temperance Spectator* (published at various dates between 1792 and 1866).

1711-14 ADDISON (*title*), The Spectator. 1711 STEELE *Spect.* No. 20 ¶ 2 Ever since the *Spectator* appear'd. 1714 ADDISON *Ibid.* No. 567 ¶ 8, I intend shortly to publish a *Spectator*, that shall not have a single Vowel in it. 1728-37 (*title*), The Universal Spectator, and Weekly Journal. 1744 ELIZA HEYWOOD *Female Spectator* I. 5 Whatever Productions I shall be favour'd with from these Ladies..will be exhibited under the general Title of *The Female Spectator*. 1755 H. WALPOLE *Lett.* (1846) III. 178 The Spectator-hacked phrases. 1828- (*title*), The Spectator. A weekly journal of news, politics, literature, and science.

Hence **Specta·tordom,** spectators collectively; **Specta·torism,** the practice of being a spectator or onlooker at sports or games.

1854 THOREAU *Walden* i. (1863) 49 He was there to represent spectatordom. 1889 *Wykehamist* No. 241. 317/1 There are distinct limits to the use of 'spectatorism'.

Spectatorial (spektătō·riăl), *a.* [f. prec.]

1. Pertaining or appropriate to, characteristic of, a spectator.

In earlier examples with reference to SPECTATOR 3.

1712 STEELE *Spect.* No. 336 ¶ 1, I hope your Spectatorial Authority will give a seasonable Check to the Spread of the Infection. *Ibid.* No. 430 ¶ 1 All which is submitted to your Spectatorial Vigilance. 1744 ELIZA HEYWOOD *Female Spectator* v. (1748) I. 257 In fine, my spectatorial capacity will permit me to approve of no other entertainments which are paid for. 1889 *Macm. Mag.* May 40 He..stood in a spectatorial attitude, watching the world through wicked humorous eyes.

2. Forming part of a spectacle.

1783 COLMAN *Prose Sev. Occas.* (1787) III. 73 To introduce a groupe of Spectatorial actors speaking in one part of the Drama and singing in another.

3. Having the characteristics of one or other of the periodicals bearing the title of *Spectator*.

1817 WHEWELL in Todhunter *Acc. Writ.* (1876) II. 21 A magazine or periodical collection of essays upon all subjects, scientific, literary, spectatorial, or any other. 1834 SOUTHEY *Doctor* lxiii. (1848) 134 A painter might describe the facial angle,..and whether the chin was in the just mean between rueful length and spectatorial brevity. 1891 *Pall Mall G.* 4 Mar. 2/2 Disposing of it in one of those airy generalizations which Spectatorial omniscience is wont to throw off from time to time.

Spectatorship (spektē·təɹʃip). [f. as prec.]

†**1.** Presentation to the eyes of spectators. *Obs.*

1607 SHAKS. *Cor.* V. ii. 71 If thou stand'st not i'th state of hanging, or of some death more long in Spectatorship.

2. The state of being a spectator or beholder; the fact of (merely) looking on.

1712 STEELE *Spect.* No. 304 ¶ 3 Moreover, your first rudimental Essays in Spectatorship were made in your Petitioner's Shop, where you often practised for Hours. 1854 MRS. OLIPHANT *M. Hepburn* III. 248 He stood.. looking forth, if not with the exulting delight of his former spectatorship, at least with..curiosity. 1881 H. JAMES *Portrait of Lady* xv, What is the use of being..restricted to mere spectatorship at the game of life? 1896 *Eng. Churchm.* 5 Nov. 745/1 England's part in such an event could not..be one of mere spectatorship.

3. Spectators collectively.

a 1836 CHALMERS *Moral Philos.* vii. Wks. V. 301 It..will be followed up by the instant and obstreperous glee of a whole host of spectatorship.

Spectatory (spektē·təri). [f. SPECTATOR: see -ORY.]

1. A body of spectators.

1831 *Blackw. Mag.* XXIX. 887 They anticipated or rather turned the tables on the audience or spectatory.

2. The part of a building intended for, or assigned to, spectators.

1836 G. CLARKE *Pompeii* I. 286 Galleries gave access to the spectatory at different elevations. 1837 *Penny Cycl.* IX. 3/2 The spectatory or saloon for the visitors is a rotunda 40 feet in diameter.

Spectatress (spektē·três). [f. SPECTATOR: see -ESS[1] and cf. next.] A female spectator.

1632 J. HAYWARD tr. *Biondi's Eromena* 101 The Princesse that stood all this while an amazed spectatresse [etc.]. 1703 ROWE *Fair Penit.* V. i, See where she stands! Spectatress of the Mischief which she made. 1759 JOHNSON *Idler* No. 42 ¶ 5 To be a daily spectatress of his vices. 1799 CAMPBELL *Pleas. Hope* I. 179 She, sad spectatress,.. Watch'd the rude surge his shroudless corse that bore. 1844 *For. Q. Rev.* XXXIII. 440 As soon as she appeared the other spectatresses were eclipsed. 1861 *Sat. Rev.* 21 Dec. 648 Was the Grand Duchess a spectatress of the atrocity?

fig. 1789 E. DARWIN *Bot. Gard.* I. 149 So should young Sympathy, in female form, Climb the tall rock, spectatress of the storm. 1791 COWPER *Iliad* XI. 89 Discord, spectatress terrible. 1836 THIRLWALL *Greece* III. xix. 92 As she had been a quiet spectatrix of the fall of Samos.

Spectatrix (spektē·triks). [a. L. *spectātrix*, fem. of *spectātor*. Cf. F. *spectatrice*, It. *spettatrice*.] = SPECTATRESS.

1611 COTGR., *Spectatrice*, a spectatrix. 1615 W. HULL *Mirr. Maiestie* 88 She (good soule) stood by the crosse as a dolefull spectatrix of that wofull Tragedy. 1651 HOWELL *Venice* 4 She [Venice] hath allwayes..chosen rather to be a Spectatrix or Umpresse, than a Gamestresse. *c* 1710 CELIA FIENNES *Diary* (1888) 15 The discription of the Coronation ..which I received the relation off from a spectatrix. 1781 EARL MALMESBURY *Diaries & Corr.* I. 390 The Dutch Ambassadors..are leaving nothing untried to prevent Her Imperial Majesty from remaining spectatrix of their quarrel. 1860 MRS. A. CLIVE *Why P. Ferrall* x, She had been spectatrix of the same scene at a play. 1866 J. B. ROSE tr. *Ovid's Met.* 264 Spectatrix of this cruel fate was I.

†**Spe·ctible,** *a. Obs.*[−1] [f. L. *spect-*, ppl. stem of *specĕre* to look.] Visible.

1581 J. BELL *Haddon's Answ. Osor.* 207 Hee added moreover Statutes and Lawes, not onely emprinted within every ones hart, but engraven also outwardly in spectible Tables.

Spectioneer, variant of SPECKSIONEER.

Spectra, pl. of SPECTRUM.

†**Spe·ctral,** *sb. Obs. rare.* [Cf. next.] An apparition; a spectre.

a 1656 USSHER *Ann.* (1658) Ep. to Rdr., Those things which I produce concerning Preesages, Spectrales, and Oracles. *Ibid.* 705 He expounded to him out of the doctrine of the Epicureans, what was to be thought concerning such spectrals.

Spectral (spe·ktrăl), *a.* [ad. L. type *spectrālis, f. *spectrum* SPECTRE and SPECTRUM. So mod.F. *spectral*.]

†**1.** Capable of seeing spectres. *Obs.*

1718 BP. HUTCHINSON *Witchcraft* v. 81 Joseph Ballard.. sent to Salem, for some of these Accusers, who pretended to have the spectral Sight, to tell him who afflicted his Wife.

2. Having the character of a spectre or phantom; ghostly, unsubstantial, unreal.

1815 SHELLEY *Alastor* 259 The mountaineer, Encountering on some dizzy precipice That spectral form. 1818 SCOTT *Br. Lamm.* xiii, Some of the spectral appearances which he had heard told of in a winter's evening. 1853 KANE *Grinnell Exp.* xxxiv. (1856) 307 The setting sun..gave us again the spectral land about Cape Adair, eighty miles off. 1877 BLACK *Green Past.* xlii, We saw through a window a wild vision of a pair of spectral horses apparently in mid-air.

fig. 1829 I. TAYLOR *Enthus.* viii. 191 A spectral resemblance of piety, unsubstantial and cold as the mists of night. 1837 DICKENS *Pickw.* xxiv, A spectral attempt at drollery.

Comb. 1840 MRS. S. C. HALL *Irish Peasantry* (1850) 138 A lean, spectral-looking gray horse..limped towards them. 1868 BOYD *Less. Middle Age* 315 A mile or two down,..tall and spectral-white, stands the Cloch lighthouse.

b. Resembling, looking like, suggestive of, a spectre or spectres. Also *spec.* in *Zool.*

1828 LYTTON *Pelham* xviii, The spectral secretary of the embassy. 1843 BETHUNE *Sc. Fireside Stor.* 110 That species of erect tombstone, which some one has somewhere designated 'spectral'. 1851 RUSKIN *Stones Ven.* (1874) I. App. 366 The old spectral Lombard friezes. 1884 COUES *N. Amer. Birds* 509 *Strix cinerea*...Spectral Owl. 1896 H. O. FORBES *Hand-bk. Primates* I. 20 The Spectral Tarsier.

3. Characteristic of, appropriate to, a spectre.

1820 BYRON *Mar. Fal.* V. ii, They form'd a spectral voice, Which shook me in a supernatural dream. 1852 MRS. JAMESON *Leg. Madonna* Introd. (1857) 25 Compared with the spectral rigidity, the hard monotony, of the conventional Byzantines. 1898 WATTS-DUNTON *Aylwin* I. vi, Crumbling cliffs, whose jagged points..had the kind of spectral look peculiar to that coast.

4. Produced merely by the action of light on the eye or on a sensitive medium.

1839 G. BIRD *Nat. Phil.* 398 If the wafer were yellow, and placed on a black surface, the spectral image will be deep violet when viewed on a white ground; in the same manner a white wafer is attended by its black spectral figure.

5. a. Of or pertaining to, appearing or observed in, the spectrum.

1832 *Nat. Philos.* (L. U. K.) II. Index 40 Spectral colours, when re-united, produce white. 1849 MRS. SOMERVILLE *Connex. Phys. Sci.* (ed. 8) xxiv. 235 A spectral image obtained by Mr. Hunt on a similar [Daguerreotype] plate. 1866 ATKINSON tr. *Ganot's Physics* (ed. 2) § 480. 424 The relative distances of the different spectral lines. 1879 ROOD *Mod. Chromatics* x. 127 By mixing three or more spectral colours no new hues were produced. 1883 *19th Cent.* Nov. 861 Its absorptive capacity for particular spectral tints.

b. Carried out or performed by means of the spectrum. Freq. in *spectral analysis*.

1862 *Amer. Jrnl. Sci.* Nov. 404 There are few branches of science which promise more magnificent results than the spectral analysis. 1879 PROCTOR *Pleas. Ways Sci.* I. 26 The inquiry seems specially suited to the methods of spectral photography pursued by Dr. Draper. 1881 *Times* 11 Mar., Spectral observations on stars.

Hence **Spe·ctralism,** a spectral or ghostly scene. **Spectra·lity,** a phantasm; ghostliness. **Spe·ctrally** *adv.*, in a ghostly manner. **Spe·ctralness,** the quality or character of being spectral.

1851 CARLYLE in *New Rev.* (1891) Oct. 299 All dreamlike, one *spectralism succeeding another. 1850 — *Latter-d. Pamph.* i. 50 Traditions now really about extinct;..still haunting with their *spectralities..almost all of us! 1880 *Scribner's Mag.* July 326 There is about it a certain vagueness and spectrality. 1837 CARLYLE *Fr. Rev.* II. II. vi, This ..did for many months..walk *spectrally,—in all French heads. 1865 DICKENS *Mut. Fr.* III. ii, The steamer's lights moved spectrally a very little. 1892 W. W. PEYTON *Memorab. Jesus* x. 235 A *spectralness, which..gives you an idea of weirdness.

Spectre (spe·ktəɹ), *sb.* Also 7–8 **specter.** [a. F. *spectre* (16th cent., = It. *spettro*, Sp. and Pg. *espectro*), or ad. L. *spectrum*, f. *specĕre* to look, see.]

1. An apparition, phantom, or ghost, esp. one of a terrifying nature or aspect.

1605 Z. JONES (*title*), A Treatise of Specters or straunge Sights, Visions and Apparitions appearing sensibly unto men. 1641 *Lords Spiritual* 15 Thus this great Goliah being handled, appeareth..rather a ghost and specter, then a body. 1703 POPE *Thebais* 133 Swift as she pass'd, the flitting ghosts withdrew, And the pale spectres trembled at her view. 1744 HARRIS *Three Treat.* Wks. (1841) 40 The superstitious have not a more previous tendency to be frightened at the sight of spectres,..than [etc.]. 1813 SCOTT *Trierm.* II. Interlude i, How should I, so humbly born, Endure the graceful spectre's scorn? 1862 *Macm. Mag.* Apr. 507 The simple..explanation of spectres is that they are our own thoughts. 1871 PALGRAVE *Lyr. Poems* 37 A terror..As when a sudden spectre at mid-day Meets us.

b. *fig.* An unreal object of thought; a phantasm of the brain.

1711 SHAFTESB. *Charac.* (1737) I. 53 When the mind is taken up in vision, and fixes its view either on any real object, or mere specter of divinity.

c. *fig.* An object or source of dread or terror, imagined as an apparition.

1774 GOLDSM. *Nat. Hist.* (1776) II. 206 Death..is a spectre which frights us at a distance. 1837 CARLYLE *Fr. Rev.* I. I. iv, That same cloud-capt, fire-breathing Spectre of Democracy. 1856 KINGSLEY *Lett.* (1878) I. 500 The glaring eye of the dark spectre of bereavement. 1893 *Black & White* 29 July 122/2 The Channel Tunnel spectre is laid.

d. *transf.* One whose appearance is suggestive of an apparition or ghost.

1807-8 W. IRVING *Salmag.* (1824) 352 [She is] a mere household spectre, neither giving nor receiving enjoyment. 1825 J. NEAL *Bro. Jonathan* I. 361 A creature like you—a spectre— ..to talk about seeking your fortune! 1891 MARIE A. BROWN tr. *Runeberg's Nadeschda* 50 Ever since a spectre From place to place he wanders.

e. A faint shadow or imitation *of* something.

1849 C. BRONTË *Shirley* xxiv, With the strangest spectre of a laugh.

2. One of the images or semblances supposed by the Epicurean school to emanate from corporeal things.

1785 REID *Intell. Powers* 26 The spectres of Epicurus were composed of a very subtle matter. 1834 SOUTHEY *Doctor* v. 11 The old atomists supposed that the likenesses or spectres of corporeal things..assail the soul when she ought to be at rest.

3. An image or phantom produced by reflection or other natural cause.

1801 *Encycl. Brit.* Suppl. II. 514/2 Spectre of the Broken, a curious phenomenon observed on the summit of the Broken. 1832 BREWSTER *Natural Magic* vi. 148 It is only within the last forty years that science has brought these atmospherical spectres within the circle of her dominion. 1860 TYNDALL *Glac.* I. ii. 22 Before each of us..stood a spectral image of a man... We stretched forth our arms; the spectres did the same. 1908 [MISS FOWLER] *Betw. Trent & Ancholme* 299, I must look again for this aerial and charming spectre.

4. *Zool.* One or other of the insects or animals distinguished by the epithet *spectre-* (see 7), esp. an insect of the family *Phasmidae*.

1797 *Trans. Linn. Soc.* IV. 190 This singular animal [sc. *Phasma dilatatum*]..belongs to that tribe of insects which Stoll has called by the title of Spectres. 1815 KIRBY & SP. *Entomol.* iii. (1818) I. 67 *note*, Orthoptera consisting of Cockroaches, Locusts,..Spectres, Mantes, &c. 1816 *Ibid.* xxiii. (1818) II. 328 The spectres..are distinguished by tarsi of five joints. 1880 *Encycl. Brit.* XIII. 152/2 *Phasmidæ* (Spectres, or Walking-Sticks).

†**5.** A horrid spectacle or sight. *Obs.*[−1]

a 1763 SHENSTONE *Elegies* xxii. 68 To see my limbs..gash'd beneath the daring steel, To crowds a spectre, and to dogs a prey!

6. a. *attrib.* (chiefly in sense 1), as *spectre-bark, -chimera, -doubt, -fashion, -horse*, etc.

1817 COLERIDGE *Anc. Mar.* III. xiii, Off shot the *spectre-bark. 1837 CARLYLE *Fr. Rev.* III. VI. i, Through some section of History, Nineteen *spectre-chimeras shall flit,.. till Oblivion swallow them. 1799 CAMPBELL *Pleas. Hope* II. 263 Ye *spectre-doubts, that roll Cimmerian darkness on the parting soul! 1822 SCOTT *Nigel* x, It were a shame to my household, thou shouldst glide out into the Strand after such a *spectre-fashion. ? 186. B. HARTE *Friar Pedro's Ride* in *Fiddletown*, etc. (1873) 112 A phantom friar, on a *spectre horse. 1805 SCOTT *Last Minstrel* VI. xxvi. Like him..Who spoke the *spectre-hound in Man. *c* 1820 S. ROGERS *Italy* (1839) 118 He had so oft beheld..The *spectre-knight. 1825 J. WILSON *Poems* II. 305 While stern beneath the chancel high, My country's *spectre monarch stood. 1777 WARTON *Poems* 61 We bid those *spectre-shapes avaunt. 1798 COLERIDGE *Anc. Mar.* III. xiv, Off darts the *Spectre-ship. 1807 BYRON *Childish Recoll.* 7 What grisly forms, the *spectre-train of woe, Bid shuddering Nature shrink beneath the blow. 1816 KIRBY & SP. *Entomol.* xxi. (1818) II. 220 The *Spectre tribe..go still further in this mimicry. 1817 COLERIDGE *Anc. Mar.* III. x. *marg. note*, The *Spectre-Woman and her Death-mate.

b. *Comb.*, chiefly in similative adjs., as *spectre-lean, -like* (also adv.), *-looking, -pallid, -staring, -thin*; also *spectre-haunted, -mongering* (adjs.), *-queller*.

1831 CARLYLE *Sart. Res.* II. viii, At worst as a *spectre-fighting Man, nay who will one day be a Spectre-queller. 1718 ROWE tr. *Lucan* 303 No Swain thy *Spectre-haunted Plain shou'd know. 1873 E. BRENNAN *Witch Nemi*, etc. 78 That dark land and spectre-haunted grove. 1887 MEREDITH *Ballads & P.* 85 He came out of miracle cloud, Lightning-swift and *spectre-lean. 1719 DE FOE *Crusoe* I. (Globe) 258 Not making quite so staring a *Spectre-like Figure as I did. 1834 *Tait's Mag.* I. 726/1 Spectre-like they stray, And soon their steps in distance die away. 1884 J. COLBORNE *Hicks Pasha* 41 The camels glided noiselessly and spectre-like over the track. 1849-50 ALISON *Hist. Europe*

VIII. lv. § 24. 580 With a few thousand miserable and *spectre-looking followers. 1809 BYRON *Bards & Rev.* 919 Let *spectre-mongering Lewis aim..To rouse the galleries. 1844 HOOD *Haunted House* III. ix, But from their tarnish'd frames dark Figures gaz'd, And Faces *spectre-pallid. 1831 *Spectre-queller [see *spectre-fighting* above]. 1826 MILMAN *A. Boleyn* (1827) 72 Thy tossing, feverish, *spectre-staring midnights. 1820 KEATS *Ode to Nightingale* 26 Where youth grows pale, and *spectre-thin, and dies.

7. Special combs.: **spectre-bat,** a tropical species of bat (*Vespertilio* or *Phyllostoma spectrum*); **spectre-candle** (see quot.); **spectre-crab,** a glass-crab (*Cent. Dict.*); **spectre insect,** an insect of the genus *Phasma* (see 4); **spectre-lemur,** = *spectre tarsier*; **spectre-mantis,** = *spectre insect*; **spectre-shell** (see quot.); **spectre-shrimp,** a slender-bodied amphipod of the genus *Caprella*; **spectre tarsier,** a small lemuroid animal (*Tarsius spectrum*).

1781 PENNANT *Hist. Quadrup.* II. 552 *Spectre Bat... Inhabits South America. 1827 GRIFFITH tr. *Cuvier* V. 71 *Phyllostoma Spectrum* (Spectre or true Vampyre Bat). 1835 *Penny Cycl.* IV. 172/2 Belemnite, Thunderstone, or Arrowhead...: we..find the term Devil's fingers bestowed on them, and not unfrequently that of *spectre-candles. 1826 KIRBY & SP. *Entomol.* III. 90 The largest egg known..is that of a *spectre insect (*Phasma dilatatum*), figured in the Linnean Transactions. 1886 GEIKIE *Class-Bk. Geol.* 359 Spectre-insects (*Phasmidæ*)..have been detected chiefly among the shales and coals of the Coal-measures. 1882 *Spectre-lemur [see TARSIER]. 1840 F. D. BENNETT *Whaling Voy.* I. 343 The insects we found here were the *spectre-mantis; a purple butterfly [etc.]. 1753 *Chambers' Cycl.* Suppl., *Concha spectrorum*, the *spectre shell, a name given by authors to a species of voluta, from some odd figures described on its surface [etc.]. 1882 *Cassell's Nat. Hist.* VI. 212 The popular name of *Spectre, or Skeleton Shrimp, seems very appropriate. 1871 *Ibid.* I. 250 The *Spectre Tarsier, which inhabits the Oriental Archipelago and the Philippine Islands.

Hence **Spe·ctre** *v. trans.*, to fill with spectres; **Spe·ctredom,** the realm or region of spectres.

1849 AYTOUN *Old Camp* ii, It hath a look that makes me old, and spectres time again. 1883 J. S. STALLYBRASS tr. *Grimm's Teutonic Myth.* III. 930 Part and parcel of this heathenish spectredom. 1897 *Daily Tel.* 20 July 7/3 The tyranny of the manager of spectredom.

Spectred (spe·ktəɹd), *a.* [f. SPECTRE *sb.* 1.] Filled with spectres; converted into a spectre; resembling a spectre.

1791 WOLCOT (P. Pindar) *Lousiad* III. Wks. 1794 I. 269 Amidst the spectred solitude of sleep. 1803 T. G. FESSENDEN *Petit. agst. Tract. Trumpery* 2 'Gainst spectred poverty still striving. 1809 E. S. BARRETT *Setting Sun* I. 69 That specter'd elf, Grim death hath seiz'd our father your viceroy.

†**Spectrene,** *a. Obs.*[−1] [f. as prec.] Spectral.

1652 GAULE *Magastrom.* 355 By malefical incantations there was brought in to him the spectrene apparition of her whom he loved.

Spectrey. *nonce-wd.* [f. SPECTRE *sb.* 1.] A place of spectres.

1822 GALT *Sir A. Wylie* I. xxiii. 207, I believe it is a huge old Ann-Radcliffe place, a spectrey surrounded by a rookery.

†**Spe·ctrical,** *a. Obs.*[−1] [f. as prec.] Spectral. Hence †**Spe·ctrically** *adv. Obs.*

1609 SIR E. HOBY *Let. to T. H[iggons]* 85 Then are you cruell comforters, who..do terrifie the departing soule of him..with such spectricall delusions. 1615 *Curry Combe for a Coxe-Combe* iii. 121 Such is the exposition of the place so spectrically raysed, and so dubitatiuely propounded by the Interpreters themselues.

Spe·ctrish, *a. rare*[−1]. [f. SPECTRE *sb.* + -ISH.] Somewhat spectral or ghostly.

1822 GALT *Sir A. Wylie* I. xx. 170, I am indeed not surprised that you should be somewhat disconcerted, for I believe that I am a little spectrish.

Spectro- (spe·ktro), combining form (on Greek analogies) of SPECTRUM, chiefly employed in a number of recent terms, as **Spectrohe·liograph, -heliogra·phic** *a.*, **-microsco·pical** *a.*, **-phone, -pho·nic** *a.*, **-photo·meter, -photome·tric** *a.*, **-photome·trically, -pyro·meter, -te·lescope.**

Others are *spectrobolograph, -bolographic* adj., *-bolometer, -bolometric* adj., *-chemistry, -colorimetry, -comparator, -photograph(y, -polarigraph, -polarimeter, -polariscope*, etc.

1892 *Athenæum* 16 July 102/1 An instrument called the 'spectroheliograph.., by means of which..photographs are now made of all the prominences visible round the entire circumference of the sun with a single exposure. 1907 *Ibid.* 6 Apr. 415/3 Dr. Lockyer showed spectroheliographs of the sun. 1905 *Ibid.* 29 Apr. 535/2 *Spectroheliographic Results explained by Anomalous Dispersion. 1885 tr. *Behrens' Micros. in Bot.* V. 139 The *spectro-microscopical apparatus..has become an important instrument in the investigation of the coloring matter of plants. 1881 A. G. BELL *Sound by Radiant Energy* 41 These substances are put in communication with the ear by means of a hearing-tube, and thus the instrument is converted into a veritable *spectrophone. *Ibid.*, Suppose we smoke the interior of our *spectrophonic receiver. 1881 *Nature* XXIV. 552 Photometric comparison of luminous sources of different colours, by M. Crova. He uses a *spectrophotometer. 1884 *Boston* (Mass.) *Jrnl.* 13 Sept., A *spectrophotometric study of pigments', by Professor Nicolls. 1897 *Allbutt's Syst. Med.* IV. 285 Normal fresh urines..examined *spectro-photometrically. 1881 *Nature* XXIII. 524 The *spectropyrometer is proved practically useful. 1880 *Athenæum* 25 Sept. 405/1 A *spectro-telescope,..the purpose of which is to enable the observer to survey large portions of the sun's disc at once in homogeneous light.

Spe·ctrogram. [f. prec. + -GRAM.] A photograph of a spectrum.

1892 *Pall Mall G.* 17 Feb. 7/2 The spectrograms of the star show two spectra, one above the other. 1900 *Edinb. Rev.* Apr. 474 There must be a suspension of judgement in the matter until spectrograms of nebular nuclei can be produced in evidence.

Spe·ctrograph. [f. as prec. + -GRAPH.]

1. An instrument used for photographing a spectrum.

1884 YOUNG in *Proc. Amer. Acad. Arts & Sci.* 238 In July, 1876, several photographs of the spectrum of Vega were taken with an apparatus which Dr. Draper called the spectrograph. 1889 *Anthony's Photogr. Bull.* II. 394 The color sensitiveness of the plate I find out with the aid of my Quartz spectrograph. 1893 *Nation* 16 Feb. 126/2 With the eleven-inch Draper spectrograph nearly a thousand photographs were taken.

2. = SPECTROGRAM.

1891 *Pall Mall G.* 26 Sept. 4/2 A few spectrographs of pure and impure blood. 1898 *Edinb. Rev.* Apr. 306 Rich harvests of photographs and spectrographs were garnered.

Hence **Spectrogra·phic** *a.*, relating to a spectrograph or the observations made with it; **Spectrogra·phically** *adv.*, in a spectrographic manner; **Spectro·graphy,** the art of using the spectrograph.

1884 *Science* III. 727/1 Spectrographic operations are.. much more sensitive to atmospheric conditions than are visual observations. 1900 *Edinb. Rev.* Apr. 458 'Spectrography' is the complement of spectroscopy. *Ibid.* 460 The spectrographic impression of a hydrogen star. *Ibid.* 474 Having spectrographically surveyed the entire heaven. 1903 AGNES CLERKE *Probl. Astrophys.* 3 Spectroscopic photography, or 'spectrography' dates from Sir William Huggins's adoption of the dry gelatine process in 1876.

Spectrolo·gical, *a.* [See next and -LOGICAL.]

1. Pertaining to spectres or apparitions.

1802 *Ann. Reg., Chron.* 387/1 This man stated that he had lately arrived from the Continent and intended to exhibit before the public his deceptions in the spectrological art.

2. 'Of or pertaining to spectrology; performed or determined by spectrology; as, spectrological analysis' (1882 *Imp. Dict.*).

Spectro·logy. *rare.* [f. SPECTRO- (in senses 1 and 3 of SPECTRUM) + -LOGY.]

1. The science or study of spectres.

1820 W. IRVING *Sketch Bk.* (1821) II. 196 The gloom of religious abstraction, and the wildness of their situation,.. had filled their imaginations with the frightful chimeras of witchcraft and spectrology. 1827 HONE *Table Bk.* I. 710 Spectrology. A Remarkable Narrative.

2. The scientific study of spectra.

1862 *Amer. Jrnl. Sci.* May 440 The attention of the French scientific world is wholly fixed on *spectrology*, for thus do they designate the experiment with the spectroscope of Bunsen and Kirchhof. [Hence in Webster (1864), etc.]

Spectro·meter. [ad. G. *spektrometer* or F. *spectromètre*.] An instrument used for measuring the index of refraction.

1874 tr. *Lommel's Light* 144 The determination of the index of refraction can be much more conveniently effected by means of Meyerstein's Spectrometer. 1878 *Smithsonian Rep.* 431 The spectrometer stands upon a plate of metal which can be made to revolve so that measurements by repetitions are practicable. 1883 *Knowledge* 18 May 297/1 Professor Clifton of Oxford has brought out a new spectrometer.

Hence **Spectrome·tric** *a.*; also **Spectro·metry** (1902 *Webster's Suppl.*).

Cf. F. *spectrométrique, -métrie* (Littré).

1891 *Cent. Dict.*, Spectrometric. 1903 AGNES CLERKE *Probl. Astrophys.* 8 The 'spectrometric' division of photometry consists in the comparative estimation of ray-intensities.

Spectroscope (spe·ktrŏskōʊp), *sb.* [ad. G. *spektroskop* or a. F. *spectroscope*.] An instrument specially designed for the production and examination of spectra.

1861 *Proc. Amer. Philos. Soc.* VIII. 279 The results obtained by the spectroscope. 1869 ROSCOE *Chem.* 153 The blowpipe flame..exhibits a characteristic series of bands when examined by means of the spectroscope. 1880 HAUGHTON *Phys. Geogr.* i. 6 By means of the spectroscope, it has been ascertained that the terrestrial elements, found in meteoric stones, may be found also in the sun.

Hence **Spe·ctroscope** *v. trans.*, to examine by means of a spectroscope.

1881 *Standard* 30 Dec. 5/2 It was photographed and spectroscoped. 1886 PIAZZI SMYTH in *Trans. Roy. Soc. Edin.* XXXII. 521 Hence a solar spectroscoping..might be expected to have some further special interest connected with our own earth.

Spectroscopic (spektrŏskǫ·pik), *a.* [f. prec. or ad. F. *spectroscopique*.]

1. Performed by means of the spectroscope.

1864 *Athenæum* No. 1929. 500/2 The spectroscopic examinations. 1870 PROCTOR *Other Worlds* ii. 38 So many of the wonders of modern science are associated with spectroscopic analysis. 1878 NEWCOMB *Pop. Astron.* III. ii. 257 Devoting special attention to the spectroscopic observations. 1883 *Science* I. 115/1 The results of spectroscopic work.

2. Presented or afforded by, pertaining or belonging to, the spectroscope.

1869 *Eng. Mech.* 31 Dec. 375/1 Data..with respect to the spectroscopic appearances of comets. 1879 PROCTOR *Pleas. Ways Sci.* i. 7 In some cases, the quantity of a material to give unmistakable spectroscopic evidence is singularly small. 1884 KNIGHT *Dict. Mech.* Suppl. 835/2 *Spectroscopic Eye-piece*,..an adaptation of the spectroscope to the microscope for the examination of minute substances.

3. Occupied or dealing with spectroscopy.

1871 tr. *Schellen's Spectrum Anal.* Pref. 4, I regret that the author has reversed the practice of the principal spectroscopic authors. 1871 *Daily News* 12 Jan., It is true the spectroscopic party..at Oran failed totally.

So **Spectrosco·pical** *a.*

1870 *Eng. Mech.* 11 Feb. 520/2 The nature of the solar atmosphere is ascertained by spectroscopical examinations of the light of the sun. 1882 *Athenæum* 4 Mar. 286/2 An interesting series of spectroscopical observations.

Spectrosco·pically, *adv.* [f. prec.] By means of the spectroscope; in respect of spectroscopic qualities, etc.

1871 tr. *Schellen's Spectrum Anal.* 16 *note*, When the light of burning magnesium is observed spectroscopically. 1879 PROCTOR *Pleas. Ways Sci.* v. 125 The part of the remaining light spectroscopically most effective. 1903 *Times* 25 Mar. 10/4 Radium..remains spectroscopically identical after many months of continuous emission of heat.

Spectroscopist (spektrǫ·skǒpist, spe·ktrǒskoᵘpist). [f. SPECTROSCOPE *sb.* + -IST.] One who pursues researches with the spectroscope.

1866 *Athenæum* 3 Mar. 304/3 The following will perhaps interest spectroscopists. 1879 PROCTOR *Pleas. Ways Sci.* i. 8 [It] would not affect those rays sufficiently for the spectroscopist to recognize any diminution of their lustre. 1893 SIR R. BALL *Story of Sun* 195 The phenomenon known to spectroscopists as the reversal of the dark lines.

Spectroscopy (spektrǫ·skǒpi, spe·ktrǒskoᵘpi). [f. as prec., after forms in *-scopy*, or ad. F. *spectroscopie.*] The art of using the spectroscope; that branch of science which involves the use of the spectroscope.

1870 W. HUGGINS *Manchester Lect.* 36 This was the state of this newly-born science of Spectroscopy when in 1861 [etc.]. 1881 M. L. KNAPP *Coming Disasters* 17 The progress made within the last few years in spectroscopy.

Spectrous (spe·ktrǝs), *a.* [f. SPECTRE *sb.* 1.] Spectral.

1652 GAULE *Magastrom.* 213 We see that men are really affected and terrified even from spectrous and ludibrious phantasmes. *Ibid.* 298 [He] was haunted mightily with a spectrous apparition of a beautiful woman. 1678 CUDWORTH *Intell. Syst.* I. ii. § 2. 61 They could have been nothing else but a certain kind of Aerial and Spectrous Men. 1809 W. BLAKE *Descr. Catal.* 22 The Plowman of Chaucer is Hercules in his supreme eternal state, divested of his spectrous shadow. 1858 SWINBURNE *Blake* 282 These, with all their flock of emanations and spectrous or vegetating shadows, let us leave to the discretion of Los.

Spectrum (spe·ktrǒm). Pl. **spectra** (also **spectrums**). [L. *spectrum*: see SPECTRE *sb.*]

1. An apparition or phantom; a spectre.

1611 SPEED *Hist. Gt. Brit.* IX. xiv. (1632) 770 Walsingham hath written of a fatall Spectrum or Apparition,..where sundry monsters of diuers colours..were seen. 1649 BULWER *Pathomyot.* II. ii. 140 Feare also, and a Sudden fright or Spectrum..hath the same effect sometimes upon the Muscles of the Face. 1684 *Case of Cross in Baptism* 14 Startled at Thunder, taken in a storm, frighted with a spectrum. 1706 BAYNARD *Cold Baths* II. 309 He would sooner believe Witch-Craft and Spectrums. 1728 *Brice's Weekly Jrnl.* 19 July 1 The Maid's seeing his Spectrum, could be no..*Deceptio Visus*, but..was a real Apparition of the Deceased. 1809 W. IRVING *Hist. New York* (1861) 182 Subject to bad dreams..in the night, when the grizzly spectrum of old Keldermeester would stand sentinel by his bedside. 1860 RUSKIN *Mod. Paint.* V. IX. xi. 326 *note*, Fuseli may wander wildly among gray spectra, but Reynolds and Gainsborough must stay in broad daylight, with pure humanity.

fig. 1657 H. PINNELL *Philos. Ref.* 67 The Spectrum, ghost, or fantasie, the Light of Nature. 1674 GREW *Anat. Pl., Disc. Mixture* (1684) 222 Their notions of Mixture..being ..so many phantastick Spectrums, serving only to affright men from coming near them. 1710 SACHEVERELL *Answ. Bp. Oxford's Sp.* 21, I was..surpriz'd..with an Apparition or Spectrum, which the Magi call a Parenthesis. 1866 HUXLEY *Physiol.* x. 247 Many persons are liable to what may be called *auditory spectra*—music of various degrees of complexity sounding in their ears, without any external cause, while they are wide awake.

2. An image or semblance. *rare.*

1693 PENN *Fruits Solitude* II. § 197 A jealous man only sees his own spectrum, when he looks upon other men, and gives his character in theirs. 1831 CARLYLE *Sart. Res.* II. viii, Two little visual Spectra of men, hovering..in the midst of the Unfathomable.

3. The coloured band into which a beam of light is decomposed by means of a prism or diffraction grating.

1671 NEWTON in *Phil. Trans.* VI. 3076 Comparing the length of this coloured Spectrum with its breadth, I found it about five times greater. 1674 *Ibid.* IX. 218 The Sunbeams..passing through a Glass Prism to the opposite Wall, exhibited there a Spectrum of divers colours. 1728 PEMBERTON *Newton's Philos.* 323 These colours shall discover themselves more perfectly..the larger the spectrum is. 1788 V. KNOX *Winter Even.* I. iii. 27 All the hues of the prismatic spectrum. 1815 J. SMITH *Panorama Sci. & Art* I. 440 It assumes an oblong shape,..and exhibits seven different colours. This oblong image is called the spectrum, and from its being produced by the prism, the prismatic spectrum. 1839 G. BIRD *Nat. Philos.* 326 The solar spectrum may therefore be regarded as composed of three spectra of equal lengths overlapping each other. 1879 *Cassell's Techn. Educ.* I. 126/1 Most of our sources of artificial light yield spectra without lines.

fig. 1860 HOLLAND *Miss Gilbert's Career* iv. 68 All the colors of the spectrum of truth. 1874 H. R. REYNOLDS *John Bapt.* viii. 453 A luminous spectrum lingers for a while in the atmosphere of Judaism.

4. The image retained for a time on the retina of the eye when turned away after gazing fixedly for some time at a bright coloured object.

1786 *Phil. Trans.* LXXVI. 313 This appearance in the eye we shall call the ocular spectrum of that object. 1829 *Nat. Philos., Optics* xvii. 46 (L.U.K.), One of the most curious affections of the eye, is that in virtue of which it sees what are called ocular spectra, or accidental colours.

1839 G. BIRD *Nat. Philos.* 398 Thus wafers, or other coloured objects, produce spectra of colours complementary to their own. 1854 *Lardner's Mus. Sci. & Art* I. 85 Unreal objects will often be perceived. These are called spectra. *Ibid.*, This object is an optical spectrum.

5. *Ent.* A spectre-insect (*Phasma*).

1838 *Murray's N. Germany* 34 The minerals and insects are also good; among the latter are various specimens of spectrum, nearly a foot long.

6. *attrib.* (in sense 3): **a.** *Spectrum analysis* (cf. SPECTRAL *a.* 5 b). Also *fig.*

1866 ATKINSON tr. *Ganot's Physics* 425 The method of spectrum-analysis is most readily applied to the alkaline metals. 1871 tr. *Schellen's Spectrum Anal.* Pref. 4 The great merit of the book as a popular treatise on Spectrum Analysis. 1873 FARRAR *Famil. Speech* ii. 39 The microscope and spectrum analysis of Philology.

b. Misc., as *spectrum-band, -line, microscope, photography, work.*

1871 tr. *Schellen's Spectrum Anal.* 101 The number of the spectrum-lines of a substance. *Ibid.* 456 Qualitative Analysis ..by means of the spectrum microscope. 1889 *Anthony's Photogr. Bull.* II. 389 The bath plate is less suitable for spectrum photography. 1891 *Ibid.* IV. 357 The yet hardly visible spectrum band. 1899 LOCKYER in *Daily News* 13 Nov. 6/7 For this spectrum work very rapid isochromatic plates..should be employed.

Spe·ctry, *a. rare.* [f. SPECTRE *sb.* 1.] Spectral.

1796 TOWNSHEND *Poems* 69 When the cowl'd monk.. Fleets o'er the seat of long past crimes; And spectry forms of cloister'd maids In sorrow bow their pensive heads.

†**Spe·culable,** *a. Obs. rare.* [ad. L. *speculābilis*, f. *speculārī* to SPECULATE. Cf. It. *speculabile.*] **a.** That admits of speculation; speculative. **b.** = SPECULAR *a.* 3.

c 1449 PECOCK *Repr.* II. i. 134 Ech treuthe knowun in mannis vnderstonding is a treuthe considerable or speculable or biholdable oonli. 1592 R. D. *Hypnerotomachia* 68 b, Beeing come to the fift mount they finde it speculable, lyke a mirrour.

Specular (spe·kiŭlǟɹ), *a.* [ad. L. *speculāris*, f. *speculum* SPECULUM; or, in senses 6 and 7, f. L. *speculārī* to spy, observe, *specula* watch-tower. Cf. F. *spéculaire* (16th c. in Godef. *Compl.*), Prov. *specular*, It. *speculare, specolare*, Sp. and Pg. *especulario.*]

I. 1. *Specular stone* (after L. *specularis lapis*), a transparent or semi-transparent substance formerly used as glass or for ornamental purposes; a species of mica, selenite, or talc; a piece or flake of this. (Cf. PHENGITE.) *Obs.* exc. *arch.*

1577 HARRISON *England* II. xii. (1877) I. 236, I find obscure mention of the specular stone to haue beene found and applied to this use [*sc.* window-making] in England. 1627 DONNE *Serm.* Wks. 1839 IV. 472 In Temples made of Specular Stone that was transparent as glass or crystal. 1677 PLOT *Oxfordsh.* 68 Unless they are particles of the specular stone, or English Talc. 1715 tr. *Pancirollus' Rerum Mem.* I. I. vi. 15 Specular Stones were a shining kind of Substance, and..transparent like the Air. 1889 tr. *Rénan's Apostles* xi. 168 The decoration of a hall which he wanted to have adorned with specular stones.

†**b.** A piece of this used as a mirror. *Obs.*⁻¹

1640 CAREW *Poems* Wks. (1824) 104 Give then no faith to the false specular stone, But let thy beauties by th' effects be knowne.

†2. Of vision: Obtained by reflection only; not direct or immediate. *Obs.*

Based upon 1 *Cor.* xiii. 12, where the Vulgate has *per speculum in ænigmate* and the Greek δι' ἐσόπτρου ἐν αἰνίγματι.

a 1619 FOTHERBY *Atheom.* II. viii. § 5 (1622) 293 Not in a specular, and ænigmaticall vision; but in a cleere, and immediate one. *a* 1677 MANTON *Transfig. Christ* ii. Wks. 1870 I. 349 Not only doth vision or immediate intuition produce this effect, but also spiritual specular vision, or a sight of God in the ordinances. 1704 NORRIS *Ideal World* II. v. 287 St. Paul says..we see through a glass darkly...This has given occasion to the schools to distinguish of a certain ænigmatical or specular vision, in opposition to that vision of God which is by his essence.

3. Having the reflecting property of a mirror; presenting a smooth, polished, and reflecting surface; of a brilliant metallic lustre. Now *Min.*

1661 BOYLE *Scept. Chem.* v. 333 From this red Body..may be obtain'd a Mercury bright and Specular as it was before. 1666 — *Orig. Forms & Qual.* 235 Divers of these Christals have..Triangles..and other Figures exquisitely Cut on their smooth & specular surfaces; and others, Bodies of Prismatical shapes. 1796 *Phil. Trans.* LXXXVI. 273 It is evident that the particles of bodies are specular. 1796 KIRWAN *Elem. Min.* (ed. 2) I. 36 The laminæ. have not a polished, or at least, not a specular surface. 1816 P. CLEAVELAND *Min.* 512 Specular native arsenic. This very remarkable variety of Arsenic possesses a metallic brilliancy. 1839 *Chapters Phys. Sci.* 281 Specular bodies are those the surfaces of which, being polished, reflect the rays in the same order as they come from other bodies. 1851 MANTELL *Petrifactions* iii. § 1. 144 Iron-glance, or specular oxide, from Elba, Stromboli, Vesuvius.

fig. 1665 BOYLE *Occas. Refl.* III. vi. (1848) 156 The fine Expressions you applaud, are commonly parts of a Sermon that have no specular Virtue in them.

b. *Specular iron* or *iron ore*, hæmatite, esp. the brilliant crystalline form of this.

(*a*) 1796 KIRWAN *Elem. Min.* (ed. 2) II. 162 Specular Iron ore. 1803 *Phil. Trans.* XCIII. 336 The primitive form of the slightly attractable oxide of iron, formerly known by the name of specular iron ore. 1859 R. HUNT *Guide Mus. Pract. Geol.* (ed. 2) 153 Specular iron ore is found throughout Asia, Corsica, Germany [etc.]. 1882 FLOYER *Unexpl. Baluchistan* 125 The blocks of specular iron ore are very heavy.

(*b*) 1804 *Phil. Trans.* XCIV. 332 The fine gray specular iron from Sweden. 1854 BAKEWELL *Geol.* 87 Iron presents itself separately as a volcanic product in the peculiar form of brilliant laminæ, called specular iron, which bears a high polish. 1879 RUTLEY *Study Rocks* x. 155 The crystallised variety, specular iron or ironglance, belongs to the rhombohedral system.

c. (See quot.)

1863 ATKINSON tr. *Ganot's Physics* 363 The reflection from the surfaces of polished bodies, the laws of which have just been stated, is called the regular or specular reflection.

4. Of a telescope: Fitted with a speculum; reflecting.

1676 *Life Paul Sarpi* in *Brent's Counc. Trent* 21 Gio. Battista Porta..makes honourable mention of Padre Paolo as of no ordinary personage, and particularly of his specular perspective.

5. Performed by means of a surgical speculum.

1898 P. MANSON *Trop. Diseases* xviii. 307 In every case in which there is probability of rectal disease digital or specular examination must be made.

II. 6. Of or pertaining to sight or vision; esp. *specular orb* (poet.), the eye.

1656 BLOUNT *Glossogr.*, *Specular*,..belonging to seeing or spying, to Spectacles or glass windows. 1708 J. PHILIPS *Cider* i. 22 Thy Specular Orb Apply to well-dissected Kernels. 1721 D'URFEY *Two Queens Brentford* v. i, Always considering the Design is for specular Instruction. 1810 SOUTHEY *Kehama* XIV. x, In the fiendish joy within his eyes, She knew the hateful Spirit who look'd through Their specular orbs.

7. *poet.* Of heights, etc.: Affording or giving a wide or extensive view. (Cf. SPECULATION 2 c.)

1671 MILTON *P. R.* IV. 236 Look once more e're we leave this specular Mount Westward. 1833 WORDSW. '*Hope smiled when your nativity was cast*', Calm as the Universe, from specular towers Of heaven contemplated by Spirits pure. 1842 IS. WILLIAMS *Baptistery* I. x. (1874) 115 This is Wisdom's specular height, from whence To view as from a watchtower things of sense. 1890 J. H. STIRLING *Philos. & Theol.* viii. 144 The specular heights of the universal.

Spe·cularly, *adv. rare*⁻¹. [f. as prec.] In a specular manner; by reflection as in a mirror.

1704 J. NORRIS *Ideal World* II. v. 288 If we have no knowledge of God at all, then we do not know him so much as specularly or ænigmatically.

†**Spe·culary,** *a. Obs. rare.* [ad. F. *spéculaire*: see -ARY ².] = SPECULAR *a.* 1.

1694 MOTTEUX *Rabelais* v. xliv. 207 She..led him..into a round Chappel made of transparent speculary Stones.

Speculate (spe·kiŭleᵗt), *v.* [f. L. *speculāt-*, ppl. stem of *speculārī* to spy out, watch, examine, observe, etc., f. *specula* a look-out, watch-tower, f. *specĕre* to see, look. Cf. It. *speculare, specolare*, Sp. and Pg. *especular*, OF. *especuler, speculer*, F. *spéculer.*]

1. *trans.* To observe or view mentally; to consider, examine, or reflect upon with close attention; to contemplate; to theorize upon.

Common in the 17th c.; now *rare* or *Obs.*

1599 SANDYS *Europæ Spec.* (1632) 62 Yet notwithstanding these are theorems which few list to speculate. 1632 J. HAYWARD tr. *Biondi's Eromena* 12 To speculate the meanes of negotiating with diversity of persons, and to put the same in practise. 1643 SIR T. BROWNE *Relig. Med.* II. § 13 If we do but speculate the folly and indisputable dotage of avarice. *a* 1706 EVELYN *Hist. Relig.* (1850) I. 54 We should not, therefore, wholly consult our senses when we speculate truth. 1788 T. TAYLOR *Proclus* I. 74 It is just, after speculating its whole and entire genus, to consider the differences of its more particular sciences, according to their species. 1793 — *Sallust* v. 24 Likewise..we should speculate providence, fate and fortune, virtue and vice. 1852 SIR W. HAMILTON *Discuss.* (1853) 21 We..conceit ourselves that we contemplate absolute existence, when we only speculate absolute privation.

b. Said of the soul, understanding, etc.

1604 T. WRIGHT *Passions* IV. ii. § 2. 129 A gluttonous stomacke..causeth such a mist before the eyes of the soul, that shee cannot possibly speculate any spirituall matters. *a* 1652 J. SMITH *Sel. Disc.* iv. 87 Whensoever it will speculate truth itself, it will not then listen to the several clamours and votes of these rude senses. 1678 NORRIS *Misc.* (1699) 157 It being..against the Nature of Understanding to make that truth which it speculates. 1816 *Pamphleteer* VIII. 65 Fables are theological which employ nothing corporeal, but speculate the very essences of the gods.

c. With obj. clause introduced by *how, what, when.*

1856 *N. Brit. Rev.* XXVI. 192 When the company were speculating what lost production of the human mind was most to be regretted. 1857 J. HAMILTON *Less. Gt. Biog.* 296 They were speculating how the stone might be moved away. 1885 'MRS. ALEXANDER' *At Bay* xi, She had begun to speculate when Glynn would join them.

d. To talk (a matter) *over* conjecturally.

1862 DICKENS *Somebody's Luggage* i, Speculating it over with the Mistress, she informed me that the luggage had been advertised.

2. To look or gaze at (something); to examine, inspect, or observe closely or narrowly. ? *Obs.*

1616 J. LANE *Contn. Sqr.'s T.* VI. 208 The troopes of horse, before, behind, theare, heere, speculates all approches, farr and neere. 1672 MARVELL *Reh. Transp.* I. 66 If he frequented their company it was only to speculate his own Baby in their Eyes. *a* 1734 NORTH *Lives* (1826) III. 350 Every morning he speculated his urine. 1805 *Spirit Public Jrnls.* IX. 244 Louis shall hold a mirror to thine eyes, Wherein thy downfal thou mayst speculate.

b. *spec.* To observe (the stars, heaven, etc.), esp. as an object of study.

1630 SHIRLEY *Grateful Servant* II. i, I shall neuer eat garlike with Diogenes in a Tub, and speculate the Starres without a shirt. 1652 GAULE *Magastrom.* 7 One contemplates them [i.e. the heavens, etc.] devoutly, and constantly;..the other

speculates them superstitiously. 1707 *Athenian Sport* (title-p.), The Eye beholds as much when it looks on a Shilling, as when it speculates the whole Heaven. 1890 J. H. STIRLING *Philos. & Theol.* iv. 73 The sun and moon, which, he [Anaxagoras] said, he was born to speculate.

†3. *intr.* To exercise spiritual contemplation.

c 1630 C. LEVER in Farr *S. P. Eliz.* (1845) II. 523 Thy heauenly presence is a faire aspect; There doth my soule delight to speculate.

4. To engage in thought or reflection, esp. of a conjectural or theoretical nature, *on* or *upon* a subject.

a 1677 BARROW *Serm.* ii. Wks. 1686 III. 28 For who would not more readily learn..to draw by setting a good Picture before him, than by merely speculating upon the laws of Perspective. 1774 GOLDSM. *Nat. Hist.* (1776) II. 67 It is all this time storing its mind with objects, upon the nature, the properties, and the relations of which future curiosity may speculate. 1790 BURKE *Fr. Rev.* Wks. 1898 II. 7, I certainly take my full share..in speculating on what has been done, or is doing, on the public stage. 1845 BAILEY *Festus* (ed. 2) 138 Here we can speculate on policy, On social manners, fashions, and the news. 1871 C. DAVIES *Metric Syst.* III. 121 Taxation and philosophy now began to speculate, at the same time, upon the weights and measures of England.

b. Const. *about, as to, concerning*, etc.

1847 HELPS *Friends in C.* I. viii. 133 Nearly every body whose death was worth speculating about. 1855 *Orr's Circ. Sci., Inorg. Nat.* 217 Adaptations, concerning the nature, object, and extent of which it would be equally foolish and impossible to speculate. 1860 TYNDALL *Glac.* I. v. 38 While speculating as to the wisdom of entering the cavern.

5. To engage in the buying and selling of commodities or effects in order to profit by a rise or fall in their market value; to undertake, to take part or invest in, a business enterprise or transaction of a risky nature in the expectation of considerable gain. Also const. *on* or *in*.

1785 JEFFERSON *Corr.* Wks. 1859 I. 472 Should any attempt be made to speculate on these papers [i.e. the public stocks]. 1787 [implied in *Speculating* vbl. sb.]. 1822 BYRON *Let. to Ellice* 12 June, I do not go there to *speculate*, but to settle. 1839 DICKENS *Nickleby* i, Would he be what he is if he hadn't speculated?

transf. 1841 THACKERAY *Gt. Hoggarty Diam.* xiii, I was not over well pleased that his lordship should think me capable of speculating in any way on my wife's beauty.

b. In the game of speculation (q.v.).

1850 *Bohn's Handbk. Games* (1864) 325 The eldest hand shews the uppermost card, which if a trump, the company may speculate on or bid for. *Ibid.*, The company speculating as they please, till all are discovered.

c. To count or reckon *on* something as probable or certain. *rare*⁻¹.

1797 COLERIDGE *Lett.* (1895) I. 215 You might safely speculate on twenty pounds a year or more from your compositions.

d. *trans.* To invest (money) in an enterprise which involves considerable risk.

1907 *Westm. Gaz.* 2 Dec. 7/1 They were compelled to own the cars privately because the railways would not speculate the money.

Hence **Spe·culated** *ppl. a.*, **Spe·culating** *vbl. sb.* (also *attrib.*) and *ppl. a.*

1787 M. CUTLER in *Life*, etc. (1888) I. 304 The speculating plan concerted between the British in Canada and New Yorkers was now well known. 1812 COMBE *Syntax, Picturesque* XXV. 232 We do not bring our learned powers To vex its speculating hours. 1820 SCOTT *Monast.* xxxi, A rash..interpretation of the Scriptures, wrested according to the private opinion of each speculating heretic. 1865 H. BUSHNELL *Vicar. Sacr.* i. (1868) 49 The innate sense of justice in men has been mocked by the speculated satisfactions of justice.

Speculation (spekiŭlēᵗ·ʃǝn). Also 4 speculacioun, 5–6 -cion, 6 -cyon, -tyon, -tione. [ad. late L. *speculātiōn-em*, noun of action f. *speculārī* to SPECULATE. Cf. OF. *speculation* (14th c.), F. *spéculation*, It. *specul-, specolazione*, Sp. *especulacion*, Pg. *especulação.*

In English, as in later L. and the Romance languages, the literal senses have been less usual than the transferred, and the earliest examples occur in the latter group.]

I. 1. The faculty or power of seeing; sight, vision, *esp.* intelligent or comprehending vision. Now *arch.*

1471 RIPLEY *Comp. Alch.* in Ashm. (1652) 121 O Hygh Yncomprehensybie and gloryous Mageste, Whose Luminos Bemes obtundyth our Speculation. 1474 *Cov. Leet Bk.* 393 O splendent Creator! In all oure speculacion, More bryghter then Phebus! 1603 BRETON *Packet Mad Lett.* I. xx. Wks. (Grosart) II. 11 Beleeue not your eyes, till they haue a better speculation. 1605 SHAKS. *Macb.* III. iv. 95 Thou hast no speculation in those eyes Which thou dost glare with. 1648 J. BEAUMONT *Psyche* XXI. lxviii, Her Speculation fix'd its Eye Upon the royal Goodness of her Lord. 1821 SHELLEY *Ginevra* 149 Open eyes, whose fixed and glassy light Mocked at the speculation they had owned. 1829 SCOTT *Anne of G.* xxxiv, His horny eye had lost the power of speculation. 1861 LD. LYTTON & FANE *Tannhäuser* 84 Her eyes Wide open, fix'd into a ghastly stare That knew no speculation.

†2. The exercise of the faculty of sight; the action, or an act, of seeing, viewing, or looking on or at; examination or observation. *Obs.*

1509 HAWES *Past. Pleas.* VII. (Percy Soc.) 27 Her goodly chambre was set all about With depured myrrours of speculacion. 1530 PALSGR. 274/1 Speculation, beholding, *speculation.* 1599 SHAKS. *Hen. V*, IV. ii. 31 Though we vpon this Mountaines Basis by, Tooke stand for idle speculation. 1648 BOYLE *Seraph. Love* (1660) 13 Whilst they liv'd Exiles here on Earth, 'twas such a speculation..'as seeing Him who is invisible'. 1693 *Phil. Trans.* XVII. 691 The square Tower in the middle fitted with Holes for Speculation. 1711 ADDISON *Spect.* No. 3 ¶ 1 In one of my late Rambles, or rather Speculations, I looked into the great Hall where the Bank is kept. 1774 JOHNSON in *Boswell* 1 Oct., Wales is so little different from England, that it offers nothing to the speculation of the traveller.

†**b.** Observation of the heavens, stars, etc. *Obs.*

In some quots. with suggestion of sense 4.

1538 ELYOT, *Astrologia*, the speculation and reasonyng concernyng the celestial or heuenly motions. 1601 HOLLAND *Pliny* I. 597 But now to goe on still with our Astrologie and Speculation of Heaven as wee have begun. 1617 MORYSON *Itin.* I. 59 He [Tycho Brahe] had a little round house of great beauty, in which he did exercise his speculation. 1652 GAULE *Magastrom.* 7 What difference betwixt a divine contemplation and a diviners speculation of the heavens!

†**c.** *Top*, or *turret, of speculation*, one from which a wide or extensive view is obtained. *Obs.*

After L. *turris speculationis* (Gregory *Moral.* xxxi. § 85).

1653 CODRINGTON *Marrow Hist.* Ep. Ded., Here, as from a Turret of Speculation, you may look down upon the Vulgar. 1667 MILTON *P. L.* XII. 589 Let us descend now therefore from this top Of Speculation.

†3. **a.** A spectacle or sight; a spectacular entertainment or show. *Obs. rare.*

c 1440 *Gesta Rom.* I. xxvi. 100 (Harl. MS.), As ofte as a man goþe to the Iolytees of worldlye speculacions, & hathe delectacion in hem. *c* 1520 *Mystery Resurr.* in *Rel. Antiq.* II. 151 It pleasid thi Godhed to tak but three To beholde and see the highe speculatioun, Of thy Godly majestye in thy transfyguratioun.

†**b.** An observer or watcher; a spy. *Obs.*⁻¹

1605 SHAKS. *Lear* III. i. 24 Seruants,..Which are to France the Spies and Speculations Intelligent of our State.

II. 4. The contemplation, consideration, or profound study *of* some subject.

Freq. in the 17th cent.; now *rare* or *Obs.*

c 1374 CHAUCER *Boeth.* v. pr. ii. (1868) 153 Þe soules of men moten nedes ben more free whan þei loken hem in þe speculacioun or lokynge of þe deuyne þouȝt. 1549 *Compl. Scotl.* vi. 62 Ane rustic pastour..distitut of vrbanite, and of speculatione of natural philosophe. *c* 1590 MARLOWE *Faustus* iii. 114 He liue in speculation of this Art, Till Mephastophilis returne againe. 1604 WRIGHT *Passions* I. xi. 45 The motions of our Passions are hidde from our eyes...Yet for the Speculation of this matter, I thinke [etc.]. 1693 CONGREVE *Old Bach.* IV. vi, Sure it is a good book, and only tends to the speculation of sin. 1788 T. TAYLOR *Proclus* I. Pref., The great object of ancient philosophy, was an accurate speculation of principles and causes.

b. Without const., or with *in, into, concerning.*

1550 BALE *Eng. Votaries* II. E iij, Other instructors he had ..whych..were most conning in that speculacyon. 1563 SHUTE *Groundes Architecture* B ij b, Optica, is properly called perspectiue, and is of a furder speculacion, then therin can or nedeth to be exprest. 1636 HEYWOOD *Challenge Beautie* II. i, *Bona.* That you may know it is not lust, but love, And the true speculation I have tane, In both these adjuncts, that proclaime you rare. 1669 CLARENDON *Ess.* Tracts (1727) 96 The end of this speculation into ourselves and conversation with ourselves. 1674 *Playford's Skill Mus.* III. 3 This kind of Counterpoint..may appear simple, ..yet the right speculation may give much satisfaction even to the most skilful. 1678 CUDWORTH *Intell. Syst.* I. iv. 416 Furthermore Aristotle declares, that this Speculation concerning the Deity, does constitute a Particular Science by it self. 1715 (*title*), The Prophecies of Michael Nostradamus...Made English for the Speculation of the Publick.

c. The conjectural anticipation *of* something.

1795 BURKE *Th. Scarcity* Wks. 1842 II. 253 Continually in a state of something like a siege, or in the speculation of it.

5. An act of speculating, or the result of this; a conclusion, opinion, view, or series of these, reached by abstract or hypothetical reasoning.

1432–50 tr. *Higden* (Rolls) V. 27 Pthtotomeus, a man nobly erudite in speculacions mathematicalle. 1575 VAUTROLLIER *Luther on Ep. Gal.* 16 There is nothing more daungerous then to wander with curious speculations in heauen. 1588 LAMBARDE *Eiren.* III. i. 328 These speculations of M. Marrowes reading, are like inough to fall in practise. 1613 PURCHAS *Pilgrimage* (1614) 512 Such are his speculations of these hidden fires, that he maketh them the causers of Windes [etc.]. 1673 TEMPLE *Let. Duke Florence* Wks. 1720 II. 286 To make the Speculations of Strangers Abroad, part of your own Diversion at Home. 1708 SWIFT *Sentim. Ch. Eng. Man* Wks. 1755 II. I. 77 It is not a bare speculation that kings may run into such enormities as are abovementioned. 1769 BURKE *Let. Marq. Rockingham* Corr. 1844 I. 219 Not that I rely much on this speculation of my own. 1793 SMEATON *Edystone L.* § 344 In consequence of these speculations, I ordered a well to be sunk near the middle of the peninsula. 1816 MACKINTOSH *Bacon & Locke* Wks. 1846 I. 332 The source of many mistaken speculations on the important subjects of government and education. 1881 *Nature* No. 618. 414 Speculations respecting their ultimate form or structure will have found a place in the science as soon as such speculations have helped to arrange the facts which are known.

†**b.** An aim, purpose, or intention. *Obs.*

1616 B. JONSON *Devil an Ass* II. v, They may..spend an houre; Two, three, or foure, discoursing with their shaddow: But sure they haue a farther speculation.

c. A conjectural consideration or meditation; an attempt to ascertain or anticipate something by probable reasoning.

1796 HORSLEY *Serm.* (1811) 189 The populace that were witnesses of the miracle 'wondered': they wondered, and there was an end of their speculations upon the business. 1833 HT. MARTINEAU *Brooke Farm* xii. 135 Our annual speculations about how so much good cheer was to be consumed. 1841 DICKENS *Barn. Rudge* i, The subject of their speculations had done due honour to the house by calling for some drink.

6. Without article: Contemplation of a profound, far-reaching, or subtle character; abstract or hypothetical reasoning on subjects of a deep, abstruse, or conjectural nature.

a 1450 tr. *De Imitatione* III. lx. 141 Neiþer þe ȝifte of prophecie, ner worching of myracles, ner speculacion, be it neuere so hye, is of eny estimacion wiþouten hir [*i.e.* grace]. *c* 1532 DU WES *Introd. Fr.* in *Palsgr.* 1062 Abstynence of Danyell, speculation of Hely, experience of saynt Paule. 1565 HARDYNG *Confut.* I. 34 The scriptures haue nede of speculation (that is to witte, to be well studied and considered) to the ende the force and power of euery argument may be knowen. 1596 SPENSER *Hymn Heavenly Beautie* 134 Thence gathering plumes of perfect speculation, To impe the wings of thy high flying mynd. 1606 BRYSKETT *Disc. Civill Life* 252 Euen as sapience or wisedom is the guide and gouernesse of speculation. 1708 SWIFT *Sentim. Ch. Eng. Man* Wks. 1755 II. I. 72 Because slavery is of all things the greatest clog and obstacle to speculation. 1749 HARTLEY *Observ. Man* II. i. § 4. 17 Men of great Speculation and Refinement may desire to have this analogical Reasoning supported. 1776 ADAM SMITH *W. N.* I. i. (1869) I. 11 Philosophers or men of speculation, whose trade it is not to do anything, but to observe everything. 1828 LYTTON *Pelham* xxxiii, If I have any fault, it is too great a love for abstruse speculation and reflection. 1857 BUCKLE *Civiliz.* i. 5 Habits of speculation..are the essential condition of all real knowledge. 1875 JOWETT *Plato* (ed. 2) V. 25 The same desire to base speculation upon history we find in the Critias.

b. As opposed to *practice, fact, action*, etc.

1530 LYNDESAY *Test. Papyngo* 30 Boith in practick and speculatioun. 1597 MORLEY *Introd. Mus.* III. 153 Now..make a lesson as I haue done, and ioine practise with your speculation. 1599 B. JONSON *Cynthia's Rev.* II. iii, Your courtier theorique, is hee, that..doth now know the court, rather by speculation, then practice. *a* 1676 HALE *Prim. Orig. Man.* (1677) 25 Usefulness in reference to Speculation or Knowledge, and Usefulness in relation to Practice or Exercise. 1777 J. ADAMS *Wks.* (1854) IX. 470 This is fact, and facts are stubborn things in opposition to speculation. 1800 *Asiat. Ann. Reg.* 28/1 His talents were much more fitted for action than speculation.

c. In more or less disparaging use, usually with adjs., as *bare, mere, pure*, etc.; also simply = conjecture, surmise.

(*a*) 1575 VAUTROLLIER *Luther on Ep. Gal.* 35 And that which he thinketh him selfe to know, he attaineth only by bare speculation. 1612 BRINSLEY *Lud. Lit.* Comm. Pref., Neither are these directions of meere speculation, whose promises are commonly as large, as the performance defective. 1665 SIR T. HERBERT *Trav.* (1677) 106 For that of Abulfæda..is no new discovery;..I know he has it onely by speculation. 1696 STANHOPE *Chr. Pattern* (1711) 87 The reason why these things are seen with so useless speculation, is because our minds are not rightly disposed. 1712 STEELE *Spect.* No. 450 ¶ 1 [Partaking] more of the Invention of the Brain, or what is styled Speculation, than of sound Judgment or profitable Observation. 1780 *Mirror* No. 107, In every art and science, practitioners complain how often they are deceived by specious theories and delusive speculation. 1812 WOODHOUSE *Astron.* xiii. 135 The enquiry into the form, since the theory is complete without it, is one of pure curiosity and speculation. 1861 LD. BROUGHAM *Brit. Const.* i. (1862) 13 The mere romantic speculation of political dreamers.

(*b*) 1791 LD. AUCKLAND *Corr.* (1861) II. 396 There is some speculation here that he may look towards the fourth princess.

d. In *matter, object, subject*, etc., *of speculation.* Also *ellipt.* for this.

(*a*) 1665 GLANVILL *Def. Van. Dogm.* 75 The little delight I have in matters that are not of very material speculation. 1736 BUTLER *Anal.* Introd. (1798) 3 This determines the question, even in matters of speculation. 1769 *Junius Lett.* xii. (1788) 75 Let me..consider your character and conduct merely as a subject of curious speculation. 1788 PRIESTLEY *Lect. Hist.* v. xlix. 369 The progress of society, is one of the most..useful objects of speculation. 1810 W. WILSON *Hist. Dissent. Ch.* iii. 63 Points of speculation, or party, he studiously avoided. 1832 BREWSTER *Nat. Magic* xiii. 340 They afford ground of curious speculation. 1847 HELPS *Friends in C.* I. i. 4 It was a matter of frequent speculation with us, whether [etc.].

(*b*) 1793 SMEATON *Edystone L.* § 111 The various Strata.. would furnish speculation to the curious naturalist.

e. *In speculation*, in conjecture or theory; not actually or practically; also, under consideration, in contemplation or view.

(*a*) 1638 MEDE *Wks.* (1672) 154 This Faith is not barely Historical and in speculation, but a Faith in motion. 1645 USSHER *Body Div.* (1647) 37 Is God every where in speculation only? 1718 *Free-thinker* No. 90. 246 It avails nothing, that a projected Change is, in Speculation, for the Better. 1777 HAMILTON *Wks.* (1886) VII. 483 As to their notion ..., I apprehend it will do better in speculation than in practice. 1793 HORSLEY *Serm. Westm.* 29 Whatever preference therefore, in speculation, he might give to the Republican form, he could not, with these principles, be practically an enemy to the Government of Kings.

(*b*) 1811 SIR WM. SCOTT *Dodson's Rep.* I. 32 Operations against Buenos Ayres were entirely in speculation, and not finally decided upon.

†7. A plan or scheme for some enterprise or undertaking. *Obs.*⁻¹

a 1700 EVELYN *Diary* 7 Sept. 1667, Came Sir John Kiviet to article with me about his brick-work speculation.

8. The action or practice of buying and selling goods, land, stocks and shares, etc., in order to profit by the rise or fall in the market value, as distinct from regular trading or investment; engagement in any business enterprise or transaction of a venturesome or risky nature, but offering the chance of great or unusual gain. Also *Comb.*

1774 H. WALPOLE *Let. to Mann* 1 May, Next to gaming, ..the predominant folly is pictures...Sir George Colbroke, a citizen, and martyr to what is called *speculation*, had

his pictures sold by auction last week. 1776 ADAM SMITH *W. N.* I. x. I. (1904) I. 127 Sudden fortunes, indeed, are sometimes made in such places, by what is called the trade of speculation. *a* 1817 T. DWIGHT *Trav. New Eng.*, etc. (1821) I. 218 The first cause..of this evil was, if I mistake not, what has been proverbially called in this country *Speculation.* 1834 *Tait's Mag.* I. 408/1 The evils produced by that species of gambling named speculation. 1897 *Daily News* 10 Apr. 5 The speculation-laden air of Johannesburg.

b. *On speculation*, on chance; on the chance of gain or profit. Cf. SPEC 1 b.

1811 MISS HAWKINS *Countess & Gertrude* (1812) II. 162 A distant relation who had married, at fifteen, in the East Indies, sent out on speculation. 1837 DICKENS *Pickw.* xxvi, Won't Mr. Dodson and Fogg be wild if the plaintiff shouldn't get it,..when they do it all on speculation?

9. An act or instance of speculating; a commercial venture or undertaking of an enterprising nature, esp. one involving considerable financial risk on the chance of unusual profit. Cf. SPEC 1.

1776 ADAM SMITH *W. N.* I. x. I. (1904) I. 127 A bold adventurer may sometimes acquire a considerable fortune by two or three successful speculations. 1787 M. CUTLER in *Life*, etc. (1888) I. 305 We obtained..the remainder for a private speculation. 1825 COBBETT *Rur. Rides* 327 The talk about 'speculations', that is to say adventurous dealings, or rather commercial gamblings,..is the most miserable nonsense. 1841 W. SPALDING *Italy & It. Isl.* III. 393 The government was to undertake a certain part of the speculation, while the remainder of the capital might be given off in shares. 1880 *Austr. Town & Country Jrnl.* 14 Feb. 314/4 A young fellow who had a speculation in pigs on hand.

fig. 1876 J. PARKER *Paracl.* II. Epil. 387 Life itself is a high and solemn speculation.

10. *Cards.* A round game of cards, the chief feature of which is the buying and selling of trump cards, the player who possesses the highest trump in a round winning the pool.

1804 MISS AUSTEN *Watsons* in J. E. A. Leigh *Mem.* (1871) 357 'What's your game?'..'Speculation I believe.' 1839 DICKENS *Nickleby* ix, They sat down to play speculation. 1868 PARDON *Card Player* 83 As a merry game for Christmas parties speculation is without a rival.

Speculatist (spe·kiŭlǝtist). [f. SPECULATE *v.*]

1. One who speculates, or indulges in abstract reasoning; a professed or habitual speculator; a theorist. (Very common from *c* 1750.)

1613 tr. *Pedro Mexio's Treas. Anc. & Mod. Times* 12/2 The Septuagint..haue commonly traduced it to be in Eden. ..Other speculatis[t]es do affirme it to be in Syria. 1681 GRANGER *Eccl.* 24 Let the profoundest speculatist, or curious practitioner, turne the edge of his wit which way he will to finde out some new thing. 1714 tr. *T. à Kempis, Chr. Exerc.* x. 15 Either a lofty Speculatist, or a subtil Disputant. 1750 JOHNSON *Rambler* No. 14 ¶ 5 The speculatist is only in danger of erroneous reasoning, but the man involved in life has his own passions, and those of others, to encounter. 1780 COWPER *Progr. Error* 490 Fresh confidence the speculatist takes From ev'ry hair-brain'd proselyte he makes. 1807 *Edinb. Rev.* X. 369 We shall..lay before our readers the opinions of this clever speculatist. 1849 DARWIN in *Life & Lett.* (1887) II. 37 This confounded variation..is pleasant to me as a speculatist, though odious to me as a systematist. 1886 A. WEIR *Hist. Basis Mod. Europe* (1889) 20 The social principles recommended by speculatists.

b. With disparaging adjs.

1693 W. FREKE *Sel. Ess.* xxxiv. 223 'Tis the Curse of dreaming Speculatists, that they not only have no taste of real Wisdom, but mispend the time that should lead them to it. 1766 ELIZ. CARTER *Let. to Mrs. Vesey* 1 July, The most visionary speculatist must sometimes awake to the cares and solicitudes of real life. 1792 W. ROBERTS *Looker-on* (1794) I. 373 An Utopian speculatist might amuse himself with planning a department..which should be called the office of advice. 1827 G. S. FABER *Orig. Expiat. Sacr.* 262 The notion of its divine institution originated..with some fantastical innovating speculatists among the modern Puritans. 1850 MᶜCOSH *Div. Govt.* 217 He is probably an idle dreamer,..or a wild speculatist. 1893 *Ch. Times* 20 Oct. 1002 The vapid and airy region of third-rate speculatists.

c. As the title of a book or periodical.

1730 (*title*), The Speculatist. A Collection of Letters and Essays, Moral and Political, Serious and Humourous, upon Various Subjects. [1787 SIR J. HAWKINS *Life Johnson* 538 Concanen, one of the Dunciad heroes, in a paper called 'The Speculatist'.]

d. With adjs. denoting the subject or sphere of speculation.

1802 BEDDOES *Hygëia* VIII. 92 The hypothesis of any medical speculatist. 1818 BUSBY *Gram. Music* 167 Among those who succeeded Rameau, as musical speculatists, was the celebrated Tartini. 1837–8 SIR W. HAMILTON in *Reid's Wks.* I. 53/2 Some of the recent physiological speculatists of Germany. 1850 GLADSTONE *Glean.* (1879) V. lxxxiii. 222 In the other case we may as political speculatists either rank with those [etc.].

2. One who speculates in commerce or finance.

1812 *Examiner* 5 Oct. 634/1 The Corn and Mealing Trade has lately got into the hands of Speculatists. 1832 *Fraser's Mag.* V. 653 Among other inducements to the cupidity of the queen and speculatists, he affirmed [etc.]. 1834 H. MILLER *Scenes & Leg.* xxx. (1857) 448 The great wealth of the speculatist proved insufficient.

Speculative (spe·kiŭlǟtiv), *a* and *sb.* Also 5 **speculatif, -ijf, -iff, -yff,** 6 **-ife, -yf(e, -yue,** 6–7 **-iue.** [a. OF. *speculatif, -ive* (mod.F. *spéculatif, -ive*, = It. *specul-, specolativo*, Sp. and Pg. *especulativo*), or ad. late L. *speculātīv-us*, f. the ppl. stem of *speculārī* to SPECULATE.]

A. *adj.* 1. Of the nature of, based upon, characterized by, speculation or theory in contrast to practical or positive knowledge: **a.** Of knowledge.

c 1380 WYCLIF *Sel. Wks.* I. 241 Þis cunnyng was not speculatif. 1555 EDEN *Decades* (Arb.) 277 They..confessed that the ordinarie pilottes and mariners ignorant in Cosmographi, are not to bee compared to men of speculatiue knowleage. 1585 BLAGRAVE (*title*), The Mathematical Iewel,..compiled and published for the Furtherance..of Gentlemen and others desirous of Speculatiue Knowledge. 1612 BRINSLEY *Lud. Lit.* xxi. (1627) 252 Other speculative or more curious knowledge in Quiddities. *a* 1674 CLARENDON *Surv. Leviath.* (1676) 117 From his speculative knowledge of man-kind. 1736 BUTLER *Anal.* I. v. Wks. 1874 I. 103 A practical sense of things, very different from a mere speculative knowledge. 1748 RICHARDSON *Clarissa* (1811) V. ix. 124 She has a world of knowledge: knowledge speculative, as I may say, but no experience. 1850 C. DAUBENY *Atom. The.* i. (ed. 2) 4 One more proof of the benefits arising from experimental science, and of the unexpected advances in speculative knowledge. 1865 DICKENS *Mut. Fr.* I. v, His knowledge of its affairs was mostly speculative and all wrong.

b. Of special sciences, or parts of these.

c 1400 *Lanfranc's Cirurg.* 15 Alle þese þingis..ben but techinge of medicyns [*v.r.* medycine] speculatijf. 1561 T. NORTON *Calvin's Inst.* Pref., An arte of brawlyng whiche these men call Speculatiue Diuinitie. 1597 MORLEY *Introd. Mus.* Annot., As for the diuision, Musicke is either speculatiue or practicall. 1601 HOLLAND *Pliny* II. 344 Chrysippus ..altered the Theoricke and speculatiue Physicke of Hippocrates and Prodicus, with all their principles. 1665 BOYLE *Occas. Refl.* v. i. (1848) 296 The diligent Studies of Speculative and Polemical Divinity. 1730 CHAMBERLAYNE *Relig. Philos.* Pref. p. xx, Euclid, Algebra, and other Speculative Parts of the Mathematicks. 1741 WATTS *Improv. Mind* (1801) 112 Endeavour to apply every speculative study, as far as possible, to some practical use. 1859 SIR W. HAMILTON *Lect.* (1877) I. vii. 111 Theoretical, called likewise speculative,.. philosophy has for its highest end mere truth or knowledge. 1881 FROUDE *Short Stud.* (1883) IV. II. i. 168 The speculative part of it [religion] was accepted because it was assumed to be true.

c. In general use.

a 1483 *Liber Niger* in *Househ. Ord.* (1790) 50 Men of worshipp, endowed with vertues, morall and speculatiff. 1526 *Pilgr. Perf.* (W. de W. 1531) 31 b, As well in matters speculatyue as practyue. 1615 CROOKE *Body of Man* 26 Many of these nice and fine points..serue rather for a speculatiue pleasure & admiration, then be of any vse in the art of physick or Chirurgery. 1677 YARRANTON *Eng. Improv.* Addr. Ld. Windsor, They have given the World sufficient Tests of the vast difference betwixt Speculative Notions and Practical Experiments. 1708 SWIFT *Sacram. Test* Wks. 1755 II. I. 127 The bare opinion of his being vicar of Christ is but a speculative point. 1761 HUME *Hist. Eng.* III. xlvi. 24 The king's despotism was more speculative than practical. 1812 SIR H. DAVY *Chem. Philos.* 17 The speculative ideas of the Arabians were more or less adopted by their European disciples. 1849 MACAULAY *Hist. Eng.* ii. I. 247 He..had a languid speculative liking for republican institutions. 1880 MᶜCARTHY *Own Times* xlv. III. 350 Even against speculative dangers a wise people will always take precautions.

2. Of persons: Given to speculation; inclined to theorize or indulge in conjectural reasoning.

c 1546 G. JOYE in Gardiner *Declar. Joye* (1546) 53 Euery speculatyue pharisay and idle hypocrite. 1555 EDEN *Decades* (Arb.) 218 If there bee any dyfference.., it canne not bee perceaued but by the iudgement of speculatiue men. 1609 J. DOWLAND *Ornith. Microl.* 5 A Speculative Musitian excels the Practick. 1660 BOYLE *New Exp. Phys. Mech.* (1682) 123 To dwell upon all the several Reflexions, that a Speculative Wit might make. 1712 ADDISON *Spect.* No. 305 ¶ 8 Six Professors, who, it seems, are to be Speculative Statesmen. 1785 REID *Intell. Powers* I. viii. 245 Why have speculative men laboured so anxiously to analyse our solitary operations? 1813 SIR H. DAVY *Agric. Chem.* (1814) 339 He is too speculative a writer to awaken confidence in his results. 1841 HELPS *Ess., Pract. Wisd.* (1842) 4 Many persons are considered speculative merely because they are of a searching nature. 1855 MACAULAY *Hist. Eng.* xix. IV. 327 The only statesman, indeed, active or speculative, who did not share in the general delusion was Edmund Burke.

absol. 1774 GOLDSM. *Nat. Hist.* I. x, The various opinions that have employed the speculative upon this subject.

b. Similarly of the soul, mind, etc.

1570 DEE *Math. Pref.* *j, Ascend, and mount vp (with Speculatiue winges) in spirit. 1599 NASHE *Lenten Stuffe* Wks. (Grosart) V. 300 The grossest kind of fire that.. illumines my speculatiue soule. 1793 T. BEDDOES *Math. Evid.* 10 They seem to promise, to speculative minds, a sort of independance upon external things. 1809–10 COLERIDGE *Friend* (1818) III. 81 A certain number of speculative minds is necessary to a cultivated state of society.

†**c.** Given to pry or search *into* something. *Obs.*

1605 BACON *Adv. Learn.* I. iii. § 7 To be speculatiue into another man, to the end to know how to worke him,..proceedeth from a heart that is double. 1612 — *Ess., Counsel* (Arb.) 322 Councellors should not be too speculatiue into their Soueraignes person.

3. Of life, etc.: Spent in, devoted to, speculation.

1579 LYLY *Euphues* (Arb.) 142 A trifold kinde of life, Actiue,..Speculatiue, which is continuall meditation and studie. 1643 MILTON *Divorce* II. xix. Wks. 1851 IV. 115 Christ himselfe hath taught us..even for a bodily healing to dispence with that holy and speculative rest of Sabbath. 1670 CLARENDON *Ess.* Tracts (1727) 167 An active and practical condition of life, or a speculative repose. 1849 MACAULAY *Hist. Eng.* vi. II. 54 There was..no walk of speculative or of active life, in which Jesuits were not to be found.

4. Of faculties, etc.: Adapted for, exercised in, speculation († or vision).

1604 SHAKS. *Oth.* I. iii. 271 When light wing'd Toyes Of feather'd Cupid, seele with wanton dulnesse My speculatiue, and offic'd Instrument. 1605 — *Macb.* v. iv. 19 Thoughts speculatiue, their vnsure hopes relate. 1678 CUDWORTH *Intell. Syst.* 408 That Perfect Happiness is a Speculative or Contemplative Energy, may be made manifest from hence. 1703 ATTERBURY *Serm.* (1734) II. 126 The other, being a mere speculative Power, hath no Contrary in the Mind of Man to struggle with. 1860 MILL *Repr. Govt.* (1865) 6/2 If any one requires to be convinced that speculative thought is one of the chief elements of social power. 1896 DK. ARGYLL *Philos. Belief* 11 Our speculative faculties are altogether untrustworthy on such subjects.

†5. Pertaining to vision; optical. *Obs.*

1656 BLOUNT *Glossogr.*, *Catopticks*, professors of the Opticks, or art speculative.

6. Suitable for observation or watching; speculatory. Chiefly *poet.*

1709 POPE *Lett.* (1735) I. 81, I have been inform'd, that you have left your speculative Angle in the Widow's Coffeehouse. 1782 COWPER *Jackdaw* 13 Fond of the speculative height, Thither he wings his airy flight. 1784 — *Task* I. 289 Now roves the eye; And, posted on this speculative height, Exults in its command. 1821 WORDSW. *Eclipse Sun* 1 High on her speculative tower Stood Science.

7. **a.** Of persons: Given to, or engaging in, commercial or financial speculation.

1763 JANSSEN *Smuggling laid open* 28 Several Persons, who go under the Denomination of Speculative Buyers, purchase Teas there, meerly on an Expectation of the Price rising afterwards. 1776 ADAM SMITH *W. N.* I. x. (1869) I. 119 The speculative merchant exercises no one regular.. business. 1799 *Hull Advertiser* 6 Oct. 3/3 To keep down the price of corn which speculative men were trying to advance. 1813 SCOTT *Let.* in *Lockhart* (1837) III. ii. 107 Any rare printed book which a speculative bookseller might purchase with a view to re-publication.

b. Of the nature of, characterized by, or involving speculation.

1799 *Hull Advertiser* 6 Oct. 3/3 Articles which ought..to be exempt from all speculative interest. 1848 MILL *Pol. Econ.* III. xxiv. § 2 (1876) 395 There are two states of the market, one which may be termed the quiescent state, the other the expectant or speculative state. 1879 H. GEORGE *Progr. & Pov.* VIII. iii. (1881) 371 How speculative rent checks production. 1907 *Standard* 19 Jan. 2/4 Heavy speculative transactions have been in progress in tin for weeks past.

c. Forming an object of speculation.

1890 *Daily News* 30 Sept. 2/5 The market for speculative beetroot continues dull and prices to decline.

B. *sb.* †1. As a book-title, = MIRROR *sb.* 4. *Obs.*

c 1430 LYDG. *Min. Poems* (Percy Soc.) 63 Vincencius in his speculatif historialle, Of this saide monk makithe ful mencyoune.

2. †**a.** Speculation; hypothetical reasoning; theory. *Obs.*

After late L. *speculātīva* sb. So F. *spéculative.*

1412–20 LYDG. *Chron. Troy* I. 3578 For-dullid is myn ymagynatif, To deme in practik or in speculatif. 1426 — *De Guil. Pilgr.* 18575 For speculatyff..With-outen good experience Avaylith lytle or ellis nought. 1474 CAXTON *Chesse* III. v. (1883) 119 The maistres of rethorique ben the chyef maistres in speculatyf. *a* 1500 in M. Cooke *Hist. Masonry* (1861) 90 Of specculatyfe he was a master and he lovyd well masonry and masons. 1509 BARCLAY *Shyp Folys* (1570) 102 Such that haue practise and nought of speculatife.

†**b.** *pl.* Speculative matters; the speculative sciences. *Obs.*

1640 SEDGWICK *Christ's Counsell* 258 In speculatives be wise to sobriety, in practicals be as good as thou canst. *a* 1670 RUST *Disc. Truth* (1682) 166 As indispensible are the mutual respects and relations of things both in Speculatives and Morals. 1678 CUDWORTH *Intell. Syst.* 416 Aristotle..concludes, that as the Speculative Sciences in General, are more Noble and Excellent than the other, so is Theology or Metaphysicks the most Honourable of all the Speculatives.

c. With *the*: That which rests only on speculation.

1877 SPARROW *Serm.* xix. 254 When..we are compelled.. to make a choice between the speculative and the practical we should give preference to the latter.

†3. A speculator or speculatist. *Obs.*⁻¹

a 1638 MEDE *Wks.* (1672) 878 If it were in Latine, it would make some of your German Speculatives half wild.

Speculatively (spe·kiŭlǟtivli), *adv.* [f. prec.]

1. In a speculative manner; in respect of, by means of, speculation.

1570 DEE *Math. Pref.* C iij b, Thus can the Mathematicall minde deale Speculatiuely in his own Arte. 1599 *Life More* in Wordsw. *Eccl. Biog.* (1853) II. 110 As [he] speculatively, so practicallie taught them to embrace vertue. 1631 R. H. *Arraignm. Whole Creature* xii. § 6. 166 Salomon, as the wisest of men speculatively: as the best experienced of men, practically. 1693 NORRIS *Pract. Disc.* (1711) III. 230 If he that is speculatively wise, did but joyn Consideration to his Notion, he would quickly become practically so. 1713 *Guardian* No. 3 ¶ 1 These Sages of Iniquity are, it seems, themselves, only speculatively wicked. 1793 BURKE *Obs. Conduct Minority* Wks. 1842 I. 623 It is not easy to state for what good end..Mr. Fox should be fond of referring to those theories, upon all occasions, even though speculatively they might be true. 1814 D'ISRAELI *Quarrels Auth.* (1867) 454 No man was more speculatively bold, and more practically timorous. 1855 MACAULAY *Hist. Eng.* xv. III. 579 The objection was, beyond all doubt, speculatively just; but..no practical inconvenience was to be apprehended. 1875 MANNING *Mission H. Ghost* ii. 37, I will endeavour then to draw this out, not speculatively, but practically.

b. With a speculative or meditative air.

1883 *Harper's Mag.* Sept. 626/1 She looked speculatively at the..linen duster.

2. Towards, by way of, commercial or financial speculation; on speculation.

1847 in WEBSTER. 1898 *Westm. Gaz.* 16 Feb. 8/1 Whether the shares..should command a premium of 250 per cent. is a question best answered by the speculatively-inclined. 1908 *Ibid.* 10 Nov. 2/1 Occasionally a solicitor may be found who will take up his case speculatively.

Spe·culativeness. [f. as prec.] The quality of being speculative; tendency towards speculation.

1727 BAILEY (vol. II), *Speculativeness*, Propenseness to Speculation, Studiousness in Observation: *Speculativeness* is the Opposite to Practicalness. 1828–32 WEBSTER, *Speculativeness*, the state of being speculative, or of consisting in speculation only. 1855 MILMAN *Lat. Chr.* XIV. ii. VI. 402 The one man who at that period..by the congenial speculativeness of his mind..was qualified to translate into Latin the mysterious doctrines of the Areopagite. 1890 *Nature* 30 Oct. 633 The subject is worked out with all Mr. Seebohm's..energy and speculativeness.

Spe·culativism. [f. as prec.] Excessive exercise of, or leaning towards, speculation.

1865 *Spect.* 30 Sept. 1094 The characteristic of the sixteenth century was a *speculativism* alike in thought and action, rather than earnest faith and resolute deed. 1878 *Pop. Sci. Monthly* July 269 Built on the quicksand of æsthetics and speculativism which was quickly swept away by the tide of barbarian invasion.

Speculator (spe·kiŭleᵗtǝɹ). Also 6–7 -our. [a. L. *speculātor*, agent-noun f. *speculārī* to SPECULATE, or ad. F. *spéculateur*, = It. *specul-, specolatore*, Sp. and Pg. *especulador.*]

1. One who speculates on abstruse or uncertain matters; one who devotes himself to speculation or theoretical reasoning.

1555 EDEN *Decades* (Arb.) 367 The philosophers, speculatours of naturall thynges, saye that it is engendered of substaunce more watery then fyerie. 1646 SIR T. BROWNE *Pseud. Ep.* III. xiii. 137 The Writers of Mineralls and naturall speculators, are of another beliefe. 1664 POWER *Exp. Philos.* III. 193 The old Dogmatists and Notional Speculators, that onely gaz'd at the visible effects and..Resultances of things. 1798 MALTHUS *Popul.* (1878) 5 The most enthusiastic speculator cannot suppose a greater increase. 1855 PALEY *Aeschylus* Pref. (1861) p. xii, Pythagoras, one of the most deep-minded speculators of the ancient world, speaks in every page of Aeschylus. 1871 C. DAVIES *Metric Syst.* III. 285 Some philosophical speculators have started doubts whether the metre is really the forty millionth part of the circumference of the earth.

b. Used as the title of periodicals.

1790 [N. DRAKE, etc.] The Speculator. 1801 The Speculator, containing essays on men and things.

2. A watchman, sentry, or look-out.

1607 TOPSELL *Four-f. Beasts* (1658) 406 It is reported by a certain Greek writer that, if their speculator do not give them the watch-word,..they tear him in pieces with their teeth. 1661 R. BURNEY Κέρδιστον Δῶρον 104, I am the speculator and sentinel that chase away all evil with my eyes. 1663 BUTLER *Hud.* I. i. 711 We,..Like Speculators, should foresee From Pharos..Portended Mischiefs [etc.]. 1725 BROOME *Observ.* in *Pope's Odyss.* XII. III. 215 All the boats had one speculator in common, to give notice when the fish approach'd. 1820 T. S. HUGHES *Trav. Sicily* I. iv. 139 The speculator or man who descries the movements of the fish.

†3. One who engages in occult observations or studies. *Obs.*

1652 GAULE *Magastrom.* 9 Diviners, Speculators, Circulators, Prognosticators,..&c. 1658 SIR T. BROWNE *Pseud. Ep.* (ed. 4) VI. xiv. 416 The Hebrew letters in the heavens, made out of the greater and lesser Stars, which put together do make up words, wherein Cabalistical Speculators conceive they read the events of future things. 1691 WOOD *Ath. Oxon.* I. 244 Dee..appointed his Friend Kelley to be his Seer or Skryer or Speculator, that is to take notice what the Spirits did.

†4. An observer, spectator. *Obs.*⁻¹

1647 NYE *Gunnery* xviii. 95 As they wriggle to and fro, they will pull one another after them, to the speculatour a great deal of content.

5. A messenger sent to consult an oracle. *rare*⁻¹.

1794 T. TAYLOR *Pausanias' Descr. Greece* III. 149 They sent speculators (*theoroi*) to Delphos.

6. One who engages in commercial or financial speculation.

1778 HAMILTON *Wks.* (1886) VII. 560 The speculators in the city have been bidding against the commissaries. 1786 JEFFERSON *Writ.* (1859) I. 578 There are even speculators in America who will purchase it. 1827 HONE *Every-day Bk.* II. 1476 He was a keen..speculator, well versed in the mystery of the bulls and bears. 1848 DICKENS *Dombey* vi, One or two bold speculators had projected streets. 1884 *Fortn. Rev.* Mar. 346 There are a class of speculators in the fag ends of leases.

Speculato·rial, *a. rare*⁻⁰. = SPECULATORY *a.*

1860 WORCESTER (citing Blount and Bailey). Hence in later Dicts.

Spe·culatory, *sb.* and *a.* Now *rare.* Also 6–7 **-orie.** [ad. L. *speculātōri-us*: see SPECULATE *v.* and -ORY. In sense 1 of the sb. from the L. fem. *speculātōria* (sc. *ars*): cf. F. *spéculatoire.*]

A. *sb.* †1. The observation or study of occult phenomena. *Obs.*

1569 J. SANFORD tr. *Agrippa's Van. Artes* 52 b, Out of the same fundation commeth Speculatorie, which doth enterprete thunder, lightning, and other impressions of the Elementes. 1676 tr. *Agrippa's Van. Arts* (1684) 99 Among the Arts therefore of Fortune-telling vulgarly professed in hope of gain, are Physiognomy,..Soothsaying, Speculatory, and Interpretation of Dreams.

†2. A place of observation. *Obs.*⁻¹

1619 J. BAINBRIDGE *Descr. Late Comet* 14 Appearing to our eye on the superficies of this terrestriall speculatorie.

†3. = SPECULATOR 2. *Obs.*⁻¹

1775 L. SHAW *Hist. Moray* v. 211 By their speculatories or scouts, they had certain intelligence of the King's approach.

B. *adj.* †1. Of the nature of, pertaining to, occult speculation. *Obs.*

1588 J. HARVEY *Disc. Probl.* 26 No Opticall, or Speculatorie Theories: no Cabalisticall, or Traditionall Suppositions. 1652 GAULE *Magastrom.* 244 Whether mythology or astrology (the poeticall or the speculatory fable) serves most to make one another good or more significant? 1676 tr. *Agrippa's Van. Arts* (1684) 105 Upon the same Grounds the Art of Speculatory Divination is founded.

†2. Inspectorial. *Obs.*⁻¹

1634 T. CAREW *Cœlum Brit.* Wks. (1824) 154 My privileges are an ubiquitary, circumambulatory, speculatory, interrogatory, redargutory immunity over all the privy lodgings.

3. Serving for observation; affording an outlook or view.

1781 WARTON *Hist. Kiddington* (1783) 58 Both these [Roman camps] were nothing more than speculatory outposts to the Akeman-street. 1791 W. GILPIN *Forest Scenery* II. 99 Another small fort..is generally supposed to have been a speculatory station to the grand camp of Buckland. 1837 CARLYLE *Fr. Rev.* II. v. ii, Extreme Left; sitting on the topmost benches, as if aloft on its speculatory Height or Mountain.

Speculatrix (spekiŭlǟ·triks). [a. L. *speculātrix*, fem. of *speculātor.*] A female speculator, in various senses.

1611 COTGR., *Speculatrice*, a speculatrix; a contemplatiue..or watchfull woman. 1744 Z. GREY *Butler's Hud.* II. iii. 1093 *note*, This Sarah Jimmers, whom Lilly calls Sarah Shelhorn, a great Speculatrix. 1841 D'ISRAELI *Amen. Lit.* III. 207 Persons even of ordinary rank in life pretended to be what they termed *speculators*, and sometimes women were *speculatrices.* 1908 *Westm. Gaz.* 29 Aug. 7/2 This.. indicates that the exploitress and speculatrix has just obtained an advantage by doing something particularly mean.

†**Specule,** *v. Obs.*⁻¹ [ad. OF. *speculer*: see SPECULATE *v.*] *trans.* To regard attentively.

1484 CAXTON *Fables of Æsop* v. vi, The he goot..speculynge and beholdynge his shadowe [in the water]..sayd suche wordes within hym self.

Speculist (spe·kiŭlist). [f. SPECUL-ATE *v.* + -IST.] = SPECULATIST.

1707 C. N. *Poem on Union* 18 No more vain Speculists your Fancies Cheat. 1788 G. A. STEVENS (*title*), The Adventures of a Speculist, or, a Journey through London. 1825 N. WOOD *Railroads* 290 The ridiculous expectations, or rather professions, of the enthusiastic speculist. 1861 I. TAYLOR *Spir. Hebrew Poetry* 198 The astute speculist shall be heard quoting the very man—who is quoting Isaiah.

†**Spe·culous,** *a. Obs.*⁻¹ Speculative.

?*c* 1600 *Distr. Emperor* IV. iii. in Bullen *O. Pl.* (1884) III. 236 *Ol.* Thys newe pyle of honor walks as if A would knocke patts with heaven. *Rich.* Tys not unlike Your owne true pryde dothe make you speculous.

‖**Speculum** (spe·kiŭlǒm). Pl. **spe·cula** and **-ums.** [L. *speculum*, f. *specĕre* to look (at), observe. So F. *spéculum*, It. *speculo, specolo*, Sp. *espéculum.*]

1. A surgical instrument of various forms, used for dilating orifices of the body so as to facilitate examination or operations.

Freq. with Latin genitive of the part for which the instrument is used, as *speculum oculi, oris*, etc.

1597 A. M. tr. *Guillemeau's Fr. Chirurg.* C ij b/1 A Dilatorye of the Eyeliddes, or the Speculum of the Eye. 1671 PHILLIPS, *Speculum oris*, an Instrument to skrew open the mouth, that the Chirurgion may discern the diseased parts of the throat. 1693 tr. *Blancard's Phys. Dict.* (ed. 2), *Dilatorium*, a Chyrurgeon's Instrument, wherewith the Womb or the Mouth is dilated or opened. It is called likewise *Speculum*, because by it one may see into the Mouth or the Womb. 1752 SMELLIE *Midwifery* Introd. p. xlix, He is the first who gives a draught of the *Speculum Matricis* for dilating the Os Internum. 1800 *Med. Jrnl.* IV. 103 Permit me to offer the model of a Speculum Oculi, for insertion in the Medical and Physical Journal. 1862 *Catal. Internat. Exhib., Brit.* II. No. 3552, *Specula*, an elegant assortment for the eye, ear, vagina, rectum and nose. 1897 *Allbutt's Syst. Med.* III. 983 Under an anæsthetic the speculum may be of service.

2. A mirror or reflector (of glass or metal) used for some scientific purpose; † a lens.

1646 SIR T. BROWNE *Pseud. Ep.* VII. xviii. (1686) 312 Archimedes burnt the ships of Marcellus with Speculums of Parabolical figures. 1666 BOYLE *Orig. Formes & Qual.* (1667) 30 The giving to a large Metalline Speculum a concave figure, would never enable it to set wood on fire. 1756–7 tr. *Keysler's Trav.* (1760) I. 401 The notes are written in a very small hand,..so that they cannot be easily read without a magnifying *speculum.* *c* 1790 IMISON *Sch. Art* I. 218 There are four of these concave specula, of different magnifying powers, to be used as objects to be examined may require. 1825 *Gentl. Mag.* XCV. I. 292/1 On opening it, it was found to contain in the lid a small convex metallic *speculum*, and in the under-part a larger one. 1860 FARADAY *Forces Nat.* (1874) 186 A single small speculum, no larger than a nut, will send it in any direction we please. 1873 SPON *Workshop Rec.* Ser. I. 317/1 Place the speculum, face downwards, in a dish.

fig. 1826 KIRBY & SP. *Entomol.* xlvii. IV. 404 The ultimate object intended to be reflected from this great speculum of creation. 1829 I. TAYLOR *Enthus.* vi. 146 The few individuals in every age to whom it has happened to live, and act, and speak under the focus of the speculum of history.

b. *spec.* A metallic mirror forming part of a reflecting telescope.

1704 NEWTON *Optics* (1721) 97 Such an Instrument,..if it be six Foot long, (reckoning the length from the Speculum to the Prism, and thence to the Focus T). 1782 J. EDWARDS in *Naut. Almanac* (1787) 52 The Springs at the Back of the great Speculum, which are every Moment varying their Elasticity. 1815 J. SMITH *Panorama Sci. & Art* I. 44 It.. is susceptible of so exquisite a polish, as to be admirably adapted for the speculums of telescopes. *c* 1865 *Wylde's Circ. Sciences* I. 73/2 The speculum is generally made of an alloy composed of variable quantities of copper and tin. 1868 LOCKYER *Elem. Astron.* § 481 The largest reflector in the world has been constructed by the late Earl of Rosse; its mirror, or *speculum*, is six feet in diameter.

c. *transf.* A telescope fitted with a speculum.

1789 HERSCHEL in *Phil. Trans.* (1790) LXXX. 10 In hopes of great success with my forty-feet speculum, I deferred the attack upon Saturn till that should be finished.

†3. A diagram or drawing. *Obs.*⁻¹

1676 COLEY *Clavis Astrol.* (ed. 2) III. 674 A Speculum of the Geniture, or Table of the Radiations of the Planets.

4. *Ornith.* A lustrous mark on the wings of certain birds; = MIRROR *sb.* 6 b.

1804 BEWICK *Brit. Birds* II. 341 The exterior webs..are glossed with gold green, which forms the speculum or beauty-spot of the wings. 1863 C. ST. JOHN *Nat. Hist. & Sport Moray* 35 The pochard has no speculum or bright bar on the wing. 1871 DARWIN *Desc. Man* I. viii. 291 The beautiful green speculum on the wings is common to both sexes.

5. *attrib.* **a.** *Speculum metal*, an alloy of copper and tin used for making specula. Also *speculum steel.*

1796 *Phil. Trans.* LXXXVI. 438 The composition in common use, which contains the greatest proportion of tin, is called speculum metal. 1807–10 TANNAHILL *Poems* (1846) 76 'Twas by the rays' reflected heat, Frae speculum steel. 1818 W. PHILLIPS *Outl. Min. & Geol.* (ed. 3) 46 If the proportion of tin [to copper] amount to one third, it forms speculum metal, used for reflecting telescopes. 1873 SPON *Workshop Rec.* Ser. I. 13/1, 2 lbs. copper, 1 lb. tin, 1 oz. arsenic, form a good speculum metal.

b. *Speculum forceps* (see quot. 1875).

1875 KNIGHT *Dict. Mech.* 2261/1 *Speculum-forceps*, long, slender forceps, used for dressing wounds or operating on parts not accessible except through speculums. 1881 *Trans. Obstet. Soc. Lond.* XXII. 47 The ovum could generally be removed by the administration of ergot and the ordinary speculum forceps.

Sped, *ppl. a.* [Pa. pple. of SPEED *v.*] Discharged, let go.

1891 H. HERMAN *His Angel* 75 No human ingenuity has yet invented the means of recalling the sped bolt.

Sped, obs. f. SPADE *sb.*[1] and *sb.*[3], SPEED *sb.*; pret. of SPEED *v.* **Spedd(e,** obs. pret. of SPEED *v.* **Spede,** obs. f. SPEED *sb.* and *v.* **Spedee, Sped(e)ful(le, Spedi,** etc., obs. ff. SPEEDY *a.*, SPEEDFUL *a.*, etc. **Speece,** variant of SPECE *Obs.*

Speech (spītʃ), *sb.*[1] Forms: α. 1–2 **spræc, sprec,** 2 **sprace, spræche.** β. 1 **spæc, spec,** 2 **spece,** 3 **spæche (spache, spiche),** 3–6 **speche** (4 **spieche**), 4–6 **spech,** 6– **speech,** 6–7 **speach, speache;** *Sc.* 6 **speitche,** 6–7 **speiche.** [OE. *spræc, sprēc* (later *spǣc, spēc*), = OFris. *sprēke, sprētse* (NFris. *sprēk, spriak*) and *sprāke* (WFris. *sprake, sprack*, EFris. *sprōk*), MDu. *sprāke, spraec* (Du. *spraak*), OS. *sprāka* (MLG. *sprāke*, LG. *sprāke, sprāk*, etc.; hence Sw. *språk*, Da. *sprog*), OHG. *sprâhha* (MHG. *sprâche*, G. *sprache*), f. *sprǣc-* the pret. pl. stem of *sprecan, specan* SPEAK *v.* As in the verb, the forms with *spr-* did not survive beyond the 12th century.]

I. 1. The act of speaking; the natural exercise of the vocal organs; the utterance of words or sentences; oral expression of thought or feeling.

c 725 *Corpus Gloss.* (Hessels) S 299 *Sermo*, spæc. *c* 897 K. ÆLFRED tr. *Gregory's Past. C.* 274 Hit is awriten.. ðætte hwilum sie spræce tiid, hwilum swigȝean. *c* 1000 *Ags. Gosp.* Matt. vi. 7 Hiȝ wenað þæt hi sin ȝehyrede on hyra menigfealden spæce. *c* 1230 *Hali Meid.* 17 Hire forme fulst is sihðe:..Speche is hire oðer help. 1297 R. GLOUC. (Rolls) 7197 Stalwarde mon of speche he was. *c* 1330 *Assump. Virg.* (B.M. MS.) 628 Oure mayne þee knewe þat ilke nyȝt Bothe bi speche & by syȝt. *c* 1386 CHAUCER *Prol.* 783 Hold up youre hond withoute more speche. *c* 1400 LOVE *Bonavent. Mirr.* (1908) 53 For moche speche with oute frute is a grete vice and displesynge to god and man. *c* 1470 *Gol. & Gaw.* 261 Than schir Spynagrose with speche spak to the king. 1500–20 DUNBAR *Poems* xx. 4 In mekle speiche is part of vanitie. 1594 T. B. *La Primaud. Fr. Acad.* II. 89 Thus the thoughtes and counsailes of the minde and spirite are discouered and manifested by speach. 1667 MILTON *P. L.* VIII. 377, I with leave of speech implor'd, And humble deprecation thus repli'd. 1690 LOCKE *Hum. Und.* III. vi. (1695) 258 This is adjusted to the true end of Speech, which is to be the easiest and shortest way of communicating our Notions. 1732 BERKELEY *Alciphr.* I. § 14 Men..express their thoughts by speech. 1751 HARRIS *Hermes* Wks. (1841) 117 Since speech, then, is the joint energy of our best and noblest faculties. 1825 SCOTT *Talism.* xxii, A movement ..attended with no speech and very little noise. 1864 *Reader* 14 May 626 The author would define human speech as a method of expressing human thought by audible sounds. 1887 BOWEN *Æneid* VI. 387 He accosts them, and first breaks silence in speech.

fig. 1611 SHAKS. *Wint. T.* v. ii. 14 There was speech in their dumbness, Language in their very gesture.

transf. 1866 B. TAYLOR *Euphorion* 273 The speech of winds. 1904 SWINBURNE *Channel Passage*, etc. 181 The speech of storm, the thunders of the soul.

b. *transf.* The speaking or sounding of a musical instrument, organ-pipe, etc.

1862 *Catal. Internat. Exhib., Brit.* II. No. 3377, Quickness of 'speech', flute-like quality of tone,..are some of the characteristics of the English harmonium. 1880 *Grove's Dict. Music* II. 578 The manner of testing the 'speech' [of an organ] by blowing the pipe with the mouth in various ways. 1881 W. E. DICKSON *Pract. Organ-building* xii. 146 The speech of the pipe will be entirely unaltered.

†**c.** *fig.* Mouth-piece; organ. *Obs.*⁻¹

1578 T. N. tr. *Conq. W. India* (1596) 34 Certainly he was the meane and speech of all their proceedings.

Supplement, p. 3873; Corrigenda, p. 4092; Spurious words, p. 4093; Books quoted, p. 4094.

2953

Speir — *Chron.* Wace (Rolls) 5790 To haue a lord þey were in *spyr*. ...

Speir², v.

Speiss (spais). Also 8–9 *speis*. [ad. G. *speise*] ... An impure metallic compound, containing nickel, cobalt, iron, etc., produced in the smelting of certain ores ...

Spele, var. SPEEL *sb.* and *v.*

Spele, *v.* ¹ Now *dial.* and *rare.*

Spald, *sb.* Also 4–5 *spelde*, 4 *spielde.*

Spelk, *sb.* [= SPEAK, SPEKE, SPEKE²] ...

Spelk-broom (African flax, ...

Speke, **Spak**, obs. ff. SPEAK, SPEEK.

Speke¹ ... A handsalve.

Speke², ² Also 4 *spok*, 7 *speak.* [a. MDu. or MLG. *spēke* ...]

Spelt, *sb.* ¹ [= MLG. *spelder* ...]

Spelk, v. ... To spread or extend oneself ...

Spele, var. SPEEL *sb.* and *v.*

Spelk, *sb.* Chiefly *north.* (and *Sc.*) ...

Spelding (spĕl'diŋ). *Sc.* Also 7–8 *spelden*, 8–9 in pl. *spak.* [f. SPELD v. + -ING¹.]

Speldring, *Sc.* Also *spel-ring, -rin, -ron.* [f. ...]

Spell (spel). *sb.* ¹ Also 1–7 *spel*, 2–5 *spelle.* [OE., *spel, spell* ...] **†1.** Without article: Discourse, narration, speech; occas. idle talk, tale. *Obs.*

Spell, *sb.* ² Now *dial.* Also 6–9 *spel*, 7 *spilte.* [perh. a form of SPELD *sb.*, but cf.]

Spell, *sb.* ³ Now *dial.* Also 6–9 *spell.* 7 *spilte.* ...

Spell (spel), *sb.* ⁴ *colloq.* [f. SPELL *v.* ⁴] ...

Spell, *v.* ¹ Also 1–5 *spellen*, 4 *spel.* [OE. *spellian* ...] **1.** *intr.* To discourse or preach; to talk, converse, or speak. *Obs.*

Spell, *v.* ² Also 3–5 *spellen.* [Of ... origin.] ...

Spell, *v.* ³ Also 4–5 *spellen*, 4 *spel.* ...

Spell, *v.* ⁴ [a. OF. *espel(l)er* ...] **1.** *trans.* To read (a book, etc.); letter by letter ...

Spellbind, *v.* [Back-formation ...] *trans.* To bind by, or as by, a spell; to fascinate, enchant.

Spellbinder (spe'lbəndŏ). *U.S.* [f. as prec.] A political speaker capable of holding an audience spell-bound.

Spell-bound, *ppl. a.* [f. SPELL *sb.* ¹ + BOUND *ppl. a.* ¹] Bound by, or as by, a spell; fascinated, enchanted.

Speller (spe'lɒ). [f. SPELL *v.* ⁴ + -ER¹.] **1.** One who spells, or spells out, words ...

Spelling, *vbl. sb.* ¹ [f. SPELL *v.* ⁴] ... The action, practice, or art of naming the letters of words, or reading letter by letter ...

Spelling, *vbl. sb.* ² [f. SPELL *v.* ¹] Speaking, talking, discourse; utterance.

Spelling-book (spe'liŋ-bŭk). [SPELLING *vbl. sb.* ¹] ...

Spellingly, *adv.* [f. *spelling*, pres. ppl. of SPELL *v.* ⁴ + -LY².] By spelling; letter by letter.

†Spelken. *Cant. Obs.* [See SPELL *sb.* ³ and KEN *sb.* ²] ...

Spellman. *Obs.* Also *spelman.* [f. SPELL *sb.* ¹ + MAN] ...

Spallican, var. SPILLIKIN.

Spelling, *vbl. sb.* ³ Speaking, talking, utterance.

Spelly, *v.* ... Full of spells or charms.

Spelk, *sb.* ² 5 *spilt*, 6 *spylt*, 6 *spelte*, 7 *spelt*: = MDu. *spelte*, *spilte*, OHG. (MHG., *spëlte*, *spilt-*), late L. *spelta* (from *c.* 400, mentioned as a foreign word among the Teutons) ...

Spelt, *sb.* ² *rare.* Now *dial.* [Connected with SPELT *v.* Cf. SPELD *sb.* and G. *spelze* husk.] A thin piece of wood or metal; a splinter. Also in *spelk*.

Spelt, *v.* [Related to SPALD *v.* Cf. G. *spalten* husk.] *trans.* To split or cleave. Hence

Spelter (spe'ltɒ). *al.* Also 6–9 *speltre*. [Cf. (M)LG. *spialter* ...] Zinc as an article of commerce ...

lamp or two of Spelter there for two or three days. **1691** J. Webster *Metallogr.* Pref. B ij b, Ores...of Antimony, Tinglass, Spelter, Tutty, and Cinnabar. **1758** Newcome *Hunt. Enk.* 139, I have often made them with a mix'd Metal of Pewter and Spelter. **1798** Boswell *Life Johnson* (1887) III. 398 note, I procured...his napkin...I have received specimens from several parts of Cornwall. **1799** G. Smith *Laboratory* I. 102 Filing into it one ounce of Spelter...

2. An alloy or solder of which zinc is the principal constituent.

1825 J. Nicholson *Operat. Mechanic* 383 The hard solder for copper, is a soft fusible sort of granulated brass, well known to artists under the name of spelter. *Ibid.*, *Method of making spelter for brazing iron, copper, etc.*

3. *attrib.* and *Comb.*, as *spelter-box, -dust, -heap, -maker, -ore.*

Hence **Spelter** *v. trans.*, to unite with spelter solder.

Speluncar (spiᵘlᵃŋkaᵊ), *a.* [f. L. *spelunca.*]

1. Having relation or reference to a cave.

2. Of the nature of a cave.

Spelunce, *n. rare* [...]. *var. prec.* + *-ess.*]

†Spelunk. *Obs.* Forms: 4–5 spelonk(e; 4–6 spelunke, spelunk(e, 6 spelunca, -ke, 7 spelunca or OF. *spelunque, spelunque.* Cf. MDu. *spelunke,* Du. *spelonck*), MHG. and G. *spelunke.*]

A cave or cavern; a grotto.

Spenceanism (spenᵃʃᵊnᵃiz'm), *n.* [f. the name of the politician Thomas *Spence* (1750–1814).] **A.** *adj.* Of or pertaining to Thomas Spence or his views.

Spenceanism (spenᵊʃᵊnᵃiz'm), *n.* [f. the name of the politician Thomas *Spence* (1750–1814).] **A.** *adj.* Of or pertaining to Thomas Spence or his views.

B. *sb.* A follower of Thomas Spence.

Spen, variant of SPEAN *sb.*

Spence¹ (spens). Also 5–7 spens(e, 6 spennye. [Aphetically f. OF. *despense* (mod.F. *dépense*), — Sp. and Pg. *despensa*, It. *dispensa*, med.L. *dispensa, dispensa* (rarely *spensa*), in the same sense: cf. DISPENSE *sb.*] So Swiss dial. *spensa.*

1. A room or separate place in which victuals and liquor are kept; a buttery or pantry; a cupboard. Now *dial. or arch.*

b. A kind of close-fitting jacket or bodice commonly worn by women and children early in the 19th century, and since revived.

2. A form of life-belt.

3. *slang.* (See quot.)

4. An inner apartment of a house; a parlour.

5. *Sc.* The part of a farm-house between the kitchen and the spence.

Spencer¹ (spenᵊsaᵊ), *sb.* [perh. Of obscure origin.] *dial.* [Of obscure origin.]

†Spencer. *Obs.* Also 4 *apense.* [Substituted for SPENCER *sb.*1, after prec.] A steward.

Spencer (spenᵊsaᵊ), *sb.2* [From the family name *Spencer.*]

Spence² (spens). Also 5–7 *spence,* 6 *spense.*

Spence³, *sb.* var. of SPEAN *sb.*

Spend (spend), *v.1* Pa. t. and pa. pple. **spent.**

Forms: 1–3 *spenden;* 3 *spende* (3 *spendyn*), 4–*spend.*

I. *trans.* **I.** Of persons : To pay out or away; to disburse or expend; to dispose of, or deprive oneself of, in this way.

b. *refl.* To exert oneself.

2. *absol.* To exercise, make, or incur expenditure of money, goods, means, etc.

Spender¹. *Obs.* In 4 *apendre,* 5 *spendere.*

Spender² (spenᵊdaᵊ). Also 4 *spendour,* 5 *spen-dyrⁱ.*

Spending, *vbl. sb.* [f. SPEND *v.1*] **1.** The disbursing, expending, paying out or away of money, etc.

Spending-money, [f. SPENDING *vbl. sb.*]

Spend-good. *Obs. rare* [f. SPEND *v.1* + *good sb.*]

†Spendible, *a. Obs. rare* [ad. late L. *spendibilis.*]

Spendless, *a. rare* — [f. SPEND *v.1* + *-LESS.*] That cannot be spent or consumed.

Spendthrift (spenᵊdθrift), *sb.* (and *a.*). Also 7 *spend-thrift.* [f. SPEND *v.1* + THRIFT *sb.*]

Spendful, *a.* *rare* — [f. SPEND *v.1* + *-FUL.*] Inclined to spend; lavish, extravagant.

Spender, *n.* One who, or that which, expends.

Spend, *sb.1* [f. SPEND *v.*] The action of spending money. Only in phrase *on* or *upon*

Spendable (spenᵊdab'l), *a.* Also 6 *-abyll.* [f. SPEND *v.1* + *-ABLE.*]

Spending, *ppl. a.* [f. SPEND *v.1*]

Spen, variant of SPEAN *sb.* and *v.*

Spene, variant of SPEAN *sb.*

2. *concr.* That which may be or is spent; money, supplies; *dial.* pocket-money. Also *pl.*

a 1225 *Ancr. R.* 350 Ne he ne bereð no garsum bute gnedeliche his spense. *c* 1290 *Beket* 1365 in *S. Eng. Leg.* 145 Þe king him fond spence i-no3 to him and alle his. 1303 R. Brunne *Handl. Synne* 6857 To þe cyte he was com late, And of spensys had he non. 1387 Trevisa *Higden* (Rolls) VII. 127 Þe duke was prayed of þe emperour for to take costage and spence for the way. *c* 1460 *Towneley Myst.* xxii. 249, I wold spende all my spence To se hym ones skelpt. 1886 H. Cunliffe *Rochdale Gloss.*, *Spence*, pocket-money.

†**3.** The expenditure or spending *of* goods, income, etc. *Obs.*

c 1400 *Destr. Troy* 13622 So he sped hym by spies, & spense of his gode. 1538 Starkey *England* II. iii. 201 Wych..ys the occasyon of the grete spens of the intrat of the monastery. 1567 Drant *Horace, Ep.* I. xv. E vj, When as with spence of parentes goddes Sir Meui once began.. for to be cawld a iolly gentleman.

†**b.** The employing, expending, consuming, or using up *of* something. *Obs.*

1555 J. Proctor *Hist. Wyat's Rebellion* 54 b, To aduenture the spense of her royall bloude in defense of them. 1563 Foxe *A. & M.* 745 Many hote argumentes were betwene them,..with muche spence of language. 1594 Lodge *Wounds Civil War* A iv b, The spence of yeares that Marius hath ore-past..Hath taught him this.

Spense, obs. form of Spence.

†**Spe·nseful,** *a. Obs.*⁻¹ [f. Spense.] Extravagant or lavish in expenditure.

1600 Sir R. Cecil in *Carew MSS.* (1869) 445, I think he is but spenceful beyond measure.

Spenser, variant of Spencer¹ *Obs.*

Spenserian (spensī°·riăn), *a.* and *sb.* [f. the name of the Elizabethan poet Edmund *Spenser* (? 1552–1599) + -ian.]

A. *adj.* Of or belonging to, characteristic of, Spenser or his work.

Spenserian stanza, the stanza employed by Spenser in the *Faerie Queen*, consisting of eight decasyllabic lines and a final Alexandrine, with the rhyming scheme *ab ab bc bcc.*

1818 Scott *Rob Roy* ii, I..was busy in meditation on the oft-recurring rhymes of the Spenserian stanza. 1853 Ruskin *Stones Ven.* II. vii. 273 The Spenserian mingling of the mediæval image..is altogether exquisite. 1890 Hosmer *Anglo-Sax. Freedom* 97 The redoubtable Spenserian giant, Kirk-rapine.

B. *sb.* **1.** A Spenserian stanza, or a poem in this metre.

1818 Keats *Lett.* (1848) I. 133, I see no reason..why I should not have a peep at your Spenserian. 1853 J. Nichol in Knight *Mem.* (1896) ii. 101, I hope to come nearer it at any rate than in these Spenserians. 1886 *Athenæum* 23 Jan. 131/2 Scarcely any poet since Spenser has written entirely successful Spenserians... Byron..failed altogether in Spenserians.

2. A follower or imitator of Spenser; a poet of Spenser's school.

1894 Gosse *Jacobean Poets* 47 His [Donne's] were the first poems which protested, in their form alike and their tendency, against the pastoral sweetness of the Spenserians.

So **Spense·ric,** *a.* [-ic.] Spenserian.

1795 Anna Seward *Lett.* (1811) IV. 113 That gay town, which Shenstone, in his Spenseric poem, the Schoolmistress, has so beautifully apostrophized.

Spent (spent), *pa. pple.* and *ppl. a.* [Spend *v.*¹]

I. In predicative uses.

1. Of material things: Expended, consumed, used up completely.

c 1440 *Promp. Parv.* 468/2 Spent, *expensus, dispensatus.* 1450 in *Rep. Hist. MSS. Comm.* Var. Coll. IV. 85 The vitailes of oure seid Towne ben al moste spent & consumed. *a* 1548 Hall *Chron., Hen. V,* 14 b, Their vitaile was in maner al spent, and newe they coulde gette none. 1591 Shaks. *1 Hen. VI,* II. v. 8 These Eyes, like Lampes, whose wasting Oyle is spent, Waxe dimme. 1632 Lithgow *Trav.* vii. 329 The..cause of our Arriuall here, was in regard of our fresh Water that was spent. 1664 Power *Exp. Philos.* I. 34 When the Liquor wherin they swim is almost spent and dried up. 1769 Sir W. Jones *Palace Fortune* Poems (1777) 12 His guards retir'd, his glimmering taper spent. 1837 Lockhart *Scott* I. xi. 417 When the lamp of his own genius was all but spent. 1849 Macaulay *Hist. Eng.* v. I. 611 Their powder and ball were spent. 1883 Browning *Jocoseria* 116 Our acquist Of life is spent.

†**b.** Wrecked; drowned. *Obs. rare.*

c 1477 Caxton *Jason* 76 b, And thus by this waye they [i.e. ships] were all lost and spent. 1626 *Whitburn Par. Reg.* 17 July, John Burne of Sheels, being casten forth of a Cobble and spent in the sea.

2. Passed, gone; come to an end; over: **a.** Of time. Also *far spent* (Far *adv.* 3 c).

1528 Gardiner in Burnet *Hist. Ref., Rec.* I. ii. (Pocock) IV. 127 The day being then spent. 1560 Daus tr. *Sleidane's Comm.* 181 The time is farre spente. 1593 Shaks. *Rich. II,* II. i. 154 His time is spent, our pilgrimage must be. 1611 Bible *Rom.* xiii. 12 The night is farre spent. 1615 Sandys *Trav.* 87 January being now well spent, we departed from Constantinople. 1667 Milton *P. L.* viii. 206 Day is yet not spent. 1724 Gay *Captives* I. (1772) 19 Is night near spent? 1841 Browning *Pippa Passes* Poems (1905) 189 New year's day is over and spent. 1860 Tyndall *Glac.* I. xi. 79 The day was already far spent.

b. Of things, material and immaterial.

c 1600 Shaks. *Sonn.* cvii, And thou in this shalt finde thy monument, When tyrants crests and tombs of brasse are spent. 1634 Sir T. Herbert *Trav.* 7 The raine is spent. 1766 Blackstone *Comm.* II. 237 Till both the immediate bloods of George Stiles, the paternal grandfather, are spent. 1818 Cruise *Digest* (ed. 2) III. 496 The lease..determined by the estate tail being spent.

3. Of persons or animals: Deprived of force or strength; tired or worn out by labour, exertion, hardship, etc.; completely exhausted.

1591 Savile *Tacitus, Hist.* I. xii. 7 Galba was spent and feeble for age. 1647 Hexham I. (*Hunting*), The Hart, Stagg, Hinde, Buck, or Doe, is spent. 1691 Ray *Creation* I. (1704) 159 Why the Hare when she is near spent makes up a Hill? 1713 Addison *Cato* IV. iv, Now thou seest me Spent, overpower'd, despairing of success. 1774 Goldsm. *Nat. Hist.* (1776) V. 33 Many..quite spent by the fatigues of their flight, drop down into the sea. 1840 Dickens *Old C. Shop* xiv, So very weak and spent she felt.

transf. 1612 Drayton *Poly-olb.* i. 319 When long-renewed Troy lay spent in hostile fire.

b. Const. *with* age, fatigue, toil, etc.

Freq. from *c* 1600 to 1730.

1603 Knolles *Hist. Turks* (1621) 137 Ertogrul now spent with age, shortly after died. 1611 Shaks. *Cymb.* III. vi. 63 Almost spent with hunger, I am falne in this offence. 1703 Pope *Thebais* 537 On the cold marble spent with toil he lies. 1760–72 H. Brooke *Fool of Qual.* (1809) III. 5 Being spent with fatigue, I..sat me down to die. 1817 Shelley *Rev. Islam* x. xxxvii, They will sleep with luxury spent. 1867 F. Parkman *Jesuits in N. Amer.* iv. (1875) 26 Spent with travel, and weakened by precarious and unaccustomed fare.

4. Of things: Exhausted of the active or effective power or principle.

1596 Lodge *Marg. Amer.* F iv b, Thy sap by course of time is blent, My sence by care and age is spent. 1633 T. James *Voy.* 85 Our tooles were all so spent, that we could cut none. 1665 Manley *Grotius' Low C. Wars* 437 For by the..long distance of place, the Shot was spent, before it came to the place, which it was intended to batter. 1697 Dampier *Voy.* I. 36 At length when the Creatures strength is spent, they ..knock it on the head. *a* 1722 Lisle *Husb.* (1757) 154 The malt is spent and wasted before it is laid in the grounds. 1774 Goldsm. *Nat. Hist.* (1776) I. 201 If this acquired velocity be quite spent. 1817 Shelley *Rev. Islam* IV. xxx, Though their lustre now was spent and faded. 1883 *Manch. Exam.* 28 Nov. 5/1 The vigour and 'go' infused into the party..would show symptoms of being spent.

b. *Naut.* Of the tide or a current.

c 1595 Capt. Wyatt *Dudley's Voy.* (Hakl. Soc.) 3 Our master thought it not good to turne downe the channell, the tide beinge soe far spent. 1616 J. Lane *Contn. Sqr.'s T.* VII. 359 Then in hee bore for land, till th' tyde was spent. 1719 De Foe *Crusoe* I. (Globe) 143 When I had made something more than a League of Way by the Help of this Current or Eddy, I found it was spent. 1743 Bulkeley & Cummins *Voy. S. Seas* 137 And the Tide being spent, we put into a small Cove, and made fast.

II. In attributive uses.

5. Of persons or animals; = sense 3.

a 1568 Ascham *Scholem.* (Arb.) 152 The talke of a spent old man. 1605 Shaks. *Macb.* I. ii. 8 It stood, As two spent Swimmers, that doe cling together. 1715 Pope *Iliad* II. 465 Let..each spent courser at the chariot blow. 1825 Hone *Every-day Bk.* I. 292, I remember the..squire and his.. chaplain casting home on spent horses. 1859 Jephson *Brittany* xii. 193 The English archers..charged down..upon the now spent and wearied French.

b. Of fish: Exhausted by spawning; having recently spawned.

1864 *Intell. Observ.* V. 363 After the performance of this function the fish is sickly and weak, and is then called a Shotten or Spent fish. 1866 *Chambers's Encycl.* VIII. 446/1 Salmon, which have completed their spawning, continue for some time..very unfit for the table... They are called 'foul fish', or more distinctively, 'spent fish', or Kelts. 1883 *Fisheries Exhib. Catal.* 69, 1 Barrel Large Full Herrings.. 1 Barrel Spent Herrings.

c. *Spent gnat*, a kind of artificial fly used in trout fishing.

1867 F. Francis *Angling* vi. (1880) 229 The black drake, or spent gnat, as it is sometimes called. 1894 *Daily News* 9 June 832/1 All kinds were tried, including the spent gnat, but the fish would have none of them.

6. Of things: Exhausted, worn out, used up; no longer active, effective, or serviceable.

1697 Dryden *Virg. Georg.* I. 108 That the spent Earth may gather heart again; And, better'd by Cessation, bear the Grain. 1830 Lyell *Princ. Geol.* I. 322 If the action of one becomes very great for a century or more, the others assume the appearance of spent volcanos. 1850 Whittier *To Avis Keene* 38 Where spent waves glimmer up the beach. 1883 Miss Broughton *Belinda* II. 1.9, 'I should like to sit down,' says Belinda, in a spent voice.

b. Of arrows, balls, or shot.

1697 Dryden *Æneid* IX. 906 Heaps of spent Arrows fall and strew the Ground. 1799 *Naval Chron.* I. 169 A spent ball ..hit him. 1802 James *Milit. Dict.* s.v., Spent balls..are frequently fatal in their effects. 1858 Carlyle *Fredk. Gt.* II. ix. I. 153 [He] declared in solemn Diet, the Pope's ban to be mere spent shot.

c. Of hops, tan, etc., from which the essential properties have been extracted.

1826 *Art of Brewing* (ed. 2) 105 If the disorder do not subside readily, a gyle of spent hops thrown in will generally be advantageous. 1842 Loudon *Suburban Hort.* 391 Coverings for the surface of the ground include dead leaves,..spent tan,..rotten dung,..&c. 1857 Miller *Elem. Chem., Org.* vi. § 1. 372 A quantity of common salt is next added to separate the spent leys. 1877 Raymond *Statist. Mines & Mining* 390 The spent liquor..is discharged into the stream.

7. In comb. with *out.*

1620 Dekker *Dream* Wks. (Grosart) III. 18 The Terrestiall Pauement burn'd, In which the Starres to spent-out Snuffes were turnd. 1848 Thackeray *Van. Fair* lxi, A spent-out, bootless life of defeat and disappointment.

Spen3e(e, -3ie, obs. Sc. varr. Spain.

‖**Speos** (spī·ǫs). *Egyptol.* [Gr. σπέος cave, grotto.] A cave temple or tomb, esp. one of some architectural importance.

1843 G. Wilkinson *Mod. Egypt & Thebes* v. II. 56 Pasht ..has always the head of a lioness, and the title, 'Lady of the excavation' or 'Speos'. 1888 C. D. Bell *Winter on Nile* xviii. 170 There is a large speos with four massive pillars.

Speowen, obs. form of Spew *v.* **Sper,** obs. var. Spar *v.*¹, Spear *sb.*¹, *v.*¹, Speer *v.*, Sphere.

†**Sperable,** *a. Obs.* [ad. L. *spērābilis* (f. *spērāre* to hope) or F. *espérable* (Sp. *esperable*, Pg. *esperavel*, It. *sperabile*).] That may be hoped for; admitting of, giving room for, hope. Of debts: = Sperate *a.* 1.

1565 Sir W. Cecil in Ellis *Orig. Lett.* Ser. II. II. 297 Wherin suerly perceaving his own cause not sperable, he doth honorably and wisely. 1571 — in D. Digges *Compleat Ambass.* (1655) 164, I am sorry that your health is not more sperable to be speedily recovered. 1591 Unton *Corr.* (Roxb.) 187 If..you yourselfe shall find the recovery [of Rouen] sperable, then..you may afterwards use the kind of speache. *c* 1615 Jas. I in *Buccleuch MSS.* (Hist. MSS. Comm.) I. 170 Debts before the 30th of Elizabeth, though they be never so sperable.

Speragas, variant of Sparagus *Obs.*

†**Spe·rage.** *Obs.* Also 7 **spirage, sperrage,** 8 **spearage.** [a. OF. *sperage*, var. of *sparage* Sparage.] Asparagus.

c 1440 *Pallad. on Husb.* III. 558 Sperages seed..Is good to sewe hem with,..For cannes & sperage haue oon tylynge. 1545 Elyot, *Asparagus*, an herbe callyd of common Apotecaries Sparagus, in englishe Sperage. 1577 B. Googe tr. *Heresbach's Husb.* 19 Sperage and such like, must be sowen in shaddowy places. 1620 Venner *Via Recta* vii. 130 Asparagus or Sperage is hot in the beginning of the first degree. 1688 Holme *Armoury* II. 99/2 Asparagus or Sperage... The Flowers are yellow, consisting of six leaves. 1731 Miller *Gard. Dict.*, *Asparagus*,..Sparagus or Sperage. 1760 J. Lee *Introd. Bot.* App. 327 Spearage, see Asparagus.

attrib. 1611 Cotgr., *Pois à visage*,..Sperage Beanes, French Beanes,..Kidney Beanes. *a* 1661 Holyday *Juvenal* 77 Thy patrone's fish, Deck'd round with sperage-buds.

b. With distinguishing adjs.

1545 Elyot, *Corruda*, an herbe called wylde sperage. 1548 Turner *Names Herbes* (E.D.S.) 17 It maye be called in englishe pricky Sperage, because it is all full of pryckes. 1601 Holland *Pliny* II. 122 The stalke is smooth, and resembleth garden Sperage. *a* 1661 Holyday *Juvenal* 214 Wild sperage too We'll have; my plow-man's wife her spindle threw Aside, to gather it. 1758 Borlase *Nat. Hist. Cornw.* 233 Marsh-asparagus or sperage, *Asparagus palustris.*

Spe·rate, *a.* ? *Obs.* [ad. L. *spērāt-us*, pa. pple. of *spērāre* to hope.]

1. Of debts: Having some likelihood of being recovered; not desperate.

1551 *Will of R. Studlaye* (Somerset Ho.), Sperate debtes. *a* 1625 Cope in Gutch *Coll. Cur.* I. 122 Which [debts] were good, which were bad, which sperate, which desperate, no man knew. 1697 in *New Jersey Arch.* Ser. I. (1901) XXIII. 83 A negro mald servant and debts sperate and desperate. 1710 in Exton *St. Q. Anne's Bounty* (1721) 108 We have therefore spent much Time..in distinguishing between the sperate and desperate Debts of the Clergy. 1798 *Washington's Reports* I. 169 Outstanding debts, distinguishing such as are sperate from such as are supposed to be desperate.

2. In general use: Giving or leaving room for hope; of a promising nature.

1808 Ld. Ellenborough in 10 *Rev. Rep.* (1893) 718 If you think there is anything sperate in it, I will save the point. 1824 *Cowen's Rep.* (N.Y. State Supreme Crt.) 106 Every vessel has a point of time at which it passes from a Sperate to a desperate state, or arrives at a situation of unseaworthiness.

†**Speratory,** *a. Obs.*⁻¹ [See prec. and -ory.] Resting in hope or expectation.

1629 Donne *Serm.* cxxxvi. Wks. 1839 V. 442 [Mammon offers] the present and possessory things of this world, God but the future and speratory things of the next.

†**Spercil.** *Obs.*⁻¹ [app. f. *sper* Spar *sb.*¹] ? The spars of a roof.

1570 Levins *Manip.* 123 Ye spercil, *subtegulaneum.*

Spercle, obs. form of Sparkle.

Spere, obs. form of Spear, Speer, Sphere.

†**Spere,** *a. Obs.* Also **speer.** [Of obscure origin.] Frail, delicate.

c 1440 *Promp. Parv.* 468 Spere, or fres (*K.* freshe or brityl, *P.* britill or brekyll), *fragilis.* *c* 1440 *Jacob's Well* 221 My chayere is my body of speer brotyl & rotyn bonys, in whiche my soule sytteth. 1486 *Bk. St. Albans*, *Hawking* e viii b, She may be callid a Spere hawke for of all the hawkys that ther be she is moost spere, that is to say moost tendre to kepe.

†**Sperel.** *Obs.* Also **sperl-.** [prob. of Flem. origin: cf. WFlem. *sperel, sperrel* door-bar, f. *sperren* Spar *v.*¹] A means of closing or fastening; a bar or bolt; a book-clasp.

13.. *S. Erkenwolde* 49 in Horstm. *Altengl. Leg.* (1881) 267 Thre sperlis of þe spelunke þat spradde [? *read* sparde] hit o lofte Was metely made of þe marbre. *c* 1440 *Promp. Parv.* 363 Ondoynge, or opynynge of schettellys, or sperellys, *aperio.* *Ibid.* 469/1 Sperel, or closel yn schetynge... *firmaculum.* *Ibid.*, Sperel, of a boke,... *offendix*,... *signaculum.*

Sperete, obs. form of Spirit *sb.*

†**Sperge**¹. *Obs.*⁻¹ [? ad. OF. *esperge*, var. of *asperge.*] ? Asparagus.

c 1400 *Lanfranc's Cirurg.* 275 He schal ete fenel, ache, persil, sperge,..& he schal ete no mustard.

†**Sperge**². *Obs.*⁻¹ [Aphetic f. Asperge *sb.*] A sprinkler.

1675 Evelyn *Philos. Disc. Earth* (1676) 143 Gently refresh'd with a dewie sperge or brush, not with the watring-pot.

‖**Spergula** (spɔ·ɹgiŭlă). [med. and mod.L. *Spergula*, of unknown origin.] One or other variety of spurrey.

1882 *Garden* 29 Apr. 297/2 Couch Grass and Spergula are at this season very troublesome. 1884 tr. *De Candolle's Orig. Cultivated Pl.* 115 Agriculturists distinguish a taller variety of spergula.

Spe·rgulin. *Chem.* [f. mod.L. *Spergula*: see prec.] (See quot.)

1881 Watts *Dict. Chem.*, 3rd *Suppl.*, *Spergulin*, a fluorescent body, occurring in the seed-coverings of *Spergula vulgaris* and *S. maxima*, and produced at the time when the seeds blacken and are nearly ripe.

Sperie, obs. var. Spurrey. **Sperit**(e, varr. Spirit *sb.* **Sperk**(e, obs. or Sc. varr. Spark. **Sperket,** obs. or dial. f. Spirket. **Sperling,** var. Sparling.

Sperm (spɔ̄ɹm), *sb.* Forms: 4–7 **sperme,** 6 **spearme, sparme,** 7 **sparm,** 6– **sperm.** [ad. OF. *esperme* (F. *sperme*), *sparme*, or L. *sperma* (hence also It. *sperma*, Sp. and Pg. *esperma*), a. Gr. σπέρμα, f. the stem of σπείρειν to sow.]

I. 1. The generative substance or seed of male animals (esp. of vertebrates).

c 1386 Chaucer *Monk's T.* 19 In the feld of Damassene With goddes owene finger wroght was he And nat bigeten of mannes sperme [*Harl. MS.* sperma] unclene. 1398 Trevisa *Barth. De P. R.* XIII. xxix. (Tollem. MS.), The whale haþ gret plente of sperme, and after þat he gendreþ with þe female, superfluite þerof fleteþ aboue þe water. *a* 1425 tr. *Arderne's Treat. Fistula*, etc. 14 Som-tyme þe sperme goþ oute by þe hole of þe 3erde infistulate. 1526 *Grete Herball* xxviii. (1529) B v b, Ambre is hote and drye... Some say that it is the sparme of a whale. 1549 *Compl. Scot.* vi. 67, I sau hemp, that coagulis the flux of the sparme. 1605 Timme *Quersit.* I. xvi. 85 We see, of bread and wine, blood to be made; of blood, sperm or seed. 1646 Sir T. Browne *Pseud. Ep.* 330 And thus may it also be in the generation and sperm of Negroes. 1725 *Fam. Dict.* s.v. *Poultry*, The Cock.. rarifies the Egg, and renders it fit to produce its Species by the Sperm or Tread he infuses into it. 1783 Justamond tr. *Raynal's Hist. Indies* V. 361 It hath since been imagined, that pearls must be the eggs or the sperm of the fish inclosed in the shell. 1822–7 Good *Stud. Med.* (1829) V. 6 The male shortly afterwards passes over the spawn or hard roe, and discharges upon it his sperm, which we call soft roe or milt. 1878 F. J. Bell *Gegenbaur's Elem. Comp. Anat.* 53 Receptacles which serve for the collection of the sperm.

b. A spermatozoon.

1904 *Brit. Med. Jrnl.* 15 Oct. 964 Gametes (eggs and sperms). 1905 G. A. Reid *Princ. Heredity* xii. 162 If these same sperms reside for a longer time [etc.].

†**2. a.** The eggs of insects. *Obs.*

1615 W. Lawson *Country Housew. Gard.* (1626) 44 The red peckled butter-flye doth euer put them [i.e. caterpillars], being her sparm, among the tender spraies for better feeding. 1747 W. Gould *Eng. Ants* 34 A just Description of the Sperm or Eggs (which is entirely answerable to what the Queen lays).

†**b.** Offspring, brood (of persons). *Obs. rare.*

1641 Milton *Animadv.* Wks. 1851 III. 237 Let not those wretched Fathers thinke they shall impoverish the Church.., though they keep back their sordid sperm begotten in the lustinesse of their avarice.

3. *transf.* The generative matter or source from which anything is formed or takes its origin:

a. Of plants.

1610 J. Davies (Heref.) *Commend. Poems, Vaughan* Wks. (Grosart) II. 3/2 His royall Trench (that..holds the Sperme of Herbage by a Spring). 1620 Markham *Farew. Husb.* (1625) 99 The worme..deuouring vp the substance or sperm, is the cause that the corne cannot grow. 1642 H. More *Song of Soul* II. I. ii. 25 I'll call't form bestiall, It makes a beast added to plantall sperm.

b. Of other material things.

1651 French *Distill.* v. 168 Water is both the Sperme, and the Menstruum of the world. 1671 J. Webster *Metallogr.* iv. 77 The Sperm of Metals is not different from the sperm of other things, to wit, an humid vapour. 1694 Motteux *Rabelais* IV. i. 3 The Fifth [ship had for its device] a famous Kan made of Sperm of Emerald. 1845 Bailey *Festus* (ed. 2) 123 The primal sperm and matter of the world.

c. Of qualities, conditions, etc.

1639 G. Daniel *Ecclus.* xxvi. 91 Infects her mind With the black Sperme of Contradiction. 1659 C. Noble *Inexpediency Exped.* 4 The Remedy that is prescribed is the very Seed and Sperm..and Vivary of that difference. 1820 Shelley *Ode Liberty* xv, 'Tis the sperm Of what makes life foul, cankerous, and abhorred.

4. a. *attrib.*, as *sperm-bag, -ball, -cell, -germ*, etc.

1849 *Phil. Trans.* CXXXIX. I. 347 The spermatozoa are distinctly seen in the *sperm-bag. 1887 *Encycl. Brit.* XXII. 424/2 Each cell..produces a large number of spermatozoa, which occur in spherical clusters or *sperm-balls. 1851 Carpenter *Man. Phys.* (ed. 2) 148 In the lower tribes, both of Plants and Animals, we find that '*sperm-cells' and 'germ-cells' are developed in the midst of the ordinary tissues of the body. 1881 Mivart *Cat* 318 The male pronucleus is a spermatozoon, which is a part of the nucleus of the original sperm-cell. 1868 Watts *Dict. Chem.* V. 397 With *sperm-corpuscles, mucus-corpuscles, and epithelium-scales. 1859 *Todd's Cycl. Anat.* V. [138] Two different organised bodies, which are respectively formed from two different cells; the ovigerm and the *spermgerm. 1856 Emerson *Eng. Traits, Ability* (1903) 56 Stall-feeding makes *sperm-mills of the cattle. 1826 Kirby & Sp. *Entomol.* IV. xlii. 146 The '*Sperm-reservoir (*Spermatheca*) is an organ connecting the vagina with the oviduct. 1883 Lankester in *Encycl. Brit.* XVI. 682/2 In other Mollusca..this formation of '*sperm ropes' is known. 1859 Huxley *Oceanic Hydrozoa* 64 The smaller contained a *sperm-sac, with incompletely developed spermatozoa. 1841 T. R. Jones *Anim. Kingd.* 280 Two long auxiliary vessels.., that have been named *sperm-vessels, gluten-vessels, and gum-vessels by different authors.

b. *Comb.*, as *sperm-forming, -like, -secreting* adjs.

1836–9 *Todd's Cycl. Anat.* II. 414/1 The principal forms of the sperm-secreting organs. 1876 Bristowe *Th. & Pract. Med.* (1878) 32 Infect them, by either growing parasitically.., or (sperm-like) imparting to them specific properties. 1878 F. J. Bell *Gegenbaur's Elem. Comp. Anat.* 53 The relation of the egg-forming and sperm-forming organs to one another varies greatly.

II. (Short for Sperm whale or Spermaceti.)

5. a. *Sperm oil*, an oil found together with spermaceti in the head of various species of whales.

1839 T. Beale *Nat. Hist. Sperm Whale* 149 There was still a gradual increase in the importation of sperm oil. 1857 Miller *Elem. Chem., Org.* vi. § 1. 358 The principal drying oils are those of linseed, walnut, hemp,..and sperm oil. 1883 *Fisheries Exhib. Catal.* 202 Crude and refined Sperm oil, used for illuminating,..and in the manufacture of spermaceti.

attrib. 1849 Cupples *Green Hand* ii. (1856) 18 Trimming up the sperm-oil lights.

b. *Sperm candle*, a spermaceti candle.

1856 *Orr's Circ. Sci., Pract. Chem.* 458, 15 sperm candles will give the light of 16·5 stearic. 1890 *Daily News* 23 Oct. 3/5 The only clean and tidy candles..were wax candles and sperm candles.

6. A sperm whale. Also *collect.* and *attrib.*

1840 F. D. Bennett *Narr. Whaling Voy.* II. 185 The commencement of the Sperm Fishery by England. 1854 *Chamb. Jrnl.* 28 Jan. 53/2 See, again! there is a sperm of the largest size, which has just leaped. 1860 Maury *Phys. Geog.* xviii. 772 The parts of the ocean..in which the sperm are found. 1895 *Pall Mall G.* 16 Dec. 2/1 He killed as many as five sperms in a single day with one harpoon.

b. *Sperm-bird* (see quot.).

1840 F. D. Bennett *Narr. Whaling Voy.* I. 10 Many ocean birds of the high south latitudes were now visible.., as nellies (*Procellaria gigantea*); blue-petrels, or sperm-birds (*Prion pachyptila*), [etc.].

7. Sperm candles or oil.

1856 *Orr's Circ. Sci., Pract. Chem.* 458 If there be any difference, the light of sperm is a little greater, and that of stearic acid a little whiter. 1890 Clark Russell *Ocean Trag.* I. iv. 68 The soft..radiance diffused by the burning sperm.

†**Sperm,** *v. Obs.*⁻¹ [f. prec.] *intr.* To spawn.

a 1425 tr. *Arderne's Treat. Fistula*, etc. 41 Þei grew to þe liknes of þe womb of a..creuyse or lopster when he spermeþ or frieþ.

‖**Spe·rma.** Now *rare.* Pl. **spermata.** [a. L. *sperma* or Gr. σπέρμα: see Sperm *sb.*] Sperm; seed.

14.. [see Sperm *sb.*¹]. 1527 Andrew *Brunswyke's Dist. Waters* M iij, The same water is good and multyplyeth the sperma. 1597 A. M. *Guillemeau's Fr. Chirurg.* 3 b/2 The patient can nether retayne his vrine, Sperma, or Stole. 1600 Pory tr. *Leo's Africa* 344 Whether the said Amber be the sperma or the excrement therof, they cannot well determine. 1668 *Phil. Trans.* III. 790 Here have been Sperma-Ceti-Whales driven upon the shore, which Sperma (as they call it) lies all over the Body of those Whales. 1728 Chambers *Cycl.*, *Sperm* or *Sperma*, the Seed whereof an Animal is form'd. 1843 R. J. Graves *Syst. Clin. Med.* xxvii. 350 By the mixture and mutual neutralization or solution of different spermata. 1886 *Lond. Q. Rev.* Oct. 129 Basilides is said to have spoken of a 'sperma' or seed-mass, from which all things have been produced.

Sperma-, combining form of prec.: see Spermaduct, etc., and cf. Spermato-, Spermo-.

Spermaceti (spɔ̄ɹmăsī·ti, -se·ti). Forms: 6–9 **sperma ceti** (5 **cete,** 7 **coeti, cetæ**); 5– **spermaceti** (5 **-cetie,** 7 **-cete, -cæty,** 8 **-cety**); 6 **sparmaceti.** [med.L., from *sperma* sperm + *cēti* gen. sing. of *cētus* (ad. Gr. κῆτος) whale, through an erroneous opinion as to the nature of the substance. Hence also F. *spermaceti*, It. *spermaceti*, Sp. *espermaceti*, Pg. *-cete.* The corrupt form Parmacety was formerly common.]

1. A fatty substance, which in a purified state has the form of a soft white scaly mass, found in the head (and to some extent in other parts) of the sperm-whale (*Physeter macrocephalus*) and some other whales and dolphins; it is used largely in various medicinal preparations, and in the manufacture of candles.

1471 Ripley *Comp. Alch.* in Ashm. (1652) 113 Use.. Sperma Cete ana with redd Wyne when ye wax old. 1525 tr. *Jerome of Brunswick's Surg.* R iij b/2 Take sperma ceti .iij. dragma, mumie an ounce. 1581 Rich *Farew.* Tj, The Doctor tooke Sparmaceti, and suche like thynges that bee good for a bruse. 1600 Dallam in *Early Voy. Levant* (Hakl. Soc.) 95 This day we saw greate store of the spane of whales, whearof they make spermaceti. 1658 A. Fox *Würtz' Surg.* IV. v. 334 When Sperma Cetæ is stale..it ought not to be used, making the medicine very unpleasant. 1747 Wesley *Prim. Physick* (1762) 53 Put a Scruple of Sperma-Ceti into the yolk of a new-laid Egg. 1774 Goldsm. *Nat. Hist.* (1824) III. 27 The first cavity or chamber of the brain, is filled with that spermaceti which is supposed of the greatest purity and highest value. 1811 A. T. Thomson *Lond. Disp.* (1818) 297 Spermaceti is demulcent and emollient. 1842 Lover *Handy Andy* ii. 26 All the spermaceti in M'Garry's shop won't cure you. 1897 F. T. Bullen *Cruise of 'Cachalot'* 51 Spermaceti exists in all the oil, especially that from the dorsal hump.

fig. 1601 B. Jonson *Poetaster* II. i. (1905) 28 Looke here, my sweet wife..., my deare mummia, my balsamum, my spermacete. *a* 1613 Overbury *Characters, Ord. Fencer* Wks. (1856) 112 For an inward bruise, lambstones and sweet-breads are his onely sperma ceti, which he eats at night next his heart fasting.

2. *attrib.* and *Comb.*, as *spermaceti-candle, -fat, -fish, manufactory, oil, -ointment, -refiner.*

1738 Chambers *Cycl.* s.v., *Spermaceti candles are of modern manufacture,..superior to the finest wax-candles. 1758 Franklin *Lett.* Wks. 1887 III. 8 The extinguisher is for spermaceti candles only. 1858 Simmonds *Dict. Trade*, *Spermaceti-candles*, fine transparent candles, used as wax lights. 1868 Watts *Dict. Chem.* V. 397 Sperm-oil appears to be isomeric with *spermaceti-fat or cetin. 1781 *Encycl. Brit.* (ed. 2) VIII. 6171 *Physeter*, or *Spermaceti-fish,..a genus belonging to the order of cete. 1748 Armstrong *Misc.* (1770) I. 216 Their filthy greasy brains, that were never fit for any thing but the *sperma ceti manufactory. 1765 *Museum Rust.* IV. 76 A taper..lamp, with four ordinary threads of cotton in the wick, consumes ·1664 oz. of *spermaceti oil in one hour. 1820 Scoresby *Acc. Arctic Reg.* II. 413 The oil..is more inflammable than spermaceti-oil. 1843 R. J. Graves *Syst. Clin. Med.* ix. 103 A piece of lint smeared with *spermaceti ointment. 1858 Simmonds *Dict. Trade*, *Spermaceti-ointment*, a pharmaceutical preparation consisting of lard, spermaceti, and bees'-wax. *Ibid.*, **Spermaceti-refiner*, a person who purifies spermaceti, chiefly by pressure and crystallization.

b. *Spermaceti whale*, the sperm whale.

1658 Sir T. Browne *Gard. Cyrus* iii, A better account.. of that prominent jowle of the Sperma Ceti Whale. 1672 *Phil. Trans.* VII. 5021 To heal Bruises and Aches with the Oyl of the Sperma-ceti-Whale. 1763 *Ann. Reg.* I. 116 Two spermaceti whales have been caught on the Essex coast. 1783 *Phil. Trans.* LXXIII. 231 They look for ambergrise in all the spermaceti-whales they catch. 1845 Darwin *Voy. Nat.* (ed. 2) x. 223 *note*, We saw..several spermaceti whales jumping upright quite out of the water.

Spe·rmaduct. *Zool.* [f. Sperma- + Duct 6 a.] A spermatic or seminal duct or passage in a male animal. Also **Spe·rmagone, Spermago·nium,** *Bot.* = Spermogone, -gonium. **Spe·rmaphore, Spe·rmaphyte,** *Bot.* = Spermophore, -phyte.

1891 *Cent. Dict.*, **Spermaduct*,..a spermatic duct, or sperm-duct [etc.]. 1905 J. McCabe tr. *Haeckel's Evol. Man* II. 823 In the male they convey the spermatozoa away from the testicles, and are called 'spermaducts', or *vasa deferentia.* 1876 *Encycl. Brit.* IV. 159/1 Embedded in the margin of the thallus in Lichens..certain hollow urn-shaped bodies are found, which have been termed *spermagones (conceptacles). 1861 H. Macmillan *Footn. Page Nat.* 73 Minute, blackish, elevated, somewhat gelatinous points called *spermagonia, occurring on various parts of the upper surface of the thallus. 1880 Bessey *Botany* 299 Minute cells (the *spermatia*), which..are permitted to escape through the small opening at the apex of the spermagonium. 1847 Webster, **Spermaphore*, in botany, that part of the ovary from which the ovules arise; it is synonymous with *Placenta.* 1891 *Cent. Dict.*, **Spermaphyte.* 1897 tr. *Strasburger's Text-bk. Bot.* 432 They are also termed Seed-plants or Spermaphytes.

†**Spe·rmal,** *a. Obs.*⁻¹ [f. Sperm *sb.* + -al, or ad. med.L. *spermāl-is.*] Spermatic.

1642 H. More *Song of Soul* II. II. i. 9 This is the nourishing Of all; but spermall form, the certain shapening.

‖**Spermarium** (spɔɹmē°·riŏm). Pl. **-aria.** [mod.L., f. *sperma* sperm.] = next.

1861 J. R. Greene *Man. Anim. Kingd., Coelent.* 40 Processes of the body-wall, within which are developed true generative organs, the 'spermaria' and 'ovaria', constitute the reproductive apparatus of the *Hydrozoa.* 1881 Lankester in *Encycl. Brit.* XII. 550 Each ovarium and each spermarium represents an aborted generative person.

Spermary (spɔ̄·ɹmări). [Anglicized f. prec: see -ary¹.] The organ or gland in which spermatozoa are generated in male animals.

1864 in Webster (citing Dana). 1885 S. F. Clarke in *Riverside Nat. Hist.* (1888) I. 76 In a limited region on the body of *Hydra*,..there appear..small out-growths of the body-wall which prove to be the spermaries.

‖**Spermatheca** (spɔɹmăþī·kă). Pl. **-thecae.** [f. Sperma- + Theca.] A receptacle in the oviduct of female insects and invertebrates, in which fecundation of the ova takes place.

1826 Kirby & Sp. *Entomol.* xlii. IV. 147 *n.*, Perhaps likewise the organ discovered by M. L. Dufour in *Scolia*..may be a *spermatheca.* 1841 T. R. Jones *Anim. Kingd.* 283 The spermatheca has a small accessory vesicle connected with it. 1888 Rolleston & Jackson *Anim. Life* 206 The female apparatus is completed by two pairs of vesicular spermathecae.

Hence **Spermathe·cal** *a.*, of or belonging to the spermatheca.

1883 Lankester in *Encycl. Brit.* XVI. 658/2 On reaching the point where the spermathecal duct debouches they are impregnated by the spermatozoa. 1900 *Proc. Zool. Soc.* June 169 In the region of the spermathecal apertures.

Spermatic (spɔɹmæ·tik), *a.* and *sb.* Also 6 **sparmatyke,** 7 **-ique,** 6 **spermaticke,** 6–7 **-ike,** 7 **-ique,** 7–8 **-ick.** [ad. med.L. *spermatic-us*, ad. Gr. σπερματικός, f. σπέρμα sperm, or OF. (also mod.F.) *spermatique* (1314), = It. *spermatico*, Sp. and Pg. *espermatico.*]

1. Containing, conveying, or producing sperm or seed; seminiferous.

1539 Elyot *Cast. Helthe* (1541) 12 Vessels spermatike, wherin mannes seede lyeth. 1597 A. M. tr. *Guillemeau's Fr. Chirurg.* 21 b/2 Not to touch the testicles, nether anye of the spermaticke vessels. 1646 Sir T. Browne *Pseud. Ep.* 189 The seminall ejaculation proceeds..from the spermatick glandules. 1730 Chamberlayne *Relig. Philos.* I. iii. § 22 The Spermatic Arteries, coming on each Side out of the great Artery. 1797 M. Baillie *Morb. Anat.* (1807) 356 A disease of the spermatic chord which is not uncommon, is an enlargement of its veins. 1857 Bullock tr. *Cazeaux' Midwifery* 69 The numerous lymphatic vessels..contribute to the formation of the spermatic plexus. 1881 Mivart *Cat* 243 Within it is a layer of membrane—the spermatic fascia.

b. Full of, abounding in, sperm; generative, productive.

1619 Drayton *Owle* Poems 407 There in soft Downe the liquorous Sparrow sat, Pamper'd with meats, full spermatike and fat. 1648 J. Beaumont *Psyche* IX. xxxiv, Spermatick Nile, which brings Choise Monsters forth. 1655 T. Vaughan *Euphrates* 32 This Primitive spermatic Ocean filled all that space which we now attribute to the Air.

2. Of the nature of sperm; resembling sperm.

1541 R. Copland *Guydon's Quest. Chirurg.* B iv b, They haue theyr breding and begynnynge of sparmatyke mater. *a* 1631 Donne *Elegies* viii. 8 Ranke sweaty froth.. Like spermatique issue of ripe menstruous boiles. *c* 1645 Howell *Lett.* III. xxix, A production of an organicall body out of the spermatic substance. 1693 Sir T. P. Blount *Nat. Hist.* 28 It would sometimes let fall a Spermatick Juice, which.. would thereupon produce another coral. 1828 Kirby & Sp. *Entomol.* (ed. 2) IV. xlii. 153 This organ was a reservoir for the spermatic fluid. 1869 H. A. Nicholson *Man. Zool.* 22 As a rule, the germ-cell is produced by one individual and the spermatic element by another.

b. *transf.* and *fig.* Resembling sperm, esp. in generative or reproductive power.

1669 Gale *Crt. Gentiles* I. III. iii. 44 The Stoics also held, there was..a spermatic efformative word, whereby the world was formed. 1671 J. Webster *Metallogr.* x. 142 Having annexed to it some slates and other spermatick matter, which detracts from the goodness of its own nature. 1741 Warburton *Div. Legat.* Wks. 1811 III. 168 You will be assumed into the Divine nature, or the spermatick reasons. 1870 Emerson *Soc. & Solit.* Wks. (Bohn) III. 80, I find certain books vital and spermatic, not leaving the reader what he was.

†**3.** Directly derived from sperm (according to old physiological views). *Obs.*

1548–77 Vicary *Anat.* ii. (1888) 18 The Grystle is a member simple and spermatike, next in hardnes to the bone. 1621 Lodge *Summary Du Bartas* I. 284 *Stomake*. The substance thereof is more spermatique then sanguine. 1670 *Phil. Trans.* V. 2077 The two sorts of Parts of the Body, Spermatick and Sanguineous. 1684 tr. *Bonet's Merc. Compit.* XIV. 498 A Membrane is a Spermatick part, which being consumed is not regenerated. 1728 Chambers *Cycl.* s.v., The Ancients made a general Division of the Parts of the Animal Body into Spermatic and Fleshy.

4. Of qualities: Characteristic of, peculiar to, derived from, sperm.

1642 H. More *Song of Soul* II. App. 101 Nought can e'er consume that centrall power Of hid spermatick life. 1669 W. Simpson *Hydrol. Chym.* 269 Water..by the spermatick efflorescence of a mineral seed becomes wrought into a mineral juyce. 1706 De Foe *Jure Div.* Introd., Spermatick Vigour spreads the poison'd Race, Conveys Hereditary Crimes apace. 1866 Shuckard *Brit. Bees* 296 This in some cases has a spermatic odour. 1896 *Allbutt's Syst. Med.* I. 203 The first theory..views the growth of a tumour as due to the spermatic influence of certain cells upon those contiguous.

5. Existing in sperm.

1837 P. Keith *Bot. Lex.* 304 According to him, they are animated substances; the analogues of the spermatic animalcules of Leuenhoeck. 1857 Bullock tr. *Cazeaux' Midwifery* 90 These minute bodies have been designated as the spermatic animalcules, or the spermatozoa.

6. As *sb.* in *pl.* The spermatic vessels.

1690 in Maidment *Bk. Sc. Pasquils* (1868) 277 Spermaticks sink, true mother of discord, Inflam'd these Hectors. 1719 Quincy *Phys. Dict.* (1722) s.v. *Semen*, In the Aorta, where the Spermaticks arise. 1857 Bullock tr. *Cazeaux' Midwifery* 63 The arteries which supply the ovary are the spermatics, and proceed directly from the aorta. 1859 *Todd's Cycl. Anat.* V. 651/1 This structure is found..in the internal spermatics, and in all the veins of the uterine substances.

†**Sperma·tical,** *a. Obs.* Also 5 **spermatycall,** 6 **sparmaticall.** [See prec. and -al.]

1. = Spermatic *a.* 2.

1471 Ripley *Comp. Alch.* vi. xviii. in Ashm. (1652) 165 Yt thus fro thyng to thyng was alterat..; And so our Mater spermatycall wythin one Glas Wythin hyt selfe must turne fro thyng to thyng. 1655 in Hartlib *Ref. Commw. Bees* 22 A tender spermatical milk enclosed in a most tender skin.

2. = Spermatic *a.* 3.

1562 Bulleín *Bulwarke, Dial. betw. Sorenes & Chir.* 22 Members, whiche Phisicians call sparmaticall, beyng ones loosed, will not be ioyned again. 1615 Crooke *Body of Man* 637 Euery Similar part is either Spermaticall or fleshie. 1633 P. Fletcher *Purple Isl.* II. xii. *marg. note*, A nerve is a spermaticall part rising from the brain and the pith of the back-bone. 1668 Culpepper & Cole *Barthol. Anat.* Introd., All these parts are commonly divided into Spermatical, Sanguine or mixt.

3. Endowed with sperm or semen.

1610 Healey *St. Aug. Citie of God* vii. ii. 260 Liber and Libera, [gods] of the distillation of seede in all spermaticall creatures.

4. = Spermatic *a.* 1.

1615 Crooke *Body of Man* 217 The spermaticall vessels which bring the seede from the whole bodye..are foure. *Ibid.* 837 The left Emulgent also is larger then the right, because of the Spermatical veine which was to arise therefrom. 1621 Lodge *Summary Du Bartas* I. 269 The spermaticall, or seede Vessels.

5. = Spermatic *a.* 4.

1642 H. More *Song of Soul* II. I. ii. 25 Both what hight form spermaticall Hath here a share, as also that we term Soul sensitive. *a* 1652 J. Smith *Sel. Disc.* VII. iv. (1660) 309 Like the Spermatical virtue of the Heavens, which spreads it self freely upon this Lower World. 1682 H. More *Annot. Glanvill's Lux Orient* 119 We have..reason..to suppose this Vital or Spermatical Law is amongst the rest.

Sperma·tically, *adv.* [f. prec. + -ly².] In a spermatic manner; in a way characteristic of sperm; seminally.

1647 Trapp *Comm. Matt.* i. 20 He..was conceived of the holy Ghost, not spermatically, but operatively. 1682 H. More *Annot. Glanvill's Lux Orient* 119 Such a spirit as contains Spermatically or Vitally all the Laws contrived by the Divine Intellect. 1822 T. Taylor *Apuleius* 324 The participations subsist in these subjects spermatically.

Spe·rmatid. *Biol.* Also **-ide.** [f. L. *spermat-*, stem of *sperma* sperm + -id.] A seminal cell which develops into a spermatozoon.

1889 Geddes & Thomson *Evol. Sex* ix. 113 The sperm or spermatozoon is differentiated from an immature cell or spermatide. 1904 *Biol. Bulletin* Feb. 150 There is the normal number of two chromosomes. The ovotid and the spermatid have each only one.

Spermati·ferous, *a.* [f. as prec. + -(i)ferous.] Bearing or conveying sperm.

1862 Ansted *Channel Isl.* II. viii. 189 His specimens were covered with spermatiferous spermogones. 1865 M. C. Cooke *Microsc. Fungi* ii. 24 The colour of this spermatiferous matter is commonly orange.

Spe·rmatin. *Chem.* Also **-ine.** [a. F. *spermatine*, f. as prec. + *-ine* -in¹.] An albuminic constituent of the spermatic fluid.

1836–9 *Todd's Cycl. Anat.* II. 458/2 In the spermatic fluid of the horse, Lassaigne has detected..Peculiar animal matter called spermatine. 1856 *Orr's Circ. Sci., Pract. Chem.* 317 The seminal principle (spermatine), is..nearly analogous to albuminous substances. 1873 Ralfe *Phys. Chem.* 176 The peculiar albuminoid substance, spermatin, is probably a mixture of globulin and lecithin.

Spermatio-, comb. form of Spermatium, as in **Spermatio·genous** *a.*, bearing spermatia. **Sperma·tiophore,** = Spermatophore 2.

1887 Garnsey tr. *De Bary's Fungi* v. 241 Some Pyrenomycetes..form layers agreeing in every respect with the spermatiophores. *Ibid.*, They are..cushion-shaped bodies with spermatiogenous surface.

Spe·rmatism. *rare*⁻⁰. [ad. mod.L. *spermatismus* (Gr. σπερματισμός) or F. *spermatisme*: cf. next.] (See quots.)

1857 Dunglison *Med. Dict.*, *Animalculism*, Spermatism. 1882 *Imp. Dict.* IV. 155/1 *Spermatism*,..1. The emission of sperm or seed.—2. The theory that the germ in animals is produced by spermatic animalcules.

Spe·rmatist. [ad. mod.L. **spermatista* or F. *spermatiste*, f. L. *spermat-*, *sperma* sperm + -ist.] One who held the view that the sperm alone was the source of animal life.

1836–9 *Todd's Cycl. Anat.* II. 427/1 According to the.. theory..of the Spermatists,..the male semen alone furnished all the vital parts of the new animal. 1899 J. A. Thomson *Sci. Life* 125 Other observers, nicknamed 'spermatists' or 'animalculists', believed them [*sc.* spermatozoa] to be the earliest stages of the young animal.

‖**Spermatium** (spɔɹmæ·ʃiŏm). *Bot.* Pl. **-atia.** [mod.L., ad. Gr. σπερμάτιον, dim. of σπέρμα seed, Sperm *sb.*] A minute linear sporule forming part of the reproductive system of lichens and fungi. (Chiefly in pl.)

1856 W. L. Lindsay *Pop. Hist. Brit. Lichens* 75 The fecundating influence of the spermatia or stylospores. 1867 J. Hogg *Microsc.* II. i. 291 The spermatia or contents of the spermagonia never germinate. 1885 Goodale *Physiol. Bot.* 440 *note*, A branch showing antheridia, *a*, and a carpogonium, *o*, with the trichogyne, *t* (*c*, spermatium).

†**Spe·rmative,** *a. Obs. rare.* Also 6 **sparmatyf.** [ad. med.L. **spermatīv-us.*] Spermatic.

1541 R. Copland *Guydon's Quest. Chirurg.* C j, I say secondly that no membres sparmatyf after the losse of theyr substaunce maye nat regenerate. 1610 Healey *St. Aug. Citie of God* 267 The brain..is the most excellent of the spermative parts.

†**Spe·rmatize,** *v. Obs.* [ad. F. *spermatiser* or med.L. *spermatizāre*, ad. Gr. σπερματίζειν to sow, etc., f. σπερματ-, stem of σπέρμα Sperm *sb.*] *intr.* To emit or produce sperm.

1611 Cotgr., *Spermatiser*, to spermatize; to shed, eiect, or iniect sperme. 1646 Sir T. Browne *Pseud. Ep.* 149 Affirming that women do not spermatize,..he deductively includes both sexes in mankinde. 1725 Bourne *Antiq. Vulg.* xxvii, In ancient Times the Dragons..did frequently ..Spermatize in the Wells and Fountains. 1777 Brand *Pop. Antiq.* xxvii. 281, I have nothing to observe here concerning Mr. Bourne's lustful Dragons, their spermatizing in the Wells,..&c.!

Spermato- (spɔ̄·ɹmăto), repr. Gr. σπερματο-, combining form of the stem of σπέρμα Sperm *sb.*, employed in a large number of terms (chiefly of very recent origin) relating to the reproductive organs or activities of animals and plants.

Some of these are employed only in L. forms, as *spermatocystidium, -cystis, -cystitis*, etc., and others have had very little currency even in special works. A number have alternative forms in *sperma-* or *spermo-*.

1. In terms denoting special reproductive organs, or parts of these, as **Spe·rmatoblast, -cyst, -cyte, -gemma, -gone, -gonium, -mere, -spore.**

Some of these are the source of adj. forms, as *spermatoblastic, -cystic, -gonial, -gonic*, etc.

1882 *Imp. Dict.* IV. 155/1 **Spermatoblast*,..certain stalk-like filaments in the seminal ducts upon which the spermatozoa are developed. 1886 *Encycl. Brit.* XX. 412/1 To the whole prolongation with its lobes he [Von Ebner] applies the term spermatoblast. 1884 *Proc. Boston Soc. Nat. Hist.* 61 The first stages in the development of the *spermatocyst of Hydra. 1886 *Encycl. Brit.* XX. 412/2 One kind.. divide into a mass or spermatogemma of small cells (*spermatocytes). *Ibid.* 413/1 The *spermatogemma meanwhile is developing a central cavity. 1898 A. S. Packard *Text-bk. Entomol.* 499 A colossal cell,..the *spermatogone, from which the entire contents of the testes originate. 1861 Bentley *Man. Bot.* 384 The spermagonia or *spermatogonia [in Lichens] were first discovered by Tulasne. 1886 *Encycl. Brit.* XX. 412/2 One kind, resembling young ovules, which he [Von La Valette St. George] terms primitive seminal cells or spermatogonia. 1886 *Q. Jrnl. Microsc. Sci.* XXVI. 597 The region where the spermatogonia are formed at the expense of their mother-cells or *spermatomeres.

2. In some other sbs. and adjs. with second elements of obvious meaning, as **Spermato·genesis, -gene·tic** *a.*, **-genic** *a.*, **-logy, -phoral** *a.*, **-phorous** *a.*, **-poe·ic** *a.*, **-rrhœ·a, -spore.**

1881 *Athenæum* 11 June 787/1 M. Mathias Duval on *spermatogenesis. 1886 *Encycl. Brit.* XX. 412/1 The process of spermatogenesis in the Bull, Dog, and Rabbit. *Ibid.*, Ascribing *spermatogenetic functions both to the spermatoblasts and to the round cells. 1880 Allman in *Linn. Soc. Jrnl., Zool.* XV. 136 These I regard as the remains of the *spermatogenic tissue. 1851 Dunglison *Med. Lex.*, **Spermatology*, a treatise on sperm. 1886 Howes & Scott *Huxley's Pract. Biol.* 291 The *spermatophoral gland or flagellum. 1851 Dunglison *Med. Lex.*, **Spermatophorous*, sperm-bearing. The cells or granules in the sperm have been so called. 1799 *Monthly Rev.* XXX. 521 A curious restorative and *spermatopoeic sugar-candy of the Japanese. 1858 Mayne *Expos. Lex.* 1180/2 **Spermatorrhœa*,..seminal flux. 1879 T. Bryant *Pract. Surg.* II. 226 Spermatorrhœa doubtless exists as a disease although rare. 1880 *Q. Jrnl. Microsc. Sci.* 83 The term *spermatospore..is applied to the constituent cells of a testis, derived from the primitive germ-epithelium.

‖**Spermatocele** (-sīl). *Path.* [med.L.: see prec. and Cele. So F. *spermatocèle*, Sp. *espermatocela.*] (See quots.)

1693 tr. *Blancard's Phys. Dict.* (ed. 2), *Spermatocele*, a Rupture caused by the Contraction of the Vessel which ejects the Seed, and its falling down into the Scrotum. 1823 Crabb *Technol. Dict.*, *Spermatocele*,..a swelling of the testes, or epididymis, from an accumulation of semen. 1874 Van Buren *Dis. Genit. Org.* 407 Spermatocele is a collection of serous fluid, containing spermatic elements.

Spermatogone, -gonium: see Spermato- 1.

Spe·rmatoid, *a. rare*⁻⁰. [f. *spermat-* sperm + -oid.] Similar to sperm.

1855 Dunglison *Med. Lex.*, *Spermatoid*, Gonoides.

Spermato·on. *Biol.* Pl. **-o·a.** [f. Spermato- + Gr. ᾠόν egg.] A spermatid.

1875 Brande & Cox *Dict. S.i.*, etc. III. 530/1 Sometimes the sperm-cell contains a single spermatoon, sometimes several spermatoa.

Spe·rmatophore. [f. Spermato- + -phore.]

1. *Biol.* In certain of the lower forms of animal life, a structure containing a compact mass of spermatozoa.

1847–9 *Todd's Cycl. Anat.* IV. I. 485/1 These fibres in the Cephalopods are..surrounded..by peculiar sack-like enclosures or Spermatophores. 1870 Rolleston *Anim. Life* 108 A packet of spermatozoa, aggregated in their passage along the convolutions of the vasa deferentia into the so-called 'spermatophore'. 1880 Huxley *Crayfish* 351 The filaments are in fact tubular spermatophores.

2. *Bot.* A part of the spermogonium of lichens or fungi, on which the spermatia are borne.

1861 Bentley *Man. Bot.* 384 The spermagonium, when mature, has its interior filled with a number of bodies called spermatia..raised on stalks, termed spermatophores.

Spe·rmatophyte. *Bot.* = Spermophyte.

1897 *Nature* 11 Nov. 46/1 In the pteridophytes and spermatophytes nutritive and assimilatory structures are developed.

Spermatozo·al, *a. Phys.* [f. Spermatozo-on + -al.] Of or pertaining to spermatozoa; of the nature of a spermatozoon. So **Spermatozo·an, -zo·ic** *adjs.*

1858 J. W. Draper *Human Physiol.* (ed. 2) 518 Spermatozoic filaments, developing in Certhea vulgaris. 1877 Huxley *Anat. Inv. Anim.* xii. 661 The ascription of a spermatozoal nature to the striæ of the modified endoplastules is not warranted. 1888 Rolleston & Jackson *Anim. Life* Introd. p. xxv, Fusion of the nuclei, often termed the male (spermatozoal) and female (ovular) pronuclei.

Spermatozo·id. [f. as prec. + -id, or ad. F. *spermatozoïde.*]

1. *Bot.* A minute fertilizing body or cell in Cryptogamia and Algæ.

1857 Henfrey *Bot.* 511 Spermatozoids are filiform bodies of various forms, mostly presenting one or more spiral curves, or minute globules. 1863 M. J. Berkeley *Brit. Mosses* iii. 13 An oblong sac..filled with cellular tissue, each ultimate cell of which..gives birth to a spermatozoid. 1877 Heath *Fern World* 11 The sperm cells contain minute, active, thread-like bodies called spermatozoids.

2. *Phys.* = next.

1861 T. R. Jones *Anim. Kingd.* (ed. 3) 156 The testicular cæca become filled with granulations,..but these do not contain spermatozoids. 1870 H. A. Nicholson *Man. Zool.* 22 A sperm-cell or spermatozoid..is enabled to develop itself into a new individual.

‖**Spermatozoon** (-zō^u·ǫn). Pl. **-zoa.** [f. Spermato- + Gr. ζῷον living thing, animal.] One of the numerous minute and active filaments present in the seminal fluid, by which the fecundation of the ovum is effected.

1836–9 *Todd's Cycl. Anat.* II. 113/1 The Spermatozoa have been detected..in the different classes of the Articulate Animals. 1844 G. Bird *Urin. Deposits* (1857) 376 Mixed with these are generally found round granular bodies, rather larger than the body of a spermatozoon. 1881 Mivart *Cat* 245 The special secretion of the testis consists of certain spermatic filaments or spermatozoa.

Spermi-, irregular comb. form of L. *sperma* Sperm *sb.*, as in **Spermidu·cal** *a.*, **Spe·rmiduct** (= Spermaduct), †**Spermifica·tion, Spermi·gerous** *a.*

1666 J. Smith *Old Age* 106, I shall only mention five; ..Chylification, Sanguification, Assimulation, Lactification, and Spermification. 1877 Huxley *Anat. Inv. Anim.* v. 240 They frequently play the part of oviducts and spermiducts. *Ibid.* viii. 481 *note*, In the common Oyster the genital cæca..are found to be either almost all ovigerous or almost all spermigerous. 1897 *Proc. Zool. Soc.* 313 The spermiducal glands are long and coiled.

Spe·rmic, *a. rare*⁻⁰. [ad. F. *spermique*: see Sperm *sb.*] Of or pertaining to sperm or seed.

1858 Mayne *Expos. Lex.* 1180/2 The interior of the Spermoderm..he [Richard] terms the *spermic cavity*. 1882 *Imp. Dict.* IV. 155/1.

Spe·rmin. *Chem.* Also **-ine.** [a. F. *spermine*: see Sperm *sb.* and -in¹.] A toxin extracted from the pancreas and some other parts of the body.

1892 *Lancet* 16 July 175/1 Professor de Poehl..had succeeded in extracting from the pancreas, thyroid body, ovaries and testes a leucomaine called spermine. 1898 *Allbutt's Syst. Med.* V. 647 A compound of phosphoric acid and a base 'Spermin'. 1899 *Ibid.* VIII. 50 Oppenheim once observed tetany after a spermin injection.

Spermo-, irregular comb. form (for Spermato-) of L. *sperma* or Gr. σπέρμα Sperm *sb.*¹, used in various terms of *Phys.*, *Zool.*, and *Bot.*

The older and more important of these are given below; many others, as *spermocarp, -centre, -coccus, -cyte, -duct, -lith, -nucleus*, etc., appear in recent Dicts. or special scientific works.

Spermoderm (spɔ̄·ɹmodɔɹm). *Bot.* [ad. mod.L. *spermoderma, -dermis* (De Candolle) or F. *spermoderme*: see prec. and Derm.] The combined outer and inner integuments of a seed, or the outer of these by itself.

1841 *Penny Cycl.* XXI. 184/1 The external coverings of the seed..are called the testa, perisperm, or spermoderm. 1861 Bentley *Man. Bot.* 337 Some writers..use the word testa in a general sense for the two integuments, and call the external one spermoderm. 1864 *New Syd. Soc. Year-bk. Med. & Surg. for 1863* 427 The spermoderm of the bean.. is also poisonous.

Spermogon-, the stem of Spermogon-ium, occurring in a few derivative adjs., as **Spermogoni·ferous, Spermo·gonoid, Spermo·gonous.**

1871 W. A. Leighton *Lichen-Flora* 126 Laciniæ..undulate, and spermogoniferous towards the centre. 1875 M. C. Cooke *Fungi* 200 The fungus never got beyond the spermogonoid stage. 1891 *Cent. Dict.*, *Spermogonous*,..having the character of spermogonia or spermogones.

Spe·rmogone. *Bot.* Anglicized form of next.

1856 W. L. Lindsay *Pop. Hist. Brit. Lichens* 72 The cavity of the spermogone is usually simple and rounded. 1862 Ansted *Channel Isl.* II. viii. 189 His specimens were covered with spermatiferous spermogones. 1882 *Encycl. Brit.* XIV. 553/1 The spermogones, which are the presumed male organs of reproduction,..differ in appearance from the apothecia in being very minute corpuscles.

‖**Spermogonium** (-gō^u·niŏm). Pl. **-gonia.** [mod.L., f. Spermo- + Gr. γον- stem of γονή, γόνος offspring, etc. Cf. Spermagonium.]

1. *Bot.* One of the receptacles in lichens and fungi in which the spermatia are produced.

1857 Henfrey *Bot.* 169 Smaller chambers, analogous in structure to the perithecia,..occur in the thallus of all Lichens..; they are called spermogonia. 1866 *Treas. Bot.* 1211/2 The pycnidia or spermogonia of different sporidiiferous lichens. 1887 W. Phillips *Brit. Discomycetes* 349 Spermogonia in the form of minute depressed tubercles.

2. *Phys.* A sperm-cell.

1913 J. W. Jenkinson *Vertebrate Embryol.* 23 In the male sex the primordial germ-cells divide to form small cells, the spermogonia.

†**Spermo·loger.** *Obs.*⁻¹ [f. Gr. σπερμολόγος gathering seeds, also *fig.* picking up news, gossiping.] A gatherer of seeds. In quot. *fig.*

1676 Marvell *Mr. Smirke* 38 Whereas there are some Few among the Few, such Spermologers, that unless a grain of Faith fall down, by the by, from Heaven, your seed is Barren.

Spermo·logist. *rare*⁻⁰. [f. as prec. or next: see -ist.] (See quots.)

1727 Bailey (vol. II), *Spermologist*, a Gatherer of Seed. 1755 Johnson, *Spermologist*, one who gathers or treats of seeds. [Hence in later Dicts.]

Spermo·logy. *rare.* [In sense 1 f. Spermo- + -logy. In sense 2 ad. Gr. σπερμολογία: cf. Spermologer.]

1. (See quot. and cf. Spermatology.)

1882 *Imp. Dict.* IV. 155/1 *Spermology*,..that branch of science which investigates sperm or seeds; a treatise on sperm or seeds.

2. An instance of babbling or trifling talk.

1890 Earle *Engl. Prose* xii. 485 For historical truth it is on a level with that favorite spermology of the Liberation Society, which seeks to diffuse the notion [etc.].

Spermophile (spɔ̄·ɹmofil). *Zool.* [ad. mod.L. *Spermophilus* (Cuvier) or a. F. *Spermophile*: see Spermo- and -phile.] A rodent belonging to the squirrel-like genus *Spermophilus*, widely distributed in the northern hemisphere; a pouched marmot.

1824 Richardson in Parry *N. W. Passage* App. 314 We know nothing..whether they are true marmots or spermophiles. 1839 *Penny Cycl.* XV. 517/2 This Spermophile inhabits the barren grounds skirting the sea-coast. 1849 *Sk. Nat. Hist.*, *Mammalia* IV. 18 Besides possessing cheek-pouches, the Spermophiles are distinguished by the closeness of the ears, the slender form of the body,..and the narrowness of the paws. *c* 1880 *Cassell's Nat. Hist.* III. 92 The Spermophiles are Squirrel-like in form and have rather short tails.

Spe·rmophore. *Bot.* [ad. mod.L. *spermophorum* or a. F. *spermophore*: see Spermo- and -phore.] The placenta in plants. Also **Spe·rmophyte** *Bot.*, a seed-bearing plant. **Spermophy·tic** *a.*, 'capable of producing true seeds' (1891 *Cent. Dict.*). **Spe·rmospore** *Phys.*, a compound cellular mass from which sperm filaments are developed. **Spermoto·xin** *Chem.*, a serum destructive to spermatozoa.

1861 Bentley *Man. Bot.* 283 The placenta is called by Schleiden the *spermophore. 1891 *Cent. Dict.*, *Spermophyte*,..a plant producing true seeds. 1881 Mivart *Cat* 245 From these cells the spermatozoa appear to be formed by subdivision of the nucleus of each *spermospore. 1902 *Brit. Med. Jrnl.* 12 Apr. 920 Metchnikoff [deals] with *spermotoxins and leucotoxins.

Spe·rmous, *a. rare*⁻¹. [f. Sperm *sb.* + -ous.] Of the nature of sperm; spermatic.

1822–7 Good *Study Med.* (1829) V. 8 The male..afterwards ejecting over them his spermous fluid.

Sperm whale. Also **sperm-whale.** [Short for *spermaceti whale*: cf. Sperm *sb.* II.]

1. The spermaceti whale, *Physeter macrocephalus*; = Cachalot.

1839 T. Beale *Nat. Hist. Sperm Whale* 3 The sperm whale is one of the most noiseless of marine animals. 1860 Gosse *Rom. Nat. Hist.* 48 In the midst of this war of the elements appear a pair of sperm-whales. 1884 Goode *Nat. Hist. Aquat. Anim.* 7 The Sperm Whale..was first described by Clusius in 1605 from specimens cast up on the coast of Holland in 1598 and 1601.

b. Applied, with distinguishing epithets, to species of whales resembling, or related to, this.

1882 *Cassell's Encycl. Dict.* s.v. *Cachalot*, The Mexican Sperm-whale (*Catodon Colneti*). *Ibid.*, The South Sea Sperm-whale, found..in the Southern Ocean. 1891 *Cent. Dict.* s.v., *Porpoise sperm-whale*, a pygmy sperm-whale, or snub-nosed cachalot.

2. *attrib.*, as *sperm-whale fishery, fishing*, etc.; **sperm-whale porpoise** (see quot. 1884).

1839 T. Beale *Nat. Hist. Sperm Whale* 136 Rise and Progress of the Sperm Whale Fishery. 1884 Goode *Nat. Hist. Aquat. Anim.* 18 The Sperm Whale Porpoise,..*Hyperaodon bidens.* 1887 — *Fisheries of U. S.* 69 The next important sperm-whale ground to be discovered was the Japan Ground. 1888 *Encycl. Brit.* XXIV. 528/1 American Fisheries..Sperm whale fishing seems to have commenced early in the 18th century.

Hence **Sperm-whaler,** a person or vessel engaged in the capture of sperm-whales; **Sperm-whaling** *pres. pple.* and *vbl. sb.*

1834 *Tait's Mag.* I. 411/1 The London sperm-whalers are generally large vessels. 1840 F. D. Bennett *Narr. Whaling Voy.* II. 202 Difficulties that oppose the Sperm-Whaler's success. 1851 *Lit. Gaz.* 11 Jan. 30/3 The graphic accounts of sperm-whaling, by Beale and Bennett. ?1863 in *Pall Mall G.* (1895) 16 Dec. 2/1 Accidentally killed while sperm-whaling off the Brazil Banks. 1887 Goode *Fisheries of U. S.* 69 Sperm-whaling at New Zealand and the offshore ground.

Spe·rmy, *a. rare*⁻¹. [f. Sperm *sb.*] Resembling, of the nature of, sperm.

1657 S. Purchas *Pol. Flying-Ins.* 29 Into those orbicular cells is injected a spermy matter thick like cream.

†**Spermyse.** *Obs.* A kind of cheese.

1542 Boorde *Dyetary* xiii. (1870) 266 Spermyse is a chese the which is made with curdes and with the iuce of herbes. *Ibid.*, I knowynge the herbes,..coulde tell the operacyon of spermyse chese.

Spern, variant of Spurn *sb.*

‖**Speronara** (speronā·ră). Forms: α. 8–9 **speronara,** 9 **-aro.** β. 8–9 **speronare.** γ. 8–9 **sparan-, sparonaro,** 9 **sparonara.** [It.] A large rowing and sailing boat used in southern Italy and Malta.

α. 1783 *Phil. Trans.* LXXIII. 175, I had a pleasant voyage in my Maltese Speronara (which are excellent boats, and the boatmen very skilful). 1838 H. G. Knight *Normans in Sicily* 135 The harbour only contains a few fishing-boats and speronaras. 1870 Disraeli *Lothair* lxxi. 378 The boat was what is called a *speronaro*; an open boat worked with oars, but with a lateen sail at the same time when the breeze served.

β. 1797 Holcroft tr. *Stolberg's Trav.* IV. xcii, We went on board a *speronare.* 1836 Marryat *Midsh. Easy* xviii, Let's get on board one of the speronares which come with fruit from Sicily. 1887 Gunter *Mr. Barnes* i. 6 A score or so of feluccas and speronares from Sardinia and Sicily.

γ. 1799 Nelson 22 May in Nicolas *Disp.* (1846) VII. p. clxxxiii, Neither of the two Sparanaroes..having joined, I cannot send this for Palermo. 1823 J. J. Blunt *Vestiges Anc. Manners Italy* ii. 33 A friend of mine who..had hired a sparonara to convey them from Naples to Rome. 1828 Duppa *Trav. Italy*, etc. 202 Here we quitted Sicily, and took a Sparanaro to visit Stromboli.

Sperow, obs. f. Sparrow. **Sperple,** var. Sparple *v. Obs.* **Sperr,** obs. var. Spar *sb.*¹, *v.*¹ **Sperrable,** obs. var. Sparable. **Sperre,** obs. var. Spar *sb.*¹, *v.*¹, Sphere, Spur.

†**Spe·rring,** *vbl. sb. Obs.*⁻¹ (Meaning obscure.)

1340 *Ayenb.* 53 Þe ilke byeþ properliche glotounes þet al uorzuelʒeþ, ase deþ þe kete of his sperringe.

Sperrowe, obs. form of Sparrow.

Sperse (spɔ̄ɹs), *v.* Now *arch.* Also 7 **spearse.** [Aphetic form of Disperse *v.*, prob. in part after It. *sperso*, pa. pple. of *spergere* to scatter.]

1. *trans.* To cause to scatter or disperse; to drive in different directions.

1580 Baret *Alv.* S. 93 That is spersed and scattered out of order. 1591 Spenser *Visions Bellay* viii, I saw the wrathfull winde..That sperst these cloudes. 1596 — *F. Q.* v. iii. 37 He..broke his sword in twaine, and all his armour sperst. 1603 Dekker *Wh. Babylon* (1607) K iv, Are those clowds sperst that stroue to dimme our light? 1614 Gorges *Lucan* II. 77 Rockes..like the sands are spearst abroad, Faster than hands can them vnload. 1642 H. More *Song of Soul* xlviii, What then shall hinder but a roscid air With gentle heat eachwhere be 'sperst and sprent.

1845 T. Cooper *Purg. Suicides* (1877) 122 Who, then, shall sperse the dark eternal mists? 1879 J. D. Long *Æneid* I. 80 Wreck their sinking boats, Or sperse and whelm their corses in the deep.

2. *intr.* To take different directions.

1819 W. Tennant *Papistry Storm'd* (1827) 125 They spers'd about in search o' beds.

Hence **Spersed** *ppl. a.*

1590 Spenser *F. Q.* I. i. 39 Making speedy way through spersed ayre. 1642 H. More *Song of Soul* II. App. 5 An inward triumph doth my soul up-heave And spread abroad through endlesse 'spersed air.

†**Spert.** *Obs.* Also 5–6 **sperte.** [OE. *sperte, spirte, spyrte*, ad. L. *sporta* basket.]

1. A basket used for holding articles or for catching fish.

c 975 *Rushw. Gosp.* Matt. xv. 37 Þara ʒebroca [hie] ʒenomen siofun sperta fulle. *a* 1000 Ælfric *Hom.* II. 402 Spyrte bið..of rixum ʒebroden, oððe of palm-twyʒum. *c* 1000 *Colloq. Ælfric* in Wr.-Wülcker 93 Hu ʒefehst þu fixas?.. Ic wyrpe..spyrtan and swa hwæt swa hiʒ ʒehæftað ic ʒenime. 1406 in *Essex Rev.* (1904) April 74 [Putting] spertes [and other fish-catching devices into the lord's river].

2. A species of willow or osier.

1578 Lyte *Dodoens* 744 That which hath reddish barke, is called..in English Red Withy, and the better sort thereof is called Red Sperte. *Ibid.*, The small lowe Withy is called.. the Sperte or twigge Withy. 1611 Cotgr., *Siler*, the hearbe ..Hartwort; some also call Spert, or the Osier Withie, so.

Spert(e, varr. Spirt *sb. Obs.* **Spertle,** obs. var. Spirtle *v.* **Speruwe,** obs. f. Sparrow.

†**Sperver.** *Obs. rare.* In 4–5 **speruer, -vyr, spreuere.** [ad. OF. *espervier, esperver* (mod.F. *épervier*) and *esprevier* (obs. F. *éprevier*), = Prov. *esparvier*, It. *sparviere* (*-eri, -ero*), of Germanic origin (OHG. *sparwari, sperwere*, G. *sperber*).] A sparrow-hawk.

c 1330 *Arth. & Merl.* 5258 (Kölbing), And Agreuein tok þat destrer, & fleiʒe þer on so a speruer. 13.. *King Alis.* 183 (Laud MS.), A speruer þat was honest, So sat on þe lefdyes fyst. *a* 1400 *Octouian* 702 A stowt squyere..bar vpon hys ryght hond gay A fayr spreuere.

†**Sperviter.** *Obs. rare.* In 5 **sper-, sparuiter** (**-uyter**). [ad. OF. **esperveteur, esprevetur*, f. *espervier*: see prec.] A keeper of sparrow-hawks.

1486 *Bk. St. Albans*, *Hawking* b v b, Tho that kepe Sperhawkys and muskettys ben called Speruiteris. *Ibid.* e viij b, The namys of a Spare hauke as Ostrigers and Sparuiters have determyned.

Sperwe, obs. f. Sparrow. **Spery,** obs. var. Spurrey. **Sperycall,** obs. f. Spherical. **Speryt,** obs. f. Spirit.

†**Sperware.** *Obs.* (Meaning obscure.)

1434 *Indenture Fotheringey* in Dugdale *Monast.* (1830) VI. III. 1414/1 Til aither isle shall be a sperware enbattailement of free-stoon throwgh out, and both the ends enbattailled butting upon the stepill.

Spessartine (spe·săɹtin). *Min.* [ad. F. *spessartine* (Beudant, 1832), f. *Spessart* a hilly district in north-western Bavaria, where it is found: see -ine⁵.] A species of manganese garnet.

1850 Ansted *Elem. Geol., Min.*, etc. 190 *Spessartine* is the name given to a deep red garnet in which protoxide of manganese replaces the lime of the usual formula, so that it becomes silicate of alumina and manganese. 1888 Rutley *Rock-Forming Min.* 112 Spessartine, or manganese-alumina garnet, occasionally exhibits a red, or yellowish-red colour.

So **Spe·ssartite.** [-ite¹ 2 b.]

1887 in *Cassell's Encycl. Dict.* 1896 in Chester.

Spet, *sb.*¹ Now *dial.* [f. Spet *v.*] The or an act of spitting; spit, spittle. Also *Comb.*

1446 Lydg. *Nightingale P.* I. 259 Hogh that the Iewes.. There all defouled with spet his blessed face. 1570 Levins *Manip.* 86 Spet or spetting, *sputum.* 1592 Nashe *P. Penilesse* Wks. (Grosart) II. 67 Would you..gesse it were possible for anie shame-swolne toad to haue the spet-proofe face to out liue this disgrace? *a* 1658 Lovelace *Lucasta, Posth.* 42 The speckl'd Toad..Defies his foe with a fell Spet. 1882 T. Hardy *Two on Tower* xxii, Well, when I found 'twas Sir Blount my spet dried up within me.

Spet, *sb.*² *U.S.* [a. F. *spet*, = Sp. *espeto*(*n*).] A species of barracuda, the *Sphyræna sphyræna* (*S. spet*) of Europe.

1896 D. S. Jordan & B. W. Evermann *Fishes N. & Mid. Amer.* I. 826 *Sphyræna sphyræna* (Linnæus). European Barracuda; Spet; Sennet.

Spet, *v.* Now *dial.* [Alteration of Spete *v.*, after pa. t. and pa. pple. *spet*(*te*.] To spit, in various senses; to expectorate. (Freq. *c* 1550–*c* 1630.)

a. *intr.*

c 1421 26 *Pol. Poems* 91 She spettes on me, and doþ me fyʒe. 1542 Udall *Erasm. Apoph.* 147 A certain saucy.. young spryngall..spetted even in the veraye face of hym. 1584 R. Scot *Discov. Witchcr.* XII. xviii. (1886) 219 Spet into the shoo of your right foote. 1617 Moryson *Itin.* III. 42 Their sumptuous Churches (in which it is a great trespasse so much as to spet). 1655 Culpepper, etc. *Riverius* VI. i. 130 They who have the Tooth-ach, do continually spet. 1867 H. J. Daniel *Muse in Motley* 43 He wud spet, Iss, spetty like a toad. 1881– in southern dial. glossaries.

Spetch (spetʃ), sb. Also 7 *spetch*, 9 *epitch*. [Related to Speck sb.²]

1. A piece or strip of uncooked leather, a trimming of hide, used in making glue or size.

Spetch, v. Obs. Forms: inf. 1 spetan, 3 spetan, 4-5 spete. Pt. t. 1 spette, 3-5 spette (4 spettid); 3-4 spatte, 4 spat. [OE. spǽtan (:- *spaitjan), 3 *speowte, 4-5 spewe.]

b. trans. Also const. in, out, up. Freq. fig.

† Spettle. Obs. Forms: 5 spetil, 6 spetill, spetly[, 7 -ell; 6-7 spotle, spottle.

Spetchel. Obs. rare. Also 7 spetchy.

Spettle, sb. Also 2 spetch, 9 epitch.

Spetchy, a. Obs. rare. Also 7 spetry.

Spetty, *spetstone*, see Spettle etc.

Spete, var. of Spit.

† Spetevil. Obs. rare. (Of uncertain origin and meaning.)

† Spetia. Obs. rare. Also 7 spetya. [? a. It. spezia.]

Speticide, obs. form of Spotticide.

Spetoviously, variant of Spitously Obs.

† Speutic, a. Obs.

Spew (spjū), v. Forms: α. 1 spiwan, spywan, spiwian, 3 speowen ; 2- spew, 4-6 spewe, 5 spewe, spyw-. [Two OE. forms are here represented : (1) the strong verb spīwan, spywan (pa. t. spāw, pl. spiwon) = OFris. spīa, spīwa, WFris. spije, EFris. spī, NFris. spï, (pret. span). OS. spīwan (MLG. spīen, spīe, spigen), OHG. spīwan (MHG. spīwen, spīen, G. speien), and Icel. spýja (Norw., Sw., Da. spy), Goth. speiwan, spiwun; the weak verb spīwjan, spīwan...]

Spewed, ppl. a. [f. Spew v. + -ED.]

† Spewiness. Obs. rare.

Spewing, ppl. a. [f. as prec.]

1. That spews, in senses of the vb.

Spacelate (sfæsǐlē-fsn), v. Path. [f. Spacelate sb.]

1. intr. To affect with sphacelus; to cause to gangrene or mortify.

2. intr. To become gangrenous or mortified.

Sphacelation (sfæsǐlē-fsn). Path. [n. of action f. prec.]

Sphacelia (sfæsī·lǐä). Bot. [mod.L., f. Gr. σφάκελος gangrene.]

Sphacelism (sfæ·sǐlǐz'm). Path. Also 7 -ismus.

Sphacelus (sfæ·sǐlɒs), sb. Path. Also 6 sphacele, 7 -us. [L., a. Gr. σφάκελος.]

1. Necrosis, mortification ; an instance of this.

† Sphacel. Obs. rare.

Spha·celate, ppl. a.

Sphacelous, a.

Sphacelacion, variant of Sphacelation.

Sphæriaceous (sfī·rǐǣfǐäs), a. Bot. [f. mod.L. Sphæriaceæ.]

Sphæriaform. Belonging to, or typical of, the Sphæriaceæ, an extensive family of Fungi.

Sphæriaform, a.

Sphæridium [mod.L. Sphæria (see def.) + -(i)form.] Having a form like that of Sphæria, the typical genus of Sphæriaceæ (see prec.).

Spherical, -ick, obs. forms of Spheric(al.

Sphæri·dium. Zool. [n. -i·dia. -ideum.]

Sphere (sfīǝr), sb. Forms: α. 4-5 sper (5 spere, spere), 4-6 spere, 5 spyre, sphere, 6- sphere, 6-7 spheere, 7 sphear(e. β. 5-6 spere, 6-7 spher, spheare. [a. OF. espere (13th c.), later sphere (mod.F. sphère) or L. sphæra, Gr. σφαῖρα ball, globe, sphere.]

1. The apparent outward limit of space, conceived as a hollow globe enclosing (and at all points equidistant from) the earth.

2. In matters of science, as Sphæ·noclase (see quot.), or of genera of animals or plants, as Sphæ·nodon, Sphenodontini, Sphenodont, etc.

Sphæriaform, etc.

Sphere (sfīr), sb.

Sphere, v.

Sphered, ppl. a.

Sphereless (sfī·rlĕs), a.

Sphereometer, rare.

Spheric (sfe·rik), a. and sb.

Spherical (sfe·rikăl), a.

Sphericality (sferikæ·liti).

Spherically (sfe·rikăli), adv.

Sphericalness.

Sphericist, Obs.⁻¹

Sphericity (sferi·siti). Also 7 **sphæricity.**

Sphero- (sfī·ro), var. of SPHERO-, used as combining form.

Spheroid (sfī·roid), sb. and a.

Spheroidal (sfīroi·dăl), a.

Spheroidical (sfīroi·dikăl), a.

Spheroidically, adv.

Spheroidicity.

Spheroidity.

Spherometer (sfīrǫ·mĕtĕr). Also **sphæro-meter.**

Spherula (sfe·rŭla).

Spherular (sfe·rŭlăr), a.

Spherule (sfe·rūl).

Spherulite (sfe·rŭləit).

Spherulitic (sferŭli·tik), a.

Sphery (sfī·ri), a.

Sphincter (sfiŋ·ktĕr).

Sphincteral.

Sphincterate.

Sphincterize, v.

Sphinx (sfiŋks).

Sphingian.

Sphingid.

Sphingine.

Sphinx-like, a.

Sphinxian, a.

Sphinxine, a.

Sphragide, rare.

Sphragistics.

Sphygmia.

Sphygmic, a.

Sphygmo- (sfi·gmo).

Sphygmogram.

Sphygmograph.

Sphygmometer.

Sphygmophone.

Sphygmus.

Spica (spəi·ka).

Spical, a.

Spicate (spəi·kĕt), a.

Spicaceous, Bot.

Spicated (spai·kéitéd), a. Now rare.

1. *Bot.* Having the form of a spike.

2. Furnished with spikelets; bristly.

Spice (spais), sb. Forms: 4 spise, 4–6 spyse, 4–6 spyce, 3– spice. [ad. OF. *espice* (mod.F. *épice*), ad. L. *speciēs* SPECIES. Cf. SPECE.]

1. One or other of various strongly flavoured or aromatic substances of vegetable origin, obtained from tropical plants, commonly used as condiments or employed for other purposes on account of their fragrance and preservative qualities.

b. *fig.*

2. Without article, as a substance or in collective sense.

3. A slight touch or trace of some physical disorder or malady. Now *dial.*

b. A slight touch, trace, or share, a dash or flavour, of some thing or quality.

4. A specimen or sample. *rare.*

Spice-box.

1. A box, usually having several compartments, to keep spices in.

2. A cake seasoned with spice; *dial.*, a rich currant cake. Also *fund.*

Spiced (spaist), *ppl. a.*

Spicer. *Obs.* [Cf. SPICE.]

Spicery (spai·səri). Forms: 3–7 spicerie ...

Spicilege.

Spiciferous.

Spicily (spai·sili), *adv.*

Spiciness (spai·sinés).

Spick, sb.[1] *Obs.* Forms: α. 1 spic, 4–5 spyk (5 spike), 6–9 spick.

Spick, sb.[2] A spike, spike-nail.

Spick, v. *Obs.*

Spick and span, sb., adv. and adv.

Spick-and-span new. Also spick-span new.

Spicknard, obs. form of SPIKENARD.

Spick-span, a, abbrev. of SPICK AND SPAN.

Spicose, a. *rare*.

Spicous, a. *Bot.* ... Also SPICOSE.

Spiculate, a.

Spicular, a.

Spiculate, v.

Spiculated, *a.*

Spicula tion.

Spicule (spi·kiūl). Pl. **spicula**.

1. A small sharp-pointed process or part of an animal or plant.

Spiculum (spi·kiŭlŏm). Pl. spicula.

Spiculi- (spi·kiŭli), combining form after L. models, of SPICULA, SPICULE, and SPICULUM.

Spiculiferous, a.

Spiculiform, a.

Spiculum (spi·kiŭlŏm).

Spider (spai·dər), sb. Forms: 1 spiþra, 5 spiþer, spyþþer, spyþþyr, 6 spyder (7 spyther), 6– spider.

1. One or other of the arachnids belonging to the order *Araneidae*.

SPIDER. 598 SPIDER-CRAB. SPIDERED. 594 SPIER

SPIER-HAWK. 595 SPIGURNEL. 596 SPIKE

Spike, sb.³ Obs. — SPIKE-HOLE.

Spike, v.¹ [f. SPIKE sb.¹] Cf. MSw. and Sw. spika to nail; also LG. spikern, Du. spijkern.

1. trans. With sp². a. To fasten or close firmly with spikes or strong nails.

2. To render (a gun) unserviceable by driving a spike into the touch-hole; also, to block or fill up (the touch-hole) with a spike.

3. To fix or secure by means of long nails or spikes.

4. a. To make sharp like a spike.
b. To provide, fit, or stud with spikes.

Spiked, ppl. a.¹ [f. SPIKE sb.¹]

Spiked, ppl. a.² [f. SPIKE v.¹]

Spike-hole. In this sense (SPIKE sb.²) occurs earlier than the compound.]

Spikelet (spaɪˈklɛt). Bot. [f. SPIKE sb.¹]

Spikelet (spaɪˈklɛt). [f. SPIKE sb.¹] A small spike or spike-shaped object; a prickle or thorn.

Spike-nail. [f. SPIKE sb.¹] Also LG. spikernagel, MHG. spîchernagel (G. dial. speichernagel.)

Spikenard (spaɪˈknɑːd). Forms: α. 4- spike-nard (4 spoke-, spyknard), 5-6 spikenarde, spyk(e)narde (5 spiknarud) 6 spekard, spyk-narde, 7 spike-, 7 spyke nardy.

Spiker (spaɪˈkər). [f. SPIKE v.¹]
1. A device for spiking a cannon.
2. One who spikes a gun; one who drives or hammers in a spike.

Spiket. Obs. [f. SPIKE sb.¹]

Spike-tackle, club: see SPIKE sb.⁴ 2.

Spiking, vbl. sb. [f. SPIKE v.¹]

Spiky (spaɪˈki). a.¹ Also 6 spike. [f. SPIKE sb.¹]

Spiky (spaɪˈki). a.² Also 8 -ey. [f. SPIKE sb.²]

Spill, sb.¹ [f. SPILL v.¹]

Spile-box, obs. form of SPEEL-BONE dial.

Spiling (spaɪˈlɪŋ), vbl. sb.¹ [f. SPILE v.¹]

Spiling (spaɪˈlɪŋ), vbl. sb.² [?]

Spilite (spaɪˈlaɪt). Min. [a. F. spilite: see -ITE.]

Spill (spɪl), sb.¹ Forms: 4 spille, 5-6 spyll(e, 6-7 spil. [Of doubtful origin; app. in some way related to SPILL v.¹]
1. A splinter; a sharp-pointed fragment of wood, bone, etc.; a slip or sliver.

Spill (spɪl), sb.² [f. SPILL v.²]

Spill (spɪl), sb.³ slang. Obs. [Of doubtful origin: perh. from SPILL v.²]

Spill (spɪl), sb.⁴ [Of doubtful origin; app. in some way related to SPILL v.¹]
1. A throw from a horse or vehicle; a fall or tumble; an upset.

Spill (spɪl), v.¹ [OE. spillan.]
1. trans. To destroy by deprivation of life; to put (or bring) to death; to slay or kill.

Spill (spɪl), sb. (later quots.)

Spill (spɪl), v.² [f. SPILL v.¹]

ourselves and to make an idol of our will.

Spilling, ppl. a. [f. SPILL v.]

Supplement, p. 3873; Corrigenda, p. 4092; Spurious words, p. 4093; Books quoted, p. 4094

SPILLED.

Spillard. Cf. SPILLER *sb.*[1]

Spilled (spild), *ppl. a.* [f. SPILL *v.* + -ED[1].]

Spiller. In quot. *attrib.*

Spiller, *sb.*[1] Chiefly Cornish *dial.*, *Ir.*, and *Amer.* [Of obscure origin.] A long fishing-line provided with a number of hooks: a trawl-line.

Spiller, *sb.*[2] *Obs. exc. arch.* [Alteration of SPELLER[2].] A branchlet on a deer's horn.

Spilling (spi'lin̄), *sb.*[1]

Spilth (spilþ), *sb.* [f. SPILL *v.* + -TH[1].]

Spillikin (spi'likin), **spellican** (spe'likăn).

SPIN.

Spit. Obs.[1]

Spilth (spilþ), *sb.*[2] That which is spilled.

Spilus (spəi'lʌs). *Path.*

Spin (spin), *sb.*[1] [f. the vb.]

Spin (spin), *sb.*[2] *Anglo-Indian.* (Abbreviation of SPINSTER.) An unmarried lady.

†Spin, *sb.*[3] *Obs.*[1] In 6 *spynne.*

Spin (spin), *v.* Pa. t. **spun**, **span**. Pa. pple. **spun**.

SPIN.

Spin (spin), *v.*[2]

Spin, *v.*[3]

Spinster ...

SPIN. 603 SPINACH. SPINAL. 604 SPINDLE.

Spinaceous. *Bot.*

Spinach (spi'nidʒ). Forms: a. 6 *spynnage*, *spynage*, 7–9 *spinnage*, 6–9 *spinage*. β. 6 *spynoch*, *spinoche*, 6– *spinach* (also *-ace*).

Spinage, obs. form of SPINACH.

Spinach-beet.

Spinal, *sb.* Also 6–7 *spinall*.

Spinal, *a.* [f. L. *spīnālis*.]

Spination (spəineĭ'ʃən). [f. L. *spīna* SPINE.]

†Spinde. *Obs.*[1]

Spindle (spi'nd'l), *sb.* Forms: a. 1 *spinl*, *spinel*, 1–5 *spindel*, 3–7 *spindle*.

Spindle (spi'nd'l), *v.*

SPINDLE. (continued)

grooves so as to act as a screw; *spec.* that by which the spindle of a hand printing-press is lowered and raised.

III. *attrib.* and *Comb.* **14. a.** In sense 1 (in use especially in comb. relating to machine-spinning), as *spindle-band*, *-box*, *-carriage*, *-hook*, *-maker*, *-production*, *-work*.

b. In sense 6, as *spindle-end*, *-gearing*, *-lathe*, *-screw*, *-volve*.

c. In sense 9, as *spindle-cell*, *-formed*, *-pointed*, *-rooted*, etc. Also *spindle-like*, *screw-*, *volve*.

15. a. Of the limbs (or person), in the sense 'thin, slender, lacking in robustness'. See also SPINDLE-SHANK.

b. Of things, in the sense 'having the form of a spindle; cylindrical with a taper towards either end'.

16. In parasynthetic adjs., as *spindle-celled*, *-formed*, *-pointed*, *-rooted*, etc. Also *spindle-like* adj., *-wise* adv.

17. Special Comb. *+spindle bud*, a bud giving rise to a short or thin spindle; *spindle cross*, *Her.* a cross having arms shaped somewhat like a spindle; *spindle-pear*, a pear having the elongated form of a spindle; *spindle-stromb* (see quots.); *spindle-twirl*, *+whirl*, *-whorl*, a whorl used for weighting a spindle; *spindle-wood*, the spindle-tree, or the wood of this; *spindle-worm*, the maize eating larva of a noctuid moth (*Achatodes zea*).

Spindle (spi·nd'l), *v.* Also *b* spindel. [f. the *sb.*; cvp. in sense 2.]

1. *intr.* Of cereals : To grow up into the slender stalks on which the ear is formed.

b. To grow (into stalk, etc.), in the sense implying too slender a growth.

2. To shoot out or up, to develop by rapid growth or attenuation, *into* something thin or unsubstantial.

b. *transf.* To become spindly or weak.

3. a. *trans.* To draw or shape into a spindle.

b. To provide with a spindle.

Spindled (spi·nd'ld), *ppl. a.* [f. prec.]

1. Drawn out into a spindle form.

2. Of plants : Run to spindle, drawn up.

Spindle-leg. [SPINDLE *sb.* + *leg.*]

1. A long and slender leg.

2. *pl.* A person who has spindle-legs.

Spindle-legged, *a.* [f. SPINDLE *sb.* 15.]

Having thin, slender, spindle-shaped legs.

Spindle-shanked, *a.* [Cf. prec.]

Having long and slender legs; spindle-legged.

Spindle-shanks, *sb. pl.* [Cf. SPINDLE-LEG.]

1. Long and slender shanks.

2. A person having spindle-shanks.

Spindle-shaped, *ppl. a.* [SPINDLE *sb.* 16.]

Having the form of a spindle; fusiform.

Spindle-tree. [SPINDLE *sb.* + *tree.*]

An ornamental European shrub (*Euonymus Europaeus*), furnishing a hard fine-grained yellow-ish wood formerly made use of for spindles.

Spindleful. [SPINDLE *sb.* + -FUL.]

As much (yarn or thread) as fills a spindle.

Spindle-legged (cont.)

Spindleful (cont.)

SPINE.

Spine (spain), *sb.* Also *5* spyne, spin. [ad. L. *spina* thorn, prickle, backbone, etc.]

1. a. A stiff, sharp-pointed process produced or growing from the wood of a plant, consisting of a hardened or irregularly developed branch, petiole, stipule, or other part ; a thorn ; a similar process developed on fruits or leaves.

b. *pl.* The natural order *Celastraceæ*, to which the genus *Euonymus* belongs.

Spindling (*sbl.*) *sb.* [f. SPINDLE *v.* + -ING.]

1. The action of providing with a spindle or spindles.

2. The formation of a stem, stalk, or shoot, in plants.

3. *attrib.* in the sense 'having spindles'.

Spindly (spi·ndli), *a.* Also *6* spinly. [f. SPINDLE *sb.*]

1. Of plants : Of a slender and weakly growth.

2. Of animals : Having long and slender legs.

Spine-shaped, *ppl. a.* [SPINE *sb.* + *shaped.*]

Spinescence (spaine·sĕns), *sb.* [ad. mod.L. *spinescentia*.]

Spinescent (spaine·sĕnt), *a.* [ad. mod.L. *spinescens*, -*entem*, pres. pple. of *spinescere* to grow thorny.]

Spinet. [dim. of SPINE *sb.*] A small spine or thorn.

Spinet (spi·nĕt), *sb.* [dim. of SPINE *sb.*]

Spine-tail. [SPINE *sb.*]

Spinous (spai·nŭs), *a.* [f. *spina* spine + -OUS.]

Spini- combining form of L. *spina* spine, thorn.

Spiniferous (spaini·fĕrŭs), *a.* [f. L. *spinifer*, f. *spina* SPINE + -FEROUS.]

Spiniform (spai·nifǫrm), *a.* Bot. and Zool. [ad. mod.L. *spiniformis*: see SPINE *sb.* and -FORM.] Having the form of a spine or thorn.

Spinigerous (spaini·jĕrŭs), *a.* [f. L. *spiniger*, f. *spina* SPINE + -GEROUS.]

Spinose (spai·nōs, spain·ōs), *a.* [ad. L. *spinōsus*, f. *spina* SPINE.]

Spinous (spai·nŭs), *a.*

Spink (spiŋk), *sb.* Also dial. *spank*, *sprink*. A local and dialect name for the chaffinch.

Spinner (spi·nǝr), *sb.*

SPINE. | 609 | SPINNING. | SPINNING. | 610 | SPINOUS

Spink, v. *Obs.* *Sc. and north.* [Of obscure origin.] The cuckoo-flower or lady-smock, *Cardamine pratensis*.

Spink, sb.2, 3 *Sc. and north. dial.* [See SPINE sb.2] Flecked, speckled, spotted. Usually of cattle.

Spinnable (spi·năb'l), a. [f. SPIN v. + -ABLE.] Capable of being spun.

Spinner (spi·năkaₓ). Also **spinnaker**. [Said to have been a fanciful formation on *spin*, mispronunciation of *Sphinx*, the name of the first yacht which commonly carried the sail.] A large three-cornered sail carried by racing-yachts, boomed out at right angles to the vessel's side, opposite to the mainsail, and used in running before the wind. Also *attrib*.

Spink, a. *Obs.* [Cf. SPINK sb.1] = next.

Spinal, Spinel, *obs. ff.* SPINALLE. Spinnel, north. f. SPINDLE sb.

Spinner (spi·naₓ). Forms : 3–4 **spinnere**, 4–9 **spynner**, 7–8, 9 **spynnare**, 6–9 **spinner**, &c.; 8 SPIN v. + -ER1. [f. SPIN v. + -ER1, MHG. *spinnære* (G. *spinner*).]

I. 1. A spider, *esp.* one which spins a web.

b. A caterpillar which spins a web or cocoon; a silkworm. *rare*.

2. *dial.* A daddy-longlegs. = JENNY-SPINNER 1. Also *spinner*-fly.

b. In specific names, as *common loach*, *shark*, *spider-crab*, *tortoise*.

1872 Tennyson *Last Tourn.* 510 She heard the feet of Tristram grind The spiring stone that scaled about her tower.

Spirit (spi·rit), *sb.* Forms: α. 3- spirit, 4-6 -ite, 4-5 -itt, 4, 6 spiryte, 5 spiryt. 9 *dial.* spirut; 4-6 spyrite, 5 -itte, -id, -ut, -ete, 5-6 -it, 4-5 spyryt, 5-6 -yte. β. 5 sperete, -ite, 5-6 speryt, 5, 7, 9 sperit, 9 sperrit. See also Spirt, Spright, and Sprite. [a. AF. *spirit* (*espirit*), *spirite*, = OF. *esperit*, *-ite*, *esprit* (mod.F. *esprit*), or ad. L. *spīrit-us* (It. *spirito*, Pg. *espirito*, Sp. *espiritu*) breathing, breath, air, etc., related to *spīrāre* to breathe.

Mod.F. has also *spirite* in the sense of 'spiritualist'. In G., Da., and Sw. the L. form *spiritus* occurs, chiefly in sense 21.

The earlier English uses of the word are mainly derived from passages in the Vulgate, in which *spiritus* is employed to render Gr. πνεῦμα Pneuma and Heb. רוּחַ *rūaḥ*. The translation of these words by *spirit* (or one of its variant forms) is common to all versions of the Bible from Wyclif onwards.]

I. **1.** The animating or vital principle in man (and animals); that which gives life to the physical organism, in contrast to its purely material elements; the breath of life.

In some examples with implication of other senses.

c 1250 *Gen. & Ex.* 203 God made Adam, and his licham of erðe he nam, And blew ðor-in a liues blast,..A spirit ful of wit and sckil. 1340 *Ayenb.* 92 Þet body of man is..þe ydeluer þet is, and þe spirit of man is þe zaule, and ys þe noblest þing an þe heȝeste ssepþe þet may by. 1382 Wyclif *Eccl.* iii. 21 Who kneȝ, if the spirit of the sonus of Adam steȝe vp aboue, and if the spirit of bestis go doun byneþe? 1582 N. T. (Rhem.) *Jas.* ii. 26 For euen as the body without the spirit is dead: so also faith without workes is dead. 1611 Bible *Wisd.* xvi. 14 The spirit when it is gone foorth returneth not; neither the soule receiued vp, commeth againe. 1667 Milton *P. L.* x. 784 Least that pure breath of Life, the Spirit of Man,..cannot together perish With this corporeal Clod. 1728 Chambers *Cycl.* s.v. *Person*, Thus, a Man, tho' consisting of two very different Things, *viz.* Body and Spirit, is not two Persons. 1850 Tennyson *In Mem.* lvi, The spirit does but mean the breath. 1853 Abp. Thomson *Laws Th.* (ed. 3) 61 When the breath is exhaled the spirit remains immortal.

transf. 1382 Wyclif *John* vi. 64 The wordis that I haue spokun to ȝou, ben spirit and lyf. 1712 J. James tr. *Le Blond's Gardening* 201 Water-Works are the Life of a Garden; 'tis these..which animate and invigorate it, and, if I may so say, give it new Life and Spirit.

b. In phrases denoting or implying diminution or cessation of the vital power, or the recovery of this. Also *transf.*, life-blood.

In various Biblical passages used with reference to profound discouragement, or recovery from this: cf. sense 13.

a 1300 *Cursor M.* 12075 And sone þe spirit þat was fledd again come in þat ilk stede. 1382 Wyclif *Luke* viii. 55 And her spirit turnyde aȝeyn, and sche roos anon. *Ibid.* xxiii. 46 And he seyinge thes things, sente out the spirit [*v.r.* ȝaf vp the goost], ether diede. a 1425 tr. *Arderne's Treat. Fistula*, etc. 38 Neþerlesse þai may..moue almost to þe breþing out of þe spirit. 1606 Shaks. *Ant. & Cl.* iv. xv. 58 Now my Spirit is going, I can no more. 1611 Bible *Judg.* xv. 19 When he had drunke, his spirit came againe, and he reuiued. 1720 Pope *Iliad* xviii. 120 Let me revenge it on proud Hector's heart, Let his last spirit smoke upon my dart.

transf. 1595 Shaks. *John* iv. i. 110 There is no malice in this burning cole, The breath of heauen, hath blowne his spirit out.

c. In contexts relating to temporary separation of the immaterial from the material part of man's being, or to perception of a purely intellectual character. Chiefly in phr. *in spirit*.

1382 Wyclif *Rev.* iv. 2 Anoon I was in spirit, and lo! a seete was put in heuen, and on the seete oon sittinge. c 1400 Maundev. (Roxb.) xiv. 61 In spirit he was rauischt intill heuen, whare he sawe heuenly priuetez. c 1440 *Alph. Tales* 451 He was ravisshid his spyrid fro his body vnto Pasch day. 1582 N. T. (Rhem.) *Rev.* i. 10, I was in spirit on the Dominical day. 1667 Milton *P. L.* xi. 406 In Spirit perhaps he also saw Rich Mexico.., And Cusco in Peru. 1850 Tennyson *In Mem.* xvii, For I in spirit saw thee move Thro' circles of the bounding sky.

d. Incorporeal or immaterial being, as opposed to *body* or *matter*; being or intelligence conceived as distinct from, or independent of, anything physical or material. (Cf. Mind *sb.*[1] 17 f.)

1382 Wyclif *John* iii. 6 That that is born of spirit, is spirit. 1611 Bible *Isaiah* xxxi. 3 Now the Egyptians are men and not God, and their horses flesh and not spirit. 1690 Locke *Hum. Und.* ii. xxiii. (1695) 164 The primary Ideas we have peculiar to Body, as contradistinguished to Spirit. *Ibid.*, The Ideas we have belonging, and peculiar to Spirit, are Thinking, and Will. 1725 Watts *Logic* (1736) 23 Modes belong either to Body or to Spirit, or to both... Modes of Spirit belong only to Minds. 1832 Brewster *Nat. Magic* ii. 10 The sentinel which guards the pass between the worlds of matter and of spirit. 1845 Bailey *Festus* (ed. 2) 19 Spirit is soul Deified. 1898 Illingworth *Div. Immanence* i. 5 If matter and spirit are thus only known in combination, it follows that neither can be completely known.

2. The soul of a person, as commended to God, or passing out of the body, in the moment of death.

c 1375 *Sc. Leg. Saints* i. (*Peter*) 730 And þis he ȝalde þe spyrit, of god in-to þe halde. 1382 Wyclif *Luke* xxiii. 46 Fadir, in to thi hondis I bitake my spirit. 1509 Fisher *Funeral Serm. C'tess Richmond* Wks. (1876) 309 Sone after ..she departed & yelded vp her spyryte in to the handes of our lorde. 1582 N. T. (Rhem.) *Acts* vii. 59 They stoned Steuen..saying: Lord Iesus, receiue my spirit. 1611 Bible *Luke* xxiii. 46 Father, into thy hands I commend my spirit. 1825 Scott *Betrothed* Concl., If you come to announce the doom of this poor frame, may God be gracious to the spirit which must be violently dismissed from it!

b. The disembodied soul of a (deceased) person, regarded as a separate entity; = Soul *sb.* 11.

1375 Barbour *Bruce* iv. 757 The Pithones..Rasit, throu hyr mekill slycht, samuell[s] sperit. 1426 Lydgate *De Guil. Pilgr.* 11960 To the body a spyryt spak,..The spyryt in the weye stood; The body..hong on a tre. 1526 *Pilgr. Perf.* (W. de W. 1531) 7 All the holy sayntes that ben saued, and also the damned spirytes in hell. 1560 Daus tr. *Sleidane's Comm.* 115 There by a signe made, he sheweth that he is the spirite of her. 1611 Bible *Heb.* xii. 23 To the generall assembly,..and to the spirits of iust men made perfect. 1632 Milton *Penseroso* 88 Where I may..unsphear The spirit of Plato. 1741-2 Gray *Agrippina* 14 Twould dash his joy To hear the spirit of Britannicus Yet walks on earth. 1790 Cowper *Mother's Picture* 23 Hover'd thy spirit o'er thy sorrowing son, Wretch even then, life's journey just begun? 1819 Shelley *Cenci* iv. i. 93 Her spirit shall approach the throne of God Plague-spotted with my curses. 1840 Hood *Open Question* 145 Spirit of Kant! have we not had enough To make Religion sad, and sour, and snubbish.

fig. 1742 Young *Nt. Th.* ii. 180 The spirit walks of ev'ry day deceas'd.

3. A supernatural, incorporeal, rational being or personality, usually regarded as imperceptible at ordinary times to the human senses, but capable of becoming visible at pleasure, and freq. conceived as troublesome, terrifying, or hostile to mankind.

a 1300 *Cursor M.* 17288+449 Spirit has nauther flesch ne bone, as I now haf sothly. c 1330 R. Brunne *Chron. Wace* (Rolls) 8072 We fynde writen..Of swylk manere of spyrites; Bytwyxte þe mone & þe erþe þei wone. 1387 Trevisa *Higden* (Rolls) III. 279 We haveþ i-lerned of Socrates, þat was alway tendaunt to a spirit þat was i-cleped demon. 1422 tr. *Secreta Secret., Priv. Priv.* 143 This Spyritte that al thy workys seyth ande parceywth. 1483 Caxton *G. de la Tour* F j, His wyf..sayd it was the fende or elles the goblyn or somme spyryte. 1560 Daus tr. *Sleidane's Comm.* 116 After that Luthers doctrine was spred abroad and knowen, those spirites..vanyshed cleane out of syght. 1596 Shaks. *1 Hen. IV*, iii. i. 52, I can call Spirits from the vastie Deepe. 1610 — *Temp.* i. ii. 409 What, is't a Spirit? ..Beleeue me sir, It carries a braue forme. But 'tis a spirit. 1646 Sir T. Browne *Pseud. Ep.* 76 The conceit is excellent, and if the effect would follow somwhat divine, whereby we might communicate like spirits. 1667 Milton *P. L.* i. 423 For Spirits when they please Can either Sex assume, or both. 1721 Young *Revenge* iii. i, Shut close the doors, That not a spirit find an entrance here. 1731-8 Swift *Polite Conv.* 110, I saw some thing in black, I thought it was a Spirit. 1799 Wordsw. *Nutting* 54 With gentle hand Touch —for there is a spirit in the woods. 1841 Browning *Pippa Passes* Poems (1905) 175 As if God bade some spirit plague a world. 1897 Mary Kingsley *W. Africa* 479 The spirit is malevolent: all native-made spirits are. 1902 J. M. Robertson *Hist. Christianity* 71 Mithra..being the first of the seven planetary spirits on whose names the week was based.

fig. 1850 Tennyson *In Mem.* cii, As down the garden-walks I move, Two spirits of a diverse love Contend for loving masterdom.

transf. 1860 Tyndall *Glac.* i. ii. 22 We had, in fact, the Spirit of the Brocken before us.

b. With qualifying terms, as *evil*, *familiar*, *guardian*, *wicked*, etc.

c 1340 Hampole *Prose Treat.* 5 For thare may na wykked spyrite noye þare Ihesu es mekyll in mynde. c 1380 Wyclif *Last Age Ch.* (1840) 34 Alas, þat no good spiryt dweilid wiþ me at my comynge into Goddis Chirche. 1382 — *1 Sam.* xxviii. 7 There is a womman hauynge a dyuynynge spirite in Endore. 1508- [see Damned *ppl. a.* 2]. a 1536 *Songs, Carols*, etc. 69 Þe sperytis infernall, all þe hole rowte. 1555- [see Evil *a.* 3 b]. 1565- [see Familiar *a.* 2 d]. 1582 N. T. (Rhem.) *Heb.* i. 14 Are they not al ministring spirits? 1611 Bible *1 Tim.* iv. 1 Giuing heed to seducing spirits. 1676 *Charge in Office of Clerk of Assize* 101 If any person have..employed any wicked spirit, to any intent or purpose whatsoever. 1711 [see Guardian 6 b]. 1785 C. Wilkins tr. *Bhagvat-Geeta* 68 The evil spirits are terrified. 1827 Scott *Highl. Widow* v, The days and hours when the wicked spirits were supposed to have especial power over man and beast. 1860 Pusey *Min. Proph.* 30 It has been thought that the evil spirits assault mankind in a sort of order or method.

transf. 1581 Pettie *Guazzo's Civ. Conv.* i. (1586) 38 The more they are in prosperitie, the more they are beset with Flatterers,..whereof it commeth that Princes are euer besieged by these euill spirites.

c. A being of this nature imagined as possessing and actuating a person.

1382 Wyclif *Matt.* viii. 16 Thei brouȝte to hym many hauynge deuelys, and he castide out spiritis by word. 1382 — *Acts* xvi. 16 Sum wenche hauynge a spirit of dyuynacioun. 1546 Langley *Pol. Verg. de Invent.* i. xviii. 33 To banish the Spirit out of yᵉ Demoniake. 1651 [see Possess *v.* 5 b]. 1711 Shaftesb. *Charac.* (1737) III. 117 He had been seiz'd with this prophesying spirit-errant, processional, and saltant. 1728 Chambers *Cycl.*, *Demoniac*,..a Person possess'd with a Spirit, or Demon. 1850 [see Possess *v.* 5].

d. In generalized sense: A being essentially incorporeal or immaterial.

c 1340 Hampole *Pr. Consc.* 3022 Bot now may som..aske how þe saul may fele payne, þat es noght elles bot a spirit. c 1380 Wyclif *Sel. Wks.* III. 502 Hit is heresye to trowe þat Crist is a spiryt and no body. 1382 — *John* iv. 24 God is a spirit. 1653 Binning *Serm.* 9 Angels and men next to God, are spirits, as He is a Spirit. a 1703 Burkitt *On N. T., John* iv. 24 God..is not a bare spiritual substance, but a pure and perfect Spirit. 1710 Berkeley *Princ. Hum. Knowl.* i. § 6 In my mind, or in that of some other created spirit..or of some eternal spirit. 1876 J. Parker *Paracl.* i. i. 9 Man *has* a body, but he *is* a spirit.

4. With *the* and qualifying term, denoting some particular being of the above nature.

1375 Barbour *Bruce* iv. 758 [She raised] in his sted þe euill spirit þat gaf grath ansueir hir to. a 1425 *Cursor M.* 170 (Trin.), Iesu..Was temptide with þe spirit of wronge. c 1440 *Alph. Tales* 281 Þer was ane hermett þat was tempid with þe spiritt of blasfemyng.

1797 Coleridge *This Lime-tree Bower my Prison* 42 Such hues As veil the Almighty Spirit, when He makes Spirits perceive his presence. 1836 *Penny Cycl.* VI. 208/2 The Indians..consider it as the dwelling of the Great Spirit, or 'Manitou'. 1842 Lytton *Zicci* 2 The Evil Spirit is pulling you towards him by the hair.

5. †**a.** One who kidnaps; an abductor. *Obs.*

1645 Whitelocke *Mem.* (1682) 140/1 An Ordinance against such who are called Spirits, and use to steal away, and take up children. 1686 *Lond. Gaz.* No. 2532/1 The frequent Abuses of a lewd sort of People, called spirits, in Seducing many of His Majesties Subjects to go on Shipboard [etc.]. 1690 J. Child *Disc. Trade* x. 170 A sort of loose vagrant People,..which Merchants and Masters of Ships, by their Agents (or Spirits, as they were called) gathered up about the Streets of London, and other places.

b. *Printing.* (See quots.)

1683 Moxon *Mech. Exerc., Printing* 373 The Press-man sometimes has a Week-Boy to take Sheets, as they are Printed off the Tympan. These Boys do..black and dawb themselves; whence the Workmen do jocosely call them Devils; and sometimes Spirits, and sometimes Flies. 1888 Jacobi *Printers' Vocab.* 129 *Spirit*, the evil genius of a chapel.

c. (See quot.)

1825 in Drewitt *Bombay in Days Geo. IV* (1907) 176, I shall gain the character here of a 'spirit',..having met several times at his house ladies of spotted reputation, and who are not visited by any one.

d. *ellipt.* The spirit duck.

1784 Pennant *Arct. Zool.* II. 558 Called sometimes the Spirit, as is supposed, from its suddenly appearing again at a distance, after diving.

II. **6.** *The Spirit of God* (or *the Lord*), the active essence or essential power of the Deity, conceived as a creative, animating, or inspiring influence.

13.. *Cursor M.* 7106 (Gött.), Sampson slou þat leon kene, þe spirit of godd in him was sene. 1382 Wyclif *Isaiah* lxi. 1 The spirit of the Lord [is] vp on me. — *1 Cor.* ii. 11 What thingis ben of God, no man knowith, no but the spirit of God. 1582 N. T. (Rhem.) *Eph.* iv. 30 And contristate not the holy Spirit of God. 1604 Hieron *Wks.* I. 480 Were these inuented by Gods Spirit Or found you them in holy writ? 1667 in *Cath. Rec. Soc. Publ.* III. 70 One of those ..happy trees vnto which the spirit of God compares a iust man. 1841 Trench *Parab.* xiii. 220 The informing Spirit of God which prompts the works and quickens the faith. 1875 Manning *Mission H. Ghost* i. 1 The Spirit of the Lord is God the Holy Ghost.

b. *The Holy Spirit*, = Holy Ghost 1.

a 1300 *Cursor M.* 19415 (Edinb.), þe hali spirite oute of him spac. c 1375 *Sc. Leg. Saints* x. (*Matthew*) 130 Eftyre cristis ascencione, þe haly spyrit of criste come done. c 1420 *Prymer* 40 Take þou not fro me þin hooli spirit. 1549 *Bk. Com. Prayer, Ord. Priests*, Laude and praise be to the father,..And to the holy spirite. 1639, etc. [see Procession *sb.* 4]. 1709 Watts *Hymn*, 'Come, Holy Spirit' 1, Come, Holy Spirit, heavenly Dove. 1881 N. T. (R. V.) *Matt.* i. 18 The Holy Ghost. *marg.* Or, Holy Spirit: and so throughout this book. 1898 Chavasse *Litton's Ch. Christ* 18 Those who by the Holy Spirit have been convinced of sin.

c. *The Spirit*, = prec.

1382 Wyclif *Mark* i. 12 Anon the Spirit puttide [Vulg. *expulit*] hym in to desert. a 1400 N. T. (Paues) *Rom.* viii. 26 Þe Spirit also helpeþ oure infirmyte. c 1520 M. Nisbet *John* i. 32, I saw the spirit cummande doun as a dow fra heuen. 1546 Gardiner *Declar. Joye* 88 Baptisme yᵉ sacrament of birth of yᵉ spirite, as ye speake, in newe englyssh, and of the holly goost as the olde english turned it. a 1619 Fotherby *Atheom.* ii. xii. § 2 (1622) 337 With diuine accents, tuning rarely right, Vnto the rapting Spirit, the rapted spright. 1679 *Establ. Test* 24 If the Spirit moves, he can disgorge himself against the Priests of Baal, the Hirelings. 1822 Shelley *Chas. I*, ii. 223 The apostolic power with which the Spirit Has filled its elect vessels.

d. So *The Spirit of truth* or †*verity*, etc.

1382 Wyclif *John* xiv. 17 He schal ȝyue to ȝou another coumfortour, the spirit of treuthe. ?a 1533 Frith *Answ. More* L ij b, That spiryte of veryte whiche is sent from God our Father through our sauyour.., to lyghten our darke ignoraunce. 1551 Bible *John* xv. 26 When the comforter is come,..which is the spirite of truthe. 1819 J. Montgomery *Hymn*, '*Lord God the Holy Ghost*' iii, Spirit of Light, explore And chase our gloom away.

7. The active or essential principle or power *of* some emotion, frame of mind, etc., as operating on or in persons.

1382 Wyclif *2 Tim.* i. 7 God ȝaf not to vs the spirit of drede, but of vertu, and of loue, and sobrenesse. c 1400 Love *Bonavent. Mirr.* (1908) 61 Knowynge hym by the spirit of prophecie. 1551 Bible *Isaiah* xix. 14 The Lorde hathe made Egypte droncken wyth the spirite of erroure, and they shall vse it. 1560 Daus tr. *Sleidane's Comm.* 129 One of them, as though he were moved with the spirite of prophecie, runeth up and downe the citie. 1591 Shaks. *Two Gent.* v. iv. 55 The gentle spirit of mouing words. 1601 — *Twel. N.* i. i. 9 O spirit of Loue, how quicke and fresh art thou. 1675 Owen *Indwelling Sin* (1732) i. 3 The effectual Power of the Spirit of Grace. 1705 in *Buccleuch Pap.* (Mont. Ho.) I. 354 The spirit of lying runs away with more torrys than ever I had the honour to know. 1779 *Mirror* No. 18, The dark and gloomy spirit of fanaticism, which prevailed so universally..during the last century. 1820 Belzoni *Egypt & Nubia* iii. 326 The spirit of contradiction excited by the illiberality of travellers. 1855 Prescott *Philip II*, ii. v. (1857) 247 The spirit of independence was fostered by the institutions of the country. 1872 Morley *Voltaire* (1886) 250 A momentary self-indulgence in the spirit of party.

b. With *a*: A tendency, inclination, impulse, etc., *of* a specified kind.

1388 Wyclif *Isaiah* xix. 14 The Lord meddlid a spirit of errour in the myddis therof. c 1430 Lydg. *Min. Poems*

(Percy Soc.) 9 God the ffulfylle withe intelligence, And withe a spyrut of goostly sapience. *Ibid.*, God send [thee] also ..A spiryt..Of connyng. 1596 Shaks. *1 Hen. IV*, v. ii. 64 A double spirit Of teaching, and 'of learning. 1765 *Museum Rust.* IV. 56 A certain spirit of improvement.. has been promoted and carried on. 1774 Goldsm. *Nat. Hist.* (1776) I. 18 If possest with a spirit of theory, his imagination will supply the rest. 1833 Ht. Martineau *Vanderput & S.* ix. 133 The old woman had infused a further spirit of thankfulness into the suffering boy. 1844 Disraeli *Coningsby* iii. i, A slight spirit of mockery played over his speech. 1859 C. Barker *Assoc. Princ.* iii. 62 To foster a spirit of comprehensive patriotism.

8. A particular character, disposition, or temper existing in, pervading, or animating, a person or set of persons; a special attitude or bent of mind characterizing men individually or collectively.

1561 Rastell *Confut. M. Ivelles Serm.* 137 Not onlye Moyses had the grace of gouerning.., but seuentie elders.. had imparted vnto them of his spirite and dignitie. 1588 Kyd *Househ. Phil.* Wks. (1901) 242 There mette vs another youth of lesse yeeres, but no lesse gentle spirit. 1611 Shaks. *Wint. T.* ii. iii. 127 Ioue send her A better guiding Spirit. 1665 Sir T. Herbert *Trav.* (1677) 62 Observing in his pupil a Spirit fitted for the Government of that Monarchy. 1682 Flavel *Fear* Ded., A dear friend from whom I have often had the fair idea and character of your excellent spirit. 1712 Addison *Spect.* No. 363 ⁋ 8 His Person, his Port, and Behaviour, are suitable to a Spirit of the highest Rank. 1754 Gray *Progr. Poesy* 81 Latium had her lofty spirit lost. 1856 Froude *Hist. Eng.* (1858) I. i. 34 By these measures the money-making spirit was for a time driven back. 1897 *Cavalry Tactics* 5 Like the quality of tact, the cavalry spirit is perceptible only by its results.

b. The disposition, feeling, or frame of mind with which something is done, considered, or viewed.

1601 Bp. W. Barlow *Serm. Paules Crosse* Pref. 10 But from what spirit these objections proceede, may soone be gessed at. c 1680 Aubrey in Ingleby *Shaks. Cent. Praise* (1880) 383 It seemed to him that he writt with the very spirit that Shakespear [did]. 1837 Carlyle *Fr. Rev.* i. i. iv, It is not thy works,..but only the Spirit thou workest in, that can have worth or continuance. 1861 M. Pattison *Ess.* (1889) I. 31 Such is the spirit in which the history of our ancestors is ordinarily propounded to us. 1864 Bryce *Holy Rom. Emp.* ix. (1875) 147 Otto laboured on his great project in a spirit almost mystic.

9. A person considered in relation to his character or disposition; one who has a spirit of a specified nature: **a.** With preceding adjs.

1591- [see Choice *a.* 1 b]. 1598 E. Guilpin *Skial.* v, Here I converse with those diviner spirits Whose knowledge and admire the world inherits. 1601- [see Master *sb.*[1] 24 a]. 1638 Junius *Paint. Ancients* 10 Many lively spirits at length are most pittifully turned away from their forward course. 1655 Fuller *Ch. Hist.* ix. 194 Thus impossible it is to please froward spirits. 1718 *Free-thinker* No. 56. 8 The Brave Spirits of France now strive to vindicate their Liberty in Religious Matters. 1746 Francis tr. *Horace, Epist.* i. xix. 11 Let thirsty Spirits make the Bar their Choice. 1808 Scott in *Lockhart* I. i. 27 He is..led to be the associate and companion of those inferior spirits with whom he is placed. 1849 Macaulay *Hist. Eng.* i. I. 34 A few regiments of household troops are sufficient to overawe all the discontented spirits of a large capital. 1883 *Manch. Guard.* 29 Oct. 5/2 That the army, at least the more active spirits within it, were discontented was notorious.

b. With other forms of qualification. *rare.*

1603 Daniel *Def. Rhime* Wks. (1717) 21 Being..in all Ages furnish'd with Spirits fit to maintain the Majesty of her own Greatness. a 1648 Ld. Herbert *Hen. VIII* (1683) 93 So haughty were the major part of the spirits in this assembly, that..they condemned Luther's Books to the Fire. 1760-72 H. Brooke *Fool of Qual.* (1809) III. 82 Our ship..was full manned, with about two hundred and seventy spirits.. ready, and desirous to go and meet death.

10. The essential character, nature, or qualities *of* something; that which constitutes the pervading or tempering principle of anything. (Common after 1800.)

1690 Temple *Ess., Poetry* Wks. 1720 I. 241 The true Spirit or Vein of ancient Poetry. 1721 Bradley *Philos. Acc. Wks. Nat.* 189 Which is enough to support the Spirit of Botany. 1746 Francis tr. *Horace, Epist.* ii. i. 224 It breathes the Spirit of the tragic Scene. 1843 Ruskin *Mod. Paint.* I. ii. iv. § 3 The spirit of the hills is action, that of the lowlands repose. 1888 Bryce *Amer. Commw.* v. xciii. III. 298 To do so would be alien to the whole spirit of American legislation.

b. The prevailing tone or tendency *of* a particular period of time.

1820 Shelley *Lett.* Wks. 1880 IV. 166 It is the spirit of the age, and we are all infected with it. 1824 Landor *Imag. Conv.* Wks. 1846 I. 144 The spirit of the times is only to be made useful by catching it as it rises. 1884 Gladstone in *Western Daily Press* 22 Sept. 3/3 This legitimate process.. conducted in the spirit of the present day. 1891 *Pall Mall G.* 6 Aug. 3/1 The Spirit of the Age is against those who put party or programme before human needs.

c. The broad or general intent or meaning *of* a statement, enactment, etc. Used in contrast to Letter *sb.*[1] 5.

Suggested by the use of the words in 2 *Cor.* iii. 6.

1802 *Med. Jrnl.* VIII. 288 Knowing..that Magistrates are generally obliged to inflict penalties according to the Letter and not according to the Spirit of an Act. 1850 Robertson *Serm.* Ser. iii. vi. (1857) 84 His faith appears to have consisted in disbelieving the letter, almost as much as in believing the spirit of the promise.

III. **11.** The immaterial intelligent or sentient element or part of a person, freq. in implied or expressed contrast to the body.

1382 Wyclif *Ps.* l. 19 Sacrifise to God [is] a spiritt holly trublid. c 1386 Chaucer *Knt.'s T.* 1907 Naught may the woful spirit in myn herte Declare a poynt of my sorwes smerte. a 1420 *Aunters of Arth.* xx, The holy goste, That enspyres alle sperites..to come to that blysse. 1551 Bible *Luke* i. 47 My spirite reioyseth in god my sauiour. 1585 T. Washington tr. *Nicholay's Voy.* iii. i. 69 b, [They] teach them to learne some art or occupation, according to the capacitie of their spirit. 1604 E. G[rimstone] *D'Acosta's Hist. Indies* ii. iv. 88 As well in the fruites of the earth, as in the bodies and spirits of men. c 1665 Mrs. Hutchinson *Mem. Col. Hutchinson* (1846) 5 But these things bounded not their great spirits. 1743 Francis tr. *Horace, Odes* ii. iii. 2 In arduous Hours an equal Mind maintain, Nor let your Spirit rise too high. 1789 Cowper *Queen's Visit Lond.* 65 That cordial thought her spirit cheer'd. 1827 Hallam *Const. Hist.* iii. (1876) I. 162 They stood the trial of their spirits without swerving from their allegiance. 1842 Tennyson *Sir Galahad* iv, My spirit beats her mortal bars. 1872 Morley *Voltaire* 7 Many new things, after which the spirits of others were unconsciously groping and dumbly yearning.

b. In generalized sense, with *the*.

1382 Wyclif *Baruch* iii. 1 The soule in anguysshes, and the spirit tormentid crieth to thee. c 1440 *Gesta Rom.* i. 4 (Harl. MS.), þi flesch, þat dispisith all werkis that þe spirite lovith. a 1450 tr. *De Imitatione* ii. viii. 48 Blesful is þat man whom..he calliþ fro teres to þe ioy of þe spirit. 1560 Daus tr. *Sleidane's Comm.* 55 Luther hath offended..in..not teaching those thinges, that are of the spirite. 1614 C. Brooke *Ghost Rich. III*, F iv, As the Catholick Spirit in Man applyes Each Sence and Organ, to their proper Ends. 1665 R. Howard *Four Plays, Committee* iii. 99 Saffron-posset-drink is very good against The heaviness of the Spirit. 1781 Cowper *Hope* 299 Hopes..that cannot..cheer the spirit, nor refresh the sight. 1875 E. White *Life in Christ* iii. xx. (1878) 293 In such cases the spiritual action must at first be directly on the spirit and not at all on the mind.

c. Without article; freq. in phr. *in spirit*.

1382 Wyclif *Rom.* xii. 11 Not slow in bisynesse, feruent..in spirit. *Ibid.* 1 *Cor.* vii. 34 And a..mayden thenkith what thingis ben of the Lord, that sche be hooly in body and spirit. c 1430 Lydg. *Min. Poems* (Percy Soc.) 48 This rose of Jericho,..Pore in spirit, parfit in pacyence. 1582 N. T. (Rhem.) *Luke* x. 21 In that very houre he reioyced in spirit. 1582 N. Lichefield tr. *Castanheda's Conq. E. Ind.* 143 The Captaine Generall was inwardly moued in spirit. 1663 Bp. Patrick *Parab. Pilgr.* xix, Losing more time by these dejections of spirit. 1670 Clarendon *Hist. Reb.* xvi. § 10 The poor man had not spirit enough to discern what was best for him. 1779 *Mirror* No. 10, Mr. Fleetwood felt an unusual elevation of spirit. 1859 Thackeray *Virgin.* vi, Saddened and humbled in spirit, the young officer presented himself after a while to his old friends. 1860 Ruskin *Mod. Paint.* V. viii. i. 167 *note*, This being the true distinction between flesh and spirit.

12. The emotional part of man as the seat of hostile or angry feeling.

1382 Wyclif *2 Chron.* xxi. 16 Thanne the Lord rerede aȝeinus Joram the spirite of the Philisteis, and of Arabes. 1607 Shaks. *Timon* iii. v. 104 And not to swell our Spirit, He shall be executed presently. 1611 Bible *Eccl.* x. 4 If the spirit of the ruler rise vp against thee, leaue not thy place. a 1715 Burnet *Own Time* (1724) I. 467 The carelessness and luxury of the court came to be so much exposed that the King's spirit was much sharpened upon it. 1862 Trollope *Orley F.* xiv, She was prepared for war and her spirit was hot within her.

13. Mettle; vigour of mind; ardour; courage; disposition or readiness to assert oneself or to hold one's own.

1596 Shaks. *1 Hen. IV*, iv. i. 101 All furnisht, all in Armes, ..As full of spirit as the Moneth of May. 1603 — *Meas. for M.* iii. i. 212 I haue spirit to do any thing that appeares not fowle. 1643 in Clarendon *Hist. Reb.* vi. § 338 They have of late taken spirit, and begun to speak big words. a 1715 Burnet *Own Time* (1734) II. 427 A man of more spirit than discretion. 1749 Fielding *Tom Jones* iv. viii, Molly had too much spirit to bear this treatment tamely. 1809 Byron *Bards & Rev.* (ed. 2) Postscr., 'The age of chivalry is over,' or, in the vulgar tongue, there is no spirit now-a-days. 1862 Stanley *Jew. Ch.* (1877) I. xv. 296 They replied with all the spirit of Arab chiefs. 1890 'L. Falconer' *Mlle. Ixe* i. 33 She consoled herself by describing what other people called disobedience as spirit.

b. In the phr. *with* (..) *spirit*.

1748 Gray *Alliance* 95 What wonder if..They guard with spirit what by strength they gain'd? 1799 Nelson 7 June in Nicolas *Disp.* (1846) VII. p. clxxxiv, Don Jose..has on several occasions conducted himself with spirit. 1816 Scott *Old Mort.* xxxii, Ere Morton or Burley had reached the post to be defended, the enemy had commenced an attack upon it with great spirit. 1830 Marryat *King's Own* xiii, The action was now maintained with spirit, but much to the disadvantage of the cutter.

c. Freq. in *a man of spirit*.

1747 Hoadly *Suspicious Husband* i. i, We Men of Spirit, Sir, are above it. 1780 *Mirror* No. 102, Youths entering on the stage of life are catched with the engaging appellation, 'a man of spirit'. 1812 *Lex. Bal.* Pref. p. vi, They may be initiated into all the peculiarities of language by which a man of spirit is distinguished from a man of worth.

14. a. A brisk or lively quality in things.

1588 Kyd *Househ. Phil.* Wks. (1901) 272 The small wynes, and those of little spirite that quickly lose their strength. 1638 Junius *Paint. Ancients* 229 Seeing..that nothing marreth the life and spirit of the invented things so much, as to force and strain them to a fore-determined purpose. 1686 Horneck *Crucif. Jesus* (1716) 190 Wine hath Briskness and Spirit in it. 1852 Mrs. Stowe *Uncle Tom's C.* xiv, So much motherliness and full-heartedness..seemed to put a spirit into the food and drink she offered. 1874 H. H. Cole *Catal. Ind. Art S. Kens. Mus.* App. 281 The action and modelling of the conventional griffin has some spirit about it.

b. Liveliness, vivacity, or animation in persons, their actions, discourse, etc. (Cf. 17 c.)

a 1700 Evelyn *Diary* 16 Aug. 1691, An honest discourse, but read without any spirit or seeming concern. 1750 Gray *Long Story* 30 Arm'd with spirit, wit, and satire. 1783 Mme. D'Arblay *Diary* 20 June, The absence of Dr. Johnson.. took off the spirit of the evening. 1867 Ruskin *Time & Tide* v. § 24 She danced her joyful dance with perfect grace, spirit, sweetness, and self-forgetfulness. 1886 *Athenæum* 30 Oct. 559/2 The twenty-second chapter..relates with some spirit the disputes between England and the United States.

IV. **15.** A movement of the air; a wind; a breath (of wind or air).

In later use *poet.* and associated with other senses.

1382 Wyclif *Gen.* viii. 1 The Lord..brouȝte to a spirit [1388 wynd] vpon the erthe. And the watris ben lessid. *Ibid.* *Ps.* x. 7 Fyr, brunston, and the spiritis [1388 spirit] of tempestis. 1561 Daus tr. *Bullinger on Apoc.* (1573) 158 Fyre, brimstone, and spirite of tempest. 1601 Holland *Pliny* I. 37 All the spirit and winde which should beare them [*sc.* birds] vp is withdrawne from them. 1626 Bacon *Sylva* § 39 All Purgers haue in them a raw Spirit, or Wind; which is the Principall Cause of Tortion in the Stomach. 1725 Pope *Odyssey* vii. 152 The balmy spirit of the western gale. 1820 Shelley *Witch Atlas* lx, With motion like the spirit of that wind Whose soft step deepens slumber.

†**b.** The act of breathing; (a) breath. *Obs.*

1382 Wyclif *2 Thess.* ii. 8 The ilke wickid man..whom the Lord Jhesu schal sle with the spirit of his mouth. 1481 Caxton tr. *Cicero, Old Age*, Their wisedom ascendyd in encreasing and contynued unto the last spirite of their lives. 1483 — *Gold. Leg.* 129/2 For all her body bycam cold and she felte that her spirite helde her in her brest. 1581 Marbeck *Bk. Notes* 55 Him shall God destroie with yᵉ spirit of his mouth. 1678 Wanley *Wond. Lit. World* 293 Forasmuch as the force of the words was sharp and that there was a succession of spirits.

c. *Gram.* An aspirate or breathing; a conventional mark indicating this; *spec.* in the writing or printing of Greek.

1555 Eden *Decades* (Arb.) 169 Ye, all suche woordes as in their tonge are aspirate, are pronounced with lyke breath and spirite as is *f.* 1612 Brinsley *Lud. Lit.* 232 Call vpon them oft to marke carefully the accents of each word, with the spirits. a 1653 Gouge *Comm. Heb.* i. 3 The Greek makes an apparent distinction by a different spirit over the head of the first letter. 1680 Dalgarno *Deaf & Dumb Man's Tutor* 126 The unnecessary and troublesome luggage of Spirits and Accents. 1751 Wesley *Wks.* (1872) XIV. 79 Every initial vowel has a spirit prefixed. 1827 Faber *Sacr. Cal. Prophecy* (1844) III. 163 The inscription in the Greek cursive character, even with the accompanying accents and spirits. 1861 Scrivener *N. T. Critic.* 39 The book has neither spirits..nor accents.

†**d.** *Mus.* An air; a melody. *Obs.*[−1]

1608 Weelkes (*title*), Ayeres or Phantasticke Spirites for three voices.

16. One or other of certain subtle highly-refined substances or fluids (distinguished as *natural*, *animal*, and *vital*) formerly supposed to permeate the blood and chief organs of the body. In later use only *pl.*

See also Animal spirits 1, Natural *a.* 12 a, and Vital *a.*

1387 Trevisa *Higden* (Rolls) I. 53 For þe son beme.. draweþ oute þe humours,..and by drawing oute of spirites makeþ hem coward of herte. c 1400 *Lanfranc's Cirurg.* 26 Þe toþer arterie..ha[s] two cootis, bi cause þat oon myȝt not aȝenstonde þe strenkþe of þe spiritis. *Ibid.* 162 Of þis clene blood þe spirit is engendrid; which spirit is..more sutil þan ony bodi. 1477 Norton *Ord. Alch.* v. in Ashm. (1652) 82 The Spirit Vitall in the Hert doth dwell, The Spirit Naturall..in the Liver.., But Spirit Animall dwelleth in the Braine. 1539 Elyot *Cast. Helthe* (1541) 12 b, Spirite is an ayry substance subtyll, styrynge the powers of the body to perfourme theyr operations. 1587 Golding *De Mornay* xiv. (1592) 206 A mans..eyes faile because the Spirites of them fayle. 1615 Crooke *Body of Man* 61 The reason is, because all the spirits are immured. a 1646 Burroughes *Exp. Hosea* vi. (1652) 266 The fatter mens bodies are, the lesse blood and the fewer spirits they have. 1697 Dryden *Virg. Georg.* iii. 155 When his Blood no Youthful Spirits move, He languishes and labours in his Love. 1725 N. Robinson *Th. Physick* 250 What Remedies will be properest to repress the Disorders of the Spirits. 1791 *Pop. Tales Germ.* I. 190 Her spirits retired inward, her cheeks grew pale, and down she sank.

transf. 1719 W. Wood *Surv. Trade* 3 It disperses that blood and Spirits throughout the Members, by which the Body Politick subsists. 1812 Cary *Dante, Parad.* xxvi. 70 With the eye's spirit running forth to meet The ray.

b. *pl.* Vital power or energy; the normal operation of the vital functions.

c 1386 Chaucer *Knt.'s T.* 514 So feble eek were hise spiritz and so lowe,..that no man koude knowe His speche ne his voys. c 1450 *St. Cuthbert* (Surtees) 6065 Fra he was vp ryght sett, he began his spirits to gett with in a litil stounde. 1617 Moryson *Itin.* i. 118 At last feeling my spirits begin to faile me, I was glad to returne. 1670 Walton *Lives* iii. 228 More he would have spoken, but his spirits failed him. 1700 Rowe *Amb. Step-Moth.* i. i, That ever will remain, And in my latest Spirits still survive. 1793 Cowper *To Mary* ii, Thy spirits have a fainter flow, I see thee daily weaker grow.

17. *pl.* The mind or faculties as the seat of action and feeling, esp. as liable to be depressed or exalted by events or circumstances.

1375 Barbour *Bruce* vi. 223 He..sumdeill affrayit wes; But in schort tym he till him tais His spiritis richt full hardely. a 1548 Hall *Chron., Rich. III*, 49 To visite his familie, and to recreate and refreshe his spirites (as he openly saide). 1592 *Arden of Feversham* i. 1 Arden, cheere vp thy spirits and droup no more. 1608 Chapman *Dk. Byron* v. i. 133 For we shall never brag That we have made his spirits check at death. 1719 De Foe *Crusoe* i. (Globe) 193 Dangers, the Sight of which, if discover'd to him, would..sink his Spirits. 1771 Smollett *Humph. Cl.* (1815) 184, I find my spirits and my health affect each other reciprocally. 1825 Scott *Betrothed* xxii, The spirits of Eveline in particular felt a depression. 1845 J. Coulter *Adv. in Pacific* xi. 135 It is one of the means of keeping up the spirits of the men on long voyages. 1893 *Law Times* XCIV. 603/2 For the last three or four days he appears to have been depressed in spirits.

b. With adjs., as *good*, *great*, *high*, *low*, etc. Freq. *in..spirits*.

1737 Gray *Lett.* (1900) I. 6 Low spirits are my true and faithful companions. 1743 Bulkeley & Cummins *Voy. S. Seas* 169 So that we are in pretty good Spirits. 1744 [see Low *a.* 8 b]. 1780 *Mirror* No. 98, I walked home in great spirits. 1802 Mar. Edgeworth *Moral T.* (1816) I. vii. 41 She had a constant flow of good spirits. 1820 Irving *Sketch Bk.* I. 49 She seems in better spirits than I have ever known her. 1884 *Daily News* 21 Feb. 5/3 The men are in high spirits at the prospect of a fight.

c. Vigour or animation of mind; cheerfulness, vivacity, liveliness. (Cf. 14 b.)

1716 Lady M. W. Montagu *Let. to Lady Rich* 16 Aug., I found myself perfectly recovered, and have had spirits enough to go and see all that is curious in the town. 1780 *Mirror* No. 81, I lost all my former spirits, as well as my former bloom. 1803 *Med. Jrnl.* IX. 211 Loss of appetite and spirits, succeeded with thirst. 1852 Mrs. Stowe *Uncle Tom's C.* xxi, The horse would roll when he was bringing him up from the stable; he's so full of spirits.

d. *In spirits*, in a cheerful mood; animated, elated, happy. *Out of spirits*, low-spirited.

1766 Goldsm. *Vicar* xxxii, His time is pretty much taken up in keeping his relation..in spirits. 1779 in Jesse *Selwyn & Contemp.* (1844) IV. 259 [She] is..so out of spirits, that she is cruelly afraid she shall never live till her dear master's return. 1826 Disraeli *V. Grey* iv. ii, I suppose he is quite in spirits at your success? 1838 Lytton *Alice* i. i, Who can be out of spirits in such weather?

†**18.** *pl.* **a.** The faculties of perception or reflection; the senses or intellect; mental powers. *Obs.*

1526 *Pilgr. Perf.* (W. de W. 1531) 57 b, That..thou gather to the thy spirytes, & be..quyet. 1604 Shaks. *Oth.* iii. iv. 63 His Spirits should hunt After new Fancies. c 1645 Howell *Lett.* (1650) II. 115 Truly the more I scrue up my spirits to reach it, the more I am swallowed in a gulf of admiration. 1697 Dryden *Virg. Past.* iv. 66 To sing thy Praise, wou'd Heav'n my Breath prolong, Infusing Spirits worthy such a Song.

†**b.** Disposition, character. *Obs.*

1602 Shaks. *Ham.* iii. ii. 63 For what aduancement may I hope from thee, That no Reuennew hast, but thy good spirits To feed & cloath thee?

19. †**a.** A subtle or intangible element or principle in material things. *Obs.*

1626 Bacon *Sylva* § 98 The Spirits or Pneumaticalls, that are in all Tangible Bodies are scarce known. 1638 Rawley tr. *Bacon's Life & Death* (1650) 57 There is in every Tangible Body a Spirit, covered and encompassed with the Grosser Parts of the Body. 1661 South *Serm.* Wks. 1823 II. 328 In the rain, it is not the bare water that fructifies, but a secret spirit or nitre descending with it. a 1722 Lisle *Husb.* (1757) 218 The spirit of the straw is washed out by the rain. 1725 *Fam. Dict.* s.v. *Cider*, The Spirits of Cider being exceedingly apt to evaporate.

b. (See quot.)

1829 *Chapters Phys. Sci.* 235 The oxygenous gas..is a kind of vivifying spirit or quality, which is necessary to continue the lives of animals.

V. †**20. a.** One or other of four substances so named by the mediaeval alchemists. *Obs.*

c 1386 Chaucer *Can. Yeom. Prol. & T.* 60 Ne eek oure spirites Ascencioun..Mowe in oure werkyng no thyng vs auaille. *Ibid.* 103 The firste spirit quyk siluer called is, The seconde Orpyment, the thridde ywis Sal Armonyak, and the ferthe Brymstoon. 1390 Gower *Conf.* II. 84 Of bodies sevene ..With foure spiritz joynt withal Stant the substance of this matiere.

†**b.** *Spirit of the world*: (see quot.).

1651 French *Distill.* v. 107 In the element of Water there is a great plenty of the Spirit of the world,..and..this Spirit hath three distinct substances, *viz.* Salt, Sulphur, and Mercury.

†**c.** *spec.* Mercury. *Obs.*

1704 J. Harris *Lex. Techn.* I, *Spirit*, which the Chymists call Mercury, is one of the 5 Principles separable from a Mixt, by Fire. 1725 Watts *Logic* i. ii. § 2 The chemist makes spirit, salt, sulphur, water, and earth, to be their five elements. 1728 Chambers *Cycl.* s.v. *Element*, Mercury, which they [*sc.* chemists] also call *Spirit*.

†**d.** (See quot.) *Obs.*[−1]

1733 W. Ellis *Chiltern & Vale Farm.* 200 The Exhalations of the Sun that draws up a moist Vapour from the Earth, by some, called the Spirit, by others, the Salt of the Earth.

21. A liquid of the nature of an essence or extract from some substance, esp. one obtained by distillation; a solution in alcohol of some essential or volatile principle.

1610 Jonson *Alch.* ii. vi, H' is busie with his spirits, but we'll vpon him. 1651 French *Distill.* v. 139 Dissolve any sulphurous..metall..in *Aqua fortis*, or any other acid Spirit. 1728 Chambers *Cycl.* s.v., The Chymists are said to draw a Spirit from Sulphur, Salt and other Bodies, when they extract the Essence..by Distillation or otherwise. 1813 Sir H. Davy *Agric. Chem.* (1814) 136 All the common spirits may, I find, be deprived of their peculiar flavour by repeatedly digesting them with..charcoal and quicklime. 1831 J. Davies *Mat. Med.* 36 The spirits have a weaker odour than the distilled waters. 1875 H. C. Wood *Therap.* (1879) 18 Spirits are alcoholic solutions of volatile principles made by direct solution or by distillation from the crude drugs.

fig. 1613 Sylvester (*title*), Lachrymæ Lachrymarum: or the Spirit of Teares, distilled for the vntymely Death of the incomparable Prince of Wales. 1639 Fuller *Holy War* ii. xxxiv. (1840) 94 These Assassins..had in them the very spirits of that poisonous superstition. 1742 Young *Nt. Th.* iv. 144 To drink the spirit of the golden day, And triumph in existence.

b. Without article: Liquid such as is obtained by distillation, *spec.* that which is of an alcoholic nature. Also *pl.*

sing. 1610 Jonson *Alch.* i. i, Haue I..Wrought thee to spirit, to quintessence, with paines Would twise haue won me the philosophers worke? 1688 Holme *Armoury* iii. xx. (Roxb.) 250/2 Wine coopers termes:..Spirits, wine double distilled. 1726 *Dict. Rust.*, *Spirit dulcified*, a choice Remedy for the Cholick in Hor-es. a 1774 Goldsm. *Surv. Exp. Philos.* (1776) I. 380 A solid that will swim in water, will sink in spirit. 1799 G. Smith *Laboratory* I. 334 In this manner are extracted from roses the three principles, spirit, oil, and salt. 1815 J. Smith *Panorama Sci. & Art* II. 576 The substances from which spirit is obtained are usually barley, wheat, oats, rye, sugar, or molasses. 1854 Ronalds & Richardson *Chem. Technol.* (ed. 2) I. 289 In this manner, by one operation, spirit containing about 60 per cent. of alcohol is obtained. 1863 Huxley *Man's Place in Nat.* i. 16 M. Palm..shot one, and forwarded it to Batavia in spirit.

pl. 1800 Southey in C. C. Southey *Life* (1850) II. 91 The head and hands were sent here; I have seen them in the Museum, in spirits.

c. orig. *pl.* Strong alcoholic liquor for drinking, obtained from various substances by distillation; *sing.* any particular kind of this.

1684 Bunyan *Pilgr.* ii. 67 He gave me also a piece of an Honey-comb, and a little Bottle of Spirits. 1742-3 Hervey in *Johnson's Deb.* (1787) II. 409 It is not to be doubted, my Lords, but that spirits will, by this additional duty, be made one third part dearer. 1833 Ht. Martineau *Vanderput & S.* vi. 95 Every body agreed that spirits were the only safeguard against the perils of ditch water. 1884 *Graphic* 29 Nov. 562/2 An exuberance of animal spirits occasionally increased by spirits of another character.

sing. 1840 Dickens *Old C. Shop* xxi, Quilp..drank three small glass-fulls of the raw spirit. 1848 Thackeray *Van. Fair* lxvii, When she was prevailed on..to take a little spirit-and-water. 1884 J. P. Quincy *Figures of Past* 265 The use of wine and spirit was practically universal at the time of which I am speaking.

d. With *of* (the name of the liquor). *rare.*

1700 T. Brown tr. *Fresny's Amusem.* viii. Wks. 1709 III. i. 77 To the Charms of Coffee the wiser sort joyn'd Spirit of Clary, Usquebaugh, and Brandy. 1831 Scott *Cast. Dang.* xiii, Wilt thou take some refreshment?—or shall we go on without the spirit of muscadel?

22. An essence, distilled extract, or alcoholic solution, *of* a specified substance. Freq. *pl.*, esp. in later use.

Only the earlier or more important of these special designations are illustrated here: see also Turpentine, Vitriol, and Wine.

a 1700 Evelyn *Diary* 27 Oct. 1675, By applying hot fire-pans and *spirit of amber to his head. 1737 [see Amber *sb.*[1] 3 b]. 1839 Ure *Dict. Arts* 1158 **Spirit of Ammonia* is, properly speaking, alcohol combined with ammonia gas; but the term is often applied to water of ammonia. 1871 Garrod *Mat. Med.* (ed. 3) 47 Aromatic Spirit of Ammonia. ..Often called Sal Volatile. 1853 Royle *Mat. Med.* (ed. 2) 599 *Spirit of Camphor..Dissolve Camphor..in Rectified Spirit. *Ibid.* 701 *Spirit of Ether..Mix Sulphuric Ether.. with Rectified Spirit. *Ibid.*, Compound Spirit of Ether. 1871 Garrod *Mat. Med.* (ed. 3) 149 Spirit of ether is employed in making the ethereal tincture of lobelia. 1683-4 Boyle *Mem. Nat. Hist. Hum. Blood* 122 The 'Sp. of Hartshorn. 1685 [see Hartshorn 2]. 1826 Henry *Elem. Chem.* II. 609 Spirit of Hartshorn. This may be counterfeited by mixing the *aqua ammoniæ puræ* with the distilled spirit of hartshorn. 1666 Boyle *Orig. Forms & Qual.* 337, I did..make a red *spirit of Nitre, by the help onely of Oyl of Vitriol. 1710 J. Clarke tr. *Rohault's Nat. Philos.* (1729) I. 113 A few Drops of Spirit of Nitre or of Oil of Vitriol. 1823 J. Badcock *Dom. Amusem.* 45 A strong solution of mercury, made with spirit of nitre. 1853 Royle *Mat. Med.* (ed. 2) 702 *Spirit of Nitric Ether. Hyponitrous Ether dissolved in Rectified Spirit. Sweet Spirits of Nitre. 1859 Mayne *Expos. Lex.* 1189/2 *Spirit of nitrous ether. 1871 Garrod *Mat. Med.* (ed. 3) 151 Spirit of nitrous ether ..is popularly known by the name of Sweet Spirits of Nitre. 1779 *Phil. Trans.* LXX. 40 Apply to the precipitate solution of volatile alkali, sold by the name of *spirit of sal ammoniac. 1651 French *Distill.* i. 36 The *Spirit of salt being rectified may serve again. 1779 *Phil. Trans.* LXX. 30 Half an ounce of muriatic acid sold by the name of spirit of salt. 1807 T. Thomson *Chem.* (ed. 3) II. 611 This residuum is usually called bittern, and sometimes in Scotland spirit of salt. 1860 Ure's *Dict. Arts* (ed. 5) II. 481 The solution of hydrochloric acid in water is the muriatic acid and spirit of salt of commerce. 1753 *Chambers' Cycl. Suppl.* s.v. *Silk*, If spirit of wine be poured upon spirit of sal armoniac, or *spirit of silk. 1704 J. Harris *Lex. Techn.* I, **Spirit of Sulphur*, commonly call'd Oil of Sulphur,..is only the acid Part of Sulphur turned into a Liquor by the means of Fire. 1651 French *Distill.* iii. 66 Dissolve Salt-Armoniack in.. *spirit of Urine. 1710 J. Clarke tr. *Rohault's Nat. Philos.* (1729) I. 129 An equal Quantity of Spirits of Wine and Spirits of Urine. 1797 *Encycl. Brit.* (ed. 3) IV. 598 (Plate), Pyroligneous acid. *Spirit of wood.

b. *Dyeing.* (See quots.)

1875 Knight *Dict. Mech.* 428/1 [In] spirit-color printing, the colors are produced by a mixture of dye extracts and solution of tin, called by the dyers *spirits of tin*. 1877 *Encycl. Brit.* VII. 574/2 The so-called nitrate of tin (sometimes called 'bowl spirits', from being prepared in an earthenware bowl). 1880 D. Smith *Pract. Dyer's Guide* (title-p.), Receipts for making all the Dye Spirits with which to dye every colour in the work.

VI. *attrib.* and *Comb.*

23. In senses 1-14: **a.** Simple attrib., in various applications, as *spirit-blow*, *-body*, *-book*, *-child*, etc.

1818 Keats *Endym.* iv. 899 But the *spirit-blow Was struck, and all were dreamers. 1848 Kingsley *Saint's Trag.* ii. ii, Spirit-love in *spirit-bodies. 1852 Bailey *Festus* (ed. 5) 500 To..strict collation of the *Spirit-book With the pretemporal volume, writ of God. 1845 S. Judd *Margaret* i. xii, Call me your child,..your *spirit-child, and so love me. 1874 Geo. Eliot *Coll. Breakf.-P.* 278 The Church as..fount of *spirit force. 1865 Miss Braddon *Sir Jasper's Tenant* iii, Shadowy as those *spirit-hands of which we hear so much nowadays. 1831 Carlyle *Sart. Res.* iii. viii, Like a God-created, fire-breathing *Spirit-host.

1845 Hirst *Poems* 157 Beyond the Vale of Shadows, lie dispread The *spirit-lands. 1859 Bartlett *Dict. Amer.* (ed. 2) 434 *Spirit-land*, an expression which, in the cant of the rappers, means the abode of departed spirits, the other world. 1869 Ruskin *Q. of Air* iii. § 157 The *spirit-life of art. 1662 Hibbert *Body Divinity* i. 127 Soul-light is not enough to make us truly wise, but there must also be *spirit-light. 1830 Mrs. Hemans *Indian w. Dead Child* ix, I saw the spirit-light From his young eyes fade away. a 1835 — *Song of Rose* Poems (1875) 550 Shall we not behold thee..In *spirit lustre clothed? 1844 Mrs Browning *Lady Geraldine's Courtsh.* liii, No new *spirit-power comprising. 1877 E. Caird *Philos. Kant* Introd. v. 79 The *spirit-monad—the monad that has consciousness of itself. a 1835 Mrs. Hemans *Painter's last Wk.* Poems (1875) 536 Purified To *spirit radiance from all earthly stain. 1858 Sears *Athan.* iii. x. 333 This tide of humanity sweeps on into the *spirit-realm. 1852 Bailey *Festus* (ed. 5) 529 So every bodily organ shall be changed Into a *spirit-sense. 1657 J. Watts *Vind. Ch. Eng.* 115 Refuse the Mother-tongue Translation, and call for the *Spirit-tongue Original. 1655 Vaughan *Silex Scint.* 40 Prayer is a *spirit-voyce. 1852 Mrs. Stowe *Uncle Tom's C.* xxiv, The voice came over him as a spirit-voice. 1847 Mary Howitt *Ballads* 266, I see on *spirit-wings, How thou hast set them high. *Ibid.* 323 My *spirit-words were all too faint. 1855 Browning *In a Balcony* Wks. 1863 II. 404 The success And consummation of the *spirit-work. a 1853 Robertson *Serm.* Ser. iii. v. 62 The reality of the *spirit-world. 1871 Tylor *Prim. Cult.* I. 131 Two of the most popular means of communicating with the spirit-world. 1878 Maclear *Celts* ii. 28 *Spirit-worship, which peopled all the objects of nature with malignant beings.

b. Appositive, as *spirit-chieftain*, *-enemy*, *-friend*, *-guardian*, *-lady*, etc.

1841 Mrs. S. C. Hall *Ireland* I. 192 A belief in the existence of the *spirit-chieftain. 1900 *Month* Jan. 96 For ages..these wild people had believed in spirit-guardians, and also in *spirit-enemies. 1839 Bailey *Festus* 50 Have I not heard thee hint of *spirit-friends? Where are they now? 1845 G. Murray *Islaford*, etc. 186 The *spirit-lady soars away. 1845 Bailey *Festus* (ed. 2) 119 There are *spirit-rulers of all worlds. 1848 *Ibid.* (ed. 3) 336 It will bear the gaze Of all the star souls and the *spirit stars Which will the living land of light indwell. 1838 Mrs. Browning *Seraphim* ii. Poems (1904) 87/2 Doth the *Spirit-wind Blow white those waters?

c. With agent-nouns, as *spirit-charmer*, *-hunter*, *-monger*, *-ridder*, *-seer*, *-wrestler*.

As the specific name of a religious sect, *Spirit-wrestlers* is a rendering of Russ. *Dukhobortsi*, f. *dukh'* spirit + *borets'* wrestler.

1711 Shaftesb. *Charac.* (1737) II. 330 In ghostly company of spirit-hunters, witch-finders [etc.]. 1832 Hood *Ode Ld. Gambier* iii, Consider The sorry figure of a spirit-ridder. 1862 S. Lucas *Secularia* 91 'How, exclaims the spirit-seer, ..'do I envy you a sight of Bristow, in the year 1480'. 1877 J. E. Carpenter tr. *Tiele's Hist. Relig.* 29 The magicians, soothsayers, and spirit-charmers. 1881 *Dr. Cheist, an Autobiogr.* 43 All the spirit-mongers are either old women or curates. 1897 (*title*), Christian Martyrdom in Russia. Persecution of the spirit-wrestlers (or Doukhobortsi) in the Caucasus. 1899 R. Whiteing 5 *John St.* 329 The real spirit-wrestlers who struggle for a new blessing with the God within.

d. With vbl. sbs. and ppl. adjs., as *spirit-cheering*, *-chilling*, *-crushing*, *-freeing*, *-healing*, etc.

1838 Mary Howitt *Birds & Fl.* 52 Raven, thou art *spirit-cheering. 1825 D. L. Richardson *Sonets* 15 This sad heart By *spirit-chilling Sorrow unrepressed. 1858 Hawthorne *Fr. & It. Jrnls.* II. 221 It is extremely *spirit-crushing, this remorseless gray. 1858 T. Guthrie *Christ & Inheritance Saints* (1859) 20 The same *spirit-freeing words. 1798 Coleridge *Fears in Solitude* 12 O! 'tis a quiet *spirit-healing nook. 1605 Sylvester *Du Bartas* ii. iii. iii. *Law* 26 It is the *spirit-inspiring Spirit. 1818 Shelley *Rosal. & Helen* 1156 His countenance..burned with radiance Of *spirit-piercing joy. 1817 — *Rev. Islam* xi. xiv, On each unwilling heart Unusual awe did fall—a *spirit-quelling dart. c 1611 Chapman *Iliad* iii. 265 Two lambs, and *spirit-refreshing wine..they bring. 1814 Scott *Lord of Isles* vi. i, The emotions of the *spirit-rousing time. 1777 Potter *Æschylus, Choephoræ* 323 Bitter constraint, and *spirit-sinking fear. a 1822 Shelley '*She was an aged woman*' vii, The spirit-sinking noise Of heartless mirth. 1817 — *Rev. Islam* iv. xxviii, The love that lies Hovering within those *spirit-soothing eyes. 1799 Campbell *Pleas. Hope* i. 98 The dauntless brow, and *spirit-speaking eye. 1817 Shelley *Rev. Islam* vii. iv, A wild, and sad, and *spirit-thrilling lay. 1830 Tennyson *Ode to Mem.* 39 Those spirit-thrilling eyes. 1777 Brand *Pop. Antiq.* 71 Mr. Bourne might have stiled this Chapter, A Sermon on *Spirit-walking. *Ibid.* 235 The Spirit-walking Time of Popery! 1809 Malkin *Gil Blas* ix. i. ⁋ 6 Six merchants.., all plodding *spirit-wearing personages.

e. With pa. pples., denoting either (*a*) 'of or by the spirit', 'by spirits', as *spirit-born*, *-guided*, *-haunted*, etc., or (*b*) 'in spirit', as *spirit-broken*, *-crushed*, *-fallen*, *-froze*, etc.

(*a*) 1602 Fulbecke *Pandects* Introd., The valiant Persians, the spirit-guided Hebrews, the prudent Grecians. 1645 Quarles *Sol. Recant.* xii. 59 And what his spirit-prompted pen did write Was truth it self, and most exact upright. 1855 Bailey *Mystic* 70 The spirit-haunted Kâf. 1850 Robertson *Serm.* Ser. iii. ii. (1857) 23 Those called the Spirit-born, and those called the world. 1897 Mary Kingsley *W. Africa* 417 Sending out long white arms..and then drawing them back as if it were some spirit-possessed thing.

(*b*) a 1628 F. Grevil *Life Sidney* (1652) 60 If not with abrupt, and spirit-fall'n tolleration, yet with that invisible web of connivencie. 1649 G. Daniel *Trinarch., Hen. V*, cccxxxvii, Stung with the Aspiche of invadeing feare, Or Spirit-froze, bound vp in bloodlesse veines. 1839 Bailey *Festus* 268 See where she flies, spirit-torn, round the heavens. 1845 *Encycl. Metrop.* XI. 375/1 The injured but spirit-broken progeny of Ali and Fatima wanted resolution or ability to assert their cause. 1865 J. H. Ingraham *Pillar of Fire* i. xxv. (1872) 423 The queen..seems heart-broken, spirit-crushed! 1880 Swinburne *Songs of Spring-t., Thalassius* 30 Death spirit-stricken of soul-sick days.

f. Similative, as *spirit-pure*, *-small*, *-wise*; *spirit-tongued*, *-winged*.

1817 Shelley *Rev. Islam* xii. xxxviii, The stream..faster bare The spirit-winged boat. 1820 — *Prometh. Unb.* ii. i. 164 The crags..mock our voices As they were spirit-tongued. 1842 Browning *By the Fireside* xxiii, The spirit-small hand propping it. 1845 — *Statue & Bust* vii, A pale brow spirit-pure. 1848 Bailey *Festus* (ed. 3) 309 Thou shalt perceive earth spirit-wise.

g. In expressions relating to the phenomena or doctrines of spiritualism, as *spirit-circle*, etc.

1858 W. M. Wilkinson (*title*), Spirit Drawings; a Personal Narrative. 1865 Masson *Rec. Brit. Philos.* 295 The heterodox science of the Swedenborgians and the spirit-manifestationists. 1867 J. H. Powell (*title*), Mediumship: ..with brief instructions for the formation of Spirit-Circles. 1871 Tylor *Prim. Cult.* I. 135 The Baron..publishes a mass of fac-similes of spirit-writings thus obtained. 1887 *Encycl. Brit.* XXII. 405/2 'Spirit-photography,' or photographing of human and other forms invisible to all but specially endowed seers. 1893 *Fortn. Rev.* Jan. 125 Can a ghost be photographed? Are all the spirit-photos frauds?

h. In specific names, as **spirit-butterfly**, **duck**, **-leaf**, **-weed**, **-wood** (see quots.).

1891 *Cent. Dict.*, **Spirit-butterfly*, a tropical American butterfly of the genus *Ithomia*. 1784 Pennant *Arct. Zool.* II. 558 *Spirit Duck...Inhabits North America, from Hudson's Bay to Carolina. 1829 Griffith tr. *Cuvier* VIII. 611 Spirit Duck, *Anas Albeola*. 1872 Coues *N. Amer. Birds* 290 Buffle-headed Duck. Butter-ball. Spirit Duck. Dipper. 1696 Sloane *Cat. Plantarum Jamaica* 52 *Spirit leaf. 1864 Grisebach *Flora Brit. W. Ind.* 787/2 Spirit-leaf, *Ruellia tuberosa*. 1866 *Treas. Bot.* 1085/1 Spirit-leaf, or Spirit-weed, *Ruellia tuberosa*, now called *Cryphiacanthus barbadensis*. 1699 Sloane in *Phil. Trans.* XXI. 119 None is more surprizing then one in Jamaica, called *Spirit-weed. 1866 [see above]. 1716 *Petiveriana* i. 259 *Spirit-wood,.. *Pucumatoxylum*.

24. In sense 21 (freq. 21 c): **a.** Simple attrib., as *spirit bubble*, *-extract*, *-flame*, *-licence*, *-trade*, etc.

1796 Burke *Regic. Peace* Wks. VIII 406 The spirit licences kept nearly the same level till the stoppage of the distilleries in 1795. 1842 *Penny Cycl.* XXII. 360/1 Spirit-trade. 1846 G. E. Day tr. *Simon's Anim. Chem.* II. 186 Spirit-extract with chloride of sodium. 1862 *Catal. Internat. Exhib., Brit.* II No. 2947, When the instrument is turned in any direction, the spirit bubble will be kept in the centre of its run. 1866 Odling *Anim. Chem.* 68 The heat of the spirit-flame..passing into the water.

b. In the sense 'used for holding, storing, or selling alcoholic spirits', as *spirit-back*, *-beck*, *-bottle*, *-case*, *-flask*, *-jar*; *spirit-cellar*, *-room*, etc.

1839 Ure *Dict. Arts* 402 The middle portion..are received into the *spirit-back. 1894 *Funk's Stand. Dict.*, **Spirit-beck*, a beck or vat for containing the spirit in a distillery. 1786 G. Frazer *Dove's Flight* 76 They have recourse to the *spirit-bottle..for consolation. 1849 R. G. Cumming *Hunter's Life S. Afr.* (1902) 78 They were both very drunk, having broken into my wine-cask and *spirit-case. 1833 Loudon *Encycl. Archit.* § 916 The *spirit cellar is to have two tiers of catacombs (bins). 1834 Marryat *P. Simple* (1863) 161 He put the *spirit-flask to his mouth. 1858 Simmonds *Dict. Trade*, **Spirit-jar*, an earthenware jar.., for sending out spirits. 1797 *Encycl. Brit.* (ed. 3) XVII. 404/2 That part of the orlop which is over the after magazine, *spirit room, and fish room. c 1850 *Rudim. Navig.* (Weale) 143 The spirit-room is built in the hold, next before the fish-room, to contain the spirituous liquors for the use of the ship's company. 1837 Ht. Martineau *Soc. Amer.* III. 202 *Spirit shops have been shut up by hundreds. 1858 Simmonds *Dict. Trade*, **Spirit-store*, a shop where spirits are kept for sale, wholesale and retail. 1863 Hawthorne *Our Old Home* (1883) I. 327 Gin-shops, or what the English call *spirit-vaults.

c. With agent-nouns, as *spirit-dealer*, *-drinker*, *-grocer*, *-merchant*, etc.

1826 *Art of Brewing* (ed. 2) 44 It would be a matter of great convenience if one instrument only were adopted by the trade, as is the case with *spirit-dealers. 1864 A. McKay *Hist. Kilmarnock* 190 He spent a social hour in the house of a spirit-dealer. 1827 *Edin. Rev.* XLVI. 69 The *spirit-drinkers..never can agree in one party. 1899 *Allbutt's Syst. Med.* VI. 685 A man, aged 41, a spirit drinker. 1872 *Act 35 & 36 Vict.* c. 94 § 81 The term '*spirit grocer'.. means any person..having an excise licence to sell spirits by retail. 1841 Dickens *Barn. Rudge* xiii, To be looked upon as a common *spirit-guzzler. 1858 Simmonds *Dict. Trade*, **Spirit-merchant*, a vender of spirits. 1896 *Daily News* 4 Mar. 8/5 Her greatest danger came from the *spirit-sellers.

d. With vbl. sbs. and ppl. adjs., as *spirit-bibing*, *-boiling*, *-drinking*, etc.

1827 *Edin. Rev.* XLVI. 69 The spirit-bibing party began to indulge in foolish..conversation. 1834 Marryat *P. Simple* (1863) 234 Mr. Apollo, who was above spirit-boiling heat with jealousy. 1897 *Daily News* 11 Feb. 5/3 Mr. Sharpe ..observed that the Celtic population are a spirit-drinking people.

e. In the sense 'that works, acts, etc., by means of spirit or spirits', as *spirit blow-pipe*, *-engine*, *-standard*, *-stove*, *thermometer*, *tube*, *weather-glass*.

1842 Francis *Dict. Arts*, *Alcoholic*, or '*Spirit Blow-pipe*, a blow-pipe which acts by the inflammation of a stream of the vapor of spirits of wine. 1858 Simmonds *Dict. Trade*, **Spirit-engine maker*, a manufacturer of the tavern, or bar, engines for drawing spirits for retail sale. 1856 Kane *Arct. Expl.* I. xiv. 154 The reduced mean of our best *spirit-standards gave -67°. 1895 *Army & Navy Price List*, Kettle and *Spirit Stove. 1902 Eliz. Banks *Newspaper Girl* 170 One day I thought I'd cook some over my spirit-stove. 1827 Faraday *Chem. Manip.* iv. (1842) 139 A large and a small bulb, or a mercury and *spirit thermometer, will take different periods to heat and cool. 1842 *Penny Cycl.* XXII. 359/1 The *spirit-tube is used in determining the relative heights

of ground at two or more stations. 1704 *Dict. Rust.* s.v., *Spirit Weather-Glass.

f. Applied to various dye-colours obtained from a mixture of dye extracts and solution of tin, as *spirit black*, *blue*, *brown*, etc. Also *spirit-colour*.

1836 *Penny Cycl.* VI. 157/1 Spirit-Colours are brilliant, but fugitive; they consist generally of decoctions of dye-woods, mixed with nitro-muriate or muriate of tin. 1867 *Ure's Dict. Arts* (ed. 6) I. 589, 2 quarts spirit pink. *Ibid.*, 1 gallon spirit yellow. *Ibid.* 590 Spirit black. 1875 Knight *Dict. Mech.* 428/1 Spirit-color printing.

g. Special combs.: **spirit fresco**, a method of fresco-painting, in which the colours are ground in a medium of wax, elemi resin, artist's copal, oil of spike or spirits of turpentine; **spirit-gum** (see quot.); **spirit-liver**, a liver affected by the drinking of spirits; **spirit varnish**, a varnish prepared by dissolving a resin in spirit; hence *spirit-varnish* vb.

1880 Gambier Parry (*title*), Spirit Fresco Painting. *Ibid.* 4 Wash over the part for the morning's work with pure spike oil, to melt the surface (hence the name 'Spirit Fresco). 1909 J. Ward *Fresco Painting* 35 The method of painting followed out in the spirit-fresco system..is almost precisely the same as that of the lime or buon-fresco process. 1891 *Cent. Dict.*, **Spirit-gum*, a quick drying preparation used by actors and others to fasten false hair on the face. 1905 Rolleston *Dis. Liver* 107 The *spirit livers appeared to be more frequently fatty [than the beer livers]. 1850 Holtzapffel *Turning* III. 1375 These resins constitute the basis of what are called 'spirit varnishes. 1887 *Pall Mall G.* 7 Mar. 6/1 The miserable, hungry appearance of the wood in all old violins known to be spirit varnished.

Spirit (spi·rit), *v.* [f. Spirit *sb.*]

I. **1.** *trans.* To make (the blood, a liquor) of a more active or lively character.

1599 Shaks. *Hen. V*, iii. v. 21 And shall our quick blood, spirited with Wine, Seeme frostie? 1644 in Hartlib *Legacy* (1655) 221 The blood being..spirited with subtle Nitre or Gunpowder. it..is distributed through the body. 1670 Evelyn *Pomona* (ed. 2) 55 Mustard made with Sack preserves boild Cider, and spirits it egregiously. 1822-7 Good *Study Med.* (1829) I. 511 We find it [*sc.* the blood] return from the lungs spirited with newness of life.

2. To infuse spirit, life, ardour, or energy into (a person); to inspirit, animate, encourage. Also const. *for* or *to*.

1608 Chapman *Dk. Byron* iii. i, Like men, that, spirited with wine, Pass dangerous places safe. 1682 N. O. *Boileau's Lutrin* iii. 28 Thy Valour firm'd the wavering Troops that day, And spirited their Files with fresh array! 1698 Fryer *Acc. E. India & P.* 14 May had now began, when..we were once more spirited with milder Weather. 1719 De Foe *Crusoe* i. (Globe) 45, I also found some Rum.., which I had indeed need enough of to spirit me for what was before me. 1736 Lediard *Life Marlborough* II. 235 The small Advantages they had obtained..spirited them to entertain several towering Projects. 1758 *Ann. Reg.* 16 Spirited with this advantage, he pushed onwards. 1844 H. Rogers *Ess.* (1874) I. ii. 69 He was further spirited to it by an anonymous letter. 1851 *Chr. Spect.* I. 100 Let the song of faith spirit thee for the fight of faith.

b. With impersonal object.

a 1652 J. Smith *Sel. Disc.* ix. (1821) 423 There is a living soul of religion in good men which..spirits all the wheels of motion. 1679 J. Goodman *Penit. Pard.* ii. ii. (1713) 164 Hope and apprehension of feasibleness spirits all industry, actuates all faculties, raises the spirits.

c. To lead or urge *on* by encouragement.

1682 *New News fr. Bedlam* 30 Give Nature a Phillip with two or three quarts of Mum, to spirit them on for any Attempt. 1792 Mme. D'Arblay *Lett.* 2 Oct., I wish to spirit him on to collect them [*sc.* notes] into a pamphlet. 1840 Lady C. Bury *Hist. of Flirt* xv, What was labour to me when my cousin James was at hand to spirit me on?

d. To excite, instigate, or stir up.

a 1680 Charnock *Attrib. God* (1834) II. 636 It is not to spirit rebellion, but to give a merciful stop to it. 1701 Swift *Contests Nobles & Comm.* Wks. 1755 II. i. 36 Civil dissentions never fail of introducing and spiriting the ambition of private men.

3. To invest with a spirit or animating principle.

1629 T. Adams *Rage Oppression* Wks. 608 God hath.. tempered all our bodies of one clay, and spirited our soules of one breath. 1642 Cudworth *Disc. Lord's Supper* Introd. 2 There is ever some Soule of Truth, which doth secretly Spirit and Enliven the dead and unweildy Lump of all Errours, without which it could not move or stirre. 1650 R. Stapylton *Strada's Low C. Wars* i. 1 A Prince (the great body of whose Empire must be spirited with a great soul. 1717 Pope *Iliad* ix. 98 Thy high commands must spirit all our wars.

b. To invest with a particular spirit, disposition, or character.

Not always clearly distinguishable from 2 and 2 b.

1654 Owen *Saints' Persev.* v. 113 The first great Promise of Christ..is that which Spirits and principles all other promises whatsoever. 1662 R. Mathew *Unl. Alch.* 63 Your rash and hasty zeal, running upon Ordinances not spirited from on high. 1685 W. Adams *Dedham Pulpit* 108 This will spirit and dispose you to practise all those counsels. 1721 R. Keith tr. *T. à Kempis, Valley of Lillies* xxxiii. 105 The holy Spirit, who..taught him, and spirited him, and adorned his whole Life with Virtues. 1728 P. Walker *Life Peden* To Rdr. (1827) p. xxviii, They were some Way fitted and spirited for Trials.

c. Const. *by* or *with* (some principle, etc.). Chiefly in passive.

1646 J. Gregory *Notes & Obs.* (1650) 33 Thus spirited with this secret power, it [the Palladium] was dispos'd of in some eminent..place of the City. 1654 Owen *Saints' Persev.* v. 112 The generall intention of God in all Gospel Promises, whereby they being equally Spirited, become as one. 1671 Temple *Ess., Constit. & Int. Emp.* Wks. 1731 I. 107 In all these Wars the People were both united and spirited by the common Love of their Country. 1704 Swift *Mech. Operat. Spirit* Misc. (1711) 300 Spirited by a noble Zeal. 1741 Betterton *Hist. Eng. Stage* i. 21 They had warm Disputes behind the Scenes, which spirited the Rivals with..a natural Resentment to each other.

d. To lead or win *over* by persuasion.

1656 Hammond *Leah & Rachel* (1844) 10, I shall abhor to spirit over any; but go along with such as are voluntarily desirous to go thither.

4. With *up*: To stimulate, animate, encourage, stir up, or excite (a person).

1712 Addison *Spect.* No. 482 ⁋ 2 She is forced..to spirit him up now and then, that he may not grow musty, and unfit for Conversation. 1743 Bulkeley & Cummins *Voy. S. Seas* 11 Not knowing..by whom the Fellow might be spirited up, I acquainted the Captain with the Affair. 1760-72 H. Brooke *Fool of Qual.* (1809) I. 70 Being encouraged and spirited up...they became, by degrees, quite happy and jovial. 1797 Jane Austen *Sense & Sens.* xxx. Well, I shall spirit up the Colonel as soon as I can. 1847 Mrs. Gore *Castles in Air* xix, 'You might live at a worse place, Charley!' said I, spirited up for Yorkshire. 1871 Browning *Balaust.* 106 We want no colony from Athens here, With memories of Salamis..To spirit up our captives.

b. Const. *against*, *into*, or *to*.

1716 Pope *Lett.* (1735) I. 288 Such a Mind as your's has no need of being spirited up into Honour. 1721 Amherst *Terræ Fil.* No. 8 (1726) 38 They made it their business to.. spirit up their neighbours to rebellion. 1728 H. Herbert tr. *Fleury's Eccl. Hist.* I. 328 The powerful party that had been spirited up against him. 1764 Goldsm. *Hist. Eng. in Lett.* (1772) II. 220 The French..continually spirited up the Indians to repel the new comers. 1809 W. Irving *Knickerb.* vi. vii. (1849) 355 Spiriting them up to heroic deeds. 1841 W. Duncan *Cicero's Sel. Orat.* ii. 32 Many very powerful nations were spirited up against us. 1857 Trollope *Barchester T.* (1861) 130 Expecting that he should find his lordship..spirited up by his wife to repeat the rebuke.

c. To instigate or promote (rebellion, etc.).

1715 in *Westm. Gaz.* (1907) 14 May 2/3 Those Incendiaries who came hither on Purpose to spirit up a Rebellion. 1751 Smollett *Per. Pic.* (1779) IV. xcvii. 258 Attempts..to spirit up suits against him. 1770 Langhorne *Plutarch* (1879) I. 255/1 He determined to spirit up a cruel war.

II. **5.** To carry off or away, to make away with or remove in a mysterious or dexterous manner: †**a.** To kidnap, in order to transport to the plantations in America. *Obs.* (Cf. 6 a.)

1666 *Lond. Gaz.* No. 107/1 Several persons escaped from the Vessel, who pretend they were spirited (as they term it) and invited upon several pretences aboard them, and then.. carried away. a 1683 Oldham *Wks.* (1686) 85 These serve for Baits the simple to ensnare, Like Children spirited with Toys at Fair. 1693 I. Mather *Cases Consc.* (1862) 241 A Servant, who was Spirited or Kidnapt (as they call it) into America.

b. In general use.

1670 *Caveat to Conventiclers* 4 They do in a manner acknowledge, that they were Spirited out of their Bogs and Woods, and transported hither with vain hopes of preferment. 1678 *Strange News fr. Wicklow* 3 Mr. Uniack demanded if she could give them any account of a Gentleman..that had been Spirited out of their Company [by fairies] about an hour before. 1837 Carlyle *Fr. Rev.* i. v. i, Leading men from all the Three Orders are nightly spirited thither. *Ibid.* ii v. v, Deserters are spirited over by assiduous crimps. 1858 R. S. Surtees *Ask Mamma* xlv. 199 [He] seemed to spirit the things off the table without sound or effort. 1889 Stevenson *Edinburgh* 46 Many a solid bulk of masonry has been likewise spirited into the air.

6. With *away* (cf. 5): **a.** To kidnap, carry off, or abduct (a person).

Freq. c 1670-c 1690, with reference to transporting boys to the West Indian plantations: cf. 5 a.

1670 Marvell *Corr.* Wks. (Grosart) II. 323 An Act.. against spiriting away Children beyond Sea. 1682 *Lond. Gaz.* 1723/4 For Spiriting or Stealing away a Young Boy, and sending him to Jamaica. 1697 Dampier *Voy.* (1729) I. 178 We anchor'd, and sent..to treat about an Exchange for our Man they had spirited away. 1749 Fielding *Tom Jones* i. ix, Some..intimated, that she was spirited away with a design too black to be mentioned. 1769 Blackstone *Comm.* IV. 219 In the civil law, the offence of spiriting away and stealing men and children..was punished with death. 1820 Scott *Monast.* iv, She was sensible that he would have neither scruple nor difficulty in spiriting away the child. 1858 Froude *Hist. Eng.* III. xvii. 443 The archbishop spirited away the preacher into Kent. 1883 *Law Rep.* 11 Q.B.D. 592 The prosecutor had spirited away..the sister of the accused person, and had shut her up in a convent.

fig. 1688 Crowne *Darius* v. Wks. 1874 III. 449 What is it spirits me away to fear?

b. To take away, carry off, by some mysterious means or power; to transport with speed.

1696 C. Leslie *Snake in Grass* (1697) 97 Their Spiriting away the Letter of the Promised Seed. 1726 Penn *No Cross* xiii. § 14 An Enemy to the State, for he [the miser] spirits their Money away. 1775 R. Chandler *Trav. Asia M.* (1825) I. Introd. p. xi. The jealousy of the papal court.. spirited away these inestimable treasures. 1794 Godwin *Caleb Williams* 63 There is no Mrs. Jakeman now to spirit you away. 1861 Hughes *Tom Brown at Oxf.* xxxii, One shake of the hand, and she was spirited away in a moment.

c. Said of the action of spirits.

1825 J. Neal *Bro. Jonathan* I. 253 Peters had been.. spirited away in a thunderstorm. 1855 W. Irving *Chron. Wolfert's Roost* 179 Others jocosely hinted that old Pluto ..had spirited away the boy to the nether regions. 1889 Barrie *Window in Thrums* 102 It was thocht next mornin' at the ghost had spirited them awa.

III. †**7.** To extract spirit from; to distil. In quot. *fig.* *Obs.*[−1]

1677 *Cleveland's Poems* Ded., Yet how many such Authors must be creamed and spirited to make up his *Fuscara*?

SPIRITAL.

8. To treat with a solution of spirits.

†Spirital, *a.* Obs. Also 7 **-all.** [a. OF. *(e)spirital,* ad L. *spiritalis*: see SPIRIT *sb.*]

1. Pertaining to sacred concerns; = SPIRITUAL *a.*

2. Of the nature of spirit; of or pertaining to the spirit in contrast to the body or matter.

†Spiritality, Obs.⁻¹ [f. prec. + -ITY.]

†Spiritually, *adv.* Obs. rare. [f. prec. + -LY².]

†Spiritate, *ppl. a.* Obs. rare.

Spiritato, Obs. rare. [It.]

†Spiritdom. Obs.⁻¹ [f. SPIRIT *sb.* + -DOM.]

Spirited, *a.* [f. SPIRIT *sb.*]

Spiritedly, *adv.* [f. prec. + -LY².]

Spiritedness. [f. as prec. + -NESS.]

Spiriter, rare⁻¹. [f. SPIRIT *v.* + -ER.]

Spiritful, *a.* — Obs. *or dial.* [f. SPIRIT *sb.*]

Spiritfully, *adv.* Obs.⁻¹

Spiritic, *a.* [f. SPIRIT *sb.* + -IC.]

SPIRITIE.

a. Of literary worth, speech, etc.

Spirit-lamp, *a.* A lamp for spirit lamp. [SPIRIT *sb.*]

Spiritless, *a.* [f. SPIRIT *sb.* + -LESS.]

Spirit-like, *a.* [f. SPIRIT *sb.* + -LIKE.]

Spiritly, *a.* Obs.⁻¹

†Spiritose, *a.* Obs.⁻¹ [f. SPIRIT *sb.* + -OSE.]

Spiritous, *a.* † Obs. Also 8 *poet.* spirt'ous.

Spiritrump. Ent. [ad F. *spiritrompe.*]

Spiritsome, *a.* [f. the nature of spirit.]

Spirit-stirring, *a.* [SPIRIT *sb.*]

SPIRITUAL.

a. G. H. TOWNSEND *Man. Dates* LV.

SPIRITUAL. 623 SPIRITUALISM. SPIRITUALIST. 624 SPIRITUALIZE.

Spiritualise, *pa. pple.* Obs.⁻¹ [Cf. next.]

Spiritualisation (spiritualiz-.)

Spiritualism (spiritualiz'm).

Spiritualist.

Spiritualistic (spiritualist'ik), *a.* (and *sb.*) [f. prec. + -IC.]

Spirituality.

Spiritualize.

Spiritualized (spiritualized), ppl. a. [f. Spiritualize v.]

1. Containing an infusion of spirits. Obs.

2. Rendered spiritual; characterized by spirituality.

3. Changed from a bodily or material condition to a spiritual one; converted into spirit.

Spiritualizer (spiritualizer), [f. Spiritualize v.] One who gives a spiritual sense to a Scriptural statement, etc.; one who interprets spiritually.

Spiritualness (spiritualnes), [f. as prec.] The action of the verb Spiritualize; a spiritual interpretation.

Spirituality (spirituæliti). Forms: 4-6 spiritualte(e), 5 -alite, eperitwalte, spyrytt, -6 spyry tualte, 5 spyryt-, epiritualite(e), 4-7 spiritualite, 5- spirituality. [ad. OF. espiri-tualité, spiritualité, -tê, etc. (F. spiri-tualité), ad. late L.]

1. The quality or state of being spiritual; spiritual character. — Spirituality 3. Obs.

2. Spirituality (spirituæliti). Also 4 spirit-uellyche, 5 spiritually. [f. Spiritual a.]

Spiritually (spiritueli), adv. Also 4 spirit-uellyche, 5 spiritually. [f. Spiritual a.]

1. In a spiritual manner; in or as to the spirit; as regards or in respect of spiritual things; in accordance with spiritual principles.

Spirituous (spiritiuas), a. [ad. mod.L. spiritu osus, f. L. spiritus spirit.]

1. Spirited, animated, lively, vivacious. Now rare.

2. Of the nature of spirit; spirituous. rare.

Spirituously (spiritiuasli), adv. In a spirituous manner; with spirit.

Spirituousness. [f. Spirituous.]

Spiritus (spiritas), sb. [L.] Chiefly dial.

Spiritvalve, a. Zool. [a. f. Spiritvalve, f. L.]

Spirket. Naut. Obs. In 8 spirkit. [Cf. next and Spirket.]

Spirketting (spirketiŋ). Naut. Also 8 spirket (prec.), var. of Spurket.

Spirling (spörliŋ). Now only Sc. Also 5-6 sperling. [var. of Sperling.]

Spiro- (spair), combining form of L. spira, spire, coil.

Spirograph. [ad. mod.L. spiroil.]

Spiroil. Chem. (See quot. and Spiroil.)

Spirometer (spairometǝr). [f. spir-, spiro-, L. spira + -meter.] An instrument for measuring the breathing power of the lungs.

Spirometric (spairmetrik), a. [f. prec.]

Spirometry (spairometri). Measurement of breathing-power or lung-capacity.

Spirous (spairas), a. rare. [f. Spire sb.]

Spirt (spört), sb. Also 5 apyrt, 6 spert. [Reduced form of Spirit.] = Spirit sb., in various senses.

Spirt, var. Spurt sb.

Spirt (spört), sb. Also 6 spyrrt. [Of obscure origin: cf. Spurt sb.]

Spirt (spört), v. Also 6 spyrt, 7 spurt. [Metathetic form of Sprit v.2 Cf. Spurt sb.3] A sprout or shoot.

Spirt (spört), sb.2 [f. Spirt v.] Cf. Spurt sb.3] A sprout or shoot.

Spirt (spört), sb.4 [f. Spirt v.1 Cf. Spurt sb.3]

Spirt (spört), v. [Of obscure origin: cf. MHG. and Gk. dial. spirtan to spit, feel.] (I of 3) (fig.) to utter. The form SPURT 3 is recorded a little earlier.]

Spirtle (spör tl), sb. [f. Spirt v.3] A small spirt or jet; a sprinkle.

Spirtle (spört l), v. Now dial. Also 7 spertle. [f. Spirt v.1 + -le.]

Spirt-net. Now dial. [f. Spirt 1.] (See quot.)

Spiry (spairi), a.1 [f. Spire sb.3] Curving or coiling in spirals.

Spiry (spairi), a.2 [f. Spire sb.1] Having the character or form of a spire; tapering up to a point. a. Of parts of buildings.

Spiss (spis), a. Obs. rare—1. [ad. L. spissus.] A thickening substance.

Spissated, ppl. a. Obs. rare—1. [ad. L. spissat-.] = Spissed.

So Spissating ppl. a., thickening. rare.

Spissation. Obs. rare—1. [ad. L. spissation-.] A thickening (1727 in Bailey, vol. ii).

Spissitive, a. Obs. rare—1. [f. prec. and -ive.] Serving to thicken.

Spissed, a. Obs. rare. [f. L. spissus.] Thickened.

Spissitude (spisitiud). [ad. L. spissitudo, f.] Density, thickness, compactness.

Spissy, a. Obs. rare—1. [f. Spiss sb.] Dense, compact.

Spit (spit). sb.1 [OE. spitu wk., corresp. to MDu., MLG. spit, spet (Du. spit), and other cognate forms.]

Spit (spit), sb.2 [f. Spit v.1]

Spit (spit), sb.4 [OE. spittan.]

Spit (spit), sb.3 Also 7 spett. [Of uncertain origin.]

Spit (spit), v.1 [OE. spittan.]

Spitting, vbl. sb. The action of Spit v.1

SPITE. 631 SPITEFUL. SPITEFULLY. 632 SPITTER.

2970

SPITTER-SPATTER. 633 **SPITTLE.** | **SPITTLE.** 634 **SPLASH.**

Spitter-spatter. *rare⁻¹.* [f. SPATTER v.]
Trifling talk.

† Spittery. *Obs.* [f. SPIT v.¹, after F. *crachoir*.]
A spittoon.

Spitting, *vbl. sb.¹* [f. SPIT v.¹] The action of piercing with, or fixing on, a spit. Also *attrib.*

Spitting, *vbl. sb.²* [f. SPIT v.²]
1. The action of ejecting saliva from the mouth; expectoration.
2. *b.* A spittle or shower of rain.
c. techn. (See quot.)
4. *attrib.* In sense 'for spitting in or on', as *spitting-box, -cup, -dish, -kettle, -mug, -pan,* etc.

Spitting, *ppl. a.* [f. SPIT v.²]
1. That spits, in various (chiefly *transf.*) senses of the verb.
2. In specific names of reptiles, etc., as *spitting adj.* *click-beetle, gecko, snake.*

Spittle, *sb.¹* *Obs.* Forms: *a.* 3, 4, 6 spittel (4 -el, -yle; 4 spyttel, 5 spytyl; 5–6 spittil, 6 -el, &c. *b.* 6 spyttle, 6–7 spittle, 7 spittle. *c.* 6 spettle, spitell. *d.* 5 spyttle. [Modification of HOSPITAL, modified on the analogy of native words in *-l.* Forms with more original ending appear in UHG. *spital (spitoul; G. spital, MLG. spetal, spittel; MHG. spit tl—, spetel, MHG. spittel; G. spital*), universally representing an aphetic form of HOSPITAL, modified on the analogy of native words in *-el.* The common source of these is app. Italian or Levantine; cf. It. *spedale, ital. spitale, mod.Gr. σπίτι*; med.Gr. *σπιτάλιον* (1342 in Du Cange), med.Gr. *σπιτάλιον* (c 1350).]
1. A house or place for the reception of the indigent or diseased; a charitable foundation for this purpose, esp. one chiefly occupied by persons of a low class or afflicted with foul diseases; a lazar-house. (Now written SPITAL.)
2. *b.* A slight sprinkle or shower of rain.

Spittle, *sb.²* *Obs.* Forms: *a.* 3–4, 6 spittel (4 -yle); 5 spettel, 6-yle; 5–6 spittil, 6-el, &c. spittaill, spyttell, -yll, 6. spittle, 6–7 spittle, 7 spittle. *b.* 6 spittle, *c.* 6 spettle, -oll. See also SPITAL. [ME. *spittel, spittel,* etc.—MLG. *spittel, spettel,* MHG. *spittel; G. spittel*), universally representing an aphetic form of HOSPITAL, modified on the analogy of native words in *-el.*
1. Saliva, spit.
b. The saliva emitted from the mouth.

Spittle, *v.¹* *rare.* [f. SPITTLE *sb.²*] To dig (*in*), to pare, etc., with a spittle. Hence **Spittling** *vbl. sb.*

Spittle-house. *Obs.* [f. SPITTLE *sb.¹*] = SPITAL-HOUSE s.v. SPITAL b.

Spittle-staff. *Obs.* [f. SPITTLE *sb.³*] A kind of spade or digging implement.

† Spitty, *a.* *Obs. rare⁻¹.* [f. SPIT *sb.¹*] Marked by the presence of spittle.

Spittoon (spitū′n). Also **spitoon.** [f. SPIT *sb.* + -OON.] A receptacle for spittle; usually a round flat vessel of earthenware or metal, sometimes having a cover in the form of a shallow inverted cone, with an opening in the middle.

Spitz (spits). Also spitzdog. [a. G. *spitz* ...] A species of dog having a very pointed muzzle; a Pomeranian dog.

SPLASH. 635 SPLASHY. | SPLAT. 636 SPLAY.

Splash (splæʃ), *sb.* [f. SPLASH *v.*]
1. *trans.* To bespatter, to wet or soil, by dashing water, mud, etc.
2. To stain, mark, or mottle with irregular patches of colour or light.
b. absol.

Splash (splæʃ), *v.* [Alteration of PLASH *v.²*]

Splashboard. Also splashboard. [f. prec.]

Splashed (splæʃt), *ppl. a.* [f. SPLASH *v.*]

Splasher. [f. SPLASH *v.* + -ER¹.]

Splashing, *vbl. sb.* [f. SPLASH *v.*]

Splashing, *ppl. a.* [f. SPLASH *v.*]

Splashy, *a.* [f. SPLASH *sb.* + -Y.]

Splat, *sb.¹* [f. SPLAT *v.*] A flat piece of wood, esp. one forming the central part of a chair-back.

Splat, *v.¹* *dial.* [Alteration of SPLIT *v.*]

Splatch (splætʃ), *sb.* Now *Sc.* and *U.S.* A large or solid splash or spatter of mud, etc.; a large or glaring patch of colour.

Splatter, *v.* [Imit., perh. a blend of SPLASH and SPATTER.]

Splay (splei), *sb.* [Aphetic form of DISPLAY *sb.*]

Splay (splei), *v.¹* [Short for DISPLAY *v.*]

Splay, *v.²* Now *dial.* [Alteration of SPAY *v.*] To spay (female animals).

| SPLAYED. | 637 | SPLEEN. | SPLEEN. | 638 | SPLEET-NEW. |

Splayed (spl**ā**d), *ppl. a.* [f. SPLAY *v.*]

Splay-ing, *ppl. a.* [f. SPLAY *v.*] Sloping or spreading outwards.

Splay-legged, *a. rare*⁻¹. [Cf. SPLAY-FOOTED *a.*] Having straddling legs.

Splay-mouth, *a. Obs.* [f. SPLAY *a.* + MOUTH.] A distorted or wry mouth.

Splay-mouthed, *a.* *Obs.* [f. prec.] Having a wide or wry mouth.

Splea-footed, obs. f. SPLAY-FOOTED. **Splea-geant**: see SPLAYGENT. **Spleat**, obs. f. SPLEET or SPLIT.

† Spleck. *Obs. rare.* [Cf. PLECK *a.*] A speck, a spot.

† Spleiced, *a.* *Obs. rare.* In 4 splobid, epleiced, 5 splebent. [Cf. MDu. *pleiken* (Verdam *v. gespekelt*) and PLECKED *a.*] Specked, spotted.

Spleen (splēn), *sb. Forms:* 4-6 splen; 4-7 splene, 5 spleene, 4-9 splene, etc., or L. *splen, a.* Gr. σπλήν, related to Skr. *plīhan*, L. *liēn.* In Romanic the word has survived in many Italian dialects, and in Roumanian *pliná*, but It. *spléne* is a learned original, with mod. F. *spléen* (+ *spline*) and Sp. *esplin* have been adopted from English in sense F.]

1. *Anat.* An abdominal organ consisting of a ductless gland of irregular form, which in mammals is situated at the cardiac end of the stomach and serves to produce certain changes in the blood; the milt or melt.

Spleen, *sb.* Now *dial.* and *rare.* [a. MDu. *splēte* (WFlem. *spleit*), *spleet* (Du. *spleet*) or MLG. (and LG.) *splēte*, NFris. *split*, related to SPLIT *v.*] A small strip of split wood or withe.

Spleet, *sb.* Now *dial. and rare.* [a. MDu. *splēte* (WFlem. *spleit*), *spleet* (Du. *spleet*) or MLG. (and LG.) *splēte*, NFris. *split*, related to SPLIT *v.*]

Spleen-stone. *Obs.* [tr. G. *milzstein*.] A stone supposed to cure disorders of the spleen.

Spleen-wort. Also 5 splen(e)-, spleenewoort, spleenwort. Gr. σπλήνιον or *asplēnon.*

Spleet-ed, *ppl. a.* [f. SPLEET *v.*¹ or *v.*²] Made wet, or consisting of, split rods.

Spleet-new. *a. Obs.* [app. f. SPLEET *v.*² + NEW *a.*] Perfectly new.

| SPLEN- | 639 | SPLENDIDLY. | | 640 | SPLENETIC. |

Spleget, var. SPLEDGET *Obs.* **Spleigh**, obs. f. SPLAY. **Spleion**: see SPLECK (*a.*). **Splen-**, comb. f. SPLEEN *sb.*

Splen-, var. of SPLENO- before vowels, occurring in a few medical terms, as **Splenæ'mia**, **-ag'ia** [cf. F. *splénalgie*], **-a'ig'ia** *a.*

† Splenatick, *a.* *Obs.* Also 7-8 -ick; spleniatick. [ad. med.L. *spleniaticus*, Roum. *splenatic*, var. of *spléniticus* SPLENETIC *a.*]

† Splenative, *a.* *Obs.* Also 6 splenatiue, 7 splen-. [ad. L. type *splīnātīvus* (cf. prec.), or independently f. SPLEEN *sb.*]

Splendacious, *a.* *Obs.* Also -atious, -aceous. [Fancifully f. SPLEND-ID *a.*] Very splendid; gorgeous, grand.

Splendent (splendént), *a.* [a. L. *splendent-*, -ēns, pres. pple. of *splendēre* to be bright, to shine.]

1. Shining brightly by virtue of inherent light.

1. With much grandeur or display; sumptuously, grandly, gorgeously : **a.** In respect of living, state or ceremony, etc.

b. Of persons : Maintaining, or living in, great style or grandeur.

2. Reflecting light with great brilliancy ; bright, gleaming, resplendent.

3. Extremely brilliant, gorgeous, or magnificent.

4. *fig.* Having qualities comparable to material brightness or brilliancy ; pre-eminently beautiful, grand, or great.

Splendidious, *a.* *Obs. rare.* [f. next + -OUS.] Splendid, magnificent, brilliant.

† Splendidous, *a.* *Obs.* Also 7 splen-, -idious, splendidious. [f. L. *splendidus* + -OUS.] Splendid, magnificent.

Splendiferous (splendī'fěɹəs), *a.* [In early use f. med.L. *splendiferus* (for late L. *splendorifer*) ; in mod. use f. SPLENDOUR + -I- + -FEROUS, after *splendiferous.*]

Splendour (splendəɹ), *sb.* [a. AF. *splendour* (14th cent., mod.F. *splendeur*), or ad. L. *splendor-, splendor,* f. *splendēre* to shine.]

Splendrous, obs. variant of SPLENDOROUS *a.*

† Splendy, *a.* *Obs.*⁻¹ [f. L. *splend-ēre.*] Lustrous, glittering.

Splenectomy. *Surg.* [ad. mod.L. *splēnectomia*, f. Gr. σπλήν SPLEEN *sb.* + ἐκτομή excision.] Excision or removal of the spleen.

Splenetic (splēnětik, spl, and -e'tik), *a. and sb.* [ad. late L. *splēneticus*, f. *splēn* SPLEEN *sb.*]

1. *Med.* Of or pertaining to the spleen ; splenic.

2. Affected with, or suffering from, disease or disorder of the spleen ; in later use, affected with melancholia or hypochondria. *Obs.*

3. Characterized by, tending to produce, melancholy or depression of spirits. *Obs.*

4. Bad-tempered, irritable, peevish, spiteful.

Supplement, p. 3873 ; Corrigenda, p. 4092 ; Spurious words, p. 4093 ; Books quoted, p. 4094

Splenetical ... (see spleen)

Splenetic, *a.* and *sb.*

Splene·tive, *a. Obs.* [f. prec.]

Splenial, *a.* and *sb. Zool. Anat.*

Splenic, *a.* and *sb.*

Splenical, *a.*

Splenification.

Splenio-, comb. form of splenic.

Splenitis. *Path.*

Splenish, *a.* = Spleenish.

Splenitive, *a. Obs.* Splenetic.

Splenium. *Anat.*

Splenius. *Anat.*

Splenial, *a.²*

Sple·niatic, *a. Obs.*

Splenisa·tion, Splenization.

Splenize, *v.* *Path.*

Splenoid.

Splenotomy. *Path.*

Splenculus.

Splenish.

Splet, *v.* Now *dial.* Also 6 **splette**.

Sple·nous, *a.*

Splenate.

Spleet, *v.*

Spleen-like.

Spleter. [*L.* SPLET *v.*] A splinter.

Splet-bone, var. form of SPLEENISH *sb.*

Splice, *sb.* Also 6- **splise**.

Splicer. [f. SPLICE *v.* + -ER.] One who splices ropes, etc.

Splicing, *vbl. sb.*

Splinter, *sb.*

Splint, *sb.*

Splint, *sb.*

Splint, *v.*

Splint-coal.

Splinted, *ppl. a.*

Splinter, *sb.*

Splinter, *v.*

Splintage.

Splinten.

Splinter-bar.

Splinter-proof, *sb.* and *a. Mil.*

Splintery, *a.*

Splinting, *vbl. sb.*

†1. The action of constructing or providing with splints or laths; the material used in this. *Obs.*

2. The action of putting into surgical splints; binding or securing by means of a splint or splints.

+3. Splintering, splitting. *Obs.*

Splinty, *a.* Now *rare*. Also **8 splinty.** [f. SPLINT *sb.* + -Y.] Of a splintery nature or texture; of the nature of splint or splint coal.

So **Splinty-splashy** *a.*, sloppy, slushy. *rare*⁻.

Split (split), *sb.*¹ Also **6 splitte, 7 splitt.** [f. SPLIT *v.* or *a.*: cf. LG. *split*, G. *splitt*, NFris. *spletti.*]

1. A narrow break or opening made by splitting; a cleft, crack, rent, or slit; a fissure.

2. A division, separation, breach, schism, or the like (in a party, etc.).

3. A rupture, breach, division, or dissension in a party or sect; or between friends.

Split, *v.* *Sc.* and *dial.* [Cf. SPLUNT *v.*] *intr.* To spirit or spout.

Splish-splash, *a.*, *rare.* [f. SPLASH *v.*¹, with usual variation of vowel.] *intr.* To splash repeatedly.

Splitter (splitter), *sb.*² Also **6 splitte, 7 splitt.**

SPLITE. 647 SPLODGE. SPLODGE. 648 SPODUMENE.

Split-ful, *Weaving.* [f. SPLIT *sb.*¹ + -FUL.] A division of the warp, consisting of the threads passing between each pair of dents or splits.

Split-new, *a.* quite new, brand-new. *Sc.* and *dial.*

†Splitted, *ppl. a.* *Obs.* [f. SPLIT *v.* + -ED.] Split.

Splitter (splitter), *sb.* [f. SPLIT *v.* + -ER¹.]

1. One who, or that which, splits or cleaves, in various senses.

2. *Zool.* One employed in splitting fish, etc.

3. Separated, divided, parted, or apportioned in some way. In special collocations, as *split draught, copy,* etc.

4. With advs., as *split-off, -up.*

b. *Split-up, long-legged.* *slang.*

Splitter, *v.* *rare.* [f. SPLIT *v.* + -ER², or *ad.*]

†Splittern. *Obs.*⁻¹ [f. SPLIT *v.*]

Splodge (splǫdʒ), *sb.* [Imitative of the sound.]

1. *intr.* To trudge or plod splashily through mud or water.

2. *trans.* To splash heavily. (Cf. SPLODGE *v.* 1.)

Splodgy (splǭdʒi), *a.* [f. SPLODGE *sb.* + -Y.] Full of splodges; showing coarse splotches of colour.

Sploit, obs. form of SPOIL.

Splore (splōɹ), *sb.* Chiefly *Sc.* [Of obscure origin.]

1. A frolic, merrymaking, revel, carousal.

2. A commotion or disturbance; a skirmish or encounter; a scrape.

3. *pl.* That which is split, cleft, or chopped.

4. *attrib.,* chiefly in the sense of 'used or adapted for splitting,' as *splitting-knife, -machine, -mill, -tool; splitting-block* (see quot. 1711), *-board*

Splotch (splǫtʃ), *sb.* Also **7 sploach, sploach.** [Onomatopoeic: cf. BLOTCH and SPLODGE.]

Splotch, *v.* [f. prec.] *trans.* To cover with splotches; to splash or stain in patches.

Splotchy (splǫtʃi), *a.* [f. prec. + -Y.] Covered with splotches or stains; having the appearance of splotches.

Splunt, obs. form of SPLINT.

Splurge (splɜːdʒ), *sb.* *U.S.* [Imitative.]

1. An ostentatious display or effort.

Splurge (splɜːdʒ), *v.* *U.S.* [f. prec.]

Splurgy (splɜːdʒi), *a.* *U.S.* [f. SPLURGE *sb.* + -Y.] Given to splurge; ostentatious.

Splutter (splʌtəɹ), *sb.* [Imitative: cf. SPUTTER *sb.* Perhaps by Johnson as 'a low word'.]

1. A noise or fuss.

Splutter (splʌtəɹ), *v.* [f. prec.]

1. *trans.* To utter hastily and indistinctly. Also *const.*

2. *intr.* To make a noise as of spitting or sputtering. Also with *out.*

Spluttering, *vbl. sb.* [f. as prec.] The action of the verb in various senses.

Spluttering, *ppl. a.* [f. as prec.] That splutters or sputters.

Spluttery, *a.* [f. as prec.] Tending to splutter; characterized by spluttering.

Spode, *sb.* [The surname of J. Spode (1754–1827).] A fine kind of English porcelain. Also *attrib.*

Spodium, *sb.* *rare.* [L. *spodium* (Pliny), ad. Gr. σπόδιον.]

Spodo-, combining form of σποδός *spode* sb., as in *Spodogenous a.*, etc.

Spodomancy, *sb.* *rare.* [f. Gr. σποδός ashes + -MANCY.] Divination by ashes.

Spodumene (spǭdjumiːn), *sb.* *Min.* [ad. F. *spodumène* (Rabelais), f. Gr. σποδούμενος burnt to ashes.] A silicate of aluminium and lithium, of varying colour, found in crystals and masses.

Spoffish (spF·fiʃ), a. slang. [Of obscure origin.] Bustling, fussy, officious.

So Spoffy a.; **Spoffiness.**

Spogourt, obs. form of SPOGOURT (scoop).

Spoil (spoil), sb. ... See also SPULZIE. [ad. OF. *espoille, espuille, f. espoillier* (see next); or directly L. *spolium*.]

...

Spoil (spoil), v.[1] Pa. t. and pa. pple. **spoiled**, **spoilt**. Forms: 4 *spoili* (4–7 *spoyle*), 4–7 *spoyl*, 4–7 *spoile* (5–7 *spoyle*), ... [ad. OF. *espoillier*, *espillier* ... = Sp., Pg. *espoliar*, It. *spogliare*, ...]

...

Spoilage (spoi·ledʒ). [f. SPOIL v.[1] + -AGE.]

Spoiler (spoi·lɐ(r)). [f. SPOIL v. + -ER.]

Spoilful, a. [f. SPOIL sb. + -FUL.]

Spoiling, vbl. sb.[1] [f. SPOIL v.[1]]

Spoiling, vbl. sb.[2] Naut. [Of obscure origin.]

Spoiling, ppl. a. [f. SPOIL v.[1]] Despoiling, plundering, robbing, etc.

Spoilless, a. [f. SPOIL sb. + -LESS.]

Spoilsman. U.S. [f. SPOILS pl. of SPOIL sb.]

Spoilsport, sb. [f. SPOIL v.[1]] One who acts so as to spoil the sport or plans of others.

Spoke (spəuk), sb.[1] Forms: a. 1 *spaca*, 3 *spoch*, 4 *speke*, 4–5 *spake*, 5 *spoke*, 5–6, 7–9 *spoak*; β. *spaak*, 8–9 *spauk*. [OE. *spáca* masc.; = OFris. *spêke*, WFris. *spaike*, *speak*, MDu. *spake*, *speke* (Du. *speek*), MLG. and LG. *spêke* (Da. *spage*), OHG. *speicha* (MHG. and G. *speiche*).]

Spoke, sb.[2] dial. [Cf. prec. and SPOG.]

Spoked (spəukt), a.

Spokeless, a. [f. SPOKE sb.[1] + -LESS.] Destitute of spokes; made without spokes.

Supplement, p. 3873; Corrigenda, p. 4092; Spurious words, p. 4093; Books quoted, p. 4094

1673 R. Head *Canting Acad.* 103 He may Spunge, and have his Leachery for nothing. a 1700 B. E. *Dict. Cant. Crew, Spunge*, to drink at others Cost. 1785 Grose *Dict. Vulgar T., To spunge*, to eat and drink at another's cost. 1849 W. Irving *Goldsm.* xxv. 222 An Irishman..who lived nobody knew how nor where; sponging wherever he had a chance. 1884 G. Moore *Mummer's Wife* (1887) 203 Fearing to look as if she were sponging, Kate insisted on..standing treat.

b. Const. *on* or *upon* (a person, etc.).

(a) 1677 Miège *Fr. Dict.*, To spunge upon one, *écornifler*. 1693 *Humours Town* 101 The poor Curate is fain to Spunge upon the Wealthier Sinners of his Parish. 1706–7 Farquhar *Beaux' Strat.* iv. iii, I had rather spunge upon Morris, and sup upon a Dish of Bohee scor'd behind the Door. 1730 Fielding *Tom Thumb* ii. i, There when I have him, I will spunge upon him. 1824 *Hist. Gaming* 41 Frequenting shabby ale-houses, sponging upon credulous persons. 1857 Ruskin *Pol. Econ. Art* 198 They will cheat the public at their shops or sponge on their friends at their houses. 1887 Miss Braddon *Like & Unlike* x, I hope I shall never be obliged to sponge upon you.

(b) 1681–6 J. Scott *Chr. Life* iii. Mortification iii, What man in his Wits would keep such a Company of devouring Lusts about him, that are perpetually spungeing upon his Estate. a 1692 Pollexfen *Disc. Trade* (1697) 155 [They] must live by preying, pilfering or spunging upon other Mens Labours. 1855 Trollope *Warden* xx, It was an easy matter to abandon his own income, as he was able to sponge on that of another person. 1902 L. Stephen *Stud. Biogr.* III. iii. 114 Humbugs, ready to..sponge upon his benevolence.

c. With *for* (something).

1719 D'Urfey *Pills* (1872) I. 200 That all Bullies should pay; And sponge no more for recreation. 1735 Sheridan *Let. to Swift* 5 Oct., Do not think to sponge upon me for anything but meat, drink, and lodging. 1837 Lytton *E. Maltrav.* i. xvii, A doubt lest I should some day or other sponge upon his lordship for a place. 1883 Stevenson *Treas. Isl.* i. v, I'm to be a poor, crawling beggar, sponging for rum, when I might be rolling in a coach!

11. To go about in a sneaking or loafing fashion, esp. in order to obtain something.

1825 Jamieson *Suppl.* s.v. 1866 *Lond. Rev.* 3 Mar. 245/2 Soldiers..loafing and spunging from tavern to tavern during the entire day.

III. 12. *intr.* (See quot.)

1881 Ingersoll *Oyster-Industr.* (Hist. Fish. Industr. U.S.) 248 *Sponge*, or *To go Sponging*.—To go on a cruise for gathering sponges.

Sponge-cake. [Sponge *sb.*[1]] A very light sweet cake made with flour, milk, eggs, and sugar.

1843 Mrs. Carlyle *Lett.* I. 269 A hot jelly, and one modest sponge cake. 1860 *All Year Round* No. 48. 514, I cannot dine on stale sponge-cakes that turn to sand in the mouth. 1874 Burnand *My Time* 97 He returned..with a bottle of lemonade..and two sponge-cakes in a bag.

attrib. 1846 Soyer *Cookery* 565 Have buttered a large sponge-cake mould. 1883 'Annie Thomas' *Mod. Housewife* 9 Some nice soup and a spongecake-pudding.

Sponged (spʌndʒd), *ppl. a.* Also 5 **spounged**, 7 **spunged.** [f. Sponge *sb.*[1] or *v.*]

†**1.** Of a spongy texture; porous. *Obs.*[−1]

1398 Trevisa *Barth. De P. R.* xiv. xxxii. (Bodl. MS.), Þouȝ cragges be neuer so hard and rouȝe and scharpe wiþoute, ȝitte wiþin þei beþ somdele sponged [1495 spounged] and holowȝe.

2. Saturated with moisture like a sponge.

1628 Feltham *Resolves* ii. xii. 31 Who can but thinke what a nastie Beast he is in his drunkennesse,..how like a nated Sop spunged, euen to the cracking of a skinne?

3. Wiped or cleansed with a sponge.

1871 Browning *Pr. Hohenst.* Poet. Wks. 1897 II. 296/1 The old plan saved, instead of a sponged slate And fresh-drawn figure?

Spongeful (spʌ·ndʒful). [f. Sponge *sb.*[1] + -ful 2.] As much as fills a sponge.

1867 Macgregor *Rob Roy on Baltic* 243 We ran the canoe into a mass of tall reeds, to see if she had got any water. There were only three spongefuls. 1871 Napheys *Prev. & Cure Dis.* ii. iv. 537 A spongeful of warm water.

Spo·ngeless, *a.* [-less.] Having no sponge.

1868 Dickens *Uncomm. Trav.* xxv. 149 My sponge being left behind at the last Hotel,..I went spongeless.

Spongelet (spʌ·ndʒlėt). [f. Sponge *sb.*[1] + -let.]

1. *Bot.* = Spongiole 1.

1835 Lindley *Introd. Bot.* (ed. 2) 36 The stigma and the spongelets of the roots. 1841 *Florist's Jrnl.* (1846) II. 210 They will push forth sponglets into the moss. 1870 *Academy* 12 Mar. 155 In the very first phases of vegetation where the primary spongelet..is clearly the absorbent of moisture.

2. A small sponge.

1887 in *Cassell's Encycl. Dict.*

Sponge-like, *a.* [f. Sponge *sb.*[1] + -like.] Like or resembling a sponge: spongy.

1594 T. B. *La Primaud. Fr. Acad.* ii. 49 The matter of Kernels is more Sponge-like. 1642 H. More *Song of Soul* iii. App. xxxix, Wherein they bathe Themselves, and sponge-like suck that vitall flood. 1798 *Hull Advertiser* 1 Sept. 3/3 Plumb-stones had an incrustation attached to them of a spunge-like substance. 1837 P. Keith *Bot. Lex.* 402 The *cutis vera*..is itself chiefly cellular and sponge-like in its structure. 1866 *Treas. Bot.* 513/2 The sponge-like masses in which the capsules of *Polyides* are immersed.

Spongeoid, *a. rare*[−1] [f. Sponge *sb.*[1] + -oid.] = Spongoid *a.* 2.

1822 J. Parkinson *Outl. Oryctol.* 61 The fructiform figures which the spongeoid fossils so frequently possess.

Spongeol, anglicized form of Spongiole.

1832 *Planting* 16 (L.U.K.) III, The fibres of the root, with the minute spongeols. *Ibid.* 32.

Spongeo-piline: see Spongiopiline.

† **Spongeosity**, obs. variant of Spongiosity.

1541 R. Copland *Guydon's Quest. Chirurg.* Ej, This bone is perced and hath great spongeosyte to purge the grosse superfluytees.

Spongeous (spʌ·ndʒəs), *a.* Also 6 **spoungeous**, 6–7 **spungeous.** [ad. L. *spongeōs-us*, f. *spongea* Sponge *sb.*[1] Cf. Spongious *a.*]

1. Of the nature or character of a sponge; porous, spongy.

a. 1398 Trevisa *Barth. De P. R.* xiv. xxxii. (Tollem. MS.), Thouȝe cragges be neuer so harde and rouȝe and scharpe without, ȝit within þey ben sumdel spongeous. 1541 R. Copland *Guydon's Quest. Chirurg.* Eiv, Fro the vaynes and arteres and the spongeous flesshe. 1548–77 Vicary *Anat.* v. (1888) 43 The Uuila is a member made of a spongeous fleshe. 1610 W. Folkingham *Art of Survey* i. viii. 19 A Wood-like rottennesse, viz. drie, spongeous, full of holes. 1698 A. Brand *Emb. fr. Muscovy into China* 21 The Agarius Tree, whose spongeous substance is..carried to Archangel. 1758 J. S. tr. *Le Dran's Observ. Surg.* (1771) 227, I..found a *Caries*..penetrating into their spongeous Texture. 1847 Ansted *Anc. World* x. 233 In the sand associated with the chalk..spongeous bodies..are also met with in a perfect state. 1889 Z. A. Ragozin *Media, Babylon, & Persia* 35 Many are the rivulets..that dribble and trickle through spongeous stone and rocky rifts.

β. 1601 Holland *Pliny* II. 514 It is spungeous and brittle, apt to break or resolue into flakes. 1658 Franck *North. Mem.* (1821) 350 A marly spungeous clay. 1683 K. Digby *Chym. Secr.* 96 To render it more Spungeous. 1728 Chambers *Cycl.* s.v. *Disease*, Spungeous Membranes of the Head.

b. Soft and yielding as a sponge. *rare*[−1].

1607 Brewer *Lingua* iv. iv, I lay my head between two spungeous pillowes.

2. Characterized by porousness or sponginess.

c 1600 T. Pont *Topogr. Acc. Cunningham* (Maitl. Club) 6 The surface of the soyle..being of it selve of a spungeous nature, sucking the humiditie. 1822 J. Parkinson *Outl. Oryctol.* 22 That spongeous state which accompanies bituminization.

Sponger (spʌ·ndʒəɹ). Also 7–9 **spunger.** [f. Sponge *v.* or *sb.*[1] + -er[1].]

1. One who lives meanly at another's expense; a parasite, a sponge.

1677 Miège *Fr. Dict.* i, *Ecornifleur*,..a Spunger, a smell feast. 1681 T. Flatman *Heraclitus Ridens* No. 74 (1713) II. 203 A Detachment of sorry Spungers from the Suburb Shovel-board Tables and Nine-pin Alleys. 1710 Swift *Lett.* (1767) III. 19, I dined with some friends that board hereabout, as a spunger. 1731 Medley *Kolben's Cape G. Hope* I. 109 My company..only listen'd to Spongers, in order to be treated with the other bottle. 1866 *Cornh. Mag.* Sept. 287 Shameless and impudent spungers. 1888 *Pall Mall G.* 3 Sept. 3/2 The spongers for free hospitality at scientific and other annual congresses.

b. Const. *on.*

a 1732 Gay *Fables* ii. viii, Crush'd in his luxury and pride, The spunger on the public dy'd. 1860 Thackeray *Lovel* i, An old sponger on other people's kindness. 1890 *N. Lindsey Star* 9 Aug. 5/3 Those spongers on the nation's earnings are quite happy without work.

2. One who uses a sponge, esp. in order to cleanse the bore of a cannon.

1828–32 Webster, *Spunger*, one who uses a sponge. 1859 Griffiths *Artill. Man.* (1862) 228, 4. The sponger. 5. The loader. 1886 *Cent. Mag.* Apr. 909/1, I was serving on one of the thirty-two pounders, and my sponger was an old man-o'-war's man.

b. One who transfers designs to pottery by means of a piece of sponge.

1881 *Instr. Census Clerks* (1885) 88 Earthenware, China, Porcelain, Manufacture:..Sponger,..Stamper.

3. A gatherer of, a diver or fisher for, sponges.

1880 N. H. Bishop *Sneak-Box* 289 An almost uninhabited region, where only an occasional fisherman or sponger is met. 1887 Goode *Fisheries U.S.* 8.6 To allow the slimy matter, called 'gurry' by the spongers, to run off easily.

b. A vessel engaged in sponge-fishing.

1885 *Harper's Mag.* Jan. 217/1 We cast longing glances at certain Nassau spongers, trim, shapely cock-boats.

Spongi- (spʌ·ndʒi), combining form, after L. types, of Sponge *sb.*[1], occurring in a few terms, as **Spo·ngiculture, Spongi·ferous** *a.*

1833–4 J. Phillips *Geol.* in *Encycl. Metrop.* (1845) VI. 656 Traces of spongiferous bodies. 1876 Page *Adv. Text-bk. Geol.* xviii. 353 The spongiferous cherts of the Portland and coralline oolites. 1902 *Encycl. Brit.* (ed. 10) XXXII. 813/2 Sponges in Commerce, Spongiculture.

Spo·ngiary. *Zool.* [ad. mod.L. *Spongiaria* (pl.), f. L. *spongia* Sponge *sb.*[1]] A sponge.

1860 *Edinb. New Philos. Jrnl.* XII. 223 The spongiaries.., or skeletons, or remains of the sponge after the death and decomposition of the live jelly, or living being. *Ibid.*, A great many spongiaries are not amorphous, but have very distinct forms.

Spongiform (spʌ·ndʒifǫɹm), *a.* [f. Spongi-.]

1. Resembling a sponge in structure; light and porous.

1805–17 R. Jameson *Char. Min.* (ed. 3) 97 *Spongiform*. In this figure the cells are cylindrical. 1841 *Penny Cycl.* XIX. 199/2 Cavernous quartz is termed Spongiform quartz or Swimming stone. 1875 *Encycl. Brit.* III. 251/2 An infinite number of minute cavities, which render the product light and spongiform.

2. Zoologically resembling a sponge.

1839 De la Beche *Rep. Geol. Cornwall*, etc. ix. 264 This view seems borne out by the alcyonic and other spongiform remains. 1876 Page *Adv. Text-bk. Geol.* xv. 280 Of spongiform organisms we may mention mammillopora.

Spo·ngily, *adv.* [f. Spongy *a.*] In a spongy manner.

1882 *Nature* XXV. 363 Increase of storage capacity can be given to corrugated or to spongily and otherwise roughened lead elements.

Spongin (spʌ·ndʒin). [f. Sponge *sb.*[1] + -in.] The horny or fibrous substance found in the skeleton of sponges: = Keratose *sb.*

1868 Watts *Dict. Chem.* V. 404 *Spongin*, Städeler's name for the organic matter of sponge. 1887 Sollas in *Encycl. Brit.* XXII. 416 An axial fibre of organic matter,—probably of the same nature as spongiolin or spongin, the chief constituent of the fibres of horny sponges. 1888 Rolleston & Jackson *Anim. Life* 252 Lamellae of Keratin or Spongin, a substance near akin chemically to silk.

Sponginess (spʌ·ndʒinės). Also 7–8 **spunginess.** [f. Spongy *a.* + -ness.]

1. Spongy or porous character, nature, or quality.

a. 1610 Markham *Masterp.* i. lxiv. 134 It through the sponginesse is apt to sucke in all manner of filth. 1659 H. More *Immort. Soul* ii. ix. 214 The sponginess & laxness of the Brain. 1815 J. Smith *Panorama Sci. & Art* II. 603 In what the soil extracts from the stream by its sponginess. 1836–41 Brande *Chem.* (ed. 5) 512 Animal Charcoal..often has a peculiar lustre and sponginess. 1883 J. Millington *Are we to read backwards?* 76 The paper should be..free from sponginess.

β. 1611 Florio, *Midollo*,..the soft or spunginesse of any thing, as of crummes of bread. 1707 Mortimer *Husbandry* (1721) II. 20 Because of its spunginess the Rain easily penetrates. 1788 *Med. Comm.* II. 209 A spunginess..of the membrane.

b. *fig.* and *transf.*

a 1631 Donne *Serm.* cii. Wks. 1839 IV. 370 For this plurality..of Sin hath first found a Sponginess in the Soule. 1670 Clarendon *Contempl. Ps.* Tracts (1727) 666 We must have all that looseness and spunginess of our hearts removed. 1852 Mundy *Antipodes* (1857) 29 The size and sponginess of the two Sydney butchers.

2. *Path.* The characteristic soft fungous condition of the gums in scurvy.

1873 F. T. Roberts *Handbk. Med.* 824 Sponginess of the gums with tendency to bleed, and rapid destruction of the teeth are frequently noticed. 1897 *Allbutt's Syst. Med.* II. 158 It..frequently begins with a simple sponginess of gums.

Sponging (spʌ·ndʒiŋ), *vbl. sb.* [f. Sponge *v.* or *sb.*[1]]

1. The action of washing or wiping with a sponge.

1575 in Feuillerat *Revels Q. Eliz.* (1908) 254 The Charges of this Office grew by meanes of..Brusshing, Spunging,..putting in order..of the garmentes, Vestures [etc.]. 1593 Nashe *Christ's T.* Wks. (Grosart) IV. 208 To see how you torture poore old Time with spunging, pynning and pounsing. 1704 J. Harris *Lex. Techn.* I, *Spunging* of a great Gun, is clearing of her Inside, after she hath been discharged, with a Wad of Sheep-skins, or the like. 1775 Ash, *Sponging*,..the act of wiping away as with a sponge. 1875 B. Meadows *Clin. Observ.* 65 Prescribed animal diet; regular exercise; cold sponging. 1898 *Allbutt's Syst. Med.* V. 1031 There should be spongings, first with warm and afterwards with cool water.

attrib. 1859 *Habits of Gd. Society* ii. (new ed.) 122 The hip-bath..or the sponging-bath.

2. The action of living parasitically on others.

1677 Miège *Fr. Dict.* i, *Ecornifleries*,..spunging, or feast smelling. 1693 *Humours Town* 37 There are others whose youthful Extravagancies have driven 'em to the wretched fate of Spunging. 1731 Swift *Let. to Gay* 29 June, This will maintain you, with the perquisite of sponging while you are young. 1838 Lockh. in *Life* (1891) I. 300, I have almost given up the Portland plan. It..would look like sponging, in these hard times. 1849 *Knife & Fork* 32 Sponging is a subtle art—so subtle, that few out of its many thousand votaries have attained to any great eminence in it.

attrib. 1707 J. Stevens tr. *Quevedo's Com. Wks.* (1709) 225 Encouraging me to follow the spunging Course of Life.

3. The practice or occupation of gathering sponges. Also *attrib.*

1868 H. D. Grant *Rep. Wrecking in Bahamas* 72 A large number of boats and men are employed in sponging. 1887 Goode *Fisheries U.S.* 823 The Key West sponging-fleet consisted in 1879 of 86 vessels. *Ibid.* 826 When on the sponging-grounds the men breakfast at daylight.

Sponging, *ppl. a.* [f. Sponge *v.* + -ing [2].] That sponges on others; parasitic.

a 1700 B. E. *Dict. Cant. Crew, A Spunging Fellow*, one that lives upon the rest and Pays nothing. 1707 J. Stevens tr. *Quevedo's Com. Wks.* (1709) 353 There is a sort of Spunging, elemosinary Travellers. 1859 Geo. Eliot *A. Bede* iii, To some of my readers Methodism may mean nothing more than..sponging preachers, and hypocritical jargon. 1889 *Times* 7 Oct. 8/3 The daughter of a 'sponging' drunkard.

Sponging-house. Also 7–9 **spunging-.** [f. Sponging *vbl. sb.* (in the sense of Sponge *v.* 8 c).] A house kept by a bailiff or sheriff's officer, formerly in regular use as a place of preliminary confinement for debtors.

a. a 1700 B. E. *Dict. Cant. Crew, Spunging-house*, a By-prison. 1722 De Foe *Moll Flanders* 60 In about two Years and a Quarter he Broke, got into a Spunging-House. 1765 *Ann. Reg.* i. 131 It was again debated by several eminent lawyers, whether spunging-houses were to be deemed prisons, and finally determined in the negative. 1802–12 Bentham *Ration. Judic. Evid.* (1827) IV. 636 In jail, or in a spunging-house, his effects..are as much in his power as if he were at home. 1871 M. Collins *Marq. & Merch.* I. ix. 283 [We] have been in a spunging-house together.

fig. 1827 Hood *Whims & Oddities, Bianca's Dream* xii, In Death's most dreary spunging-house to lie.

β. 1838 Jas. Grant *Sk. Lond.* 21, I have been arrested, and now locked up in a sponging-house for a debt I am wholly unable to pay. 1855 Thackeray *Newcomes* I. 251 He had made himself much liked in the sponging-house. 1874 L. Stephen *Hours in Library* (1892) II. iv. 135 His creditors..become more pressing, and at last he gets into a sponging-house.

Spongio- (spʌ·ndʒio), combining form, on Greek analogies, of Gr. σπογγιά, L. *spongia*,

Sponge *sb.*[1], as in **Spo·ngioblast** *Biol.*, one of the embryonic cells of the brain and spinal cord from which the neuroglia is formed; **Spongio-fi·brous** *a.*, provided with sponge-like fibres; **Spongio·logist, -logy,** = Spongologist, -logy; **Spo·ngioplasm** *Biol.*, a fibrillar or protoplasmic network pervading the cell-substance and forming the reticulum of the cell; hence **Spongiopla·smic** *a.*

1902 *Science* 17 Jan. 103 Mitotic figures are occasionally found in multipolar nerve cells and in *spongioblasts. 1822 J. Parkinson *Outl. Oryctol.* 56 *Alcyonium incrustans.*—Lobated; *spongio-fibrous within. 1873 *Ann. Nat. Hist.* XI. 245 *note*, The later *spongiologists..almost unanimously refer the sponges to a place among the Protozoa. 1892 *Athenæum* 13 Aug. 228/1 The arguments of other spongiologists. 1895 *Funk's Stand. Dict.*, *Spongiology. 1886 Nansen *Histol. Elem. Nervous Syst.* 38 The contents of the cells consists, also, of the same two substances of *spongioplasm and hyaloplasm. *Ibid.* 86 What he called fibrillæ, are the *spongioplasmic walls between the real 'primitive fibrillæ'.

Spo·ngioid, *a.* [f. L. *spongi-a* sponge. Cf. Spongeoid *a.*, Spongoid *a.*] Like that of a sponge.

1884 *Proc. Zool. Soc.* 178 The curious translucent gelatinous substance known as spongioid tissue so eminently characteristic of rickets.

Spongiole (spʌ·ndʒ-, spʌ·ndʒiōul). [a. F. *spongiole* (De Candolle), ad. L. *spongiola* asparagus-root (Columella), rose-gall (Pliny), dim. of *spongia* Sponge *sb.*[1]]

1. *Bot.* The tender extremity of the radicle of a plant, characterized by loose sponge-like cellular tissue: a spongelet.

1832 Lindley *Introd. Bot.* 77 In Pandanus the spongioles of the aerial roots consist of numerous very thin exfoliations of the epidermis. 1850 Daubeny *Atomic The.* viii. (ed. 2) 244 The spongioles of the roots always contain an azotized material, which is from them transmitted to all the other parts of the plant. 1870 tr. *Pouchet's Universe* (1871) 264 The water-lentil, which spreads its carpet of verdure on the surface of our pools, possesses nothing but spongioles.

2. = Sponge *sb.*[1] 6 b. *rare*[−1].

1884 *Evang. Mag.* June 252 There are often seen in rose-bushes, small green mossy-looking tufts called 'spongioles', ..produced by a small insect.

Spongiolin: (see Spongin, quot. 1887).

Spongiopiline (spʌ·ndʒiopəi·ləin, -in). Also **spongio-pilene, -pyline, spongeo-piline.** [f. Spongio- + Gr. πῖλ-os felt + -ine.] (See quot. 1858.)

1851 *Catal. Gt. Exhib.* I. 263 Impermeable Spongio-pilene. 1858 Simmonds *Dict. Trade, Spongiopiline*, a substitute for the ordinary poultice, made of small pieces of sponge and wool or cloth felted together, on an impermeable back. 1862 *Catal. Internat. Exhib., Brit.* II. No. 3578, Electro conducting spongeo-piline. 1876 Harley *Royle's Mat. Med.* 250 Soft linen, or spongiopiline, may be saturated with the warm solution and worn as a poultice.

Spongiose (spʌndʒiōu·s), *a.* [ad. L. *spongiōs-us* spongy, f. *spongia* Sponge *sb.*[1]] Of a spongy texture; porous.

1755 *Dict. Arts & Sci.* IV. s.v., The spongiose or ethmoide bone of the nose. *Ibid.*, The spongiose bodies of the penis. 1826 Kirby & Sp. *Entomol.* IV. xlvi. 259 *Spongiose*...A soft elastic substance resembling sponge. 1859 W. H. Russell in *Times* 24 Mar. 9/4 Mango, peepul, and other spongiose and heartless timbers are of no good.

† **Spongio·sity.** *Obs.* Also -iosite(e. [ad. F. *spongiosité* (14th cent.), ad. med.L. *spongiositas* (13th cent.), f. L. *spongiōsus*: see prec.]

1. Spongy or porous nature; = Sponginess 1.

1543 Traheron *Vigo's Chirurg.* 65 b/1 It is conuenient, to applie a mollifycatiue..playster,..bycause of the Spongiosite of the dugge. 1678 R. Russell tr. *Geber* ii. i. 66 Flowing through the Bowels of the Minera and Spongiosity of the Earth.

2. A sponge-like part.

1543 Traheron *Vigo's Chirurg.* i. iii. 4 Thys bone hathe manye holes and spongiositees whych serve to purge the superfluities of the brayne.

Spongious (spʌ·ndʒiəs), *a.* Now *rare.* Also 5 **spongyouse**, 6 **-yous, -ius, -iouse,** 7–8 **spungious.** [ad. L. *spongiōsus* (see Spongiose *a.*). Cf. F. *spongieux*, † *espongieux*, It. *spugnoso*, Sp. *esponjoso*.]

1. Of the nature of a sponge; spongy.

Very common c 1550–1700.

a. c 1400 *Lanfranc's Cirurg.* 108 Þei [bones] ben sumwhat spongious [v.r. spongyouse] in þe myddis. 1543 Traheron *Vigo's Chirurg.* ii. xv. 60 Uvula (as the Anatomystes say) is a spongyous membre. 1597 Gerarde *Herbal* i. xxiv. 35 They are full stuft with a spongious substance. 1652 French *Yorksh. Spa* vii. 70 The ground..is spongious, and drinks in water apace. 1678 R. Russell tr. *Geber* ii. i. 98 Solid Woods give a strong Fire, spongious a weak. 1709 *Phil. Trans.* XXVII. 121 There are several spongious *Laminæ* which arise from its lower part. 1778 *Ibid.* LXVIII. 672 In the spongious bones of the upper jaw. 1825 *Examiner* 732/2 Soft, fluid, porous, spongious, but withal tenacious matter. 1869 Blackmore *Lorna D.* ii, He came up to me..with a piece of spongious coralline.

β. 1604 E. G[rimstone] *D'Acosta's Hist. Indies* iv. xii. 245 In weight it is diminished five partes of that it was, and is spungious. 1657 Heylin *Ecclesia Vind.* 177 An oake..which was of an hollow or spungious body. 1758 J. S. *Le Dran's Observ. Surg.* (1771) 236 This *Caries* more commonly attacks those Bones that are Spungious.

2. Of or pertaining to a sponge.

1846 *Proc. Berw. Nat. Club* II. 196 Of a..spongious texture. 1851 G. F. Richardson *Geol.* 214 Many of the moss agates are of spongious origin.

Hence † **Spo·ngiousness**, sponginess. *Obs.*

1597 A. M. tr. *Guillemeau's Fr. Chirurg.* 37 b/1 The fleshe in that place is not of such a crassitude and spongiousnes as in the ioyncte. 1611 Cotgr., *Spongiosité*, sounginesse, or spungiousnesse; a spungie lightnesse. 1727 Bailey (vol. II), *Spongiousness*, Spunginess.

Spo·ngite. [a. F. *spongite*: see Sponge *sb.*[1] and -ite[1] 2.] 'A fossil apparently identical in structure with sponge' (*Imp. Dict.* 1882).

Spongo- (spʌŋgo), a. Gr. σπογγο-, combining form of σπόγγος sponge, as in **Spo·ngoblast, -clast** *Biol.* (see quots.); **Spo·ngolith,** a fossil sponge; **Spongo·logist,** an authority on sponges; a spongiologist; **Spongo·logy,** the science or knowledge of sponges; **Spo·ngotype** (see quot.).

1888 Rolleston & Jackson *Anim. Life* 252 The hyaline lamellae [in sponges] are secreted by pear-shaped cells or **spongoblasts*.., which are probably modified connective tissue or mesodermic cells. *Ibid.* 798 *note*, According to von Lendenfeld,..these cells..are destructive in nature,—hence *spongoclasts. 1860 Maury *Phys. Geog. Sea* xiv. § 614 *note*, It would not be strange if these fifty-two forms were *spongoliths. 1883 in Adderley *Fisheries Bahamas* 43 Three distinct..Mediterranean forms are usually recognised, both by the trade and scientific *spongologists. 1889 *Athenæum* 13 July 67/3 No more fascinating branch of natural history exists than the new *spongology. 1892 Herkomer *Etching* 104 A '*Spongotype'. Enough can be seen in this imperfect illustration to gauge the possibilities of the process. It is printed from the untouched (steel-surfaced) electrotype.

Spongoid (spʌ·ŋgoid), *a.* Also **spungoid.** [f. Gr. σπόγγ-os Sponge *sb.*[1] + -oid. Cf. Gr. σπογγοειδής, σπογγώδης, and Spongeoid *a.*]

1. *Spongoid inflammation*, a kind of soft cancer or morbid growth. (Cf. Fungus *sb.* 2.)

1808 *Med. Jrnl.* XIX. 431 A disease totally different from that affection named by them Fungus Hæmatodes, or Spongoid Inflammation. 1834 Cooper *Good's Study Med.* (ed. 4) II. 579 *note*, The medullary sarcoma of Abernethy,..the spongoid inflammation of John Burns, and the soft cancer of several other writers.

2. Having the form or structure of a sponge.

1833–4 J. Phillips *Geol.* in *Encycl. Metrop.* (1845) VI. 659 The abundance of spongoid fossils is a very remarkable character of the English and Westphalian chalk. 1843 *Penny Cycl.* XXVI. 245/1 *Ventriculites*, a genus of spongoid Zoophyta.

3. Resembling that of a sponge.

1847–9 *Todd's Cycl. Anat.* IV. i. 29/2 Its thickness becomes considerably augmented, its texture spungoid.

Spongy (spʌ·ndʒi), *a.* Forms: a. 6–9 **spungy**, 6 **-ye,** 6–7 **-ie.** β. 6–7 **spongie,** 7–9 **spongey,** 7– **spongy.** [f. Sponge *sb.*[1] + -y.]

1. Having a soft elastic or porous texture resembling that of a sponge; deficient in solidity or firmness, so as to be readily compressible: **a.** Of flesh, animal tissue, etc., sometimes with special reference to morbid conditions.

a. 1539 Elyot *Cast. Helthe* 31 b, The tounge is of a spungy & sanguine substance. 1545 Raynald *Byrth Mankynde* 45 Leuing al the grosser part in yᵉ spungye body of the houpecall. 1612 Woodall *Surg. Mate* Wks. (1653) 15 If the disease be a Kinde of spungie flesh. 1695 J. Edwards *Perfect. Script.* 245 The lower part of the ear..is spungy and flexible. 1712 S. Sewall *Diary* 4 Jan., Major Walley's Left foot is opened underneath, and found to be very hollow, and spungy.

fig. a 1628 F. Grevil *Alaham* ii. iii, The spungie hearts of men Their hollowes gladly fill with women's love.

β. 1646 Sir T. Browne *Pseud. Ep.* (1658) 158 It hath in the tongue a spongy and mucous extremity. 1774 Goldsm. *Nat. Hist.* (1776) V. 250 The muscular, spongy flesh of the tongue. 1809 *Med. Jrnl.* XXI. 339 The other parts..were very pulpy, soft, spongy, and broken down. 1843 R. J. Graves *Syst. Clin. Med.* xvi. 192 His mouth became very sore,..his gums spongy. 1898 *Allbutt's Syst. Med.* V. 204 Islets of spongy tissue separate the individual nodules.

b. Of parts of plants, timber, etc.

a. 1589 *Pappe w. Hatchet* C iv, Elders..being fullest of spungie pith, proue euer the driest kixes. 1613 Purchas *Pilgrimage* (1614) 506 The wood is of a spungie substance. 1710 Whitworth *Acc. Russia* (1758) 135 Timber..cut in the spring after the sap is run up, which makes the wood spungy. 1769 E. Bancroft *Guiana* 47 Their internal substance is white, spungy, and saponaceous. 1807 Crabbe *Birth Flattery* 301 Where spungy rushes hide the plashy green.

β. 1578 Lyte *Dodoens* 181 The roote is white and of a spongie substance. 1671 Grew *Anat. Pl.* (1682) 47 This Inner Coat..is a very Spongy and Sappy body. 1784 Cowper *Task* iii. 522 Then rise the tender germs, upstarting quick, And spreading wide their spongy lobes. 1842 Loudon *Suburban Hort.* 182 The shoots there are generally more luxuriant and spongy. 1860 Ruskin *Mod. Paint.* V. vi. vi. § 4. 43 A root [of a tree], properly so called, is a fibre, spongy or absorbent at the extremity. 1884 Bower & Scott *De Bary's Phaner.* 410 Lamellar cavernous parenchyma.., which from this spongy character has also been called 'spongy parenchyma'.

c. Of ground or soil, esp. through excess of moisture.

a. 1652 Earl Monm. tr. *Bentivoglio's Hist. Relat.* 10 The scituation of all the other Provinces is low and spungie. 1677 *Lond. Gaz.* No. 1224/3 The ground about the place being very spungy in wet weather. 1708 J. C. *Compl. Collier* (1845) 25 It must of necessity rise through the Spungy Earth. 1799 *Scotland Descr.* (ed. 2) 16 The morasses, of which the soil is either a spungy turf, or a black consistent peat-earth. c 1853 Kingsley *Misc.* (1859) I. 151 The soft tread of..horse-hoofs upon the spungy vegetable soil.

β. 1732 *Ray's Disc.* (ed. 4) 12 A spongey kind of Earth. 1796 Withering *Brit. Plants* (ed. 3) III. 793 Rotten spongy ground. 1818 Shelley *Marenghi* xxiv, The coarse bulbs of iris-flowers he found Knotted in clumps under the spongy ground. 1844 H. Stephens *Bk. Farm* I. 507 Where clay is..very spongy, tough, and wet. 1889 F. Cowper *Capt. of Wight* 259 There is not a hole or a spongy place anywhere.

d. In miscellaneous applications.

1616 Surfl. & Markh. *Country Farme* v. xx. 577 Neither must it [manchet bread] be made too light or spungie. 1672 Petty *Pol. Anat.* 375 The art of making the excellent, thick, spungy, warm coverlets, seems to be lost. 1713 Gay *Rur. Sports* 135 When floating Clouds their spongy Fleeces drain. 1716 — *Trivia* i. 45 The Frieze's Spongy Nap is soaked with Rain. 1753 Hanway *Trav.* v. lxix. (1762) I. 314 Their cloths are spungy, but they are thin, light, and soft. 1834 *Brit. Husb.* I. 340 The ashes..produced from soft soap..will be found light and spongy. 1836–41 Brande *Chem.* (ed. 5) 109 The rising of fluids in porous and spongy bodies.

2. Of hard substances: Having an open porous structure resembling that of a sponge: **a.** Of bones, *spec.* of certain bones of the skull.

1591 Sylvester *Du Bartas* i. vi. 573 Whereby the moist Brain's spongy boan doth sup Sweet-smelling fumes. 1594 T. B. *La Primaud. Fr. Acad.* ii. 123 It is called by the phisicions the siue-bone, or otherwise (& that more properly) the spungy bone. 1607 Topsell *Four-f. Beasts* 401 A Splent is a spungy harde grissell or bone, growing fast on the inside of the shin-bone of a Horse. 1753 *Chambers' Cycl. Suppl.* s.v. *Bone*, Bones..which have thin solid sides, and a thick intermediate spongy part. 1854 Owen in *Orr's Circ. Sci., Org. Nat.* I. 166 Most of the bones of fishes are solid or spongy in their interior. 1876 *Quain's Anat.* (ed. 8) I. 53 The inferior turbinated, *maxillo-turbinal*, or spongy bone, is a slender lamina, attached [etc.].

b. Of stone, ice, minerals, etc.

1615 G. Sandys *Trav.* 22 The walls..consisting of great square stone, hard, blacke, and spongie. 1694 *Marten's Voy. Spitzbergen* in *Acc. Sev. Voy.* II. 44 This Ice becometh very spungy by the dashing of the Sea. 1796 Kirwan *Elem. Min.* (ed. 2) I. 13 When it [silex] is exceedingly comminuted, ..it is light and spungy. 1800 tr. *Lagrange's Chem.* I. 333 Hence those tender calcareous, cellular stones, and perhaps also the spungy tufs. 1834 L. Ritchie *Wand. by Seine* 74 Such stones as were most spungy and defective, and, of course, most easily cut. 1856 Kane *Arct. Expl.* II. xxiii. 231 The falling of some of the party through the spongy ice.

c. Of metals, esp. platinum.

1807 T. Thomson *Chem.* (ed. 3) II. 64 Spongy alumina, when exposed to a red heat, loses 0·58 parts of its weight. 1827 Faraday *Chem. Manip.* xiv. (1842) 314 Spongy platina ..causes the union of oxygen and oxide of carbon at common temperatures. 1849 D. Campbell *Inorg. Chem.* 246 [This] leaves the metal, in a highly divided state, as a greyish-black powder, and known as spongy platinum. 1884 Knight *Dict. Mech.* Suppl. 845/2 The production of spongy platinum..is a task more easy in appearance than in reality.

3. a. Resembling a sponge in respect of moisture or capacity for containing this.

1598 Sylvester *Du Bartas* ii. i. iv. *Handicrafts* 759 With th' other hand he gripes and wringeth forth The spungy Globe of th' execrable Earth. 1602 Marston *Ant. & Mel.* iv, Even this brinish marsh Shall squeaze out teares from out his spungy cheekes. 1611 Shaks. *Cymb.* iv. ii. 349, I saw ..the Roman Eagle wing'd From the spungy South, to this part of the West. 1659 S. Titus *Killing no Murder* 5 Had not his Highnes had a faculty to be fluent in his teares..: Had he not had spungie eyes [etc.]. 1872 *Echo* 10 Aug., After plenty of rain, with leaden water and a dismal, spongy look everywhere.

fig. 1599 B. Jonson *Ev. Man out of Hum.* Prol., With a gripe, [to] Crush out the humour of such spongie sooles. 1611 Cotgr. s.v. *Mer*, When Princes doe squeeze out of their spungie Officers the moisture which they haue purloyned from them.

b. Resembling a sponge in absorptive qualities; absorbent. Chiefly *fig.*

1605 Shaks. *Macb.* i. vii. 71 What [can we] not put vpon His spungie Officers? 1606 — *Tr. & Cr.* ii. ii. 12 There is no Lady..More spungie, to sucke in the sense of Feare. 1697 Dryden *Virg. Georg.* i. 438 Oft whole sheets descend of slucy Rain, Suck'd by the spongy Clouds from off the Main.

c. Of the nature or character of a sponger or parasite; = Sponging *ppl. a.*

1602 Marston *Ant. & Mel.* iv, Blowne up with the flattering puffes Of spungy sycophants.

4. *fig.* Deficient in substance or solidity.

1603 Florio *Montaigne* iii. v. 524 The wordes: no longer windie or spungie, but of fleshe and bone. 1665 J. Webb *Stone-Heng* (1725) 82 To set a petty Gloss upon a spungy Conjecture. 1680 H. More *Apocal. Apoc.* 273 R. H. in his answer..is plainly not so much copious as loose and spungy, and not at all solid. 1829 Best *Pers. & Lit. Mem.* 171 The puffy, spungy,..washy, style that prevails at the present day. 1896 *St. James's Gaz.* 6 Jan. 4/2 Mr. Olney's English is, as usual, rather spongy.

5. Of texture or other qualities: Resembling that of a sponge.

1611 Cotgr., *Spongiosité*,..a spungie lightnesse. 1633 P. Fletcher *Purple Isl.* iv. xxvii, [The lungs] Built of a lighter frame, and spungie mold. 1733 W. Ellis *Chiltern & Vale Farm.* 84 Hollow, spungy Texture of Parts. 1765 A. Dickson *Treat. Agric.* (ed. 2) 69 The soil may be of a spungy nature. 1800 *Med. Jrnl.* III. 199 The sore had an ugly, spungy aspect. 1827 Faraday *Chem. Manip.* xiv. (1842) 315 The platina in the spongy state. 1860 Tyndall *Glac.* ii. xxvi. 372 The ice on which the dirt-bands rest..appears to be of a spongier character.

fig. 1865 Geo. Eliot *Ess.* (1884) 202 A spongy texture of mind that gravitates strongly to nothing.

6. Resembling that pressed from a sponge.

1605 G. Ellis *Lament. Lost Sheep* lxxvii, That spungy moysture, that in deadly thrall For thy pale lips the sonnes of men thought meete. a 1864 Hawthorne *Amer. Note-bks.* (1879) II. 191 With a spongy moisture diffused through the atmosphere.

7. *Comb.*, as *spongy-flowered, -footed, -looking, -wet, -wooded* adjs.

1825 *Greenhouse Comp.* II. 26 A spongy-wooded greenhouse shrub. 1829 Loudon *Encycl. Plants* (1836) 600 *Adlumia cirrhosa*; spongy-flower'd. 1835 Willis *Pencillings* II. lv. 130 The small donkey..pricking back his long ears as if he were counting his spongy-footed followers. 1855 Tennyson *To Rev. F. D. Maurice* xi, The lawn as yet Is hoar with rime, or spongy-wet. 1870 H. A. Nicholson *Man. Zool.* xiv. (1875) 143 It forms spongy-looking, orange-coloured crusts.

Sponk, obs. form of Spunk.

† **Spon-new,** *a. Obs. rare.* [Southern form of Span-new *a.*] Perfectly new.

13.. *K. Alis.* 4055 Richeliche he dob him schrede, In spon neowe knytis wede. a 1400 *Minor Poems fr. Vernon MS.* 75/386 Heil whos sone has wrouht Al vr hele sponnewe.

Sponsal (spǫ·nsăl), *a.* [ad. L. *sponsāl-is*, f. *sponsus, -a*, spouse.] Of or pertaining to marriage: spousal; wedded, wedding.

1656 Blount *Glossogr.*, *Sponsal*, belonging to betrothing or marriage. [Hence in Bailey, etc.] 1840 *Penny Cycl.* XVIII. 197/1 A vase, executed for her majesty, as a sponsal present by her. 1866 J. B. Rose tr. *Ovid's Fasti* ii. 595 O maidens fair, Choose not a sponsal day. *Ibid.* iv. 1097 Tithonia thrice must leave the sponsal bed.

Sponsalia (spǫnsē¹·liă). [L., neut. pl. of *sponsālis*: see prec.] Espousals, marriage.

1535 Stewart *Cron. Scot.* III. 390 That quietlie..Betuix thame seiffis *sponsalia* tha maid, Syne in his place ressauit hir as wyfe. 178. R. Watson *Chem. Ess.* V. 376 (Jod.), An order, equally determined, is observable in the times of accomplishing the sponsalia of plants.

† **Sponsali·tious,** *a. Obs.*[−0] [ad. late L. *sponsālitius, -ĭcius*, f. *sponsālia*: see prec.] = Sponsal *a.*

1656 in Blount *Glossogr.*

Sponsibi·lity. *rare*[−1]. [f. next: see -ity.] Responsibility, respectability.

1767 Cowper *Let. to Mrs. C.* 3 Apr., Though my friend,.. before I was admitted an inmate here, was satisfied that I was not a mere vagabond, and has since that time received more convincing proofs of my sponsibility, yet [etc.].

Sponsible (spǫ·nsib'l), *a.* Now only *dial.* [Aphetic f. Responsible *a.*: cf. next.] Responsible, reliable, respectable.

1721 Wodrow *Hist. Suff. Ch. Scot.* (1830) III. 439/1 Till caution was found, by two sponsible persons, [that] she should present herself to the sheriff when called. 1765 Cowper *Let.* 3 July, My woollen-draper, a very healthy, wealthy, sensible, sponsible man. 1810 S. Green *Reformist* I. 120 'My Lord,' replied the creditor, 'I am an honest, sponsible shoemaker.' 1836–8 Haliburton *Clockm.* Ser. ii. xxii. (1839) 276 But John Bull is like all other sponsible folks; he thinks 'cause he is rich he is wise too. 1856 G. Henderson *Pop. Rhymes* 97 One of the decent neighbours, and most sponsible man in the company.

Sponsion (spǫ·nʃən). [ad. L. *sponsio*, noun of action f. *spondēre* to promise solemnly, give assurance, etc.]

1. A solemn or formal engagement, promise, or pledge, freq. one entered into or made on behalf of another person.

1677 Owen *Justif.* vii. Wks. 1850 III. 170 The apostle interposeth himself by a voluntary sponsion to undertake for Onesimus. 1692 Burnet *Disc. Pastoral Care* vi. 54 No Church before ours..took a formal Sponsion at the Altar from such as were ordained Deacons and Priests. 1709 Strype *Ann. Ref.* I. xxxiv. 345 Because in the Initiation of Baptism we stuck not to the Abrenuntiations and Sponsions made for us. 1737 Waterland *Eucharist* 16 A kind of Sponsion and Security for the present and future Performance of the whole Duty of Man. 1801 Napleton *Advice Minister Gosp.* 35 This is a great and weighty sponsion. 1850 R. D. Hampden *Charge Visit. Diocese Heref.* 39 Many children have not been baptized in the Church—have never had those sponsions made for them, which the instructions of the Church Catechism presuppose.

b. *spec.* (See quot. 1853.)

1776 in Sparks *Corr. Amer. Rev.* (1853) I. 258 The agreement entered into by Gen. Arnold was a mere sponsion on his part, he not being invested with powers for the disposal of prisoners not in his possession. 1853 Whewell *Grotius* II. 130 *Sponsions* is the term we may use when any persons not having a commission from the Supreme Authority make any engagement which properly touches that authority.

2. *Rom. Law.* An engagement to pay a certain sum to the other party in a suit, in the event of not proving one's case.

1632 Sanderson *Serm.* 207 The Defendant also making the like sponsion and entring the like bond, in case he should be cast. 1880 Muirhead *Gaius* iv. § 13 In the same way as..the action for a definite sum of money due is perilous for a defender rashly denying his liability, on account of his sponsion.

Hence † **Spo·nsional** *a.*, entering into an engagement or pledge. *Obs.*

a 1684 Leighton *Serm.* Wks. (1859) 526 It is evident that he is righteous, even in that representative and sponsional person he put on.

Sponson (spǫ·nsən), *sb.* Also 9 **sponsing, sponcing.** [Of obscure origin.]

1. One or other of the triangular platforms before and abaft the paddle-boxes of a steamer.

a. 1835 *Naut. Mag.* IV. 154 The 'Lightning' was ran into by a collier, which struck her just abaft her paddle-box... Her sponcings and sponcing-timbers were broken. 1846 A. Young *Naut. Dict.* 292 *Sponsings*, or *Sponcings*, in a steam-ship, the curve of the timbers and planking towards the outer part of the wing before and abaft each of the paddle-boxes.

β. 1838 *Civil Eng. & Arch. Jrnl.* I. 384/2 Breadth over the sponsons, 43 ft. Ditto over the paddle boxes, 48 ft. 1871 Kingsley *At Last* i, Then had come..a day of..watching..the water from the sponson behind the paddle-boxes.

attrib. 1835 [see above]. 1867 Smyth *Sailor's Word-bk.* 644 *Sponson-Rim*, the same as *wing-wale*. 1875 Knight *Dict. Mech.* 2287 *Sponson-beam*, one of the two projecting beams uniting the paddle-box beam with the ship's side.

2. A gun platform, standing out from the side of a vessel. Also *attrib.*

1862 W. H. Russell *Diary North & S.* I. 291 The ship.. is armed..with rifled field-pieces and howitzers on the sponsons. 1887 *Daily News* 24 Oct. 5/5 The system..of carrying heavy guns..in sponson ports so high on the poop and forecastle. 1897 *Ibid.* 28 July 8/5 Their construction (five sponsons on each side of the upper deck) causes them to roll heavily.

Hence **Spo·nson** *v. trans.*, to support, or set *out*, on a sponson. Also **Spo·nsoned** *ppl. a.*

1895 *Morn. Post* 10 Aug. 4/5 The same may be said of cruisers, part of whose most important armament is sponsoned out on the broadside. 1897 *River & Coast* 4 Sept. 13/1 The sponsoned deck acts as a guard to the hull.

Sponsor (spǫ·nsǫɹ), *sb.* [a. L. *sponsor*, agent-noun f. *spondēre*: cf. Sponsion.]

1. *Eccl.* One who answers for an infant at baptism; a godfather or godmother.

1651 Baxter *Inf. Bapt.* 153 How could the Sponsors be indangered while there were Parents? a 1700 Evelyn *Diary* 6 Oct. 1687, I was godfather to Sir John Chardin's sonn...The Earle of Bath and Countesse of Carlisle, the other Sponsors. 1737 *Gentl. Mag.* VII. 21/1 It is well known, that the Business of Sponsors at Baptism is in general brought to a very scandalous Pass. 1807 Crabbe *Par. Reg.* iii. 959 Here, with an infant, joyful sponsors come. 1850 R. I. Wilberforce *Holy Baptism* 103 The practice of requiring sponsors at Baptism is of ancient date. 1907 *Verney Mem.* II. 237 When her daughter was born nothing would satisfy Lady Abdy but that Sir Ralph should stand sponsor.

fig. 1848 Thackeray *Van. Fair* xxiii, His Lordship.. was a credit to his political sponsor.

2. One who enters into an engagement, makes a formal promise or pledge, on behalf of another; a surety.

1677 Miège *Fr. Dict.* ii, Sponsor, or surety that undertaketh for another. 1681 J. Scott *Chr. Life* i. iv. (1684) 207 Our Mediator is called the *Sponsor*, or Surety of a better Covenant. 1741 C. Middleton *Cicero* viii. II. 197 Magius, oppressed with debts,..had been urging Marcellus, who was his sponsor for some part of them, to furnish him with money to pay the whole. 1800 *Asiat. Ann. Reg.* V. 58/1 Sponsors also are of two kinds, one for appearance, the other for payment. 1864 D. G. Mitchell *Sev. Stor.* 107, I found it requisite..to become sponsor for his good conduct. 1880 Muirhead *Gaius* iii. § 118 The positions of sponsor and fidepromissor are much the same. *Ibid.* Dig. 535 All.. who failed..to relieve sponsors (sureties) who had paid for them.

b. One who stood surety for the appearance and good faith of either party in a trial by combat.

1825 Scott *Talism.* xxviii, The sponsors of both champions went, as was their duty, to see that they were duly armed, and prepared for combat. *Ibid.*, The sponsors, heralds, and squires now retired to the barriers.

3. *transf.* Of things (after sense 1 or 2).

1846 Landor *Hellenics* Wks. II. 486 We are what suns and winds and waters make us; The mountains are our sponsors. 1870 Emerson *Soc. & Solit.* Wks. (Bohn) III. 134 All the good days behind him are sponsors, who speak for him. 1889 Gretton *Memory's Harkback* 233 In Essex, especially, the aguish climate stood sponsor for the absence of clerics as a rule.

Spo·nsor, *v.* [f. prec.] *trans.* To be surety for, to favour or support strongly. (Common in recent use.)

1884 *L'pool Mercury* 6 June 5/8 The eldest daughter, who has ever sponsored her father's cause. 1888 *Standard* 24 Feb. 5/1 The Company is to be most powerfully sponsored.

Spo·nsoress. [f. Sponsor *sb.* + -ess.] A female sponsor.

1871 G. A. Lawrence *Anteros* xxi, Lady Montfort, another relative,..offered to be the bride's sponsoress at St. James'.

Sponsorial (spǫnsō³·riăl), *sb.* and *a.* [f. Sponsor: see -orial.]

A. *sb.* A baptismal sponsor or name-father.

1836 Marryat *Pirate* vii, You will now on the coast meet with a Blucher, a Wellington, a Nelson, &c., who will wring swabs..without feeling that it is discreditable to sponsorials so grand.

B. *adj.* Of or pertaining to a sponsor.

1847 in Webster. 1853 *Chr. Rememb.* No. 79. 62 The clause just quoted of the sponsorial exhortation. 1862 Wilberforce in Hopkins *Hawaii* Pref., She..sends out sponsorial gifts befitting England's Queen. 1897 *Daily News* 12 May 4/4 He would rather regard the former in their sponsorial function.

Sponsorship (spǫ·nsǫɹʃip). [f. Sponsor *sb.* + -ship.] The state of being a sponsor; the office of a sponsor.

1809 Malkin *Gil Blas* xi. i, The governor's lady, wishing to draw the bonds of sponsorship still closer in this friendly party, stood for Scipio's daughter. 1848 Kingsley *Saint's Trag.* ii. v, It knits them unto me, and me to them, That bond of sponsorship. 1895 *Daily News* 16 Feb. 2/4 To undertake the sponsorship of a resolution which asks the House to put aside this measure.

† **Spo·ntal,** *a. Obs.*[−0] [ad. L. *spontāl-is.*] (See quot.) Also † **Spo·ntane** *a. Obs.*[−0] (Cf. next.)

1656 Blount *Glossogr.*, *Spontal, Spontane*,..that doth or is done willingly, naturally, without help or constraint, voluntary.

† **Spontaneal,** *a. Obs.* [f. L. *spontāne-us* + -al.] Spontaneous, in various senses.

1602 Fulbecke *1st Pt. Parall.* 58 But curtesie is a free, spontaneal and ingenious quality, to which no inforcement can be used. 1653 R. G. tr. *Bacon's Hist. Winds* 361 Let the seventeenth Motion be the Spontaneall or Willing Motion of Rotation or wheeling. 1669 W. Simpson *Hydrol. Chym.* 82 The occasional and spontaneal depravations of their ferments.

Spontaneity (spǫntănī·iti). [ad. L. type **spontāneitas*, f. *spontāne-us*. So F. *spontanéité*, It. *spontaneità*, Sp. *espontaneidad*, Pg. *-idade*.]

1. Spontaneous, or voluntary and unconstrained, action on the part of persons; the fact of possessing this character or quality.

1651 C. Cartwright *Cert. Relig.* i. 181 Thus we see how Bernard doth agree with Calvin in making the freedome of mans will to consist in a spontaneity, and a freedom from coaction. 1681 Flavel *Meth. Grace* xxix. 504 He laid down his life with the greatest chearfulness and spontaneity that could be. 1702 tr. *Le Clerc's Prim. Fathers* 348 Freedom, in his Opinion, is only a meer Spontaneity, and doth not imply a Power of not doing what one doth. 1789 Belsham *Ess.* I. ix. 171 Physical liberty; by which he means the principle of spontaneity. 1804–6 Syd. Smith *Mor. Philos.* xvii. (1850) 251 Actions performed without the spontaneity of the agent, are automatic. 1851 Carlyle *Sterling* iii. vii, The general aspect of him indicated freedom, perfect spontaneity, with a certain careless natural grace. 1899 *Allbutt's Syst. Med.* VIII. 302 There is less energy and less spontaneity and originality.

2. Spontaneous or voluntary action or movement on the part of animals (or plants); activity of physical organs in the absence of any obvious external stimulus.

1721 J. Clarke *Orig. Mor. Evil* 113 Because they [animals] have not the Power of abstract Reasoning..we call it generally Spontaneity. 1789 E. Darwin *Bot. Gard.* ii. (1791) 153 See note on Collinsonia for other instances of vegetable spontaneity. 1793 Cowper *Let.* 23 Feb., Considering more nearly, I found it [a minnow] alive, and endued with spontaneity. 1837 P. Keith *Bot. Lex.* 340 We regard the term Spontaneity as being less exceptionable than that of Instinct; but still it is a spontaneity that feeling has nothing to do with. 1866 J. Martineau *Ess.* I. 168 The instincts and spontaneities of animals. 1877 M. Foster *Physiol.* iii. v. (1878) 472 How absolutely devoid of spontaneity or irregular automatism is the spinal cord of the frog.

3. The fact or quality in things of being spontaneous in respect of production, occurrence, etc.

1751 Johnson *Rambler* No. 131 ¶ 12 Community of possession must include spontaneity of production. 1794 Mrs. Piozzi *Synon.* II. 361 We cannot commend the opulence of the ground, but its richness and spontaneity. 1833 Chalmers *Serm.* I. 129 Every constitutional desire would run out in the unchecked spontaneity of its own movements. 1899 *Allbutt's Syst. Med.* VI. 546 The most conspicuous feature of these [tabetic] fractures is their spontaneity.

b. The fact or quality of coming without deep thought or premeditation.

1826 J. Gilchrist *Lect.* 35 *note*, Many remarks..to which we had given some credit for originality and spontaneity. 1839 Hallam *Hist. Lit.* iii. v. § 7 Poets who, delighted with the spontaneity of their ideas, never reject any that arise. 1873 Symonds *Grk. Poets* i. 2 Those poems of nascent nations,..marvellous in their infantine spontaneity.

Spontaneous (spǫntē¹·nīəs), *a.* [f. L. *spontāne-us*, f. *sponte* of one's own accord, freely, willingly. So F. *spontané(e*, It. *spontaneo*, Sp. and Pg. *espontaneo*.]

1. Of personal actions: Arising or proceeding entirely from natural impulse, without any external stimulus or constraint; voluntary and of one's own accord.

1656 Hobbes *Liberty*, etc. (1841) 79 That all voluntary actions, where the thing that induceth the will is not fear, are called also spontaneous, and said to be done by a man's own accord. 1690 C. Nesse *Hist. & Myst. Test.* I. 43 Her eating therefore was a spontaneous act. 1727 De Foe *Hist. Appar.* i. (1840) 16 By apparition also I am to understand such appearances of these superior beings, as are spontaneous and voluntary. 1781 J. Moore *View Soc. It.* (1790) I. ix. 91 The spontaneous respect paid to the antiquity of their families. 1839 Hallam *Hist. Lit.* ii. i. § 29 The resemblance of natural disposition made it a spontaneous act of Muretus to fall into the footsteps of Cicero. 1868 M. Pattison *Academ. Org.* 6 The movement was by no means a spontaneous one on the part of the House.

b. Of persons: Acting voluntarily and from natural prompting.

1732 Berkeley *Alciphr.* ii. § 21 It was needless to establish professors..while there are so many spontaneous lecturers in every corner of the streets. 1829 I. Taylor *Enthus.* iv. 79 The ranks of a numerous body of men can never be filled up by spontaneous labourers of this sort.

c. Of utterances, etc.: Coming freely and without premeditation or effort.

1856 *N. Brit. Rev.* XXVI. 52 The privileged visitor..would ..have heard from him..similar spontaneous expositions of Scripture. 1870 Burton *Hist. Scot.* lxxii. (1873) VI. 265 A spontaneous thought which he could not help uttering. 1885 *Manch. Exam.* 9 Sept. 3/1 The fun is never strained or beaten out, but is always fresh, spontaneous, and luxuriant.

2. Of motion: Arising purely from, entirely determined by, the internal operative or directive forces of the organism.

1659 H. More *Immort. Soul* ii. ii. 126 Sense..must likewise Imagine, Remember, Reason, and be the fountain of spontaneous Motion. 1695 J. Edwards *Perfect. Script.* 334 Things that had sense and spontaneous motion. 1750 G. Hughes *Barbados* iii. 61 Animals are sensitive organic Bodies, endued with spontaneous Motion. 1807 J. E. Smith

Phys. Bot. 2 Vegetables..have in some instances spontaneous, though we know not that they have voluntary, motion. 1848 Carpenter *Anim. Phys.* 17 These two functions,—sensibility and the power of spontaneous motion,—being peculiar to animals, are called the functions of animal life. 1880 Bessey *Botany* 106 Living protoplasm has everywhere, under proper conditions, the power of spontaneous movement. 1882 Vines tr. *Sachs' Bot.* 871 These movements were termed 'spontaneous nutations'.

3. Of natural processes: Occurring without apparent external cause; having a self-contained cause or origin.

In 19th cent. use esp. of chemical or physical changes: see quots. under (*b*).

(*a*) 1664 Power *Exp. Philos.* ii. 117 The Spontaneous Dilatation and Elastick Rarefaction of that little remnant of Ayr. 1692 Bentley *Boyle Lect.* iv. 114 A spontaneous production of Mankind may not possibly have been true. 1751 Johnson *Rambler* No. 163 ¶ 3 He expects every moment to be placed in regions of spontaneous fertility. 1765 *Museum Rust.* IV. 200, I suppose there was no corn on it of spontaneous growth. 1831 Scott *Cast. Dang.* v, The old man looked with horror at the spontaneous motion of the book. 1859 Mill *Liberty* iv. (1865) 45/2 He suffers these penalties only in so far as they are..the spontaneous consequences of the faults themselves. 1860 Tyndall *Glac.* ii. 292 The spontaneous falling of the stones appeared more frequent this morning.

(*b*) 1805 Saunders *Min. Waters* 338 The spontaneous changes which this water undergoes. 1813 J. Thomson *Lect. Inflam.* 51 When inflammation occurs..without our being able to trace its production to the action of any obvious cause, it is termed spontaneous inflammation. 1836–41 Brande *Chem.* (ed. 5) 561 The aqueous solution..is subject to spontaneous decomposition. 1861 J. R. Greene *Man. Anim. Kingd., Cœlent.* 182 The mode in which spontaneous fission occurs among many other forms of *Actinozoa*.

† **b.** *spec.* Of lassitude. *Obs.*

1675 Owen *Indwelling Sin* ix. (1732) 105 A spontaneous Lassitude, or a causeless Weariness and Indisposition of the Body. 1732 Arbuthnot *Rules of Diet* in *Aliments*, etc. 378 Its Symptoms are a spontaneous Lassitude or Sensation of Weariness.

4. a. *Spontaneous generation*, the development of living organisms without the agency of preexisting living matter, usually considered as resulting from changes taking place in some inorganic substance. (Cf. Equivocal *a.* 3.)

The possibility of such development, once generally accepted as a fact and subsequently rejected, has been a subject of debate in more recent times.

1656 Cowley *Pindar. Odes, Notes* Wks. 1710 I. 278 The Generation of Serpents, which is Spontaneous sometimes. 1665 Hooke *Microgr.* 141 For the Sea..affords as many Instances of spontaneous generations as either the Air or Earth. 1728 Chambers *Cycl.* s.v. *Equivocation*, Equivocal Generation,..which we also call spontaneous, was commonly asserted and believed among the antient Philosophers. 1835 J. Duncan *Beetles* 194 Admitting the doctrine of spontaneous generation, it was necessary [etc.]. 1857 Henfrey *Bot.* 543 The idea of a spontaneous generation of organic bodies is now exploded. 1882 Vines tr. *Sachs' Bot.* 944 The first and simplest plants had no ancestors; they arose by spontaneous generation.

fig. 1870 Max Müller *Sci. Relig.* (1873) 377 You see the spontaneous generation of mythology with every new name that is formed.

b. *Spontaneous combustion*, the fact of taking fire, or burning away, through conditions produced within the substance itself; *spec.* the alleged occurrence of this fact in persons addicted to the excessive use of alcohol.

(*a*) 1809 *W. Nicholson's Jrnl. Nat. Philos.* XXIII. 278 The spontaneous combustion of a large quantity of charcoal. 1863 Watts *Dict. Chem.* I. 1093 The spontaneous combustion..of masses of tow, cotton, or rags saturated with oil. 1876 Voyle & Stevenson *Milit. Dict.* 397/1 New-burnt charcoal, and particularly new ground charcoal, is very liable to spontaneous combustion.

(*b*) 1795 *Repertory of Arts* II. 424, I shall not pass over in silence the spontaneous combustions of human bodies. 1799 *W. Nicholson's Jrnl. Nat. Philos.* III. 305 The apparently spontaneous Combustion of living Individuals of the human Species. 1832 Brewster *Natural Magic* xiii. 321 The extraordinary phenomenon of the spontaneous combustion of living bodies. 1853 Dickens *Bleak Ho.* Pref., It was shewn upon the evidence that she had died the death to which this name of spontaneous combustion has been given. 1882 *Syd. Soc. Lex.* s.v. *Combustion, Spontaneous combustion*...In most of the cases recorded,..either they have been near a fire, or some suspicious circumstances suggestive of murder have been present.

5. Growing or produced naturally without cultivation or labour.

1665 Hooke *Microgr.* 214 Spontaneous Vegetables seeming a food proper enough for spontaneous Animals. 1684 Penn in *Academy* (1896) 11 Jan. 37/1, I have observed three sorts [of vines]...Thes are spontaneous. 1705 R. Beverly *Virginia* ii. iv. (1722) 127 Whence they had their Indian Corn, I can give no Account; for I don't believe that it was spontaneous in those Parts. 1725 Pope *Odyss.* ix. 125 Spontaneous wines from weighty clusters pour. 1760–2 Goldsm. *Cit. W.* xxxi, Spontaneous flowers take place of the finished parterre. 1805 Saunders *Min. Waters* 333 Except the turf, and some scanty heath, no spontaneous vegetation is to be seen. 1837 Ht. Martineau *Soc. Amer.* II. 49 We passed 'a spontaneous rye-field'. 1883 Day *Indian Fish* 8 Fish cured with salt-earth, or spontaneous but untaxed salt.

b. Freq. with *fruits, products, productions*.

a 1727 Newton *Chronol. Amended* i. (1728) 183 These several colonies..fed on the spontaneous fruits of the earth. 1751 Johnson *Rambler* No. 169 ¶ 4 There are regions of which the spontaneous products cannot be equalled in other soils by care and culture. 1826 Syd. Smith *Wks.* (1859) II. 67/2 If the English were in a paradise of spontaneous productions, they would continue to dig and plough. 1839 Hallam *Hist. Lit.* iii. iv. § 96 When men lived on the spontaneous fruits of the earth. 1872 Morley *Voltaire* 6 The self-raised spontaneous products of some miraculous soil.

c. Produced, developed, coming into existence, by natural processes or changes.

1732 Arbuthnot *Rules of Diet* in *Aliments*, etc. 290 Constitutions abounding with a spontaneous alkali, ought to avoid alkaline Substances. 1779 *Encycl. Brit.* (ed. 2) IV. 2671/2 Mr. Wilcke..distinguishes it by the name of spontaneous electricity. 1826 *Art of Brewing* (ed. 2) 28 Leaving a portion of matter unattenuated, to produce briskness, and, consequently, spontaneous fineness and flavour. 1846 G. E. Day tr. *Simon's Anim. Chem.* II. 249 The urine which threw down a spontaneous sediment. 1862 Marsh *Eng. Lang.* iii. 59 All the gorgeous spontaneous hues of sun-lit cloud.

6. Quasi-*adv.* = next.

1667 Milton *P. L.* vii. 203 Chariots wing'd..now came forth Spontaneous. 1720 Pope *Iliad* xvii. 248 The stubborn arms..Conform'd spontaneous, and around him closed. 1780 Cowper *Progr. Error* 364 But we, as if good qualities would grow Spontaneous, take but little pains to sow. 1810 Scott *Lady of L.* i. xxxii, Till to her lips in measured frame The minstrel verse spontaneous came.

Spontaneously (spǫntē¹·nīəsli), *adv.* [f. prec. + -ly.] In a spontaneous manner.

1. By natural impulse; of a free and unconstrained will; of one's own accord.

1660 R. Coke *Justice Vind.* 7 Therefore Children..have will, and do things spontaneously. 1670 G. H. *Hist. Cardinals* iii. ii. 266 Considering the offers many had spontaneously made him. 1751 Johnson *Rambler* No. 175 ¶ 10 He who is spontaneously suspicious, may be justly charged with radical corruption. 1794 R. J. Sulivan *View Nat.* I. 130 For what is power or energy? Is it not a disposition to act, either spontaneously, or in consequence of some impression? 1809 Syd. Smith *Wks.* (1859) I. 161/2 Monk spontaneously sent down some confidential letters, which turned the scale of evidence. 1856 Dove *Logic Chr. Faith* i. § 2. 37 This is correct so long as the mind acts..spontaneously. 1877 Brockett *Cross & Crescent* 456 The Sublime Porte spontaneously informed the prince..that it would spare no effort [etc.].

b. Without thought or premeditation.

1800 S. & Ht. Lee *Canterb. T.* (ed. 2) III. 167 [The apology] sprang spontaneously to his lips. 1831 D. E. Williams *Life & Corr. Sir T. Lawrence* II. 383 In his letters, his opinions and sentiments are poured forth warmly and spontaneously as they arose. 1870 J. H. Newman *Gram. Assent* ii. viii. 331 Taste, skill, invention in the fine arts..are exerted spontaneously, when once acquired.

2. By natural action; without apparent or obvious external cause or influence.

1658 Evelyn *Fr. Gard.* (1675) 85 The unripe figs,..if they stay till they spontaneously quit the trees [etc.]. 1664 Power *Exp. Philos.* ii. 143 You shall see the water spontaneously arise..in the Tube. 1764 Reid *Inquiry* vi. § 24 Truth goes forth spontaneously if not held back. 1776 Adam Smith *W. N.* ii. v. (1869) I. 364 If [the capital] was produced spontaneously, it would be of no value in exchange. a 1806 Horsley *Serm.* xvii. (1816) II. 68 As the inquiry is of the highest importance, and spontaneously presents itself, it is to this that I shall devote the remainder of the present discourse. 1825 J. Neal *Bro. Jonathan* III. 188 A great bell..far below me, rang out, spontaneously, of itself. 1875 Jowett *Plato* (ed. 2) I. 206 If only wisdom can be taught, and does not come to man spontaneously.

b. *spec.* By natural chemical or physical change or development.

1771 *Encycl. Brit.* II. 120/1 Some earths and stones abound so with nitre, that it effloresces spontaneously. 1794 G. Adams *Nat. & Exp. Philos.* I. xii. 501 It takes fire spontaneously by the contact of air. 1804 Abernethy *Surg. Obs.* 91 It is no uncommon circumstance to meet with wens, that have burst spontaneously. 1837 P. Keith *Bot. Lex.* 35 The nascent bulbs, which..spontaneously detach themselves from the parent plant. 1878 Huxley *Physiogr.* xv. 251 In other cases the coral animal spontaneously splits in two halves. 1892 *Photogr. Ann.* II. 517 This remarkable group of crystals was produced..quite spontaneously.

3. By natural growth; without being specially planted or cultivated.

a 1682 Sir T. Browne *Tracts* (1683) 52 This same plant may grow naturally and spontaneously in several countries. 1733 W. Ellis *Chiltern & Vale Farm.* 84 Young Oaks.. that spontaneously grow up from the Acorns. 1765 *Museum Rust.* IV. 242 Common hay which is mixed with burnet growing spontaneously. 1836 Macgillivray *Trav. Humboldt* xxv. 384 It is supposed by botanists that it grows spontaneously in the mountainous regions.

b. By natural production; without tillage.

1700 Evelyn *Diary* 13 July, Some foreign country which would produce spontaneously pines, firs,..yew, holly, and juniper. 1748 *Anson's Voy.* i. v. (ed. 4) 61 The soil of the Island is truly luxuriant, producing fruits of most kinds spontaneously. 1830 Herschel *Study Nat. Philos.* 2 The coarse aliments which the earth affords spontaneously.

Spontaneousness (spǫntē¹·nīəsnės). [f. as prec.] The state or quality of being spontaneous.

a 1649 in *N. & Q.* Ser. i. X. 357 Spontaniousnes, and readines to helpe those who are in distress or suffer injury. a 1676 Hale *Prim. Orig. Man.* i. ii. (1677) 49 It is impossible to resolve the spontaneousness of many of their animal motions into those Principles. 1837 Ht. Martineau *Soc. Amer.* III. 267 This can only be done by those who do approve and reverence spontaneousness. 1872 Spurgeon *Treas. Dav.* Ps. liv. 6 The spontaneousness of our gift: is a great element in their acceptance.

† **Spontany,** *a. Obs.*[−1] [ad. L. *spontāne-us.*] Spontaneous.

1387–8 T. Usk *Test. Love* iii. iv. (Skeat) l. 33 Voluntarie or spontanye it is; for by spontanye wil it is do, that is to saye, with good wil not constrayned.

Spontoon (spǫntū·n). Now only *Hist.* [a. F. *sponton* (also *esponton* Espontoon), = Sp. *esponton* (Pg. *espontão*), ad. It. *spontone, spuntone*, f. *puntone, punto* point.] A species of half-pike or halberd carried by infantry officers in the 18th century (from about 1740).

The It. form *spontone* is used as a foreign word by Barret *Theor. Warres* (1598) iv. iv. 113.

1746 Dr. Cumb'ld in *10th Rep. Hist. MSS. Comm.* App. I. 443, I dare say there was neither Soldier nor Officer.. who did not kill their one or two Men with their Bayonets & Spontoons. 1746 *Lond. Mag.* 242 The Spontoon..is a Weapon used of late Years by the Officers of Foot instead of the Half-Pike. 1769 Pennant *Brit. Zool.* III. 64 The nose was very long, narrow, and sharp-pointed, not unlike the end of a spontoon. 1786 *Gentl. Mag.* Apr. 350/1 The officers who mounted guard..were paraded with their swords drawn instead of spontoons, for the first time since the regulation took place. 1802 James *Milit. Dict.* s.v., When the spontoon was planted, the regiment halted; when pointed forwards, the regiment marched; and when pointed backwards, the regiment retreated. 1819 Scott *Leg. Montrose* xxi, I am just now like the half-pike or spontoon of Achilles, one end of which could wound, and the other cure. 1841 Emerson *Ess.* Ser. i. xii. (1876) 284 Like the spontoons and standards of the militia, which play such pranks in the eyes and imaginations of school-boys.

transf. 1785 Burns *Jolly Beggars* xiii, From the gilded spontoon to the fife I was ready; I asked no more but a sodger laddie.

Spoof (spūf), *sb. slang.* [Invented by A. Roberts (1852–), comedian.]

1. A game of a hoaxing and nonsensical character. Also, a trivial round game of cards in which certain cards when occurring together are denominated 'spoof'.

1889 *Pall Mall G.* 14 May 5/1 'The Adelphi Club was the birthplace of the mysterious game called "Spoof", was it not?'—'Yes, I invented the pastime.' 1894 D. C. Murray *Rising Star* II. 235 There is in theatrical circles an amusement which is known as the game of spoof. 1895 Mrs. Croker *Village Tales* 89 We..were sitting in our dining-room tent fanning ourselves vigorously and playing 'spoof'.

2. Hoax, humbug; an instance of this.

1897 *Westm. Gaz.* 23 Apr. 2/1 There seems just a little too much 'spoof' about the long-talked-of Trickoli. 1905 *Sat. Rev.* 16 Sept. 370 One sees that the whole thing is a clumsy spoof.

3. *attrib.* Hoaxing, humbugging.

1895 A. Roberts in *Daily News* 26 Aug. 6/3 My 'spoof French' has often been the subject of amusement. 1899 *Westm. Gaz.* 27 June 7/2 Asking him to..send a 'spoof wire'—meaning any sort of nonsense.

Hence **Spoof** *v. trans.*, to hoax or humbug.

1895 *Punch* 28 Dec. 301/1, I 'spoof' him—to use a latter-day term. 1901 *Daily Mail* 2 Apr. 5/7 The House gave the willing tribute of laughter to the fact that it had been 'spoofed'.

Spook (spūk), *sb.* [ad. Du. *spook*, G. *spuk* (also † *spuch*), app. of LG. origin, appearing first in MLG. *spôk, spoek, spouk, spûk* (whence MSw. *spok*, Da. *spøg*), and older Du. *spoocke* (Kilian); other modern forms are LG. *spôk, spok*, WFris. *spoek*, NFris. *spøok, spuk*, Sw. *spöke*. No certain cognates have been traced.] A spectre, apparition, ghost.

First in American usage, which is illustrated separately in the first set of quotations.

(*a*) 1801 *Mass. Spy* 15 July (Thornton), By mine dunder I fly so swift as any spook. 1833 Paulding *Banks Ohio* III. iii. 40 Who ever heard of a spook eating? a 1853 'Dow, Jr.' *Patent Serm.* iii. 158 (Thornton), There did I see a Spook, sure enough,—milk-white, and moving round. 1878 W. H. Daniels *That Boy* i, The corners of New England which spooks and spirits were the last to leave.

(*b*) 1859 Aytoun & Martin tr. *Goethe's Poems and Ball.*, *Magician's Apprentice* 102 Broom, avaunt thee! To thy nook there! Lie, thou spook, there! 1873 Stephens *Black Gin*, etc. 11, I am haunted by a spook with oblique eyes and a pigtail. 1891 *Tablet* 19 Sept. 446 To what particular order of spook or spectre may he be assigned?

attrib. 1842 *Spirit of Times* (Philad.) 7 Mar. (Thornton), A-clatterin' the ghosts of dishes..as tho' he was bringin' in a spook-dinner. 1878 Aylward *Transvaal To-day* 213, I became acquainted with a 'spooke story',.. which [etc.]. 1896 *Westm. Gaz.* 10 Jan. 3/3 An alleged spook-photo.

Hence (as more or less colloquial or nonce-formations) **Spoo·kery, Spoo·kic(al** *a.*, **Spoo·kiness, Spoo·kish** *a.*, **Spoo·kism, Spookolo·gical** *a.*, **Spooko·logy, Spoo·ky** *a.*

1893 *Athenæum* 18 Feb. 214/1 The writer drags in sundry 'hauntings' and '*spookeries' of a mild nature. 1894 *Contemp. Rev.* LXVI. 651 The spookery business could not have saved him. 1887 *Sat. Rev.* 11 June 823/2 The new *spookic studies have come to stay. 1885 *Ibid.* 11 Dec. 771/2 Those who have watched..the recent outburst of *spookical activity. 1886 *Athenæum* 25 Dec. 858/2 The great thing in the book is the creation of the 'spookical' uncle. 1890 *Critic* 4 Jan. 3/2 An air of *spookiness pervades the volume. 1893 *Athenæum* 18 Mar. 343/2 There is some *spookish mystery about a reappearance. 1886 *Ibid.* 25 Dec. 858/2 By his own rash act he resolved himself into *spookism. 1897 *Westm. Gaz.* 6 July 2/3 Everything happened in the most orthodox *spookological manner. 1893 *Ibid.* 15 July 5 *Spookology in Vienna. 1883 *Harper's Mag.* Nov. 929/1 Tis a *spooky place, that grave-yard.

Spook (spūk), *v.* [f. Spook *sb.* Cf. MLG. *spôken*, Du. *spoken*, G. *spuken* (dial. *spuchen*); also WFris. *spoekje*, NFris. *spooke*, Sw. *spöka*, Da. *spøge*.]

1. *trans.* To haunt (a person or place).

1883 Olive Schreiner *Afr. Farm* i. ii. She heard a rustling,..and knew it was your father coming to 'spook' her.

2. *intr.* To play the spook; to 'walk' as a ghost. Also with *it*.

Spool, *sb.* Sc. *Obs.* In 5 *apule*. [app. an alteration of *apune* SPOOL *sb.* 1 b.] *collect.* Wooden roofing-shingles. Also *attrib.*

Spool (spūl), *sb.* Forms: 4–7 *spole*, 7 *spoole*, *spowle*, 7– *spool*. *β. north.* and *Sc.* 5– *apule* (6 *spewle*). 7. 8–9 *spoole* (8 *spoaol*). 6 *apoyle*, 8–9 *dial. spewl*, &c. [ad. ONF. *espole* (13th cent.) or the source of this, MDu. *spoele*, *spuele*, *spoule* (Du. *spoel*), MLG. and LG. *spôle* (hence Da. and Sw. *spôle*), OHG. *spuola* fem. (G. *spule*) and *spuolo*, *spuolo* (mod. G. *spul*).]

1. A small cylindrical piece of wood or other material on which thread is wound as it is spun, esp. for use in weaving; a bobbin.

Spooler. Also 6 *spullar*, 7 *-er*. [Cf. prec.]

Spool, *v.* Also 6 *spoole*, 6–7 *spool-*. [f. SPOOL *sb.*]

Spooling, *vbl. sb.* Also 6 *spool*, 6–7 *spol-*, *spool-*. [f. SPOOL *v.*]

Spoom, *v. Obs.* [Alteration of SPOON *v.*]

Spooming, *vbl. sb.* [f. prec.]

Spoon (spūn), *sb.* Forms: 1– 4 *spon*, 3–5 *spone*, 4–7 *spone*, 4– *spoon*; 6–7 *spoon-* (6 *spowne*); *β. spowne*, 6–7 *spoone*; *north.* 6 *spone*, 7– *spoon*, 5 *spune*, 6–7 *spune*, 9 *spuin*, *spyune*; *spean*, etc. (Common Teutonic: OE. *spôn-*, OFris. *spôn* (WFris. *spoen*, *spoan*, EFris. *spôn*, NFris. *spân*, *spôn*, *spun*), MLG. and LG. *spôn*, ON. and Icel. *spânn* (Norw. *spôn*); the original *spânn* is differently (not normally) represented in ON. *spânn*...

6. *fig.* The stomach, the pit of the stomach. *Obs.*

Spoon, *v.* [f. SPOON *sb.*]

Spoonage.

Spooner.

Spoonerism [f. the name of the Rev. W. A. *Spooner* (1844–).] An accidental transposition of the initial sounds, or other parts, of two or more words.

Spoonery, *moon-wort*. [f. SPOON *sb.* 7 + -ERY.] Foolishness, silliness.

Spoon-fed, (spūn'fed), *a.* [f. SPOON *sb.* + FED.]

Spoonful (spūn'ful), *sb.* [f. SPOON *sb.* + -FUL.]

Spoon-shaped, *ppl. a.* [SPOON *sb.*] Having the shape of a spoon; cochleariform.

Spoonwort. *Bot. Obs.* [f. SPOON *sb.* + WORT.]

Spoony (spū'ni), *a.* Also *spooney*, *spoonie*. [f. SPOON *sb.* 7.]

Spoony, *sb.* Also *spooney*, *spoonie*. [f. SPOON *sb.*]

Spoonyism.

Spoor (spūr, spō·ər), *sb.* [a. Du. *spoor* (in South African use), repr. MDu. *spor* (Du. *spoor*, = OE., MLG., OHG. and MHG. *spor*)...

1. The trace, track, or trail of a person or animal, esp. as followed in hunting.

Spoor, *v.* [f. SPOOR *sb.* and Du. *spoor en*.]

Spoorer. (spū'rər). [f. prec.] One who follows an animal, etc., by the trace or trail; a tracker.

Sporadic (spŏræ·dik), *a.* Also 7 -ick. [ad. mod.L. *sporadicus*, a. Gr. σποραδικός...

Sporadical, *a.* Also 7 -all. [f. prec.]

Sporadically, *adv.* [f. prec. + -LY.]

Sporangiophore. *Bot.* [See -PHORE.] A structure bearing sporangia.

Sporangite. *Fossil* [next : see -ITE.]

Sporangial, *a.* [f. SPORANGIUM.] Of or pertaining to a sporangium.

Sporangiferous, *a.* [f. SPORANGIUM + -FEROUS.] Bearing sporangia.

Sporangium (spŏræ·ndʒiǔm). Pl. **-gia**. *Bot.* [mod.L., f. Gr. σπορά + ἀγγεῖον vessel.]

Spore (spō·ər, spōər), *sb.* [ad. mod.L. *spora*, a. Gr. σπορά sowing, seed.]

Spore-blind, variant of SPUR-BLIND *a. Obs.*

Spore-case. *Bot.* [f. SPORE *sb.*]

Sporidium (spŏri·diŭm). Pl. **-dia**. *Bot.* [mod.L., dim. of SPORA.]

Sporidiferous, *a.* [f. next + -FEROUS.]

Sporidiole, **Sporidiolum** (spŏridiō·lŭm). *Bot.* [mod.L., dim. of next.]

‖ Sporidium (spŏrĭ·dĭŭm). *Bot.* [mod.L., dim. (after Gr. types of σπορα Spore.] **a.** A case or cell containing sporules. **b.** a sporule.

Sporiferous, *a.* [f. mod.L. *spor-a* Spore + -(i)ferous.] Bearing spores. Also **Sporifica·tion,** the process of form'ng spores. **Spori·genous** *a.*, producing spores. **Sporo·genous** *a.*, bearing spores.

‖ Sporinwood. *Obs.* [ad. older Flem. *sporckenhout* (Kilian).] The black alder.

Sporo·cyst. *Bot.* [f. prec. + Gr. κυστ-ις fruit.] **1.** *Zool.* A cyst or capsule containing spores.

Sporo·carp. *Bot.* [f. prec. + Gr. καρπ-ός fruit.] A fructification containing sporangia; a spore-fruit or spore-case.

Sporo·gen. *Bot.* [f. Sporo- + Gr. γέν-ος.] A simple form of gonophore.

Spo·rosac. *Zool.* [f. Sporo-.] A simple form of gonophore.

Spo·rous (spō·rəs), *a.* [f. Gr. σπορα Spore, combining form of Gr. σπορά Spore, adopted in a considerable number of recent scientific terms relating to the spores of plants or elementary forms of animal life, as **Sporoblast,** **-cyte,** **-derm,** **-dont,** **-gonous,** **-gone,** **-gonic** *a.*, **-gonium,** **-gony,** **-phorous** *a.*, **-phyll,** **-phyllary** *a.*, **-phyte,** **-phytic** *a.*, **-zoal**, **-zoan,** **-zoa** *n. pl.*, etc.

Sport (spōɹt), *sb.*[1] Also **3–6 sporte.** [Aphetic form of Disport *sb.*]

I. Pleasant pastime; entertainment or amusement; recreation; diversion.

Sport (spōɹt), *v.*[1] Also **3–5 sporte.** [Aphetic form of Disport *v.*]

1. *refl.* To amuse, divert, recreate (oneself):

Spo·rtance. *rare.* [f. Sport *v.* + -ance.] Sport, play; sportive or amorous activity.

Spo·rter. *Obs.*[1] [f. Sport *sb.*[1]] One who is given to sport.

Spo·rter (spō·rtəɹ). Also **5 sportour.** [f. Sport *v.* + -er.[1] Cf. Disporter.]

Spo·rtful, *a.* [f. Sport *sb.*[1] + -ful.] **1.** Full of sport or play; playful, sportive; given to sport or pastime.

Spo·rtfully, *adv.* [f. prec. + -ly.[2]]

Spo·rtfulness. Now *rare.* [f. as prec.] The quality or state of being sportful; sportiveness.

Spo·rtiness. *colloq.* [f. Sporty *a.*] Sporty quality or tendency.

Spo·rting (spō·rtiŋ), *vbl. sb.* [f. Sport *v.*] **1.** The action of the verb; engagement or participation in sport.

Spo·rtingly (spō·rtiŋli), *adv.* [f. prec.] **1.** As a matter of amusement or diversion; in or as sporting words or speech; not earnestly or seriously.

Spo·rting-wise, *adv.* = prec.[1] [f. Sporting *ppl. a.* + -wise.]

Spo·rtive (spō·rtiv), *a.* and *sb.* [f. Sport *sb.* or *v.* + -ive.] **1.** Inclined to jesting or levity; disposed to a playful manner or expression.

Spo·rting (spō·rtiŋ), *ppl. a.* [f. Sport *v.*] **1.** Engaged in sport or play.

Sporting, *vbl. sb.* [f. SPORT *sb.*[1] or *v.* + -LING[1].]

Sportively, *adv.* [f. prec. + -LY[2].]

Sportiveness. [f. as prec.] The fact, quality, or condition of being sportive.

Sportless, *a.* [f. SPORT *sb.*[1] + -LESS.] Destitute or devoid of sport; marked by the absence of sport.

†Sportlet. *Obs.*—[1] [Cf. SPORT *sb.*[2] and -LET.] A small basket or hand-basket.

Sportsman (spōǝ·tsmæn). [f. SPORT *sb.*[1]]

Sportsmanlike (spōǝ·tsmənlǝik), *a.* Also **sportsman-like**.

Sportsmanly (spōǝ·tsmənli), *a.* [f. as prec. + -LY[1].]

Sportsmanship (spōǝ·tsmænʃip). [f. as prec. + -SHIP.]

Sportula. *Obs.*—[1] [L. *sportula* little basket, dole, gift, dim. of *sporta* SPORT *sb.*[2]]

†Sportule. *Obs.*—[1] [ad. L. *sportula*: see prec.]

Sposh. *U.S.* [Imitative.] Slush, mud.

Sposh, *v.* *U.S.* [f. prec.]

Sportswoman (spōǝ·tswumæn). [f. SPORT *sb.*[1]]

Sporty (spōǝ·ti), *a.* *colloq.* or *slang*. [f. SPORT *sb.*[1] + -Y[1].]

Sporular (spōrū·lăǝ), *a.* [f. SPORULE + -AR[1].]

Sporulate (spōrū·lē[1]t), *v.* [f. as prec. + -ATE[3].]

Sporulation (spōrūlē[1]·ʃən). [n. of action f. prec.]

Sporule (spōrū[1]l). *Bot. and Zool.* [a. F. *sporule* or ad. mod.L. *sporula* (Hedwig): see SPORE and -ULE.]

Spot (spŏt), *sb.*[1]

Spot, *sb.*[2] [f. SPOT *v.* B.]

Spot (spŏt), *v.* [f. SPOT *sb.*[1]]

Spotless (spŏ·tlɛs), *a.* Also -4 *-les*, 6-7 *-lesse*. [f. SPOT *sb.*[1] + -LESS.]

Spotlessly (spŏ·tlɛsli), *adv.* [f. prec. + -LY[2].] In a spotless manner; without spot or stain; immaculately.

Spotlessness (spŏ·tlɛsnɛs). [f. as prec. + -NESS.] The quality or state of being spotless.

Spotsman. [f. SPOT *v.*] A smuggler.

Spotted (spŏ·tɛd), *a.* and *ppl. a.* Also 5 *spottid*, *-yd*, 6 *-id*, *-ȝt*, 7 *spotede*. [f. SPOT *v.* + -ED[1].]

Spottedness (spŏ·tɛdnɛs). [f. prec. + -NESS.]

Spotter (spŏ·tǝ[1]). [f. SPOT *v.* or *sb.*[1] + -ER[1].]

Spottily, adv. [f. SPOTTY + -LY.] In a spotty manner; without uniformity.

Spottiness (spŏ'tines). [f. SPOTTY a. + -NESS.]

Spotting (spŏ'tiŋ), vbl. sb. [f. SPOT v. + -ING¹.]
1. The action or process of making spots; the fact of becoming spotted.
2. Patchy; lacking in uniformity or harmony.

Spotty (spŏ'ti), a. [f. SPOT sb. + -Y¹.]
1. Full of, marked with, spots; spotted.

Spouch, obs. form of SPOUSE.

Spousage. Obs. rare. arch. Forms: 4 spousage, (5-6 spowsage). [ad. AF. *espousage, OF. espousage: cf. ESPOUSAGE.] 1. espo(u)ser SPOUSE v.

Spouse (spauz), sb. Forms: 1-4 spus, spuse, 3-4 spuse, 4 spouce; 4 spowes, 5-8 apowse, 6 spowse; also Sc. 5 spoys, 6 spousa. 3-4 spuse. etc.

Spouse (spauz), v. Obs. exc. arch. Forms: 3-4 spuse (4 spusi), 3-4 spousen (3 spowen).

Spouseage, sb. and a. Obs. rare.

Spouse-bed, sb. arch. Forms: 4 spouse-bed.

Spouse-break, sb. and a. Obs. rare.

Spoused, ppl. a. [f. SPOUSE v.]

Spousehead. Obs. Forms: 4 spousehede, 5 spowsede.

Spousess. Obs. rare. [f. SPOUSE sb.]

Spousing, vbl. sb. Obs. [f. SPOUSE v.]

Spout (spaut), sb. Forms: 4-6 spowte, 6-7 (9 Sc. spowtt-, spowtt); 5-7 spoute (5 spute).

Spout (spaut), v. Forms: 4-6 spowte (5 Sc. spowt, spowte), 5-7 spoute; 6-8 spoute.

Spouter (spau·tər). [f. SPOUT v.]

Spout-hole. [f. SPOUT sb.] The blow-hole or spiracle of a whale or other cetacean.

Spoutiness. rare. [f. SPOUTY a.] Tendency to discharge water.

Spouting, sb. [f. SPOUT sb.] Roof-spouts collectively; material for these.

Spouting, vbl. sb. [f. SPOUT sb.]
1. The action of issuing or discharging in a spout or stream.
2. Declamation or recitation; speech-making, speechifying.

Spouty, a.² Sc. [f. SPOUT v.] Given to spouting.

Spow, Obs. [f. Scand. origin: cf. Icel. spói, Norw. spove, spue, Da. spove, Sw. spof.] A curlew or whimbrel.

Spowl, obs. f. SPOIL.

Spowy, Obs. var. of SPILE sb.²

Spoyl(e, Spoyll, obs. forms of SPOIL sb. and v.

Spoylle, variant of SPOIL v.² Obs.

Sprach (spræx). Also sprauch, sprach. [Of obscure origin.]

Sprachel, sb.

Sprack, a. Now dial. Also asprack.

Sprackle, v.² Sc. Also 9 sprackle.

Spracklin (spræ'klin).

Sprack-barley, Obs. variant of SPRAT-BARLEY.

Sprackle, sb.³ Sc. Also 9 sprackle.

Spraich, Sc. Now rare. Also 6 spreich, 6-7 spreach, 6 sprauch. [Imitative.]

Spraick, sb.

Spraik, sb.

Spra'ckly, adv. rare. [Cf. SPRACK a.] Actively, smartly.

Spracle, obs. f. SPRACKLE.

Spra'ddle, v. Now chiefly dial. [f. SPRAD, pple. of SPREAD.] intr. To sprawl.
Hence **Spra'ddling** ppl. a.

Sprag, sb.¹ Now dial. [Of obscure origin: cf. Sw. dial. sprag, spragg; in the same sense.] A slip; a twig or spray.

Sprag, sb.² A lively young fellow.
1. A lively young fellow.

Sprag, sb.³ A young salmon.

Sprag, a. rare. Smart, clever.

Sprag, sb.⁴ Mining. A prop used to support the coal or roof during the working of a seam.

Sprag, v. [f. SPRAG sb.⁴]
1. Mining.

Sprag, a. rare = A mispronunciation of SPRACK a.

Sprag, v. Now rare or Obs. Also 5 spreyne.

Spraich. Sc. Now rare. Also 6 spreich, 6-7 spreach, 6 sprauch. [Imitative.]

Spraickle, v.

Sprack (spræk).

Sprain (spreᵻn), sb. Also 7 sprein. [prob. f. SPRAIN v.]
A severe wrench or twist of the ligaments or muscles of a joint, causing pain and swelling of the part.

Sprain (spreᵻn), v. Also 7 sprein. [Of doubtful origin. Connexion with OF. espreign-, espreindre to squeeze out, is not clear.] trans. To wrench or twist (a part of the body) so as to cause pain or difficulty in moving.

Spraints, sb. pl. [a. OF. espraintes.] The excrement of the otter.

Sprainch, v. Obs.

Sprai'nt, ppl. a. Obs.

Spraith, variant of SPREATH Obs.

Sprankle, v. [Du. sprankelen, WFris. spranckelje: cf. prec. and SPRANK sb.²]
1. intr. To throw out sparks; to sparkle.

Sprangle, sb.

Sprankling, vbl. sb. Obs.

Spranky, a. [f. SPRANK sb.¹] Showy.

Sprant, v. ? Error for SPRUNT v.

Sprash, v.

Sprat (spræt), sb.¹
1. A small sea-fish, Clupea Sprattus, common on the Atlantic coasts of Europe.
2. transf. and fig.

Sprat, sb.² [Of obscure origin.]

Spratt, v.¹ = SPRAT v.

Spratt, sb.³

Sprait, Obs. f. SPREAD.

Sprangle, v. U.S. [f. SPRANGLE sb.]
1. intr. To spread out in branches or ramifications.
2. To straggle; to spread out in branches or ramifications.

Sprangle, sb. U.S. [f. prec.]
A branching border; a ramification, a sprawl.

Sprangly, a. U.S. [f. SPRANGLE v.] Spreading.

Sprat, form of SPRAING sb. and v.

Sprag, var. SPRAG sb. and v.

Sprat-barley. Also 6 sprot, 8 sprack. [f. SPROT and SPRAT sb.¹] A species of barley, Hordeum distichon, with short broad ears and long awns.

Spratling, vbl. sb.

Spratkin, sb.

Spratt, obs. f. SPRAT sb.

Spratter, sb.

Sprattle, v. Sc. [f. SPRATTLE v.²] A struggle or scramble.

Spratty, a.¹ Sc. [f. SPRAT sb.³]

Spraty, a.² Sc. [f. SPRAT sb.³] Producing rushes; rushlike.

Sprauchle, Spraughle, later sf. SPRACKLE v.

Sprawl (sprɔl), v.

Sprawl (sprɔl), sb. [f. prec.]

Sprawler (sprɔ'lər).

Sprawling, ppl. a. [f. SPRAWL v.]

Sprawling (sprɔ'liŋ), vbl. sb. as prec.]
The action of the verb in various senses.

Sprawl'ing, ppl. a. [f. as prec.] That sprawls, in senses of the verb.
b. Of animals or persons, their actions, etc.

Spray (spreᵻ), sb.¹ [Of obscure origin.]
1. collect. Small or slender twigs or trees or shrubs, either as still growing or as cut off and used for fuel, etc.; fine brushwood.

Spray (spreᵻ), sb.² Water blown or driven in minute particles.

Spray, v.¹ trans. To sprinkle.

Spray, sb.³ Obs. Also sprey. [f. SPREE sb.] A kind or drinking-bout; frolic.

Spray, v.² [f. SPRAY sb.²]
1. trans. To diffuse or send in the form of spray; to scatter in minute drops.

Sprayed, ppl. a.¹ [f. SPRAY sb.¹]

Sprayed, ppl. a.² [Of obscure origin, common in south-western dialects, chiefly in the pa. pple.] Roughened or made uneven.

Sprayey (spreᵻ·i), a.¹ [f. SPRAY sb.¹] One who or that which sprays; a machine for diffusing insecticides over plants and trees.

Sprayey (spreᵻ·i), a.² [f. SPRAY sb.²]

SPRAYING. 681 SPREAD. SPREAD. 682 SPREAD.

Spraying, vbl. sb. [f. SPRAY v.¹] The action of dispersing as, or sprinkling with, spray; concr. a liquid used as a spray.

Spray·ing, ppl. a. [1. prec.] Casting up or scattering spray.

Spray·less, a. [f. SPRAY sb.²] Having no spray.

Spread (spreḍ), sb. Also ‡ spredde. [f. the verb. Cf. I.G. spredde, spreide, G. spreite.]

1. † A bitter spread, a hard experience. Obs.

2. The act of spreading in space; degree or extent of this.

a. With a. or about.

b. With the: The extent, expanse, or superficial area of something.

c. Capacity for spreading or extension; tendency to spread or go apart.

3. With a. or concr.: A spreading of something. Also, a spread-out layer or stream (quot. 1747).

b. A feast, a display of viands.

4. The act of being spread abroad, diffused, or made known; diffusion, dispersion. With a.

5. Without article.

6. A feast, a display of viands.

Spread, ppl. a., pa. pple. [f. SPREAD v.]

a. Extended, expanded; displayed; displaced.

b. Of tidings, rumour, fame, etc.

Spread (spreḍ, ppl. a. Also 6–7 spred.)

Spread·-eagle, sb. 1. Also spread-eagle. [SPREAD ppl. a.]

Spread-englism sb. [f. SPREAD EAGLE sb. 4 b.]

Spread-eagled, ppl. a. [f. SPREAD-EAGLE sb.]

Spreader (spre·dəɹ). [f. SPREAD v.]

Spreading (spre·diŋ), vbl. sb. [f. SPREAD v.]

Spreading, ppl. a. [f. SPREAD v.]

Spread·ingly, adv. [f. prec.] In a spreading manner.

Spread·ingness. [f. prec.] Tendency to spread.

Spreath, spreagh (spreɪθ). [Alteration of SPREATH sb.] Booty, plunder, spoil. Obs.

Spread·ation, rare. [irreg. f. SPREAD v. 8 b.]

Spread-bat. [f. SPREAD sb. + BAT sb.]

'Sprecious. Obs. Also a'pretious, sprecious. [See GOD sb. 1, 4, and PRECIOUS a. 2 b.]
Shortened form of *God's precious* used as an
asseveration of oath.

Spreckle. Sc. and north. Also 6 sprinkle.
—MHG. sprechel, sprekel, obs. or dial. G. sprechel,
sprächel, sprankel, Sw. spräckla, Norw. sprikl-
et, next.] A spot or speckle.

Speckled (sprek'ld), ppl. a. Now dial. Also
6 spreckled. [Cf. prec. and G. (obs. or dial.)
gesprechelt (also sprechlicht, -ig, etc.), Du. spreg-
kel, MSw. sprecklott, Norw. sprekluht, Icel. sprekl-
öttr.] Speckled.

Spred (e, obs. forms of SPREAD sb. and v.

Spree (sprī), sb. Chiefly collog. [A slang word
of obscure origin; cf. Spray sb.4]

Spreckle, variant of SPRIT sb. Spreet(e, obs. var.
Sprite. Spreet-sail, obs. f. SPRIT-SAIL. Sprein,
obs. form of SPRINKLE v. Spreit, obs. var. SPRITE.
Spreitless, v. f. SPRITELESS a. Obs. Spreinole,
obs. f. SPRINKLE v.

Sprendle. Obs.—1 [Cf. WFlem. sprendel

Sprenge, sb. [f. next.] Sprinkling.

Sprenge, v. Obs. exc. arch. in pa. t. and
pa. pple. sprent. Forms: Inf. 1 sprengan,
sprængan, 3–5 sprengen, 4–5 sprenge (5
sprentche). Pa. t. 1 sprende, 3 sprende,

Sprenges. Obs.—1 [Of doubtful origin.] A
disease of cattle.

Sprengle, Sprenkyll. Obs. rare. [App. var.
of SPRINKLE.]

Sprent, sb.2 Obs. rare. [Of obscure origin.]
A young turbot or other flat-fish.

Sprent, ppl. a.¹ north. and Sc. [f. SPRENT v.
Cf. Lovel. of fresh of rush, esp. the joint-leaved

welefulnesse is 3yspraid [ric] manye bitternesse.

Hence † Spret·ting vbl. sb.

Spret (spret), v.¹ Obs. rare.
† a. To sprout or shoot. Obs. rare⁻¹.
† 2. To spring by breaking or splitting; to shiver
into or into splinters. Obs.

Spret, sb.² Sc. and north. dial.
[Obscurely related to SPART sb.³ Also so SPREAT
and SPRIT sb.⁴] A kind of rush, esp. the joint-leaved

Sprig, sb.¹ Also 4–5 sprigge, 5–6
sprygge. [Of obscure origin; relationship to LG. sprick, dry twig, is doubtful.]
1. A shoot, twig, or spray of a plant, shrub, or
tree; a rod.

and a satchel not so very many years ago.

Sprig, sb.² [f. prec.]
1. A branch of a nerve, vein, etc. Obs.

Sprig, sb.³ Also 4–5 sprigge (6
spryggo). [Of obscure origin; relation-

Sprig, v.¹ [f. SPRIG sb.¹]
1. trans. To furnish with sprigs of brads. Also

Sprig, v.² [f. SPRIG sb.³]
¶ 1. a. trans. To form roots(s. Obs.—¹

Spriggan. Cornish dial. [prob. Cornish.]
A sprite, a goblin.

Sprigged (sprigd), ppl. a. [f. SPRIG sb.¹ or v.²]
1. Adorned or ornamented with sprigs.

Sprigger. [f. SPRIG sb.¹ or v.¹] One who
or that which drives in sprigs.

Sprigger.² [f. SPRIG sb.¹ or v.²] One who
ornaments a textile fabric or other material with
sprigs.

Sprigging, vbl. sb. [f. SPRIG sb.³]
1. The action or occupation of making sprigs
or on textile fabrics. Also attrib.

Spriggy, a. [f. SPRIG sb.¹] Abound-
ing in sprigs or small branches; suggestive of a
sprig or sprigs.

Spright, sb. and v., obs. forms of SPRITE
sb. and v.

Spright, sb.² [f. SPRIGHT sb.¹]

Spright, v. Obs. rare. [f. SPRIGHT sb.¹]

Sprightful, a. Now rare. Also
4 sprightfull. [f. SPRIGHT sb.¹]

Sprightless, a. [f. SPRIGHT sb.¹]

Sprightly (spraitli), a. and adv. [f. SPRIGHT
sb.¹ + -LY.]
1. Of persons: Full of vivacity or animation; cheerful, gay, brisk.

Sprightliness (spraitlines). [f. next + -NESS.]
The character or state of being sprightly; lively-
ness, vivacity, animation.

Spriglet. [f. SPRIG sb.¹ + -LET.]
A short pointed tail.

Sprig-tailed, a. [f. as prec.] Having a sharp-
pointed tail.

Sprind, a. Obs. rare. [OE. sprind, of obscure origin.] Active, vigorous.

Springe, obs. form of SYRINGE.

Sprindge, obs. form of SPRINGE.

Spring (sprin), sb.¹ Forms: 1 spring,
4–7 springe, 5 spring, 3–4 sprong,
4 spreng, 6 sprenge. [OE. spring and sprung,
f. SPRING v., whence a number of the later
senses are directly derived.]

Spring (sprin), sb.²
4. attrib. and Comb., as spring-level, -nymph,
etc.; spring-grass, -mattress,

SPRING.

Mast to spring.

II. To issue or come forth suddenly, to break out, esp. in a jet or stream. Freq. with *forth* or *out*.

III. Of vegetation: To grow; to arise or develop by growth.

b. In fig. contexts.

b. *trans.* Of water: To rise or flow in a stream out of the ground. Freq. with *out* or *up*.

7. Of morning, dawn, etc.: To come above the horizon; to begin to appear.

SPRING.

c. *c* 1440 *Jacob's Well* 283 Þt springeth out of compassioun.

b. In fig. contexts.

III. Of vegetation (continued).

b. Without const. In later use commonly with *up.*

c. To come into being. With additions as *forth*, *to life*, etc.

II. To grow (*up*): to increase or extend in height or length; to grow *out* from some thing or part.

b. To attain to a certain height or point by growth.

c. Of arches, etc.: To take a curving or slanting direction from some point of support. Also *without const.*

10. Of persons (or animals): To originate by growth; to issue or descend. Usn. const. *from*, *of*, *out of*. &c.

11. With *up.* Of a breeze: To begin to blow.

IV. 13. †**a.** To sprinkle (a liquid, etc.).

b. In fig. contexts.

Transitive senses.

SPRING.

b. To sprinkle (a person or thing). —SPRENGE.

c. In other parts.

†14. a. To grow (a beard). *Obs.*[-1]

†b. To produce, bring forth. *Obs.*

b. In fig. use. Also with *up.* *Obs.*

c. To come into being. Also with additions as *forth*, *to life*, etc.

†15. To cast out of; to drain off. *Obs.*

†16. To cause to well up or flow out of the ground. *Obs.*

17. To cause (a spring) to appear.

†b. To utter or pass (bad coin); to let off (a joke). *Obs.*

18. To cause (a bird, *esp.* a partridge) to rise from cover.

b. *colloq.* To give, pay, or disburse (a sum of money).

c. Of arches, etc.: To take a curving or slanting direction.

d. To bring (a ship) to spring, move suddenly, with a jerk, etc.

e. To cause (a thing) to spring.

f. To make (a horse) gallop.

g. *Mil.* To explode (a mine).

19. *Naut.* Of a vessel, or those on board: To have (a mast, yard, etc.) split, cracked, or strained.

c. To cause (some mechanism, etc.) to work with a sudden movement; to force open by pressure.

2. To apply or adjust by force applied to some elastic or resilient body.

b. To bend or deflect from a straight line.

23. *techn.* &c. *Arch.* To commence the curve of (an arch).

V. †24. —LEAP TO *v. Obs.*

Spring, *v.*[2] Now *arch.* [f. SPRING *sb.*[2]] *trans.* (See quot.)

Spring, *sb.*[1] in various senses.

†1. *trans.* To allow (timber or ground) to send up shoots from the stools of felled trees. *Obs.*

2. *intr.* To pass or spend the season of spring at a place.

3. *trans.* To give spray or elasticity to.

4. To provide or fit with a spring or springs.

Spring-, the verbal stem used in a few specific names, as spring-beetle (see quot.); spring-hare, the jumping hare of South Africa; spring-jack, lobster (see quots.).

Spring-: see SPRINGLE *sb.*[2]

Springal: see also *Obs. Hist.* Forms: 4. springalle (5 -al), 4 spryngalde, -elle, 5 -oll; 4 sprengal (-oll), 4-6, 5 -all. 6-5 sprynggald (5 -olde), 4-6 (9) springald (5 -alt). [a. OF. *espringalle* (cf. ESPRINGAL), or a. AF. *springalde* (Anglo-Lat. *springaldus*), f. OF. *espringuer* (cf. SPRING *v.*[1]) Hence also MDu. and MHG. *springal*, MLG. *springolt*.] A species of engine or catapult, used in medieval warfare for throwing heavy missiles; also, a missile thrown by an engine of this kind.

Springal(d[2], Now *arch.* Forms: a. 5 sprynghold, 6 sprynggald, 6-7 springaldo, 6 -hold, -olte, -ol (sprynghaldy). 7. 6 spryngald, 6-9 springal, -aid; 8 springaldo. [Of doubtful origin; perh. a formation from SPRING *v.*[1] suggested by *prce.*] A stripling, a youth.

Springback. Anglicised form of—

Springbuck. *1775 Phil. Trans.* LXVI. 371 They informed us, they had seen great flocks of the spring bucks.

Spring-cleaning. [f. SPRING *sb.*[1] 6 b.] The general cleaning of a house, etc., usually performed in the spring. Also *attrib.*

Hence **Spring-clean** *v.*; **Spring-cleaner.**

Springe (sprindʒ), *sb.* Also 3, 6 sprenge, 5 spryngge, 7-8 springe. [app. repr. OE. *spreng*, related to SPRENGE *v.* SPRING *v.*[1] Cf. the later SPRING *sb.*[2]]

1. A snare for catching small game, esp. birds.

b. *fig.* In allusions to the catching of woodcocks.

2. *Zool.* The springing tail of a springtail.

3. Some contrivance with a spring.

Springe (sprindʒ), *v.*[1] [f. SPRINGE *sb.*]

1. *trans.* To catch in a springe or snare.

2. *intr.* To set snares.

Springe (sprindʒ), *v.*[2] [var. of SPRING *v.*]

1. To sprinkle water.

Springed (sprind), *ppl. a.* [f. SPRING *v.*[1] or *sb.*] Provided with a spring or springs.

†Springed. *Obs.*[-1] [SPRING *sb.*[2] 9 +-ED.] A small or young shoot.

SPRINGEL.

†Springel, *Obs.* Also 5 springaill, sprynggill. [app. f. SPRING *v.*[1] The suffix may be after med.L. *aspergillum.*] A sprinkler for holy water. Also (in *springel-stick*).

Springhalt. Also SPRING-HALT. [f. SPRING *sb.*[1] + HALT *sb.*] = STRINGHALT.

Springer[1] (sprind). [f. SPRING *v.* + -ER[1].] One who or that which springs.

†Springer[2]. *Obs.* [f. SPRING *sb.*[2] + -ER[1].] An instrument for sprinkling (holy) water.

Springer[3]. [f. SPRING, *Trade, Springer* and *Liner*, a work-man who puts springs in.]

†Springet. *Obs.*[-1] [SPRING *sb.*[2] 9 +-ET.]

Spring-flood. [f. SPRING *sb.*[1] +FLOOD.]

†1. = SPRING-TIDE 2. Also in fig. context. *Obs.*

Springer. [f. SPRING *v.*[1] 8] So MDu. (and Du.), MLG., MHG. (and G.), Da. *springer*, MSw. (and Sw.) *springare*.

1. A source or origin. *Obs.*

2. A growing tree or plant. *rare*[-1].

3. A nursery for young plants.

b. A variety of marguerite.

c. A garden having concealed jets of water to be set in action by persons treading on the mechanism.

Spring-headed, *a.* [f. SPRING *v.*[1]] Having heads which spring afresh.

Springily, *adv.* [f. next + -LY[2].]

SPRINGING.

Spring-gun. [f. SPRING *sb.*[1]] A gun capable of being discharged by one coming in contact with it, or with a wire or the like attached to the trigger; formerly used as a guard against trespassers or poachers, and in concealment for this purpose.

Springhead. Also *attrib.*

1. The source or fountain of a stream; a well-head; = SPRING-HEAD 2.

Springing (sprin), *vbl. sb.*[1] [f. SPRING *v.*[1]] The action, on the part of seeds, plants, etc., of sprouting or growing.

Spring-water. Also spring water. [SPRING *sb.*]

Spring-well. [f. SPRING *sb.* + WELL *sb.*]

Spring-wood. [f. SPRING *sb.* and 6 b.]

Spring-time. Also springtime, spring time. [SPRING *sb.* 6 b.]

Spring-lock, *a.* [f. SPRING *sb.*]

Spring-locked, *a.* [SPRING *sb.*]

Spring-tail. *Zool.* Also springtail, spring tail. [SPRING *sb.*]

Spring-tide, spring-tide. [SPRING *sb.*]

Spring-tree. [f. SPRING *sb.*]

Springle (spri'ng'l), *sb.1* [f. SPRING *sb.*]

Springle, *sb.2* [f. SPRING]

Springle, *v.1* Now *rare* or *arch.*

Springle, *v.2*, *var.* SPRINKLE *v.*

Springless (spri'ngles), *a.* [f. SPRING *sb.*]

Spring-ling, *rare.* [-LING.] (See quots.)

Springling, *vbl. n.* [f. SPRING *v.*]

Sprink. *Obs.* rare.

Sprink, *a.* *Obs.1* Smart, spruce.

Sprink, *v.* *Obs. exc. dial.* [Cf. SPRINKLE *v.*]

Sprinkle (spri'ng'k'l), *sb.* [Imitative.] A light, tinkling sound.

Sprinkle, *sb.2* [f. the vb.]

Sprinkle (spri'ng'k'l), *v.* [Frequent.]

Sprinkled (spri'ng'k'ld), *ppl. a.* [f. SPRINKLE *v.*]

Sprinkler (spri'ng'klə). [f. SPRINKLE *v.* + -ER.]

Sprinkling, *vbl. sb.* [f. SPRINKLE *v.*]

Sprinkling, *ppl. a.* [f. SPRINKLE *v.*]

Sprinklet. [SPRINKLE *sb.* + -LET.] A slight sprinkle.

Sprint (sprint), *sb.* [f. SPRINT *v.*]

Sprint (sprint), *v.* [Cf. SPRENT *v.*]

Sprinter (spri'ntə). [f. SPRINT *v.*] One who sprints or engages in sprint-racing.

Sprisle, Sprissel, forms of SPRITSAIL.

Sprit (sprit), *sb.1* [OE. *spréot.*]

Sprit, *sb.2* *dial.* [var. of SPRENT *sb.*]

Sprit, *sb.3 techn.* (See quot. 1880.)

Sprit, *sb.4* = SPRET, SPRIT.

Sprit (sprit), *v.* [f. SPRIT *sb.1*, or aphetic f. ASPRIT *v.*]

Sprit, *v.2 dial.* [OE. *spryttan.*]

Sprit, *sb.*[2] *? Obs.* [Of obscure origin: cf. SPRIT *v.*[3]] *intr.* To spring; dart.

Sprite (sprəit), *sprit*, *sb.* Forms: 4–6, 5–7 *Sc.*, *spreit* (5 *spreyt*, *spreyte*), 5–6 *sprede*, 5–6 *spret*, 6 *spreete*, 6 *spryte*. Also *Sc.* 5 *spryt* (6 *spryttl*), 5–7 *apryte* (6 *apryte*), 5–7 *apryte*, 5–6 *apryte*, 6 *aprite* (6 *aprit*), 5–7 *spryte*, 5–6 *sprite*. (See also SPRIGHT *sb.*) [Of *sprit*, or similarly reduced from OF. *esperit* (e, AF. *espirit*; cf. SPIRIT *sb.*)]

†Sprited, *a. Obs.* [f. SPRITE *sb.*]

†Sprithood. *As prec.* The condition or state of being a sprite.

†Spritish, *a. Obs.* [f. as prec.] = SPRITE-LESS *a.*

Sprite, *a. Obs.* [f. as prec.] = SPRIGHTLY.

†Sprite-less, *a. Obs.* Resembling a sprite or that of a sprite.

Sprite-liness. Now *rare.* [f. SPRITELY *a.*]

†Spritely, *a.* Now *arch.* [f. SPRITE *sb.* + -LY[1]] = SPRIGHTLY *a.*

†Spritely, *adv. and a.* Obs. Also 6 *apritly*, 7–9 *aprightly.* [f. SPRIGHTLY *a.*]

†Spritish, *a. Obs.* [f. SPRITE *sb.* 2 b and 3, SPRIGHT *sb.* 2]

Sprite, *sb.* Also 7 *sprite.* [f. SPRITE *sb.*]

†Sprits, *v. Obs.* [f. as prec.]

Spritsail, sprit-sail (sprit'sə'l, sprit'sl). *Naut.* Forms: see SPRIT *sb.*[1] and SAIL *sb.*[1]; also) 7 *sprisael*, *sprislo.* [f. SPRIT *sb.*[1] Cf. Du. *sprietzeil*, Da. *sprijlsejl*, Sw. *sejl*, G. *prietzsegel*.]

Spritsman, *Obs. rare.* [f. SPRIT *sb.* + MAN *sb.*]

†Spritted, *Obs. rare.* [f. as prec.]

Sprittle, *sb. Obs.* exc. *dial.* [Of obscure origin.]

Sprittle, *v. Obs.* exc. *dial.*

Sprittly, *adv.* [f. SPRITTLE *a.*] Sprightlily.

Spritous, *a. Obs.* [f. as prec.] Impish, malicious, mischievous.

†Spritale, *a. Obs.* [f. as prec.]

†Spritty, *a.[1]*, *Sc.* [f. SPRIT *sb.*[3] + -Y[1].] Abounding in sprits or rushes.

†Spritty, *a.[2]* [f. SPRITE *sb.*] Spirited.

Spritsail-yard. *Naut.*

†Sprittle, *v. Obs.* [f. the stem of SPRIT *v.*]

Spritual, obs. form of SPIRITUAL.

Sprity, obs. form of SPRIGHTY.

Sprod, *north. dial.*

Sproat, obs. variant of SPRAT.

Sprote[1], *Obs.* exc. *dial.* [= MLG. and LG.) *sprote*, -s, 5–9 *sprots*, 5 *sprote* = MDu. *sprote*, *sprot* (Du. *sproot*), ON. *sproti*, related to SPROUT *sb.*]

Sprote[2], *Obs.* rare. [? Related to SPROUT *sb.*]

Sprog, obs. form of SPRAG.

Sproggle, obs. variant of SCROGGLE.

Sprong, obs. pa. t. and pa. pple. SPRING *v.*

Sproty, *a. Obs.[1]* [f. SPROTE[1]]. Small, thin, weak.

Sprouting, *vbl. sb.* [f. SPROUT *v.*] Spouting.

Sprout (sprout), *sb.[1]* [Related to SPROUT *v.*]

Sprout[2], *Obs. exc. dial.* and *pa. pple.* SPROUT *v.*

Sprout[3], *rare.* [Of obscure origin.] (See quot.)

Sprout (sprout), *v.[1]* Forms: 3 *spruten*, 4 *sproute*, 6 *sprut*, *sproyte*, 6–7 *sprowte*, *sprowt*, 6–7 *sproute*, Also 4 *sprote* (3 *sprowtte*, 4–9 *sproten*), *WFris. sprute* (NFris. *sprut*), MDu. *spruyten*, *spruten* (Du. *spruiten*), MLG. *spruten*, MHG. *spruzzen* (+*prossen*). Cf. OE. *sprytan* (rare) and *spryttan* SPRIT *v.*[1] The vbl. stem *sprout, sprowt,* are due to D2.

†Sprout, *v.[2]* Obs. rare. [Of obscure origin.]

Sprouting, *ppl. a.* [f. SPROUT *v.*] That sprouts.

Sprout-age, *rare.* [f. SPROUT *v.*[1] + -AGE.]

Sprout-hole, *Obs.*

Sprouting, *vbl. sb.[2]* [f. SPROUT *v.*]

Sprouting, *ppl. a.* [f. SPROUT *v.*]

Spruce (sprūs), *a.* Also 6–7 *apruse*, 7 *spruse*, 8–9 *sprews.* [perh. from SPRUCE *sb.* in the collocation *spruce (leather) jerkin*, etc.]

Spruce (sprūs), *sb.* Also 4 *Sprws*, *Sprwys*, 5 *sprewse*, 6 *Spreuwse*, 6–7 *Spruse*, 7 *Spruse.* [Alteration of PRUCE, Prussia: cf. SPRUCE *a.*]

Spruce (sprūs), *v.* Also 7 *apruse.* [f. prec.]

Column 1

SPRUCE BEER. 705

Himselie he sproutch, studieth to be fine. 1683 11. *Evans. Mariae Encomium* 44 Another shall spruce himself in a light periwig. 1709 *Rules Civility* 57 An old Man or Woman trimm'd up like young People of Eighteen, would make us believe they had spruced themselves so for no other end. 1895 J. GUTHRIE & HUBERT ROMANCE 10. 66 Star Spruce up himself a bit.

b. With refl. 1596 EDWARDE *Man of Mode* III. iii, I took particular notice of one that is alwaies spruc'd up with a deal of dirty sky-colour'd Ribband. 4701 E. BROWN *I. Estt. Serv.* 54 We dress'd, and spruc'd up, and decoy'd Persons. 1798 J. LAIV *LUXBORUGH Lett. Shenstone* 27 June, My slovenly garden, which cannot be weeded, nor in the least spruced up, till my hay is all in. 1829 FELTON *Fann. Life* viii. (1865) 336, I do not think you would have known your cad, hardly one, so spruced up was he in his Sunday's best. 1886 H. NISBET *Bush Girl's Rom.* 135 When washed and spruced up they looked and talked not unlike gentlemen.

tg. 1679 *Bachard Lect.* viii. III. ii. 11, Salmacis would not be seen of Hermaphroditus, till she had spruced up her self first. 1890 D. in *Schaffler's Lapland* 171 Woollen Cloth-Garments (such as they use to spruce themselves withal, at their public Festivals, or more solemn affairs). 1791 Mrs.DELANY *Life & Corr.* (1861) II. 131 Mrs. Foley's, where I was to spruce myself up a little before dinner. 1862 SALA *Seven Sons* II. v. 138 (She) spruced herself up to the extent of putting on. a black silk jacket. 1890 SHAIRP *Mistress Dorothy Marvin* xli, Go spruce yourself up a bit.

†2. *intr.* With *it*: To be spruce or trim. *Obs. rare.* 1621 COPE, *Palre* to *out* (1662 II. 13) Mr. Hubble. It is a grandmother... profess'd Sparks, and spruce up in Clary Stockings. 1798 M. DELANY *Life & Corr.* (1861) II. 447 We return home at two and have after two. 1833 SERRA LETT. 7. *Drawing* ii. (1835) 3 To right wee join to a quilt at Uncle Jodi's. Miss Wilbeby...is spruced up for it. 1869 Mrs. STOWE *Old Town* xvii. All of a sudden, Dench...seemed to kind o' spruce up and have a deal of money to spend.

Spruce beer. Also spruce-beer. [SPRUCE *sb.*] The modern use is app. due to rather the source of, the synonymous G. *sprossenbier, f. sprosse* shoot, sprout.] **1. a.** Beer from Prussia. *Obs.* **b.** A fermented beverage made with an extract from the leaves and branches of the spruce fir. *c.*1500 *Ortus Hawkiuh Test.* 331 in Hazl. *E.P.P.* I. 106 Spruce beer, and the beer of Hanbur, Whycine makyth of tymen men to stumber. 1829 NAASH *Progenitits Albion* 11 Many shall haue more Spruce Beere in their bellie, then wit in their heads. 1668 PHILLIPS (ed. Kersey), *Spruce-Beer*, a kind of Physical Drink, good for inward Brui- ses. 1708 BERKELEY *Sat. of Amer.* (1724) 11 A Spruce made of molasses, and the black spruce-fir. 1769 M. STONE *Acc. East-Florida* 4 The spruce fir here is quite a differ- ent tree from that to the northward, but answers the same end for making the spruce beer. 1823 J. GRAHAM *Pract. Med.* 601 d to Spruce beer is a powerful diuretic and anti-scorbutic, and is a wholesome beverage for the summer. 1845 LELAND *Mem.* I. 389 Stone beer, and ginger-bread.

Spruce fir. Also spruce-fir. [SPRUCE *sb.*] **1.** A distinct species of fir (*Pinus* or *Abies*) com- prising several clearly-marked varieties. (Cf. SPRUCE *sb.* 4); one or other of these varieties. 1670 *Phil. Trans.* V. 1101 The Common Fir, or Pitch Tree; sometimes called, The Norway or Spruce Fir. 1799 J.A. YOUNG *Agric. Lincoln.* 114 The spruce fir also grows well and large. 1823 J. SMITH *Panerat.* (Calcutta) II. 111 r 83 This essence is extracted from the small twigs or sprouts of the black and white Spruce Fir. 1881 BENTLEY *Man. Bot.* 209 The whole will be shaped like a cone or pyramid, as in the Spruce Fir.

2. A tree belonging to this species. 1768 PENNANT *Brit. Zool.* II. 262 The last spring we dis- covered the nest of this bird in a spruce fir. 1894 CRAIG *Corr.* (184.) 173 There you may see larches, Weymouth pines, and spruce firs that have risen by magic. 1842 LOUDON *Suburban Hort.* 317 Those remarkable rows of spruce-firs which line some of the avenues at Meudon. 1866 *Lloyd's Nat. Hist.* 18 The ordinary Crossbill devours the seeds of the larch and spruce-firs.

Spruce (sprös·ali), *adv.* [f. SPRUCE *a.* +-LY[2].] In a spruce manner; smartly, trimly, neatly. 1599 MARSTON *Pygmal. Sat.* iii, Under that faytre Rufle so spruce-ly set Appeares a fault, a false demeanour well. 1640 H. HAWKINS *Causist's Holy Crt.* 186 We see men...who wast all their tyme...in trining to haue their stockings spruceal-ly set. 1618 G. BROWN *Trav. Germ.* (1677) 159 Every Station is braucely set and couered within with green Turf. 1861 BERESFORD *Miseries Hum. Life* II. xxii, A yew walk forth briskly and smartly (thou) EMERSON *Lett. & Soc. Aims. Poet. & pros* Wks. (Bohn) III. 160 A small, well-sewn, sprucely brushed vocabulary serves him.

Spruceness (sprös·mes). [f. SPRUCE *a.*] The character or quality of being spruce; neatness. 1631 MIDDLETON & DEKKER *Roaring Girl* To Rdr. Now in the time of spruceness, our plays follows the niceness of our Garments. 1653 W. RAMESAY *Astrol. Restd.* 60 An exceeding well shaped body throughout, louing meanes, spruceness, trimming and the like. 1848 CHREVSTREY. *Lett. Ord.* (1792) II. 57 A spruceness of dress is also very proper and becoming at your age. 1833 H. MARTINEAU *Briery Creek* v. 108 Not all his spruceness could hide it, if he was as spruce as ever.

Column 2

refl. 1697 HEYWOOD *Pleas. Dial.* No. 4 Wks. 1874 VI. 191 Himselie he sproutch, studieth to be fine.

1683 *Sat. Rev.* 1 June 345/4 There is an offensive spruce- ness about the whole picture.

Spru·cery. *rare.* [f. as prec. + -ERY.] = prec. 1844 *Fraser's Mag.* XXX. 322/1 There is a sprucery about almost every thing he did.

† Spru·cia. *Obs.* Also 8 Sprusia. [Altera- tion of *Prussia* PRUCE *s.f.* SPRUCE *sb.*] The coun- try of Prussia; also *attrib.* in *Sprucia deals.* In Latin context the form occurs as early as 1419 in *North Country Wills* (Surtees) 19. 1664 GENTLEMAN *Engl. Way to Wealth* 6 For the Hol- landers...are compelled to fetch...their hopes and Barrell- boards out of Norway and Sprucia. 1799 *Lend. Gaz.* No. 3477/4 Spruce Deals, for Plank and Sprucia Deals.

†Spru·cier. *Obs.* [f. med. L. *Sprucia* (see prec. or SPRUCE *sb.*).] A Prussian. 1644 LITHGOW *Trav.* (1632) V. 133 My Lord Tres. hath declared...that you be Spruciers & Hansers both freer here in England pan be Kyngen subjects.

Spru·cify, *v. Obs.* [f. SPRUCE *a.*] *trans.* To make spruce. Also with *it* in refl. sense. 1611 COTGR., *Pimper,* to spruncle, or finifie it; curiously to pranke, trimme, or tricke vp himselfe. 1661 K. W. *Conf. Charac., Counter. Minion* (1860) 78 Of thinkeé he pufficeth himselfe with the gorgeous trappings of a lofty breast- phalos. 1890 *Poor Robin's Intell.* 15-22 Aug. 1/2 Sprucify- ing himself like a Country Bridegroom he came up to her brush'd and powder'd.

†Spru·cle, *v. Obs.* [Of obscure origin.] *trans.* ? To attract, secure. 13-- E. E. Allit. P. C. 104 Cables bay fasten, Witt at ye wynden wyten her makes, Spale spak to be sorne & spare spare.

Spru·e[1] (sprö). *Chem.* Also **8. sprow,** Sc. **sproo.** [ad. Du. *spruw, sprouw* (older Flem. *sprouwe,* W.Flem. *sprew* = MLG. and LG. *sprüwe*), perh. related to Du. *sprouwen, sprocies* to sprinkle (cf. SPREW[1]).]

1. = THRUSH[2] 1. *Obs.* Erroneously defined by Webster (1828-30) as 'a matter formed in the mouth in certain diseases.' 1825 *MASON Supp., Sp*-oo, a disease affecting the mouths of very young children. 1837 WEBSTER, *Sprew,* a disease of the mucous membrane, consisting in a specific in- flammation of the mouparoral glands. *Ibid., Spruw,* ...tis is sometimes a vicious orthography of *Sprew,* the name of the disease otherwise called thrush. 1859 *Syd. Soc. Lex., Thrush, Parasitic stomatitis.* Also called *Aphtha, Aphlth, sprew, spruce.*

2. A disease characterized by sore throat, raw tongue, and digestive disturbance, occurring esp. in tropical countries; psilosis.

1888 DAVY (title), Psilosis or 'Sprue': its nature and treat- ment. 1890 ALLbutt's *Syst. Med.* III. 777 Amongst the remoter causes of sprue prolonged residence in hot climates must be reckoned as the first.

attrib. 1897 *Allbutt's Syst. Med.* III. 778 One who has resided in a sprue country. *Ibid.* 790 In the debilitated con- dition of sprue patients. *Ibid.* 799 The sprue tongue is but a by a class of charlatans who profess to be "sprue doctors".

Spru·e[2] (sprö). *Founding.* [Of obscure origin.] Webster's definition is probably erroneous.

1828-30 WEBSTER, *Spew,* in Scotland, that which is thrown off in casting metals. 1875 KNIGHT *Dict. Mech.* 2254/2 *Head*...the *sprue,* sullage-piece, or riser of a casting, which is knocked off. 1881 *Ibid. Suppl., Sprew Hale,* a gate, ingate, or pouring-hole in a mold. 1884 W. H. GREENWOOD *M'f'g & Iron* 160 The smaller passages, often two or three in number, leading from the channel or gate to the mould are called sprues or sprue gates.

† Sprug[1], *v. Obs.* [Of obscure origin.] A poor or inferior quality of asparagus. Also *sprug grass.* 1846 SOYER *Cookery* 41 Throw in the sprue and let it b.il for only a few seconds. 1862 *Lett. fr. Madras* (1843) 219 They are tolerably fine, not quite like the English asparagus, commonly known as the sprue. 1899 *Times* 3 April 3/4 Sprue, 12 to 2s. ; asparagus, 10.6l. to 5s. per bundle.

Sprug[1] (sprÖg), *sb. Sc. and north. dial.* Also **sprog, sprag** [Of obscure origin: the form *sprug* (with variant *sprag*) is also common in Sc. and Eng. dial.] A sparrow. 1825 SCOTT *Guy M.* ii, Mrs. Mac-wasa a blustering kind of shield, without the heart of a sprug. 1886 -in *Eng. Dial. Dict.*

Sprug[2], *v. dial.* [cf. Sussex dial. *sprug* adj., smart, spruce ; cf. SPRIG *a.*] *trans.* To deck or dress up smartly ; to make smart or trim.

**†1821 T. STOUGHTON *Chr. Sacrif.* ir. 72, Some dainitie Dames, euen spruggd vp of nothing, that are so long in dressing, and striring themselues in the morning. 1847 HALLIWELL, *Sprug,* to dress neatly. Sussex. 1885 *Sussex Gloss.*, 112 *Sprug,* to smarten.

†Spruit (spröit, sprout), *s. African.* [Du. *sprsit* SPROUT sb.] A small stream or water- course, usually almost or altogether dry except in the wet season. 1805 W. C. BALDWIN *Afr. Hunting* 307, I scraped my finger-nails off in making large holes in the dry spruits, but not one drop came. 1876 LADY BARKER *Year's House- keeping S. Africa* 116, In dry weather it-it a sandy spruit, sometimes a lake. 1887 *Pall Mall G.* 13 Sept. 4/1 They go off in search of the missing spruit, and sometimes a lake. 1889 *Scots Observ.* 8 June 74 Wonderfully spruit did the parched veldt look. 1897 *Westm. Gaz.* 18 Oct. 1/2 We we outspanned the boys made a fire in the hollow bed of a spruit.

Sprule, *north.* or *Sc.* variant of SPRAWL *v.*

Column 3

SPRUNT. 705

Sprun. *north. dial.* [? A metathetic var. of SPURN *sb.*] (1 b.) [See quot. 1828.] Also *attrib.* in *sprun-tree.* 1737 BACKEN *Farriery Instr.* (1736) I. 338 Bleeding in the Sprun-Vein. 1825 JAMIE CROSS GLOSS., *Sprun,* 1. The fore part of a horse's hoof. 2. A sharp piece of iron fixed to the fore part of a horse's shoe to prevent him slipping up a hill.

Sprung (spröng), *ppl. a.* [pa. pple. of SPRING *v.*] **1.** That has sprung up ; arisen. Also with *up.* 1723 GREGORING *Flowers, Stan Bartholomew* Wks. 1907 I. 101 God be knoweth...who pluckt his first sprung rose. 1832 LITTLOW *Prol.* to, 213 he had so dropt vpon all: Liue on now wel-threne, wel-sprung, wel-threatening the clouds. 1865 J. DAVIES *Chal Werare* 313 This vtterly dissipated the power of the new sprung Committee of Safety. 1842 J. AITON *Domest. Econ.* (1857) 150 The progress of his crops, from the scarce sprung-braird to the whitening har- vest.

2. Cracked, split. 1597 J. PAYNE *Royal Exch.* 23 Besyde myne acquaytanus with your spryng masts, rotne sailes from the yarde. 1866 DRYDEN *Ann. Mirab.* cliii, Tall Norway Fir, their masts in Battel spent, And English Oak sprung Leaks and Planks restore. 1859 HARDY *Voyage* v. 300 The main mast has a sprung mast. 1833 H. NEWMAN *Tractariansim* 13 Some mixing mortar...some strengthening the sprung beam. 1890 EGAN *Philolotte's Human Boy* 12 Browne...made that noise in his throat like a sprung bar.

3. Made to fly up. 1885 SYLVESTER *Du Bartas* II. ii. 111 *Colonies* 431 Our amaz'd first Grand-sires faintly fled, And like a timorous Pheasant, to their next shrowde flye.

†Sprunk, *v. Obs.* [app. f. Du. *pronk,* or G. *prunk* ; cf. next.] A display of wealth or grandeur. *c.*1725 *The King's Disguise* xli. in *Child Ballads* III. 101/1 With gryars and monks, with their fine sprunks, I mak my child a king.

†Sprunking, *vbl. sb. Obs.* [f. Du. *pronken* or G. *prunken* : cf. prec.] Personal adornment or beautifying. Also *attrib.* in *sprunking glass.* 1890 LINWOOD *Munden Mulidetic* 6 Ten Pocket Sprunking Looking-Glass. *Ibid.* 9 The Table, Toilet, or Pocket Sprunking-Glass. 1894 N. H. *Lambard Diary* 11 Sprunking Glass, this sprunking is a Dutch word, the first as we hear of that Language, that euer came to Germany is called a mirror.

Sprunny. *Now dial.* [Of obscure origin : some dialects have *sprawny* adj., spruce, smart.] A sweetheart.

1762 *Collins's Mist.* 111 Where if good Satan lays her on like thee, Whipp'd to some Purpose will thy Sprunny be. 1800 PEAKE *Suppl. Grose, Sprunny,* a sweetheart of either sex. 1824 -in midland and eastern dialects.

†Sprunt[1], *v.[1]* [SPRUNT *v.*] A convulsive movement ; a start ; a spring or bound. 1793 *Phil. Trans.* XVII. 896 Then (having just only opened her Eyes and made Two Sprunts, without speaking one word) [she] dyed immediately. 1800 *Pocket Suppl. Grose, Sprunt,* or *Sprint,* a spring in leaping, and the leap itself. *Ibid.* 1847-78 in dial. glossaries (Derby, Northampt., Shropsh., Warw.).

†Sprunt[1], *sb.[1]* [cf. next.] That which a tie is short and will not easily bend ? (Johnson, 1755). In the quot. applied to an obstinately curly lock of hair. 1700 COCKRAVE *Venus Ann.* 13 Sprunts, or stumps as of a *Tree* ; short-hair. 1759 JOHNSON *Idler* No. 6, with sprunt, cleft, or slip, and she drest his.

Sprunt, *v.* ? *Obs.* [next.] Brisk, active, smart, spruce. 1590 *quoted in SPRUNTLY adv.* 1848 DICKENS *Dombey* 2 A midnight.

Column 4

Hence **Spru·nting** *vbl. sb.* 1893 TRAPP *Gen.* 271/1 Spuddle, all their faint oppositions, and sprungings before death. 1897 —*Rev.* xii. 8 Their late great instant endeavours ; never has as the last sprungings, or bitterdelves of dying beasts.

Spruntly (spröntl·), *adv.* [f. SPRUNT *a.*] Smartly, sprucely, trimly. 1596 R. JOHNSON *Devil an Ass* IV. ii, How do I look to-day? Am I not drest Spruntly? 1651 H. MORE *Enthus.* 7 ff. (1656) 193 Provided *thou* wilt not prick up thy ears too, and look too spruntly upon the Sumptes. 1700 D'URFEY *Hell beyond Hell* 75 The pup appear'd, well jaunty dress'd, Powder'd all o'er, hop, trim, and smug, And spruntly.

†Spruceadog. *Obs.* [f. prec. SPRUCE *a.* +-ADO 1.] A smartly-dressed person.

3. a. A digging or weeding implement (of the spade-type, having a narrow chisel-shaped blade. 1697 *Poor Diary* to Oct., We...began with a spud to lift up the ground. 1798 SMITH *Poet. Dial.* Wks. 1755 III. n. 203 My spud close nettles from the stones can part ; No knife so keen to weed them from my heart. 1775 King. DELANY *Life & Corr.* I. 570, I sallyd out in a rage, arm'd with a spud. 1809 W. DICKSON *Pract. Agric.* II. 748 In eating the pies to the bottom with a spade or spud. 1830 ANDREWS *Righteblels Gloss., Spud,* all kinds of the 'spud', as agricultural weapon which old farmers persist in carrying about with them in their war upon weeds, till they have fulfilled the help of his favourite spud, managing to get along.

fig. **4.** 1878 M. COLLINS *Yen Six Stitches* (1891) II. 21 To reappear inevitably, through the heavy harrow of argument, and the light spud of wit have both been thrown at them. *Coml.* 1893 *Miss Dowie Girl in Karp.* 206 She shook a wise chair on which they sit, while they rest their knobby hands on their knees.

Spud, variant of SPEW *v.*

†Spuffle, *v. E. Angl. dial.* [Imitative.] *intr.* To fuss or bustle ; to be in a flurry or in breathless haste.

c.1825 FORBY *Voc. E. Anglia.* 321 I saw Mr. A. spuffling along. 1887 BURNE *Wks.* 113 He spuffled and sputtered about in a most extraordinary manner. 1835 *Sylvester* II. Jinks. 1829 ROBINSON *such* had means to tell his friend that he is making a too much fuss about anything...he says, quietly, 'Now don't spuffle.'

Spug (sprög), variant of SPROG. **Spugnie** (spög·ni). *Sc.* Also variants of SPULYIE.

Spule. *Sc.* [Of obscure origin : not a normal variant of SPAULL.]

1. A shoulder, esp. of an animal. 1807 SCOTT *Christie's Will* II. in *Minstrelsy,* The spule of the deer on the board he beat. 1845 *Complaynt Sc.* (E.E.T.S.) 64 The fattest that ran the Huton Law.

b. in *spule-blade,* -bone. 1813 DOUGLAS *Aeneid* v. ii. 40 (1553) His spule bone. Then for-iower's no double breasts will a help. 1870 — *Ibid.* ii. xii 54 Wounded in his spule. 1790 BURNS *Caled. Hunt,* When first I bore the little Fellow.

Spulyie (spöl·yi), *sb. Sc. and north. dial.* Forms : 5 spuilye, 5-6 spulye, -yie, 6 spoylie, -zie, 7 spuilyie, 6-7 spulzie, -lye, -lie ; 6 spuilye (spuill-), 6 spullie, 7 spuilyie (spuill-), 6 spullie, 8 spuilyie, 9 spulleziO ; 5 spuilyie, -lze, 7 spuilye (spuil-), 8 spuilzie, 9 spulzie. [ad. OF. *espeiller* SPOIL *v.*]

1. *trans.* To dig up or out, to remove, by means of a spud.

1653 URQUHART *Rab. I. xli.* ii, I have found out a more certain way which will destroy the acre once, spudding up...I caused them to be spudded up by the root.

2. To dig up (a plant) by the root, etc. ; to root out, clear away.

Column 5 (bottom row)

[Second row of columns - dense dictionary text continues with entries for SPULYIE, SPUME, SPUMEOUS, SPUMESCENCE, SPUMIFORM, etc.]

Column 6 (bottom)

[Entries for SPUN, SPUNG, SPUNGE, SPUNK, SPUNKILY, SPUNKY, etc.]

SPUR.

Spur-gall.

Spurge.

Spurging.

Spuriosity. *rare*. [f. next : see -OSITY.] The state or condition of being spurious ; a spurious thing or production. *Also Const.*

Spurious, *a.* [f. L. *spuri-us* illegitimate, bastard, Sp. *espuria*.]

1. Of persons : Begot or born out of wedlock ; illegitimate, bastard, adulterous.

2. *gen.* : Not really proceeding from its reputed origin, source, or author ; not genuine or authentic ; forged.

4. Of a writing, etc. : Not really proceeding from its reputed origin, source, or author ; not genuine or authentic ; forged.

b. Similarity of words or passages.

5. Characterized by spuriousness or falseness.

Spuriously, *adv.* [f. prec.] In a bastard or spurious manner ; with pretence or simulation ; falsely.

Spuriousness. [f. as prec.]
1. Bastardy, illegitimacy. *rare*.
2. Irregular or abnormal condition.
3. The state or quality of being spurious, false, or counterfeit ; the falseness of a thing.
4. *Bot.* Having no spur or calcar.

Spurk, *v.* *E. Anglian.* [Of obscure origin.]

†Spurket. *Obs.* Also **-ett, -it.** (See quots.)

Spurless (spɜ̄·les), *a.* Also **4 sporeles, 5 spureles.** [f. SPUR *sb.*1 + -LESS. Cf. G. *spornlos.*]
1. Lacking a spur ; having no spurs. Also in *fig.* context.
2. Of birds or their legs : Devoid of spurs.
3. *Bot.* Having no spur or calcar.
4. Of branches : Destitute of fruiting-spurs.

Spurlet, *rare*⁻¹. [f. SPUR *sb.*1 + -LET.] A small spur of a mountain or mountain-range.

Spur-like, *a.* [f. SPUR *sb.*1 + -LIKE.] Like or resembling a spur.

Spurling, ⁴ *Obs.* [var. of SPIRLING.]

Spurling-line. *Naut.* (See quot.)

Spur-maker. [f. SPUR *sb.*1 + MAKER. Cf. MDu. and Du. *spoormaker, spoornmaker*, G. *spor(e)nmacher*, Da. *sporemager*, Sw. *sporrmaker*.] One who makes spurs ; a spurrier.

Spurn (spɜ̄rn), *sb.*1 Also **4-7 spurne, 4-5 sporn.** [f. SPURN *v.*1]
1. A trip or stumble.
†2. A kick ; an act of spurning.
b. A pace or course (on horseback). *Obs.*⁻¹
†3. A stroke with the foot ; a kick. *Obs.*

Spurn, *v.*1 Also **4-7 spurne, 4-5 sporn, 5 spwrn.** [OE. *spurnan, spornan* str. v. = OS. *spurnan*, OHG. *spurnan*, ON. *sporna*, etc.]

†1. To trip or stumble.
b. To strike against something with the foot ; to trip or stumble. *Also fig. Obs.*
†c. To encounter, fray. *Obs. rare.*
2. To strike with the foot ; to kick.
b. To reject with contempt or disdain ; to treat contemptuously ; to scorn or disdain.
3. *intr.* To kick ; to strike out with the foot.

Spurner. [f. SPURN *v.*1 + -ER.]
1. One who or that which spurns.
b. One who kicks or strikes with the foot.

Spurning, *vbl. sb.*1 [f. SPURN *v.*1] The action of the verb, in various senses.

†Spurning, *vbl. sb.*2 *Obs.*⁻¹ [f. SPURN *v.*2]

Spurning, *ppl. a.* [f. SPURN *v.*1] That spurns.

†Spurn-point. *Obs.* [f. SPURN *v.*1 + POINT.] An old game, perch, of the nature of hop-scotch.

Spurn-water. *Naut.* [f. SPURN *v.*1] (See latest quot.)

Spurred (spɜ̄rd), *ppl. a.* [f. SPUR *sb.*1]
1. Wearing or provided with a spur or spurs.
2. Furnished with sharp and hard spikes, claws, or the like.
b. In specific names, as **spurred** *centropys*, etc.
3. Affected with ergot or spur.
4. *Bot.* Of the nature of, provided with, a spur or calcar.

Spur-rial. *Now Hist.* Forms: **6 spurr royall, 6 spur-rial, 7-8 spuriall (8 -al), 7 spurryal.** [f. SPUR *sb.*1 + RIAL *sb.*]

Spurrier (spə̄·riər). Forms: **4-6 sporyer, 5 -ier, sporyiere, 6 sporryere, 6 -ier, 7-8 spuryer.** [f. SPUR *sb.*1 + -IER.] A spur-maker.

Spurring, *vbl. sb.* [f. SPUR *v.*1]
1. The action of pricking with a spur or spurs. *Also transf.*

Spurring, *ppl. a.* [f. SPUR *v.*1] That spurs.

Spur-rowel (-rowel). [f. SPUR *sb.*1 + ROWEL *sb.*]
The rowel or revolving pricking-wheel of a spur.

Spur-royal. *Now Hist. or arch.* Forms: **7 spur(re) royal, 7-8 spur royal ; 6-7 spuri-all, 7-spur-royal (7-8 -al, spurroyal), (7 riole), 8 -ROYAL *sb.* Cf. SPUR-RIAL.** A gold coin of the value of fifteen shillings.

Spurry (spə̄·rī), *sb.* [ad. MDu. *spurie, sporie* (mod.Du. *spurrie*, whence G. *spörgel*), etc.]
One of various species of herbaceous plants or weeds belonging to the genus *Spergula*.

Spurry (spə̄·rī), *a.* [f. SPUR *sb.*1 + -Y.]

Spurt (spɜ̄rt), *sb.*1 [f. SPURT *v.*1]
1. *intr.* Freq. with *out* and *up.*

Spurt, *v.*1 Cf. SPIRT *v.*1
1. *intr.* To sprout or shoot.

Spurting, *ppl. a.* [f. SPURT *v.*2] The action of the vb., in various senses.

Spurtle, *sb.* Now *dial.* and *rare*. [f. SPIRT *sb.*]

Spurtle (spɜːˈtl), sb. [Cf. SPURT v.¹ + -LE. Cf. SPIRTLE sb.]
The action or an act of spurtling.

Spurtle (spɜːˈtl), v. [f. SPURT v.¹ + -LE. Cf. SPIRTLE v.]

1. trans. a. To besprinkle or bespatter. rare.

b. To cause to spurt or spatter. rare.

2. intr. a. To burst or fly out in a small quantity or stream with some force or suddenness; to spirt or spurt.

Spurtled, a. Sc. Obs. [Metathetic form of SPIRTLED q.v.] Speckled, spotted, variegated.

Spurvey, a. rare. [f. SPURT sb.⁴ + -Y.] Characterized by spurts; intermittent, spasmodic.

Spur-wheel. Also **spur wheel.** [SPUR sb.¹]
A gear-wheel which has cogs or teeth on the periphery, projecting radially from the centre; a cog-wheel.

Spur-winged, a. Ornith. [f. The Spur Wheel.]

Spur-winged, a. Ornith. [f. SPUR sb.¹]
Having one or more stiff claws or spurs projecting from the pinion-bone of the wing. In specific names (see quots.)

Spurway, variant of SPARWAY Obs.

Sput, v. Obs. rare. [Of obscure origin.] trans.
To urge, incite.

†Sputa, pl. Of SPUTUM.

†Sputaminous, a. Obs. rare. [f. L. spūtāmin-, spūtāmen, l. spūtāre to spit.] Of the nature of spittle; characterized by the presence or flow of saliva.

†Sputania. Obs. Also -ania. (See quots.)

†Sputation. Obs. [a. F. sputation, ad. L. spūtātiō, -ōnem, f. spūtāre, frequentative of spuĕre to spit.]
The action of spitting : expectoration.

†Sputative, a. Obs. rare. [f. L. spūtāt-: see -ATIVE.] Of, characterized by, given to (excessive) spitting or salivation.

Sputchcon (spɜːˈtʃən). [Of obscure origin.]
(See quots.)

Spute, obs. form of SPOUT sb.

Spute, v.¹ Obs. or dial. Also 4 spoute, 6 speut. [Aphetic form of DISPUTE v.] intr. To dispute ; to contend in disputation.

Spute, v.² Obs. rare. [Aphetic form of DISPUTE v.] trans. To dispute.

Sputher, variant of SPUDDER.

†Sputinoun. Obs.⁻¹ [Aphetic form of DISPUTISOUN.] Disputation.

†Sputous, a. Obs.⁻¹ [var. of SPITOUS a., perh. under the influence of SPUTE v.¹] = DESPITOUS a. Hence **†Spu'tously** adv. Obs.⁻¹

Sputter (spɜːˈtə(r)), sb. [f. SPUTTER v.]

1. Noisy or violent and confused speech or discourse; angry, excited, or fussy argument or protest; fuss, clamour; = SPUTTER sb. 1.

b. An instance or occasion of this.

2. A state of bustling confusion or excitement.

Sputter (spɜːˈtə(r)), v. [f. SPUTTER v.]

1. intr. In Spirit Publ. Trnds. 750 He will live in a sputter. And die in a gutter.

2. Matter ejected in or by sputtering. rare.

3. The action or an act of sputtering; the emission of small particles with some amount of explosive sound; the sound characteristic of or accompanying this.

b. A spattering or sprinkling.

Sputter (spɜːˈtə), v. [-Du. sputteren, WFris. sputterje, NFris. sputteri, spütere, of imitative origin.]

1. trans. To spit out in small particles and with a characteristic explosive sound or a series of such sounds.

b. transf. To scatter, throw up or about, in small particles.

2. To utter hastily and with the emission of small particles of saliva; to ejaculate in a confused, indistinct, or uncontrolled manner.

3. Of speech, etc., or of persons with reference to this: (see SPUTTER v. 4).

4. To speak or talk hastily and confusedly or disjointedly.

Sputterer (spɜːˈtərə(r)). [f. SPUTTER v. + -ER.] One who or that which sputters.

Sputtering, vbl. sb. [f. as prec.] The action of the verb in various senses; an instance of this.

b. pl. Small particles sputtered out or emitted with some force and noise.

Sputtering, ppl. a. [f. as prec.]

1. Emitting or ejecting saliva or spittle. rare.

2. Characterized by, burning with, making or giving out, a succession of explosive sounds accompanied by the emission of small particles, sparks, or bursts of flame.

Sputtery, a. rare. [f. SPUTTER v. + -Y.] Inclined to sputter or burst out explosively; of a sputtering nature.

†Sputum (spɪ'tūm). Med. Pl. **sputa** (spɪ'tə). [L. spūtum spittle, neut. pa. pple. of spuĕre to spit.] Saliva or spittle mixed with mucus or purulent matter, and expectorated in certain diseased states of the lungs, chest, or throat; a mass or quantity of this.

Spy (spaɪ), sb. Forms 3–4 spie, 4–7 spie (4 spye), 4–6 spye 4, 5 spye, 5 spy, 4–7 spy. Also 5 pl. spyne. [ad. OF. espie (mod. espion), MLG. spȳe, MSw. spēja, spyia (Sw. spejare, spia).]

1. trans. 1. To watch (a person, etc.) in a secret or stealthy manner; to keep under observation with hostile intent; to act as a spy upon.

Spy, v. Forms 3–4 spie, etc. [ad. OF. espier (mod. espier), f. espie SPY sb.]

1. trans. To catch sight of, perceive, discern, observe.

Spy, sb. Also 4–7 spie, spye, spye. [ad. OF. espie.] A person employed to obtain secret information regarding the enemy; in early use esp. one venturing in disguise into the enemy's camp or territory.

b. Of a candle, fire, etc. (Cf. the ppl. a. 2.)

Spytterer. rare.⁻⁰ [f. SPUTTER v.] One who or that which sputters.

Spy-glass, sb. [f. prec.]
1. = SPY-GLASS sb.

Spy-glass, sb.
1. A telescope; a field-glass.

Spy-glass. Also SPY-GLASS. [f. SPY v. + GLASS.]

Spyder, variant of SPIDER int. Obs.

Spying, vbl. sb. [f. SPY v. + -ING.] Spying; espionage.

Spy-money, sb. Obs. Money paid to or for spies.

Spire, obs. form of SPICE.

Spy-dom. [f. SPY sb.]
The world of spies.

Squab (skwɒb), sb. Also 7 squabb. [Cf. Sw. dial. squabb loose fat flesh, squabba a soft wet mass.]

1. A raw, inexperienced person.

A. A newly-hatched, unfledged, or very young bird. Also fig.

Squab, a. [Cf. prec.]

1. Short and stout; squat and plump.

Squab, v. [f. SQUAB sb.]

1. trans. To knock or press (something); to squeeze flat. Now dial.

b. Const. with (another or others).

Squab, adv. Also 7 squob. [f. SQUAB sb.]

Squabash (skwɒ'bæʃ), v. [f. SQUAB a.] trans. To crush, demolish.

Squabble (skwɒ'bl), sb. [f. SQUABBLE v.] A noisy quarrel about something trivial; a petty or noisy contention.

Squabble (skwɒ'bl), v. [prob. imitative; cf. next and Sw. dial. skvabbel.] A wrangle, dispute, brawl; a petty quarrel.

Squabbler (skwɒ'blə(r)). [f. as prec.] One who squabbles.

Squabbling, vbl. sb. [f. as prec.]

Squabbling, ppl. a. [f. as prec.]

Squabbly, adv. [f. SQUAB a.] Bluntly.

Squab-pie, sb. [f. SQUAB sb. or a.]

Squa·cco. Ornith. Also 7–9 aguscoo. [Local Italian *squacco*.] A small crested species of heron, *Ardea ralloides* or *comata*.

Squash, variant of SQUATCH *v.* Obs.

Squad (skwǫd), *sb.*[1] [f. F. *escouade*, earlier *esquade* (*esquouade*), var. of *esquadre* SQUADER.]

1. *Mil.* A small number of men, a subdivision or section of a company, formed for drill or told off for some special purpose.

2. To assign or allocate to a squad.

3. A small number, group, or party of persons.

Squa·dding, *vbl. sb.* [f. SQUAD *sb.*[1] or *v.*] The action of forming into or drawing up in squads.

†Squa·dme, *v.* Now *dial.* and *U.S.* [Cf. SQUAD *sb.*[1]]

†Squa·drate, *a.* Obs. rare. [ad. L. *squadrāt-us*, pa. pple. of *squadrāre* to square.]

†Squa·drat, *sb.* and *a.* Obs. [ad. It. *squadrante*, pres. pple. of *squadrare* to square.]

2. A squadron of soldiers or ships.

†Squa·draic, *a.* Obs. rare. [f. SQUADRO + -IC.]

Squadron (skwǫdrən), *sb.* [ad. It. *squadrone*, f. *squadra* SQUADER.]

1. *Mil.* A body of soldiers drawn up or arranged in square formation.

†Squad, *v.* Obs. [f. F. *escouade*, earlier *esquade*.]

Squad (skwǫd), *v.* [f. prec.]

1. *trans.* To divide or form into squads; to draw up in a squad.

2. *intr.* [?]

Squa·dron, *v.* rare. [f. the *sb.*] *trans.* To form into, or as into, a squadron or squadrons.

Squa·dronal, *a.* [f. SQUADRON *sb.* + -AL.] Of or pertaining to a squadron or squadrons.

†Squa·drone (skwǫdrōn·), *sb.* Now *Hist.* Also 8 *-rony*.

Squa·droned, *ppl. a.* [f. SQUADRON *v.*] Formed into squadrons; drawn up in a squadron. Also *transf.*

†Squa·dronist. Obs. [ad. F. *squadroniste* or It. *squadronista*, f. SQUADRON *sb.*]

Squall (skwǫl), *sb.*[1] Also 8 squawl. [f. SQUALL *v.*[1]]

1. A discordant or violent scream; a loud, harsh cry.

Squall (skwǫl), *sb.*[2] [Of obscure origin: perhaps connected with prec.]

1. A sudden and violent gust, a blast or short sharp storm, of wind. *Naut.*

Squall (skwǫl), *v.*[1] Also 8 squawl (8 squawll). [imitative: cf. SQUEAL *v.*]

1. *intr.* To scream loudly or discordantly; to utter cries or shrieks.

Squall (skwǫl), *v.*[2] [Of obscure origin.]

Squa·ller. [f. SQUALL *v.*[1] + -ER.] One who squalls or screams; one addicted to squalling.

Squa·lling, *vbl. sb.*[1] [f. SQUALL *v.*[1]] Loud and shrill singing.

Squa·lling, *ppl. a.*[1] [f. SQUALL *v.*[1]] That squalls or screams.

†Squa·lm. Obs. [Cf. QUALM.]

†Squa·lor. Obs. rare. [L. *squalor*.]

†Squally, *a.*[1] Obs. [Of obscure origin.]

Squally, *a.*[2] [f. SQUALL *sb.*[2] + -Y.] Characterized by the prevalence of squalls.

Squall (skwǫl), *sb.*[3] [In many of these fields they are troubled with squalls.]

Squall (skwǫl), *v.*[3] Also 7–9 squawl (8 squawll). [imitative: cf. *squabby.*]

Squama (skwēˑmă), *sb.* Pl. *squamæ*. [L. *squama* scale.]

Squamaceous, *a.* Also 7 squammaceous. [f. L. *squama* + -ACEOUS.]

Squa·mate, *a.* [ad. L. *squāmāt-us*, f. *squama* scale.] Provided or covered with scales.

Squamation. *Zool.* [f. SQUAMA. See -ATION.]

Squa·me. *Zool.* Also 8 squam. [f. L. *squāma*.]

Squamella (skwămeˑlă), *sb.* Pl. *squamellæ*. [L., dim. of *squama* SQUAMA.]

Squami·ferous, *a.* [f. L. *squāmi-ger* + -OUS.] Scale-bearing; squamigerous.

Squami·form, *a.* [ad. mod.L. *squāmiformis.*] Having the shape of a scale.

Squami·gerous, *a.* [f. L. *squāmiger*: see SQUAMEROUS.] Scale-bearing; squamiferous.

Squamo-, used as combining form of SQUAMA *a.*, in the sense 'squamous and'.

Squa·mose, *a.* Also 6 squamous. [ad. L. *squāmōs-us*, f. *squama* scale.]

Squamosal (skwămōuˑsăl), *a.* and *sb.* Anat.

Squa·mose, *v.* rare. [f. SQUAMA *sb.*]

Squa·mous, *a.* Also 6 squamous. [ad. L. *squāmōs-us*, f. *squama* scale.] 1. Covered or furnished with scales; scaly.

Squa·mula (skwæˑmiˑûlă). *Zool., Ent., and Bot.* [L., dim. of *squama* SQUAMA.] A small scale.

Squa·mulate, *a.* [ad. mod.L. *squāmulāt-us*: see SQUAMULA and -ATE.]

Squamulation. [f. prec. or *mod.L. squāmulātiō.*]

Squa·mule. *Zool.* and *Bot.* [Anglicized f. SQUAMULA, = SQUAMULA.]

Squamuliform, *a.* [ad. mod.L. *squāmuliform-is.*]

Squamulose (skwæˑmiˑûlōus), *a.* [ad. mod.L. *squāmulōs-us*: see SQUAMULA and -OSE.] Furnished or covered with little scales.

Squamy ... Covered with scales; scaly.

Squander, v. ...

Squandering, ppl. a.

Squarable (skwēˑrăbˑl), a. and sb. [f. SQUARE v.] a. Capable of being squared. b. sb.

Square (skwēr) ...

IV. In various phrases.

Square (skwēr), a. Also 4–7 sqware, 5 sqwayre, 6 squear, &c. squair, squayr; 4–5 sware (4 suare), 5 pp. of esquarre= SQUARE v., assimilated to this and to SQUARE sb.]

SQUARE. ... SQUARE.

Square (skwēə). ... Also 5 squarn, sqvare, sqware, 6 sqware, squarre, 7 squarre; *sqvarre*, 9 dial. *squadrer*. [a. OF. *esquarrer* (*escarrer*, *escarrer*), ... F. *équarer*; *tjo*, *cxsadrur*. It. squadrar: — pop.L. *exquadrāre*, f. L. ex *out*+ *quadrāre* to make square: cf. *quadrus* (*escarrir*, etc., mod.F. *équarrir*).]

Square (skwēə), *sb.* ...

Squarelike, *a.* ...

Squarely (skwē·rli), *adv.* ...

Squarer (skwē·rəɹ). ...

SQUARE CAP. 731 SQUARE-RIGGED. SQUARE SAIL. 732 SQUARSONAGE.

Square cap. ...

Square-headed, *a.* ...

Square-leg. ...

Squarable (skwē·rəb'l), *a.* ...

Square-rigged, *a.* ...

Square sail. ...

Squareman. ...

Squareness (skwē·rnes). ...

Square-sterned, *a.* ...

Square-tailed, *a.* ...

Square-toe. ...

Square-toed, *a.* ...

Square-toes. ...

Squaring (skwē·riŋ), *vbl. sb.* ...

Squarewise, *adv.* Also *square-wise*, 6 *squre-*, 6–7 *squarewise*. [f. SQUARE *sb.* + WISE.]

Squarier. *Obs. rare.*

Squarish (skwē·riʃ), *a.* ...

Square-toed, *a.* ...

Squaring (skwē·riŋ), *ppl. a.* [f. SQUARE *v.*]

Squarish. ...

Squarrose (skwɒ·rōs), *a.* ...

Squarrous, *a.* = SQUARROSE *a.* 1.

Squarrulose, *a. Bot. rare.* [Dim. of SQUARROSE.]

Squarson (skwā·ɹsən). [A jocular combination ...] Hence **Squarsonage**, **Squarsonocracy.**

Squary (skwɛ̄·ri), a. [f. SQUARE sb. + -Y.]
Square-shaped; squarish.

Squash, sb.[1] [Related to, or directly from, SQUASH v.[1]]

1. I. **1.** The unripe pod of a pea. Also applied contemptuously to persons. Obs. exc. arch.

+2. Squash pear, a variety of pear.

Squash (skwɔʃ), sb.[2] Also 8 squosh. [Abbreviation of Narragansett Indian asquutasquash, f. asq raw, uncooked: cf. SQUANTER-squash. (The -ash is a plural ending, as in succotash.)]

Squash (skwɔʃ), v.[1] Also 8 squosh. [ad. OF. esquasser (esquacer, esquacier), = It. squassare:—pop. L.]

Squashable (skwɔ·ʃăbl), a. [f. SQUASH v.[1]]
Capable of being squashed. Hence **Squashabi·lity**, capability of being crushed together.

Squashiness (skwɔ·ʃĭnes), sb. [f. SQUASHY a.] The condition or character of being squashy.

Squash pear: see SQUASH sb.[1]

+Squashy (skwɔ·ʃi), a. [f. SQUASH sb.[1] + -Y.]
Of fruit, etc.: Having a soft or pulpy consistency; lacking in firmness.

Squass, obs. form of SQUAW.

Squassation. Obs.—[1] [f. squassare to shake severely: see SQUASH v.[1]]

Squat (skwɔt), sb.[1] Also 4 squatte, 5, 7 squate. [f. SQUAT v.]

1. A heavy fall or bump; a severe or violent jar or jolt. Now north. dial.

2. A bruise, contusion, or wound, esp. one caused by a fall; a dent or indentation. Now dial.

Squat (skwɔt), sb.[2] Comm. [Perh. the same word as prec.]

Squat (skwɔt), sb.[3] U.S. [Of doubtful origin.] The angel-fish, Squatina angelus.

Squat (skwɔt), pa. pple. and (ppl.) a. Also 5 squatte, 7, 9 dial., squat, 9 dial. swat. [Pa. pple. of SQUAT v.]

Squat (skwɔt), v. Also 4 squatte, 5, 7 squatte, squate. [ad. OF. esquatir, var. of esquater, f. es- (L. ex) + quater to press.]

I. **1.** trans. To crush, flatten, or beat out of shape; to smash or squash severely. Now dial.

Squatter (skwɔ·tə(r)), sb.[1] [f. SQUAT v.]

1. U.S. A settler having no normal or legal title to the land occupied by him, esp. one thus occupying land in a district not yet surveyed or apportioned by the government.

Squatter (skwɔ·tə(r)), v.[1] [A variant of SWATTER v.]

Squatterarchy. Austr. [SQUATTER sb.[1] + -ARCHY.] = SQUATTOCRACY.

Squatterdom. Austr. [SQUATTER sb.[1] + -DOM.] The collective body of squatters.

Squattering, vbl. sb. [f. SQUATTER v.] The action of the verb, in various senses.

Squatting, ppl. a. [f. SQUAT v.] That squats or crouches.

Squaw (skwɔ), sb. Also 7 squa, squae, squae. [a. Narragansett Indian squaws, Massachusetts squa, woman, female; related forms in nearly all other Algonquin dialects.]

1. In North American Indian usage, or with reference to North American Indians: A woman or wife.

Squawberry. U.S. [SQUAW sb. + BERRY.]

Squaw-duck. U.S. [SQUAW sb. + DUCK.]

Squawk (skwɔk), v. [A word of imitative origin: cf. SQUEAK, SQUAWL.]

Squawking, ppl. a. [f. SQUAWK v.] That squawks, or utters hoarse squeaks; characterized by squawks or squawking.

Squawky, a. [f. SQUAWK sb. or v. + -Y.] Of the voice: Loud and harsh; hoarsely squeaky.

Squawroot. U.S.

Squayt, Squaysome, obs. forms of SQUEASY, SQUEASOME.

Squddle, obs. f. SQUIDDLE.

Squeak (skwīk), v. Also 8 squeek.

1. intr. To call or cry with a loud harsh note; to squall or screech hoarsely.

Squeak, v. Also 4-6 squeake, 6-7 squeake, 7 squeeke, etc.

Squeaker (skwī·kəɹ). [f. the vb.]

Squea·klet. [-LET.] A little squeak.

Squeaky (skwī·ki), a. [f. SQUEAK sb. or v.] Characterized by squeaking sounds; tending to squeak.

Squeal (skwīl), sb. [f. the vb.]

Squeal, a. s.w. dial. [? Related to QUEAL v.] Feeble, frail.

Squealer (skwī·ləɹ). [f. SQUEAL v.]

Squeal, v. Also 6-7 squele, squeale.

Squea·ling, vbl. sb. [f. SQUEAL v.] The action of the verb, in various senses.

Squea·ling, ppl. a. [f. as prec.]

Squeal (skwēl), v. Forms: 4-5, 7 aquele (north., 4 squele, 4 swele), 6 3c. squeli(l), 7-9 aquel, 7 -squeal. [Imitative.]

Squeamish (skwī·miʃ), a., adv., and sb. Forms: 4-5 squaymous, 6-7 squaymish, 6 -yah, -ich, 6-7 squaimish(e, 7 squemish, north. dial. 8-9 swaimish, 8-9 sweamish, 7, 9 sweemish, 7-9 squeamish. [var. of squaymous, squeamous, q.v.; see alteration of suffix.]

Squeamishly, adv.

Squeamishness.

Squea·mous, a. Now north. dial. Forms: a. 4-5 squaymous, 5-os, -os, -ous; 4-5 squaymouse; 4-5 sqwaymous, 4-6 -ous, 4-6, 5-7 a -ous; 5 skeymous, -e ; 4-6 -ous, north. dial. 8 swaims, 9 swaymous, 7-9 -us, swaim, swamous, 9 -ua, swaim, swaymous. 7. a. AF. escumous, escouet, of obscure origin. Cf. ESCUAYMOUS (b.

Squeeze (skwīz), v. Also 7 squees, squease, squeaze, 7-8 squeese, squeeze, 7-9 squeize. [f. SQUEEZE v.]

Squeeze (skwīz), sb. [f. the vb.]

Squegee, sb. and v.: see SQUEEGEE.

Squeeze (skwīz), v. Also 8-9 squeedge. [Strengthened form of SQUEEZE v.]

Squeezable (skwī·zăb'l), a. [f. SQUEEZE v.] Capable of being compressed or squeezed.

Squeezer (skwī·zəɹ). [f. SQUEEZE v.]

Squeeze·ness, nonce-wd. [f. SQUEEZE.]

Squeegee (skwī·dʒī), sb. Also 8-9 squeegee. [f. prec.]

Squeeze, *v.* (continued)

Squeezed, *ppl. a.* 1. Subjected to pressure or compression.

Squeezer (skwī·zǝɹ). 1. One who squeezes, in various senses.

Squee·zing, *vbl. sb.* 1. The action of pressing or compressing; the fact of being compressed.

Squee·zekin. [f. Squeeze *v.* + -kin.] A slight squeeze or pressure.

Squee·zy (skwī·zi), *a.* [as prec.]

Squelch (skwelʃ, skwelj), *sb.* [Imitative.]

Squelch (skwelʃ, skwelj), *v.* [as prec.]

Squelcher. One who, or that which, squelches.

Squelching, *vbl. sb.*

Sque·lching, *ppl. a.*

Squelchy, *a.*

Squelchily, *adv.*

Squelchiness, *sb.*

Squelet, obs. form of Scullery.

Squelt, var. Swelt.

Squench, *v.* Now *dial.*

Squentin, obs. variant of Squinancy.

Squeteague (skwetē·g), *sb.* *U.S.* [Narragansett Indian.]

Squib (skwib), *sb.* 1. A common species of firework.

Squib (skwib), *v.*

Squibbish (skwi·biʃ), *a.* [f. Squib *sb.*]

Squibber. One who writes or utters squibs.

Squibbery (skwi·bǝri), *sb.* [f. Squib *v.* + -ery.]

Squibbing, *vbl. sb.*

Squibbling, *ppl. a.* — *Obs.*

Squiblet, *rare* — [. Squib *sb.* + -let.]

Squibling, *rare* — [-ling.] = Squiblet.

Squibster. *Obs.*

Squibchary. *Obs.*

Squid (skwid), *sb.* 1. One of various species of cephalopods.

Squidge (skwidʒ), *v.* [as prec.]

Squidgy (skwi·dʒi), *a.* [as prec.]

Squiery, obs. form of Squiry.

Squiffy, *sl.* 1. Intoxicated; drunk.

Squiggle, *sb.* [Imitative.] A giggle or titter.

Squi·ggle, *v.*

Squi·ggly, *a.*

Squilgee (skwilʒī·), *sb.*

Squill (skwil), *sb.*

Squiller, *Obs.* Forms: 4 squyler.

Squillitic, *a.* *Obs.* [ad. L. *squilliticus.*]

Squillitical, *a.* *Obs.*

Squilla (skwi·la), *sb.* Pl. **squillæ.**

Squinant. *Bot.* Also 6 squinant.

Squinance (skwi·năns), *Obs.*

Squinancy (skwi·nănsi), *Obs.*

Squinant, var. Squinance.

Squinch (skwinʃ), *sb.* *Arch.* Also 6 squynch.

Squirm (skwɜːm), *v.*

Squirming *vbl. sb.* and *ppl. a.*

Squirmy (skwɜːmɪ), *a.* [f. SQUIRM *v.*]

Squiracy, *var.* SQUIREARCHY.

Squirocracy, *rare.* [f. SQUIRE + -OCRACY.]

Squirr, *v.* Also *squir.* [var. of SKIRR *v.*]

Squirrel (skwɪrəl), *sb.* Forms: α. 3 squirel, squyrel, squyrell, -ylle, 4–5 squyrel, -elle; β. 4–7 squirel, 5 squyrell, -ell, 6–7 squirrell, -il, 6–7 -il, squerell, &c. skurel (6 skarale).

Squirrel, *v.* Obs. [f. the sb.] *a. intr.*

Squirrel-tail.

Squirrel-tailed, *a.*

Squirrelite, -*ility*, obs. *vars.* SCURRILITY.

Squirr-ity, -*var.* → SQUIRR *v.*

Squirt (skwɜːt), *sb.* Forms: 5 soqwyrt, 6 skuert, squyrte, 6 squyrt, -yrte, 6–quirt, 6 (*north. dial.* swirt), 6–quirt (9 *north. dial.* swirt).

Squirt (skwɜːt), *v.* Also 5–6 squyrt, squyrte, squrte, 6 *north. dial.* swirt. [f. SQUIRT *sb.*]

Squirter.

Squirtful. [f. SQUIRT *sb.*]

Squirrel, *var.* → SQUIRREL.

Squirrical, *a. nonce-word.* [f. as prec.]

Squirting, *vbl. sb.*

Squirting, *ppl. a.*

Squish (skwɪʃ), *v.* Also *dial.* [f. the vb.]

Squish (skwɪʃ), *sb.* [Imitative: cf. SQUISH-SQUASH.]

Squishop: see note to SQUARSON.

Squish-squash, *adv., sb.,* and *v.* [Imitative.]

Squit (skwɪt), *sb.* *rare.* [Of obscure origin.]

† Squize, *v. Obs.* *rare.*

Squit, *int. dial.* [perh. related to SQUIT *v.*]

Squit (skwɪt), *v.* Now *dial.* [Imitative. Cf. SQUITTER.]

Squitch (skwɪtʃ), *sb.* [Altered form of QUITCH *sb.*]

Squitch, *v. U.S.* [f. SQUITCH *sb.*]

Squitchineal, obs. *var.* of COCHINEAL.

† Squiry, *Obs.* Forms: 4–6 squierie, 4 squyrye, *Sc.* squyary, 6 squyry. [ad. OF. *escuirie, esquierie.*]

Squitter (skwɪtər), *sb.* Now *dial.* [f. the vb.]

Squint, *var.* → SQUINT.

Squitter, *v.* Now *dial.* [Imitative of SQUIT *v.*, or alteration of SKITTER *v.*]

Squitter-, the verbal stem used in comb.

† Squitter, *Obs.* Forms: 6 squyse, 6–7 squize, 7 squize. [Of obscure origin: cf. squeeze.]

Squoyle, local *var.* of SQUAIL *sb.*

St, the nineteenth letter of the English alphabet.

St.

St (st), *int.* Also 7 'st. [repr. a checked sibilation, instinctively felt as expressive; less exactly rendered by HIST, † ISP *int.* Cf. L. *st* (Plautus, Terence, etc.).]

St. Abbreviation of SAINT.

Staal, var. STALE *sb.*

Staale, obs. var. of STALE *sb.*

Staare, obs. form of STARE *v.*

Staat, Staately, obs. ff. STATE *sb.*, STATELY.

Stab (stæb), *sb.* Also 7 stabbe, 6 stabe.

Stab (stæb), *v.* [Related to the synonymous STAB *sb.*]

Stab (stæb), *sb.* Printers' *slang.* Also 'stab. [f. ESTABLISHMENT 10.]

Stab, obs. form of STAFF *sb.*

Stabado. *Obs. rare*⁻¹. In pl. **stabadoes.**

† Stabat Mater. A sequence, composed by Jacobus de Benedictis in the 13th c., in commemoration of the sorrows of the Blessed Virgin Mary. Also a musical setting of this sequence.

Stabbed, *ppl. a.* [f. STAB v. + -ED¹.]
1. Wounded by stabbing.
2. Of pain: Sharp and sudden, characterized by twinges comparable to the effect of a stab.
3. *Bookbinding.* [See STAB v. 6.]

Stabber. [f. STAB v. + -ER¹.]
1. One who stabs.
2. Something which stabs, a knife, dagger, etc.
3. *Naut.* Rigging & Seamanship.
4. (See quot.)

Stabbing, *vbl. sb., ppl. a.* [-ING¹.]
1. The action or an act of STAB in various senses.
2. Something which gives stability or firmness; stay, support.

Stabilimeter (stæbili·miː·təɹ). *Aeronautics.*

Stability (stăbi·liti). Forms: 4 stabilite, etc. [ME. stabilite, a. OF. (e)stableté, semi-popular ad. L. stabilitāt-, f. stabilis STABLE a.]

† Stabilate, *v. rare.* [L. stabilāt-, ppl. stem of stabilīre, f. stabilis STABLE.]

Stabilitate, *v. rare.* [L. stabilitāt-, ppl. stem of stabilitāre, f. stabilitāt-: see STABILITY.]

Stabilization (stæbilaɪzeɪ·ʃən). [f. STABILIZE v. + -ATION.] = STABILIER.

Stabilize (stæ·bilaɪz), *v.* [ad. F. stabiliser, f. L. stabilis STABLE a.]

Stabilizer (stæ·bilaɪzəɹ). [f. STABILIZE v. + -ER¹.]
1. *Aeronautics.* A stabilizing apparatus or device.

Stabilizing, *ppl. a.* [f. STABILIZE v.]

Stabling (stæ·bliŋ). [ad. F. stable + -ING.] The action of placing or accommodating (horses) in a stable.

Stable, *sb.*¹ [a. OF. estable, F. étable.]

† Stablement. *Obs.* [a. OF. establement, f. establir to ESTABLISH.]

Stableness. [f. STABLE a. + -NESS.] The quality or condition of being stable; = STABILITY.

Stabler (stæ·bləɹ). Now *Sc.* Forms: 5 stabyler, (stabyller), 6 stabulare, stabillar, etc. [f. STABLE sb. + -ER¹.]

Stable door. The stable door: whence the proverb.

Stable-stand. [STAND sb.]

Stablish (stæ-blif), v. Now *arch.* Forms: 3–5 stablis, 4 stablis, stablice, 4–5 stablisse, -esshe, -ysh, -ish, 4–6 stablysche, -ysshe, 4 stablysshe, -ishe, (stablyssahe), 4–7 **'stablish**, 4–stablish; also *pa. t.* and *pa. pple.* 3–stablissed, 4–stablissht (*Sc.* stablisait). 4, 6 **-stablish** *v.* = ESTABLISH *v.* in various senses.

†Sta'blisher. *Obs. rare.* One who stablishes.

Stablishment (stæ-blifment), *arch.* [var. of ESTABLISHMENT. Cf. STABLISH *v.* and -MENT.]

†Stabstuate, v. *Obs. rare⁻¹.* [f. L. *stabiliā-re*, *stabilit-*, pa. pple. of *stabilire*.] To make stable.

†Sta'bulate, v. *Obs.⁻⁰.* [f. L. *stabulāt-*, *stabulā-*, *-ári*, f. *stabulum* = see STABLE *sb.*]

Stabula'tion. *rare.* [ad. L. *stabulātiōn-*, *-ātiō.*]

Sta'bulist. *rare⁻¹.* [f. L. *stabulum* STABLE *sb.*]

†Stacca'do. *Obs.* Also 7–8 stacado.

†Sta'blishness. *Obs. rare⁻¹.* [f. STABLISH *a.* + -NESS.] Stability.

†Sta'bly, *a¹. Obs.* Also 4–5 stable.

†Staccato (stǎkā'to), *a.* (*adv., sb.*) *Mus.* [It., pa. pple. of *staccare*, shortened form of *distaccare* = DETACH *v.*]

†Sta'bly, *a². Obs. rare.* [f. STABLE *sb.*]

Stably (stē'bli), *adv.* Forms: see STABLE *a.* + -LY²

Stachys (stē'kis). [L. *stachy-* (Pliny), a. Gr. στάχυς.]

Stacioner, -dour, obs. f. STATIONER, STATION.

Stack (stæk), *sb.¹* Forms: 1, 3–stac, 3–7 stak (4 stakke), 4–stack, 6 stakke, 6 stayke, 4–stack. 6 ON. *stakk-r* hay-stack, 6 stacke, 6 stayke, 4–stack.

†Sta'blick, *Sc. Obs. rare⁻¹.* [f. STACK *sb.¹ + -LE.*] A small stack (of wheat, etc.).

†Staco', obs. f. STUCCO.

Stack (stæk), *v.¹* Forms: see the sb. [f. STACK *sb.¹*]

Stacker (stæ-kǝr), *sb.¹* Also *f.²* stakers, 9 stacker. [f. STACK *v.¹* + -ER¹.]

Stacker (stæ-kǝr), *sb.²* *Obs. exc. dial.* Forms: 3–6 staker, 4–6 stakere, 5 stakyer, 3 stacker; (*Sc. dial.*) 8–9 stagher; freq. of *stack* to push, to stagger. [f. STACKER *v.*]

Stack (stæk), *v.¹* Forms: see the sb.

Stackering (stæ-kǝriŋ), *vbl. sb.¹* [f. STACKER *v.* + -ING¹.]

Stackering (stæ-kǝriŋ), *ppl. a.* [f. STACKER *v.* + -ING².]

Stocklons (stæ-klǝnz), *sb. pl.* [f. STACK *sb.* + -LESS.]

Stacket (stæ-ket). *Obs. rare⁻¹.* [f. STACK *sb.*]

Sta'cklet. *Obs. rare⁻¹.* A small stack of wheat, etc.

Stacte (stæ-kti). [a. L. *stacte*, a. Gr. στακτή.]

†Sta'cket, *sb.* *Sc.* Forms: 6 stacat, 6 stackat, 7 stacket. [f. Du. *staket* (whence G. *stacket*) or Fr. *estacade*, *estacade* see STACCADO.]

Stackful (stæ-kful). Forms: see STACK *sb.* + -FUL.]

Stack-garth, *north.* Also 6–9 staggarth; *f. dial.* stagarth. [f. *stack sb.* + GARTH¹.]

Stacking (stæ-kiŋ), *vbl. sb.* [f. STACK *v.* + -ING¹.]

Staddle (stæ-d'l), *sb.* Forms: 1 staðol, 1–3 staðel, 6 stathell (6 stadel), 7 stad-del, 6, 6–9 staddle, 9 staddel, stadle; (for dial. forms see STADDLE.) [OE. *staðol* masc., *staðol* neut. = MLG. *stadel* = OHG. *stadal* (MHG. *stadel*, G. *stadel*) barn, storehouse, ON. *stöðull* masc., milking-place (Norw. *stöl*) :—OTeut. *staðlo-*, f. *sta-*, root of STAND *v.*]

Staddle (stæ-d'l), *v.* Forms: see the sb.

Staddlerian, *sb.* and *a.* Pertaining to or the office of stadtholder; *sb.* A partisan of the stadtholder.

Staddow (stæ-dǝu). [Anglicized form of STADIUM. Cf. *stade* and STADE *sb.*]

Stade (stēd). *Obs. rare⁻¹.* [Anglicized form of STADIUM.]

†Stade⁴. *Obs.* [f. *Stade*, name of a town in Eng. textile place.]

Stadthodler, stadtholder (stæ-thǒudǝr). *Hist.* Forms: 6–8 stadholder, 7 state-holder, (8 stadhouder), 7 – stadtholder, 8 stadtholder. [a. Du. *stadhouder* (= G. *statthalter*) one who occupies another's place.]

Stadho'lderate. *Obs. rare.* Also stadt-.

Stadho'lderian, *a.* and *sb.* Pertaining to or the office of stadtholder.

Stadho'ldership. [f. STADHOLDER + -SHIP.]

Stadia (stē-diǎ). [Of obscure history; prob. derived from STADIUM, and perhaps from the plural of stadium.]

Stadium (stē-diǒm). Pl. stadia (stē-diǎ); also 6 stadies, 7 stadio, 8 stadia's, 7 stadiums, stadium's, 8 stadias, stadium's.

or space of ground, conteining 625. foote. 1676 H. Vernon in *Phil. Trans.* XI. 579 There is the stadium yet to be seen. 1749 G. West *Pindar's Odes, Diss. Olympic Games* i. (1753) II. 10 Homer..introduces his greatest Heroes contending in the very same kind of Exercises, with those practised in the Stadium of Olympia. *Ibid.* vii. 61 The simple Foot-Race, named the Stadium, from the Length of the Course. 1833 Sir H. Ellis *Elgin Marbles* I. 26 One of the greatest of the public works of Athens was the stadium of Herodes Atticus. 1834 Baron Berenger (*title*) Particulars and Recommendations of the Stadium, or British National Arena for Manly and Defensive Exercises, Equestrian, Chivalric and Aquatic Games..at the Residence of the late Lord Cremorne. 1847 Grote *Greece* II. xxviii. IV. 96 Kylon..had gained the prize in the Olympic stadium. 1866 Alger *Solit. Nat. & Man* II. 51 We always think of the oracles of the gods as dropping in grove and grotto, not in street and stadium. 1901 *Westm. Gaz.* 27 Feb. 8/2 The stadium for sports, covering ten acres, is one of the chief features of the [Pan-American] Exposition [at Buffalo].

3. A stage of a process, disease, etc.

1659 W. Simpson *Hydrol. Chym.* 190 The several Stadiums of this Salt gives the various apparencies of growth, maturity, and old age of Plants. 1725 *Phil. Trans.* XXXIII. 391 Hence those Deliriums, Coma's, &c. so frequently threatening at this Stadium of the Disease. 1822–29 *Good's Study Med.* (ed. 3) IV. 77 Hence different stadia of life seem to exercise some control [over insanity]. 1860 Geo. Eliot in Cross *Life* (1885) II. 282 We are still far off our last stadium of developement. 1876 Bartholow *Mat. Med.* (1879) 176 Its good effects are limited, however, to that stadium of these maladies in which the morbid action is confined to the nasal passages. 1878 Dowden *Stud. Lit.* 36 A new stadium in the advance of the revolutionary idea commenced. 1888 J. Martineau *Study Relig.* II. ii. II. 26 As the later stadia of her [Nature's] developments rise above the earlier. 1895 D. Sharp *Insects* I. 158 The intervals between the ecdyses are called stadia, the first stadium being the period between hatching and the first ecdysis.

4. *Surveying.* (See quots.) Cf. Stadia.

1861 in *Abridgm. Specif. Patents, Opt.* etc. *Instrum.* (1875) 363 An improved stadium or telemetre. 1871 Heather *Math. Instrum.* III. 79 The Stadium for measuring distances in rifle practice. 1884 Knight *Dict. Mech.*, Suppl., *Stadium*, the leveling rod of a surveyor.

Stadt, variant of Stad.

‖**Stadthaus** (stat,haus). [G., f. *stadt* town + *haus* House *sb.*] A German town-hall. Cf. Stadthouse.

1839 Barham *Ingold. Leg.*, *St. Gengulphus*, They stuck up placards on the walls of the Stadthaus. 1848 Thackeray *Van. Fair* lxiii, Georgy Osborne..came to the Stadthaus' ball in company of his uncle's courier.

Stadtholder, variant of Stadholder.

Stadthouse (stæ·t,haus). Also: 7 **stat-**, 8 **stad-house.** [ad. G. *stadthaus* and Du. *stadhuis*, f. G. *stadt*, Du. *stad* town + G. *haus*, Du. *huis* House *sb.*] A town-hall, esp. one in a Dutch town (or Dutch colony).

1646 Howell *Lewis XIII*, ii. 42 A Stat-House in Delph in Holland, which had bin burnt in like maner and reedified. 1673 Temple *Observ. United Prov.* ii. 86 The Magnificence of their Publique Buildings, as Stadthouse and Arsenals. 1704 *Lond. Gaz.* No. 4077/3 Having shewn his Grace their Famous Stadhouse. 1766 *Ann. Reg.*, *Chron.* 94/1 A most terrible fire at Muskau in Upper Lusatia, which reduced to ashes, two churches, the stadthouse [etc.]. 1809 W. Irving *Knickerb.* (1861) 131 A great banquet was served up in the stadthouse. 1849 Macaulay *Hist. Eng.* v. I. 550 The Stadthouse of Amsterdam.

Stagg, obs. form of Stag *sb.*[1]

†**Sta·fador.** *Obs. rare*[−1]. [ad. Sp. *estafador*, agent-n. f. *estafar* to swindle.] An impostor.

1638 W. M. *Garcia's Sonne Rogue* 246 For the first are the Robbers, next the Stafadours, then the Grumets, after these the Hobgoblins. *Ibid.* 249 A Robber, Staffador or Grumet.

Stafesagro, obs. form of Stavesacre.

Staff (staf), *sb.*[1] Pl. **staves** (stēvz), **staffs** (stafs). Forms: 1 **stæb**, (**stab-**, **stob-**), 1–2 **stef**, 1–4 **stæf**, 1–6 **staf**, 3 *oblique* **stæve**, **steave**, 3–4 *oblique* **stave**, 4–7 **stafe**, 4–8, (9 *arch.*) **staffe**, 5–6 *Sc.* **staif**, 6 **stayffe**, *Sc.* **stalf**, (**stafte**), 4–7 *genit. sing.* **staves**, 3– **staff**; *pl.* 1 **stafas**, 2 **stafen**, 2–5 **stafes**, 3 **staven**, *Ormin* **stafess**, 4 **stafs**, **steves**, (**stavenes**), 4–5 **stafis**, **stawis**, 4–6 **stavis**, **-ys**, 5–6 **staffes**, 6 **stavez**, *Sc.* **staiffis**, **sta(l)ffis**, 3–9 **staves**, 8– **staffs.** [Com. Teut.: OE. *stæf* masc. corresponds to OFris. *stef*, OS. *-staf* (MLG., MDu., Du. *staf*), OHG., MHG. *stap*, genit. *stabes*, mod.G. *stab*), ON. *staf-r* (Sw. *staf*, Da. *stav*):—OTeut. **stabo-z*; a variant type **stabi-* appears in Goth. **staf-s* (in dat. pl. *stabim* rendering στοιχεῖον element; a third type, possibly ancient, is represented by early mod. Du. *stave*, now *staaf* fem., bar. Other probable derivatives from the Teut. **stab-* (? to be firm or fixed) are Da. *stabbe* (Icel. *stabbi*) Stab *sb.*[1]; ON. *stef* neut. (:—**stabjon-*) set or recurring time, refrain, *stefja* (:—**stabjon-*) to prevent, *stefna* fem. appointed time (:—**stabnjōn-*). Steven *sb.*; OHG. *stabēn* (MHG. *staben*) to become stiff. The pre-Teut. type might be either **stapo-* (? f. **stā-* to stand, with suffix of causative import as in Sk. *sthāpāyati* makes to stand), or **stabho-*.

The plural form *staves* is now somewhat archaic, exc. in certain senses in which a sing. form Stave has been developed from it; but it is still preferred in those senses that are confined to literary use.]

I. 1. A stick carried in the hand as an aid in walking or climbing. Now chiefly *literary* (e.g. in reference to 'pilgrims').

c 725 *Corpus Gloss.* 1441 *Olastrum*: stæb. *c* 888 Ælfred *Boeth.* xxxvi. § 6 Ða cild ridað on hiora stafum. *c* 897 — *Gregory's Past. C.* xvii. 126 Mid ʒierde mon bið beswungen, and mid stæfe he bið awreðed. *c* 1205 Lay. 30754 Þene staf he nom an honde and ferde ouer þan londe. *c* 1250 *Gen. & Ex.* 3149 Stondende, and staf on hond. 1377 Langl. *P. Pl.* B. xvii. 36 Þe gome þat goth with o staf, he semeth in gretter hele þan he þat goth with two staues to syʒte of vs alle. *a* 1533 Berners *Huon* cxlvi. 545 Huon..aparelyd hymselfe lyke a pylgryme, with a stafe, and a bage abought his necke. *c* 1539 in Aungier *Syon* (1840) 131 They bare small staves in their honds to lepe over the watery play-shes. 1590 Spenser *F. Q.* I. viii. 30 An old old man..That on a staffe his feeble steps did frame. 1666 Pepys *Diary* 20 July, He did present me with a varnished staffe, very fine and light to walk with. 1760–72 H. Brooke *Fool of Qual.* (1809) IV. 139 With their staffs in their hands. 1803 Jane Porter *Thaddeus* i, When we possessed no other property than the staffs which we hold in our hands. 1860 Tyndall *Glac.* I. xiv. 95, I..dug my staff deeply into the snow. 1857 J. G. Holland *Bay Path* vi. 78 Two or three pedestrians..swinging their sturdy staves. 1907 *Verney Mem.* I. 50 A curious pilgrim's staff.

b. *jocularly* as a type of thinness or leanness.

c 1386 Chaucer *Prol.* 592 Ful longe were his legges and ful lene, Ylyk a staf, ther was no calf ysene. 1597 Shaks. *2 Hen. IV*, v. i. 71 If I were saw'de into Quantities, I should make foure dozen of such bearded Hermites staues, as Master Shallow.

†**c.** Applied to a crutch. *Obs.*

1483 Caxton *Gold. Leg.* 432/2 He coude not goo ne stande wythoute he had two crutches or staues under hys armes.

†**d.** A stick or rod, esp. one with a hooked end, used for tending sheep; a shepherd's crook. *Obs.*

For *shepherd's staff* used as a plant-name, after L. *virga pastoris*, see Shepherd *sb.* 7 d.

c 1475 *Pict. Voc.* in Wr.-Wülcker 814 *Hoc pedum*, a scheperdes stafe. 1530 Palsgr. 266/2 Schepherdes staffe, *houlette*. 1538 Elyot *Dict.*, *Agolum*, a staffe to dryue cattell with. 1577 Googe *Heresbach's Husb.* III. 141 They must be well ware in the driuing of them..that they guide them with theyr voyce, and shaking of theyr staffe.

e. A rod or wand used as an instrument of magic or divination.

1610 Shaks. *Temp.* v. 54 I'le breake my staffe. 1656 S. Holland *Don Zara* 67 Her Rod, Staff, and other implements of Sorcery stood by her on a Table of Abstersive Ebony. 1770 Langhorne *Plutarch*, *Camillus* (Rtldg.) 109/2 They discovered under a great heap of ashes the augural staff of Romulus. This staff is crooked at one end, and called *lituus*. 1836 Thirlwall *Greece* xiv. II. 197 Diviners..who drew their knowledge of the future from the position of staves thrown on the ground.

f. *By staff and baton*: a formula of Scots Law, used when the vassal resigns his feu into the hands of his superior. (Cf. Rod *sb.*[1] 1 c.)

1499 *Reg. Privy Seal Scot.* I. 43/2 Resignit be his procuratouris in our soverane lordis handis..be staf and bastoun. 1596 in T. Morris *Provosts of Methven* (1875) 86 Thair in my name..be staff and bastoun, as vse is, to resigne..in our said Souerane lordis handis..my mansioun. 1762 in *Nairne Peerage Evid.* (1874) 92 To resign surrender overgive and deliver duely and lawfully by staff and baton as use is all and haill the foresaids parts and portions of his baronies.

2. A stick, pole or club used as a weapon. (Cf. Quarterstaff.)

The constable's staff (quot. 1583, etc.) is at once a weapon and a badge of office: see sense 7 and Tipstaff 1.

c 1000 Ælfric *Gram.* ix. (Z.) 55 *Fustis* saʒol oððe stæf. *c* 1250 *Owl & Night.* 1167 Her-uore hit is þat me þe shuneþ, & þe to-toruep & to-buneþ Mid staue & stone & turf & clute. *c* 1290 *St. Lawrence* 114 in *S. Eng. Leg.* 343 He het heom with grete staues leggen on him to grounde. *a* 1300 *Cursor M.* 7528 His arms fra him did he suing, And tok bot a staf and a sling. 1340 *Ayenb.* 156 Þe sergons..nome steues and byete þane asse riʒt to þe uolle. 1382 Wyclif *Mark* xiv. 48 As to a thef ʒe han gon out with swerdis and staues, for to take me. *c* 1386 Chaucer *Knt.'s T.* 1652 Yemen on foote and communes many oon With shorte staues. 1421 *Cov. Leet Bk.* 28 That no bocher..ber no billys, ne gysarnez, ne no grett stauys within the Cite..Saue leefull be hit to euery bocher and othur man..comyng to market to dryve hur beestis with smale stavys and non othur. 1470–85 Malory *Arthur* I. ix. 47 Thenne the comyns of Carlyon aroos with clubbis and stauys and slewe many knyghtes. 1583 *Nottingham Rec.* IV. 201, xxx. Cunstable stavez at xvd. a pece. 1663 Killigrew *Parson's Wedd.* IV. i, Constables staff, and Lanthorn. 1671 Milton *Samson* 1123, I only with an Oak'n staff will meet thee. 1742 *Col. Rec. Pennsylv.* IV. 621 The Constables interposing with their Staves for some time kept off the Rioters. 1778 *Learning at a Loss* I. 103 In his Hand [was] a very inimical Oak staff of at least two Inches diameter. 1821 Combe *Syntax*, *Wife* I. (1869) 267 But warrants, staves and mastiffs wait To guard the approaches to his gate. 1847 Mrs. A. Kerr tr. *Ranke's Hist. Servia* 32 We find them armed only with long staves.

fig. 1541 Crome in Strype *Eccl. Mem.* (1721) III. xi. 104 But, alack! this bold Beggar's Staf hath this Beggar of Rome left here behind him. Which Staf beateth both the Bodies and Souls of Men. 1577 *F. de Lisle's Legendarie* G vij, She looked to finde in him a new staffe wherewith to suppresse the Guisians.

3. a. The shaft of a spear or lance. *arch.* †**b.** A spear, lance, or similar armed weapon. *To break a staff*, to tilt or contend *with* (an antagonist). *Obs.*

c 1205 Lay. 8155 Euelin..mid þan stæue to-draf, and smat Herigal a þon ribben þat þe stæf to-bræc amidden. *c* 1330 R. Brunne *Chron. Wace* (Rolls) 14806 Eyþer þorow pleyn bataille in feld, Or wyþ chaumpion staf & scheld. *c* 1400 *Brut* ccxxiii. 276 He fonde in a chambre aboue v C of grete stafes [Caxton staues] of fyne oke, with longe pikes of yren and of stele. 1471 Caxton *Recuyell* (Sommer) 157 Ther was ..many an arowe shotte and many a staffe and guysarme broken. 1513 Douglas *Æneis* VIII. xi. 45 Twa javilling speris, or than gyssarn stavis. *a* 1548 Hall *Chron.*, *Hen. VIII*, 6 There wer broken many staues and great praise geuen to the twoo straungers. 1597 Shaks. *2 Hen. IV*, IV. i. 120 Their armed Staues in charge, their Beauers downe. 1599, 1624 [see Taint *v.* A. 5 b]. 1600 Holland *Livy* VIII. vii. 285 Wilt thou then..break a staffe with me in the meane time. 1605 Shaks. *Macb.* v. iii. 48 Come, put mine Armour on: giue me my Staffe. 1611 Bible *1 Sam.* xvii. 7 The staffe of his speare was like a weauers beame. 1611 Cotgr. s.v. *Manche*, *Le manche d'un espieu*, the staffe of a Borespeare. 1868 Morris *Earthly Par.*, *Man born to be King* 1226 Who bore armed staves and coats of fence.

†**c.** with defining word, indicating some kind of spear or javelin, as *horseman's*, *hunter's*, *hunting*, *Jedburgh* (*Jedworth*, *Jedwood* etc.) *staff*. *Obs.*

1515–6 *Exchequer Rolls Scot.* XIV. 141 Halbertis, Leith axis, et Jedworth stauis [*printed* stanis]. 1538 Elyot *Dict.*, *Venabulum*, a huntynge staffe. *a* 1547 Surrey *Æneid* IV. 167 The hunting staues with their brod heads of steele. 1560 Whitehorn *Ord. Souldiours* xl. 45 Howe to make certayn fyreworke to tye at the poinctes of pykes or horsemen staues. 1561 in *Maitland Club Misc.* III. 278 And for ye sam caws of set purpos ye person had Jedwod staiffis in ye qweyr. 1567 *Reg. Privy Council Scot.* I. 578 Stryking and schuting of culveringis and Jedburgh staffis. 1579–80 North *Plutarch*, *Pelopidas* (1595) 309 Taking houndes with them, and hunters staues in their handes. 1611 Cotgr., *Espieu*, a Boare-speare; a hunting staffe, or Iauelin. *a* 1625 Fletcher *Hum. Lieut.* I. i, And on Our Horsemans Staves, Death lookes as grimly as on your keene-edgd Swords. 1680 *Lyon Office Register of Arms* (MS.), A kynde of Launce (called the Jedburgh staff). 1708 Motteux *Rabelais* v. ix. (1737) 35 Troutstaves,..and Hunting Staffs.

†**d.** *Judas staff* [cf. Mark xiv. 43] = Judas 2.

1488 in *Archæologia* XLV. 119 Ther bith vi Judas Staves for torches peynted.

4. *fig.* Something which serves as a support or stay.

1390 Gower *Conf.* II. 145 Therof the Jelous takth non hiede, Bot as a man to love unkinde, He cast his staf, as doth the blinde, And fint defaulte where is non. *a* 1489 Caxton *Blanchardyn* 213 And is she gon, the comfort of my youth, the staffe of my age. *a* 1591 H. Smith *Serm.* (1637) 496 Take heed is a good staffe to stay upon. 1596 Shaks. *Merch. V.* II. ii. 70 The boy was the verie staffe of my age, my verie prop. 1606 — *Ant. & Cl.* III. xiii. 68 It much would please him, That of his Fortunes you should make a staffe To leane vpon. 1642 Fuller *Holy & Prof. St.* v. xiv. 415 Having lost his own legs, he relyes on the staff of his kinred. 1721 De Foe *Mem. Cavalier* (1840) 256 They were the staff of the party. 1820 W. Irving *Sketch Bk.* I. 223 They had one son, who had grown up to be the staff and pride of their age. 1830 Scott *Introd. Last Minstrel* P 13, I determined that literature should be my staff, but not my crutch. 1876 Hardy *Ethelberta* xiii, Long before he adopted music as the staff of his pilgrimage.

b. In the Biblical phr. *to break the staff of bread* (literally from Heb. *mattēh leḥem*, Vulg. *baculum panis*), to diminish or cut off the supply of food.

1382, 1388 Wyclif *Lev.* xxvi. 26. 1560 Bible (Geneva) *Lev.* xxvi. 26. *Ps.* cv. 16. *Ezek.* iv. 16. [And so 1611.] *c* 1586 C'tess Pembroke *Ps.* cv. iv, Scarse had he spoken, When famine came, the staff of bread was broken. 1596 Barlow *Three Serm.* i. 121 God in his lawe threatneth that he will breake the staffe of bread, that is, bread shall not nourish them that eate it.

c. Hence *the staff of life* = bread (or similar staple food).

1638 Penkethman *Artach.* A j b, Bread is worth all, being the Staffe of life. 1656 J. Hammond *Leah & Rachel* (1844) 9 Corn (the main staffe of life). 1698 Fryer *Acc. E. India & P.* 35 For Corn, they have Rice the Staff of the Land. 1860 *All Year Round* No. 45. 440 Barley bannocks and oat cake long remained the staff of life in villages in Scotland. 1901 D. Sladen *In Sicily* I. 372 Broad beans form one of the staves of life in Sicily.

d. *Staff and staple*: the chief elements or ingredients.

1869 Buckle *Civiliz.* II. 171 Events of this sort though neglected by ordinary historians are among the staff and staple of history.

5. In proverbs and proverbial phrases. †**a.** Various phrases of obvious meaning. *Obs.*

a 1300 *Cursor M.* 7322 Þat þai desire, þai sal it haue, To þair aun heued a staue. 1444 Lydg. in *Pol. Poems* (1859) II. 219 Whoo hath noon hors on a staff may ride. *a* 1450 *Knt. de la Tour* xv. 21 And sum saide it hadd be beter for her to holde her pees..and that she had bete her selff with her owne staffe. 1508 Dunbar *Tua Mariit Wemen* 384 All thus enforsit he his fa And maid a stalwart staff to strik him selfe doune. 1546 J. Heywood *Prov.* (1867) 21 The walkyng staffe hath caught warmth in your hand. 1579 Fulke *Heskins' Parl.* 515 These be all as good reasons as yt comon iest: The staffe standeth in the corner, therefore ye good man is not at home. 1593 Shaks. *2 Hen. VI*, III. i. 171 A Staffe is quickly found to beat a Dogge. 1594 Nashe *Unfort. Trav.* Wks. (Grosart) V. 27, I warrant you are made while you liue, you neede not care which waie your staffe falles. 1659 N. R. *Prov.*, *Eng. Fr.*, etc. 67 If you would know a knave give him a staff. *Ibid.* 74 Lean not to a broken staff. 1681 Foulis *Rom. Treasons* 82 And though the Rule be but obscure, they are apt to take the staff by the wrong end, and apply it to their own pleasures.

†**b.** *At* (*the*) *staves end* or *staff-end*: at a distance, away from close quarters or familiarity, on unfriendly terms. Chiefly in phr. *to keep* or *hold* (a person) *at staves end*, *to stand at staves end with* (a person). (Cf. *at arm's end*, Arm *sb.*[1] 2 b.) *Obs.*

c 1374 Chaucer *Anel. & Arc.* 184 (Fairf. MS.) His new lady holdeth him vp so narowe Vp by the bridil at the staves ende, That euery worde he dred hit as an arowe. 1546 J. Heywood *Prov.* I. xi. (1867) 34 And now without them, I liue here at staues end. 1602 Dent *Pathw. Heauen* 175 So that

wee both keepe Satan at the staues end, and also much sinne out of our soules. 1601 Shaks. *Twel. N.* v. 292. 1640 Harsnet *God's Summons Repentance* 218 Hee keepes them a-while at the staves end, and speakes harshly unto them. 1650 I. Ambrose *Ultima* (1654) 193 Whosoever they are that stand at the staffes end, he desires them to lay aside their weapons and come in. 1657 S. Purchas *Pol. Flying-Ins.* II. 322 Vaine and wicked thoughts..will presse..into the heart, but a good heart will not owne them,..but stands at staves end with them. 1680 Bunyan *Mr. Badman* (1905) 66 Had I been his Father, I would have held him a little at staves-end, till I had had far better proof of his manners to be good. *a* 1780 Shirrefs *Poems* (1790) 215 Fowks that ha'e power to mak' an' men', Sud keep sic lads at the staff-en'. 1816 Scott *Antiq.* xvi, I expect him here one of these days; but I will keep him at staff's end, I promise you.

†**c.** *To have*, *get*, etc., *the better* (or *worse*) *end of the staff*: to come off best (or worst) in a contest, disputation, etc.; to have the advantage or the contrary. *Obs.* (Now Stick *sb.*)

1542 Udall *Erasm. Apoph.* 306 As often as thei see theim selfes to haue the wurse ende of the staffe in their cause. 1546 J. Heywood *Prov.* II. iii. (1867) 48 Who had the wurs ende of the staffe (quoth I) now? 1616 in *Cal. Colon. Papers, E. Ind.* 465 If others will be so foolish to cut their beilies for love (or rather lust) after whores, the worst end of the staff will be their own. 1626 Jackson *Creed* VIII. viii. 71 He having gotten (as wee say) the better end of the staffe, did wrest our wills at his pleasure. *c* 1645 Howell *Lett.* (1650) II. II. 20 He was sure to keep the better end of the staff still to himself. 1688 Bunyan *Christ as Advocate* 94, I am ashamed my self of mine own doings, and have given mine Enemy the best end of the Staff. 1753 Richardson *Grandison* (1754) II. ii. 12 Miss Byron, I have had the better end of the staff, I believe?

†**d.** *To set down* (*the* or *one's*) *staff*: to take up a fixed or settled position; to abide stedfastly by an opinion, decision, etc.; similarly *to fix the staff* (obs.). *To set up* (or † *in*) *one's staff* (*of rest*): to settle down in a place, take up one's abode.

1584 Greene *Arbasto* Wks. (Grosart) III. 217 Setting downe the staf therefore on this secure periury thus it fell out. *a* 1610 Healey *Epictetus* (1636) 61 But sette downe thy staffe at this, whateuer the end bee, it noway concerneth thee. 1642 D. Rogers *Naaman* 175 Yet till she rests there, and sets downe her stafe upon the promise, shee shall haue no rest. 1667 O. Heywood *Heart-Treasure* xiv. 165 A sober solid wel-taught Christian hath fixt the Staffe, and you know where to finde him, and he knows where to finde his own Principles. 1828 [Carr] *Craven Gloss.* s.v., 'To put down one's staff in a place', to settle or take up his residence in it.

1590 Shaks. *Com. Err.* III. i. 51 Haue at you with a prouerbe, Shall I set in my staffe. 1594 Nashe *Unfort. Trav.* Wks. (Grosart) V. 46 Here I was in good hope to set vp my staffe for some reasonable time. 1609 Bodley *Life* (1647) 15, I concluded at the last to set up my Staffe at the Library doore in Oxford. 1760–72 H. Brooke *Fool of Qual.* (1792) III. 71 This gentleman who has done us the honour to set up his staff of rest in our house. 1765 H. Walpole *Let. to Earl Strafford* 3 Sept., The Countesses of Carlisle and Berkeley..will set up their staves there [in Paris] for some time. 1815 Scott *Guy M.* xix, Here, then, Mannering resolved, for some time at least, to set up the staff of his rest. 1840 Dickens *Sk. Yng. Couples* 75 Old Mrs. Chopper, when her daughter married,..set up her staff of rest with Mr. and Mrs. Merrywinkle. 1860 Trollope *Framley P.* xlviii, They appeared in London and there set up their staff.

†**e.** (*One's*) *staff stan is next the door*: it is (one's) turn next. *Obs.*

1548 Hall *Chron.*, *3 Hen. VII.* (1550) 13 The Prouerbe that sayth, when thy neighboures house is a fyer, thy staffe standeth nexte the dore. 1577–87 Harrison *England* II. iii. 152/2 in *Holinshed*, For when the lands of colleges be gone, it shall be hard to saie, whose staffe shall stand next the doore.

†**f.** *To argue from the staff to the corner*: to shift a discussion to another issue. *Obs.*

1656 Bramhall *Replic.* ii. § 9. 107 This is an argument from the Staffe to the Corner. I speak of a succession of holy Orders, and he of a succession of Opinions.

g. *To have the staff in* (*one's*) *own hand*: see quot. 1828.

1828 [Carr] *Craven Gloss.* s.v., 'To have the staff in one's own hand', to keep possession of his property, and, of consequence, to retain authority and obedience. 'To part with one's staff', the very reverse of the former phrase. 1852 Mrs. Stowe *Uncle Tom's C.* xviii, And, of course, they know the staff is in their own hands. 1854 Miss Baker *Northampt. Gloss.* s.v., To keep the staff in your own hand.

6. (Cf. sense 1 c.) Part of the insignia of the episcopal office, consisting of a rod or pole of wood, metal or ivory supporting a crook, or, in the case of metropolitans, a cross. See Crose, Crosier, Cross-staff 1, and cf. Pastoral *a.* 3.

The staff represents the possession of jurisdiction and was one of the insignia connected with Investiture.

a 1122 *O. E. Chron.* (Laud MS.) an. 1047 Vif biscop com þær to, & for neah man sceolde tobrecan his stef. *Ibid.* an. 1102, Manige Frencisce & Englisce þær heora stafas & rice for luron. *c* 1205 Lay. 22105 Þene ærchebiscopes staf þer he Piram aʒaf. *c* 1400 *Apol. Loll.* 56 Prelats, wiþ þer stafis & oþer ornaments. 1535 Stewart *Cron. Scot.* II. 424 How the Bischopis Stalf tuke Neidfyre. 1535 Bp. Hilsey in Ellis *Orig. Lett.* Ser. III. II. 352 Yff hytt may plese your Mastershypp to be soe good unto me as to geve my predecessours Mytre, Staff, and Seale. 1643 Baker *Chron.*, *Hen. I*, 55 That the King should receive homage of Bishops elect; but should not invest them by Staffe and Ring. 1851 Mrs. Browning *Casa Guidi Wind.* I. 1006 With his pastoral ring and staff.

7. A rod or wand, of wood or ivory, borne as an ensign of office or authority; *spec.* as the badge of certain chief officers of the Crown.

Cf. *leading-staff* s.v. Leading *vbl. sb.*[1] 6.

1535 Coverdale *Ezek.* xix. 11 Hir stalkes were so stronge, that men might haue made staues therof for officers. 1593 Shaks. *Rich. II*, II. ii. 59 The Earle of Worcester Hath broke his staffe, resign'd his Stewardship. 1605 *1st Pt. Jeronimo* I. i. 8 For honering me..With this high staffe of office. *a* 1618 Raleigh *Prerog. Parl.* 32 In his fifth yeare was the Treasurer againe changed, and the Staffe giuen to Segraue, and the Lord Chancellour was also changed, and the staffe giuen to the Lord Scroope. 1640 in *3rd Rep. Hist. MSS. Comm.* 80/2 Mr. Treasurer would not accept of the secretary's place until he was assured of holding his white staff also. 1642 G. Mountagu in *Buccleuch MSS.* (Hist. MSS. Comm.) I. 299 These Lords, Holland and Essex, ..accordingly delivered their key and staff respectively to the Lord Falkland. 1711 Swift *Jrnl. to Stella* 31 May, I was bit about the two staves, for there is no new officer made to-day. 1716 Hearne *Collect.* (O.H.S.) V. 283 By this Resignation of the..place..of Beadle..I kept Possession of the Library, laying down the Staff before I went out. 1813 Geo. [IV] in Gurw. *Wellington Desp.* (1838) X. 552 You have sent me..the Staff of a French Marshal, and I send you in return that of England. 1827 Hallam *Const. Hist.* (1876) I. iv. 204 He kept the white staff of treasurer down to his death. 1843 Pugin *Apol. Rev. Chr. Archit.* 52 A verge or cantor's staff. 1863 H. Cox *Instit.* III. vii. 694 Lord Godolphin, the Earl of Oxford, and the Duke of Shrewsbury successively received the Treasurer's staff.

8. A pole from which a flag is flown.

a 1613 [see Flag-staff]. 1667 Milton *P. L.* I. 535 Who forthwith from the glittering Staff unfurld Th' Imperial Ensign. 1702 [see Jack *sb.*[2]]. 1769 Falconer *Dict. Marine* (1780) *Staff*, a light pole erected in different parts of a ship, whereon to hoist and display the colours. 1774 M. Mackenzie *Maritime Surv.* 39 Setting perpendicular in a level Ground three Poles, or Staves, between four and five Feet high, with Flags flying at each, so as to form a Triangle. 1816 Byron *Siege Cor.* xi, The banners droop'd along their staves. 1836 W. Irving *Astoria* III. 228 They would willingly have nailed their colours to the staff, and defied the frigate. 1894 *pl.* staves [see Jack *sb.*[2]].

b. A rod or pole on which a processional cross was borne.

1431 *Rec. St. Mary at Hill* 27, ij staues [*printed* stanes] for þe principall crosses. *a* 1529 Skelton *Ware the Hauke* 114 Cros, staffe, lectryne, and banner.

†**9.** A strong stick, pole, bar, rod or stake used for various purposes; e.g. for carrying burdens, to support a canopy, the stems of plants, etc. *Obs.*

c 1000 *Lamb. Psalter* cvi. 16 *Vectes ferreos confregit*, stafas *vel* sahlas isenne tobræc. 1297 R. Glouc. (Rolls) 2677 Ac some þat ofscapede..mid staues of hegges defended hom aboute. 1382 Wyclif *Exod.* xxv. 13 And thow shalt make berynge staues of the trees of Sychym. 1390 Gower *Conf.* II. 294 Doun goth the corde into the pet, To which he hath at ende knet A staf, wherby, he seide, he wolde That Adrian him scholde holde. 1485 in *Rutland Papers* (Camden) 5 A seele of cloth of gold baudekyn with iiij staves gilte, to be borne alweis by iiij noble knights. 1523–34 Fitzherb. *Husb.* § 21 Than muste ye haue a weddynge-hoke with a socket set vpon a lyttel staffe of a yarde longe. 1530 Palsgr. 275/1 Staffe to beare two peyles on, as they do in Fraunce, *une courge*. 1538 Elyot *Dict.*, *Phalangæ*, staues, whereon men doo carye packes, playne staues. 1552 in Daniel-Tyssen *Invent. Ch. Goods Surrey* (1869) 14 Item a canype with iiij staves. 1572 Mascall *Plant. & Graff.* (1592) 13 How to set small staues by, to strengthen your Cions. 1643 Baker *Chron.*, *Rich. II*, 1 To beare the Kings Canopy, upon foure staves of silver, over the Kings head. 1688 Holme *Armoury* III. 320/1 A Bearing Staff by which empty Barrels are carried by Servants from place to place. 1708 *Constit. Watermen's Co.* xxv, No Waterman..shall stick up and lay his Boat at his Staff, so as to hinder..due and orderly passing..but shall..stick up their said Staves clear of the said Stairs or Landing places.

†**b.** A Churn-staff; also = *pump-staff* (see Pump *sb.*[1] 6). *Obs.*

1559 in *Richmond Wills* (Surtees) 134 A chirn with a staf. 1593 [see Shor *sb.* 5 b]. 1609 *Balliol Coll. Acc.* (MS.), Item, staffe for mendinge the quadrangle pumpe.

†**c.** = Plough-staff. *Obs.*

1538 Elyot *Dict.*, *Rulla*, the staffe, wherwith the ploughman clenseth his culter. 1565 Cooper *Thesaurus*, *Rallum*, the staffe wherewith plough men in tillyng put the earth from their share. 1577 Googe *Heresbach's Husb.* I. 21 With the Rodde or Staffe well poynted, the plowman maketh cleane his Coulter.

†**d.** = Bowstaff. *Obs.*

1545 Ascham *Toxoph.* II. (Arb.) 116 The boole of ye tree is..best for a bow, yf the staues be euen clouen. 1583 *Rates Custom Ho.* A vj, Bowestaues the bundel containing xvi staues vs. 1688 Holme *Armoury* III. 105/2 A Staff, the first cleeving out of the Timber, to make the Shaft. 1868 Kirk *Charles the Bold* III. IV. viii. 136 And 'bowiers' [were ordered] to make their staves into bows with all possible haste.

e. ? Each of two sticks fastened to the extremities of a fishing-net.

1823 J. F. Cooper *Pioneers* xxiii, Benjamin prided himself greatly on his skill in throwing the net...A loud splash in the water, as he threw away the 'staff', or 'stretcher'. *Ibid.*, 'I see the "staffs",' shouted Mr. Jones;—'gather in, boys, and away with it'...Elizabeth strained her eyes and saw the ends of the two sticks on the seine.

10. *Surveying.* A rod for measuring distances and heights. Cf. Jacob's staff 2 b; also *levelling staff* s.v. Levelling *vbl. sb.* 4.

[1538 Elyot *Dict.*, *Pertica*, a staffe, a cogell, a perche or polle, wherwith grounde is mette.] 1556 Digges *Tecton.* (1592) title-p., An Instrument called the profitable Staffe. 1571 — *Pantom.* I. xiv. D iv b, Heightes are ingeniously searched out by a staffe. 1590 Blagrave (*title*) Baculum Familliare, Catholicon siue Generale. A Booke of the making and vse of a Staffe, newly invented by the Author, called the Familiar Staffe. As well for that it may be made vsually and familiarlie to walke with, as for that it performeth the Geometrical mensurations of all Altitudes, Longitudes, Latitudes, Distances and Profundities. 1610 A. Hopton (*title*) Baculum Geodæticum, sive Viaticum. Or The Geodeticall Staffe. 1753 *Chambers' Cycl.* Suppl., *Staff*. This is used as an instrument for taking accessible, or inaccessible heights. *Ibid.* s.v., *Station-Staff*, in surveying. 1835 *Lond. Jrnl. Arts & Sci.* Conj. Ser. VI. 330 The graduated staffs or measuring rods being thus placed at the stations. 1880 L. D'A. Jackson *Aids Surv.-Practice* 11 Telemetrical observation on graduated staves. A graduated staff is held vertically at the required distant point [etc.].

†**b.** (See quot. and cf. Jacob's staff 2 c.)

For other uses see Backstaff, Cross-staff 2, Fore-staff, Jacob's staff 2 a.

1728 Chambers *Cycl.*, *Staff*, in Surveying, a kind of Stand, whereon to mount a Theodolite, Circumferentor, plain Table, or the like, for use. It consists of Three Legs of Wood, joyned together at one End, whereon the Instrument is placed; and made pecked at the other, to enter the Ground.

†**c.** = *half-breadth staff* (see Half- II. f).

1797 *Encycl. Brit.* (ed. 3) XVII. 407/1 The half breadth staff may be one inch square, and of any convenient length. ..Two sides of the staff are marked half breadths, and the other two sides heights of the sheer.

d. The gnomon of a sun-dial.

1669 Sturmy *Mariner's Mag.* VI. iii. 123 The shadow being 83, the Gnomon or Staff 100. 1829 *Chapters Phys. Sci.* ix. 89 The sun dial, which marks the time by the shadow of a stile or staff.

11. *Her.* A representation of a stick, stake, bar, etc.; *spec.* = Baton 3, Fissure *sb.* 2 c. See also Ragged staff 1.

1486 *Bk. St. Albans*, *Her.* e vij b, Ther be fyssuris or stauys playn ingradyt inueckyt and fusyllatit. 1874 Papworth & Morant *Dict. Coats of Arms* s.v. *Staff*, Arg. a hawk ppr...standing on a staff couped and raguled vert. *Ibid.*, Az. eight staves fretty and raguly or.

12. *Surg.* †**a.** The piston of a syringe. *Obs.*

1653 T. Brugis *Vade Mecum* (ed. 2) 148 In dangerous fluxes when we give comfortable Clysters, we oftentimes force them up as far as we can, I mean the Liquor by thrusting the staffe harder.

b. A grooved steel instrument used to guide the knife in lithotomy.

1698 Lister *Journ. Paris* (1699) 233 He boldly thrusts in a broad Lancet..till he joins the Catheter or Staff, or the Stone betwixt his Fingers. 1720 J. Douglas *Lithotomia Douglas.* 14 That [operation] which Surgeons call Cutting on the Staffe, i.e. when a furrow'd Probe is pass'd into the Bladder, upon which they afterwards Cut. 1726 — *Hist. Lateral Operation* 30 The Instruments he made Use of were first a Catheter or Staff. 1839 *Hooper's Lex. Med.* (ed. 7) 1216. 1895 *Arnold & Sons' Catal. Surg. Instrum.* 572 Stricture Staff (Syme's). *Ibid.* 625 Lithotomy Instruments ..Six Staffs, grooved.

13. *Arch.* **a.** = Rudenture.

1817 Rickman *Styles Archit.* 95 The square pedestal of the pinnacle being set with an angle to the front, is continued down, and on each side is set a small buttress of a smaller face than this pedestal, thus leaving a small staff between them..this small staff at each set-off has the moulding to it.

b. (See quot. 1812.)

1812 P. Nicholson *Mech. Exerc.* 202 *Staff*, a piece of wood fixed to the external angle of the two upright sides of a wall for floating the plaster to, and for defending the angle against accidents. 1902 Sturgis *Dict. Archit.* III. 593.

14. a. A rung of a ladder. ? *Obs.* Cf. Stave.

c 1325 *Gloss. W. de Bibbesw.* in Wright *Voc.* 168 (Camb. MS.) [En les reideles vount les roilouns *glossed*] staves. *a* 1400–50 *Wars Alex.* 1438 On ilka staffe of a staire stike wald a cluster. *c* 1440 *Gesta Rom.* xlvi. 367 The goldyn laddere; of the which the fyrste staffe is contricion of herte. 1526 *Pilgr. Perf.* (W. de W. 1531) 68 b, Saynt Bernarde compareth them to a ladder of vii staues. 1563 *Homilies* II. *Repentance* II. 279 The first staffe or steppe of this ladder. *a* 1657 R. Loveday *Lett.* (1663) 273 How many mount Fortunes ladder, and break the staves as they go up. 1657 J. Watts *Scribe, Pharisee*, etc. III. 99 They fall off the Ladder at the lower staffe or step again. 1850 G. L. Banks (*title*) Staves for the Human Ladder. 1858 Simmonds *Dict. Trade*. 1875 Knight *Dict. Mech.*

b. A round cross-bar connecting the handles or stilts of a plough, or the legs of a chair; = Round *sb.*[1] 3 d. Also, each of the handles of a plough. *Obs.* or *dial.* Cf. Stave.

1523–34 Fitzherb. *Husb.* § 3 There be two roughe staues in euery ploughe in the bynder ende, set a-slope betwene the ploughe-tayle and the stilt, to holde out and kepe the plough abrode in the hynder ende, and the one lenger than the other. 1652 Blith *Eng. Improver Improv.* II. xxviii. (1653) 190 But for the Plough-handles, some call them.. Hales, and some Staves. 1851 Sternberg *Northampt. Gloss.*, *Staff*, the spar or 'round' of a chair.

†**c.** A spoke of a wheel. *Obs.* exc. *Her.* (also applied to the 'rays' of a carbuncle).

1642 D. Rogers *Naaman* 296 As then the spokes and staves cannot be wanting to a wheele. 1754 Boyer *Gt. Theat. Honour* (ed. 2) 116 Staves (is said of the Rays of the Carbuncle), *Rais, ou Bâtons d'Escarboucle*. 1847 *Gloss. Heraldry* 294 *Staff*, a word applied by some to the rays of an escarbuncle, and the spokes of a wheel.

†**d.** *Weaving.* = Lam *sb.*[2]

1338 in Dugdale *Monasticon* (1819) II. 585/2 Item pro weblomes emptis xx[s]. Et pro staves ad easdem vj[d]. 1797 *Encycl. Brit.* (ed. 3) XVIII. 835/1 The lams..or, as they are called in some parts of Scotland, the hiddles, and in others the staves.

†**e.** A bar or rail used in the construction of a gridiron, gate, cart, cage, etc. *Obs.*

1459 *Paston Lett.* I. 468, j. roste iren with vij. staves. 1523–34 Fitzherb. *Husb.* § 5 The bodye of the wayne of oke, the staues..the keys and pikstaues. *Ibid.* § 70 Make

standynge cratches, to caste theyr fodder in, and the staues set nyghe ynough togyther, for pullynge theyr fodder to hastely out. *Ibid.* § 141 If any gate be broken down, or want any staues. 1596 Mascall *Cattle, Horses* 120 When thou dost take any iourney, with thy horse and cart, thou must..see the rath staues and struts be whole and sound & wel furnished, with staues of good strong holly, hasell, or oak. 1601 Holland *Pliny* XXX. x. II. 388 The staves and windings, whereof the said cages are made.

†**f.** Each of the thin narrow pieces which compose a cask, barrel, tub, etc. *Obs.* (Now Stave *sb.*)

The sing. has always been rare; for examples of pl. from 1398 onwards, see Stave *sb.*

1531–2 *Act 23 Hen. VIII*, c. 4 § 8 If any personne..do mynysshe..any maner of barrell..by reason of..takyng oute of any Staffe out or frome any suche vessell. 1599 Dallam in *Early Voy. Levant* (Hakl. Soc.) 35 Ther weare marvalus greate peecis that weare made of hammered Iron, everie stafe at the leaste 3 inches square, and houped aboute lyke a barrell.

†**g.** The shank of an anchor. *Obs. rare*[−1].

1611 Cotgr., *Stangue d'un' ancre*, the staffe of an Anchor.

h. *Mech.* Each of the cylindrical bars forming the teeth of a trundle or lantern; cf. Stave *sb.*

1659, 1812–16 [see Lantern *sb.* 7 d]. 1764, 1805 [see Round *sb.*[1] 3 d]. 1825 J. Nicholson *Oper. Mech.* 24 The semidiameter of a staff of the trundle.

i. *Watchmaking.* An arbor or axle.

1860 E. B. Denison *Clocks & Watches* (ed. 4) 285 The staff or arbor of the balance. 1885 Lock *Workshop Rec.* Ser. IV. 339/1 Centre the point so that the body of the staff runs perfectly true. 1902 *Daily Chron.* 13 May 10/5 All Jobbers requiring pivots, staffs, cylinders, and complicated watch repairs.

†**15.** A pair (of cocks), a set of three (hawks).

1688 Holme *Armoury* II. 252/2 Four staves of Cocks (or 16 Cocks). *Ibid.* 311/1 Three a staff of Hawks. 1691 Ray *S. & E. C. Words* 115 A Staffe of Cocks, a pair of Cocks. 1790 Grose *Prov. Gloss.* (ed. 2), A *staffe* of cocks; a pair of cocks.

16. A bundle of 50 bunches of the heads of the teasel (*Dipsacus fullonum*) used for teasing cloth. (See also Staves *sb.*, which occurs in Mortimer 1707.)

1794 Griggs *Agric. Essex* 19 These heads [of teasel] are.. bound up in small bunches, or gleans, of five and twenty heads each; the like number of which bunches, or gleans, constitute half a staff; which, after a few days sun, to harden and dry them, are tied together upon a stick or staff, of two feet and a half long, and in this form, carried to market. 1856 Morton *Cycl. Agric.* II. 1126/2 *Staff*, of teazles (Essex), 50 bunches, or gleans of 25 each = 1250.

17. a. An enclosure or plot of pasture ground. **b.** A measure of nine feet.

1786 *Jackson's Oxf. Jrnl.* 3 June 1/3 A Ham or Staff of rich Meadow Ground, in Kelmscott, containing ten Acres and a Half. 1796 W. H. Marshall *West Eng.* I. 330 *Staff*: a measure of nine feet; half a customary rod.

II. Letter, verse, musical staff.

These senses are here placed together because of their similarity of application, but it is doubtful whether they have any immediate connexion.

†**18.** A written character, a letter. *Obs.* Cf. Bocstaff, Rune-stave.

c 888 Ælfred *Boeth.* xix, Hwæt is heora nu to lafe, butan ..se nama mid feaum stafum awriten? *c* 1000 Ælfric *Gram.* ii. (Z.) 4 Littera is stæf on englisc. *c* 1200 Ormin 16403–5 & off þatt name toc Drihhtin An staff Allfa ʒehatenn, To timmbrenn till þe firrste mann Hiss name off stafess fowwre.

†**b.** A mark made by, or as by writing. *Obs.*

c 1050 *Voc.* in Wr.-Wülcker 346/27 *Apicibus*, stafum. *c* 1205 Lay. 21154 Þer wes innen igrauen mid rede golde stauen an on-licnes deore of drihtenes moder.

19. †**a.** A line of verse. *Obs.*

c 1450 in *Herrig's Archiv* CIV. 309 All be it the frenssh in foure staves be, The ynglissh sevyn kepith in degree. *c* 1475 *Partenay* 6555 As ny as metre can conclude sentence, Cereatly by rew in it haue I go. Nerehand stafe by staf. *Ibid.* 6581 Als the frensh staffes silabled be More breueloker and shorter also Then is the english lines. *c* 1540 *Pilgryms T.* 739 in Thynne *Animadv.* (1875) App. i. 98 Thes vi stauis..whiche be chaucers own hand work.

†**b.** A stanza or set of lines. *Obs.* Cf. Baston 2.

[There is no ground for the common statement that this is from ON. *stef* set or recurring time, refrain of a poem.]

a 1530 J. Heywood *Weather* (Brandl) 179[a] At thende of this staf the god hath a song played in his trone. *a* 1577 Gascoigne *Certayne Notes* P 14 Wks. 1907 I. 471 Rythme royall is a verse of tenne sillables, and seven such verses make a staffe. *Ibid.*, The firste twelve do ryme in staves of foure lines by crosse meetre. 1582 T. Watson *Hekatompath.* lxxxviii. (Arb.) 124 The two first staffes (excepting onely the two first verses of all). 1586 W. Webbe *Eng. Poetrie* (Arb.) 59 Some of many rymes in one staffe (as they call it). *Ibid.* 62 The diuersities of the staues (which are the number of verses contained with the diuisions or partitions of a ditty). 1607 R. C[arew] tr. *Estienne's World of Wonders* 199 *marg.*, A staffe of eight verses. 1656 Cowley *Pindaric Odes*, *To Dr. Scarborough* Note ii, In the ninth staffe of the Nemeæan Ode. 1697 Dryden *Æneid* Ded. (f) 1 b, Mr. Cowley had found out that no kind of Staff is proper for a Heroick Poem; as being all too lirical.

c. A 'verse' or stanza of a song. Now Stave.

1598 Yong *Diana* 257 These two last staeffs [sic] so liuely touched Parthenius that sung them. 1601 Holland *Pliny* x. xxix. I. 286 Yee shall have them listen attentively to the old birds when they sing, and to take out lessons as it were from them, whom they would seem to imitate staffe by staffe. 1601 B. Jonson *Poetaster* II. ii, I can sing but one staffe of the dittie neither. 1667 C. Simpson *Compend. Mus.* 21 The second Staff or Stanza is the same as the first; only it is broken into Crochets.

20. *Mus.* A set of horizontal lines (now five in number) on which, and in the spaces between, notes are placed so as to indicate pitch. Also Stave.

In harmonic or concerted music two or more staffs are used together, connected by a brace.

1662 Playford *Skill Mus.* I. i. 4 But [for all] Lessons for the Organ, Virginals, or Harp, two staves of six lines together are required. 1688 Holme *Armoury* III. 157/1 [Follows Playford and adds:] They are called a Staff or Stansa. 1776 Burney *Hist. Mus.* (1789) II. 87 The regular staff of four lines. 1806 Calcott *Mus. Gram.* 1 The lines and spaces of the Staff are counted upwards. 1842 *Westm. Rev.* Jan. 34 *note*, There is a schism among musicians, whether this should be *staff* or *stave*, pronounced by some *staaf*. Authorities are mostly in favour of 'stave' but custom may be pleaded for 'staff' and 'staves' in the plural. 1873 H. C. Banister *Mus.* 2 Musical characters are written upon a series of parallel lines, termed a Stave or Staff.

attrib. 1881 Broadhouse *Mus. Acoustics* 365 The ordinary musical notation, or, as it is called, the 'staff notation'.

III. (Pl. always *staffs*.)

21. *Mil.* A body of officers appointed to assist a general, or other commanding officer, in the control of an army, brigade, regiment, etc., or in performing special duties (as the *medical staff*). *General staff*, a body of officers controlling an army from headquarters under the commander-in-chief. [App. of continental Teut. origin. Cf. the like use of G. *stab* (also *generalstab*, *regimentsstab*, etc.), Du. *staf*; prob. developed from the sense 'baton' (= 7 above).]

[1700 J. A. Astry tr. *Saavedra Faxardo* II. 249 The Germans call a Regiment, and all that belongs to it, the Colonel's Staff, (den Regiment oder Colonelstab,) for with that Soldiers are to be ruled.]

1781 Simes *Milit. Guide* (ed. 3) 7 Staff of the Army. *Ibid.*, The Staff properly exists only in the time of war. 1790 *Debates in Congress* 18 Jan. (1834) 2146 The legionary staff ..the brigade staff..the regimental staff. *Ibid.* 2152 The United States to make an adequate provision..for the following general staff. 1795 in *Ld. Auckland's Corr.* (1862) III. 328 My destiny is finally to act on the staff in the island of Corsica. 1801 *Med. Jrnl.* V. 185 The Medical Staff of the Armies acting in the West Indies. 1844 *Queen's Regul. Army* 5 Any Officer of the Regimental Staff. 1844 H. H. Wilson *Brit. India* II. 112 Several conferences ensued, not only with the Governor-General, but with members both of his civil and military staff. 1871 *Ann. Reg.* II. 95 The Duke of Cambridge, with his staff and the foreign officers attending the manœuvres, looked on from Bisley Common. 1875 *Encycl. Brit.* II. 577 Officers for the General Staff are selected exclusively from the regular army, and except in cases of proved abilities in the field, must have passed through the Staff College...Officers appointed to the Personal Staff are not required to pass through the Staff College.

22. *gen.* A body of persons employed, under the direction of a manager or chief, in the work of an establishment or the execution of some undertaking (e.g. a newspaper, hospital, government survey).

1837 Carlyle *Fr. Rev.* II. v. v, Subterranean Rivarol has Fifteen Hundred Men in King's pay..; what he calls 'a staff of genius': Paragraph-writers, Placard Journalists;.. one of the strangest Staffs ever commanded by man. 1849 J. J. Blunt *Four Serm.* iii. (1850) 84 With what a staff would our colleges be furnished to carry on the same work! 1857 Trollope *Barchester T.* xliii, Those caterers for our morning repast, the staff of the Jupiter. 1875 Dawson *Dawn of Life* iii. 38 One of the explorers on the staff of the Survey. 1879 M. Arnold *Mixed Ess.* 152 The teaching staff have to furnish guarantees of their capacity to teach the matters of instruction confided to them. 1884 *Times* (weekly ed.) 26 Sept. 13/1 Besides their staff of clerks, bookkeepers, &c., they employed about 300 ordinary hands. 1894 Conan Doyle *Mem. S. Holmes* 149 A coachman and two maids form the staff of servants.

23. *Staff* (*of Government*): in the Isle of Man, a court of justice presided over by the governor; since 1883 a Division of the High Court.

a 1700 *34th Customary Law* in Keble *Life Bp. Wilson* xvi. 511 No appeal shall be made from Church censures to the Staff, and none to be privileged from them. 1900 A. W. Moore *Hist. Isle of Man* 836 The courts existing prior to 1883, viz., the Staff of Government, Chancery, Exchequer ..[etc.] were united and formed into 'Divisions' of the 'High Court of Justice of the Isle of Man'...The 'Staff of Government Division'..was deprived of all its original jurisdiction, and is now solely an appellate court.

IV. *attrib.* and *Comb.*

24. Objective, as *staff-bearer*, *-holder*, *-maker*; instrumental, as *staff-supported* adj.

1553 in Kempe *Losely MSS.* (1836) 44 Touching the staffmaker..I wyll see hym contented. 1611 Cotgr., *Bastonnier*, a staffe-bearer, or Vergier. 1814 Wordsw. *White Doe* I. 217 That bearded, staff-supported Sire. 1880 L. D'A. Jackson *Aids Surv. Pract.* 98 The staff-holders must..be capable of holding the staff truly vertical.

25. In sense 'of or belonging to a military staff' (see 21), as *staff appointment*, *duty*, *parade*, *pay*, *surgeon*, *uniform*; **staff cap**, a flat-topped cap with a peak, such as forms part of various uniforms: **staff college**, a school in which officers are trained for staff appointments; **staff corps**, a body of officers and men organized to assist the commanding officer and his staff in various special departments; in India, a corps formed in each of the three presidencies to supply officers for service; **staff-ride** (see quot. 1902); hence *staff-rider*; **staff sergeant** (see quot. 1876). Also Staff officer.

1825 T. Hook *Sayings* Ser. II. *Passion & Princ.* iii. II. 303 The Captain, habituated to India, 'held on', with *staff appointments, as long as he could. 1875 *Encycl. Brit.* II. 577/2 Staff appointments are held for five years only. 1902 *Westm. Gaz.* 26 June 8/2 His Majesty,..with hand raised to *staff-cap, in military salute. 1904 *Daily Chron.* 23 Aug. 8/1 The woman who depends upon a motor-car for recreation..wears a staff-cap just as much as she who goes yachting. 1868 *Queen's Regul. Army* § 220 No Officer will be appointed to the Staff, who shall not have passed the final examination of the *Staff College. 1811 *Regul. Army* 121 The Royal *Staff Corps. 1813 Wellington in Gurw. *Disp.* (1838) XI. 122, I have therefore had cut out the sheets..containing the maps of the country immediately in my front, which I have had pasted upon linen by the Staff corps. 1853 Sir H. Douglas *Milit. Bridges* (ed. 3) 241 Two companies of the Staff Corps were accordingly sent, with a strong working party, to Baragona, to make a bridge across the Tietar. 1880 Gen. Adye in *19th Cent.* No. 38. 698 All officers now seeking what is called an Indian career in any capacity—regimental, staff, or civil —must enter one of the three Staff Corps. 1909 *Blackw. Mag.* Apr. 568/2 The adjutant inspected the *Staff parade. 1876 Voyle & Stevenson *Milit. Dict.* 401/1 **Staff Pay*, pay given to officers and soldiers in the government service, who perform duties either on the permanent staff of an army or in regimental or departmental employment. 1898 E. S. May *Field Artillery* 25 We have done the same sort of thing in this country in the form of '*staff-rides'. 1902 *Encycl. Brit.* (ed. 10) XXXIII. 7/1 'Staff-rides', as exercises on the ground without troops have come to be called, are just as effective a means of teaching strategy as field-days are of teaching tactics. 1910 *Contemp. Rev.* Jan. 46 No one had seen the alleged *staff riders. 1811 *Regul. Army* 147 *Staff Serjeants. 1851 *Ord. Royal Engin.* § 26. 121 On no account is any Non-Commissioned Officer acting as a Staff-Serjeant to be employed as a Pay-Serjeant. 1876 Voyle & Stevenson *Milit. Dict.* 401/1 *Staff Sergeants*, non-commissioned officers employed on the staff of a regiment, district, or division. 1794 *Gentl. Mag.* Nov. 995/2 Whilst the regimental surgeons are thus engaged in the field of battle ..the new *staff-surgeons..are to be found at the general hospital, perhaps..20 or 30 miles..from the scene of action. 1803 Wellington in Gurw. *Disp.* (1844) I. 539 Mr. Gilmour, the Staff surgeon with this division of the army. 1809 Byron *Ch. Har.* II. lxii. *note*, I was dressed in a full suit of *staff uniform.

b. In the Navy used to designate a senior grade of officers, as *staff captain*, *commander*, *surgeon*.

1867 Smyth *Sailor's Word-bk.*, *Staff-Captain*, a designation conferred in 1863 upon masters of the fleet. *Ibid.*, *Staff-Commanders*, a designation conferred in 1863 on masters of fifteen years' seniority. 1875 Bedford *Sailor's Pocket Bk.* v. (ed. 2) 150 *note*, Staff-Commander Thomas A. Hull, R.N. 1913 *Times* 13 Aug. 4/1 The first paper..was read by Staff-Surgeon Stewart, R.N.

c. In sense 'belonging to the staff of a hospital, hotel, or other large establishment' (see 22).

1888 Honnor Morten *Sk. Hosp. Life* 6 An intelligent and capable woman can expect to rise by gradations from 'staff-nurse' to 'sister'. 1902 *Daily Chron.* 13 May 10/7 Woman (Strong, active) as staff maid...Apply Housekeeper, Hotel Windsor.

26. Special comb. (see also 25): **staff-angle**, **-bead** = 13 b (cf. *angle-staff*, *angle-bead* s.v. Angle *sb.*[2] 8); hence **staff-beaded** *a.*; **staff-bismar**, a kind of steelyard; †**staff-drive** *v.* = *staff-herd*; **staff-head**, the upper end of a staff, carved, tipped with metal, etc.; the top of the tripod which supports a theodolite or other measuring-instrument; **staff-herd** *v. trans.*, to depasture sheep in charge of a shepherd upon common or forest land; **staff-hook**, 'a sharp hook fastened to a long handle to cut peas and beans and to trim hedges' (*I. of Wight Gloss.* 1881); **staff-land** *Isle of Man* [= med.L. *terra de baculo*], certain land in the parish of St. Maughold, also formerly in that of St. Patrick, the holder of which had the custody of the patron saint's pastoral staff; **staff-man** †(*a*) a man who wields a staff or cudgel; (*b*) a workman employed in silk-throwing (Simmonds *Dict. Trade* Suppl. 1883); †**staff-shide**, a billet of wood for fuel; †**staff-striker**, a sturdy beggar, tramp; †**staff-torch**, a tall thick candle used for ceremonial purposes; **staff-tree**, the genus *Celastrus*; **staff-vine**, *Celastrus scandens* of U.S.

1875 Knight *Dict. Mech.*, **Staff-angle*. 1833 Loudon *Encycl. Archit.* § 239 The angles of the chimney breasts to have proper *staff beads. 1842 Gwilt *Archit.* Gloss., Angle Bead, or Staff Bead. 1833 Loudon *Encycl. Archit.* § 1198 Fix 1-inch deal tongued and splayed and *staff-beaded linings to three windows. *a* 1733 *Shetland Acts* 31 in *Proc. Soc. Ant. Scot.* (1892) XXVI. 200 That none use *staff bismers, nor any other save such as are adjusted and marked to buy and sell on. 1566 in Hyslop *Ch. Stretton* (1904) II. 178 [John Nichols, who had taken cattle] cum baculis, videlicet, *Staff-dryve [over Whittington Heath to the injury of the township]. 1506 *Acc. Ld. High Treas. Scot.* III. 355, xij *staf hedis. 1766 *Complete Farmer* s.v. *Surveying* 7 I 1/2 Turn about the table upon the staff-head. 1862 *Catal. Internat. Exhib.*, *Brit.* II. No. 2947 (Theodolite) The tripod and its staff-head. 1888 in *Archæologia* LI. 373 A staff-head of wood, coloured and gilded. 1563 in W. Nicolson *Leges Marchiarum* (1705) 138 If it shall happen the Cattel or Sheep of the one Realm to be *staff-herded, or to remain depasturing upon the ground of the opposite Realm. *Ibid.*, *marg.* Staffherding of Cattel. 1595 in C. W. Hatfield *Hist. Notices Doncaster* (1866) I. 168 Doncaster time out of mind have made drives..and staff hearded upon the moor. 1828 [Carr] *Craven Gloss.*, *Staff hird*, to have sheep under the care of a shepherd. 1523 Fitzherb. *Husb.* § 29 Pees and benes be..reped or mowen some with sickles, some with hokes, and some with *staffe-hokes. 1890 A. W. Moore *Surnames* etc. *Isle of Man* 122 *Staff lands. 1659 Torriano, *Bastonière*..also a cudgeler, a *staff-man. 1411 *Rolls of Parlt.* III. 665/2 Tout le maresme & fuaile, autrement apelle *Staffes-hides [*sic*] & Kides. 1376 *Ibid.* II. 340/2 Et plusours de eux deveient

*stafstrikers. 1468 *Maldon* (Essex) *Liber B.* lf. 12 b, Nyghtwalkeres, stastrykeres [*sic*], and evesedropperes. 1532–3 *Rec. St. Mary at Hill* 361 Item, paid for iij *staf torches of wex, to hold at the levacion ijs vjd. 1556 *Chron. Grey Friars* (Camden) 54, ij C. powre men in blacke gownes holdynge staffe torches. 1580–1 *Act 23 Eliz.* c. 8 § 3 Wares wrought with Waxe, as in Lightes, Staftorches. 1633 Johnson *Gerarde's Herbal* App. 1600 *Celastrus Theophrasti*. The *staffe tree. 1771 J. R. Forster *Flora Amer. Septentr.* 11 Celastrus bullatus. Staff tree, elegant. Virginia. 1884 W. Miller *Plant-n.* 130 *Staff-vine, *Celastrus scandens*.

Staff (staf), *sb.*[2] [Of obscure origin.] A building material consisting of plaster mixed with fibre, used for temporary ornamental work.

1892 *Advance* (Chicago) May 19 When mixed the staff is rolled out into slabs to be nailed to the sides of buildings, or made up in blocks..for statues, friezes or cornices. 1892 *Times* (weekly ed.) 21 Oct. 10/1 They [the Exhibition buildings at Chicago] are..covered with the composition of plaster, cement, and hemp, or similar fibre, known as 'Staff'. *Ibid.*, The sculpture and decorations on the buildings are also chiefly of 'staff', being first modelled in clay. 1893 *Offic. Guide World's Columbian Expos.* 21 Staff was invented in France about 1876, and was first used in the buildings of the Paris Exposition in 1878.

Staff (staf), *v.* [f. Staff *sb.*[1]] *trans.* To provide with a staff of officers, teachers, servants, etc.

1859 *Times* 20 Aug. 7/6 We end by being efficiently and sensibly equipped, commanded and staffed. 1881 *19th Cent.* Apr. 656 Two or three such women, a care-taker, and a cook would adequately staff each home. 1888 Mrs. H. Ward *R. Elsmere* v. xxxiii, A powerful church of the new type, staffed by friends and pupils of Pusey. 1895 *Naturalist* 132 It is a satisfaction to note how well the museum is staffed. 1904 *Catholic Times* 1 Jan. 8/3 To furnish and staff some three or four first class day schools for boys.

Hence **Sta·ffing** *vbl. sb.*

1882 *19th Cent.* Nov. 788 The Board schools..have..many advantages, derived from..their superior staffing, and more highly paid teachers. 1901 *Scotsman* 30 Oct. 12/4 The staffing of the offices at Castle Terrace.

‖**Staffage** (sta·fāʒ). [Ger.: a pseudo-Fr. formation after G. *staffiren* to fit out, garnish, believed to be corruptly ad. OF. *estoffer*, f. *estoffe* Stuff *sb.*] The accessories of a picture. Also *transf.* and *fig.*

1878 B. Taylor in *Life & Lett.* (1884) II. 594 A forge where he [Schiller] studied the *staffage* for his ballad of 'Fridolin'. 1887 *Pall Mall Gaz.* 22 Nov. 3/1 The *staffage* to the little love-story is a fertile little oasis in the wide, bleak Cossack steppes. 1906 *Academy* 10 Nov. 480/1 But the seated figure is a needless piece of *staffage*. 1908 A. M. Hind *Short Hist. Engraving* 230 The *staffage* of some of Piranesi's dullest subjects..discloses an irrepressible instinct for life.

Staffage, Sc. variant of Staffish *a. Obs.*

Staffed (staft), *ppl. a.* [f. Staff *sb.*[1] + -ed[2].] In *Her.* (see quot. and Staff *sb.*[1] 11).

1891 *Century Dict.* s.v., An amulet staffed, a ring from which staffs or scepters radiate.

†**Sta·ffer.** *Obs. rare*[−1]. [? f. Staff *sb.*[1] + -er[1].] ? A kind of peashooter.

1688 Holme *Armoury* III. xvi. (Roxb.) 82/2 Playes with Instruments...Shooting in a trunk staffer or spitter.

Staffette (stæfe·t). *Obs.* exc. *Hist.* Also 7 **staffett**, **staffeto.** [ad. It. *staffetta*, dim. of *staffa*, stirrup. Cf. Estafette.] A mounted courier.

1545 Wotton in *St. Papers Hen. VIII*, X. 487, I have written thryse to you, twyse by the ordynarye staffette that goith weekelye to Andwerpe. 1633 *Cal. St. Papers, Dom.* 28 Jan. 521 [Orders..to erect] staffette [or packet posts at fit stages]. *Ibid.* Apr. 39 [That letters should be sent by] staffeto. 1635 in *Rep. Secret Comm. Post-Office* App. (1844) 55 A Proposition for setling of Staffets or pacquet posts betwixt London and all parts of his Maiesties dominions. 1714 *Lond. Gaz.* No. 5263/2 We have Advices from Vienna which say, that a Staffette was arrived there with Letters from Constantinople. 1858 Carlyle *Fredk. Gt.* IV. v. (1865) I. 307 Brief weekly report to his Majesty will be expected; staffettes, should cases of hot haste occur.

†**Staff-full**, *a. Obs.* [? f. Staff *sb.*[1] + Full *a.* The original notion was perh. 'full to the brim but not heaped up', as when a staff has been passed across the brim. But cf. Norw. *stappfull* crammed full (Aasen), f. *stappa* to stamp, crush.] Quite full.

13.. *Gaw. & Gr. Knt.* 494 Now ar þay stoken of sturne werk staf-ful her hond. *a* 1400–50 *Wars Alex.* 1543 A Mitre..Stiʒt staffull of stanes þat straʒt out bemes. *c* 1420 *Liber Cocorum* 34 And do hit in a barel þenne; Þe barel staf ful as I þe kenne.

Sta·ffian, *a. nonce-wd.* [f. Staff *sb.*[1] + -ian.] Suited for making staffs.

1820 L. Hunt *Indicator* No. 35 (1822) I. 279 The ash..hath been famous, time immemorial, for its staffian qualities.

†**Staffier.** *Obs.* Forms: 6 **stafyre**, 7–8 **staffier.** [ad. It. *staffiero*, *-ere*, f. *staffa* stirrup, a. OHG. *stapho*: see Step *v.* Cf. F. *estafier*.] 'A lacquey, that attends the stirrup' (Blount *Glossogr.*, 1674); a footman. Chiefly with reference to Italy.

1532 Boner in *St. Papers Hen. VIII*, VII. 396 The said old Abbot of Ferfa..hath been of late at Rome with 3 score in companye, besides 20 stafyres. 1664 Butler *Hud.* II. ii. 650 Before the Dame, and round about, March'd Whifflers, and Staffiers on foot. *a* 1668 Lassels *Voy. Italy* I. (1670) 12 The Italians..value no bravery but that of Coach and Horses and Staffiers. 1673 Ray *Journ. Low C.*, *Charac. Italians* 396 The Nobility..chuse..to spend their revenues in..keeping coaches and horses and a great retinue of servants and staffiers. *a* 1734 North *Exam.* III. vii. § 89. 574 These figures were brought by the Mob in grand Procession, from the further End of London, with honourable Attendance of Staffiers and Link-Boys.

†**Sta·ffish**, *a. Obs.* Also 6–9 *Sc.* **staffage.** [f. Staff *sb.*[1] + -ish.] **a.** Rigid, stiff, hard. **b.** *fig.* Stubborn, unmanageable.

1500–20 Dunbar *Poems* lx. 17 Stuffettis, strekouris, and stafische strummellis. 1513 Douglas *Æneis* XII. vi. 134 Thymetes, a man of full gret fors, Castyn from hys staffage, skeich and hedstrang hors. 1545 Ascham *Toxoph.* II. (Arb.) 118 An unfit and staffysh bow. *a* 1568 — *Scholem.* I. (Arb.) 34 A witte in youth, that is not ouer dulle, heauie, knottie and lumpishe, but hard, rough, and though somwhat staffishe. *a* 1568 A. Scott *Poems* xxi. 17, I fand hir of ane staffage kynd, Bath staitly, strange, and he. 1802 J. Sibbald *Chron. Scot. Poetry* IV. Gloss., *Staffage*, *Staffisch*, obstinate, obdurate, dry in the mouth, or not easily swallowed, like pease meal bannocks.

Sta·ffless, *a. rare.* Without a staff.

a 1661 Fuller *Worthies*, *Kent* (1662) 67 Hereat the Queen in some passion snatching the staff out of his hand...The Lord waited Staffless almost a day..before the same was reconferred upon him.

†**Sta·ffly**, *a. Obs.* [OE. *stæflic*: see Staff *sb.*[1] and -ly[1]. Cf. ON. *stafligr.*] Literal. So †**Sta·ffly** *adv.* [see -ly[2]], literally.

c 1000 Ælfric *Saints' Lives* xxv. 73 Hi..nellað understandan butan þæt steaflice [*v. r.* stæflice] andgit. *c* 1200 Ormin 11117 Forr to drinnkenn gastliʒ witt Ut off staffike fetless. *Ibid.* 14419 Aʒʒ whil þatt menn þurrh flæshliʒ witt Stafflike itt unnderrstodenn. *Ibid.* 15055 Þa takesst tu gastlike witt Off staffliʒ witeʒhunnge.

Staff officer.

†**1.** A high officer of the royal household, or minister of state, bearing a white staff. See Staff *sb.*[1] 7. *Obs.*

1702 *Lond. Gaz.* No. 3862/1 The Duke of Ormond, being the Staff-Officer in waiting. 1728 Chambers *Cycl.* s.v. *Officer*, *Staff Officers* are such as in the King's Presence bear a white Staff; and at other times, going abroad, have a white Staff borne before them by a Footman bare-headed. Such are the Lord Steward, Lord Chamberlain, Lord Treasurer, &c.

2. *Mil.* †**a.** A non-commissioned officer. *Obs.*

1702 *Milit. Dict.* (1704) s.v. *Officer*, *Warrant, and Staff-Officers*, those who have not the King's Commission, but are appointed by the Colonels and Captains, as Quartermasters, Serjeants, Corporals. [*ed.* 4, 1711, *adds*: and in the same Number are included Chaplains and Surgeons]. 1706 Farquhar *Recruiting Officer* v. v, *Kite.* [A sergeant, addressing a constable] And then we are both staff-officers. 1709 *Lond. Gaz.* No. 4590/3 Forty-four Staff-Officers. 1727 H. Bland *Milit. Discipl.* v. 61 The Staff-Officers, viz. Chaplain, Adjutant, Quarter-Master, Surgeon and Mate.

b. An officer doing duty with the general or departmental staff of an army, division, or brigade. Cf. G. *stabsoffizier*.

1777 Sheridan *Sch. Scand.* IV. i, Why then, he shall have him for ten pounds, and I'm sure that's not dear for a staff-officer. 1802 C. James *Milit. Dict.* Fff 3/1 No officer must ride between the divisions on a march, except General and Staff officers. 1811 *Regul. & Orders Army* 29 Aides-de-Camp, Brigade-Majors, and other Staff Officers. 1864 [see Sashery]. 1912 Trevelyan *Geo. III & Fox* I. iii. 112 When he was a young staff officer on active service.

c. In the United States navy, an officer not exercising military command. 1891 in *Century Dict.*

Staffold. *dial.* [Corrupt form (? after *scaffold*) of *stavel* Staddle *sb.*] = Staddle *sb.*

a 1722 Lisle *Husb.* (1757) 182 This method is not to be used where the wheat is designed for a staffold. 1764 *Museum Rust.* II. 221 Your said correspondent justly recommends the reek staval, or staffold, a frame of wood for the mow, placed on stones.

Stafford (stæ·fəɹd). The name of a town in England (the county town of Staffordshire); also a surname derived from this. Used *attrib.* as in †**Stafford blue**, some kind of blue cloth; **Stafford('s) knot** *Her.*, a knot used as a badge of the Stafford family; hence, a form of knot resembling this; †**Stafford law**, 'club law', with pun on *staff*; so †*Stafford court*. Also used for Staffordshire, as in **Stafford brick** (see quot. 1908).

c 1460 *Towneley Myst.* iii. 200 Thou were worthi be cled In *stafford blew; ffor thou art alway adred. 1908 *Animal Management* (Vet. Departm., War Office) 48 'Candy', 'blue *Stafford', 'Dutch', and 'adamantine clinkers' being the names of familiar varieties [of vitrified bricks]. 1611 Cotgr. s.v. *Festin*, *Il a esté au festin de Martin baston*, He hath had a triall in *Stafford Court. 1552 *Invent. Ch. Goods York*, etc. (Surtees) 49, iij sewtes of vestmentes with *Staforde knotes. 1828–40 Berry *Encycl. Her.* I, *Stafford Knot*, a badge used by the family of *Stafford*. 1847 *Gloss. Heraldry* 197 *Stafford's Knot*. 1868 Walcott *Sacred Archæol.* 507 A true-love-knot..was the well-known Stafford knot. 1589 *Hay any Work* Aiij, I threatned him with blowes, and to deale by *stafford law. 1599 Breton *Will of Wit*, etc. (Grosart) 29/1 And among souldiours Stafford law, martiall law, killing or hanging is soone learned. 1615 Bedwell *Moham. Impost.* I. § 26 The Alkoran of Mohammed established by Stafford law. 1647 M. Corbet *Sp.* 31 July 5 We have unlawfully erected Marshall Law, Club Law, Stafford Law, and such lawless Laws as make most for Treason.

Staffordshire (stæ·fəɹdʃəɹ). The name of a county of England, used *attrib.* as **Staffordshire coke**, **slack** (see quots.); **Staffordshire ware**, earthenware and porcelain made in Staffordshire, hence *Staffordshire warehouseman*. Also **Staffordshire knot** [? error for *Stafford knot*], 'a knot used to ligature the pedicle in ovariotomy' (*Syd. Soc. Lex.* 1898).

1784 H. Walpole *Descr. Strawberry H.* Wks. 1798 II. 414 Four green leaves of Staffordshire-ware. *Ibid.* 501 A Staffordshire Etruscan vase. 1813 *Examiner* 22 Feb. 119/1 J. Clarke, Tottenham-court-road, Staffordshire warehouseman. 1827 Faraday *Chem. Manip.* iv. (1842) 99 Of this kind is the Staffordshire coke, which may be obtained at some of the wharfs on the canals near London. 1857 J. Marryat *Pottery & Porcelain* (ed. 2) 149 The earliest specimens extant of the Staffordshire ware are the 'Butter-pots', and the Tygs or Tiggs. 1869 Day *Puddling* 4 in Rankine *Machine & Hand-tools*, The thick coal called 'Staffordshire slack'.

b. *ellipt.* = *Staffordshire ware*. Also *sb. pl.* = *Staffordshire bricks*.

1898 *Daily News* 8 Feb. 3/5 Little stacks of various kinds of bricks—from London stocks to Staffordshires. 1908 *Daily Report* 25 Aug. 8/3 The 'Fitz-Gerald' sale of Staffordshire ware..came as a revelation, both as to the quality of old Staffordshire and the prices it now obtains.

Staff-sling. *Obs.* exc. *Hist.* [f. Staff *sb.*[1] + Sling *sb.*[1] Cf. OHG. *stapaslinga*, G. *stabschlinge*.] A sling (Sling *sb.*[1] 1) the cords or strings of which are attached to the end of a staff, used for hurling larger stones than the ordinary 'cord-sling'.

13.. *Coer de L.* 5226 (W.), With staffe-slynges that smyte wel. 1375 Barbour *Bruce* XVII. 344 Instrumentis..As scaffatis, ledderis..Pykis, howis, and ek staff-slyngis. *c* 1386 Chaucer *Sir Thopas* 118 This geant at hym stones caste Out of a fel staf slynge. 1432–50 tr. *Higden* (Rolls) I. 297 Vsenge dartes and crosse bawes or staffe slynges. 1530 Palsgr. 275/1 Staffe slyng made of a clyftestycke, *ruant*. *c* 1550 Rolland *Crt. Venus* II. 226 Alswa he slew the Giant Golyas, In the foirheid with ane stane and stafsling. 1557–8 *Acc. Ld. High Treas. Scot.* X. 336 To big dikis and fowseis and to have stafe slungis in the reddines to the portis thairof. 1825 Fosbroke *Encycl. Antiq.* 780 The Staff-sling, the Classical *Fustibalum*.

Hence †**Staff-slinger.**

13.. *Coer de L.* 4454 (W.), Foremeste he sette hys arweblasteres, And aftyr that hys good archeres And aftyr hys staff-slyngeres And othir with scheeldes and with speeres.

†**Staff-sword.** *Obs.* [Cf. OHG. *stapaswert*, MHG. *stab-*, *stapswert*, Du. *stafsweerd* (Kilian), etc.] A sword-stick.

c 1000 Ælfric *Voc.* in Wr.-Wülcker 143/21 *Dolones*, stæfsweord. *c* 1470 Henry *Wallace* III. 178 With a staff suerd Boyd stekit him that tyde. *Ibid.* VI. 737 With a staff suerd off steill. *a* 1603 T. Cartwright *Confut. Rhem. N. T.* (1618) 543 Neither Aristotles..one shooe for both feet, nor Platoes staffe-sword.

Stafisagre, obs. form of Stavesacre.

Stag (stæg), *sb.*[1] Forms: α. ? 2 *accus.* **staggon**, 4–7 **stagge**, (4 **staghe**), 6–8 **stagg**, 4– **stag.** β. 5–7 **stage**; also (sense 2 only) 6 *north.* **staige**, 7 **staeg**, 5– *Sc.* **staig.** [Prob. repr. OE. **stacga* (*stagga*) wk. masc.; cf. various other names of animals, *docga* dog, *frocga* frog, **picga* pig, *wicga* beetle. The word seems to have meant properly a male animal in its prime; cf. the various senses below and the cognate ON. *steggi*, *stegg-r* (Norw. *stegg*) male bird, mod. Icel. *stegg-r* tom-cat, formerly also male fox: see Steg *sb.*

There is no ground for the current statement that *stag* is of Scandinavian origin, though some of the senses below may be due to confusion with Steg.]

1. The male of a deer, esp. of the red deer; spec. a hart or male deer of the fifth year. (In the 15th c. † *stag of a hart*.)

α. ? *c* 1185 Pseudo-Cnut *Constit. de Foresta* xxiv. in Liebermann *Gesetze der Ags.* (1903) I. 624 (Stowe MS., late 16th c.) Regalem feram, quam Angli a staggon [*Camb. MS. c.* 1570 Astaggon, *Harrison* 1577 staggon] appellant. *c* 1400 *Master of Game* (MS. Digby 182) ii, Þe first yere þat thei [harts] be calfede, þei be ycalle a calfe þe secund yere a bulloke..þe thred yere a broket, þe iiii. yere a stagard, þe v. yere a stagge, þe vi. yere an herte of .x. 14.. *Chaucer's Sqr.'s T.*, *heading of Part II*, *MSS. Petworth & Corpus*, The Stag of an hert. 1473 *Rolls of Parlt.* VI. 98/2 Oure Graunte..., of a Tonne Wyne, and a Stagge of an Hert. 1576 Turberv. *Venerie* xxii. (1908) 62 If you find together the footing of two stagges. *Ibid.* lxxix. 237 An Hart is called the firste yeare a Calfe.. the fourth a Staggerd, the fifth a Stagge, and..the sixth..an Hart. 1584 Powell *Lloyd's Cambria* 157 William Rufus was slaine by an Arrowe shot at a Stagge. 1596 Shaks. *Tam. Shr.* Induct. ii. 50 Thy gray-hounds are as swift As breathed Stags I fleeter then the Roe. 1613 Drayton *Poly-olb.* XII. 523 Those fallow Deere, and huge-hancht Stags that graz'd Vpon her shaggy Heaths. *c* 1643 Ld. Herbert *Autobiog.* (1824) 88 Forests and Chases which were well stored with wild Boar and Stag. 1667 Milton *P. L.* VII. 469 The swift Stag from under ground Bore up his branching head. 1735 Somerville *Chase* I. 283 [The] stately Stag, that o'er the Woodland reigns. 1821 Shelley *Hellas* 537 The tiger leagues not with the stag at bay Against the hunter. 1863 Lyell *Antiq. Man* 23 Venison, or the flesh of the stag and roe, was more eaten. 1877 *Encycl. Brit.* VII. 23/2 The Red Deer or Stag..the largest of the British deer, is a native of the temperate regions of Europe and Northern Asia. 1908 *Blackw. Mag.* July 105/2 A herd of fourteen reindeer was seen...The horns of the entire band —for the hinds carry them as well as the stags—were still in velvet.

β. 1546 *Plumpton Corr.* (Camden) 250, I must..ride to Tankerslay..& se a showt at a stage, as my keper hath sent me wourd. *c* 1550 *Battle of Otterburn* iii. in Child *Ballads* III. 295/1 Vpon Grene Lynton they lyghted dowyn, Styrande many a stage [*rime* crage].

b. *fig.* Also in phrases † *To go in stag*: To go naked. † *To make* (a husband) *a stag*, *to make to wear the stag's crest* = to cuckold. (*Obs.*)

1591 Florio *2nd Fruites* 143 What dooth she make him weare the staggs crest then? 1602 Dekker *Satirom.* F 3, No, come my little Cub, doe not scorne mee because I goe

Staged, *ppl. a.* [f. STAGE *sb.* and *v.* + -ED.]

Stage-manager. One whose office it is to superintend the production and performance of a play, and to regulate the arrangements of the stage. Also *fig.*

Stage-play. A dramatic performance; also, a dramatic composition adapted for representation on the stage.

Stage-player.

Stage-playing. Playing on the stage as an actor; play-acting.

Stager.

Stag head, stag's head.

Stag-headed.

Stag-horn. Also *stag's horn.*

Staging, *vbl. sb.* Also 9 *stageing.*

Stagiary, *sb.* (and *a.*)

Stagirite.

Stagma.

Stagnal.

Stagnancy.

Stagnant, *a.* (*sb.*)

Stagnate, *v.*

Stagy, Stageous, see STAGEY, STAGINESS.

Staggard (stæ·gǎd). *arch.* Also 5 *stagard, 6-7 stagguard, 7 staggarde, 9 staggart.*

Staggart.

Stagger, *v.* [f. STAGGER *sb.* + -ER.]

Staggeringly, *adv.*

Staggery.

| STAGNATED. | 773 | STAIDNESS. | STAIN. | 774 | STAIN. |

Stagnated (stæ'gn,ētĕd), *ppl. a.* [f. STAGNATE *v.* + -ED.] Rendered stagnant.

Stagnature, *nonce-wd.* [f. STAGNATE *v.* + -URE.] The state or condition of being stagnant.

†Stagne, *v. Obs.* [a. F. *stagner*, ad. L. *stagnā-re.*] *intr.* To become stagnant; to stagnate.

Stagnicolous (stægni'kŏlŏs), *a.* [f. mod.L. *stagnicol-a* + -OUS.] Of animals: Living in or inhabiting stagnant water.

†Stagninous, *a. Obs. rare⁻¹.* [f. L. *stagnin-*: see -INE².] *trans.* To render stagnant.

‡Stagnum. *Obs. rare.* [a. late OE. *stagnen* (11th c.), *a. L. *stagn-um*.] A stag or stag-pool.

Stagy, stagey (stē'dʒi), *a.* [f. STAGE *sb.* + -Y.] Theatrical in appearance, manner, style, etc.

Staid (stēd), *ppl. a.* [Pa. pple. of STAY *v.*] Of beliefs, institutions, etc.: Fixed, permanent; settled, unchanging.

Staidness (stē'dnēs). [f. STAID *a.* + -NESS.] The quality or fact of being staid.

Stain (stēn), *sb.* Forms: 4-6 steyne, 5 stayn, stene, steane, 5-7 staine, 7 staine, 6- stain. [f. STAIN *v.*]

Stain (stēn), *v.* Forms: 4-6 steyne, steyn, 5 steyn, steyne, 6-7 staine, 6- stain. [ME. *steynen*, a. F. *desteindre.*]

Stainable (stē'nǎb'l), *a.* Capable of being stained. Hence **Stainability**.

Stained (stēnd), *ppl. a.* [f. STAIN *v.* + -ED¹.] Discoloured with blood, dirt, etc.; having stains or blemishes. Also *fig.*, tainted with guilt, disgraced, etc.

Stainer (stē'nǎr), *sb.* Forms: 4-6 steynour, 5 staynour, stener, steynoure, 6 steyner, 7 stayner, 8- stainer. [agent-n. f. STAIN *v.*]

†Stainful, *a. rare⁻¹.* [f. STAIN *sb.* + -FUL.] Polluting, disgraceful.

Staining (stē'niŋ), *vbl. sb.* [f. STAIN *v.* + -ING¹.] The action of the verb STAIN, in various senses.

Stainless (stē'nlēs), *a.* [f. STAIN *sb.* + -LESS.] Without stain, spot, or blemish.

Stair (stēǎr), *sb.* Forms: 1 stǽger, 5 stayer, steyer, steyr, steier, 3-5 steir, 3-6 steyr, steyre, 4-7 steyr, 4- stair. [OE. *stǽger*: — OTeut. type *staigri-*, f. *staig-*, ablaut-var. of *stig-* to climb.]

STAIR.

degrei]; There shall ye find the clothes. 1548 UDALL *Erasm. Par. Acts* xxi. 31-6 As Paule came to the stayghere of the castell. *Ibid.*, The multitude...folowed, euen to the stayre.

4. *pl.* (rarely † *sing.*). **a.** A landing-stage, esp. on the Thames in and near London.

b. A flight of stone steps, or a steep lane or alley with steps at intervals, forming a passage from one street to another at a different level.

5. *attrib.* and *Comb.* **a.** simple attrib. as *stair-arch, -baluster, -carpet, -carpeting, -door, -newel, -rail, -top*, etc. ; *stair-like* adj. ; *stair-voise* adv. ; *stair-insider*, *building*, *-climbing*. (Rarely *stairs-*.)

b. Special *comb.*: **stair-beak**, a Brazilian bird of the genus *Xenops* ; **stair-cloth**, a fabric for covering stairs ; **stair-maid**, a maid-servant employed about the staircase in an hotel ; **stair-pit** *Mining* (see quot. 1883) ; **stair-rod** (see quot. 1858) ; † **stairs-shell** = *staircase-shell* ; † **stair-stele** *b.* the side-piece for a stair-case ; **stair-step** *n.*, the piece in a flight of stairs, also *attrib.* in *stair-step carpet* ; **stair-step** *v.*, to furnish with a range of steps ; **stair-tower**, a stair-turret ; **stair-tree**, † *(a)* the sloping timber on or in which the ends of the steps of a wooden stair-case are fixed ; *(b)* (see quot. 1688) ; (*c*) a tree with steps in it to serve as a staircase ; **stair-turret**, a turret with a staircase in it ; **stair-wire**, a slender rod used to keep a stair-carpet in position on or in connexion with stairs. See also STAIRCASE, STAIR-FOOT, STAIR-HEAD, STAIRWAY.

Staircase (stēᵊ·rkēs). [f. STAIR *sb.* + CASE *sb.* 8.]

1. Originally, 'The inclosure of a pair of Stairs, whether it be with Walls, or with Walls and Railes and Bannisters, &c.' (Moxon *Mech. Exerc.*, 1679. p. 172) ; now usually a flight (or sometimes a whole series of flights) of stairs with their supporting framework, balusters, etc.

b. *transf.*

2. *Phys.* A continuous series of responses to nerve stimuli, varying from a minimal to a maximal intensity. (*Syd. Soc. Lex.* citing Romanes.)

Stairway (stēᵊ·rwē). [f. STAIR *sb.* + WAY *sb.*] A way up a flight of stairs, a staircase.

Staithe (stēθ), *sb.* *dial.* [f. prec. *sb.*] *trans.* To furnish with a staithe ; to embank.

Staithman (stēθmăn). Also **staithesman**. [f. STAITH *sb.* + MAN *sb.*] (See quots.)

Staitly, obs. Sc. form of STATELY *adv.*

Staive, **Staiver** : see STAVE, STAVER *vbs.*

Stake (stēk), *sb.¹* Forms : 1 staca, 3 stake, 4-5 *sc.* and *north.* staike (6 stayke), 6 staik, 5-6 *Sc.* and *north.* stack, 4-6 (6 staye), 4-6 stake. [OE. *staca* wk. masc. corresponds to OFris., MDu. *stake* masc. and fem. (Du. *staak* masc.), (M)LG. *stake* (whence MHG., mod.G. *stake*, *staken*), and prob. MSw. *stak*, Sw., Norw. *staka*, Da. *stage* ; f. *stak-* ablaut-var. of *stek-* to pierce, thrust in : see STEKE, STICK *vbs.*

1. A stout stick or post, usually of wood, with a pointed end for driving into the ground ; used, e.g. to mark a boundary or site, to support a plant, to secure an animal, to form one of the component parts of a fence, hedge, or the like.

b. Stake and band, bond, bound : see quot. 1805.

Staking (stēᵊ·kiŋ), *vbl. sb.* [f. STAKE *v.¹* + -ING¹.] The action of driving a stake, or the action of piercing with or impaling on a stake.

Stalactic (stălæ·ktik), *a.* (*sb.*) [f. Gr. σταλακτ-ός dropping, dripping + -IC.] = STALACTITIC.

Stalactical (stălæ·ktikăl), *a.* [f. STALACTIC + -AL.] = STALACTITIC.

Stalactite (stălæ·ktəit), *sb.* [mod.L. *stalactitēs* (Olaus Wormius : see STALAGMITE) f. Gr. σταλακτός dropping (see prec.).]

Stalactitic (stælæktiʹtik), *a.* [f. STALACTITE + -IC.] Having the form or structure of a stalactite.

Stalactitical (stælæktiʹtikăl), *a.* [f. prec. + -AL.] = STALACTITIC.

Stalactitiform (stælæktiʹtifǭ̈m), *a.* [f. STALACTITE + -I- + -FORM.] Having the form of a stalactite.

Stalagma (stălæ·gmă). [mod.L., a. Gr. σταλαγμός a dropping.]

Stalagmite (stă·lăgmăit). [a. mod.L. *stalagmitēs* (Olaus Wormius : see STALACTITE).]

STALAGMITIC.

1. An incrustation or deposit, more or less like an inverted stalactite, on the floor of a cavern, formed by the dropping from the roof of some material in solution.

Stalagmitic (stælægmi′tik), *a.* [f. STALAGMITE + -IC. Cf. F. *stalagmitique.*] Formed in the same way as a stalagmite; consisting of or having their form or character.

Stalagmitical, *a.*

Stalagmite (stæ′lægməit), *a.* [f. STALAGMITE + -METER.] An apparatus for measuring drops. So **Stalagmometry** [-scope], an apparatus.

Stalan(d, stalɑn)n't, *sb.*

Stalboat, obs. form of STALE-BOAT.

Stalch, *Mining. Obs. rare.* [Of obscure origin.] A piece of ground left uncut though all around has been worked.

Stalder (stɔ′ldər). Also † **staulder.**

† Stale, *sb.¹ Obs.* Forms: 1 stalu, *Northumb.* stalo, 2 stale, 3–4 stal.

Stalding; errors, from STEAL *sb.*

Stale (stēᵊl), *sb.² Now dial.* Forms: 1 stalu, 7 stale, stayl, 7, 9 stail, 3–5 stale. See also STEAL *sb.²*

Stale, *sb.³* [Prob. a. AF. *estale, estal* (only in Bozon, 13th c.), applied to a pigeon used to entice a hawk into the net; that this word is not an adoption from English is rendered probable by the occurrence of the extended form *estalon* in continental Fr. with the same sense]

1. A decoy-bird; a living bird used to entice other birds of its own species, or birds of prey, into a snare or net.

† **4.** More fully **common stale**: a prostitute of the lowest class, employed as a decoy by thieves. Often (? associated with STALE *v. a.*) a term of contempt for an unchaste woman. *Obs.*

† **5.** A person or thing made use of as a means or tool for inducing some result, as a pretext for some action, or as a cover for sinister action.

† 6. A lover or mistress whose devotion is turned into ridicule for the amusement of a rival or rivals.

Stale, *sb.⁴* Also 4–6 **stail**, 6 **stayl, staile**; (6–7 **stal**). [f. OE. *estal,* used in many specific applications of the senses]

Stale, *sb.⁵* Also 4–6 **stall.** [f. STALE *v.²* or *sb.*]

Stale, *sb.⁶ Chess. Obs.* [f. AF. *estale,* perh. vbl. n. *f. estaler* to STALE *v.*]

Stale, *a.* [Stale *adj.¹*] Obs.

†1. Of malt liquor, mead, wine: That has stood long enough to clear; freed from dregs or lees; hence, old and strong. *Obs.*

2. That has lost its freshness; altered by keeping.

b. *Comb.* **stale-born,** (Decoy) *Stale birds,* that have frequently visited the decoy, but have lost interest in the actions of the dog.

7. *Comb.*

†Stale, *a.² Chess. Obs.* [f. STALE *sb.⁶*] Stale-mated.

Stale (stēᵊl), *v.¹* Also 3–4 **stale**, 6 **stail**, 7 **staill,** etc. [Cf. MDu. *stolen.* See STALE *sb.³*]

†Stale, *v.²* [f. STALE *a.*] *trans.* To render (beer or ale) 'stale'.

Stale (stēᵊl), *v.³* [f. STALE *sb.⁴*] *trans.* To put rungs in a ladder.

Stale, *v.⁴* Also *stail.* [f. STALE *sb.³*] *trans.* To decoy, lure.

Staled (stēᵊld), *ppl. a.* [f. STALE *v.*]

Staleless, *a. rare.*

Stalely, *adv. rare.* [f. STALE *a.¹ + -LY².*]

Stalemate (stēᵊl′mēᵊt), *sb. Chess.* [f. STALE *sb.⁶* + MATE *sb.²*]

Stalemate (stēᵊl′mēᵊt), *v. Chess.* [f. STALE-MATE *sb.*] *trans.* To subject to a stalemate.

Stalemated, *ppl. a.*

† Staling, *sb.¹ Obs. rare—¹.* [f. STALE *a.¹ + -ING².*]

Stalewort, Stalworth; = STALWORTH.

† Staling, *sb.² Obs. rare—¹.* [f. STALE *v.³ + -ING¹.*] The action of urinating.

Stalk (stɔk), *sb.¹* Forms: 4–7 **stalke**, 6 *Sc.* **staok,** 7 **stauk.** [ME. *stalk-e,* dim. form, with *d* suffix, of STALE *sb.²* (OE. *stæl-).* The exact formal equivalent does not occur in the other Teut. langs., but a parallel formation from the ablaut-variant *stel-* (in OE. *stela* STEAL *sb.,* stem, handle, etc.) is found in NFris. *stidl,* MSw. *stiälk,* stiälkar (mod.Sw.sjelk, själk), Norw. *stylk, stilk,* Icel. *stilk,* mod.Icel. *stilk-ur.* Cl. Eng. dial. *stilk-t,* post, stake.]

1. The main stem of a herbaceous plant, bearing the flowers and leaves; also, a scape or flower-stem rising directly from the root.

2. A straw.

Stalk (stɔk), *sb.²* Also 4–7 **stalke,** 7 *Sc.* **stawk,** 8 *Sc.* **stauk.** [ME. (14th c.) *stalke,* app. a dim. with *d* suffix in STALE *sb.²* (O.E. *stælu*). The exact equivalent formation does not occur in the other Teut. langs., but a parallel formation from the ablaut-variant *stel-*]

Stalk (stɔk), *sb.³* Also 7–8 **stauk,** 8–9 *dial.* **stawk.** [f. STALK *v.²*]

1. An act of stalking game.

Stalk (stɔk), *v.¹* Forms: 1 **-stealcian,** 4–7 **stalke,** 7 **stauk.** [Partly repr. OE. *-stealcian* (in *bestealcian* to move stealthily).]

1. *intr.* To walk softly, cautiously, or stealthily.

2. *trans.* To pursue (game) by stealthy approach.

Stalk (stɔk), *v.²*

Stalkable (stɔ′kăb'l), *a.* [f. STALK *v.² + -ABLE.*]

Stalked (stɔkt), *a.² dial.* [f. STALK *v.² + -ED².*]

Stalker (stɔ′kər). Forms: 1 **stealcere,** 5–7 **stalker.** [f. STALK *v.¹ + -ER¹.*]

Stalking (stɔ′kiŋ), *vbl. sb.* [f. STALK *v.¹ + -ING¹.*] The action of STALK *v.¹*

Stalking, *ppl. a.* [f. STALK *v.¹ + -ING².*]

Stalking, vbl. sb. [f. STALK v.¹ + -ING².] That stalks.

Stalkless (stǫ·kles), a. [STALK sb.¹ + -LESS.] A small stalk; in Bot.

Stalk-like, Anglo-Irish.¹ Obs. [a. Irish stácach.]

Stalky (stǫ·ki), a. [f. STALK sb.¹ + -Y.] Consisting of or abounding in stalks; of the nature of a stalk or stalks; long and slender like a stalk.

Stall (stǫl), sb.¹ Forms: 1 steall, steal, stal, 3–7 stal, stalle, 3 steal, 3–4 stel, 4–6 stale, (5 stayle, stawll), 6 staull, stawle, stawyll, 6–7 staule, 7 staul, 7–9 stall; 6–9 staw, 7– stall.

Stall-fed, a. Also 6 stauled, stalfed, (7 stall-feed) to be fatened.

Stalla·ge (stǫ·lėdż). Obs. [a. AF. estalage.]

Staller. Obs. Also -ere. [a. Norman F. estaler.]

Stallion (stæ·lyǫn), sb. Forms: 4 stalun, 4–5 stalon, stalond, -ound, stalion, 5 stalyon, 6–9 stallon, 6– stallion.

Stallionize ... To stallionize it, to act the stallion.

Stallion (stǣ'li̯ən). [f. STALL sb.¹ + -IZE.] ...

Stall-net. *Obs.* [= stalnets, 0 stalnette, 7 stale-net, small nett. [Prob.1. STALL sb.¹ + ...

Stalor. ... Misspelling of STOLON.] A slip, scion.

Stalloy (stǣloi). [? App. arbitrarily f. ST(EEL) + ALLOY. (See quots.)

Stalworth, Stalwart. See STALWORTH a.

† **Stalment.** *Obs.* Also **stallment.** [a. AF. *estallement* ...

Stalworth(e, a. *Now arch.* and *literary.* ...

† **Stalp,** *Sc. Obs.*⁻¹. [Cf. WFris. *stap* trap, and STAMP sb.²] ? Some kind of trap.

Stalth, (e, obs. forms of STEALTH.

Sta'tic, a. *Obs.* ...

Stalwart (stǣ'lwərt), a. and sb. *Now literary.*

Stalwartise, -ize ...

Stalwartness. ...

Stalworth, a. and sb. *Obs. exc. arch.*

Stalworthiness. ...

Stalworthly, adv. *Obs.*

Stalworthhead. *Obs.* In 3 stalwardhede.

Stalworthly, adv. *Obs.*

Stam (stæm), sb.¹ dial. [Belongs to STAM v.; possibly *stagm.* OE. *stamm*.]

Stam, sb.² *dial.* [See STAM sb.²]

Stam (stæm), v. dial. [See STAM sb.²]

Stamin (stæ'min). ... The thread spun by the Fates ...

Stamin (stæ'min), sb. *pl.* stamens, stamin, stamyn(e ...

Stam, sb.³ *dial.* Also stom, staum. ...

Stamina (stæ'minǎ). 1. ...

Staminal (stæ'minǎl), a. [f. L. *stāmin-* + -AL.]

Stamineal, a. [f. L. *stāmineus* ...]

Stamineous, a. [f. L. *stāmineus* ...]

Staminate (stæ'minět), a. *Bot.* [f. L. *stāmin-*]

Staminode, sb. *Bot.* Anglicized form of next.

Staminodium (stæminǒ'diǔm). *Bot.* [f. L. *stāmin-* STAMEN, after PHYLLODY.]

Staminody (stæ'minǒdi). *Bot.* [f. L. *stāmin-* STAMEN, after PHYLLODY.]

Staminode, sb.

Stammel¹ (stæ'měl). *Now only arch.* or *Hist.* ...

Stammel², *slang. Obs.*

Stammer (stæ'mər), v. [OE. *stamerian* ...]

Stammerer (stæ'mərə). ...

Stammering (stæ'məriŋ), vbl. sb. [-ING¹.]

Hence **Stampe·ded** ppl. a.; **Stampeding** vbl. sb. and ppl. a. Also **Stampede·er**.

Stampee. Obs. [Corruptly a. F. estampille stamp, seal, a. Sp. estampilla dim. of estampa STAMP sb.] A counterfeit coin formerly circulated in the West Indies.

Stamper (stæ·mpəɹ), sb. [f. STAMP v. + -ER¹.]
1. One who stamps with the feet; who treads (grapes). Also with out (cf. STAMP v. 3 d).

b. Med. (See quot.)

Stamper, Obs. [ad. Sp. estampador a person affected with locomotor ataxia] so called because of the peculiar stamping gait of that disease.

Stampinated, a.

Stampian (stæ·mpiən), a. Geol. [f. mod.L. Stamp- æ Etampes (France).] = RUPELIAN.

Stamping (stæ·mpiŋ), vbl. sb. [-ING¹.]
1. The action of STAMP v., in various senses.

Stamp̓er, sb. Obs. rare⁻¹. [? var. of STAMP-MER.]

Sta·mping-ground. Now dial. and U.S.

Stanch, staunch (stanʃ, stɔnʃ), sb.¹ Also
Stance (stæns, stɑːns), sb. [a. OF. estance.]

Stanch, staunch, v. [a. OF. estancher.]

Stanchel (stæ·nʃel). Sc. and north. ? Obs. Also **stanchil**.

Stancher (stɑ·nʃəɹ). [f. STANCH v. + -ER¹.]

STAND.	801	STAND.
STAND.	802	STAND.
STAND.	803	STAND.
STAND.	804	STAND.

stand much longer than they do in England. 1883 Greslky Gloss. Coal-mining 237 Stand, does not break down or require timbering. A rock or coal roof generally stands better than one composed of shale or clay.

fig. 1805 Wordsw. *Prelude* II. 280 The props of my affections were removed, And yet the building stood, as if sustained By its own spirit! 1834 J. Wilson *Noctes Ambr.* xxxvii. Wks. 1856 IV. 198 The Church doesna deserve to staun when sic atrocities are rife beneath its shelter.

b. Of the world: To exist; to remain stable, last. Chiefly in phrase: cf. quot. 1526.

c 1205 Lay. 18850 Þe wile þe þis world stænt [c 1275 steond] ilæsten scal is worðmunt. a 1225 *Leg. Kath.* 1490 Of marbrestan a temple, þet schal aa stonden, hwil þet te world stont. 1340–70 *Alex. & Dind.* 587 3e were alle..bred of þat modur þat is stable to stonde. 1526 Tindale 1 *Cor.* viii. 13 Whill the worlde stondeth [So 1611; Gr. εἰς τὸν αἰῶνα]. 1598 R. Bernard tr. *Terence, Adelphos* I. ii, Neuer was there since the world stood, any thing more vnreasonable.

c. Of any mechanism or contrivance: To hold together, resist wear or damage, keep its place.

1768 Sterne *Sent. Journ., The Wig*, But I fear, friend! said I, this buckle won't stand.

24. Naut. *To let all stand*: to leave a ship fully rigged. *All standing*, i. e. without dismantling or unrigging; *transf.* with one's clothes on, dressed. *To be paid off, brought up all standing*: see quot. 1867.

1669 Sturmy *Mariner's Mag.* I. 17 Shall we get down our Top-masts? No, let all stand. 1791 Smeaton *Edystone L.* (1793) § 259 We began to heave in our ground chain,..and, it being nine P.M. concluded to let all stand till the next morning... Found all standing as we had left it. 1802 *Naval Chron.* VIII. 172 The Fisgard..was paid off all standing, directly recommissioned. 1867 Smyth *Sailor's Word-bk.* s.v. *All*, *To be brought up all standing*, is to be suddenly checked or stopped, without any preparation. *Paid off all standing*, without unrigging or waiting to return stores; perhaps recommissioned the next day or hour. 1893 Dunmore *Pamirs* II. 62, I dined, and after smoking a pipe, turned in all standing for the night.

25. Of a pigment or dye: To keep its colour; also, not to blot or run.

1811 *Self Instructor* 531 All these three colours stand. 1815 J. Smith *Panorama Sci. & Art* II. 731 Vermilion... Stands tolerably well if perfectly pure. 1883 R. Haldane *Workshop Rec.* Ser. II. 336 Most of the black Indian ink.. blots when a damp brush is passed over it; or, as draughtsmen say, 'it does not stand'.

26. *Farriery.* Of the eye: To preserve its sight, to keep good sight.

1737 Bracken *Farriery Impr.* (1757) II. 13, I must return to a Description of the Eye that I think most likely to stand (as we term it).

*** To be still or stationary.

27. Of liquids: To cease flowing; *esp.* of water, to collect and remain motionless, be stagnant (cf. Standing *ppl. a.*). (See also Still *adv.*)

c 888 Ælfred *Boeth.* xxxv. § 7 Se hearpere [*sc.* Orpheus].. hearpode ðæt..þa ea stodon. 1382 Wyclif *Luke* viii. 44 And anon the flix of hir blood stood [*v.r.* ceesed]. 1538 Elyot *Dict.*, *Stagno*, proprely of water is to stande and not to flowe. 1585 Higins *Junius' Nomencl.* 401/2 *Lacuna*,..a ditch wherein water standeth. 1697 Dryden *Æneid* VII. 1093 Where Ufens glides along the lowly Lands, Or the black Water of Pomptina stands. 1852 *Jrnl. R. Agric. Soc.* XIII. I. 80 The stagnant water being permitted year after year to stand on the surface during the winter. 1882 *Unexpl. Baluchistan* 41 The water appeared to stand here some time, judging by the presence of many water weeds.

transf. 1899 Mrs. E. Cotes *Path of Star* xv. 160 The garden where heavy scents stood in the sun.

fig. 1842 Tennyson *Sir Galahad* 10 When the tide of combat stands.

b. Of land, a ditch, etc.: *To stand with*, to be full of (stagnant water). (Cf. 17 c.)

1601 Holland *Pliny* VI. xxvii. I. 138 The countrey Elemais is so fennie, and standeth with water so wet, that there is no way through it to Persis. 1718 Hearne *Collect.* (O.H.S.) VI. 229 The Ditch about the Camp stands with water, except in a dry time. 1848 *Jrnl. R. Agric. Soc.* IX. I. 242 It is not at all uncommon to see a clay pit stand with water.

28. Of tears: To remain collected (in the eyes) without falling. Of a humour, esp. perspiration: To remain in drops (*on* the skin, etc.).

1530 Palsgr. 733/1 He dyd nat wepe that I sawe, but the water stode in his eyes. 1581 A. Hall *Iliad* VI. 119 She smiles therewith, yet in hir eyes the water ful doth stand. 1627 May *Lucan* VI. L 3, She..gathers poisonous filth, and slime that stands On the cold ioynts. 1675 Hannah Woolley *Gentlew. Comp.* 71 Do not venture to eat Spoon-meat so hot, that the tears stand in your eyes. 1719 De Foe *Crusoe* I. (Globe) 230 This he spoke so earnestly, that I saw Tears stand in his Eyes. 1841 Longf. *Excelsior* v, A tear stood in his bright blue eye. 1849 *Tait's Mag.* XVI. 226/1 Cold drops stood on my brow. 1891 *Strand Mag.* II. 509/2 The sweat stood in beads on his forehead.

†**b.** Of the eyes, *To stand a-water*: to be filled with tears. *Obs.*

1605 Chapman, etc. *Eastw. Hoe* II. C 3 b, *Gyr.* Gods my dignitie! as I am a Lady, if he did not make me blush so that mine eyes stood a water.

29. Of a liquid, etc.: To be kept in a vessel without shaking.

c 1467 *Noble Bk. Cookry* (1882) 101 Sye it throughe a clothe and let yt stond and setelle. c 1550 Lloyd *Treas. Health* liii. R ij, Such thynges are neuer mynystred excepte they haue stonde [1585 N iij b, stoode] setteled a good whyle after commixtion. 1675 Hannah Woolley *Gentlew. Comp.* 136 Strain it [the Jelly], and so let it stand for your use. 1827 Faraday *Chem. Manip.* xii. (1842) 275 The whole is to be closed up, and suffered to stand until cold. 1852 *Jrnl. R. Agric. Soc.* XIII. I. 37 The first milk is set..to stand for cream. 1862 Miller *Organ. Chem.* (ed. 2) 165 The liquid portion is removed by pressure, and after standing over chloride of calcium is rectified.

†**30.** Of a mixture or confection: To be stiff, have a firm consistence. (Cf. Standing *ppl. a.* 8 b.)

c 1450 *Two Cookery-bks.* 88 Loke that hit stonde well, with Gynger, Sugur. *Ibid.* 109.

31. Of a star: To appear fixed in the heavens. Of the sun or a planet: To be seen apparently motionless at any point of its course.

1382 Wyclif *Josh.* x. 13 And the sunne and the mone stoden, to the tyme that [etc.]. 1398 Trevisa *Barth. De P. R.* VIII. xxi. (1495) 331 Stelle ben callyd sterres and haue that name of stando, stondyng, for though they moue alwaye, alwaye it semyth that they stonde. 1577 Kendall *Flowers of Epigr.* 86 In heuen where starres do stand. 1629 Milton *Nativity* 70 The Stars with deep amaze Stand fixt in stedfast gaze. 1833 Tennyson *Lotos-Eaters* 7 Full-faced above the valley stood the moon.

32. Of a piece of machinery, an implement, a vehicle, etc.: To remain still or motionless; not to move or be operated; to cease moving, working, turning, etc. Of a timepiece: To cease 'going', to have stopped. Now somewhat *rare*. Cf. *to stand still*: see Still *adv.*

1362 Langl. *P. Pl.* A. VII. 105 At heiȝ prime perkyn lette þe plouȝ stonde. c 1386 Chaucer *Friar's T.* 243 Deepe was the wey, for which the Carte stood. c 1400 *Anturs of Arth.* 266 Maye no mane stere hym of strenghe, whilles þe whele standis. 1549 Latimer *Ploughers* (Arb.) 25 The ploughe standeth, there is no worke done. a 1696 P. Henry in M. Henry *Life* x. (1825) 247 When the weight is off, the clock stands. 1772 Foote *Nabob* I. (1778) 22, I..told him, the dog was mad, the parrot dead, and the clock stood. 1820 Scoresby *Acc. Arctic Reg.* II. 476 During an hour.. the pumps were allowed to 'stand'. 1885 'Mrs. Alexander' *At Bay* viii, Before his astonished companion could reply he was beside the vehicle, which was still standing.

b. Of a ship: To ride at anchor.

a 1300 *K. Horn* 1021 He let his schup stonde, & ȝede to londe. *Ibid.* 1437 His schup stod vnder ture. c 1350 *Will. Palerne* 2728 Þan hiȝed þei hem to þe hauen..þer stoden fele schippes.

c. Of a vehicle: To remain in a customary place waiting for a fare or for the time to start.

1665 in *Verney Mem.* (1907) II. 241 The Black Swan in Holborn where the Alisbury and other coaches stand. 1676 in J. Playford *Vade Mecum* (1679) 197 All Merchants..may chuse what Carr they please, except such as stand for Wharf-work [etc.]..which are to be taken in turn.

d. Of a mine, factory, etc., also of the men employed: To stop working; to be at a standstill.

1733 *N. Riding Rec.* VIII. 202 The Treasurer to pay £22.15/ for the Milne standing tenn weeks. 1789 J. Williams *Min. Kingd.* I. 170 Several Cornish mines are now standing ..because they cannot be carried on with profit while coal is so dear. 1892 *Black & White* 12 Mar. 331/1 If they [the colliers] 'stand' for a fortnight. 1892 *Standard* 28 Apr. 7/5 Works which stood all last week for holidays being now restarted.

**** With some notion of motion or direction in a fixed or steady course.

†**33.** Of light (also rarely of vapour): To issue in a beam or shaft. *Obs.*

Beowulf 726 Him of eagum stod..leoht unfæger. c 900 *Bæda's Hist.* v. xxiii. (1890) 476 Stod se leoma him of, swilce fyrenbecele. c 1000 Ælfric *Hom.* (Th.) I. 86 Him stod stincende steam of ðam muðe. a 1300 *Cursor M.* 8160 A lem fra þe wandes stode. c 1300 *Havelok* 591 Of hise mouth it stod a stem, Als it were a sunnebem. c 1400 *St. Alexius* 439 (Laud 463) Out of his mouþ þer stoed a leom Brighter þan þe sonne beom.

†**34.** Of a weapon: To be fixed *at* or *on* the place to which it penetrates in wounding; to penetrate *through, unto*. Said also of the stroke or 'dint'. *Obs.*

Beowulf 1434 Sumne Feata lœod of flanbogan feores getwæfde,..þæt him on aldre stod herestræl hearda. a 1300 *Cursor M.* 11371 Þe suerd o soru thoru hir stode. *Ibid.* 24760 Þe nails þat him fest on rode, thoru mi hend and fete þai stode. 13.. *King Alis.* 3709 Hesmot anothir,..That he clef his basnet, At his chyn stod the dunt. c 1330 *Arth. & Merl.* 8134 King Malgar on þe heued he gert, Þat þe dent stode at þe hert. 1390 Gower *Conf.* III. 268 With his swerd droppende of blod, The which withinne his douhter stod.

35. Of the wind: To blow from a quarter indicated; also simply, to blow favourably, to continue to blow. Similarly of the weather. ? *Obs.* (Cf. Sit *v.* 13 d.)

c 1205 Lay. 1780 Wind stod on willen. *Ibid.* 25537 Weder stod on wille, wind wex an honde. c 1300 *Cursor M.* 24834 Forth þai floted on þat flod, For al to will þair bir þam stode. c 1300 *K. Horn* 784 (Laud MS.), Þe whyȝt him gan stonde And drof tyl hirelonde. 1338 R. Brunne *Chron.* (1810) 145 Þe next Marche folowand He suld take þat way, if wynde wild with him stand, At Marsile to aryue. 1412–20 Lydg. *Chron. Troy* I. 4392 Whan þei seye þat þe wedir stood, þe wynde also þat lust þei hadde, Þei gan to saille. 1546 J. Heywood *Prov.* (1867) 56 If the winde stande in that doore, it standth awry. 1635 Brereton *Trav.* (Chetham Soc.) 77 The wind stood most easterly. 1669 Sturmy *Mariner's Mag.* I. ii. 16 The Wind is fair, though but little; he comes well, as if he would stand. 1699 Dampier *Voy.* II. I. 155 If the gale stood. 1708 *Lond. Gaz.* No. 4417/2 [They] will sail for the River, as soon as the Wind stands fair.

36. *Naut.* Of a vessel (hence of the commander, sailors, etc.): To sail, steer, direct one's course (in a specified direction, to sea, into harbour, etc.).

See also *stand along, away*, etc. in branch VII; also *stand for* 71 k, *stand with* 79 d. (Note the pa. t. *stowed* in the 17th c., prob. due to misapprehension.)

1627 J. Taylor (Water P.) *Famous Fight* Wks. (1630) III. 39/1 We gaue him a whole broad-side..tacking forthwith, and standing after him. 1633 T. James *Voy.* 18 Wee stowed alongst it [floating ice], hoping to weather it. 1633 T. Stafford *Pac. Hib.* II. x. 189 The Spanish fleete..standing to the Northward. a 1700 Evelyn *Diary* 16 Oct. 1644, The weather being still so fowle that for two houres at least we durst not stand into the haven. 1707 *Lond. Gaz.* No. 4312/2 They stood to Sea. 1745 P. Thomas *Jrnl. Anson's Voy.* 280 We immediately..stood towards her, and I believe if she had..stood from us, we should have found it very difficult to have come up with her. 1748 *Anson's Voy.* III. ix. 386 This entrance he proposed to stand through next day. 1769 Falconer *Dict. Marine* (1789) D 4 b, We discovered a fleet..standing *athwart* us, i.e. steering across our way. 1823 W. Scoresby *Jrnl.* 2 We took sail, and stood into the river. a 1860 in *Temple Bar* LVI. 353 We passed the bank, stood round the light, and sailed away to sea. 1867 Smyth *Sailor's Word-bk.*, *Stand in Shore*, to sail directly for the land. 1878 Bosw. Smith *Carthage* 107 The Roman fleet.. stood right across the Mediterranean to the nearest point of Africa. 1892 *Black & White* 16 Jan. 78/1 The whole fleet put on good speed, and stood nearly due west.

With cognate object. 1705 tr. *Bosman's Guinea* 13 The Ship..being bound to..touch at Curacao before it stands its course homewards.

b. *transf.* Of a person: To go, proceed (in a specified direction).

a 1300 *K. Horn* 1179 Ifond horn child stonde To schupeward in londe. 1829 Shipp *Mem.* II. 87 They bowed a hundred times..; then stood towards their village.

37. *Archery.* Of an arrow (see quot.).

1801 T. Roberts *Eng. Bowman* 294 An arrow is said to stand (or to stand in) a bow, when it flies from it steadily, and without shaking or flirting. *Ibid.*, To Stand in the wind, to stand across the wind.

***** Of immaterial things.

38. With adv., advb. phr., or adj. predicate: To be or remain in a specified condition, relation, situation, etc.

a 1122 *O. E. Chron.* an. 1093 Þæt arcebrice on Cantwarbyriȝ, þe ær on his agenre hand stod. c 1315 Shoreham *Poems* I. 231 For ȝef þat water his kende lest, Þat cristning stant te tealte. 14.. 26 *Pol. Poems* 20/194 A cheuenteyn may fyȝte o day, Þe victorye wiþ hym stande. c 1420 ? Lydg. *Assembly of Gods* 1887 Thy wytte stant a crooke. c 1470 *Gol. & Gaw.* 1056 Ane sair stonayand stour at thair hartis standis. 1548 Hall *Chron., Hen. IV*, 12 b, My life stoode in ieopardie. 1603 Shaks. *Meas. for M.* v. i. 108 His Integritie Stands without blemish. 1688 *Lett. conc. Pres. State Italy* 170 The greatest part of the Revenue of this State stands engaged for the Interest that they pay. 1870 Rogers *Hist. Glean.* Ser. II. 102 No reputation stood higher than that of Selden. 1875 Jowett *Plato* (ed. 2) IV. 8 He cannot tell the relation in which abstract ideas stand to one another. 1891 *Standard* 16 June 3/2 Mr. Balfour's plan stands condemned in his eyes.

b. With a relative or demonstrative adv. as predicate; e.g. *the case stands thus, as things or matters stand* (= under present circumstances). Also impersonally, as *it stands well*, †*how stands?, how does it stand?* (*with*, †*by*, †*of* a person or thing; †also with dat., *him stands well*).

a 1000 *Boeth. Metr.* i. 28 Stod þrage on ðam. c 1300 *Havelok* 2983 Him stondes wel þat god child strenes. c 1380 Wyclif *Sel. Wks.* III. 346 And þus it stondiþ in þe Chirche of þes newe servauntis þat ben brouȝt in. c 1386 Chaucer *Shipman's T.* 114 It stant not so with me. c 1485 *Digby Myst.* (1882) IV. 1505 Sister! how standes with yow? a 1578 Lindesay (Pitscottie) *Chron. Scot.* II. 25 The erle of glencairne returnit..to the erle of lennox and schew him how all studd. 1591 Shaks. *Two Gent.* II. v. 21 *Spee.* Why then, how stands the matter with them? *Lau.* Marry thus, when it stands well with him, it stands well with her. 1600 *Weakest goeth to Wall* H 3, My Lord of Bulloigne, thus then stands my case. 1612 *Benvenuto's Passenger* I. ii. 137 Sure sir, if it stood with you as he pleased, you should be in an euill case. 1672 Petty *Pol. Anat.* (1691) 68 As things now stand. 1709 Berkeley *Ess. Vision* § 45 The truth of the matter, I find, stands thus. 1826 Lamb *Pop. Fallacies* xi, A hare, as the law now stands, makes many friends. 1837 Carlyle *Fr. Rev.* III. VII. viii, Ill stands it with me if I have spoken falsely. 1862 *Temple Bar* VI. 401 How does it stand with your..studies? 1898 'Merriman' *Roden's Corner* vii. 75 People did not know how matters stood between Joan Ferriby and Tony Cornish.

†**39. a.** With dative of person: To exist, be present (to one); e.g. *me stondeþ rape* = I am in haste. Chiefly in (*me*, etc.) *stands awe, need*: see 45, 46. *Obs.*

a 1300 *K. Horn* 554 For þi me stondeþ þe more rape. a 1300 *Cursor M.* 24220 Quen he þe sagh þis murning mak, sumthing to þe iwiss he spak if him stode ani steuen.

†**b.** *impers.* To be the case (*that*). *It cannot stand but*, it cannot but be that... *Obs.*

1377 Langl. *P. Pl.* B. XIV. 251 A strawe for þe stuwes! it stode nouȝt, I trowe, Had þei no þyng but of pore men, her houses were vntyled. 1561 *Reg. Privy Council Scot.* I. 173 It mycht stand that I had ressavit sum of the gudis libellit fra the thrid hand. 1644 Maxwell *Prerog. Chr. Kings* ix. 99 It cannot stand but..the like should hold.

c. *impers.* To behove (a person) *to do* (something). *rare.*

? A cutting down, or confused recollection, of *stand* (one) *in hand* (see 47) or *stand* (one) *upon* (see 78 q).

1857 Trollope *Barchester T.* xlvi, He knew that it depended solely on his own wit whether or no he could throw the joke back upon the lady. He knew that it stood him to do so if he possibly could, but he had not a word. 1911 Webster s.v., 19. To concern; to be of interest or advantage (to); as, it stood him to leave the country for a time.

40. Of a condition, process, or the like: To remain stationary or unchanged, neither progressing nor receding; to be at a standstill.

c 1386 Chaucer *Merch. T.* 519 (Harl.). Now wolde God that it were woxe night, And that the night wold stonder [*v.r.* lasten] evermo. 1436 *Pol. Poems* (Rolls) II. 202 For whiche they muste dresse hem to pease in haste, Or ellis there thrifte to standen and to waste. c 1530 *Judic. Urines* II. xii. 40 But comynly in Homotheus, the sekenes is stondyng tyll the seke man passe other to deth or to lyfe. 1658 Sir T. Browne *Hydriot.* v. 27 Every houre addes unto that current Arithmetique, which scarce stands one moment. 1723 Swift *Poems, Pethox* 52 And while his Fate is in thy Hands, The Bus'ness of the Nation stands.

41. To endure, last; to continue unimpaired; to flourish.

c 1000 *Ags. Gosp.* Matt. xii. 26 Hu mæȝ þonne bys rice standan. c 1200 Ormin 18190 Þatt ȝet ta stod stafflike witt Amang Judisskenn þede Off Moysæsess laȝheboc. a 1300 *Cursor M.* 9221 Þair kingrik..þat had four hundret yeir stand. 1399 Langl. *Rich. Redeles* III. 249 Iche rewme..Sholde stable and stonde be þese þre degrees. 1553 T. Wilson *Rhet.* (1580) 28 If in other thynges we should bee as negligente, this Realme could not long stande. 1865 M. Arnold *Ess. Crit.* ii. 60 Work done after men have reached this platform is classical; and that is the only work which, in the long run, can stand. *Ibid.* vii. 223 How little either of his poetry, or of his criticism, or of his philosophy, can we expect permanently to stand!

42. To be or remain valid or of force, hold good.

c 888 Ælfred *Boeth.* xxi, Þa gesetennesse þa he læt standan þa hwile þe he wile. a 1122 *O. E. Chron.* (Laud MS.) an. 656 Ic bidde ealle þa ðe æfter me cumen..þæt ure ȝyfe mote standan. c 1275 Lay. 397 After þan hiþene lawe þat stot in þan ilke dawe. c 1315 Shoreham *Poems* I. 238 For bote þat water his kende haue, Þat cristnynge may nauȝt stonde. 1377 Langl. *P. Pl.* B. XV. 573 Owre lorde wrote it [the Law] hym selue, In stone, for it stydfast was and stonde sholde eure. c 1400 *Pilgr. Sowle* (Caxton) I. xxx. (1859) 34 Yf he byquethe al his good to his owne lord, standyth the testament? 1544 tr. *Littleton's Tenures* 39 The last deuyse and wyl made by him shal stande and abyde. 1568 Grafton *Chron.* II. 100 The yonger sort which had chosen Reignold their Subprior, would have that election to stande. a 1578 Lindesay (Pitscottie) *Chron. Scot.* I. 343 Gif all promeisis had stand quhilk was maid be the king of scotland. 1719 De Foe *Crusoe* II. (Globe) 432 A written Contract..would stand. 1758 S. Hayward *Serm.* Introd. 19 The promise yet stands. 1855 Macaulay *Hist. Eng.* xii. III. 211 No English Parliament..would permit such laws as were now passing through the Irish Parliament to stand. 1879 *Nature* 20 Nov. 62/2 This result is so utterly opposed to fact that a theory which leads to it cannot stand for a moment. 1885 *Law Times Rep.* LII. 625/1, I think..that the nonsuit ought not to stand. 1894 Hall Caine *Manxman* III. xiii. 172 It was taken for granted that the old relations would stand.

b. With complement or predicative extension, as *to stand good, in force*, (†*for*) *law*, etc.

a 1300 *Cursor M.* 6746 Qua stelis scep, or ox, or cu..Oxen fiue for an he pai, For a scep four, it stand for lai. 1581 Allen *Apol.* 42 No statute then that stood in force. 1586 in J. Morris *Troubles Cath. Forefathers* Ser. III. (1877) 87 Which common presumption always standeth good by their own law until the contrary be plainly and evidently proved. 1633 Bp. Hall *Hard Texts, Rom.* ix. 11 That the decree and purpose of God..might stand in force. 1667 Milton *P. L.* v. 602 Hear my Decree, which unrevok't shall stand. 1747 in *Nairne Peerage Evid.* (1874) 148 The said obligation was..to stand in full force and virtue. 1890 *Chamb. Jrnl.* 27 Dec. 826/1 That charge of murder will not stand law. 1893 *Sat. Rev.* 11 Feb. 164/1 The chapter on planting..stands good for all time.

43. Of a ceremony: To be performed, take place. *Sc.* ? *Obs.*

1649 Lamont *Diary* (Maitl. Club) 5 The mariage feast stoode at the place of the Weyms in Fyfe. 1828 *Burd Isabel* ix. in Child *Ballads* IV. 420 Her kirking and her fair wedding Shall baith stand on ae day. a 1868 *Earl of Errol* i. ibid. V. 269 An they hae made a marriage o't, It stood at Earlstoun, O.

III. 44. To cost. (Cf. L. *stare, constare*.)

a. *To stand* (one) *high*, to cost a high price. (Cf. G. *einem hoch zu stehen kommen*.) *rare.*

1362 Langl. *P. Pl.* A. III. 49 We han a wyndow in worching wol stonden [*B. text* sitten] vs ful heiȝe. 1864 Carlyle *Fredk. Gt.* XV. iii. IV. 41 His father and he have stood these Bavarian Countries very high. *Ibid.* XX. x. VI. 243 Carlos's War of ten months had stood him uncommonly high.

†**b.** *To stand* (one) *on, upon, to* (a price). *Obs.*

c 1440 *Jacob's Well* 38 Þe seed stondyth þe on ij. s., þe rente stante þe on vj. d, þe gaderyng & þe repyng standyth þe on xij. d. 1471 *Paston Lett.* III. 31 The fense must stand yow over on xij. mark by the lest wey. 1641 Best *Farm Bks.* (Surtees) 76 Sheepe that are fedde all the summer longe in our closes stande us to three shillings..a peece. 1764 *Museum Rust.* III. 11 His stakes will not stand him, besides his labour, to more than half a farthing each.

c. *To stand* (one) *in* (a price, etc.). The ordinary construction; now restricted in currency, being partly fashionable slang, partly dialectal.

Also *to stand* (a person) *in at* (an amount).

c 1460 Fortescue *Abs. & Lim. Mon.* vi. (1885) 122 Yet his highnes shall þan haue therfore a bouute his persone.. lordes, knyghtes, and sqviers..to his charges peraduentur also gretly, as his houshold well ruled was wonned to stonde hym inne. 1488–9 *Act 4 Hen. VII*, c. 9 Where an hatte standeth not theym in xvj d. they woll sell it for iij s. or xl d. 1544 in *Lett. & Pap. Hen. VIII* (1903) XIX. I. 445 Here they shall stand the King not in one penny. 1551 Robinson tr. *More's Utopia* II. iv. (1895) 150 The same standeth them in muche lesse coste. 1625 in *Cosin's Corr.* (Surtees) I. 71 Boording and breakfest will stand him in 16[li] per annum. 1651 H. L'Estrange *Answ. Mrq. Worcester* Ep. Ded., It will be in some sort an Answer to God for the time it stood me in. 1713 *Guardian* No. 84 ¶ 2 It has not stood me in above a Button. 1778 Mme. D'Arblay *Early Diary* (1889) I. 160 Do you know, it stands me in a hundred a year for chaises? 1837 Dickens *Pickw.* xli, It'll stand you in a pound a week. 1848 Thackeray *Van. Fair* xiii, It stands me in eight shillings a bottle. 1875 Miss Braddon *Hostages to Fortune* II. viii. 168 It only stands me in seven and sixpence. 1886 Mrs. Randolph *Mostly Fools* III. iv. 116 His town house..stood him in at fifteen hundred a year.

d. With prep. as in b or c, but without indirect obj. of person. *rare.*

1457 *Paston Lett.* I. 414 That my maister shud be lerned whate hys housold standyth uppon yerlye. 1546 Johnson in Ellis *Orig. Lett.* Ser. II. II. 174 Thay stond in above 4[li] sterling a peise. 1583 Stubbes *Anat. Abus.* I. (1877) 61, I haue knowen the very nedle work of some one payre of these bootehose to stand, some in iiij pound, vj. pound, and some in x. pound a peece. 1737 Bracken *Farriery Impr.* (1756) I. 167 This Ball would stand in five or six Shillings a Day. 1845 *Jrnl. R. Agric. Soc.* VI. II. 526 This concern stands in 70l.

e. Without prep. before the word which denotes the price or cost. *rare.*

1542 in J. H. Glover *Kingsthorpiana* (1883) 82 An acre of lande sown in reye stondeth the tenant in sowing vii shillings at the lest. 1671 Lamont *Diary* (Maitl. Club) 224 The new bake howse..stood in workmanship, dales, iyronworke, and nayls, above 300 merks Scots. 1710 Luttrell *Brief Rel.* (1857) VI. 545 The company [were] ordered to bring in a modest computation of what their forts and castles have stood them. 1713 *Lond. Gaz.* No. 5137/10 The first..will stand the Importer near 9s. and 6d. the Gallon. 1801 *Farmer's Mag.* Jan. 110 Good soup is delivered out at 1d. per quart, which stands the subscribers 2¼d. 1808 Jamieson, To *Stand* one, to cost; as, *It stood me a groat*, it cost fourpence. 1872 S. De Vere *Americanisms* 552 This horse stands me two hundred dollars at least.

IV. Phrases and idiomatic uses.

45. To stand in awe.

†**a.** Orig. 'awe' was the nominative and the person affected in the dative: *him* (*them, men*, etc.) *stands awe*; const. *of*, also *from, to, with* (the object of dread). Occas. with some other sb. of kindred meaning, as *doubt*. *Obs.*

c 1000 Ælfric *Hom.* (Th.) I. 64 Swa micel eȝe stod deoflum fram eow. c 1200 *Trin. Coll. Hom.* 73 Þer hem stod eie, þer hem ne sholde, þat is of idele þing. c 1205, c 1250 [see Awe *sb.*[1] 4 a. α, β]. a 1300 *Cursor M.* 14805 Of him þam stod selcut gret agh. c 1320, c 1380 [see Awe *sb.*[1] 4 a. β, α].

13.. *K. Alis.* 3426 (Laud MS.), At þat half stant hem no doute Of Alisaunder ne al his route. c 1330 *Arth. & Merl.* 4341 Þat hem no stondeþ no doute Of þe payens no of her route.

†**b.** By inversion of const. the dative of the person became the subject and 'awe' the object of the verb: *to stand awe* (*of*, also *to do* something). Similarly *to stand dread*. *Obs.*

c 1200 *Trin. Coll. Hom.* 39 He þat is recheles and non eiȝe ne stand of louerde. *Ibid.* 139 And te king stod eie of him for his holinesse. a 1300 *Cursor M.* 12091 Þan suld þou sett him to sum scole, Þar he moght lere o man stand agh. 1330, c 1460 [see Awe *sb.*[1] 4 a. α, β]. c 1470 Henry *Wallace* IX. 851 The Scottis defens so sykkyr was and keyn, Sotheroun stud aw to enter thaim amang. 1535 Lyndesay *Satyre* 2520 Of na man we sould stand aw. 1597 Montgomerie *Cherrie & Slae* 1053 Of vs ȝe stand na aw.

14.. 26 *Pol. Poems* 19/140 Holy chirche stant of hem drede.

c. The modern const., *to stand in awe*. Similarly *to stand in dread, fear*, etc.

1413 [see Awe *sb.*[1] 4 a. β]. a 1425 *Cursor M.* 12091 (Trin.) Þou most do sett him to þe scole For to lerne & stonde in awe. 1535 Coverdale *Ps.* xcvi. 9 Let the whole earth stonde in awe of him. 1581 A. Hall *Iliad* IV. 70 Of whom stand you in awe? 1771 Burke *Corr.* (1844) I. 325 He stood in some awe, though in no sort of fear of you. 1885 Mrs. Lynn Linton *Christ. Kirkland* I. x. 271, I stood in wholesome awe of him.

14.. 26 *Pol. Poems* xiii. 6 Falsed stondis ay in drede. 1701 W. Wotton *Hist. Rome* 302 The Brothers stood in fear of their Lives. 1885 J. Payn *Luck of Darrells* I. XIV. 246 His aunt stands rather in fear of him.

46. To stand in need.

†**a.** Orig. in the form (*me, him*, etc.) *stands need* = I (etc.) have need. Const. *till, to* (the thing required). (Corresponds to *need is, is need*: see Need *sb.* 4, 5.) *Obs.*

a 1300 *Cursor M.* 23983 Wede o welth wil i namar, Clething wil i me tak o care, Þar-til [*Fairf.* þer-to] me standes nede. a 1400 *Sir Perc.* 184 A maydene scho tuke hir withalle, That scho myȝte appone calle, Whenne that hir nede stode.

b. In inverted const. (cf. 45 b), of a person, *to stand need* = to be in need (*of, to do* something). *Obs.* exc. *dial.*

1551 Crowley *Pleas. & Payne* Wks. 109 For aye, when I Stode nede of meate, ye gaue me fode. 1578 T. Lupton *All for Money* 699 If you stoode neede of me you should finde me your friende. 1627 R. Sibthorpe *Apostol. Obed.* 28 These, I say, and infinite others, neither will time permit, nor doth your experience stand need. 1657 J. Sergeant *Schism Dispach't* 260 Though we have better grounds then to stand need to build upon it. 1664 Marvell *Corr.* Wks. (Grosart) II. 180 If I stood need of witnesses, I would cite only Your own merits. 1877 *N. W. Linc. Gloss.*, *Stan' need*, stand in need of, ought [to do something]. 1886 *S. W. Linc. Gloss.* s. v., One stans need to tak' care of one's lasses nowa-days.

c. Now (cf. 45 c), *to stand in need*. Const. *of*, †*to do*.

1530 Palsgr. 733/2 If you stande in nede of me you shall fynde I am your frende. 1597 Hooker *Eccl. Pol.* v. xlviii. § 2 Petitionarie prayer belongeth only to such as..stand in need of relefe from others. 1600 J. Pory tr. *Leo's Africa* VI. 277 Their fields stand in neede of continuall watering. 1630 W. T. *Justif. Relig. now Professed* ix. 66 Who themselues stand in neede to bee saued. 1701 W. Wotton *Hist. Rome* i. 15 His Mind truly stood in need of Instruction. 1849 Macaulay *Hist. Eng.* x. II. 658 A realm of which these were the fundamental laws stood in no need of a new constitution. 1887 Westall *Capt. Trafalgar* xix. 245, I felt very tired and stood much in need of sleep.

47. To stand (one) in (†on) hand. Now *dial.*

Cf. the phrases *to lie* (one) *upon hand, in hand*: see Hand *sb.* 32 a, quot. 1548, 29 d quot. 1627.

a. Of the wind: To be favourable. *rare*[−1].

c 1205 Lay. 22313 Wind heom stod an honde.

b. To behove, concern; to be needful or necessary to; to be of importance or advantage to. Chiefly *impers.* with *it* and inf.

c 1400 *Beryn* 3173, I take no reward of othir mennys case, But oonlich of myne own, that stont me most an hond. 1470 *Paston Lett.* II. 400 Look that ye spare for no cost to do serche for itt, for it wyll stand yow on hand. 1523 Berners *Froiss.* I. ccxxii. 289 [They] fought valiantly, the whiche stode them well in hand to do, for ye naueroyse had caused them somwhat to recule. 1587 Golding *De Mornay* i. 9 To lay forth the proofes..it would stand me in hand to ransacke the whole world. 1654 H. L'Estrange *Chas. I* (1656) 89 The King..conceived it stood him in hand to stand upon his guard. 1667 O. Heywood *Heart-Treas.* vii. 54 It stands us all in hand to try our selves. a 1825 Forby *Voc. E. Anglia* s. v., 'To stand in hand', to concern, behove, or interest. Ex. 'It stands you in hand to look to that'. 1848 Bartlett *Dict. Amer.*, *To stand in hand*, to concern, to behoove... This phrase is a colloquial one in New England. Ex. 'It stands you in hand to attend to your business'.

48. To stand in stead.

†**a.** To be of use or advantage, to be serviceable or profitable. Also with adj. qualifying *stead*, to be of (little, no, good) avail or service. *Obs.*

a 1300 *Cursor M.* 26512 It sal stand in sted sumquar. 13.. *Ibid.* 4114 (Gött.) Lat vs do him to dreri dede. Loke quat his drem sal stand in-sted. 1340 Hampole *Pr. Consc.* 3648 His helpe thurgh hym-selfe standes in na stede, For he es als a lym þat es dede. 1399 *Pol. Poems* (Rolls) I. 365 The busch is bare and waxus sere, Hit may no lengur leves bere; now stont hit in no styde. c 1430 *Freemasonry* (Halliw. 1840) 679 They schul be told to stonde yn stede, When thou hast therto gret nede. 1544 Betham *Precepts War* I. cxci. I iv b, But yf we must warre in playne and champyon countryes, then horsemen be moost necessarye. For fotemen wyll stande in lytle steade and vse. c 1645 Howell *Lett.* (1650) III. 12 If Love be fire, to light this Indian weed, The Donor's Love of fire may stand in steed. 1659 Hammond *On Ps.* lxii. 9 It standeth in no stead, and so disappoints those that depend on it. 1772 Whitefield *Serm.* xxxii. Wks. VI. 11 Thy wealth and grandeur will stand in no stead.

b. More usually with indirect obj. († rarely with *to*). *To stand* (one) *in stead, in* (*good*, etc.) *stead*: to be of service or benefit to; to help or avail. Now only with adj. (*good*, etc.), and that in literary rather than familiar use.

When without epithet, *in stead* was sometimes written or printed as one word.

1387 Trevisa *Higden* (Rolls) VII. 267 But for it stood hem but litel in stede [orig. *sed quia parum profecerunt*]. c 1440 *Sir Gowther* 658 He..stode poure men in stede. 1513 More in *Grafton's Chron.* (1568) II. 785 Suche as they thought..able to stande them in stead, eyther by power or by policie. 1577 Kendall *Flowers of Epigr.*, *Trifles* 5 The weake may stand the strong in sted. 1603–26 Breton *Poste Mad Lett.* (Grosart) 39/1 Your kind promise vpon any urgent occasion to stand me instead. 1662 Gerbier *Principles* 1 Some Principles thereon, which may stand the lovers of it instead. 1730 *Lett. to Sir W. Strickland rel. to Coal Trade* 25 It will therefore stand them in stead to consider, whether they be likely to gain anything by the Exchange. 1802 Mar. Edgeworth *Moral T.*, *Forester* (*The Bet*), That excuse sha'n't stand you in stead. 1826 Disraeli *Viv. Grey* III. v, Your boasted knowledge of human nature shall not again stand you in stead.

1338 R. Brunne *Chron.* (1810) 202 Better is holy bede of man þat right lyues, & standes vs in more stede, þan alle þe gode he gyues. 13.. *Minor Poems fr. Vernon MS.* 674/90 Strengþe stont vs in no stide. c 1449 Pecock *Repr.* v. vi. 514 If thilk gouernaunce..stondith to him in miche goostli stide. 1539 Wriothesley in *St. Papers Hen. VIII*, VIII. 160 Soo that his advise therein could stand them in small stede. 1577 Hanmer *Anc. Eccl. Hist.*, *Euseb.* III. ix. (1585) 44 Josephus him selfe, that hath stoode vs in so great stead, for the furnishing of this our present history. 1665 *Extr. St. Papers rel. Friends* Ser. III. (1912) 241 Our good intentions stand us in little stead. 1749 Fielding *Tom Jones* v. viii, It is then he will find in what mighty stead that heathen goddess..will stand him. 1848 Thackeray *Van. Fair* liv, A Johnson's Dictionary, which stood them in much stead. 1887 Westall *Capt. Trafalgar* i. 13 Continual practice stood me in better stead than whole volumes of theory. 1891 *Temple Bar* Oct. 177 His early training.. stood him in good stead.

†**c.** Similarly *to stand* (one) *to* (good) *stead*. Also without prep., *to stand* (one) *stead*. *Obs. rare.*

1549 Chaloner *Erasm. Praise Folly* B j, If ye aske me, what stede these stande me to? I aunsweare [etc.]. 1577 Stanyhurst *Descr. Irel.* 1/2 in *Holinshed*, Thersites..being in outwarde feature so deformed, and in inwarde conditions so crooked, as he seemed to stande to no better steede, then to leade Apes in hell. 1581 A. Hall *Iliad* v. 95 What stead canst thou the Troyans stand?

†**d.** In various other phrases of like meaning, as *to stand* (a person) *in force, in profit, in vail, at* or *to avail. To stand stall, in stall*: see Stall *sb.*[1] 2 b. *Obs.*

c 1400 *Pilgr. Sowle* (Caxton) I. xiii. (1859) 9 It maye hym stande nought in profite ne at none auaile. 1428 in *Engl. Misc.* (Surtees 1890) 7 For y[t] yair praiers suld stand John Lyllyng to availl. c 1450 *Mirk's Festial* 76 What maner vertu þat a man haue, but yf he be yn charyte, hit stondys hym in no vayle. 1563 *Homilies* II. *Passion* II. 201 b, So the death of Christ shall stande vs in no force, vnlesse we applye it to our selues in suche sort, as God hath appoynted.

49. To stand in stead of, to take the place of, represent, do duty for; also *instead of, in the stead of, in lieu of*. Also with indirect object.

a 1500 *Gest of Robyn Hode* lxxxi. in Child *Ballads* III. 60 In a yeman's stede he may the stande, If thou greate nede haue. 1530 Palsgr. 733/2 Syns my lorde can nat be here him selfe to day, who shall stande in his stede. 1583 Melbancke *Philotimus* F iv b, Their banquet was ready..and Parmenio & Antigone stoode in steade of sewer and seruitours. 1612 *Benvenuto's Passenger* II. i. 395 Will stands instead of power, where wee cannot performe. 1847 C. Bronte *J. Eyre* ii, To stand in the stead of a parent to a strange child she could not love. 1849 *Tait's Mag.* XVI. 58/1 Chemistry does not stand a man instead of dinner. 1870 Dickens *E. Drood* xvii, I have undergone some mental distress..which has stood me in the stead of illness. 1881 Stevenson *Fam. Stud.* 283 The rigidity of intricate metrical forms stood him in lieu of precise thought. 1893 *Temple Bar* XCIX. 68 A down-drawing of the corners of her mouth that stood her instead of a smile.

50. To let...stand. a. *lit.* To leave (a person or thing) undisturbed in an erect position. **b.** *fig.* To leave for the time without notice or discussion; to leave in abeyance, let alone.

For other literal examples, see 29, 32, 32 b.

c 1205 Lay. 27159 An his riht honde he lette Lengres stonde. 1297 R. Glouc. 1276 Þe king þe wule londone bisegede uaste ..Ac þo he hurde þat þe romeins icome were to þis londe, To hom he wende hasteliche & let londone stonde. a 1300 *Cursor M.* 19601 Lat we nu þe prechurs stand, For to spek of a warraiand. a 1300 *Harrow. Hell* 136 Ich lete hem [the gates of Hell] stonden and renne away. 1377 Langl. *P. Pl.* B. XX. 101 Deth cam dryuende after and al to doust passhed ..Lered ne lewed, he let no man stonde. c 1400 *Beryn* 157 Pese, quod the hoost of Southwork, let stond þe wyndow glasid. 1535 Coverdale 1 *Sam.* xxiii. 13 Whan it was tolde Saul that Dauid was escaped from Cegila, he let his iourney stonde. a 1810 Tannahill *Poems* (1846) 25 She has my vows, but aye I let her stan', In hopes to win that bonnie lassie's han'. 1888 *Times* (weekly ed.) 22 June 13/3 To ask the Court to let the case stand. 1889 Conan Doyle *Micah Clarke* xi. 97 For my own claim, I let it stand for some time. 1898 H. Newbolt *He fell among Thieves* ii, Let the reckoning stand till day.

†**51.** The pres. pple. **standing**, placed before a sb. with which it agrees, or before a clause, has been used in certain 'absolute' constructions (cf. *during, pending*). **a.** = While (so-and-so) subsists, is retained, remains what it was. *Obs.*

c 1380 Wyclif *Sel. Wks.* III. 115 He [Christ] becom man, stondynge his godhed, þat he myȝt not lese. c 1400 *Pilgr. Sowle* (Caxton) I. xiii. (1859) 9 Yet ouer this will I [Satan] preue by reson, that standing this filthe and dishoneste of synne with whiche he is entachyd, this lauure rather causeth hym to be juged to oure company. c 1449 Pecock *Repr.* v. xiii. 554 Not eny yuel, which mai not eesili be remedied, stonding al the good which bifore is rehercid to come bi the same bildingis. 1526 *Pilgr. Perf.* (W. de W. 1531) 205 b, For otherwyse (standynge the ordynate iustyce of god) he myght neuer haue..goten by meryt suche hye..dignitie. 1569 Abp. Parker in *Corr.* (1853) 353, I think he should do this thing..better cheap than they may be bought from beyond the seas, standing the paper and goodness of his print.

†**b.** = While (so-and-so) lasts; during. *Obs.*

c 1500 Medwall *Nature* I. 323 (Brandl) Standyng the nonage of thys gentylman. 1512 in Willis & Clark *Cambridge* (1886) I. 609 Duryng the contynuaunce of the seid werkes and standyng the lyff and helth of the said John Wastell.

†**c.** = When (so-and-so) is taken into account; considering, in view of. (The examples might be referred to a; but cf. d.) *Obs.*

c 1528 Wolsey in *Burnet's Hist. Ref.* (1679) I. Rec. II. 52 Which I suppose neither his Holiness nor any true Christian Man can do, standing the manifest occasions, presumptions, and apparent evidences to the contrary. 1532 More *Confut. Tindale* Wks. 720/1, I can not..perceyue what counsayle Tyndall can geue any manne towarde saluacion, standyng his frantike heresies agaynst free will.

†**d.** As the first word of a clause (with or without *that*): The fact being that, considering *that*, since.

c 1450 *Cov. Myst.* 190 Stondynge that ȝe be so wytty and wyse, Can ȝe owth tellyn how this werde was wrought? *Ibid.* 218 Stondynge ȝe wyl not graunt me grace, But for my synne that I xal dye, I pray ȝow kylle me here in this place. 1513 More *Rich. III* Wks. 59/1 And y[t] he could not well otherwise do, standing that y[e] Earle of warwik had so far moued already. 1526 *Pilgr. Perf.* (W. de W. 1531) 17 Thynkynge that it was impossyble for them to optayne and wynne the sayd lande, standynge that the people were so myghty and stronge.

V. Transitive senses.

* Originating from the conversion of an indirect into a direct object, from the omission of a prep., or from intrans. uses with cognate object.

52. To confront, face, oppose, encounter; to resist, withstand, bear the brunt of.

†**a.** an opponent. *Obs.*

c 1325 *Chron. Eng.* 72 (Ritson) Yef the word of the spronge That eny mon the stode so longe,..Al thyn honour were leid adoun. c 1435 *Torr. Portugal* 81 Full Euyll thow dourst hyme stond. c 1450 Holland *Howlat* 500 Was nane so stur in the steid micht stand him a start. 1470–85 Malory *Arthur* x. lxxiv. 543 There myghte none stande hym a stroke. 1591 Shaks. 1 *Hen. VI*, I. i. 123 Hundreds he sent to Hell, and none durst stand him. c 1611 Chapman *Iliad* XXI. 508 This last heart, made him bold, To stand Achilles. 1615 — *Odyss.* VI. 225 All but Nausicaa fled; but she fast stood...And still she stood him, as resolued to know What man he was. 1719 De Foe *Crusoe* II. (Globe) 393 They resolved to stand them there. 1770 Langhorne *Plutarch*, *Crassus* (Rtldg.) 385/2 The young man cried out, 'They dare not stand us', and followed at full speed.

b. a blow or stroke, shot, attack, assault, siege, or the like; also laughter, raillery, indignation, etc.

c 1330 *Arth. & Merl.* 9282 Non no miȝt stond his dent. 13.. *Adam Bel* 145 There myght no man stand hys stroke. 1605 Shaks. *Lear* III. vii. 54, I am tyed to' th' Stake, And I must stand the Course. 1625 Massinger *New Way* IV. i, I, that haue liu'd a Souldier, And stood the enemies violent charge vndaunted. a 1630 J. Taylor (Water P.) *Dog of War* B 2 b, He durst t'haue stood sterne Aiax frowne. 1670 Dryden *2nd Pt. Conq. Granada* III. i, The shock of such a curse I dare not stand. 1712 Tickell *Spect.* No. 410 ¶ 4 My good Friend could not well stand the Raillery which was rising upon him. 1748 *Anson's Voy.* II. xiv. 286 Supposing that the troops..should..resolve to stand a general assault. 1803 *Pic Nic* No. 9 (1806) II. 87 Cecilia had stood a siege more than half as long as that of Troy. 1823 Byron *Age of Bronze* xi, What is the simple standing of a shot, To listening long, and interrupting not? 1837 Carlyle *Fr. Rev.* II. VI. i, He busy meanwhile training a few thousands to stand fire and be soldiers. 1890 *Illustr. Lond. News* 13 Sept. 331/1 These virgin walls have stood unmoved a hundred assaults. 1891 *Murray's Mag.* Sept. 382 She was ready to stand fire rather than retreat.

†**c.** To be exposed to (stress of weather, or the like). *Obs.*

1583 Stubbes *Anat. Abus.* II. 41 If the poore come to their houses, their gates be shut against them, where they standing frost and snow, haile, wind or raine whatsoeuer, are forced to tary two houres. 1607 Shaks. *Cor.* v. iii. 74 Like a great Sea-marke standing euery flaw. 1726 Leoni *Alberti's Archit.* I. 45 a, Those parts..which stand all the changes of Weather..very soon decay.

53. To endure, undergo, be submitted to (a trial, test, ordeal, or the like). Usually (cf. sense 54), to come through or sustain successfully, (be able) to bear (a test, etc.). Said also of things.

1606 Shaks. *Ant. & Cl.* I. iii. 74 And giue true evidence to his Loue, which stands An honourable Triall. 1610 — *Temp.* IV. i. 7 All thy vexations Were but my trials of thy loue, and thou Hast strangely stood the test. 1712 Addison *Spect.* No. 409 ¶ 4 The celebrated Works of Antiquity, which have stood the Test of so many different Ages and Countries. 1742 Blair *Grave* 666 Pure as Silver from the Crucible, That twice has stood the Torture of the Fire And Inquisition of the Forge. 1824 Mrs. J. West *Alicia de Lacy* IV. 217 'Of what shall we hereafter stand question', said the Earl of Hereford. 1822 Lamb *Elia* Ser. I. *Artif. Comedy* (init.), The business of their dramatic characters will not stand the moral test. 1825 *New Monthly Mag.* XV. 201 He has stood the ordeal of a London audience. 1890 *Blackw. Mag.* CXLVIII. 749/1 It would not be easy to get up a grievance which would stand a rigid examination.

b. spec. *To stand one's trial*: to be tried by a court for an offence. Also *slang*, in the same sense, *to stand the patter*. †*To stand suit*: to allow oneself to be sued.

1667 Pepys *Diary* 27 Aug., Desiring that he may stand his trial in Parliament, if they will accuse him of any thing. 1685 P. Henry *Diaries & Lett.* (1882) 344 Hee..sayes, hee wil stand suit, which if he doe, I know who wil get the better. 1726 Swift *Gulliver* I. vii, I sometimes thought of standing my trial. 1812 [see Patter *sb.*[1] 1 b]. 1891 *Chamb. Jrnl.* 5 Sept. 571/1 He was obliged to stand his trial for forgery.

c. To submit to, offer to abide by (a judgement, decision, vote); to expose oneself to the chances of (a contested election: cf. 12).

a 1700 Evelyn *Diary* 30 Nov. 1682, I was exceedingly indanger'd and importun'd to stand the election [for President of the R. S.]. 1713 Addison *Cato* II. ii, Bid him..Submit his actions to the publick censure, And stand the judgment of a Roman Senate. 1754 A. Murphy *Gray's Inn Jrnl.* No. 86 ¶ 10 They would not be at a Loss for a proper Representative..whenever the Author of the *Polymetis* should be willing to stand the Poll. 1774 Johnson *Let. to G. Steevens* 21 Feb. in *Boswell*, I am desirous of nominating you, if you care to stand the ballot. 1789 Mrs. Piozzi *Journ. France* I. Pref. 5 [It] induces authors to venture forth, and stand a public decision. 1858 J. Martineau *Stud. Chr.* 122 He who claims by the law, must stand the judgment of the law. 1889 Gretton *Memory's Harkback* 244, I thought that the Prince Consort was lowering his position by standing a contest for the office. 1892 *Blackw. Mag.* CL. 147/1 All through his career he never stood a contested election.

d. *To stand one's chance*: to take one's chance, submit to what may befall one.

1796–7 Jane Austen *Pride & Prej.* ii, Mrs. Long and her nieces must stand their chance.

†**e.** To abide by, obey, remain loyal to (an ordinance, etc.). *Obs. rare.*

c 1450 *Merlin* vi. 99 The wise men and the high barouns ..a-corded to stonde the ordenaunce of the archebisshop. 1573 *Reg. Privy Council Scot.* II. 265 Obleissis thame to stand and fulfill the injunctionis and articles quhilk wer aggreit be thame.

54. To face, encounter without flinching or retreating (an issue, hazard, etc.). Also in weaker sense, to be exposed or liable to (hazard, fortunes). (Cf. *stand to* 76 f.)

1594 Shaks. *Rich. III* v. iv. 10 Slaue, I haue set my life vpon a cast, And I will stand the hazard of the Dye. 1607 — *Timon* v. ii. 5 We stand much hazard, if they bring not Timon. a 1619 Fletcher *Knt. Malta* IV. ii, I am sorry ye are so poor, so weak a Gentleman, Able to stand no fortune. 1667 Pepys *Diary* 2 Sept., He that serves a Prince must expect, and be contented to stand, all fortunes. 1705 Collier *Ess. Mor. Subj.* III. *Pain* 16 'Twas a noble Act of Faith to throw themselves upon Providence, to stand the Event, and face Death under the most frightful Form. 1792 Charlotte Smith *Desmond* I. 255 A gallant fellow, who had been in the former wars with the English, and stood the hazards of many a bloody day.

†**55.** To withstand, disobey, hold out against (a command). *Obs. rare.*

1605 Shaks. *Lear* IV. i. 71 (Qo.) The superfluous and lustdieted man That stands [*Fo.* slaues] your ordinance. c 1800 *Bob Norice* vii. in Child *Ballads* II. 267 How daur you stand my bidding, Sir, Whan I bid you to flee?

56. *To stand one's ground*: to maintain one's position against attack or opposition. Also *fig.*

1621 T. Williamson tr. *Goulart's Wise Vieillard* 99 Thou ..wilt not from thy coullers flie, But stand thy ground couragiously. 1688 *Lett. conc. Pres. State Italy* 116 He could not have stood his ground in the Dispute. 1785 Jefferson *Corr.* Wks. 1859 I. 379, I have now no further fears of that Arret's standing its ground. 1804 Nicholl in Owen *Wellesley Despatches* (1877) 530, I directed the picquets to stand their ground. 1849 Macaulay *Hist. Eng.* vi. II. 115 He could not stand his ground against competitors who were willing to pay such a price for the favour of the court. 1891 *Strand Mag.* Jan. 77/1 The donkey..bravely stood his ground.

57. *To stand a chance* (also *a good, poor, small*, etc. *chance*; *some, little, no chance*): to be likely to meet with some (specified or implied) piece of fortune, some danger, some good or ill luck. Const. *of* (something, doing something), *for*.

1725 *New Cant. Dict.* s. v. *Lay*, He stands a queer Lay; He stands an odd Chance, or is in great Danger. 1736 Lediard *Life of Marlborough* I. 319 The Duke stood a very ticklish Chance. 1803 *Pic Nic* No. 13 (1806) II. 211 They stood a fair chance of going to hell. 1845 M. Pattison *Ess.* (1889) I. 18 Under such circumstances an obnoxious criminal stood..small chance of justice. 1848 *Jrnl. R. Agric. Soc.* IX. II. 281 He would have stood a fair chance for a prize. 1861 *Temple Bar* II. 539 Grey will stand no chance. 1889 F. C. Philips *Ainslie's Courtship* I. vii. 100 He would stand no chance over the snow against your snow-shoes.

58. To endure (a physical trial, hardship, etc.) without hurt or damage, without succumbing or giving way: **a.** of persons and animals.

1839 T. Mitchell *Frogs of Aristoph.* 73 *note*, A trumpet,.. by which horses are proved, as to whether they will stand noises. 1853 Lytton *My Novel* I. ix, 'But this climate—she could never stand it', said Riccabocca. 1887 *J. Coleman's Cattle* etc. *Gt. Brit.* 349 The Shropshire is a hardy sheep,.. standing moisture better than severe cold. 1891 *Chamb. Jrnl.* 19 Sept. 608/1 Drivers have to stand all weathers. 1903 Sir M. G. Gerard *Leaves fr. Diaries* ii. 47 The great heat renders the tiger comparatively helpless—as he cannot stand the sun.

b. of things.

1756 C. Lucas *Ess. Waters* I. 56 Common glass stands the utmost degree of fire without waste. 1777 [W. Marshall] *Minutes Agric.* 28 Apr., The green-cole and brown-cole stood the winter very well. 1864 *Jrnl. R. Agric. Soc.* XXV. II. 360 Turnips will stand almost any amount of frost. 1875 F. J. Bird *Dyer's Hand-bk.* 45 Very fine shades of blue that will stand soaping. 1890 *Temple Bar* July 420 These dyes will not stand water.

fig. 1885 *Manch. Exam.* 13 July 5/3 These luxuriant growths of Liberal aspirations will stand pruning. 1885 *Law Times Rep.* LIII. 480/2 To avoid..the consequences of having sent in a bill which would not stand taxation.

59. To put up with, tolerate; (to be able or willing) to endure.

1626 G. Sandys *Ovid's Met.* x. 198 A Stag..who..well pleas'd would stand The gentle strokings of a stranger's hand. 1710 Steele *Tatler* No. 225 ¶ 2 It is often said, such an one cannot stand the Mention of such a Circumstance. 1750 Chesterf. *Lett.* III. ccxxxvi. 76 Till I am satisfied in these particulars, you and I must by no means meet: I could not possibly stand it. 1816 Scott *Antiq.* xliv, Weel, I thought there was naething but what your honour could hae studden in the way o' agreeable conversation. 1821 [see Nonsense 1 c]. 1831 Palmerston in Bulwer *Life* II. viii. 93 England never would stand the occupation of the Tagus by the French. 1858 Carlyle *Fredk. Gt.* II. iv. (1872) I. 66 Baiern ..could not stand to be balked after twenty-years possession. 1869 Trollope *He Knew*, etc. lxv. (1878) 361 She..declared that she was not going to stand that kind of thing. 1891 *19th Cent.* Dec. 859 The Court cannot and will not stand.. journalistic personalities about its members.

b. Familiarly in more trivial sense (with negative expressed or implied): To reconcile oneself to, be favourably disposed to, feel any liking for (a repugnant or distasteful object).

1879 Mrs. Oliphant *Within Precincts* xx. II. 60 She could not stand that Manager fellow. I could not stand him myself.

60. *To stand watch, to stand a* or *one's watch*: to keep watch, perform the duty of a watch. Now chiefly *Naut.*, to take part in the duty of a 'watch' during a prescribed time.

1605 Shaks. *Macb.* v. v. 33 As I did stand my watch vpon the Hill. c 1730 Ramsay *Vision* iv, My wakryfe mynd..still stude watch. 1883 *Century Mag.* XXVI. 911/1 Fenton stood the first watch. 1890 *Chamb. Jrnl.* 21 June 389/1 He's the ship's carpenter, and stands watch as second officer.

61. colloq. *To stand shot* (*to*), rarely *to stand the shot*: to meet the expenses, pay the bill (for all): see Shot *sb.*[1] 23. Similarly *to stand Sam, treat*: see Sam *sb.* 1, Treat *sb.*[1] 4 d. Also *to stand one's hand* (*to*).

1821 [see Shot *sb.*[1] 23]. 1823–1887 [see Sam *sb.* 1]. 1837–1885 [see Treat *sb.*[1] 4 d]. 1883 J. Purves in *Contemp. Rev.* Sept. 356 At the one year's end and the beginning of the other, he must stand his hand like the rest. 1890 *Sat. Rev.* 3 May 61/2 Mr. Lowther..requested that his speech might be published..offering to take the consequences and stand the shot. 1892 H. Nisbet *Bushranger's Sweetheart* viii. 58, I used to see her..'standing her hand' liberally to all who happened to be in the bar.

b. To bear the expense of, make a present of, pay for (a treat). Const. *to* or dative of the recipient. *colloq.*

1835 Dickens *Sk. Boz, Dancing Academy*, Mr. Augustus Cooper..'stood' considerable quantities of spirits-and-water. 1840 Thackeray *Shabby-genteel Story* ii, I'll stand glasses round to his jolly good health! 1848 — *Van. Fair* xiii, I know my father will stand something handsome. 1890 *Lippincott's Mag.* May 633 I'll stand you a dinner. 1891 *Sat. Rev.* 18 Apr. 482/1 They..stood drinks promiscuously to all-comers.

c. With indirect obj. only = to stand drink for (a person or persons). *colloq.*

1894 Mrs. Dyan *All in Man's Keeping* (1899) 173 Sit down here, and I'll stand you both.

62. *To stand the market*: to attend market in order to sell goods or to hire oneself out. *dial.*

Cf. *to overstand one's market* s. v. Market *sb.* 6.

1866 W. Dobson *Diary of P. Walkden* 42 *note*, It was customary for carts with cannel to 'stand the market'. 1886 *Cheshire Gloss.* s. v., Farmers' wives call it *standing the market* when they sell their butter, eggs, &c., in the open market instead of taking them to shops or from house to house. 1886 *Ripon Chron.* 4 Sept. 3/5 The first harvest hirings were held at Malton on Saturday, when there was a good number of men 'standing the market'.

63. *Racing*, etc. **a.** To bet, wager (a sum of money) *on* or *about* a result. ? *Obs.*

1804 Chifney *Genius Genuine* 155 The fellow had asked him to stand fifty guineas with him on the match. 1825 *New Monthly Mag.* XVI. 375 Made up my mind..to stand something about the double event, if I could get any thing worth having.

b. To bet on the success of, 'back' (a horse).

1890 *Daily News* 10 Dec. 3/7 Backers were also well on the mark in standing Alfred for the Park selling Hurdle. 1891 *Standard* 9 Mar. 3/7, I shall stand Flower of the Forest for the..Hunters' Steeplechase. 1892 *Ibid.* 25 July 2/5, I shall stand him to carry his 12lb. penalty successfully.

64. *Hunting.* Of a dog: To set (game). Cf. 4 c.

1863 W. C. Baldwin *Afr. Hunting* viii. 333 Juno returns and stands them one after another. 1892 *Field* 7 May 671/3 He finds his birds, and stands them well.

** Causative.

65. To cause to stand; to place or leave standing; to set (a thing) upright; to place firmly or steadily in a specified position. Also with advs., as *up*. Only colloq. or in familiar writing.

1837 Dickens *Pickw.* xxvi, The pretty house-maid had stood the candle on the floor. 1848 — *Dombey* ii, A plump and apple-faced boy, whom he stood down on the floor. 1848 *Jrnl. R. Agric. Soc.* IX. II. 560 Sharpen the pole.. and stand it in the ground. 1850 Dickens *David Copp.* xxxii A low iron [fender], with two flat bars at top to stand plates upon. 1873 M. Collins *Squire Silchester* I. i. 17 She would..stand her in a corner if she gave herself airs. 1878 *Scribner's Monthly* XV. 763/1, I stood my rifle against a tree. 1889 'Mrs. Alexander' *Crooked Path* I. v. 153 I've stood them [a chest of drawers] open all last night. 1892 *Illustr. Sporting & Dram. News* 17 Dec. 494/3 We recommend the driver to stand his horse in running water. 1894 *Jrnl. R. Agric. Soc.* June 230 Owners were compelled to resort to the fields near the borough to stand their horses. 1905 Wastell & Bayley *Hand Camera* 126 The negatives ..may be stood up to dry... They must not be stood close together in a rack.

b. *refl. rare.*

1848 Dickens *Dombey* xxv, The Captain then stood himself up in a corner, against the wall.

VI. With prepositions. (The more literal and obvious meanings are left to be inferred from the simple senses above and those of the various prepositions.)

66. Stand about —.

a. *lit.* To surround; = L. *circumstare*.

c 1368 Chaucer *Compl. Pity* 36 Aboute hir herse there stoden lustely..Bounte parfyt [etc.]. 1535 Coverdale *Job* xxix. 4 When my housholde folkes stode aboute me. 1849 M. Arnold *Sick King Bokhara* 105 They who stood about the King.

†**b.** *fig.* To spend time upon, stay to consider, wait for (something to be done). *Obs.*

c 1555 Towrson in Hakluyt *Voy.* (1599) II. II. 30 As for their arrowes, I haue not as yet seene any of them, for they had wrapped them vp close, and because I was busie I could not stand about it, to haue them open them. 1579 Fulke *Refut. Rastell* 708, I will not stand about this trifling cauil.

67. Stand against, †again(s —.

a. To stand and face (an antagonist, etc.); to withstand, oppose, resist. Also, to resist successfully, hold one's ground against. Said also of things. (Cf. 10 and Again-stand *v.*)

a 1122 *O. E. Chron.* (Laud MS.) an. 1048 Þæh him lað wære þæt hi onȝean heora cyne-hlaford standan sceoldan. c 1200 Ormin 2785 He maȝȝ stanndenn wel onnȝæn Þe deofell wiþ swillc wæpenn. a 1300 *Cursor M.* 4096 Þi bod i aght noght agains to stand. c 1330 *Arth. & Merl.* 4842 Armes non, ywrouȝt wiþ hond, Oȝain his dent no miȝt stond. a 1400–50 *Wars Alex.* 1322 Was nane sa stiffe in þat stoure miȝt stand him agayn. c 1450 *Merlin* i Our strengthes.. may nought..again him stonde in no diffence. 1593 Abp. Bancroft *Dang. Posit.* IV. xii. 173 That the people are inflamed with zeale, and that it is impossible to stand against it. 1687 Burnet *Contin. Reply to Varillas* 102 He finding that he was not able to stand against so strong a Party, submitted himself to them. 1820 Scott *Monast.* Introd. Ep., I hae fund something now that stands again' the spade, as if it were neither earth nor stane. 1833 Nyren *Yng. Cricketer's Tutor* 114 He [Aylward] had to stand against the finest bowling of the day—that of Lumpy. 1881 Mrs. Lynn Linton *My Love* II. viii. 156, I will not stand against your happiness. 1890 Conan Doyle *Firm of Girdlestone* xi. 85 No firm could stand against such a run of bad luck.

†**b.** To feel repugnance for. *Obs.*

1551 Robinson tr. *More's Utopia* I. (1895) 36 [Ought I to advance myself] to a weithyer condition..by that meanes that my mynde standethe cleane agaynst [*a qua abhorret animus*]?

68. Stand at —.

†**a.** To abide by, obey (a decree, etc.) (Cf. *stand to* 76 a.) *Obs.*

c 1290 *S. Eng. Leg.* 160/1874 Þat heo don sikernesse for-to stonde at holi churche lawe And to þe lokinge of holi churche. c 1386 Chaucer *Prol.* 778 And if yow lyketh alle, by oon assent, ffor to stonden at my Iuggement. c 1480 Henryson *Fables, Fox, Wolf & Husbandman* 81 Ȝe sall be sworne to stand at my decreit. 1581 *Exch. Rolls Scot.* XXI. 551 Bayth the saidis parties oblissis thame to stand and abyid thairat bot any reclaming.

†**b.** To assist or be present at. *Obs. rare*[−1].

1746 Hervey *Medit.* (1818) 79, I..must stand at the dissolution of all terrestrial things, and be an attendant on the burial of nature.

c. To stick, hesitate or scruple at; to allow oneself to be deterred, impeded or checked by.

1756–7 tr. *Keysler's Trav.* (1760) I. 2 Men of large fortunes stand at no price for Swiss cattle. 1808 *Sporting Mag.* XXXII. 122 We don't stand at a trifle. 1837 Carlyle *Fr. Rev.* III. v. v, To stand at no obstacles; to heed no considerations, human or divine. 1890 F. C. Philips & Wills *Sybil Ross* xx. 147 He is not a man who stands at trifles.

69. Stand before —.

a. To continue in the presence of, attend upon (a lord). Chiefly *Biblical*: see concordances.

c 1200 Ormin 206 Witt tu þatt icc amm Gabriæl þatt æfre & æfre stannde Biforenn Godd, to lutenn himm. c 1400 *Rule St. Benet* (Prose) 19 Loke ye do yure seruise als ye stode by-fore god almihti. c 1440 *Gesta Rom.* xlviii. 211 (Addit. MS.) [He] stode atte borde before the Erle, and served hym curtesly [*Harl.* gentilmanly stode afore him].

b. To come or be brought into the presence of, to confront (a person or assembly, a king, judge, tribunal, etc.).

a 1225 *Leg. Kath.* 632 Hwen ȝe stondeð biforen kinges & eorles, ne þenche ȝe neauer hwet ne hu ȝe schulen seggen. 1377 Langl. *P. Pl.* B. Prol. 183 A mous..Stroke forth sternly and stode biforn hem alle. c 1386 Chaucer *Man of Law's T.* 520 For as the lomb toward his death is brought So stant this Innocent bifore the kyng. c 1450 tr. *De Imitatione* I. xxiv. 32 In all þinges biholde þe ende, & how þou shalt stonde before þe rightwise Juge. 1526 Tindale *Rev.* xx. 12 And I sawe the deed, both grett and smale stonde before God. 1819 S. Rogers *Human Life* 586 Alone before his judges in array [He] Stands for his life.

c. To confront (an adversary). Usually with *can* etc. negatively or interrogatively: To maintain one's ground against. (Cf. 10.)

For Bible examples (lit. from Heb.), see concordances.

c 1205 Lay. 21377 Her stondeð us biuoren vre ifan alle icoren. 1652 Needham tr. *Selden's Mare Cl.* 51 None was able to stand before him either by Sea or Land. 1721 De Foe *Mem. Cavalier* (1840) 87 Nothing could stand before them; the Spanish army..was everywhere defeated. 1879 M. J. Guest *Lect. Hist. Eng.* xlviii. 485 The Cavaliers could not stand before them.

†**d.** To protect, shield (a person) by placing oneself in front of him. *Obs. rare.*

c 1205 Lay. 25938 For ȝif he cumeð a-bolȝen mid his balu ræsen, nes he neuere iboren þe maȝen stonden þe biuoren.

e. *Hunting.* Of a fox: To hold out when pursued by (hounds). Cf. *stand up* 103 h.

1892 *Illustr. Sporting & Dram. News* 26 Nov. 400/3 A bag fox stood before hounds for two hours and a quarter till the pack were called off.

70. Stand by —.

a. *lit.* To station oneself or remain stationed beside (a person); usually as a helper, advocate, sympathizer, or the like (passing into sense c).

c 1250 *Gen. & Ex.* 3666 Ches ðe nu ðer seuenti Wise men to stonden ðe bi. c 1275 *Passion of our Lord* 163 in *O. E. Misc.* 42 Þer com of heuene on engel and stod hym vaste by. 14.. 26 *Pol. Poems* 53/77 And euere by trouþe stondes wreche, For wreche is goddis champioun. 1611 Bible *Zech.* iv. 14 These are the two annointed ones, that stand by the Lord of the whole earth. a 1700 Evelyn *Diary* 7 Dec. 1680, He had likewise the assistance of what Counsel he would, to direct him in his plea, who stood by him. 1849 Macaulay *Hist. Eng.* v. I. 666 His son and daughter stood by him at the bar.

b. *Naut.* To prepare to work (a gun, rope, etc.).

1669 Sturmy *Mariner's Mag.* v. xii. 46 When they be required to stand by a great Gun in time of Fight. 1867 Smyth *Sailor's Word-bk.*, To *stand by* a rope, is to take hold of it; *the anchor*, prepare to let go. 1897 Ansted *Dict. Sea Terms*, *Stand by*.—An order to be ready to do something; as 'Stand by the anchor', *i.e.* make ready to let go the anchor.

c. *fig.* (cf. a). To support, assist, protect, defend (a person, a cause, etc.); to uphold the interests of, take the side of, be faithful or loyal to.

1530 Palsgr. 733/1, I stande by, or I asyste a man in an acte, *je assiste*. Go to it, man, be nat a frayde, I wyll stande by the who so ever come. a 1586 Sidney *Ps.* x. vii, Lift up thy heav'nly hand, And by the silly stand. 1681 Nevile *Plato Rediv.* 263 That if they could make an honest Government, they should be stood by (as the Word then was) by the Army. 1687 Jas. II in *Magd. Coll.* (O. H. S.) 218, I will stand by them who stand by me. 1768 Boswell *Corsica* ii. 100 The house of Matra in Corsica, which stood by the republick. 1855 Macaulay *Hist. Eng.* xvii. IV. 54 To stand by the liberties of England and the Protestant religion, and, if necessary, to die for them. 1855 Trollope *Warden* iii, Surely he was bound to stand by his order. 1874 Stubbs *Const. Hist.* I. x. 316 The clergy stood by the king in his struggle with the feudatories.

†*Of a thing*. a 1770 Jortin *Serm.* (1787) IV. 35 This amiable quality will stand by him, will be a protector and benefactor to him in all stations.

d. To adhere to, maintain, abide by (a statement, agreement or the like).

c 1386 Chaucer *Wife's T.* 159 Thy lyf is sauf, for I wol stond therby, Vp-on my lyf, the queene wol seye as I. c 1400 *Brut* 329, & þese þinges þey profered hem self, if þe King wold, certey[n]ly to preue & stonde by. 1693 in Picton *L'pool. Munic. Rec.* (1883) I. 300 Whatever Ald[m] Clayton shall do..y[e] town will confirme and stand by. 1849 *Tait's Mag.* XVI. 158/1 We mean to stand by the assertion. 1891 *Review of Rev.* 15 Sept. 229/2 The Queen has..avowed her serious purpose to stand by her oath.

†**e.** To rest or depend upon; to be caused by, derived from, or owing to. *Obs.*

1471 *Paston Lett.* III. 31 And ther ayenst ye shold loose iij *li.* of the ferme of the maner yerly, whych standyth by undyr wood. 1477 *Rolls of Parlt.* VI. 188/1 The defense of this Lond stondeth moche by Archers. 1530 Palsgr. 733/1 This towne standeth by artificers: *ceste ville se mayntient par gens mecanicques.* 1547 Boorde *Introd. Knowl.* iv. (1870) 137 Muche of theyr lyuyng standeth by stelyng and robbyng. 1589 Puttenham *Eng. Poesie* II. i. (Arb.) 78 It is said by such as professe the Mathematicall sciences, that all things stand by proportion.

†**f.** To approach in character or quality; to be nearly related to. *Obs. rare.*

c 1530 *Judic. Urines* II. vii. 26 b, Vryne that is Ielowe and standet most by whyttenes. *Ibid.* II. viii. 32 b, Color Citrine standith by color rubea & by fleume, but more by color rubea than by fleume.

71. Stand for —.

a. To uphold, defend (a cause, etc.); to support, take the part of (a person). Also, †*to stand hard for*.

a 1300 *Cursor M.* 18933 To stand ai stitli for þe fai, And thrali preche al crist lai. c 1380 Wyclif *Wks.* (1880) 24 For to meyntene goddis lawe and stond for his worschipe. 1567 *Gude & Godlie B.* (S. T. S.) 142 For Christis word se ȝe stand for it. 1593 Abp. Bancroft *Dang. Posit.* IV. xiv. 179 Certaine..men..would shortly take vpon them the defence of the cause, which he and his brethren in prison stood-for. 1642 *Prince Rupert his Declaration* 6 The Lord prosper the worke of their hands who stand for God and King Charles. 1711 Addison *Spect.* No. 34 ¶ 10 Every Man at first stood hard for his Friend. 1842 Browning *Cavalier Tunes* I. i, Kentish Sir Byng stood for his King. 1847 Tennyson *Princess* IV. 169, I beheld her, when she rose.. and storming in extremes, Stood for her cause.

†**b.** To insist on, urge (a view, proposal, etc.); to support, maintain (a theory, thesis); to strive for, try to obtain or bring about, insist on having. Also, *to stand hard for*. *To stand for't*, ? to defend one's claim as against others. *Obs.*

1531 *Abstr. Protocols Town Clerks of Glasgow* (1897) IV. 39 Gaef sa beis that ther be ony mair Anwell tane nor fyf crownis..the sayd Robert or his airis sall pas to the toder part and stand for raleyf of the samyne. 1616 B. Jonson *Devil an Ass* I. vi. 36 All that pretend, to stand for't o' the Stage. 1618 Bolton *Florus* III. xii. (1636) 212 What cause was there why the People of Rome should stand so hard for fields or food [*agros et cibaria flagitaret*]? 1643 Trapp *Comm. Gen.* xlviii. 19 The Jewish converts stood hard for a mixture of Christ and Moses. 1676 H. More *Remarks* Contents b v, That Experiment of Regius..can be no instance of such an Attraction and Rarefaction as this Author stands for. 1690 Norris *Beatitudes* (1694) I. 41 But that which I stand for is this, That we ought not [etc.]. 1726 Shelvocke *Voy. round World* 165 He stands more for his honour than any money.

†**c.** *I stand for it* (written also *foird, forde*), as parenthesis = I warrant, I'll go bail for it. *Sc.*

c 1480 Henryson *Mor. Fab.* III. (*Cock & Fox*) xxiv, Than will thay stint, I stand for it, and not steir. 1535 Lyndesay *Satyre* 3982 Thou art an limmer, I stand foird. 1570 *Satir. Poems Reform.* xiv. 103, I stand forde.

†**d.** *To stand in wax for*: to be legal security for (another). *Obs.*

1608 *Yorksh. Trag.* i, He has consumed al, pawnd his lands, and made his vniuersitie brother stand in waxe for him – Thers a fine phrase for a scrivener.

†**e.** Of custom, sentiments: To be on the side of. *Obs.*

1581 Mulcaster *Positions* xxxviii. (1887) 168 Seeing my countrie giues me leaue, and her custome standes for me. 1788 *New London Mag.* 428 The King's affections standing for this disposition of the crown, he was gained at last to overlook his sisters and break through his father's will.

f. To be reckoned or alleged for; to be counted or considered as; to serve in lieu of. *To stand for nothing*, to be worthless, of no avail; *to stand for something*, to have some value or importance. Also with dative of person.

a 1300 *Cursor M.* 9972 It es vs sett als in þe marche, And standes vs for sceild and targe Agains all vre wiþerwyns. *Ibid.* 26601 And for þe scam man thinc scriuand, It sal for part o penance stand. c 1374 Chaucer *Boeth.* IV. pr. ii. (1868) 112 Yif power fayleþ þe wille nis but in ydel and stant for nauȝt. 1563 Becon *Reliques of Rome* 211 b, For that daye ye he heareth a masse,..if a man die: it shall stand hym for hys housell. 1579 Gosson *Sch. Abuse* (Arb.) 51 Iupiter himself shall stand for example. 1659 N. R. *Prov., Eng. Fr.* etc. 54 He stands for a Cipher. 1686 tr. *Chardin's Trav. Persia* 23 The two Audiences which he had receiv'd should stand for nothing. 1863 Mrs. Oliphant *Salem Chapel* ii. 28 He began to divine faintly,..that external circumstances do stand for something.

†**g.** Of a money-payment: To be reckoned sufficient for, to free from obligation. *Obs.*

1389 in *Eng. Gilds* (1870) 10 And ȝif þe man wil haue his wyf a suster, þan schal þ[e] paiement stonde for hem bothe.

h. To represent, be in the place of, take the place of, do duty for.

1567 Sanders *Rocke of Churche* ii. 31 According to the

STAND. 809 **STAND.** 810 **STAND.**

72. Stand in—

73. Stand of—

74. Stand on—

75. Stand over—

76. Stand to—

77. Stand under—

78. Stand upon—

STAND. 811 **STAND.** 812 **STAND.**

80. Stand beside.

81. Stand again.

82. Stand along. *Naut.*

83. Stand aloof.

84. Stand apart.

85. Stand aside.

86. Stand back.

87. Stand away.

88. Stand behind.

89. Stand behind.

90. Stand beside.

91. Stand by.

92. Stand up.

93. Stand forth.

94. Stand forward. *Naut.*

95. Stand in. *Naut.*

96. Stand off. *Naut.*

97. Stand off and on. *Naut.*

98. Stand on.

99. Stand out.

transf. 1806–7 J. Beresford *Miseries Hum. Life* (1826) x. lxi, The pullies resolutely standing out against all your efforts to turn them.

d. *To stand it out* = prec.

1607 Topsell *Four-f. Beasts* 571 When the fight is once begunne, there is none of both that may runne awaie, but standeth it out vntil one or both of them bee slaine to the ground. *a* 1694 Tillotson *Serm.* xxxv. (1742) III. 17 He is in good earnest, and will execute these threatnings upon them if they will obstinately stand it out with him. 1718 Ockley *Saracens* (1848) 219 Knowing very well how hard it would go with them if they should stand it out obstinately to the last, and be taken by storm. 1837 Carlyle *Fr. Rev.* I. vii. xi, He, tough as tanned leather..will stand it out for another year. 1866 Ruskin *Crown of Wild Olive* iv. § 148, I..stood it out to the end, and helped to carry four of my fellow students..down stairs.

e. *To stand out for*: to declare oneself for, contend on behalf of.

a 1600 *Raid of Reidswire* xviii. in Scott *Border Minstrelsy* (1869) 74 None stoutlier stood out for their laird, Nor did the lads of Liddisdail. 1633 Bp. Hall *Hard Texts* Hos. v. 13 When Ahaz..was in distresse, he sends to Tiglath Pileser, that should stand out for him. 1891 *Chamb. Jrnl.* 19 Sept. 593/2 He has not grit enough to stand out for justice and honesty.

f. To haggle, make difficulties about striking a bargain; to make an obstinate demand *for* (certain terms).

1766 Goldsm. *Vic. W.* xii, He always stands out and higgles. 1816 Scott *Antiq.* xxiv, 'If the secret were mine,' said the mendicant, 'I wad stand out for a half.' 1889 Rider Haggard *Col. Quaritch* xliii. 325, I am not going to stand out about the price. 1890 *Sat. Rev.* 20 Sept. 337/1 They stood out partly for more wages.

†g. Of a bill, debt, etc.: To remain unsettled or unpaid. (Cf. Outstanding *ppl. a.* 4.) *Obs.*

1723 *Lond. Gaz.* No. 6183/2 Exchequer Bills (which are all that are now standing out and undischarged). 1736 *Gentl. Mag.* VI. 563/1 An Account of all the publick Debts..due or standing out at Christmas, 1735.

h. *Naut.* (See sense 36.) To sail in a direction away from the shore. Usually *to stand out to sea.* Hence *gen.*, to start on a journey.

1718 Rowe *Lucan* iv. 717 *note*, Octavius stood out to sea. 1834 M. Scott *Cruise Midge* vi, The signal to weigh and stand out, sir. 1885 *Times* 18 Sept. 13/2 We stood out through the thickening rain. 1891 *Longman's Mag.* Oct. 596 They cut their cables..and stood out into the Channel.

i. To jut out, project, protrude (*from* a surface); to be prominent.

1540 Palsgr. *Acolastus* ii. i. H ij b, My chynne standynge out lyke as aged folkes lyppes do, that be totheles. 1558 Phaer *Æneid* viii. (1562) Cc ij b, Agrippa loftie prince whose pendaunt streamers proud stand out. 1560 Bible (Geneva) *Ps.* lxxiii. 7 Their eyes stand out for fatnes. 1585 Higins *Junius' Nomencl.* 206/1 *Striæ*,..those partes in furrowed pillers which stand out and swell as it were. *c* 1643 Ld. Herbert *Autobiog.* (1824) 100 The Pier of Dover, which stands out in the Sea. 1680 Moxon *Mech. Exerc.* xi. 202 The work..is required to stand out free from the outer Flat of the Cheeks of the Coller. 1742 Blair *Grave* 274 Oh! how his Eyes stand out, and stare full ghastly! 1889 Mrs. Lynn Linton *Thro' Long Night* I. i. xiii. 207 Her ears stood out from her head like jug-handles. 1890 W. C. Russell *Ocean Trag.* I. i. 6 The veins stood out like whipcord.

j. To be conspicuous; to be seen in contrast or relief *against* a dark object or background. Of figures in painting: To appear as if in relief.

1856 Whyte Melville *Kate Coventry* ix, Lucy's white face stood out in the lamplight. 1884 *Times* (weekly ed.) 29 Aug. 14/1 The white houses, sparkling in the sunshine, stood out against the dark background of woods. 1889 Mrs. E. Kennard *Landing a Prize* II. iv. 65 Red flannel shirts..stood out in the distance as a brilliant spot of colour.

k. *fig.* To be prominent or conspicuous to the mental gaze.

1826 Lamb *Elia* Ser. ii. *Genteel Style in Writing*, The man of rank is discernible in both writers; but in the one it is only insinuated gracefully, in the other it stands out offensively. 1874 Green *Short Hist.* viii. § 6. 518 John Pym..stands out for all after time as the embodiment of law. 1891 *Chamb. Jrnl.* 7 Feb. 81/1 Two facts stand out in bold relief.

l. *trans.* To remain standing throughout (a performance). Also *Naut.* To 'stand watch' (see sense 60) during (a specified time).

1840 R. H. Dana *Bef. Mast* vii, We were then divided into three watches, and thus stood out the remainder of the night. 1890 Constance Smith *Riddle Lawr. Haviland* II. iii. iv. 90 He propped himself in an angle of the doorway, and prepared to stand out the performance.

m. To endure to the end, hold out under or against (a trial, ordeal, severe weather, etc.); to last out (a period of time).

1623 *Shaks. Wks.* To Rdrs., These Playes have had their triall alreadie, and stood out all Appeales. 1649 Jer. Taylor *Gt. Exemp.* i. Ad Sec. vi. 105 Jesus fled from the persecution; as he did not stand it out, so he did not stand out against it. 1676 Phillips *Purchasers Pattern* 18 Houses..many times cannot well stand out a long Lease. 1821 Scott *Kenilw.* vii, It is a sunburnt beauty,..well qualified to stand out rain and wind. 1827 — *Jrnl.* 28 Mar., I..went out in as rough weather as I have seen, and stood out several snow blasts. 1855 Flor. Nightingale in Sir E. Cook *Life* (1913) I. 283, I am ready to stand out the War with any man.

n. With object-clause: To maintain, insist, persist in asserting (*that*). Also *to stand it out* (*that*): cf. d.

1664 H. More *Myst. Iniq.* i. xiii. 42 They..will stand it out as stoutly for their justification, as these professors of Christianity that they are no Idolaters. 1726 Berkeley *Lett.* Wks. 1871 IV. 120 The latter still stands out. that she never received..any of Mrs. Mary's money. 1863 Mrs. Gaskell *Sylvia's Lovers* xxxix, It were only yesterday at e'en she were standing out that he liked her better than you. 1898 Besant *Orange Girl* ii. xii, He..stoutly stood it out that he was a gentleman of Cumberland.

o. *Sport.* To stick to (a bet) without hedging. (Cf. sense 63.)

1892 *Illustr. Sporting & Dram. News* 28 May 382/2 Personally I would not take 100 to 1, to stand it out. *Ibid.* 406/3 Still, mark my words, he will stand that bet out, if only for Julia's sake.

p. *dial.* To force or try to force (a person) by pertinacious assertion to believe or admit (the fact expressed by an object-clause).

1895 Alicia A. Leith *Plant of Lemon Verbena* v. 105 He tried t' stand me out 'twas a white caaf or a cow I'd zeen. 1895 Jane Barlow *Strangers at Lisconnel* ii. 26, I question would any raisonable body stand me out I don't own her be rights.

100. **Stand over.**

a. *Naut.* (See sense 36.) To leave one shore and sail towards another.

1699 Dampier *Voy.* II. i. 171 Yet we did not stand over towards Sumatra, but coasted along nearest the Malacca shore. 1855 Macaulay *Hist. Eng.* xv. III. 604 He now stood over to the English shore.

b. To be left or reserved for treatment, consideration or settlement at a later date. (See Over *adv.* 9.)

1824 *Examiner* 67/1 [He] directed the trial to stand over until the next morning. 1853 *Jrnl. R. Agric. Soc.* XIV. i. 30 Many acres..are left unsown, and must stand over for Lent corn. 1884 *Law Rep.* 25 Chanc. Div. 707 The motion was ordered to stand over for a fortnight. 1891 *Sat. Rev.* 22 Aug. 219/1 His accounts are balanced at the close of each season, and no bad debts are allowed to stand over.

101. **Stand to.**

†a. To be present, 'assist'. *Obs.*

1540 Palsgr. *Acolastus* Peroration Bb iij b, You al.. whiche stand to here .i. all you, whiche stande here at this presente tyme.

†b. To set to work, fall to; *esp.* to begin eating. (See To *adv.* 6.) *Obs.*

1605 Shaks. *Macb.* ii. iii. 38. 1610 — *Temp.* iii. iii. 49, 52, I will stand to, and feede..: my Lord, the Duke, Stand too, and doe as we.

102. **Stand together.**

†a. To agree, be consistent, harmonize. *Obs.*

1387–8 T. Usk *Test. Love* iii. ix. (Skeat) l. 26 As I was lerned how goddes before-weting and free choice of wil mowe stonden togider. *c* 1449 Pecock *Repr.* ii. xvi. 246 And so these ij. thingis whiche Scripture seith of ydolatrers stonden to gidere and ben trewe. 1565 Harding *Answ. Jewel's Challenge* 137 Sith both these verities may well stande together. 1629 Burton *Babel no Bethel* 96 The Arke and Dagon cannot stand together. 1711 Felton *Diss. Classics* (1718) 9 Sprightly Youth and close Application will hardly stand together.

†b. To consist *in*, *of*. (Rendering L. *constare* with ablative.) *Obs.*

c 1400 *Apol. Loll.* 47 We..striue to proue þe sacrifice of þe kirk to stond to gidre in two þingis, and to be maad in two þingis to gidre:..as þe persoun of Crist stondiþ to gidre of God and man.

103. **Stand up.**

a. To assume an erect position; to rise, get up on one's feet.

a 1122 *O. E. Chron.* (Laud MS.) an. 656 Þa stod seo kyning up toforen ealle his ðegna & cwæd luddor stefne [etc.]. *c* 1200 Ormin 16138 Hat lufess fir..Iss kinndledd i þatt herrte þatt..stanndeþþ upp biforenn follc,..To niþþrenn woh wiþþ all hiss mahht. *a* 1300 *Cursor M.* 16415 Pilate stode vp on his fete mid-ward þat gret gadring. 1535 Coverdale *Song Sol.* v. 5, I stode vp to open vnto my beloued. 1667 *Answ. to Quest. out of North* 12 If any person coming to Church..do not Stand Up at the Creed. 1711 Addison *Spect.* No. 112 ¶ 3 He..sometimes stands up when every Body else is upon their Knees. 1787 'G. Gambado' *Acad. Horsem.* (1809) 34 The standing up in your stirrups, whilst trotting..has a most elegant and genteel effect. 1877 Miss Yonge *Cameos* Ser. iii. xxxvi. 391 He stood up in the waggon and began to sing.

b. To remain erect and firm *under* (a crushing weight, or the like). (Cf. 77 b.)

1682 Bunyan *Holy War* 164 For the grace, the benefit, the pardon, was sudden, glorious, and so big, that they were not able without staggering to stand up under it.

c. To take part in a dance; to dance *with* (a partner).

1766 Goldsm. *Vic. W.* xxi, We were here interrupted by a servant who came to ask the Squire in to stand up at country-dances. 1796 Jane Austen *Pride & Prej.* xviii, In vain did she entreat him to stand up with somebody else. 1804 — *Watsons* (1879) 328, I thought you were to stand up with Mr. Tomlinson the two last dances.

d. To take up one's position to play an athletic game.

1884 *J. Marshall's Tennis Cuts* 169 He had a twist in his spine, which rendered him physically incapable of standing up to play more than one game a day. 1896 A. E. Housman *Shropsh. Lad* xxvii, Is football playing.., With lads to chase the leather, Now I stand up no more?

e. *dial.* (See quots.)

1886 *W. Somerset Word-bk.*, *Stand up for*, to undertake the office of God-parent at a baptism. 1891 *Century Dict.*, *To stand up with*, to act as groomsman or bridesmaid to: as, I stood up with him at his wedding. (Colloq.)

f. *colloq.* and *dial.* To take shelter from rain.

1887 'Mark Rutherford' *Revol. Tanner's Lane* xviii. (ed. 8) 271 Thomas, however,..proposed that they should stand up in a shed which had been used for faggot-making. The rain, which now came down heavily, enforced his arguments. 1893 in Cozens-Hardy *Broad Norf.* 13 Let us stand up out of the wet. 1908 G. K. Chesterton *Man who was Thursday* 126 Hoping..that the snow-shower might be slight, he stepped back..and stood up under the doorway of a..shop.

g. colloq. *To stand up in*, to be actually wearing. (Cf. *stand in* 72 a.)

1901 Alldridge *Sherbro* xxvii. 309 The boat returned.. bringing down Miss Mullen with only such things as she stood up in.

h. Of an animal: To hold out, endure (in a race or chase). †Also in *imper.* as a cry to urge on a horse.

1656 Earl Monm. tr. *Boccalini's Advts. fr. Parnass.* i. xxxi. (1674) 36 Coach-men..whipping their Horses, and.. crying, Stand up. 1891 *Field* 7 Nov. 695/3 A baker's dozen struggled on to the finish..but if our deer had stood up for another mile or two, the number would have been still further reduced. 1893 *Sat. Rev.* 7 Jan. 16/1 A dog who would lap after a course would have no chance of standing up in subsequent rounds.

i. Of things: To be set upright; to be or become erect. Of hair, spines, etc.: cf. sense 17 d.

a 1300 *Cursor M.* 3779 In slepe he sagh stand vp a sti, Fra his heued right to þe ski. *c* 1460 *Towneley Myst.* xxiii. 232 Vp with the tymbre fast on ende!..A, it standys vp lyke a mast. 1549 *Compl. Scot.* xii. 102 And ane vthir speyr set & bundyn athort betuix the tua speyris that stude vp fra the eyrd lyik ane gallus. 1667 Milton *P. L.* vii. 321 Up stood the cornie Reed Embattell'd in her field. 1815 J. Smith *Panorama Sci. & Art* II. 182 Its apex rests upon the point of a steel pin standing up in the centre of the box. 1889 G. Gissing *Nether World* III. xii. 253 His hair stood up like stubble. 1896 tr. *Boas' Text-bk. Zool.* 391 The Sea Hedgehog (*Diodon*) is beset with bony spines, which stand up when the animal puffs itself out.

†j. Of flame, vapour: To rise up, issue upwards. (Cf. sense 33.) *Obs.*

c 1290 *S. Eng. Leg.* 233/501 Þe leiȝe stod op on heiȝ ase þei it a wal were. *c* 1330 R. Brunne *Chron. Wace* (Rolls) 1818 Þe stem stod vp, so þey blew.

†k. Of a door: To remain open. *Obs.*

1550 Crowley *Epigr.* 118 In service tyme no dore standeth up, Where such men are wonte to fyll can and cuppe.

†l. *Naut.* Of a number of ships: To form up, assemble *together* in a given place or position. *Obs.*

1585 T. Washington tr. *Nicholay's Voy.* iv. xv. 130 The Cicilians..beeing acquainted with the seas,..Coursaries, and Skummers of the sea, stood vp in so great number, [etc.]. 1623 *Cal. St. Papers, Col.* 1622–4, 213 [The ships] Stood up altogether [in the road of Swally].

m. *Naut.* (See quot.)

1867 Smyth *Sailor's Word-bk.*, *Standing up*, a ship in good trim, and well attended to, is said to stand well up to her canvas.

n. To hold oneself boldly erect to confront an opponent; to make a stand *against*. *lit.* and *fig.*

1601 Shaks. *Jul. C.* ii. i. 167 We all stand vp against the spirit of Cæsar. 1605 — *Lear* iii. vii. 80 Giue me thy Sword. A pezant stand vp thus? 1855 Macaulay *Hist. Eng.* xv. III. 506 With the same spirit with which he had stood up against the Stuarts he had stood up against the Cromwells. 1890 Tout *Hist. Eng. fr.* 1689 156 Lord Liverpool was not strong enough to stand up against Canning. 1897 A. E. Houghton *Gilbert Murray* xvii. 273 The smaller boy, who, though still standing up pluckily, was getting decidedly the worst of it.

o. *To stand up for*: to defend, support, take the part of, champion (a person, a cause, etc.).

1605 Shaks. *Lear* i. ii. 22 Now Gods, stand vp for Bastards. 1645 T. Coleman *Hopes Deferred* 30 His subjects stood up for their liberties. 1768–74 Tucker *Lt. Nat.* (1834) II. 317 They..stand up for the honour of the nation. 1867 Trollope *Chron. Barset* I. xvi. 136, I liked her for standing up for her husband. 1879 M. J. Guest *Lect. Hist. Eng.* xxi. 208 All swore that they would stand up for their rights.

p. *To stand up to*: to confront or encounter boldly. Also *U.S.*, 'to meet fairly and fully (an obligation, one's word or promise)' (Webster, 1911).

1624 Fletcher *Rule a Wife* iii. i, He stood up to me And mated my commands. 1823 'Jon Bee' *Dict. Turf* s.v., 'Stand up to him' (ring); do not flinch from the blows. 1827 Scott *Two Drovers* i, He found few antagonists able to stand up to him in the boxing ring. 1848 Bartlett *Dict. Amer.* 331 *To stand up to the rack*, a metaphorical expression of the same meaning as the like choice phrases, 'to come to the scratch', 'to toe the mark'. 1889 'M. Gray' *Reproach of Annesley* I. i. vi. 136 How pluckily he stood up to the kicking horse! 1892 *Blackw. Mag.* CLI. 102/1 Few men..ventured to stand up boldly to such terrific bowling. 1894 *Speaker* 9 June 640/1 He knuckled under to any one who chose to stand up to him.

VIII. 104. Comb. in phrases used subst. or attrib., as **stand-easy**, an assumption of the attitude directed by the command 'stand easy'; *fig.* a period of relaxation; also *attrib.*; †**stand far** (or **further**) **off**, a kind of cloth (see quots.); **stand-over**, a plant that has been left standing beyond the normal time; **stand-to-arms**, the action of standing to arms. Also Stand-by, Standfast, Stand-off, Stand out, Stand-still, Stand-up.

1613 J. Taylor (Water P.) *Eighth Wond.* Wks. (1630) ii. 62 Certaine sonnets,..fashioned of diuers stuffs, as mockado, fustian, stand-further-off, and Motly. 1619 — *Kicksey Winsey* B 8 b, I muse of what stuffe these men framed be, Most of them seeme Muckado vnto me: Some are Stand-further off, for they endeauer, Neuer to see me. *a* 1661 Fuller *Worthies, Norwich* (1662) 274 In my child-hood there was one [stuff] called *Stand-far-of*,..which seemed pretty at competent distance, but discovered its courseness when nearer to the eye. 1837 Carlyle *Fr. Rev.* III. vii. iii, Whereupon also, on the Republican side, there will be rapid stand-to-arms. 1847 *Simmonds's Colon. Mag.* Dec. 374 Old standover rattoons. *Ibid.* 375 The crop of sugar from these standovers is entirely lost for at least two years. 1898 *Daily News* 15 Feb. 8/3 The blue-jackets had by no means been idle in their 'stand easy' moments. 1899 F. M. Holmes *Firemen* 97 Allowing for a 'stand easy' of fifteen minutes at eleven. 1906 *Daily Chron.* 14 July 6/2 They need holidays far more than civilians,..A 'stand-easy' is necessary to everyone.

☞ *Key to phrases, etc.*

Followed by an inf. 5 b, 12, 16; to let stand 50; to let all stand, all standing 24; as it stands 20 b; as things stand 38 b; how do you stand (financially)? 15 e; standing 51.

Stand aback 88; *s* about (*prep.*) 66, (*adv.*) 80; *s* again 81; *s* against 12, 67; *s* ajar 20; *s* alone 15 d; *s* along 82; *s* aloof 83; *s* and (do something) 5 c; *s* and deliver! 4 b; *s* and fight 10; *s* apart 84; *s* aside 85; *s* astrut 86; *s* at 68; *s* at (a figure or amount) 21 b; *s* at (a level or height) 22; *s* at attention 5; *s* at avail 48 d; *s* at bay, at defiance 10; *s* at ease, at gaze 5; *s* at livery 3; *s* a-water 28 b; *s* away 87; *s* awe 45 b; *s* back 88; *s* before 69; *s* behind 89; *s* beside 90; *s* by (*prep.*) 70, (*adv.*) 91; *s* candidate 12; *s* captain 15 a; *s* a chance 57; *s* one's chance 53 d; *s* committed, corrected 15 d; *s* deep in 17 c; *s* double 12 b; *s* down 92; *s* dread 45 b; *s* fair (for, to do) 15 e; *s* fast 4, 9, 10, 23; *s* fire 52 b; *s* firm 9, 10, 20; *s* for 71; *s* (= fish) for 6 a; *s* for (an office, a constituency, etc.) 12, 12 b; *s* for law 42 b; *s* forth 93; *s* forward 94; *s* free 15 d; *s* (one's) friend 15 c; *s* godfather 15 b; *s* good 42 b; *s* (one's) good lord, prince 15 c; *s* one's ground 56; *s* one's hand 61; *s* a hazard 54; *s* high 17 b, 20; *s* (one) high 44 a; *s* high with 15 e; *s* in (*prep.*) 72, (*adv.*) 95; *s* (one) in (a price) 44 c, d; *s* in awe 45; *s* in the breach 10; *s* in danger 15 e; *s* in defence 10; *s* in doom 11 a; *s* in doubt 15 e; *s* in dread, in fear 45 c; *s* in force 42 b, 48 d; *s* (one) in hand 47; *s* in judgement 11 a, b; *s* in lieu of 49; *s* in one's light 2; *s* in need 46; *s* in profit 48 d; *s* in a (certain) relation 15 e, 38; *s* in (another's) shoes 2; *s* in stall 48 d; *s* in stead 48; *s* in stead of 49; *s* in vail 48 d; *s* in the way 2; *s* indebted 15 d; *s* instead of 49; *s* king 15 a; *s* law 42 b; *s* the market 62; *s* model 5 e; *s* mute 15 d; *s* (= consist) of 73; *s* off 96; *s* off and on 97; *s* officer 15 a; *s* on (*prep.*) 17, 74, (*adv.*) 98; *s* (one) on (a price) 44 b; *s* on one's own bottom 5; *s* on the defensive 10; *s* on end 17 d; *s* on one's own feet, on (upon) a foot, footing 2; *s* on one's guard 10; *s* (one) on hand 47; *s* on one's head 8; *s* on one's own legs 2; *s* on the offensive 10; *s* open 20; *s* or fall 9 c; *s* out 99; *s* over (*prep.*) 75, (*adv.*) 100; *s* pad 5 e; *s* pat 14; *s* the patter 53 b; *s* perdu 5; *s* pledged, reproved 15 d; *s* Sam 61; *s* security 15 a; *s* sentinel, sentry 5 e; *s* shot 52 b, 61; *s* sound 23; *s* sponsor 15 b; *s* stable 23; *s* stall 48 d; *s* stiff 9; *s* still 4, 27, 32; *s* suit 53 b; *s* surety 15 a; *s* thick 17 b, c; *s* till 76; *s* to (*prep.*) 76, (*adv.*) 101; *s* to (the knees, etc.) in 1 c; *s* (one) to (a price) 44 b; *s* to avail 48 d; *s* to the bar 11 a; *s* to lose, win 16 d; *s* together 102; *s* treat 61; *s* one's trial 53 b; *s* umpire 5 e; *s* under 77; *s* until, unto 76; *s* up 17 d, 103; *s* up to (the knees, etc.) in 1 c; *s* upon 17, 78; *s* (one) upon (a price) 44 b; *s* upon game 4 c; *s* upon one's trial 11 a; *s* upright 5, 17 d; *s* (a) watch 60; *s* well 15 e, 38 b; *s* whole 23; *s* with 79; *s* with water 27 b.

Standage (stæ·ndédʒ). In 6 **stannage**. [f. Stand *v.* + -age.]

1. Arrangements or accommodation for standing. Also, a charge for permission to stand.

1777 *Barmby Inclos. Act* 10 Settling the standage for the crops. 1848 *Jrnl. R. Agric. Soc.* IX. i. 120 The object is to give a firm standage for cattle drinking at the pond. 1896 *Times* 18 Dec. 13/5 The action was to recover..in respect of sidage or standage charged upon trucks..which remained more than four days upon..sidings. 1907 *Advt.* [Northumbld.], Standage for Motors and Cycles.

†b. A standing, stall. *Obs.*

1600 S. Forman *Autobiogr.* (1849) 8 They kept a stannage at our Ladie faier, and ther were many knavishe boies which were at play behinde the stannage, and often thruste downe their ware.

2. *Mining.* An underground reservoir for water.

1842 *1st Rep. Comm. Employmt. Childr. Mines* 59, 15 fathoms lower being sunk for 'standage', or for a reservoir of water. 1875 J. H. Collins *Princ. Metal Mining* 53 The space underneath serves as a water channel and standage or sump. 1883 Greslev *Gloss. Coal-mining* 237.

Standage, obs. variant of Standish.

Standard (stæ·ndǎɹd), *sb.* Also 4–6 **standarde**, 4–5 **stondard**, 4–6 **standerde**, 4–7 **standerd**, (6 **standred**), 4–7, 8 *rare* **standart**, 5–6 **standert** (5 **estandert**, 6 **standertt**), **stondart(e** (5 **stondert**), 6 **stander**, 7 *Sc.* **stender**. See also Estandard. [aphetic a. OF. *estandard*, *-art*, *-estendard*, *-art* (mod.F. *étendard*) = med.L. *standardum*, *-us*, *standarium*, etc., Pr. *estandard*, *-art*, Sp., Pg. *estandarte*, It. *stendardo*; according to most scholars f. com. Rom. *estend-ere* (L. *extend-ĕre* to stretch out: see Extend *v.*) + -ard; a parallel synonymous formation with different suffix is It. *stendale*, late OF. *estandale*, *-deille* (med.L. *standale*, *-ālis*). The Fr. word has passed into all the living Teut. langs.: MHG. *stanthart* (by popular etymology, as if 'stand hard'), later *standart*, *standert* (mod.G. *standarte*), MDu. *standaert* (mod.Du. *standaard*, *standerd*), Da. *standart*, Sw. *standar*.

The origin of sense 9 ('standard of measure or weight'), whence the other senses in branch II are derived, is somewhat obscure. It appears in AF. (*estaundart*) and Anglo-L. (*standardus*) in the 13th c., two centuries earlier than our earliest vernacular instance. It has not been found in continental OF.; the use of Du. *standaard* in this sense is believed to be imitated from English. It is noteworthy that in early instances the standard of measure is always either expressly or by implication called 'the king's standard', an expression which belongs to the older sense 1. It seems probable that sense 9 is a fig. use of sense 1; the king's standard being the point of reunion of the army, and the centre from which commands are issued.

The senses grouped as branch III are of doubtful, probably of various and in some instances of mixed origin. The notion of 'something conspicuously erected', involved in sense 1, would account for several of them; others may be referred to the idea of 'something permanent, fixed, or stationary', generalized from sense 9. Etymological association with Stand *v.* has, however, certainly affected the whole group, and it is possible that in some uses the word should be regarded as an alteration of Stander. The senses of this branch are almost confined to English: OF. has *estandart* some kind of torch (*rare*⁻¹), and WFlem. has *standaart* mill-post (De Bo; *standaert*, Kilian); but the relation of these to the English uses is obscure.]

I. A military or naval ensign.

1. A flag, sculptured figure, or other conspicuous object, raised on a pole to indicate the rallying-point of an army (or fleet), or of one of its component portions; the distinctive ensign of a king, great noble, or commander, or of a nation or city.

†*Standard-general*: the principal standard of an army.

In Eng. the word appears first with reference to the 'Battle of the Standard' in 1138. A contemporary writer, Richard of Hexham, relating the story of the battle, describes the 'standard' there used as a mast of a ship, with flags at the top, mounted in the middle of a machine which was brought into the field. He quotes a Latin couplet written on the occasion, which says that the standard was so called from 'stand', because 'it was there that valour took its stand to conquer or die'.

1154 *O. E. Chron.* (Laud MS.) an. 1138, Him [*sc.* king David of Scotland] com to ȝænes Willelm eorl of Albamar..mid fæu men &..flemden þe king æt te Standard. 1297 R. Glouc. (Rolls) 6175 Edmond diȝte is stondard ware he ssolde him sulue abide. 13.. *K. Alis.* 2377 (Laud MS.), To ymagu hij turneden pas þer þe kynges standarde was. 1338 R. Brunne *Chron.* (1725) 115 Þise men lift ther standard, that stoute was & grim Ageyn Dauid wandelard, & disconfite him. *c* 1425 ? Lydg. *Assembly of Gods* 825 All these seuyn capteynes had standardes of pryce. 1483 *Cath. Angl.* 359/1 A Standerd or A bekyn, *statela.* *a* 1548 Hall *Chron., Hen. V*, 64 b, Banners, standers and penons of the kynges armes. 1588 Parke tr. *Mendoza's Hist. China* 165 A watch towre ..who had discouered our shippe, and knew the standard or flagge to bee the kings. 1594 Shaks. *Rich. III.* v. iii. 263 Then in the name of God and all these rights, Aduance your Standards, draw your willing Swords. 1609 Holland *Amm. Marcell.* xv. vii. 43 An high banke above which stood the maine standerds of Eagles and other ensignes. 1609 Bible (Douay) *Jer.* vi. 1 In Thecua sownd with the trumpet, and over Bethacarem lift up the standart. 1611 Bible *Num.* ii. 3. 1630 *R. Johnson's Kingd. & Commw.* 314 Every Citie hath his principall Standard, with their peculiar armes and devices therein, to distinguish one people from another. 1633 T. Stafford *Pac. Hib.* ii. xxv. 252 The Burgesses.. came to the Lord President, to beseech him to render unto them their Charter, Seale, Mace, and Standard. 1656 Earl Monm. tr. *Boccalini's Advts. fr. Parnass.* i. lxxxv. (1674) 112 Francisco Pico..was made Standard-bearer; and, in his Standard-General, bore the famous Ensign of an open Book. 1660 Waterhouse *Arms & Arm.* 45 *Vexilla* properly signifies the Standers of Kings and Chiefs. 1737 Pope *Hor. Ep.* ii. ii. 41 He..Tore down a Standard, took the Fort and all. 1781 Cowper *Table T.* 454 The standards of all nations are unfurl'd. 1804 *Med. Jrnl.* XII. 46 The late dispute respecting the capture of the standard of the *Invincibles* before Alexandria. 1808 Pike *Sources Mississ.* ii. App. 23 They gave up the Spanish flag, and we had the pleasure to see the American Standard hoisted in its stead. 1831–3 E. Burton *Eccl. Hist.* xxx. (1845) 643 From this time the imperial standards bore a device, which was composed of the two first letters of the name of Christ in Greek. 1864 Pusey *Lect. Daniel* (1876) 114 The black eagle is the standard of Prussia. 1891 Farrar *Darkn. & Dawn* iii, The tents and standards of the soldiers had been struck with fire from heaven.

transf. 1761 *Ann. Reg.*, *Char.* 8/2 Every raja..appears ..mounted on an elephant, and is at once the general and ensign, or standard of that corps, who keep their eyes constantly on him.

b. In many phrases used with pregnant sense, the standard being taken as typifying the army or its leaders; e.g. *to raise one's standard*, take up arms; *under the standard of*, serving in the army of; so *to join the standard of*; and the like.

c 1500 *Melusine* xxiv. 164 Your vassall & seruaunt shal I euer be vnder the standart of your gouernance. 1667 Milton *P. L.* vii. 297 As Armies at the call Of Trumpet.. Troop to their Standard. 1697 Dryden *Virg. Georg.* iv. 102 With hoarse allarms the hollow Camp rebounds,..Then to their common Standard they repair. 1738 Glover *Leonidas* i. 155 They with dread Will shrink before your standards. 1838–43 Arnold *Hist. Rome* II. xxxvii. 481 All the nations of southern Italy..were ready to join his standard. 1840 Thirlwall *Greece* VII. lvii. 241 In a short time he.. had a body of more than 2000 horse under his standard. 1842 W. C. Taylor *Anc. Hist.* xvii. § 2 (ed. 3) 500 Wearied by the tyranny of Domitian, Lucius Antonius..raised the standard of revolt in his province. 1845 James *Arrah Neil* vi, He would raise his standard at once, and march to London. 1852 Sir J. Graham in C. S. Parker *Life & Lett.* (1907) II. 149 The rival camps under hostile standards will thus be pitched.

c. *fig.*

1532 More *Confut. Tindale* ii. 105 Some that were heretyques in dede, and wolde..auaunce theyr owne heresyes forwarde vnder the name and standard of his [Origen's] famouse authoryte. 1613 Purchas *Pilgrimage* (1614) 87 No crueltie or sacriledge against God, or man, so irreligious ..but Religion was pretended to be the cause, and bare the Standard to Destruction. 1688 Jas. II in Gutch *Coll. Cur.* I. 339, I tell you this is a Standard of Rebellion: I never saw such an address! 1856 *N. Brit. Rev.* XXVI. 250 [They] if they did not vote against him, at least deserted their standard, and did not vote at all. 1888 Bryce *Amer. Commw.* II. lxx. 566 The gain of even twenty or thirty votes..is so likely to bring fresh recruits to his standard.

2. In a more restricted sense, a military or naval flag of some particular kind.

Ordinarily, the *standard* is understood to be distinguished from a banner by being long and tapering instead of square, and from a pennon by its greater breadth. The British *royal standard*, however, which is flown when the king or a member of the royal family is present, is now a square flag (thus technically a 'banner'), divided into four compartments bearing the emblems of England (twice), Scotland, and Ireland. In the British army, the regimental flags of the cavalry are called *standards*, those of the infantry being 'colours'. In the U.S. army the flag of a cavalry regiment is called its *standard*.

1375 Barbour *Bruce* xi. 465 Thai saw so fele browdyn baneris, Standartis, pennownys apon speris. 1471 Caxton *Recuyell* (Sommer) 199 And than made dysplaye banyers, standardes & penons. 1523 Berners *Froiss.* I. xviii. 22 Euery man mounted, and the baners and standers folowed this new made knyght. *a* 1548 Hall *Chron., Hen. VII* 53 b, Barges garnished with standardes, stremers and penons. *a* 1577 Sir T. Smith *Commw. Eng.* i. xviii. (1589) 33 Knights bannerets are made in the field, with the ceremonie of cutting off the poynt of his standert, and making it as it were a baner. 1644 [Walsingham] *Effigies True Fortitude* 12 His Majesties Banner Royall, vulgarly called the Standard. 1700 Tyrrell *Hist. Eng.* II. 765 The Victors carried off his Standard Royal. 1811 *Regul. & Orders Army* 11 A Field Marshal is to be saluted with the Colours and Standards of all the Forces. 1814 Wellington in Gurw. *Desp.* (1838) XII. 75 A request..that the brigade of cavalry consisting of the 5th dragoon guards, the 3rd and 4th dragoons.. should be permitted to bear the word 'Salamanca' on their Standards. *c* 1860 H. Stuart *Seaman's Catech.* 12 Who attends the standard? 1868 *Queen's Regul. Army* § 6 The Standards of Regiments of Dragoon Guards are to be of silk damask.

†b. In certain occasional uses. *Standard of trade*: a merchant ensign. *Standard of truce*: a flag of truce hoisted on a pole. *Obs.*

1449 *Paston Lett.* I. 85 Then they lonchyd a bote, and sette up a stondert of truesse. 1653 H. Cogan tr. *Pinto's Trav.* xvii. 59 A Standart of Trade hung out..to the end they might be taken for Merchants.

3. = Standard-bearer.

13.. *K. Alis.* 1995 Sendith Ymagu, youre standard, And Archilaus in the furst ward! *c* 1400 *Sowdone Bab.* 2717 'Go forth' quod the stondart, 'thou getist noon here'. 1481 Caxton *Godfrey* xcix. 150 Theyr estandart had ben longe seke by thoccasion of his hurte. 1610 Shaks. *Temp.* iii. ii. 19 Thou shalt bee my Lieutenant Monster, or my Standard. 1796 *Cavalry Instr.* (1813) 14 The standard must take care never to oblige the wheeling man to exceed a moderate gallop. 1832 *Prop. Reg. Instr. Cavalry* iii. 101 The Standard and his Coverer resume their posts.

†4. A body of troops kept in reserve in the earlier part of an engagement. *Obs.*

1297 R. Glouc. (Rolls) 8252 Þes tueye adde þe meste ost. Þat as standard was þere Vor to helpe hor felawes, wanne hii weri were.

†5. A company of cavalry. *Obs.*

1580 Hollyband *Treas. Fr. Tong*, *Vne Cornette de chevalliers*, a cornet or standard of horsemen. 1678 *Lond. Gaz.* No. 1313/3 The French have received a reinforcement of 15 Standards.

†6. Head-quarters. *Obs.*

1481 Caxton *Myrr.* ii. xviii. 106 There [in helle] deth holdeth his standard whiche sendeth out thurgh all the world for to fetche them that ben his.

7. *Bot.* The uppermost petal of a papilionaceous corolla: = Vexillum.

1776 J. Lee *Introd. Bot.* (ed. 3) 396 Papilionacea, butterfly shaped...Vexillum, the Standard, or upper Petal ascending. 1785 Martyn *Lett. Bot.* iii. (1794) 35 A large petal, covering the others, and occupying the upper part of the corolla [of a pea-blossom]; it is called the standard or banner. 1806 J. Galpine *Brit. Bot.* 329 Legumes sessile..: standard villous. 1870 Hooker *Stud. Flora* 103 Lathyrus hirsutus.. Flowers ½ in.; standard crimson.

8. *Ornith.* Each of the two lengthened wing-feathers characteristic of certain birds. Cf. Standard-wing.

1859 G. R. Gray in *Proc. Zool. Soc.* xxvii. 130 It has, springing from the lesser coverts of each wing, two long shafts, both of which are webbed on each side at the apex. It is the possession of these peculiar winged standards that induces me to propose for it the subgeneric appellation of *Semioptera*. 1862 — in *Ann. & Mag. Nat. Hist.* Ser. iii. X. 445 The ninth feather (or, as it has been termed, 'standard feather') is the longest of all. 1864 P. L. Sclater in *Ibis* VI. 115 The long 'standard feather'. 1903 W. L. Sclater *Stark's Birds S. Africa* III. 42 The ninth [primary] is prolonged to about three times the length of the first and forms the so-called streamer or standard.

II. Exemplar of measure or weight.

9. The authorized exemplar of a unit of measure or weight; e.g. a measuring rod of unit length; a vessel of unit capacity, or a mass of metal of unit weight, preserved in the custody of public officers as a permanent evidence of the legally prescribed magnitude of the unit.

Original standard: the standard of which the others are copies, and to which the ultimate appeal must be made.

1429 *Rolls of Parlt.* IV. 349/1 Weistis..acordant to ye standard of ye Chekier. *c* 1450 *Eng. Misc.* (Surtees) 61 The sayd Burgese schall haffe yᵉ standard, that is to say, the buschell, halff a buschell [etc.]..the qwhyche mesures schuld agre with the kynges standard. 1530 Palsgr. 276/2 Stondart to mesure bye, *maistresse mesure*. 1588 Lambard *Eiren.* iv. iv. 456 If they of the towne where the kings Standerd is appointed to remaine, haue not their common weights and measures signed. 1622 Bacon *Hen. VII* 201 There was also a Statute, for the dispersing of the Standard of the Exchequor, throughout England; thereby to size Weights and Measures. 1624 Massinger *Renegado* iii. iv, Let but any Indifferent gamester measure vs inch, by inch, Or waigh vs by the standard, I may passe I haue beene prou'd againe, true mettall. 1658 Phillips, *Standard*.. also the standing measure of the King, or State, to which all other measures are framed. 1681 *Peace & Truth* 7 'Tis equally Treason to serve a Usurper, and to Usurp the Regalities of the Lawful Prince by forging new Standards of Commerce. 1694 J. Smith *Horolog. Disquisit.* 45 A Royal Pendulum already Rectified, for a Standard to Adjust other Clocks by. 1728 Chambers *Cycl.* s.v. *Measure*, The sealed Gallon at Guildhall, which is the Standard for Wines, Spirits, Oils, &c. 1764 Burn *Poor Laws* 244 The statute for ascertaining the measure of ale quarts and pints according to the standard, is seldom put in execution. 1856 W. H. Miller in *Phil. Trans.* CXLVI. 753 History of the Standards of English Weight. 1870 *Pall Mall Gaz.* 2 Sept. 5 The annual report of the Warden of the Standards lately issued. 1871 C. Davies *Metric System* iii. 101 These standards were kept in the royal exchequer.

fig. 1736 Butler *Anal.* ii. viii. 399 An original standard of right and wrong in actions.

b. In abstract sense: The legal magnitude of a unit of measure or weight.

1540 *Act 32 Hen. VIII*, c. 13 § 2 Euery handfull to contein .iiii. inches of the standerde. 1609 *Ev. Wom. in Hum.* i. C, *Citty wife.* I haue a Ruffe is a quarter deepe, measured by the yard. *Hostis.* Indeede by the yard! *Citty w.* By the standard.

c. A normal uniform size or amount; a prescribed minimum size or amount.

1625 Bacon *Ess., Greatness Kingd.* (Arb.) 477 Making Farmes, and houses of Husbandry, of a Standard; That is, maintained with such a Proportion of Land vnto them, as may breed a Subiect, to liue in Conuenient Plenty. 1694 Falle *Jersey* ii. 68 Almost all our Trees are Pollards;..The Husbandman being obliged to bring his Trees to a Standard, by Lopping of those..Luxuriant branches which..would cover his little Plots.

†d. A unit of measurement. *Obs. rare.*

1646 Sir T. Browne *Pseud. Ep.* vi. iii. 284 As for the divisions of the yeare, and the quartering out this remarkable standard of time, there have passed especially two distinctions. 1830 Herschel *Study Nat. Phil.* 125 As a first preliminary towards effecting this, we fix on convenient standards of weight, dimension, time, &c.

¶ e. Sometimes misused for: Actual stature.

1833 Nyren *Yng. Cricketer's Tutor* (1902) 135 John was a stoutly-made man; his standard about five feet ten inches.

f. The substance or thing which is chosen to afford the unit measure of any physical quantity, such as specific gravity.

1805 R. Jameson *Char. Min.* (1817) 266 Water is the standard with which all other bodies are compared. 1815 J. Smith *Panorama Sci. & Art* II. 486 Water..is employed as the standard of comparison in all tables of specific gravities. 1869 C. H. Gill *Chem. for Sch.* xxii. 274 Dalton ..adopted it [*sc.* hydrogen] as the unit or standard of atomic weight.

g. *Bowls.* A light reed or cane used to measure the distance of rival bowls from the jack.

1876 *Encycl. Brit.* IV. 180/2. 1897 *Encycl. Sport* I. 123/2.

10. (Originally *fig.* from 9.) An authoritative or recognized exemplar of correctness, perfection, or some definite degree of any quality.

1477 Norton *Ord. Alch.* Proem., in Ashm. (1652) 9 This Boke; Named of Alkimy the Ordinall, The Crede mihi, the Standard perpetuall. 1665 Boyle *Occas. Refl.* v. v. (1848) 316 Men will be asham'd to be unlike those, whose Customs and Deportments pass for the Standards, by which those of other Men are to be measur'd. 1676 Hale *Contempl.* i. 304 He was exhibited, as the common standard and pattern of a Christian's condition. 1691 T. H[ale] *Acc. New Invent.* p. cvii, These Draughts of the Rivers serving as the Standards by which all future Enlargements or Diminutions ..may be guided. 1709 Felton *Diss. Classics* (1718) 147 Among the Romans, Horace is the Standard of Lyric, and Virgil of Epic Poetry. 1710 *Caldwell Papers* (Maitl. Club) I. 219 They [at Hanover] believe themselves a standart that mankind should be guided by. 1742 West *Let.* in *Gray's Poems* (1775) 136 [Racine's] language is the language of the times, and that of the purest sort; so that his French is reckoned a standard. 1777 Sir W. Jones *Poems*, etc. Pref. 14 We always return to the writings of the ancients, as the standard of true taste. 1789 Mrs. Piozzi *Journ. France* II. 139 Let us learn better than to set up self, whether nation or individual, as a standard to which all others must be reduced. 1838–9 Hallam *Hist. Lit.* IV. iv. vii. § 11. 299 The Academy rendered this dictionary the most received standard of the French language.

b. A rule, principle, or means of judgement or estimation; a criterion, measure.

1563 Winȝet *Bk. 83 Quest.* Wks. (S. T. S.) I. 53 At Pasche ..thai..ministrate the sacramentis til ws on the Catholik manere; and be Witsonday thai change thair standart in our plane contrare. 1673 Dryden *Amboyna* Ep. Ded. A 3 b, You have serv'd Him..: making His Greatness, and the true Interest of your Country, the standard and measure of your actions. 1681 — *Abs. & Achit.* 785 Nor is the people's judgment always true:..What standard is there in a fickle rout, Which, flowing to the mark, runs faster out? 1779 *Mirror* No. 30 ¶ 8 Let them [the inexperienced] not believe that the scale of fortune is the standard of happiness. 1781 Gibbon *Decl. & F.* xx. (1787) II. 201 Personal interest is often the standard of our belief, as well as of our practice. 1790 Burke *Fr. Rev.* 61 The degree of estimation in which any profession is held becomes the standard of the estimation in which the professors hold themselves. 1836 J. Gilbert *Chr. Atonem.* ii. (1852) 37 Without a prior standard somewhere presupposed, who shall ascertain the quality of what is willed? 1837 Lockhart *Scott* II. iii. 86 Scott had by no means measured..the character..of great public functionaries, by the standard with which observation and experience subsequently furnished him. 1888 Bryce *Amer. Commw.* I. x. 126 The English reader must be cautioned against applying his English standards to the examination of the American system.

c. *pl.* The books or documents accepted by a church as the authoritative statement of its creed. Hence *occas.* in *sing.*

1841 *Penny Cycl.* XXI. 175/1 All the divisions of the Seceders..agree in adopting as their standards, in addition to the Westminster Confession of Faith [certain works of their founders]. 1848 G. Struthers *Hist. Relief Ch.* 293 These considerations..induced them simply to proclaim their adherence to the Westminster standards. 1881 J. Macpherson *Westm. Confess. of Faith* (1882) 1 A Confession of Faith..is accepted by members of churches acknowledging it, simply as a subordinate standard.

11. Legal rate of intrinsic value for coins; also, the prescribed degree of fineness for gold or silver.

1463 *Ir. Acts*, 3 *Edw. IV*, c. 32 Forasmuche as the said moneis of silver may not continually be made according to his right estandert. 1551 Sir J. Williams *Accompte* (Abbotsf. Club) 91 Golde..coyned into crownes of vs a pece, according to the standerde apperteyninge to the mynte. 1568 Grafton *Chron.* II. 121 At thys tyme was vsed to be coyned that standard and finenesse that was called sterling money. 1601 in *Stafford's Pac. Hib.* ii. iv. (1633) 149 Being meerely dependant of our Prerogatiue to alter the Standerd of our Moneys at our pleasure. 1638 *Charter Goldsm. Co.* in A. Ryland *Assay Gold & Silver* (1852) 28 The standards for gold are 22 and 18 carats of pure metal in every ounce...The coinage is of the higher standard...The lower standard is used for all manufacturing purposes...The standards for silver are 11 oz. 10 dwt., and 11 oz. 2 dwt. of pure metal in every pound troy. ..The higher standard is never used. 1691 Locke *Consid. Raising Value Money* Wks. 1714 II. 68 That precise Weight and Fineness, by Law appropriated to the Pieces of each Denomination, is called the Standard. *a* 1700 Evelyn *Diary* 19 Sept. 1683, He said it must be finer than the standard, such as was old angel gold. 1702 *Lond. Gaz.* No. 3863/4 Lost.., a wrought Silver-Candlestick, old Standard. 1722 De Foe *Col. Jack* (1840) 78 Good tower standard. 1757 Harris *Money & Coins* 36 Trade requires..an indelible standard of money. 1772–3 *Act* 13 *Geo. III*, c. 52 § 4 Plate, being of the standard of eleven ounces ten pennyweight of fine silver per pound troy [shall be marked with] the figure of..Britannia.

fig. 1672 Marvell *Reh. Transp.* i. 271 The wit of France and England..hath at all times gone much after the same current Rate and Standard.

b. (Originally, †*standard of commerce.*) A commodity, the value of which is treated as invariable, in order that it may serve as a measure of value for all other commodities.

1683 *Brit. Spec.* 47 Some one or other Commodity was every where found out to be the Standard of Commerce and Traffick. 1757 Harris *Money & Coins* 84 In these parts of the world, silver is, and time immemorial hath been, the money standard. 1776 Adam Smith *W. N.* i. v. 43 Labour..is..the only standard by which we can compare the values of different commodities at all times and at all places. 1825 McCulloch *Pol. Econ.* i. 25 Having been used ..as standards whereby to measure the relative value of different commodities.

12. A definite level of excellence, attainment, wealth, or the like, or a definite degree of any quality, viewed as a prescribed object of endeavour or as the measure of what is adequate for some purpose.

Standard of living, of comfort: the view prevailing in a community or class with regard to the minimum of material comfort with which it is reasonable to be content.

1711 Shaftesbury *Charact.* (1732) III. 138 'Twas thus they [the Greeks] brought their beautiful and comprehensive Language to a just Standard...The Standard was in the same proportion carry'd into other Arts. 1748 Melmoth *Fitzosborne Lett.* lvii. (1749) II. 86 For may not publick happiness be estimated by the same standard as that of private? 1766 Fordyce *Serm. Young Women* (1767) I. i. 11 Act up to the best standard of your sex. 1780 *Mirror* No. 79 ¶ 18 We are told that those manners should be painted, not as they are found in nature, but according to an ideal standard of perfection in what is called the golden age. *c* 1800 Pegge *Anecd. Eng. Lang.* (1803) 38 During his translation of Quintus Curtius..it [*sc.* the French language] had varied so much that he was obliged to correct the former part of the work to bring it to the standard of the other. 1827 Lytton *Falkland* i. 45 Neither in person nor in character was he much beneath or above the ordinary standard of men. 1903 A. McNeill *Egregious English* xx. 186 The standard of living in England is an..artificial standard. Practically every Englishman lives, or longs to live, beyond his means.

b. In British elementary schools: Each of the recognized degrees of proficiency, as tested by examination, according to which school children are classified.

The sixth is the highest standard which children are ordinarily required to pass, the seventh being intended mainly for those who are to become teachers.

1876 Lubbock *Elementary Educ.* in *Contemp. Rev.* June 79 The classes from which the children are examined in Standards II–VI. 1894 *Times* 22 Mar. 4/6 He..was in the class of which defendant was teacher—viz., the seventh standard. 1899 *Allbutt's Syst. Med.* VIII. 204 In some schools there is a standard o..for dull or backward children. 1902 Violet Jacob *Sheep-Stealers* xv, When the village urchins..are still wrestling with the fourth 'standard'.

attrib. 1891 Hardy *Tess* xix, She was expressing in her own native phrases—assisted a little by her Sixth Standard training—feelings which [etc.]. 1903 A. McNeill *Egregious English* i. 9 Nature, like the seventh-standard boy in a board school, 'can get no higher'.

c. *Sporting.* (See quot.)

1897 *Encycl. Sport* I. 62/2 (Athletics) *Standard*, the time or distance assigned to each event at a championship meeting, by beating which a competitor becomes entitled to a medal.

13. †a. Some fixed numerical quantity. (? A quarter hundred, 25.) *Obs.*

1545 *Rates Custom Ho.* b vj, Knyues of collayne the groce xxx. s. Knyues of roue the standerde v. s.

b. A definite quantity of timber, differing in different countries. (Cf. *standard deal*, B 1 c.)

1858 Simmonds *Dict. Trade*, *Standard*,..a solid measure by which hewn timber is estimated, varying in different timber countries. 1864 *Daily Tel.* 17 Aug., A 'Petersburgh Standard'..consists of 120 deals of 12 feet long by 11 inches wide and 1½ inch thick. [This = 165 cubic feet.] 1891 *Law Times* XCI. 192/2 The vessel contained about 1000 standards...A standard was 165 cubic feet of timber.

†14. A kind of arrow (distinguished from 'bearing arrow' and 'flight'). *Obs.*

Perh. short for 'standard arrow', which occurs in later citations of 16th c. documents. See quot. 1465.

[1465 *Ir. Acts*, 5 *Edw. IV*, c. 4 (1786) I. 29 It is ordeyned ..That every Englishman..shall have an English bow.. with twelve shafts of the length of three quarters of the standard.] 1557 *City of Lond. Jrnl.* 17 lf. 46 in *Vicary's Anat.* (1888) App. iii. 177–8 Who will comme..and take a longe bowe in his hande—having the standarde therin therefore prouyded,..shall haue for the best game a Crown of golde...And for the best game of the bearing arrowe, he shall haue [etc.]...And for the best game of the flight, he shall haue [etc.]...And..there shalbe a trumpett blowen at eueryе shott, aswell of the standarde, as of the arrowe or flight. 1598 Stow *Surv. Lond.* 77 Of old time..the Officers of the Citie..were challengers of all men..to shoote the Standarde, broade arrow, and flight, for games. [1682 W. M. (W. Wood) *Remembr. Show & Shooting*, 1583, 51 Then came the Duke..bearing a Standard Arrow in his hand.]

15. The market price per ton of copper in the ore.

1855 Leifchild *Cornwall* 233 The term 'standard of copper'..denotes the estimated value of the fine copper per ton, considered from the various assays to be in the ores sold; less a fixed sum per ton..deducted for the cost of smelting... When I began this book the standard of copper was £125, 5s., but it has since varied considerably. 1913 *Times* 13 Sept. 18/5 London, Sept. 12.—Copper...Standard continued its advance on Monday.

16. Short for: a. *standard book* (see Standard *a.* 3 b); b. (*Dyeing*) *standard solution* (see Standard *a.* 1 b).

1882 Crookes *Dyeing & Tissue-Printing* 379 A set of so-called 'standards'. These are mixtures of colouring matters and mordants not liable to undergo change or decomposition, and which merely require the addition of a thickener ..to be ready for printing. 1889 *Amer. Publ. Weekly* 30 Mar. 462 The old-fashioned book-store, with its supply of standards on the shelves tempting a customer to increase his library.

III. Senses associated with the verb *stand*.

†17. A lofty erection of timber or stone, containing a vertical conduit pipe with spouts and taps, for the supply of water to the public. *Obs.*

'The Standard in Cornhill' continued as the name of a point from which distances were measured, long after the 'standard' had disappeared.

1434 *Cov. Leet Bk.* 157 Þat þe stondard of þe cundyte in þe Smythford-strete..shall not be doon awaye. 1517 *Chron. Grey Friars* (Camden) 30 At the stondert in Cheppe. 1580 *Memoriall W. Lumbe* c ij, A standart with one cocke at Holborne bridge. 1598 Stow *Surv. Lond.* 316 A standard of timber with a cocke or cockes, deliuering fayre spring water to the inhabitants. 1616 B. Jonson *Devil an Ass* i. i, I will fetch thee a leape From the top of Pauls-steeple, to the Standard in Cheepe. 1665 Sir T. Herbert *Trav.* (1677) 164 Towers, most of which are terrassed near the top like the Standard in Cheap-side. 1854 Thackeray *Newcomes* ii, This paradise, five miles from the standard at Cornhill.

18. A tall candlestick. Now *spec.* a tall candlestick (or, in recent use, an upright gas candelabrum) rising directly from the floor of a church.

a 1420 *Aunters of Arthur* 451 (Thornton MS.) Sythene he..clathes gune calle, Sanapes and salers..Preketes and broketes, and standertes [*Douce* stondardes, *Irel.* stondartis] by-twene. 1488 in *Archæologia* XLV. 116 A payre of Candelstyckks, greate standards for grete tapers, of tynne. 1538 *Ibid.* XLIII. 218, ij greate standers of laten; ij lampes. 1553 in Daniel-Tyssen *Surrey Ch. Goods* (1869) 97 Item ij stondardes of lattyn. 1605 Treswell *Journ. Earl Nottingham* 51 The roome was garnished with three hundred and twenty lights of wax, al set in standerds of siluer, of diuers fashions. 1851 Pugin *Chancel Screens* 23 This screen is surmounted by standards for wax tapers. 1860 *Ecclesiologist* XXI. 72 The church is lighted with brass gas standards.

†b. (See quot.) Cf. OF. *estandart*, a kind of torch. *Obs.*

1611 Florio, *Doppione*, a great torch of waxe, which we call a standard or a quarrier.

19. An upright timber, bar, or rod; e.g. †a tall pole erected for display on an occasion of rejoicing or festivity (*obs.*); an upright scaffold pole; an upright bar for a window: an upright support or pedestal in various machines. In recent use often, a slender and lofty iron pillar carrying an electric or gas lamp, overhead electric wires, or the like.

c 1450 *Brut* 487 At the Ledenhall in Cornhill..a standard of tre was set in myddys of the pavement fast in the grounde, nayled with holme and Ive, for disport of Cristmasse to þe peple of the Cite. 1477–9 *Rec. St. Mary at Hill* (1905) 85 For xxv foote of Elmyn borde, for steppes and standardis for the same steyre, vj d. 1486 *Nottingham Rec.* III. 257 To ij. sawers for sawyng of þe standerdes of the chymney. 1502 *Privy Purse Exp. Eliz. York* (1830) 25 Item..to John Coneway smyth for foure transoms and xij standerdes. *c* 1580 in *Fabric Rolls York Minster* (Surtees) 118 For helping to carry into the wryghte housse standerdes, powles and boordes. 1587 Mascall *Cattle* (1596) 72 Their standarts and posts to fasten them [oxen] by, would be round and smooth. 1609 Holland *Amm. Marcell.* xxiii. iii. 222 Whereupon the standard [of a ballista: L. *stilus*] being now at libertie with that quicke stroke..hurleth out the stone. 1627 in *Maitl. Club Misc.* III. 369 *note*, For gilting the Cok and thanis and culloring of the same yallow with the glob and standart and stanes above the steiple heid. 1703 Moxon *Mech. Exerc.* 251 Fir Poles, of several lengths for Standards and Ledgers for Scaffolding. 1813 *Gentl. Mag.* LXXXIII. 227/2 The pyramidal iron lamp standards in the outer court. 1823 P. Nicholson *Pract. Build.* 593 Standards; the upright poles used in scaffolding. In joinery, the upright pieces of a plate-rack. 1839 Ure *Dict. Arts* 268 An apparatus with cutters attached to a standard. 1840 F. Whishaw *Railw. Gt. Brit. & Irel.* 128 The mile-standards are of wood,..and are placed at intervals of a quarter of a mile. *Ibid.* 391 The distances are marked from either end of the line on stone standards. 1856 Hurlstone & Gordon *Exch. Rep.* XI. 183 The wires..for the..use of the railway company rest upon all the posts or standards in the respondent's township. 1869 Rankine *Machine & Hand-tools* Pl. D 5, The same turning table also carries the standard, F, which supports the main gearing. 1883 *Law Times Rep.* XLIX. 139/1 The scaffolding in front was constructed of five standards or uprights and one ledger. 1885 *Act* 48 & 49 *Vict.* c. 50 § 4 (iv), The purchase and erection of lamp standards. 1892 *Labour Commission Gloss.*, *Standards*, two standards, *i.e.*, two wooden legs with feet, which are often used instead of four legs to support the top frame of a table. 1907 H. Wyndham *Flare of Footlights* xxxiii, At intervals [along the Embankment] rose the tall standards of the electric lights.

b. *Naut.* An inverted knee-timber, having the vertical portion turned upwards.

1748 *Anson's Voy.* ii. iv. 158 Two standards were broken. 1750 Blanckley *Nav. Expositor*, Standards are a Sort of Knees fay'd from the Deck to the Sides of the Ship withinboard, to strengthen her in the same Manner as Knees, but are bigger. 1769 Falconer *Dict. Marine* (1780) s.v. *Architecture* D, The standard of the head which fastens it to the stem. 1874 Thearle *Naval Archit.* iii. xiii. 222 Standards are knees for connecting the stern posts to the deck beams of screw ships...Standards were fitted in sailing ships connecting the fore side of inner post with the after end of the keelson.

†c. *Coachmaking.* ? Each of the four corner posts of a coach. *Obs.*

1659 Pepys *Diary* 26 Apr., I..do resolve upon having the standards of my coach gilt with this new sort of varnish. *Ibid.* 1 May, We went alone through the town with our new liveries..and the standards thus gilt with varnish.

d. In a plough: = Sheath *sb.*⁴

1652 Blithe *Eng. Improver Impr.* ii. xxix. (1653) 205 By a Standard put into the end of it [*sc.* the plough-beam]. 1727 R. Bradley *Compl. Body Husb.* 43 in *Compl. Farmer* (1766) s.v. *Plough*, CC are the sheaths or standards.

e. *Figure-weaving.* (See quot.)

1831 G. R. Porter *Silk Manuf.* 284 The leaves [of heddles in a gauze loom] numbered 1 and 2 which are called standards.

f. (See quot.)

1866 J. H. Parker *Concise Gloss. Terms Archit.* 251 *Standard*..was also applied to the ends of the oak benches in churches, and that is the common use of the term now.

20. a. *Forestry.* A tree or shoot from a stump left standing when a coppice is cut down.

1473 Sir J. Paston in *P. Lett.* III. 86 That the standardes off suche mesur as he and I comonyd off maye also be reservyd. I suppose it was xxx. inche, abowt a yerde from the grownde. 1577 B. Googe *Heresbach's Husb.* ii. (1586) 95 b, I sette them on the outside of my Orchard, as standards to defend their fellowes from tempest and weather. 1669 Worlidge *Syst. Agric.* vi. 94 Felling of Coppices...Trimming up such as you spare for standards, as you go. 1677 Plot *Oxfordsh.* 206 That ancient Standard in the high-Park, known of all by the name of the Kings Oak. 1799 J. Robertson *Agric. Perth* 238 If the advantage of the copse alone is attended to, no standard should be left, except such seedlings as appear necessary to renew the stocks. 1832 *Planting* 91 in *Husbandry* (*Libr. Usef. Knowl.*) III, Standard.—The shoots of a coppice stool, selected from those cut down as underwood to remain for large poles or timber-trees.

transf. 1776 [W. Marshall] *Minutes Agric.* 31 July 1775, This pulled up the running weeds; the standards left, were readily drawn by hand.

b. *Gardening.* A tree or shrub growing on an erect stem of full height, not dwarfed or trained on a wall or espalier.

1625 Bacon *Ess., Gardens* (Arb.) 562 Part of which Heapes, to be with Standards, of little Bushes, prickt upon their Top...The Standards to be Roses; Iuniper; Holly [etc.]. 1685 Temple *Gardening* Wks. 1770 III. 218 [Gardens] part laid out for flowers, others for fruits; some standards, some against walls or palisadoes. 1688 Holme *Armoury* ii. 86/2 Standards are trees standing of themselves, not on Wall sides. 1713 *Guardian* No. 173 (1756) II. 359 The trees, which were standards, and suffered to grow to their full height. 1846 Baxter *Libr. Pract. Agric.* (ed. 4) I. 261 The fig-tree may be grown either as a standard, espalier, or against a wall. 1903 *Q. Rev.* Oct. 430 The only material difference between the experiments on dwarfs and standards respectively is that [etc.].

†21. A kind of collar of mail or plate armour. *Obs.* exc. *Hist.*

[1371–3 *Acc. Exch. K. R.* 397/10 m. 3 Cxliiij standardis pro loricis.] 1465 *Will of T. Packet* in *Fairholt's Costume* (1885) II. 379 A standard of gesserant garneshed with silver. 1465 Marg. Paston in *P. Lett.* II. 190 Sertyn harnys...Inprimis;..a standard of mayle [etc.]. *c* 1490 in *5th Rep. Hist. MSS. Comm.* 445/1 Fower standardys with two gossetts of mayl. 1530 Palsgr. 275/2 Standart of mayle, *gorgerin*. 1885 *Fairholt's Costume* (ed. 3) I. 205 [On monuments 1391 and 1412] the camail is replaced by, or covered over with, a standard of plate.

†22. Some kind of service-book. *Obs.*

c 1400 in *Fabric Rolls York Minster* (Surtees) 244 Super librum vocatum standard. 1409 *Ibid.* 245 Standerdes, ac eciam libri processionales, [etc.]. 1503 *Visit. Southwell* (Camden) 71 Libri in choro vulgariter vocati le Standarıbs.

†23. A large packing-case or chest. *Obs.*

1371–3 *Acc. Exch. K. R.* 397/10 m. 3, j. standard magn[um] ferro ligatum, vj. Ciste magne ferro ligate. 1454 *Inv.* in *T. H. Turner's Dom. Archit.* (1859) III. 113 A square standarde, & covered with blaak letheir, & bowden with yrne, with 2 lokys...A grete red standerd, full of stuff. ..A gret standard of the chapell, bounde wth ierne, with 2 lokks. 1530 *Privy Purse Exp. Hen. VIII* (1827) 43 For ij standardes for to cary plate fro yorke place to hampton courte. *a* 1562 G. Cavendish *Wolsey* (1893) 183 The kyng caused to be sent hyme iii or iiii cartloods of stuffe, and most parte thereof was lokked in great standerds. 1663 *Cheque Bk. Chapel Royal* (Camden) 83 The Sergeant shall ..deliver the Gentlemen their surplices out of the standard. *Ibid.* 93 Item, three standards, whereof one is for the song books of our sayd Chapell.

†24. *Coining.* ? = Pile *sb.*⁴ 1. *Obs.*

1473 *Chancery Enrolments, Durham* 3/49 m. 6 (P.R.O.), We..haue..licencid..William Omorighe..to make graue and prynte ij dosene Trussellys and j dosene Standerdys for penys and .iiij. Standerdys and viiij. Trussellys for half penys. 1477 *Ibid.* 3/52 m. 4 (P.R.O.), To make..iij. dosen Trussels and .ij. dosen Standerdys for penys, and ij. dosen trussels and j. dosen Standerdys for halfpenys.

25. *s.w. dial.* 'A large standing tub used for washing purposes, for containing salted meat, etc.' (*Eng. Dial. Dict.*).

1535 in Weaver *Wells Wills* (1890) 116, ii. vates, a standerde, a barell and a kole.

26. †a. Something permanent; something that has lasted a long time. In *plural*, Permanent or necessary furniture or apparatus (of a household, etc.). *Obs.*

1492 *Deed* A. 8331 in *Catal. Anc. Deeds P. R. O.* (1902) IV. 292 [She to have all the goods and chattels of the said Sir William] except the stondardys of howseholde [and all his growing corn, etc.]. 1506 *Will J. Cornewallis* in *Privy Purse Exp. Eliz. York* (1830) 224/2 All the brewyng vessells and standards in the brewhouse and bakehouse. 1639 Fuller *Holy War* i. xxiii. (1640) 35 The mountains..are standards too great..for either time or warre to remove. 1650 — *Pisgah* v. 191 So there are certain standards in all visions, being the materiall and corporall ground-work, for a spirituall flourish..to improve itself thereupon. 1655 H. L'Estrange *Reign K. Charles* 157 The Queen was loath to proscribe so long a standard as Episcopacy, to entertain such an upstart in-mate as Presbytery.

b. One who has been long in a position; an old resident, official, servant, etc. Now only *old standard* (rare exc. dial.).

a 1661 Fuller *Worthies, Gen.* xi. (1662) i. 38 The Ficklenesse and Fugitivenesse of such Servants, justly addeth a valuation to their Constancy, who are Standards in a Family. 1665 Wood *Life* (O.H.S.) II. 45 This Dʳ. was an old standard ..and at leisure times he would entertaine A. W. with old stories relating to the universitie. 1768 in *10th Rep. Hist. MSS. Comm.* App. i. 410, I believe [the new Cabinet will harmonize] well.., the old standards are usefull & I think makes every office better.

†27. *Cookery.* (Of somewhat obscure meaning; usually explained as 'principal or standing dish'.)

1513 *Bk. Kervynge* in *Babees Bk.* 157 For standarde, venyson roste, kydde, fawne & cony [etc.]. *Ibid.* 166 The seconde course. Gelly whyte and rede..samon, dorrey, brytte, turbot, halybut; for standarde, base, troute [etc.]. 1526 in J. Croft *Excerpta Ant.* (1797) 79 Item, a Roe roasted for Standart. *Ibid.* 80 Item, for a Standart Cranes, two of a Dish.

†28. A suit (of clothes): = Stand *sb.*¹ 23 a. *Obs.*

1630 B. Jonson *New Inn*, Argt. ii, The Lady had commanded a standard of her owne best apparrell to bee brought downe. *Ibid.* ii. ii, We ha' brought a standard of apparrell, down, Because this Taylor fayld vs i' the maine.

†b. ? A set (of plumes). *Obs.*

1578 *Invent. R. Wardr.* (1815) 238 Foure standeris of fedderis for the toppis of beddis.

IV. *attrib.* and *Comb.*

29. Simple attrib. a. in sense 1, as *standard-car*, *-flag*, *-guard*, *half-squadron*, *-pole*, *-shaft*, *-sheet*, *-spear*, *-staff*.

1848 *W. Hemingburgh's Chronicon* I. 59 *note*, The carroccio, or great *standard-car, is said to have been invented ..in the year 1035. 1821 *Sporting Mag.* VII. 106 When potent nature her *standard-flag rears. 1750 *Phil. Trans.* XLVII. 6 A soldier being confin'd to a tent call'd the *standard-guard. 1796 *Cavalry Instr.* (1813) 227 The commanding officer in the rear of the *standard half squadron. *a* 1700 Evelyn *Diary* 23 Nov. 1644, The ropes and cables which support the *standard-pole. 1497 *Naval Acc. Hen. VII* (1896) 89 *Standard shaftes. 1799 Campbell *Pleas. Hope* ii. 180 The stormy showers..Freeze every *standard-sheet. 1825 Scott *Talism.* xi, [He] laid his hand on the *standard-spear, as if to pluck it from the ground. 1560 Phaer *Æneid* ix. (1562) E e ij b, His fyriesmoking bronds on *standard-staff Mezentius shooke. 1802 C. James *Milit. Dict.*, *Soc*, a machine..fixed near the stirrup, to receive the end of the standard staff. 1855 Kingsley *Westw. Ho!* xx, His left hand on the standard-staff, his sword pointed in his right.

b. in sense 9, as *standard mark*.

1858 Simmonds *Dict. Trade*, *Standard-mark*, a legal assay mark for gold of 22 carats fine, and for silver of 11 oz. 2 dwts. 1884 F. J. Britten *Watch & Clockm.* 116 The Standard Mark of the London Hall is a lion passant for sterling silver. 1889 Gretton *Memory's Harkback* 73 In stature and in grasp of mind rather below standard-mark.

c. in sense 12 b.

1882 S. C. Buxton in *19th Cent.* Nov. 792 The standard subjects are the three R's, while the class subjects include English grammar, geography..and needlework.

30. Special comb.: **standard-bred** *a.*, of horses, etc., bred up to the standard of excellence prescribed by some authority; **standard-high** *a.*, of the height of a standard shrub (see B. 5); **standard lamp**, a lamp with a tall standard resting on the floor (either moveable, as a lamp for domestic use, or fixed, as in churches).

1891 *Century Dict.*, *Standard-bred. 1901 *Westm. Gaz.* 28 Sept. 4/3 The standard-bred mare. 1842 Loudon *Suburban Hort.* 555 Standard cherry trees are generally budded *standard high, on free stocks of three years' growth from the seed. 1900 G. Swift *Somerley* 124 [He] came and stood with me under the light of the tall *standard-lamp.

B. *adj.* [Attributive use of the sb.]

I. 1. Serving as a standard of measurement, weight or value; conformed to the official standard of a unit of measure or weight.

1622 Malynes *Anc. Law-Merch.* 306 If it bee appointed of make a Standard peece of tenne ounces fine. 1669 Beale in *Phil. Trans.* IV. 1113 A measure, taken exactly from the standard-foot of London. 1827 Faraday *Chem. Manip.* iii. (1842) 67 The standard or imperial pint now to be used is larger than the wine pint. 1862 H. Spencer *First Princ.* ii. vi. § 61 (1875) 192 a, From the standard-measure preserved at Westminster, are derived the measures for trigonometrical surveys. 1870 Jevons *Elem. Logic* xxxiii. 290 A yard or foot has no meaning unless there be a definite standard yard or foot which fixes the meaning. 1871 B. Stewart *Heat* (ed. 2) § 25 The difference between mercurial and the standard air thermometer becomes very considerable at high temperatures. 1873 J. C. Maxwell *Electr. & Magn.* (1881) II. 322 When it is intended to measure a current [electric] with the greatest accuracy in terms of standard units, it is called a Standard Galvanometer. 1878 Jevons *Primer Pol. Econ.* 108 In the English system of money, gold is the standard money and the legal tender. 1879 *Cassell's Techn. Educ.* II. 175 The *unit* of calculation adopted in practice is a sperm candle one-sixth of a pound in weight and burning 120 grains per hour; this is called a 'standard candle', and the 'standard burner' in use in London is Sugg's London Argand, Number 1. 1884 Knight *Dict. Mech.* Suppl., *Standard Battery* (Electricity). One to be used as a standard, having a perfectly constant electro-motive force.

b. Having the prescribed or normal size, amount, power, degree of quality, etc.

Standard gauge (Railways): see quot. 1884; also *attrib.*

1807 T. Thomson *Chem.* (ed. 2) 165 He calculated, that the increase of density, on mixing different quantities of standard acid and water, was [etc.]. 1813 J. Thomson *Lect. Inflam.* 113 In hectic fever the temperature seldom rises two or three degrees above the natural or standard temperature. 1825 J. Nicholson *Oper. Mech.* 550 The standard thickness of a brick wall is 1½ brick laid lengthwise...A rod of standard brick-work..will require 4500 bricks. 1826 *Art of Brewing* (ed. 2) 17 To..evaporate the unnecessary quantity to a standard gravity. 1857 Miller *Elem. Chem., Org.* 60 For the preparation of the standard copper solutions. 1878 Stewart & Tait *Unseen Univ.* iii. § 107. 120 That of boiling water under the standard pressure is 374°. 1881 *Chicago Times* 12 Mar., A standard-gauge railroad. 1884 Knight *Dict. Mech.* Suppl. s.v., 'Standard gage' means 4′ 8½″ between centers of rails. 1889 *Hardwicke's Science-Gossip* XXV. 184/2 They are rectangular in shape, and are made of one standard size. 1900 P. N. Hasluck *Model Engin. Handybk.* 43 All the small parts..would be made to some standard measurement. 1904 D. J. Shackleton *Sp. Ho. Comm.* 23 Mar. in *Hansard* 553 In using the words standard rate of wages in his Resolution, he desired the House to understand that he meant the trade union rate. *Ibid.* 557 That this House is of opinion that the wages paid to the unskilled workers in Government factories..should be not less than the standard rate of wages.

c. *Standard deal*: see quots.

1834 McCulloch *Dict. Comm.* (ed. 2) 1150, 36½ Russian stand[ard] deals 12 ft. long, 1½ inch thick, 11 inch broad, make 1 load timber. 1867 Smyth *Sailor's Word-bk.*, *Standard-Deals*, those planks of the pine or fir above 7 inches wide and 6 feet long.

d. Of bread (see quot.).

1851 Mayhew *Lond. Labour* I. 178 Previously to 1815 bakers were restricted..to the baking of three kinds of bread—wheaten, standard wheaten, and household. The wheaten was made of the best flour, the standard wheaten of the different kinds of flour mixed together.

2. Of precious metals, coins: Conforming to the legal standard of fineness or intrinsic value. Also said of value or fineness.

1677 W. B. *Touchst. Gold & Silver* (title-p.), Discovering ..how to know Adulterated Wares from those made of the True Standard Alloy. 1691 Locke *Consid. Raising Value Money* Wks. 1714 II. 68 The Fineness of Standard Silver in England is eleven parts Silver, and one part Copper, near. 1706 Phillips (ed. Kersey), *Jacobus*,..a Gold-coin..of two sorts, viz. the Broad Piece of Twenty Shillings Standard-value..and the 22s. Broad-Piece. 1790 Keir in *Phil. Trans.* LXXX. 370, I added 144 grains of standard silver. 1809 R. Langford *Introd. Trade* 38 Standard Gold contains 11 parts of pure Gold, and 1 part of alloy. Standard Silver contains 37 parts of pure Silver, and 3 parts of alloy. 1866 Crump *Banking* x. 230 The standard purity of the sovereign underwent many changes. 1879 *Cassell's Techn. Educ.* IV. 308/2 Standard gold which implies the quality used for coinage..is..what is called twenty-two carat.

3. Serving or fitted to serve as a standard of comparison or judgement.

1724 A. Collins *Gr. Chr. Relig.* 103 It seems incredible, that Origen..and other Christians of his time..should receive an Old Testament (and that with the greatest applause for its integrity, and as a standard Text) from enemies.

STANDARD.

Standard-bearer.

Standard-wing.

Standard-winged, a. Ornith.

Stand-by.

Standardbearing.

Standardism.

Standardization.

Standardize, v.

Standardee, Standee.

Standel.

Standelwelks. Obs. Also standweks.

Standelwort. Obs. Also standelwort.

Standen-gurse, Standergrass.

Stander.

STANDER.

Standerful, Standful.

Standergrass.

Standful.

Standing.

Standfast.

Standgale.

STANDING.

STANDING.

Standing lottery, one that remains open and redrawn for a specified long period. *Obs.*

Standing stone. [STANDING *ppl. a.*] A large block of stone set upright; a menhir, monolith.

Standing-place.

A place prepared or assigned for a person or thing to stand in; a place to accommodate persons standing.

Standish.

Obs. exc. Hist. or arch. A stand containing ink, pens and other writing materials and accessories (see quots.); an inkstand.

Stand-out.

[f. vbl. phr. *stand out* (after lock-out): see STAND v. 99.] A workmen's strike.

Stand-pipe, sb.

A vertical pipe for the conveyance of water, gas, steam or the like to a higher level.

Standpoint.

A fixed point of standing; the position in which a person stands to view an object, scene or the like.

Stand-still, sb. and a.

A state of cessation of movement; a halt.

Stand.

A stand-up fight.

STANG.

A long pole or bar. Now dial.

Stangster.

STAP.

Stangster.

Stanhope.

Stank.

Stannary.

Stannate.

Stannine.

Stannite.

Stanno-.

Stannotype.

Stannous.

Stannum.

Stanza.

STAP. — 825 — STAPLE.

Stap, affected pronunciation of Stop v., in the phrase *Stap my vitals*, used as an exclamation of surprise, anger, etc., or as an asseveration.

Stap, Sc. form of Stop sb. and v.

Stape, obs. f. Step.

Stapedectomy (stæpidéktŏmi). *Surg.* [f. mod.L. staped- Stapes + Ectomy.] Excision of the stapes.

Stapedial (stăpī·diăl), a. Anat. [f. mod.L. staped-es (see Stapedius) + -al.] Pertaining to the stapes.

Stapediform (stăpē·difŏɹm), a. Anat. [f. staped- Stapes + -(i)form.] Stirrup-shaped.

Stapedius (stăpī·diŏs). Anat. [mod.L.] A muscle.

Stapes (stæ·pīz). [mod.L. use of med.L. stapes (stirrup)] Stirrup (sense 1).

Staphisagria (stæfisā·griă). *Bot.* Also -agre, -agris: see Stavesacre.

Staphisagriated (stæfisā·griĕtĕd), a. *Pharm.* [f. staphisagria (see next) + -ate + -ed[1].]

Staphisagrine (stæfisā·grin). *Chem.* Also -ine. [f. mod.L. staphisagria, which is abnormally formed.]

Staphisaine (stæfisæ·in). *Chem.*

Staphyle (stæ·fili), a. [ad. late Gr. σταφυλώμα, pertaining to a bunch of grapes, f. σταφυλή + -ηωμα.]

Staphylectomy. *Surg.*

Staphylic (stăfī·lik), a. and n. Ent.

Staphylinid (stăfī·linid), a. and n.

Staphylococcus (stæfilokŏ·kŏs). *Bacteriology.*

Staphyloma (stæfilŏ·mă). *Path.*

Staphyloplasty (stæ·filoplæ̆sti). [f. Gr. σταφυλή + -plasty.]

Staphylorrhaphy (stæfilŏ·răfi). *Surg.* Also -o·rynghy.

Staphyloraphy, rare. [f. Gr. σταφυλή + ῥαφή sewing, suture.]

Staphylotomy, rare. [ad. mod.L. staphylotomia, a. Gr. σταφυλοτομία.]

Staphylotoxin (stæfilŏ·tŏksin). *Bacteriology.*

Staple (stē·p'l), sb.[1] Forms: 1, 4 stapol, 1–5 stapul, stapel, 3 stapil, stapple, 5 stapill, stapyl[l], 6 stapulle, 5–6 stapulle, 6 stappell, 4–7 stayple, 4–7 staple. [OE. stapol str. masc. (a wk. form stapole is doubtful)]

Staple (stē·p'l), sb.[2] Also 5–6 stapell, stapyll, 5–6 stapill, 6 estapell, estaple. [a. OF. estaple (estaple-place) — med.L. staptla, staple.]

Staple, sb.[3] Also 5–7 stapel, 5tn. stable, stapel. [f. Staple sb.2]

Staple (stē·p'l), sb.[4] rare. [Of obscure origin.]

Staple (stē·p'l), sb.[5] Also staple-fish.

Staple (stē·p'l), a. [From the attributive use of Staple sb.2, as in adj. senses 1 b), 2 b).]

Stapled (stē·p'ld), a.[1] [f. Staple sb.3 + -ed[2].]

Stapled, a.[2] [f. staple sb.5 + -ed[1].]

† Staple-fish. Obs.

Stapler (stē·p'lăɹ). [f. Staple sb.2 + -er[1].]

Staple (stē·p'l), v.[1] [f. Staple sb.4]

Stappe, obs. f. Step sb. and v.

Star (staɹ), sb.[1] Forms: 1 steorra, steorre, Northumb. steorra, sterra, 3 steorre, storre, 3–4 sterre, 2–6 sterre, 3 sterr, stirre, 4–6 starre, 5–7 stare, 6–7 starr, (6–star, 6–star, steerre), 6– star.

Star-chamber, †starred chamber, -la (nonce-form) **chamber of stars.** [f. STAR sb.]

Starched (stäːtʃt), ppl. a. [f. STARCH v. + -ED.]

Starcher. [f. STARCH v. and sb. + -ER.]

Starching, vbl. sb. [f. STARCH v. + -ING.]

Starchly (stäːtʃli), a. [f. STARCH sb. + -LY.]

Starchness (stäːtʃnes). [f. STARCH a. + -NESS.]

Starchy (stäːtʃi), a. [f. STARCH sb. + -Y.]

Stare, sb.1 Also 5-6 sc. stair.

†Stare, sb.2 [OE. stær.]

Stare (steəɹ), v.1 [OE. starian.]

Stare-blind, a. [OE. stær-, steru-blind.]

Staring (steəɹiŋ), vbl. sb. [-ING.]

Staring, ppl. a. [f. STARE v. + -ING.]

Staringly (steəɹiŋli), adv. [f. prec. + -LY.]

Stark (staːk), a. and adv. Forms: 1-4 stearc, 1 starc, 2-6 stare, 3-6 starke, 4-6 starc, etc. [OE. stearc.]

Stare-dust, ppl. a.

Star-gazer.

Star-gazing, ppl. a.

Star-grass. [STAR sb.]

Supplement, p. 3873; Corrigenda, p. 4092; Spurious words, p. 4093; Books quoted, p. 4094

Starting-hole

Startish

Startle

Starting, ...

Startle-brain

Startled, ppl. a.

Startish

Startful

Startling, vbl. sb.

Startless

Startling, ppl. a.

Startler

Start naked

Startmeal

Start-up

Starty

Start up

Starve, v.

Starve, v.

Starved, ppl. a.

Starvedly

Starvel

Starveling, sb. and a.

Starver

Starving, vbl. sb.

Starving, ppl. a.

Starving, *ppl. a.* [f. STARVE *v.* + -ING 2.]

† 1. Of death : † Lingering, languishing. *Obs.*

2. Causing death, killing. *Obs.*

3. That is dying of hunger; that lacks the necessaries of life; also *absol.*

4. That causes or entails starvation or famine; also, that treats disease by stinting the patient of food.

b. That causes one to starve with cold. *rare.*

Starvy, *a.*, *Obs. rare.* [f. STARVE *v.* + -Y.] Poor in quality, starved. — *a. 1400.* b. of *frost.*

Starward, *adv.* [-WARD.] Towards the stars. Also *attrib.* or *adj.*

Starwort (stä'zwuot). Also 6-8 ster-, sterre-, 6-7 (*erron.*) atir(e-. [f. STAR *sb.*1 + WORT *sb.*]

1. The genus *Stellaria*, with starry flowers; esp. *S. Holostea.*

2. A book-name for the genus *Aster*; esp. *A. Tripolium*, Sea Starwort; *A. Amellus*, Italian Starwort.

3. Water starwort, the genus *Callitriche.*

4. The name of a moth, *Cucullia Asteris.*

Stash (stæʃ), *v.* *slang.* [Of obscure origin.] *trans.* To bring to an end, stop, desist from (a matter, a practice); to quit (a place). Often *imp. stash it!* *stash that!* † To stash the glim: to cease using the light. To stash up: to bring to an abrupt end.

Statable (stä'tăb'l), *a.* Also **stateable.** [f. STATE *v.* + -ABLE.] Capable of being stated.

† **Statarism.** *Obs. rare.* [ad. Gr. σταταρισμός, f. στατός standing.] One or more trifling alterations made, and with time to cure the disable reasons for thus acting.

† **Statary**, *a.* *Obs.* Also *7 erron. statory.* [ad. L. *statāri-us*, f. *stat-* *ppl. stem* of *stāre* to stand.]

1. Standing fast or firm, established; stated, fixed; having a fixed position, stationary.

2. Of soldiers : Equip'd for stationary combat as opposed to skirmishing.

State (stä't), *sb.* Forms : 3-6 *stat,* *pl.* **stas** (?), 4-5 **staat,** 4-5, 7 **statt,** 4-6 **stade,** 4, 5-7 *Sc.* **stait,** 6 *Sc.* **stayte,** 6 *Sc.* **steat,** 7 *Sc.* **steit,** 4- **state.** [a. OF. *estat* (*état*) = Pr., *etc.* Sp., Pg. *estado,* It. *stato,* ad. L. *status* (u stem), manner of standing, condition, *n.* of action f. *stat-* *ppl. stem* of *stāre* to stand.]

I. Condition, manner of existing.

1. A combination of circumstances or attributes belonging for the time being to a person or thing; a particular manner or way of existing, as defined by the presence of certain circumstances or attributes; a condition. Sometimes qualified by *adj.* or a following phrase.

b. *collog.* Used for 'a dreadful state' (of dirt, untidiness, etc.).

2. *A condition (of mind or feeling);* the mental or emotional condition in which a person finds himself at a particular time.

b. *The state or form of existence of a particular mode or phase of (spiritual) existence.

II. A class, rank; a person of rank.

III. A class, rank : a person of rank.

STATE (continued columns...)

STATE. 853 STATE.

STATE. 854 STATE.

STATE. 855 STATEHOOD. STATE-HOUSE. 856 STATELY.

5. Of speech or writing or its style; hence of a speaker or writer: Elevated in thought or expression, dignified, majestic.

†6. Powerful, effectual. *Obs.*

†7. Pertaining to the state or body politic. *monte-state.*) *Obs.*

8. *Comb.*

†b. With splendid ceremonial or surroundings; in state. *Obs.*

†2. In a domineering or arrogant manner. *Obs.*

†3. In a noble or dignified form or style; so as to have a stately appearance. *Obs.*

4. With stately or dignified bearing, movement, or expression.

†5. In a fitting manner, properly. *Obs.*

6. *Comb.*

Statement (stēɪtmɛnt). [f. STATE *v.* + -MENT.]

1. The action or an act of stating, alleging, or enunciating; the manner in which something is stated.

b. *Mus.* A presentation of a subject or theme in a composition.

State-monger, states-monger *Obs. exc. arch.* [See MONGER.] A projector of political constitutions; a pretender to political science.

Stater¹ (stēɪtə). *Antiq.* [L. *stater*, a. Gr. *στατήρ*, f. στα-, ίστάναι (see STAND *v.*) in the sense 'to weigh'.]

1. An ancient weight.

b. *Mus.* [f. STATE *v.* + -ER¹.] One who states: *alterage stater* = average-adjuster.

Statement (stēɪtmɛnt). [f. STATE *v.* + -MENT.]

Statal (stēɪtal). *Law.* [f. STATE *sb.* + -AL.]

State-room.

1. A state apartment; a room in a palace, great house, hotel, etc., splendidly decorated and furnished, and used only on ceremonial occasions.

2. A captain's or superior officer's room on board ship. (*Cf. state-cabin, STATE sb.* 41.)

3. *U.S.* A sleeping apartment with one or two berths on a passenger steamer.

b. *Boating.* (See quot.)

†State-room *rare⁻¹.* [See STATE sb.] The art of statesmanship.

Statesmanlike, *a.* [f. STATESMAN + -LIKE.] Having the qualities characteristic of a statesman; befitting or worthy of a statesman.

Statesmanly, *a.* [f. STATESMAN + -LY¹.] Pertaining to or characteristic of a statesman; befitting a statesman.

Statesmanship. [-SHIP.] The activity or skilful management of public affairs.

Statement

State-general. *Hist.* Also ◊ general **states.** [= F. *états généraux*, Du. *staaten generaal.*] A legislative assembly representing the three estates, viz. clergy, nobles, and commons or burghers of a whole realm, principality, or commonwealth (distinguished from *states provincial*); in France before the Revolution; b. in the Netherlands from 1216 to 1796.

Statesman² *Obs.* [f. STATES (see STATE sb. 23) + -MAN.] A subject of the States of Holland.

Statesmanship.

Statement.

Stateswoman (stēɪtswʊmən). [f. STATE sb. + WOMAN.] A woman who takes part in the conduct of public affairs; a woman with statesmanlike ability.

1. One who takes a leading part in the affairs of a state or body politic; esp. one who is skilled in the management of public affairs.

Stathe, *v.* *Obs.* [f. STATHE.]

Stathe, Stathel. *Obs.*

Stathel (stēɪðəl). *Obs.* [OE. *staðol*.]

Stathelness, *b.* *Obs.* [f. prec. + -NESS.] Solidity, firmness.

Stathely, *a.* *Obs.* [f. STATHEL + -LY.] Firm, steadfast.

Stathmograph. [f. Gr. σταθμός = *'weighing', + -GRAPH*.]

Static (stætɪk). *a.* and *sb.* Also 7-8 **statick.** [ad. mod.L. *staticus*, a. Gr. στατικός causing to stand, also pertaining to or skilled in weighing. The sb. is a. Gr. στατική, *statike*] in ad. mod.L. *statica*, ad. Gr. στατική.]

A. *adj.*

1. Of or pertaining to weighing or the use of the balance: = STATICAL *a.* 1. *Obs.*

2. Of bodies: Characterized by STASIS.

3. Pertaining to forces in equilibrium, or to bodies at rest: opposed to *dynamic.*

B. *sb.* = STATICS.

Stathe, *v.* *Obs.*

Stathe, *sb.* *Obs.* (local, *staithe.*)

STATICAL. 859 STATION. STATION. 860 STATION.

Statical (stætɪkəl). *a.* Also 6 **-all.** [formed as prec. + -AL.]

†1. Pertaining to the action or process of weighing: = STATIC *a.* 1. *Obs.*

2. Of or relating to the science of statics, or to forces in equilibrium, or to bodies at rest.

3. Pertaining to weight or the equilibrium of weight. *Obs.*

4. *Astr.* The apparent standing still of a planet at its apogee and perigee. *Obs.*

Statically (stætɪkəli), *adv.* [f. STATICAL *a.* + -LY².] With reference to static conditions; by means of static electricity.

Statics (stætɪks), *sb.* [f. STATIC: see -ICS.]

2. Of or pertaining to the metrology of weight. *Cf.* STATIC *sb.* 2.

Statice (stætɪsɪ). *Bot.* [a. L. *statice*.]

Station (stēɪʃən), *sb.* Forms: 4-6 stacio(u)n, 5 stascyon, stacyon, stasyon, 5-6 stacyon, 7- station. — F. *station* (12th c. = L. *statio*-onem, noun of action f. sta-, *stare* to stand. Cf. Sp. *estación*, It. *stazione*, and the popular form It. *stagione* season.]

I. Action or condition of standing.

1. The action or posture of standing on the feet; manner of standing. Now only in scientific and technical uses: see quots. 1891 and 1913.

2. The condition or fact of standing still; assumption of or continuance in a stationary condition. Now *rare.*

b. The height at which the barometer stands.

†3. *Arith.* = PLACE *sb.* 10. *Obs.*

4. An intermediate stopping place on a journey.

II. Standing-place, position.

5. A place to stand in; a position assigned to a man on duty, or in games.

6. *Path.* The stationary point, crisis, a height (of a disease). *Cf.* STATE sb. 31. *Obs.*

7. A place to stand in; a position assigned to a man on duty, or in games.

8. *Surveying*, etc. Each of the selected points at which observations are taken. Formerly *†place, point of station.*

b. The place in which a thing stands or is appointed to stand. Now *rare* or *Obs.*

9. *Path.* The stationary point, crisis, a height (of a disease). *Cf.* STATE sb. 31. *Obs.*

10. *Naut.* A more fully *naval station.* In modern use, a place at which ships of the Navy are regularly stationed.

b. *Police-station.*

c. *Preaching-station.*

11. *gen.* A metaphorical standing-place or position, e.g. in a case of estimation or value; a point of view.

12. *Eccl.* Each of the places where processions halt, esp. in the Roman Catholic Church, on the way of the Cross; *stations of the cross.*

13. A place where men are stationed and apparatus set up for some particular kind of industrial work, scientific research, or the like.

b. A place where railway-trains stop.

14. *Astr.* (See quot.)

15. *gen.* Rank or position in life.

STATION. 861 STATION. 862 STATIONARY.

STATIONED. 863 STATIONING. STATIONIZE. 864 STATIVE.

Statization — **Statue**

Statize, v. Obs. [f. STATE sb. + -IZE.] intr. In depreciative sense : To meddle in state-affairs.

Statizes, Obs. [f. STATE + -IZE.] 1. One who meddles in state-affairs. 2. A partisan.

Stato- (state), repr. Gr. στατο- = standing, set (mainly as virtual combining form of STATIC, STATION) in scientific words, chiefly Biol., as **Statoblast**, a reproductive gemmule developed in some Polyzoa and Sponges and liberated after the death of the parent organism; hence **Stato'blastic** a. **Sta'tocyst**, -cyte, each of the cells or cysts containing statoliths. **Sta'togene'tic, Sta'togene'tic** adj. **Statogene'tic** a. **Sta'togene'tically** adv. **Sta'tolith** [Gr. λίθος rod] = TENTACULOCYST. **Sta'tomorph**, an instrument for measuring the degree of exophthalmos. **Sta'toplast** [Gr. πλαστός]. **Sta'tosphere** (see quot.). **Sta'tospore** (see quot.).

Statoblast

Statocyst

Statolith

Statuarism

Statuary

Statue

Statuesque

Statuette

Status

Status quo

Statutable

Statute

Statutorily

Statutory

Statute, v.

Statute-book

Statute merchant. *Law.* Now only *Hist.* [STATUTE *sb.* + MERCHANT *a.*] An elliptical use of the designation of the *Statute of Merchants* of 1283, (Anglo-L. *statutum de mercatoribus*, also *statutum mercatorium*, Aff. *estatut marchaund* whence the powers of summary execution of this kind of instrument were derived.]

A bond of record, acknowledged before the chief magistrate of a trading town, giving to the oblige power of seizure of the land of the obligor if he failed to pay his debt at the appointed time.

Statutable (stæˈtiutăb'l), *a.* and *sb.* [ad. assumed L. type *statūtorius*, f. *statuto* to decree, enact; see -ORY. Cf. STATUTORY.]

Statutary (stæˈtiutări), *adv.* [f. next + -LY 2.] In a statutory manner; by statute; enactment; in accordance with the provisions of the statutes.

Statutory (stæˈtiutări), *a.* and *sb.* [ad. assumed L. type *statūtorius*, f. *statuto* to decree, enact; see -ORY. Cf. STATUTORY.]

Statute staple. *Law.* Now only *Hist.* Also *statute of the staple.* An elliptical use of *statute of the staple* as the name of the ordinance of 1353 (see STAPLE *sb.* 1 1).

Staulanche, Stalanche, obs. forms of STALLION.

Staule, obs. f. STALE *v.* 2, STALL *sb.* and *v.* 1

Staull, obs. form of STALL *sb.* 1

Staum, variant of STAM *sb.* 3 dial.

Staumer (stǫˈmrel), *a.* and *sb.* Sc.

Staumrel, staumrel, [f. *staumer*, dial. var. of STAMMER *v.* + -EL 1 *adj.* Stupid, half-witted.

Staunch, stanch (stǫntʃ, stǫnʃ), *a.* Forms: (1 stavnche, staunche), 6-7 stanche, (6 stansho), 5-6 stanch, 7- staunch. [a. OF. *estanche* tem. of *estanc*- (mod.F. *étanche*)]

Staunch, stanch, *sb.* 1 : see STANCH *sb.*

Staunchon, -(i)on, var. ff. STANCHION.

Staunge, staunk (o, obs. ff. STANK, STANCH.

Staup, obs. or dial. form of STOUP.

Staupe, var. STAP *sb.* and *v.* north. *Obs.*

Staupings (stǫˈpingz), *sb. pl.* north.

Staura-, comb. form of Gr. σταυρός cross.

Staurolatry (stǫrǫˈlætri). *Obs. rare.* [ad. late L. *staurolatria* (Tertullian), f. Gr. σταυρο- cross + λατρεία worship: see -LATRY.] The worship of the Cross.

Staurolite (stǫˈrǫlait). *Min.* [f. *staurolite* (Delamétherie 1792) : see STAURO- and -LITE.]

Staurolitic (stǫrǫˈlitik), *a.* Min. [f. *staurolite* + -IC.]

Stauroscope (stǫˈrǫskōp). *Min.* [f. σταυρός cross (see STAURO- + -SCOPE.] An instrument used for the microscopic examination of rocks (see quot. 1879).

Stauroscopic (stǫrǫˈskōpik), *a.* pertaining to or made by means of the stauroscope.

Staurotide (stǫˈrǫtaid). *Min.* = STAUROLITE.

Stauroti'di-ferous (-FEROUS.] Containing staurotide.

Staurus (stǫˈrʊs). *Zool.* [mod.L. ad. Gr. σταυρός cross.] A type of sponge spicule of the form of a cross.

Staval(l, stavel, dial. ff. STADDLE *sb.*

Stave (stēv), *sb.* A back-formation from *staves* pl. of STAFF *sb.* 1

Stave (stēv), *v.* Pa. t. and pa. pple. *staved*; also (chiefly *Naut.*), 8-9 stove. [f. STAVE *sb.*]

Stave, *sb.* 2 *Obs. rare.* [for *staven*, var. of STAFF *sb.* 1]

Stave, *sb.* 3 [var. STAFF *sb.* 1]

Staver (stēˈvər), *sb.* Chiefly *dial.* in *staver*.

Stavesacre (stēˈvzēˌkər). Forms: 4 *scaffisage*, 5 staphisagre, 5-7 *staf-sage*, *staffisacre*, 6 stafisagre, stavysagre, stavis aloes, 6-8 stavesaker, *stavire sacre*, *stavire sacre*. [ad. L. *staphisagria*, a. Gr. σταφὶς ἀγρία wild raisin.]

Staveless (stēˈvlĕs), *a.* Having no staves. *rare.*

Staver (stēˈvər), *v.* 1 dial. Sc. In 6 stavir. [f. STAVE *v.*]

Staver (stēˈvər), *v.* 2 Chiefly Sc. In a staver.

Stavewise (stēˈvwaiz), *adv.* In the form of a stave.

Staving (stēˈviŋ), *vbl. sb.* [f. STAVE *v.* + -ING 1.] The action of the verb STAVE.

Staving (stēˈviŋ), *ppl. a.* [f. STAVE *v.* + -ING 2.]

Stavrel, var. STAUMREL.

Staw, Sc. and dial. form of STALL *sb.* 1 and *v.*

Stawbote, variant of STALK BOAT. *Obs.*

Stawe, obs. pa. t. of STEAL and STY.

Stawl, obs. Sc. N. DIAL. STALKER.

Stawnche, -ing, obs. forms of STANCH *v.*, -ING.

Staxis (stæˈksis), *Path.* [mod.L., a. Gr. στάξις a dripping, f. στάζειν to drop, drip.] 'Slight defluxion of any humour, as nasal hæmorrhage' (Syd. Soc. Lex.).

Stay (stē), *sb.* 1 Also 4-5 steye, 5 stye, 5-6 staie, 6 stayo. [OE. stæg (neut.) corresp. to Du. stag, (neut.) stag (neut.) stag, ON. stag neut. (Da., Sw., Norw. stag). Naut. A large rope used to support a mast, and leading from its head forward or aft to some other mast or spar, or to some part of the ship.

Stay (stē), *sb.* 2 Also 4-5 steye, 5 stye, 6 staie, 6 staye, 8 *pl.* steas. [Prob. f. STAY *v.* 1; but in sense 1 perh. in part ad. OF. *estaye* tem. (mod. F. *étaie*), whence also STAY *v.* 1]

Stay, *sb.* 3 Also 7 *pl.* staies.

Stay, *v.* 1

Stay, *v.* 2

Stave (stēv), *sb.* 1797 MRS. A. M. BENNETT *Beggar Girl* (1813) III. 10 One fair day the old barrel staved, over her poor dear tipped, and broke his neck.

2. *trans.* To break a hole in (a boat); to break *to pieces*; also, to break (a hole in a boat). To *stave in*, to crush inwards, make a hole in.

3. *trans.* To burst in, crush inwards. Chiefly with *in*.

4. To renew the staves of (a bucket); to put together the staves of (a cask, etc.).

5. To fit with a staff or handle.

6. To drive off or beat with a staff or stave; esp. *in stave off*, to beat off (a dog in Bear- or Bull-baiting; also *transf.* a human combatant); to keep back (a crowd). Now only *arch.*

7. *To break up* (a cask) into staves; to put the staves asunder or apart.

8. *intr.* To fight with staves; to lay down his arms.

9. *trans.* To drive with a heavy blow. *Obs.*

10. *intr.* To go with a rush or dash; to 'drive'. *Sc.* and *U.S.*

Staver (stēˈvər), *v.* Also, 'one of the bars of a hay-rack' (E. Anglian *Gloss.*); 'a stake for a hedge, etc.' (*Sheffield Gloss.*).

Staver (stēˈvər), *sb.* 2 Chiefly *Sc.* In a stavir.

Staver (stēˈvər), *sb.* 3 To be continually 'staving' about; an active, energetic person.

Stavesacre (stēˈvzēˌkər). *a* 1400 *Stockholm Med. MS.* 26 Seabage *stafisagre*. 1400 *Lanfranc's Cirurg.* 162 Medicyn (*quod coll.*) IV. 262 [He took sauerei of Stafisagre, an aloes, antifol of Wormode, etc.]

Staveless (stēˈvlĕs), *a.* Having no staves.

Stavewise (stēˈvwaiz), *adv.* In the form of a stave.

Stavring (stæˈvriŋ), *ppl. a.* [f. STAVER *v.* + -ING.] Addicted to fighting with staves, quarrelsome. *Obs.*

Staw, Sc. and dial. form of STALL *sb.* 1 and *v.*

Staxis. 1693 *Blancard Phys. Dict.* (ed. 2), *Staxis*, a Distemper which Farriers call the Staggers.

Stay (stē), *sb.* 1 Naut. A large rope used to support a mast, and leading from its head forward or aft to some other mast or spar, or to some part of the ship.

3. *Comb.*, stay-block, a block buried in the ground as an attachment for a stay; stay-bolt; stay-light, a rolling light (Cent. Dict. 1891); †stay-nail, a nail for securing a stay; stay-peak (see quot. 1815); stay-wire, a wire forming part of a stay for a telegraph post.

Stay, *sb.* 2 **1.** Naut. A general name for the strong ropes which support the masts of a ship.

2. *transf.* A supporting prop. A prop, pedestal, buttress, bracket, or the like.

STEAD. 879 STEAD. STEAD. 880 STEAD.

Steadable ... *Obs.*

Stead, obs. form of SPEED.

Steadfast (ste'dfăst), *a. (adv.)* and *sb.* Forms: 1, 3 stedefæst, 4 stedefast, 5 stedfast (3 Ormin -fast), 3 stedevast, 4 stecnfaste, 3-4 studefast, 3 studevast, -vest, 4 studfaste, 4-5 stid(e)fast, stydfast, 6, 7 stedefast, faste, 5-6 stedfaste, 4-9 stedfast. [OE. *stedefæst, stede* (see STEAD sb.) + *fæst*, FAST *a.*]

1. Fixed or secure in position.

STEADFASTNESS.

1. Constancy or fixity in purpose, belief, fidelity, affection, etc.

2. Established or permanent condition.

3. In physical sense: Fixity in position. *arch.*

Steadfastship. *Obs.* [-SHIP.] — prec.

Steadful, *a. Sc.* and *north. Obs. rare.*

Steading (ste'diŋ), *sb. Sc.* and *north. Also* 6 steding, stedding, stidding, steden. [f. STEAD]

1. A farm-house and outbuildings; often, the outbuildings in contrast to the farm-house.

Stead-less, *a. Obs. rare.*

Steadship. *Obs. rare⁻¹.* ? Security of position.

Steady (ste'di), *a.* Forms: 6 steddy, 7 stydie, -y, stady, studdie (*Sc.*), steedy, 7- STEADY. [First in Palsgrave 1530; app. f. STEAD *sb.* + -Y.]

A. adj.

1. Fixed or immovable in position; not liable to give way or become displaced. *Obs.*

STEADY.

8. Regular in habits; not given to dissipation or looseness in conduct.

STEAK.

Steak (stēk), *sb.* Forms: 4 steke, steyke, stylke, 5-6 steyk, 4-6 steike, 5, 6-7 steake, 7- steak. [a. ON. *steik*; cf. *steikja* to roast on a spit, *stikna* to be roasted.]

STEAK RAID.

STEAL.

Steal (stēl), *sb.¹* [? f. foshound]

Steal (stēl), *sb.²* [f. STEAL *v.*]

Steal (stēl), *v.* Pa. t. stole, stale. Pa. pple. stolen. [Com. Teut.]

1. trans. To take away dishonestly (portable property, cattle, etc.)

STEAL (continued)

d. In wider sense: To take or appropriate dishonestly (anything belonging to another, whether material or immaterial).

e. *cp.* To plagiarize; to pass off (another's work) as one's own; to 'borrow' improperly (words, expressions).

f. To derive obscurely and dishonourably. *nonce-use.*

2. *absol.* and *intr.* To commit or practise theft. † Const. *dat.* of person.

3. *trans.* To take away by stratagem or eluding observation (something that is in the possession or keeping of another).

b. *with away:* rarely with other advs., as † *down*, † *out.*

c. Of an impersonal agent.

d. To carry off (young animals) from the dam.

e. *refl.* To take (oneself) away secretly.

f. To capture (a fortress, a military position) by surprise. *Obs.*

g. To carry off, abduct, kidnap (a person) secretly. Now *rare.*

4. In various applications with immaterial obj.

b. To cause the loss of, take away (something valued, e.g. happiness, a person's life, etc.).

c. To direct (a look), breathe (a sigh) furtively.

d. *Also* (cf. sense 6) to give (a kiss) to a person.

†e. To gain, win over (something) stealthily.

†f. To take (time) by contrivance *from* its ordinary employment, sleep, etc. to devote to some other purpose.

†g. To take by fraud or unobtrusive means. *Obs.*

†h. To gain, or attain to (an end, etc.) stealthily. *Obs.*

5. To go or come secretly or stealthily; to walk or creep softly so as to avoid observation.

b. Of a person: to go stealthily; to depart furtively.

†c. Of a net: To make (her nest) in a concealed place.

†d. Of a ewe: To bring forth (lambs) out of season.

6. *techn.* To omit or suppress (some out of a natural number of parts of a structure). *A. Nind.*

7. *intr.* To depart unobserved secretly or surreptitiously from a place. Chiefly with *adv.*

8. *intr.* To come stealthily *on* or *upon* a person for the purpose of attack or injury.

9. To come stealthily; to creep; to glide or flow.

10. To go or come secretly or stealthily; to walk or creep softly so as to avoid observation.

11. Of change, a disease, etc.: To come insensibly *over* or *on* a person.

b. Of a condition, etc.: To come insensibly *over* or *on* a person.

12. *Hunting.* To steal away.

13. Of a stream, tears, a body of vapour, a ship, etc.: To glide, or move gently and almost imperceptibly.

II. To proceed secretly or stealthily; to walk or creep softly so as to avoid observation.

III. The verb-stem in combination: steal-clothes, steal-counter, steal-placard, steal-truth, etc.

STEALABLE. 887 STEALTHILY. 888 STEAM.

Stealable (stī'labl), a. [f. STEAL v.[1] + -ABLE.] That can be stolen.

Stealage (stī'lėdʒ). [f. STEAL v.[1] + -AGE.] Loss due to stealing.

Stealed, *pa. pple.* & *ppl. a.* = STOLEN.

Stealer (stī'lər). [f. STEAL v.[1] + -ER.] One who steals; a thief; now only, one who steals something specified.

b. *slang.* The ten stealers: the fingers.

2. *Naut.* Also *stealer.*

Stealing, *vbl. sb.* [f. STEAL v.[1] + -ING.] The action of STEAL v.[1] in its various senses. Also *Comb.* with advbs., as *stealing-forth,* etc.

†b. An instance of stealing; a theft. *Obs.*

c. Plagiarism.

2. Something stolen; something to steal; plunder.

Stealing, *ppl. a.* [f. STEAL v.[1] + -ING.] That steals or moves stealthily; that eludes observation.

†b. Plagiarism.

Stealth (stelþ). Forms: 3–4 stalðe, 4–6 stelthe, 4–7 stelth, 5 stelth, 6 stealth. [f. STEAL v.[1] + -TH.]

1. The action or practice of stealing or taking secretly and wrongfully; theft. *Obs.*

2. *By stealth.* †a. With reference to taking or appropriating.

b. In modern use, the phrase has ordinarily no conscious association with *steal* vb., or sense 1 of the sb., and the neutral sense: Secretly, clandestinely.

3. †a. A sneaking or coming by surprise upon a person.

b. A stealthy action or an act accomplished by stealing observation or discovery. *Obs.*

Stealthful (stelþ'fǔl), a. Obs. rare.

Stealthfulness.

Stealthily (stelþ'ili), adv. [f. STEALTHY a. + -LY.] In a stealthy manner.

Stealthiness.

Stealthy (stelþ'i), a. [f. STEALTH sb. + -Y.] 1. Characterized by or acting with stealth.

2. Proceeding with, or characterized by, imperceptible degrees; furtive.

†3. A ray or beam of light; a flame. *Obs.*

Steam (stīm), sb. Forms: 1 stéam, stém, 3–4 stem, 4–7 steme, 4–5 steme, 5–7 steam. [OE. *stéam = *WFris. staem, Du. stoom = OTeut. type *staumoz.]

I. 1. A vapour or fume given out by a substance when heated or burned.

b. The visible vesicles produced by condensation of watery vapour.

†b. A noxious vapour generated in the digestive system.

2. The visible moist vapour into which water is converted when heated. In popular language, applied to the water when hot.

3. An exhalation or watery vapour rising from the earth or sea.

4. *techn.* The vapour into which water is converted when heated.

5. A fume, an odorous exhalation or fume.

6. The vapour into which water is converted when heated.

7. The vapour of boiling water used, by confinement in specially constructed engines, for the generation of mechanical power. Hence, the mechanical power thus generated.

b. Energy, 'go', driving power, etc.

c. *Phr. By steam,* (to travel) by steamer. *Under steam.* To get up steam. To let off steam. Full steam ahead.

8. An exhalation or watery vapour rising from the earth or sea.

II. *attrib.* and *Comb.*

| STEAM. | 889 | STEAM. | STEAMBOAT. | Steamer | 890 | STEAMSHIP. |

STEAM (continued) ... arrangement in which a saucepan is converted into a temporary steam chamber. ... steam-chaise, a chaise driven by steam; †steam-coach = steam-carriage; steam-coal, coal suitable for heating water in steam-boilers; steam-colour Calico-printing, a colour developed and fixed in the cloth by steaming; †steam-doctor, one who treats diseases by vapour-baths; steam-horse, a kind of traction-engine; steam-jacket, a jacket or casing filled with steam in order to preserve the heat of the vessel round which it is placed; hence steam-jacketed pa. pple. and adj., steam-jacketing vbl. sb.; steam-navvy, a machine for digging or excavating by steam; steam-niggar U.S. the lump cylinder with piston and rod by which the log is forced up to the saw in a saw-mill; steam-organ = Calliope; steam-road, a road prepared for steam-traction; U.S. a railroad; steam-room, -space, the space above the water-level in a steam-boiler; steam-tight, -tight enough to resist the ingress or egress of steam; also quasi-adv.; steam-tug, a steam-boat specially constructed for towing vessels; †applied jocularly to a railway-engine; †steam-wagon, a wagon drawn by steam on a railway or on a common road; †steam-wheel, the rotary steam-engine; also fig.

13. In the names of the various contrivances for containing, conveying, or regulating the steam in a steam-engine, as steam-box, -case, -chamber, -chest, -cock, -valve, -cylinder, -dome, -gauge, -pipe, -port, -valve, -way, etc.

14. In the names of implements, machines, processes, etc. operated by steam or by a steam-engine, as steam-crane, -gun, -hammer, -mill, -milling, -plough, -ploughing, -pump, -thresher, -threshing, -whim, -winch, etc.

15. With reference to locomotion by steam-power, and in names of vehicles and vessels propelled by steam, as steam-ferry, -flat, -frigate, -launch, -navigation, -navy, -omnibus, -packet, -ram, -train, -tram, -trawler, -tug, -vessel, etc. See also steam-car, -carriage, -tug, etc. in 17, and the main-words STEAM-BOAT, etc.

16. Instrumental, with ppl. adjs., as steam-driven, -going, -ridden (fig.), -wrought. Also steam-like adj.

17. Special comb.: steam-boiler, a vessel in which water is heated to generate steam, esp. for working a steam-engine (BOILER 2); steam-car, a car driven or drawn by steam, e.g. a motor-car worked by steam instead of petrol; U.S. a railway-carriage; †steam-carriage, a carriage driven or drawn by steam (a) on a railroad or tramway, (b) on common

Steam (stīm), v. [OE. stēman, stýman :—pre-Teut. *steumjan, f. *staum- STEAM sb.]

†1. To emit a scent or odour. Of a scent: To be emitted or exhaled. Also with advs., as out.

2. To apply steam to; to expose to the action of steam; to treat with steam for the purpose of softening, cooking, heating, disinfecting, etc.

3. To fill with 'steam' or water-vapour.

†b. fig. (Cf. evaporate.)

4. To expose (a gummed packet) to the action of steam in order to soften the gum. To steam open, to open by this method.

b. Calico-printing. To fix (colours) by the steam-process.

5. To convey on a steam-vessel. collog.

d. To bedew (a surface) with vesicles of condensed vapour.

6. Of a surface: To become covered or bedewed with condensed vapour.

Steamboat. A boat propelled by steam; esp. a coasting or river steamer of considerable size, carrying either passengers or goods. Also attrib.

Steam-engine. An engine in which the mechanical force of steam is made available as a motive power for driving machinery, etc.

Steamer (stī·məɹ). [f. STEAM v. and sb. + -ER¹.]

1. One who steams, a person employed in some process of steaming.

2. An apparatus for steaming (in various technical processes); a vessel in which articles are subjected to the action of steam, as in washing, cookery, etc.

b. attrib., steamer-chair, a lounge-chair such as is used on the deck of a steamer.

Steamship. A ship propelled by steam.

| STEAM'-VESSEL. | 891 | STEATO-. | STEATOID | 892 | STEEK. |

Steam'-vessel. †1. A vessel for holding steam; esp. one in which the steam is formed. 2. A steamboat or steamship.

Steam-whistle. A powerful whistle worked by a jet of steam (usually from a steam-boiler); used as a signal.

Steamy (stī·mi), a. [f. STEAM sb. + -Y¹.] 1. Consisting of, abounding in, or emitting steam; resembling steam.

Steapsin (stī·æpsin). Physiological Chem. [f. Gr. στέαρ fat, after PEPSIN.] A ferment of the pancreatic juice which saponifies fat (Syd. Soc. Lex. 1893).

Stear: see STAIR, STARE sb.¹, STEER.

Stearate (stī·ərēt). Chem. [formed as STEAR-IC + -ATE⁴.] A salt of stearic acid.

Stearin (stī·ərin). Chem. [a. F. stéarine, f. Gr. στέαρ fat.]

Stearic (stiæ·rik), a. [f. F. stéarique (see STEARIN) + -IC.]

Stearo-, combining form of Gr. στέαρ fat.

Steatite (stī·ətəit). Min. [ad. L. steatītēs, a. Gr. στεατίτης, f. στέαρ, στεατ- fat.]

Steato-, before a vowel steat-, combining form of Gr. στέαρ, στεατ- fat.

Steatoid (stī·ətoid), a. [f. STEAT- + -OID.] Resembling fat.

Steatoma (stiatō·ma). Path. Also anglicized steatome. [L., a. Gr. στεάτωμα.]

Steatopygia (stiatopi·dʒiǎ). Path. Also anglicized steatopygy. [mod.L.]

Steatopygous (stiatopī·gəs), a.

Steatornis (stiatō·ɹnis). [mod.L.]

Steatosis (stiatō·sis). Path.

Ste边- ...

Steek (stīk), sb.¹ Obs. exc. dial. Also steik. [a. ON. stik neut.] A thrust with a rapier.

Steek (stīk), v. Sc. and north. [Of obscure origin.] To fill (the stomach); to replenish; to cram (food) into (the stomach). Also refl.

Steedless, a. Without a steed.

Steek, sb.² Sc. Obs. rare. Also stoik. [a. MDu.] A stitch.

Steek, v.³ To stitch.

STEEK.
(6 steke), 8-9 north. steek : Sc. and north. 6-9 steak, 7, 9 steick, 7- stuck ; Pa. t. 3, 4 steak, 4 north. steok, 4-5 steke, 5 stekyt, 7 stekid, 9 north. steak'd ; 6- 4-5 stekyte, stekit, 9-, steikit, 7 steeked, 9 stiket, steekit | Pa. pple. 3-4 stoken, (4 stokin), 4 stoky'n, (4-5c stoken), 4-5 -stoke, y-stoke, stoke ; 4-5 ystekyd, (4 istekid, 5 steekit, steeked), 5-9 steekid, stekith, stekit; 6 y-stokit, 9 stikket, steekit | Pa. pple. 3-4 steeked.

1. *trans.* To set fast, close, enclose, imprison (a person *in* a place); also *with up*. Also *refl.*

2. To enclose. Also *refl.*

3. To shut, close, to close securely, to lock *up*.

4. *trans.* To shut (the mouth, eyes, ears, heart).

5. To full (up) of something.

6. *intr.* To pierce and remain fixed (in something).

7. To remain fixed where placed; to adhere.

8. Of thoughts, memories, etc.: To remain fixed and immovable in one's mind, heart, etc.

9. To be hindered from proceeding.

10. Of a person: To cling tenaciously to.

STEEK.
Steek, *v.* Obs. exc. dial. Forms: 4-6 steke, 5-6 Sc. steik, 6 steek, 7 steak, 9 north. steak, *etc.*

STEEKING.
Steeking (*strˈkɪŋ*), *vbl. sb.³ dial.* [f. STEEK.]

1. The action of the verb; stitching; also *concr.*

2. *concr.* A fastening, lock.

Steeking, *ppl. a.* dial.

Steekan (*strˈk,kæn*). Also 8 stekan, stekkan. [f. stokan, stockan, 9 steohkanne : Du. stekkan.] A Dutch liquid measure containing half an anker or about 5 gallons English measure.

STEEL.
Steel (stīl), *sb.¹* Forms: 1 stéli, steeli, stéli, 1-4 styli, stél, (1 stiel), 3-5 stel, 4 styl, Sc. stele, 4-6 stele, stele, styl, 4-6 stele, stele, steyle, stiell, stéill, 5-6 steele, (steiele), 5-7 steele, 4 steel, 7 steele. [OE. stéli, stéli (WFris. stél, NFris. stiel), OTeut. *stax̂ija- (literally), something made of steel, but in OE. simply, the metal itself, as in late L. acitrium superseded acit) =-L. OTeut. *stax̂lo- steel, Germanic steel.]

I. A general name for certain artificially produced varieties of iron, distinguished from those known as 'iron' by certain physical properties.

II. A piece of steel: usually, iron chloride (but used also for the sulphate or other salts of iron).

STEELBACK.
2. *fig.* To cause to resemble steel in some quality.

Steel boy, Irish Hist.

Steel (stīl), *sb.²* [f. STEEL *v.¹* + BACK *sb.*] A name for Alicant wine, from its supposed property of strengthening the back.

Steel-bow, *Sc. Law. Obs. exc. Hist.* Forms: 5-7 steelbow, 6 steille ; 7 steelbow. [f. STEEL *sb.¹* + Bow.]

Steeled (stīld), *ppl. a.* [f. STEEL *v.¹* + -ED.]

Steelify (stīlɪfaɪ), *v. rare-¹* [Anglicized form of L. *stylif., stylifer.*]

Steel glass. Obs.

Steel-head, *a.* Having a head, tip or top of steel.

Steel-hearted, *a.*

Steely (stīlɪ), *a.* [f. STEEL *sb.¹* + -Y(1).]

Steeliness (stī'lĭnes). [f. STEELY a. + -NESS.] The quality or condition of being steely.

Steeling (stī'lĭŋ), vbl. sb. [f. STEEL v. + -ING.] 1. The action of stiffening (a bodice, etc.) with steel, etc.

2. The giving a steely edge or point to iron, etc.

3. Conversion into steel.

4. In *Engraving*, the process of covering a metal plate with steel to render it more durable.

5. The steel part of a machine.

6. *attrib.* †**steeling-box**, a box-iron (cf. STEEL v. 7).

Steeling (stī'lĭŋ), ppl. a. [-ING 2.] That steels, in quot. hardening, strengthening.

Steeling, obs. var. STELLING, stand for a cask.

Steells, obs. form of STEAL v.

Steelless (stī'lles), a. [f. STEEL sb. + -LESS.] Of an article: Containing no steel.

Steel mill. 1. A device for producing a stream of sparks by the rapid revolution of a steel disc in contact with a flint; used for light in coal-mines before the invention of the safety-lamp.

2. *attrib.*

Steel pen. A pen made of steel, split at the tip like a quill. (In quot. 1636 *transf.*)

2. *colloq.* Applied to the 'swallow-tail' or evening-dress tail-coat.

Steel spring. A spring made of steel

Steel-plated -plater, -plating.

Steely (stī'lĭ), a. Also 6 **stely**. [f. STEEL sb.]
1. Of or belonging to steel; made or consisting of steel.

2. Resembling steel in appearance, colour, hardness, or some other quality.

3. Of iron: see quot.

4. Of a person, his qualities, etc.: a. Hard and cold as steel, unimpressionable, inflexible, obdurate.

b. In physical sense: Strong as steel.

5. *Comb.* with names of colours, as **steely-blue**, etc. b. in parasynthetic formations, as **steely-hearted**, **-stomached**, **-tongued** adjs.

Steelyard (stī'lyaɑd). *Hist.* [Curt. var. 5 stiljeyerd, etc., styliarde, -ierd, -yerd, 6 stilliard, (stuliard -yard), 6-7 stilyard, (6 styliard), stillyard, -e, 6 styliliarde, (stellzard, stilliart, stillyar, stilliyard), 6-7, 9 stillyard (6-yarde). 8. 6 steel(e)-yard, 6-7, 9 steel-yard, 7-9 steel-yard. 6-9 steelyard.]

1. The place on the north bank of the Thames above London Bridge where the Merchants of the Hanse had their establishment. Also, the merchants collectively.

b. A similar establishment in a provincial town.

2. A tavern within the precincts of the Steel-yard where 'rhenish wine' was sold.

Steelyard (stī'lyaɑd). Forms: e.7-8 stilliard, -yard, stilli(art), (7 stilard), 8 still-yard, 7 steelyard, 8- steelyard, steel-yard. [f. STEEL sb.1 + YARD sb.2; the formation was prob. suggested by the existence of STEELYARD1.]

1. An instrument for weighing by means of a lever with unequal arms, which moves on a fulcrum.

Steem, sb. Obs. Also 6 **steeme**. [Aphetic var. of ESTEEM sb.]
It is noteworthy that the first two examples are much earlier than any known instance of the fuller form.

Steem, sb. Obs. To stain (goods) on credit; to order in advance, bespeak. Also, to pay a deposit upon goods bought.

Steem, obs. form of STEAM.

Steen (stīn), sb.1 Forms: 1 stænan, 2 steanen, 3-5 stene, 3 steane, 5 stoyn(e, 8-9 steen, stein, 9 stean, stayn(e, [OE. stǽnan = OHG. (MHG.) steinīn, Goth. stainein, f. stǽn, OTeut. *stain- STONE sb.]
In certain dialects this and STONE are formally coincident.

†1. *trans.* To stone (a person); to put to death by stoning. *Obs.*

2. To line (a well or other excavation) with stone, brick or other material. Also with up.

Hence **Steened** ppl. a.

Steen (stīn), sb.2 [f. STEAN1.]

Stenbrass (stē'nbras). *S. Afr.* Also 8 **steenbras**, 9 **-brasem**, **steembrasa**. [Cape Du., f. Du. steen stone + brasem bream.]

Steenbok, steinbuck (stī'nbŏk, -bŭk). *Hist.* Also 8 **stinkirk**. [a. F. (cravate à la) Steinkerke, Steinkerque, from the victory of Steenkerke (Belgium) gained by the French over the English and their allies on 3 Aug. 1692.]

Steenbok (stī'nbŏk), Alsosteenbo(k-, buck, steinbo(c(k-, buck, steem-, steen-bok, l steen Stone sb. + bok BUCK sb.] Cf. STEINBOCK.] A small South-African, Rhaphiceros campestris.

Stone, obs. form of STEAN.

Steening (stī'nĭŋ), vbl. sb. [f. STEEN v.1 + -ING1.]
1. *concr.* The lining of a well or other excavation.

2. *dial.* A paved kerb across a river.

3. *attrib.*

Steenkirk (stī'nkĕɑk). *Hist.* Also 8 **stinkirk**. [a. F. (cravate à la) Steinkerke, Steinkerque, from the victory of Steenkerke (Belgium) gained by the French over the English and their allies on 3 Aug. 1692.]

Steep (stīp), a. Forms: 1 stéap, 5 steepe, (steppe), 6-7 steepe, 7- steep.
1. Extending to a great height; elevated, lofty.

2. Of eyes: Projecting; prominent (also *steep-out*); staring; glaring with passion.

Steep (stīp), sb.1 [f. STEEP v.1]
1. The process of steeping or soaking; the state of being steeped, esp. in phr. (to lay) a steep (obs.)

†2. The steep; the midday plunge taken by a stag in hot weather.

Steep (stīp), sb.2 [f. STEEP a.]
1. The declivity or slope of a mountain, hill, cliff; a steep or precipitous place.

2. A steep or precipitous place.

Steep (stīp), v.1 Forms: 3-6 stepe, 4-5 stype, 5 stipe, 6- steep. [ME. stepen.]
1. With a steep slope, abruptly.

2. To run steep = to run high (HIGH adv. 9).

3. With the eyes wide open. *Obs.*

Steep (stīp), v.2 Forms: 5-6 steppe, 5-7 steepe, 6 stepe(n, stype, (steyp), 6- steep, 6-7 steep, 6- steepe. [Of difficult etymology.]

1. *trans.* To soak in water or other liquid; chiefly, to do so for the purpose of softening, altering its properties, cleansing, or the like, or for that of extracting some constituent. Const. in; rarely with.

2. *fig.*

3. In various metaphorical applications.

Steeped (stīpt), ppl. a. [f. STEEP v.2 + -ED1.]
Hence **Steeped** ppl. a.

Steepen (stī'p'n), v. [f. STEEP a. + -EN5.]
1. *intr.* To become steep or steeper.

2. *trans. fig.* To increase ('pile on', 'heap up', also with up).

Steeper (stī'pəɑ). [f. STEEP v.2 + -ER1.]
1. One who steeps; *spec.* one who carries out the operation of steeping flax, wool, etc.

2. *Comb.* **Steep-down**, a. [STEEP a. + adv.]

Steep-down, a. [STEEP a. + DOWN.] Precipitous.

Steepish (stī'pĭʃ), a. [f. STEEP a. + -ISH1.]
Somewhat steep, rather steep.

Steeple (stī'p'l), sb. Forms: 1 stépel, stípel, 2-5 stepel, 4-5 stepil, 4-7 steple, 6 stepell, steeple, (5 stepul), 6-7 steple, stepyll, 7 steipil, steple, 6-7 stiple, steipel. [OE. stépel, -styple.]
1. A tall tower; a building of great altitude in proportion to its length and breadth.

2. A lofty tower forming part of a church, temple, or other public edifice (often serving to contain the bells); such a tower together with the spire or other superstructure by which it is surmounted.

Steeping (stī'pĭŋ), vbl. sb.1 [f. STEEP v.1 + -ING1.]
1. The action of tilting or giving an inclination.

Steeping (stī'pĭŋ), vbl. sb.2 [f. STEEP v.2 + -ING1.]
1. The action or process of STEEP v.2

Steeplish, a.

Steem, sb.

Steeple. [Cl. Du. *stapel* heap.] — PACK *sb.*[1] 9.

1. *trans.* To pack (a bell) in a steeple.

†2. To imprison in a steeple.

3. *intr.* To rise or tower like a steeple. Hence **Steepling** *ppl. a.*

Steeplechase, *sb.* [f. STEEPLE + CHASE.]
1. A horse-race across country or over a course furnished with hurdles, ditches, and other obstacles.

2. *transf.* A foot-race across country or over a course furnished with hurdles, ditches, and other obstacles.

3. A parlour game played on a board representing a steeplechase, each player having a metal figure of a horse.

Steeplechase, *v.* [f. STEEPLECHASE *sb.*] *intr.* To ride or run in a steeplechase; to practise riding in steeplechases. Also *transf.* and *fig.* So **Stee-plechasing** *vbl. sb.*

Stee·plechaser.

Steepled (stī·p'ld), *ppl. a.* [f. STEEPLE *sb.*[1] + -ED[2].]
1. Having the form of a steeple. *Obs.*
2. Furnished with, or having a steeple.

Steeplet (stī·p'let), *sb.* [Altered form of STAPLE *sb.* ... perh. influenced by prec.]

Steepless (stī·p'les), *a. nonce-word.* [f. STEEP *sb.* + -LESS.]

Steepwise, *adv.* [f. STEEP *sb.*[1] + -WISE.]

Steeply (stī·p'li), *adv.* [f. STEEP *a.* + -LY[2].]

†Steeple fair. *Obs.* In sarcastic use, an imaginary fair or market for church livings.

Steeple-house. A building with a steeple.

Steep-lo, *a. Naut.*

Steep-up, *a.* [f. STEEP *a.* + UP *adv.*] Precipitous; perpendicular.

Steepy (stī·pi), *a.* Obs.

Steer (stī·r), *sb.*[1] Forms: 1 stéor, stýr, 2 steore, 2–5 ster, 3–6 stere, 4 steer, 4–7 steere, 5 steyr, 4 steir, etc.

Steer (stī·r), *v.*[1] Obs. exc. in Comb.

Steer (stī·r), *sb.*[2] [Origin unknown; perh. some error.] ? A pile of wood.

Steer (stī·r), *v.*[2] Forms: 1 stéoran, (stéoran), stíeran, stíoran, 3 stiren, styran, 2 stire, stiren, stýre, steore, etc.
1. *trans.* To guide the course (of a vessel) by means of a rudder, or of an oar or paddle used like a rudder.

2. *intr.* In passive sense. Of a ship: To admit of being steered; to answer the helm (well or ill).

3. *trans.* To guide, conduct, lead (a person).

4. *intr.* To guide one's course (on land, in the air). Also *transf.*

†5. To check, restrain, control. In OE. also ... To rebuke.

†6. To govern, administer (government); to conduct (business, negotiations, etc.).

†7. To govern, rule. *Obs. exc.* as conscious metaphor (figurative use of sense 1).

Steerable (stī·rab'l), *a.* That may be steered or guided; dirigible.

Steerage (stī·rėdʒ), *sb.* Forms: 5–7 storage, 6 sterage, 7 steirage, (stirage, sterege), ... 7– steerage.

Steer-board, -bord, obs. ff. STARBOARD.

Steered (stī·rd), *ppl. a.* Guided.

Steerer (stī·rə(r)), *sb.*

2. One who steers, a steersman ; a coxswain (of a rowing boat).

Steering (stī·riŋ), *vbl. sb.* [f. STEER *v.*¹ + -ING¹.]

1. The action of the verb, in various senses.

2. Short for *steering-gear*.

3. *attrib.* and *comb.*: a. simple attrib., as *steering-apparatus, -fan, -fork, -gear, -handle.*

Steering, Sc. variant of STIRRING.

†Steerish, *a. Obs.* [f. STEER *sb.*¹ + -ISH¹.]

†Steeress. *Obs.* [OE. *stéorlas*: see STEER *sb.*² and -LESS.]

†Steersman, *rare.* [Formed as STEERS-MAN + WOMAN *sb.*] A woman who steers.

Steerling, *sb.* [f. STEER *sb.*¹ + -LING.] A young steer.

Steersman (stī·smăn). Forms: 1 stéoresman, *etc.*

†Steert, *var.* STEART, *a point of land.*

Steeve (stīv), *sb.*¹ *Naut.* Also 8-9 ative, 9 steeve.

Steeve (stīv), *sb.*² *Naut.* Also 7 stive, 8 steeve, stive, stieve. *Obs.*

Steeve (stīv), *v.*¹ *trans.* To make 'steeve' or firm; to strengthen, fix, secure.

Steeve (stīv), *v.*² *Naut.* In 6 steeve, 9 steave.

Steeve, variant of STEEVEN.

†Steever (stī·vez), *sb. jewish.* Also *stever, shtibivz.* [Yiddish pronunciation of LG. *stiver*.]

Steevy (stī·vi), *adv.* Now only Sc. Forms: see STEEVE *a.* [f. STEEVE *a.* + -LY².] Firmly, un-yieldingly.

†Stegh, obs. form of STECH *v.*

†Stegno·tic, *a.* and *sb. Med. Obs.* [ad. mod.L. *stegnoticus*, ad. Gr. στεγνωτικός.]

Stego (stego), used as combining form of Gr. root στέγος of στέγειν to cover, στέγη covering, στέγος (neut.) roof, in certain modern scientific terms.

Stegocarpous *a.* [Gr. *-καρπος* fruit.]

Stego·cephalous *a.*

†Steg, obs. form of STEEVE *a.*

Steganography (steganŏ·grăfi), *Obs. exc.*

So Steganogram, a cryptogram; **Steganographer, Steganographist**, one expert in steganography, a cryptographer; **Steganogra·phical** *a.*, pertaining to steganography.

Steganopod (stegă·nopŏd), *sb.* and *a. Ornith.*

So Stegano·podan, Steganopodous *adj.*

Stegh, var. of STCH *v.*

Steinmannite

Stegoid (stē·goid), *a. Craniometry.*

Stegosaur, Stegosaurus (stegosô·rus), *Palæont.*

Stein (Stīn), *sb.* [G. *stein*.]

Steiner, Steier, var. STEAD, STEER, STAIR.

Stein, rare obs. form of STRAN.

†Steinbock (stī·nbŏk), Also **steinbok**, (7 stein-boke). [G. *steinbock*.]

Steining, variant of STENING.

Steinkle, sb. f. STEINKLE.

†Steinmannite (stai·nmănait), *Min.* [Named (*steinmannit*) by Zippe 1833 after Prof. J. Steinmann: see -ITE².]

Steke, obs. f. Stela. 907 STELLARY. STELLASCOPE. 908 STELLIGERATE

Steke, obs. f. STELA. 2 ; variant of STEEK *v.*²

Stokelyng, Stel, obs. ff. STICKLING, STALL *sb.*¹

†Stela (stī·lă). Pl. **stelæ** (stī·lī), *rarely* **stelas.**

Stelar (stī·lar), *a.* [f. *stel-* mod. structure.]

Stele (stil), *stī·li, Antiq.* [= A dissyllable, repr. Gr. στήλη standing block or slab, f. Indo-germanic root *stā-* to stand.

Steliferous, Stell, obs. f. STELLIFEROUS, STELL.

Stele·chite, *Obs.* [ad. Gr. στηλεχίτης.]

†Ste·lion. *Obs. rare.*¹ [ad. Gr. στηλίον.]

Steliteutio·n, *rare.* [ad. Gr. στηλιτεύειν.]

Stell (stel), *sb.* and *north.* Also 2 stello, (7 stel-, 6-7 stell, 8 stelle), 9 stale, 7-9 still.

Stella (ste·lă), *a. Obs.*¹ [L. *stella* star.]

Stellar (ste·lar), *a.* [ad. late L. *stellāris*, f. *stella* star: see -AR¹.]

†Stellary (ste·lări), *a.* [L. *stellāris*: see -ARY.] STELLAR.

†Stellate (ste·lět), *a.* [ad. L. *stellātus*, pa. pple. of *stellāre* to set with stars.] **A.** *adj.*

So Ste·llated *a.*, f. STELLATE + -ED.

Stella·scope *Obs.* [+ -SCOPE.]

†Stellate (ste·lět), *v.* [L. *stellāt-*, ppl. stem of *stellāre* to cover or set with stars.] *trans.* To make stellate or star-shaped.

Stellated (ste·lětid), *a.* [f. STELLATE *a.* + -ED.]

†Stellatúre. *Obs. rare.*¹

Stelleffer. *Obs.* [f. L. *stella* star + *-fer* bearing.]

†Stelleferal *a. Obs.* [f. L. *stelliferal-* : see prec. + -AL.] STELLIFEROUS.

†Stellifer *a. Obs.* [ad. L. *stellifer-*.]

Stelliferous (steli·ferăs), *a.* [f. L. *stellifer-* + -OUS.] Bearing stars.

Stellify (ste·lifai), *v.* [a. OF. *stellifier*, ad. med.L. *stellificāre*.]

Stellify (ste·lifai), *trans.* To place among the stars.

Stellifo·rmly *adv.*

Stellifica·tion (stelifikē·ʃăn).

Stelliform (ste·lifôrm), *a.* [ad. mod.L. *stelliformis*.]

†Stelliferate (steli·jerāt), *a. Obs. rare.*¹ [ad. L. *stelligerāt-*.] ? Exalted to the heavens.

Stelling (ste'liŋ), sb. Brit. Guiana. [a. Du. stelling scaffolding, landing-stage, f. stellen to place.] A wooden pier or landing-place.

‖**Stellio** (ste'li·o). Zool. Now rare. [L.] A kind of lizard with star-like spots, mentioned by ancient writers.

Stellion (ste'ljŏn). Forms: a stellioun, (6 errom. stelon), 6- stellion. [a. L. stellionem.]

Stellionate (ste'ljŏnĕt). Civil Law. Also 7 -at. [ad. L. stelliōnātus (n stem), f. stellion-em, a fraudulent person, perh. a. transl. use of stelliōn-em a kind of lizard (see STELLION). See quot. 1754.]

Stellite (ste'lait), sb. [f. L. stella star + -ITE.]

Stell-net (see STELL sb.⁴)

Stellular (ste'liŭlăr), a. [ad. late L. stellula, dim. of stella star + -AR.] Having the form of a small star or small stars.

Stelography (stĭgra·fi). Also 6 St- Gr. στηλογραφία, f. στήλη STELE + -γραφία writing. [f. -GRAPH.]

Stem (stem), sb.¹ Forms: 1 stefn, stemn, 6-7 stemme, 7 stemne, stemm, 4- stem. [OE. stefn, stefn wk. masc. (for the corresponding forms in continental Teut. see STEM sb.²)]

Stem (stem), sb.² [ad. ON. stamn, stafn masc.]

Stemma (ste'mă), sb. [L. a. Gr. στέμμα garland.] Pl. **stemmata** (ste'mătă).

Stemmatiform (ste'mătifōrm), a. Zool. [f. L. stemmat-, STEMMA + -FORM.] Having the form of stemmata.

Stemmation (ste'mătās). a Zool. [L. stemmatus.]

Stemmed (stemd), a. [f. STEM sb.¹ + -ED².]

Stemmer (ste'măr). [f. STEM v.¹ + -ER¹.]

Stemming, vbl. sb.

Stemless (ste'mlĕs), a.¹ [f. STEM sb.¹ + -LESS.] Having no stem.

Stemless (ste'mlĕs), a.² [f. STEM sb.² + -LESS.]

Stemlet (ste'mlĕt). [f. STEM sb.¹ + -LET.]

Stemlike, a.

Stemming, vbl. sb.

Stemmy (ste'mi), a. [f. STEM sb.¹ + -Y.]

Stemple (ste'mp'l). Mining. Also **stempel**. [Of obscure origin; = MHG. stempfel (Lexer), mod.G. stempel, etc. Cf. MDu. stumpel hole of furniture.]

Stemplar (ste'mplăr). [f. STEMPLE.]

Stemson (ste'msŏn). Naut. [f. STEM sb.² after keelson.]

Stemware (ste'mwĕăr).

Stench (stenʃ), sb. Also 6-7 stinch, 7 stanch. [OE. stenc masc.]

Stench (stenʃ), v. Also 6-7 stinch, 7 stanch. [OE. stencan.]

Stenched, a. rare. [Alteration of stanched.]

Stenchel, variant of STANCHEL.

Stencher, variant of STANCHER.

Stenchful (ste'nʃfŭl), a. [f. STENCH sb. + -FUL.] Full of stench, smelling offensively, stinking.

Stenchy (ste'nʃi), a. [f. STENCH sb. + -Y.] Emitting a stench, foul-smelling.

Stencil (ste'nsĭl), sb. Also 8 stensil, 9 stencel. [app. f. ME. stanselen, stansel to ornament with various colours.]

Step (step), v. Pa. t. and pa. pple. **stepped** (stept), formerly also **stept**; pa. pple. **stapen**, **steppen**, etc.

Stepdaughter. Occasional forms of the prefix in ME. are stip- (styp-), ste-, stæ-, stappe-

Stepdame (ste·pdēm). Now arch. Also **stedame**. [f. STEP- + DAME (sense 2).] A stepmother.

Stepfather. Forms: 1 stéopfæder, stéopfædor, 4 stiffader, -dre, steofader...

Stepbrother (ste·pbrŏðər) sb. [See STEP-. OHG. stiofbruoder (mod.G. stiefbruder).] A son, by a former marriage, of one's stepfather or stepmother.

Stepchild (ste·ptʃəild) sb. [OE. stéopcild (MHG. stiefchint). An orphan.

Stephan, obs. form of STEVEN.

Stephane (ste·fănē) [Gr. στεφάνη.] A kind of diadem or coronet, represented in statuary as worn by the goddess Hera and other deities; also worn by military commanders.

Stephanial, etc. Of or pertaining to the stephanion.

Stephanion (stĕfā·niǫn). [Gr.] Craniometry. Pl. **-ia, -ions**. A point on the cranium.

Stephanite (ste·fănǝit). Min. [ad. G. *stephanit* (Haidinger, 1845), named after the Archduke Stephan of Austria.] Sulphantimonide of silver, black in colour and very brittle.

Stephanophore (ste·fănǫfōǝr). One wearing a crown.

Stephanotis (stefǎnō·tis). [mod.L., a Gr.] fit for a crown or wreath.

Step, sb. [A Com. Teut. word.] A motion made by lifting the foot and setting it down again in a new position.

Stepdame, -mother.

Stepladder. [STEP sb.] A ladder which has flat steps instead of rungs.

Stepless, having no step or steps.

Stepmother, etc.

1. A woman who has married one's father after one's mother's death.

Steppage (ste·pėdʒ). Path. [a. F. steppage.]

Steppe (step). [a. Russian *step'*.] One of the vast comparatively level and treeless plains of south-eastern Europe and Siberia.

Stepped (stept), ppl. a. [STEP sb. and v. + -ED.] Having a step or steps; formed in a series of steps.

Stepper (ste·pǝr). 1. A horse with good paces and showy action.

Stepping (ste·piŋ), vbl. sb. [-ING.] The action of STEP v.; an instance of this.

Stepony. Also 7 stepponi, copy, stipona, stipponie, 8 steponey, stepany, stepney. [Of obscure origin.]

Stepping-stone. Also 4 steppyngston, 7 Sc. stopping stane, stapping ston. [STEPPING.]

1. A stone for stepping upon. a. A stone placed in the bed of a stream or on muddy or swampy ground, to facilitate crossing on foot.

2. attrib., as stepping-board, -line, -piece, -place, -wheel; stepping-off place jocular, the place at the end of the world, whence one steps off into vacancy; stepping-stile = STEP-STILE.

Stepson (ste·psǫn). Also 1 step-, 5 stepp-, OE. stéopsunu; see STEP-. Cf. Du. stiefzoon, MLG. stēpsone, etc. A son of one's husband or wife.

Stercoraceous (stɜːkǫrē·ʃǝs) a. [f. L. stercor-, stercus dung + -ACEOUS.] Consisting of, containing, or pertaining to fæces. Also stercoral, stercorary.

Stercoraceously, adv.

Stercoremia, **-aemia**. Path. [f. L. stercor-, stercus dung, form + Gr. αἷμα blood.] Contamination of the blood by absorption from retained fæces.

Stercoral (stɜː·kǫrăl), a. [f. L. stercor-, stercus dung + -AL.] = STERCORACEOUS. Stercoral dung.

Stercorary (stɜː·kǫrări), a. and sb. [ad. L. stercorari-us.] Of or pertaining to dung. Also, a place where dung is stored.

Stercorate (stɜː·kǫrēt), v. [ad. L. stercorāt-, stercorāre.] To manure with dung.

Stercorean (stɜːkǫrī·ăn), a. [f. L. stercor-, stercus + -EAN.] = STERCORACEOUS.

Stercorianist (stɜːkǫrī·ănist), sb. Eccl. Hist. [ad. med.L. stercorianista.]

Stercorin (stɜː·kǫrin), sb. [a. F. stercorine.]

Stercorist (stɜː·kǫrist). Eccl. Hist. Also -ite. = STERCORIANIST.

Stercorous (stɜː·kǫrǝs), a. Obs. [ad. L. stercorōs-us.]

Stercory (stɜː·kǫri), sb. Obs. Also stercorie. [ad. L. stercor-ium.] Dung, ordure.

Stercus (stɜː·kǝs), sb. [L.]

Stereo- (ste·rio, stī·rio), before a vowel **stere-**, combining form repr. Gr. στερεός solid, in various (chiefly recent) scientific and technical terms (for the more important of these see below).

Stereobate (ste·riobēt). Arch. [ad. L. stereobat-a, a. Gr. στερεοβάτης.]

Stereochemistry (sterio·ke·mistri). [f. STEREO- + CHEMISTRY.] The branch of chemistry which deals with theoretical differences in the relative position in space of atoms in a molecule.

Stereochromatic (steriokrǫmæ·tik), a.

Stereochromy (sterio·krǫmi). [ad. mod.G. stereochromie.]

Stereogram (ste·riogræm), sb. [f. STEREO- + -GRAM.] A diagram representing a solid object on a plane.

Stereograph (ste·riograf), sb. [f. STEREO- + -GRAPH.] A picture (or pair of pictures) representing the object so that it appears (or may be made to appear) solid.

Stereographic (steriogræ·fik), a. [ad. mod.F. stéréographique.] Pertaining to or effected by stereography.

Stereographical. ... Now *rare.* ...

Stereographically, *adv.* In a stereographic manner; by stereographic projection.

Stereography. 1. The art of delineating or representing the forms of solid bodies on a plane, as in perspective; in quot. 1860, stereoscopic photography.

Stereogram.

Stereome (ster'iŏm). Also (after Ger.) -om.

Stereometer (steriŏ'mĭtər), *sb.* ... 1. An instrument for measuring the specific gravity of porous or equivalent bodies, invented by Say, a French officer of engineers, in 1797. Also *attrib.* 2. An apparatus consisting of a frame of bars and columns with sliding rods and wires, for illustrating problems in solid geometry.

Stereometric (steriŏmĕ'trik), *a.* [ad. mod.L. *stereometricus* (Fergius 1583), f. Gr. *stereometr-ĭkos*, f. *stereometría* STEREOMETRY.] Pertaining to stereometry or solid geometry; relating to or existing in three dimensions of space.

Stereometrical ... Now *rare.* [f. prec. + -AL.]

Stereometrically, *adv.* Now *rare.* [f. prec. + -AL.]

Stereometry (steriŏ'mĕtri), *sb.* ... 1. The art or science of measuring solids; that branch of geometry which deals with solid figures, solid geometry; the practical application of this to the measurement of solid bodies.

Stereomonoscope.

Stereomould (ste'riŏ,mŏuld), *v.* [f. STEREO- + MOULD *v.*, after STEREOTYPE *v.*: cf. STEREO-.] *trans.* To stereotype by casting in a mould.

Stereopticon (steriŏ'ptikŏn). [f. Gr. *stereo-* + *optikon*, neut. of *optikós* OPTIC.]

Stereoscope (ste'riŏskōp, *often ster'iō-*), *sb.* [f. Gr. *stereo-* + -SCOPE.] 1. An instrument for obtaining, from two pictures (usually photographs) of an object, taken from slightly different points of view (corresponding to the positions of the two eyes), a single image giving the impression of solidity or relief, as in ordinary vision of the object itself.

Stereoscopic (steriŏskŏ'pik), *a.* [f. prec. + -IC.]

Stereoscopical, *a.*

Stereoscopically, *adv.*

Stereoscopist.

Stereoscopy (steriŏ'skŏpi).

Stereotomic.

Stereotomy (steriŏ'tŏmi).

Stereotype (ste'riŏtaip, *often ster'iō-*), *sb.* [ad. F. *stéréotype* (1795), f. Gr. *stereo-* solid + *type* TYPE.] 1. *trans.* To cast a stereotype plate (from a forme of type); to prepare (literary matter) for printing by means of stereotypes.

Stereotyped (-taipt), *ppl. a.*

Stereotyper.

Stereotypic.

Stereotyping, *vbl. sb.*

Stereotypography.

Steril.

Sterile (ste'ril, steril), *a.* [ad. F. *stérile* ... or ad. L. *sterilis*.]

Sterilely, *adv.*

Sterility (sterĭ'liti). [ad. L. *sterilitās*, or ad. F. *stérilité*.]

Sterilization (sterilaiz'eiʃən).

Sterilize (ste'rilaiz), *v.*

Sterilizer.

Sterin, Stering, obs. ff. STERN *a.*, STIRRING.

Sterisol.

Sterk, obs. form of STARK.

Sterlet (stə'rlet). Also 6 **sterledy**, 7 **sterledt**, 6-8, *sterlady*, 7-8 *sterlet*, 8-9 *sterlin*, 9 *sterlet*.

Sterling (stə'rliŋ), *sb.* and *a.* Forms: 1-4, 6 **steorling**, **styrling**, 4-5, 6 **sterling**, 4 *starling*, etc. [Early ME. *sterling*, whence OF. *esterlin*, med.L. *esterlingus*, *sterlingus*, etc.] 1. The English silver penny of the Norman and subsequent dynasties.

Sterlingness.

Stern (stə:n), *sb.* 1 **stearn**, **stearno**, **stern**, *starn*, 7 *stern* (*stern*), *etc.*

Stern, starn (stə:n), *sb.* 2

Stern, sb.[1] Forms: α. 4–8 sterne, 4 stoerne, 5–6 stearne, 6 sterane, 6–7 stearne, 4– stern. β. 6, 9 starn dial., 7 starne dial. γ. 6 stern. *

1. The steering gear of a ship, the rudder and helm together; but often applied to the helm only, less commonly to the helm itself. *Obs.*

†b. *transf.* An apparatus which controls a horse, machine, etc. as a rudder controls a ship. *Obs.*

†c. *fig.* That which guides or controls affairs, actions, etc.; also, from (the metaphor of the ship of state), government, rule.

†d. In various phrases, with literal or figurative meaning. *To be, sit, at the stern*, to stand (to conduct, guide, hold, keep, possess, rule, steer, turn the stern:* to steer, govern, control, to occupy the seat of government. *To take in hand the stern*, to assume the government. *Obs.*

2. The hind part of a ship or boat (as distinguished from the *bow* and *midships*); in restricted sense, the external rear part of a ship's hull; also *spec.* in vessels of ordinary type, the overhanging portion of the hull abaft the sternpost. Often in collocation with STEM, HEAD.

b. Phrases with *stern*: *On stern, a stern, by stern*; etc.

8. Special comb.: †stern-bearer, a rudder-bearer, ship; stern-boat, (of a boat hanging at a ship's stern; (b) an attendant boat following a stern; stern-frame, (b) the framework of a ship's stern, stern-gallery (see GALLERY sb.[1]); stern-line = STERNFAST; stern-looker (see LOCKER sb.[1] III.); stern-notch, a notch in the topmost plank of a boat's stern to receive an oar used in sculling or steering; stern-port, (a) an ornament on a vessel's stern; (b) *pecularly*, the rail of an animal; stern-shot, (a) of wood to which the side planks of a ship or boat are brought, so that it terminates the hull behind; stern-port, a port or window in the stern of a vessel; stern-race, race in which one boat closely follows another without being able to overtake it; stern-shot, a shot; stern-rudder, the rudder at the stern, as distinguished from the *bow-rudder* with which some craft are fitted; stern-sea, a sea which beats on a ship's stern; a following sea; stern shot, a shot at the buttocks of a fleeing animal; stern speed, the speed of a vessel travelling stern-foremost with engines reversed; stern-timber (see quots.); stern tube, (a) the tube in which the propeller-shaft works; (b) a tube fitted in the stern of a war-ship from which torpedoes are discharged; stern-wager = stern-race; stern-walk (see quot. 1867); stern-way, the movement of a ship going stern-foremost; also *transf.*; stern-ways arts, *n.*, jocularly, the buttocks. Also STERN-BOARD, -CHASE, -CHASER, -FAST, -MAN, -POST, -SHEET, -WHEEL.

Stern (stɔ̄rn), *a.* (*sb.*[4] *and adv.*) Forms: α. 1 styrne, 3–5 sturne, 3 stuyrne, 4–5 stourne, 4 sturen, 5 sturun; β. 3 Orm. stirne, 4–5 stirn, 4–5 stirne, stiern; 3 Orm. stirne, stourne, 4–5 sternne, styerne, stierne; 4–5 storen(e, -in, -yn(e, -ynne; 6 stearne, 8–9; 3–7 stern, 1 OE. (WS.) styrne, earlier *stierne* evidenced by *sternlice*; see STERNLY *adv.*

The ME. forms, particularly Ormin's *stirne* (cf. *hirde* from Anglian *hierde*), point to an OTeut. type *sternjo*-, which is represented only in English.

A. *adj.*

1. Of persons and things personified, their dispositions and temper: Severe, strict, inflexible; rigorous in punishment or condemnation; not inclined to leniency.

†3. In a bad sense: Merciless, cruel. *Obs.*

2. Hard or severe to endure or bear; grievous, distressing, violent. *Obs.*

3. Having a grave aspect or manner; grave, austere, forbidding.

b. *Const. with, to, towards.* (OE. dative.)

c. Rigorous in morals or principles; uncompromising, austere.

d. Of personal attributes, utterances, feelings, etc.: Severe, strict, hard, grim, harsh.

4. Of the voice: Harsh, menacing.

†d. Of the weather: Severe, causing hardship.

7. Of a country, or its physical features, the soil, etc. (with fig. notion of senses 1 and 4): Unkindly, inhospitable; destitute of amenity; forbidding in aspect, frowning, gloomy.

B. *adv.* Sternly.

†3. In alliterative verse: A stern or bold man.

Stern (stɔ̄rn), *v.*[1] [f. STERN sb.[2]; cf. ON. *stjórna*.]

†1. *trans.* and *intr.* To steer. *Obs.*

STERN. 931 STERNNESS STERNO- 932 STERNUTATORY.

Sternboard. *Naut.* [f. STERN sb.[2] + BOARD.]

†Sterneess. *Obs. rare.* [f. STERN *a.* + -NESS.] Sternness; severity.

Sterniform (stɔ̄·nifɔ̄m), *a. Ent.* [f. (as STERNUM) + -FORM.] Having the form of a sternum or sternite.

Sterning (stɔ̄·niŋ), *vbl. sb. Ornith.* [f. STERN *a.*] Belonging to or having the characters of the *Sterninæ* or terns, a subfamily of *Laridæ*, typified by the genus *Sterna*.

Sternite (stɔ̄·nit). *Zool. and Comp. Anat.* [f. STERN-UM + -ITE.] The under or ventral part of each somite or segment of the body of an insect or other arthropod; correlated with *tergite* and *pleurite*. *b.* = STERNEBRA. *rare.*

†Sternman. *Naut.* [STERN *sb.*[2] + MAN.]

Sternnness (stɔ̄·nnes), *sb.* [f. STERN *a.* + -NESS.]

†Sterno-. *Comb.* The stem of Gr. στέρνον, the breast, used in combination with another element.

Sterno-costal (stɔ̄·nokɒ·stal), *a. Anat.* [f. STERN-O + COSTAL.]

Sternum (stɔ̄·nǒm). *Anat. and Zool. Pl.* **sterna.** [mod. L., ad. Gr. στέρνον chest, breast. Cf. STERN *sb.*[2]]

Sternutament. *Obs. rare.* [ad. L. sternūtāmentum, f. sternūtāre: see next.]

Sternutation (stɔ̄·nuti·ʃen), sb. [ad. L. sternūtātiōn-em, n. of action f. sternūtāre to sneeze.]

Sternutative (stɔ̄·niutātiv), *a.* and *sb.*

Sternutatory (stɔ̄·niutātŏri), *a.* and *sb.*

Sternutory ...

Stern-wheel ... A paddle-wheel placed at the stern of a small river or lake steamer.

Stern-wheeler ...

Sterny, starny, a. Sc. Starry.

Sterop(e, -oppe, obs. forms of STIRRUP.

†Sterquil'inan, a. Obs. rare⁻¹. [Formed as next + -AN.] ...

†Sterquil'inous, a. Obs. rare⁻¹. [f. L. sterquilīn-ium (see quot.) + -OUS.] Of or belonging to the dunghill.

Sterrā variant of STARRA.

Sterrate (star'eit), ppl. a. Sc. A stellate sponge-spicule ...

Hence **Sterra'tral** a., pertaining to, or composed of STERRASTERS.

Sterre, obs. f. STAR sb.¹, STEER n., STIR v.

Starred, -id, -it, obs. forms of STARRED.

Sterrep, obs. form of STIRRUP.

Sterrile, -ill, obs. forms of STERILE.

Sterro-metal [Gr. στερρό-ς stiff, hard.] An alloy of copper and zinc, with a small amount of iron and tin. Also shortened sterro.

Sterrop, -up, obs. forms of STIRRUP.

Stert(e, obs. forms of START.

Stertle, stertle, obs. forms of STARTLE.

Stertel, stertelt, obs. forms of STITHY.

†Stertor (ster'təz). [mod.L., f. L. stertĕre to snore. Cf. F. stertor.] A heavy snoring sound accompanying inspiration in profound unconsciousness. Path.

Stertorous (ster'tərəs), a. [f. STERTOR + -OUS. Cf. F. stertoreux.] Characterized by, of the nature of, stertor or snoring.

Stertorously, adv.

Stertorousness.

Sterve, obs. f. STARVE.

Steryne, -yrne, obs. forms of STEER sb.

Stet (stet). Printing. [3rd sing. pres. subjunct. of L. stāre to stand.] 'Let it stand'; a direction in the margin of a proof or MS. ...

Stetch: see STITCH sb. dial.

†Stete, v. Obs. Only in pa. t. and pple. stett, stettid (wettie). [Perh. repr. OE. *stētan = OFris. stēta (EFris. stâte), NFris. stiate, WFris. stjitte), ON. steyta (Sw. stöta, Da. stöde):—pre-Teut. *staujan, related to the stv. v. Goth. stautan, Du. stooten, OHG. stōzan (MHG. stōzen, mod.G. stossen), to push] ...

To push, shove, kick; to throw or fling violently.

Stetho-, before a vowel **steth-**, combining form repr. Gr. στῆθος breast, chest, occurring in medical terms. **Ste·tho·gra·phy**, the photographic representation of the movements of the chest ...

Stethograph (ste'θəgræf). [f. STETHO- + -GRAPH.] An instrument for automatically recording the movements of the chest in breathing ...

Stethom'eter (stɪθɒ'mɪtəɹ). [f. STETHO- + -METER. Cf. F. stéthomètre (from Eng.).] An instrument for measuring the extent of the movement of the walls of the chest in breathing.

Stethophone (ste'θəfoʊn). [f. STETHO- + -PHONE.] A name given independently to two improved forms of stethoscope: see quots.

Stethoscope (ste'θəskoʊp). [f. STETHO- + -SCOPE. Cf. F. stéthoscope (Laennec, the inventor, 1819).] An instrument used for examining the chest or other part by auscultation ...

Stetho·scope v. trans., to apply a stethoscope to, examine with a stethoscope. **Stetho·scopic** (-skɒ'pɪk) [= F. stéthoscopique], adj., pertaining to, or used or obtained by a stethoscope. **Stetho·scopically** adv., by means of the stethoscope. **Stetho·scopist** (stɪθɒ'skəpɪst), one who uses a stethoscope. **Stethoscopy** (stɪθɒ'skəpɪ), examination of the chest or other part with a stethoscope; the use of the stethoscope.

Stet Processus (stet pro'sesəs). Law. [L. let process (i.e. proceedings) stand] ...

Stethy, obs. form of STITHY.

†Stet proce·ssus. Law. [L.—let process stand.]

Steuard, -art, obs. forms of STEWARD.

Steuch, variant of STEW sb.² Sc.

Studiant, Steure, obs. ff. STUDENT, STIR v.

Steven ... A workman employed either as overseer or labourer in loading and unloading the cargoes of merchant vessels.

Stevedorage ...

Stevedore (ste'vɪdɔːɹ), sb. [a. Sp. estivador, agent-n. (1 Dicts.) estivador. a. Sp. estivador, agent-n. f. estivar to stow a cargo: see STEEVE v.¹ A med. L. stivator in the same sense, together with the verb stivare, occurs A.D. 1263 in Las Matrès Trinitè de Pais (J886) Docum. 39, 60.] ...

Stevedore v. trans.

Stevedoring vbl. sb.

Stevel, obs. f. STAVEL.

Steven (ste'v'n), sb.¹ Obs. exc. dial. Forms: 6 stevin, -yn, 6-7 steven. [Either repr. OE. stefn var. of stemn (see below), or ad. the equivalent Du. or LG. steven.] ...

†Steven, sb.² Obs. Forms: 6 stewin, -yn, 6-7 steven. ... Money.

†Steven, v.¹ [OE. stefnan, stafnan, f. stefn, stafn STEVEN sb.¹] intr. In sense 'to appoint, constitute.'

†Steven, v.² [OE. stefnan, ...] To appoint, constitute.

Steven (ste'v'n), sb.³ Sc. slang. Money.

†Steven, stevene, stevin, etc.: see STEVEN.

Stevin, stevns, stevon, etc.: see STEVEN.

Stew (stiū), sb.¹ Forms: 4- stew, 4- stewe. ... OF. estui (mod.F. étui) case, sheath, also tub for keeping fish in a boat, verbal noun f. estuier to stow up, keep ...

Stew, sb.¹ ... 2. A pond or tank in which fish are kept until needed for the table.

3. An artificial oyster-bed.

Stew v.¹ ... †b. transf. A pond of any kind; also, a moat.

3. An artificial oyster-bed.

4. A brewing place (or cistern).

Stew (stiū), sb.² Forms: 4 stu, stuwe, stuyue, styue, 5 stywe, 5 stw, stywe, 4-6 stuw, 4-7 stewe (-ue). [OF. estuve (mod.F. étuve), f. estuver ...] ...

†Stew, sb.³ Obs. Forms: 4 stywe, 4 steowen, 5 steowin. [Early ME. steowi, steve: the compound stiwarde occurs ...]

Stew (stiū), v.² Forms: 4 stue, stuwe, stowyn, stuwyn, stuyn, 5-6 stewe, 5-7 stue, styue, stywen, 5-6 steuwe, -y, 5-7 stewe, 4-7 stew. [a. OF. estuver (mod.F. étuver) ...]

Stewable (stiū'ab'l), a. [f. STEW v.² + -ABLE.] Capable of being stewed.

Steward (stiū'əd), sb. Forms: 1 stigweard, stiweard 1-3 stiward, 3-5 stywarde, 4-6 steward(e, 4-7 stuard, 5 stywarde, 4-6 stuardwarde, 5-6 steuart, 5-6 stewartde, etc.; 7 sewart ... [OE. stíweard, stígweard ...]

rente and fond Of any lord that is in Engelond. c1420 Sir Amadace (Camden) i, The stuard sayd, Sir, ȝe awe wele mo..ne ȝe may of ȝour londus rere, In faythe this seuyn ȝere. 1488 Maldon (Essex) Liber B. fol. 39 Robert Plomer, chefe Styward of landis on-to lord Henry, Erle of Essex. 1577 Googe tr. Heresbach's Husb. i. 11 Ouer my Gate I haue laide my Steward, from whence he may looke into the Court..and ouersee his neighbour the Bayly. 1741 Middleton Cicero I. vi. 456 The principal manager or steward of all his affairs. 1821 D'Oyly Life Sancroft I. 463 On the following day, the servants of his establishment were dismissed by the steward. 1846 McCulloch Acc. Brit. Emp. (1854) I. 451 We believe that the stewards of England, though inferior, perhaps, to the factors of Scotland, are a..useful body of men. 1892 Lady Verney Verney Mem. I. 14 The estate had been so long without a head, under the management of the steward. 1910 C. Shorter Highw. & Byways Buckingh. xvi. 177 The present Manor House..has long been given over to the Duke of Bedford's steward.

b. *Steward of the manor*: one who transacts the financial and legal business of a manor on behalf of the lord; he holds the manor-court in the lord's name and keeps a copy of its rolls, whence the name *steward of copyhold*. *Steward of the leet, steward of the hundred, steward of the haven-court*, an official with similar functions in the leet, hundred, and haven courts.

1303 R. Brunne Handl. Synne 5421 Stywardes..þat lordyngs courtys holde. 1377 Langl. P. Pl. B. Prol. 96 In stede of stuwardes sytten and demen. 1425 Rolls of Parlt. IV. 306/2 Stuardus of Letus and Hundredis. 1531 Star Chamber Cases (Selden Soc.) II. 186 William Marchall gentleman than being Steward of the seid Manour. c1537 in W. Rye Cromer (1889) 52 Henry Erle of Surrey High Steward of the Kyngs Haven Courts in Cromer. 1577 Leigh Armorie 44 b, Yerely Fees to any Receiuour..high Stewarde, or vnder Stewarde..to bee goyng out of a Mannour,..are called Reprises. c1600 Mannor & Crt. Baron (1909) 200 The Stewarde ys an offycer named by the Lorde, and his office ys to directe the sewtors by order of lawe to recorde and regester the plees and Judgements of the Courte...And there is no Judge there but Recorder or clerke as shalbe sayde ..[he] cannot quash an Essoin nor doe any other thinge without the assente of the Sewtors. 1791 Ritson Jurisd. Crt.-Leet Introd. p. viii, The Leet is a court of record... held..before the Steward..of the Lord. 1864 Miss S. P. Fox Kingsbridge Estuary 3 The Manor of Kingsbridge belongs to John Scobell, Esq...whose Steward holds a Court Leet and Court Baron here. 1897 E. Howlett in W. Andrews' Legal Lore 93 The steward also usually presides over the copyhold courts of the manor.

c. The title of: The administrator, often with merely nominal duties, of certain estates of the Crown, as *Steward of Blackburn Hundred*, † *the Duchy of Lancaster*. For *Steward of the Chiltern Hundreds*, see Chiltern 1.

1444 Rolls of Parlt. V. 106/1 The Styward of the Duche of Lancastre. c1472 Plumpton Corr. (Camden) 26 To our right trustie & welbeloved Sir William Plompton, knight, steward of the lordshipp of Spofford. 1499 N. Riding Rec. N.S. (1894) I. 130 To..Sir Ric' Chomley, Stuard of oure lordship of Pykeryng. 1600 in Cath. Rec. Soc. Publ. V. 383 Out of Blacborne hundreth, whereof yt maiestie haith made him the stuarde.

d. In Scotland: A magistrate originally appointed by the king to administer the crown lands forming a Stewartry, *q.v.*; see quot. 1754. *Principal stewart*, such an official as distinguished from the *stewart-depute*, to whom part of the duties were usually delegated. *Obs.* exc. *Hist.*

1432 Sc. Acts Jas. I (1814) II. 21 Þe lorde of þe Regalite or his stewart or balȝe. 1473-4 Acc. Ld. High Treas. Scot. I. 5 In the..of the Stewarte of Kirkcudbrith lxli. c1575 Balfour Practicks (1754) 16 Stewartis and Stewartreis. ..Strathearne, Lord Drummond. 1678 Sir G. Mackenzie Crim. Laws Scot. I. xxvii. § x. (1699) 143 The Sheriffs, Lords of Regalities, and Stewarts, are declared Judges competent to this crime. a1688 J. Wallace Descr. Orkney (1693) 88 The Government of the Stewart is in the Kings Bounds, the Manner and Procedure of his Jurisdiction is after the form of Sheriffship, the Title only differing. 1708 Procl. 18 Aug. in Lond. Gaz. No. 4464/4 We..ordain..Our Solicitor to send Copies thereof to the Sheriffs of the several Shires, Stewarts of Stewartries. 1754 Erskine Princ. Sc. Law (1809) 38 The stewart was the magistrate appointed by the king over such regality lands as happened to fall to the crown by forfeiture, &c.; and therefore the stewart's jurisdiction was equal to that of a regality. a1768 — Inst. Law Scot. I. iv. § 10 (1773) 55 Regality-deputes were sometimes called stewards; but steward, in the strict sense, signified a magistrate appointed by the King over special lands belonging to himself. 1901 R. De B. Trotter Galloway Gossip 256 Davie..summons't the laird for the price o' the horse, but he made naething o't, for the Steward said he hadnae writins on't. 1912 A. Porteous Hist. Crieff ii. 32 The office of dapifer, seneschal, or steward, of Strathearn.

e. *Steward of the High Peak*: see quot. 1851.

1653 Manlove Cust. Lead-mines 199 (E.D.S.) The Dutchie Court..may appoint a Steward, that may try The Cause that's hurt on the minery. 1851 Act 14 & 15 Vict. c. 94 § 3 To be holden by the Steward of the High Peak Barmote Courts, ..and such Steward shall hold his Office during the Will and Pleasure of Her Majesty.

6. *fig.* (from senses 1 and 5.) An administrator and dispenser of wealth, favours, etc.; esp. one regarded as the servant of God or of the people.

Partly after Biblical uses, in which the word represents Gr. οἰκονόμος, L. *dispensator*.

?c900 Soliil. Augustine in Cockayne Shrine (1864) 176 Me þincð betere þæt ic forlete þa ȝyfe and folȝyȝe þam ȝyfan ðe me exðer ys stiward ȝe ðas welan ȝe eac hys freonscypes. a1225 Ancr. R. 386 Luue is heouene stiward. c1430 How Good Wyf tauȝte Douȝ. 21 in Babees Bk., Ȝeue of þin owne good, and be not to hard, For seelden is þat hous poore þere god is steward. 1539 Bible (Great) 1 Cor. iv. 1 Let a man thys wyse esteme vs, euen as ye minysters of Christ, and stewardes of the secretes of God. 1575-85 Abp. Sandys Serm. x. 167 God hath made him rich, that he as a faithful steward might bestowe those riche blessings vpon the familie..of God. 1594 A. Hume Poems (S.T.S.) 147 The Lord is a wise and discreet stewurt, and dispensator of his benefits. 1597 Shaks. 2 Hen. IV, v. iii. 137 Master Shallow, my Lord Shallow, be what thou wilt, I am Fortunes Steward. 1615 G. Sandys Trav. i. 32 Luxury being the steward, and the treasure vnexhaustable. 1765 Blackstone Comm. i. vii. 257 He [the king] is the steward of the public, to dispense it [justice] to whom it is due. 1769 Harte Eulogius 203 Just steward of the bounty he receiv'd, And dying poorer than the poor reliev'd! 1849 Macaulay Hist. Eng. vi. II. 19 A man of business and a vigilant steward of the public money.

7. An officer in a gild, usually ranking next to the alderman; also *Hist.* often as a rendering of L. *senescallus*, ONF. *eskevein*: see Skevin.

10.. in Kemble Cod. Dipl. IV. 278, & ȝyf he on neawyste forðfaren sy warniȝe man þone stiwerd to hwylcere stowe þæt lic sceole & se stiwerd warniȝe syððan ða ȝeȝyldan. 1432 in F. A. Hibbert Orig. Eng. Gilds (1891) 46 The Stywardes and Maistres of the saide Crafte. 1494 in Eng. Gilds (1870) 188 The Stuarde off the Gilde for the tyme beyng shall truly countrolle them yt ben absente. 1870 Toulmin Smith English Gilds Introd. p. ciii, There was an alderman at the head of the Gild, and often stewards by his side as assistants.

b. In certain City companies: One of two or more officers, who are charged with the arrangements for the annual dinner. Cf. sense 10.

1614 in W. M. Williams Ann. Founders' Co. (1867) 90 That..Master Wardens, Assistants, and Livery should pay to the Stewards for the providing of dynner on the day of the Master's Feast the some of Two Shillings each. a1700 Evelyn Diary 21 Sept. 1671, I din'd..at the fraternity feast in Yron-mongers Hall, where the 4 stewards chose their successors. 1796 in W. M. Williams Ann. Founders' Co. (1867) 165 That as two stewards, properly enabled to serve the office, cannot be immediately fixed upon, the annual dinner, on Lord Mayor's day, be omitted.

c. In various societies, the title of certain officers forming an executive committee. Cf. sense 10.

1831 in J. C. Whyte's Hist. Brit. Turf (1840) I. 145 At a meeting of the Stewards and Members of the Jockey Club, it was stated that [etc.]. 1910 Encycl. Brit. (ed. 11) XIII. 732/2 Sport is carried on under the auspices of the Jockey Club...Three stewards, one of whom retires each year,..govern the..work of the club...The stewards of the Jockey Club are ex officio stewards of Ascot, Epsom, Goodwood and Doncaster. All other meetings are controlled by stewards, usually well-known patrons of the Turf invited to act by the projectors of the fixture.

8. A corporation official, whose rank and duties vary widely in different municipalities; often with a defining word, as *Capital steward, city steward, town steward*.

1433 Rolls of Parlt. IV. 477/1 The Styward of the seid Town. 1835 App. Munic. Corpor. Rep. i. 186 The Steward [of Cardiff]..is required to be learned in the law. Ibid. 613 The Capital Steward [of South Molton]..has neither duties nor emoluments. Ibid. ii. 1275 The Town Steward [of Dorchester] is the treasurer of the corporation. Ibid. iii. 1741 Previous to the year 1714, the city steward [of York] was appointed by the upper house.

9. **High steward** (see also 3).

a. In the Universities of Oxford and Cambridge, the title (in academic Latin *seneschallus*) of a judicial officer, in whom is vested the jurisdiction belonging to the university in causes of treason and felony.

1459 in Munim. Acad. (Rolls) I. 345 If the same prisoner be claymed by the said Chaunceller or his styward..within iv. wykes next after his takyng and imprisonyng in the common prison of the town. c1674 Wood Fasti Oxon. (1790) 180 The Office of Steward in this University concerning the capital and chief causes of Scholars and privileged persons, King Henry IV..did institute. 1714 Ayliffe Ant. & Pres. St. Univ. Oxf. II. 166 The Lord High Steward.. is to hold and keep the University Court-Leet..either by himself, or his Under-Steward,..and on account of this Office, the High Steward receives the yearly Fee of five Pounds from the University. 1797 Encycl. Brit. (ed. 3) XVIII. 684 The trial of treason, felony, and mayhem, by a particular charter, is committed to the university jurisdiction in..the court of the lord high steward of the university. 1824 Encycl. Metrop. (1845) XVI. 184 art. Cambridge [Officers of the University] 2 A High Steward, who has special power to take the trial of scholars impeached of felony, and to hold and keep a court-leet within the university. 1845 G. R. M. Ward tr. Oxf. Univ. Statutes I. 178 The office of High Steward or Deputy High Steward of the University. 1895 Rashdall Universities II. ii. 409 Henry IV [in 1406] gave the University [of Oxford] the right to claim the surrender of 'privileged persons' indicted for felony, who were thereupon to be tried by a newly-constituted officer of the University, the Seneschal or Steward, to be appointed by the Chancellor. Ibid. 790 The jurisdiction of the Court of the High Steward of the University [of Oxford]..remains intact, but the privilege has never been claimed for a century or more.

† b. An official having at the inthronization of an archbishop ceremonial functions similar to those of the Lord High Steward at a coronation. *Obs.*

15.. in Dugdale Monast. (1817) I. 118/1 He shoulde be the hye stewarde of the sayde archbyshop, and of his successors, at their great feast, when it shoulde fortune the sayde archbyshoppe to be intronizated.

c. In certain English cities, a municipal title of dignity, usually borne by a nobleman or royal prince.

1563 in W. H. Turner Select Rec. Oxford (1880) 306 Sir Francis Knollis, Knyght, was chosen stuarde of this Cytie of Oxford this the third day of February, 1563. 1582 Nottingham Rec. IV. 199 The Earle of Rutland beinge Highe Steward. 1835 App. Munic. Corpor. Rep. i. 59 The present lord high steward [of Gloucester] is His Royal Highness the Duke of Gloucester. 1914 Kelly's Oxf. Directory 142 High Steward [of the city of Oxford], the Right Hon. the Earl of Jersey.

10. A person appointed to supervise the arrangements or maintain order at a race meeting, exhibition, dinner, ball, concert, public gathering, etc.

1703 Lond. Gaz. No. 3949/4 The Horses to be shewn at the George in Amsbury.., and to be entred by the Steward. 1709 Bp. Atterbury Serm. Sons of Clergy Ded., To the Worshipful Mr. John Tenison [and others] Stewards for the Late Feast of the Sons of the Clergy. 1751 Laws of Mus. Soc. at Castle-Tavern, Pater-noster-row 13 The Stewards shall observe the Directions herein after mentioned..for preserving good Order at the Concerts. 1812 Examiner 24 Aug. 542/1 He himself was one of the Stewards of that dinner! 1841 Orderson Creoleana vi. 62 It was customary for the stewards..to arrange the order of the minuets. 1854 Poultry Chron. II. 330/2 Fill up the delivery order, stating how the birds are to be returned. The stewards will pack them after the show. 1910 [see 7 c]. 1915 Morn. Post 7 Dec. 4/3 The meeting was perfectly quiet..until one or two of the stewards..attempted to remove four or five Colonial soldiers.

11. An overseer of workmen. In mod. use, the 'underlooker' of a colliery, 'who receives his orders from the manager, and to whom the overmen and deputies report upon the state of the mine' (Gresley *Gloss. Coal-mining*, 1883); also, in Scotland, the foreman of a workshop.

a1300 Cursor M. 5525 On þam þe king sett sere stuward [magistros operum] To hald þam in-to werkes hard. 1708 J. C. Compleat Collier (1845) 38 Six Pence per Corfe,..which is Deducted..by the Steward or Pay-Master. 1916 Observer 9 Jan. 12/2 The fact that Logan had strong trades union views is nothing exceptional for a shop's steward.

12. Among Methodists, a layman appointed to manage the financial affairs of a congregation (*society* or *chapel steward*) or of a circuit (*circuit steward*). Also *book steward*, the manager of the Book-room or publication department of the Wesleyan Methodist Society; *poor steward*, a person appointed in a congregation to administer the funds collected for the poor.

1741 Wesley Jrnl. 23 May (1749) 85 The Stewards of the Society (who receive and expend what is contributed weekly). 1771 — Jrnl. 31 Mar. (1777) 22 In the Methodist discipline, the wheels regularly stand thus: the assistant, the preachers, the stewards, the leaders, the people. 1896 Daily News 10 Mar. 5/3 The Rev. C. H. Kelly, the book steward, who is still prosecuting his searches in the Archives of the Wesleyan Book Room. 1904 Daily Chron. 15 Feb 3/5 Mr. Slack is an active member of the Wesleyan Methodist body...He is circuit-steward of the West London Mission.

13. *attrib.* and *Comb.*, as (sense 1 d) *steward boy*; (sense 5 d) *steward-clerk*; also † **stewart-compt**, *Sc.* the statement of the accounts of a stewartry; **stewart-, steward-court**, *Sc.* the court having jurisdiction within a stewartry; also *attrib.*; **steward-depute**, see 5 d; **steward's mate**, the assistant of a ship's steward; **steward's room, steward-room**, see quots.; **steward's table** (see quot.).

1897 Mary Kingsley W. Africa 613 Assisting Idabea and the *steward boys in chivying this pig. 1912 A. Porteous Hist. Crieff ii. 48 Other officials connected with the Steward Court were: the Judge or Judex, the Steward Depute, the *Steward Clerk, the Doomster or Deemster. 1580 Exch. Rolls Scot. XXI. 549, I am restand awand in my *stewart compt of Menteyth the sowme of 32 pundis. 1475 in 3rd Rep. Hist. MSS. Comm. 418/1 Vylȝam reyd, dempstar of the *stewart curt of Stratherne. a1600 in W. Nicolson Leges Marchiarum (1705) 202 First that he.. charge him within the Stewart-Court Book. 1752 J. Louthian Form of Process (ed. 2) 287 The several Officers in the Sheriff or Stewart-courts are prohibited to take..any other or higher Fees. a1600 in W. Nicolson Leges Marchiarum (1705) 202 Ane wise and famous Gentleman,..to be *Stewart Deput. 1824 G. Chalmers Caledonia III. iii. v. 247 In 1747 this stewartry was placed under a stewart-depute. 1708 Lond. Gaz. No. 4440/1 The..*Stewards Mate, Cooks Mate,..and Marine-Soldiers, two Eighth Parts. 1627 Capt. Smith Sea Gram. ii. 13 The *Stewards roome. 1644 Manwayring Seamans Dict. 102 Stewards-Roome, is that part of the Howlde, wherein the Victuals are Stowed. c1850 Rudim. Navig. (Weale) 153 Steward's room, an apartment built on the larboard side of the after platform, whence the purser's steward issues the provisions to the ship's company, and where he makes up his accounts. 1758 (title) Treatise on the Use and Abuse of the Second, commonly called the *Steward's Table, in Families of the First Rank.

Steward (stiū·ərd), *v.* [f. Steward *sb.*]

1. *trans.* To manage, administer.

1621 Bp. H. King Serm. 25 Nov. To Rdr. L 3 b, Whether I haue vprightly stewarded his honour, and my owne faith, I leaue to the strict judgement of any who are able to..discerne Truth from Imposture. 1626 J. Yates Ibis ad Cæsarem i. To Rdr., The Athenian Commander,..having ill stewarded the Treasury of the Commonwealth. 1639 Fuller Holy War ii. xxxi. (1640) 83 Did he thus requite his mothers care in stewarding the State? 1905 Daily Chron. 22 Sept. 4/5 A race..who may..steward aright the mighty heritage which is passing into their hands.

2. *intr.* To do the duties of a steward.

1897 J. Chalmers in R. Lovett Autobiog. & Lett. (1902) 434 We have with us two boys to cook and steward for us.

Hence **Stew·arding** *vbl. sb.*

1548 Udall Erasm. Par. Luke vi. 17-19 To whom the dispensacion & stewardyng of goddes woorde is to be committed. 1602 Archpriest Controv. (Camden) I. 232 Every baker or brewer, for stewarding and treasuringe..must, by this newe device, be made equall with you. 1865 Dickens Mut. Fr. iv. xii, As for stewarding, I think it's time my brother gave that up.

Stewardess (stiū·ərdės). [f. Steward *sb.* + -ess1.] A female who performs the duties of a steward; also *fig.*

1631 Celestina xxi. 198 O variable fortune..thou Ministresse and high Stewardesse of all temporal happinesse. 1827 Carlyle Germ. Rom. III. 212 She was his..Castle-Stewardess. 1865 Gladstone in Morley Life v. x. (1903) II. 160 Her [sc. the church's] high office as stewardess of divine truth.

b. Now chiefly: A female attendant on a ship whose duty it is to wait on the women passengers.

1837 Ht. Martineau Soc. Amer. II. 2 Mrs. F. and I were the only ladies on board; and there was no stewardess. 1885 Times 21 Sept. 10/1 There were five females among the passengers, including the stewardess.

Stewardly (stiū·ərdli), *a.* [f. Steward *sb.* + -ly1.]

†1. Pertaining to or administered by a steward; of the nature of a stewardship. *Obs.*

1642 Bridge Wound. Consc. Cured iv. 26 If abused that he do not perform his Stewardly trust as hee should, the people..are to looke to it. 1643 J. Cotton Doctr. Ch. 2 The Government of his Kingdome is not Lordly, but Stewardly and Ministeriall. a1683 Owen Holy Spirit (1693) 256 They are sufficient of themselves for the Stewardly Dispensation of the Mysteries of the Gospel.

2. *dial.* Skilled in household management.

1746 Exmoor Courtship 569 Tha stewardlest vittest Wanch that comath on tha' Stones o' Moulton. c1750 Mrs. Palmer's Devon. Dial. i. (1839) 11 A notable, thorough-paced stewardly body. 1874 Miss S. P. Fox Kingsbridge (E.D.D.) A good stewardly wife.

Stewardly (stiū·ərdli), *adv. rare.* [+ -ly2.] Like a steward; with the care of a steward.

1604 Tooker Fabric of Ch. iv. 48 Euery dispensation..is to be stewardely dispensed not wastfully spent or powred vpon euery ones head or altogether.

Stewardry, variant of Stewartry.

Stewardship (stiū·ərdʃip). [f. Steward *sb.* + -ship.]

1. The office of steward; also *fig.*

1465 Mann. & Househ. Exp. (Roxb.) 178 Item, the bayly off Hadley owyth hym ffor hys ffe off the stewardsheppe off the same town. 1491 Act 7 Hen. VII, c. 20 § 8 Any Stiwardshippes offices fees wages or annuities..to him graunted. 1593 Shaks. Rich. II, iii. iii. 78 Shew vs the Hand of God, That hath dismiss'd vs from our Stewardship. 1601 [? Marston] Jack Drums Entert. i. A 4 b, No, I do loue my Girles should wish me liue, Which fewe do wish that haue a greedy Syre: But still expect and gape with hungry lip, When heele giue vp his gowtie stewardship. 1709 Bp. Atterbury Serm. Sons Clergy Ded., There are, I believe, Two hundred Persons now living, who have gone before You in the Stewardship. 1839 John Bull 11 Aug. 382/2 A new writ was..issued for Perth, in the room of Mr. Kinnaird, who vacated by accepting a stewardship of the Chiltern Hundreds. 1862 Goulburn Pers. Relig. i. iv. (1871) 41 Each one of us has a stewardship somewhere in the great social system. 1886 Manch. Exam. 1 Oct. 5/3 At a meeting of the Jockey Club..H. W. Fitzwilliam was appointed as successor in the stewardship to the Marquis of Londonderry. 1907 Outlook 19 Jan. 91/1 The origin and development of the Stewardship of England.

2. Conduct of the office of steward; administration, management, control.

1526 Tindale Luke xvi. 2 Geve a comptes off thy stewardshippe. 1684 Norris Poems etc. 46 Among all the Talents which are committed to our Stewardship, Time..is the most precious. 1791 Cowper Iliad xix. 52 Those who held In stewardship the food. 1915 Morn. Post 22 Dec. 4/4 We want further such a stewardship of the economic resources of the country as will enable us to lift and to carry the financial burden.

†3. Used for Stewartry 1. *Obs.*

1796 Morse Amer. Geog. II. 97 Scotland is divided into 31 shires and two stewardships.

Stewart: see Steward.

Stewartry, stewardry (stiū·ərtri, stiū·ərdri). Chiefly *Sc.* [See Steward *sb.* and -ry.]

1. A former territorial division of Scotland under the jurisdiction of a steward: see Steward 5 d.

Two of the stewartries, that of Orkney and Shetland and that of Kirkcudbright, were identical with the present counties, and the term is still used instead of *county* as the official designation of these districts. Elsewhere the stewartry was of smaller extent than the county. As an administrative division, the stewartry was abolished in 1748.

α. 1473-4 Acc. Ld. High Treas. Scot. I. 5 His landis of Barnagehane within the Stewartry of Kirkcudbrith. 1491 in Acta Dom. Concil. (1839) 199/2 Landis..liand in the stewartry of straitherne. 1685 Sc. Procl. 28 Apr. in Lond. Gaz. No. 2032/2 All the Heretors, Liferenters, Feuars and Wodsetters in the Shires of Air, Renfrew, Clidsdale, Wigtoun, Dumfreis, and Stewartries and Bailliaries within the same. 1747 Act 20 Geo. II, c. 43 § 4 All Stewartries not hereby before taken away and extinguished. 1806 Gazetteer Scot. (ed. 2) 140 Dumfries-shire..comprehends 3 districts or stewartries, viz. Annandale, Eskdale or Wauchopedale, and Nithsdale. 1837 Act 7 Will. IV & 1 Vict. c. 39 The Words..'Shire', 'Sheriffdom', and 'County' [shall be deemed] to comprehend and apply to any Stewartry in Scotland. 1884 Manch. Exam. 9 Dec. 5/6 Sir John proposes to..add to it..the stewartry of Kirkcudbright. *attrib.* 1792 Copper-Plate Mag. No. ix, The stewartry (or county) courts are held at this place [Kirkcudbright].

β. 1495-6 Acc. Ld. High Treas. Scot. I. 219 Vmquhill M'Lelane of Garrochcragow wythin the steuardry of Kirkcowbrycht. 1708 Lond. Gaz. No. 4434/1 The Barons, Freeholders and Gentlemen of the Stewardry of Kirkcudbright. 1862 J. Grant Capt. Guard xix, Sir Herbert Herries..had large possessions in the stewardry.

2. The office of steward in such a territory.

1483 in Acts Parlt. Scot. (1875) XII. 33/1 Þe office of the steuartry of Kirkcwbrich with þe keping of þe castel of þe treif. 1563 Ibid. 44/2 Þe said office of stewartrie of Menteith with all feis and dewities pertening thairto. 1711 in Nairne Peerage Evid. (1874) 142 To use and exerce the said office of steuartrie. 1746-7 Act 20 Geo. II, c. 43 § 2 The possessors of the seid heretable baillieries, stewartries, or constabularies.

3. = Stewardship 3.

a1763 Byrom Poet. Version Let. Earl of Essex 37 You have them [sc. Talents], not as Things your own..; But as an human Stewartry, or Trust, Of which Account is to be giv'n, and just. 1877 Blackie Wise Men 341 The statesman..skilled by faithful stewartry to give Increase to money wisely husbanded.

Stewarty (stiū·ərti). *Sc.* Also 8 **stuarty**. [f. *stewart*, Steward *sb.* + -y.] = Stewartry.

Chiefly used by English writers, though one or two Scottish examples are found.

1610 Holland Camden's Brit. ii. 6 Counties which they cal Shiriffdomes, Seneschalsies commonly Stewarties and Bailiwickes. 1708 Lond. Gaz. No. 4473/1 The Head Burghs of the several Shires and Stuarties in Scotland. 1747 Gentl. Mag. XVII. 556 These jurisdictions are either regalities, justiciaries, sheriffalties, stewarties, bailliaries. 1752 J. Louthian Form of Process (ed. 2) 171 The Sheriffs or Stewarts of the Shires or Stewarties. 1796 Morse Amer. Geog. II. 97 Caithness, and the two stewarties.

†**Stewat.** *Sc. Obs.* [app. f. Stew *v.*3 + *-art, -ard*.] A stinker, stinkard.

1535 Lyndesay Satyre 2486 Thou art ane stewat, I stand foird. Ibid. 2489 Thir stewats stinks as thay war Broks.

Stewdyent, obs. form of Student.

Stewed (stiūd), *ppl. a.*1 Also 5 **stwed**, 6 **stude, stued(e, stuyd**, 6-7 **stewd**, 7 **stu'd**. [f. Stew *v.*2 + -ed1.] Of meat, fruit, vegetables: Cooked by slow boiling in a closed vessel. Of tea: Made strong and bitter by being kept too long in the pot.

c1450 Two Cookery-bks. ii. 72 Stwed Beef..Stewed Mutton. 1538 Elyot Dict., Offella,..also a potage made with pieces of fleshe, as stuyd brothe or forced gruell. 1555 in W. H. Turner Select. Rec. Oxford (1880) 230 Item, stude meate..xd. c1596 Henslowe Diary (1904) i. 32 Then take a stewed pryne and plucke owt the stone. 1664 F. Hawkins Youths Behav. ii. 178 A dish of stu'd Oysters. 1747 Mrs. Glasse Cookery ii. 48 A stewed Pheasant. 1816 Tuckey Narr. Exped. R. Zaire iv. (1818) 138 A repast..consisting of a stewed fowl, a dish of stewed beans, and cassava bread named Coanga. 1915 Blackw. Mag. May 600/2 We had a great meal off lunch-tongue, bread, wine and stewed pears. *absol.* 1861 [Trevelyan] Horace at Univ. Athens (1862) 24 I'm..tightly filled With roast, and boiled, and stewed, and pulled, and grilled.

b. *Comb.* † **stewed-pot**, a stew of various ingredients (cf. Stewpot 2); **stewed quaker** *U.S.* (see quot. 1890).

1596 Nashe Saffron Walden S 2 b, Neither are these parts seuerally distinguished in his order of handling, but, like a Dutch stewd-pot iumbled altogether. 1785 Grose Dict. Vulgar T., Stewed quaker, burned rum with a piece of butter, an American remedy for a cold. 1890 Century Dict. s. v. Quaker, Stewed Quaker, a posset of molasses or honey, stewed with butter and vinegar, and taken hot as a remedy for colds. (Colloq.)

¶ c. With pun on Stewed *ppl. a.*2

1596 Shaks. 1 Hen. IV, iii. iii. 128 There's no more faith in thee then in a stu'de Prune. So 1597-1603 — 2 Hen. IV, ii. iv. 158, Merry W. i. i. 296, Meas. for M. ii. i. 92. 1606 — Tr. & Cr. iii. i. 44 Sodden businesse, there's a stewed phrase indeede. 1609 Dekker Gull's Horn-bk. v. 25 When your Knight is vpon his stewed Mutton, be you presently.. in the bosome of your goose.

†**Stewed,** *ppl. a.*2 *Obs.* [f. *stew vb. (f. Stew *sb.*2) + -ed1.] Belonging to the stews. *Stewed whore, strumpet*: vaguely used as opprobrious epithets imputing unchastity.

1532 More Confut. Tindale Wks. 772/2 This good scholer of Tindalle..findeth in his heart written by the spirit of God, yt freres & monkes..may..vnder the name of weddyng, make stewed strumpettes of nunnes. 1532 Lett. & Pap. Hen. VIII, V. 425 The King's grace was ruled by one common stued huer, Anne Bullan. 1549 Latimer 3rd Serm. bef. Edw. VI (Arb.) 82 There is more open whoredome more stuede whoredome then euer was before. 1556 Olde Antichrist 140 b, That Sodomitical stewed state. 1575 Gamm. Gurton iii. iii, Where is the strong stued hore?

Stewfe, variant of Stufe *Obs.*, hot bath.

†**Stew-house.** *Obs.* [Stew *sb.*2] A stews.

1436 Rolls of Parlt. IV. 511/1 Other strange persones.. have set up Stywehouses, and houses of Bordell. 1572 R. T. Discourse 49 Sixtus the fourth pope of that name builded stuehouses of both the kindes. 1651 J. F[reake] Agrippa's Occ. Philos. 96 To hide them in a stew house.

Stewin, variant of Steven.

Stewing (stiū·iŋ), *vbl. sb.* [f. Stew *v.*2 + -ing1.] The action of the vb. Stew in various senses; an instance of this.

1398 Trevisa Barth. De P. R. vii. lviii. (1495) 272 The pacyent shall haue stewynges and bamynges and oynementes hote other colde. 1618 J. Taylor (Water P.) Pennyles Pilgr. F 2, Such Baking, Boyling, Rosting, and Stewing. 1778 Cook 3rd Voy. iii. xii. (1784) II. 235 We met with no utensil there that could be applied to the purpose of stewing or boiling. 1877 Encycl. Brit. VI. 333/2 The lid of a vessel used for stewing should be removed as little as possible. 1899 Allbutt's Syst. Med. VIII. 497 Remembering to warn him against heated rooms, violent changes of temperature, stewing in bed, and any possible irritation by vestments.

b. *attrib.* and *Comb.*

1833 Loudon Encycl. Archit. § 1484 The fundamental principles of the construction of stewing-hearths. 1837 Civil Engin. & Arch. Jrnl. I. 60/1 The kitchen..containing an oven, stewing-stoves, &c. 1860 Hogg Fruit Man. 156 A stewing pear, in season from November to April.

Stewing (stiū·iŋ), *ppl. a.* [f. Stew *v.*2 + -ing2.] That stews; very hot.

1856 Emerson Eng. Traits, Voy. Eng., Wks. (Bohn) II. 12 Nobody likes to be treated ignominiously,..rolled over, suffocated with bilge, mephitis, and stewing oil. 1911 J. Masefield Everlasting Mercy (1912) 24 Jane brought the bowl of stewing gin And poured the egg and lemon in.

b. *Comb.* **Stewing-hot** *a.*

1711 Swift Jrnl. to Stella 7 June, 'Tis stewing hot, but I must rise and go to town between fire and water. 1897 Mary Kingsley W. Africa 684 The sudden fall of temperature that occurs after a tornado coming at the end of a stewing-hot day, is sure to tell on any one.

†**Stew·ish**, *a. Obs.* [f. Stew *sb.*2 + -ish.] Of or pertaining to the stews.

a1555 R. Taylor in Foxe A. & M. (1583) 1528/1 This Babylonicall stewish spirituall whoredome. 1597 Bp. Hall Sat. i. ix, Rymed in rules of Stewish ribaldry. 1609 Sir E. Hoby Let. to T. H[iggons] 91 Your..Reliques,..Stewish Pardons, Indulgences.

Stewpan (stiū·pæn). [f. Stew *sb.*2 or *v.*2 + Pan *sb.* Cf. Du. *stoofpan*.] A saucepan for stewing (see quot. 1858).

1651 T. Barker Art of Angling (1820) 14 Taken out of the stew-pan and dished. 1674 Engl. & Fr. Cook 2 Put him [the Carp] in a Stew-pan with a quart of White-wine. 1747 Mrs. Glasse Cookery ii. 14 Then butter your Stew-pan, and shake some Flour into it. 1853 Soyer Pantropheon 66 Each piece was well washed before putting it into the stewpan. 1858 Simmonds Dict. Trade, Stew-pan, a shallow sauce-pan of iron, copper, or block tin. 1915 Daily Tel. 14 Aug. 10/2 Next lay the prepared fish..in a large, deep stewpan.

b. *transf.* and *fig.*

1771 Smollett Humph. Cl. 5 May (1815) 66 To lead a weary life in this stewpan of idleness and insignificance. 1863 G. H. Kingsley Sport & Trav. (1900) 397 That tideless stewpan of a harbour can be little less unwholesome than that of Naples.

c. *attrib.*

1839 Mag. Dom. Econ. IV. 174 When onions are fried as a flavouring substance in stewpan-cookery. 1846 Soyer Cookery 545 Turn it over upon the bottom of a stewpan-lid.

Stewpot (stiū·pǫt). [f. as prec. + Pot *sb.*]

1. A covered pot for stewing meat, etc.

1628 Ford Lover's Mel. iv. ii, He chafes hugely, fumes like a stew-pot. 1806 Culina 236 Put these into a stew-pot. 1883 'Annie Thomas' Mod. Housewife 108 She is a venerable bird, and would have become the stew-pot better than the spit.

fig. 1899 Westm. Gaz. 5 Apr. 2/3 The very air, damp with the pestilential steam from the fever stew-pots of the slimy swamps and lagoons, is poison.

†2. A dish of meat cooked in a stewpot; a stew. (Cf. *stewed-pot*.) *Obs.*

1542 Boorde Dyetary xii. (1870) 263 Sewe and stewpottes, and grewell made with otmell..can do lytel displeasure. 1605 Rowlands Hell's broke loose To Rdr., They were constrayned to frie..Bootes in Steakes, and Stew-pottes of old Shoes.

¶ b. *allusively*. (See Stew *sb.*2) A prostitute.

a1613 Overbury Characters, Sargeant (1618) N 7, Vpon one of the Sheriffs custards he is not so greedy, nor so sharp set, as at such a stew-pot.

†3. (See quot.) *Obs.*

1688 Holme Armoury iii. 424/1 A Stew or Stove or Stew pot covered...This is a Vessel made of either Brass, Iron, or Copper; with high Feet and Rings on the sides by which it is removed..from place to place; in which a Fire is put.. by which Rooms are made warm.

Stewth, variant of Stouth.

Stewy (stiū·i), *a.* [f. Stew *v.*2 + -y.] Suggestive of being stewed; having a stewed flavour.

1895 Pall Mall Gaz. 30 Dec. 4/3 The beverage she doles out is too frequently repellantly cold and detestably stewy.

Stewyn(e, variant forms of Steven.

Stey (stēi), *a. Sc.* Forms: 4- **stay**, 6- **stey**, 9 *erron.* **steigh**. [? repr. OE. *stǽge (:—prehistoric *staigjo-), f. OTeut. *staig-: *stīg- to climb: see Sty *v.* Cf. OE. *stǽgel* steep.]

1. Of a mountain, cliff, etc.: Approaching the perpendicular, difficult of ascent, steep.

1375 Barbour Bruce x. 25 On the owthir half ane montane was So cumrouss, and ek so stay, That it wes hard to pas that way. c1375 Sc. Leg. Saints xvi. (Magdalene) 813 Þat roche hey & stay. 1513 Douglas Æneis iii. viii. 56 A port thair is,..With rochis set forgane the streme full stay. 1533 Bellenden Livy II. 214/24 Þai mycht þe more eslie be dung doun agane be þe stay brayis þareof. c1590 J. Stewart Poems (S.T.S.) II. 208 The entres is so strait and stay, Quhilk leeds to lyf. 1597 Montgomerie Cherrie & Slae 357 The craige was vgly, stay and dreich. 1710 Ruddiman Gloss. Douglas' Æneis, Stay,..steep: As we say Scot. a stay brae. 1721 Kelly Sc. Prov. 287 Set a stout Heart to a stay Brea. 1786 Burns To Auld Mare xiv, The steyest brae thou wad hae fac't it. 1826 J. Wilson Noct. Ambr. Wks. 1855 I. 250 They gang swinging up the stey streets without sweetin. 1893 Stevenson Catriona xv. 168 There was he hingin' by a line an' speldering on the craig face, whaur it's hieest and steighest.

†2. *transf.* Unbending, upright. Also of a person: Reserved, haughty. *Obs.*

a1586 Sat. Poems Reform. xxxvii. 47 Gif ȝe beir strange, þai ȝow esteme our stay. a1605 Montgomerie Misc. Poems xxvii. 36 Nou I must rot, vha some tym stoud so stay. a1605 — Sonn. xxxii. 2, I love the lillie as the first of flours, Vhose staitly stalk so streight vp is and stay. 1632 Lithgow Trav. x. 503 This Patroness Crescent stands so stay.

Stey(e, obs. forms of Stay, Sty.

Steyer, Steyg: see Stair, Steg.

Steyl(e, Steyll, obs. ff. Steal, Steel, Stile.

Steylling, obs. form of Stilling.

Steyme, Sc. form of Stime.

Steynch, obs. form of Stanch *v.*

1573-5 Gascoigne Adv. Mr. F. J. Wks. 1907 I. 391 Ye Lady..felt hir bleeding began to steynch. Ibid. 395 For that you have so clerkly steynched my bleeding.

Steyn(e, var. forms of Stain *v.*, Steen *v.*

Steyp(e, Steyr, obs. ff. Steep, Steer.

Steyre, obs. form of Stair, Stir.

Steyvyne, -wyne: see Steven *sb.*3, *sb.*2

St. Foin(e, St. Foyne, obs. forms of Sainfoin.

‖ **Sthenia.** *Path. Obs.* [mod.L. (Brown) irreg. f. Gr. σθέν-ος strength, after Asthenia.] Used by Brown (see next) for: Normal or excessive 'excitability' or vital power. Opposed to *asthenia*.

1788 J. Brown tr. Elem. Med. II. 43 In every sthenia, in all sthenic diseases,..an universal criterion is encreased excitement over the whole system. 1833 Cycl. Pract. Med. II. 702/1 [Dr. Brown] maintained..that both sthenia and asthenia could never exist together in the same individual.

Sthenic (sþe·nik), *a. Path.* [ad. mod.L. *sthenic-us* (Brown), f. Gr. σθέν-ος strength: after *asthenicus* Asthenic *a.*] Applied by Dr. John Brown (1735-88) and his followers to diseases characterized by a normal or excessive accumulation of 'excitability' or vital power in the system. Similarly in later use, of diseases, symptoms, etc.: Marked by normal or excessive vital or nervous energy. Opposed to *asthenic*.

1788 J. Brown tr. Elem. Med. I. Pref. p. xii note, Sthenic diseases..are such as depend upon an excessive application of the several powers that otherwise produce health. 1793 T. Beddoes Let. Darwin 49 It had before occurred to me that air of a reduced standard would be extremely beneficial in sthenic inflammation. 1874 Maudsley Mental Dis. iii. 83 Idiopathic insanity divisible into two varieties,—sthenic and asthenic, according to the strong or feeble condition of the bodily health. 1877 F. T. Roberts Handbk. Med. (ed. 3) I. 6 The sanguineous temperament is believed to predispose to fevers of a sthenic type. 1880 Barwell Aneurism 94 When the too sthenic symptoms are somewhat subdued, a dry diet is preferable.

b. In extended sense: Belonging to, tending to produce, vital or nervous energy.

1797 Monthly Mag. III. 350/2 M. Humboldt concludes his letter with some observations on the sthenic or asthenic virtue of chemical agents, that is to say, their ability or impotence to produce irritation. 1899 Allbutt's Syst. Med. VII. 372 The cerebellum normally exerts on the apparatus of movement, a sthenic, tonic, and static influence.

Sti, Stian: see Sty, Styan.

Stiarne, obs. form of Stern *a.*

Stib-, used in *Chem.* as combining form of Stibium, before both a vowel and a consonant: see quots. Cf. Stibio-.

1852 Fownes' Chem. (ed. 4) 438 A curious substance, which MM. Loewig and Schweizer have described under the name of stibethyl. 1857 Miller Elem. Chem., Org. 226 Stibethyl, or Stibiotriethyl. 1863 Watts Dict. Chem. I. 339 Antimonides of Amyl, or Stibamyls..Stibdiamyl..Stibtriamyl. Ibid. 341 Stibtriethyl.., commonly called Stibethyl. Ibid. 344 Stibtrimethyl. 1865 Mansfield Salts 317 The compounds called Stibmethyl and Stibethyl.

Stibble, Sc. form of Stubble.

†**Sti·bbler.** *Sc. Obs.* Also 8 **stibler**. [Of obscure origin; for suggestions see Jamieson.] A licensed probationer who has not yet received a call to a settled ministerial charge.

1721 Ramsay Morning Interview 211 Not the long 'tending stibler, at his call;..E'er knew such raptures as thy joyful swain. 1815 Scott Guy M. xlvi, Ye sticket stibbler [addressed to Dominie Sampson]. 1865 R. Paul in B. Bell Mem. (1872) 335 Mr. Burns..is away for six weeks, and only a set of young stibblers in his place.

†**Sti·bial**, *a. Obs. rare*−1. [ad. mod.L. *stibiāl-is*: see Stibi-um and -al.] Having the qualities of antimony, antimonial.

1666 G. Harvey Morbus Angl. xv. (1672) 33 An adust Stibial or Æruginous Sulphur.

Stibialism (sti·biăliz'm). *Med. rare*−0. [f. prec. + -ism.] (See quot.)

1857 Dunglison Med. Lex., Stibialism, the aggregate phenomena produced by antimonials, when given in large quantities:—antimonial intoxication or poisoning.

†**Stibia·rian.** *Obs. rare*−1. [f. Stibi-um + *-arian*, denoting an adherent of a doctrine or practice.] One who administers antimony (as an emetic); in quot. *fig.*

1635 F. White Sabbath-day Ep. Ded. 3 This Stibiarian ..tendereth a bitter pill of sacriledge and cruelty: but when the same was rejected because it was violent, then he presents his Antimonian potion, to the States of the Kingdome.

†**Sti·biate**, *a. Obs.* [ad. mod.L. *stibiāt-us*: see Stibi-um and -ate2.] Impregnated or combined with antimony.

1625 Hart Anat. Ur. ii. ix. 113 Strong stibiate vomits are vsed. 1684 tr. Bonet's Merc. Compit. xiv. 487 They place the chief stress of the Cure in Stibiate Emeticks. 1754 Huxham Antimony in Phil. Trans. XLVIII. 853 'Tis also of some consequence how long the stibiate lixivium stands before the acid is poured on. Ibid. 868 As stibiate medicines are now so much in vogue.

Sti·biated, *a. rare*−0. [f. prec. + -ed.] = prec.

1828-32 in Webster; and in later Dicts.

Stibic (sti·bik), *a. rare.* [f. Stib-ium + -ic.] Of or belonging to antimony; antimonic.

† *Stibic stone*, 'black antimony': see Stibium.

1609 Bible (Douay) 2 Kings ix. 30 Jezebel..paynted her face with stibike stone [Vulg. depinxit oculos suos stibio]. 1839 Hooper's Lex. Med. (ed. 7) 1221 Stibic Acid, Berzelius's name for the yellow oxide of antimony.

Stibiconite (sti·bikŏnəit). *Min.* [f. Stibi-um + Gr. κόνις dust + -ite. Originally named *stibiconise* (Beudant 1832).] A hydrous oxide of antimony, sometimes found in a pulverulent form. Cf. Stiblite.

1843 E. J. Chapman Pract. Min. 70 Stibiconise. 1868 Dana Min. (ed. 5) 188 Stibiconite.

†**Stibie.** *Obs.* Anglicized form of Stibium.

1548 Udall Erasm. Par. Luke vii. 36-39 Hir iyes..she was woont..to payncte with Stibie.

Stibilite: see Stiblite.

Stibine (sti·bəin). [f. Stib-ium + -ine.]

1. *Min.* = Stibnite. (Named by Beudant 1832.)

1843 E. J. Chapman Pract. Min. 124. 1860 Piesse Lab. Chem. Wonders 2 Native sulphuret of antimony or stibine.

2. *Chem.* Any of the antimony-compounds on the type of ammonia, SbH_3.

1852 Fownes' Chem. (ed. 4) 568 Triethylstibin. 1878 Abney Photogr. (1881) 34 Antimoniuretted hydrogen or stibine. 1878 Tidy Mod. Chem. 667 Stibines. Trimethyl stibine $Sb(CH_3)_3$. Triethyl stibine (Stibethyl) $Sb(C_2H_5)_3$.

Stibio- (sti·bio), combining form of Stibium, used in *Chem.* and *Min.* (see quots.). Cf. Stib-.

1857 Miller Elem. Chem., Org. 225 The radicles stibiotrimethyl and stibiotriethyl. 1874 Amer. Jrnl. Sci. Ser. iii. VII. 152 Stibioferrite from Santa Clara Co., California. 1868 Dana Min. (ed. 5) 591 Stibiogalenite.

Sti·bious, *a. rare*−0. [f. Stibi-um + -ous.] Of or belonging to antimony; antimonious.

1839 Hooper's Lex. Med. (ed. 7) 1221 Stibious, antimonial. Stibious Acid. So Berzelius calls the white oxide of antimony.

Stibium (sti·biŏm). Also 6 **stebium**, 7 **stybium**. [a. L. *stibium*, also *stibi, stimmi* = Gr. στίβι, στίμμι.] 'Black antimony', i.e. trisulphide of antimony calcined and powdered, used as a cosmetic for blackening the eyelids and eyebrows. † Formerly used also for metallic antimony or any of its salts, esp. as a poison or an emetic.

1398 Trevisa Barth. De P. R. xix. xxxv. (1495) 879 Stibium is a feyned colour made of Cerusa and of other thynges medlyd therwyth, wymmen paynted theyr faces therwyth. c1596 Henslowe Diary (1904) i. 32 Take stebium & beate yt in powder verey fine. 1612 Webster White Devil ii. i. 281, I will compound a medicine out of their two heads, stronger then garlick, deadlier then stibium. 1633 T. Adams Exp. 2 Peter ii. 22. 1094 Sinne, like Stibium, will tarry with no body: up it must, either here by a humble confession, or hereafter by a wretched confusion. 1634 W. Wood New Eng. Prosp. ii. vi. 67 Their belly-timbers, which I suppose would be but stibium to weake stomacks as they cooke it, though never so good of it selfe. 1660 J. H. Basil Valentine's Tri. Chariot of Antimony 81 The Antimony thus melted in the Crucible, Take a plain and broad dish..; poure in the stibium by litle and litle. 1699 Garth Dispens. v. 122 Of temper'd Stibium the bright Shield was cast. 1842 Bonar & M'Cheyne Narr. Mission to Jews ii. (1843) 59 Their eyes painted with stibium. 1874 Birch 1st & 2nd Egypt. Rooms Brit. Mus. 27 Vase for holding stibium,.. called by the Arabs kohl.

Stibler, variant of Stibbler.

Sti·blite. *Min.* Also **stibi(o)lite**. [f. Stib-ium + -lite.] Obsolete synonym of Stibiconite.

1854 Dana Min. (ed. 4) II. 142 Stiblite. 1858 Greg & Lettsom Man. Min. 372 Stiblite.

Stibnite (sti·bnəit). *Min.* [f. Stibine + -ite.] Native trisulphide of antimony, 'gray antimony', the most common ore of the metal.

1854 Dana Min. (ed. 4) II. 33. 1878 Tidy Mod. Chem. 388.

Stibogram (sti·bŏgræm). *rare*−0. [f. Gr. στίβο-ς footprint + γράμμα written character: see -gram.] A graphic record of footprints.

1891 Century Dict. 1898 Syd. Soc. Lex.

Stiborn(e, -ourne, -urn(e, obs. ff. Stubborn.

Stica: see Styca.

Sticados, variant of Stechados *Obs.*

Sticca·do. *Mus.* Also **-ato**. [? ad. It. *steccato*.] A kind of xylophone (see quot. 1875).

1776 Burney Hist. Mus. (1789) I. ii. 33 A kind of Sticcado, consisting of bars of wood of different lengths as sonorous as if they had been of metal. 1794 Mrs. Radcliffe Myst. Udolpho xxxii, If I can but steal out into the woods, and play upon my sticcado, I forget it all directly. 1811 Busby Dict. Mus. (ed. 3) Sticcado. 1875 Stainer & Barrett Dict. Mus. Terms, Sticcado or Sticcato, an instrument composed of pieces of wood of graduated lengths, flat at the bottom and rounded at the top, resting on the edges of an open box, and tuned to a diatonic scale. The tone is produced by striking the pieces of wood with small hard balls at the end of a flexible stick.

Stiche, obs. form of Stitch *sb.* and *v.*

Stich (stik). [ad. Gr. στίχ-ος row, line, verse, or the collateral form στίχ-ες (pl.).] A portion or division of prose or verse writing, of a measured or average length; a line. verse.

1723 S. Mather Vind. Holy Bible 67 In some ancient Greek New Testaments, at the close of the epistles, there were some numeral letters added, signifying how many Stichs were in the epistle...The Jewish and Christian writers have computed these Stichs in scripture books, and added them at the end of each book. 1883 Schaff Encycl. Relig. Knowl. III. 1955 Trying whether these pauses have a like or symmetrically correspondent number of stichs.

Stich(e, obs. forms of Stitch.

Stichados, variant of Stechados *Obs.*

Sti·chering, *vbl. sb. dial.* [Of obscure origin.] A method of catching eels. **Sti·cherer**, one who catches eels by this method. (See quot. 1885.)

1867 F. Francis Angling iii. (1880) 92 Stichering is yet another method of catching eels...An unskilful sticherer will sometimes chop off his neighbour's ear. 1885 Sat. Rev. 21 Nov. 673/1 'Stichering', a Hampshire method, is perhaps one of the most amusing...The only apparatus used is an old sickle,..tied firmly on a light pole about 12 ft. long. The object of the sticherer is to thrust the sickle under the eel's body, and, with a sudden hoist, to land him on the bank.

Stichewort, -wurt, obs. ff. Stitchwort.

Stichic (sti·kik), *a.* [ad. Gr. στιχικ-ός, f. στίχος: see Stich, Stichos.]

1. Pertaining to or consisting of verses or lines.

1864 Webster. 1883 Jebb Œdipus Tyr. p. lxxii, Two rhythmical sentences of equal length..form a 'stichic' period. 1897 W. H. Stevenson in Eng. Hist. Rev. XII. 490 Coote completed Palgrave's stichic re-arrangement of the text.

2. *Prosody.* Consisting of successive lines of the same metrical form.

1886 Amer. Jrnl. Philol. VII. 399 The stichic portions of the cantica of Terence are divided into strophes. 1900 H. W. Smyth Grk. Melic Poets 219 Lesser Asclepiads in stichic arrangement.

So **Sti·chical** *a.* = prec. 1.

1787 A. Geddes Let. Bp. London 43 No one will..assert the same of any stichical version made from the Hebrew.

Stichid (sti·kid). Anglicized form of next.

1891 Century Dict.

Stichidium (stiki·diŏm). *Bot.* Pl. **stichidia** (-iă). [mod.L. f. Gr. στίχ-ος Stichos + dim. suffix *-idium* (= Gr. -ίδιον).] A pod-like receptacle for tetraspores in some rose-spored Algæ.

1855 Ogilvie Suppl. 1857 Henfrey Elem. Bot. § 337 Transformed branches containing imbedded tetraspores are called stichidia.

Stichle ([illegible]), *v. Sc. intr.* To rustle, make a rustling sound. Hence **Sti·chling** *vbl. sb.*

1500-20 Dunbar Poems xlii. 78 Sik straikis and stychling wes on steir. 1501 Douglas Pal. Hon. i. xx, The stichling of a mouse out of presence. 1788 Picken Poems 166 Ithers dose, While, stichlan, whis'les through their nose The eldritch snore.

Stichochrome (sti·kokrōum). *Phys.* [f. Gr. στίχο-ς Stichos + χρῶμα colour.] 'Any nerve-cell having the stainable substance (chromophilic bodies) arranged in more or less regular striæ or layers' (*Dorland's Med. Dict.* 1913). Also *attrib.*

1899 Allbutt's Syst. Med. VII. 261 The stichochrome granules disappear from the cells, to reappear once more when the animal recovers. 1901 Jrnl. Exper. Med. 1 Oct. 552 Nissl..recognizes three subgroups [of nerve cells]:.. Stichochromes or cells in which the chromatic substance is arranged in more or less distinctly parallel rows.

Stichoi, pl. of Stichos.

Stichology (stikǫ·lŏdʒi). *rare.* [ad. Gr. *στιχολογία, f. στίχος: see Stichos and -logy.] The science or theory of poetic metres.

1737 E. Manwaring (title) Stichology: or, a recovery of the Latin, Greek and Hebrew numbers. 1895 Lambros in Athenæum 6 July 16/3 His exact acquaintance with Byzantine melody and the Neo-Hellenic stichology.

Sti·chomancy. *rare*−1. [a. F. *stichomantie* (Rabelais), f. Gr. στίχο-ς Stichos + -mancy.] Divination by lines of verse in books taken at hazard.

a1693 Urquhart's Rabelais iii. xxv. 209 By a Sibylline Stichomancy.

Stichometric (stikome·trik), *a.* [f. Stichometr-y + -ic.] = next.

1881 Scribner's Monthly Feb. 614 Euthalius..published portions of the New Testament, broken up into longer or shorter clauses, for the convenience of the reader, and to avoid the use of punctuation. The clauses terminated at the more important pauses. Manuscripts written in this style are called 'stichometric'. 1883 J. R. Harris in Schaff's Encycl. Relig. Knowl. III. 2245 The actual number of lines in the manuscripts never tallies with the stichometric record. 1883 — in Amer. Jrnl. Philol. IV. 134 [heading] Nature of Stichometric data.

Stichometrical (stikome·trikăl), *a.* [f. prec. + -al.] Of or pertaining to stichometry; characterized by measurement by *stichoi* or lines.

1845 W. Wright in Kitto Cycl. Bibl. Lit. s. v. Vulgate (1849) II. 926/1 The beautiful Lindisfarne book of the Gospels (Nero D. 4) is a stichometrical uncial MS. of the seventh century. 1885 G. Salmon Introd. N. T. xxi. 537 note, Then follows a stichometrical catalogue of the books both of Old and New Testament. 1904 M. Rule in Athenæum 9 Apr. 464/3, I find..upon making a careful stichometrical analysis of the Libellus, that it resolves itself into thirty-eight sections. 1909 Times Lit. Suppl. 11 Feb. 52/? The stichometrical note in the margin of Frag. 58.

Hence **Stichome·trically** *adv.*

1871 G. V. Smith Bible & Pop. Theol. App. 320 The six clauses may be arranged stichometrically. 1882 G. C. Macaulay in 19th Cent. Dec. 908 Passages from this preface have been introduced word for word, or with insignificant changes, into subsequently published poems, being divided stichometrically into lines by the natural pauses of the sentence. 1882 Schaff Encycl. Relig. Knowl. I. 268 Written stichometrically, i.e., in single lines containing only so many words as could be read, consistently with the sense, at a single inspiration.

Stichometry (stikǫ·mĕtri). *Palæography.* [ad. late Gr. στιχομετρία, f. στίχο-ς Stichos + -μετρία -metry.] a. The measurement of a manuscript text by *stichoi* or lines of fixed or average length into which the text is divided. Also, a list or appendix stating this measurement. b. Occas. used for: The practice of writing a prose text in lines of nearly equal length corresponding to divisions in the sense. Also, *stichoi* collectively.

a. 1754 N. Lardner Credib. Gosp. Hist. ii. XI. 248 A Stichometrie is a Catalogue of books of sacred Scripture, to which is added the number of the verses, which each book contains. This Stichometrie [of Nicephorus] contains a Catalogue of the books of the Old and New Testament. 1855 Westcott Canon N. T. 522 note, Credner has examined the Stichometry of Nicephorus in connexion with the Festal Letter of Athanasius. 1883 J. R. Harris in Schaff's Encycl. Relig. Knowl. III. 2245 The data of stichometry consist chiefly of subscriptions at the close of manuscripts, expressing the number of lines which are contained in the book.. copied. 1884 D. Hunter Reuss's Hist. Canon ix. 159 The Codex Claromontanus..presents at the end of the text the copy of an old complete list of the books of the Old and New Testaments, with the number of lines in each book, what was then called a stichometry. 1885 G. Salmon Introd. N. T. xxv. 617 note, It appears from the Claromontane stichometry, as well as from that of Nicephorus, that in length this Apocalypse was less than a quarter of that of St. John.

b. 1875 W. R. Smith in Encycl. Brit. III. 645/2 Another system was to write the text in short lines (στίχοι) accommodated to the sense. The author of this stichometry was Euthalius of Alexandria in the second half of the 5th century, who applied it to the epistles and Acts. 1875 Scrivener Lect. Text N.T. 69 Stichometry, that is, the division of prose sentences into lines of about equal length corresponding as nearly as possible to the sense. Ibid. 71 Another manuscript in which the prose text..is broken up into stichometry. 1881 Scribner's Monthly Feb. 614 Stichometry was really nothing but a cumbrous substitute for punctuation.

‖ **Stichomythia** (stikomi·þiă). Also *rarely* **stichomuthia** (-miū·þiă). [mod.L. a. Gr. στιχομυθία, f. στίχο-ς Stichos + μῦθ-ος speech, talk.] In classical Greek Drama, dialogue in alternate lines, employed in sharp disputation, and characterized by antithesis and rhetorical repetition or taking up of the opponent's words. Also applied to modern imitations of this.

1861 Paley Æschylus (ed. 2) Prometh. 640 It is not unlikely that a verse has been lost, which preserved the continuity of the stichomythia. 1914 Blackw. Mag. June 855/1 Take..the passage of dialogue between Richard and Queen Elizabeth in 'Richard III,' as vivid a piece of stichomuthia as the English drama has to show.

Stichomythic (stikomi·þik), *a.* [f. prec. + -ic.] Of the nature of stichomythia.

1866 Felton Anc. & Mod. Gr. I. xii. 222 This is shown particularly in those parts called stichomythic or line for line dialogues, responding like alternate strokes of hammers on the anvil. 1908 Saintsbury Engl. Prosody II. 14 Much of it [the Comedy of Errors]..is devoted to..stichomythic bandying of speech.

‖ **Stichos** (sti·kǫs). Pl. **stichoi** (sti·koi). [a. Gr. στίχος row, line, verse. Cf. Stich.]

1. In the Greek Church, a verse or versicle.

1863 Littledale Offices East. Ch. 248 At the Praises, we recite six stichoi. 1868 Walcott Sacred Archæol. 555 Stichos, a short varying versicle and response in the Greek liturgy...The koinonikon is a sacramental hymn and stichos, sung a little before the Communion.

2. *Palæography.* A line of a stichometrically written text; a line of average length assumed in measuring the contents of a text or codex.

1885 G. Salmon Introd. N. T. xi. 236 note, According to the Stichometry of Nicephorus, it [this Gospel] contained 1300 stichoi. 1911 Jrnl. Manch. Oriental Soc. 2 The amount assigned to a stichos is determined, as in all the old inscriptions, by the sense.

Sticht, pa. t. of Sty *v.*

Stichwort(e, obs. forms of Stitchwort.

Stick (stik), *sb.*1 Forms: 1 **sticca**, 3-7 **sticke**, 3-5 **stikke**, 4-5 **stykke**, 4-6 **stik, styke**, 5 **stike**, 5-6 **styk, stycke**, 6 **styck, stykk**, 6- **stick**. [OE. *sticca* masc. = ? OS. *stekko* (Gallée), MDu. *stecke* masc., fem. also *stec* masc., neut. (mod.Du. *stek* fem.), OHG. *stecko* (MHG. *stecke*, mod.G. *stecken*):—OTeut. type *stikkon- (a synonymous *stikon- is represented by the parallel forms OHG. *stehho*, MHG. *steche* masc.; cf. also ON. *stika* fem., stick, yardstick, *kerta-stika* candlestick, MSw. *stikka*, mod. Sw. *sticka* fem. stick, chip), f. Teut. root *stik- to pierce, prick: see Stick *v.*]

I. A rod or staff of wood.

1. A short piece of wood, esp. a piece cut and shaped for a special purpose, usually with defining word indicating its use, as in *bung-stick*, Potstick, Setting-stick, *tooth-stick*, etc.

In OE. also in the specific applications 'tent-peg' and 'pointer of a dial': see Bosworth-Toller.

c1000 Sax. Leechd. I. 386 Ȝenim twegen..sticcan federegede & writ on æȝðerne sticcan..an pater noster. c1450 Bk. Curtasye 94 in Babees Bk. (1868) 180 Clense not thi tethe at mete sittande, Withe knyfe ne stre, styk ne wande. 1707 Mortimer Husb. (1721) I. 334 The next Morning pluck out the Bung-stick or Plug. 1913 M. W. H. Beech in Man XIII. 5 [It] can be used as either the female, i.e., the passive stick of the fire drill or for the male or active stick.

† b. A piece of wood used as a tally. Also White stick. *Obs.* as specific sense.

c1380, c1400 [see White stick]. 1500 God Speed Plough (E.E.T.S.) 30 And to the kyngis courte we moste it lede, And our payment shalbe a styk of A bough. 1523-34 Fitzherb. Husb. § 141 Yf he [the husbandman] canne not wryte, let hym nycke the defautes vppon a stycke, and shewe his bayely. 1664 Marq. Newcastle in M'ness Newcastle Sociable Lett. To Author, Each Tavern-token, Nick'd Sticks for Merchants [etc.]. 1737 Pope Hor. Epist. i. i. 84 To him who notches sticks at Westminster. 1784 Cowper Tiroc. 559 Th' indented stick, that loses day by day Notch after notch. 1846-8 Lowell Biglow P. Ser. i. ix. 61 Wy, into Bellers's we notched the votes down on three sticks.

c. *Mining.* (See quot. 1899.)

1708 J. C. Compl. Collier (1845) 37 The..chief Banck's-Man takes an Account..by Sticks or Pieces of Wood. 1797 J. Curr Coal Viewer 20 Nogs and boxes for mottys, or sticks, to distinguish the Corf, o. o. 6. 1899 Dickinson & Prevost Cumbld. Gloss., Stick, the wooden token whereon was branded the distinguishing number of the hewer in the coal pit.

d. *The* (*sixty* or *sixty-four*) *sticks of fate*: the apparatus employed in a Chinese method of divination.

?c1850 Lady Dufferin (title of poem) Consulting the 'Sticks of Fate'. 1860 Cobbold Pict. Chinese 14. 1884 Friend Flowers & Flower-lore I. 268.

2. A slender branch or twig of a tree or shrub esp. when cut or broken off. Now *rare*.

c1000 Sax. Leechd. II. 142 Læt yrnan þæt blod on grennne [sic] sticcan hæslenne. c1200 Vices & Virtues 135 Ne lat hie nawht ðe hande pleiȝende mid stikke, ne mid strawe—nis þat non god tocne of ripe manne. 13.. K. Alis. 4425 (Laud MS.), Þe speres crakeþ also þicke So on hegge sere stykke. c1369 Chaucer Dethe Blaunche 423 So grete trees ..of..fourty fifty fedme lengthe Clene withoute bowgh or stikke. c1400 Maundev. (Roxb.) vii. 25 Þe preste..lays þerapon spiceries..and stikkes of þe iunipre tree. 1593 Shaks. 2 Hen. VI, i. ii. 33 He that breakes a sticke of Glosters groue, Shall loose his head for his presumption. 1620 Quarles Feast for Worms K 4, Thou, in whose distrustfull brest Despayre hath brought in sticks to build her nest. 1735 Dict. Polygraph. s. v. Verdegris, This [crystallised verdegrease] commonly comes from Holland..on sticks in form like our sugar-candy. To be good, these crystals must be..as free from sticks as possible.

b. *pl.* Pieces of cut or broken branches, also pieces of cut and chopped wood, used as fuel.

c1200 Ormin 8651, & her I gaddre stikkess twa..To ȝarrkenn þatt to fode. c1300 Havelok 914 Stickes kan ich breken and kraken, And kindlen ful wel a fyr. 1382 Wyclif Numb. xv. 32 Thei fonden a man gederynge stikkis in the holi day. c1450 St. Cuthbert (Surtees) 807 Stikkes to a fyre þai gadird fast. 1653 Walton Angler xi[xvi]. 209 Come, Hostis,..lay a few more sticks on the fire. 1737 Pope Hor. Epist. ii. ii. 242 Such large-acred men..Buy every stick of wood that lends them heat. 1821 Clare Vill. Minstr. II. 117 Seeking..her harmless sticks from hedges hung with rime. 1902 A. Symons Stud. Prose & Verse (1904) 251 Mr. Phillips has laid the paper, the sticks, and the coals neatly in the grate.

† c. A piece of wood from the hearth, a brand. *Stick of fire*, a firebrand. *Obs.*

1538 Elyot Dict., Torris, a stycke of fyre. 1607 Dekker Jests to make Merry 33 Your Glimerer, shees vp in the morning betweene 5 or 6 of the clock..and with a black brand in her hand...If she but perceiue a light..she desires to haue leaue to kindle her stick.

d. A twiggy bough or long rod stuck in the ground for a plant to 'run' upon, more definitely *bean-stick, pea-stick*.

1577 Googe tr. Heresbach's Husb. 33 There are two sortes of Pease, the one sort..runneth vp vppon sticks. 1741 Miller Gard. Dict. s. v. Phaseolus, [The Scarlet Bean] being supported either with Sticks or Strings, grows up to a good Height.

3. A stem or thick branch of a tree cut and trimmed and used as timber for building, fencing, etc.; a stave, stake. Also *fig.* Cf. sense 6.

c1386 Chaucer Nun's Pr. T. 28 A yeerd she hadde, enclosed al aboute With stikkes. 1577 Googe tr. Heresbach's Husb. 41 b, They vse a greater Sythe with a long Snath, and fenced with a crooked frame of stickes, wherwith with both their hands they cut downe the Corne, and laye it in Swathes. 1644 [see Hedge *sb.* 6]. 1707 Fountainhall Decis. (1761) II. 408 The pursuer had no inclosure..neither was their a stick of planting or hedging therein.

b. *Every stick*, the whole materials of a building: used (sometimes *advb.*) to emphasize total destruction or ruin. Also negatively: (*to leave*) *not a stick*.

1338 R. Brunne Chron. (1725) 113 Carro, Lodelow toun,.. Dunford & Maltone, Steuen wan þam ilk a stik. a1400-50 Wars Alex. 1311 Þus þe strenth [of Alexander's towers] ilk stike was in a stounde wasted. c1450 Brut 577 Thai brake vp al þe lede of the halle and of þe toures, and brent vp euery stykke. 1557-71 A. Jenkinson Voy. & Trav. (Hakl. Soc.) II. 339 One of ye dukes howses..was consumed with fyer and not one stick left. 1596 Spenser State Irel. Wks. (Globe) 616/2 Of all townes, castels, fortes, bridges, and habitations, they left not any stick standing. 1625 in Foster Eng. Factories India (1909) III. 80 The Sultan suffaringe not a sticke to bee puld downe out of aney house.

c. Similarly in alliterative expressions, esp. (*every, both*) *stick and stone*. *stick and stour* dial., *stick and stow* Sc. and north. (cf. *stab and stow*, Stab *sb.*2), *stick and stock*.

c1436 Brut 583 Þe Calisers..bare lxiii clene away, Euery stikke & stone, & lafte not ther one log. 1459 Sir J. Fastolf Will in Paston Lett. I. 462 That thanne the said John Paston shulde doo poule down the said mansion and every stone and stikke therof. 1542 Udall Erasm. Apoph. 232 b, [He] to declare hym selfe [free from the assumption of kingly power], was fain to pul down his hous sticke and stone euen to ye plain grounde. 1600 Fairfax Tasso ix. ix, Godfrey meane-while to ruine sticke and stone Of this faire towne, with battrie sore, assaies. 1611 Beaum. & Fl. Knt. Burn. Pestle ii. i, Shee swore, neuer to marry, But such a one, whose mighty arme could carry..Her bodily away through sticke and stone. 1792 Wolcot (P. Pindar) Lyric Ep. Ld. Macartney xxxvii. Wks. 1816 II. 355 For troops.. May, like wild meteors, pour into mine east, And leave my palace neither stick nor stone. 1904 Athenæum 27 Aug. 271/3 Every stick and stone of Beau Nash's Pump Room [at Bath] has long since passed away.

c1450 St. Cuthbert (Surtees) 7177 Þe place was brynt, styk and stoure, Abbay and house. 1877 N. W. Linc. Gloss., Stick and stour,..Often used to signify all a person's goods and chattels. 'They've sell'd him up, stick an' stour'.

1786 Burns To W. Simpson Postscr. ix, Folk thought them ruin'd stick-an-stowe. 1862 C. C. Robinson Dial. Leeds 422 A nasty, thratching hussey!—shoo wants bundling art o't' street stick an' stow.

1880 Baring-Gould Mehalah xii. (1884) 161 Cousin Charles is not the man to see his relatives sold up stick and stock.

d. *Stick and rag*: see quot.

1911 Encycl. Brit. XXI. 786/1 Fibrous plaster is given by plasterers the suggestive name 'stick and rag',..for it is composed of plaster laid upon a backing of canvas stretched on wood.

e. *Over the sticks*: in steeplechasing and hurdle-racing.

1898 T. Haydon Sporting Reminisc. 67 The quality of the competitors, both in flat races and 'over the sticks' was of the highest class.

4. A long and relatively slender piece of wood, whether in natural form or shaped with tools, cut or broken of a convenient length for handling.

Cleft stick: see Cleft *ppl. a.*

c1386 Chaucer Can. Yeom. Prol. & T. 712 In his hand he bar An holwe stikke..In the ende of which an Ounce..Of siluer lemaille put was as bifore. 1523-34 Fitzherb. Husb. § 21 And in his other hande he hath a forked stycke a yarde longe, and with his forked stycke he putteth the wede from hym. 1526 Pilgr. Perf. (W. de W. 1531) 30 b, Whiche by theyr enchauntementes made serpentes of styckes. 1590 Lucar Lucarsolace i. iv. 11 Take vp your Geometricall table, ..leauing an arrow or sticke set vpright in the point of grounde directly vnder B. 1662 Stillingfl. Orig. Sacræ iii. i. § 17 So in the sight of a stick, when under water, the representation of it by the sense to imagination is as crooked. 1784 Cowper Task i. 561 A Kettle, slung between two poles upon a stick transverse. 1889 Doyle Micah Clarke v, Like the turnip on a stick at which we used to throw at the fairs.

b. A staff, club, cudgel used as a weapon.

1377 Langl. P. Pl. B. xii. 14 Al-þough þow stryke me with þi staffe with stikke or with ȝerde. 1547 Boorde Brev. Health (1870) 84 For the Feuer lurden..Take me a stycke or wan[d] of a yerde of length and more..and with it anoynt the bake. 1605 Shaks. Lear ii. iv. 125 She knapt 'em o'th' coxcombs with a sticke, and cryed downe wantons, downe. 1664 in Verney Mem. (1904) II. 214 [If the] Whelps meddle with Sheepe, they must be..whipped soundly, but not beaten with Stickes. 1847 W. C. L. Martin Ox 139/2 Contusions, and the blows of cattle-drivers, merciless in the use of their sticks about the heads of the poor beasts. 1850 A. M'Gilvray Poems 69 For he has laid, with their own sticks, The strongest watchmen down.

fig. phr. (*U.S.*) 1848 Bartlett Dict. Amer., Sharp stick. He's after him with a sharp stick; i.e. he's determined to have satisfaction or revenge. 1871 Trenton State Sentinel 26 May in Schele de Vere Americanisms 631 We are pleased to see that the New York Tribune is still after Senators Carpenter, Conkling and others, with a very sharp stick, for [etc.].

c. (Chiefly *the stick*.) A beating with a stick. *To eat stick*: see Eat *v.* 2 d.

1856 Miss Yonge Daisy Chain i. viii, Come in, ye bad girls, or I'll give you the stick. 1884 Sir S. St. John Hayti iii. 81 The productiveness of the north [of Hayti] was founded on the liberal application of the stick. 1886 'Maxwell Gray' Silence Dean Maitland I. v. 125 He'll do what he is told now without the stick. 1892 Mrs. H. Ward David Grieve i. iv, Mak her behave...She'll want a stick takken to her, soon, I can see.

d. = Walking-stick.

1680 E. Blount's Horæ Subs. 33 Some had rather bee lame ..of a legge, then lose the grace of carrying a French sticke. 1792 Charlotte Smith Desmond II. 285, I tapped at the old, thick, carved door with my stick. 1892 Rider Haggard Nada the Lily xviii. 145 We went on in silence, the king leaning on my shoulder as on a stick.

e. A rod of dignity or office, a baton; also the bearer of such a stick. Cf. Gold stick, White stick.

1688 Lond. Gaz. 22 Oct. 7 He had the Honour to be in Waiting upon the King with the Stick. 1833 Hood Publ. Dinner 14 Twelve sticks come attending A stick of a Chairman. 1876 Voyle & Stevenson Milit. Dict. 409/2 Stick, Silver, the field officer of the life guards, when on duty, is called silver stick. 1892 Huxley in L. Huxley Life (1900) II. 328 Then waiting about while the various 'sticks' were delivered. 1897 Westm. Gaz. 25 June 4/1 One of the 'Sticks' now doing duty at Buckingham Palace.

f. *Basket-making.* (See quot. 1910.)

1907 Jrnl. Soc. Arts 11 Jan. 190/1 A dog or commander for straightening the sticks. 1910 Encycl. Brit. III. 482/1 Rods..known as 'sticks', are used to form the rigid framework of the bottoms and lids of square work.

g. In *Candlemaking*, the rod to which the wicks are attached in order to be dipped: = Broach *sb.* 2 b. Hence, the candles made at one dipping.

1711 Act 10 Anne c. 26 § 106 Every Chandler..shall.. declare..the Number of Sticks which he designs to make.. and also the Sizes of the Candles whereof each Stick is to consist. 1751 Chambers' Cycl. s. v. Candle, The workman ..takes two sticks [ed. 1727 rods], or broches, at a time, strung with the proper number of wicks.

h. The rod of a sky-rocket (see quot. 1886).

1651 J. White Rich Cabinet (1677) 83 Rockets whose sticks are longer than the staffe. 1792 T. Paine Let. to Addressers

Stickleback (stiˈklbak). Forms: 5 stykylbak, 6 stickelbanke, -banok, 6–7 stickle bag(ge, 7 stit(i)cle bag(ge, 8 stittle-back, 7–8 stickle-back. [f. OE. sticel prick, sting + BACK sb.[1] Cf. the synonymous bansticle, stanstickle, stickling, tittlebat, prickleback, -bag [N. Irel. sprickleback].] A small spine-based fish, of the genus Gasterosteus or family Gasterosteidæ. The common three-spined stickleback, G. aculeatus, is found in both fresh and salt water.

Stickler (stiˈklr). Also 6 styckler, stickler, 7 stickler. Cf. STICKLE v.[1] + -ER[1]. Cf. the earlier STIFFLER, STIGHTLER.]

1. A moderator or umpire at a tournament, a wrestling or fencing match, etc., appointed to see fair play, and to part the combatants when they have fought enough (obs. exc. Hist. dial.). Hence, †One who intervenes as a mediator between combatants or disputants.

Stickling (stiˈklŋ). Obs. Also 4 stikeling-, 5 styk(e)lyng(e, stekelyng, 6 styokelyng, stik-lyng. [ME. stikeling(e n'(M)Du. stikeling, MLG. stickelinc; from STICKLE v.] Stickleback.

Stick-out, a. and sb. [f. vbl. phrase stick out.]

†Stickpenny. Obs. [STICK sb.[1]] (See quot.)

†Stidy, a. Obs. rare—¹. [Ormin's spelling implies app. related to STITHE a. (Ormin's spelling implies app. related to STITHE a.

Stiff, v. [f. STIFF a. + -EN[5].] To make or become stiff or rigid.

Stiffen (stiˈfn), v. [f. STIFF a. + -EN[5].] To make or become stiff or rigid.

†Stiffen-bodied, a. Obs. [prob. for † STIFFENED ppl. a.] Having the body (esp. as stiffened with whalebone, etc.) stiff.

†Stif-ler. Obs. [Alteration of stifler STIGHTLER, by substitution of (l for t'.)] a. A mediator or umpire.

Stiffener (stiˈfnr). [f. STIFFEN v. + -ER[1].] A workman who stiffens (cloth, hats, etc.).

Stiffish (stiˈfiʃ). [f. STIFF a. + -ISH[1].] Rather stiff.

Stiffly (stiˈfli), adv. [f. STIFF a. + -LY[2].] In a stiff manner; so as to be stiff; (in various senses of the adj.).

Stiffness, variant of STIFFENER.

Stiffness (stiˈfnes). [f. STIFF a. + -NESS.] The state or quality of being stiff (in any sense).

Stifle. [Of obscure origin.] The joint at the junction of the hind leg and the body (between the femur and the tibia) in a horse or other quadruped; corresponding anatomically to the knee in man.

Stifle, sb.² In a **stifle.** [f. STIFLE v.¹]

Stifle, sb.³ Forms: 4 stuf(f)le, 5–6 stifil, 6 styfel, stifle, stiffel, 6–7 stiffle, stifel, 6–8 … stifle, 6–stifle. [Of obscure origin.]

Stifle (stəiˈfl), v.¹ [Of obscure origin.]
1. trans. To kill by stopping respiration; to kill or deprive of consciousness by covering the mouth and nose, by depriving of pure air or by introducing an irrespirable vapour into the throat and lungs; to suffocate.

2. To choke by compressing the windpipe; to strangle, throttle.

3. To suffocate by immersion; to drown.

4. To stop the passage of (the breath); to suppress, prevent the escape of, check or stop.

5. To make mute or inaudible through intervening space or obstructing medium.

6. To make faint or exaggerated sense.

Stifle-burn, v. in Agric. [f. STIFLE sb.²] trans. To burn (field-crisse and surface-soil) in heaps pressed down with small coal.

Stifled (stəiˈfld), ppl. a. [f. STIFLE v.¹ + -ED¹.]

Stifler (stəiˈflər). [f. STIFLE v.¹ + -ER¹.] One who or something which stifles, suffocates, smothers, suppresses, etc.

Stifling (stəiˈflɪŋ), vbl. sb.¹ [f. STIFLE v.¹ + -ING¹.]

Stifling, vbl. sb.² Farriery. [f. STIFLE-sb.²]

Stifling (stəiˈflɪŋ), ppl. a. [f. STIFLE v.¹ + -ING².] That stifles or tends to stifle; suffocating, smothering.

Stigma (stɪgˈma). Pl. **stigmata** (stɪgˈmātə), **stigmas.** [L. stigma, Gr. στίγμα, mark made by a pointed instrument, brand, f. root *stig-in στίζειν (= *stig-) to prick, puncture: see STICK v.]

Stigmata

Stigmata (stɪgˈmātə), sb. pl. [ad. mod.L. stigmatica (occurring in some MSS. of De Off. iii. 7. 25, where the true reading is stigmatias), f. L. stigmat- STIGMA and -ic.]

Stigmatic (stɪgˈmætɪk), a. and sb. [ad. med.L. stigmaticus, f. Gr. στιγματικ-ός, f. στίγμα, στιγματ-.]

Stigmatical, a. Obs. [f. prec. + -AL.]

Stigmatiferous (stɪgmætɪˈfərəs), a. Bot. [f. stigmat- STIGMA 6. In quot. 1902, having a character of a stigma: see STIGMA 6.]

Stigmatiform (stɪgˈmætɪfɔːm), a. Nat. Hist. [f. stigmat- STIGMA + -(I)FORM.]

Stigmatism (stɪgˈmætɪz'm), n. [f. Gr. στίγμα, στιγματ- + -ISM.]

Stigmatist (stɪgˈmætɪst). [f. Gr. στίγμα, στιγματ- + -IST.]

Stigmatization (stɪgmætaɪˈzeɪʃən), vbl. sb. [f. next + -ATION.]

Stigmatize (stɪgˈmætaɪz), v. [ad. F. stigmatiser (1552 in Hatz.-Darm.), It. stigmatizzare, Sp., Pg. estigmatizar.]

Stigmatose (stɪgˈmætəʊs), a. [ad. mod.L. stigmatosus.]

Stigmatospermous

Stil, Stile, obs. forms of STEEL, STILE, STYLE.

Stilb (stɪlb). [G., a bishopric.]

Stilbite (stɪlˈbaɪt). Min. [ad. F. stilbite (Haüy 1796), f. Gr. στίλβειν to glitter: see -ITE.]

Stilboestrol

Stile (stəil), sb.¹ [OE. stigel.]

Stile (stəil), sb.² Carpentry. Also 9 style. [Of uncertain origin.]

Stile, sb.³: see STYLE.

Stiletto (stɪˈletəʊ). [It., dim. of stilo STILE, STYLE.]

Supplement, p. 3873; Corrigenda, p. 4092; Spurious words, p. 4093; Books quoted, p. 4094

961 — STILLATION. | STILLICIDE. | STILLICIDIOUS. | **962** — STILL WATER.

Stillation. Stillatitious. Stilbumb. Still-house. Stilled. Stillicide. Stillicidious. Stillidium. Stilliform. Stillish. Stilling. Stilliness. Stillstand. Stillworth.

Still-birth. Still-born. Still-brunt. Stillen. Stiller. Stillery. Still-green. Still-head. Stillhunt. Stillicidous. Stilliard. Stilliardois. Stillish. Stilly.

963 — STILT. | **964** — STILTED. | STIMULATE.

Stilt. Stilted. Stilter. Stiltify. Stiltish. Stimance. Stimie. Stimmer. Stimpart. Stimulable. Stimulance. Stimulancy. Stimulant. Stimulate.

Still-yard. Stillyard's. Stilo novo. Stilpnomelane. Stilpnosiderite. Stilt. Stily. Stithy. Stith.

Stimulating, *ppl. a.* ... [The action of stimulating or condition of being stimulated.]

Stimulation. The action of stimulating or condition of being stimulated.

Stimulative.

Stimulator (sti·miǔlētər).

Stimulatory (sti·miǔflātŏri), *a.*

Stimulatress.

†Stimulatrix, *Obs.*

†Stimule. *Obs. rare*⁻¹. [Anglicized form of STIMULUS.]

Stimulose (sti·miŭlōus), *a.* *Nat. Hist.*

Stimulus (sti·miŭləs). Pl. **stimuli** (sti·miŭlai). [(Originally a mod. L. use (in medical books) of L. *stimulus* goad, of doubtful origin; perh. f. root *sti- in *stīva* : see STIVE.]

1. A pole, staff.

2. A sharp-pointed organ in certain insects and other animals (e.g. bees, wasps, scorpions) capable of inflicting a painful or dangerous wound.

Stimy, variant of STIMIE (*Golf*).

Stinch(e, obs. ff. STENCH v., STENCH.

Stinck(e, obs. ff. STINK sb. and v.

†Stine. *Obs. rare*⁻¹.

Sting, *sb.*¹ *Sc. and north.* Forms:
1 **steng**, (-nəg), 1, 4 **steng** (1 -nog, -ngo, -no,
5 **steyng**, 5-6 **stang**, 6-7 **steing**, 7-8 **stang**, ... : see STANG sb.¹

1. A pole, staff.

Sting, *sb.*² *Sc. and north.* Forms: 1 **steng**, 5-6 **styng**, 5-7 **stinge**, 1, 4 **styng**, 1, 4, 6- **sting**. [f. STING v.]

1. The act of stinging. The fact or effect of being stung; the wound inflicted by the *aculeus* of an insect, the telson of a scorpion, the fang of an adder, etc.; the pain or smart of such a wound.

2. A sharp-pointed organ in certain animals (as the bee, scorpion, etc.) by which a wound is inflicted; a stinging hair.

Sting (stiŋ), *v.* Pa. t. and pa. pple. **stung** (stʌŋ). Forms: *Inf.* 1 **stingan**, stingan, 3 **stingen**, 4-6 **stinge**, 4-5 **stynge**, 5 **styng**, 3-6 **sting**. [A Com. Teut. str. vb.]

1. To prick or pierce (the skin, flesh, etc.) with a sting.

Sting (stiŋ), *sb.* *slang.* Forms: 1 stineg, 3 stinke, etc.

6. The tapering point of a pointer's tail. Cf. *sting-tail* in sense 8.

STING. 967 STINGING. STINGLE. 968 STINK.

Stingare, **Stingaree** (stiŋgə·rī), *sb.* *Austral.* [Corrupt f. STING-RAY.] A sting-ray.

Stinge, obs. form of STING.

Stinger (sti·ŋər). [f. STING v.¹ + -ER¹.]

1. One who stings; applied *fig.* to Death. Also, one who goads or instigates; one who has a sharp tongue.

Stinger². **Stinger**³ (sti·ŋər, stiŋəz). *Sc. and dial.*

Stinging (sti·ŋiŋ), *vbl. sb.* [f. STING v.¹ + -ING¹.]

Stinging, *ppl. a.* [f. STING v.¹ + -ING²]

Stingily (sti·ndʒili), *adv.* [f. STINGY a.¹ + -LY².]

Stinginess (sti·ndʒinɛs). [-NESS.] The quality of being stingy; niggardliness, meanness.

Stingingly (sti·ŋiŋli), *adv.* [f. STINGING a.]

Stingless (sti·ŋlɛs), *a.* [f. STING sb.² + -LESS.]

Stingle, *sb.* and *v.* [Obs.? exc. *dial.*]

Stingo (sti·ŋgou). *slang.* [f. STING sb.²] Strong ale or beer.

Stingray, **Sting ray**. [STING sb.²]

Stingy (sti·ndʒi), *a.*¹ [STING sb.² + -Y¹.]

Stingy (sti·ŋi), *a.*² Also 7 **stingie**. [f. STING sb.²]

STINK. thrown among the enemy (see quot. 1802); stink berry.

Stink (stiŋk), *sb.* Forms: 3-4 **stinc**, 3 **stinke**, 4 **stenk**, **stink**, 4-5 **stynk**, 4-5 **stynke**, 4, 7 **stinke**, 6- **stink**.

1. A foul, disgusting, or offensive smell; stench.

2. Evil-smelling quality; offensive odour; STENCH *sb.* 2.

Stink (stiŋk), *v.* Forms: 1 **stincan**, 3 **stinke-n**, 4 **stenk**, **stink**, stynke, (4-5 **sting**, **stynk**), 4-6 **stynk**, 4-6 **stinke**, 6-7 **stincke**, 7- **stink**.

1. *intr.* To emit a strong offensive smell; to smell foully or offensively.

Stinker (stiŋkəɹ). [f. STINK v. +-ER¹.] One who or something which stinks.

Stink-horn (stiŋk‚hǫɹn). [f. STINK sb. + HORN sb.] A name for various ill-smelling fungi.

†Stinkibus. slang. Obs. Also -ubus. [f. STINK sb. + obscure Latin ending of dat. pl. ; cf. circumbendibus, recumbentibus, muckibus.] Bad liquor, gin.

Stinking (stiŋkiŋ), vbl. sb. [-ING¹.] The action of the verb STINK ; an instance of this.

Stinking (stiŋkiŋ), ppl. a. [-ING ².] 1. That stinks ; offensively smelling.

Stinkingly (stiŋkiŋli), adv. [f. STINKING ppl. a. + -LY².] In a stinking manner.

Stinkingness (stiŋkiŋnes). [f. STINKING ppl. a. + -NESS.] The quality of being stinking.

Stink-pot. [f. STINK sb. + POT sb., after Du.]

Stinkstone. Min. [f. STINK sb. + STONE sb.] A name given to various limestones which give out a fetid odour on being scratched or struck.

Stinkweed. [f. STINK sb. + WEED sb.] A name for various ill-smelling plants.

Stinkwood. [f. STINK sb. + WOOD sb., partly after Du. stinkhout.] A name given in certain colonies to various trees the wood of which has an unpleasant odour.

Stint (stint), sb.¹ Forms: α. 4-6 stynt, (5 stynt), 6 stynte, (6 styntte), 7 stinte, 4-stint. 8 4-stent. [f. STINT v.]

Stint (stint), sb.² [Of obscure origin.] A common name for any of the smaller Sandpipers (genus Tringa), esp. the Dunlin. Also a provincial name for the Sanderling (Calidris arenaria).

Stint (stint), v. Forms 1-2 stintan, (1-3 stint-), 3 stunte, 3 stunten, 4-6 stynte, stynt, (3 stynt) 4-7 stint, 3-stint; β.3-5 stente, 6-7 stent, 4-6 stent, 6-7 stent. Pa. t. (contracted forms) 1, 6 stenten, 5 stent, 5 stynt ; (weak forms) 4-6 stynted, stented, 6 stented. Pa. pple. (contracted forms) 3 stent, 4 stunt, i-stunt, y-stynt, stynte, 4-6 stynt, i-stinte ; β 3 stunde ; (weak forms) 4 i-stented. [OE. styntan to blunt, dull; to check, stop (ME. ASTINT v.).]

STINT. 971 STINT. STINT. 972 STINT. STINTED.

Stintance. Obs. rare⁻¹. [f. STINT v. + -ANCE.] Cessation, limitation.

Stinted, ppl. a. [f. STINT v. + -ED ¹.] 1. a. Stopped, checked, etc.

Stinter (stĭ·ntəɹ). [f. STINT v. + -ER¹.] One who or something which stints, in the senses of that verb.

Stinting, vbl. sb. [f. STINT v. + -ING¹.]
1. The action of the verb STINT in various senses; † stopping, ceasing, coming or bringing to an end (obs.); limiting, apportioning within limits; scant limitation, scant supply.
2. concr. (See quot. 1889.)

Stinting, ppl. a. [-ING².] That stints.

Stintless (sti·ntlĕs), a. [f. STINT sb.¹ + -LESS.] That may not be assuaged or satisfied. Obs.

Stinty (sti·ntĭ), a. rare⁻¹. [f. STINT sb.¹ + -Y.] Stinted, meagre, niggardly.

Stip, Stipand, obs. ff. STEEP sb.¹, STIPEND.

Stipate (stəɪ·pət), a. Bot. [ad. L. stipātus, pa. pple. of stipāre] to crowd.

† Stipate, v. Obs. rare. [f. L. stipāt-, pa. ppl. stem of stipāre, to crowd, to accompany in crowds.]

Stipation (stəɪpēɪ·ʃən). [ad. L. stipātiōnem, f. stipāre: see prec. and -ATION.]
1. ‡ A guarding or entraining about' (Cockeram 1623). Obs.
2. † An accumulation in the tissues or cavities' (B. D. Jackson Gloss. Bot. Terms, 1900).

Stipe (stəip). [a. F. stipe, ad. L. stipes (stipiti-)-log, post, tree-trunk (in mod.L. = sense 1).]
1. Bot.
2. Anat.

† Stiped, Bot. Obs. [f. STIPE + -ED².] = STIPITATE d.

Stipel (stəɪ·pĕl). Bot. Also q. stipelle. [ad. F. stipelle, ad. mod.L.: see next.]

† Stipella (stəɪpe·lă). Bot. [mod.L., dim. of L. STIPULA.] = prec.

Stipellate (stəɪpe·lᵉt), a. Bot. [ad. mod.L. stipellātus, f.: see prec. and -ATE².]

Stipend (stəi·pĕnd, -pent). Forms: 5 stipende, -e, 6 stipeande, 6 stipand, 6 stipaunt, -6 stypend, -6 stipond, -6 stipend.
1. A salary or fixed periodical payment, made (annually or at shorter intervals) to a clergyman, teacher, or public official, in requital of his services.
2. † Income. Obs.
3. Mil. Obs.
5. attrib. as † stipend coin, wage(s.

† Stipend, v. Obs. Also 7 stipen. [f. STIPEND sb. Cf. F. stipendier (15th c. in Hatz.-Darm.), Sp. estipendiar, It. stipendiare; also L. stipendiārī to be in receipt of pay.]
1. trans. To pay as a reward.
† b. In generalized sense. Obs.

† Stipendary, a. and sb. Obs. Also 6 stependare. [f. STIPEND sb. + -ARY.]
A. adj. = STIPENDIARY a.
B. sb. = STIPENDIARY B.

Stipendia·rian, a. rare. [f. L. stipendia- + -RIAN.]

Stipendiary (stəɪpe·ndiəri), a. and sb. Also 6-7 stipendiarie. [ad. L. stipendiārius, f. stipendium: see STIPEND sb. and -ARY. Cf. F. stipendiaire.]
A. adj.
B. sb.
1. One who receives a stipend; a salaried clergyman or teacher; † a pensioner.
2. Stipendiary magistrate.

Stipe·ndious, a. Obs. rare⁻¹. [f. L. stipendi- + -OUS.]

Stipe·ndiumless, a. [f. next + -LESS.]

Stipe·ndium. Obs. [L., = STIPEND sb.]

Stiper, obs. exc. dial. (see Eng. Dial. Dict.)

Stipes (stəɪ·pīz). Pl. stipites (sti·pĭtīz). [a. L. stipes: see STIPE.]

Stipitate (sti·pĭtᵉt), a. Bot. and Zool. [ad. mod.L. stipitātus, f. stipit-, STIPES.]

Stipitiform (sti·pĭtifɔːm), a. Bot. and Zool. [f. mod.L. stipit-, STIPES + -(I)FORM.]

Stiple, obs. form of STIPPLE.

Stipone, -onie, -ony, var. f. STEPONY Obs.

Stipound, obs. f. STIPEND sb.

Stipple (sti·p'l), sb. [f. the verb STIPPLE: see the verb.]
1. Painted, engraved, etc. with dots: see the verb.
2. The method of painting, engraving, etc. by means of dots or small spots, so as to produce gradations of tone.

Stipple (sti·p'l), v. [f. Du. stippelen, frequent. of stippen to prick, speckle, f. stip, a point.]
1. trans. To paint, engrave, or otherwise design in dots; to produce gradations of shade or colour in a design by means of dots or small spots.
2. intr. or absol.

Stippled (sti·p'ld), ppl. a. [f. prec. + -ED¹.]

Stippler (sti·plər). [f. STIPPLE v. + -ER¹.]
1. One who stipples; an artist who paints, engraves, etc. in stipple.
2. An instrument by means of which stippling is done.

Stippling (sti·plin), vbl. sb. [f. STIPPLE v. + -ING¹.] The action of the verb STIPPLE; the process or art of painting, engraving, etc. in dots; the design or display so produced; dotted work.

Stipply (sti·plĭ), a. [f. STIPPLE sb. + -Y.]

Stiptic, var. STYPTIC.
Stiptio, -ik, -ike, etc., obs. ff. STYPTIC etc.
† Stipula (sti·piŭlă). Pl. stipulæ. [L. stipula.]

Stipulaceous (stipjŭlēɪ·ʃəs), a. [f. mod.L. stipulāceus.]

Stipulane (sti·pjŭlᵉn), a. Bot. rare⁻⁰.

Stipulant (sti·pjŭlănt), ppl. a. and sb. Roman Law. [ad. L. stipulant-, stipulāri: see STIPULATE v.]

Stipular (sti·pjŭlər), a. Bot. [ad. mod.L. stipulāris, f. STIPULA: see -AR.]

Stipulary (sti·pjŭlări), a. Bot. rare. [ad. mod.L. stipulārius, f. STIPULA.]

Stipulate (sti·pjŭlᵉt), a. Bot. and Zool. [ad. mod.L. stipulātus, f. STIPULA: see -ATE².]

Stipulate (sti·pjŭlēɪt), v. [f. L. stipulāt-, ppl. stem of stipulārī to bargain, to demand a formal engagement.]
1. intr. a. Roman Law. To make an oral contract in the verbal form (of question and answer) necessary to give it legal validity.
2. intr. To make an express demand for something as a condition of agreement.
† b. absol. To become surety or bail (for some one).
† 2. trans. Of an agreement, or of both contracting parties: To specify (something) as an essential part of the contract.
3. trans. To contract, make a bargain, settle terms, covenant (with a person or persons). Obs.
4. trans. To make an express demand.

Stipulated (sti·pjŭlēɪtĕd), ppl. a. [f. STIPULATE v. + -ED¹.] That has been specified in the conditions of a contract or agreement.

Stipulation¹ (stipjŭlēɪ·ʃən). [ad. F. stipulation or L. stipulātiōnem, f. stipulārī: see STIPULATE v. and -ATION.]
1. Roman Law. (See quots. and STIPULATE v. 1.)

Stipulation² (stipjŭlēɪ·ʃən). Bot. [ad. mod.L. stipulātiō, -ōnem, f. STIPULA.] The arrangement of the stipules.

Stipulator (sti·pjŭlēɪtər). [L., agent-n. f. stipulārī: see STIPULATE v.]

Stipule (sti·pjūl). Bot. [ad. F. stipule, ad. L. stipula straw, stubble.]

Stipuled (sti·pjūld), a. Bot. [f. STIPULE + -ED².] Having very pointed stipules.

Stir (stəːɹ), sb.¹ Forms: see STIR v. [partly f. STIR v.; partly of Norse origin, ON.]
1. Movement, considered in contrast to or as interruption of rest or stillness; slight or momentary movement; a moving. On the stir (rare): astir, stirring.
2. One who makes a formal promise or pledge. Obs.

STIR. 977 STIR. STIR. 978 STIR. STIR. 979 STIRABOUT. STIRE. 980 STIRRAH.

Stir, sb.¹

Stir, sb.² slang.

Stir, v. Inflected **stirred**, **stirring**. Forms: α. 1 *styrian*, 3–4 *sturie* (4 *styry*), 3–5 *sture*, 3–8 *styre*, 4–7 *styrre*, 6–9 *sturre*, 4–8 *styr*, 5 *styrr*, 6–7 *stur*, 4–9 *stirre*, 4 *stirr*, 4– *stir*.

I. **Transitive senses.**

1. To move, set in motion; *esp.* to give a slight or tremulous movement to; to move to and fro; to shake, agitate.

b. To move (a limb or member); to move almost always, in negative or similar expressions: to make any or the slightest movement with.

c. To stir a liquid, etc.; a pole, etc.

d. To send forth, utter, cause to be heard (a voice or sound); also, to make (a gesture). *Obs.*

e. To cause to move up or away; to drive, convey, impel; also *fig. Obs.*

f. To move (something) from its place; to shift, displace.

g. To move or disturb with a push.

2. **Fig.** To move from a fixed or quiet condition; to disturb, trouble, molest; to put into tumult or commotion.

b. To rouse to action, activity, or emotion; to rouse from indifference or sloth; to incite, instigate, stimulate.

3. To agitate with the hand or an implement so as to alter the relative position of the parts of: a. a liquid, or a soft or semi-liquid mass.

b. To affect with strong emotion; to move strongly (a person, his spirit, 'blood', etc.).

c. To excite, provoke (passion); to prompt, evoke or occasion (anger, hatred, affection, suspicion, etc.).

II. **Intransitive senses.**

11. To move (continuously, or in general sense); *spec.* to move as a living being.

12. To stir one's self: to make vigorous use of one's opportunity.

b. To bestir oneself; to be active; to act briskly or energetically.

Stirk (stɜːk). Forms: 1 *stirc*, *steorc*, *styrc*, 3 *sterk*, *stirk*, 5–7 *styrk*, 6 *sterck*, *stirk*, 5–9 *styrk*, 6 *stirk*, *steirk*, *steirke*, *stierke*, *sterck*, 4– *stirk*. [OE. *stirc*, *styrc*, *steorc*.] A young bullock or heifer.

Stirless (stɜː·lɪs), a. Motionless.

Stiricide (stɪ·rɪsəid). rare. [ad. L. *stīricīdium*.]

Stirious, a. Obs. [ad. L. *stīria* + *-ous*.]

Stirk, obs. form of STIRRING.

Stirkling, obs. form of STARLING.

Stirabout (stɜː·rəbaut). Also α *stirrabout*. A porridge made by stirring oatmeal (or occas. some other meal) in boiling water or milk.

Stire, obs. f. STEER, STIR, STOUR.

Stire, Obs. Also α *styre*, α *styre*. [Of obscure origin. Cf. the synonymous STIROM.] A kind of cider apple; also the cider made from it.

Stirop, obs. form of STIRRUP.

Stirp (stɜːp), a. Law. [Badly f. L. *stirps* (see STIRPS), the correct form would be *stirped*.]

Stirpital (stɜː·pɪtæl), a. Law.

Stirps (stɜːps). Pl. **stirpes** (stɜː·piːz). [L.] 1. Law. A branch of a family; the person who with his descendants forms a branch of a family.

Stirra, **Stirrah**, obs. ff. SIRRAH.

Stirrage (stɜː·rɪdʒ), sb. dial. Also 6 Sc. *storage*. [f. STIR v. + -AGE.] Stirring, movement, commotion.

Stirrance. *Obs. rare⁻¹.* In 7 stirrance. [f. STIR v. + -ANCE.] Disturbance.

Stirred, *ppl. a.* [f. STIR v. + -ED¹.] Moved, agitated, excited, etc.: see the various senses of the verb. Also with *up*: see STIR v. 16.

Stirrer (stə̄'rəʌ). Forms: see STIR v. 7 stirrier (sense 3 b). [f. STIR v. + -ER¹.] One who or something which stirs, in various senses.

1. One who or something which excites or provokes something, as strife, passion, etc., or incites a person to something; an inciter, instigator; a promoter (*obs.*); † an exhorter (*obs.*).

2. A beginning to move; a slight or momentary movement; (with negative) any of the least movement.

Stirring (stə̄'riŋ), *vbl. sb.* [f. STIR v. + -ING¹.] The action of the verb STIR in various senses.

1. The action of moving (in general sense); movement, motion. *Obs. or arch.*

2. A beginning to move; a slight or momentary movement; (with negative) any of the least movement.

3. The action of rousing or exciting to activity or emotion; incitement, instigation, provocation; prompting, suggestion, inducement, persuasion.

Stirring, *ppl. a.* [f. STIR v. + -ING².] That stirs, in various senses of the verb.

1. Moving; that is in motion, or capable of motion; moving about or along; moving lightly or tremulously.

2. Moving briskly, active, lively, agile; energetic in action; actively occupied, busy, bustling.

Stirringly (stə̄'riŋli), *adv.* [f. prec. + -LY².] In a stirring manner.

Stirrow, Stirrun: see STIRRAH, STERN *a.*

Stirrup (sti'rŏp), *sb.* Forms: see below. [OE. *stigráp*, f. *stigan* to climb + *ráp* ROPE.]

1. A contrivance suspended from the side of a saddle to serve as a support for the foot of the rider; in modern times, an arched piece of metal (rarely of wood, leather, etc.) closed by a flat plate to receive the sole of the foot.

Stirrup-leather. The strap by which a stirrup hangs from the saddle.

Stirch: see STITCH.

Stitch (stitʃ), *sb.* Forms: 1 *stice*, 3-6 *stiche*, 4-6 *styche*, 5 *styche*, 5-6 *stytche*, 6-8 *stitche*, 6- *stitch*. [OE. *stice* masc., corresp. to OFris. *steke* prick, stab, OS. *stiki* (Galilee), point, OHG. *stih* (MHG., mod.G. *stich*) prick, puncture, stitch, sting, stab, pitch (LG. *stik*), etc.]

I. A thrust, stab.

1. † A prick, puncture, or stab, inflicted by a pointed implement. Only *OE.*

2. A sharp sudden pain, like that produced by the thrust of a pointed weapon; *esp.* (now only) an acute spasmodic pain in the intercostal muscles, called more fully a *stitch in the side.* Also in generalized or collective sense.

II. A single movement of a threaded needle in and out of a fabric which is being sewn. Also, the like movement with the awl in shoemaking.

Stitch, *v.* [f. prec.] trans. To work upon with a needle; to sew.

Stitch. [See Stitch sb.] ... Obs. To fasten or attach (something) by sewing.

Stitchback. Obs. [f. Stitch v.¹ + Back sb.]

Stitched, ppl. a. [f. Stitch v.¹ + -ed¹.] Embroidered, worked with ornamental stitches.

Stitchel. Obs. [Etymology unknown.]

Stitchel, *stitchell*, -il. [Etymology unknown.]

Stitcher (stitʃəɹ). [f. Stitch v.¹ + -er¹.] One who stitches or sews.

Stitchery (stitʃəɹi). [f. Stitcher + -y.] Needlework.

Stitching (stitʃiŋ), vbl. sb. [f. Stitch v.¹ + -ing¹.] 1. The action of the verb, in different senses. Obs.

Stith (stiθ), a. Obs. exc. Sc. north.

Stith, adv. Obs. Forms: 1-2 stiðe, 4 stiðe.

Stithe, Obs. rare⁻¹. A sty in the eye.

Stithily, adv. Obs. [f. Stith a. + -ly².]

Stithy (stiði), sb. Forms: 4 stiþi, 4 stethie, 4-5 stiþ, 4 stithie, 4-7 stithe, 4-7 stithy, 5-6 stethy, 6 stythie, 5 stethye. [a. ON. steði wk. masc.]

Stive, sb.¹ [app. a variant of Stew v., a OF. estiver.]

Stive, sb.² dial. [ME. stīven, OE. stīfian.]

Stive (stəiv), sb.³ dial. rare⁻¹. In 4 styue. [Var. of Stew v.²]

Stive, v.¹ [f. Stive sb.¹]

Stive (stəiv), v.² Now chiefly Sc. [a. OF. estiver, otherwise adopted as Stive v.¹]

Stiver (stəivəɹ), sb. [a. MDu. stiver.] A small coin (originally silver) of the Low Countries.

Stiver (stəivəɹ), v. dial. In 4 styuer, 5 stiver, 6 -steuer, 9 stiver, 5 stiuer, 9 -stiver.

Stoat (stəut), sb.¹ Forms: 5 stote, 6-9 stoate, 7 stote, 9 stoat. Obs. exc. dial.

Stoat, sb.² Tailoring. [Of obscure origin.]

Stoater (stəutəɹ). Racing. [Of obscure origin.]

Stoat, v. [f. Stoat sb.²]

Stob (stɒb), sb.¹ Now only Sc. and dial.

Stob, sb.² [f. Stob sb.¹ + -er.] Stumpy.

Stob, v.¹ [f. Stob sb.¹]

Stob, v.² dial. [Prob. f. Stob sb.¹]

Stoborn, obs. form of Stubborn.

Stoccado, Stoccata. see Stoccado, Stoccata.

Stock (stɒk), sb.¹ Forms: 1 stocc, 3 stok, 4-6 stoc, 4-6 stokke, 4-7 stocke, 4- stock. [OE. stocc.]

STOCK. | 993 | STOCK. | STOCK. | 994 | STOCK.

STOCK. | 995 | STOCK. | STOCK. | 996 | STOCKER.

Stock-exchange. A market for the buying and selling of public securities; the place or building where this is done; an association of brokers and jobbers who transact business in a particular place or market.

Stock-fish, stockfish. For forms see STOCK *sb.*[1] and FISH *sb.*[1]

Stockey, variant of STOCKY.

Stock-gillyflower. Forms: see STOCK *sb.*[1] and GILLYFLOWER.

Stockholder.

Stockish.

Stock-job. [Formed as next.]

Stock-job, *v.*

Stock-jobber.

Stock-jobbing, *vbl. sb.* and *ppl. a.*

Stock-keep, *v.*

Stock-keeping, *vbl. sb.*

Stockless.

Stockman.

Stock-market.

Stock of trade, stock-still, *a.*

Stocky, *a.*

Stodge.

Stodgy, *a.*

Stoic.

B. adj.

1. Of or belonging to the school of the Stoics or to its system of philosophy.

2. Of temper or disposition, or its manifestations: Conformable to the precepts of the Stoic philosophy; characterized by indifference to pleasure and pain.

Hence † Sto'icly *adv.* (*rare*) = STOICALLY.

Stoical (stōu'ikăl), *a.* Also 6–7 -all. [f. L. *stoic-us* (see prec.) + -AL.]

1. Of or belonging to the Stoics; characteristic of the Stoic philosophy.

2. a. Of temper or disposition, or its manifestations: Conformable to the precepts of the Stoic philosophy; characterized by indifference to pleasure and pain.

b. Of persons: Resembling a Stoic in austerity, indifference to pleasure and pain, repression of all feeling, and the like.

Stoicheiometry (stoikaiŏ'mĕtri), **stochiometry** (stŏkiŏmetri). *Chem.* Also † **stechi-**, † **stoechi-**, **stoichiometry**. [f. Gr. στοιχεῖο-ν element + -METRY.] The process or art of calculating or determining the equivalent and atomic weights of the elements participating in any chemical reaction; the science of estimating chemical elements; the branch of science concerned with the determination of atomic weights. (See also quot. 1869.)

Hence Stoicheio-, stochiome'tric, -al *adj.*

† Stoicheio'tical, *a.* *Obs. rare*⁻¹. In 7 erron. stechio-. [f. mod.L. *stoicheiomatic-us* (as prec.)] Pertaining to the casting of nativities.

† Stoi'cism. *Obs.* = STOICISM. In 7 erron. stechio-. [f. late Gr. στοιχείωσις (f. στοιχειό-ειν element) + -AL.] Pertaining to stoichiology.

† Stoi'cism. *Obs.* Also 7 stoicke. [ad. stem Stoicos, Stoyen, 6en, Stoisen, 5 Stoycen. [f. L. *stoic-us*; see Stoic and -IAN.]

Stoicism (stōu'isiz'm), *sb.* [f. Stoic + -ISM.]

Hence Stoi'cness.

Stoically (stōu'ikăli), *adv.* [f. prec. + -LY.]

1. In the manner of a Stoic; like the Stoics of old; in accordance with the principles of the Stoical philosophy.

2. With the indifference or fortitude of a stoic.

Hence Stoi'calness.

Stoicheiology (stoikaiŏ'lŏdʒi), **stochiology** (stŏkiŏlŏdʒi). *rare*. [f. Gr. στοιχεῖο-ν element +

+ -LOGY. Orig. ad. the G. form *stöchiologie*.] The science of elements. In Oken's use: see quot.

b. Logic. (See quot.)

† Stoi'city. *Obs. rare*⁻¹. [ad. L. *stoicitāt-, stoicitas.* f. *stoic-us*.] Stoicism.

Stoi'cal. *Obs.* In 4 stoy, Stoyen, 5en, Stoisen, 5 Stoycen.

Stoicism (stōu'isiz'm), *sb.* [f. Stoic + -ISM.]

1. The philosophy of the Stoics.

2. Conduct or practice conformable to the principles of the Stoics; austerity, repression of feeling, fortitude.

stoicism of the savage.

Stoi'city. *Obs. rare*⁻¹.

Stoiter (stoi'tə), *v.* *Sc.* and *north.* [Frequentative f. STOIT v. Cf. stolter, stalter, stolter in similar senses (see *Eng. Dial. Dict.*).]

Stokeghe. *Obs.* In Johnson and later Dicts. stoach. [Irish *stéach*: cf. the later STALKO.]

† Stoke, *sb.¹* *Obs.* [f. STOKE *v.¹*] A thrust with a weapon.

† Stoke, *sb.²* *Obs.* [cf. STOCK *sb.*] A stump.

† Stoke, *sb.³* *Obs.* [Perh. a. OF. *estoquier* = to stop.]

Stoke (stōuk), *v.¹* [Back-formation from STOKER.]

1. *trans.* To feed, stir up, and poke the fire in (a furnace), to tend the furnace of (a boiler). Also *absol.*

2. *intr.* To make a thrust (*at*).

3. *trans.* To thrust, drive home (a sword).

b. *Fig.*

Stoke (stōuk), *v.²* Also ‡ **stoak.** [Back-formation from STOKER.]

1. *trans.* To feed, stir up, and poke the fire in (a furnace), to tend the furnace of (a boiler). Also *absol.*

b. *intr.* To rebound, bounce (*Eng. Dial. Dict.*).

Stoke-hole. [Partly an adoption, partly a transl. of Du. *stookgat*, f. *stoken* to stoke + *gat* hole.]

after the Fire and some other Concerns in a Brew-house.

Stokehold (stōu'khould). [f. STOKE *v.²* + HOLD *sb.²*] An apartment containing the ship's boilers, where the stokers tend the furnaces.

Stoker (stōu'kə), *sb.* [a. Du. *stoker*, f. *stoken* to stoke.]

Stoke-hole.

Stokage. *Obs.*

Stokery (stōu'kəri). [f. STOKE *v.²* + -ERY.] A place where stoking is done.

† Sto'king, *vbl. sb.¹* [f. STOKE *v.¹* + -ING¹.] The action of thrusting with a weapon.

Stoking (stōu'kiŋ), *vbl. sb.²* [f. STOKE *v.²* + -ING².] The action of the verb; the operation of tending a furnace and feeding it with fuel.

b. *transf.* and *fig.*

Stokehold.

Stoker (stōu'kə), *sb.* Also 8 stoaker. [f. STOKE *v.²* + -ER¹.]

1. One who feeds and tends a furnace.

2. A mechanical contrivance for automatically feeding fuel into a furnace.

Stokerage. *Obs.*

Stoke (stōuk), *v.³* [? a. ON. (Norw.) *stauka*) Stealth.

Stokehold.

xix. Some little corn by stoldred brought to him, Each pound was valued at half a crown.

Stole (stōul), *sb.¹* Forms: 1 stol, 4, 6 stole, 4–6 stoole, 4, 7 stool, 3–6 stole, 6 stoale, stoole, stolie, stoill, stoyle, stoyll, 7 stoale, 4–stole. [a. L. *stola*, ad. Gr. στολή, orig. equipment, array; f. *stel-* root (cf. στέλλειν to place, array). Cf. OF. *estole* (mod.F. *étole*), Sp., Pg. *estola*, It. *stola*.]

1. A long robe.

2. *pl.* Small particles of black gritty matter which escape through the funnel of a steam-engine.

Stokerage (stōu'kərədʒ), *sb.* [f. STOKER + -AGE.] The action or the services of a stoker.

Stokery (stōu'kəri), *sb.* [f. STOKER + -Y.] The action of thrusting; the simplicity of construction of furnaces.

Stokeless (stōu'kləs), *a.* [f. STOKE *sb.*] Without a stoker.

Stole-hole.

3. Eccl. A vestment consisting of a narrow strip of silk or linen, worn over the shoulders (by deacons over the left shoulder only) and hanging down to the knee or lower.

Stolated (stōu'lātəd), *a. rare*⁻¹. [f. L. *stolāt-us* (f. *stola*) + -ED.] = next.

Stolate (stōu'lāt), *a.* and *sb.* [ad. L. *stolāt-us*, f. *stola*: see -ATE².]

† Sto'lled. *Obs.* In 4–5 stolde. [f. ME. *stolen* (a. ON. *stolla*) + -ED.]

Stoker (stōu'kə), *sb.* Also 8 stoaker. [f. STOKE + -ER¹.]

Stoole upon his left shoulder.

b. Sto'le *sb.²* [Irregularly ad. L. *stolo*: see STOLON.]

Stole (stōul), *sb.³* [Irregularly f. L. *stolo*: see STOLON.]

Stole (stōul), *sb.⁴* [? f. plant: To provide (an altar, a church) with altar-stoles: see STOLE *sb.²* 3.]

Stole (stōul), *v.¹* [f. STOLE *sb.¹*]

Stole, pa. t. and pa. pple. of STEAL *v.*; obs. f. STOOL.

Stoled (stōuld), *ppl. a.* [f. STOLE *sb.¹* 3 + -ED²] Wearing a stole (in various senses of the sb.).

Stolen (stōu'lən), *ppl. a.* Forms: see STEAL *v.*

Stolid (stŏ'lid), *a.* [ad. L. *stolidus*, related to *stultus* foolish, f. root *stel-* to stand or cause to stand still: cf. STALL *sb.* STOLL 1.] Dull and impassive; having little or no sensibility; incapable of being excited or moved.

Stolidity (stŏli'diti), *sb.* [ad. L. *stoliditāt-em*, f. *stolidus* STOLID: see -ITY.]

Stolidly (stŏ'lidli), *adv.* [f. STOLID + -LY.] In a stolid manner.

Hence Sto'lidly *adv.*, **Sto'lidness.**

Stolisma (stŏli'sma), *v. rare*⁻¹. [f. L. *stolid-us* + -IZE.] *trans.* To render stolid.

Lett. lxv. 398 The stolen goods were found upon him.

Stolle or **Stolled**, *obs. f.* STOLE *sb.²*, STOOL.

Stolo (stōu'lo), *sb.* Pl. **stolones** (stŏlōu'niz). [L.]

1. *Bot.* = STOLON 1. *rare*.

2. *Zool.* = STOLON 2. *Stolo* developing, the germ-stock of certain compound organisms.

Stolon (stōu'lən), *sb.* [ad. L. *stolon-, stolo* a shoot, sucker, sprout, etc.]

1. *Bot.* A sucker or shoot.

2. *Zool.* (See quot. 1880.)

Stolonate (stōu'lonāt), *a.* and *sb.*

Stoloniferous (stŏlŏni'fərəs), *a.* *Bot.* and *Zool.* [f. mod.L. *stolonifer*, f. *stolon*-, *stolo* STOLON + -FEROUS.] Bearing, having stolons.

Hence Stoloni'ferously *adv.*

Stoma (stōu'mă), *sb.* Pl. **stomata** (stŏ'mătă). [mod. use of L. *stoma*, a. Gr. στόμα mouth.]

1. *Anat.* and *Zool.* A small opening in an animal body; an aperture, orifice, pore (as of a lymphatic or other vessel, an air-tube, etc.).

2. *Bot.* One of the minute orifices in the epidermis of plants, especially of the leaves, occurring as a

slit between two (or in some cases more) cells of special structure (guard-cells), and opening into intercellular spaces in the interior tissue so as to afford communication with the outer air; a breathing-pore. (Sometimes used for the whole structure, including the guard-cells.)

Stomacace (stŏ'măkəsi), *sb.* [a. Gr. στομακάκη (Strabo), in the MSS. στομακάκκη, prob. f. στόμα mouth + κάκη bad.]

Stomach (stŏ'măk), *sb.* Forms: 4–6 stomak, 4–7 -ake, -ok, 6 stommok, stomacke, stomacque, 7 stomacke. 6 Pl. stomaches, 5 stomakes, 6–7 stomackes. [a. OF. *estomac*, *stomaque* (mod.F. *estomac*), ad. L. *stomachus*, a. Gr. στόμαχος orig. the throat, gullet, hence the mouth or orifice of any organ, esp. of the stomach, and later the stomach itself.]

1. In a human or animal body: The internal pouch or cavity in which food is digested.

b. The belly, abdomen.

c. as the seat of hunger, nausea, discomfort from disease, etc.

Stomacal (stŏ'măkəl), *a.* = STOMACHAL.

transf. 1848 THACKERAY *Van. Fair* lxii, With..his hand in the stomach of a voluminous white waistcoat. 1902 CORNISH *Naturalist Thames* 8 Barometers, if tapped violently in the centre of their mahogany stomachs.

†4. *Sc.* = STOMACHER. Also, a chest-covering for a horse. *Obs.*

1473–4 *Acc. Ld. High Treas. Scot.* I. 38 Deliuerit to Caldwele..j elne of satyne for stomokis to the Quene. 1488–92 *Ibid.* 80 Item, in the same box, a stomok. 1500–20 DUNBAR *Poems* xxvii. 11 With mony lymmar loun,..Off stomok steillaris and clayth takkaris. 1506 [see SHAKER 6]. 1508 *Acc. Ld. High Treas. Scot.* IV. 22 Item for vj quartaris quhilk dames to be foure stomo[k]is for hors housouris, xlij s. 1540–1 *Ibid.* VII. 423 The litill copburd of silver witht certane stomokkis, perle bedis, [etc.]. 1558 *Extracts Aberd. Reg.* (1844) I. 309 The wrangous reiffing and away taking fra hir of ane plyd,..ane bukrame approwne, ane stomak.

5. Appetite or relish for food. *Obs.* exc. (somewhat *arch.*) with const. *for*.

c1386 CHAUCER *Sompn. T.* 139 The body is ay so redy and penyble To wake, that my stomak is destroyed. 1514 BARCLAY *Cyt. & Uplondyshm.* (Percy Soc.) 1 A lordes stomake & a beggers pouche Full yll accordeth. 1555 EDEN *Decades* (Arb.) 182 They haue no stomacke to their meate. 1560 T. WILSON *Rhet.* (1563) 72, I haue no liste to eate now, it is to early for me, my stomacke is not yet come to me. 1590 SHAKS. *Com. Err.* I. i. 49 You haue no stomacke, hauing broke your fast. 1642 FULLER *Holy & Prof. St.* III. xiii. 185 A rich man told a poore man that he walked to get a stomach for his meat. a1654 SELDEN *Table-T.* (Arb.) 88 'Tis a good rule, eat within your Stomach, act within your Commission. 1674–7 J. MOLINS *Anat. Observ.* (1896) 19 The Boy came to his Stomack, and would goe. a1722 LISLE *Husb.* (1757) 271 Such working every other day..would get them a stomach to their meat. 1726 SWIFT *Gulliver* II. iii, I had quite lost my stomach, and was almost reduced to a skeleton. 1746 *Oxf. Sausage* (1764) 34, I..Rode for a Stomach. 1766 *Complete Farmer* s.v. *Purging*, Horses that fall off their stomach, ..should have a mild purge or two. 1841 JAMES *Brigand* v, Heaven send us all as good food as I have a good stomach. 1855 THACKERAY *Newcomes* II. xxxvii. 334 'You must go back to your dinner.' In vain I pleaded that I had no stomach for it. 1859 TENNYSON *Enid* 1062 And Enid took a little delicately, Less having stomach for it than desire To close with her lord's pleasure. 1867 HOWELLS *Ital. Journ.* 95 The lions had no stomach for Glaucus on the morning of the fatal eruption.

b. *fig.* Relish, inclination, desire (for something immaterial).

1513 DOUGLAS *Æneis* XIII. vi. 76 Agane his stomak..the contrak is ybrokken. 1596 SHAKS. *Merch. V.* III. v. 92 Nay, let me praise you while I haue a stomacke. 1610 — *Temp.* II. i. 107 You cram these words into mine eares, against the stomacke of my sense. 1610 HOLLAND *Camden's Brit.* (1637) 313 These matters, I assure you, it goes against my stomacke to relate. 1622 BACON *Hen. VII*, 38 It was an Act against his stomacke, and put vpon him by necessitie and reason of State. a1660 *Contemp. Hist. Irel.* (Ir. Archæol. Soc.) II. 27 The captain against his stamocke condescended. 1682 BUNYAN *Holy War* (1905) 369 The Captains..did do such execution with their stones, that they made him, though against stomach, to retreat. 1722 DE FOE *Plague* 65, I had no stomach to go back again to see the same dismal scene over again. 1793 DR. BURNEY in *Mme. D'Arblay's Diary & Lett.* (1891) III. 479, I have little stomach to write. 1870 EMERSON *Soc. & Solit., Books* Wks. (Bohn) III. 82 And if one lacks stomach for Mr. Grote's voluminous annals, the old slight and popular summary of Goldsmith..will serve. 1902 BUCHAN *Watcher by Threshold* 186, I had no stomach for more mysteries.

†6. Used (like 'heart', 'bosom', 'breast') to designate the inward seat of passion, emotion, secret thoughts, affections, or feelings. *Obs.*

1482 *Cely Papers* (Camden) 131 The wyche y onderstond ye taked sor at yowre stomak. 1537 STARKEY in Strype *Eccl. Mem.* (1721) I. App. lxxxi. 197, I trust..your bounden duty to your Sovereign Lord & Master shal so prevail in your stomac, that you [etc.]. 1537 CRANMER *Let. to Crumwell* Misc. Writ. (Parker Soc.) II. 348 Your good mind towards me concerning my debts to the king's highness, which of all other things lieth most nigh unto my stomach. a1548 HALL *Chron.*, *Hen. VIII*, 164 b, They knew nothyng of all his doynges, whiche sore greved their stomackes. 1571 WALSINGHAM in Digges *Compl. Ambass.* (1655) 151 The common people ease their stomacks onely by uttering certain seditious words. 1599 CHAPMAN *Hum. Day's Mirth* E 2 b, Nay I do not cry, but my stomacke waters to thinke that you should take it so heauily. 1642 D. ROGERS *Naaman* 346 Evill which causeth such a fulsomenesse and wearinesse in Gods stomacke. 1663 BUTLER *Hud.* I. iii. 222 This said, his grief to anger turn'd, Which in his manly stomach burn'd. 1707 ADDISON *Rosamond* II. ii. 16 My Stomach swells with secret Spight To see my fickle, faithless Knight..So little his own Worth to know. 1721 STRYPE *Eccl. Mem.* I. I. xi. 98 Nor cared they to meddle openly against the Emperor, especially in this, which he took so much to Stomach.

†b. *To utter (the bottom of) one's stomach*: to disclose one's inmost thoughts. Similarly, *to fish out the bottom of a person's stomach*. *Obs.*

1537 CROMWELL in Merriman *Life & Lett.* (1902) II. 92 As you may therby fishe out the botom of his stomake, and aduertise his Maieste howe he standethe disposed towardes him. 1538 *Ibid.* 128, I cannot but..be glad, that ye so frankely utter your stomache to me. 1604 HIERON *Preachers Plea* 28 But such as I am shall often heare them talke at libertie, and vtter the very bottome of their stomackes.

†c. In various phrases, *To pierce one's stomach, sink (deep) into one's stomach, to stick in one's stomach*: said of something that makes a lasting (esp. painful) impression on the mind. *Obs.*

1387–8 T. USK *Test. Love* II. viii. (Skeat) l. 15 It may not sinke in my stomake til I here more. 1509 FISHER *Funeral Serm. C'tess Richmond* Wks. (1876) 298 Dauyd sayth.. *zelaui super iniquos*..it perceth my stomacke to se the rest & ease that synners often haue. c1536 in *Priory of Hexham* (Surtees) I. App. p. clix, There is somewhat that stykkes in their stomakkes. a1548 HALL *Chron.*, *Edw. IV*, 207 These reasons..sancke in the Dukes stomacke. 1565 COOPER *Thesaurus* s.v. *Mordeo*, Thy letters did much greue me, or pinche me at the stomake. 1579 RICE *Invect. agst. Vices* H j b, Now, therefore do I sore muse, how this question..could sinke into any honest, & specially, into any Christian mans stomake, to demaunde, what [etc.]. 1643 BAKER *Chron.*, *Eliz.* (1653) 558 For this new Earl [of the Holy Empire] stuck in the stomachs of the English Barons, who inwardly grudged to give him place. 1691 WOOD *Athenæ Oxon.* (1817) III. 369 Which usage sunk so deep into his stomach, that he [Selden] did never after affect the bishops and clergy. 1708 MRS. CENTLIVRE *Busy Body* v. iv, Does not your hundred pounds stick in your stomach? 1781 COWPER *Madan's Answ. Newton* 8 Which stuck in M.'s stomach as cross as a bone. 1809 MALKIN *Gil Blas* x. vii. (Rtldg.) 356 This declaration stuck in his stomach. 1828 *Carr Craven Gloss.*, 'To stick in the stomach,' to remain in the memory with angry resentment.

†7. Temper, disposition; state of feeling with regard to a person; *occas.* friendly feeling, friendliness. *Obs.*

1476 SIR J. PASTON in *Paston Lett.* III. 160 He also hathe tolde me moche off hys stomake and tendre faver that he owythe to yow. c1489 CAXTON *Sonnes of Aymon* xii. 288 And I behelde vpon my bredern, & knewe their stomackes. 1535 COVERDALE *Prov.* xi. 17 He yt hath a gentle liberall stomacke, is mercifull. 1553 BRENDE *Q. Curtius* VI. 98 Antipater therefore which knew ful wel his stomake, durst not vse the victory accordinge to his owne will. 1565 COOPER *Thesaurus* s.v. *Animus*, *Nec vnus in te ego hos animos gessi*, Not only I had that stomake towarde you. 1607 TOPSELL *Four-f. Beasts* 307 When he had gotten perfect intelligence and vnderstanding of the Horsses stomacke, he.. addressed himselfe to mount on his backe. 1610 HOLLAND *Camden's Brit.* (1637) 51 The auxiliarie souldiers likewise were of the same stomach.

b. With various adjs. (e.g. *bold, high, proud, malicious*) or other qualifying words. (The combination of adj. and sb. is sometimes equivalent to the sb. in sense 8.)

c1510 MORE *Picus* Wks. 5/1 He was verie quicke, wise, and subtile in dispicions, and had great felicitee therein, while he had that high stomak. 1535 COVERDALE *Prov.* xvi. 18 After a proude stomake there foloweth a fall. 1536 in *Priory of Hexham* (Surtees) I. App. p. cxxxi, He did nothyng..but of a willyng malicys stomak. 1548 HALL *Chron.*, *Edw. IV*, 218 Erle of Warwicke, whose stoute stomacke, and invincible corage,..caused death before..old age. 1565 COOPER *Thesaurus*, *Sublimitas animi*, lofty stomake or courage. 1573 G. HARVEY *Letter-bk.* (Camden) 14 A wurthi pattern of a noble stummock. 1576 RALEGH in Gascoigne *Steele Glas* (Arb.) 47 For spyteful tongs, in cankred stomackes plaste, Deeme worst of things, which best (percase) deserued. 1617 HIERON *Penance for Sin* xix. (1619) 283 It is scarcely to be thought that that mans soule is truely taught of God, who is backward, especially out of height of stomake, to bee a Teacher vnto others. 1631 QUARLES *Samson* iii, Great God! whose power hath so oft prevail'd Against the strength of Princes, and hast quail'd Their prouder stomackes. a1661 FULLER *Worthies*, *Durh.* (1662) 294 This Ralph was a Prelate of High Birth, haughty Stomach, great Courtship, [etc.]. 1697 DRYDEN *Virg. Georg.* III. 322 Before his Training, keep him poor and low: For his stout Stomach with his Food will grow. 1709 STRYPE *Ann. Ref.* I. xxxv. 348 But Bourne, notwithstanding, had an angry Stomack against the Bishop. 1772 J. FLETCHER *Logica Genev.* 29 The proud and haughty stomachs of the daughters of England are so maintained with divers disguised sorts of apparel, that [etc.]. 1835 LYTTON *Rienzi* v. v, His stomach is too high for that now. 1881 BLACKIE *Lay Serm.* viii. 263 Middleton, soon after this hasty provocation of the stout old Scottish stomach, fell into discredit.

8. In various senses relating to disposition or state of feeling.

†a. Spirit, courage, valour, bravery. *Obs.*

Phrase, *to take stomach* (often with dat. of refl. pron.).

c1532 DU WES *Introd. Fr.* in *Palsgr.* 904/2 The stomake, *le courage*. 1534 MORE *Comf. agst. Trib.* II. Wks. 1171/1 A merye tale wyth a frende, refresheth a manne..and amendeth his courage and hys stomake. 1538 STARKEY *England* (1878) 27 Yet the grete frute..wych may..yssue of the same may somewhat encorage vs and gyue vs stomake. 1540 HYRDE tr. *Vives' Instr. Chr. Wom.* (1592) I 3, Against these darts of the divell..let her take the buckler of Stomacke. 1544 BALE *Exam. Oldcastle* 26 b, He toke stomake vnto him agayne. 1565 COOPER *Thesaurus*, *Afferre animum alicui*, to encourage; to geue stomake. 1569 UNDERDOWNE *Heliodorus* IV. 55 After shee knewe her selfe, and had taken stomake vnto her, shee..saide [etc.]. 1571 *Homily agst. Disobedience* II. D j b, Lustie and couragious captaines, valiaunt men of stomacke. 1579 FENTON *Guicciard.* VII. (1599) 270 The king of Romains also taking stomack by the greatnesse of his son, solicited to passe into Italy. 1606 SHAKS. *Tr. & Cr.* II. i. 137 Hector..Will with a Trumpet,..To morrow morning call some Knight to Armes, That hath a stomacke. 1611 CHAPMAN *Iliad* IX. 335 Let him take stomacke to repell Troyes firie threatenings. 1645 FULLER *Good Th. in Bad T.* 172 John Courcy, Earl of Vlster, was chosen Champion for the English; A Man of great Stomack and Strength. 1663 BUTLER *Hud.* I. ii. 107 Instead of Trumpet and of Drum, That makes the Warrier's stomach come; A squeaking Engine be apply'd.

†b. Pride, haughtiness; obstinacy, stubbornness.

a1513 FABYAN *Chron.* VII. 643 For yᵉ great stomake of the father, yᵗ he wolde not be condycioned with of yᵉ sone. 1575–85 ABP. SANDYS *Serm.* x. 169 Zeale without knowledge is not zeale but stomacke. 1590 SPENSER *F. Q.* II. vii. 41 Sterne was his looke, and full of stomacke vaine. 1613 SHAKS. *Hen. VIII*, IV. ii. 34 He was a man Of an vnbounded stomacke, euer ranking Himselfe with Princes. 1641 MILTON *Animadv.* Wks. 1851 III. 239 They were..for stomach much like to Pompey the great, that could indure no equall. 1674 J. HOWARD *Engl. Mounsieur* II. i. 26 Oh—is your stomack come down. 1692 R. L'ESTRANGE *Fables* ccxv. 188 Now 'tis not Courage but Stomach, that makes many People Break, rather then they will Bend. 1765 FOOTE *Commissary* I. Wks. 1799 II. 9 Oh ho! what, I suppose his stomach's come down.

†c. Anger, irritation; malice, ill-will, spite; vexation, pique. *Obs.*

c1540 *Life Bp. Fisher* (E.E.T.S.) p. xlix, Whereat the Cardinall tooke such hartie displeasure against the Emperour that ever after he bare him in stomacke. 1559 ABP. PARKER in N. Johnston *King's Visit. Power* (1688) 116, I shall be bold in secretys to Wright it..to avoid som Stomake that ellys might be taken. 1568 T. HOWELL *Newe Sonets* (1879) 139 Wordes be but winde, to purge his heate, His stomacke to abate. 1592 WOTTON *Let.* 10 July *Reliq. W.* (1685) 675 Having left a stipend..of 1200 Crowns, upon Stomach to see himself cross'd in the Court by the Archbishop of Pisa. 1603 KNOLLES *Hist. Turks* (1621) 440 Zemes more upon stomacke and desire of revenge, than [etc.]. 1611 SPEED *Hist. Gt. Brit.* IX. xiii. § 67 But the King vpon a stomacke doth it. 1633 BP. HALL *Hard Texts* Eccl. x. 4 If the Prince be angry with thee, doe not in a stomach or froward pettishnese give up thine office. 1641 MILTON *Ch. Govt.* II. Wks. 1851 III. 140 Not suddenly to condemn all things that are sharply spoken, or vehemently written, as proceeding out of stomach, virulence and ill nature. 1643 BAKER *Chron.*, *Edw. I*, 131 Others of the nobility..took stomach against him. a1825 FORBY *Voc. E. Anglia*, *Stomach*, anger.

9. *Brewing.* See quot. [Perhaps a corruption of some other word; perh. a fanciful use of 8 a.]

1835 W. BLACK *Brewing* 52 What is technically called the stomach or vinous vapour begins to be smelt, and continues to acquire strength until the process [of fermentation] is concluded. *Ibid.* 204 Stomach means the pungency, but more particularly the odour of the vapour evolved during fermentation; by which an experienced brewer should at all times be able to judge how the process is going on. 1882 E. G. HOOPER *Man. Brewing* (ed. 2) 240 The proper cleansing point is fixed in different ways, and whilst one judges by the heat of the wort ceasing to rise, another goes by the diminution in pungency of the odour or 'stomach' exhaled.

10. *attrib.* and *Comb.* a. Simple attrib., pertaining to the stomach, as *stomach-blood, -catarrh, -complaint, -digestion, †fit, -wall, -wound*; good for the stomach, as *stomach-drink, -essence, -pill, -wine*; b. objective and locative, as *stomach-stretching*; *stomach-hating, -healing, -qualmed, -sick, -soothing, -turning, -twitched, -whetting, -worn*, adjs.; c. special comb., †**stomach-anger** *nonce-wd.*, concealed anger; **stomach-bag** = CHEESELIP[1] 2; **stomach cough**, a cough supposed to proceed from indigestion; †**stomach grief**, bitter anger; †**stomach-gut**, the duodenum; **stomach-piece** *Naut.* (see quot.); **stomach pocket** *Zool.*, in Medusæ, a cavity serving as a stomach; **stomach-pouch**, (*a*) the protuberant abdominal pouch found in certain ducks and geese; (*b*) = prec.; **stomach-pump**, a kind of pump or syringe for emptying the stomach (esp. in cases of poisoning) or for introducing liquids into it; **stomach-staggers**, a variety of staggers (STAGGER *sb.*[1] 2) caused by distension of the stomach; **stomach sweetbread**, the pancreas, as distinguished from the 'throat sweetbread' or THYMUS; **stomach-syringe** = *stomach-pump*; †**stomach-tight** *a. Sc.*, hungry; **stomach-tooth** (see quot.); **stomach-tube**, (*a*) 'a siphon used in washing out the stomach'; (*b*) 'a feeding tube' (Dorland *Med. Lex.*); **stomach-warmer**, a flat vessel of tin-plate, to be filled with hot water and applied to the pit of the stomach; **stomach-wise** *adv.* (*nonce-wd.*), (crawling) on one's stomach; **stomach-worm**, (*a*) a common intestinal round worm, *Ascaris lumbricoides*, sometimes found in the human stomach (= MAW-WORM), (*b*) *slang* (see quot. 1788).

1640 BP. REYNOLDS *Passions* xxxi. 317 Neither can I like that close and dissembled, that politick and *stomacke anger, which cunningly shrowds it selfe under a calme and serene countenance. 1717 *Dict. Rust.* s.v. *Cheeslip-bag*,.. 'Tis the *Stomach-bag of a young Sucking Calf that never tastes any other food than Milk. 1847 W. C. L. MARTIN *Ox* 37 The first thing to be done is to clear the stomach-bag. 1666 G. HARVEY *Morbus Angl.* xxx. (1672) 90 If the evacuated blood be florid, it's *Stomach-blood. 1910 *Daily Chron.* 5 Apr. 9/2 Niemeyer,..speaking of the value of this fluid in *stomach-catarrh, is found saying [etc.]. 1824 SCOTT *St. Ronan's* iii, The gentlemen were as liable to *stomach complaints, as the ladies to nervous disorders. 1875 T. K. CHAMBERS *Man. Dict* 287 '*Stomach cough' and 'Stomach sore throat'..are best treated by [etc.]. 1899 *Allbutt's Syst. Med.* VIII. 369 The sensations accompanying *stomach and intestinal digestion are felt excessively. 1903 *Daily Chron.* 20 Feb. 3/5 Thus tea and coffee both retard stomach-digestion powerfully. 1766 *Complete Farmer* s.v. *Purging*, When horses lose their appetites after purging, it is necessary to give them a warm *stomach drink. 1672 G. THOMSON *Let. to H. Stubbe* 25 A Vindication of the Author's *Stomach-Essence, and other effectual Remedies. a1700 B. E. *Dict. Cant. Crew*, *Qualm*, a *Stomach-Fit. 1533 T. WILSON *Rhet.* 106 b, *Stomake grief [margin, *Iracundia*], is when we will take the matter as hote as a tost. 1585 HIGINS *Junius' Nomencl.* 31/1 *Intestinum primum*,..the *stomach gutte, or maw gut. 1620 J. TAYLOR (Water P.) *Praise Hemp-seed* (1623) 21 Iniunctions for some *stomacke hating Fast. 1735 SOMERVILLE *Chace* I. 378 Each *Stomach-healing Plant Curious they crop. 1846 A. YOUNG *Naut. Dict.* 14 *Apron*, or *Stomach-piece, a piece of curved timber which is bolted on the inside of a vessel's main-stem, to strengthen it and to give shifts to its scarphs. 1875 KNIGHT *Dict. Mech.*, *Stomach-piece*, a compass-timber fayed to the stem and keel. An apron. 1662 J. DECHAVERE *Thesaurus Remed.* (ed. 2) 35 First clense downward with the *stomack pills. 1885 W. K. BROOKS in *Mem. Boston Soc. Nat. Hist.* III. 361 The Narcomedusæ..Radial canals absent, or present as flat radial *stomach pockets. 1854 *Poultry Chron.* I. 498 The duck of this kind has at a very early age a great development of its '*stomach pouch.' 1871 ALLMAN *Gymnobl. Hydroids* 84 The fact of their having twelve tentacles and twelve stomach-pouches instead of eight. 1822–9 *Good's Study Med.* (ed. 3) I. 119 Until Dr. Physic proved the utility of the *stomach pump in the case of a child poisoned with laudanum, the invention gained little attention. 1899 CAGNEY tr. *von Jaksch's Clin. Diagn.* v. (ed. 4) 151 The handle is removed and the sound connected with a stomach-pump. 1611 SHAKS. *Cymb.* III. iv. 193 If you are sicke at Sea, or *Stomacke-qualm'd at Land, a Dramme of this Will driue away distemper. 1613 PURCHAS *Pilgrimage* (1614) 289 He proued *stomack-sick to his expedition also. 1657 W. RAND tr. *Gassendi's Life Peiresc* I. 98 He withdrew himself [to sit by the Mainmast] that he might not be Stomach-sick. 1664 H. MORE *Exp. 7 Epist.* ix. 149 Christ here expresseth how nauseous and stomack-sick he is against his Church under this Intervall and Title of Laodicea. 1876 BRISTOWE *Th. & Pract. Med.* (1878) 201 Spirits of chloroform, bismuth, or other *stomach-soothing drugs. 1831 YOUATT *Horse* vii. 103 In *Stomach-staggers the horse stands dull, sleepy, staggering. 1648 G. DANIEL *Eclog* iii. 79 T'allay The *Stomacke-Stretchings of the former Day. 1822–9 *Good's Study Med.* (ed. 3) I. 119 A *stomach syringe, for diluting and washing away various poisons introduced into the stomach..was first suggested by Renault. 1715 RAMSAY *Christ's Kirk Gr.* II. xviii, But ithers that were *stomach-tight, Cry'd out, [etc.]. 1890 BILLINGS *Nat. Med. Dict* II. 594 **Stomach tooth*, canine tooth of lower jaw of first dentition, so called because of gastric disturbance frequently accompanying its eruption. 1857 DUNGLISON *Med. Lex.* s.v. *Tube*, *Tube Œsophageal*, **Stomach Tube*, a long elastic gum tube, capable of being passed into the œsophagus or stomach. 1897 *Allbutt's Syst. Med.* III. 437 Emetics..may be given when the use of the stomach-tube is inadvisable. 1875 BROWNING *Aristoph. Apol.* 197 The *stomach-turning stew. 1804 COLERIDGE *Lett.* (1895) 457, I am as asthmatic and *stomach-twitched as when with you. 1871 ALLMAN *Gymnobl. Hydroids* 84 The internal surface of the *stomach walls. 1835 DICKENS *Sk. Boz*, *River*, A flat bottle like a *stomach-warmer. 1858 SIMMONDS *Dict. Trade*, *Stomach-warmer* a metal vessel for holding hot water to place on the stomach. 1631 QUARLES *Samson* x, Their *stomacke-whetting Sallats. 1677 J. BEALE *Nurseries*, etc. ii. 24 Poitiers (where I always met with excellent *stomach-wine). 1750 J. THEOBALD *App. Medulla Med. Univ.* 67 Stomach Wine. Take Half an Ounce of Gentian-root, [etc.]. 1893 K. GRAHAME *Pagan Ess.* 131 Where a rabbit could go, a boy could follow, albeit *stomach-wise, and with one leg in the stream. 1647 TRAPP *Comm. Mark* ix. 50. 27 *Stomach-worms are killed with salt. 1666 G. HARVEY *Morbus Angl.* xvii. (1672) 35 Whence they are called Stomach or Maw-worms. 1788 GROSE *Dict. Vulgar T.* (ed. 2) s.v., The stomach worm gnaws; I am hungry. 1812 [SOUTHEY] *Omniana* I. 229 The same man, sick, dyspeptic, and *stomach-worn. 1905 *Brit. Med. Jrnl.* 4 Mar. 471 The upper part of the *stomach wound was closed.

Stomach (stʊ·măk), *v.* Forms: see the sb. [f. STOMACH *sb.* Cf. L. *stomachārī* to be resentful, to be angry with, F. *s'estomaquer* to take offence.]

†1. *trans.* To be offended at, resent. *Obs.*

1523 CROMWELL in Merriman *Life & Lett.* (1902) I. 36, I stomak as a sory Subiect may doo, the high iniuries done by the saide Francoys. 1560 DAUS tr. *Sleidane's Comm.* 382 Than began he to stomack the matter, & was right sore offended. a1591 H. SMITH *Restit. Nebuchadnezzar* 33 So God doth stomacke sinnes in those that beare his owne person. 1611 B. JONSON *Catiline* III. F 1 b, Publicke report, That giues you out, to stomacke your repulse. 1649 MILTON *Eikon.* 110 Parlament is call'd, not by the King, but by the Law, to be his Counselers & Dictators, though he stomac it. 1678 *Lively Oracles* II. ix. 246 We daily..receive those things with contentment..from an intimate..which if spoken by a stranger or enemy, would be despis'd or stomach'd. 1739 GRAY *Let.* Poems (1775) 47 Moreover I think I have reason to stomach your last piece of gravity. 1741 RICHARDSON *Pamela* (1824) I. 115 In such a manner as might show I would not disoblige on purpose, though I stomached this matter very heavily too. 1780 JOHNSON in *Boswell* (1904) II. 341 An Englishman would have stomached it, and been sulky. a1825 FORBY *Voc. E. Anglia*, *Stomach*, to resent.

†b. with clause or infinitive as obj. *Obs.*

1587 NORTON tr. *Calvin's Inst.* IV. vii. (ed. 4) 377 *marg.*, The Bishop of Rome stomoking that the Bishop of Constantinople should come so neere as to bee made by a councell next him in authoritie. 1594 *Mirr. Policy* (1599) K ij, When as Iulius Cæsar scorning a superior, and Pompey stomacking to haue any equall to himself, did both striue for the principality. a1641 BP. MOUNTAGU *Acts & Mon.* (1642) 289 Alexander..stomached that Antipater was all in all with his Father.

c. To be offended with (a person).

a1548 HALL *Chron.*, *Hen. IV*, 30 Jhon duke of Burgogn.. stomaked and envied the Duke of Orliance. 1583 STOCKER *Civ. Warres Lowe C.* IV. 52 b, The Magistrate and all the Citezeins did wonderfully stomacke the Catholickes, in so muche, that [etc.]. 1652–62 HEYLIN *Cosmogr.* III. (1676) 222/1 Both Nations hated by the Natives..but of the two the Spaniard looked on by the people as the more a Gentleman; the other stomached and despised for their sordid dealings. 1671 WOODHEAD *St. Teresa* II. ii. 6, I was very much stomached by all my Monastery, because I would erect another, more recluse.

†d. *intr.* To take offence, feel resentment. *Obs.*

1567 PALFREYMAN *Baldwin's Mor. Philos.* To Rdr. (1600) A vj b, Not as though I..should swell or stomack against any man. 1591 SAVILE *Tacitus, Hist.* II. xxviii. 69 The Auxiliaries mourned the Legions stomacked. 1648 GAGE *West Ind.* 208 The good Archbishop..corrected some things in it..which we already hear they have stomached at. 1650 S. CLARKE *Eccl. Hist* (1654) I. 142 Herodias rageth afresh, stomacketh anew. a1662 HEYLIN *Laud* (1668) 359 The Archbishop had long stomackt at the Insolencies of Matthews. 1706 PHILLIPS (ed. Kersey), To *Stomach* or *Stomach at*, to be angry at, to resent a thing. 1706 J. SERGEANT *Acc. Chapter Bp. Chalcedon* (1853) 85 The Cardinals..who.. stomached at the authority of the chapter.

†2. *trans.* To excite the indignation of, to offend, vex. *Obs.*

1588 A. MUNDAY *Palmerin of Eng.* I. xi. (1639) E 1 b, Palmerin was chosen chiefe Defendant, which somewhat did stomack the sonnes of Primaleon. 1652–62 HEYLIN *Cosmogr.* III. (1676) 136/1 These insolent and unsufferable pranks committed so commonly by these masterful slaves so exceedingly stomached Bajazet the second, that [etc.]. 1675 ALSOP *Anti-Sozzo* 693 But the Apostle has said enough in this Chapter to stomach the Pride and Restifness of humane Wisdom.

3. To turn the stomach of, to nauseate. *rare.*

1796 ELIZA HAMILTON *Lett. Hindoo Rajah* (1811) II. 298 Some of us were so much stomached, that we did not much like to go. 1866 HOWELLS *Venet. Life* 76 It is not that the restaurants are very dirty—if you wipe your plate and glass carefully before using them, they need not stomach you.

†4. To inspire with resentment, fury or courage; to incite. *Obs.*

1541 PAYNEL *Catiline* xxxix. 56 b, Tell me I pray you, wherto serueth that oration? was it to stomake you ageynst the conspiracy [L. *an uti vos infestos conjurationi faceret*]? 1545 BALE *Image Both Ch.* I. vi. (1550) F j, When he had stomaked theim by the holy ghost, to shote forth his worde without feare. a1548 HALL *Chron.*, *Hen. VII*, 7 To encourage, stomacke and entyce many other to be aiders, assisters & partakers of the same conspiracy. *Ibid.*, *Hen. VIII*, 163 b, Which fordele might perchance so stomacke him yᵗ he would agre to no new condicions nor agrementes.

5. To brook, endure, put up with, tolerate.

1677 SIR H. CAPELL in *Essex Papers* (Camden) II. 128 Treas[urer] ill stomachs Ormond's carrying this businesse. 1814 LADY BURGHERSH *Lett.* (1893) 232, I confess I cannot stomach treating these people *de princes*. 1814 SCOTT *Wav.* lvii, So that Fergus was compelled to stomach this supposed affront. 1845 JAMES *Arrah Neil* vi, Dry stomached the affront till the time came for his revenge. 1861 HUGHES *Tom Brown Oxf.* xlii, In the end he could not stomach such a backsliding. 1862 *London Rev.* 30 Aug. 190 He cannot stomach 'a filthy compound of bones and alum'. 1874 *Slang Dict.* 311 *Stomach*, to bear with, to be partial to. Mostly used in a negative character,—as, 'I can't stomach that.' 1880 L. TENNYSON in *19th Cent.* Jan. 67 The first two evils he was obliged to stomach as best he might. 1887 BESANT *World went* iii, The study of the Latin language..he could not stomach. 1894 BARING-GOULD *Kitty Alone* III. 49 But that Pepperill's niece..should have the temerity to refuse his son was a fact he could not stomach.

6. To take into or retain on the stomach, to digest. *nonce-use.*

1822 PRAED *Poems* (1866) I. 66 Iron and steel, for an early meal, He stomached with ease. 1854 S. DOBELL *Balder* i. 3 Vales, mountains, trees, And stones of home,..anon Are stomached by mine hunger.

7. To climb by laying the stomach against.

1884 *Century Mag.* Dec. 195/1 Now creeping under an uprooted tree..; then 'stomaching' a prostrate log three or four feet in height.

Stomach-ache (stʊ·măk,ēik). Pain in the stomach or abdomen. Also *fig.*

1763 BICKERSTAFF *Love in Village* III. ix, Well, aunt, you have been complaining of the stomach-ach all day. 1839 J. H. NEWMAN *Lett.* (1891) II. 286, I must confess it has given me a stomach-ache. 1897 *Allbutt's Syst. Med.* IV. 241 In lead colic the more or less persistent 'stomach ache' ..will usually assist in the diagnosis.

Hence **Stomach-achey** *a.* (*nonce-wd.*) productive of stomach-ache.

1860 H. MAYHEW *Upper Rhine* ii. 65 A pickle that may be excellent..but which is sad stomach-achey wash. 1885 'L. MALET' *Col. Enderby's Wife* III. ix, What a windy, stomach-achy sort of reward it promises to be!

Stomachal (sto·măkăl), *a.* [ad. mod.L. *stomachālis*, f. L. *stomach-us* STOMACH *sb.*: see -AL. Cf. F. *stomacal* (in 16th c. *-chal*), Sp. *estomacal*, It. *stomacale*.]

1. Pertaining to the stomach, gastric; of the nature of or serving the purpose of a stomach.

1582 HESTER *Secr. Fiorav.* I. xxxviii. 45 Flebothomie euacuateth the stomochall humors that are cause of that corruption [in gout]. 1683 SNAPE *Anat. Horse* I. ix. (1686) 18 The Stomachal Arteries are twigs from the Coeliacal branch of the *Arteria magna*. 1841 *Penny Cycl.* XXI. 425/2 A curved longitudinal furrow, which circumscribes laterally the stomachal region. 1859 G. H. LEWES *Physiol.* I. iii. 201 Our knowledge of the stomachal process has been rendered more accurate. 1860 *Encycl. Brit.* XXI. 1000/1 Near the middle of the body the canal is dilated into a stomachal cavity. 1861 HULME tr. *Moquin-Tandon* II. VII. ii. 344 The alimentary canal [of the Oxyurus] has the appearance of three stomachal dilatations which succeed each other. 1871 W. A. HAMMOND *Dis. Nerv. Syst.* 49 In stomachal vertigo the attacks of dizziness are often severe. 1896 A. WILLEY in *Q. Jrnl. Microsc. Sci.* XXXIX. 336 The stomachal axis of Ctenoplana.

2. Of remedies: Good for the stomach.

1599 A. M. tr. *Gabelhouer's Bk. Physicke* 117/1 An excellent stomacalle pouldre. 1603 FLORIO *Montaigne* II. xxxvii. 436 Let her hardly remit this vocall lithernesse vnto evill, if it be neyther cordiall, nor stomacall. 1612 WOODALL *Surg. Mate* Wks. (1653) 63 They are very stomachal, for they refresh much the stomack. 1707 *Curios. Husb. & Gard.* 235 Balm..is..stomachal and diuretick.

†**Sto·machate**, *a. Sc. Obs.* In 6 -chat, -chait, -kat. [ad. L. *stomachātus*, pa. pple. of *stomachārī*: see STOMACH *v.*] Indignant, angry.

c1550 ROLLAND *Crt. Venus* II. 563 Richt stomakat in hart ay haiffand dreid. *Ibid.* III. 253 Than Venus said in mind half stomachat, Of the assyis nane salbe alterat. *Ibid.* IV. 237 For I lang eir was sa hie stomachait At Desperance for his greit rebellioun.

Stomached (stʊ·măkt), *a.* and *ppl. a.* Forms: see STOMACH *sb.* [f. STOMACH *sb.* and *v.* + -ED.]

1. Having a stomach. In quots. only as the second element of parasynthetic formations, having a stomach of the specified kind or condition.

1540 HYRDE tr. *Vives' Instr. Chr. Wom.* (1592) R 2, Likewise as of men, he who is most like stomacked unto a woman, nor lusty couraged, wil remember injurie longest. 1567 MAPLET *Gr. Forest* 83 b, There are some so eger and stout stomaked that they haue [etc.]. 1589 GREENE *Menaphon* (Arb.) 86 And with that Carmela was so full stomackt that she wept. 1615 S. WARD *Coal fr. Altar* 79 This want of reformation makes the queasie stomacked Brownists cast them selues out of our Church. 1710 FULLER *Pharm. Extemp.* a 3, When Patients are so weak Stomach'd..that they cannot..admit of the Bark. 1843 JAMES *Forest Days* (1847) 66 A jolly, large-stomached personage.

†2. In senses of STOMACH *v.*: Offended; incited, encouraged. *Obs.*

1599 JAS. I *Basil. Doron* To Rdr. (1603) A 4 b, I will the more narrowly rippe up the wordes, whereat they seeme to bee somewhat stomacked. 1623 COCKERAM I, *Stomaked*, angered, hartened. c1712 G. GUTHRIE in *Monogr.* (1900) 10 Alexander suggested to his father that if he would allow him he could make money by his skill in musick, which the stomached father resented with no less than a pistoll.

Stomacher[1] (stʊ·mătʃəɹ, stʊ·măkəɹ). Forms: 5 **stomakere, stomechere, stomachyr**, 5–6 **stomachere**, 5–6, 8 **stomager**, 6 **stomackger**, (8 **stomatcher**), 6– **stomacher** [app. f. STOMACH *sb.* + -ER[1]: but see below.

The alleged F. *estomachier* appears to be recorded only by Palsgrave. If it be genuine, and the source of the Eng. word, it would account for the pronunciation (stʊ·mătʃəɹ), which is given in the pronouncing dictionaries of Kenrick (1773), Sheridan (1780), Walker (1791), Smart (1836), Worcester (1860), in Cassell's *Encyclopædic Dict.* (1888), and in *Webster's Dict.* (1828–1886). The genuineness of this pronunciation is attested by the spellings *stomager* (1450, 1727), *stomackger* (1575), *stomatcher* (17..), and *stomacher* (c1450 onwards): the spelling with *k* is evidenced only once (c1466), though the word occurs frequently in writers who wrote the word *stomach* with *k*. The pronunciation (stʊ·măkəɹ) was given by Ogilvie *Imperial Dict.* (1850) and appears in later editions of that work and in recent U.S. dicts. It is not impossible that *estomachier* was really formed in late Anglo-French, and is the source of the Eng. word. For the sense cf. the misuse of *stomach* for 'chest' (STOMACH *sb.* 3).]

†1. ? A waistcoat or pectoral of mail. *Obs. rare*⁻¹.

1450 in *Rep. MSS. Ld. Middleton* (1911) 114, I will..my felowe John Shipton for to have my dubbelet of mayell, my stomager of mayell, and a salet.

†2. A kind of waistcoat worn by men. *Obs.*

c1450 *Coventry Myst.* (Shaks. Soc.) 241 A stomachere of clere reynes. 1466 *Mann. & Househ. Exp.* (Roxb.) 382 Item, the same day my mastyr paid fore a stomakere of velvet, ij.s. iiij.d. 1478 *Paston Lett.* III. 237, I beseche yow to sende me a bose clothe..and a stomechere and ij schyrtes. 1508–13 *Bk. Kervynge* in *Babees Bk.* (1868) 282 Than warme his petycote, his doublet, and his stomachere. 1530 PALSGR. 276/2 Stomacher for one's brest, *estomachier*. 1575 TURBERV. *Falconrie* 16 The furryers doe vse their skynnes for stomackgers, to guard and defend the brest against the force of feruent colde. 1617 MORYSON *Itin.* III. 167 They use large stomachers of furre or lambe skinnes. a1625 FLETCHER *Mad Lover* III. i, Talking to an old man is like a stomacher, It keeps his blood warm. 1693 CONGREVE *Double Dealer* III. i. (1694) 33 The first Favour he receiv'd from her was a piece of an old Scarlet Petticoat for a Stomacher. a1700 EVELYN *Diary* May 1645 (Lucca), Embroidred stomachers generaly worn by gentlemen in these countries. 1702 BAYNARD *Cold Baths* II. (1709) 375 He wore a quilted Stomacher. 1715 tr. *Pancirollus' Rerum Mem.* I. IV. ii. 147 They wore also Stomachers, but in cold Weather most commonly woollen Shirts.

†b. A medicated cloth applied to the chest. *Obs.*

1577 FRAMPTON *Joyfull Newes* I. 7 In griefes of the Stomake, it [this plaister] doth a merueilous effect, applied after the maner of a Stomacher. 1584 COGAN *Haven Health* xlviii. 56 The herbe..put in a lynnen bagge and laide as a stomager next the skinne comforteth a colde stomacke well. 1682 *Digby's Chym. Secr.* II. 243 Take Wormwood..; of these make a Stomacher, and apply it.

3. An ornamental covering for the chest (often covered with jewels) worn by women under the lacing of the bodice.

1535 COVERDALE *Isa.* iii. 24 Instead of a stomacher [so 1560 (Geneva), 1611, 1884 (Revised), a sack cloth. 1566 *Engl. Ch. Furniture* (Peacock 1866) 56 Wherof his wiel made of one a stomacher for her wench. 1580 LYLY *Euphues Eng.* To Ladies (Arb.) 222 If a Tailour make your gowne too little, you couer his fault with a broad stomacher. 1611 SHAKS. *Wint. T.* IV. iii. 226 Golden Quoifes, and Stomachers For my Lads, to giue their deers. 1653 H. COGAN *Diodorus Sic.* 161 The Goddesse Minerva..killed this cruell monster, and of her skinne made her selfe a stomacher. 1688 HOLME *Armoury* III. 94/2 The Stomacher is that peece as lieth under the lacing or binding on of the Body of the Gown. 1702 *Lond. Gaz.* No. 3806/8 Lost.., a Diamond Stomacher with a row of Rose Diamonds down the middle. c1710 CELIA FIENNES *Diary* (1888) 252 Their stomatchers some were all Diamonds. 1727 DORRINGTON *Philip Quarll* 163 Which seem'd to adorn her Bosom far more than the richest Stomager made of Diamonds or Pearls could do. 1731 *Gentl. Mag.* I. 189 Sometimes the stomacher rises almost to the chin. 1737 *Ibid.* VII. 513/2 The Princess of Wales had on an exceeding rich Stomacher. 1761 *Brit. Mag.* II. 446 The rich diamond stomacher for our intended queen is quite finished. 1837 DICKENS *Pickw.* xlix, An old-fashioned green velvet dress, with a long waist and stomacher. 1868 *Morn. Star* 7 Mar., Ornaments: Diamond necklace and stomacher. 1880 *Cassell's Family Mag.* VI. 758/2 Several of the winter dresses are laced in front over a stomacher.

attrib. 1753 *Lond. Mag.* Sept. 396/2 Before, for your breast, pin a stomacher bib on.

†b. *transf.*

1611 SHAKS. *Cymb.* III. iv. 86 Away, away Corrupters of my Faith, you [*sc.* letters that she had carried in her bosom] shall no more Be Stomachers to my heart. 1613 DONNE *Epithalam.* 8 The houshold Bird with the red stomacher. 1717 J. DENNIS *Orig. Lett.* (1721) I. 33 You look full over Box Hill, and see the Country beyond it,..and, over the very Stomacher of it, see St. Paul's at five and twenty Miles Distance.

†**Sto·macher**[2]. *Obs.* In 7 **stomaker**. [f. STOMACH *v.* + -ER[1].] One who 'stomachs' or resents.

1608 CHAPMAN *Byron's Trag.* v. R 3, By my loue..command them To..proue no stomakers of my misfortunes.

Stomacher[3] (stʊ·măkəɹ). *Pugilism.* [f. STOMACH *sb.* + -ER[1].] A blow on the stomach.

1814 *Sporting Mag.* XLIII. 68 B. gave C. a stomacher. 1831 *Blackw. Mag.* XXX. 979 [He] seems to have given his adversary a facer and a stomacher, right and left. 1832 MARRYAT *N. Forster* xlvii, A stomacher, and both down!

Stomachful (stʊ·măkful), *sb.* [f. STOMACH *sb.* + -FUL[2].] As much as will fill one's stomach.

1865 G. MACDONALD *Alec Forbes* II. xxv. 238 Ye'll be laid up yersel' gin ye dinna get a stammachfu' o' the cailer air noo and than. 1891 HERMAN *His Angel* viii. 179, I guess you've had your stomachful of the law.

†**Sto·machful**, *a. Obs.* [f. STOMACH *sb.* + -FUL[1].] Full of 'stomach' (STOMACH *sb.* 8).

1. Obstinate, self-willed. (Often said of horses; also of children.)

1600 SURFLET *Country Farm* I. xxiii. 130 If he [the ox] be stomackfull,..cause him to smell your hande oftentimes, that so hee may be acquainted with you. 1610 HOLLAND *Camden's Brit.* I. 623 A very shrewd, stout, and malapert stomackfull woman. 1633 T. ADAMS *Exp. 2 Peter* ii. 12. 835 A stomackfull horse, that will not be stopp'd in his carrier with the sharpest bit. 1643 T. GOODWIN *Trial Chr. Growth* 154 Like a stomachfull boy, that cryes he cannot have the victory, yet is weak, and easily laid on his back. 1676 MARVELL *Mr. Smirke* 61 (bis) But the few sincere or stomachful Bishops..expiated so in some measure, what they had committed in the Nicene Council. 1690 LOCKE *Educ.* § 112 The obstinate or stomachful crying [of children] should by no means be permitted. 1710 M. HENRY *Expos. O. & N. T.* (1725) III. 522/2 A stomachful high-spirited Child must be subdued betimes. 1778 FOOTE *Trip to Calais* II. Wks. 1799 II. 361 You sullen, sulking, stomachful slut! 1797 MRS. A. M. BENNETT *Beggar Girl* (1813) V. 38, I suppose you was too stomachful to wait on her after the gentleman died. 1828 *Carr Craven Gloss.*, *Stomach-full*, proud, obstinate.

2. Resentful, angry, malignant.

1610 BP. HALL *Apol. agst. Brownists* Ep. Ded. 2 From the other, I received..a stomakful Pamphlet. 1625 PURCHAS *Pilgrims* II. 1216 Thomas Becket was slaine in his Church at Canterburie..by..Courtiers..which had heard some stomackfull speeches of the King, touching the said Archbishop. 1765 J. ADAMS *Diary* 29 Dec., Wks. 1850 II. 169 Major Miller, forsooth, is very fearful that they will be stomachful at home, and angry and resentful.

3. Spirited, courageous.

1610 GUILLIM *Heraldry* III. xiv. (1660) 172 The Males are more stomachfull, and of greater courage than the Females. 1658 tr. *Porta's Nat. Magick* II. vi. 37 We see, how to generate a dog as stomackful as a Lion. 1676 WYCHERLEY *Pl. Dealer* III. i. (1677) 39 Nay, but if I had but any Body to stand by me, I am as stomachful as another. 1809 W. IRVING *Knickerb.* v. viii. (1861) 173 In the interim the stomachful heroes of Pyquag would have been choked with their own onions.

Hence †**Sto·machfully** *adv.*; †**Sto·machfulness**.

1611 COTGR., *Ireusement*, irefully, wrathfully, stomackefully. 1614 BP. HALL *Contempl.* v. *Golden Calf* 117 While so many thousand Israelites were slaine, that had stomachfully desired the Idoll. 1621 T. GRANGER *Eccles.* ix. 17. 248 Pride, stomachfulnesse, headinesse,..auaile little. 1664–5 PEPYS *Diary* 28 Feb., I..did give her very provoking words, ..which she took very stomachfully, and reproached me justly with mine. 1682 BUNYAN *Holy War* (1905) 302, I have often heard him say, and that with great stomachfulness, that he believed that there was neither God, Angel, nor Spirit. 1747 RICHARDSON *Clarissa* (1749) II. 113 Only this Miss, That your stomachfulness has swallowed up your stomach. 1755 JOHNSON, *Chuffily*, surlily, stomachfully.

Stomachic (stomæ·kik), *a.* and *sb.* [ad. L. *stomachicus*, a. Gr. στομαχικός, f. στόμαχ-ος STOMACH *sb.*: see -IC. Cf. F. *stomachique*, Sp. *estomáquico*, Pg. *estomachico*, It. *stomachico*.] A. *adj.*

1. Of or pertaining to the stomach; gastric.

1656 BLOUNT *Glossogr.* s.v. *Vein*, Stomachick vein (*vena stomachica*). 1677 tr. *Groenevelt's Treat. Stone* 33 The stomachic branch of the sixt pair. 1690 J. EDWARDS *Demonstr. Exist. God* II. (1696) 60 Others hold that this stomachick ferment proceeds immediately from the blood. 1771 *Encycl. Brit.* I. 254/2 The stomachic plexus, formed by the eighth pair [of nerves]. 1799 *Med. Jrnl.* II. 398 The author ..treats..of the great stomachic gland. 1808 SCOTT in *Lockhart* I. i. 49, I have..only had to complain of occasional headaches or stomachic affections. 1856 EMERSON *Eng. Traits*, *Manners* Wks. (Bohn) II. 46 The Englishman speaks with all his body. His elocution is stomachic—as the American's is labial. 1875 H. C. WOOD *Therap.* (1879) 51 The nitrate of silver is..useful in stomachic..diseases. 1881 *Encycl. Brit.* XII. 630/2 Whilst the mullet has a fleshy stomach like a bird, others have no stomachic dilatation.

b. Of an ailment: Caused by disorder of the stomach.

1878 A. M'L. HAMILTON *Nerv. Dis.* 123 Stomachic Vertigo is common, and is produced, directly after a hearty meal, or else when the stomach is entirely empty.

†2. Having or subject to disorder of the stomach.

1656 BLOUNT *Glossogr.* 1661 LOVELL *Hist. Anim. & Min.* 238 Partridge,..it helps the cœliack and stomachick persons.

3. Good for the stomach.

1665 G. HARVEY *Disc. Plague* (1673) 146 Likewise Pestilential stomachick Emplasters applied to the Stomach. 1732 J. MARTYN tr. *Tournefort's Hist. Plants* I. 91 The root is stomachick, pectoral, diuretick, and provokes the menses. 1754–64 SMELLIE *Midwifery* II. 45 He ordered..three or four ounces every morning of the following Stomachick wine. 1833 L. RITCHIE *Wand. by Loire* 110 A red wine celebrated for its rich colour and stomachic qualities. 1846 SOYER *Cookery* 58 This potage, though complicated, is very easily made with a little practice; it is entirely new, very stomachic and wholesome. 1876 DUNGLISON *Med. Lex.*, *Tinctura Absinthii Composita*..Tonic, stomachic, vermifuge, and carminative. 1899 *Allbutt's Syst. Med.* VIII. 550 A stomachic or febrifuge mixture.

B. *sb.* A stomachic medicine.

1735 BRACKEN in *Burdon's Pocket Farrier* 41 *note*, It is a better Stomachick than most Compounds out of an Apothecary's Shop. 1850 DICKENS *Dav. Copp.* vii, It was exactly the compound one would have chosen for a stomachic.

Hence **Stoma·chicness**. *rare*⁻⁰.

1727 BAILEY vol. II, *Stomachickness*, stomachick Quality, or Helpfulness to the Stomach.

Stomachical (stomæ·kikăl), *a.* and *sb.* [f. STOMACHIC + -AL.] A. *adj.*

1. = STOMACHIC *a.* 1.

1601 HOLLAND *Pliny* XX. xvii. II. 66 Dieuches used..to give also the seed beaten to pouder with Mints in wine, for ..the defluxion Stomachicall. 1651 BIGGS *New Disp.* § 285 Whatsoever is taken in a surfet, above the native power of the stomachicall ferment. 1708 *Brit. Apollo* No. 38. 3/2 You must Chasten your Belly, And forbear the Stomachical Prizes. 1822 L. STURGEON (*title*) Essays, Moral, Philosophical, and Stomachical, on the..Science of Good-living.

2. = STOMACHIC *a.* 3.

1603 F. HERING *Cert. Rules* (1625) B 2, Take three or foure cordiall and stomachicall pilles. 1725 *Bradley's Family Dict.* s.v. *Balm*, Balm-mint..is stomachical, cordial, and excites the Appetite and Wind.

†B. *sb.* = STOMACHIC B. *Obs.*

1657 *Physical Dict.*, *Stomachicals*, medicines peculiar to the stomach. 1689 J. MOYLE *Abstr. Sea Chyrurg.*, These are inferiour to no stomachicals in the whole World.

Hence **Stoma·chically** *adv.*

1684 tr. *Bonet's Merc. Compit.* XVI. 565 As when they say, A Man swoons stomachically. 1898 *Daily News* 12 Jan. 6/6 He seemed to suddenly double up as if stomachically stricken.

Stomaching (stʊ·măkiŋ), *vbl. sb.* [f. STOMACH *v.* + -ING[1].] The action of STOMACH *v.*; †feeling or cherishing indignation or bitterness.

1549 CHEEKE *Hurt Sedit.* (1641) 14 Where disobedience is thought stoutnesse, and sullennesse is counted manhood, and stomaking is courage. 1582 N. T. (Rhem.) 2 *Cor.* xii. 20 Contentions, emulations, stomakings. 1606 SHAKS. *Ant. & Cl.* II. ii. 9 Tis not a time for priuate stomacking. 1671 WOODHEAD *St. Teresa* II. 99 When it is with Perturbation, and Passion, Stomacking, and repining at the Prioress, let them take it for a manifest Temptation.

†**Sto·maching**, *ppl. a. Obs.* [f. STOMACH *v.* + -ING[2].] Full of malignity; given to cherish anger or resentment.

1577–87 HOLINSHED *Hist. Scot.* 260/2 The whole nation, against which the chiefest part of his booke seemeth to be a stomaching inuectiue. 1579 TOMSON *Calvin's Serm. Tim.* 859/1 Wee are so stomaking of nature, that if a man displease vs we woulde that God shoulde straight wayes lighten against him.

†**Stoma·chious**, *a. Obs.* [f. STOMACH *sb.* + -IOUS.] = STOMACHOUS.

1611 SPEED *Hist. Gt. Brit.* IX. vi. § 69 A Lady no lesse proud, and stomachious then himselfe.

Stomachless (stʊ·măklės), *a.* [f. STOMACH *sb.* + -LESS.]

†1. a. Having no appetite. b. Unresentful. *Obs.*

1626 in *Cosin's Corr.* I. (Surtees) 87 You will say this is nothing. I feele it some thing yet, being weake and stomacklesse. 1697 R. PIERCE *Bath Mem.* I. ii. 31 He was Stomachless, nautiated every thing they offer'd him to eat. 1722 *Phil. Trans.* XXXII. 30 This Application produced no considerable Alteration in the Dog; he neither appear'd sleepy nor stomachless. 1727 BAILEY vol. II, *Stomachless*, wanting an Appetite; also, not apt to resent.

2. Destitute of a stomach.

1865 H. J. SLACK in *Intell. Observer* VII. 96 A stomachless, organless thing, like the Gregarina.

Hence **Sto·machlessness**.

1657 TRAPP *Comm. Job* xxxiii. 21. 292 What marvel if.. extreme stomacklesness cause leaness and deformity.

†**Stomacho·sity**. *Obs.*⁻⁰ [ad. assumed L. *stomachōsitās*, f. *stomachōs-us*: see STOMACHOUS *a.* and -ITY.] 'Anger, indignation, disdain.'

1656 BLOUNT *Glossogr.*, *Stomachosity*.

†**Sto·machous**, *a. Obs.* [ad. L. *stomachōsus*, f. *stomach-us* STOMACH *sb.*: see -OUS.] a. Spirited, courageous. b. Resentful, bitter, irascible; stubborn, obstinate.

1547 RECORDE *Judic. Uryne* A iii, Stomachouse horses, whiche contemptuously passe by the barkynge of curres. 1590 SPENSER *F. Q.* II. viii. 23 Who..with sterne lookes, and stomachous disdaine, Gaue signes of grudge and discontentment vaine. a1641 FINETT *Philox.* 163 These and other the like Stommachous Speeches he let fall in my hearing. 1658 PHILLIPS, *Stomachous*, angry, disdainfull.

Hence †**Sto·machously** *adv.*

1593 G. HARVEY *New Lett.* A 3, I haue often bene compassionatly sory (or shall I say? stomachously angry) to read how [etc.].

Stomachy (stʊ·măki), *a. dial.* [f. STOMACH *sb.* + -Y.]

1. Ready to take offence, irritable.

1825 JENNINGS *Observ. Dial. W. Eng.* 73 *Stomachy*, obstinate, proud, haughty. 1829 BROCKETT *N. C. Gloss.* (ed. 2), *Stomachy*, easily offended, resentful—stomachful. 1876 HARDY *Ethelberta* xlvi, 'Now never be stomachy, my good soul,' cried Sol from the fireplace.

2. High-spirited.

1896 BARING-GOULD *Broom-Squire* i. 3 'He's a stomachy (sturdy) young chap,' she said, patting the babe with the now disengaged hand.

3. Big-bellied, paunchy.

1889 STEVENSON *Ballantrae* 21 A little, bald, solemn, stomachy man, a great professor of piety.

Stomager, obs. form of STOMACHER.

Stomapod (stǫ·măpǫd), *a.* and *sb. Zool.* [f. mod.L. *Stomapoda* neut. pl. (Latreille, 1817), irreg. f. Gr. στόμα mouth + ποδ-, πούς foot.] = STOMATOPOD.

1833 GRIFFITH tr. *Cuvier* XIII. 240 The Squillæ have received the denomination of Stomapods. a1843 *Encycl. Metrop.* (1845) VII. 275/2 The two most highly developed Orders [of Crustaceans], viz. the Decapod and Stomapod. 1857 AGASSIZ *Contrib. Nat. Hist. U.S.* I. 110 In the classification of Dana, his first type embraces Decapods and Stomapods.

So **Stomapo·diform** *a.*, having the form of, or resembling, a stomapod: applied to certain insect larvæ. **Stoma·podous** *a.* = *stomapod*; also applied to the mouth in certain arachnids, etc. when resembling or analogous to that of a stomapod crustacean.

1826 KIRBY & SP. *Entomol.* III. xxx. 165 [Primary Forms of Larvæ.] Stomapodiform...Ex. *Mantis*. *Ibid.* IV. xlvi. 309 Mouth...Stomapodous...When the Legs and Sternum act the part of Maxillæ, Labium, and Palpi. Ex. *Araneidæ*, *Scolopendra*, &c.

Stomata, plural of STOMA.

Stomatal (stǫ·mătăl), *a. Bot.* and *Zool.* [f. Gr. στοματ-, στόμα (see STOMA) + -AL.] Pertaining to or connected with a stoma or stomata; of the nature of a stoma; *loosely*, having stomata, stomatous.

1861 BENTLEY *Man. Bot.* 43 Generally..the stomatal cells are placed nearly or quite on a level with those of the epidermis. In other cases,..the stomatal cells are below the epidermal ones, while in some rare instances again they are above them. 1894 F. DARWIN & ACTON *Physiol. Plants* 93 Stomatal transpiration. 1897 *Nature* 17 June 167/1 The stomatal surface of a leaf.

Stomate (stōᵘ·mĕt), *sb. Bot.* [app. formed as an Eng. sing. for the pl. **stomata**: see STOMA. Cf. F. *stomate*, and STIGMATE.] = STOMA 2.

1835 LINDLEY *Introd. Bot.* (1848) I. 137 In most plants the cuticle has..openings..called Stomates, Stomata, or Stomatia. *Ibid.* 141 Another singular kind of stomate. 1877 HUXLEY & MARTIN *Elem. Biol.* 73 Stomates are absent in the epidermis of the root.

Stomate, *a. rare*⁻⁰. [app. f. STOMA + -ATE[2]; but prob. a fiction of mod. Dicts. due to mistaking the sb. (see prec.) for an adj.] 'Having stomata' (Ogilvie *Suppl.* 1855: hence in later Dicts.).

Stomatic (stomæ·tik), *a.* and *sb.* [ad. mod.L. *stomaticus*, a. Gr. στοματικός, f. στοματ-, στόμα mouth: see STOMA and -IC. Cf. F. *stomatique*, It. *stomatico*, Sp. *estomático*. (The sb. is in L. *stomaticē*, a. Gr. στοματική, fem. of the adj.)]

1. a. *adj.* Of a medicine: Good for diseases of the mouth. b. *sb.* A 'stomatic' medicine. ? *Obs.*

The explanation in quot. 1656 is app. an error. In the bracketed quots. the word is misused for *stomachic*; the same blunder has been common in Fr., Sp., and It.

1656 BLOUNT *Glossogr.*, *Stomatick*..that hath a sore or swelling in the mouth. 1657 TOMLINSON *Renou's Disp.* I. vi. 10 *Stomatick* [medicaments] to the mouth. [1676 SALMON *Lond. Disp.* 588 1 It is designed for a Stomatick to comfort and warm a cold and weak Stomach. 1683 — *Doron Med.* II. 174 It is a good Cephalick, 'Stomatick' and hysterick. 1699 — *Bate's Disp.* (1713) 242/1 Besides all this, it is an excellent Stomatick, strengthens the Ventricle, causes..a quick Digestion. 1741 *Compl. Family-Piece* I. i. 3 Take of the Stomatick-Pill with Gums.] 1857 DUNGLISON *Med. Lex.* s.v., Dentifrices, masticatories, &c., are stomatics.

2. *Bot.* and *Zool.* = STOMATAL.

1835 LINDLEY *Introd. Bot.* (1848) I. 141 The stomatic apparatus. 1890 *Hardwicke's Sci.-Gossip* XXVI. 172/2 The stomatic cells.

So †**Stoma·tical** *a. Obs.*

In the bracketed quots. the word is misused for *stomachical*; cf. the similar misuse of STOMATIC.

[1547 BOORDE *Brev. Health* ccclviii. 115 Let the pacient purge hym selfe..with pylles stomatical.] 1601 HOLLAND *Pliny* XXIII. vii. II. 170 This was the stomaticall medicine [L. *Hæc erat stomatice*] of the auncients. [1662 CHANDLER *Van Helmont's Oriat.* 201 This is a sharp, hungry, stomatical [L. *stomachicum*], specifical, and humane ferment.]

Stomatiferous (stǫmăti·fĕrəs), *a. Bot.* [f. mod.L. *stomat-* STOMA + -(I)FEROUS.] Bearing stomata.

1866 *Treas. Bot.* 1101/2 *Stomatiferous*, bearing stomates.

‖**Stomatitis** (stǫmătəi·tis). *Path.* [mod.L. f. Gr. στοματ-, στόμα mouth + -ITIS.] Inflammation of the mucous membrane of the mouth.

1859 J. TOMES *Dental Surg.* 508 Follicular stomatitis is commonly associated with eruptions about the face and lips. 1899 *Allbutt's Syst. Med.* VIII. 527, I have traced the connection of impetigo with..ulcerative stomatitis [etc.].

Hence **Stomatitic** (-i·tik) *a.*, pertaining to or affected with stomatitis.

1901 *Lancet* 20 July 133/1 Those unhappy children who are born with teeth—blighted probably by stomatitic inflammation in utero—which are teeth but in name.

‖**Stomatium** (stomēⁱ·ʃiŏm). Pl. -ia. [mod.L. dim. of STOMA, on Gr. type *στομάτιον.] = STOMA. 1835 [see STOMATE]. 1866 *Treas. Bot.*, *Stomate*, *Stomatium*.

Stomato- (stǫ·măto), repr. Gr. στοματο-, combining form of στοματ-, στόμα mouth (see STOMA): occurring in modern scientific terms, chiefly zoological. ‖**Sto:matode·ndron** (pl. -dendra) [Gr. δένδρον tree], each of the dendritic branches bearing minute polyps in the family *Rhizostomidæ* of hydrozoans. **Sto:matoga·stric** *a.* [GASTRIC], pertaining to or connected with the mouth and stomach; applied to a system of visceral nerves in invertebrates. **Sto·matogna:th** [Gr. γνάθος jaw], a generic term for the hard structures or 'teeth' in the stomodæum of various classes of animals, as molluscs, crustaceans, annelids, rotifers, etc. **Stomato·logy** [-LOGY], the scientific study of the mouth; hence **Sto:matolo·gical** *a.*, relating to stomatology; **Stomato·logist**, one versed in stomatology. **Sto:matomo·rphous** (-mǭ·ɹfəs), *a. Bot.* [Gr. μορφή form], mouth-shaped. **Sto·matopla:sty** [-PLASTY], plastic surgery of the mouth (or of the *os uteri*); hence **Sto:matopla·stic** *a.*, pertaining to stomatoplasty. **Stomato·poroid** *a.* [f. mod.L. *Stomatopora* (f. Gr. πόρος pore) + -OID], resembling or characteristic of a coral of the fossil genus *Stomatopora*. **Sto·matosco:pe** (-skōᵘp) [-SCOPE], an instrument for examining the interior of the mouth. See also STOMATOPOD.

1859 HUXLEY *Oceanic Hydrozoa* 18 In the *Rhizostomidæ*, a complex tree-like mass, whose branches, the *stomatodendra, end in, and are covered with, minute polypites..is suspended from the middle of the umbrella. 1848 CARPENTER *Anim. Phys.* 342 Other small ganglia and nerves, connected with..mastication and digestion..are called *stomato-gastric. 1895 D. SHARP *Insects* I. 120 Stomato-gastric nerves of Cockroach. 1900 W. B. BENHAM in *Proc. Zool. Soc.* 982 *note*, I would suggest..'*stomatognath' as a convenient term by which to refer to the various chitinous, or calcified, or siliceous 'teeth' or 'jaws' occurring as specialized thickenings of the lining of the stomodæum. 1913 *Times* 13 Aug. 3/3 At the final session of the *Stomatological Section the subject of dental disease as a cause of pain in remote parts of the body was discussed. 1913 *Publ. Opinion* 15 Aug. 166/2 The *stomatologists of the Medical Congress held a meeting in the Dental Hospital. 1895 *Westm. Gaz.* 22 June 8/1 The Science of *Stomatology. 1866 *Treas. Bot.* 1101/2 *Stomatomorphous*, mouth-shaped. 1857 DUNGLISON *Med. Lex.*, **Stomatoplastic*, **Stomatoplasty*. 1860 R. FOWLER *Med. Vocab.*, *Stomatoplasty*, the operation for remedying a contracted aperture of the mouth. 1880 *Brit. Med. Jrnl.* 27 Mar. 483/2 Stomatoplasty.—Dr. Mapother described a case of contracted mouth and nostrils from cicatrices after lupus. 1889 E. A. WALFORD in *Q. Jrnl. Geol. Soc.* XLV. III. 566 The interweaving of the *Stomatoporoid branches gives rise to another phase of growth, Tubuliporoid. 1855 DUNGLISON *Med. Lex.*, *Stomatoscope. 1866 *Sci. Rev.* July 62/3 The Stomatoscope..promises to be very useful in dental surgery,..It consists of a spiral wire of platinum..enclosed in a box-wood cup, and..brought to a red heat by the current..from a small galvanic battery; and a small mirror which reflects the light.

Stomatodæ·um. *Embryology.* [Intended as a correction (after *Stomato-*) of the irregularly-formed STOMODÆUM.] = STOMODÆUM. Hence **Stomatodæal** *a.* = STOMODÆAL.

1887 A. M. MARSHALL & HURST *Jun. Zool.* 141 The stomatodæum or anterior portion of the [alimentary] canal [of a crayfish]. 1888 HUXLEY & MARTIN *Elem. Biol.* (ed. 2) 171 The stomatodæum; a sac-like involution of the epidermis abutting against [the mesenteron]. 1893 A. M. MARSHALL *Vertebr. Embryol.* 148 The stomatodæal pit rapidly deepens.

Stomatode (stǫ·mătōᵘd), *a.* and *sb. Zool.* [f. mod.L. *Stomatōda* neut. pl., irreg. f. Gr. στοματ-, στόμα mouth, on the supposed analogy of names like *Cestoda*, *Nematoda*.] a. *adj.* Pertaining to the *Stomatoda*, a group of *Protozoa* characterized by having a mouth. b. *sb.* A member of the *Stomatoda*.

1870 H. A. NICHOLSON *Man. Zool.* I. 59 The Infusoria, or Stomatode Protozoa.

Stomatopod (stǫ·mătopǫd), *a.* and *sb. Zool.* [f. mod.L. *Stomatopoda* neut. pl., later and more correct form for Latreille's *Stomapoda*: see STOMAPOD.] a. *adj.* Belonging to the *Stomatopoda*, an order of malacostracous crustaceans, orig. (in form *Stomapoda*: see STOMAPOD) synonymous with *Gastrura*, now restricted to the family *Squillidæ*. b. *sb.* A stomatopod crustacean.

1877 HUXLEY *Anat. Inv. Anim.* vi. 361, I believe that the tergum of the seventh (or first thoracic) somite is obsolete, as in a Stomatopod.

So **Stomatopodous** (-ǫ·pŏdəs), *a.* = prec. a.

Stomatous (stǫ·mătəs), *a.* [f. mod.L. *stomat-* STOMA + -OUS.] Having or furnished with stomata. Also **Sto·matose** *a.*

1880 WEBSTER Suppl., *Stomatous*. 1909 *Cent. Dict.* Suppl., *Stomatose*.

Sto·mber, *v. Obs.* exc. *dial.* [var. of *stamber*, STAMMER *v.*]

1. *intr.* To stumble.

1568 A. KING tr. *Canisius' Catech.*, *Certane Prayers* 34 Thame that hes stombered thow liftes vp agane. 1879 MISS JACKSON *Shropsh. Word-bk.*, *Stombering*, walking in a heavy, stamping, stumbling way.

2. *trans.* To confuse. (Cf. STAMMER *v.* 4.)

1841 HARTSHORNE *Salop. Ant.* Gloss., *Stomber*, to confuse. 1879 MISS JACKSON *Shropsh. Word-bk.*, *Stombered*, confused. 'I got stombered o'er it.'

Stomble, stomel(e, obs. forms of STUMBLE.

Stomere, var. STUMMER *v. Obs.*, to stumble.

Stomle, obs. form of STUMBLE *v.*

Stommok, obs. form of STOMACH.

Stomochord (stǫ·mokǭɹd). *Zool.* [f. Gr. στόμα mouth + χορδή CHORD *sb.*[1], after *notochord*.] Name proposed by Willey for the so-called 'notochord' of *Enteropneusta*: see quots. Hence **Stomocho·rdal** *a.*, pertaining to or having a stomochord.

1899 WILLEY in *Q. Jrnl. Microscop. Sci.* XLII. 234 MM. Delage and Hérouard retain the designation notochord applied by Bateson to the diverticulum from the throat which projects into the proboscis, where it acquires a rigid consistency and sustaining properties. I prefer to call this structure by a non-committal name, and propose the term stomochord. 1902 G. H. FOWLER in *Encycl. Brit.* XXIX. 251/1 The stomochord is a forward dorsal diverticulum of the gut in the collar region, which pushes before it the wall of the præ-oral body cavity or protocœle.

Stomocke, -ok, -oke, obs. ff. STOMACH.

‖**Stomodæum, -eum** (stǫmodī·ŏm). *Embryology* and *Zool.* Pl. **-æa, -ea** (-ī·ă). [mod.L. irreg. f. Gr. στόμα mouth + ὁδαῖος that is on or by the road.] The anterior portion of the digestive tract, beginning as an invagination of the epiblast.

1876 RAY LANKESTER in *Q. Jrnl. Microsc. Sci.* XVI. 64 A second invagination forms the true mouth and the stomodæum. [*Foot-note*] This term and its correlative 'proctodæum' I propose for the oral and anal invaginations. 1900 G. C. BOURNE in *Ray Lankester's Treat. Zool.* II. *Anthozoa* 7 The elongation of the mouth and stomodaeum confers a bilateral symmetry on the Anthozoan zooid.

Hence **Stomodæal, -eal** (-ī·ăl) *a.*, belonging to or constituting a stomodæum.

1883 RAY LANKESTER in *Encycl. Brit.* XVI. 637/1 (Mollusca) Both behind and before the stomodæal invagination. 1892 E. B. WILSON in *Jrnl. Morphol.* VI. 418 The stomodæal arc rapidly enlarges. *Ibid.*, The stomodæal glands.

Stomok, obs. form of STOMACH.

Stomp, *v.* Used by Browning (to obtain a rime) for *stump* or *stamp*.

1845 BROWNING *Englishm. Italy* 272 And then will the flaxen-wigged Image Be carried in pomp Thro' the plain, while in gallant procession The priests mean to stomp.

Stomp, dial. pronun. of STAMP.

Stompe, obs. form of STUMP.

†**Sto·mper**, *v. Obs. rare*⁻¹. [f. STAMPER *sb.* (see sense 3 a).] *trans.* To pound with a pestle.

c1430 *Liber Cocorum* (1862) 30 Take mustarde and let hit drye..Stomper hit in a morter fyne.

‖**Stompneus** (stǫ·mpnös). *S. Africa.* [Du. = blunt nose.] A fish, *Chrysophrys globiceps*, caught in great abundance round the Cape during summer (Pettman *Africanderisms* 1913). Also *stump-nose* (see STUMP *sb.*).

1705 tr. *Bosman's Guinea* 261 Several sorts of Bream, Stompneuses, or flat Noses. 1792 tr. *Le Vaillant's Trav. Africa* I. 22 There are plenty of fish at the Cape. Among those most valued..are..the stompneus [etc.].

Ston, obs. form of STONE, STUN.

Stonage (stōᵘ·nėdʒ). [f. STONE *sb.* + -AGE.]

†1. Stones collectively. *Obs.*

1618 CHAPMAN *Hesiod* II. 29 Draw ashore Thy Ship; and fence her round with stonage store, To shield her ribs against the humorous Gales.

2. Weight measured in stones. *nonce-use.*

1882 H. C. MERIVALE *Faucit of B.* II. II. i. 149 Six good feet of height, and a stonage coming nearer to fourteen than to thirteen on the average.

Stonage, obs. form of STONEHENGE.

Stonch, obs. form of STANCH *v.*

†**Stond**. *Obs.* [App. a dial. variant of STAND *sb.*, adopted by certain writers in special uses.]

1. *Falconry.* Cf. STAND *sb.*[1] 7.

1580–3 GREENE *Mamillia* I. 4 b, The hawke that commeth at the first cal, wil neuer be stedfast on the stond. 1587 — *Carde of Fancie* (1593) E 3 b, The Hawke that bates at euerie cast of the Lure will neuer be stedfast on the stonde.

2. Impediment, stoppage. (Only in Bacon.)

1605 BACON *Adv. Learn.* II. xxii. § 10 That..you may work out the knots and stondes of the mind. 1612 — *Ess.*, *Studies* (Arb.) 11 Nay, thear is no stond or impediment in the wit, but may be wrought out by fit studies. a1626 — *Disc. touching Helps Intell. Powers* Resusc. (1657) 277 The Removing of the Stonds, and Impediments, of the Mind, doth often clear, the passage, and Current, to a Mans Fortune.

Stond(e, obs. forms of STAND, STOUND.

Standard, -art(e, obs. forms of STANDARD.

Stondenegosse, -gousse: see STANDENGUSS.

Stonderde, -ert, obs. forms of STANDARD.

c1550 *Battle of Otterburn* lvii, The stonderdes stode styll on eke a syde.

Stone (stōᵘn), *sb.* Forms: 1–3 (4–5 *Sc.* and *north.*) **stan**, 3 **stæn**, 3–5 **ston**, 4–5 **sten**, 4–6 **stoon** (5–6 **stoone**), 4–9 (*Sc.* and *north.*) **stane**, 5 *Sc.* **stayne**, (**stein**), 5–7 **stonne**, 6 **stoan(e**, **steane**, 6–7 *Sc.* **stain(e**, 7 *Sc.*, 8–9 *dial.* **stean**, 4– **stone.** [Common Teut.: OE. *stán* str. masc. corresponds to OFris. *stēn*, (WFris. *stien*, *stien*, NFris. *stīn*, *stīæn*), OS. *stēn* (LG., Du. *steen*), OHG. (MHG., mod.G.) *stein*, ON. *stein-n* (Sw., Da. *sten*), Goth. *stain-s*:—OTeut. **staino-z*, cogn. w. OSl. *stěna* (Russ. стѣна) wall, and Gr. στία, στῖον pebble.]

1. A piece of rock or hard mineral substance (other than metal) of a small or moderate size.

c888 ÆLFRED *Boeth.* xxxiv. § xi, Ȝif þu þonne ænne stan toclifst, ne wyrð he næfre ȝegadrod swa he ær wæs. c1175 *Lamb. Hom.* 9 Me þe sculde nimen and..þe al to-toruion mid stane. c1250 *Gen. & Ex.* 1604 He lay bi luran ut on niȝt, A ston under hise heued riȝt. a1300 *Cursor M.* 7581 He tok fiue stans rond. c1412 HOCCLEVE *De Reg. Princ.* 1805 A stoon no thyng ne felith. 1573 TUSSER *Husb.* (1878) 80 The sticks and the stones go and gather vp cleene. 1686 W. HARRIS tr. *Lemery's Course Chem.* 214 There have been who gazing too earnestly upon the Stars above, have not perceived the stone at their feet, that caused them to stumble. 1798 COLERIDGE *Anc. Mariner* 17 The Wedding-Guest sat on a stone. 1812–16 PLAYFAIR *Nat. Phil.* (1819) I. 323 The Stones which have..been ascertained..to fall down from the air. 1833 *Penny Cycl.* I. 150/1 Aerolites, called also Meteoric Stones. 1875 JOWETT *Plato* (ed. 2) III. 54 A dog who..quarrels with the stones which are thrown at him.

†b. A rock, cliff, crag; a mass of rock; rocky ground. *Obs.*

c825 *Vesp. Psalter* xxvi. 6 [xxvii. 5] In stane upahof mec. c1000 *Rule St. Benet* (1888) 5 Hit ne feoll forþam þe hit wæs ȝestaðelod ofor þam stane. c1200 *Trin. Coll. Hom.* 155 Sum of þe sed ful uppe þe ston and dride þere. a1300 *Cursor M.* 16762+83 þe son wex merke, þe erth quoke, þe stons clef. c1400 *Laud Troy Bk.* 4133 Lest thei..breke her schippus on cragges and stones. c1430 *Prymer* (1895) 65 He ordeyned my feet on a stoon. 1513 DOUGLAS *Æneis* IX. vii. 174 Quhil the famyl and ofspring of Enee The stane immovable of the Capitolie Inhabitis. a1700 EVELYN *Diary* Apr. 1646, Some of these vast mountaines were but one entire stone.

fig. a1220 *Vices & Virtues* (1888) 27 And uppe þese stane ðe ðu hier hafst ȝenamd, Crist, godes sune, ich wille araren mine cherche. c1400 *Rule St. Benet* 189 Þis stone es crist, þat we on call. 1535 COVERDALE *Deut.* xxxii. 4 Perfecte are the workes of the Stone for all his wayes are righteous.

2. The hard compact material of which stones and rocks consist; hard mineral substance other than metal.

1154 *O. E. Chron.* (Canterb. MS.) an. 1020, Se cyng..let timbrian ðar an mynster of stane & lime. c1200 ORMIN 4129 Þatt cnif wass..Off stan, & nohht off irenn. a1225 *Leg. Kath.* 266 Maumez of treo oðer of stan. 13.. *K. Horn* 505 (Harl.) A chirche of lym & ston. c1384 CHAUCER *H. Fame* 70 The god of slepe..That dwelleth in a cave of stoon. c1400 MAUNDEV. (Roxb.) i. 4 A brigg of stane þat es ouer þe ryuer. 1542 BOORDE *Dyetary* viii. (1870) 249 Stand nor syt long bareheed vnder a vawte of stone. 1590 in *Rep. Hist. MSS. Comm.*, *Var. Coll.* IV. 284 Perceiving as well muche sand as stone..fetched from the sea-side. 1613 PURCHAS *Pilgrimage* (1614) 229 Mount Sinai..whose top..is hard stone of yron colour. 1774 GOLDSM. *Nat. Hist.* I. 27 We find layers of stone often over the lightest soils. 1826 *Art of Brewing* (ed. 2) 193 In Gloucestershire, and other parts of England, where stone is abundant. 1869 LOWELL *Cathedral* 283 Imagination's very self in stone!

b. as material for lithography.

c1806 in *Archæol. Jrnl.* (1894) Ser. II. I. 111 The art of printing from stone called Polyautography. 1838 W. C. HARRIS *Narr. Exped. S. Africa* frontisp., Moselekatse, King of the Amazooloo. On Stone by W. C. Harris. 1864 *Scott. Metr. Psalter of 1635* title-p., Printed from stone, by Maclure and Macdonald, Lithographers to the Queen.

c. A particular kind of rock or hard mineral matter.

c1400 tr. *Secreta Secret.*, *Gov. Lordsh.* 87 Of propertez of stones, and of vertuz of herbes. 1480 CAXTON *Mirr. World* 92 In Archade is a stone whiche in no wyse may be quenchyd after it is sette a fire. 15.. in *Dunbar's Poems* (1893) II. 306 He knew the vertew of erb and stone. 1731 *Historia Lit.* III. 353 Semitransparent Stones, as Agat. 1796 KIRWAN *Elem. Min.* (ed. 2) I. 2 Stones differ from earths principally in cohesion and hardness. 1800 tr. *Lagrange's Chem.* I. 154 Many stones contain silex. 1841 *Penny Cycl.* XXI. 173/2 The material is a white calcareous stone, obtained in the neighbourhood.

d. *spec.* = PHILOSOPHERS' STONE.

1390 GOWER *Conf.* II. 88 This Ston..makth multiplicacioun Of gold. 1450 LYDG. *Secrees* 986 Al worldly tresour breeffly shet in Oon, Is declaryd in vertu of this stoon. 1610 B. JONSON *Alch.* Argt. 11. 1822 BYRON *Werner* III. i. 328 Thou more than stone of the philosopher!

e. = STONEWARE. Chiefly attrib.: see 17 b.

1642 *Rates of Merchandizes* 57 Whistles, cocks or Birds of stone. 1851 [see STONE-FRUIT 2].

†f. A mirror. *Obs. rare*⁻¹. Cf. *specular stone*, SPECULAR *a.* 1, 1 b.

1605 SHAKS. *Lear* v. iii. 262 Lend me a Looking-glasse, If that her breath will mist or staine the stone, Why then she liues.

3. a. As a type of motionlessness or fixity; esp. in phr. (*as*) *still as a stone*. ? *Obs.* (Cf. STONE-STILL.)

a1225 *Leg. Kath.* 1253 Þᵗ nan ne seide na wiht, ah seten stille ase stan. 1390 GOWER *Conf.* I. 102 He lay stille as eny ston. 1535 COVERDALE *Exod.* xv. 16 Let feare and drede fall vpon them..that they maye be as styll as a stone. 1657 FULLER *Serm.*, *Best Employm.* 12 Sit not there as a stone upon a stoole.

†b. As an emblem of stability or constancy; in phr. *sad, stable, steadfast, true as stone*. *Obs.*

c1320 *Sir Tristr.* 115 Roháud, trewe so stan. c1425 *Hampole's Psalter* Metr. Pref. 46 Euery word is sad as stone and sothly sayd, ful sykerly. c1440 CAPGRAVE *Life St. Kath.* IV. 1251 He hath made hir hardy and stable as þe stoone. c1450 *Godstow Reg.* 22, I wyl be as stedfast as any stone.

c. As a type of hardness, and hence as an emblem of insensibility, stupidity, deadness or the like; esp.

in phrases of comparison with various adjs. as *blind, cold, dead, deaf, dumb, hard*, etc. (Cf. 19.)

a 1300 *Cursor M.* 12028 He fel dun ded as ston. 13.. *Seuyn Sages* (W.) 2359 He bicam blind so ston. c 1400 *Rom. Rose* 2409 Dom as a stoon. c 1400 *Pety Job* 318 in *26 Pol. Poems* 131 Me thynketh myn hert ys harder than a ston. 1500–20 Dunbar *Poems* xv. 9 He that dronis ay as ane bee Sowld haif ane heirar dull as stane. 1599 Shaks. *Hen. V*, II. iii. 26 All was cold as any stone. 1601 — *All's Well* II. i. 76 A medicine..able to breath life into a stone. 1791 Hampson *Mem. Wesley* II. 133 The man continued as blind as a stone. 1837 P. Keith *Bot. Lex.* 116 The albumen..in the seed of the coffee plant..is horny, and in that of the Date-palm it is said to be as hard as a stone. 1841 Hood *Tale Trumpet* 42 She was deaf as a stone.

4. *transf.* and *fig.* Something resembling stone or a stone: **a.** in physical sense: A hard concretion.

1893 Baring-Gould *Cheap Jack Zita* III. 119 The frost had set in..and..the Lark was turned to stone within its embankments.

b. in figurative sense, chiefly as the supposed substance of a 'hard' heart; also, a 'hard' or unfeeling person, or heart; † also, a stupid person, blockhead; a silent person.

1388 Wyclif *Ezek.* xxxvi. 26 Y schal do awei an herte of stoon [1382 a stonen herte] fro 3oure fleisch. a 1400 *Minor Poems fr. Vernon MS.* 618/266 þe Iewes weoren harde stones. 1500–20 Dunbar *Poems* lxxv. 40 3our mvsing wald perss ane hairt of stane. 1591 Shaks. *Two Gent.* II. iii. 11 He is a stone, a very pibble stone, and has no more pitty in him then a dogge. 1598 R. Bernard tr. *Terence, Heauton-tim.* v. i, Signes..whereby I might haue perceiued it, had not I beene a very stone [*ni essem lapis*]. 1613 *Two Noble K.* I. i. 140 Your sorrow beates so ardently upon me, That it shall make a counter reflect gainst My Brothers heart, and warme it to some pitty, Though it were made of stone. a 1659 T. Pestel *Psalm for Christmas Day Morning*, Joyn then all hearts that are not stone,..To celebrate this holy One. 1746 Hervey *Medit.* (1818) 147 The heart of stone is taken away, and a heart of flesh..is introduced in its stead. a 1771 Gray *Dante* 54 Nor wept, for all Within was Stone. 1837 Dickens *Pickw.* xiv, Tom Smart said the widow's lamentations when she heard the disclosure would have pierced a heart of stone. 1852 Mrs. Stowe *Uncle Tom's C.* xxxiv, He..said he should come back; but it didn't deceive me, I knew that the time had come. I was just like one turned into stone.

5. A piece of stone of a definite form and size (usually artificially shaped), used for some special purpose. (Often as the second element of a compound: cf. definitions below.)

a. for building, or as a part or element of a building. (See also Coping-stone, Corner-stone, Foundation-*stone*, etc.)

c 825 *Vesp. Psalter* ci. 15 [cii. 14] Forðon welgelicad hefdun ðeowas ðine stanas his. c 1200 Ormin 16285 Swa þe33 stodenn..To wirkenn o þe temmple, þatt draghenn swerd wass inn an hannd, & lim & stan inn oþerr. c 1400 *Laud Troy Bk.* 3374 Noble Troye..A-doun is throwen, with ston an[d] wal. 1427 in Heath *Grocers' Comp.* (1869) 4 In here tyme..was the furste stoon leyd of the Groceres place in Conyhoope-lane. 1552 Abp. Hamilton *Catech.* (1884) 28 A Mason can nocht hew ane evin aislair staine without directioun of his rewill. 1594 Shaks. *Rich. III*, IV. i. 104 Looke backe with me vnto the Tower. Pitty, you ancient Stones, those tender Babes, Whom Enuie hath immur'd within your Walls. 1610 Holland *Camden's Brit.* (1637) 696 With the stones hewed out of it..Sant Peters at Yorke was reedified. 1796 H. Hunter tr. *St. Pierre's Study Nat.* (1799) II. 132 Water..diffused..through the air..attaches itself, to the glass-windows and the polished stones of our houses. 1833 Loudon *Encycl. Archit.* § 79 To build all the foundations..with stones properly headed. 1867 H. Macmillan *Bible Teach.* xii. (1870) 232 It is built up, stone by stone, from the level of the earth.

b. for paving.

(See also Hearthstone, Pavingstone, etc.)

1427–8 *Rec. St. Mary at Hill* (1905) 68 Also for a goter ston for þe same gate, xiiij d. 1613 *Two Noble K.* v. iv. 63 On this horse is Arcite Trotting the stones of Athens. 1682 *Lond. Gaz.* No. 1694/4 An Iron Grey Gelding,..a little tender-footed on the Stones. 1738 *Gentl. Mag.* VIII. 549/1 He was driven over the Stones in a Hackney Coach. 1840 Dickens *Old C. Shop* xix, Horses clattered on the uneven stones. 1841 [see Pauper 1 c]. 1851 Mrs. Browning *Casa Guidi Wind.* I. 601 On the stone Called Dante's,—a plain flat stone, scarce discerned From others in the pavement.

c. A block, slab, or pillar of stone set up as a memorial, to impart information, or for some ceremonial purpose: *e.g.* as an altar, a monument, a boundary-mark, etc.

See also Hoar-stone 2, Milestone, Shire-*stone*, Standing stone.

847 *Charter* in *O. E. Texts* 434 On ðone stan æt ðære flodan. c 1205 Lay. 9959 He lette a-ræren anan enne swuðe sæleuð stan: he lette þer on grauen sælcuðe run-stauen hu he Rodric of-sloh. 1297 R. Glouc. (Rolls) 138 Evene vp riȝht & swiþe heiȝ, þat wonder hit is to se, Þe stones stondeþ þere so grete. a 1300 *Cursor M.* 979 3ee sal do bren it on a stan. 1450–80 tr. *Secreta Secret.* lviii. 33 It was founde writen in a stone of þe tunge of Caldee. c 1470 Henry *Wallace* I. 121 The croune he tuk apon that sammyne stane At Gadalos send with his sone fra Spane. 1581 *Cov. Leet Bk.* 822, & so Crosse ouer to the corner of Babethorp-wast vnto another stone there sett. 1598–1603 Stow *Surv.* (1908) I. 224 On the south side of this high streete..is pitched vpright a great stone called London stone. 1716 Addison *Freeholder* No. 18 ᴘ 5 As ridiculously puzzled..as a man that counts the stones on Salisbury-plain, which can never be settled to any certain number. 1827 G. Higgins *Celtic Druids* 212 Some of these stones-erect have crosses cut upon them. 1831 Scott *Ct. Robt.* xx, The troth I had plighted to Hereward at the stone of Odin.

d. *spec.* = Gravestone 2, Tombstone.

13.. *Cursor M.* 193 (Gött.) Lazar þat ded lay vnder stan. 1303 R. Brunne *Handl. Synne* 8780 Lordes are besy aboute to haue Proude stones lyggyng an hye on here graue. 1436 *E. E. Wills* 105, I woll þat there be leyde vpon my body a stone of Marble. a 1585 Montgomerie *Cherrie & Slae* 567 Than sall be graud vpon the stane Quhilk on thy graue beis laid [etc.]. 1687 A. Lovell tr. *Thevenot's Trav.* I. 58 When the Grave is filled up, they erect a stone over the head of the deceased. 1750 Gray *Elegy* 116 The lay, Grav'd on the stone beneath yon aged thorn. 1767 Jago *Edge-hill* IV. 332 Alike the simple Stone And Mausoleum proud, his Pow'r attest, In wretched Doggrel, or elab'rate Verse. 1850 Thackeray *Pendennis* lxxi, The stone closes over Harry the Fourth, and Harry the Fifth reigns in his stead. 1900 Bp. W. How *Lighter Moments* 21 A stone-mason..brought a stone to put into the churchyard.

e. As an object of idolatrous worship; chiefly *pl.* in conjunction with *stocks*: see Stock *sb.* 1 d.

c 1400 *Apol. Loll.* 89 Wat honor of God is þis, to ren about bi tre, and stone, and formis, and honor as God veyn figeris?

† f. A gun-flint. *Obs.*

1611 Beaum. & Fl. *Knt. Burning Pestle* v. i, *Ralph.* Wheres the stone of this Peece? 2 *Sold.* The Drummer took it out to light Tobacco.

g. A rounded stone or pebble formerly used as a missile in war, being thrown with the hand, discharged from a sling, or shot from a fire-arm (cf. Gunstone); † *stone of iron*, a cannon-ball (*obs.*).

c 1205 Lay. 626 Mid stocken & mid stanen stal fiht heo makeden. c 1330 R. Brunne *Chron. Wace* (Rolls) 3030 Grete stones wyþ slynges [they] caste. c 1450 *Brut* 434 A traitour..shotte a Gonne, and the stone smot this good Erle of Salusbury. 1511 *Guylforde's Pilgr.* (Camden) 8 An other pece..shoteth a stone of irron of .ij. fote depe. a 1548 Hall *Chron., Hen. VIII*, 113 The Frenchemen shot out ordinaunce, quarelles and stones. 1573–5 Gascoigne *Flowers* Wks. 1907 I. 81 The harquebush doth spit his spight, with prety persing stones. 1581 A. Hall *Iliad* III. 47 The Greekes cease not to martch, their stones & darts at random flye. 1705 *Lond. Gaz.* No. 4097/1 They..ply the Enemy ..with Bombs and Stones, from 6 Mortars. 1745 P. Thomas *Jrnl. Anson's Voy.* 288 Each of those they had loaded with ..Flint Stones and Shot. 1867 A. L. Gordon *Poems* (1912) 94 Like a bird on the wing, or a stone from a sling.

h. A shaped piece of stone for grinding or sharpening something, as a Grindstone, Millstone, Whetstone.

1578 *Invent. R. Wardr.* (1815) 260 Ane man mylne with hir stanys and hir haill tymmer werk. 1599 Breton *Wil of Wit* (Grosart) 11/1 The stone, that Wit must whet himselfe uppon. 1751 *N. Jersey Archives* XIX. 1 A Large..gristmill, with two pairs of stones. 1886 Stevenson *Kidnapped* xxvi, Shearers worked all day in a field..and we could hear the stones going on the books.

i. A flat slab or tablet for grinding something upon, or for smoothing or flattening something (see also Flattening-*stone*, Sleekstone, etc.); in *Printing* = Imposing-*stone*; also a slab of stone for lithography (see 2 b).

14.. *Crafte of Lymnynge* in *E. E. Misc.* (Warton Club) 72 Grynde vermelone one a stone with newe glayre. a 1550 [see *mustard-stone*, Mustard *sb.* 3 c]. 1573 *Art Limming* 5 b, Grind Synapour lake & Synapour topes ech by him selfe on a Painters stone. 1683 Moxon *Mech. Exerc., Printing* xvii. ᴘ 2 The Stone is commonly about eighteen Inches diameter, having both its Sides truly Rub'd flat and smooth. *Ibid.* xxiv. ᴘ 17 They are to be Ground with a Mullar on a smooth Marble Stone. c 1806 in *Archæol. Jrnl.* (1894) Ser. II. I. 112 A drawing..intended to be printed is made on a stone with a pen and a particular ink or with a kind of chalk. 1827 Faraday *Chem. Manip.* xix. (1842) 535 Glass may be ground on almost any flat stone with a coarse grain, by means of a little sharp sand and water. 1886 Furnivall in *Shaks. Ven. & Ad.* (1st Qo. facs.) p. xix, *Troilus and Cressida* is partly on the stone.

j. A heavy stone used in athletic sports. Phrases, *to cast, put*, or *throw the stone*: see also Put *v.*[1] 2, *v.*[2] 2.

c 1300–1816 [see Put *v.*[1] 2, *v.*[2] 2]. 1518 H. Watson *Hist. Oliver of Castile* (Roxb.) C 1 b, Dysportes..vsed by noble men..as..tennys, lepe, sprynge, wrastle, cast the stone, cast the barre, or ony other games. 1561 Hoby tr. *Castiglione's Courtier* I. (1577) D vj, It is meet for hym also to haue the Arte of swymming, to leape, to runne, to caste the stone. 1620 [see Curling-stone]. 1638 Nabbes *Totenham-Court* II. ii. (Bullen) I. 120 He pitcheth the barr and throws the stone. 1849 *Chambers's Inform.* II. 649/2 Each person.. causing his stone to slide towards the opposite end of the rink. 1891 [see Curling-stone].

† 6. A vessel of stone, or of stoneware; a stone jar, cistern, etc. *Obs.* (Cf. Stean.)

c 1450 Lovelich *Grail* lv. 165 Thanne let he fyllen a ston [Fr. *vne cuue*]..Ful of water. c 1450 *Mirk's Festial* 52/8 Þen bade Ihesus seruandus full syxe stones þat stoden þer wyth watyr. 1470–85 Malory *Arthur* IV. viii. 128 Oute of that pype ranne water..in a stone of marbel. a 1722 Lisle *Husb.* (1757) 206 The maltsters used to fling the barley out of the cistern or stone into the floor.

7. A precious stone: see Precious *a.* 6 a.

c 825 *Vesp. Psalter* xviii. 11 [xix. 10] Wilsum ofer gold & stan. c 1200 Ormin 8170 E33whær bisett Wiþþ deorewurrþe staness. c 1300 *Havelok* 1633 A gold ring drow he forth anon, An hundred pund was worth þe ston. 1340 *Ayenb.* 140 He louede betere þe bestes þet god him made þanne he dede gold oþer stones of pris. c 1386 Chaucer *Clerk's T.* 1062 With a coroune of many a riche stoon Vp on hire heed. c 1475 *Rauf Coilȝear* 468 His Basnet was bordourit and burneist bricht With stanes of Beriall cleir, Dyamountis and Sapheir, Riche Rubeis in feir. 1503 Dunbar *Thistle & Rose* 102 This lady..crownit him with dyademe Off radyous stonis. 1568 Grafton *Chron.* II. 383 A riche crowne of gold garnished with stone and pearle. 1594 Shaks. *Rich. III*, I. iv. 27 Inestimable stones, vnvalewed Iewels. 1611 — *Cymb.* II. iv. 40 Sparkles this Stone as it was wont? 1753 *Lond. Mag.* Oct. 480/2 His buckles of stones, of five guineas price. 1910 H. A. Miers in *Encycl. Brit.* VIII. 161/2 The River Diggings on the Vaal river are still worked upon a small scale...The stones, however, are good.

8. A lump of metallic ore. *Obs.* exc. in *stone of tin*, a lump of tin ore.

c 888 Ælfred *Boeth.* xxxiv. § 8 Þa gyldenan stanas, & þa seolfrenan, & ælces cynnes ȝimmas. 1778 W. Pryce *Min. Cornub.* 81 A few Stones of Tin are found. 1895 *Times* 7 Jan. 3/4 The agents report good stones of tin coming from Trevannance engine shaft.

† b. = Loadstone. *Obs.*

1390 Gower *Conf.* III. 293 He bath his rihte cours forth holde Be Ston and nedle, til he cam To Tharse. 1436 *Libel Eng. Policy* in *Pol. Poems* (Rolls) II. 191 Of Yseland to wryte is lytille nede,..Men have practised by nedle and by stone Thider-wardes wythine a lytel whylle. 1631 W. Foster *Sponge Weapon-salve* 25, I deny that the Loadstone doth worke upon the North-pole. The pole rather workes upon the stone.

9. = Hailstone.

1422 Yonge tr. *Secreta Secret.* 198 God keste ham dovne wyth grete Stonys of hawle. 1606 Shaks. *Ant. & Cl.* III. xiii. 160 If I be so, From my cold heart let Heauen ingender haile, And poyson it in the sourse, and the first stone Drop in my necke. 1753 *Scots Mag.* June 307/1 Some of the stones measured three inches about.

10. A hard morbid concretion in the body, esp. in the kidney or urinary bladder, or in the gall-bladder (Gall-stone); also an intestinal concretion in some animals (*bezoar stone*: see Bezoar 2 a): = Calculus 1. Also, the disease caused or characterized by the formation of such a concretion; lithiasis. (In hawks = Cray 2.)

c 1000 *Sax. Leechd.* II. 238 On þære blædran stanas weaxað. 1398 Trevisa *Barth. De P. R.* VII. lv. (1495) 268 Of gleymy humours in the reynes and in the bledder comyth the stone. 1483 Caxton *Cato* e viij b, [Mustard] purgeth.. the brayne and heyleth and breketh the stone. 1486 *Bk. St. Albans* C vij b, When yowre hawke may not metese then she hathe thatt sekenes calde the stoon. 1533 Elyot *Cast. Helthe* (1541) 23 Chese ingendreth yll humours, and bredeth the stone. 1597 Gerarde *Herbal* II. ccccliii. 888 The seede and roote of Saxifrage drunken with wine.. breaketh the stone in the kidneies and bladder. 1620 Venner *Via Recta* viii. 177 To liue fettered with gouts,..& tormented with stones. 1621 Burton *Anat. Mel.* II. v. I. v. 474 Bezoar stone...I haue seene [some] that haue beene much displeased with faintnesse,..& taking the weight of three grains of this stone..haue beene cured. 1628 in Foster *Eng. Factories India* (1909) III. 206 Very sick, being newly cutt for the stone. 1709 Steele *Tatler* No. 27 ᴘ 2 In the Pangs of the Stone, Gout, or any acute Distemper. 1797 M. Baillie *Morbid Anat.* (1807) 373 Stones have sometimes been found in the cavity of the uterus. 1846 G. E. Day tr. *Simon's Anim. Chem.* II. 442 Of 59 small stones taken from a man aged 45 years, 24 consisted of urate of ammonia and 35 of uric acid. 1859 Jephson *Brittany* vii. 89 Mineral waters, said to be beneficial in cases of stone and dropsy. 1897 *Allbutt's Syst. Med.* IV. 233 The stones may have passed into the bowel.

b. A hard natural formation in an animal.

See also *crab-stone* (Crab *sb.*[1] 11), *ear-stone* (Ear *sb.*[1] 10). 1605 [see Crab's-eye]. 1661 Lovell *Hist. Anim. & Min.* Isagoge d 6, All kinds of stones found in the heads of fishes, powdred and drunk in wine, help the collick. *Ibid.* 190 Crab...The eyes or stones..breake the stone.

11. A testicle: chiefly in *pl.* *Obs.* exc. in vulgar use. (See also Ballock-*stone*.)

1154 *O. E. Chron.* an. 1124 ad fin., Six men spilde of here æȝon & of here stanes. 1387 Trevisa *Higden* (Rolls) IV. 289 Þe rotynge of his priue stones. a 1450 *Knt. de la Tour* 71 They toke a knyff, and cutte awey the monkes stones. 1542 Boorde *Dyetary* xviii. (1870) 277 The stones of a cockrell, & the stones of other beestes that hath not done theyr kynde, be nutrytyue. 1617 Moryson *Itin.* I. 163 The Toscanes hold Rammes stones fried for a great daintie. 1668 Culpeper & Cole *Barthol. Anat.* Introd., The action of the Liver is blood-making, of the Stones, Seed-making. 1713 J. Warder *True Amazons* 10 In the very shape of the Stones of a Lamb.

† b. In old names of various species of orchis, as Dogstones, *fool's stones* (Fool *sb.*[1] 7 c), *foxstones* (Fox *sb.* 16); hence used in *plural* as a generic term for 'orchis'. *Obs.*

1562 Turner *Herbal* II. 152 Y^e^ other kindes [of orchis] ar in other countrees called fox stones or hear stones, & they may after ye Greke be called dogstones. 1597 Gerarde *Herbal* I. xcvii. 155, I haue placed it..next vnto the Lillies, before the kinds of *Orchis* or stones. *Ibid.* xcviii. 156 *Tragorchis*, or Gotes stones:..*Testiculus odoratus*, or sweete smelling stones:..*Testiculus Pumilio*, or Dwarffe stones.

12. The hard wood-like endocarp of a *stone-fruit* or drupe, inclosed by the pulpy pericarp, and inclosing the seed or kernel. Also applied to the hard seeds of some pulpy fruits, as the grape.

1523–34 Fitzherb. *Husb.* § 140 Cheryes..maye be sette of stones. 1591 A. W. *Bk. Cookrye* 10 b, Great Raisins, the stones taken out. 1603 Shaks. *Meas. for M.* II. i. 110 Cracking the stones of the foresaid prewyns. 1620 Venner *Via Recta* vii. 120 In the eating of Grapes..that neither the skinnes, nor the kernels or stones in them be swallowed downe. 1796 Withering *Brit. Plants* (ed. 3) I. 252 Prunus. ..S[eed] Vessel nearly globular, pulpy, including a nut or stone. 1870 Hooker *Stud. Flora* 108 Bird Cherry..Stone globose. 1882 Vines tr. *Sachs' Bot.* 122 The stone is the inner layer of the fundamental tissue of the same foliar structure of which the outer layers form the succulent flesh of the fruit.

13. A name for a domino.

1865 *Compl. Domino-player* 19 [At vingt-et-un] the dealer then slides the players one domino or stone each. 1870 *Routledge's Ev. Boy's Ann.* 274 Stones...The name by which the domino is called at vingt-et-un.

14. A measure of weight, usually equal to 14 pounds avoirdupois ($\frac{1}{8}$ of a hundredweight, or half a 'quarter'), but varying with different commodities from 8 to 24 pounds. The stone of 14 lb. is the common unit used in stating the weight of a man or large animal. (Collective pl. usually *stone*.) See also Stone-weight.

139. *Earl Derby's Exp.* (Camden) 76/16 Pro x stone lini. a 1400 *Sir Perc.* 2024 The clobe wheyhed reghte wele,..The hede was of harde stele, Twelve stone weghte! There was iryne in the wande, Ten stone of the lande. 1465 *Manners & Househ. Exp.* (Roxb.) 200 Item, in aparayll of the said shippe; ropes for hyr srowde, the wyche weyid xv. stone .ij. li., prise the stone, xxj.d. 1474 *Stat. Winch.* in *Cov. Leet Bk.* 396 The wich kepes weyght & mesure I li. the halfe C, xxv^ti^ li. the quartern, xij li. & halfe the halfe quartern, þe wich was called of olde tyme beyng Stone of London, & vj li. & a quartern ys the halfe Stone, as it appereth in Magna Carta. 1483 in *Acta Dom. Concil.* (1839) 83*/2, ix stane of chese,..ten stane of butter. 1495 *Act 11 Hen. VII*, c. 4 § 2 Be it also enacted that ther be but only..xiiij lb. to the stone of Wolle. 1520 *Cov. Leet Bk.* 668 That no taloo be solde by-twene this & the next lete a-bove ij s. the Stonne. 1542 Recorde *Gr. Artes* (1575) 203 In woolle..the 14 pounde is not named halfe quarterne, but a Stone. 1609 Skene *Reg. Maj., Stat. Robt. III*, 56 b, The stane to wey woll and other things, sould haue fiuetene punds. Ane stane of walx, aucht. Twelue London punds makes ane stane. 1674 Josselyn *Two Voy.* 15 Of Sugar and Spice 8 pound make the stone. 1730 Cheny *List Horse-Matches* 68 Fourteen Hands to carry Nine Stone. 1825 R. P. Ward *Tremaine* I. xviii. 123 He rose up, as well as sixteen stone would permit. 1845 G. Dodd *Brit. Manuf.* IV. 96 The wool comes in bags containing about ten stones each—a 'stone' in this commodity being twenty-four pounds. 1846 *Baxter's Libr. Pract. Agric.* I. 213 A calf..eighteen weeks old, weighing..33 stone. 1887 'M. Rutherford' *Revol. Tanner's Lane* I. (ed. 8) 7 A drayman weighing about eighteen stone. 1913 *Times* 19 Aug. 14/5 Quotations per stone of 8 lb...Beef.. Mutton.

b. A piece of metal of this weight, used in weighing, or (as in quot.) as a standard.

1556 *Peebles Burgh Rec.* (1872) 235 The commoun stane to be put in sure keping in the commoun Kist.

15. In collectors' names of certain moths: see also Mocha[1] 2.

1775 M. Harris *Engl. Lepidoptera* 45 Phalæna...Stone, mocha...Stone, pale mocha. 1832 J. Rennie *Consp. Butterfl. & Moths* 64 *Xylina*...The Stone (*X. petrificata*..) Wings ..pale grey brown. *Ibid.* 114 *Ephyra*...The Mocha Stone (*E. porata*..).

16. Proverbial phrases.

† a. *To boil, roast*, or *wash a stone*: to labour in vain, expend effort with no result. *Obs.*

1522 Skelton *Why not to Court* 109 They may..elles go rost a stone. 1546 J. Heywood *Prov.* II. ii. (1867) 46, I doo but roste a stone. In warmyng hir. c 1548 in Strype *Eccl. Mem.* (1822) II. II. 316 Or els he washeth a stone, that is to say, he laboureth in vayne. 1895 *Westm. Gaz.* 22 May 6/1 Like the old saying:—'Boil stones in butter and you shall sup the broth.'

b. *To kill two birds with one stone*: to accomplish two different purposes by the same act or proceeding.

1656 [see Bird 6]. 1696 *Growth of Deism in Eng.* 11 Thereby they kill two or three Birds with one stone. 1847 Mrs. Sherwood *Fairchild Fam.* III. xxi. 273 So..she will be killing two birds with one stone.

c. *To leave no stone unturned* (also formerly *to move, roll*, or *turn every stone* or *all stones*): to try every possible expedient in order to bring about a desired result.

c 1550 *Dice-Play* B vj, He wil refuse no labor nor leaue no stone vnturned, to pick vp a penny. 1569 Underdowne *Heliodorus* VIII. 108 b, Now turne euery stoane, deuise al maner of meanes. 1600 Holland *Livy* xxv. xxiii. 565 Hee would leave no stone unrolled, but trie all waies that could be devised. 1637 Gillespie *Eng. Pop. Cerem.* Epist. B 1 b, They make so much adoe, and move every stone against us. 1648 J. Beaumont *Psyche* x. lxx, Still he persever'd all stones to roll, Which might that one in Judas' Bosom move. 1670 G. H. tr. *Hist. Cardinals* II. III. 190 [He] has left no stone unturn'd to arrive at his designs. 1791 Burke *Corr.* (1844) III. 349 We shall not be negligent; no stone will be left unturned. 1873 Stanley *Serm. East* 108 He left no stone unturned to do the work which was set before him.

d. (*a*) † *To roll the stone*: to discuss a matter (*obs.*). (*b*) *To set* († *put*) *a stone rolling*: to start a course of action which may lead to unforeseen, esp. disastrous, consequences. (*c*) Prov. *A rolling stone gathers no moss*: see Moss *sb.* 3 b, Rolling stone 1. (*d*) † *To stand on a rolling stone* (etc.): to be in a precarious position where one is likely to fall or suffer disaster (*obs.*).

1581 R. Goade in *Confer.* III. (1584) Q iiij, This stone hath bene rowled enough. 1592 Kyd *Spanish Trag.* I. iii. 317 Whose foote is standing on a rowling stone. 1602 Fulbecke *Pandectes* 78 How murther hath beene punished...I haue shewed I hope sufficientlie..so that I shall not need here to rowle the same stone. 1613 Shaks. *Hen. VIII* v. iii. 104, I told ye all When we first put this dangerous stone a rowling, 'Twold fall vpon our selues.

† e. *To spring* or *be sprung of* (*a, the*) *stone*: used in similative expressions indicating the absence of any known ancestry or kinsfolk. *Obs.*

1297 R. Glouc. (Rolls) 6720 Seint Edward in normandie was þo bileued al one As bar, as wo seiþ, of þe kunde as he sprong of þe stone. a 1300 *K. Horn* (Camb.) 1026 Horn him 3ede alone, Also he sprunge of stone. a 1400 *Sir Perc.* 1043 Als he ware sprongene of a stane, Thare na mane hym kende.

† f. *To take a stone* (*up*) *in the ear*: (of a woman) to lapse from virtue. *slang*. *Obs.*

1691 Shadwell *Scowrers* II. 19 Did you see who went off with your Aunt! is she given to stumble? will she take a Stone in her Ear? 1702 T. Brown *Lett. fr. Dead* Wks. 1730 II. 92 Madam, I much rejoice to hear, You'll take a stone up in your ear; For I'm a frail transgressor too.

g. *To throw* (*cast*) *a stone* or *stones* (*at*): to make an attack (upon), or bring an accusation (against). So *to cast the first stone* (in allusion to John viii. 7).

1568 *Sat. Poems Reform.* xlvii. 83 Quhat cummer castis the formest stane,..At tha peure winschis 3e wrangulie suspect. 1579 Fulke *Heskins' Parl.* 325 Will not all the Grammarians, Logicians, and Rhetoricians..throwe stones at him? a 1633 [see Glass *sb.*[1] 1]. 1670 [see Glass window]. 1674 Hickman *Hist. Quinquart.* (ed. 2) 109 The Doctor, as if he were perfectly free from this crime, thus throweth his stones at others. 1754 Shebbeare *Matrimony* (1766) II. 102 Thee shouldst not throw stones, who hast a Head of Glass thyself. 1827 Scott *Chron. Canongate* v, It is not, however, prudent to commence with throwing stones, just when I am striking out windows of my own. 1869 [see Glass-house 2].

h. *Stone of stumbling* († *scandal*, † *slander*, etc.): an occasion of scandal or stumbling, a stumbling-block (Vulgate *petra scandali*). † *Stone of touch* = Touchstone (*obs.*).

1382 Wyclif *Isa.* viii. 14 The Lord..shal be..in to a ston ..of offencion [1388 a stoon of hirtyng], and in to a ston of sclaunder [Coverd. stone to stomble at, y^e^ rock to fall vpon]; 1611 for a stone of stumbling and for a rocke of offence] to the two houses of Irael. 1604 A. Craig *Poet. Ess.* (1873) 13 Be thou the stone (precellent Prince) of tuch, For to secerne the honest mindes from such. 1639 S. Du Verger *Camus' Admir. Events* 111 She was accounted as a stone of scandall which ought to bee cast forth of the City. 1695 tr. *Misson's Voy. Italy* II. 107 His Authority has been always a Stone of Stumbling to those who are wont to make Prejudice their Rule of Faith. 1911 B. Nightingale *Ejected of 1662 in Cumbld. & Westmld.* I. 701 Hutchinson's error has..been quite a stone of stumbling to subsequent writers.

i. Phrases of comparison, with adjs. (*cold, dead, hard*, etc. *as* (*a*) *stone*): see 3 c.

17. *attrib.* passing into *adj.* **a.** Consisting of stone; made or built of stone.

a 1000 *Cædmon's Gen.* 1700 (Gr.) Him on laste bu stiðlie stantorr. a 1000 *Ruin* 39 (Gr.) Stanhofu stodan. 1402–3 *Durham Acc. Rolls* (Surtees) 217, 1 stanetrogh et 1 tretrogh. 1420 *Engl. Misc.* (Surtees) 17 The stane house toward the kynges strete. c 1483 in Nicolas *Chron. Lond.* (1827) 7 In this yere the stone brigge of Londone was first begoune to make. 1552 Huloet, Stone crosse, *pyramis*. a 1578 Lindesay (Pitscottie) *Chron. Scot.* (S.T.S.) I. 176 [He] bigit money stain house. 1610 Holland *Camden's Brit.* (1637) 333 A very goodly stone bridge of arch-work. 1663 Gerbier *Counsel* 18 The Stone or wooden Figure. a 1672 Wood *Life* (O.H.S.) I. 43 M. Anthony Wood..was borne in an antient stone-house opposite..Merton Coll. a 1728 Woodward *Fossils Method* II. 39 The Stone-Weapons,..were all cut out, and made, before the Discovery of Iron. 1766 Smollett *Trav.* I. 351 The olives..are..ground into a paste by a mill-stone, set edge-ways into a circular stone-trough. *Ibid.* II. 46 A range of antient Roman stone-coffins. 1776 G. Semple *Building in Water* 89 The Water that had fallen on the Urn from the Lime-stone..had petrified and made a Stone-crust on the outside thereof. 1805 R. W. Dickson *Pract. Agric.* I. Plate XIII, A common stone roller..for rolling arable lands. 1829 Scott *Anne of G.* xiv, The sword, escaping from his hold, rolled on the stone floor with a heavy clash. 1833 Tennyson *Lady Clara* 23 The lion on your old stone gates. 1837 Dickens *Pickw.* xxii, At last he reached a stone hall. 1841 Brees *Gloss. Civil Engin.* 24 Stone blocks were introduced in place of wooden sleepers. 1908 [Miss E. Fowler] *Betw. Trent & Ancholme* 29 A stone quern.

b. Made of stoneware; also *transf.* of ginger-beer contained in stoneware bottles.

c 950 *Lindisf. Gosp.* Mark xiv. 3 & mið-ðy gebrocen wæs þæt stan fæt to-dælde..ofer heafud his. 1479–81 *Rec. St. Mary at Hill* (1905) 101 Item, for a stone potte to put in oyle, j d ob. 1547 *Test. Ebor.* (Surtees) VI. 256 My stone cup withe the silver cover. c 1600 *Acc. Bk. W. Wray* in *Antiquary* XXXII. 80 Beate them well in a stone morter. 1626 in Jewitt *Life Wedgwood* (1865) 37 To grant vnto them our royall priveledge for 'The sole making of the Stone Potte, Stone Jugge, and Stone Bottle', within our Dominions. 1642 *Rates of Merchandizes* 54 Stonebirds or Whistles. [Cf. *Ibid.* 57 Whistles, cocks or Birds of stone.] 1676 Worlidge *Vinet. Brit.* 103 Glass-bottles are preferr'd to Stone-bottles, because that Stone-bottles are apt to leak. a 1756 Eliza Haywood *New Present* (1771) 215 Always keep your pickles in stone jars. 1782 Cowper *Gilpin* 66 Mistress Gilpin...Had two stone bottles found, To hold the liquor that she lov'd. 1851–4 Tomlinson *Cycl. Arts* (1867) II. 196/2 The contents of the basket are turned into a stone or iron vessel. 1884 *B'ham Daily Post* 28 July 3/4 Mineral-water Trade..stone beer. 1904 H. Beswick *Last Karkawber* etc. 37 While I sipped my stone-ginger.

c. Applied to substances in a solid or massive (as distinct from liquid or powdered) form, as *stone alum*, Stone-blue, *stone ochre*, Stone-pitch.

1608 Topsell *Serpents* 42 Mustard-seede three scruples, ..Stone-Allom and Opoponax, of either halfe an ounce. 1815 J. Smith *Panorama Sci. & Art* II. 802 A thin coat of gold size..composed of stone ochre ground in fat oil.

d. Of, pertaining or relating to stone or stones (in various senses).

1826 A. C. Hutchinson *Pract. Observ. Surg.* 313 The paucity of stone cases occurring in tropical climates. 1833 Loudon *Encycl. Archit.* § 1244 Constructing them..either on the wooden model or the stone model. 1879 Ruskin *Hortus Incl.* (1887) 67 It is delightful of you to be interested in that stone book. 1911 W. W. Skeat in *Folk-lore* (1912) XXIII. 60 The best-known stone superstition is that the celt was a thunderbolt.

e. *ellipt.* Belonging to the Stone age.

1864 J. Hunt tr. *Vogt's Lect. Man* xii. 340 The stone skull ..is still narrower than the Lapp skull. *Ibid.* 368 The stone people of Europe knew of no metal. 1880 Dawson *Fossil Man* i. (1883) 7 The earlier Stone folk are known to us only by their graves.

f. (from 11.) Of male domestic animals: Not castrated, entire, as *stone-ass, -colt, -ram*, Stone-horse; † hence allusively of men = lascivious, lustful, as *stone-priest, -puritan*.

1602 Chettle *Hoffman* II. (1631) C 3, I could helpe you now to a stone mule, a *stone-asse. a 1722 Lisle *Husb.* (1757) 355 A mare takes a stone-ass. 1691 *Lond. Gaz.* No. 2710/4 A Cream-coloured young *Stone-Colt. 1778 *Eng. Gazetteer* (ed. 2), Benager..near Mendip-hills; has a fair for stone colts at Whitsuntide. 1608 *Merry Devil Edmonton* IV. i. (facs.) E 1, The *stone Priest steales more venison then halfe the country. 1663 Dryden *Wild Gallant* v. ii, Who have I got, a Stone-Priest by this good Light. 1614 B. Jonson *Barth. F.* III. ii, Fine ambling hypocrites! and a *stone-puritane. 1764 *Ann. Reg.* II. 10/1 Their winter garment is made of deer or *stone-ram skins with the hair on.

g. With preceding numeral, forming an attrib. or adj. phrase, in sense (*a*) set with a (specified) number of (precious) stones; (*b*) weighing (so many) stone; hence *transf.* applied to the prize in a race in which the horses carry the specified weight.

1683 *Lond. Gaz.* No. 1865/8 A Seven Stone Diamond Ring. 1705 *Ibid.* No. 4149/4 A 12 Stone Plate..will be run for..by Hunters.

18. Obvious Combinations (unlimited in number): **a.** attrib. as *stone-heap, -marl* (Marl *sb.*[1] 1 b), *-merchant, -quarry, -ship, -volley, -worship*, etc. **b.** objective, etc., as *stone-caster, -digger, -gatherer*, † *-graver, -hewer, -setter, -shooter, -worshipper*; *stone-casting, -cleaving, -darting, -eating, -moving, -rolling, -throwing, -worshipping* sbs. and adjs.; *stone-like* adj.; **c.** instrumental, locative, and parasynthetic, as *stone-builder*; *stone-arched, -bladed, -built, -coated, -edged, -faced, -floored*, † *-living* (living in stone), *-paved, -pillared, -ribbed, -roofed*, etc., adjs.; *stone-face* vb.

1822 Scott *Nigel* x, The old *stone-arched hall. 1893 H. Balfour in *6th Ann. Rep. Univ. Mus. Oxford* 24 *Stone-bladed axe. 1837 Carlyle *Fr. Rev.* II. I. x. Spade-men, barrow-men, *stone-builders. 1913 Sir H. Johnston *Pioneers Australasia* viii. 266 This vanished race of stone-builders whose works stretch across the Pacific. 1798 *Times* 28 June 4/1 A large *stone-built Farm House. 1598 Grenewey *Tacitus, Ann.* II. v. (1622) 39 The Captaine..commaunded the sling-casters and *stone-casters to let freely at them. a 1400 *Octovian* 895 At wrestelyng, and at *ston castynge, He wan the prys. 1644 Digby *Nat. Soul* Concl. 457 In halfe yeare nights;..in perpetuall *stonecleauing coldes. 1884 Knight *Dict. Mech.* Suppl. 866/2 Stone cleaving Machine..for dividing granite. 1767 *Phil. Trans.* LVII. 411 A clean *stone-coated retort. 1769 Pennant *Brit. Zool.* III. 145 The stone-coated worms which the fishermen call hadock meat. 1599 Nashe *Lenten Stuffe* 12 Their *stondarting engines. 1562 in *Archæologia* XXXVI. 301 To Dorye the *stone dyggere..for xxxiij. dayes dyggynge of stone and chalke. 1864 in *Life W. Pennefather* (1879) 389 Including stone-diggers, there were representatives from more than thirty..villages. 1815 Kirby & Sp. *Entomol.* xii. (1818) I. 391 The *stone-eating caterpillars recorded in the Memoirs of the French Academy..are now known to erode the walls..solely for the purpose of forming their cocoons. 1895 K. Grahame *Golden Age* 45 Terrace of shaven sward, *stone-edged. 1852 Wiggins *Embanking* 125 The cost of *stone-facing a sea-bank. 1632 Lithgow *Trav.* VIII. 375 Where huge and hilly lands Haue *stone-fac'd scurrile bounds. 1874 *Contemp. Rev.* Oct. 762 The churches are proud of their stone-faced interiors. 1841 Dickens *Barn. Rudge* lviii, A *stone-floored room. 1875 Knight *Dict. Mech.* 2396/2 **Stone-gatherer*, a machine for picking up loose surface stones in fields. 1894 Lady M. Verney *Verney Mem.* III. 132 Stone-gatherers should be set to work on some of the fields. 1530 Tindale *Exod.* xxviii. 11 After the worke of a *stonegrauer..shalt thou graue the .ii. stones with the names of the children of Israel. 1904 Spencer & Gillen *North. Tribes Central Australia* xxiii. 671 A *stone-headed spear. 1382 Wyclif *2 Kings* x. 8 Puttith hem at the two *stone hepis [Vulg. *ad duos acervos*]. 1579–80 North *Plutarch, Alcib.* (1595) 217 Many carpenters, masons, *stone hewers, and other workmen. 1837 Carlyle *Fr. Rev.* II. vi. viii, Heavy Monge the Mathematician, once a stone-hewer. 1776 Da Costa *Elem. Conchol.* 2 A Shell..a kind of *stone-like calcareous covering..in which the whole animal..lives included as in a house. 1855 Lynch *Rivulet* xxvi. i, While the law on stone is written, Stone-like is the mighty word. 1631 W. Foster *Sponge Weapon-salve* 25 But of *Saxanimalia* *stone-living creatures never did I heare. 1760 R. Brown *Compl. Farmer* II. 44 Cow-shut or *stone-marle is commonly found under clay. 1805 R. W. Dickson *Pract. Agric.* I. 238 It is distinguished..into shell, clay, and *stone* marle..the stone marle has different proportions of sand united with the calcareous matter and the clay. 1610 Healey *St. Aug. Citie of God* XVIII. xiii. 678 The fiction..of Amphion and his *stone-mooving musicke. a 1593 Marlowe *Ovid's Elegies* III. i. 3 A *stone-pau'd sacred spring. 1819 Scott *Leg. Montrose* xiii, On the floor of a damp and stone-paved dungeon. 1601 Holland *Pliny* VII. lvi. I. 188 Cadmus..found out *stone quarries first. 1837 Carlyle *Fr. Rev.* III. VI. iii, He has to fly again, to skulk, round Paris, in thickets and stone-quarries. 1817 Scott *Harold* IV. i. 2 The long Gothic aisle and *stone-ribb'd roof. 1606 Sylvester *Du Bartas* II. iv. I. *Tropheis* 1045 *Stone-rowling Tay. 1903 *Daily Chron.* 31 Mar. 9/1 Wheelbarrow races and stone-rolling competitions. 1825 R. Wilson *Hist. Hawick* 56 The building.. being *stone-roofed, was preserved. 1725 *Lond. Gaz.* No. 6432, 5 Simon Dyer,..*Stone-setter. 1849 W. R. O'Byrne *Naval Biog. Dict.* 850/2 An attempt to sink two *stone-ships at the entrance of the harbour. 1875 Jowett *Plato* (ed. 2) III. 700 Two archers, two slingers, three *stone-shooters. 1598 Grenewey *Tacitus, Ann.* XIII. ix. (1622) 191 The sling-

casters and *stone-throwers had a place appointed them. 1880 Goldw. Smith *Cowper* ii. 32 He..became the mark for a little *stone-throwing. 1881 W. E. Forster in T. W. Reid *Life* (1888) II. 321 An obstructing, stone-throwing mob. 1861 M. Pattison *Ess.* (1889) I. 45 A *stone-vaulted kitchen. 1837 Carlyle *Fr. Rev.* I. III. viii, It has passed from..duelling..to street-fighting; to *stone-volleys and musket-shot. 1838 Akerman in *Numism. Jrnl.* II. 216 The *stone-worship of the ancients illustrated by their coins. 1844 Lingard *Anglo-Sax. Ch.* (1858) I. iv. 152 *note*, We forbid *stone-worshippings.

19. In adverbial comb. with adjs. or pples., in similative sense (cf. phrases in 3), and hence occas. as a mere intensive (= very, completely): as in *stone-asleep*, † *-astonied, -cold, -dead, -deaf, -dumb, -hard*, † *-naked*, † *-old* (Sc. *stane-auld*), *-silent*; Stone-blind, also Stone-still *adv.* and *adj.* Also with adjs. of colour (which may also be used as sbs.), as *stone-brown, -buff, -grey*.

1826 Hood *Last Man* 64 The folks were all *stone-asleep. 1596 R. L[inche] *Diella* (1877) 60 *Stone-astonied, like a Deare at gaze. 1894 R. B. Sharpe *Birds Gt. Brit.* I. 65 Eggs.—Four to six in number. Ground-colour, *stone-brown..scribbled and blotched all over with black. 1882–4 *Yarrell's Brit. Birds* (ed. 4) III. 561 The nestling is of a *stone-buff on the upper parts. 1592 Breton *Pilgr. Paradise* (Grosart) 12/1 Thou *stone-colde hart. 1836 T. Hook *G. Gurney* I. 139 The lamb was stone cold, and the fish boiled to pieces. 1855 Milman *Lat. Chr.* XIV. iii. (1864) IX. 123 His text-book was the rigid, stone-cold Sentences of Peter the Lombard. c 1290 *St. Agnes* 76 in *S. Eng. Leg.* 183 He fel a-doun *stan-ded. 1531 Tindale *Expos. 1 John* (1537) 55 We were stone dead and wythout lyfe or power to do or consent to good. 1590 Spenser *F. Q.* II. xi. 43 As when Ioues harnesse-bearing Bird from hie Stoupes at a flying heron.. The stone-dead quarrey fals. 1719 De Foe *Crusoe* II. (Globe) 331 He dropt down stone-dead. 1888 Bryce *Amer. Commw.* lxxxix. III. 217 Keep up the fight until it [the power of corruption] is stone dead. 1837 Lockhart *Life Scott* (1839) IX. 197 A man almost literally *stone-deaf could not discharge..the highest duties of a parish-priest in a satisfactory manner. 1872 A. J. C. Hare *Story My Life* (1900) IV. xvi. 50 She is quite stone-deaf, so we..correspond on a slate. 1888 F. R. Stockton in *Century Mag.* Feb. 622, I did say to myself..Now Elizabeth is so *stone dumb that she'll jus' stay here an' do the little I tell her to do. 1878 Trimen *Regiments Brit. Army* 21 Its uniform when raised was *stone-grey. 13.. *E. E. Allit. P.* B. 884, & steken þe 3ates *ston-harde wyth stalworth barrez. a 1400 *Minor Poems fr. Vernon MS.* 618 222 Iewes ston-hard in sinnes merk. 1594 Shaks. *Rich. III*, IV. iv. 227 The murd'rous Knife was dull and blunt, Till it was whetted on thy stone-hard heart. 1875 Tennyson *Q. Mary* I. v, He is..Stone-hard, ice-cold—no dash of daring in him. c 1450 *Mirour Saluacioun* (Roxb.) 77 3e tirvid hym *stone naked a3einward scornfully. c 1800 *Johnnie o Cocklesmuir* xi. in Child *Ballads* III. 9 By there came a *stane-auld man. 1862 Carlyle *Fredk. Gt.* XII. x. (1865) IV. 235 Friedrich..was *stone-silent on this matter.

20. Special comb.: † **stone-bag**, ? a bag carried on board ship, containing stones to be used as shot; **stone-bark** *Bot.*, bark consisting chiefly of hardened and thickened cells (cf. *stone-cell*); **stone-barrow** [Barrow *sb.*[3]], a barrow for carrying stones; † **stone-binder** = Osteocolla; **stone-boiler**, one who practises *stone-boiling*; **stone-boiling**, the process of boiling water by putting hot stones in it, as practised by certain primitive tribes; **stone-brash** [Brash *sb.*[2]], a subsoil consisting of loose broken stone; also *attrib.*; **stone-breaker**, a person employed in, or a machine used for, breaking stones; so **stone-breaking**; **stone-broke** *a. slang*, 'hard up', ruined (cf. *stony-broke*, Stony *a.* 6 c); **stone-buckle**, a buckle set with precious stones; **stone-butter** [after G. *steinbutter*; cf. *rock-butter* Butter *sb.*[1] 3], a name for alum occurring in soft masses greasy to the touch; **stone-canal** *Zool.*, a canal forming part of the water-vascular system in Echinoderms, usually with calcareous walls, leading from the madreporic plate to the circumoral water-vessel; † **stone-case**, (*a*) ? an enclosed millstone for grinding apples for cider; (*b*) a case to contain a stone; **stone-cell** *Bot.*, one of a number of greatly hardened and thickened cells occurring in certain plants; **stone-china**, a kind of stoneware (see quot. 1825); **stone circle** *Archæol.*, = Circle *sb.* 12; † **stone-colic**, colic attributed to the presence of a stone in the kidneys (see 10); **stone-colour**, the (usual) colour of stone, a yellowish or brownish grey, also *attrib.*; so **stone-coloured** *a.*; **stone-crusher**, a machine for crushing or grinding stone, a stone-breaker; **stone-delf** (now *dial.*) a stone-quarry; † **stone-doublet** *slang*, a prison; † **stone-drawer**, (*a*) a surgical instrument for extracting a stone from the bladder; (*b*) a man who digs stone from a quarry, a quarryman; **stone-dresser**, one who dresses or shapes stone for building; also, a machine for this purpose; so **stone-dressing** (also *attrib.*); **stone-drop** (*nonce-wd.*), poetic name for a stalactite; **stone-eared** *a.*, 'hard of hearing', deaf (in quot. in *fig.* sense); **stone-eater**, a conjuror who pretends to swallow stones (see also 20 b); **stone-element** *Bot.*, a hard element of tissue (cf. *stone-cell*); **stone-engraving**, the art or process of engraving on stone, lithography; **stone era** = *stone period*; **stone-etching**, the art or process of etching on stone; **stone-eyed** *a.*, (*a*) ? having the eyes fixed or motionless; (*b*) dull-sighted, 'blind' (*fig.*); **stone-fall**, a fall of meteoric stones, or of loose stones on a mountain slope; **stone fence**, (*a*) a fence made of stones, a stone wall; (*b*) *U.S. slang*, name for various intoxicating drinks (see quots.); **stone-gall** [Gall *sb.*[2] 4]: see quot.; **stone-getter**, a workman who gets stone from a quarry, a quarryman; † **stone-glass** = *glass-stone* (see Glass *sb.*[1] 16); **stone-grave**, † (*a*) = *stone-pit*; (*b*) a prehistoric grave containing stone implements (also *attrib.*); † **stone-grist**, ? the privilege of using a grindstone; **stone-ground** *a.*, ground by means of millstones: cf. *stone-mill* (*c*); † **stone-gun**, a gun for firing stone shot; **stone-hammer**, a hammer for breaking or rough-dressing stones; **stone hand** (*Printing*) = Stoneman[1] 1; **stone harmonicon**: see quot., and cf. *rock harmonicon* (Rock *sb.*[1] 9); **stone-head**, the top of the stratum of solid stone or bed-rock beneath the loose or soft superficial deposit; also = next; **stone-heading** *Coal Mining*, a heading driven through stone or rock; **stone-hearted** (now *rare*) = Stony-hearted; **stone-heled** (**-healed, -hilled**) *a.* [Hele *v.*[2] 2], covered or roofed with stone (*obs.* or *dial.*); **stone-honey** (see quot.); † **stone-hook**, ? one of a pair of hooks for lifting blocks of stone; **stone-knife** *House-painting*, a larger form of palette-knife used for mixing colours on the slab; **stone-layer** (? *obs.*), a workman who lays stones in building (cf. *bricklayer*); **stone-laying**, the laying of stones in building; *spec.* the ceremonial laying of the foundation-stone of a public building, esp. a church; **stone-lifter**, (*a*) a machine for hoisting stones; (*b*) a name for the Australian fish *Kathetostoma læve*, of the family *Uranoscopidæ*; **stone-lime**, lime made from limestone (as distinguished from *chalk-lime*); **stone-marble** *Bookbinding*, one of the many ways of marbling books; † **stone marl** = next; **stone marrow** [after G. *steinmark*, latinized by Agricola as *stenomarga*], name for a kind of spongy limestone (= Lithomarge); **stone-mill**, (*a*) a mill for grinding stone, a stone-crusher; (*b*) a machine for dressing stones; (*c*) a mill in which millstones (not rollers) are used for grinding the flour; so **stone-milled** *a.* = *stone-ground*; † **stone-mushroom**, ? = *mushroom coral* (Mushroom 6 c); † **stone-nail**, ? a nail for fixing stone slates (cf. Stone-brod); **stone-oil**, a name for a kind of bitumen (see quot. 1838), or for petroleum or rock-oil; also erron. applied to a mixture of petrosilex and water used as a glaze for pottery; **stone period** *Archæol.*, = Stone age; also, a portion of the stone age; also *attrib.*; **stone-pit**, a pit from which stones are dug, a quarry; **stone-plant**, † (*a*) a fossil or petrified plant (= Rock-plant 1); (*b*) a plant growing in stony or rocky places (= Rock-plant 2); **stone-pock** *Path.*, a hard suppurating pimple; a disease characterized by such pimples, as acne; **stone-polisher**, one engaged in polishing stones for building or other purposes; also, a machine for this purpose; so **stone-polishing** (also *attrib.*); **stone-printer**, a lithographic printer; **stone-put** *Sc.* [Put *sb.*[1] 2] = Stone's throw; † **stone-roche** = Rock *sb.*[1] 2 a; **stone-saw**, a saw, usually without teeth, for cutting stone into blocks or other shapes for building or other purposes; **stone-sawyer**, a man who works a stone-saw; **stone-sclerenchyma** *Bot.*, sclerenchyma or hard tissue formed of *stone-cells*; **stone-shower**, a shower or fall of meteoric stones; † **stone-shrub**, name for a kind of coral; **stone-slate**, a roofing slate made of thin stone; **stone-square** *Brewing*, a square fermenting-tank made of stone; **stone-squarer**, one who squares or shapes stone for building, a stone-cutter, stone-dresser; **stone tint** = *stone-colour*; **stone-turf**, ? a hard or compact kind of turf; **stone-user**, one who uses stone for weapons, etc., a man of the Stone age; so **stone-using** *a.*; † **stone-wring** (*Sc.* **stane-**), ? = *stone-colic*; **stone-yard**, a yard in which stone-breaking or stone-cutting is done; *fig.* a part of the sea full of rocks. See also Stone age, Stone-ax, Stone-blind, Stone-boat, Stone-bow, etc.

1346 *MS. Acc. Exch. K. R.* 25/7 no. 2 In emendacione..iiij. anulorum ferri pro iiij. *stonbagges et ij. ligulis ferreis pro le topcastel. 1388 in Nicolas *Hist. Royal Navy* (1847) II. 476, iii. stonebagges febles. 1884 Bower & Scott *De Bary's Phaner.* 540 In other cases [these cells] form larger groups, ..inserted in the soft tissue, the number and size of which may increase in the older parts of the cortex..so that the old cortex has been appropriately termed '*stone-bark' by Hartig. c 1470 Henryson *Mor. Fab.* XIII. (*Frog & Mouse*) xx, To the war better beir the *stane barrow, Than to be matchit with ane wickit marrow. 1480–1 *Durham Acc. Rolls* (Surtees) 96 Pro factura unius hollbarowe et 2 stanebarowes, 6d. 1791 G. Wallis *Motherby's Med. Dict.* (ed. 3) 563/2 *Osteites, Osteocolla*, called also..*stone-binder. 1865 Tylor *Early Hist. Man.* ix. 262 A North American tribe,..the Assinaboins or '*Stone-Boilers'. *Ibid.*, This intermediate process, which I propose to call *Stone-Boiling. 1883 tr. *Joly's Man before Metal* II. i. 204 *note*, The process known as 'stone-boiling', which consists in obtaining boiling water by means of stones heated directly in the fire and then dropped in the water. 1677 Plot *Oxfordsh.* 242 Another sort of Land they call *Stone-brash, consisting of a light lean Earth and a small Rubble-stone. 1794 T. Davis *Agric. Wilts* 149 The stone-brash land in the north-west part of the district. 1860 *Times* 4 Jan. 10/5 A flinty soil sucks its surface dry, a thin Stonebrash soil lets the rain run through it. 1843 Bethune *Scott. Peasant's Fireside* 127 My attention was arrested by one of the *stonebreakers. 1868 *Rep. U.S. Commissioner Agric.* (1869) 355 The cost.. has..been..reduced by the introduction of the 'Blake Stone-Breaker'. 1851 Mayhew *Lond. Labour* I. 357 We found that we could obtain employment at *stone-breaking. 1873 *Spons' Dict. Engin.* VII. 2544 Blake's Stone breaking Machine. 1888 Rutley *Rock-Forming Min.* 12 Not every kind of hammer..is suitable for stone-breaking. 1888 F. Hume *Mme. Midas* I. ii, I'm nearly *stone broke. 1889 Besant *Bell St. Paul's* I. 7 The stone-broke sporting man. 1748 Smollett *Rod. Random* xliv, A set of *stone buckles for the knees and shoes. 1756 A. Murphy *Apprentice* I. i, Wearing stone-buckles, and cocking his hat. 1796 Kirwan *Elem. Min.* (ed. 2) II. 14 [Alum] is found in soft brittle masses, that feel somewhat greasy, and thence called by the Germans *Stone Butter. 1887 H. Bury in *Phil. Trans.* CLXXIX. II. 277 The tube thus formed..is the equivalent of the '*stone-canal' of other Echinoderms. 1664 Dr. Smith in *Evelyn's Pomona* 46 The Cider that is ground in a *Stone-case is generally accused to taste unpleasantly of the Rinds, Stems and Kernels of the Apples. 1664 Pepys *Diary* 27 Aug., Thence to my case-maker for my stone case. [Cf. 19 Aug. *ante*..a case, for to keep my stone, that I was cut of, in.] 1884 Bower & Scott *De Bary's Phaner.* 540 '*Stone-cells' in the external cortex. 1825 J. Nicholson *Oper. Mech.* 479 *Stone-china is formed of a compound of Cornish-stone and clay, blue clay, and flint. 1847 Dickens *Haunted Man* i, It's surprising how stone-chaney catches the heat, this frosty weather. 1827 Higgins *Celtic Druids* 234 From these stones, the place became called the place of the *stone circle. 1831 Scott *Ct. Robt.* xx, The practice of youths and maidens plighting their troth at the stone circles dedicated, as it was supposed, to Odin. 1901 *Scotsman* 12 Mar. 4/8 Six distinct varieties of stone circles. 1603 Florio *Montaigne* III. xiii. 651 Since I have had the *stone-chollike. 1695 *Phil. Trans.* XIX. 77 Nephritick Pains, commonly called, the Stone-Colick. 1663 Gerbier *Counsel* 83 A fair *Stone-colour in oyl. 1762–71 H. Walpole *Vertue's Anecd. Paint.* (1786) II. 193 In a corner in stone colour is a statue of peace. 1808 *Fashionable Biogr.* 75 Light stone-colour musquito pantaloons. 1894 R. B. Sharpe *Birds Gt. Brit.* I. 34 In some specimens the ground-colour of the egg is yellowish or creamy stone-colour. 1770 *Phil. Trans.* LXI. 254 A kind of light *stone-coloured varnish. c 1850 Lytton in *Life & Lett.* (1883) I. 117 A comely plump matron in a stone-coloured silk gown. 1875 Knight *Dict. Mech.* 2391/1 **Stone-crusher*, a mill for grinding stone or ore. 1912 *Blackw. Mag.* Aug. 265 These wagons are emptied direct into a stone-crusher. ? 972 *Charter of Eadgar* in Birch *Cartul. Sax.* III. 586 Andlang sices to lan *stan 3edelfe. 1356 in Owen & Blakeway *Hist. Shrewsbury* (1825) II. 462 Versus le Whyte stanydelf. 1894 *Yorks. Weekly Post, Xmas No.* 1, Boggart Hole is a forsaken stone-delf. 1694 Motteux *Rabelais* IV. xii, In danger of miserably rotting within a *stone Doublet. 1767 Thornton tr. *Plautus* II. 322 *note*, He talks of the prison as of a garment; like as the cant-word is with us,..a Stone-doublet. 1775 Jekyll *Corr.* (1894) 19 A stone doublet, which fathers have a legal right to clap upon their sons for extravagance. 1597 A. M. tr. *Guillemeau's Fr. Chirurg.* 16 b/2 A little *stone-drawer, may be vsed to drawe out a bullet. 1703 T. N. *City & C. Purchaser* 19 An ancient experienced Stone drawer. 1858 Simmonds *Dict. Trade*, *Stone-dresser*, one who tools, smooths, and shapes stone for building purposes. 1875 [see Stone-cutter 1 b]. 1845 *Builder* 15 Feb. 83/2 *Stone Dressing Machinery. 1897 *Allbutt's Syst. Med.* IV. 728 Constant exposure to dust.. as in..stone-dressing. 1810 Southey *Kehama* XIII. v, Hung Like *stone-drops from the cavern's fretted height. 1895 *Dublin Rev.* Apr. 356 Had Mr. Swinburne been less stone-eyed and less *stone-eared. 1820 Scott *Monast.* Answ. Introd. Ep., The guisards, the *stone-eater, and other amusements of the season. 1884 Bower & Scott *De Bary's Phaner.* 127 The *stone-elements ('stone-cells' of the Pharmacologists), so called after the stony bodies in the flesh and stalk of many pears, which are composed of them. 1891 *Century Dict.*, *Stone-engraving. 1911 McEwen *Hist. Ch. Scot.* I. vii. 144 The Scottish type of Stone-engraving. 1873 Math. Blind tr. *Strauss' Old Faith & New* 231 This *stone-era already bears a certain stamp of civilization. 1807 J. Landseer *Lect. Engraving* 143 The *Stone-etching is calculated..to render a faithful fac-simile of a painter's sketch. 1890 Hall Caine *Bondman* I. v, Stephen Orry grew woebegone and *stone-eyed. 1895 [see *stone-eared* above]. 1868 Lockyer *Elem. Astron.* § 316 A third *stonefall occurred at Orgueil, in the south of France, on the..14th of May, 1864. 1901 *Westm. Gaz.* 26 July 5/3 The mountain this year is more difficult than usual...Stone-falls have been frequent. 1809 *Stone-fence [see Cobbler 3]. 1844 'Jon. Slick' *High Life New York* I. 37, I might as well a been talking to a stun fence. 1856 Kingsley in *Life & Lett.* xiv. (1879) II. 29 Climbing cliffs, and showing down stone fences. 1859 Fowler *Southern Lights* 52 A Stone-fence. Ginger-beer and brandy. 1872 Schele de Vere *Americanisms* 217 Now he is asked to take a Stone Fence, and now a Railroad, but both are simple whiskey. 1889 *Pall Mall Gaz.* 20 June 3/2 'Stone fence' is the euphonious cognomen given to whisky which is drunk with cider instead of water. 1850 Ogilvie, *Stone-gall*, the name given by workmen to a roundish mass of clay, often occurring in variegated sandstone. Stone-galls lessen the value of stones for building. 1688 Holme *Armoury* III. 394/1 The Mattock..is much used with *stone

Getters in Quarries. 1870 *Inquiry Yorksh. Deaf & Dumb* 4 He has been employed as a stone-getter, and stone-dresser. 1585 Higins *Junius' Nomencl.* 413/2 Glasse stone, or *stone glasse, which may be cut into very small and thin panes, which in old time they vsed in stead of glasse windowes. c 1205 Lay. 31881 Þat folc flah in to wuden..leien in þa *stan-graffen. 1878 J. C. Southall *Epoch of Mammoth* xv. 264 Another find of this sort..occurring in a large stone-grave near Stubnitz. 1883 *Science* II. 25/1 Mound-builders and stonegrave people. 1235–52 *Rentalia Glastonb.* (Somerset Rec. Soc.) 224 Henricus Faber pro j *stanegrist xijd. per annum. 1905 *Macm. Mag.* Nov. 50 It is hoped the public are beginning to insist upon having *stone-ground flour. 1495 *Naval Acc. Hen. VII* (1896) 194 *Stone gonnes of yron in the Wast of the seid Shipp. 1411 in *Finchale Priory Charters* etc. (Surtees) p. clviii, Item ij *stanehammers. Item ij hamers pro sclattis. 1533–4 in W. H. St. John Hope *Windsor Castle* (1913) I. 264 For iij stone hamors ffor the bryklayers to work wyth...xviij^d^. 1875 Knight *Dict. Mech.* 2398/1 *Stone-hammer*, a chipping hammer used by stone-masons in rough-dressing stone. 1896 *Daily News* 7 Dec. 12/5 Overseer wanted for Evening and Weekly. Must be a..smart *stone hand. 1875 Knight *Dict. Mech.*, **Stone Harmonicon*, a musical instrument consisting of a number of bars or slabs of stone,..played like the dulcimer. 1708 J. C. *Compl. Collier* (1845) 15 To dig till we sink down to the *Stone head. 1883 Gresley *Gloss. Coal-mining* 242 *Stone-head.* 1. A heading driven in stone. 2. (N.) The first hard stratum met with underlying quicksand. 1892 *Labour Commission* Gloss., **Stone Headings*, Drivages other than coal formed in stone. 1569 T. Norton *Warn. agst. Papists* A ij, He is obstinately *stone harted. 1640 J. Taylor (Water P.) *Differing Worships* 9 St. Steven..prayd..For his stone-hearted stony enemies. 1899 *Daily News* 11 Oct. 8/4, I would not be stone-hearted. 1578 Lyte *Dodoens* I. xxxii. 46 Tyled, or *stone healed houses. *Ibid.* II. iii. 151 Olde walles & stonehilled houses. 1623 G. Markham *Eng. Housew.* 47 Take the iuice of red Fennell, and the iuyce of Sen greene and *stone hony, and mixe them very well together. 1623 C. Butler *Fem. Mon.* vi. (1634) 108 While it continueth liquid,..it is called Live-hony, when it is turned white and hard (euen like unto sugar) it is called Corn-hony, or Stone-hony. 1814 tr. *Klaproth's Trav. Cauc.* 263 The stone-honey..is dissolved in water, and drunk. 1909 *Westm. Gaz.* 14 Apr. 4/1 The Chinese histories of 1,800 years ago, ..frequently speak of 'stone honey' as coming from Tonquin and the various States of India. 1396–7 *Durham Acc. Rolls* (Surtees) 214, 1 par de *stanhokes. 1426–7 *Rec. St. Mary at Hill* (1905) 66 A peire stone hokis. 1875 E. A. Davidson *House-painting*, etc. I A *Stone Knife. 1562 in *Archæologia* XXXVI. 301 To one other *stone leyere for .x. dayes,..iiij s. ij d. 1669 *Canterb. Marriage Licences* (MS.), John Mathewes,..stonelayer. 1562 in *Archæologia* XXXVI. 302 In Masonrye worke and *stone leynge. 1898 J. T. Fowler *Durham Cathedral* 22 On the occasion of the stone-laying. 1884 Knight *Dict. Mech.* Suppl. 867/1 **Stone lifter*, Shepherd's lifter..has a pair of eccentric lever griping jaws, pivoted in a frame. 1898 Morris *Austral Eng.* 441 *Stone-lifter*, a Melbourne name for the fish *Kathetostoma læve*. 1707 Mortimer *Husb.* (1721) I. 86 The *Stone-Lime is much the best for Land. 1847 A. Smeaton *Builder's Man.* 27 Builders are accustomed..to use more sand with stone-lime than with chalk-lime. 1818 *Art Bookbinding* 82 *Stone marble. 1681 Grew *Musæum* III. § iii. iii. 347 *Stone Marrow. *Stenomarga Agricolæ*, i. e. *Saxi Medulla*: because found between the Commissures of great Stones. 1839 Ure *Dict. Arts* 771 Spongy limestone, usually called Agaric mineral, stone marrow, etc. 1875 Knight *Dict. Mech.* 2398/2 *Stone-mill. 1901 *Daily Chron.* 7 Aug. 7/6 Bread composed of *stone-milled flour. 1687 *Stone-Mushromes [see *stone-shrub*]. 1469–70 in Swayne *Churchw. Acc. Sarum* (1896) 13 Et in iiij m^l^ clauis voc' *stone nayle occupatis supra Capellam be' Marie. 1586 *Shuttleworths' Acc.* (Chetham Soc.) 31 For a quarterone of a thousand of stone nalles, vj^d^. 1612 *Ibid.* 201 Twoe hundreth of stone naile for the leades, vij^d^. 1688 Holme *Armoury* III. 300/1 Stone Nails, or Lath Nails. 1838 T. Thomson *Chem. Org. Bodies* 721 This bitumen [found at Bechelbronn (Bas Rhin)]..is known in the neighbourhood under the name of *stone oil. 1880 Janvier *Practical Keramics* 154 The proportions..for the best glaze are about ten of petrosilex and water (stone-oil) to one of lime and water (fern oil, lime oil). 1849 W. J. Thoms tr. *Worsaae's Primeval Antiq. Denmark* II. iii. 106 The cromlechs of the *stone-period. 1864 J. Hunt tr. *Vogt's Lect. Man* xii. 342 The Lapps present..in their cranial structure a greater affinity with the stone-period people than with the Romanic-type. 1880 Dawson *Fossil Man* i. (1883) 11 A still earlier Stone period, that more properly named the Palæolithic, appears to be indicated by [etc.]. c 1325 in *Kennett's Par. Antiq.* (1818) I. 570 Quatuor rodæ terræ jacent super le *Staneputtes. 1525 in *Archæologia* XXV. 478 For dyggyng of xliij lode of stone & for makyng of the stone pytte. a 1728 Woodward *Nat. Hist. Fossils* I. (1729) 107 Found frequently in the Stone-pits about Oxford. 1859 *Sporting Mag.* Jan. 4 [The fox] went to ground in a stone-pit. 1676 *Phil. Trans.* XI. 736 In a Mine where the *Stone-plants grow. 1883 Stevenson *Silverado Squatters* 236 About the spurs of the tall pine, a red flowering stone-plant hung in clusters. 1818–20 E. Thompson *Cullen's Nosol. Meth.* (ed. 3) 332 Acne; *Stone Pock. 1822–9 *Good's Study Med.* (ed. 3) V. 584 When this species becomes inflamed, it lays a foundation for a varus or stone-pock. 1704 *Collect. Voyages & Trav.* III. 656/1 The *Stone-Polishers make them thinner. 1875 Knight *Dict. Mech.*, *Stone-polishing Machine*, a machine for giving the final dressing and gloss to the surface of stone. 1819 J. Hodgson in J. Raine *Mem.* (1857) I. 260, I called..at a *stoneprinter's in Lincoln's Inn Fields. 1896 N. Munro *Lost Pibroch* (1902) 70 A *stone-put further. c 1300 *Vices & Virtues* 45 For us eft to warnin wið ðo *stanroches of ðe harde hierte. 1843 Holtzapffel *Turning* I. 169 The *stone-saw, a smooth iron blade fed with sand and water. 1890 'M. Rutherford' *Miriam's Schooling* etc. 155 He sat at one end of the heavy stone-saw, with David Trevenna,..at the other. 1845 G. Dodd *Brit. Manuf.* IV. 17 If we watch..a *stone-sawyer, we shall..see that the saw frequently 'jars'. 1884 Bower & Scott *De Bary's Phaner.* 540 The formation of *stone-sclerenchyma. 1687 A. Lovell tr. *Thevenot's Trav.* I. 166 We bought of these poor Greeks several Stone-Mushromes, which in that place are got out of the Red-sea; as also small *Stone-shrubs, or branches of Rock, which they call white Coral. 1530 Palsgr. 706/1, I sclate a house with *stone slates, *je couuers de pierre*. 1880 Sir E. Beckett *Bk. Building* (ed. 2) 183 In some places a thin kind of stone slates are used,..they make picturesque roofs but rather heavy. 1882 E. G. Hooper *Man. Brewing* (ed. 2) 237 There is another system of fermentation..known as the *stone-square system. The fermenting tank here is a large square, constructed of stone. 1888 F. Faulkner *Mod. Brewing* (ed. 2) 187 The original closed box, denominated a Yorkshire stone square. 1611 Bible *1 Kings* v. 18 And Solomons builders, and Hirams builders, did hewe them, and the *stone-squarers. 1833 Loudon *Encycl. Archit.* § 235 The cement chimney shafts to be coloured..of a good warm *stone tint. 1797 *Encycl. Brit.* (ed. 3) XII. 105/2 That called in England by the name of *stone-turf contains a considerable proportion of peat. 1915 H. R. Hall *Anc. Hist. Near East* ii. 32 The earlier Greeks..were still *stone-users. 1870 Greenwell in *Jrnl. Ethnol. Soc.* (N. S.) II. 420 The supply of flint [at Grime's Graves], in itself a mine of wealth to a *stone-using people. c 1500 *Rowlis Cursing* 61 in Laing *Anc. Poet. Scot.*, The *stane-wring, stane and stane blind. 1858 Simmonds *Dict. Trade*, **Stone-yard*, a contractor's or other yard where paupers are set to break stones. 1886 Stevenson *Kidnapped* xiii. 115 If I had kent of these reefs..it's not sixty guineas..would have made me risk my brig in sic a stoneyard! 1899 A. C. Benson *Life Abp. Benson* I. v. 161 A small walled garden..with a rockery of broken carvings from the stone-yards.

b. In names of animals, as **stone-bass**, † (*a*) a fish of the genus *Pagrus*, found in the West Indies; (*b*) a fish of the genus *Polyprion* (family *Serranidæ*), characterized by a bony ridge on the operculum, and serrated spines on the anal and ventral fins; **stone-bird**, (*a*) the vinous grosbeak = Moro[3]; (*b*) = *stone-snipe* (*a*); **stone-biter**, (*a*) the hawfinch; (*b*) *Orkney & Shetl.* the common cat-fish or wolf-fish [= Icel. *steinbítr*, Da. *stenbider*, Norw. *steinbit*, Du. *steenbijter* (Kilian)]; **stone-borer**, a bivalve mollusc that bores into stones or rocks; **stone-cat**, a N. American fresh-water cat-fish of the genus *Noturus*; **stone-centipede**, a centipede of the family *Lithobiidæ*, found in stony places; **stone-coral**, hard or sclerodermatous (as distinguished from sclerobasic), or massive (as distinguished from branching) coral; **stone-crab**, (*a*) name for various species of crab (see quots.); (*b*) applied locally in *U.S.* to the dobson or hellgrammite, the larva of a neuropterous insect, used as a bait in angling; **stone-crawfish**, a European species of crawfish or crayfish, *Astacus torrentium*; **stone-cricket**, a wingless insect of the genus *Ceuthophilus* or other genera of *Locustidæ*, found under or among stones; **stone curlew**, see Curlew 3; **stone-eater**, = *stone-borer*; **stone falcon** [G. *steinfalke* (Gesner)], a name for the merlin; **stone-fish**, a name for various fishes harbouring under stones (see quots.); **stone-flower** = Stone-lily; **stone-fox** [= Du. *steenvos*], the Arctic fox, *Canis lagopus*; † **stone-grig** [Grig *sb.*[1] 3], local name for a species of eel or lamprey; **stone hawk** = *stone falcon*; **stone-lifter** (see 20 a); **stone-loach**, a species of loach, *Cobitis barbatula*; **stone-lugger** = *stone-roller*; **stone-marten**, the beech-marten (*Mustela foina*), or its fur; **stone-owl**, *U.S.* the saw-whet owl, *Nyctala acadica*, which frequents quarries or rocks; **stone-pecker** (*Sc.* **stane-**), local name for the Turnstone, and for the purple sandpiper, *Tringa striata* or *maritima*; **stone-perch**, a small fish allied to the perch (= Pope *sb.*[1] 4, Ruff *sb.*[1] 2); **stone-piercer** = *stone-borer*; **stone-plover**, see Plover 2; **stone-roller**, name for two N. American fresh-water fishes (see quots., and cf. *stone-lugger* and *stone-toter*); **stone-runner**, a name for the ringed plover, or the dotterel; also applied to some species of sandpiper; **stone-snipe**, (*a*) the stone-curlew, *Œdicnemus scolopax*; (*b*) a large N. American bird of the snipe family, *Totanus melanoleucus*; also applied to other species of *Totanus*; **stone-sponge**, a lithistid sponge; **stone-sucker**, a fish belonging or allied to the genus Petromyzon, a Lamprey (see the etymologies of these words); **stone-thrush**, a local name of the missel-thrush; † **stone-tivet** [? Tewhit], ? the lapwing; **stone-toter** [Tote *v.*], a N. American fresh-water fish, *Catostomus* or *Hypentelium nigricans*, also called *stone-lugger* or *stone-roller* (see quot. 1817); also applied to the genus *Exoglossum*. See also Stonebuck, Stonechat Stone-fly, Stonehatch, Stone-smatch.

1698 Fryer *Acc. E. India & P.* 12 There is another Fish they call a *Stone-Bass,..of a Colour sandy, but has a Relish equal to our Soles. 1725 Sloane *Jamaica* II. 286 *Pagrus totus argenteus*..A Stone-Basse. This is taken in all the Rivers of this Island,..they are altogether of a white Colour, and are..one of the best sort of Fish they have in Jamaica. 1822 Couch in *Trans. Linn. Soc.* XIV. 81 Sciæna..Stone Basse—This species, which is common in more southern latitudes..approaches the Cornish coast under peculiar circumstances. When a piece of timber covered with Barnacles is brought by the currents from the regions which these fishes inhabit, considerable numbers of them sometimes accompany it. 1883 *Fisheries Exhib. Catal.* 270 Special Line, ..used in fishing for Stone Bass or Wreck-fish. 1731 Medley *Kolben's Cape G. Hope* II. 157 There are in the Cape countries great numbers of Haw-Finches...They are call'd likewise *Stone-Biters. 1743 *Phil. Trans.* XLII. 612 Other Fish, as Sharks, Holly-butts,..Stone-biters. 1854 A. Adams etc. *Man. Nat. Hist.* 153 *Stone-borers (Saxicavidæ). 1882 Jordan & Gilbert *Syn. Fishes N. Amer.* 97 *Noturus*, *Stone Cats. 1854 A. Adams etc. *Man. Nat. Hist.* 266 *Stone-Centipedes (Lithobiidæ). 1880 F. P. Pascoe *Zool. Classif.* 32 Sclerodermata. (*Stone-corals.) 1713 Petiver *Aquat. Anim. Amboinæ* Tab. i, *Cancer saxatilis*..*Stone Crab. 1853 T. Bell *Stalk-eyed Crustacea* 165 Northern Stone-crab. *Lithodes Maia*. 1884 Goode *Nat. Hist. Aquat. Anim.* 772 The Stone Crab, *Menippe mercenarius*,..is one of the two edible species of Crabs occurring upon the Southern Atlantic coast of the United States. 1815 S. Brookes *Conchol.* 157 *Stone Eater. *Mytilus lithophagus*. 1854 Woodward *Mollusca* II. 243 The boring shell-fish have been called 'stone-eaters' (lithophagi). 1656 Blount *Glossogr.*, *Stonefaulcon (*Lithofalcus*..) so called from the stones and rocks where she *eyries*, or builds her nest. 1678 Ray *Willughby's Ornith.* II. ix. 80 The Stone-Falcon,..*Falco Lapidarius*. 1862 Wood *Illustr. Nat. Hist.* II. 77 The Merlin..from this habit of perching on pieces of stone..has derived the name of Stone Falcon. 1668 Charleton *Onomast.* 135 *Alphestes*..Belgis Stein-Fish, i. e. *Stone-fish. 1710 Sibbald *Hist. Fife* 51 *Gunnellus Cornubiensium*, the Butter Fish of the English, our Fishers call it the Stone-fish. 1881 Day *Fishes Gt. Brit.* I. 204 Shanny or shan:..Stone-fish, Parnell. 1896 *Strand Mag.* XII. 354/2 Another fish that is unpleasant to meet is that known as the stone-fish. It is small,..but its bite is poisonous. Apparently, it makes its home under the pearl shell, for it is only when picking up a shell that a diver is bitten. 1847 Ansted *Anc. World* iii. 49 The simple forms of the crinoids or *stone-flowers. 1832 J. Bree *St. Herbert's Isle* 48 Through the night the hungry *stone-fox howls. 1884 *Chamb. Jrnl.* 5 Jan. 10/1 The stone-foxes and wolverines having destroyed the provision depôts. 1666 Merrett *Pinax* 188 *Lampetra parva fluviatilis*.. *Herefordiensibus*, a *Stone Grig. 1736 Ainsworth, The *stone hawk, *lithofalco*. 1863 H. G. Adams *Birds of Prey* 46 The Merlin..makes its..nest..in the holes generally amid pieces of rock, hence one of its common names, Stone or Rock Hawk. 1825 Hone *Every-day Bk.* I. 697 When he essay'd to war on dace, bleak, bream, *stone-loach or pike. 1883 Day *Fishes Gt. Brit.* II. 204 Stone-loach, due to its fondness for secreting itself beneath a stone. 1882 Jordan & Gilbert *Syn. Fishes N. Amer.* 130 *Catostomus nigricans*, Stone Roller, Hammer-head; *Stone lugger. *Ibid.* 149 *Campostoma anomalum*, Stone-roller; Stone-lugger. 1841 J. H. Fennell *Nat. Hist. Quadrupeds* 106 *note*, Besides beech marten, it is called *stone marten, martern, marteron, martlett, and mouse-hunt. 1882 Caulfeild & Saward *Dict. Needlework* 463/1 Stone Marten..This fur is much esteemed throughout Europe. 1869–73 T. R. Jones *Cassell's Bk. Birds* II. 87 The *Stone Owls (*Athene*). *Ibid.* The Stone Owl Proper (*Athene noctua*). 1904 *Brit. Med. Jrnl.* 17 Sept. 644 Transformations undergone by a blood parasite of the stone-owl when taken into the stomach of a mosquito. 1731 Medley *Kolben's Cape G. Hope* II. 157 The *Stone-pecker. The Dutch call this Bird *Strand Loper*, i. e. Shore-Courser. 1885 Swainson *Prov. Names Birds* 187 Turnstone ..Stanepecker (Shetland Isles). *Ibid.* 194 Purple Sandpiper (*Tringa striata*)..Stanepecker (Shetland Isles). 1888 Goode *Amer. Fishes* 2 The *Stone-perch, Pope, Ruffe,..which somewhat resembles the Perch,..is..not found in America. 1713 Petiver *Aquat. Anim. Amboinæ* Tab. 19/13 *Pholas*.. *Stone Peircer. 1768 Pennant *Brit. Zool.* (1776) I. 293 This [red-headed Linnet] seems to be the species known about London under the name of *stone redpoll. 1802 Montagu *Ornith. Dict.*, s. v. *Redpole*, Lesser, Numbers [are] frequently taken about London..: it is there called Stone Redpole. 1882 *Stone Roller [see *stone-lugger*]. 1681 Grew *Musæum* I. § 4 iv. 77 The Egg of a *Stonerunner. 1802 Montagu *Ornith.* s. v., *Stone-runner*, many of the Sandpipers so called. 1849 *Zoologist* VII. 2392 The ringed plovers are 'stone-runners'. 1785 Pennant *Arct. Zool.* II. 468 *Stone Snipe. With a black bill: head, neck, and breast spotted with black and white...Double the size of a Snipe. 1864 Webster, *Stone-snipe*,..a large snipe (*Gambetta melanoleuca*), common in the United States. 1887 *Cassell's Encycl. Dict.*, *Stone-snipe*, stone-curlew,..*Œdicnemus scolopax*. 1753 *Chambers' Cycl.* Suppl., *Petromyzon*, the *stone sucker,..a genus..comprehending the lamprey, etc. 1851 Gosse *Nat. Hist., Fishes* 319 *Petromyzonidæ*. (Stone-suckers.) 1885 Swainson *Prov. Names Birds* 2 Missel Thrush...*Stone thrush (Dorset). 1579 Hake *Newes out of Powles* iv. (1872) D ij b, *Stonetiuets, Teale, and Pecteales good, with Busterds fat and plum. 1817 Paulding *Lett. fr. South* (Bartlett), The most singular fish in this part..is..the *Stone-toter, whose brow is surmounted with several little sharp horns, by the aid of which he totes small flat stones..in order to make a snug little inclosure for his lady. 1868 Sir J. Richardson etc. *Mus. Nat. Hist.* II. 123 The species of *Exoglossum* are named 'Stone-toters,' because they pile up little heaps of small stones, among which they deposit their spawn.

c. In names of plants (either growing in stony places, or having some part hard like stone), or their fruits, etc.: as † **stone apple** = *stone pippin*; **stone basil**, the wild basil, *Calamintha Clinopodium*, or basil-thyme, *C. Acinos*; **stone-beech**, a variety of the common beech (see quot.); **stone-berry**, the dwarf cornel of N. America, *Cornus canadensis*; **stone-brake**, the rock-brake or parsley-fern, *Allosorus crispus*; **stone bramble**, a species of bramble, *Rubus saxatilis*, growing in stony places, with bright red fruit; **stone-clover**, = Hare's-foot 1; **stone-fern**, *Asplenium Ceterach*; also applied to other ferns growing in stony places (see quots.); † **stone-grape**, ? a grape with stones or hard seeds; **stone-leek**, the rock or Welsh onion, *Allium fistulosum*; in quot. 1904 app. misused for Houseleek; **stone-lichen**, any lichen growing on stones or rocks; spec. *Parmelia*

Stone (sb.) ...

Stone-ax ...

Stone-blind ...

Stone-cart ...

Stone-boat ...

Stone age ...

Stone-brod ...

Stonebreak ...

Stonehawk ...

Stone-coal ...

Stonecrop ...

Stone-cutter ...

Stone-chacker, -chatter, -chat, -chock ...

Stone-cast, stone's cast ...

Stone-fern ...

Stone-fly ...

Stone-fruit ...

Stone-cutting ...

Stoned ...

Stonegall ...

Stonehatch ...

Stonehenge ...

Stonehore ...

Stonemason ...

Stone-horse ...

Stone-lath ...

Stoneless ...

Stone-lily ...

Stoneman ...

Stone-parsley ...

Stone-pine ...

Stone-pitch ...

Stoner ...

Stone's throw ...

Stonesfield ...

Stone-shot ...

Stone-smatch, -smitch ...

Stone-still (adv. and predicative adj.) ...

Stone-wall (sb.) ...

Stoneware ...

Stonework ...

Stone-weight ...

Stone-working ...

Stonewort ...

Stoning (vbl. sb.) ...

+ Stonish, a. Obs. [f. STONE sb. + -ISH 1.] Resembling, or having the character of, stone. *Chiefly fig.*

+ Stonish, obs. form of STANDARD a.

Stonish, stonisch, 5–6 Sc. stonis, -ys, -nis, 6 Sc. stwnys, stunnys; 5 ston-a(y)sch, 6, 7 stonish. [aphetic f. ASTONISH v.] To stun mentally, shock, surprise. = ASTONISH v. 2–4.

+ Stonishment.

+ Stonishing, ppl. a., **+ Stonishing** vbl. sb. Also **+ Stonishment.**

Stonk(e, -en, obs. pa. t. and pple. of STINK v.

Stonkerd, obs. form of STONKARD a.

Stonne, obs. form of STONE.

Stonore, variant of STONEHORE.

Stont, variant of STOUND a., STUNT a.

Stont(e, see STOUND v., STUNT a.

Stony (stōˑni), a. Forms: 1 stánis, 3 stoni, 3–4 stani, 4–5 stone, 5–6 stonye, 6 stoany, 5 Sc. stoany, 6 stonie, 7 stoanie, 6–9 stony, 4– stony. [OE. stániᵹ, stæniᵹ, stæin-haⁱ—OTeut. *stainiᵹ—, *staino-STONE sb.) + -Y. (OE. had also stæniht, type *stainigo-.]

1. Abounding in, or having the character of, stone or rock; full of rocks; rocky. *Now rare* or *Obs.*

2. Made of stone. rare.

+ 3. Of a quality (as hardness, colour): like that of stone.

+ 4. fig. a. 'Hard', insensible, or unfeeling, as if consisting of stone; petrified or petrifiable.

b. *fig. as sb.*

5. Rigid, fixed, motionless; destitute of movement or expression: esp. of the eyes or look.

6. Of fear, grief, etc. 'Petrifying', stupefying: having no relief.

c. *slang*: Short for *stony-broke* (see 6).

d. *slang*: Short for *stony-hearted* (see 6).

6. Combinations, as *stony-, with* adj., as *+ stony-blind*: b. Parasynthetic formations, as *stony-eyed, -pointed, -toed, -winged* adjs. c. Special comb. and collocations: *+ stony bone* (in med.), *+ stony broke* (= *STONE-BROKE*, *slang*) = *stone-broke* (see 6); *+ stony cool* = *stone-cold* (see 6); *+ stony coral* = *stone-coral* (STONE sb. 21 b); *+ stony-hearted* (at w.f.), 'hard', *unfeeling*, merciless.

Stony-hearted (at w.f.], adj. Having a stony heart; cruel, unfeeling, merciless.

+ Stoo, an exclamation used to incite an hound. Cf. STABOY, SPEEDY, STIDDY.

Stoober, Stood, obs. ff. STUBBER, STUD.

+ Stony, v. Obs. Forms: 4–5 stoney, stonay, stunay, -y, 4 stonay, 5 stony, stonyry, (*Prond, l'aro.*), 7 stunny, 4–7 stony. *Th. 1. 4* stoneyd, stoneȝed; *Sc.* stonait, -ayit, 5 stonayd, stonᵹed, *Sc.* stonait, -ayt, 6 stoned, -yd, *Sc.* stonayt, 5–6 stonyd, (6 stonied), 7 stunied. *Th.* (Prob. sometimes confused with STUN v.)

1. trans. To stupefy with noise or with a shock to the mind or feelings, benumb the faculties of (a person); to confound, amaze.

2. To amaze or stupefy with a blow.

3. refl. To be stupefied with wonder or terror.

4. intr. To be stupefied with wonder or terror.

+ 3. A cock (of hay). Obs.

Stony-hearted.

Stook (stuk), sb. Forms: 5–6 stowk, stouke, 5–7 stowke, 5–6, 8–9 dial. stouk, 9 dial. stuck, 6– stook. [ME. stook, a. ?MDu., MLG. stûke (WFlem. stuik) — HG. dial. stauche fem.; formally coincident (though etymological identity is doubtful on account of the difference of meaning) with a widespread Teut. word meaning sleeve: MLG. stûke, OHG. stûhha MHG. stûche, mod.G. (dial.) stauche.] [O'Teut. stûkō (? from Ger.).]

I. = SHOCK sb.[1] 1.

b. Comb. and Collocations.

Stook, dial. variant of STOUK sb. handle.

Stooke, pple. pa. t. and pa. pple. of STICK v.

Stooker (stuˑkɐ:). [f. STOOK sb. + -ER[1].] One who arranges sheaves in stooks.

Stookless, a. [f. STOOK sb. + -LESS.] Without a stook or stooks.

Stool (stūl), sb. Forms: 1 stool, 1–3 stōl, 3–6 stole, 4–6 stoole, 3–9 stoole, 4–7 stoule, -lle, stoale, storwle, 6 stoull, 5–8 stowll, 5 stuell, -le, stewle, (6 stuill, 5–6 stuell, -yll, stwyll, stuul), 5 stowle, 6 stollε, 7–8 stoul, 4– stool.

Stool-ball.

STOOP

+ d. A seat for an offender. See *CUCKING-STOOL, CUTTY-STOOL, PINING-STOOL, stool of REPENTANCE.*

+ d. A wooden seat (for one person) without arms or a back; a piece of furniture consisting in its simplest form of a piece of wood (or a seat) set upon legs, usually three or four in number, to raise it from the ground.

2. A wooden seat (for one person) with arms or a back; a piece of furniture.

Stooker (stuˑkɐ:). = STOOKER.

3. A high seat of this kind for convenience of writing at a high desk; more fully *office stool*. Hence, a situation as clerk in an office.

4. A low short bench or form upon which all of would use and sit [or stool.]

+ 5. Stool and ball, the implements used in the game of STOOL-BALL. Obs.

6. *fig.* a. Proverb. *To fall, come to the ground, sit between two stools*: to incur failure through vacillation between two different courses of action.

b. *Phrases.*

STOOL. 1019 STOOL. STOOL. 1020 STOOL. STOOP

Hare seek her lodging...Then let him [the hunter] draw his nets round about them.

A. seat enclosing a chamber utensil; a commode; more explicitly *stool of ease*. Also, a privy.

b. In phrases originally meaning 'the place of evacuation', (now without *the*) the action of evacuating the bowels.

c. The action of evacuating the bowels; an act of discharging faeces. *By stool* by faecal as distinguished from other means of evacuation.

d. A discharge of faecal matter of a specified colour, consistency, etc.; the matter discharged (chiefly *pl.*).

+ 6. A frame upon which to work embroidery or tapestry. Obs.

7. *Naut.* a. (See quot. 1867.) Cf. CHANNEL sb.[2]

b. = STOOL sb. 5 b.

8. Brickmaking. A brick-moulder's shed or workshop; also, the gang of workmen employed in one shed; also, a moulder's bench.

9. Arch. The sill of a window. Obs.

STOOP

Stool (stūl), v. Also 6, 9 stole. [f. STOOL sb.]

1. trans. To put or set (a person) on a stool.

2. To condemn (a person) to the stool (of repentance), unce-unc. In quot. *absol.*

b. The 'eye' of an apple, pear or quince.

+ 15. The head or cap of a mushroom. (Cf. *stool* in *TOADSTOOL, Obs. rare?*)

16. *U.S.* (See quot.)

17. *+ a.* Some part of a plough. Obs. rare?. (Possibly an error.) **b.** The rail of a hay-fork (*Northumb.* Gloss. 1893–4.)

18. *U.S.* A decoy-bird (perh. short for *stool-pigeon*), esp. one used in shooting wildfowl; also a perch upon which a decoy-bird is set. (Cf. STALL sb.[3]?)

19. *attrib.* and *Comb.* (sense 2) as *stool cover* (sense 5), as *stool door*), *stool-seat* (sense 1), as *stool-foot, -leg, -pan, -post, -seat*; *stool-bearer, -bearing*, *-casting*; similative, as *stool-borne, -bearing* etc.; objective, as *stool-bearer, -bearing*, *casting*; similative, as *stool-borne, -bearing* etc.

Stool-ball. [f. STOOL sb. + BALL.] An old country game somewhat resembling

STOOP

cricket, played chiefly by young women or, as an Easter game, between young men and women for a 'tansy' (TANSY 2) as the stake. Still played (in modified forms) by women and children in some districts, esp. in Sussex. (Quite distinct from *STOW-BALL*.)

Stool-ball.

Stooling (stūˑliŋ), vbl. sb. [f. STOOL v. and -ING.]

1. The action or process of evacuating the bowels; also, concr. the matter evacuated.

2. The action of throwing up young shoots; stems, of corn, etc., the forming of a thick head from lateral shoots.

+ Stool-work. Obs. [f. STOOL sb.[1] + WORK sb.] Embroidery or tapestry work of the kind made on a 'stool'.

Stoop (stūp), sb.[1] Forms: 1 stēap, stēop.

Stoop (stūp), sb.[2]

Stoop, v. Also 6, 9 stowpe. [f. STOOP v.]

STOOP.

†c. To give the **stoop**: to bow; *fig.* to yield, give way. *Obs.*

†3. Descent, declivity (of a mountain); a downward slope or incline. *Obs.*

4. The action of descending from a height; *spec.* the swoop of a bird of prey on its quarry, or the descent of a falcon to the lure. Also *fig.*

5. *Comb.*: **stoop-necked** *a.*, having the neck bent downwards; **stoop-shouldered** *a.*, having a stoop in the shoulders.

Stoop (stūp), *sb.[2]* *U.S. and Canada.* Also *9* **stoup.** [a. Du. *stoep*: see STOEP.] 'An uncovered platform before the entrance of a house, raised, and approached by means of steps.

Stoop (stūp), *v.[1]* Pa. t. and pp. *ppl.* **Stooped** (stūpt). Forms: *1* **stūpian**, *3-4* **stupe**, *4-7* **stoupe** (*4* **stoupe**), *7* **stoup**, 6 **stoope**, 6- **stoop.** [OE. *stūpian* wk. vb., corresp. to MDu. *stūpen* (WFlem. *stuipen*, now conjugated strong), ON. *stúpa* (*onct.* in inf.), MSw., Sw. *stupa* wk. vb., Norw. *stupa* str. vb.); related by ablaut to OTeut. *staup-* STEEP *adj.* For the phonology of the mod. Eng. form cf. *coop*, *droop*, where ME. ō before *p* has similarly remained unchanged instead of becoming (ū).]

I. To bow down, to descend.

1. *intr.* Of a person: To lower the body by inclining the trunk or the head and shoulders forward, sometimes bending the knee at the same time. Often *with down*.

†b. *trans.* To lower or degrade oneself morally, to descend or condescend unworthily. *Obs.*

3. Of a thing: To incline from the perpendicular; to bend down; to slope; to hang over.

d. To lower (a part of one's person) to a stooping position. *Obs.*

II. Causative uses.

7. *trans.* To cause to bow down, bring to the ground; *fig.* to humiliate, subdue. Now *rare*.

13. To train (a dog) to 'stoop' for a scent. Cf. 1 *v.*

¶10. To put (roses, stake (money)) on a game.

14. *Comb.*: **stoop-frog** (? *nonce-wd.*), an oppressor of frogs (the King Stork of the fable).

Stoop, *v.[2]* *Sc.* and *north. dial.* [f. STOOP *sb.[1]*] *trans.* To mark *and with* 'stoops' or posts.

Stoop and roop, roop and stoop, *adv., phr. Sc. and north. dial.* Of obscure origin.

Stooped (stūpt), *ppl. a.* [f. STOOP *v.[1]* + -ED[1].]

1. Of a person, animal, etc.; also of the posture: Bowing down, inclining or leaning forward; chiefly, having a habitual stoop.

2. Of things: Inclined from the perpendicular.

3. Of a vessel: Tilted, inclined.

†9. To let down, lower, 'vail'. Often *Naut.* and *Mil.* to lower (a sail, an ensign). *Obs.*

Stooper (stū'pər). [f. STOOP *v.[1]* + -ER[1].]

1. One who or that which stoops.

2. One who stoops or bends down; one who has a stoop.

†Stoop-gallant, *a.* [f. STOOP *v.[1]* + GALLANT *sb.*] *= Frauce-gallant*, recorded *c.*1590 in *Dark Æntyrs* XXII. v. (1641) 530.

Stoo'py, *a. rare.* [f. STOOP *sb.[1]* *v.[1]* + -Y.] Having a stoop.

Stoor(e: see STIR, STORE, STOUR.

Stoot(e: see STOAT, SHUT.

†Stoo'ter. Obs. In *6-7* **stoter.** [Du. *stooter.*] A Dutch coin worth two stuivers and a half.

Stooth (stūþ), *dial.* Forms: *3-9* **stooth**, *5* **stothin**, *stoyt*, *9* **stooth**, **storys**, *9* **stooth**, [Either repr. OE. *stūðu* var. of *studu* STUD *sb.*, or a. the equivalent ON. *stoð*.]

1. A post, an upright lath; now only one of the upright battens in a lath-and-plaster wall.

Stooth, *v.* *dial.* [f. prec.]

1. *trans.* To garnish with studs or knobs. *Obs.*

2. To furnish (a wall) with the framework on which the lath-and-plaster is fixed; to build with lath and plaster.

Hence **†Stooth**ed *a.*, having studs. **†Stoothing** *vbl. sb.*, the action of the vb.; *concr.* a wall or partition of lath and plaster; also *attrib.*

Stoove, **Stoover**: see STOVE, STOVER.

Stoovre, etc. form of STOWER[1].

†Stop, *sb.[1]* Obs. Forms: *4-6* **stoppe**, *5-6* **stopp**, *4-9* **stoppe**. OS. *stoppo* — WGer. *stoppon-*. [f. OTeut. *stup-ablaut*-var. of *stupp.*: see STOP *sb.[2]*]

1. A pail or bucket.

Stop, *sb.[2]*

I. Action of stopping.

1. The action or an act of impeding, obstructing, or arresting; the fact of being impeded or arrested; a check, arrest, or obstruction (of motion or activity).

2. *trans.* A halt or stay occupying some considerable space of time; a stay or sojourn made at a place, esp. in the course of a journey.

c. A place at which a halt is made; a stopping-place (for carriages, etc.).

II. Something that stops, arrests, or blocks.

b. A projection at the upper part of a mast.

11. *Shipbuilding.*

12. *Optics.* A perforated plate or diaphragm used to cut off marginal rays of light round a lens. Cf. DIAPHRAGM *sb.* 4 b.

13. Something that stops an aperture; a plug.

III. *Music.*

IV. *Grammar.*

17. A mark or point of punctuation.

18. *Phonetics.* A consonant in articulating which the passage of the breath is completely obstructed.

V. Miscellaneous specific and technical senses.

STOP.

Stop off, trans. (a) in *Moulding*, to adapt (a mould) to a new design by shortening or obliterating some part of it; also *refl.* of a mould. (b) In *Etching, Electroplating,* etc. = *stop out.*

Stop out. trans. (a) in *Etching*, to obliterate or cover with a varnish (the marks, lines, or other parts of a plate which are to be kept from the acid in the process of biting). Also *absol.* (b) In *Electrotyping, Calico-printing,* etc.: see quots.

III. To come to a stand, cease to move or act.

34. intr. To cease from onward movement, to come to a stand or position of rest. Now emphatically to *stop dead, stop short* (see DEAD, SHORT *advs.*). Said of a person or other living creature, also of an inanimate thing driven or propelled.

35. To make a halt on a journey, to halt and remain for rest and refreshment. Of a coach, train, boat, or other public conveyance: To halt at a specified place to pick up and set down passengers, etc.

III. 4. [From STOP *sb.*] trans. To furnish with stops or punctuation-marks, to punctuate. Also in the phrase *stop a moment*.

STOP. 1029 **STOP.**

it is not hand.

38. To lease off... to shed (in a course of action or a pursuit, or from one's customary action or employment). Const. *from,* to *with inf.* Also to *stop short.*

39. Of a thing: To cease its motion or action. Of a process: To cease activity; to come to a pause.

40. Of an immaterial thing: To have its limit of operation at a specified point. Of a series: To come to an end.

41. Of a machine, etc.: To cease working or going. Also to *stop dead.*

b. Of an immaterial thing: To have its limit of operation at a specified point. Of a series: To come to an end.

IV. 41. [From STOP *sb.*] trans. To furnish with stops or punctuation-marks, to punctuate. Also in the phrase *stop a moment.*

42. Versification. To conclude or divide (a line of verse) with a stop. Cf. STOP *sb.* 17 c, STOPPED *ppl. a.* 8. Also *intr.* (cf. 37 b).

STOPCOCK.

V. 43. Combinations of the verb with a *sb.* in objective relation: † **stop-gamble,** a game, a situation that ends or interrupts the game; † **stop-hole,** a plug; **stop-loss,** *a.* (of or with or to sell stock, etc.) intended to save further loss that has been already incurred by falling prices; **stop-motion,** a device for automatically stopping a machine or engine when something has gone wrong; **stop-mouth** *a. nonce-wd.,* intended to keep people silent; **stop-ship** *sb.* (see quot. 1888); also *attrib.* (of an issue of a newspaper... etc.) containing late news inserted after printing has begun; † **stop-ship** [tr. Gr. ἐχενηΐς], the remora; † **stop-thrust,** *a.* (app. cogn.w. STEP *sb.*) the phonological relation is obscure.]

† **Stope,** *sb.1* Obs. Also 6 **stoppe.** [a. OF. *estoupe* *f. L. stuppa* L. *stuppa* tow, oakum.]

Stope (stōʊp), *sb.2 Mining.* [app. related to STEP *sb.* and vb.]

1. A step or notch in the side of a pit, or in an upright beam, to receive the end of a stemple or cross-piece. Also *attrib.*

2. A step-like working in the side of a pit.

b. *attrib.,* in *stope-working;* **stope-drill,** a portable rock-drill, used in stoping; **stope-hole,** a portable rock-drill, used in stoping.

Stope (stōʊp), *v.* [f. STOPE *sb.2*] trans. To cut (mineral ground) in stopes; to excavate horizontally, layer after layer; to work by this process. Also *with out.* Also *absol.*

Stopeable, *a.* [f. STOPE *v.* + -ABLE.] Capable of being stoped.

Stopel. Obs. rare. [f. OTeut. *stōp-*: ablaut-variant of *stap-*: see STEP *v.* and -EL.] **a.** A foot-print.

Stopell, obs. form of STOPPLE *sb.1*

Stopen, obs. pa. pple. of STEP *v.*

Stoper. [f. STOPE *v.* + -ER.] One who stopes.

Stop-gap (stō·pgap). [f. STOP *v.* + GAP *sb.* (From phr. *stop a gap.*)]

1. An argument in defence of some point attacked. *Obs.*

2. Something that temporarily supplies a need; a makeshift. Also, of a person: One who temporarily occupies an office, etc. until a permanent appointment can be made.

Stope, *sb.3* See STOOP *sb.3*

Stopel. *Obs. rare.* [f. OTeut. *stōp-...*]

Stoppance. Obs. [f. STOP *v.* + -ANCE.]

Stoppage (stō·pēdʒ). [f. STOP *v.* + -AGE.]

1. The action or condition of stopping or blocking up; obstruction or discontinuance of movement or activity; a stop or halt in a journey.

2. Discontinuance of supply.

3. Cessation of movement or activity; a stop or halt in a journey.

4. Obstruction of a passage, etc.

Stopped (stopt), *ppl. a.* [f. STOP *v.* + -ED.]

Stopper (stō·pə(r)), *sb.* [f. STOP *v.* + -ER.]

1. A person who stops or checks the course of (a river); one who stops or fills up holes or chinks.

Stopper (stō·pə(r)), *v.* [f. STOPPER *sb.*]

1. trans. *Naut.* To secure with a stopper.

2. To close or secure (a bottle, etc.) with a stopper.

Stoppered (stō·pə(r)d), *ppl. a.*

STOPPER. 1032 **STOPPLE.**

Stoppering (stō·pərɪŋ), *vbl. sb.* [f. STOPPER *v.* + -ING.]

Stopping (stō·pɪŋ), *vbl. sb.* [f. STOP *v.* + -ING.]

1. The action of the vb. STOP in various senses.

10. *Comb.* **stopper-berry tree,** the Barbados cherry, *Malpighia glabra;* **stopper-bolt** *Naut.* (see quots.); **stopper-hitch** *Naut.* (see quot.); **stopper-hole;** **stopper-knot** *Naut.,* a kind of knot used for the ends of stoppers; **stopper-net** (see quot.).

Stopping (stō·pɪŋ), *vbl. sb.*

II. Concrete uses.

Stopping (stō·pɪŋ), *ppl. a.* [f. STOP *v.* + -ING.]

Stopple (stō·p'l), *sb.1* [? Related to STOP *v.* ...]

Stopple, *v.* To close with a stopple.

Storied, *ppl. a.* [f. STORY *sb.*]

Storie, form of STIE *v.*

Storiated, *ppl. a.*

1. Ornamented with scenes from history or legend or other art; also, inscribed with a legend or memorial record.

2. Celebrated or recorded in history or story.

Storier (stō-riə̆r). Also 5–7 storyer. [In sense 1, altered variant of HISTORIER; in senses 2, 3 f. STORY *sb.* or v.3 + -ER1.]

1. A chronicler, historian, etc.

2. The teller of a story; a story-teller.

3. *dial.* One who tells "stories" for fun.

Storiette, storyette (stōri̯e̱t). [f. STORY *sb.* + -ETTE, Cf. NOVELETTE.] A very short story.

Storify (stō-rifai), *v.* [f. STORY *sb.* + -FY.] *trans.* To picture, delineate or historical event or fact; to celebrate in history or story. Hence **Storifying** *vbl. sb.* (attrib.)

Chr. Relig. Appeal...

Storify (stō-rifai), v.² [-FY.] *trans.* To arrange (beehives) in stories. Hence **Stori-fying** *vbl. sb.*

Storiologist (stōri̯o̱lŏdʒist). [f. next + -IST.] A student of storiology.

Storiology (stōri̯o̱lŏdʒi). Also **storology**. The systematic study of popular tales and legends, with regard to their origin and development.

+Storise, *Obs. rare*−1. [aphetic f. HISTOR-IZE.] *trans.* To represent in imagery.

Storjon, obs. form of STURGEON.

Stork (stǭk). Forms: 1 storc, 3 (storo), (MLG., MDu.), stork, ... [Common Teut. *sturk-.]

1. A large wading bird of the genus *Ciconia*, allied to this and heron; characterized by having long legs and a long stout bill.

2. *Comb.*, as **stork-assembly**, -**flight**, -**kind**, -**migration**, -**tribe**; *parasynthetic* and *similative*, as **stork-billed** adj., **stork-fashion** adv., **stork-like** adj. and adv.

Storken (stǭ·k'n), *v.* Sc. and north. Also 5–6 storkyn, 7– sturken. [a. ON. *storkna* to coagulate, corresp. to OHG. *kistorcan* to become rigid, Goth. *gastaurknan* to dry up. f. Teut. root *stark-* ablaut-var. of *stork-*: see STARK *a.*]

1. *intr.* To become stout, sturdy, strong; to grow, thrive, gain strength.

2. To be stiffened with cold; to congeal. (Said esp. of blood or melted fat.)

Storkish (stǭ·kiʃ), *a.* [f. STORK + -ISH.] Of, pertaining to, or resembling a stork; like that of a stork.

Storkling (stǭ·kliŋ). [-LING.] A young stork.

Stork's-bill.

1. A book-name for a plant of the genus *Erodium* (N.O. *Geraniaceæ*), esp. *E. cicutarium* or *E. mos-chatum*. † Also in corrupt forms **stocks-bill** (Ray

Storm (stǭm), *sb.* Also 1 **starm** *north.*), 3–7 **storme** (4 **sturme, etarme**). [Com. Teut. (not recorded in Gothic):...]

1. A violent disturbance of the atmosphere, manifested by high winds, often accompanied by heavy falls of rain, hail, or snow, by thunder and lightning, and as by turbulence of the waves.

2. *attrib.* as **storm-assembly**, **-flight**, **-kind**, **-migration**, **-tribe**; *parasynthetic* and *similative*, as **storm-billed** adj., **storm-fashion** adv., **storm-like** adj. and adv.

b. *fig.* and in figurative context. A violent disturbance of affairs whether civil, political, social or domestic; commotion, sedition, tumult.

3. *fig.* and in figurative context. A violent disturbance of affairs whether civil, political, social or domestic; commotion, sedition, tumult.

4. A violent assault on a fortified place.

II. 6. *Mil.* A violent assault on a fortified place.

b. A tumultuous rush (of sound, tears, etc.); a vehement utterance (of words, etc.).

7. *transf.* A heavy discharge or downfall (of missiles, blows).

storm obtained by meteorological observation; **storm-water**, (*a*) an abnormal amount of surface water resulting from a heavy fall of rain or snow; also *attrib.*; (*b*) *poet.*, water agitated by a storm; **storm-wave**, an abnormally heavy wave due to cyclonic disturbance which rolls across the ocean and frequently causes the inundation of low-lying coast lands; also *fig.*; **storm-wind**, the wind which accompanies a storm; also *fig.*; **storm-window**, (*a*) *storm-hind* window; (*b*) an outer window to protect the inner from the effects of storms (Cassell 1888); † **storm-winnock** (-win-dŏk) Sc. *prec.* *dial.*; **storm-zone** = storm-belt.

d. *Special comb.*: **storm-area**, the area of the earth's surface over which a storm spreads itself; **storm-bell** (see quot.); **storm-bell** (*a*) [G. *sturmglocke*] an alarm-bell; (*b*) *fig.* (see quot. 1910); **storm-belt**, a belt or zone in which storms occur periodically; **storm-breeder** (see quot.); **storm-card**, a transparent disc marked with lines representing the wind-directions of a cyclonic storm, to be placed over the ship's position on the chart in order to ascertain the course of the storm-centre; **storm-centre**, the central area of a cyclonic storm, characterized by comparative calmness; *fig.* the central point around which a storm of controversy, trouble, etc. rages...

Storm (stǭm), *v.* [f. STORM *sb.* (OE. had *styrman*, early ME. STURME *v.*)]

1. *intr.* Of the elements or weather: To be tempestuous or stormy; to rage.

2. *trans.* To make stormy. Also *pass.*

3. *intr.* To complain with rough and violent language; to rage, scold, *or* against (a grievance or person).

b. *trans.* To rush with the violence of a storm.

c. *transf.* To rush with the violence of a storm.

Stormable (stǭ·mǎb'l), *a.* [f. STORM *v.* + -ABLE.] That can be taken by storm.

Stormer (stǭ·mǎr). One who storms or rages; one who makes a wild agitation.

2. One who takes part in a storming party.

Stormful (stǭ·mful), *a.* [f. STORM *sb.* + -FUL.] Abounding in or subject to storms; tempestuous, stormy. *fig.* and *transf.*

Stormily (stǭ·mili), *adv.* [f. STORMY + -LY2.] In a stormy manner.

Storminess (stǭ·mines). [f. STORMY + -NESS.] The state of being stormy; stormy character.

Storming, *vbl. sb.* [-ING1.] The action of the vb. STORM.

Stormless (stǭ·mles), *a.* [f. STORM *sb.* + -LESS.] Free from storms.

Stormling (stǭ·mliŋ). [f. STORM *sb.* + -LING1.] That storms or rages.

Stormy (stǭ·mi), *a.* [-Y1.] 1. Of the weather, season, air, sky, sea, etc.: Characterized by storm or tempest; tempestuous. Of a place or region: Subject to storms.

b. *Path.* of inflammation.

Stornello (stǫrne̱lo). Pl. **stornelli** (-li). [It.] A short popular Italian lyric, usually improvised.

Storoppe, obs. form of STIRRUP.

Storre, obs. form of STAR *sb.* STIR *v.*, STOUR.

Storrie, obs. form of STORY sb.[2]

Storrope, obs. form of STIRRUP.

Stort, error for START sb.[3] (cormorant).

Storthing (stōr'tiŋ). [Norw. *storting*, formerly *-thing*, f. *stor* great + *ting*, thing assembly (see THING sb.[1]; cf. ON. *stórþing* œcumenical council.] The Norwegian parliament.

† Stortykn, sto tteryky. Obs. [Form uncertain; perh. a corruption of some Du. word; see -KIN.] Some measure of liquid.

† Storven, obs. pa. pple. of STARVE v.

Story (stōō'ri), sb.[1] Pl. **stories** (stōō'riz). Forms: 3-7 storie, 4-5 stoury, 4-6 story, 4 storye, 5 storii, 5-7 storye, 5-7 storie, 6 storrie, 6 storij, 6 storye, 7 storee, 6 story. Pl. 4 storijs, -yes, 4-5 storys, -yies, stories, storije, stories, storyes, 4 stories. [a. AF. *estorie* (OF. *estoire*, later in *un*-learned form *histoire*):—L. *historia* HISTORY. Cf. It. and med.L. *storia*.]

I. † 1. A narrative, true or presumed to be true, relating to important events and celebrated persons of a more or less remote past; a historical relation or anecdote. *Obs.*

Story (stōō'ri), sb.[2] *Obs.* [f. STORY sb.[2]] *trans.* To arrange in 'storeys' or strata one over the other.

Storyette: see STORIETTE.

Story'ful, *a. nonce-wd.* [-FUL.] Rich in story.

Storying (stōō'riin), vbl. sb. [f. STORY sb.[1] + -ING[1].] Having no story or stories.

Story-teller. [f. STORY sb.[1] + TELLER.] One who tells stories.

Story-telling, sb. The action of telling stories.

Story (stōō'ri), sb.[3] Forms: 3 storie, storye, 6 storie, storye, 6 storie, storey. [f. STORY sb.[2]]

1. Each of the stages or portions one above the other of which a building consists; a room or set of rooms on one floor or level.

2. Each of a number of tiers or rows (of orders, columns, window mullions or lights, etc.) disposed horizontally one above another.

Story (stōō'ri), v.[1] *trans.* In early use, to record historically; in later use, to tell as a story, to tell the story of. Often with clause as obj.

2. To decorate with paintings or sculpture; to illustrate by a series of pictures.

Stot (stot), sb.[1] Also 1, 3-9 stott, 5-7 stotte.

Stote, obs. form of STOAT, var. STOT sb.[1]

† Stotay e, obs. Forms: 4 stotaye, etc.

Stoter, variant of STOOTER n.

Stotoye, obs. form of STOTAYE.

Stotter, variant of STUTTER v.

Stoun d (stound), sb.[1] Forms: 1-3 stund, 2-5 stound, 4-5 stunde, 4-6 stownd, 4-6 stond, 5-6 stounde, 5-7 stownde, 6 stoond, 6-7 stownd, stound, north. Also stownd, stund.

Stound (stound), v.[1] *trans.* To stun, stupefy, as with a blow; to benumb.

STOUND. 1045 STOUR. STOUR. 1046 STOUR.

STOUR. 1047 STOUT. STOUT. 1048 STOUT.

Supplement, p. 3873; Corrigenda, p. 4092; Spurious words, p. 4093; Books quoted, p. 4094

Stout (stout, *n.*). [f. STOUT *a.*]

Stout, *a.* (and *adv.*). [a. OF. *estout*, *estolt*...]

Stouten (stou′t'n), *v.* [f. STOUT *a.* + -EN.] **1.** *trans.* To make stout. **2.** *intr.* To grow stout.

Stou·ter. (See quot.) ? *Obs.*

Stout·ness. [f. STOUT *a.* + -NESS.]

Stoutly (stou′tli), *adv.* [f. STOUT *a.* + -LY.] Stoutly.

Stoutish, *a.* [f. STOUT *a.* + -ISH.] Somewhat stout, in senses of the adj.

Stout-hearted, *a.* Having a stout heart; courageous, undaunted; ? stubborn, intractable. Hence **Stout-heartedly** *adv.*; **Stout-heartedness**.

Stove (stōv), *sb.*[1] Forms: 6 stofe, stouf(e, 7–9 stove. [Common Teut.] **I.** A heated chamber or box for some special purpose.

Stove, *v.*[1] [f. STOVE *sb.*[1]] **1.** *trans.* To heat in a stove.

Stove, *sb.*[2] [? f. STOVE *v.*[2]]

Stove, *v.*[2] [a. Du. *stoven*.] *trans.* To stew.

Stoved (stōvd), *ppl. a.*[1] [f. STOVE *v.*[1] + -ED[1].]

Stovel, corrupt form of STOVER.

Stoveless, *a.* [f. STOVE *sb.*[1] + -LESS.] Having no stove.

Stoven (stō′v'n). [OE. *stofa* masc. and fem.] = STOVE *sb.*[1]

Stover (stō′vəɹ), *sb.*[1] [a. AF. *estover*, *estovoir*.] Food, provision.

Stover, *sb.*[2] [f. STOVE *sb.*[1]] *intr.* To stand up like stubble, to bristle up.

Stoving (stō′viŋ), *vbl. sb.* [f. STOVE *v.*[1] + -ING[1].] The action of STOVE *v.*[1] in various senses.

Stow (stou), *sb.*[1] Also 7–9 stowe, 9 stow. [App. a. sing. form evolved from STOWCE (to which the first quot. may belong).]

Stow, *sb.*[2] *Mining.* Also 7–9 stowe, 9 stow.

Stow (stou), *v.* [OE. *stówian*, f. STOW *sb.*[1]] **1.** To place in a receptacle to be stored or kept in reserve.

Straight-away, *adv.* *rare*. [-WISE.]

Straightway, *adv. rare.*

Straik (strēk), *sb.*[1] *Sc. and north.* Also 9 strake, straike, straick. [f. STRAIK v.]

Straik (strēk), *sb.*[2] *Sc. rare*. A narrow channel in a stream.

Straik (strēk), *sb.*[3] *Sc. Also* strake. [Normal]

Straik (strēk), *v. Sc. Also* straike. [f. OE.]

†**Strai·ken, strai·king.** *Sc. and north. Obs.*

Strain (strēn), *sb.*[1] Forms: 1 strēl, strēlai, strēl, 4-5 straite, strayt, 4-6 straylte, stralyke, [OE. *strǣl*]

Strain (strēn), *sb.*[2]

Strain (strēn), *sb.*[3] *Obs.* Forms: 2-3 strēon, atrion, 2-3 streon, 3-4 stren, 7 strene, 4 streone, 4-5 streon, 3-4 strene, 5 streen, strēne, stręne, 6-7 straine, strȳne, 6-7 straine. [OE.]

Strain (strēn), *sb.*[4] *Obs.* Forms: 1 strēon, atrion.

STRAIN. 1063 STRAIN. STRAIN. 1064 STRAIN.

Strain, *sb.*[5] Forms: 1 strēn, 5 strēnte, strȳnte, 4 streyt, strȳnt, 6-7 straine, 6-7 straine. [STRAIN v.]

†**Strain**, *sb.*[6] *Obs.* Forms: 4 strayn, strayny, 4-5 streyny, streyn, 4-5 strayne, 4-5 strȳne, stręne, 4-5 strȳne, strenge, strēyne, 6-7 strain. [ME.]

†**Strain**, *sb.*[7] *Obs. rare*[-1]. In 6 strayne.

†**Strain**, *sb.*[8] *Obs. rare*[-1]. In 6 strayne.

STRAIN. 1065 STRAIN.

STRAIN. 1066 STRAIN.

STRAIN. 1067 STRAINED.

STRAINER. 1068 STRAIT.

† **d.** Tense, not lax. *Obs.*

3 Scanty or inadequate in quantity; affording little room; narrow. Of bounds, limits: Narrow.

II. Strict, rigorous.

† **6.** Of conditions, sufferings, punishment, etc.: Pressing hardly, severe, rigorous. *Obs.*

7. Of a religious order, its rules, etc., also of a sect: Rigorous, strict. *Obs.*

† **8.** Of a siege: Close. *Obs.*

III. Limited in nature, degree, or amount.

† **10.** Scanty, poor in degree. *Obs.*

† **11.** Of fortune, means, circumstances: Limited so as to cause hardship or inconvenience; inadequate. *Obs.*

12. Of words: Limited in application or signification. *Obs.*

† **b.** Of a legal instrument: Stringently worded, peremptory. *Obs.*

13. Strictly specified, exact, precise, definite; esp. of an account, exactly rendered. *Obs.*

14. Of friendship, alliance, etc.: Close, intimate.

† **15.** Reluctant and chary in giving; close, stingy, illiberal. *Obs.*

16. In parenthetic adjs., as strait-bodied, -broasted, -brreched, -cheekd, -clothed, -coated, -necked, -sleeved, -toothed, -waisted.

17. Special comb.: † strait-handed a., close-fisted, grasping, stingy; hence † strait-handedness; † strait-hearted a., ungenerous, exacting, mean; hence † strait-heartedness; † strait-winded a., short of breath.

Strait, *adv.* Forms: see the adj.

1. narrow confined place or space or way generally. *Now rare or Obs.*

2. *fig.* narrow or tight place, a time of need or of awkward or straitened circumstances, a difficulty or fix. *Now rare in sing.*; still common in *plural*.

b. *spec.* Short for *Straits Settlements*, the name given to the British possessions in the Malay peninsula collectively.

3. A dilemma; a difficulty of choice. † *Obs.*

4. A narrow pass or gorge between mountains; a defile, ravine.

5. A narrow strip of land with water on each side, an isthmus. *Now rare.* (*poet.*)

6. Naut. Strait of time: pressure or insufficiency of time.

7. In generalized sense: Privation, hardship.

STRAIT. 1071 STRAITEN. STRAITEN. 1072 STRAITENED.

Strait, *v.* Forms: see the adj. [f.]

1. *trans.* To brace up to restraint.

2. As rendering of Vulg. *coartare, artare,* lit. to press together, contract.

Straiten, *v.* Forms: 6 straighten, 7 straiten, 6-8 straighten, 9-4 straighten, 7 straiten, straighten, 7-9 strayten.

1. *trans.* To render strait or narrow; to narrow, contract (an opening, a passage, road, stream, etc.).

5. To narrow or restrict the freedom, power, or privileges of (a person). *Obs.*

6. To narrow or restrict in range, scope, or amount.

b. *Phrase,* To straiten (a person's) quarters.

c. To restrict *from* doing something.

7. To bind stringently. *Obs.*

8. To straiten one's hand: to become niggardly. *Obs.*

9. To narrow or restrict in range, scope, or amount.

Straitened, ppl. a. [STRAITEN v.] In various senses of the verb.

1. Contracted, narrowed; insufficiently spacious.

2. Confined in narrow space; having too little room.

3. Drawn tight / straightened.

Straithead, **Straiting**, **Strait-lace**, **Strait-laced**, **Straitly**, **Straitness**, **Strait waistcoat**, **Strak**, **Strake**

Strake, **Straked**, **Straky**, **Strall**, **Stram**, **Stramash**, **Stramazo**, **Stramazon**, **Stramel**, **Stramineous**, **Stramison**, **Stramonium**, **Stramony**, **Stramp**, **Strand**

Strand ... Three strand shroud-laid rope.

Strand, v.² 1. intr. Of a rope: To break one or more of its strands. Also transf., to break one or more of the strands (of a rope).

Strander. [f. STRAND v.² + -ER¹.] spec. An operative employed in electric cable manufacture.

Strandless (strændlès), a. [f. STRAND sb.¹ + -LESS.] Without a strand or beach.

Stranding, vbl. sb.

Strandling. Obs. Forms: stranlyne, -ling, -lyng, strenlyng, strandling(e, -lynge. [Of obscure origin.] Some kind of fur; ? the fur of the squirrel taken at Michaelmas.

Strandlooper. S. Africa. [Du., f. strand STRAND sb.¹ + looper runner.] A Hottentot who picks up such living as he can by the sea shore.

Strand (strænd), v.¹

Strang: see STRAND sb.¹, STRANGE a., STRONG a.

Strange (strēⁿdʒ), a. Also 3–7 straunge, 4–6 straunge, 4–7 strainge, 5 strawnge, straunche, 6 strenge, straynge, straing, Sc. strenge, 6–7 strainge. [a. OF. estrange (mod.F. étrange) = Pr. estranh, Sp. estraño, Pg. estranho, Rum. strǎin, It. strano adj., stranio, stranju sb., a L. extrāneus external, foreign (see EXTRANEOUS), f. extrā adv. outside, without.]

1. Of persons, language, customs, etc.: Of or belonging to another country; foreign, alien. Obs.

2. Belonging to some other place or neighbourhood; unknown to the particular locality spoken of.

3. Of a place or locality: Other than one's own.

9. Exceptionally great (in degree, intensity, amount, etc.), extreme. (Now tending to merge in 10.)

10. Unfamiliar, abnormal, or exceptional to a degree that excites wonder or astonishment; queer, surprising, unaccountable.

4. Strange woman: a harlot. (With the, as denoting an individual.)

5. Added or introduced from outside, not belonging to the place or person where it is found.

6. quasi-adv., qualifying an adj.: Very, extremely. Also strange and = Now dial.

11. Unfamiliar, abnormal, or exceptional to a degree that excites wonder.

12. Of a person: Unfamiliar or unacquainted with something (expected or implied); fresh or unaccustomed to unskilled at.

13. To make (it) strange : to make difficulties, refuse to assent or comply, be reluctant or unwilling; to hold back, keep a stand-off attitude; to be distant or unfriendly; to affect or feel surprise, indignation, etc. Const. of (= about) a matter, etc.; to (do something); to make strange at.

14. A strange person, stranger; in pl. sense, strangers. Also rarely a.

STRANGE. 1079 STRANGER. STRANGER. 1080 STRANGER.

III. 16. Comb., forming adjs.

Strange, v. Also 5–6 straunge, 5 straunche. [ad. OF. estranger: see ESTRANGE v.]

1. trans. To remove, banish, keep apart from an association, condition, relations, etc.

2. To make (a person) a stranger (to something).

3. To alienate in feeling or affection, estrange (one party) from (another).

4. To grudge (something valuable) to (a person); refl. to refuse (a grant something).

5. intr. To depart, estrange oneself from; to be removed or become estranged from.

6. quasi-Comb. (The adv. qualifying a ppl. adj.)

7. To become strange or changed. Obs.

8. To be surprised, wonder. Const. at, dependent clause, or to and inf.

Strangeful, ppl. a., made strange; wondering.

Strangely (strēⁿdʒli), adv. [f. STRANGE a. + -LY².]

1. In a foreign or unfamiliar manner.

2. In an unfriendly or unfavourable manner; with cold or distant bearing.

3. In an uncommon or exceptional degree; very greatly, extremely. Obs.

4. In an uncommon or exceptional manner by the outer of hours for the wonder.

Strangeness (strēⁿdʒnès). [STRANGE sb.]

1. The quality of being strange, foreign, unfamiliar, uncommon, unusual, extraordinary, etc. (See the adj.)

Stranger (strēⁿdʒər), sb. (and a.). Forms: 4 strangere, 4–5 straungere, 4 strawnger, strangiere, 5 strawngere, 5–6 straunger, -iere, 6 strawnger, straungoure, strongere, stronger, 6 strangeour, a. strange, straunger. See also EXTRANEUS. [Aphetic a. OF. estrangier (mod.F. étranger) = Pr. estrangier, Sp. estrangero, It. straniero, stranguero, extraneo : — popular L. *extrāneārius.]

1. One who belongs to another country; a foreigner; chiefly (now exclusively), one who resides in or comes to a country to which he is a foreigner; an alien.

2. One who is not a native of, or who has not long resided in, a country, town, or place.

3. Absence of friendly feeling or relations; disobliging or uncomplying attitude towards others; coldness, aloofness. Obs.

b. Something that comes from abroad; esp. an exotic plant.

4. An unknown person; a person with whom one has not become, or is not known or acquainted.

5. One who is not privy or party to an act.

6. One who is not a member of the household. Now chiefly with mixture of sense 4.

7. One who has no share in (some privilege or business). Const. of, from. ? Obs.

8. A guest or visitor, in contradistinction to the members of the household.

7. Vocatively. (Said to be, in rustic use in the U.S., the customary mode of address to one whose name is unknown.)

8. In parochial registers: A person not belonging to the parish. Obs.

9. Predicatively, and of one whose visits have long ceased. Also, one who never visits (a place), an absentee.

b. quasi-adj. With pl.: Something strange; a strange circumstance, object, event, or the like.

Strangering, vbl. sb.

Stranger ...

Strangle (stræŋ'g'l), sb. [f. STRANGLE v.]

Strangle (stræŋ'g'l), v. [a. OF. estrangler (mod.F. étrangler) = Pr. estrangular ...]

Strangleable (stræŋ'g'lăb'l), a. nonce-wd. [f. STRANGLE v. + -ABLE.] Capable of being strangled.

Strangled (stræŋ'g'ld), ppl. a. [f. STRANGLE v. + -ED.]

Strangler (stræŋ'glăr). [f. STRANGLE v. + -ER.]

Strangles (stræŋ'g'lz). [Orig. pl. of STRANGLE sb.]

Strangling (stræŋ'gliŋ), vbl. sb. [f. STRANGLE v. + -ING.]

Strangling, ppl. a. [f. STRANGLE v. + -ING.]

Strangulate (stræŋ'giŭlēt), v. [f. L. strangulāt-, ppl. stem of strangulāre to STRANGLE.]

Strangulation (stræŋgiŭlē'ʃən). [ad. L. strangulātiōn-em, n. of action f. strangulāre: see prec.]

Strangulative (stræŋ'giŭlătiv), a. Obs. rare. [f. L. type *strangulātīvus, f. strangulāre: see STRANGULATE v. and -IVE.] That strangles or stops respiration.

Strangullion (stræŋ'gŭliŏn). Forms: 5-6 strangulyon, (6 -guillyon, -guil'l)ion, -guo-gyon, straŋ(o)n, 6 strangulyon, 6-7 stran-gulion, 6- strangullion. [a. OF. estranguillon (mod.F. étranguillon), f. L. stranguliōnem, f. L. strangullionem; -popular L. *strangulliōnem, f. L. strangu-lāre to STRANGLE.]

Strangurion Obs. Also 6 -yon, 6-7 -ian. [A confusion of STRANGURY and STRANGULLION.] = STRANGURY.

Strangurious (stræŋgiŭr'iəs), a. rare⁻¹. [ad. late L. strangūriōsus, f. strangūria STRANGURY: see -OUS.] Of, pertaining to, or characteristic of strangury; affected with strangury.

Strangury (stræŋ'giŭri). Path. Forms: 6-7 stranguria, 6-ye, 7 stranguery, 7-9 stranguary, 4- strangury. [ad. L. strangūria, a. Gr. στραγγ-ουρία, f. στράγξ, -γγός strip or drop squeezed out ...]

Strany (strænĭ). A local name of the Common Guillemot.

Strap (stræp), sb. [var. of STROP sb.]

Strap (stræp), v. [f. STRAP sb.]

Strappado (stræpē'dō, stræpā'dō). Also 6 strapado, strapadoe, strappadoe, 7 strappada, strappada, 7 strappado, strappa- (-do, -does), 6- strappado. [f. It. strappata, f. strappare to pull, snatch.]

Strappado, v. Obs. [f. STRAPPADO sb.]

1. trans. To torture or punish with the strappado.

Strapped (stræpt), ppl. a. [f. STRAP v.¹ + -ED².]

1. Furnished with a strap, bound or fastened with a strap or with straps.

Strapper (stræpə(r)).

1. A 'strapping' or tall and robust person; one above the average stature and strength of build. (Chiefly applied to women. Cf. STRAPPING ppl. a.)

Strapping (stræpiŋ), vbl. sb.² dial. [f. STRAP v.² + -ING¹.]

Strapping (stræpiŋ), ppl. a. Also 8 Sc. strapan, 8–9 Sc. strappan. [f. STRAP v.¹ + -ING².]

Cf. **STRAPPER**.] Originally of a young woman:

Strappet. Obs. rare⁻¹. [f. STRAP sb. + -ET.]

Strapple, v. Obs. exc. dial. [f. STRAPPLE sb.]

Strapple, sb. Obs. exc. dial. [Belonging to the family of words with 'strapples' or coverings for the legs.]

Strap-shaped, a.

Strapwork, sb.

Strapwort, sb. Bot.

Strass (stræs). [a. G. strass, F. stras (Dict. Acad. 1762); said to be from the name of the inventor, Josef Strasser.] A vitreous composition used as a basis in the manufacture of artificial stones. = PASTE sb.³ 5.

Strass², strasse (stræs(ə)).

+Strapple, sb. Obs. Forms: 1 strapul, 3 strapol, 4–5 strapple, 5 strapil, strapple, stra-.

Strasburg, **Strassburg**, **Strasbourg**, etc. Also 7 Strass-burgh, Strassburgh (G. Strassburg, F. Strasbourg.) The name of the principal town of Alsace, used attrib. in the names of various articles.

Strata, pl. of STRATUM.

Stratagem (strætədʒem). Forms: 5–7 stratagem, 6 -geme, 7 strata-, 6–8 strata-gem. [a. F. stratagème (= Sp., Pg. estratagema, It. stratagemma), ad. L. stratēgēma.]

1. An operation or act of generalship; usually, an artifice or trick designed to outwit or surprise the enemy.

2. Any artifice or trick; a device or scheme for obtaining an advantage.

Stratagematic, a. Obs. Also 7 strate-gematick.

Stratagematist. Obs. [C. (with alteration of the second vowel) Gr. στρατηγηματ-, στρατήγημα.]

Strategemical, a. Obs. rare.

Strategemitor. Obs. rare. [irreg. f. STRATAGEM + L. agent-suffix -(I)TOR.]

+Strategeme, a. Obs. rare⁻¹.

Stratal, a. Geol.

Strarchy, **stratarchy**. Obs.

+Stratarithmetry. Obs. rare⁻¹.

Strateuma. Obs. rare⁻¹.

Strategetic, a. rare.

Strategetical, a. rare.

Strategic (strætiːdʒik, -dʒaik), a. and sb.

A. adj. Of or belonging to strategy; useful or important in regard to strategy.

Strategical, a. rare. [Formed as prec.]

Strategically, adv.

Strategician, rare⁻¹.

Strategist (strætidʒist).

Strategus (strætiːdʒəs). Gr. Hist. Pl. -gi (-dʒai). Also with Gr. ending strategos (strætiːgɒs), pl. -oi. [L. strategus, a. Gr. στρατηγός (Doric στραταγός), f. στρατ-ός army.]

1. Used by Holland to render Pliny's provincia (στρατηγία), a government or province. Cf. STRA-TEGY.

2. A strategist.

A. adj. Of or belonging to strategy.

Strategy (strætidʒi). Also 7 strategie. [a. F. stratégie (In Pinet's tr. Pliny, 1562), ad. Gr. στρατηγία office or command of a general, generalship, f. στρατηγός = STRATEGUS.]

1. The office of a commander-in-chief or chief magistrate at Athens and in the Achæan league (also in Harrington's imaginary commonwealth).

2. The art of a commander-in-chief; the art of projecting and directing the larger military movements and operations of a campaign.

3. transf. and fig., chiefly with reference to the geological use.

Straticle (strætiːkl).

Straticulate (strætikiʊleit), a. Geol. and Min.

Stratification (strætifikeiʃən). [ad. med.L. stratificātiōn-em, n. of action f. STRATIFY v.]

Stratified (strætifaid), ppl. a. [f. STRATIFY v. + -ED¹.] Disposed in strata or layers.

Stratiform (strætifɔ:m), a. [ad. F. stratiforme, f. L. strātum STRATUM + -FORM.]

Stratify (strætifai), v. [ad. F. stratifier, f. mod.L. strātificāre; f. strātum STRATUM + -FICARE.]

Stratigrapher (strætigrəfə(r)). [f. STRATI-GRAPHY + -ER¹.]

Stratigraphic (strætigræfik), a. [f. STRATI-GRAPHY + -IC: cf. F. stratigraphique.]

Stratigraphical (strætigræfikal), a.

Stratigraphy (strætigrəfi). [f. L. strāti- + -GRAPHY.] Military science.

Strati-pedarch. Hist. rare.

Stratiote (strætiəʊt), rare. [a. Gr. στρατιώτης soldier.]

Stratiotic, -ical, a. Obs. rare.

Stratonic, a. rare⁻¹.

Stratocracy (strætɒkrəsi). [f. Gr. στρατός army + -CRACY.] Government by the army; military rule; a polity in which the army is the controlling power.

Stratocrat. rare.

Stratography (strætɒgrəfi). Military science.

Stratonic, a. rare⁻¹.

Strato-cumulus (streitəʊ-kʌmiʊləs).

Strato-cirrus.

Stratose (strætəʊs), a.

Stratosphere (strætəsfiə(r)).

Stratous (strætəs), a.

Stratum (streitəm, strætəm). Pl. **strata** (streitə). Also rarely **stratums**. [mod.L., a mod.L. use of L. strātum neut.—lit. something spread or laid down (in classical use with the senses 'bed-cloth', 'pavement'), neut. pa. pple. of sternĕre to throw down, strew, etc. Cf. STRATE, STREW v.]

1. The branch of geology that is concerned with the order and relative position of the strata of the earth's crust.

2. A bed of sedimentary rock, usually consisting of a series of 'layers' or 'laminæ' of the same kind, representing continuous periods of deposition.

Stratus (strē·tŏs). *Meteorol.* [a. L. *strātus* (*u* sterm), f. *strā-, sternĕre* to spread, lay down. (See quot. 1803, and cf. STRATUM.] One of the simple forms of cloud, having the appearance of a broad sheet of nearly uniform thickness, usually existing at low elevations.

Strauch·t: see STRAIGHT, STRETCH *v.*

Straugh·t, *a., Obs.* [Apheric f. DISTRAUGHT *a.*] Distraught, out of one's mind. Also, *beref t* (one's wits, mind).

Straught: see STRAIGHT *a.* and *v.*, STRETCH *v.*

Strauhe, Strauht, obs. ff. STRAW, STRAIGHT.

Straunge, obs. f. STRANGE.

Straunde, obs. form of STRAND *sb.*

Straungeour, -or(e, *etc.,* obs. ff. STRANGER.

Straungle, obs. form of STRANGLE *v.*

Strauth, obs. f. pple. of STRETCH *v.*

† **Stra·vagant,** *a.* and *sb. Obs.* [ad. L. *stra- vagant-*, f. L. *extrāvagant-*: see EXTRAVAGANT.] *A. adj.* Irrelevant, unsuitable, extraordinary: = EXTRAVAGANT *a.* 4, 5, 6.

Straw (strǭ), *sb.1* Forms: 1– † straw, strau, 3 strau, straugh, 3–7 strawe, straw (*pl.* strais), 6–9 *Sc.* straw; *e.* 5 strowh, 5–6 *Sc.* north. *strēe* (*not found in Gothic*): OE. *strēaw* neut. = OFris. *strē*(*h*, *w*)*Fris. strie*(*h*), OS. MDu. *strō* (Du. *stroo*) neut., OHG., MHG. *strō* neut., gen. *strawes, strewes* (mod.G. *stroh*), ON. *strá* neut. (Sw., Da. *strå*):—OTeut. **strawo-*, f. root **straw-* : see STREW *v.*

STRAW. 1091 STRAW. STRAW. 1092 STRAWBERRY

Strawberry (strǭ·beri). Forms: see STRAW *sb.* and BERRY *sb.1* [OE. *strēaw*-, *strēo- berig(e*, = 4–6 *strauberie*, -*bery*, 5 *strau-*, etc.]

Strawberry leaf. The leaf of the strawberry plant. Also, † the plant itself (obs.). Also attrib.

Hence **Strawberry-leaved.**

Straw-breadth, straw's breadth. Now rare. The breadth of a straw. Chiefly in contexts referred to as a typically small distance.

† Straw brede, Obs. Also 6-7c. strawbrede.

Strawcloth, etc. [= pa.ppl. of STRETCH v.]

Straw colour. The colour of straw, a pale yellow. Also attrib. or adj. = STRAW-COLOURED.

Straw-coloured, a. Of the colour of straw; pale light yellow.

Strawed, obs. form of STROWED.

Strawen, 6-7 strawne. [f. STRAW sb.¹ + -EN⁴.] Made of straw.

† Strawer, Obs. [f. STRAW sb.¹ + -ER¹.] One who strews; (see quot.).

Straw-er², Obs. [STRAW v.² + -ER¹.] (See quot.)

Strawhat. (Formerly often hyphened.) A hat made of plaited or woven straw.

† Straw-ish, a. Obs. [f. STRAW sb.¹ + -ISH¹.] Resembling straw.

Strawless (strōˈles), a. [f. STRAW sb.¹ + -LESS.] Made without straw, containing no straw.

Strawnge, -er, etc., obs. ff. STRANGE, STRANGER.

Strawt(e, obs. Sc. form of STRAIGHT; obs. pa. t. and pa. pple. of STRETCH v.

Strawy (strōˈi), a. Also 8-9 strawey. [f. STRAW sb.¹ + -Y¹.]

1. Consisting of, the nature of, full of straw.

2. Made with straw; filled, thatched, or strewed with straw.

3. Resembling straw in texture, colour, etc.

STRAY

Stray, strowen, 6-7 strawne. [f. STRAW sb.¹ + -EN⁴.] Made of straw.

Straw-yard. A straw littered with straw, in which horses and cattle are wintered.

Straw-yarder sing. (See quot.)

Stray (strē), sb. Also 6 streyi, 6 pl. straies. See also STREAK. [Two formations: (1) a. AF. stray, estrai, verbal noun f. AF., OF. estraier STRAY v.²: (2) f. STRAY v.²]

† Stray, v.¹ [Partly an aphetic variant of ASTRAY (cf. LONE a. from ALONE); partly attrib. use of STRAY sb.]

Stray (strē), v.² Also 5-6 strey, 6 pl. strayes. [a. OF. estraier, estreier.]

Strayaway. [f. STRAY v.² + AWAY adv.] An animal that strays away; a straggler.

Strayed (strēd), ppl. a. [f. STRAY v.² + -ED¹.]

Strayer (strēˈər). [f. STRAY v.² + -ER¹.] One who strays, in the senses of the verb.

Straying (strēˈiŋ), vbl. sb. [f. STRAY v.² + -ING¹.] The action of the verb, in various senses; also, an instance of this.

Straying (strēˈiŋ), ppl. a. [f. STRAY v.² + -ING¹.] That strays, in the senses of the verb.

† Strayling. In a-straying. Obs. rare⁻¹.

Stray-line. Naut. [STRAY a. (or STRAY sb.²) + LINE sb.²]

Streak (strīk), sb. Also 6 streke, strick. [OE. strica wk. masc.; f. weak-grade of the Teut-root *strīk-: see STRIKE v. The a and forms represent a difference of dialectal phonetic development: in the a forms the ĭ remained.]

Streak (strīk), v. Also 6-7 streake. [OE. strician wk.: OHG., mod.G. strichen wk.:—OE. striccan.]

Streaked (strīkt), ppl. a. [f. STREAK v.² + -ED¹.] Marked with streaks; striped, striate. Often fig.

Streaker (strīˈkər). 1. One who streaks.

Streaking (strīˈkiŋ), vbl. sb. the action of the verb.

Streaky (strīˈki), a. Also 7 streeky. [f. STREAK sb. + -Y¹.]

Streal, variant of STREEL.

Streale, *Obs. exc. dial.* Also 3 stral. [OE. *strǽl* (Anglian *strēl*), *strále* masc. and fem.; MDu. *straal* masc., *strael* masc. and fem., MLG. *strāl*, *strāle* masc. and fem.; OHG. *strāla* fem. (MHG. *strāl*, mod. G. *strahl*); OS. *strāla*, *strála*, cogn. w. OSl. *Russian* orphta arrow.] An arrow.

Stream (strīm), *sb.* Forms: 1 *stréam*, *stráam*, *strǽm*, 2–6 *strem* (5 *streem*, (stram), 3 *streame*, (*streome*), 4–7 *streeme* (5, 6–7 *streme*), 5–7 *stream*, 5–9 *streme*, *strēme*, 7–9 *stream*.

A course of water flowing continuously along its bed on the earth, forming a river, rivulet, or brook.

Streamer (strīˈmə(r), *sb.* Forms: 3–7 *streamer*, (5, 6 *stremour*), 4 *streamer*, *stremer* (5, *stremour*), 7 *stremour* (*S. stroyme*), *strym-*, 5–9 *streamer*.

STRECK.

Streck, adv. Obs. exc. dial. Forms: 4 strik, 4–5 streke, 4–6 strek, 8–9 strick, 9 streck. [f. STRECK v.] In a straight course, directly; immediately, straightway. Also with away. Also streck up, in upright posture.

Streck, sb. Obs. form of STREAK sb.

Strecto, obs. form of STRAIT a.

Stred, Strede var. of STREET, STRIDE.

Stree(s, e, obs. var. of STRAW sb.

Streek, streak (strīk), v. Now Sc. and dial. Forms: see STRETCH v.

Streeker (strī·kəɹ). dial. [f. STREAK v. + -ER¹.] A layer-out of the dead.

Stree·king, vbl. sb. [f. STREAK v. + -ING¹.]

Streel (strīl), v. Chiefly Anglo-Irish. Also streal.

Stree·ling, ppl. a.

Street (strīt), sb. Forms: 1–2 strǽt, strēt, (3–5 strate,) 3 street, 4 streete, OE. strǣt, etc.

Street (strīt), v. [f. STREET sb.] trans. To furnish or provide with streets; to lay out in streets.

Streeter (strī·təɹ). [f. STREET + -ER¹.]

Street-orderly. the system of employing street-orderlies for scavenging.

Street-walker. 1. One who walks in the street.

Street-coach, a hackney-coach; **street-manure; street-dog,** an ownerless dog living in the streets; **street-farer** *nonce-wd.,* one who passes through the streets; **street-firing,** discharge of musketry in order to defend or secure a street; **street-gadder,** one who 'gads' about the streets; **street-light,** a window opening on the street; **street-lamp; street-manure,** horse-dung and road-scrapings used for manure; **street-parlour,** a sitting-room on the ground-floor, fronting the street; **street-porter,** a porter employed to lift or carry heavy packages in the street (in early use = ticket-porter); **street price** Stock Exchange, see quot.; **street-railway,** a tramway; **street-refuge,** a. Sc., that wanders about the streets; **street-refuge** = REFUGE sb. 3; **street-room,** sufficient space in the streets; **street-scroll** (?ash); **street-thread,** **street-thread-net,** a mischievous little street-boy; **street-web** (dial.), see quot. 1854; **street-yarn** (U.S., see quot.).

Streetage. U.S. [STREET sb. + -AGE.] A charge or toll for the use of a street or street facilities.

Street-car. U.S. A passenger car, running through the streets, usually on rails; a tram-car.

Street-door. The chief external door of a house or other building, giving immediate access to the street.

Street-keeper. A parish or district official appointed to keep order in the streets. Also see quot. 1748.

Streetless (strī·tles), a. [-LESS.] Destitute of streets, having no street or streets.

Streetlet (strī·tlet). [STREET sb. + -LET.] A diminutive street.

Street·ling. [STREET sb. + -LING.]

Streetman. [STREET sb. + MAN sb.]

Street·ward, sb., adv. Also adv. [STREET sb. + WARD.] a. adv. Towards the street. Also in phr. to the streetward. b. adj. Facing or opening on the street.

Streetway. A paved road or highway, the roadway of a street.

Streety (strī·ti), a. [-Y.] Of, pertaining to, or characteristic of the street.

Strength (streŋþ), sb. Forms: 1–2 streŋ(o, strengu, strenðu, etc. [OE. *strengþu*. 1. The quality of being strong, whether in physical or immaterial sense.]

Strengly (streŋ·li), adv. more strongly.

Strengthen, v. Obs. Forms: 3–5 strengen, strengðen, 4 strengthen.

Strengh, obs. form of STRENGTH.

†Strenghfully, adv. Obs. [f. STRENGH sb. + -FUL + -LY 2] Strongly in power.

Strengine (strenjīn'). Min. [a. G. strengin]

†Strengly, adv. Obs.

Strength (streŋþ), sb. Forms: 1 strengðu, -o, strengð, strencð, strenhð, oblique cases strengðe etc., 2-3 strengðe, 2 streongðe, strenðe, 2-6 ætrengðe, 2 streinðe, 3 (5, 5c) strenþe, 3 strengðe (Orm.), strenðe, 3-4 strenncþe, strenþe, strench, 3-5 strengthe, 4 strenþ, 4 streonþe, strinth (4, atrenthe, streiþ), strenþhe, 4-5 strenkeȝt, strynth, strengthe...

I. The quality or condition of being strong.

II. Thus has Time mellowed the Works of Antiquity...

k. Vigour, intensity (of feeling, conviction, etc.)

l. Intensity of the specific property, or proportionate quantity of the active ingredient in a substance; potency (of drugs, liquors).

m. Of soil: Firmness.

n. Demonstrative force or weight (of arguments, evidence); amount of evidence.

o. Energy or vigour of literary or artistic conception or execution; forcefulness (of delineation, versification, expression).

p. Cards: Of a hand (or the player holding it)...

q. Billiards.

r. Comm. Firmness, absence of lowering tendency, in prices.

2. Phrases. †a. By or with strength of: by force of. Cf. FORCE sb.1 16. Obs.

†b. On the strength of: †(a) with the strength derived from, fortified by (food or drink) (obs.)...

3. Used for: A source of strength; that which makes strong. (Not now in pl.)

†9. Legal power: authority. Cf. 1 b.) Obs.

10. A stronghold, fastness, fortress. Now arch. or Hist., chiefly with reference to Scotland.

†b. A defensive work, munition, fortification. Also fig. Obs.

†c. A strong position; the place within which one is most secure; spec. in Wrestling (see quot. 1714). Obs.

11. †a. collect. sing. Troops, forces. Obs.

†b. A body of soldiers; a force. Obs.

12. Mil. and Naval. The number of men on the muster-roll of an army, a regiment, etc.; the body of men enrolled; the number of ships in a navy or fleet.

†Strength, v. Obs. Forms: see STRENGTH sb. [f. STRENGTH sb.]

1. trans. To give strength to, strengthen; to make strong, fortify, confirm.

†Strengthen (streŋþ'n), v. [f. STRENGTH sb. + -EN 5.]

1. trans. To make strong or stronger; to confirm, establish.

o. To increase the strength (of the mind or its faculties).

10. intr. To become strong or stronger; to grow in strength or intensity.

4. To make stronger in influence, authority, or security of position.

5. To reinforce (some material thing) by an additional support, added thickness, or covering.

6. To furnish with something to augment, intensify.

7. To increase the strength of (reasons, obligations); to support (a case, an opinion) by additional evidence; to give increased strength or vigour of style to (a composition).

8. To make more effective or powerful by reinforcement of numbers or resources.

Strengthful (streŋþfŭl), a. [f. STRENGTH sb. + -FUL.] Full of or characterized by strength.

Strengthfully, adv. rare. Also **Sc. strenthfully**, 6 Sc. **strenthfilly**.

Strengthily, adv. rare. Also 5 Sc. **strenthilly**, 6 Sc. **strenthfully**.

Strengthener (streŋþnər). Also 6-8 **strengthner**. [f. STRENGTHEN v. + -ER 1.] One who or something which strengthens.

Strengthening (streŋþ'niŋ), vbl. sb. [f. STRENGTHEN v.] The action of the vb. STRENGTHEN, in various senses; an instance of this.

Strengthening, ppl. a. [-ING 2.] That strengthens or makes stronger.

Strengthless (streŋþlĕs), a. [f. STRENGTH sb. + -LESS.] Destitute of strength; without strength.

†Strengthly, adv. Sc. Obs. rare. [f. STRENGTH sb. + -LY 2.] Strongly. With force. Also **strenthly**.

Strength silver. Sc. Obs. App. a sum of money which the tenant of a shieling paid to the landlord for entering, on the same conditions as the farming stock.

Strengthy (streŋþi), a. Chiefly Sc. and north. Forms: 4 strenkithi, 7- strengthi, -pl., 4-6 strenthi, 6 strinthy, 8- strengthy. [f. STRENGTH sb. + -Y 1.]

1. Of a person: Strong to act or to withstand attack; mighty, powerful. Obs.

†b. Of a position or structure: Strong against assault.

STRENK.

Strenk, v. Obs. rare. [Early ME. *strenken*, of obscure origin. Cf. *strenkle* STRINKLE v.] trans. To sprinkle.

Strenkel(l, **kit**(h, **-kyght**, obs. ff. STRENGTH.
Strenkle, var. STRINKLE sb. and v. Obs.
Strenlyug, var. STRANDLING Obs.
Strenth(e, obs. ff. STRENGTH.

Strenuity (strĭniū·ĭti). Now rare. Also 5-6 strenuite, 6 -uyte, strenewite, 7 strenuiti. [ad. L. *strēnuitā*, f. *strēnu-us*: see STRENUOUS a. and -ITY.] The quality of being strenuous, strenuousness.

Strenuosity (streniŭo·sĭti). [f. STRENUOUS a.: see -OUS and -ITY.] Strenuousness (somewhat disparaging in use).

Strenuous (stre·niŭĭs), a. [f. L. *strēnu-us* brisk, active, vigorous (related to Gr. στρηνής strong, hard, rough, στρῆνος haughtiness, arrogance) + -OUS. Cf. L. *strenuus* a.]

Strenuously (stre·niŭĭsli), adv. In a strenuous manner.

Strenuousness (stre·niŭĭsnes). [f. STRENUOUS a. + -NESS.] The quality of being strenuous.

Strep, Mining. Obs.⁻¹. Corruption of or mistake for STRAKE sb.?

Strepe, obs. form of STRIP sb. and v.

Strepent (stre·pĕnt), a. rare. [L. *strepent-em*, ppl. stem of *strepĕre*: see next.] Noisy.

Strepera·tion. rare. Obs.⁻¹.

Strepitant (stre·pĭtănt), a. [ad. L. *strepitant-em*, pr. pple. of *strepitāre*: see next.] Making a great noise, noisy.

Strepitate, v.

Stre·pitate, v. Obs.⁻¹.

Strepitation (strepitēi·ʃən). rare. [f. prec.] A repeated noise, clattering.

Streptious (stre·ptiŭs), a. [ad. mod.L. type *streptiōsus*, f. L. *streptus* noise, clatter, f. *streptere* to make a noise.

Streptitous.

Streptitous (stre·ptĭtŭs), a.

Strepsipterous (strepsi·ptĕrɒs), a. [f. mod.L. *Strepsiptera* neut. pl. + -OUS.] Belonging to the order *Strepsiptera* of insects (named by Kirby from the twisted front wings).

Also Strepsi·pteral a.; **Strepsi·pteran** a., sb. an insect of the order *Strepsiptera*.

Strepto- (stre·ptɒ), before a vowel **strept-**, combining form of Gr. στρεπτός twisted (f. στρέφειν to turn, twist), used in many scientific terms, as **Strepto·ster** [Gr. ἀστήρ star], a form of sponge-spicule (see quot. 1888). **Strepto·bacte·ria** [BACTERIUM] sb. pl., bacteria linked together like a chain. **Strepto·coccy·sin**, also (in shortened form) **strepto·lysin**, 'a hemolysin destructive to streptococci, formed when virulent streptococci are grown in blood serum' (Dorland Med. Dict. 1913). **Strepto·gyre** [-CYTE], an amœbiform body occurring in bead-like strings from the vesicles of foot-and-mouth disease. **Strepto·lysin** [LYSIN] = *Streptococcolysin*.

Also Strepto·spiral a.; **Strepto·zyma** a., also sb. an insect of the order *Streptozyma*.

Streptococcus (streptɒko·kŏs). *Bacteriology*. Pl. **-cocci** (-ko·ksəi, -koksī), [f. Billroth), f. Gr. στρεπτός = twisted (see STREPTO- b) + κόκκος berry. A form of bacterial organism in which the cells are arranged in chains or clusters.

Hence Streptoco·ccal (-kp·kăl), **-coccic** (-kp·ksik), adjs., pertaining to or produced by streptococcus.

Streptothrix (stre·ptŏθriks). *Bacteriology*. Pl. **-thricous** (-θrəi·sɒs), [mod.L., f. Gr. στρεπτός twisted (see STREPTO- b) + θρίξ, τριχ- hair].

Hence streptothri·cial a., of or relating to *streptothrix*.

Stress (stres), sb. Forms: 4-6 stres, 4-7 stresse, 5 stresce, strest, 6 Sc. straisse, 6 stress. [Prob. an aphetic form of DISTRESS sb., which occurs earlier in all the older senses; in ME. *destresse* and *streste* often appear as variant readings.

Stress (stres), v. [f. STRESS sb.]

STRESS.

Streful (stre·ful), a. [f. STRESS sb. + -FUL.]

Stressful (stre·sfŭl), a. [f. STRESS sb. + -FUL.] Full of, or subject to, stress or strain.

Stressless (stre·sles), a. [f. STRESS sb. + -LESS.] Having no stress, unstressed. Hence **stre·sslessness**.

Strēstrel, var. form of THESTLE.

Stretch (stretʃ), sb. Also 6 stretche, 7 stretch, Sc. stretch, stratch. [f. STRETCH v.]

STRETCH.

Stretch (stretʃ), v. Forms: see below.

Stretch (stretʃ), *v.*

Stretchable (stretʃabᵊl), *a.*

Stretched (stretʃt), *ppl. a.*

Stretcher (stretʃə(r)).

Stretching (stretʃiŋ), *vbl. sb.*

Stretching (stretʃiŋ), *ppl. a.*

Stretchless (stretʃles), a. [f. STRETCH sb. or v. + -LESS.] Incapable of being stretched.

Stretchling mince-veal. [f. STRETCH sb. or v. + -LING.] A minute quantity of space.

Stretchy, a. colloq. [f. STRETCH + -Y.]
1. Having the quality of stretching; elastic.
2. Liable to stretch unduly.
3. Inclined to stretch oneself or one's limbs.

Strete, aphetic f. ESTREAT; obs. f. STREET.

†Stretta (stre'ta). Mus. [It., fem. of stretto adj.: see next.]

Stretto (stre'to), adv. and sb. Mus. [It. = narrow]
A. adv. A direction to perform a passage.
B. sb. (See quot. 1869.)

Streugh, Streum: see STRAIGHT, STREAM.

Streven, -yn, -yng: see STRIVE v.

Strew (strū), sb. rare. [A number of things strewed over a surface or scattered about.]

Strew (strū), v. Also now arch. and dial. strow (strou). Pa. t. and pa. pple. strewed, strown; pa. pple. strewn.

Strewer (strū'ər). Also strower (strou'ər). [f. STREW v. + -ER.]

Strewing (strū'iŋ), vbl. sb. Also now arch. strowing (strou'iŋ). [f. STREW v. + -ING.]

Strewingly (strū'iŋli), adv. Obs. rare⁻¹. [f. strewing ppl. a. of STREW v. + -LY.]

Strewment (strū'mənt). rare. [f. STREW v. + -MENT.] Something strewed or for strewing.

Stria (strai'a). Pl. striæ (strai'ī). [L. stria a furrow; flute of a column. Cf. L. stria.]
1. Arch. A fillet between the flutes of columns, pilasters, and the like.
2. Chiefly in scientific use. A small groove, channel, or ridge; a narrow streak, stripe, or band of distinctive colour, structure, or texture.

Striated (strai'ēted), a. [f. prec. + -ED.]
1. In scientific use: Marked or characterized by striæ, furrowed, streaked.
2. Arch. Chanelled, grooved.
3. Constituting striæ.

Striation (strai'eijən). [f. action of STRIATE v.: see -ATION.]

Strick (strik), sb. Also 5 stryche, striche.

Strick, v. Sc. Chiefly in form strict. [perh. related to STRIKE v., cf. STRIKE v.]

Strick(e, obs. forms of STREAK sb., STRIKE v.

Stricken (stri'k'n), pa. pple. and ppl. a. [pa. pple. of STRIKE v.]

Strickland (strik'lənd).

Strickle (stri'k'l), sb. 1. Founding. 2. Also assol.

Strickling, vbl. sb.

Strict (strikt), a. Forms: 6 strykct, 6-7 strict, stricte, 7 (8-9 dial.) strick.
1. Drawn or pressed tightly together; tight, close. Obs.
2. Restricted or limited in amount, meaning, application, etc. Obs.
3. Accurately determined or defined; exact, precise, not vague or loose. † Of particulars: Enumerated or described in exact detail.
4. Of quality or condition, an attitude or line of action: Maintained to the full, admitting no deviation or abatement; absolute, entire, complete, perfect. (Cf. 13.)
5. With defining word: Restricted to the exact use or definition indicated by the word.
6. Of a calculated or measured result: Precise, exact; opposed to approximate.
7. Strict settlement: see quot. 1841.
8. Of truth, accuracy, etc.: Exactly and rigidly observed; exactly answerable to fact or reality.
9. Of confinement or imprisonment: Rigorous; severely restricted in regard to space or liberty of movement.
10. Of watch and ward, authority, discipline, obedience, etc.: Rigorously maintained, admitting no relaxation or indulgence.
11. Of a law, ordinance, etc., or its execution: Stringent and rigorous in its demands or provisions, allowing no evasion.

Striction (strik'ʃən). [ad. L. striction-em, n. of action f. stringere to draw tight, strain.]

Strictive (strik'tiv), a. [ad. L. strictiv-us.]

Strictly (strik'tli), adv. [f. STRICT a. + -LY.]
1. The action of straining.

Strictness (strĭktnĕs). [-NESS.] The quality or condition of being strict.

Strictures (strĭktŭrɪz).

Stricturation (strĭktūreɪʃən).

Strictured (strĭktūrd), a. Also 5 **stricture**.

Stricture (strĭktūr). Obs. rare.

Stricturotomy (strĭktūrŏtŏmɪ). Surg. rare.

Strid (strĭd). app. repr. OE. stride.

Straddle (strædl), sb. [f. the verb.] A stride.

Straddle (strædl), v. Obs. exc. dial. [Back-formation from STRADDLING adv.]

Straddling (strædlɪŋ), vbl. sb.

Straddling (strædlɪŋ), ppl. a.

Stride (straɪd), sb. Pa. t. **strode** (strəʊd).

Stride (straɪd), v. Pa. t. **strode** (strəʊd), pa. pple. **stridden** (strĭdn).

Striding (straɪdɪŋ), vbl. sb.

Striding (straɪdɪŋ), ppl. a.

Stridelong, adv. Obs. rare.

Strider (straɪdə(r)). [f. STRIDE v. + -ER.]

Stridence (straɪdĕns). [f. STRIDENT.]

Stridency (straɪdĕnsɪ). [f. STRIDENT.]

Strident (straɪdĕnt), a.

Striding (straɪdɪŋ), vbl. sb.

Striding (straɪdɪŋ), ppl. a.

Stridling, adv.

Stridor (straɪdə(r)). Also 7 **stridour**.

Stridulant (strĭdiūlănt), a.

Stridulate (strĭdiūleɪt), v.

Stridulation (strĭdiūleɪʃən).

Stridulator (strĭdiūleɪtə(r)).

Stridulatory (strĭdiūleɪtərɪ), a.

Stridulous (strĭdiūləs), a.

Strife (straɪf), sb.

Strifeful, a.

Strifeless, a.

Strift, obs. form of STRIFE v.

words] Pray for me—It is a strift, but I am safe.

Strift: see STRIF Obs., a measure for wine.

Strig (strig), sb. Also 6 **strigge**. [Of obscure origin.]

1. The stalk of a leaf, fruit or flower; a petiole, peduncle, or pedicel. Also, the stem of a fruit.

2. *Bot.* A row of stiff bristles; now, a stiff bristle (chiefly *pl.*).

† Strigate, a. *Obs.* [f. mod. L. *strigāt-us*, *strigillāt-us* ppl. a. of *strigāre*.] (See quot.)

Strigiate, a. *Obs.* [f. mod. L. *strigāt-us*.]

† Strigiliform, a. [ad. mod. L. -*FORM*.] Having the form of a strigil.

Strigillose (strī'dʒiləus). *Bot. rare.* [f. mod. L. *strigilla*, dim. of *STRIGA*.] Finely strigose.

† Strigment, *dim.* (see quot. in STRIGIL.)

Strigose (straigōus'), a. [f. mod.L. *strigōs-us*, f. L. *striga*: see STRIGA and -ATE ².] = STRIGOSE ² ².

Strigose (straigōus'), a. [f. *strig-, striga*, prec.] + ATE ².] Having a channelled surface.

a. *Min.* In Zool. (in specific name of a snake).

‡ Strigose (straidʒous'), *pl.* [L. *strigēs* (Vitruv.), synon. with *strix*, *strigae*: if the word be not a misreading, the sing. would normally be *striga*.] The channels of a fluted column.

Strigil (stri'dʒil). [ad. L. *strigil-is*, t *strigere* to touch lightly: see STRICTURE *sb.*]

1. *Rom. Antiq.* An instrument with a curved blade, for scraping the sweat and dirt from the skin in the hot-air bath or after gymnastic exercise. Also *applied transf.* to a flesh-brush or other instrument used for the same purpose.

Strigae (strai'dʒī). *Pl.* **strigae** (strai'dʒī). [L. *striga* furrow, swath of hay or corn, flute of a column (= *stria*).]

1. *Arch.* Obs.

2. *Bot.* A row of stiff bristles; now, a stiff hair.

3. *Ent.* (See quot.)

Strigilate (stri'dʒilət), a. [ad. mod. L. *strigilātus*, f. L. *strigil-is*: see STRIGIL.] (See quot.)

Strigillose (stri'dʒiləus), a. [f. mod. L. *strigilla*.]

† Striginous, a. *Obs. rare.* [f. mod. L. *strig-*, *striga* screech-owl + -OUS.]

Strigose ... see STRIGA and -OSE.]

Strigous (strai'dʒəs), a. Obs. rare. [f. mod. L. *striga* + -OUS.]

Strigula (stri'ɡjūlə). *Bot. rare.* [ad. L. *strigula*, dim. of STRIGA.] (See quot.)

Strigulose (strī'ɡjūlous'), a. [f. mod. L. *strigula* + -OSE.]

STRIKE.

Strike (straik), v. Pa. t. struck; also *arch.* stroke, struck; also *arch.* stricken.

STRIKE. 1129 STRIKE. STRIKE. 1130 STRIKE.

STRIKE. 1131 STRIKE. STRIKE. 1132 STRIKE.

STRIKE. 1133 STRIKE. STRIKE. 1134 STRIKE.

STRIKE. 1135 STRIKE. STRIKE. 1136 STRIKER.

Striking (strī·kiŋ), vbl. sb. [f. STRIKE v. + -ING¹.]

1. The action of STRIKE v., in various senses.

2. a. *Building, Carpentry, etc.* (see quot.).
 b. *Electr.* (see quot. 1893); **striking-earth** *Agric.*, soil for roots to strike in; **striking gear**, in a saw-mill; **striking-house** (a) *Mining* (see quot.); (b) *Agric.*, a house in which seeds, etc. are placed to 'strike', before they are planted out; **striking-iron**, a kind of harpoon; **striking knife**, (a) a triangular steel knife for sharpening saws; (Knight *Dict. Mech.* 1875); (b) *Carpentry*, a knife for marring or scribing (cf. sense 1 c); **striking-line**, a harpoon line; **strik·ing magnet** *Electr.* (see quot.); **striking-plate**, the metal plate against which the end of a spring-lock bolt strikes, when the door or lid is being closed; **striking-plough** (see quot. 1805); **strik·ing-reed** *Mus.*, a percussion reed (Stainer & Barrett); **striking-ring** *Billiards*, the D or half-circle in which a player whose ball is in hand must place it to make a stroke; **striking-tache** (see TACHE sb.² 2).

3. *striking* (strī·kiŋ), ppl. a. [f. STRIKE v.² + -ING².]

STRIND sb. Obs. In later use only sb. Forms: 1 (s)strend, 3 strund, strend, 5-6 strynd, 3-6 strond, 7, 9 strine, 9 strynne, strynde. See STREND v.

STRING (striŋ), sb. Forms: 1-6 streng, (pl. 3 strengen, -an, 5-6 strenges), 4-6 strang, strenge, 4-6 string, 5 streeng, 5-string. [OE. strenge = MLG. strenk, strenge, MDu. strenghe, strange, Du. streng...]

1. A line for binding or fastening anything; normally one composed of twisted threads of spun vegetable fibre.

STRING. 1139 STRING.

7. To empty, make bare, clear out (a place, thing) of its contents, ornaments, etc.

II. To doff, take off, peel away.

9. To remove (the clothes, a garment, trappings, hair) from a person, body, etc.

10. To disrobe, undress.

11. To remove (an adhering covering of skin,

Strip (strip), *sb.*[1]

Stripe (straip), *sb.*[1]

Stripe (straip), *v.*[1]

Striped (straipt), *ppl. a.*

Stripeless, *a. rare.*

Striping (straipin), *vbl. sb.*

Striplet, *a small strip.*

Stripling (striplin), *sb.*

Stripper[1] (stripar), *sb.*

Stripper[2]

Stripped (stript), *ppl. a.*

Strippage (stripedg), *rare.*

Stripping (stripin), *vbl. sb.*[1]

Stripping, *vbl. sb.*[2]

Stripping (stripin), *ppl. a.*

Strippy (stripi), *a. rare.*

Stript, variant of STRIPPED *ppl. a.*

Stripy (straipi), *a.*

Strit (strit), *Obs. exc. dial.*

Stritch (stritʃ), *Obs. exc. dial.*

Strive (straiv), *v.*

STRIVE.

Strivingly, *adv.* form of STERLING.

† Strivous, *a. Obs.* [f. STRIFE *sb.* + -OUS.] Full of strife.

Stro, obs. form of STRAW.

Stroak(e, obs. forms of STROKE *sb.* and *v.*

Stroaken, obs. pa. pple. of STRIKE *v.*

Stroam, strome (stroum), *v. Obs. exc. dial.* [Formed after *stroll* and *roam*.] To walk with long strides. Also to wander about idly.

10. To make one's way in effort.

Stroan, variant of STRONE.

Stroan, strone (stron), *v. Sc.* To make water, urinate.

Stroap, Sc. variant of STROUP *sb.* gullet.

Strobic (strō'bik), *a.* [ad. Gr. στροβό-s.] That has a spinning motion. *Strobic circles*: sets of concentric circles, toothed wheels, and the like, which appear to revolve when the surface on which they are inscribed is moved about.

Strobil, variant of STROBILE *sb. Obs.*

Strobila (strō'bilă). Pl. **strobilæ** (-lī). *Zool.* [mod.L. *strobila*, a. Gr. στροβίλη plug of lint twisted into the shape of a fir-cone.]

1. A stage in the development of certain Hydrozoa. *Also attrib.*

2. One who makes strenuous effort or endeavour.

Strobilaceous (strɒbilā'ʃəs), *a. Bot.* [f. mod.L. *strobilāce-us*, f. STROBIL-US: see -ACEOUS.] Relating to, or resembling, a strobilus.

Strobilation (strɒbilē'ʃən). *Zool.* [f. STROBILA + -ATION. Cf. STROBILIZATION.] The formation of strobilæ in Hydrozoa, tapeworms, etc.

Striving, *ppl. a.* [-ING¹.] That strives (in senses of the verb).

Striving, *vbl. sb.* [-ING¹.] The action of the verb STRIVE; an instance of this.

Strobile (strɒ'bil, -bail, -bil). Also 8–9 strobil. [a. F. *strobile* or ad. L. *strobil-us*, Gr. στρόβιλος.]

1. *Bot.* = STROBILA 1.

2. *Zool.* = STROBILA 2.

Strobiliform (strɒbi'lifɔːm), *a. Bot.*

Strobiline (strɒ'bilain), *a. Zool.* and *Bot.* [ad. Gr. στρόβιλ-os.] Shaped like a strobilus.

Stroboscope (strɒ'bəskoʊp). [f. Gr. στρόβος a whirling round + -SCOPE.]

Stroboscopic (strɒbəskɒ'pik), *a.* [f. prec. + -IC.] Relating to, or the nature of, the stroboscope.

Strobile (strɒ'bail). Also (in Dicts.) 7–9 stroosal, 8–9 strokal, 9 strocle,

strokle, strockle. [Of obscure origin.] (See quot.)

Strodle, strockle, see STRADDLE.

Stroddle, -in, obs. ff. of pa. t. STRIDE.

Stroddling, *Sc. Obs.* Also 9 stroddlyng. [Of obscure origin.] A foundling.

Stroe: see STRAW *sb.¹*, STREW *v.*

Strof, obs. pa. t. of STRIVE *v.*

Strog(e)l, strog(g)le, obs. ff. STRUGGLE.

Stroil (stroil), *v. = dial.* [Related origin.] Couch-grass.

Strok, obs. pa. t. of STRIKE *v.*

Strokal: see STROBILE.

Stroke (stroʊk), *sb.¹* Forms: α. 3–4 stroc, 4–7 strok, 4–5 strook, 5–8 strooke, 6 stroeke, 6–7 stroake, 7 strok, 4–6 strake, 5–9 strak, 6 strack, 4–6 strake, 5–9 strak, 6 strak, 6 strokke, 6 strake, Sc. 5–9 straik, 6 strack, 6 strake, 6 strak; γ. 4 struck, 6 strucke. [OE. *strác* = MHG., mod.G. *strich*.]

STROKE.

† 7. Smith *Panorama Sci.* § Art II. 745 Draperies are to be done with broad strokes of the pencil. 1869 Fortescue *Malietha* 85 It would seem laid on purposely with a coarse brush the strokes of which are very apparent.

† 10. Manner of handling the pencil, graver, etc.

† 12. Evelyn *Chalcogr.* 64 The imitations of the graver...

17. A linear mark : a mark traced by the moving point of a pen, pencil, etc. ; a component line of a written character (cf. *up-stroke*, *down-stroke*) ; also, a dash (in writing or print).

† 18. Lineament ; line of face or form.

† b. *fig.* A constituent feature ; a characteristic ; a trait of character. Obs.

c. *fig.* A felicitous or characteristic expression or thought in literary composition ; a 'touch' of description, satire, pathos, or the like. Cf. 15.

† d. *Stroke above* : 'a cut above' (Cut 2b. 17).

19. *To have a good stroke* (at eating) : to have a hearty appetite. Obs.

† 22. Transom 2. Obs. rare.

23. denomination of thy measure, varying in capacity according to locality : = Strike 2b. 4.

24. Geol. = Strike 2b. 8. rare.

25. attrib. & Golf, in terms relating to the method of scoring by strokes (sense 1 d) instead of by holes, as *stroke-competition*, *-game*, *-play* ; b. *Electricity* (sense 17 c), as *stroke-cultivation*, *-culture*, *-inoculation*; c. special combinations, † **stroke-bias**, an obsolete game resembling 'prisoners' base' ; † **stroke engraving**, a line engraving ; **stroke-hand**, an apparatus used for illegal capture of fish, formed of three hooks joined back to back, and weighted with lead ; hence **stroke-haul** v., **stroke-hauling** *vbl. sb.* ; **stroke-oar** (a) the oar nearest the stern of a rowing-boat ; (b) the rower who handles this oar (= sense 13 d) ; **stroke-oarsman** = sense 13 d ; **stroke-side**, the side of a rowing-boat on which the stroke-oarsman sits ; *stroke-stitch Needlework* (see quot.).

Stroke, *sb.* † ? Anglo-Irish. Obs. rare.

Stroke (str∂uk), *v.* Forms : 1 strácian, 3-4 straken, 6- stroke. [OE. strácian.]

1. *trans.* To rub (a surface) softly with the hand...

Stroke, *sb.* Obs. rare dial. Also 8 stroak. [Altered form of Strake *sb.*[1] = Strake *sb.*[1]]

Stroker (str∂u·kər). [f. Stroke *v.* + -er[1].] One who strokes.

Stroking (str∂u·kiŋ), *vbl. sb.* [f. Stroke *v.*]

Stroll (str∂ul). Also 7 stroule, strowle, 9 *rare* stroul. [Belongs to Stroll *v.*]

1. A stroller. Obs. U.S. (rare.)

2. A walk or ramble taken leisurely, a saunter.

Stroll (str∂ul), *v.* Also 7 stroule, strowle, stroule, strowl. [Of obscure origin...]

STROLLER.

Stroller (str∂u·lər). [f. Stroll *v.* + -er[1].] One who strolls.

1. A vagabond, vagrant ; an itinerant beggar or pedlar. Now *chiefly* U.S.

2. An itinerant actor ; a strolling player.

3. One who strolls or rambles ; a saunterer.

4. A parasitic insect.

5. A casual traveller or visitor.

Strolling (str∂u·liŋ), *vbl. sb.* [f. Stroll *v.* + -ing[1].] The action of the verb Stroll.

Strolling (str∂u·liŋ), *ppl. a.* [f. Stroll *v.* + -ing[2].] That strolls ; wandering, roving, itinerant.

STROMB.

Strom (strɒm), **strum.** Also 7 stroam, 8 strawm, 8-9 stroom. [f. a strumme v.] Obs. exc. dial.

1. *Brewing.* An oblong basket of wicker work placed over the bung-hole within the mash-tub to prevent the grains and hops passing through when the liquor is drawn off.

2. *Mining.* A kind of iron sieve placed round the suction-pipe of a pump to prevent obstruction.

Stroma (str∂u·ma), *sb.* Pl. **stromata.** [mod.L. *strōma*, a. Gr. στρῶμα bedding, fr. στρωννύναι to spread.]

1. *Anat.* The fibrous connective tissue or substance of a part or organ.

b. *Bot.* A structure containing the organs of fructification are immersed.

Stromal (str∂u·mal), *a.* [f. Stroma + -al.] Of or pertaining to a stroma.

Stromatic (strʊmæ·tik), *a.* rare. [f. Gr. στρωματ-, στρῶμα + -ic.] Bearing or producing a stroma.

Stromb (strɒm). [Anglicized form of Strombus.]

STROMBIFORM.

Strombiform (strʊ·mbifɔəm), *a. Zool.* [ad. mod.L. *strombiform*(*is*, f. L. *strombus* : see Strombus and -form. Cf. F. *strombiforme*.] Shaped like a stromb or strombus ; belonging or related to the Strombidæ.

Strombite (strɒ·mbəit). [f. Stromb + -ite.] A fossil stromb or strombus.

Strombid (strɒ·mboid), *a.* and *sb.* [f. Strombus + -oid.] *a.* sb. Resembling or related to a stromb or strombus.

Stromboid (strɒ·mboid), *a.* [f. Strombus + -oid.]

Strombolian (strʊmbō·liæn), *a.* [f. the name *Stromboli*, one of the Lipari Islands + -an.] Of, pertaining to or characteristic of Stromboli, a family of fishes of which the genus *Stromateus* is the type.

Strombus (strɒ·mbəs), *sb.* [mod.L., a. Gr. στρόμβος anything spiral, spiral snail-shell.]

Stromatiform (strʊmæ·tifɔəm), *a.* [f. Stromat-, Stroma + -form.] Having the form of a stroma.

Stromatoporid (strʊmatō·pərid), *a.* and *sb.* [f. mod.L. *Stromatoporid*a pl.] *sb.* A member of the Stromatoporidæ.

Stromatoporoid (strʊmatō·pərɔid), *a.* and *sb.* [f. mod.L. *Stromatopora* + -oid.]

Stromeyerine (strɒ·maiərin), *sb. Min.* prec. and -ine.] named after Fr. *Stromeyer*, the German chemist who first analysed it : see -ine.

Stromeyerite (strɒ·maiərəit), *sb. Min.* [f. the name *Stromeyer* + -ite.] Sulphide of silver and copper, of steel-gray colour and metallic lustre.

Stromming (strɒ·miŋ), *sb.* Also 8 *Sw.* *strömming*, 9 *Sw.* strömming, 8-9 **stromling.** [f. Sw. *strömming*.]

Stromnite (strɒ·mnəit), *sb. Min.* [Named by T. S. Traill 1819, from *Stromness*, Orkney Isl., its locality : see -ite.] A variety of strontianite.

Stromb, variant of Strumpet.

STRONG.

Strone[1]. Obs. rare. [Of obscure origin.]

Strone[2] (str∂un), *a. Sc. rare.* [ad. Gael. *srōn*, nose, promontory.] A hill that terminates a range, the end of a ridge ; (Sc.).

Strong (strɒŋ), *a.* Forms : 1-2 strang, strong, 3-6 *a*-strang ; 4-6 stronge, 4 strang. [OE. *strang*, *strong*, = OFris. *strang*, OS. *strang*, MLG. *strank*, etc.]

I. *a.* 379 He ran no risk but of a sound ducking, being, of course, a strong swimmer.

1. Physically strong or robust ; capable of physical endurance or exertion ; not readily affected by disease, fatigue, etc. ; specifically (of a person) who has regained his normal health and vigour after illness.

b. Of living beings, or their limbs : Physically powerful ; able to exert great muscular force.

2. *Strong meat* : solid food.

b. of the vital organs and their functions, the nerves, brain, etc.

Strong, v. Obs. Forms: 1–2 strangian, strongian, 3 strange-n, 3–5 stronge-n.

Strong-box. A strongly made chest or safe for money, documents, or other valuables.

Strong-breathed ppl. a. Obs.

Strong drink. Intoxicating liquor, alcoholic liquors generally.

Strongful, a. Obs. rare—¹.

Strongish (strǫ̆ŋiʃ), a.

Strongle, obs. var. STRANGLE v.

Strong-handed, a.

Stronghead (strǫ̆ŋhĕd), a.

Stronghold (strǫ̆ŋhōld). A strongly fortified place of defence, a secure place of refuge or retreat, a fastness.

Strongish (strǫ̆ŋiʃ), a. (1–)

Strongle, obs. var. STRANGLE v.

Strongly (strǫ̆ŋli), adv. Forms: see STRONG a. and -LY2.

Strong-minded (strǫ̆ŋmaind), a.

Strong-mt ndedness.

Strong-ness (strǫ̆ŋnes). rare. The quality of being strong.

Strong room. A room made specially secure for the custody of persons or things; esp. a fire- and burglar-proof room in which valuables are deposited for safety.

Strong water. [Rendering of med.L. aqua fortis.]

†**1.** = AQUAFORTIS 1, 2. Obs.

2. Any form of alcoholic spirits used as a beverage.

3. Comb. With ppl. adjs., as strongly-bound, -drawing, -made, -marked, -scented, -shod, -worded; also occas. with adjs. in -ED2, forming combs.

Strongyle (strǫ̆ŋil). Zool. [ad. Gr. στρογγύλος round.] A thread-worm of the genus Strongylus (of which this is the type), common as a disease-producing parasite in various animals.

Strongyloid (strǫ̆ŋiloid), a.

Strontian (strǫ̆nʃi·an). Min. [f. Strontian, name of a parish in Argyllshire.]

Strontianic, a. Obs. [f. piec. + -IC.]

Strontianiferous, a.

Strontianite (strǫ̆nʃi·anait). Min. Native strontium carbonate.

Strontic (strǫ̆ntik), a. Chem. [f. STRONTI-UM + -IC.] Of or pertaining to strontium.

Strontites. (Said of salts: now superseded by the attrib.)

†**Strontites.** Obs. Strontic oxide.

Strontium (strǫ̆nʃiǒm). Chem. [f. STRONTIAN + -IUM.] The metallic base of strontia; a dark-yellow metal, fusible at red heat.

Stronk(e, -onk: see STRINK v., STRUNK v.

†Strontiane. Chem. Obs. [f. STRONTIUM + -ANE.]

Struntia (strǫ̆nʃiǎ). Chem. [f. STRONTIAN-.]

Stroke(, -or: see STRIKE v., STROKE.

Stroop(, obs. form of STROUP dial.

Strook(e, obs. form of STRUCK, STROKE.

Stroop, sb. Forms: 5–6 stroupe, 5–6 strop, strope. [ad. ON. strúpi (also strjúpe) MSw., mod.Sw. strupe, Da. strube, throat.]

Strop, sb.¹ dial. form [Cf. STRAP sb.¹]

Strop (strǫp), v.² dial. [Cf. STRAP v.², STRIP v.²]

†Strope, v. Obs. rare.

Strophanthus (strǫfa·nþǒs). [mod.L. (De Candolle 1802), f. Gr. στροφός twisted cord + ἄνθος flower.]

Strophe (strǫ̆fi). Pl. strophes (-īz), strophæ (strǫ̆fī). [a. L. from στροφή, a. Gr. στροφή, lit. 'turning', f. στρέφ-ειν, στροφεύ-ειν to turn.]

Strophiolate (strǫ̆fiǒleit), a. Bot. [ad. mod.L. strophiolatus.]

Strophiole (strǫ̆fiǒl). Bot. [a. mod.L. strophiolum.]

Strophoid (strǫ̆foid). Geom. [ad. F. strophoïde, f. Gr. στροφός twisted cord : see -OID.]

Strophula (strǫ̆fiūlǎ). Path. [mod.L. ('Kedlogoworde, strophulus' Huloet 1552, and later Lat.-Eng. Dicts.)]

Stroppe, obs. form of STROUP.

Stropper (strǫ̆pǎr). [f. STROP v.¹ + -ER¹.]

Strother. north. Obs. Also 3 strothre, stroudyr, strowthr, struther, struthyr. [OE. strōd marsh.]

Strothir. Obs. rare—¹.

Stro-thir. Obs. rare.

Stroubance, -ulance, 5–6 -lana, 6 lens. [Aphetic f. DISTROUBANCE.]

Stroublance, obs. form of DISTURBANCE.

Strouble, a. Obs. rare—¹.

Strouble, v. Obs. [Aphetic f. DISTROUBLE v.]

Strous, obs. var. STROUSE.

Strout, v. Obs. Also strowte.

Strout, sb. Obs. rare. Also stroute.

Stroud (stroud). ? Obs. Also 8 strowd. [f. Stroud in Gloucestershire.]

Strounce, obs. va. STROUP.

Stroy (stroi), v. Obs. and arch. Forms: a. 2–3 stroye, 3–4 stroie, 4 stroy, stroi, 4 atray(e, 4–5 stroi-e, 5–6 stroye, 6 stroye. [Aphetic f. DESTROY v.]

Struction. Obs. Forms: 3 strucion, 4 stru-ccioun, 4 structioun.

Strucken, obs. pa. pple. of STRIKE v.

Struction, v. Obs. [Aphetic f. DESTROY v.]

Struck (strǫk), ppa. t. and pa. pple. of STRIKE v.

Strucken, obs. pa. pple. and pa. t. of STRIKE v.

Structor. Obs. rare⁻¹. [a. L. structor, agent-n. from struĕre to build.] A builder.

Structural (strŭ'ktiŭrăl), a. [f. STRUCTURE sb. + -AL.] Of or pertaining to structure.

1. Of or pertaining to the art or practice of building.

2. Of or pertaining to the structure of a building as distinguished from its decoration or fittings. *Structural load* (see quot. 1883).

3. Of or pertaining to the arrangement and mutual relation of the parts of any complex unity.

4. In various scientific uses.

Structure (strŭ'ktiŭr), sb. [ad. L. structūra, i. struĕre, structus to build : see STRUCT- f. structure, Sp., Pg. estructura, It. struttura.]

1. The action, practice, or process of building or construction. Now *rare* or Obs.

2. Manner of building or construction ; the way in which an edifice, machine, implement, etc. is made or put together.

3. The mutual relation of the constituent parts or elements of a whole as determining its peculiar nature or character ; make, frame.

4. Of a branch of a science : Concerned with the study of the structures of natural products.

5. Geol., Min., etc.

6. In a wider sense : A fabric or framework of material parts put together.

b. A building or edifice of any kind, esp. a pile of building of some considerable size and imposing appearance.

Structure (strŭ'ktiŭr), v. [f. prec.]

Structured (strŭ'ktiŭrd), ppl. a.

Structureless (strŭ'ktiŭrlĕs), a. [f. STRUCTURE sb. + -LESS.] Lacking organic structure.

Structurer (strŭ'ktiŭrĕr). rare⁻¹. [f. STRUCTURE v. + -ER.] An architect, a builder or constructor.

Structurist (strŭ'ktiŭrist). rare. [f. STRUCTURE sb. + -IST.] A builder.

Struggle (strŭ'g'l), v. Also 8 struggle. [f. STRUGGLE v.]

1. An act of struggling ; a resolute contest, whether physical or otherwise ; a continued effort to resist force or free oneself from constraint ; a strong effort under difficulties.

b. A strong effort to continue to breathe, as in the death-agony or under conditions tending to produce suffocation.

Struggle (strŭ'g'l), v. Also 8 struggle. [f. STRUGGLE sb.]

1. intr. To contend (with an adversary) in a close grapple as in wrestling ; also, in wider use, to make violent bodily movements in order to resist force or free oneself from constraint ; to exert one's physical strength in persistent striving against an opposing force.

2. intr. To contend (with difficulty) ; to contend resolutely with (a task, burden) ; to strive to do something difficult. Also const. at.

3. fig. To contend (with) or against ; to contend resolutely, esp. with or for obstinate resistance; to make violent efforts to escape from constraint. Const. with, against, for.

4. To make great efforts in spite of difficulties ; to contend resolutely with (a task, burden).

Struggle-for-lifer. slang. [The phrase struggle for life (see STRUGGLE sb. 1 d) + -ER.]

Struggler (strŭ'glĕr). [f. STRUGGLE v. + -ER.] One who struggles.

Struggling (strŭ'gliŋ), vbl. sb. [f. STRUGGLE v. + -ING.]

1. The action of STRUGGLE v.

2. Effervescence. (Cf. STRUGGLE sb. 1 c.) Obs.

Struggling (strŭ'gliŋ), ppl. a. [f. STRUGGLE v. + -ING.] That struggles ; in recent use, of a lawyer, etc., struggling to keep themselves alive.

Strugling, var. of STRUGGLING.

Struke, obs. pa. t. of STRIKE v.

Strullbrug (strŭ'lbrŭg). Also 8 (Swift) -brug : (wrongly 8, 9 Struldbrug) [Arbitrarily formed.] In Swift's Gulliver's Travels, given as the native appellation of the "immortals" in the kingdom of Luggnagg, who were incapable of dying, but after the age of eighty continued to age legally dead, and receiving a small pittance from the state. Hence in allusive uses.

Hence **Strŭldbrŭ'ggian** a., of or pertaining to a Struldbrug. **Strŭldbrŭggism**, the condition or practice of a Struldbrug.

Strum (strŭm), sb.¹ [Abbreviated form of STRUMPET.] A strumpet, prostitute.

Strum (strŭm), sb.² = STROM.

Struma (strū'mă), sb. Pl. strumæ ; also 6 strumas, 7 -ans, 7-8 -a's. See also STRUME. [mod.L. use of L. strūma scrofulous tumour.]

1. Path. = SCROFULA. Also applied to tubercular disease, esp. in mod.L. specific designations as Struma aberrata, etc.

2. Bot. = STRUMA.

3. Hair.

4. Nat. Hist. Having a natural protuberance on some part of the body. Struma Lizard [see quot.].

Strumatic (strumæ'tik), a. rare⁻¹. [ad. late L. strūmaticus.] = STRUMOUS.

Strumat'cal, var. STRUMMEL a. and sb.²

Strumble, var. STRUMMEL a. and sb.²

Strume (strūm), sb. Obs. rare. [? Altered form of STRUMA.] = STRUMA.

Strumiferous (strumi'fĕrŭs), a. rare. Bearing a struma.

Strumiform (strū'mifŏrm), a. [ad. mod.L. strūmiform-is.] Having the appearance of a struma.

Strumose (strū'mōs), a. [ad. L. strūmōs-us.]

Strumous (strū'mŭs), a. [ad. L. strūmōs-us.]

1. Affected with struma ; characteristic of or indicative of a scrofulous disposition.

2. Bot. Having a struma.

3. Nat. Hist. Having a protuberance.

Strumpery. Obs. Also 6 strumperie.

Strumpet (strŭ'mpĕt), sb. Forms : 4 strumpat, strompet, 4-5 -ette, 5 strompett, 6 strompet, 6 strumpat, stromppet, 7 strumpett, (6-7), 7 strumpet, 5- strumpet.

1. The action of the verb STRIKE.

2. A woman who is sexually promiscuous, a harlot, prostitute.

b. fig. and in figurative contexts.

Strumpet (strŭ'mpĕt), v. To make a strumpet of.

Hence **Strŭ'mpeted** ppl. a. ; **strumpet-blood**, flattery ; **strumpet-wise** adv. ; **strumpet-like** adj.

Strumpet, obs. form of TRUMPET.

Strumpetly, *a.* and *adv. Obs. rare.* [f. 1 and 3] Like a strumpet.

Strumphause, *Obs.*—¹ (of obscure origin).

Strumple. *Obs.* In 6 strumpell. [Alteration of STRIPPLE (? influenced by STRUT).] The fleshy stem of a horse's tail.

Strumstrum. *Obs. rare.* [Echoic reduplication: see STRUM.] A rude stringed instrument.

Stramulose (strǣ'miŏləs), *a.* [f. L. *stramul-* as *stramulosa* dim. of *stramen*: see STRAMINEOUS.] Having a small straw.

Strund(e: see STRAND *sb.,* STRIND¹ and V.

Strung (strụŋ), *ppl. a.* [pa. pple. of STRING *v.*] Furnished or fitted with strings or a string.

Strunt, *a. north. Obs.* [Cf. STRUM *sb.*, *north.*] A fit of ill-humour or sulks; *esp.* in phr. *to take the strunt.*

Strunt (strǫnt), *v.*¹ *trans.* To cut short; *esp.* to dock the tail (of a horse or sheep). Hence Stru'nted *ppl. a.*

Strunt, *v.*² *Sc.* [Cf. STRUT *v.*; also Norw. *strunta* to walk stiffly as under a burden; to be haughty and stiff in manner (Ross).] *intr.* To move with a self-important air.

Struntian (strǫ'ntian), *north. Obs.* [Of obscure origin.]

Strunty (strǫ'nti), *a. Sc.* and *north.* [f. STRUNT *a.* or *v.*¹ + -Y¹.] Stunted, short.

Struse. *Obs.* Also 7 strusse. [? rep. Russian *strugǔ*, *struskǔ*, dim. of *strug*, a kind of large boat (see quot. c 1531).] (See quots.)

Strusion. *Obs. rare.*—¹ Meant to represent an illiterate corruption : *for* destruction.

Strust, *v. Obs.* Also 5 strost. [An unexplained alteration of TRUST *v.*], *trans.* and *intr.* To trust. So **Strust'y**, *a.*—TRUSTY.

Strut (strǫt), *sb.*¹ Forms : 3-4 strut, 4 strot, 5 strutt, 3-4,7- strut. See also STRUT *sb.*² and STRUT-*v.*² [Cf. STRUT *v.*] The act of strutting; deflection (of the spoke of a wheel) from the perpendicular.

Strut (strǫt), *sb.*² Also 7-9 strutt. [Proximate origin obscure ; from the root of STRUT *sb.*¹ or Cf. LG. *strutt*, rigid.]

Strut (strǫt), *v.*¹ Infected strutted, strutting. Forms: *a.* 1 strútian, 3-7 stroute, 4-7 strute, 6 strutte, 6-9 strout, 6-7 strute, 6 strutte, 7 strutt, 6- strut. [The forms represent OE. *strútian*, prob. f. **strút* STRUT *sb.*²; corresponding formations are mod.G. dial. *straussen* to wrangle, Da. *strude* to strut ; also with difference of conjugation, MHG. *striuzen* wk. v. to contend, struggle (mod.G. dial. *sträussen*).]

Strut, *v.*² *Sc.* [Cf. STRUT *v.*¹; also Norw. *strutt* to walk stiffly as under a burden.]

Strut (strǫt), *sb.*³ The act of strutting ; a strutting gait.

Strut, *sb.*⁴ [f. STRUT *v.*¹] The act of strutting ; also ellipt. for strut-belliied adj.

Strutting (strǫ'tiŋ), *vbl. sb.* [f. STRUT *v.*¹ + -ING¹.] The action of strutting or bulging out, or swaggering.

Strutting (strǫ'tiŋ), *ppl. a.* [f. STRUT *v.*¹ + -ING².]

Struttle (strǫ't'l), *dial.* Corruption of *stuttle* (bar²), dial. var. of STICKLEBACK.

Struverite (strū'vərǝit), *Min.* [ad. G. *strüverit* (A. Brezina 1876), f. name of Prof. G. Strüver, of Rome : see -ITE.]

Struvite (strū'vǝit), *Min.* [ad. G. *struvit* (G. L. Ulex 1846), f. name of *Struve*, Russian minister at Hamburg : see -ITE.] Hydrous phosphate of ammonium and magnesium, found in small yellowishbrown or greyish crystals.

Stry, obs. form of STROY *v.*

Strychnia (strik'niă), *Chem. Obs.* see -IA.] = STRYCHNINE.

Strychnic (strik'nik), *a.* = STRYCHN-OS.

Strychnine (strik'nǝin, -in), *Chem.* [a. F. *strychnine*, f. L. *strychnos*, a. Gr. *στρύχνος*, nightshade : see -INE.]

Strychnin-ize, *v. trans.*, to poison by strychnine.

Strychnos (strik'nɒs), *Bot.* Also strychnus, pl. strychni. [mod.L., *Linnæus* 1737) use of L. *strychnos* (Pliny), a. Gr. *στρύχνος*, a kind of nightshade.]

Stub (stǫb), *sb.* Forms : 1 stubb, styb(b, (steb), 3-7 stubbe, 4-9 stubb, 6 stoube, 4- stub. [OE. *stubb*, *styb(b* masc.—(M)LG., MDu. *stubbe* stump, MHG. *stübbe*, G. *stübben* (cf. MSw., stubbe, Sw., stubbe, Norw., stubbe, OE. dial. *stub*; related to Gr. *στύπος* stem, stump.]

Stub (stǫb), *v.* Forms : 1 stubb, styb(b, (steb), 3-7 stubbe, 4-9 stubb, 6 stoube, 4- stub. [f. STUB *sb.*] To grub up by the roots; to clear of stubs.

Stub-iron. [f. STUB *sb.* 6] A tough, fibrous, wrought iron obtained from stub-nails, horseshoe nails, etc., used for making gun-barrels.

Supplement, p. 3873; Corrigenda, p. 4092; Spurious words, p. 4093; Books quoted, p. 4094

(dictionary text, STUDY entry, continued)

Study (stŭdi), *v.* Pa. t. and pa. pple. **studied**. Forms: 3–7 **studie**, 4 **studie**, studie, 4–6 **studye**, 5 **studyen**, 4–5 **stodie**, 4–6 **stodye** (6 pres. pple. **stoding**), 7–8 **studdy**, etc. See also **Estudy**. [ME. *studie*, a. OF. *estudie* (semi-popular *estudier* (mod.F. *étudier*)), f. L. *studēre*.]

I. *Intransitive uses.*

1. To apply the mind to the acquisition of learning, whether by means of books, observation, or experiment.

2. To exercise oneself, employ one's thought or effort in.

3. To meditate, reflect, or cogitate.

Studyaunt(e, -**ent(e,** obs. forms of **Student.**

Studying (stŭdiiŋ), *vbl. n.* [f. Study *v.* + -ing.] The action of the verb Study.

Studyism, *rare*⁻¹. [f. Study + -ism.] Not addicted to study.

Stue, obs. var. Stew *sb.*¹, *sb.*², Stew *v.*

Stuer, var. Sture, a sturgeon.

Stuerd, e, Stuerne, obs. f. Steward, Stern *a.*

Stufa, obs. f. Stove.

Stuff, *sb.* Forms: 4–5 *stof*, 5–6 *stoffe*, 5–6 *stuffe*, 4 *stuff*. [ME. *stuff*, *stof*, a. OF. *estoffe* (mod.F. *étoffe*) fem., material, furniture, provision (mod.F. *étoffe*), = Pr., Sp., Pg. *estofa*, It. *stoffa*; cf. also *estoffer* vb., textile material) = Pr., Sp., Pg.

Stuffer, obs. f. Stiver.

Supplement, p. 3873; Corrigenda, p. 4092; Spurious words, p. 4093; Books quoted, p. 4094

STUFF.

1185

Cycl. XVII. 208/1 The pulp, or *stuff*, as it is technically called, is now ready to be made into paper. ...

d. Mining. Material of rock, earth, or clay containing ore, metal, or precious stones.

5. Material for making garments; woven material of any kind.

II. In particular sense: A kind of stuff; a textile fabric.

6.a. A woollen fabric (see quot.).

b. *attrib.* A woollen manufacture.

c. As the material for the gown worn by a junior counsel. Hence *rarely*, A stuff-gownsman; i.e. a junior counsel, as distinguished from a 'silk' (see SILK *sb.* 3 d).

III. Matter of an unspecified kind.

6. The general designation for solid, liquid, or rarely) gaseous matter of any kind: used indefinitely instead of the specific designation, or where no specific designation exists. Often applied to a preparation or composition used for some special purpose.

7. *transf.* and *fig.* in non-physical sense.

8. Literary or artistic matter; compositions, productions. Now *rare* exc. with disparaging implication (cf. 8), and *colloq.* among journalists and professional authors = 'copy'.

8.b. *colloq.* The material of which a person is made.

STUFF.

1186

11. *attrib.* and *Comb.*

a. *attrib.* passing into *adj.* Made of stuff or woollen cloth (see sense 5c).

b. *simple attrib.*, as *stuff-goods*, *-manufacture*, *-mercer*, *-trade*; *objective*, as *stuff-finisher*, *-maker*, *-manufacturer*, *-seller*, *-weaver*; *stuff-weaving*-vb. *sb.*; *parasynthetic*, as *stuff-bottomed*, *adj.*

Stuff,

sb.[2] Now S. African. Also *5 stuf* [a. Du. *stof* dust; powder (...)].

Stuff,

v.[1] Forms: 4–5 stoff, 6 stuffe, 7–9 stuff [a. OF. *estof(f)er* (NE dial. *stofier*: Anglo-Latin *stuffare*) to furnish, equip, garrison (mod.F. *étoffer*, to furnish with what is necessary...)].

STUFF.

1187

10. To fill (oneself, one's stomach, etc.) to repletion with food. Also *said* of the food.

11. To fill (something, esp. loose materials) tightly into a receptacle or cavity. Also *fig.*

12. To thrust (something, esp. loose materials) tightly into a receptacle or cavity.

13. To treat (something, esp. loose materials) tightly into a receptacle or cavity.

14. *Leather-manuf.* The process of stuffing.

STUFFAT.

1187

To cause stuffiness (in the head or nose).

Stuffed,

ppl. a. [f. STUFF *v.[1]* + -ED [1].]

1. † a. Well stored or provided (*obs.*).

2. Of a person, the like: Filled out with some distending or stiffening material.

3. Filled with forcemeat or minced seasoning before cooking.

4. Of a fowl, joint, fish, etc.: Filled with forcemeat or minced seasoning before cooking.

5. Filled out or distended.

Stuffer

(stə'fər). [f. STUFF *v.[1]* + -ER [1].]

1. A person who stuffs or fills; one whose trade it is to stuff (...).

Stuffat,

-et. *Obs.* [ad. F. estuve (...).]

STUFFED.

1188

3. The state or sensation of stoppage or obstruction in the throat or nose.

Stuffing,

vbl. sb. [f. STUFF *v.[1]*]

1. The action of the vb. STUFF in various senses.

2. *concr.* The material with which anything is stuffed.

3. *Leather-manuf.* The process of rubbing a mixture of fish-oil and tallow; the mixture used for this.

Stuffy,

a. [f. STUFF *sb.[1]* + -Y.]

1. Of material used for furnishing; made of or consisting of stuff.

2. Cookery. Stuffing, forcemeat.

Stuffily,

adv. [f. next + -LY [2].]

Stuffiness.

[-NESS.] The quality or state of being stuffy.

† Stug, sb.[1] Obs. rare. In 5 stugg(e)r. [Cf. STOCK sb.[1] 22.] A pig-trough.

Stug (stɒg), sb.[2] Sc. [Cf. STOG sb.[2]]
1. A stab, thrust.
b. A Scot. Form of (E.D.D. s.v. Stag.[1]) Quo' he, let's steely gie's a stug.
2. Curling. (See quot.)

Stug (stɒg), v. Sc. [Cf. STOG v.[2]] trans. To stab, pierce with a weapon.

Stuggy (stɒgi), a. dial. [Related to stug, STUCK a.]

† Stülage, stü'ling, Sc. Obs. rare. (Sense obscure: explained by editor as 'ballast'.)

Stülify, var. STULTIFY, Obs.

Stulk, var. of STALK sb.

Stull (stʌl), sb.[1] Mining. [Perh. a. G. stollen (OHG. stolla, MHG. stolle) a support, prop.

Stull (stʌl), sb.[2] Mining. [Perh. a. G. stolln (stolln) of the same meaning.]

Stull, var. of error for STALKO Anglo-Irish.

Stulko, var. of STALKO Anglo-Irish.

Stull-piece (stʌl-piːs), sb. Mining. [f. STULL sb.[1] + PIECE sb.]

Stulm (stʌlm), sb. Mining. [f. as prec., in another form.]

Stulp (stʌlp), sb. [Cf. STOOP sb.[5]]

† Stult. Obs. rare. A derisive name for a tailor.

Stultification (stʌltɪfɪkeɪʃən). [f. STULTIFY + -ATION.] The action of stultifying; an instance of this.

Stultify (stʌltɪfaɪ), v. [ad. L. stultificāre, f. stultus foolish, fool + -FY.]
1. trans. Law. To allege or prove to be of unsound mind
b. To render nugatory, worthless, or useless.
2. To regard as a fool or fools.

Stülti-loquence (stʌltɪləkwens). [ad. L. stultiloquentia.] Foolish talking.

Stulti-loquent (stʌltɪləkwent), a. [f. L. stultiloqu-us + -ENT.] Talking foolishly.

Stulti-loquy (stʌltɪləkwi). [L. stultiloquium.] Foolish talking.

Stulti-tious a. Obs. rare. [f. L. stulti-loqu-us + -OUS.] Foolish, ridiculous.

Stu-lty, a. Obs. [app. f. L. stult-us foolish + -Y.] Foolish, stupid.

Stum (stʌm), sb. Also 8 stumm, stume. [Du. stom, subst. use of stom foolish. Cf. STUM v.]

Stum (stʌm), v. [f. prec.] trans. or partly fermented grape-juice, must.

Stumble (stʌmb'l), v. Also 6 stumble. [f. STUMBLE sb.]
1. intr. To miss one's footing, or trip over an obstacle, in walking or running, so as to fall or be in danger of falling.
2. To fumigate (a cask) with burning sulphur.

Stumble (stʌmb'l), sb. Also 6 stumble. [f. STUMBLE v.]
1. An act of stumbling.
a. A missing one's footing, a partial fall.
b. fig. An instance of erring.

Stumbling (stʌmblɪŋ), vbl. sb. [f. STUMBLE v. + -ING[1].] The action of STUMBLE v. in various senses.

Stumbling, ppl. a. [f. as prec. + -ING[2].] That stumbles, in various senses of the verb.

Stumbling-block, sb. [STUMBLING vbl. sb.]

Stumblingly (stʌmblɪŋli), adv. [f. STUMBLING ppl. a. + -LY[2].]

Stumbly (stʌmbli), a. [f. STUMBLE v. + -Y.] Addicted to stumbling.

Stumer (stjuːmə(r)), sb. slang. Also stumor. [Of unknown origin.] A forged or dishonoured cheque; a counterfeit bank-note or coin.

Stume, obs. form of STUM.

Stumie, stummel, obs. forms of STUMBLE v.

Stumm, stummed, var. STUMBLE v.

Stummer (stʌmə(r)), v. Obs. [? exc. dial.] intr. To stumble (lit. and fig.).

Stummy (stʌmi), sb. Also stum, + -Y.]

Stummmel, obs. var. of STOMACH.

Stummy, var. STUMMY sb.

Stump (stʌmp), sb. Also 3–6 stumpe, 4 stompe, 6– stump. [First in 14th c. a. or cogn. w. MLG. stump masc., stumpe fem., = MDu. stump, (M)Du. stomp ...]
1. The part of a tree-trunk remaining in the ground.
2. The portion of the trunk of a felled tree-trunk.
3. Something (as a pencil, quill pen, cigar) that has been reduced by wear or consumption to a small part of its original length; a fag-end.
4. A broken-off end of something. Also a splinter (cf. STUB sb.).
5. A rudimentary limb or member, or one that has the appearance of being mutilated.
6. The stalk of a plant (esp. cabbage) when the leaves are removed.
7. A post, a short pillar not supporting anything.

Stump (stʌmp), v. Also 4–6 stumpe. [f. STUMP sb.]

Stumper (stʌmpə(r)), sb.

Stumping (stʌmpɪŋ), vbl. sb.

Stump (stɒmp), *sb.*3 [f. STUMP *v.*1]

1. A heavy step or gait, as of a lame or wooden-legged person.

Stump (stɒmp), *v.* [Partly from the attrib. use of STUMP *sb.*1, but perh. partly an original vb., corresponding to or adopted from Du., LG. *stump*.]

1. Worn down to a stump.

Stump (stɒmp), *sb.*2 [Of obscure history.]

Stump (stɒmp). Also 7 stompe, 5–6, 9 *dial.* stomp. [f. STUMP *sb.*1]

1. To stumble over a tree-stump or other obstacle. Also, to walk stumblingly (in quot. *fig.*).

Stumpy (stɒ·mpi), *sb.* [f. STUMP *sb.*1 + -Y.]

1. A spiritual party.

Stumpy (stɒ·mpi), *a.* [f. STUMP *sb.*1 + -Y.]

1. Like a stump; short and thick. Of grass, etc. Full of stumps or short hard stalks.

Stun (stɒn), *v.* [ME. *stunie*, *stonie*, OE. *stunian*, ad. a stem *stun-* : cf. STOUND *sb.* and STONE *v.*]

1. The act of stunning or dazing; a stunning effect; the condition of being stunned.

Stundist (stɒ·ndist). Also 9 Stundist, of which this is a doublet. Cf. also STONY, STOYNE *vbs.*

Stunkard, *a.* *Sc.* Also -kert, -kerd, stonkard, -art. [Of obscure origin.] Sulky, sullen.

Stunner (stɒ·nəɹ). [f. STUN *v.* + -ER.]

1. Something that stuns or dazes; something that amazes or astounds.

Stunning (stɒ·niŋ), *vbl. sb.* [-ING.1] The action of the verb STUN; the state of being stunned.

Stunning (stɒ·niŋ), *ppl. a.* [-ING.2]

1. That stuns or stupefies; dazing, astounding.

Stunningly (stɒ·niŋli), *adv.* [-LY.2]

Stunning-flash sb.

Stunt (stɒnt), *sb.*1 [f. STUNT *v.*1]

1. A check in growth; also, a state of arrested growth or development.

Stunt (stɒnt), *sb.*2 [Of obscure origin.]

Stunt (stɒnt), *v.*1 [f. STUNT *a.*]

1. To be or become angry. (Cf. STUNT *a.* 3.) To bring to an abrupt stand; to nonplus. *Obs.*

Stunt (stɒnt), *a.* [OE. *stunt* foolish, corresp. to MHG., stunt stupid, short. OE. *stunt* = earlier *stunt* (also *sturt*)...]

1. Foolish. *Obs.*

Stunted (stɒ·nted), *ppl. a.* [f. STUNT *v.*1 + -ED.1]

Stuntly, *adv.* *Obs.* [OE. only.]

1. Foolishly.

Stuntness. *Obs. rare*−1. [f. STUNT *a.* + -NESS.] Stupidity.

beora lac to eorðfæstum stane..And nellað under-standan hu stuntlice hi doð.

2. ? Arrogantly.

1581 A. HALL *Iliad* x. 174 Their state recite and eke their race, and doe not stuntly talke, Still with a lowe and courteous grace let there the speeches walke.

Stu·ntness. [f. STUNT *a.* + -NESS.]

†**1.** Foolishness, stupidity. *Obs.*

c 1000 ÆLFRIC *Saints' Lives* i. 228 Þysses middan-eardes wysdom is stuntnis [L. *stultitia*] ætforan gode. *Ibid.* xvii. 23 Se rihtwisa soðlice ne þearf him ondrædan..ȝif he him sylfum styrð fram eallum stunt-nyssum. *c* 1175 *Lamb. Hom.* 117 Feia stuntnesse beoð, þer nan steore ne bið.

2. Abrupt brevity.

1871 J. EARLE *Philol. Eng. Tongue* x. 497 Short sentences are prevalent in our language, as long ones are in German. In all things we incline to curtness and stuntness.

Stunty (stʌ·nti), *a.* [f. STUNT *a.* + -Y.]

1. Stunted in growth, short in stature.

1828 H. ANGELO *Remin.* I. 287 Two stock-broker's clerks, the one six feet two in height; the other, a stunty Jew, performed the parts of Pierre and Jaffier. 1868 *Cleveland Gloss.*, *Stunty*, 1. Short in growth or stature; of Ling, or any other shrubby plant: of a person also, who is short in stature.

2. Sulky, obstinate; curt, blunt. *dial.*

a 1825 [see STUNT *a.* 3]. 1861 AGNES STRICKLAND *Old Friends* Ser. II. 69 Their hoss..had kicked her own fetlock, and then she turned both lame and stunty (sulky stubborn).

Hence **Stu·ntiness**, the condition of being stunted.

Latham quotes from 'Cheyne *Philosophical Conjectures*' a passage identical with quot. 1740 s.v. STUNTEDNESS.

a 1878 SIR G. SCOTT *Lect. Archit.* (1879) II. 179 While walls and pillars might avail themselves to the full of this upward striving, it was hard that the arch should be condemned to unalterable stuntiness.

Stuny, Stunys: see STONY *v.*, STONISH *v.*

†**Stuorie.** *Obs. rare*-1. [ad. It. *stuora* (in the orig.), repr. L. *storea.*] A mat.

1555 EDEN *Decades* (Arb.) 257 They founde the kyng in his pallaice sittynge vppon a floure or stuorie made of the leaues of date trees.

‖**Stupa**1 (stiū·pă). Also **stuppa**. [L. *stūpa*, more correctly *stuppa*, tow = late Gr. στύππη.]

1. = STUPE *sb.*1 Only in Dicts.

1693 tr. *Blancard's Phys. Dict.* (ed. 2), *Stupea*, *seu stupa*, a piece of linnen dipt in a liquor, and applied to the part affected. *Ibid.*, *Stuppa* or *Stupa*, the same with *Stupea*. 1706 PHILLIPS (ed. Kersey), *Stupa* or *Stupea*, the course part of Flax, Tow, Hards, Ockam to calk Ships with; also a Stupe us'd by Surgeons. 1875 KNIGHT *Dict. Mech.*, *Stupa*, tow used as a pledget, compress, or as a wad in fomentations.

2. *Bot.* (See quots.) Only in Dicts.

1856 HENSLOW *Dict. Bot. Terms*, *Stupa*, a tuft or mass of hair or fine filament matted together. 1866 *Treas. Bot.*, *Stupa*, tow; a tuft of long hairs. 1900 B. D. JACKSON *Gloss. Bot. Terms*, *Stupa* or *Stuppa*.

‖**Stupa**2 (stū·pă). [Skr. *stūpa.*] A Buddhist monument; = TOPE *sb.*5

1876 FERGUSSON *Ind. & East. Archit.* I. iii. 57 The difficulty was met by assigning a portion [of the remains of Buddha] to each of the contending parties, who are said to have erected stupas to contain them. 1882 *Edin. Rev.* Oct. 356 Monasteries in ruins, and stupas in a dilapidated condition.

Stupe (stiūp), *sb.*1 Also 5 **stuppe**, 6 **stoupe**, 7 **stoup, stuphe**, 7–8 **stuph**. [ad. L. *stūpa*, *stuppa*: see STUPA1. Cf. F. *étoupe* tow.] A piece of tow, flannel, or other soft substance, wrung out of hot liquor and medicated, for fomenting a wound or ailing part.

c 1400 *Lanfranc's Cirurg.* 53 Wiþinne þe wounde leie þe ȝelke of an ey, wiþ oile of rosis, with stupis, or ellis wiþ lint. *a* 1425 tr. *Arderne's Treat. Fistula*, etc. 87 Stuppez of lyne or coton. 1543 TRAHERON *Vigo's Chirurg.* 94 b, Applye it with stoupes moysted in water. 1612 WOODALL *Surg. Mate* Wks. (1653) 96 A large hot stupe wet in a good lixivium, and wrung out. 1634 T. JOHNSON *Parey's Chirurg.* XI. xii. (1678) 286 These stoups I stayed and held to the part with double cloaths. 1684 tr. *Bonet's Merc. Compit.* III. 76, I rolled up his head upon a Stuphe, dry wrung from the fomentation. 1743 tr. *Heister's Surg.* I. xv. (1768) 110 Foment the Eye with Stuphs wrung out of the Decoctions which we prescribed above. 1896 *Allbutt's Syst. Med.* I. 435 Fomentations and stupes are conveniently made of a length of flannel doubled.

Stupe (stiūp), *sb.*2 *colloq.* Now chiefly *dial.* [Shortened f. STUPID.] A stupid person, a fool.

1762 BICKERSTAFFE *Love in Village* II. ii, Was there ever such a poor stupe! 1813 *Sketches of Character* (ed. 2) I. 11 How could they think of bringing that stupe of a Miss Newton? 1840 LADY C. BURY *Hist. Flirt* v, Of all the silent stupes, commend me to Captain Thelwal. 1876 BLACKMORE *Cripps* xxxv, 'What a stupe I must be,' she continued to herself, 'to imagine that the boy could be in love!'

Stupe (stiūp), *v.* Also 8 **stoop**. [f. STUPE *sb.*1]

†**1.** *trans.* To moisten (lint, tow, etc.) in some hot liquid so as to form a stupe. *Obs. rare*-1.

c 1540 *Pract. Cyrurgyons* A i, Roulettes, stupes, or plagettes made of lynte,..stuped or dypped in hote Oyles.

2. To foment with a stupe or stupes.

1670 NARBOROUGH *Jrnl.* in *Acc. Sev. Late Voy.* I. (1694) 52 They use bathing and stuping those places. 1735 *Phil. Trans.* XL. 426 The Abdomen was stuped twice a Day with an emollient Fomentation. 1747 WESLEY *Prim. Physick* (1762) 100 Stoop it [a sprain] with one spoonful of Brandy, two of Vinegar and four of Water. 1843 in R. J. Graves *Syst. Clin. Med.* xxix. 390, I..stuped the part with warm water and laudanum. 1892 *Cassell's Fam. Mag.* Mar. 211/1 [She] developed a tiresome face-ache, which no amount of stuping with poppy-heads could bring into visiting shape.

Stupe, obs. form of STOOP *v.*1

Stupefacient (stiūpǐfēi·ʃěnt), *a.* and *sb.* *Med.* Also 7 **stupi-**. [ad. L. *stupefacient-em*, pres. pple. of *stupefacĕre*: see STUPEFY *v.*] **A.** *adj.* Stupefying, producing stupor. ? *Obs.*

1669 ROWLAND *Schroder's Chym. Disp.* I. xxx. 40 Stupefacient, Narcotick. 1675 GREW *Anat. Plants*, *Lect.* VI. i. 280 Stupifacient [is a kind of Taste] as in the Root of Black Hellebore. 1748 HARTLEY *Observ. Man* I. ii. § 2. 155 Very nauseous and stupefacient Tastes may perhaps arise from violent and irregular Vibrations. 1849 in CRAIG; 1850 in OGILVIE; and in later Dicts.

B. *sb.* A medicine producing stupor. *rare*-0.

1855 in OGILVIE Suppl. (and in later Dicts.). 1898 in *Syd. Soc. Lex.*

†**Stupefact**, *v.* *Obs. rare*-1. [f. L. *stupefact-*, ppl. stem of *stupefacĕre.*] *trans.* = STUPEFY.

1598 FLORIO, *Alloppiare*,..to stupefact ones sences.

†**Stupefact**, *pa. pple.* *Obs.* Chiefly *Sc.* Also 6 **stupifact, stupe-, stupifak**. [ad. L. *stupefact-us*, pa. pple. of *stupefacĕre*: see STUPEFY *v.*] Stupefied.

1513 DOUGLAS *Æneis* v. xi. 87 Of Troiane wemen the myndis worth agast, And all thair hartis sum deill stupifak. 1549 *Compl. Scot.* 6 Bot ȝit i vas lang stupefact ande timide, for falt of ane peremptoir conclusione. *a* 1578 LINDESAY (Pitscottie) *Chron. Scot.* (S. T. S.) I. 116 The king hearand this was stupefact in his mynd. 1590 BARROUGH *Meth. Physick* III. xi. (1596) 118 The senses be astonied and stupefact by cooling things.

Stupefaction (stiūpǐfæ·kʃən). Also 7 **stupi-**. [a. F. *stupéfaction* (15–16th c.), or ad. mod.L. *stupefactiōn-em*: see STUPEFY *v.* and -FACTION.]

1. The action of stupefying or state of being stupefied; numbness, torpor, or insensibility, of body or mind.

1543 TRAHERON *Vigo's Chirurg.* II. xvi. 26 b, The extremitees of theyr bodyes..were reduced to suche colde, and congelation or stupefaction. 1677 tr. *Groeneveldt's Treat. Stone* 32 A stupefaction in the Thigh and Leg. 1756 BURKE *Subl. & B.* Introd., Wks. I. 103 Tobacco is the delight of Dutchmen, as it diffuses a torpor and pleasing stupefaction. 1865 DICKENS *Mut. Fr.* II. i, Half the pupils dropped asleep, or fell into a state of waking stupefaction. 1911 RIKER *Henry Fox Ld. Holland* viii. II. 98 The activity of Fox..seemed the result of long pent-up energy that had suffered stupefaction under an arbitrary over-lord.

¶ **b.** Used for STUPEFACIENT *sb.*

1651 WITTIE tr. *Primrose's Pop. Err.* 327 Stupefactions [L. *stupefacientia*] being applyed outwardly, doe [etc.].

2. Overwhelming consternation or astonishment.

1597 A. M. tr. *Guillemeau's Fr. Chirurg.* 52 b/2 This foresayed stupefactione and feare. 1634 SIR T. HERBERT *Trav.* 189 Which ceremony is so hideously acted that it raises no small stupefaction in the beholders. 1831 CARLYLE *Sartor Res.* III. viii, The deceptions, and wonder-hiding stupefactions, which Space practises on us. 1865 DICKENS *Mut. Fr.* III. vi, What was the stupefaction of the friendly movers when this object at last emerging proved to be a much-dilapidated dark lantern!

Stupefactive (stiūpǐfæ·ktiv), *a.* and *sb.* ? *Obs.* Also 7 **stupi-**. [a. F. *stupéfactif*, *-ive* adj. (16th c.), ad. med.L. *stupefactīv-us*, f. L. *stupefact-*, ppl. stem of *stupefacĕre*: see STUPEFY *v.* and -IVE.]

A. *adj.* **1.** *Med.* Having the property of producing stupor or insensibility.

1527 ANDREW *Brunswyke's Distyll. Waters* c j b, The water of Nenufara floure..is half poyson or venym thrughe his great coldenes or stupefactyfe. 1543 TRAHERON *Vigo's Chirurg.* Interpret. Words, Stupefactiue: That, that hathe strength to astoynie, and take awaye felynge. 1626 BACON *Sylva* § 98 Opium hath a Stupefactiue Part, and a Heating Part. 1649 E. REYNOLDS *Hosea* iii. 14 Some affections and motions of the heart..are of a cold stupefactive, and constringent nature. 1669 FLAVEL *Husb. Spiritual.* I. vi. 57 Opium and such-like stupifactive ingredients. 1789 W. BUCHAN *Dom. Med.* xlvi. (1790) 473 Those [sc. poisons] of the vegetable kind are generally of a narcotic or stupefactive quality. 1797 *London Compl. Art Cookery*, *Brewing* 219 Cocculus Indicus..is poisonous, stupefactive, and unlawful.

2. *gen.* Stupefying, astounding. *rare.*

1689 T. PLUNKET *Char. Good Commander* 45 What dire Catastrophe's impending are? What stupefactive things we daily hear?

B. *sb.* A stupefactive medicine.

1562 BULLEYN *Dial. Sorenes & Chir.* 33 b, Superfactiues or dedde things, as Opium. 1626 BACON *Sylva* § 74 This we see in the Operation of Opium, and Stupefactiues, vpon the Spirits of liuing Creatures. 1668 E. REYNOLDS *Serm.* 24 Thereby teaching us..to refuse any Anodynes or Stupefactives which might take away the sense of sinne from us.

Hence **Stupefa·ctiveness**. *rare*-0.

1727 BAILEY, vol. II.

Stupefica·tion. *rare*-1. In 7 **stupi-**. [f. STUPEFY *v.*: see -FICATION.] = STUPEFACTION.

1650 JOHN HALL *Paradoxes* 35 What other is this..but selfe stupification.

Stupefied (stiū·pǐfəid), *ppl. a.* [f. STUPEFY *v.* + -ED1.] In senses of the verb.

1639 J. TAYLOR (Water P.) *Crabtree Lect.* 12 Goe, thou art a stupified Asse. 1654 POWER *Exp. Philos.* I. 70 Thirdly, in the return of the Spirits into the stupefied Leg, we plainly perceive by the prickling, what a slow motion the Spirits have. 1673 BUNYAN *Diff. Judgem. Water-Baptism* 44, I will not suppose you so much stupified. 1790 BURKE *Refl. Rev. France* Wks. 1792 III. 100 Several English were the stupified and indignant spectators of that triumph. 1825 MACAULAY *Milton* Ess. (1897) 27 To break the ties which bound a stupefied people to the seat of enchantment. 1908 C. BIGG *Orig. Christianity* xxi. (1909) 285 Herodian..speaks of Severus with an almost stupefied admiration.

Hence **Stu·pefiedness**.

c 1647 BOYLE *Disc. Swearing* Wks. 1772 VI. 6 We know that insensibility of pain may..proceed from the deadness and stupifiedness of the part.

Stupefier (stiū·pǐfəiəɹ). [f. STUPEFY *v.* + -ER1.] Something that stupefies; a medicine that produces stupor.

1684 tr. *Bonet's Merc. Compit.* VIII. 280 The violence of the Pain sometimes forces us of necessity to apply Stupefiers. 1735 BERKELEY *Querist* § 348 Wks. 1871 III. 384 Whether the natural phlegm of this island needs any additional stupifier? 1831 J. DAVIES *Manual Mat. Med.* 43 Narcotics, soporifics or stupefiers.

Stupefy (stiū·pǐfəi), *v.* Also 7 **stupefie**, 7–8 **stupifie**, 6–9 **stupify**. [a. F. *stupéfi-er* (16th c.), ad. L. *stupefacĕre* to make stupid or senseless, f. *stupēre* to be struck senseless, be amazed: see -FY.

The spelling with *i* (cf. *liquify*) was common until the latter half of the 19th c. 'This word should..be spelled *stupefy*; but the authorities are against it' (Johnson).]

1. *trans.* To make stupid or torpid; to deprive of apprehension, feeling, or sensibility; to benumb, deaden.

? *a* 1600 in *Lyly's Wks.* (1902) III. 497 Twas not Tobacco stupifyed yᵉ braine. 1611 SHAKS. *Cymb.* I. v. 37 Those [drugs] she ha's, Will stupifie and dull the Sence a-while. 1652 *Hermeticall Banquet* 69 This by the narcoticall Sulphur of the Opium, stupefied the Nerve. 1709 T. ROBINSON *Vindic. Mosaick Syst.* 56 That any one..should be so stupified by the Prevalency of his Lusts, as to deny the Being of that God, whose [etc.]. 1732 ARBUTHNOT *Rules of Diet* (1736) 365 Opiate and anodyne Substances which stupify and relax the Fibres. 1806–7 J. BERESFORD *Miseries Hum. Life* (1826) VI. xxx, Your fingers being..stupefied by the cold. 1849 MACAULAY *Hist. Eng.* v. I. 666 The prisoner, stupified by illness, was unable..to understand what passed. 1889 MRS. OLIPHANT *Poor Gentl.* xlv, His anxiety stupefied instead of quickening his senses.

fig. 1874 SPURGEON *Treas. David* lxxxi. IV. 26 No dulness should ever stupify our psalmody.

b. *absol.*

1691 HARTCLIFFE *Virtues* 81 As nothing doth restore us more to our selves, when we faint and are weary, than Sleep soberly taken, so nothing doth more stupifie, than its Excess. 1707 FLOYER *Physic. Pulse-Watch* 81 If the Bath be so long continu'd as to stupifie. *a* 1848 W. A. BUTLER *Serm.* ix. (1849) 149 Satan,..who deceives that he may destroy, stupifies that he may deceive.

2. To stun with amazement, fear, or the like; to astound. [So L.]

1596 SPENSER *F. Q.* V. iii. 17 With great amazement they were stupefide. 1622 MALYNES *Anc. Law-Merch.* 337 The apprehension of the continuance of intollerable Vsurie in England, is able to stupifie a mans senses. 1779 *Mirror* No. 11. ¶ 13 He sat, stupified with shame and remorse. 1796 MME. D'ARBLAY *Camilla* VI. iii. III. 175 'If she is not in the rooms to-night,' said Sir Sedley, 'I shall be stupified to petrifaction.' 1845 DARWIN *Voy. Nat.* viii. (1879) 171 The mind is stupified in thinking over the long, absolutely necessary, lapse of years. 1909 *Engl. Rev.* Feb. 602 All these people seem stupefied by the immensity of the calamity which has befallen them.

†**3.** To deprive (a material substance) of mobility. *Obs. rare*-1.

a 1626 BACON *Physiol. Rem.* Baconiana (1679) 100 This stupifieth the Quick-silver that it runneth no more. *Ibid.* 122 When it..is not fluent, but stupified.

4. *intr.* To become stupid or torpid; to grow dull or insensible. Now *rare.*

a 1631 DONNE *Let. to Sir H. G.* v, Poems (1633) 365, I which live in the Country without stupifying, am not in darknesse, but in shadow. 1803 MARY CHARLTON *Wife & Mistress* III. 47 Do not go and stupify with such an old *illuminée* as the Dowager Lady Melville. 1844 SYD. SMITH in Lady Holland *Mem.* (1855) II. 523, I always fatten and stupefy on such diet; I want to lose flesh and gain understanding.

Hence **Stu·pefying** *vbl. sb.* and *ppl. a.*

1611 COTGR., *Noix vomique*..is of a poisonous, deadly, and stupifying qualitie. 1637 B. JONSON *Sad Sheph.* II. viii, The dead-numming Night-shade! The stupifying Hemlock! 1673 PENN *Chr. Quaker* xx. 585 The Stupifyings of Sin. 1731 MILLER *Gard. Dict.* s.v. *Wine*, The Effects they have upon the human Body are rather stupifying than inebriating. *a* 1768 SECKER *Serm.* (1770) IV. 27 The benumbing and stupefying of so important a Principle of their Nature. 1863 MARY HOWITT tr. *F. Bremer's Greece* II. xvi. 155 A cave, out of which..a stupefying exhalation ascended. 1916 *Blackw. Mag.* May 607/1 The views obtained are almost stupefying in their majesty and grandeur.

Stupen, stuppin, dial. (Kent) ff. STEWPAN.

1617 in W. F. Shaw *Mem. Eastry* (1870) 227 Fowr brass potts three brass stupens. 1736 J. LEWIS *Hist. Isle Tenet* (ed. 2) 39 *Stuppin*, a Stew-pan or Skillet.

Stupend (stiūpe·nd), *a.* *Obs.* in serious use. [ad. L. *stupend-us*: see STUPENDOUS. Cf. *horrend*, *tremend.*] Stupendous.

1621 BURTON *Anat. Mel.* I. i. II. vii. 35 In time of sleepe this faculty is free, & many times conceaues strange, stupend, absurd shapes. *Ibid.* II. ii. II. 314 The Romanes had their publike Bathes, very sumptuous and stupend. 1676 *Doctrine of Devils* 25 That stupend miracle of Christ's Incarnation. 1702 C. MATHER *Magn. Chr.* III. II. xix. 122 The stupend Variety of Human Faces. 1864 LOWELL *Fireside Trav.* 127 A lobster..of experience so stupend, His claws were blunted at the end, Turning life's iron pages o'er.

Hence †**Stupe·ndly** *adv.*

1621 BURTON *Anat. Mel.* III. iv. I. i. 717 The Brittaines are so stupendly superstitious in their ceremonies, that [etc.].

Stupendio·sity. *rare*-1. [f. next, in imitation of *religiosity*, etc.: see -ITY.] Stupendousness.

1830 H. ANGELO *Remin.* I. 174 Gresse..could not patiently endure the least observations upon the stupendiosity of his figure

†**Stupe·ndious**, *a.* *Obs.* [irreg. f. L. *stupend-us* (see STUPENDOUS), after adjs. in *-ious*; cf. *tremendious*, vulgar form of *tremendous.*] Stupendous.

Our numerous instances show that this was the accepted form until the latter part of the 17th c., when the correct *stupendous* began to be used.

1547 BOORDE *Introd. Knowl.* 133 Yet in Ierland is stupendyous thynges; for there is neyther Pyes nor venymus wormes. 1591 HARINGTON *Orl. Fur.* Apol. Poetrie ¶ ij b, As witnes the huge Theaters, and Amphitheaters, monuments of stupendious charge. 1611 CORYAT *Crudities* 184 A most stupendious summe of money. 1667 MILTON *P. L.* X. 351 At sight Of that stupendious Bridge his joy encreas'd. 1712 STEELE *Spect.* No. 472 ¶ 7 That stupendious Machine [the Eye]. 1768 BOSWELL *Corsica* i. (ed. 2) 29 Craggy cliffs of so stupendious a height, that [etc.]. *a* 1800 PEGGE *Anecd. Eng. Lang.* (1814) 55 On the other hand, they [*sc.* Londoners] say *stupendious*, for *stupendous*.

Hence †**Stupe·ndiously** *adv.*, **Stupe·ndiousness**.

1630 PRYNNE *Anti-Armin.* 198 Can any elected persons heart be found so stupendiously obdurate, as to withstand this omnipotent working. 1656 EARL MONM. tr. *Boccalini's Advts. fr. Parnass.* I. v. 9 The stupendiousness of the Venetian liberty. 1662 H. MORE *Enthus. Tri.* 14 There may be such a due dash of Sanguine in the Melancholy, that the Complexion may prove stupendiously [*ed.* 1712 stupendously] enravishing. 1676 *Doctrine of Devils* 54 This is..an Axiomatical Truth among the Doctors of Demonology, That a Devil or Witch can, for stupendiousness of the work do as much as ever Christ did. 1711 in *10th Rep. Hist. MSS. Comm.* App. v. 113 The Jewes..remained so stupendiously incredulous, that they putt him to death for an imposter.

Stupendous (stiūpe·ndəs), *a.* [f. L. *stupend-us* 'that is to be wondered at, amazing', gerundive of *stupēre* to be struck senseless, be amazed at: see -OUS.] Such as to cause stupor or astonishment; amazing, astounding; marvellous, prodigious; amazingly large or great.

1666 PEPYS *Diary* 21 May, It is stupendous to see how favourably..my Lord Ashly carries himself to Mr. Yeabsly. 1669 GALE *Crt. Gentiles* I. I. iii. 22 The strength of these Anakims was stupendous. 1697 DRYDEN *Æneis* IX. 705 There stood a Tow'r..of stupendous height. 1732 POPE *Ess. Man* I. 267 All are but parts of one stupendous whole. 1798 SOPHIA LEE *Canterb. T.*, *Young Lady's T.* II. 412 They reached the foot of that stupendous natural barrier, the Alps. 1863 COWDEN CLARKE *Shaks. Char.* x. 261 The man who thinks to outwit three women, who are aware of his purpose, must indeed be a stupendous ass. 1863 MISS BRADDON *Aurora Floyd* iii, The young officer laughed aloud at the stupendous joke. 1914 *Eng. Hist. Rev.* Jan. 135 He is apt to attribute to his opponents stupendous oversights and elementary misunderstandings.

Hence **Stupe·ndously** *adv.*, **Stupe·ndousness**.

1712 Stupendously: see STUPENDIOUSLY, quot. 1662. 1727 BAILEY vol. II, *Stupendousness*, Astonishingness. 1742 *Lond. & Country Brew.* I. (ed. 4) 37, I have known some of the little Victualling Brewers, so stupendously ignorant, that [etc.]. 1743 J. ELLIS *Knowl. Div. Things* 219 Those very Works, which, from their Stupendousness, should have taught them the Greatness of the former. 1824 J. W. CROKER in *C. Papers* (1884) 7 Oct., Be..sure to make it [a column] stupendously high. 1848 DICKENS *Dombey* i, Her nose, stupendously aquiline. 1890 *Voice* (N.Y.) 17 July, This generation so familiar with stupendousness of all kinds.

†**Stupe·nduous**, *a.* *Obs.* [irreg. f. L. *stupend-us* (see STUPENDOUS), after adjs. in *-uous*: cf. *tremenduous.*] Stupendous.

1736 *Mrs. Manley's Secret Mem.* III. 17 Horatio, named *immortal* from his stupenduous [*ed.* 1720 III. 15 stupendous] Conquests in Iberia. 1760–72 H. BROOKE *Fool of Qual.* (1792) III. 241 Travellers..are apt to enquire by whom the stupenduous pile was erected. 1794 MORSE *Amer. Geog.* (1796) II. 12 A torrent, precipitating itself from stupenduous rocks.

Stupent (stiū·pěnt), *a.* *rare.* [ad. L. *stupent-em* pres. pple. of *stupēre* to be stupefied or astounded.] That is in a state of stupor or amazement.

1843 CARLYLE *Past & Pr.* III. viii, We stand speechless, stupent, and know not what to say! 1851 — in Froude *C.'s Life in Lond.* (1884) II. xix. 68 Poor Simeon..sat stupent in the whirlpool of heterodox hail. 1912 G. B. SHAW *Pygmalion* II. (1916) 120 *Higgins* [*stupent*] Well!!! (*Recovering his breath with a gasp*) What do you expect me to say to you?

Stupeous (stiū·pi,əs), *a.* *Zool.* and *Bot.* Also **stuppeous** (stʌ·pi,əs). [f. L. *stūpe-us*, *stuppe-us* made or consisting of tow, f. *stūpa*, *stuppa*: see STUPE *sb.*1 and -OUS.] Having, or covered with, matted or tufted hairs or filaments.

1826 KIRBY & SP. *Entomol.* IV. xlvi. 275 *Stupeous*, covered with long loose scales resembling tow. Ex. The *Palpi* of *Lepidoptera*. 1871 W. A. LEIGHTON *Lichen-flora* 104 Medulla stuppeous. 1900 B. D. JACKSON *Gloss. Bot. Terms*, *Stupeous*, woolly.

†**Stupex.** *Obs.* App. a jocular improvement on STUPE *sb.*2

1853 SURTEES *Sponge's Sp. Tour* (1893) 338 'The little stupexes!' exclaimed Miss Glitters. 1864 MISS YONGE *Trial* I. 81 The light of nature would show that to any one but a stupex.

Stuph(e, variant ff. STUFE *Obs.*, STUPE *sb.*1

Stupid (stiū·pid), *a.* and *sb.* [ad. L. *stupid-us*, f. *stup-ēre* to be stunned or benumbed. Cf. F. *stupide* (Rabelais), Sp., Pg. *estúpido*, It. *stupido.*]

A. *adj.*

1. Having one's faculties deadened or dulled; in a state of stupor, stupefied, stunned; esp. *hyperbolically*, stunned with surprise, grief, etc. *Obs.* exc. *arch.* (*poet.*)

Very common in Dryden.

1611 SHAKS. *Wint. T.* IV. iv. 409 Is not your Father growne incapeable Of reasonable affayres? Is he not stupid With Age, and altring Rheumes? Can he speake? heare? Know man, from man? 1656 BLOUNT *Glossogr.*, *Stupid*, dismaid, abashed, astonied, amazed, senceless. 1675 *Machiavelli's Prince* xix. Wks. (1883) 123 These remained..stupid and astonished. 1697 DRYDEN *Æneis* VII. 1104 Men, Boys, and Women stupid with Surprise, Where ere she passes, fix their wond'ring Eyes. 1725 POPE *Odyss.* XVIII. 114 Down drop'd he stupid from the stunning wound. 1737 in H. T. Waghorn *Cricket Scores* (1899) 19 The latter..receiving..so smart a blow by the ball that he was knocked down and lay stupid for a long time. 1859 TENNYSON *Geraint & Enid* 753 And Enid could not say one tender word, She felt so blunt and stupid at the heart.

†**b.** Belonging to or characterized by stupor or insensibility. *Obs.*

1607 CHAPMAN *Bussy d'Ambois* V. 64 Reuiue those stupid thoughts, and sit not thus, Gathering the horrors of your seruants slaughter,..Into an idle fancie. 1697 DRYDEN *Virg. Georg.* III. 781 His Eyes are settled in a stupid peace. 1708 POPE *Sappho* 128 No sigh to rise, no tear had pow'r to flow, Fix'd in a stupid lethargy of woe. 1818 KEATS *Endymion* I. 678 My sweet dream Fell into nothing—into stupid sleep.

†**c.** Of a part of the body: Paralysed. *Obs.*

1638 A. READ *Chirurg.* xi. 82 Touch the stupid parts [of a paralytic person] with quick nettles.

d. *Path.* ? *Obs.*

1822–9 GOOD *Study Med.* (ed. 3) IV. 519 *Cephalæa gravans*. Stupid head-ache. Pain obtuse; with a sense of heaviness extending over the whole head.

†**e.** Emotionally or morally dull or insensible; apathetic, indifferent. Const. *to* [cf. F. *stupide à*].

1605 BACON *Adv. Learn.* II. xxii. § 17 As for pleasure, wee haue likewise determined, that the minde oughte not to bee reduced to stupide, but to retayne pleasure. 1641 J. JACKSON *True Evang. T.* II. 148 The Stoicks..patience..was..onely a stupid senselessnesse, and wretched carelessnesse. 1653 H. MORE *Antid. Ath.* II. vi. § 5 He is as stupid to these things [the beauties of nature] as the basest of Beasts. 1713 *Guardian* (1756) I. No. 19. 86 It was a cause of great sorrow and melancholy to me..to see a crowd in the habits of the gentry of England stupid to the noblest sentiments we have. 1758 S. HAYWARD *Serm.* xvii. 530 Oh stupid creatures that are not raised with the descriptions of his person! *a* 1770 JORTIN *Serm.* (1787) II. x. 199 Vice begets the dread of punishment, unless it be constantly attended with unbelief, and with a stupid carelessness about futurity.

†**2.** As the characteristic of inanimate things: Destitute of sensation, consciousness, thought, or feeling. *Obs.*

1626 BACON *Sylva* § 98 Tangible Parts in Bodies are Stupide things; And the Spirits doe (in effect) all. 1642 H. MORE *Song of Soul* II. iii. III. 60 Yet if the Earth stand stupid and unmov'd, This needs must come to passe. 1660 BOYLE *New. Exp. Phys.-Mech.* xxxiii. 251 And as for the Care of the Publique Good of the Universe ascrib'd to dead and stupid Bodies; wee shall only demand, why [etc.]. *a* 1664 KATH. PHILIPS *Poems* (1667) 40, *In Mem. of F. P.* 14 Alas! in vain, in vain on thee I rave; There is no pity in the stupid Grave. *a* 1694 TILLOTSON *Serm.* (1743) IX. 4110 The stone is stupid, and is not in the least conscious of any of those impressions, does not perceive what is done to it. *a* 1718 PRIOR *2nd Hymn of Callimachus* 141 Euphrates..copious runs, but Muddy; And carries forward with his stupid Force Polluting Dirt. 1722 WOLLASTON *Relig. Nat.* v. 74 Matter is incapable of acting, passive only, and stupid. 1744 BERKELEY *Siris* § 190 Were it not for this [fire], the whole wou'd be one great stupid inanimate mass. But this active element is supposed to be every where.

3. Wanting in or slow of mental perception; lacking ordinary activity of mind; slow-witted, dull.

1541 R. COPLAND *Galyen's Terap.* 2 B iij b, For the fyrste speake ouer lyghtly and to imprudently,..and the other are all togyther stupydes, sturdy, & lytygious. 1616 BULLOKAR *Eng. Expos.*, *Stupid*, blockish, without wit: dull. 1649 MILTON *Tenure of Kings* 8 No man who knows ought, can be so stupid to deny that all men naturally were borne free. 1657 — *P. L.* XII. 116 O that men..should be so stupid grown While yet the Patriark liv'd, who scap'd the Flood, As to forsake the living God. 1692 DRYDEN *St. Euremont's Ess.* 290 But I esteem the Faith of a stupid Peasant, more than all the Lessons of Socrates. 1712 ADDISON *Spect.* No. 291 ¶ 8 A Man, who cannot write with Wit on a proper Subject, is dull and stupid. 1778 MISS BURNEY *Evelina* (1791) II. xxvii. 161 'Why is Miss Anville so grave?' 'Not grave, my Lord,' said I, 'only stupid.' 1819 SHELLEY *Peter Bell* VII. iii, His lordship stands and racks his stupid brains. 1829 HOGG *Sheph. Cal.* Wks. (1865) 368/2 'What a stupid idiot I was!' exclaimed Wat. 1838 LYTTON *Alice* II. iii, How stupid in Caroline not to show it to you. 1842 LOVER *Handy Andy* xliii, She felt the pique which every pretty woman experiences who fancies her favours disregarded, and thought Andy the stupidest lout she ever came across. 1855 MACAULAY *Hist. Eng.* xv. III. 560 Anne, who, when in good humour, was meekly stupid, and, when in bad humour, was sulkily stupid. 1865 CARLYLE *Fredk. Gt.* XXI. viii. (1872) X. 160 He knew how to listen..which no stupid man was ever capable of. 1875 JOWETT *Plato* (ed. 2) I. 29, I remain as stupid as ever; for still I fail to comprehend. 1879 HARLAN *Eyesight* viii. 108 Children with astigmatism often appear stupid.

absol. 1692 R. L'ESTRANGE *Fables* xviii. 19 But Good Council is cast away, upon the Arrogant, the Self-conceited, or the stupid.

b. Of attributes, actions, ideas, etc.: Characterized by or indicating stupidity or dullness of comprehension.

1621 T. WILLIAMSON tr. *Goulart's Wise Vieillard* 131 Christians willingly lay downe their neckes vnder the light yoke..not with a stupid, or hastie mad braine-sicke, or fond toying ioy. 1687 A. LOVELL tr. *Thevenot's Trav.* I. 145, I went to that Burying-place on the Holy Friday of the Greeks ..that I might see what Ground they had for this stupid Belief. 1707 PATRICK *Disc. Prayer* II. xviii. 197 Let us not ..persist in such a stupid error. 1711 STEELE *Spect.* No. 2 ¶ 3 It is a stupid and barbarous Way to extend Dominion by Arms. *a* 1770 JORTIN *Serm.* (1771) IV. ix. 184 Great reason have we to be thankful that we are not educated in such stupid and inhuman principles. 1819 SHELLEY *Peter Bell* VI. xxxii, 'Twould make George Colman melancholy To have heard him, like a male Molly, Chanting those stupid staves. 1871 C. GIBBON *Lack of Gold* ii, This cursed frenzy makes me say and think the stupidest things. 1891 E. PEACOCK *N. Brendon* I. 122 Our stupid passion for snugness.

†**c.** Of the lower animals: Irrational. Also of an individual animal, its propensities, etc.: Lacking intelligence or animation, senseless, dull. *Obs.*

a 1680 BUTLER *Rem.* (1759) I. 203 And trains him up with Rudiments more false, Than Nature does her stupid Animals. 1774 GOLDSM. *Nat. Hist.* (1776) IV. 328 [The badger] is a solitary stupid animal. 1815 STEPHENS in *Shaw's Gen. Zool.* IX. I. 19 The birds of this genus [*Bucco*]..are a solitary stupid race. 1867 MORRIS *Jason* VIII. 64 A monstrous cage, Of iron bars, shut in the stupid rage Of those two beasts.

4. Void of interest, tiresome, boring, dull.

1778 MISS BURNEY *Evelina* (1791) I. xxxiii. 179 Of all the stupid places ever I see, that Howard Grove is the worst; there's never no getting nothing one wants. 1832 LYTTON *Eugene A.* I. iii, 'I am sorry, dear Ellinor, my awkwardness should occasion you so stupid an evening', answered Madeline. 1845 MISS G. JEWSBURY *Let. to Mrs. Carlyle* (1892) 161, I..was getting quite fat till within the last few days, when I caught cold on the stupid Rhine. 1854 WHYTE MELVILLE *Gen. Bounce* xviii, For the first time in her experience of a London season, Blanche begins to think it a 'stupid ball.' 1862 MISS BRADDON *Lady Audley* ii, We were quartered at a stupid sea-port town. 1884 M. CREIGHTON *Let.* 22 May, in L. Creighton *Life & Lett.* (1904) I. 269 If my letter is very stupid, forgive me. 1901 W. R. H. TROWBRIDGE *Lett. her Mother to Eliz.* xviii. 89 We went once to the Empire, but it was awfully stupid, and I never want to go again.

5. Obstinate, stubborn. *north. dial.*

1788 W. H. MARSHALL *Yorksh.* II. 357 *Stupid*; obstinate (the common epithet). 1829 BROCKETT *N. C. Gloss.* (ed. 2), *Stupid*, obstinate, though possessing good talents. 1866 MRS. LYNN LINTON *Lizzie Lorton* xii, 'So Miss Lizzie, my dear, divn't be stupid'—she meant obstinate—'but let yersel be guided by them as knaws best.' 1877 *Holderness Gloss.*, *Stupid*, obstinate. 'As stupid as a mule.' 1893 J. K. SNOWDEN *Tales Yorksh. Wolds* 170 Kit Harpur were main stupid ower it.

6. *Comb.*, as *stupid-looking* adj.; adverbial with another adj., as *stupid-honest*, *-sure* (nonce-wds.); **stupid-head**, a blockhead.

1838 DICKENS *O. Twist* xxxi, Think it's the same boy, *Stupid-head? 1877 TENNYSON *Harold* III. i, Be thou not *stupid-honest, brother Gurth! 1815 J. CAMPBELL *Trav. S. Africa* 502 How such a *stupid looking animal [as the turtle] finds out this speck of land [Ascension island]..is truly wonderful. 1877 TENNYSON *Harold* IV. iii, The people *stupid-sure Sleep like their swine.

B. *sb.* A stupid person. *colloq.*

1712 STEELE *Spect.* No. 468 ¶ 6 Thou art no longer to drudge in raising the Mirth of Stupids..for thy Maintenance. 1819 *Metropolis* I. 222 His loudest applauders were..stupids, like Sir G. W. who scarcely could speak a word of French. 1880 MRS. PARR *Adam & Eve* II. 17 Ain't there no place else for us to go to, eh, stupid? 1885 'MRS. ALEXANDER' *Valerie's Fate* v, You do not know what a thoughtless, heartless stupid I have been.

†**Stupi·dious**, *a.* *Obs.* [f. STUPID + -IOUS. Cf. STUPIDOUS.] Stupid, grossly unintelligent, dull. Hence †**Stupi·diously** *adv.*

1600 G. ABBOT *Jonah* 109 The Saracens and Turkes, who ..may not so much as dispute of any point of their religion, and so do beleeve in Mahomet, most grossly and stupidiously. 1615 J. TAYLOR (Water P.) *Taylor's Rev.* Wks. (1630) II. 144/2 Can you, O can your senses be stupidious And see your selues abused thus perfidious!

Stupidish (stiū·pidiʃ), *a.* [f. STUPID *a.* + -ISH.] Somewhat stupid.

1806 LOUISA GURNEY in A. J. C. Hare *Gurneys of Earlham* (1895) I. 153 On Monday we had a stupidish dinner at the Fellowes'. 1813 JANE AUSTEN *Lett.* (1884) II. 178 It was stupidish; Fanny did her part very well, but there was a lack of talk altogether. 1864 CARLYLE *Fredk. Gt.* XVI. xiii. IV. 463 Much can be done in that way with stupidish populations.

Stupidita·rian. *nonce-wd.* [f. STUPIDITY, after *humanitarian* etc.] One whose ruling principle is stupidity.

1846 WHIPPLE *Lit. & Life* (1851) 73 A heavy-headed stupiditarian in official station, veiling the sheerest incompetency in a mysterious sublimity of carriage!

Stupidity (stiupi·diti). [ad. L. *stupiditās*, f. *stupid-us*: see STUPID and -ITY. Cf. F. *stupidité*, It. *stupidità.*]

†**1.** Numbness, incapacity for sensation. *Obs.*

Stupidity of the teeth = late L. *stupor dentium*: see STUPOR 1.

1607 TOPSELL *Four-f. Beasts* 83 It is also good against the inflammation of the eares, the stupidity and dulnesse of the teeth. 1653 R. SANDERS *Physiogn.* 186 A dull stupidity of the head and sences. 1661 R. LOVELL *Hist. Anim. & Min.* 201 The signes of their wounds are great paine,..blacknesse, and stupidity of the part. 1702 FLOYER *Cold Bathing* I. (1709) 139 The Nature and Cure of a Torpor or Stupidity of the Limbs. 1737 BRACKEN *Farriery Impr.* (1757) II. 273 Those Things which take away Pain by causing a Stupidity.

†**2.** The condition of being deprived of the use of the faculties; a state of stupor. *Obs.*

1604 R. CAWDREY *Table Alph.*, *Stupiditie*, dulnesse: astonishment. 1608 WILLET *Hexapla Exod.* 257 Pharaoh was taken with such stupiditie that..hee had no power. 1615 CHAPMAN *Odyss.* VI. 252 As now thee To view (O Virgin) a stupiditie Past admiration strikes me. 1621 G. SANDYS *Ovid's Met.* V. (1626) 102 Stone-like stood Ceres at this heauy newes;..When griefe had quicknèd her stupiditie, Shee

tooke her Chariot, and ascends the skie. 1622 WOTTON in L. P. Smith *Life & Lett.* (1907) II. 236 One of my gondoliers ..was suddenly strucken with a silent stupidity, his feet going from him. 1627 DRAYTON *Agincourt* 39 The dreadfull bellowing..sounded like the dreadfull doome, And them with such stupidity benummes, As though [etc.]. 1684 tr. *Bonet's Merc. Compit.* VI. 169 Causing onely a gentle Sleep, in no wise a Stupidity. 1684 W. RUSSELL *Phys. Treatise* 117, I ..found her drowsie, tho the Cold and Stupidity were somewhat less. 1806 *Med. Jrnl.* XV. 381 The pain in her head became so acute, as to produce at times, actions of violence, which rendered confinement necessary, and the intervals were marked by stupidity. 1831 *Examiner* 764/2 'Locus' was a cant word to describe the act of putting a man in a state of stupidity.

†**3.** Incapacity for emotion; lack of feeling or interest, apathy, indifference. *Obs.*

1568 G. SKEYNE *Pest* (Bannatyne Club) 15 The cause quhairby few ar preseruit..is maist euident..the negligence & Stupiditie of mankynd, contemptioun of medicine, [etc.]. 1597 HOOKER *Eccl. Pol.* V. lxvii. § 3 Shall I wish that men would more giue themselues to meditate with silence what we haue by the Sacrament, & lesse to dispute of the manner how? If any man suppose that this were too great stupiditie and dulnes, let vs see whether [etc.]. 1668 CLARENDON *Contempl. Ps.* Tracts (1727) 688 The stupidity of the heart alone is the cause of all desperate incogitance. *a* 1672 WILKINS *Nat. Relig.* 387 It supposes them to have..such a stupidity upon their consciences, as makes them past feeling. 1701 G. STANHOPE *Medit. St. Aug.* xl. (1720) 105 Awaken my stupidity, quicken my deadness. 1719 DE FOE *Crusoe* I. (Globe) 89 A certain Stupidity of Soul, without Desire of Good, or Conscience of Evil, had entirely overwhelm'd me. 1724 BOLINGBROKE *Let.* 12 Sept., in *Swift's Lett.* (1766) II. 37 It is neither sickness, nor journies, nor ill humours, nor age, nor vexation, nor stupidity, which has hindered me from answering sooner your letter. 1748 HARTLEY *Observ. Man* II. iv. § 4. 412 If indeed a Man's Despair should make him ..harden himself in a careless Stupidity with respect to his future Condition.

†**b.** Insensibility to pain or sorrow; blameable absence of resentment under injury or insult. *Obs.*

1627 DONNE *Serm.* xliv. (1640) 443 Without this [belief in the Trinity], all morall vertues are but diseases;..Active valour is but a fury, whatsoever we do, and passive valour is but a stupidity, whatsoever we suffer. 1661 COWLEY *Cromwell* Ess., etc. (1906) 362 The continuance of those oppressions upon the people, which will at last tire out their patience, though it be great even to stupidity. *a* 1672 STILLINGFL. *Serm.* VI. (1673) 110 Stupidity then under sufferings can be no part of the excellency of a man; which in its greatest height is in the Beings the most beneath him.

4. Dullness or slowness of apprehension; gross want of intelligence.

1541 R. COPLAND *Galyen's Terap.* 2 C ij b, Nowe we must esteme the stupydyte or audacyte of the man. I say the stupidite yf he thynke to say well and the boldnes yf he fele hym selfe culpable to saye nothynge. 1598 B. JONSON *Ev. Man in Hum.* III. v, I forgive Mr. Stephen, for he is stupiditie it selfe! 1640 T. GRANGER *Div. Logike* 110 Stupiditie a naturall impotencie to vnderstand easily. 1675 in *Verney Mem.* (1907) II. 292 God watt his stupiditie will find it a hard Taske to learn one [*sc.* a trade]. 1690 LOCKE *Hum. Und.* II. x. § 8. 67 It moves slowly, and retrieves not the Ideas, that it has, and are laid up in store, quick enough to serve the Mind upon occasions. This, if it be to a great degree, is Stupidity. 1759 GOLDSM. *Pres. St. Pol. Learn.* iv, But let the Germans have their due: if they are dull, no nation alive..better understands all the decorums of stupidity. 1774 H. WALPOLE *Let. to C'tess Upper Ossory* 14 June, Mr. Anstey..has published the most complete piece of stupidity I ever read. It is a satire on a parson who [etc.]. 1831 CARLYLE *Sartor Res.* II. vii, With Stupidity and sound Digestion man may front much. 1880 'MARK TWAIN' *Tramp Abr.* viii. 58 'Have you engaged a hearse?' 'Bless my stupidity, I never thought of it!' 1896 *Law Times* CI. 516/1 On the average, stupidity in the Church gets better paid than brains at the Bar. 1913 WOODROW WILSON *New Freedom* iii. 70 In public affairs stupidity is more dangerous than knavery.

b. A stupid idea, action, etc.

1633 G. HERBERT *Temple*, *Ch. Militant* 153 Their hearts Are given over..To such Mahometan stupidities, As the old heathen would deem prodigies. 1707 *Curios. in Husb. & Gard.* 245 There..is an infinity of learned Men, who would think themselves Hereticks in Philosophy, if they..thought to search after Truth elsewhere...This is so great a Stupidity, that [etc.]. 1851 *N. Brit. Rev.* XV. 467 The dull stupidities and senseless flippancies of Roman architecture. 1868 E. EDWARDS *Ralegh* I. xxiii. 525 To..enlightened persons ..such themes..are of course, mere obsolete stupidities. 1870 DASENT *Ann. Eventful Life* III. iv. 74 Of all our escapades and stupidities on the journey I decline to dwell. 1874 MICKLETHWAITE *Mod. Par. Churches* 115 One of the stock stupidities of modern times is belief in a *vista*.

5. Obstinacy. *dial.*

1885 *S. W. Linc. Gloss.*, *Stupidity*, obstinacy, not dullness. They understood it well enough; it was stupidity, and nowt else.

Stupidly (stiū·pidli), *adv.* [f. STUPID *a.* + -LY2.] In a stupid manner.

1. In a condition of stupor. Now *rare.*

1661 GLANVILL *Van. Dogm.* vii. 62 They that feel it not, are not less sick, but stupidly so. 1899 *Allbutt's Syst. Med.* VIII. 143 When ailing he sleeps long and stupidly.

†**b.** In consequence of stupefaction. *Obs.*

1667 MILTON *P. L.* IX. 465 That space the Evil One abstracted stood From his own evil, and for the time remained Stupidly good, of enmity disarmed.

†**2.** Apathetically, indifferently. *Obs.*

1647 CLARENDON *Hist. Reb.* II. § 127 Their wariness and wisdom could not be great enough to preserve them, if they did not stupidly look on without seeming to understand what they could in no degree control or prevent.

3. With gross lack of intelligence; foolishly; in a manner indicative of stupidity.

c 1611 CHAPMAN *Iliad* XIV. 199 Comment., How stupidly soeuer all his interpreters would haue Hector (being strooke into a trembling, and almost dead) turne about like a whirlewind. 1699 BENTLEY *Phalaris* 250 Would a person of Learning..be..so stupidly negligent as not to examin the Stone-Cutter's Work. 1700 DRYDEN *Fables* Ded. C 1, There was engraven on it, Plans of Cities, and Maps of Countries, which Ajax could not comprehend, but look'd on them as stupidly as his Fellow-Beast the Lion. 1719 DE FOE *Crusoe* II. (Globe) 445 They were all stupidly ignorant as to Matters of Religion. 1743 WESLEY *Jrnl.* 27 June, I preach'd at Awkborough, on the Trent-side to a stupidly-attentive congregation. 1819 SHELLEY *Peter Bell* VII. xxi, And every neighbouring cottager Stupidly yawned upon the other. 1851 W. WHEWELL *Let.* 26 Jan. in Mrs. Stair Douglas *Life* (1881) 414 We English are as stupidly servile in looking with reverence on all German philosophy, as we are stupidly conceited about our social institutions and manners. 1865 LECKY in Eliz. Lecky *Mem.* i. (1909) 39 The only printed review I have seen is an exceedingly stupidly written one. 1865 E. C. CLAYTON *Cruel Fortune* I. 259 It stared at her, stupidly, its round, chubby face streaked with tears and dirt. 1885 *Manch. Exam.* 25 Mar. 5/1 Nothing could be more stupidly false than such an impression.

4. Obstinately. *dial.*

1884 *Methodist Mag.* 52 Moffat stuck stupidly (this last word, in Lancashire, means resolute persistence in either a wise or foolish saying, or course) that he would go and hear Roby.

Stupidness (stiū·pidnės). Now *rare.* [f. STUPID *a.* + -NESS.] The quality of being stupid (in various senses of the adj.): = STUPIDITY.

a 1628 LD. BROOKE *Treat. Hum. Learning* lxiii, Therefore ..to refine Her stupidnesse, as well as ostentation, Let vs set straight that Industrie againe. 1645 MILTON *Tetrach.* 17 What a stupidnes then is it, that in Mariage,..wee should deject our selvs to such a sluggish and underfoot Philosophy, as to esteem the validity of Mariage meerly by the flesh. 1656 J. SMITH *Pract. Physick* 110 Stupidnesse in the Legs and the whole Body, that they can scarse feel the prick of a needle. 1689 SHERLOCK *Death* iii. § 6 (1731) 139 We may be cut off by a sudden Stroke, or seized with Distraction or Stupidness. 1725 *Bradley's Family Dict.* s.v. *Lethargy*, A Person is threaten'd with this Distemper, when..he grows sluggish, and percieves a Stupidness upon himself and is always inclin'd to Sleepiness.

†**Stu·pidous**, *a.* *Obs. rare*-1. [f. STUPID *a.* + -OUS.] = STUPID.

1597 A. M. tr. *Guillemeau's Fr. Chirurg.* f iij, We shewe our selves stupidouse and involuntary to helpe, the one the other.

†**Stu·pnet.** *dial.* *Obs.* In 7 **stuppnett**, ? **stuppenet, stufnet**. [? dim. of STUPEN: see -ET.] A saucepan.

1600 in W. F. Shaw *Mem. Eastry* (1870) 226 Two chafing dishes fower stuppuetts [? *read* stuppnetts] five brass candlesticks [etc.]. 1649 in *Archæologia Cantiana* XVI. 205 It' rec'd for a Brass Stugpenet [? *read* stuppenet] 00 02 00. 1674 RAY *S. & E. Country Wds.* 76 *Stufnet* [correctly placed, alphabetically, but erroneously printed *stusnet* (long ſ)]: a posnet or skillet. Suss. [Correctly printed in 1691.]

Stupor (stiū·pɔɹ; as scientific Latin ‖ stiū·pǫɹ). Also 5, 7 **stupour**. [a. L. *stupor*, f. *stup-ēre*: see STUPID. Cf. F. *stupeur*, Sp., Pg. *estupor*, It. *stupore.*]

1. A state of insensibility or lethargy; spec. in *Path.*, a disorder characterized by great diminution or entire suspension of sensibility.

Stupor of the teeth: tr. med.L. *stupor dentium*, the rendering, in the ancient translation of Galen, of Gr. αἱμωδία, 'a scorbutic affection of the gums' (L. & Sc.).

1398 TREVISA *Barth. De P. R.* VII. vii. (1495) 227 Stupor is a lettynge and stonyenge of lymmes and crokynge of the vtter partyes of the body for colde so that it semyth that the lymmes shrynke and slepe. 1656 tr. *Hobbes' Elem. Philos.* (1839) 395 For what is stupor but that which the Greeks call ἀναισθησία, that is, a cessation from the sense of other things? 1666 G. HARVEY *Morbus Angl.* x. (1672) 28 Various Diseases, as Catarrhs, stupors, [etc.]. 1678 GALE *Crt. Gentiles* IV. III. iii. 91 By the spirit of deep sleep, must be understood such a stupor of spirit as leaves men without al sense. 1746 R. JAMES *Moffet's Health Improv.* Introd. 12 Acid Eructations, which have in some Cases been so sharp as to induce a Stupor of the Teeth. 1752 *Phil. Trans.* XLVII. 413 There appear'd some signs of stupor from the medicine. 1822–9 GOOD *Study Med.* (ed. 3) IV. 500 The pricking pain like that of pins, or of a limb awaking from stupor. 1843 R. J. GRAVES *Syst. Clin. Med.* v. 71 An expergefaciant..was employed to rouse a patient from the lethargic stupor brought on by a large dose of opium. *a* 1849 POE *Tales*, *Oval Portrait* Wks. 1874 I. 281 The first flashing of the candles upon that canvas had seemed to dissipate the dreamy stupor which was stealing over my senses. *a* 1859 MACAULAY *Hist. Eng.* xxv. V. 289 James sank into a stupor which indicated the near approach of death. 1899 CONAN DOYLE *Duet* viii. 111 She had drunk herself into the stupor in which she had been found.

b. = DEMENTIA 1.

Anergic stupor, a form of dementia in which the patient is quiet, listless, and non-resistant. *Delusional stupor*, stuporous insanity or acute dementia. (Dorland *Med. Dict.* 1913.)

1899 *Allbutt's Syst. Med.* VIII. 297 Stupor, both in its melancholic and anergic varieties, is found much more frequently during the age of adolescence than in any other period of life.

2. A state of mental stupefaction; apathy or torpor of mind (now only, torpor or prostration of mind due to sorrow, painful surprise, or the like).

a 1672 WILKINS *Nat. Relig.* 267 That stupor and benummedness of spirit, whereby men are made unapprehensive of their afflictions. 1784 COWPER *Task* IV. 283 Laugh ye, who boast your more mercurial pow'rs, That never feel a stupor, know no pause, Nor need one. 1786 BURNS *Lament* x, Oh! scenes in strong remembrance set!..Scenes, if in stupor I forget, Again I feel, again I burn! 1837 CARLYLE *Fr. Rev.* I. II. iii, Our Church stands..like a dumb ox..with dumb stupor, expecting its further doom. 1838 DICKENS *Nick. Nick.* xv, The back parlour sat with her mouth wide open, staring vacantly at the collector, in a stupor of dismay. 1841 ELPHINSTONE *Hist. Ind.* XII. iii. II. 633 The inhabitants of Delhi remained in a sort of stupor. They had not yet recovered the terror of the past. 1850 GROTE *Greece* II. lx. VII. 457 A downcast stupor and sense of abasement possessed every man. 1863 MRS. OLIPHANT *Salem Chapel* xxii, It was very different from the stupor of agony.

transf. 1772 BURKE *Let. to W. Dowdeswell* (1844) I. 346, I do not suppose that there was ever anything like this stupor in any period of our history. 1855 DISRAELI in G. E. Buckle *Life* (1916) IV. i. 23 There has been a great stupor over affairs since we parted,..but there are now indications of events. 1879 MORLEY *Burke* iv. 62 The war with the American colonies was preceded by an interval of stupor.

b. Admiring wonder. Also (after med.L. *stupor mundi*), the object of wonder, 'the marvel *of*' (the world, etc.).

1482 *Monk of Evesham* (Arb.) 26 Yet beyng holde in a certeyn stupour and wondyr of mynde of suche thinges that he had seyne. 1599 *Broughton's Lett.* viii. 26 You Cynosura and Lucifer of nations, the stupor and admiration of the world. 1619 PURCHAS *Microcosmus* lxxiii. 727 What shall we say of Him,..the great Stupor and Wonder of Diuines? 1633 'H. A.' (H. Hawkins) *Parthenia Sacra* 237 That Cæsar of Cæsars in captiuing..Caligula the Roman Monark, to the stupour and amazement of the world. 1706 PHILLIPS (ed. Kersey), *Stupor*,..Astonishment, Amazement; ..Wonder, Surprise.

3. Stupidity, dullness of comprehension. *rare.*

1845 CARLYLE *Cromwell* (1871) III. 126 One stupid Annotator..says [etc.]; which is evidently downright stupor and falsehood.

4. *Comb.*

1823 SCORESBY *Jrnl.* 376 A dripping stupor-struck sailor, clinging by the weather-raill, comes aft at the moment. 1833 LAMB *Elia*, *Product. Mod. Art*, Bowed, bent down, so would they have remained, stupor-fixed, with no thought of struggling with that inevitable judgment.

†**Stu·porific**, *a.* *Obs. rare*-1. [f. L. *stupōr-em* STUPOR + -IFIC.] That causes stupor.

1771 J. GILES *Poems* 169 Then she presents a stuporific draught.

Stuporose (stiū·pĕrōᵘs), *a.* [ad. med.L. *stupōrōsus* (Diefenb.) f. L. *stupōr-em*: see STUPOR and -OSE.] = STUPOROUS *a.*

188. BUCK *Med. Handbook* V. 53 (*Cent. Dict.* Suppl.). 1899 *Allbutt's Syst. Med.* VIII. 297 The other 20 per cent. of the cases were mostly melancholic in character, seldom being deeply suicidal, but often tending to be stuporose. *Ibid.* 317 Chloral hydrate, if taken in very large doses, may cause stuporose dementia. 1901 *Brit. Med. Jrnl.* 29 June 1604 The amount of free hydrochloric acid was high when they were in a torpid and stuporose state.

Stuporous (stiū·pĕrəs), *a.* [ad. med.L. *stūpōrōsus*: see prec. and -OUS.] Affected with or characterized by stupor.

1892 E. C. SPITZKA *Insanity* II. v. 158 (Funk) Stuporous insanity consists in the simple impairment or suspension of the mental energies, unmarked by any emotional or other perversion. 1897 *Allbutt's Syst. Med.* III. 357 The stuporous form of melancholia, occurring in young adults. 1899 *Ibid.* VIII. 353 The patient is less responsive to questions and appears to be more profoundly stuporous.

Stupose (stiū·pōᵘs), *a.* *Bot.* [ad. med.L. *stūpōsus*, *stuppōsus* (Diefenb.), f. L. *stūpa*, *stuppa* tow: see -OSE.] (See quots.)

1835 LINDLEY *Introd. Bot.* I. ii. 125 In Anthericum [the filament is] bearded or stupose. 1849 BALFOUR *Man. Bot.* § 60 Bearded, or stupose,..when hairs occur in small tufts. 1900 B. D. JACKSON *Gloss. Bot. Terms*, *Stupose*, tow-like, with tufts of long hairs.

Stuppenet, variant of STUPNET.

Stuppeous: see STUPEOUS *a.*

Stuppin: see STUPEN.

†**Stupple.** *Obs. rare*-1. [Prob. related in some way to STEP *sb.* and *v.*; cf. STOPEL.] ? A row of stepping-stones.

1611 CORYAT *Crudities* 89 [Vercellis] hath many faire streets through which diuers riuers doe runne, with many stupples to passe ouer from one side of the street to the other as in Sarisbury.

Stuppnett, variant of STUPNET.

†**Stu·prate**, *v.* *Obs.* Pa. pple. 6 *Sc.* **stuprat**. [f. L. *stuprāt-* ppl. stem of *stuprāre*, f. *stuprum*: see STUPRE and -ATE3.] *trans.* To violate (a woman).

a 1548 HALL *Chron.*, *Rich. III*, 56 Richarde..hath..compased all the meanes and waies yᵗ he coulde inuent how to stuprate and carnally know his awne nece vnder the pretence of a cloked matrimony. *a* 1560 ROLLAND *Crt. Venus* III. 582 Sichem..Had hir stuprat. 1624 HEYWOOD *Gunaik.* III. 143 Sextus had stuprated the faire Lucretia. 1647 LILLY *Chr. Astrol.* xlix. 318 There may be just suspition..the Mother was stuprated.

Hence †**Stu·prated** *ppl. a.*

1727 BAILEY vol. II, *Stuprated* [*stupratus*, L.] ravished.

†**Stupra·tion.** *Obs.* [a. OF. *stupration* or ad. L. *stuprātiōn-em* noun of action f. *stuprāre*: see STUPRATE *v.*] Violation (of a woman).

1533 BELLENDEN *Livy* III. xv. (S. T. S.) II. 2 The stupratioun and deforcement of lucres. 1535 STEWART *Cron. Scot.* (Rolls) II. 121 Stupr[at]ioun to him wes sic plesour. 1646 SIR T. BROWNE *Pseud. Ep.* v. xxi. 270 Incest, adultery, or stupration. 1656 BLOUNT *Glossogr.*

†**Stupre,** *sb.* *Obs. rare.* [a. OF. *stupre* (revived in 18th c.), ad. L. *stuprum.*] Defilement or violation (of a woman).

1382 WYCLIF *Gen.* xxxiv. 13 The sones of Jacob..waxynge cruel for the stupre of the sister. *Ibid.* 27. 1563 BECON *Demands Script.* Wks. III. 457 Stupre, inceste, fornicacyon, and lyke abhominacyons.

†**Stupre,** *v.* *Obs. rare*-1. [a. OF. *stupre-r*, ad. L. *stuprāre*: see STUPRATE *v.*] *trans.* = STUPRATE *v.*

a 1548 HALL *Chron.*, *Hen. VIII*, 172 b, Thei violated Virgins, and stupred matrones.

†**Stu·prous**, *a.* *Obs. rare*-1. [ad. L. *stuprōsus*, f. *stuprum*: see STUPRE *sb.* and -OUS.] 'Corrupt, naught, given to adultery or whoredom, whorcish' (Blount *Glossogr.* 1656).

1603 FLORIO *Montaigne* II. xxxiii. 418 [Her father] seeing himselfe engaged in so stuprous a necessity [Fr. *en si vilaine necessité*], resolved vpon a haughtie enterprize.

Stupulose (stiū·piŭlōᵘs), *a.* *Ent.* [= mod.L. *stūpulōsus* (Kirby), f. **stūpula* dim. of L. *stūpa*, *stuppa*: cf. STUPOSE.] (See quot.)

1826 KIRBY & SP. *Entomol.* IV. xlvi. 276 *Stupulose*..Covered with coarse decumbent hairs. 1848 MAUNDER *Treas. Nat. Hist.* 807.

†**Stur.** *Obs. rare.* Also 6 **sture**. [? subst. use of STOUR *a.* 7.] A hard variety of apple. Only in comb. *stur-apple*, *-tree.*

1483 *Cath. Angl.* 370/2 A Sturtre, *Duracenus*. 1500 *Ortus Vocab.* (W. de W.) M ij, *Durascenus*, a sture tree. *Durascenum*, a sture appell.

Stur, obs. form of STIR, STOUR, STURE2.

†**Sturb**, *v.* *Obs.* Also 4–5 **storb, stourb**, 5 **sturbe, stourbe**. [Aphetic var. of DISTURB *v.*] *trans.* To disturb, trouble, upset.

a 1225 *Ancr. R.* 428 Al so efter þe ancre cumplie uort midmorwen ne don no þing, ne ne siggen, hwarc þuruh hire silence muwe beon i-sturbed. 1382 WYCLIF *Gen.* xlii. 28 And thei stonyed al aboute and sturbed, seiden togideres, What forsothe is this that God hath doon to vs? *a* 1400–50 *Wars Alex.* 513 Þan was ser Philip of þat fare ferly mekill sturbid. *c* 1400 *Rule St. Benet* (1902) 34 Sho ne sal make noise for to sturbe the othir. *c* 1425 *Eng. Conq. Ireland* xlix. 124 (Dubl. MS.) Throgh that thynge, al the contrey forth ther-aftyr worth so I-storbet, that [etc.]. *a* 1450 MYRC *Par. Pr.* 686 We accursen al them that broken the pece of holy church or sturben hit. *Ibid.* 1459 Hast þou I-storbet prest or clerk þat were bysy in goddes werk? *a* 1450 in *Eng. Gilds* (1870) 448 And þat no brother presume to take vp-on him..to lette, stourbe, ne geynseye, þat elleccioun.

Hence †**Stu·rbing** *vbl. sb.*

a 1225 *Ancr. R.* 154 Heo fluwen monne sturbinge, & wenden bi ham one. *c* 1230 *Meidan Maregrete* 48 Wo þe hider sende, to maken stourbing. 13.. *Guy Warw.* 5751 (Auchinleck MS.) Gij werd him fast in þat sturbing.

†**Stu·rbance.** *Obs. rare.* In 5 **sturbans**. = DISTURBANCE.

c 1450 *Mirk's Festial* 185 Herod..schapute..how Ion myght be don to deth wythout sturbans of þe pepyll.

†**Stu·rblance.** *Obs. rare.* In 5 **sturbelans**. Aphetic form of DISTURBLANCE (cf. STROUBLANCE).

1435 MISYN *Fire of Love* I. xxiii. 50 And in [in]warldly rest, all sturbelans put bak, swetely to byde.

†**Stu·rble**, *v.* *Obs.* Also 5 **sturbyl, sturbel**. [Aphetic var. of DISTURBLE *v.* Cf. STROUBLE *v.*] *trans.* To disturb, trouble.

1303 R. BRUNNE *Handl. Synne* 4713 So was he sturbled with þe mynstral, Þat he hadde no grace to sey with-alle His graces ryght deuoutely. *c* 1330 — *Chron. Wace* (Rolls) 4764 When þe kyng þys chaunce herd seye, Þe feste was sturbled & aweye. 1382 WYCLIF *Ezek.* xxvi. 18 And ylis in the see shulen be sturblid [1388 disturblid]. 1435 MISYN *Fire of Love* 97 Oftyms also odyr noys happyns þat gaynes & swetnes of lufars sturbyls. *c* 1440 *Promp. Parv.* 481/2 Sturbelyn, or turbelyn, *conturbo*, *turbo*, *perturbo.*

Hence †**Stu·rbling** *vbl. sb.* Also †**Stu·rbler.**

13.. *St. Marg.* 223 in Horstm. *Altengl. Leg.* (1881) 231 Who þe hider sent to make me sturbling. 1382 WYCLIF *Ezek.* xxi. 15 In alle the ȝatis of hem Y ȝaue togidre sturblynge [1388 disturbling] of swerd [Vulg. *conturbationem gladii*]. — *Acts* xix. 23 Therfore ther was maad in that day a sturbling [1388 troubling, Vulg. *turbatio*] not leest, of the wey of the Lord. *c* 1440 *Promp. Parv.* 481/2 Sturbelare, or turbelare (or stroblare, sturblar or trowblar) *turbator*, *turbatrix*. *Ibid.*, Sturbelynge, or turbelynge, [sturblinge or troublynge] *turbacio*, *perturbacio.*

Sturdied (stǝ̄·ɹdid), *a.* [f. STURDY *sb.* + -ED2.] Of sheep or cattle: Afflicted with 'sturdy'.

1807 *Prize Ess. & Trans. Highl. Soc.* III. 408, I catched every sturdied sheep that I could lay my hands on. 1822 SCOTT *Nigel* vi, I would as soon set out, with hound and horn, to hunt a sturdied sheep. 1844 H. STEPHENS *Bk. Farm* III. 877 The complaint may be cured, though it is seldom attempted, the sturdied hogg being killed whenever it is seen to be affected.

Sturdily (stǝ̄·ɹdili), *adv.* Forms: see STURDY *a.*; also 4–6 **sturdely**. [f. STURDY *a.* + -LY2.] In a sturdy manner; † with reckless daring (*obs.*); ruthlessly, cruelly, violently (*obs.*); † surlily, rudely, harshly, mutinously, rebelliously (*obs.*); obstinately, unyieldingly, resolutely.

c 1374 CHAUCER *Compl. Mars* 82 Til him fel a drede, Through Phebus, that was comen hastely Within the paleys-yates sturdely. 1375 BARBOUR *Bruce* II. 363 Thai.. Swappyt owt swerdis sturdyly. *c* 1440 *Partonope* 6154 The wind..blew so sturdely. *c* 1470 HENRY *Wallace* II. 42 Full sturdely he coud befor him stand. 1538 ELYOT *Dict.*, *Toruè*, sturdyly in looke. 1544 in *Sel. Cases Crt. Requests* (Selden Soc.) 107 The whiche to doo the said complaynaunte..obstynatly and sturdyly then & there refusyd. 1549 CHEKE *Hurt Sedit.* (1569) H ij b, What say ye to the number of vagabonds and loytring beggers, which..will..stande sturdely in Cities, and begge boldly at euery dore. *a* 1674 CLARENDON *Hist. Reb.* x. § 68 The Scots now begun again to talk sturdily. 1674 PRIDEAUX *Lett.* (Camden) 13, I assure you they dispute the case most sturdyly. 1810 SCOTT *Lady of Lake* IV. xxv, It was a stag, a stag of ten, Bearing his branches sturdily. 1858 FROUDE *Hist. Eng.* III. xvii. 456 Wyatt answered sturdily that Brancetor was his master's subject. 1893 J. EDGAR *Hist. Early Scott. Educ.* 211 The University of Aberdeen held out sturdily against the reformers. 1901 RASHDALL & RAIT *New College* vi. 115 The soul of the sturdily Protestant Bishop Horne was moved by the tidings which reached him from Oxford.

Sturdiness (stǝ̄·ɹdinės). Forms: see STURDY *a.*; also 4 **stordenesse**. [-NESS.] The quality or condition of being sturdy.

1. The condition (in animals) of being 'sturdy' or dizzy; *spec.* in sheep. = STURDY B. 1.

1552 HULOET, Sturdynes or desynes of a beast,..*gangilion*. 1756 *Compl. Body Husb.* 695 Sturdyness..is a kind of vertigo or giddiness in the Head of Sheep.

†**2.** Fierceness, violence; harshness, sternness.

1382 WYCLIF *2 Cor.* xii. 20 Sturdynessis [Vulg. *animositates*]. *c* 1386 [see STURDY *a.* 4]. *c* 1430 LYDG. *Min. Poems* (Percy Soc.) 198 Tempest on se, and wyndes sturdynesse.

†**3.** Refractoriness, rebelliousness, contumacy, obstinacy. *Obs.*

a 1400 *Gloss* in *Rel. Ant.* I. 7 *Contumacia*, a sturdynesse. *c* 1440 *Jacob's Well* 77 Þe laste cornere of wose in pride is sturdynesse, þat is, whanne þou excusyst þin opyn or pryue synne,..& wylt noȝt knowyn þi defawte, ne wylt noȝt suffryn to ben vndertakyn. *c* 1440 *Promp. Parv.* 481 2 Sturdynesse, *rebellio*, *inobediencia*, *contumacia*. 1544 BETHAM *Precepts War* II. xvii. K iij, Of disobedience and sturdynesse. 1549 CHEKE *Hurt Sedit.* (1569) C ij b, What counsayle taketh place, where sturdinesse is lawe, and churlishe aunsweres be counted wisedome? 1673 *Ladies Calling* I. ii. § 10 The stupid sturdiness of an asse has rendered it proverbial for folly.

4. Strength of character; firmness, resoluteness.

1675 J. SMITH *Chr. Relig. Appeal* I. 70 Their Nurture and Education..had..so much effeminated their innate sturdiness, as they were not able to sustain the sharpness of that War. *a* 1716 SOUTH *Serm.* (1727) VI. 273 The natural Sturdiness of some Tempers might be sufficient to enable some Persons to endure such exquisite Torments. 1727 BAILEY vol. II, *Sturdiness*, Lustiness, Resoluteness. 1768–74 TUCKER *Lt. Nat.* (1834) II. 287 What degree of sturdiness we can acquire, to maintain the determinations of our impartial judgment. 1822 HAZLITT *Table-t.*, *Knowl. Charac.* II. 346 All they want is imagination and sturdiness of moral principle! 1914 *Q. Rev.* Apr. 487 The virility and sturdiness of the Cretan Greeks.

5. Rough vigour of body; solidity of build. Also of things.

1863 GEO. ELIOT *Romola* xxx, His limbs had got back some of their old sturdiness. 1916 *Glasgow Herald* 1 Sept. 8 Craft that, despite their sturdiness, move in rough weather like buck-jumping ponies.

Sturdy (stǝ̄·ɹdi), *a.* and *sb.* Forms: 4 **stourdi, sturdi, (stourde)**, 4–6 **stourdy, stordy**, 6 **stourdie, sturdye**, 6–7 **sturdie**, 7 **stirdy**, 4– **sturdy**. [a. OF. *estourdi*, *estordi*, *esturdi*, stunned, dazed, reckless, violent (mod.F. *étourdi* feather-brained, thoughtless), = Pr. *estordit*, It. *stordito*, Sp., Pg. *aturdido*; pa. pple. of OF. *estourdir* (mod.F. *étourdir*) to stun, daze, = It. *stordire*, Sp., Pg. *aturdir* (? from Fr.):—vulgar L. **exturdire*, of obscure origin.

Some scholars think that it is f. *ex-* (see EX-) + *turd-us* thrush (for the sense cf. the Fr. proverbial phrase *soûl comme une grive*, 'drunk as a thrush'); some regard it as a contraction of **extorpidire* (L. *torpidus* TORPID) or of **exturbidire* (L. *turbidus* TURBID). All these conjectures are open to grave objection; another hypothesis, of derivation from Teut. **sturtjan* to overthrow (see START *v.*), is on phonological grounds inadmissible.]

A. *adj.*

I. 1. In the primary etymological sense: Giddy. Said of sheep affected with the 'sturdy': see B. Now *dial.* (see *Eng. Dial. Dict.*).

1641 BEST *Farm. Bks.* (Surtees) 73 If there bee any of the hogges that bee sturdy, lame, weake.

II. †**2.** Impetuously brave, fierce in combat.

1297 R. GLOUC. (Rolls) 7936 Þe heyemen of engelond..mid gret ost wende uorþ & mid stourdi [*v.r.* stourde] mod. *c* 1300 *K. Horn* 893 (Laud MS.) We neuere ne hente Of man so harde dunte Bute of þe king Mory Þat was so swyþe stordy. 1375 BARBOUR *Bruce* V. 506* He sa sturdy wes and stout, That he wes the mast vorthy man That in-to Carrick liffit than. *c* 1425 *Engl. Conq. Ireland* xlvi. 116 The northeren men ben stordyer & smerter to fyght than other. *Ibid.* 118 Thegh he wer yn wepne vnmetly stordy, & sterne, out of wepne natheles, he was meke and sobre. 1630 R. JOHNSON *Kingd. & Commw.* 23 Able, and hardy bodies, and stout and sturdy stomacks. 1684 BUNYAN *Pilgr.* II. (1900) 258 They so belabored him, being sturdy men at Arms, that they made him make a Retreat.

†**b.** Of a battle: Fierce, violent. *Obs.*

c 1450 LOVELICH *Grail* xliii. 782 Therfore was that stour ful Stordy. 1579 E. K. *Gloss. to Spenser's Sheph. Cal.* Feb. 149 Sterne strife, said Chaucer, s. fell and sturdy.

†**3.** Recklessly violent, furious, ruthless, cruel.

1297 R. GLOUC. (Rolls) 3842 He adrou sire calibourne, is suerd..& anowarde þe helm, mid wel stourdy mod, Þen oþer he smot. *c* 1374 CHAUCER *Boeth.* III. met. ii. (1868) 68 Þe liouns of þe contre of pene..dreden her sturdy maystres [L. *trucem..magistrum*] of whiche þei ben wont to suffren betinges. *a* 1513 FABYAN *Chron.* VII. (1811) 643 Lewys the ..xi..of Gaguinus is callyd the sturdy or fell Lewys. 1531 ELYOT *Gov.* III. ix. (1883) II. 272 So no violence or sturdye mynde lackynge reason and honestie is any parte of fortitude. 1589 PUTTENHAM *Eng. Poesie* I. iii. (Arb.) 22 To redresse and edifie the cruell and sturdie courage of man.

†**b.** Of waves, a stream, a storm, etc.: Violent, rough. *Obs.*

1375 BARBOUR *Bruce* III. 698 And entryt sone in-to the rase, Quhar that the strem sa sturdy was. 1426 LYDG. *De Guil. Pilgr.* 16670 Fordryven with many sturdy wawes off adversyte. 1569 T. NEWTON *Cicero's Old Age* 33 In the sturdy and nipping cold of winter. 1588 CHURCHYARD *Spark Friendship* Ep. Ded. A 3 b, The brute beastes that auoydes a sturdie storme, vnder the sauegard of a strong and flourishing tree. 1648 *Kentish Serm. to Commons* 10 The highest Houses are subject to the sturdiest storms. 1660 RIDERS *Brit. Merlin* Oct., Sturdy storms of rain or snow, with extream ill weather, to the moneths end. 1823 COBBETT *Rur. Rides* (1885) I. 226 A pretty decent and sturdy rain began to fall.

†**c.** Of movement: Furious. Of a blow: Violent.

c 1386 CHAUCER *Sompn. T.* 454 And forth he gooth, with a ful angry chere..A sturdy [*v.rr.* stourdy, stordy] paas doun to the court he gooth. 1579 SPENSER *Sheph. Cal.* Feb. 201 But to the roote [he] bent his sturdie stroke, And made many wounds in the wast Oake. 1603 KNOLLES *Hist. Turks* (1638) 40 With many wounds and sturdy blows both giuen and receiued.

†**4.** Of or with regard to countenance, speech, demeanour: Stern, harsh, rough, surly. *Obs.*

1297 R. GLOUC. (Rolls) 3287 After mete he nom is wif mid stourdi mod ynou, & wiþoute leue of þe kinge toward is contreye drou. *c* 1386 CHAUCER *Clerk's T.* 642 What koude a sturdy housbonde moore deuyse To preeue hire wyfhod or hir stedefastnesse, And he continuynge euere in sturdinesse? *c* 1440 *Partonope* 2573 And to my men dyspitous and sturdy. 1531 ELYOT *Gov.* I. vii. (1883) I. 40 Retaynyng his fiers and stourdie countenance. *Ibid.* II. v. II. 48 Litle and litle he withdrewe from men his accustomed gentilnesse, becomyng more sturdy in langage, and straunge in countenance, than euer before had ben his usage. 1552 HULOET, Sturdy, *superbus*, *superciliosus*. 1611 SPEED *Hist. Gt. Brit.* VIII. ii. § 13 Their sturdy behauiour, and Lord-like carriage against the English.

†**5.** Hard to manage, intractable, refractory; rebellious, disobedient. *Obs.*

13.. *K. Alis.* 1332 Thider he wendith with gret pres, This stordy citeis for to dres. *c* 1400 *Master of Game* (MS. Digby 182) xv, Alauntes beeth inly fell and euyl vndrestondynge and more fooliche and more sturdy þan any oþer manere of houndes. *c* 1440 *Promp. Parv.* 481/2 Sturdy, vnbuxum, *rebellis*, *contumax*, *inobediens*. *c* 1440 *Jacob's Well* 236 To be sturdy to fadyr & modyr. 1514 BARCLAY *Cit. & Uplondyshman* (Percy Soc.) 17 The fyrste plowman and tyller of the grounde, Was rude and sturdy, dysdaynynge to be bounde. 1603 DRAYTON *Bar. Wars* I. 1, Sturdie to manage, of a haughtie Spright. 1604 F. HERRING *Mod. Defence Caveat* 6 A sturdie horse requires a rough rider. 1611 SPEED *Theat. Gt. Brit.* II. xiii. 121 The ancient Inhabitants of this Country [Flint] were the Ordouices, a sturdy people against the Romans, but now most kinde and gentle towards the English. *c* 1635 in *Verney Mem.* (1907) I. 122 My soun doth begine to be toe sturdie for my government. 1655 FULLER *Ch. Hist.* IX. 187 The most sturdy and refractory Non-conformists. 1688 PENTON *Guardian's Instruct.* (1897) 10 Beware of setting up that stirdy Resolution which some make, never to give off what they have once begun. 1781 COWPER *Hope* 182 Man is the genuine offspring of revolt, Stubborn and sturdy—a wild ass's colt.

†**b.** Obstinate, immovable in opinion. *Obs.*

1664 H. MORE *Myst. Iniq.* Apol. 522 If men would not bring their own sturdy Preconceptions, but listen to the easy and natural aire of the Text. 1680 *Tides* (MS. Bodl. Add. A. 202) 10 Seafareing men..grow as sturdy and deafe to all the reason and argument that can be employed to undeceive them, as the Eliments wherein they converse. 1687 R. L'ESTRANGE *Answ. to Dissenter* 4 If they be not either too Sturdy, or too Stately, to Hearken to Reason. 1780 COWPER *Progr. Error* 539 Your blund'rer is as sturdy as a rock. 1781 — *Expost.* 298 Where obstinacy takes his sturdy stand, To disconcert what policy has plann'd.

c. [With mixture of sense 7.] Epithet of beggars or vagabonds who are able-bodied and apt to be violent: see BEGGAR *sb.* 1 b., VALIANT *a.* 1 b. Also *sturdy and valiant*.

1402 *Jack Upland* in *Pol. Poems* (Rolls) II. 96 For in many places thai dampnen suche sturdy beggyng. 1535–6 *Act 27 Hen. VIII*, c. 25 § 1 Suche poore creature or sturdie vacabund. 1556 in *Vicary's Anat.* (1888) 174 *note*, Sturdie & valiente Beggers. 1577 tr. *Bullinger's Decades* II. iii. (1592) 129 The sturdie roag vnworthie of almes. 1656 BEALE *Heref. Orchards* (1657) 39 Where Trade thrives not,..all doors and highways are oppressed with idle and sturdy vagabonds. *a* 1680 BUTLER *Lady's Answ.* 43 Like sturdy Beggars, that intreat For Charity at once, and threat. *a* 1700 B. E. *Dict. Cant. Crew*, *Sturdy-beggers*, the fifth and last of the most ancient Order of Canters. 1789 J. WILLIAMS *Min. Kingd.* I. 202 When I reprove a sturdy beggar for being idle, he tells me roundly, that he cannot get employment.

6. Of material things: Refractory, defiant of destructive agencies or force; strong, stout.

c 1374 CHAUCER *Troylus* II. 1380 Þe sturdy ok On which men hakketh ofte for þe nones. *c* 1400 *Rom. Rose* 4155 Vpon the whiche also stode Of squared stoon a sturdy wall. 1575 *Gammer Gurton* I. ii. 16 Chwold rend it, though it were stitched wath sturdy pacthreede. 1577 B. GOOGE *Heresbach's Husb.* I. 41 b, Suche Grayne as hath the sturdiest strawe. 1600 FAIRFAX *Tasso* XV. ii, Euerie tender lim In sturdie steele and stubburne plate they dight. 1663 BUTLER *Hud.* I. i. 305 His Doublet was of sturdy Buff. 1671 MILTON *P. R.* IV. 417 On the vext Wilderness, whose ..sturdiest Oaks Bow'd their Stiff necks. 1697 EVELYN *Numism.* i. 10 Foliated with Silver upon this sturdy and inflexible Metal [Iron]. 1841 DICKENS *Barn. Rudge* xxxiii, A violent gust of wind and rain..seemed to shake even that sturdy house to its foundation. 1858 HAWTHORNE *Fr. & It. Jrnls.* (1871) I. 141 The old triumphal arch of Drusus—a sturdy construction, much dilapidated [etc.]. 1870 BRYANT *Iliad* XIII. 359 Hasten thou And bring a sturdy javelin from the tent.

†**b.** Of wine: Rough or harsh to the taste. *Obs.*

c 1440 *Pallad. on Husb.* XI. 390 Also a man may in oon dayes while So trete a stordy wyn that hit shal smyle, And of a rough drynker be cleer and best.

†**c.** Of an ailment: Refractory to treatment. *Obs.*

Supplement, p. 3873; Corrigenda, p. 4092; Spurious words, p. 4093; Books quoted, p. 4094

STYING

3. Black as the river Styx; dark or gloomy as the region of the Styx.

†4. *Stygian water, liquor* [tr. mod.L. *aqua Stygia*]: in Old Chemistry, a name for nitro-hydrochloric acid and strong mineral acids. Also applied to virulent poisons. Also *Stygian liquor* (jocularly): a black manseous drink. *Obs.*

Styin, styill, obs. forms of STEEL, STILL.

† Sty·ing, *vbl. a. Obs.* [f. STY v.[2] + -ING[1].]
The action of ascending; ascent.

Styin·g, *ppl. a. Obs.* That ascends.

Stying, obs. f. STYE *sb.*, enclosure for swine.

Styk, **Stykn**, obs. forms of STICK, STYCCA.

Styl, obs. form of STEEL, STILL.

Sty lagalma·tic, *a. rare. Arch.* (In Dicts. erron. -ale.) [f. Gr. στῦλος column + ἄγαλμα, -ματ- image + -IC.] Pertaining to, containing, or supported by, figures serving as columns.

I. Stylus, pin, stalk.

† Stylar, *a.* Also **stilar**. [f. mod.L. type *stylāris*, f. *stylus*: see STYLE *sb.* and -AR.]

† Stylate *a. rare. Obs.* [ad. L. *stylātus*.]

†1. Stylator (stəla·rɑtə), *n. Obs.* [mod.L. (Gray 1821), f. Gr. στῦλος column + φόρος-bearing.]

II. [Developed in L. from sense 1.] Writing; manner of writing (hence also of speaking).

†12. A written work or works; literary composition; in later use occas. a composition spoken or read. *Obs.*

† b. An inscription or legend. *Obs.*

† c. An entry, clause, or section in a legal document. Also *†* the heading or introductory formula of a will, a writ, or other document. *Obs.*

13. The manner of expression characteristic of a particular writer (hence of an orator), or of a literary group or period; a writer's mode of expression considered in regard to clearness, effectiveness, beauty, and the like.

† 16. A form of words, phrase, or formula, by which a particular idea or thought is expressed.

† b. A particular manner of life or behaviour.

†20. Condition with regard to convenience, etc. *Obs.*

21. A particular mode or form of skilled construction, execution, or production; the manner in which a work of art is executed, regarded as characteristic of the individual artist, or of his time and place; one of the modes recognized in particular art as suitable for the production of beautiful or skilful work.

STYLE. 1207

Syst. Med. VII. 649 The 'style' of the symptoms, as I am in the habit...

STYLELESS

Styleless (stəi·lȝes), *a.* [f. STYLE *sb.* + -LESS.] Devoid of style, in various senses. Hence **Sty·lelessness**.

STYLET. 1208

Stylet (stəi·let). Forms: 7 -* o*-*tille*, 8 **stillet**, 9 **stilette**, 9 **stylet**. [a. F. *stylet*, ad. It. *stiletto*.]

1. *Surg.* A slender probe. Also, a wire run through a catheter or canula in order to stiffen it or to clear it.

2. *Ent.* = STYLE *sb.* 8.

Stylo- (stəi·lo), before a vowel *styl-*, the combining form of Gr. στῦλος column, used in various scientific words.

Stylobata. ... pertaining to the styloid process and the tongue ; *sb.* = *styloglossus* (in recent Dicts.). ‖ **Stylo-glo'ssus** (†-*glossum*), a muscle arising from the styloid process and inserted in the tongue.

Stylohyal (stailə̄·hăi·ŏid), *a.* and *sb. Anat.* [ad. mod.L. *stylohyoīd-eus* (see below), f. STYLO- + *hyoídeus* (see HYOIDEAN and HYOID).] **A.** *adj.* Of or pertaining to the stylohyal and the hyoid bone.

Stylobate (stai·lŏbăt). *Arch.* [a. L. *stylobata*, ad. Gr. στυλοβάτης, f. στῦλος pillar + -βατης, f. βαίνειν to walk, step.] = next.

Stylolite (stai·lŏləit). *Geol.* Also *attrib.*

Stylomastoid (stailomæ·stoid), *a. Anat.* [f. STYLO- + MASTOID.] Common to the styloid and mastoid processes of the temporal bone.

Stylopized (stai·lŏpəized), *ppl. a.*

Stylop (stai·lŏp), *Ent.* Anglicized form of *Stylops*.

Stylopod (stai·lŏpŏd), *Bot.* Pl. **-podia** (-pōu·diă). [mod.L. (Hoffmann), f. Gr. στῦλο- + πίλλαρ (Gr. πούς, πο̄δ-) + πούς, root-foot.]

Stylopodium (stailopōu·diŭm), *Bot.* Pl. **-podia** (-diă). [mod.L. f. Gr. στῦλο- + ...]

Stylops (stai·lŏps), *Ent.* Pl. **Stylopes** (-pīz).

Stylospore (stai·lŏspoə̄r). *Bot.*

Stylostixis (stailostikˑsis). *Med.*

Stylostegium (stailostē·dziŏm). *Bot.*

Stylobata (cont.) ...

Styloid (stai·loid), *a.* and *sb. Anat.*

Stylite (stai·ləit). *Eccl. Hist.*

Stylograph (stai·lŏgraf). [f. mod.L. *styl-us*, incorrect form of L. *stil-us* STYLE + -GRAPH.]

Stylographic (stailŏgræ·fik), *a.* [Formed as prec. + -GRAPHIC.]

Stylography (stailŏ·grăfi). 1 *Obs.*

Stylote (stai·lŏut), *a. Zool.*

Stylus (stai·lŏs). Also *stilus.* [a. L. *stylus*, incorrect form of L. *stilus* : see STYLE *sb.*]

Stylotegium (stailotē·dziŏm). *Bot.* [mod.L.] = the source of STYLE *sb.* + στέγιον roof.]

Stylote (cont.) ...

Style, **stime** (stəim, stī·m). Chiefly *Sc.* and *north.* Forms: 3-4, 7 **stime**, 5 **styme**, 6 **steyme**, *etc.*

Stymie (stai·mi), *sb.* Also *steimie*. [Of obscure origin : cf. prec. and STYME *sb.*]

Stymie, *v.* *Golf.*

Stymphalian (stimfē·liăn), *a. Myth.*

Stymphalid (sti·mfălid), *sb.*

Stymphalid (cont.) ...

Stymphalist (sti·mfălist).

Stymphalize (sti·mfăləiz).

Stych, Styche: see STREICH, STYANY.

Styng(e, **Styngill**: see STINGE, STINGLE.

Stynie, -y, *etc.* ff. STANY.

Stypand, -ond, *etc. obs.* ff. STIPEND.

Styphate (sti·fŏt), *sb. Chem.* [f. STYPHN-IC + -ATE.]

Styphnic (sti·fnik), *a. Chem.*

Stythe (staiðð), *sb. north.* Forms : 5 **stithe**, 8 **styth**, *north.* Also 8 **stith**.

Styptic (sti·ptik), *a.* and *sb.* Forms : 5 **stip-tike**, 6 **styptike**, 6-7 **stiptike**, *etc.*

Styptical (sti·ptikăl), *a.* ? *Obs.* [f. as prec. + -AL.]

Stypticity (stiptiˑsiti). *Min.*

Stypticity (cont.) ...

Styptus (sti·ptŭs). ? *Obs.*

Styrax (stai·ræks). *Chem.* Also -ine.

Styracin (sti·răsin). *Chem.*

Styrax (cont.) [a. L. *styrax*, a. Gr. στύραξ.]

Styrian (sti·riăn), *a.* and *sb.* [f. *Styria* (see below : in Ger. *Steier, Steiermark*) + -AN.]

Styrol (stai·rŏl), *Chem.* Also **styrole**. [f. STYR-AX + -OL.]

Styrolene (stai·rŏlīn). *Chem.*

Styrone (stai·rŏn). *Chem.*

Styryl (stai·ril). *Chem.* Also **-yle**. [f. STYR-AX + -YL.]

Styth, **styth**: see STITHE.

Stythe (staiðð). *Obs.* ...

Styx (stiks). Also -ine. [L. *Styx*, a. Gr. Στύξ (Στυγ-).]

Su—Sz.

Su, dial. f. SHE; obs. f. SUE. **Sua**, obs. f. So.

Suabian: see SWABIAN.

Suability (siŭābi·liti). *U.S.* [f. next : see -ITY.] Liability to be sued.

Suable (siŭ·ăb'l), *a.* Now chiefly *U.S.* [f. SUE *v.* + -ABLE.] Capable of being sued, liable to be sued.

Suada, **Suade**: see SUASION, SUADE.

Suade (swēd), *v.* Now *rare* or *dial.* Also 6 **swade**, 9 'swade. [Partly ad. L. *suadēre*, f. root SWAD-; partly a syncopation from PERSUADE.]

Suant (siū·ănt), *a.* Now *dial.* Forms : 6 **suaunt**, 6-9 **sewant**, 8 **suent**, 9 **suant**, **S-uant**. [a. AF. *su(a)nt*, OF. *suiant*, *sivant*.]

Suasible (swē·sib'l), *a. rare.* [f. L. *suādi-bilis*, f. *suādēre*, to persuade.]

Suasion (swē·ʒən). [a. F. *suasion*, ad. L. *suāsiōn-em*, n. of action f. *suādēre*.]

Suasive (swē·siv), *a.* and *sb.* [ad. late L. *suāsīvus*, f. *suās-*.]

Suasory (swē·səri), *a.* Now *rare.* [ad. L. *suāsōri-us*.]

Suave (swāv, swēv), *a.* [ad. F. *suave* or L. *suāvis*.] **1.** Pleasing or agreeable to the senses or the mind ; sweet.

SUAVELY

and well-bred equanimity. **1865** GEO. ELIOT *Romola* xxxi. Doubtless the suave secretary had his own ends to serve.

Suavely (swēvˑli), *adv.* [f. SUAVE *a.* + -LY²]

1. In a suave manner; with urbanity.

2. Agreeably, sweetly, gently.

Suaveness. [f. SUAVE *a.* + -NESS.] The quality of being suave.

Suavescent, *a. rare.* [ad. L. *suāvēscent-*, *-ēns*, f. *suāve* advb. neut. of *suāvis* SUAVE + *olēns*, *-ent-*, pr. pple. of *olēre* to smell.]

† Suaviate, *v. Obs. rare.* [f. L. *suāviāt-*, ppl. stem of *suāviārī*, f. *suāvium*, altered f. *sāvium* kiss, by assimilation to *suāvis* sweet.] *trans.* To kiss. So **Suaviˑation**, kissing.

Suavify (swēˑvifai), *v. rare.* [f. SUAVE *a.* + -FY.] *trans.* To make suave or affable (Webster 1847).

Suaviloquence (swēviˑlŏkwĕns), *rare.* [ad. L. *suāviloquentia*, f. *suāviloquens*, f. *suāvis* SUAVE + *loquens*, pres. pple. of *loquī* to speak.] Pleasing or agreeable speech or manner of speaking. So **Suaviˑloquent**, **Suaviˑloquious** (in Dicts.), *adj.*, of sweet speech; **Suaviˑlogy** [L. *suāviloquium*], suaviloquence.

Suavitude. *Obs. rare.* [ad. L. *suāvitūdin-*, *-tūdo*.] Sweetness, gentleness.

Suavity (swēˑviti), *also* **3 suavitee, 6 suavitude**. [ad. L. *suāvitās*, f. *suāvis* SUAVE + -TY².] Sweetness, pleasantness.

† 1. Sweetness or agreeableness to the senses: *esp.* sweetness (of taste), fragrance (of odour). *Obs.*

b. Sweetness (of sound, harmony, expression).

2. Pleasurableness agreeableness; *pl.* delights, amenities. Now only in coloured by sense *4.*

SUB-

Sub (sŏb). The Latin prep. *sub* (with the ablative) 'under', enters in to a few legal and other phrases, now or formerly in common use, the chief of which are given below.

sub camino (?).

2. sub dio, under the open sky, in the open air.

sub finem, towards the end.

sub judice, lit. 'under a judge'; under the consideration of a judge or court; undecided, not yet settled, still under consideration.

† sub pœna, lit. 'under penalty', i.e. upon the penalty.

sub rosa, lit. 'under the rose'.

† sub sigillo, under the seal (of confession); in confidence, in secret.

14. sub silentio, in silence, without remark being made, without notice being taken.

15. sub voce (abbreviated *s.v.*): under the word (so-and-so); abbreviated *s.v.*

Sub- (sŏb, səb) *prefix*, repr. L. *sub-* = the prep. *sub* under, close to, up to, towards, used in composition (cf. UNDER): with the various meanings detailed below. (The related Skr. *upa-*, Gr. *ὑπο-* have a similar range of meaning.)

SUB-. 6 SUB-.

SUB-. 7 SUB-.

SUB-. 8 SUBACT. SUBACTION. 9 SUBALTERN

had other subaltern modes that were dependent on them. 1839 Hallam *Lit. Eur.* III. iv. § 55 All causes of wealth, except those he has enumerated, Serra holds to be subaltern or temporary. 1866 Whipple *Char. & Char. Men* 22 The power and working intelligence of the subaltern natures it uses. 1893 in J. H. Barrows *World's Parl. Relig.* I. 256 Not a subaltern science to dogmatic theology.

†**d.** Of material things. *Obs.*

1733 tr. *Winslow's Anat.* (1756) I. 302 The Composition of the Fibres of this Muscle, and its division into several subaltern Muscles.

3. *Subaltern officer*: an officer in the army of junior rank, i.e. below that of captain. Hence *subaltern rank*, etc.

1688 *Lond. Gaz.* No. 2396/3 Count Strozzi..was..Shot dead..and two or three Subalterne Officers wounded. 1702 *Milit. Dict.* (1704) s. v. *Officer, Subaltern-Officers.* The Lieutenant, Ensigns, and Cornets of Horse, Foot, and Dragoons, are so call'd. *a* 1721 Prior *Dial. Dead* (1907) 208 Had not I equally my Captains, and Subaltern Officers? 1807 *Med. Jrnl.* XVII. 222 The cries of the soldier were heard by the subaltern officer. 1811 *Regul. & Orders Army* 248 The Subaltern Officers, Non-Commissioned Officers, and Men, are to be divided into Watches. 1859 W. Collins *Q. of Hearts* iv, Have you any ears left for small items of private intelligence from insignificant subaltern officers?

4. Of a vassal: Holding of one who is himself a vassal. Hence of a feu or right.

1681 Stair *Inst. Law Scot.* I. xiii. 252 The Vassals of the King, who only might grant subaltern Infeftments of their Ward Lands. *Ibid.* xxi. 420 If the major part be not alienate, Subaltern Infeudations..infer not recognition, when these rights are *disjunctim* of parts of the Fee. *Ibid.* 424 Seing all other Rights fall in *consequentiam*, as was found in Subaltern-rights in the said case. *Ibid.* 429 Omitted not only by the immediat Vassal, but by all subaltern Vassals. 1723 *Bibl. Literaria* No. vi. 17 Reliefs, Fines, Duties upon the several subaltern Manors. 1765–8 Erskine *Inst. Law Scot.* II. vii. § 8 Subaltern infeftments soon recovered force after the statute of Robert which abolished them. 1838 W. Bell *Dict. Law Scot.* 88 Suppose A to hold of the Crown blench, and that he subfeus his lands to B, to be held in feu...A's right is termed a public one; B's a base or subaltern right.

5. *Logic.* Of a proposition: Particular, in relation to a universal of the same quality.

Subaltern opposition: opposition between a universal and a particular of the same quality. (Cf. Subalternant, Subalternate.)

1656 tr. *Hobbes' Elem. Philos.* I. iii. 30 Subaltern, are Universal and Particular Propositions of the same Quality; as, Every Man is a Living Creature, Some Man is a Living Creature. 1725 Watts *Logic* II. ii. § 3 Both particular and universal Propositions which agree in Quality but not in Quantity are call'd Subaltern. 1860 Abp. Thomson *Laws Th.* § 84. 151 Subaltern opposition is between any pair of affirmative or negative judgments, when the one has fewer terms distributed, that is, taken entire, than the other. 1864 Bowen *Logic* vi. 162, I can immediately infer the truth of its Subaltern Opposite.

B. *sb.*

1. A person († or thing) of inferior rank or status; a subordinate; *occas.* † a subaltern genus; † a subordinate character in a book.

1605 Camden *Rem.* (1623) 4 When all Christianity in the Counsell of Constance was diuided into Nations, Anglicana Natio was one of the principall and no subalterne. *a* 1619 Fotherby *Atheom.* II. iii. § 3 (1622) 219 The subalternes, are both, in their diuers relations; Genera, to their inferiors; and Species, to their superiors. *a* 1628 F. Grevil *Life of Sidney* (1652) 14 They..both encourage, and shaddow the conspiracies of ambitious subalternes to their false endes. 1706 Phillips (ed. Kersey), *Subalterns*, inferiour Judges, or Officers. 1765 H. Walpole *Otranto* (1886) 10 The art of the author is very observable in the conduct of the subalterns. 1787 Charlotte Smith *Rom. Real Life* II. 133 If the subalterns of the law once seize on the property. 1816 'Quiz' *Grand Master* I. 3 Passive obedience under wrongs, 'Tis thought, to subalterns belongs. 1860 Emerson *Cond. Life, Power* Wks. (Bohn) II. 332 The geologist reports the surveys of his subalterns. 1885 'Mrs. Alexander' *At Bay* v, The *chef de la sûreté* and his subaltern.

2. A subaltern officer in the army.

1690 *Lond. Gaz.* No. 2616/3 The Marquis de St. George,..with his Lieutenant-Colonel, Major, 10 Captains, and 25 Subalternes are arrived here. 1760 *Caut. & Adv. Off. Army* 77 A Subaltern will find it extremely difficult to live upon his Pay, and support the Appearance of a Gentleman. 1796 Morse *Amer. Geog.* I. 431 The respective companies choose their captain, and subalterns. 1811 *Gen. Regul. Army* 37 No Officer shall be promoted to the Rank of Captain, until he has been Three Years a Subaltern. 1846 Browning *Luria* III. 4 How could subalterns like myself expect Leisure or leave to occupy the field?

attrib. 1898 'Merriman' *Roden's Corner* x, Major White had, in his subaltern days, been despatched from Gibraltar on a business quest into the interior of Spain.

b. **subaltern's butter**, the fruit of *Persea gratissima* = Avocado, called also *midshipman's butter*; **subaltern's luncheon** (see quot. 1904).

1829 Marryat *Fr. Mildmay* xviii, Abbogada pears (better known by the name of subaltern's butter). 1904 A. Griffiths *50 Yrs. Public Serv.* 50 The traditional 'subaltern's luncheon'—'a glass of water and a pull at the waistbelt'.

3. *Logic.* A subaltern proposition.

1826 Whately *Logic* II. ii. § 3, 1st. the two universals (A and E) are called contraries to each other; 2d. the two particular, (I and O) subcontraries; 3d. A and I, or E and O, subalterns; 4th. A and O, or E and I, contradictories. *Ibid.*, Subalterns differ in quantity alone; Contraries, and also Subcontraries, in quality alone. 1870 Jevons *Elem. Logic* ix. 78 Of subalterns, the particular is true if the universal be true.

Hence **Su·balternhood, -ship**, the status or period of service of a subaltern.

1857 *Fraser's Mag.* LVI. 172 The Indian officer has to serve a long subalternhood. 1861 *Cornh. Mag.* Jan. 74 James Outram soon obtained the grand reward of efficiency in regimental subalternship, the adjutancy of a corps.

†**Subaltern**, *v. Obs. rare.* [ad. med.L. *subalternāre*, f. *subalternus* (see prec.). Cf. OF. *subalterner*.] *trans.* To subordinate.

c 1400 *Pilgr. Sowle* (Caxton) I. xxx. (1859) 31 Al other worldly lawes ben..subalterned to gods lawe.

†**Subalte·rnal**, *a.* (*sb.*) *Obs.* [a. OF. *subalternal* (15th c.) or its source med.L. **subalternālis*, f. *subalternus* Subaltern: see -al.]

1. Subordinate, inferior. Const. *to*.

c 1400 *Pilgr. Sowle* (Caxton) I. xxx. (1859) 33 Alle other lawes ordeyned of man be not subalternal for to serue the lawe of oure lord. 1588 Fraunce *Lawiers Logike* I. ii. 10 b, It were against..all arte to jumpe abruptly from the highest and most generall to the lowest and most speciall, without passing by the subalternal. 1607 Topsell *Four-f. Beasts* 714 Sundry Beastes haue not onely their diuisions, but subdeuisions, into subalternal kinds. 1625 Darcie *Annales* a 4, Those subalternal Deities who, for putting themselues in Iupiters bedde, were..metamorphosed into strange shapes. 1628 R. Heath *Discov. Jesuit's Coll.* (Camden) 29 They acknowledg subjection to a foren power, and have setled a government amongst themselves subalternal thereunto.

b. *sb.* A subordinate.

1673 Marvell *Reh. Transp.* II. 227, I am not at all doubtful but that he [the Supreme Magistrate] may punish any such transgression in his Subalternals and Substitutes.

2. Succeeding in turn, alternating.

1588 J. Harvey *Disc. Probl.* 23 There should euery 7000 yeere, insue a certaine subalternall time of peaceable calmeties, and transitory rest. 1657 *Penit. Conf.* v. 72 [74] Where the disease is sin, the remedy confession and prayer; the Physicians and Patients subalternal.

Subalternant (sɒbǫltɜ·ɹnănt). *Logic.* (More freq. in L. form.) [ad. mod.L. *subalternans, -ant-*, pr. pple. of *subalternāre* Subaltern *v.*] See quots.

1826 Whately *Logic* Index (1827) 347 Subaltern opposition, is between a Universal and a Particular of the same Quality. Of these, the Universal is the Subalternant, and the Particular the Subalternate. 1867 Atwater *Logic* 109 In each pair of these the Universal is called the Subalternans, the Particular the Subalternate.

Subalternate (sɒbǫltɜ·ɹnĕt), *a.* (*sb.*) [ad. late L. *subalternātus* (*subalternātum genus* in Boethius), pa. pple. of *subalternāre*: see Subaltern *v.* and -ate².] **A.** *adj.*

†**1.** Subordinate, inferior. Also const. *to*: Subordinate or subservient *to*. *Obs.*

1432–50 tr. *Higden* (Rolls) III. 123, iiij. principalle realmes, ..x. other realmes, subalternate to theyme. 1595 in *12th Rep. Hist. MSS. Comm.* App. IX. 173 What ministers of state and subalternat governors, as counsaile and magistrats. 1611 in *10th Rep. Hist. MSS. Comm.* App. I. 546 In putting so muche difference between an absolute king and a subalternate Queen. 1638 Baker tr. *Balzac's Lett.* (vol. II) 79 As though the present time, were but subalternate to the future. 1670 Clarke *Nat. Hist. Nitre* 51 Medicine being a subalternate Art to Philosophy. 1686 Spence tr. *Varillas' House of Medicis* 15 The Enditement was drawn up by the Subalternate Judges. 1701 Norris *Ideal World* I. ii. 204 So only the subalternate sciences suppose their objects, as taking them from the superior science wherein they are proved. 1704 *Phil. Trans.* XXV. 1702 An account of the several kinds of subalternate Species of Plants. 1874 in Manning *Ess. Relig. & Lit.* III. 317 Theology is a science subalternate to Revelation.

†**2.** Successive, succeeding by turns. *Obs.*

1706 Phillips (ed. Kersey), *Subaltern* or *Subalternate*, that succeeds by turns.

†**b.** *Logic.* = Subaltern *a.* 1 b.

1658 E. Phillips *Myst. Love* (1685) 285 The subalternate genus, as also the subalternate species, is that which is the species of this, but the genus of that.

3. [A new formation from Sub- 20 d and Alternate *a.*] *Nat. Hist.* Alternate, but with a tendency to become opposite.

1829 Loudon *Encycl. Plants* 571 Leaves pinnat[ifid]: segm[ents] stalked subalternate. 1846 Dana *Zooph.* (1848) 655 Polyps few and at distant intervals on the branches, subalternate. 1851 Mantell *Petrifactions* iii. § 5. 309 The subalternate arrangement and reversed position of the upper and lower series of teeth.

B. *sb. Logic.* A particular proposition.

1826, 1867 [see Subalternant].

Hence †**Subalte·rnately** *adv.*, subordinately, successively.

1606 B. Barnes *Foure Bks. Offices* 19 Subalternately respecting the purse. 1727 Bailey (vol. II), *Subalternately*,..successively.

Suba·lternating, *ppl. a.* [f. **subalternate* vb. (cf. prec.) + -ing².] Succeeding by turns (1855 in Ogilvie Suppl.).

Subalternation (sɒbǫltəɹnē·ʃən). [ad. med. L. *subalternātio, -ōnem*, n. of action f. *subalternāre*: see Subalternate.]

†**1.** Subordination. *Obs.*

1597 Hooker *Eccl. Pol.* v. lxxiii. (1617) 397 Whereunto it was not possible they could concurre, vnlesse there were subalternation betweene them, which subalternation is naturally grounded vpon inequalitie.

†**2.** Succession by turn. *Obs.*

1616 Bullokar *Eng. Expos.*, *Subalternation*, A succeeding by course. 1627 Donne *Serm.* xliv. (1640) 441 That use of Subalternation in the service of God, of that, which we have called Antiphones, and Responsaries.

3. *Logic.* The relation between a universal and a particular of the same quality; the opposition which exists between propositions alike in quality but differing in quantity; also, 'an immediate inference from a universal to a particular under it' (*Cent. Dict.*).

1650 Eldersfield *Civ. Right Tythes* 35 It may be..needful to consider her [the law's] several species, or indeed not so much their contradiction, as subalternation. 1677 Gale *Crt. Gentiles* Proem. 8 The Relate Affections of a Proposition are Conversion, Equipollence, Subalternation, and Opposition. 1697 tr. *Burgersdicius his Logic* I. xxxii. 127 By Subalternation we express our Meaning when we would signifie that one Enunciation is subordinated to another, and does necessarily follow from it. 1813–21 Bentham *Ontology* Wks. 1843 VIII. 203 Subalternation, viz. logical subalternation, opposition, and connexion, or the relation between cause and effect. 1864 Bowen *Logic* vi. 155 But of these less perfect expressions some may more properly be regarded as inferences by Subalternation. 1867 Atwater *Logic* 116 This is U, and by subalternation will give I also.

Subalternity (sɒbǫltɜ·ɹnĭti). [f. Subaltern + -ity. Cf. F. *subalternité*.] Subordinate position.

1620 T. Granger *Div. Logike* 178 Which respecteth not suppartitions, anatomical diuisions, or subalternities of members. 1773 H. Walpole *Let. to Mann* 4 Nov., I am sure I have none of the symptoms but the age and the subalternity. 1831 Southey in *Q. Rev.* XLV. 443 Christianity, they say, has raised the sex from servitude, but has condemned them to subalternity. 1850 tr. *Mazzini's Royalty & Republ.* Pref. 8 Redeeming by brilliant personal qualities the vice of subalternity, to which his position condemned him.

Subalternize (sɒ·bǫltəɹnəiz), *v. rare.* [ad. F. *subalterniser*, f. *subalterne*: see Subaltern *a.* and -ize.] *trans.* To subordinate.

1905 *19th Cent.* July 24 France was subalternised, domesticated everywhere; she suffered her greatest interests to be subordinated to those of an alien Power.

†**Subalternly**, *a. Sc. Law. Obs.* [f. Subaltern *a.* + -ly².] By subinfeudation.

1681 Stair *Inst. Law Scot.* I. xiii. 263 If the Lands..be Disponed..by the Vassal to others Subalternly Infeft.

Subanco·neal, *a. Anat.* [See Sub- 1 b and next.] Situated beneath the anconeus.

1891 *Cent. Dict.* 1898 *Syd. Soc. Lex.*

‖ **Subanconeus** (sɒbæŋkonī·ɒs). *Anat.* Also -æus. [mod.L. (sc. *musculus*), f. *sub-* Sub- 1 d + *ancōn* = Gr. ἀγκών elbow.] A small muscle arising from the triceps and humerus above the elbow-joint and inserted in the posterior ligament of the elbow. Hence **Su·bancone·ous** *a.*

1848 *Quain's Anat.* (ed. 5) I. 330 On removing the triceps from the lower part of the humerus, some muscular fibres will be found connected with the capsule of the elbow-joint. Two slips extending from the bone above the fossa for the olecranon to the capsule have been described as distinct from the triceps, under the name sub-anconæus. 1887 *Buck's Handbk. Med. Sci.* V. 45 Subanconeous [muscle]. This consists of a few muscular fibres.

Suba·ngular, *a.* [ad. mod.L. *subangulāris*: see Sub- 20 c and Angular.] Somewhat or slightly angular; having a blunt angle.

1777 Pennant *Brit. Zool.* IV. 51 Ast[erias] with five rays depressed; broad at the base; sub-angular. 1849 Dana *Geol.* App. I. (1850) 685 Mesial fold large and subangular. 1873 Geikie *Gt. Ice Age* xvi. 202 Sprinkled with loose angular and subangular stones. 1894 *Geol. Mag.* Oct. 434 Each tubercle gives rise to three..subangular ribs.

So **Suba·ngled, -a·ngulate**(d *adjs.*

1819 Samouelle *Entomol. Compend.* 423 *Geometra*..*strigilata.* The subangled Wave. 1822 J. Parkinson *Outl. Oryctol.* 207 Turreted, with subangulated keels. *Ibid.* 210 Whirls round, but subangulate.

Subapennine (sɒbæ·pĕnəin), *a.* (*sb.*) *Geol.* Also -appen(n)ine. [Sub- 12.] Applied to a series of strata of Pliocene age, such as are characteristic of the formation of the flanks of the Apennines in Italy; belonging to or characteristic of these strata.

1822 *Edin. Rev.* XXXVII. 50 Subappennine alluvial soils. 1833 Lyell *Princ. Geol.* III. 110 Throughout a great part of Italy, where the marls and sands of the Subapennine hills are elevated to considerable heights. 1851 Richardson *Geol.* viii. 248 The subapennine beds of Piedmont. 1861 P. P. Carpenter in *Rep. Smithsonian Instit.* 1860, 159 The Subappenine tertiaries of Piedmont.

b. *sb. pl.* The geological series bearing this name; a low range of hills skirting the slopes of the Apennines in Italy.

1830 Lyell *Princ. Geol.* I. 137 *note*, The newest tertiary strata of the age of the Subapennines. 1833 *Ibid.* III. 155 Brocchi, the first Italian geologist who described this newer group in detail, gave it the name of the Subapennines.

Suba·pical, *a. Nat. Hist.* [Sub- 1 b, c, 11.] Beneath or near the apex; nearly apical.

1846 Dana *Zooph.* (1848) 445 The subapical calicles becoming very small. 1870 Hooker *Stud. Flora* 78 Carpels hairy with an eglandular subapical pit. 1913 *Oxf. Univ. Gaz.* 4 June 955 The orange subapical bar to the fore wing.

Su·baposto·lic, *a.* [Sub- 18.] Belonging to or characteristic of the period in the history of the Church immediately following that of the apostles.

1880 *Encycl. Brit.* XI. 854/2 The history of the apostolic and subapostolic ages. 1881 Westcott & Hort *Grk. N. T.* II. 296 Stray relics surviving from the apostolic or subapostolic age.

†**Subaqua·neous**, *a. Obs. rare*⁻⁰. [f. late L. *subaquāneus* (Sub- 1 a, *aqua* water) + -ous.] = next, 1.

1656 Blount *Glossogr.*

Subaqua·tic, *a.* [Cf. F. *subaquatique*.]

1. [Sub- 1 a.] = Subaqueous 1. Also, pertaining to plants growing under water.

1789 E. Darwin *Bot. Gard.* II. 146 *note*, The subaquatic leaves of this plant..are cut into fine divisions. 1800 — *Phytol.* 76 The roots of..water-plants, which might..become articles of subaquatic agriculture. 1828 *Blackw. Mag.* XXIV. 316 Subaquatic paths for crossing the Nile. 1849 *Sk. Nat. Hist., Mammalia* III. 111 Tearing up the strong-fibred vegetables from their subaquatic bed by means of its tusks. 1874 Coues *Birds N. W.* 11 Ability to progress under water ..by a sort of subaquatic flying and scrambling.

2. [Sub- 20 c.] *Zool.* and *Bot.* Partly aquatic.

1844 H. Stephens *Bk. Farm* I. 483 Subaquatic plants, such as rushes. 1880 A. R. Wallace *Isl. Life* II. xiii. 268 The large number of allied forms [*sc.* tortoises] which have aquatic or sub-aquatic habits. 1889 — *Darwinism* 29 A large sub-aquatic dock.

Subaqueous (sɒbē̆ⁱ·kwĭəs), *a.* [f. L. type **subaqueus*: see Sub- 1 a. Cf. It. *subaqueo*.]

1. Existing, formed, or constructed under water.

1677 Plot *Oxfordsh.* 28 Terrestrial and subaqueous Plants. *a* 1711 Ken *Edmund* Poet. Wks. II. 26 As if sub-aqueous Fires..Had boil'd the Waves. 1774 Pennant *Tour Scot. in 1772*, 33 In some places are vast subaqueous precipices. 1776 — *Brit. Zool.* I. 345 For the purpose of plunging into their subaqueous winter quarters. 1829 Landor *Imag. Conv.* Wks. 1853 I. 573/1 That dark colour which subaqueous weeds are often of. 1855 Kingsley *Westw. Ho!* xxxii, Tarn David, one of those strange subaqueous pebble-dykes. 1862 Townsend *Man. Dates* s. v. *Submarine telegraph*, In 1848 successful subaqueous telegraphs were laid across the Rhine. 1903 Myers *Hum. Pers.* I. 77 There is a rush upwards as of a subaqueous spring.

b. Performed or taking place under water; adapted for use under water.

1774 A. Campbell *Lexiphanes* (ed. 4) 25, I risqued a subaqueous voyage. 1839 *United Service Jrnl.* June 189 Subterraneous or subaqueous explosions. 1847 Barham *Ingol. Leg.* Ser. I. *Grey Dolphin*, As though the River god and Neptune were amusing themselves with a game of subaqueous battledore. 1875 Knight *Dict. Mech.*, *Sub-aqueous Helmet*, a diver's head-dress, supplied with air by pump from above.

c. *jocular.* That constructs works under water.

1844 Thackeray *Contrib. to Punch* Wks. 1898 VI. 83 It weds the tunnel of the subaqueous Brunel with the mystic edifice of Cheops.

2. Below the sea-level. *nonce-use.*

1724 Ramsay *Health* 397 Ye Dutch..You scarce dare sleep in your subaqueous bowers.

3. Reflected as if in depths of water.

1798 W. Mavor *British Tourists* V. 260 The shelving hills..with their subaqueous images were of a faint grape-like hue. 1843 Wordsw. *Prose Wks.* (1876) III. 167 These specks of snow reflected in the lake, and so transferred, as it were, to the subaqueous sky.

So **Suba·quean** *a. rare*⁻¹.

1782 W. Stevenson *Hymn to Deity* 19 Subaquean monsters multiform in size.

Subara·chnoid, *a.* (*sb.*) *Anat.* and *Path.* [Sub- 1 b.] Situated or taking place beneath the arachnoid membrane. Also *sb.*, the subarachnoid space (between the arachnoid membrane and the pia mater).

1839–47 *Todd's Cycl. Anat.* III. 641/2 In apoplexy the blood escapes from the ventricle into the sub-arachnoid space. *Ibid.* 673/2 The subarachnoid fluid. 1843 R. J. Graves *Syst. Clin. Med.* ix. 97 Extensive thickening of the membranes of the brain, with subarachnoid effusion. 1893 W. R. Gowers *Man. Dis. Nerv. Syst.* (ed. 2) II. 390 Subarachnoid hæmorrhage. 1896 *Allbutt's Syst. Med.* I. 189 The perivascular lymphatic sheaths and subarachnoid are filled with fatty products. 1902 Hughes & Keith *Man. Pract. Bot.* III. 305 To this subarachnoid tissue is given the name of Pia mater.

So **Su·barachnoi·dal, -oi·dean** *adjs.*

1844 Hoblyn *Dict. Terms Med.* (ed. 2) 293 *Sub-arachnoidean fluid*, an abundant serous secretion, situated between the arachnoid and the pia mater. *Sub-arachnoidean space*, the space between the arachnoid and the spinal cord. 1871 W. A. Hammond *Dis. Nerv. Syst.* 51 Sub-arachnoidean effusion. 1876 tr. *Wagner's Gen. Pathol.* 229 The sub-arachnoidal connective-tissue bands and meshes.

Subarbis, obs. pl. Suburb.

Su·b-arch. *Archit.* [Sub- 3, 5 b.] A subsidiary or secondary arch; one of two or more arches grouped in a larger arch; the lowest member in an arch of two or more 'orders'.

1835 R. Willis *Archit. Mid. Ages* vii. 91 The square body of the pier sustains the pier arches, while its lateral half shafts are appropriated to the sub-arches. 1849 Parker *Introd. Gothic Archit.* iii. 133 Three or more lancet-lights under one arch, the points of the sub-arches touching the enclosing arch. 1879 *Cassell's Techn. Educ.* III. 40 The first of the three orders, or 'sub-arch'.

Suba·rctic, *a.* (*sb.*) [Sub- 12 b.] Nearly arctic; somewhat south of the arctic circle or regions; belonging to such a region. Also *sb. pl.*, subarctic regions.

1854 H. Miller *Sch. & Schm.* (1858) 460 When sub-arctic molluscs lived in her [*sc.* Scotland's] sounds and bays. 1875 Croll *Clim. & Time* xv. 236 As the ice began to accumulate during the cold periods in subarctic and temperate regions. 1892 Stevenson *Across the Plains* vi. 204 It was still broad day in our subarctic latitude [in Caithness]. 1898 J. W. Tyrrell (*title*) Across the Sub-Arctics of Canada.

Suba·rcuate, *a. Nat. Hist.* [Sub- 20 c.] Somewhat arcuate or bowed.

1819 Samouelle *Entomol. Compend.* 87 Thumb subarcuate. 1846 Dana *Zooph.* (1848) 471 Branches..subarcuate.

Suba·rcuated, *a.*

1. [Sub- 20 c.] *Nat. Hist.* = prec.

1777 Pennant *Brit. Zool.* IV. 71 Solen Pellucidus..subarcuated and sub-oval.

2. [f. next.] *Archit.* Having two or more subordinate arches under a main arch.

1881 Parker *ABC Gothic Archit.* 195 The mullions are carried up to the architrave, and the side lights only are sub-arcuated. 1886 Willis & Clark *Cambridge* I. 582 Each of the three main divisions of the window is sub-arcuated.

Su·barcua·tion. *Archit.* [Sub- 2.] The construction of two or more subordinate arches under a main arch; the system of arches so constructed.

1845 J. Ingram in *Builder* III. 465/2 The principle of subarcuation; that is the mode of constructing two inferior and subordinate arches under the third or main arch. *a* 1878 Sir G. Scott *Lect. Archit.* (1879) II. 112 The round pillar has lateral shafts to carry the sub-arcuation.

‖ **Subarmale** (sɒbaɹmē̆ⁱ·li). [L., neut. of *subarmālis*, f. *sub-* Sub- 1 a + *arma* Arms: see -al. Cf. F. *subarmale*.] A coarse coat worn to protect the body from the pressure of the cuirass.

1825 Fosbroke *Encycl. Antiq.* I. 784 The gambeson or wambais, or *subarmale*. 1849 [Jas. Grant] *Mem. Kirkaldy* x. 97 The constable received a bullet through his steel cuisses and subarmale.

Subarrhation (sɒbarē̆ⁱ·ʃən). Also -arration. [ad. med.L. *subarr(h)ātio, -ōnem*, n. of action f. *subarr(h)āre*, f. *sub-* Sub- 1 g + *arr(h)a* pledge.] An ancient form of betrothal in which pledges in the form of money, rings, etc. were bestowed by the man upon the woman.

a 1623 Swinburne *Treat. Spousals* (1686) 207 Forasmuch as Subarration, that is the giving and receiving of a Ring, is a Sign of all others, most usual in Spousals and Matrimonial Contracts. 1710 Wheatly *Bk. Com. Prayer* x. § 5. 1839 Palmer *Orig. Liturg.* II. 211 Subarrhation.

‖ **Subashi** (sū̆bā·ʃi). Forms: 6 subbassi, 6–7 subassi, 7 subashie, -sha, subbashaw, -bassawe, -bassa, sou-bashi, sous-basha, 8 sous-bachi, 9 soo-bashee, subasche, súbáshí. [Turkish سوباشى *sūbāshī* and صوباشى *çūbāshī*, f. مو *çū* water + باش *bāsh* head, chief. (Some of the Eng. forms indicate an attempt to analyse the word as Sub- 6 + Bashaw.)] A Turkish official in command of a district or village; a 'police magistrate under the timariot system' (Redhouse).

1599 Hakluyt *Voy.* II. I. 106 Ye Subassi, & the Meniwe, with the Padre guardian. *Ibid.* 292 The Admirall..appointeth the Subbassas. 1613 Purchas *Pilgrimage* (1614) 302 The Cadi and Subassi, if they finde any shops open, or any body eating in the day, set him on an Asse backwards. 1615 Sandys *Trav.* 63 The Subashie is as the Constable of a Citie, both to search out and punish offences. 1632 Lithgow *Trav.* IV. 136 In this Prison, are Bassawes, and Subbassawes imprisoned. 1687 Sous-basha [see Sous-]. 1688 *Lond. Gaz.* No. 2336/5 The Sub-Bassa of this City. 1718 Ozell tr. *Tournefort's Voy.* II. 279, I promis'd them to pay the Tax for them, if the Sous-Bachi should demand it. 1819 T. Hope *Anast.* (1820) II. 377 A Tchawoosh..summoned me before the Soo-bashee. 1823–4 *Encycl. Metrop.* (1845) XV. 509 A Jeri-báshi (Captain), Jeri-surejí (Corporal), and Súbáshí (Sergeant)..who have particular lands assigned to them on which they are obliged to reside. 1847 Mrs. A. Kerr tr. *Ranke's Hist. Servia* 115 In the villages, Subasches appeared as executors of the judicial and magisterial power.

Subastri·ngent, *a.* and *sb.* [Sub- 20 b.]

A. *adj.* Somewhat astringent.

1694 Salmon *Bate's Dispens.* (1713) 99/2 The Spirit of Mint,..stomachick, cephalick,..and subastringent. 1719 Quincy *Lex. Physico-Med.* (1722) 40 A soft, healing, subastringent Balsamick. 1788 *Phil. Trans.* LXXX. 280 It had a slight saline, sub-astringent taste. 1887 Moloney *Forestry W. Afr.* 304 The plant yields a sub-astringent gum.

B. *sb.* A sub-astringent substance.

1756 P. Browne *Jamaica* 208 All the plants of this tribe are mild subastringents and vulneraries.

Su·b-atom. *Chem.* [Sub- 7.] A constituent part of an atom.

1880 Cleminshaw *Wurtz' Atomic Theory* 51 A primordial matter, the sub-atoms of which were grouped in different numbers to form the chemical atoms of hydrogen and the various simple bodies. 1904 A. J. Balfour *Refl. New Th. Matter* 9 There are those..who think that the elementary atom of the chemist..is but a connected system of monads or sub-atoms.

Hence **Subato·mic** *a.*

1903 *Edin. Rev.* Oct. 385 Sub-atomic physics. 1905 *Athenæum* 27 May 661 Experiments have been made with sub-atomic particles from one or other of these sources.

Subaud (sɒbǫ·d), *v. Gram. rare.* [ad. late L. *subaudīre* (tr. Gr. ὑπακούειν), f. *sub-* Sub- 24 + *audīre* to hear.] *trans.* To supply mentally or 'understand' (a word or words) to complete the sense or the construction. 1864 in Webster.

Subaudition (sɒbǫdi·ʃən). [ad. L. *subauditio, -ōnem*, n. of action f. *subaudīre* (see prec.). Cf. F. *subaudition*.]

†**1.** Hearing a little. *Obs. rare*⁻⁰.

1658 Phillips.

2. Chiefly *Gram.* The act of mentally supplying something that is not expressed; something that is mentally supplied or understood; implied or understood meaning.

1798 Tooke *Purley* II. (1805) 17 If it must have a name, it should rather be called *subaudition* than *abstraction*. *Ibid.* 121 Bond Band Bound—however spelled, and with whatever subaudition applied, is still one and the same word. 1839 *New Monthly Mag.* LVI. 455 There is a subaudition of so many ifs. 1859 Trench *Study of Words* (ed. 9) iii. 87 'Policeman' has no evil subaudition. 1859 Thackeray *Virgin.* lix, Taking the business-part for granted, and leaving it as it were for subaudition. 1905 *Sat. Rev.* 11 Mar. 311 A glorified subaudition of social control is also behind the Tudor despotism.

‖ **Subauditur** (sɒbǫdəi·tɒɹ). [L. = 'it is understood', 3rd pers. sing. pres. ind. pass. of *subaudīre* to Subaud.] = prec. 2. Phr. *In a subauditur*: by implication.

1803 Beddoes *Hygëia* XI. 95 It will not pass for a *subauditur* in grammar. 1880 *Contemp. Rev.* Feb. 256 Our fiction..is as much occupied, though in a subauditur, with the skeleton in the cupboard of daily life as [etc.]. 1886 J. Martineau *Types Eth. Th.* I. I. ii. (1886) 313 You cannot tack on the word 'modes' immediately to 'substance' without a subauditur of attribute.

Suba·xillary, *a.* (*sb.*) [Sub- 1 b, c.]

1. *Zool.* Situated beneath the axilla; *Ornith.* = Axillary. **b.** *sb. pl.* Axillary feathers or wing-coverts (*Cent. Dict.*).

1769 Bancroft *Guiana* 304 Together with an inflammation and tumefaction of the lymphatic subaxillary glands. 1776 Pennant *Brit. Zool.* II. 421 The subaxillary feathers [of the eared grebe].

2. *Bot.* Beneath the axil or the angle made by a branch with the stem or a leaf with the branch.

a 1802 E. Darwin (Webster 1828–32). 1857 A. Gray *First Less. Bot.* (1866) 232.

†**Sub-bai·liff, -baily.** *Obs.* [a. AF. = OF. *sub(b)aillif, -balif* (cf. *southbaily* s. v. South-²) = med.L. *subballīvus*: see Sub- 6 and Bailiff.] An under-bailiff.

14.. *Customs of Malton* in *Surtees Misc.* (1890) 59 The Balyffes or Subbalyffes of þe said Burgage. 1456 *Cov. Leet Bk.* (1908) 293 To take suerte of theire subbaily & officers. *Ibid.* 322 The subbayliy and Constable. 1572 in Picton *L'pool Munic. Rec.* (1886) II. 149 The sheriffs and sub-bailiffs.

Hence †**Subbai·liwick**, the office or jurisdiction of an under-bailiff.

1452 *Cov. Leet Bk.* (1908) 274 Ye shall not set ony of your subbayliwikkes to eny certeyn ferm.

Subbarbes, -ardes, obs. pl. Suburb.

Sub-ba·sal, *a.* [Sub- 1 b, 11.] Situated near or below the base of a part or organ. Also *sb.*, a subbasal plate (*Funk's Standard Dict.* 1895).

1848 *Proc. Berw. Nat. Club* II. vi. 276 Nostrils subbasal. 1870 Hooker *Stud. Flora* 172 Cornus sanguinea..lateral nerves subbasal. 1902 *Proc. Zool. Soc.* I. 48 The basal area of these wings irrorated with pearl-grey indicating two vague subbasal bands.

Sub-base.

1. [Sub- 3.] **a.** *Archit.* The lowest part of a base which is divided horizontally.

1826 Britton *Exeter* 91 A charge of 5*l.* 6*s.* 8*d.* for four columns, with bases, sub-bases, and capitals. 1851 Pugin *Chancel Screens* 29 [The screen] of S. Mark [Venice] is open above the subase [*sic*].

b. A base placed under the bottom of a machine or other apparatus to raise it higher from the ground.

1904 *Electr. Rev.* 24 Sept. 489 The whole turbine is mounted on a sub-base.

2. [Sub- 5 b.] A secondary base.

1903 *Science* 9 Oct. 478 Mr. Peary..will..after establishing a sub-base there, force his way northward to the northern shore of Grant Land.

†**Subbasmont.** *Sc. Obs.* [a. OF. *soub-, subbassement* (mod.F. *soubassement*), app. f. *soubasser*.] The valance (of a bed).

1539 *Inv. Roy. Wardrobe* (1815) 45 Four grete beddis viz. ane of grene..with ane subbasmont of grene velvet.

Subber(be)s, obs. ff. pl. of Suburb.

Subbing: see Sub *v.*

†**Sub-bois.** *Obs.* [AF. *subbois* = Law-Latin *subboscus*, f. *sub-* Sub- 3 + *boscus* wood. (Mod.F. has *sous-bois*; cf. *south bois* s. v. South-².)] = Underwood.

1677 N. Cox *Gentl. Recreat.* (ed. 2) 15 Of Sub-bois, some for Browse and Food of the Game, and for Shelter and Defence; as Maples, &c. Some for Browse and Defence; as Birch, Sallow, Willow. 1706 [see *south-bois* s. v. South-²]. 1708 *Les Termes de la Ley* 519 *Sylva cædua*..is Subbois or Coppice Wood.

Subborn, obs. form of Suborn.

†**Subbosco.** *Obs.* Also subosco. [f. Sub- 3 + It. *bosco* wood.] A jocular word for: The hair that grows upon the lower part of the face.

1579 G. Harvey *Letter-bk.* (Camden) 61 The clippinges of your thrishonorable mustachyoes and subboscoes. 1596 Gayton *Pleas. Notes* II. iii. 42 The boscos, and subboscos (I mean,) the duiapes and the jawy part of the face.

Subbra·chial, *a.* [ad. mod.L. *subbrachiālis*; see Sub- 1 b and Brachial.]

1. *Ichth.* Situated under or near the pectoral fins; (of a fish) having the ventral fins so situated.

1836 *Partington's Brit. Cycl. Nat. Hist.* II. 556/2 *Gadoidæ.* ..A family of soft-finned fishes with sub-brachial fins. 1840 *Cuvier's Anim. Kingd.* 324 *Echeneis.* This genus, like Pleuronectes, might form a distinct family of Sub-brachial Malacopterygii.

2. Under the pectoral muscles.

1898 *Syd. Soc. Lex.*

3. Beneath the brachium (in cerebral anatomy).

1913 Dorland *Med. Dict.* (ed. 7).

Subbra·chian, *a.* and *sb. Ichth.* [As prec. + -an.] **A.** *adj.* = prec. 1. **B.** *sb.* A subbrachial fish; one of the *Subbrachiati* (formerly *-ata*).

1842 Brande *Dict. Sci.*, etc. 1183 *Subbrachians*, the name

of the order of Malacopterygious fishes comprising those which have the ventral fins situated either immediately beneath and between, or a little in front or behind the pectoral fins. *a* 1843 in *Encycl. Metrop.* (1845) VII. 293/2 The Fish is designated Jugular or Subbrachian when the ventral fins are immediately beneath the pectoral and connected with their girdle, as the Cod.

So **Subbra·chiate** [mod.L. *subbrachiātus*].

1859 Mayne *Expos. Lex.*, *Subbrachiatus*,..subbrachiate.

Su·b-branch, *sb.* [Sub- 7.] A subdivision of a branch (in any sense).

1859 Darwin *Orig. Spec.* iv. 124 In our diagram, this is indicated by the broken lines, beneath the capital letters, converging in sub-branches downwards towards a single point. 1875 Jevons *Money* xx. 258 The National Bank of Ireland has about 114 branches and sub-branches.

So **Su·b-branch** *v.*, **Su·b-branched** *ppl. a.*

1676 Grew *Anat. Plants* Lect. iv. (1682) 266 Sprigs made up of four chief Branches standing crosswise, and those subbranched. 1857 Darwin in *Life & Lett.* (1887) II. 125 Species..always seem to branch and sub-branch like a tree from a common trunk.

Su·b-brigadier. [Sub- 6. Cf. F. *sous-brigadier*.] Formerly, an officer in the Horse Guards with the rank of a cornet.

1684 E. Chamberlayne *Angl. Notitia* (ed. 15) I. 200 Sub-Corporals, or Sub-Brigadiers. 1738 *Gentl. Mag.* VIII. 109/2 Mr Rastall,—Eldest Sub-brigadier of the first Troop of Horse-guards, in room of Capt. Prew decd. 1802 James *Milit. Dict.* 1852 Burn *Naval & Milit. Dict.* (1863), *Sub-brigadier*, (second corporal of cavalry).

Su·bcartila·ginous, *a.*

1. [Sub- 20 b.] Somewhat, partly, or incompletely cartilaginous.

1541 Copland *Guydon's Quest. Cyrurg.* E iv, The subcartylagynous [substance of the nose; orig. L. *pars cartilaginosa*] is dowble one outwarde that maketh the typ of the nose and the other inwarde deuydeth the nosethyrlles. 1787 tr. *Linnæus' Fam. Plants* 487 The Fruit is a tongue pedicel'd, slender, subcartilaginous. 1835–6 *Todd's Cycl. Anat.* I. 37/1 Body..gelatinous, supported by an internal, solid, subcartilaginous body. 1887 W. Phillips *Brit. Discomycetes* 42 Perizæ..differs..from Bulgaria: by not being..subcartilaginous.

2. [Sub- 1 b.] Lying beneath the cartilage; hypochondrial.

1775 Ash, *Subcartilagenous*, lying under the gristles.

So **Subcartilagi·neous** *a. rare*⁻⁰. [late L. *subcartilāgineus*] = sense 2 above.

1727 Bailey (vol. II), *Subcartilagineous*, under the Gristles.

Subcau·dal, *a.* (*sb.*) [Sub- 1 b, 11, 20 d.] Situated under or near the tail; not quite or almost caudal. **b.** *sb.* A subcaudal part; *esp.* a subcaudal plate in a serpent.

1777 Pennant *Brit. Zool.* IV. 16 The sub-caudal fins. 1841 *Penny Cycl.* XIX. 404/2 All serpents which have abdominal scuta and subcaudal scales. 1877 Coues *Fur-Bearing Anim.* I. 16 In the Badgers..a particular subcaudal pouch..which produces a peculiar liquid. 1899 *Proc. Zool. Soc.* 671 The anterior subcaudals are purplish grey.

Subcele·stial, *a.* and *sb.* [Sub- 1 a. Cf. OF. *sousceleste*.] **A.** *adj.* Situated or existing beneath or below the heavens; *rare* in literal sense; chiefly *transf.* Terrestrial, mundane, sublunary.

1561 Eden *Arte Nauig.* I. v. 7 b, The Emperial heauen, conteyneth three..*Hierarchias*,..the fyrste..called supercelestiall...The second is called Celestiall...The thyrde called Subcelestiall, conteyneth Virtues, Archangels and Angels. 1627 Hakewill *Apol.* (1630) 45 All subcelestiall bodies..consist of matter and forme. 1661 Glanvill *Van. Dogm.* 4 The most refined glories of subcœlestial excellencies are but more faint resemblances of these. 1678 Cudworth *Intell. Syst.* I. iv. § 32. 497 The *Dii Consentes*, were understood by Apuleius neither to be Celestial nor Subcelestial Bodies, but a certain higher Nature perceptible only to our Minds. 1741–70 Eliz. Carter *Lett.* (1808) 35 Whether Mrs. Montagu may not be delighting herself with a tour through the coal mines, and have lost all remembrance of her subcelestial friends. 1911 Webster, *Subcelestial*,.. *Astron.*, exactly beneath the zenith.

B. *sb.* A subcelestial being.

1652 Benlowes *Theoph.* Pref., Sub-cœlestials, or Sublunaries have their Assignment in the lowest Portion of the Universe. 1708 H. Dodwell *Expl. Dial. Justin* 61 Speaking of the Difference between the Cœlestials and Subcœlestials, he makes their Life to be a Death to us, and our Life to be a Death to them.

†**Subce·llarer.** *Obs.* [f. Sub- 6 + Cellarer, after med.L. *subcell(er)ārius*, or obs.F. *soubscellerier*. Cf. ME. *sowcelerere* s. v. Sous-, *sowthselerer* s. v. South-².] An under-cellarer in a convent.

c 1475 *Pict. Voc.* in Wr.-Wülcker 780/23 *Hic subselarius*, a subselerer. *c* 1700 in *Cath. Rec. Soc. Publ.* IX. 374 She was imployed..as subcellerere; Mrs of Novices, Conseler, and ward-robe.

Subce·ntral, *a.*

1. [Sub- 11, 20 d.] Nearly or not quite central; near or close to the centre.

1822 J. Parkinson *Outl. Oryctol.* 124 The mouth beneath, subcentral. 1836 *Penny Cycl.* V. 313/2 Fissure of adhesion in the lower valve subcentral. 1870 Hooker *Stud. Flora* 461 Asplenium Trichomanes..midrib subcentral.

2. [Sub- 1 a.] Being under the centre.

1828–32 in Webster.

3. [Sub- 1 b.] *Anat.* Beneath the central sulcus of the brain; beneath the centrum of a vertebra.

1882 *Quain's Elem. Anat.* (ed. 9) I. 23 The precentral or subcentral parts or hypapophyses. 1890 Billings *Nat. Med. Dict.*, *Subcentral arch*, hæmal arch. 1901 *Amer. Anthropologist* (N.S.) III. 461 The subcentral sulci of Eberstaller.

Hence **Subce·ntrally** *adv.*, under or near the centre or centrum. Also **Subce·ntrical** *a.* = 1 above.

1824 Du Bois *Lamarck's Arrangem.* 30 The interior [of the Orthocera] is divided into many cells, transversely separated by septa, which are traversed by a subcentrical syphon. 1870 Rolleston *Anim. Life* 12 Several of the anterior.. vertebræ, have low hypapophysial ridges developed subcentrally. 1872 H. A. Nicholson *Palæont.* 173 A pair of large compound eyes placed marginally or subcentrally.

†**Subce·rnicle.** *Obs. rare.* [ad. late L. *subcerniculum*: see Sub- 5 b and Cernicle.] ? A small sieve.

1657 Tomlinson *Renou's Disp.* 484 Sieves made of Horses hairs..called seraceous subcirnicles.

Subcesive, obs. variant of Subsecive.

Su·bcha·nter. [f. Sub- 6 + Chanter. Cf. OF. *sou(b)chantre*, F. *sous-chantre*.] A precentor's deputy, succentor; now, a vicar choral or lay-clerk of a cathedral, who assists in chanting the litany.

The title is retained in York and Lichfield cathedrals.

1515 in W. Fraser *Sutherland Bk.* (1892) III. 60 Schir William Nory, subchantour of Murray. 1546 *Yks. Chantry Surv.* (Surtees) II. 438 Denis Heckylton, subchaunter there. *a* 1578 Lindesay (Pitscottie) *Chron. Scot.* I. 200 The..chanter and subchanter witht all kynd of wther officeis pertaining to ane colledge. 1637 Gillespie *Eng. Pop. Cerem.* III. viii. 161 Deanes, Vice-Deans,..Sub-deacons,..Chantours, Subchantours. 1703 M. Martin *Descr. W. Isl. Scot.* 362 A Sub-Chanter, who was bound to play on the Organs each Lords Day, and Festivals. 1825 (*title*) Expository Discourses, by the late Rev. Wm. Richardson, Subchanter of York Cathedral. 1876 J. Grant *Burgh Sch. Scot.* I. 19 There are four principal persons in that cathedral [*sc.* Sarum], namely, the dean, chanter, chancellor, treasurer, besides a subdean and subchanter. 1898 *Daily News* 1 Apr. 7/6 Sub-chanter and priest vicar of Lichfield Cathedral.

transf. *a* 1618 J. Davies *Wittes Pilgr.* (1878) 52/2 That Holy, Holy, Holy, which They crie That are Sub-chaunters of Heau'ns Hermony.

Hence †**Subcha·ntership**, †**Subcha·ntress.**

14.. *Rule Syon Monast.* xiii. in *Collectanea Topogr.* III. (1836) 31 The chauntres and sub-chauntresses, the sexteyne and undersexteyne. 1546 *Yks. Chantry Surv.* (Surtees) II. 439 For his subchauntershipe, iiʲ.

Su·bcharge. [Sub- 5 b, c.]

†**1.** A second dish or course. Also *fig. Sc. Obs.*

c 1480 Henryson *Mor. Fab.* II. (*Town & C. Mouse*) xviii, Till eik thair cheir ane subcharge furth scho brocht, Ane plait of grottis [etc.]. *Ibid.* xxvii, The subcharge of thy seruice is bot sair. 1513 Douglas *Æneid* XIII. ix. 118 All ar expert, efiir new mariage, On the first nycht quhat suld be the subcharge.

2. Subordinate charge.

1900 *Century Mag.* Feb. 503/2, I have seen M. Clémenceau as storm-fiend-in-chief, and M. Clovis Hugues in subcharge of the Cave of the Winds.

Subche·la. [f. Sub- 22 + Chela¹.] A form of chela characteristic of certain crustaceans, in which the terminal segment is bent back upon the next.

Subche·late, *a.* **a.** [Sub- 20 c.] Imperfectly chelate. **b.** [f. prec.] Having a subchela.

1852 Dana *Crust.* II. 802 Four anterior legs subchelate. 1877 Huxley *Anat. Inv. Anim.* vi. 272 *Corycæus* has.. subchelate antennæ, and a rudimentary abdomen. 1893 Stebbing *Crust.* 45 The limb is..said to be subchelate, the claw being in that case partial.

Subche·liform, *a.* [Sub- 20 c.] = prec. **a.**

1835–6 *Todd's Cycl. Anat.* I. 762/1 In the first instance these instruments are denominated subcheliform claws, in the second chelæ simply, or cheliform claws. 1856 W. Clarke *Van der Hoeven's Zool.* I. 649 First and second pairs of feet terminated by a large moveable hook, subcheliform.

Subchet, ? error for Subcharge.

1500–20 Dunbar *Poems* lxvii. 19 Of quhais subchettis [*v.r.* surcharge] sour is the sals.

†**Subcineri·tious**, *a. Obs.* [f. L. *subcinericius*, var. *succinericius*: see Sub- and Cineritious.]

1. [Sub- 1 a.] Baked under ashes. *rare*⁻⁰.

1656 Blount *Glossogr.*

2. [Sub- 20 a.] Somewhat ash-coloured, greyish. Hence **Subcineri·tiously** *adv.*

1657 Tomlinson *Renou's Disp.* 353 Subcineritiously virid. *Ibid.* 672 Balm flows from a..Tree..of a subcineritious colour. 1670 H. Stubbe *Plus Ultra* 130 A subcineritious or dirty-coloured putrilage.

‖ **Subci·ngulum.** [med.L.; see Sub- 3.] A broad belt or girdle worn beneath another.

1824 Meyrick *Ant. Armour* Gloss., *Subcingulum*, when one belt was worn below another it was thus called. 1849 Rock *Ch. Fathers* I. v. 492 Besides the girdle, our Anglo-Saxon bishops were girt with the sub-cingulum or broad belt.

Suboisive, obs. variant of Subsecive.

†**Subcitrine**, *a. Obs.* [ad. mod.L. *subcitrinus*: see Sub- 20 a and Citrine *a.*] Of a somewhat yellow or greenish-yellow colour.

c 1530 *Judic. Urines* I. iii. 6 b, Theyr vryne is faynt of colour, as subcitrine or ʒelowysshe. 1572 J. Jones *Bathes Ayde* III. 26 b, Chaffie, or subcitrine coloure. 1637 Brian *Pisse-prophet* (1679) 85 Taking the Urinal out of the case, (perceiving it to be of a subcitrine or pale colour). 1702 *Phil. Trans.* XXIII. 1281 Of subcitrin colour.

Subclass (sɒ·bklɑs). [Sub- 7 b. Cf. F. *sous-classe*.] A subdivision of a class; *Nat. Hist.* a group of orders ranking next to a class.

1819 G. Samouelle *Entomol. Compend.* 77 Dr. Leach considered the Malacostraca and Entomostraca as subclasses. 1857 A. Gray *First Less. Bot.* (1866) 177 Series, Class, Subclass, Order, or Family, Suborder, Tribe, Subtribe, Genus, Subgenus or Section, Species, Variety. 1880 Günther *Fishes* 65 The lowermost sub-class of fishes, which comprises one form only, the Lancelet. 1882 Vines tr. *Sachs' Bot.* 161 Dividing this class of structures into two sub-classes, hairs and emergences.

attrib. 1869 Dk. Argyll *Primeval Man* II. 61 One of Cuvier's sub-class divisions.

So **Su·bclass** *v. trans.*, to place in a subclass.

1894–5 *16th Ann. Rep. Bur. Amer. Ethnol.* 72 The motive must be subclassed as sortilegic.

‖ **Subcla·via.** *Anat.* [mod.L. *subclāvia* (sc. *artēria* artery), fem. of *subclāvius* (see below).] The subclavian artery.

1733 tr. *Winslow's Anat.* (1756) II. 10 The Trachealis.. runs up from the Subclavia, in a winding Course. 1771 *Encycl. Brit.* I. 227/1 The Carotid arteries..arise near each other,..the left immediately, the right most commonly from the trunk of the subclavia on the same side.

†**Subcla·vial**, *a.* and *sb. Anat. Obs.* [ad. mod.L. *subclāviālis*, f. Subclavius.] = next.

1666 J. Smith *Old Age* (1676) 236 The subclavial branch of the *Vena Cava*. 1670 *Phil. Trans.* V. 2078 Part of the Chyle is by the *Ductus Thoracicus* conveyed into the Subclavials, and so into the Cistern of the Breasts. 1674 *Ibid.* IX. 115 Whether through his *ductus* all the Chyle passeth to the subclavial vessel.

Subclavian (sɒbklē̆ⁱ·viăn), *a.* and *sb. Anat.* [f. mod.L. *subclāvi-us* (see below) + -an. F. has *sousclavier* (from 16th c.).] **A.** *adj.*

1. Lying or extending under the clavicle.

Subclavian artery, the principal artery of the root of the neck, being the main trunk of the arterial system of the upper extremity. *Subclavian muscle* = Subclavius. *Subclavian vein*, the continuation of the axillary vein from the first rib till it joins the internal jugular vein.

1681 tr. *Willis' Rem. Med. Wks.* Vocab., Subclavian vessels; the vessels that belong to the little ribs of the breast. 1688 Holme *Armoury* II. xvii. 423/1 The right Subclavian Arterie. 1702 *Phil. Trans.* XXIII. 1188 That part of the Axillary-Arteries, by some called the Subclavian Arteries. 1705 *Ibid.* XXV. 2010, I found the same Tumor comprehending the intercostals, Deltoides, Subclavian, and Subscapulary Muscles. 1770 Fordyce in *Monthly Rev.* 310 The thoracic duct..commonly terminates in the left subclavian vein. 1808 Barclay *Musc. Motions* 239 The difference of manner in which the carotid and subclavian arteries, on the two sides, arise from the aorta. 1834 J. Forbes *Laennec's Dis. Chest* (ed. 4) 19 Subclavian region. This includes merely the portion of the chest covered by the clavicle. 1887 Conan Doyle *Study in Scarlet* I. i, I was struck on the shoulder by a Jezail bullet, which shattered the bone and grazed the subclavian artery.

b. Pertaining to the subclavian artery, vein, or muscle, as *subclavian groove*, etc. (see quots.).

1646 Sir T. Browne *Pseud. Ep.* IV. iv. 188 The Liver, which though it be seated on the right side, yet by the subclavian division doth equidistantly communicate its activity unto either arme. 1870 Rolleston *Anim. Life* 15 The right arteria innominata is seen to divide into its common carotid and subclavian trunks. 1890 Billings *Nat. Med. Dict.*, *Subclavian glands*, lymphatic glands under the arch of the right subclavian artery. *Subclavian groove*, 1. That in which the subclavian artery lies on upper surface of first rib. 2. That into which the subclavius muscle is inserted on under surface of clavicle.

2. [As if f. L. *sub* under + *clāvis* key.] (See quot.) *rare*⁻⁰.

1656 Blount *Glossogr.*, *Subclavian*, pertaining to that which is under lock and key.

B. *sb.* A subclavian vessel, nerve, or muscle.

1719 Quincy *Lex. Physico-Med.* (1722) 241 The Vein [*Vena Pneumonica*] opens into the Subclavian. 1771 *Encycl. Brit.* I. 226/2 The subclavian on each side terminates at the upper edge of the first rib. 1888 Rolleston & Jackson *Anim. Life* 365 The sub-clavians and carotids arise from the aortic arch in various ways.

Subclavi·cular, *a. Anat.* and *Surg.* [ad. mod.L. *subclāviculāris*: see Sub- 1 b and Clavicular.] Situated, occurring, or performed below or beneath the clavicle.

1656 Blount *Glossogr.* s. v. *Vein*, *Subclavicular vein*, one of the two maine ascendant branches of the hollow veine, divided into six parts. 1853 Markham *Skoda's Auscult.* 80 Weak bronchophony heard in the interscapular and subclavicular regions. 1872 Bryant *Pract. Surg.* 228 The subclavicular operation. 1878 Walsham *Handbk. Surg. Pathol.* 151 Dislocation of the humerus...The head of the bone may be displaced..Forwards and inwards beneath the clavicle (subclavicular).

Subclavio- (sɒbklē̆ⁱ·vio), used as combining form of next, as in **Subcla·vio-a·xillary**, pertaining to the subclavian and axillary arteries.

1815 J. Gordon *Syst. Hum. Anat.* I. 69 The Subclavio-Jugular Veins. 1880 Barwell *Aneurism* 38 A subclavio-axillary aneurism.

‖ **Subclavius** (sɒbklē̆ⁱ·viɒs). *Anat.* [mod.L. *subclāvius* (sc. *musculus*, f. *sub-* Sub- 1 b + *clāvis* key (cf. Clavicle¹ etym.).] In full *subclavius muscle*: A small muscle extending from the first rib to the clavicle.

1704 J. Harris *Lex. Techn.* I, *Subclavius*, is a Muscle of the Thorax. 1733 tr. *Winslow's Anat.* (1756) I. 288 The Subclavius..is a proper Depressor of the Clavicula. 1831 Knox *Cloquet's Anat.* 31 Its anterior extremity [*sc.* of the first rib]..sometimes affords insertion above to the sub-clavius muscle. 1835–6 *Todd's Cycl. Anat.* I. 360/1 The thickened edge of the fascia which covers the subclavius.

Subcolle·ctor. [Sub- 6. OF. *soub(s)collecteur*, Sp. *subcolector*.] A deputy or assistant collector.

1558–9 *Act 1 Eliz.* c. 21 § 22 No..Commissioner, shalbe named or assigned to any Collector or Subcollector or presentor of the said Subsidie. 1687 *Lond. Gaz.* No. 2306/4 The Sub-Collector of the Tenths of the said Diocess due to His Majesty. 1758 J. Blake *Mar. Syst.* 29 The collector,

or sub-collector, of the customs. 1837 *Lett. fr. Madras* (1843) 93 A Mr. Macdonald, the sub-collector. 1902 Gairdner *Engl. Ch. 16th c.* i. 12 Polydore Vergil was a native of Urbino, sent to England by Alexander VI. as sub-collector to Adrian.

Subcommi·ssion. [Cf. F. *sous-commission*.]

1. [Sub- 5 c.] An under-commission.

1629 *Reg. Privy Council Scot.* Ser. II. III. 21 The commissioners..have ordained sub-commissiouns to be granted to some selected persouns. 1648 Heylin *Relat. & Observ.* I. 119 Skippon..authorized the said Commissioned Apprentices to grant Sub-commissions again to other Apprentices under them.

2. [Sub- 7 b.] A division of a commission.

1882 *Macm. Mag.* XLVI. 253 The President..and the Minister..name commissions, these name sub-commissions, and so we go on from day to day.

Subcommi·ssioner. [Sub- 6.] An assistant or subordinate commissioner.

1629 *Sc. Acts Chas. I* (1870) V. 199/2 The commissioners and subcommissioners alreadie appointed. 1696 *Lond. Gaz.* No. 3183/3 The Association of the Sub-Commissioners for Prizes, of the Port of Dover and its Districts. 1697 *View Penal Laws* 14 Offences against this Act..to be determined by the Chief Commissioners..then by the Subcommissioners. 1846 McCulloch *Acc. Brit. Empire* (1854) II. 289 The valuation was devolved on commissioners and sub-commissioners.

Subcommi·t, *v. rare.* [Sub- 8.]

1. *trans.* To commit (something entrusted to one) to another.

1818 Ranken *Hist. France* V. v. ii. 286 He subcommitted the publication of this dispensation..to the friars of the Dominican order.

2. To refer to a sub-committee.

172. Wodrow *Corr.* (1843) II. 582 At night the Instructions met, and we had a fast before us, which was subcommitted.

Subcommi·ttee. [Sub- 7 b.] A committee formed from and acting under a main committee; a part of a committee appointed for special purposes.

1610 in *Crt. & Times Jas. I* (1848) I. 113 This day a subcommittee is appointed to consider [etc.]. 1621 Elsing *Debates Ho. Lords* (Camden) 98 Referred to the Sub-comittees of the priviledges. 1666 Pepys *Diary* 5 Oct., The Subcommittee have made their report to the Grand Committee. 1790 Burke *Fr. Rev.* 4 By acting as a sort of sub-committee in England for extending the principles of the National Assembly. 1823 Jefferson *Writ.* (1830) IV. 376 The committee of five met; no such thing as a sub-committee was proposed. 1898 'Merriman' *Roden's Corner* vii. 69 The meeting of the lady committees of the bazaar and ball subcommittees.

Subconscious (sɒbkǫ·nʃəs), *a.* [Sub- 19.]

1. *Psych.* **a.** Partially or imperfectly conscious; belonging to a class of phenomena resembling those of consciousness but not clearly perceived or recognized. **b.** Belonging to that portion of the mental field the processes of which are outside the range of attention.

1832–4 De Quincey *Cæsars* Wks. 1862 IX. 137 *note*, The Emperor Hadrian had taken one solitary step..in the elevation of human nature; and not..without some subconscious influence received directly or indirectly from Christianity. *a* 1841 — *Pope* Wks. 1858 IX. 42 How much grander and more faithful to that great theme [Christianity] were the subconscious perceptions of his heart than the explicit commentaries of his understanding. 1886 Myers *Phantasms of Living* II. 285 There exist sub-conscious and unconscious operations of many kinds; both organic, as secretion, circulation, &c.,..and also mental, as the recall of names, the development of ideas, &c. 1886 *Encycl. Brit.* XX. 48/1 Subconscious presentations may tell on conscious life..although lacking either the differences of intensity or the individual distinctness requisite to make them definite features. 1899 *Allbutt's Syst. Med.* VIII. 151 To cultivate the highest powers of the body and mind is to strengthen self-control and that subconscious inhibition which governs us in our habits of life.

absol. with *the*. 1886 *Encycl. Brit.* XX. 48/1 We cannot fix the limit at which the subconscious becomes the absolutely unconscious.

c. *transf.*

1893 *Min. 8th Nat. Council Congr. Ch. U. S.* 54 This spirit that has always existed in the sub-conscious life of the Church is now rising into the light of consciousness. 1899 *Daily News* 7 Jan. 6/4 A sketch of himself..has a subconscious humour one would not have suspected.

2. Partly or imperfectly aware.

1864 Hawthorne *Septimius* (1883) 352 He was subconscious that he was trying a bold experiment. 1879 Lewes *Probl. Life & Mind* Ser. III. vii. 204 While obeying the prevailing impulse we are conscious and sub-conscious of simultaneous solicitations in different directions.

Subco·nsciously, *adv.* [f. prec. + -ly².] In a subconscious manner; with imperfect or feeble consciousness; in the region of subconsciousness.

1823 De Quincey *Language* Wks. 1858 IX. 78 Whilst the finest models of style exist, and sub-consciously operate effectively as sources of delight, the conscious valuation of style is least perfectly developed. 1895 *Times* 17 Oct. 3/2 You do not feel as if you had had enough, but you are subconsciously aware of having had too many. 1903 Myers *Hum. Pers.* I. 378 Some of the associative consequents of the writing on the other [fragment of stone] were sub-consciously involved.

Subco·nsciousness. [f. as prec. + -ness.]

1. Partial or imperfect consciousness; a state of consciousness in which perception is indistinct; that part of the mental field which is on the border of consciousness.

1879 Lewes *Probl. Life & Mind* Ser. III. v. 88 There all the processes are blended, integrated, and in certain relative intensities become states of Consciousness; in lesser intensities, states of Subconsciousness. 1886 *Encycl. Brit.* XX. 47 The hypothesis of unconscious mental modifications, as it has been unfortunately termed,—the hypothesis of subconsciousness, as we may style it to avoid this contradiction in terms. 1904 *Brit. Med. Jrnl.* 17 Sept. 692 He probably projects into the mental life of others what is present in his own subconsciousness.

2. A condition of imperfectly realizing or being aware *of* something.

1881 *Nation* (N.Y.) XXXII. 290 Brady's consciousness or subconsciousness of the shortness and uncertainty of his own tenure. 1896 F. M. Crawford *Corleone* xxxiii, He drove away the sub-consciousness that the thing was not yet done.

Sub-co·nstable. Now *Hist.* [Sub- 6.] An under-constable, *esp.* in the Royal Irish Constabulary (see quots. 1814, 1883).

1512 *Act 4 Hen. VIII*, c. 19 § 6 Preceptes to the Constables Hedbouroghes Thirdbouroghes Subconstables. 1558–9 *Act 1 Eliz.* c. 21 § 16. 1814 *Act 54 Geo. III*, c. 131 § 6 To appoint, for the Aid and Support of any such Chief Magistrates,..a Clerk, and also a Chief Constable, and any Number of Sub Constables, not exceeding Fifty in the whole. 1839 *Penny Cycl.* XIII. 25/2 The police..in 1836, consisted of.. 155 chief constables of the first and 59 of the second class; 1232 constables; 6233 subconstables. 1883 *Act 46 Vict.* c. 14 § 12 After the first day of October one thousand eight hundred and eighty-three the sub-inspectors, constables, acting constables, and sub-constables of the Royal Irish Constabulary, shall respectively be styled district inspectors, sergeants, acting sergeants, and constables. 1886 Brophy *Sk. R. I. C.* i. 7 Sub-Constable D—— was a scion of a family that were ruined chiefly by horse-racing. 1907 *Westm. Gaz.* 4 July 1/2 Sir Thomas Echlin..served..as sub-constable and constable in the ranks of the Royal Irish Constabulary.

Su·bco·ntinent. [Sub- 5 b.] A land mass of great extent, but smaller than those generally called continents; a large section of a continent having a certain geographical or political independence; in recent use, *spec.* South Africa.

1863 Huxley *Man's Place Nat.* III. 154 From central Asia eastward to the Pacific islands and subcontinents on the one hand, and to America on the other. 1902 *Scotsman* 16 Oct. 11/1 In South Africa..the inhabitants of the sub-continent. 1911 *United Empire* June 389 Rhodesia might have seemed the Never-never-land of the sub-continent, a Cinderella among South African States.

Su·bcontine·ntal, *a.*

1. [Sub- 1 a.] Situated or occurring under a continent.

1900 Sollas in *Nature* LXII. 487/1 The sub-continental excess of temperature.

2. [Sub- 19.] Partly continental.

1897 *Pop. Sci. Monthly* L. 329 The occurrence of what are stated to be subcontinental or terrigenous deposits.

†**Subconti·nuative**, *a. Gram. Obs.* [ad. late L. *subcontinuātīv-us* (in *conjunctiōnēs subcontinuātīvæ*): see Sub- 8 and Continuative. Cf. Gr. παρασυναπτικός applied to conjunctions used to introduce clauses implying a fact.] (See quots.)

1530 Palsgr. 148 Some [conjunctions] be subcontinuatyves whiche serve to contynue a mater whan..begon, or to begyn a mater at the first, as *pour autant*..*si*..*combien*..*encore*. *Ibid.*, I have..called one of the vii modes..the subjunctyve mode or subcontinuatyve mode. 1798 Tooke *Purley* (ed. 2) I. vii. 111 We shall get rid of that farrago of useless distinctions into *Conjunctive, Adjunctive, Disjunctive, Subdisjunctive*,..*Continuative, Subcontinuative*.

Sub-conti·nued, *a. Med.* [Sub- 20 g.] Of a fever: Almost continuous, remittent.

1836 J. M. Gully *Magendie's Formul.* (ed. 2) 60 Twenty-seven sub-continued, and eight remittent fevers, were cured. 1898 P. Manson *Trop. Diseases* xxxvi. 543 Fever of an irregular, intermitting, or even of a sub-continued type.

So **Sub-conti·nual** *a.*

1890 Billings *Nat. Med. Dict.*, *Subcontinual fever*, malarial fever.

Subco·ntract, *sb.* [Sub- 9.] A contract, or one of several contracts, for carrying out a previous contract or a part of it.

1817 Selwyn *Law Nisi Prius* (ed. 4) IV. 1037 If the defendant was not liable, the plaintiff might be obliged to sue all the parties who had subcontracts before he could obtain redress. 1885 *Law Rep.* 15 Q. B. Div. 87 The contract with the plaintiff was to enable him to fulfil a subcontract with his customer.

attrib. 1887 *Pall Mall Gaz.* 25 Nov. 11 Making it a condition of all Government clothing contracts that they must not be worked out under the sweating or sub-contract system.

Subcontra·ct, *v.* [Sub- 9.]

†**1.** *pass.* To be betrothed for the second time.

1605 Shaks. *Lear* v. iii. 86 'Tis she is sub-contracted to this Lord.

2. *intr.* To make a subcontract.

1842 Burn *Naval & Milit. Dict.* (1863) s. v. *Sous, Soustraiter*, to sub-contract. 1889 *Lancet* 9 Mar. 498 He.. hands over what he cannot do himself to others with whom he subcontracts.

3. *trans.* To make a subcontract for.

1898 *Westm. Gaz.* 26 Aug. 7/2 As to the food arrangements, they were not worked from London, but sub-contracted by people in the locality.

Hence **Subcontra·cted** *ppl. a.*, **Subcontra·cting** *vbl. sb.*; **Sub-contra·ctor**, one who enters into a subcontract.

1842 *Civil Engin. & Arch. Jrnl.* V. 85/2 The sub-contractor ..had to..lay down the temporary road. 1900 *Westm. Gaz.* 22 Oct. 8/1 Direct employment and no sub-contracting. 1902 *Daily Chron.* 29 Apr. 3/4 The conditions under which the sub-contracted work is carried out.

Su·bcontrari·ety. *Logic.* [f. next: see Contrariety.] The relation existing between subcontrary propositions.

1697 tr. *Burgersdicius his Logic* I. xxxiii, Subcontrariety is between two Particulars; Opposition Indefinite between two Infinites. 1864 Bowen *Logic* vi. 162 It was convenient for Logicians to consider the relations of Subalternation and Sub-Contrariety.

Subco·ntrary, *a.* and *sb.* [ad. late L. *subcontrārius*, as a term of logic transl. Gr. ὑπεναντίος: see Sub- 19 and Contrary *a.* Cf. OF. *subcontraire*, F. *sous-contraire*.]

A. *adj.* **1.** Somewhat or partially contrary.

1603 Holland *Plutarch's Mor.* 1038 The other [number] which surmounteth, and is surmounted by the same parts of their extremities, is named *Hypenantia*, that is to say, subcontrary. 1697 J. Sergeant *Solid Philos.* 314 Finding his Discourse in other Places Sub-contrary to what he said in his Thoughts. 1897 Blackmore *Dariel* xxix, A manner not directly counter, but sub-contrary..to the view which her husband had ventured to form.

2. *Logic.* **a.** Applied to particular propositions (or the relation of opposition between them) agreeing in quantity but differing in quality.

1656 tr. *Hobbes' Elem. Philos.* I. iii. 31 Subcontraries, are Particular Propositions of different Quality; as Some Man is learned. Some Man is not learned. 1826 Whately *Logic* (1827) Index 347 Subcontrary opposition—is between two particulars, the affirmative and the negative. 1870 Jevons *Elem. Logic* ix. 78 Of subcontrary propositions..both can be false, and both may be true.

b. 'Applied to the relation between two attributes which co-exist in the same substance, yet in such a way that the more there is of one, the less there is of the other' (Webster 1864).

3. *Geom.* **a.** Applied to the relative position of two similar triangles having a common angle at the vertex and their bases not parallel, so that the basal angles are equal but on contrary sides. Also in a generalized sense (see quot. 1842).

1704 J. Harris *Lex. Techn.* I, *Subcontrary Position*, (in Geometry). 1842 *Penny Cycl.* XXIII. 185/1 When a line or solid is symmetrical, so that equal lines or polygons can be drawn on two different sides, those equal lines or polygons may be called subcontrary.

b. Applied to any circular section of a quadric cone in relation to the base or to another circular section not parallel to it.

1706 W. Jones *Syn. Palmar. Matheseos* 254 If the Cone be cut by a Plane Parallel or Subcontrary to the Base, the Section will be a Circle. 1842 *Penny Cycl.* XXIII. 185/1 The generating circle ABCD has a subcontrary circle EBFD, made by taking the line EF subcontrary to AC. 1877 *Encycl. Brit.* VI. 283/1 If the cone be cut by a plane which does not pass through the vertex, and which is neither parallel to the base nor to the plane of a subcontrary section.

B. *sb.* **1.** *Logic.* A subcontrary proposition.

1697 tr. *Burgersdicius his Logic* I. xxxiii, Subcontraries, are, some man is just, some man is not just.., where only the negation added or taken away, contradict subcontraries. 1725 Watts *Logic* II. ii. § 3 If two particular propositions differ in quality, they are subcontraries. 1826 [see Subaltern *sb.* 3]. 1864 Bowen *Logic* vi. 164 Sub-Contraries..are called 'opposites' only in a qualified and technical sense.

2. *Geom.* A subcontrary section of a cone.

1842 *Penny Cycl.* XXIII. 185/1 In a right cone, every section has its subcontrary, except only the circle which generates the cone, and its parallels.

Hence **Subco·ntrarily** *adv.* (see quot.).

1728 Chambers *Cycl.* s. v. *Subcontrary*, If the Scalenous Cone BVD be so cut by the Plane CA, as that the Angle at C = D; the Cone is then said to be cut Subcontrarily to its Base BA.

Subco·rtical, *a.* [Sub- 1 a.]

1. Lying, situated, or formed under the bark of a tree; (of insects) living or feeding under the bark.

1815 Kirby & Sp. *Entomol.* (1818) I. 212 Wood-lice, earwigs, spiders, field-bugs, and similar subcortical insects. 1832 Lindley *Introd. Bot.* 113 To facilitate the development of the subcortical fibres of the growing buds. 1851 Mantell *Petrifactions* i. 43 These are not produced by the attachment of petioles, but are sub-cortical protuberances. 1866 Rye *Brit. Beetles* 89 *Omalium planum*..is, perhaps, as good an example of a subcortical insect as could be seen.

2. Situated under or pertaining to the region underlying (*a*) the cortex of a sponge, (*b*) the cortex of the brain.

1887 *Encycl. Brit.* XXII. 415 The roots of the canals and sinuses form widely open spaces immediately beneath the cortex and are the rudiments of subcortical crypts. 1899 *Allbutt's Syst. Med.* VI. 810 Supra-nuclear paralysis (including the cortical and subcortical varieties). *Ibid.* VII. 318 The lesion was an essentially subcortical one.

Hence **Subco·rtically** *adv.*, with reference to the region underlying the cortex.

1871 W. A. Leighton *Lichen-flora* 150 The sub-cortically albo-maculate thallus.

‖ **Subcosta** (sɒbkǫ·stă). *Entom.* [Sub- 1 f.] The subcostal vein of the wing of some insects; the vein just behind the costa.

1861 H. Hagen *Synopsis Neuroptera N. Amer.* 343.

Subco·stal, *a.* and *sb.* [ad. mod.L. *subcostālis*: see Sub- 1 b and Costal.]

A. *adj.* **1.** *Anat.* Situated below a rib or beneath the ribs; lying on the under side of a rib, as a groove for an artery.

1872 Humphry *Myology* 10 The under or sub-costal parts of the broad pelvic shield. 1876 *Quain's Elem. Anat.* (ed. 8)

Subcrureal, *a.* Also **-eal**. [f. next.] Situated under the crureus; pertaining to the subcrureus.

Subcrureus (s-). *Anat.* Also **-eus**.

Subcutaneous (sʊbkiuˈteinəs), *a.* [f. late L. *subcutāneus*, f. *sub-* SUB- 1 + *cutis* skin + *-aneus*: see *-ous.* Cf. F. *subcutané*.]
1. Lying or situated under the skin.
2. Living under the skin.
3. Of operations, etc.: Performed or taking place under the skin; characterized by application of a remedy beneath the skin; hypodermic.
Hence **subcutaneously** *adv.*, under the skin, hypodermically; **subcutaneousness**.

Subdane, *-dayn*, obs. forms of SUDDEN.

Subdeacon (sʌbˈdiːkən). *Eccl.* Forms: α. 4 *side.kne*, 4-5 *sodeken*, 5 *-ken*, 4-7 *sub-diacon*, etc. (see DEACON *sb.*). β. *subdeacon*.
1. The name of an order of ministers in the Christian church next below that of deacon.
2. *transf.*

Subdeaconry, the office, position, or residence of a subdeacon.

Subdeanery, the office, position, or residence of a subdean.

Subdeacanal, *a. rare.* [f. med.L. *subdecānalis*] Of or pertaining to a subdean or subdeanery.

Subdecanal, *a. rare.*

Subdelegate (-ət), *v.* Obs. [f. SUB- 6 + DELEGATE *sb.*] *trans.* To appoint (a person) to act as a subdelegate; to transmit (power) to a subdelegate.

Subdelegate (-ət), *sb.* [f. SUB- 6 + DELEGATE, after AF. *subdelegat*, med.L. *subdelegā-tus*.] A subordinate delegate; a delegate of a delegate.

Subdelega·tion. The action of subdelegating.

Subdenomination. [SUB- 7 b.] A subordinate denomination.

Subdialect. A subordinate dialect; a division of a dialect.

Subdistich. [SUB- 10 c.] Consisting of almost two rows. So **Subdistichous** *a.*

Subdistinction [in sense 1, ad. late L. *subdistinctiō* = Gr. ὑποστιγμή, f. *subdistinguere* = Gr. ὑποστίζειν, f. *sub-* SUB- + *distinguere* to DISTINGUISH.]

Subdistinguish, *v.* [SUB- 9 + DISTINGUISH *v.* Cf. L. *subdistinguere*, Gr. ὑποστίζειν.] *trans.* To distinguish by subordinate kinds, classes, species, etc.

Subdi·strict. [SUB- 7 c.] A division or subdivision of a district.

Subdi·vidable, *a. rare.* [f. SUBDIVIDE *v.* + -ABLE.] Capable of being subdivided.

Subdi·vidant. [f. SUB- 5 + DIVIDANT *a.*]

Subdistinction [SUB- ; see SUBDIVISION.] A subordinate division between rivers and their branches.

Subdi·visible, *a.* [after *divisible*, q.v.] Capable of being subdivided.

Subdi·vision. [f. SUBDIVIDE *v.* + *-ion*, after *division*; = F. *subdivision*, Sp., Pg. *subdivisão*; also It., Sp., Pg. *subdivisione*.]
1. The act or process of subdividing, or fact of being subdivided.
2. A subordinate division; one of the parts into which a thing is divided.

Hence **Subdivi·sional** *a.*; **Subdivi·sive** *a.*

Subdivi·sional, *a.* [f. prec. + -AL.] Of the nature of subdivision; pertaining to subdivision, or a subdivision; consisting of a subdivision.

Subduce, *v. Obs.* [ad. L. *subdūcĕre*, f. *sub-* SUB- 23 + *dūcĕre* to lead, bring.]
1. *trans.* To take away; withdraw (lit. and *fig.*).
2. To subtract.

Subdual, *sb.* Now *rare.* [f. SUBDUE *v.* + -AL.] The act of subduing, or state of being subdued; subjection.

Subduable (sʌbˈdjuːəb'l), *a. rare.* [ad. late L. *subduābilis* or f. its source *subdolēre*, f. *sub-* + *dolus* cunning.] Crafty, cunning, sly.

Subdolous (sʌˈbdoʊləs), *a. Now rare.* [ad. L. *subdolus* f. *sub-* SUB- + *dolus*.] Marked by subdolousness; crafty, cunning, sly.

Subdominant. *Mus.* A., C. f. *sous-dominante*.] The note next below the dominant or a scale; the fourth note in ascending and the fifth in descending a scale. Also *attrib.*

Subdominant, *a.* Subordinately dominant, not quite dominant.

Subdorsal, *a.* [SUB- 14.] Less than dorsal; situated towards the back.

Subdu·plicate, *a. Math.*

Subdue (sʌbˈdjuː), *v.* Forms: α. 4 *so-dewe*, *so-*, *suddewe*, *sodewe*. β. 5-6 *sub-dewe*, 5-6 *subdue*. γ. 6 *subdue*. [Of difficult etymology. M.E. *sodewe*, *subdewe*, represents chiefly AF. *soduer*, *sodue* (= OF. *sub-* or *sous-duire*), f. Latin *subducere*.]
1. *trans.* To conquer (an army, an enemy, a country or its inhabitants) in fight and bring them into subjection.
2. To take away or remove surreptitiously or fraudulently. Also *absol.*
3. To draw up, lift.
4. *Med.* To overcome or overpower (a person) by physical strength or violence. *Obs.*
5. To reduce the intensity, force, or vividness of (sound, colour, light); to render less prominent or salient.
6. To bring under cultivation.

Hence **Subdued** *ppl. a.*, reduced to subjection; brought under control; lessened in intensity, force; toned down.
Subduedly *adv.*, in a subdued manner.
Subduement *sb.*, the act of subduing.
Subduer, one who subdues.
Subduing *ppl. a.*; **Subduingly** *adv.*

Sub-edit, *v.* [Back-formation f. next.] To edit (a paper, periodical, etc.) under, to prepare

Sub-editor. Sub-editorship. Sub-editorial. Sub-element. Sub-elemental. Subequal. Suberiferous. Suberification. Suberiform. Suberin. Suberine. Suberize. Subero-. Suberone. Suberose. Suberous. Suberate. Subereous. Suberic. Suberiform.

Suberic. Suberin. Suberization.

Subfactor. Subfamily. Subfebrile. Subfeu. Subfeudation. Subfeudatory. Subfief. Subfigure. Subfoliaceous.

Subglobular. Subgovernor. Subhastation. Subhead. Subhuman. Subindicate. Subindication. Subincision. Subinfer. Subinfeud. Subinfeudate. Subinfeudation.

Subintroduce. Subinvariant. Subitaneous. Subitany. Subito. Subject.

Subjectively, adv. [f. prec. + -LY.]

Subjectiveness. [Formed prec. + -NESS.] The quality or condition of being subjective.

Subjectivism. [f. SUBJECTIVE + -ISM.] The philosophical theory according to which all our knowledge is merely subjective and relative, and which denies the possibility of objective knowledge.

Subjectivist. One who believes in or advocates subjectivism. Also attrib.

Subjectivity. [f. as prec.: see -ITY.] So mod. L. subjectivitas, G. subjectivität, F. subjectivité.

Subjectivize. [f. as prec. + -IZE.]

Subjectless, a. [f. SUBJECT sb. + -LESS.]

†Subjectly, adv. or adv. rare. [-LIKE.] Like a subject; submissively.

Subject-matter. [Earlier matter subject: see SUBJECT sb. + MATTER.]

Subject-object. Philos.

Subjoin, v. [f. SUB- + JOIN.]

Subjoinder (sbdgdoindər). rare⁻¹. [f. SUBJOIN after rejoinder.] A remark subjoined to another.

Subjugable, a. rare⁻¹. [f. L. subjugare: see -ABLE.]

Subjugate, pa. pple. and a. [ad. L. subjugat-us, pa. pple. of subjugare: see next.]

Subjugate, v. [f. L. subjugat-, ppl. stem of subjugare.]

Subjugation (sbdgugeiʃən). [ad. late L. subjugātio, -ōnem, n. of action f. subjugare: see SUBJUGATE. Cf. F. subjugation.]

Subjugator (sb·dgugeitər). [ad. late L. subjugātor, agent-n. f. subjugare to SUBJUGATE.]

Subjugation (sbdgugeiʃən).

Subjunction (sbdgʌŋkʃən). [ad. late L. subjunctiō, -ōnem, n. of action f. subjungere to SUBJOIN.]

Subjunctive (sbdgʌŋktiv), a. and sb. [ad. late L. subjunctīv-us, f. subjunct-, ppl. stem of subjungere to SUBJOIN.]

Sub-lease, sb. [SUB- 6.]

Sub-lease, v. [f. prec.]

Sublate, pa. pple. and a. [ad. L. sublāt-us: see next.]

Sublate, v. [f. L. sublāt-, taken as pa. ppl. stem of tollere to take away.]

Sublation (sbleiʃən). [ad. L. sublātiō, -ōnem, n. of action f. sublāt-: see SUBLATE.]

Sublieutenancy.

Sub-let, v. [SUB- 6.]

Sub-let, sb. A sub-lease.

Sub-lieutenant. [SUB- 6. Cf. F. sous-lieutenant.]

Sublimable (sblaiməb'l), a. Now rare. [f. SUBLIME v. + -ABLE.]

Sublimate (sb·limeit), v. [f. L. sublīmāt-, ppl. stem of sublīmāre to SUBLIME.]

Sublimate (sb·limət), sb. [See SUBLIMATE v.]

Sublimate (sb·limət), a. Also -ATED.

Sublimation (sblimeiʃən). [ad. med. or mod. L. sublīmātiō, -ōnem, n. of action f. sublīmāre to SUBLIME.]

Sublimate, v.

Sublimation (sublimēˈʃən). ...

Sublime (sŏblaiˈm), a. and sb. ...

Sublimable ...

Sublimity (sŏbliˈmĭti). ...

Sublimize (sŏbˈlimaiz), v. ...

Sublingual ...

Subluxation ...

Submarginal, a. ...

Submarine (sŏbmărīˈn), a. and sb. ...

B. *sb.*

1. A submarine creature; †a submarine plant, coral, etc.

1753 *Phil. Trans.* XLVIII. 1419 A Description of some Corals, and other curious Submarines.

2. A submarine boat.

3. A submarine boat: see A 2.

Submarshal. [SUB-6.] A deputy or under-marshal; an official in the marshalsea acting as the knight-marshal's deputy.

Submaster. [SUB-6. Cf. med.L. *submagister*, F. *sous-maître*, formerly †*soubs-maistre*.] A subordinate, deputy, or assistant master.

Submaxilla (sᵘbmækˈsila). [mod.L.: see SUB-3 and MAXILLA.] The lower jaw or jaw-bone.

Submaxillary, *a.* [SUB-1 and MAXILLARY.]

1. Situated beneath the inferior maxilla.

2. *Anat.* Pertaining to the submaxilla.

Submedial, *a.* [SUB-11, 21.] Near the middle or median line; almost medial.

2. *Geol.* [SUB-1 a.] Lying below the middle group of rocks.

Submedian, *a.* [SUB-11, 21.]

Submental, *a.* [SUB-1 b, MENTAL.] Situated beneath the chin or under the edge of the lower jaw; chiefly in *submental artery, vein.* Also, pertaining to the submentum.

Submentum. [F. *sous-menton*, mod.L.] The basal part of the labium.

Submerge (sᵘbmɜ˕ˈdʒ), *v.* [ad. L. *submergĕre*, var. of *submergĕre*; see SUB-2 and MERGE.]

1. *pass.* To be covered with water; to be sunk under water.

2. *trans.* To cause to sink or plunge into water; to place under water.

3. *intr.* To sink or plunge under water; to undergo submersion. Now *rare.*

Submergement. [f. SUBMERGE v. + -MENT.] Submersion.

Submergence (sᵘbmɜ˕ˈdʒəns). [f. as prec.: see -ENCE.]

Submerse, *v.* [L. *submers-*, ppl. stem of *submergĕre*.] To plunge or sink into water; to submerge, drown.

Submersed (sᵘbmɜ˕ˈst), *ppl. a.* [f. L. *submers-*, pa. pple. of *submergĕre* + -ED.]

Submersible, *a.* and *sb.* [f. L. *submers-*, pa. pple. stem of *submergĕre* to SUBMERGE, prob. after F. *submersible.* Cf. mod.L. *submersibilis* and INSUBMERSIBLE (1865).]

Submersion (sᵘbmɜ˕ˈʃən). [ad. L. *submersio, submersiōn-*, n. of action f. *submergĕre* to SUBMERGE. Cf. F. *submersion.*]

Sub-minister, *sb.* Now *rare* or *Obs.* [SUB-6 MINISTER *sb.*]

Subminister, *v.* [L. *subminister-*, f. *sous-ministre*, formerly †*soubministre.*]

Chr. *Heaven* (N.Y.) *ay. Apr.* 76/1

Submenagōgue, *a. rare.*

Submaristic, *a.* [SUB-7.]

Sub-ministrant. *Obs. rare.* [ad. med.L. *subministrant-*: see prec.] Subordinate.

Submistrant, *a. Obs. rare.* [ad. med.L. *subministrant-* (see prec.).] Subordinate.

Submistrate, *v.* [L. *subministrāt-*, ppl. stem of *subministrāre* to SUBMINISTER.]

Submministration. [ad. late L. *subministrātio, -ōn-*, n. of action f. *subministrāre* to SUBMINISTER. Cf. OF. *-ation, subministration* (Cotgr.).] The action of subministering; ministering support; provision, supply.

Submine, *v. Obs. rare.* (Chiefly Caxton.) Also *sub-.* [OF. *sousminer*, var. of *sousmenĕr.*]

Submisal (sᵘbˈmaizəl), *sb. Obs. rare.*

Submis (sᵘbmiˈs), *a.* Also 6-7 *-is, -isse.* [a. F. *submis*, pa. pple. of *submettre* to SUBMIT. Cf. SUBMISS.]

1. SUBMISSIVE. (Const. *to*) *Obs. exc. arch.*

Submissible, *a.* [f. SUBMIT + -IBLE.] Capable of being submitted.

Submission (sᵘbmiˈʃən). Also 5-7 *-ysyon, -tion* (var. *summ-*), n. of action f. *submittĕre* to SUBMIT, F. *soumission*, etc.: see SUBMIT, SUBMISSION.)

1. *Law.* Agreement to abide by or to obey an authority; reference to the decision or judgement of a (third) party; in recent use *spec.*, the referring of a matter to arbitration.

2. The condition of being submissive, yielding, or deferential; submissive or deferential conduct or attitude; of bearing; deference; †*occas.* humiliation.

Submissioner. *Obs. rare⁻¹.* [f. SUBMISSION + -ER¹.] One who makes his submission.

Submissionist. [f. SUBMISSION + -IST.] One who advocates submission; *spec.* in Spanish and U.S. history.

Submissive (sᵘbmiˈsiv), *a.* [f. L. *submiss-*, ppl. stem of *submittĕre* to SUBMIT. Cf. F. *soumissive.*]

1. Disposed or inclined to submit; yielding to power or authority; marked by submissive or humble and ready obedience.

2. Of deference or homage; demonstrative of submissiveness. *arch.*

3. Of material things.

†c. *Phr.* With (*great*) *submission*: subject to correction. *Obs.*

Submissively, *adv.* [-LY².] In a submissive manner, with submission.

Submissiveness. [f. as prec. + -NESS.] The quality or condition of being submissive.

Submissness. *arch.* [f. as prec. + -NESS.] Submissiveness.

Submissly, *adv.* [f. SUBMISS + -LY².] In a submissive manner, submissively.

Submit (sᵘbmiˈt), *v.* Also 4-6 *-mytte, -4 pa. t. -mytte, 5 pa. pple. -myt(t), 5-ment, 5-6 -myt, 5-7 -mitte, 6-7 -mitt.* [ad. L. *submittĕre*, var. of *summittĕre* (see SUB-2 and note), mod.F. *soumettre*, and Pr. *sots-, sosmetre*, It. *sottomettere* beside *sottomettĕre*, Sp. *someter*, Pg. *submeter.*]

1. *refl.* and *intr.* To place oneself under the control of a person in authority or power; to become subject, surrender oneself, or yield to a person or his rule, etc.

†a. Const. *under*; *refl.* *unto. Obs.*

b. Const. *to* (†*unto*) a person, his government, rule, will, etc.

c. Without const.

2. *refl.* To subject oneself to judgement, criticism, correction, a condition, treatment, etc.

3. To subject *to* an operation or process.

4. To present for consideration, judgement, decision, etc.

5. *Sc. Law.* One who makes a "submission".

Submitter. [f. SUBMIT + -ER¹.] One who submits.

Submittal. *rare.* [f. SUBMIT + -AL.] The act of submitting.

Submittance. *Obs.* [f. as prec. + -ANCE.]

Submittingly, *adv.* [f. SUBMITTING + -LY².]

Submocous, *a.* = SUBMUCOUS a (1913 *Dorland Illustr. Med. Dict.*)

Submoccasin, *a.* = SUBMUCOUS a.

Submontane, *a.*

1. *Path.* [SUB- b.] Passing under, or existing below, mountains.

2. [SUB-12 a.] Lying about the foot of mountains; belonging to the foot-hills of a range; also, belonging to the lower slopes of mountains.

Submove, *v. Obs. rare.* [ad. L. *submovēre* (var. *summ-*), f. *sub-* SUB- 2 + *movēre* to MOVE.] *trans.* To remove.

Submucosa (sᵘbmiukōˈsa), *sb. Anat.* [mod.L., fem. (*sc. membrāna*) of *submucōsus*: see next.] The layer of areolar tissue lying beneath a mucous membrane; the submucous layer.

Submucous, *a.* [SUB- + MUCOUS.]

1. *Path.* [SUB- a.] Somewhat mucous; partly consisting of or attended by mucus; of an indistinctly mucous character.

Submormal, *a.* [SUB- b.] Situated beneath the mucous membrane; pertaining to the submucosa.

Submultiple, *sb.* and *a.* [ad. late L. *submultiplus*: see SUB-10 and MULTIPLE.]

Submultiplication, *vbl. sb.* [f. as next + -ING¹.] That submits or makes a submission.

Submunition. *Obs.* [ad. L. *submunitio, -ōnem*, n. of action f. *submunīre.*] Under-munition, suggestion.

Submundane, *a.*

Subnascent, *a.* [SUB-2 and NASCENT.] Growing underneath or up from beneath. *Obs. rare⁻¹.*

Subnect, *v. Obs.* [ad. L. *subnectĕre*, f. *sub-* SUB-2 + *nectĕre* to knit.]

Subnex, *v. Obs.* [L. *subnex-*, pa. ppl. stem of *subnectĕre*: see prec. †]

Subnormal, *sb. Geom.* [ad. mod.L. *subnormālis (sc. linea line)*: see SUB-1 and NORMAL.]

Subnormal, *a.* [ad. mod.L. *subnormālis.* Less than normal; below the normal.]

Subnotochordal, *a.* [f. SUB- + NOTOCHORDAL.] Somewhat of the nature of a notochord.

Subnotochordal, *a.* [SUB-1 b.] Situated beneath the notochord.

Subobscure, *a. Obs.* [SUB-11 a.] Somewhat obscure.

Subobscurely, *adv.* Somewhat obscurely.

Suboccipital, *a.* [ad. mod.L. *suboccipitālis.*]

Subocular, *a.* [ad. mod.L. *suboculāris.*] Situated below or under the eye.

Subnex, *v. Obs.* [L. *subnex-*, pa. ppl. stem of *subnectĕre*: see prec.]

Subocellar, *a.* Situated below or under the eye.

Suboctave, *sb.* [SUB-1.] An eighth part. *Obs. rare.*

2. *Mus.* [SUB- 4 (1).] The octave below a given note. Also *attrib.* in *suboctave coupler.*

Subocular, *a.* [SUB- 4.] Situated below or under the eye.

Subodorate, v. rare.

Subo'dorous, a.

Suboffice.

Suborbicular.

Suborbital, a. (sb.) Ichth.

Subopercular, a. (sb.) Ichth.

Subopercle.

Suboperculum.

Suborbicular, a. Nat. Hist.

Suborbital, a.

Subordinal, a.

Subordinary, sb.

Subordinate, a. (sb.)

Subordinate, v.

Subordinately, adv.

Subordinateness.

Subordinating, ppl. a.

Subordination.

Subordinationism. Theol.

Subordinationist. Theol.

Subordinative, a. rare.

Suborn, v.

Subornate.

Subornation.

Suborned, ppl. a.

Suborner.

Subovate, a.

Subpœna, sb. and v.

Subpolar, a.

Subprincipal, a.

Subprior.

Subrogate, v.

Subrogate (sū'brŏgēt), v. [f. L. subrogāt-, ppl. stem of L. subrogāre (var. narr-), f. sub- SUB- 26 + rogāre to ask, offer for election.]

1. trans. To elect or appoint in the place of another; to substitute in an office. Obs.

2. To substitute (a thing) for another; const. in stead of, into the place of, occas. to. Now rare.

3. Law. To put (a person) in the place of, or substitute (him) for, another in respect of a right or claim; to cause to succeed to the rights of another: see SUBROGATION 2.

Hence **Su'brogated** ppl. a.

Subrogation (sŭbrŏgē'ʃən). [ad. L. subrogātiō-, -ōnem, n. of action f. subrogāre to SUBROGATE. Cf. F. subrogation, Pg. subrogação, and see SUBROGATION.]

†L. Substitution.

Subround, a. [SUB- 20 d.] Subrotund.

Subsalt, sb. Chem. (Not in use.) [f. SUB- 21 + SALT sb.] Cf. F. sous-sel.] A basic salt.

Subsaltatory (sŏbsæ'ltătŏri), a. rare⁻⁰. [f. SUB- 21 + SALTATORY.] Characterized by a slight dancing motion.

Subsannate, v. Obs. [f. late L. subsannāt-, ppl. stem of subsannāre, f. sub- SUB- 31 + sannæ mocking grimace.] trans. To deride, mock. Hence **†Subsanna'tion**, mockery, derision.

Subscapular (sŏbskæ'piŭlăr), a. Anat. [mod.L.: see SUBSCAPULAR.] Situated below, or on the under surface of, the scapula.

†Subscapularis (sŏbskæpiŭlæ'ris). Anat. [mod.L.: see SUB- 1 d and SCAPULAR.]

Subscapulary (sŏbskæ'piŭlări), a. Anat. rare. [f. mod.L. subscapularis: see SUB- 1 and SCAPULAR.] = SUBSCAPULAR.

Subscribable (sŏbskrai'băb'l), a. [f. SUBSCRIBE + -ABLE.] Capable of being subscribed.

So Subrotu'nde, -rotu'ndous adjs. in the same sense; **Subrotu'ndo**, combining form of SUBROTUND.

1. trans. To write (one's name or mark) on, or at the bottom of, a document, esp. as a witness or consenting party; to sign (one's name) to. Now rare.

b. To write, set down, or inscribe below or at the conclusion of something. Now rare.

2. With compl. a. refl. To put oneself down as so-and-so at the foot of a letter or document. Now rare.

b. Occurring under the scapula.

3. To sign one's name to; to signify assent or adhesion to, by signing one's name; to attest by signing. Cf. SUBSCRIPTION 3.

4. To give (one's) word so-and-so.

5. To agree or be a party to a course of action or condition of things; to give approval, sanction, or countenance to; also occas. to consent or engage to; to agree that.

6. To give one's adhesion or allegiance, make one's submission to another; gen. to submit, yield, give in. Now rare or Obs.

b. Of a bookseller: to take beforehand to take (a certain number of copies of a book).

c. intr. Of a book: to be taken by this trade.

1. trans. To write (one's name or mark) to (a sum of money) for shares in an undertaking, or to or towards a particular object; to contribute (money) in support of any object. Also, to take up (shares) = subscribe for (see 12).

b. With compl. Esp. in Milton C[omus].

7. To give one's assent to a statement, opinion, proposal, scheme, or the like; to express one's agreement, concurrence, or acquiescence.

8. To agree to be a party to.

b. To submit or subject oneself to law or rule; to conform or defer to a person's will, etc. Obs.

†3. To give one's assent or adhesion to; to countenance, support, favour, sanction, concur in.

9. intr. Admit no other way to save his life (As I subscribe not that, nor any other, But in the loose of question).

†c. To admit one's inferiority or defeat, confess oneself in the wrong. Obs. rare.

†5. To sign away, yield up. Obs. rare.

6. intr. To write one's signature, esp. to put testimony; to sign one's name as a witness, etc. Also in indirect pass.

†c. To admit or concede the force, validity, or truth of. Now rare or Obs.

11. trans. To promise over one's signature to pay (a sum of money); to give to or towards an undertaking, or to or towards a particular object; to contribute (money) in support of any object. Also, to take up (shares) = subscribe for (see 12).

12. absol. or intr. To undertake to contribute money to a fund, to a society, party, etc.

13. Book trade. †a. trans. To expose (books) to subscribers. Obs.

b. Of a bookseller: to agree beforehand to take (a certain number of copies of a book): also subscribe for. Now occas. intr. Of a book: to be taken by this trade.

Subscribed (sŏbskrai'bd), ppl. a. [f. prec. + -ED¹.]

1. One who subscribes, or affixes his signature to, a letter or document, articles of religion, etc.

2. To make acknowledgement or admission of.

†10. To write under the undertaking for, vouch or answer for a person. Obs.

Subscribing (sŏbskrai'biŋ), vbl. sb. [f. SUBSCRIBE + -ING¹.] The action of the verb SUBSCRIBE.

Subscribing v. + -ING¹.] That subscribes, attests or assents to a document, etc.

Subscript (sŏ'bskript), sb. and a. [ad. L. subscript-us, -a, -um, pa. pple. of subscribere to write underneath, SUBSCRIBE.] A.

1. That which is written underneath; a writing at the bottom or end of a document, etc.; a signature.

B. A subscript letter or symbol.

B. adj. Written underneath; chiefly in iota subscript (see IOTA 1), the small written underneath in ᾳ, ῃ, ῳ.

Subscription (sŏbskri'pʃən). [ad. L. subscriptiō-, -ōnem, n. of action f. subscrip-, subscrībere to SUBSCRIBE. Cf. OF. sub-, subscription, mod.F. souscription, (Pr. sotzscriptio), It. soscrizione, Sp. subscripcion, Pg. subscripção.]

1. A piece of writing at the end of a document, e.g. the concluding clause or formula of a letter with the writer's signature, the colophon of a book, etc., the note appended to the epistles in the New Testament, etc.

†b. Something written or inscribed underneath, e.g. a number written under another, an inscription or title underneath.

2. A signature, name.

3. In sc. sign (or signet) and subscription manual w[riting].

4. The act or fact of subscribing; the signing of one's name or of a document.

5. A declaration of one's assent to articles of religion, or some formal declaration of principles, etc. by signing one's name; spec. in the Church of England, assent to the Thirty-nine Articles.

†6. Assent, approval. Also, an instance of this.

7. The action or an act of subscribing money to a fund or for assent; the raising of a sum of money for a certain object by collecting contributions from a number of people; †a scheme for raising money in this way. Also, an undertaking or agreement to subscribe to such.

b. spec. A share in a commercial undertaking or a loan. Also collect. sing. Obs.

8. a. A sum of money subscribed by several parties; a fund: formerly spec. in Stock Exchange language. Now U.S. in phr. to make or take up a subscription, to make a collection.

b. (a) The taking up of a book by the trade.

(b) The offering of a book to the trade.

c. U.S. The house-to-house sale of books by canvassers. Freq. attrib.

9. Mus. attrib., as subscription ball, charity-school, club, concert, cricket-match, dance, house, library, masquerade, music, night, school.

Subscriptive (sŏbskri'ptiv), a. rare. [f. L. subscript-: see prec. and -IVE.]

1. Pertaining to the 'subscription' of a letter.

2. Pertaining to the subscribing of money.

†Subscrive, v. Sc. Obs. [f. OF. subscrivre, souscrivre, ad. L. subscrībere to SUBSCRIBE.]

Subsecutive, a. Obs. rare⁻⁰. [f. as prec. + -IVE.] Subsequent.

Subsection (sŏ'bsekʃən, sŏbse'kʃən), sb. [f. SUB- 7 + SECTION.] A division or subdivision of a section; a part of a section.

Subsecutive, a. Obs. rare⁻⁰. [as prec.]

Subsequent (sŏ'bsĭkwĕnt), a. and sb. [a. F. subséquent or ad. L. subsequent-em, pr. pple. of subsequī to follow.] A. adj.

1. Following in order or succession; coming or placed after, esp. immediately after.

2. The condition or fact of being subsequent.

Subsequently adv. In a subsequent manner; afterwards; later.

Subsession...

this Charter by many others Subsequent. **1855** MACAULAY *Hist. Eng.* xvi. IV. 38 The day from which all his subsequent years took their colour. **1862** TYNDALL *Glac.* i. iii. 23 My subsequent destination was Vienna. **1905** R. BAGOT *Passport* xxvii. Concetta delivered the letter, and another subsequent one.

b. *Comb.*, as *subsequently to*. (Also *advb.* — *subsequently to*.)

1647 CLARENDON *Hist. Reb.* ii. § 12 The ill Consequences of it, or the Actions which were subsequent to it. **1794** SMITH *Some Remarks on Barrier Treaty* Wks. 1842 I. 430/1 This prodigious article is introduced as subsequent to the treaty of Munster. **1816** *Med. Jrnl.* XV. 141, I have not heard of any death but one shortly subsequent to cow-pox inoculation. **1822** HAZLITT *Table-t.* (1869) I. 5, I, Subsequent to the suppression ..he was..at large. **1891** SMILES *Charac.* ii. (1876) 37 It was subsequent to the death of both his parents.

c. Forming a sequel to. (*rare*)
1779 JOHNSON *L. P., Pope* (1868) 402 He had planned a work, which he considered as subsequent to his 'Essay on Man'.

d. *Phys. Geog.* (See quots.)
1880 JUKES in *Q. Jrnl. Geol. Soc.* XVIII. 400 That the lateral valleys are the first formed... while the longitudinal valleys are of subsequent origin, gradually produced by atmospheric action on the softer and more easily eroded beds that strike along the chains. **1890** W. M. DAVIS in *Geogr. Jrnl.* (R.G.S.) V. 132 The peculiarity of subsequent streams is...that they run along the strike of weak strata; hence the distinction between the dip, crossing harder and softer strata alike. **1898** L. C. RUSSELL *River Development* vi. 185 Streams originate..the downward affects are regulated by the hardness and solubility of the rocks. Such streams appear subsequently to the main topographic features in their environment, and are termed subsequent streams.

e. *Geol.* = INTRUSIVE *a.* 2.
1888 TEALL *Brit. Petrogr.* 449.

+ B. *sb.* A person or thing that follows or comes after. *Obs.*
1663 HOWARD *Montaigne* II. xii. 294 Deeming all other apprentishipps as subsequents and of superarogation in regard of that [orig. *estiment tout aprentissage reciproqué à celà-ci à suprerogation*]. **1677** GALE *Crt. Gentiles* II. iv. 464 This conceit...is quite dissonant from the conceit, both in regard of the precedents, and subsequents. **1696** PHILLIPS (ed. 5), *Subsequents of their holy History*, those *Jan-2t.* [Ibreadside]. **1691** T. H[ALE] *Acc. New Invent.* 18 Whether all the subsequents need but heir Ladies, Her Subsequents need it but heir Maidens. **1724** T. MURRAY *Engl. Gram.* (ed. 5) II. 247 As the relative pronoun, when used interjectively, refers to the subsequent word or phrase containing the answer to the question, that word or phrase may properly be termed the subsequent to the interrogative.

+ b. *These subsequents:* the persons or things mentioned immediately afterwards. *Obs.*
1622 STUBBYVANT *Metallica* 57 These subsequents are not necessarie, as namely: byrners, Carpenters, Smithes, Brickelayers, Masons. **1851** *90 New Hist. Kirk* (*Wodrow Soc.*) 13 These subsequents: to be observed in this Realme concerning Doctrine.

Subsequential, *a.* (sɒbsɪˈkwɛnʃæl). *Obs.*
1670 W. P[enn] *Case Lib. Consc.* 19 No Temporary Subsequential Law whatever, to our Fundamental Rights, ..can invalid so essential a part of the Government. **1691** JOHN FLATMAN *Jodie. Avid.* (1837) III. 580 Whether in their original character of advocates or in their subsequential character of Judges. **1809** — *Justice & Col. Petit.* 150 In another, say a subsequential judicatory, to which...the inquiry is..transferred. **1879** STEVENSON *Across the Plains* (1892) 9 It seems to fit some subsequential, evening epoch of the world.

Hence **Subsequen•tially** *adv.*, subsequently.
1829 BENTHAM *Justice & Col. Petit.* 127 Subsequentially subordinated to the main doctrine.

Subsequently (sɒ'bsɪˈkwɛntlɪ), *adv.* (Fig. SUBSEQUENT *a.* + -LY 2.) At a subsequent or later time. Const, *to*.
1611 COTGR., *Subacutivement*, subsequently. **1657** COMWELL *Sp. 17 Apr.* (Carlyle), If any be [subsequently] named, after the Other House is set. **1685** SOUTH *Serm.* I. ii. 314 Johnzon is grander in his reasonings, and to write in with things as they fall out. **1790** R. J. SULLIVAN *View Nat.* II. 74 From the same cause, the natural character of nations may arise, however subsequently moulded. **1845** DARWIN *Voy. Nat.* viii. 174 In North America..the large quadrupeds lived subsequently to that period. **1863** LYELL *Antiq. Man* 2 The remains of living beings which have peopled the district of the globe since man was born..may have subsequently been mingled in such caverns. **1890** *Law Times* XCI. 1/1 Cases where a man becomes a soldier subsequently to the making of the order.

‖ **Subserosa** (sɒbsɪˈroʊsə). *Anat.* (*mod.* L.) (*sc. membrana*; see SUB- 1 *d.* and *cf. next.*) Serous tissue.
1899 THALL *Med. Dict. Dict.* 1899 Nov. No. 135.

Subserous (sɒb'sɪərəs), *a. Anat.* and *Path.* [f. SUB- + SEROUS.]
[SUB- 1 *b.*] **a.** *Anat.* Situated or occurring beneath a serous membrane, as *subserous tissue*. *b. Path.* Affecting the subserous tissue.
1813 *Cycl. Fract. Med.* II. 131/1 Its bloodvessels and those of the sub-serous cellular tissue are de-ply injured. **1879** T. G. THOMAS *Dis. Women* (ed. 3) 276 Neoplasms, whether they be subserous, subserous or mural, keep up a constant nervous irritation. **1875** in *two Aitermar's Cycl. Med.* X. 279 The subserous flood being comparatively soft.

found wandering far and wide in the submucosa, the muscularis, etc.

2. [SUB- 20 *b.*] Somewhat serous. *In rare Dicts.*

+ **Subser•vant**, *Obs. rare.* [SUB- 5 *a.*] An inferior servant, under-servant.
1611 W. C[nef.] *Charaxc.*, *Detracting Empirick* (1860) 64 A poor apothecaries subservant, whose work is to tend to the still, and sweep the shop.

Subserve (sɒb'sɜːv), *v.* [ad. L. *subservire*, f. *sub-* SUB- 8 + *servire* to SERVE *v.*]
1. = SUBSERVIENCE 2. A. § 8 (1601) 186 Arts belonging to all there; and yet all of them subserving unto the Art of Riding. **1646** H. LAWRENCE *Communis.* 69 All creatures shall subserve to that composition of which God is a part. **1897** GALE *Crt. Gentiles* iv. 3 The manner of our disquisitions...is irregular...When we...make that subservient which should be ultimate, and that ultimate which should subserve. **1795** HUNTER *Nat. Hist.* II. 317 It subserves...to the Trade of this Place. **1822** L. HUNT *Indicator* No. 25 (1822) I. 273 Merely subservient to the worst taste of the times. **1865** WESTCOTT *Introd. Study Gosp.* v. 197 The historical framework of their writings subserved to a doctrinal development.

2. *trans.* To be instrumental in furthering or assisting (a purpose, object, action, function, or condition); to promote or assist by supplying an instrument or means.
1657 GALE *Crt. Gentiles* IV. 430 Is there not a world of men, which...subserve the Glorie of their Maker? **1689** BAXTER *Paraphr. N. T.* Matt. vi. 9 That thou wilt...cause us to subserve thy Providence by our war and diligent labours. **1867** *Contemp. Rev.* No. 2030/3 The true Exercise of Religion...will...truly subserve the Interest of our Majesties Power. **1741** WATTS *Impr. Mind* i. vi. (1801) 135 [The memory] uses all their parts..which subserve our sensations. **1836** W. *Sockford's World* I. 45 Even insensible matter showed a forwardness to subserve his designs. **1845** KIRBY & Sr. *Entomol.* x. (1818) I. 305 It might subserve the double purpose of riding to aid a nuisance, and relieving the public pressure. **1874** NEWMAN *Hist. Sk.* (1876) I. iv. 417 The cause of Protestantism...the Catholic Fathers certainly do not subserve. **1891** *Cent. Dict.* 1893 *Org. Nat.* I. 107 The ribs...subserve locomotion. **1897** *Allbutt's Syst. Med.* I. 109 The peripheral nervous system subserves sensation alone.

b. To be instrumental in furthering the purpose, interest, or function of (a person or thing). *rare.*
1661 BAXTER *Last Wk. Believer* (1688) 67 Christ will not take it ill...to have his Ministers subserve him in so glorious a work. **1865** GALE *Crt. Gentiles* I. v. § You see how the matter subservent subserve the perfect; the inanimate the animate; as the earth the plant... these subserve to protect and subserve subserve the organs of the senses.

+ **3. a.** *intr.* To act in a subordinate position.
1657 MILTON *Samson* 57 Not made to rule, But to subserve where wisdom bears command.

b. *trans.* To serve under, be subordinate to. *Obs. rare.*
1709 E. BANCROFT *Guiana* 319 The Bushmen takes a second [wife]..who lives and subserves the former in all domestic employments.

c. *refl.* To avail oneself of. *rare.*
1792 COKBRIDGE *Comm.* Lat. Elem. 1826 I. 373, I not merely subserve myself of them, but I employ them.

Subserviate (sɒb'sɜːvɪeɪt), *v.* [f. SUB- + SERVIAT + -ATE 2.] *trans.* To make subservient or subordinate.
1661 CROMWIGORT-SCHLEISEN in Farrelly *Settlem. S. Africa* (19,02 p0 They would solidify and foolishly subserviate the interests of the whole Colony to their own benighted wishes. **1906** CHURCHILL *Crisis* 11 v. x. Ja, the time would come when this people and its eternal subordinate interests in their subserviate bis the sublimation of.

+ b.
1681 Urquhart's *Rabelais* III. I. 401 The uses and subserviences they were for. **1802** PALEY *Nat. Theol.* xii. The plan is attended, through all its varieties and difficulties, by subserviences i. special circumstances and utilities. **1879** MILTON *Ch. Govt.* II. v. 198 No subservient to another. **1701** S. CLARKE *Serm.* (1730) L. 16 § An example of subserviate to another. **1800** *Westmr Rev.* July 273 They wanted the singer to remain subserviate to the composer.

this excess of subservience, because she was a stranger to the nearness of mind...by which it was dictated. **1863** GEO. ELIOT *R. Holt* I. v. 49 A young Persian monarch, corrupted by universal subservience around him. **1879** HARRISON *Autobi.* § 124 xxiv. 314 Johnston, is grander in his neglect of fashion than Goldsmith in his ruinous subservience. **1900** MATHERSON *Pol. in Relig.* I. x. 293 His subserviance to the Pope, and also in part to the external weakness of his position.

2. = SUBSERVIENCE 2. A. § 8 (1601) 186 Acts belonging to all there; and yet all of them subserving unto the Art of Riding. **1646** H. LAWRENCE.

3. Of persons, character, etc. : Slavishly submissive; truckling, obsequious.
1794 Mrs. RADCLIFFE *Myst. Udolpho* xlviii. Emily was... obliged by the subservient manners of those persons, who [etc.]. **1807** SCOTT *Marmion* i.x. This foreigner came here poor, beggarly, cringing, and subservient. **1813** JANE LOUIS *Mansf. P.* x.vii. 207 He contrived to ally the ranks subservient vovation which unworthy assemblies around the Crown.

B. *sb.* A subservient person or thing.
1863 D. PAGE *Man* 143 The primitive notion that this earth was the centre of the universe, and the sun, moon, and stars, formed merely to be its subservients. **1626** MASSINGER *Rom. Actor* IV. i. Whatever subservient of our Imperial Fact.

Subserviently (sɒb'sɜːvɪ əntlɪ), *adv.* [f. *prec.* + -LY 2.] In a subservient manner.
1878 H. MORE *Conject. Cabbal.* (1713) 15 It is reasonable we should conclude their in subserviency to the Good and Perfection of the Whole. **1795** A. M. *Reg. Hist.* 28 They acted subserviently to this purpose. **1795** SCODREN *Treal.* p. xv. Discovery was an object, therefore, that could only be pursued subserviently to this. **1865** MARCH. *Exton.* 31 Aug. 5 4 Unless it [sc. the Government] complies subserviently with the Nationalist demands.

50 **Subserviventness** *rare*⁻¹ (1727) Bailey Vol. II.

Subserving (sɒb'sɜːvɪŋ), *ppl. a.* [f. SUBSERVE *v.* + -ING²] That subserves; subservient.
1681 BURTON *Anat. Mel.* I. i. ii. iii, Ligaments, are they that tye the bones together, and other parts to the Bones, with their subserving tendons. **1891** *Advance* (Chicago) 9 Nov. Combine...against the ring and its boss and its subserving tool that now fills the Mayor's chair, [1882] W. H. HURLTON *Spencer's Philos.* 124 In non-gregarious creatures, the only conflict is between self-subserving and race-subserving activities.

Subsessile (sɒb'sɛsɪl), *a. Zool.* and *Bot.* [f. mod.L. *subsessilis*: see SUB- 20.] Not truly sessile ; almost sessile.
1760 J. LEE *Introd. Bot.* iii. (1765) 174 Verticillus, a Whorl, expresses a Number of Flowers that are subsessile. **1777** S. ROBSON *Brit. Flora* 154 Snow Saxifrage... Leaves obovate, crenate, subsessile. **1865** W. CLARKE *Unto der Heerd's Zool.* I. 341 Abdomen subsessile, conico-acuminate. **1794** MARTYN *Rousseau's Bot.* xii. 158 The corolla is mono-petalous...subsessile, or, sessile.

Sub•sext, *sb.* [f. SUBSET + -ING *sb.*¹] A subordinate set.
1900 *Encycl. Brit.* XXIX. 292/1 It may be possible to divide the set into a number of subsets, each of which can contain a common object.

Subset (*sub*'sɛt), *v.* intr. [f. SUB- 9 (8) + SET *v.*] *trans.* To underlet, sublet.
1828 STAIN *Inst. Laws* vi. xiii. 253 As the half may be sub-sett, so any other right less than the value of the whole; for if lands be set at an Indefeasement of warrandice. **1752** *Scots Mag.* Nov. 553/2 A small farm...which had been sub-let at four-fold beyond its former worth. **1867** SMILES *Husw. Man. Brit. Mag.* Nov. 382 A minute of tack,..which made no mention of assignees,... was..found, neither capable of being assigned, nor subset. **1847** HARDY *Lon. Ren.* xx. § 25, I have subset the whole of the sheep farm. **1881** W. BELL *Dict. Law Scot.* 261 To assign or subset a lease of the ordinary endurance of nineteen years.

Subsettle, *Obs.* [f. SUB- 14 + -LE, *cf. underset•tle*.] An under-tenant ; a sub-tenant.
1651 in J. GUEST *Rotherham* (1879) 361 Andrew Robinson sub-settell for a house on the common contrary to a statute therein made.

Subseyd, variant of SUBSIDE *v.*

Subshire *Obs. rare*⁻¹ [SUB- 9 (*b*) + SHIRE.] A division of a shire.
1721 *Fountainhall* *Decis.* I. 454 The axiom against sub-setting is only against an assignation... But a sub-lease is lawful, and was so found 10 March 1686. **1598** R. BERNARD *Terence, Andr.* iv. ii. § 33 (1572) 163 It means a Sub-shire,..for the whole Shire is divided into Sub-shires. [By a subset the principal tackman is not changed.] **1695** *Farmer's Mag.* Nov. 379 All tacks, likewise, that is, subleases for a great length of time, are also as-signable, as well as subsettible.

Subsh•ell, *Obs. rare*⁻¹ [SUB- 14 + -EL ; *cf. underset•tle*.] An under-tenant ; a sub-tenant.
1574 J. MILTON *Ch. Govt.* II. Wks. 1851 III. 109 Copies out from the furrow'd manuscript of a subservient scrowl. **1626** TUCKER *Reg. in Micst. Scott.* (Bannat.) 63 The towne is a mercat towne, but subservient and belonging..to the towne of Lydington. **1687** DRYDEN *Hind & P.* i. 68 Superior faculties are set aside,..Shall their subservient organs be my guide? **1709** POPE *Ess. Crit.* ii. 180 And made them keep their place, still made the Whole depend upon a part, then all in order, due or not. **1616** MILTON *Ch. Govt.* II. Wks. 1851 III. 109 Copies out from the furrow'd manuscript.. the subservient scrowl. **1685** BULWER *Anthropomet.* 177 The water in the number of them that perform an action, but of those that are subservient. **1691** J. FLAVELL *Husb. Spirit.* ix. xii. xxiv. (1674) 127, 5 Thou in the house of God hast made subservient the inferior... to the superior. **1753** HARTLEY *Observ. Man.* I. ii. 12. 134 Ideas of these..are subservient to, as are subordinate and things subservient.

+ **Subsidary**, *a. Obs.* Erron. f. SUBSIDIARY.
1646 W. THUNDER *Israel's Fast* Ded. p. v. Who doe more hinder or protecte the King in his necessarie and Royall subsidary Imports. **1658** SUCKLING *Aglaura* xvii. 1957/2 Suffragan or Subsidary Bishops.

+ **Subsid•iate**, *v. Obs. rare*⁻¹ [irreg. f. L. *subsidiāri* to SUBSIDE.] *intr.* To sink in.
1677 R. GILPIN *Dæmonol.* 172 The eyes, being modest, subsided in.

Subsidation (sɒbsɪˈdeɪʃən), *a.* depression. [SUB-SIDE.]

Subside (sɒb'saɪd), *v.* Also *-sede, -seyd, -syde.* [ad. L. *subsīdere*, f. *sub* SUB- 9 + *sidere* to settle down, related to *sedēre* to SIT.]

1. *intr.* To sink to the bottom, pre-cipitate. Also *with* down.
1681 WILLIS *Rem. Med. Wks.* Vocab., *Subside*, to sink down, or below. **1729** T. SWIFT *Ld. Lieut. Instr.* (1730) 278 Their Shells were buried among the other Bodies of Maure, which subsided down. **1707** CURIOS. in *Husb. & Gard.* 241 A thin Solution must subside, and leave..the subsiding fluids, and become firm and solid matter. **1751** JOHNSON *Rambl.* No. 119 § 3 Let the clear water be poured off, and let the feces subside, and leave at last an equal height to both. **1799** *Comm. Bd. Agric.* III. 254 If the water will subside,... **1826** HENDERSON *Hist. Anc.* & *Mod. Wines* i. 12 The gravel is the first to fall : then the sand subsides, and finally the mud settles down.

2. To sink to a lower level, *esp.* of liquids or soil sinking to the normal level; (of valleys) to form a depression; (of a swelling or something inflated) to be reduced so as to become flat.
1706 PHILLIPS (ed. Kersey), x. 2, The Streams Subside from their Banks. **1749** T. COOKE *Tales*, etc. 46 Were shaky Mountains rise, and Vales subside. **1732** ARBUTHNOT *Aliments* iii. (1735) 249 When air would Air-bladders subside, the air..would the earth both fully subdued, and become sick, and solid matter. **1843** LYELL *Travels N. Amer.* II. 196, I have seen the whole surface of the ground in Tasco como to be an equal heights of its Subsidences. **1878** HUXLEY *Phsiogr.* 189 Deltas are formed..by the sea; is subsiding, so that the sea-water invades the land.

3. *Of a mass of earth, etc.* : To fall or give way as the result of pressure, disturbance, etc.
1773 *Cook's Voy.* I. xiv. (1842) I. 370 A large tract of country, of which it was part, subsided or sunk under the continuity of nature. **1803** MILLAR *Elem. Chem.* (1809) 150 A force of subsidence, the natural consequence of gravity...has reduced this enormous mass into one wide level, almost imperceptibly declining. **1817** *Full Hall Cen.* 23 July 2/2 Its whole breath..was subsided. **1831** BREWSTER *Nat. Magic* iii. 56 Here the wave of the deep to subside, and sea and the subsided more and more...; the *Full Hall Cen.* 22 July 2/2 its whole breath..was subsided. **1837** CARLYLE *Fr. Rev.* II. ii. viii. Subsided into privacy, into obscurity.

4. *Of strong feeling, excitement, clamour, and the like* : To cease from agitation, fall into a quieter state.
1749 *Ld. Chesterf.* *Lett. to Son* 9 Nov. 1746 My anger would subside. **1759** STERNE *Tr. Shandy* I. ix. Before his passion could subside. **1781** GIBBON *Decl. & F.* xxvi. III. 40 Then did the rage of the discontented subside. **1793** DEVOE *Family's Lett.* 6 June The subsidies subside. **1855** MACAULAY *Hist. Eng.* xvii. IV. 155 The excitement has subsided ; the anxiety is over.

5. *Of persons* : To fall into an inactive or less active or efficient state.
1732 *Young Love of Fame* vi. 196 His swelling and sublimes to nature and the King's favour, ..that subsides into a humbler state. **1823** LAMB *Elia* i. 2 xxiv. Your elder brother..fixing his eye upon some remote object. **1784** COWPER *Task* III. 676 The subsidence of a quiet and inactive solid state. **1855** MACAULAY *Hist. Eng.* xvi. IV. 133 The excitement has subsided.

+ **6. trans.** To cause to sink in. *Obs. rare*⁻¹.
1657 TOMLINSON *Renou's Disp.* 58 The humour raises the abscess, and then subsides it again.

Subsided (sɒb'saɪded), *ppl. a.* [f. *prec.* + -ED 1.] Sunk ; precipitated.
1732 TULL *Horse-hoeing Husb.* xiii. 194 The Earth sinking away from the Roots, leaves the bottom of the Stalk higher than the subsided Ground.

Subsidence (sɒb'saɪdəns, 'sʌbsɪdəns), *sb.* [ad. L. *subsidentia* sediment, f. *subsidere* to SUBSIDE : see -ENCE. Cf. it. *subsidenza* sediment.]

1. A sediment, precipitate. ? *Obs.*
1626 BACON *Sylva* § 24 A Chalky earth, which ..steeped in water, afforded a certain...on the top, and a gross subsidence at the bottom. **1656** JEAN. FRENCH's *Labrynthe* 31 The Earth was an impious, and...from the causes of pure mortar of the Creation. **1657** GRANT in *Tvrel. 8. Aprvl. Sis. V.* 150 The Oil of the whole subsidence, or substance.

2. The settling (of solid or heavy things) to the bottom, formation of sediment, precipitation.
1697 BOYLE *Christ. Virtuoso*, *Subsidence*, a resting or settling in the bottom of a liquor. **1745** DE SAUSSURE *Hist.* xx. 85 In this manner the Shells of Fishes...being absorbed in the subsidence of the Shells of these Fishes. **1790** *Monthly Rev.* XXX. 175 A force of subsidence, the natural consequence of gravity,..has reduced this enormous mass. **1855** MACAULAY *Hist. Eng.* xvi. IV.

c. Sinking into decline or decay.
1856 MERIVALE *Rom. Emp.* xxiii. (1865) IV. 67 It was precisely that subsidence of the old aristocracy of birth began first to be renewed.

d. (*Geol.*) A gradual lowering or settling down of a portion of the earth due to dynamic causes, mining operations, or the like.
1802 PLAYFAIR *Hutton.* 774. 440 Though a local subsidence, or setting of the ground, could hardly account for this change...yet a subsidence that has extended to a great tract...will agree very well with the appearance. **1833** NEWMARCH *Solaria* ii. 132 The rock is..subject to slides or subsidences. **1842** DARWIN *Struct. & Distr. Coral-Reefs.* vi. 149 Subsidences occasioned by earthquakes and volcanic convulsions. **1872** *Standard* 10 Sept. 6/3 Streets and buildings ..are being damaged by subsidences due to disused subterranean ground workings.
transf. **1884** *Morning Post* 27 Nov., They reached the door, but found it fixed by the subsidence of the walls.

6. *attrib.*, applied to vessels in which liquids are put in order to precipitate their suspended solid matter, as *subsidence reservoir, road*.
1837 SIMMONDS *Dict. Trade, Subsidence*, a dyer's settling-vat. **1891** *Pall Mall Gaz.* 9 Sept. 7/1 All the companies supplying river water..have subsidence reservoirs, into which the water is first turned for the purpose of allowing such of the suspended solid matter to subside..as will subside naturally.

Subsidency (sɒb'saɪdənsɪ, 'sʌbsɪdənsɪ). Now *rare*. [f. L. *subsidentia* : see *prec.*]
1655-87 H. MORE *App. Antid.* (1712) 215 Bodies..in a confused state may very likely go together, as we not alone..in the subsidency into the dregish part of the World, the Earth. **1686** PLOT *Staffordsh.* x. 146 Those who judiciously impute the subsidency inundation of the Earth in the interstice should so undergo some underground burrows. **1719** WATERLAND *Vind.* (1739) xl. 80 So to cause a subsidency the cavity there. **1775** *Phil. Trans.* LXIX. 259 A strong and regular current confined in a river is the best of all means...for preventing the formation of banks in the bed by the subsidency of mud. **1811** PENNANT *Petrol.* I. 181 Throughout all the space many features appeared and subsidences of the ground. **1844** S. JUDD *Margaret* ii. ix. In the subsidency and departure of love, the moral system is broken up.

Subsident (sɒb'saɪdənt, 'sʌbsɪdənt), *a.* [ad. L. *subsident-, -entem,* pr. ppl. of *subsidere* : see SUBSIDE *v.*] Precipitating.
1620 VENNER *Via Recta* iii. 59 Whether by subsequent treatment of the precipitated and subsident matter.

Subsidentical, *a. Obs. rare*⁻¹. [SUB- 11 + -AL.] Subcelestial, sublunary.
1656 in *Ann. Dubrensia* (1877) 57 This subside-iall rundle. **1672** *Ibid.*, 88.

Subsi•dial, *a. Obs.* [f. SUBSIDY + -AL.] = SUBSIDY *sb.*
1798 PENNANT *Hindoostan* II. 13 A subsidial ally of the English, who receive from its monarch the annual sum of £700,000.

Subsidi•arily (sɒbsɪˈdɪærɪlɪ), *adv.* [f. next + -LY 2.] In a subsidiary manner or position; subordinately, secondarily. (*occas.* const. *to*.)
1651 STANLEY *Montaigne's Ess.* xviii. At first sight he addresseth himself to this means, which they never embrace but subsidiarily. **1605** DAGON, *Inqueck.* III. iii. (Camden Soc.) 309 There only should speak, subsidiarily one to another. **1811** PALEY *Testc. iv.* 112 This Court was first brought in Subsidiarily, when Causes grew too numerous for Land. **1826** H. J. COLERIDGE *Obligations* 141 He is not bound subsidiarily for the remainder, in the event of insolvency of his debtor. **1899** BENSON *Stalky's Lett. I. Bened.* Ron. (1887) 7 Subsidiarily to the human interest of his work. **1897** MAITLAND *Domesday Bk.* 8 *Beyond* 248 The hundred being not subsidiarily liable.

Subsidiary (sɒb'sɪdɪərɪ), *a.* and *sb.* [ad. L. *subsidiarius*, f. *subsidium* : see SUBSIDY. Cf. F. *subsidiaire*, It. *sussidiario*, Sp., Pg. *subsidiario*.]

A. *adj.* 1. Serving to help, assist, or supplement; furnishing additional or supplementary supplies; auxiliary, tributary, supplementary. (Chiefly of things.)
1543 JOYE *Q. confuteth Winch. Arct.* fol. ij. Justified by theonlye faith in him, and by nothinge els as subsidiarie to that faith, for this mulle thei justification in christe. **1597** SHAKS. *Richard III*, *Subsidiarie* that is given or to aide another. **1615** CROOKE *Body of Man* 24 A blood-like vapor which returneth into the hollow venae, by Anastomosis.. of the parts. **1647** DONNE *Serm.* xliii. (1640) 440 In these our subsidiary prayers, the subsidiary gods, there could be no See. **1774** GOLDSM. *Nat. Hist.* (1776) I. vii. (1833) 63, I, shall not be obliged here to mention, at all these subsidiary methods of hypotheses, be superfluous. **1844** H. STEPHENS *Bk. Farm* III. 1119 The subsidiary supplies which these measures subsidiarie always at hand to be mortgaged in aid of any other subsidiarie fund. **1807** GIFFORD *Q. Rev.* I. 543 [A subsidiary fund] always at hand to be mortgaged in aid of any other subsidiarie fund. **1836** WHEWELL *Hist. Induct. Sc.* (1837) II. 243 Subsidiarie parts of our systems of scientific thought. **1840** DICKENS *Barn. Rudge* ii. on these last facts are considered as subsidiary to the action of the principal document. **1818** BREWSTER *Nat. Mag.* viii. (1833) 214 The inflammation of the ignited gas will be sustained by these four subsidiary flames. **1819** SHELLEY in *two Loci's* (1879) Illustrate the nature of the principal process by subordinate and subsidiary processes. **1847** YEATTS *Techn. Hist. Comm.* Oct. 5/3 Dulce Subsidiary of Cabeson.

B. *sb.* 1. Const. *to*.
1597 HOOKER *Eccl. Pol.* V. ii. 3 The Good. *Lragure Anglia* 98 The Crmmoners of England being Sword and the Commons of England being Lord to subsidiary to their Princes and Laws in all kinds of rights. **1674** EVELYN *Sylva* (ed. 3) To Rdr. ii. 45, A son seems to be a kind of subsidiarie. **1790** WATERLAND *Resp. 2. conf. of** *Cometu.* v. A son soon became impaired, the Use of the Eucharist had grown...

to come in as subsidiary, or supplemental to it. **1626** KECBLE *Serm.* viii. (1848) 2 A system of tradition, subsidiary to the Scriptures, might yet exist in the commonwealth or city of God. **1888** STEVENSON *Black Arrow* IV. i. 360 This was his first object, to which every thing else was subsidiary. **1897** R. WALLASCHEK *Primitive Music* 229 The Cymbal is subsidiary to this... **1808** LANGSTONE *Gibson* Wks.

+ 3. A subsidized state. *Obs.*
1630 *Mumeler* No. 30 i. 975 The immense treasure paid for those subsidiaries, which by their treaties are engaged to cover their and the suicide states of Great Britain.

2. Technical use.
Subsidiary cells (Bot.) : certain epidermal cells which are less thickened or striated lower than the guard-cells which they surround. *Subsidiary axis* (cons of the subsequent branching or inflorescence, etc.); (of inflorescence other than the dichot. *Subsidiary quantity or symbol* (Math.) : one quot. 1836.
1842 *Penny Cycl.* XXIII. 118 *Subsidiary.* A quantity or problem used in the investigation to help on the solution. The term is particularly applied to angles, since the trigonometrical tables give a greater power over their magnitude, which causes their frequent introduction. **1863** FARADAY *Fxt. Econ.* xiii. vi. 1(1856) 480 Our copper and silver ..are merely subsidiary coinage. **1881** GREENER *Gun* 241 A steel spiral spring is obtained in the same way as a true coal, except that to score a subsidiary coat the ball must pass between the subsidiary coil mark and the graph post which is nearest to it. Subsidiary goods are to be measured of feet from each goalpost on the outside.

d. Of a stream : Tributary. Similarly of a river.
1843 PENCILLY *Afr.* 54 xli. 546 We piept one night at the mouth of a subsidiary dell. **1881** CARLYLE *Fr. Rev.* II. i. All manner of subsidiary streams and brooks of bitterness tributary to them. **1846** *McCULLOCH Acc. Brit. Empire* ch. I. In tributary subsidiary streams they fell into the Trent. **1894** JAMES *Daly* S. D. in *Times* 29 Oct. 9/6 The general plateau on the south is divided by a subsidiary valley of much the same character, from which that little River Welle flows to the main stream.

2. With the notion of helping or supplementing weakened or obscured : Subordinate, secondary.
1847 CHAMB. *Laws. Crt.* (1828) 171 The three are only the subsidiary parts of a subsidiary conquest. **1850** MICHELET *ii.* xxiii. When systems of ideas were with men, with obstacle, subsidiary systems of subsidiary will be subservient. *Western Life Lang.* 66. 206 In begin of subsidiary dialectic forms. **1863** M.H. STILLE *R. Nettervly.* 380 Lesser subsidiaries about the outline of the original degrees..At times these latter 'subsidiary', 'auxiliaries', or 'satellites' impositions, as they are called, develop greater energy than their primaries.

3. Consisting of a subsidy or subsidies. **1608** WILLET *Hexapla Exod.* Ded. I The reasonable assemble hath..presented to your Maiestie a subsidiarie benevolence. **1897** *Salzonymy, Rasha's Constantine* 3 The most royall Emperour after their present subsidiarie contributions, those against that had sent in their Subsidiary monie. **1640** CULPEPER in *Rushw. Hist. Coll.* (1692) 11. 34 As soon as the House was settled, a Subsidiary Aid and Supply was propounded.

c. Depending on a subsidy of subsidies : in a subsidiary treaty (Cf. SUBSIDY 3 *b.*).
1755 H. WALPOLE *Lett.* (1846) II. 479/2 That old Subsidiary scheme. **1766** JONES *Eccl.* 96 iii. 51 [Sir that the more cruel of Randolstan]fee the stupid ignis Hambone's subsidiary treaty. **1853** POCOCKE *Observ. as to Antiquities* I. 92 He did so at a subsidiary treaty..that old subsidiary scheme.

b. To furnish (a country, nation, princes) with a subsidy for the purpose of securing their assistance or their neutrality in war.
1797 H. WALPOLE *Mem. Reign Geo. III.* (1845) I. vii. 109 Little Princes are subsidized..with worthy of reciproca-tion. **1849** *Spirit Publ. Jrnls.* I. 1. 374, I have sought relief in hearing the cousent of Administration for subsidizing the continent. **1882** A. HARCOURT *Exam.* G. *Rev.* I. 56 To subsidize one power against another.

2. *trans.* a. To secure the services of by pay-ment or bribery.
1825 W. H. IRELAND *Scribblemonia* 26 note, Deigning to subsidize a vennl pen in order to throw a gloze over the flagrant dereliction. **1809** *Daily News* 8 Nov., If a man no sustain..from subsidizing the Press. **1848** KINGSLEY *Saint's Tragedy* II. iii. not his conscience subsidize. **1887** *Cent. Dict.*, a Subsidized journal.

b. To furnish funds for (a scheme or course of action).
1794 PAINE *Rights of Man* II. iv. 432 Like so many of the northern allies, he might have been hoarding a fund to subsidize insurrection.

c. To support by grants of money : now *esp.* of the government or some public authority contributing to the upkeep of an institution, etc.
1826 CANTU *Papers* 48 vii. 398 For the British Government to pay the Roman Catholic clergy would be to subsidize the Court of Rome against itself. **1891** *Pall Mall G.* The encouragers and subsidizers of the slavers. **1893** *Globe* 30 May 5/1 The question of the value of Enolioceicun fish... .the whole question of the value of Raailoncican fish, in the way of which its subsidisation turns out. **1897** *Daily News* 14 June 8/3 [Subsidizers will not be lost sight of them. **1899** SIDGWICK *Elem. Polit.* II. iv. § 8 note, The State may subsidize an industry.

introduction of a countervailing rush. **1 Jan.** 5/2 The statement as to Mr. Schiff's subsidization of the ..and Galveston scheme is inaccurate. **1908** *Athenæum* 31 Oct. 545/1 In a smaller case as a subsidized publi-cation of the French Government.

+ Subsiduous, *a. Obs. rare*⁻¹. [irreg. f. L. *subsidium* SUBSIDY + -ous. *cf. subside* SUBSIDE 20. F. *subside* SUBSIDE *a.* (Fr.)... .see -UOUS.] Assisting, subsidizing.
1675 BOYLE *New Exper. Flame & Air* 13 The subsiding of the Mercury. **1720** HALE *Prim. Orig. Man* II. viii. 190 [whereof it] were indeed Flood: and insinuations in the elevation and subsiding of the idiolec terrestrii. **1791** MONRO *Amal. Bones* iii. 3/2 A regular alternate Elevation and subsiding, or as apparent in.. .*Mag.* § J. BADCOCK *Philos. Recr.* (1820) 64 Then subsiding; a blowing a small quantity of alum with the water accelerates the subsiding of the starch. *attrib.* (cf. SUBSIDIDE 6.) **1665** *Phil. Mag.* (5) 325, 1/1. Observing a small quantity of alum with the water, gave it the subsiding power. **1897** *Westmr Gaz.* 12 July 2/1 A small subsiding dam were provided so that the fluid passing in the river was alone supplied to the consumers.

Subsiding (sɒb'saɪdɪŋ), *ppl. a.* [f. SUBSIDE *v.* + -ING²] 1. That subsides, in various senses of the verb.
1646 Sir T. BROWNE *Pseud. Ep.* 98 The subsiding powder retains some magnetical vertue. **1644** SALMON *Doit.'s Disp.* 117/3 355/1 Educate the subsiding Powder, by many affusions of fair Water. **1770** R. JAMESON *Treat. Commerce* 8 Having allowed the subsiding froid, and dross... **1783** BLAIR (1818) xvii. 3/ That class of widely-encircling reefs, which indicate a subsiding land. **1842** DARWIN *Struct. & Dist. Coral-Reefs* vi. 147 Whereever the sea is of less extent than the Plateau of the subsiding island.

2. Subsidence (sɒb'saɪdəns), *a.* [f. SUBSIDE + -ANCE.] A help, aid, subsidy.
1640 H. MORE *Def. Philos. Cabbala* (1713) 50/2 It was reasonable that in Gendenite they should contrive some help to their Neighbours. **1678** HALE *Prim. Orig. Man* 170 If left it self without the concurrent *Subsidiance* and *Influence* of the Divine Providence. **1859** SMYTH *Lat. Dic.* *Subsidiance*, that doth give succour or aid.

b. To furnish (a country, nation, princes) with a subsidy for the purpose of securing their assistance or their neutrality in war.

Subsidy (sʌb'sɪdɪ), *sb.* Also 4-7 subsidie, 5 -sidye, 5-6 -sidye, 5-7 -sedy, -sydy, -sedie, -sidie ; *pl.* -sidies. [ad. OF. *subside*, ad. L. *subsidium* aid, help, support, *sub-* SUB- + sed-, stem of *sedēre* to SIT + -ium.]

I. Help, aid, assistance. Also *with a* and *pl.*
1. *gen.* A help or assistance. Also *with a* and *pl.*
1387 TREVISA *Higden* (Rolls) VII. 429 Subsidie [printed subsidye] of help and socour. **1598** FLORIO, *Sussidio*, a subsidie, ...a subside...help or succour. **1667** MILTON *P. L.* xi. 256 So Angel-forms. **1677** HALE *Prim. Orig. Man.* 300. A sum of money paid by one country to an-other for the promotion of war or the preservation of neutrality.

Subsist (sʌb'sɪst), *v.* Also *-cyst, -syst.* [ad. L. *subsistere* to stand still, stand firm, cease, be adequate to, sup-port, f. *sub-* SUB- 5 + *sistere* to cause to stand (f. root of *stāre* to STAND).]

I. 1. *intr.* To have an existence as a reality ; to exist as a substance or entity. (Cf. SUBSISTENCE 1.)
1398 TREVISA *Barth. De P. R.* xix. xxxvii. (Bodl. MS.) The formes and likenesse of elementis ben not in the elementis but in the mynde and thought. **1646** Sir T. BROWNE *Pseud. Ep.* vi. 11 Some things exist, and others only subsist. **1647** H. MORE *Song of Soul* II. ii. xvi. 11. xvi. That which subsisteth of itself. **1678** CUDWORTH *Intell. Syst.* I. iv. § 35 That which doth Subsist by Itself. **1690** LOCKE *Hum. Und.* II. xxxiii. § 6, I make the colour of gold to subsist in a certain manner.

2. To have its being in ; to reside or inhere in.
1600 HOOKER *Eccl. Pol.* v. § 51 in which essential whole exist in a certain manner.

Subsist

III. 10. *trans.* To provide sustenance for; to support or maintain with provisions or funds; to maintain, support, keep; said of provisions, funds, etc., or of the persons dispensing them.

4. To preserve its existence or continue to exist; to remain in existence, *as, to exist.*

5. *b.* of physical objects.

6. Of physical objects: To be or live in a certain place or state. *Obs.*

8. Of a condition or quality: To exist.

Subsistence (sŏbsistĕns). Also, *- (now erron.) substance.* [ad. late L. *subsistentia*, f. *subsistĕnt-*, ppl. stem of *subsistĕre*: see SUBSIST.]

I. 1. Existence as a substance or entity; substantial, real, or independent existence.

2. A thing that has substantial or real existence.

b. The substance of a thing. *Obs.*

4. Continued existence; continuance. Now *rare.*

b. Continuation or quality of inhering or residing in something. *Obs.*

5. *b.* A state of continued existence. *Obs.*

6. *Theol.* Any of the three Persons of the Trinity; = HYPOSTASIS 2. *Obs.*

7. *Theol.* The provision of support for animal life; the furnishing of food or provender. Now *rare.*

8. *Sediment;* = HYPOSTASIS 1 *a. Obs.*

III. 9. The means of supporting existence; means of support or livelihood.

Subsistence money.

1. Money paid in advance to soldiers, workmen, etc., to supply their needs until regular pay-day.

Subsistent (sŏbsistĕnt), *a.* and *sb.* Now *rare* or *Obs.* [ad. L. *subsistĕnt-, -ens*, pr. pple. of *subsistĕre* to SUBSIST. Cf. F. *subsistant.*]

A. *adj.*

1. Existing substantially or really; existing or by itself.

2. Existing at a specified or implied time.

3. Inherent or residing in. *Obs.*

4. Subsisting at a specified or implied time.

5. Having means of subsistence. *nonce-use.*

Subsisting, *ppl. a.* [-ING 2.]

1. Existing substantially, substantial.

Subsoil (sŏbsoil), *sb.* [f. SUB- 3 + SOIL *sb.*]

1. The stratum of soil lying immediately under the surface soil.

2. *transf.* and *fig.*

3. *trans.* and *fig.*

Subsoil (sŏbsoil), *v.* [f. prec.] *trans.* To plough so as to cut into the subsoil, use a subsoil plough upon.

Subsoil plough, *sb.* A kind of plough used in subsoiling.

Subsoiling

Subsolar, *a.*

Subspecies. [mod.L.; f. SUB- + *species* SPECIES.] A subdivision of a species, a more or less permanent variety of a species.

Subspecific, *a. Nat. Hist.*

Subspinous, *a.*

Substage (sŏbsteidʒ), *sb.*

Substance (sŏbstăns). Also *4-6 substaunce,* (5 sobstance, 6 suppstance), [a. OF. (mod.F.) *substance,* = Pr., Sp., It. *sostanza, sustanza,* ad. L. *substantia.*]

I. That which underlies phenomena; the permanent substratum of things; that which receives modifications and is not itself a mode; that in which accidents or attributes inhere.

4. That which underlies or supports; a basis, foundation; a ground, cause. *Obs.*

5. The matter, subject-matter, subject (of a study), discourse, written work, etc.

6. That of which a physical thing consists; the material of which a body is formed and in virtue of which it possesses certain properties.

10. A solid or real thing, as opposed to an appearance of shadow. Also, reality.

12. The vital part.

13. That which gives a thing its character; that constitutes the essence of a thing.

Supplement, p. 3873; Corrigenda, p. 4092; Spurious words, p. 4093; Books quoted, p. 4094.

† Substa·nder. *Obs.* [Rendering of L. *substans* (see SUBSTANCE sb.).] That which subsists. So **Substa·nding** ppl. a., subsisting.

Substantial (sǝbstǽnʃǎl), a. (adv.) and sb. Forms: 4–8 **substancial**, (4 -cial, 5 -cyal, 5–6 -aunce, -ciall; 4 -cyall, 6 -5 -tiall). So **-cial** substantial, ... **substantial** [ad. late L. *substantiālis* (f. *substantia* SUBSTANCE), whence also F. *substantiel* (from 13th c.), Pr. *substancial*, Sp. *substancial*, It. *sostanziale, sustanziale*. A., *adj.*

I. **1.** That is, or exists as, a substance; having a real existence, self-subsisting.

Substantia·lity. Error for SUBSTANTIALITY.

Substa·ntially (sǝbstǽnʃǎli), *adv.* [f. as prec. + -LY².]

1. In substance; in or as a substantial nature or existence; as a substantial thing or being.

Substa·ntialness (sǝbstǽnʃǎlnɛs). [f. prec. + -NESS.] The condition or quality of being substantial; solidity, firmness, soundness.

Substa·ntiate (sǝbstǽnʃieit), v. [f. mod.L. *substantiāt-*, ppl. stem of *substantiāre*, f. L. *substantia* SUBSTANCE.]

1. *trans.* To give substance or substantial existence to and realize.

Substantia·tion (sǝbstanʃiei·ʃǝn). [f. SUBSTANTIATE: see -ATION.]

1. Embodiment. *rare.*

Substa·ntious, a. Chiefly L. *Obs.* Also substantial; with substance.

† Substa·ntious, a. *Obs. rare.*

Substa·ntive (sǝbstǎntiv), a. and sb. [ad. late L. *substantīvus*, f. *substantia* SUBSTANCE: see -IVE. Cf. OF. *substantif*, F. *substantif*, Sp., It., *sustantivo*, Pr. *substantiu*.]

A. *adj.*

I. **1.** Of persons, nations, etc.: That stands of or by itself; independent, self-existent, self-subsisting.

Substantively, adv.

Substantiveness.

Substantivity.

Substantivize, v.

Substantivo, a.

Substantize, v.

Sub stantive v.

Substituable.

Substitute (sŭ·bstĭtiūt), sb.

Substitute (sŭ·bstĭtiūt), v.

Substituent, a. and sb.

Substituted, ppl. a.

Substituteless, a.

Substituter.

Substituting, ppl. a.

Substitution (sŏbstĭtiū·ʃən).

Substitutional, a.

Substitutionalism.

Substitutionally, adv.

Substitutionary, a.

Substitutive, a.

Substract, v.

Substraction.

Substractor.

Substragulous.

Substrate, sb.

Substrate, v.

Substratose.

Substratous.

Substraction.

Substrative, a.

Substractor.

Substructor.

Substructory.

Substructure.

Substylar, a.

Substyle, sb.

Subsultive, a.

Subsultory, a.

Subsultus.

Subsumable, a.

Subsume, v.

2. *intr.* (*Logic.*) To state a minor premiss: freq. with the words of the proposition following.

1589 R. Bruce *Serm.* 1 *Cor.* xi. 28 (1843) 110 There is not a law that ever was..devised, but of all the laws that ever was made, it is leisome to us to have a care of our health. Now, subsume; but the health of thy saull stands in the health of thy conscience..; therefore, be all laws, thou aught to attend to thy conscience. 1624 F. White *Repl. Fisher* 323 Now then I subsume, no religious worship..is due to Saints...Inuocation of Saints is religious worship...*Ergo*, Inuocation is not due to Saints. 1644 Digby *Nat. Soul* ii. § 6. 371 If any body..take this proposition rigorously and peremptorily, that what wise men affirme is true; and should there vpon subsume with evidence, that wise men say such a particular thing [etc.]. 1670 *Comenius' Janua Ling.* 156 The Major proposeth the basis or ground of the reasoning thus;..the Minor subsumeth,..the conclusion follows. 1733 W. Crawford *Infidelity* (1744) 84 God..may unmake again what he has already made...But then I add, much more may he..annihilate an Offender...But I further subsume, if God can eternally annihilate even an innocent Being, he may do more eternally to the Guilty.

b. *spec.* in *Sc. Law* (see Subsumption 1 b).

1745 [H. Home] *Ess. upon Several Subj.* iii. (1747) Suppl. Note, An Act of the 7th Parliament,..bearing That the Lands of Doun, &c. were feued by Queen Mary to Sir James Stewart..subsuming, that the said Sir James being descended of the Royal Blood [etc.]. 1747 in *Nairne Peerage Evid.* (1874) 148 Subsumeing that for the said James Fothringhame pursuer his greater security..they bound and obliged them..to warernd free relieve harmless and skaithless keep the said James Fothringhame.

3. *trans.* (*Logic.*) To state as a minor proposition or concept *under* another.

1697 J. Sergeant *Solid Philos.* 427 It will not follow, from the Equal Application of it, by the respective Minors, to this or that Particular, Subsum'd under them, that the Assent to the two Conclusions,..will be Equal. 1828 De Quincey *Rhet.* Wks. 1859 XI. 42 To judge, that is to subsume one proposition under another. 1838 [F. Haywood] tr. *Kant's Crit. Pure Reason* 271 In every syllogism I first think a rule (major), by means of the understanding. Secondly, I subsume a cognition under the condition of the rule (minor), by means of the faculty of judgment. 1864 Bowen *Logic* x. 319 Isolated cognitions..are not entitled to be called Sciences, until they are arranged in some Class, or subsumed under some comprehensive Law. 1876 W. Fleming *Vocab. Philos.* (ed. 3) s.v. *Subsumption*, In the judgment, 'all horses are animals', the conception 'horses' is subsumed under that of 'animals'. 1887 Adam *Platonis Apol. Socr.* Introd. (1889) p. xvi, No sooner has it [*sc.* induction] been attained than we ought (as in the practical syllogism) to subsume under it the special case.

4. To bring (one idea, principle, term, etc.) *under* another, (a case, instance) under a rule; to take up *into*, or include *in*, something larger or higher.

(*a*) 1825 Coleridge *Aids Refl.* (1848) I. 177 Under some one or other of these forms, the resemblances and differences must be subsumed in order to be conceivable. 1846 De Quincey *Christ. Org. Pol. Movem.* Wks. 1859 XII. 279 In subsuming the given case proposed under the Scriptural principle. 1877 E. Caird *Philos. Kant* i. 138 To subsume the complexities of knowledge under its simplest principles. 1884 tr. *Lotze's Logic* 247 We must know beforehand that μ and ν can be subsumed under the species *m* and *n* of which the equation has been proved to be true. 1885 Pater *Marius* xv, A principle under which one might subsume men's most strenuous efforts after righteousness. 1887 W. T. Martin *Evol. Hypoth.* 42 A law may be subsumed under a higher law. 1899 Mackail *Morris* II. 197 Every form of decorative art could be subsumed under the single head of architecture. 1910 *Edin. Rev.* Apr. 461 Perhaps the wider term Aegean will come into general use; under it Minoan and Mycenean may be subsumed to describe successive stages in European developement.

(*b*) 1812 Coleridge *Friend* (1818) III. 255 Man in his idea, and as subsumed in the divine humanity, in whom alone God loved the world. 1871 Mivart *Gen. Spec.* 23 'Natural Selection' itself must be capable of being subsumed into some higher law. 1890 A. Moore *Ess. Mental Evol.* 58 The child subsumes in its intellectual life the processes of the lower animals, but it rises above them. 1906 Saintsbury *Hist. Engl. Prosody* I. 288 The literature of the fifteenth century, with that first quarter of the sixteenth which is by pretty common consent to be subsumed in it for Southern England.

(*c*) 1869 *J. Austin's Jurispr.* (ed. 3) I. 506, I must correctly subsume the specific case as falling within the law. 1871 Huxley *Wks.* (1893) II. 182 These forces..operate according to definite laws..in accordance with some general law which subsumes them all. 1882 Stevenson *Men & Bks.* 107 His cosmology must subsume all cosmologies. 1906 *Hibbert Jrnl.* Apr. 553 [Idealism] has shown how Spirit subsumes the world as its own.

b. *absol.*

1896 *Fortn. Rev.* July 146 Why continue to subsume when the only result will be to produce a formula which..may utterly fail?

†5. *gen.* To assume; to infer. *Obs.*

1643 Hammond *Serm.* vii. Wks. 1684 IV. 511 A Piece of the Philosopher there hath..had a great stroke in debauching the Divine, that the Understanding doth necessarily and irresistibly move the Will..from whence the Divine subsumes, that when Faith is once entered..these Works must ..follow. 1678 *Hist. Indulgence* To Chr. Rdrs. 5 They must give me leave to assert and subsume..That..I beleeve the Right that Christ hath bought, to be sole and supreme. 1694 S. Johnson *Notes Past. Lett. Bp. Burnet* i. 13 His Axiom or Postulatum is in the first Sentence, which I will allow..at present...But what he subsumes in the next Sentence is begging the Question.

†6. To resume, summarize. *Obs.*

a 1677 Barrow *Serm.* Wks. 1687 I. 123 The Apostle, after the proposing divers enforcements of this duty, subsumeth in the 8. verse, I will therefore, that men pray every-where [etc.]. 1678 R. Barclay *Apol. Quakers* ii. § 4. 26 The Proposition..comprehendeth divers unquestionable Arguments, which I shall in brief subsume. *Ibid.* iii. § 2. 72 The Sum whereof I shall subsume in one Argument.

Hence **Subsu·ming** *vbl. sb.*

1652 Urquhart *Jewel* 277 The pregnancy of the State, whose intuitive spirits can at the first hearing discerne the strength of manifold conclusions (without the labour of subsuming) in the very bowels and chaos of their principles. 1897 tr. *Fichte's Sci. Ethics* 116 In the first mode of proceeding, our judgment is what Kant calls *subsuming*, and in the latter work, what he calls *reflecting*.

Subsumption (sŏbsʊ·mᵖʃən). [ad. mod.L. *subsumptio*, *-ōnem*, n. of action f. *subsūmĕre* to Subsume.]

1. *Logic.* A proposition subsumed under another; a minor premiss; *gen.*, an assumption.

1651 Biggs *New Disp.* ⁋ 182 Galen himself proveth the subsumption. 1662 J. Chandler *Van Helmont's Oriat.* 57 They shall sweat more than enough, before they will prove the subsumption or second Proposition. 1672 G. Mackenzie *Pleadings* Pref. A iij b, It is the nature of a syllogisme to haue the subsumption in the second proposition. 1704 *Lond. Gaz.* No. 4037/5 This is not offered as an Elogie..on Her Majesty: She is far above what I can say, but it is an Antecedent to the following Subsumption. 1838 Sir W. Hamilton *Logic* xvi. (1866) I. 295 The proposition in which is expressed the relation of the middle term to the minor, is the Subsumption or Minor Premise. 1876 W. Fleming *Vocab. Philos.* (ed. 3) s. v., Thus, if one were to say, 'No man is wise in all things', and another to respond, 'But you are a man', this proposition is a subsumption under the former.

b. *Sc. Law.* In full *subsumption of the libel*: a narrative of the alleged crime, specifying the manner, time, and place of the crime, the person injured, etc. *Obs.* exc. *Hist.*

1639 *Declar. conc. Tumults Scot.* 256 The subsumptions of the particular faults committed by the Bishop of the Diocese. 1678 G. Mackenzie *Crim. Laws Scot.* ii. xxi. § i. (1699) 232 The Subsumption of the Libel, is the matter of Fact, which should condescend upon the Actors Names, and Designations. 1720 Wodrow *Corr.* (1843) II. 491 Probably you will have heard the contents of it, and whether the subsumption relates to the stipend, or the five hundred pounds, or both. 1727 *Ibid.* III. 304 The whole of Mr. Dundas' arguments run upon this supposition, that heresy was to be the subsumption of the libel. 1838 in W. Bell *Dict. Law Scot.* 951.

2. Chiefly *Logic* and *Philos.* The bringing of a concept, cognition, etc. *under* a general term or a larger or higher concept, etc.; the instancing of a case *under* a rule, or the like.

1652 J. Pawson *Vind. Free Grace* 7 The term (as many παν ὁ quotquot) is too comprehensive and large to be restrained to so few as the Apostles; especially considering 'tis put as a sutable subsumption under that general term (all flesh) immediately foregoing. 1816 Coleridge *Lay Serm.* (Bohn) 339 The understanding..is the science of phenomena, and their subsumption under distinct kinds and sorts (genus and species). 1823 De Quincey *Lett. to Yng. Man* Wks. 1860 XIV. 33 The minor is..distinguished from the major by an act of the judgment, namely, a subsumption of a special case under a rule. *Ibid.* 34 A casuistry, that is, a subsumption of the cases most frequently recurring in ordinary life. 1838 [F. Haywood] tr. *Kant's Crit. Pure Reason* 290 The subsumption of the condition of another possible judgment under the condition of the rule, is the minor. 1855 Sandars in *Oxford Ess.* 244 The administrative power, or the subsumption of different spheres and particular cases under the universal. 1864 Bowen *Logic* vii. 188 The Judgment that a given 'Subject is contained under that intermediate Term or part', is the Subsumption of this Subject under the condition of that Rule. 1892 *Athenæum* 25 June 829/2 Is not the subsumption of fetishism under animism, as by Dr. Tylor, a self-contradictory confusing of two essentially different conceptions?

Subsumptive (sŏbsʊ·mᵖtiv), *a. rare.* [ad. mod.L. *subsumptīvus*, f. *subsumpt-*, pa. ppl. stem of *subsūmĕre* to Subsume: see -ive.] Involving subsumption.

a 1834 Coleridge (Webster). 1884 tr. *Lotze's Logic* 97 Circle in the subsumptive syllogism.

Subsuperparticular, etc.: see Sub- 10.

Subsurface (sɒ·bsɒːfės). [Sub- I.]

I. 1. That which lies immediately below the surface, e.g. the subsoil.

1778 [W. Marshall] *Min. Agric.* 12 Dec. 1776, Rough harrows, which tore up the plits, and shook still more of the seed down to the sub-surface. 1884 H. Spencer in *Contemp. Rev.* July 31 The will of the majority is valid respecting the modes in which..parts of the surface or subsurface, may be utilized.

2. *Math.* In five-dimensional geometry, a three-dimensional continuum.

1873 Cayley *Math. Papers* (1896) IX. 79 *note*, In explanation of the nomenclature [*sc.* five-dimensional space], observe that in 5 dimensional geometry we have: space, surface, subsurface, supercurve, curve, and point-system, according as we have between the six coordinates 0, 1, 2, 3, 4, or 5 equations.

II. as *adj.* [see Sub- 1 e.] Existing, lying, or operating under the surface (as of the earth or water).

1875 Croll *Clim. & Time* App. 553 Subsurface-water, or the stratum immediately below it. 1885 L. Oliphant *Sympneumata* 101 The subsurface world. 1888 *Athenæum* 18 Aug. 215/1 Sympneumatic and subsurface consciousness. 1894 *Q. Rev.* Apr. 371 They are abundant in all surface and subsurface waters. 1894 *Geol. Mag.* Oct. 466 The downward creep of the surface and sub-surface soil. 1900 *Pop. Sci. Monthly* Mar. 533 Where sewers and subsurface pipes have not yet been laid. 1902 *Westm. Gaz.* 31 Dec. 6/3 The construction of sub-surface torpedo boats.

Su·btack. *Sc. Law.* [f. Sub- 9 (*b*) + Tack *sb.*²] A tack or lease granted by a superior to an inferior tenant.

1681 Stair *Inst. Law Scot.* i. xix. § 22. 384 A Sub-tack is that which is granted by the principal Tacks-man to his Subtennent. 1765–8 Erskine *Inst. Law Scot.* ii. vi. § 34 A subtack requires the same solemnities as a principal tack. 1792 Spalding *Hist. Scot.* I. 338 He had already set in subtack these customs of Aberdeen and Banff to the town of Aberdeen. 1838 in W. Bell *Dict. Law Scot.* 951.

Hence **Su·btacksman**, one who holds a subordinate tack at the hands of a tacksman.

1681 Stair *Inst. Law Scot.* i. xix. § 22. 385 The Heretor is not oblieged to know the Sub-tack, nor to call the Subtacksmen, in the Reduction of the principal Tack. 1733 P. Lindsay *Interest Scot.* 213 The Sub-tacksman of this Duty can easily put the Law in Execution against them. 1765–8 Erskine *Inst. Law Scot.* ii. vi. § 34 The subtacksman is tenant, not to the proprietor, but to the principal tacksman.

Su·btangent. *Math.* [ad. mod.L. *subtangens*, *-entem*: see Sub- 1 and Tangent.] That part of the axis of a curve which is contained between the tangent and the ordinate.

1715 *Phil. Trans.* XXIX. 196 He determines the Proportion of the Subtangent to the Ordinate. 1798 Hutton *Course Math.* II. 306 The Method of Tangents, is a method of determining the quantity of the tangent and subtangent of any algebraic curve; the equation of the curve being given. 1816 tr. *Lacroix' Diff. & Int. Calc.* 75 The line PS will constantly tend to become equal to the subtangent PT. 1827–8 Hamilton in *Encycl. Metrop.* (1845) I. 740/1 The subtangent is bisected by the curve, whether the coordinates are rectangular or oblique.

Su·btarget. [Sub- 5 b.] (See quots.)

1904 *Westm. Gaz.* 6 July 10/2 The 'Sub-Target Gun Machine' is the latest invention whose object is to afford indoor practice in rifle-shooting...The technical description of the invention defines it as 'a firearm holder with no aiming-point-of-rest, having the capacity to move with the firearm carried by it, and electrically controlled recording mechanism including a miniature target offset from the trajectory of the firearm, to record the direction of trajectory. 1906 *Ibid.* 9 May 5/2 A miniature rifle range provided with the sub-target rifle.

Subtartarean, -ian, *a.* [tr. Gr. ὑποταρτάριος: see Sub- 1 a and Tartarean *a.*¹, Tartarian *a.*²] Being or living under Tartarus.

1675 Hobbes *Iliad* xiv. (1686) 211 Then Juno, as she was required sware By all the Subtartarian Gods. 1718 Pope *Iliad* xiv. 314 The queen..from the infernal bowers Invokes the sable subtartarean powers. 1794 T. Taylor *Pausanias' Descr. Greece* III. 280 Some [of the mundane gods] are.. subtartarean. 1820 *Blackw. Mag.* VII. 358 Invoking from the realms below The subtartarean gods, the Titan train.

So **Subtartarus'd** *a.*

1856 S. R. Maitland *False Worship* 36 It was the place of the Titans; of those whom Hesiod calls 'Subtartarus'd Titans', τιτῆνες θ' ὑποταρτάριοι.

†Subte·ctacle. *Obs. rare.* [f. L. *sub* under + *tectum* roof, probably after *tabernacle*.] Covering, protection.

1609 J. Davies *Holy Roode* (1878) 20/1 This is true Faiths intire Subtectacle; Propitiatorie Sacrifice for Sinne: This is God crucifi'd. 1612 — *Muse's Sacr.* (1878) 10/1 Th' abuse of Men, and Shames Subtectacle.

Subtegulaneous: see Sub- 1 a.

Subtelitie, obs. form of Subtility.

Su·btenancy. [f. next.] The status, right, or holding of a subtenant.

a 1861 Palgrave *Norm. & Eng.* (1864) III. 405 The others who received their rewards by Vavassories or Subtenancies. 1882 *Encycl. Brit.* XIV. 276/1 The determination of a lease by forfeiture has the same effect as its determination in any other way, in destroying subtenancies or other rights created under it.

Subtenant (sɒ·bte·nănt). Chiefly *Sc.* Also 5 -ten(n)and, 6 -tenent, sibtennend, 6–7 -tennent, 7 -tennant. [Sub- 9 (*b*). In med.L. *subtenens*.] One who holds of a tenant; an undertenant.

1445 in *14th Rep. Hist. MSS. Comm.* App. III. 12 Twenty schillingis..to be pait to me be the Saide Androu Kere or his facturis or subtenandis. 1474 in *Acc. Fam. of Innes* (Spalding Cl.) 81 To be haldin and had all and hale the saidis landis..to the foresaid James his airis assigneis and subtennandis for al the termis of thretein yeris. 1541 *Rec. Elgin* (New Spalding Cl. 1903) I. 66 Tha that ar sibtennendis to the burgh for the landis of Duuellegrene. 1586 in *Exch. Rolls Scot.* XXI. 418 Sett in assedatioun for the space of fyve yeiris.. to Uthrid Makdowell of Garthland, his airis, assignais, and subtenentis. 1681 Stair *Inst. Law Scot.* i. xix. § 23. 385 Where the Sub-tennent was warned, tacite Ralocation alledged by the Sub-tennent, was not sustained without producing a standing Tack to the principal Tacks-man. 1703 in M. A. Mills *Stat. Laws I. of Man* (1821) 175 The said Tennants and Inhabittants dwelling in and possessing those Cottages and Intacks shall henceforward become Subtennants to the said Farmers, Tennants, and other Persons. 1846 McCulloch *Acc. Brit. Empire* (1854) II. 215 Subtenants or assignees to the leases specified in the article immediately preceding..can also vote. 1861 Brougham *Brit. Const.* x. 136 There were smaller owners or sub-tenants, holding of the eleven thanes, as these held of the Crown.

b. *fig.*

1804 Bewick *Brit. Birds* II. Introd. p. vi, They [*sc.* land birds] are the subtenants of the cultivated world.

Subtend (sŏbte·nd), *v.* [ad. L. *subtendĕre*, f. *sub-* Sub- 2 + *tendĕre* to stretch, Tend. Cf. Sp., Pg. *subtender*.]

1. *trans.* (*Geom.*) To stretch or extend under, or be opposite to: said *esp.* of a line or side of a figure opposite an angle; also, of a chord or angle opposite an arc.

1570 Billingsley *Euclid* i. iv. 14 That angle is said to subtend a side of a triangle, which is placed directly opposite, and against that side. 1571 Digges *Pantom.* i. xviii. F j, This done conioyne their endes together and the angle subtended of the longest staffe is a right. 1646 Sir T. Browne *Pseud. Ep.* i. vii. 25 In rectangle triangles the square which is made of the side that subtendeth the right angle, is equall to the squares which are made of the sides containing the right angle. 1681 Colvil *Whigs Suppl.* (1710) 13 The truth is, they [*sc.* a man's legs] in every thing Resemble do a Bow and String. The one strait to the other bending, Is like a Chord an Arch subtending. *c* 1791 *Encycl. Brit.* (1797) VII. 666/2 An angle at the circumference is measured by half the arc it subtends. 1798 Hutton *Course Math.* I. 292 In any Triangle, the square of the Side subtending an Acute Angle, is Less than the Squares of the Base and the other Side, by Twice the Rectangle of the Base and the Distance of the Perpendicular from the Acute Angle. 1862 Todhunter *Euclid* 19 The greater angle of every triangle is subtended by the greater side or has the greater side opposite to it. 1885 Leudesdorf *Cremona's Proj. Geom.* 227 The angle subtended at any point on the curve by a fixed diameter will be a right angle. 1885 Watson & Burbury *Math. Th. Electr.* I. 137, 2β is the angle of the cone subtended by the disc at *M'*.

b. in *Astron.* and *Optics.*

1722 Wollaston *Relig. Nat.* iii. 54 He must be a brute.. who does not know, that the same line (*v. g.* the diameter of the Sun) at different distances subtends different angles at the eye. *c* 1790 Imison *Sch. Arts* I. 196 The best eye can hardly distinguish a particle of matter that subtends at the eye an angle less than half a minute. 1821 Craig *Lect. Drawing*, etc. vi. 362 The same angle which the picture subtends with the eye. 1833 M. Arnott *Physics* (ed. 5) II. 241 The fly then would subtend a larger visual angle than he, that is to say, would be forming on the retina a larger image than the man. 1835 Poe *Adv. Hans Pfaall* Wks. 1864 I. 36 Whose apparent diameter subtended at the balloon an angle of about sixty-five seconds. 1907 Hodges *Elem. Photogr.* (ed. 6) 24 The visual angle subtended on the plate.

c. *transf.* and *gen.*

1859 Murchison *Siluria* (ed. 3) iii. 53 The Llandeilo formation is subtended on the north, south, and west by younger Silurian deposits. 1860 Motley *Netherl.* (1868) I. 140 The river..subtends the arc into which the place [*sc.* Antwerp] arranges itself. 1867 Murchison *Siluria* (ed. 4) xx. 493 The chalk-cliffs which subtend the Wealden area. 1868 Kinglake *Crimea* III. vii. 117 Standing upon a semicircular tract of ground, subtended by the great bay or roadstead. 1873 Symonds *Grk. Poets* ix. 282 This large arc was subtended by a long straight line—the σκηνή, or background of the stage. 1880 *Nature* XXI. 212/2 Tracts such as the great deserts or prairies might subtend a sufficient angle to preserve their natural hue.

d. *fig.*

1866 Felton *Greece, Anc. & Mod.* I. 33 It takes but a few moments to tell in outline this traveller's story; but how many ages does it subtend. 1869 Spencer *Princ. Psychol.* (1872) I. ii. iv. 217 The angle it subtends in consciousness when we are reminded of it a year after, is very small. 1898 P. Manson *Trop. Dis.* Introd. p. xiv, When this third animal happens to be a tropical species, the disease it subtends, so to speak, is in natural conditions, necessarily tropical also.

†2. *pass.* Of an angle, a side of a figure: To be extended *under*, to be opposite *to*. *Obs.*

1570 Billingsley *Euclid* i. iv. 14 Euery angle of a triangle is contayned of two sydes of the triangle, and is subtended to the third side. 1660 Barrow *Euclid* i. iv, The remaining angles B, C, shall be equal to the remaining angles E, F, each to each, under which the equal sides are subtended.

3. *trans.* (*Bot.*) To extend under, so as to embrace or enfold.

1871 W. A. Leighton *Lichen-flora* 94 Apothecia..subtended by the very short deformed divaricate extremities of the laciniæ. 1872 Oliver *Elem. Bot.* ii. 237 A 3-lobed bract, subtending a single nut.

Hence **Subte·nded** *ppl. a.*, (*a*) stretched underneath; (*b*) of an angle opposite a side.

1679 Evelyn *Sylva* (ed. 3) 56 To clip, and let the leaves fall upon a subtended sheet. 1824 Smyth in Duppa *Trav. Italy*, etc. (1828) 185 *note*, The subtended angles carefully corrected. 1884 tr. *Lotze's Logic* 248 The formula we are seeking must mention the subtended angle.

†Subte·ndent, *a.* and *sb. Obs.* Also 7 -ant. [ad. L. *subtendens*, *-entem*, pr. pple. of *subtendĕre* to Subtend.]

A. *adj.* That subtends.

1571 Digges *Pantom.* i. vi. C iij b, In equiangle triangles, al their sides are proportional aswel such as conteyne the equall angles, as also their subtendente sides. *Ibid.* xx. F ij b, The subtendent staffe or side of the triangle. 1688 Holme *Armoury* iii. iii. 139/2 A *Cord*, *Chord*, or *Subtendant Line*; is a streight Line which joyns to an Arch or Bow by its ends.

B. *sb.* A subtending line or side.

1570 Dee *Math. Pref.* 30 Square then, halfe the Subtendent of that watry Superficies. 1673 in Rigaud *Corr. Sci. Men* (1841) II. 569 *A*, *E*, are the subtendants of two arches which together make up ½ the circumference.

Subte·nding, *ppl. a.* [-ing ².] That subtends.

1571 Digges *Pantom.* i. xx. F ij b, Make a fyne notche, or marke vpon that subtending staffe. 1660 R. Coke *Justice Vind.* 20 What proportion..the subtending side of an isosceles right-angle triangle hath to one of the comprehending sides. 1859 R. F. Burton *Central Afr.* in *Jrnl. Geogr. Soc.* XXIX. 237 The Tanganyika cannot be drained eastward by rents in a subtending mountain ridge. 1882 Vines tr. *Sachs' Bot.* 599 If..the subtending leaf (bract) is developed later than the axillary branch (inflorescence). 1900 B. D. Jackson *Gloss. Bot. Terms* 250/2 *Subtending Leaf*, that leaf whose axil gives rise to a bud or peduncle.

‖Subte·nia. *Arch. rare.* [f. Sub- 1 + *tenia*, Tænia.] The narrow listel under the lower tænia of the Doric entablature; the guttæ band.

1563 Shute *Archit.* c iij b, Geue Tenia..the seuenth parte, and geue Subtenia, and Gutta pendante..the sixte part of a modulus to their height.

Subtense (sŏbte·ns). *Geom.* [ad. mod.L. *subtensa* (sc. *linea* line), fem. pa. pple. of *subtendĕre* to Subtend. Cf. Sp., Pg. *subtensa*.] A subtending line; *esp.* the chord of an arc.

1614 Handson tr. *Pitiscus' Trigonom.* 31 A subtense is a right line, inscribed in a Circle, dividing the whole Circle into 2. Segments. 1656 tr. *Hobbes' Elem. Philos.* (1839) 193 The subtenses of equal angles in different circles..are to one another as the arches which they subtend. 1678 Cudworth *Intell. Syst.* i. iv. 653 Nor doth every one, who hath an Idea of a Rectangular Triangle, presently understand, that the Square of the Subtense, is Equal to the Squares of both the Sides. 1713 Derham *Phys. Theol.* i. iv. (1727) 30 *note*, The whole Diameter of the Orb, viz. 20000, made the Subtense but of one Minute to one of the fix'd Stars. 1733 Tull *Horse-hoeing Husb.* xxi. 305 Plow-Wrights always take this Subtense at the Fore-End of a Beam, whether it be a long Beam or a short one. 1803 *Phil. Trans.* XCIII. 396 The total extent of the arch is about 15°, having half of its subtense on each side zero.

b. *attrib.*: **subtense method**, a method of tacheometry in which the angle at the instrument is variable and the distance base is either constant or specially measured.

1897 *Geogr. Jrnl.* (R. G. S.) X. 469 We..then made a traverse of the valley on the bar-subtense method. 1902 *Encycl. Brit.* XXXIII. 143/2 Subtense method. 1905 C. F. Close *Topogr. & Geogr. Surv.* 51 The general principle of subtense work and tacheometry is the measurement of the angle subtended at the observer by a short measured length at a distance.

†Subte·ntion. *Obs.* [f. L. *subtent-*, pa. ppl. stem of *subtendĕre* to Subtend: see -tion.] = Subtense.

1610 Horton *Baculum Geodæt.* vii. ii. 297 Any right lines being applied to a circle is called a subtention, which may be Sines, Tangents, or Secants.

Subtenure (sɒ·bte·niŭɹ). [f. Sub- 9 (*b*) + Tenure.] The subfeudation of land; the holding of land, or land held, by a lease from a superior tenant.

1839 *Penny Cycl.* XIV. 105/1 Owing to the extensive system of subfeudation, or subtenure. 1862 H. Beveridge *Hist. India* III. vii. iv. 125 The sale of a zemindary abolished all sub-tenures. 1911 E. Beveridge *N. Uist* 24 It became necessary for King Alexander III. to deal with the subtenure of the Hebrides.

Subter- (sɒ·btəɹ) *prefix*, repr. L. *subter-* = the adv. and prep. *subter* below, underneath, used in composition = (1) below, beneath; (*a*) advb. as in *subterfluĕre* to flow beneath (see Subterfluous), (*b*) prep. as in *subtercutāneus* lying under the skin (*cutis*); (2) secretly, as in *subterfugĕre* to flee secretly (see Subterfuge); and, in some rare Eng. compounds, = (3) lower or less than (cf. Sub- 14). The following are instances either of little-used adoptions of L. compounds or mere nonce-words (in some cases suggested by antithesis to compounds of *super-*).

Subtera·nnuating *vbl. sb.*, the placing of an event later than its actual date. **Subter-bru·tish** *a.*, lower than (that of) the brutes. **Su·bter-cele·stial** *a.*, below the heavens. **Subter-co·nscious** *a.*, = Subconscious. **†Subtercu·bant** [L. *cubāre* to lie down] (meaning unknown). **Su·btercuta·neous** L. *-eus*], = Subcutaneous. **Subterdu·ction** [cf. L. *subterdūcĕre*], a carrying away secretly. **Su·bterero·gation**, the performance of less than is required. **Su·bterethe·rial** *a.*, subaerial. **†Subterflu·ent**, **†Subte·rfluous** *adjs.*, flowing underneath. **Subterhu·man** *a.*, below what is human. **Subterja·cent** *a.* [L. *subterjacēre*], underlying, subjacent. **Su·bterlapsa·rian** [properly **subtersublapsarian*] *a.*, pertaining to a view of redemption which conceived a sufficiency of grace for all, but a positive decree to save restricted to some. **Su·btermarine**, one who works under the sea. **Subterse·nsual**, **-se·nsuous** *adjs.*, = Subsensual, -sensuous. **Su·btersupe·rlative**, a degree lower than that expressed by an ordinary superlative of inferiority. **Su·btersu·rface** *a.*, lying below the surface, subsurface.

1656 Heylin *Extraneus Vapulans* 102 The superannuating in the business of the Councel of Dort, (a *subterannuating call'd in the true sense of the thing). 1831 Carlyle *Sart. Res.* i. viii, O *subter-brutish! vile! most vile! 1665 Sir T. Herbert *Trav.* (1677) 253 By the Fiat of the Almighty the *subter-celestial waters were separated from the supercelestial. 1856 Bagehot *Biogr. Studies* (1880) 15 There is a kind of eruption of ideas from a *subter-conscious world. 1597 Harvey *Trimming of Nashe* Wks. (Grosart) III. 69 The..grand Commander of all the superrants & *subtercubants of Englands great Metropolis. 1748 tr. *Vegetius Renatus' Distemper of Horses* 9 There are seven Species of this Maul: The moist, the dry, the *subtercutaneous, the articular [etc.]. 1656 Blount *Glossogr.*, **Subterduction*, a private stealing or leading away. 1617 Collins *Def. Bp. Ely* ii. ix. 346 It is certaine that Supererogation there can be none, though praetererogation we should graunt you, howbeit *subtererogation were the fitter word. 1686 Goad *Celest. Bodies* iii. iii. 456 The *Subter-Ætherial Globe. 1755 Johnson, **Subterfluent*, running under. 1656 Blount *Glossogr.*, **Subterfluous*, which runs or flows under. 1833 Carlyle *Misc. Ess.*, *Cagliostro* (1888) 88 He were no man but some other kind of creature, superhuman or *subterhuman. 1839 J. Sterling *Ess.*, etc. (1848) I. 264 The universe presents itself to them as a conflux of forces, subterhuman, human, and superhuman. 1597 A. M. tr. *Guillemeau's Fr. Chirurg.* 25/2 As then not parte of the corrosive fall on any of the *subteriacent partes. 1762 tr. *Busching's Syst. Geog.* III. 29 A delightful prospect over the subterjacent plain. 1893 Fairbairn *Christ Mod. Theol.* i. viii. 173 The *Subterlapsarian School, which had hypothetical universalism as its note. 1891 Meredith *One of our Conq.* xxvi, A diver's wreck, where an armoured livid *subtermarine, a monstrous puff-ball of man, wandered seriously light in heaviness. 1885 — *Diana* III. xii. 219 To pursue the thing would be to enter the *subtersensual perfumed caverns of a Romance of Fashionable Life. 1878 P. W. Wyatt *Hardrada* 43 Sailing on one vast *subtersensuous greed Their smuggling life-craft ply. 1655 Fuller *Ch. Hist.* vi. 271 The Apostles words of himself, who am lesse than the least of all saints...As I may say, a *subter-subterlative [*sic*] in his humility. 1659 — *App. Inj. Innoc.* iii. 18 Because he was Ελαχισ[τ]ότερος, (and if there be a more subtersuperlative) the least of the least of his brethren. 1831 *Fraser's Mag.* IV. 322 He never fails to sink to the *subtersurface level of Joseph Hume.

Subteraquean (sɒbtəɹēⁱ·kwĭăn), *a. rare.* [Formed as next + -an.] = next.

1865 *Morning Star* 21 July, The people ascended from the subteraquean chamber.

Subteraqueous (sɒbtəɹēⁱ·kwĭəs), *a. rare.* Also *erron.* subterr-. [f. L. **subteraqueus*: see Subter- (1) and Aqueous.] Living, situated, performed, etc. under water.

1682 H. More *Annot. Glanvill's Lux O.* 139 By those inevitable Laws of the subteraqueous Sandalphon. 1733 Tull *Horse-hoeing Husb.* iii. 26 The Effect the vicissitudes of Winter and Summer have upon Subterraqueous Vegetables. 1823 Byron *Juan* xiv. lxxxi, An oyster may be cross'd in love,—and why? Because he mopeth idly in his shell, And heaves a lonely subterraqueous sigh.

Subterfuge (sɒ·btəɹfiūdʒ), *sb.* [ad. L. *subterfugium*, f. *subterfugĕre*, f. *subter-* Subter- (2) + *fugĕre* to flee. Cf. F. *subterfuge*, It. *sutterfugio*, Sp., Pg. *subterfugio*.]

1. An artifice or device to which a person resorts in order to escape the force of an argument, to avoid condemnation or censure, or to justify his conduct; an evasion or shift. Chiefly of discourse, argument, debate, but also of action in general.

1573 J. Tyrie *Refut.* in *Cath. Tractates* (S.T.S.) 29, I dout na thing, gif thay ansver directlie without all subterfuge,.. that it salbe easie to everie man to espy quha defendis the richt caus. 1611 Cotgr., *Subterfuge*, a subterfuge; a shift; a priuie slip, craftie euasion, cunning escape. 1637–50 Row *Hist. Kirk* (Wodrow Soc.) 268 That no such subterfuge be left unto impious and wicked men. 1651 Chas. II. *Let.* 24 May in *10th Rep. Hist. MSS. Comm.* App. i. 42 That without delays or subterfuges the goods be restored. 1659 H. More *Immort. Soul* iii. xiv. 475 The Fifth and last is rather a Subterfuge then an Objection. 1665 Glanvill *Scepsis Sci.* vii. 39 All their shifts, subtilties, newly invented Words and Modes, sly subterfuges and studyed evasions. 1741 Watts *Impr. Mind* i. x. (1801) 87 Do not affect little shifts and subterfuges to avoid the force of an argument. 1781 Cowper *Friendship* 189 No subterfuge or pleading Shall win my confidence again. 1784 — *Task* ii. 670 By forgery, by subterfuge of law. 1829 Lytton *Disowned* vi By what subterfuge, or cavil, does the present claimant of these estates hope to dislodge their rightful possessor. 1843 R. J. Graves *Syst. Clin. Med.* x. 106, I speak here without any subterfuge. 1849 Macaulay *Hist. Eng.* v. I. 564 It was answered that the earl was asleep. The privy councillor thought that this was a subterfuge, and insisted on entering. 1895 Rider Haggard *Heart of World* xvi, I will answer you, and, scorning subterfuge or falsehood, set out the whole matter in the hearing of the people.

b. contextually: A means of escape (*from* censure, etc.); an excuse.

1755 Smollett *Quix.* (1803) 122 You have no subterfuge, nor the least room to say you was deceived. 1761 Hume *Hist. Eng.* II. xxxix. 377 The queen of Scots had no other subterfuge from these pressing remonstrances. 1828 Scott *F. M. Perth* xxxiv, You seek but a subterfuge, that you may say when you are defeated..that it was for want of the number of your band fully counted out.

†2. A place to which a person escapes; a retreat, refuge. *Obs.*

1616 Bullokar *Engl. Expos.*, *Subterfuge*,..A place to hide or saue one in. 1660 in *Sel. Harl. Misc.* (1793) 379 My lord of Derby had taken this place for a subterfuge, after the defeat given him by Colonel Lilburn. 1665 Manley *Grotius' Low C. Wars* 363 There were in the Castle Subterfuges and Scluces, to prevent the inraging [orig. *iram*] of the Enemy. 1737 Whiston *Josephus* ii. vi. vii. 941 They depended on these under ground subterfuges.

fig. 1780 Welton *Suffer. Son of God* I. iv. 68 We have now a Subterfuge to flee to; under which, we are sure to be shelter'd from the Justice and Wrath of God. 1844 Thirlwall *Greece* lxvi. VIII. 426 This proposal drove the senate out of its last subterfuge.

†3. That which conceals; a 'cloak'. *Obs.*

1635 Brathwait *Arcadian Princ.* 55 Connivence gives impunity to impiety, and greatnesse becomes a Subterfuge to guiltinesse. *a* 1718 Prior *Knowledge* 710 They..sculk behind the Subterfuge of Art. 1733 Cheyne *Engl. Malady* ii. viii. § 3. 194 The Spleen or Vapours..is a common Subterfuge for meer Ignorance of the Nature of Distempers.

†Su·bterfuge, *v. Obs. rare.* [ad. L. *subterfugĕre* (see prec.).]

1. *intr.* To employ subterfuges.

1637 in *Prynne's Disc. Prel. Tyrr.* (1641) ii. 95 Upon paine of suspention of the parties offending, or subterfuging.

2. *trans.* To escape, evade, get out of.

1641 J. Shute *Sarah & Hagar* (1649) 59 Jonah had a ploc to subterfuge his employment to Nineveh. *a* 1643 — *Judgem. & Mercy* (1645) 80 Whatsoever plea he hath before thought of to subterfuge the judgement.

So **†Su·bterfuging** *ppl. a.*, employing subterfuges; evasive.

1802 in *Ann. Rev.* (1803) I. 391/2 No little, narrow policy, will do; no partial meanness, no monopoly, no jobbing business, nor subterfuging tricks of avarice!

†Su·bterfugy. *Obs. rare.* [ad. L. *subterfugium*: see Subterfuge *sb.*] A subterfuge.

1637 Gillespie *Engl. Pop. Cerem.* Ord. C 3 The lurking places of their elaborate subterfugies. 1655 Fuller *Ch. Hist.* xi. xvii. 230 Many more are their subterfugies.

Subterna·tural, *a.* [Subter- (3).] Below what is natural, less than natural.

1870 Lowell *Among my Bks.* Ser. i. (1873) 87 We must be content to call hypochondria subternatural, because the tone of the instrument is lowered. 1880 Gladstone in W. O'Brien *Recoll.* (1905) 262 The expression of subternatural glee which sits upon the visage of the hon. member for Cavan. 1890 *Q. Rev.* Apr. 296 Shakspere's preternatural or subternatural creations.

Subterpose (sɒbtəɹpōᵘ·z), *v. rare.* [f. Subter- (1) + *-pose*, as in *superpose*, *impose*.] *trans.* To place underneath.

1894 Baring-Gould *Deserts S. France* I. 149 Their remains may be discovered at a lower level, though not subterposed.

So **Su·bterposi·tion**, a placing below, position underneath.

1833 Lyell *Princ. Geol.* III. 388 Subterposition in the plutonic, like superposition in the sedimentary rocks, being.. characteristic of a newer age. 1851 Gladstone *Let. to Manning* 26 Jan., It will bring about a great shifting of parts, much super- and much subter-position.

Sub-terra, *a. rare*⁻¹. [L. *sub* under + *terra* ground.] Subterranean.

1841 Catlin *N. Amer. Ind.* x. (1844) I. 76, I have subjoined a sketch of one of these sub-terra communities.

Subterrane (sɒ·btĕrēⁱn), *a.* and *sb.* Now *rare.* Also 9 -ain. [ad. L. *subterrāneus*, f. *sub-* Sub- 1 a + *terra* earth. Cf. OF. *soub-*, *subterrain* (F. *souterrain*), It. *sotterrano*, *-aneo*.]

A. *adj.* = Subterranean *a.* 1.

1614 Raleigh *Hist. World* ii. 650 By this secret subterrane vault, Zedechias making his stealth, recouered..the plaines or deserts of Iericho. 1633 T. Adams *Exp. 2 Peter* ii. 4. 513 Hell is a subterrane treasure of hidden fire. 1712 *Phil. Trans.* XXVII. 481 As to the Age in which those Trees were interred, it is hard to determine. Many think they have lain in that Subterrane State ever since Noah's Flood. 1824 Byron *Def. Transf.* i. i. 79 The waters stir, Not as with air, but by some subterrane And rocking power of the internal world. 1830 W. Phillips *Mt. Sinai* i. 550 From all its vasty antres subterrane. 1831 Keightley *Mythol. Greece & Italy* 68 Hades, the brother of Zeus and Poseidon, was lord of the subterrane region, the abode of the dead. 1842 J. F. Watson *Ann. Philad. & Penn.* (1877) I. 412 A subterrane tunnel. 1861 D. Greenwell *Poems* 95 Some echo subterrain.

B. *sb.* = Subterranean *sb.* 3.

1774 J. Bryant *Mythol.* I. 116 It was a cave in the rock, abounding with variety of subterranes, cut out into various apartments. 1816 G. S. Faber *Orig. Pagan Idol.* III. 260 Like the subterrain of mount Olivet, it resembled the mouth of an oven or a well. 1830 W. Phillips *Mt. Sinai* ii. 34 Mystic subterrane From surface down to centre is commoved. 1843 tr. *Custine's Empire of Czar* II. 18 The submarine dungeons of Kronstadt,..and..many other subterranes.

†Subterra·neal, *a.* (*sb.*) *Obs.* [f. L. *subterrāneus* (see prec.) + -al.]

A. *adj.*

1. Underground; = Subterranean *a.* 1.

1592 R. D. *Hypnerotomachia* 30 Feareful vaultes, and subterraneal buttresses. 1639 G. Plattes (*title*) A Discovery of Subterraneall Treasure: viz. of all manner of Mines and Minerals. 1651 J. F[reake] *Agrippa's Occ. Philos.* 404 Subterraneall and dark Demons. 1671 Bohun *Disc. Wind* Contents, The 2ᵈ Locall Origine of Winds in Generall from the Earth or Seas, as from Submarine or Subterraneall Eruptions. 1673 Boyle *Ess. Effluviums* iii. 51 The more agile Corpuscles of Subterraneal Salts. 1681 Grew *Musæum* i. § ii. i. 14 He catcheth Ant's by scratching open their subterraneal Hives. 1690 C. Nesse *Hist. & Myst. O. & N. Test.* I. 7 Mountains not cast up by the flood, nor by the subterraneal spirits. 1741 *Phil. Trans.* LV. 239 The subterraneal damps and mineral spirit of fountains seem.. exactly to resemble each other.

2. Belonging to the lower regions; infernal; = Subterranean *a.* 2.

1651 T. Stanley *Plat. Disc. Love* 222 The World her self being one, can have but one soul; which as it animates the subterraneal parts, is called Pluto; the sublunary Neptune; the celestial, Jupiter. 1803 Shaw tr. *Bacon's Fables Anc.* xi, [Pluto] hurrying her to his chariot, carried her with him to the subterraneal regions.

B. *sb. pl.* Underground strata.

1652 French *Yorksh. Spaw* iii. 32 How variously subterraneals communicate their vertues to this Element [*viz.* water].

Subterranean (sɒbtĕrēⁱ·nĭăn), *a.* and *sb.* [f. L. *subterrāneus* (see Subterrane) + -an.]

A. *adj.*

1. a. Of inanimate objects: Existing, lying, or situated below the surface of the earth; formed or constructed underground, either by nature or by the hand of man; underground.

1610 Holland *Camden's Brit.* 747 Their further inquiery, whether there are not Subterranean trees growing under earth. *a* 1625 Chaloner *Six Serm.* (1629) 24 Even the Labyrinthes of Dedalus haue left their subterranean habitations. 1634 Sir T. Herbert *Trav.* 95 [The Caspian Sea] has no..entercourse with any Sea, except (as is credible) it be subterranean, into the Euxine. 1712 Blackmore *Creation* i. 34 Tell, by..what subterranean Ways, Back to the Fountain's Head the Sea conveys The refluent Rivers. 1718 Lady M. W. Montagu *Lett.* II. xlix. 64, I was..led into one of the subterranean apartments, which they call 'The Stables of the Elephants'. 1835 Lyell *Princ. Geol.* (ed. 4) IV. 6 The relative date of rocks formed in the subterranean regions during the Newer Pliocene ages. *Ibid.* Index 450 Subterranean lava causes elevation of land. 1849 Macaulay *Hist. Eng.* iii. I. 316 In 1685 the tin of Cornwall..was still one of the most valuable subterranean productions of the island. 1856 Macaulay *Johnson* in *Encycl. Brit.* (ed. 8) XII. 795 His taste in cookery, formed in subterranean ordinaries and *Alamode* beefshops, was far from delicate. 1856 Stanley *Sinai & Pal.* xiv. (1858) 439 The subterranean vault, over which..the whole structure was erected. 1860 Prescott *Electr. Telegr.* 169 The idea of building subterranean lines in this country! 1863 Dana *Man. Geol.* 647 Subterranean streams, which have their rise in hills and mountains, and are fed, like the surface-rivers, by the rains and snows. 1877 Northcote *Rom. Catac.* i. v. 71 The ceilings of their subterranean chapels. 1876 *Encycl. Brit.* VIII. 685/1 Along the French coast several subterranean affluents of the Mediterranean have been discovered.

b. Of animate beings: Living or working under ground.

1621 Burton *Anat. Mel.* i. ii. i. ii, Of these sublunary Diuels, *Psellus* makes six kindes, fiery, aeriall, terrestriall, watery, and subterranean Diuels. 1642 Howell *Twelve Treat.* (1661) 50 Ther were subterranean invisible troups (at Ragland Castle) mustered under-ground in Wales. 1753 Richardson *Grandison* (1754) VI. ix, Subterranean colliers, tinners, [&c.] 1835 Kirby *Creat. Anim.* II. 420 Baron Humboldt has given an account of a wonderful eruption of subterranean fishes.

c. Of physical phenomena, forces or movements, actions, etc.: Operating or performed under ground.

1603 Holland *Plutarch's Mor.* 1190 The casting up aloft into the aire of stones & cinders by subterranean windes under the earth. 1667 Milton *P. L.* i. 231 When the force Of subterranean wind transports a Hill Torn from Pelorus. 1813 Bakewell *Introd. Geol.* Pref. 6 All rocks or strata have been either formed or consolidated by central subterranean fire. 1825 Scott *Betrothed* xxiv, Immured as he seemed to be, to perish by a strange and subterranean death. 1829 — *Anne of G.* ii, A noise like subterranean thunder. 1855 J. Phillips *Man. Geol.* 585 The same localities..were during later periods influenced by more gradual and continual subterranean expansion. 1877 Huxley *Physiogr.* 186 This region is peculiarly subject to subterranean disturbances.

d. *Bot.* Of parts of a plant: Growing under ground.

1839 Lindley *Introd. Bot.* (ed. 3) 491 *Subterranean*.., growing under the earth. 1849 Balfour *Man. Bot.* § 70 Stems have been divided into *aerial*, or stems which appear wholly or partially above ground; and *subterranean*, or those which are entirely under ground. 1884 Bower & Scott *De Bary's Phaner.* 349 The subterranean shoots of the rhizome.

e. Of trees or a forest: Buried in the earth.

1813 Bakewell *Introd. Geol.* 11 On the coast of Lincolnshire and part of Yorkshire there is a subterranean forest about seventeen feet under the present high-water mark.

2. Existing under the earth; belonging to the lower regions or underworld; infernal.

1619 Googes tr. *Bacon's Wisd. Anc.* 156 He [Pluto] caught vp Proserpina..and caried her away with him in his Coach to the Subterranean dominions. *a* 1700 Evelyn *Diary* 20 Feb. 1645, The celestial, terrestrial, and subterranean deities. *a* 1806 Horsley *Serm.* xx. (1816) II. 176 The consolation which the preaching of our Lord in the subterranean regions afforded to these prisoners of hope. 1837 Carlyle *Fr. Rev.* i. i. i, And ye, as subterranean Apparitions are wont, vanish utterly,—leaving only a smell of sulphur!

3. *fig.* Existing or working out of sight, in the dark, or secretly.

1651 Jane Εἰκων Ακλαστος 230 They never pretended priviledge of Parliament further then the subterranean junto. 1855 Motley *Dutch Rep.* vi. i. (1866) 782 His subtle, unscrupulous, and subterranean combinations of policy. 1879 Farrar *St. Paul* I. 570 They saw through the subterranean injustice and virulent animosity of the Jews in bringing false charges against innocent men. 1882 Lecky *Eng. in 18th Cent.* III. 68 The subterranean and more ignoble works of faction. 1892 Hall Caine *Scapegoat* xxvi, The entire town..was honeycombed with subterranean revolt.

B. *sb.*

1. One who lives under ground; a cave-dweller.

1625 B. Jonson *Staple of News* i. vi. 44 Her Graces Grandfather, Was Duke, and Cousin to the King of Ophyr, The Subterranean. 1691 R. Kirk *Secret Commw.* i. (1815) 5 These Subterraneans eat but little in their Dwellings. 1833 L. Ritchie *Wand. Loire* 61 An anecdote..will convey a better idea..of the habitations and manners of the subterraneans.

2. An inhabitant of the lower regions.

1836 I. Taylor *Phys. Theory* xvi. 219 That very ancient, and may we not say biblical classification of all intelligent orders, under the three heads of celestials, terrestrials, and subterraneans.

3. An underground cave, chamber, or dwelling.

1797 in C. K. Paul *W. Godwin* (1876) I. 259 We proceeded to about the middle of the subterranean. *c* 1800 R. Cumberland *John de Lancaster* (1809) III. 251, I have..a subterranean of strong beer to assist the antient Britons a-dancing on their heads. 1836 Wiseman *12 Lect. Sci. & Rev. Relig.* II. 146 The hypogeæ, or subterraneans of Eilithyia. 1855 Newman *Callista* (1890) 333 The passage..was only one of several natural subterraneans..opening into each other. 1906 R. Whiteing *Ring in the New* 66 Prue found an ample subterranean, neatly furnished.

b. *fig. pl.* Depths.

1912 *Engl. Rev.* Dec. 27 Down into subterraneans within myself that were positively frightening.

Subterraneanly (sɒbtĕrēⁱ·nĭănli), *adv.* [-ly ².] Under the ground.

1888 Rolleston & Jackson *Anim. Life* 534 Eyes are absent in some Crustaceans which live subterraneanly. 1892 Agnes M. Clerke *Fam. Stud. Homer* x. 259 They are commonly disguised under some form of ore, subterraneanly bestowed.

†Subterrane·ity. *Obs. rare.* [f. next + -ity.] The condition of being subterraneous; *concr.*, a place or thing found under ground.

1686 *Sir T. Browne's Pseud. Ep.* ii. i. 42, I fear we commonly consider subterraneities [*earlier edd.* subterranities], not in Contemplations sufficiently respective unto the Creation. 1721 Bailey, *Subterraneity*, a being subterraneous. 1807 tr. *Three Germans* I. 69 The flight of steps by which they had been conducted to the subterraneity.

Subterraneous (sɒbtĕrēⁱ·nĭəs), *a.* Now *rare.* [f. L. *subterrāneus* (see Subterrane) + -ous.]

1. a. = Subterranean *a.* 1 a.

1607 J. King *Serm.* 5 Nov. 29 They saie to the ground couer vs, and to a subterraneous vault, keep vs close. 1646 Sir T. Browne *Pseud. Ep.* ii. i. 55 Yet are they not to be closed up in the generall name of concretions, or lightly passed over as onely Elementary, and Subterraneous mixtions. 1662 Stillingfl. *Orig. Sacræ* iii. iv. § 6 Those subterraneous waters which pass up and down through the bowels of the earth. 1667 *Decay Chr. Piety* xii. ⁋ 1 There are many subterraneous springs which feed this ocean. 1712 E. Cooke *Voy. S. Sea* 84 The River..having run subterraneous for two Leagues, rises again. 1725 Pope *Lett.* (1737) VI. 69 In my garden..I have happily finished the subterraneous way and grotto. 1775 Johnson *West. Isl.* 164 Being subterraneous, they must be always damp. 1776 Gibbon *Decl. & F.* ii. I. 45 The subterraneous prisons were abolished. 1813 Southey *Nelson* II. 28 Lady Hamilton.. explored..a subterraneous passage, leading from the palace to the sea side. 1842 Loudon *Suburban Hort.* 227 The sources of cold..are, rain at a lower temperature than the soil,..and where draining has been neglected, subterraneous water. 1875 Jowett *Plato* (ed. 2) V. 332 Let them bring together the streams in subterraneous channels. 1900 *Q. Rev.* July 93 The area of those subterraneous riches is limited.

b. = Subterranean *a.* 1 b.

1727 Swift *Wonder Wond.* Wks. 1755 II. ii. 52 Certain subterraneous nymphs. 1832 G. Downes *Lett. Cont. Countries* I. 193 The *Proteus anguineus*—a creature, which is in a manner both subaqueous and subterraneous. 1832 J. Rennie *Butterfl. & M.* 51 The Subterraneous Rustic (*Agrotis annexa*). 1860 Smiles *Self Help* ii. 29 Occupying an underground cellar, over which he put up the sign, 'Come to the subterraneous barber'.

c. = Subterranean *a.* 1 c.

1658 Sir T. Browne *Hydriot.* 34 The Stoicks who thought the souls of wise men had their habitation about the Moon, might make slight account of subterraneous deposition. 1664 Power *Exp. Philos.* i. 63 Subterraneous Damps do sometimes..grow to that over-height of fermentation, that they fire of themselves. *a* 1682 Sir T. Browne *Tracts* (1683) 154 There can be no assured decision without an ocular exploration and subterraneous enquiry. 1703 *Phil. Trans.* XXIII. 1327 Venomous Steems and Damps..are frequent in Countries that abound with Minerals or Subterraneous Fires. *a* 1774 Tucker *Lt. Nat.* (1834) II. 121 The subterraneous thumps of the miner's spade and pickaxe. 1803–5 Wordsw. *Matron of Jedborough & her Husb.* 27 He breathes a subterraneous damp. 1832 Brewster *Nat. Magic* ix. 240 Camels are..rendered furious when they hear these subterraneous sounds. 1855 *Orr's Circ. Sci.*, *Inorg. Nat.* 49 This matter, in a melted state, has been from time to time agitated, disturbed, and forced out by subterraneous forces.

d. = Subterranean *a.* 1 d.

1777 S. Robson *Brit. Flora* 136 *Trifolium subterraneum*, ..Subterraneous Trefoil. 1829 T. Castle *Introd. Bot.* 45 Subterraneous—when they are in the ground, as with the snow-drop and most plants. 1833 Hooker in Smith's *Engl. Flora* V. i. 117 Perianth subterraneous oblong fleshy.

e. = Subterranean *a.* 1 e.

1704 J. Harris *Lex. Techn.* s.v., Those Trees, which being left there at the Universal Deluge, are so plentifully found buried in the Earth, in many Countries, are called Subterraneous Trees, and by some Fossile-wood. 1712 *Phil. Trans.* XXVII. 478 The Subterraneous Trees, uncovered by an Inundation of the River of Thames in Dagenham and Havering Marshes. 1728 Chambers *Cycl.* s.v., Mr. Boyle gives us an Instance..of a huge Subterraneous Oak dug out of a Salt Mine in Transylvania. 1830 Herschel *Study Nat. Phil.* 346 The subterraneous 'Flora' of a geological formation. 1887 Cassell s.v., Subterraneous forest.

f. (See quot.)

1781 *Ann. Reg.* iii. 248/2 The application of the principles of ordinary geometry to the working of mines is what the author of this work calls subterraneous geometry.

2. = Subterranean *a.* 2.

1633 Prynne *Histrio-m.* i. 260 She obtained the subterraneous places of Hell in stead of an inheritance. 1678 Cudworth *Intell. Syst.* i. i. § 19. 19 [Pluto's] Subterraneous Cave. *Ibid.* iv. § 17. 308 Calling him in the Starry Heaven and Æther, Jupiter; in the Air, Juno; in the Winds, Æolus; in the Sea, Neptune; in the Earth and Subterraneous Parts Pluto.

3. = Subterranean *a.* 3.

1660 R. Burney Κέρδιστον Δῶρον 130 All other leagues and combinations are subterraneous, when they either trust to or fear the Arm of flesh. 1682 *2nd Plea Nonconf.* 44 It was as cunning a Subterraneous Conveyance for Popery, as could be thought of. 1735 H. Walpole *Let.* 9 Sept. in *10th Rep. Hist. MSS. Comm.* App. i. 259 These dark & subterraneous negociations wᵗʰ yᵉ promise of secrecy in all events. 1759 — *Mem. Geo. II* (1847) III. vii. 176 He might have discovered some of Legge's subterraneous intrigues. 1856 De Quincey *Confess.* Pref. Notice, So obstinately has this malady pursued its noiseless, and what I may call subterraneous, siege.

Subterra·neously, *adv.* [-ly ².]

1. Below the surface of the ground.

1859 R. F. Burton *Central Afr.* in *Jrnl. Geogr. Soc.* XXIX. 218 An edible white fungus growing subterraneously. 1890 *Hardwicke's Science Gossip* XXVI. 73 At no great depth beneath London and the south-eastern counties there lay the continuation subterraneously of the chain of hills represented by the Mendips in the West of England, and the Ardennes of Belgium.

2. Secretly; in the dark.

1791–1823 D'Israeli *Cur. Lit.*, *Buckhm.'s Pol. Coquetry* III. 349 He winded the duke circuitously,—he worked at him subterraneously. 1833 T. Hook *Parson's Dau.* ii. xi, From the elder Miss Lovell to her brother this news was thus as it were subterraneously conveyed. 1856 De Quincey in H. A. Page *Thomas De Quincey* (1877) II. 123 What more, then, was it, my dear girls, that you were subterraneously seeking? 1912 A. Harrison in *Engl. Rev.* Mar. 676 It is a force growing subterraneously.

Subterra·neousness. *rare.* [-ness.] The quality of being subterranean.

1727 Bailey (vol. II), *Subterraneousness*, the being under the Earth, or inclosed within the Surface, Bowels, or hollow Parts of the Earth. 1851 G. S. Faber *Many Mansions* 345 We find the same character of Centrical Subterraneousness given to the Locality of Hades in two Cognate passages of the Apocalypse.

Subterra·nity. *Obs.* or *rare.* Irreg. var. of Subterraneity.

1646 Sir T. Browne *Pseud. Ep.* ii. i. 55, I feare we commonly consider subterranities not in contemplations sufficiently respective unto the creation. 1656 Blount *Glossogr.*, *Subterranity*, the being under ground. 1877–8 Henley in *Ballades & Rondeaus* (Canterb. Poets) 83 We search the stars for Fame, Or sink her subterranities; The legend's still the same:—'O Vanity of Vanities!'

†Su·bterrany, *a.* (*sb.*) *Obs. rare.* [ad. L. *subterrāneus* (see Subterrane): cf. *momentany*.] = Subterranean.

1626 Bacon *Sylva* § 326 The Making of Gold did require a very temperate Heat, as being in Nature a Subterrany worke, where little Heat commeth. *Ibid.* 354 We see that in Subterranies there are, as the Fathers of their Tribes, Brimstone and Mercury: In Vegetables, and Liuing Creatures there is Water and Oyle. 1651 R. Child in *Hartlib's Legacy* (1655) 73 It is necessary for him to know all subterrany things. 1651 J. F[reake] *Agrippa's Occ. Philos.* 393 Innumerable unclean spirits..; under these they place a kind of spirits, subterrany or obscure, which the Platonists call Angels that failed. 1656 Blount *Glossogr.*

Subterrene (sɒbtĕrī·n), *a.* and *sb.* Also 7-en. [ad. L. *subterrēnus*: see Sub- 1 a and Terrene.]

A. *adj.*

1. Underground; = Subterranean 1.

1610 Healey *St. Aug. Citie God* x. ix. 372 Sixe kindes of Dæmones. First the fiery,..5. the subterrene, that liue in caues. 1615 G. Sandys *Trav.* 302 The earth is full of subterrene fires. *a* 1711 Ken *Hymnarium* Poet. Wks. II. 127 Shew me the Gulph, that's fix'd between The upper Hades, and the sub-terrene. 1829 I. Taylor *Enthus.* ix. 228 Those dungeons of dimness,..those labyrinths of subterrene communication. 1862 *Macm. Mag.* May 64 The inconvenience of the subterrene trains. 1878 Proctor *Pleas. Ways Sci.* ix. (1879) 181 The activity thus exhibited..had its origin in the same subterrene or submarine region as the Peruvian earthquake.

2. Infernal; = Subterranean 2.

1836 I. Taylor *Phys. Theory* xvi. 219 *note*, The three great orders of the intelligent economy—the heavenly, the earthly, and the subterrene. 1858 Caswall *Poems* 80 Dread Angels subterrene Mighty in works of ill.

B. *sb.* An underground dwelling, etc.; (with *the*) the underworld.

1854 S. Dobell *Balder* xviii. 75 Have we shut thee forth, poor child, And wist not of thy journey, nor the end And exit of that gloomy subterrene Which thou didst enter? 1856 *Tasso & Leonora* 95 Being as transparent as Montesino's glass Castle, while he fancied himself as impenetrable as the said Montesino's Subterrene. 1867 J. B. Rose tr. *Virg. Æneid* Notes 404 The urns and sarcophagi in these subterrenes bear purely native mythological subjects. *c* 1873 J. Addis *Eliz. Echoes* (1879) 94 Th' uncertain hum Of hosts upsweeping from the subterrene.

†Subterre·nean, *a. Obs. rare*⁻¹. [Formed as prec. + -an.] Subterranean.

1670 Pettus *Fodinæ Reg.* Introd., Many do write of Subterrenean Trees, Serpents, Fishes, &c.

Subterrestrial (sɒbtĕre·striăl), *a.* and *sb.* Now *rare.* [See Sub- 1 a and Terrestrial.]

A. *adj.*

1. = Subterranean 1. Now *rare.*

1613 M. Ridley *Magn. Bodies* Pref. 2 For searchers of minerals, mettals, sea-coles, and other subterestrial bodies. 1658 Rowland tr. *Moufet's Theat. Ins.* 891 Bees subterrestrial have another form and nature. 1686 Plot *Staffordsh.* 87 Hot Springs or subterrestrial Exhalations. 1730 Fielding *Tom Thumb* Pref., Wks. 1882 VIII. 351 Those two extremities of style Mr. Dryden illustrates by the familiar image of two inns, which I shall term the aërial and the subterrestrial. 1885 W. K. Parker *Mammal. Desc.* vi. 148 The mole did not become subterrestial just lately.

†2. = Subterranean 2. *Obs.*

1615 W. Hull *Mirr. Maj.* 68 The Popes pretended Supremacie ouer coelestiall, terrestriall, and subterrestriall creatures. 1643 R. O. *Man's Mort.* v. 27 Angels that are highest in dignitie, and so coelesteiall;..Divels and Death the lowest, and so subterrestriall. *a* 1653 Gouge *Comm. Heb.* ii. 8 Every creature, invisible or visible,..celestiall or supercelestiall, terrestriall or subterrestriall. 1702 T. Brown *Lett. fr. Dead to Living* Wks. 1760 II. 209 The most reputable way of entring into this subterrestrial country [*viz.* Hell] is to come in at the fore-door.

B. *sb.* A creature living under ground.

1800 Coleridge *Piccolom.* i. xi. 91 Mole-eyed, thou mayest but burrow in the earth, Blind as that subterrestrial.

Subtile (sɒ·til, sɒ·btil), *a.* (*sb.*) Forms: 4–6 subtyl, -yll, 4–7 -ill, (4 soubtil, -tiel, 5 subtille, 5–6 -tyle, 6 -tylle, *Sc.* -tel(l, sobtyll, suptel), 4– subtil, subtile. [a. F. *subtil* (from 14th c.), latinized refashioning of OF. *s(o)util* Subtle *a.*]

1. Chiefly of fluids: Not dense, thin, rarefied; penetrating, etc. by reason of tenuity; = Subtle *a.* 1.

1390 Gower *Conf.* III. 92 This soubtil water myhtely.. The strengthe of therthe perceth ofte. 1398 Trevisa *Barth. De P. R.* iii. xvii. (1495) 63 Subtyl humour temprith and purith that that is in the lymmes of the syȝte. *Ibid.* v. xix. 124 The ayre and brethe drawen in by the mouth is amended and puryd, and made subtyll therin. *a* 1425 tr. *Arderne's Treat. Fistula* etc. 59 If it be for humour, þat is..for it is scharp, or subtile, or watrye. 1509 Fisher *Funeral Serm. C'tess Richmond* Wks. (1876) 304 It [*sc.* the risen body] shall be subtyle that it shall perce thorowe the stone walles. *c* 1530 *Judic. Urines* ii. xii. 41 b, It maketh the vryne subtyle and thynne. 1533 Elyot *Cast. Helthe* 33 The rayne water..is most subtyl & penetratiue. 1590 Spenser *F. Q.* iii. vii. 39 An Egle, that with plumy wings doth sheare The subtile ayre. 1616 Surfl. & Markh. *Country Farm* 630 The..red-like wines which are of a thin and subtile substance. *c* 1645 Howell *Lett.* (1655) IV. i. 120 As if they had som subtile invisible Atomes wherby they [*sc.* thoughts] operat. 1661 Lovell *Hist. Anim. & Min.* 150 The fat, is hot, subtile and better than the rest. 1742 *Lond. & Country Brewer* iii. (ed. 2) 233 By the subtile Salts of the Lime, it will make its Way into the Pores..of the Wood. *a* 1774 Goldsm. *Surv. Exp. Philos.* (1776) II. 4 Some have thought that air is nothing more than earth or water expanded and assuming a more subtil form. 1784 Cowper *Task* vi. 135 The vital energy that mov'd..the pure and subtile lymph Through th'imperceptible meand'ring veins Of leaf and flow'r. 1839 Hallam *Lit. Eur.* iii. iii. § 149 The belief in ghosts, or spirits of subtile bodies. 1858 Sears *Athan.* xviii. 160 The luminiferous ether is still more subtile, and eludes the analysis of the chemist. 1872 J. G. Murphy *Comm. Lev.* vii. 37 The fat and the flesh turned by the fire of the altar into a subtile fume.

transf. 1642 H. More *Song of Soul* ii. ii. iii. 18 Corporeall wight such subtile virtue never has. 1844 Emerson *Nature*, *Discipline* Wks. (Bohn) II. 158 The air resembles the light which traverses it with more subtile currents.

fig. 1681–6 J. Scott *Chr. Life* (1747) III. 628 The Arguments of it would be too thin and subtil for vulgar Capacities. 1829 I. Taylor *Enthus.* ii. (1867) 22 The region of abstract conceptions..has an atmosphere too subtile to support the health of true piety.

b. *Subtile matter*: see Matter *sb.*¹ 5 b.

†c. Of a voice: Thin. *Obs.*

1398 Trevisa *Barth. De P. R.* xix. cxxxi. (1495) 942 In subtyll voys the spyryte is not stronge.

2. Of fine or delicate texture; also, delicately formed or moulded; = Subtle *a.* 2.

c 1381 Chaucer *Parl. Foules* 272 A subtyl couerscheif of valence. 1398 Trevisa *Barth. De P. R.* iii. ix. (1495) 54 The soule that yeueth felynge hathe place in the moost subtill chambres of the brayne. 1474 Caxton *Chesse* iii. i. (1883) 79 More subtile & more deyntous metes. 1481 Caxton *Myrr.* ii. x. f viij, Trees the whiche in stede of leues bere wulle of whiche is made cloth right fair & subtyle. 1579 Langham *Gard. Health* 535 Rose water..maketh the skinne subtill and thinne. 1599 Sir J. Davies *Nosce Teipsum* ii. 12, I do distinguish plaine Each subtill line of her immortall face. *Ibid.* 11 Her subtile forme thou onely canst define. 1608 B. Jonson *Masques*, *Beauty* Wks. (1616) 906 A thinne subtile vaile ouer her haire. *a* 1648 Digby *Closet Opened* (1677) 90 Strain the[m] clean through a subtil strainer. 1668 Culpepper & Cole *Barthol. Anat.* i. xiv. 33 A certain little lobe..compassed with a thin and subtile Membrane.

3. Of small thickness, thin, fine; = Subtle *a.* 3.

a 1425 tr. *Arderne's Treat. Fistula* etc. 68 Wolle y-tesed or subtile stupez of line. 1555 Eden *Decades* (Arb.) 222 He putteth his toonge to one of the ryftes..being as subtyle as the edge of a swoorde. 1612 Shelton *Quix.* (1620) I. iii. 18 Some slight and subtill wallets, which could scarce be perceived. 1616 B. Jonson *Devil an Ass* Prol. 5 Though you presume Satan a subtill thing, And may haue heard hee's worne in a thumbe-ring. 1665 Boyle *Occas. Refl.* iv. iv. 69 The subtil threds of Silk-worms. 1742 Pope *Dunc.* iv. 590 Arachne's subtile line.

fig. 1870 Lowell *Among my Bks.* Ser. i. (1873) 158 Every subtilest fibre of feeling.

†b. Of ships: Narrow, slender. Cf. OF. *galere subtile*. *Obs.*

c 1489 Caxton *Blanchardyn* 151, xxx grete shyppes and four score galeys subtyl. 1599 Hakluyt *Voy.* II. i. 78 Gallies, aswell bastards as subtill mahonnets.

4. Of powder, etc.: Fine, minute; = Subtle *a.* 4.

a 1425 tr. *Arderne's Treat. Fistula* etc. 41 Þe moste subtile mele of barly. 1513 *Life Hen. V* (1911) 110 Many heapes of sand, wᶜʰ was so subtill and smale, that it mooued wᵗʰ everie wynde. 1545 Raynalde *Byrth Mankynde* (1552) 136 b, Beynge fyrst beaten to subtyle powdre. *c* 1600 Chapman *Iliad* ix. 620 The subtile fruit of flax. 1683 K. Digby *Chym. Secrets* 77 Take Antimony Mineral..in subtil Powder. 1697 Headrich *Arcana Philos.* 30 Of this Marchasite.. make a subtile Powder. 1797 *Encycl. Brit.* (ed. 3) XI. 447/2 Beat your ore into a most subtile powder.

5. Involving careful discrimination or fine points; †difficult, abstruse; = Subtle *a.* 5.

c 1386 Chaucer *Man of Law's T.* 80 Many a subtil resoun forth they leyden. 1390 Gower *Conf.* III. 331 In proverbe and in probleme Sche spak, and bad he scholde deme In many soubtil question. 1456 Sir G. Haye *Law Arms* (S. T. S.) 14 It be sum part subtile to understand. 1560 Daus tr. *Sleidane's Comm.* 13 b, Let vs not throughe a subtill interpretation accompt king Charles a Germaine. 1565 Cooper *Thesaurus* s. v. *Abstrusior*, *Disputatio abstrusior*, a more subtill, hard, or obscure disputacion. 1598 Stow *Surv.* 44 Halfe pence and Farthinges, the account of which is more subtiller then the pence. 1610 Holland *Camden's Brit.* 352 [Odo] was committed to prison by a subtile distinction, as Earle of Kent, and not Bishop of Baieux. 1651 Hobbes *Leviathan* i. xv. 79 This may seem too subtile a deduction of the Lawes of Nature, to be taken notice of by all men. 1664 *Comenius' Janua Ling.* 755 The study of the Mathematicks is as profitable, as subtil (deep). 1788 Reid *Active Powers* iii. iv. 162 There has been much subtile disputation in ancient and modern times.

6. Fine, delicate; = Subtle *a.* 6.

1599 Sir J. Davies *Nosce Teipsum* ii. Introd. xxiv, But of that clocke within our breasts we beare, The subtill motions we forget the while. 1625 B. Jonson *Staple of N.* ii. iv. 164 Like a knitting needle, To serve by subtill turnes. 1634 W. Tirwhyt tr. *Balzac's Lett.* (vol. I.) 205 Those other more fine, and subtile vertues I cannot learne at Court. 1752 Hume *Pol. Disc.* i. 3 Some principles..which may seem too refin'd and subtile for such vulgar subjects. 1858 Longf. *M. Standish* vi. 4 As if thought had the power to draw to itself..Whatsoever it touches, by subtile laws of its nature. 1871 *Edin. Rev.* Apr. 428 The subtilest differences of perception and emotion. 1885 F. B. Van Vorst *Without a Compass* 20 Those intricate questions that possess so subtile a charm. 1888 E. Clodd *Story Creation* xi. 216 Their subtile shades of meaning.

†7. Of persons: Clever, dexterous, skilful; = Subtle *a.* 7. *Obs.*

c 1374 Chaucer *Anel. & Arc.* 88 He was..subtill in þat Crafte. *c* 1385 — *L. G. W.* 672 Sci e..made hire subtyl werkemen make a schryne. 1390 Gower *Conf.* III. 114 It causeth yit A man to be scubtil of wit To worche in gold. *c* 1450 *Merlin* i. 21 This Blase was a nobill clerk and subtile. 1456 Sir G. Haye *Law Arms* (S. T. S.) 38 [He] was rycht subtile in spech of Latyn. *c* 1489 Caxton *Sonnes of Aymon* xi. 277 He was the subtillest nygramancer that ever was in the worlde.

†8. Cleverly devised; ingeniously contrived; ingenious; = Subtle *a.* 8. *Obs.*

c 1384 Chaucer *H. Fame* 1188 Many subtile compassinges Babewynnes and pynacles Ymageries and tabernacles I say. 1390 Gower *Conf.* III. 40 A wonder soubtil thing he wroghte. *c* 1391 Chaucer *Astrol.* ii. § 40, I tok a subtil compas. 1484 Caxton (*title*) Here begynneth the book of the subtyl historyes and Fables of Esope. 1577–87 Holinshed *Chron.* III. 833/2 Blew veluet and cloth of siluer, all to cut in subtill knots. 1585 T. Washington tr. *Nichelay's Voy.* i. viii, By great artifice and subtill architecture builded. 1659 Leak *Waterwks.* 23 A very Subtile Engin, to raise a standing Water, by means of the Sun.

9. Of persons, animals, their actions, etc.: Crafty, artful, sly, cunning; = Subtle *a.* 10.

c 1385 Chaucer *L. G. W.* 2559 Be war ȝe wemen of ȝoure subtyl fo. 1386 *Rolls of Parlt.* III. 225/1 Many wronges subtiles, and also open oppressions. 1390 Gower *Conf.* I. 231 To voide with a soubtil hond The beste goodes of the lond And bringe chaf and take corn. 1513 Douglas *Æneis* vi. ii. 43 In subtell wordis of obscurite Involupand the trewth and verite. 1549 Latimer *Ploughers* (Arb.) 32 He goeth aboute bi his sleyghtes and subtyle meanes, to frustrate the same. 1575 Gascoigne *Kenelworth* Wks. 1910 II. 108 In sweetest flowres the subtyll Snakes may lurke. 1591 Shaks. *Two Gent.* iv. ii. 95 Thou subtile, periur'd, false, disloyall man. 1611 *Bible* Gen. iii. 1 The serpent was more subtill [Coverdale sotyller] then any beast of the field. 1628 Feltham *Resolves* ii. ix. 23 Taken with the subtile cozenages of Vice. 1634 Sir T. Herbert *Trav.* 199 Their [crocodiles'] condition is subtile (such their bloudie teares when they haue deuoured a man proue them for). 1646 Sir T. Browne *Pseud. Ep.* i. iii. (1686) 8 They are mocked into Error by subtiler devisors. 1719 De Foe *Crusoe* i. 71 The Goats were so shy, so subtile, and so swift of Foot. 1814 Southey *Roderick* x. 346 And with such subtile toils enveloped him. 1850 Hare *Mission Comf.* 137 To overcome sin's fiercest and subtilest temptations.

†b. Of looks: Sly. *Obs.*

c 1386 Chaucer *Squire's T.* 277 Swich subtil lookyng and dissymelynges. 1500–20 Dunbar *Poems* lxxxiv. 35 Be subtill winkis, and thair desaitfull talis. 1513 Douglas *Æneis* vii. Prol. 100 Hir subtell blenkis sched and wattry lycht.

10. Characterized by sagacity or penetration; discriminating, discerning; = Subtle *a.* 9.

1474 Caxton *Chesse* ii. v. (1883) 65 Ther was a kynge of so subtyll engyne That [etc.]. *a* 1533 Berners *Huon* lvii. 194 Frenchemen are ryght subtyl in gyuyng of good counsell. *Ibid.*, Gerames, who was subtyl, wel perceyued the mynde of the lady. 1600 Shaks. *A. Y. L.* i. iii. 79 She is too subtile for thee. 1611 *Bible* 2 Sam. xiii. 3 Ionadab was a very subtill man. 1612 Bacon *Ess.*, *Studies* (Arb.) 11 Histories make men wise, Poets wittie, the Mathematickes subtill [1598 subtle]. 1691 Ray *Creation* i. (1692) 71 How or why that should have such influence upon the Spirits..I am not subtil enough to discern. 1718 Prior *Solomon* ii. 224 With subtil Wit and fair Discourse. 1741 Betterton *Hist. Engl. Stage* iii. 34 This was a Nicety in Acting that none but the most subtile Player could so much as conceive. 1826 Disraeli *Viv. Grey* v. vi. 200 The most subtile diplomatist. 1875 Stedman *Vict. Poets* (1887) xi. 411 A subtile observer would perceive how truly he [*sc.* Shelley] represents his own time.

11. Of feeling, sense: Acute, keen.

1610 Guillim *Heraldry* iii. v. (1660) 123 By reason that our sight is far more subtill and apprehensive than is our hearing. 1662 J. Davies tr. *Olearius' Voy. Ambass.* 2 The stinch also offends it, and makes those heart-sick whose smelling is subtile. 1718 Prior *Solomon* iii. 136 Pass we the slow Disease, and subtil Pain. 1721 Bradley *Philos. Acc. Wks. Nat.* 54 In which I suppose there is contained their most Subtile sense of feeling. 1847 Longf. *Evang.* ii. iv, A secret Subtile sense crept in of pain. 1913 Dorland *Med. Dict.* (ed. 7) 917/2 *Subtile*, keen and acute, as, a subtile pain.

12. †a. Of weight, after tare has been deducted. Cf. Subtle *a.* 12. *Obs.*

1502 Arnolde *Chron.* (1811) p. xvi, The rekenynge of grocery, and weight sobtyll and grosse. 1660 T. Willsford *Scales Comm.* 107 What those gross or subtile summes do make in pence.

†b. Of a quantity: Belonging to a lower denomination. *Obs.*

15.. *MS. Harl.* 660 lf. 81 b, Euery subtylle grayne [doth]

Subtile, *v.* Obs. Also 6 suptyle.

Subtileness. Obs. [f. SUBTILE *a.* + -NESS.]

Subtiliate, *pa. pple.* and *ppl. a.* Obs. rare.

Subtiliation. Obs.

Subtilization.

Subtilize (sĕ·b)tilaiz), *v.* Also 6 subtilise.

Subtilizer.

Subtiling, *vbl. sb.*

Subtilly, *adv.*

Subtilty.

Sub-title, *sb.*

Sub-title, *v.*

Subtle (sĕ·t'l), *a.*

Subtlehead. Obs.

Subtleness. (arch.)

Subtleship. Obs. rare⁻¹. [-SHIP.]

Subtlety (sĕ·t'lti).

Subtly (sĕ·t'li), *adv.*

Subtone, *sb.*

Subtonic, *a.* and *sb.*

Subtract, *v.*

Subtracter. *rare.* [f. prec. + -ER¹.]
1. One who subtracts.

†2. = SUBTRAHEND. *Obs.*

Subtraction (sŏbtræ·kʃən). Forms: 4 subtracioun, 4-6 subtraccio(u)n, 5-6 subtraccion, 6 subtractioun. [ad. late L. *subtractiō*, -*ōnem* (in Vulgate Jer. v, ūṣoraṇ), f. *subtrahĕre* to SUBTRACT. Cf. L. *subtractiōne*, F. *soustraction*.]

†1. Withdrawal or removal from a place. *Obs.*

2. The withdrawal or withholding of something due, necessary, or useful. Also, an instance of this. *Obs. exc. arch.*

3. *Law.* The withdrawal or withholding from a person of any right or privilege to which he is lawfully entitled.

4. *Arith.* The taking of one quantity from (it out of) another; the operation of finding the difference between two quantities, the result being termed the *remainder*. Also, an instance of this.

Compound subtraction: see COMPOUND *a.* 6.

Subtractive (sŏbtræ·ktiv), *a.* [ad. med.L. *subtractīvus*, f. *subtract-*: see SUBTRACT *v.* and -IVE. Cf. F. *soustractif*, *subtractive*.] Involving or denoting subtraction, deduction, or diminution; (of a mathematical quantity) that is to be subtracted, negative, having the minus sign.

Subtrahend (sŏ·btrăhend). *Math.* [ad. L. *subtrahendum* (sc. *numerus* number), gerundive of *subtrahĕre* to SUBTRACT.] The quantity or number to be subtracted.

†Subtray, *v. Obs.* Also 5-6 subtrahe, 6-7 -trah. [f. impr. sing. *subtrahe* or stem *subtrah-* of L. *subtrahĕre* to SUBTRACT. Cf. SUBTRA.] To subtract (*trans.* and *intr.*).

Subtreasurer. [SUB-6.] An assistant or deputy treasurer.

Subtreasury. [SUB-7 d.] A subordinate or branch treasury. *U.S.* the organization by which the separate safe-keeping of the public funds is entrusted to specially appointed officers; any of the branches of the Treasury established in certain cities of the States for the receipt and safe-keeping of public moneys.

Subtribe. Chiefly *Zool.* and *Bot.* [SUB-7 b.] A subdivision of a tribe.

Subtriangular *a.*, with combining form **Su·btriangula·to-**.

Subtriple, *a. Math.* [SUB-10.]

Subtripli·cate, *a. Math.* [SUB-10.]

Subtuberance, *Subtu·berant*. [See SUB- and SUBER, SUBEROUS.]

Subtype. [SUB-5 c.] A subordinate type; a type included in a more general type.

Subty·pical, *a.* Of the character of a subtype.

Subucula (sŏbiū·kiŭla). Also anglicised (rare) subuoule. [L. dim. of *sub* under + *sū(e)re* to put, as in *exuĕre*, *induĕre*.] A kind of shirt or undertunic worn by the ancient Romans.

Subulate (siū·biŭleit), *a. Bot.* and *Zool.* [ad. mod.L. *subulātus*, f. *subula* awl: see -ATE².] Awl-shaped; slender and tapering to a point.

Subuliform (siū·biŭlifōrm), *a.* [ad. mod.L. *subuliformis*, f. *subula* awl: see -FORM.] Awl-shaped.

†Subulous, *a. Obs. rare⁻¹.* [ad. late L. *subulōsus*, f. *subula* awl.] A young heart with straight unbranched horns.

Subumbonal, *a. Zool.* (A misuse.)

Subtriplicated, *a.* [SUB-20 b.] Imperfectly divided into three sections.

Suberist (siū·bərist), *a.* and *sb.* [L. *subtilis*, f. *sub* + *tristis* sad.] Somewhat sad.

Suber, **Suberic** etc.: see SUB-, SUB-.

Submer·ber, *v. Obs. rare⁻¹.* [f. L. *sub-* + *umbra* shadow. Cf. SUBUMBRAGE *v.* SUB-2.] *trans.* To shelter.

Submumbrella. *Zool.* [mod.L.; see SUB-1 f.] The internal ventral or oral disk of a hydrozoan; the concave muscular layer beneath the umbrella of a jelly-fish.

Subrovince, *a.* [SUB-10.] Bordering on the tropics.

Subu·nion, *v. Obs. rare.* [ad. L. *subūnio*, rendering late Gr. ὑφέν = ὑφ', ὑπό under + ἕν one (*syllables*).

Suburb (sŏ·bərb), *sb.* [a. OF. *suburbe*, -*es* (13th c.), or ad. L. *suburbium*, -*is*, f. *sub* near + *urbs*, *urbis*, city.]

Suburban (sŏbŏ·rbăn), *a.* and *sb.* [ad. L. *suburbānus*, f. *suburbium*: see SUBURB.]

1. Of or belonging to a suburb or the suburbs of a town; living, situated, operating, or carried on in a suburb.

2. Any of such residential parts, having a definite designation, boundary, or organization.

Suburbars. *sb. pl.* †Error for *suburbans* (cf. prec. B. 1.). But cf. SUBURBANS.

†Suburbed, *a. Obs. rare⁻¹.* [f. SUBURB + -ED².] Having a suburb or suburbs.

Suburbia (sŏbŏ·rbiă). [L. SUBURB + -IA².] A quasi-proper name for the suburbs (*esp.* of London).

†Suburbial, *a. Obs. rare.* [f. L. *suburbium* SUBURB + -AL¹.] = SUBURBAN.

Suburbian, *a.* and *sb. Obs.* [f. L. *suburbium*, SUBURB + -AN.] *a.* Suburban; in the 17th cent. often with reference to the licentious life of the (Lon'don) suburbs (cf. SUBURB *d.* b).

Suburbican, *a. Obs. rare.* [ad. L. type *suburbicānus*, f. *suburbium*, after *suburbicārius*.] = SUBURBICARIAN.

Suburbicarian (sŏbŏ·rbikĕ·riăn), *a.* [f. late ecclesiastical L. *suburbicārius*, f. *suburbium*.] Applied to the dioceses (now six in number) around Rome, and to their churches, etc., which are subject to the jurisdiction of the Pope as metropolitan and the bishops of which form the body of cardinal bishops.

Suburbicary, *a.* = prec.

Subvassor. *Sc. Obs. rare⁻¹.* Also sub-vavasour. [ad. med.L. *subvassor*; see SUB-and VAVASOUR.] A subvassal.

Subvert, *v. Obs. rare⁻¹.* [f. L. *subvect-*, ppl. stem of *subvehĕre*, f. *sub*-SUB-12 + *vehĕre* to carry.] *trans.* To bring forward.

†Subvene, *v. Obs. rare⁻¹.* [L. *subvenīre*, f. *sub*-SUB-23 + *venīre* to come.] = SUBVENE.

Subveral, *v.* [f. L. *subvenīre*.] (see next), after *subveral*.

Subverse, *v.* [f. L. *subvers-*, ppl. stem of *subvertĕre*.] *trans.* To come to the help of.

†Subventaneous, *a. Obs. rare.* [f. L. *subvent-*, ppl. stem of *subvenīre* to come to the help of.]

Subvention (sŏbve·nʃən), *sb.* [a. OF. *subvencion*, -*tion*, or Pr. *subventio*, *-onem*, ad. late L. *subventio*, *-ōnem*, f. *subvenīre* to assist.]

1. A subsidy levied by the state. *Obs. exc. Hist.*

†2. The provision of help, support, or relief. Also, an instance of this. *Obs.*

3. A grant of money for the support of an institution; a grant out of necessitous persons.

Subvari·ety. [SUB-7 b.] A subordinate or minor variety, *esp.* of a domestic animal or cultivated plant.

Subversion (sŏbvǝ·rʃən). Also 4-5 -cioun, -sioun, 4-6 -cion. [a. OF. *subversion*, -*cioun*, ad. L. *subversiōnem*, f. *subvert-*: see SUBVERT.]

1. Overthrow, demolition (of a city, stronghold, etc.).

Subversionary, *a. rare.* [f. prec. + -ARY¹.] Of the nature of a subversion.

Subversionist. [f. SUBVERSION + -IST.] One who advocates or promotes subversion.

Subversive (sŏbvǝ·rsiv), *a.* [ad. med.L. *subversīv-us*, f. *subvert-*: see SUBVERT.] Having a tendency to subvert or overthrow; tending to subversion.

Subvert (sŏbvǝ·rt), *v.* [ad. OF. *subvertir*, or ad. L. *subvertĕre*, f. *sub*-SUB-2 + *vertĕre* to turn. Cf. *pervert*.]

1. *trans.* To overthrow, raze to the ground (a town or city, a structure, edifice). *Obs.*

Subway. [SUB-10.] 1. An underground passage for conveying water-pipes, gas-pipes, telegraph wires, etc. 2. An underground tunnel by which pedestrians cross beneath a road or railway.

Subzonal ... *Anat.* ...

Subzone *(sŭbzōn).* Geol. [SUB- 7 c.]

Suc, *obs.* ... *suc.* Juice, sap.

Succade *(sŭkē·d).* Also 6 sucade, 6 suckade, ... [a F. *succade*, ...]

Succanéous, *a. Obs.* [L.]

Succate, do. Obs. [See prec. and -ADO 2.]

Succeed *(sŭksī·d),* v. Forms: ...

Succeedable, *a. Obs. rare.*

Succeeded, *ppl. a.* [SUCCEED v. + -ED 1.]

Succeeder *(sŭksī·dǝr).* Also 5 succidor, 6 -ceder, 7 -ceder.

Succeeding, *vbl. sb.* ...

Succeeding, *ppl. a.* ...

Succeeding-ly, *adv.*

Succent, *a.* [L.]

Succenturiation.

Succenturiate, *v.*

Succentor *(sŭkse·ntǝr).*

Succès *(süksè),* sb. Obs. rare.

Success *(sŭkse·s),* sb. Also 6 sukses.

Successful *(sŭkse·sfŭl),* a.

Successfully, *adv.*

Successfulness.

Succession *(sŭkse·shǝn),* sb. Also 4-5 -oun, ...

Succour.

Succour (sɒ̆ˈkəʊər), v. Forms: 3–5 socur(e, socour, sokere, soukur, socoure, sokour, 4 suckur, sokere, 7 sucurre; 5–6 succoure, 6 socoure, 7 succur, 6– succour. [a. OF. (i) socorre, sec-(curre, secourre—L. succurrere, f. suc- = SUB-25 + currere to run; (ii) suc(c)urir (mod. secourir), of changed conjugation), mod.F. secourir. Cf. Pr. secorre, securrer, It. soccorrere, Sp. Pg. socorrer.]

Succour, obs. form of SUGAR sb.

Succous, obs. form of SUCCOUS.

Succoury, obs. form of CHICORY.

†Succourable, a. Obs. In 5 socourable.

Succourance, Obs. rare. In 5 socourance.

Succourer (sɒ̆ˈkərər). [f. SUCCOUR v. + -ER¹.]

†Succourful, a. Obs. rare.

Succouring, vbl. sb.

Succourless, a.

Succourment, Obs. rare.

Succuba (sɒ̆ˈkjʊbə). Pl. succubae (-bī), also succubas. [med.L. succuba, f. succub- stem of succumbere.] = SUCCUBUS.

Succube (sɒ̆ˈkjuːb). rare. Also succub. [ad. F. succube or L. succuba.] = SUCCUBUS.

Succubine (sɒ̆ˈkjʊbaɪn), a. rare. [f. SUCCUBA or SUCCUBUS + -INE¹.]

Succubous (sɒ̆ˈkjʊbəs), a. Bot. [f. L. suc- + SUB-2 + cumbere to lie + -OUS.]

Succubus (sɒ̆ˈkjʊbəs). Pl. -bi (-baɪ). [med.L., masc. form (with fem. meaning) corresp. to SUCCUBA, after INCUBUS.]

Succulence (sɒ̆ˈkjʊləns). [ad. med.L. succulentia, f. succulent-us.]

Succulency (sɒ̆ˈkjʊlənsɪ). [ad. med.L. succulentia (succulent-): see prec.]

Succulent (sɒ̆ˈkjʊlənt), a. and sb. [ad. L. succulentus (suculentus), f. succus (sucus) juice.] A. adj.

Succumb (sɒ̆ˈkʌm), v. Also 5 succombe, socumbe, 5–7 succumbe, 7–8 succomb. [a. OF. succumber, also subcomber, (sub-), f. suc- = SUB-2 + cumbēre to lie. Cf. It. soccombere.]

Succumbence (sɒ̆ˈkʌmbəns). rare. [f. SUCCUMB: see -ENCE.]

Succumbency. rare. [see -ENCY.]

Succumbent (sɒ̆ˈkʌmbənt), a. [ad. L. succumbent-em, pr. pple. of succumbere to SUCCUMB.] A. adj.

Succurrance, obs. form of SUCCOURANCE.

†Succurse, sb. Obs. In 5 succourse.

†Succursal, a. rare.

Succuss (sɒ̆ˈkʌs), v. rare. [f. L. succuss-, pa. ppl. stem of succutĕre, f. suc- = SUB-25 + quatĕre to shake.] trans.

†Succussation. Obs. [ad. L. *succussātiō, -ōnem (altered in med.L. to succursātiō in the sense 'trotting'), n. of action f. succussāre, f. suc-cuss- (see Succuss). Cf. F. succussation (Cotgr.).]

Succussion (sɒ̆ˈkʌʃən). [ad. L. succuss-iō, -ōnem, n. of action f. succutĕre: see SUCCUSS.]

Succussive (sɒ̆ˈkʌsɪv), a. rare. [f. L. succuss-: see SUCCUSS.]

Such (sɒtʃ), a. and pron. Forms: see below.

A. Illustration of Forms.

B. Signification.

have gain'd his Immortality by the Milk he suckt from her. 1774 Goldsm. *Nat. Hist.* (1776) IV. 70 The weasel, where it once fastens, holds, and continuing also to suck the blood at the same time, weakens its antagonist. 180. in Dickson *Pract. Agric.* (1805) II. 1058 If an ewe gives more milk than its lamb will suck. 1825 Scott *Talism.* xxi, Suck the poison from his wound, one of you. 1848 Steinmetz *Hist. Jesuits* I. 212 Ignatius..even applied his mouth to their ulcers, and sucked the purulent discharge. 1848 Thackeray *Van. Fair* lxii, The knowing way in which he sipped, or rather sucked, the Johannisberger.

b. Of flies, etc. drawing blood, bees extracting honey from flowers; also of flowers 'drinking' the dew, etc.

1340 *Ayenb.* 136 Þe smale uleȝe þet..of þe floures zoucþ þane deau huerof hi makeþ þet hony. 1422 Yonge tr. *Secr. Secr.* 180 The flyes thyke lay on hym that his blode soke. 1474 Caxton *Chesse* II. v. (1883) 66 Many flyes satte vpon the soores and souked his blood. 1593 Shaks. *2 Hen. VI*, IV. i. 109 Drones sucke not Eagles blood, but rob Bee-hiues. 1637 Milton *Lycidas* 140 Throw hither all your quaint enameld eyes, That on the green terf suck the honied showres. c 1645 Howell *Lett.* III. iv. (1892) 517 The Bee and the Spider suck honey and poison out of one Flower. 1820 Shelley *Prometh. Unb.* III. iii. 102 Night-folded flowers Shall suck unwithering hues in their repose. 1833 Wordsw. *Warning* 33 Like the bee That sucks from mountain-heath her honey fee.

c. *To suck the blood of* (fig.): to exhaust the resources of, drain the life out of. (Cf. Blood-suck *v.*)

1583 Stubbes *Anat. Abus.* II. (1882) 7 He meaneth to sucke thy bloud. 1584 Greene *Mirr. Modestie* Wks. (Grosart) III. 17 These two cursed caitifes..concluded when they might finde hir alone, to sucke the bloude of this innocent lambe. 1610 Holland *Camden's Brit.* (1637) 49 The Lieutenant, cruelly to suck their bloud, and the Procuratour as greedy to preie upon that substance. 1819 Scott *Ivanhoe* vii, The wealth he had acquired by sucking the blood of his miserable victims, had but swelled him like a bloated spider.

d. *To suck one's fill*: see Fill *sb.*[1] 1.

c 1475 *Songs & Carols* xlvi. (Percy Soc.) 50 He toke hyr lovely by the pape,..And sok hys fyll of the lycowr. 1798 Wordsw. '*Her Eyes are Wild*' 84 My little babe! thy lips are still, And thou hast almost sucked thy fill. 1805 Dickson *Pract. Agric.* II. 981 Young calves when permitted to suck their fill are often seized with a looseness. 1818 Scott *Hrt. Midl.* xxxix, I wad wuss ye, if Gowans, the brockit cow, has a quey, that she suld suck her fill of milk.

e. *transf.* and *fig.* or in fig. context.

13.. *Bonaventura's Medit.* 277 Þys sermoun at crystys brest slepyng he soke. 1393 Langl. *P. Pl.* C. XIII. 55 Crist ..bad hem souken of hus brest sauete for synne. 1580 J. Stewart *Poems* (S. T. S.) II. 103/5 Thocht source I souck not on the sacred hill. a 1586 Sidney *Astr. & Stella* Sonn. lxxiii, Because a sugared kiss In sport I suckt. 1592 Shaks. *Rom. & Jul.* v. iii. 92 Death that hath suckt the honey of thy breath. 1592 — *Ven. & Ad.* 572 Had she then gaue ouer, Such nectar from his lips she had not suckt. 1600 *Cath. Tract.* 245 Ye may sie what venemous poyson thay souk out of the Ministers breists. 1601 Shaks. *Jul. C.* II. ii. 87 From you great Rome shall sucke Reuiuing blood. 1602 Marston *Antonio's Rev.* IV. i, Studious contemplation sucks the juyce From wisards cheekes. 1604 Earl Stirling *Crœsus* I. i, Faire Citie, where mine eyes first suck't the light. 1842 Tennyson *Will Waterproof* 213 Thou shalt from all things suck Marrow of mirth and laughter.

2. To imbibe (qualities, etc.) *with* the mother's milk. (Cf. 5.)

1586 T. B. *La Primaud. Fr. Acad.* I. 166 As if we had sucked iniquitie togither with our nurses milke. 1588 Kyd *Househ. Philos.* Wks. (1901) 259 That first and tender age of infancie..oftentimes with the milke sucketh the conditions of the Nursse. 1607 Shaks. *Cor.* III. ii. 129 Thy Valiantnesse was mine, thou suck'st it from me. 1639 Massinger *Unnat. Comb.* I. i, I think they suck this knowledge in their milk.

3. To extract or draw (moisture, goodness, etc.) *from* or *out of* a thing; to absorb into itself.

1398 Trevisa *Barth. De P. R.* XVII. cxxvi. (1495) 686 The pyth of the russhe is good to drawe water out of the erthe for it soukyth it kyndly. 1585 Jas. I *Ess. Poesie* (Arb.) 14 Fra tyme that onis thy sell [Phœbus] The vapouris softlie sowkis with smyling cheare. 1593 Shaks. *Rich. II*, III. iv. 38 The noysome Weedes, that..sucke The Soyles fertilitie from wholesome flowers. 1657 Austen *Fruit Trees* 71 Great and large Trees do suck and draw the fertility of the ground exceedingly. 1697 Dryden *Virg., Georg.* I. 438 Oft whole sheets descend of slucy Rain, Suck'd by the spongy Clouds from off the Main. *Ibid.* III. 222 Let 'em [*sc.* Mares] suck the Seed with greedy Force; And close involve the Vigour of the Horse. 1847 Tennyson *Princ.* VII. 24 She..sees a great black cloud..suck the blinding splendour from the sand. 1880 *Scribner's Mag.* Mar. 736 Treat all suckers as weeds, cutting them down..before they have sucked half the life out of the bearing hill.

†4. To draw or extract (money, wealth) from a source. Also in early use *intr.* with partitive *of*. *Obs.*

c 1380 Wyclif *Serm.* Sel. Wks. II. 187 Þes prelatis..cunnen summone þe Chirche..from oo place to anoþer, to sooke of her moneye. c 1386 Chaucer *Cook's T.* 52 To sowke Of that he brybe kan or borwe may. 1399 Langl. *Rich. Redeles* IV. 9 Sellynge, þat sowkid siluer rith ffaste. 1610 Holland *Camden's Brit.* (1637) 756 Having first cunningly suckt a great masse of money from the credulous king.

5. To derive or extract (information, comfort, profit, etc.) *from*, †*of*, or *out of*. (Cf. 2.)

1535 Coverdale *Ps.* lxxii. 10 There out sucke they no small auauntage. 1539 Cromwell in Merriman *Life & Lett.* (1902) II. 176 Communications at large sucked of hym. 1565 T. Stapleton *Fortr. Faith* 10 He made those notes sucked out of John Bale. c 1600 Chalkhill *Thealma & Cl.* (1683) 95 Ægypt Schools..From whence he suckt this knowledg. 1605 *1st Pt. Jeronimo* II. iii. 8 Hast thou worne gownes in the Uniuersity, Tost logick, suckt Philosophy? 1625 Bacon *Ess., Travel* (Arb.) 523 In Trauailing in one Country he shall sucke the Experience of many. 1715 Hearne *Collect.* (O.H.S.) V. 109 Spinosa..suck'd the first Seeds of Atheism from the famous Francis Vanden Ende. 1784 Cowper *Task* IV. 111 He sucks intelligence in ev'ry clime. 1822 Lamb *Elia* I. *Compl. Decay of Beggars*, Much good might be sucked from these Beggars. 1908 M. S. Rawson *Easy go Luckies* xxi, Had he been a scholar he might have sucked a sort of delicately pungent comfort from an epigram of Tacitus. 1914 Marett in *Folk-Lore* XXV. 20 The active conditions that enable us to suck strength and increase out of the passive conditions comprised under the term environment.

†6. To draw (air, breath) into the mouth; to inhale (air, smoke, etc.). *Obs.*

1590 Shaks. *Com. Err.* II. ii. 194 They'll sucke our breath, or pinch vs blacke and blew. ? 1614 D. Murray in Drumm. of Hawth. *Poems* (S. T. S.) I. 95 To them who on their Hills suck'd sacred Breath. 1634 Sir T. Herbert *Trav.* 150 Tobacco suckt through water by long canes or pipes. 1712–14 Pope *Rape Lock* II. 83 Some [spirits]..suck the mists in grosser air below. 1717 — *Eloisa* 324 See my lips tremble, and my eye-balls roll, Suck my last breath, and catch my flying soul!

7. To draw (water, air, etc.) in some direction, esp. by producing a vacuum. Also *intr.* for *pass.* of the wind.

1661 Boyle *Certain Physiol. Ess.* (1669) 216 Having by a certain Artifice out of a large glass..caus'd a certain quantity of air to be suck'd, we [etc.]. 1730–46 Thomson *Autumn* 768 Old Ocean too, suck'd thro' the porous globe, Had long ere now forsook his horrid bed. 1847 Tennyson *Princ.* v. 339 Right and left Suck'd from the dark heart of the long hills roll The torrents. 1849 Cupples *Green Hand* ii, The [gulf] stream *sucks* the wind with heat. *Ibid.* xiii, The air aloft appeared in the mean time to be steadying and *sucking*. 1857 Miller *Elem. Chem., Org.* i. 17 Instead of sucking air through the apparatus, heat is to be very cautiously applied to the chlorate.

8. To draw in so as to swallow up or engulf.

1523 Fitzherb. *Husb.* § 2 The lande is verye toughe, and wolde soke the ploughe into the erthe. c 1590 *Sir T. More* (Malone Soc.) 1306 As when a whirle-poole sucks the circkled waters. 1697 Dryden *Æneid* III. 538 Charibdis..in her greedy Whirl-pool sucks the Tides. 1817 Shelley *Rev. Islam* XII. ix, Like the refluence of a mighty wave Sucked into the loud sea.

b. *fig.* To draw *into* a course of action, etc.

1771 Smollett *Humphry Cl.* (1815) 266, I am insensibly sucked into the channel of their manners and customs. 1779 J. Moore *View Soc. Fr.* (1789) I. i. 9 Small chance will remain of his being sucked into the old system. 1840 De Quincey *Essenes* Wks. 1862 IX. 287 He is now rapidly approaching to a torrent that will suck him into a new faith. 1899 Ld. Rosebery in *Daily News* 6 May 4/1 We were sucked into a house dinner.

II. 9. To apply the lips to (a teat, breast, the mother, nurse, or dam) for the purpose of extracting milk; to draw milk from with the mouth.

c 1000 Ælfric *Saints' Lives* viii. 125 Ne sceamode þe to ceorfanne þæt þæt ðu sylf suce? c 1000 *Ags. Gosp.* Luke xi. 27 Eadiȝ is se innoð þe þe bær & þa breost þe ðu suce. c 1205 Lay. 5026 Þa tittes þet þu suke [c 1275 soke] mid þine lippes. *Ibid.* 12981, & Vther his broðer þa ȝæt sæc [c 1275 soc] his moder. c 1275 *XI Pains of Hell* 135 in *O. E. Misc.* 151 Neddren heore [*sc.* the women's] breosten sukeþ. 1303 R. Brunne *Handl. Synne* 546 Hyt shulde a go, and sokun ky. c 1350 *Will. Palerne* 2702 For þe blissful barnes loue þat hire brestes souked. 1387 Trevisa *Higden* (Rolls) III. 267 Hir moder..schewed hir brestes þat eiþer of hem hadde i-soke. a 1400 *Octouian* 566 We segh..a wonder happe; A manchyld swoke a lyones pappe. c 1450 *Merlin* 88 To put youre owne childe to sowken a-nother woman. 1538 *Test. Ebor.* (Surtees) VI. 85 The foll that soukes olde maire. 1588 Shaks. *Tit. A.* IV. ii. 178 Ile make you..feed on curds and whay, and sucke the Goate. 1697 J. Lewis *Mem. Dk. Gloucester* (1789) 6 He ordered her to go to bed to the young prince, who soon sucked her. 1781 Cowper *Expost.* 473 Thou wast born amid the din of arms, And suck'd a breast that panted with alarms. 1805 Dickson *Pract. Agric.* II. 986 When the calf is suffered to suck the mother, it should have the first of the milk.

b. of bees, etc., as in 1 b.

1426 Lydg. *De Guil. Pilgr.* 17560 As an yreyne sowketh the flye, And hyr entroylles draweth oute. 1665 Boyle *Occas. Refl.* 67 How busie the Bees are in sucking these [blossoms]. 1812 Kirby in K. & Spence *Introd. Entom.* (1816) I. 164 *note*, A small Melitta, upon which some of these creatures were busy sucking the poor animal. 1889 *Science-Gossip* XXV. 270/2 Union of many flowers on one inflorescence, which is therefore more conspicuous, and more easily sucked by insects, than single flowers.

10. To apply the lips and tongue (or analogous organs) to (an object) for the purpose of obtaining nourishment; to extract the fluid contents of by such action of the mouth; to absorb (a sweetmeat) in the mouth by the action of the tongue and the muscles of the cheeks.

To suck a person's brains: see Brain *sb.* 4 b. *To teach one's grandmother to suck eggs*: see Egg *sb.* 4 b. †*To suck the eggs of*: to extract the 'goodness' of, cause to be unproductive. *To suck the monkey*: see Monkey *sb.* 11.

1340 Hampole *Pr. Consc.* 6764 Þai sal for threst þe hevedes souke Of þe nedders þat on þam sal rouke. c 1450 *Cov. Myst.* (Shaks. Soc.) 28 That sory appyl that we han sokyn To dethe hathe brouth my spouse and me. 1576 Gascoigne *Philomene* Wks. 1910 II. 179 Such unkinde, as let the cukowe flye, To sucke mine eggs. 1599 Shaks. *Hen. V*, I. ii. 171 The Weazell (Scot) Comes sneaking, and so sucks her Princely Egges. 1602 *2nd Pt. Return fr. Parnass.* IV. ii, This sucks the eggs of my inuention. 1658 Rowland tr. *Moufet's Theat. Ins.* 1067 When he hath his belly full, he laies up the rest of his provant, and hangs them up by a thred to suck them another time. 1706 E. Ward *Wooden World Diss.* (1708) 81 They may suck their Paws at Home in a whole Skin. 1750 Gray *Long Story* 48 A wicked Imp.. Who prowl'd the country far and near,..And suck'd the eggs, and kill'd the pheasants. 1774 Goldsm. *Nat. Hist.* (1776) IV. 322 It is a common report, that during this time, they [*sc.* bears] live by sucking their paws. 1780 Cowper *Progr. Err.* 530 If some mere driv'ler suck the sugar'd fib, One that still needs his leading-string and bib. 1851 Mayhew *Lond. Labour* I. 204/2 The old ones wants something to suck, and not to chew. 1852 Thackeray *Esmond* I. iii, A grand, languid nobleman in a great cap and flowered morning-gown, sucking oranges. 1908 M. S. Rawson *Easy go Luckies* xviii, The policeman's five children (all sucking sweets).

b. To apply the tongue and inner sides of the lips to (one's teeth) so as to extract particles of food.

1595 Shaks. *John* I. i. 192 When my knightly stomacke is suffis'd Why then I sucke my teeth. 1901 W. R. H. Trowbridge *Lett. her Mother to Eliz.* xxii. 106 The people at Croixmare couldn't have eaten worse than Mr. Sweetson;.. he sucked his teeth when he had finished.

11. *transf.* **a.** To draw the moisture, goodness, etc. from.

1693 Evelyn *De la Quint. Compl. Gard.* I. 51 Without doubt the Earth would not grow Lank, Meagre, and Hungry, as it does, if the Plants did not Suck it just as Animals do their Dams. 1733 Tull *Horse-hoeing Husb.* xvi. 246 'Tis certain that Turneps, when they stand for Seed, suck and impoverish the Ground exceedingly. 1879 E. Arnold *Lt. Asia* v. 134 In forest glades A fierce sun sucked the pools.

b. To work (a pump) dry. (Cf. 19.)

1753 *Scots Mag.* Mar. 156/2 About four in the afternoon the pump was sucked. 1857 in *Merc. Marine Mag.* (1858) V. 8 After sucking the pumps, I had to keep one pump..at work.

c. To cling closely to.

1859 Tennyson *Marr. Geraint* 324 Monstrous ivy-stems.. suck'd the joining of the stones.

12. To draw money, information, or the like from (a person); to rob (a person or thing) of its resources or support; to drain, 'bleed'.

1558 in Feuillerat *Revels Q. Eliz.* (1908) 17 He will..make waiste, sucke the Quene, or pynche the poore or all thre. 1617 Sir T. Roe in *Embassy* (1899) 419 In hope to gett, no man can escape him [the King]; when hee hath suckd them, hee will not knowe them. 1752 Chesterf. *Lett.* cclxxii, When you are with *des gens de robe*, suck them with regard to the constitution and civil government. a 1774 Fergusson *Plainstanes & Cawsey* Poems (1845) 48 And o' three shillin's Scottish suck him. 1847 Emerson *Repr. Men, Napoleon* Wks. (Bohn) I. 374 The land sucked of its nourishment, by a small class of legitimates. 1856 Kingsley in *N. Brit. Rev.* XXV. 22 Fathers became gradually personages who are to be disobeyed, sucked of their money, [etc.]. 1874 Geo. Eliot *Coll. Breakf.-P.* 617 Who..suck the commonwealth to feed their ease.

13. With predicative adj.: To render so-and-so by sucking.

1530 Palsgr. 742/2 You shall se hym sucke him selfe asleepe. 1606 Shaks. *Ant. & Cl.* v. ii. 313 Dost thou not see my Baby at my breast, That suckes the Nurse asleepe. 1607 Topsell *Four-f. Beasts* 302 In the next morning let them [*sc.* foals] be admitted to sucke their belly full. 1715 F. Slare *Vindic. Sugars* 54 This Liquor invited all Sorts of Flies to it,..many of them did suck themselves drunk. 180. in Dickson *Pract. Agric.* (1805) II. 1058 [The ewes] are..held by the head till the lambs by turns suck them clean. 1879 Burroughs *Locusts & Wild Honey* 11 Bees will suck themselves tipsy upon varieties like the sops-of-wine.

b. *To suck dry*, to extract all the moisture or liquid out of by suction; *fig.* to exhaust.

1592 *Arden of Feversham* II. ii. 119 When she is dry suckt of her eager young. 1593 Shaks. *3 Hen. VI*, IV. viii. 55 My Sea shall suck them dry. 1598 Stow *Surv.* 470 London felt it most tragicall; for then he both seysed their liberties, and sucked themselues dry. 1647 H. More *Poems* 206 Abhorred dugs by devils sucken dry. a 1719 Addison tr. *Virg. Fourth Georg.* 195 Wks. 1721 I. 24 Some [bees].. Taste ev'ry bud, and suck each blossom dry. 1771 *Ann. Reg.* 207/1 After one had sucked the bones quite dry,.. I have seen another take them up,..and do the same. 1865 Dickens *Mut. Fr.* III. v, A crew of plunderers, who would suck me dry by driblets.

14. To produce as by suction. *rare.*

1849 T. Woolner *My Beautiful Lady, My Lady in Death* xvi, The heavy sinking at her heart Sucked hollows in her cheek.

III. 15. *intr.* Of the young of a mammal: To perform the action described in sense 1; to draw milk from the teat; to feed from the breast or udder.

c 1000 [see Sucking *ppl. a.* 1]. c 1175 *Lamb. Hom.* 5 He mihte ridan..uppon þa lutthle fole þat ȝet hit wes sukinde. c 1205 Lay. 13194 Vther wes to lutel þa ȝet he moste suken. c 1290 *Beket* 1460 in *S. Eng. Leg.* 148 Ne womman þat was with childe, Ne þe children þat soukinde weren. 1303 R. Brunne *Handl. Synne* 6022 Com a pore womman..And bare a chylde..Þe pappe yn þe mouþe as hyt had soke. c 1375 *Sc. Leg. Saints* xvi. (*Magdalena*) 679 Þai..fand þe child at þe pape, lyand rycht as he sukit had. c 1440 *Sir Gowther* 113 He sak so sore thei [*sc.* the nurses] lost here lyfes. 1513 Douglas *Æneis* III. vi. 74 A grete sow fereit of grysis thretty heid, Liggin on the ground..About hir pappis sowkin. 1523 Fitzherb. *Husb.* § 39 Let them sucke as longe as the dammes wyll suffre theym. 1542 Boorde *Dyetary* xvi. (1870) 275 All thynges the whiche dothe sucke, is nutrytyue. 1600 Shaks. *A. Y. L.* III. ii. 81 To see my Ewes graze, & my Lambes sucke. 1606 — *Tr. & Cr.* I. iii. 292 Tell him of Nestor, one that was a man When Hectors Grandsire suckt. 1687 A. Lovell tr. *Thevenot's Trav.* I. 167 There we saw a great many Women, and little Children, most of them Sucking. 1799 *Med. Jrnl.* II. 44 The wet-nurse having presented it the breast, it took it with avidity, but it could suck but little, in consequence of its weak state. 1820 Shelley *Œd. Tyr.* I. 51, I suck, but no milk will come from the dug. 1858 Churchill *Dis. Childr.* 30 It is desirable that a child should not be weaned before nine months, nor suck after twelve.

b. *at*, †*of*, †*on* the breast or the mother.

c 1330 *Arth. & Merl.* 8466 Þou souke of hir tat. 1377 Langl.

P. Pl. B. XI. 116 He..badde hem souke for synne saufly at his breste [1393 C. XIII. 55 Souken of hus brest]. c 1386 Chaucer *Prioress' Prol.* 6 Children..on the brest soukynge. a 1400 *Octouian* 555 A man chyld..Sok of her as of a woman That wher hys dame. c 1460 *Towneley Myst.* xxi. 57 Of my dame sen I sowked had I neuer sich a nyght. 1486 *Bk. St. Albans, Hunting* e iv, A fawne sowkyng on his dam. 1549 *N. Country Wills* (Surtees 1908) 204 Two mares ..and two feles sucking upon theym. a 1578 Lindesay (Pitscottie) *Chron. Scot.* (S.T.S.) II. 53 The zoung babe of hir breist sucand. 1590 Spenser *F. Q.* I. i. 15 A thousand yong ones..Sucking vpon her poisonous dugs. 1645 *Relation late Witches* 19 The said Anne offered to give unto her daughter Sarah Cooper an Impe in the likenes of a gray Kite, to suck on the said Sarah. 1691 Ray *Creation* I. (1692) 117 Such as are nourished with Milk, presently find their way to the Paps, and suck at them.

c. of flies drawing blood, etc., as in 1 b.

1610 Shaks. *Temp.* v. i. 88 Where the Bee sucks, there suck I. 1728 Pope *Dunc.* I. 130 How there he plunder'd snug, And suck'd all o'er, like an industrious Bug. 1780 Cowper *Progr. Err.* 326 These flesh-flies of the land; Who fasten without mercy on the fair, And suck, and leave a craving maggot there. 1870 Wilson *Austral. Songs* 99 Honey-birds loitered to suck at the wattle.

†d. *transf.* and *fig.* *Obs.*

a 1548 Hall *Chron., Edw. IV*, 229 b, Suche other as daily flatered hym for their peculier profites (as he had many in deede that daily sucked at his elbowe). 1571 Digges *Pantom.* A iv, Such two footed Moules and Todes whom.. nature hath ordayned to craule within the earth, and suck upon the muck. a 1626 Bacon *Hen. VIII* in *Misc. Wks.* (1629) 165 The Crowne, which had sucked too hard, and now being full,..was like to Draw lesse.

16. To give suck (occas. †*to give to suck*): to give milk from the breast or udder, to suckle. Const. simple dat. or *to*. Now *arch.*

Suck, properly infin. (cf. G. *zu saugen geben*, Du. *te zuigen geven*), is now felt as a sb.; cf. Suck *sb.*[1] 1 a.

c 1330 *Arth. & Merl.* 2694 Late..þi wiif it loke Of hir milk & ȝiue it souke. 1340 *Ayenb.* 60 Þe blondeeres byeþ þe dyeules noriches þet his children yeueþ zouke. c 1386 Chaucer *Reeve's T.* 237 To rokken and to yeue the child to sowke. c 1400 *Pilgr. Sowle* (Caxton 1483) IV. xx. 65 Eke the to sowken of my brestes yafe I. 1471 Caxton *Recuyell* (Sommer) 12 Am y not he that ye bare and gaf me souke of your brestes? 1588 Kyd *Househ. Phil.* Wks. (1901) 237 Mothers ought to giue their owne Children sucke. 1653 H. Cogan tr. *Pinto's Trav.* lxiv. 257 If a mother hath a child which she cannot give suck unto for some valuable consideration. 1786 J. Hunter *Treat. Ven. Dis.* VII. i. 388 She gave suck to this second child. 1801 *Med. Jrnl.* V. 504 A poor woman, who gave suck to a child about a year old. 1858 Churchill *Dis. Childr.* 30 The mother may give the child suck during the night or day only.

b. without personal obj. Now *arch.*

1382 Wyclif *Luke* xxiii. 29 Wombis that han not gendrid, and the teetis whiche han not ȝouun souke. 1526 Tindale *Matt.* xxiv. 19 To them that are with chylde, and to them that geve sucke [Wyclif noryschinge]. 1605 Shaks. *Macb.* I. vii. 54, I haue giuen Sucke, and know How tender 'tis to loue the Babe that milkes me. 1674 tr. *Scheffer's Lapland* 131 Those [does] that have young ones never are housed, but give suck without. 1691 Ray *Creation* I. (1692) 107 Seeing it would be for many reasons inconvenient for Birds to give Suck.

17. *To suck at*: (*a*) to take a draught of; to inhale; (*b*) to take a pull at (a pipe, drinking vessel).

1584 Cogan *Haven Health* ccxxi. (1636) 256 Mervaile it is to see how the Welchmen will lye sucking at this drinke [*sc.* Metheglin]. 1607 Dekker *Knt.'s Conjur.* (1842) 49 Snakes euer sucking at thy breath. 1815 J. Smith *Panorama Sci. & Art* II. 124 Drawing out the air with the mouth by sucking at the orifice *c*. 1855 Browning *Grammar. Funeral* 96 Back to his studies..He..Sucked at the flagon. 1872 E. Yates *Castaway* I. ix, He sat quietly sucking away at his long pipe.

18. Of inanimate objects: To draw by suction.

c 1220 *Bestiary* 568 Ðer ðe water sukeð [*MS.* sinkeð], sipes ge sinkeð. [*Cf.* suk *in l.* 578.] 1573 Tusser *Husb.* (1878) 47 Weede and the water so soketh and sucks, that goodnes from either it vtterly plucks. 1871 *Trans. Amer. Inst. Mining Eng.* I. 53 If the stamps are left..standing in the pulp, between blows, the material settles around them and they 'suck' when the lift commences.

19. Of a pump: To draw air instead of water, as a result of the exhaustion of the water or a defective valve.

1627 Capt. J. Smith *Sea Gram.* ii. 9 The Pumpe sucks, is when the water being out, it drawes vp nothing but froth and winde. 1769 Falconer *Dict. Marine* (1780) s.v. *Pompe*, The pump sucks, or is dry. 1831 Jane Porter *Sir E. Seaward's Narr.* I. 61 It [*sc.* the pump] sucked, that is no more water remained within reach. 1899 F. T. Bullen *Log Sea-waif* 170 Of course she leaked..but still in fine weather the pumps would 'suck' in ten minutes at four-hour intervals.

fig. 1854 Lowell *Jrnl. in Italy* III. Prose Wks. 1890 I. 129 Even Byron's pump *sucks* sometimes, and gives an unpleasant dry wheeze. 1854 Emerson *Lett. & Soc. Aims, Resources* Wks. (Bohn) III. 197 This pump [*sc.* our globe] never sucks; these screws are never loose.

transf. 1710 C. Shadwell *Fair Quaker Deal* II. 27 The Bowl sucks; Empty is the Word.

†IV. 20. *trans.* To give suck to, suckle. *Obs.*

1607 Topsell *Four-f. Beasts* 671 So is this beast enabled by nature to beare twice in the yeare, and yet to sucke her young ones two monthes together. 1612 [see Opossum 1]. 1680 R. L'Estrange *Erasm. Colloq.* ii. 29 He had the Happiness to taste the Milk of the same Breast that suck'd our Saviour.

†V. 21. In trans. senses of Soak *v.*: **a.** To cause to sink in, instil. **b.** *To suck one's face*, to drink. *Obs.*

a. 1549 Coverdale, etc. *Erasm. Par. 1 Tim.* 16 Not bryngynge the sentence with the, that fauoure or malyce or dyspleasure or any other affeccion hath secretlye sowked into thee, but of the thing selfe in dede knowen.

b. a 1700 B. E. *Dict. Cant. Crew* s.v., *We'll go and Suck our Faces*,..let's go to Drink...*He loves to Suck his Face*, he delights in Drinking.

VI. Specialized uses with advs.

22. *trans.* With various advs.: To draw by suction in some direction.

1570 *Satir. Poems Reform.* xxiv. 80 That bludy Bouchour ever deit of thrist, Soukand the soules furth of the Sanctis of God. 1599 Shaks. *Hen. V*, IV. ii. 17 Your faire shew shall suck away their Soules, Leauing them but the shales and huskes of men. 1687 A. Lovell tr. *Thevenot's Trav.* I. 3 Two contrary Eddies.., which making Vessels turn round for some time, suck them down to the bottom without remedy. 1784 Cowper *Task* II. 103 The fixt and rooted earth, Tormented into billows,..with..hideous whirl Sucks down its prey. 1806 J. Beresford *Miseries Hum. Life* (ed. 3) II. x, One shoe suddenly sucked off by the boggy clay. 1873 G. C. Davies *Mount. & Mere* ii. 7 A head would pop up to suck some insect down. 1879 Browning *Ivan Ivanovitch* 26 The monstrous wild a-hungered to resume Its ancient sway, suck back the world into its womb.

23. Suck in.

a. *trans.* To draw into the mouth by suction; to inhale (air, etc.); *occas.* to draw in (one's breath), etc.

c 1220 *Bestiary* 514 Ðis cete ðanne hise chaueles lukeð, ðise fisses alle in sukeð. c 1400 Maundev. (1839) 205 Whan thei schulle eten or drynken, thei taken thorghe a Pipe..and sowken it in. c 1460 *Promp. Parv.* (Winch.) 461 Sokyn in diuers þyngis, or drynkyn yn, *imbibo*. 1686 tr. *Chardin's Trav. Persia* 341 There they suck in the fresh Air. 1706 E. Ward *Wooden World Diss.* 85 He sucks in Smoak like a Virginia-Planter. 1845 Disraeli *Sybil* (1863) 282, I have breathed this air for a matter of half a century. I sucked it in when it tasted of primroses. 1885 E. Greey *Bakin's Captive of Love* iv. (1904) 28 Sucking in his breath as he bowed respectfully.

b. To imbibe (qualities, etc.) *with* one's mother's milk, *with* a draught.

1622 Fletcher *Beggar's Bush* II. iii, I suck'd not in this patience with my milk. 1732 Berkeley *Alciphr.* I. v, The notions you first sucked in with your milk. 1781 Cowper *Hope* 518 The wretch, who once..suck'd in dizzy madness with his draught. 1848 W. K. Kelly tr. *L. Blanc's Hist. Ten Y.* II. 201 That fatal diversity which these different races had sucked in with their mother's milk.

c. *gen.* To draw or take in (*lit.* and *fig.*); to absorb.

1597 Donne *Lett. Sev. Pers., Storme* 62 Pumping hath tir'd our men, and what's the gaine? Seas into seas throwne, we suck in againe. 1603 B. Jonson *Sejanus* I. ii, Those deeds breath honor, that do suck in gaine. 1606 Shaks. *Tr. & Cr.* II. ii. 12 There is no Lady..More spungie, to sucke in the sense of Feare. 1678 Bunyan *Pilgr.* I. (1900) 56 These infirmities possessed me in thy Country, for there I suckt them in. 1728 Pope *Dunc.* III. 58 As..whirligigs twirl'd round by skilful swain, Suck the thread in, then yield it out again. a 1774 Goldsm. *Surv. Exp. Philos.* (1776) I. 64 Sometimes electric bodies suck in the electric fire, and sometimes they throw it out.

d. To take in by means of the perceptive faculties.

c 1600 Chalkhill *Thealma & Cl.* (1683) 10 With desire Her ears suck'd in her speech. 1667 Pepys *Diary* 17 Aug., I have sucked in so much of the sad story of Queen Elizabeth,..that I was ready to weep for her. 1669 Gale *Crt. Gentiles* I. II. viii. 116 This Persian Idolatrie, which the Israelites had suckt in. 1745 P. Thomas *Jrnl. Anson's Voy.* 240 They could not shake off the Prejudices they had sucked in. 1780 Mme. D'Arblay *Lett.* 27 April, The portion you allowed me of your..Journal, I sucked in with much pleasure and avidity. 1793 D'Israeli *Cur. Lit.* II. 112 He [*sc.* Jonson] would sit silent in learned company, and suck in (besides wine) their several humours into his observation.

e. To draw in, as into a whirlpool or vortex.

1616 J. Lane *Contn. Sqr.'s T.* IX. 273 Which..bothe sokes and bringes men in, Wheare none, at last, shall either save or winn. 1663 S. Patrick *Parab. Pilgr.* xxxvii. (1687) 486 The waters began to suck him in. 1728 Pope *Dunc.* II. 332 Sinking to the chin, Smit with his mien the Mud-nymphs suck'd him in. 1807 Wordsw. *Blind Highland Boy* 155 The tide retreated from the shore, And sucked, and sucked him in. 1849 Lyell *2nd Visit U.S.* (1850) II. 168 He had seen the water rush through the opening at the rate of ten miles an hour, sucking in several flat boats. 1856 Emerson *Eng. Traits, Wealth* Wks. (Bohn) II. 75 The poor-rate was sucking in the solvent classes.

f. *dial.* and *slang.* To take in, cheat, deceive.

1842 'Mrs. Clavers' *Forest Life* I. xiii. 135, I a'n't bound to drive nobody in the middle of the night,..so don't you try to suck me in there. c 1850 'Dow jr.' in Jerdan *Yankee Hum.* (1853) 113 The British got pretty nicely sucked in, when our Dutch grandaddies went to smoking on the Battery, and concealed it beneath a cloud of tobacco fume. 1909 *Westm. Gaz.* 15 May 2/3 You've tried to run a ship on the cheap and been sucked in.

g. *intr.* To curry favour *with*. *Sc.*

1899 Crockett *Kit Kennedy* 239 He tells tales on the rest of the scholars, to sook-in wi' the maister.

24. Suck out.

a. *trans.* To draw out or extract by or as by suction. Also in fig. context.

c 1375 *Sc. Leg. Saints* xi. (*Symon & Judas*) 321 Þa..bad þe edris suk owt faste al þe venyme. 1398 Trevisa *Barth. De P. R.* IV. vii. (1495) 90 Flyes and wormes that sytt on flesshe and sucke out the blode. c 1440 *Pallad. on Husb.* XI. 16 Sowe hit not, hit sowkith out the swete Of euery lond. 1535 Coverdale *Ps.* lxxiv. 8 As for the dregges therof, all yͤ vngodly of the earth shal drynke them, & sucke them out. 1563 T. Gale *Antidot.* I. ii. 2 It [a medicine] sucketh oute superfluous moysture in dropsyes. 1611 *Bible* Ezek. xxiii. 34 Thou shalt euen drinke it and sucke it out. 1618–19 Fletcher, etc. *Q. Corinth* II. iv, They look like potch'd Eggs with the souls suckt out Empty and full of wind. a 1700 Evelyn *Diary* 24 Aug. 1678, The flannell sucking out the moisture. 1753 *Chambers' Cycl.* Suppl. s. v. *Sucking*, The tip [of the tongue] is again employed to the sucking out more milk. 1843 Carlyle *Past & Pr.* II. iv. 78 Every fresh Jew sticking on him like a fresh horseleech, sucking his and our life out. 1865 Tylor *Early Hist. Man.* xiii. 363 They pretend to cure the sick by sucking out stones through their skin.

†b. To extract (information or profit). *Obs.*

1546 *St. Papers Hen. VIII*, XI. 14 His Majestes pleasure is, that sucking out as moche as ye may to what other condicions they will descende, you shall [etc.]. 1604 E. G[rimstone] *D'Acosta's Hist. Indies* To Rdr., Every one may sucke out some profit for himselfe.

†c. To drain. *Obs.*

1687 Miège *Gt. Fr. Dict.* II. s.v., He suckt out (or suckt up) the Bottle.

25. Suck up.

a. *trans.* To draw up into the mouth by suction. Also, †to drain the contents of.

a 1450 Myrc (1902) 1811 Ȝef a drope of blod..Falle vp-on þe corporas, Sowke hyt vp a-non-ryȝt. 1560 *Bible* (Geneva) Job xxxix. 33 His yong ones also sucke vp blood. 1577 B. Googe *Heresbach's Husb.* IV. (1586) 188 The Toade bloweth them, and sucketh them [*sc.* bees] vp at their owne doores. 1601 Shaks. *Jul. C.* II. i. 262 Is it Physicall To walke vnbraced, and sucke vp the humours Of the danke Morning? 1668 Wilkins *Real Char.* II. ix. § 2. 236 Sucking up the breath. 1687 [see 24 c]. 1774 Goldsm. *Nat. Hist.* (1776) IV. 264 The elephant dips the end of its trunk into the water, and sucks up just as much as fills that great fleshy tube. 1840 *Cuvier's Anim. Kingd.* 207 The Sun-birds..subsist on the nectar of flowers, which they suck up.

b. To draw up as by suction or the creation of a vacuum; to absorb (liquid); to draw up (moisture) by heat; also, to draw up moisture from.

1530 Palsgr. 742/2 As the yerthe, or a sponge sucketh up water. 1590 Shaks. *Mids. N.* II. i. 89 The Windes..haue suck'd vp from the sea Contagious fogges. 1604 Jas. I. *Counterbl. to Tobacco* (Arb.) 104 The smoakie vapours sucked vp by the Sunne. 1630 Drayton *Muses Eliz., Noah's Flood* 106 By this the Sunne had suckt vp the vaste deepe. 1683 Moxon *Mech. Exerc., Printing* xxiv. ₱ 19 He rubs it [*sc.* the sponge] over..the Tympan, to Suck up the Water. 1825 J. Nicholson *Oper. Mech.* 102 To prevent the formation of a vacuum in the rising bucket, or what is called by the miller 'sucking up the tail-water'. 1863 Kingsley *Water-Bab.* (1874) 55 The burning sun on the fells had sucked him up; but the damp heat of the woody crag sucked him up still more. 1877 Huxley *Physiogr.* 71 The thread constantly sucks up the liquid.

†c. To absorb by a mental process; to drink in.

1602 Marston *Antonio's Rev.* v. vi, May his stile..have gentle presence, and the sceans suckt up By calme attention of choyce audience. c 1610 *Women Saints* 89 The holie virgin..sucked vp and exhaled her maisters..praises of her celestiall Loues excellencie.

d. To swallow up.

1611 Shaks. *Cymb.* III. i. 22 Roaring Waters, With Sands that will not beare your Enemies Boates, But sucke them vp to' th' Top-mast. 1650 *Contemp. Hist. Irel.* (Ir. Archæol. Soc.) II. 101 This good service they haue don to his Majestie after shokinge up the sweete and substance of his Catholicke subjects of Monster. 1795 Gouv. Morris in Sparks *Life & Writ.* (1832) III. 52 Britain will suck up that commerce which formerly flowed to Amsterdam. 1869 Lowell *Dara* v, Wise Dara's province, year by year, Like a great sponge, sucked wealth and plenty up.

e. *intr.* *To suck up to*, to curry favour with; to toady to. (Also without *to*.) *Schoolboy slang.*

1860 *Hotten's Slang Dict.* (ed. 2) 231 *Suck up*, 'to suck up to a person', to insinuate oneself into his good graces. 1876 Annie Thomas *Blotted out* xvi, I can't suck up to snobs because they happen to be in power and to have patronage. 1899 E. Phillpotts *Human Boy* 203 Fowle sucked up to him..and buttered him at all times. 1905 H. A. Vachell *Hill* vi, 'Afterwards', John continued, 'I tried to suck-up. I asked you to come and have some food.'

Suck-, the verb-stem used in combination: **suck-fish** = Sucker *sb.* 11; †**suck-fist** [Fist *sb.*[2]], a toady; †**suck-giver** [f. phr. *give suck*: see Suck *v.* 16], a wet-nurse; †**suck-hole**?; **suck-jack** [partial transl. of Pg. *papa-jaca*, f. *papar* to swallow + *jaca* (locally) little crab], a fish (see quot.); **suck-lamb** [tr. G. *sauglamm*; cf. Sock-lamb], a sucking lamb; †**suck-nurse**, a wet-nurse; †**suck-pint** = Suck-bottle 2; †**suck-purse**, an extortioner; †**suck-spigot** = Suck-bottle 2; also *attrib.*; †**suck-stone**, a remora or sucking-fish; **suck-(a)-thumb**, a child that sucks its thumb; also *attrib.*

1753 *Chambers' Cycl.* Suppl., **Suck-fish*,..an English name for the *remora*, or *echeneis* of Artedi. 1758 W. Borlase *Nat. Hist. Cornw.* 269, I found on Careg-killas, in Mount's Bay, a particular kind of suck-fish [*Lepadogaster cornubiensis*]. 1876 Goode *Fishes of Bermudas* 61 *Leptecheneis naucrates* ..and *Ptheirichthys lineatus*..are probably the most common species of 'Suck-fish' found here. 1611 Cotgr., *Humevesne* [read *vesse*], a *sucke-fist. 1551 T. Wilson *Logic* (1580) 80 b, Wee Englishemen knowe (not onely by hearesaie, but also by good experince) that custome is the mother, and the *sucke giuer vnto all erroure. 1626 Middleton *Mayor of Queenb.* III. iii, I will learn the villany of all trades;..if in the brewer, I will taste him throughly, and piss out his iniquity at his own *suckhole. 1843 Lowe *Fishes Madeira* 177 *Sebastes Maderensis*..Little Rock-fish, or *Suck-jack. *Ibid.* 178 Its second Portuguese name of 'Papa-Jaca', or Suck-jack, it has earned by its troublesome addiction to hooks baited with the little crab 'Jaca'. 1887 *Daily News* 20 June 2/6 German *suck lamb, 5s 4d. c 1640 H. Bell *Luther's Colloq. Mens.* (1652) 315 They compelled women with childe and *suck-nurses to fast. 1611 Cotgr., *Humeux*, a *sucke-pinte, or swill-pot; a notable drunkard. 1586 Sir E. Hoby tr. *Coignet's Polit. Disc. Truth* 41 [They] winde themselues out of the handes of these *suckpurses [orig. *succebourses*]. 1585 Higins *Junius' Nomencl.* 425 *Ebriosus*,... a dronkard: a *suckspigget. 1639 Horn & Rob. *Gate Lang. Unl.* lxxxiv. § 823 A common drunkard (a suck-spiggot, swill-bowl) that is alwaies bibbing. 1661 K. W. *Conf. Charac., Cambr. Minion* (1860) 32 She's a fine finacle Cambridge production, got by and aiming no higher then some suckspicket sophister. 1602 *Withals' Dict.* 37 A little Fishe called a *Suckstone, yͭ staieth a ship vnder saile. 1661 Lovell *Hist. Anim. & Min.* 235 Suckstone. *Remora*. They are said by their magnetick vertue to stop ships. 18.. *Shock-headed Peter*, I said the Scissors Man would come, To disobedient *Suck-a-Thumb. 1890 E. Warren *Laughing Eyes* 50 A helpless suck-thumb infant.

Suckable (sʊ·kăb'l), *a.* and *sb. rare.* [f. Suck *v.* + -able.] **A.** *adj.* That can be sucked. **B.** *sb.* A suckable kind of food.

1846 M. Williams *Sanscr. Gram.* p. 9 This division of food into four kinds, lickables, drinkables, chewables, and suckables, is not unusual in Indian writings. 1865 *Morn. Star* Sept. 25 They sucked the sweets of all that was suckable.

Suckabob (sʊ·kăbǫb). *rare.* [f. Suck *v.*] A sweetmeat that is sucked in the mouth.

1888 J. Payn *Myst. Mirbridge* v, The British lollipop or suckabob.

Su·ck-bottle. [f. Suck- + Bottle *sb.*]

1. An infant's feeding-bottle. (Cf. Sucking-bottle.)

1641 Brome *Joviall Crew* v. Wks. 1873 450 Nephew Martin, still the Childe with a Suck-bottle of Sack. 1674 tr. *Scheffer's Lapland* xxvi. 123 Rain-deers milk..is grosser and thicker then they can well draw out of a suck-bottle. 1709 [W. King] *Usef. Trans. Philos.* Mar. & Apr. 56 The Child must have Presents of Silver Caudle-Cups, Porringers, Spoons, and Suck-Bottles. 1853 *Househ. Words* VIII. 146/1 They will furnish you with every assistance you can want; a valet-de-chambre,..a nurse-maid, and, thanks to the suck-bottle, even a nurse.

2. A tippler. Also as a quasi-proper name.

a 1652 Brome *Love-sick Crt.* v. ii, What sayes old Suck-bottle? 1707 Ward *Terræ-filius* No. 2. 9 Such a Swill-Belly'd Suck-Bottle.

Sucked (sʊkt), *ppl. a.* [f. Suck *v.* + -ed[1].] In various senses of the verb; extracted, absorbed, or depleted by suction.

Sucked orange: see Orange *sb.*[1] 1 b.

1600 Shaks. *A. Y. L.* IV. iii. 127 Did he leaue him there Food to the suck'd and hungry Lyonnesse? 1667 Milton *P. L.* x. 633 Nigh burst With suckt and glutted offal. 1824 Miss Ferrier *Inher.* lxxii, Pretty!—what makes her pretty?—wi' a face like a sooket carvy! 1857 W. E. Gladstone in Morley *Life* (1903) I. IV. viii. 561 But for Disraeli, who could not be thrown away like a sucked orange. 1881 Ensor *Journ. Nubia* viii. 73 The sucked and marrowless bones. 1904 *Brit. Med. Jrnl.* 17 Sept. 665 Some half dozen [maggots] which were filled with recently sucked blood. 1906 C. Mansfield *Girl & Gods* xxiii, The streets seemed filled with drunkards, sucked oranges, hot chestnuts, sore noses and chilblains. 1909 Oxenham *Great-Heart Gillian* xliii. 310 Baby Gillian..waved a sucked pink thumb at him and his men.

b. *Sucked stone*, a honeycombed stone occurring in the tin lodes of Cornwall.

1778 Pryce *Min. Cornub.* 90 The Lode itself..is cavernous, and full of holes, thence called a Sucked Stone by the Tinners. 1814 W. Phillips in *Trans. Geol. Soc.* II. 118.

Su·ck-egg. [f. Suck- + Egg *sb.*[1]] **a.** An animal that is reputed to suck eggs, e.g. a weasel, cuckoo; *fig.* an avaricious person. **b.** A young fellow; *slang*, 'a silly person' (Barrère & Leland).

1609 Armin *Maids of More-Cl.* Ciij b, Where's this suck-egge, where's Jack a boy? 16.. Middleton, etc. *Old Law* III. ii, This beard cannot get children, you lank suck-eggs, Unless such weasels come from court to help us. c 1640 [Shirley] *Capt. Underwit* v. i. in Bullen *Old Pl.* (1883) II. 395 Con. Is there not a weesill crept into your Chamber, lady?..A Mounsier sucklegge [*sic*]. *Sis.* Do you take my Chamber for a henns neast? 1685 Crowne *Sir C. Nice* II, A Scholler Madam? a Schollers Egg—emptyed by old suck-Eggs, of all that Nature gave me. 1836 Haliburton *Clockm.* Ser. I. v. (1839) 12, I guess, said he, if General Campbell knew what sort of a man that are magistrate was, he'd disband him pretty quick, he's a regular suck-egg. 1851 Sternberg *Dial. Northants.* 109 *Suck*, *Suck-egg*, the cuckoo; also applied to a stupid fellow.

c. *attrib.* That sucks eggs.

1631 Quarles *Hist. Samson* Wks. (Grosart) II. 141 The suck-egge Weasell. 1658 Rowland tr. *Moufet's Theat. Ins.* 934 Of the first kinde is the Flesh-fly, Horse-fly, Oxe-fly, the Suck-egge-fly.

Sucken (sʊ·kən), *sb.*[1] *Sc.* Forms: 5 **sukkin**, **swken**, 5–7 **suckin**, 6 **su(c)kyn**, 9 **shucken**, 7– **sucken**. [Variant of Soken. The orig. meaning is 'resort' (*sc.* to a particular mill).]

1. The duty and liability of tenants within a district astricted to a mill. (See Thirlage 2 and cf. Soken 2 b.) †Also *occas.* the meal ground at such a mill.

1423 *Charters, etc. of Edinb.* (1871) 55 With the suckins, thryl multris, and al freedomes langand thairto. 1488 *Acta Dom. Audit.* (1839) 124/2 þe wrangwis withhalding of þe þrell multure and sukkin awing to þe said alexandris mylne. 15.. *Aberd. Reg.* V. 16 (Jam.), He com nocht to grynd his quhyt in thair mill as he that aucht suckyn thareto. 1641 *Acts Parl. Scot., Chas. I* (1814) V. 657/1 Sex bollis of moulter or suckin quhilkis perteinet to the Carmelite freires of the said burcht. 1711 in *Nairne Peerage Evidence* (1874) 138 All and haill the lands of Hardhaugh and Chimieshill with yͤ multures suckens sequells and knaveship therof. 1806 R. Jamieson *Pop. Ballads* I. 294 Her daddie, a cannie ald carl, Had shucken and mouter a fouth.

2. The lands astricted to a mill; = Thirl *sb.*[2] 1 c; also, the population of such lands.

Cf. Insucken, Outsucken.

1754 Erskine *Princ. Law Scot.* II. ix. (1757) 210 The lands astricted, (which are called also the thirle or sucken). 1799 J. Robertson *Agric. Perth* 397 The greatest difficulty arises, where the mill belongs to one proprietor and the sucken to another. 1820 Scott *Monast.* xiii, Those of the Sucken, or enthralled ground, were liable in penalties, if, deviating from this thirlage,..they carried their grain to another mill. 1872 Innes *Lect. Scot. Legal Antiq.* ii. 47 The sucken, as we call the population thirled to a mill.

b. *transf.* The area of a bailiff's jurisdiction; the district within which one practises or carries on business.

a 1688 J. Wallace *Descr. Orkney* (1693) 93 Sucken, A Bailiffrie, so much ground as is vnder the Bailiffs Jurisdiction. 1871 W. Alexander *J. Milne's Songs & Poems* Introd. p. ix, He afterwards commenced business as a shoemaker..in the parish of Durris, where he had a sufficient 'sucken' to employ two men besides himself. 1871 — *Johnny Gibb* (1873) 117 The younger Dr. Drogemweal, who had settled 'doon throu'', so as to be beyond the limits of his father's 'sucken'.

Hence **Su·ckener**, a tenant of a sucken; **Su·ckening**, the astriction of tenants to a mill.

1636 *Reg. Mag. Sig. Scot.* 215/2 In *lie suckning, thirling*, et astringendo burgenses. 1754 Erskine *Princ. Law Scot.* II. ix. (1757) 214 Where there is neither an explicite constitution of thirlage, nor proof of services of any sort, performed by the suckeners, the dominant tenement can claim none. 1797 *Statist. Acc. Scot.* XIX. 67 The millers..oppress the suckeners. 1820 Scott *Monast.* xiii. *note*, Perquisites demanded by the miller, and submitted to or resisted by the Suckener as circumstances permitted.

Su·cken, *sb.*[2] *dial.* Also -an. [Obscure formation on the root of Suck *v.*] Wet, moisture; liquid manure; = Sock *sb.*[3] 2, 2 b. Hence **Su·ckeny** *a.*

1615 W. Lawson *Country Housew. Garden* (1626) 7 The sucken of your Dwelling-house, descending into your Orchard (if it be cleanly conueighed) is good. *Ibid.* 41 The earth that feeds them decaying..must either haue supply of sucken, or else leaue thriuing and growing. 1878 *Cumberld. Gloss.*, *Suckan* [mispr. *Suckam*]..*Suckeny land*, moist land of good quality.

Su·cken, *a. rare.* [Short for *bond-sucken* (cf. *love-soken* s.v. Love *sb.* 16), properly a sb. = compulsory resort of a tenant to a mill for the grinding of his corn.] Astricted *to* a mill; = Thirl *a.*

[1523 Fitzherb. *Surv.* 9 b, The lordes tenauntes be called bonde socon. 1859 Dickinson *Gloss. Words & Phr. Cumberld.* 11 Some farms are bound by tenure to carry their corn to the manorial mill to be multured and ground, and are 'bond-sucken' to that mill.]

1878 J. Davidson *Inverurie* Introd. 7 The corns sucken to the mill. *Ibid.* v. 178 Conglass and Drumnies were sucken to the very ancient Mill of Inveramsay. 1882 in *Jamieson's Sc. Dict.*

†**Sucken,** obs. Sc. pa. pple. of Sink *v.* (Cf. *drucken*.)

1535 Stewart *Cron. Scot.* (Rolls) I. 20 His cristell eyne wes suckin in his heid.

Su·ckeny. *Hist.* Also 4 **sukkenye**, 7 **surkney**, 9 **suckeney**. [a. OF. *soucanie*, also *sor-*, *surquanie* (earlier *soschanie*, *sousquenie*, cf. med.L. *soscania*) of Slavonic origin (cf. Polish *suknia* coat), whence also MHG. *sukkenîe*.] A smock.

? a 1366 Chaucer *Rom. Rose* 1232 She hadde on a sukkenye [16th c. edd. suckeny; orig. F. *sorquanie*] That not of hempe ne heerdis was. 1658 Phillips, *Surkney*, a kind of white garment like a rotchet. [1834 Planché *Brit. Costume* 113 The sosquenie, surquayne, or suckeney was an exterior garment at this period [viz. temp. Edw. I]. 1885 Dillon *Fairholt's Costume Eng.* II. 387 *Sukkenye*, a loose frock.]

Sucker (sʊ·kəɹ), *sb.* Forms: 4 **souker(e**, 5 **sokare**, **-ere**, **sowker**, **sucour**, 6 **socar**, *Sc.* **soukar**, 6–7 **succor**, **suckar**, 7 **soker**, **succur**, **shucker**, 9 (in sense 4) **succour**, *dial.* **sooker**, 6– **sucker**. [f. Suck *v.* + -er[1].]

I. 1. A young mammal before it is weaned; †a child at the breast (*even-sucker*, see Even- 2); now *spec.* a sucking-pig; a young whale-calf.

See also Rabbit-sucker (†*rabbit's sucker*).

1382 Wyclif *2 Macc.* ix. 29 Philip, his euen souker [Vulg. *collactaneus ejus*]. c 1440 *Promp. Parv.* 463/1 Sokere, or he þat sokythe, *sugens*. c 1460 [see Rabbit-sucker 1]. a 1549 in *Gentl. Mag.* (1813) May 417 Rabetts socars the dozen, xviij d. 1591 Percivall *Sp. Dict.*, *Mamanton o mamon*, a sucker. 1607 Topsell *Four-f. Beasts* 673 Although the fœcundity of Swine bee great, yet it is better to kil off two or three,..for this multitude of suckers do quickly draw away all nourishment from the dam. c 1614 Fletcher *Wit at Sev. Weapons* III. i, *Sir Gr.* I promise you, not a house-Rabbit, Sir. *Old K.* No sucker on 'em all. 1701 C. Wolley *Jrnl. New York* (1860) 38 Their [*sc.* whales'] young Suckers come along with them their several courses. 1836 *Uncle Philip's Convers. Whale Fishery* 253, I saw the whale with its sucker. 1878 *Ure's Dict. Arts* IV. Suppl. 380 Racks, or young rabbits about two months old..and suckers, or very young rabbits. 1883 *Standard* 11 June 6/3 The inquiry [for pigs] was restricted, at less money for suckers. 1908 T. F. Dale *Riding & Polo Ponies* iii. 45 Fillies should be taken off the moors as suckers.

b. *fig.* A greenhorn, simpleton. *U.S.*

1857 *San Francisco Call* 5 Dec. (Thornton *Amer. Gloss.*), You may think I'm a sucker. 1904 E. Robins *Magnetic North* viii. 153 Goin' out to stir up a boom, and sell his claim to some sucker.

2. One who or that which sucks with the mouth.

Cf. the animal-names Blood-sucker, Goatsucker, Honey-sucker.

c 1440 *Promp. Parv.* 463/1 Sokare of mylke, or sokerel that longe sokythe, *mammotrepus*. 1596 *Extr. Aberd. Reg.* (1848) II. 168 Devoraris and suckeris of the blude and substance of the pure. 1611 Cotgr. s.v. *Tetard*, A great sucker, a child that sucketh much. 1861 *Jrnl. R. Agric. Soc.* XXII. I. 147 The fastest sucker will have an undue share of the milk.

3. One who lives at the expense of another; one who draws profit or extorts subsistence from some source; *U.S. slang*, a sponger, parasite.

1500–20 Dunbar *Poems* lxiii. 41 Soukaris [*pr.* sonkaris], groukaris, gledaris, gunnaris. a 1548 Hall *Chron., Hen. VI*, 159 Flatterers to the kyng.., suckers of his purse and robbers of his subiectes. 1589 [? Lyly] *Pappe w. Hatchet* To Rdr., I knowe there is none of honour so carelesse..that wil succor those that be suckers of the Church. 1728 Ramsay *Gen. Mistake* 140 This sucker thinks nane wise, But him that can to immense riches rise. 1856 Dow *Serm.* III. (Bartlett) Those suckers belonging to the body loaferish, whose sole study appears to be to see how much they can get without the least physical exertion.

4. A shoot thrown out from the base of a tree or plant, which in most cases may serve for propagation; now *esp.* such a shoot rising from the root under ground, near to, or at some distance from, the trunk; also (now *rare*), a runner (as of the strawberry); also, a lateral shoot; in the tobacco plant, an axillary shoot (cf. Sucker *v.* 2).

1577–82 Breton *Toyes of Idle Head* Wks. (Grosart) I. 54/1 If suckers draw the sappe from bowes on hie, Perhaps in tyme the top of tree may die. 1591 Percivall *Sp. Dict.*, *Pimpollo*, a succor that groweth out of the bodies of trees, *Stolo*. 1615 W. Lawson *Country Housew. Garden* (1626) 4 The roots of Apples and Peares..will put forth suckers, which are a great hinderance. 1669 Worlidge *Syst. Agric.* (1681) 129 Filberds are generally drawn as Suckers from the old Trees. 1682 G. Rose *Sch. Instruct. Officers Month* 154 Take the Succors or Stalks of these Roman Lettice, and peel of the leaves and skins. 1686 *Phil. Trans.* XVII. 982 When the top-bud [of the tobacco plant] is gone, it puts forth no more Leaves, but Side-branches, which they call Suckers. a 1700 Evelyn *Diary* 12 Sept. 1641, Out of whose stem, neere the roote, issue 5 upright and exceeding tall suckers or boles. 1707 Mortimer *Husb.* (1721) II. 188 Spanish Broom is not much unlike the yellow Jessamine...It..is increased by Seeds or Suckers. 1766 *Complete Farmer* s.v. *Quince-tree*, Suckers are the worst to raise them from; and cuttings are generally preferred to layers. 1772–84 *Cook's Voy.* (1790) I. 279 Pine-apples..grow so luxuriantly that seven or eight suckers have been seen adhering to one stem. 1807 *Med. Jrnl.* XVII. 374 Stem upright,..bare at base, at top leafy, branched, never throwing out succours. 1815 J. Smith *Panorama Sci. & Art* II. 688 Clear the strawberries from suckers. 1842 Loudon *Suburban Hort.* 239 Plants are propagated either by seed, or by division: the latter mode including cuttings, joints, leaves, layers, suckers, slips, budding, grafting, and inarching. 1870 Hooker *Stud. Flora* 107 The Dwarf Cherry forms a bush with copious suckers. 1877 Aug. Morris *Tobacco* 45 The tobacco plant shoots up its stalk at top, sending out some four or five main suckers branchwise.

b. *fig.* (freq. with reference to the withdrawal of nourishment from the parent stem).

1591 Greene *2nd Pt. Conny Catch.* Ep. Ded., Wks. (Grosart) X. 73 If the honorable and worshipfull of this land looke into their liues, and cut off such vpstarting suckars that consume the sap from the roote of the Tree. 1642 Fuller *Holy & Prof. St.* III. v. 163 If thou payest nothing, they will count thee a sucker, no branch. 1688 Norris *Theory & Regul. Love* II. iii. 113 This [*sc.* self-love] is the great Sucker of Society, and that which robbs the Body Politick of its due nourishment. 1777 Sheridan *Sch. Scandal* II. iii, For my part I hate to see prudence clinging to the green suckers of youth. 1792 in *Ld. Auckland's Corr.* (1861) II. 428, I have no olive-branches round my table, and I stand like a blasted pollard without a sucker to survive me. 1818 Hallam *Mid. Ages* VIII. ii. (1819) III. 382 A manufacturing district..sends out, as it were, suckers into all its neighbourhood. 1827 J. F. Cooper *Prairie* III. v. 160, I am a sycamore, that once covered many with my shadow...But a single succour is springing from my roots. 1858 Stanley *Life of Arnold* I. v. 215 A living sucker from the mother country. 1876 Geo. Eliot *Dan. Der.* xxx, This woman whose life he had allowed to send such deep suckers into his had a terrible power of annoyance in her.

5. An organ adapted for sucking or absorbing nourishment by suction, *e.g.* the proboscis of an insect, the mouth of a cyclostomous fish, a siphonostomous crustacean, etc.

1665 *Phil. Trans.* XV. 1158 The Sucker or Proboscis.. wherewith the Bee sucks the Honey from the flowers. 1771 *Ann. Reg.* II. 169/1 Corals and sea-pens protrude or draw back their suckers. 1817 Kirby & Sp. *Entomol.* xvii. II. 88 Their sucker being inserted in the tender bark, is without intermission employed in absorbing the sap. 1868 Stark *Elem. Nat. Hist.* II. 247 The mouth consisting of a rostrum, from which a syphon or sucker is protruded at will. *Ibid.*, Pediculus..; mouth consisting of a rostrum, inclosing an exsertile sucker. 1899 *Allbutt's Syst. Med.* VIII. 866 When the sucker [of the louse] is taken out a tiny blood mark appears on the surface [of the human skin].

6. Any fish having a conformation of the lips which suggests that it feeds by suction; *esp.* North American cyprinoid fishes of the family *Catostomidæ*.

1772 *Phil. Trans.* LXIII. 155 The fourth and last fish brought from Hudson's Bay is there called a Sucker, because it lives by suction. 1806 Pike *Sources Mississ.* (1810) 60 They..raise plenty of Irish potatoes, catch pike, suckers, pickerel, and white fish in abundance. 1848 Bartlett *Dict. Amer.*, *Sucker*, a very common fish of the genus *labeo*, and of which there are many varieties, including the Chub, Mullet, Barbel, Horned Dace, etc. 1888 Goode *Amer. Fishes* 16 The destructive inroads of sturgeon, cat-fish and suckers upon the spawning beds in Lake Pepin.

b. *U.S.* An inhabitant of the state of Illinois.

For the alleged origin of the term see quot. 1833.

1833 C. F. Hoffman *Winter in Far West* (1835) I. 207 There was a long-haired 'hooshier' from Indiana, a couple of smart-looking 'suckers' from the southern part of Illinois, a keen-eyed leather-belted 'badger' from the mines of Ouisconsin. [*note*, So called after the fish of that name, from his going up the river to the mines, and returning at the season when the sucker makes its migrations]. 1838 Haliburton *Clockm.* Ser. II. xix. (1839) 258 There's the hoosiers of Indiana, the suckers of Illinoy, the pukes of Missuri [etc.]. 1856 Emerson *Eng. Traits, Race*, I found abundant points of resemblance between the Germans of the Hercynian Forest and our 'Hoosiers', 'Suckers', and 'Badgers', of the American woods.

7. Used as a book-rendering of *Suctoria*, the name of various groups of animals having a sucking apparatus.

1835–6 *Todd's Cycl. Anat.* I. 771/1 The suckers..live almost invariably attached to their prey. a 1843 South *Zool.* in *Encycl. Metrop.* (1845) VII. 275/1 Edwards.. arranges the Crustaceans in the three sub-classes: 1. Suckers ..; 2. Xyphosures..; 3. Masticators.

8. The embolus, piston, or rising-valve of a pump; the piston of a syringe or an air-pump.

1611 Cotgr., *Soupape*,..the Supper, or Sucker of a Pumpe. 1634 J. B[ate] *Myst. Nat.* 7 No engine for water workes.. can be made without the help of Succurs, Forcers, or Clackes. 1653 H. More *Antid. Ath.* II. ii. § 9 The Sucker of the Air-pump, the Cylinder being well emptied of the Air, should draw up above an hundred pound weight. 1712 J. James tr. *Le Blond's Gardening* 192 Almost all Water-Engines are reducible to the Bucket and Sucker. 1837 W. B. Adams *Carriages* 113 If the sucker of a pump be allowed to get dry it fails to draw up the water. 1862 Smiles *Engineers* III. 10 When the pump descends, there is heard a plunge..: then, as it rises, and the sucker begins to act [etc.].

9. †a. *Anat.* = Emulgent *sb.* *Obs.*

1615 Crooke *Body of Man* 145 The other veine, of his office is called the emulgent or sucker.

†b. An absorbent substance. In *fig.* context.

1605 Bacon *Adv. Learn.* II. 34 The entrie of doubts are as so many suckers or sponges, to drawe vse of knowledge.

†c. One of a number of 'buckets' attached to a moving chain. *Obs.*

1686 Plot *Staffordsh.* 148 The chain is made with leather suckers upon it at little distances, which bring up water, and discharge themselves into a trough.

d. A pipe or tube through which anything is drawn by suction; *locally*, a hood over a fire-place.

1755 *Churchw. Acc. Wolsingham* (MS.) Sucker in yͤ Vestery Chimnay, 3s. od. 1838 T. Thomson *Chem. Org. Bodies* 602 All the oil passed over with the water...It was separated from the water by means of a sucker. 1848 Bartlett *Dict. Amer.*, *Sucker*, a tube used for sucking sherry-cobblers. They are made of silver, glass, straw, or sticks of maccaroni. 1876 *Whitby Gloss.*, *Sooker*, in old dwellings, a brick hood or canopy..projecting over the fire for focalizing the air current.

e. An air-hole fitted with a valve; a valve for the regulation of the flow of air.

1797 *Monthly Mag.* III. 303 When the bellows is opened, one of its sides becomes filled with ordinary air, by means of a sucker placed next to the moving leaf. 1833 Loudon *Encycl. Archit.* § 1975 In long conduit pipes, air-holes.. terminating in inverted valves or suckers, should be made at convenient distances. 1881 C. A. Edwards *Organs* 42 In the middle-board are placed suckers, *i.e.*, holes provided with leather valves on the top.

f. *Bot.* = Haustorium.

1849 Balfour *Man. Bot.* § 122 In parasites..such as Dodder..,roots are sometimes produced in the form of suckers, which enter into the cellular tissue of the plant preyed upon. 1856 Henslow *Dict. Bot. Terms*, *Sucker*,..a tubercular process..on the stems of certain flowering parasites.

II. 10. A part or organ adapted for adhering to an object; the adhesive pad of an insect's foot, etc.; a suctorial disk, foot, etc.

1681 Grew *Musæum* I. 105 This Fish [*i. e.* Remora] is able to fasten himself to any great Fish, Boat, or Ship, with the help of the Coronet or Sucker on his Head. 1817 Kirby & Sp. *Entomol.* xxiii. II. 320 Those [insects] that climb by the aid of suckers, which adhere..by the pressure of the atmosphere. 1851 Carpenter *Man. Phys.* (ed. 2) 521 The arms of the Cuttle-fish, which are furnished with great numbers of contractile suckers. 1897 *Allbutt's Syst. Med.* II. 1007 These, the suckers and hooklets, serve to attach the parasite to the mucous membrane of the alimentary canal of the host.

11. Any fish characterized by a suctorial disk by which it adheres to foreign objects; *e.g.* fishes of the genus *Cyclopterus* (cf. *lump-sucker* s.v. Lump *sb.*[2]), the genus *Liparis* (sea-snails or snail-fishes), the remora (*Echeneis*).

1753 *Chambers' Cycl.* Suppl. App., *Sucker*, or *Suck-fish* [i. e. *Remora*]. 1776 Pennant *Brit. Zool.* III. pl. xxi, Unctuous Sucker. *Ibid.* pl. xxii, Bimaculated Sucker. Jura Sucker. 1828 Fleming *Hist. Brit. Anim.* 189 *L[epadogaster] cornubiensis*. Cornish Sucker. 1863 Couch *Brit. Fishes* II. 195 Network Sucker..*Liparis reticulatus*. 1898 Morris *Austral Eng.* 443 *Sucker*, name given in New Zealand to the fish *Diplocrepis puniceus*.

12. A toy, consisting of a round piece of leather with a string attached at the centre, which, laid wet upon a solid surface and drawn up by the string, adheres by reason of the vacuum created.

1681 Grew *Musæum* I. 105 Those round Leathers, wherewith Boys are us'd to play, called Suckers, one of which, not above an inch and ½ diametre, being well soaked in water, will stick so fast to a Stone [etc.]. 1832 Brewster *Nat. Magic* x. 260 The leathern suckers used by children for lifting stones. 1906 O. Onions *Drakestone* xxix, The lad was..cutting a round sucker of leather.

III. 13. *local.* A sweet, a 'suck'.

1823 E. Moor *Suff. Words* 408 *Suckers*, a longish sort of a sweety. 1893 Kipling *Many Invent.* 168 We've played 'em for suckers so often. 1898 *Tit-Bits* 30 Apr. 85/2 'Young bloods' of the town who buy their 'Suckers' and weeds at the shop.

IV. 14. *attrib.* and *Comb.*, as (sense 10) *sucker-bearing*, *-like*, *-shaped* ppl. adjs.; **sucker-cup**, **-foot** = *sucking-cup*, *-foot* (see Sucking *vbl. sb.* 3 b); **sucker-fish** = senses 6 and 11, Sucking-fish; **sucker-rod** (see quots.).

1857 Gosse *Omphalos* vii. 171 In the adult the *sucker-bearing shoots frequently run to a considerable distance. 1883 *Encycl. Brit.* XVI. 674/2 The sucker-bearing arms of male Dibranchiate Siphonopods. 1845 Gosse *Ocean* vi. (1849) 306 There is placed in each *sucker-cup of the long feet [of squids, etc.], a sharp projecting hook. 1867 Smyth *Sailor's Word-bk.* 568 The *sucker-fish. It has a long oval plate on the top of the head, by which..it clings to a ship's bottom. 1889 *Nature* 17 Jan. 285/2 The Employment of the Sucker-fish (Echeneis) in Turtle-fishing. 1898 *Proc. Zool. Soc.* Nov. 589 A small sucker-fish of the genus *Lepadogaster*. 1870 Rolleston *Anim. Life* 141 The water-vascular canal supplying the ambulacral *sucker-feet. 1846 Dana *Zooph.* iv. (1848) 31 Tentacles, which affix themselves by a *sucker-like action. 1875 Knight *Dict. Mech.* 2442/2 **Sucker-rod*, a rod connecting the brake of a pump with the bucket. 1881 Raymond *Mining Gloss.*, *Sucker-rod*, the pump-rod of an oil-well. 1840 *Cuvier's Anim. Kingd.* 471 *Limnocharis*, Latr., has the mouth *sucker-shaped.

Sucker (sʊ·kəɹ), *v.* Also 8 **succour**. [f. prec.]

†1. *trans.* To fit or provide with a sucker or valve. *Obs. rare*[−1].

1660 R. D'Acres *Elem. Water-drawing* iv. 33 The water will not follow after, though you suck never so strongly, and sucker it never so closely.

2. To remove superfluous young shoots from (tobacco or maize plants); † also, to remove (the shoots).

a 1661 Fuller *Worthies, Glouc.* (1662) 349 Many got great estates thereby, notwithstanding the great care and cost in.. suckering, topping,..making and rowling it [*sc.* tobacco]. 1705 R. Beverley *Virginia* II. § 20 (1722) 128, I am inform'd they [*sc.* Indians] used to let it all run to Seed, only succouring the Leaves, to keep the Sprouts from growing upon, and starving them. 1779 *Ann. Reg.* 107/1 Care must be taken to nip off the sprouts that will be continually springing up at the junction of the leaves with the stalks. This is termed 'suckering the tobacco'. 1817–18 Cobbett *Resid. U.S.* (1822) 94 Fifteen acres of good Indian corn, well planted, well suckered, and well tilled in all respects. 1908 Mary Johnston *Lewis Rand* xiv. 162 I've wanted power ever since I went barefoot and suckered tobacco.

3. *intr.* To throw up suckers. Also occas. *pass.*, to be thrown up as a sucker.

1802 *Trans. Soc. Arts* XX. 369 When those [plants] I have now planted begin to sucker. 1894 *Times* 21 Feb. 4/3 Plants of Sisal hemp suckered in fourteen months. 1894 Blackmore *Perlycross* 256 As straight as a hazel wand sucker'd from the root.

Hence **Suckering** *vbl. sb.* in sense 2 (also *attrib.*).

1817–18 Cobbett *Resid. U.S.* (1822) 138 Where would the hands come from to do the marking; the dropping and covering of the Corn;..the suckering when that work is done, as it always ought to be? 1877 Aug. Morris *Tobacco* 44 In suckering, the work is done with both hands, commencing at the top of the plant. 1881 *Encycl. Brit.* XII. 235/1 The soil should be carefully opened and the shoots removed with a suckering iron.

Sucker: see Succour, Sugar.

Suckered (sʊ·kəɹd), *ppl. a.* [f. Sucker *sb.* + -ed[2].] Of an organ: Provided with suckers.

1855 Kingsley *Glaucus* (1878) 163 Small cuttle-fish..with a ring of suckered arms round their tiny parrots' beaks. 1879 Spencer *Data of Ethics* ii. § 4. 12 The cephalopod ..using its suckered arms at one time for anchoring itself and at another for holding fast its prey.

Suckered, Sc. form of Sugared.

Suckerel (sʊ·kĕrĕl). Also 5 **sokerel**. [f. Suck *v.*: see -rel.]

1. A suckling; *esp.* a sucking foal.

c 1440 *Promp. Parv.* 463/1 Sokare of mylke, or sokerel that longe sokythe, *mammotrepus*. 1813 *Sporting Mag.* XLI. 37 Six suckerels averaged the sum of 37l 16s 8d each.

2. A catostomous fish, *Sclerognathus* (*Cycleptus*) *elongatus*, of the Mississippi and Ohio Rivers.

1888 Goode *Amer. Fishes* 436 The Black Horse,..also called 'Missouri Sucker',..'Suckerel' and 'Shoenaber'.

†Su·cket. *Obs.* Forms: 5 **soket**, 6 **suckitte**, **-otte**, **sucoet**, **suk(k)ett**, **sok(k)ett**, 6–7 **socket**, **suckett**, 6–8 **sucket**. [Altered form of Succate after Suck *v.* and -et.] = Succade.

1481–90 *Howard Househ. Bks.* (Roxb.) 42 Item, soket viij. li. vj. onces viij.s. vj.d. 1509 *Test. Ebor.* (Surtees) V. 5 Comfettes, sugir plattes, and suckittes. 1542 *Ibid.* VI. 167 A longe silver spone for sokett, a longe forke of silver for sokett. 1544 Phaer *Regim. Lyfe* (1553) E.ij, Sucket of citrons. 1611 Cotgr., *Carbassat*, wet sucket, made of the vpper part of the long white Pompion, cut in slices. 1615 Markham *Eng. Housew.* ii. 78 Your preserued fruites shall be disht vp first, your Pastes next, your wet Suckets after them, then your dried Suckets. 1662 Hibbert *Body Div.* I. 77 Pope Alexander poysoned the Turks brother in candid suckets. 1688 Holme *Armoury* III. iii. 80/1 Dried Sweetmeats & Suckets of Oranges. 1751 *Affect. Narr. H.M.S. Wager* 7 Here is plenty of Citrons, of which they make a fine Sweet-meat, or Sucket.

b. *transf.* and *fig.*

1607 Walkington *Optic Glass* 27 This made the Castalianist..to bee esteemed..the Marmalade and Sucket of the Muses. 1635 Brathwait *Arcadian Princ.* III. 214 Celsus a theevish Poet..was arraign'd..For stealing Suckets from an others hive. 1654 Cleveland *Poems* 4 Natures confectioner, the Bee, Whose suckets are moist Alchimie.

c. As a term of endearment.

1605 *Tryall Chev.* II. i, Peace, good Thomasin, silence, sweet socket.

d. *attrib.* and *Comb.*

1575 Laneham *Let.* (1871) 23 The bridecup, foormed of a sweet sucket barrell. 1636 Davenant *Witts* II. i, Now does my blood wamble! you! Sucket eater!

¶ Reliable evidence for the survival of *sucket* in mod. dialects is wanting. Halliwell's entry *sucket*, a young rabbit, is clearly an error for *sucker*.

†Su·ckey, *a. slang. Obs. rare*[−0]. [f. Suck *sb.*[1] or *v.* + -ey, -y.] (See quot.)

a 1700 B. E. *Dict. Cant. Crew*, *Suckey*, drunkish, maudlin, half Seas o'er.

Suck-eye, variant of Sockeye.

†Sucking, *sb. Obs.* [f. Suck *sb.*[2]] (See quot.)

1499 *Placitum* in Blount *Law Dict.* (1691) s. v., Per *Sucking*, hoc est fore quiet. de illis americiamentis, quando *in Burlimen*, id est, supervisores del Ringyord,..præmonit. fuerint ad imparcand. & faciend. clausuras illas simul cum vicinis suis, ille qui non venit ad talem præmonitionem amerciatus erit ad pretium unius vomeris, Anglice a *Suck*, prætii quatuor denar.

Sucking (sʊ·kiŋ), *vbl. sb.* [f. Suck *v.* + -ing[1].]

1. The action of the verb Suck; suction. Also, an instance of this.

c 1375 *Sc. Leg. Saints* xi. (*Symon & Judas*) 324 Þai wechis, þat had mare care of þat swkyne þan þai had yare. 1382 Wyclif *Gen.* xxi. 8 Thanne the child growide and was don awey fro sowkyng. 14.. *Tundale's Vis.* 123 Thou blestful quene of kyngis emperes That gaf thi son sowkyng in a stall. c 1440 *Jacob's Well* 231 Whan þe modyr wanyth here child, sche wetyth here tetys wyth sum byttere thyng, & so þe chyld felyng ofte þat bytternes leuyth his soukyng. 1573 Tusser *Husb.* (1878) 84 Otes with hir sucking a peeler is found. 1581 *Satir. Poems Reform.* xliii. 44 Preseruit from slauchter be sucking of a beir. 1596 Dalrymple tr. *Leslie's Hist. Scot.* I. 91 Meil quhilke throuch souking thay fed vpon. 1599 A. M. tr. *Gabelhouer's Bk. Physicke* 267/2 Nether must we afther his meates and suckinges, dandle it much. 1688 Holme *Armoury* III. xx. (Roxb.) 234 An Instrument or pipe..made of this forme, will cause the water by sucking to rise vp and run forth. 1727 *Philip Quarll* (1816) 61 Reserving only one for sucking of the old ones, to keep them in milk. 1885 *Daily News* 13 Feb. 5/1 There are very powerful engines which do the blowing and the sucking through these tubes. 1892 Carmichael *Dis. Children* 387 The child should be fed at regular intervals from both breasts at each sucking.

†b. *transf.* = Suction 1 c. *Obs.*

1656 Ridgley *Pract. Physick* 10 Appetite wanting. If there be no sucking, the forces cannot fail, and there are signs of repletion.

2. *pl.* What is obtained by suction. *rare.*

1387–8 T. Usk *Test. Love* I. iv. (Skeat) l. 27 The olde soukinges whiche thou haddest of me arn amaystred and lorn fro al maner of knowing. 1809 Malkin *Gil Blas* X. x. (Rtldg.) 371 To dip in my four fingers and thumb, and then to sup like a bear upon suckings.

3. *attrib.* and *Comb.*, as *sucking operation*, *power*; †**sucking-bone**, ? a marrowbone; **sucking-cushion**, **-pad**, a lobulated mass of fat occupying the space between the masseter and the external surface of the buccinator; †**sucking-pipe**, a pipe used for drawing air or water in some direction; †**sucking-pot** = Sucking-bottle 1; †**sucking-tooth** = Milk-tooth; **sucking-tube**, a tube through which liquid is sucked into the mouth; †**sucking-young** *adj.*, young enough to be still sucking the dam.

1648 Hexham II, *Een Zuygh-been*, a *Sucking-bone. a 1907 Sutton in *Piersol's Human Anat.* 493 The *sucking cushions sometimes enlarge in adults. 1896 Hardy *Jude* I. vi, She had managed to get back one dimple by..repeating the odd little *sucking operation before mentioned. 1889 Macalister *Human Anat.* 566 The buccal fat in the child forms a lobulated..*sucking-pad. 1699 *Phil. Trans.* XXI. 228 [In a Draught of Savery's Engine] *G* The Force Pipe. *H* The *sucking Pipe. 1731 *Ibid.* XXXVII. 7 A Sucking Pipe and Grate..going into the Water, which supplies all the four Cylinders alternately. 1735 *Ibid.* XXXIX. 42 The Sucking-Pipe receives its Air only from the Room where the Machine stands. 1552 Huloet, *Suckyng pot for chyldren, *aliphanus*. 1774 Goldsm. *Nat. Hist.* (1776) VI. 272 On this occasion their *sucking power is particularly serviceable. 1601 Holland *Pliny* I. 338 A guelding never casts his teeth, no not his *sucking teeth, in case he were guelded before. 1875 Knight *Dict. Mech.* 2442/2 The *sucking-tube was used by the ancients as a domestic utensil, and also in the temples. 1657 W. Rand tr. *Gassendi's Life Peiresc* II. 110 It was a most swift Beast, and such as could not be taken, save when it was *sucking-young.

b. Applied to various organs in fishes, crustaceans, etc. adapted for use as suckers, e.g. *sucking-bowl*, *-cup*, *-disk*, *-foot*, *-mouth*, *-spear*, *-tube*.

1841 T. R. Jones *Anim. Kingd.* § 171 In the male *Actheres*, the *sucking-bowl possessed by the female does not exist. 1840 *Cuvier's Anim. Kingd.* 446 The two anterior [legs].. exhibiting, on the inside, a kind of rosette, formed by the muscles, and seeming to act as a *sucking-cup. 1830 J. E. Gray in *Encycl. Metrop.* (1845) XXI. 592/1 A dorsal tail, ending in a *sucking disk. 1883 *Science* I. 195/2 Ambulatory tentacles..terminating..in expanded sucking-disks. 1855 Kingsley *Glaucus* (1878) 167 The bird's foot star.. which you may see crawling by its thousand *sucking-feet. a 1843 South *Zool.* in *Encycl. Metrop.* (1845) VII. 279/2 The *Sucking Mouth exhibits..three different forms, the proboscis, the promuscis, and the antlia. 1895 D. Sharp *Insects* in *Cambr. Nat. Hist.* V. 467 The *sucking-spears of this Insect are so long and slender as to look like hairs. 1868 *Rep. U. S. Commissioner Agric.* (1869) 310 The *sucking tube, or tongue [of hymenoptera].

Sucking (sʊ·kiŋ), *ppl. a.* [f. Suck *v.* + -ing[2].]

1. That sucks milk from the breast; that is still being suckled, unweaned.

†*Sucking fere* [Fere *sb.*[1], companion], a foster brother. (Cf. *even-sucker* s.v. Sucker *sb.* 1.)

Sucking-fish. *Obs.*

Sucking-pig. A new-born or very young pig; a young milk-fed pig suitable for roasting whole.

Sucking-pump.

Sucking-stone.

Suckle, sb.

Suckle, v.

Sucket.

Suckling (sŭ·kliŋ), vbl. sb.

Suckling, ppl. a.

Suckling (sŭ·kliŋ), sb.

Sucrate.

Sucre (sū·krě).

Sucro-, combining form of F. sucre sugar.

Sucrose (siū·krōs).

Sudan (sudā·n, -en).

Sudanese (sudăni·z).

Sudanic, a.

Sudary. *Obs.*

Sudation. *Obs.*

Sudatorium (siūdătō·riǔm).

Sudatory (siū·dătŏri).

Sudd (sʌd).

Sudden (sʌ·d'n), a., adv. and sb.

Sudden death (slang).

Suddenly (sʌ·d'nli), adv.

Suddenness.

Suddenly (sŏd'nli). Chiefly *Sc. Obs. exc. arch.* Forms: see SUDDEN. [f. *soudeinel*(*l*), f. *sodein* SUDDEN: see -LY.]

Suddenness (sŏd'nnĕs). Forms: see SUDDEN *a.*; also 4 sodenesse, 7 suddaness. [f. SUDDEN *a.* + -NESS.]

†Sudder (sŏd'əɹ), *a. Obs. exc. Anglo-Indian.* [Urdu = Arab. *ṣadr* foremost or highest part of a thing, chief place or seat, etc., used in comb. with adj. sense.] Chief, superior: applied esp. to high government departments or officials.

Sudding (sŏd'iŋ), *vbl. sb.* [f. SUD(s) + -ING1.] The action of putting through a sud.

† Budding, *ppl. a. Obs.* [f. SUD *v.* + -ING2.] Foaming.

Sudite (sŏd'əit). [f. SUDD + -ITE1.] A kind of fuel manufactured from sudd.

Suddle (sŏd'l), *sb. Sc.* [f. the vb.] A stain, spot.

Suddle, *v. Sc. Obs.* [f. prec.] To soil, sully, defile.

† Sudly, *a. Obs. Sc.* In 5 soudly, 6 sudly. Soiled, dirty.

Sudorous, **Sudoration**, obs. ff. SOUTHRON.

† Sudly, *a.* [f. SUD(s) + -Y.] Turbid, thick; *also fig.* "muddy".

† Sudoriferous (sᵘ'dŏrī'fĕrəs), *a.* [f. late L. *sūdōri-fer* + -OUS.] Producing or secreting sweat.

Sudoriferous (sᵘdŏrī'fĕrəs), *a.* [f. late L. *sūdōri-fer*: see -FEROUS. Cf. F. *sudorifère*.]

Sudorific (sᵘ'dŏri'fik), *a.* and *sb.* Also 7 -iphicke, 7-8 -ifick. [ad. mod.L. *sudorificus*: see -FIC. Cf. F. *sudorifique*, It. Sp., Pg. *sudorifico*.]

Suds (sŏdz), *sb. pl.* Forms: 6 sudes, 6-7 suddes, 7 sudds, 6- suds. Also *sing.* sud.

Sue (siū), *v.* Forms: 3-5 sewe, 3-7 suwe, 4-5 suw, 5-6 sywe, 3 siuwe, 3 suu, aiu, subu, aiwi, aywi, siwy, 4 siue, 5 sywe, seurwe, suite, 5 0, siuew, seewe, sieux, syewr, avyn, 6 siuw, seyy, 4- sue. [a. AF. *suer*, *siwer*, *sure*, *su*(*i*)*r* = OF. *sivre*, also *seure*, *seore*, (pres. stem *siu-*, *seu-*, *sew-*), *suivre* (= F. *suivre*) (cf. Pr. *segre*, *seguir*, It. *seguire*, Sp., Pg. *seguir*), f. L. *sequī* to follow.]

Sue (siū), *sb. Obs.* Forms: 3-5 sywe, 3-7 sewe, 4-5 suw, 4-7 siew, 5 suew, 7 sue, shue, etc. [a. AF. *sywe*, *sewe*.]

Sueable, obs. form of SUABLE.

Suede (swēd), *sb.* and *a.* [Fr. *Suède* Sweden.]

Suer (siū'əɹ). Forms: 4-5 suere, 6-7 suer, etc. [f. SUE *v.* + -ER1.]

Suet (siū'et), *sb.* [a. AF. *suet*, dim. of OF. *seu*, *sieu* (mod.F. *suif*), L. *sēbum*.]

Suety (siū'eti), *a.* [f. SUET + -Y1.]

Sueve ... **Sueven**, variant of SWEVEN, dream.

Suevian (swīˈviăn), a. and sb. [L. *Suēvī*.] **A.** adj. Of or belonging to a confederation of Germanic tribes called by the Romans *Suēvī* (*Suēbī*), which inhabited large territories in Central Europe to the east of the Rhine. **B.** Any individual of these tribes.

Suey, *see* SUWE.

†Suff. Obs. Also 6–7 suffe, 7 suff (?). [Of unascertained origin; the relation to *suff* is obscure.]

Suffer (sΩˈfəɹ), v. Forms: 3–4 so-, suffri, 3–6 sofre, 3–7 suffre, 4–5 suffere, -yr, soofre, 4–6 soffur, -ir, 4–7 suffer, -yr, -ur ... etc.

Suffect (sΩˈfekt), a. rare⁻⁰. Rom. Antiq. [ad. L. *suffectus*.]

Suffete (sΩˈfiːt). Rom. Antiq. [ad. L. *suffetēs*.]

(The remaining entries — **Suffer**, **Sufferable**, **Sufferably**, **Sufferance**, **Sufferant**, **Suffered**, **Sufferer**, **Suffering**, **Suffice**, etc. — appear in the Oxford English Dictionary columns of this page.)

SUFFICE.

106

c. Const. for in the same sense.

d. Const. for (a thing): To be of sufficient quantity, capacity, or scope for; to provide enough material or accommodation for.

†e. Const. to: To be adequate or equal to; to avail for. Obs.

f. Const. for with a noun of action or gerund.

g. Const. to with inf.

h. impers. It is enough. Obs.

i. Const. inf. or clause with, or (formerly) without, anticipatory subject it. Now chiefly in the subjunctive, suffice it, sometimes short for Suffice it to say.

†2. To suffice to oneself: to be self-sufficient. Obs.

SUFFICIENCE.

2. To do something.

†3. To have the necessary ability, capacity, or resources for doing something; to be competent or able to do something. Chiefly const. inf. Obs. (to later use coloured by 1 g.)

†4. trans. To make or be sufficient; to suffice for. Obs.

†5. trans. To be capable of. Obs.

†6. intr. Consectually, of a quality or condition: To provide adequate means or opportunity; to allow or admit of a certain thing being done. Also trans. Obs.

‖Suffi·ced, *ppl. a. Obs.* [f. prec. + -ED¹.] Satisfied.

Suffi·cer, *rare.* [as prec. + -ER¹.] A satisfier.

†Suffi·cience, *sb.* (*pron.*) *Forms: 4-6 suffi-ciens, 5 suffisance, suffycyence, 5-6 suffisauns, 5-7 -aunce, 6 suficiens, sufficence, sufficent, -ent, SUFFICIENT: var. -ENCE; cf. next and SUFFISANCE.*

1. *The quality or condition of being sufficient or enough; sufficient supply, means, or resources.*

2. *A sufficient number or quantity of; enough.*

3. *A sufficient manner or quantity; sufficiency, ability, competence.*

4. *Sufficient capacity to perform or undertake something; adequate qualification; ability, competency. Obs. or arch.*

5. *Contentment, satisfaction. Obs.*

SUFFICIENCY.

107

Sufficiency (sŏfi·ʃĕnsi). *Also 5-7 -encie, 8 -entcy.* [ad. L. sufficientia (see prec. and -ENCY). Cf. It. sufficienza, etc. Sp. suficiencia.]

†1. Sufficient means or wealth; ability or competence to meet pecuniary obligations. Obs.

†2. To satisfy, meet the 'calls' of a desire, need, sense, emotion, etc.; Obs.

†9. trans. To make or be sufficient provision for; to supply with something. Also, to replenish (a supply). Obs.

10. To supply, furnish (a product, etc.). Obs.

2. *The quality or condition of being sufficient or enough; sufficient supply, means, or resources.*

3. *A sufficient number or quantity of; enough.*

4. *Sufficient capacity to perform or undertake something; adequate qualification; ability, competence.*

5. *Contentment, satisfaction. Obs.*

= SELF-SUFFICIENCE 1. Obs.

= SELF-SUFFICIENCY 1. Obs.

SUFFICIENT.

d. Const. to with inf.

Sufficient (sŏfi·ʃĕnt), *a. (adv., sb.) Forms: 4 Sc. suffoyand, -yoiand, 4-5 -icia(u)n(e, 4-6 -ioyent, Sc.-ioiand, 5-laia(u)nt, -yoeant, -yoient, -yçeunt, -yeyant, -eoant, 5-6 -yoeant, 6-icient, 6-7 -itient, (7 sophytient), 4- sufficient.* [a. OF. sufficient, -or ad. its source L. sufficient-, -ens, pr. pple. of sufficere to SUFFICE. Cf. It. sufficiente, Sp. suficiente, Pg. sufficiente.]

A. *adj.*

1. *Of a quantity, extent, or scope adequate to a certain purpose or object.*

†b. Theol. Sufficient grace: see GRACE sb. II.

B. *Const. for: (a) to furnish means or material*

†2. Capacity; ability; competence. Also, a competent person. Obs.

†Sufficientize, *v. Obs. rare⁻¹.* [f. prec. + -IZE.] To make 'sufficient' or competent.

Sufficiently (sŏfi·ʃĕntli), *adv. (sb.)* [f. SUFFICIENT + -LY².]

1. In a manner or to an extent calculated to satisfy the circumstances of the case or adequate to a certain purpose or object; enough for the purpose (expressed or implied).

†Suffi·cientise, *v. Obs. rare⁻¹.*

SUFFISANCE.

108

†Suffi·sance, *Obs.* [a. F. suffisance.]

Suffisant, *Obs.*

SUFFISANT.

109

Suffisant, *a. Obs.*

Suffite, *sb.* [ad. L. suffītus, f. suffīre to fumigate.]

Suffi·tion, *Obs.*

Suffla·tion. [ad. L. sufflātiōn-em.]

Suffl·ate, *v. Obs. rare⁻¹.*

Suffla·tion.

Suflia·tion.

Suffocate.

SUFFOCATE.

Suf·focate (sŏ·fŏkēt), *v.* [f. L. suffōcāt-, ppl. stem of suffōcāre, f. sub- + faucēs.]

1. *trans.* To kill (a person or animal) by stopping the supply of air through the lungs, gills, or other respiratory organs.

2. *intr.* To suffer or undergo suffocation, to be suffocated.

Suf·focate, *ppl. a. and pa. pple. Obs.* [ad. L. suffocātus, pa. pple. of suffocāre.]

suffocated himself with this pleasantry. 1854 J. S. C. Abbott *Napoleon* (1855) II. xxii. 418 The soldiers were suffocated with sorrow.

3. To destroy as if by the exclusion of air; to smother, overwhelm, extinguish.

a. something material or physical.

1584 R. Scot *Discov. Witchcr.* xii. vi. 223 Manie lewd persons..with incantations..doo..extinguish, suffocate, and spoile all vineyards, ortchards, medowes [etc.]. 1614 T. Adams *Diuells Banket* iii. 109 The thicke spumy mists, which vapour vp from the..earth, doe often suffocate the brighter aire. 1651 French *Yorksh. Spaw* iv. 46 The use of cold baths is not..for old men, because that little heat which they have is thereby suffocated. 1758 Reid tr. *Macquer's Chym.* I. 122 By distillation..it [sc. acid of Vinegar] may be freed..from the great quantity of water which in a manner suffocates it. 1793 *Trans. Soc. Arts* V. 54 The plants..will suffocate every kind of weed near them. 1797 *Phil. Trans.* LXXXVII. 421 A mass sufficiently thick to suffocate the whole of the light which enters it. 1807 J. Barlow *Columb.* ii. 330 His fleet high flaming suffocates the skies. 1842 Loudon *Suburban Hort.* 386 The roots are suffocated and rotted from their delicacy.

b. something immaterial, esp. a mental attribute.

1526 *Pilgr. Perf.* (W. de W. 1531) 76 b, Labour..to expell the same venym..or..to suffocate or smere it within y^e. c 1550 Rolland *Crt. Venus* ii. 720 Thay wald him mak sum aid,..Or his sorrow in sum part suffocat. 1644 Prynne & Walker *Fiennes' Trial* 39 It being a meere artifice..to suffocate the truth. 1664 H. More *Myst. Iniq.* 257 The being inveigled in idolatrous Worship does not quite suffocate and dead that Divine sense. 1749 Hartley *Observ. Man* i. i. § 1. 44 Blood and Serum..lying in the Ventricles, suffocate Sensations. 1868 Milman *St. Paul's* vi. 112 That ..superstition which..had suffocated the higher truths of religion.

4. *intr.* To become stifled or choked. *rare.*

1702 De Foe *Mock Mourners* (ed. 3) 77 Convulsions follow, and such Vapours rise, The Constitution Suffocates and Dies. 1730 *Phil. Trans.* XXXVI. 419 The Disease continued so obstinate, and the Patient so like to suffocate, that [etc.]. 1883 *Harper's Mag.* Jan. 237/2, I suffocate in a stuffy room. 1888 *Daily News* 9 July 5/7 Whilst he was suffocating he remained calm and still.

Hence **Su·ffocated** *ppl. a.*, **Su·ffocating** *vbl. sb.*

1621 T. Williamson tr. *Goulart's Wise Vieillard* 23 Death is a suffocating and quenching of the naturall heate of the body. 1737 Whiston *Josephus, Hist.* v. xi. § 4 As the suffocated materials were now gradually consumed. 1793 Beddoes *Scurvy*, etc. 50 In suffocated animals the left cavities of the heart are full of venous blood. 1898 G. B. Shaw *Plays* II. *Candida* 148 In a suffocated voice.

Su·ffocating, *ppl. a.* [-ing ².]

1. That causes suffocation; stifling.

1604 Shaks. *Oth.* iii. iii. 389 If there be Cords, or Kniues, Poyson, or Fire, or suffocating streames, Ile not indure it. 1667 *Phil. Trans.* II. 416 The hot winds blowing..with such a suffocating heat. 1764 Harmer *Observ.* i. § 16. 39 These hot winds are not deadly at Aleppo...They are very incommoding and suffocating in Barbary and Egypt too. 1807 T. Thomson *Chem.* (ed. 3) II. 172 The dense and suffocating odour of muriatic acid. 1817 Shelley *Rev. Islam* i. xiii. 3 Would the Snake Relax his suffocating grasp. 1829 Lytton *Disowned* lxxxiv, Throwing, as it were, in that exclamation, a whole weight of suffocating emotion from his chest. 1860 Tyndall *Glac.* i. xviii. 133 The dead suffocating warmth of the interior of an oven. 1879 Froude *Cæsar* xxii. 391 The hills were waterless, the weather suffocating.

fig. 1875 Helps *Soc. Press.* viii. 101, I hope he told you of the suffocating interest I take in your present subject.

†**b.** *Suffocating damp*, = Choke-damp. So *suffocating shaft*. *Obs.*

1695 Woodward *Nat. Hist. Earth* iv. (1723) 227 One is called the *Suffocating*, the other the *Fulminating Damp*. 1778 Pryce *Min. Cornub.* 201 If faggots on fire..be thrown into a suffocating Shaft, it will rarify the bad air.

2. Accompanied by suffocation.

1748 *Anson's Voy.* ii. v. 184 That uneasy and suffocating sensation. 1818–20 E. Thompson *Nosologia* (ed. 3) 222 Convulsive suffocating cough. 1838 Thackeray *Yellowpl. Corr.* iv. (1887) 26 She gev a suffycating shreek. 1900 *Westm. Gaz.* 10 Sept. 6/2 A hoarse, suffocating sound.

3. That undergoes suffocation. *rare.*

1869 *Daily News* 2 July, The mute agonies of the suffocating lobster before he is boiled alive in a pot.

4. as *adv.* = Suffocatingly. *rare.*

1737 Whiston *Josephus, Hist.* iii. ix. § 1 It was suffocating hot.

Hence **Su·ffocatingly** *adv.*, so as to cause suffocation.

1822 *Blackw. Mag.* XII. 434. I never felt more suffocatingly hot. 1854 Dickens *Hard T.* ii. iv, The..suffocatingly close Hall. 1885 'Mrs. Alexander' *Valerie's Fate* vi, Her heart suddenly waking from its torpor to beat wildly, suffocatingly.

Suffocation (svfǒkē¹·ʃən). Also 6 -cion. [ad. L. *suffōcātio-*, *-ōnem*, n. of action f. *suffōcāre* to Suffocate. Cf. F. *suffocation*.] The act of suffocating or condition of being suffocated.

a 1577 Sir T. Smith *Commw. Eng.* ii. xxiii. (1589) 95 He ..that violently commeth to his death, whether it bee by knife, poison, cord, drowning, burning, suffocation, or otherwise. 1598 Shaks. *Merry W.* iii. v. 119 It was a miracle to scape suffocation. 1620 Venner *Via Recta* viii. 190 They ..that..surcharge their bodies with ouer-much meat..incurre suddaine and perilous suffocations. 1737 Whiston *Josephus, Antiq.* vi. viii. § 2 Some..demoniacal disorders.. brought upon him such suffocations as were ready to choke him. 1819 Scott *Leg. Montrose* xiii, Departing quietly by suffocation, like your ancestors before you. 1846 J. Baxter *Libr. Pract. Agric.* (ed. 4) I. p. xxiv, The large ball room..was crammed to suffocation. 1875 A. S. Taylor *Poisons* (ed. 3) 107 A lady who had been rendered unconscious by chloroform died from suffocation, as a result of the food finding its way into the air passages.

b. *transf.* and *fig.*

1567 Fenton *Trag. Disc.* i. (1898) I. 76 To dye afore my tyme by suffocacion of pynnynge dolloür. 1651 Wittie tr. *Primrose's Pop. Err.* iii. 150 The suffocation of heat. 1744 *Phil. Trans.* XLIII. 130 Blackness is brought on, by an Extinction or Suffocation of those same mixed Rays. 1824 Loudon *Encycl. Gard.* (ed. 2) § 893 *Suffocation* [in plants]. Sometimes it happens that the pores of the epidermis are closed up, and transpiration consequently obstructed. 1837 Carlyle *French Rev.* ..iv. iv, Is it not..the very murkiness, and atmospheric suffocation, that brings the lightning?

†**c.** [medical L. *suffocatio hysterica* or *uterina*.] In full *suffocation of the womb, matrix, mother* (see Mother *sb.*¹ 11 b), *bairn's bed* (see Bairn *Comb.*): hysteria. *Obs.*

1549 *Compl. Scot.* vi. 67 Muguart, that is gude for the suffocatione of ane vomans bayrnis hed [*read* bed]. 1578 Lyte *Dodoens* 19 The same is good against the Suffocation of the Matrix (that is the stopping and hardnesse of the Mother). 1603 E. Jorden (*title*), A Briefe Discovrse of a Disease called the Suffocation of the Mother. 1607 Topsell *Four-f. Beasts* 652 The fat of a sheep..cureth the suffocation of the womb. 1719 Quincy *Lex. Physico-Med.* (1722), *Suffocation*, Choaking. This is used in Hysterick Cases, wherein the Uterus is imagined to be..as it were suffocated with ill Humours.

Suffocative (sv·fǒke¹tiv), *a.* [ad. mod.L. *suffōcātīvus*, f. *suffōcāt-*: see Suffocate *v.* and -ive.] Tending to suffocate; causing or inducing suffocation; attended by suffocation.

Chiefly *Med.*, esp. in *s. catarrh* = capillary bronchitis.

1605 Timme *Quersit.* iii. 157 Violent catarres which are called suffocatiue. 1753 *Chambers' Cycl.* Suppl., *Suffocative catarrh*,..the name of a disease, which consists in a copious eruption of a serous and mucous humor into the vesicles of the lungs. 1758 *Monthly Rev.* 507 Nervous suffocative asthmas. 1791 E. Darwin *Bot. Gard.* i. iv. 64 The fell Syroc's suffocative breath. *Ibid.* ii. iii. 61 With quick sighs, and suffocative breath, Her interrupted heart-pulse swims in death. 1869 E. A. Parkes *Pract. Hygiene* (ed. 3) 114 Sextons..are subject to..suffocative catarrhs. 1876 *Trans. Clinical Soc.* IX. 129 She has suffocative attacks, in which she can hardly breathe. 1908 G. W. E. Russell *Threepenny Bits* vii. 47 Forging their way through suffocative crowds.

†**Suffoke,** *v. Obs. rare*⁻¹. [a. F. *suffoquer*, = Pr. *sofogar*, ad. L. *suffōcāre* to Suffocate.] *trans.* To suffocate, drown.

1490 Caxton *Eneydos* xxi. 77 Wythout to suffoke me now ..in-to the depe see of amaritude.

Suffolk (sv·fək). The name of one of the counties of East Anglia; used attrib. in designations of things produced in or peculiar to the county, as *Suffolk butter, cheese, cow, dumpling, dun, pig*; **Suffolk bang** (see quot.); **Suffolk coprolite**, a phosphatic nodule occurring in the Red Crag of Suffolk; **Suffolk crag**, a Pliocene formation occurring in Suffolk (see quot. 1852); **Suffolk grass**, the annual meadow grass, *Poa annua*; **Suffolk punch**, a small but strong and hardy horse bred largely in Suffolk; **Suffolk thump** = *Suffolk bang*.

1867 Smyth *Sailor's Word-bk.*, *Suffolk Bang, a very poor and hard kind of cheese. 1735 J. Kirby *Suffolk Trav.* 2 In this Part is made the *Suffolk Butter, so managed by the Neat Dairy-Wife, that it is justly esteemed the pleasantest and best in England. 1636 Davenant *Wits* iii. i, Some *Suffolk Cheese. 1661 Pepys *Diary* 4 Oct., I found my wife vexed at her people for grumbling to eat Suffolk cheese. 1797 Young *Agric. Suffolk* 203 Cheese 5d., but Suffolk 3½d. and 4d. 1867 Sibson *Agric. Chem.* 249 *Suffolk Coprolites are amongst the first known phosphatic minerals. 1797 T. M. in Young *Agric. Suffolk* 180 *note*, The true *Suffolk polled cow. 1834 [Youatt] *Cattle* (Lib. Usef. Knowl.) 175 The milking properties of the Suffolk cow. 1852 Lyell *Man. Elem. Geol.* (ed. 4) 162 The *Suffolk crag is divisible into two masses, the upper of which has been termed the Red, and the lower the Coralline Crag. 1824 *New Syst. Cookery* (new ed.) 234 Yeast or *Suffolk Dumplings. 1834 [Youatt] *Cattle* (Lib. Usef. Knowl.) 174 The *Suffolk Dun used to be celebrated ..on account of the extraordinary quantity of milk that she yielded. 1875 *Encycl. Brit.* I. 389/1 A polled breed of cattle, the prevailing colour of which is dun or pale red, from which they are known as the *Suffolk Duns*. 1759 B. Stillingfleet *Observ. Grasses* in *Misc. Tracts* (1762) 367 What is known in some few counties by the name of the *Suffolk grass. 1846 J. Baxter *Libr. Pract. Agric.* (ed. 4) I. 368 The *Pôa dunna*, or Suffolk grass, is so short of growth..as to render it an encumberer of the soil. 1842 *Penny Cycl.* XXIII. 214/1 *Suffolk pigs are perhaps..the most profitable breed in England. 1784 Cullum *Hist. Hawsted* 222 This breed is well known by the name of *Suffolk Punches. 1816 J. Smith *Panorama Sci. & Art* II. 644 The Suffolk-punches, which are common in the district called High Suffolk. 1850 Dickens *Dav. Copp.* xix, A Suffolk Punch, when he's a good 'un, is worth his weight in gold. a 1825 Forby *Voc. E. Anglia* s.v. *Bang*, *Suffolk Thump.

†**b.** **Suffolk powder**: see quot. *Obs.*

1753 *Chambers' Cycl.* Suppl., *Suffolk powder*, the name of a medicinal powder, good for the bite of a mad dog. It had its name from a Countess of Suffolk, who used to give it with great success.

c. *absol.* = Suffolk cow, pig

[1797 in Young *Agric. Suffolk* 185 The Suffolk milk gave two and one-third ounces more cream than the horned one.] 1834 [Youatt] *Cattle* (Lib. Usef. Knowl.) 173 In no part of the kingdom were the farmers more careless as to the breed, providing only that the cows were true Suffolks. 1846 — *Pig* 66 A cross between the Suffolk and Lincoln.

Hence **Suffolkian** (in 7 -cean), *a.*, of or belonging to the county of Suffolk; **Su·ffolkism** (-cism), a Suffolk idiom or peculiarity.

1622 Drayton *Poly-olb.* xix. 399 From the Suffolcean side yet those which Stour prefer Their princely Orwell praise. 1823 E. Moor *Suffolk Words* 23 Where words occur, not readily understood by the Unsuffolked reader, he is to take them as Suffolcisms.

†**Suffo·ssion.** *Obs. rare.* [ad. L. *suffossio*, *-ōnem*, f. *suffodĕre*, f. *suf-* = Sub- 3, 25 + *fodĕre* to dig.] Digging under or up; undermining.

1623 Cockeram, *Suffossion*, an undermining. c 1625 Bp. Hall *St. Paul's Combat* i. Wks. 1634 II. 440 Those suffossions of walls [etc.]. 1648 — *Select Th.* i. § 32 What is it to tell of the suffossion of her vineyards? vastation of her tents?

†**Suffounge,** *v. Obs. rare*⁻¹. [a. OF. **suffongier* (cf. AF. *fungier* to smoke):—L. *suffūmigāre*, f. *suf-* = Sub- 25 + *fumigāre* to Fumigate.] *trans.* To fumigate.

1490 Caxton *Eneydos* xxiv. 87 [She] toke herself for to encence it, and to suffounge the place.

Suffragan (sv·frăgăn), *sb.* and *a.* Forms: 4 **suffrigane, soffragan**, 4–7 **suffragane**, 5 **suffragann, -igan(n, -ygane, -ann, sofregann**, 5–6 **suffrygan**, 6 **suffregan(e, -ragene, (suffryngham)**, 4– **suffragan**; β. 5 **suffrecan, -ykayn, soffrycan**, 5–6 **soffrecan**, 6 **suffrecane, -ykane, soufrecan.** [a. AF., OF. *suffragan* (13th c.), occas. *-ain* (mod.F. *suffragant*), corresp. to It. *soffraganeo, -ano*, Sp. *sufraganeo, -ano*, Pg. *suffraganeo*, repr. med.L. *suffrāgāneus*, f. stem of *suffrāgium* Suffrage.

The earliest OF. examples, being in the pl. *suffragans*, are ambiguous for the form of the sing., but it is probable that **suffragan* was the older form (cf. MDu. *suffragaen*), and that *suffragant* (1451 in Du Cange) is due to etymologizing alteration (see -ant); cf. however Pr. *suffraguant*, It. *suffragante*.]

A. *sb.*

1. A bishop considered in regard to his relation to the archbishop or metropolitan, by whom he may be summoned to attend synods and give his suffrage.

c 1383 *Concl. Loll.* xxvii. in *Eng. Hist. Rev.* (1911) Oct. 746 Decrees..þat 3euen þe chesigne of þe erchebisshop to alle his suffragans. 1387 Trevisa *Higden* (Rolls) II. 115 Þe primat of 3ork haþ but tweie suffragans in Engelond, þat beeþ þe bisshopis of Caerlile and of Duram. c 1440 *Jacob's Well* 17 Which sentence was 3ouyn..be Boniface, erchebysschop of cauntyrbury, and be v. oþere bysschopys, his suffraganys. 1534 *Lyndewode's Const. Provinc.* 3 We..commaunde all and euerye our Cobysschoppes and suffragans. 1611 Coryat *Crudities* 532 He had no lesse then sixteene Bishops vnder him that were subiect to his iurisdiction as his Suffragrans [*sic*]. 1716 M. Davies *Athen. Brit.* III. 28 The two High-flying Suffragans to AB. Laud. 1768 Boswell *Corsica* iii. (ed. 2) 164 The Corsican bishops, who are..suffragans of the archbishop of Pisa. 1862 Hook *Lives Abps.* II. ii. 121 The suffragans of the province were summoned as usual to assist at the consecration of their metropolitan. 1876 Freeman *Norm. Conq.* V. xxiii. 214 The Bishop of Orkney, more strictly a suffragan of Trondhjem, is seen acting as a suffragan of York.

transf. 1877 C. Geikie *Christ* lii. (1879) 619 The Jewish primate and his suffragans kept steadily in view his arrest.

2. An assistant or subsidiary bishop, performing episcopal functions in a certain diocese but having no jurisdiction; in the Church of England, since the passing of Act 26 Hen. VIII, c. 14, a bishop appointed to assist a diocesan bishop in a particular part of his diocese.

Suffragan bishops take their title from certain towns named in the above act or (according to the Suffragans Nomination Act of 1888) from 'such other towns as Her Majesty may..by Order in Council direct shall be taken'.

c 1380 Wyclif *Wks.* (1880) 225 Þat þei ben not maad bischopis of heþene men..& þanne meyntened to be suffragans & sellen sacramentis. 14.. *S. E. Leg.* (MS. Bodl. 779) fol. 102 Suþþe he made him bysschop..& makid him his soffragan & in his stede prechour. 1483 *Cath. Angl.* 371 Suffragane, *Coepiscopus*. 1511–12 *Rec. St. Mary at Hill* 277 Paid the Suffregan for haloyng of a Chales [etc.]. 1534 *Act 26 Hen. VIII*, c. 14 § 1 Everie Archebysshope and Byshop of this Realme,..beynge dysposed to have any Suffragane. 1536 Boorde *Let.* in *Introd. Knowl.* (1870) 58, I was..dyspensyd with þe relygyon by the byshopp of Romes bulles, to be suffrygan off chychester. 1587 Harrison *England* ii. ii. 49 in *Holinshed*, Which function peraduenture he [sc. the Bishop] committed to his suffragane. 1615 Wadsworth in Bedell *Lett.* (1624) 13 One Hodgeskin Suffragan of Bedford. 1654 Gataker *Disc. Apol.* 101 Dr. Stern..was at that time Suffragane of Colchester. 1885 *Life & Lett. A. Monod* 58 M. Charles Barde of Geneva who had been called to act as suffragan at Lyons. 1912 *Cath. Encycl.* XIV. 324/2 It is presumed that the cardinal-bishop has given his suffragan all the faculties necessary for the government of his diocese.

β. 1470–85 Malory *Arthur* xii. xiv. 611 Thenne the suffrecan lete fylle a grete vessel with water. 1493–4 *Rec. St. Mary at Hill* 198 Payd to þe soffrycan of london for halowyng of sentt stevyn ys autyr, x s. iij d. 1530 Palsgr. 273/1 Soufrecan, *suffragan, penitencier*. 1556 *Chron. Grey Friars* (Camden) 78 There the suffrecane gave them their dyscipline.

†**3.** A coadjutor, assistant; a deputy, representative. *Obs.*

1481 in Legg *Clerk's Bk.* 1549, 66 Howe the Clerke And the Suffrigann of Seynt Nicholas Church Aught to do...The suff[r]ygann Augh to fastenn the Church Dorys[etc.]. 1500–20 Dunbar *Poems* xlviii. 173 The nychtingaill song [to the rose], 'Haill, naturis suffragene'. *Ibid.* lxxxv. 68 Oratrice, mediatrice, salvatrice, To God gret suffragane! 1577 B. Googe tr. *Heresbach's Husb.* 3, I haue..my maide, so skilfull in huswyferie, that she may well be my wyues suffragan. 1647 C. Walker *Myst. Two Junto's* 6 The remaining part of the House are but..Suffragans to ratify what is forejudged. 1687 *Lond. Gaz.* No. 2242/3 The Elector of Trier has named the Bishop his Suffragan to go and compliment the King.

1748 Richardson *Clarissa* (1768) VIII. xix. 53 Her [sc. a strumpet's] bed-side, surrounded..by her suffragans and daughters. 1760 H. Walpole *Let. to Mann* 7 May, She made her suffragan, Whitfield, pray for and preach about him.

†**b.** Of things: A help, aid. *Obs.*

1644 Bulwer *Chiron.* 16 So these suffragans of speech [sc. hands] by a lively sense afford that shadow which is the excellencie of the vocall pourtraicture. 1693 *D'Emilianne's Hist. Monast. Orders* 35 The Canons of those times..frequently..were Helps and Suffragans to the Bishops.

B. *adj.*

1. *Bishop suffragan, suffragan bishop*: = A. 1, 2.

1475 *Voc.* in Wr.-Wülcker 629 Prelatte or byschop suffrygane. 1534 *Act 26 Hen. VIII*, c. 14 § 1 Everie suche personne..shalbe callyd Byshop Suffragane of the same See wherunto he shalbe namyd. 1538 Audley in *Lett. Suppr. Monast.* (Camden) 240 William More, clerk, byshopp suffragan of Colchester. 1671 F. Phillips *Reg. Necess.* 442 The Arch-bishop of York, and his Suffragan Bishops. c 1676 T. Barlow *Rem.* (1693) 162 A Co-adjutor or Suffragan Bishop is, *quoad Ordinem*, really and properly a Bishop. 1726 Ayliffe *Parergon* 69 No Suffragan Bishop shall have more than one riding Apparitor in his Diocess. 1846 McCulloch *Acc. Brit. Empire* (1854) II. 301 The total income of the two archbishops, and of their ten suffragan bishops, will then be 70,938*l.* 1888 *Act 51 & 52 Vict.* c. 56 It was enacted that the towns therein named should be taken..for sees of bishops suffragans. 1907 *Cath. Encycl.* I. 691/2 In regard to his suffragan bishops the metropolitan may compel them to assemble in provincial council every three years.

2. Of a see or diocese: Subordinate *to* a metropolitical or archiepiscopal see.

1712 E. Cooke *Voy. S. Sea* 399 Valladolid, a Bishoprick, suffragan to Mexico. 1907 *Cath. Encycl.* I. 692/1 To-day archbishops cannot visit a suffragan diocese, unless [etc.]. 1913 T. F. Tout in *Reg. J. de Halton* Introd. 24 The see of Sodor, which, until the fifteenth century, was supposed to be suffragan to..Trondhjem.

fig. 1784 H. Walpole *Let. to H. S. Conway* 14 Aug., That the King of Spain, now he has demolished Algiers, the metropolitan see of thieves, will come and bombard Richmond, Twickenham, and all the suffragan cities that swarm with pirates and banditti.

Hence **Su·ffraganal** *a.*, pertaining to a suffragan bishop; **Su·ffraganate**, the seat of a suffragan bishop; **Su·ffragancy**, the office or tenure of a suffragan; **Su·ffraganship**, the office or status of a suffragan.

1892 *Times* 14 Oct. 11/2 The *suffraganal or nominal sees are as absolute shams as Wiseman's original Bishopric of Melipotamos *in partibus infidelium*. 1879 *Echo* 11 July 2/5 Bedford is the town nearest to London that is mentioned in the Act of Henry VIII. as a suitable place for a *suffraganate. 1888 *Guardian* 8 Feb. 186/2 The appointment of Sir Lovelace Stamer to the Suffraganate of Shrewsbury. 1864 *Spectator* 25 June 742 The refusal of the Presbyteral Council of Paris to renew the '*suffragancy' of the younger Athanase Coquerel. 1549 Latimer *5th Serm. bef. Edw. VI* (Arb.) 135, I meane not hallowers of belles, nor Christiners of belles, that is a popysh *suffraganship. 1583 Stocker *Civ. Warres Lowe C.* i. 5 b, There were certaine Suffraganeships of cathedral churches conuerted into Bishopricks. a 1661 Fuller *Worthies, Cumbld.* (1662) 220 He was..made *Episcopus Pissinensis*..and therewith held the Suffraganeship under Henry Beaufort Bishop of Lincoln.

Suffraga·nean, *a. rare.* [f. med.L. *suffrāgāneus* (see prec.) + -an.] Suffragan. So **Suffraga·neous** *a.*, pertaining to a suffragan.

1704 *Collect. Voy.* (Churchill) III. 641/1 The Patriarch.. has eight..Suffraganean Bishops. 1904 *Times, Lit. Suppl.* 4 Nov. 338/2 The dreary round of suffraganeous functions.

†**Su·ffragant,** *sb.* and *a. Obs.* [a. F. *suffragant*, ad. L. *suffrāgans*, *-ant-*, pr. pple. of *suffrāgārī* (see next).] **A.** *sb.* **1.** = Suffragan *sb.* 2.

1611 Cotgr., *Suffragant*, a Suffragant, or Suffragan, a Bishops deputie.

2. One who gives his suffrage or vote; a voter; hence, a supporter, witness.

1627 Jackson *Holy Cath. Faith* i. xxi. 181 Wee haue euery member of the Romish Church a suffragant or witnesse for vs. 1656 *Artif. Handsom.* 118 Hoping to find them more friends and suffragants to the virtues..of sober women than enemies to their beauty. 1678 R. L'Estrange *Seneca's Mor.* ii. xx. 161 When they are no longer Candidates, they are Suffragants. 1697 Potter *Antiq. Greece* i. ix. (1715) 44 The Prytanes, who were also oblig'd to provide a sufficient number of Stones for the Suffragants.

B. *adj.* **1.** Auxiliary, subordinate.

1603 Florio *Montaigne* i. lvi. (1632) 175 She [sc. Divinity] ought to be chiefe ruler..and not suffragant and subsidiary.

2. Giving support or witness.

a 1656 Bp. Hall *Rem. Wks.* (1660) 302 If..I should let my pen loose to the suffragant testimonies..I should trye your patience.

†**Su·ffragate,** *v. Obs.* [f. L. *suffrāgāt-*, pa. ppl. stem of *suffrāgārī*, f. stem of *suffrāgium* Suffrage.]

1. *trans.* To delegate, appoint.

1600 W. Watson *Decacordon* (1602) 273 Suffragating Arrian Bishops and others in their places.

2. *intr.* To testify, to bear witness *to*.

1620 T. Granger *Div. Logike* 233 Verbes, to witnes, testifie, ..Suffragate. 1629 Prynne *Old Antith.* 73 All these doe fully suffragate to this our third Ante-Arminian Conclusion. 1633 — *Histrio-m.* 77 All Times, All Ages..Subscribe, and Suffragate with these our Authors to our Minor. 1665 Glanvill *Scepsis Sci.* viii. 45 Now this seems bigg of repugnancies, though Sense it self suffragate to its truth. a 1676 Hale *Prim. Orig. Man.* i. ii. (1677) 62 Unless there were some common consonancy and congruity of somewhat inherent in Nature which suits, corresponds and suffragates to that Tradition.

3. To vote (*for*).

1630 Prynne *Anti-Armin.* 2 If all these suffragate or passe their Verdict for the Arminians. 1691 Wood *Fasti Oxon.* (1820) II. 345 Michael Ward..was incorporated in the said degree, with liberty given him to suffragate in congreg. and convoc.

Hence †**Su·ffragating** *ppl. a.*, voting; assenting.

1684 Dryden *Prol. to Univ. Oxford* 31 Nations su'd to be made free of Rome: Not in the suffragating Tribes to stand, But in your utmost, last, Provincial Band. 1850 Blackie *Æschylus* II. 119 These words the Argive people Answered with suffragating hands.

†**Suffraga·tion.** *Obs. rare.* [ad. L. *suffrāgātio*, *-ōnem*, n. of action f. *suffrāgārī* to Suffragate.] The giving of a vote.

1576 Fleming *Panopl. Epist.* 12 Our suffragation, or consenting voices. 1652 Gaule *Magastrom.* 176 A diabolicall ..contract, sacrament, suggestion, suffragation, operation, and delusion. 1656 in Blount *Glossogr.*

So †**Su·ffragator** [L. *suffrāgātor*], a voter, supporter; witness; †**Su·ffragatory** *a.* [L. *suffrāgātōrius*], exercising a right to vote.

1617 Collins *Def. Bp. Ely* ii. vii. 262 Did euer any man make them his suffragators or spokes-men to god? 1618 T. Morton in *Ussher's Lett.* (1686) 67 The Synod..is held at Dort, the most of their Suffragators are already Assembled. 1813 *Monthly Mag.* XXXV. 427/1 Suffragatory institutions were to be solicited.

Suffrage (sv·frĕdʒ), *sb.* Also 5 **souffrage, sofrage**, 6 *Sc.* **suffeagh**, 6–7 **sufferage**, 7 **suff'rage.** [ad. L. *suffrāgium*, partly through F. *suffrage* (from 13th c.). Cf. It., Pg. *suffragio*, Sp. *sufragio*. An earlier anglicization of the L. pl. is Suffragies.]

1. *collect. pl.* and *sing.* Prayers, *esp.* intercessory prayers, intercessions. *arch.*

c 1380 Wyclif *Wks.* (1880) 303 In alle þise wordis ben feyned of gostliche suffrage wiþ-oute grounde. 1432–50 tr. *Higden* (Rolls) I. 431 Vn til thei aske the suffrage and helpe of Seynte Wenefride. c 1450 *Godstow Reg.* 182 In massys, in matyns, in oþer owrys, suffrages, almys, fastynges. 1513 Bradshaw *St. Werburge* i. 3259 Also by her merite, suffrage and peticion Euery humble creature had helpe and succour. 1553 Becon *Reliques of Rome* (1563) 197* The Suffrages and sacrifices of the Masse. 1602 Warner *Alb. Eng.* xiii. lxxvii, Not tedious suffrages they ask't, nor Sacrifices strate. 1660 Wood *Life* (O.H.S.) I. 345 The chappell being onlie for privat or secret suffrages. 1681 Burnet *Hist. Ref.* ii. i. 64 That the Sacrifice might bring to them a greater Indulgence, being offered up by the Suffrages of the Saint. 1865 Kingsley *Herew.* i, Of what use to you then the suffrages of the saints? 1904 M. Hewlett *Queen's Quair* i. viii. 110 The Queen was at prayers—which is more than can be said for the priest who should have lifted up her suffrages.

b. *spec.* Prayers for the souls of the departed: *esp.* in phr. *to do suffrage*. *arch.*

c 1440 *Alphabet of Tales* 58 He..garte do message & oders prayers & suffrage of halie kurk for hym. c 1450 *Godstow Reg.* 206 So þat þey scholde haue in mynde the sowlys Afore in alle here prayeris suffrages & benefettes for euer. 1483 Caxton *Gold. Leg.* 348/2 That generalle Suffrages temporal myght be done for them. 1521 *Extr. Burgh Recs. Stirling* 14 Oct. (1887) 13 Twa markis of obit silver..for sufferagh to be doun for the saullis of wmquhill Allexander lord Elphinstoun and Sir Johen Elphinstoun, his fader. c 1554 in *10th Rep. Hist. MSS. Comm.* App. i. 87 To do suffrage for the sawll of the deid. 1584 R. Scot *Discov. Witchcr.* xv. xxii. 434 Whose soule art thou?..Wantest thou any suffrages, masses, or almes? 1596 R. H. tr. *Lavaterus' Ghostes & Spir.* 107 Whether he require any aide by prayers and suffrages? 1848 K. H. Digby *Broad Stone Hon.* III. *Morus* 280 Their prayers and suffrages for the dead.

†**c.** phr. *Suffrages of prayers*; cf. med.L. *orationis suffragium*, OF. *suffrages d'oroisons*. *Obs.*

The original sense was prob. 'help given by (intercessory) prayer': cf. sense 2.

1447 in Anstey *Epist. Acad. Oxon.* (O.H.S.) I. 261 We commend us unto 3owr goode lordschipe w^t the gostly suffrages of oure prayers. c 1613 in *Cath. Rec. Soc. Publ.* (1914) XIV. 34 We humbly request the Suffrages of your Devout Prayers of Charity.

d. *pl.* Liturgical intercessory petitions; *esp.* in the Book of Common Prayer, (*a*) the intercessory petitions pronounced by the priest in the Litany (also *sing.*, any one of these); (*b*) a series of petitions pronounced by the priest with the answers of the people, a set of versicles and responses.

Also by some writers (see quots. 1657, 1732, 1796) used for a responsive petition (or response to a versicle, etc.).

1532 Elyot *Let.* in *Gov.* (1880) I. p. lxxix, [In Germany] the Preest [at mass] in vestmentes after oure manner singith everi thing in Latine as we use, omitting suffrages. 1548–9 (Mar.) *Bk. Com. Prayer, Evensong*, Then the suffrages before assigned at Matins. *Ibid., Litany*, The Letany and Suffrages. 1587 Harrison *England* ii. i. 138/1 in *Holinshed*, After morning praier also we haue the letanie and suffrages. 1657 Sparrow *Bk. Com. Prayer* 95 These Forms of prayers, (where the peoples devotion is so often excited..by continual Suffrages, such as *Good Lord deliver us*; *We beseech thee to hear us good Lord*,) were called ἐκτενεῖς δεήσεις, earnest or intense Petitions. 1662 *Bk. Com. Prayer, Form of Prayer 5 Nov.*, In the Suffrages after the Creed, these shall be inserted and used for the King. 1697 J. Lewis *Mem. Dk. Glocester* (1789) 78 He..would answer very properly at prayers, in the Suffrages and different parts of the Liturgy. 1714 *Order in Council* 1 Aug. in *Lond. Gaz.* No. 5247/3 In the Suffrages next after the Creed, instead of *Queen* read *King*. 1732 Neal *Hist. Purit.* I. 54 They compiled a Litany consisting of many short petitions interrupted by Suffrages. 1796 Pegge *Anonym.* (1809) 145 *Tu autem*..is the beginning of the suffrage, which was supposed to follow the reading of the Scripture, which the reading scholar was to continue, by saying, *Miserere mei, Domine*. 1855 Procter *Bk. Com. Prayer* 235 After the suffrage for the Church, those for the ecclesiastical orders usually come first. 1882–3 *Schaff's Encycl. Relig. Knowl.* II. 1327 A brief litany, in which the people continually respond to the various suffrages, 'Lord, have mercy upon us'. 1885 *Pall Mall Gaz.* 23 May 7/2 Installation of the Dean of Gloucester...The Bishop then said some suffrages. 1885 Dixon *Hist. Ch. Eng.* III. 496 The Suffrages which the clerks were wont to sing in the time of the communion [*viz.* the Agnus Dei, etc.].

transf. 1701 Norris *Ideal World* i. ii. 35 This great and solemn suffrage of the adorable Trinity, Let us make man.

†**2.** Help, support, assistance. Also, one who helps, a support. *Obs.*

c 1460 *Promp. Parv.* 483/2 K.,P. Suffrage, or helpe, *suffragium*. c 1480 Henryson *Orpheus & Eurydice* 174 And had noucht bene throu suffrage of his harp, Wyth scharp pikis he had bene schorne & schent. 1513 Bradshaw *St. Werburge* i. 420 Moost blessed Werburge..Our synguler suffrage, and sterre of our clerenes. *Ibid.* 3055 Than she requyred with humylyte The spyrytuall sufferage of holy vnccyon. 1528 Roy *Rede me* (Arb.) 86 Thorowe his passion, For vs he made satisfaccion, Withoute eny mans suffrage. 1613 R. C. *Table Alph.*, *Suffrage*, consent, or voyce, or helpe.

3. *orig.* A vote given by a member of a body, state, or society, in assent to a proposition or in favour of the election of a person; in extended sense, a vote for or against any controverted question or nomination.

1534 More *Comf. agst. Trib.* iii. xxvi. Wks. 1259/2 Euery mans assent was called his suffrages:..one kinde of those suffrages, was by certayn thynges that are in latine called *calculi*. 1588 Shaks. *Tit. A.* i. i. 218 People of Rome, and Noble Tribunes heere, I aske your voyces and your Suffrages. c 1600 Drayton *Miseries Q. Margaret* cliv, The Spirituall Lords, and Temporall,..who farre more ready are To giue, then be their suffrages to craue. 1651 Hobbes *Leviath.* iii. xlii. 290 The manner of choosing Magistrates..was by plurality of suffrages. a 1707 S. Patrick *Autobiog.* (1839) 43 The fellows came up one by one, and in a paper wrote their suffrages. 1765 Blackstone *Comm.* i. 170 In all democracies ..it is of the utmost importance to regulate by whom, and in what manner, the suffrages are to be given. 1781 J. Moore *View Soc. It.* (1790) I. viii. 79 When the election took place, all the suffrages fell upon Paul Lue. 1809–10 Coleridge *Friend* (1865) 127 Each of these [sc. inhabitants] has a right to a suffrage. 1848 Mill *Pol. Econ.* ii. i. § 2 (1876) 125 A magistrate or magistrates, whom we may suppose elected by the suffrages of the community. 1873 C. Robinson *N. S. Wales* 91 Those whose suffrages are to determine its [*i. e.* the State's] future should be able to give an intelligent vote.

b. An object, as a pebble, a marked paper, or the like, used to indicate a vote given. *rare.*

1534 More *Conf. agst. Trib.* iii. Wks. 1259/2 Vnto him which ouercometh, he will geue a white suffrage. 1665 J. Buck in Peacock *Stat. Cambr.* (1841) App. B. p. lxxviii, The Scrutators..put their suffrages into one of the Hats. 1819 Scott *Ivanhoe* xxxvii, The Grand Master had collected the suffrages. 1835 T. Mitchell *Acharn. of Aristoph.* 543 *note*, ψηφίζεσθαι, to vote by suffrages thrown into jars.

4. *gen.* A vote in support of or an opinion in favour of some person or thing; hence (now *Obs.* or *arch.*), in neutral sense, an opinion.

1594 *Selimus* E, The loue I beare to my deare Acomat, Commands me giue my suffrage vnto him. 1610 B. Jonson *Alch.* To Rdr., If it were put to the question..the worse would finde more suffrages. 1640 Hall *Episc.* ii. xiii. 166 Tertullian was..not at all below him [sc. Irenæus] in the clearnesse of his suffrage, *Edant origines &c.* 1653 *Nicholas Papers* (Camden) II. 24, I have herein sent you an Extract of the Substance of that Elector's Suffrage there concerning his Majesty. 1660 H. More *Myst. Godl.* To Rdr. 25 He that is a perfect Papist being of one mind and suffrage with his Church. 1726 Pope *Odyss.* xix. 181 My anxious parents urge a speedy choice, And to their suffrage gain the filial voice. 1750 Johnson *Rambler* No. 11 ⁋ 9 He that finds his knowledge narrow,..and by consequence his suffrage not much regarded. c 1804 Jane Austen *Watsons* in Austen-Leigh *Mem.* (1871) 322 'Oh uncle! do look at my partner; she is so pretty!'..Charles was hurried off without being able to receive his uncle's suffrage. 1822–7 Good *Study Med.* (1829) I. 423 It has not fallen to my lot..to add my suffrage in its favour. 1850 Whipple *Ess. & Rev.* (ed. 3) I. 13 He has the hesitating suffrages of men of taste, and the plaudits of the million. 1883 'Ouida' *Wanda* I. 216 The world would not be as much so if I really wanted its suffrages.

5. Approval, sanction, consent. Const. *to*. *arch.*

1598 Chapman *Iliad* viii. 7 That God nor Goddesse may attempt, t' infringe my soueraigne mind: But all giue suffrage. 1609 B. Jonson *Sil. Wom.* i. ii, I'll giue no suffrage to't. a 1652 Brome *Novella* v. i, Let me beg Your suffrage Lady, I may bid them welcome. 1668 *Rolle's Abridgm.* Publ. Pref. a 2, The Common-Law of England..hath had the suffrage of the whole Kingdome in all Ages. 1704 Evelyn *Diary* Dec., My Lord of Canterbury wrote to me for suffrage for Mr. Clarke's continuance..in the Boyle Lecture. 1787 J. Barlow *Oration 4th July* 12 The system to be established by his suffrage is calculated for the..purposes of extending peace. 1825 Scott *Jrnl.* 20 Nov., To gain your suffrage to his views, he endeavours [etc.]. 1873 H. Rogers *Orig. Bible* ii. (1875) 80 Those religious systems which happen to have the suffrage of the government.

†**b.** An instance of this; an expression or token of approval. *Obs.*

1603 Knolles *Hist. Turks* (1621) 304 Such was the glorie and valour of Huniades..as..procured vnto him the generall fauour and suffrages of all. 1607 Topsell *Four-f. Beasts* 470 The man was pardoned, and the lion was giuen vnto him for a reward or suffrage. 1610 Heywood *Gold. Age* i. i, The Queene, the Peeres, And all the people with lowd suffrages, Haue shrild their Auees. 1788 T. Taylor *Proclus* I. 9 They openly presaged, that this gift..was a future suffrage of his succession confirmed by divine events. 1829 I. Taylor *Enthus.* viii. 195 A system..which had won for itself a suffrage so general if not universal.

†**6.** The support or assurance of evidence or testimony in favour of something. *Obs.*

1606 S. Gardiner *Bk. Angling* 30 We list first to conclude our iudgement by suffrages of scriptures. 1650 Bulwer *Anthropomet.* 4 In the opinion of Claramontius, the reason of the thing gives a suffrage unto it. a 1677 Barrow *Serm.* (1686) III. ii. 17 Precepts are delivered in an universal and abstracted manner,..without any intervention, assistence, or suffrage of sense. a 1718 W. Penn *Tracts* Wks. 1726 I. 570 We herein are not without the Suffrage of the Scriptures to our Defence.

7. The collective vote of a body of persons.

1610 Heywood *Gold. Age* i. i, I choose it as my right by gift of heauen, The peoples suffrage, the dead Kings bequest. a 1700 Evelyn *Diary* 6 Jan. 1661, I was now chosen (and nominated by his Majestie for one of the Council) by suffrage of the rest of the Members, a Fellow of the Philosophic Society. 1776 Gibbon *Decl. & F.* (1782) I. xii. 384 The election of a new emperor was referred to the suffrage of the military order. 1823 Bentham *Not Paul but Jesus* 221 Philip,..one of the seven trustees, who..had been chosen by universal suffrage.

8. The collective opinion of a body of persons; hence, contextually, consensus of opinion; (common or general) consent.

1576 Fleming *Panopl. Epist.* 111 In this suffrage or voyce of consent. 1611 Coryat *Crudities* 627 Mercator..who by the vniuersall suffrage of all the learned is esteemed the most excellent cosmographer. 1662 Gunning *Lent Fast* 79 The Apostles by their common suffrage sanctified..these 7 weeks of fastings. 1697 Evelyn *Numismata* vii. 240 Head..cut in Onyx, comparable by universal Suffrage to any of the Old Masters. 1794 R. J. Sulivan *View Nat.* II. 232 To prefer their own judgment to the general suffrage of mankind. 1861 Mill *Utilitar.* ii. 16 What means are there of determining which is the acutest of two pains..except the general suffrage of those who are familiar with both? 1882 Hinsdale *Garfield & Educ.* ii. 361 He draughted a paper,..and submitted it to the suffrage of the republic of scientific scholars.

†**b.** Repute; = Opinion 6. *Obs.*

1667 Waterhouse *Narr. Fire in London* 90 She hath the suffrage abroad to be one of the most August..Governments in the world.

9. The casting of a vote, voting; the exercise of a right to vote; election by voting.

1665 Manley *Grotius' Low C. Wars* 907 They..should have right of suffrage in their Dyets and Assemblies. 1667 Milton *P. L.* ii. 415 Here he had need All circumspection, and wee now no less Choice in our suffrage. 1709 Strype *Ann. Ref.* I. xxix. 299 They went to the Suffrage in the Afternoon, and such of the House as were against the Six Articles..carried it. 1760–72 J. Adams tr. *Juan & Ulloa's Voy.* (ed. 3) II. 45 In the former [university] are chairs for all the sciences, and filled by suffrage. 1850 Marsden *Early Purit.* (1853) 300 A successor was chosen by general suffrage. 1887 Lowell *Democracy* etc. 32 The right of suffrage is not valued when indiscriminately bestowed.

†**10.** A voice or voting power in a matter. *Obs.*

a 1662 Heylin *Laud* (1668) 375 The Covenanters had so laid the Plot, that none but those of their own Party should have Suffrage in it. 1673 *Lady's Call.* Pref., The Gynecæum has still had a rival suffrage with the Senate.

11. The right or privilege of voting as a member of a body, state, etc. (orig. *U.S.*)

1789 *Constit. U. S.* v, No state shall be deprived of its equal suffrage in the Senate. 1817–8 Cobbett *Resid. U. S.* (1822) 220 The suffrage, or qualification of electors, is very various. 1840 Arnold *Hist. Rome* II. 313 The survivors.. were obliged to become Roman citizens without suffrage. 1867 Latham *Black & White* 114 No territories shall be admitted as States in which there is not an equal suffrage of all races and colours.

b. With prefixed word denoting the extent, as *female, household, manhood, universal, woman('s, women's suffrage*.

1798 W. Nares *Jacobin* vi. in *Anti-Jacobin* No. 22, I pant and sigh for univers—al suffrage. 1866 [see Household 8]. 1873 [see Manhood 7]. 1877 Gladstone *Glean.* (1879) I. 147 Is not Mr. Lowe a little hard on the universal suffrage of France, when he charges on it a protective tariff, seeing that the no-suffrage of Russia has one tenfold more protective? 1884 [see Female *a.* 4 b].

†**Su·ffrage,** *v. Obs.* [f. prec. or ad. L. *suffrāgārī* (see Suffragate).]

1. *intr.* To vote *for* or *against*; hence, to agree or side *with*, to give support *to*.

1613 T. Godwin *Rom. Antiq.* (1614) 97 Neither children.. nor old men..were allowed to suffrage in these assemblies. 1652 L. S. *People's Liberty* ix. 60 They are not to be permitted to suffrage in state affairs. 1657 Tomlinson *Renou's Disp.* 237 Yet Matthiolus will not suffrage herewith, but contends [etc.]. 1657 W. Morice *Coena quasi Κοινη* ix. 93, I never voted for exorbitant Episcopacy, nor should I have ever suffraged against a regulated. *Ibid.* Diat. vi. 309 Some, that suffrage for the Presbyterial Government. 1661 Glanvill *Van. Dogm.* 179 What he hath of this, was never learnt from his Hypotheses; but forcibly fetch'd in to suffrage to them.

2. *trans.* To elect by vote; hence, to give support to; to side with.

1641 Milton *Reform.* ii. Wks. 1851 III. 57 As well as their worldly wisedomes are priviledg'd as members of the State in suffraging their..Burgesses. 1641 *Anc. Customs Eng.* in *Harl. Misc.* (Malh.) IV. 368 Every particular subject, who is either present personally, or consenting by his assignee, suffraged by himself. 1838 S. Bellamy *Betrayal* 17 When the false god call'd Upon her tempest breath to suffrage him.

Hence †**Su·ffrager** *Obs. rare*, a voter.

1613 T. Godwin *Rom. Antiq.* (1614) 98 Little coffers, into which the suffragers which did approue the law did cast in the first table; those that disliked it, did cast in the second. 1701 *Eng. Inconv. Public & Adv. Priv. Elect.* 22 An Election ..is a Majority of Votes including the Sense of a Majority of Suffragers.

Suffragette (svfrădʒe·t). [f. Suffrage *sb.* + -ette.] A female supporter of the cause of women's political enfranchisement, *esp.* one of a violent or 'militant' type.

Attrib. uses, and derivatives such as *suffragettish, -ism* are frequent in newspapers.

1906 *Daily Mail* 10 Jan., Mr. Balfour and the 'Suffragettes'...It was not surprising that Mr. Balfour should receive a deputation of the Suffragettes. 1907 *Athenæum* 28 Sept. 358/2 [Aristophanes] who represented Cleon as noisy, Euripides as sentimental, Socrates as pedantic, and women as 'suffragettes'.

Suffragial (sǒfrē¹·dʒiăl), *a. nonce-wd.* [f. L. *suffrāgium* Suffrage + -al.] Pertaining to voting.

1844 Mozley *Ess.* (1878) II. 40 The two rights, commercial and suffragial.

†**Suffragies,** *sb. pl. Obs.* Also 3 -iis, 4–5 -ijs, 5 -iez, -yes, -is, 6 -ees. [ad. L. *suffrāgia*, pl. of *suffrāgium* Suffrage *sb.*]

1. Prayers, *esp.* on behalf of the departed.

a 1225 *Ancr. R.* 22 A morwen, oþer a niht efter þe suffragiis of Uhtsong, sigge Commendacium. c 1380 Wyclif *Sel. Wks.* III. 259 No prelat may assoylle, ne graunte hevenely suffragies. 1432–50 tr. *Higden* (Rolls) VI. 195 Suffragyes doen for dedde men. 1450 *Rolls of Parlt.* V. 188/1 A solempne Obite..to be..founden with other certayn observauncez and suffragiez. a 1533 Frith *Disput. Purgat.* i. Wks. (1573) 17 He shal lye in the paynes of purgatory, vntill he be deliuered thence by Masse pence, the Popes pardon or certaine other Suffragies. 1555 Eden *Decades* (Arb.) 293 They..thinke that the soules of deade menne are not helped with the suffragies of preestes.

2. Votes, opinions, testimonies.

1587 D. Fenner *Def. Ministers* 26 Lett him neither be a Commaunder or Lorde, nor a slaue vnto the suffragies, but a fellowe & a discerner. 1593 R. Harvey *Philad.* 9 If nothing be true in one country which hath not suffragees from another Countrey, I cannot tell what historie may stand.

†**Su·ffraging,** *vbl. sb. Obs.* [f. Suffrage *v.* + -ing ¹.] The exercise of the suffrage, voting.

1613 T. Godwin *Rom. Antiq.* (1614) 101 They also having freedome of suffraging. 1691–2 Wood *Fasti Oxon.* II. 107 An equal power of suffraging did not now pertain to all masters.

†**Suffra·ginous,** *a. Obs. rare*⁻¹. [ad. L. *suffrāginōsus*, f. *suffrāgin-*, Suffrago.] Of, belonging to, or affecting the hocks of animals.

1646 Sir T. Browne *Pseud. Ep.* iii. i. 106 The bought of the fore-legs [in the elephant] not directly backward,..the hough or suffraginous flexure behinde rather outward. 1656 Blount *Glossogr.*, *Suffraginous*, that is diseased in the houghes or pasterns.

Suffragism (sv·frădʒiz'm). [f. next + -ism.] The advocacy of an extension of the suffrage, e.g. to women (*women's suffragism*).

1888 Bryce *Amer. Commw.* xciii. III. 301 Women's suffragism is thought 'bad form'. 1908 *Lit. Guide* 1 Aug. 123/2 He does, indeed, make a remark on feminine achievement in those spheres, but we dare not repeat it in this year of suffragism.

Suffragist (sv·frădʒist). [f. Suffrage + -ist.] An advocate of the extension of the political franchise, *esp.* (since about 1885) to women. Often with prefixed word (cf. Suffrage *sb.* 11 b), as *complete suffragist, universal suffragist, woman suffragist*.

1822 *Blackw. Mag.* XII. 156 If they come back Universal Suffragists, we offer to turn Radicals. 1845 *Tait's Mag.* XII. 67 The Complete-suffragists, will say, that..the League are practically admitting the truth of what they have always urged...Which..furnishes one reason the more why the Suffragists should help the League. 1865 *Pall Mall Gaz.* 17 Oct. 5 The anti-negro-suffragists in Connecticut. 1883 *American* VI. 7 The most persistent suffragist claims no more than this. 1900 *N. Eng. Hist. & Gen. Reg.* Suppl. cxxi, The cause of the woman suffragists. 1914 *Daily Mail* 8 June 6/6, I am a woman and a suffragist.

‖**Suffrago** (sǒfrē¹·go). *Anat.* [L.] The 'heel' at the junction of the tibia and the tarsus in quadrupeds and birds.

1842 Brande *Dict. Sci.* etc., *Suffrago*, in Mammalogy and Ornithology, the joint of the tibia with the tarsus. 1872 Coues *N. Amer. Birds* 240 The feathers rarely reach the suffrago.

Suffraine, -ayn(d, obs. forms of Sovereign.

†**Suffre·te.** *Obs.* Also 5 -aite. [a. OF. *s(o)uffrete, -aite* = Pr. *sofracha*, It. †*soffratta*:— L. *suffracta-m*, pa. pple. fem. (used as sb.) of *suffringĕre* to break up, f. *suf-* = Sub- 25 + *frangĕre* to break.] Want, need.

c 1450 *Merlin* iii. 59 Many provertees [*sic*] and grete suffraites suffred oure lorde her in erthe for oure sake. 1481 Caxton *Godfrey* xciii. 144 Vytayll began to faylle, And was grete suffrete and scarsenes in thoost.

†**Suffretous,** *a. Obs.* Also 5 **suffretouse, -ateuse, -atous.** [a. OF. *suffretous, -aitous* (mod. F. *souffreteux*), = Pr. *sofrachos*; f. *suffraite* (see prec.).] Needy, in want, miserable.

c 1450 *Merlin* xiii. 201 He knoweth beste the pore and the suffretouse. 1481 Caxton *Godfrey* ccix. 306 The hoost.. were but fewe and suffretous by cause they had no shippes. 1490 — *Eneydos* i. 13 Now was that pyetous cyte..putte in desolacyon suffretous. 1491 — *Vitas Patr.* (W. de W. 1495) i. xli. 64 b/2 Tyll that thou haste dystrybuted alle thyse goodes..to the suffretous, poore and nedy.

Suffreyn, obs form of Sovereign.

14.. in *Tundale's Vis.* (1843) 149 Fyrst hyle to hym honowre That suffreyn is and socowre.

†**Su·ffriate,** *v. Obs. rare*⁻⁰. [f. pa. ppl. stem of L. **suffriāre*, f. *suf-* = Sub- 25 + *friāre* (see Friable).]

1623 Cockeram, *Suffriate*, to crumble bread.

†**Suffricate,** *v. Obs. rare*⁻⁰. [f. pa. ppl. stem of L. *suffricāre*, f. *suf-* = Sub- 25 + *fricāre* to rub.] 1623 Cockeram, *Suffricate*, to rub off.

†**Suffront.** *Obs.* [app. f. *suf-* = Sub- 3 + Front *sb.* (9 b).] ? An altar-frontal.

1526 in G. Oliver *Lives Bps. Exeter* etc. (1861) 364 Suffront, stayned de blodio bokeram cum ymagine Crucifixi. 1668 Bp. Hacket *Let.* in T. T. Carter *Life J. Kettlewell* (1895) 49 In velvet, purple and azure, fifty pounds worth.. to serve as paraphront or suffront, and carpet for the Altar. a 1670 — *Abp. Williams* ii. (1693) 107 Paraphront, Suffront, for the Hangings above and beneath the Table.

Suffrutescent (svfrute·sĕnt), *a. Bot.* [ad. mod.L. *suffrutescens, -ent-*, f. *suf-* = Sub- 20 c + *frutescens* Frutescent. So F.] Somewhat woody or shrubby at the base.

1816 *Edwards' Bot. Reg.* II. 130 *Arctotis maculata*. White tawny-stained suffrutescent Arctotis. 1829 Loudon *Encycl. Plants* (1836) 729 Stem suffrutescent. 1880 A. Gray *Struct. Bot.* iii. § 3. 50 Undershrubs or Suffruticose plants, are woody plants of humble stature...If less decidedly woody, they are termed Suffrutescent.

‖**Suffrutex** (sv·fruteks). *Bot.* Pl. **suffrutices** (svfrū·tisīz); also 7 *erron.* -ages (but cf. Fruitage 3). [mod.L., f. *suf-* = Sub- 22 + Frutex.] A plant having a woody base, but a herbaceous annual growth above.

1567 Maplet *Gr. Forest* 27 A fourth kind [of plant] which they cal Suffutrex [*sic*] a mean betwene the Herbe and the shrub. 1691 Ray *Creation* i. (1692) 154 Odoriferous and ever-green Shrubs and Suffrutices. a 1706 Evelyn *Silva* (1776) 509 Herbaceous Suffrutages. 1726 *Dict. Rust.* (ed. 3), *Suffrutex*, is a low Woody perennial Plant, that sends out no leaves from its Roots; and beginning to be branch'd from the very bottom of the Stalk, as Lavender, Sage, Rue, and the like. 1866 in *Treas. Bot.*

†**Suffruti·ceous, -ious,** *a. Bot. Obs.* [f. mod. L. *suffrutic-* (see prec.) + -eous, -ious.] = next.

1657 Tomlinson *Renou's Disp.* 283 Kermes..is the name of a Suffruticeous Plant. 1657 *Physical Dict.*, *Suffruticious*, between a shrub and an herb.

Suffruticose (svfrū·tikōs), *a. Bot.* [ad. mod. L. *suffruticōsus*, f. *suffrutic-*, Suffrutex + -ose.] Of the character of a suffrutex; woody at the base but herbaceous above.

1793 Martyn *Lang. Bot.*, *Suffruticosus*, Suffruticose, Undershrubby. 1842 Loudon *Suburban Hort.* 430 Raspberries being suffruticose plants. 1842 Brande *Dict. Sci.* etc. s. v., Lavender is an instance of a suffruticose plant. 1876 Harley *Mat. Med.* (ed. 6) 362 Litmus Lichens are rigid suffruticose lichens.

So †**Suffru·ticous** *a. Obs. rare.*

1776 J. Lee *Introd. Bot.* Explan. Terms 378 *Suffruticosus*, suffruticous, half-shrubby.

†**Suffu·lce,** *v. Obs. rare.* [ad. L. *suffulcīre*, f. *suf-* = Sub- 25 + *fulcīre* to prop, but ? confused with *suffarcināre* to stuff.] *trans.* To stuff.

1599 A. M. tr. *Gabelhouer's Bk. Physicke* 106/2 For Asthmasye..Take 14 or 15 figges, suffulce, or fille the same with Mustard seed. *Ibid.* 111/2 Gird the bodye..with the suffulced little pillowes.

†**Suffu·lt,** *v. Obs. rare*⁻¹. [f. L. *suffult-*, pa. ppl. stem of *suffulcīre* (see prec.).] *trans.* To support.

c 1540 tr. *Pol. Verg. Eng. Hist.* (Camden 36) 181 Hee minded to have suffultid and releeved religion with his goods.

Suffulted (svfv·ltĕd), *a. Ent.* [f. L. *suffultus*, pa. pple. of *suffulcīre* (see above) + -ed.] See quot.

1826 Kirby & Sp. *Entomol.* IV. xlvi. 287 Suffulted Pupil (*Pupilla suffulta*). When the pupil shades into another colour.

†**Suffu·me,** *v. Obs. rare*⁻¹. [ad. L. **suffūmāre*, f. *suf-* = Sub- 2, 25 + *fūmāre* to Fume.] *trans.* To suffumigate. Hence †**Suffu·me** *sb.*, a suffumigation.

1540 R. Jonas *Byrth Mankynde* 19 b, It shalbe also verye profytable for her to suffume the nether places with muske. 1656 Ridgley *Pract. Physick* 20 Resolving suffumes are profitable.

Suffumigate (svfiū·migeⁱt), *v. rare.* Also 6 *pa. pple.* (*Sc.*) **suffumigat.** [f. pa. pple. of L. *suffūmigāre*, f. *suf-* = Sub- 2, 25 + *fūmigāre* to Fumigate.]

1. *trans.* To fumigate from below.

1588 Alex. Hume *Hymns* vii. 35 Suffumigat with nard and cinnamon. 1612 Woodall *Surg. Mate* Wks. (1653) 202 The patients hinder parts well suffumigated with the same decoction. 1623 Cockeram, *Suffumigate*, to smoake underneath. 1910 Kipling *Rewards & Fairies* 270, I sprinkled sulphur on the faggots whereby the on-lookers were as handsomely suffumigated.

†**2.** *intr.* To rise in smoke or vapour. *Obs.*

1599 A. M. tr. *Gabelhouer's Bk. Physicke* 219/2 Take greene Corne or seede, lay it on coales, and it will suffumigate.

Suffumigation (svfiūmigē¹·ʃən). Now *arch.* or *Hist.* [ad. L. *suffūmigātio, -ōnem*, n. of action f. *suffūmigāre* to Suffumigate. Cf. OF. *subfumigation*, F. *suffumigation*.] The action of suffumigating or fumigating from below; an instance of this; chiefly *concr.* (usually *pl.*): fumes or vapours generated by burning herbs, incense, etc.; also *occas.*, a substance used for this purpose.

a. *Med.* used to produce a therapeutic effect by penetration of the body.

1422 Yonge *Secr. Secr.* lxiii. 239 Aftyr that man sholde vse suffumygacionys of herbis. a 1425 tr. *Arderne's Treat. Fistula* etc. 74 Afterward be þer done suffumigacion or

fomentacion. 1540 R. Jonas *Byrth Mankynde* 26 Yf this profet nothynge, then vse this suffumigation. Take myrrhe, galbanum, castorium [etc.]. 1599 A. M. tr. *Gabelhouer's Bk. Physicke* 65/1 Let the suffumigatione therof ascende to thy Eares. 1601 Holland *Pliny* II. Expl. Wds. Art, *Suffumigation*, is the smoke that is received into the body from under a stoole, for the diseases of the guts, fundament, or matrice. 1604 Jas. I *Counterbl. to Tobacco* (Arb.) 100 The stinking Suffumigation whereof [sc. of tobacco] they yet vse against that disease. 1635 Brathwait *Arcadian Princ.* 235, I meane by sweatings and suffumigations to extract all those viscid and oily humours. 1684 tr. *Bonet's Merc. Compit.* xiv. 494 A Phthisical Person [cured]..by a Suffumigation of Amber. 1769 E. Bancroft *Guiana* 87 The Indians..often use it by way of suffumigation, for rheums, bead-achs etc. 1835 Browning *Paracelsus* iii. 442 Such a suffumigation as, once fired, Had stunk the patient dead ere he could groan.

b. used in incantations, in the offering of sacrifices, and in witchcraft to excite evil spirits.

[1390, 14..: see Subfumigation.]

1565 Jewel *Repl. Harding* (1611) 427 The Sacrifices, that in Old times were made vnto Fides, and Terminus,..consisted only in Suffumigations, and Odors. 1567 Fenton *Trag. Disc.* iii. (1898) 153 Diverse suffumigacions incident to witchecrafte. 1614 Selden *Titles Hon.* 9 To these were ..giuen diuine worship and ceremonies with suffumigations, crownes of flowers, and other rites. 1646 J. Gregory *Notes & Obs.* (1650) 97 They observed such a place of the Moone, made such a suffumigation, uttered such and such words at the graffing of one Tree upon another. 1652 Gaule *Magastrom.* 222 A suffumigation made with the congealed blood of an Asse, and the fat of a wolfe, and Storax. 1696 Aubrey *Misc.* (1721) 172 Evil Spirits are pleased and allured and called up by Suffumigations of Henbane &c. stinking Smells, &c. 1830 Scott *Demonol.* i. 46 The nostrils are made to inhale such suffumigation, as well as the mouth. 1856 R. A. Vaughan *Mystics* (1860) II. viii. iii. 119 *note*, The sympathetic influence..of stones and metals, ointments and suffumigations.

†**c.** *gen.* A fume, vapour. *Obs.*

1567 Maplet *Gr. Forest* 72 Suffumigation of Brimstone. a 1618 Harington *De Valet. Conserv.* (1624) 43 Your parlors or Chambers being first purged and ayred with suffumigations. 1614 T. Adams *Diuells Banket* iii. 109 As the suffumigations of the oppressed stomach, surge vp and cause the head-ach. 1651 H. More *Enthus. Tri.* (1712) 5 A little reek or suffumigation.

Hence †**Suffumiga·tious** *a.*, used for suffumigation.

1688 Holme *Armoury* ii. vi. 119/3 Suffumigatious Gums, or such as are for Perfumes.

†**Suffumige.** *Obs. rare.* [ad. med.L. *suffūmigium* (whence It., Pg. *suffumigio*), f. *suffūmigāre* to Suffumigate.] = Suffumigation.

1666 G. Harvey *Morb. Angl.* xx. 245 Drying suffumiges or smoaks are oft prescribed with good success. [1855 Dunglison *Med. Lex.*, *Suffimentum*, a perfume; suffumige; fumigation.]

†**Suffu·nd,** *v. Obs. rare*⁻¹. [ad. L. *suffundĕre* (see Suffuse).] *trans.* To suffuse.

1657 Tomlinson *Renou's Disp.* 68 Many stones may be ignified..and still suffunded with a certain humour.

†**Suffurate,** *v. Obs. rare.* [f. pa. ppl. stem of L. *suffūrārī*, f. *suf-* = Sub- 25 + *fūrārī*, f. *fur* thief.] *trans.* To steal away.

1549 E. Becke *Bible* Pref. A A vi, If all magistrates..wolde ..vouchsafe to suffurate & spare an houre or ii in a day, from theyr worldly busines. a 1564 Becon *Nosegay* Pref., Wks. (1843) 195 At such hours as I could conveniently suffurate and steal away from the..teaching of my scholars.

Hence †**Suffura·tion**, a drawing away.

1651 Biggs *New Disp.* ⁋ 297 The Spagyrick art..doth debilitate many things by a privie and insensible suffuration.

Suffuse (sǒfiū·z), *v.* [f. L. *suffūs-*, pa. ppl. stem of *suffundĕre*, f. *suf-* = Sub- 2, 25 + *fundĕre* to pour.]

1. *trans.* To overspread as with a fluid, a colour, a gleam of light.

a. of tears, moisture. Chiefly *pass.*

1590 [see Suffused 1]. 1600 Fairfax *Tasso* xii. lxxiv, His eies vnclos'd, with teares suffused. 1754 Hume *Hist. Eng., Chas. I*, x. I. 461 Hamilton long followed him with his eyes, all suffused in tears. 1773–83 Hoole *Orl. Fur.* xviii. 1162 While tears his cheeks suffuse. 1797 S. & Ht. Lee *Canterb. T.* (1799) I. 352 His whole frame [was] suffused with a cold dew. 1838 Prescott *Ferd. & Is.* xiii. II. 115 Every eye was suffused with tears.

b. of light, air, fire, colour. Often in fig. context.

1728–46 Thomson *Spring* 1086 Dark looks succeed; Suffus'd, and glaring with untender fire. 1786 tr. *Beckford's Vathek* (1883) 33 To hide the blush of mortification that suffused their foreheads. 1813 Shelley *Q. Mab* vi. 25 A kindling gleam of hope Suffused the Spirit's lineaments. 1828 Wordsw. *Even. Volunt.* ix. 45 Yon hazy ridges..Climbing suffused with sunny air. 1860 Tyndall *Glac.* i. xxv. 184 The glorious light..suffused with gold and crimson the atmosphere itself. 1877 Black *Green Past.* xxxv. 283 The beautiful colour that for a second suffused her blushing face. 1882 *Garden* 5 Aug. 119/1 Sepals and flowers white, suffused at base with rosy lilac.

c. *transf.* and *fig.*

1813 Coleridge *Night-scene* 43 Eyes suffused with rapture. 1848 W. H. Bartlett *Egypt to Pal.* v. (1879) 101 The life and literature of the nation were suffused with these reminiscences. 1867 J. B. Rose tr. *Virg. Æneid* 160 The crowded ranks Of disembodied Shades suffused the banks. 1868 Helps *Realmah* ii. (1876) 10 The most commonplace objects being suffused with beauty. 1876 Holland *Sev. Oaks* xv. 234 The amused expression suffused the lawyer's face.

2. To pour (a liquid) over a surface. (Also *refl.*) Chiefly in fig. context.

1734 tr. *Rollin's Roman Hist.* (1827) III. vii. 328 Suffusing over the study of philosophy the dye of rhetoric. 1825 *Ann. Reg., Chron.* 92/2 Water, sugar, &c. from the boiler and pans..suffused thickly upon the trees. 1829 I. Taylor *Enthus.* x. 282 The healing flood of Christian truth shall suffuse itself in all directions. 1854 *Jrnl. R. Agric. Soc.* XV. ii. 427 Springs, suffused from higher grounds.

Suffused (sǒfiū·zd), *ppl. a.* [f. prec. + -ed ¹.]

1. Overspread as with fluid, light, colour, etc.

1590 Spenser *F. Q.* iii. vii. 10 Wiping the teares from her suffused eyes. 1629 Quarles *Argalus & Parthen.* ii. Wks. (Grosart) III. 264/2 Which strongly did importune A world of teares from these suffused eyes. 1805 *Med. Jrnl.* XIV. 201 The eyes became more suffused and dull. 1878 Browning *La Saisiaz* 71 How suffused a cheek You had turned me had I sudden brought the blush into the smile.

2. Spread over a surface like water. Also *fig.*

1851 Mrs. Browning *Casa Guidi Wind.* i. 817 The deep look which shall drain Suffused thought into channelled enterprise. 1873 Black *Pr. Thule* xxvi. 432 There was a faint suffused sense of joy in her heart.

Hence **Suffu·sedly** *adv.*, in a suffused manner.

1895 Meyrick *Brit. Lepidopt.* 461 Forewings whitish.. dorsum suffusedly fuscous.

Suffusion (sǒfiū·ʒən). Also 7 -tion. [ad. L. *suffūsio, -ōnem*, n. of action f. *suffūs-* (see Suffuse). Cf. F. *suffusion*, It. *suffusione*, etc.]

1. The defluxion or extravasation of a fluid or 'humour' over a part of the body; † *concr.* the fluid itself; *spec.* in *Old Med.*, cataract.

1398 Trevisa *Barth. De P. R.* xvii. xli. (Bodl. MS.) An oynemente þat..helpeþ a3ens suffusion of y3en. 1575 Turberv. *Faulconrie* 235 Ther is a cataract which doth light upon the eyes of a hawke whome we may tearme a suffusion. 1608 Topsell *Serpents* 209 The braine [sc. of lizards] is profitable for suffusions. 1667 Milton *P. L.* iii. 26 So thick a drop serene hath quencht thir Orbs, Or dim suffusion veild. 1674 W. Bates *Harmony Div. Attrib.* vii. 140 As the Eye that is clouded with a Suffusion, so that all things appear yellow to it. 1688 Boyle *Vit. Sight* 251, I have observed them [sc. flyes in the eye] to continue many years without being more than a bastard suffusion, as Physicians speake. 1726 *Dict. Rust.* (ed. 3), Suffusion of the Eye, in a Horse, is a Sort of Pin and Web. 1728 *Chambers' Cycl.* s. v., The Jaundice is a Suffusion of Bile over the whole Body. 1748 V. Renatus *Dis. Horses* 70 A Suffusion or Defluxion in their Feet. 1859 Mayne *Expos. Lex.* s.v., A suffusion, or extravasation of some humour, as of blood in the eye.

2. The action of suffusing a surface with fluid, moisture, or colour; the condition of being suffused or overspread. Also, an instance of this.

1611 Cotgr., *Suffusion*, a suffusion, or powring vpon; a spreading abroad. 1642 H. More *Song of Soul* ii. iii. 49 Miry clods of this accursed earth; Whose dull suffusions make her often sown. 1789 E. Darwin *Bot. Gard.* ii. (1791) 65 In dim suffusion lies The glance divine, that lighten'd in their eyes. 1813 Scott *Trierm.* iii. xxx, The golden glow..O'er which in slight suffusion flows A frequent tinge of paly rose. 1843 R. J. Graves *Syst. Clin. Med.* xi. 127 He had..a furious aspect, suffusion of the eyes..and perfect sleeplessness. 1872 Darwin *Emotions* viii. 218 The suffusion of the eyes with tears.

fig. 1676 Cudworth *Intell. Syst.* i. iv. 224 Because he.. being deeply tinctured, as it were, with the Suffusions of it [sc. a doctrine], every thing which he look'd upon, seem'd to him coloured with it. 1792 A. Young *Trav. France* I. 251 There is in this painting such a suffusion of grace, and such a blaze of beauty [etc.]. 1852 Ld. Cockburn *Life Jeffrey* I. 91 A clear sweet voice, and a general suffusion of elegance.

3. A colouring or tint spread over a surface, *esp.* over the skin by the action of the blood, etc.; *freq.* a flush of colour in the face, a blush.

1700 Dryden *Ovid's Met.* xv. 287 The Disk of Phœbus when he climbs on high, Appears at first but as a bloodshot Eye; And when his Chariot downward drives to Bed, His Ball is with the same Suffusion red. 1712 Steele *Spect.* No. 390 ⁋ 1 Would she not be much more modest without that ambiguous Suffusion? 1745 Akenside *Odes, Agst. Suspicion* ii, Already in your eyes I see a pale suffusion rise. 1763 *Phil. Trans.* LIII. 232 He..had a yellow suffusion over his skin. 1777 G. Forster *Voy. round World* I. 102 A beautiful suffusion of purple. 1818 Scott *Br. Lamm.* ix, The deadly paleness..gave place to a deep and rosy suffusion. 1843 R. J. Graves *Syst. Clin. Med.* viii. 93 The tunica adnata was of a pearl-white colour, without the slightest suffusion.

Suffusive (sǒfiū·siv), *a.* [f. L. *suffūs-* (see Suffuse) + -ive.] Tending to suffuse or spread.

1889 J. M. Robertson *Ess. Crit. Meth.* 152 Interest in the love-stories and satisfaction in the minor character-drawing have passed into retrospection and suffusive musing. 1891 *Harper's Mag.* June 65/1 Purple and saffron and a suffusive blood-red flush.

‖**Sufi** ¹ (sū·fi). Forms: 7 **Sufi**, 7, 9 **Sofee**, 8 **Souffee**, 8–9 **Sofi**, 9 **Soof(f)ee, Soofi, Soophee**, 9 **Sufi.** [a. Ar. صوفي *çūfī* lit. 'man of wool', f. صوف *çūf* wool (see Margoliouth *Early Devel. Mohamm.*, 1914, 141). Cf. F. *sofi, soufi*. It has often been erron. associated with Sophy ¹, q.v.] One of a sect of Mohammedan ascetic mystics who in later times embraced pantheistic views.

1653 Greaves *Seraglio* 178 Those Turks which..would be accounted Sofees [*marg.* Puritans] do commonly read, as they walk along the streets. 1796 Morse *Amer. Geog.* II. 571 Some of them called Souffees, who are a kind of quietists. 1815 Elphinstone *Acc. Caubul* (1842) I. Introd. 83 The mystical doctrines of the Sofees. 1872 Lowell *Dante* Prose Wks. 1890 IV. 149 A Soofi who has passed the fourth step of initiation. 1875 *Encycl. Brit.* II. 677/2 The Persian Sufis specially distinguished themselves by their practice of abstinence and solitary meditation.

attrib. 1815 Elphinstone *Acc. Caubul* (1842) I. 273 The beauty of the Soofee system. 1886 Conder *Syrian Stone-Lore* ix. (1896) 342 *note*, The 'path', the final 'unity' with God, the disbelief in all creeds, [etc.]..which form the great Sufi doctrines, are purely Buddhist.

Sufi ², erron. form of Sophy ¹.

1876 *Encycl. Brit.* IV. 707/1 The Sophi or Sufi of Persia. *Ibid.* V. 175/1 The palace of the Sufi princes.

†**Su·fian,** *a.* and *sb. Obs.* Also 6 **Sophian**, 7 **Suffean.** [f. Sufi ¹ + -an.] **A.** *adj.* Belonging to the Sufis. **B.** *sb.* A Sufi.

1585 T. Washington tr. *Nicholay's Voy.* iii. xx. 108 For that in the Arabian tongue wool is called Sophy, those which are of this sect are called Sophians...The Sophians whiche are the Persians, weare redde ones [sc. turbans]. 1698 Fryer *Acc. E. India & P.* 268 One of the Suffean Creed is Constituted Governor.

Sufic (sū·fik), *a.* [f. Sufi ¹ + -ic.] Pertaining to the Sufis or their mystical system.

1884 *Encycl. Brit.* XVII. 522/2 There are frequent Sûfic allegories [in the *Iskandarnâma*], just as in the *Makhzan*. 1914 Margoliouth *Early Devel. Mohamm.* 153 To a certain extent the Ṣūfic fasting and simplicity of diet was based on medical theory.

Sufiism (sū·fiiz'm). Also **Soofeeism, Sufyism, Suffeeism, Sufeism.** [f. Sufi ¹ + -ism.] = next.

1817 C. Mills *Hist. Muhammedanism* 407 The..visionary doctrines of Soofeeism. 1844 H. H. Wilson *Brit. India* I. 101 The blended abstractions of Sufyism and the Vedanta. 1864 *Lond. Rev.* 28 May, Hafiz, with his mystic Suffeeism. 1880 *Encycl. Brit.* XI. 368/1 The system of philosophy professed by Persian poets and dervishes..is called Sufiism.

So **Sufii·stic** *a.*, pertaining to Sufiism.

1880 *Encycl. Brit.* XI. 368/1 The Sufiistic system of philosophy.

Sufism (sū·fiz'm). Also **Sofism.** [f. Suf(i) ¹ + -ism.] The mystical system of the Sufis.

1836 *Partington's Brit. Cycl. Lit.*, etc. III. 854 Sufism, the pantheistic mysticism of the East. 1847 in Webster. 1898 E. P. Evans *Evol. Ethics* iv. 126 In Persia a highly mystical and poetical sofism has grown up.

Also **Su·fist** = Sufi ¹ (in quot. *attrib.*); **Sufi·stic** *a.*, pertaining to Sufism.

1854 Lowell *Journ. Italy* Prose Wks. 1890 I. 199 He should take his motto from Bishop Golias's '*Mihi est propositum in tabernâ mori*', though not in the sufistic sense of that misunderstood Churchman. 1913 *Everyman* 13 June 269/1 The Sûfist mystic, Jelalu' d' Din Rumi.

Sufon, obs. form of Seven.

†**Sug,** *sb.*¹ *Obs.* Variant of Sog *sb.*

1578 Lyte *Dodoens* 511 The Rushes grow in low moyst sugges [*edd.* 1595, 1610 sugs], or waterie places.

†**Sug,** *sb.*² *Obs.* Also 7 **sugg.** [Origin unknown.] A species of fish-louse parasitic on the trout.

1653 Walton *Angler* iii. 90 Many of them [sc. trout] have sticking on them Sugs or Trout lice, which is a kind of a worm, in shape like a Clove or a Pin with a big head. 1668 Wilkins *Real Char.* ii. v. § 2. 125. 1688 Holme *Armoury* ii. ix. 190. 1758 Binnell *Descr. Thames* 176.

Sug (svg), *v. dial.* (chiefly west-country). Also **sugg.** [Variant of Sog *v.*] To soak (*trans.* and *intr.*).

1633 T. Adams *Exp. 2 Peter* ii. 5 As land by long sugging under the waters hath the heart of it eaten out. 1706 Phillips (ed. Kersey), To *Sug*, to soak in Water. 1733 W. Ellis *Chiltern & Vale Farm.* 276 Its spungy, deep Roots will sugg, rot, and die here in a few Years.

Sugan, variant form of Suggan *sb.*

Sugar (ʃu·gəɹ), *sb.* Forms: see below. [a. OF. *çucre* (12–14th c.), *çuquere, zuchre, sukere*, north-east. *chucre*, mod.F. *sucre* (from 13th c.), = Pr. *sucre*, It. *zucchero*, ad. (prob. through OHG.) med.L. *succarum, zuccarum*, ad. Arab. سكر *sukkar* (with prefixed article *assukkar*, whence Sp. *azucar*, Pg. *assucar*). The phonological history of the Eng. forms is in several points obscure. (1) The *g* of the modern form (see γ-forms below) cannot be accounted for by any known OF. or AF. forms (but med.L. *zugurum* occurs); cf., however, AF. *segerstaine*, Norman F. *segrestein* = OF. *secrestain* (see Sexton), and Eng. *flagon* representing F. *flacon*. (2) The quantity of the vowel of the first syllable appears to have been variable from early times (cf. the spellings *suigur, sewger, seukere*, and *suggur*), but the development of initial (si) into (ʃ) makes it probable that the long *ū* prevailed (cf. *sure*), and that shortening took place afterwards; (siu·gəɹ) survives in some north midl. districts. (3) The Sc. forms (δ) pronounced (sv·kər) show a survival of the short vowel type from F. (sükr), but LG. influence is also possible.

The relation of Arab. *sukkar* to Gr. σάκχαρον, σάκχαρ (whence L. *saccharon*, Saccharum), Pers. *shakar*, Skr. *śarkarā* (Prakrit *sakkara*) ground or candied sugar, orig. pebble, grit (cf. Jaggery), is not clear. Forms representing one or other of the types are found in most European languages: e.g. MLG. *sucker*, MDu. *sucker, sûker, suycker* (mod. Du. *suiker*), OHG. *sucura* (MHG. *zuc(k)er*, G. *zucker*), Icel. *sykr*, MSw. *so(c)ker, sucker* (Sw. *socker*, Da. *sukker*), Lit. Russ. *cukor*, Serb. *cukar*, Boh. *cukr*, Pol. *cukier*, Turk. *sukker*; Rum. *zahăr*, Russ. *sakharŭ*, Serb. *šećer*, †*cahara*, †*cakarn*, Bulg. *sheker, zahar'*, Turk. *sheker*.]

1. A sweet crystalline substance, white when pure, obtained from a great variety of plant juices, but chiefly from those of the sugar-cane and sugar-beet, and forming an important article of human food.

Sugar-candy

Sugar-cane.

Sugar-loaf.

Sugared (ppl. a.)

Sugariness

Sugaring

Sugarish

Sugarly, *adv. Obs. rare*—1. In 5 **sugerlie**.

Sugar-maple. The North American *Acer saccharinum*, which yields maple-sugar.

Sugar-plate. *Obs.* [orig. *sucre in* Plate *sb.*] A dainty kind of a flat cake; see Plate *sb.*

Sugar-roset: see Roset *sb.* 1 a.

Sugar-sop. [Sugar *sb.* 8 *Sc.* suear-sap, *sb. dial.* sugar-sop.] Cf. Sugar *sb.* + -able Cf. Subjectable.

Sugar-plum (**†-loaved**) *ppl. a.*, shaped like a sugar-loaf.

Sugar-plum *v. trans.*, to reward or pacify with sweetmeats; hence, to pet, cosset.

Suggan, (*sə'gæn, sʌ'gæn*). *Anglo-Irish.* Also 5 **suggin**, 9 soo-, **s(o)ugan**, suggaun, -awn.

Suggest *v.* [ad. L. *suggest-*, ppl. stem of *suggerĕre*, f. *sug-* = Sub- + *gerĕre* to bear, carry, bring.]

Suggested, *ppl. a. Obs.*

Suggester. *Obs.* One who suggests.

Suggesting, *vbl. sb.* [-ing 1] The action of the vb. Suggest; an instance of this, a suggestion.

Suggesting, *ppl. a.* [-ing 2] Prompting to evil, tempting.

Suggestingly, *adv.*, in a suggesting manner.

Suggestion (*sə'dʒestʃən, -tjən*). Forms: 4–5 suggestioun, -tioune, -tioun, suggestion[i], 4–6 suggestyon, (5 suggestyoune), -cioun, 6 suggestion. [a. F. suggestion.]

Suggestibility (*sə'dʒestə'biliti*). [f. next + -ity.] Quality or condition of being suggestible.

Suggestible (*sə'dʒestib'l*). [f. Suggest *v.* + -ible.]

Suggestionable, *a. rare.* [f. prec. + -able] = Suggestibility 1.

Suggestionism. [f. Suggestion + -ism.]

Suggestive (*sə'dʒestiv*). [ad. L. *suggestivus*, f. *suggest-*: see Suggest *v.* and -ive.]

Suicidal (*sjuːi'said'l*), *a.* Also 7 *sui*-cide. [ad. mod. L. *suicidium*, f. *sui* of oneself + *-cīdium* -CIDE.]

Suicide (*sjuːi'said*), *sb.* Also 7 sui-cide. [ad. mod. L. *suicidium.*]

Suicide, *v.* [f. prec. Cf. F. *se suicider.*]

Suicidical, *a. Obs. rare*—1.

Suicidism (*sjuːi'saidiz'm*). The doctrine or practice of suicide.

Su'icidist. One who commits suicide.

Su'icism. *Obs.* [In sense 1, app. f. L. *sui* of oneself + -ism, with intercalated *c*; in sense 2, f. Sui-cide + -ism.]

Sui juris (*sjuːai dʒuːris*). *Law.* [L. — of one's own right.]

Suing (*sjuːiŋ*), *vbl. sb.* [f. Sue *v.* + -ing 1.]

Suint (*swint*). [a. F. *suint*, earlier *† suin*.] The natural greasy substance in the wool of sheep, consisting of fatty matter combined with potash salts.

Suiogothic (*swiːo'gɒθik*), *a.* and *sb.* Also 8 Suo-gothic, Sueo-gothic. [f. *Sviar* (Swedes), + Gothic.]

Suist (*sjuːist*). [f. L. *sui* of oneself + -ist.] One who seeks his own interest.

Suite (*swiːt*). [Fr.]

Suivte, *obs.* past t. Swipe.

Suix, obs. f. Six.

Suisse (*swiːs*). [F. = 'Swiss'.] The porter of a large house; the beadle of a church (in France).

†Suist. *Obs.* [f. L. *sui* of oneself + *-ist*.] One who follows his own inclinations; a self-pleaser.

Suit (*siūt*), *sb.* Forms: 3–4 sywte, 3–8 sute, 4–6 seute, sewte, suyt, 4–8 suyte, 4–9 suite, sewte, sywte, suyte, soute, 4–5 suyt, 5–7 suet, 5–6 sut, 6–8 sutte, soytt, Sc. soitt, soyt, soyte, 6–7 Sc. suitt, 6–8 shute, 7 suet, sout, shutte, sutet, *dial.* illiterate shoot, 5–7 **suit**.

1. *Feudal Law.*
1. a. In full, *suit of court*: Attendance by a tenant at the court of his lord.

2. *Suit and service*: attendance at court and personal service.

3. The resort of tenants to a certain mill to have their corn ground; the obligation of such resort.

†4. A due paid in lieu of attendance at the court of a lord.

†5. Pursuit, chase; also, a pursuit. Phr. *to follow, make suit.*

†6. The pursuit of an object or quest. *Obs.*

7. The action of suing in a court of law; legal prosecution; hence, a litigation. *Obs. or arch.*

†8. To follow a suit: to prosecute a legal action.

†9. *In suit.*
a. Engaged in a legal prosecution or lawsuit. *Obs.*

†b. Of a person: Being prosecuted. *To have.*

†c. Of a matter: Being in dispute. *Obs.*

†d. *Put of suit* (*q.v.*): *to put* (an instrument) *in force in a court of law*; also, *to set the law in motion concerning a matter.*

10. A process instituted in a court of justice for the recovery or protection of a right, the enforcement of a claim, or the redress of a wrong; a prosecution before a legal tribunal.

11. The action or an act of suing, supplicating, or petitioning; (a) petition, supplication, or entreaty; (b) a petition made to a prince or other high personage. *Now* rare.

†12. To make (one's) suit: to supplicate, petition; to sue to a person for something to be done, etc.

†13. *In suit with*: in company with, hence, out of favour with. *Obs.*

14. Condition, state. *Obs. rare.*

15. Of various objects (chiefly in phr. with preps., *cf. loc.*): Pattern, style of workmanship or design; *occas.* colour; hence = set (see V).

†16. Kind, sort, class. *Obs.*

IV. Following, train, suite.
16. A company of followers; a train, retinue, Suite. Also, a company of disciples. Now *arch.* or *dial.* (superseded by *suite*).

17. Wooing or courting of a woman; solicitation for a woman's hand. Also, an instance of this, a courtship.

†18. Offspring, progeny; *spec.* the offspring of a villein. *Obs.*

III. Livery, garb; sort, class.

18. A livery or uniform; also, in wider use, a dress, garb: chiefly in phr. *in* or *of a suit* = clothed in the same garb or colour, as the members of a retinue or fraternity; also, *in suit with*, in the same dress or uniform as. *Obs.*

19. A set of garments or habiliments intended to be worn together at the same time. (Cf. 1.)
a. of church vestments, caps, chasuble and dalmatics, cope, etc. of the same colour and material.
b. of men's or boys' outer garments; in full, *suit of apparel, of clothes.*
c. of women's attire: in earlier use, an entire set of garments for wear at one time; now a costume (i.e. coat and skirt).
d. of armour.
e. *transf.* Earnest assertion for or endeavour to obtain something.

IV. Following, train, suite.

17. Offspring, progeny; *spec.* the offspring of a villein.

18. A number of objects of the same kind or pattern intended to be used together or forming a definite set or series.
a. A group. **b.** A set of tools, plate, furniture, locks, etc. **c.** The whole of the sails required for a ship or for a set of spars. **d.** A set of musical pieces, pictures, etc. A suite. **e.** A batch of biscuits, weights, coins, or one charge of the oven (Simmonds *Dict. Trade*). U.S. The whole complement of hair, whiskers, etc. (of a person). A complete set.

20. Any of the four sets (distinguished by their several marks, as spades, clubs, hearts, diamonds) of which a pack of playing-cards consists. Also, the whole number of cards belonging to such a set held in a player's hand at one time. *In technical and allusively.*

b. *To follow suit* (earlier †*to suit*): to play a card of the same suit as the leading card; hence *often fig.*, to do the same thing as somebody or something else. (Cf. 15.)

VI. Sequence; agreement.
† 21. A succession, sequence. *Obs. rare.*

†22. *For suit of*: on account of. *In consequence of.* *Obs.*

23. Pursuit in agreement or harmony with. *Of a suit with*: of a piece with.

24. *attrib.* and *Comb.*: † suit-breeder, a promoter of legal prosecutions; † suit-broker, one who made a business of procuring a favourable hearing for suits; suit-call, a card, or a lead from a particular suit; suit-case, a small portmanteau designed to contain a suit of clothes; suit-coat (*sc. coat*); suit-country, obligation to give suit at a mill; † suit-groat, a due paid in lieu of suit at court; suit-hold (see HOLD *sb.*[1] b), tenure by suit and service to the superior; † suit-jogger, a promoter of lawsuits; † suit-maker, one who institutes a suit; suit-mark, any of the marks distinguishing suits of cards; suit-roll *Hist.* a roll of persons bound to give suit at a particular court; suit-service *Feudal Law*, service required by attendance at a lord's court; also *fig.*; † suit-worth, worthy of imitation.

Suit (*siūt*), *v.* Forms: 5–6 suyt, 6 sewt, shute, 4–6 suite, suyte, 6–8 suite, *prec.*]
† 1. *intr.* 'to do suit' to a court; hence, to have recourse to. *Obs.*
† 2. To prefer a suit; to sue to a person for something. *Obs.*
† 3. *tr.* To follow (a person) as a suitor; to make suit to. *Obs.*

4. To dress or attire oneself. *Obs. or arch.*

5. To provide with a suit of clothes; to clothe, attire, dress. Chiefly *pass. arch.*

6. *trans.* To arrange in a set, sequence, or series; to set in order, sort out. Also *with forth. Obs.*

† 7. To pursue, aim at; to seek to obtain. *Sc.*

8. To arrange in a set, sequence, or series; to set in order, sort out. Also *with forth. Obs.*

9. *trans.* To provide with a suit of clothes; to clothe, attire, dress. Chiefly *pass. arch.*

10. To make appropriate or agreeable to; to adapt or accommodate in style, manner, or proportion to; to make consonant or accordant with; to render suitable. Also *refl.*

11. To provide (oneself) with (*orig.* clothing); hence, to fit in with; to be suitable to; *accas.* to match in colour, etc. *Obs. or arch.*

† b. *intr.* To range oneself. *Obs. rare.*

8. *trans.* To agree, accord with (a person, his inclinations, etc.); to fall in with the views or wishes of.

12. To find a parallel to; match. *Obs. rare.*

13. To be agreeable or convenient to (a person, his inclinations, etc.); to fall in with the views or wishes of.

14. To be suitable to; to be fit or fitting for; to become. *Obs.*

15. To be in keeping with; to accord or be consistent with; to fit or be proper to; to befit, become, beseem.

16. To be suitable, fitting, or convenient.
17. To be suitable, fitting, or convenient. *Obs.*

18. To be good for, 'agree with'; *esp.* to be salubrious to. *Obs.*

19. To be fitted or adapted to; to be suitable for, answer the requirements of.

Suitability (*siūtabíl·iti*). [f. next + *-ity.*] The quality or condition of being suitable; an instance of this. Const. *to, for.*

Suitable (*siū·tab'l*), *a.* (*adv.*) Also 6–8 *sutc(e)*-able, 7–8 *suitable.* [f. SUIT *v.* + -ABLE, agreeable. Earlier synonyms were *suit-like, -suitly.*]

1. Of or belonging to the same class or kind; of the same nature, order, or quality as; corresponding to; in keeping, accordant, or agreeing with.

2. To be adapted to; to be suitable for; fit.

3. To be good for, 'agree with'; *esp.* to be salubrious.

Suitableness. [-NESS.] The quality or condition of being suitable; suitability; conformity.

Suit-tableness, *sb. rare.*

Suite (*swīt*). Also 7 *suitte.* [a. F. *suite*: see SUIT *sb.*]

1. A train of followers, attendants, or servants; a retinue. Also *sing. (collog.)* = members of a suite.

2. of two or more things: That are in agreement or accord.

3. A company or series; in earlier use (rare), a succession or series of publications.

4. A connected series or set, as in a *suite* of rooms.

5. *Comb.*, as *suitable-sized* adj.

Stanton Grange 295 A suite of tree-sparrow's eggs, not less than 20 in number. 1874 Westropp Prec. Stones 3 The colour suite [of diamonds] is, however, extensive.

b. A number of rooms forming a set used together by a person, a family or company of persons. Also *in a suite* = 5 b (below).

1716 Lady M. W. Montagu Let. to C'tess Mar 8 Sept., A suite of eight or ten large rooms. 1794 Mrs. Radcliffe Myst. Udolpho xliv, A room that opens beyond the saloon, and terminates the suite. 1809 Miss Mitford in L'Estrange Life (1870) I. iii. 80 Five splendid rooms open in a suite. 1824 W. Irving T. Trav. I. 103 My suite of apartments were in a proud melancholy palace. 1885 Mabel Collins Prettiest Woman i, Her home was a pretty little suite on the second floor.

c. A set of furniture of the same pattern.

1851 Catal. Gt. Exhib. III. 824/1 Suite of sculptured decorative furniture. 1883 Miss Broughton Belinda II. 286 The early English suite of rush-bottomed chairs.

d. *Mus.* †(*a*) A set or series of lessons, etc. (cf. Suit *sb.* 18 c); (*b*) a series of dance tunes arranged for one or more instruments and composed in the same key or related keys.

1801 Busby Dict. Mus., Suite, (French) The name formerly given to a set, or course, of lessons, sonatas, concertos, &c. [1811 adds Also applied to a single piece when consisting of several movements.] 1886 A. Weir Hist. Basis Mod. Europe (1889) 548 The grand cyclic forms of modern art, the offspring of the suites. 1887 H. C. Banister Mus. Anal. 15 The Suites and Partitas of Bach.

3. A sequel, result. *rare.*

c1800 H. K. White My own Character 27 And so in the suite, by these laudable ends, I've a great many foes. 1862 Thackeray Philip xxiv, In case the battle of the previous night should have any suite.

4. A sequel to a literary work. *rare.*

1839 W. Irving in Ticknor Prescott (1864) 181, I had always intended to write an account of the 'Conquest of Mexico', as a suite to my 'Columbus'.

5. ‖ **En suite** (aṅ sẅīt). a. In agreement or harmony (*with*).

1797 Mrs. A. M. Bennett Beggar Girl (1813) II. 79 The decorations..were not even *en suite* with the polish of the owner's mind. 1860 Once a Week 3 Nov. 520/1 She was an antique gem, was this concierge, and we thought if everything in the establishment were *en suite* [etc.].

b. Of rooms: In a series leading from one to the other.

1818 Mrs. Opie New Tales I. 24 Elegant rooms thrown open *en suite*. 1837 J. F. Cooper Europe I. 321 The state apartments lie *en suite*, in the main body of the building.

Suited (s¹ū·tėd), *ppl. a.* [f. Suit *sb.* or *v.* + -ed.]

†1. ? Belonging to a group or set. *Obs. rare.*

1621 G. Sandys Ovid's Met. vi. (1626) 109 Twice six Cœlestialls..Ioue in the midst. The suted figures tooke Their liuely formes: Ioue had a regall looke.

2. With qualifying word: Wearing a suit or attire of a specified kind.

1632 Milton Penseroso 122 Till civil-suited Morn appeer. 1638 Ford Fancies I. iii, Enter Livio, fresh suited. 1842 Tennyson You ask me why ii, It is the land that..sober-suited Freedom chose. 1901 Westm. Gaz. 12 Nov. 9/2 The grey-suited brigade.

Suiter, shooter (siū·təɹ, ʃū·təɹ). *local.* Forms: 6 **shewter**, 7, 9 **shooter**, 9 **suiter, -or**. [f. Suit *v.* + -er¹. Cf. Follower 5 a (Voller), and *suity-board* s.v. Suity *a.* 3; *suitel* is a variant in Northamptonshire (Baker N'hampton Gloss.).] a. A round board placed between two cheeses in the press. b. A square board in a cider-press placed on the top of the pile of must or 'cheese'. More fully, *suiter-board*.

1586 Shuttleworths' Acc. (Chetham Soc.) 29 Fyffe chef-fates [i.e. cheese-vats]..and one shewter vjᵈ viijᵈ. 1625 in Miss Jackson Shropsh. Word-bk. s.v., Eleven chefats, five shooters. 1833 Loudon Encycl. Archit. § 1316 [In a cider-press] A square board, termed a shooter. 1870 in Miss Jackson Shropsh. Word-bk. s.v. Follower, Cheese-vats, followers, and suitors. 1886 Cheshire Gloss., Shooter boards or suiter boards.

Suiter, obs. or dial. f. Suitor.

Sui·terer. *rare.* [? f. Suitor *v.* + -er¹.] One who 'goes after' another: applied to a sodomite.

1720 J. Johnson Collect. Eccl. Laws Ch. Eng. I. Excerp. Ecgb. lxvii, A Suiterer of young Boys [orig. adolescentium consectator].

Suith, Sc. form of Sooth.

Suipe, variant of Swithe.

Suiting (s¹ū·tiŋ), *vbl. sb.* [f. Suit *v.* + -ing¹.]

†1. The action of doing suit at a court. *Obs.*

c1540 in J. R. Boyle Hedon (1875) App. 71 Yf anye tenante make defaulte of sewtinge of the said courte at two tymes in the yere.

†2. The action of suing for something; suing out a writ; petitioning, supplication; paying court to a woman. *Obs.*

1561 Reg. Privy Council Scot. Ser. I. I. 163 To charge..all utheris personis fra all suting or persewing of the saidis confirmationis. 1572 Knox in Calderwood's Hist. Kirk (Wodrow Soc.) III. App. 767 For suting of justice of the kirk's actions in the session. 1579–80 Reg. Privy Council Scot. Ser. I. III. 269 The suitting of redres. 1591 R. Bruce Serm. (Ps. xl.) V vij b, Our suddantie is so greate..that wee cannot continue in suting. 1631 Brathwait Eng. Gentlew. 130 There is no time that exacts more modesty of any woman, than in her time of suiting.

attrib. 1690 C. Nesse Hist. & Myst. O. & N. T. I. 158 Mark well who carrieth it in this suiting work.

3. Fitting or adaptation of one thing *to* another.

1707 Mortimer Husb. (1721) I. 89 In the suiting of the Land and Marle together, lies the chief advantage. Ibid. II. 276 The third occasion of Unfruitfulness is the not suiting of your Fruit and Soil together. 1898 Westm. Gaz. 3 Feb. 3/1 The suiting of one thing to another.

†4. The action of clothing or attiring. *Obs.*

a1637 B. Jonson Discov. (1641) 92 That though the nakednesse would shew deform'd and odious, the suiting of it [sc. a lie] might draw their Readers.

5. *concr.* Trade name for: Material for making suits of clothes; usually *pl.*

1883 Daily News 10 Sept. 2/6 The..demand for..fancy tweed suitings continues good.

†**Sui·ting**, *ppl. a.* *Obs.* [f. Suit *v.* + -ing².] Fitting, suitable.

1643 Declar. Lords & Comm. 9 Jan. 3 Some suting course how to have the want of Armes..to be supplyed. 1708 J. Philips Cyder II. 415 Now sportive Youth Carol incondite Rhythms, with suiting Notes. 1801 Eliz. Helme St. Marg. Cave (1819) IV. vii. 95 For my honour and her own it is necessary that all should be suiting. 1821 Clare Vill. Minstr. (1823) I. 113 Wildness is my suiting scene.

Hence †**Sui·tingly** *adv.*, fittingly.

1540 Palsgr. Acolastus I. i. D j, Lyke as it is in maner sutyngly or throughly agreinge betwene vs, so must it nedes cause mutuall loue betwene vs.

†**Sui·t-like**, *a.* *Obs.* [f. Suit *sb.* + -like. Cf. next.] = Suitable 1, 2.

1570 Foxe A. & M. (ed. 2) II. 1126/1 Being sute like to his glorious life. 1579–80 North Plutarch (1595) 54 She put her into mans apparell, and gaue her all thinges sute like to the same. 1583 Golding Calvin on Deut. xxviii. 59–64 We must vnderstande that all the bodie must be sutelike.

†**Sui·tly**, *a.* *Obs.* [f. Suit *sb.* + -ly¹.] = Suitable 1, 2, 3.

1459 Paston Lett. I. 477, j. pece of skarlot for trappars..with rede crossis and rosys. Item, ij. stripis of the same trappuris sutly. Ibid. 479 Item, iij. curtaynys sutely. Ibid. 480 Item, iij. clothis of grene and whyte, withe braunchis sutely to the other wreten before. 1532 More Confut. Tindale Wks. 342/2 Frythes Prologue..is ryght sutely, and a verye mete couer for suche a cuppe. 1595 Southwell Mæoniæ 29 All pangs and heauie passions here may find A thousand motiues suitly to their griefes.

†**Sui·tly**, *adv.* *Obs.* [f. Suit *sb.* + -ly².] Fittingly, suitably.

1388 Wyclif 1 Kings vi. 18 Al the hows..hadde hise smethenessis, and hise ioynyngis maad suteli. 1422 Yonge tr. Secr. Secr. 209 Thow shalt sutely and besely auise the, whych of ham beste consaill yewyth to the. 1533 More Apol. xxxiii. Wks. 896/2 If this pacifier..wil saythat we be not sewtly the temporalti and spiritualty of this realme.

Suitor (s¹ū·təɹ), *sb.* Forms: 3 **syutor**, 4 **sewtour, suytour**, 4–5 **sutere**, 4–7 **-er, -our**, 5–6 **sewter**, 5–7 **sutor**, (5 **soutoure, sutter**, 6 **sueter, sutar, swttar, shu-, shewter, suitour, -ore**; *Sc.* 6 **soytor(e**, 6–7 **soytour**, 7 **swotar**), 6–8 **suiter**, 6– **suitor**. [a. AF. *seutor, suitour, sut(i)er, -or*, ad. late L. *secūtor, -ōrem* (f. *secūt-, sequī* to follow, Sue), with assimilation to *suite* Suit *sb.*]

†1. A frequenter (*of* a place). *Obs. rare.*

c1290 S. Eng. Leg. 413 He wax a syutor of tauernes.

†2. One of a retinue or suite; hence, an adherent, follower, disciple. *Obs.*

c1380 Wyclif Serm. Sel. Wks. II. 141 Þat Crist is every-where..wiþ his apostlis and her suters. c1380 — Wks. (1880) 292 He þat hatiþ blamynge is sutere of þe fend. 1398 Trevisa Barth. De P. R. IX. iii. (Bodl. MS.), Plato and his suytors. c1450 Cov. Myst. (Shaks. Soc.) 201 Oure Lorde God, that comyth me to, Hese pore servaunt and his sutere. a1483 Liber Niger in Househ. Ord. (1790) 23 Lordes & gentyls & other comyn sutors. 1509 Barclay Shyp of Folys (1874) I. 262 Yet dyvers suters suche folysshe wytches have. 1517 in Ellis Orig. Lett. Ser. I. II. 4 note, So that who shall be a suitour to him may have no other busynesse but give attendaunce upon his plesure. 1586 Holinshed's Chron. III. 920/2 Other officers, seruants, reteiners, and suters, that most commonlie dined in the hall. 1601 F. Tate Househ. Ord. Edw. II (1876) § 94. 56 None of the kinges meignee..Knight or clarke serjant, esquier,..page or sutor. 1830 Tennyson How & Why 1, I am any man's suitor, If any will be my tutor.

3. One who owed suit (see Suit *sb.* 1) to a court, and in that capacity acted as an assessor or elector. Now only *Hist.*

14.. Customs of Malton in Surtees Misc. (1890) 60 All maner of playutties..schall be..jugyd be yᵉ sutterys of yᵉ sayd cowrte. 1506 in Exch. Rolls Scotl. XII. 704 All officeris and ministeris of court sic as baillie and juge,..sutour, dempstar. 1541 Act 33 Hen. VIII, c. 24 § 3 Any Mayres Sheriffes Recorders, Stewardes Bayliffes Sewters or other officers..within any Cittie Boroughe or Towne. c1550 Rolland Crt. Venus III. 4 Great membres of Court baith mair & les All is Sutour, to gif finall sentence. 1597 Skene De Verb. Signif. s.v. Sok, Na judge aucht of law, or of reason, to accept ony man in court as Soytour, bot gif he can make sufficient and lauchfull reporte of processe. 1609 — Reg. Maj. 79 Ilke soytour before the Schiref represents the person of ane Baron, for quhom he was soytour in that court. Ibid. 93 That the court (the soytours of court) be lawfull. 1846 McCulloch Acc. Brit. Emp. (1854) II. 87 By directing the election to be made by *all* the suitors,..this statute secured the constituency from undue practices. 1863 [see Suit *sb.* 1].

†b. A tenant who owes suit to a mill. *Obs.*

1602 Carew Cornwall 13 This casualtie may be worth the owner some ten pound, by the yeere, or better if his mil have store of sutors.

4. One who sues or petitions; a petitioner, suppliant. *arch.*

?1402 Quixley Ball. in Yorksh. Arch. Jrnl. (1908) XX. 48 Se, lo! How sche [sc. Fortune] tourneth þe face hir sutoure fro. c1460 Fortescue Abs. & Lim. Mon. xx. (1885) 157 The kyng shal..be wele defended ageyn suche importune suters. 1533–4 Act 25 Hen. VIII, c. 21 § 6 All Suters for dispensacions, faculties, licences and other wrytynges. 1576 Gascoigne Kenelworth Castle Wks. 1910 II. 131 That you would..be a suter for him unto the heavenly powers. 1581 H. Walpole in Allen Martyrdom Campion (1908) 56 He stands before the throne with harmonie, And is a glorious suter for our sinne. 1607 Hieron Wks. I. 178 The apostle is a suter to God on the behalfe of the Ephesians. 1651 Walton Life Wotton in Reliq. Wotton. c 4 b, The Provostship of..Eton became Void..., for which there were..many..powerfull suiters to the King. 1718 Free-thinker No. 147. 310 The frank Philosopher shall be the favourite Suiter. 1822 Scott Nigel iii, Those suitors who shall be so bold as to approach the Court. 1878 C. Gibbon For the King xvii, The officers stared in amazement at the importunate suitor. 1892 A. E. Lee Hist. Columbus I. 195 The colonies of Worthington and Franklinton became rival suitors for the location of the Capital of the State.

†b. One who seeks earnestly. *Obs.*

1548 Udall Erasmus Par. Pref. 18 Studentes and suters to atteigne to the philosophye of the gospell.

5. A petitioner or plaintiff in a suit.

1503–4 Act 19 Hen. VII, c. 28 Preamb., The seid sueters & peticioners were..in dispayre of expedicion of ther suetes. 1560 Daus tr. Sleidane's Comm. 108 b, Lawes, whiche concerned partly the judges, partly the advocates, and partly the suters. a1577 Sir T. Smith Commw. Eng. II. viii. (1584) 50 In all iudgements necessarily being two parties, the first we call the impleader, suiter, demaunder or demaundaunt and plaintiffe. a1660 Contemp. Hist. Irel. (Ir. Archæol. Soc.) II. 108 Amonge sutors in love and in lawe money is a comoun medler. 1856 Emerson Eng. Traits, Ability, In the courts, the independence of the judges and the loyalty of the suitors are equally excellent. 1883 Law Times 20 Oct. 410/2 The effect of the rule will be to deprive the suitor of the right of conducting his case as he thinks most conducive to his own interest.

6. One who seeks a woman in marriage; a wooer.

a1586 Sidney Arcadia I. xi, My court quickely swarmed full of suiters; some perchaunce loving my state, others my person. 1588 Kyd Househ. Philos. Wks. (1901) 273 That noble Grecian dame that bated in the night As much as she had wouen by day, to bleare her sutors sight. 1637 T. Heywood Emblem. Dial. xxxvii, Merry Suiters, make mad Husbands. 1781 Cowper Retirem. 237 The suitor's air indeed he soon improves, And forms it to the taste of her he loves. 1870 L'Estrange Life Miss Mitford I. 5 She was rich—her fortune was at her own command—of course she had suitors. 1888 Fergus Hume Madame Midas I. i, Miss Curtis soon brought crowds of suitors around her.

7. *attrib.*, as (sense 6) *suitor-crowd*, etc.; †*suitor-fee*, a fine paid in lieu of suit at court.

1725 Pope Odyss. I. 353 To their own districts drive the *suitor-crowd. 1601 Reg. Mag. Sig. Scot. 425/1 Necnon 6s. 8d. pro sectis curie de Rescobie vulgo lie *suotar-fie.

Suitor (s¹ū·təɹ), *v.* Now chiefly *dial.* Also 7 **suter, souter**, 9 **suiter, sooter**. [f. prec.]

1. *trans.* To court, woo.

1672 Shadwell Miser I, How did you go to work to suitor my Mother? 1706 Phillips (ed. Kersey) s.v., He Suitor'd her in vain several Years. 1824 Scott Redgauntlet ch. v, The miller's son..suitored me.

2. *intr.* To be a suitor or wooer (*to*): chiefly in gerund (*to come* or *go a suitoring*). Also *fig.*

1668 Sir C. Sedley Mulberry Gard. II. ii, You are over-serious For a man that comes a Sutering. 1730 Fielding Tom Thumb II. v, In vain to me a suitoring you come, For I'm already promis'd to Tom Thumb. 1777 Franklin Lett. Wks. 1889 VI. 83 A virgin State should preserve the virgin character, and not go about suitoring for alliances. 1817 Scott Let. to Terry 12 Mar. in Lockhart, A daughter, suitored unto by the conceited young parson. 1838 Barham Ingol. Leg. Ser. I. St. Nich. vii, Counts a many, and Dukes a few, A suitoring came to my father's Hall.

Hence **Sui·toring** *vbl. sb.*, wooing, courtship; also *attrib.*

1671 Mrs. Behn Amorous Prince IV. iv, Well, I see there is nothing but soutering I' this Town; wo'd our Lucia were here too for me. 1746 (title) Exmoor Courtship, or A Suitoring Discourse, in the Devonshire Dialect and Mode. 1847 Halliwell, Sootering... Devon. 1886 Elworthy W. Somerset Word-bk., Suitering. 1889 Athenæum 14 Dec. 816/3 The usual 'suitorings', sulkings, makings-up, of various couples.

Suitor, var. Suiter.

Sui·torcide, *a. nonce-word.* [Badly f. Suitor *sb.* + -cide¹.] Fatal to suitors.

1839 Syd. Smith Wks. (1859) Pref. p. vii, To say a word against the suitorcide delays of the Court of Chancery..was treason against the Plousiocracy.

Suitorship (s¹ū·təɹʃip). [f. Suitor *sb.* + -ship.] The state or condition of being a suitor.

c1800 R. Cumberland John De Lancaster (1809) I. 6 This distinguished personage was now in the fifth year of his suitorship. 1878 Morley Diderot I. 125 They revolted..against the old system of suitorship and protection. 1886 T. Hardy Mayor Casterbr. II. iii. 33 The sense of occult rivalry in suitorship was..superadded.

Suitress (s¹ū·trės). *rare.* [f. Suitor *sb.* + -ess¹.] A female suitor.

1714 Rowe Jane Shore III, 'Twere Pity of his Heart, That could refuse a Boon to such a Suitress. 1791 Cowper Iliad I. 686, I noticed her a suitress at thy knees. 1894 Daily Tel. 1 Dec. 5/4 Both suitresses are of some position and worldly prospects.

Suity (s¹ū·ti), *a.* [f. Suit *sb.* or *v.* + -y¹.]

†1. Appropriate, fitting. *Obs.*

1609 J. Davies Holy Roode F ij, In loue, in care, in diligence and dutie, Be thou Her Sonne, sith this to Sonnes is sutie.

2. Of hounds: Matching those of a pack.

1856 'Stonehenge' Brit. Sports I. II. iv. ¶ 344. 124/2 Many men draft young hounds from their looks not pleasing the eye, or from their being too high or too low, or not being 'suity', as it is called.

3. *Suity-board*, in cheese-making: = Suiter a.

c1830 Glouc. Farm Rep. 30 in Husbandry (L. U. K.) III, Round boards, called 'suity boards',..are occasionally necessary to place on the cheeses.

Suitzer, obs. form of Switzer.

‖ **Suivante** (sẅivaṅt). *Obs.* [F., pres. pple. fem. of *suivre* to follow.] A confidential maid.

1698 Vanbrugh Short Vindic. 51 Mademoiselle brings to mind what may often be expected from a *Suivante* of her Countrey. 1782 [T. Vaughan] Fashionable Follies I. xci. 139 The more secrets Madame had to keep, the better for her suivante. 1812 Scott Let. in Lockhart (1837) III. i. 17 Lady Douglas's *suivante*.

Suiymme, Sujee, Sujet, Sujorn(e, Suk, Sukcade, Sukces, Suke(n, Sukere, Sukett: see Swim, Soojee, Subject, Sojourn, Suck, Succade, Success, Suck, Succour, Sucket.

†**Sukkarke.** *Obs. rare*⁻¹. [prob. AFr.] app. = Subcharge 1, Surcharge *sb.*¹

c1400 Maundev. (1839) xxxi. 310 He ȝevethe of the Flesche to his most specyalle Frendes, in stede of Entre Messe, or a Sukkarke [Roxb. for a dayntee].

Suk-kegh, variant of Sockeye, salmon.

Sukkelyng, Sukkenye, Sukkett, Sukkin, Sukle, Suklinge, -lynge, Sukour, Sukudry, Sul: see Suckling, Suckeny, Sucket, Sucken¹, Suckle, Suckling, Succour, Succudry, Shall.

‖ **Sula** (siū·lă). [mod.L. (Willughby, 1676), a. ON. *súla*.] Applied by Hoier and others to a supposed variety of sea-fowl; in modern *Ornith.* a genus of gannets (family *Sulidæ*).

1678 Ray Willughby's Ornith. III. 331 The Sula of Hoier,..near of kin to, if not the same with the Soland-goose. 1688 Holme Armoury II. xii. 262 The Sula is like the Soland Goose for Bodily shape. 1766 Pennant Brit. Zool. 162.

Sulayne, variant of Solein *Obs.*

Sulcal (sɒ·lkăl), *a.* *Anat.* [f. Sulcus + -al.] Belonging to or connected with a sulcus.

1889 Buck's Handbk. Med. Sci. VII. 300 (Cent. Suppl.). 1901 Dorland Med. Dict., Sulcal artery, a branch of the anterior spinal artery in the anterior median fissure, or sulcus, of the spinal cord.

So **Su·lcar** *a.*

1900 Trans. Linn. Soc., Zool., March 527 The zooids so oriented that their sulcar (ventral) aspects are abaxial, their asulcar (dorsal) aspects axial.

Sulcate (sɒ·lkeᵗt), *a.* *Nat. Hist.* [ad. L. *sulcātus*, pa. pple. of *sulcāre* (see next).] Marked with (parallel) furrows or grooves.

1760 J. Lee Introd. Bot. II. xxxiii. (1765) 160 Cucurbita, with a sulcate Fruit. 1828 Stark Elem. Nat. Hist. II. 15 Shell thin, hyaline, transversely sulcate. 1872 Coues N. Amer. Birds 187 The bill is more or less depressed with smooth, rounded or sulcate, culmen.

†**Sulcate**, *v.* *Obs.* [f. L. *sulcāt-*, pa. ppl. stem of *sulcāre* to plough, f. Sulcus. Cf. Sulk *v.*¹] *trans.* To plough (*esp.* the seas).

1577 Hanmer Anc. Eccl. Hist. 327 A mightie Easterne winde, which draue the ship with violence, swiftely for to sulcate the seas. a1604 — Chron. Irel. (1633) 85 The Irish nation..would not sulcate the seas, neither give themselves to merchandise. 1656 Blount Glossogr.

Sulcated (sɒ·lkeᵗtėd), *ppl. a.* *Nat. Hist.* [f. L. *sulcātus* Sulcate + -ed.] Sulcate.

1694 Phil. Trans. XVIII. 178 The sides of the Astroites are always sulcated, or a little furrow'd. 1753 Chambers' Cycl. Suppl. s.v. Leaf, Sulcated Leaf, one which has a great number of ridges all round it, with obtuse sinuses. 1768 Pennant Brit. Zool. I. 39 Their lower part is sulcated lengthways. 1828 Stark Elem. Nat. Hist. II. 41 The plaits distant, black, transversely sulcated with white. 1897 W. F. Kirby in Mary Kingsley W. Africa 722 All the tibiæ sulcated, front tibiæ with conspicuously open foramina.

Sulcation (sɒlkēᵗ·ʃən). *rare.* [f. L. *sulcāre* Sulcate *v.*: see -ation.]

1. Furrowing, grooving.

1658 Phillips, Sulcation, a making furrows.

2. A sulcus or set of sulci.

1852 Dana Crust. II. 856 The sculpturing of the male being represented in the female by merely a few faint sulcations.

Sulcato-, used as comb. form (see -o) of L. *sulcātus* Sulcate *a.* in the sense 'sulcate and...', as *sulca·to-a·reolate, -co·state, -ri·mose* adjs.

1852 Dana Crust. II. 855 Epimerals and coxæ of six posterior legs slightly sulcato-areolate. 1866 Treas. Bot. 1110/2 Sulcato-rimose, furrowed and cracked like the cotyledons of a Spanish chestnut. 1887 W. Phillips Brit. Discomycetes 11 Stem..sulcato-costate, and lacunose.

Sulch, obs. form of Such.

Sulciform (sɒ·lsifǫɹm), *a.* [ad. mod.L. *sulciformis*: see Sulcus and -form.] Having the form of a sulcus or groove.

1822 J. Parkinson Outl. Oryctol. 222 Hinge very broad, furrowed with numerous long sulciform teeth. 1836–9 Todd's Cycl. Anat. II. 533/1 The sulciform depression..in the vestibule [of the ear].

†**Su·lcous**, *a.* *Obs. rare*⁻¹. [f. Sulcus + -ous.] Sulcate.

1750 G. Hughes Barbados 116 The bark..is rough and shagged, if not sulcous.

‖ **Sulculus** (sɒ·lkiŭlŭs). *Anat.* and *Zool.* [mod. L., dim. of Sulcus. Cf. F. *sulcule*.] A small sulcus or groove. Hence **Su·lculate** *a.*, having small grooves.

1848 Proc. Berw. Nat. Club II. 338 Longitudinally striate or sulculate. 1859 Mayne Expos. Lex. 1226/1. 1900 Trans. Linn. Soc., Zool., March 533 One cannot speak of a sulcus and sulculus in this case.

‖ **Sulcus** (sɒ·lkŏs). Pl. **sulci** (sɒ·lsəi). [L. = furrow, trench, ditch, wrinkle.]

1. a. A groove made with an engraving tool. b. A trench. c. A hollow or depression in the land. *rare.*

1662 Evelyn Sculptura 126 Monsieur Bosse's invention of the *Eschoppe*, does render the making of this *Sulcus*, much more facile. 1675 — Terra (1729) 14 The *Sulcus* or Trench be made to run from North to South. 1901 A. Trotter East Galloway Sk. 158/2 The house..is situated in a sulcus of fertile land.

2. *Anat.* A groove or furrow in a body, organ, or tissue.

1744 tr. Boerhaave's Inst. III. 297 The sensible Papillæ lie concealed in the Sulci formed by the Cuticle. 1766 Complete Farmer s.v. Shoeing, The sulcus of the inner surface of the hoof. 1822–7 Good Study Med. (1829) V. 252 Hydatids have found the means of forming a nidus in some one of the sulci of the womb. 1872 Coues N. Amer. Birds 27 Sulci, like carinæ, are of all shapes, sizes and positions. 1897 Allbutt's Syst. Med. IV. 227 A distinct sulcus between the liver and gall-bladder is nearly always perceptible to the touch.

b. *spec.* A fissure between two convolutions of the brain.

1833 Cycl. Pract. Med. I. 286/2 The sulci which separate the convolutions. 1840 G. V. Ellis Anat. 15 On its under surface, near the median fissure of the brain, is a sulcus, which lodges the olfactory nerve. 1899 Allbutt's Syst. Med. VII. 273 That portion of the cerebral hemisphere which lies anterior to the precentral sulcus.

3. *Bot.* The lamella in some fungi.

1856 Henslow Dict. Bot. Terms 90.

Sulcup, Suld, Suldan, Suld(e)art, Sulder: see Selcouth, Shall, Soldan, Suddart, Shoulder.

†**Sule** *sb.*, var. of Soil *sb.*¹; cf. Sulye.

c1440 Promp. Parv. 484/1 Sule erthe.., solum, tellus.

†**Sule**, *v.* *Obs.* [OE. *sylian* (also *besylian*), f. *sul-*, related to *sol-*: see Sole *sb.*⁴, Sol *a.*, Sole *v.*³, Soll *v.*, Solwe *v.*, Sowl *v.*¹, and cf. OFris. *sulenge* soiling, MHG. *süln* to sully.] a. *trans.* To soil, sully.

c897 K. Ælfred Gregory's Past. C. liv. 419 Sio sugu hi wille sylian on hire sole æfterðæmðe hio aðwæȝen bið. a1000 Boeth. Metr. ix. 60 He on unscyldgum eorla blode his sweord selede swiðe ȝelome. a1225 Ancr. R. 396 Þet weren so sike of sunne, & so isuled þer mide. c1230 Hali Meid. 35 Þis is sunne,..& unwurðeð þi bodi, Suleð þi sawle.

b. *intr.* To be defiled.

a1250 Owl & Night. 1240 Sum blynd mon..To þare diche his dwele voleweþ, & falleþ, & þar-onne sulieþ.

Sulement, variant of Soulement *adv.* *Obs.*

†**Sulf.** *Obs.* ? Toadflax, *Linaria vulgaris*.

c1450 Alphita (Anecd. Oxon.) 104/1 Linguarium, assimulatur herbe Sti. I[ohannis] in foliis et in stipite sed fetat. gall. lignarie, angl. sulf [v. r. gulf].

Sulf, obs. form of Self.

Sulf-: see Sulph-.

Sulfatara, variant form of Solfatara.

1884 Pall Mall Gaz. 23 Feb. 4/2 The internal fires that still spurt and hiss in the sulfataras.

Sulfer, obs. form of Silver.

Suling (sū·liŋ). *Hist.* Forms: 1 **swulung, sulung** (*rare* **sulong**), *Domesday Bk.* **solin**, 2 **solling**, (also 7 *Hist.*) **swuling**, (also 9 *Hist.*) **swilling**, 2–3 (also 7–9 *Hist.*) **sulling, suling**, 4 **swol(l)ing, -yng, swyling, suyling**, 4–5 **swylling**, 9 *Hist.* **sullung**. [OE. *swulung, sulung*, probably vbl. sb. of an unrecorded vb. **swul(h)ian, *sul(h)ian* to plough, f. **swulh, sulh* plough, Sullow. The generally accepted view that *sulung* is f. *sulh* + *lang, long* long (Sweet in Anglia III. 151) and that it is therefore parallel to *furlong* (f. *furh* furrow + *long*) cannot be maintained in face of the divergent form-history and meaning of the two words.] In Kent, the fiscal unit corresponding to the hide (see Hide *sb.*²) and the *carucata* (see Carucate) of other counties.

In Latin documents relating to Kent it is called *aratrum*: cf. Plough *sb.* 3 a.

A term that has been erron. identified with this word is *solanda, scolanda, scotlanda* in Domesday of St. Paul's (Camden Soc.) 58, 93, 99, 142, 145, 151: see J. H. Round in Eng. Hist. Rev. VII. 708 foll.

805 in Birch Cart. Sax. (1885) I. 449 Aliquam in Cantia partiunculam terræ hoc est duorum manentium, ubi Sueordhlincas vocitantur Iuxta distributionem suarum utique terrarum ritu saxonica *dn sulung* seu in alia loco mediam partem unius mansiunculæ id est *dn geocled* ubi ab incolis Ecgheanng lond appellatur. 805 Charter in O. E. Texts 442 Þisses londes earan ðrie sulong æt hæȝyðe ðorne. 805–31 Ibid. 443 Ðæt lond æt stanhamstede, xx swulunga. 835 Will in Thorpe Dipl. Angl. Sax. (1865) 470, & him man sælle an half swulung an Ciollandene. 973 in Birch Cart. Sax. (1893) III. 610 Decem mansas, quod Cantigene dicunt, x. sulunga. 1086 Domesday Book (1783) I. 2 De communitate Sancti Martini habent simul iii. canonici unum solin & xvi. acras. c1140 Inst. Cnuti (Liebermann) 295 (MS. H) Scotum ad luminaria..ter in anno detur de unaquaque hyda (id est suling, c1160 Colbert MS. sulinghida). 11.. Bk. Battle Abbey in Selden Titles Honor (1631) 636 Cum omnibus apenditijs suis septem Swillingarum id est, Hidarum. 1196 in Archæol. Cant. I. 234 De una sollinga terræ et dimidia, cum pertinenciis, in Estrelling. 1209–10 in Archæol. Cant. V. 284 De medietate unius sullinge terre. 13.. MS. Cott. Vesp. A. xx. 69 b, Svthfliet defendit se per v sulingos cum dimidio sulingi de pole. 1364 W. Thorne Chron. in Twysden Hist. Angl. Script. (1652) 2140 Et debent pro quolibet Swollinge xivd. per annum pro Schippeshere, timberlode, & bordlode. a1667 Skinner Etymol. Ling. Angl. (1671), Swoling vel Suling. 1706 Phillips (ed. Kersey), Swoling or Suling of Land. 1867 C. J. Elton Tenures of Kent vi. 124 Opinions have been much divided on this point, viz. whether the Kentish suling corresponded in size to the Norman carucate. 1897 Maitland Domesday & Beyond 124 At Peckham the Archbishop had an estate which had been rated at six sullungs.

b. *attrib.*: † *suling-land* = Plough-gate; † *suling-man*, (*a*) a man chosen from the tenants of a suling to collect the dues belonging thereto; (*b*) a service due from tenants of a suling.

1364 W. Thorne Chron. xxvii. § 1 in Twysden Hist. Angl. Script. (1652) 2140 Quae servicia & consuetudines ipsi tenantes annuatim faciunt & solummodo præter corporale servicium quod vocatur Swollyngman. Ibid., iij. rodas dimidiam de terra vocata Swollyngland quæ tenentur per diversa servicia subsequentia. 1440–1 in Twysden Hist. Angl. Script. (1652) Gloss. s.v. Sulinga, Singuli tenentes omnium & singularum prædictarum Swyllingarum, & 38. acrar. terræ de Swyllingland..eligent & eligere debent de qualibet Swyllinga, unum de seipsis qui nominetur Swyllingmannus. [1887 Parish & Shaw Dict. Kent. Dial., Swilling-land, a plough land.]

†**Sulk**, *sb.*¹ *Obs. rare*⁻¹. [ad. L. *sulcus* furrow. Cf. Sulk *v.*¹] A hollow or trough of the sea.

1578 Sidney Wanstead Play in Arcadia (1629) 619 When he soiourned in the surging sulkes of the sandiferous seas.

Sulk (sɒlk), *sb.*² [f. Sulk *v.*²]

1. *pl.* A state of ill-humour or resentment marked by obstinate silence or aloofness from society. Often with *the* and in phr. *in the sulks* (occas. *in one's sulks*); also *to take (the) sulks* (Sc., to turn sulky.

1804 J. Grahame Sabbath (1839) 13/2 A child of about ten months old took sulks, and would not eat. 1818 Todd s.v., We use also, as a colloquial term, to be in *the sulks*; which formerly was, in *the sullens*. 1824 Miss L. M. Hawkins Annaline I. 177 A fit of the sulks. 1831 Greville Mem. 8 Dec. (1874) II. 224, I never had the advantage of seeing the Chancellor before in his sulks. 1839 Dickens Nickleby xxvii, Her pretty sulks and peevishness. 1885 Spurgeon Treas. Dav. Ps. cxxxi. 2 The child..frets and worries,..or sinks into sulks. 1890 D. Davidson Mem. Long Life iv. 93 Ram Bukhs took the sulks. 1894 W. E. Norris St. Ann's II. 208 When you are tired of being in the sulks, let me know.

b. *sing.* A fit of sulking; the action of sulking.

1837 Disraeli Venetia I. xiii, Mrs. Cadurcis remained alone in a savage sulk. 1888 Contemp. Rev. LIV. 383 Rodbertus had lived for a quarter of a century in a political sulk against the Hohenzollerns. 1898 Daily News 20 June 4/7 To try and force those proposals by a policy of sulk.

2. A person who sulks (*rare*); an obstinate horse (*dial.*)

1883 Lord R. Gower Reminisc. II. xxiv. 125 If one reads away from the others, one appears to avoid the rest and is considered a sulk. 1888 Berks. Gloss., Zulk, a term applied to a horse that will not try to do what is required of him.

†**Sulk**, *v.*¹ *Obs. rare.* Also 6 **sulke, sulck**. [ad. L. *sulcāre* to plough, furrow, f. *sulcus* furrow.] *trans.* To plough (the seas). Also *intr.*, sometimes with *it*.

1579 Poor Knight's Palace, etc. K iv b, To sulke the seas and furrow foming floods. Ibid. L ij b, While saylers sulke upon the seas. 1582 Stanyhurst Æneis II. (Arb.) 50 Two serpents monsterus ouglye Plasht the water sulcking to the shoare moste hastelye swinging. 1612 Drayton Poly-olb. i. 422 They..keep Upon the lee-ward still, and (sulking up the deep) For Mauritania make. 1682 Earl Argyle To Lady Lindsay in Law's Mem. (1818) 213 Our admirall, though tide and wind say nay, He'll row and work, and sulk it all the way.

Hence †**Su·lking** *ppl. a.*, ploughing (the land).

1582 Stanyhurst Æneis I. 1 (I) forced Thee sulcking swincker thee soyle, thoghe craggie, to sunder.

Sulk (sɒlk), *v.*² [Source uncertain; perhaps related to Sulke *a.* Cf. NFris. (Sylt) *sulke*.] *intr.* To keep aloof from others in moody silence: to indulge in sullen ill-humour; to be sulky.

1781 Mme. D'Arblay Diary May, I still sulked on, vexed to be teased. 1794 W. Blake Songs Exp., Inf. Sorrow 8, I thought best To sulk upon my mother's breast. 1852 W. Jerdan Autobiog. I. xi. 82 My uncle..sulked a little at my not having made myself celebrated. 1861 Reade Cloister & H. lxv, He sulked with his old landlady for thrusting gentle advice and warning on him. 1880 Daily Tel. 4 Oct., It is now thirteen years that we have been sulking with the Republic of Mexico.

b. *transf.* and *fig.* Of a fish: To remain in biding and motionless when hooked. Of tea-plants: see quot. 1891. In quot. 1860 *refl* with *out*: To go out 'sulkily'.

1860 O. W. Holmes Elsie V. (1887) 75 The lamps..sulked themselves out. 1873 Browning Red Cott. Nt.-cap 154 Sorrowful Sulked field and pasture with persistent rain. 1873 W. C. Prime I go a-fishing ii. 21 He started down stream, over a low fall and into a deep hole, where he sulked like a salmon. 1884 Sat. Rev. 12 July 61/1 [He] was occupied two hours and twenty minutes in landing an eight-pound trout which sulked. 1891 T. C. Owen Tea Planting in Ceylon, When the foliage becomes too luxuriant, and they [sc. tea-bushes] sulk and no longer send out vigorous flushes. 1905 Sir F. Treves Oth. Side Lant. II. ii. (1906) 33 Sluggish streams, sulking through a gully of sand and stones.

Hence **Su·lker**, one who sulks; **Su·lkery** (*nonce-wd.*), = Boudoir; **Su·lking** *vbl. sb.* (also *attrib.* in *sulking-room* = Boudoir) and *ppl. a.*

1888 Library Mag. June 313 He called upon the *sulkers to come to the front. 1906 Month July 72 *Sulkery, as they translated *boudoir*. 1816 Lady Byron in Ld. Broughton's

Recoll. Long Life (1909) II. 203 Such a sitting-room or *sulking-room, all to yourself. 1880 Daily Tel. 4 Oct., Not all the sulking of which diplomacy is capable can restore Maximilian to life. 1778 Foote Trip Calais II. Wks. 1799 IV. 58 You sullen, *sulking, stomachful slut!

Sulk(e, variants of Suck, Swilk.

†**Sulke**, *a.* *Obs. rare*⁻¹. [? Related to Sulk *v.*, Sulky *a.*] Hard to sell; slow in going off.

1636 Heywood Challenge Beautie III. i, Never was thrifty trader more willing to put of a sulke commodity, than she was to truck for her maydenhead.

Sulkene, obs. form of Silken *a.*

Sulkily (sɒ·lkili), *adv.* [f. Sulky *a.* + -ly².] In a sulky manner; with silent or moody ill-humour.

1796 Colman Iron Chest Pref. p. ii, Here is a scowling, sullen, black Bull,..he stands sulkily before. 1855 Macaulay Hist. Eng. xv. III. 560 Anne, who, when in good humour, was meekly stupid, and, when in bad humour, was sulkily stupid. 1865 Flo. Marryat Love's Confl. I. xviii. 317 Agnes took the sulkily-granted leave joyfully. 1874 Green Short Hist. viii. § 9 (1882) 560 The stricter Covenanters retired sulkily from the Royal army.

fig. 1823 Byron Juan XIV. xxviii, When..sulkily the river's ripple's flowing. 1839 Kemble Resid. in Georgia (1863) 69 The eagle..hovered sulkily a while over the river.

Sulkiness (sɒ·lkinės). [f. Sulky *a.* + -ness.] The state or quality of being sulky.

1760 Gray Let. to Dr. Clarke 12 Aug., Three women that laughed from morning to night, and would allow nothing to the sulkiness of my disposition. 1818 Scott Hrt. Midl. xix, Driven into pettish sulkiness by the persecution of the interrogators. 1885 Manch. Even. News 2 Feb. 2/4 Their sulkiness manifests itself in the most peevish manner.

Sulkup, variant form of Selcouth *Obs.*

Sulky (sɒ·lki), *sb.* Also 8–9 **sulkey**, 9 **sulkee, sulkie**. [subst. use of Sulky *a.*]

1. A light two-wheeled carriage or chaise (sometimes without a body), seated for one person: now used principally in America for trials of speed between trotting-horses. (So called because it admits only one person. Cf. Désobligeant.)

1756 Connoisseur No. 112 ¶ 4 A formal female seated in a Sulky, foolishly pleased with having the whole vehicle to herself. 1775 J. Adams in Fam. Lett. (1876) 55 My mare..ran and dashed the body of the sulky all to pieces. 1796 Southey Lett. fr. Spain (1797) 118 Many sulkies drawn by three mules abreast. 1860 O. W. Holmes Elsie V. xi, The doctor turned and looked through the little round glass in the back of the sulky. 1882 Standard 1 Dec. 5/4 (Canada) The din and noise of waggons,..buggies, sulkees, and ox teams. 1884 B'ham Daily Post 23 Feb. 2/5 American Trotting Sulkie, weighs 56 lb.; to carry 180 lb.

2. *transf.* a. A bathing-machine for one. *jocular.*

1806–7 J. Beresford Miseries Hum. Life (1807) XIV. vi, On re-entering your Sulky in your new character,..you discover, for the first time, that your own towel is safely locked up at home.

b. (See quot.)

1862 Mrs. Speid Last Years India 129 A little silver 'sulky',..a small spherical box, pierced all over with small holes [etc.]. This pretty apparatus is intended for brewing a single cup of tea, by the morosely inclined.

3. Short for *sulky-plough* (see 4).

1891 C. Roberts Adrift Amer. 37 Two single-furrow sulkies with three horses each.

4. *attrib.* passing into *adj.*, applied to (*a*) a set of articles for the use of a single person, (*b*) an agricultural implement having a seat for the driver (*U.S.*).

1786 Mackenzie Lounger No. 89 ¶ 7 A dispute about the age of a sulky set of China. 1875 Knight Dict. Mech. 2452 Sulky-cultivator, one having a seat for the rider, who manages the plows, moving them to the right or left as the plants in the rows may require. Ibid., Sulky-rake, a horse-rake having an elevated seat for the driver. 1879 Scribner's Mag. Nov. 137/1 Next spring I..bought me a sulky-plow.

Sulky (sɒ·lki), *a.* [app. f. Sulk *v.*² Cf. NFris. (Sylt) *sulkig*.]

1. Of persons and their actions: Silently and obstinately ill-humoured; showing a tendency to keep aloof from others and repel their advances by refusing to speak or act.

1744 M. Bishop Life & Adv. vi. 45 It is often seen in press'd Men that they are stubborn and sulky. 1790 Burns Tam o' Shanter 10 Our hame, Whare sits our sulky sullen dame, Gathering her brows like gathering storm. 1821 Scott Kenilw. iii, He has sulky ways too, breaking off intercourse with all that are of the place. 1834 James J. Marston Hall xi, My companion generally rode on in sulky silence. 1856 Ruskin Elem. Drawing ii. (1857) 134 The true zeal and patience of a quarter of an hour are better than the sulky and inattentive labour of a whole day. 1880 W. Harris Serm. Boys & Girls (1881) 40 They were like..sulky children who would be pleased with nothing.

b. Of animals; *spec.* of a fish (cf. Sulk *v.*² b).

1810 Scott Lady of L. I. x, Back limp'd..The sulky leaders of the chase. 1823 Lamb Elia I. Dream children, A great sulky pike hanging midway down the water. 1828 Davy Salmonia 30, I thought after a fish had been hooked, he remained sick and sulky for some time.

2. Of inanimate natural objects, the weather, etc.: Gloomy, dismal. Of things, with respect to their growth, progress, or movement: Sluggish. Also, *dial.* difficult to work.

1817 W. Irving in Life & Lett. (1864) I. 380 The weather is still sulky and threatening. 1825 Scott 11 Oct. in Fam. Let. (1894) II. xxiii. 350 One's friends are not so easily entertained on such a sulky day as this. 1849 Cupples Green Hand ix. (1856) 85 A sulky patch of dark-gray sky. 1867 F. Francis Angling vii. 223 Some, again, are termed 'sulky lakes', and are very hard to get fish from at all. 1886 Cheshire Gloss., Sulky,..applied to..rock which has no cleavage and is difficult to quarry, very cross-grained timber, &c. 1889 E. E. Green in Ceylon Indep. (Cent. Dict.), The condition called sulky as applied to a tea-bush is unfortunately only too common on many estates. 1890 Clark Russell Marriage at Sea viii, The sulky undulations of the water. 1905 Daily News 31 Aug. 6 The cream..gets 'sulky', or it 'goes to sleep', and then you may churn all day and get no result.

3. *Comb.*, as *sulky-looking* adj.

1828 Lytton Pelham II. xxv, A few dull and sulky-looking fir-trees. 1844 H. Stephens Bk. Farm II. 692 The dull sulky-looking colt.

Sull. Chiefly *w.* and *s.w. dial.* Also 7, 9 **sul**, 9 **zull**; 7 **soule**, 8 **sewl**, 9 **sole, sowle, zowl, zarl**. [repr. the stem of the oblique cases (*sule, sulum*, etc.) of OE. *sulh* Sullow, or the later nom. *sul, sūl*. Somerset *zill* repr. OE. oblique *syl(l* for *sylh* (cf. *sillow*, etc. s.v. Sullow).] A plough.

1607 J. Carpenter Plaine Mans Plough 109 The Soule..that Instrument wherewith being fastened to the Oxen, the Husbandman rippeth up his land. 1669 Worlidge Syst. Agric. (1681) 36 The Sun and the Sull are some Husbandmens Soil. Ibid. 332 A Sull, a term used for a Plow in the Western parts. 1766 Willy in Complete Farmer s.v. Turnep, Ploughing the intervals with a small sull, drawn by one horse. 1791 W. H. Marshall W. England (1796) II. 276 The plowman carries, in the body of his sewl, a parcel of small rods. 1825 Jennings Observ. Dial. W. Eng. 86 Zull,..a plough. 1883 Hampsh. Gloss., Zarl (zaal), a plough.

b. *attrib.* and *Comb.*, as *sull-breaking*; *sull-paddle* = Plough-staff.

1669 Worlidge Syst. Agric. (1681) 331 A Sulpaddle, a small Spade-staff or Instrument to cleanse the Plough from the clogging Earth. 1766 Compl. Farmer, Sull-paddle, a plough paddle. 1791 W. H. Marshall W. England (1796) II. 276 A field..which has long been noted for sewl-breaking.

‖ **Sulla** (sɒ·lă). [Sp. *sulla*.] A leguminous plant, *Hedysarum coronarium* (also called French honeysuckle), with flowers resembling those of the red clover, found in some Mediterranean countries. Also *attrib.*

1787 Jefferson Writ. (1859) II. 202 The sulla of Malta, or Spanish St. Foin. 1818 Mrs. Iliff Poems (ed. 2) 129 Lovely May Wreathing the sulla-flowers of brightest red, With ears of barley. 1895 Atlantic Monthly Mar. 340 The *sulla*, a sort of pink vetch.

Sullabub, obs. form of Sillabub.

Sullage (sɒ·lėdʒ). Forms: 6 **sollage**, 7 **sulledge**, 7–8 **suillage**, 8 **sulli(d)ge, swillage**, 7– **sullage**. [Of uncertain origin. ? a. AF. **souillage*, **soullage*, **suillage*, f. *souiller* Soil *v.*¹, Sully *v.*: see -age. The synonymous Soilage is perhaps due to a variant **soillage*. In the 17th and 18th cent. the spelling was influenced by Sully: see Sulliage.]

1. Filth, refuse, *esp.* such as is carried off by drains from a house, farmyard, or the like; sewage.

1553 in Vicary's Anat. (1888) App. iii. 176 To caraye awaye the Sollage of the Clensinge of the saide Stretes. 1609 in Sussex Archæol. Coll. (1867) XIX. 199 Annoying the Bowrne wᵗʰ the sulledge of his hoggs by a dyke. 1624 Wotton Elem. Archit. (1672) 18 Under-conducts and Conveyances, for the Suillage of the House. 1748 Dousley Preceptor (1763) I. 180 The Apertures..are either Doors..or conduits for the Suillage. 1750 W. Ellis Mod. Husbandm. I. i. 39 (E. D. S.) If..highway sullidge and dung are mixed together. 1879 Flor. Nightingale in Jrnl. Indian Assoc. Art Educ. Oct., The people themselves feel the misery of having no channels to remove sullage away clear from every habitation.

†2. *fig.* Filth, filthiness, defilement, pollution.

1641 S. Hinde in W. Hinde J. Bruen To Rdr., Free from the sullage of Envie, and detraction. 1673 Lady's Call. II. i. § 7. 59 The lightest act of dalliance leaves somthing of stain and sullage behind it. 1697 Evelyn Numismata ix. 309 The Soul contracts no sullage from the deformity of the Body.

3. The silt washed down and deposited by a stream or flood.

1691 T. H[ale] Acc. New Inv. p. lxi, Such Shelfes arising in our River from the Gravel and Sullage that are wash'd into it. 1725 Henley tr. Montfaucon's Antiq. Italy (ed. 2) 28 Several Strata of this Kind were form'd by the Suillage of Rivers and Torrents. 1733 W. Ellis Chiltern & Vale Farm. 236 Sullidge which the Waters leaves on the Ground. 1755 Gentl. Mag. XXV. 396 The swillage of rivers. 1800 W. Chapman Witham & Welland 62 The bottom was found quite hard, and without sullage, from the Grand Sluice to Fishtoft-jetties. 1867 Smyth Sailor's Word-bk. 665.

4. *Founding.* Metal scoria or slag.

1843 Holtzapffel Turning I. 349 The metal is..free from the scoria or sullage, which sometimes renders the upper surface very rough.

5. *Comb.*: **sullage-piece** (see quot. 1875); **sullage-pipe**, a drain-pipe.

1852 Burn Naval & Milit. Dict. II. 276/2 *Sullage piece, or dead head, masselotte. 1875 Knight Dict. Mech. 2452/2 Sullage-piece,..a dead-head, or feeding-head. A piece of metal on a casting which occupies the ingate at which the metal entered the mold...In this piece the sullage rises, hence its name. 1907 'J. Halsham' Lonewood Corner 214 He reckons it's better for a man to be on the top of a stack than down a *sullage-pipe.

†**Sullayne**, ? erron. form of Sewin.

1570 Levins Manip. Q iv, A sullayne, fishe, salmo parvus.

Sulle, obs. f. Sell *v.*, Shall *v.*, Sill *sb.*¹

Sulledge, obs. form of Sullage.

Sullen (sɒ·lən), *a.*, *adv.*, and *sb.* Also 6 **solen, sulleyne**, 6–7 **sollen**, 7 **sull(a)in, sulen**. [Later form of Solein.] A. *adj.*

1. Of persons, their attributes, aspect, actions: Characterized by, or indicative of, gloomy ill-humour or moody silence.

In early use there is often implication of obstinacy or stubbornness.

1573–80 Tusser Husb. (1878) 180 Be lowly not sollen. if ought go amisse. 1592 Arden of Feversham I. i. 510 Who would haue thought the ciuill sir so sollen? 1641 'Smectymnuus' Vind. Answ. To Rdr., Wee are called..sullen and crabbed peices. 1668 Extr. St. Papers rel. Friends Ser. III. (1912) 279 They Saintᵉ Penn..is divelishly cryed vp amongest that pervers sullen Faction. 1680 C. Nesse Church Hist. 55 Because they might not have what they would, grew sullain, and would have nothing. 1713 Steele Guard. No. 18 ¶ 2 These contemplations have made me serious but not sullen. 1718 Free-thinker No. 149. 323 In the Middle sits Cato, with a sullen Brow. 1795 Burke Corr. (1844) IV. 315 If the better part lies by, in a sullen silence, they still cannot hinder the more factious part both from speaking and from writing. 1814 Wordsw. Excurs. VI. 459 Here..they met,..flaming Jacobite And sullen Hanoverian! 1849 Macaulay Hist. Eng. vi. II. 28 The answer of James was a cold and sullen reprimand. 1879 Froude Cæsar xxvi. 438 Some were still sullen, and refused to sue for a forgiveness.

b. *transf.* Of animals and inanimate things: Obstinate, refractory; stubborn, unyielding.

1577 B. Googe Heresbach's Husb. III. 128 b, Which being well punished with hunger, and thyrst, wyll teache him [sc. a plough-ox] to leaue that sullen tricke. 1648 Gage West Ind. 89, I got up again and spurred my sullen jade. 1678 Cudworth Intell. Syst. I. v. 888 Things are Sullen, and will be as they are, what ever we Think them, or Wish them to be. 1691 Ray Creation I. (1692) 38 The stupid Matter..would be as sullen as the Mountain was that Mahomet commanded to come down to him. 1725 De Foe Voy. round World (1840) 339 The other [bull] proved untractable, sullen, and outrageous. 1859 Tennyson Geraint & Enid 862 As sullen as a beast new-caged.

†c. Holding aloof. *Obs.*

1628 Earle Microcosm., Acquaintance (Arb.) 86 Friendship is a sullener thing, as a contracter and taker vp of our affections to some few.

†d. *fig.* Baleful, malignant. *Obs.*

1676 Dryden Aurengz. I. i. 360 Such sullen Planets at my Birth did shine, They threaten every Fortune mixt with mine. 1679 Dryden & Lee Œdipus III, Ye sullen Pow'rs below. 1703 Rowe Fair Penit. II. i, Some sullen Influence, a Foe to both.

†2. Solemn, serious. *Obs.*

1583 Melbancke Philotimus M iij b, So was he free from sulleyne sterne seueritie. a1586 Sidney Apol. Poetrie (Arb.) 30 Morrall Philosophers, whom me thinketh, I see comming towards me with a sullen grauity. 1640 Ep. Reynolds Passions iv, Some plausible Fancy doth more prevail with tender Wills than a severe and sullen argument. 1719 Young Busiris I. i, In sullen Majesty they stalk along, With Eyes of Indignation, and Despair.

3. Of immaterial things, actions, conditions: Gloomy, dismal, melancholy; sometimes with the notion of 'passing heavily, moving sluggishly'.

1593 Shaks. Rich. II, I. iii. 265 The sullen passage of thy weary steppes. 1604 — Oth. III. iv. 51 (Q¹), A salt and sullen rhume. 1605 Daniel Philotas Ep. 59 To sound The deepe reports of sullen Tragedies. 1648 Milton Sonn. xvii, Where shall we sometimes meet, and by the fire Help wast a sullen day. 1712–14 Pope Rape Lock IV. 19 No cheerful breeze this sullen region knows. 1775 Johnson Let. to Mrs. Thrale 1 Aug., The place [sc. Oxford] is now a sullen solitude. 1816 Byron Pris. Chillon xiv, With spiders I had friendship made, And watch'd them in their sullen trade. 1858 Kingsley Lett. (1878) I. 21 It was an afternoon of sullen Autumn rain. a1864 Hawthorne Amer. Note-bks. (1879) II. 52 A bleak, sullen day.

b. Of a sound or an object producing a sound: Of a deep, dull, or mournful tone. Chiefly *poet.*

1592 Shaks. Rom. & Jul. IV. v. 88 Our solemne Hymnes, to sullen Dyrges change. 1632 Milton Penseroso 76, I hear the far-off Curfeu sound,..Swinging slow with sullen roar. 1742 Collins Ode ix. 12 Where the beetle winds His small but sullen horn. 1819 Scott Ivanhoe xliv, The heavy bell..broke short their argument. One by one the sullen sounds fell successively on the ear. 1849 Kingsley North Devon in Misc. (1859) II. 264 The sullen thunder of the unseen surge.

4. Of sombre hue; of a dull colour; hence, of gloomy or dismal aspect. (Also qualifying an adj. of colour = dull-.) Cf. Sad *a.* 8.

a1586 [implied in Sullenly 2]. 1592 Arden of Feversham III. i. 45 Now will he shake his care oppressed head, Then fix his sad eis on the sollen earth. 1596 Shaks. 1 Hen. IV, I. ii. 236 Like bright Mettall on a sullen ground. 1647 Harvey Sch. of Heart XXI. i, Take sullen lead for silver, sounding brass Instead of solid gold. 1665 J. Rea Flora 130 A dark sullen violet purple colour. 1710 Steele Tatler No. 266 ¶ 3 Two apples that were roasting by a sullen sea coal fire. 1713 Phil. Trans. XXVIII. 224 A sort of sullen greenish Wood-like rust. 1784 Cowper Task II. 212, I would not yet exchange thy sullen skies..for warmer France With all her vines. 1811 Scott Don Roderick II. i, All sleeps in sullen shade, or silver glow. 1818 Keats Sonn. Ben Nevis 6, I look o'erhead, And there is sullen mist. 1855 Tennyson Maud I. x. i, The sullen-purple moor. 1894 Hall Caine Manxman V. iii. 286 The sky to the north-west was dark and sullen.

†b. **Sullen lady**, ? *Fritillaria nigra*. *Obs.*

1688 Holme Armoury II. iv. 74/1 The sullen Lady, hangeth her head down..and is of an umberish dark hair colour, without any checker or spots. Some call it the black Fritillary.

5. Of water, etc.: Flowing sluggishly. *poet.*

1622 Drayton Poly-olb. xxviii. 91 Small Cock, a sullen Brook, comes to her succour then. 1628 Milton Vac. Exerc. 95 Sullen Mole that runneth underneath. 1814 Scott Wav. xxii, The larger [stream] was placid, and even sullen in its course. 1818 Shelley Rosal. & Helen 398 Each one lay Sucking the sullen milk away About my frozen heart.

6. *Comb.*: parasynthetic adjs., as *sullen-browed, -hearted*; complementary, as *sullen-seeming*; with other adjs., as *sullen-sour, -wise*.

1831 Scott Cast. Dang. ii, This *sullen-browed Thomas Dickson. 1909 R. Bridges Par. Virg. Æn. VI, 434 The *sullen-hearted, who..Their own life did-away. 1855 Tennyson Maud I. XVIII. vi, *Sullen-seeming Death. 1849 J. A. Carlyle tr. Dante's Inf. p. xliv, The *Sullen-sour or Gloomy-sluggish. 1710 Steele Tatler No. 149 ¶ 5 A *sullen-wise Man is as bad as a good-natured Fool.

B. *adv.* = Sullenly. *rare.*

1718 Prior Solomon II. 201 Sullen I forsook th' Imperfect Feast. 1810 Scott Lady of L. II. xxxiv, Sullen and slowly they unclasp.

C. *sb.* (in *pl.*, usually *the sullens*; rarely *sing.*) A state of gloomy ill-humour; sullenness, sulks. Phr. *in the sullens, sick of the sullens*.

1580 Lyly Euphues (Arb.) 285 She was solitaryly walking, with hir frowning cloth, as sick lately of the solens. 1631 R. H. Arraignm. Whole Creature xvi. 280 So long he is sicke in the suds, and diseas'd in the sullens. 1633 Marmion Fine Comp. I. iii. B 2, They can doe no more good upon me, then a young pittifull Lover upon a Mistresse, that has the sullens. 1662 Hibbert Body Divinity I. 142 Its a dangerous thing to sit sick of the sullens, or be discontented. a1670 Hacket Abp. Williams I. (1692) 84 If his Majesty were moody..he would fetch him out of that Sullen with a pleasant Jest. 1671 Wood Life (O. H. S.) II. 215 When William Lenthall was troubled with the sullins. 1679 Dryden Troil. & Cress. IV. ii, I'll e'en go home, and shut up my doors, and die o' the sullens, like an old bird in a cage. 1747 Richardson Clarissa (1811) I. xviii. 134 No sullens, my Mamma; no perverseness. 1819 Scott Leg. Montrose xxiii, Annot Lyle could always charm Allan out of the sullens. 1864 Carlyle Fredk. Gt. XVI. viii. IV. 362 Russian Czarina evidently in the sullens against Friedrich. 1868 'Holme Lee' B. Godfrey xxxvi, Gerrard was in a fit of sullens.

b. *Comb.*, †**sullen-sick** *a.*, 'sick of the sullens', ill from ill-humour.

1614 T. Adams Sinners Passing Bell Wks. (1629) 247 If the state..lie sullen-sicke of Naboths vineyard. 1650 Fuller Pisgah II. vii. § 7. 158 On the denyall Ahab falls sullen-sick.

Sullen (sɒ·lən), *v.* *rare.* [f. Sullen *a.*]

1. *trans.* To make sullen or sluggish.

1628 Feltham Resolves II. xlviii, The Idle man..like a member out of joynt, sullens the whole Body, with an ill disturbing lazinesse. 1894 Amyand Only a Drummer Boy iv. 47 [They] prevented Douglas's happy nature getting completely crushed and sullened.

†2. *intr.* To be sullen; to sulk. *Obs.*

a1652 Brome Covent Gard. I. i, Keeping her chamber whole weeks together, sullenning upon her Samplery breech-work.

Sullen, obs. form of Sell *v.*, Shall *v.*

Sullenly (sɒ·lənli), *adv.* [f. Sullen *a.* + -ly².] In a sullen manner.

1. With gloomy or morose ill-humour.

1650 Fuller Pisgah III. xi. § 15. 434 If any..sullenly say, with Judas Iscariot, To what purpose is this wast? 1668 Dryden Secr. Love III, While jealous pow'r does sullenly o're spy. 1784 Cowper Task III. 393 His book, Well chosen, and not sullenly perus'd In selfish silence, but imparted oft. 1841 Dickens Barn. Rudge xvii, 'Give me meat and drink', he answered sullenly. 1879 Spectator 13 Sept. 1148 That if the Viceroy were only sufficiently persistent, Afghans, like Turks, would sullenly give way.

2. With sombre or gloomy aspect; with a dull or dismal sound.

a1586 Sidney Arcadia III. x. (1912) 402 The colours for the grounde were so well chosen, neither sullenly darke, nor glaringly lightsome. 1794 Mrs. Radcliffe Myst. Udolpho li, The wind..groaned sullenly among the lofty branches above. 1841 W. Spalding Italy & It. Isl. I. 295 The volcanic fires..smoulder sullenly at the present day. 1860 Tyndall Glac. I. xiv. 93 The clouds..sailed sullenly from the west. 1898 H. Newbolt He fell among Thieves iv, The ravine where the Yassin river sullenly flows.

Sullenness (sɒ·lənnės). Also 7 **solennesse**, **sulliness**, 8 **sulleness**. [f. Sullen *a.* + -ness.]

1. The condition or quality of being sullen in behaviour, aspect, or temper. Also, an instance of this.

a1586 Sidney Arcadia III. (1912) 379 Fearing least silence would offend her sullennes. 1644 Milton Educ. Wks. 1851 IV. 392 When the air is calm and pleasant, it were an injury and sullennesse against nature not to go out. 1663 Patrick Parab. Pilgr. xxxii. (1687) 393 His seriousness gives no disgust, his silence is without sullenness. a1721 Prior Cromwell & his Porter 20 Wks. 1907 II. 262 By..the sulleness of his brow it should be my old Porter. 1784 Cook's 3rd Voy. I. viii. I. 154 The countenance..has..sometimes a sullenness or reserve. 1825 Scott Betrothed iii, They are..a mixed breed, having much of your German sullenness. 1879 Froude Cæsar xiv. 205 After a few vicious efforts, they subsided into sullenness.

†2. Slowness, reluctance. *Obs.*

1619 Lushington Resurrection I. (1659) 34 No removing of the Tombestone; that besides its weight & sullenness to give way, was rib'd and clasped down with Iron barrs and bonds.

3. Dismalness, gloom.

1885 Pater Marius IV. xxiii, The long winter had been a season of unvarying sullenness.

†**Su·llenwood.** *Obs.* Altered f. Southernwood, with play on *sullen*.

1632 W. Rowley New Wonder III, I'l make you eate Sorrill to your supper, though I eate Sullenwood my selfe.

Sullepe, variant of Serelepy *Obs.*

a1400–50 Wars Alex. 4305 Þat sullepe sire at sett all þe werde.

Sullepsis, variant of Syllepsis.

Suller(o, obs. forms of Seller¹.

Su·llerye. ? Misprint for *sullinge* = Suling.

1628 Coke On Litt. 5 Vna Hida seu carucata terræ, which is all one as a plow-land,..sullerye also signifieth a plow-land.

Su·llevate, var. Sollevate *v.* (Cf. Sublevate.)

1595 Daniel Civ. Wars I. xlviii, How he his subiectes sought to sulleuate.

Sulleva·tion, var. Sollevation *Obs.* (Cf. Sublevation.)

1611 Sir D. Carleton in 10th Rep. Hist. MSS. Comm. App. I. 533 To furnish the Albanesi with weapons for a suddaine sullevation. 1623 Cockeram, Sullevation, a murderous intent. 1637 Earl Monm. tr. Malvezzi's Romulus & Tarquin 97 To suffocat sullevations in their cradle.

Sulli, variant form of Selly *Obs.*

a1290 Pains of Hell 213 in Herrig's Archiv LXII. 403 Neren nowiȝt hoe þerof adrad: ffor-þi hoe slepeþ in sulli bed.

Sulliage (sɒ·liėdʒ). Variant of Sullage influenced by Sully *v.*

1667 Decay Chr. Piety xi. § 2 Though we wipe away with never so much care the dirt thrown at us, there will be left some sulliage behind. 1793 W. H. Marshall Rural Econ. W. Eng. (1796) II. 358 The sulliage which such places are ever accumulating. 1853 Bill to establish Metrop. Board Sewers Preamble 2 The Sewage, Filth, Soil, and Sulliage issuing from the Sewers and Drains. 1879 R. Fletcher Dickens xv. 13 No taint or sulliage falls on all he writ. 188. R. G. H[ill] Voices in Solit. 111 Oft have I watched and proved her perfidy, And chid with bitter words her sulliage.

Sullibib, -bub, obs. forms of Sillabub.

Sullic, -ich(e, var. forms of Selly *Obs.*

Sullidge, var. Sullage.

Sullied (sɒ·lid), *ppl. a.* Also 6 **solyed**, 7 **sully'd**. [f. Sully *v.* + -ed¹.] Soiled, polluted (*lit.* and *fig.*); †made gloomy or dull.

1571 [implied in Sulliedness]. c1600 Shaks. Sonn. xv, To change your day of youth to sullied night. 1612 Drayton Poly-olb. x. 294 Her sullied face. 1683 Tryon Way to Health 320 A loathsomly sullied Soul, and an indisposed distempered Body. 1695 A. Telfair New Confut. Sadd. (1696) 7 Seven small Bones..wrapp'd up in a piece of old sullied Paper. 1734 tr. Rollin's Anc. Hist. xv. viii. (1827) VI. 132 The moon..appeared afterwards quite sullied and as it were tinged with blood. 1824 Scott Redgauntlet ch. xiii, He wore a smart hanger and a pair of pistols in a sullied sword-belt. 1870 Dickens E. Drood i, The choir are getting on their sullied white robes. 1889 R. Bridges Growth of Love lii, Let the true Muse rewrite her sullied page.

b. *Sullied white*, dirty white.

1681 Lond. Gaz. No. 1676/4 A very large Irish Greyhound being of a sullied White, with some pale yellowish spots. 1817 Stephens in Shaw's Gen. Zool. X. II. 493 The under parts of the body sullied white: the tail greenish black.

Hence †**Su·lliedness**, defilement.

1571 Golding Calvin on Ps. lxviii. 15 Although the land were covered with solyednesse throughe the troublous invasion of the enemies: yit..it recovered hir whitenesse, so as it became as whyte as snowe.

Sulliva·tion, variant of Sollevation *Obs.*

1605 Daniel Philotas II. i, How can that be donne, Without some sulliuation to insue?

Su·llow. Chiefly *w.* and *s.w. dial.* Forms: 1 **sulh**, 1, 3 **suluh**, 3 **solh**, (**sul(o)h-, sulȝ-, solȝ-, solw-**), 4 **soluȝ, -ou**, *Kent.* **zuolȝ**, 4–5 **solouȝ, -ow**, 5 **-ouh, -owe, -oȝ**, 6 **zolow**, 7– **sullow** (9 **zullow, sillow, silla, zilla**). [OE. *sulh* str. fem., for **swulh*, the *w* being preserved in Kentish ME. *zuolȝ* and OE. *swulung*, ME. *swoling*, etc. (see Suling); ultimately cogn. with L. *sulcus* furrow.

The local variant *sillow* represents OE. dat. sing. or nom. pl. *sylh, sylg*. The oblique forms without umlaut (*sule*, etc.) are represented by forms s.v. Sull.]

1. A plough. (Also in *fig.* context.)

c897 K. Ælfred Gregory's Past C. li. 403 Ðæt nan mon ne scyle don his hond to ðære sylȝ, & hawian underbæc. c900 tr. Bæda's Hist. V. ix. (1899) 594 For þon þe heora sylh unrihte gangað. c950 Lindisf. Gosp. Luke ix. 62 Ne ænig sende hond his on sulh [Rushw. suluh] & behaldas on bæcg. c1000 Sax. Leechd. I. 404 Þonne man þa sulh forð drife. c1205 Lay. 4260 Þe[t] ælc cheorl æt his sulche hæfde grið al swa þe king sulf. Ibid. 31811 Þer cheorl draf his sulȝe i-oxned swiðe fæire. a1225 Ancr. R. 384 Ȝif eax ne kurue, ne þe spade ne dulue, ne þe suloh [MS. T. ploh] ne erede. 1340 Ayenb. 242 Þe ilke þet zet þe hand ope zuolȝ and lokeþ behinde him. 1340–70 Alex. & Dind. 295 Hit is no leue in oure lawe þat we..sette solow on þe feld ne sowe none erþe. 1387 Trevisa Higden (Rolls) VII. 445 Þe solouȝ of holy cherche schal nouȝt goo aryȝt. 14.. Ibid. App. 535 (Harl. MS. 1900) This day is my solowe y-come to the laste forowe. 1535 in F. W. Weaver Wells Wills (1890) 178 A zolow with all other apparell for vj oxen. 1636 H. Sydenham Serm. Sol. Occ. (1637) 265 The spirituall Plough is not halfe so well manag'd by any, as one that was yesterday conversant with the Goade and the Sullow. c1640 J. Smyth Lives Berkeleys (1883) I. 303 What waynes, carts, sullows, harrowes..remained. 1893 Wilts. Gloss., Sillow, Sullow,..Sylla, a plough, was used at Bratton within the memory of persons still living.

†b. A plot of land is described as being 'of so many sullows'; hence *sullow* = Plough *sb.*¹ 3 a, Plough-land 1. *Obs.*

c1205 Lay. 13176 Twenti sulhene [c1275 sulȝene] lond. Ibid. 18779 Þritti solh of londe. Ibid. 18780.

2. *attrib.* and *Comb.*, as *sullow-beam, -board, -handle, -share* (all *Obs.*).

a1000 in Wr.-Wülcker 196/1 Burris, curuamentum aratri, *sulhbeam. 14.. Metr. Voc., Ibid. 628/5 Buris, solowbeme. Ibid. 628/7 Barcha, *solowborde. c1000 Ælfric Gloss., Ibid. 104/11 Stiba, *sulhhandla. 14.. Metr. Voc., Ibid. 628/5 Stiua, solowhanddul. 14.. Trevisa's Higden (Rolls) VII. App. 527 (Harl. MS. 1900) Heo wole go barfot..uppon nyne *solow schares brennyng and fuyre hote.

†**Su·lly**, *sb.* *Obs.* Also 7 **sulley**. [f. Sully *v.*] An act of sullying, soiling, or polluting (*lit.* and *fig.*); a stain, blemish.

1602 Shaks. Ham. II. i. 39 You laying these slight sulleyes on my Sonne, As 'twere a thing a little soil'd i' th' working. 1683 Moxon Mech. Exerc., Printing xxiv. ¶ 19 The Gold or Silver will stick to the least Sully that the Varnish may chance to make. 1711 Addison Spect. No. 256 ¶ 4 These little Spots and Sullies in its Reputation. 1742 Fielding J. Andrews I. iv, Without the least sully of their virtue. 1762 Franklin Lett., etc. Wks. 1840 V. 393 After the explosion, I could find neither any moisture nor any sully from the ink.

Sully (sɒ·li), *v.* Also 6, 8 **sulley**, 7 **sullie**. [app. ad. F. *souiller*: see Soil *v.*¹]

1. *trans.* To pollute, defile; to soil, stain, tarnish.

a. in material sense. Now *rare* or *poet.*

1611 Shaks. Wint. T. I. ii. 327 Sully the puritie and whitenesse of my Sheetes? 1615 G. Sandys Trav. 295 The roofe and sides are..sullied..with the smoke of torches. 1756 C. Lucas Ess. Waters II. 164 A sky colored pellicule, sullied with dark spots. 1818 Wordsw. Near Spring of Hermitage 12 Rains, that make each rill a torrent, Neither sully it nor swell. 1885 Manch. Exam. 25 Mar. 3/2 The delicate white of the vellum cover which a careless touch might sully.

absol. 1601 Holland Pliny II. 473 [How] that if one rule paper..therewith [sc. silver], it will draw blacke lines, and sullie as it doth.

b. in immaterial sense.

1591 Shaks. 1 Hen. VI, IV. iv. 6 The ouer-daring Talbot Hath sullied all his glosse of former Honor By this vnheedfull..adventure. 1612 Two Noble K. I. ii. 5 Before we furthur Sully our glosse of youth. 1657 Sparrow Bk. Com. Prayer (1661) 33 Christmas and Epiphany..holy Church held for such high times of joy and Festivity, that they would not have one day among them sullied by..sorrow and fasting. 1706 Phillips (ed. Kersey) s.v., To Sully the Fancy, to fill it with nasty, filthy, or impure Thoughts. 1729 Shelvocke Artillery v. 355, I will not sully my Page with any Rehearsal of them. 1781 Gibbon Decl. & F. xxiv. II. 475 The purity of his virtue was sullied by excessive vanity. 1849 Macaulay Hist. Eng. v. I. 529 His life had been sullied by a great domestic crime. 1874 Green Short Hist. v. § 2 (1882) 226 A merciless massacre sullied the fame of his earlier exploits.

†2. *intr.* To become soiled or tarnished. *Obs.*

1596 Shaks. 1 Hen. IV, II. iv. 84 Looke you Francis, your white Canuas doublet will sulley. 1654 Z. Coke Logick Pref., The Enamel of these Gayeties and Gauds, Sully and soon grow Dusky. 1670 Sir Sackville Crow in 12th Rep. Hist. MSS. Comm. App. v. 15 The silke sleizie and not Naples, which will soone grow rough, gather dust and sullie.

Hence **Su·llying** *vbl. sb.* and *ppl. a.*

1628 Ford Lover's Mel. II. ii, The purest whitenesse is no such defence Against the sullying foulenesse of that fury. 1659 C. Noble Mod. Answ. to Immed. Queries To Rdr., They are also sullyings and discolorings of the sacred memory of the dead. 1707 Mortimer Husb. (1721) I. 327 The sullying and foulness of the Floor. 1715 Gay Trivia II. 32 Three sullying trades avoid with equal care. 1842 Manning Serm. vi. (1848) I. 84 He that leaves upon driven snow a dark and sullying touch. 1871 Tennyson Last Tourn. 679 Thro' that sullying of our Queen.

Sullybub, obs. form of Sillabub.

1663 Pepys Diary 12 July, Then to Commissioner Pett's and had a good sullybub.

†**Sulp**, *v.* *Obs.* Also 4–5 **solp**. [Etym. obscure. Possibly related to G. dial. *sulper, solper* bog, mud, (? orig.) brine, pickle, *sölpern* to soil, sully.] *trans.* To defile, pollute. Hence **Su·lping** *vbl. sb.* (= defilement) and *ppl. a.*

a1350 St. Laurence 210 in Horstm. Altengl. Leg. (1881) 110 [He] makes it clene, þat no solping þaron es sene. 13.. E. E. Allit. P. A. 726 With-outen..mascle of sulpande synne. Ibid. B. 550 If he be sulped in synne. Ibid. 1135 Sulp no more þenne in synne þy saule. a1400–50 Wars Alex. 4292 All þe syn at solp may þe saule. 1412 26 Pol. Poems 49 Sulpid in synne derk as nyȝt.

Sulph- (sɒlf) *Chem.*, variant of Sulfo- before a vowel, as in *sulphacetic* (*-ate*), *-acetone*, *-amic* (*-ate*), *-amidate*, *-amide*, *-amine*, *-aminic*, *-amylic* (*-ate*), *-anilic* (*-ate*), *-antimonic* (*-ate*, *-iate*), *-ious* (*-ite*), *-arsenic* (*-ate*, *-iate*), *-ious* (*-ite*), *-arsin*, *-ethamic* (*-ate*), *-ethylic* (*-ate*), *-imide*, *-iodide*: see quots. and the second elements.

1843 Chem. Gaz. I. 598 *Sulphacetate of silver. Ibid. 507 On decomposing the lead salt [sc. carbonate of lead]..with sulphuretted hydrogen, an acid is obtained, to which the author [sc. M. Melsens] has applied the name of *sulphacetic acid. 1879 Watts Dict. Chem., Suppl. 1047 *Sulphacetone ..is formed by the action of 1 mol. phosphorus trisulphide on 6 mol. acetone. 1868 Ibid. V. 476 Neutral *Sulphamate of Ammonium. 1857 Miller Elem. Chem., Org. iv. § 1. 244 *Sulphamic Acid. 1868 Watts Dict. Chem. V. 477 Sulphamic ethers. 1844 Chem. Gaz. II. 461 The *sulphamidate of ammonia is prepared by leaving the corresponding *sulphammonate in cold water for some hours. 1868 Watts Dict. Chem. V. 482 Sulphamidate..formed from the sulphammonate by the action of water. 1838 T. Thomson Chem. Org. Bodies 601 We may represent the compound thus:— SO^2+H^2Az+HO, or an atom of sulphurous acid, an atom of amide, and an atom of water, and distinguish it by the name of *sulphamide. 1888 Morley & Muir Watts' Dict. Chem. I. 186/2 Toluene *sulphamine..got by heating *p* amido-toluene sulphinic acid with conc HCl. 1902 Encycl. Brit. XXVI. 728/2 Acetanilide..when cautiously dissolved in moderately strong fuming sulphuric acid..is..converted into the *sulphaminic acid $C_6H_5.N(C_2H_3O)(SO_3H)$. 1862 Miller Elem. Chem., Org. (ed. 2) iii. § 1. 164 Both the *sulphamylates of baryta. 1852 W. Gregory Handbk. Org. Chem. 233 *Sulphamylic Acid...This compound is formed exactly like sulphovinic acid. 1856 Q. Jrnl. Chem. Soc. IX. 260 *Sulphanilate of Silver. Ibid., M. Gerhardt's well-known *sulphanilic acid. 1896 Allbutt's Syst. Med. I. 825 A saturated solution of sulphanilic acid. 1863 Watts Dict.

Supplement, p. 3873; Corrigenda, p. 4092; Spurious words, p. 4093; Books quoted, p. 4094

Sulphacid.

Sulphate (sɐˈlfeɪt), sb. Chem. Also sulfate, sulphat. [ad. F. *sulphate* (De Morveau, etc. *Nomenclature chimique*, 1787), ad. mod. L. *sulphātum*, *acidum* ACID), f. *sulphur*: see SULPHUR, -ATE¹ ¹ c.]

A salt of sulphuric acid: usually with term indicating the base, as *sulphate of ammonia*, of *lime*, *ferrous sulphate*.

Sulphated (sɐˈlfeɪtɪd), ppl. a.

Sulphatic (sɐˈlfætɪk), a. Chem.

Sulphating (sɐˈlfeɪtɪŋ), vbl. sb.

Sulphation (sɐˈlfeɪʃən). Chem.

Sulphatize (sɐˈlfətaɪz), v.

Sulphide (sɐˈlfaɪd, -ɪd), sb. Chem. [f. SULPH- + -IDE.]

A compound of sulphur with another element (usually denoted by a qualifying term).

Sulphindigotic (sɐlfindɪˈɡɒtɪk), a. Chem. [f. SULPH-.]

Sulphindigotate (sɐlfinˈdɪɡɒteɪt).

Sulphinic (sɐlˈfɪnɪk), a. Chem.

Sulphine (sɐlˈfaɪn). Chem. [f. SULPH- + -INE.]

Sulphinic (sɐlˈfɪnɪk), a. Chem. [f. SULPH- + -IC.]

Sulphion (sɐˈlfaɪən). Chem. [f. SULPH- + ION.]

Sulphite (sɐˈlfaɪt). Chem. Also § sulfite. [a. F. *sulphite* (Morveau, etc. 1787): arbitrary alteration of *sulphate*: see -ITE¹ 4 b.]

A salt of sulphurous acid: usually with a qualifying term indicating the base.

Sulpho-, before a vowel **sulph-** (sɐlf-), used as combining form of SULPHUR, in names of chemical compounds containing sulphur, or (in modern use) produced by the substitution of sulphur for oxygen (etc.) in a compound: now superseded extensively by THIO-, q.v.

Sulpho-acid. Chem. [f. SULPHO- + ACID.]

An acid obtained from another acid by substituting sulphur for oxygen.

Sulpho-cyanic (sɐlfəʊsaɪˈænɪk). Chem.

Sulphocyanic (sɐlfəʊsaɪˈænɪk), a. Chem.

Sulphocyanogen (sɐlfəʊsaɪˈænədʒɛn), sb. Chem. [f. SULPHO- + CYANOGEN.]

Sulpho-indigotic, a. Chem.

Sulphonal (sɐˈlfəʊnæl). Chem. Also sulf-.

Sulphonate (sɐˈlfəʊneɪt), sb. Chem. [See SULPHONIC ACID, -ATE⁴.]

A salt of sulphonic acid.

Sulphone (sɐˈlfəʊn). Chem. Also -on. [ad. G. *sulfon*, f. *sulfur*: see -ONE.]

Sulphonic (sɐlˈfɒnɪk), a. Chem.

Sulphopurpuric (sɐlfəʊpɜˈpjʊərɪk), a. Chem.

Sulpho-salt (sɐˈlfəʊsɔːlt). Chem.

Sulphovinic (sɐlfəʊˈvɪnɪk), a. Chem.

Sulphoxide (sɐlˈfɒksaɪd). Chem.

Sulphur (sɐˈlfə(r)), sb. Forms: ... Also -our, sulfur.

A greenish-yellow non-metallic substance, found abundantly in volcanic regions, and occurring free in nature as a brittle crystalline solid, widely distributed in combination with metals and other substances. In popular and commercial language it is otherwise known as BRIMSTONE.

Sulphurate (sɐˈlfjʊəreɪt), v. [f. SULPHUR sb. Cf. F. *sulfurer*.]

Sulphurated (sɐˈlfjʊəreɪtɪd), ppl. a. [f. prec. + -ED.]

Sulphurate, a. Obs. rare. [ad. late L. *sulphurātus*.]

Sulphuration (sɐlfjʊəˈreɪʃən). [f. SULPHURATE v. and -ion.]

Sulphurator (sɐˈlfjʊəreɪtə(r)). [f. SULPHURATE v. + -OR.]

Sulphure, Chem. Obs. Also F. *sulphure*, *sulfure* (*Nomencl. Chimique*, 1787): = SULPHIDE sb.

Sulphured (sɐˈlfjʊəd), ppl. a. [f. SULPHUR sb.]

Sulphureity (sɐlfjʊˈriːɪtɪ), v. rare. [f. SULPHUREOUS + -ITY.]

Sulphureous (sɐlˈfjʊərɪəs), a. Also 6 sulphureus, 8 sulfureous. [f. L. *sulphureus*, f. *sulphur*: see -EOUS.]

Of or pertaining to sulphur; full of, consisting of sulphur.

Sulphuric (sɐlˈfjʊərɪk), a. [ad. F. *sulfurique* (= SULPHUR sb. and -URIC. (Now only in Materia Medica and Mining.)]

sulphuric acid, a highly corrosive oily fluid (hydrogen sulphate, H_2SO_4), also called *oil of vitriol*, in its pure state a liquid without colour or smell.

† 2. Consisting of or containing sulphur. *Obs. rare.*

Sulphuriferous (sŭlfūri·fĕrəs), *a. rare.* [f. SULPHUR *sb.* + -(I)FEROUS.] Containing sulphur; sulphurous.

† Sulphurine, *a. Obs. rare⁻¹.* [f. SULPHUR *sb.* + -INE¹.] Of or pertaining to, like or of the quality of sulphur.

Sulphuring (sŭ·lfŏriŋ), *vbl. sb.* [f. SULPHUR *v.* + -ING¹.]

† 1. The action of dipping in sulphur. *Obs. rare⁻¹.*

2. Exposure to the fumes arising from burning sulphur, to produce whiteness in fabrics, to prevent fermentation in casks, to disinfect, etc.

3. The sprinkling of plants with flowers of sulphur to prevent or destroy mildew.

Sulphurious, *a. Obs.* Also 5 sulphuryous.

Sulphurize (sŭ·lfŭrəiz), *v.* [f. SULPHUR *sb.* + -IZE.]

1. *trans.* To cause to combine chemically with, or to be impregnated by, sulphur; to convert into a sulphur compound.

2. To treat or dress with sulphur; to vulcanize (rubber).

Sulphurous (sŭ·lfŏrəs), *a.* (and *sb.*)

1. = SULPHUREOUS 1.

2. = SULPHUREOUS 2.

3. *allusively* and *fig.* Pertaining to sulphur or brimstone as an adjunct of hell or the infernal regions; hellish, satanic.

b. = SULPHUROUS 2 b.

4. = SULPHUREOUS 4. The sulphurous acid.

Sulphury (sŭ·lfŏri), *a.* [f. SULPHUR *sb.* + -Y¹.]

† Sulphur vif, vive. *Obs.* [a. OF.]

† Sulphur virum (sŭ·lfŏr vai·rŭm), [L.; = living sulphur.] Native or virgin sulphur; also, in a fused, partly purified form (see quot. 1855).

Sulphurwort (sŭ·lfŏrwɜ̄t). [f. SULPHUR *sb.* + WORT. Cf. G. *schwefelwurz.*] An umbelliferous plant, *Peucedanum officinale*, having pale-yellow flowers; hog's fennel.

Sulphury (sŭ·lfŏri), *a.* Also 6 sulphry, sul-phrie, 6–7 sulphirie, sulphry, 7 sulfrie, sulphory, 7, 9 (*U.S.*) sulfury. [f. SULPHUR *sb.* + -Y¹.]

1. Consisting of, containing, or impregnated with sulphur; sulphureous 1.

2. = SULPHUREOUS 2.

b. = SULPHUROUS 2 b.

Sulphuryl (sŭ·lfŏril). *Chem.* Also -yle. [f. SULPHUR *sb.* + -YL.] The radical SO_2.

Sulphydrate (sŭlfəi·drət), *sb.* Also sulf-, sulph-hydrate. [f. SULPH- + HYDRATE *sb.*] = HYDROSULPHIDE.

Sulphydric (sŭlfəi·drik), *a.* Also sulf-, sulph-hydric. [f. SULPH- + HYDRIC, after F. *sulfhydrique.*] hydrogen sulphide, sulphuretted hydrogen. **Sulphydric ether** (see quot. 1852).

Sultan (sʊ·ltăn), *sb.* Also 6 soltane, 6–7 soltan, sultane, 7 soultan, sultaine (6, sulthan, 6–9 soldan). [a. F. sultan.]

1. The sovereign or chief ruler of a Mohammedan country; in recent times, *spec.* the sovereign of Turkey.

2. A mistress; concubine.

4. = SULTANA 6.

5. The seventh chief of a magnificence; also attrib.

6. Any bird belonging to either of the genera *Porphyrio* and *Notornis*.

Sultanic (sʊltæ·nik), *a.* [f. SULTAN *sb.* + -IC.] Of, belonging to, or characteristic of a sultan; hence, despotic, tyrannical.

Sultan, *obs.* form of SULTAN.

Sultanin (sʊ·ltănin), *sb.* Also 7 sultanine, -an. [ad. It. sultanino, or F. sultanin.] A former Turkish gold coin valued at about 8s.

Sultanism (sʊ·ltăniz'm), *sb.* [f. SULTAN *sb.* + -ISM.] Rule like that of a sultan; absolute government; despotism, tyranny.

Sultanize, *v.* [f. SULTAN *sb.* + -IZE.]

Sultan't, *var.* SULTANRY.

Sultanate (sʊ·ltănət), *sb.* [f. SULTAN *sb.* + -ATE.] The position or dominion of a sultan.

Sultane, *obs.* form of SULTAN.

Sultaness. Obs. form of SULTANESS.

Sultany (sʊ·ltăni), *sb. Obs.* [f. SULTAN *sb.* + -Y.]

Sultanship (sʊ·ltănʃip). [Formed as prec. + -SHIP.]

† Sultany, *sb. Obs.* Also 6–7 sultrie, 7 soultry, -ie, soultry. [f. SULTRY *v.* + -Y. Cf. SULTRY.]

1. Of the weather, the atmosphere, etc.: Oppressively hot and moist; sweltering.

b. Characterized by sultry heat.

2. Of places, seasons of the year, etc.: Characterized by such weather.

c. Of the sun, etc.: Producing oppressive heat.

2. *transf.* Of persons, their blood, etc.: Hot, heated, inflamed.

(b) Characterized by the heat of temper or passion; hot with anger or lust.

3. *fig.* 'Spicy', 'smutty'.

Sum (sʊm), *sb.* Forms: 3–4 summe, sume, 4–5 soume, 4–6 somme, chiefly *Sc.* sowm, 4–6 soume, sowme, 5–6 soum, 6 soume, swowme, 7 soum), 4–9 sum, *Sc.* somme. [a. F. *somme* (Du. som).]

1. A quantity or amount of money.

2. A number, company, or body (of people); a host, band. *Obs.*

3. *Arith.* A number; *occas.* a whole number as distinguished from a fraction. *Obs.*

Sum-total. Also *fig. Obs.*

Sum. Obs. form of SUMACH.

Sulver, *obs.* form of SILVER.

Sulvey, Sulwine: see SOLVE, SOLWINE.

Sulz, *obs.* form of SOUSE.

Sum (sʊm), *v.* [f. SUM *sb.*]

2. A number, company, or body (of people).

3. *Arith.* A whole number.

6. *Math.* The number, quantity, or magnitude resulting from the addition of two or more numbers, quantities, or magnitudes; †in early use also, the result of multiplication; a product.

Sumach, **sumac** (siūˈmæk, ʃiūˈmæk), sb. Forms: 4 *sumac*, *sumack*, 5 *sumak*, [s]*ymak*, 6 *sumache*, shomacko, 6-7 *shoemake*, shoom-a(o)ko, shewmake, 6-7, 7 *shumach*, -ach, -ack, *Sc.* shoomack, 7-8 *shemach*, 8 shomach, 9 shu-mac(k), 4 *sumac*. [a. OF. *sumac*, *sumach* (mod.F. *sumac*) or med.L. *sumac(h*, a. Arabic سمّاق *summāq*.]

Sumation, obs. form of SUMMATION.

Sumatran (sūmæˈtrɑn), a. and sb. [f. the name of a large island of the Malay archipelago; used *attrib.* in specific names of animals or products of the island, as Sumatra *benzoin*, *cat*, *dog*, *monkey* (cf. SUMATRAN).]

Sumba, **Sumbal**, **mic**, **Sumbu'lic**, **Sumbulo'lic acid**, *obs.* vars. (see quots.).

Sumbul (sŭˈmbul, sǝˈmbul). Also **sambal**, **sumbul**. [a. F. *sumbul*, a. Arab. سنبل *sunbul*.]

Sumen (sūˈmen). [L. *sūmen*; *sūgmen*, f. *sūgere* to suck.]

Sumerian (sūˈmɪ·rɪǝn), a. and sb. Also Sumirian, Shumerian. [ad. F. *sumérien* (Oppert, 1872, in *Journal Asiatique* Ser. VII. I. 114), f. *Sumer* (see def.).]

Summable (sŭˈmǎb'l), a. [f. SUM sb. + -ABLE.]

Summage (sŭˈmedʒ). *Obs. exc. Hist.* Also †*sommage* (13 in *Cotgr. Lat.*), †*sumage*. [a. AF. *sumage*, f. *sume*, *somme* SUM sb.]

Summand (sŭˈmænd). *rare*. [ad. med.L. *summandum* (sc. *numerus*), gerundive of *summāre* to SUM.]

Summar (sŭˈmǎr), a. *Sc.* Chiefly *Law.* Also 6 *summair*, *summare*, 7 *summer*. [a. F. *sommaire*, with subsequent assimilation to its source, L. *summārius* SUMMARY.]

Summarily (sŭˈmǎri·li), adv. [f. SUMMAR + -LY.]

Summariness, rare. [f. SUMMARY a. + -NESS.]

Summarist (sŭˈmǎrist). [f. SUMMARY + -IST.]

Summarization. [f. next + -ATION.]

Summarize (sŭˈmǎrǎiz), v. [f. SUMMARY sb. or a. + -IZE.]

Summary (sŭˈmǎri), a. (adv.) and sb. [ad. L. *summārium*, neut. sb. of *summārius* SUMMAR.]

Summate (sǝˈmeit), v. *rare*. [f. L. *summāt-*, ppl. stem of *summāre* to SUM.]

Summation (sŭˈmeiʃǝn). [ad. mod.L. *summātio*, -ōnem, n. of action, f. *summāre* to SUM. Cf. F. *sommation*.]

Summational (sŭˈmeiʃǝnǎl), a. [f. SUMMATION + -AL.]

Summative (sŭˈmǎtiv), a. [f. SUMMATE + -IVE.]

Summatory, a. *rare.* [f. med.L. *summāt-*, ppl. stem (see SUMMATE) + -ORY.]

Summer (sŭˈmǝr), sb.[1] [OE. *sumor*, (*-er*), = OS. *sumar* (MDu., Du. *zomer*), OHG. *sumar* (MHG. *sumer*, G. *sommer*), ON. *sumar* (Sw. *sommar*, Da. *sommer*).]

Summer (sŭˈmǝr), sb.[2] Forms: *β* *yeomed*, *somerd*, 6 *sommerd*, 6 *soom'd*, *summ'd*, 7 *sommr'd*, *summ(er)d*, 7 *somer'd*, 9 *summer*. [In branch II, f. SUM sb.]

a 1400–50 *Wars Alex.* 4343 Make we na salues for na sares ne na somir-bathis. *c* 1480 HENRYSON *Mor. Fab.* xi. (*Fox & Wolf*) xviii, It is somer cheis, baith fresche and fair. 1481 *Cely Papers* (Camden) 71, j pack lyeth upprest and sum of that packe ys somer felles. 1536 *Acc. Ld. High Treas. Scot.* VI. 280 Ane pair symmir buttis to the Kingis grace. 1585 T. WASHINGTON tr. *Nicholay's Voy.* I. xvi. 17 Sommer cloathing of the women of Malta. 1588 SHAKS. *L. L. L.* v. ii. 916 When..Maidens bleach their summer smockes. *c* 1620 *Hatton Corr.* (Camden) 3 At my returne I will make you a sommer sute. 1693 DRYDEN *Juvenal* i. 40 Charg'd with light Summer-rings his fingers sweat. 1697 — *Virg. Georg.* III. 665 A Snake..in his Summer Liv'ry rouls along. 1765 *Museum Rust.* IV. 367 It lies extremely convenient for my summer-pasture. 1797 *Encycl. Brit.* (ed. 3) XVIII. 63/2 The melasses may..compose the basis of a pleasant summer beer. 1801 *Farmer's Mag.* Aug. 325 The summer cheese, which is the best, is made of the evening milk. 1834 *Encycl. Metrop.* (1845) XXII. 366/1 Such is its Summer coat, and.. we distinguish it by the name Stoat. 1881 BESANT & RICE *Chapl. Fleet* I. 33 Sir Robert is calling every day for a summer sallet to cool his blood.

(*c*) of places or buildings. (Cf. OE. *sumerselde*, SUMMER-HOUSE.)

1382 WYCLIF *Judg.* iii. 20 Forsothe he sat in the somer sowpynge place [Vulg. *in æstivo cœnaculo*] alone. 1596 *Edw. III*, II. i. 61 Then in the sommer arber sit by me. 1611 *Bible* Judg. iii. 24 Surely he coucreth his feet in his Summer chamber. 1611 — Dan. ii. 35 [They] became like the chaffe of the summer threshing floores. 1612 WEBSTER *White Devil* I. ii, Tis iust like a summer bird-cage in a garden. 1708 *Lond. Gaz.* No. 4447/1 The Heat of the Weather obliges both sides to retire..into their Summer Quarters. 1783 COWPER *Faithf. Friend* 1 The green-house is my summer seat. 1837 LOCKHART *Scott* I. ix. 307 To establish his summer residence in Lanarkshire. 1847 TENNYSON *Princ.* I. 146 A certain summer-palace which I have.

(*d*) of times and seasons. (See also SUMMER-DAY, -TIDE, -TIME.)

c 1440 *Alphabet of Tales* 170 Sho wolde gar hur maydyns gader þe dew on sommer mornyngis. *a* 1578 LINDESAY (Pitscottie) *Chron. Scot.* I. 228 Wpoun ane summar morning ..ane of the Inglishe scheipis persaueit tua schipis command wnder saill. 1586 W. WEBBE *Eng. Poetrie* Ep. Ded. (Arb.) 15 A sleight somewhat compyled for recreation, in the intermyssions of my daylie businesse, (euen thys Summer Eueninges). 1592 *Arden of Feversham* I. i. 58 Sommer nights are short, and yet you ryse ere day. 1599 SHAKS., etc. *Pass. Pilgr.* 159 Youth like summer morn, age like winter weather. 1626 BACON *Sylva* § 606, I left once, by chance, a Citron cut, in a close Roome, for three Summer-Moneths. 1632 MILTON *L'Allegro* 130 Such sights as youthfull Poets dream On Summer eeves by haunted stream. 1725 POPE *Odyss.* IV. 55 The dazzling roofs,..Resplendent as the blaze of summer noon. 1785 BURNS *Holy Fair* 1 Upon a simmer Sunday morn. 1815 SCOTT *Guy M.* xlv, All the tints of a summer-evening sky. 1821 SHELLEY *Hellas* 13 Sweet as a summer night without a breath. 1833 TENNYSON *Pal. of Art* 62 A gaudy summer-morn. 1892 *Photogr. Ann.* II. 621 Excursions are made during the summer months.

(*e*) of conditions, qualities, or actions.

1594 SHAKS. *Rich. III*, IV. iii. 13 Their lips were foure red Roses on a stalke, And in their Summer Beauty kist each other. 1617 WITHER *Abuses* II. iv. 275 Their ancient drunken-summer-reuelings Are out of date. 1636 H. BURTON *Div. Trag.* 22 One in Glocestershire being very forward to advance a solemne sommer-meeting [for sports]. 1641 BROME *Joviall Crew* I, After so many Sommer vagaries. 1684 T. BURNET *Th. Earth* I. ix. 123 This reason is a Summer-reason, and would pass very ill in Winter. 1707 MORTIMER *Husb.* (1721) I. 194 Towards the end of May, you must give your Ground the Summer-Digging. 1725 *Fam. Dict.* s.v. *July*, Vines..will be satisfy'd with a single winter and one summer Pruning. 1726–46 THOMSON *Winter* 644 A gay insect in his summer shine..spreads his mealy wings. 1787 BURNS *Petit. Bruar Water* i, Saucy Phœbus' scorching beams, In flaming summer-pride. 1813 SCOTT *Rokeby* I. i, The Moon is in her summer glow. 1819 KEATS *Indolence* ii, The blissful cloud of summer-indolence Benumb'd my eyes. 1826 LAMB *Pop. Fallacies* xii, [The talk] is not of toys, of nursery books, of summer holidays. 1836–9 *Todd's Cycl. Anat.* II. 768/2 The summer-sleep of hibernating animals. 1854 *Poultry Chron.* I. 34/2 Birds that have taken prizes at London Summer Meeting. 1868 *Rep. U.S. Commissioner Agric.* (1869) 255 During this interval of rest..is the best time for summer trimming. 1878 B. TAYLOR *Deukalion* III. i, My bed of long delight and summershine.

(*f*) with descriptive designations.

1611 BEAUM. & FL. *King & No K.* v. i, *Lyg.* I know you dare lie. *Bes.* With none but Summer Whores.., my means and manners never could attempt above a hedge or haycock. 1645 G. DANIEL *Scattered Fancies* XXIII. iv, You are but weake, Meere summer Chanters. 1888 *Encycl. Brit.* XXIII. 45/1 Three if not four species are common summer immigrants to some part or other of the United States. 1897 *Appleton's Ann. Cycl.* 806/1 The statistics of the summer-boarder industry are very incomplete.

(*g*) in superlative *summerest* (nonce-formation).

1772 H. WALPOLE *Let. to Mann* 3 Aug., The summerest summer that I have known these hundred years.

b. The possessive *summer's* is similarly used, but now chiefly with *morning*, *evening*, and *night*. (See also SUMMER'S DAY, SUMMER'S TIDE.)

c 1369 CHAUCER *Dethe Blaunche* 821 As the somerys sonne bryghte. 14.. *Sir Beues* 4138 (Pynson) M iv, And so lasted that cruel fyght, Al that longe somers nyght. 1513 DOUGLAS *Æneis* x. vii. 109 In the symmeris drouth, Quhen wyndis rysis of the north or south. 1592 *Soliman & Pers.* I. v. 64 The humming of a gnat in Summers night. 1596 SHAKS. 1 *Hen. IV*, III. i. 210 Ditties highly penn'd, Sung by a faire Queene in a Summers Bowre. 1601 — *Jul. C.* III. ii. 176 'Twas on a Summer's Euening. 1613 JACKSON *Creed* I. xxiii. 136 Diseases, neuer perceiued in their Summers growth, vntill they be ripe of death in the Autumne. 1654 WARREN *Unbelievers* 22 The Sodomites..shall have a Summers parlour in hell over that soule. 1667 MILTON *P. L.* III. 43 The ..sight of vernal bloom, or Summers Rose. *Ibid.* IX. 447 As one..Forth issuing on a Summers Morn. 1721 RAMSAY *Keitha* 45 Her presence, like a simmer's morning ray. 1780–2 COWPER *Cricket* 21 Their's is but a summer's song. 1808 J. MAYNE *Siller Gun* I. i, Ae Simmer's morning. 1855 MILLER *Elem. Chem.*, *Chem. Phys.* iii. § 4. 112 If the right rhombic crystals [of sulphate of nickel] be placed in the summer's sun for a few days they become opaque.

c. Applied to crops, etc. that ripen in summer, as *summer fruit*, more particularly to such as ripen in the summer of the year in which they are sown, as *summer barley*, *corn*, *grain*, *rye*, *seed*, *vetch*, *wheat*; also *spec.* in popular names of early-ripening apples and pears, as *summer apple*, *pearmain*, *poppering*, etc. (cf. also 6 b).

1398 TREVISA *Barth. De P. R.* XVII. lxv. (Bodl. MS.) Winter seede is sone isowe and somer sede is late isowe. 1535 COVERDALE *Amos* viii. 1 Beholde, there was a maunde with sommer frute. 1577 B. GOOGE *Heresbach's Husb.* 26 Sommer seedes, whiche are sowed before the risyng of the seuen starres, and in the Spring, as Beanes. *Ibid.*, Sommer Barley..and suche other, are sowed in the Spring time. *Ibid.* 27 b, Rye.. is sowed..in Februarie, and called Sommer Wheate. *Ibid.* 34 Pease..are sowed among Sommer Corne. 1578 LYTE *Dodoens* IV. i. 453 A sommer wheate or grayne. *Ibid.*, Men sow their winter corne in September, or October, & the sommer corne in March, but they are ripe altogither in July. 1676 WORLIDGE *Cyder* (1691) 214 The Denny-pear, Prussia-pear, Summer-Poppering..are all very good table-fruit. 1681 GREW *Musæum* II. III. iii. 235 Summer Wheat of New England. *a* 1722 LISLE *Husb.* (1757) 174, I spoke..of the husbandry of sowing goar or summer-vetches. 1722 *Phil. Trans.* XXXII. 231 The Apple, that produces the Molosses, is a Summer-Sweeting. 1764 *Ann. Reg.* II. 2 Several trials of summer-corn ..in which both barley and oats have succeeded. 1765 *Museum Rust.* IV. 435 He was..obliged to wait till Mr. Rocque's summer-seed was reaped. 1812 SIR J. SINCLAIR *Syst. Husb. Scot.* I. 244 The real spring or summer wheat, has been of late introduced in various districts in Scotland. 1834 *Penny Cycl.* II. 190/1 Summer golden pippin. Summer Thorle. 1854 MAYNE *Expos. Lex.* 352/1 Summer-fruits; as cherries, currants, gooseberries, raspberries, strawberries, etc.

†**d.** = Having a sunny or southerly aspect; so *summer-east*, *-west* = south-east, -west. *Obs.*

c 1440 *Pallad. on Husb.* I. 491 Thyn oilcelar sette on the somer side. 1555 EDEN *Decades W. Ind.* (Arb.) 328 Towarde the sommer East, it confineth with the Tartars. 1604 E. G[RIMSTONE] *D'Acosta's Hist. Indies* III. v. 135 They do call lower windes those..which blowe from the South to the summer-weast. 1676 *Phil. Trans.* XI. 585 A kind of Solar stove, made in a Summer-wall.

e. *fig.* with reference to prosperous, pleasant, or genial conditions; said *esp.* of friendship that lasts only in times of prosperity, = FAIR-WEATHER 2.

1592 NASHE *Strange Newes* Wks. 1904 I. 291 His low-flighted affection (fortunes summer folower). 1611 SHAKS. *Cymb.* III. iv. 12 If't be Summer Newes Smile too't before. 1624 QUARLES *Job Militant*, *Digestion* iv, If Winter fortunes nip thy Summer Friends,..despaire not, but be wise. 1632 MASSINGER *Maid of Hon.* III. i, Summer-friendship, Whose flattering leaves, that shadowed us in our Prosperity..drop off In the Autumn of adversity! 1727–46 THOMSON *Summer* 347 Luxurious Men, unheeding, pass An idle summer-life in fortune's shine. *c* 1800 R. CUMBERLAND *John De Lancaster* (1809) III. 93 We are but summer soldiers. 1805 *Ann. Rev.* III. 584 He was in the Fleet.. deserted by his three Summer friends. 1818 *Ibid.* XIX. 42 He was the frequent visitor of Clarendon, when that admirable man was abandoned by the swarm of summer followers. 1842 TENNYSON *Locksley Hall* 164 Summer isles of Eden.

5. *Comb.*: objective, as *summer-breathing*, *loving* ppl. adjs.; instrumental, as *summer-blanched*, *-dried*, *-shrunk*, *-stricken* pples. and ppl. adjs.; similative, as *summer-seeming* adj.; 'in or during summer', as *summer-brewed*, *-felled*, *-flowering*, *-leaping*, †*-lived*, *-made*, *-ripening*, *-staying*, *-swelling*, *-threshed* pples. and ppl. adjs.; *summer-feed*, *-graze*, *-prune*, *-till*, *-yard* vbs.; *summer-curer*.

1864 TENNYSON *Aylmer's F.* 152 One [*sc.* hut] that, *summer-blanch'd, Was parcel-bearded with the traveller's-joy. 1806 M. A. SHEE *Rhymes on Art* 68 In calmer seas, and *summer-breathing gales. 1826 *Art of Brewing* (ed. 2) 32 Imperfect fermentation..causes acidity and other faults in *summer-brewed beers. 1881 *Chicago Times* 14 May, It is to the interest now of the leading *summer-curers [*sc.* of pork] to get values down. 1810 SCOTT *Lady of L.* III. xvi, A *summer-dried fountain. 1799 A. YOUNG *Agric. Linc.* 190, 13 acres of marsh at Grimsby, that *summer-feeds 14 bullocks. 1838 HOLLOWAY *Prov. Dict.*, To *skeer*, to mow lightly over, applied to pastures, which have been summer fed. 1804 *Phil. Trans.* XCV. 92 Proper marks were put to distinguish the winter-felled from the *summer-felled poles. 1897 MRS. VOYNICH *Gadfly* i, In one corner stood a huge *summer-flowering magnolia. 1900 *Daily News* 5 May 4/5 Summer-flowering chrysanthemums. 1799 A. YOUNG *Agric. Linc.* 354 He..in April *summer-grazed them, taking the wool. 1596 *Edw. III*, II. i. 107 To musicke euery *sommer leaping swaine Compares his sunburnt louer when shee speakes. 1594 NASHE *Unfort. Trav.* Wks. 1904 II. 275 *Summer liude grashoppers gaping after deaw. 1875 *Zoologist* Ser. II. X. 4693 They [*sc.* starlings] fly into the air with swallows, &c., and catch insects similar to that *summer-loving tribe. 1842 J. AITON *Dom. Econ.* (1857) 206 This.. increases the quantity of your *summer-made manure. 1786 ABERCROMBIE *Gard. Assist.* 174 *Summer prune by displacing all fore-right productions. 1840 J. BUEL *Farmer's Companion* 44 They are cropped with small grains or *summer-ripening crops. 1605 SHAKS. *Mach.* IV. iii. 86 This Auarice..growes with more pernicious roote Then *Summer-seeming Lust. 1825 SCOTT *Betrothed* ii, A maiden smiles at the *summer-shrunk brook while she crosses it. 1868 LYNCH *Rivulet* CLX. iii, Can..The *summer-staying birds forget The winter's force to shun? 1827 SCOTT *Hight. Widow* v, You do but resemble the *summer-stricken stream, which is turned aside by the rushes. 1591 SHAKS. *Two Gent.* II. iv. 162 Lest the base earth Should..Disdaine to roote the *Sommer-swelling flowre. 1812 SIR J. SINCLAIR *Syst. Husb. Scot.* I. 346 It enables the farmer to make his *summer-threshed straw into dung. 1847 HALLIWELL s.v., 'That field was *summer-tilled last year', i.e. lay fallow. 1840 J. BUEL *Farmer's Comp.* 198 Feeding these crops with the long manure of the yards and stables, instead of *summer-yarding it.

6. Special combs.: †**summer-ale**, (*a*) ale brewed in summer, new or heady ale; (*b*) a summer festival (see ALE 3); **summer-barm** *v. intr.*, to ferment in warm weather; †**summer-blink**, a short spell of sunshine in dull weather; †**summer-broach**, a maypole decked; **summer catarrh** = HAY-FEVER; **summer cholera** = CHOLERA 2; **summer-colt** (usually *pl.*) *local*, the undulating appearance of the air near the ground on a hot day; see also quot. 1825; **summer complaint** *U.S.*, summer diarrhœa of children; also, infantile cholera and dysentery; **summer diarrhœa** = *summer cholera*; **summer-dream**, a pleasant or happy dream; **summer-eat** *v. trans. dial.*, to use as summer pasture; **summer-eggs** = *summer ova* (Cassell, 1887); **summer fever**, hay-fever; **summer-field**, †(*a*) rendering L. *æstiva area* = *summer floor*; (*b*) a field with the summer crop; (*c*) *dial.* a summer-fallow; †**summer floor** [FLOOR *sb.*1 6], a thrashing-floor; **summer-fold** (now *dial.*), a freckle; **summer-gauze**, **-goose** *local*, gossamer; †**summer hall**, (*a*) rendering L. *æstiva area* = *summer floor*; (*b*) = SUMMER-HOUSE 2, 2 b; **summer-heat** [OE. *sumorhǣte*], the heat of summer; *spec.* an arbitrary maximum summer temperature commonly marked on thermometers; †**summer lady**, the queen of the 'summer-game'; **summerlay** *sb. dial.*, land lying fallow in summer; in East Anglia, a turnip fallow; **summerlay** *v. trans. dial.*, to lay fallow; †**summer lea-land** = SUMMER-FALLOW; **summer-lease** *dial.* (see quots.); **summer-leding** *pseudo-arch.* [f. OE. *sumorlida* summer expedition (*O.E. Chron.* an. 871)], see quot.; **summer lightning**, sheet lightning without audible thunder, often seen in hot weather; also allusively and *attrib.*; †**summer-lord**, a youth chosen as president of the 'summer-game'; cf. MAY-LORD; **summer meal** *Sc.*, meal for use until harvest; **summer number**, a summer issue of a periodical, with special features; **summer-ova**, eggs produced by certain freshwater invertebrates in spring and summer; **summer parlour** *Obs.* or *arch.*, an apartment for summer use; †**summer-pole**, a pole decked with flowers erected during the 'summer-games'; †**summer('s) queen** = *summer lady*; **summer rash**, prickly heat, *Lichen tropicus*; †**summer-ripe** *a.*, fully ripe; †**summer-room** = SUMMER-HOUSE 2; **summer-sob** *Sc.*, a summer shower; **summer spot**, a freckle; †**summer-stirring**, summer ploughing; hence †**summer-stir** *v. trans.*; †**summer top** *v. trans.*, to cut off as in summer pruning; †**summer tree** *Sc.* = *summer-pole*; **summer-work** *sb.* and *v.*, **-working** = SUMMER-FALLOW *sb.* and *v.*; **summer-yellow**, a variety of cotton-seed oil.

1586 A. DAY *Eng. Secretary* I. (1625) 109 The superfluities of *summer-ale, that hath wrought in his giddie braine. 1636 H. BURTON *Div. Trag.* 21 The people..prepared for a solemne summer-ale. 1828 *Craven Gloss.* (ed. 2) s.v., When malt liquor begins to ferment, in warm weather, before the application of the barm, it is said to be *summer-barm'd. 1637 RUTHERFORD *Let. to R. Gordon* 1 Jan., Yet I am in this hot *summer-blink, with the tear in my eye. 1619 *Pasquil's Palin.* B 3, A *Sommer-broach, Ycleap'd a May-pole. 1828 *Medico-Chirurg. Trans.* XIV. 437 Of the Catarrhus Æstivus, or *Summer Catarrh. 1862 *Chamb. Encycl.* III. 6/1 The milder forms of C[holera]..termed by some..British or *Summer C[holera]. 1685 *Phil. Trans.* XV. 993 An undulating motion [which] our Countrie People call by the name of *Summer Colts in the Air. 1768 ROSS *Helenore* 21 The summer cauts [*mispr.* cauls] were dancing here an' there. 1796 W. H. MARSHALL *Rural Econ. Yorks.* (ed. 2) II. 349 When the air is seen in a calm hot day to undulate,..the phænomenon is expressed by saying, 'the summer colt rides'. 1825 JAMIESON, *Summer-couts*, ..the gnats which dance in clusters on a summer evening. 1847 E. HALLOWELL in *Amer. Jrnl. Med. Sci.* XIV. 40 On the endemic gastro-follicular enteritis, or '*summer complaint' of children. 1855 DUNGLISON *Med. Lex.*, *Summer complaint*, ..is often..made to include dysentery and cholera infantum. 1883 F. T. ROBERTS *Th. & Pract. Med.* (ed. 5) 196 The so-called sporadic, bilious, or English cholera, or *summer diarrhœa, the symptoms of which sometimes closely resemble those of true cholera. 1820 CLARE *Poems Rural Life* (ed. 3) 60 Ye gently dimpled, curling streams, Killing as smooth as *summer-dreams. 1905 *Westm. Gaz.* 1 July 14/2 Delighting in the summer-dream of love. 1788 W. H. MARSHALL *Rural Econ. Yorks.* II. 357 *Summer-eat, to use as pasture. 1870 *Zoologist* Ser. II. V. 2335 A field of summer-eaten clover, from which the sheep had a few days been removed. 1867 PIRRIE *Hay Asthma* 25 It appears to us, that in many instances, *Summer Fever or Summer Illness, would be more applicable than Hay Fever. 1382 WYCLIF *Dan.* ii. 35 The yren,..syluer, and gold, ben..dryuen as in to a qwenchid brond of *somer feeld [1388 somer halle; Vulg. *æstivæ areæ*]. 1594 SHAKS. *Rich. III*, v. ii. 8 The wretched, bloody, and vsurping Boare, (That spoyl'd your Summer Fields, and fruitfull Vines). 1794 T. DAVIS *Agric. Wilts* 59 In the four-field husbandry, where the clover is sown the second year, and mowed the third, the field becomes in the fourth year what is called in Wiltshire 'a summer field'. 1535 COVERDALE *Dan.* ii. 35 Like the chaffe off corne, that the wynde bloweth awaye from yᵉ *somer floores. 1668 *Lond. Gaz.* No. 281/4 With some Freakles, or *Summer foldes in the Face. 1876 *Whitby Gloss.*, **Summer-gauze*, gossamer; quantities of which, blown from the land to the sea, adheres to the rigging of ships. *a* 1800 PEGGE *Suppl. Grose*, **Summer-goos*, the gossamer. *North.* 1388 *Somer halle [see *summer field*, 1382]. *a* 1400–50 *Wars Alex.* 2922 So silis he furth..in-to a somere-hall, þare sesonde was a soper. 1429 in *Munim. Magd. Coll. Oxf.* (1882) 16, j somerhalle cum iij cameris ibidem annexis. 1583 STUBBES *Anat. Abuses* M 3 b, They straw the grounde rounde about, binde green boughes about it [*sc.* the May-pole], set vp sommer haules, bowers, and arbors. 1781 COWPER *Retirem.* 196 Her [*sc.* Nature's] *summer heats, her fruits, and her perfumes. 1815 J. SMITH *Panorama Sci. & Art* II. 319 If the instrument is..intended chiefly to measure the higher degrees of heat, as from a summer-heat to that of boiling water. 1853 M. ARNOLD *Scholar Gypsy* vii, In my boat I lie Moor'd to the cool bank in the summer heats. 1877 HUXLEY *Physiogr.* 64 The Summer-heat may never be strong enough to melt all the ice. 1571 *Summer lady [see *summer lord*]. 1782 W. H. MARSHALL *Rural Econ. Norfolk* (1795) II. 320 Lambs..bought up by the East Norfolk 'graziers' in order to pick among their *summerlies, and their stubbles, after harvest. 1467 *Paston Lett.* II. 302 He wolde *somerlay and tylle the londe, otherwise then it is. *c* 1503 *Ibid.* III. 402 The seide x. acres londe, sowen with barly and peson, wherof v. acres were weel somerlayde to the seid barly. *c* 1440 *Promp. Parv.* 464/1 *Somyr laylond, *novale*. 1863 W. BARNES *Dorset Gloss.*, *Leäze*, or **Zummer leäze*, a field stocked through the summer, in distinction from a mead which is mown. 1886 *W. Som. Gloss.*, *Summerleys*, *summerleaze*, pasture fed only in summer. 1865 KINGSLEY *Herew.* iii, A certain amount of '*summer-leding' (*i.e.* piracy between seed-time and harvest). 1833 TENNYSON *Miller's Daughter* 13 Gray eyes lit up With *summer lightnings of a soul So full of summer warmth. 1856 MRS. GORE *Life's Lessons* xxiv, Like summer lightning gleaming from a thunder-cloud. 1872 *Daily News* 7 Nov., When a pheasant is flushed you only catch a summer-lightning glimpse of him. 1888 *Encycl. Brit.* XXIII. 330/1 What is called 'summer lightning' or 'wild-fire'...In the majority of cases it is merely the effect of a distant thunderstorm. It is also often due to a thunderstorm in the higher strata of the atmosphere overhead. 1571 GRINDAL *Injunc.* II. § 19 That the Minister and churchwardens shall not suffer any Lordes of misrule, or *sommer Lordes, or Ladies..to come vnreuerently into any Church, or Chapel. 1589 *Marprel.*, *Hay any Work* 3 The sommer Lord with his Maie game. *a* 1500–20 DUNBAR *Poems* xxxix. 30 Lairdis in silk harlis to the eill, For quhilk thair tennentis sald *somer meill. 1877 HUXLEY *Anat. Inv. Anim.* 190 In some Rotifers, the eggs are distinguishable, as in certain *Turbellaria*, into *summer and winter ova. 1388 WYCLIF *Judg.* iii. 20 He sat aloone in a *somer parlour. 1684 BUNYAN *Pilgr.* II. 26 So he left them a while in a Summer Parler below. 1732 BERKELEY *Alciphron* I. 95 As we sate round the Teatable, in a Summer-Parlour which looks into the Garden. 1829 SCOTT *Guy M.* Introd., The old man led the way into a summer parlour. 1617 WITHER *Abuses* II. iv. 277 They know how to discommend A May-game, or a *Summer-pole dene. 1619 *Pasquil's Palin.* B 3 b, Since the Sommer-poles were ouerthrowne, And all good sports and merryments decayd. *c* 1400 *Destr. Troy* 1627 *Somur qwenes, and qwaintans, & oþer qwaint gaumes. 1590 GREENE *Mourning Garm.* C 3 b, Faire she was as faire might be..Beautious, like a Sommers Queene. 1820 GOOD *Nosology* 466 Lichen ..Tropicus..Attacks new settlers in the West Indies, and other warm regions..Prickly heat. *Summer-rash. *a* 1670 HACKET *Abp. Williams* II. (1693) 228 It is an Injury..upon Corn, when it is *Summer-ripe, not to be cut down with the Sickle. 1748 *De Foe's Tour Gt. Brit.* (1753) I. 307 On the Summit of this Hill his Lordship built a *Summer-room. 1797 JANE AUSTEN *Sense & Sens.* xiii, One of the pleasantest Summer-rooms in England. 1768 ROSS *Helenore* 69 Yon *summer sob is out, This night looks weel,..The morn, I hope, will better prove. 1876 DUNGLISON *Med. Lex.*, **Summer Spots*, Ephelides. 1669 WORLIDGE *Syst. Agric.* (1681) 332 To **Summer-stir*, to Fallow Land in the Summer. 1766 *Complete Farmer*, *To Summer-land*, or *To Summer-Stir*, to fallow land in the summer. 1616 SURFL. & MARKH. *Country Farm* 555 At mid-May you shall manure it, and in Iune you shall giue it the second earing, which is called *Sommer-stirring. *a* 1548 HALL *Chron.*, *Hen. VII*, 43 The head of thys sedicion was *sommer topped, that it coulde haue no tyme to sprynge any higher. 1555 *Acts Parl. Scot.*, *Mary* (1814) II. 500/1 Gif ony wemen or vthers about *simmer treis singand makis perturbatioun to the Quenis liegis in the passage throw Burrowis. 1886 *Cheshire Gloss.*, **Summer-work*, a summer fallow. 1682 MARTINDALE in Houghton *Coll. Lett. Impr. Husb.* No. 11. 125 If it [*sc.* land] grow weedy or grassie, we sometimes Fallow or *Summer-work it. 1793 J. H. CAMPBELL in *Young's Annals Agric.* XX. 124 The fallows (or **Summer-workings*) are tumbled over by the plough, and jingled over by harrows. 1801 *Farmer's Mag.* Aug. 263 Rotation of different crops, fallowing, summer-working. 1912 *Standard* 20 Sept. 8/7 Cottonseed oil irregular, *summer yellow spot 10 up, October option 9 points down.

b. In names of animals and plants which are active or flourish in summer (often rendering L. *æstivus*, *æstivalis* as a specific name): **summer cock** *dial.*, see quots.; **summer cypress** = BELVEDERE 2; **summer duck**, a North American duck, *Æx sponsa*, the wood-duck; **summer finch** *U.S.*, a popular name for birds of the genus *Peucæa*; †**summer fool**, a species of *Leucojum*; **summer grape**, a North American wild grape, *Vitis æstivalis*; **summer grass**, (*a*) the grass of summer; (*b*) the Australian hairy finger-grass, *Panicum sanguinale*; **summer haw**, *Cratægus flava*; **summer hemp** = FIMBLE *sb.*1 1; **summer-herring**, (*a*) a herring taken in summer; (*b*) *U.S.* applied to some fishes resembling the herring, as the alewife, *Clupea serrata*; **summer rape**, *Brassica campestris* (*Treas. Bot.* 1866); **summer red-**

bird, the rose tanager, *Pyranga æstiva*, which summers in N. America; **summer rose**, (*a*) a rose of summer; (*b*) an early kind of pear; **summer savory** (see SAVORY 1); **summer snake** = GREEN SNAKE 1; **summer snipe**, the common sandpiper, *Tringoides hypoleucus*; **summer snowflake** (see SNOWFLAKE 3); **summer squash**, a pumpkin (*Treas. Bot.* Suppl. 1874); **summer tanager** = *summer redbird*; **summer teal**, the garganey; †**summer-whiting** = PELAMYD 1; **summer-worm**, a worm or maggot that breeds in summer; **summer yellowbird**, a N. American wood-warbler, *Dendrœca æstiva*.

1790 GROSE *Provinc. Gloss.* (ed. 2) Suppl., **Summer-cock*, a young salmon at that time. York City. 1882 DAY *Fishes Gt. Brit.* II. 69 In Northumberland a 'milter' or spawning male is known as a summer-cock or gib-fish. 1767 ABERCROMBIE *Ev. Man his own Gardener* (1803) 735/2 Belvidere or *Summer Cypress. 1829 LOUDON *Encycl. Plants* (1836) 226 *Kochia scoparia*..summer Cypress. 1732 *Phil. Trans.* XXXVII. 449 The *Summer Duck..is one of the most beautiful of Birds. 1743 M. CATESBY *Nat. Hist. Carolina* (1754) I. 97 The Summer Duck..is of a mean size, between the common Wild Duck and Teal. 1860 GOSSE *Rom. Nat. Hist.* 199 The Summer-duck of America..delights in woods. 1884 COUES *N. Amer. Birds* 373 *Peucæa æstivalis illinoensis*, Illinois *Summer Finch. 1597 GERARDE *Herbal* I. lxxviii. 121 *Leucoium Bulbosum præcox*. Timely flowring Bulbus violet..In English we may call it..after the Dutch name *Somer sottekens*, that is, *Sommer fooles. 1629 PARKINSON *Parad.* (1904) 16 Diuers sorts of Crocus or Saffron flower will appeare, the little early Summer foole or Leucoium bulbosum. 1814 PURSH *Flora Amer. Septentr.* I. 169 *Vitis æstivalis sinuata*..is known by the name of '*Summer-grape. 1599 SHAKS. *Hen. V*, I. i. 65 Which..Grew like the *Summer Grasse, fastest by Night. 1882 'OUIDA' *Maremma* I. 3 The rich loads of summer-grass or grain. 1889 MAIDEN *Usef. Pl. Australia* 102 *Panicum sanguinale*,..Summer Grass. 1856 A. GRAY *Man. Bot.* (1860) 124 C[ratægus] *flava*, Ait. (*Summer Haw). 1707 MORTIMER *Husb.* 118 The light *Summer-hemp, that bears no Seed, is called Fimble hemp. 1614 T. GENTLEMAN *England's Way* 20 A barrell of *Summer-herrings, worth 20 or 30 shillings. 1883 WALLEM *Fish Supply Norway* 17 The catch of Summer-herring and Sprat in the Fisheries of the years 1876–1881. 1743 M. CATESBY *Nat. Hist. Carolina* (1754) I. 56 *Muscicapa rubra*. The *Summer Red-Bird. This is about the size of a Sparrow..and..is of a bright red. 1872 COUES *N. Amer. Birds* 111 Summer Red-bird, rich rose-red, or vermilion, including wings and tail. 1727–46 THOMSON *Summer* 354 Full as the *summer-rose Blown by prevailing suns, the ruddy maid. 1841 WHITTIER *Lucy Hooper* 3 All of thee we loved and cherished Has with thy summer roses perished. 1860 HOGG *Fruit Manual* 214 Pears..Summer Rose (Epine Rose; Ognonet; Rose; Thorny Rose). 1802 SHAW *Gen. Zool.* III. II. 551 *Summer Snake. *Coluber Æstivus*...Native of many parts of North America, residing on trees. 1802 MONTAGU *Ornith. Dict.*, *Sandpiper —Common*...It is known in some places by the name of *Summer Snipe. 1849 KINGSLEY *Misc.* (1859) II. 251 The summer snipes flitted whistling up the shallow. 1783 LATHAM *Gen. Synop. Birds* II. I. 220 *Summer Tanager. A little bigger than an House Sparrow. 1884 COUES *N. Amer. Birds* 317. 1668 CHARLETON *Onomast.* 101 *Querquedula Cristata..ab aucupibus dicta*, the *Summer-Teal. 1766 [see GARGANEY]. 1879 *Encycl. Brit.* X. 80/1 *n.* 1624 MIDDLETON *Game Chess* v. iii, The pelamis Which some call *summer-whiting, from Chalcedon. 1658 ROWLAND tr. *Moufet's Theat. Ins.* 1130 The English call them [*sc.* water-worms] *Summer-worms, either because they are seen only in Summer, or they die in Winter. 1668 CHARLETON *Onomast.* 59 *Lumbrici aquatici*, Summer-Worms. 1820 SHELLEY *Prometh. Unb.* IV 313 The jagged alligator, and the.. behemoth..multiplied like summer worms On an abandoned corpse. 1872 COUES *N. Amer. Birds* 97 Blue-eyed Yellow Warbler. Golden Warbler. *Summer Yellow-bird.

Summer (sʊ·məɹ), *sb.*2 Also 4 sumer, 4–5 swmmer, somere, 4–8 somer, (6 somor), 5 sommere, 6–9 sommer; *Sc.* 6–7 (9) symmer, 9 simmer, (shimmer). See also SOMMIER2. [a. AF. *sumer*, *somer*, = OF. *somier* (mod.F. *sommier*) pack-horse, beam = Pr. *saumier*, It. *somaro*, *somiere*:—pop.L. *saumārius*, for *sagmārius*, f. *sagma* (see SUM *sb.*2). For the sense-development cf. *horse* and F. *cheval*.

The OF. word was adopted in MLG. *somer* long thin pole or tree.]

I. †**1.** A pack-horse. (Cf. SOMER 1, SOUMER.)

1375 BARBOUR *Bruce* XIX. 746 [They] tynt bot litill of thar ger, Bot gif it war ony swmmer [*v.r.* summer] That in the moss wes left liand. 14.. *Guy Warw.* (ed. Copland ? 1560) Cc j b, His neck is great as any sommere; he renneth as swifte as any Distrere [*MS. Auch.* I. 7163 As a somer it is brested bifore in þe brede & swifter ernend þan ani stede]. *c* 1470 *Love's Bonavent. Mirr.* xiv. (Sherard MS.), 3oure.. knyghtes,..horses and herneyes, charyotes and summeres.

II. 2. †**a.** *gen.* A main beam in a structure. *Sc.* (in genuine use). *Obs.*

1324 *Acc. Exch. K. R.* Bd. 165 No. 1. m. 4 (P.R.O.), Pro iiij^{xx} xvij. somers pro springaldis..xij li. xviij. s. viij. d. 1375 BARBOUR *Bruce* XVII. 696 The stane..hyt the sow in sic maner, That it that wes the mast summer..In-swndir with that dusche he brak. 1533 in Pitcairn *Crim. Trials* (1833) I. *163 [Breaking their] dooks, [and Fishing in the water of Dee,..and destruction of the] symmeris [and] hekkis [thereof]. 1654 EARL MONM. tr. *Bentivoglio's Wars Flanders* 219 That they might place their Summers in the parts nearest the banks..and in the middle where it was deepest their boats. 1658 tr. *Porta's Nat. Magick* IV. i. 113 Binde [the vines] fast to the summers or beams with the sprigs of Broom. 1715 LEONI *Palladio's Archit.* (1742) I. 85 These summers were join'd with other summers across them.

b. A horizontal bearing beam in a building, *spec.* the main beam supporting the girders or joists of a floor (or *occas.* the rafters of a roof). (When on the face of a building it is properly called BREAST-SUMMER.)

1359–60 *Sacrist Rolls Ely* (1907) II. 193 In xij lapidibus pro pendauntz postes portandis iij someres et xx linteles. 1448 in Willis & Clark *Cambridge* (1886) II. 8 The Someres of the seid hows shall be one side xij inch squar and on the other part xiiij inch squar. 1532 in Bayley *Tower Lond.* (1821) App. I. p. xviii, A roffe of tymber, and a bourde made complete, wᵗ a somer and joystes. 1594 T. B. *La Primaud. Fr. Acad.* II. To Rdr. b 3, The saide roome beganne to shake againe, so that one of the sommers of the chamber sprang out of the mortesse, and bowed downeward two feete, but fell not. 1623 *Something Written Occ. Accid. Blacke Friers* 25 At an instant the maine Summer or beame brake in sunder. 1663 GERBIER *Counsel* 42 Double Mortises, which doe but weaken the Summers. 1733 W. ELLIS *Chiltern & Vale Farm.* 96 Mortaises made ready for Plates, Chimney Pieces, and also for Somer and Joysts. 1836 PARKER *Gloss. Archit.* (1850) I. 431 In a framed floor the summers were the main beams, the girders were framed into the summers, and the joists into the girders.

¶ The senses 'large stone laid over a column in beginning a cross vault' and 'lintel of a door, window, etc.', which are given in Dicts., do not appear to be in genuine English use, but are from French: see 1728 CHAMBERS *Cycl.* (copying *Dict. de Trévoux*) and 1842 GWILT *Archit.* Gloss.

3. In various other technical applications.

a. *pl.* The framework of stout bars fitted with cross rails or staves, which is added to a cart or wagon to extend its capacity. **b.** A beam in the bed or body of a cart or wagon. †**c.** The sound-board of an organ. *Obs.* **d.** *Sc.* (see quot. 1825). **e.** In the old hand-press, a rail or cross-bar mortised into the cheeks of the press, to prevent them from spreading. **f.** *Tanning.* A horse or block on which skins are pared, scraped, or worked smooth. †**g.** In the spinet, any of the ribs supporting the board holding the tuning-pins. *Obs.* **h.** In a lapidary's mill, each of two opposite bars supporting the bearings of the wheels. **i.** 'The large beam on the top of a cider-press..which sustains all the pressure' (*W. Som. Gloss.* 1886).

a. 1510 STANBRIDGE *Vocabula* (W. de W.) C iij, *Epyredia*, the somors or the rauys [*mispr.* rauye]. 1530 PALSGR. 272/2 Somers or rathes of a wayne or carte. 1802 JAMES *Milit. Dict.*, *Sommers*, in an ammunition waggon, are the upper sides, supported by the staves entered into them with one of their ends, and the other into the side pieces.

b. 1523 FITZHERB. *Husb.* § 5 The bodye of the wayne of oke, the staues, the nether rathes, the ouer rathes, the crosse somer. 1886 *West Som. Gloss.*, *Summer*,..(tech.) the longitudinal parts of the bottom of a wagon.

c. 1659 LEAK *Waterwks.* 29 The 12 holes that are in the Summer serves to conveigh the wind of the said Summer.. to the Organ Pipes. 1728 CHAMBERS *Cycl.* s.v. *Sound-board*, The Sound-board, or Summer, is a Reservoir, into which the Wind..is conducted.

d. 1662 LAMONT *Diary* 15 Jan. (1810) 179 The whole roofe and symmers of that said kill were consumed, and only about 3 bolls oatts saffe. 1809 *Edinb. Even. Courant* 21 Dec. (Jam.) As some servants..were..drying a quantity of oats on the kiln, the mid shimmer gave way, when three of them were precipitated into the killogy. 1825 JAMIESON, *Simmer*, *Symmer*,..one of the supports laid across a kiln, formerly made of wood, now pretty generally of cast metal, with notches in them for receiving the ribs, on which the grain is spread for being kiln-dried; a hair cloth, or fine covering of wire, being interposed between the ribs and the grain.

e. 1662 EVELYN *Sculptura* II. (1906) 13 Upon the Summer or head of the Press marked C let the paper prepared and moistned for the impression lye ready. 1683 MOXON *Mech. Exerc.*, *Printing* x. ¶ 4 This Summer is only a Rail Tennanted, and let into Mortesses made in the inside of the Cheeks.

f. 1728 CHAMBERS *Cycl.* s.v. *Parchment*, The Skin, thus far prepared by the Skinner, is taken..by the Parchment-Maker; who first scrapes or pares it dry on the Summer. 1837 WHITTOCK, etc. *Bk. Trades* (1842) 370 (*Parchment-maker*) The workman then stretches the skin to dry in the sun, ..being done enough, it is..placed on the *summer*, or horse, to be again pared and smoothed with the stone. 1860 TOMLINSON *Cycl. Useful Arts*, *Parchment Making* (1867) II. 275/2 The parchment maker..stretches it tail downwards upon a machine, called the sumner, consisting of a calf-skin mounted on a frame.

g. 1797 *Encycl. Brit.* (ed. 3) XVII. 692/2 [The spinet] consists of a chest or belly..and a table of fir glued on slips of wood called summers, which bear on the sides.

h. 1839 URE *Dict. Arts* 739 In each of these summers a square hole is cut out..which receives the two ends of the arbor [of the cutting wheel]. 1882 *Encycl. Brit.* XIV. 299/1.

4. *attrib.*, as (sense 1) †*summer-saddle*; (sense 2): **summer bar**, the upper summer of a lapidary's wheel; **summer-beam**, **-tree** = sense 2 b; †**summer-piece**, **summer-stone** (see quot. 1833); †**summer-trestle**, ? a railed rack on a trestle-like stand.

1839 URE *Dict. Arts* 739 Every thing that stands above the upper *summer-bar has been suppressed in this representation. 1519 HORMAN *Vulg.* 241 b, The carpenter or wryght hath leyde the *summer bemys [*trabes*] from wall to wall, and the ioystis a crosse. 1766 *Complete Farmer* s.v. *Balk*, The summer-beam, or dorman of a house. 1859 PARKER *Dom. Archit.* III. II. vii. 322 The summer-beam well moulded. *c* 1429 in Willis & Clark *Cambridge* (1886) II. 445 Et iij *somerpecys xijᵈ. 1398–9 *Durham Acc. Rolls* (Surtees) 215 Uno *sumersadill et 2 hakenaysadilles. 1792 J. WOOD *Cottages* (1806) 9 The *summer stone..becomes an abutment..and support to the rest of the tabling. 1833 LOUDON *Encycl. Archit.* § 209 Summer stones (stones placed on a wall, or on piers, for the support of beams, or on the lower angle of gable ends,..as an abutment of the barge stones). *Ibid.* § 1368 Ridge-tiles, gutter-tiles, valley-tiles, and barge and summer-stone tiles. 1458 in Willis & Clark *Cambridge* (1886) I. 282 Principalls with *somere trees conuenient vnto the werk. 1623 *Nottingham Rec.* IV. 388 For takinge vp two summertrees. 1706 PHILLIPS (ed. Kersey), *Summer-Tree*, (among Carpenters) a Beam full of Mortises, for the ends of Joists to lie in. 1875 KNIGHT *Dict. Mech.* 2453/2. 1605 *Shuttleworths' Acc.* (Chetham Soc.) 170 A waller, iiij days fillinge the holles aboute the endes of the *somer trisle in the cowhowse, xijᵈ.

Summer (sʊ·məɹ), *sb.*3 [f. SUM *v.*1 + -ER1.] One who sums or adds; esp. in *summer-up*, one who or that which sums up; *colloq.* or *dial.* one who does sums, an arithmetician.

1611 COTGR., *Nombreur*, a numberer, reckoner, teller, summer, counter. 1643 DIGBY *Observ. Relig. Med.* (1644) 50 This last great day (the summer up of all past dayes). 1828 D'ISRAELI *Chas. I*, I. iii. 29 That aptitude..which made him so skilful a summer-up of arguments. 1830 *Blackw. Mag.* XXVIII. 140 A summer-up of the tottle of the whole. 1863–5 STATON *Rays Loominary* (1867) 68 Awm but a bad summer at th' best o toimes.

Summer (sʊ·məɹ), *v.*1 Forms: 5–7 somer, 6–7 sommer, (5 someryn, somoryn, 6 soommer, *Sc.* 6 symmer, 9 simmer), 5– summer. [f. SUMMER *sb.*1 Cf. MLG. *som(m)eren*, LG. *sommern*, MHG. *sumer(e)n*, *summern*, G. *sommern* and *sömmern*, ON. *sumra*.]

1. *intr.* To pass or spend the summer, to dwell or reside during the summer (now chiefly *Sc.* and *U.S.*); (of cattle, etc.) to be pastured in summer.

c 1440 *Promp. Parv.* 464/2 Somoron [*Winch. MS.* someryn], or a-bydyn' yn' somyr, *estivo*. 1560 *Bible* (Geneva) Isa. xviii. 6 The foule shal sommer vpon it, and euerie beast of the earth shal winter vpon it. 1610 HOLLAND *Camden's Brit.* I. 806 The Ancient Nomades,..who from the moneth of Aprill unto August, lyout skattering and sommering..with their cattaile. 1819 SOUTHEY *Let. to N. White* 14 Oct., A great many Cantabs have been summering here. 1842 E. FITZGERALD *Lett.* (1889) I. 100 He is summering at Castellamare. 1880 *E. Cornw. Gloss.* s.v. *Summering*, Store cattle..are sent summering under the care of the moorland herdsmen. 1895 ANNA M. STODDART *J. S. Blackie* II. 154 A short stay with Dr and Mrs Kennedy, who were summering at Aberfeldy. 1899 MARK TWAIN *Mancorr. Hadleyb.*, etc. (1900) 93 A lady from Boston was summering in that village.

†**b.** *transf.* To pass one's time pleasantly. *rare*$^{-1}$.

1568 C. WATSON *Polyb.* 82 After they had ben vexed with long warres in Scicilie, & concluded a league with the Romans, they hoped to soommer and keepe holydaie.

2. *trans.* To keep or maintain during summer; *esp.* to provide summer pasture for (cattle, etc.): said of the land or the grazier. Also *transf.*

Cf. SUMMERING *vbl. sb.*1 1.

1599 SHAKS. *Hen. V*, v. ii. 335 Maides well Summer'd, and warme kept, are like Flyes at Bartholomew-tyde, blinde, though they haue their eyes. 1601 *Account Bk. W. Wray* in *Antiquary* XXXII. 119 For sommeringe ii stirkes, xs. 1610 FOLKINGHAM *Feudigr.* II. x. 63 How many Cattell such a Plot will Winter and Sommer, feed or keepe. 1707 MORTIMER *Husb.* (1721) I. 208 If your Colts be not well weaned, well summered and wintered. 1765 *Museum Rust.* IV. xliv. 190, I am obliged to allow three acres to summer a cow. 1810 J. T. in *Risdon's Surv. Devon* p. ix, Dartmoor summers an immense number of..sheep. 1883 *Standard* 3 Apr. 3/5 It should be the aim of the grass-land farmer to summer as many and winter as few animals as possible.

b. *spec.* in the management of hunters.

1825 *Sporting Mag.* N.S. XV. 343 Now for summering the hunter. 1862 WHYTE-MELVILLE *Inside Bar* v, The fascinating pursuit for which they [*sc.* hunters] have been bought, and summered, and got into condition. 1879 FEARNLEY *Less. Horse Judging* 114 Our present plan of summering hunters in boxes instead of out in the open.

†**c.** *fig.* To give (a person) a 'sunny' or happy time. *Obs.*

1622 J. TAYLOR (Water P.) *Sir Greg. Nonsence* Wks. (1630) II. 3/2 Time now that summers him, wil one day winter him.

d. *refl.* or *intr.* To sun oneself, bask. Chiefly *fig.*

1837 C. LOFFT *Self-form.* II. 133 Summer house indeed:— and truly my best feelings..summered themselves there most complacently. 1848 AIRD *Devil's Dream* xxx, Thou shalt summer high in bliss upon the hills of God. 1906 J. HUIE *Singing Pilgr.* 18 To sun and summer in the smile of God.

3. *To summer and winter*: **a.** To spend the whole year; also *transf.* to remain or continue permanently (*with*).

1650 ELDERFIELD *Civ. Right Tythes* 210 The best and usefullest Constitutions of State are those experienced firm ones, that have lived, summered and wintered with us, as we say. 1809 W. IRVING *Knickerb.* (1861) 276 Grey-headed negroes, who had wintered and summered in the household of their departed master for the greater part of a century. 1832 — *Alhambra* II. 209 The ruined tower of the bridge in Old Castile, where I have now wintered and summered for many hundred years.

b. *trans.* To maintain one's attitude to or relations with at all seasons; to associate with, be faithful to, or adhere to constantly; hence, to be intimately acquainted with; also, to consider or discuss (a subject) constantly or thoroughly; †*occas.* to continue (a practice) for a whole year. Chiefly *Sc.*

a 1626 BRETON *Packet Mad Lett.* I. § 15 Wks. (Grosart) II. 10 Shake of such acquaintance as gaine you nothing but discredit, and make much of him that must as well winter as summer you. 1644 RUTHERFORD *Serm. bef. H. of Comm.* 31 Jan. 1643 To Chr. Rdr. A 2 b, Whatever they had of Religion, it was never their mind both to summer and winter Jesus Christ. *a* 1670 HACKET *Abp. Williams* II. (1693) 197 [Presbyterianism] was not suitable to the eternal gospel, for the fautors of it did scarce summer and winter the same form of discipline. 1726–8 P. WALKER *Life Peden* To Rdr. (1827) p. xxxv, These have been my Views and digested Thoughts, that I have summer'd and winter'd these many Years. 1816 SCOTT *Antiq.* xliv, We couldna think o' a better way to fling the gear in his gate, though we simmered it and wintered it e'er sae lang. 1849 LONGF. *Kavanagh* xx. Prose Wks. 1886 II. 370, I know the critics root and branch,—out and out,— have summered them, and wintered them,—in fact, am one of them myself. 1865 MRS. STOWE *Little Foxes* (1866) 29 Mrs. Crowfield, who..has summered and wintered me so many years, and knows all my airs and cuts and crinkles so well. 1891 MRS. LYNN LINTON *Let. to H. Spencer* 28 Mar., I am always afraid of 'summering and wintering' a subject too much.

c. *intr.* To consider or discuss a matter at great length; to be tediously long in discourse. *Sc.*

1822 GALT *Sir A. Wylie* xcviii, I'm for no summering and wintering about the matter. 1832 *Blackw. Mag.* XXXII. 651 The Provost was thus summering and wintering to me. 1833 GALT *Gudewife* in *Fraser's Mag.* VIII. 654/1 What would you be at, summering and wintering on nothing?

4. *trans.* To make summer-like, summery, balmy, or genial.

1863 S. DOBELL *An Autumn Mood* Poet. Wks. 1875 II. 332 Myself a morning, summer'd through and lit With light and summer. 1868 G. MACDONALD *Ann. Q. Neighb.* xi. (1878) 228 His rough work-worn face, summered over with his child-like smile. 1896 A. AUSTIN *England's Parting* I. iii, Till your name Soared into space and summered all the air.

Hence **Su·mmered** (with adv. prefixed), **Su·mmering** *ppl. adjs.*

1804 ANNA SEWARD *Mem. Darwin* 337 The seas of glass, the noble rocks, the ever-summered gales. 1836 *Fraser's Mag.* XIII. 233 Regularly Nimrodded, as the term for a well summered hunter now is. 1887 SWINBURNE *Locrine* I. i. 10 Seas that feel the summering skies.

†**Summer**, *v.*2 *Archit. Obs. rare.* In 8 sommer. [Back-formation from SUMMERING *vbl. sb.*2] *intr.* To radiate from or converge towards a centre, like the joints of an arch.

1703 MOXON *Mech. Exerc.* 279 Let the breadth of the upper part of the Keystone be the height of the Arch, *viz.* 14 Inches, and Sommer, from the Centre at I. 1703 T. N. *City & C. Purchaser* 9 The Key-stone..ought to..Sommer (or point with its 2 edges) to the Centre.

Summer bird.

1. A bird that makes its appearance in summer, a summer migrant; locally applied *spec.* (see quots.). Also *fig.* (cf. SUMMER *sb.*1 4 e).

1597 SHAKS. 2 *Hen. IV*, IV. iv. 91 O Westmerland, thou art a Summer Bird, Which euer in the haunch of Winter sings The lifting vp of day. 1607 — *Timon* III. vi. 34, 2 [*Lord*]. The Swallow followes not Summer more willing, then we your Lordship. *Tim.* Nor more willingly leaues Winter, such Summer Birds are men. 1784 COWPER *Task* VI. 921 He cannot skim the ground like summer birds Pursuing gilded flies. 1821 SHELLEY *Epipsych.* 208 The singing of the summer-birds. 1885 SWAINSON *Prov. Names Birds* 103 Wryneck..Summer bird (Northumberland). 1895 MORRIS *Austral Engl.*, *Summer-bird*, the Old-Colonists' name for the Wood-swallows [*Artamus sordidus*, Lath.]. In Tasmania it is applied to a species of Shrike, *Graucalus melanops*, Lath. 1913 *Melbourne Argus* 27 Dec. 5 The bee martin or summer bird.

†**2.** With allusion to the cuckoo as the 'summer bird': A cuckold. Also *summer's bird*. *Obs.*

Cf. SHAKS. *Merry W.* II. i. 127, *L. L. L.* v. ii. 911.

1560 *Scholeh. Women* (1572) B ij, Some other knaue Shall dub her husband a summer bird. ? *a* 1600 *Sack-full of Newes* (1864) 171 The poore man was cruelly beaten, and made a Summers Bird.

†**Summer-castle.** *Obs.* In 4–6 somer-, 5 -yr, 6 sommer-. [? f. SUMMER *sb.*2 + CASTLE *sb.*]

1. A movable tower used in sieges. (Also SUMMER-TOWER.)

? *a* 1400 *Morte Arth.* 3033 The kynge than to assawte he sembles his knyghtez, With somercastelle and sowe appone sere halfes. 1408 CLIFTON tr. *Vegetius' De Re Milit.* IV. viii. (Digby MS. 233) lf. 219 b, 3if þyn enemye sette to þy walles a somercastel oþere a bastyle, þat be muche herre þan þe walles. *c* 1440 *Promp. Parv.* 464/1 Somyr castell, *fala*.

2. An elevated structure on a ship. (Also SUMMER-HUTCH.)

1346 *Acc. Exch.*, *K. R.* Bundle 25. No. 7. m. 2 (P.R.O.) In ij haucers emptis..pro j castello vocato somercastel eadem naui. 1496 *Naval Acc. Hen. VII* (1896) 176 Forcastell the overloppe the somercastell the dekke ovyr the somercastell & the pope. *c* 1500 *Three Kings' Sons* 44 They that were in the somer Castells & toppis of the shippis, that might easely se alle them that were a londe. 1530 PALSGR. 272/2 Sommer castell of a shyppe.

Summer-cloud. (Also summer's cloud.) A cloud such as is seen on a summer day, *esp.* one that is fleeting or does not spoil the fine weather. Also *allusively*.

1605 SHAKS. *Macb.* III. iv. 111 Can such things..ouercome vs like a Summers Clowd, Without our speciall wonder? 1671 MILTON *P. R.* III. 222 A shelter and a kind of shading cool Interposition, as a summers cloud. 1727 WATTS *Hope in Darkness* i. in *Horæ Lyricæ* I. (1743) 133 What tho' a short Eclipse his [*sc.* God's] Beauties shrowd 'Tis but a Morning Vapour, or a Summer-Cloud. 1792 S. ROGERS *Pleas. Mem.* Poems (1839) 3 As summer-clouds flash forth electric fire. 1820 SCOTT *Abbot* xxxvi, Floating in the wind, as lightly as summer clouds. 1893 E. PHILLPOTTS *Summer Clouds* 54 There are people in the world..who would say that we had had a row to-day...I should describe the matter myself as—well, merely a passing summer-cloud.

Summer-day. [Cf. WFris. *simmerdei*, (M)LG. *sommerdach*, MHG. *sum(m)ertac* (G. *sommertag*).] = SUMMER'S DAY.

a 1300 *Cursor M.* 9946 A tron of iuor..Þat es o gretter light and leme þan somer dai es son bem. 1390 GOWER *Conf.* I. 184 This was upon a Somer dai. *c* 1450 *St. Cuthbert* (Surtees) 5634 In þe hete of somyr day. *a* 1578 LINDESAY (Pitscottie) *Chron. Scot.* (S.T.S.) I. 229 Frome the sone ryssing quhill the sone zeid to in ane lang sommer day. 1608 SHAKS. *Per.* IV. i. 18 While Sommer dayes doth last. 1711 ADDISON *Spect.* No. 128 ¶ 10 The Lady..hates your tedious Summer Days. *a* 1774 GOLDSM. *Surv. Exp. Philos.* (1776) I. 329 He calculated that it [*sc.* the Mediterranean sea] would lose by evaporation, every summer day, fifty-two thousand and eighty millions of tons. 1823 SCOTT *Quentin D.* v, To spend summer-day and winter-night up in yonder battlements. 1848 LYTTON *K. Arthur* I. 6 This soft summer-day.

b. *fig.* and *allusively*. Also *attrib.*

1605 ERONDELL (*title*) The French Garden:..Or, A Sommer dayes labour. Being an instruction for the attayning vnto the knowledge of the French Tongue. 1806 *Ann. Rev.* IV. 466 The summer days of Naples were over. 1833 TENNYSON *May Queen* vi, There's many a bolder lad 'ill woo me any summer day. 1867 AUGUSTA WILSON *Vashti* xxii, No mere gala barge..was his religion; no fair summer-day toy.

Su·mmer-fa·llow, *sb.* [See FALLOW *sb.* 2.] A lying or laying fallow during the summer; also, land that lies fallow during the summer.

1733 TULL *Horse-hoeing Husb.* vii. 78 This sort of Hoeing has ..every Year the Effect of a Summer-fallow. 1765 *Museum Rust.* IV. 143 The ill consequence of not giving it a summer-fallow to clean the ground thoroughly. 1801 *Farmer's Mag.* Jan. 85 The quantity of ground under Summer-fallow this year. 1844 H. STEPHENS *Bk. Farm* III. 990 The sowing of the fallow-crop on the summer-fallow is delayed to autumn. 1875 *Encycl. Brit.* I. 340/1 That prolonged form of it [*sc.* the fallowing process] called a summer or naked fallow.

b. as *adj.* Lying fallow during the summer.

1801 *Farmer's Mag.* Jan. 105 The months of November and December were very favourable for getting the Summer-fallow land seed-furrowed. 1844 H. STEPHENS *Bk. Farm* III. 990, I..trenched 13 acres of my summer-fallow break in the months of June and July.

Su·mmer-fa·llow, *v.* [See FALLOW *v.*2] *trans.* To lay (land) fallow during summer. Also *absol.* Hence **Summer-fallowing** *vbl. sb.* and *ppl. a.*

1669 WORLIDGE *Syst. Agric.* (1681) 9 For the same reason are the Summer-Fallowings advantageous to the Husbandman. 1760 BROWN *Compl. Farmer* II. 11 In Staffordshire, they often give their lands a winter-fallowing, besides the three summer-fallowings. 1765 A. DICKSON *Treat. Agric.* (ed. 2) 271 The English writers on agriculture, when giving directions about the opening up of grass-ground, always suppose that the land is to be summer-fallowed. 1778 [W. MARSHALL] *Minutes Agric.* 6 Feb. 1776, The summer-fallowing Farmer. 1813 VANCOUVER *Agric. Devon* 158 In the division of Meshaw, it is common to plough clean before Christmas, and summer-fallow for wheat. 1844 H. STEPHENS *Bk. Farm* III. 990 That part of the fallow-break which is summer-fallowed.

†**Su·mmerful**, *a. Obs. rare*$^{-1}$. [f. SUMMER *sb.*1 + -FUL.] Having the summer development or quality.

1614 T. GENTLEMAN *England's Way* (1660) 5 They do sell them for Sprats, the which, if that they were let live, would all be, at Midsummer, a Fat Summerfull Herring.

Summer-game. (Also 4 somere(s) gamen.)

†**1.** A festival held at Midsummer, celebrated with dancing, games, dramatic performances, etc.

1303 R. BRUNNE *Handl. Synne* 4681 Daunces, karols, somour games, Of many swych come many shames. *a* 1340 HAMPOLE *Psalter* xvi. 12 Þai haf vmgifen me in þe crosse hyngand, as foles þat gedirs til a somere gamen. *c* 1380 WYCLIF *Wks.* (1880) 246 A wilde pleiere of someres gamenes. *c* 1440 *Promp. Parv.* 464/1 Pley, or somyr game, *spectaculum*. 1469 *Test. Ebor.* (Surtees) V. 103 *note*, Accessit cum Thoma Barker..et Margareta More, in regem et reginam ipsius villæ in ludo suo æstivali, Anglice Somer-game, forte electis. 1583 BABINGTON *Commandm.* (1590) 166 Whether carding,..stage plaies, and summer games..be exercises commanded of God for the sabaoth day or no. *a* 1629 HINDE *J. Bruen* xxxiii. (1641) 104 Profane exercises of May-games, and Summer-games [*mispr.* greenes].

†**b.** *attrib.* **Summer-game light**: a light burnt in church on the feast of the Nativity of St. John Baptist (Midsummer Day, June 24). *Obs.*

[1438 *Test. Ebor.* (Surtees) V. 103 *note*, Lumini Æstival in eadem ecclesia vs.] 1464 *Ibid.*, Lumini vocato Somergame light. 1519 *Ibid.* 103 To the Somer-game lyght in my parishe chirche ijs.

2. *U.S. slang.* (See quot.)

1890 BARRÈRE & LELAND *Slang Dict.* (1897), *Summer game* (American gamblers), playing merely for amusement or benefit of another person, but with his money.

Summerhead, Anglo-Indian corruption of SOMBRERO, sun-umbrella.

1797 S. JAMES *Narr. Voy.* 88 Not one European was able to stir outside his door without his summerhead. 1886 YULE & BURNELL *Hobson-Jobson* Suppl. s.v. *Sombrero*, *Summer-head* is a name in the Bombay Arsenal (as M.-General Keatinge tells me) for a great umbrella.

Su·mmer-hou·se. [Cf. WFris. *simmerhûs*, MDu. *somerhuys* (Du. *zomerhuis*), MHG. *sum(m)erhaus* (G. *sommerhaus*).]

1. A summer residence in the country. Now *rare*.

1... *Cust. of Newington by Sittingbourne* in *Cowel's Interpr.* (1701), *Homines quoque de walda debent unam domum æstivalem quæ Anglice dicitur* Sumer-hus *invenire*, *aut viginti solidos dare*. 1382 WYCLIF *Amos* iii. 15 Y shal smyte the wyntyr hous with the somer hous [Vulg. *domo æstiva*]. 1596 SHAKS. 1 *Hen. IV*, III. i. 164, I had rather liue With Cheese and Garlick in a Windmill farre, Than feede on Cates, and haue him talke to me, In any Summer-House in Christendome. 1654 GATAKER *Disc. Apol.* 50 The Doctor making onelie a Summer-House of it. 1688 HOLME *Armoury* III. xii. 453/1 *Summer Houses*, *Bowers*, Places to which the Gentry resort, and abide there dureing the Summer season, for their Recreation and pastime. *a* 1709 J. LISTER *Autobiog.* (1842) 35 At present her summer-house is in Highgate. 1797 W. JOHNSTON tr. *Beckmann's Invent.* II. 38 [Privies] are at present considered to be so indispensably necessary, that few summer-houses are constructed without them. 1881 *Daily News* 26 Sept. 5/2 Its very nearness to London perhaps has made it less of an actual residence and more of a holiday summer-house than it would otherwise have been.

fig. 1754 FIELDING *Voy. Lisbon* Wks. 1882 VII. 82 The wind..slyly slipped back again to his summer-house in the south-west.

2. A building in a garden or park, usually of very simple and often rustic character, designed to provide a cool shady place in the heat of summer.

c 1440 *Pallad. on Husb.* I. 347 Lest the sonne in somer do hit harm, Thi somer hous northest & west let wrie. 1577 B. GOOGE *Heresbach's Husb.* 34 b, Frenche Beanes..climeth aloft,..seruyng well for the shadowyng of Herbers and Summer houses. 1585 HIGINS *Junius' Nomencl.* 389/2 *Horti adonidis*,..a banketting summer house made of trees, herbs, flowers, &c. 1624 WOTTON *Archit.* II. 100 [Paintings of] Land-schips, and Boscage..in open Tarraces, or in Summer houses. 1721 MORTIMER *Husb.* II. 206 Summer-Houses may..be erected at each Corner [of the garden], and made so as to let in the Air on all sides, or to exclude it. 1762–71 H. WALPOLE *Vertue's Anecd. Paint.* (1786) IV. 275 At the end of the terras-walk are two summer-houses. 1824 SCOTT *St. Ronan's* xxxvii, One of her gloves lay on the small rustic table in the summer-house. 1888 MISS BRADDON *Fatal Three* I. vi, There was an old stone summer-house in each angle of that end wall.

†**b.** An arbour or the like used in connexion with the 'summer-game'. *Obs.*

1519 *Test. Ebor.* (Surtees) V. 103 In quo..horreo..loco adtunc vulgariter dicto Somer-house, prædicta Margareta More,..permansit..jocundam se faciendo in eodem.

†**Summer-hutch.** *Obs.* In 5 -hoche, -wiche, -wyche. = SUMMER-CASTLE 2.

1417 in *For. Acc.* 8 *Hen. V*, D/1 *dorso* (P.R.O.), In..ij batellis pro eadem Naui j grapnelle j Somerwyche. *Ibid.* G/1 De..iiij cordis paruis..j Grapnelle j Somerwiche. 1420 in *For. Acc.* 3 *Hen. VI*, H *dorso* (P.R.O.), j. pompe pro aqua haurienda..j Grapnelle j. somerhoche.

Summering (sʊ·məriŋ), *vbl. sb.*1 [f. SUMMER *v.*1 or *sb.*1 + -ING1.]

1. a. The pasturing of cattle in summer. †Also *attrib.*, as *summering ground*, *place*, *plain*.

1477 *Churchw. Acc. Tintinhull* (Somerset Rec. Soc.) 193 For wynteryng and summering of the chyrche cowe, iijᵈ. 1580 *Records of Elgin* (New Spald. Club) I. 156 Fyve s. for the symmering of tua ky to him in symmer last wes. 1595 *Wills & Inv. N. C.* (Surtees 1860) 254. I will that my wiffe be fre to all my sommering places. 1607 TOPSELL *Four-f. Beasts* 605 The Romans had a speciall regard to chuse some places for the summering of their sheepe, and some place for their wintering. 1615 G. SANDYS *Trav.* I. 45 Aladin.. assigned him this village to winter in, and the mountaines adioyning for the sommering of his cattell. 1664 in *Northumb. Gloss.* s.v. *Summering*, All my summering grounds in the parish of Symonburne. 1688 WALTER SCOT *Hist. Name Scot* (repr. 1776) 33 All our south-parts was wood and forrest, Except here and there a summering plain. 1801 *Farmer's Mag.* Apr. 197 Summering on grass, being the customary payment for a cow, L. 3 10 0. 1888 DOUGHTY *Trav. Arabia Deserta* I. 24 When nearly all the villagers lie encamped..for the summering of their cattle.

b. Spending the summer, summer residence. †Also *attrib.*, as *summering-house*, *place*. Now *U.S.*

1565 COOPER *Thesaurus* s.v. *Confectus*, When they had done restinge in their summering places. 1675 COVEL in *Early Voy. Levant* (Hakluyt Soc.) 238 The G. Sr. nourishes severall [English mastiffs], and hath here hard by our house a sommering-house for them. 1817–18 COBBETT *Resid. U.S.* (1822) 272 After a long summering upon wild flesh. 1856 MISS WARNER *Hills Shatemuc* x, The young ladies' summering in the country had begun with good promise. 1883 *Harper's Mag.* Aug. 331/2 Altoona..is a summering place. 1892 KIPLING in *Times* (weekly ed.) 25 Nov. 13/2 You in England have no idea of what Summering means in the States.

c. The summer treatment of hunters.

1856 'STONEHENGE' *Brit. Rural Sports* II. III. ii. § 2. 404/2 In the middle of September the training for the hunting season begins, and at that time the summering may be considered at an end. 1881 *Encycl. Brit.* XII. 194/1 It will probably be nearly a month after the last hunting day before the summering treatment is adopted.

†**2.** A summer excursion, festivity, or revelling.

1606 JAS. VI in *Reg. Privy Council Scot.* VII. 489 Thair forbearing ony suche lyke sommering heirefter. 1630 BRATHWAIT *Eng. Gentlem.* 166 Both Southward in their Wakes, and Northward in their Summerings, the very same Recreations are to this day continued. 1631 — *Whimzies*, *Ruffian* 82 His soveraignty is showne highest at May-games, wakes, summerings, and rush-bearings. 1781 J. HUTTON *Tour to Caves* Gloss. (E.D.S.), *Summering*, a rush-bearing.

3. *dial.* **a.** *pl.* Summer apples or pears.

1847 HALLIWELL, *Summerings*,..very early apples and pears. 1877 *N. W. Linc. Gloss.*

b. Summer pasture or feed.

1894 *Morning Post* 3 Feb. 2/1 If the meadow land which belonged to the farm was cut off, leaving only the summering. 1894 *Northumb. Gloss.* s.v., *Summerings*, *Sommerings*, pastures on the moors; so-called from their being occupied only in the summer months.

c. *pl.* Cattle of one year old.

Cf. ON. *sumrungr*.

1828 *Farm. Jrnl.* 9 June (E.D.D.). 1847 in HALLIWELL.

Summering (sʊ·məriŋ), *vbl. sb.*2 *Archit.* Also 8 som(m)ering. [app. f. SUMMER *sb.*2 + -ING1.]

a. *collect.* The beds of the stones or bricks of an arch considered with reference to their direction. **b.** The radial direction of the joints of an arch. **c.** The degree of curvature of an arch.

The term perhaps originally indicated the support given by the impost from which the arch springs (cf. F. *sommier*) and which by its mould determines the curve of the arch, but there is no evidence for a sense (given in some recent Dicts.) 'the first mass of masonry laid upon a pier, column, etc. when it begins an arched construction'.

1703 T. N. *City & C. Purchaser* 9 The Centre for the Skew-back or Summering to point to...By Sommering, is to be understood the level Joints betwixt the Courses of Bricks in the Arch. 1703 MOXON *Mech. Exerc.* 279 According to the breadth of the Piers between the Windows, so ought the Skew-back or Sommering of the Arch to be. 1751 HALFPENNY *New Des. Chinese Bridges* II. 8 The middle Pieces are taper, according to the summering of the Arch. 1823 P. NICHOLSON *Pract. Builder* 329 In arching, the beds are, by some, called summerings. *Ibid.* 593 *Sommering*, the continuation of the joints of arches towards a centre.

attrib. 1703 MOXON *Mech. Exerc.* 275 Divide the upper Hanse from the centre O, making a right Angle from each sommering Line to the Ellipsis.., this will be the Sommering Mould for the Hanse;..then make another Sommering Mould to fit between two of these Lines. 1725 W. HALFPENNY *Sound Building* 55 Cut the Arch on the End of the Brick, as also the Summering Joint.

Summerish (sʊ·məriʃ), *a.* [f. SUMMER *sb.*1 + -ISH1.] Somewhat summer-like.

1726 LEONI *Alberti's Archit.* I. 15/1 In Places subject to much Snow, the Coverings shou'd have a very steep Slope..; but in more Summerish Climates (to use such an Expression) they laid their Coverings less oblique. 1754 H. WALPOLE *Let. to J. Chute* 30 Apr., To-day looks summerish, but we have no rain yet. 1847 JEFFREY *Let. to Mrs. A. Rutherfurd* 21 June, Our weather has been summerish of late, but never quite summer. 1856 HAWTHORNE *Eng. Note-Bks.* (1870) II. 80 In wide-awake hats and loose, blouse-like, summerish garments.

Summerize (sʊ·məraiz), *v. nonce-wd.* [f. SUMMER *sb.*1 + -IZE.] *intr.* To spend the summer.

1797 *Monthly Mag.* III. 460 A Series of Familiar Poetical Epistles, from Mr. Simkin Slenderwit, summerising at Ramsgate, to his dear Mother in Town. 1799 *Monthly Rev.* XXX. 350 In this summerising tour from Wisbech to Scarborough.

Su·mmer-land, su·mmerland, *sb.* Also 8 somerland.

1. A summer-fallow. *dial.*

1695 KENNETT *Par. Antiq.* Gloss. s.v. *Warectare*. 1723 LEWIS *Hist. Tenet* 8 The tilth for this grain is either Somerland, Bean- or Pease gratten, or Clover, or Trefoil-lay. 1765 *Museum Rust.* IV. 145, I make no summer-land on this light land, but plough sufficiently to get out the grass. 1846 *Jrnl. R. Agric. Soc.* VII. II. 589 To make a summerland only for swede turnips.

2. A land where it is always summer; in the language of spiritualists applied to the intermediate state of the departed.

1895 WORKMAN *Algerian Mem.* 44 The summer-land of oranges, lemons and figs. 1896 MRS. BESANT in *Daily News* 31 Oct. 6/3 The purgatory of the Roman Catholics, the summerland of the spiritualists, the intermediate states of the Hindus and Buddhists. 1901 'LUX AUREA' (*title*) Light from the Summerland. Being a Series of Articles illustrating the Truth and Teachings of Spiritualism.

Hence **Summerland** *v. trans.*, to lay fallow.

1674 RAY *S. & E. C. Words*, *To Summerland* a ground; to lay it fallow a year, *Suff.* 1723 LEWIS *Hist. Tenet* 10 They are forc'd to Somerland or lay fallow their ground.

Su·mmerless, *a.* [f. SUMMER *sb.*1 + -LESS.] Having no summer; not summery.

1879 *Mem. G. S. Arnold* 104 A summerless tomorrow. 1882 MORRIS in Mackail *Life* (1899) II. 77 The summerless season.

Summer-like (sʊ·məlaik), *a.* [f. SUMMER *sb.*1 + -LIKE.] Like, or like that of, summer; summery. †Also = SUMMERLY *a.* 1.

1530 PALSGR. 325/1 Sommerlyke, belongyng to the sommer season, *estival*. 1610 HOLLAND *Camden's Brit.* (1637) 220 In summer time it is a right summer-like Country. 1772 T. SMITH *Jrnl.* (1849) 278 Several summer-like days this month [Dec.] 1842 LONGFELLOW in *Life* (1891) I. 413 The weather for ten days past has been delicious and summer-like. 1912 *World* 7 May 681/1 The King..attended the races on Thursday, when the weather was almost summer-like.

Su·mmerling. [f. SUMMER *sb.*1 + -LING.] A beast put out to graze in summer.

1889 *Glover's Hist. Derby* I. 204 Large pasture fields, for the taking in of summerlings or ley cattle, at fixed prices per week.

Summerly (sʊ·məli), *a.* [OE. *sumerlic* = OHG. *sumarlih* (MHG. *sumerlich*, G. *sommerlich*), ON. *sumarligr*; see SUMMER *sb.*1 and -LY1.]

†**1.** Of or pertaining to summer; taking place in summer. *Obs.*

c 1000 *Sax. Leechd.* III. 250 Se sumerlica sunnstede. *Ibid.* 252 Þære sumerlican hætan. *c* 1050 *Suppl. Ælfric's Gloss.* in Wr.-Wülcker 176/18 *Æstinus dies*, sumorlic dæg. 1559 W. CUNNINGHAM *Cosmogr. Glasse* 34 After this somerlye reuerting, the Sonne is not perceiued to decline farther North. 1576 FLEMING *Panopl. Epist.* 227 The grassehopper ..leapt and chirpte..among the greene herbes and summerlie plantes. 1749 H. WALPOLE *Let. to Mann* 4 June, As summerly as June and Strawberry Hill may sound, I assure you I am writing to you by the fire-side. 1771 — *Let. to J. Chute* 9 July, The weather is but lukewarm, and I should choose to have all the windows shut, if my smelling was not much more summerly than my feeling.

2. Having the qualities of summer; summer-like, summery.

a 1225 *Leg. Kath.* 1678 Euch strete..bute sloh & slec, eauer iliche summerlich. *a* 1661 [implied in SUMMERLINESS]. 1850 T. T. LYNCH *Theoph. Trinal* xi. 210 A quiet, most summerly, September day. 1858 *Times* 15 Dec. 6/1 Whenever the season is summerly and the weather is damp and mild. 1894 JEAFFRESON *Bk. Recoll.* I. iv. 57, I journeyed in summerly weather..to Oxford.

Hence **Su·mmerliness**, summeriness.

a 1661 FULLER *Worthies*, *Somerset.* (1662) 17 Some will have it [*sc.* Somersetshire] so called from the Summerlinesse, or temperate pleasantnesse thereof.

Summerly (sʊ·məli), *adv. rare.* [f. SUMMER *sb.*1 + -LY2.] In a manner or condition befitting summer.

1600 NASHE *Summer's Last Will* Wks. 1905 III. 247 Let the prodigall childe come out in his dublet and hose all greasy, his shirt hanging forth, and ne're a penny in his purse, and talke what a fine thing it is to walke summerly. 1839 LD. HOUGHTON *Treasure-Ship* i, The wind is blowing summerly. 1902 *Rime* in *Daily Chron.* 3 Jan. 5/2 If the January calends be summerly gay, It will be winterly weather till the calends of May.

Summersault, -saut, var. of SOMERSAULT.

Summer's day. [Cf. OFris. *sumersdey* Midsummer day.] A day in summer: often put typically for a very long day.

a 1300 *K. Horn* 29 Hit was vpon a someres day. 1340 HAMPOLE *Pr. Consc.* 715 Als a shadu on þe somers day. 1426 LYDG. *De Guil. Pilgr.* 11613 Vp-on the glade somerys dayes. *a* 1536 *Songs*, *Carols*, etc. (E.E.T.S.) 117 Lyke a meyny of bullokkis..on a whot somers day, when they be mad all. 1588 SHAKS. *Tit. A.* v. i. 14 Like stinging Bees in hottest Sommers day. 1667 MILTON *P. L.* I. 449 To lament his fate In amorous dittyes all a Summers day. 1743 BLAIR *Grave* 107 Oh! then the longest summer's day Seemed too too much in haste. 1853 M. ARNOLD *Scholar Gypsy* ii, All the live murmur of a summer's day.

b. Phr. *In* (†*upon*) *a summer's day*, used in various commendatory phrases; *some summer's day*, some day or other, 'one of these fine days'.

1590 SHAKS. *Mids. N.* I. ii. 89 A sweet-fac'd man, a proper man as one shall see in a summers day. 1594 LYLY *Mother Bombie* I. iii, As goodly a youth as one shall see in a Summers daie. 1697 H. WANLEY in *Bodl. Q. Rec.* (1915) Jan. 112 [The] Vice-Chancellor..with the other Curators, upon some Somers day, might call them all over. 1742 FIELDING *J. Andrews* IV. xv, As fine a fat thriving Child as you shall see in a Summer's Day. 1823 BYRON *Juan* XIV. lxxxii, There's another little thing..Which you should perpetrate some summer's day. 1848 THACKERAY *Van. Fair* xxxvii, You won't see a prettier pair, I think, *this* summer's day, sir.

Summer season. Now *rare*. The season of summer.

1362 LANGL. *P. Pl.* A. Prol. 1 In A somer sesun whon softe was þe sonne. *a* 1400 *Stockholm Med. MS.* i. 107 in *Anglia* XVIII. 297 Late take a gres in somer-sesoun. 1530 PALSGR. 703/1 In the sommer season I love to shyfte me often. 1588 A. KING tr. *Canisius' Catech.* i vij, Giff he [*sc.* the sun] be in ony of ye sowth signes in ye simmer sessone. 1688 HOLME *Armoury* III. xii. 453/1 Places to which the Gentry resort, and abide there dureing the Summer season. 1712 ADDISON *Spect.* No. 477 ¶ 1 In the Summer-Season the whole Country blooms. 1821 SHELLEY '*She was an aged woman*' 66 When the time of summer season smiled. 1812 *New Bot. Gard.* I. 88 The cuttings should be made in the summer season.

Summerset, var. form of SOMERSET.

Summer solstice. The time at which the sun reaches the summer tropic, *i.e.* in the northern hemisphere, the tropic of Cancer, in the southern hemisphere, the tropic of Capricorn; †*occas.* applied to the tropic itself.

1549 *Compl. Scot.* vi. 37 Distant fiue degreis fra oure symmyr solstice, callit the borial tropic of cancer. 1601 HOLLAND *Pliny* II. 245 About the Summer solstice it sheweth a red floure. 1698 FRYER *Acc. E. Ind. & P.* 23 Five days after our Summer Solstice we had soundings 14 Fathom. 1837 BREWSTER *Magnet.* 217 The declination has never diminished between the vernal equinox and the summer solstice. 1868 LOCKYER *Guillemin's Heavens* (ed. 3) 119 From the 21st of June to the 22d of September, the Earth passes from the Summer solstice to the autumnal equinox.

†**Summer's tide.** *Obs.* [Cf. G. *sommerszeit*.] = next.

a 1000 *Phœnix* 209 (Gr.) On sumeres tid sunne hatost ofer sceadu scineð. *a* 1250 *Owl & Night.* 489 Sumerestyde is al wlonk. 1303 R. BRUNNE *Handl. Synne* 2127 Hyt was yn þe somerys tyde, whan þe hete ys al yn pryde. *a* 1352 MINOT *Poems* (ed. Hall) x. 7 Þai sailed furth in þe Swin in a somers tyde. *c* 1465 *Pol. Rel. & L. Poems* (1903) 1 Erly in a sommeristide. 1513 DOUGLAS *Æneis* VI. xi. 57 The byssy beis in schene symmeris tyde.

Su·mmer-tide. Now chiefly *poet.* [Cf. WFris. *simmertiid*, NFris. *sumartidj*, MLG. *sommertyd*, LG. *sommertitt*, OHG. *sumarzît* (MHG. *sumerzît*, G. *sommerzeit*).] = SUMMER-TIME 1.

c 1250 *Gen. & Ex.* 1224 He flemede agar and ysmael In sumertid. 1303 R. BRUNNE *Handl. Synne* 903 Whan hyt come to somer tyde,..Here vynys florshede feyre & weyl. 1390 GOWER *Conf.* II. 328 Whan the world is woxe grene And comen is the Somertide. *c* 1420 ? LYDG. *Assembly of Gods* 334 Grene as any gresse in the somertyde. *a* 1513 FABYAN *Chron.* VII. (1811) 482 In this yere, folowynge the somertyde in Guyan. 1566 STERNHOLD & H. *Ps.*, *Benedicite*, Ye winter and the sommer tyde.

1800 WORDSW. *Hart-leap Well* 150 Asleep he sank, Lulled by the fountain in the summer-tide. 1873 GEIKIE *Gt. Ice Age* x. 125 The arctic sun, which shines day and night during the whole summertide. 1891 MORRIS *Poems by the Way* 123 Ask the Summer-tide to prove The abundance of my love.

Su·mmer-time. Also †summer's time.

1. The season of summer; the time that summer lasts.

1377 LANGL. *P. Pl.* B. xv. 94 In somer tyme on trowes, Þere somme bowes ben leued and somme bereth none. *c* 1380 WYCLIF *Sel. Wks.* II. 400 Hete of somer tyme. *c* 1440 *Pallad. on Husb.* x. 153 In somer tyme hym liketh wel to glade. 1596 DALRYMPLE tr. *Leslie's Hist. Scot.* II. 345 To Dondei, and S. Johnestoune quhair al that selfe seasone of the 3eir and sommer tyme he consumet. *c* 1600 SHAKS. *Sonn.* xcvii, And yet this time remou'd was sommers time. *a* 1660 *Contemp. Hist. Irel.* (Ir. Archæol. Soc.) I. 87 About 8 o'clock in the afternoone (somer time) he comaunded the horse to come home and make readie. 1778 MISS BURNEY

Ecline sl., I prefer'd my cousin would not..have come to town in the summer-time, since I don't like it.

2. The standard time (in advance of ordinary time) adopted in some countries during the summer months (in the British Isles, in 1916, from 21 May to 30 September).

†Summer-tower. *Obs.* [See TOWER *sb.*]

Summerward, *adv.* [f. SUMMER *sb.*¹: see -WARD 2.] Towards summer.

Summery, *a.* [f. SUMMER *sb.*¹ + -Y¹.] Resembling or pertaining to summer; characteristic of or appropriate to summer; summer-like.

Hence **Su·mmeriness**, summery character or quality.

Summet, obs. form of SUMMIT *sb.*

Summer, var. of SUMMON *Obs.*, beam.

Summing (sŏ·miŋ), *vbl. sb.* [f. SUM *v.*² + -ING¹.]

1. The calculation of a total amount; computation.

2. With (rarely without) *up.* The stating of the sum and substance of a matter; summarizing; a summary account or statement.

3. With (rarely without) *up.* A judge's address to a jury; in which he reviews and comments upon the evidence adduced in the case before him: see SUM *v.*² 5.

4. Doing 'sums' or arithmetical problems; the act of performing arithmetical operations.

Summing, *ppl. a.* [f. SUM *v.*² + -ING².] That sums or sums up; summarizing.

Su·mmist, *v. Obs. rare.* In 5 -*zen.* Variant of SUMMIE *v.*, to summon.

†Su·mmiss, *a. Obs. rare.* [ad. L. *summissus*, pa. pple. of *summittĕre* SUBMIT *v.*] = SUBMISS 2.

†Summi·ssion. *Obs.* [ad. L. *summissiō*, *-nem*, or ad. late L. *summissio*, *summittĕre* SUBMIT *v.*] = SUBMISSION.

Su·mmist. [f. SUMMA.] [ad. med.L. *summista*, Sp. *summista*, Pg. *summista*.]

1. The author of a summa of religious doctrine, etc.

†b. An epitomizer; abridger; *transf.* an epitome, abridgement.

†Su·mmister. *Obs.* [f. med.L. *summister*: see prec. and *-ER*¹.] = prec. 1, 2 b.

Summit (sŏ·mit), *sb.* Forms: 4 *sommet*, 5 *somette*, *sommet* (6 *-ete*, 6 8 *summet* (7 *-en*, *sommet*), dim. of *som*, *sum-* = L. *summum*, neut. sing. of *summus* (see SUM *sb.*¹). The modern spelling with *-it* is due to assimilation to SUMMITY, *q. v.*

1. The topmost part, top; the vertex, apex; † the crown (of the head), boss (of a shield), umbo (of a shell).

†b. *Bot.* An etymological alteration of Grew's *summit*, for 'anther'; and hence for 'stigma.' *Obs.*

2. The topmost point or ridge of a mountain or hill. Also, the highest elevation of a road, railway, or canal.

3. The highest point or degree; the acme.

†b. The highest point in particularized use.

†Summit, *v. Obs.* In 4-5 *summyt(e*, 5 *summitte*, *summittit*, assimilated f. *submittin* to SUBMIT.] *trans.* To submit, subject.

Su·mmister, *sb.* [f. med.L. *summister*: = prec. 1, 2 b. In Taylor *Artemidy* Note to i. iv 1, Hist. outlines, mountains summettics, grey warren.

†Su·mmity. *Obs. or arch.* Forms: 5-7 summitie, (5 summittie, 6 -yt(i), sumite, 6 sumitie, summittye, summittie, 8 *errron.* summaty), 7-9 summity, *summity*. [a. OF. *sommet*, *summitee* (F. *sommité*), *ad.* late L. *summitas, -ātem,* f. *summus* highest, the top (cf. SUM *sb.*¹).]

1. *trans.* To call together by authority for action or consultation. † *Occas.* with *up.* (See SUMMONS *sb.* 1, 7 b.)

2. *fig.* With immaterial or inanimate subject: To call, but come or go. Often with *up.*

Summon, (sŏ·mən), *sb. Obs.* Forms: 4 *somun*, *sumun*, *sommoun*, 5 *sumone*, *somone*, *summoune*, *sowmone*, 6 *somon*, *-own*, *sowmon*, 6-7 *somon*, *-oun*, 6-7 *sommon*, *-own*, *sowmon*, 4-5 *somyn*, *somn-*; 4-5 *sompne*, *-y*. (See SONNE *v.*², *Somne v.*) 7, 3-4 *summi*, *-y*, *-e*, 5 *sumne*, (6. AF. *somne*, *semoune*, 3-6 *soman*, 4-5 *somyn*, *-nd* 5 *somene*, *semondre* (see SUMMON *v.*): — Pr. *somon(dyre*, *semondre* (f. *semondre*, *summonĕre*, in earlier L., to give a hint, suggest), in med.L. to call, cite, summon, L. *sub*- (see SUB- 24) + *monĕre* to warn (see MONITION).

†Su·mmonance. [a. AF. *somon'saunce*, *semoun'saunce* = OF. *somonse*, *semonse* = SUMMON *v.* To summon. Hence **Su·mmoning**, *a.*

Summonds. *Sc. and north. Obs.* Forms: 5 *summondis*, 6-7 *summonds*, 6 *summons* dis, *ad.*, *summands*, 5 *summonds*. Variant of SUMMONS assimilated to SUMMOND *v.*

Summond (sŏ·mənd), *ppl. a.* [f. SUMMON *v.* + -ED.] In sense of the verb.

Summoner (sŏ·mənər). Forms: 1 *somnour*, *-on(o)ur*, 6 *-oner*, 6-7 *summoner*, 5 *-ur*, *mono-*. See also SOMNER, SOMONER, SOMPNER and SUMMONITOR. [a. AF. *-as sumenour*, *-d* med. L. *summonitor*.]

Summoning (sŏ·məniŋ), *vbl. sb.* [f. SUMMON *v.* + -ING¹.] The action of the vb. SUMMON; the act of summons; † calling to arms; calling to surrender.

Summoning, *ppl. a.* [f. SUMMON *v.* + -ING².]

†Su·mmonister. *Obs.* [SUMMONER + -ISTER.] = SUMMONITOR.

†Summoni·tion. *Obs.* Also 5 *somon-*, 6 *sommon-*: 5 *-yciou*, 6-7 *somoni-*, *sommoni-*, *summoni-*. [ad. med.L. *summonitiōn-*, *-ōnem*, n. of action f. *summonĕre* to SUMMON.] A summons.

†Summoni·tor. *Obs.* Also 7 *somoniter*, *-menitor*. [a. med.L. *summonitor*, agent-n. f. *summonēre* to SUMMON.] An officer of the Court of Exchequer in Ireland who assisted in collecting the royal revenues by citing defaulters.

Summons (sŏ·mənz), *sb.* Forms: 3-6 *som-oune*, *-ounce*, 3-6 *somona*, 4-5 *somone*, 5 *sommaunce*, 5 *sommons*, 4 *somon-*, *-ouns*, 4 *-unes*, *-ona*, *sumouns*, 6 *summons*, 6-7 *-monce*, 7 *sumonce*, 5-6 *summons*, 5-6 *somon(a)s* (*red*, *med.L.*), *somo(u)ns* (*red. semmondis*), pa. pple. fem. (used subst.) of *summodēre* to SUMMON.]

1. An authoritative call to attend at a specified place for a specified purpose.

b. *attrib.* (see quot.).

c. *fig.* An authoritative or urgent call or command; a summoning sound, knock, or the like.

2. A call or citation by authority to appear before a court or judicial officer; also (in full *writ of summons*), the writ by which the citation is made.

a. A citation or writ apprising a defendant that an action has been begun against him and citing him to appear to the action, in default of which the court may proceed to give judgement and award execution against him.

b. *attrib.* (see quot.).

3. *Sc. Law.* A citation or writ issuing from the Court of Session under the royal signet, or, if in a sheriff court, in the name of the sheriff.

4. *Mil.* The act of summoning a place to surrender. Also, now only, with *inf.* (cf. 3 b.)

Summons (sŏ·mənz), *v.* [f. prec. Cf. obs. F. *semonse*.]

1. *trans.* = SUMMON *v.* 1, 2, 4, 5, 6. Now *rare.*

†Summo·perous, *a. Obs. nonce-wd.* In 7 *suno-.* [f. L. *summopere* with the greatest labour + -OUS.] Highest, utmost.

†Summo·tion. *Obs.* [ad. mod.L. *summotio, -ōnem*, f. *summovēre* to remove, f. *sub-* SUB- 25 + *movēre* to MOVE.] Removal.

†Su·mmulary. *Obs. rare.* [ad. med.L. *summulārius*, f. *summula*, dim. of *summa* SUM *sb.*¹.]

1. = SUMMULIST.

2. A summary, compendium.

Summulist (sŏ·mjŭlist). [ad. mod.L. *summulista*, f. *summula*: see prec. and -IST.] A writer of a *summula* or small compendious treatise of science; an abridger. b. A commentator on the *Summulæ Logicales* of Petrus Hispanus (13th cent.).

Sump (sŏmp), *sb.* Also 4-5 *sompe*, 7 *sumpe*; 6-9 *sump(p)e* and dial. 7 *somp*; 7 *soomp*, *sump* of MD4, *somp*, *sumph*, Flem. *sompe* (WFris. *somp*); or ad. (in the mining sense) the related MHG., G. *sumpf* marsh, swamp; cf. SWAMP *sb.*.]

1. A marsh, swamp, morass; (now only) a dirty pool or puddle.

2. A pit or well for collecting water or other fluid; *spec.* a cesspool; a pool of filth which sea-water is collected for salt-making.

Summony, obs. form of SUMMON *v.*

Summy, obs. form of SUMMA.

Sump. Variant of SUMMONER, assimilated to prec.

Sumph (sŏmf), *sb.* [Echoic.] The sound of something heavy and limp falling.

Sumph, *sb.*² [Echoic.] A dolt; a stupid, spiritless person.

SUMPHION.

Sumph. *Obs. rare⁻⁰.* Altered form of **Symphan.**

Sumpit: see after Sump *sb.*

Sumpit (sŭ'mpit). [a. Malay *sumpit* (*sempit*), blowpipe, properly = narrow.] = Sumpitan; also *erron.* one of the darts blown from the sumpit.

Sumpitan (sŭ'mpitan). Forms: 7 sempitan, sampitan, 9 sumpitan, sumpitan. [a. Malay *sumpitan*, f. *sumpit* (see prec.): in Du. *sompitan.*]

A blow-gun made by the Malays from a hollowed cane, from which poisoned arrows are shot.

Sumpter (sŭ'mptəɹ), *sb. arch.* Forms: 4-7 sompter, 4, 8 somter, 5 sometour, 6 somter, 7 sompter. See also Sumpitan².

Sumpter, variants of Sumter.

Sumptuary (sŭ'mptiŭari), *a.* (*sb.*) Also 7 somptuarie. [ad. L. *sumptuāri-us*, f. *sumptus* expense: see -ary.] Pertaining to or regulating expenditure.

Sumptuous (sŭ'mptiŭəs), *a.* Also 5 sompttuous, 5-6 sumptuouse, 6 somptous, sumptuose, 7 sumtuous, 6-7 somptuous, sumtuous. [a. OF. *sumptueus,* sumptueux = Pr. sumptuos, It. sontuoso, ad. L. sumptuōsus, f. sumptus expense.]

Sumption (sŭ'mpʃən). Also 4 sumpcion. [a. L. sumptio, -ōnis, n. of action f. sumpt-, sūmĕre to take. Cf. OF. sumpcion, somption.]

Sumptuosity (sŭmptiŭɒ'siti). Also 5 sumptuosite. [ad. L. type *sumptuōsitās,* f. sumptuōsus Sumptuous. Cf. F. sumptuosité.]

Sumptuously, *adv.* [f. prec. + -ly²] In a sumptuous manner; at great cost, with great expenditure of money; with magnificence or pomp of living, equipment, decoration, entertainment, etc.

Sumptuousness. [Sumptuous + -ness.] The condition or quality of being sumptuous; costliness and magnificence of living, production, etc.

Sumpture. *Obs.* Altered form of Sumpter after *words in* -ure.

Sumpy (sŭ'mpi), *a.* dial. [Sumpi sb. + -y¹.] Boggy, swampy.

Sumy, variant of Summit.

Sum-total (sŭ'm-tou·tal). Also **sum totall, sum totalis.** [med.L. *summa tōtālis* see Sum *sb.*¹]

Sun (sŭn), *sb.* Forms: 1-7 sunne, (1 sunna), 4-9 sonne, 4-6 (9 dial.) sunn, 3 (9 chiefly dial.) sun, 6-8 soone, Sc. soun, sune, 5 soon, swne, Sc. sonne, Sc. soun, 5 soun, *etc.* [Com. Teut. wk. fem.: OE. sunne = OFris. sunne, sonne (WFris. sinne, MLG., LG. sunne), MDu. sonne (Du. zon), OHG. sunna (MHG. sunne, sun, mod. G. Sonne), ON. sunna (poet.), Goth. sunnō: also wk. masc. OE. sunna, = OFris. sonna, OS. sunno, OHG. sunno.]

Sun, v. [f. SUN sb. Cf. G. sonnen.]

1. trans. To place in or expose to the sun; to subject to the action of the sun's rays; to warm, dry, etc. in sunshine.

 b. To sun salmon: see SUNNING vbl. sb. 3.

2. refl. To expose oneself to or bask in the sun.

 3. intr. To shine as or like the sun. rare.

 b. intr. or pass.; also fig.

Sun-baked, a.
 1. Baked by exposure to the sun; as bricks, pottery, etc.
 2. Excessively heated by the sun; dried up, parched, or hardened by the heat of the sun.

Sunbeam (snˈbīm). [OE. sunn(b)ēam, also sunne bēam: see SUN sb. and BEAM sb.] The form sunnebeme was current until c 1430; sunbeame became frequent from c 1500 in modern texts.]
 1. A beam of sunlight.

Sunbird, sun-bird.
 1. = DANTER a 2 (Plotus anhinga).
 2. Any bird of the passerine family Nectariniidæ, which comprises small birds with brilliant and variegated plumage, found in tropical and subtropical regions of Africa, Asia, and Australia; also applied to similar birds of other families.

Sun-blink. Sc. [BLINK sb.] A gleam of sunshine. Also attrib.

Sun-bright, a. Chiefly poet. [OE. sunbeorht occurs in sense 2.]
 1. Bright as the sun; supremely bright.
 2. Used as a literal rendering of a native word applied to a radiant-coloured humming-bird.

Sunburn (snˈbॴn), sb. [f. SUNBURN v.] The condition of being sunburnt; discoloration of superficial inflammation of the skin caused by exposure to the sun's rays; the brown or tan thus produced.

Sunburn, v.
 1. trans. To burn, scorch, or discolour (usually the skin) by exposure to the sun; to affect with sunburn.

Sun-burning, vbl. sb.

Sunburnt, ppl. a.
 1. Discoloured, tanned, or superficially inflamed by exposure to sunshine; chiefly of the skin or complexion.

Sunday (snˈdi), sb. Forms: see below.

Sunday, variant of SUNDAY.

Sunday-school. A school in which instruction is given on Sunday; esp. such a school for children held in connection with a parish or congregation; such schools are now intended only for religious instruction, but originally instruction in secular subjects was also given.

Sunder (snˈdə), a. and adv. Forms: see below.

Sunder, v. [OE. sundrian, syndrian, Northumb. sundria, sundren, -rn, 3–5 sundre, 4–5 sondre, -ri, sonder, (sunder, sundar).]
 1. trans. To dissolve connexion between two or more persons or things; to separate or part one from another.
 2. To separate in thought, distinguish. Obs.
 3. To separate into two or more parts; to split, break up, cleave.
 4. To keep apart, separate by an intervening space or distance, from something. rare.
 5. To be torn, break, or split in pieces.

Sunderable, a.

Sunderer, one who sunders or severs.

Sundering, vbl. sb.

Sunderling, adv.

Sunderly, a.

Sun-dial.

Sunderlepes (Sunderlepe), a.

So Sundering (ppl. a.)

Sunderment.

Sunderness.

Sunderwise, adv.

Sundew (sundiu).

Sun-dried.

Sundown, sun-down.

Sun-dog.

Sunderly, adv.

Sundri (sundri).

Sundries.

Sundrily, a.

Sundry, a.

Sundriness.

Sundrop.

Sunlet (sunlet).

Sundry, adv.

Sun-fish.

Sunny-hazy.

Sundog.

Sunegild.

Sunen, obs.

Sunfall.

Sun-flower.

Sunga, sanga.

Sungar, sangar.

Sunflower.

Sungle.

Sunk (sǫŋk), a. and north. dial.

Sunk, ppl. a.

Sunken (sǫŋk'n), a.

Sunfoile, obs.

Sung (sǫŋ), ppl. a.

Sunga, obs.

Sun-gleam.

Sungod.

Sunglie.

Sunk, n. obs.

Sunlet (sunlet).

Sunlight (sunlait).

Sun-lighted, sun-lighted, ppl. a.

Sunket, north. dial.

Sunkie.

Sunkland.

Sunless, a.

Sunlit (sunlit), ppl. a.

Sunly, a.

Sunna.

Sunned.

Sunner.

Sunning.

Sunnite.

Sunni.

Sunnah.

Sunniness.

Sunnily.

Sunnud.

Sunnian.

Sunny.

Sunnyasee, sunyasi.

Sun-ray.

Sunrise.

Sunrising.

Sunset.

Sunshade.

Sunshine.

Sunshining.

Sunshiny.

Sun-spot.

Sunstead.

Sunstone.

Sunstricken.

Sunstroke.

Sun-struck.

Sunt.

Sunuol, -uolliche.

Sun-up, sunup.

Sunward.

Sunwards.

Sunway.

Sunways, sunwise.

Sup.

6-sup. [a. OF. *soper*, *super*, (also mod.F.) *souper* = Pr. *sopar*; of obscure origin.]

1. *intr.* To eat one's supper; to take supper.

Supars (sipə̄z). *n. pl. U.S.* Also S-9 *suppawn*, 9 *supon* (*suppone*), *sipawn*, *sepon*, -awn. [Native *suahpaun* softened, t. *saupan*; softened from Abenaki *nt͡sa͞ba͞m* (Rasles), *nsobon* (Laurent), Narragansett *nasaump* (see SAMP). Cf. Du. *aapaen*, *supaen* (17th c.).] A kind of porridge made of maize flour boiled in water until it thickens. Also *attrib.*

Supe (si̇up). *slang.* Short for SUPER *sb.*

† **Supellectious**, *a. Obs. rare⁻⁰.* [f. L. *supellectīlis*: see next, -IC, and -ABIOUS.]

Supellectile (si̇upelek'til), -*tily*, *a.* and *sb.* [ad. L. *supellectīlis*, prob. i. *super*, SUPER-] *+lectus* (see -ILE.)]

† **Supellective-rious**, *a. Obs. rare⁻⁰.* [f. L. *supellectīcārius*: see next, -IC, and -ABIOUS.]

Super (si̇u'pər), *sb.* [Short for various adjs. compounds in SUPER-. Short for various uses.]

1. = SUPERFICIAL 2. (Usually following the sb.)

2. = SUPERFINE 2.

Super (si̇u'pər), *v.*

† 1. † [Short for INSUPER.] Something 'standing in super'; a balance remaining over. *Obs.*

II. Short for various subst. compounds in SUPER-. Chiefly *colloq.*, *slang*, or *commercial*.

2. a. = SUPERSALT. b. = SUPERPHOSPHATE 2.

3. = SUPERNUMERARY. a. *Theatr.*

Supari (supā'rĭ). *East Indian.* Also 7-9 *supatee*, 9 *soopari*, etc. [Hindi *supārī* betel nut.] The areca palm; also, the areca leaf which is chewed with the leaves of the betel palm. Also *attrib.*

Supra-, combining form of L. *supra*. See SUPER- I. Over, above, at the top (of); on, upon.

II. Short for various subst. compounds in SUPER-.

Super-, prefix, repr. L. *super*, adv. and prep., above, over, beyond.

I. Over, above, at the top (of); on, upon.

1. Forming adjs. in which *super-* is prepositional relation to the sb.

a. Compounds of a general character (chiefly nonce-wds.) and miscellaneous scientific and technical terms.

Super-aerial, situated above the air or atmosphere. **Supra-aqueous**, situated above the surface of water. **Superacromial**, situated above the acromion.

Superintendent

Superfine

Superscrewing, watch-stealing.

Thieves' slang. A watch. *Comb.*

b. *Anat.* In same sense as b (varying with SUPRA-), as *supera xillary* (mod.L. *superaxillāris*), *superfoliāceus*; also in terms relating to the geographical distribution of plants, as *supra-arctic* (see SUPRA).

a. Compounds of a general character (chiefly nonce-wds.) and miscellaneous scientific and technical terms.

Superaerial

b. *Anat.* Forming adjs. (with *-ar* in adj. relation to the sb. or subst. phr. implied in the second element: cf. I b): (*a*) derivatives from sbs. in b, as *supramaxillary* (= pertaining to the upper jaw); (*b*) = situated in, or forming, the upper part of, e.g. *supraglenoid*, *-cerebellar*, *cerebral*, *-dural* (see from the cavernous.

b. *Anat.* Designating the upper of two parts or members; superior: e.g. *super-axilla* the upper maxilla or jaw (Dorland), *superfemoral*.

4. Prefixed to adjectives: = Above or beyond, more or higher than, above the range, scope, capacity, etc. of (what is denoted or expressed by the radical part), after *excel*. L. *superessentiālis* SUPER-ESSENTIAL, *supersubstantītuus* supermaterial: e.g. *supererogatic*, †*-icial* = more than angelic, beyond that of an angel), *-earthly*, †*-elementary* (see ELEMENTARY 2), *-intellectual*, *-organic*, *-regal*, *-secular*, *worldly*.

c. In recent (chiefly nonce) formations after SUPERMAN used to designate a person, animal, or thing which markedly surpasses all others, or the generality, of its class: e.g. *super-brute*, *-critic*, *-dramatist*, *-goddess*, *-race*, *-tramp*, *-woman*; **Super-Dreadnought**, an all-big-gun ship with no armament superior to that of the Dreadnought class.

b. *Mus.* Designating a note next above some principal note, as SUPERDOMINANT, SUPERTONIC.

c. *Nat. Hist.* In classification, denoting a group or division next higher than, or including a number of those denoted by the radical part; as *super-family*, *-order*, *-species*, *-suborder*. So **Super-molecule**, *Chem.*, a complex molecule formed by the combination of several different substances.

8. Before in time, prior to; as in SUPERLAPSARIAN (= SUPRALAPSARIAN = next above, usual as adj.), derived before the Creation.

9. a. Prefixed to adverbs, with relation to adjs.: Exceedingly, very high, extremely, supremely, extraordinarily; over-: as in late or mod.L. *supergloriōsus* (Vulgate) exceedingly glorious, *superfluously* very illustrious (see *Superillustrious* below), *superlaudābilis* (Vulgate) worthy to be praised; e.g. *superlative* (= highly active), *-ceremonious* (= highly ceremonious), *-dainty*, *-glorious*, *-ingenious*, *-sufficient*, *superabundantly*, *-gloriously*, *-curious*.

† **Superbenedict** [L. *benedictus* blessed], supremely blessed.

Superbi-, *-ty* (of high degree), **Superilluster-ious**

Superfidel, *-a*. believing too much. † **Superillustrious**, knowing title of certain kings and other exalted personages.

b. with nouns of action or condition, etc.: e.g. *supera dequately*, *artificially*, *-cathedrally*, *-diabolically*.

c. much of that great wits as *supercivilised*. 1661 GAUDEN ... (= actualized to excess), *-civilised*, *-elated*, *-excited*, *-faced* (FACED *ppl. a. 2.*), *-peopled* ...

b. With prepositional force, in mod.L. *superannitus*, † *super annō* beyond the year; as in *superannuate*, *-ation*, *-ated*.

7. Beyond in time, later; as in L. *supervīvere* to outlive, SUPERVIVE, SURVIVE; † **Superla'st** *v.* trans., to last beyond, outlast.

6. In geometry of more than three dimensions, designating a locus or figure having one more dimension than the simple word: e.g. *super-solid*, *-surface*.

III. In or to the highest or a very high degree; hence, in excess of what is usual, or of what ought to be; superabundant [L. *super-*].

9. a. Prefixed (with relation to adjs.): Exceedingly, very highly, extremely, supremely, extraordinarily, over-: as in late or mod.L.

Superfetation. ... **Superfluity** ...

Superable, a. [ad.L. *superābilis*.]

Superabound, v.

Superabundance, sb.

Superabundant, a.

Superabundantly, adv.

Superacid, a. and sb.

Superacute, a. and sb.

Superaddition, sb.

Superaltar, sb.

Superancy ...

Superannate, v.

Superannuate, v.

Superannuation, sb.

Superarrogation, sb.

Superation, sb.

Superate, v.

Superbiate, v.

Superbience ...

Superbient ...

Superbious ...

Superbifical ...

Superb, a.

Superbity ...

Superbly, adv.

Supercargo ...

Supercelestial, a.

than supercelestial, crabbed, and Seraphical. **1576** KNEWSTUB *Confut.* vii. (1579) 39 Hee hath ..ouerthrowen al H. N. his spirituall instructions, and supercelestiall [etc] interpretations.

†B. sb. A supercelestial being. *Obs. rare⁻¹.*

1604 BREWOOD *Treach.* viii. 73 This spirituall Pærs, which treateth on Supercelesticals, Celestials and Super-celestials.

†Supere·lical, a. *Obs. rare⁻¹.* [See SUPER-1 and CELICAL] Supercelestial.

1654 VILVAIN *Theorem. Theol.* i. 28 Mans Soul for excellence hath a far sublimer supercelical efficient.

Supereoncion, var. (now erron.) of SUPERSESSION.

Su·percharge, *rare.* [SUPER-3, 10.]

1. *Her.* A charge borne upon another charge.

1768 HENRY *Hist. Brit.* (1771) T viij b3o. **1910** EDMONDSON *Heraldry* II. Gloss., *Super-charge,* is a term that hath been applied by some to express any figure borne on another. ..N. B. This word, *Super-charge,* is now seldom or ever used, *surmounted* being a better term.

2. An excessive charge ; an overcharge.

1898 J. HUTCHINSON *Archiv. Surg.* IX. 95, I generally detect the *surcharge* in a super-charge.

Superchar·ged, *ppl. a.* [see prec.]

1. *Her.* Charged to excess ; overcharged.

1876 PAGE *Adv. Text-bk. Geol.* vii. 163 Shallow seas super-charged with saline matter. **1889** *Athenæum* 19 Oct. 499/1 The story is supercharged with the frolicsome spirit and delicate humour that [etc.]. **1909** *Q. Rev.* Oct. 469 Our supercharged imagination.

†Superchery (sū·pər-tshə·ri), *v.* In form *superchery* (see SUPER-). Also **6-chierie, 7-chiery, 7-8-cherie.** *[a., misread in* It. *supercheria* (var. *soverchiera*), f. *soverchiare* (mod.It. *soverchio*) superfluous, f. *super* over, above.]

1. An attack made upon one at a disadvantage ; (a piece of) foul play.

Geometry, the outside or exterior surface of any body. This is considered as of two dimensions, viz. length and breadth.

2. The surface of a body or object ; **— SUPERFICES 2.**

Superficialize, v.

Superficially, adv.

Superficiary, a. (sb.)

Superficies, sb.

Superfine, a.

Superfinely, adv.

Superfineness.

Superfluence.

Superfluent, a.

Superfluitance.

Superfluity, sb.

Superfluous, a.

Superfull, adv.

Superfluously, adv.

Superfluousness.

Superflux, sb.

Superfrontal, sb.

Superfuse, v.

Superfusion.

Superhuman, a.

Superheat, v.

Superheated, ppl. a.

Superhumanity.

Superhumanize, v.

Superhumanly, adv.

Superhumanness.

Superimperial, a.

Superimpose, v.

Superimposed, ppl. a.

Superimposition.

Superinduce, v.

Superinduce, ... v.

Superinduced, ppl. a.

Superinducement [-MENT.]

Superinduction, sb.

†Superinduct, v. Obs. [late L. superindūct-, ppl. stem of superindūcere.]

Superinduced ppl. a.

Superintend (siū·pərinte·nd), v. [ad. eccl. L. superintendĕre ... f. Super- 2 and Intend v.]

1. trans. To have or exercise the charge or direction (of operations or affairs); to look after, oversee, supervise the working or management (of an institution, etc.).

2. absol.

3. Law. Insertion of a word or letter in a document.

†Superinduce, v. Obs. rare⁻¹.

Superinfuse, v. Obs. [Super- 13.] trans. To infuse in addition.

Superinfusion.

Superinspect, v. Now rare or Obs.

Superintelligence.

Superinstitute, v. Now rare or Obs.

So Superinstitution, institution of a person to a benefice to which another is already instituted.

Superintendence. Also 6-7 -ance, 7-8 -ancy. [ad. med. L. superintendentia, f. superintendent-, super-intendēns: see -ence.]

1. The office or position of a superintendent; the function, authority, or right of superintending; the exercise of this function, superintendence; oversight, control, direction of, f. over (rare: that which is controlled), in reference to a definite business, institution, etc.

2. Eccl. a. Adopted as an etymological rendering of Gr. ἐπίσκοπος 'overseer' (see Bishop) of the N. T. ...

Superintendent (siū·pərinte·ndənt), sb. and a. Also 6-9 -ant. [ad. eccl. L. superintendēns, -ent, pr. ppl. of superintendĕre to Superintend. Cf. obs. F. superintendant (mod.F. surintendant), Sp., Pg. superintendente.]

A. sb. One who superintends.

1. An officer or official who has the chief charge, oversight, control, or direction of some business, institution, or works; an overseer. Const. of, † over.

†2. trans. To keep a watch upon. Obs. rare.

Superintendency. Also 6-7 -ance, 7-8 -ancy.

Superintendentship [-SHIP.] The office or position of a superintendent.

Superintender, rare. [f. Superintend v. + -ER1.]

Superintendress, a female superintendent.

Superior (siū·pī·ˈə̯r), a. and sb. Also 4-9 -iour, 6 -ioure, -your. [ad. OF. superior, -iour (mod.F. supérieur) ... a. L. superior, -ōrem, compar. of superus that is above, f. super above.]

1. Higher in local position; situated above or further up than something else; upper; † belonging to the upper regions, heavenly, celestial ... Now chiefly in technical use: see senses 9-13.

2. Higher in rank or dignity; more exalted in social or official status.

3. Superintendent-general [General a. 10], an officer exercising supreme control over a number of superintendents.

Superior (continued).

4. Logic. Having greater extension.

5. Higher in degree, amount, quality, importance, or other respect; of greater value or consideration.

6. Const. to († occas. with, than). a. Higher in status or quality than; hence, greater or better; 'formerly' also adv. — more or better than, above, beyond.

B. sb. **1.** A person of higher rank or dignity; one who is above another or others in social or official station; esp. a superior officer or official. (Commonly with possessive pronoun.)

2. In a positive or absolute sense (admitting comparison with more and most): Supereminent in degree, amount, or (most commonly) quality; surpassing the generality if its class or kind.

7. Printing. A superior letter or figure: see A. 12.

Superiorate, sb. rare⁻¹. [ad. med.L. superiorātus.] The position or rank of a superior.

Superioress (siū·pī·ˈə̯res). Also 6 Sc. -rise, + -ess. [f. Superior sb. + -ess.] A female superior; the head of a convent or order of nuns; a mother superior. Also superiors-general.

Superiority (siūpī·ˈo·rı̆tı̆). Also 6 Sc. -atie, superioritie. [a. OF. superiorité = It. superiorità, Sp. -idad, Pg. -idade; or ad. med.L. superioritās: see Superior and -ity.] The quality or condition of being superior.

Superiority, a. [f. Superior sb.]

2. Feudal Law. The position or right of the superior (see Superior B. 3) of an estate; the lordship of an estate.

Superiorship [-SHIP.] = Superiority, superiority. nonce⁻¹.

Superlapsarian, a. and sb. = Supra-lapsarian.

Superlation. Obs. rare⁻¹. [ad. L. superlātiō, -ōnem, n. of action f. superlātus: see next.] Exaggeration.

Superlative (siūpэ̄·ˈlɑ̄tı̆v), a. and sb. Also ... [ad. late L. superlātīvus, f. superlāt-, ppl. stem of superferre: see Super- 11 + late L. -ive.] A. adj.

1. Gram. Applied to that inflexional form of an adjective or adverb used, in comparing a number of objects, to express the highest degree of the quality or attribute denoted by the simple word.

2. Exaggerated, hyperbolical.

3. Raised above or surpassing all others; extremely high, great, or excellent; supereminent, supreme.

B. sb.

1. Gram. The superlative degree of comparison.

2. fig. That which is highest or supreme.

Superjacent, a. [ad. L. superjacēns, -ent, pr. ppl. of superjacēre: see Super- 7 and Jacent.] Lying above; overlying; superincumbent.

†Superjection. Obs. rare⁻¹. [ad. L. superjectiō, -ōnem, n. of action f. superjacĕre: see Super- 7 and Jacent.] Exaggeration, hyperbole.

Superlatively, adv.

Superlativeness.

Superleather.

Superlucration.

Superliminary.

Supernacular.

Supernaculum. [Formed as next, after *sub-lunar*.]

Superlunar, a.

Superlunary (sɪūpərlūˈnări), a. (sb.)

Superman (sɪūˈpərmæn).

Supermaterial.

Supermediocre.

Supermercial.

Supermundane, a.

Supernal, a.

Supernatant, a.

Supernatation.

Superne.

Supernacle.

Supernal, a. [SUPER- 4 a.]

Supernally, adv.

Supernatant, a. (sb.) [ad. L. *supernatant-*, *-ans*, pr. pple. of *supernatāre* : see next.]

Supernatation.

Supernatural, a. (sb.) [ad. med.L. *supernātūral-*, -is, f. L. *supernātūra* NATURE : see -AL.]

Supernaturalism.

Supernaturalist, sb. and a. [f. prec. + -IST.]

Superi.

Supernaculum.

Supernaturalize, v. [f. as prec. + -IZE.]

Supernaturally, adv. [f. as prec. + -LY[2].]

Supernaturalness.

Supernature.

Supernatural, a. [SUPER- 4 b.]

Super-

Supernumeral.

Supernumerary, a. and sb. [ad. late L. *supernumerārius* applied to soldiers added to a legion after it is complete, f. *super numerum* : see SUPER- 11 and NUMERAL. Cf. F. *surnuméraire*.]

Supero-, combining form of L. *superus*.

Superoccipital, a. and sb. Anat. and Zool.

Superordinal.

Superordinary.

Superordinate, a. (and sb.) [SUPER- 4 a.]

Superordinary.

Superordinate, v. trans.

Supero-external, a.

Superorganic.

Superovarian.

Superior.

Superterranean, a.

Superterrestrial, a.

Supero-internal, a.

Superous, a.

Superoxidize.

Supero-posterior.

Superparticular, a. (sb.) Arith. Obs.

Superpartient, a. (sb.) Arith. Obs.

Superperson.

Superphosphate.

Superphosphite.

Superphysical, a.

Superplant.

Superplus. Chiefly Sc. Obs.

Superposable (sɪūpərpōˈzăbl), a. [f. next + -ABLE.]

Superpose (sɪūpərpōˈz), v. [a. F. *superposer* = to POSE, after L. *superpositus*, *-pose* (see SUPERPOSITION).]

Superpolitic, a. Obs.

b. *Geom.* To transfer (one magnitude) ideally to the space occupied by another, esp. so as to show that they coincide.

Superpo´sit, *ppl. a.* [f. prec. + -ED¹.]

1. Placed above or upon something else, or (loosely, of two or more things) one above or upon another.

Superpo´sition (sɪ̄ūpərpɒzɪʃən). [ad. F. *superposition,* or late L. *superpositiōn-em,* n. of action f. *superpōnĕre,* f. *super-* SUPER- 2, 13 + *pōnĕre* to place (see POSITION).] The action of superposing or condition of being superposed.

Superra´tional, *a.* [SUPER- 4.] That is above, or beyond the scope of, reason; higher than what is rational. So **Superra´tionally** *adv.*

Super-ro´yal, *a.* [SUPER- 4.]

1. That is above royal or kingly rank; higher than royal. *rare.*

Superscribe (sɪ̄ūpərskrəiˈb), *v.* [ad. L. *superscrībĕre,* f. *super-* SUPER- 2 + *scrībĕre* to write. Cf. It. *soprascrivere,* Sp. *sobrescribir,* Pg. *sobrescrever.*]

1. *trans.* To inscribe or mark *with* writing on the surface or upper part; to write upon; to put an inscription on or over.

Supersa´liency, *rare.* [f. SUPER- 2 + SALIENCY.]

Supersa´turate, *v.* [SUPER- 2.]

Supersa´turation. [SUPERSATURATE + -TION.]

Superscri´ption (-skrɪ̄pˈʃən). [f. L. *superscrīpt-,* ppl. stem of *superscrībĕre,* see prec. and cf. SCRIPT.]

b. with the document as obj. (also with compl.)

Superscri´pt, *a.* and *sb.* [f. late L. *superscrīptus,* pa. pple. of *superscrībĕre:* see prec. and cf. SCRIPT.]

Superscribed (sɪ̄ūpərskrəiˈbd), *ppl. a.* [f. SUPERSCRIBE *v.* + -ED¹.]

Supersede (sɪ̄ūpərsɪ̄ˈd), *v.* [ad. L. *supersedēre* to sit above, preside over, refrain from, f. *super-* SUPER- 1 + *sedēre* to sit.]

Superse´dable, *a.* [f. prec. + -ABLE.] That may be superseded.

Superse´deal.

Superse´dence (sɪ̄ūpərsɪ̄ˈdəns).

Superse´deas.

Supersede, *v.* (cont.)

Supersede´able.

Supersedere (-sɪ̄dɪ̄ˈrɪ). *Sc. Law.* Also **s -cedere.** [f. SUPERSEDE *v.*]

Superse´ding, *vbl. sb.* [f. SUPERSEDE *v.* + -ING¹.] The action of the verb SUPERSEDE.

Superse´nsual, *a.*

Supersede´ment. *Sc. Obs. rare.* [f. SUPERSEDE + -MENT, after med.L. *supersedimentum.*]

Superse´der (-sɪ̄dərˈ). [f. SUPERSEDE *v.* + -ER¹.]

Supersedure (sɪ̄ūpərsɪ̄ˈdjūr). *Sc. Law.* Also **8 -cedere.**

Supersemina´tion. *Obs.* [ad. late L. *superseminātion-em,* n. of action f. *superseminā-re.*]

Superse´minator, *rare.* [SUPER- 4.]

Superse´nsible, *a.* [SUPER- 4 2.]

Supersensibi´lity, *rare.* [SUPER- 10.]

Supersensual.

Supersensua´lity.

Supersensua´lism.

Supersensua´lity, *rare.* [f. next + -ITY.]

Supersensuous, *a.* [SUPER- 4 a.]

Superservice´able, *a.* [SUPER- 9 a.]

Supersensitive.

Supersessor.

Supersession (sɪ̄ūpərseʃˈən). [ad. med.L. *supersession- (cessio),* -ōnem, n. of action f. *supersēdēre, supersedēre* to SUPERSEDE.]

Supersolid.

Supersessive.

Superspend, *v.* *Sc. Obs.* Variant of SUPER-EXPEND.

Superstita´tion.

† Supersti´tious, *a.* [f. L. *superstitiōs-us,* f. *superstitiōn-em* SUPERSTITION: see -OUS.]

Supersti´tion (sɪ̄ūpərstɪʃˈən). [ad. L. *superstitiōn-em,* n. of action f. *superstāre* to stand over or upon.]

Superstition.

Superstitious (sɪ̄ūpərstɪʃˈəs), *a.* Also 4-7 **-cious,** 5 -cyous, 5-6 -cious, 6 -tyous, -cyous, -tious, -stious, Sc. -stius. [a. OF. *supersticios, -cieus,* F. *superstitieux,* or ad. L. *superstitiōs-us:* see SUPERSTITION and -OUS.]

1. Of the nature of, involving, or characterized

ellis be takith awey the newe supplement [*glos* or pacche; Vulg. *supplementum*], and a more brekynge is maad. 1398 TREVISA *Barth. De P. R.* VIII. xxi. (Bodl. MS.) lf. 85 b/2 But þeiȝe sterres haue liȝte of here owne. Ȝitte to perfeccioun of here liȝt þei fongeth supplemente [1495 supplyment; orig. *complementum*] and help of þe sonne. 1544 *St. Papers Hen. VIII*, I. 764 The Lord Chauncelour..shall..admit and swere..Mr. Cox to be his Aulmoner,..and Mr. Cheke as a suppliment to Mr. Cox. 1594 HOOKER *Eccl. Pol.* III. viii. § 10 Vnto the word of God..we do not add reason as a supplement of any maime or defect therin. 1628 FELTHAM *Resolves* II. [I.] xxxvii. 114 Minerva cur'd Vlysses of his wrinkles and baldnesse; not that she tooke them away by supplements. 1664 H. MORE *Myst. Iniq.* 94 God would have afterwards raised other persons of Apostolical purity.. to have made a Supplement to the former. 1698 FRYER *Acc. E. India & P.* 250 Fording the River without such a Suppliment [as a bridge]. 1728 YOUNG *Love Fame* I. 12 Instructive Satire,..Thou shining supplement of public laws! 1856 J. RICHARDSON *Recoll.* I. vi. 142 As supplements to this bowl, small cups, brimming with milk punch were placed upon the table. 1861 PALEY *Æschylus* (ed. 2) *Supplices* 154 *note*, Hermann's supplement σάε completes the anapaestic verse. 1893 G. H. PEMBER *Earth's Earliest Ages* 67 How wonderful a supplement may, in the World to Come, be added to our present scanty information.

b. A part added to complete a literary work or any written account or document; *spec.* a part of a periodical publication issued as an addition to the regular numbers and containing some special item or items.

1568 GRAFTON *Chron.* I. 3 As Iames Philip of Bergamo sayth, in the suppliment of his Chronicles. 1576 FLEMING tr. *Caius' Dogs* (1880) 44 The winding vp of this worke, called the Supplement. 1650 ROW (*title*) A Supplement of the Historie of the Kirk of Scotland. 1683 WOOD *Life* (O.H.S.) III. 35 He died Sunday 21 Jan. (20 Jan., saith the suppliment to his will). 1696 RAY in *Lett. Lit. Men* (Camden) 202 To speed the finishing and fitting my Supplement for the Presse. 1779 JOHNSON *L. P.*, *Cowley* Wks. 1787 II. 22 His work, to which my narration can be considered only as a slender supplement. 1863 LYELL *Antiq. Man* i. 5 In my 'Elements or Manual of Elementary Geology' and in the Supplement to the fifth edition of the same. 1868 FREEMAN *Norm. Conq.* II. App. 577, I accept his account..as a supplement, to the account in the Chronicles. 1887 (Nov. 5) Special Literary Supplement to The Spectator.

c. *Math.* (*a*) † *Supplements of a parallelogram* = *complements of a parallelogram* (COMPLEMENT *sb.* 5 b). *Obs.* (*b*) *Supplement of an arc* or *angle*, the amount by which an arc is less than a semicircle, or an angle less than two right angles; also *attrib.*, as *supplement-chord*. (*c*) An additional term introduced in certain cases in an equation or expression (abbreviated *Supp.*).

1570 BILLINGSLEY *Euclid* I. Theorem xxxii. 53 In euery parallelograme, the supplementes of those parallelogrammes which are about the diameter, are equall the one to the other. *Ibid.* Prop. xliii. 53 b, Supplementes or Complementes are those figures which with the two parallelogrammes accomplish the whole parallelogramme. 1704 J. HARRIS *Lex. Techn.* I, *Supplement* of an Ark, in Geometry or Trigonometry. 1747 T. SIMPSON *Elem. Plane Geom.* 138 If the Measure of the Supplement-chord of any Arch be increased by the Number 2, the Square-root of the Sum will be the Supplement-chord of half that Arch. 1801 *Encycl. Brit.* (ed. 3) Suppl. II. 630/2 The supplement of 50° is 130°; as the complement of it is 40°. 1842 GWILT *Archit.* § 1038 ADE being a semicircle, BDE is the supplement of the arc AB, which arc, reciprocally, is the supplement of BDE. 1861 FERRERS *Trilinear Co-ordinates* vi. 112 The angle between the asymptotes of the reciprocal hyperbola will be the supplement of that between the tangents. 1868 CAYLEY *Math. Papers* (1893) VI. 263, I introduce into the equation a term called the 'Supplement' (denoted by the abbreviation 'Supp.')...The expression of the Supplement should in every case be furnished by the theory. 1884 tr. *Lotze's Logic* 278, *k.f*²*x.dk*..is the general term of this second series, and is what we must add as supplement to the general term of the first series.

†**2.** The action of supplying what is wanting; the making good *of* a deficiency or shortcoming.

1483 CAXTON *Gold. Leg.* 345/1 The feeste of all the saynttes was establysshed..Fyrste for the dedycacion of the Temple secondly for supplement of offences done. 1523 SKELTON *Garl. Laurel* 415 *Mayster Chaucer to Skelton*...Your besy delygence Of that we [*sc.* Chaucer, Gower, and Lydgate] beganne in the supplement. 1575 in *Reg. Mag. Sig. Scot.* 1585. 261/1 Our said kirk..haveand neid and mister of beitment and supplement. 1586 A. DAY *Eng. Secretorie* II. (1625) 76 For better supplement of the learners knowledge. 1592 *Reg. Privy Council Scot.* IV. 611 Ane new gift of the saidis landis grantit with all dew solempniteis and with supplement of all faultis. 1610 DONNE *Pseudo-martyr* 21 Councels submitted their decrees to the Emperours for Authoritie, and supplement of defects. 1660 R. COKE *Power & Subj.* 135 Equity is..either a remission or moderation of the laws..or ..a supplement of the law in cases wherein things in conscience ought to be done.

b. Sc. Law. *Letters* (or *writ*) *of supplement*, a writ issuing from the Court of Session to compel the appearance before an inferior court of a person who resides out of its jurisdiction. *Oath in supplement*, an oath of a party on his own behalf, admitted to confirm imperfect evidence, such as the oath of a single witness, so as to constitute sufficient legal proof: cf. *suppletory oath* s.v. SUPPLETORY *a.* b.

1672 in G. J. Bell *Comm. Laws Scot.* (ed. 5) I. 331 *note*, The count-book, with the merchant's oath in supplement, was sufficient to make it a full probation. 1693 STAIR *Inst. Law Scot.* (ed. 2) IV. xlv. § 17. 710 Whosoever is cited by a Messenger, to Compear and Depone by an Oath of Calumny, Verity or Supplement, if he do not Depone, he is holden as Confest. 1765-8 ERSKINE *Inst. Law Scot.* I. ii. § 17 The pursuer must apply to the court of session..for letters of supplement..containing a warrant to cite the defender to appear before the judge of the territory where the controverted subject lies. 1826 G. J. BELL *Comm. Laws Scot.* (ed. 5) II. 66 *note*, If the original creditor do not live within the jurisdiction in which the arrestee resides,..he must be summoned by a writ of supplement from the Court of Session. 1838 W. BELL *Dict. Law Scot.* 378 s.v. *Evidence*, The oath in supplement is admitted to supply deficiences in legal evidence, where the party whose oath is allowed has brought what is called a *semiplena probatio*.

†**3.** The reinforcement *of* troops; chiefly *concr.* (*sing.* and *pl.*), reinforcement(s). *Obs.*

a 1548 HALL *Chron.*, *Hen. VI*, 137 Twoo M. archers, and foure hundred speres, was sente into Gascoyne, as a suppliment to the countrey. 1549 *Acts Privy Council* (1890) II. 273, xvj Albanoys horsmen, to him allotted for the suplement of his band. 1600 HOLLAND *Livy* XLII. x. 1121 The Pretors also, who required to have a supplement with them into Spain. 1665 MANLEY *Grotius' Low C. Warrs* 421 Souldiers both of Horse and Foot were..drawn together..as a Supplement to the old exhausted Militia.

†**4.** The action of supplying or providing; that which is supplied; supply, provision. *Obs.*

1544 *St. Papers Hen. VIII*, I. 766 We see manifest occasion of moche greatter charge, then was att the begynnyng consideryd;..and..as We cannot use any other present meanes, for the supplement hereof, thenne [etc.]. 1545 *Ibid.* III. 519 Supposing that they have of His Majestie sufficient supplyment for ther furnyture. *Ibid.* 543 We coulde have no supplement of caske for their victualles, but suche as we had from..Waterforde. 1588 PARKE tr. *Mendoza's Hist. China* 77 Generall purueier and president of the counsell of warre: whose office is..for the suppliment of garrisons. 1615 CHAPMAN *Odyss.* IX. 242 We had not spent Our ruddie wine aship-boord: supplement Of large sort, each man to his vessell drew. 1658 OSBORN *K. James* Wks. (1673) 494 The People, if they denied him supplement or inquired after the disposure of it, were presumptuous peepers into the sacred Ark of the State.

† **Supplement**, *sb.*² *Obs. rare*⁻¹. [f. SUPPLE *v.* + -MENT.] Suppleness.

1583 STUBBES *Anat. Abus.* I. 54 It [*sc.* whoredom]..consumeth the moysture and supplement of the bodie.

Supplement, var. SUPPLIMENT.

Supplement (sʊ·plĭment, sʊplĭme·nt), *v.* (First in Sc. writers.) [f. SUPPLEMENT *sb.*¹] *trans.* To furnish a supplement to, supply the deficiency in; also, to supply (a deficiency).

In recent story-writing, to add as a supplementary statement or remark.

1829 JAS. MILL *Hum. Mind* (1869) II. 62 Clusters of sensations, supplemented by possibilities of sensation. 1833 CHALMERS *Power of God* I. vi. (1834) I. 224 The strong appetite of hunger supplements the deficiency of the rational principle of self-preservation. 1857 J. W. DONALDSON *Chr. Orthod.* Introd. p. viii, This work is a continuous essay, supplemented by a number of special disquisitions on certain important subjects. 1863 GLADSTONE *Financ. Statem.* 442 The spiritual food is to be supplemented, as Scotchmen say, by something which finds a shorter way to their perceptions and their appetites. 1868 G. DUFF *Pol. Surv.* 23 The two sets of dissimilar conditions supplement and throw light upon each other. 1875 ROSSETTI *Hood's Poet. Wks.* Ser. II. Pref. p. xv, It is now thought desirable to supplement that by a second volume. 1878 MISS BRADDON *Open Verdict* i, If I am a poor creature as a parson, you supplement me so well, Selina, that, between us, I think we do our duty to the parish. 1888 'J. S. WINTER' *Bootle's Childr.* xi, 'Yes, a disparity,' answered Maud..'It means age!' 'And not less than twenty years,' supplemented Pearl.

Hence **Supplemented** *ppl. a.*, **Supplementing** *vbl. sb.* and *ppl. a.*

1865 W. KAY *Crisis Hupfeldiana* 80 Their cancellings, supplementings, and arbitrary assumptions. 1901 *Westm. Gaz.* 30 Nov. 2/1 'You love the garden?' she hazarded.. 'And everything in it,' was his supplemented answer. 1904 R. SMALL *Hist. Congreg. U. P. Ch.* I. 529 A winding-up was insisted on by the Supplementing Board.

Supplemental (sʊplĭme·ntăl), *a.* (*sb.*) Also 7–8 **suppli-**. [f. SUPPLEMENT *sb.*¹ + -AL.] = SUPPLEMENTARY. Const. *to*, *of*.

Supplemental air, the air that remains in the lungs after an ordinary expiration: cf. quot. 1855 s. v. SUPPLEMENTARY *a.* b.

1605 BACON *Adv. Learn.* II. ii. § 7 Wee speake nowe of parts of Learning supplementall, and not of supererogation. 1629 GAULE *Holy Madn.* 134 Womens Supplimentall Art, does but the rather bewray Natures Defects. 1668 HALE *Pref. to Rolle's Abridgm.* c j b, An Appendix was intended that might have been supplemental of some Titles. 1768 BLACKSTONE *Comm.* III. xxvii. 448 If new matter arises, which did not exist before, he [*sc.* the plaintiff] must set it forth by a supplemental bill. 1795 MASON *Ch. Mus.* II. 153 All those supplemental graces which really serve to assist musical expression. 1866 LIDDON *Bampton Lect.* v. (1875) 220 Viewed in its historical relation to the first three Gospels it is supplemental to them. 1866 HUXLEY *Physiol.* iv. (1869) 104 About as much more in addition to this remains in the chest after an ordinary expiration, and is called *Supplemental air*. 1872 T. BRYANT *Pract. Surg.* (1878) I. 563 Supplemental teeth are occasionally developed in both temporary and permanent sets.

b. *Math.*

Supplemental angle, either (in relation to the other) of two angles which are together equal to two right angles. *Supplemental arc*, either of two arcs which are together equal to a semicircle. *Supplemental chord*, the chord of a supplemental arc. *Supplemental triangle*, either (in relation to the other) of two spherical triangles in which the angular points of the one are the poles of the sides of the other, and each side of the one is the supplement of the corresponding angle of the other.

1796 HUTTON *Course Math.* (1827) I. 315 Let C and D be two angles..standing on the supplemental arc AEB; then will the angle C be equal to the angle D. 1827 AIRY *Trigon.* in *Encycl. Metrop.* (1845) I. 683 Suppose great circles EF, FD, DE..to be described, of which A, B, C are respectively the poles; they will intersect in the points D, E, F, and form a spherical triangle, called the polar or supplemental triangle. 1840 LARDNER *Geom.* vii. 78 If a quadrilateral figure be inscribed in a circle, its opposite angles will be supplemental. 1842 *Penny Cycl.* XXIII. 300/1 Chords or arcs of a circle or other curve which have a common extremity, and together subtend an angle of two right angles at the centre, are sometimes called supplemental chords or arcs.

c. *sb.* A supplementary fact, etc. *rare.*

1670 BLOUNT *Law Dict.* Pref. (1691) (a) ij, In the Supplementals, Bracton, Britton,..and divers other Authors have been my Guides. 1836 SOUTHEY *Lett.* (1856) IV. 454 There are three works which I shall want for our supplementals. 1852 DE MORGAN in Graves *Life Sir W. R. Hamilton* (1889) III. 344 You do not see how I get my supplementals.

Hence **Suppleme·ntally** *adv.*, by way of supplement.

1768 *Woman of Honor* III. 254 Clara, in her turn, or supplementally for her sister, would bless me with her company. 1853 G. S. FABER *Downfall Turkey* 77 The cities of the Medes are only subjoined supplementally.

Supplementary (sʊplĭme·ntări), *a.* (*sb.*) [f. SUPPLEMENT *sb.*¹ + -ARY ¹. Cf. F. *supplémentaire*.] Of the nature of, forming, or serving as, a supplement. Const. *to*.

1667 *Decay Chr. Piety* xviii. 399 Divinity would not then pass the Yard and Loom,..nor Preaching be taken in as an easier supplementary Trade, by those that disliked the pains of their own. 1770 PENNANT *Brit. Zool.* IV. Ded. p. iv, To you therefore I address this little supplementary work. 1793 BEDDOES *Lett. Darwin* 9 These I shall from time to time submit..as supplementary to the knowledge accumulated by former experience. 1823 LAMB *Elia* Ser. II. *Old China*, Competence to age is supplementary youth. 1855 MACAULAY *Hist. Eng.* xiii. III. 287 To this Claim..was added a supplementary paper containing a list of grievances. *a* 1862 BUCKLE *Civiliz.* (1864) II. vi. 437 Each is supplementary to the other; so that in order to understand either, it is necessary to study both. 1908 *Athenæum* 15 Aug. 182/2 A supplementary volume of whose memoirs was published a few years ago.

b. In various technical uses.

1796 *Act 37 Geo. III*, c. 3 § 2 If a sufficient Number of Officers..cannot be found to accept of Commissions in the Supplementary Militia..it shall be lawful for the said Lieutenants..to appoint for that Service, such a Number of the Officers in the Army..as his Majesty shall approve. 1826 G. J. BELL *Comm. Laws Scot.* (ed. 5) II. 214 Of Supplementary Deeds or Acts.—These are certain acts and steps of conveyancing necessary for supplying the links of a defective conveyance. *Ibid.* 409 Of the method of affecting the acquisitions of the bankrupt subsequent to sequestration... The best method..is, that the trustee..shall apply to the Court for a supplementary sequestration. 1838 W. BELL *Dict. Law Scot.* s.v., When all the parties interested have not been called, or where the original summons requires amendment, and the defender has not appeared, a supplementary or auxiliary summons is necessary. 1842 *Penny Cycl.* XXII. 343/2 The supplementary triangle. [Cf. SUPPLEMENTAL b.] 1848 CAYLEY *Math. Papers* I. 362 The supplementary cone (i.e. the cone generated by lines through the vertex at right angles to the tangent planes of the cone in question). 1855 DUNGLISON *Med. Lex.* (1857) s. v. *Respiration*, The supplementary or reserve air or that which can be expelled by a forcible expiration, after an ordinary outbreathing. 1875 KNIGHT *Dict. Mech.* 2455/1 *Supplementary Engine*, an auxiliary steam-engine, for feeding the boiler when the main engine is at rest. 1891 F. TAYLOR *Man. Pract. Med.* (ed. 2) 347 Increased vesicular murmur happens..over one lung or part of a lung, when another part of the lung is not properly in use. It is then called compensatory or supplementary breathing.

c. *sb.* A supplementary person or thing.

In recent parliamentary use, a question supplementary to that put down on the question-paper.

1812 SOUTHEY in *Edinb. Ann. Reg.* III. I. 485/2 Supplementary deputies were then to be chosen, who were to take their seats in case of any vacancy by death; the supplementaries were, as nearly as could be, in the proportion of one to three. 1879 *Scribner's Monthly* Dec. 304 The prayers ..are simply preliminaries and supplementaries to the sermon. 1902 ALICE TERTON *Lights & Shadows in Hosp.* i. 3, I was called a 'supplementary', which was a dignified title for a charwoman. 1904 *Westm. Gaz.* 16 May 1/2 Lord Cranborne..did not altogether ignore supplementaries, but he came one or two bad croppers over them.

Hence **Suppleme·ntarily** *adv.*, by way of supplement.

1862 F. HALL *Hindu Philos. Syst.* 205 To indicate, supplementarily, the object denied. 1899 *Pop. Sci. Monthly* Sept. 677 Those we propose to tax supplementarily are mostly wealthy.

Supplementation (sʊplĭmentē¹·ʃən). [f. SUPPLEMENT *v.* + -ATION.] The action of supplementing; also, an instance of this, a supplementary addition.

1854 FERRIER *Inst. Metaph.* 430 To redeem from contradiction a centreless circle or a stick with only one end, two supplementations are required. 1873 A. W. WARD tr. *Curtius' Hist. Greece* I. II. i. 218 The war had made great gaps in the military body itself, and it was in the interest of the state to fill these up...This supplementation miscarried. 1903 G. E. UNDERHILL in *Eng. Hist. Rev.* Oct. 736 The shortest supplementation [of lines in a fragmentary papyrus] is always the most probable.

Supplementer (see the vb.). Also -or. [f. SUPPLEMENT *v.* + -ER¹.] One who supplements.

1644 FEATLY *Roma Ruens* 12 The author and supplementer of Catalogus testium veritatis. 1697 DRYDEN *Virgil*, *Life* **j b, Franshemius, the Learn'd Supplementor of Livy, has inserted this Relation into his History. 1869 BONAR *Life J. Milne* xix. 409 Not one minister out of a thousand would have borne such supplementing, however needful, or would have so cordially thanked the supplementer. 1873

G. W. KITCHIN *Hist. France* I. III. x. 380 'Which thing', says the Supplementor to William of Nangis, 'came not to pass'. 1906 ORR *Probl. O. T.* x. 344 So long as the Jehovist was regarded as a mere supplementer of the Elohist.

Suppleness (sʊ·p'lnės). [f. SUPPLE *a.* + -NESS.] The quality or condition of being supple.

1. Flexibility and elasticity: sometimes with implication of nimbleness of movement (cf. 2).

1626 BACON *Sylva* § 610 The Supplenesse and Gentlenesse of the Iuyce of that Plant, being that which maketh the Boughes also so Flexible. 1707 *Curios. Husb. & Gard.* 69 There is no part..in which the Subtility and Suppleness of the Sap more claim our Admiration, than in Trees that are grafted. 1782 SIR J. REYNOLDS *Disc.* xi. (1876) 29 That suppleness which is the characteristic of flesh. 1791 HAMILTON *Berthollet's Dyeing* I. I. ii. 134 By scouring, silk acquires its suppleness and whiteness. 1858 O. W. HOLMES *Aut. Breakf.-t.* ix. (1883) 186 Hair like the fibrous covering of a cocoa-nut in..suppleness as well as color. 1858 CARLYLE *Fredk. Gt.* v. ii. (1872) II. 68 You have beaten Louis XIV. to the suppleness of washleather.

2. Of the body or limbs: Capability of bending easily.

1768 TUCKER *Lt. Nat.* I. II. xx. 47 Nature may have prepared one man for a dancer by giving him strength and suppleness in his joints. 1774 GOLDSM. *Nat. Hist.* (1776) VII. 165 Serpents..have the length and the suppleness of the eel. 1838 DICKENS *Nich. Nick.* xiii, Giving his right arm two or three flourishes to try its power and suppleness. 1893 ECCLES *Sciatica* 80 Elderly persons from whom feats of suppleness could not be expected.

3. Flexibility or adaptability of mind, character, etc.

1594 CAREW *Huarte's Exam. Wits* v. (1596) 62 Children ..through the great supplenesse of their braine, abound in memory. 1638 BAKER tr. *Balzac's Lett.* (vol. II.) 160 He hath both the substance and the suppleness which are necessary in dealing with the brains of that country. 1665 BOYLE *Occas. Refl.* (1848) 35 Bringing those that use to write their Thoughts to what may be call'd a certain Suppleness of Style. 1807 KNOX & JEBB *Corr.* (1834) I. 328 A certain suppleness in your mental powers, by virtue of which they will bend to all occasions and subjects, with an ease and readiness [etc.]. 1878 O. W. HOLMES *Motley* xxi. 187 As a diplomatist his great want is suppleness.

4. Yielding disposition or character, compliantness, complaisance. ? *Obs.* exc. as in b.

1629 DONNE *Serm. Whitsunday* (1640) 309 God findes a better disposition, and souplenesse, and maturity, and mellowing, to concurre with his motion in that man. 1671 WOODHEAD *St. Teresa* I. xxv. 172 There never remains any sweetness, or softness, or suppleness in the Soul; but she is, as it were, frighted. 1752 JOHNSON *Rambler* No. 189 ¶ 11 A governess, whom misfortunes had reduced to suppleness and humility.

b. Servile or obsequious compliance or complaisance.

c 1727 HARTE *Eulogius* 398 He smooth'd his voice to the Bizantine note, With courtly suppleness unfurl'd his face. 1838 LYTTON *Alice* III. i, Naturally dictatorial and presumptuous, his early suppleness to superiors was now exchanged for a self-willed pertinacity. 1855 PRESCOTT *Philip II*, I. ii. I. 13 He had none of the duplicity or of the suppleness which often marks the character of the courtier. 1879 FARRAR *St. Paul* (1883) 207 The ever-rising tide of Roman sensuality and Græco-Syrian suppleness.

Suppler (sʊ·plər). *rare.* [f. SUPPLE *v.* + -ER¹.] A person or thing that supples.

1620 SHELTON *Quix.* II. I. xiii. 78, I haue suppler [orig. *despegador*] hangs at the pummell of my horse, as good as touch.

† **Supplete**, *v.* *Obs. rare.* In 7 **suppleat**. [f. L. *supplēt-*, pa. ppl. stem of *supplēre*: see SUPPLY *v.*¹] *trans.* To supplement.

1664 EXTON *Maritime Dicæol.* I. iv. 20 Laws..which sprang from the Rhodes, suppleated out of several other titles in the body of the Civil Law.

† **Supple·tion**. *Obs. rare.* Also 4 **supplecioun**, 5 **-plecion, supplexion**. [a. OF. *sup(p)letion*, *suppletion*, ad. L. **supplētio*, *-ōnem*, f. *supplēre* SUPPLY *v.*¹] Supplementation, supplement.

a 1325 *MS. Rawl. B. 520* lf. 47 b, Ware fore diuerse supplecious of lawe ant newe forlokinges bihoues. 1483 CAXTON *Gold. Leg.* (1892) 33 The quinquagesme..is instituted for supplecion & fulfyllyng. *c* 1485 *Digby Myst.*, *Conversion of St. Paul* 359 The compyler here-of shuld translat veray so holy a story, but with fauorable correccyon of my fauorable masters of þer benygne supplexion.

Suppletive (sʊplī·tiv), *a. rare.* [ad. med.L. *suppletivus*, f. *supplēt-*: see SUPPLETE and -IVE. Cf. F. *suppletif*.] Having the attribute of supplying deficiencies.

1816–30 BENTHAM *Offic. Apt. Maximized, Extract Const. Code* 52 His functions will be exercised by a depute of his, as per Ch. viii. Prime Minister, § 4. Self-suppletive Function. 1862 F. HALL *Hindu Philos. Syst.* 53 Cognition is here denoted by the suppletive expression after 'will'.

So † **Supple·tively** *adv.*, so as to supply deficiencies.

1644 MAXWELL *Prerog. Chr. Kings* x. 104 This tenet, that a King hath his Soveraigne power, *communicativè*, not *privativè*, from the people, that he is so invested with it, that the people have it habitually, suppletively, and may resume it in some exigent cases. [Cf. 1660 BONDE *Scut. Reg.* 71 The people..still retaining the same [government] in the collective body, that is to say, in themselves *suppletive*.]

Suppletory (sʊ·plĭtəri), *a.* and *sb.* [ad. late L. *supplētōrius* (neut. sing. as sb. = supplement), f. *supplēt-*: see SUPPLETE and -ORY ².]

A. *adj.* Supplying a deficiency; supplementary. Const. *to*, *of*. † In first quot., expletive. Now *rare*.

1628 DONNE *Serm. Christmas Day* (1640) 52 Many men have..certaine suppletory phrases, which fall often upon their tongue, and..have certaine suppletory Oathes, with which they fill up their Discourse. 1656 BRAMHALL *Replic.* ix. 372 Let him that dare..say that it is a suppletorie Sacrifice, to supply the defects of the Sacrifice of the Cross. 1659 FULLER *App. Inj. Innoc.* I. 42 A Book..which..will be suppletory of all such defects. 1673 *Lady's Call.* I. i. § 7 As a suppletory ornament to the deckings of gold and pearl and costly aray. 1778 JOHNSON 15 Apr. in *Boswell*, His hope of salvation must be founded on..obedience; and where obedience has failed, then, as suppletory to it, repentance. 1802 PALEY *Nat. Theol.* xiv. § 1 This double or suppletory provision [of teeth]. 1818 CRUISE *Digest* (ed. 2) IV. 305 By suppletory or explanatory evidence. 1856 A. BUTLER *Hist. Anc. Philos.* I. 114 The genus 'pronoun' does not more truly classify the words in a language that are suppletory of nouns. 1874 STEPHEN *New Comm. Laws Eng.* v. viii. (ed. 7) III. 446 Equity..a..portion of our juridical system —distinct from and suppletory to the common law.

b. Law. *Suppletory oath*, an oath (given by a party in his own favour) admitted to supply a deficiency in legal evidence: cf. *oath in supplement* s.v. SUPPLEMENT *sb.*¹ 2 b.

1726 AYLIFFE *Parergon* [305] If I can only prove the Tenor thereof by one Witness, I shall not be admitted to the Suppletory Oath through a Defect of Evidence. 1768 BLACKSTONE *Comm.* III. xxiii. 369 Abroad..a man's own books of accounts..with the suppletory oath of the merchant, amount at all times to full proof. 1802–12 BENTHAM *Ration. Judic. Evid.* (1827) V. 563 The suppletory oath is admitted in default of other sufficient evidence.

† **B.** *sb.* A supplement. *Obs.*

1649 JER. TAYLOR *Gt. Exemp.* II. Disc. viii. § 20. 70 The rite of confirmation..is an admirable suppletory of an early Baptisme. 1672–5 COMBER *Comp. Temple* (1702) 475 A Suppletory for any particular omitted. 1698 NORRIS *Pract. Disc.* IV. 86 Force must be made use of as a Suppletory to the defects of Reason. 1707 — *Treat. Humility* iv. 162, I look upon grace as the suppletory of corrupt nature.

Hence † **Su·ppletorily** *adv.*, by way of, or as a, supplement.

1622 DONNE *Serm. Christmas Day* (1640) 4 This personall name of the Father (*It pleased the Father*) is but added suppletorily by our Translators, and is not in the Originall.

Supplexion, variant of SUPPLETION *Obs.*

† **Suppliable**, *a.*¹ *Obs. rare.* [f. SUPPLY *v.*³ + -ABLE.] Supple.

1599 A. M. tr. *Gabelhouer's Bk. Physicke* 114/2 He causeth the sayede Image to be overdeckede with an Oxehyde..& ..glueth on the sayede skinne a suppliable Dogges skinne.

Suppliable (sŏplai·ăb'l), *a.*² *rare.* Also **supplyable**. [f. SUPPLY *v.*¹ + -ABLE.] Capable of being supplied or supplemented.

1667 WATERHOUSE *Narr. Fire in London* 23 If suppliable elsewhere, yet with more charge. 1681 *Acts Parl. Scot.*, *Chas. II* (1820) VIII. 243/1 That all such writs..wherin the Writer & witnesses are not designed, shall be null, And are not supplyable by condescending upon the Writer. 1754 ERSKINE *Princ. Sc. Law* (1809) 11 Where statutes establish certain solemnities as requisite to deeds, such solemnities are not suppliable by equivalents.

Supplial (sŏplai·ăl). Now *rare* or *Obs.* [f. SUPPLY *v.*¹ + -AL.] The act of supplying.

1752 WARBURTON *Princ. Nat. & Rev. Relig.* iv. Wks. 1788 V. 58 For the supplial of our imaginary..wants. *a* 1779 — *Div. Legat.* IV. v. Wks. 1788 II. 560 To form the principal members of his demonstration with an unornamented brevity, and leave the supplial of the small connecting parts to his reader's sagacity. 1801 MASON *Suppl. Johnson's Dict.* Pref. p. iii, The supplial of omissions. 1819 G. S. FABER *Dispensations* (1823) I. 276 The..supplial of all the wants of life.

b. A thing that supplies the place of another.

1837 C. RICHARDSON *Dict.* Pref. iii, It may be deemed a supplial of many books.

Suppliance¹ (sŏplai·ăns). Now *rare.* [f. SUPPLY *v.*¹ + -ANCE; cf. SUPPLIANT *a.*²] = SUPPLY *sb.*

1598 CHAPMAN *Iliad* IV. [VIII.] 321 When he..lookt vp for helpe to heauen, Which euer at command of Ioue, was by my suppliance geuen. 1604 SHAKS. *Ham.* I. iii. 9 (Qo.), A Violet in the youth of Primy Nature;..sweet not lasting The perfume and suppliance of a minute. 1664 POWER *Exper. Philos.* 118 In suppliance of that seeming Vacuity. 1786 ANNA SEWARD *Lett.* (1811) I. 160 To leave something to the suppliance of the heart and the fancy. 1845 TRENCH *Huls. Lect.* Ser. I. v. 95 What a man wins by his labour, be it inward truth, or only some outward suppliance of his need. 1884 BROWNING *Ferishtah, The Sun* 160 To lack is not to gain Our lack's suppliance.

Suppliance² (sʊ·pliăns). *rare. poet.* [f. SUPPLIANT *a.*¹: see -ANCE.] The action of a suppliant; supplication.

c 1611 CHAPMAN *Iliad* XVIII. 402 Mightie suppliance, By all their graue men hath bene made. 1615 — *Odyss.* VI. 211 If..He should..trie with words of grace, In humblest suppliance, if he might..gaine Her grace. 1773 J. ROSS *Fratricide* I. 4 (MS.) Smile on the suppliance of an humbler Bard. 1873 W. S. MAYO *Never Again* xii, The Kaiser smiled, then lifts his child From suppliance at his knee.

So **Su·ppliancy**, the condition of a suppliant.

1837 *Fraser's Mag.* XVI. 588 The living image of abject suppliancy!

Suppliant (sʊ·pliănt), *sb.* and *a.*¹ In mod. use *poet.* or *rhet.* Also 5 **-eant**, 5–6 **-iaunt**, 6–7 **-yant**. [a. F. *suppliant* (superseding older *so(u)pleiant*, *-oiant*), pr. pple. of *supplier* SUPPLY *v.*²

In early use sometimes stressed *supplia·nt*.]

A. *sb.* One who supplicates; a humble petitioner.

1429 *Rolls of Parlt.* IV. 346/2 The seide Suppliauntz doubten hem of damage and prejudice. 1480 *Cov. Leet Bk.* 429 Albe-it your pore suppleant to his gret coste & charge hath demaunded the contentacion therof, ȝit be in no wyse can be satisfied. 1549–62 STERNHOLD & H. *Ps.* XXVIII. ii, The voice of thy supplyant heare. 1555 EDEN *Decades* (Arb.) 125 The blessed virgin..with her redde loosed bandes of her suppliant. 1594 SHAKS. *Rich. III*, I. iv. Heard you not what an humble Suppliant Lord Hastings was, for her deliuery? 1667 MILTON *P. L.* X. 917 Thy suppliant I beg, and clasp thy knees. 1738 WESLEY *Ps.* God of my Righteousness Thy humble Suppliant ... 1814 BYRON *Ode Napoleon* v, The Arbiter of others' fate A Suppliant for his own! 1848 LYTTON *Harold* VIII. iii, ... mother is a suppliant to the son for the son.

Comb. 1669 DRYDEN *Tyr. Love* IV. i, She Suppliant-like, e're long, thy succour shall implore.

B. *adj.* Supplicating, humbly petitioning.

a 1586 SIDNEY *Arcadia* III. (1912) 418 One might see his eyes (humbly lifted up to the window where Philoclea stood) that he was rather suppliaunt, then victorious. 1591 SHAKS. *Two Gent.* III. i. 234 When she for thy repeale was suppliant. 1666 DRYDEN *Ann. Mirab.* ccl, The Rich grow suppliant, and the Poor grow proud. 1781 GIBBON *Decl. & F.* xxvii. (1787) III. 46 The tribunal of the magistrate was besieged by a suppliant crowd. 1818 SCOTT *Rob Roy* xi, I had..seen the followers of this man commit a cruel slaughter on an unarmed and suppliant individual. 1859 TENNYSON *Guinev.* 656 She look'd and saw The novice weeping, suppliant.

b. *transf.* Expressing or involving supplication.

1667 MILTON *P. L.* I. 112 To bow and sue for grace With suppliant knee. 1697 DRYDEN *Virg. Georg.* IV. 775 With Vows and suppliant Pray'rs. 1767 WILKES *Corr.* (1805) III. 193 Was it possible for me after this to write a suppliant letter to lord Chatham? 1800 WORDSW. *Hart-leap Well* II. 22 With suppliant gestures. 1870 BRYANT *Iliad* I. vi. 389 Stretched forth their suppliant hands To Pallas.

Hence **Su·ppliantness** (Bailey, vol. II. 1727).

† **Suppli·ant**, *a.*² *Obs. rare*⁻¹. [f. SUPPLY *v.*¹ + -ANT.] Supplying deficiencies; supplementary.

1611 SHAKS. *Cymb.* III. vii. 12 Those Legions..whereunto your leuie Must be suppliant.

† **Suppliant**, *a.*³ *Obs. rare*⁻¹. [f. SUPPLY *v.*³ + -ANT.] Suppling, emollient; = SUPPLE *a.* 7.

1631 R. H. *Arraignm. Whole Creature* xiii. § 2. 202, To thinke to heale a green wound with suppliant oyles, and yet the poysoned bullet stick still in the flesh.

Suppliantly (sʊ·pliăntli), *adv.* [f. SUPPLIANT *a.*¹ + -LY ².] In a suppliant manner, or as a suppliant; in the way of supplication; beseechingly.

1565 STAPLETON tr. *Bede's Hist. Ch. Eng.* 158 Entreating as suppliantly as I could to have licence to galloppe my horse ..with the other younge men. 1605 CAMDEN *Rem.* (1637) ... His brother John..came in..and suppliantly besought Richard, brotherly to pardon his..offences. 1750 *Student* I. 139 Can [he]..not prostrate himself..before the throne of grace, and suppliantly implore the divine mercy for his ..sins? 1842 G. S. FABER *Prov. Lett.* (1844) I. 230 Suppliantly invocating the saints. 1895 *Daily News* 10 May 6/3 Two hundred members of the House of Commons called at his private house..suppliantly to ascertain how they stood with him.

‖ **Supplica·mus**. *Obs. nonce-wd.* [L., = 'we supplicate', 1st pers. pl. pres. indic. of *supplicāre*: to SUPPLICATE: after legal terms such as *mandamus*, etc.] A petition, entreaty.

1574–5 G. HARVEY *Mercy Harvey* Wks. (Grosart) III. 89 Swearing that she should haue any thing he had at commaundiment, and vse him as familiarly..as her owne brother, with a many sutch goodly supplicamussis.

† **Su·pplicancy**. *Obs. rare*⁻¹. [f. next: see -ANCY.] Suppliant quality, beseechingness.

1728 GORDON *Tacitus*, *Ann.* XV. 408 The first letter..contain'd nothing of supplicancy or abasement.

Supplicant (sʊ·plĭkănt), *sb.* and *a.* Now rare exc. *arch.* Also 7 **suplicant**. [ad. L. *supplicantem*, *-ans*, pr. pple. of *supplicāre* to SUPPLICATE. Cf. It., Pg. *supplicante*, Sp. *suplicante*.]

A. *sb.* = SUPPLIANT *sb.*

1597 HOOKER *Eccl. Pol.* V. xxiv. § 1 The Prince and people of Nineueh assembling themselues as a maine army of supplicants. 1650 ROW *Hist. Kirk* Suppl. (Wodrow Soc.) 509 The supplicants [in 1638] gave in a Supplication to his Majestie's Commissioners for a free Generall Assemblie and Parliaments. 1693 tr. *Dupin's Hist. Eccl. Writers* II. 109 The Third Rank of Catechumens was, that of those who were present at the Prayers, who were called the *Supplicants* or the *Prostrati*. 1834 K. H. DIGBY *Mores Cath.* vi. 184 The pious supplicants, who repair to the church. 1873 BURTON *Hist. Scot.* VI. lxix. 161 The Supplicants treated the king's person with great reverence.

b. *spec.* One who supplicates for a degree: see SUPPLICATE *v.* 3.

1649 LAMONT *Diary* (Maitl. Club) 6 Ther was 12 [scholars] in euery colledge, and two supplicants laureat. 1901 RANDALL & RAIT *New College* 220 When a Fellow of New College takes any degree, his name is omitted from the list of supplicants.

B. *adj.* = SUPPLIANT *a.*¹

1597 SHAKS. *Lover's Compl.* 276 All these hearts that doe on mine depend,..supplicant their sighes to you extend. 1605 CAMDEN *Rem.*, *Epigr.* 16 One did write this supplicant Verse to the Emperour. 1705 BULL *Corrupt. Ch. Rome* III. 268 [They] offer'd to this Council their Letters supplicant, confessing that they had sinn'd. 1787 *Phil. Trans.* LXXVII. 259 Pricking up the ears when anxious,..depressing them when supplicant. 1807 J. BARLOW *Columb.* II. 338 A sovereign supplicant with lifted hands. 1834 K. H. DIGBY *Mores Cath.* v. iii. 85 The supplicant people.

Hence **Su·pplicantly** *adv.* = SUPPLIANTLY. 1864 in WEBSTER.

‖ **Supplicat** (sʊ·plĭkæt). Also 7–9 **-ate**. [L., = he supplicates, 3rd pers. sing. pres. ind. of *supplicāre* to SUPPLICATE. Formerly often assimilated in form to abstract nouns in -ATE ¹;—L. *-ātus* (cf. med.L. *supplicātus*).

In university use arising from its occurrence as the first word in the formula used by the proctor in presenting the petition. In quots. 1660 and 1859², perh. an independent formation in -ATE ¹.]

A supplication, petition; *spec.* (now only) in English universities, a formal petition for a degree or for incorporation (cf. SUPPLICANT b, SUPPLICATE *v.* 3, SUPPLICATION e).

1660 Z. CROFTON *Fastening of St. Peter's Fetters* 133 The servants query..was not a supplicate for an Authoritative Release; but a scrutiny into the Extent of the Oath. 1665 J. BUCK in Peacock *Stat. Cambr.* (1841) App. B. p. xc, There are no supplicats put up for King's College Fellows. 1691 WOOD *Ath. Oxon.* I. *Fasti* 637 This year was a Supplicate made in the venerable Congregation of Regents for one Tho. Dalby to be admitted to a Degree in Decrees. *Ibid.* 642 Supplicat. *Ibid.* 662 This year..there was a kind of a Supplicate made for one Magnus a Doctor beyond the Sea, to be incorporated here. 1715 M. DAVIES *Athen. Brit.* I. 23 This Supplicat being granted, he was..crown'd ..with a Wreath of Lawrel; that is, doctorated in the Arts of Grammar and Rhetorick. 1859 *Cambr. Univ. Cal.* 2 No degree is ever conferred without a Grace for that purpose. The Grace in this instance is termed a Supplicat. 1859 MASSON *Milton* I. vii. 678 The king has hitherto shown his displeasure by leaving the supplicates substantially unanswered. 1906 WELLS *Oxf. Degree Ceremony* 8 One of the Proctors reads out the *supplicat*.

Supplicate (sʊ·plĭkeᶦt), *v.* (Also 7 *pa. pple.* **-ate.**) [f. L. *supplicāt-*, pa. ppl. stem of *supplicāre*, f. *sup-* = SUB- 2 + *plic-*, root of *plicāre* to bend (cf. *supplex*, *supplic-* SUPPLE). Cf. SUPPLY *v.*²]

1. *intr.* To beg, pray, or entreat humbly; to present a humble petition. Const. *to* or *unto* a person (*obs.*), *for* a thing; also with dependent clause introduced by *that*, or inf.

1417 in Ellis *Orig. Lett.* Ser. II. I. 55 Wee..have supplicated unto him..to attend heare. 1625 BACON *Ess.*, *Friendship* (Arb.) 181 A Man cannot sometimes brooke to Supplicate or Beg. 1625 USSHER *Answ. Jesuit* 457 Doe we supplicate vnto these, because by these we supplicate vnto God? 1652 NEEDHAM tr. *Selden's Mare Cl.* 34 Giacomo Croato..was..assailed by an armed Bark of Pirates..and supplicate's that som order might bee taken therein. 1654 in *Verney Mem.* (1907) I. 556, I supplicate to non for there good word. *a* 1700 EVELYN *Diary* 23 Feb. 1645, Supplicating for a victory over the Turks. 1771 tr. *Horstius' Parad. Soul* App. 7 O holy Mary..supplicate for the devout Female Sex. 1791 MRS. RADCLIFFE *Rom. Forest* ix, I supplicated to know what was designed me. 1805 WORDSW. *Ode to Duty* v, I supplicate for thy control. 1862 R. VAUGHAN *Eng. Nonconformi.* 44 He urged..that the rubric should not supplicate that the bread and wine might become the body and blood of Christ to the recipient. 1864 TENNYSON *En. Ard.* 263 Annie..Besought him, supplicating, if he cared For her or his dear children, not to go. 1876 MISS BRADDON *J. Haggard's Dau.* II. 19, I have thought of you often..and have supplicated for you in my prayers.

2. *trans.* To petition humbly. **a.** with the person addressed as obj.; also with compl. clause or inf.

1643 *Decl. Lords & Comm. Gen. Assemb. Ch. Scot.* 11 The Assembly has humbly supplicate the Kings Majesty. *a* 1696 in Aubrey *Misc.* 165 They have supplicated the Presbyterie, who judicially appointed publick Prayers to be made. 1835 LYTTON *Rienzi* I. iv, To supplicate Clement VI to remove the Holy See from Avignon to Rome. 1864 TENNYSON *Boadicea* 9 Shall I brook to be supplicated?

b. with the thing sought as obj.

1660 R. COKE *Power & Subj.* 244 The Church..did supplicate protection from the temporall powers. 1779 *Mirror* No. 35 ¶ 3, The blessings which a fond father should supplicate from Heaven for his offspring. 1791 MRS. RADCLIFFE *Rom. Forest* vi, I supplicate of you a few moments' private discourse. 1838 JAS. GRANT *Sk. Lond.* 242 Supplicating a crust of bread for her famishing children. 1854 MISS M. S. CUMMINS *Lamplighter* xxiii, To supplicate Heaven's blessing upon them.

3. *spec. intr.* In Oxford University, to present a formal petition for a degree or for incorporation. † Also *trans.*, to present such a petition to (Congregation).

1691 WOOD *Ath. Oxon.* I. *Fasti* 638 Thom. Beaumont..did supplicate to be licensed to proceed in Divinity. *Ibid.* 639 John Newland..supplicated for a Degree in Divinity. *Ibid.* 642 James Denton..sometimes Fellow of Kings Coll. in Cambridg, did..supplicate to be incorporated. *Ibid.* 643 Richard Ede,..Scholar in Musick, did supplicate the ven. Congregation to be admitted Bachelaur of that Faculty. *Ibid.* 644 Eight [men] supplicated to oppose. 1830 *Oxf. Univ. Cal.* 16 In the sole instance of supplicating for Graces ..every Member of the House is invested..with a suspending negative upon each Grace for three times. 1891 *Ibid.* 76 No Graduate in any Faculty can supplicate for incorporation without..having obtained express permission from the Hebdomadal Council.

Hence **Su·pplicated** *ppl. a.*

1861 WARDLAW *Lect. Romans* (1869) I. ii. 26 Under the supplicated guidance of the Holy Spirit.

Supplicating (sʊ·plĭkeᶦtiŋ), *ppl. a.* [f. SUPPLICATE *v.* + -ING ².] That supplicates, or expresses supplication; humbly petitioning or entreating.

1649 MILTON *Eikon.* iv. Wks. 1851 III. 362 As for that supplicating People they did no hurt either to Law or Authority. 1726 SWIFT *Gulliver* III. i, I then put myself into the most supplicating postures, and spoke in the humblest accent. 1797 MRS. RADCLIFFE *Italian* xvi, 'Do not leave me,' said she, in accents the most supplicating. *a* 1859 MACAULAY *Hist. Eng.* xxiv. (1861) V. 177 A request made ..in earnest and almost supplicating terms. 1880 MEREDITH *Tragic Com.* (1881) 72 She would not have listened..to a silly supplicating girl.

Hence **Su·pplicatingly** *adv.*

1865 MEREDITH *Rhoda Fleming* xliv, Rhoda..turned her eyes supplicatingly on Robert. 1884 GOLDSMID *Wright's Pol. Songs* II. 45 *Song of Lewes*, Those whose aid he will ask supplicatingly.

Supplication (sʊplĭkeᶦ·ʃən), *sb.* Also 5 **supl-**. [a. OF. (mod.F.) *supplication* (= It. *supplicazione*, Sp. *suplicacion*, Pg. *supplicação*), ad. L. *supplicātio*, *-ōnem*, n. of action f. *supplicāre* to SUPPLICATE.] The action, or an act, of supplicating; humble or earnest petition or entreaty.

1384 in Arnolde *Chron.* (1811) 36 At the supplicacion of the Mayre Sherefs and Communalyte of the cite of London to vs mekely Imade. *c* 1390 CHAUCER *Purse* 26 Ye that mowen alle myn harme amende Haue mynde vpon my supplicacion. 1417 in Ellis *Orig. Lett.* Ser. II. I. 58 Hee dayly made supplication to have peace. 1432–50 tr. *Higden* (Rolls) III. 227 His moder and his wife..made a supplicacion to hym for the savegarde of the cite. *a* 1513 FABYAN *Chron.* v. cxxxi. (1811) 114 He ..ordeyned such meanes as byllys of supplicacion,..that the causes and maters of poore men myght come to his knowlege. 1555 EDEN *Decades* (Arb.) 80 They made humble supplication to the Admirall. 1671 MILTON *Samson* 1459, I have attempted..the Lords..With supplication prone and Fathers tears To accept of ransom for my Son. 1781 GIBBON *Decl. & F.* xviii. (1787) II. 94 Peace was at length granted to their humble supplications. 1855 MACAULAY *Hist. Eng.* xiv. III. 475 Pathetic earnestness of supplication. 1856 FROUDE *Hist. Eng.* II. viii. 301 In a moment the noise and bravado..was hushed into a supplication for forgiveness.

b. A written or formal petition. *Obs.* exc. *Hist.*

1390 GOWER *Conf.* III. 352 Whanne I this Supplicacioun ..Hadde after min entente write Unto Cupide and to Venus. *c* 1460 FORTESCUE *Abs. & Lim. Mon.* xiv. (1885) 143 Þat all supplicacions wich shalbe made to þe kynge..be sende to be..counsell. *a* 1578 LINDESAY (Pitscottie) *Chron. Scot.* (S.T.S.) I. 90 Schir patrick gray..passit haistelie with the said wreitting and supplicatioun of the kingis to the erle of douglas. 1592 KYD *Sp. Trag.* III. xiii. 78 Whats heere? 'The humble supplication of Don Bazulto for his murdred Sonne.' 1606 DEKKER *Newes fr. Hell* Wks. (Grosart) II. 91 Great wagers were layd..that when the Supplication was sent, it would not be receyued; or if receyued, it would not be read ouer. 1690 [see SUPPLICANT *sb.*]. 1816 SCOTT *Old Mort.* xxx, A paper, termed a Remonstrance and Supplication. 1822 — *Nigel* iii, To have the Supplication put into his Majesty's own hands.

c. (A) humble prayer addressed to God (or a deity); chiefly *pl.*, esp. in phr. *prayers and supplications*; *spec.* the petitions for special blessings in litanies.

1490 CAXTON *Eneydos* xiii. 46 Bifore the aulters thei offred sacrifices with grete supplycacyons and prayers. 1526 TINDALE *Acts* i. 14 These all continued with one acorde in prayer and supplicacion. — 1 *Tim.* ii. 1 That..prayeers, supplicacions, peticions, and gevynge of thankes be had for all men. 1526 *Pilgr. Perf.* (W. de W. 1531) 3 The sayd Moyses..made supplicacyon to God. 1549 *Bk. Com. Prayer*, *Communion* ad fin., Assist us mercifully, O Lord, in these our supplicacions and praiers. *Ibid.*, *Litany* ad fin., With one accorde to make our commune supplicacions unto thee. 1643 SIR T. BROWNE *Relig. Med.* II. § 6. 154, I cannot see one say his Prayers, but in stead of imitating him, I fall into a supplication for him. 1657 SPARROW *Bk. Com. Prayer* 100 These Collects after the Letany, though the matter of them hath been prayed for before particularly in the Supplications foregoing [etc.]. 1663 PATRICK *Parab. Pilgr.* xxv. (1687) 278 In devout supplications to Jesus. 1678 CUDWORTH *Intell. Syst.* I. iv. § 27. 455 We conclude, that this *Kyrie Eleeson*, or *Domine Miserere*, in Arrianus, was a Pagan Litany or Supplication to the Supreme God. 1817 SHELLEY *Rev. Islam* X. xxvi, Each among the train To his own Idol lifts his supplications vain. 1837 CARLYLE *Fr. Rev.* I. I. i, The churches resounded with supplications and groans. 1882 *Encycl. Brit.* XIV. 696/1 From an early period the special written litanies of the various churches all showed the common features which are now regarded as essential to a litany, in as far as they consisted of (1) invocations, (2) deprecations, (3) intercessions, (4) supplications.

d. *Rom. Antiq.* A religious solemnity decreed on the occasion of some important public event, esp. in thanksgiving for victory.

1606 HOLLAND *Sueton.* 10 By reason that his affaires sped well..hee obtained in regard thereof solemne Supplications both oftner, and to hold more daies than ever any man did (before himselfe). 1741 MIDDLETON *Cicero* (1742) II. vii. 229 After the contemptible account which Cicero gives of Bibulus's conduct in Syria, it must appear strange to see him honored with a supplication, and aspiring even to a Triumph. 1753 *Chambers' Cycl.* Suppl., App. s.v., On subduing the Sabines, in the year of the city 304, a supplication of one day only was ordained.

e. *spec.* In Oxford University, a formal petition for a degree or for incorporation: cf. SUPPLICAT.

1691 WOOD *Ath. Oxon.* I. *Fasti* 640 This year was a Supplication made in the ven. Congregation of Regents for one Rich. Bere..to be graduated in Divinity. *Ibid.* 670 Richard Bryncknley..Dr. of Divinity of Cambridge...His supplication..was granted..and his incorporation..set down..under this year (1524). 1810 *Oxf. Univ. Cal.* 3 In the Congregation degrees are conferred, graces or supplications for them having been there previously proposed and passed. 1895 RASHDALL *Univ. Europe* II. 508 This abstention on the part of Wykehamists from the 'supplications', which had come to be regarded as essential to all other candidates.

Hence **Supplica·tion** *v.*, *trans.* to make supplication to; **Supplica·tioner**, a petitioner.

1585 in *Cath. Rec. Soc. Publ.* V. 106 Against th'untruth of such libellers and supplicationers. 1589 [? NASHE] *Almond for Parrat* N.'s Wks. 1905 III. 365 The Protestationer, Demonstrationer, Supplicationer, Appellationer. 1593 — *Christ's T.* Wks. (Grosart) IV. 61, I haue..humbly supplicationd you, to accept of my largesse.

† **Supplicative**, *a.* *Obs. rare.* [f. L. *supplicāt-*: see SUPPLICATE and -IVE.] Supplicatory.

1600 W. WATSON *Decacordon* (1602) 120 A very formall letter, petitionall or supplicatiue.

Supplicator (sʊ·plĭkeᶦtəɹ). [ad. late L. *supplicātor*, agent-n. f. *supplicāre* to SUPPLICATE.] One who supplicates; a suppliant, petitioner.

1634–5 BRERETON *Trav.* (Chetham Soc.) 81 This is a pretty supplicator. 1687 [SHIELDS] *Hind let loose* 57 Our sneaking Supplicators, & Petitioners, & Pardon-mongers. 1794 T. TAYLOR *Pausanias' Descr. Greece* II. 195 Other ambassadors and supplicators were sent to the Romans. 1843 LYTTON *Last Bar.* IV. ii, The supplicators then withdrew from the royal presence.

Supplicatory (sʊ·plĭkătəri), *a.* [ad. med.L. *supplicātōrius*, f. *supplicātor*: see prec. and -ORY ². Cf. F. *supplicatoire*.] Expressing, consisting of, or containing supplication.

Letters supplicatory, *supplicatory letters* = F. *lettres supplicatoires*, mod.L. *supplices litteræ*. (*Obs.* exc. *Hist.*)

c 1450 *Mankind* 866 in *Macro Plays* 32 Wyth-owte deserte & menys supplicatorie, ȝe be compacient to my inexcusabyll reprowe. 1550 *Reg. Privy Council Scot.* I. 92 Heraldis with lettres supplicatiouris. 1579 STUBBES in *Harington's Nugæ Ant.* (1804) I. 151 To offer this supplicatorye submission and peticion into your Majesties handes. 1583 TRAVERS (*title*) An Answere to a Svpplicatorie Epistle of G. T. for the pretended Catholiqves. 1699 BURNET *39 Art.* xxv. 283 The Pardon that we give in the Name of God, is only declaratory of his Pardon, or supplicatory in a prayer to him for Pardon. 1732 NEAL *Hist. Purit.* I. 203 They framed a supplicatory letter. 1742 RICHARDSON *Pamela* III. 289, I..laid my Hand upon her Ladyship's in a supplicatory Manner. 1880 SOUTHEY *Wesley* II. 553 A supplicatory hymn for his recovery was sung in the church. 1876 BANCROFT *Hist. U. S.* V. xxii. 578 The Vermont council of safety despatched supplicatory letters for aid to the New Hampshire committee.

b. Of persons: Suppliant. *rare.*

1880 MEREDITH *Tragic Com.* (1881) 287 After the manner of supplicatory ladies appealing to lawyers.

Hence **Supplicatorily** *adv.*, in a supplicatory manner.

1625 DONNE *Serm. 26 Apr.* (1649) II. 289 Having the dignity of a Parent upon her, she [*sc.* the Church] does not proceed supplicatorily,..but..imperatively, authoritatively.

‖ **Supplicavit** (sʊplĭkē¹·vit). *Law.* [L., = he has supplicated, 3rd pers. sing. perf. ind. of *supplicāre* to SUPPLICATE.] A writ formerly issuing out of the King's Bench or the Court of Chancery for taking surety of the peace against a person: so called from the first word in the writ.

1507 in Leadam *Sel. Cases Star Chamber* (Selden Soc.) 260 By virtue of the kynges writt of supplicauit to them directed. 1518 — *Sel. Cases Crt. Requests* (Selden Soc.) 14 Robert..sued oute of the kynges chauncry a wrytte of supplicauit ayenst your seid besechour. 1623 BACON *Ordinances* § 87 No *Supplicavit* for the good behaviour shall be granted, but upon Articles grounded upon the Oath of two at the least. 1682 LUTTRELL *Brief Rel.* (1857) I. 162 Articles were exhibited, in a speciall supplicavit formerly granted in the court of Kings bench..by the court of arches..against Edmund Hickeringill, minister, for severall indignities offered to that court. 1769 BLACKSTONE *Comm.* IV. xviii. 250 If the justice is averse to act, it may be granted by a mandatory writ, called a *supplicavit*.

Supplice. *rare.* [ad. L. *supplicium*, f. *supplic-*, *supplex* (see SUPPLE *a.*). In quot. 1911 ad. F. *supplice*.] Punishment; torture.

1656 BLOUNT *Glossogr.*, *Supplice*.., punishment, correction, pain, torment; it is also used for Prayer or Supplication, and sometimes for Sacrifice. *Mr. Montagu.* 1911 MRS. OLIPHANT *Salem Chapel* I. 12 It is easier to play the victim under the supplice inflicted by a pretty girl than by two mature matrons.

Supplie, obs. form of SUPPLY.

Supplied (sŏplai·d), *ppl. a. rare.* [f. SUPPLY *v.*¹ + -ED ¹.] In senses of the verb: usually with prefixed adv., as *well-supplied*.

1609 CHAPMAN *Tears of Peace*, *Addr. Death* 31 The river needes the helpfull fountaine ever, More then the fountaine the supplyed river. 1900 *Westm. Gaz.* 29 May 4/1 A well-supplied advance depôt.

Supplier (sŏplai·əɹ). Forms: 5–6 *Sc.* **supplear**, 7 **-yer**, 7– **supplier**. [f. SUPPLY *v.*¹ + -ER ¹.]

† **1.** One who takes the place of or acts as substitute for another. *Obs.*

1491 *Cartular. S. Nicholai Aberdon.* (New Spalding Club) I. 255 Ilkane chaplane writin to ye haly bluide mess..falȝeande in ye doinge of þame sal pay iiii d to ye supplear.

† **2.** A helper, supporter; an assistant. *Obs.*

1515 in Pitcairn *Crim. Trials* (1833) I. 231* Makand him and his assignais Keparis ouersearis, correkaris, and suplearis of the Isle of Litill Comeray..becaus Robert Huntare ..Forrestar of beretage of þe said Ile, is nocht of power to resist þe personis þat waistis þe samyn, without suplé and help. 1525 *St. Papers Hen. VIII*, IV. 418 Togither with yair part takaris, assistaris, supplearis. 1586 *Reg. Privy Council Scot.* IV. 71 Ressavaris, supplearis and intercommonaris with the Kingis rebellis. 1654 tr. *Scudery's Curia Pol.* 69 His neighbour Princes will censure his ambition, and rather be spectators of his successes, then be supplyers.

3. One who makes up a deficiency.

1607 CHAPMAN *Bussy d'Ambois* II. i. 103 All vaunt themselves Law-menders and suppliers. 1737 STACKHOUSE *Hist. Bible* v. v. (1752) I. 745/2 Saul might set up for..a Supplier of the Default of Joshua.

4. One who (or that which) furnishes something needed; a provider, purveyor.

c 1630 RISDON *Surv. Devon* § 202 (1810) 211 Dartmore, our daily supplier. 1796 MORSE *Amer. Geog.* II. 440 Brundusium..was the great supplier of oysters for the Roman tables. 1827 *Examiner* 99/1 The suppliers of intellectual gratification. 1858 GEN. P. THOMPSON *Audi Alt.* lxxvi. II. 28 To reduce Asia to be the supplier of the European slave-market. 1897 MARY KINGSLEY *W. Africa* 665 Van Huytemers

and Peters are the two great suppliers of the gin that goes to West Africa. 1907 O'GORMAN *Motor Pocket Bk.* (ed. 2) 463 You cannot have too many spares, though the supplier will tell you the contrary.

b. An apparatus for supplying something; a feeder.

1823 J. BADCOCK *Dom. Amusem.* 147 A kind of funnel-shaped supplier.

Su·ppliment. *dial.* Also **-ement**. [Corruption of SUBLIMATE.] Corrosive sublimate. Also *silver suppliment*.

1809 PARKINS *Culpepper's Eng. Phys. Enlarged* 385 How to take away little red pimples from the face. Take two ounces of lemon juice, two ounces of rose water, two drachms of silver suppliment. 1886 *Cheshire Gloss.* s.v., A chemist, if asked for supplement, would perfectly well understand what was wanted.

Suppliment, obs. form of SUPPLEMENT *sb.*

Suppline, obs. Sc. form of SIPLING.

Suppling (sʊ·pliŋ), *vbl. sb.* [f. SUPPLE *v.* + -ING ¹.] The action of SUPPLE *v.*; making supple.

a. in literal senses.

1577 B. GOOGE *Heresbach's Husb.* II. (1586) 87 b, Of Oyle, some part serueth for meate, and other for the sowpling of the bodie. 1655 MOUFET & BENNET *Health's Improv.* (1746) 221 The Butter..is most thin, liquid, moist and penetrating, whereby such a suppeling is procured, that their Cheeses do rather ripen than dry with long lying. 1668 WILKINS *Real Char.* II. vi. § 5. 173 That Cavity or Glandule ..containing an unctuous substance for the suppling of the Feathers. 1676 MACE *Musick's Mon.* 56 That part..will ask good Suppleing with Water and Heat, before it will yield. 1720 W. GIBSON *Dict. Horses* x. (1731) 163 The suppling of the Joints [of a horse], which is generally first practised, is very reasonable. 1802 C. JAMES *Milit. Dict.*, *Siguette*,..a sort of nose-band..which is put on the nose of a horse, to forward the suppling or breaking of him. 1889 BADEN-POWELL *Pigsticking* 124 A few hours of quiet suppling and bending will amply repay the trouble.

b. in fig. senses.

1617 R. FENTON *Treat. Ch. Rome* 64 It cureth by way of suppling, to teach them to be gracious Soveraignes, to establish their royal thrones by mercy. 1625 DONNE *Serm.* *3 Apr.* 26 For the suppling of boysterous, and for the becalming of tempestuous humours. 1853 RUSKIN *Stones Venice* II. vi. § 59 That quickening and suppling of the dull spirit that cannot be gained for it but by bathing it in blood. 1865 LOWELL *Scotch the Snake* Prose Wks. 1890 V. 245 We doubt if any substantial excellence is lost by this suppling of the intellectual faculties.

Suppling (sʊ·pliŋ), *ppl. a.* [f. SUPPLE *v.* + -ING ².] That renders the skin or the joints of the body supple; also, softening, emollient.

1562 TURNER *Herbal* II. 101 The rosin..of the popler is meuged oft tymes with softenyng and souplyng emplasters. 1562 *Burnynge of Paules Ch. in Lond.*, Nothinge..does more ease the paines of the sicke bodye than these supplinge oiles. 1638 RAWLEY tr. *Bacon's Life & Death* (1650) 64 Onely three Set Diets: The Opiate Diet, the Diet Malacissant, or Suppling; and the Diet Emaciant, & Renewing. 1639 T. DE GREY *Compl. Horsem.* 272 Mollifie the heeles of the horse with suppling things. 1648 HERRICK *Hesper.*, *To the King to cure Evill*, All those suppling healing herbs and flowers. 1650 VENNER *Via Recta*, *Baths of Bathe* 356 The Crosse-bath is an excellent temperate soupling bath. 1710 T. FULLER *Pharm. Extemp.* 422 By means of suppleing Oils, those Fibrillae are..lubricated, and relaxed. 1871 *Daily News* 11 Apr. 6 Good marching..tells of weary but necessary hours over the goose step, of laborious and oft-repeated 'suppling' motions.

b. in fig. context or allusively.

1563 *Form Medit.* in *Liturg. Serv. Q. Eliz.* (Parker Soc.) 505 Mollify..O Lord, our flinty hearts with the suppling moisture of thy Holy Spirit. 1595 SOUTHWELL *St. Peter's Compl.* lxxx, Pour suppling showers upon my parched ground. 1633 G. HERBERT *Priest to Temple* xviii, Mollifying and suppling words. 1659 W. CHAMBERLAYNE *Pharonnida* II. 154 If ere thy sober Reason did submit To suppling Mirth. 1713 C'TESS WINCHELSEA *Misc. Poems* 380 Employ my Hand, yet warm, to close the Wound, And with my suppling Tears disperse the anguish. 1727 P. WALKER *Life R. Cameron* in *Biogr. Presbyt.* (1827) I. 194 In the 1719, there was a softning, soupling, sweetning Oil, composed and made up by the cunning Art of carnal Wit, and State-policy.

† **Supplo·de**, *v.* *Obs. rare*⁻⁰. [ad. L. *supplōdĕre*, f. *sup-* = SUB- + *plaudĕre* PLAUD *v.*] *intr.* To stamp with the feet. So † **Supplo·sion** [L. *supplōsio*].

1599 *Broughton's Lett.* xii. 42 It deserueth a supplosion or an hissing. 1623 COCKERAM, *Supplode*, to stampe with the foot. 1656 BLOUNT *Glossogr.*, *Supplosion*.., a stamping or noise with the feet.

† **Supplusage**. *Obs.* Variant of SURPLUSAGE.

c 1475 *Pol. Poems* (Rolls) II. 283 With the supplusage of oone of thyse iij. thynges. 1507–8 *Rec. St. Mary at Hill* 262 We haue Resseyuyd of the Supplorâgiis [? Supplusagis] of the last yere ix li viij s iiij d.

Supply (sŏplai·), *sb.* Forms: 5 **supplye** (6–7 *pl.* **supplyes**), 5–6 *Sc.* **supple**, 6–8 **supplie**, 7– **supply**. [f. SUPPLY *v.*¹ (In early use mainly *Sc.*)]

I. The action of supplying, or condition of being supplied.

† **1.** Assistance, succour, support, relief. Also predicated of a person or thing that is the means of assistance or support. *Obs.*

Phr. *to make* (*a*) *supply*, to give assistance.

1423 JAS. I *Kingis Q.* xv, Ryght as the schip that sailith sterelee Vpon the rokkis most to harmes hye, For lak of It that suld bene hir supplye. *Ibid.* cxii, In this case sche [*sc.* Minerva] may be thy supplye. *c* 1480 HENRYSON *Fables*, *Fox, Wolf, & Cadger* xiv, Ȝe man tak trauell and mak vs sum supple. 1513 DOUGLAS *Æn.* III. x. 105, I Isis..all supple of our travale and pane. 1549 *Compl. Scot.* Ep. Queen: The langorius desolat & affligit pepil, quhilkis ar al mast disparit of mennis supple. 1567 *Gude & Godlie B.* (S.T.S.) 46 Quhair I culd nocht the Law fulfill, My warkis maid me na supplie. *Ibid.* 162 Thow art..My hope, support, and haill supplie. 1587 TURBERV. *Trag. Tales* (1837) 32 When he sawe Nastagio bent For her supplie, whom he would reave of life. 1598 R. BERNARD tr. *Terence, Phormio* I. iv, Heere will I lie in a bush to make a supply, if you shall faile in anything. 1602 SHAKS. *Ham.* II. ii. 24 To expend your time with vs a-while, For the supply and profit of our Hope. *c* 1614 MURE *Dido & Æneas* I. 566 See how Penthesilea leads Her Amazonian trowpes to Troye's supplie! 1697 DRYDEN *Virg. Georg.* II. 597 Apple Trees..Want no Supply, but stand secure alone.

2. The act of making up a deficiency, or of fulfilling a want or demand.

Phr. † *To make* (*a*) *supply*, to fill up a deficiency.

1500–20 DUNBAR *Poems* xxviii. 35 Supportand faltis with ȝour supple. 1596 BACON *Max. & Use Com. Law* II. (1635) 61 The maner of making supply when the part of the heire is not a full third. 1638 QUARLES *Hieroglyph.* I. Epigr. i. 3 Thy wants are far more safe then their supply. 1662 H. MORE *Philos. Writ.* Pref. Gen. (1712) 17, I omitted to set down the Succession of the Pythagorick School..and therefore I will here make a supply out of Diogenes Laertius. 1768 TUCKER *Lt. Nat.* I. xxvii. 186 Why are usefull things good? because they minister to the supply of our wants and desires. 1824 L. MURRAY *Eng. Gram.* (ed. 5) I. 317 The supply of the ellipsis..gives an uncouth appearance to these sentences. 1835 T. MITCHELL *Acharn. of Aristoph.* App. 245 A system..which drew..upon the purses of the tributary states for a supply of those pecuniary demands, which the native resources of Athens were unable to furnish.

† **3.** The act of supplying something needed; the filling up *of* a place or position; the provision *of* a person or thing in the place of another; the substitution *of* a thing for something else. *Obs.*

1585 in *Presbyt. Movem. Eliz.* (Camden) 53 Mr. Tay.. desired the brethren to helpe him..for the supplie of his place. 1607 SHAKS. *Timon* II. i. 27 My releefe Must not be tost and turn'd to me in words, But finde supply immediate. 1608 J. KING *Serm. St. Mary's, Oxf.* 5 Two partes, first the cession or decease of the one, secondly the succession and supply of the other. 1667 MILTON *P. L.* XI. 736 The Southwind..all the Clouds together drove..; the Hills to their supplie Vapour..Sent up amain. 1673 TEMPLE *United Prov.* Wks. 1731 I. 34 This Course seems to have been instituted by way of Supply or Imitation of the Chamber of Mechlyn.

b. Now only in reference to persons: The act, or position, of supplying a vacancy, or officiating temporarily instead of another, esp. as a minister or preacher; *on supply* = acting in such a capacity.

1580 CAMPION in Allen *Martyrdom Campion* (1908) 23 Such as..are to be sent for supplie,..let them be well trained for the pulpit. 1896 'IAN MACLAREN' *Kate Carnegie* 248 A 'probationer', who on Saturdays can be seen at any country junction, bag in hand, on his patient errand of 'supply'. 1905 *Daily Chron.* 1 Sept. 1/6 Wanted, an Assistant Schoolmaster, on 'Supply.' 1912 *Universe* 16 Aug. 12/1 Southwark...Father Hallett [stationed] on supply at Melior Street.

4. The provision or furnishing *of* a person, etc. with necessaries.

1781 COWPER *Charity* 251 These have an ear for his paternal call, Who makes some rich for the supply of all. 1805 COLLINGWOOD 7 Oct. in Nicolas *Disp. Nelson* (1846) VII. 83 *note*, The active part he takes in everything that relates to the supply of the Fleet. 1848 DICKENS *Dombey* xx, The Native then handed him separately, and with a decent interval between each supply, his wash-leather gloves, his thick stick, and his hat. 1876 VOYLE & STEVENSON *Milit. Dict.* (ed. 3) s.v., In time of peace the method of supply is by contract for the principal articles of sustenance.

II. That which is supplied.

† **5.** *coll. sing.* or *pl.* An additional body of persons, esp. reinforcements of troops. *Obs.*

c 1470 HENRY *Wallace* v. 87 Butleris men so stroyit war that tide, In to the stour he wald na langar bide. To get supple he socht on to the staill. 1591 SHAKS. *1 Hen. VI*, I. i. 159 The Earle of Salisbury craueth supply. 1597 — *2 Hen. IV*, IV. ii. 45 Though wee here fall downe, Wee haue Supplyes, to second our Attempt. *a* 1624 in *Capt. J. Smith's Virginia* III. vi. 59 There we found the last Supply [of colonists] were all sicke. 1633 T. STAFFORD *Pac. Hib.* III. x. (1821) 335 The two thousand supplyes, that were now landed out of England. 1685 STILLINGFL. *Orig. Brit.* v. 297 The Romans..sent them speedy Supplies. 17.. *Outlaw Murray* xliii. in Child *Ballads* V. 196/1 Word is gane to Philiphaugh, ..To meet him the morn wi some supply.

† **6.** A substitute. Const. *of*. *Obs.* exc. as in b.

1567 FENTON *Trag. Disc.* xiii. (1898) II. 279 Usinge the pointe of a sharppe bodkyn as a supplie of a steeled cherell.

b. One who supplies a vacancy or acts as substitute for another; *esp.* a minister or preacher who temporarily officiates in a vacant charge or pulpit.

1584 in *Presbyt. Movem. Eliz.* (Camden) 36 Mr. Newman moued whether he might get a standing supply for his place. 1697 in W. S. Perry *Hist. Coll. Amer. Col. Ch.* (1870) I. 10 To give notice what number of ministers was wanting, and earnestly to solicit for a suitable Supply. 1718 BP. ROBINSON *Ibid.* 200, I should be glad to hear from you what vacant Churches are in your parts, to the end I may..procure you a supply. 1888 HOWELLS *Annie Kilburn* xxx, Supply after supply filled his pulpit. 1892 *Pall Mall G.* 8 Oct. 7/2 Some servants..will only stay in situations for short periods... These would make excellent supplies.

† **7.** A supplement or appendix *to* a literary work.

1585 BANISTER *Chyrurg.* Title-p., Encreased and enlightened with certaine Annotations, Resolutions, and Supplyes, not impertinent to this Treatise. 1596 DANETT tr. *Comines* (1614) 225 (*heading*) A Supply to the Historie of Philip de Commines from the death of King Lewis the XI. 1638 BAKER tr. *Balzac's Lett.* (vol. III.) 1 A Supply to the Second part; or The Third Part of the Letters of M. de Balzac.

† **b.** *gen.* Something supplementary, additional, or auxiliary; a supplement, adjunct. *Obs.*

1620 [G. BRYDGES] *Horæ Subs.* 21 To make himselfe an encreasing figure, whilst the rest serue but for supply. 1625 BURGES *Pers. Tithes* 49 All these Defects are supplied in this Statute of Edw. the 6. For, (passing ouer the supply touching Prædiall Tithes) wee may finde these supplies for Personal Tithes. *a* 1626 BP. ANDREWES *96 Serm.*, *Holy Ghost* (1661) 488 To do that was to be done, Christ is enough; needs no supply. 1752 HUME *Ess. & Treat.* (1777) I. 197 Municipal laws are a supply to the wisdom of each individual.

8. A quantity or amount *of* something supplied or provided.

1607 SHAKS. *Timon* II. ii. 201, I am proud, say, that my occasions haue found time to vse 'em toward a supply of mony. 1665 MANLEY *Grotius' Low C. Warrs* 241 The Queen of England..ordered a supply of mony to the King of France, together, with four thousand English Souldiers. 1703 DAMPIER *Voy.* III. 16 Till..the greatest part of the Salt-water is congeal'd..or till a fresh Supply of it come again from the Sea. 1710–11 ATTERBURY *Serm.*, *1 Cor.* ... (1734) I. 108 What is Grace, but an Extraordinary Supply of Ability and Strength to resist Temptations? 1832 H. MARTINEAU *Life in Wilds* ix. 117 The greatest possible supply of human labour. 1837 DICKENS *Pickw.* ii, The bottle was passed, and a fresh supply ordered. 1846 J. BAXTER *Libr. Pract. Agric.* (ed. 4) I. 34 Certain crops..require a particular alkali; the vine, for example,..and sorrel,..needs have supplies of potash. 1849 MACAULAY *Hist. Eng.* v. I. 592 The duke had brought..but a scanty supply of pikes and muskets. 1898 G. B. SHAW *Plays* II. *Candida* 95 Carrying..a handbag, and a supply of illustrated papers.

† **b.** *spec.* (*absol.*) A collection of materials to form the basis of an argument or treatise. *Obs.*

1662 MORE *Antid. Ath.* II. xi. heading, A Supply of ordinary and known Examples as convictive..of a directing Providence. 1714 SWIFT *Pres. St. Aff.* Wks. 1755 II. I. 203 Systems, that..are supplies for pamphlets in the present age.

9. *absol.* (A) provision of funds or food; (a quantity of) money or provisions supplied or to be supplied: now chiefly *spec.* the food and other stores necessary for an armed force. **a.** *sing.* (Now rare exc. as *attrib.* of b: see 12.)

1611 *Bible* 2 *Cor.* viii. 14 That now at this time your abundance may be a supply for their want, that their abundance also may be a supply for your want. 1622 FLETCHER *Span. Cur.* I. i, When this is spent, Seek for supply to me. 1769 FALCONER *Dict. Marine* (1780), *Supply*, a fresh recruit of provisions or stores sent to a ship or fleet. 1825 P. BUCHAN *Gleanings*, *Willie Wallace* xi, If ye be a captain as gcod as ye look Ye'll give a poor man some supplie. 1831 SCOTT *Ct. Rob.* xx, Judging that it was full time to carry some supply to Count Robert, who had been left without food the whole day. 1836 W. IRVING *Astoria* xlix. III. 107 The slaughter of so many buffaloes had provided the party with beef for the winter, in case they met with no further supply.

b. *pl.*

?*c* 1650 *Hist. Tom Thumb* III. in Hazl. *E. P. P.* II. ... Finding all retir'd and gone, His hunger to suffice In cause sort he moves along; Nature wants some Supplies. *a* 1687 PETTY *Pol. Anat.* (1691) 6 England..sent Money and other Supplies into Ireland. 1690 C. NESSE *Hist. & Myst. O. & N. Test.* I. 26 After other losses..there may be found some supplys for repairing them. 1777 ROBERTSON *Hist. America* v. (1783) II. 267 Notwithstanding the supplies which they received from the Tlascalans, they were often in want of provisions. 1875 *Encycl. Brit.* II. 582/1 The Surveyor-General of Ordnance, assisted by a director of supplies and transport, and a director of artillery and stores. 1881 JOWETT *Thucyd.* I. 169 The invaders remained until their supplies were exhausted.

10. *coll. sing.* or *pl.* A sum of money granted by a national legislature for expenses of government not provided for by the revenue.

1626 SIR J. ELIOT *Sp. in Ho. Comm.* in *Apol. Socrates* etc. (Grosart) I. 152 Yᵉ extraordinary resort to yᵉ sub[jec]ᵗˢ for supplies. 1670 *Hatton Corr.* (Camden) ... this I suppose they waite the parlimᵗˢ results for supplyes. 1689 *Acts Parlt. Scotl.* (1875) XII. 56/2 Þe collecting of the supply in the schyre of Edinburgh. 1735 BOLINGBROKE *On Parties* 77 After these Invasions were over ... They voted a Supply. 1817 EARL GREY in *Parl. Deb.* ... The supplies of last year were 35 millions, and the ways and means did not exceed 20 millions. 1827 HALLAM *Const. Hist.* viii. (1876) II. 19 As the ordinary revenues might prove quite unequal to great exigencies, the constitution has provided another means..parliamentary supply. 1867 *Chambers' Encycl.* IX. 218/1 All bills authorising the expenditure of public money must originate in the House of Commons, and be based on resolutions moved in a Committee of Supply. 1874 GREEN *Short Hist.* viii. § 5. 517 The Commons declared ..that redress of grievances must precede the grant of supplies.

b. *Commissioners of Supply*: see quots. (*Sc.*)

a 1768 ERSKINE *Inst. Law Scot.* I. iv. § 31 The commissioners of supply are the persons appointed by parliament in their yearly acts of supply, to levy the land-tax within the county to which they are named. 1838 W. BELL *Dict. Law Scot.* 184 Under the militia acts the commissioners of supply have also power to assess for failures to make up their *quota* for allowances to the families of militiamen.

11. *Pol. Econ.* The amount of any commodity actually produced and available for purchase: correlative to DEMAND *sb.* 4 b.

1776–1878 [see DEMAND *sb.* 4 b]. 1878 JEVONS *Prim. Pol. Econ.* 103 The labour which is required to get more of a commodity governs the supply of it. 1900 LD. ALDENHAM *Colloquy on Currency* 82 If the demand exceeds the supply the price will rise. If the supply exceeds the demand, the price will fall.

III. 12. *attrib.* and *Comb.*: in sense 3 b *supply teacher*; in sense 9, esp. = having charge of

Supported, ppl. a. [f. SUPPORT v. + -ED.] Upheld, sustained, maintained, etc.; see the verb.

Supporter, sb. Also 5 -our. [f. SUPPORT v. + -ER.] One who or that which supports.

Supportful, a. Obs. rare. [f. SUPPORT sb. + -FUL.] Affording support.

Supporting, vbl. sb. [f. SUPPORT v. + -ING.]

Supporting, ppl. a. [f. as prec. + -ING.]

Supportive, a. [f. SUPPORT v. + -IVE.]

Supportless, a. Obs. rare. [f. SUPPORT sb. + -LESS.]

Supportment. Obs. [f. SUPPORT v. + -MENT.]

Supportress, Obs. [f. SUPPORT + -ESS.] A female supporter.

Supporture. Obs. [f. SUPPORT v. + -URE.]

Supposable, a. [f. SUPPOSE v. + -ABLE.]

Supposal, sb. [f. SUPPOSE v. + -AL.]

Supposably, adv. (chiefly U.S.), as may be supposed; presumably.

Suppose, v. [a. OF. supposer.]

Supposed, ppl. a. [f. prec. + -ED.]

Supposedly, adv. [f. prec. + -LY.]

Supposer. [f. SUPPOSE v. + -ER.] One who supposes.

Supposing, vbl. sb. [f. SUPPOSE v. + -ING.]

Supposita, pl. of SUPPOSITUM.

Supposital, a. Metaph. Obs. [ad. mod.L. suppositālis, f. suppositum: see SUPPOSITUM.]

Supposititious, a. [f. L. supposītīcius.]

Suppositive, a. [ad. L. suppositīvus.]

Supposititial, a. Obs. rare.

Suppository, sb. [ad. med.L. suppositōrium.]

Supposition, sb. [a. F. supposition.]

SUPPOSITIONAL. 214 SUPPOSITUM. SUPPOST. 215 SUPPRESSED.

SUPPRESSEDLY. 216 SUPPRISSION. SUPPULLULATE. 217 SUPRA-

its [*sc.* the aspirate's] having passed into a mere *supra-lineal mark in classical Greek suggests the question whether it had not even in those days become an unmeaning symbol. 1832 LYELL *Princ. Geol.* II. 195 The effects..of subterranean action on *supramarine land. 1863 — *Antiq. Man* xiii. (ed. 3) 232 Difficulty in distinguishing between the effects of the submarine and supramarine agency of ice. 1855 J. PHILLIPS *Man. Geol.* 157 Millstone grit (*supramedial group). 1826 KIRBY & SP. *Entomol.* IV. xlix. 485 Beginning at 84° N. L. he [*sc.* Latreille] has seven Arctic ones [*sc.* climates], which he names polar, subpolar, superior, intermediate, *supratropical, tropical, and equatorial.

b. *Anat.* and *Zool.* Extensively used to form adjectives (some of which are also used *ellipt.* as sbs.) in the sense 'Situated above, or on the dorsal side of (sometimes, upon the upper surface of) the part or organ denoted by the second element': as in mod.L. *suprācostālis* (*costa* rib), *suprārēnālis* SUPRARENAL. = SUPER- 1 b.

Numerous compounds of this class appear in recent Dicts., general and technical; the following is a selection of the more important. The meaning can usually be inferred from that of the second element; where necessary, a brief explanation or reference is added in parentheses. (Cf. SUB- 1 b.)

Supra-abdo·minal, supra-acro·mial, supra-a·nal, supra-a·ngular (the angular bone of the lower jaw in some vertebrates: cf. ANGULAR 2 a, quot. 1855), *supra-aryte·noid, supra-au·ditory, supra-auri·cular, suprabra·nchial, suprabu·ccal, supracæ·cal, supracau·dal, supraco·ndylar, -co·ndyloid* (= above a condyle or condyles of the humerus, femur, etc.), *supraco·stal, supraco·xal, supracra·nial* (= on the upper surface of the cranium), *suprado·rsal, supradu·ral* (= above the dura mater), *supra-e·thmoid, supraglo·ttic* (above the glottis), *suprahepa·tic* (on the upper surface of the liver), *suprahy·oid, supra-i·liac* (= on the upper surface of the ilium), *suprama·rginal* (*spec.* above the upper edge of the Sylvian fissure), *suprama·stoid, suprana·sal, supranervian, supraneu·ral* (= above a neural axis), *supranu·clear* (NUCLEUS 6 b), *supra-o·cular* (= above the ocular region, *spec.* of the small scales in reptiles above the superciliaries; also *sb.*), *supra-œsopha·geal* (= on the dorsal side of the œsophagus, applied to a nervous ganglia in invertebrates), *suprapapi·llary* (= above the biliary papilla), *suprape·dal* (= above the 'foot' of a mollusc), *suprapharyngeal* (= *supra-œsophageal*), *suprapu·bian, -pu·bic* (hence *suprapu·bically* adv., above the pubis), *suprapy·gal* (of plates of the carapace in tortoises; also *sb.*), *suprari·mal* (RIMA), *suprase·ptal* (SEPTUM), *suprastape·dial, supraste·rnal, supratro·chlear* (TROCHLEA *a, b*), *supratympa·nic, supraventri·cular* (VENTRICLE 2).

1835–6 *Todd's Cycl. Anat.* I. 114/1 Two *supra-abdominal nervous columns generally extend along the middle of the back. 1840 G. V. ELLIS *Anat.* 130 The *transversalis humeri* artery..ends by dividing into the *supra-acromial and supra-scapular arteries. 1893 H. MORRIS *Treat. Hum. Anat.* 831 The supra-acromial branches cross the clavicular insertion of the trapezius and the acromion process. 1867 LANKESTER in *Ann. & Mag. Nat. Hist.* Nov. 335 The *supra-anal organ is very small. 1835–6 *Todd's Cycl. Anat.* I. 277/1 The anterior extremities of the angular and *supra-angular pieces are wedged into corresponding grooves of the symphyseal element. 1896 NEWTON *Dict. Birds* 872 The bones forming the right and left Mandibulæ..namely, the Dentals, Splenials, Supra-angulars, Angulars and Articulars. 1872 COHEN *Dis. Throat* 48 The arytenoid and the *supra-arytenoid cartilages, with their connecting muscle. 1866 HUXLEY *Laing's Preh. Rem. Caithn.* 87 The mastoid processes are large, the *supra-auditory ridges strong. 1890 BILLINGS *Nat. Med. Dict.*, **Supra-auricular diameter*, parietal diameter, inferior. 1916 KEITH in *Man* XVI. 101 Skull of an aged man. Maximum length, 195 mm.; width, 140 mm.;..height (supra-auricular), 116 mm. 1889 DUNMAN & WINGRAVE *Gloss. Terms*, **Supra-branchial*, applied to the dorsal division of the pallial chamber in the Lamellibranchiata..above the gills, which separate it from the infra-branchial chamber. 1883 *Encycl. Brit.* XVI. 665/1 Large special ganglia (optic, stellate, and *supra-buccal) are developed in the higher forms (Siphonopoda). 1901 P. C. MITCHELL in *Trans. Linn. Soc., Zool.* Oct. 188 In *Spheniscus* the portion between the supra-duodenal loop and the rectum..is expanded into a minor fold,..to which I give the name '*supra-cæcal kink'. 1890 *Proc. Zool. Soc. Lond.* 180 The *supracaudal muscle is the direct continuation backwards of the *spinalis dorsi*. 1881 MIVART *Cat* 91 An elongated opening..called the *supracondylar foramen which transmits the median nerve and brachial artery. 1899 *Allbutt's Syst. Med.* VI. 659 Supracondylar fracture may readily implicate the nerve. 1866 *Quain's Elem. Nat.* (ed. 7) II. 385 The occasional prominence called the *supracondyloid process. 1884 T. BRYANT *Pract. Surg.* (ed. 4) II. 634 Mr. W. Stokes, of Dublin, advocates..the supra-condyloid amputation of the thigh. 1855 OGILVIE *Suppl.*, **Supra-costal*,..the supra-costal muscles, which raise the ribs. 1890 BILLINGS *Nat. Med. Dict.*, *Supracostal groove*, light furrow sometimes found along upper edge of the body of a rib, at its posterior extremity. 1872 HUMPHRY *Myology* 21 The *supra-coxal part of the pelvis. 1848 OWEN *Homol. Vertebrate Skel.* 48 The frontals and parietals, being ossified in *supra-cranial fibrous membrane. 1889 *Nature* 20 June 172/1 The ..details of the mouth-plates, the *supradorsal membrane,..and other..portions. 1889 *Buck's Handbk. Med. Sci.* VIII. 232/2 *Supradural branch or *ramus parietalis*. 1888 ROLLESTON & JACKSON *Anim. Life* 96 In the Salmon this region [*sc.* the mesethmoidal cartilage]..is covered by a *supra-ethmoid bony plate. 1890 *Retrospect Med.* CII. 302 The narrowing of the *supraglottic portion of the larynx. 1848 DUNGLISON *Med. Lex.* s.v. *Hepatic*, Hepatic Veins or *Suprahepatic veins..open into the vena cava inferior. 1904 *Brit. Med. Jrnl.* 17 Sept. 672 In suprahepatic abscess the pus occurs between the layers of the coronary ligament. 1882 *Quain's Elem. Anat.* (ed. 9) I. 292 *Suprahyoid muscles. 1870 FLOWER *Osteol. Mammalia* xvii. 285 The ilium is flattened and expanded, and has a greatly extended..*supra-iliac border. 1872 H. A. NICHOLSON *Palæont.* 109 Ananchytidæ..anus..marginal, or *supramarginal. 1899 *Allbutt's Syst. Med.* VII. 433 The left visual word-centre..is now..supposed to be situated in the angular and possibly in part of the supramarginal convolution. 1893 H. MORRIS *Treat. Hum. A*[illegible] 37 A ridge of bone, the *supra-mastoid crest, runs imme[illegible]ately above the external auditory meatus. 1865 *Reader* No. 145. 409/1 The *supranasal notch. 1903 *Proc. Zool. Soc. Lond.* II. 125 Nostril pierced in a single nasal; no supranasal. 1888 *Supranervian [see *subnervian*, SUB- 1 b]. 1899 *Allbutt's Syst. Med.* VII. 623 The *supranuclear connections of the nerve. 1897 GÜNTHER in Mary Kingsley *W. Africa* 696 Two large *supraoculars on each side. 1835–6 *Todd's Cycl. Anat.* I. 524/1 The..*supra-œsophageal ganglions are protected by a dense membrane. 1840 *Penny Cycl.* XVI. 112/2 The brain, or supracesophageal mass. 1897 *Allbutt's Syst. Med.* III. 723 The duodenum is more extensively dilated [in infra-papillary carcinoma] than in *supra-papillary carcinoma. 1888 ROLLESTON & JACKSON *Anim. Life* 110 A *supra-pedal gland appears to be present in all *Pulmonata*. 1878 BELL tr. *Gegenbaur's Comp. Anat.* 351 There is but one buccal ganglion in the Dibranchiata, and behind it there is a large *supra-pharyngeal ganglion. 1848 DUNGLISON *Med. Lex.*, **Supra-Pubian Nerve*, is the internal ramus of the inguino-cutaneous branch of the first lumbar nerve. 1835–6 *Todd's Cycl. Anat.* I. 507/1 The shortest route by which the bladder can be reached at this early age is according to the method of the *suprapubic operation. 1847–9 *Ibid.* IV. 280/1 In the turtles..the suprapubic muscle divides into two fasciculi. 1887 *Brit. Med. Jrnl.* I. 1098/2 A suprapubic abscess. *Ibid.* 1214/2 Suprapubic lithotomy in a boy. *Ibid.* 204/2, I..proceeded to open the bladder *suprapubically upon the point of an ordinary lithotomy-staff. 1889 NICHOLSON & LYDEKKER *Palæont.* II. 1086 While..the nuchal is a cartilage bone, the pygal and *suprapygals are of purely dermal origin. 1893 H. MORRIS *Treat. Hum. Anat.* 948 The cavity is naturally divided into two portions—*supra- and infra-rimal—divided by the glottis. 1890 *Q. Jrnl. Microsc. Sci.* XXX. 137 The smaller division of the cœlom, the *supraseptal cavity, is continued into the tentacles. 1875 W. K. PARKER in *Encycl. Brit.* III. 710/2 The short, notched *supra-stapedial..the slender, combined infra-stapedial and stylo-hyal..are still cartilaginous. 1862 H. W. FULLER *Dis. Lungs* 4 The *supra-sternal is the hollowed space which lies immediately above the notch of the sternum. 1876 *Quain's Elem. Anat.* (ed. 8) I. 27 The occurrence of suprasternal bones in some animals. 1882 *Ibid.* (ed. 9) I. 27 The upper end [of the sternum] is marked by the deep suprasternal notch. 1836–9 *Todd's Cycl. Anat.* II. 280/1 It [*sc.* the frontal nerve]..ascends round the superciliary arch,..and is thenceforth called by some the external frontal nerve in contradistinction to a branch from itself, the *supra-trochlear, or internal frontal. 1870 FLOWER *Osteol. Mammalia* x. 157 The large *supratympanic or mastoid bulla [of *Pedetes caffer*]. 1865 *Reader* 11 Mar. 288 The *supraventricular masses of the hemispheres [of the brain].

c. With sb., denoting a part situated above that denoted by the second element, as mod.L. *suprāclāvicula*, SUPRACLAVICLE.

2. In adverbial relation to the second element: = SUPER- 2. † **Suprano·minated** *ppl. a.*, above-named. **Su:praposi·tion**, the action of placing or state of being placed above or upon something; position above; in quot. 1788 = SUPERPOSITION 2. **Su:prasori·ferous** *a.*, *Bot.*, bearing sori on the upper surface.

1599 A. M. tr. *Gabelhouer's Bk. Physicke* 344/2 Take..of the *supra-nominatede poudre 3 qu. of an ownce. 1683 E. HOOKER *Pref. Pordage's Mystic Div.* 105 The Architypous Globe, or Original Beeing is the Basis..of all other Essences, ..brought forth out of the Womb of pure Nature supranominated. 1788 in E. H. Barker *Parriana* (1829) II. 64 Coincidence can only be proved by *supraposition. 1855 T. R. JONES *Aquarian Nat.* 9 Their..steady supraposition upon each other should ensure..stability. 1857 T. MOORE *Handbk. Brit. Ferns* (ed. 3) 46 Crenato-lobate above, *suprasoriferous.

3. In adjectival relation to the sb. constituting or implied in the second element: = SUPER- 3. **a.** *Anat.* and *Zool.* = Superior, upper; (a structure) situated above some other, or forming or belonging to the upper part of (that denoted by the second element): chiefly in mod.L. terms, as *supramamma*. Also **Supraco·mmissure**, a commissure of nerve-fibres above and in front of the pineal body.

1889 *Buck's Handbk. Med. Sci.* VIII. 132/1 The diatela.. is..continuous with the supracommissure. 1901 DORLAND *Med. Dict.* (ed. 2), Supramaxilla..Supra-obliquus..Supraturbinal. 1902 *Amer. Anthropol.* IV. 172/1 The significance of the '*supramamma' (a sort of rudimentary mamma).

b. *Anat.* and *Zool.* Prefixed to adjs., or forming derivative adjs. from sbs. in *-al* (sometimes used ellipt. as sbs.): = Pertaining to or situated on the upper... or the upper part of (what is expressed by the second element), as *supralabial* (the upper lip), *supramaxillary* (the upper jaw).

1891 *Cent. Dict.*, *Supralabial. 1904 *Biol. Bulletin* Nov. 293 A black spot, just above the sixth supralabial. *Ibid.*, The supralabials are dusky yellow. 1847–9 *Todd's Cycl. Anat.* IV. 548/1 Its *supra-maxillary part is constituted by one or two large branches. 1872 HUMPHRY *Myology* 46 The supra-maxillary, or second division of the fifth [nerve].

II. Above (in various figurative senses); higher in quality, amount, or degree. (Cf. SUPER- 4, 5, 6.)

4. a. Prefixed to adjectives: = SUPER- 4 a, as *supra-Christian, -conscious, -historical, -intellectual, -legal, -local, -mechanical, -moral, -national, -normal* (= SUPERNORMAL), *-ordinary, -rational*; † **Supravu·lgar**, that is above the common or ordinary. Also in derived sbs., as *supra-rationalism*, and advs., as *supra-locally*.

1867 SWINBURNE *Blake* (1868) 266 Thus prophesies Blake, in a fury of *supra-Christian dogmatism. 1891 JAS. ORR *Chr. View God & World* ii. (1893) 70 Hartmann..speaks..of his Absolute..as *supra-conscious. 1902 *Contemp. Rev.* Mar. 385 Experimental psychical research is throwing great light on..the importance of the subconscious and supraconscious, or the 'Subliminal' self. 1908 *Hibbert Jrnl.* Jan. 436 The intelligence..tries to apprehend the *supra-corporeal in terms of the corporeal. 1894 N. BUCHANAN tr. *Harnack's Hist. Dogma* I. ii. 97 History and doctrine are surrounded by a bright cloud of the *suprahistorical. 1885 SETH *Scot. Philos.* vi. 188 The hungering and thirsting of men's hearts after..some *supra-intellectual union..with the source of all. 1875 DIGBY *Real Prop.* vi. (1876) 289 He would..be restrained..by the extra-legal, or, if the expression may be allowed, *supra-legal power of Chancellor. 1852 BP. FORBES *Nicene Creed* viii. 146 Immensity..and *supralocal existence, are the qualities of the true God. *Ibid.* xiii. 227 The supra-local Presence of His Body in the Sacrament of the Altar. 1866 *Clerical Jrnl.* 3 May 422/1 Jesus Christ..offers, and.. is offered, on all earthly altars supernaturally and *supra-locally. 1740 CHEYNE *Regimen* 3 Impossible..that an Animal Body could have been..formed without a *Supra-mechanical Organisation. *a* 1894 ROMANES *Thoughts Relig.* I. ii. (1895) 81 Without being *supra-moral..He may be unmoral. 1908 *Dublin Rev.* Oct. 384 One great *Supranational body, in which there should be 'neither Jew nor Greek'. 1897 LANG in *Contemp. Rev.* Dec. 774 *Supranormal phenomena. *a* 1683 SWINBURNE *Treat. Spousals* (1686) 22 Yet doth their *supraordinary Understanding..supply that small defect of Age. 1651 N. BACON *Disc. Govt. Eng.* II. xxx. (1739) 136 The Pope had now usurped a power supra-ordinary over all Appeals. 1894 N. BUCHANAN tr. *Harnack's Hist. Dogma* I. App. iii. 346 The Divine Original Essence is *supra-rational. 1882–3 *Schaff's Encycl. Relig. Knowl.* III. 1995 Their..views were designated as supranaturalism, and not as *suprarationalism or irrationalism. 1697 COLLIER *Ess. Mor. Subj.* I. (1703) 81 To furnish himself with *supravulgar and noble qualities.

b. Prefixed to a sb., forming an adj., as *supra-state* (cf. SUPER- 4 b).

1914 *Contemp. Rev.* Aug. 200 If there is an inter-State life there is also a supra-State life.

5. Prefixed to a sb. = SUPER- 5; as *supra-entity*.

1647 HERRICK *Noble Numb.*, *Upon God*, God is not onely said to be An Ens, but Supraentitie.

6. = Higher, superior (cf. SUPER- 6 b), as *supra-consciousness*, † *supra-passion*, *supra-world*.

1914 *19th Cent.* July 121 This *supra-consciousness..is seen..to be independent of the material senses. 1624 F. WHITE *Repl. Fisher* 538 The merits and *supra-passions of Saints. 1907 E. E. FOURNIER D'ALBE (*title*) Two New Worlds. I. The Infra-World. II. The *Supra-World.

7. Above in degree or amount, beyond, more than (what is expressed by the second element): with sbs., as *su:pra-centena·rian* (so *su:pracentena·rianism*), or adjs., as *suprama·ximal, supra-o·ptimal* (also ellipt. as sbs., *sc.* temperature); **Su:praquanti·valent** *a.*, more than equivalent, higher in ideal than real value; so *su:praquanti·valence*.

1870 SCOFFERN *Stray Leaves Sci. & Folk-lore* 470, I do not find that women figure as *supra-centenarians in any way comparable to men. 1881 W. D. MACRAY *Index Registers Ducklington* Pref., One case of *supra-centenarianism is recorded; the 'old widow Knapp' was buried 10 March 1727, at the age of 105. 1905 *Science* 23 June 948 Death at the *supramaximal or subminimal may be due to changes of a very definite nature. 1904 *Ibid.* 2 Dec. 751 This reaction is repeated as long as an effective *supraoptimal or suboptimal temperature continues. 1903 *Alien. & Neurol.* Feb. 50 (Cent. D., Suppl.) Occupation is very especially suited to produce a *supraquantivalence of certain ideas. *Ibid.*, We had previously considered as the basis of the *supraquantivalent idea the frequent repetition..of definite trains of thought.

8. Before in time; = SUPER- 8; as in SUPRALAPSARIAN; so † **Su:pra-creata·rian**, one who believes that in the divine decrees the purpose of election and reprobation was antecedent to that of creation; also as *adj.*

1660 HEYLIN *Hist. Quinquart.* III. 61 According to the Supra-lapsarian, or Supra-creatarian way. *Ibid.* 64 The Supra-lapsarians..(or Supra-creatarians rather, as a late judicious Writer calls them).

III. In the highest or to a very high degree.

9. Very highly, extremely, = SUPER- 9 a, b: as *supra-censorious, supra-feminine, supra-fine* (= SUPERFINE), *supra-sensitive* (= SUPERSENSITIVE), *supra-subtle* (= SUPERSUBTLE), adjs.; *supragravitate, supra-parasite* (with *it*, to play the parasite to excess), *supra-saturate* (= SUPERSATURATE), vbs.

1901 *Westm. Gaz.* 31 Aug. 5/2 This *supra-censorious censorship of minor news. 1883 *Fortn. Rev.* July 117 A *supra-feminine love of softness and splendour. 1819 SYD. SMITH *Game Laws* Wks. 1859 I. 259/1 The *supra-fine country gentleman. 1672 FLAMSTEED in Rigaud *Corr. Sci. Men* (1841) II. 139 The apogæon part of the system may contain more of matter..and consequently..may *supragravitate and incline the axis towards the synodical line. 1654 GAYTON *Pleas. Notes* III. vi. 108 The slave Sancho doth *supra-parasite it. 1770 *Phil. Trans.* LXI. 341 Till the fluids are (if I may use that expression) *supra-saturated with the acid. 1893 W. H. HUDSON *Idle Days Patagonia* xii. (1899) 194 *Suprasensitive retinae. 1894 *Athenæum* 13 Jan. 47/2 The same *supra-subtle unraveller of mysteries.

IV. 10. Expressing addition; involving addition or repetition (cf. SUPER- 13, 14, 15): as † *supra-addition* (= SUPERADDITION 2), *supra-compound*

(= a compound of a compound, a compound of more than two elements). † **Su:prabipa·rtient** = *superbipartient* (see SUPER- 14). **Su:pradeco·mpound, Su:pradeco·mposite** *adjs. Bot.*, additionally decompound; triply or more than triply compound.

a 1706 EVELYN *Hist. Relig.* (1850) II. 46 These..were the doctrines and *supra-additions of the Scribes and Pharisees. 1753 HOGARTH *Anal. Beauty* xi. 136 The length of the foot .., in respect to the breadth, makes a double *suprabipartient, a diapason, and a diatesseron. 1791 HAMILTON tr. *Berthollet's Dyeing* I. I. i. 22 At other times they unite with the salts and form *supracompounds. 1816 J. SMITH *Panorama Sci. & Art* II. 532 Acids, alkalies, [etc.]..may sometimes form supra-compounds with the cloth, and thereby change its colour. 1753 *Chambers' Cycl.* Suppl. s.v. *Leaf*, **Supradecomposite Leaf*, one which has the common petiole divided more than twice. *Ibid.* s.v. *Leaf* (*Compound*), The *supradecompound [leaf]. 1777 S. ROBSON *Brit. Flora* 204 Hemloc Dropwort. Leaves supradecompound. 1874 GARROD & BAXTER *Mat. Med.* 225 The leaves are supra-decompound, the leaflets oblong and ovate.

† **Supraca·rgo.** *Obs.* Also 7 **sopracargo.** [ad. Sp. *sobrecargo* (f. *sobre* over + *cargo* CARGO), whence F. *subrécargue*, also † *supercarge* (Voltaire), Pg. *sobrecarga*.] = SUPERCARGO.

1667 DENHAM *Direct. Painter* I. xiii. 12 Though Clifford in the Character appear Of Supra-Cargo to our Fleet and their. 1674 J. COLLINS *Introd. Merchants-Acc.* E 3, Journal of the Sopracargos Accounts. 1719 DE FOE *Crusoe* I. (Globe) 198 What Business had I to..turn Supra Cargo to Guinea, to fetch Negroes? 1813 MILBURN *Oriental Commerce* II. 533 The Company's instructions to the supracargoes of their ships are very particular as to the mode of package and stowage. 1824 *Encycl. Metrop.* (1845) XVI. 589/1 The black [teas]..or boheas, [are brought] from Fŏ-kyen, called the Bohea country by the Supra-cargoes at Canton. 1844 H. H. WILSON *Brit. India* I. 321 The supracargoes..at last counselled acquiescence.

Su:pracele·stial, *a. rare.* [f. late L. *suprācælestis*: see SUPRA- 1, 4 a, CELESTIAL.] = SUPERCELESTIAL 1, 2.

1432–50 tr. *Higden* (Rolls) II. 291 Abraham, experte in astronomy,..folowede in erthe that he vnderstode by the disposicion of bodies supracelestialle. 1811 R. HINDMARSH tr. *Swedenborg's Coronis* 110 If I have told you earthly things, and ye believe not, how shall ye believe if I shall tell you supra-celestial things? [Cf. John iii. 12 τὰ ἐπουράνια.]

Supraciliary (s[i]ūpräsi·liări), *a.* (*sb.*) *Anat.* and *Zool.* [f. SUPRA- 1 b, after *superciliary*.] = SUPERCILIARY; as *sb.* applied *spec.* to the small scales attached to the eyelids in reptiles, below the supra-oculars.

1828–32 in WEBSTER (citing URE). 1863 HUXLEY *Man's Place Nat.* II. 76 In the Man..the supraciliary ridges or brow-prominences usually project but little. 1874 COUES *Birds N. W.* 450 A yellowish suffusion about the head, and especially along the supraciliary stripe. 1903 *Proc. Zool. Soc. Lond.* II. 125 Five supraoculars,..10 or 11 supraciliaries.

Supraclavicle (-klæ·vik'l). *Anat.* and *Zool.* Also in L. form **su:praclavi·cula.** [See SUPRA- 1 c and CLAVICLE[1].] A superior bone of the scapular arch in some fishes, above the clavicle.

1873 MIVART *Elem. Anat.* 162 In bony Fishes, where the clavicles..may not only be provided with a distinct inter-clavicle, but also each with a distinct portion above—the supra-clavicle. 1880 GÜNTHER *Fishes* iii. 59 The scapular.. arch is suspended from the skull by the (suprascapula) post-temporal..Then follows the (scapula) supraclavicula. 1888 ROLLESTON & JACKSON *Anim. Life* 416 The *Ganoidei* and *Teleostei* have investing bones known as supra-clavicle, clavicle, inter-clavicle, and post-clavicle.

Supraclavicular (-klăvi·kiŭlăɹ), *a.* *Anat.* and *Zool.* [In sense 1, ad. mod.L. *suprāclāviculāris*, f. *suprā* SUPRA- 1 b + *clāvicula* CLAVICLE[1]; in sense 2, f. SUPRACLAVICLE: see -AR.]

1. Situated above the clavicle or collar-bone.

1847–9 *Todd's Cycl. Anat.* IV. 753/2 The supra-clavicular and acromial nerves, form the termination of the cervical plexus. 1876 *Trans. Clinical Soc.* IX. 193 Forced breathing called into play the diaphragm far more than the supraclavicular muscles. 1886 FAGGE *Princ. Med.* I. 715 In one of my cases, these supraclavicular swellings were much larger than hen's eggs.

2. Pertaining to the supraclavicle.

In recent Dicts.

Suprahu·man, *a. rare.* [SUPRA- 4 a.] = SUPERHUMAN.

1740 CHEYNE *Regimen* 40 Outward and inward Means may be..bestow'd, by external Providences, suprahumane..Aid and Grace. 1809 J. FOSTER *Contrib. Eclectic Rev.* (1844) I. 379 No believer in any supra-human means, in any immediate interposition of the Almighty. 1840 DE QUINCEY *Rhetoric* Wks. 1859 XI. 42 Any supra-human intelligence, divine or angelic.

So **Su:prahuma·nity** = SUPERHUMANITY.

c 1810 COLERIDGE in *Lit. Rem.* (1838) III. 253 An essential supra-humanity in Christ.

Supralapsarian (s[i]ūprălæpsē·riăn), *sb.* and *a.* *Theol.* [f. mod.L. *suprālapsārius*, f. *suprā* SUPRA- 8 + L. *lapsus* fall, LAPSE: see -IAN. Cf. F. *supralapsaire*.]

A. *sb.* A name applied to those Calvinists who held the view that, in the divine decrees, the predestination of some to eternal life and of others to eternal death was antecedent to the creation and the fall: opposed to INFRALAPSARIAN.

1633 HOARD *Gods Love to Mankind* 13 The Maintainers of the Absolute Decree do say..eyther that all actions..and all events..are absolutely necessary; so the Supralapsarians: or that all mens ends (at least) are unalterable and indeterminable by the power of their wills; so the Sublapsarians. 1674 HICKMAN *Quinquart. Hist.* (ed. 2) 75, I believe, with the Supralapsarian, that God hath decreed, not to bestow converting Grace upon many whom he could easily (had he so pleased) have converted. 1674 BOYLE *Excell. Theol.* I. i. 50 Some few Theologues..have got the name of Supralapsarians, for venturing to look back beyond the fall of Adam for God's decrees of election and reprobation. 1797 *Encycl. Brit.* (ed. 3) XVIII. 84/1 According to the supralapsarians, the object of predestination is, *homo creabilis et labilis*; and, according to the sublapsarians and infralapsarians, *homo creatus et lapsus*. 1849 MACAULAY *Hist. Eng.* iii. I. 400 The young candidate for academical honours..was strictly interrogated by a synod of louring Supralapsarians as to the day and hour when he experienced the new birth.

B. *adj.* Of or pertaining to the Supralapsarians or their doctrine; that is a Supralapsarian.

1633 HOARD *Gods Love to Mankind* 2 The rest of that side, thinking to avoyd the great inconveniences, to which that supralapsarian way lyeth open,..present man to God in his decree of Reprobation, lying in the fall. 1733 NEAL *Hist. Purit.* II. 79 A treatise of Beza's upon the Supralapsarian scheme of Predestination. 1764 MACLAINE tr. *Mosheim's Eccl. Hist.* XVII. (1833) 639/1 The Supralapsarian and Sublapsarian divines forgot their debates and differences. 1831 MACAULAY *Ess.*, *Pilgr. Progr.* (1897) 191 An absurd allegory written by some raving supralapsarian preacher who was dissatisfied with the mild theology of the Pilgrim's Progress. 1839 HALLAM *Lit. Eur.* III. ii. § 32 The supra-lapsarian tenets of Calvin. 1885 *Encycl. Brit.* XIX. 670/2 The supralapsarian view was..adopted by Beza and other Calvinists, as it had been held by some of the Augustinian schoolmen.

Hence **Su:pralapsa·rianism** [cf. mod.L. *suprālapsāriismus*], the doctrine of the Supralapsarians. So † **Suprala·psary** *sb.* and *a.* = SUPRALAPSARIAN.

1728 CHAMBERS *Cycl.*, *Supralapsary*, in Theology, a Person who holds, that God, without any Regard to the good or evil Works of Men, has resolv'd, by an eternal Decree, to save some, and damn others. 1755 JOHNSON, *Supralapsary*, antecedent to the fall of man. 1775 ASH, Supralapsarianism. 1841 *J. Evans' Sk. Denom. Chr. World* 80 Recent divines who have gone to the height of Supralapsarianism. 1874 GREEN *Short Hist.* viii. § 1. 458 Whitgift strove to force on the Church the supralapsarianism of his Lambeth Articles.

Supraliminal (s[i]ūprăli·minăl), *a.* *Psych.* [f. SUPRA- 1 a + L. *līmin-*, LIMEN threshold: after *subliminal*.] Above the limen or threshold of sensation or consciousness; belonging to the ordinary or normal consciousness: opp. to SUBLIMINAL.

1892 MYERS in *Proc. Soc. Psychical Res.* Feb. 306, I hold ..that this subliminal consciousness..may embrace a far wider range..of..activity than is open to our supraliminal consciousness. *Ibid.* [see SUBLIMINAL].

Hence **Suprali·minally** *adv.*

a 1901 MYERS *Hum. Personality* I. 87 We need not postulate any direct or supernormal knowledge,—but merely a subliminal calculation,..expressing itself supraliminally.

Supralunar (s[i]ūprăl[i]ū·năɹ), *a.* [See SUPRA- 1 a and LUNAR, and cf. SUBLUNAR.] = next: cf. SUPERLUNAR.

1719 STEELE *Old Whig* No. 2. 12 Comets, said he, are Two-fold, Supra-lunar, and Sub-lunar. 1848 KINGSLEY *Yeast* ii, I am..utterly deficient in that sixth sense of the angelic or supralunar beautiful, which fills your soul with ecstasy. 1856 — *Misc.* (1859) II. 114 The most supralunar rosepink of piety, devotion, and purity.

Supralunary (s[i]ūprăl[i]ū·nări), *a.* [See SUPRA- 1 a and LUNARY, and cf. SUBLUNARY.] = SUPERLUNARY.

1635 SWAN *Spec. Mundi* (1670) 84 The admittance of terrene Exhalations to join their forces towards the effecting of supralunary Comets. *a* 1656 HALES *Gold. Rem.* (1673) 276 Certain strange supralunary arguments, which never fell within the sphere of common action. 1691 NORRIS *Pract. Disc.* 216 If it be once granted that there is a Providence, 'tis an absurd..conceit, to confine it..to the Supralunary Regions. 1903 *Blackw. Mag.* Nov. 628/1 His head full of these supralunary matters.

Supramundane (s[i]ūprămʊ·ndeⁱn), *a.* [ad. mod.L. **suprāmundānus*, f. *suprā* SUPRA- 1 a, 4 a + *mundus* world. Cf. F. *supramondain*, It. *sopramondano*.] = SUPERMUNDANE.

1662 STANLEY *Hist. Chaldaick Philos.* (1701) 8/2 The Supramundane Light, an Incorporeal Infinite luminous Space, in which the intellectual Beings reside. 1678 CUDWORTH *Intell. Syst.* I. iv. § 14. 243 These Eternal Gods of Plato, called by his Followers θεοὶ ὑπερκόσμιοι, the Supramundane Gods. 1744 HARRIS *Three Treat.* II. (1765) 363 Beings divine, supramundane, and..unchangeable. 1829 CARLYLE *Misc.* (1857) II. 52 The supramundane, divine nature of Virtue. 1872 LIDDON *Elem. Relig.* iii. 83 Revelation has familiarized Christians with the angels, as supramundane beings. 1884 *Manch. Exam.* 10 Oct. 5/3 Free trade is..suitable rather for an ideal and supramundane existence than for the present state of society.

Supranatural (s[i]ūprănæ·tiŭrăl, -tʃŭrăl), *a.* (*sb.*) *rare.* [See SUPRA- 4 a and NATURAL. Cf. F. *supranaturalisme, -iste*.] = SUPERNATURAL.

1857 P. FREEMAN *Princ. Div. Serv.* II. 32 To express.. their..conceptions of the divine and supranatural element in the subject. 1874 J. H. BLUNT *Dict. Sects* 125/1 A mechanical Deity that is only so far supra-natural as that Infinite Substance must always stand in antagonism with the finite. 1908 *Hibbert Jrnl.* July 808 We measure the change from the standpoint of the supranatural.

So **Suprana·turalism, Suprana·turalist, Su:pranaturali·stic** *a.*, **Su:pra-na·ture** (= SUPERNATURALISM, etc.).

1828–32 WEBSTER (citing MURDOCK), Supranaturalism. 1842 BRANDE *Dict. Sci.*, etc., *Supranaturalists*, a name given of late years to the middle party among the divines of Germany, to distinguish them from the Rationalists,..and from the Evangelical party. 1846 GEO. ELIOT tr. *Strauss' Life Jesus* Introd. § 11. I. 46 Those theologians..who think to unite both parties by this middle course—a vain endeavour which the rigid supranaturalist pronounces heretical, and the rationalist derides. 1846 WORCESTER (citing *P. Cyc.*), Supranaturalistic. 1856 R. A. VAUGHAN *Mystics* (1860) II. XIII. i. 250 They sought..for a sign; and in their credulous incredulity, grew greedy of every supranaturalism except the scriptural. 1866 *Chambers' Encycl.* VIII. 120/2 The struggle between Rationalism and Supranaturalism. 1890 J. F. SMITH tr. *Pfleiderer's Developm. Theol.* II. ii. 122 The difficulties of the supranaturalistic theology. 1908 *Hibbert Jrnl.* July 808 It is increased knowledge of nature which has made supra-nature incredible.

Su:pra-occi·pital, *a.* and *sb.* *Anat.* and *Zool.* [ad. mod.L. *suprā-occipitālis*: see SUPRA- 1 b and OCCIPITAL.] = SUPEROCCIPITAL.

1846 OWEN in *Rep. Brit. Assoc.* I. 319 The flattening..of the human supraoccipital, parietal and frontal bones. 1848 — *Homol. Vertebrate Skel.* 5, I..regard the supraoccipital as the serial homologue of the parietal and the midfrontal. 1851 MANTELL *Petrifactions* iv. § 3. 390 The horns being placed more anteriorly in relation to the supra-occipital ridge. 1880 GÜNTHER *Fishes* 56 The supraoccipital separates the parietals, and forms a suture with the frontals.

Supra-o·rbital, *a.* (*sb.*) *Anat.* and *Zool.* [ad. mod.L. *suprā-orbitālis*: see SUPRA- 1 b and ORBITAL.] Situated or occurring above the orbit of the eye. Also as *sb.* a supra-orbital artery, vein, bone, or nerve.

1828 QUAIN *Elem. Anat.* 648 The external, or supra-orbital branch [of the frontal nerve]. 1846 OWEN in *Rep. Brit. Assoc.* I. 283 The bones of the dermo-skeleton are:—The Supratemporals; The Supraorbitals; The Suborbitals; The Labials. 1868 DARWIN *Anim. & Pl.* I. iv. 117 The supra-orbital plates or processes of the frontal bones are much broader than in the wild rabbit. 1876 TOMES *Dental Anat.* 39 Pain..is often referred to the point of emergence of a nerve, as..in supra-orbital neuralgia.

Also **Supra-o·rbitar, Supra-o·rbitary** [mod.L. *suprā-orbitārius*], *adjs.*

1782 MONRO *Anat.* 287 The sight may be lost by an injury done to the supra-orbitar branch. 1844 SIR C. BELL *Anat. Expression* ii. (ed. 3) 49 The prominences over the orbits (the supra-orbitary ridges), which are peculiar to a more advanced age. 1856 TODD & BOWMAN *Phys. Anat.* II. 7 The fissure which bounds the supra-orbitar convolution.

Suprarenal (s[i]ūprărī·năl), *a.* (*sb.*) *Anat.* [ad. mod.L. *suprārēnālis*: see SUPRA- 1 b and RENAL.] Situated above the kidney; applied to a pair of ductless glands (*suprarenal bodies, capsules, corpuscles, glands*), one immediately above each kidney; also to other structures connected with these.

1828 QUAIN *Elem. Anat.* 500 The kidneys and supra-renal capsules. 1840 W. J. E. WILSON *Anat. Vade M.* (1842) 309 The Supra-renal are sometimes branches of the phrenic or of the renal arteries. *Ibid.* 350 The Supra-renal veins terminate partly in the renal veins, and partly in the inferior vena cava. 1876 tr. *Wagner's Gen. Pathol.* 154 The connective tissue corpuscles of the supra-renal glands. 1883 *Encycl. Brit.* XV. 365/1 The 'suprarenal bodies' or 'adrenals'. 1905 H. D. ROLLESTON *Dis. Liver* 271 The various preparations of suprarenal gland substance.

b. *transf.* Of, pertaining to, or affecting the suprarenal capsules.

1876 BRISTOWE *Theory & Pract. Med.* (1878) 583 There are no lesions..which are constantly associated with the suprarenal affection. *Ibid.* 585 Supra-renal degeneration.

B. *sb.* A suprarenal capsule (in quot. 1841, a suprarenal artery).

1841 R. E. GRANT *Outl. Comp. Anat.* 512 The aorta gives off..the two small phrenic arteries..to the diaphragm; two or more minute supra-renals to the supra-renal capsules. 1895 *Athenæum* 7 Dec. 795/2 The supra-renal bodies of fishes...There was no relation..between the supra-renals and the lymphatic head-kidney. 1897 *Allbutt's Syst. Med.* III. 313 Glands without ducts, such as the..suprarenals.

Hence **Suprare·nalin, Suprare·nin,** a substance extracted from suprarenal capsules, used as a hæmostatic.

1904 *Brit. Med. Jrnl.* 17 Sept. 681 The constitution of suprarenin. 1909 *Chem. & Druggist* 20 Feb. 316/2 Novocain-Suprarenin Dental Tablets..contain..Suprarenin borate. 1909 *Cent. Dict.*, Suppl., Suprarenalin.

‖ **Suprascapula** (s[i]ūpräskæ·piŭlă). *Anat.* and *Zool.* Pl. **-æ.** [mod.L.: see SUPRA- 3 a and SCAPULA.] A bone (or cartilage) in the upper or anterior part of the scapular arch or shoulder-girdle, in fishes, and in some batrachians and reptiles.

1854 OWEN in *Orr's Circ. Sci.*, *Org. Nat.* I. 175 The special names of the above elements of the hæmal arch of the occipital vertebra are, from above downwards, 'suprascapula',..'scapula',..'coracoid'. 1888 ROLLESTON & JACKSON *Anim. Life* 81 [The dorsal scapular] consists of a broad semicartilaginous supra-scapula and an ossified scapula.

Suprasca·pular, *a.* *Anat.* and *Zool.* [ad. mod.L. *suprāscapulāris*: see SUPRA- 1 b, 3 b and SCAPULAR *a.*] Situated above or upon the scapula; belonging to or connected with the upper or anterior part of the scapular arch, or the suprascapula.

1828 QUAIN *Elem. Anat.* 160 A foramen, for the transmission ..of the supra-scapular nerve. *Ibid.* 401 The supra-scapular and posterior-scapular arteries. *Ibid.* 416 The nerve passes through the supra-scapular notch, or foramen. 1854 OWEN in *Orr's Circ. Sci.*, *Org. Nat.* I. 190 The suprascapular plate remains long cartilaginous, and always partly so. *Ibid.* 210 The upper or suprascapular piece..retains..its cartilaginous state. 1878 T. BRYANT *Surg.* I. 479 The suprascapular artery and vein will always be seen behind the clavicle.

Also † **Suprasca·pulary** *a.*

1693 tr. *Blancard's Phys. Dict.* (ed. 2), *Infra Spinatus Musculus*, or *Supra Scapularis Secundus*, proceeds under the Spine, from the Basis of the Scapula, with the Second, Supra Scapulary, Carnous and Thick, and runs into the Ligament of the Shoulder. 1828–32 WEBSTER.

Suprascript (s[i]ū·präskript), *a.* [ad. late L. *suprāscriptus*, f. *suprā* above + *scriptus* written.] Written above: = SUPERSCRIPT *a.*

1896 W. M. LINDSAY *Introd. Latin Textual Emend.* 36 In the original the *h* was expressed by this suprascript sign. 1902 *Scotsman* 5 Nov. 11/7 To have one's attention, at the height of a tragic climax, hitched up by a suprascript cipher.

† **Supra-sedeas,** error for SUPERSEDEAS.

1615 BRETON *Char. Ess.* Wks. (Grosart) II. 10/1 It is a *supra sedeas* for all diseases.

Suprase·nsible, *a.* (*sb.*) [SUPRA- 4 a. So F.] = SUPERSENSIBLE; also *absol.* with *the*.

1839 *Penny Cycl.* XIII. 177/1 Kant applies the term of *noumenon* to the notion of God, and generally to all supra-sensible objects, which may be conceived of. *Ibid.*, The acceptance of this postulate [of the practical reason] as true and legitimate does not constitute a scientific certainty,..which indeed does not exist for the supra-sensible. 1855 KINGSLEY *Westw. Ho!* ii, Your Platonical 'eternal world of supra-sensible forms'. 1901 A. M. FAIRBAIRN *Philos. Chr. Relig.* I. vi. 200 Religion is, subjectively, man's consciousness of relation to suprasensible Being.

Suprase·nsual, *a.* [SUPRA- 4 a.] = SUPERSENSUAL.

1857 KINGSLEY *Two Y. Ago* I. 10 Of him, too,..I presume, an ideal exists eternally in the supra-sensual Platonic universe. 1868 LIGHTFOOT *Philippians* 198 The star is the suprasensual counterpart, the heavenly representative; the lamp, the earthly realisation. 1889 SKRINE *Mem. E. Thring* 79 The touch of supra-sensual things, the breath of religious mystery.

So **Suprase·nsuous** *a.* = SUPERSENSUOUS.

1866 WESTCOTT *Ess.* I. (1891) 2 An inherent communion with a divine and suprasensuous world.

Supraspe·ctive, *a. rare*$^{-1}$. [f. L. *suprā* above, after *introspective*.] Surveying from above.

1864 SALA in *Temple Bar* Mar. 483 Tranquilly supraspective of the bustle and clamour.

Supraspinal (s[i]ūpräspəi·năl), *a.* *Anat.* [ad. mod.L. *suprāspīnālis*: see SUPRA- 1 b and SPINAL.] Situated above or upon a (or the) spine.

a. Situated above the spine of the scapula: opp. to *infraspinal* (see INFRA- B.).

1733 G. DOUGLAS tr. *Winslow's Anat.* III. iv. § 7 (1756) I. 183 *Supra-Spinatus*..is a thick narrow Muscle,..filling all the Supra-Spinal Cavity of the Scapula. 1835–6 *Todd's Cycl. Anat.* I. 569/2 The spine is..so placed as to divide the dorsum of the scapula into a supra-spinal and infra-spinal depression. 1847–9 *Ibid.* IV. 435/1 The supra-spinal branch [of the supra-scapular artery]..is distributed to the supra-spinatus muscle.

b. = SUPRASPINOUS b.

1835–6 *Todd's Cycl. Anat.* I. 374/1 On the lips of the spinous processes of the neck some fibres may be shown, to which the name supra-spinal muscles has been given. 1855 DUNGLISON *Med. Lex.*, Supra-spinal ligaments, are..1. The Dorso-lumbo-supra-spinal ligament,..extending above the spinous processes of the dorsal and lumbar vertebræ... 2. Cervical-supra-spinal ligament,..which extends above all the cervical spinous processes.

c. (See quot.)

1836–9 *Todd's Cycl. Anat.* II. 980/1 A distinct vascular canal..is extended along the upper surface of the abdominal portion of the cerebro-spinal cord in perfect Lepidopterous insects...We have designated this structure the *supra-spinal vessel*.

‖ **Supraspinatus** (s[i]ūpräspəinē·tŏs). *Anat.* [mod.L., f. L. *suprā* SUPRA- 1 b + *spīna* SPINE: see -ATE[2].] A muscle arising from the supraspinal fossa of the scapula, and inserted into the greater tuberosity of the humerus, serving to raise and adduct the arm.

[1704 J. HARRIS *Lex. Techn.* I, *Supra Spinatus*, or *Supra Scapularis*, is a Muscle..placed above the Spine of the Shoulder-blade.] 1733 G. DOUGLAS tr. *Winslow's Anat.* (1756) I. 291 The Supra-Spinatus is commonly supposed to join with the Deltoides in lifting up the Arm. 1828 QUAIN *Elem. Anat.* 161 It [*sc.* the capsular ligament] receives additions from the tendons of the supra and infra spinatus muscles. 1875 SIR W. TURNER in *Encycl. Brit.* I. 838/2 The muscles which cause these movements are inserted into the humerus; the supra-spinatus, infra-spinatus, and teres minor into the great tuberosity; the sub-scapularis into the small tuberosity.

Supraspinous (s[i]ūpräspəi·nəs), *a.* *Anat.* [ad. mod.L. *suprāspīnōsus*, f. L. *suprā* SUPRA- 1 b + *spīna* SPINE.] Situated above or upon a spine.

a. = SUPRASPINAL a.

1828 QUAIN *Elem. Anat.* 374 The *supra-spinatus* is placed at the superior part of the shoulder in the supra-spinous fossa of the scapula. 1876 *Trans. Clinical Soc.* IX. 151 On percussion there was absolute dulness in the left sub-clavian and supra-spinous regions.

b. Situated above or upon the spinous processes of the vertebræ.

1828 QUAIN *Elem. Anat.* 152 The supra-spinous ligament consists of small, compressed bundles of longitudinal fibres, which connect the summits of the spinous processes. 1875 SIR W. TURNER in *Encycl. Brit.* I. 835/1 Inter- and supra-spinous ligaments connect adjacent spinous processes, and in the neck the supra-spinous ligament forms a broad band.

Supratemporal (s[i]ūpräte·mpŏrăl), *a.*[1] (*sb.*) *Anat.* and *Zool.* [See SUPRA- 1 b and TEMPORAL *a.*[2]] = SUPERTEMPORAL *a.*[2] (*sb.*).

1846 [see SUPRA-ORBITAL]. 1854 OWEN in *Orr's Circ. Sci.*, *Org. Nat.* I. 187 The suborbital, superorbital, and supra-temporal scale-bones are removed. 1866 HUXLEY *Laing's Preh. Rem. Caithn.* 95 The..supra-temporal ridges are but little marked. 1888 ROLLESTON & JACKSON *Anim. Life* 95 [In the perch] a forked bone, the supra-temporal scale, connects the fore-limb to the skull.

Suprate·mporal, *a.*[2] [See SUPRA- 4 a and TEMPORAL *a.*[1]] = SUPERTEMPORAL *a.*[1]

1882 FARRAR *Early Chr.* II. 404 That life is..eternal, i.e. spiritual, supratemporal, Divine. 1882 WESTCOTT *Hist. Faith* xi. (1883) 144 The 'eternal' does not in essence express the infinite extension of time but the absence of time: not the omni-temporal but the supra-temporal.

Su:praterra·neous, *a. rare.* [f. L. *suprā* SUPRA- 1 a + *terra* land, earth; after *subterraneous*.] = SUPERTERRANEOUS.

1666 *Phil. Trans.* I. 186 The things, to be observ'd..may be..divided..into Supraterraneous, Terrestrial, and Subterraneous. *a* 1900 SPRUCE in B. D. Jackson *Gloss. Bot. Terms* s.v., Supraterraneous Perianth.

So **Su:praterre·strial** *a.* = SUPERTERRESTRIAL 1.

1887 *Andover Rev.* Jan. 42 She might find her first supra-terrestrial experience in some dim subjacency of aromatic spiritual forest, in which she might smoke a spiritual pipe in peace. 1908 ORR *Resurrect. Jesus* vii. 198 That supra-terrestrial sphere to which it [*sc.* Christ's resurrection body] now more properly belonged.

Supravagi·nal, *a.* *Anat.* [See SUPRA- 1 b and VAGINAL.] Situated above or outside a sheath or sheathing membrane; situated, or performed, above the vagina.

1891 in *Cent. Dict.* 1893 H. MORRIS *Treat. Hum. Anat.* 890 The supravaginal space around the optic nerve. *Ibid.* 1083 The cervix..may be divided into..an upper supravaginal zone, a middle zone of vaginal attachment, and a lower intravaginal zone, the os uteri. 1901 *Lancet* 5 Oct. 917 Arguments..in favour of supra-vaginal amputation of the uterus rather than total hysterectomy.

† **Supravi·se,** *v. Obs.* [f. med. or mod.L. *suprāvīs-*, pa. ppl. stem of *suprāvidēre* (in med.L. to reconnoitre), f. *suprā* SUPRA- 2 + *vidēre* to see.] *trans.* = SUPERVISE *v.* 2. Also *absol.*

1606 HOLLAND *Sueton.* 231 Surveying and supravising the publick works. 1618 S. WARD *Jethro's Justice* (1627) 7 If God supravise not, Samuell the Seer shall take seuen wrong before one right. 1640 in Carlyle *Misc. Ess.* (1872) VII. 65 No man did supravise all the clerkes.

† **Supravi·sion.** *Obs.* [ad. med.L. *suprāvīsio, -ōnem*: cf. prec. and VISION.] = SUPERVISION 1.

1642 JER. TAYLOR *Episc.* (1647) 107 There comes upon me (saith S. Paul) daily the care or Supravision of all the Churches. 1651 — *Clerus Domini* iii. § 15 Taking supravision or oversight of them willingly. 1667 — *Gt. Exemp.* Disc. xix. § 12. (ed. 4) 477 The supravision of a Teacher over him.

† **Supravi·sor.** *Obs.* Also 6 -our. [ad. med.L. *suprāvīsor*: cf. prec.] = SUPERVISOR 1, 1 b, c, 3.

1566 GASCOIGNE *Supposes* v. ii, I make thee supra visour of this supper. 1609 W. M. *Man in Moone* (Percy Soc.) 2 What false orthographie escapeth in the print, impute to the hast of the supravisor of the proofes. 1614 in *Trans. Cumbld. & Westmld. Archæol. Soc.* III. 116 To take panes as supravisors to see the performinge of all things accordinge to this my will and testament. 1653 JER. TAYLOR *Serm. for Year* I. xxiii. 297 They made Aræus titular [admiral] and Lysander supravisor of him. *a* 1677 BARROW *Serm. Heb.* xiii. 17 Wks. 1686 III. 270 The Curators, or Supravisors of the Church. 1694 in Picton *L'pool Munic. Rec.* (1883) I. 320 The Supravis[rs] of the Highway.

Supremacy (s[i]upre·măsi). Also 6 supremasie, -isie, 6–7 -acie, -icie, 7 -acye, supreamacie, 8 supreamacy. [f. SUPREME *a.* + -ACY 2. Hence F. *suprématie*, It. *supremazia*, Sp., Pg. *supremacia*.]

1. The condition of being supreme in authority, rank, or power; position of supreme or highest authority or power.

a. with reference to the position of the sovereign (*royal* or *regal supremacy*) as supreme head in earth of the Church of England (as declared in the statute 26 Hen. VIII, c. 1, an. 1534), or as supreme governor of England in spiritual and temporal matters (as in 1 Eliz. c. 1, an. 1558–9). Also used retrospectively of the more indefinite authority claimed by earlier sovereigns.

Act of Supremacy (or *Supremacy Act*), any of the acts of parliament in which this is laid down. *Oath of* (*the King's*) *Supremacy*, the oath in which this is acknowledged.

1549 *Bk. Com. Prayer, Ord. Deacons*, The Othe of the Kynges Supremacie. I from henceforth shal utterly renounce..the Bysshop of Rome, and his auctoritie, power, and iurisdiction...And I from hencefoorth wyll..take the Kynges Maiestie, to be the onely Supreme head in earth, of the Church of Englande. 1554 *Act 1 & 2 Philip & M.* c. 8. § 42 Albeit the Title or Stile of Supremacye or Supreme Hedd of the Churche of Englande and of Irelande..never was..lawfully attributed..to any King..of this Realme. 1603 *Const. & Canons Eccles.* ii, Whosoeuer shall hereafter ..impeach in any part his [the King's] regal Supremacy in the said causes [ecclesiastical] restored to the Crowne. 1626 in Ellis *Orig. Lett.* Ser. I. III. 243 All three of them have taken the Oath of Allegiance, some say of Supremacy also. 1710 *Managers' Pro & Con* 62 If the Party will allow the Queen her Supremacy. 1769 BLACKSTONE *Comm.* IV. 53 The statute 1 W. & M. st. 2. c. 18..which exempts all dissenters..from all penal laws relating to religion, provided they take the oaths of allegiance and supremacy. 1839 KEIGHTLEY *Hist. Eng.* I. 103 [William the Conqueror] asserted his royal supremacy over the clergy of England. 1880 *Encycl. Brit.* XI. 664/2 Sir Thomas More and Fisher..were executed for refusing to accept the Supremacy Act (1535). 1884 *Encycl. Brit.* XVII. 701/1 Statutes of Charles II. and George I. enacted that no member should vote or sit in either house of parliament without having taken the several oaths of allegiance, supremacy, and abjuration.

b. with reference to the supreme authority of the see or bishop of Rome (*papal supremacy*).

1560 DAUS tr. *Sleidane's Comm.* 222 Those places of scripture, which the Bishop [of Rome] doeth vsurpe to establyshe hys supremacie [orig. *ad sui primatus confirmationem*]. 1561 T. NORTON *Calvin's Inst.* I. Pref., So that no man lift vp hys fynger agaynst the supremicie of the Apostolike sea. 1624 GATAKER *Transubst.* 132 So long as he acknowledgeth the Popes Supremacie. 1714 FORTESCUE-ALAND *Pref. Fortescue's Abs. & Lim. Mon.* 69 Possibly Rome had not then resolved to derive her Supremacy from St. Peter. 1757 in *Cath. Rec. Soc. Publ.* VII. 189 The learned Bossuett makes it an article of faith, the Supremacy of y[e] pope, as does the Councill of Trent.

c. *gen.* in the relation of one person, sovereign, state, etc. to another, or of God to the universe.

1547 TONSTALL in Burnet *Hist. Ref.* (1681) II. I. *Collect. Rec.* 107, I fortuned to find many Writings for the Supremacy of the King to the Realm of Scotland. 1584 B. R. tr. *Herodotus* I. 31 Determining to atchieue y[e] supremisie. 1596 SHAKS. *Tam. Shr.* v. ii. 109 Peace it boads, and loue, and quiet life, An awfull rule, and right supremicie. 1614 RALEIGH *Hist. World* III. xii. § 5. 150 They (who had beene accustomed vnto such a supremacie, as they would in no wise communicate with..Athens..). 1667 MILTON *P. L.* III. 205 Man disobeying..sinns Against the high Supremacie of Heav'n. 1782 PRIESTLEY *Corrupt. Chr.* I. I. 150 The divine being cannot give his own supremacy. 1835 THIRLWALL *Greece* viii. I. 291 The steps by which Sparta rose to a supremacy above the rest of the Dorian states. 1847 PRESCOTT *Peru* (1850) II. 170 The Indian lords then tendered their obeisance..after which the royal notary read aloud the instrument asserting the supremacy of the Castilian Crown. 1848 R. I. WILBERFORCE *Doctr. Incarnation* iv. (1852) 74 A supremacy over them [*sc.* the inferior creatures], had been the result of Adam's likeness to their Creator. 1856 DOVE *Logic Chr. Faith* vi. § 4. 354 Revelation exhibits.. the Supremacy of God.

d. With possessive as a mock title.

1760–72 H. BROOKE *Fool of Qual.* (1809) II. 14 Truth, so please your supremacy, has been sunk in..a well.

e. *fig.* Said of qualities, influences, etc.

1583 MELBANCKE *Philotimus* G iij, I giue you the supremasie of my soule, vse it as you list. 1663 PATRICK *Parab. Pilgr.* xxxii. (1687) 387 It suffers reason to retain its throne, or rather exalts..its Supremacy..to a greater height. 1809–10 COLERIDGE *Friend* I. vi. (1865) 25 The disbelief of essential wisdom and goodness..prepares the imagination for the supremacy of cunning with malignity. 1874 GREEN *Short Hist.* iii. § 4. 133 Abelard claimed for reason the supremacy over faith.

2. Supreme position in achievement, character, or estimation.

1589 GREENE *Menaphon* (Arb.) 35 Iuno for maiestie, Pallas for wisedome, and Venus for beautie had let my Samela haue the supremacie. 1693 DRYDEN *Juvenal* Ded. (1697) p. viii, That your Lordship is form'd by Nature for this Supremacy, I cou'd easily prove..from the distinguishing Character of your Writing. 1836 HOR. SMITH *Tin Trumpet* (1876) 335 The discovery that water would resist being boiled above 212 degrees has conferred upon England its manufacturing supremacy. 1872 YEATS *Techn. Hist. Comm.* 250 To secure the naval supremacy of Athens over the rest of the Greek states. 1879 *Cassell's Techn. Educ.* III. 154 English gunpowder has long held almost undisputed supremacy as to excellence of quality and strength.

Supreme (s[i]uprī·m), *a.* and *sb.* Also 6 suppreme, 6–7 supreame, 7–8 supream. [ad. L. *suprēmus*, superl. of *superus* that is above, f. *super* above. Cf. F. *suprême*, It., Sp., Pg. *supremo*.

In poetry, esp. when attrib., freq. stressed *su·preme*.]

A. *adj.*

1. Highest (in literal sense), loftiest, topmost. Now only *poet.*

1523 SKELTON *Garl. Laurel* 694 What thynge occasionyd the showris of rayne, Of fyre elementar in his supreme spere. 1653 R. SANDERS *Physiogn.* 115 The supream angle not joyned..predicts loss of the eyes. 1661 LOVELL *Hist. Anim. & Min.* 299 The venters are the inferiour, or abdomen; the middle, or thorax; or the supreame, which is the head. 1695 WOODWARD *Nat. Hist. Earth* I. (1723) 89 The supreme or outmost Stratum of the Globe. 1808 MACAULAY in Trevelyan *Life & Lett.* (1876) I. i. 32 Day set on Cambria's hills supreme. 1878 BROWNING *La Saisiaz* 75 Blanc, supreme above his earth-brood.

2. Highest in authority or rank; holding the highest place in authority, government, or power.

Chiefly in technical collocations, and first used in the expressions *supreme head* and *supreme governor* in the enactments of Henry VIII's and Elizabeth's reigns (respectively) dealing with the position of the sovereign as the paramount authority (as against the bishop of Rome). (Cf. SUPREMACY 1 a.)

Supreme Court of Judicature: (*a*) in India (see quot. 1773); (*b*) in Great Britain and Ireland (see JUDICATURE 1).

1532–3 *Act 24 Hen. VIII*, c. 12 Preamble, Where by dyvers sundrie olde autentike histories and cronicles it is manifestly declared and expressed that this Realme of Englond is an Impire..governed by oon Supreme heede and King. 1534 *Act 26 Hen. VIII*, c. 1, That the Kyng our Soveraign Lorde ..shalbe..reputed the onely supreme heed in erthe of the Churche of England callyd Anglicana Ecclesia. 1558–9 *Act 1 Eliz.* c. 1. § 19 (Form of Oath), I..doo..declare in my Conscience, that the Quenes Highnes is thonelye supreme Governour of this Realme..aswell in all Spirituall or Ecclesiasticall Thinges or Causes as Temporall. 1560 DAUS tr. *Sleidane's Comm.* 66 b, Geuyng hym his faythe as to his supreme Magistrate. 1597 SKENE *De Verb. Sign.* s.v. *Scaccarium*, Some callis it [*sc.* the Exchequer] the soveraigne and supreame court. 1611 *Bible* 1 Pet. ii. 13 Submit your selues to euery ordinance of man..whether it be to the King, as supreme, Or vnto gouernours. 1656 J. HAMMOND *Leah & Rachel* Postscr. (1844) 30, I..will abide such censure..as the supreame power of England shall find me to have merited. 1672–5 COMBER *Comp. Temple* (1702) 119 Such Miscreants..who should thirst so vehemently for the blood of its Supream Governor. 1765 BLACKSTONE *Comm.* I. ii. 146 Of magistrates also some are supreme, in whom the sovereign power of the state resides; others are subordinate, deriving all their authority from the supreme magistrate. 1770 *Junius Lett.* Ded., When we say that the legislature is supreme, we mean, that it is the highest power known to the constitution. 1773 *Act 13 Geo. III*, c. 63 § 13 That it shall..be lawful for his Majesty,..to..establish a Supreme Court of Judicature at Fort William [in Bengal]. 1790 A. J. DALLAS (*title*), Reports of Cases adjudged in the Courts of Pennsylvania, namely, the Common Pleas, Supreme Court, and the High Court of Errors and Appeals. 1844 H. H. WILSON *Brit. India* III. ix. III. 535 The Supreme Council..was to consist of six members, of whom four were to be officers of the four Presidencies. 1861 BROUGHAM *Brit. Const.* xvii. 255 The judicial power exercised by the Lords as a supreme Court of Judicature in all matters of law. 1873 *Act 36 & 37 Vict.* c. 66. § 4 The said Supreme Court shall consist of two permanent Divisions, one of which, under the name of 'Her Majesty's High Court of Justice', shall have and exercise original jurisdiction..and the other of which, under the name of 'Her Majesty's Court of Appeal', shall have and exercise appellate jurisdiction. 1881 *Encycl. Brit.* XIII. 789/2 In the United States the supreme court consists of a chief justice and eight associate justices.

†Const. *to.* 1642 JER. TAYLOR *Episc.* § 36 The king is supreme to the bishop in impery.

b. Said of the authority, command, etc.

1539 TONSTALL *Serm. Palm Sund.* (1823) 61 Faustinus.. alleged..that the byshop of Rome ought to haue the orderynge of all Great Matters..by his supreme auctoritie. 1594 SHAKS. *Rich. III*, III. vii. 118 It is your fault, that you resigne The Supreme Seat, the Throne Maiesticall. 1659 HAMMOND *Dispatcher Disp.* iv. § 4 What the rights are, which are peculiar to the Supreme Pastourship. 1667 MILTON *P. L.* III. 659 Uriel,..thou..here art likeliest by supream decree Like honour to obtain. 1726 POPE *Odyss.* XIX. 170 He, long honour'd in supreme command. 1754 ERSKINE *Princ. Sc. Law* (1809) 13 Jurisdiction is either supreme, inferior, or mixed. 1840 THIRLWALL *Greece* lvi. VII. 185 When they had joined their forces, Craterus resigned the supreme command to his colleague. 1863 H. COX *Inst.* I. i. 2 The supreme power of making and abrogating laws.

c. *transf.* and *fig.* (chiefly predicative).

1656 BRAMHALL *Replic.* iv. 159 In a great Family there are several offices, as a Divine, a Physitian, a Schoolmaster, and every one of these is supreme in his own way. 1667 MILTON *P. L.* IV. 91 The lower still I fall, onely Supream In miserie. *a* 1680 BUTLER *Rem.* (1759) I. 238 Man is supreme Lord and Master Of his own Ruin and Disaster. 1726 BUTLER *Serm. Rolls Chap.* ii. 26 Which Principle..being in Nature supream,..ought to preside over and govern all the rest. 1838 DICKENS *Nich. Nick.* xxi, The temple of fashion where Madame Mantalini reigned paramount and supreme. 1876 STUBBS *Const. Hist.* III. xviii. 158 During the session parliament was supreme. 1884 F. TEMPLE *Relat. Relig. & Sci.* ii. (1885) 59 To believe that the rule of duty is supreme over all the universe, is the first stage of Faith. 1892 WESTCOTT *Gospel of Life* 89 Each science is supreme within its own domain.

ellipt. 1718 PRIOR *Solomon* II. 36 The spreading Cedar, that an Age had stood, Supreme of Trees, and Mistress of the Wood. 1774 BRYANT *Mythol.* II. 125 He seems to have been the supreme of those..spirits described above.

3. Of the highest quality, degree, or amount.

1593 SHAKS. *Lucr.* 780 Let their exhald vnholdsome breaths make sicke The life of puritie, the supreme faire, Ere he arriue his wearie noone-tide pricke. 1609 DANIEL *Civ. Wars* IV. xli, Hee could not meane t' haue peace with those, Who did in that supreame degree offend. *a* 1631 DONNE *Paradoxes* (1652) 17 If these kil themselves, they do it in their best and supream perfection. 1649 E. REYNOLDS *Hosea* vi. 81 The supreame end and happinesse of the soule. 1751 JOHNSON *Rambler* No. 110 ¶ 1 That to please the Lord and Father of the universe, is the supreme interest of created ..beings. 1847 HELPS *Friends in C.* I. vi. 96, I have a supreme disgust for the man who at the hustings has no opinion beyond..the clamour round him. 1849 MACAULAY *Hist. Eng.* iii. I. 412 In no other mind have the demonstrative faculty and the inductive faculty coexisted in such supreme excellence. 1856 EMERSON *Eng. Traits, Race* Wks. (Bohn) II. 20 They have sound bodies, and supreme endurance in war and in labour. 1872 LIDDON *Elem. Relig.* I. 5 The needs of the human mind, and among them..its supreme need of a religion. 1878 R. W. DALE *Lect. Preach.* vii. 212 The death of Christ, which is the supreme revelation of the Divine love.

b. Of persons: Highest or greatest in character or achievement.

c 1611 CHAPMAN *Iliad* v. 1 Then Pallas breath'd in Tydeus sonne: to render whom supreame To all the Greekes,..she cast a hoter beame, On his high mind. 1837 CARLYLE *Fr. Rev.* I. I. ii, The Supreme Quack. 1874 CREIGHTON *Hist. Ess.* i. (1902) 1 In..the reflective and analytic class, Lionardo and Dante stand supreme. 1878 GLADSTONE *Prim. Homer* 138 Homer exhibits Odusseus as a supreme master of the bow. 1891 FARRAR *Darkn. & Dawn* xvii, You are a supreme artist.

ellipt. 1814 WORDSW. *Laodamia* ix, Supreme of Heroes—bravest, noblest, best!

c. Of a point or period of time: Of highest or critical importance.

1878 BOSW. SMITH *Carthage* 170 The Carthaginian government managed, even in this supreme hour, to thwart Hamilcar. 1883 *Manch. Examiner* 26 Nov. 5/1 The generals have been at loggerheads at the supreme moment of the battle.

d. *spec.* applied to highly excellent varieties of fruits or vegetables.

1706 LONDON & WISE *Retir'd Gard'ner* I. xi. 48 Summer Pears. The Little Muscat, The Supreme, The Cuisse-Madame. [1860 HOGG *Fruit Man.* 221 Pears...Windsor (Bell Tongue..Summer Bell; Suprême).] 1882 *Garden* 21 Jan. 38/1 Supreme [a variety of pea]..gives large successional pickings.

4. *spec.* applied to God (or his attributes), as the paramount ruler of the world, or the most exalted being or intelligence; also to the most exalted of heathen deities.

1594 SHAKS. *Rich. III*, II. i. 13 Take heed you dally not before your King, Lest he that is the supreme King of Kings Confound your hidden falshood. 1607 — *Cor.* v. iii. 71 With the consent of supreame Ioue. 1634 MILTON *Comus* 217 He, the Supreme good, t' whom all things ill Are but as slavish officers of vengeance. 1667 — *P. L.* x. 70 Mine both in Heav'n and Earth to do thy will Supream. 1672–5 COMBER *Comp. Temple* (1702) 93 That Supream Lord, the Creator of Heaven and Earth. 1699 BURNET *39 Art.* i. 38 The Supream and Increated Being. 1711 SHAFTESB. *Charac.* (1737) II. 274 Whether there be really that Supreme-One we suppose. 1751 HARRIS *Hermes* Wks. (1841) 235 Original truth having the most intimate connexion with the Supreme Intelligence. 1820 SHELLEY *Œd. Tyr.* I. i. 1 Thou supreme Goddess! 1836 THIRLWALL *Greece* xiii. II. 165 When the victim was to be offered to the supreme God, it was taken up to the top of the highest hill. 1854 *Orr's Circ. Sci.*, *Org. Nat.* I. 29 The proposition..that human science is..adverse to the belief in a Supreme Intelligence. 1902 *Encycl. Brit.* XXXII. 824/1 The Festival of the Supreme Being, decreed by the National Convention, designed by David and conducted by Robespierre.

5. Last, final, as belonging to the moment of death. Now only a gallicism: cf. F. *le moment suprême*.

1606 HOLLAND *Sueton.* 66 The supreme iudgments & testimonies of his friends..delivered at their deaths. 1648 [see 6 b]. 1894 SIR E. SULLIVAN *Woman* 37 When Queen Elizabeth was dying she had her band summoned to her ante-chamber..when she felt the supreme moment approaching she told the musicians to strike up her favourite air.

6. In comparative and superlative.

a. Comparative *supremer*. *rare.*

1683 KENNETT tr. *Erasm. on Folly* (1709) 125 After their reign here they must appear before a supreamer judge. 1748 RICHARDSON *Clarissa* (1811) VIII. xxiv. 109 Having given way to supremer fervours.

b. Superlative *supremest*, *most supreme*.

1631 MASSINGER *Emperor East* IV. i, Fate..appointed you To the supremest honour. 1648 HERRICK *Hesper.*, *Upon a Maide* 6 Virgins, come, and in a ring Her supreamest requiem sing. *a* 1674 TRAHERNE *Chr. Ethics* (1675) 11 There are many degrees of blessedness beneath the most supream. 1725 POPE *Odyss.* IV. 325 Throned in omnipotence, supremest Jove Tempers the fates of human race. 1772–84 *Cook's Voy.* (1790) V. 1637 This man felt the most supreme pleasure. 1862 MISS BRADDON *Lady Audley* xxxiv, In her supremest hour of misery.

B. *sb.* †**1.** A person having supreme authority, rank, or power; a supreme authority, ruler, or magistrate; sometimes = superior. *Obs.*

1553 CROME in Strype *Eccl. Mem.* (1721) III. App. x. 24 That they that be prohybyte of the byshops,..ought to cease from preachyng..till they haue purgyd them byfore the supreme of soche suspicion. *a* 1578 LINDESAY (Pitscottie) *Chron. Scot.* (S. T. S.) I. 98 He wald nocht enter his sone into his landis the said Earle being supreme thairof. 1592 SHAKS. *Ven. & Ad.* 996 She clepes him..Imperious supreme of all mortall things. 1631 CHAPMAN *Cæsar & Pompey* II. i. Plays 1873 III. 148 This day had proud him the supreame of Cæsar. 1654–66 EARL ORRERY *Parthen.* (1676) 349 There ought to be a Supreme above the Law. 1660 WATERHOUSE *Arms & Arm.* 177, I return to London which I find of great consequence to her Supremes. 1671 MILTON *P. R.* I. 99 Their King, their Leader, and Supream on Earth. 1677 W. HUGHES *Man of Sin* I. vi. 27 Was it not a fine cast of his office, that one of them [*sc.* popes] practised upon one of these Supremes [*sc.* emperors]? 1725 POPE *Odyss.* XIII. 144 Old Ocean's dread Supreme. 1807 E. S. BARRETT *Rising Sun* III. 100 By the act of Reformation, the lord was declared to be the supreme of the church.

2. The highest degree or amount *of* something.

1760–72 H. BROOKE *Fool of Qual.* (1809) II. 20 The qualities that intitle a man to this supreme of denominations. 1817 KEATS *Sleep & Poetry* 236 A drainless shower Of light is poesy; 'tis the supreme of power. 1858 GEN. P. THOMPSON *Audi Alt. Part.* lxv. I. 249 The Native Indian term for the supreme of folly, is 'monkey business'.

3. As a title of God (or an exalted deity). *The Supreme*: the Supreme Being, God.

[1667 MILTON *P. L.* VI. 723 O Father, O Supream of heav'nly Thrones. *Ibid.* VIII. 414 To attaine The highth and depth of thy Eternal wayes All human thoughts come short, Supream of things.] 1702 ROWE *Tamerl.* I. i, O thou Supream! 1711 ADDISON *Spect.* No. 257 ¶ 7 It is the greatest Folly to seek the..Approbation of any Being, besides the Supreme. *a* 1766 MRS. F. SHERIDAN *Nourjahad* (1767) 197 May the Supreme grant thy petition. 1820 SHELLEY *Hymn Merc.* i, Heaven's dread Supreme. 1884 *Contemp. Rev.* Feb. 256 That aboriginal law of self-sacrifice which links the Supreme to His creatures.

† **4.** The highest or topmost part. *Obs. rare*$^{-1}$.

1660 F. BROOKE tr. *Le Blanc's Trav.* Ded. A 2 b, One, who..took not his information at the shore or Suburbs, but ..visited the intestines and supreme, whence he might the better look below, and round about him.

Supremely (s[i]uprī·mli), *adv.* [f. prec. adj. + -LY[2].]

1. In a supreme degree, to a supreme extent.

1615 CHAPMAN *Odyss.* XXIV. 24 The supremely strenuous Of all the Greeke hoast. 1696 TATE & BRADY *Ps.* C. iv, For He's the Lord, supreamly good. 1718 PRIOR *Solomon* I. 53 The fair Cedar, on the craggy Brow Of Lebanon nodding supremely tall. 1726 POPE *Odyss.* XXIII. 62 How blest this happy hour, should he appear, Dear to us all, to me supremely dear! 1781 COWPER *Ep. Lady Austen* 34 The hand of the Supremely Wise. 1865 E. C. CLAYTON *Cruel Fortune* I. 123 That young person..was supremely jealous of every new pet her mistress took a fancy to. 1870 LOWELL *Among my Books* Ser. I. (1873) 169 More supremely incapable [of this] than any other man who ever wrote English. 1885 'MRS. ALEXANDER' *Valerie's Fate* vi, Those [moments]..dwelt forever in the memory of both as supremely blissful.

† **2.** By or with supreme authority or power. *rare.*

1687 A. LOVELL tr. *Thevenot's Trav.* I. 65 All suits are there supreamly decided. 1734 tr. *Rollin's Anc. Hist.* (1827) I. II. iii. 301 The senate decided supremely, and there lay no appeal from it.

So **Supre·meness,** the quality of being supreme; supreme degree.

1843 POE *Premature Burial* Wks. 1864 I. 331 The supremeness of bodily and of mental distress. 1896 A. WHYTE *Bible Char.* x. I. 112 An amazing elevation, detachment, supremeness, and sweetness of soul.

† **Supre·mist.** *Obs. rare.* [f. SUPREME *a.* + -IST.] One who takes upon himself supreme authority.

1649 HEYLIN *Relat. & Observ.* II. 200 The Junto of Tituler Supremists at Westminster..are very unwilling to quit their long-held Dominion. 1651 C. WALKER *Hist. Independ.* III. 18 Our Self-created Supremists.

Supremity (s[i]upre·miti). Now *rare*. [ad. late L. *suprēmitās, -tātem*, f. *suprēmus* SUPREME: see -ITY. Cf. OF. *supremité*.]

1. = SUPREMACY 1. ? *Obs.*

1538 in *Lett. Suppr. Monast.* (Camden) 186 The Welsh rudenes decreasynge, Christian cyvilitye maye be introduced to the famous renowne of the kynges supremytye. 1540–1 ELYOT *Image Gov.* (1549) 146 Whether theyr natures were obstinate or proude, aspiryng vnto supremitee. *a* 1548 HALL *Chron.*, *Rich. III*, 51 Victorie and supremitie ouer his enemies. *a* 1661 FULLER *Worthies* (1662) I. vi. 19 The Pope (whose Supremity he [*sc.* Henry VIII] had suppressed in his Dominions). 1716–20 *Lett. Mist's Jrnl.* (1722) I. 292 You here stand fair for the Supremity; for Men in their Dotage generally yield an implicite Obedience to their Wives.

2. = SUPREMACY 2.

1882 W. SHARP *Rossetti* viii. 408 Such sonnets..and others of like supremity.

† **3.** = SUPREME *sb.* 4. *Obs.*

1584 B. R. tr. *Herodotus* I. 57 In the top or supremity of the highest turret is another Chappell.

Sup. versed: see SUVERSED *Math.*

Sur, obs. form of SIR *sb.*

Sur- (sŏr, sŭɹ), *prefix*, a. (O)F. *sur-*, earlier *sour-*, *sor-*, *soure-* (repr. L. *super*), used in various senses of SUPER-, as in *surcharger* to burden excessively, overburden, SURCHARGE, *surcot* upper coat, SURCOAT, *surnom* additional name, SURNAME, *surpasser* to pass beyond, SURPASS, *surseoir* (:—L. *supersedēre* to SUPERSEDE) to suspend, delay (cf. SURCEASE), *survivre* to live beyond, SURVIVE. As a living suffix, *sur-* is or has been used in a few compounds, chiefly (*a*) nonce-words formed after existing words, as † *surburdened* [after SURCHARGED], † *surgirdle* [after SURCINGLE]; esp. after the legal terms SURREBUTTER, SURREJOINDER, q. v., as *surrebend*, *surrebrite*, † *surrecompounded*, † *surrecountermand* vbs., † *surregaining*; (*b*) variants of technical terms compounded with SUPER- or SUPRA-, as *surci·liary* = SUPERCILIARY, *suroccipital* = SUPEROCCIPITAL, *surre·nal* = SUPRARENAL; also † **Suranna·tion** = SUPERANNUATION; † **Su:r-azota·tion** *Chem.* = *superazotation* in SUPER- 12 a; † **Surclose,** ?a final close; † **Sur-clou·ded** *pa. pple.*, shaded from above; † **Surco·ntract**, a contract following upon a previous contract; **Surcu·rrent** *a.* *Bot.*, 'the opposite of decurrent; when a leafy expansion runs up the stem' (*Treas. Bot.* 1866); † **Surfeo·ff** *v.* [after med.L. *super(af)feudare*] *trans.*, to invest (a person) with an estate which one already holds from another (cf. *super(in)feudation* in SUPER- 13); † **Surflux**, overflow, flood; **Sur-inve·st** *v.* *trans.*, to provide with outer clothing; † **Surma·tch** *v.* *trans.*, to excel, surpass; † **Surpay·** *v.* *trans.*, to more than compensate for; **Surprecia·tion**, enhancement of price or value; † **Surrebou·nd** *v.*, to echo repeatedly; † **Sursa·turated** *a.* *Chem.* = SUPERSATURATED; † **Surstre·tching** *ppl. a.*, extending far; **Sursty·le** *v.* *trans.*, = SURNAME *v.*

1656 BLOUNT *Glossogr.*, **Surannation*..a growing old, stale or above a years date. 1802 *Med. Jrnl.* VIII. 534 Their different degree of virulence depends on the different degree of *sur-azotation. 1577 HARRISON *England* I. iii. 3/2 in *Holinshed*, They were not now able to remooue the importable loade of the Normanes from our *surburdened shoulders. 1874 DAWKINS *Cave Hunt.* vi. 219 The *surciliary ridges are strongly marked. 1589 PUTTENHAM *Engl. Poesie* III. xix. (Arb.) 225 The Epigrammatist will vse to conclude ..his Epigram with a verse or two, spoken in such sort, as it may seeme a manner of allowance to all the premisses, and that with a ioyfull approbation, which the Latines call *Acclamatio*, we therefore call this figure the *surcloze or consenting close. 1632 LITHGOW *Trav.* x. 494 This Ile of Arrane is..*sur-clouded with Goatfield Hill. 1584 *Leycesters Commw.* (1641) 30 Hee will alwayes yet keepe a voyd place for a new *surcontract with any other. *c* 1482 in *Cal. Proc. Chanc. Q. Eliz.* (1830) II. Pref. 70 Affermyng that the same Piers Bank should have *surfeffed the same Robert Scrop of trust in divers parcells of londes. 1660 F. BROOKE tr. *Le Blanc's Trav.* 217 The *surfluxes and inundations which fertilize all Egypt. 1483 *Cath. Angl.* 372/1 A *Surgyrdyle,..*succingula*. 1819 W. TENNANT *Papistry Storm'd* (1827) 95 The plumes, that *sur-invest her skin. 1636 *Montgomerie's Cherrie & Slae* 76 (Wreittoun's ed.), Poets..Whose Muse *surmatches mine. 1848 OWEN

Surd.

Müller *Sci. Lang.* Ser. ii. vii. (1868) 197 No longer mere interjections...

6. *Arabic Gram.* (tr. Arab. *aṣamm* lit. deaf.) Applied to verbs in which the second and third letters of the root are the same.

Surd, *v. Obs.* To deaden or dull the sound of, as by a 'sordine' or mute.

Surdal, variant of SIRDAR.

Surden, obs. form of SORDINE.

† **Surdesolid**, *sb.* (*a.*) *Math. Obs.* Also surdesolid. [ad. mod.L. *surdesolidus*. Cf. It. *surde-solido*, G. *surdsolidisch*.]

‡ **Surdity** (sə̄ˈrdĭti). [*ad.* L. *surditāt-, -tem*, n. of quality f. *surdus* deaf : see SURD *a.* and -ITY. Cf. F. *surdité*.] Deafness. (Now Path.)

Surdomute (sə̄domɪuⁱt), *a.* and *sb. rare⁻⁰.*

Sure (ʃuər), *a.* and *adv.* Forms: 4– sure; also 4–6 sur, seur, (5 sowr, suere, sewer, sowrn, suyre, suyr), 5–6 seure, sewre, sewer, 5–7 sewr, (6 suar, swer, syure), shure, suore, 4– sure, (6 suar, swer, syure), shure.

Surefire, *a.* and *adv.*

SURE. ... (dense dictionary text continues)

Sure-footed (stress variable), *a.*

Sure-footing, vbl. sb.

Surely (ʃuəˈli), *adv.* Forms: see SURE *a.* and -LY².

Surement, *Obs.* Also secure-, surment.

Sureness (ʃuəˈnes). Forms: see SURE *a.* [f. SURE *a.* + -NESS.] The quality or condition of being sure.

Surety (ʃuəˈrĭti), *sb.* Forms: 4–6 surte, seurte, -tee, sourte, 4–6 suerte, surete, surtee, (5 suertie, suertye, sewrte, 5–6 suretye, surtie), 5–7 suertie, (6 suer-, soerte), surtye, 6–7 suretye, surtie, 7 surtie, surity, 4– surety.

Supplement, p. 3873; Corrigenda, p. 4092; Spurious words, p. 4093; Books quoted, p. 4094

II. Means of being sure. (See also 1 c.)

5. A formal engagement entered into, a pledge, bond, guarantee, or security given for the fulfilment of an undertaking. Chiefly in phr. *to do, make, find, give, put in, take surety* or *sureties*; *in, to, under, upon surety.* Now superseded by SECURITY 8.

†b. A document embodying such an agreement or pledge. *Obs.*

c. *Surety of the (the) peace*, a bond entered into for the maintenance of peace between parties; *spec.* in *Law*, a security entered into to the king by the offending party and taken by a justice for keeping the peace. Now only in *St. Law*: *so surety for (the) good behaviour*: see quot. 1808.

Suretyship (ʃʊ·ətiʃip). Forms: see prec.; also 6 suretishyp, shyp, suretishipp, suretiship, 7-9 suretiship. [f. prec. + -SHIP.]

The position or function of a surety (see prec. 7); responsibility or obligation undertaken by one person on behalf of another, as for payment of a debt, performance of some act, etc.

Surf (sɜːf), *sb.* Also 8 *sorf.* [Continues SUFF *sb.* in chronology and meaning, but the relation between the forms is not clear. (Not in general Dicts. before Todd, 1818.)]

1. The swell of the sea which breaks upon a shore, esp. a shallow shore. (In recent use usually with implication of sense 2.)

2. The mass or line of white foamy water caused by the sea breaking upon a shore or a rock.

Surface (sɜː·fis), *sb.* [ad. F. *surface* (from 16th c.), f. *sur-* SUR- + *face* FACE *sb.*, after L. *superficies*: cf. obs. Sp. *superfice*, Sp. *sobrefaz*, Pg. *sobreface*, and SUPERFICE, SUPERFICIES, SUPERFICIES.]

1. The outermost boundary (or one of the boundaries) of any material body, immediately adjacent to the air or empty space, or to another body.

2. *Geom.* A magnitude or continuous extent having only two dimensions (length and breadth, without thickness), such as constitutes the boundary of a material body (sense 1) or that between two adjacent portions of space; a superficies.

3. The outermost part of a material body, considered with respect to its form, texture, or extent;

Surfacer (sɜː·fisəɹ). [f. SURFACE *v.* + -ER[1].] One who or that which produces a smooth or even surface.

Surfacing (sɜː·fisiŋ), *vbl. sb.* [f. SURFACE *v.* + -ING[1].]

1. The action or process of giving a (smooth or even) surface to something; the coating with which a body is surfaced.

Surfaceman (sɜː·fismæn). Pl. **-men.** [f. SURFACE *sb.* 3 + MAN *sb.*] A workman whose business is to attend to the surface of something; esp. a railway workman who keeps the permanent way in repair.

Surface (sɜː·fis), *v.* [f. SURFACE *sb.*]

1. *trans.* To give a (particular kind of) surface, esp. a smooth or even surface, to; to smooth or polish the surface of; also, to cover the surf: ce (with something).

2. *intr.* To bring or raise to the surface.

†3. *intr.* To mine beneath the surface; to wash the surface deposit or 'dirt' for a valuable mineral.

Surfeit (sɜː·fit), *sb.* Forms: 4 surfayte, sor-fait, 4-5 surfait, -feit, sorfete, 5-6 surfait, 4-8 surfet, 5-fayte, -fett, -ffete, -phette, 5-6 -fete, 6-fete, 6 -fayt, -fit, -foote, 5c.-date, 6-7 surfit, 7-8 -feat, 8 surfeit. [a. OF. surfait, -fet, vbl. sb. from *surfaire* to overdo, etc.]

1. Excess, superfluity; excessive supply or something. (In later use only as *fig.* from 4.)

2. An eruptive disease in horses and other animals, arising from immoderate feeding and other causes.

Surfeit, *v.* Forms: see the sb. [f. SURFEIT *sb.*; cf. FORFEIT *v.*]

1. *trans.* To feed to excess or satiety; to sicken or disorder by overfeeding († or as unwholesome food). Also *refl.*

2. *intr.* To feed to excess or satiety; to surfeit oneself.

Surfeited, *ppl. a.* [f. SURFEIT *sb.* or *v.* + -ED.]

1. Fed to excess or satiety; oppressed or disordered by excess of feeding.

Surfeiter (sɜː·fitəɹ). Forms: § surfeitour, 6 surfetter, surfeiter, 7 -feiter. [f. SURFEIT *v.* + -ER[1].] One who surfeits; a glutton.

Surfeiting, *vbl. sb.* [f. SURFEIT *v.* + -ING[1].] The action of the vb. SURFEIT.

Surfeiting, *ppl. a.* [f. SURFEIT *v.* + -ING[2].]

Surfeitless, *a.* Obs. rare. [f. SURFEIT *sb.* + -LESS.]

Surfet, obs. form of SURFEIT.

Surfle. Obs. rare⁻¹. [a. F.] 1. An embroidered border or hem; also, one of the pleats made in hemming.

†Surfle, v. Obs. [f. prec.] 1. An embroidered border or hem; also, one of the pleats made in hemming. 2. transf. To paint or wash (the face, etc.) with a cosmetic. Hence Surfled ppl. a., Surfling vbl. sb.

† Surfoil, Obs. In 7 -foyl. [f. Sur- + Foil sb.¹] To build up? Grew for a structure serving to cover and protect the leaves, as a bud-scale or a cotyledon.

† Surfoot, a. Obs. rare. [Formed after Sur-rate by substitution of foot in the second syllable, with reminiscence of sure-footed.]

Surfuil, variant of Surfle Obs.

Surfuse (sə̄·fiūz), v. Physics. [f. Sur- + Fuse v.] = Surfusion 2. Hence Surfused (-fiūzd) ppl. a. So Surfusion (-fiū·ʒən), the duration or state of fusion.

Surfy (sə̄·fi), a. [f. Surf sb. + -y.] Abounding in surf; consisting of or resembling surf.

†Surgal, sb. Obs. form of Surcoat.

†Surgat, erron. form of Surgeon.

Surgent, erron. form of Surgeon.

†Surgation. Obs. rare⁻¹. [irreg. f. Surge v.; rising of the interment of Surgeon.]

Surge (sə̄dʒ), sb. Forms: 5-7 sourge, 6 sowrge, shourge, pl. surgies, 7 surdge, 4?9?. 6- surge. Of obscure origin. In the earliest examples (sense 1 a.) used with ref. to water.

† a. A fountain, stream. Obs.

† b. Naut. The part of a capstan or windlass upon which the rope surges.

Surge (sə̄dʒ), v. Also 6-7 sourge. [Partly f. OF. sourge- (see prec.), or a. early mod.F. surgir (F. surgir), = Pr. surgir, surgir, It. surgere, Sp., Pg. surgir, ad. L. surgere to rise; partly L. Sp.] 1. intr. To rise and fall or toss on the waves.

Surge, obs. form of Clerge, Serge.

Surgeand, -ant, obs. forms of Surgeon.

Surgeant, obs. form of Sergeant, or Sergeant.

Surged (sə̄dʒd), ppl. a. rare. ? Obs. [f. Surge sb. or v. + -ed.] a. Raised or moved as in swelling waves. b. Attrib. = Using, Wavy.

Surgeful (sə̄·dʒfūl), a. poet. rare. [f. Surge sb. + -ful.] Full of surges or billows.

Surgeless, a. rare. [f. as prec. + -less.] Free from surges.

Surgent (sə̄·dʒənt), a. and sb. [ad. L. surgentem, surgens, pr. pple. of surgere to rise: see Surge v.] 1. Rising or swelling in waves, or as a flood or spring: surging. lit. and fig.

b. gen. Rising, ascending, mount.

Surgeon (sə̄·dʒən), sb. Forms: a. 4 sorgien, surgeyn, 4-5 surgyon, -yne, 4-6 surgien, surgen, 4-5 surgion, 5-7 -ien, -eon, 6 -ién; 4 (3 abjian); 8. 5 surgeonn, surgion, 5-6 surgyon, 5-7 -ion, -eon, sowrgeon, 7 surgon. 7- surgeon. y. 5 surgiand, 6 -iant, 5-6 -iane, -yon; 6 surgain, -ayne, -aine, yne, -en. 4. AF. surgien (13th c.), also sirogien, sur-i-ygian, contracted form of OF. serurgien, cirurgien, mod.F. chirurgien; see Chirurgeon, Cf. OF. surgeon (fem. mod.Pg. cirurgião), MDu. surgijn, -ijn, cursiien were also from OF.]

1. One who practises the art of healing by manual operation; a practitioner who treats wounds, fractures, deformities, or disorders by surgical means.

Surgeon. Chiefly Sc. Obs. Forms: 6 sor-, surgiour, surrigiare, surigeoner, sur-inger; [f. Surgeon v.]

b. A medical officer in the army or the navy (on board ship — 'a ship's doctor').

† Surgeoner. Obs. rare⁻¹. In 5 surioner. [f. Surgeon sb. + -er.]

Surgeonship. [f. Surgeon sb. + -ship.]

Surgeony, Sc. Obs. Forms: 4-5 surgerie, surgenrie, surgeonrie; (1 cirurgiunrerie (l chirurgie).

† Surger. Obs. [a. OF. surgie, by-form of Surgeon sb.]

Surgery (sə̄·dʒəri), sb. Also 4 surgerie, 4-7 surgerie, 6 surgrerie, surcerie. [ad. OF. surgerie, contracted form of cirurgerie (mod.F. chirurgie): see Chirurgery.] 1. The art or practice of treating injuries, deformities, and other disorders by manual operation or instrumental appliances; surgical treatment.

b. A room, office, etc. where a surgeon treats his patients.

Mayne Expos. Lex. 369/1 They [sc. general practitioners] are also called Surgeon-Apothecaries. **Surg.** v. **a.** surge. **b.** Comb. as surgeon-like adv.; surgeon-bird, the jacana; surgeon-fish, a fish of the genus Acanthurus.

Surgiant, a. Her. [irreg. f. F. surger to rise + -ant.] = Roussant.

Surgian, obs. form of Surgeon.

Surgical (sə̄·dʒikăl), a. [Alteration of Chi-rurgical, after surgeon, surgery. Cf. med.L. sur-gicus.] Pertaining to, dealing with, or employed in surgery or the surgeon's art.

Surgically (sə̄·dʒikăli), adv. [f. prec. + -ly.] In a surgical manner; by the application of, or in relation to, surgical treatment.

Surginess (sə̄·dʒinĕs), rare. [f. Surgy + -ness.] The quality or condition of being surgy.

Surging (sə̄·dʒiŋ), vbl. sb. [f. Surge v. + -ing.] The action of the verb Surge.

Surging, ppl. a. [f. as prec. + -ing².] Rising, swelling, rolling or tossing heavily, as waves.

Surgy (sə̄·dʒi), a. [f. Surge sb. + -y.] 1. Rising, swelling, or rolling of great waves; impetuous movement of the sea or any body of water; also transf. and fig.

† Surgy, obs. form of Surgery.

Surgial, obs. Sc. form of Surgeon.

Surgian, a. rare⁻¹. [f. Surge sb. + -ian.] Of or pertaining to a surge.

Surhound, error for Surround v.

Suric, ans, obs. form of Syrian.

Suric, obs. form of Surah.

Suricate (siū·rikĕt). Also -kate, -cat. [a. F. suricate, of native African origin.] An animal of the genus Suricata, esp. S. zenik or S. tetradactyla, a viverrine burrowing carnivore of Cape Colony; the meerkat or zenick.

Surian, Sc. form of Surgeon.

Surinam (siū·rinam). Also attrib. [The name of a country in S. America also called Dutch Guiana; used attrib. in specific names of animals, plants, and products, as Surinam bunting, darter, falcon, grass, medlar, quassia, rat, sturm, sprat, tern; Surinam bark, the bark of species of Andira, or that of Cinchona magnifolia, used in medicine; Surinam cherry, (a) a edible aromatic fruit; (b) a Brazilian tree, Eugenia uniflora, or its red cherry-like fruit; Surinam poison, a tropical leguminous plant, Tephrosia toxicaria, or the poison derived from the leaves; Surinam toad (also S. water toad), a large flat toad, the Pipa.

Suring, obs. var. of Souring sb.¹

Surinamine (siū·rinamin), Chem. an alka-loid supposed to be contained in Surinam bark.

† Suring, vbl. sb. Obs. [f. Sure v. + -ing¹.] Betrothal.

† Surinament, sb. and a. Obs. Also 8-sant. ad. F. surintendant: see Sub- and Intendant. **A.** sb. = Superintendent sb. and a.

† Surine, v. Obs. rare. [ad. L. surenare.] To surmount.

Surion, -yn, -yon, obs. forms of Surgeon.

Surly (sə̄·li), a. Forms: 6 sirrly, 6-7 surley, sur-lie, 7-8 surely, 7- surly. [Altered spelling of Sirly a.]

† 1. Lordly, majestic. Obs.

† 2. Masterful, imperious; haughty, arrogant; superciliou, Obs.

b. With gloomy ill-humour or churlish morose-ness.

Surling. Obs. nonce-wd. [app. f. Surly a. (or the (lake) surl) of a lordly or lordling.] A surly fellow.

Surloin, var. of Sirloin.

Surly (sə̄·li), adv. Obs. 6-li, 7-lie, -ley. [Altered spelling of Sirly a.]

Surma, soorma (siū·rmă). E. Ind. Also surmah, sulma. [Urdu sūrma = Pers. surma.] A black powder consisting of sulphide of antimony or of lead, used by Indian women for staining the eyebrows and eyelids.

Surmaistre, -master, var. of Sermaster.

Surmulot (sə̄·mūlŏt), Obs. [a. F.] = Surmullet.

Surma, Surmark, var. of Stirma, Surmark.

Surmaster, var. of Sermaster.

Surma, -men, -mah, var. of Surma.

Surment, Surmet, var. of Subemenet, Summit.

Surmia, var. of Surma.

Surmisable (sə̄rmei·zăb'l), a. Also surmiz-able. [f. Surmise v. + -able.] That may be surmised or conjectured.

† Surmisal. Obs. Now rare. [f. as prec. + -al.]

Surmisant (sə̄rmei·zănt), nonce-wd. [f. sur-mise v. + -ant², after surmisant.]

Surmise (sə̄rmei·z), sb. Also 5-6 -mise, -myse, 6 -mize, 7 singile-(?- surmis. 6-8 -mise, -mize. [a. AF., OF. surmise, fem. of surmis, pa. pple. of surmettre (mod.F. surmettre) to accuse, allege, f. sur- over + mettre to put.]

Surmise (sə̄rmei·z), v. Also 5-6 -myse, -myze, 6 -mize, ? singile-(?- surmis. [a. AF. surmiser, f. OF. surmis, pa. pple. of surmettre: see prec.]

Surmised, ppl. a.

†Surmisal. Obs.

†Surmisant, pr. pple. of Surmount. Obs.

†Surmisaunce, sb. Obs. rare.

Surmiser.

Surmising, vbl. sb.

Surmising, ppl. a.

†Surmit, v. Obs.

Surmount, sb.

†Surmount(e, v.

Surmountable.

Surmounted, ppl. a.

Surmounter.

Surmounting, ppl. a.

Surmounting, vbl. sb.

Surmullet.

Surn.

†Surnai. Obs.

Surname, sb.

Surname, v.

Surnamed, ppl. a.

Surnamer.

Surnominal, a.

†Surnoun. Obs.

Surnumber.

Surpass, v.

Surpassable, a.

Surpassant, a.

Surcordial. see Sur-.

†Surot. Obs.

Surpassed, ppl. a.

Surpassing, ppl. a.

Surpassing, vbl. sb.

Surpassingly, adv.

Surpeal. see Sur-.

Surpeol. anglicised form of Serpico.

Surplice, sb.

Surpliced, a.

Surplician.

Surplis, obs. form of Surplice.

Surplus, sb. and a.

Surplusage.

Surpay.

†Surpcloth. north. Obs.

Surpeual. see Sur-.

†Surpench. Obs.

Surpeue.

Surplicial.

Surplus. see Surplus.

Surprint.

†Surpose, v. Obs.

Surprisable, a.

Surprisal.

Surprise, sb.

Surprise, v.

Surprisedly, adv.

[Dictionary columns — dense lexicographic text covering the entries **Surprise** *(sb. and v.), with numbered senses, followed by* **Surprised** *ppl. a.,* **Surpriser,** **Surprisement,** **Surprising** *vbl. sb. and ppl. a.,* **Surprisingly** *adv.,* **Surprisal,** **Surquidance,** **Surquidous,** **Surquidry,** **Surquidant,** **Surquidous,** **Surquidour,** **Surra,** **Surrebound,** **Surrebut,** **Surrebutter,** **Surreptitious,** *and* **Surrect.*]*

[Lower columns cover the entries **Surrection,** **Surreine,** **Surreined,** **Surrejoin,** **Surrejoinder,** **Surrender** *(v. and sb.),* **Surrendered,** **Surrenderee,** **Surrenderer,** **Surrenderor,** **Surrentine,** **Surrepent,** **Surreption,** **Surreptitious.*]*

† **Surrepti-tious**, a. Obs. rare. [f. SURREPTION 2: also pref.] Characterized by or of the nature of 'surreption'; stealthily suggested to or introduced into the mind.

Surrepti-tiously, adv. In a surreptitious manner.

Surre-verence, sb. Obs. Also 7 sur-reverence. [Variant of SIR-REVERENCE.]

1. = SIR-REVERENCE 2.

2. by extension with Sub- prefix, used for: Great reverence.

† **Surre-verently**, adv. Obs. nonce-wd. [f. SUB- + REVERENTLY, after prec.] Very reverently: ironically with reference to SURREVERENCE 2.

Surrey (sᵊ·rɪ). An American four-seated pleasure carriage, the seats being of similar design and facing forwards; also, a motor-carriage of similar structure.

Surrigate, -lan, -ine, obs. ss. SURGEON, **Surrip**, obs. form of STRIP.

Surrogacy (sᵊ·rŏgăsɪ). 1. The office of a surrogate; surrogateship.

Surrogate (sᵊ·rŏgĕt), sb. [ad. L. surrogātus, pa. pple. of surrogāre: see SUBROGATE v.]

1. A person appointed by authority to act in place of another; a deputy. a. gen.

2. To put instead of another; to substitute: = SUBROGATE v. 3.

Surrogateship (sᵊ·rŏgĕtʃip). 1. The office of a surrogate.

Surrogation (sᵊrŏgēɪ·ʃ(ᵊ)n), sb. Now rare. [ad.med. L. surrogātiō, -ōnem.]

1. Appointment of a person to some office in place of another.

2. fig. and gen. A person or (usually) a thing that acts for or takes the place of another; a substitute. Const. for, of.

Surrogatum (sᵊrŏgēɪ·tᵊm), Sc. Law. [L., neut. sing. of sur-rogātus, pa. pple. of surrogāre to SUBROGATE.] A thing put in the place of another; a substitute.

Surrole, obs. form of SURAIL.
Surround, v. pa. pple. SURROUNDED. [f. the vb.]

Surround (sᵊraᵘ·nd), v. Now rare or Obs. Also 7 (Sc.) -at, 6 (Sc.) f. -ate, pa. pple. -at, -aitt, surrogat, 6-7 pa. pple. -ate. [f. L. superundāre, pa. pple. of surrogāre, assimilated f. subrogāre to SUBROGATE.]

1. trans. To appoint as a successor, substitute, or deputy: = SUBROGATE v. 1.

2. trans. To substitute in respect of a right or claim: = SUBROGATE v. 2.

Surrounded (sᵊraᵘ·ndĕd), ppl. a. [f. SURROUND v. + -ED.]

1. Overflowed, flooded, sub-merged. Obs.

Surrounder (sᵊraᵘ·ndᵊɹ). One who or that which surrounds.

Surrounding (sᵊraᵘ·ndiŋ), vbl. sb. [-ING.]

I. The action of the verb SURROUND.

II. That which surrounds.

Surrounding, ppl. a. [-ING.] That which surrounds.

Surroundings, sb. pl. Things surrounding or attending upon a person.

Surroyal, Forms: 5 surroyal, 5 sureall, sureaile, surriall, 7 surroyall, sur-royal, 7- surroyal, sur-royal. [L. SUR- + ROYAL sb. (REAL sb.).] An upper or terminal branch of a stag's antler, above that called 'royal' (ROYAL B. 3). Also attrib.

Sursanure (sᵊrsᵊnɪᵘᵊɹ), sb. Obs. rare. Also 4 saunsure, 5 surensaure, 6 sursaunure. [a. OF. sursaneure, -ure = med.L. supersanātūra.] The healing over of a wound; a wound healed outwardly or superficially.

Sursault, sb. Obs. rare. Also 4 sorsault, 5 sursaut. [a. F. sursaut, OF. sorsalt, -saut.] A sudden start or movement.

Surse, obs. form of SOURCE, **Sursingle**, obs. form of SURCINGLE.

Sur-sharp, a. Obs. [SUR- + SHARP.] Very sharp.

Sursise, obs. form of CESS (Hist.) surcise.

Sursolid (sᵊrsŏ·lid), sb. and a. Math. Obs. [app. etymologizing alteration of SUPERSOLID, by reference to SOB- prefix; surd-solid was app. an intermediate form. Cf. F. sursolide, It. supersolido.]

A. sb. The fifth power of a number or quantity; also, an equation of the fifth degree.

B. adj. Of the fifth degree; that is a fifth power or root; involving the fifth power of a quantity.

Sursurrara, obs. corruption of CERTIORARI: see SISERARA.

Surtax (sᵊ·ɹtæks). sb. [ad. F. surtaxe: see SUR- and TAX.] An additional or extra tax on something already taxed.

Surtax, v. trans., to tax additionally, charge with a surtax.

Surturbrand (sᵊ·ɹtᵊɹbrand). Also 8 surtur-, surturbrandur. [. (Jastur)brand, ad. Icel. surtarbrandr, f. (Surtar-, genit. of Surtr (related to SWART a.), name of a fire-giant + brandr BRAND sb.) name of a mine occurring in Iceland.

Surveigh, obs. form of SURVEY.

Surveillance (sᵊrvēɪ·lăns, -lyăns, F. sûrveɪyɑ̃s). [ad. F. surveillance, tr. of action f. surveiller: see next and -ANCE.] Watch or guard kept over a person, etc., esp. over a suspected person, a prisoner, or the like; often, spying, supervision; less commonly, supervision for the purpose of direction or control, superintendence.

Surveillant (sᵊrvēɪ·lănt), sb. and a. [F. surveillant, pr. pple. of surveiller.]

A. sb. One who keeps watch over another; a superintendent, e.g. of a prison.

B. adj. Exercising surveillance.

† **Surveillant**, Obt. rare⁻¹. [f. F. survenant, pr. pple. of survenir: see next.] One who comes up, or to a place; a comer.

† **Survene**, v. Obs. [a. after SUPERVENE by substitution of prefix SUR-.] = SUPERVENE 1.

† **Survenient**, a. Obs. rare⁻¹. [f. next.] = SUPERVENIENT.

† **Survenue**, sb. Obs. rare⁻¹. [a. F. survenue, vbl. sb. f. survenir.] A later or subsequent arrival.

Survey, -vewe, obs. forms of SURVIEW.

Survey (sᵊrvēɪ·, sᵊ·ɹveɪ), v. Also 6-7 -vay, -veigh, 7 servey. [a. AF. surveier, -veer, etc., = OF. so(u)rvoir.]

1. The act of viewing, examining, or inspecting in detail, esp. for some specific purpose; usually spec. a formal or official inspection of the particulars of something, of an estate, of a ship or its stores, of the administration of an office, etc.

2. The process († or art) of surveying a tract of ground, coast-line, or any part of the earth's surface; the determination of its form, extent, and other particulars, so as to be able to delineate or represent it on a map; also, a plan or description thus obtained; a body of persons or a department engaged in such work.

3. fig. A comprehensive mental view of, or (usually) literary examination, discussion, or description, of something.

Survey (sᵊrvēɪ·), v. Also 6 survaye, survaye, 6-7 survay, surveigh, 7 surveɪ, pa. t. surveied. [a. AF. surveier, -veer, -voir; = OF. so(u)rvo(e)ir (Pr. sobreveire), med.L. supervidere to SUPERVIDE.]

1. trans. To examine and ascertain the condition, situation, or value of, formally or officially, e.g. the boundaries, tenure, value, etc. of an estate, a building or structure, accounts, or the like; more widely, to have the oversight of, supervise, inspect.

Surveyal (sᵊrvēɪ·ăl), rare. [As prec. + -AL.] The act of surveying; a survey.

Surveyance (sᵊrvēɪ·ăns), rare. Also 5 sur-veyance, 7 surviance. [a. OF. *surveance.] Survey; superintendence; inspection.

Surveying (sᵊrvēɪ·iŋ), vbl. sb. [f. SURVEY v. + -ING.] The action of the verb SURVEY (in various senses): esp. (officially) the exploration of a country.

Surveyor (sᵊrvēɪ·ᵊɹ). Forms: 4-5 sur-veyoure, 5-7 surveyour, survoior, 6-7 surveour, survaiour, -veiour, -veyour, -vyour, 7 surveyer, surveyor, 6- surveyor. [a. AF. surveour, f. surveier to SURVEY v.]

1. One who has the oversight or superintendence of a person or thing; an overseer, supervisor.

SURVEYOR.

†e. One who had the oversight of the lands and boundaries of an estate and its appurtenances. *Obs.*

5. Surveyor-general, *† general surveyor* (see GENERAL a. 10): a principal or head surveyor (see the control of a body of surveyors, or the general oversight of some business. Often *surveyor-generalship.*

6. *attrib.* and *Comb.*, as *surveyor-general*, *surveyorship*; *surveyor-general-ship*.

Surveyorship.

The office of surveyor.

Surview (sərvˈiū), v. Forms: 4 survue, 5-6 -vewe, 6-7 -vew, 6 -view, 6- surview.

b. *A name for certain caterpillars:* = GEOMETER 4. LOOPER 2 † 1.

c. One whose business is to inspect and examine land, houses, or other property and to calculate and report upon its actual or comparative value or productiveness for certain purposes.

2. One whose business is to view a whole, or in its details; the action of taking such a view; consideration, contemplation.

Surview (sərvˈiū), v. Forms: 3 seepenc. [f. prec.]

1. *trans.* To take a general view of, to view as a whole; also, to command a view of, overlook; to survey.

Survivalist.

by the captaine of the Ianisars.

Hence **† Survi·wer**, a surveyor, supervisor.

Surviour, obs. form of SURVEYOR.

† Survise, v. *Obs. nonce-wd.* [Formed by substitution of prefix SUR- in SUPERVISE.] *trans.* To look upon, behold.

† Survisor. *Obs.* [a. By-form (see SUR-) of SUPERVISOR (t b.)]

Survivable (sərvʌivˈăbl), a. *rare.* [f. SURVIVE + -ABLE.] Capable of surviving. Hence Survivability, capability of surviving.

Survival (sərvʌivˈăl). [f. SURVIVE v. + -AL. See SUR-VIVAL 2.]

1. The continuing to live after some event (*spec.* the soul after death); remaining alive, living on.

b. *Survival of the fittest* (Biol.): a phrase used to describe the process of *natural selection* (q. v.).

2. *transf.* Continuance at the end of cessation of something else, or after some event; *spec.* the continuance of a custom, observance, etc. after the circumstances or conditions in which it originated or which gave significance to it have passed away.

Survivance (sərvʌivˈăns). [ad. early mod.F. survivance, f. survivant : see next and -ANCE.]

1. = SURVIVAL 1. Now *rare* or *Obs.*

2. The succession to an estate, office, etc. of a survivor nominated before the death of the existing occupier or holder; the right of such succession in case of survival.

So † Survivancy.

† Survivant, a. *Obs.* [a. F. *survivant*, pr. pple. of *survivre*; cf. SURVIVE.] Surviving.

Survive (sərvʌivˈ), v. Also 6 survyve, 7 Anglo-Irish surveyve. [a. AF. *survivre*, OF. *sorvivre*, f. L. *supervivere* to live.]

1. *trans.* To continue to live after the death of another, or after the end or cessation of some thing or condition or the occurrence of some event (expressed or implied); to remain alive, live on.

2. *intr.* To continue to exist after some person, thing, or event; to last on.

† Surviver [2]. *Obs.* In 6 -oure, 6-7 -or. [f. SURVIVE + -ER [1]. Cf. SUPERVIVOR.] = SURVIVORSHIP.

Surviving (sərvʌivˈiŋ), *vbl. n.* [f. as prec. + -ING [1].] That survives. a. Still living after another's death.

Survivor (sərvʌivˈər). [f. SURVIVE v. + -OR. See SUR-VIVOR.]

1. One who survives, outlives, or lives on after another.

Survivorship. [f. SURVIVOR + -SHIP.]

1. *Law*, etc. a. The condition of a survivor, or the fact of one person surviving another or others, considered in relation to some right or privilege depending on such survival or the period of it.

Surwan.

Surviyour, -overe, obs. ff. SURVEYOR.

Surwan (sə̄rˈwan). *India.* Also -aun, ser-sirwan. [a. Urdū = Pers. چ sārbān, f. چār camel + bān keeper.] A camel-driver.

Sury, variant of SURREY.

Susannite (sŭzˈanˌaiт). *Min.* Also susannite. [ad. Ger. *susannit* (Haidinger, 1845), f. proper name *Susanna* (see below): see -ITE [1].] A mineral found in the Susanna mine at Leadhills in Scotland, chemically identical with the rhombohedral lanarkite.

Susceptibility (sŭsɛptibˈiliti). [f. next: see -ITY. Cf. med.L. *susceptibilitas* (Abelard), F. *susceptibilité* (from 18th c.).] The quality or condition of being susceptible; capability of receiving, being affected by, or undergoing something.

1. *Const.* of (now *rare*) or *to*.

a. Capability of undergoing a specified action or process.

Susceptible (sŭsɛptibˈl), a. [ad. med.L. *susceptibilis* (Boethius, Thomas Aquinas), f. *suscepi-*: see SUSCEPTION and -IBLE. Cf. F. *susceptible*.]

1. *Const.* of or *to*: Capable of taking, receiving, being affected by, or undergoing something.

a. *with of*: Capable of undergoing, admitting of (some action or process).

Susceptive (sŭsɛptiv), a. [ad. med.L. *susceptivus* (Aquinas), f. *suscept-*: see prec. and -IVE. Cf. *susceptivo.* So *susceptive.*]

1. Having the quality of receiving, receptive; in later use *esp.* disposed to receive and be affected by impressions: = SUSCEPTIBLE 2 a 2.

Susceptiveness. [f. prec. + -NESS.] = next.

Susceptivity (sŭsɛptivˈiti). [f. as prec. + -ITY.] The quality of being susceptive; susceptibility.

Susception (sŭsɛpˈʃən). [ad. L. *susception-*, *suscepti*, n. of action f. *suscipere*: see SUS- [2] + *capere* to take. Cf. F. *susception.*]

Suscitate (sŭsˈitˌeit), v. *rare.* Now *rare.* [ad. L. *suscitāt-*, ppl. stem of *suscitāre*.]

Suscitation (sŭsitˈeiʃən). [ad. L. *suscitātion-*, *-io*, n. of action f. *suscitāre*: see prec. and -ATION. Cf. F. *suscitation*, OF. resuscitation.] The action of suscitating or exciting; quickening; incitement.

Susliccoty, obs. form of SOOT.

Suslik (sŭsˈlik). [a. Russ. сусликъ. Cf. F. *souslik*, -lik.] A species of ground-squirrel, *Spermophilus citillus* (or similar).

Suspect (sŭspɛkt), a. and *sb.* [a. OF. *suspect*, -ect and mod.F.] *suspect* (= Pr., Sp. *sospecha*, It. *sospetto*).

1. The or an act of suspecting, or the condition of being suspected.

Suspect (sŭspɛkt), v. [ad. L. *suspect-*, ppl. stem of *suspicere.*]

Suspect. (continued)

As for ..conplexions in diuinitie it is not to be sought, which makes this course of artificall diuinitie the more suspecte.

† b. *Suspected to (a person): mistrusted by; — suspect of*, SUSPECT *a. c. Obs.*

2. To imagine or fancy something, esp. something wrong, about (a person or thing); to suspect; with or no proof: with various const. expressing that which is so imagined. **a.** const. *of*; rarely *for*.

b. with *obj.* and *compl.* (sometimes introduced by *as* or *for*), and in corresp. passive use. Now rare.

7. With *obj.* To think in the least, have any idea of (doing something). *Obs. rare*[−1].

Hence **Suspē·cting** *vbl. sb.* and *ppl. a.*

Suspectable, *a.* Also 8 *erron.*

Suspe·ctant, *a.* [f. *L. suspectant-, -ans*, *pr. pple.* of *suspectāre*.] — *suspect-* = see SUS-PECT *v.* and *-ANT.* [See *quot.*]

Suspē·cted, *ppl. a.* [f. SUSPECT *v.* + -ED[1].]

1. That suspects or suspected of (someting evil or wrong); regarded with suspicion; imagined guilty or faulty; suspect.

b. with *obj.* clause; also parenthetically, with *as* or *to*, or *ellipt.*

Hence **Suspē·ctedly** *adv.*, so as to be suspected; **Suspē·ctedness**, state of being suspected.

Suspecter. One who suspects. — **Suspectful**, *a. Now rare.* — **† 1.** Having regard or respect for something; mindful of. *Obs. rare*[−1]. **2.** Full of suspicion; inclined to suspect; mistrustful; suspicious.

Suspēction. *Obs.* Also 4 *supiciun*, *-ecciun*, 4-5 *suspecion*, 5-6 *-eccion*, *-ectyon*, 5, 6-, *-ection*. [a. OF. *suspection*, ad. L. *suspectiōn-, -tio* (subst.).] = SUSPICION.

Suspectious, *a. Obs.* [f. *suspectiōus*, f. *suspection*: see prec. and -IOUS.] = SUSPICIOUS.

Hence **† Suspē·ctiousness**. *rare*[−1].

† Suspē·ctless, *a.* [f. SUSPECT *sb.*[1] + -LESS.] **1.** Having no suspicion; unsuspecting. **2.** Not suspected; unsuspected.

Suspectly, *adv.* *Obs. rare.* [f. SUSPECT *a.* + -LY[2]. Cf. OF. *suspectement.*] In a way open to suspicion; suspiciously, *rare*—.

Suspector *Obs.* = -KER]. *Obs. rare*.

† Suspē·ctress, *a. Obs. rare*[−1]. [f. *suspicere*, ad. L. *suspicax*: see -IOUS and -ACIOUS.] Suspicious.

Suspend (sŏspe·nd), *v.* Also 3 *sos-*, 5-6 *-pende or ad.*, 4 *-ponde.*

I. 1. *trans.* To debar, usually for a time, from the exercise of a function or enjoyment of a privilege; esp. to deprive (temporarily) of rank or office. Const., *† of.*

† 3. Exciting or deserving suspicion; = SUSPICIOUS 1. *Obs. rare.*

Hence **† Suspectuousness**, proneness to suspicion.

Suspend (continued)

2. To put a stop to, usually for a time; *esp.* to bring to a (temporary) stop; to intermit the use or exercise of, put in abeyance. Chiefly *sit passive* without implication of a definite agent.

b. To cause (the action or operation of a law or rule) to be temporarily inoperative; to abrogate. *Obs.*

Suspend (continued)

† b. To defer dealing with; to put off consideration of; to pass over for the time; hence *gen.* to disregard. *Obs.*

4. *trans.* To keep (one's judgement) undetermined; to refrain from forming (an opinion) or giving (assent) decisively.

† occas. to withhold (assent) *from.*

5. *trans.* To hang up, attach to some point above; to cause to hang freely downward.

Suspende

6. *Sc. Law. trans.* To defer or stay (execution of a sentence) pending its discussion in the Supreme Court. **b.** *intr.* To present a bill of suspension, SUSPENSION 4.

II. 6. Supported by attachment above; hanging.

II. 6. Supported by attachment above; hanging. = SUSPENSION-BRIDGE.

Suspendee. [f. SUSPEND *v.* + -EE.] One suspended.

Suspender. **1.** One who or that which suspends or puts a stop to something, esp. temporarily.

† 2. One who suspends his judgement; a doubter; hesitator. *Obs. rare*[−1].

3. *Sc. Law.* One who presents a bill of suspension; = SUSPENDER 6. **b.** *pl.* The clasps by which the garments are suspended.

4. One of a pair of straps passing over the shoulders to hold up the trousers.

5. An apparatus or a natural structure which supports something suspended.

Suspendible (sŏspe·ndibl'), *a.* Also *-able.* [f. SUSPEND *v.* + -IBLE.] Capable of being, or liable to be, suspended.

Suspending (sŏspe·ndiŋ), *vbl. sb.* [f. SUSPEND *v.* + -ING[1].] = SUSPENSION.

Suspense (sŏspe·ns), *sb.* Also 5-9 *suspense*, 6-7 *-sens.* [a. AF. *suspens*, in phr. *en suspens*, *et suspens* (Rolls Parl., *an.* 1306) in abeyance, *OF. suspense* f. deterring, delay, repr. med.L. *suspensum*, etc.]

† 1. (Chiefly *Law.*) *In suspense*, being suspended, remitted, or held in abeyance; *put in suspense*, to defer or interrupt the execution, payment, etc. of, *Obs.*

2. Discontinuance, cessation.

3. A state of mental uncertainty, with expectation of or desire for decision, and usually some apprehension or anxiety; the condition of waiting, of being kept waiting for decision; suspension, in contemplation, attentive. (Cf. SUS-PEND *v.* 5 **b**, SUSPENSE 7.)

Suspense, *a. Now rare or Obs.* Also 5-7 *suspens*.

† 1. Held in contemplation, attentive. (Cf. SUSPEND *v.* 5 **b**, SUSPENSE 7.)

2. The state of being suspended or kept undetermined (chiefly *to hold*, *keep in suspense*); hence, the action of suspending one's judgement; = SUSPENSION 2.

3. Something that is suspended.

4. = SUSPENSION 9.

| SUSPENSE. | 258 | SUSPENSION. | SUSPENSION-BRIDGE. | 259 | SUSPICABLE. |

SUSPENSE.

SUSPENSIBLE.

SUSPENSIBLE.

Suspensely.

Suspension.

SUSPENSION-BRIDGE.

Suspensive.

Suspensively.

Suspensorial.

Suspensorium.

Suspensory.

Suspicable.

| SUSPICIENCY. | 260 | SUSPICIOUS. | SUSPICIOUSLY. | 261 | SUSQUE DEQUE. |

SUSPICIENCY.

Suspiciency.

Suspicion.

Suspicionable.

Suspicionless.

Suspicious.

Suspiciousness.

Suspicable.

Suspicate.

Suspicion.

Suspicious.

Suspiciously.

Suspiral.

Suspiration.

Suspiratious, Suspirative.

Suspire.

Suspired.

Suspiring.

Suspirious.

Suspiry.

Susque deque.

Susreal, var. *surreal*: see SURROYAL.

c 1410 *Master of Game* (MS. Digby 182) ii, þe first tynde that is next þe heed is ycleped aunteleer, and þe secund reiall, and þe .III. above susreall.

Suss (sʌs). *dial.* Also 6 **sose.** [Variant of SOSS *sb.*[1] (sense 3); cf. SOSS-.] A slattern, slut.

15.. *Smyth & his Dame* 251 in Hazl. *E. P. P.* III. 210 He hath amended well thy ble; For yester day,..Thov were a fovle sose [*rimes* thus, Jesus, vs]. 1865 R. HUNT *Pop. Rom. W. Eng.* Ser. I. 97 A great, nasty Suss of a woman.

† Su·ssapine. *Obs.* ? mispr. for GOSSAMPINE.

1594 GREENE & LODGE *Looking Gl.* (1598) D 4, Ile deck my Aluida, In Sendall and in costly Sussapine.

Sussarara, var. SISERARY (senses 2, 4).

1770 GOLDSM. *Vicar W.* (ed. 4) xxi, Gentle or simple, out she shall pack with a sussarara [*edd.* 1766, 1767 sass-]. 1884 *Athenæum* 3 May 578/1, I..at last gave such a sussarara on the bell that I thought the deafest person must hear.

†Sussemy, *a. Obs.* [a. AF. *sussemé, OF. sonssemé, var. soursemé, = med.L. *supersēminātus* lit. 'sown over' (see SUPERSEMINATE), applied to measly swine because of their tongues being covered with spots.] Of swine's flesh: Measly.

1421 *Cov. Leet Bk.* 25 Þat no bocher sell..no roten Schep, ne Sussemy flesche, ne non swyn of bryne.

Sussex (sʌ·seks). The name (OE. *Súþseaxe* 'South Saxons') of a maritime county in the south-east of England; used attrib. in designations of things produced in or peculiar to the county, as breeds of cattle, agricultural implements, etc.

1704 *Dict. Rustic.* (1726) s.v. *Plough*, The Sussex single Wheel-Plough. 1818 *Compl. Grazier* (ed. 3) Introd. 3 The Sussex and Hereford breeds [of cows]. 1834 YOUATT *Cattle* 41 The loins of the Sussex ox are wide. 1837 *Brit. Husb.* (Libr. Usef. Knowl.) II. Index, Sussex waggon [described I. 155]. 1846 YOUATT *Pig* (1847) Index, Sussex pigs. 1855 *Poultry Chron.* III. 534/2 My declining to adopt the name of Hamburg for the Bolton Greys and Bays, or that of Dorking for the Sussex fowls. 1856 'STONEHENGE' *Brit. Rural Sports* 59 A good, useful team of the Sussex spaniels. 1875 *Encycl. Brit.* I. 392/2 These sheep are now usually classed as Sussex Downs and Hampshire Downs. 1885 *Ibid.* XIX. 645/2 The Surrey and Sussex fowls are four-toed.

† b. *Sussex crest*, a name for the cuckold's 'horn'. *Obs.*

1681 T. FLATMAN *Heraclitus Ridens* No. 8. (1713) I. 49 A Cuckold is always to be the last Man that knows he has got a Sussex Crest.

c. **Sussex marble**, a marble occurring in thin beds in the Wealden clay of Sussex and Kent, formerly much used for pillars in churches.

1753 *Chambers' Cycl.* Suppl. 1850 ANSTED *Elem. Geol., Min.*, etc. 379 Weald clay, with subordinate limestone (called Sussex marble) and sand.

Hence † **Sussexan,** † **Sussexian** *adjs. rare*, belonging to Sussex.

1612 DRAYTON *Poly-olb.* xvii. 423 Clear Lavant, that doth keep the Southamptonian side (Dividing it well-near from the Sussexian lands). 1614 *Disc. Strange & Monstrous Serpent* B 2 b, I will conclude this generall discovrse of Serpents, and come to the particular description of our Sussexan Serpent.

† **Sussing,** *vbl. sb. Obs. rare.* [Echoic.] The 'spitting' of a cat.

a 1693 *Urquhart's Rabelais* III. xiii. 107 Barking of Curs, bawling of Mastiffs..sussing of Kitnings.

Sussingle, obs. form of SURCINGLE.

Sussite, var. SUSCITE *v. Obs.*, to resuscitate.

Susspecion, -pitioun, etc., obs. ff. SUSPICION.

† **Sussy,** *sb. Sc. Obs.* Also 6 **sussie, sowcy.** [a. OF. *soussy* (mod.F. *souci*), vbl. sb. f. *soussier*: see next.] Care, trouble.

1513 DOUGLAS *Æneis* IV. Prol. 236 Quhat sussy, cuir, and strang ymagynyng? a 1578 LINDESAY (Pitscottie) *Chron. Scot.* (S.T.S.) I. 307 My lord of Angus tuik lyttill sussie of the samin. 1587 W. FOWLER *Wks.* (S.T.S.) I. 120 He..who hes of his state ones sowcy, cair, and feare. 1591 R. BRUCE *Serm.* iii. G 6, Ane King that hath na kind of cair, nor sussie [*ed.* 1843 soucie] of his subjectis.

† **Su·ssy,** *v. Sc. Obs.* Also 6 **sussie.** [a. OF. *soussier*:—L. *sollicitāre* to rouse, excite, SOLICIT.]

1. *intr.* To care, trouble.

c 1550 ROLLAND *Crt. Venus* II. 428 Sussie not, for thow will get reskew. 1570 *Satir. Poems Reform.* xvi. 76 He susseis not thre strais Quha suld be rewlar. a 1609 ALEX. HUME *Ep. G. Moncrieff* 318, I sussie not how viuely they be tuitched.

b. With negative and const. inf.: *Not* to refuse *to do* something.

1567 *Gude & Godlie B.* (S.T.S.) 171 Thou susseit nocht to suffer deid. 1570 *Satir. Poems Reform.* xiii. 38 Cain aganis his brother did Rebell, And susseit not to sched his saikles blude. 1580–90 J. STEWART *Poems* (S.T.S.) II. 113 The fengʒeit freind..susseis not to leif his freind in smart.

2. *trans.* To care for, regard.

c 1560 A. SCOTT *Poems* (S.T.S.) xxx. 22 Thay sussy not thair God abufe.

Sussy, obs. f. SOOSY, E. Indian fabric.

† **Sustain,** *sb. Obs. rare.* [f. next.] That which sustains; means of sustenance.

1653 MILTON *Ps.* iii. 14, I lay and slept, I wak'd again, For my sustain Was the Lord.

Sustain (sŏstē^i^·n), *v.* Forms: 3 **susteni, -eini, -einy, -eyni, -eyny, costeine, souste(i)ne,** 3–6 **susteyne,** 3–7 **susteine, sustene,** 4–5 **sustyne, -teene,** 4–6 **sust(e)igne, susteyn, -tayn,** (4 **sostene, suste(e)n, -tyene,** 5 **sousteyne,** 6 **swstene**), 4–7 **sustaine, sustayne,** 6–7 **sustein,** 4– **sustain.** [a. AF., OF. *sustenir, so(u)stenir* (mod.F. *soutenir*), pres. stem *sus-, so(u)stein-, -eign-*, corresp. to Pr., Sp. *sostener*, It. *sostenere*, Pg. *soster*, ad. L. *sustinēre*, f. *sus-* SUB- 25 + *tenēre* to hold, keep.]

† 1. *trans.* To support the efforts, conduct, or cause of; to succour, support, back up. *Obs.*

c 1290 *Beket* 1507 in *S. Eng. Leg.* 149 And bote heo wolden him bi-leue and ne susteyni him non-more. 13.. *Cursor M.* 22102 (Gött.) Bethaida and corozaim, Þir tua cites sal susten [*Cott.* foster] him [*sc.* þe anticrist]. a 1450 *Knt. de la Tour* lxv, The wiff of the said Amon was not wise..to susteyne hym in his foly. c 1500 *Melusine* 111 That..ye..worship with all your power holy church, beyng her champyons, the same to susteyne & withstand ayenst alle her euyl wyllers. 1525 LD. BERNERS *Froiss.* II. clxxxvii. 572 That was the duke of Bretaygne, who susteynd the traytour syr Peter of Craon. a 1578 LINDESAY (Pitscottie) *Chron. Scot.* (S. T. S.) I. 333 No man sould foster, succour or sustene no Douglasses within thair boundis. 1614 RALEIGH *Hist. World* v. i. § 6. 349 The Romans resolue to sustaine him, and put themselues in order. 1697 DRYDEN *Æneid* VI. 1122 His Sons, who seek the Tyrant to sustain. 1711 in *10th Rep. Hist. MSS. Comm.* App. I. 143 They brought all the Grenadiers of their army, well sustain'd by a good body of other foot. 1757 W. WILKIE *Epigoniad* I. 16 While Thebes secure our vain attempts withstands, By daily aids sustain'd from distant lands. 1802 JAMES *Milit. Dict.* s.v., To sustain is to aid, succour, or support, any body of men in action, or defence.

† b. To uphold, back up, give support to (a person's conduct, a cause, a course of action). Also, to stand by (one's own action or conduct).

1297 R. GLOUC. (Rolls) 7354 Þo willam hurde þat he wolde susteini is tricherie. a 1300 *Cursor M.* 29275 Þam..þat sustens..Fals trout gain cristen state. c 1368 CHAUCER *Compl. Pite* 111 And netheles yit my troth I shall susteen vnto my deth. c 1374 — *Troylus* II. 1686, I wole right fayn with al my myght ben oon. Haue god my trouþe here cause to susteyne. 1483 CAXTON *Gold. Leg.* 154/2 He began to susteyn the feyth to whiche he had ben contrarye. a 1575 *Diurn. Occurr.* (Bannatyne Cl.) 281 Johne Knox minister requyrit the lordis to sustene ane book, quhairinto wes contenit that thay suld ordane..xij superintendentis. 1671 FLAVEL *Fount. Life* vii. Wks. 1701 I. 44/1 His [*sc.* Christ's] Death and Sufferings..must respect others, whose Persons and Cause he sustained in that suffering Capacity. 1752 YOUNG *Brothers* III. i, I'll go; Sustain my part, and echo loud my wrongs.

c. Const. clause or (rarely) acc. and inf.: To support the contention or argument, maintain (that ...). Now *rare.*

c 1366 CHAUCER *A. B. C.* 22 As bi riht þei mihten wel susteene. Þat j were wurþi my dampnacioun. c 1380 WYCLIF *Sel. Wks.* III. 175 Þes freres..seyde..þat it is an erroure to susteyne þat dymes ben pure almes. a 1450 *Knt. de la Tour* xii, Ther was moche speche whiche be shulde take, mani folke susteninge to take the elder [daughter]. 1456 SIR G. HAYE *Law Arms* (S.T.S.) 209 How it may be sustenyt that the king of Fraunce has na soverane. c 1550 R. BIESTON *Bayte Fortune* B ij, With wordes thou wouldest susteine that no good dede is doen without thee. 1609 HUME *Admonit.* in *Wodrow Soc. Misc.* (1844) 570 On the other part, otheris of you..sustene, that, among pastoris, thair sould be imparitie. 1678 G. MACKENZIE *Crim. Laws Scot.* I. xi. § 3. (1699) 59 The Justices would not sustain, *mina per se*, to be a sufficient qualification of self-defence. 1899 *Westm. Gaz.* 8 Sept. 3/1 What patriotic Englishman can for a moment sustain that [etc.]?

2. To uphold the validity or rightfulness of; to support as valid, sound, correct, true, or just.

1415 HOCCLEVE *To Sir J. Oldcastle* 183 Fro Cryst þat right first greew, & if þat we Nat shuln susteene it, we been ful vnwyse. 1425 *Rolls of Parlt.* IV. 271/2 Such possession ..ought not to be sustened ne affermed. 1689 *Sc. Acts Will. & Mary* (1875) XII. 47/2 The objectione þerafter putt to the vote and sustained to reject the Commissione be 24 votes. 1754 in *Nairne Peerage Evid.* (1874) 60 [They] sustained and hereby sustain the claim and fand and hereby find that she is a just and lawful creditor. 1756 C. LUCAS *Ess. Waters* II. 67 In the Thesis which I sustained for the degrees in physic at Leyden. 1793 LD. ESKGROVE in Lockhart *Scott* (1837) I. vii. 215 Sustain the Sheriff's judgment, and decern. 1807 LD. ELDON in Vesey *Reports* (1827) XIII. 601 The trustee, having..proved, that he had removed himself from the character of trustee, his purchase may be sustained. 1855 *Poultry Chron.* III. 412 If an objection be made to any entry as being a false one, and such objection be sustained within ten days.

3. To keep (a person or community, the mind, spirit, etc.) from failing or giving way.

13.. *Minor Poems fr. Vernon MS.* xxxii. 984 Þat sacrament reconsileþ him ay, Susteyneþ him, þat he ne falle may. c 1386 CHAUCER *Man of Law's T.* 62, I prey to god in honour hire susteene. a 1400–50 *Wars Alex.* 1749 All þe gracious godis & gudnes..Þat..sustaynes þe erth. 1535 COVERDALE *Ps.* iii. 6, I layed me downe and slepte, but I rose vp agayne, for the Lorde susteyned me. 1662 ROWLEY *Birth Merlin* I. ii. 10 That hope alone sustains me. 1742 YOUNG *Nt. Th.* IV. 401 He tunes My voice (if tun'd): the nerve, that writes, sustains. 1837 LOCKHART *Scott* III. x. 334 [He] who, more perhaps than any other master of the pen, had contributed to sustain the spirit of England throughout the struggle. 1843 WORDSW. *Grace Darling* 49 Inwardly sustained by silent prayer.

4. To keep in being; to cause to continue in a certain state; to keep or maintain at the proper level or standard; to preserve the status of.

c 1290 *St. Kath.* 68 in *S. Eng. Leg.* 94 Þis Aumperour sende ..is sonde þat þe gretteste maistres of clergie to him comen ..for to susteinen op heore lawe þoru strencþe of clergie. c 1290 *Beket* 1605 *ibid.* 152 He þat sosteinez vuele lawes. 1297 R. GLOUC. (Rolls) 6507 He..muche louede holi chirche & susteinede al so. *Ibid.* 7697 No time nas Þet pes bet isusteined þan bi his time was. 1340 *Ayenb.* 57 Þo þet þe tauernes sustyeneþ byeþ uelaʒes of alle þe zennen þat byeþ y-do ine hare tauernes. 1377 LANGL. *P. Pl.* B. IX. 108 Trewe wedded libbing folk..mote worche & wynne & þe worlde susteyne. c 1386 CHAUCER *Man of Law's T.* 294 The honour of his regne to susteene. c 1430 LYDG. *Min. Poems* (Percy Soc.) 210 Trewe juges and sergeauntis of the lawe,..Holde trouthe and sustene rightwisnesse. 1483 CAXTON *Cato* d j, He deyed for to holde and susteyne the lawe and trowthe. 1590 SPENSER *F. Q.* II. ii. 40 That great Queene..That with her soueraigne powre,..All Faery lond does peaceably sustene. 1666 DRYDEN *Ann. Mirab.* xlvii, Two Chiefs..Each able to sustain a Nations fate. 1697 — *Æneid* I. 400 Remus with Quirinus shall sustain The righteous Laws. 1700 PRIOR *Carm. Sec.* 10 Happy Pow'r sustain'd by wholesom Laws. 1836 J. GILBERT *Chr. Atonem.* vi. (1852) 154 The rule of good, no longer enforced by its proper penalties, requires to be sustained by some equivalent expedient. 1841 MYERS *Cath. Th.* IV. § 45. 406 If it [*sc.* Protestantism] has destroyed much it has also created much, and is now sustaining much. 1875 MANNING *Mission Holy Ghost* viii. 211 We are creatures who have come forth from His omnipotence, and are sustained by His almighty power.

5. To keep going, keep up (an action or process, † *occas.* a material object); to keep up without intermission; (with mixture of sense 8 or 9), to carry on (a conflict, contest).

c 1330 *Arth. & Merl.* (Kölbing) 9026 Four geauntes,..Þat sustend þat bataile. 1405 *Lay Folks Mass Bk.* (1879) 65 Any other anourment whare-wit godes seruys es sustend. c 1407 LYDG. *Reason & Sens.* 771 Vertu sensityf..hir quarel doth sustene Ageyns hir ful Rigorously. c 1420 ? LYDG. *Assembly of Gods* 1093 Whyle these pety-capteynes susteynyd thus the feelde. c 1450 *Godstow Reg.* 602, ij lampes to be susteyned with oyle. 1500–20 DUNBAR *Poems* xlvii. 22 To turne to trew luve his intent, And still the quarrell to sustene. 1544 BETHAM *Precepts War* I. lxxvii. E ij, Men refreshed wyth hote meates, bene hable to susteyne battayle an whole daye. 1553 PAYNELL tr. *Dares' Phryg. Destr. Troy* F ij, Aiax Thelamonius valiantly sustained yᵉ thinge vntill the night departed yᵉ battel. 1697 DRYDEN *Virg. Past.* III. 86 Menalcas shall sustain his under Song. 1760–2 GOLDSM. *Cit. W.* xci, Their perseverance is beyond what any other nation is capable of sustaining. a 1774 — *Hist. Greece* I. 292 At last, the Athenian fleet, after sustaining a long battle, ..was put to flight. 1816 SCOTT *Old Mort.* xxxvi, He felt no sort of desire..to sustain a correspondence which must be perilous. 1817 JAS. MILL *Brit. India* IV. v. II. 205 It was the severest conflict which the English had yet sustained with an Indian army. 1827 FARADAY *Chem. Manip.* iv. (1842) 96 The fire is lighted by a piece of brown paper and a little small coal, and is sustained..with coke and small coal. 1848 DICKENS *Dombey* xxx, The conversation was almost entirely sustained by Mrs. Skewton. 1850 HAWTHORNE *Scarlet L.* iii. (1879) 71 By the Indian's side, and evidently sustaining a companionship with him. 1875 JOWETT *Plato* (ed. 2) III. 46 The arts by which he sustains the reader's interest. 1883 GROVE *Dict. Mus.* III. 638/1 Comical..effects might be got by sustaining such sounds as 'z-z'..'r-r'..or 'ū'. *Ibid.* 639/1 By giving the pianoforte this power of sustaining sound, the special character of the instrument is transformed.

† b. To maintain the use, exercise, or occupation of. *Obs.*

1601 B. JONSON *Poetaster* IV. vi, If you thinke gods but fain'd, and vertue painted, Know, we sustaine an actuall residence. 1612 CHAPMAN *Rev. Bussy d'Ambois* III. iv. 5 Since I see You still sustain a jealous eye on me. 1623 *Shakspere's Wks.* Ep. Ded., When we valew the places your H. H. sustaine.

† 6. To support life in; to provide for the life or bodily needs of; to furnish with the necessaries of life; to keep. *Obs.*

c 1290 *St. Edmund* 552 in *S. Eng. Leg.* 447 Swiþe faire under-fongue, And isusteyned in his anuy. 1297 R. GLOUC. (Rolls) 2354 He nadde noʒt inou is kniʒtes to soustene. *Ibid.* 7755 Hom þoʒte in engelond so muche folc neuere nas þat it was wonder ware þoru isousteined it was. 1340–70 *Alex. & Dind.* 797 Alle þe godus þat ʒe geten..Seruen for to sustaine ʒour vnsely wombe. 1377 LANGL. *P. Pl.* B. XV. 275 Þorw þe mylke of þat mylde best þe man was susteyned. c 1400 MAUNDEV. (Roxb.) xv. 68 Of concubines ilke man takes als many as he may sustene of his gudes. *Ibid.* xxxii. 145 Meet and drink wharwith þe feble body myght be susteynd. 1483 CAXTON *Cato* A iij b, Thou oughtest to loue thy fader and moder nexte after god, and to..susteyne them in theyr necessytees. 1653 HAMMOND *On Matth.* iv. 4 21 Bread or ordinary means of susteining men. 1667 MILTON *P. L.* v. 415 Whatever was created, needs To be sustaind and fed. a 1700 EVELYN *Diary* 26 Oct. 1685, The daughter of a poore labouring man, who had sustain'd her parents..by her labour.

† b. Said of the means of support. *Obs.*

1538 STARKEY *England* (1878) 75 Other cuntreys in lyke space or les, dothe susteyn much more pepul then dothe thys ourys. a 1578 LINDESAY (Pitscottie) *Chron. Scot.* (S.T.S.) I. 3 Ane hes that micht ane hundreith weill susteine. 1615 G. SANDYS *Trav.* 7 Their territories though large and fruitfull, too narrow to sustaine so populous a State. 1697 DRYDEN *Virg. Georg.* II. 743 Enough remains..His Wife and tender Children to sustain.

† c. *refl.* To keep oneself; *occas.* to take food, feed. *Obs.*

a 1300 in *E. E. P.* (1862) 20 Sum þer beþ þat swinkiþ sore winne catel to hab more ham silf fair to susteni. 1380 in *Eng. Gilds* (1870) 40 He may nought ne haue nouʒhe to susteyne him self. ? a 1550 *Freiris Berwik* 226 in *Dunbar's Poems* (1893) 293 That na apperance of feist be heir sene, Bot sobirly our selfis dois sustene. 1640–1 *Kirkcudbr. War-Comm. Min. Bk.* (1855) 157 Thair..families are reducit to extreme miserie..not haveing quhairupon to sustein thame. 1650 W. D. tr. *Comenius' Gate Lat. Unl.* § 385 A husbandman that..mainteineth (susteineth) himself with the crop (incom) of his yearly corn.

† d. To support (life, nature) with necessaries.

1402 *Pol. Poems* (Rolls) II. 17 Neither they tillen ne sowen,..neither nothing that man should helpe, but onely themselves, their lives to susteine. 1483 CAXTON *Cato* h j b, Thou oughtest not to requyre..of god but that whyche is vtyle and prouffytable for to susteyn nature humayn. 1591 SYLVESTER *Du Bartas* I. iii. 694 O sacred simples that our life sustain. 1697 DRYDEN *Virg. Georg.* IV. 82 They..labour Honey to sustain their Lives.

† e. To supply (a person's need). *Obs. rare.*

1601 SHAKS. *Twel. N.* IV. ii. 135 Ile be with you againe: In a trice, like to the old vice, Your neede to sustaine.

† 7. To provide for the upkeep of (an institution, establishment, estate, etc.). *Obs.*

1338 R. BRUNNE *Chron.* (1810) 20 Þre þousand marke he gaf..To Petir & Paule of Rome, to susteyn þer light. 1431 *Rec. St. Mary at Hill* (1905) 15 That the same Wardeyns & their Successours fynde & susteyn v tapers of wexe..to brenne vpon my candylstyk. c 1450 *Godstow Reg.* 491 And they shold susteyne the seid mese, with ther owne costis, in al so good state or better than they resceived hit. 1544 tr. *Littleton's Tenures* I. viii. 16 Yf a house be let, to holde at wyl, the lessee is nat holden to susteyne or repayre the house. 1592 WEST *1st Pt. Symbol.* § 103 C, The saide J. shall well..sustaine & maintaine the houses & buildings which be..builded.

8. To endure without failing or giving way; to bear up against, withstand.

c 1330 *Arth. & Merl.* (Kölbing) 7132, & he bihinde to ben bi cas, To susten þe paiems ras. 1382 WYCLIF *1 Cor.* xiii. 7 Charite..hopith alle thingis, it susteyneth alle thingis. a 1400 CHAUCER *Merciles Beaute* 2 Your yen two wol slee me sodenly, I may the beauté of hem not sustene. 1474 CAXTON *Chesse* I. ii. (1883) 12 The euyll lyf..of the kynge is the lyf of a cruell beste and ought not longe to be susteyned. 1577 GOOGE tr. *Heresbach's Husb.* 125 Asses ..able to susteyn blowes, labour, hunger, and thyrst. 1667 MILTON *P. L.* II. 209 This is now Our doom; which if we can sustain and bear, Our Supream Foe in time may much remit His anger. 1817 JAS. MILL *Brit. India* IV. viii. II. 281 He sustained the attack, which, for the space of an hour was vigorously maintained. 1849 MACAULAY *Hist. Eng.* iii. I. 290 Scarce one [of the cities] was now capable of sustaining a siege. 1875 JOWETT *Plato* (ed. 2) V. 263 There is no soul of man..who will be able to sustain the temptation of arbitrary power. 1889 A. R. WALLACE *Darwinism* (1890) 17 Each species [of plant] can sustain a certain amount of heat and cold.

b. † *intr.* (also with *it*) To bear up, hold out (*obs.*). Also occas. *refl.*

1382 WYCLIF *Ps.* cxxix. [cxxx.] 3 If wickidnessis thou shalt al aboute kepe, Lord; Lord, who shal sustene? 1382 — *Isaiah* lxiv. 3 Whan thou shalt do merueiles, wee shuln not sustene. 1412–20 LYDG. *Chron. Troy* IV. 2029 *heading*, The Troyans and þe Grekes resumede the felde, in þe which the Grekis might not susteyne against þe swerde of Troylus. 1546 LANGLEY tr. *Pol. Verg. De Invent.* I. iii. 5 Other that suppose this worlde had both an originall cause of being, and shall also sustein and ende by putrifaccion. 1573 *Satir. Poems Reform.* xli. 139 In deid that ʒe suld not susteind [= sustain it] He thunderit threitnings to the air. 1598 CHAPMAN *Iliad* II. 287 Sustaine a little then my friendes, that we the trueth may trie: Of reuerend Chalchas prophesy. 1864 TENNYSON *Aylmer's F.* 544 Tho' Averill wrote And bad him with good heart sustain himself.

c. *trans.* To bear, stand the force of (criticism, etc.).

1790 GIBBON *Misc. Wks.* (1814) III. 502 Their opinion will not sustain the rigour of critical enquiry. 1855 MACAULAY *Hist. Eng.* xii. III. 142 The Cathedral..ill qualified to sustain a comparison with the awful temples of the middle ages.

9. To undergo, experience, have to submit to (evil, hardship, or damage; now chiefly with *injury, loss* as obj., † formerly also *sorrow, death*); to have inflicted upon one, suffer the infliction of.

In mod. journalistic use (orig. *U.S.*), to suffer the injury of (a broken limb, or the like).

c 1400 *Destr. Troy* 7179 Why Sustayn ye þat sorow, þat Sewes for euer..? Why proffer ye not pes, or ye payne thole? c 1407 LYDG. *Reason & Sens.* 3570 Iason..Fortunyd was for to sustene Al the perells oon by oon. 1426 in *Surtees Misc.* (1890) 10 After þe grete losses þat I have had and susteined. 1531 ELYOT *Gov.* I. xxvi, The most noble emperour Octauius Augustus,..only for playing at dise and that but seldome, sustaineth a note of reproche. 1542–3 *Act* 34 & 35 *Hen. VIII*, c. 3, The Offendoures..to susteyne suche further punisshement as shall seme expedient. 1555 EDEN *Decades* (Arb.) 172 The princes are determyned noo longer to susteyne theyr oppressions. 1582 N. LICHEFIELD tr. *Castanheda's Conq. E. Ind.* I. ii. 6 In which time they susteined many and great tempests. 1583 STUBBES *Anat. Abus.* II. (1882) 62 The host of Pharao..who all sustained one kinde of death. 1601 SHAKS. *Twel. N.* I. v. 186 Good Beauties, let mee sustaine no scorne. 1628 DIGBY *Voy. Medit.* (Camden) 3 If either should chance to breake or spring mast or yarde or sustayne any leake or other damage. 1653 R. SANDERS *Physiogn.*, *Moles* 13 She shall sustain thefts, and suffer by fugitive servants. a 1700 EVELYN *Diary* 21 Sept. 1674, I went to see the greate losse that Lord Arlington had sustain'd by fire at Goring house. 1771 GOLDSM. *Hist. Eng.* IV. 163 He died of a gangrene, occasioned by the bruises which he had sustained. 1793 SMEATON *Edystone L.* § 322 The storms which the building had now sustained, without material damage. 1823 SCOTT *Quentin D.* xvii, He was relating the story of the bastinading which he had sustained. 1825 — *Betrothed* xiii, Recollecting the loss she had so lately sustained on that luckless spot. 1833 HT. MARTINEAU *Three Ages* ii. 46 His Majesty had sustained a signal defeat abroad. 1865 MORLEY *Mod. Characteristics* 62 A provincial hostess, whose entertainment has gone off flatly, sustains about as much mortification as if her firstborn had been attacked by the small-pox. 1880 *Troy* (U.S.) *Daily Times* 28 Aug., [He] fell from a pile of lumber yesterday afternoon and sustained a broken arm.

† *const. inf.* 1559 AYLMER *Harborowe* N iij b, Was it no wronge..that she susteyned..to be first a prysoner..and garded with a sorte of cutthrotes?

† b. With neutral obj. *Obs.*

1575 GASCOIGNE *Glasse Govt.* Wks. 1910 II. 9 Having susteyned like adventures. 1577 HARRISON *England* II. ii. (1877)

I. 47 Shireburne also susteined the sub-diuision. 1663 *Rec. Meeting of Exercise, Alford* (1897) 9 Mr. John Mair sustained his questionarie tryall, and his tryall in the Languages, and is approven. 1697 DRYDEN *Virg. Georg.* I. 73 That Crop ..Which twice the Sun, and twice the Cold sustains. *Ibid.* III. 99 The Bull's Insult at Four she [*sc.* the cow] may sustain.

c. To bear (a burden, charge); † to bear (expense).

1433 *Rolls of Parlt.* IV. 425/1 Ye charges yat he most bere and susteigne. 1530 in W. H. Turner *Select. Rec. Oxford* (1880) 89 The Towne susteyneth nott one peny of the sayd charges. 1533 BELLENDEN *Livy* II. iv. (S.T.S.) I. 142 He was sa fer rvn in age, þat he mycht nocht sustene þe charge of þe consulate. 1601 R. JOHNSON *Kingd. & Commw.* (1603) 106 Neither coulde the King of Spaine sustaine the burden of so many warres. 1651 HOBBES *Leviath.* II. xxiv. 129 That such portion [in the distribution of land] be made sufficient, to susteine the whole expence to the common Peace. 1738 WESLEY *Hymns* LXXIII. iv, The Burthen for me to sustain Too great, on Thee, my Lord, was laid. 1833 HT. MARTINEAU *Manch. Strike* ix. 106 It has enabled us to sustain burdens which would have crushed any other people.

† d. To support (a part or character); to play the part of. Also *occas.* to bear (a title). *Obs.*

1560 DAUS tr. *Sleidane's Comm.* 107 Where as they susteyne the persones of intercessours. 1588 KYD *Househ. Philos.* Wks. (1901) 252 [He] ought principally to haue care in choosing of his wife, with whom hee must sustaine the persoune of a Husbande. 1596 DALRYMPLE tr. *Leslie's Hist. Scot.* I. 116 Thay susteine the persone of honest sitizenis. 1643 PRYNNE *Sov. Power Parl.* App. 198 Christ our Saviour, who although he were the King of Kings, yet because he then sustained a private person, he payed tribute willingly. 1700 WALLIS in *Collect.* (O.H.S.) I. 325 From him that..sustains that title. 1731 A. HILL (in *Sotheran's Catal.* No. 12. (1899) 26), I am at a loss, how those characters will be sustain'd wᵗʰ they were to have represented. 1782 COWPER *Parrot* 35 Each character in ev'ry part Sustain'd with so much grace and art.

† 10. Const. inf., or acc. and inf., chiefly in negative, conditional, or interrog. use: To reconcile oneself to doing, to bear to do, something; to tolerate or bear that something should be done.

14.. in *Tundale's Vis.* (1843) 113 O who is alas that may sustene To be prowd, consider her mekenes. 1426 LYDG. *De Guil. Pilgr.* 4432, I swepe, I make yt clene, For fylthe noon I may sustene Ther tabyde. 1540–1 ELYOT *Image Gov.* xxvi. 58 b, She coulde not susteyne hyr sonnes wyfe to be called Augusta. 1567 *Gude & Godlie B.* (S.T.S.) 110 We may not sustene To heir thame say, [etc.]. 1700 DRYDEN *Ceyx & Alc.* 19 Can Ceyx then sustain to leave his Wife? a 1726 SEWELL *Rich. I* II, He who leads Armies in the Cause of Heaven.. Yet can sustain to wrong a King—a Friend.

11. To hold up, bear the weight of; to keep from falling by support from below; often simply, to carry, bear. † Also with *up.* Now *rare.*

a 1330 *Roland & V.* 338 Mahoun..dede mani fendes þer in..For to susten þe ymage, & sett him on heiʒe stage. 1390 GOWER *Conf.* III. 108 Whos condicion Is set to be the foundament To sustiene up the firmament. 1470–85 MALORY *Arthur* XVI. ii. 667 Gawayne..lepte vp behynde hym for to sustene hym. 1481 CAXTON *Myrr.* I. xvi. 50 That one [of the four elements] susteyned that other in suche manere, as therthe holdeth hym in the myddle. 1590 SPENSER *F. Q.* II. x. 43 Next whom Morindus did the crowne sustaine. 1592 KYD *Sp. Trag.* II. i. 3 In time the sauuage Bull sustaines the yoake. 1594 — *Cornelia* II. 339 What e're the massie Earth hath fraight. Or on her nurse-like backe sustaines. 1606 SHAKS. *Ant. & Cl.* III. xi. 45 Well then, sustaine me: Oh. 1697 DRYDEN *Virg. Georg.* III. 256 To harrow Furrows, and sustain the Plough. 1756 E. MOORE *Trial Selim* 27 Her left hand clench'd, her cheek sustain'd. 1759 TOPLADY *Poems* (1860) 96 Each a Palm sustain'd In his victorious Hand. 1794 MRS. RADCLIFFE *Myst. Udolpho* xxvi, Here again she looked round for a seat to sustain her. 1831 SCOTT *Cast. Dang.* viii, He found the minstrel seated at a small table, sustaining before him a manuscript. 1832 BREWSTER *Nat. Magic* x. 253 The difficulty..really consists in sustaining the anvil. 1850 MRS. JAMESON *Leg. Monast. Ord.* (1863) 394 Sustained in the arms of two sisters of her Order.

fig. 1390 GOWER *Conf.* III. 136 Pes sustiened up alofte With esy wordes and with softe Wher strengthe scholde lete it falle. 1680 T. GRANGER *Div. Logike* 66 The Adiunct receiued of the Subiect by inherence is infixed, infused, ingrafted, sustained of the subiect.

b. To be the support of, as in a structure or building; to have resting upon it.

c 1386 CHAUCER *Knt.'s T.* 1135 For to make it strong Euery pyler the temple to sustene. c 1489 CAXTON *Sonnes of Aymon* xxiv. 505 A forke that susteyned vp their lodges, that was grete and stronge. 1611 CORYAT *Crudities* 325 Two exceeding great Lyons in red marble, that sustaine two goodly pillars. 1697 DRYDEN *Æneid* x. 1189 A Bough his Brazen Helmet did sustain. a 1700 EVELYN *Diary* 12 July 1654, The ample Hall and columne that spreads its capital to sustaine the roofe. 1717 PRIOR *Alma* II. 277 The swelling Hoop sustains The rich Brocard. 1784 COWPER *Task* IV. 544 Her head..Indebted to some smart wig-weaver's hand For more than half the tresses it sustains. 1828 SCOTT *F. M. Perth* xxiii, The bier was so placed, as to leave the view of the body it sustained open [etc.]. 1856 STANLEY *Sinai & Pal.* x. (1858) 365 The Galilean hills..contain or sustain green basins of table-land just below their topmost ridges.

c. To bear, support, withstand (a weight or pressure). Also in fig. context.

c 1386 CHAUCER *Prioress' T.* 31 My konnyng is so wayk.. That I ne may the weighte nat susteene. 1697 DRYDEN *Virg. Georg.* I. 164 Lest the Stem..Shou'd scarce sustain the Head's unweildy weight. 1774 GOLDSM. *Nat. Hist.* (1776) VI. 91 Though they have but a small weight of body to sustain. 1781 COWPER *Flatting Mill* 9 This process achiev'd, it is doom'd to sustain The thump after thump of a gold-beater's mallet. 1800 VINCE *Hydrost.* ii. (1806) 23 The same pressure must sustain the same weight. 1836 J. GILBERT *Chr. Atonem.* ix. (1852) 268 This external pressure has nothing substantial to sustain it from within. 1860 TYNDALL *Glac.* II. xxx. 404 When the pressure applied becomes too great for the glass to sustain, it flies to pieces.

† d. To hold in position, hold erect, etc.; also, to be sufficient to bear the weight of. *Obs.*

1398 TREVISA *Barth. De P. R.* v. xxv. (Bodl. MS.), Þe nekke..bereþ and susteyneþ þe heed. 1481 CAXTON *Myrr.* II. xvii. 104 The quyck syluer is of suche nature..that it susteyneth a stone vpon it. 1538 STARKEY *England* (1878) 49 Bycause they [*sc.* the feet] by theyr labour susteyne and support the rest of the body. 1599 ALEX. HUME *Hymns* II. 81 The feit ar swift and members meit, for to susteine the rest. 1668 CULPEPPER & COLE *Barthol. Anat.* IV. vii. 165 If all eight [muscles] act, they hold the Back straight, and do as it were sustain a man.

† e. *refl.* and *intr.* To hold oneself upright; also, to be in or maintain a fixed position. *Obs.*

c 1374 CHAUCER *Anel. & Arc.* 177 She ne hath foot on which she may sustene. c 1450 *Merlin* 354 He myght no lenger sustene on his feet for the traueile. 1604 SHAKS. *Oth.* v. ii. 260 Behold, I haue a weapon: A better neuer did it selfe sustaine Vpon a Soldiers Thigh. 1728 R. MORRIS *Ess. Anc. Archit.* 35 The Solidity becomes of less Power to sustain in Proportion to its Height.

† f. Const. inf. To have sufficient strength to do, be equal to doing, something. *Obs.*

1430–40 LYDG. *Bochas* IX. ii. (MS. Bodl. 263) 408/1 To stonde upriht be myhte nat susteene. 1481 CAXTON *Myrr.* I. xv. 50 No bodyly man may not susteyne for to see hym [*sc.* an angel] in no manere.

12. To be adequate as a ground or basis for. (Cf. SUPPORT *v.* 3 c.)

1828–32 WEBSTER s.v., The testimony or the evidence is not sufficient to sustain the action, the accusation, the charges, or the impeachment. 1866 SEELEY *Ecce Homo* v (ed. 8) 40 We go beyond what the evidence is able to sustain. 1869 J. MARTINEAU *Ess.* II. 361 This passage undoubtedly sustains Mr. Grote's assertion.

¶ 13. To wait for. (A literalism of translation.)

1382 WYCLIF *Ecclus.* xxxvi. 18 ʒif meede, Lord, to men sustenende thee. 1382 — *Mark* viii. 2 Now the thridde day thei susteynen [*gloss* or abyden] me.

Sustainable (sŏstē^i^·năb'l), *a.* [f. prec. + -ABLE. Cf. SUSTENABLE.]

† 1. Capable of being borne or endured; supportable, bearable. *Obs. rare.*

1611 COTGR., *Soustenable*, sustainable,..abideable.

2. Capable of being upheld or defended; maintainable.

1845–6 DE QUINCEY *Gilfillan's Lit. Portr.* Wks. 1859 XII. 304 From the verdict of a jury,..no candid and temperate man will allow himself to believe any appeal sustainable. 1857 TOULMIN SMITH *Parish* 130 It is the duty of the constable to apprehend offenders taken in the fact, or on sustainable presumption. 1875 *N. Amer. Rev.* CXX. 463 Religion may be morally useful without being intellectually sustainable. 1884 *Law Rep.* 27 Chanc. Div. 69 The Defendant has taken several technical objections to the order, none of which..are sustainable.

Sustained (sŏstē^i^·nd), *ppl. a.* [f. SUSTAIN *v.* + -ED[1].]

1. Kept up without intermission or flagging; maintained through successive stages or over a long period; kept up or maintained at a uniform (esp. a high) pitch or level.

1796 BURKE *Regic. Peace* I. Wks. 1907 VI. 144 A vehement and sustained spirit of fortitude. 1826 SCOTT *Old Mort.* xxxii, His marksmen, commencing upon the pass a fire as well aimed as it was sustained and regular. 1837 CARLYLE *Fr. Rev.* I. IV. iv, Next day, with sustained pomp, they are ..installed in their *Salle des Menus.* 1853 LYTTON *My Novel* XII. xxxiii, Harley's compassion vanished before this sustained hypocrisy. 1860 *All Year Round* No. 67. 396 Mr. Hyde Clarke is the only man who has attempted a sustained biography of him. 1873 SYMONDS *Grk. Poets* v. 126 The Dorian poets, inspired by a graver and more sustained imagination, composed long and complex odes.

2. Of a note or tone: **a.** Maintained at the same pitch. *rare.*

1775 T. SHERIDAN *Art Reading* I. 197 That interruption ought to make no change in the proper manner of delivering it, which should be in a sustained note.

b. *Mus.* Maintained (in its full force) through its whole length; see also quot. 1876.

1801 BUSBY *Dict. Mus.* s.v., Notes are said to be *sustained* when their sound is continued through their whole power, or length. 1845 G. DODD *Brit. Manuf.* IV. 156 Unless..it were possible to obtain the sustained tones of the organ. 1876 STAINER & BARRETT *Dict. Mus. T.*, *Sustained note*, a name given to prolonged notes which partake of the character of a pedal-point by their immunity from ordinary harmonic rules, but which cannot with propriety be called pedal-points owing to their occurrence in the middle or upper part.

3. Endured, borne.

1819 BYRON *Mazeppa* ii, This [horse] too sinks after many a league Of well sustain'd but vain fatigue.

4. *Her.* (See quot.)

1882 CUSSANS *Her.* 130 *Sustained*: Usually applied to a Chief or Fess, when a narrow fillet or fimbriation occupies the base of the Charge. This term is seldom used in modern Armory, nor..is it necessary.

Hence **Sustai·nedly** *adv.*, in a sustained manner.

1842 E. FITZGERALD *Lett.* (1889) I. 119, I think Beethoven is rather spasmodically, than sustainedly, grand. 1857 SPENCER *Ess.* (1858) I. 376 More consistently, more unitedly, and more sustainedly.

Sustainer (sŏstē^i^·nəɹ). Forms: 4 **sosteynere,** 5 **suste(y)nour, -tener,** 6– **sustainer.** [Partly a. AF. *sustenour, OF. *sosteneor, sousteneur*, f. *sostenir* to SUSTAIN; partly directly f. SUSTAIN + -ER[1].] One who or that which sustains.

1. One who or that which upholds, supports, or keeps in being; an upholder, supporter.

a 1400 in *Eng. Gilds* (1870) 349 Principal sosteynere of þe fraunchyse. c 1412 HOCCLEVE *De Reg. Princ.* 2856 Honour, long lyfe,..Mot haue oure sustenour, our prince & kyng! 1429 *Rolls of Parlt.* IV. 360/1 Ye seid Inhabitauntz ben sustenors and supportours. 1547–64 BAULDWIN *Mor. Philos.* (Palfr.) 126 The sustainers of wrong. a 1680 CHARNOCK *Attrib. God* (1682) 70 God is the Lord of all, as he is the sustainer of all by his power. 1726 BUTLER *Serm. Rolls* xiv. 283 When they shall have a Sensation, that He is the Sustainer of their Being, that they exist in him. 1845 *Encycl. Metrop.* II. 861/1 Almighty Creator and Sustainer of all things. 1909 *Q. Rev.* Apr. 657 The aim of our politics can be no other than that the Bohemian people should again become the sustainers of the idea of the State.

† b. *pl.* Military supports. *Obs. rare.*

1708 *Lond. Gaz.* No 4468/2 [They] had for the Attack on the Right 800 Grenadiers,..and for the Left 1600 Grenadiers, with the like number of Sustainers.

c. A thing or circumstance that sustains a condition.

1818 SHELLEY *Rosal. & Helen* 337 The very hope of death's dear rest; Which, since the heart within my breast Of natural life was dispossessed, Its strange sustainer there had been. 1831 LYTTON *Godolphin* ix, It is not always a sustainer of the stage delusion to be enamoured of an actress.

2. † a. One who supports or holds a thing. *rare.*

c 1616 CHAPMAN *Homer's Hymn to Vesta & Merc.* 17 Of Heauens golden Rodd The sole Sustainer.

b. A supporting structure or device.

1893 *Westm. Gaz.* 25 Apr. 7/3 The weight of the carriage was 60lb., of the engine 200lb., and of the grating of sustainers 70lb. 1909 *Cent. Dict., Suppl.*, *Sustainer*.., a little disk,..which serves to support in an upright position the wick of a night-light.

† 3. A sufferer. *Obs. rare.*

c 1611 CHAPMAN *Iliad* XXIII. 524 Thy selfe, hast a sustainer bene Of much affliction in my cause.

4. One who provides another with the necessaries of life. *rare.*

1678 SIR G. MACKENZIE *Crim. Laws Scot.* I. xix. § 16. (1699) 106 By sustainers, are meant such as entertain the Thief at bed and board. 1866 J. G. MURPHY *Comm. Exod.* xxii. 22 The decease of the father leaves both the widow and the child without their natural protector and sustainer.

Sustai·ning, *vbl. sb.* [f. SUSTAIN *v.* + -ING[1].] The action of the verb SUSTAIN, in various senses; sustenance, maintenance, support, etc.

c 1383 in *Eng. Hist. Rev.* Oct. (1911) 749 Susteynininge [*sic*] of felowis bi forme of þe gospel þat ben able to performe þe office of þe gospel in good lyuynge. 1398 TREVISA *Barth. De P. R.* XVII. ii. (Bodl. MS.) lf. 188 b/1 For sadnes of þe.. grounde þe herbe hathe greneneș in rote and susteynynge of þe stalke in þe reringe þereof. c 1400 *Rom. Rose* 2765 Though he lye in strawe or dust, In Hoope is alle his susteynyng. c 1450 *Godstow Reg.* 393 They graunted to hym and to his wyf..a corrodye of oon seruaunt to ther susteynynge. *Ibid.* 438 To the susteynyng of the masse of oure lady seynt marye. 1495 *Naval Acc. Hen. VII* (1896) 159 The Susteynyng & fortyfying of the seid dokke & gates of the same. 1541 COPLAND *Guydon's Quest. Cyrurg.* D ij, Demaunde. Wherfore are the bones made? Answere. Bycause they shulde be the foundacyon of all the body and susteynynge therof. 1593 SHAKS. *Lucr.* 1573 Short time seems long, in sorrowes sharp sustayning. 1607 HIERON *Wks.* I. 170 Without Whose gracious sustaining he should soone returne vnto his first nothing. 1726 LEONI *Alberti's Archit.* I. 76/1 Provisions necessary for the sustaining of a Siege. 1850 McCOSH *Div. Govt.* II. i. (1874) 89 Every one knows how needful the atmosphere is for the sustaining of animal and vegetable life. 1893 *Athenæum* 2 Dec. 767/3 The sustaining of her strong personality..is no easy task.

Sustai·ning, *ppl. a.* [f. SUSTAIN *v.* + -ING[2].] That sustains, in various senses; supporting.

1605 SHAKS. *Lear* IV. iv. 6 Darnell, and all the idle weedes that grow In our sustaining Corne. 1610 — *Temp.* I. ii. 218 On their sustaining garments not a blemish, But fresher then before. 1817 SHELLEY *Rev. Islam* V. lvi. 6 Melons, and dates, and figs, and many a root Sweet and sustaining. 1820 — *Prometh. Unb.* III. iii. 91 The many children fair Folded in my sustaining arms. 1828 D'ISRAELI *Chas. I*, I. vi. 163 Mary of Scotland was long the sustaining hope of France, of Spain, and of Rome. 1855 MACAULAY *Hist. Eng.* XV. III. 594 The sustaining power of high religious principle.

b. In technical use.

1839 NOAD *Electricity* iii. 105 The introduction of the 'sustaining' or 'constant' batteries of Messrs. Daniell and Mullins, has..entirely superseded the employment of these simple circles in electro-magnetic investigations. 1842 *Civil Eng. & Arch. Jrnl.* V. 95/1 The meaning of the technical terms of 'retaining' and 'sustaining' walls was—when a wall was used either to support water or earth artificially put together. a 1878 SIR G. SCOTT *Lect. Archit.* (1879) I. 281 A narrow vault..which is not necessarily of the same curvature as the sustaining arches.

Hence **Sustai·ningly** *adv.*

1640 G. ABBOT *Job Paraphr.* Argt., A little chinke of light whereby he was able to see, and sustainingly to remind himselfe of God's former favours. 1875 *Toxie* I. vi. 101 Holding my soft gloved hand sustainingly to his side.

Sustainment (sŏstē^i^·nmĕnt). Also 5 **sustene-.** [In earliest quot. a. OF. *sus-, sostenement*, f. *sostenir* to SUSTAIN; later f. SUSTAIN *v.* + -MENT.]

1. Means of support; chiefly = SUSTENANCE 1, 2.

c 1450 *Merlin* xxix. 591 Whan Arthur hadde slain Magloras the kinge that was the sustenement of the saisnes. 1588 PARKE tr. *Mendoza's Hist. China* 351 They haue no other sustainement, but onely that which this tree yeeldeth. 1670 MILTON *Hist. Eng.* III. Wks. 1851 V. 104 They betook them to the Woods, and liv'd by hunting, which was thir only sustainment.

2. The action of sustaining; *esp.* maintenance in being or activity, in a certain condition or at a certain level; sustentation. (Cf. SUSTENANCE 3.)

1568 HACKET tr. *Thevet's New found World* lxxxii. 135 b, They began to..till the earth, for to receive the fruits therof for the sustainment of their liues. a 1680 CHARNOCK *Attrib. God* (1834) I. 459 God..not..receiving from any place any thing for his preservation or sustainment. 1816 *Q. Rev.* XV. 70 An unnatural and artificial sustainment of the language and imagery. 1833 J. MARTINEAU *Misc.* (1852) 45 In Priestley's case there was not merely a sustainment—but a positive advancement of character in later years. 1857 DICKENS *Lett.* (1880) II. 16 In an impossible attitude for the sustainment of its weight. 1876 LOWELL *Among my Bks.* Ser. II. 50 The Hebrew forerunners, in whose society his soul sought consolation and sustainment.

† **Sustantive,** *a. Obs. rare.* In 5 **-yf.** [? irreg. formed as adj. to SUSTAIN; cf. SUSTENABLE.] Having the function of sustaining physical life.

c 1400 tr. *Secr. Secr., Gov. Lordsh.* 96 Strengthe nutrityf, and infirmatyf, and sustantyf [orig. *nutritiua informatiua & vegetatiua*]. Þe wirkynge of þis last, þat þe Auctour clepys vegetatyf, & I here strenght sustantyf, [etc.].

† **Sustenable,** *a. Obs.* Also 5 **-tin-.** [a. OF. *sus-, sostenable*, f. *sostenir* to SUSTAIN.]

1. Capable of being or that is maintained in physical life and growth: in quots. used as synonym for VEGETABLE *a.* 1.

c 1400 tr. *Secr. Secr., Gov. Lordsh.* 90 Some þinges vegetables or sustenables er..by sedys, & with-outen plantyng. *Ibid.* 95 Þe composicioun vegitable þat is sustinable is mor noble þan þe originale.

2. Capable of being endured; = SUSTAINABLE *a.* 1.

1471 CAXTON *Recuyell* (Sommer) 320 Hys strookes were not sustenable.

† **Sustenal.** *Obs. rare.* [a. OF. *soustenal*, f. *soustenir* to SUSTAIN: see -AL.] A support.

c 1400 *Pilgr. Sowle* (Caxton 1483) IV. xxxi. 80 The necke next vnder the hede is set aboue al the body ryght as the sustenal and the piler.

Sustenance (sʌ·stĭnăns). Forms: 3–4 **sustynance,** 3–6 **-tinaunce,** 4 **sust-, sostnaunce, sostinonce, -tenaunse, sustenauns,** 4–5 **-tiena(u)nce,** 4–6 **-ten-, -tynaunce,** 5 **-tinens, -tenence, -tenaunse,** 5–6 **-tinance,** 6 **-tynans, -tenans, -teynaunce, -tainance,** 7–8 **sustinence,** 3– **sustenance.** [a. AF. *sustenaunce*, OF. *sos-, soustenance*, mod.F. *soutenance* (= Pr. *sostenensa*, It. *sostenenza*, OPg. *sustinencia*: cf. late L. *sustinentia*), f. *sostenir* to SUSTAIN: see -ANCE.]

1. Means of living or subsistence; livelihood; † phr. *to find, win (a) sustenance.*

1297 R. GLOUC. (Rolls) 975 Hii..swonke & tylede hor lifiode..Hii founde hom sustenance inou & liuede þus vorþ. 1303 R. BRUNNE *Handl. Synne* 1326 Ʒyf þou þurgh wykked ordynaunce Fordost pore mannys sustynaunce Þat aftyrward he may nat lyue. 13.. *Coer de L.* 3757 Kyng Richard gaff castels and touns, To hys eerlys and to barouns, To have therinne her sustynaunce. 13.. *Sir Beues* (A.) 3916 Iosian euericke a day ʒede aboute þe cite wiþ inne. Here sostenaunse for to winne. c 1385 CHAUCER *L. G. W.* 2041 (*Ariadne*), And for myn sustenaunce, yet wil I swynk. c 1400 MAUNDEV. (Roxb.) vii. 24 In þis deserte I dwell and gase to gete my sustinaunce. c 1460 FORTESCUE *Abs. & Lim. Mon.* xviii. (1885) 154 Þe clarkes off is chapell..[shall] be rewarded with pencions..ffor þer rewardes or sustenance. 1568 GRAFTON *Chron.* II. 350 To haue sufficient for their necessarie sustenance. 1687 A. LOVELL tr. *Thevenot's Trav.* I. 243 There is..all that is necessary for the Service of the Church, and the sorry sustenance of the Religious. 1710 PRIDEAUX *Orig. Tithes* i. 30 They reap from them a sustenance in Earthly things. 1836 W. IRVING *Astoria* I. 2 It was the fur trade..which gave early sustenance and vitality to the great Canadian provinces. 1864 TENNYSON *En. Ard.* 258 She..Gain'd for her own a scanty sustenance.

2. Means of sustaining life; food, victuals.

c 1290 *St. Francis* 229 in *S. Eng. Leg.* 60 Miseyse huy hadden þare i-novʒ..For defaute of heore sustinaunce and for defaute of bokes. 13.. *Gaw. & Gr. Knt.* 1095 Nauþer of sostnaunce ne of slepe, soþly I knowe. 1377 LANGL. *P. Pl.* B. XX. 7 To clothes and to sustenance. 1390 GOWER *Conf.* II. 83 The cornes and the wynes Ben sustenance to mankinde. 1470–85 MALORY *Arthur* VII. xxvi. 253 Many.. merueilled that he desyred his sustenaunce for a twelf monethe. c 1491 *Chast. Goddes Chyld.* 13 It is nedeful to take bodily sustenaunce..in resonable manere. 1549 LATIMER *Ploughers* (Arb.) 25 If the ploughemen..were..negligente..we shoulde not longe lyue for lacke of sustinaunce. 1626 BACON *Sylva* § 360 [The Chameleon] feedeth not onely vpon Aire, (though that be his principall Sustenance;) For sometimes hee taketh Flies. 1691 RAY *Creation* I. (1692) 71 Water is one part, and that not the least of our Sustenance. 1760–72 H. BROOKE *Fool of Qual.* (1809) II. 144 Having sold all our moveables..for sustenance. 1808 SCOTT in Lockhart *Life* I. i. 47, I had all the appetite of a growing boy, but was prohibited any sustenance beyond what was absolutely necessary for the support of nature. 1864 TENNYSON *En. Ard.* 550 No want was there of human sustenance, Soft fruitage, mighty nuts, and nourishing roots. 1873 BROWNING *Red Cott. Nt.-cap* II. 1103 Now dying and in want of sustenance!

† b. A kind or a quantity of food; *pl.* eatables.

c 1450 *Mirk's Festial* 254 Þay..toke no hede what þat þay haden but a sympull sustenaunce. 1528 PAYNEL *Salerne's Regim.* D iij, Nothynge more daungerous than to myngle diuers sustinances to gether. 1615 G. SANDYS *Trav.* 89 Fortie saile of ships..by the trading whereof they bring in that sustenance which the soile affordeth not. 1677 in *Ray's Corr.* (1848) 128, I am apt to believe that water cannot be a competent sustenance for them.

c. *gen.* and *fig.* Nourishment.

c 1489 CAXTON *Sonnes of Aymon* xix. 437 They ete all a lityll therof, whiche gaaf theim grete sustenaunce. 1577 GOOGE tr. *Heresbach's Husb.* I. (1586) 18 b, Those [thinges] that require more sustenaunce, are sowen in richer ground. 1671 MILTON *P. R.* I. 429 Lying is thy sustenance, thy food. 1686 W. HOPKINS tr. *Ratramnus* Dissert. v. (1688) 93 This Spiritual virtue [of the Sacrament]..ministering to it the sustenance of Eternal Life. 1742 YOUNG *Nt. Th.* v. 466 Some reject this sustenance divine. 1830 HERSCHEL *Study Nat. Phil.* 65 That dry bones could be a magazine of nutriment,..ready to yield up their sustenance in the form best adapted to the support of life. a 1831 A. KNOX *Rem.* (1844) I. 66 The taste once revived, its due sustenance would not be difficult to find. 1849 HELPS *Friends in C.* II. iv. 95 The plants draw most of their sustenance from the air.

3. The action of sustaining life by food; the action of supporting with the means of subsistence; the fact or state of being so sustained.

Tends to merge in sense 2.

c 1386 CHAUCER *Pars. T.* ¶ 298 Euery tyme that a man eteth or drynketh moore than suffiseth to the sustenaunce of his body. 1389 in *Eng. Gilds* (1870) 46 Ilke broþer and sistir shal ʒeuen..j.d to his sustenauns and releuynge. c 1400 *Brut* I. 11 Brut..done mow medes for sustinaunce of hym & of his peple. a 1513 FABYAN *Chron.* VI. (1533) 101/2 Other viii. houres he spent in his naturall reste, sustinaunce of his body, & the nedes of the realme. 1538 STARKEY *England* (1878) 74 When ther ys of vytayl ouerlytyl for the necessary sustenans and maynteynyng of the same. 1586 B. YOUNG *Guazzo's Civ. Conv.* IV. 224 They take but small refection, a thing most natural for sustainance of life. 1719 DE FOE *Crusoe* I. (Globe) 78 That it was so directed purely for my Sustenance on that wild miserable Place. 1842 COMBE *Digestion* 249 Only two-thirds of the quantity now ascertained to be requisite for human sustenance. 1870 YEATS *Nat. Hist. Comm.* 117 In Europe large spaces are covered with food-grasses and other plants, for the sustenance of the inhabitants. 1913 *Act* 3 & 4 *Geo. V*, c. 20 § 74 Payment ..to the bankrupt..of such sum out of the estate as they shall think proper for sustenance.

† 4. Endurance. *Obs.*

1390 GOWER *Conf.* II. 131 It is to kinde no plesance That man above his sustienance Unto the gold schal serve and bowe. 1393 LANGL. *P. Pl.* C. IV. 208 Vnsyttynge suffraunce [*v. r.* sustienance]. a 1677 BARROW *Serm.* Wks. 1716 I. 350 The willing susception and the cheerful sustenance of the cross.

† 5. The action of sustaining, supporting, or upholding. *Obs.*

c 1400 LOVE *Bonavent. Mirr.* xliii. (1908) 238 So hongeth oure lorde onely by thoo two nayles..with outen sustenaunce of the body. c 1460 FORTESCUE *Abs. & Lim. Mon.* xiv. (1885) 144 Savynge to hym selff sufficiant ffor the sustenance off his estate. 1836 J. GILBERT *Chr. Atonem.* iv. (1852) 99 Upheld not merely by unreasoning instinct, but by a sustenance of their understandings.

6. Something that sustains, supports, or upholds; a means or source of support.

c 1400 tr. *Secr. Secr., Gov. Lordsh.* 53 Þe maners and þe goodis sustinancez of vertues er to guerdon olde trauailles, to reles wrongys, [etc.]. 1526 *Pilgr. Perf.* (W. de W. 1531) 137 b, Whiche two that is grace & the Sacrament..be all our sustenaunce and supportacyon. 1571 GOLDING *Calvin on Ps.* I. 13 Meate and drinke, which are but sustenances of mans infirmitie. a 1613 OVERBURY *A Wife*, etc. (1638) 70 The sustenance of his discourse is Newes. 1871 SMILES *Charac.* i. (1876) 6 Simple honesty of purpose..gives him strength and sustenance.

b. Applied to a person.

c 1400 *Beryn* 1176 He toke hir in his armys..And seyd, 'myne ertly Ioy..my lyvis sustenaunce!' a 1450 *Knt. de la Tour* xcv, The childe that God gaue me..whiche was alle my ioye and sustenaunce.

7. *attrib.*: **sustenance diet** = *subsistence diet* (SUBSISTENCE 11); **sustenance money** = SUBSISTENCE MONEY 2. (*rare.*)

1886 C. SCOTT *Sheep-farming* 59 The system of carrying on animals to a certain age on merely sustenance diet, before commencing to fatten them. 1905 *Edin. Rev.* Oct. 468 The sustenance-money which was allowed to many *émigrés.*

Hence **Su·stenanceless** *a.*, devoid of sustenance or food.

1630 *R. Johnson's Kingd. & Commw.* 87 You have sauce and no sustenance; and so *mich God dich you* with your sustenancelesse sauce.

Sustenant (sʌ·stĭnănt), *pr. pple.* and *a. rare.* [In A., a. OF. *sustenant*, pr. pple. of *sustenir* to SUSTAIN; in B., f. SUSTENANCE: see -ANT.]

† A. *pr. pple.* Supporting, encouraging. *Obs.*

c 1386 CHAUCER *Pars. T.* ¶ 366 (MS. Egerton 2726) Sustenaunt [*Ellesm.* susteynynge] the theft of her Ostillers.

B. *adj.* Sustaining. Const. *to, of.*

1874 M. COLLINS *Transmigr.* II. vi. 106 The flowers are sustenant and medicinal. 1897 F. THOMPSON *Poems, Anthem of Earth* 147 Mother, I at last Shall sustenant be to thee. 1908 *Edin. Rev.* Oct. 486 So as to make them congruous with it and sustenant of it.

† **Sustenate,** *v. Obs. rare*[−1]. ? Error for SUSTENTATE; but cf. next.

1712 in G. Fox *Hist. Pontefract* (1827) 343 The said lands be granted..for the sustenating an afternoon lecturer.

† **Sustena·tion.** *Obs. rare.* [f. *sustene*, SUSTAIN *v.* + -ATION, after *sustenance.*] Sustentation; sustenance.

1606 in Davidson *Inverurie* v. (1878) 171 For the uphoildin and sustenation of the said scole. a 1635 NAUNTON *Fragm. Reg.* (Arb.) 58, 1000 Marks *per annum*, wherewith he lived plentifully in a fine way and garb, and without any great sustenation. 1675 BAXTER *Cath. Theol.* I. I. 25 As he was to dye by Gods withdrawing his Vital influx or sustenation.

Sustension, erron. spelling of SUSTENTION.

† **Sustent,** *sb. Obs. rare.* [? Shortening of SUSTENTACLE, after OF. *soustien.*] That which sustains or supports.

1664 EVELYN tr. *Freart's Archit.* 125 The Base..imports the sustent, prop or foot of a thing.

† **Sustent,** *v. Obs. rare.* [f. L. *sustent-* or ad. L. *sustentāre*: see SUSTENTATE.] *trans.* To sustain.

1512 *Helyas* in Thoms *Prose Rom.* (1858) III. 68 The which..myraclusly there had be nourisshed and sustented by the divine prouidence of God. 1591 SYLVESTER *Du Bartas* I. vii. 518 No firmer base her burthen to sustent Then slippery props of softest Element.

† **Sustentable,** *a. Obs. rare.* [f. L. *sustentāre* (see SUSTENTATE) + -ABLE.] Capable of being sustained or maintained; maintainable.

a 1623 SWINBURNE *Spousals* (1686) 81 Howsoever the singular Opinion doth seem more probable or more sustentable in the very point of Law.

Sustentacle (sŏste·ntăk'l). [ad. L. *sustentāculum* (whence OF. *su(b)stentacle*, It. *sostentacolo*, etc.): see SUSTENTACULUM.]

† 1. That which sustains or upholds; a support.

1432–50 tr. *Higden* (Rolls) II. 219 Bestes and other creatures, whiche were create to the solace of man, to the sustentacle of recreacion. c 1450 CAPGRAVE *Life St. Gilbert* vi, Whan he slept his hed hing down with-outen sustentacle and touchid sumtyme his brest. 1545 BALE *Image Both Ch.* I. x. (1550) K vij, Strong sustentackles and sure stayes hath God made the vpholders of his true churche. 1642 H. MORE *Song of Soul* II. i. III. xxv, That God's the sustentacle of all Natures. 1653 — *Conject. Cabbal.* (1713) 189 It will be ἕδρα and ὑποβάθρα,..and, being thus a Sustentacle or Foundation, be fitly represented by the term Earth.

2. = SUSTENTACULUM.

In recent Dicts.

Sustentacular (sʌstentæ·kiŭlăɹ), *a.* [f. next + -AR.] Pertaining to or of the nature of a sustentaculum; supporting.

1890 BILLINGS *Nat. Med. Dict.*, *Sustentacular fibres*, Müller's fibres. 1897 *Allbutt's Syst. Med.* III. 676 The sustentacular ligaments of the peritoneum.

‖ **Sustentaculum** (sʌstentæ·kiŭlŏm). Pl. **-a.** [L., f. *sustentāre*: see SUSTENTATE and -CULE.] **a.** *Anat.* A sustaining or supporting part or organ (only in L. phr., as *s. lienis, s. tali*). **b.** *Zool.*: see quot. 1838.

1838 BLACKWALL in *Trans. Linnean Soc.* (1841) XVIII. 224 *note*, A strong, moveable spine inserted near the termination of the tarsus of each posterior leg, on the under side, in spiders belonging to the genus *Epeira*, which I propose to denominate *sustentaculum.* 1882 *Cassell's Nat. Hist.* VI. 178 In this operation many species are aided by peculiar spines (called *sustentacula*) attached to the last joints of the posterior legs.

Su·stentate, *v. Obs.* or *arch. rare.* [f. L. *sustentāt-*, pa. ppl. stem of *sustentāre*, f. *sustent-*, pa. ppl. stem of *sustinēre* to SUSTAIN: see -ATE[3].] *trans.* To sustain.

a 1564 BECON *Policy War* Pref., Wks. I. 124 Our countrey doeth not onely receaue and ioyfullye sustentate it [*sc.* the body], but also opulently adourne..both that and the minde with most goodly..vertues. 1631 A. B. tr. *Lessius' De Prov. Num.* I. ix. 143 All things being first created by diuyne power, need to be sustentated by the said power. 1861 READE *Cloister & H.* ii, Who have by this divine restorative been sustentated, fortified,..and consoled.

Sustentation (sʌstentē^i^·ʃən). Also 4–5 **-acioun,** 5–6 **-acyon,** etc. [a. AF., OF. *sustentacion* = Pr. *sustentacio*, It. *sostentazione*, Sp. *sustentacion*, Pg. *sustentação*, ad. L. *sustentātio, -ōnem*, n. of action f. *sustentāre*: see prec.]

† 1. The action of bearing or enduring; endurance.

In first quot. transl. Vulg. *sustentatio* (= Gr. ἀνοχή).

1382 WYCLIF *Rom.* iii. 26 In the sustentacioun [*gloss* or beringe vp] of God. 1607 J. CARPENTER *Plaine Mans Plough* 131 Patience,..a voluntarie and daily sustentation and tolleration. 1653 BAXTER *Meth. Peace Consc.* 244 Their [*sc.* martyrs'] sufferings and strange sustentations.

† b. The bearing *of* a pecuniary charge. *Obs.*

1553 in Strype *Eccl. Mem.* (1721) III. App. ii. 4 For sustentation of your charges in this behalf.

2. The action of keeping up or maintaining an institution, establishment, building, or the like; upkeep, maintenance.

1389 in *Eng. Gilds* (1870) 67 He schal payen, to the sustentacion of this gylde v.s. c 1450 *Godstow Reg.* 190 Which rent he assigned vnto the sustentacion of the kechyn of the forsaid mynchons. 1486 *Rec. St. Mary at Hill* (1905) 7 The said xx s for the sustentacion of the said v tapers. *Ibid.* 16 Than I bequethe all..to the vse and sustentacion of london Brigge. 1557 in *10th Rep. Hist. MSS. Comm.* App. v. 385 The maynteyninge and sustentacion of the same housse and Colladge. 1667 SIR R. COTTON *Hen. III.* 46 Councellors..are but as accessaries, not principals, in sustentation of the State. 1635 SWAN *Spec. Mundi* (1670) 280 The Stars..stand in need of daily sustentation, like a lamp. 1837 J. D. LANG *New S. Wales* II. 165 The sustentation and maintenance of agriculture and commerce. 1860 HOOK *Lives Abps.* II. ii. 139 The Peter-pence had..been..a charge laid upon the private estates of the king..for the sustentation of the English College at Rome. 1869 RAWLINSON *Anc. Hist.* 49 The taxes, which he imposed on the provinces for the sustentation of his enormous court.

b. The keeping up or preservation *of* a condition or state, esp. human life; also, maintenance of something at a certain level.

1425 *Rolls of Parlt.* IV. 174/1 For ye better sustentation of ye said stile, title, name and worship. c 1460 FORTESCUE *Abs. & Lim. Mon.* xiv. (1885) 142 Howe the kyng mey best haue sufficient..livelod ffor the sustentacion off his estate. 1533 CROMWELL in Merriman *Life & Lett.* (1902) I. 356 A certeyn Annuytie of xxvi s. viii d. toward the Sustentacion of his lyvyng for terme of his Naturall life. 1538 STARKEY *England* (1878) 56 Al thyngys necessary and plesaunt for

the sustentatyon and quyetnes of mannys lyfe. 1607 J. CARPENTER *Plaine Mans Plough* 68 To till..their fieldes for the better sustentation of mans life. 1785 PALEY *Mor. Philos.* (1818) I. 99 Applied to the sustentation of human life. 1850 W. R. WILLIAMS *Relig. Progr.* iv. (1854) 89 A nation..eager..for the sustentation and diffusion of freedom. 1856 OLMSTED *Slave States* 279 The improvement, or even the sustentation of the value of his lands became a matter of minor importance. 1878 STUBBS *Const. Hist.* III. xviii. 244 Royal progresses for the sustentation of peace and justice.

3. The action of maintaining a person or concrete thing in being or activity, or of keeping it from failing or perishing; esp. in the 17th cent. of divine support. Now *rare.*

1477 EARL RIVERS (Caxton) *Dictes* 11 b, Slepe no more than shall suffyse onely for the Sustentacion of thy body. 1555 WATREMAN *Fardle Facions* App. 325 If menne shal not onely haue regard to their owne priuate profecte, but also to the sustentacion of other. a 1617 [see SUAVITY 2 b]. 1644 DARCIE *Birth of Heresies* xxii. 105 The Sunne..by his force and calidity giues sustentation to whatsoeuer liues vpon the earth. 1645 USSHER *Body Div.* (1647) 378 That he would not take his holy Spirit from us in our trialls, but give us sustentation in our temptations. 1675 BROOKS *Gold. Key* Wks. 1867 V. 164 'The preservation and sustentation of all things': Col. i. 17. 1847 GROTE *Greece* II. xxxi. IV. 235 The fruit of the fresh-planted democracy as well as the seed for its sustentation and aggrandisement.

† b. *fig.* A prop, stay, support. *Obs.*

1585 T. WASHINGTON tr. *Nicholay's Voy.* III. xiii. 95 b, They haue some small peeces of money giuen vnto them which is their onely aduantage and sustentation [orig. *soustien*] of their pouerty. 1642 H. MORE *Song of Soul* I. III. xlviii, God ..Who is our lifes strong sustentation. a 1734 NORTH *Lives* (1826) I. 18 His family was not in a posture to sustain any of the brothers, by estates to be carved out of the main sustentation of the honour.

4. The provision of a person with a livelihood or means of living; maintenance or support with the means of subsistence; livelihood.

Very common in the 16th century.

1428 *E. E. Wills* (1882) 79, I be-quethe to the sustentacion of that..preest..xx.li. 1530 *Proper Dyaloge* in Roy *Rede me*, etc. (Arb.) 138 Artificers and men of occupacion Quietly wanne their sustentacion. 1547 *Act 1 Edw. VI*, c. 14 § 7 Mooeye..payed..abowte the fyndyng, mayntenaunce, or sustentacion of any preistes. 1558 T. WATSON *Seven Sacr.* xxvi. 168 The payment of tythes..for so much as perteineth to..the sustentacion of Gods ministers. 1563 FOXE *A. & M.* 112 The patronages and almoise bestowed by them..for the sustentation of the poore of the realme. 1601 R. JOHNSON *Kingd. & Commw.* (1603) 35 So much [land] was allotted to euery man, as was thought sufficient for the sustentation of his familie. 1609 SKENE *Reg. Maj.* 2 They ordeined to the Justitiar for his sustentation, ilk day of his justice air, fiue pounds. 1677 SCOUGAL *Praise & Thanksgiving* (1770) 14 He that brought it into the World, hath already provided for its Sustentation in it. 1845 STEPHEN *Comm. Laws Eng.* (1874) II. 695 For the proper sustentation and payment of licensed curates, the law has made a variety of provisions. 1852 GLADSTONE *Glean.* (1879) IV. 176 As there is no poor-law under which nations can be rated in proportion to their means, for the sustentation of the impotent.

† b. With *a* and *pl.* A provision or allowance for maintenance; also, one who provides maintenance for others. *Obs.*

1461 *Rolls of Parlt.* V. 473/2 Eny Graunte of a Corrodye or Sustentacion made..by th'abbot and Convent. 1568 GRAFTON *Chron.* II. 174 The reuenues..shall be well kept by the handes of the treasurer of Scotlande..sauyng a reasonable sustentation of the lande, Castelles, and ministers of the kingdome. 1622 DONNE *Serm., John xi. 35* (1640) 156 Lazarus, the staffe and sustentation of that family was dead. 1671 J. WEBSTER *Metallogr.* i. 23 To seek for a sustentation by such slavish and drudgery Work.

5. The action of sustaining the life of an animate being; the provision of the means of sustenance; feeding, nourishment. Also applied to spiritual nourishment.

c 1440 *Gesta Rom.* xlviii. 218 The water shalle seye..I brynge forþe diuerse kynde of Fishis for thi sustentacioune. a 1483 EDW. IV. in Ellis *Orig. Lett.* Ser. II. I. 141 Yeving unto hir for the sustentacion of hir houshold half a beef and ii motons. 1543 *Necessary Doctr.* I iij b, A perpetual fode ..for our spiritual sustentation. 1549 LATIMER *Ploughers* (Arb.) 25 It is necessarie for to haue thys ploughinge for the sustentacion of the bodye. 1586 CAMDEN *Rem.* (1637) 190 All manner of prices of things in this Realme, necessary for sustentation of the people, grew daily excessive. 1658 ROWLAND tr. *Moufet's Theat. Ins.* 903 Unlesse you see that there is not so much Honey left as may serve for the sustentation of the Parents or elder Bees. 1741 WARBURTON *Div. Legat.* IV. v. II. 266 The Country..was rocky and mountainous: which, therefore,..was unfit for the Breed and Sustentation of Horse. 1825 COLERIDGE *Aids Refl.* (1848) I. 193 The part of the plant..suited..to the deposition of its eggs, and the sustentation of the future larva. 1861 HOLLAND *Less. Life* iv. 62 That peculiar element on which the germ must rely for quickening and sustentation.

b. *Phys.* The action of those vital functions or processes (as digestion, etc.) which sustain the life and normal activity of an organism.

1877 HUXLEY *Anat. Inv. Anim.* Introd. 24 The apparatuses by which certain operations, subsidiary to sustentation and generation, are carried on. 1881 MIVART *Cat* 10 The study of the actions of the system of organs which nourish and support the body: i. e., the study of the function of sustentation.

6. *concr.* That which sustains life; sustenance, food, nourishment. Also applied to spiritual food. (Cf. 5.) Now *rare.*

1537 *Inst. Chr. Man* I v, The sacrament of the Altare..is the very spirituall fode, and the very necessarye sustentation ..of all christen men. 1549 *Compl. Scot.* vi. 38 Beystis.. quhilk past besyde burnis & boggis on grene bankis to seik ther sustentatione. 1552 ABP. HAMILTON *Catech.* (1884) 21 We may lesumlie desyre of God our necessarie sustentatioun. 1630 LENNARD tr. *Charron's Wisd.* I. Pref. 2 To meditate.. therein..is the food, sustentation, life, of the spirit. 1646 SIR T. BROWNE *Pseud. Ep.* III. xxi. 163 It is..a very abstemious animall, and such as..will long subsist without a visible sustentation. 1668 WILKINS *Real Char.* II. x. § 3. 259 By Sustentation Ordinary..is intended such kind of Food as is usual for ordinary persons, and ordinary times. 1774 T. WEST *Antiq. Furness* (1805) 195 Sustentation and commodities for themselves and their children. 1866 *Reader* 26 May 513 The soil from which they derive their supplies and sustentation.

7. The action of holding up or keeping from falling; the condition of being so supported. † Also *concr.*, a support. Now *rare.*

c 1400 *Lanfranc's Cirurg.* 23 It is nessessarie summe lymes to han a sustentacioun. 1482 *Monk of Evesham* (Arb.) 27 And so [he] came to chirche..and without sustentacion or helpe of any thing entrid into the quire. 1555 EDEN *Decades* (Arb.) 349 The most notable pyllers or sustentacions that the earth hath in heauen. 1612 WOODALL *Surg. Mate* Wks. (1653) 93 A convenient Fascia..for the sustentation of the arm. 1650 BULWER *Anthropomet.* 189 Since the Tonique motion of the Muscules is not sufficient for sustentation of the Body. 1669 BOYLE *Contn. New Exper.* I. xxvi. 91 An ordinary School-philosopher would confidently have attributed this sustentation of so heavy a Body to Nature's fear of admitting a Vacuum. 1893 BENT in *Geogr. Jrnl.* II. 140 In difficult places the rocks have been cut [for the old roadways]; walls of sustentation are visible at many points.

8. *attrib.*: **sustentation fund**, a fund in the Free Church of Scotland and other bodies for providing adequate support for ministers.

1843 CHALMERS *Consid. Free Ch. Scot.* in Hanna *Mem.* (1852) IV. 564 That the General Fund shall be separated into two parts—a Building and a Sustentation Fund. 1869 *Daily News* 21 Oct., The Free Church of Scotland in 20 years had..raised a sustentation fund of 132,000*l.* per annum, so that every minister should have not less than 150*l.* a year.

Sustentative (sʌ·stentētiv, sŏste·ntătiv), *a.* [f. L. *sustentāt-*: see SUSTENTATE and -IVE.]

1. Having the quality of sustaining.

a 1640 JACKSON *Creed* XI. vi. § 4 Unless our Being be supported and strengthned by his power sustentative. 1652 URQUHART *Jewel* 278 Dialogismes, displaying their Interrogatory part with communicatively-Pysmatick and Sustentative flourishes.

2. *Phys.* Pertaining to sustentation.

1877 HUXLEY *Anat. Inv. Anim.* Introd. 24 Each cell.. must needs retain its sustentative functions so long as it grows. 1880 J. COOK *Boston Monday Lect.* 203 Sustentative, generative and correlative functions in the lower forms of life are exerted indifferently.

Sustentif, v.r. in some MSS. of Langl. *P. Pl.* C. IV. 338, 345, 355, for *su(b)stantif*, SUBSTANTIVE.

Sustention (sŏste·nʃən). Also *erron.* **-sion.** [A modern formation coined, after the analogy of *retain, retention, detain, detention*, to express senses derived immediately from certain spec. senses of SUSTAIN *v.*, and with the purpose of avoiding the general implications of *sustentation.*

Sustencyon in ed. 1542 of Boorde's *Dyetary* vi. (1870) 241 is app. a misprint; edd. 1557 (?) and 1562 read *sustentacion*, *-tion.*]

1. The action of sustaining or keeping up a condition, feeling, etc.; the holding-on of a musical note.

1868 *Pall Mall Budget* 20 Oct. 66 In the very highest orator, an unlaboured sustention of passion or emotion naturally expresses itself in long and sustained form. 1870 LOWELL *Study Wind.* 277 Pity, a feeling capable of prolonged sustention. 1883 *19th Cent.* May 863 The emission and sustension of sound are subjects of extreme difficulty to singers.

2. The quality of being sustained in argument or style.

1871 MORLEY *Condorcet* in *Crit. Misc.* Ser. I. 98 Condorcet becomes rapturous as he tells in a paragraph of fine sustention [etc.]. 1876 *Macm. Mag.* XXXIV. 94 'Sustained,' in this fashion, Macaulay certainly is not. But in another and a better form of sustension Macaulay is a master.

Sustentive (sŏste·ntiv), *a. rare.* [f. L. *sustent-*, pa. ppl. stem of *sustinēre* to SUSTAIN + -IVE.] Having the quality or property of sustaining.

1662 STANLEY *Hist. Chaldaick Philos.* (1701) 18/2 These Powers the Oracle calls ἀνοχῆας, Sustainers, as sustaining the whole World. The Oracle saith, they are immoveable, implying their setled Power; sustentive, denoting their Guardianship. 1863 DE MORGAN *Pref.* in *Fr. Matter to Spirit* p. xliv, Experiences..of a character not sustentive of the gravity and dignity of the spiritual world.

† **Suste·ntment.** *Obs. rare.* [a. OF. *sustentement*, ad. med.L. *sustentāmentum*, f. *sustentāre*; see SUSTENTATE.] Sustentation, support.

c 1400 tr. *Secr. Secr., Gov. Lordsh.* 50 Sustentement of kynges. It most nede be of force þat ilk a kyng haue two helpes to susteyn his kyngdome.

Suster, obs. form of SISTER.

Su·stinent, *a.* and *sb. rare.* [ad. L. *sustinent-, -ens*, pr. pple. of *sustinēre* to SUSTAIN.]

A. *adj.* Sustaining. † B. *sb.* Support.

1603 J. DAVIES *Microcosmos* (1878) 70/1 And our right Arme the Weedowe's Sustinent. 1876 DOWDEN *Poems* 13 Gather me close in tender, sustinent arms.

Sustren, -yn, Sustyr: see SISTER.

‖ **Susu** (sū·sū). Also **soosoo, sousou.** [Bengali.] The Gangetic dolphin, *Platanista gangetica.*

1801 ROXBURGH in *Asiatic Res.* VII. 171 Delphinus

Susurr, *v. rare.* [f. L. *susurrāre*, or its source *susurrus*, L. *susurrus* a whisper.] *intr.* to whisper.

1592 W. Knight *Let. to Wolsey* (MS. Cott. Vit. B. xiii. 13) The Cæsarians that susurred dayly in the popes ear. 1828 J. Lake *Contn. Spc't* f. x. 401 To susurre and murmure. 1808 *Busw. Theatr.* Sermon.

So **Susurrant** *a.*, whispering, softly murmuring; also *irreg.* **Susurrent** *a.* **Susurrose** = Susurrous; **Susurratio** *rare*[—0], whispering; **Susurringly** *adv.*

1792 E. Darwin *Bot. Card.* i. 160 With soft 'susurrant voice. 1822 Montgomery *Pelican Isl.* i. 99 Sweet accord of natural sounds. 1725 *Temple Stoic Mag.* July 303 A soft susurrant echo. 1903 *Academy* 24 Apr. 407/3 The clm "susurrence of cicalas in the trees.

Susurration (*siusurā'fṇ*). Also 5–6 -acy-, o(*c*)i-, 6 *erron. suserus-*. [ad. L. *susurrātiōn-, -ōnem, susurrātiō*, *-ōne*, whispering; *occas.* a whisper, in early use, malicious whispering, tattle.

c 1400 *Paulina Epistles* 3 co Disconnyuous, bacbytyngis, susurryouns. 1529 *Cromwell in State Papers* 3 co Disconious murmuracons and susurracions. 1598 *Pilgr. Perf.* (W. de W. 1531) 50 b Susurracons or privy whisperes.

Susurrous, *a. rare.* [f. L. *susurrus* (see next) + -ous.] Full of whispers. 1850 W. H. Russell *Diary in India* (1860) II. xiii. 247 There were eyes peering around, and a gentle susurrous whispering.

Susurrus (*siusurā'tis*). [L., – humming, muttering, whispering.] A low soft sound as of whispering or muttering; a whisper; a rustling. 1832 Scott *Ct. Rob.* Introd. Adde. § 13 The first thing which alarmed me was a rumour in the village. 1844 whatever alarmed in this susurrus. 1895 C.

So **Sutile**, *a. Obs.* Forms: 1 *sutol*, *-el*, *sutol*, 2 *sutel*, 3–4 *sotel*. [OE. (late WS.) *sūtol* Anglian *sūtol*, f. *sēoðan* to seethe.] Clear, manifest, evident.

Sutile, *a. Obs.* [L. *sūtilis*, f. *suĕre* to sew.] Made or done by stitching or sewing.

1688 Sir T. Browne *Tracts* ii. (1683) 59 These (crowns and garlands) were made up after all ways of Art, Contexile, Pactile. 1708 *Dawson Idler* No. 13 § 8 Half the crowns are adorned with a kind of sutile pictures, which imitate tapistry.

Sutler (*sutlēr*). Also 7 *suttler*, *suckler*, *shuttler*, *suttler*; 7–9 *sutter*, *drudge*, *sutler* in an army (*mil.L. sut'lár*, *sudler*), *sootelen* to befoul, to perform mean duties, follow a mean or low occupation or trade (cf.LG. *suddeln*, early mod.G. *sudeln* to sully: see Suddle).

1590 (Dec. 30) *Ordinances 9 Jas. Masters*. The Provost Marschal and Serjeant Major of every garrison shall keepe a perfect rolle of all such English victuallers called in church Sutlerell paymar chants, and other loose persons of the English nation. 1599 Nashe *Lenten Stuffe* (1871 E. D. S.) 57 Sutlers, botches and taberdces. 1599 Nashe *Hen. V*. ii. i. 116, I shut Sutler be vnto the Campe.

One who follows an army or lives in a garrison town and sells provisions to the soldiers.

1590 (Dec. 30) *Ordinances 9 Jas. Masters.* The Provost Marschal and Serjeant Major of every garrison.

†o. *slang.* (See quot.) *Obs.*

1790 B. E. *Dict. Cant. Crew. Suttler*, one that Pockets up Gloves, Knives, Handkerchiefs, Snuff and Tobacco-boxes, and all the lesser Moveables.

Hence (all *rare*) **Su'tlerage** = Sutlery; **Sut'leress**, a female sutler; **Su'tlership**, the office or occupation of a sutler.

Sutlery (*su'tlēri*). Also 7 *suttlery*, *suttlory*. [f. Sutler + -y. Cf. early mod. Du. *soeteterije* 'vile opus, sordidum artificium', etc. (Kilian).]

1. The occupation of a sutler; victualling.

2. A sutler's establishment; a victualling establishment or department, for the supplying of soldiers with food and drink.

1826 Davenant *Wits* vi. I. A new Plantation. Is made in

Suttee, *sb.* Also 7–9 *suttu*, 9 *satti, suttu, satti, abusive*. [a. Skr. (Hindi, Urdu) *satī* faithful or virtuous wife, in *sat* good, wise, honest, lit. being, pr. pple. of *as* to be (see as q.).]

1. A Hindu widow who immolates herself on the funeral pile with her husband's body.

1786 in *Parl. Papers E. India 1821, Hindu Widows* (1821) 3 We were informed the suttee (for that is the name given to the person who so devotes herself) had just been told she was married by the godde and that beel she saw scattered as she went along. *Ibid.* a 1 the suttee ascends the pile, she is furnished with a lighted taper. 1787 Sir W. Jones in *Parl. Papers E. India* (1821) 265 the suttee, or widow who burns herself to expiate sins.

Suttee, *a.* (Hindi, Urdu). Of, pertaining to, or connected with, the suttee or rite of suttee.

an account of the proceedings of these European suttees. 1829 Merideth R. *Fouverel* xxxix. He had become resigned to her perpetual lamentation and living Suttee for his defunct rival. 1880 Mrs. Beaconsf. IV. 74 Suttee-dom.

Hence **Suttee'ism**, the practice of suttee.

1846 in Worcester. 1869 *Eclectic Rev.* (N.S.) XIII. 94 The Suttee ism of Christian. 1880 Webster, *Suppl.* 6 Oct., The mistaken condition of Hindoo widows after the custom of sutteeism was done away with.

Suttle (sut'l), *a. Comm. Obs.* [Old variant spelling of Subtle *a*. retained in a technical use. Cf. AF. *sotil*, *sutil*.]

Suttle, *sb.* Also 9 *suttling*. [f. Suttle *v.*] 1. Sewing, stitching; also, a stitch or seam; of clownish life; a common term of abuse. 1541 Copland *Galyen's Terap.* s (K) We suture. 1596 Shakes.

Suture (*siū'tiūr, -tjur*). Also 7 *erron. sutor*. [ad. F. *suture* or L. *sūtūra*, f. action of *sū-*, pa. ppl. stem of *suĕre* SEW *v.*: see -URE.]

1. *Surg.* The joining of the lips of a wound, or the ends of a severed nerve or tendon, by stitches; also, an instance of this; a stitch used for this purpose.

skif of sutured skins or bark To the three-decker with its thundering guns, The floating castle of the world of war.

Suture, *v. rare.* [f. prec.]

1. *trans.* To join together by, or as by, a suture; to close up, draw together the edges of; to unite by suture.

Suty, *v. Obs.* [f. Suti *sb.*] *Obs.*

Suwar, Suwarree, variant of Sowar, Sowarry.

Suwe, obs. pa. t. of Saw *v.*; obs. f. Sow *sb.*

Suy, obs. form of Sew *v.*

Suz-, obs. form of Suss-.

Suzerain (*siū'zerein*, older *s(e)useran*, *sqp*. f. *suserein*, older *s(e)useran*, *spp*. f. [ad. F. *suzerain*, older *s(o)userain*, spp. f.: from *sus* above, up (L. *sūsum*, *sursum*, f. *sub* from below, up + *vorsum*, *versum*, pa. pple. of *vertĕre* to turn), after *sovereign* SOVEREIGN.] A feudal overlord.

Suzeraine (*siū'zereɪn*), *sb. U.S.* – Sirs i: see Sir § 7 b. Also *suz-*. The wife of the minister was careful always to acknowledge the Queen of Fashion as her suzeraine. 1829 Kay in *Lond.* *a* 1847 Thackeray *Van. Fair* xxiii. The power of a vassalage which really existed in the social system of his time.

Suzeraine (*siū'zerein*), *a. U.S.* Also *suz-*. 1828 Disraeli *Eng. Lit.* i. 61 To acknowledge the queen suzerain. a 1890 *Cassell's Encycl. Dict.* s.v., female head of a state.

Suzerainty (*siū'zerēnti*). Also 5 suserenite. [In sense 1, a. OF. *suzerainete, souverainete*, *-te*, after mod. F. *suzeraineté*.]

†1. ? Supremacy. *Obs.*

2. The position, rank, or power of a suzerain.

†Svelte (svelt). Also *svelt*. [F. (– I. *svelto*), = Pg. *esvelte*, Sp. *esvelto*, Pr. (= *s*vel-tire, t. *ex* out + *vellĕre* to pluck.] Slim, slender, willowy.

Swa, obs. form of So.

Swab (swob), *sb.* Also 6 *swobbe*, 7 *swab*. With sense c, *swab*, *swobb* mop. With sense 4, *swab*, *swobb* dirty person.

1. A mop made of rope-yarn, etc. used for cleaning and drying the deck, etc. on board ship.

Swab (swob), *v.* Also 8 Swab *v.* With sense 1, *swab*, *swabb* to swab; also 6–7 mop; also 7 to splash, to water with sense, as dirt.

1. To clean or dry (a deck, etc.) with a swab or mop.

1855 Marryat *Jacob Faithful* xx. He said 'other day I was a drunken old swab. 1890 *All Year Round* No. 66. 384 Look there, you swab! 1899 Besant *The World Wont* xxii. Luke was a grass comber and a nasal swab.

Swabber (swo'bar). Also 6 *swabber*, 7–8 *swobber*, [a. early mod.Du. *swabber*, f. *swabben*: see Swab *sb.* and v.] Cl. LG. *swabber* (G. *schwabber*) mop, f.Wris. *swabber* mop, also roving fellow, vagabond, beggar.]

Swa-bie, *sb.* [Shortening of Swartback.] The greater black-backed gull.

Swabble, *v.* (and *sb.*). *dial.* Also *swobble*. [f. Swab *v.* + freq. suffix *-le*.]

vibrate with a noise, like liquids in a bottle: 'I heard the water swabble in her throat.' 1876 *Whitby Gloss.*, *Swabble*, to be moved about to the required portion.

Swa'bby, *a.* [f. Swab *sb.* + -Y. Cf. Swaddy.] Having pods or husks.

Swabian (*swē'biɑn*), *a.* and *sb.* [f. *Suabia*, latinized f. G. *Schwaben* + -AN.]

1. *a. adj.* Belonging or pertaining to, or native of Swabia (Schwaben), a former German duchy, now a province including Württemberg and part of Bavaria. *b. sb.* A native of Swabia.

Swabyn, *sb.* – Swawsin.

Swab, *v.³ dial.* (*eastern*). Also *swawb*. [Local variant of Swarp *a.* Cf. Swathe.] = Swarp *v.*

Swack, *a.* and *adv. Sc.* and *dial.* Also 6 *swawk*, *-ck*. [App. related to SWAK *a.*]

Swack, *sb. Sc. and north. dial.* Also 4–6, 9 *swak*, 9 *swawk*. [Echoic; cf. Swack *sb.*]

Swad (swod), *sb.¹ dial. (eastern)*. Also *swawd*. [Local variant of Swarp *a.* Cf. Swathe(R.².] = Swarp *v.*

Swad, *sb.² dial.* Also 5–6, 9 *swadd*. [Origin obscure; perhaps related to SWARP *sb.¹* or SWATH.]

†Swad, *sb.³ Obs.* [Perhaps the same word as Swad *sb.²*] Also **Swad-gill**. A clownish fellow, a country bumpkin, a lout.

Swaddle (*swo'd'l*), *sb.* Forms: a. 5 *swabele*, *swathele*, *swadel*, 7 *swadle*. [f. next. Cf. MDu. *swadel* and Swaddle *v.*]

1. Swaddling-clothes. *rare.*

Swaddle (*swo'd'l*), *v.* Forms: a. 1 *swaðelian*, 4–5 *swathelen*, *swadil*, *swadelen*. [OE. *swaðelian*, f. *swaðel*, Swaddle *sb.*]

1. *trans.* To bind (an infant) in swaddling-clothes.

Swaddleband. Forms: *a.* 2 swabel-, 6 swathel-, swathie-, 6–7 swaddel-, 7–8 swaddel-, 6–7 swaddil-, swaddle-, 7 swaddle-.

Swaddler (swŏ'dlər). *sb.*

Swaddling (swŏ'dlɪŋ), *vbl. sb.*

Swaddling-band.

Swaddling-clothes, *sb. pl.*

Swaddling-clouts, *sb. pl.*

Swaddy (swŏ'di), *sb. slang.*

Swadeshi (swədē'ʃi). *Indian.*

Swag, *sb.*

Swage, *sb.*

Swagement. *Obs. rare.*

Swa'ger. *Obs. rare.*

Swagged (swægd), *ppl. a.* 2

Swagger (swæ'gər), *v.*

Swagger, *sb.*

Swagger-cane

Swaggerer (swæ'gərər).

Swaggering, *vbl. sb.*

Swaggering, *ppl. a.*

Swaggeringly, *adv.*

Swaggie (swæ'gi). *Also -y. Austral. colloq.*

Swagging (swæ'gɪŋ), *vbl. sb.*

Swagging, *ppl. a.*

Swaggy (swæ'gi), *a. rare.*

Swahili (swəhī'li). *Also Souahili, Suaheli, -ahe, Swaheli.*

Swaible, *var. of* SWIVEL.

Swaile, *obs. form of* SWALE.

Swaily, *obs. f. of* SQUEAMISH.

Swain (swein), *sb.*

Swainish (swei'niʃ), *a.*

Swainling. *Obs. Also -lin.*

Swaip, -e. *Obs.*

Swaird, *obs. form of* SWARD, SWORD.

Swale (sweil), *sb.*

Swale, sb.[1] ... *Also Northern.*

Swall, var. SWALE sb.[1]; obs. or dial. f. SWELL.

Swall, var. SWALE sb.[1]; obs. or dial. f. SWELL.

Swale (swēl), sb.[3] *local.* Also 6 Sc. swaill, swayll, 9 swall, Sc. swyle. (Origin unknown. Prob. conveyed to America from the eastern counties, where it is still in use.) A hollow, low place; esp. U.S., a moist or marshy depression in a tract of land, esp. in the midst of rolling prairie.

Swale (swēl), v.[1] [app. of dial. origin (see swail in Eng. Dial. Dict.); prob. frequent. f. SWAL v. +-L, but parallels are wanting. Cf. Shropsh. dial. swayl-bole = swoy-pole.] intr. To move or sway up and down or from side to side. Hence **Swa'ling** vbl. sb. and ppl. a.; also **Swa'lingly** adv., with a swaying motion.

Swale, sb.[2] north. dial. [a. ON. svalr (MSw., Sw., Norw.) = cool.] Shade; a shady place.

Swale, sb.[3] the cool, the cold.

Swale, sb.[5] north. dial. [a. ON. svalr (MSw., Sw., Norw.) = cool.] Shade; a shady place.

Swaler (swē'lər), north-midl. dial. Also 6 swaller, 8–9 swealer, 9 sweeler. [f. SWALE v.[1]+-ER[1].] One who swales.

SWALLOW

Swallow (swo'lōu), sb.[1] Forms: 1 sƿalwe, swealwe, swealuwe, -uwe, -uwe, 1, 4 swalewe, swalwe, swelewe, 4 swalouȝe, swalwe, 5–7 swallowe, -e, swalou, swalowe, swalo, 5–7 swal-lowe, 6– swallow. [Com. Teut. (not recorded for Gothic): OE. sƿealwe wk. fem. = OS. swala (Du. zwaluw), OHG. swalawa, swalwa (MHG. swalwe, G. schwalbe), ON. svala (or *svalwa = *sƿalwa) (Da. svale, Sw. svala):—OTeut. *swalwōn-.]

1. A bird of the genus *Hirundo*, esp. H. rustica, a well-known migratory bird with long pointed wings and forked tail, having a swift curving flight and a twittering cry, building mud-nests on buildings, etc., and popularly regarded as a harbinger of summer (*cf.*)

c. Prov. *One swallow does not make a summer* (and allusions to it.)

2. In extended sense, any bird of the swallow kind, or the family *Hirundinidæ*, e.g. a martin; often misapplied to (and in earlier scientific use including) the swifts, now reckoned as a distinct and unrelated family (*Cypselidæ*).

Swallow (swo'lōu), sb.[2] Also swalla, swalloe, -ow. [a. Malay *swallo* ...] = SEA-SLUG ...

3. + a. = SEA-SWALLOW 1. b. Collector's name for a species of moth: see quot. 1832. d. A variety of domestic pigeon: see quot. 1867.

Swallow (swo'lōu), v. Forms: 1 swelgan, swelȝan, 3 swolwen, swolȝen, 3–4 swolewen, swolwe, swolȝe, swoluȝe, 4 swolwe, swolȝe, swelȝe, swolewen, 4–5 swelwen, swelowe, swolowe, swallow, 6– swallow.

I. 1. trans. To take into the stomach through the throat and gullet, as food or drink. In early use and still *fig.*

Swallower (swo'lōuər). Also 1 swelgere, 6 Sc. sweillar. [f. as prec.+-ER[1].] One who or that which swallows.

Swallow-hole. [f. SWALLOW v. or sb.[2]+HOLE sb.] ... = SWALLET 1.

Swallowing (swo'lōuiŋ), vbl. sb. Also 4 swelȝing, swolȝing, swolowing, swelwyng[?], swoluȝing, etc. [f. SWALLOW v.+-ING[1].] The action of the verb SWALLOW ...

Swallowable (swo'lōuəb'l), a. [f. SWALLOW v.+-ABLE.] Capable of being or fit to be swallowed (*lit.* and *fig.*).

Swallow-tail, swallowtail (swo'lōutēl). Also in some senses swallow's tail. [f. SWALLOW sb.[1]+TAIL sb.]

1. The tail of a swallow ...

Swallow-pipe. rare[-1] [f. SWALLOW v.+ PIPE sb.[1]] The gullet.

Swallow-tailed.

Swallow-tailed *a.*

Swallow-tailed *a.*

Swallow-wort (swo'lowwort). [f. prec. + -ed².]

Swamp (swomp), *sb.* Also 8 *swomp*. [First recorded as a term peculiar to the N. American colony of Virginia, from pop. in local use before it in England]

Swamp (swomp), *v.* [f. SWAMP *sb.*]

Swamper (swo'mpər). [f. SWAMP *sb.* or *v.*]

Swampine (swo'mpain). *U.S.* [ad. mod.L. *Swampina*]

Swampish (swo'mpiʃ), *a.* [f. SWAMP *sb.* + -ISH¹.]

Swamp-oak.

Swampy (swo'mpi), *a.* [f. SWAMP *sb.* + -Y.]

Swan (swon), *sb.*

Swanherd (swo'nhərd). [f. SWAN *sb.* + HERD.]

Swanimote.

Swank (swæŋk), *sb.* dial.

Swank, *v.*

Swank, *a.*

Column 1 (headwords):
Swank, *a.* Sc.
Swank, *v.*
Swanker, *dial.*
Swanking.
Swan-like, *a.* (*adv.*)
Swank, *v.*, *slang*.

Column 2 (headwords):
Swan-like, *a.* (*adv.*)
Swan-mark. [MARK *sb.*]
So Swan-marker, *sb.*
†Swannage. *Obs.* Also 4 wanadge.
Swan-neck. Also swan's neck.
Swan-pan.
Swan-necked.
Swanner.

Column 3 (headwords):
Swannery. Also 8 swanery.
Swan's feather.
Swan's-down, swansdown.
Swanish, *a.*
Swan-upping.
Swan-pan.
Swannish, *a.*
Swanskin.
Swan-white, *a.*
Swanwort.
Swanyeard, *obs.* form of SWANHERD.
Swap, swop (swop).

Column 4 (headwords):
Swap, swop, *sb.*
Swap, swop, *v.*

Column 1 (headwords):
Swap, swop, *sb.*
Swap, swop, *v.*
Swapper, swopper.
Swapping, swopping, *ppl. a.*
Swaping, swoping, *ppl. a.*
Swap, swop, *adv.* (*int.*)

Column 2 (headwords):
Swapper, swopper (swop-pa).
Swapping, swopping, *ppl. a.*
Swapping, swoping, *vbl. sb.*
Swap-ple, swopple.
Swappit, *a.* *dial.*
Swap that.
Swar, *var.* SWARE *sb.*, *Obs.*
Swarbout *v.* *var.* SWORBOTE *Obs.*

Column 3 (headwords):
Sward (swǝd), *sb.*
Swarded (swǝ·ded), *ppl. a.*
Swarding (swǝ·diŋ), *vbl. sb.*
Swardy (swǝ·di), *a.*
†Sware.
Swards, *v.*
Swarf.

Column 4 (headwords):
Swarl, *v.* *rare*.
Swarm (swǝm), *sb.*[1]
Swarf, *v.*[2]
Swarl, *v.*
Swarm (swǝm), *sb.*[2]
Swarm, *v.*[1]
Swarmish, *a.*

which are very hurtfull both to man and beast. *Ibid.* 51 Swarmes of a kinde of fowles of the bignes of duckes. 1684 *Contempl. St. Man* I. x. (1699) 116 Locusts..in great swarms shall disperse themselves over the Face of the whole Earth. 1780 COWPER *Progr. Err.* 481 The wriggling fry soon fill the creeks around, Pois'ning the waters where their swarms abound. 1842 TENNYSON *Locksley Hall* 10 Many a night I saw the Pleiads..Glitter like a swarm of fire-flies tangled in a silver braid. 1914 *Brit. Mus. Return* 197 A swarm of cockroaches..in a house at Chislehurst.

(*c*) of inanimate objects or abstract things.

1582 BENTLEY *Mon. Matrones* I. 1 My sinnes..are so manie, that the infinit swarme of them [etc.]. 1596 SHAKS. *1 Hen. IV*, v. i. 55 This swarme of faire aduantages. 1684 BUNYAN *Pilgr.* II. 6 Upon this, came into her mind by swarms, all her unkind, unnatural, and ungodly Carriages to her dear Friend. 1698 FRYER *Acc. E. India & P.* 2 Such a swarm of Vessels of greater bulk. 1785 BURKE *Sp. Nabob of Arcot's Debts* Wks. 1842 I. 340 He is overpowered with a swarm of their demands. 1866 WHITTIER *Snow-bound* 33 A night made hoary with the swarm And whirl-dance of the blinding storm. 1890 *Nature* 20 Mar. 473/2 There are swarms of dust travelling thro' space.

(*d*) *Biol.* A cluster of free-swimming cells or unicellular organisms moving in company.

1900 B. D. JACKSON *Gloss. Bot. Terms.*

3. *attrib.* and *Comb.*: **swarm-cell** *Biol.* = *swarm-spore* (*a*); **swarm-movement** *Biol.*, the movement of swarm-spores in 'swarming' (SWARM *v.*[1] 1 c); **swarm-spore** *Biol.* (cf. SWARM *v.*[1] 1 c), (*a*) a motile spore in certain Algæ, Fungi, and Protozoa, a zoospore; (*b*) the free-swimming embryo or gemmule of freshwater sponges.

1882 VINES tr. *Sachs's Bot.* 38 Much quicker movements ..occur in cells either before their growth, as in 'swarm-cells, or when it is nearly completed. 1898 PORTER tr. *Strasburger's Bot.* I. i. 50 The swarm-spores of the Myxomycetes soon lose this characteristic 'swarm-movement. 1859 J. R. GREENE *Man. Anim. Kingd., Protozoa* 41 Ciliated 'swarm spores, similar to those which are found in Spongilla. 1874 A. W. BENNETT in *Pop. Sci. Rev.* XIII. 29 The production of spontaneously motile zoospores, or 'swarm-spores'. 1880 BESSEY *Botany* 36 The swarm-spores ..are naked masses of freely moving protoplasm.

Swarm (swǭɹm), *v.*[1] Also 4-7 **swarme**, (5 **swermo**), 6 *Sc.* **suarm**, 7 *Sc.* **swairme**. [f. SWARM *sb.*: cf. MLG., MHG. *swarmen*; also, with mutation, OE. **swierman*, *swirman*, MLG., MDu. *swermen* (Du. *zwermen*), MHG. *swärmen* (G. *schwärmen*), Sw. *svärma*, Da. *sværme*.]

1. *intr.* Of bees: To gather in a compact cluster and leave the hive in a body to found a new colony: see SWARM *sb.* 1. Also with *off*.

c 1386 CHAUCER *Sompn. Prol.* 29 Right so as bees out swarmen [*Corpus & Camb. MSS.* swermen] from an hyue. 1573 TUSSER *Husb.* (1878) 114 Take heede to thy bees, that are readie to swarme. 1609 C. BUTLER *Fem. Mon.* v. (1623) I 3. Those that swarme before the blowing of knap weed come in very good time. 1697 DRYDEN *Virg. Georg.* IV. 28 The youthful Prince, with loud allarm, Calls out the vent'rous Colony to swarm. 1818 SCOTT *Rob Roy* xvii, Ye see this is the second swarm, and whiles they will swarm off in the afternoon. The first swarm set off sune in the morning. 1875 *Encycl. Brit.* III. 502/1 It often happens that bees give every indication of an intention to swarm, and cluster idly outside the hive..for..weeks before they really emigrate.

b. *allusively*: cf. SWARM *sb.* 1 b.

1609 *Bible* (Douay) 2 Macc. i. 12 He made them swarme out of Persis. 1745 *Season. Adv. Protest.* 17 Protestants, who from a common Ancestor..have swarmed into many Stocks. 1821-30 LD. COCKBURN *Mem.* vii. (1874) 401 Jealousies and dissensions..induced the artists to swarm off, and begin the Academy. 1909 J. T. FOWLER in *Yorks. Archæol. Jrnl.* XX. 1 The number of monks increased so rapidly that they were soon obliged to swarm off, like bees, into new monasteries of the same Order.

c. *Biol.* Of certain spores or reproductive bodies: To escape from the parent organism in a swarm, with characteristic movement; to move or swim about in a swarm, as zoospores ('swarm-spores') do in the cell just before escaping, and in the water after escaping.

1864, 1867, 1875, 1882 [see SWARMING *ppl. a.* 4, *vbl. sb.* 2]. 1875 BENNETT & DYER tr. *Sachs's Bot.* 674 In Algæ of simple structure..the swarmspores are also formed in the night, but swarm only with access of daylight.

d. *trans.* in causative sense.

1827 J. F. COOPER *Prairie* iv, 'Swarm your own hive', returned the discontented bee-hunter.

2. *intr.* To come together in a swarm or dense crowd; to collect, assemble, or congregate thickly and confusedly; to crowd, throng; also, to go or move along in a crowd.

c 1386 CHAUCER *Sqr.'s T.* 181 Greet was the prees þat swarmeth to and fro To gauren on this hors that stondeth so. 1513 DOUGLAS *Æneis* VI. v. 23 Thiddir to the bray swarmit all the rout Of deid gaistis. 1515 BARCLAY *Egloges* II. (1570) B iv/2 If the dishe be pleasaunt,..Ten handes at once swarme in the dishe. 1526 TINDALE *Acts* xxi. 30 All the cite was moved, and all the people swarmed togedder. 1551 ROBINSON tr. *More's Utopia* II. (1895) 179 All the people were swarmed furth into the stretes. 1604 DEKKER *Honest Wh.* Wks. 1873 II. 96 They swarme like Crickets to the creuice of a Brew-house. 1764 BURN *Poor Laws* 205 The religious houses sent abroad their friers mendicant, who swarmed about the kingdom. 1847 TENNYSON *Princess* Concl. 37 The crowd were swarming now, To take their leave, about the garden rails. 1867 LADY HERBERT *Cradle L.* iv. 126 The English were swarming out of this inn. 1875 JOWETT *Plato* IV. 233 The ideas swarming in men's minds.

3. To occur or exist in swarms or multitudes; to be densely crowded or congregated; to be very numerous, abound excessively. (Often in reproach or contempt, esp. when said of persons.)

1399 LANGL. *Rich. Redeles* II. 21 Signes þat swarmed so thikke þoru-oute his lond..þat [etc.]. a 1548 HALL *Chron., Hen. V*, 54 Their bodies whiche swarmed euery day about thenglishe shippes. 1570 GOOGE *Pop. Kingd.* IV. (1880) 47 b, Puddings every wheare Do swarme. 1594 GREENE & LODGE *Looking Gl.* III. ii, When falshood swarmeth both in old and youth. 1634 BRERETON *Trav.* (Chetham Soc.) 13 Arminians, Brownists, and Anabaptists, and Manists, do lurk here and also swarm. a 1700 EVELYN *Diary* 19 Aug. 1641, The Sectaries that swarm'd in this Citty. 1721 BAILEY, To *Swarm* ..to abound, spoken of Vermin. 1742 YOUNG *Nt. Th.* IX. 765 Bright legions swarm unseen, and sing..the glorious Architect. 1849 MACAULAY *Hist. Eng.* vii. II. 239 Roman Catholics already swarmed in every department of the public service. 1883 GILMOUR *Mongols* xv. 167 Native doctors swarm in Mongolia.

4. *To swarm with*: to be crowded or thronged with; to contain swarms or great numbers of; to abound greatly in. Now only in material sense.

a 1548 HALL *Chron., Hen. V*, 46 The countree swarmed with men of warre. 1548 UDALL, etc. *Erasm. Par. Matt.* vii. 49 They that swarme with much greater vices. a 1592 GREENE *Jas. IV*, v. ii, Oh, what are subtile meanes to clime on high, When euery fall swarmes with exceeding shame? 1593 SHAKS. *Rich. II*, III. iv. 47 Her wholesome Herbes, Swarming with Caterpillers. 1667 MILTON *P. L.* VII. 400 Each Creek & Bay With Frie innumerable swarme. 1732 BERKELEY *Alciphr.* II. § 13 All kinds of animals, with which the creation swarms. 1849 MACAULAY *Hist. Eng.* ix. II. 484 A market-place swarming with buyers and sellers. 1893 FORBES-MITCHELL *Remin. Gt. Mutiny* 269 The river swarmed with alligators.

† **b.** Similarly, *to swarm full of*, *to swarm in*.

1482 *Monk of Evesham* (Arb.) 40 The lenthe of that valey ..was so full of fowyls, as hyues swarmyn ful of bees. 1560 DAUS tr. *Sleidane's Comm.* 35 They shall not onely not take awaye theyr sectes, but increase and swarme in the same. 1561 T. NORTON *Calvin's Inst.* II. iii. (1634) 127 The soule..while it swarmeth full of such diseases of vices. 1694 ATTERBURY *Serm., Prov.* xiv. 6 (1726) I. 198 The Great Lords of the Earth, who swarm in all the Delights of Sense.

5. *trans.* To fill or beset as, or with, a swarm; to crowd densely, throng. Chiefly *pass.*

1555 EDEN *Decades* III. (Arb.) 188 The barbarians..came swarmyng the bankes on bothe sydes the ryuer, to the number of syxe thousande men. 1559 *Mirr. Mag., Induct.* lxxv, The rout Gan all in heapes to swarme vs round about. a 1586 SIDNEY *Ps.* XXXII. vii, Who on God his trust invokes With mercies shall be swarmed. 1647 FANSHAWE *Æneid* IV. Poems 287 How did thy sences quayle Seeing the shoares so swarm'd. 1810 *Sporting Mag.* XXXV. 8 Your house is so swarmed with rats. 1823 MOORE *Mem.* (1853) IV. 121 Poor wretches, who marry upon the strength of this pied-à-terre, and swarm the little spot they occupy with children. 1847 *Zoologist* V. 1399 Brighton was swarmed with ladybirds on Saturday and Sunday. 1886 R. L. DE BEAUFORT *Lett. Geo. Sand* I. 130 You will also see the towers of Notre Dame; they are swarmed with swallows.

6. To breed or produce a swarm of. *rare*[—1].

1842 TENNYSON *Will Waterproof* xxv, Ere days, that deal in ana, swarm'd His [*sc.* the Poet's] literary leeches.

Swarm (swǭɹm), *v.*[2] [Of unascertained origin. Perh. orig. a sailor's word borrowed from the Continent, but no trace of the meaning has been discovered for phonetically corresponding words. Cf. the synonymous SWARVE *v.*[1] and etymol. remarks s. v. SWARM *sb.*

Connexion with *squirm* is out of the question, on historical and phonological grounds.]

1. *intr.* To climb *up* († *upon*) a pole, tree, or the like, by clasping it with the arms and legs alternately.

15.. *Sir A. Barton* in *Surtees Misc.* (1890) 72 Then he swarmd up the maine mast tree [cf. SWARVE *v.*[2], quot. a 1650]. c 1550 [see SWARVE *v.*[1]]. 1607 DEKKER *Knt.'s Conjur.* B j b, The waues..boylde vp to such heigth, as if they meant that all men should swarm in heauen, and shippes to sayle in the Skie. 1653 H. MORE *Antid. Ath.* III. iv. § 3 Swarming upon Trees as nimbly as Cats. 1701 C. WOLLEY *Jrnl. New York* (1860) 41 We follow'd a Bear from Tree to Tree, upon which he could swarm like a Cat. 1804 *Naval Chron.* XI. 103 He swarms up to his seat. 1872 CALVERLEY *Fly Leaves, Changed* v, They fright me, when the beech is green, By swarming up its stem for eggs. 1893 SELOUS *Trav. S. E. Africa* 433. I..could have swarmed up the branchless stem of the sapling.

b. *transf.* To climb a steep ascent or the like by clinging with the hands and knees, or in some way compared to this.

1681 COTTON *Wond. Peak* (ed. 4) 17 Having swarm'd sevenscore paces up..you find a kind of Floor. 1848 DICKENS *Dombey* ii, The smallest boy but one divining her intent, immediately began swarming upstairs after her—if that word of doubtful etymology be admissible—on his arms and legs. 1851 HELPS *Comp. Solit.* vi. (1874) 93 People who are swarming up a difficult ascent. 1890 W. CLARK RUSSELL *Ocean Trag.* II. xviii. 107 Onward she held her course, swarming steadily forward in long gliding curtseyings over each frothing surge.

2. *trans.* with the pole, etc. as obj.

1668 H. MORE *Div. Dial.* I. II. vi. 207 Endowing them with such..Nimbleness in swarming of trees, as Apes..have now. a 1769 JOHNSON in Boswell *Life* (1831) IV. 451 Why, I can swarm it now. [replied Dr Johnson,..on which he ran to the tree, clung round the trunk, and ascended to the branches]. 1787 'G. GAMBADO' *Acad. Horsemen* (1809) 23 Like swarming the bannisters of a stair-case. 1859 F. E. PAGET *Curate of Cumberworth* 72 She rushed towards a clean-stemmed beech, apparently with the intention of swarming it.

Swarmer[1] (swǭ·ɹmǝɹ). [f. SWARM *v.*[1] + -ER[1].]

1. One of a number that swarm; one of a swarm (as of insects); in *Biol.* a swarm-spore.

1844 DICKENS *Mart. Chuz.* lii, 'Oh, vermin!' said Mr. Pecksniff. 'Oh, bloodsuckers!..vermin and swarmers.' 1872 J. G. MURPHY *Comm. Lev.* xi. 20 Winged creepers or swarmers are so called from their minuteness and their multitude. 1898 H. M. WARD in *Ann. Bot.* XII. 301 The obvious suspicion arose that an intruding swarmer had got into my hanging-drop. 1900 *Nature* 21 June 191/1 The beetles are late swarmers, appearing chiefly in July.

2. A bee-hive adapted for swarming, or from which a swarm is sent forth.

1855 *Poultry Chron.* III. 300/1, I have found hives in which the combs ranged in the way most common, from front to back, indifferently swarmers or non-swarmers. 1883 in *Standard* 15 Feb. 5/2 'Artificial swarmers'..have displaced the old-fashioned 'skep'.

† **Swarmer**[2]. *Pyrotechny.* *Obs.* [ad. G. *schwärmer* or Du. *zwermer*, f. *schwärmen*, *zwermen* to rove, stray.] A cracker or serpent.

1765 R. JONES *Fireworks* iv. 149 Rockets which go under the denomination of swarmers, are those from two ounces downwards. 1799 G. SMITH *Laboratory* I. 7 Cases for Swarmers, or Rockets.

Swarming (swǭ·ɹmiŋ), *vbl. sb.* [f. SWARM *v.*[1] + -ING[1].] The action of SWARM *v.*[1]

1. The action of assembling in a swarm or dense crowd; *spec.* the gathering and departure from the hive of a swarm of bees; also *transf.* of persons (usually with *off*).

1550 BALE *Engl. Votaries* II. 77 b, A myddle swarmynge of Antichristes sectes in England. 1573 TUSSER *Husb.* (1878) 110 Watch bees in May, for swarming away. 1661 CHILDREY *Brit. Baconica* 26 The chief time of the swarming (as one would say) of Pilchards about the shores of Cornwall, is from July to November. 1675 GEDDE *New Discov. Bee-houses* 16 When Bees are at the Swarming. 1707 MORTIMER *Husb.* (1721) I. 271 Observe what you can of the usual Signs that precede their Swarming. 1817 KIRBY & SP. *Entomol.* xix. (1818) II. 167 Sometimes, when every thing seems to prognosticate swarming, a cloud passing over the sun calms the agitation. 1911 J. H. ROSE *W. Pitt* vii. 168 The divisions, by the process of swarming-off, rapidly extended the organisation.

2. *Biol.* The movement characteristic of swarm-spores; reproduction by swarm-spores.

1867 *Chambers's Encycl.* IX. 234/2. 1875 BENNETT & DYER tr. *Sachs's Bot.* 673 The swarming of zoospores. 1882 VINES tr. *Sachs's Bot.* 4 *note*, The term 'swarming' is applied to any apparently spontaneous motion imparted to a naked protoplasmic body by vibratile cilia.

3. *attrib.*, as *swarming-place*, *season*, *time*.

Used spec. in names of apparatus for transferring a swarm of bees to a new hive, as *swarming-bag*, *-basket*, *-box*, *-hook* (in recent Dicts.).

1707 MORTIMER *Husb.* (1721) I. 270 In Swarming time the Hives that you are minded to use, rub with sweet Herbs. 1855 *Poultry Chron.* III. 206/2 Watching and hiving for several weeks in the swarming season. 1892 ZANGWILL *Childr. Ghetto* I. 3 At last it [*sc.* the Ghetto] becomes only a swarming-place for the poor and the ignorant.

Swa·rming, *ppl. a.* [f. SWARM *v.*[1] + -ING[2].]

1. Assembling or moving in a swarm; forming a swarm or dense crowd; thronging; very numerous.

1590 SPENSER *F. Q.* II. x. 63 Those spoilefull Picts, and swarming Easterlings. 1725 POPE *Odyss.* XIII. 179 The swarming people hail their ship to land. 1784 COWPER *Task* III. 555 Moisture and drought, mice, worms, and swarming flies. 1817 SHELLEY *Rev. Islam* v. xxxviii, To see Earth from her general womb Pour forth her swarming sons to a fraternal doom. 1856 FROUDE *Hist. Eng.* I. i. 40 Barges pursuing their now difficult way among the swarming steamers.

2. *spec.* of bees; also *transf.* of persons: see SWARM *v.*[1] 1, 1 b.

1553 GRIMALDE *Cicero's Offices* I. (1558) 60 Being swarming [orig. *congregabilia*] by kinde they work their combes. 1697 DRYDEN *Virg. Past.* VII. 18 See..How black the Clouds of swarming Bees arise. 1713 YOUNG *Last Day* II. 51 Swarming bees..Charm'd with the brazen sound. 1869 FREEMAN *Norm. Conq.* III. xii. 147 Whence Ambigatus had sent forth his swarming colonists.

3. Filled with a swarm or multitude; densely crowded; thronged; very populous.

1810 MONTGOMERY *West Indies* II. 117 That stock he found on Afric's swarming plains. 1842 TENNYSON *Talking Oak* 213 The swarming sound of life. 1858 HAWTHORNE *Fr. & It. Note-bks.* (1872) I. 16 A swarming city.

4. *Biol.* Emerging as swarm-spores, or moving in the way characteristic of them: see SWARM *v.*[1] 1 c.

1864 *Reader* 30 Apr. 548/3 The swarming-spores of certain Algæ. 1882 VINES tr. *Sachs's Bot.* 232 In many of the more highly developed Thallophytes this power of motility is however limited to the male 'swarming' fertilising elements.

Swarmy (swǭ·ɹmi), *a.* *rare*[—1]. [f. SWARM *sb.* + -Y.] Swarming, thronged.

1858 HAWTHORNE *Fr. & It. Note-bks.* (1872) II. 192 This market is the noisiest and swarmiest centre of noisy and swarming Florence.

Swarne, obs. pa. pple. of SWEAR *v.*

Swarry (swǭ·ri). Also **-ee**, **-ey**. Humorous spelling of SOIRÉE (repr. a vulgar or careless Eng. pronunciation).

1837 DICKENS *Pickw.* xxxvii, A friendly swarry, consisting of a boiled leg of mutton with the usual trimmings. 1848 THACKERAY *Van. Fair* xlii, At one of her *swarrys* I saw one of 'em speak to a dam fiddler. 1884 *Illustr. Lond. News* 15 Nov. 467/2 The complaint of the 'English Hostess' that ladies and gentlemen invited to dinner have become so ..unpunctual that, as the lady calls it: 'There will be no dinners in London and we shall be reduced to cold swarries.'

Swart (swǭɹt), *a.* (*sb.*) Now only *rhet.* or *poet.* (or *dial.*) Forms: 1 **sweart**, 2 **sward**, 3 **swært**, **sweort**, **sword**, **suart**, 5 **swertt**, 5-6 **swarte**, 5, 7 **swert**, 1- **swart**. [Com. Teut.:

OE. *sweart*, = OS., OFris. *swart* (NFris. *sẅart*, EFris. *suurt*, WFris. *swart*), MLG.; LG. *swart*, MDu. *swart* (Du. *zwart*), OHG., MHG. *swarz* (G. *schwarz*), ON. *svartr* (Sw. *svart*, Da. *sort*), Goth. *swarts*; f. root *swart-* 'dark', of which another grade is found in ON. *sorta* black dye, *sorti* black cloud, *sortna* to grow black, *Surtr* (see SURTURBRAND).

While surviving as the regular colour-word in the Continental languages, it has been superseded in ordinary use in English by *black*.]

1. Dark in colour; black or blackish; dusky, swarthy. **a.** *gen.*

Beowulf 167 (Gr.) Heorot eardode, sincfaze sel sweartum nihtum. *Ibid.* 3145 Wudurec astah sweart. c 1000 *Sax. Leechd.* I. 310 Ðeos wyrt..ys þyrnihton stelan..& bradran leafon þonne leac & sweartran. 1122 *O. E. Chron.* (Laud), Þa wearð swiðe mycel wind fram þa undern dæies to þa swarte nihte. a 1200 *Moral Ode* 278 in *O. E. Hom.* I. 177 Nis þer neure oþer liht þanne þe swarte leie. c 1205 LAY. 11974 Swurken vnder sunnen sweorte weolcnen. 1297 R. GLOUC. (Rolls) 10049 Vor he vel of is palefrey & brec is fot..So suart so eni crowe amorwe is fot was. 13.. *E. E. Allit. P.* C. 363 To be swolȝed swyftly wyth þe swart erþe. c 1430 *Hymns Virg.* etc. (1895) 119 Hitt shalle be swarte as any pyche. 1578 LYTE *Dodoens* 38 It is smaller, smother, and of a swarter colour. 1601 HOLLAND *Pliny* XXIII. i. II. 149 Foule and unseemly swert skars, it reduceth to the fresh and naturall colour. 1602 MARSTON *Antonio's Rev.* I. i. Wks. 1856 I. 73 You horrid scouts That centinell swart night. 1682 SIR T. BROWNE *Chr. Mor.* III. § 6 Nor deepen those swart Tinctures, which Temper, Infirmity, or ill habits have set upon thee. 1794 COLERIDGE *Koskiusko* 4 Through the swart air.. on the chill and midnight gale Rises..The dirge of murder'd Hope! 1811 SCOTT *Don Roderick* I. liii, Swart as the smoke from raging furnace. 1890 'R. BOLDREWOOD' *Col. Reformer* (1891) 283 The trees upon the swart hillsides were visible.. as at midday.

b. *spec.* Of the skin or complexion, or of persons in respect of these.

a 1395 HYLTON *Scala Perf.* (W. de W. 1494) II. xii, Beholde me not that I am swart [*ed.* 1533 blacke] for the sonne hath defaded me. a 1400-50 *Wars Alex.* 3970 Þa swart men of ynde. c 1407 LYDG. *Reason & Sens.* 3791 Vulcanus..For his smotry swarte face He stood clene out of hir grace. 1568 GRAFTON *Chron.* II. 197 This king was of stature talle, somewhat swarte or black of colour. 1590 SHAKS. *Com. Err.* III. ii. 104 *Anti.* What complexion is she of? *Dro.* Swart like my shoo, but her face nothing like so cleane kept. 1614 SYLVESTER *Bethulia's Rescue* III. 36 The swelting coasts of swartest Abyssine. 1613-16 W. BROWNE *Brit. Past.* I. iv, The swart ploughman for his breakfast staid. 1634 MILTON *Comus* 436 No goblin, or swart faëry of the mine. 1810 SHELLEY *Solitary* ii, The swart Pariah in some Indian grove. 1825 SCOTT *Talism.* xxvii, Their countenance swart with the sunbeams. 1901 E. L. ARNOLD *Lepidus* 154 This swart adventurer made love to the girl that was all in all to me.

† **c.** Livid through suffering or emotion. *Obs.*

a 1400 *Sir Beues* (S.) 1012 For teene he wexe al swert. c 1485 *Digby Myst., Mary Magdalene* 780, I wax alle swertt! 1567 GOLDING *Ovid's Met.* XII. (1593) 288 Al his body waxt starke cold and died swart. 1581 in Farr *S. P. Eliz.* (1845) II. 395 Who alwaies thinkes of death Shall neuer looke with cheerful face, But swarte, and wan. 1590 BARROUGH *Meth. Phisic* I. iii. (1639) 5 Their face is..full and pale, and their eyes are swolne and swart.

d. quasi-*adv.* qualifying an adj. of colour.

In first quot. *swarte* is a disyllable, as if repr. OE. *swearte* adv.

c 1384 CHAUCER *H. Fame* III. 557 Blak blo grenyssh swarte Red. c 1530 *Judic. Urines* II. xiv. 45 b, Lyke as we see whan a thyng that is swart grene. 1578 LYTE *Dodoens* 82 Small round beries of a swarte redde colour. 1841 BROWNING *Pippa Passes* II. 51 An Almaign Kaiser,..Swart-green and gold, with truncheon based on hip.

2. *transf.* Producing swarthiness of complexion.

Applied by Milton to some heavenly body, perhaps the dog-star (cf. Hor. *Od.* III. xxiii. 9), in reference to the heat of summer; hence in echoes of Milton, sometimes in sense 'malignant' (cf. 3 b).

1637 MILTON *Lycidas* 138 Ye valleys low..On whose fresh lap the swart Star sparely looks. 1759 MASON *Caractacus*, *Ode* II. iii, From the sultry south alone The swart star flings his pestilential fire. 1818 KEATS *Endym.* II. 15 Swart planet in the universe of deeds! 1862 TRENCH *Poems* 254 (*Sonnet*) The swart sun's blaze Down beating with unmitigated rays. 1892 HENLEY *Song of Sword* etc. 15 From swart August to the green lap of May.

b. Dressed in black.

Cf. MLG. *swartbroder*, ON. *svartmunkr*, etc., a Dominican, black friar.

1688 MRS. BEHN *Fair Jilt* Plays etc. 1871 V. 206 Canonesses, Begines, Quests, Swart-Sisters, and Jesuitesses. 1856 AYTOUN *Bothwell* II. ix, There he stood,..Swart in the Congregation's garb.

3. *fig.* **a.** 'Black', wicked, iniquitous. **b.** Baleful, malignant.

a 900 CYNEWULF *Juliana* 313 (Gr.) Wraþra fela..bealwa.. sweartra synna. c 1000 ÆLFRIC *Hom.* (Th.) I. 54 Swa lange swa he hylt ðone sweartan niþ on his heortan. a 1225 *Ancr. R.* 304 A domesdei schulen ure swarte sunnen bicleopen us stronchiche of ure soule murðre. 1594 CAREW *Tasso* IV. xx. (1881) 78 Whereto booted this, if they ne mote Of these vncertaine broyles the issue cleere?..Nor hels swart cunning could to truth direct? 1852 ROCK *Ch. Fathers* III. ix. 222 Whenever any swart evil had betided this land. 1867 EMERSON *Poems, The Past* 3 Nor haughty hope, nor swart chagrin, Nor murd'ring hate.

4. *Comb.*, as *swart-coloured*, *-complexioned*, *-faced*, *-featured*, *-visaged* adjs. (Cf. OE. *sweartheswen*.)

1620 T. GRANGER *Div. Logike* 67 Vnder the North pole they are browne, and *swart coloured. c 1600 SHAKS. *Sonn.* xxviii, The *swart complexiond night. 1821 SCOTT *Kenilw.* xi, A..*swart-faced knave of that noble mystery. 1905 TUCKWELL *Remin. Radical Parson* xii. 181 A great gathering of swart-faced enthusiasts in the Black Country. 1837 CARLYLE *Fr. Rev.* II. IV. iv, So many *swart-featured haggard faces. 1858 O. W. HOLMES '*This is it*' 57 in *Aut. Breakf.-t.* ii, Bare-armed, *swart-visaged, gaunt, and shaggy-browed.

† **B.** *sb.* A person of swarthy complexion; in quot. c 1425 *fig.* as a term of reproach. *Obs. rare.*

c 1425 *Cast. Persev.* 2211 in *Macro Plays* 143 Charyte, þat sowre swart, with fayre rosys myn hed gan breke. 1867 SMYTH *Sailor's Word-bk.*, *Swarts*, a name formerly applied by voyagers to Indians and negroes.

† **Swart**, *v.* *Obs.* [f. SWART *a.* In OE. *sweartian*, corresp. to MLG. *swarten*, also *swerten*, OHG. *suarzên*, MHG. *swarzen*, also OHG. *suarz(i)an*, *suerzen*, MHG. *swerzen* (G. *schwärzen*); cf. ON. *svartaðr* dyed black.]

1. *intr.* To become swart, dark, or dusky.

c 1000 ÆLFRIC *Saints' Lives* xviii. 151 Efne ða aras se wind and ða wolcnu sweartodon. c 1000 *Sax. Leechd.* III. 104 Þanne sweartigeð hy [*sc.* the teeth] & fealleð.

1581 A. HALL *Iliad* v. 86 Hir colour gay So bright that was, beginnes to swarte.

2. *trans.* To make swart; to darken (esp. the skin or complexion).

1577 GRANGE *Golden Aphrod.* N j, Vulcane beyng..swarted with the..smoke of his forge. 1614 GORGES *Lucan* VI. 217 The skinne it scorching swarts. 1628 *Brittain's Ida* in *Spenser's Wks.* (1862) 502/2 Jove upon him downe his thunder darted, Blasting his splendent face, and all his beauty swarted. 1646 SIR T. BROWNE *Pseud. Ep.* VI. x. 326 The heate of the Sun, whose fervor may swarte a living part, and even black a dead or dissolving flesh.

Swart, obs. form of SWARD.

Swartback, **swarthback**. *local.* Also 5 **suerthbak**, 7 **swarth bag**. [ad. Icel. *svartbakur* (whence Norw. *svartbak*, Da. *svartbagmaage*): see SWART *a.*, SWARTH *a.* + BACK *sb.*[1] Cf. SWABIE.] The great black-backed gull, *Larus marinus*.

c 1450 HOLLAND *Howlat* 180 The Goule was a gryntar, The Suerthbak a sellerar. 1676 STERPIN *Descr. Færoe* 141 The Swarth bag is a great Bird like a Kite, it is white all over, but the back. 1678 RAY *Willughby's Ornith.* 344 In the Feroe Islands it is called, The Swarth-back. 1805 BARRY *Orkney* III. i. 304 The Great Black and White Gull..our black-backed maw, or as it is sometimes called swartback, is the largest of the gull kind in our seas. 1821 SCOTT *Pirate* x, Thy foot had been on the Maiden-skerrie of Northmaven, known before but to the webbed sole of the swartback. *Ibid.* [see SWABIE].

Swarth (swǭɹþ), *sb.*[1] Now only *dial.* Also 7 **sworth**, 8 **swarthe**. [OE. *swearþ*: see SWARD *sb.* and cf. SWARF *sb.*[3]]

1. Skin, rind; *fig.* the surface, outside.

c 725 *Corpus Gloss.* C 198 *Cater*, suearth. c 1050 *Ags. Voc.* in Wr.-Wülcker 363/9 *Catrum*, swearð. c 1450 *St. Cuthbert* (Surtees) 2280 For oft knelyng his knees boun, A grete swarth was on þaim groune. 1807 STAGG *Poems* 49 Lest for the swarth I past retrievan, The substance torfeit. 1869 *Lonsdale Gloss.*, *Swarth*,..any outward covering, as the rind of bacon. 1878 *Cumbld. Gloss.*, *Swarth*, the skin of hams and bacon.

2. Green turf, grass land, greensward.

? a 1400 *Morte Arth.* 1126 One the erthe [he] hittez A swerde lenghe with-in þe swarthe. *Ibid.* 1466 Swyftly with swerdes, they swappene there-aftyre,..That alle swelltez one swarthe. a 1552 LELAND *Itin.* (1906) VI. 79 In Cairarvonshire..is Llinedwarchen, wher [is] the Swymming Island, and ther of it hath the name as of a suimming swarth of yerth. 1594 PLAT *Jewell-ho.* I. 19 Cloddes of earth..such as are full of swarth. 1616 SURFL. & MARKH. *Country Farme* v. vi. 523 New broken swarthes. 1664 EVELYN *Sylva* 18 The swarth par'd first away, and the earth stirred a foot deep or more. 1770-4 A. HUNTER *Georg. Ess.* (1803) I. 141 Two acres of rich sand land, which the year before had been ploughed out of swarth. 1794 VANCOUVER *Agric. Cambridge* 93 The old swarthe produces a very indifferent herbage, but may be much improved, by breaking up, [etc.]. 1798 *Trans. Soc. Arts* XVI. 242 He has it in contemplation to leave the rest to swarth without sowing seeds on it.

b. qualified by *green* (or *grassy*).

1616 SURFL. & MARKH. *Country Farme* III. i. 335 As soone as you see these bankes firme, and beginning to grow to haue a greene swarth vpon them. 1637 B. JONSON *Sad Shepherd* I. v, On every greene sworth, and in every path. 1751 R. PALTOCK *P. Wilkins* xi. (1883) 34/1, I walked over the green swarth to the wood. 1784 COWPER *Task* I. 110 Through lanes, Of grassy swarth close cropt by nibbling sheep.

† **c.** *transf.* Applied to the top layers of soil. *Obs.*

1649 BLITHE *Eng. Improv.* vii. 38 This..cold hungry water is found, beneath the first and second swarth of thy Lands.

d. *attrib.*

1598 *Fitzherbert's Husb.* viii. (1882) 132 If you sowe Winter-corne..vpon swarth ground. 1607 MARKHAM *Caval.* VI. ii. 5 Some plaine leuell Meddowe or such like greene swarth ground. 1794 *Act for inclosing South Kelsey* 26 Any old Green Swarth Ground. 1876 *Mid-Yorks. Gloss.* s.v., 'Swarth-balks', the end portions of a field, left unploughed, for a cart-way.

Swarth (swǭɹþ), *sb.*[2] Now *dial.* [Obscure altered form of SWATH[1].]

1. = SWATH[1] 3.

1552 HULOET, Swarth of grasse newe mowen. 1688 HOLME *Armoury* III. 72/2 The Swarth..are the rows of the cut Grass as the Sithe leaves it. 1706 *Phil. Trans.* XXV. 2237 The Waves came rolling down, like long Swarths of Grass, one upon another. 1713 *Ibid.* XXVIII. 91 When it is cut, it must in most Years lie 5 or 6 Days in swarth. a 1722 LISLE *Husb.* (1757) 277, I could have no prospect of mowing a good swarth in the French-grass. 1763 *Museum Rust.* (ed. 2) I. 236 In Buckinghamshire they cannot use a cradle, their crops being in general so heavy, that the workmen could not carry over the swarth. 1817-18 COBBETT *Resid. U.S.* (1822) 181 They mow four acres of oats, wheat, rye, or barley in a day, and, with a cradle, lay it so smooth in the swarths, that it is tied up in sheaths with the greatest neatness and ease. 1861 HUGHES *Tom Brown at Oxf.* xxiii. (1889) 221 There were groups of children in many parts of the field, and women to look after them, mostly sitting on the fresh swarth.

attrib. 1813 VANCOUVER *Agric. Devon* 171 The barley is gathered from the swarth into sheaves,..and, after the swarth-corn is secured, the fields are carefully raked.

b. *To mow in swarth*: see quots.

1763 *Museum Rust.* (ed. 2) I. 235 Horse-beans..they usually mow with a bare scythe, in swarth, as they term it; that is, they mow the beans towards the beans. 1764 *Ibid.* III. lxxvi. 336 As to mowing wheat in swarth, I think it will litter about very much, for beans do so.

c. Applied to growing grain: cf. SWATH[1] 3 b.

1880 SIR J. B. PHEAR *Aryan Village* i. 4 These open spaces..are..covered..by green waving swarths of rice.

2. *transf.* and *fig.* = SWATH[1] 4 a, b.

† *At full swarth*: (app.) 'in full swing' (Davies), like a scythe making swaths.

1601 SHAKS. *Twel. N.* II. iii. 162 An affection'd Asse, that cons State without booke, and vtters it by great swarths. 1713 *Gentl. Instructed* III. iii. (ed. 5) 403 Tho' his Design miscarried, his Malice was at full swarth. 1847 LE FANU *T. O'Brien* 267 Old time sweeps in his swarth. 1854 J. S. C. ABBOTT *Napoleon* (1855) II. ix. 139 He sees the course of his heroes by the black swarth of dead men.

Swarth (swǭɹþ), *sb.*[3] Variant of SWARF *sb.*[2]

With quot. 1596 cf. quot. 1566 s.v. SWARF *sb.*[2]

1596 *Wills & Inv. N. C.* (Surtees 1860) 259 In dieng stuffe ..In brasell, half a hundreth and xj poundes, 46s. 8d. In galles, viij poundes, 6s. In swarthe, iiij poundes, 8d. 1783-4 *London Sessions Papers* 472 He told me that there was some swarth, that is iron file dust. 1892 RIGBY in *Min. Proc. Inst. Civ. Engin.* CXI. 140 A capillary brass tube [in a drilling-machine], supplying soap-and-oil emulsion at a pressure of 80 lbs. on the inch. This washes out the 'swarth' and cools the cutting-edge.

Swarth, *sb.*[4] *dial.* [perh. subst. use of SWARTH *a.* But cf. Sc. *warth*, var. *wraith*.] The apparition of a dying person; a wraith.

1674 RAY *N. C. Words* 47 A *Swarth*, Cumb., the Ghost of a dying man. 1790 GROSE *Provinc. Gloss.*, *Pop. Superstitions* 13 These apparitions are called Fetches, or Wraiths, and in Cumberland, Swarths.

Swarth, *a.* (*sb.*[5]) [Obscure variant of SWART *a.*; cf. SWARTHY *a.*[1], and SWARF *a.*, SWARFISH, SWARFY.] Dusky, swarthy, black.

c 1530 [implied in *swarthness*]. 1569 C. T[YE] *Nastagio & Traversari* A vj b, A knight, of colour swarthe. 1600 SURFLET *Country Farm* VI. xxii. 787 Such women as..are subject to pale and swarth colours. 1600 E. BOLTON *Palinode* in *Eng. Helicon* B iv b, Swarth clowdes. 1613 FLETCHER, etc. *Captain* II. ii, He looks Of a more rusty swarth Complexion Than an old arming Doublet. 1784 COWPER *Task* IV. 749 A swarth Indian with his belt of beads. 1814 SCOTT *Ld. of Isles* I. vii, Where thwarting tides, with mingled roar, Part thy swarth hills from Morven's shore. 1851 MAYNE REID *Scalp Hunters* vii. 55 The complexion, from tan and exposure, was brown and swarth.

fig. 1621 FLETCHER *Isl. Princess* v. i, Foule swarthe ingratitude.

b. *sb.* Swarthiness; dusky complexion or colour. *rare.*

a 1661 HOLYDAY *Juvenal* (1673) 258 The skies Face and black swarth of cloud threaten no ill: 'Tis summer-thunder. 1872 BROWNING *Fifine* xv, First Let me..pourtray you..The gypsy's foreign self, no swarth our sun could bake.

Hence **Swa·rthish** *a.*, somewhat swarthy; **Swa·rthness**, swarthiness, duskiness.

c 1530 *Judic. Urines* II. ii. 11 b, A swarthnes, a derknes & dymnes in the vryne, most to blaknesse warde. 1653 RAMESEY *Astrol. Restored* 86 A..long visage, and a swarthish complexion.

Swarth, *v.*[1] Now *dial.* [f. SWARTH *sb.*[1]] *trans.* and *intr.* = SWARD *v.* 1, 2.

1620 FOLKINGHAM *Feudigr.* I. vi. 13 With what Herbage the Crust or Sword is matted, mantled and swarthed. 1765 *Museum Rust.* IV. xxi. 95 If, through..some mischance in the hay-seeds, it should not swarth well. 1858 *Jrnl. R. Agric. Soc.* XIX. I. 256 Where land is of a rich loamy character, there is no difficulty in getting it to swarth over with grass of good quality.

Swarth, *v.*[2] *rare.* [f. SWARTH *a.*] *trans.* To make swarthy, to darken.

1846 G. WARBURTON *Hochelaga* II. 161 Complexion fresh and ruddy but swarthed over by sun and wind.

Swarth, obs. var. SWARF *v.*, to faint.

Swarthback: see SWARTBACK.

Swarthily (swǭ·ɹþili), *adv.* *rare*[—0]. [f. SWARTHY *a.*[1] + -LY[2].] With a swarthy colour.

1755 JOHNSON, *Swarthily*, blackly; duskily; tawnily. [Hence in later Dicts.]

Swarthiness (swǭ·ɹþinės). [f. as prec. + -NESS.] The quality of being swarthy; duskiness; darkness of colour or complexion.

1577 B. GOOGE *Heresbach's Husb.* II. (1586) 67 b, The ripenesse whereof is deemed by the swarthinesse and the softnesse of the berrie. 1628 FELTHAM *Resolves* II. [I.] xxxvi. 111 It thickens the complexion, and dyes it into an vnpleasing swarthinesse. 1668 WILKINS *Real Char.* II. viii. 224 Yellowness and Swarthiness of colour, accompanied with faintness. 1758 *Descr. Thames* 179 The Fat is thought excellent against Redness, or Swarthiness. 1823 SCOTT *Quentin D.* v, The complexion of the face..in its ordinary state of weather-beaten and sunburnt swarthiness. 1884 JEFFERIES in *Pall Mall Gaz.* 8 Aug. 4/2 A clear swarthiness —a translucent swarthiness—clear as the most delicate white.

Swarthish, **Swarthness**: see after SWARTH *a.*

Swarthy (swǭ·ɹði, swǭ·ɹþi), *a.*[1] [Obscure

variant of SWARTY: cf. SWARTH *a.*, SWARF *a.*, SWARFISH, SWARFY.] Of a dark hue; black or blackish; dusky.

a. *gen.* = SWART *a.* 1 a.

1577 [implied in SWARTHINESS]. 1596 GOSSON *Quippes Upstart Gentlewom.* 99 in Hazl. *E. P. P.* IV. 254 The swarthie-blacke, the grassie-greene, The pudding-red, the dapple graie. 1602 MARSTON *Ant. & Mel.* I. Wks. 1856 I. 16 Swarthy darknesse popt out Phoebus eye. 1697 DRYDEN *Virg. Georg.* III. 596 Search his Mouth; and if a swarthy Tongue Is underneath his humid Palate hung [etc.]. 1786 tr. *Beckford's Vathek* (1868) 35 From a swarthy crimson to a bright rose colour. 1827 HEBER *Europe* 270 The swarthy vintage. 1842 TENNYSON *Morte d'Arthur* 269 Like some full-breasted swan That..takes the flood With swarthy webs.

b. of or in reference to the complexion: = SWART *a.* 1 b.

1591 SHAKS. *Two Gent.* II. vi. 26 Siluia..Shewes Iulia but a swarthy Ethiope. 1601 B. JONSON *Poetaster* v. i, Let our Roman eagles flie On swarthy Ægypt. 1634 SIR T. HERBERT *Trav.* 14 The people are of a swarthy darke colour. 1638-56 COWLEY *Davideis* III. 178 Your Name..That to rich Ophirs rising Morn is knowne, And stretcht out far to the burnt swarthy Zone. 1744 MITCHELL in *Phil. Trans.* XLIII. 122 If we proceed from the swarthiest white Person to the palest Egyptian, from thence to the fairest Mustee, Molatto, Moor, &c. to the darkest Indian. 1833 TENNYSON *Dream Fair Wom.* xxxii. A queen, with swarthy cheeks and bold black eyes. 1879 S. C. BARTLETT *Egypt to Pal.* xxv. 493 Six swarthy Arabs pulled our oars as we headed north.

c. *fig.* 'Black', 'dark', malignant, dismal: cf. SWART *a.* 3.

1651 J. S. *Prince of Priggs Revels* III. 9 You (Parson).. Black best becomes your swarthy function Whose Doctrine ..damns more souls Then Lucifer by all his stratagems. 1756 AMORY *Buncle* (1825) I. 2 My lot has been a swarthy one in this first state.

d. *Comb.*

1587 TURBERV. *Trag. Tales* (1837) 31 A hydeous knight, to seeming swarthie hewde. 1689 *Lond. Gaz.* No. 2433/4 A swarthy Complexioned Boy. 1891 DOYLE *White Company* xxiv, A raw-boned, swarthy-cheeked man.

Hence † **Swarthy** *v. trans.*, to make swarthy.

1663 COWLEY *Cutter Colman St.* IV. vi, Now will I and my Man John swarthy our Faces over as if that Country's Heat had made 'em so.

† **Swarthy**, *a.*[2] *Obs. rare*[—1]. [f. SWARTH *sb.*[1] + -Y.] = SWARDY.

1613 [STANDISH] *New Direct. Planting* 8 The best way to inclose, is (if it be in swarthy grounds) to set [etc.].

Swartish (swǭ·ɹtiʃ), *a.* Also 6 **swerttysshe**. [f. SWART *a.* + -ISH[1].] Somewhat swart, dusky, or dark-coloured. Also *advb.*

1483 *Chaucer's H. Fame* III. 557 Black, blo, grenyssh, swartysh [*MSS.* swart(e) rede. c 1530 *Judic. Urines* I. iii. 8 The womans vryne is more swartyshe..than is mannes vryne. *Ibid.* III. v. 50 A vapourus superfluyte, swerttysshe and dymmysshe. 1545 RAYNALDE *Byrth Mankynde* 43 The couloure swartisshe blacke. 1630 *R. Johnson's Kingd. & Commw.* 59 The Tartars are swartish, illfavoured, with a great thick lip. 1647 LILLY *Chr. Astrol.* viii. 58 His complexion pale, swartish or muddy.

Swa·rtly, *adv. rare.* [f. as prec. + -LY[2].] So as to be or become swart; swarthily.

1582 STANYHURST *Æneis* IV. (Arb.) 111 When she the gift sacrifice with the incense burned on altars..thee moysture swartlye was altred. 1607 *Puritan* IV. ii. 16 How do's hee looke..? very swartlie, I warrant, with black beard, scorcht cheekes, and smokie eyebrowes.

Swartness (swǭ·ɹtnės). [f. as prec. + -NESS.] The quality of being swart; swarthiness, duskiness.

a 1100 *Aldhelm Gloss.* I. 4681 (Napier 121/1) *Nigredine*, sweartnysse. a 1395 HYLTON *Scala Perf.* (W. de W. 1494) II. xii, The swartnesse [1533 blackenes] that I haue is all wythoute. 1530 PALSGR. 278/1 Swartnesse, *estalleure*. 1584 B. R. tr. *Herodotus* II. 75 The blacknesse and swartnesse of the people. 1590 BARROUGH *Meth. Phisick* III. xix. (1639) 133 It chanceth sometime the face to be made very red..but this colour turneth againe into swartnesse. 1823 SCOTT *Peveril* xxvi, She..denounced the plague of swartness to the Eden, of leanness to the poultry, of dearth and dishonour to the housekeeping.

Swartrutter. *Obs.* exc. *Hist.* Also 6 **swart-roter**, **swart(e) rutter**, **swartrytter**, **swarthrutter**. [a. early mod. Du. *swartrutter* (in Kilian *swerte ruyters* pl.): see SWART *a.* and RUTTER.] One of a class of irregular troopers, with black dress and armour and blackened faces, who infested the Netherlands in the 16th and 17th centuries.

1557 in *Cecil Papers* (Hist. MSS. Comm.) I. 144 A number of our Swartroters took Scheney. 1558 in Feuillerat *Revels Q. Eliz.* (1908) 94 The performaunce of A Maske of swartrutters. 1572 BUCHANAN *Detection Mary Q. Scots* D iij b, Put on ane lose cloke, sic as the Swartrytters weare. 1598 E. GUILPIN *Skial.* (1878) 36 Like a Swartrutters hose his puffe thoughts swell, With yeastie ambition. 1634 W. TIRWHYT tr. *Balzac's Lett.* I. 128 The novelty of these barbarous faces, and of those great lubberly Swa[r]t-rutters, might easily have affrighted us. 1657 REEVE *God's Plea* 81 Fitter for Swartrutters and Ruffians, then for true Penitents. [1706 PHILLIPS (ed. Kersey), *Swart-Reyter*, (Dutch) a Horseman with black Armour.] 1900 F. W. MAITLAND in Fisher *Biog.* (1910) 122 The English government's one idea of carrying on a big war..was that of hiring German 'swart-rutters'.

Hence † **Swartrutting** *a. nonce-wd.*, behaving like a swartrutter.

1590 GREENE *Upst. Courtier* D 4, Making no brawles to haue wounds, as swartrutting veluet breeches dooth.

Swarty (swǭ·ɹti), *a.* Now *rare* or *Obs.* [f. SWART *a.* + -Y[1].] = SWARTHY *a.*[1]

1572 J. JONES *Bathes Buckstone* 1 b, It should not onely bee of another collour marly yellow, or swarty greene. 1582 STANYHURST *Æneis* III. (Arb.) 72 With black weede the altar is hanged, With tree swartye Ciperʒ. 1600 SHAKS. *Tit. A.* II. iii. 72 (Q.) Your swartie [*Folios* swarth] Cymerion. 1609 HEALEY *Discov. New World* I. xii. 55 A stonie, swartie, barren, Grass-lesse, sandie soyle. 1613-16 W. BROWNE *Brit. Past.* I. v, The swarty Smith spits in his Buckhorne fist. 1656 HEYLIN *Surv. France* 205 A beard..black and swarty. 1888 DOUGHTY *Trav. Arabia Deserta* II. 69 Before us appeared that great craggy blackness—the Harra, and thereupon certain swarty hills and crests.

Comb. 1635 R. N. tr. *Camden's Hist. Eliz.* II. 189 Frobisher..under the Latitude of 63 degrees..found men.. swarty coloured.

Swarve (swǭɹv), *v.*[1] *local* (Kent and Sussex). Also 5-6 *pa. pple.* **swared**. [Cf. the synonymous QUAR *v.*[1]] Chiefly *pass.*, to be choked *up* with sediment, to be silted *up*. Hence **Swa·rving** *vbl. sb.*

1485 *Rolls of Parlt.* VI. 331/1 The said Ryver, at the said place called Sarre..is so swared, growen, and hyghed with wose,..that nowe no Fery..may be there. 1548 *Act 2 & 3 Edw. VI*, c. 30 The Channell there is so choked swared and fylled uppe, that there cannot lye in the same Harborowe [of Camber, near Rye] above thirtie or fowrtie saylle of Shippes. 1562 in *W. Holloway's Hist. Romney Marsh* (1849) 141 A creek or waterway swawed [*sic*] or dried up. 1587 FLEMING *Contn. Holinshed* III. 1545/2 The hauens mouth would..hane soone beene swarued vp. 1603 KNOLLES *Hist. Turks* (1621) 544 A narrow way almost swarved up with rubbidge. 1665 in *W. Holloway's Hist. Romney Marsh* (1849) 165 When the ditches and bounds be swarved up. 1701 WALLIS in *Phil. Trans.* XXII. 978 At Hythe in Kent (which is one of the Cinq-Ports) there was..a Convenient Harbour for small Vessels; which is now swarved up. 1904 MAUD S. RAWSON *Apprentice* 17 The swarving of river channels with sand and shingle.

† **Swarve**, *v.*[2] *Obs.* [Of doubtful origin; see the synonymous SWARM *v.*[2] (North. dialects have *swarble* beside *swarmle* in the same sense.)] = SWARM *v.*[2] (*intr.* and *trans.*).

15.. *Isumbras* 351 (Douce MS. 261, lf. 7) He swarued [*ed. Copland* (c 1550) swarmed] vp in to a tree Whyle ether of them myght other see. a 1613 OVERBURY *A Wife*, etc. (1638) 107 He swarves up to his seat as to a saile-yard. a 1650 *Sir A. Barton* liii. in Child *Ballads* (1889) III. 341/2 With that hee swarued the maine-mast tree [*another version, ibid.* 345/1 Then up the mast-tree swarved he]. 1844 *M. A. Richardson's Historian's Table-bk., Leg. Div.* II. 393 Now leaping, now swarving the slipp'ry steep.

Swarve: see SWARF *v.*, SWERVE.

Swash (swǫʃ), *int.* or *adv.* and *sb.*[1] Also **swosh**. [Imitative of the sound of splashing or agitated water, or of a resounding blow. Cf. *swish*.]

A. *int.* or *adv.* Expressive of the fall of a heavy body or blow: With a crash.

1538 BALE *Thre Lawes* 393 Haue in than at a dash, With swash myry annet swash. 1582 STANYHURST *Æneis* II. (Arb.) 58 Pat fals thee turret, thee Greeks with crash swash yt beapeth. 1863 MRS. GASKELL *Sylvia* xv. II. 7 If a hadn't been too quick for her, it would have a' gone swash down i' t' litter.

B. *sb.*

I. 1. Pig-wash; also, wet refuse or filth.

1528 TINDALE *Parable Wicked Mammon* Wks. (1573) 65/1 His stomacke abhorreth longyng after slibbersause and swashe, at which a whole stomacke is readye to cast hys gorge. 1634 MERES *Wits Commonw.* II. 50 Swine..refuse partriges and delicats, and doe greedily hunt after Acornes and other swash. 1847 HALLIWELL, *Swash*..(4) Refuse; hog-wash. 1878 *Cumbld. Gloss.*, *Swash*, wet stuff. 1893 *Times* (weekly ed.) 10 Feb. 114 The well-filled troughs of swash and potatoes round which I have seen pigs crowd.

2. A body of water moving forcibly or dashing against something.

An alleged sense 'stream, puddle of water', entered in Phillips's *World of Words*, ed. Kersey, 1706, is not otherwise authenticated.

1671 SKINNER *Etymol.*, Swash, a great Swash of water, *magnus & cum magno impetu ruens aquarum Torrens*. 1844 W. H. MAXWELL *Wanderings in Highlands* xviii. II. 5 Some 'swash' in the Goodwins. 1852 HAWTHORNE *Blithedale Rom.* xxvii, Up came a white swash to the surface of the river. It was the flow of a woman's garments. 1860 *Wilts. Archæol. Mag.* VI. 380 *note*, A man in answer to my question of how the rain seemed to fall, said 'It came down in swashes'.

3. Chiefly *U.S.* = SWATCH *sb.*[3]

1670-1 NARBOROUGH *Jrnl.* in *Acc. Sev. Late Voy.* I. (1694) 46 It drains into salt Water-swashes. *Ibid.* 52, I sent the Boat for Water to a Swash on the East-side. 1775 ROMANS *Florida* App. 78 As the bank is bound with a reef here, you must pick your way through that, which you may, as there are several swashes, which though they are narrow, have no less than 11 or 12 feet thro'. 1788 JEFFERSON *Writ.* (1859) II. 453 Having got themselves near the swash, at the mouth of the Boristhenes. 1869 *New Orleans Bee* in Schele de Vere *Americanisms* (1872) 556 It is said they took refuge in the swash behind the house.

4. A heavy blow, esp. of, or upon, some yielding substance; the sound of this.

1789 DAVIDSON *Seasons, Spring* 32 Forthwith amain he [*sc.* the salmon] plunges on his prey, Wi' eager swash. 1853 KANE *Grinnell Exp.* xxvi. (1856) 211 The voices of the ice and the heavy swash of the overturned hummock-tables. 1865 G. MACDONALD *Alec Forbes* 29 The cruel serpent of leather went at him, coiling round his legs with a sudden, hissing swash. 1866 GREGOR *Banffsh. Gloss.*, *Swash*, (1) a severe blow. (2) A severe dash. 1898 J. PATON *Castle-braes* ii. 49, I laid ma Heezel Rung, a second swash, athwart the safter pairts.

5. The action of water dashing or washing against the side of a cliff, ship, etc. or of waves against each other; the sound accompanying this.

1847-54 WEBSTER, *Swash*..2. Impulse of water flowing with violence. 1849 CUPPLES *Green Hand* ix, The lazy swash of the water round our fore-chains. 1849 W. S. MAYO *Kaloolah* ii. (1850) 21 The captain fancied that he heard the swash of the water against the sides of a ship. 1863 HAWTHORNE *Our Old Home* (1879) 279 The swash and swell of the passing steamers. 1883 G. H. BOUGHTON in *Harper's Mag.* Feb. 393/1 We were steaming along splendidly now, sending up a fine wash and swash along the banks. 1891 H. HUTCHINSON *Fairway Island* 25 The swash of the sea at the cliff foot.

6. A watery condition of land; ground under water.

1864 CARLYLE *Fredk. Gt.* XVI. xiv. IV. 478 Waters all out, ground in a swash with December rains. 1891 *The Auk* Jan. 65 Here [*sc.* Andros in the Bahamas] the ground is soft, and in wet weather almost entirely under water; hence the peculiar appropriateness of the local term *swash*.

II. 7. A swaggerer; a swashbuckler; now *Sc.* an ostentatious person: cf. SWASH *a.*[1], SWASHING *ppl. a.* 1.

1549 CHALONER *Erasm. on Folly* D iij b, Commonly thei that bringe any valiant feate to passe, are good blouddes, venturers, compaignions, swasshes. 1579 GOSSON *Sch. Abuse* (Arb.) 46 Every Duns will be a Carper, every Dick Swash a common Cutter. 1584 R. WILSON *Three Ladies Lond.* (1592) A 3, I will flaunt it and brave it after the lusty swash. 1593 G. HARVEY *Pierce's Super.* 117 The noddy Nash, whom euery seruing Swash With pot-iestes dash, and euery whipdog lash. 1637 I. JONES & DAVENANT *Brit. Triumphans* 17 With Courtly Knights, not roaring country swashes, Hath beene her breeding still. 1659 T. PECKE *Parnassi Puerp.* 16 Two Swashes did the fair Camilla court. 1693 SOUTHERNE *Maid's last Prayer* II. ii, I remember your Dammee-boys, your Swashes, your Tuquoques. 1824 MISS FERRIER *Inher.* xviii, A great gormandizing swash. 1866 GREGOR *Banffsh. Gloss.*, *Swash*..(4) A vapouring dandy.

8. Swagger; swashbuckling.

1593 G. HARVEY *Pierce's Super.* ***j, If nothing can the booted Souldiour tame..But Swash will still his trompery aduaunce. 1605 A. WARREN *Poor Man's Pass.* E 3, I would elect, Flaunt, Cut, and Swash for mates, For choise Companions, pleasure, mirth, delight. 1822 MAGINN in *Blackw. Mag.* XI. 370 The stamping, ramping, swaggering, staggering, leathering swash of an Irishman. 1854 MISS BAKER *Northampt. Gloss.* s. v., What a swash he cuts! 1866 GREGOR *Banffsh. Gloss.*, *Swash*..(3) The act of walking with a haughty, silly air.

III. 9. *attrib.*: **swash bank** (see quot.); **swash channel**, **swash-way**, 'a channel across a bank, or among shoals, as the noted instance between the Goodwin Sands' (Smyth *Sailor's Word-bk.*, 1867).

1852 WIGGINS *Embanking* 25 The *swash bank, which, having only to sustain the broken tops of the waves, is but 2½ feet high and 2½ feet wide at top. 1885 *Century Mag.* XXIX. 742 The *Minnesota*, taking the middle or *swash channel. 1839 *Civil Engin. & Arch. Jrnl.* II. 221/1 Forming track-paths across *swash-ways in Loch Dochfour. 1883 *Chambers's Jrnl.* 18 Aug. 525/2 Certain narrow fareways which seam the sands at low tide,..are called on the south side of the Roach 'swatch'-ways, but beyond the Crouch 'swash'-ways.

Swash, *sb.*[2], **swesh**. *Sc.* *Obs.* exc. *Hist.* Forms: 6 **swasche**, (**suasche**, **squasche**, **swach(e**, **swass**, **sc(h)osche**?), 6, 9 **swash**; 6 **swesch(e**, **swech(e**, (**suech**, **suis**, **suishe**, **swische**), 6, 9 **swesch**, **swesh**, 7 **swy(s)che**. [Perh. orig. in full *swasche*, *swesche*, or *swische ta(l)burne* (see TABORN *sb.*), but the orig. meaning and source of *swasche*, etc. are unknown.] A kind of drum. Also *attrib.* **swash-head**, a drum-head; **swash-man** = SWASHER[1].

1533 *Acc. Ld. High Treas. Scot.* VI. 159 For ane swasche talburne to the futmen xx s. 1541 *Ibid.* VII. 478 The twa Toddeis that playis upoun the Swische taburn. 1543-4 *Ibid.* VIII. 250 Thre playarris upon the swesche. 1560 ROLLAND *Seven Sages* 20 With trumpet, schalme, drum, squasche & clarioun. 1562 *Extr. Aberd. Reg.* (1844) I. 343 Passing throw the toun with ane swech. 1571 *Extr. Burgh Rec. Lanark* (Burgh Rec. Soc.) 55 That thei nychtly wache with the balleis fra the strak of the secund strak of the suishe. 1574-5 *Burgh Rec. Glasgow* (1876) I. 455 Item, to Thomas Downy for inputting of the schoscheheid vs. Item, for ane perchement skyn to Robert Muir to cover the scosche iij s. vj d. 1576 in *Maitl. Club Misc.* (1840) I. 343 For ane swasche to our moustiris iiijli. 1593 *Extr. Aberd. Regr.* (1848) II. 81 Andro Inglis, sweschman, commoun servand to the toun. 1598 in Pitcairn *Crim. Trials* II. 30 'Stryke þe swasch' and 'Ryng þe commoun bell'! 1625-6 *Charters* etc. *Peebles* (1872) 414 Item, gewine John Robeine for striking of the swyche, xij s. 1672 *Burgh Rec. Peebles* (1872) 336 At the stryking of the swysche.

¶ Misused for: A trumpet. Also *swash-trump*.

This is the only meaning given by Jamieson, 1808, on the authority of quot. 1609; cf. also the following, where the Latin original would seem to warrant such a meaning:—

1533 BELLENDEN *Livy* II. lxiv. (S. T. S.) 238 Horsmen with swasche and taberne [orig. *cornicinus tubicinesque in equis impositos*]. 1609 SKENE *Reg. Maj.*, *Stat. Gild* 143 After they heare the striak of the swesch (or the sound of the trumpet). 1819 TENNANT *Papistry Storm'd* (1827) 47 Wi' swesch-trump in his hand. 1871 WADDELL *Ps. in Scottis* xlvii. 5 God has gane up wi' a sugh; the Lord wi' the tout o' a swesch.

† **Swash** (swǫʃ), *sb.*[3] *Obs.* [Derived from or forming the radical of ASWASH *adv.* = aslant. Cf. SWASH *a.*[2]] **a.** *Turning*, etc., A figure or ornament the lines or mouldings of which lie obliquely to the axis of the work. **b.** *Printing.* The flourished extension characteristic of swash letters (see SWASH *a.*[2] 2).

1680 MOXON *Mech. Exerc.* xiv. 241 You set it to that Slope you intend the Swash on your Work shall have. *Ibid.* Explan. Terms L1 2 b, *Swash*. A *Swash* is a Figure whose

Circumference is not Round, but Oval; and whose Moldings lye not at Right Angles, but Oblique to the Axis of the Work. 1683 *Ibid.*, *Printing* xiii. ¶ 4 𝒬, whose Swashes come below the Foot-Line,..ought to have the..Sholder of that Swash Sculped down straight.

Swash, *a.*[1] [f. SWASH *sb.*[1]]

† **1.** = SWASHING *ppl. a.* 2. *Obs.*

1599 MINSHEU *Sp. Dict.*, *Dial.* (1623) 30 This wound hurts me not much, for it is giuen with the hand vpward, but beware of the swash blow [Spanish *el revés*], for I will draw it with the hand downwards.

2. † **a.** ? Swashbuckling, swaggering: = SWASHING *ppl. a.* 1. *Obs.* **b.** 'Swell', 'swagger', showy. *dial.*

c 1600 DAY *Begg. Bednall Gr.* II. ii. (1881) 39 Old Simsons son..that wears his great gall gaskins o' the Swash-fashion, with 8 or 10 gold laces of a side. 1635 J. GOWER *Pyrgomachia* A 3 b, Some others..Are of the rash-swash-fellowes band. 1713 S. SEWALL *Diary* 5 Nov., I first see Col. Tho. Noyes in a swash Flaxen Wigg. 1866 GREGOR *Banffsh. Gloss.*, *Swash*, (1) gaudy; showy..(2) Of ostentatious manners. 1877 *Holderness Gloss.*, *Swash*, showy; gaudy.

Swash (swǫʃ), *a.*[2] [app. SWASH *sb.*[3] used attrib.]

1. *Turning*, etc. Inclined obliquely to the axis of the work.

Swash-work, work in which the cuttings or mouldings traced round a cylinder are inclined to the axis; also called *pumped work*. *Swash-engine*, an apparatus for turning swash-work. *Swash-board*, *swash-plate*, 'a rotating, circular plate, inclined to the plane of its revolution so as to give a vertical reciprocation to the rod, whose foot rests thereupon, and which moves between lateral guides' (Knight *Dict. Mech.*, 1875); also called *pumping-plate*.

1680 MOXON *Mech. Exerc.* xiv. 241 To the Turning of Swash-Work you must have two such Puppets as the Fore-puppet described in § 22. *Ibid.*, Upon both the Flat sides of this Swash Board in a Diametrical Line is fastned upright an Arch of a Quadrant made of a Steel Plate... The convex edges of these Quadrants are cut into Notches,.. that according as you may have occasion to set the Swash-Board more or less a slope, you may be accommodated with a Notch or Tooth to set it at. *Ibid.* 242 These Oval-Engines, Swash-Engines, and all other Engines. 1688 HOLME *Armoury* III. 360/1 The Turning Engine [is] for the turning of Oval Work, Rose Work, and Swash Work. 1703 *Lond. Gaz.* No. 3887/4 A Gold Watch in a Grav'd Case..; with a Moco Stone Swash. 1812 P. NICHOLSON *Mech. Exerc.* 356 Turning is also of different kinds, as Circular Turning, Elliptic Turning, and Swash Turning.

2. *Printing.* Applied to old-style capital letters having flourished strokes designed to fill up unsightly gaps between adjacent letters.

1683 MOXON *Mech. Exerc.*, *Printing* xiii. ¶ 4 Swash-Letters, especially 𝒬. 1867 BRANDE & COX *Dict. Sci.*, etc., *Swash Letters*..have been revived of late years with the reintroduced old-fashioned types. 1899 DE VINNE *Pract. Typogr.* (1902) 271 *note*, An excellent form of old-style italic of bold face, with the swash letters and other features of quaintness.

Swash, *a.*[3] *dial.* [Cf. SWASHY.] Soft; also, fuddled.

1711 RAMSAY *On Maggy Johnstoun* vi, We did baith.. pish and spew, and yesk and maunt, Right swash I true. 1728 *Ramsay's Poems* II. Gloss., *Swash*, squat, fuddled. a 1800 PEGGE *Suppl. Grose*, *Swash*, and *Swashy*, soft, like fruit too ripe. Derb. 1888 *Sheffield Gloss.*

Swash (swǫʃ). *v.* [Echoic. Cf. SWASH *sb.*[1]]

1. *trans.* To dash or cast violently.

1577 HOLINSHED *Chron.* II. 444/2 The Archbyshop of Yorke..swasht him down, meaning to thrust himselfe in betwixt the Legate, and the Archb. of Canterbury. 1582 STANYHURST *Æneis* I. (Arb.) 19 This Queene wyld lightninges from clowds of Iuppiter hurling Downe swasht theyre nauy. 1710 RUDDIMAN *Douglas' Æneis* Gloss. s. v. *Squat*, Scot. *swash*, Ang. *squat* is to cast against the ground. 1866 GREGOR *Banffsh. Gloss.*

2. *intr.* To dash or move violently *about*; also occas. *refl.*

1583 GOLDING *Calvin on Deut.* cxxxi. 807/1 As a swyne when he hath once winded his meat, runnes on to swash himself in it [orig. *se fourrer là*]. 1609 HOLLAND *Amm. Marcell.* XXXI. vii. 413 On all sides swords swashed and darts flew as thicke as haile.

1831 CARLYLE *Sart. Res.* II. ii, If..your House fell, have I not seen five neighbourly Helpers appear next day; and swashing to and fro,..complete it again before nightfall? 1837 — *Fr. Rev.* II. IV. vi, Your dusty Mill of Valmy..may furl its canvas, and cease swashing and circling. 1879 STEVENSON *Trav. Donkey* 139 A jolting trot that set the oats swashing in the pocket of my coat. 1889 'MARK TWAIN' *Yankee at Crt. K. Arthur* vii, The gusts of wind were flaring the torches and making the shadows swash about.

3. To make a noise as of swords clashing or of a sword beating on a shield (cf. SWASHBUCKLER); to fence with swords; to bluster with or as with weapons; to lash *out*; hence, to swagger.

1556 [see SWASHING *vbl. sb.* 1 and *ppl. a.* 1]. 1565 COOPER *Thesaurus* s.v. *Concrepo*, *Concrepare gladiis ad scuta*, to swashe, or make a noyse with swoordes agaynst tergattes. 1593 LODGE *Will. Longbeard* C 3 b, He overmaistered [them] by his attendants, swashing out in the open streets upon everie light occasion. 1593 *Bacchus Bountie* in *Harl. Misc.* (Malh.) II. 265, I giue them right to sweare it out with wordes, I giue them might to swash it out with swerdes. 1600 BRETON *Pasquil's Fooles Cap* xl, Shee that..Ruffin-like, will sweare, and swash it out. 1611 FLORIO, *Cortellare*, to fence, to swash with swords, to swagger. 1649 Z. BOYD *Last Battell* 673 [They], in hight of stomacke, ruffling & swashing, did tread vpon God's turtles. a 1825 FORBY *Voc. E. Anglia*, *Swash*, to affect valour; to vapour or swagger. 1837 CARLYLE *Fr. Rev.* I. VII. ii, Captains of horse and foot go swashing with 'enormous white cockades'. 1850 — *Two-hundred & Fifty Y. Ago* Ess. 1857 IV. 321 Bucklers went out..'about the twentieth of Queen Elizabeth'; men do not now swash with them, or fight in that way. 1890 *Pall Mall G.* 1 July 2/2 When Mr. Caine joined Lord Randolph in swashing at the Government. 1893 BARING-GOULD *Cheap Jack Zita* xxxv. III. 111 He will swash about with his toasting-fork as if 'twere a cutlass.

4. *trans.* To dash or splash (water) about; to dash water upon, souse with water or liquid; (of water) to beat with a splash against.

1589 FLEMING *Virg. Georg.* IV. 64 *note*, Gargarise, or swash in and about the mouth. 1656 [? J. SERGEANT] tr. *T. White's Peripat. Inst.* 67 As it happens in liquids when they are swash'd up and down. 1721 BAILEY, To *Swash*, to make fly about, as Water. 1828 MOIR *Mansie Wauch* xix. 281 Having a bucket..I swashed down such showers on the top of the flames. 1836 W. IRVING *Astoria* v. (1849) 61 For three hours and a half did they tug..at the oar, swashed occasionally by the surging waves of the open sea. 1862 G. H. KINGSLEY *Sport & Trav.* (1900) 375 Men swishing and swashing and brooming about. 1863 W. W. STORY *Roba di R.* II. i. 1 The boards on which the meats are laid are swashed constantly with water. 1876 R. BRIDGES *Growth of Love* xxvii, What grisly beast of scaly chine That champ'd the ocean-wrack and swashed the brine. 1887 *Pall Mall G.* 28 Sept. 8/1 He added that the excursion boats also swashed the *Thistle*, damaging her to a certain extent.

5. *intr.* Of water or of an object in water: To dash with a splashing sound; to splash *about*.

1836 W. IRVING *Astoria* lviii. (1849) 477 The next wave threw their bodies back upon the deck, where they remained swashing backward and forward. 1843 CARLYLE *Misc.*, *Dr. Francia* (1857) IV. 269 You have all got linen bathing-garments, and can swash about with some decency. 1847 H. MELVILLE *Omoo* x, The water fairly poured down in sheets..swashing about. 1876 HOLLAND *Sev. Oaks* v. 65 Flocks of ducks..swashed down with a fluttering ricochet into the water. 1891 H. HUTCHINSON *Fairway Island* 25 The sea at the cliff foot—swashing ever louder and louder.

† **Swasha·do**. *nonce-wd.* [f. SWASH *v.* + -ADO.] A swashbuckler.

1663 *Proposal to use No Conscience* 4 A company of Swashado's beat the Watch.

Swashbuckler (swǫ·ʃbɒklǝɹ). [f. SWASH *v.* + BUCKLER *sb.*[2]; hence *lit.* one who makes a noise by striking his own or his opponent's shield with his sword.] A swaggering bravo or ruffian; a noisy braggadocio.

1560 PILKINGTON *Expos. Aggeus* ii. 8-9 (1562) 266 Too be a dronkarde,..a gamner, a swashe-buckeler he hath not alowed thee one mite. 1593 NASHE *Christ's T.* Wks. 1904 II. 148 No Smithfield ruffianly Swashbuckler will come of with such harshe hell-raking othes as they. 1648 JENKYN *Blind Guide* i. 14 He speaking..more like a swash-buckler than a Bishop. a 1680 BUTLER *Charact.*, *Hermetic Philos.*, Make those spiritual Swash-Bucklers deliver up their Weapons, and keep the Peace. a 1721 PRIOR *Dial. Dead*, *Charles & Clenard* Wks. 1907 II. 218 When ever You have Thought and Conquered with your Ruyters & Swashbucklers. 1809 W. IRVING *Knickerb.* VI. i. (1861) 184 He had a garrison after his own heart..guzzling, deep-drinking swashbucklers. 1828 SCOTT *F. M. Perth* iv, Neither did his frank and manly deportment..bear the least resemblance to that of the bravoes or swash-bucklers of the day. 1899 E. GOSSE *Life J. Donne* I. 32 He shows himself..a daring..young swash-buckler of poetry.

attrib. 1680 MELTON *Astrolog.* 13 What a quarrelling Swash buckler Mars. 1672 MARVELL *Reh. Transp.* I. 260 Men..do..cut and slash about vestments..rather in a swash-buckler and Hectoring way, than..like..Christians. 1816 SINGER *Hist. Cards* 258 *note*, The swash-buckler manners of the youth of fashion in the reign of Elizabeth. 1896 GEN. H. PORTER in *Century Mag.* Nov. 25 The most approved swashbuckler style of melodrama.

Hence (*nonce-wds.*) **Swa·shbu·cklerdom**, **-ism**, **-bu·cklery**, the conduct of a swashbuckler; also **Swa·shbu·cklering** = SWASHBUCKLING *a.*

1862 MRS. SPEID *Last Years Ind.* 91 A sort of paralytic attempt at *swashbucklerdom and swagger. 1884 *19th Cent.* Dec. 1023 The *swash-bucklering and speculative fashion which the Republican supporters..extolled. 1914 G. K CHESTERTON *Flying Inn* 180 Such swashbucklering comedy. 1892 *Review of Rev.* 14 Apr. 360/1 Mr. Gladstone has..been so sedulous an opponent of *swashbucklerism. 1889 D. HANNAY *Life F. Marryat* 21 He would have condemned..such a piece of frantic *swashbucklery as the last fight of the *Revenge*.

Swa·shbu·ckling, *a.* [f. SWASHBUCKLER (apprehended as an agent-n. in -ER[1]) + -ING[2].] Acting like, or characteristic of the conduct of, a swashbuckler; noisily swaggering, blustering. So **Swa·shbu·ckling** *sb.*

a 1693 *Urquhart's Rabelais* III. xlii. 349 The huff, snuff, ..swash-buckling High Germans. 1863 SALA in *Temple Bar* IX. 65 The Hungarian are stout wines, of a swashbuckling flavour. 1865 KINGSLEY *Herew.* xxxii, A swashbuckling ruffian. 1888 *Boston* (Mass.) *Transcript* 7 July 4/4 Swashbucklers are generally satisfied with swashbuckling. 1889 T. B. REED in *Boy's Own Paper* 3 Aug. 696/1 A score or more of swashbuckling 'prentices were on board the ship. 1894 *Athenæum* 27 Oct. 565/3 The one occasionally degenerates into artifice, and the other into literary swashbuckling.

Hence (back-formation) **Swa·shbu·ckle** *v.*, to swagger noisily, act like a blustering bravo.

1897 *Westm. Gaz.* 6 Jan. 3/1 He strikes one as a bravo, he swashbuckles and swaggers.

Swasher[1], **swesher**. *Sc.* *Obs.* exc. *Hist.* In 6 **swasche(a)r**, **swacher**, **suescher**, **swescher**, **-eour**. [f. SWASH *sb.*[2], SWESH + -ER[1].] A drummer.

15.. *Aberd. Reg.* (Jam.) Commoun tabernar and swescher. 1576 in *Maitl. Club Misc.* (1840) II. 340 Gevin Carsane the swaschear that day we moustirit xxx s. 1600 in Pitcairn *Crim. Trials* II. 245 To the townes twa swascheris.

Swasher[2] (swǫ·ʃǝɹ). [f. SWASH *v.* + -ER[1].] A swashbuckler; a blustering braggart or ruffian; *Sc.* a swaggerer, showy fellow. See also quot. 1866.

1589 [? NASHE] *Almond for Parrat* Ded. 3 Neither must you thinke his worship is to pure to be such a swasher. 1599 SHAKS. *Hen. V*, III. ii. 28 As young as I am, I haue obseru'd these three Swashers. 1619 A. NEWMAN *Pleas. Vis.* 30, I no blaspheming Roarer was, No Swasher, no Repent-too-late. 1621 BURTON *Anat. Mel.* I. ii. III. xv. 170 They cannot ..make congies, which euery common swasher can doe. 1821 SCOTT *Kenilw.* iii, Known for a swasher and a desperate Dick. 1866 GREGOR *Banffsh. Gloss.*, *Swasher*, (1) a person of tall stature, and somewhat ostentatious manners. (2) Anything whatever large and attracting attention. 1889 T. STODDART *Angling Songs* 300 Sic a swasher I ween Is rare to be seen.

Swashing (swǫ·ʃiŋ), *vbl. sb.* [f. SWASH *v.* + -ING[1].]

1. Ostentatious behaviour; swaggering.

(Cf. SWASH *sb.*[1] 7, 8, SWASH *a.*[1] 2, SWASH *v.* 3, SWASHER[2], SWASHING *ppl. a.* 1.)

1556 OLDE *Antichrist* 138 b, The ruffling and ioyly swashing of a princes courte. 1587 GREENE *Carde of Fancie* Wks. (Grosart) IV. 14 To see my sonne,..consume his time..in swearing and swashing.

2. Violent or noisy striking.

a 1661 FULLER *Worthies, London* II. (1662) 199 Swash-Buckler [so called] from swashing, or making a noise on Bucklers.

3. Dashing or splashing of water.

1829 C'TESS SPENCER *Let.* 3 Nov. in *Corr. Lady Lyttelton* viii. (1912) 215 Only that we still keep up that rare and useless custom of washing and swashing, we should pig it as comfortably as they wallow in Italy. 1864 CARLYLE *Fredk. Gt.* XVII. v. IV. 558 The primordial diluviums and world-old torrents,..with such storming, gurgling, and swashing. 1870 J. SHARPE in *Eng. Mech.* 4 Mar. 608/3 'Rushing' and 'swashing' in millstones is caused by not driving the stone from its centre. 1872 O. W. HOLMES *Poet Breakf.-t.* xi. (1885) 287 Sparrows..keep up such a swashing and swabbing and spattering round..the water basins.

Swashing (swǫ·ʃiŋ), *ppl. a.* Also 7 **swassing**. [f. SWASH *v.* + -ING[2].]

1. Characterized by ostentation, or by showy or blustering behaviour; swaggering; swashbuckling; dashing. (Cf. prec. 1.)

1556 OLDE *Antichrist* 147, I speake not now of mytred bishoppes, and swashing abbottes. 1600 SHAKS. *A. Y. L.* I. iii. 122 Weele haue a swashing and a marshall outside. c 1600 DAY *Begg. Bednall Gr.* IV. i. (1881) 77 The name and habit of some swashing Italian or French Noble-man. 1665 G. HAVERS *P. della Valle's Trav. E. India* 181 By profession Souldiers, sufficiently swashing and brave. 1684 OTWAY *Atheist* IV. i, A blustering, roaring, swashing Shark. 1809 MALKIN *Gil Blas* IV. iii. ¶ 4 With the swashing outside of a gay spark. 1821 SCOTT *Kenilw.* iv, Lay aside your swashing look. 1885 STEVENSON *Prince Otto* I. iv, The song went to a rough, swashing, popular air.

2. Applied to a particular stroke in fencing, perh. the 'stramazon'; also of a weapon: Slashing with great force. In mod. use only in reminiscences of Shakspere. (Cf. SWASH *a.*[1] 1, WASHING.)

1611 BEAUM. & FL. *Philaster* v. iv, With this swashing blow,..I could hulk your Grace, and hang you up cross-leg'd. c 1615 *Shaks.'s Rom. & Jul.* I. i. 70 (Qo. 4) Gregorie, remember thy swashing [Qq. 2 & 3, *Fo.* washing] blowe. 1670 MILTON *Hist. Eng.* II. Wks. 1851 V. 70 The Britans had a certain skill with their broad swashing Swords and short Bucklers. 1882 G. A. LAWRENCE *Barren Honour* I. x. 210 Even 'Lanky Jem' recovered after a while from Somers' swashing blow. 1876 TREVELYAN *Life & Lett. Macaulay* II. xii. 253 *note*, He soon showed that he had not forgotten his swashing blow. 1905 *Times* 17 June 4/6 [He] is a swashing foe of all accepted or debated theories but his own.

3. Of water, etc.: Dashing and splashing.

1620 J. TAYLOR (Water P.) *Praise Hemp-seed* (1623) 31 Drencht with the swassing waues, and stewd in sweat. 1853 KANE *Grinnell Exp.* xiv. (1856) 101 Rendered dangerous.. by the swashing ice and a growing fog.

Hence **Swa·shingly** *adv.*, swaggeringly; in a swashbuckling style.

1664 COTTON *Scarron.* IV. (1741) 79 He wore a Hat Instead of Sattin lac'd with Fat, Which being limber grown we find Most swashingly pinned up behind. 1891 *Sat. Rev.* 15 Aug. 179/2 Mr. Balfour spoke..swashingly about Sir William Harcourt.

† **Swa·shly**, *adv.* *Obs.* [f. SWASH *int.* or *a.*[1] + -LY[2].] With a sound of dashing or splashing.

1582 STANYHURST *Æneis* II. (Arb.) 50 Their tayls with croompled knot twisting swashlye they wrigled.

Swash-man: see SWASH *sb.*[2]

Swash-pen. [f. SWASH *v.* + PEN *sb.*[1], after *swashbuckler*.] A literary braggadocio.

1593 G. HARVEY *Pierce's Super.* 135 Meridarpax..neuer made such a hauocke of the miserable frogges: as this Swash-pen would make of all English writers.

† **Swashruter**. *Obs.* If not a misprint, ? a combination of SWASHBUCKLER and SWARTRUTTER.

1582 STANYHURST *Æneis* I. 15 Then sootherne swashruter [orig. *procacibus Austris*]..Flundge vs on high shelueflats.

Swash-work: see SWASH *a.*[2]

Swashy (swǫ·ʃi), *a.* [f. SWASH *sb.*[1] or *v.* + -Y.] Sloppy, watery. Also *fig.* 'watery', 'washy'.

1796 J. OWEN *Trav. Europe* I. 70 Some part of the track ..was piled into heaps of swashy clay. 1803 J. BUNTING *Let.* 23 Sept., in *Life* (1859) I. x. 182 When I hear such preaching as Mr Jay's, I..wonder that the people should ever like to listen to my poor swashy sermons. 1876 *Whitby Gloss.*, *Swashy*, wet ground. 'Swashy stuff', poor beverage. 1890 *Temple Bar* Sept. 127 The pavement was swashy with three inches of half-melted snow.

Swasion, **-ive**, obs. ff. SUASION, SUASIVE.

†Swa·sivious, a. Obs. rare—¹. [f. It. suasivo SUASIVE + -IOUS.] Agreeably persuasive.

1592 R. D. Hypnerotomachia 39 b. With pleasurable action, magnetly gestures, swasivious behaviours.

Swass, Swassing, var. SWASH sb.², SWASHING ppl. a.

[Swastika (swæ·stĭkă). Also svast-, -ica. [Skr. svastika, f. svasti well-being, fortune, luck, f. sū good + astĭ being (l. as to be).] A primitive symbol or ornament of the form of a cross with equal arms with a limb of the same length projecting at right angles from the end of each arm, all in the same direction and (usually) clockwise; also called GAMMADION and FYLFOT. Also attrib.

1871 ALABASTER Wheel of Law 397 On the great toe is the Trisul. On each side of the others a Swastika. 1883 E. B. C. ROBERTSON in Proc. Berw. Nat. Club IX. No. 3. 516 In Japan...the cross-like symbol of the sun, the Swastika, is found...

Swat (swɒt), sb.¹ north. dial. and U.S. Also **swot**. [f. SWAT v.¹ Cf. SQUAT sb.¹] A smart or violent blow. Also, a lump.

Swat, a., adv. and dial. var. SQUAT a.

Swat, sb.³ dial. var. of SQUAT v.

Swat (swɒt), v.¹ Also 7 swatt, 9 swot. [north. dial. and U.S. variant of SQUAT v.]

1. intr. To sit down; to squat.

2. trans. To hit with a smart slap or a violent blow; also, to dash. Chiefly U.S.

Swat, sb.² & v.², hard worker: see SWOT sb.

Swat, a., obs. and dial. var. SQUAT a.

Swatch (swɒtʃ), sb.¹ Sc. and north. Also 6–7 swache, 7 suasche, swacch. [Origin unknown.]

1. †The 'foil' or 'counterstock' of a tally (obs.)

2. The space covered by a sweep of the mower's scythe; the width of grass or corn so cut.

3. As a measure of grass-land: a longitudinal division of a field, reckoned by the breadth of one sweep of the scythe. local.

Swatch (swɒtʃ), sb.² Obs. exc. dial. [app. an irreg. variant of SWATH v.] Cf. dial. swatch = SWATHE v.] A row (of corn or grass) cut.

Swatch (swɒtʃ), sb.³ [In local English use chiefly in eastern counties. Its relation to SWASH sb.¹ 3 is not clear.] A passage or channel of water lying between sandbanks or between a sandbank and the shore.

Swatch, v. Obs. rare. Variant of SQUATCH v.

Swatching (swɒ·tʃɪŋ), vbl. sb. [Origin unknown.] A method of taking sea(s): see quot. (1901).

Swath (swɒθ, swɔθ), swathe (sweɪð). Forms: 1 swæþ, swaþu, 3 swaðe, (4 swethe, 6 swaþde, 7 swaithe, swath, 7 swathe, 9 dial. swod, sweath). [OE. swæþ (d-), n., swaþu str. f.]

1. A track, trace. lit. and fig. Obs.

2. The space covered by a sweep of the scythe; the width of grass or corn so cut.

Swath (swɒθ), v. Sc. and north. Also 6–7 swache, 7 suasche, swacch. [Origin unknown.]

Swathe (sweɪð), sb. Forms: 1 swaþu, 3–4 swaþde, 7 swath. [OE. swæþ (d-), n.]

Swathe (sweɪð), sb.² Also 7–8 swath, swathe. [Obs. rare.]

Swathe (sweɪð), v.¹ [f. SWATHE sb.²]

†Swath-band, swathe-band. Obs. Forms: 4 suæsbend, 6 swathband, swabband, 6–7 swathe-band, (9 dial.) swath-band. [f. SWATHE sb. + BAND sb.²] Cf. SWATHING-BANDS.]

Swath-clouts, sb. pl. Obs. Also 4 clout; 6 swathe. [f. stem of SWATHE v. + CLOUT sb.] Cf. SWATHING-CLOUTS. Swaddling-clothes.

Swathe (sweɪð), sb.³ 2–3 swaith, swaþ. [OE. *swaeþ (?), prob., only in dat. pl. swaþum; for related forms see SWATHE, SWADDLE, SWEDDLE.]

1. A band of linen, woollen, or other material in which something is enveloped; a wrapping; sometimes, a single fold or winding of such; also collect. sing. & pl.

†Swathe-band, sb. Obs. = SWATH-BAND.

Swathed (sweɪðd, poet. sweɪð·id), ppl. a.¹ SWATHE v.¹ + -ED¹.]

Swathel (sweɪð·əl), sb. Obs. rare. [Cf. SWADDLE.]

Swather¹ (sweɪð·ər), sb. rare. [f. SWATHE v.¹]

Swatt, Swatte: see SWEAT v., SWOTE Obs.

Swatter (swɒt·ər), v. Sc. and north. dial. [Echoic. Cf. SQUATTER.] Also intr. to swadder, swodder (of serpents), to splash in water (Kilian), dial. swadderin in the latter sense.

Swathing (sweɪð·ɪŋ), vbl. sb.

Swathing-band. Usually pl.

Swathing-clothes, sb. pl. Obs. = SWADDLING-CLOTHES.

Swathing-clouts, sb. pl. Obs. = SWADDLING-CLOUTS.

Swattle (swɒt·əl), v. Sc. and north. dial. [f. the root as prec. + frequent. suffix -LE. Cf. G. dial. schwatteln to splash, etc.]

1. intr. To make a splashing or spluttering noise in or with water. (Cf. prec. 1.)

2. To fritter away (as time, money).

Swattle (swɒt·əl), sb. Obs. rare. [Etym. dub.]

Swatty (swɒt·ɪ), a. U.S. slang. [f. SWAT sb. + -Y¹.]

Swaty: see SWEATY a.

Swauk, Sc. form of SWALK sb.

Swaule, obs. variant of SWALE sb.¹

Swave, obs. form of SUAVE; variant of SWATHE v.

Swaver (sweɪ·vər), v. north. dial. Also 4 swafre. [? f. Scand. stem of SWALE.] intr. To stagger, totter. Also fig. to decline away from.

Swavigerent: see SWAVILOQUENT.

Swaviloquent, the variant of SWASILOQUENT.

Swavile, obs. variant of SWALE sb.¹

Sway (sweɪ), sb.¹ Forms: 4–5 sweghe, 4–5 swegh, 4–6 swey, 5 sweigh, swey, 6 suegh, swawe, swagh, 5 sway, dial. swee, sweye. [f. SWAY v., with sense f. cf. EFris. zwei movement in a curve. In branch II partly of different origin: for sense 12 cf. SWEY sb.²; for sense 13, prob. a. ON. sveigr a switch.]

I. The action of the verb SWAY.

Swale, obs. variant of SWALE sb.

Sway (sweɪ), sb.² Forms: 4–5 sweighe, 4–5 sweigh, 4–6 sey (5 dial.) swey, 5 swegh, swegh, swey, 6 swey, 7 sway, swow, sweyo, 6 swaye. [In branch I f. SWAY v.; with sense f. cf. EFris. swei movement in a curve.]

Swinger, f. Sc. Florence v. ii. This is the man that carries The sway, and swinge of the Court.

Sway (sweɪ), v. Forms: 4 swegȝe, 4–5 sweye, 4–7 (8–9 dial.) sweye, (6 swaie, swaye, 4–6 sweghe, 6 swowe, 6–7 sway, 7 swey; pa. t. and pple. 4 sweyed, (6 sweye, swawe), 6 swayed. [? a. ON. sveigja to swing, bend, make to bend.]

I. 1. intr. To move or swing first to one side and then to the 'other, as a hanging or pivoted object: often amplified by phr., e.g. backwards and forwards, to and fro, from side to side.

II. 2. intr. To go, move. Obs.

Sway, obs. Sc. form of SWA.

Sway-, the combining form of SWAY sb. used in comb. sway-bar, a circular piece of timber or iron; the fore-bounds of a carriage.

Sway-able, *a. rare.* [f. SWAY *v.* + -ABLE.] Capable of being swayed or influenced.

Sway-backed, *a.* [Of Scandinavian origin: cf. obs. Da. *sveiryget*, also Da. *sveiryget*, † *svegrygget*, Sw. *thai. ryggoryg.* in the same sense.] Of an animal, esp. a horse: Having a downward curvature of the spinal column; strained in the back, as by overwork. Also *transf.*

So **Sway-back**; also as *sb.* = sway-backed condition (Dorland *Med. Dict.*).

Swayed, *ppl. a., pa. pple. of* SWAY *v.*

† **I.** Of a horse: Having a depression in the spinal column, caused by strain. Also *back-swayed*, SWAY-BACKED.

Swayer (swē'ŏr). [f. SWAY *v.* + -ER.] One who or that which sways, wields, or rules.

Swayful, *a.* [f. SWAY *sb.* + -FUL.] Able to exercise sway, powerful.

Swayl, swayle, obs. ff. SWALE, SWEAL.

Swaying (swē'iŋ), *vbl. sb.* [f. SWAY *v.* + -ING¹.]

1. The action of the verb SWAY; movement to and fro; vacillation; influencing, controlling, etc.

2. Swaying *Obs. or arch.*

3. Exercising power, influence, or control; influential, controlling. *Obs. exc. as* the second element of compounds, as *all-swaying*.

Swaying, *ppl. a.* [f. SWAY *v.* + -ING².]

Swayl, swale (swāl), *sb. dial.* Also *swalle, sweel.* [f. next.] A blaze, flame; the guttering of a candle.

Sweal, swale (swīl, swēl), *sb. dial.* Also *swaile, sweel.* [f. next.] A blaze, flame; the guttering of a candle.

Sweal, swale (swīl, swēl), *v. Now dial.* Forms: 1 swelan, swelen, *pa. t.* swelde, 3-4 swele, 4 swale, (also 9 swele, 4, 7-9 swale, 5 swelle, sweyle, 6-7 sweale, 7-9 sweal, 8-9 sweel, (9 squall, swele, sweel, etc.), 6-9 sweal, 7- swale. OE. *swelan* wk. trans. to burn, related to OE. *swelen* str. intr. to burn (which may be in part also the source of this word) = (M)LG. *swelen* to singe, wither (of grass), make hay, etc. (whence G. *schwelen*, *schwülen* to burn slowly without flame, NFris. *swäl* to singe, EFris. *smil* to glow), OHG. *swilizzon* to burn, smoulder.

Swealing, swaling, *ppl. a.* [f. SWEAL *v.* + -ING¹.] Burning; singing : for special uses see quots. and SWEAL.

Swealing, swaling, *vbl. sb.* [f. SWEAL *v.* + -ING¹.] Burning, singing : (of a candle) guttering.

Swealt, obs. form of SWELT.

† **Sweam, swem**, *sb.* Forms: 3 swem, 5 swayme, swemm, sweme, 6 swaime, 7 swaim, sweam. [? SWEAM *v.*] (Cf. SWINE.)

† **Sweam, swem**, *v. Obs.* [OE. *sweman*, found only in the compound *ásweman* to grieve or afflicted. Cf. prec.]

1. *trans.* To afflict, grieve. Hence **Sweam'mand** *ppl. a.*, afflicting, grievous.

2. *intr.* To grieve, mourn. Also in *refl.* and *vbl. sb.*

3. *pass.* and *intr.* To overcome with faintness.

Sweam, dial. form of SQUEAL.

Sweamish, dial. form of SQUEAMISH.

Sweande, obs. pr. pple. of SWAY *v.*

Sweap, variant of SWAPE *v.*, SWEEP.

Sweaple, variant of SWIPPLE.

Swear (swēŏr), *sb. non colloq.* [f. SWEAR *v.*]

An act of swearing; an oath.

I. A form of swearing; an oath.

Swear (swēŏr), *v.* Pa. *t.* swore, (*swore, sware*); pa. pple. sworn (swōŏn). Forms: 1-2 swerian; pa. t. *swær* (1)gan, suerian, 1 swerigan); pa. pple. sworen. ...

Swearer (swē'rŏr). Forms: 4 sweryer, swerrer, sweorer, 4-6 swerer, swerar, 5 swerar, sweriere, 6 sweare, 7- swearer. [f. SWEAR *v.* + -ER¹.] One who swears.

1. One who takes an oath; *spec.* one who takes or has taken an oath of allegiance; a juror; a perjurer. Also *non-swearer*.

2. *attrib.*

Swearing, *ppl. a.* [-ING².] That swears.

1. That takes or has taken an oath, esp. an oath of allegiance.

2. That utters profane oaths. Also with *objective of*.

Swearing, *vbl. sb.* [f. SWEAR *v.* + -ING¹.] The action of the verb SWEAR.

1. The action of taking an oath; affirmation by oath.

2. The uttering of a profane oath; the use of profane language.

Hence **Swea'ringly** *adv.*

Swear-word, *colloq.* (orig. *U.S.*) [f. SWEAR *v.* + WORD *sb.*] A profane or obscene word; an oath.

Sweat (swet), *sb.* Forms: 4 suet, 4, (8 *Sc.*) sweet, 4-6 swete, swote, swote-, swoot, swot, 4-7 swet, 6-9 swete, sweat, *Sc.* swat, 5 swat. [ME. *swet*, *swote*, alteration of *sweot* (see SWOT) after SWEAT *v.*]

1. The moisture that is excreted through the pores of the skin.

Swedenborgian ... Hence **Swedenborgianism**.

Swedge, ... Also **attrib.** So **Swedge** v., = SWAGE v.

Swedian, obs. rare.

Swedish (swī′diʃ), a. and sb. Also **Swethish**, **Sweedish**. [f. SWEDE n. + -ISH.]

Swedle, obs. variant of SWEDDLE.

Swee (swī). [Echoic.] A South African species of waxbill (*Estrilda dufresnii*), so called from its call.

Swee, dial. form of SWAY.

Sweek, obs. form of SWEEK.

Sweel (swīl), v. Sc. Forms: 6 sweil, 7 swill, 7-8 swyle, 8 swayl, 9 sweal, sweel.

Sweel, obs. form of SQUAIL.

Sweel, dial. f. SQUEAL; Obs. f. SWELL; dial. f. SWILL, SWIVEL.

Sweem, Sc. f. SWIM. **Sweem-**, var. SWEEM; dial. var. SWEEM. **Sweens**, var. SOWENS.

Sweeny (swī′ni). U.S. Also **swinny**.

Sweep (swīp), v. Forms: 4 swepe, 5-7 swepe, 6-7 sweep, 7 sweep.

SWEET.

Sweetbread (swī′bred). (Also formerly as *sweetbread sb.*, but the reason for the name is not obvious.)

1. The pancreas, or the thymus gland, of an animal, esp. as used for food (distinguished respectively as *heart*, *stomach*, or *belly sweetbread* and *throat*, *gullet*, or *neck sweetbread*): esteemed a delicacy.

+2. a Obs. rare.

Sweet-brier, briar. (Also as two words.) Forms: see SWEET and BRIER *sb.* A species of rose, the Eglantine, *Rosa rubiginosa* (and some other species, as *R. micrantha*), having strong hooked prickles, pink single flowers, and small aromatic leaves; freq. cultivated in gardens.

Sweeten (swī′t'n), *v.* [f. SWEET *a.* + -EN [1].]

1. *trans.* To make sweet to the taste; *esp.* to add sugar or other sweet substance (to food or drink) so as to impart a sweet flavour; also *absol.*

Sweetened (swī′t'nd), *ppl.a.* [f. prec. + -ED [1].]

Sweetener (swī′t'naz). [f. as prec. + -ER [1].]

Sweetening, *vbl. sb.* [f. as prec. + -ING [1].]

Sweetful, *a.* Now dial. [f. SWEET *a.* + -FUL [1].]

Sweet-gale. Also 7 -gaule. [f. SWEET *a.* and GALE *sb.* [1].] The bog myrtle, *Myrica Gale*.

Sweet-grass. Any kind of grass (or herb called 'grass') of a sweet taste serving as fodder.

Sweetheart, *sb.* Forms: see SWEET *a.* and HEART *sb.*

Sweetheart, *v.* [f. prec.]

Sweet-hearted, *a.* [f. SWEET *a.* + HEART *sb.* + -ED [2].] Hence **Sweet-heartedness**.

Sweetie. usually in *pl.* sweeties. orig. and chiefly *Sc.* Also **sweety**. 8 -ie. Earlier than SWEET *sb.* 9. [f. SWEET *a.* or *sb.* + -IE, -Y.] A sweetmeat, lollipop. Also, sweet cake or the like.

Sweet John. *Obs.* A name for the narrower-leaved varieties of a species of pink, *Dianthus barbatus*.

Sweetish (swī′tiʃ). *a.* [f. SWEET *a.* + -ISH [1].] Somewhat or slightly sweet.

Sweetkin. *Obs. rare*. [f. SWEET *sb.* or *a.* + -KIN.] A term of endearment.

Sweeting (swī′tiŋ). Also 4-6 sweting, 4 suetyng, 5 swetyng. [f. SWEET *a.* + -ING [3].]

1. A 'sweet' or pleasant person; a dear, a darling, a sweetheart. Chiefly as an endearing form of address.

Sweetheartship (*nonce-wd.*): see -DOM, -SHIP.

Sweetleaf (swīt'līf). A tree or shrub, *Symplocos tinctoria*, of the southern U.S., having sweet-flavoured leaves eaten by horses and cattle.

Sweeting (swīt'iŋ), rare. [f. SWEET a. + -ING 1.]

1. A term of endearment for a beloved person : = SWEETING 1.

2. A small sweet thing.

Sweetly (swīt'li). Forms : see SWEET a. and v.; MHG. *swâ ́tlîche*, MHG. *swetlîche*, MHG. *swetlîche* as ME. *swotelîche*, SOOTLY.] In a sweet manner; with sweetness.

1. With a sweet taste or smell.

2. With a sweet sound or voice.

3. So as to be pleasing to the mind or the feelings; pleasurably; comfortably.

4. Qualifying pres. and past participles.

5. So as to be pleasing to the sight or the æsthetic sense; delightfully, charmingly.

b. ironically, esp. with *pay*, *cost*.

Sweetmeat (swīt'mēt), *sb*. [See SWEET *a*. and MEAT *sb*. Cf. OE. *swôtmêtas*, *swôtmêttas* delicacies.]

1. *collect. pl.* (and † *sing*) +Sweet food, as sugared cakes or pastry, confectionery (*obs.*); preserved or candied fruits, sugared nuts, etc.; also globules, lozenges, 'drops,' or 'sticks' made of sugar and fruit or other flavouring or filling; *sing.* one of these.

2. Of smell or odour : Fragrance.

3. Of sound : Melodiousness, musical quality.

4. Of wound : Pleasantness, agreeableness.

b. A sweet sound or tone, *rare*.

Sweetness (swīt'nes). Forms : see SWEET *a*. [OE. *swêtnes*. Cl. MDu. *soetnisse*; also SOOTNESS (OE. *swôtness*).] The quality of being sweet, *concr.* something sweet.

1. Sweetness of taste.

b. *Phr.* (sweetness and light, taken from Swift as quot. 1704 above) and used with æsthetic or moral reference (cf. 7.).

c. *concr.* Something sweet to the taste; a sweet substance.

d. Of smell or odour : Fragrance.

2. Pleasantness to the mind or feelings; delightfulness.

3. Pleasant feeling, delight, pleasure; also, a source of delight or pleasure. Now *rare* or merged in other senses.

4. In specific uses, denoting various desirable physical qualities, *e.g.* freshness (as opp. to saltness, putridity, etc.), mellowness (of soil), etc.

7. § 8. Addiction to sweet things; self-indulgence. *Obs. rare.*

Sweet pea. The common *Lathyrus odoratus*, a climbing annual leguminous plant, indigenous to Sicily, cultivated in numerous varieties for its showy variously-coloured sweet-scented flowers.

Sweet-scented (stress variable), *a*. Having a sweet scent; sweet-smelling, fragrant.

Sweet-sop. An imitation of the musical chirp of a bird (with suggestion of SWEET *a*.).

Sweet-water, sweet-water.
1. (as two words) Fresh water.
2. *attrib.* (usually with hyphen or as one word).

Sweet rush.
1. The lemon-grass or camel's hay, *Andropogon Schœnanthus*; also the allied species *A. laniger*.
2. The sweet flag, *Acorus Calamus*.

Sweet-smelling (stress variable), *a*. Smelling sweetly.

Sweetwort (swīt'wort), *sb*. [Wort *sb*.] A sweet-flavoured wort; *esp.* the infusion of malt, before the hops are added in the manufacture of beer.

Sweetish (swīt'iʃ), *a*. [f. SWEET *a*. + -ISH.] Somewhat sweet.

Sweety (swīt'i). *sb*. *Sc.* *dial.* A piece of confectionery.

Sweetwood (swīt'wūd). A name for various trees and shrubs, chiefly lauraceous, of the West Indies and tropical America, some of which furnish valuable timber; also the timber itself.

Swell (swel), *sb*. [f. SWELL *v*.]

Swell (swel), *v*. Pa.t. **swelled** (sweld). pa.pple. **swelled** (sweld), **swollen** (swōu'l'n), **swoln** (swōln). Forms : 1 **swelan**, 3–7 *pa.pple.* **swelle**, 5 **swal**, 5–6 **swell**, 6– **swell**. pa.t. 1 **sweal**, **sweol**, 3–4 **swal**, **swol**, 3–6 **swalle**, 4 **swelle**, *dial.* **swal**, 4 **swole**, 5 **swal**, 6–7 **swole**, 6–9 **swoll**, *dial.* **swal**. pa.pple. 1 **swollen**, **swollen**, 4–5 **swolle**, 4–7 **swollen**, 6–9 **swoln**, **OE.** **swelan**, **swellan**.

1. To become larger in bulk, increase the size of, cause to expand; to enlarge morbidly, affect with tumour. *Obs.*

2. *trans.* (see also 3) : To make larger in bulk, increase the size of, cause to expand; to enlarge morbidly, affect with tumour. Also *with out*, *up*.

b. *fig.* To make greater in amount, degree, intensity; to increase, add to. Also *with out*, *up*.

3. To cause (the sea, a river, etc.) to rise in waves, as the wind, or of a condition.

4. *intr.* To become swollen in size, expand; to become distended or full.

Swerve ... Crest vp straight, or els mak it leane to that side from whence it swerveth.

†4. To give way; to sway, totter; *fig.* to shrink from action. *Obs.*

5. *intr.* To deviate from (a path). *Obs. rare.*

6. *intr.* To turn away or be deflected from a (right) course of action, a line of conduct, an opinion, etc.; to swerve, vacillate.

7. *intr.* To turn aside; to sway. Also *fig.* to digress.

†8. *trans.* To cause to turn aside or deviate (lit. and *fig.*).

Swerver (swɜ·ɹvəɹ). [f. SWERVE v. + -ER¹.]

Swerving (swɜ·ɹvɪŋ), *vbl. sb.* [f. SWERVE v. + -ING¹.] The action of the vb. SWERVE; deviation.

Swerving, *ppl. a.* [f. SWERVE v. + -ING².]

Swesh, Swesher; see SWASH sb.³, SWASHER. **Swet(e**, obs. ff. SUET, SWEAT, SWEET. **†Sweth.** *Obs.* Misprint for *sweth*, var. of CIVET sb.², chive.

†Swethe, v.¹ *Obs.* Also 5 *sweethe*. [OE. *swæþian* (in *beswæþian*), related to *swaþian* to SWATHE (*q.v.*).] *trans.* To swathe.

Swethe, obs. form of SWATHE.

Swethel, var. SWEDDLE.

Swetter, obs. f. SUIT, SWEAT, SWEET.

†Swetter, v. *Obs.* [Variant of SWATTER.] *intr.* To wallow.

Swettely, *adv.*; see SWEET sb.³, SWABBER.

†Swere, v. *Obs.* Also 5 *sweothe*.

†Swethe, v. *Obs.* Also 5 *sweethe*. [OE. *swæþ.*]

†Sweven, v. *Obs.* [OE. *swefnian* trans. to appear to in a dream, intr. to dream, f. *swefn* sb.] *intr.* To dream.

Swevening, *vbl. sb. Obs.* Forms: 2 *swevening*, (4 *swev-*, *4-5 swef-*), 5 *swefnyng(e*. [f. SWEVEN v. + -ING¹.]

†Swevenise, v. *Obs.* [f. SWEVEN sb.] *intr.* To dream.

†Swevet, *Obs.* Forms: 1 *swefot, sweofot*, 3 *swevet, sweoueð*, 7 *swivot*. [OE. *swefot*, *swefoþ*.] Sleep, slumber.

Swevicai, *a. Obs.* [f. mod.L. *Suēvicus*, f.] = SWABIAN.

Sweven, sb. Obs. exc. arch. Forms: 1 *swefn*, *swefen*, *swefon, swefun*, etc.... A dream, vision.

Swevning, sb. *Obs.* var. SQUAMMOUS.

Swewn, sweyne, obs. ff. SWAIN, SWINE.

†Swey(t, *ppl. a.* [pa. pple. of SWEIGH v.] Wearied, tired, inactive.

Swiable (swoi·əb'l). [f. SWAY v. + -ABLE.]

Swib, var. SWIPE sb.¹

Swibber-swill. *Obs. rare.*

Swibble, obs. form of SWIVEL.

Swic, var. SWASH sb.³

Swicc, -le. See SWIKE.

†Swiccle, sb. *Obs.* [f. SWIKE sb.² + -LE.]

Swift, a. and adv. Forms: 1 *swift*, *swyft*, 3 *swift*, *swuft*, *swofte*, *suofte*, (7 *swifte*), Anglo-Ir. *shwift(e*). [OE. *swift* = prehistoric *swuptá-*.]

I. *a.* (Now chiefly *poet.*)

1. Moving far in a short time (*J.*); moving, or capable of moving, with great speed or velocity; going quickly or at a great rate; rapid, fleet.

2. Coming on, happening, or performed without delay; prompt, speedy.

3. Done or finished within a short time; passing quickly, of short continuance; that is soon over, brief. Chiefly *poet.*

4. *b. Acting*, or disposed to act, without delay; prompt, ready.

5. Coming on, happening, or performed without delay; prompt, speedy.

B. *sb.*

1. Special collocations of the adj.: *swift* *out-speedy* (see SPEEDY 7); also in names of species of animals distinguished by swift running or flight.

2. Combs. of the adj.: parasynthetic, as *swift-footed, -handed, -heeled* (= SWIFT-FOOTED), *-hoof'd* (= *-hooved*), *-paced, -streamed, -tongued*; also *swift-flight-a, -flying* swiftly; with other adjs., expressing a combination of two qualities, as *swift-frightful, -slow*. Also *swift horse-running, horse-racing.*

Swifter, sb. *Naut.* [f. SWIFT v.]

Swifter, v.¹ *Naut.* [f. prec.] *trans.* To make swift or soften.

Swift, v.² *Naut.* [f. SWIFT a.] *intr.* To move swiftly; to hasten.

Swift, v.¹ *Naut.* [f. SWIFT sb.]

Swift-foot, *a.* = SWIFT-FOOTED.

Swift-footed, *a.* [f. the name of the satirist Jonathan Swift (1667–1745) + -IAN.] Pertaining to or characteristic of Swift or his works. Hence **Swiftianism**, a piece of writing or an expression characteristic of Swift.

Swifting tackle: see SWIFT v.

Swiftlet (swi·ftlet). [f. SWIFT sb.² + -LET.] A little or young swift; a small species of swift, as those of the genus *Collocalia*, which construct edible nests.

Swiftly (swi·ftlɪ), *adv.* Forms: see SWIFT a. and LY². [OE. *swiftlíce*. f. SWIFT a.] In a swift manner; with swift movement or action.

Swiftness (swi·ftnes). [f. SWIFT a. + -NESS.]

1. The quality of being swift; rapidity.

2. The fact of happening, or acting, without delay; promptitude; haste, eagerness.

Swift-winged, *a.* Having swift wings, flying swiftly; rapid in flight (*lit.* and *fig.*).

Swig (swig), *sb.*¹ [Origin unknown.]

1. A drink, draught; a draught or copious draught of a beverage, esp. of intoxicating liquor; "a pull".

2. *Naut.* To pull at the bight of a rope which is fast at one end to a fixed object and at the other to a movable one; to pull.

Swig (swig), *v.*¹ *trans.* [f. SWIG sb.¹]

Swig, *v.*² *Naut.* Also *swagg*. [f. SWIG sb.²]

†Swig, *sb.*¹ *Cards.* Also *swigg*. *Obs.*

†Swig, *v.*² *Cards.* *Obs.*

Swiggle (swig'l), v. rare. [f. SWIG v. + -LE.] intr. To sway about, waver; to move with a swaying motion.

Swiggle (swig'l), v. rare. Also 7 **swigle**.

Swike, sb.[1] Obs. (exc. dial.) Forms 1-2 **swica**, 3 **swice**, 3-4 **swike**, **suike**, 3 **sweoke**, **swoke**, (swiche). [OE. swíce = swic a deceiver; a traitor.

Swike, sb.[2] 3-4 **swike**, 3-4 **swike**, (swiche), 4 **suike**, **suike**, (suiche), **squike**, 4-5 **swyke**, 5 **swyk**, 4-5 **swyke**. [OE. swic a trap; cf. MHG. swich.] 1. Deceit, deception, treachery; an act of deception, a trick.

Swike, v. Obs. ruice (Genesis 1996, where the meaning is doubtful; see Swik.) Deceitful; treacherous; traitorous.

Swiker, sb. Obs. exc. dial. A deceiver; a scullion.

Swill, sb.[1] north. and E. Anglian. Also 1 **sgwill**, 4 7 **swille**. [Origin unknown.] 1 A large shallow basket, made roughly with strips of oak, unpeeled willows, or the like.

Swill, sb.[2] Also 6 **swyl**, **swyll**, 6-7 **swill**. [f. SWILL v.] 1. Liquid, or partly liquid, food, chiefly kitchen refuse, given to swine; hog-wash, pig-wash.

Swill, v. north. and E. Anglian. Also 4 **swyll**, 4-6 **swyll**, **swille**, 7 **swill**. [OE. swillan, swilian, of which no certain cognates are known.] 1. trans. To wash or rinse out (a vessel or cavity), or, now usually, to cause water to flow freely upon (a surface, floor, etc.) in order to cleanse it.

Swill, v.[2] Forms: 1 **swilian** (suillan), 2-5 **swyle**, 4 **swile**, 6 **swyl**, **swell**, 7 **swille**, 6- **swill**. [OE. swillan, swilian.]

Swill-bowl (swilbōl). Obs. or arch. Forms: see SWILL v. and BOWL sb.[1]; also 6 **swilbolle**.

Swiller (swil'əɹ). [f. SWILL v. + -ER.] One who habitually 'swills the bowl' or drinks to excess; a toper, drunkard.

Swilling (swil'iŋ), vbl. sb. Forms: see SWILL v. + -ING.] The action of the verb SWILL.

Swilly, a. rare.[1] [f. SWILL sb.[2] + -Y.] Addicted to swilling or heavy drinking.

Swilly, a. rare.[2] [f. SWILL sb.[1] + -Y.]

Swilly-hole, sb. local.

Swill-tub (swil'tᴜb). [f. SWILL sb.[2] + TUB sb.] A tub for swill or hog-wash. Occas. attrib.

Swim (swim), sb.[1] [f. SWIM v.] **Swim**, sb.[2] Forms: 1 **swimman**, (swymman), 7 **swimman**, 3-7 **swimme**, 4 **swemme**, 4-6 **swym**, **swyme**.

Swim (swim), v. Pa. t. **swam** (swæm); pa. pple. **swum** (swᴜm). Forms: 1 **swimman** (swymman), 7 **swimman**, 3-7 **swimme**, 4 **swemme**, 4-6 **swym**, **swyme**, 5-6 **swymme**. I. 1. intr. To move along in or on water by movements of the limbs or other natural means of progression.

Swim-bladder. [f. SWIM sb. + BLADDER.] A fish's swimming-bladder (see SWIMMING sb. 6).

Swimble, v. Obs. rare. [f. SWIMBLE.]

Swime, sb. Obs. Forms: 1 swima, 3–4 suīm(e, suīm, 4 suūme, 4 squyme, 4–5 swym(e.

Swimmel, v. rare. Obs.

Swimmer (swi'maɹ). [f. SWIM v. + -ER1.]

Swimmeret (swi'maɹet). [f. SWIMMER + -ET.]

Swimming (swi'miŋ), vbl. sb. [f. SWIM v. + -ING1.] 1. The action of the verb SWIM.

Swimming, ppl. a. [f. SWIM v. + -ING2.] 1. That swims, in various senses.

Swimmingly (swi'miŋli), adv. [f. prec. + -LY1.] In a swimming manner.

Swimmingness (swi'miŋnes). [f. SWIMMING + -NESS.]

Swimmy (swi'mi), a. [f. SWIM v. + -Y1.]

Swinch. Obs. Forms: 2 swinche, swinch, 4 swynch, swynche.

Swind, v. Obs.

Swindle (swi'nd'l), sb. [f. SWINDLE v.]

Swindle (swi'nd'l), v. [Back-formation f. SWINDLER.] 1. intr. To act the swindler; to practise fraud.

Swindler (swi'ndləɹ). [ad. G. schwindler.]

Swindling, ppl. a. [f. SWINDLE v. + -ING2.]

Swine (swoin). Pl. swine. Forms: 1 Singular and Plural swín.

Swinebread (swoi'nbred). Also 6–7 swine-bread.

Swine-cote. Now only Hist. or dial.

Swinery (swoi'nəri). [f. SWINE sb. + -ERY.] 1. A place where swine are kept.

SWINE'S CRESS. 334 SWING. SWING. 335 SWING.

Swine's cress. Also 5 swynescaere, 6 swinaskeros, swine caroe. [Cf. *G. schwein(s)-kresse.* Through the phonetic similarity of such like form...]

Swine's feather. *Mil.* (now only *Hist.*) Also swine-feather; sweynes-feather, swan's-feather. [Cf. *G. schweinsfeder* (1 boat-spear)...]

Swine's grass. Also 5 swynes gres, 5 swyneagrasse, swyneasgaroe, 6 swyne gyrs; 7 *Polygonum aviculare*; also, local, ...

Swinestone (swainstoun). Also [cf. *G. schwein-stein* (see SWINE and STONE sb.)], = local, *lapis suillus*.] An early name for ANTHRACONITE, a variety of limestone containing bituminous matter...

Swine-stie (swainstai). Now chiefly *dial.* Forms: see SWINE and STY: also 5 swinzaty, swynesty, 6 swines-stie. [f. SWINE + STY sb.]

Swineyard, sb.: see SWINEHERD.

Swing, sb.[1] *Obs.* [OE. *swing* in form and origin identical with *getswing* SWING sb.[2] (sense 1, 4. Teut. *swangw-*; see SWING sb.[1]) cf. the same sense as the parallel form *swingðu-* (see SWINK v., to toil).] Labour, toil.

SWING. 336 SWING-. SWINGE. 337 SWINGEBREECH.

Swing. (continued) ...

†Swing, v.[2] *Obs.* Pa. t. 3 *zwang*, 4 *swange*, *wwong*. [OE. *swingan*, corresp. in form and meaning with SWINK n.[1].]

Swinge ... **swing** (in combination).

Swinge (swind3), sb. Also 6–8 *swindge*, 7 *swinge*...

Swinge (swind3), v.[1] Also 6 *swindge*, 6–8 *swinging*, 7 ...

Swingebreech. *Obs. nonce-wd.* [f. *swinge,* ...]

Swing v. ... ? One who struts or flaunts about.

Swingeing, swinging (swiˈndʒiŋ), ppl. a.

Swinger (swiˈndʒər). Also 6–9 swynger, swounger.

Swinger (swiˈŋər).

Swinging (swiˈŋiŋ), vbl. sb.

Swingle (swiˈŋg'l), sb.

Swingle-hand.

Swingletree (swiˈŋg'ltrī).

Swing-swang (swiˈŋswæŋ).

Swing-tree (swiˈŋtrī).

Swinish (swaiˈniʃ), a.

Swink (swiŋk), sb.

Swink (swiŋk), v.

Swinker (swiˈŋkər).

Swip, sb.

Swipe (swaip), sb.

Swipe (swaip), v.

Swiper (swaiˈpər).

Swipy (swaiˈpi), a.

Swirl (swərl), sb.

Swirl, v.

Swirl (swō̆il), *a.* [f. SWIRL *sb.* + -Y.] Twisted; knotty, gnarled (cf. SWIRL *sb.* 3.).

Swirler, north. dial. f. SQUIRREL.

Swirt, north. dial. f. SQUIRT.

Swirtle, obs. Sc. form of SURETY.

Swis, obs. 3 sing. pres. ind. of SUE.

Swish (swiʃ), *int.* or *adv.* Expressive of the sound made by the kind of movement defined in B. 1 *v.* with a swish. — Also reduplicated *swish, swish*.

Swish, *sb.*1 [? Native name.] A native mortar of West Africa. Also *attrib.*

Swish, *sb.*2 [Native name.] A native mortar of West Africa. Also *attrib.*

Swish (swiʃ), *v.* [Imitative. Cf. prec.]

Swishing, *vbl. sb.* [f. SWISH *v.* + -ING.]

Swish-swash (swiʃ·swɒʃ). [Reduplicated f. SWASH with alternating vowel.]

Swishy (swi·ʃi), *a.* [f. SWISH *sb.* or *v.* + -Y.] Characterized by swishing.

Swiss (swis), *sb.* and *a.* Forms: 6 Swyce, *pl.* Swisses, Swysses, 6-7 Swisse, 7 Swiss, 7-8 Suisse, 7- Swiss. [ad. F. *Suisse*, ad. MHG. *Swîz* (cf. MDu. *Swits*, *Suits*).]

†Swissener. *Obs.* In 6 Buyoener.

†Swisser. *Obs.* Forms: 6 Swyser, Swyches, Swisser, Swiser, 6-7 Swisser, 6-8 Swiasser, 7 Swisar, Swiser. *var.* MHG.

Swissing (swi·siŋ), *vbl. sb.* Also swissing.

Swit, obs. Sc. form of SOOT *sb.*1

Switch (switʃ), *sb.*1 Also 7 swittse, swytche, switch. [In branch I., early forms *swits, swyts* (*see next*): prob. ad. Flem. or LG. word.]

Switch (switʃ), *v.* Also 7 *swits*, *swytch*. [f. prec.]

Switchback (switʃ·bæk), *a.* and *sb.* [f. SWITCH *v.* 6 + BACK *adv.*]

Switchboard (switʃ·bɔ̄ɹd). [f. SWITCH *sb.* + BOARD.]

Switching (switʃ·iŋ), *vbl. sb.* [f. SWITCH *v.* + -ING.]

Switchman (switʃ·mæn). [f. SWITCH *sb.* + MAN.] A man who works a switch or set of switches in a railway; a pointsman.

Switchel (switʃ·el). *U.S.* [Origin unknown.] A drink made of molasses and water, sometimes with vinegar, ginger, or rum added.

Switcher (switʃ·əɹ). [f. SWITCH *v.* + -ER.] One who or that which switches, in any sense.

Switchy (switʃ·i), *a.* [f. SWITCH *sb.* + -Y.]

Swith (swiθ), *adv.* arch. or dial. [In later use chiefly Sc.]

†Swithe, *v.* Obs. exc. dial. Also 6 *swithe*, *sweeven*, 4 *swipe*, *pa. t.* *swath*, *swythe*. [OE. *swíðan*.]

Swither (swiðəɹ), *v.* arch. or dial. Also 6 *swidder*, *swudder*, *swydder*, 8 Sc. *swither*, Fris. *Swithern*, *Zwidder*; cf. MDu. *Swidder*, *Zwidder*, Fris. *Swither*.

Swither (swiðəɹ), *sb.* arch. and dial. Also 8-9 *swidder* (*see pa.t. and dial.* [f. SWITHER *v.*]

Swithen, *v.* Sc. exc. dial. (swidden, swissen). [5 ON. *sviða* to be singed (cf. ON. *svíðing*-clearing of land made by burning. Da. *svidning* (burning, singeing): see prec.]

Swither (swiðəɹ), *v.*2 dial. [a. ON. *svithra* to burn. Hence SWITHERING *ppl. a.*1 scorching, parching.

Switzer (swi·tsəɹ). arch. Also 6 Switzer, Zwitzer, 7 Switzar, Switsard, Zwitser. *var.* MDu. *Switzer*, *Zwitzer*; Fris. *Sweitser*, Du. *Zwitser*; cf. MDu. *Switzer*. [ad. G. *Schweizer*, now *Schweitzer*, f. *Schweiz* Switzerland.]

Swivel, v.

Swivel-bridge, **swivel-chair**, **swivel-eye**, etc.

Swizzle, sb. and v.

Swizzle-stick.

Swob, variant of SWAB.

Swink, **Swoln**, ppl. a.

Swolne, obs. pa. t. of SWELL.

Swoll, obs. pa. pple. of SWELL.

Swollen, **Swoln**, ppl. a.

Swolten, ppl. a.

Swoln-hot, a.

Swolve, obs. form of SWALLOW.

Swoln, sb. and a.

Swomp, obs. form of SWAMP.

Swon, obs.

Swoon, sb.

Swoon, v.

Swooning, ppl. a.

Swoony, a.

Swoop, sb.

Swoop, v.

Swooping, ppl. a.

Swoosh, sb.

Swoosh, v.

Swop: see SWAP.

Swope, obs. form.

Sword, sb.

Supplement, p. 3873; Corrigenda, p. 4092; Spurious words, p. 4093; Books quoted, p. 4094

SWORDLET. 352 Sword-player. SWOT. SWOT. 353

Swung, *ppl. a.* and *pple.* of SWING *v.*

Swupple, Swuttle: *see* SWIFFLE, SCOTT *a.*

Swy, Swyar: *see* SWISE, SWISER.

Swych(e, Swychor, Swycht, Swye, Swyear, *advs.* SWAY *v.*, SQUARE, SQUIRE, SWIVE

Swyfe, swyfl: *see* SWALE *sb.*3, SWEAL *v.*

Swyk, Swykil, Swyl(l)ing, obs. forms of SWEEL *v.*, SWILING. Swynacy(e, -asy, -ayay, -eaye, obs.

Swya, Swyar, Swyer, Swyfte, Swyk, Swyke, Swyl, Swyll, Swyn: *see* SWAY, SQUARE, SWIRE, SWYTE, *obs.* form of SWEET.

-sy, hypocoristic dim, suffix added to (i) proper names, as *Patsy, Patty, Topsy,* also in the form *-sy,* as *Nancy,* (ii) common nouns, as *baby, ducksy, Mopsy, petsy, Popsy (popsy-wopsy).*

Syagush (sī'ăgŭsh). *Also* †**syah-ghush**, 8 siagush, showpoose, shah goose, shaugoss, 9 syah-gush.

Sybarite (sĭ'bărəit), *sb.* *and* *a.*

Sybaritic (sĭbărĭ'tĭk), *a.* Also 7 errom. **Sabaritica**.

Sybaritical (sĭbărĭ'tĭkăl), *a.* *Now rare.*

Sybotic (sĭbŏ'tĭk), *a. rare* (*affected*).

Sybow (sɑɪ'bəu), 7 *pl.* sybeia, 8 *pl.* sybouse, 8–9 sybow, sybbow, 7 *pl.* sybeia, 8 *pl.* sybouse, 8–9 sybow, sybbow.

Sybritical, *a.* *and* *adv.* *errom.* Sabari...

Sycamore (sĭ'kămɔː), *sycomore* (sĭ'kŏmɔː).

Sycamore-tree, *sb.*

Sycamine (sĭ'kămaɪn, -ĭn). Also 4 sico-...

Syce (sɑɪs). *Anglo-Ind.* Forms: 7 seis, 7–8 saice, 9 syce, sais, sice, saice, sice, syce.

Syce, Sycee: *see* SICE, SIZE *sb.*2, 3.

Sycer, obs. form of SICKER *a.*

Sychnocarpous (sĭknŏ'kɑːpəs), *a. Bot.*

Sychon: *see* SICON *sb.*

Sycite (sɑɪ'sɑɪt). Also 7 sycites.

Sycoceric (sɑɪkŏsē'rĭk), *a. Chem.*

Sycomancy (sɑɪ'kŏmænsɪ). *Obs.*

Sycomore: *see* SYCAMORE.

Sycomorus (sɑɪkŏmɔː'rəs). *Bot.*

Syconium (sɑɪkəu'nɪəm). *Bot.*

Syconus (sɑɪ'kŏnəs). *Bot.* = prec.

Sycophancy (sɪ'kŏfănsɪ).

†Sycophant, *sb.* *Obs.*

Sycophant (sɪ'kŏfănt), *sb.*2

Sycophantic (sĭkŏfæ'ntĭk), *a.*

Sycophantical, *a.* [See prec.]

Sycophantically (sĭkŏfæ'ntĭkălɪ), *adv.*

Sycophantish (sɪ'kŏfăntĭʃ), *a.*

Sycophantism (sɪ'kŏfăntĭz'm). [as prec. + -ISM.] = SYCOPHANCY 2.

Sycophantize (sɪ'kŏfăntaɪz), *v.*

†Sycophantly, *a.* *Obs.* *rare*. [f. SYCOPHANT *sb.*2 + -LY2.]

†Sycophantly, *adv.* *Obs.* *rare*. [f. SYCOPHANT *sb.*2 + -LY2.]

†Sycophantry, *sb.* *Obs.* *rare*. [f. as prec. + -RY.]

Sycoretin (sɑɪkŏrē'tĭn). *Chem.*

Sycosis (sɑɪkəu'sĭs). *Path.* [mod.L., a. Gr.]

Sye, *sb.*1 *Obs.* exc. *dial.*

Sye, *v.*1 *Obs.* exc. *dial.* Forms: 1 sīan, 3 syen, sie, 3 syȝe, 4–5 sye, sie.

Sye, sie, *v.*2 *Obs.* exc. *dial.* Forms: 1 sion, seon, 3 syȝe, etc. sing. sīth), 3 *pa. t.* seh, 4–5 *pa. pple.* (*y)sien, syen, cy(e, sigh, 6 sighe), 7 sie.

Syenite (sɑɪ'ɪnaɪt). Also **sienite.** [ad. F. *syénite*, G. *syenit*, ad. L. *Syenītēs (lapis),* (stone) of Syene.]

Syenitic (sɑɪ'ɪnĭtĭk), *a.* Also *a.* [f. prec. + -IC.]

Syepoorite (sɑɪɪpɔː'rɑɪt). *Min.* [f. *Syepoor* or *Saipūr,* in N.W. India, where found: see -ITE1.]

Sygale, sie, *v.*3 *Obs. exc. dial.*

Sygaldry, -drye, var. SIGALDER, -DRY *Obs.*

Sye, Syed, Syeg, Syell, Syen, etc.: *see* SICKLE, SAYYID, SIEGE, SILE *sb.*1 *and* *v.*, Syen.

Syenoury, *sb.* *and* *v.*: *see* SIGNORY.

Syfe, syffe, *obs.* ff. SIEVE *sb.*

Syg: *see* SIGHT, SITH, SICKLE, SIGN.

Syhedrite (sɑɪ'hɪdraɪt). *Min.* [Improperly for *syhedrite,* f. the Syhedree Mountains in Bombay, where found: see -ITE1.]

Syllabarium (sɪlăbɛə'rĭəm). *Pl.* **-a.** [mod.L.]

Syllabary (sɪ'lăbărɪ). [ad. mod.L. *syllabārium.*]

Syllabatim (sɪlæ'bătĭm), *adv.* *rare.* [L.]

Syllabic (sɪlæ'bĭk), *a.* *and* *sb.*

Syllabical (sɪlæ'bĭkăl), *a.* Now *rare* exc. *Pros.*

Syllabically (sɪlæ'bĭkălɪ), *adv.*

Syllabicate (sɪlæ'bĭkeɪt), *v.* *rare.*

Syllabication (sɪlæbĭkeɪ'ʃən).

Syllabicity (sɪlăbĭ'sĭtɪ).

Syllabification (sɪlăbĭfĭkeɪ'ʃən). [f. next + -ATION.]

Syllabify (sɪlæ'bĭfaɪ), *v.* [irreg. f. SYLLABLE *sb.* + -(I)FY.]

Syllabism (sɪ'lăbĭz'm).

Syllabize (sɪ'lăbaɪz), *v.*

Syllable (sɪˈlæb'l), *sb.* Forms: 4–7 sillable, 4 silable, 5 sillabil–byl, sylable, sbul, sylle, bylle, cyllable, 7 syllabill, 6–syllable. *b. dial.* 5, 9 sinnable, 9 sennable. [a. AF. *sillable* = OF. *sillabe* (11th c.), mod.F. *syllabe*, ad. L. *syllaba*, a. Gr. συλλαβή, f. συλλαμβάνειν to take, put, or bring together, f. σύν SYN- + λαμβάνειν (stem λαβ-) to take.]

1. A vocal sound or set of sounds uttered with a single effort of articulation and forming a word or an element of a word; each of the elements of spoken language comprising a sound of greater sonority (vowel or vowel-equivalent) with or without one or more sounds of less sonority (consonants or consonant-equivalents); also, a character or set of characters forming a corresponding element of written language.

b. Used pregnantly of a word of one syllable, or in reference to a part of a word, considered in relation to its significance.

2. The least portion or detail of speech or writing (or of something expressed or expressible in speech or writing; the least mention, hint, or trace of something; esp. in phrases.

Syllabize (sɪˈlæbɪz), *v. rare⁻¹.* [f. SYLLABLE *sb.* + -IZE.] *trans.* = SYLLABLE *v.* 1 a.

Syllabub: see SILLABUB.

Syllabus (sɪˈlæbəs). Pl. syllabi (sɪˈlæbaɪ) or syllabuses (sɪˈlæbəsɪz). [mod.L. *syllabus*, usually referred to as alleged Gr. συλλαβος.]

1. A concise statement or table of the heads of a discourse, the contents of a treatise, the subjects of a series of lectures, etc.; a compendium, abstract, summary, epitome.

2. *R. C. Ch.* A summary statement of points decided and errors condemned by ecclesiastical authority; *spec.* that annexed to the encyclical *Quanta cura* of Pope Pius IX, 8 Dec. 1864.

†Syllepsis (sɪˈlɛpsɪs). Pl. syllepses (-iːz). Also 6 silli-. [a. Gr. σύλληψις, f. συλλαμβάνειν to take together.]

1. *Gram. and Rhet.* A figure by which a word, or a particular form or inflexion of a word, is made to refer to two or more other words in the same sentence, while properly applying to or agreeing with only one of them (e.g. a masc. adj.), qualifying two *sbs.*, masc. and fem.), or the verb serving as predicate to two subjects, sing. and pl.), or applying to them in different senses (e.g. literal and metaphorical). Cf. ZEUGMA.

Syllogism (sɪˈlɒdʒɪz'm). Forms: 4 silogime, 4–6 silogisme, 4–5 sylogyme, 5–7 sillogisme, 6 silogysme, mellogisme, 5–7 syllogisme, 7 sylogisme, 7– syllogism. [ad. OF. *silogime*, *sillogisme* (Fr. *syllogisme*), ad. L. *syllogismus*, a. Gr. συλλογισμός, f. συλλογίζεσθαι to SYLLOGIZE.]

1. *Logic.* An argument expressed or to be expressible in the form of two propositions called the premisses, containing a common or middle term, with a third proposition called the conclusion, resulting necessarily from the other two. Example: *Omne animal est substantia, omnis homo est animal, ergo omnis homo est substantia.*

Syllogistic (sɪlədʒɪstɪk), *a.* and *sb.* [ad. L. *syllogisticus* (Quintilian) or Gr. *syllogistikos*, f. συλλογίζεσθαι to SYLLOGIZE: see -IC and -ISTIC.]

Syllogistical (sɪlədʒɪstɪkal), *a.* Now *rare*. [f. prec. + -AL: see -ICAL.]

Syllogize (sɪˈlɒdʒaɪz), *v.* [ad. F. *syllogiser* (13th c.), ad. L. *syllogizāre*, a. Gr. συλλογίζεσθαι: see SYLLOGISM.]

†c. Corresponding or agreeing like the propositions of a syllogism; consistent. *Obs.*

Syllogistically (sɪlədʒɪstɪkalɪ), *adv.* [f. prec. + -LY².] In a syllogistic manner; by means of a syllogism or syllogisms; by the method of syllogisms.

Syllogizer (sɪˈlɒdʒaɪzər). [f. SYLLOGIZE *v.* + -ER¹.] One who reasons by syllogisms; one versed in syllogisms.

†Syllogistry. *Obs. nonce-wd.* [f. SYLLOGIST-ICAL, after *sophistry*.] Sophistical syllogistic reasoning.

Syllogization. [ad. med.L. *syllogizātiō*.] The action of syllogizing; syllogistic reasoning.

Sylph (sɪlf). [ad. mod.L. (pl.) *sylphes*, G. *sylphe*, F. *sylphe*, mod.L. *sylphi* (Paracelsus *De Nymphis*, etc.), mod.L. *sylphi* (Ibid. Wks. 1658 II. 391). Cf. F. *sylphe*, Sp. *silfo*, Pg. *sylpho*, etc.]

1. One of a race of beings or spirits supposed to inhabit the air (orig. in the system of Paracelsus).

Sylphid (sɪlfɪd). [ad. F. *sylphide*: see SYLPH.] A young or little sylph.

Sylva, silva (sɪlvə). [L. *silva* a wood, forest.]

1. A title for a collection or forest trees, or a descriptive list or catalogue of trees.

Sylvan, silvan (sɪlvən), *a.* (*sb.*) Also *silvan*. [ad. L. *silvānus*, f. *silva* a wood.]

Sylvanite (sɪlvənaɪt). *Min.* [f. *Sylvania* in *Transylvania*, where found: see -ITE¹.] Cf. *sylvanium*.

Sylvanity (sɪlˈvænɪtɪ), *v. trans.*, to render sylvan; *b.* Sylvan quality or character.

Sylvate, silvate (sɪlˈveɪt). *Chem.* [f. SYLVIC + -ATE⁴.] A salt of sylvic acid.

Sylvatic, silvatic (sɪlˈvætɪk), *a. rare.* Also 5 silvatike (after St. *sebastico*). [ad. L. *silvāticus*: see SYLVESTRINE.]

Sylvester (sɪlˈvɛstər). *sb.* [Proper name.]

Sylvestral, -estrial (sɪlvɛstrəl), *a. Bot.,* growing in woods or woodland places of a type found in woods.

Sylvestrian, *a²* and *sb.* *Eccl. Hist.* [L. *Silvestrīnus* (see SYLVESTRINE *a.*) + -AN.]

Sylvestrine, sil- (sɪlvɛstraɪn), *a.* [f. L. *silvestris* (see SYLVESTRIAN) + -INE¹.] Belonging to or occurring in woods.

Sylvia (sɪlvɪə). *Ornith.* [mod.L. *Sylvia* var. of *silva* a wood.]

†Sylvian, a. *Obs. rare⁻¹.* Incorrectly for SYLVAN.

Sylvicoline (sɪlˈvɪkəlaɪn), *a. Ornith.* [ad. *Sylvicola* + -INE¹.] *a.* Of or belonging to the *Sylvicolinæ.*

†Sylvicultural. [f. next + -AL.] = SILVICULTURAL.

Sylviculture, silvi- (sɪlvɪkʌltʃər). [ad. F. *sylvi-, silviculture*, f. L. *sylva, silva* a wood + F. *culture* cultivation.] The cultivation of woods or forests; the growing and tending of trees as a department of forestry.

Sylvic (sɪlvɪk), *a. Chem.* [ad. F. *sylvique* (1836), f. L. *sylva, silva* a wood + -IC.] Sylvic acid...

Sylvin, sylvine (sɪlvɪn). *Min.* [a. F. *sylvine* (Beudant, 1832), from the med. name of the substance *sal digestivum Sylvii*: see -IN¹.] Native potassium chloride, occurring in some salt-mines and on Mount Vesuvius. Also called *sylvite.*

Sylvite (sɪlvaɪt). *Min.* [ad. F. *sylvite* (Beudant), and E. *sylvine* + -ITE¹.] = prec.

Sym- (sɪm), *prefix,* repr. Gr. συμ-, assimilated form of σύν SYN- before b, m, p. Symbol, sympathy, etc.

Symblepharon, **Symbly**, **Symbol**, **Symbolaeography**, **Symbolatry**, **Symbolic**, **Symbolical**, **Symbolically**, **Symbolics** ...

Symbiont (si'mbipnt, -boi-). *Biol.* (in Diels.) symbion. [Irreg. f. Gr. σύμβιον, pr. pple. of συμβιοῦν: see next.] Either of two organisms living in symbiosis; a commensal.

Symbiosis (simbiə'sis, -bai-). [mod. L., ad. Gr. συμβίωσις a living together, companionship, f. συμβιοῦν, συμβιόειν to live together, f. σύμβιος adj. living together, sb. companion, f. σύν together + βίος life.]

Symbolist, **Symbolization**, **Symbolize**, **Symbolized**, **Symbolizer**, **Symbolizing**, **Symbolled**, **Symbolling**, **Symbology**, **Symbolology**, **Symbolatry**, **Symboliology** ...

Symmetral, **Symmetrical**, **Symmetric**, **Symmetrize**, **Symmetry** ...

Symmetricality. ... **Symmetrically** (sime'trikǎli), adv. Also 6-7 -iclly. [f. SYMMETRICAL + -LY.] In a symmetrical manner; so as to be symmetrical; with symmetry.

Symmetrician (simetri'ʃǎn), Obs. rare—1. Also 6 simmetrian. [f. SYMMETRY, after geometrician.] = SYMMETRIAN, SYMMETRIST.

Symmetrious, a. Obs. rare. [f. SYMMETRY + -OUS.] Symmetrical; corresponding. Hence **Symmetriously** adv., symmetrically.

Symmetrist (si'mitrist), rare—1. [f. SYMMETRY + -IST.] An advocate of, or one studious of, symmetry.

Symmetrize (si'mitrəiz), v. [ad. F. symmétriser (in sense 1 below), or f. SYMMETRY + -IZE.]
1. intr. To be symmetrical; to correspond symmetrically. rare—1.
2. trans. To make symmetrical; to reduce to symmetry.

Hence **Symmetrizing** ppl. a.; also **Symmetrization,** the action or process of symmetrizing.

Symmetroid (si'mitroid). Geom. [irreg. f. SYMMETRY + -OID.] Cayley's name for a certain surface of the fourth order: see quot.

Symmetrophobia (simetrofo'bia). Also **symmetriphobia.** [irreg. f. SYMMETRY + -(O)PHOBIA.] Dread or avoidance of symmetry, as shown or supposed to be shown in Egyptian temples, Japanese art, etc.

Symmetry (si'mitri). Also 6 symmetrye, simetrie, 6-7 symetry, sym(m)etrie, 7 simmetry, -ia, 7 symmetrie (1539), mod. symetrie (= it. simme-, Sp. sia, Pg. symetria), or ad. late L. symmetria, a. Gr. συμμετρία, l. σύμμετρος: see SYMMETRAL, symmetral.
1. Mutual relation of the parts of something in respect of magnitude and position; relative measurement and arrangement of parts.
2. Geom., etc. Exact correspondence in position of the several points or parts of a figure or body with reference to a dividing line, plane, or point...
3. Due or just proportion; harmony of parts with each other and the whole...
4. of natural objects or structures, esp. the human or animal body: often (esp. in early use) = regularity and beauty of form, fair or fine appearance, comeliness.

Symmetral (si'metrǎl), a. rare. [f. SYMMETRY + -AL.] ... **Symmetric** (sime'trik), a. [ad. mod.L. symmetricus, a. Gr. συμμετρικός.]

Symmetrical (sime'trikǎl), a. [f. prec. + -AL.]
1. Pertaining to, involving, depending on, acting or effected by 'symmetry', or a (real or supposed) affinity, correspondence, or mutual relation; esp. in sympathetic powder = 'powder of sympathy': see SYMPATHY 1. Now chiefly Hist.

Symmon (si'mǒn). local. [var. SIMNEL sb.] Name for a kind of red shale; also attrib. Symon fault, an interruption of a seam of coal by shale or other material (see quots.).

Symmorph (si'mǒrf), Anat. or Phys. [ad. Gr. σύμμορφος, f. σύμ, SYM- + μορφή form.] ... **Symmorphy** (si'mǒrfi), sharing of form.

Symmory (si'mǒri). Gr. Antiq. [ad. Gr. συμμορία, f. συν, σύμ-, SYM-, together + μόρ-.] Each of the companies or classes into which the citizens of Athens and other cities were divided for purposes of taxation.

Symmyst (si'mist). [ad. late L. symmysta, symmystēs (Jerome), mod.L. symmystēs (Apuleius), colleague in the priesthood, ad. Gr. συμμύστης fellow-initiate, f. σύν, SYM- + μύστης one initiated into mysteries: cf. MYST.] An associate in the same or kindred belief or mysteries; a fellow-initiate.

Symon, obs. form of SIMON, CINNAMON.

Sympatheal, a. Obs. rare—1. [f. Gr. συμπαθ-ής + -AL.] Sympathetic.

Sympathectomy (simpathe'ktǒmi), Surg. [f. SYMPATHETIC etc. + Gr. ἐκτομή excision.] Excision of a sympathetic ganglion or other part of the sympathetic nerve. Also **sympathectomize.**

Sympathetic (simpǎþe'tik), a. (sb.) [ad. mod.L. sympatheticus, a. Gr. συμπαθητικός, f. συμπαθεῖν: see SYMPATHY, SYMPATHIZE.]
1. Pertaining to, involving, depending on, acting or effected by 'sympathy', or a (real or supposed) affinity, correspondence, or mutual relation; esp. in sympathetic powder = 'powder of sympathy': see SYMPATHY 1.
2. Sympathetic ink: a name for various colourless liquid compositions used as ink, the writing with which remains invisible until the colour is developed by the application of heat or some chemical reagent. Also fig.
3. Feeling or susceptible of sympathy; having or showing a fellow-feeling; sympathizing, compassionate. (With various shades of meaning: cf. SYMPATHY 3 a-d.)
4. Agreeing, harmonious, befitting, consonant, accordant (obs.); according with one's feelings or inclinations, congenial. (Now only as coloured by transf. from 3.)

Sympathetical (simpǎþe'tikǎl), a. Now rare or Obs. [f. prec. + -AL.] = SYMPATHETIC.

Sympathetically (simpǎþe'tikǎli), adv. [f. prec. + -LY.] In a sympathetic manner; by, with, or in the way of sympathy (in various senses).

Sympatheticism (simpǎþe'tisiz'm), Now rare or Obs. [f. as prec. + -ISM.] Sympathetical principle, practice, or feeling. Hence **Sympatheticist.**

Sympathic (sim'pǎþik), a. Now rare or Obs. [ad. mod.F. sympathique, -icq, Sp. sim-patico, Pg. sympathico, ad. mod.L. *sympathicus (whence also G. sympathisch), f. sympathia SYM-PATHY.] = SYMPATHETIC a. 1, 1 c, 3. Obs.

B. sb.
1. Anat. Short for sympathetic nerve or system: see I above.
2. A person affected by 'sympathy' (SYM-PATHY 1 b); one who is susceptible of or sensitive to hypnotic or similar influence. b. A sympathetic person, sympathizer. rare.

Hence **Sympatheticism** (-siz'm), sympathetic tendency, susceptibility to sympathy (some discrediting); **Sympatheticness,** the quality of being sympathetic.

Sympathin (si'mpǎþin). Physiol. A substance concerned in the transmission of nerve impulses...

Sympathize (si'mpǎþaiz), v. Also 6-7 sim-, 6-8 -ise. [ad. F. sympathiser (16th c.), f. sympathie SYMPATHY.]
1. intr. To suffer with or like another; to be affected in consequence of the affection of some one or something; else; to be similarly or correspondingly affected; to respond sympathetically to some influence; spec. in Path. to be or become disordered in consequence of the disorder of some other part: cf. SYMPATHY 1, 1 b. Const. with.
2. To agree or accord in nature or qualities; to be similar, akin to or like each other; to correspond, harmonize.
3. To feel sympathy with another; to have a fellow-feeling; to share the feelings of another or others; to be affected with pity for the suffering or sorrow of another; to feel compassion.
4. intr. To feel sympathy; to have a fellow-feeling...

Hence **Sympathizing** ppl. a., sympathizing in any of the senses of the verb; esp. feeling or expressing sympathy; **sympathizingly** adv.

Sympathism (si'mpǎþiz'm). [f. Gr. συμπαθ- + -ISM.] ... **Sympathist** ... **Sympathizer** ...

Sympathy (si'mpǎþi). Also 6 sym-, 6-7 sim-, 7 -ie, -ye. [ad. L. sympathīa, a. Gr. συμπάθεια, f. συμπαθής: see SYMPATHETIC.]
1. Being mutually affected, or having an affinity, with something else: see SYMPATHIZE 1, 2.
2. Feeling sympathy; sympathetic: see SYM-PATHIZE.
3. a. Conformity of feelings, inclinations, or temperament, which makes persons agreeable to each other; community of feeling; harmony of disposition.
b. The quality or state of being affected by the condition of another with a feeling similar or corresponding to that of the other.

Sympathin, obs. var. SYMPATHY.

Symphilism (si'mfiliz'm), philous, etc.: see SYMPHON-.

Symphonia. ...

Symphonion, Symphonium ...

Symphonious (simfou'niǎs), a. [f. L. symphonia SYMPHONY + -OUS, after harmonious.]
1. Full of or characterized by 'symphony' or harmony of sounds (SYMPHONY 2); sounding together in harmony.
2. transf. and fig. Agreeing, accordant; concordant; harmonious. = HARMONIOUS.

Symphonize (si'mfǒnaiz), v. Also sim-, -ise. [ad. Gr. συμφωνίζειν, f. συμφωνία SYMPHONY.] To be in harmony, agree, harmonize.

Symphonous (si'mfǒnǎs), a. rare. [f. L. symphon-us, Gr. σύμφωνος + -OUS.] Of or pertaining to symphony; harmonious, consonant, in a consonant manner.

Symphony (si'mfǒni). [ad. OF. sim-, symphonie, ad. L. symphonia, a. Gr. συμφωνία, f. σύμφωνος: see prec.]
1. Agreement or harmony of sounds, esp. of musical sounds; harmony, concord.
2. An instrumental composition in three or more movements, for a full orchestra.

Symphonous. *intr.* To sing or sound together, in concert, or in harmony.

Symphony. Harmony of sound, esp. of musical sounds; concord, consonance. Also occas. of speech-sounds, as in verse.

Symphysis (Bot.) Coalescence or fusion of parts of a plant normally distinct.

Symphysy. *Obs.* A growing together.

Symphyseal, **Symphysial** Of or pertaining to, situated at, or forming a symphysis.

Symphystome

Symphytism, **Symphytize**

Symphytum An advocate of symphysistomy.

Symphysion

Sympiesometer, also **-pies-**. A form of barometer in which the column of liquid in the tube has above it a body of confined air or other gas.

Sympiezometer

Sympiesis

Sympodia (Anat.) A malformation in which the legs or lower limbs are fused together.

Sympodium (Bot.) Pertaining or relating to, of the nature of, or producing a sympodium.

Sympolar, -polity

Symposiac Of or pertaining to, or suitable for a symposium; of the nature of a symposium; convivial.

Symposial

Symposiarch The master, director, or president of a symposium.

Symposiast A member of a drinking-party; a banqueter.

Symposion

Symposium A drinking together, in a symposium. A member of a drinking-party.

Symposiac

Sympathetic, **Sympathic**

| SYMPTOM. | 372 | SYN-. | SYN-. | 373 | SYNAGOGICAL. |

Symptom. [In early use, in med.L. form *synthoma, sinthema*, corrupt fl. late L. *symptōma*, a. Gr. *σύμπτωμα*.]

1. *Path.* A (bodily or mental) phenomenon, circumstance, or change of condition arising from and accompanying a disease or affection, and constituting an indication or evidence of it; a characteristic sign of some particular disease.

2. *gen.* A symptom of something; accompanying and indicating some condition, quality, etc.; a characteristic and indication of something.

3. *transf.* The symptoms of a disease collectively (as a subject of study).

Symptomatic Of the nature of, or constituting, a symptom of disease; *spec.* applied to a secondary disease.

Symptomatology The study of symptoms; that branch of pathology which treats of the symptoms of disease.

Symptomatize

Symptomatical

Symptomatically

Symptomatist

Symptomatize

Symptomical

Symptomless Destitute of symptoms; exhibiting no symptoms.

Symptomatomates

Symptosis

Synaeresis (Gram.) Contraction, esp. of two vowels into a diphthong or a single vowel.

Synagogue

Synagogical Of or pertaining or relating to the Synagogue.

Synagogian

Supplement, p. 3873; Corrigenda, p. 4092; Spurious words, p. 4093; Books quoted, p. 4094

Synagogue (si'năgŏg). Forms: 2-6 sinagoge, 3-6 sinagogue, (4 sinnagoge), 4-7 sinagogue, (5 synagoge), 5-6 synagoge, 8 sinagoge, seongog; 3- synagogue. [a. OF. sinagoge (11th c.), mod.F. synagogue, or ad. its source late L. synagoga, a. Gr. συναγωγή meeting, place of meeting, f. σύν SYN- + ἄγειν to lead, bring.]

1. The regular assembly or congregation of the Jews for religious instruction and worship apart from the service of the temple, constituting, since the destruction of the temple, their sole form of public worship; hence, the religious organization of the Jews as typified by it, the Jewish synagogue.

Synagogism. *Obs.* [f. prec.]

2. *transf.* in hostile controversial use, often in phr. *synagogue of Satan* (in allusion to Rev. ii. 9).

3. A building or place of meeting for Jewish worship and religious instruction.

Synallactic (sinælæktik), a. rare. [ad. Gr. συναλλακτικός, f. συναλλάσσειν.]

Synallagmatic (sinæləgmætik), a. [ad. Gr. συναλλαγματικός.]

Synallaxine (sinælæ'ksin, -in), a. *Ornith.*

Synalœpha (sinælī'fă), -phe (-fī), sb. *Gram.* Also -lo-. [late L., a. Gr. συναλοιφή, f. συναλείφειν to smear or melt together, f. σύν SYN- + ἀλείφειν to anoint.]

Synanthereous (sinænθē'rĭəs), a. *Bot. rare.*

Synanthy (si'nænθi), sb. *Bot.* [f. SYN- + ANTHERA.]

Synaphe (si'năfī). *Pros.* [a. Gr. συναφή touching, f. συνάπτειν to fasten, fix.]

Synapse (sinæps). *Anat.* [f. Gr. σύναψις junction.]

Synapheia, **Synaphia** (sinæfī'ă). *Pros.* [a. Gr. συνάφεια.]

Synapar, see SINOPER *Obs.*

Synaptase (sinæptēs). *Chem.* [ad. F. synaptase (Robiquet, 1838).]

Synaptic (sinæptik), a. *Biol. & Anat.*

Synapticula (sinæptiku'lă). Zool. Pl. -æ (-ī). [mod.L. dim. suffix -icula.]

Synaptychus (sinæptikəs). Palæont.

Synarchy (sinɑ'ki). [ad. Gr. συναρχία.]

Synarthrodia (sinɑ'rθrō'diă). *Anat.* [mod.L., f. Gr. συναρθροῦν.]

Synarthrosis (sinɑrθrō'sis). *Anat.* Pl. -oses. [mod.L., a. Gr. συνάρθρωσις.]

Syncarp (si'nkɑrp). *Bot.* [ad. mod.L. syncarpium.]

Syncarpous (si'nkɑ'rpəs), a. *Bot.*

Syncarpy (si'nkɑrpi). *Bot.* [Formed as prec.]

Syncategorem (sinkætegŏ'rem). *Logic.* [ad. late Gr. συγκατηγόρημα.]

Syncategorematic (sinkætegŏrĭmætik), a. *Logic.*

Syncategorematical, a. *Obs.*

Synchondrosis (sinkŏndrō'sis). *Anat.* Pl. -oses (-ō'sīz). [a. Gr. συγχόνδρωσις.]

Synchondrotomy (sinkŏndrŏ'tomi).

Synchronal (si'nkrŏnăl), a. and sb. *Obs.*

Synchronic (sinkrŏ'nik), a.

Synchronism (si'nkrŏniz'm). [ad. mod.L. synchronismus, a. Gr. συγχρονισμός.]

1. The quality of being synchronous; coincidence or agreement in point of time; concurrence of two or more events in time; contemporary existence or occurrence.

2. Arrangement or treatment of synchronous events, etc. together or in conjunction, as in a history; agreement in relation to the time of the events described.

Synchronistic (sinkrŏni'stik), a.

Synchronize (si'nkrŏnəiz), v.

1. *intr.* To occur at the same time; to coincide in point of time; to be contemporary or simultaneous. Const. *with.*

2. *trans.* To cause to be, or represent as, synchronous; to assign the same date to; to bring together events, etc. belonging to the same time.

3. *intr.* To occur at the same successive instants of time; to keep time *with*; to go on at the same rate and exactly together; to have coincident periods, as two sets of movements or vibrations.

Hence **Synchronized** ppl. a., **Synchronizing** vbl. sb. and ppl. a.; also **Synchronization**, the action of synchronizing; **Synchronizer**, one who or that which synchronizes; a device for synchronizing clocks, etc.

Synchronograph (sinkrŏ'nŏgrăf). [irreg. f. Gr. συγχρονο- SYNCHRONO- + -γραφ -writing.]

Synchronology (sinkrŏnŏ'lŏdʒi). [f. SYN- + CHRONOLOGY.]

Synchronological (sinkrŏnŏlŏ'dʒikăl), a.

Synchronous (si'nkrŏnəs), a. [ad. late L. synchronus, a. Gr. σύγχρονος.]

1. Existing or happening at the same time; coincident in time; belonging to the same period, or occurring at the same moment, of time; contemporary; simultaneous.

2. *Path.* Recurring at the same time.

3. *Electr.* applied to alternating currents having coincident periods; also to a machine or motor working in time with the alternations of current.

Hence **Synchronously**, adv.

Syncarp — **Synchysis** (si'nkisis). *Med.* [Properly *hypochysis*, f. Gr. σύγχυσις confusion.]

Synchroscope, **Synchronoscope**, obs. ff. SIN-.

Synclastic (sinklæstik), a. *Geom.* [f. Gr. σύν SYN- + κλαστός, f. κλᾶν to break.]

Synclinal (sinkləi'năl), a. and sb. *Geol.* [f. Gr. σύν together + κλίνειν to lean.]

Syncline (sinkləin), sb. *Geol.*

Synclinical (sinkli'nikăl), a. *Geol.*

Synclinorium (sinklinō'riəm). *Geol.* Pl. -ia.

Synclitic (sinkli'tik), a. *Obs.*

Syncopal (si'nkŏpăl), a. [f. SYNCOPE.]

Syncopate (si'nkŏpeit), v. [f. ppl. stem of late L. syncopare.]

1. *Gram.* To contract (a word) by omitting one or more syllables or letters in the middle.

2. *Mus.* To begin (a note) on an unaccented part of the bar.

Hence **Syncopated** ppl. a.

SYNCOPATION.

Syncopation (siŋkŏpē·ʃən). Also 6-8 sin-. [ad. med.L. *syncopātiōn-em*, n. of action f. *syncopāre*: see SYNCOPATE.]

1. *Gram.* Contraction of a word by omission of one or more syllables or letters in the middle; *transf.* a word so contracted.

2. *Mus.* Characterised by syncopation.

† 2. *Path.* = SYNCOPE sb. 1. *Obs. rare.*

3. *Mus.* The action of beginning a note on a normally unaccented part of the bar and sustaining it into the normally accented part, so as to produce the effect of shifting back or anticipating the accent; the shifting of accent so produced.

Syncope (siŋ·kŏpi), *n.* *Path.* [C. SYNCOPE-.]

Syncopate (siŋkŏpēt), *v.* *Path.* [f. SYNCOPE.]

Syncopic (siŋkŏ·pik), *a.* *Path.* [f. SYNCOPE.]

Syncopist (siŋ·kŏpist), *sb.*

† Syncope (siŋ·kŏpi), *sb.* Forms: 5 syn-, 5-6 sincopis, 6 sincopis (5-6 -in, 6 -yne); 6-7 syn-. [a. OF. *syncope*, ad. L. *syncopē*, a. Gr. *συγκοπή*.]

Syncopate (siŋ·kŏpēt), *v.*

SYNCYTIUM.

Syncytium (sinsi·ʃiŏm), *Biol.* [mod.L. *syncytium* (D. Parona, 1875), a. Gr. *συν-* together + *κύτος* vessel.]

Syncretism (si·ŋkrĕtiz'm), [ad. Gr. *συγκρητισμός*.]

Syncretist (si·ŋkrĕtist), *sb.*

Syncretistic (siŋkrĕti·stik), *a.*

Syncretize (si·ŋkrĕtəiz), *v.*

Syncretic (sinkrē·tik), *a.*

Syncrisis (si·ŋkrisis), *sb.*

Syncrasy (si·ŋkrasi), *sb.*

Syndactyl (sindæ·ktil), *a.* and *sb.* Also -yle.

Syndactylism (sindæ·ktiliz'm), *sb.*

Syndactylous (sindæ·ktiləs), *a.*

Syndactyly (sindæ·ktili), *sb.*

Syndesis (si·ndēsis), *sb.*

Syndesmitis (sindĕsməi·tis), *sb.*

Syndesmosis (sindĕsmōu·sis), *sb.*

Syndic (si·ndik), *sb.* and *a.*

Syndactyl...

SYNDICALIST.

Syndicalism (si·ndikæliz'm), *sb.*

Syndicalist (si·ndikælist), *sb.* and *a.*

SYNDICATE. 380 SYNECDOCHE. SYNECDOCHIC. 381 SYNERGY.

Syndicate (si·ndikēt), *sb.*

Syndication (sindikē·ʃən), *sb.*

Syndicator (si·ndikē·təʳ), *sb.*

Syndicship (si·ndikʃip), *sb.*

Syndrome (si·ndrŏm), *sb.*

Syne (səin), *adv.*

SYNECDOCHE.

Synecdoche (sinĕ·kdŏki), *sb.*

Synecdochic (sinĕkdŏ·kik), *a.*

Synecdochical (sinĕkdŏ·kikal), *a.*

Synecdochically (sinĕkdŏ·kikali), *adv.*

Synecdochism (sinĕ·kdŏkiz'm), *sb.*

Synechia (sinĕ·kiă), *sb.*

Synectic (sinĕ·ktik), *a.*

SYNERGY.

Synergia (sinəʳ·dʒiă), *sb.*

Synergic (sinəʳ·dʒik), *a.*

Synergism (si·nəʳdʒiz'm), *sb.*

Synedral (sinē·dral), *a.*

Synedrial (sinē·drial), *a.*

Synedrian (sinē·drian), *a.*

Synedrion (sinē·driŏn), *sb.*, **synedrium** (-drium).

Synedry (si·nĕdri), *sb.*

Synergist (si·nəʳdʒist), *sb.*

Synergistic (sinəʳdʒi·stik), *a.*

Synergistical (sinəʳdʒi·stikal), *a.*

Synergy (si·nəʳdʒi), *sb.* [mod.L. SYNERGIA.] = SYNERGISM.

Supplement, p. 3873; Corrigenda, p. 4092; Spurious words, p. 4093; Books quoted, p. 4094

SYNGAMETE.

Syngamete (si'ŋgamiːt). Biol. [f. SYN- + GAMETE.] The cell produced by the union of two gametes in reproduction.

†**Syngamical**, a. Obs. rare. [f. Gr. σύν + γάμος marriage + -ICAL.] Pertaining to sexual union or copulation.

Syngamy (si'ŋgami). [f. Gr. σύν YN- + γάμος marriage.] a. Free interbreeding between organisms. b. The fusion of two cells, or of their nuclei, in reproduction.

Hence **Syngamic** (singæ'mik), **Syngamous** (si'ŋgaməs) adjs.

Synge, obs. form of SIGN, SING, SINGE.

‡**Syngenesia** (sindʒiniˈziːə). Bot. [mod.L. (Linnæus 1730), f. Gr. σύν SYN- + γένεσις production, GENESIS, with ending as in Decandria, etc. : see -IA.] The ninth class in the Linnæan Sexual System, comprising plants having stamens coherent by the anthers, and flowers (florets) in close heads or capitula; corresponding to the Natural Order Compositæ.

Syngenesious (sindʒiniːˈziəs), a. Bot. [f. prec. + -OUS.] a. Belonging to the class Syngenesia; having the stamens united by their anthers. b. Of the stamens : United by the anthers so as to form a tube, as in the Syngenesia (and in some plants of other classes); also said of the anthers.

Syngenesis (sindʒe'nisis). Biol. [mod.L.: see SYN- and GENESIS.] Formation of the germ in sexual reproduction by fusion of the male and female elements, so that the substance of the embryo is derived from both parents.

Hence **Syngenetic** (sindʒine'tik), a. [f. prec.: see GENETIC.] 1. Biol. Of or pertaining to syngenesis. 2. Geol. Applied to mineral deposits formed at the same time as the enclosing rocks.

Syngenite (si'ŋdʒinəit). Min. [ad. G. syngenit (Zepharovich, 1872), f. Gr. σύν SYN-, cognate + -ITE.] A hydrous sulphate of calcium and potassium, occurring in colourless or white tabular crystals; also called KALUSSITE.

Syngli, obs. form of SINGLE a.

Synglar, -er(e, var. SINGLER a. Obs.

Synglere, var. SANGLIER, wild boar.

Syngnathous (si'ŋnaθəs), a. Zool. [f. mod.L. Syngnathus (L. Gr. σύν SYN- + γνάθος jaw) + -OUS.] Belonging to the genus Syngnathus or allied genera of fishes, characterized by the jaws being united into a tubular snout, and including the pipe-fishes and sea-horses.

Syngne, obs. form of SIGN, SING, SINGE.

Syngne, Syngnefiaunce, Syngnett(e, Syngnory: see SIGN, SIGNIFIANCE Obs., CYGNET, SIGNORY, SIGNIORY.

Syngraph (si'ŋgraf). Also in L. form syngrapha, -gr. ad. Gr. συγγραφή, f. συγγράφειν to write together, compile, draw up, f. σύν SYN- + γράφειν to write.] A written contract or bond signed by both of the parties.

Syni, obs. form of SIN, SINE.

Syniresis, Synizesis: see SYNÆRESIS.

Synod (si'nəd). Forms: 4-6 sinod, 4-7 synode (6 senod), 6-7 sinode, 4-7 synod [ad. late L. synodus, a. Gr. σύνοδος assembly, meeting, astronomical conjunction, f. σύν SYN- + ὁδός way, travel; reinforced later by F. synode (16th c.). (Cf. It., Sp. sinodo, Pg. synodo.)]

Synodal (si'nədal), a. and sb. Also 5-7 synodall, sinodall, 6 sinodal, -alle, synodalle, -ole, 7 synodale, -ol, 6-7 synod, 7 synodalis. [ad. late L. synodālis (f. synod-us SYNOD: see -AL. Cf. F. synodal (from 14th c.).] A. adj. 1. Done or made by, or proceeding from a synod (or general council).

Synod·ian, a. = SYNODAL a. 3. b.] **Synodalist**, a member of a synodal assembly: **synodally** adv. [f. med.L. synodāliter, f. prec.], by the action or authority of a synod.

SYNODITE.

Synglar, -er(e, var. SINGLER a. Obs.

Synodsman (si'nədzmən). [f. SYNOD + genitive -s + MAN sb.] 1. Pseudo-etymological alteration of SIDESMAN, q.v. (sense 1), after med.L. testis synodalis in synodal witness, a representative of a parish attending a synod.

Synoeciosis (sinɜːsiˈəʊsis), Rhet. Also syne-, synoi-, -œci-, -cœ-. [ad. Gr. συνοικείωσις, n. of action f. συνοικειοῦν to associate (persons) as kinsmen or friends, f. σύν SYN- + οἰκείουν to make one's own, f. οἰκεῖος domestic, one's own, f. οἶκος house.] A figure by which contrasted or heterogeneous things are associated or coupled, e.g. contrary qualities attributed to the same subject.

Synœcious (sinɜːsi'əs), a. Bot. [f. SYN- after Diœcious, Monœcious; cf. Gr. συνοικία a dwelling together.] Having male and female flowers in the same flower-head, as some Compositæ, or male and female organs in the same receptacle, as some mosses.

Synonym (si'nənim). Gr. Antig. Also synok-. [ad. Gr. συνώνυμον, n. of action f. συνώνυμος to cause to dwell with, to unite under one capital city, f. σύν SYN- + οἰκίζειν to found as a colony, to colonize, f. οἶκος house.] The union of several towns or villages into one capital city. So **Synœcize** (si'nɜːsəiz) v. [ad. Gr. συνοικίζειν : see above], trans. to unite into or under one capital city.

Synonym (si'nənim), sb. Forms : see below. [ad. late L. synonymum, -on, a. Gr. συνώνυμον, neut. sing. subst. of συνώνυμος, f. σύν SYN- + ὄνομα (in comb. -ώνυμος) name. Cf. F. synonyme (12th c.), Pr., Sp. synonymo.] The earliest instances are plural synonyms, L. synonyma, Gr. συνώνυμα, anglicized synonymes.

Synonymical (sinəni'mikal), a. [f. SYNONYM sb. + -ICAL.] †I. = SYNONYMOUS 1. Obs.

Synonymically (sinəni'mikali), adv. [f. prec. + -LY.] In a synonymical manner; as a synonym; with the same meaning; **synonymously.**

Synonymist (sinɔ'nimist). [f. SYNONYM sb. + -IST.] One who treats of, or makes a list of, synonyms.

Synonymity (sinəni'miti). [f. as prec.: see -ITY.] The quality or fact of being synonymous, or having the same meaning.

Synonymize (sinɔ'nəmaiz) v. rare. [f. late L. synonym-on + SYNONYM sb. + -IZE.] 1. trans. To give the synonyms of. 2. intr. To be synonymous with.

Synonymous (sinɔ'niməs), a. (sb.) Also 7 synonymus-. [f. SYNONYM (from L. synonym-us) + -OUS. Cf. F. synonyme.] 1. Having the character of a synonym; equivalent in meaning: said of words or phrases denoting the same thing or idea. Const. to, (now usually) with.

Synonymy (sinɔ'nimi). Also 6-9 synonymie, 7-9 synonymy. [ad. L. synonymia, a. Gr. συνωνυμία, f. συνώνυμος SYNONYMOUS: see -Y.] 1. Having the character of a synonymy; equivalence in meaning: said of words or phrases denoting the same thing or idea.

Synopsis (sinɔ'psis). Pl. synopses (-siːz). [late L., a. Gr. σύνοψις, f. σύν SYN- + ὄψις view (cf. συνοπτικός).]

Synoptic (sinɔ'ptik), a. (sb.) [ad. mod.L. synopticus, f. Gr. συνοπτικός, f. σύνοψις SYNOPSIS. Cf. F. synoptique.] 1. Of a table, chart, etc.: Pertaining to or forming a synopsis; furnishing a general view of a subject.

Synoptical (sinɔ'ptikal), a. [f. as prec. + -AL.]

Synoptistial a. — Synoptic: see -ist.

Synoptist (sinŏ'ptist). 1. Any one of the writers of the Synoptic Gospels.

2. One who compiles a synopsis. rare—.

Synopty. In recent Dicts.

Synocchism, orthographic: see Syn-.

Synostosis, combining forms made up from Gr. ὀστέον bone, jointed (or alleged) to mean 'articulation of bones, joint', in several words instanced only from mod. Dicts.: see quots.

Synostosis (sinŏstō'sis). rare—. [f. Gr. ὀστέον bone + -osis.] — Synostosis.

Synostose (sinŏstō's). [Contracted from Synostosis.] Union or fusion of adjacent bones by growth of bony substance (either normal or abnormal).

Synotus (sinō'tŭs). Zool.

Synovia (sinō'vĭă). Also 8–9 sin-. [mod.L. sinovia, synovia, also synophia, an invention, prob. arbitrarily formed, of Paracelsus.]

Synovial (sinō'vĭăl). [f. Synovia + -al.] Pertaining to, consisting of, containing, or secreting synovia.

Synoviparous (sinŏvi'părŭs). Producing or secreting synovia.

Synovitic (sinŏvi'tik). Pertaining to synovitis.

Synovitis (sinŏvai'tis). Inflammation of a synovial membrane.

Synovy (si'nŏvi). Obs. The form of mucin occurring in synovia.

Syntactic (sintæ'ktik). [f. Gr. συντακτικός, f. συντάσσειν to arrange.]

Syntactical (sintæ'ktikăl). Belonging or relating to grammatical syntax.

Syntactitian (sintæktiti'an). One versed in syntax.

Syntagm (si'ntæm). Obs.

Syntagma (sintæ'gmă). Pl. -ata or -as. [mod.L., a. Gr. σύνταγμα, f. συντάσσειν (see Syntaxis).]

Syntaxis (sintæ'ksis). Also 7 sin-. [ad. F. syntaxe, † sintaxe. Ad. late L. syntaxis, a. Gr. σύνταξις Syntaxis.]

Syntax (si'ntæks). Also 7 syntaxe. [ad. F. syntaxe, † sintaxe, ad. late L. syntaxis, a. Gr. σύνταξις.]

Syntaxist (sintæ'ksist). rare—. [f. Syntax + -ist.]

Syntectic (sinte'ktik). a. [ad. late L. synthecticus.]

Syntexis (sinte'ksis). [Gr. σύντηξις.]

Synteresis (sintĕrī'sis). Pl. -eses (-sēz). [med.L. synthēresis (Thomas Aquinas), a. Gr. συντήρησις.]

Syntaxarion (sintæksā'riŏn).

Synthete (si'nþīt). [a. F. synthétique (1653 in Hatz.-Darm.), or mod.L. synthetica, a. Gr. συνθετικός, f. σύνθετος, vbl. adj. of συντιθέναι (see Synthesis).]

Synthetic (sinþe'tik), a. [ad. F. synthétique (1651 in Hatz.-Darm.), or mod.L. syntheticus, a. Gr. συνθετικός.]

Synthetical (sinþe'tikăl), a.

Synthetically (sinþe'tikăli) adv.

Synthetism (si'nþĕtiz'm).

Synthetist (si'nþĕtist).

Synthetize (si'nþĕtaiz), v.

Synthetical geometry.

Syntonic (sintŏ'nik), a. [f. Gr. σύντονος, f. σύν together + τόνος tone.]

Syntonical (sintŏ'nikăl), a.

Syntonin (si'ntŏnin). Chem.

Syntonize (si'ntŏnaiz), v. Electr.

Syntonizer (si'ntŏnaiză).

Syntonous (si'ntŏnŭs), a. Mus.

Syntony (si'ntŏni). Electr.

Syntomy (si'ntŏmi).

Syntone, -tone, obs. forms of Symptom.

Syntonize (si'ntŏnaiz) v.

Syntonous (si'ntŏnŭs), a.

Syntrip (sintrip), a. Anat. [f. Gr. σύν + -tripos.]

Syntrope (si'ntrōp).

Syntype (si'ntaip). Nat. Hist.

Syntony (si'ntŏni). Obs.

Syntonous — see Syntone.

Syntomize.

Synusiast. Obs.

Syphilis (si'filis). Path. Also 8 syphilia, 9 niphilis, syphylis. [mod.L. syphilis (syphilitus), orig. the title (sc. morbus) of a poem, published 1530, by Girolamo Fracastoro or Hieronymus Fracastorius.]

Syphilize (si'filaiz), v. Med. and Path. [ad. F. syphiliser.]

Syphilitic (sifili'tik), a. and sb.

Syphilization (sifilaizē'shŏn).

Syphilo-, combining form of Syphilis.

Syphiloid, *a.* (*sb.*) *Path.* [f. SYPHILIS + -OID.] Resembling syphilis.

Syphiloma. *Path.* A syphilitic tumour. Hence **Syphilomatous** *a.*

Syphilosis (sifilō·sis). *Path.* [f. SYPHILIS + -OSIS.] Syphilitic condition.

Syphir, syphyr, obs. Sc. ff. CIPHER.

Syphon, etc., *var.* SIPHON, etc.

Sypits, sypress, *var.* CYPRESS.

Syr, Syra, obs. ff. SIR, SIRE, SIRRAH.

Syracusan (si·rǎkiūz·ǎn), *a.* and *sb.* [ad. L. *Syrācūsānus,* f. *Syrācūsæ*, *Syracuse,* a city in Sicily. b. *sb.* A native or inhabitant of Syracuse.

Syracuse (si·rǎkiūz), *sb.* [Name of Sicilian city: see prec.] A luscious oval muscadine wine made in Italy. See also quots. 1858, 1883.

Syraite, *var.* SYRIAC.

Syre, etc., see SIRE, SIRRAH.

Syriac (si·riæk), *a.* and *sb.* Also *7 -aque, -ack.* [ad. L. *Syriacus* = Gr. Συριακός, f. Συρία, *Syria.*]

Syriacal, *a.* Of or pertaining to Syria.

Syriacism (si·riæsiz'm). [f. SYRIAC.] A Syriac idiom or expression.

Syrian (si·riǎn), *a.* and *sb.* [f. SYRIA.]

Syriarch (si·riärk), *sb.* The director of public games in Syria under the Romans.

Syriasm (si·riæz'm). [f. SYRIAC, after a Gr. type ΣΥΡΙΑΣΜΟΣ.] = SYRIACISM.

Syringa (sirī·ŋgǎ). [mod.L. *syringa,* f. Gr. σῦριγξ, σύριγγ-ος pipe.] First applied (by Lobel, 1576) to the mock-orange, now applied to the lilac.

Syringe (si·rindʒ), *sb.* [ad. late L. *syringa,* a. Gr. σῦριγξ.] An instrument for drawing in a quantity of liquid and ejecting it in a stream or jet.

Syringe (si·rindʒ), *v.* To treat with a syringe.

Syringeal (sirī·ndʒiăl), *a.* *Ornith.* Of or pertaining to the syrinx in birds.

Syringin (sirī·ndʒin). *Chem.* A glucoside.

Syringo-, combining form of Gr. σῦριγξ, σύριγγ-ος.

Syringomyelia (sirī·ŋgomaiī·liǎ). *Path.* A disease of the spinal cord.

Syrinx (si·riŋks), *sb.*; *pl.* **syringes** (sirī·ndʒīz). 1. An ancient musical instrument: = PAN-PIPE.

Syro- (sai·ro), combining form of Συρο-, Syro, combined with other peoples, countries, etc.

Syrphus (sö·rfŭs), *sb.* *Ent.* A fly of the genus *Syrphidæ.*

Syrt (söt), *sb.* Now *arch.* [a. L. *Syrtis,* Gr. Σύρτις.] A quicksand.

Syrtic (sö·tik), *a.* [f. prec., L. *syrticus,* f. *Syrtis.*] Of, pertaining to, or of the nature of a quicksand.

Syrtis (sö·tis). *Pl.* **syrtes** (-ēz). Also *6-7 sirtis.* A quicksand.

Syrup (si·rǎp), *sb.* Forms: *4-6 syrupe.*

Syrupy (si·rǎpi), *a.* Of the consistence of syrup.

Syruped (si·rǎpt), *ppl. a.,* **Syruping** *vbl. sb.* and *ppl. a.*

Syrupe, *var.* SYRUP *sb.*

Syrupical, *a. Obs.* = next.

Syrup-like, *a.*

Syrurge, obs. form of SURGERY, CHIRURGEON.

Syry, *a. Obs.* Also *4 siry, 5 sire.*

Syse, see SEE *sb.*, SIZE, SISE, SIZE.

Syser, syser, *var.* of SCISSORS.

Syskenne, Sysme, Sysoure(s, *var.* SISKIN.

Sysm, obs. f. of SCHISM *sb.*

Syssarcosis (sisärkō·sis). *Anat.* A connexion of bones by means of intervening muscle.

Syssition. The custom of eating at a common table.

Systaltic (sistæ·ltik), *a.* [ad. L. *systalticus* = Gr. συσταλτικός.] *Phys.* Contracting.

Systasis (si·stǎsis). *Obs.* [mod. or mock L.] A political union or confederation.

Systatic (sistæ·tik), *a.* [ad. mod. and mock L.] Bringing together.

Systema (sistē·mǎ), *sb.* [L. *systema,* a. Gr. σύστημα.] *Obs.* A system.

System (si·stĕm), *sb.* [ad. late L. *systēma* musical interval, f. Gr. σύστημα.] 1. A set or assemblage of things connected, associated, or interdependent.

2. *Mus.* In ancient Greek music, a compound interval.

(1782) I. p. xxxii, It will be..advisable, that he give his lectures from a short text or system, written,..that they may have an opportunity of perusing it. 1896 Allbutt (title) A System of Medicine.

9. An organized scheme or plan of action, esp. one of a complex or comprehensive kind; an orderly or regular method of procedure. Now usually with defining word or phrase.

1663 Heath Flagellum (1672) 17 That there might no vice be wanting to make his Life a systeme of Iniquity. 1734 in 10th Rep. Hist. MSS. Comm. App. 1. 251 The generous system, that his Maty has always pursued. 1746 Francis tr. Hor., Epist. i. vi. 99 Farewel, and if a better System's thine, Impart it frankly. 1769 Junius Lett. viii. (1788) 63 What system of government is this? 1781 Cowper Expost. 91 He found..Their piety a system of deceit. 1790 Jefferson Writ. (1895) V. 228 The conduct of Spain has proved that the occlusion of the Mississippi is system with her. 1842 Tennyson Audley Court 33 We..discuss'd the farm, The four-field system, and the price of grain. 1873 Morley Struggle Nat. Educ. 55 Subsidising the denominational system. 1882 Nature 9 Feb. 351/1 The system of dredging introduced..on the rivers of France. 1896 Badminton Mag. Dec. 708 Straight bets over single events are losing their popularity in favour of 'systems'. A system is a kind of patent safety insurance policy.

b. A formal, definite, or established scheme or method (of classification, notation, or the like).

1753 [see Linnæan]. 1760 [see Sexual 2 d]. 1797 [see Metrical a.[2] 1]. 1831 [see Notation 5 c]. 1849 Balfour Man. Bot. § 719 A natural system endeavours to bring together plants which are allied in all essential points of structure. 1850 [see Morse sb.[3]]. 1864 [see Metric a.[2]]. 1866 Watts Dict. Chem. IV. 136 The system of chemical notation now in use. 1867 [see Numeration 1 b]. 1893 Times 26 July 12/1 The T. A. system of signalling invented by Admiral Tryon.

c. Cryst. Each of the six different general methods in which different minerals crystallize, constituting the six classes of crystalline forms.

1820 Edinb. Philos. Jrnl. III. 173 We call every simple form, from which other simple forms are derived, a fundamental form; and the class of figures derived from that fundamental form, a system of crystallisations. 1863 Fownes' Chem. (ed. 9) 259–262 All crystalline forms may be arranged in six classes or systems:..1. The regular system...2. The square prismatic system...3. The right prismatic system...4. The oblique prismatic system...5. The doubly oblique prismatic system...6. The rhombohedral system. 1868 Dana Min. (ed. 5) Introd. p. xxi, The systems of crystallization are as follows: 1. Having the axes equal. The Isometric system. 2. Having only the lateral axes equal. The Tetragonal and Hexagonal. 3. Having the axes unequal. The Orthorhombic, Monoclinic, and Triclinic.

10. In the abstract (without a or pl.): Orderly arrangement or method; systematic form or order.

1699 T. Baker Refl. Learn. vi. 68 Aristotle is more noted for his order, in bringing Morality into System, and distinguishing vertues into their several kinds, which had not been handled Systematically before, than for any improvement he made in this sort of knowledge. 1748 W. Horsley Fool (1748) II. 47 It [sc. government] consists of too many detach'd Parts to be easily reduced into System. 1875 Jowett Plato (ed. 2) I. 426 There is more of system in the Phaedo than appears at first sight. 1876 Trevelyan Macaulay II. xv. 474 Macaulay, even during his hours of leisure, began to read on system.

III. 11. attrib. and Comb. **a.** attrib. Of or pertaining to, or involving a system, systematic, as system-name; belonging to or affecting a system of bodily organs (esp. the nervous system: cf. Systemic 1 b), as system degeneration, disease, tract. **b.** objective, chiefly in sense 8 or 9 (often with unfavourable implication), as system-builder, -building, -destroyer, -maker, -making, -monger, -writer.

1776 Mickle tr. Camoens' Lusiad vii. 313 note, Tristram Shandy tells us, that his father was a most excellent *system-builder, was sure to make his Theory look well. 1837 Carlyle Fr. Rev. I. iv. iv, This is the Sieyes who shall be System-builder, Constitution-builder General; and build Constitutions..which shall all unfortunately fall before he get the scaffolding away. 1899 Allbutt's Syst. Med. VII. 99 The degeneration of the posterior columns of the spinal cord is a *system degeneration. 1905 J. Brierley Eternal Relig. vi. 48 The system-maker is by an equal necessity the *system-destroyer. 1899 Allbutt's Syst. Med. VI. 494 The chief indication of a *system disease of the neuron is its intrinsic nervous origin. 1717 Prior Alma iii. 330 We *System-makers can sustain The Thesis, which, You grant, was plain. a 1721 — Cromwell & his Porter Wks. 1907 II. 267 Your System-Makers and World-wrights. 1749 Hartley Observ. Man I. Pref. p vi, I think,..that I cannot be called a System-maker, since I did not first form a System, and then suit the Facts to it. 1826 [see Methodist 2 b]. 1836 H. Rogers J. Howe ii. (1863) 21 Where Scripture speaks, or seems to speak, in consonance with the opinions of the system-maker, well and good. 1884 Century Mag. XXVII. 915 There were many independent centers of movement and *system-making. 1750 Chesterf. Let. to Son 6 Aug., A *system-monger, who, without knowing any thing of the world by experience, has formed a system of it in his dusty cell. 1836 H. Rogers J. Howe iii. (1863) 45 There would be no lack of system-mongers and theorists. 1896 Badminton Mag. Dec. 711 The system-monger is apt to derive encouragement from the fact that long runs on a colour are rare, the longest known at Monte Carlo being a series of 28 reds. 1888 Clodd Story Creation iv. 32 The stratified rocks are subdivided into the systems shown on fig. 4..No uniform principle has governed the choice of the *system-names. 1899 Allbutt's Syst. Med. VII. 79, I have seen sclerosis so situated in *system tracts, as to be mistaken for a tract-degeneration. 1711 Shaftesb. Charac. III. Misc. iii. ii. 187 A formal and profess'd Philosopher, a *System-Writer.

Systemad (si·stĕmæd), adv. Anat. [f. System + -ad: see Dextrad.] To or towards the (general) system of the body.

1808 [see Pulmonad].

†Sy·stemary, a. Obs. rare[−1]. [f. System + -ary.] ? Constituting a system (System 2).

1726 De Foe Hist. Devil i. vi. (1840) 76 One devil in a place would be enough for a whole systemary world.

Systematic (sistĕmæ·tik), a. and sb. [ad. late L. systēmaticus, a. late Gr. συστηματικός (both relating to systems of metres), f. σύστημα System. Cf. F. systématique (1584).] **A.** adj.

†1. = next, 1 b. Obs. rare.

a 1680 Glanvill Serm. Luke xiii. 24 Disc., etc. (1681) 7 All this I must confess,..because Experience constrains me; and I do not know why Systematick Notions should sway more than that.

2. = next, 1. (Passing into sense 3.)

1725 Watts Logic ii. iii. § 4 (1726) 219 Now we deal much in Essays, and most unreasonably despise systematic Learning. 1812 Sir H. Davy Chem. Philos. 10 The first Arabian Systematic Works on Chemistry are said to have been composed by Geber. a 1821 V. Knox Ess. Writing Wks. 1824 I. 5 Systematic books of morality. 1830 Herschel Study Nat. Phil. 110 The necessity of saying something learned and systematic, without knowing what to say. 1836 H. Rogers J. Howe ii. (1863) 21 Systematic theology..has..been of questionable benefit. 1847 Emerson Repr. Men, Swedenborg Wks. (Bohn) I. 316 Swedenborg is systematic..in every sentence. 1865 Tylor Early Hist. Man. i. 2 A systematic treatise on the subject.

3. gen. Arranged or conducted according to a system, plan, or organized method; involving or observing a system; (of a person) acting according to system, regular and methodical.

1790 Burke Rev. France 84 These gentlemen value themselves on being systematic. 1796 — Regic. Peace ii. Wks. VIII. 244 The systematick proceedings of a Roman senate. 1833 Alison Hist. Eur. (1849) III. xvii. § 18. 300 A systematic and uniform line of conduct. 1863 Lyell Antiq. Man i. 2 The facts brought to light..during the systematic investigation of the Brixham cave. 1867 Dickens Lett. (1880) II. 273 He is very systematic with the luggage. 1910 Encycl. Brit. II. 28/2 Though it will occasionally take a large fly, a worm or other ground-bait, its systematic capture is only essayed with small fish or artificial spinning-baits.

b. Qualifying nouns of action of unfavourable meaning: Carried out with a regularity such as to indicate intention or habitual action; regularly organized (for an evil purpose), or carried on as a regular (and reprehensible) practice. Also said of the agent.

1803 Brougham Colon. Policy I. 123 The house of Brandenburg seized this opportunity of prosecuting the systematic views of unprincipled aggrandisement, which have presided over its councils since the name of Prussia was known in Europe. 1828 D'Israeli Chas. I, I. vi. 163 The systematic intrigues of the Papal Court. 1867 Freeman Norm. Conq. I. iv. 195 After so many years of systematic devastation. 1874 L. Stephen Hours in Libr. (1892) I. iii. 106 Pope..was a systematic appropriator..of other men's thoughts. 1874 Green Short Hist. viii. § 3. 489 They turned religion into a systematic attack on English liberty.

4. Nat. Hist., etc. Pertaining to, following, or arranged according to a system of classification; of or pertaining to classification, classificatory. Also of a writer: Composing or adhering to a system of classification.

1796 Kirwan Elem. Min. (ed. 2) I. 23 The distinctive Characters, and systematic Arrangement, of Earths and Stones. 1800 Shaw (title) General Zoology or Systematic Natural History. 1809 T. Castle Introd. Bot. 12 Endeavouring to perfect systematic botany. 1835 J. Duncan Beetles (Nat. Lib.) 86 Beetles..such as burrow in the earth,..(the Geodephagi of some modern systematic writers). 1839 Yarrell Brit. Fishes I. Suppl. 11 Trigla lyra, the systematic name of our English Piper Gurnard. 1863 Huxley Man's Place Nat. ii. 102/3 This is a very noteworthy circumstance..but it has little systematic value.

5. Consisting of systems of heavenly bodies. rare.

1829 Chapters Phys. Sci. 415 Those numerous hosts of systematic universes.

6. = Systemic 1 b. rare.

1899 Allbutt's Syst. Med. VII. 3 The 'systematic' lesions [of myelitis].

B. sb. **1.** Nat. Hist., etc. A systematist.

1771 T. Percival Ess. (1777) I. 9 Salt, sulphur, acrimonies, caustics, volatiles, ferments,..have each..by different systematics, been received as the..principia morborum. 1788 J. Brown tr. Elem. Med. I. 287 note, Nothing is more artificial and arbitrary than the arrangements either of Systematics or Nosologists.

2. pl. **Systematics** [see -ic 2]: the subject or study of systems, esp. of classification.

1888 Nature 20 Dec. 177/2 Huxley's classification..in 1867, marked an epoch in the systematics of birds. 1909 E. B. Poulton in Q. Rev. July 14 Many hundreds of naturalists..devote their lives to systematics—to the study of the differences between species.

Systema·tical, a. Now rare or Obs. [f. late L. systēmaticus: see prec. and -ical.]

1. Of a writing or treatise: Containing or setting forth a system or regular exposition of some subject. Of a subject or study: Set forth, or pursued, in the way of a system or regular scheme. Of a writer: Dealing with a subject in this way; cf. 4.

1661 Boyle Style Script. 111 Such Precepts..are not Express'd and Rang'd in the Bible, as they are wont to be in Systematical Composures. 1698 Norris Pract. Disc. (1707) IV. 239 But 'tis New Philosophy, and..he likes the company of his Systematical Divines better. 1767 Blackburne (title) The Confessional; or, A Full and Free..Inquiry into the Right..Of Establishing Systematical Confessions of Faith and Doctrine in Protestant Churches. 1781 De Lolme Const. Eng. Advt. (1817) p. vi, The book..met..with approbation,..which..was no small luck for a book on systematical politics. 1782 Priestley Corrupt. Chr. I. i. ix. 124 Anselm, though he writes with wonderful acuteness, is not systematical.

b. Belonging to, or dealing in, a 'system' or theory; theoretical: cf. System 8 c.

1748 Chesterf. Let. to Son 25 Mar., They are not the laboured reflections of a systematical closet politician, who, without the least experience of business, sits at home and writes maxims. 1794 R. J. Sulivan View Nat. I. 57 Too much pertinacity in the support of systematical conjecture.

2. gen. = prec. 3.

1692 Bentley Boyle Lect. vii. (1693) 7 A brief account of some of the most principal and systematical Phænomena. 1749 Hartley Observ. Man i. Pref., Adding such things as were necessary to make the Whole appear more complete and systematical. 1763 J. Brown Poetry & Mus. v. 66 Their [sc. the ancients'] Divisions of the Musical Art are precise and systematical. 1804–8 Foster Life & Corr. (1846) I. 283 A plan of systematical reading. 1820 Scoresby Acc. Arctic Reg. II. 214 The systematical movements of the whales. 1853 Ruskin Stones Venice II. viii. § 51. 320 To arrange their ideas in systematical groups.

b. = prec. 3 b.

1750 Miss Talbot in Eliz. Carter's Lett. 26 Nov. (1809) I. 364 Some books of French, Morale Mondaine,..full of a systematical profligateness, veiled with delicacy of expression. 1755 Monitor No. 20. I. 77 The grand systematical corrupter. 1783 Burke Rep. Aff. India Wks. 1842 II. 81 In systematical contradiction to the company's orders. 1816 F. H. Naylor Hist. Germany I. i. viii. 290 The Jesuits, those systematical foes to every liberal sentiment.

†3. Belonging to the system of the universe, or to the solar system; cosmical. Obs.

1688 Boyle Final Causes Nat. Things i. 8 These Ends, may,..be call'd Cosmical or Systematical, as regarding the Symmetry of the great System of the world. 1782 Herschel in Phil. Trans. (1782) LXXII. 104 This new kind of systematical parallax, if I may be allowed to use that expression, for signifying the change arising from the motion of the whole solar system. 1797 — in Encycl. Brit. II. 480/2 The greatest..systematical parallax of the fixed stars will fall upon those that are in the line..at rectangles to the direction..of the sun's motion.

4. Nat. Hist. = prec. 4. Now rare or Obs.

1813 Sir H. Davy Agric. Chem. iii. (1814) 118 Some distinctions have been adopted by systematical authors which I have not entered into. 1817 Kirby & Sp. Entomol. xvii. (1818) II. 48 Gould..though no systematical naturalist, was a man of sense and observation. 1829 T. Castle Introd. Bot. 2 That part of the science, which refers to..the classification of plants..is denominated systematical botany.

Hence **Sy·stematica·lity,** the quality of being systematic.

1872 H. Nicol in Westm. Rev. XLI. 45 The symbols of foreign [sounds] will, from the systematicality of the alphabet, in most cases explain themselves.

Systematically (sistĕmæ·tikăli), adv. [f. prec. + -ly[2]: see -ically.]

1. In a systematic manner; according to a system or organized plan; regularly and methodically.

1661 Boyle Physiol. Ess. (1669) 7 Far from having such a stock of Experiments and Observations, as I judge requisite to write Systematically. 1699 [see System 10]. 1753 Warburton Princ. Nat. & Rev. Relig. v. Wks. 1788 V. 71 Urging those truths systematically,..which the Evangelists proposed singly and without connection. 1809–10 Coleridge Friend (1818) I. ii. 15 The majority of mankind learn nothing systematically, except as schoolboys or apprentices. 1837 Lockhart Scott IV. v. 143 Every case and shelf was accurately lettered, and the works arranged systematically. 1860 Mrs. Carlyle Lett. (1883) III. 45 The silence I systematically observe on the shortcomings of servants. 1880 L. Stephen Pope iv. 93 Pope..knew the value of independence well enough to be systematically economical.

b. With unfavourable implication: With a regularity indicating (evil) design or habit: cf. Systematic a. 3 b.

1829 F. Glasse Belgic Past. ii. 39 He systematically gains his ends By sacrifice of principles and friends. 1855 Macaulay Hist. Eng. xviii. IV. 144 The enemies of Child had ..accused him of systematically publishing false intelligence. 1858 Froude Hist. Eng. (ed. 2) II. x. 411 The pope..had heard..that abbots and monks in many places were systematically faithless to their vows. 1878 Lecky Eng. 18th Cent. I. i. 134 Officers of known Whig tendencies were systematically laid aside.

†2. By means of a 'system' or theory, theoretically: cf. prec. 1 b. Obs.

1749 Chesterf. Let. to Son 19 Dec., This knowledge is not to be gotten systematically; you must acquire it..by your own observation and sagacity.

Systematician (si:stĕmăti·ʃăn). rare. [f. Systematic + -ian, after mathematician.] One who constructs, or who adheres (esp. unduly) to, a system.

1886 19th Cent. July 73 A 'thought-mathematician', a systematician, a slave to the consistent application of his own theories. 1903 J. C. Lambert Sacraments N. T. ix. 382 He thinks it necessary to apologise for this lack of consistency on the part of the apostle, by reminding us that Paul was 'no correct systematician'.

Systema·ticness. [f. as prec. + -ness.] The quality of being systematic.

1836 F. W. Faber Lett. (1869) 58 To contrast the systematicness of the Primitive Church with..the modern worship about us.

Systematism (si·stĕmătiz'm). rare. [f. Systemat-ize + -ism. Cf. next.] The practice of systematizing: addiction to system.

1846 W. H. Mill Five Serm. (1848) 48 We see harmoniously combined those several aspects of the same great object, in which modern systematism sees only elements of contradiction. 1872 Lowell Dante Prose Wks. 1890 IV. 261 He [sc. Dante] combines the..more abstract religious sentiment of the Teutonic races with the scientific precision and absolute systematism of the Romanic.

Systematist (si·stĕmătist). [f. Gr. σύστημα, -ατ- System + -ist.] One who constructs, or adheres to, a system, esp. a system of classification in natural history; a classifying naturalist.

In Kirby's use, an advocate of a natural in preference to an artificial system of classification (opp. to Methodist 2 b).

1700 S. Parker Six Philos. Ess. 46 Your peremptory Systematist boldly distorts Nature. 1753 Chambers' Cycl. Supp., Systematists, in botany, those authors, whose works in this science are principally employed about the arranging plants into certain orders, classes, or genera. 1836 Penny Cycl. V. 248/2 Grew..was no systematist; it was reserved for another Englishman [sc. John Ray] to discover the true principles of classification. 1840 Whewell Philos. Induct. Sci. (1847) II. 557 The Fishes, in which province Cuvier has..been the great systematist. 1902 Edin. Rev. Oct. 370 Kaspar Bauhin (1550–1624), the first great botanical systematist.

Systematize (si·stĕmătəiz), v. [f. Gr. σύστημα, -ατ- System + -ize.] trans. To arrange according to a system; to reduce to system.

1764–7 Lyttelton Hen. II ii. (1769) III. 203 The eastern and western Goths had some general notions of the feudal policy, which were gradually systematised. 1780 Harris Philol. Enq. ii. xii. (1781) 224 Many things have been done in the best and purest taste, long before Rules were established, and systematized in form. 1828 D'Israeli Chas. I, I. viii. 250 His restless ambition..had systematised intrigue. 1830 Mackintosh Eth. Philos. Wks. 1846 I. 35 The vast collection of laws enacted or systematised by Justinian. 1899 Allbutt's Syst. Med. VIII. 343 Hallucinations, which are systematised into delusions.

b. absol. or intr. To construct a system (e. g. of philosophy, classification, etc.).

1891 in Cent. Dict. 1911 J. Oman in Expositor Oct. 362 The moment he proceeds to systematise,..he knows, just as little as any other systematiser, what to do with personality.

Hence **Sy·stematized** (-əizd) ppl. a., **Sy·stematizing** vbl. sb. and ppl. a. (in quot. 1827 = 'scheming'); also **Sy:stematiza·tion** (-ē¹·ʃən), the action or process of systematizing; a systematic arrangement, statement, etc.; **Sy·stematizer,** one who systematizes.

1811–13 Bentham Univ. Gram. Wks. 1843 VIII. 356/2 *Systematization; i.e. placing the several denominations.. in systematic order. 1838 [F. Haywood] tr. Kant's Crit. Pure Reason 490 The systematization of cognition—that is, the connexion thereof according to a principle. 1854 Max Müller Sci. Lang. Ser. ii. iii. 98 note, English Phonetics, containing an original systematisation of spoken sounds. 1904 Duckworth Morphol. & Anthropol. x. 232 The accompanying scheme..has been found of practical use in the further systematisation of observations. 1797 Burke Regic. Peace iii. Wks. 1808 VIII. 393 The relations of peace and amity with *systematised regicide. 1827 Lytton Pelham lxxviii, The systematised roguery of London. 1878–9 J. Caird Philos. Relig. (1880) 106 A living organism is not a mere aggregation of independent parts, but a systematised unity of members. 1884 F. Temple Relat. Relig. & Sci. v. (1885) 127 The systematised experience which we call Science. 1780 Harris Philol. Enq. i. i. (1781) 8 Aristotle ..may be called the *Systematizer of his Master's Doctrines. 1854 R. H. Patterson Ess. Hist. & Art (1862) 371 Auguste Comte..is but a systematiser of the doctrines of Confucius and the old philosophers of China. 1828 Sewell Oxford Prize Ess. 18 That mad fondness for *systematizing..which overthrows all the creations of nature. 1837 Whewell Hist. Induct. Sci. I. i. ii. § 2. 42 The treatises on the various subjects of Natural History..manifest a wonderful power of systematising. 1827 Southey in Q. Rev. Oct. 312 A cool, crafty, calculating, *systematizing knave. 1883 Sayce in Contemp. Rev. Sept. 391 The later age of systematizing philosophy.

Systemed (si·stĕmd), pa. pple. and a. rare. [f. System sb. + -ed.] Made into a system, systematized; arranged in a system or systems; composed according to system, systematic.

1748 W. Horsley Fool (1748) II. 47 Men of but middling Genius should keep to plain Rules, system'd to their Hands; acting in right Order by prescrib'd Method. 1807 J. Barlow Columb. x. 275 Social and system'd worlds around him shine. 1836 Mrs. Browning Poet's Vow i. xvii, Hear me forswear man's sympathies...His answering looks, his systemed books.

Systemic (siste·mik), a. [irreg. f. System + -ic; used for differentiation of meaning instead of the regular systematic.]

1. Physiol. and Path. Belonging to, supplying, or affecting the system or body as a whole; orig. and esp. in reference to the general circulation as distinguished from that supplying the respiratory organs (pulmonary or branchial).

1803 Barclay New Anat. Nomencl. 122 Let the vessels which convey it [sc. blood] from the lungs to the system be called the Systemic, and those which convey it from the system to the lungs be named the Pulmonic. 1835–6 Todd's Cycl. Anat. I. 794/1 The cessation of these actions, and the consequent solution of connection between the various parts of the body, is systemic death. 1841 R. E. Grant Comp. Anat. 498 The great systemic artery issuing from the left ventricle. 1858 Blackw. Mag. LXXXIII. 326 The..systemic sensation of Hunger. 1889 Bartholow Mat. Med. (ed. 7) 489 Systemic effects may be produced by such an application. 1896 Newton Dict. Birds 1008 The Systemic Circulation..divisible into Arterial and Venous.

b. Belonging to or affecting a particular system of bodily organs, esp. the nervous system or special parts of it: see quot. 1890.

1887 W. F. Revell Ethical Forecasts 81 Certain molecular movements of nerve-substance marshal themselves, or are marshalled, into such order as..gives rise to orderly sequences of thought...Does there not seem to be..a systemic intelligence, or a systemic grouping of forces which secures the results that intelligence might be expected to secure? 1890 Billings Nat. Med. Dict. s.v., S[ystemic] lesion, a lesion limited to one set of homologous parts, such as the posterior columns or the anterior cornua of the spinal cord. 1896 Allbutt's Syst. Med. I. 181 Systemic sclerosis of a small but defined tract of the spinal cord.

2. gen. Of or pertaining to a system. rare[−0].

1850 in Ogilvie; hence in later Dicts.

So **†Syste·mical** a. (obs. rare), systematic; hence **Syste·mically** adv., (a) systematically; (b) in relation to the bodily system.

1724 A. Collins Gr. Chr. Relig. Concl. 273 The commentaries on Scripture, and systemical books of all modern theologues. 1888 Centen. Confer. Missions (U.S.) II. 265 What general would dare systemically to fight without reserves? 1889 Lancet 4 May 882/1 It seems likely that it [sc. corrosive sublimate] acts as much systemically as locally.

Sy·stemist. rare. [irreg. f. System + -ist.] = Systematist.

1796 Eliza Hamilton Lett. Hindoo Rajah (1811) II. 236 But little pain did the sorrows of the mourners give to the young systemist. 1868 Peard Water-farm. xv. 151 The genus Cyprinus as now restricted by modern systemists contains the common carp and allied species.

Systemize (si·stĕməiz), v. [irreg. f. System + -ize.] trans. = Systematize.

1776 [W. Marshall] Minutes Agric., Digest 2 He continued to systemize what he thought worthy of his System. 1828–32 Webster. 1846 Worcester, Systemize, to systematize. Hiley. A word rarely used by good writers. 1908 Westm. Gaz. 27 June 13/2 Learning made easy and systemised from thirty years' experience.

Hence **Sy·stemized** (-əizd) ppl. a., **Sy·stemizing** vbl. sb. and ppl. a.; also **Sy:stemiza·tion,** systematization; **Sy·stemizer,** a systematizer.

1835 I. Taylor Spir. Despot. v. 204 Nothing cou'd have prevented this systemizing of functions. 1853 Tait's Mag. XX. 456 The improved systemization and conduct of Assurance. 1880 Ruskin Elem. Engl. Prosody § 8. 9 The whole subject of Prosody has been confused, and its systemization for English readers made virtually impossible, by the want of clearly understanding the difference between accent and time. 1895 Advance (Chicago) 370/3 The intellectualism of the reformers asserts itself in the systemizer of the school. 1907 R. J. Thompson Proofs of Life after Death 34 The amassed, severely tested and systemized knowledge that is ..essential to effect a universal conviction.

Systemless (si·stĕmlĕs), a. [-less.]

1. Devoid of system or orderly arrangement; unsystematic.

1851 Ruskin Stones Venice I. xxv. § 20 Dreading to be called upon..to admire a systemless architecture, because it may happen to have sprung from an irrational religion. 1883 Science I. 521/2 In upper Swabia, glacial deposits present their peculiar landscape of systemless hills and hollows.

2. Biol. Having no differentiated systems of organs; structureless.

1862 Dana Man. Geol. 597 If..these simple species existed in the Azoic era, they were systemless life.

System-wise, adv. [See -wise.] In relation to things as they are connected in a system.

1799 Lamb Let. to Southey 15 Mar., I never judge system-wise of things, but fasten upon particulars.

Systerne, obs. f. Cistern.

Systolated (si·stŏlē¹tĕd), a. rare[−1]. [f. next + -ate[2] + -ed[1].] Contracted by systole.

1820 Blackw. Mag. VII. 324, I therefore give him leave to alter my systolated preterites into preterpluperfects.

‖Systole (si·stŏlĭ). Also 6 sistole. [mod.L., ad. Gr. συστολή, f. Gr. σύν Syn- + στολ- (: στέλλειν to place), after συστέλλειν to draw together, contract. Cf. F. systole, † cistole (c 1600), It. sistole, Sp. sístole, Pg. systole.]

1. Phys. The regular contraction of the heart and arteries that drives the blood outward: opposed to Diastole.

1578 Banister Hist. Man vii. 92 b, Sistole is, when the hart by constriction putteth forth the same [spirit]. 1605 Daniel Queen's Arcadia iii. ii. (1606) F j b, The Systole, and Dyastole of your pulse, Do shew your passions most hystericall. 1664 Power Exp. Philos. i. 41 In this Animal [sc. lamprey] the heart in every diastole is of a fair purple and ruddy colour, and in every systole pale and wan. 1669 W. Simpson Hydrol. Chym. 76 The systole of the left ventricle. 1707 Floyer Physic. Pulse-Watch 18 When the Heart is in its Systole, the Arteries are dilated. 1806 H. K. White Let. to Maddock 17 Feb., The systole and diastole of my heart seem to be playing at ball—the stake, my life. 1835–6 Todd's Cycl. Anat. I. 655/2 The systole of each cavity [of the heart] is immediately followed by its diastole or relaxation. 1877 M. Foster Physiol. i. iv. (1879) 145 Practically speaking, there is no interval between the auricular and ventricular systole [of the heart].

b. Applied to similar rhythmical contraction in other organs, as the lungs, the intestines, the pulsatile vesicles in protozoans, the contractile vesicles in certain algæ, etc.

1578 Banister Hist. Man viii. 99 Not onely to the hart belongeth the same Diastole, and Sistole, but likewise to the brayne. 1657 Trapp Comm. Job x. 8 He was amazed at the manner of the motion of the lungs by Systole and Diastole. 1660 [see Diastole 1]. 1826 Kirby & Sp. Entomol. xxxix. IV. 81 A long dorsal vessel, the first step towards a heart, which alternately contracts and dilates with an irregular systole and diastole. 1855 T. R. Jones Anim. Kingd. (ed. 2) 306 The contraction or systole in any given [branchial] tuft occurs at frequent but irregular intervals. 1882 W. S. Kent Man. Infusoria II. 874 Systole, a term applied to the contracting action of the structure known as the contractile vesicle of Infusoria and other Protozoa.

c. fig.

1831 [see Diastole 1 fig.]. 1849 De Quincey Eng. Mail Coach i. Misc. (1854) 300 To interrupt the great respirations, ebb and flood, systole and diastole, of the national intercourse. 1872 Geo. Eliot Middlem. lxiii, There must be a systole and diastole in all inquiry. 1899 W. R. Inge Chr. Myst. i. 28 A systole and diastole of the spiritual life.

2. Pros. The shortening of a vowel or syllable long by nature or position.

1577 Peacham Gard. Eloquence E ij b, Systole, when a long Sillable is made shorte, contrary to the nature therof, Dartus for Darius, Diāna for Diāna, Iosēphus for Iosēphus. 1639 J. Bird Grounds of Gram. (1641) 183. 1657 J. Smith Myst. Rhet. 176. 1704 J. Harris Lex. Techn. I, Systole, in Grammar, is part of the Poetical Licence, whereby a long Syllable is made short: As in that of Virgil.—Tulerunt fastidia Menses.

Systolic (sistǫ·lik), a. [ad. mod.L. systolicus, f. systole: see prec. and -ic. Cf. F. systolique (Rabelais).] Pertaining to or marked by systole.

a 1693 Urquhart's Rabelais iii. iv, The Heart, which by its agitation of Diastolick and Systolick Motions so neatly subtilizeth and inflames it [sc. choler]. 1817 tr. Swedenborg's Heaven & Hell § 445 The systolic motions of the heart. 1853 Markham Skoda's Auscult. 158 Systolic murmurs heard in the left ventricle. 1875 H. C. Wood Therap. (1879) 136 The diastole generally becomes imperfect, one portion of the ventricle maintaining its systolic spasm, while the rest dilates. 1877 Huxley Anat. Inv. Anim. ii. 77 This systolic and diastolic movement usually occurs at a fixed point in the protoplasm. 1899 Allbutt's Syst. Med. VII. 241 The cardiac systolic expansion of the brain within the closed cranium is rendered possible by the ebb of the cerebro-spinal fluid.

Systren, obs. pl. of Sister.

Systyle (si·stəil), a. and sb. Arch. [ad. Gr.-L. systȳlos (Vitruvius), a. Gr. σύστυλος, f. σύν Syn- + στῦλος column, pillar. Cf. F. systyle.] adj. Applied to architecture in which the columns are close together, viz. at a distance from each other of twice their thickness; sb. a building characterized by such intercolumniation.

[1563 Shute Archit. F j, Sistylos,..whose pillers standeth distant one from the other .2. Diameters, or .2. and a halfe at the fourdest.] 1704 J. Harris Lex. Techn. I, Systyle.. is a Building where the Pillars stand thick, but not altogether so close as in the Pycnostyle. 1771 W. Newton tr. Vitruvius' Archit. iii. iii. (1791) 52 note, The eustyle intercolumns may likewise be two and a half diameters, as the mean between those of the dyastyle and systyle, instead of two and a quarter, which is nearer to the systyle. 1789 P. Smyth tr. Aldrich's Archit. (1818) 147 Whose intercolumniations in the middle are systyle, on each side pycnostyle. 1844 Civil Eng. & Arch. Jrnl. VII. 23/2 The Pantheon at Rome is a systyle.

Systylous (si·stiləs), a. Bot. [f. mod.L. systylus (f. Gr. σύν Syn- + στῦλος column) + -ous.] **a.** In mosses, having the lid permanently fixed to the columella. **b.** Having the styles united into a single column.

1863 M. J. Berkeley Brit. Mosses Gloss. 313 Systylous, used when the lid adheres to the columella.

Syt: see Set v., Sight, Sit v., Site.

Sytalle, obs. form of Citole.

14.. Nom. in Wr.-Wülcker 738/18 Hic psalmatus, the sytalle.

Syte, obs. form of Cite v.

1485 Acc. St. Dunstan's Canterb. in Archæol. Cant. (1886) XVI. 292 Payde to John Horsley for sytyng of dyuerse persons for the dutis of the Churche viij d.

Syte, obs. form of City.

1340–70 Alex. & Dind. 9 No syte nor no sur stede soþli þei ne hadde. 1a 1400 Arthur 71 Arthour bysegeþ þat Syte & town. c 1440 Promp. Parv. 457/1 Syte, urbs.

Syte: see Sight, Site, Syth.

†Syteer. Obs. (?)

1433 Rolls of Parlt. IV. 476/2 That the said xxv persones sworen in maner above seid, shall chese vi Men that been called Syteers,..and that they be true Burgeys and resseauntes within the seid Town, to have and occupie..the Office of resceite. 1444 Ibid. V. 123/1.

Syter, -wurt, obs. var. Setter v., Setterwort.

†Syth, sb. Sc. Obs. Also 6 syith, 8 site, syte. [Aphetic form of Assyth sb.] Satisfaction, compensation.

To get one's heart's syth of: see quot. 1710.

1567 Gude & Godlie Ball. (S.T.S.) 104 3our bludie boist sa syith can satisfie. 1661 in Cramond Records of Elgin (1908) II. 295 The said John wes suire that he wold get his heart syth of everie one that wronged him. 1710 Ruddiman Gloss. Douglas' Æneis s.v. Site, syte, I have gotten my heart's syte on him, i.e. my heart's desire on him, or all the evil I wish'd him.

†Syth, v. Sc. Obs. Also 5 syþ, 6 syith, sith, cythe. [Aphetic form of Assyth v.] trans. To satisfy, give satisfaction to.

c 1425 Wyntoun Cron. v. xii. 3970 (Wemyss MS.) [Scho] gaif hame siluer or payment, Or claiþ to syþ thare entent. 1513 Douglas Æneis ix. vii. 116 He mycht do stanche his ire, and syth his thocht. 1536 Bellenden Cron. Scot. (1821) II. 120 The king was nocht full sithit with his justice. c 1550 Rolland Crt. Venus iii. 774 That pane may be in put to Forfaltouris: The Partie sythit, as Law will lat it be. absol. 1583 Reg. Privy Council Scot. III. 599 He forgevis thame..of quhat degre sa evir thay be of. Quhilk as his majestie heir promittis, sa sall he mak it to cythe in gud effect heirefter.

b. ? intr. for pass. To be satisfied.

1650 in W. Ross Aberdour & Inchcolme (1885) 326 [He had called her] a trumpous [cross-tempered] witch, [and her heart] sythed [glowed with satisfaction, when she saw him coming home in his hurt condition].

Syth: see Scythe, See v., Sight, Sith, Sithe.

Sythar, var. Siquare Obs., moment.

Sytharist, obs. f. Citharist, player on the cithara; in quot. misused for the instrument.

c 1450 Holland Howlat 757 The psaltery, the sytholis, the soft sytharist.

Sythe: see Saithe, Scythe, Sight, Sith, Sithe.

Sythen, -yn, Sythence, Syther: see Sithen, Sithence, Cider.

†Sythment. Sc. Obs. Also 6 syithment, 6–7 sith(e)ment. [f. Syth v. + -ment. Cf. Assythment.] Satisfaction, compensation, indemnification.

1536 Bellenden Cron. Scot. (1821) II. 394 In sithement of his ransoun. 1560 Rolland Seven Sages 58 This is na mendis to me, Howbeit it be ane syithment to my hart. 1572 Satir. Poems Reform. xxx. 218 The Lord..send vs ane sythment of yis suddane slauchter. 1633 W. Struther True Happines 66 When we seeke a sithment and revenge on our selves for angring him we take Gods part against our selfe. 1667 in Cramond Ann. Cullen (1887) 51, £20 to be peyt to the toune for..disturbing the peace theroff with £12 of sythment to the pairtie wronged.

Sythol(l, sytole, -olphe, var. Citole Obs.

Sythpe, Syth(t)ware, Sytizin: see Sith, Siquare, Citizen.

Sythyohe, var. of so thee ich: see Thee v.[1]

Sytt, variant of Site sb.[1] Obs.

c 1560 A. Scott Poems (S.T.S.) xv. 9 So neides thow nocht now sussy, sytt, nor sorrow.

Sytyca, obs. form of Sciatica.

‖Syud (səi·əd). Also 8 syed, 9 syeud. = Sayyid.

1788 Syed [see Sayyid]. 1799 Edmonstone in Owen Wellesley's Desp. (1877) 82 The respected and accomplished Syuds..are now nominated and deputed with this friendly letter. c 1813 Mrs. Sherwood Ayah & Lady v. 29 There is but one God, whatever you Hindoos may say. Our syeuds always say so. 1850 Directions Rev. Off. N. W. Prov. 47 There is a great tendency..to be more lenient towards the powerful or the indolent, such as Syuds, Brahmans, or Goojurs.

Syue, var. Civy Obs., onion sauce.

c 1440 Anc. Cookery in Househ. Ord. (1790) 449 Turbot, and congur, and plays, and soles in syne [sic].

Syue, syve, Syuer, Syun, obs. ff. Sieve, Sure, Scion.

Syver (səi·vəɹ). Sc. Forms: 7–9 siver, 9 syvo(u)r, syver. [? ad. (north-eastern) OF. sewiere Sewer sb.[1]] = Syre.

1606 Charter in Dallas Stiles (1697) 774 Lie sinks, sivers, guttars, eyes,..airholls [etc.]. 1793 Statist. Acc. Scot. VII. 145 The manse..lies in a swamp, the inconvenience of which the present clergyman has..remedied by sivers, as they are here called. 1834 J. Wilson Noctes Ambr. Aug., Wks. 1856 IV. 99 She [sc. a hare] made for the mouth o' the siver. 1867 J. K. Hunter Retrospect Artist's Life vii. (1912) 66 He has faun wi' a clash in the syvour. 1894 P. H. Hunter James Inwick v. 62 There was Jess an' the kimmers a' stan'in wi' their boynes an' pails at the siver. 1900 J. G. Campbell Superstit. Scottish Highl. 209 An opening like the syver of a drain.

attrib. 1889 H. Johnston Chron. Glenbuckie 81 These guileless laddie-weans, sitting..by the syver-edge. 1906 N. Munro Daft Days xiii, He stood on the syver-side. Ibid. xvi, The gulls that quarrelled in the syver sand.

Sywe, Sywester(e, Syw(e)te, -yte, obs. ff. Sue, Sewster, Suit sb. **Syx(e, Syxt(e,** etc., obs. ff. Six, Sixth, etc. **Syxt,** obs. 2nd sing. ind. pres. of See v.; obs. f. Sext. **Syyk,** obs. f. Sick.

Syzygant (si·zigănt). Math. [irreg. f. Syzygy + -ant, after invariant, etc.] (See quots.)

1882 Sylvester in Amer. Jrnl. Math. V. 87 Irreducible syzygants and irreducible invariantive derivatives of the same type, to the same quantic cannot coëxist. 1882 Hammond in Amer. Jrnl. Math. V. 221. 1885 Cayley Math. Papers XII. 251 A seminvariant may be expressible as a sum of products (of a higher degree) of perpetuants of lower degrees, and of perpetuants of lower degrees, and it is not on this account reducible: a seminvariant so expressible is said to be a 'syzygant'.

Syzygetic (sizidʒe·tik), a. Math. [Loosely f. Syzygy + -etic (cf. Gr. συζυγεῖν to yoke together, be correlative).] Of, pertaining to, or constituting a syzygy (Syzygy 5). Hence **Syzyge·tically** adv.

1850 Sylvester in Camb. & Dubl. Math. Jrnl. V. 276 [U, V, W] are..capable of being connected by integral multipliers U′, V′, W′, such that U′U + V′V + W′W = 0. Any number of functions U, V, W so related, I call syzygetic functions, and U′, V′, V″ [sic: ? W′] I term the syzygetic multipliers. 1852 — Ibid. VII. 75 note, Rational integer functions which admit of being multiplied severally by other rational integer-functions such that the sum of the products is identically zero, are said to be 'syzygetically related'. 1853 — in Phil. Trans. CXLIII. 407.

†Syzygiacal, a. Obs. rare. [f. Gr. συζυγία or late L. syzygia Syzygy + -ac + -al.] = next.

1672 Flamsteed in Rigaud Corr. Sci. Men (1841) II. 140 Let MP be the line of the mean apogæon making an acute angle with the syzigiacal line SCO.

Syzygial (sizi·dʒiăl), a. Astron. and Zool. [f. late L. syzygia Syzygy + -al.] Pertaining to a syzygy or syzygies; having the character of a syzygy (senses 1 b, 3).

1863 Fitz Roy Weather Bk. xviii. 253 The moon's greatest tidal action being syzygial, and the least at quadrature. 1873 C. W. Thomson Depths of Sea ix. 452 The first brachial is united to the second by a syzygial joint. 1879 Carpenter in Trans. Linn. Soc. Ser. ii. II. i. 48 The number of segments composing the syzygial interval is..three.

‖Syzygium (sizi·dʒiŏm). Biol. [mod.L., alteration of syzygia (see next).] = Syzygy 3 b.

1883 Encycl. Brit. XIX. 855/2 The term 'syzygium' is applied to such a conjunction of two Gregarinidea. 1898 P. Manson Trop. Diseases i. 12 [The crescent body of malaria] is the result of the conjugation of two ordinary plasmodia—a syzygium, in fact.

Syzygy (si·zidʒi). Also 7 sys-, syzigie, 7–8 sys-, syzygie, 8–9 syzigy, 9 syzigee. [ad. late L. syzygia, a. Gr. συζυγία yoke, pair, copulation, conjunction, f. σύζυγος yoked, paired, f. σύν Syn- + ζυγ- : ζευγνύναι to yoke. Cf. F. syzygie (1584 in Hatz.-Darm.).]

1. Astron. **† a.** Orig. = Conjunction 3. Obs.

1656 Blount Glossogr., Syzigie (syzigia), a conjunction, a coupling. The conjunction of the Moone with the Sunne; the new moone. 1686 Goad Celest. Bodies i. xi. 43 The Great and Leading Syzygie, or human Aspect with the ☉. 169x Leybourn Curs. Math. 758 So that in every true Syzygy, the Centre of the Deferent agrees with the Centre of the Earth. 1704 J. Harris Lex. Techn. I, Syzygie, in Astronomy, is the same with the Conjunction of any two Planets, or Stars, or when they are both referred to the same Point in the Heavens; or when they are referred to the same Degree of the Ecliptick, by a Circle of Longitude passing through them both.

b. Now extended to include both conjunction and opposition (Opposition 3) of two heavenly bodies, or either of the points at which these take place, esp. in the case of the moon with the sun (new and full moon). Often opposed to Quadrature 4 b, c.

1715 tr. Gregory's Astron. (1726) I. 123 If the Nodes of the Orbit of the Body L, be in the Syzygies of the Body S. 1728 Chambers Cycl. s.v., On the Phænomena and Circumstances of the Syzygies, a great Part of the Lunar Theory depends. 1749 Phil. Trans. XLVI. 150 The greatest Spring-Tides, and least Neap-Tides, are commonly on the third or fourth Day, after the Syzygies and Quadratures. 1833 Herschel Astron. xi. 325 Suppose the disturbing body to be fixed in the line of nodes, or the nodes to be in syzygy. 1869 Phillips Vesuv. iv. 112 The eruptions were sensibly strengthened at the syzigies and weakened at the quadratures of the moon. 1882 Nature 27 July 292/1 The sunspot maxima..are nearly always associated with configurations in which Venus and Earth in conjunction or opposition, have Jupiter in or near syzygy or quadrature.

†2. Anat. pl. The pairs of cranial nerves. Obs.

1681 tr. Willis' Rem. Med. Wks. Vocab., Syzygies, are the nerves that carry the sense from the brain to the whole body.

3. Biol. **a.** A suture or immovable union of two joints of a crinoid; also, the joints thus sutured. **b.** The conjunction of two organisms without loss of identity, as in the genus Diplozoon; a syzygium.

1873 C. W. Thomson Depths of Sea ix. 440 The first of the brachial joints..is..split in two by a peculiar kind of joint, called, by Müller, a 'syzygy'. Ibid., When the animal is dying it generally breaks off its arms at these syzygies. 1888 Rolleston & Jackson Anim. Life 572 (Crinoidea) The lines of union..may be obliterated...The ligamentous connections may become very close...Two joints thus connected are termed a syzygy. Ibid. 573 The ..ligaments between brachials not united by syzygy appear to be contractile.

4. Anc. Prosody. A dipody, or combination of two feet in one metre (Metre sb.[1] 4).

[1706 Phillips (ed. Kersey), Syzygia..Among Grammarians, the coupling or clapping of different Feet together in Greek or Latin Verse.] 1836 J. R. Major Guide Grk. Trag. 109 Some grammarians, in speaking of anapæstic, iambic, and trochaic verse, use the term syzygy (συζυγία) or dipodia (διποδία) instead of metre.

5. Math. A group of rational integral functions so related that, on their being severally multiplied by other rational integral functions, the sum of the products vanishes identically; also, the relation between such functions.

1850 Sylvester in Camb. & Dubl. Math. Jrnl. V. 276 The members of any group of functions, more than two in number, whose nullity is implied in the relation of double contact,..must be in syzygy. Thus PQ, PQR, QR, must form a syzygy. 1867 Cayley Math. Papers VI. 147 While for the degree 5 we obtain 3 covariants and a single syzygy, for the degree 6 we obtain only 2 covariants, but as many as 7 syzygies. 1869 W. K. Clifford in Proc. Lond. Math. Soc. 11 Nov. 11 If the 12th powers of the nil-facta in the tangential equations of 43 points are connected by a linear syzygy, the 43 points are on a quartic curve. 1886 Hammond in Amer. Jrnl. Math. VIII. 19 Syzygy Tables for the Binary Quintic.

6. A pair of connected or correlative things; in Gnostic theology, a couple or pair of opposites, or of æons.

1838 Sir W. Hamilton Logic xx. (1866) I. 402 The Greek logicians after Aristotle, looking merely to the two premises in combination, called these Syzygies. 1853 J. Martineau Ess. (1891) III. 470 Ourselves and the external world we know..only under relation; of subject, for example, to object;..of phenomenon to cause. Yet, in pursuing this relative course of cognition, we are apt to be struck with the belief that one of the two terms in each of the primary syzygies transcends relation at the very moment of creating it. 1875 Lightfoot Comm. Col. 166 The system of syzygies, or pairs of opposites, is a favourite doctrine of this work [sc. Clementine Homilies], and in these John stands contrasted to Jesus, as Simon Magus to Simon Peter, as the false to the true. 1890 J. Martineau Seat Author. Relig. ii. ii. 237 The fourth Gospel..is..itself a Gnosticism, only baptized and regenerate: no longer lingering aloft with the divine emanation in a fanciful sphere of æons and of syzygies. 1909 Gwatkin Early Church Hist. xv. II. 37 Valentinus, says Victorinus, teaches a pleroma and thirty æons, and these he arranges in syzygies or couples.

Szaboite (sæ·boˌəit). Min. [ad. G. szaboit (1878), named in honour of Prof. J. Szabo of Budapest.] A variety of hypersthene.

1883 Encycl. Brit. XVI. 417/1. 1892 Dana Min. 350 Szaboite occurs in thin tabular crystals..; it was first described as triclinic and a relation to babingtonite suggested, but its identity with hypersthene was later fixed by Lasaulx.

Szaibelyite (sebe·lyəit). Min. [ad. G. szaibelyit (1861), named after Szajbelyi, a Hungarian.] A hydrous borate of magnesium, found in nodules in limestone.

1866 Brande & Cox Dict. Sci., etc. II. 532/1. 1868 Dana Min. (ed. 5) 594.

Szkippe, obs. f. Skip sb.[1]

Szmikite (smi·kəit). Min. [ad. G. szmikit (1887), named after Szmik, a Hungarian.] A hydrous sulphate of manganese.

1892 Dana Min. 933 Szmikite...Amorphous, stalactitic... Color whitish, on the fracture reddish white to rose-red.

T.

T (tī), the twentieth letter of the English and other modern alphabets, the nineteenth of the ancient Roman alphabet, corresponding in form to the Greek Τ (tau), from the Phœnician (and ancient Semitic) ✛ ✕ X X (tau), in Phœnician, and originally also in Greek, the last letter of the alphabet. It represents the point-breath-stop consonant of Bell's 'Visible Speech', or surd dental mute, so called, but in English is gingival or alveolar rather than dental. Several varieties of a t-sound occur in different languages, according as the flow of the breath is stopped by bringing the tip or front of the tongue into contact with different points between the edge of the upper teeth and the roof of the palate. Thus, contact of the tip of the tongue with the teeth gives the true dental t, which is common in continental European languages, very distinct in Anglo-Irish, and heard in north-western English dialects before r, where it is often represented in dialect specimens by spelling thrue or t'hrue for true, and the like (though the consonant is not actually th or þ). The Indian languages, Aryan as well as Dravidian, distinguish two kinds of t, the dental, and the retracted or 'cerebral' (mūrdhanya), in Sanskrit त and ट, of which the latter is formed by contact of the retracted tip of the tongue with the roof of the palate. The English t is formed between these two extreme positions, the contact being with the back of the gum or the front margin of the palate; its sound is much closer to the cerebral than to the dental, and in the Tamil or Telugu representation of English words, the cerebral is regularly put for English t. In the Roman transliteration of Indian words it is usual to write t for the dental, and to distinguish the cerebral as ṭ, as is done in this dictionary. The Semitic languages also distinguish two t-sounds, one, the Hebrew tau (ת), Arabic ta (ت) dental; the other, Hebrew teth (ט), Arabic ṭa (ط), said to be formed by contact of the blade of the tongue with the palate; this also has been romanized as ṭ, though distinguished in Urdū from the cerebral ṭ.

In modern English, besides its proper sound as above described, t in the combinations -tion, -tious, -tial, -tia, -tian, -tience, -tient, after a vowel or any consonant except s, has the sound of sh (ʃ), in which the following i is absorbed, as in nation (nē¹·ʃən), factious (fæ·kʃəs), partial (pā·ɹʃăl), militia (mili·ʃă), patience (pē¹·ʃĕns); but in -ia, -ian, i is sometimes more or less preserved, especially in proper names, as in inertia, Portia, Gratian, Dalmatian. In these combinations Latin (t) became (ts), usually written z, and then (s), written c, in French, as in L. grātia, It. grazia, F. grâce, L. nātiōnem, It. nazione, OF., Sp. nacion. In French and English spelling the Latin t was subsequently in most cases restored, e. g. nation; but the living sound was (s), and it is this s which combining with the following i (= y consonant) as (sy-), passed in English into (ʃ), in the same way as written c or s has done in gracious, Asia, emersion: see S the letter, par. 4. Strictly, therefore, what we have is not ti pronounced as (ʃ), but (ʃ) derived from ci, spelt ti after its Latin source. After s, the original sound of t has remained, as in bestial, Christian, Erastian, question.

A much more recent change, as yet scarcely recognized by orthoepists, is the development in southern England of the sound ch (tʃ) from t followed by u with its diphthongal or name sound (yu, iu, ɪu), in such combinations as -tual, -tue, -tuous, and especially -ture, as in nature (nē¹·tiŭɹ), whence (nē¹·tyəɹ, nē¹·tʃəɹ). In those English dialects in which u has not become (yū), the original t remains, as in 'critter' = creature, 'pictur' = picture. In rapid speech ti after s often passes similarly into tʃ, as (kwe·stʃən) for (kwe·styən).

T between s and syllabic l or n (en), as in bustle, castle, epistle, christen, fasten, hasten, is now usually mute; so between s and m in Christmas, and between f and syllabic n in often, soften.

Th is a consonantal digraph representing two simple sounds (þ, ð), for which the Roman alphabet has no simple symbols, and is thus phonetically a distinct letter (or two letters), inserted between Te- and Ti-, where see its history and pronunciation.

I. 1. The letter and its sound. The plural is variously written t's, t's, ts (tīz). See also Tee sb.[1]

c 1000 [see B]. c 1374 Chaucer Boeth. i. pr. i. 2 (Camb. MS.) Abouen þat lettre in the heyeste bordure a grekyssh t þat signifieth the lyf contemplatyf. 1487 Act 4 Hen. VII, c. 13 Every Person so convicted..for any other Felony.. to be marked with a T in the same Place of the Thumb. 1736 Ainsworth Lat.-Eng. Dict. s.v., With a design to hang T on her own gibbet, as Lucian jocosely says. 1847 Proc. Philol. Soc. III. 45 Thus the Aztecs of Mexico, though able to pronounce an l in the middle of a word, at the commencement find it necessary to prefix a t-sound to the liquid. 1859 Life E. Henderson vi. 353 Before the little inmate of the Linn could have known a T from a craw's tae. 1861 Dickens Gt. Expect. xvi, Everything producible that began with a T, from tar to toast.

b. In phrase to cross the t's: to make the horizontal stroke of t (often omitted in hasty writing); fig. to be minutely exact or particular in one's account; to make the meaning more distinct; to particularize and emphasize the points. Cf. to dot the i's in I (the letter) 1.

1865 E. C. Clayton Cruel Fortune II. 220 To ascertain whether it was..properly spelt, and had all the i's dotted, and the t's crossed. 1882 Mrs. Houstoun Recomm. to Mercy xx, Please not to cross the t's. 1885 Dunckley in Manch. Exam. 15 June 6/2 To dot his i's and cross his t's and polish up his manuscript.

c. Phr. To a T (also to a tee): exactly, properly, to a nicety.

[The original sense of T here has not been ascertained. Suggestions that it was the tee at Curling, or at Golf, or a T square, appear on investigation to be untenable; it has also been suggested that it referred to the proper completion of a t by crossing it (see b); or that it was the initial of a word; in reference to this it is notable that to a tittle (i.e. to a prick, dot, jot) was in use nearly a century before 'to a T', and in exactly the same constructions: see Tittle.]

1693 Humours Town 102 All the under Villages and Towns-men come to him for Redress; which he does to a T. 1700 Labour in Vain viii. in Harl. Misc. (1810) X. 473 Harry cajoled my inquirer, and fitted his humour to a t—. 1772 J. Giles Poems 155 I'll tell you where You may be suited to a tee. 1815 Zeluca I. 385, I knew my man to a T. 1828 Life Planter Jamaica 161, I understand the practice to a tee. 1840 R. H. Dana Bef. Mast xxii. 66 The yards were squared 'to a T' by lifts and braces. 1856 Mrs. Stowe Dred ii, All these old-fashioned goings on would suit you to a T.

2. The shape of the letter; an object having the shape T. See also Tee sb.[1], Tau. Also short for T beard, T iron, T rail: see 3.

a 1619, a 1654 [see 3 b]. 1707 Mortimer Husb. (1721) II. 262 Slit the Bark or Rind about an Inch long, in form of a T. 1733 Tull Horse-Hoeing Husb. xxii. 330 Made..with a Head like a T. 1875 Sir T. Seaton Fret-Cutting 69 Then see whereabouts to put them through the upright part or T of the bracket. 1891 Daily News 27 Apr. 2/5 Plate iron, angles, T's, and bars for railway waggon building are in large request. 1891 Scott. Leader 21 Sept. 3 Inquiries for old material are reviving, rails being chiefly in demand. Some holders are now asking 21 dols. for old T's. 1893 F. Adams New Egypt 237 The tongue of this inverted T, i.e., the entrenchments, had been carried out some two miles.

3. attrib. (sometimes hyphened): Shaped like the letter T; having a cross piece at the top; as T bandage, bar, chain, end, fish, handle, head, hinge, iron, joint, key, pattern, piece, spot, tap, tube, wharf. Also comb., as T-formed, -headed, -shaped adjs. See also Tee sb.[1], Tee-piece, etc.

1783 Bentley in Med. Commun. (1784) I. 257 The canula ..was left in the puncture, secured with a double *T bandage. 1882 Nares Seamanship (ed. 6) 84 Secured by a *T chain. 1842 Penny Cycl. XX. 465/2 The *T-formed or arrow-shaped bone [of the Saurians]. 1778 [W. Marshall] Minutes Agric. 20 Apr. an. 1775, A light beam of seven feet long, drawn by a *T handle, by one man, walking backwards. 1844 Stephens Bk. Farm III. 849 They are always attached..by a *T headed nail and spike. 1844 Ibid. I. 198 The inside doors should be hung with *T hinges, 18 inches long. 1858 Civil Eng. & Arch. Jrnl. I. 126/1 The roof.. is further supported and braced by struts of *T iron and suspension rods. 1906 Westm. Gaz. 16 Mar. 8/1 The main cable..is always connected with the consumer's house by means of a *T-joint, which is enclosed in a box filled with bitumen. 1895 Parkes Health 54 Lead *T pieces, as they are called [in water-pipes] must be used. 1860 Biog. & Crit. fr. 'The Times' 235 *T-shaped traps for the wheatear. 1896 Farrier's Price List, *T taps and other tools. 1881 Tyndall Floating Matter of Air iii. 188 One end..of a glass *T-tube was connected with an air-pump.

b. Special Combs. (sometimes hyphened). **†T beard,** a beard worn in the 17th c., grown or cut in the form of a T. **T branch,** in piping, a right-angled joint of a small pipe to a main; a T joint. **T cart,** an open phaeton, so called from its ground-plan resembling the letter T. **T cloth,** a plain cotton cloth exported to India, China, Africa, etc., so called from the large letter T stamped on it. **T rail,** a railway metal or rail having a T section. **T square,** a square of the form of a T or rather ⊢ (with a long stem), used by mechanics and draughtsmen for drawing lines parallel, or at right angles, to each other. (See also Tee sb.[1]) **T-totum:** see Teetotum.

a 1619 Fletcher, etc. Q. Corinth iv. i, Strokes his beard, Which now he puts i' th' posture of a T, The Roman T, your *T beard is the fashion. [a 1654 J. Taylor (Water P.) Superb. Flagellum, [Beards] Some with the hammer-cut, or Roman T.] 1873 Miss Broughton Nancy II. 24 The butler took the housekeeper a driving-tour in my *T-cart, and threw down one of my best horses. 1882 Daily News 30 May 3/1 Stanhope phaetons (generally called by the absurd name of T cart). 1883 F. M. Crawford Dr. Claudius xvi, A very gorgeous conveyance, called in America a T-cart, and resembling a mail phaeton in build. 1865 Manch. Guard. 2 Mar., *T cloths, 9d. and long-cloths, 6d. to 1s. per piece. 1880 Plain Hints Needlework 72 'T cloths' are lengths of 20 yards of calico, specially used as barter with native tribes in Africa. 1837 Civil Eng. & Arch. Jrnl. I. 39/2 The pattern..is by American engineers called the inverted *T rail. 18.. Whitman To Working Men vi, The strong, clean-shaped T-rail for railroads. [1701 Moxon Math. Instr. 19 Tee, a double Square in the form of a T.] 1785 Peacock in Phil. Trans. LXXV. 369 A common *T square..will answer most purposes. 1862 Smiles Engineers II. 76 His trace, his T square, his augers, his gouges, and his engraving tools.

II. 4. Used like the other letters of the alphabet to denote serial order: applied e.g. to the twentieth (or more usually the nineteenth) of any series, to the nineteenth sheet of a book, etc.

5. A mediæval symbol for the numeral 160, and with a stroke over it ($\bar{T}$) for 160,000.

6. Abbreviations: for various proper names, as Thomas, Timothy, Titus, Theresa, etc.; officially stamped on a letter, = taxed, i.e. postage to be paid; in music, = tasto, tempo, tenor, tutti; in a ship's log-book, = thunder; in Math., = time, terms, etc.

1724 Short Explic. For. Wds. in Mus. Bks., The Letter T. is often used as an Abbreviation of the Word Tutti. 1743 Emerson Fluxions 15, t = Number of Terms in V.. Continu'd to t Terms. 1872 Tait & Steele Dynamics of Particle (ed. 3) iii. § 80 Let P be the position of the particle at any time t. Ibid. § 86 If T be the time of descent down AC. 1894 Westm. Gaz. 12 Oct. 3/2 'England' stamps the cards with a 'T', an initial which, with St. Martin's-le-Grandiose conciseness stands for 'taxed'.

III. 7. T at the end of a word has sometimes been attached to the word following when this begins with a vowel: hence the To, the Tone, the Tother; cf. also 'tis, 'twas, etc. in 'T. The final t of Saint has in several cases been popularly prefixed to the name, as in Tandrew, Tandry = St. Andrew; Tann = St. Ann, hence Tanswell; Tantolin = St. Antholin; Tooly = St. Olave; see also Tanton, Tantony, Tawdry.

c 1450 Mankind 75 in Macro Plays 4, I gyff no force, by Sent Tanne! 1673 Hickeringill Greg. F. Greyb. 264 Our Tantlin Lectures. 1726 F. Howgrave Stamford 33 The Corruption that has been made of St. Anthony into Tantony, and St. Olave into Tooly. 1872 Hardwick Trad. Lanc. 260 Cakes baked for the lace-makers' feasts in honour of St. Andrew ..are locally termed 'Tandry Cakes'. 1880 W. Cornw. Gloss., 'T Andrew's dance, St. Vitus' dance.

8. In early ME., t took the place of initial þ, th, after a word ending in a dental or s, esp. in the demonstratives the, that, this, tha, there, then, thus, etc., and the 2nd personal pronoun thou and its cases. Already in OE., þæt þe became þætte, That.

c 1200 Ormin 325 Þiss streon þatt tuss wass sibb Wiþþ preostess & wiþþ kingess. Ibid. 12760 Nu shallt tu ben nemmnedd Cefas. a 1240 Wohunge in Cott. Hom. 271 Hwa is ta largere þen þu. c 1400 Rule St. Benet 23 Þis sais sain benet, þat ta þat ere of elde and vnderstandis, þai sal haue þaire mesur.

T'[1], shortened form of To, before a vowel, formerly in use, often combined with the following word, as tabandon to abandon, tabyde to abide; so taxe to ask, tescape, t'attempt; also, with omission of h, tave, tafe, to have, ta to hae, to have; tadwellyd to have dwelt, talyved to have lived, etc.

c 1200 Ormin 3679 Þatt doþ uss tunnderrstanndenn. c 1330 R. Brunne Chron. Wace (Rolls) 4334 Ffair folk to fighte, Cesar tabyde. 1426 Lydg. De Guil. Pilgr. 1019–22 He gaff to hem..Talyved euere,.. Neuer tave had necessyte Off deyyng. Ibid. 9392 Taxe and lerne, thow art wys. Ibid.

Supplement, p. 3873; Corrigenda, p. 4092; Spurious words, p. 4093; Books quoted, p. 4094

T

T, t, the twentieth letter of the English and all the modern European alphabets...

Ta, taa, in the *ta*, early ME. and north. form of *To a, i, in the ta to that o* = the one : see T 7.

Ta, taa, obs. forms of TOE A, TOAD.

Taa, in various words: earlier spelling of TA-.

Taal (tāl), sb. I. TALE. *Taald*, obs. pa. pple. of TELL v. *Taar*, obs. f. *tare*, pa.t. of TEAR D.7.

Tab (tæb), sb. Also 7 **tabb**, 8 **tabe**. [Origin obscure. At first, and still largely, a dialect word. Not in Johnson. In some senses it may be short for *tablet*; in others it interchanges with *tag*.]

Tabac, tabacco, tabacco, obs. ff. TOBACCO.

Tabachir, var. spelling (properly French) of TABASHEER.

† Tabaccosis (tabǎkōsis). *Path.* [f. mod.L. *tobac-um* TOBACCO + -OSIS.] Disease of the lungs produced by the inhalation of tobacco dust.

Tabagie (tabāzī). [F. irreg. deriv. of *tabac* (see TOBACCO).] A group of smokers who meet in club fashion; a 'tobacco-parliament'.

† Taban (tæ'ban). The Malay name of the tree, *Isonandra Gutta* (or *I. Tabau*), that yields gutta-percha. Hence *taban-tree*.

Tabanid (tæ'banid), a. and sb. [f. L. *tabānus* a gad-fly or horse-fly (adopted by Linnæus as a generic name) + -ID.] a. *adj.* Belonging to the family *Tabanidæ* of flies, of which *Tabanus* is the typical genus. b. *sb.* A fly of this family, a gad-fly.

Tabard (tæ'bard), sb. Forms: *tabard*, *tabarde*, etc.

Tabaret (tæ'bǎret). [mod. trade name, prob. f. TABBY + -ET.] A fabric of alternate satin and watered silk stripes used in upholstery.

Tabarine, tabarin. *See* TABORIN, TABORINE.

Tabasheer, tabashir (tæbasī'ǎr, -ī'r). Also 6-7 (fr. Pg.) *tabaxir*, 8 (fr. Fr.) *tabaschir* [Arab., Pers., Urdū *tabāshīr* chalk, mortar.] A siliceous substance, white or translucent, occasionally formed in the joints of the bamboo...

† Tabasheer (tæbǎshī'r). Also 6-7 (fr. Pg.)

Tabasco (tǎbæ'sko). [From *Tabasco*, name of a river and state of Mexico.] More fully *Tabasco* (*pepper*) *sauce*. A very pungent sauce made from the pulp of the ripe fruit of a variety of *Capsicum annuum*.

Tabber, Tabbern, obs. ff. TABOR, TABERN.

Tabbied (tæ'bid), *ppl. a.* [f. TABBY v. + -ED.] Having a wavy or streaky appearance.

Tabbinet, variant of TABINET.

Tabby (tæ'bi), sb. and a. Forms: 7 *tabi*, 7-8 *tabby*, etc.

Tabefy (tæ'bifai), v. [ad. L. *tābefacĕre* (Vulgate), to cause to waste (f. *tābe-re* to waste away, pine) + -FY: cf. also late L. *tābificāre* (Cassiod.) in same sense (f. *tābific-us* TABIFIC), whence F. *tabéfier* (Cotgr., Oudin).]

Tabernacle (tæ'bǎrnǎk'l), sb. Forms: 2 *tabernacle*, 3-5 *tabarne*, 4-5 *tabernacle*, *taburn*, etc.

Taberd, obs. form of TABARD.

Tabernacular (tæbǎrnæ'kiūlǎr), a. rare. [f. L. type *tabernāculāris*: see TABERNACLE + -AR.] Of or pertaining to a tabernacle.

Tabitha (tæ'bithǎ). [The scriptural name Tabitha (Acts ix. 36), rendered 'Dorcas'...]

Supplement, p. 3873; Corrigenda, p. 4092; Spurious words, p. 4093; Books quoted, p. 4094

Hence **Ta′bleau**, *v. trans.*, to put into a tableau.

Ta′ble-board.

Ta′ble-book.

Table-cloth.

Ta′ble-cloth-wise, *adv. Obs.*

Table-cover.

The table diamond.

Tableful.

Ta′ble-land.

Ta′ble-flatty. *Obs.*

Ta′bler.

Ta′ble-talk.

Ta′ble-turning.

So **Ta′ble-cutter**, a lapidary who cuts precious stones in 'tables': **Table-cutting** = B.

Tabled (tē′b'ld), *a.*

Tableau (tæ′blō), *sb.* [-LESS.] Without a table; unfurnished with a table.

Table d'hôte.

Tablement. [f. TABLE *v.* + -MENT.]

Ta′bleman. *Obs.*

Ta′bler. *Obs.*

Ta′blet.

Ta′ble-ru′by. A ruby cut with a large flat upper surface surrounded by small facets.

Ta′ble-round = ROUND TABLE *sb.*

Ta′ble-spoon.

Ta′ble-stone.

Tablet (tæ′blĕt), *sb.* Forms: 4-6 tablette, 5 tablitte, -elet, 6- (taplet), 5-6 tablett, tabellet(t, 6 tabilitte, 6c tablet, tabulatt.

Tablet (tæ′blĕt), *v.* [f. prec. *sb.*]

Tableware (tē′b'l-wēr). Ware for the service of the table.

Tablewise (tē′b'l-wəiz), *adv.* [f. TABLE *sb.* + -WISE.]

Tabling (tē′blĭŋ), *vbl. sb.* [f. TABLE *v.* + -ING.]

Tabloid, *sb.* registered on 14 March, 1884, by Messrs. Burroughs, Wellcome & Co.

Taboo, tabu (tabū′), *a.* and *sb.*

Taboo, tabu (tabū′), *v.* [f. prec.]

Ta′bor, tabour (tē′bŏr), *sb.*

Ta′bor, tabour, *v.*

Ta′borer.

Ta′born, tabroun, *obs.*

Tabourin, *var.* TABORINE *Obs.*

Tabouret (tæ′bŭrĕt, or as Fr.).

Ta′boring, *vbl. sb.*

Tabret (tæ′brĕt), *sb.* Forms: 4-5 tabrett, 4-6 tabrette, (6- tabrett, 7 tabret).

TABULA.

Tabret; β. 6 taberttle, -orde, -arte, -arde; 7, 5 taborette, 6-7 tabouret. [f. TABOR +-ET.]

1. A small labor : a timbrel.

Tabret, the form of TABOURET.

Tabro(u)n, Tabronar, etc., var TABORN, -ER.

Tabul, obs. form of TABLE.

Tabu, variant spelling of TABOO.

Tabule, (tæ-biūl). Pl. -æ (-ē). [The L. word *tabula* TABLE in particular senses.]

1. An ancient writing-tablet ; see TABLE 2 b, c, TABLET sb. 1.

Tabula rasa = scraped tablet; a tablet from which the writing has been erased, and which is therefore ready to be written upon again ; a blank tablet: usually fig.

2. Eccl. A wooden or metal frontal for an altar.

Tabula. (tæ-biūlă). [L.] = TABLE.

Tabular (tæ-biūlǎr), a. Now rare. [ad. L. *tabulār-is*, *tabula* table : see -AR².]

1. Of, pertaining to, contained in, or of the nature of a table : see TABULAR 2 b.

Tabulaʳⁱᵒᵘˢ, a. Obs. rare⁻¹. [f. L. *tabulari-us* or belonging to written documents (f. *tabula*) + -OUS. (See quot.)]

Tabularize, v. [f. TABULAR + IZE.] trans. To put into a tabular form, to tabulate. Hence **Tabularization**.

Tabulary (tæ-biūlări), a. rare. [ad. L. *tabulāri-us* a record-office, archives, f. *tabula* table, tablet : see -ARIUM.]

Tabulate, v. [f. L. *tabulāt-* ppl. stem of *tabulāre* to board, floor, f. *tabula* table, board, plank, floor : in other senses directly from mod. senses of TABLE.]

1. Shaped with or having a flat upper surface ; flat-topped: cf. TABULAR 1.

2. Arranged or exhibited in the form of a table, scheme, or synopsis: cf. TABULAR 2.

Tabulation (tæbiūlēⁱ·ʃǝn), [n. of action from TABULATE v. : cf. L. *tabulātio* a flooring over, a floor or story.]

Tabulatory (tæ-biūlǎtǝri), a. rare. [f. TABULATE v. + -ORY.]

Tabule (tæ-biūl), sb. Obs. [mod. ad. L. *tabula* table.]

Tabulet, var. of TABLET.

Tabuliform (tæbiū·lifǭrm), a. rare. [f. L. *tabula* + -(I)FORM.]

TABULIFORM.

Tabulate (tæ-biūslĕt), v. † late L. *tabulāt-*, ppl. stem of *tabulāre* [...]

Ta·burnism, Obs. rare. In 4 -yster, -yatir. [f. *taburn*, Taburn.]

Taby, Tabyl, tabylᵉ, v. obs. var. of TABBY, TABLE, TABOO. Tboⁱ: see TAKE v.

Tacamahac (tæ·kămăhak). Also 7-8 tacamahaca, 8 tacaamahaca, tacaha, tacamahacca, 8 tacoamahaca, tacamahaca, tacamahacca, mobacoa. [ad. obs. Sp. *tacamahaca*; In Hernandez 1614 *thecamahaca*; ad. Aztec *tecomahaca*.]

Tacand (tæ·kǎnd), obs. var. of TACKAND.

TABULOUS.

Ta·bulous, a. Obs. rare⁻¹. [as prec. +-OUS.]

Ta·burnist, Obs. rare. In 4 -yster.

TACHE.

Tache, (tæ·tʃ). Forms : 4-5 tache, 4-5 tachee, teche, teachie, taoche, 4-7 tachie, 4-8 tach, 5 totch, 6, tasche, tache. [a. OF. *teche*, *tache*, *techie*, *teche*, *tasche*.]

1. A spot, blotch, blot. Obs. exc. as in b.

Tache, sb.² Obs. rare⁻¹. Also 5 tach.

Tache, (tæ·ʃ), sb.³ Now dial. Forms : (4 tass), 5-6 tach, 6-7 tasch, 6, 7 tasche. [OF. *tasche* to stain, soil, f. *tache*, *tasche* sb.¹]

Tachina (tæ·kinǎ). Ent. [mod. L.]

TACHE. 16 TACHYGRAPHY TACHYLITE. 17 TACK.

Tachistoscope (tăki·stŏskoup). [mod. f. Gr. ταχιστ- swiftest + -σκοπ.]

Tacho- (tæ·ko), combining form of Gr. ταχος swift.

Tachograph, **Tachometer**.

Tachy- (tæ·ki), combining form of Gr. ταχυς swift, used in the formation of some scientific terms. **Tachydrite**, **Tachydrᵗite**, Min. [ad. Gr. *tachydor̄os* (Rammelsberg 1856), contr. for *tachyhydrite*, f. Gr. ὕδωρ water + -ITE²]

Tachygraphy (tăki·grăfi), n. [as prec., ad. Gr. ταχυγραφια, f. ταχυ-γράφος.]

Tachyphagia, **Tachyphylaxis**.

Tachytelic, **Tachytype**.

Tachylyte, **-lyte**. Min. [ad. Ger. *tachylit* (Breithaupt 1826), f. Gr. ταχυ- swift + λυτός soluble, in reference to its easy fusibility.]

Tachymeter, **Tachyscope**.

Taciturn (tæ·sitǝrn), a. [ad. F. *taciturne*, ad. L. *taciturn-us*, f. *tacit-us* TACIT.]

Taciturnity (tæsitǝ·rniti).

Tacit (tæ·sit), a. [ad. L. *tacit-us* silent, f. *tacēre* to be silent.]

Tacitly (tæ·sitli), adv.

Tacitean (tæsi·tiǎn), a. [f. the name of the Roman historian Tacitus (c 54–117) : see -AN.]

TACK.

Tack (tæk), sb.¹ Forms : 4-6 tak, takk(e, and 7- 90 together, and are doublets of TACHE sb.³ 4-7 (9-), though, and form but [...] with the stake.]

1. A small sharp-pointed nail of iron or brass, usually with a flat and comparatively large head, used for fastening a light or thin object to something more solid, especially in a slight or temporary manner, so as to admit of easy undoing.

2. Without stating or expressing it ; by implication: cf. TACIT a. 2.

TÆNIO-. 24 TAG. TAG. 25 TAG.

Tag. *v.* [f. TAG *sb.*] ...

Tagrag. ...

Tagger ...

Tagging (tæ·giŋ), *vbl. sb.* [f. TAG *v.*]

Tagnicati ...

Tagua (tā·gwă). [Native name in Guarani.] ...

Taguan ...

Tahali ...

Tahona ...

Tahsildar ...

Tail (teɪl), *sb.* Forms: ...

TAIL. 28 TAIL. TAIL. 29 TAIL.

Tail ...

TAITE. 36 TAKE. 37

III. Weakened sense of 'seize', with elimination of the notion of force or art: the ordinary current sense. I. With a material object.

* with physical action distinct.

12. *trans.* To perform the voluntary physical act by which one gets (something) into one's hand or hold; to transfer to oneself by one's own physical act. (Now the main sense.)

a. with the instrumentality of the hand or hands explicitly or implicitly indicated.

b. with the instrumentality not expressed or considered.

† c. To take *hold* of (grasp).

13. To receive into one's body by one's own act; to eat or drink, to swallow (food, drink, medicine, opium, etc.); to inhale (snuff, tobacco-smoke, etc.).

(For *tobacco*, the ordinary expression is now *to smoke*.)

b. *absol.* To take possession; *spec.* in *Law*, to enter into actual possession.

14. a. *refl.* To take oneself off (to) ... to betake oneself ... to resort to. Also (with *to*) *to take the air*, to walk out in the open air (*now* rare or arch.); see *Air* sb. 5. To take *a bath*, to bathe, esp. in a place or vessel prepared for the purpose; but the phrase is also used in sense 52 (cf. *Bath* sb. 6).

b. To expose oneself (air) so as to inhale it or get the physical benefit of it; chiefly in *phr.* to take the air, to walk out in the open air (now rare or arch.); see *Air* sb. 5.

c. To secure beforehand by payment or contract; e.g. to take a *house*, etc., to engage (a house or other place) for the purpose of occupying it.

d. To get or procure regularly by payment (something offered to the public, as a periodical, a commodity). See also *take in* 61.

e. To obtain by purchase, to derive.

30. To get, obtain, or derive by one's act from some source (something material or non-material); to adopt, copy, 'borrow' (also *absol.*, *quot.* 1493); to take *example* of, 'get' or 'learn' from some one (*quot.* 1544). See also ENSAMPLE sb. 2, EXAMPLE sb. 7.

31. To derive, 'draw' (origin, name, character, etc.) from some source. Const. *from*, *in*, *of*.

32. To get as a result or product by some special process.

33. a. To obtain in writing, write down, make (notes, a copy, etc.); to write down (spoken words).

34. To receive (something given, bestowed, or administered); to have conferred or imposed upon one: a sacrament; office, order of merit, etc.; to swear, or receive as true (a pledge, etc.); to gain, acquire (experience, etc.; see also *to take success*, s.v. SUCCESS). Also *absol.*

35. To enter into the enjoyment of (pleasure, recreation, rest, or the like). See also EASE sb. 2.

36. To receive or get in payment, as wages, etc., or by way of charge or exaction as a fine, tribute; sometimes with connotation 'accept' (*quot.* 39), or charge, exact, demand (cf. 37, 38½).

37. To exact (satisfaction or reparation for an offence); hence, to execute, inflict (vengeance, revenge; punishment, justice). Const. *on*, *of*.

38. To receive, exact, or accept (a promise, engagement, oath, or the like); hence, to administer or witness (an oath).

39. To receive (something offered), not to refuse or reject; to receive willingly; to accept.

43. To face and attempt to get over, through, etc. (something that presents itself in one's way), or actually to do so; to clear (an obstacle, as a fence, ditch, wave, space, etc.); to mount (a slope); get round (a corner); clear (the points on a railway line, etc.).

44. a. To admit, let in; to receive something fitted into it.

40. To accept (a wager, or the person who offers to lay the wager). So also in reference to a proposal, etc.: see also *to take any one at his Word*.

41. To accept and act upon (advice, a hint, warning, etc.).

42. To accept with the mind or will in some specified way (*well*, *ill*, *in earnest*, etc.). See also *to take a thing hardly*, *to take to heart*.

VII. Senses related to VI, denoting intellectual action.

46. To apprehend mentally, to conceive, understand, consider.

47. With *adv.* or *adv.b. phr.* To understand or apprehend in a specified way. Also with some word expressing the manner; *as*, *for*, etc.

48. *To take ... for.* a. To suppose to be, consider, imagine, assume (*to be* or *to do* something).

or alleged..shalbe taken but as voide plee. 1534 WHITINTON *Tullyes Offices* I. (1540) 49 He was take as a gret and a famous man. 1605 CAMDEN *Rem.* 36 This is to be take as a granted veritie. 1820 *Examiner* No. 620. 130/2 We are to take the word *liberal*..as a piece of irony. 1893 *Eng. Illustr. Mag.* X. 310/2 An average length of stroke may be taken at about six yards.

†**b.** *pa. pple.* (with qualifying adv.) Reputed, esteemed. *Obs.*

1518 in Ld. Berners *Froiss.* (1812) Pref. 17 Sir John Style ..well beloued and well takyn in theis partes. 1526 TINDALE *Rom.* xvi. 7 Andronicus and Junia my cosyns.. which are wele taken amonge the apostles. 1535 COVERDALE *Judith* xvi. 21 Iudith was..right honorably taken in all the londe of Israel. 1597–8 BACON *Ess., Followers & Fr.* (Arb.) 34 A thing ciuile, and well taken euen in Monarchies.

** *To conceive and exercise.*

50. To begin to have or be affected by (a feeling or state of mind); to conceive; hence, to experience, entertain, feel (*delight, pleasure, pride*, etc.). See also DELIGHT *sb.* 1 b, FRIGHT *sb.* 1, HUFF *sb.* 2 b, INTEREST *sb.* 7, OFFENCE *sb.* 5 c, PET *sb.*[2], PLEASURE *sb.* 5 f, PRIDE *sb.*[1] 4, UMBRAGE, etc.

c 1200 ORMIN 19558 Þatt tatt Farisewisshe folle Strang wraþþe takenn haffde. a 1300 *Cursor M.* 448 Agains him [God] he tok a pride. 1390– [see OFFENCE *sb.* 5 c]. 1390 GOWER *Conf.* II. 100 Wherof the king gret hevynesse Hath take. 1470–85 MALORY *Arthur* IV. i. 119 Take none heuynesse, said Merlyn. *Ibid.* VI. xv. 207 She took suche sorou that shee dyed. 1535 COVERDALE *Ezek.* xxxvi. 31 Ye shal take displeasure at youre owne selues, by reason of youre synnes and abhominacions. a 1553 [see GRIEF *sb.* 4 b]. 1694 *Acc. Sev. Late Voy.* Introd. 6 Upon some disgust taken at his Master. 1773 *Lift N. Fronde* 15 Persons to whom I had taken so much Dislike. 1888 LESTER *Hartas Maturin* III. ii. 41 Women do take prejudices.

b. *absol.* or *intr.* To take a fancy or liking: cf. *take to*, 74 g, *take with*, 75 c.

1600 DYMMOCK *Treat. Irel.* (1843) 6 They are quicke and capable, kind harted where they take. 1874 HARDY *Madding Crowd* xviii, Mistress and man were engaged in the operation of making a lamb 'take', which is performed whenever a ewe has lost her own offspring, one of the twins of another ewe being given her as a substitute.

†**c.** *To take on oneself*: to become distressed or disturbed in mind: = *take on*, 84 j. *Obs.*

1632 J. HAYWARD tr. *Biondi's Eromena* 121 The Prince,.. because he found him not, tooke on him like a mad man.

51. *trans.* **a.** To conceive and adopt with the will (a purpose, resolution, etc.), or with the intellect (an estimate, view, etc.); to form and hold in the mind. See also PURPOSE *sb.* 2 b, REDE *sb.*[1] 2 b.

a 1300 *Cursor M.* 11151 He..tok his redd al for to fle, Priuelik and latt hir be. 1375– [see PURPOSE *sb.* 2 b]. 1513 DOUGLAS *Æneis* v. i. 10 The Troianis in thare breistis tuk ane ges Quharfor it was. 1652 NEEDHAM tr. *Selden's Mare Cl.* 37 A conclusion [was] taken to refer all to their several Princes. 1660 BARROW *Euclid* Pref. (1714) 2, I took a Resolution to make use of most of the Schemes of the said Book. 1749 FIELDING *Tom Jones* VII. ii, Having taken a resolution to leave the Country. 1891 *Law Times* XC. 462/2 We do not take the alarmist view of our correspondent.

b. To conceive and exercise (*courage, heart*, etc.; †*mercy* (obs.), *pity*, etc.); to form in the mind and exhibit in action. (Sometimes nearly coinciding with sense 16 a, to assume: cf. also branch VIII.) See also COURAGE *sb.* 4 d, HEART *sb.* 49, HEART OF GRACE, PITY *sb.* 2.

13.. *Guy Warw.* (A.) 4636 Now, sir, take þerof pite. 13.., 1530 [see HEART *sb.* 49]. 13.. *Cursor M.* 27136 Quen þou tas to þe baldhede O gretter mans sinful dede. 1483 CAXTON *G. de la Tour* A viij, Wherfore God took mercy on them. c 1490–1841 [see COURAGE *sb.* 4 d]. 1530–1890 [see HEART OF GRACE]. 1593 ABP. BANCROFT *Dang. Posit.* II. vii. 54 They haue taken greater boldnesse, and growen more rebellious. a 1715 BURNET *Own Time* an. 1672 (1823) I. 538 No popish priest had ever taken the confidence to speak to her of those matters. 1888 *Times* (weekly ed.) 18 May 3/4 The Arabs would have taken fresh heart.

c. To exercise with the mind, in thought (*note, notice*, †*intent*, etc.), or with the mind and will, in action (*care, heed*, †*diligence*, etc.). Cf. branches VIII, IX. See also CARE *sb.* 3 c, HEED *sb.* 1 b, INTENT *sb.* 2, KEEP *sb.* 1, 2, NOTE *sb.*[2] 20 b, NOTICE *sb.* 6, 7, REGARD *sb.* 6 b, TENT *sb.*[2], THOUGHT *sb.*

a 1225 *Leg. Kath.* 1379 Þe deore Drihtin areaw us, & toc read to ure alde dusischipes. a 1300– [see KEEP *sb.* 1, 2]. c 1305– [see HEED *sb.* 1 b]. 13.. *Cursor M.* 27225 Ilk man þat will ta ȝeme. c 1368 CHAUCER *Compl. Pite* 82 But ye the rather take cure To breke that perilouse alliaunce. c 1375 *Cursor M.* 12592 (Fairf.) Hamward þai went & to ihesu toke nane entent. c 1425 *Ibid.* 7937 (Trin.) Son he seide take good gome ȝyuen þou hast þin owne dome. c 1475 *Songs & Carols 15th C.* (Percy Soc.) 54 To here song then tok I intent. 1564–5 *Reg. Privy Council Scot.* I. 320 Quhairunto hir Hienes and hir Counsall mon tak ee and regard. 1588– [see CARE *sb.* 3 c]. 1592– [see NOTICE *sb.* 6, 7]. 1596– [see NOTE *sb.*[2] 20 b]. 1724 R. BAGE *Barham Downs* I. 230, I took no concern about any of them.

VIII. Various senses, nearly = make, do, perform (some action). (See also senses 19, 37, 51 b, c.)

52. To perform, make, do (an act, action, movement, etc.): usually with some notion of undertaking or taking upon one, and carrying out or carrying on; sometimes with that of getting.

Often it forms with the object merely a periphrastic equivalent of the cognate vb.: e.g. *to take a leap* = *to leap* (*once*), *to take a look* = *to look* (*once*), *to take one's departure* = *to depart*. (See also *take aim* in Phrases, 64; ACTION 7, JOURNEY *sb.* 3, STEP *sb.*, TURN *sb.*, WALK *sb.*)

c 1380 *Sir Ferumbras* 4029 To-morwe let ous our iorne take, Hamward aȝen to ryde. c 1412 HOCCLEVE *De Reg. Princ.* 3400 The kyng took a laghtre, and wente his way. c 1449 PECOCK *Repr.* 156 At which men mowe lawȝe and take bourde for her symplenes. 1477 EARL RIVERS (Caxton) *Dictes* 1, I determyned me to take that voyage. 1483 CAXTON *Cato* C vj b, Thou oughtest not to stryue ne take noyse wyth them that ben ful of superfluous wordes. c 1489 — *Sonnes of Aymon* xiv. 341 Thei toke grete debate for me wyth Charlemagn wythin his pavylion. 1491 *Churchw. Acc. St. Dunstan's, Canterb.*, They took an axion ageynst the executores of Wyllyam Belser. 1556 *Chron. Gr. Friars* (Camden) 13 Thys yere the kynge..toke his viage towarde Normandy. 1590 SPENSER *F. Q.* III. xi. 42 Like a winged horse he [Neptune] tooke his flight. 1617 *Acc. Bk. W. Wray* in *Antiquary* XXXII. 214 King James..tooke his progresse towards Scotland. 1678 BUNYAN *Pilgr.* I. 43 How many steps have I took in vain. 1693 *Humours Town* 3 Take a last farewel-look of this overgrown City. *Ibid.* 6 You might take a survey of the Rarities. 1711 BUDGELL *Spect.* No. 77 ¶ 1 We took a turn or two more. 1719 DE FOE *Crusoe* (1840) II. xiv. 287 Without measuring the windings and turnings it takes. *Ibid.* xv. 315 He takes a great circuit about. 1766 GOLDSM. *Vic. W.* xxviii, My wife, my daughter and herself were taking a walk together. 1845 M. PATTISON *Ess.* (1889) I. 24 When Queen Brunchilde took her departure from Rouen. 1867 AUG. J. E. WILSON *Vashti* xxiv, I came to-day to beg you to take a trip somewhere, by sea or land. 1889 MRS. E. KENNARD *Landing Prize* III. viii. 148 The salmon took a great leap. 1893 J. ASHBY STERRY *Naughty Girl* vii, I'll just take a turn down to the club and see what's going on.

†**b.** *To take beginning*: to begin, start, commence. (See also 31.) *Obs.* [= ON. *taka upphaf*, to begin.]

a 1300 *Cursor M.* 12887 Þe ald testament hir-wit nu slakes, And sua þe neu bigining takes. 1557–75 *Diurnal Occurr.* (Bann. Club) 61 Vpoun the first day of August, the Parliament tuke begyning. 1601 DOLMAN *La Primaud. Fr. Acad.* (1618) III. 641 We must all beleeue..that time tooke beginning with the world.

53. *To take counsel* (†*advice*, †*advisement*): to get advice, to consult, deliberate; †to devise; †to decide: see ADVICE 4, ADVISEMENT 3, COUNSEL 1.

a 1300 *Cursor M.* 4790 Þar of es god we ta consail. c 1386 CHAUCER *Melib.* ¶ 760 Thanne Dame Prudence..delibered and took auys in hir self. 1480 CAXTON *Chron. Eng.* cxcvii. 173 The barons token counceyll bytwene hem. 1483 — *G. de la Tour* D iv b, Withoute takyng ony counceylle of her husbond. 1537 T. CUMPTON in Ellis *Orig. Lett.* Ser. II. II. 92 After that they had communiked together and taken avisement. 1609 BIBLE (Douay) *Judg.* xx. 32 Who..tooke advise to draw them away from the citie. 1879 M. J. GUEST *Lect. Hist. Eng.* xxxvi. 359 She took counsel with witches and magicians.

†**b.** *intr.* ?ellipt. for *take advisement*. *Obs.*

c 1400 *Emare* 799 Grete lordes toke hem be-twene, That þey wolde exyle þe quene.

†**54.** *trans.* To arrange, fix, agree upon, conclude (a truce, peace, league, etc.). [Cf. OF. *prendre treve*, 13th c.] *Obs.*

1375 BARBOUR *Bruce* XIV. 96 Quhill trewis at the last tuk thai. c 1400 *Laud Troy-Bk.* 8474 It was seyde to the Emperoure..How ffight was taken hem be-twene. c 1400 *Destr. Troy* 9072 The Troiens to the tenttes tristy men send, For a tru to be tan. c 1470 [see PEACE *sb.* 1 b]. 1523 LD. BERNERS *Froiss.* I. xxxiii. 48 So y[t] they wolde take no peace, nor truse, with y[e] kyng of Englande. c 1600 SHAKS. *Sonn.* xlvii. 1 Betwixt mine eye and heart a league is tooke. 1656 S. HOLLAND *Zara* (1719) 135 Having taken a Truce with his Enemy, he would not be the first should break it.

55. *To take adieu, farewell*: to bid farewell, say good-bye, take one's leave. Const. *of*. Cf. *to take leave*: see LEAVE *sb.* 2. So †*to take good night* (*obs.*).

c 1560 ROLLAND *Seven Sages* Prol. ii, I..tuke gude nicht, and said gude schirs adew. 1617 J. TAYLOR (Water-P.) *Trav.* (1872) 2 We all went to the Christopher where we took a Bacchanalian farewell one of another. 1665 PEPYS *Diary* 28 Aug., I think to take adieu to-day of the London Streets. 1700 DRYDEN *Cock & Fox* 256 Last he drew A piteous sigh, and took a long adieu. 1821 SCOTT *Kenilw.* vii, Thus saying, he at length took farewell. 1840 THIRLWALL *Greece* VII. 195 [He] besought Demosthenes to forgive his temporary estrangement,..and took a last farewell of him.

56. To lay hold of, raise, put forth, make (an objection, an exception, a distinction, etc.). See also EXCEPTION *sb.* 7 c, OBJECTION 1 b.

1542– [see EXCEPTION *sb.* 7 c]. 1830 HERSCHEL *Nat. Phil.* 7 The objection which has been taken. 1830 MONK *Life R. Bentley* (1833) I. 303 Instead of doing so, they take a dilemma, and intimate a belief that either by the old statutes, or by the 40th of Elizabeth's, the Master is subject to the jurisdiction of the Bishop of Ely. 1849 MACAULAY *Hist. Eng.* vii. II. 265 Between punishments and disabilities a distinction was taken. *Ibid.* x. 556 The distinction which they took was..ingenious. 1864 BP. WILBERFORCE *Sp. Missions* (1874) 46, I know well the objections men can take.

IX. Senses denoting movement or removal (lead, convey, remove, deliver, etc.), and related senses.

* *To convey, carry, conduct, remove.*

57. a. To carry, convey; to cause (a person or animal) to go with one, to conduct, lead, escort. Also said of a vehicle, etc.: To convey, carry (a person) to some place. Also of a road, way, etc.: = LEAD *v.*[1] 6; so of a journey, etc.

c 1200 ORMIN 8355 Josæp, ris upp & tacc þe child, & tacc þe childess moderr. a 1300 *Cursor M.* 5117 Tas Ruben þan wit yow. *Ibid.* 23814 Es þar na wai..Cun tak us better. a 1400–50 *Alexander* 4886 Syne tas he with him titly his twelue tried prince[s]. 1503 in *Trans. Roy. Hist. Soc.* (1902) 153 Walter Robardes tooke this Alex[r] apart. 1590 SHAKS. *Com. Err.* IV. i. 36 Take the stranger to my house. 1665 MANLEY *Grotius' Low C. Warres* 832 Taking through the marshy Fields of Cazant Twelve hundred Walloons and Irish with him. 1719 DE FOE *Crusoe* (1840) I. xiv. 246, I took my man Friday with me. 1848 THACKERAY *Van. Fair* xlviii, Being obliged to take four of us in his carriage to wait upon His Majesty. 1878 *Scribner's Mag.* XV. 897/1 The second stage of the journey takes the traveler through Egypt. 1908 *Betw. Trent & Ancholme* 55 A yard or two further takes us to the N.E. corner. *Mod.* Will this road take me to Abingdon?

b. To carry or bear (a thing) with one; to carry to some place or person. In quot. 1883, to draw (something) *through* a liquid.

1390 GOWER *Conf.* III. 217 [Eche] hath A pot of Erthe, in which be tath A lyht brennende in a kressette. a 1400 *Sir Perc.* 478 He..Tuke with hym his schorte spere. c 1470 HENRY *Wallace* II. 85 Thow Scot, to quhom takis thow this thing? 1590 SHAKS. *Com. Err.* IV. i. 37 And with you take the Chaine. 1605 — *Macb.* V. iii. 19 Take thy face hence. 1768 J. BYRON *Narr. Patagonia* (ed. 2) 221 They will take from the ground a glove or handkerchief. 1858 RAMSAY *Scot. Life & Char.* v. (1870) 118 She went out and did not take the door with her [*i.e.* shut it after her]. 1883 R. HALDANE *Workshop Receipts* Ser. II. 227/1 Take [the yarn] through dilute sulphuric acid, and wash very well.

c. *fig.* To induce (a person) to go; to be the cause of his going. (Cf. BRING *v.* 1 c.)

1848 THACKERAY *Van. Fair* lxvii, 'Particular business', she said, took her to Bruges. 1856 J. H. NEWMAN *Callista* (1890) 114 What takes you into the city this morning? 1883 P. GREG *Sanguelac* II. xi. 223 What took you out so late? *Mod.* The business that took me to London.

58. With *from, off* (hence sometimes *simply*): To carry away, to remove; to extract; to deprive or rid a person or thing of (with various shades of connotation): = *take away*, 78 a, *take off*, 83 a, *take out*, 85 a: see also *take out of*, 86.

To take off one's feet: to carry off one's feet by force, as a wind or wave; also *fig.* So *to take off one's balance*, etc.

a 1272 *Luue Ron* 64 in *O. E. Misc.* 95 Al deþ hit wile from him take. a 1300 *E. E. Psalter* i. 5 Als duste þat winde þerthe tas fra. a 1400 *Cursor M.* 29546 (Cott. Galba) It takes [Cott. steres] his cristendom him fra. c 1489 CAXTON *Sonnes of Aymon* 19 Saying, that they should take the head from the body of hym. 1535 COVERDALE *Ps.* l[i]. 11 Take not thy holy sprete fro me. 1567 *Gude & Godlie B.* (S.T.S.) 147 He fra me my Sin hes tane. 1610 HOLLAND *Camden's Brit.* (1637) 73 He..tooke from the towne the benefit of their haven. 1655 SIR E. NICHOLAS in *N. Papers* (Camden) II. 235 His decree is annulled and taken of y[e] file. 1678 BUTLER *Hud.* III. III. 693 The Law severely contrabands Our taking business off Mens hands. 1818 SCOTT *Hrt. Midl.* xv, The doing so would..take the case from under the statute. 1825 J. NICHOLSON *Operat. Mechanic* 560 A plane, which takes a thin shaving off the surface of the wood. 1867 TROLLOPE *Chron. Barset* i, John did take his eyes off his book. *Mod.* The sea was so rough when I was bathing that the waves took me off my feet.

b. *To take the life of*: to deprive of life, to kill.

[13.. *Cursor M.* 25831 His lijf þan sal be fra him tane. c 1489 CAXTON *Sonnes of Aymon* xii. 306, I praye you..that yourselfe wyl take the liff fro me, and cut of my hede.] 1591 SHAKS. 1 *Hen. VI*, III. i. 22 Thou layd'st a Trap to take my Life. 1766 GOLDSM. *Vic. W.* xxx, You imagine, perhaps, that a contempt for your own life gives you a right to take that of another. 1847 TENNYSON *Princ.* v. 397 Take not his life: he risk'd it for my own.

c. To remove by death.

1552 *Bk. Com. Prayer, Burial of Dead*, Forasmuche as it hath pleased almightie God of his great mercie to take vnto hym selfe the soule of our dere brother here departed, we therefore commit [etc.]. 1593 SHAKS. 3 *Hen. VI*, I. iv. 167 Hard-hearted Clifford, take me from the World. 1626 S. MOUNTAGU in *Buccleuch MSS.* (Hist. MSS. Comm.) I. 247 God hath taken to himself my brother Walter Mountagu. 1632 HEYWOOD *1st Pt. Iron Age* v. i. Wks. 1874 III. 338 Since the Fates Haue tane him from vs. 1864 TENNYSON *North. Farmer* iii, 'The amoighty's a taäkin o' you to 'issén, my friend', a said.

d. To subtract, deduct.

1611 SHAKS. *Cymb.* II. i. 60 This her Sonne, Cannot take two from twenty for his heart, And leaue eighteene. 1806 HUTTON *Course Math.* (1827) I. 8, 6 – 2, denotes that 2 is to be taken from 6. 1876 E. JENKINS *Blot Queen's Head* 28 Every one took 50 per cent. off Bobby's expletives. 1890 *Sat. Rev.* 16 Aug. 192/1 Twopence in the pound was taken off the tea-duty.

e. *absol.* with *from*: To detract from, lessen, diminish. Cf. 78 c, 83 k.

1625 MASSINGER *New Way* IV. i, [Ne'er] sullied with one taint or spot That may take from your innocence and candour. a 1700 DRYDEN (J.), It takes not from you, that you were born with principles of generosity. 1891 *Temple Bar Mag.* Oct. 254 It takes greatly from the pleasure.

f. *intr.* for *pass.* (with adv. or advb. phr.) To be capable of being, or adapted to be, taken *off, out, to pieces*, etc.; to be removable, detachable, etc.

So, by extension, *to take in and out* = to be capable of being put in and taken out; so *to take on and off*.

1669 STURMY *Mariner's Mag.* II. ii. 53 A Brass pair of Compasses..and four Steel Points to take in and out. 1703 MOXON *Mech. Exerc.* 227 The Stop-screw, to take out when the Hollow Axis moves in the Moving-Coller. 1881 GREENER *Gun* 78 Guns..so constructed as to take to pieces and stow away in a small compass. 1890 *St. James' Gaz.* 8 Feb. 6/2 Yours [i.e. hair] takes off at night.

59. in various *fig.* senses. **a.** To carry, draw, or lead in thought, etc.; with *from, off*, to distract.

1611 SHAKS. *Wint. T.* IV. iv. 356 Your heart is full of something, that do's take Your minde from feasting. 1670 COTTON *Espernon* II. v. 238 An accident fell out that soon took the Duke off all thoughts of that Solemnity. 1742 *Lond. & Country Brew.* I. (ed. 4) 41 These deluded People are taken into an Approbation of indeed an Ignis fatuus. 1890 *Murray's Mag.* VII. 65 Love..took her out of herself, and soothed her sorrows.

†**b.** *To take* (a person) *with one*: to speak so that (he) can 'follow' or apprehend one's meaning; to enable (him) to understand one; to be explicit. (Usu. in *imper.*) *Obs.*

1592 SHAKS. *Rom. & Jul.* III. v. 142 Soft, take me with you, take me with you, wife. 1695 CONGREVE *Love for L.* V. ii, Ay, but pray take me along with you, sir!

†**c.** *To take* (a thing) *with one*: to bear in mind, keep in remembrance, take note of. *Obs.*

1599 MASSINGER, etc. *Old Law* II. ii, Oh! you are too hot, sir; Pray cool yourself, and take September with you. 1610 HOLLAND *Camden's Brit.* 715 Yet take here with you, that which William Newbrigensis..writeth. 1746 CHESTERF. *Lett.* (1792) I. 295 Take this along with you that the worst authors are always most partial to their own works. 1808 SCOTT *F. M. Perth* v, Take it with you that I will never listen to them.

†**d.** To render, translate. *Obs. rare.*

c 1430 *Syr Gener.* (Roxb.) 25 A clerk itt in to latyn tooke Att hertford out of a booke.

e. To bring or convey to a higher or lower degree; to raise or lower; to advance or put back. See also *take down*, 80; PEG *sb.*[1] 3.

1589– [see PEG *sb.*[1] 3]. 1890 *Field* 24 May 730/3 By steady play the score was taken to 18.

** *To deliver, give, commit, give up.*

†**60.** *trans.* To deliver, hand over; to give; to give in charge, commit, entrust. (= BETAKE 1, 1 b, 2.) Const. *to* or dative. *Obs.*

[In Layamon, in the early version rarely (2 instances), but in the later very commonly (22 instances), *bitake* is used as equivalent to *bitæche, biteche* (BETEACH, to deliver); in 19 cases *biteche* of the earlier text becomes *bitake* in the later. In 4 cases the later version has in the same sense the simple *take*; this became from 1300 to 1530 quite established, and continued in some writers to c 1560. This use was not in Norse, and is absent from northern ME. For the history see BETAKE *v.*]

c 1275 LAY. 54 He..wrot..And þane hiike boc tock us to bisne. *Ibid.* 3361 And takeþ [c 1205 bitacheþ] hit his child. *Ibid.* 22378 And ich wolle..To hostage take þe mine sone [c 1205 biteche þe mine þreo sunen]. c 1290 *S. Eng. Leg.* I. 99/254 To Ihesu crist ich habbe al-so al min heorte i-take. 1297 R. GLOUC. (Rolls) 2027 Some sede þat him betere were take is neueu conan þe kinedom of þis lond. 1340 *Ayenb.* 171 Þe castel of his herte and of his bodye þet god him heþ ytake to loki. 1377 LANGL. *P. Pl.* B. xv. 575 Owre lorde wrote it hym-selue In stone..And toke it moyses to teche men til Messye com. 1387 TREVISA *Higden* (Rolls) II. 323 Moyses..took his wif [*uxori tradidit*] þe ryng of forȝetnesse. c 1400 *Prymer* (1894) 78 We biseche þee þat þe soule of þi seruaunt..be not take in-to þe hondis of oure enemy. c 1425 *Cursor M.* 15411 (Trin.) In to youre hondes I shal him take [*earlier MSS.* teche]. 1436 *Let.* in Burton & Raine *Hemingbrough* 393, I writte no more..at this tyme, so I tak ȝow to þe Holy Trinite. c 1440 *Promp. Parv.* 485/2 Takyn, or delyueryn a thynge to a-nother, *trado*. c 1440 *Gesta Rom.* xlvi. 183 (Add. MS.) Take me the Ryng, and I shalle kepe it as my lyf. a 1533 LD. BERNERS *Huon* lxvi. 226 Al that ye take me to kepe shalbe sauely kept to your behoue. 1533 MORE *Answ. Poysoned Bk.* Wks. 1063/1 When he tooke them the bread and bode them ete it. a 1553 UDALL *Royster D.* I. v. (Arb.) 31 Who tooke thee thys letter?

†**61.** *refl.* **a.** To commit or devote oneself (to God, to Christ, etc.); also, to commit or betake oneself *to* one's legs, heels, weapons, or other means of protection or safety. *Obs.* exc. as in b.

c 1200 ORMIN 356 Aȝȝ fra þatt Adam Godd forrlet & toc himm to þe deofell. c 1220 *Bestiary* 98 in *O. E. Misc.* 4 He..forsaket ðore satanas,..Takeð him to ihesu crist. a 1300 *Cursor M.* 23046 Þat al þis werld welth for-sok, And anerli to godd þam tok. c 1475 *Rauf Coilyear* 938, I will forsaik Mahoun, and tak me to his micht. 1530 PALSGR. 749/1, I take me to my legges, I flye a waye. 1548 [see HEEL *sb.*[1] 19]. 1606 G. W[OODCOCKE] *Hist. Ivstine* VIII. 38 Which people perceiuing them selues entrapped..fearefully tooke them to their weapons. 1607 TOPSELL *Four-f. Beasts* (1658) 19 The Gyants..took them to their heels and so were overcome.

b. *refl.* To devote or give oneself up; to betake or apply oneself *to* (some pursuit, action, or object).

a 1300 *Cursor M.* 4032 Þir breþer tuain þam tok to red To dele þair landes þam bi-tuixs. c 1425 *Ibid.* 13429 (Trin.) Of wif forsoke he hondbonde And toke [*earlier MSS.* turned] him to þe better honde. c 1440 *Alphabet of Tales* 350 He lefte all his gude and tuke hym to pouertie. 1530 PALSGR. 749/1, I take me to relygyon, or any other Kynde of Lyvynge wherein I must contynue. 1570 T. WILSON tr. *Demosthenes' Olynth.* Epist. *j b, Such are contented..to weare our Countrie cloth, and to take them selues to hard fare. 1576 GASCOIGNE *Steel Gl.* (Arb.) 67 Art thou a craftsman? take thee to thine arte. 1707 *Curios. in Husb. & Gard.* 296 One of these Leaves..took it self to walking as soon as he touch'd it. 1888 SOPHIE VEITCH *Dean's Daughter* I. viii. 155, I..took myself to the Chase. 1890 E. L. ARNOLD *Phra* v, She would not eat and would not speak, and at last took her to crying.

c. *intr.* with *into*: To give oneself up to: = *take to*, 74 e. *rare.*

1756 J. CLUBBE *Misc. Tracts* (1770) I. 105 Men had better read but few books at large, than take into this short and fallacious method of attaining..imperfect knowledge. 1765 *Ibid.* II. 10 Some men taking into life of pleasure, others into an easy chair of sleep and indolence. 1864 CARLYLE *Fredk. Gt.* XV. vi. (1872) VI. 25 Taking deeply into tobacco.

*** *To set oneself, begin, to apply oneself.*

62. *intr.* with *inf.* To set oneself, to begin (*to do* something). [After ON. *taka at*, e.g. *taka at ganga* to begin to go.] *Obs.*

1154 *O. E. Chron.* (Laud MS.) an. 1135, Dauid king of Scotland toc to uerrien him. c 1200 ORMIN 223 [Zacarije] toc to becnenn till þe follc. *Ibid.* 4772 Swa..þatt hiss bodiȝ toc to rotenn bufenn eorþe. *Ibid.* 8332 Off þa fowwre riche menn þatt tokenn þa to rixlenn. c 1300 *Sir Tristr.* 1000 Now haþ tristrem y-tan Oȝain morannt to fiȝt.

b. In later use, To apply oneself *to* a habitual action (cf. 61 b and 74 e).

1677 YARRANTON *Eng. Improv.* 157 Since the Welsh took to break up their Mountains, and sow them with Corn, they have Corn sufficient for themselves. 1839 *Times* 5 Oct., He took to cultivate his genius by reading political economy. 1856 FREEMAN in W. R. W. Stephens *Life* (1895) I. iv. 132, I have taken to write a little in a penny paper called the *Star*. 1890 *Blackw. Mag.* CXLVII. 262/2 Their taking to smoke tobacco. 1891 G. MEREDITH *One of our Conq.* III. xi. 233 She has taken to like him.

†**c.** *refl.* in same senses. *Obs. rare.*

c 1489 CAXTON *Sonnes of Aymon* i. 54 The duke Beues toke hym selfe for to wepe strongly. 1605 VERSTEGAN *Dec. Intell.* vi. (1628) 165 They tooke themselues first to rob vpon the sea coastes. a 1677 BARROW *Serm.* Wks. 1716 II. 63 A state..which they took themselves peculiarly to enjoy.

**** *To take one's course, to go.*

63. *intr.* To make one's way, go, proceed; = NIM *v.* 2, FANG *v.* 7. In early use chiefly with *to*; in later use with any prep. or adv. of direction: usually implying prompt action, cf. 'start', 'strike'. See also *take to*, 74 b; *take away*, 78 d, *take back*, 79 e, *take in*, 82 p, *take off*, 83 n.

c 1250 *Gen. & Ex.* 1751 He toc, and wente, and folwede on. c 1330 R. BRUNNE *Chron. Wace* (Rolls) 13566 So harde þe parties to-gidere tok. 13.. *St. Erkenwolde* 57 in Horstm. *Altengl. Leg.* (1881) 267 Quen tithynges tokene to þe tone [= town]. ?13.. *Cast. Love* 1686 In good tyme the[i] were i-bore, That to that feste mowe takyn [F. *peuent venir*]. a 1400 *Gosp. Nicod.* 1122 (Cott. Galba) On þe morn furth gan þai pas, to þaire iorne þai ta. c 1435 *Torr. Portugal* 598 A lytyl whyll before the day, He toke into a Ryde Wey. c 1489 CAXTON *Sonnes of Aymon* ix. 224 Whan they were all mounted, they toke on theyr way. 1606 G. W[OODCOCKE] *Hist. Ivstine* III. 19 They tooke on their way to seeke a new place of habitation. 1615 G. SANDYS *Trav.* 193 Turning backe, we tooke vp the said streete to the West. 1622 MABBE tr. *Aleman's Guzman d'Alf.* II. 282 They tooke downe through a groue of Alder trees. c 1645 T. TULLY *Siege of Carlisle* (1840) 5 Most of the fugatives took streight for Carlisle. 1707 FREIND *Peterborow's Cond. Sp.* 221 My Lord took along the edge of the Hills. 1801 tr. *Gabrielli's Myst. Husb.* III. 74, I took across some fields for the nearest way. 1863 W. C. BALDWIN *Afr. Hunting* vi. 212 He [the elephant] gave chase, and I took up the hill. 1892 MRS. E. STEWART in A. E. Lee *Hist. Columbus, Ohio* I. 264 A gang of wolves took after her.

b. *intr.* Of a road, a river, etc.: To proceed, go, run, strike off (in some direction). *Obs.* or *dial.*

1610 HOLLAND *Camden's Brit.* (1637) 731 Where it [the high road] taketh Northward, it leadeth by Caldwell and Aldburgh. 1865 CARLYLE *Fredk. Gt.* XVIII. ii. (1872) VII. 110 [The river] Moldau..takes straight to northward again. 1894 CROCKETT *Raiders* 175 At this point the drove-road took over the Folds Hill.

c. *refl.* In same sense as a; also = to betake oneself, repair, resort to. See also *take off*, 83 c.

1470–85 MALORY *Arthur* I. viii. 45 He took hym to a strong towre with v c good men with hym. c 1489 CAXTON *Sonnes of Aymon* xvi. 385 After all thyse wordes, they toke theym selfe on their waye. 1822 BYRON *Werner* I. i. 600 He will take himself to bed. 1865 TROLLOPE *Belton Est.* xxx, I am to pack up, bag and baggage, and take myself elsewhere.

X. In idiomatic phrases with special obj.

64. Take aim. To direct a missile at something with intention to strike it; to aim.

1590 [see AIM *sb.* 3]. 1697 DRYDEN *Æneid* x. 479 The Sabine Clausus came, And, from afar, at Dryops took his aim. 1719 DE FOE *Crusoe* (1840) II. iv. 92 He took a sure aim. 1850 *Tait's Mag.* XVII. 546/1 He was in the act of taking aim with a carbine.

65. Take alarm. To accept and act upon a warning of danger; hence, to become alarmed or roused to a sense of danger.

1624, 1772 [see ALARM *sb.* 8]. 1689 T. R. *View Govt. Europe* 38 The people took the Alarm, and clamour'd for a Parliament. 1825 *New Monthly Mag.* XIII. 398 His *amour propre* takes the alarm. 1893 *Nat. Observer* 7 Oct. 535/2 The pirate took the alarm in time.

66. Take charge. To assume the care or custody *of*; to make oneself responsible.

1389 [see CHARGE *sb.* 13]. 1495 *Act 11 Hen. VII*, c. 22 § 1 A maister Ship Carpenter taking the charge of the werke. 1613 SHAKS. *Hen. VIII*, I. iv. 20 Place you that side, Ile take the charge of this. 1848 THACKERAY *Van. Fair* xli, The Baronet promised to take charge of the lad at school.

†**67. Take day.** To appoint or fix a day for the transaction of some business; to make an appointment; to put off to another day. Also *fig.*

a 1400 *Octouian* 1499 They..toke day at the monthys ende Of playn batayle. c 1477 CAXTON *Jason* 123 She accorded to her this request and toke daye for to do hit. 1523 LD. BERNERS *Froiss.* I. xxxii. 46 Then they toke day to come agayn a thre wekes after the Feast of saynt John. 1565 STAPLETON tr. *Bede's Hist. Ch. Eng.* 171 To make quick confession of their sinfull actes and not to take dayes with God. 1642 FULLER *Holy & Prof. St.* II. xix.* 126 He had rather disburse his life at the present, then to take day, to fall into the hands of such remorslesse creditours.

68. Take fire. a. *lit.* To become kindled or ignited; to begin to burn, to kindle, ignite: = *catch fire* (CATCH *v.* 44).

1526 *Pilgr. Perf.* (W. de W. 1531) 263 b, At the last they take fyre & brenne. 1590 SIR J. SMYTH *Disc. Weapons* 21 Through the moystnes of the weather..the powder will take no fire. 1669 STURMY *Mariner's Mag.* V. 69 Dip therein one end of your short Pieces, least they take Fire at both ends together. 1771 SMOLLETT *Humph. Cl.* 4 July, The soot took fire. 1885 *Cent. Mag.* XXIX. 874/1 These.. chimneys..often took fire.

b. *fig.* To become 'inflamed' with some emotion or the like; to become excited, esp. with anger; to become enraged, to 'fire up'.

1607 G. WILKINS *Mis. Inforced Marr.* I. in Hazl. *Dodsley* IX. 473 On which tinder he soon takes fire, and swears you are the man. 1608 *Merry Devil of Edmonton* ibid. X. 239 How this jest takes fire. 1761 HUME *Hist. Eng.* III. liv. 171 The Commons took fire, and voted it a breach of privilege. 1844 THIRLWALL *Greece* VIII. lxii. 177 Cleomenes took fire at the affront. 1890 *Temple Bar Mag.* June 17 Lithgow's soul took fire with sympathy.

69. Take hold. a. To get something by one's own act into one's (physical) hold; to grasp, seize: = *catch hold* (CATCH *v.* 45), *lay hold* (LAY *v.* 22). Const. *of*; *on, upon* (arch.). Also said of things.

1530 PALSGR. 748/2, I take holde apon one, *je empoygne*. 1611 *Vestry Bks.* (Surtees) 161 To picke forth the ould lyme and morter that the new migtt better take hold. 1613 PURCHAS *Pilgrimage* (1614) 19 [The Indian] Figge-tree.. whose branches..doe bend themselves downewards to the earth, where they take holde, and with new rooting multiply. 1754 SHEBBEARE *Matrimony* (1766) II. 193 [She] fell on her Knees..taking hold on the Skirt of his Coat. 1816 [see HOLD *sb.*[1] 2].

b. *fig.* To get a person or thing into its (or one's) 'hold' or power; usually with *of* (*on, upon* arch.); of a feeling, a disease, etc.: to seize and affect forcibly and more or less permanently; of fire, to 'lay hold' *of* (something), begin to burn. Also, to seize, avail oneself of (an opportunity).

1577 HARRISON *England* II. vi. (1877) I. 164 A thing latelie sproong vp, when pampering of the bellie began to take hold. 1605 SHAKS. *Lear* IV. vi. 238 Hence, Least that th'infection of his fortune take Like hold on thee. 1708 J. C. *Compl. Collier* (1845) 23 Another dangerous sort of bad Air, but of a fiery Nature like Lightning,..if it takes hold of the Candle. 1725 N. ROBINSON *Th. Physick* 292 When the Disease has taken any Hold of the Patient. 1889 M. GRAY *Reproach Annesley* III. vi, A sense of her bitter bereaval took hold of her.

c. (with *of*) To take possession and management of, take under one's control. ? *U.S.*

1877 RAYMOND *Statist. Mines & Mining* 222 They..know that a company of moneyed men taking hold of their camp will have to spend a considerable amount of money before they can expect to recoup their investment. 1897 KIPLING *Captains Courageous* ix, No, I only capt—took hold of the 'Blue M.' freighters—Morgan and M'Quade's old line—this summer.

†**d.** To attach itself, take root. *Obs. rare*[−1].

a 1300 *Cursor M.* 9350 It tok neuer in þer hertes hald. 13.. *Ibid.* 10009 (Gött.) Þat er four vertus principalys,.. All oþer vertus of þaim tas [*Cott.* has] hald.

e. To apply oneself to action; to set to; to take an active part. *dial.* and *U.S.*

1868 ATKINSON *Cleveland Gloss.*, *Tak' hold*, to undertake; an office, or specified performance or duty. 1870 MISS ALCOTT *Old-fashioned Girl* xi, I'm in despair, and shall have to take hold myself, I'm afraid. 1888 BRYCE *Amer. Commw.* III. IV. lxxxvi. 153 To believe that things will come out right whether he 'takes hold' himself or not.

70. Take horse. a. To mount a horse; to get on horseback (esp. for a journey): see sense 24 c.

[c 1450 *Brut* (E.E.T.S.) 450 On þe morow he toke hys hors and rode to Wyndysore vn-to our Kyng. c 1475 *Harl. Contin. Higden* (Rolls) VIII. 544 He toke his hors with a pryvy meyney. a 1533 LD. BERNERS *Huon* vii. 18 After masse [they] toke theyr horsses.] 1675 BROOKS *Gold. Key* Wks. 1867 V. 10 Bajazet,..Tamerlane took prisoner,..and used him for a footstool when he took horse. 1743 WESLEY *Jrnl.* (1749) 9 Just as I was taking horse, he return'd. 1889 *Univ. Rev.* Oct. 263 The princes..took horse and fled.

b. *Mining.* (See quot.) *local.*

1855 J. R. LEIFCHILD *Cornwall Mines* 88 When a lode divides into branches, the miners say it has taken horse.

c. Of a mare: see sense 39 b, and HORSE *sb.* 1 c.

1577 B. GOOGE *Heresbach's Husb.* III. (1586) 118 The Mare will not take the Horse. 1688 *Lond. Gaz.* No. 2378/4 A brown bay Filly,..being locked from taking Horse.

71. Take possession. a. To get something by one's own act into one's possession; to enter into possession. With *of*: to take into one's possession, make oneself possessor of, take for one's own, appropriate: see POSSESSION *sb.* 1 c.

1535 COVERDALE 1 *Kings* xxi. 15 Vp, and take possession of the vynyarde of Naboth the Iesraelite. 1591 SHAKS. *Two Gent.* v. iv. 130 Take but possession of her, with a Touch. a 1641 BP. MOUNTAGU *Acts & Mon.* i. (1642) 21 They entred upon, and took possession of the Land of Promise. 17.. *Rem. Reign Will. III* in *Harl. Misc.* (1809) III. 359 The troops..would, in all likelihood, have took possession of White-hall. 1852 MRS. STOWE *Uncle Tom's C.* xxxiv, Then he came, the cursed wretch! he came to take possession.

b. *fig.* (with *of*) To begin to 'possess', dominate, or actuate: cf. POSSESSION *sb.* 5, 6.

1595 SHAKS. *John* IV. i. 32 His words do take possession of my bosome. 1849 MACAULAY *Hist. Eng.* vi. II. 63 Another fatal delusion had taken possession of his mind.

72. In many other phrases, as *to take* ACCOUNT, ACQUAINTANCE, ARMS, BREATH, *the* CAKE, *one's* CHANCE, *the* CHANGE *out of*, CHRISTENDOM, COUNT, *one's* CROSS, EFFECT, END, FLIGHT, FORCE, HEAD, HEELS, *the* INITIATIVE, KNOWLEDGE, *the* LAW, *the* LEAD, LEAVE, ORDER, RECORD, RISE, ROOT, SHARE, STOCK, WITNESS, etc., for which see the sbs. (See also 91.)

XI. Intransitive uses in idiomatic combination with prepositions.

73. Take after —. a. To follow the example of; to imitate; hence, to resemble (a parent, ancestor, predecessor, superior, etc.) in nature, character, habits, appearance, or other quality.

1553 T. WILSON *Rhet.* (1580) 112 If the Nurse be of a noughtie nature, the childe must take thereafter. 1657 HEYLIN *Ecclesia Vind.*, Gen. Pref., His Followers all take after him in this particular. 1678 PHILLIPS (ed. 4) s.v. *Imitatives, Patrissare*, to take after the Father, or imitate his actions, humor, or fashion. 1892 *Gd. Words* Nov. 784/2, I take after my mother's family.

†**b.** ? To conceive a desire for or inclination to.

1707 *Curios. in Husb. & Gard.* 6 Men take strangely after this their first Employment.

Take against —, take for — (= take part against, with): see 20 b.

74. Take to —. (See also 62, 63.)

a. To undertake, take in hand; to take charge of, undertake the care of. *Obs.* exc. *dial.*

[*Toc tō þe rīce* in quot. 1154 is the equivalent of the earlier *feng tō* (*þam*) *rīce* of the Chronicle: cf. anno 488, Her Esc feng to rice; 1066 Her forðferde Eadward king, and Harold eorl feng to ðam rice. Cf. also 62 with inf.]

1154 *O. E. Chron.* an. 1140 (MS. E), & te eorl of Angæu wærd ded, & his sune Henri toc to þe rice. c 1230 *Hali Meid.* 5 He wile carien for hire þat ha haueð itaken to of al þat hire biheoueð. c 1375 *Cursor M.* 5639 (Fairf.) Þis wommon bleþely toke þer-to [to þe childe; *Cott. & Gött.* it vnderfang] & fedde hit. c 1430 *Freemasonry* 120 That the mayster take to no prentysse, But he have good seuerans to dwelle Seven ȝer with hym. 1863 KINGSLEY *Water-Bab.* v. 199 All the little children whom the good fairies take to, because their cruel mothers and fathers will not. [See *Eng. Dial. Dict.* s.v.]

b. To betake oneself to, have recourse to (esp. some means of progression, as in *take to the boats, take to flight, take to wing, to one's heels* (HEEL *sb.*[1] 19); also (now *dial.*) *to* some resource or means of subsistence).

(The intr. use here and in c comes close in sense to the *refl.* use in 61 a, 63 c, and the trans. in 24 c, 25 a.)

c 1205 LAY. 23688 He hit wende þat Arður hit wolde forsaken And nawiht to þan fehte taken. c 1400 *Melayne* 1148 At þe laste þay tuke to flyinge. a 1450 *Le Morte Arthur* 1380 Madame, how may thou to us take? 1591 SHAKS. *Two Gent.* IV. i. 42 Haue you any thing to take to? *Val.* Nothing but my fortune. 1596 DANETT tr. *Comines* (1614) 32 The King tooke to barge and returned to Paris. 1693 J. DRYDEN, jun. *Juvenal* xiv. 98 The callow Storks..soon as e'er to Wing they take, At sight those Animals for Food pursue. 1708 *Lond. Gaz.* No. 4453/2 They took to their Oars, and got from us. 1761 HUME *Hist. Eng.* II. xxvii. 130 They immediately took to flight. 1786 tr. *Beckford's Vathek* (1883) 121 They all without ceremony took to their heels. 1873 HOLLAND *A. Bonnic.* i. 19, I should have alighted and taken to my feet.

c. To betake oneself to (a place); to repair, resort, or retire to; to take refuge in; to enter.

c 1275 LAY. 7976 He droh to on oþe[r] half and tock to herboreȝe. c 1425 *Cursor M.* 2832 (Trin.) No dwellyng here þat ȝe make Til ȝe þe ȝondir feld to take. 1707 FREIND *Peterborow's Cond. Sp.* 211 Take to the Mountains on the right. a 1851 MOIR *Bass Rock* iii, The rabbit..Took to its hole under the hawthorn's root. 1879 MISS YONGE *Cameos* Ser. IV. ix. 110 He took to his bed and there lay almost without speaking. [Cf. 25, and BED 6 c.]

†**d.** To attach oneself to, become an adherent of; to direct itself to. *Obs.* (Also with *till, unto.*)

c 1205 LAYAMON 29188 Crist seolue he for-soc and to þan wursen he tohc. c 1330 R. BRUNNE *Chron.* (1810) 96 Þe maistres of þe portes for gyftes tille him toke. c 1425 *Cursor M.* 17533 (Trin.) Raþer shulde þei to vs take, Þen to ihesu for oure sake. 1625 BACON *Ess., Goodness* (Arb.) 201 If it [goodness] issue not towards Men, it will take vnto Other Liuing Creatures.

e. To devote or apply oneself to; to adopt or take up as a practice, business, habit, or something habitual: cf. 61 b, c. See also ROAD *sb.* 5 b.

a 1300 *Cursor M.* 14114 O mani thing sco [Mary] tok til an, Wit-vten quam es beute nan. 1382 WYCLIF *Gen.* xxxviii. 14 The which, the clothis of widewhed don down, toke to [Vulg. *assumpsit*] a roket. c 1430 *Freemasonry* 462 Aȝayn to the craft they schul never take. 1610 HOLLAND *Camden's Brit.* (1637) 692 Clothing (a trade which they tooke to). 1707 J. STEVENS tr. *Quevedo's Com. Wks.* (1709) 319 If you take to Begging, I will take to give nothing. 1834 LYTTON *Pilgr. Rhine* vi, He has since taken to drinking. 1843 *Fraser's Mag.* XXVIII. 203 She..took to wearing caps. 1845 FORD *Handbk. Spain* I. 199 In Madrid..the men have taken to..Parisian *paletots*. 1887 [see DRINK *sb.* 3]. 1893 *Scribner's Mag.* Aug. 227/2 She has taken to society as a duck takes to water.

f. To apply oneself (*well, kindly*); to adapt oneself: leading to sense g.

c 1375 *Cursor M.* 8436 (Fairf.) Þen was þis childe sette to boke; Ful wele I wis þer-to [*Cott.* bar-wit] he toke. 1625 BACON *Ess., Parents & Childr.* (Arb.) 277 Thinking they will take best to that, which they haue most Minde to. 1766 J. W. BAKER in *Compl. Farmer* s.v. *Turnip*, [The bullock] took kindly to the turnips. 1820 *Examiner* No. 637. 413/2 A tree which is late transplanted seldom takes well to the soil. 1885 in *Manch. Weekly Times* 6 June 5/5 The new members may not take kindly to the work.

g. To take a liking to, conceive an affection for. (For absolute use: see 50 b.)

1748 H. WALPOLE *Corr.* (1837) II. 239, I took to him for his resemblance to you. 1796 LAMB *Let. to Coleridge* 3 Oct., They, as the saying is, take to her very extraordinarily. 1844 LADY FULLERTON *Ellen Middl.* (1884) 23 To use a familiar expression, we took to each other instantaneously. 1885 *Manch. Exam.* 22 July 3/2 When first the idea was suggested, Doré did not take to it.

75. Take with —. †**a.** To receive, to accept; = sense 39. [= ON. *taka við* to receive.] *Obs.*

1127 *O. E. Chron.* (Laud MS.), Þet landfolk him wið toc. c 1200 ORMIN 104 To ȝarrkenn follc onnȝeness Crist To takenn wiþþ his lare. *Ibid.* 1316 Hu wel he takeþþ aȝȝ wiþþ þa þatt sekenn Godess are. a 1300 *Cursor M.* 820 For-þi yett wald he wit him tak. *Ibid.* 5977 Vr lauerd wil tak na wirscip wiþ þat man him don in cursd kyth. 1456 SIR G. HAYE *Law Arms* (S.T.S.) 68 The barnis..will nocht tak with the doctryne of the faderis. 1538 BALE *God's Promises* in Dodsley *O. Pl.* (1780) I. 9 Yet shall they not with hym take.

†**b.** To take up with; to have to do with. *Obs.*

1597 BACON *Ess., Followers & Friends* (Arb.) 36 It is better to take with the more passable, then with the more able.

c. To be pleased with, put up with. ? *dial.* Cf. 50 b; also *take up with* 90 z (*c*).

1632 RUTHERFOORD *Lett.* (1862) I. 97 The silly stranger, in an uncouth country, must take with a smoky inn and coarse cheer. 1638 BRATHWAIT *Barnabees Jrnl.* II. (1818) 59 Thence to Kidgelay, where a black-smith, Liquor being all hee'd take with, Boused with me. 1825 JAMIESON s.v. *Tak with*, 'How does the laddie like the wark?' 'Indeed ..he taks unco ill wi't'. 1844 STEPHENS *Bk. Farm* II. 609 In a little time she [a ewe] will take with both [twin lambs].

†**d.** To take part with, agree with. Cf. 20 b.

1654 J. BRAMHALL in *Ussher's Lett.* (1686) 612 Those of the King's Party asking some why they took with the Parliament's side. 1828 SCOTT *F. M. Perth* xxix, I would MacGillie Chattachan would take [*later edd.* agree] with me ..instead of wasting our best blood against each other.

†**e.** To admit, acknowledge, own. *Obs.*

a 1653 BINNING *Serm.* (1845) 607 Few of you will take with this, that ye seek to be justified by your own works. 1786 A. GIB *Sacr. Contempl.* I. VII. i. 157 A person is therefore brought to see and take with this sin, only when his conviction issues in conversion.

f. To contract or become affected by; to catch (fire), absorb (water): = 44 b, c (cf. also d). *dial.*

1822 GALT *Steam-boat* xvi. 347 The kill took low, and the mill likewise took wi't,..and nothing was left but the bare wa's. 1847 *Jrnl. R. Agric. Soc.* VIII. II. 380 When it [the flax] begins to ferment, or 'take with the water', the latter becomes turbid and discoloured.

XII. In combination with adverbs, forming the equivalents of compound verbs, chiefly transitive.

76. Take aback *trans.*: see ABACK *adv.* 3 (*lit.* and *fig.*).

1748 *Anson's Voy.* II. vii. 215 We were obliged to ply on and off..and were frequently taken aback. 1796 in Nicolas *Disp. Nelson* (1846) VII. p. xxxix, At ½ past 8 taken flat aback with a strong wind and a high sea from the N.E.b.E. 1844 J. T. HEWLETT *Parsons & W.* liii, I never saw a man more 'taken aback' as the sailors say. 1889 J. K. JEROME *Three Men in Boat* xvii, Blest if it didn't quite take me aback.

77. Take again. a. *trans.* To resume: see simple senses and AGAIN *adv.* †**b.** To withdraw, recall; = *take back*, 79 b: cf. AGAIN *adv.* 3. *Obs.*

1474 CAXTON *Chesse* III. i. (1883) 78 He began to take agayn his vertuous werkis and recyued pardoun and so retourned to god agayn. 1728 RAMSAY *Bob of Dunblane* ii, Lest I grow fickle, And take my word and offer again.

78. Take away. a. *trans.* To remove, withdraw, abstract; to remove by death; to subtract: see sense 58 and AWAY *adv.*

a 1300 *Cursor M.* 297 If þou ta þe light awai. 1388 WYCLIF *Ps.* l. 13 [li. 11] Take thou not awei fro me thin hooli spirit. 1415 SIR T. GREY in 43 *Dep. Kpr. Rep.* 583 A sefenneghte after that Murdok of Fyche was take away. 1477 EARL RIVERS (Caxton) *Dictes* 75 To cut the vynes & take awey the euil branches therof. 1509 HAWES *Past. Pleas.* xliv. (Percy Soc.) 215 Do not I, Tyme, take his lyfe away? 1585 T. WASHINGTON tr. *Nicholay's Voy.* IV. xxxiii. 156 To take away or mittigate some of [these laws]. c 1600 *Timon* III. i, Yee theeues, restore what yee have tane away! 1736 LEDIARD *Life Marlborough* I. 131 It pleased God to take away His Majesty. 1886 AD. SERGEANT *No Saint* ix, It took away his appetite. 1890 *Jrnl. Educ.* 1 June 341/1 Take away 4 cows from 17 cows.

b. *absol.* To clear the table after a meal.

c 1450 *Bk. Curtasye* 820 in *Babees Bk.* 326 Whenne þay haue wasshen and grace is sayde, Away he takes at a brayde. 1768 STERNE *Sent. Journ.* (1775) II. 118 *Mon Dieu!* said Le Fleur,—and took away. 1809 MALKIN *Gil Blas* XI. v. (Rtldg.) 402 The servants..had taken away and left us to ourselves. 1872 S. BUTLER *Erewhon* viii. 64 She returned in about an hour to take away.

c. *absol.* To detract *from*: = 58 e, 83 k.

1875 FREEMAN *Venice* (1881) 257 The slight touch of Renaissance in some of the capitals..in no sort takes away from the general purity of the style. 1889 STEVENSON *Master of B.* iv, This takes away from the merit of your generosity.

d. *intr.* To go away, make off: see 63.

1850 R. G. CUMMING *Hunter's Life S. Afr.* (1902) 125/1 They set the dogs after him, when he took away up the river.

79. Take back. a. *trans.* To take possession of again, resume: see simple senses and BACK *adv.*

a 1771 GRAY *Dante* 68 Take back, what once was yours. 1908 *Daily Chron.* 26 Oct. 4/6 Molière never said, 'I take my goods where I find them', but 'I take back my goods where I find them'.

b. To withdraw, retract, recall, unsay (a statement, promise, etc.): cf. BACK *adv.* 7.

1775 ABIGAIL ADAMS in *Fam. Lett.* (1876) 86, I had..made some complaints of you, but I will take them all back again. 1873 M. COLLINS *Squire Silchester* I. ix. 131, I shall take back my yes if you are troublesome.

c. To carry back in thought to a past time; cf. BACK *adv.* 4.

1889 MALLOCK *Enchanted Isl.* 251 These churches took me back to the crusaders. 1890 *Temple Bar Mag.* May 43 The boy's letter has taken me back ten years.

d. = *take aback* (fig.): see ABACK *adv.* 3. ? *dial.*

? a 1860 MRS. H. WOOD *Ho. Halliwell* (1890) II. i. 6 Hester was never so taken back in her life. *Ibid.* v. 116 She was 'taken back', as the saying runs.

e. *intr.* To go back, return. ? *Obs.* exc. *dial.*

1674 N. FAIRFAX *Bulk & Selv.* To Rdr., Being quite lost in a wilde and a frightful on and on, I e'en took back again where I was. 1889 STEVENSON *Master of B.* xi. 284 Having ..forgot my presence, he took back to his singing.

80. Take down. a. *trans.* To remove from a higher to a lower, or from an upright to a prostrate, position; to lower; to carry down; to cut down, fell (a tree); to pull down (a house, etc.: implying also 'take to pieces'); to distribute (type).

a 1300 *Cursor M.* 11664 'Ioseph', sco said, 'fain wald I rest'..Son he stert and tok hir dun. c 1435 *Torr. Portugal* 1426, I rede we take down sayle & rowe. 1548 in E. Green *Somerset Chantries* (1888) 116 One of theis ij churches maye well be spared and taken downe. a 1653 BINNING *Serm.* (1845) 425 It taketh down the tabernacle of mortality. 1751 LABELYE *Westm. Br.* 81 Whilst the Arches were unbuilding and taking down. 1818 in Willis & Clark *Cambridge* (1886) I. 573 Taking down three trees. 1886 *Troy* (U.S.) *Daily Times* 2 Jan. 1/3 A boat's crew..was taken down by a whale near the Cape Verde islands. 1909 R. RENWICK in Marwick *Edinb. Guilds* Pref. 6 The printers, seeing no early prospect of the release of their type.., took it down.

b. With various implications: (*a*) to swallow; †(*b*) to cause (a speaker) to sit down (*obs.*); (*c*) in *Falconry*, to cause (a hawk) to fly down; (*d*) in a school, to get above (another scholar) in class; so of a boat in a race, to get in front of (another boat); (*e*) to lead (a lady) down to dinner at a party.

1607 B. JONSON *Volpone* III. v, I will take down poison, Eat burning coals, do any thing. 1656 in *Burton's Diary* (1828) I. 45 Captain Hatsel was speaking to have the debate put off till Monday, but Colonel Purefoy took him down. 1667 FAIRFAX in *Phil. Trans.* II. 549 Mr. Morley..was advised by some to take down a spoonfull of good English Honey. 1828 SIR J. S. SEBRIGHT *Observ. Hawking* 36 They are always taken down after having flown unsuccessfully at their game. 1844 DICKENS *Mart. Chuz.* xix, I took him down once, six boys, in the arithmetic class. 1848 THACKERAY *Van. Fair* v, Dobbin..was 'taken down' continually by little fellows. 1887 MRS. J. H. PERKS *Heather Hills* II. xviii. 308 A quiet dinner-party, with a nice, sensible man to take you down.

c. *fig.* To abase, humble, humiliate, abate the pride or arrogance of. In quot. 1562, ?to rebuke, reprimand.

1562 *Child-Marriages* 112 She had spoken to the said Custance, and taken her downe for the same. 1593 PEELE *Chron. Edw. I*, Wks. (Rtldg.) 395 I'll take you down a button-hole. 1608 TOPSELL *Serpents* (1658) 755 For revenge, and taking down the pride of this young man. 1796 MRS. M. ROBINSON *Angelina* II. 27 He seems to experience..satisfaction in what he calls taking me down. 1857 MAURICE *Ep. St. John* i. 4 Whatever takes down a young man's conceit must be profitable to him.

d. To lower, diminish, lessen, abate, reduce; to lower in health or strength, bring low, depress. Now *Sc.* and *north. dial.*

1697 DRYDEN *Virg. Georg.* III. 209 As for the Females,.. Take down their Mettle, keep 'em lean and bare. 1719 BAYNARD *Health* (ed. 2) 22 By Degrees take down your Heat. 1811 *Self Instructor* 539 Olive colours..are first put in green, and taken down again with soot. 1836–7 SIR W. HAMILTON *Metaph.* (1877) I. xviii. 342 Taken down with a bilious fever. [See *Eng. Dial. Dict.*]

e. To write down so as to use or preserve (what is said); to take a written report or notes of.

1712 W. ROGERS *Voy.* 248, I took down the Names of those that had any. 1793 *Trans. Soc. Arts* (ed. 2) V. 121 The precision with which you took down their answers. 1883 MORFILL *Slavonic Lit.* iii. 48 These ballads had been taken down about the middle of the eighteenth century. 1885 C. H. EDEN *G. Donnington* I. xii. 240 Reporters would take down the speeches.

81. Take forth. a. *trans.* To lead forth, conduct out of a place; to bring forth, take out of a receptacle, produce; *fig.* to further, advance.

a 1300 *Cursor M.* 2693 (Cott.) Abram tok forth his men. c 1460 *Battle of Otterburn* xxxvi. in Child *Ballads* III. 297/1 The letters fayre furth hath he tayne. 1530 PALSGR. 748/1, I take forthe a man, I avaunce hym. 1890 BESANT *Demoniac* xv, When he [Damien] was taken forth to have his flesh wrenched off with red-hot pincers.

†**b.** *Take forth* one's *way*: to go forth, set forth (see 25 b); also *absol.*, to proceed. *Obs.*

1523 LD. BERNERS *Froiss.* I. x. 10 On the iiii. day they toke forth theyr way. 1674 N. FAIRFAX *Bulk & Selv.* 187 We shall take forth to our last.

†**c.** To learn; *transf.* to teach: = *take out*, 85 f.

1530 PALSGR. 748/1, I take forthe, as a childe, or a scoler dothe a newe lesson, *je apprens*..Take hym forthe a newe lesson. 1549 T. SOMR *Latimer's 2nd Serm. bef. Edw. VI* To Rdr. (Arb.) 50 The gettynge of goodes and rytches, before thou hast well learned and taken furth of the lesson, of well vsyng the same. 1581 SAVILE *Tacitus, Hist.* II. lxxxiv. (1591) 102 Taught by ill masters, hee tooke foorth [L. *didicit*] a bad lesson.

82. Take in.

* *trans.* **a.** To take, draw, or receive into itself, or into something (see simple senses and IN *adv.*); to admit, absorb, imbibe; to receive as a tributary; to eat or drink, to swallow; to breathe in, inhale; to take on board (a ship). In quot. 1583 *absol.* to admit or let in water, to leak.

13.. *Cursor M.* 6066 (Cott.) Siþen sal ilk hus in take A clene be-lambe, wit-vten sake. c 1400 MAUNDEV. (Roxb.) i. 4 It takes in to him xl. oþer ryuers. 1495 *Trevisa's Barth. De P. R.* XVII. ii. (W. de W.) N j b/2 Full of holys to take in ayre. 1583 *Leg. Bp. St. Androis* Pref. 104 in *Sat. P. Ref.* (S.T.S.) 350 He lattis his scheip tak in at luife and lie. 1585 T. WASHINGTON tr. *Nicholay's Voy.* I. x. 12 b, We took in fresh water out of a wel. 1610 HOLLAND *Camden's Brit.* (1637) 547 The River Trent..taking in the River Soure from the field of Leicester. 1737 BRACKEN *Farriery Impr.* (1757) II. 103 The first of these takes in their Nourishment by their external..Absorbent Vessels. 1777 HAMILTON *Wks.* (1886) VII. 510 The ships are taking in water and provisions for two months. 1890 *Chamb. Jrnl.* 10 May 292/1 She took in amazingly little water. 1892 *Harper's Mag.* Sept. 596/2 It..readily takes in and yields moisture.

b. To receive (money) in payment, subscriptions, etc.; to receive and undertake (work) to be done in one's own house for pay.

1699 in *Millington's Sale Catal. Skinner & Hampden Libraries*, Subscriptions are taken in by John Hartley, over against Gray's-Inn in Holborn. 1832 *Examiner* 403/1 She took in washing only for her amusement. 1889 MRS. E. KENNARD *Landing Prize* II. xii. 209 We supported ourselves..by taking in plain needle-work. 1892 *Idler* June 547 He was taking in more money than he had ever taken in before.

c. To subscribe for and receive regularly (a newspaper or periodical): = sense 15 d.

1712 ADDISON *Spect.* No. 488 ¶ 2 Their Father having refused to take in the Spectator. 1779 MACKENZIE in *Mirror* No. 2 ¶ 3 A coffee-house, where it is..taken in for the use of the customers. 1882 *Blackw. Mag.* CL. 704/1 Many of them take in the French paper just as they buy 'Punch'.

d. *Cards.* To take (a card) into one's hand from the pack.

1879 'CAVENDISH' *Card Ess.*, etc. 69 The holder of the ace of trumps ruffed, i.e. he put out four cards and took in the stock. 1891 *Field* 28 Nov. 843/1 If the non-dealer takes in the king, he ought..to lead it.

e. To lead or conduct into a house, room, etc.

c 1450 *Cov. Myst.* xxvii. (Shaks. Soc.) 268 Take hym in, serys, be the honde. 1893 *Temple Bar Mag.* XCVIII. 469 John took Miss Everard in to supper.

f. To receive or admit as inmate or guest.

1530 BIBLE (Great) *Matt.* xxv. 35, I was herbourlesse, and ye toke me in [WYCL. herboriden me: TINDALE, *Geneva*, lodged me]. 1562 J. MOUNTGOMERY in *Archæologia* XLVII. 231 Hospitalles..then the poore souldior..shoulde be taken yn, cured,..and healed. 1702 ROWE *Tamerl.* IV. i, Why stand thy..Doors still open To take the wretched in? 1840 *Jrnl. R. Agric. Soc.* I. III. 265 Invalid horses are taken in ..and treated at the hospital. 1849 *Ibid.* X. II. 413 No tenant-cottager shall take in any lodger.

†**g.** To receive or accept into some relation (e.g. into surrender, or as hostage or ally). *Obs.*

1602 LD. MOUNTJOY *Let.* in Moryson *Itin.* II. (1617) 214 By the generall advice of the Counsell I tooke in Turlough mac Henry. 1606 MARSTON *Sophonisba* II. i, Her father.. on suddain shall take in Revolted Syphax.

†**h.** To capture, take prisoner, conquer (in war); to 'take' a town. Cf. sense 2. *Obs.*

1387 TREVISA *Higden* (Rolls) VI. 285 Leo..wente to Seynt Peter..wiþ þe letayne, and was i-take in, and his eyȝen i-put out, and his tonge i-kut of. 1535 COVERDALE *Jer.* xlix. 1 Why hath youre kynge then taken Gad in? 1684 *Scanderbeg Rediv.* v. 109 His Majesty took in Raskaw, a Considerable place on the Deinster. 1709 H. FELTON *Diss. Classics* (1718) 10 Open Places are easily taken in.

i. To bring into smaller compass, draw in, reduce the extent of, contract, make smaller; to shorten, narrow, or tighten; to furl (a sail).

Take in a reef: to roll or fold up a reef in a sail so as to shorten the sail: see REEF *sb.*[1] 1.

c 1515 *Cocke Lorell's B.* 12 Mayne corse toke in a refe byforce. 1641 J. JACKSON *True Evang. T.* II. 133 But I must contract my selfe, and take in this saile of speech. a 1800 COWPER *Horace* II. Ode x. vi, If fortune fill thy sail.. Take half thy canvas in. 1837 DICKENS *Pickw.* ix, Strapping a buckle here, and taking in a link there. 1841 R. H. DANA *Seaman's Man.* ix. [*heading*] Making and taking in sail. 1848 THACKERAY *Van. Fair* xliii, Sure every one of me frocks must be taken in,—it's such a skeleton I'm growing. 1889 DOYLE *Micah Clarke* xxvii. 281, I took in one hole of my sword-belt on Monday. 1897 *Outing* (U.S.) XXX. 255/1 Take in leaders when about a team's length from corner; then take in wheelers a bit, off-wheeler more than near—in fact, many only take in off-wheel rein a couple of inches.

j. To enclose (a piece of land, etc.); to take into possession (a territory, a common), or into cultivation (a waste); to include; to annex.

c 1539 in G. J. Aungier *Syon Mon.* (1840) 131 To dyche in and take in our comyn. 1633 G. HERBERT *Temple, Sunday* vi, Christ hath took in this piece of ground, And made a garden there. 1697 in Picton *L'pool Munic. Rec.* (1883) I. 288 Others have a design to take in some Commons near Mosse Lake. 1845 *Jrnl. R. Agric. Soc.* VI. II. 301 Numerous waste patches along the sides of wide roads have been taken in. 1893 *Nat. Observ.* 5 Aug. 290/2 France is determined to take in all Siam. 1897 D. SLADEN in *Windsor Mag.* Jan. 278/1 A new alcove [has been] formed by taking in one of the..landings.

k. To admit into a number or list; to include, comprise, embrace; *spec.* to include in the consideration, take into account (quot. 1752); to include in a journey or visit (*U.S.*).

1647 HAMMOND *Power of Keys* iii. 23 He hath taken in all the antient Church-writers into his catalogue. 1697 DRYDEN *Virg., Life* (1721) I. 30 Virgil was a great Mathematician, which in the Sense of those times, took in Astrology. 1752 HUME *Ess. & Treat.* (1777) I. 106 In the former case, many circumstances must be taken in. 1870 FREEMAN *Norm. Conq.* (ed. 2) I. App. 712 Writers who..did not understand that his jurisdiction took in Kent. 1879 LUBBOCK *Addr. Pol. & Educ.* iii. 55 Attention will be concentrated on the four subjects taken in. 1883 BACON *Dict. Boston, Mass.* 359 The out-of-towner who fails to take-in a trip to Taft's.

l. To receive into or grasp with the mind; to apprehend, comprehend, understand, realize; to absorb or imbibe mentally, to learn; to conceive.

a 1677 HALE *Prim. Orig. Man.* I. i. 12 A created Understanding can never take in the fulness of the Divine Excellencies. 1685 BAXTER *Paraphr. N. T.* Matt. xiii. 18–19 By not understanding is meant also, Not considering it to take it in. 1711 STEELE *Spect.* No. 79 ¶ 5 There is no end of Affection taken in at the Eyes only. 1810 LADY GRANVILLE *Lett.* (1894) I. 16 She plays..on the pianoforte, and takes in science kindly from Mr. Smart. 1877 FREEMAN *Norm. Conq.* (ed. 3) I. App. 731 Writers who do not take in the position of an Earl of the West-Saxons. 1887 BARING-GOULD *Gaverocks* III. li. 140 Sluggish minds..require time to take in new notions.

m. To comprehend in one view (physical or mental); to perceive at a glance.

1727–41 CHAMBERS *Cycl.* s.v. *Eye*, In man..the eye is.. so ordered, as to take in nearly the hemisphere before it. 1800–24 CAMPBELL *View St. Leonard's* 18 The eagle's vision cannot take it in. 1878 *Scribner's Mag.* XV. 583/2 We..turned our heads from side to side,..the better to take in the full force of the effect.

n. To believe or accept unquestioningly.

1864 *Spectator* No. 1875. 640 The Undergraduates took it all in and cheered Lord Robert Cecil as their future representative. 1888 FARJEON *Miser Farebrother* II. xiii. 169 Jeremiah listened and took it all in.

o. To deceive, cheat, trick, impose upon. *colloq.*

1740 tr. *De Mouhy's Fort. Country-Maid* (1741) I. 132 The Griparts were never taken in yet, and never more never will. 1745 FIELDING *True Patriot* No. 9 Wks. 1775 IX. 310 They are fairly taken in, and imposed upon to believe we have..as much money as ever. 1754 E. MOOR in *World* No. 96 III. 234, I am almost of opinion that (in the fashionable phrase) he is 'taking me in'. 1809 W. IRVING *Knickerb.* V. iv. (1849) 277 A contest of skill between two powers, which shall overreach and take in the other. 1846 LANDOR *Imag. Conv.* Wks. II. 228/1 Nobody shall ever take me in again to do such an absurd and wicked thing. 1884 GEO. DENMAN in *Law Rep.* 29 Ch. Div. 473 The Plaintiff has..been taken in and misled.

p. To offer (a subject) for examination.

a 1890 LIDDON *Life Pusey* (1893) I. 20 The poets and historians who, at that time, were taken in by candidates for Classical Honours at Oxford.

** *intr.* †**q.** To go in, 'put in', enter. *Obs.*

1654 H. L'ESTRANGE *Chas. I* (1655) 88 Taking in at a Cooks shop where he supt. 1677 JOHNSON in *Ray's Corr.* (1848) 127 Great shoals of salmon, which often take in at the mouths of our rivers.

†**r.** *Take in with*: to take part with, side with, agree with. *Obs.*

1597–8 BACON *Ess., Faction* (Arb.) 80 It is commonly seene that men once placed, take in with the contrarie faction to that by which they enter. 1646 SIR T. BROWN *Pseud. Epid.* I. vii. (1686) 20 Justinian took in with Hippocrates and reversed the decree. 1647 N. BACON *Disc. Govt. Eng.* I. xxxiv. (1739) 51 Kings doubting to lose their Game, took in with the weaker. a 1734 NORTH *Lives* (1826) I. 3 If he had acted in these mens measures, and betraying his master, took in with them.

83. Take off. * *transitive senses.*

a. To remove from the position or condition of being *on* (with various shades of meaning); to lift off, pull off, cut off, rub off, detach, subtract, deduct: see simple senses and OFF *adv.*

a 1300 *Cursor M.* 14318 He bad..Of þe tumb tak of þe lidd. 1495 *Ledger-bk. A. Halyburton* 40 Som of that sek, the bat of-tan is 17li. 15s. 2. c 1530 H. RHODES *Bk. Nurture* in *Babees Bk.* 67 With your Trenchour knyfe take of such fragmentes. 1644 WINTHROP *Hist. New Eng.* (1825) II. 199 He took off all her commodities, but not at so good rates as they expected. 1703 *Art & Myst. Vintners* 57 Take off the skim, and beat it together with 6 Eggs. 1709 STEELE *Tatler* No. 5 ¶ 8 A Cannon Ball took off his Head. 1780 COXE *Russ. Disc.* 267 M. Engel..takes off twenty-nine degrees from the longitude of Kamtchatka, as laid down by the Russians. 1852 *Jrnl. R. Agric. Soc.* XIII. I. 80 Repeated crops of hay are taken off without any return. *Mod.* Isn't his name on the list? No, it has been taken off.

(*b*) *spec.* To remove from the person, divest oneself, or another, of, doff (a garment, etc.).

a 1300 *Cursor M.* 9070 (Cott.) 'Tas of', he said, 'mi kinges croun'. 13.. *Ibid.* 8116 (Gött.) Wiþ þis þe king tok of his gloue. 1485 CAXTON *Chas. Gt.* 212 He..took of hys clothes. a 1548 HALL *Chron., Edw. IV* 234 He toke of hys cappe, and made a low and solempne obeysance. 1662 J. DAVIES tr. *Olearius' Voy. Ambass.* 140 A little Cap like a Callotte..they never take off. 1736 LEDIARD *Life Marlborough* III. 422 The Armour was taken off. 1840 *Tait's Mag.* XVII. 465/1 She took off her shawl. 1891 *Murray's Mag.* Apr. 531 He never takes off his boots and spurs.

(*c*) To remove or convey (a person) from on shore, from a rock, or from on board ship.

1883 BUCHANAN *Love me for Ever* v. ii. 261 He had arranged..to be taken off one night, and to sail with them right away. 1889 *Eng. Illustr. Mag.* Dec. 267, I might be able to support life on board of her until the *Ruby* took me off. 1890 *Standard* 12 Dec. 5/7 The passengers were taken off and landed safely.

(*d*) *absol.* To clear the table after a meal: = *take away*, 78 b. (*e*) *intr.* for *pass.*: see sense 58 f.

1828 J. T. SMITH *Nollekens* I. 91 Nor do I think wine was even mentioned until the servants were ordered to 'take off'.

b. *trans.* To drink to the bottom, or at one draught; to drink off, 'toss off'.

1613 PURCHAS *Pilgrimage* III. xv. 271 She dranke to him a cup of poysoned liquor: and hauing taken off almost halfe, she reached him the rest. 1662 J. DAVIES tr. *Olearius' Voy. Ambass.* 83 Many Muscovian women took off their Cups as smartly as they [their husbands] did. 1724 RAMSAY *Steer her up*, etc. ii, See that shining glass of claret..Take it aff, and let's have mair o't. 1850 HAWTHORNE *Scarlet L.* iv, And, that thou mayest live, take off this draught.

c. To lead away summarily; *refl.* to go away, take one's departure, be off.

1838 DICKENS *O. Twist* xxiv, He..took himself off on tiptoe. 1850 *Tait's Mag.* XVII. 609/1 The guilty parties had taken themselves off. 1894 PARRY *Stud. Gt. Composers, Schubert* 230 In dread of being taken off as a soldier. *Mod.* He was arrested and taken off to prison. The child was taken off to bed.

d. To lead away or draw off (in *fig.* sense); to divert, distract, dissuade; †to free, rid (const. *from*); †to remove the opposition of by bribery or corruption, to buy off (*obs.*).

1605 SHAKS. *Macb.* II. iii. 36 It makes him, and it marres him; it sets him on, and it takes him off. a 1626 BACON *New Atl.* (1900) 24 And hee..in great Courtesie tooke us off, and descended to aske us Questions of our Voyage and Fortunes. 1670 H. STUBBE *Plus Ultra* 11 This Philosophy..taking us off from the Pedantism of Philology. 1702 tr. *Le Clerc's Prim. Fathers* 27 Having not undertaken to take them off from this Opinion. a 1704 *Compl. Servant-Maid* (ed. 7) 58 You must endeavour to take off your Mistress from all the care you can. a 1715 BURNET *Own Time* (1823) I. 467 The chief men that promoted this were taken off (as the word then was for corrupting members). 1890 FENN *Double Knot* vii, The conversation took off his attention.

e. To remove or withdraw from office, or from some position or relation; to dismiss; to withdraw (a coach, train, etc.) from running.

1745 WARD in *Lett. Lit. Men* (Camden) 369 Whom the Emperor had appointed governour..but afterwards..designed to have taken him off. 1768 J. BYRON *Narr. Patagonia* (ed. 2) 189 The centinel was taken off, and we were allowed to look about us a little. 1858 *Jrnl. R. Agric. Soc.* XIX. I. 144 My early calves..I allow to suck the cows for a fortnight, then take them off. 1892 *Field* 28 May 779/3 The coaches..will be taken off for one or more days. *Mod.* Several trains will be taken off on Bank Holiday.

f. To remove by death, put to death, kill, 'carry off', cut off: said of a person (esp. an assassin), of disease, devouring animals, etc.

1605 [see TAKING *vbl. sb.* 6]. 1608 SHAKS. *Per.* IV. Prol. 14 To take off by treasons knife. 1618 BOLTON *Florus* (1636) 224 Himselfe taken off by sudden death. 1683 BURNET tr. *More's Utopia* Pref., The hiring of Assassinates to take off Enemies. 1701 W. WOTTON *Hist. Rome, Alex.* ii. 487 Diseases..took off very many of them. 1770 LANGHORNE *Plutarch* (1879) II. 828/2 Ptolemy of Cyprus..took himself off by poison. 1832 *Examiner* 6/2 Up to the 20th of November about thirty people had been taken off by cholera. 1840 *Jrnl. R. Agric. Soc.* I. III. 258 The mangold-wurzel was..taken off early by the fly.

g. To remove (something imposed), esp. so as to relieve those subject to it.

1593 SHAKS. *Rich. II*, III. iii. 135 Oh God, oh God, that ere this tongue of mine, That layd the Sentence,..should take it off againe. 1660 INGELO *Bentiv. & Ur.* II. (1682) 147 You think to take off this Inconvenience. 1726 'PHILALETHES' in J. Ker *Mem.* p. iii, If he would agree to the taking off the Penal Laws. 1737 *Gentl. Mag.* VII. Mar. 172/1 To give immediate Ease to his Majesty's Subjects, by taking off some of the Taxes which are most burthensome to the Poor. 1840 *Penny Cycl.* XVII. 399/2 The ecclesiastical courts may..take off the penance. 1879 M. J. GUEST *Lect. Hist. Eng.* xiv. 127 He pleased the people greatly by taking off a heavy tax. 1889 M. GRAY *Reproach Annesley* III. ii, The three months' embargo was now taken off.

h. To remove or do away with (a quality, condition, etc.).

1605 SHAKS. *Macb.* V. viii. 71 Who..by selfe and violent hands, Tooke off her life. 1611 — *Cymb.* V. ii. 2 The heauinesse and guilt within my bosome, Takes off my manhood. 1652 FRENCH *Yorksh. Spa* x. 90 They..should take the water a little warm'd first..the cold being just taken off. 1691 CONSET *Pract. Spir. Crts.* (1700) To Rdr., Which thing.. may..take off the Edge of Detraction. 1737 BRACKEN *Farriery Impr.* (1756) I. 227 One or two Purges will take off the Running at his Mouth. 1885 MRS. LYNN LINTON *Chr. Kirkland* II. vi. 189 The smartest and prettiest kind of cap..took off the severity of her smoothly braided hair.

†(*b*) To do away with, disprove, confute. *Obs.*

1630 PRYNNE *Anti-Armin.* 147, I must needs take off two principall draggs objections. 1682 CREECH tr. *Lucretius* (1683) Note 26 After that I shall take off his exceptions against Providence. 1695 J. EDWARDS *Perfect. Script.* 478 To take off this seeming argument.

i. (*a*) To make or obtain (an impression) from something; to print off. In quot. 1660, to receive as an impression (in *fig.* sense).

1660 tr. *Amyraldus' Treat. conc. Relig.* III. viii. 480 These [languages] which live..take off better the impression and graces of the language of the Prophets. 1707 HEARNE *Collect.* 24 Jan. (O. H. S.) I. 320 The Stationers were obliged ..to take off 200 Copies of any Book. 1817 G. ROSE *Diaries* (1860) I. 19 *note*, He had an impression of 500 taken off. 1825 *New Monthly Mag.* XV. 234/1 The expedient..of taking off an impression in some soft substance.

(*b*) To make (a figure of something); *transf.* to draw a likeness of, to portray: = sense 33 b.

a 1719 ADDISON (J.), Take off all their models in wood. 1835–40 HALIBURTON *Clockm.* (1862) 306 A native artist of great promise..that is come to take us off. 1855 THACKERAY *Newcomes* xliv, Then Clive proposed..to take his head off; and made an excellent likeness in chalk of his uncle. 1890 'R. BOLDREWOOD' *Col. Reformer* (1891) 182 A young lady who could take off a horse like that—the dead image of him —could do anything.

(*c*) To measure off; to determine or mark the position of: cf. sense 32 c.

1793 SMEATON *Edystone L.* § 97 In this way I took off 35 ..of the most remarkable points,..These 35 primary points having been determined as above.

j. To imitate or counterfeit, esp. by way of

mockery; to mimic, caricature, burlesque, parody; to make a mock of. *colloq.*

1750 Chesterf. *Lett.* (1792) III. 85 He has since been taken off by a thousand authors: but never really imitated by any one. 1760–72 H. Brooke *Fool of Qual.* (1809) II. 120 He so perfectly counterfeited or took off, as they call it, the real Christian, that many looked to see him..taken alive into Heaven. 1789 Mrs. Piozzi *Journ. France* I. 240 At the hazard of being taken off and held up for a laughing-stock. 1809 Malkin *Gil Blas* II. vii. ¶ 20, I can take off a cat to the life: suppose I was to mew a certain number of times? a 1845 Hood *Faithless Nelly Gray* v, She made him quite a scoff; And when she saw his wooden legs, Began to take them off! 1879 Minto *Defoe* 40 One of the pamphlets which he professed to take off in his famous squib.

k. *absol.* with *from*: To detract from, diminish, lessen: = 58 e, 78 c.

1701 W. Wotton *Hist. Rome* 264 This gradual Advancement took off from the Obscurity of his Birth. 1753 Chambers *Cycl. Supp.* s. v. *Sal*, A defect or flaw, which took off very much from the value of the gem. 1773 [J. Richardson] tr. *Wieland's Agathon* Pref. 14 There are many allusions in it to modern customs..which take off in a great measure from the antique cast.

l. To close the stitches in knitting; to knit off. Also *absol.*

1849 Esther Copley *Knitting-bk.* 12 By reversing the right hand pin, so inserting it in two stitches, not in front but at the back of the left hand pin, and knitting them off as one. This [way of reducing the number of stitches] is called 'taking off at the back'.

** *intr.* **m.** To abate, grow less, decrease; (of rain) to cease.

1776 Cook in *Phil. Trans.* LXVI. 447, I judged it was about high water, and that the tides were taking off, or decreasing. 1854 H. Miller *Sch. & Schm.* xxi. (1858) 463 No sooner had it [the hurricane] begun to take off than I set out for the scene of its ravages. 1878 Stevenson *Inland Voy.* 20 The rain took off near Laeken. 1899 F. T. Bullen *Log Sea-waif* 93 The breeze now began to take off a bit, and more sail was made.

n. To go off, start off, run away; to branch off from a main stream. (Cf. 63, 63 b.)

c 1813 Mrs. Sherwood *Stories Ch. Catech.* xiii. (1873) 112 Dick ran out..and took off into the great bazar. 1825 Waterton *Wand. S. Amer.* III. iv. 265 The Indian took off into the woods. 1888 *19th Cent.* Jan. 44 The second [headwater of the Hugli] takes off from the Ganges about forty miles eastward from the Bhagirathi.

(*b*) To start in leaping; to commence a leap. (Opp. to Land *v.* 8 b.)

1814 *Sporting Mag.* XLIII. 287 The spot where the horse took off to where he landed, is above eighteen feet. 1889 *Boy's Own Paper* 7 Sept. 780/3 Competitors should be encouraged to take-off with accuracy. 1892 *Strand Mag.* III. 633/2 The last attitude one would imagine a horse to adopt in 'taking off' for a jump.

(*c*) *Croquet.* To make a stroke from contact with another ball so as to send one's own ball nearly or quite in the direction in which the mallet is aimed: cf. Take-off *sb.* 4.

1872 Prior *Notes on Croquet* 48 It were an improvement ..to tether a ball in the centre of the ground, which at starting should be hit by the players from a spot in the middle of the left-hand boundary. Taking off from this tethered ball, they might go to any part of the lawn.

84. Take on. **transitive senses.*

a. See simple senses and On *adv.*: in quot. 1877, to take on board (opp. to *take off*, 83 a (*c*)).

c 1579 Montgomerie *Misc. Poems* xlviii. 140 Tak on ȝour babert luif abuird. 1839 Ure *Dict. Arts* 258 (Cards, Playing) The ink or colour..is..laid on the types and blocks..and the impressions [are] taken-on to thick drawing paper by means of a suitable press. 1877 *Scribner's Mag.* XV. 14/1 He took on the passengers who stood clustered on the wharf.

(*b*) †To put on, don (clothing, etc.) *obs.*; to 'put on' or add (flesh, etc.): see Put *v.* 46 f (*a*).

1389 in *Eng. Gilds* (1870) 56 Þe den xal warn alle þe gylde breþeren þt be in toune, for to takyn on here hodis..and comen to messe. c 1489 Caxton *Sonnes of Aymon* xxii. 494 Thenne they went, & toke on the beste clothyng that they had. 1583 *Satir. Poems Reform.*, *Life Bp. St. Androis* 1069 On a gray bonnet he tackis. 1847 *Jrnl. R. Agric. Soc.* VIII. II. 392 Sheep..thrive very well and take on flesh rapidly. 1850 *Ibid.* XI. II. 610 The animal being thus gradually prepared to take on that increased amount of muscle and fat.

†(*c*) To take up (arms); to arm oneself: see 90 a (*c*). *Sc. Obs.*

1565 *Reg. Privy Council Scot.* I. 355 Thair rebellis ar planelie conspyrit togidder, takin on arms. 1567 *Ibid.* 524 Thai have takin on armes to puneis the authouris of the said cruell murthour.

b. To assume, 'put on' (a form, quality, etc.) = sense 16 a: to assume, begin to perform (an action or function) (cf. 17); to contract, begin to be affected by, 'catch' (cf. 44 b, c).

1799 Kentish in Beddoes *Contrib. Phys. & Med. Knowl.* 258 He took on that peevish irritability so unhappy for the individual. 1842 *Jrnl. R. Agric. Soc.* III. II. 331 The blanched leaves soon take on the appearance of frost-bitten celery. 1869 G. Lawson *Dis. Eye* (1874) 41 The ulcer.. took on a healing action, and soon cicatrized. 1893 M. Gray *Last Sentence* III. v, The deep, mysterious eyes would take on a deeper charm.

(*b*) To adopt (an idea, etc.); to accept mentally.

1890 *Pict. World* 4 Sept. 298/2 That belonged to the days before its author 'took on religion', as the Methodists term it. 1893 *Nat. Observ.* 23 Sept. 471/2 He is prepared to throw over all his convictions pretty much as he took them on.

(*c*) To apprehend with the senses; to perceive, 'catch'. *rare.*

1827 D. Johnson *Ind. Field Sports* 45, I have heard the natives assert that they take on the scent of the deer many hours after they have passed.

c. To take (a person) into one's employment, or upon one's staff, to engage (also *fig.*); to accept in marriage; to receive into fellowship.

1611 G. Blundell in *Buccleuch MSS.* (Hist. MSS. Comm.) 97 If Holland take any companies on. 1625 Massinger *New Way* II. iii, I'll not give her the advantage..To..say she was forced To buy my wedding-clothes, and took me on With a plain riding-suit and an ambling nag. 1826 *Examiner* 631/1 The large manufacturers are about taking on a considerable number of hands. 1893 J. B. Thompson in *Chicago Advance* 20 July, A number of catechumens were taken on during the year.

d. To undertake; to begin to handle or deal with, to 'tackle'.

[c 1325 *Spec. Gy Warw.* 267 Allas! what sholen hij onne take, Þat wolden here her god forsake Þurw sinne of fleschly liking?] 1422 [see Taking *vbl. sb.* 6]. 1885 *Graphic* 3 Jan. 11/3 He..so frightened the other..coward that..they did not care to 'take him on'. 1898 *Daily News* 10 Mar. 7/1 We cannot take on both jobs. 1900 Sir R. Buller *ibid* 12 Nov. 3/4, I had taken on a task, and I was bound to see it through.

e. To undertake the management of (a farm, etc.), esp. in succession or continuance.

1861 *Temple Bar Mag.* III. 474 When I was twenty-two, my father died, and I took on the farm. 1889 Mrs. Comyns Carr *Marg. Maliphant* II. xix. 70, I want him to take on another small farm. 1892 *Cornh. Mag.* Oct. 346 It will be quite impossible for me to take on the lease again.

†**f.** To assert, asseverate (cf. 17 c). *Obs. rare.*

1583 Stubbes *Anat. Abus.* II. (1882) 26 Yet will they sweare, protest, and take on wonderfully, that it is very new, fresh and tender. *Ibid.* 48 If they sell you a cow,.. will protest and take on wonderfullie, that hee is but this olde, and that olde.

g. To buy on credit. *Sc.*

1808 Jamieson, *To tak on*, to buy on credit, to buy to accompt. 1866 J. H. Wilson *Our Father in Heaven* (1869) 180, I have heard of young people..going to shops and 'taking on' things, as it is called.

†**h.** To begin, commence (with *inf.*, or *intr.*); = sense 62. *Obs.*

c 1200 Ormin 2553 Ȝho toc onn ful aldeliȝ To fraȝȝnenn Godess enngell. *Ibid.* 11260 Ȝiff þu takesst onn att an & tellesst forþ till fowwre.

** *intransitive senses.*

†**i.** To act, proceed, behave, 'go on'. *Const.* dative, to a person. *Obs.*

c 1205 Lay. 3333 Ȝef ferrene kinges hiherde þa tidinde, þe we swa takede him on. *Ibid.* 5592 Þat word come to Belinne..heo he hauede itaken on. *Ibid.* 10175 Þa þis wes al idon þa token heo oðer weise on. *Ibid.* 31619 Whet Penda king hafueð iseid and hu he wulle taken on. c 1305 *Pilate* 149 in *E. E. Poems* (1862) 115 Ou liþere man,..haþ he itake on so, Assentede he to þe gywes? 1362 Langl. *P. Pl.* A. III. 76 For toke þei on trewely þei timbrede not so hye. c 1450 Lovelich *Grail* lvi. 505 And thus these lyowns Gonnon On to take Til the tyme that Cam Lawncelot de lake.

reflexive. c 1205 Lay. 30680 On alle wissen he toc him on swulc he weore a chepmon.

j. To 'go on' madly or excitedly; to rage, rave; to be greatly agitated; to make a great fuss, outcry, or uproar; now *esp.* to distress oneself greatly. Now *colloq.* and *dial.*

c 1430 *Syr Gener.* (Roxb.) 5200 That yondre knight on the white stede Taketh on as a deuel in dede. 1472 *Paston Lett.* III. 57 My modyr wepyth and takyth on mervayllously. 1530 Palsgr. 750/1, I take on lyke a madde man, *je mesnrage*. 1535 Coverdale *Num.* xiv. 1 Then the whole congregacion toke on and cryed, and the people wepte. 1600 Holland *Livy* II. xxvii. 61 All this while Appius raged and tooke on, inveying bitterly against the nicetie and popularitie of his brother Consul. 1668 Pepys *Diary* 8 Apr., Her mother and friends take on mightily. 1767 *Woman of Fashion* I. 157 You'll make me cry too, if you take on in this Manner. 1830 Galt *Lawrie T.* I. ix, He took on like a demented man. 1852 Thackeray *Esmond* II. i, She took on sadly about her husband.

k. To assume airs; to behave proudly or haughtily; to presume; to take liberties. (Cf. 18 e.)

1668 R. Steele *Husbandman's Calling* vi. (1678) 143 If a worm should take on, lift up itself, and be proud, then anything may be proud. 1851 *Beck's Florist* 180 'Pride goeth before destruction, and a haughty spirit before a fall'. I began to take on; and if the squire gave me any orders, I did not take 'em as I ought to have done.

l. To take service or employment, to engage oneself; to enlist.

a 1670 Spalding *Troub. Chas. I* (1851) II. 335 Diuerss daylie took on [to serve in the army]. 1748 Smollett *Rod. Rand.* xvi, If you take on to be a soldier. 1778 Foote *Trip to Calais* III. Wks. 1799 II. 377, I am engaged to take on with Miss Lydy. 1890 *Lippincott's Mag.* Mar. 336 At the end of their term of enlistment [they] would refuse to 'take on' again in D Troop. 1892 *Field* 7 May 698/3 'Then', replied one of the men, 'I will take on at 4s.'

(*b*) With *with*: to engage oneself to; to begin to associate with, to consort with; = *take up with*, 90 z; to adopt as a practice, etc.

1737 Bracken *Farriery Impr.* (1757) II. 51 Such a Drake has been more used to a Hen when he was young, and.. will the sooner take on with her when he grows older. 1844 *Fraser's Mag.* XXX. 104/1 The mistress is going to take on with Mister Jowles the praacher. 1886 M. Gray *Silence Dean Maitland* i, I liked Charlie Judkins well enough before he took on with this love-nonsense. 1894 G. Moore *Esther Waters* 154 His young woman must be sadly in want of a sweetheart to take on with one such as him.

m. To 'catch on', become popular: = sense 10 c. *colloq.*

1897 'Ouida' *Massarenes* xvii, He saw how greatly these musical entertainments 'took on'.

85. Take out. *trans.* **a.** To remove from within a place, receptacle, or inclosure; to extract, withdraw, draw forth: see simple senses and Out *adv.*

13.. *Cursor M.* 20564 (Gött.), I toke þaim vte on [*v.r.* with] mi right hand. 1382 Wyclif *Ps.* lxviii. 15 [lxix. 14] Tac me out fro clei, that I be not inficchid. c 1450 *Merlin* i. 1 Whan that oure lorde..had take oute Adam and Eve, and other [from hell]. 1597 Shaks. *2 Hen. IV*, IV. v. 206 Their stings, and teeth, newly tak'n out. 1711 Addison *Spect.* No. 91 ¶ 9 He had only dipped his Head into the Water, and immediately taken it out again. 1889 F. M. Crawford *Greifenstein* II. xx. 280 Rex took out his purse and gave him a gold piece. *Mod.* I asked for the book at the library, but it had been taken out the day before.

(*b*) To remove, extract (a stain, etc.).

1727 Gay *Begg. Op.* I. ix, Money..is the true fuller's earth for reputation, there is not a spot or a stain but what it can take out. *Mod.* Ammonia will take out the grease-spots.

(*c*) *intr.* for *pass.* See sense 58 f.

b. *trans.* To withdraw from a number or set (actually or mentally); to leave out, except, omit.

c 1200 Ormin 8601 Þatt ȝer þatt he wass takenn ut Þurrh Drihhtin Godd fra manne. c 1315 Shoreham *Poems* i. 552 Þaȝ he ne toke iudas out, Þe worste man on erþe. *Mod.* There are 91 festivals in the Prayer Book Calendar; but if you take out those that have no special Collects, there are only 24.

c. To lead or carry out or forth: with various special implications, as: to lead (a partner) out from the company for a dance; to summon (an opponent) to a duel, to 'call out'; to lead (a person or animal) into the open air for exercise, etc.

1613 Shaks. *Hen. VIII*, I. iv. 95, I were vnmannerly to take you out, And not to kisse you. 1665 Pepys *Diary* 13 Apr., When the company begun to dance, I came away, lest I should be taken out. 1749 Fielding *Tom Jones* VII. xiii, When a matter can't be made up, as in a case of a blow, the sooner you take him out the better. 1811 Jane Austen *Lett.* 29 May, Mrs. Welby takes her out airing in her barouche. 1877 *Scribner's Mag.* XV. 65/1 He had even promised to take her out on the ice. 1893 J. Ashby Sterry *Naughty Girl* ii, It was awfully good of you to take the children out, Charlie. *Mod.* Take the dog out for a run.

(*b*) *Cricket.* *To take out one's bat*: said of a batsman who is 'not out' at the end of the innings.

1890 *Standard* 9 May 3/8 He was batting nearly four hours and eventually took out his bat for 90. 1892 *Sat. Rev.* 16 July 63/2 The captain..took out his bat for 60.

†**d.** (*a*) To give vent to, utter. (*b*) To announce, give out (a text). *Obs.*

1678 Dryden *All for Love* Pref., Ess. (Ker) I. 197 He took out his laughter which he had stifled. 1697 Burghope *Disc. Relig. Assemb.* 6 They will take care to come before the text is taken out.

e. To make a copy from an original; to copy (a writing, design, etc.); *esp.* to extract a passage from a writing or book.

1530 Palsgr. 750/1, I take out a writyng, I coppy a mater of a boke, *je copie*. 1573 *Art of Limming* 11 A pretie deuise to take out the true forme & proporcion of any letter, knott, flower, Image, or other worke. 1604 Shaks. *Oth.* III. iii. 296, I am glad I haue found this Napkin:..Ile haue the worke tane out. *Ibid.* III. iv. 180 Take me this worke out..I would haue it coppied. *Mod.* To read a book and take out quotations for the dictionary.

(*b*) To extract from data.

1881 *Times* 10 Nov. 4/2 The surveyor employed..to take out the quantities on the architect's plan—that is, to estimate the quantities of materials and labour which will be required to carry out the proposed plans. 1896 [see Quantity 13].

†**f.** To learn (a lesson); *transf.* to teach. (See also 81 c.) *Obs.*

a 1591 H. Smith *Wks.* (1866) I. 499 If we be negligent and slack, and never take out his lessons, but stand at a stay. 1629 Earle *Microcosm.* lxv. (Arb.) 89 He hath taken out as many lessons of the world, as dayes. 1642 *Strangling Gt. Turk*, etc., in *Harl. Misc.* (1745) IV. 37 The Discipline of War must take you out other Lessons of Fury.

g. To apply for and obtain (a licence, patent, summons, or other official document) in due form from the proper authority.

1673 *Essex Papers* (Camden) I. 93 Yr vacating their charter, & forcing them to take out a new one. 1687 Burnet *Cont. Reply to Varillas* 76 The Bishops were obliged to take out new Commissions from the King..for holding their Bishopricks. 1726 Berkeley *Let. T. Prior* 27 Jan., Wks. 1871 IV. 123, I have not yet taken out letters of administration. 1840 *Jrnl. Roy. Agric. Soc.* I. III. 351 Patents have been recently taken out for supposed improvements. 1892 *Sat. Rev.* 30 Apr. 497/1 [He] took out a summons against him.

h. To obtain or enjoy completely. ? *Obs.*

1631 *Celestina* 217, I will goe downe and stand at the doore, that my Master may take out his full sleepe.

i. To obtain, receive, use up, spend, the value of (something) *in* another form. Const. *in*.

1631 Heywood *Fair Maid of West* Wks. 1874 II. 280 Because of the old proverbe, What they want in meate, let them take out in drinke. 1763 Foote *Mayor of G.* I. Wks. 1799 I. 168 When he frequented our town of a market day, he has taken out a guinea in oaths. 1828 *Examiner* 794/1 [He] has no objection, when a poor tradesman cannot advance the fee, to take it out in goods. 1891 *Review of Rev.* 15 Sept. 236/2 The prize was one guinea, which had to be taken out in books.

86. Take out of. *trans.* **a.** To withdraw or remove from within (*lit.* and *fig.*); to extract (a stain) from: see simple senses and Out of.

To take the words out of one's mouth: see Mouth *sb.* 3 l.

c 1200 Ormin Ded. 209 To tàkenn ut off helle wa Þa gode sawless alle. 1387 Trevisa *Higden* (Rolls) II. 133 While he dwellede longe in Fraunce..Chedde was i-take out of his abbay of Lestynge. c 1425 *Cursor M.* 16442 (Trin.) Þe monsleer þat barabas was take out of prisoun. 1535 Stewart *Cron. Scot.* (Rolls) II. 660 [He] Out of the erth his deid bodie hes tone. 1659 in *Burton's Diary* (1828) IV. 451 Take heed you take not the thorn out of another's foot, and put it in your own wholly. 1771 Mrs. Haywood *New Present* 246 To take Ink out of Linen. 1882 Miss Braddon *Mt. Royal* III. iv. 59 He took the cartridges out of the case himself.

b. To get, derive, or obtain from.

1579 W. Wilkinson *Confut. Familye of Loue* B iv, Out of their knowledge, whiche they take out of the Scriptures. 1650 J. French tr. *Paracelsus' Nat. Things* II. 17 Any flint taken out of River water. 1821 Scott *Kenilw.* i, There were as good spitchcocked eels on the board as ever were ta'en out of the Isis.

c. To subtract or deduct from. Now *rare.*

1593 Fale *Dialling* 14, I take the complement of the Elevation, which is 38d. out of the reclination of the plat which is 55d., and there remain 17d. 1703 Moxon *Mech. Exerc.* 127 A setting off of 8 Foot broad and 10 Foot long taking out of the Yard.

d. To deprive a person or thing of (some quality, etc.); *spec.* to deprive of (energy or the like); usu. *to take it out of*, to exhaust, fatigue.

1847 S. Wilberforce in *Life* (1879) I. 402 There is so much of interest in a Confirmation, that it takes a great deal out of one. 1858 Hawthorne *Fr. & It. Note-Bks.* II. 68 Rome..takes the splendor out of all this sort of thing elsewhere. 1884 H. Smart *Post to Finish* xxxii, Now you say you cannot come, and all the salt is taken out of my holidays. 1890 Mrs. Laffan *L. Draycott* II. i, The sort of day that takes it out of a man.

e. To remove from the jurisdiction of; to prove not to come under (a statute).

1885 Sir C. S. C. Bowen in *Law Rep.* 29 Ch. D. 810 The burthen of taking the case out of the Statute of Limitations rests on the Appellant. 1891 *Law Times* XCII. 105/2 All lawyers are familiar with the doctrine of part performance to take a case out of the statute.

f. To take (something) from a person in compensation: *to take it out of*, to exact satisfaction from.

1851 Mayhew *Lond. Labour* I. 31/2, I take it out of him on the spot. I give him a jolly good hiding. 1888 McCarthy & Praed *Ladies' Gallery* I. iv. 91 What we have to miss in sight-seeing we try to take out of the people in the cars. 1901 *Scotsman* 29 Nov. 8/2 In the olden days the villages 'took it out' of each other with club and spear.

87. Take over. *trans.* †**a.** = Overtake 1. *Obs.*

c 1330 *Arth. & Merl.* 7163 The paiens token ouer our men, And fast leyd upon hem then.

b. To take by transfer from, or in succession to another; to assume possession or control of (something) from or after some one else.

1884 A. Forbes *Chinese Gordon* ii. 36 The army whose command he took over in its headquarters. 1887 Wrstall *Capt. Trafalgar* xiv, [He] took service with us when we took over the *Eureka*. 1890 H. S. Merriman *Suspense* viii, Brenda took over all the smaller household duties. 1891 *Law Reports, Weekly Notes* 43/1 The..company was formed..for the purpose of taking over the business..carried on by the plaintiff.

c. To carry or convey across, to transport.

Mod. The ferry-boat will take you over.

88. Take to. In passive *to be taken to* = to be taken aback: see 76. *dial.*

1865 Mrs. H. Wood *Mildred Arkell* xxxii, Mr. Van Brummel, considerably taken-to at being addressed individually, lost his head completely. 1872 *Argosy* Sept. 183 Mr. T. might possibly have been slightly taken to.., but there was no symptom of it in his voice. [See *Eng. Dial. Dict.*]

89. Take together.

a. *trans.* See simple senses and Together.

†**b.** To collect: cf. Pull *v.* 30 b. *Obs.*

c 1489 Caxton *Sonnes of Aymon* xix. 429 But he toke togyder his strengthes, & stode vpryghte.

c. To consider or reckon together (cf. 26 c), or as a whole; to reckon as a group or collection.

1678 Cudworth *Intell. Syst.* I. iv. § 14. 258 Plato in his Cratylus taking these two words, Ζῆνα and Δία, both together, etymologizeth them as one. 1742 Richardson *Pamela* IV. 107 Numps, his Son, is a Character, take it all together, quite of Nature and Probability. *Mod.* Taken together, there cannot be more than a dozen.

90. Take up. **transitive senses.*

a. To lift, raise (from the ground, etc., or from a lying or prostrate position); to pick up; also, to lift or raise (something hanging down) so as to expose what is covered by it. Somewhat *arch.*

a 1300 *Cursor M.* 3064 (Cott.) Drightin has herd þi barn cri, Rise and tak it up for þi. 1382 Wyclif *John* v. 9 The man is maad hool, and took vp his bed, and wandride. c 1420–30 *Prymer* (1895) 9 Þi riȝthond took me vp. 1596 Shaks. *Tam. Shr.* III. ii. 164 The Priest let fall the booke, And as he stoop'd againe to take it vp [etc.]. 1610 Holland *Camden's Brit.* (1637) 278 The garter..which fell from her as she daunced, and the King tooke up from the floor. 1720 De Foe *Capt. Singleton* v. (1906) 83 Ten men with poles took up one of the canoes and made nothing to carry it. 1844 Hood *Bridge of Sighs* 5 Take her up tenderly, Lift her with care. 1890 *Univ. Rev.* Feb. 232 Martin..had taken up a stone to throw at him.

(*b*) *spec.* To raise or lift from some settled position, e. g. (plants) out of the ground, (a corpse) out of the grave, (a carpet) from the floor, etc.; to break up the surface of (a field, road, etc.).

† *To take up the table*: to clear the table after a meal (*orig.* to remove the board off the trestles: see Table *sb.* 6 b). *Obs.*

13.. *Cursor M.* 8045 (Cott.) Quen þe king þam [þaa tres] had vp-tan, His ost þam honurd þan ilkan. 15.. [see Table *sb.* 6 b]. 1513 More in Hall *Chron.*, *Rich. III* (1548) 27 b, Some saye that kynge Richard caused the priest to take them vp,..and to put them in a coffyne. 1585 T. Washington tr. *Nicholay's Voy.* I. xxi, The table being taken vp, the Ambassador..entred into the pauilion. 1612 [see Table *sb.* 6 b]. 1625 Massinger *New Way* I. ii, 'Tis not twelve o'clock yet, Nor dinner taking up. 1836–9 Dickens *Sk. Boz*, *Sentiment*, The carpet was taken up. 1841 *Jrnl. R. Agric. Soc.* II. II. 229 The turnips were taken up and carted. 1895 *Times* 5 Feb. 8/2 That would mean taking up all the streets in South London.

(*c*) With special obj., implying a purpose of using in some way: as, *to take up one's pen*, to proceed or begin to write; *to take up a book* (i. e. with the purpose to read): *to take up the* (or *one's*) *cross* (see Cross *sb.* 4, 10): *to take up* Arms, *the* Cudgels, *the* Glove, *the* Hatchet (see the sbs.).

c 1420 *Brut* ccxlii. 355 Þay waged batayle & cast doun her gloues; & þanne þey were take vp and seled. 1481, 1579 [see Glove *sb.* 1 d]. 1590– [see Gauntlet *sb.*[1] 1 c]. 1621 T. Williamson tr. *Goulart's Wise Vieillard* A ij b, I tooke up my Pen againe, and at starts and tymes finished it. 1660 tr. *Amyraldus' Treat. conc. Relig.* II. iv. 216 He took up arms for the conservation of his Country. 1712 Steele *Spect.* No. 514 ¶ 1 Not finding my self inclined to sleep, I took up Virgil to divert me. 1816 Scott *Old Mort.* xxx, That the cause of his country, and of those with whom he had taken up arms, should suffer nothing from being entrusted to him. 1866 G. Macdonald *Ann. Q. Neighb.* i, A man had to take-up his cross.

(*d*) To raise, lift (one's hand, foot, head, etc.). Now of a horse or other beast.

c 1425 *Cursor M.* 15227 (Trin.) Vp he toke his holy hond & ȝaf þe benesoun. c 1489 Caxton *Sonnes of Aymon* ix. 249 Rycharde that lay a grounde thus wounded..toke up his hede, and sayd [etc.]. 1737 Bracken *Farriery Impr.* (1757) II. 73 He steps boldly, and takes up his Fore-Feet pretty high. *Ibid.* 77 A Horse should take up his Feet moderately high.

(*e*) To take (a person) from the ground into a vehicle, or on horseback, etc. Said of a person, or of the carriage, horse, train, etc. Also *absol.* of a vehicle, a train, etc. To take up its occupants.

1689 *Lond. Gaz.* No. 2511/4 A Hackney-Coachman took up 3 Persons at Mark-Lane-end. 1710 *Ibid.* No. 4735/4 A Hackney Coach..that took up his Fair in Southwark. 1831 Scott *Ct. Robt.* xiii, We should not criticise the animal [elephant] which kneels to take us up. 1857 Trollope *Barchester T.* x, Carriages..were desired to take up at a quarter before one. 1893 *Eng. Illustr. Mag.* X. 257/2 Our coach..duly took us up, and set us down. 1898 *Westm. Gaz.* 27 June 10/1 All carriages will take up on the Embankment and Savoy-hill. 1909 *Bradshaw's Railway Guide* Aug. 21 Stops to take up 1st class Passengers for London. *Ibid.*, Stops to take up for Reading or beyond.

†(*f*) *fig.* To 'raise' (a siege). *Obs. rare.*

c 1489 Caxton *Sonnes of Aymon* xxiii. 493 Charlemagne.. receyued theim honourably, and toke vp his siege, and went agen to parys.

b. To lead, conduct, convey, or carry (a person or thing) to a higher place or position.

a 1300 *Cursor M.* 17547 (Cott.) Þat helias in ald dais, Was taken up als vnto heuen. 1526 Tindale *Acts* i. 9 Whyll they behelde he was taken vp, and a cloude receaued hym vp out of their sight. 1748 *Anson's Voy.* II. viii. 219 The taking up oysters from great depths..by Negro slaves. *Mod.* He took me up into the belfry. You needn't walk up the stairs; they will take you up in the lift.

(*b*) *spec.* To bring (a horse, ox, etc.) from pasture into the stable or stall.

1482 *Cely Papers* (Camden) 122 Lette hym [a horse] ron in a parke tyll Hallowtyd and then take hym wpe and ser hym and lette hym stand in the dede of whynter. 1688 R. Holme *Armoury* III. xix. (Roxb.) 184/2 Take vp your horse, is to take him from grasse to be kept in the stable. 1844 *Jrnl. R. Agric. Soc.* V. I. 75 Calves..are taken up at night about the latter end of October. 1846 *Ibid.* VII. II. 394 Sixteen polled beasts..were taken up.

c. To pull up or in, so as to tighten or shorten; to make fast in this way, as a dropped stitch. In quot. 1882 *intr.* for *pass.* to become shortened, shrink.

1804 Mar. Edgeworth *Pop. Tales*, *To-Morrow* 340 This operation of taking up a stitch..is one of the slowest. 1882 Nares *Seamanship* (ed. 6) 226 The longer the rope the more it takes up. 1891 Miss Dowie *Girl in Karp.* iii. 33 Each girth was altered to its last hole, the stirrup-leather taken up half a yard, but nowhere could it grip the little beast. 1892 *Field* 8 Oct. 545/3 The direction to the groom would be 'take up' (or 'let down', as the case may be) the near-side horse's coupling rein.

(*b*) To tie up or constrict (a vein or artery); 'to fasten with a ligature passed under' (J.).

1565 Blundevil *Horsemanship* IV. iii. (1580) 2 b, Most diseases are healed either by letting of blood, by taking vp of vaines, by purgation, or else by cauterisation. 1737 Bracken *Farriery Impr.* (1757) II. 41 The Absurdity of taking up the Veins for the Cure of Spavins. 1840 *Jrnl. R. Agric. Soc.* I. III. 322 Should any considerable [blood] vessel be opened, it will be necessary to take it up by passing a thread underneath it, and tying it tightly.

d. To take into one's possession, possess oneself of; with various shades of meaning, as: to purchase wholesale, buy up; to get, receive, or exact in payment; to levy; to borrow (at interest); to hire.

1421 *Coventry Leet Bk.* 29 Þat no maner of fresche fysher by, ne take up, no maner of fresche fysche of men of the contrey by way of regratry. c 1440 *Jacob's Well* 40 And þou apeyryst & lessyst þat tytþe in takyng vp þi cost, here þou makyst þe cherche thrall. 1528 *Bill* in R. G. Marsden *Sel. Pl. Crt. Adm.* (1894) I. 41, I Thomas Thorne..have taken up by exchange of Thomas Fuller merchaunt..the sum of [xli] sterling. 1589 Puttenham *Eng. Poesie* III. xii. (Arb.) 179 He that standes in the market way, and takes all vp before it come to the market in grosse and sells it by retaile. 1655 tr. *Com. Hist. Francion* IV. 23, I must buy me a Cloak lined with plush, or take one up at the Brokers. 1760–72 H. Brooke *Fool of Qual.* (1809) II. 130 He took up all the money he could, at any interest. 1838 T. Mitchell *Aristoph. Clouds* 6 Strepsiades had for the purchase taken up money with two usurers, Pasias and Amynias. 1890 *Pict. World* 2 Jan. 11/3 The whole of the limited edition.. was taken up by the booksellers on the day of publication.

(*b*) To take (land) into occupation; to begin to occupy, settle upon. Cf. also v (*b*).

1478 *Acta Dom. Conc.* (1839) 6/1 He occupijt and tuke vp sa mekle of þe said landis of þe ȝeris forsaide. 1682 S. Wilson *Acc. Carolina* 16 Rent to commence in two years after their taking up their Land. 1890 'R. Boldrewood' *Col. Reformer* (1891) 76 Persons..could 'take up', that is merely mark out and occupy, as much land as they pleased.

(*c*) To accept or pay (a bill of exchange); to advance money on (a mortgage); to subscribe for (stock, shares, a loan) at their original issue.

1832 *Examiner* 283/1 It was not convenient for her husband to take up the bill. 1847 C. G. Addison *On Contracts* II. v. § 1 (1883) 771 A person who takes up a bill *supra protest* for the benefit of a particular party to the bill succeeds to the title of the party from whom..he receives it. 1873 Spencer *Stud. Sociol.* x. 251 Not one of the thousand shares was taken up. 1888 Rider Haggard *Col. Quaritch* xi. 84, I am disposed to try and find the money to take up these mortgages. 1890 *Chamb. Jrnl.* 10 May 294/1 Sums of money could be remitted for the purpose of taking up bills on the last day of grace. 1891 *Harper's Mag.* Nov. 946/2 He persuaded the citizens to take up the Queen's loans themselves.

(*d*) To make (a collection). *Sc.* and *U. S.*

1892 'Mark Twain' in *Idler* Feb. 15 They take up a collection and bury him. 1908 *Daily Chron.* 21 Dec. 4/7 The tambourine..still serves its notable purpose for 'taking up', as the Scotch say, a collection.

†**e.** To obtain or get from some source; to adopt, 'borrow' (= sense 30); to apprehend with the senses, perceive (quot. 1607); to deduce, infer (= 31 b); to contract, 'catch' (= 44 b). *Obs.*

1607 Topsell *Four-f. Beasts* (1658) 454 Presently the wilde beasts take it [the scent] up, and follow it with all speed they can. 1628 Earle *Microcosm.* ii. (Arb.) 22 Notes of Sermons, which taken vp at St. Maries, hee vtters in the Country. 1662 Stillingfl. *Orig. Sacr.* III. ii. § 5 That the general conclusions of reason..were taken up from the observation of things as they are at present in the world. 1700 Dryden *Pref. Fables* Ess. (ed. Ker) II. 255, I find..I have anticipated already and taken up from Boccace before I come to him. 1848 *Jrnl. R. Agric. Soc.* IX. II. 360 We can conceive that an animal..should take up the disease, and afterwards communicate it to others.

†(*b*) ? To receive, get, have accorded to one.

1639 Fuller *Holy War* v. xxvi. (1647) 274 A chronologer of such credit that he may take up more belief on his bare word than some others on their bond.

f. To receive into its own substance or interstices; to absorb (a fluid); to dissolve (a solid); also, to receive and hold upon its surface (quot. 1840).

1682 *Art & Myst. Vintners* xxxviii. 20 Dip in it [*printed* it in] so many cloaths as will take it up, and put the cloaths in your Hogshead. 1737 Bracken *Farriery Impr.* (1757) II. 105 Nutritive Juices, taken up by the absorbent Vessels. 1758 Reid tr. *Macquer's Chym.* I. 47 An acid cannot take up above such a certain proportion thereof as is sufficient to saturate it. 1805 W. Saunders *Min. Waters* 29 Water, at a moderate temperature, will readily take up its own bulk of carbonic acid gas. 1840 Gosse *Canadian Nat.* xvi. 251 Capable of taking up and holding a large quantity of water. 1877 *Scribner's Mag.* XV. 141/2 The elastic roller thus takes up the color from the pores of the wood. 1892 *Cornh. Mag.* Sept. 257 Water will take up 2 lb. 10 oz. of salt to the gallon.

g. To grasp with the mind; to apprehend, understand: = sense 46; *take in*, 82 l. Also with the speaker as obj. (= 46 b). *Obs.* exc. *Sc.* in general sense; now only in restricted sense: To apprehend, appreciate (points in discourse, etc.).

1659 W. Guthrie *Christian's Gt. Interest* viii. (1724) 88 A Man may take up his gracious State by his Faith, and the Acting thereof on Christ. 1741 Watts *Improv. Mind* I. vi. § 6 A student should never satisfy himself with bare attendance on the lectures of his tutor, unless he clearly takes up his sense and meaning. 1825 Jamieson s.v., He taks up a thing before ye have half said it. 1867 N. Macleod *Starling* I. v. 55, 'I do not take you up, sir', replied the Sergeant. *Mod.* He is a humorous speaker, and his jokes were well taken up by the audience.

h. To accept. †(*a*) To accept mentally (*upon credit* or *trust*), believe without examination, take for granted. *Obs.* (*b*) To accept (anything offered, esp. a challenge, a bet: also the person who offers it). Cf. 40. See also Gauntlet *sb.*[1] 1 c, Glove *sb.* 1 d: see a (*c*).

1626 Bacon *Sylva* § 34 It is strange how the ancients took up experiments upon credit, and yet did build great matters upon them. 1662 Stillingfl. *Orig. Sacr.* I. iv. § 8 Greek writers..took up things upon trust as much as any people in the world did. 1711 Addison *Spect.* No. 126 ¶ 9 Notwithstanding he was a very fair Bettor, no Body would take him up. 1880 G. Meredith *Tragic Com.* xviii, Marko..had taken up Alvan's challenge. 1892 *Sat. Rev.* 8 Oct. 403/2 Mr. Stanley (on taking up the freedom of Swansea) spoke very vigorously on the subject. 1893 *Temple Bar Mag.* XCVII. 21 It don't concern you who takes up the bets.

i. To take (a person) into one's protection, patronage, or other relation; to adopt as a *protégé* or associate; to begin to patronize.

1382 Wyclif *Luke* i. 54 He, hauynge mynde of his mercy, took vp Israel, his child. 1482 *Monk of Evesham* (Arb.) 35 That worshipfull olde fader the whiche..had take me vp to be a felow with him of his wey. 1530 Palsgr. 751/2, I take up, as a man taketh up his frende that maketh hym curtesye. a 1635 Naunton *Fragm. Reg.* (Arb.) 26 The blow falling on Edward late Earl of Hereford, who to his cost took up the divorced Lady, of whom the Lord Beauchamp was born. 1848 Thackeray *Van. Fair* li, When the Countess of Fitz-Willis..takes up a person, he or she is safe. 1877 *Scribner's Mag.* XV. 62/2 He is just the man to take up a girl whom everybody neglected. 1892 *Black & White* 10 Dec. 679/1 A great art patron took him up and he became 'the fashion'.

†**j.** To levy, raise, enlist (troops). *Obs.*

1560 Daus tr. *Sleidane's Comm.* 219 b, He toke vp all that were able to weare armure. 1597 Shaks. *2 Hen. IV*, II. i. 199 You are to take Souldiers vp, in Countries as you go. 1632 Lithgow *Trav.* III. 91 He was taken vp as a souldier.

†(*b*) *intr.* for *refl.* To enter (military or naval) service; to enlist; = *take on*, 84 l. *Obs.*

1689 Shadwell *Bury F.* I. ii, The top of their fortune is to take up in some Troop.

k. *trans.* To capture, seize. †(*a*) *Chess.* = sense 2 d. *Obs.*

c 1440 *Gesta Rom.* xxi. 71 (Harl. MS.) Þe rook..holdith length & brede, and takith vp what so is in his way. c 1470 *Treat. Chess* (MS. Ashmole 344 lf. 5), Then he takith hym vpp with his knight.

(*b*) *Falconry.* To bring under restraint (a young hawk 'at hack') in order to train it: see quot. and Hack *sb.*[2] 1. Cf. b (*b*).

1826 J. Sebright *Observ. Hawking* 8 When..[Hawks] have omitted to come for their food at the accustomed hour, for two or three successive days,..it will be necessary to take them up, or they would in a short time go away altogether. 1881 E. B. Michell in *Macm. Mag.* Nov. 40 An experienced falconer will 'take up' a young merlin from hack and have him trained in three or four days.

†(*c*) *To take up for hawks*: (app.) to seize and slaughter (an old or useless horse) as meat for hawks; hence allusively, *taken up for hawks* = done for, ruined. *Obs.*

1471 J. Paston in *P. Lett.* III. 7, I beseche yow, and my horse..be not takyn up for the Kynges hawkys, that he may be had hom and kept in your plase. a 1553 Udall *Royster Doyster* III. iii, Ye were take vp for haukes, ye were gone, ye were gone. [Cf. 1632 Brome *Northern Lasse* I. iv, 'Slid I'le marrie out of the way; 'tis time I think: I shall be tane up for Whores meat else.]

l. To seize by legal authority, arrest, apprehend; in quot. 1821, to summon as a witness.

1596 Spenser *State Irel.* Wks. (Globe) 679/1 Though the sherriff have this authoritye..to take up all such stragglers, and imprison them. 1682 Wood *Life* 25 Nov. (O.H.S.) III. 31 Duke of York hath brought an action against one Arrowsmith..upon the statute of *Scandalum magnatum*, who is taken up for it. 1796 Southey *Lett. fr. Spain* (1799) 303 The Alcayde took up all the inhabitants of the village where it happened. 1821 Galt *Ann. Parish* xii, It was thought she would have been taken up as an evidence in the Douglas cause. 1861 *Temple Bar Mag.* II. 358 [He] was taken up for sacrilege, and brought before a magistrate.

†**m.** To arrest the progress or action of; to check, stop, 'pull up'. *Obs.*

1631 Weever *Anc. Fun. Mon.* To Rdr. 7, I haue beene taken vp in diuers Churches by the Churchwardens..and not suffered to write the Epitaphs. 1699 Dampier *Voy.* II. I. iv. 78 For a small piece of Money a man may pass quiet enough, and for the most part only the poor are taken up.

n. *intr.* for *refl.* To check oneself, stop short, 'pull up'; to slacken one's pace; to restrain oneself; to reform, mend one's ways. *Obs.* exc. *dial.*

1613 Fletcher, etc. *Captain* IV. iii, Take up quickly; Thy wit will founder of all four else, wench, If thou hold'st this pace: take up, when I bid thee. 1661 Pepys *Diary* 13 Nov., My expensefull life..will undo me, I fear,..if I do not take up. a 1700 B. E. *Dict. Cant. Crew* s. v. *Oats*, One that has sown his wild Oats,..begins to take up and be more Staied. 1832 *Examiner* 611/1 She longs to make her fortune by her trade, that she may 'take up and live godly'. 1868 Atkinson *Cleveland Gloss.*, *Tak' up*,..to reform one's ways.

(*b*) Of weather: To improve, mend, become fair.

1845 *Jrnl. R. Agric. Soc.* VI. II. 570 The weather took up immediately afterwards. 1889 Froude *Two Chiefs Dunboy* xiv, On the second evening the weather began to take up.

(*c*) '*Mech.* To close spontaneously, as a small leak in a steam-pipe or water-pipe' (*Cent. Dict.*).

o. *trans.* To check (a person) in speaking; to interrupt sharply, esp. with an expression of dissent or disapproval; to rebuke, reprove, or reprimand sharply or severely. Also *to take up short*: see Short.

1530 Palsgr. 750/1 It pityed my herte to here howe he toke hym up. 1573 L. Lloyd *Marrow of Hist.* (1653) 241 His wife Xantippe began to take her husband up with taunting and opprobrious words. 1645 T. Coleman *Hopes Deferred & Dashed* 2 [He] rebukes him sharply, takes him up roundly. 1768 Tucker *Lt. Nat.* (1834) I. 80 Those, who would find fault with us for attributing colour, heat, and cold, to inanimate bodies, take us up before we were down. [illegible]

†**p.** To oppose, encounter, cope with (Schmidt *Shaks. Lex.*). *Obs.*

[illegible]

them. 1641 Baker *Chron.* (1660) 274 King Henry..in June kept a solemn Just at Greenwich, where he and Sir Charles Brandon took up all commers.

†**q.** (?) To touch up; to urge on, incite. *Obs.*

1565 Stapleton tr. *Bede's Hist. Ch. Eng.* v. vi. 158 But when I sawe them take their horses vppe with the spurres [L. *concitatis..equis*].

†**r.** To begin, commence (an action); *esp.* to begin to utter, set up, raise (laughter, lamentation, etc.). *Obs.* In quot. 1689 with *inf.* (obs.); in 1878 *absol.* (*dial.*).

c 1400 *Brut* 131 The Kyng his hondes lifte vp an hye, and a grete laughter toke op. c 1425 *Cursor M.* 15990 (Trin.) Þe cok toke vp his flizt. c 1500 *Merch. & Son* 103 in Hazl. *E. P. P.* I. 139 The goste toke up a gresely grone, with fendys awey he glode. a 1610 Healey *Theophrastus* (1636) 70 Then hee would take up a great laughter, as if some prodigy or ominous thing had happened. 1689 Aubrey *Lives* (1898) I. 150 (2nd *Ld. Falkland*) 'Twas not long before he tooke-up to be serious. 1878 *Scribner's Mag.* XV. 653/1 Meanwhile the 'animal show' at the appointed time 'took up', as the country people expressed it.

†(*b*) To start, raise, or begin a song; hence (*Sc.*) to lead the singing of (a psalm) in church. *Obs.* (Cf. also *to take up one's parable*: Parable *sb.* d.)

a 1380 *Minor Poems fr. Vernon MS.* xxiii. 1089 We han taken vp þe song Of Iubilacion. 1577 *Burgh Rec. Edinb.* (1882) IV. 60 The oulklie pentioun of ten schillingis is appoyntit to Edwerd..Hendersoun, for all the dayis of his lyfe for taikin vp of the spalmes. 1637 in Cramond *Ann. Cullen* (1888) 39 To read in the kirk and take up the psalm every Sabbath. 1825 Jamieson s. v., 'He tuke up the psalm in the kirk', he acted as precentor.

s. *trans.* To begin afresh (something left off, or begun by another); to enter anew upon; to resume.

1654–66 Earl Orrery *Parthen.* (1676) 692 With Atasernes I joyfully took up our way to the Camp. 1712 Addison *Paraphr. Ps.* xix, Soon as the evening shades prevail, The moon takes up the wondrous tale. 1833 Ht. Martineau *Manch. Strike* i. 5 When at last she lost her voice..he took up the word. 1850 *Tait's Mag.* XVII. 482/2 Mr. Ward's diary takes up the history..just where Lord Malmesbury's memoirs leave it. 1879 M. Pattison *Milton* xii. 161 He took up all the dropped threads of past years. 1902 O. Wister *Virginian* xxxii, We took up our journey, and by the end of the forenoon we had gone some distance.

t. To adopt (a practice, notion, idea, purpose, etc.); to assume (an attitude, tone, etc.); to engage in, 'go in for' (a study, profession, business, etc.).

a 1450 *Knt. de la Tour* (1906) 64 She wolde not take hede to abyde unto her neygheboures..haue taken up the guyse or array that she wold haue. 1589 Puttenham *Eng. Poesie* II. xii. (Arb.) 122 They of late yeares haue taken this pastime vp among them. 1611 Bible *Transl. Pref.* 6 To haue the Scriptures in the mother-tongue is not a quaint conceit lately taken vp. 1660 tr. *Amyraldus' Treat. conc. Relig.* II. ii. 163 He seem'd to have took up a resolution of trampling upon those superstitions. 1712 Arbuthnot *John Bull* I. iv, Lewis Baboon had taken up the trade of Clothier. 1821 Southey in *Q. Rev.* XXV. 289 Whatever part indeed Cromwell took up would be well maintained. 1890 *Sat. Rev.* 20 Sept. 355/1 Those parts of the Ethics which they are obliged to take up for 'Greats'.

(*b*) To take in hand, proceed to deal practically with (a matter, question, etc.); to interest oneself in, espouse, embrace (a cause).

1502 *Star Chamber Proc.* Michaelm. 18 Hen. VII, The said late Shireffes..caused two of her frendes to take up this haynouse matier betuix theym as arbitrours. 1771 Mrs. Harris in *Priv. Lett. Ld. Malmesbury* I. 221 This [conflict with the City] was taken up yesterday in the House; the Speaker gave a detail of the fact. 1820 *Examiner* No. 618. 109/1 How generous to take up the cause of the afflicted! 1869 Freeman *Norm. Conq.* III. xiii. 312 The cause of William was eagerly taken up. 1892 *Law Times* XCIII. 459/2 Mr. Bros..suggested that the Public Prosecutor should take the matter up.

†**u.** To make up, settle, arrange amicably (a dispute, quarrel, etc.). In quot. 1666, to make up temporarily, 'patch up'. *Obs.*

1560 Daus tr. *Sleidane's Comm.* 21 b, He had done as much as lay in him that the matter might be taken vp. 1600 Shaks. *A. Y. L.* v. iv. 104, I knew when seuen Iustices could not take vp a Quarrell. 1605 *Lond. Prodigal* II. ii, If you come to take up the matter between my master and the Devonshire man. 1666 Pepys *Diary* 24 Oct., The thing is not accommodated, but only taken up.

†(*b*) To make up, make good. *Obs.*

1662 Gurnall *Chr. Arm.* III. 302 If you be hindred of your rest one Night by business, you will take it up the next.

v. To proceed to occupy (a place or position, *lit.* or *fig.*): to station or place oneself in; = sense 27.

1565 Stapleton tr. *Bede's Hist. Ch. Eng.* 86 Taking vpp his inne, and finding the neighbours of the parish at feast with the oste. 1589 Puttenham *Eng. Poesie* II. v. (Arb.) 88 He taketh vp his lodging, and rests him selfe till the morrow. a 1672 Wood *Life* (O. H. S.) I. 109 When they were going to their..beds, two or 3 houres after he had taken up his rest. 1736 Wesley *Wks.* (1872) I. 26 Mr. Delamotte and I took up our lodging with the Germans. 1840 Thirlwall *Greece* lviii. VII. 307 He cleared the defiles and took up his quarters for the rest of the winter at Celænæ. 1888 McCarthy & Praed *Ladies' Gallery* II. 29, I did [illegible]

(*c*) *Take up house*: †to take or rent a house (*obs.*); to start housekeeping; become a householder. *Sc.*

1612 *Shetland Act* in *Scotsman* 29 Jan. (1886) 7/2 It sall not be lesum for servile persones not worth .. 72 punds Scottis to tak up houssis. 1850 *Tait's Mag.* XVII. 13/1 He was unwilling to incur the expense of taking up house. 1876 Smiles *Sc. Natur.* i, John Edward and his wife 'took up house' in the Green, one of the oldest quarters of the city.

†(*d*) *absol.* or *intr.* To take up one's quarters, lodge, 'put up'. *Obs.*

1626 B. Jonson *Staple of N.* IV. ii, How much 'twere better, that my Ladies Grace Would here take vp Sir, and keepe house with you. 1662 Pepys *Diary* 14 Oct., To Cambridge..., whither we come at about nine o'clock, and took up at the 'Beare'. 1724 De Foe *Mem. Cavalier* (1840) 14, I was..forced to take up at a little village.

w. *trans.* To occupy entirely; to occupy the whole of, fill up (space, time, etc.); to occupy exclusively (quot. 1615); to occupy so as to hinder passage, to obstruct (quots. 1607, 1631). Cf. 28.

1607 Shaks. *Cor.* III. ii. 116 My throat of Warre be turn'd ..into a Pipe.., and Schoole-boyes Teares take vp The Glasses of my sight. 1610 Holland *Camden's Brit.* (1637) 633 It tooke up in compasse above a mile. 1615 G. Sandys *Trav.* 69 The men take them [the public baths] up in the morning, and in the afternoone the women. 1631 Weever *Anc. Fun. Mon.* 11 Tombes are made so huge great, that they take vp the Church, and hinder the people from diuine Seruice. 1640 S. D'Ewes in *Lett. Lit. Men* (Camden) 167 Some petitions..tooke upp our time a great parte of the morning. 1705 tr. *Bosman's Guinea* 490 The sixteen Red Cliffs, which take up in all about three Miles in length. 1719 De Foe *Crusoe* (1840) I. v. 85 The 7th..I took wholly up to make me a chair. 1825 *New Monthly Mag.* XIV. 392 The first quatrain..is taken up with a list of rivers. 1885 Mrs. Lynn Linton *Christ. Kirkland* II. ix. 274 It took up his time and bored him.

(*b*) To use up, consume (labour, material): cf. 28. ? *Obs.*

1679 Moxon *Mech. Exerc.* viii. 142 The Fraiming work will take up more labour. 1712 J. James tr. *Le Blond's Gardening* 121 You may fill up the Holes to the Level of the Ground.., to take up the Earth that may possibly remain to be disposed of. 1719 De Foe *Crusoe* (1840) I. iv. 80 The prodigious deal of time and labour which it took me up to make a plank or board.

(*c*) To occupy or engage fully, engross (a person, his attention, mind, etc.). Chiefly in *pass.* (const. *with*, sometimes *in*); also in *Sc.* and *north. dial.* = to be taken with, take an absorbing or engaging interest in.

1599 B. Jonson *Cynthia's Rev.* v. ii, He is taken up with great persons. a 1617 Bayne *Lect.* (1634) 201 To take our selves up with some behoofefull duty. 1624 Massinger *Renegado* IV. i, I am so wholly taken up with sorrow. 1712 Budgell *Spect.* No. 301 ¶ 8, I was wholly taken up in these Reflections. 1832 Ht. Martineau *Hill & Valley* v. 76 She is taken up with making her husband comfortable. 1886 Ruskin *Præterita* I. vi. 174, I was extremely taken up with the soft red cushions of the armchairs. 1892 Mrs. H. Ward *D. Grieve* II. vii, I think he feels he must make his way first. His business takes him up altogether.

** *intransitive senses.*

(See also subordinate uses in j (*b*), n, n (*b*, *c*), r, v (*d*).)

x. *Take up for*: to stand up for, take the part of, side with. *U. S.* Cf. *to take for*, 20 b.

1878 *Scribner's Mag.* XV. 760/2 To Amanda's surprise her father took up for Mark. *Ibid.* XVI. 627/2 Twonnet thought..that it was a shame for..Mr. Whittaker to take up for Bonamy.

y. † *Take up in*, to interest oneself or itself in, concern itself with, have reference to. *Obs.*

1665 J. Spencer *Vulg. Proph.* 120 Hath not the World out-grown the follies of Auguries..and took up in the resolves of Reason, as the best Oracle to consult in a civil business? c 1666 South *Serm.*, *John* vii. 17 (1697) I. 246 The former Articles, that took up Chiefly in Speculation and Belief.

z. *Take up with.* (Cf. *take with*, 75 a–c.) (*a*) To associate with (a person); to begin to keep company with; to consort with (esp. with a view to marriage). Cf. i.

a 1619 Fletcher *Wit without M.* I. i, He's taken up with those that woo the Widow. 1693 *Humours Town* 28 The man of Mode takes up with a damn'd Jilt. 1815 Scott *Guy M.* xi, To see his daughter taking up with their son. 1824 *Examiner* 250/2 Having..absconded and taken up with another woman. 1887 Miss E. Money *Dutch Maiden* (1888) 329 If you cannot marry her, you won't care to take up with another.

(*b*) To adopt, espouse (esp. as a settled practice); to assent to, agree with, accept. *arch.*

1692 Bentley *Boyle Lect.* 58, I could as easily take up with that senseless assertion of the Stoicks. 1724 A. Collins *Gr. Chr. Relig.* 275 Taking up with all manner of false proofs in behalf of Christianity. 1825 Froude in *Rem.* (1838) I. 178 My lately having taken up with reading sermons. 1885 J. Martineau *Types Eth. Th.* I. 127 We take up at once with the belief that the space around us is empty.

†(*c*) To be satisfied with; to content oneself with, put up with, tolerate. *Obs.*

[illegible]

and the joint stock company must take up with the refuse of the market.

†(*d*) To betake oneself to: = *take to*, 74 c. *Obs.*

1785 Miss Fielding *Ophelia* I. iv, At night he again took up with his Couch.

XIII. 91. In various idiomatic phrases (besides those mentioned under the senses to which they belong), as *take into* Account, *in* (*into*) *one's* Head, *in* (*to*) Pieces, *to* Task, *in* Tow, *upon* Trust, *in* Vain, *to* Witness, *at one's* Word, *in* Worth, etc., for which see the sbs.

☞ Key to phrases treated under the senses.

Not including the adverbial combinations 76–90, nor all phrases referred to the sb. or other leading word in them; see also 72, 91.

Take an accent 22, *t* adieu 55, *t* after 73, *t* against 20 b, *t* aim 64, *t* the air 13 b, *t* alarm 65, *t* assizes 32, *t* the attention 10 d, *t* a bath 13 b, *t* beginning 52 b, *t* blind 7 d, *t* one a blow 5 b, *t* buck, bull 39 b, *t* the chair 27, *t* charge 66, *t* in charge 17, *t* cold 44 b, *t* with compasses 32 c, *t* credit 21, *t* at cards, at chess 2 d, *t* the crown 16 c, *t* day 67, *t* one's death 40 b, *t* a degree 34, *t* one's dick 17 b, *t* diligence 51 c, *t* a disease 44 b, *t* drink 13, *t* in earnest 42, *t* end 72, *t* an examination 32 a, *t* the eye 10 d, *t* farewell 55, *t* a fence 43, *t* fire 63, *t* flight 72, *t* to flight 74 b, *t* food 13, *t* for 20 b, 48, *t* form 16 a, *t* fright 50, *t* in good part 42, *t* good-night 55, *t* the gown, the habit 16 c, *t* to a habit 74 e, *t* by the hand 3, *t* in *or* on hand 17, *t* a hint 41, *t* hoarse 7 d, *t* hold 69, *t* horse 39 b, 70, *t* house 15 c, *t* in idle 26 b, *t* ill 7 d, e, 42, *t* an inflexion 22, *t* inn 25, *t* inquisition 32 a, *t* intent 51 c, *t* interest 50, *t* into 4, *t* it 17 c, 47 c, *t* a journey 52, *t* knighthood 34, *t* labour 19 b, *t* lame 7 d, *t* a lease 15 c, *t* leave 21, 72, *t* leg 24 c, *t* the life of 58 b, *t* in marriage 14 b, *t* medicine 13, *t* mercy 51 b, *t* to mercy 14, *t* minutes 33 a, *t* an oar 16 c, *t* an observation 32 b, *t* an obstacle 43, *t* off one's feet 58, *t* on 50 c, 84, *t* on oneself 16, 18, *t* a paper, periodical 15 d, *t* a photograph, picture 33 b, *t* the points 43, 46, *t* possession 71, *t* punishment 37, *t* a resolution 51 a, *t* salt 13, 44 c, *t* satisfaction 37, *t* ship 24 c, *t* short 8 b, *t* a size (in gloves, etc.) 28 b, *t* snuff 13, *t* in snuff 42, *t* (so much) 28, *t* one's stand 27, *t* a step 52, *t* a stick to 24 b, *t* temperature 32 b, *t* thought 51 c, *t* to 74, *t* one's time 28, *t* toil 19 b, *t* a trip 52, *t* trouble 19 b, *t* truce 54, *t* a turn 52, *t* upon oneself 18, *t* the way 25 b, *t* on one's way 25 c, *t* well 42, *t* (to) wife 14 b, *t* wing 24 c, *t* to wing 74 b, *t* with 75, *t* with one 59 b, c.

Take (tēⁱk), *sb.* Also 6 tayke, 9 *Sc.* and *north. dial.* tak, takke: cf. Tack *sb.*[2] [f. Take *v.*]

1. †**a.** = Tack *sb.*[2] 2, a lease of land or of a farm for a term of years. *Obs.*

1511 *Test. Ebor.* (Surtees) V. 24, I will that my wif & my childre have my take in my fermhold in Kendale. 1542 *Ibid.* VI. 157 Also I give to my wif my take of yeres of the parsonadge of Kellyngton. 1599 *Knaresb. Wills* (Surtees) I. 220 All the tayke of my farmehold to bringe up my children withall.

b. The act of taking or leasing (land); the land taken; a holding; cf. Tack *sb.*[2] 2 b. *dial.*

1805 Dickson *Pract. Agric.* I. 80 The quantity of land he must till, would occupy so much of his time, that the *take* would..be injurious to him. c 1850 *Northampt. Dialect*, This is my neighbour's take that we are on now, and that yonder is Lord B.'s. 1896 *Daily News* 19 Sept. 2/5 A few new 'takes' have been at less money, but old tenants have had to be content with a 10, 5, and..1 per cent. allowance. 1905 Tuckwell *Remin. Radical Parson* xi. 157 He..will increase his take, build a cottage on it through a building society [etc.].

2. That which is taken or received in payment, or as proceeds of some business or transaction; *pl.* takings, receipts. In quot. 1654, ? impost, contribution imposed.

1654 *Nicholas Pap.* (Camden) II. 41 The take off 200,000 crownes is now sett, and the Emperor declared his present shallbe apart. 1891 *Daily News* 14 Sept. 2/1 Confident of large 'takes' for to-day and Sunday. 1892 Stevenson *Across the Plains* 193 [They] depart, if the 'take' be poor, leaving debts behind them. 1905 *Westm. Gaz.* 15 June 11/2 The current [railway] returns include the long-distance Whitsuntide takes.

†**3.** A seizure; a spell of magic or witchcraft; enchantment. *Obs. rare.*

[Cf. Take *v.* 7, quot. 1598.] 1678 *Quack's Academy* 7 He has a Take upon him, or is Planet-struck.

4. 'Taking' or captivating quality, charm. *rare.*

1794 Mrs. A. M. Bennett *Ellen* IV. 179 Her face..had that kind of harmony and take in it, which when it has once pleased, will not cease to do so.

5. An act of taking or capturing an animal, or (usually) a number of animals (esp. fish) at one time; also the quantity so caught; a catch.

1753 *Scots Mag.* Aug. 422/1 There was a great take of herrings. 1851 Mayhew *Lond. Labour* (1861) II. 60/1 The yearly 'take' of larks is 60,000. 1854 Badham *Halieut.* 339 Of late years..greater takes have been effected off those of New England alone, than from the great fishery of Newfoundland itself. 1859 Bain *Emotions* x. 189 The pleasure of each successful throw..rendering it easy [for the angler] to go on for a long time without a take. 1876 Smiles *Sc. Natur.* vi. 101 The weather..gave promise of an abundant 'take' of moths. 1883 *Daily Tel.* 25 June 7/1 Small boats being used to ferry the takes of fish to the smacks or steamers.

b. The action or process of catching fish, etc.

[illegible]

6. An act, or the action, of taking (in general).

[illegible]

b. *Chess*, etc. The taking of a piece or pieces.

[illegible]

actual play. 1903 *Times*, *Lit. Suppl.* 31 July 236/3 A good problem seldom commences with a check or take.

7. *Printing.* A portion of copy taken at one time by a compositor to be set up in type; = Taking *vbl. sb.* 5 c.

1864 in Webster. 1871 *Printers' Register* 6 Nov., The first 'take' of copy which fell to our share was about two and a half pages of 12mo Long Primer. 1882 J. Southward *Pract. Print.* (1884) 146 The compositor is bound to write his name on his copy, with a mark showing where he began to set...Each of these portions is..called a 'take'. 1890 W. J. Gordon *Foundry* 192 In the small hours of the morning..the last speech is coming in on relays of flimsy telegrams, and the compositors are working short 'takes' of half a dozen lines apiece.

b. The amount taken down at one time by each one of a staff of reporters.

1872 J. S. Jeans *West. Worthies* 98 The take of reporters became very much shortened, until they now seldom exceed a quarter of an hour or twenty minutes.

[**Take**, error for Fake, a coil of rope.

1658 in Phillips, whence in various later dicts.]

Take-, the verb-stem in combinations and phrases used as sbs. or adjs. (mostly *nonce-wds.*): **take-all**, local name in Australia for a disease in wheat; **take-down**, an act of taking down (in quot. in sense 80 b (*d*)); **take-downable** *a.*, capable of being taken down; **take-for-granted** *a.*, that takes something for granted, involving unproved assumptions; †**take-heed**, the action of taking heed, caution; a warning to take heed, a caution; **take-it-easy** *a.*, that takes things easily, easy-going; adapted for making oneself at ease, comfortable; **take-it-or-leave-it** *a.*, allowing acceptance or rejection; showing indifference; **take-leave**, *a.* of or pertaining to taking leave, parting, 'farewell'; *sb.* an act of taking leave, leave-taking; **take-on**, a state of 'taking on' (Take *v.* 84 j) or mental agitation, a 'taking'. See also Take-in, Take-off, Take-up.

1880 *Silver's Handbk. Australia* 72 That terrible foe to wheat known as the 'take-all in South Australia, has spread beyond the Adelaide plains. 1893 *Westm. Gaz.* 12 June 6/3 In the second division [of Cambridge boat-races] as many as six 'take-downs were effected, First Trinity III going sandwich boat instead of Christ's [etc.]. 1815 Lamb *Let. to Southey* 6 May, It will be a 'take-downable book on my shelf. 1833 Coleridge *Lett., to T. H. Green* (1895) 767, I feel a 'take-for-granted faith in the dips and pointings of the needle. 1853 Lynch *Self-Improv.* ii. 26 You must talk of many things in a take-for-granted style in order to talk at all to the purpose. 1611 Cotgr., *Mesgarde*,..carelesnesse, lacke of good-'take-heed. 1622 Fletcher & Massinger *Span. Curate* IV. v, I know ye want good diets,..And, in your pleasures, good take-heed. 1648 Ward (*title*) Mercurius Anti-Mechanicus, or the Simple Coblers Boy, with his Lap-full of Caveats (or Take-heeds). 1872 *Routledge's Ev. Boy's Ann.* 500/2 The good-humoured 'take-it-easy South-Sea Island nature. 1897 *Westm. Gaz.* 24 June 4/2 The walls and roofs of this take-it-easy room were draped with broad stripes of scarlet and white bunting. 1897 Mary Kingsley *W. Africa* 251, I affected an easy 'take-it-or-leave-it-manner, and looked on. 1902 *Monthly Rev.* Aug. 155 England..sets out her exhibits with a 'take-it-or-leave-it' air, with a disregard of their possibilities which seems almost wilful. 1799 Mrs. J. West *Tale of Times* II. 93 In his 'take-leave visit he made some further discoveries. c 1815 Jane Austen *Persuas.* v, Going to almost every house in the parish, as a sort of take-leave. 1837 *Lett. fr. Madras* (1843) 81, I was prevented from finishing this..by take-leave visits, &c. 1893 *Cornh. Mag.* June 566 The governor is in a dreadful 'take on about you. 1894 Baring-Gould *Kitty Alone* III. 142 Zerah's..in a fine take-on.

Takeable, takable (tēⁱ·kăb'l), *a.* [f. Take *v.* + -able.] Capable of being taken; that may or can be taken; in various senses; in first quot., comprehensible, intelligible (see Take *v.* 46).

c 1449 Pecock *Repr.* I. ii. 11 Which..is not takeable of mannis witt. 1665 Boyle *Occas. Refl.* II. vi. (1675) 116 Necessary to the rendring these Medicines takable by me. 1803 *Hist. Europe* in *Ann. Reg.* 21/1 In the last war we had taken every thing that was takeable. 1826 *Examiner* 772/1 Every take-able seat in the house had been taken. 1893 *Temple Bar Mag.* XCVII. 608 It is the only one takable, and I take it.

Take-in (tēⁱ·kˌiˈn), *sb.* (*a.*) *colloq.* [The verbal phrase *take in* used as sb. or adj.] An act of taking in (Take *v.* 82 o); a cheat, swindle, deception; a thing or person that takes one in, a 'fraud'.

1778 Miss Burney *Evelina* (1791) I. xxi. 105, I find it's as arrant a take-in as ever I met with. 1814 Jane Austen *Mansf. Park* v, What is this but a take in? 1818 *Blackw. Mag.* II. 398 There are..at least twenty take-ins (as they are called) for one true heiress. 1858 Lytton *What will he do* I. xii, Comedians are such takes in.

b. *attrib* or *adj.* That takes in; deceptive.

1819 *Metropolis* III. 119 Tales of a take-in match and a vicious mother-in-law.

Takel, -ell, obs. forms of Tackle.

Taken (tēⁱ·k'n), *ppl. a.* [pa. pple. of Take *v.*, where see Forms.] In various senses corresponding to those of Take *v.*, q. v.

[illegible]

xxviii, Did not my heart throb in my bosom with all the agitation of a taken bird?

b. With adv. or advb. phr., as *taken-for-granted*, *taken-in*, *taken-on*, etc.: see Take *v.*

a 1586 Sidney *Arcadia* III. (1622) 377 Keeping still her late taken-on granitie. 1585–7 T. Rogers 39 *Art.* (Parker Soc.) 186 Our liturgies..they call foolishness of taken-on services. 1901 *Daily Chron.* 24 Dec. 7/1 The bitter cry of the average taken-in tenant, emitted from a chilly residence, mean in furniture. 1907 *Morn. Post* 12 Aug. 2/3 Many of our taken-for-granted notions are seen to be meaningless.

Taken, OE. and obs. northern f. Token.

Ta·ke-note. A licence empowering the holder to explore for gold in a defined district.

1889 *Daily News* 18 July 7/1 The cost of the take-note amounted altogether to 5*l.* It gave the licensee the right to explore for gold in a certain area for one year. 1895 *Westm. Gaz.* 4 Nov. 6/1 (Gold found in Wales) 'Take notes' of various areas have been secured.

Take-off (tēⁱ·kˌǫ·f), *sb.* and *a.* [The verbal phrase *take off* (see Take *v.* 83) used as sb. or adj.]

A. *sb.* **1.** A thing that 'takes off' or detracts from something (see Take *v.* 83 k); a drawback.

1826 Miss Mitford *Village* Ser. II. 214 (*French Emigrants*) Notwithstanding these take-offs, our good duchess had still the air of a lady of rank. 1868 Ld. R. Gower *Remin.* (1883) I. xvi. 304 The only take-off to being perfectly happy is the state of my dearest mother's health.

2. An act of 'taking off' or mimicking (see Take *v.* 83 j); a mimic; a caricature. *colloq.*

1855 Robinson *Whitby Gloss.*, A *tak off*, a descriptive burlesque...A mimic, or satirical person. 1884 G. H. Boughton in *Harper's Mag.* Sept. 526/1 He trotted beside the car.., roaring with glee at his 'take off'.

3. The act of 'taking off', or springing from the ground, in leaping (see Take *v.* 83 n (*b*)); usually *transf.* a place or spot from which one takes or may take off. Also *fig.*

1869 Blackmore *Lorna D.* x, Is she able to leap sir? There is a good take-off on this side of the brook. 1889 *Boy's Own Paper* 7 Sept. 780/3 It..also encourages the habit of judging the take-off with accuracy. 1905 *Westm. Gaz.* 15 May 4/1 The true basis of offensive strategy is to ensure a sound 'take-off'. 1906 *Ibid.* 27 Aug. 4/1 The Great Western adopted Milford Haven as the 'take-off' for its service of steamers to Ireland.

4. *Croquet.* A stroke made from contact with another ball so as to send one's own ball nearly or quite in the direction of aim, the other ball being moved only slightly or not at all.

1874 J. D. Heath *Croquet-Player* 39 This is a take-off, and a sharp tap is made. The direction C, in which the mallet is aimed, has approached very near to B, the direction to be taken by the striker's ball Y. *Ibid.* 57 When the latter either is likely to miss his partner, or will have a long take-off to separate you.

B. *attrib.* or *adj.* **1.** From which one 'takes off' or makes the spring in leaping: cf. A. 3.

1889 *Boy's Own Paper* 7 Sept. 780/3 The ground on the further side of the take-off line. 1896 *Harper's Mag.* Apr. 731 It was a species of hurdle-racing, with the softest of take-off and landing sides [snow].

2. Applied to a part of mechanism for taking something off. *Take-off board*: see quots.

1896 *British Printer* 138 The sheets should not be allowed to accumulate on the take-off board. 1907 *Cambr. Mod. Hist. Prospectus* 97 So soon as the whole sheet is clear of the take-off drum, flyers..waft the sheet through a semi-circular arc, and drop it on to the take-off board..fixed at the end of the press opposite that from which the sheet started.

Taker (tēⁱ·kəɹ). Also 4–6 *Sc.* takar (5 -are, 6 taikar, takkar); 6 takere, tacker. [f. Take *v.* + -er [1].] One who or that which takes.

1. One who takes, in various senses of the verb.

1486 *Act 3 Hen. VII*, c. 2 Where Wymmen..been oft tymes taken by mysdoers [etc.] and after maried to such mysdoers..Such mysdoers, takers, and procuratours to the same [etc.]. 1514 in *Eng. Hist. Rev.* (1900) XV. 450 The payne sessed as well to the Taker as to the gever. 1552 Abp. Hamilton *Catech.* (1884) 11 Takaris of ouir mekil mail or farme, to the herschipe of the tenentis. 1579–80 North *Plutarch* (1676) 203 We read of Alcibiades, that he was a great taker, and would be corrupted with Money. 1602 Marston *Ant. & Mel.* I. Wks. 1856 I. 13 A great tobacco taker too. 1615 G. Sandys *Trav.* 66 The Turkes are also incredible takers of Opium. 1737 Chamberlayne *St. Gt. Brit.* (ed. 33) II. 93 Layers and takers of paper on and from the rolling-presses. 1875 Jowett *Plato* (ed. 2) I. 101 The best taker to pieces of words of this sort. 1885 *Law Times* 7 Feb. 266/1 The taker of a railway ticket must know what is on the face of it.

2. *spec.* †**a.** One who takes another into his protection, etc.: cf. Take *v.* 14. *Obs.*

a 1325 *Prose Psalter* xlv[i]. 7 Þe Lord of vertuz ys wyþ vs; our taker [Vulg. *susceptor*] ys God of Jacob. *Ibid.* liii[i]. 4 Our Lord is taker of my soule.

b. One who captures or seizes; a captor, seizer, catcher, apprehender: cf. Take *v.* 2.

c 1375 *Sc. Leg. Saints* xxxi. (*Eugenia*) 512 [A lynx] Quhen hir qwhelpis are tan hir fra, To chas þe takaris, þaim to sla. 1454 *Cal. Anc. Rec. Dublin* (1889) 281 Halfe of that ransom [illegible]

†**c.** An officer who took or exacted supplies of necessaries for the sovereign: = Purveyor 3. *Obs.*

Supplement, p. 3873; Corrigenda, p. 4092; Spurious words, p. 4093; Books quoted, p. 4094

Given the extreme density of this dictionary page, the following reproduces the principal headwords and structure of the entries as printed, column by column.

TAKER (continued)
Rolls of Parlt. V. 115/1 That no man of this Roialme have Taken but onolye the Kyng and the Quene. ... One who takes something from another by force or wrongfully; a robber, thief, plunderer, pillager; hence, a literary plunderer, a plagiarist. ...

b. One who takes possession, esp. of land: often *with first or mere.*

c. *Derbyshire Lead Mines.* A miner who has taken possession of a mere, after the 'founder' has taken his mere.

Take-up (*tēˑkˌɒp*), *sb.* and *a.* [The verbal phrase *take up* (see TAKE 90) used as sb. or adj.] The act of taking up, or a contrivance for taking up.

Takin (*tāˑkin*). [Native name in Mishmi.] A horned ruminant (*Budorcas taxicolor*) of south-eastern Tibet on the northern frontier of Assam.

Taking (*tēˑkiŋ*), *sb.* [f. TAKE *v.* + -ING¹.]

Taking (*tēˑkiŋ*), *ppl. a.* [f. TAKE *v.* + -ING².]

Takingly, *adv.*, in a taking manner.

Takingness, attractiveness.

†Talapoin (tæˑlăpoin). Forms: 6 tallipoie, 7-8 tallapoi(e, 7 talapoi, talopoy, talipoy, talapoi; 8 talapoin, 9 telapoon, 7 – talapoin. [ad. Pg. *talapão*, *-poi*.] A Buddhist monk or priest, properly of Pegu; extended by Europeans to those of Siam, Burmah, and other Buddhist countries.

Talar (tā‧lăr), [ad. L. *tālār-is*, f. *tālus* ankle: see -AR.] A long garment or robe, reaching down to the ankles.

Talaria (tălē‧riǎ), *sb. pl.* [L. *talāria*, neut. pl. of *tālāris*: see prec.] The winged sandals or small wings attached to the ankles of the deities.

†Talaric, *a.* [f. L. *talāri-* (see TALAR) + -IC.] Of or pertaining to the ankles; reaching down to the ankles.

Talaric, *sb.* [as prec. + -IC.]

Talbot (tǭˑlbŏt). A dog of a breed formerly used for tracking and hunting; a large white or light-coloured hound, having long hanging ears, heavy jaws, and great powers of scent.

Talc (tælk), *sb.* [a. F. *talc*, Sp. *talco*, etc.; ad. med.L. *talc*, *talch*, Arab. *ṭalq*.] A mineral.

Talcoid (tæˑlkoid), *a.* and *sb.* [See -OID.] Resembling or having the form of talc.

Talcose (tæˑlkōus), *a.* [a. Ger. *talkoid* (Naumann 1859).] Abounding in or consisting largely of talc.

Talcous (tæˑlkǝs), *a.* [f. TALC + -OUS.] Of the nature of talc.

Talcum (tæˑlkǝm). Also 6 talchum [med.L.] Talc; talcum powder, a preparation of powdered talc or French chalk.

Talcy (tæˑlki), *a.* [f. TALC + -Y.] Of the nature of talc.

Tale (tēl), *sb.* Forms: 1 tæl, *talu*, 3 tale (4 taile), 3-5 tale, 4 tal, taly, 4-5 tayl(e, 4-6 tayle, etc. [OE. *talu* = OFris. *tale*, OS., MDu. *tale*, MLG., ON. *tala*, etc.]

Talebearer (tēˑlˌbɛərǝ). [f. TALE *sb.* + BEARER.] One who officiously carries reports of private matters to gratify malice or idle curiosity.

Talebearing (tēˑlˌbɛəriŋ). The carrying of tales.

Taleful (tēˑlfʊl), *a.* [f. TALE *sb.* + -FUL.] Full of tales; relating a long story.

†Talebook, a book of tales.

Tale (tēl), *v.* Now *rare.* Forms: 1 *talian*, *tale*, 3 *tale*, *telen*. [OE. *talian* to reckon, impute, enumerate = OS. *talōn* to reckon.]

Talent (tæˑlent). Forms: 1 *talente*; 3-4 *talent* (4 *taland*(e, 4-6 -ente, -ant, 6-7 *talent*). [In OE. *talente*, *-a*, ad. L. *talentum*, a. Gr. *τάλαντον* balance, weight, sum of money.]

I. A denomination of weight, used by the Assyrians, Babylonians, Greeks, Romans, and other nations; varying greatly with time, people, and locality.

b. The value of a talent weight of gold, silver, or other metal.

II. Inclination, disposition (OF. *talent*).

TALENT

Talent, *sb.*

Talented, *a.*

Tales, *sb.* (Law)

Talentive, *a. Obs.*

Talentless, *a.*

Taleavose, *Obs.*

Ta'le-teller. [f. TALE *sb.* + TELLER.]

Tali-douce, -duce, *var.* TAILLE-DOUCE.

Taliacra (talik-), *sb.*

Talion, (tæ'liən), *sb.*

Taliacotian, *a. Surg.*

Talionic (tæli'nik), *a. rare.*

Taliped, *a.* and *sb.*

Talipes (tæ'lipiz), *sb.*

Talion, variant of TALLIAR, Indian watchman.

Tali-ation, *Obs. rare. Hist.*

Taliar, *a. Obs. rare*

Talliacotian.

Talisman, *sb.*

Talisman, (tæ'limæn), *sb.*

Talisman, (tæ'limæn), *sb.* [mod.L. *talīptı, pedem,*

Talipot (tæ'lipt, -pat), *sb.*

Talismanic, (tælismæ'nik), *a.* [f. TALISMAN²]

Talismanical, *a.* [See -ICAL.]

Talismanically, *adv.*

Talismanist, *rare.* [f. TALISMAN² + -IST.]

Talismanize, *nonce-wd.* [irreg. f. TALISMAN².]

Talith, talith, variants of TALLITH.

Talk, *sb.*

Talk, *v.*

Talkable (tɔ·kab'l), *a.* [f. TALK *v.* + -ABLE]

Talk-able, *nonce-wd.* [f. TALK *v.* + -ABLE.]

Talkee-talkee (tɔ·ki tɔ·ki). [A reduplicated derivative of TALK, with childish reduplication.]

Talker (tɔ·kəɹ), *sb.* [f. TALK *v.* + -ER¹.]

Talkful, *a.*

Talking (tɔ·kiŋ), *vbl. sb.* [f. TALK *v.* + -ING¹.]

Talking, *ppl. a.* [f. TALK *v.* + -ING².]

Talkative (tɔ·kativ), *a.* [f. TALK *v.* + -ATIVE.]

Talkatively, *adv.*

Talkativeness, *sb.*

Talky (tɔ·ki), *a.*

Tall (tɔl), *a.* Also 4-7 *tal,* 4-6 *tawl, talle*.

Talk, variant of TALCKY *a.*

Tall (*continued*)

7. Of things, etc., as ships, trees, mountains: High, lofty; esp. of things high in proportion to their width, as a *tall chimney*.

8. *fig.* **a.** Lofty, grand, eminent. *Obs.*

b. *absol.* as *sb.*

Tallage (tæ·lėdȝ), *sb.* **1.** Forms: a. 3–8 taillage, 4–5 taylage, 4–7 tailage, 5–7 tallage (7–8 taillage), etc. A toll or tax levied by Norman and early Angevin kings upon the towns and demesne lands of the Crown; hence, a tax levied upon feudal dependants by their superiors; also, by extension, a municipal rate; a toll or customs duty; a grant, levy, imposition, aid.

2. A tall chest of drawers (often raised on legs).

Tallaged, *ppl. a.* *Obs.*

Tallager. *Obs. rare—¹* *see* -ER¹.

Tallagium, *Obs.* [ad. med.L. *tallagium.*] = TALLAGE *sb.¹*

Tall, *obs. variant of* TAIL *sb., v.²*

Tallagier, *Obs.* [a. OF. *taillier.*] = TALLAGER.

Tallant, *obs. variant of* TALON.

Talard, *obs.* = FILANDER.

Tallboy (tô·boi). [*cf.* TALL *a.* + (app.) BOY.]

Tallet, tallat (tæ·lᴇt). *dial. Also* † **tavelott,** *9 dial.* **tallot,** **-ut, -art.**

Tallow (tæ·lŏ). *sb.* Forms: 4–5 talwgh, 4–5 talwȝ, 5 talgh, *Sc.* 5–6 talch, 6 tawlche, tawȝh, tawoht, 6–7 tauch, 6–7 tallowe, 6–tallow. [ME. *talgh, talwh, talwy*; corresponds to MLG. *talg, talch* (LG. *talg*), in early mod.Du. *talg, talch* (6th c.), Du. *talk* (6th and 7th c.), Da., Sw. *talg,* Norw. *talg, tælg,* Icel. *tólg;* Sw. *talg(k)er(t)*, mod.Icel. *tólg;* Norw., Da., Sw. *talg,* etc.]

Tallowy (tæ·lŏi), *a.* Resembling, or of the nature of, tallow.

TALLY

Tally, *v.*

Tally, *adv.* Now *rare* or *Obs.* [f. TALL *a.* + -LY².]

Tallying, *vbl. sb.* [See -ING¹.]

Tallyman.

Tallying, *ppl. a.* [See -ING².]

Tallywoman.

TALMUD

Talm, *v.*

Talma, *sb.*

Talman.

Talmouse. *Obs.*

Talmud (tălmŭd, talmŭd), *sb.*

Talmudic, *a.* [as prec. + -AL.]

Talmudical, *a.*

Talmudist.

Talmudistic, *a.*

Talo-, combining form of L. *tālus* ankle-bone.

Talon (tælŏn), *sb.*

TALSHIDE

TALUK — 64 — TAMARIND — 65 — TAMARINE — TAMBOUR.

Taluk, taluq. *East Ind.*

Talukdar, taluqdar (tălŭkdär), *East Ind.*

Talus (tēˈlŭs, tālŭs). *Also* **talud.**

Talus (tēˈlŭs, tālŭs). *Also applied to* an ankylosen part in birds, and beasts.

TAMARIND

Tamable, variant of TAMEABLE.

Tamal (tămäl'). *Also* tamaul, *etc.*

Tamandua (tămănˈdūă). *Also* tamendon.

Tamanoir (tæˈmănwār). *Also* tamandoi.

Tamarack (tæˈmărăk).

tamarisk.

Tamarin (tæˈmărĭn). [F.]

Tamarind (tæˈmărĭnd). *Forms:* 6–7 tamarinde, 7 *pl.* tamerind, tamarind, 5–8 tamarind, *etc.*

TAMARINE

Tamarine. *Obs.* *rare.*

Tamarisk (tæˈmărĭsk). *Forms:* a. 5 thamarike, -ryke, 7 tamarice, 6–8 -is, -isk, tamerisk, 7 tamariske; b. 7 tamerisk, tamarisque.

Tamasha (tămäˈshă). *East Ind.* [a. Arab., Pers., Urdu *tamāśā* walking about for recreation.]

TAMBOUR

Tambour (tæˈmbūr), *sb.*

Tambourin (tămˈbūrĭn).

Tamboura, tamboora.

Tambouki (tămbōˈkĭ), *a.*

Tamboura, tamboura.

Tambourine (tæmbŏrēˈn). *Var. of* TAMBOUR *sb.*

Tambour (tæˈmbūr), *v.*

Tambour.

Tambourin.

Tambourine.

Tambour-work.

Tamboura.

Tambourer.

Tambouret.

Tambouret.

Tamburin.

Tamburlaine.

Tamin.

Tambour.

Tame, a.

Tameable, **tamable**, a.

Tamil, Tamul.

Tameless, a.

Tamely, adv.

Tamin.

Tameness.

Tamine.

Tamis.

Tamenos.

Tamer.

Tamerlane-like, adj. or adv.

Tamis.

Tamisage.

Tamkin.

Tamise.

Tammany.

Tammanyism.

Tammanyite.

Tammy.

Tammy.

Tam o' Shanter.

Tamp.

Tamp.

Tampan.

Tamper.

Tamper.

Tampering.

Tampin.

Tampion.

Tamping.

Tamping-machine.

Tampon.

Tampon.

Tamponade.

Tamponment.

Tampoy, *Obs. rare.* [? Malay.] (See quots.)

Tan, *sb.*1 Also 7 tanne. [prob. a. F. *tan* (13th c. in Littré, also in Cotgr. 1611 *tan*, the bark of a young Oake, wherewith, being small beaten, leather is tanned') – med.L. *tannum*, app. of Celtic origin; cf. Breton *tann* masc., oak, Cornish *glas-tannen* evergreen oak, Irish (Thorneysen). Thence the vb., med.L. *tannāre*, OF. *tanner* to tan; cf. also Du. *tanen*, late MDu. *tāne* tan, *tānen* to tan.]

I. 1. The crushed bark of the oak or of other trees, an infusion of which is used in converting hides into leather.

2. The astringent principle contained in oak-bark, etc.; tannin; also the solution of this, tan-liquor, *'ooze*.

II. 3. The brown colour of tan.

4. *adjs. from* **3.** a. Of the colour of tan.

Tanager (tæˈnadʒə). *Ornith.* Also 7 tangara. [ad. mod.L. *Tanagra* (Linnæus 1758), for Tupi *tangará* (used by Brisson 1760).]

Tanagrine (tæˈnagrin), *a. [f. *tanager* ...] resembling the tanager; belonging to the *Tanagra*, or subfamily *Tanagrinæ*.

Tanagroid (tæˈnagroid), *a.* see TANAGER.

Tand, *obs. f. tanned*, pa. pple. of TAN.

Tandem (tæˈndem), *sb.*2 and *adv.* [mod.L. *errom.* tandem, L. = at length (of time) used punningly.]

Tandle, tanle (tæˈnd'l, tæˈn'l). *Sc. and north. dial.* [an altered form of TINDLE, tannel. = OHG. *zantaro, zantro*, MHG. *zanter, zander*.]

Tandour (tæˈndūə). Also 7 tenur, tenure, 8 tandoor; 9 tanour. [Hindi, a. Pers. *tanūr* oven, portable furnace, a. Aramaic *tannūr*.]

Tandrock, var. of TANDROC.

Tandry, tandy, *obs. form of* TAWNY.

Tang (tæŋ), *sb.*1 Forms: α. 4–7 tange, 7–8 tongue, 8–9 *dial.* taing. β. 5–6 tong(e. [Known in literature from 14th c., but prob. in Eng. use much earlier.]

I. 1. A projecting pointed part or instrument.

Tang (tæŋ), *sb.*2 [Origin uncertain: perh. from a place-name.] Name of some kind of linen.

Tang (tæŋ), *sb.*3 and *adv.* Also 8–9 *erron.* tandem. [q.v. tandem at length (of time) used punningly.]

Tangle (tæŋg'l), *sb.*1 Also 6–7 tangle, 7 tangyll. [Of Norse origin.] A collective name for large coarse seaweeds.

Tang (tæŋ), *sb.*4 [f. native name] = TANGO.

Tang (tæŋ), *v.*1 Also 5 taang, 7–9 *dial.* tang. [f. TANG *sb.*1]

Tang (tæŋ), *v.*2 [Mainly echoic, like TANG *sb.*3; cf. TING *v.*] In some instances affected by TAN *sb.*]

Tang (tæŋ), *v.*3 A word sometimes app. purely echoic, denoting the strong ringing note produced when a large bell or any sonorous body is suddenly struck with force, or a tense string sharply plucked.

Tang, *sb.* and *v.* see TANGHIN.

Tanga, var. of TONGA, an Indian cart.

Tangalung (Malay *tanggalong*). The civet cat of Sumatra, etc., *Viverra tangalunga*; the Sumatran civet.

Tangaroid: see TANAGER.

Tango, *obs. form of* TANG, TANGA, TONG.

Tanged (tæŋd), *ppl. a.* [f. TANG *sb.*1 and *v.*1 + -ED.] Having a tang; furnished with a tang to fix in a handle; barbed; forked.

Tangene: see TANGHIN.

Tangence (tæˈndʒens), *rare*. [a. F. *tangence* (1835 in Dict.) or ad. *tangent* adj.; see -ENCE.] The act or fact of touching; contact.

Tangency (tæˈndʒensi). [f. L. type *tangentia*, f. *tangent-em* TANGENT: see -ENCY.] The quality or condition of being tangent; state of contact.

Tangent (tæˈndʒent), *a.* and *sb.* [ad. L. *tangent-em*, pr. pple. of *tangĕre* to touch.]

Tangental (tæˈndʒental), *a.* see TANGENTIAL.

Tangential (tænˈdʒenʃəl), *a.* [f. prec. + -IAL.] 1. Of or pertaining to a tangent.

Tangentially (tænˈdʒenʃəli), *adv.* [f. prec. + -LY.] In a tangential way; in the manner, position, or direction of a tangent.

Tangerine (tændʒəˈriːn), *a.* and *sb.* Also 8 *erron.* tangierine. [f. *Tangier, Tangjer* + -INE.] A. *adj.* Of or pertaining to, or native of, Tangier, a seaport in Morocco, on the Strait of Gibraltar. B. *sb.* 1. A native of Tangier. 2. A tangerine orange.

Tanghan (tæˈngan). *East Ind.* [Hindi *tāghan*.] A strong breed of ponies found in Tibet and neighbouring hills.

Supplement, p. 3873; Corrigenda, p. 4092; Spurious words, p. 4093; Books quoted, p. 4094

Tanghin. see after next.

Tanghin (tæ·ŋgin). Also **8 tanguin, 9 tanguen, tanguin, tangena, 9 tangin,** ad. Malagasy *tangena, tangan'j.*

1. A poison obtained from the kernels of *Tanghinia venenifera*, N.O. *Apocynaceæ*, a shrub of Madagascar, the fruit of which is a large purplish drupe.

2. The shrub itself; more properly *tangena* or *tanghina*. Also *attrib.*

Tangibility (tændʒibi·liti). [f. as TANGIBLE: see -ILITY.] The state or quality of being tangible; perceptibility to the touch; tangibleness.

Tangible (tæ·ndʒib'l), *a.* [ad. L. *tangibilis* that may be touched; f. *tangĕre* to touch: see -BLE. So F. *tangible* (16th c. in Littré).]

1. Capable of being touched; affecting the sense of touch; touchable.

b. With a *n.* and *pl.*: A tangible thing or matter.

2. *fig.* That can be laid hold of or grasped by the mind, or dealt with as a fact: hence, that can be realized or shown to have substance; real, actual.

3. *fig.* Capable of being touched or affected emotionally.

Hence **Ta·ngibleness**, the quality or state of being tangible; **Ta·ngibly** *adv.*, in a tangible manner.

Tangina, tangini: see TANGHIN.

Tangle, obs. Sc. form of TONGS.

Tangle (tæ·ŋg'l), *sb.*[1] = Norw. *taangel, tongul,* ON. and Icel. *þöngull* (-gulr) the stalk of *Laminaria digitata*, app. deriv. of *þang* bladder-wrack, TANG *sb.*[3]

1. A general term for the larger seaweeds, species of *Fucus* and allied genera.

2. *spec.* Either of two species described, *Laminaria (Fucus) L. digitata* and *L. saccharina*, having long leathery fronds, the young stalk and fronds of which are sometimes eaten.

3. *Comb.*, as **tangle-picker, tangle-fish,** a popular name of the needle-fish or pipe-fish, *Syngnathus acus;* **tangle-fish** *(U.S.),* the Torontose *(Strypilus interpret);* **tangle-knit,** in surgery, a tent or pledget of seaweed; **tangle-wrack, -wrass** = sense 1.

Tangle (tæ·ŋg'l), *sb.*[2] Also 4-5 **tangil, -yl, 4-6 -le, 6 -ell.** [Known first in later 14th and early 15th c. MSS. of Hampole's *Psalter* (c 1340), as a variant reading for *tayfl, -yl,* the forms in the earliest MSS., used also in other works attributed to Hampole: see TAGLE *v.*, of which *tangle* was app. a nasalized variant.

Tangle (tæ·ŋg'l), *v.* Also 4-5 **tangil, -yl, 4-6 -le, 6 -ell.** [Known first in later 14th and early 15th c.]

1. To involve or bring together (hair, threads, etc.) confusedly.

2. *intr.* for *refl.* To be or become tangled or confusedly intertwined.

Hence **Ta·ngling** *vbl. sb.*[1] complicated or confused intertwining; complication; *† contention.*

Tank (tæŋk), *sb.*[1] Forms: 7 **tanke, tanque, taneke, tanck, 7- tank.** [In sense 1, perh. immediately from an Indian vernacular: cf. Guz. *tānkh* an underground reservoir for water (Wilson); Marāthī *tānkēṃ, tānṭeṃ,* a reservoir of water, a tank (Wilson); *tānkī* a cistern of stone in a house, a reservoir for rain-water.

Tank (tæŋk), *v.* [f. prec.]

1. *trans.* To lift or measure in a tank.

Tankage (-dʒ), *sb.* [f. TANK *sb.*[1] or *v.* + -AGE.]

Tankard (tæ·ŋkəd), *sb.* Also 4-5 **tancard, 5-7 -kard, 6-7 -kerde, -kerd,** Sc. **7 tankert.** [Known first in 14th c.]

Tanked (tæŋkt), *ppl. a.* [f. TANK *v.* + -ED[1].]

Tanker (tæ·ŋkəɹ). [f. TANK *sb.*[1] or *v.* + -ER[1].]

Tankful (tæ·ŋkfŭl). [f. TANK *sb.*[1] + -FUL.]

Tankia, variant of TANKA.

Tankle, sb. The second element in the reduplicated TINKLE-TANKLE.

Tankle, *v.* = TANGLE.

Tanna, obs. form of TAWNY.

Tannable (tæ·nəb'l), *a.* [f. TAN *v.*[1] + -ABLE.]

Tannate (tæ·neit). *Chem.* [f. TANNIC + -ATE.]

Tanned (tænd), *ppl. a.* [f. TAN *v.*[1] + -ED[1].]

Tanner (tæ·nəɹ). Also 7 *tannere.*

Tannic (tæ·nik), *a. Chem.* [= F. *tannique,* f. *tan* TAN + -IC.]

Tanniferous (tæni·fĕrəs), *a.* [f. TANNIN + -FEROUS.]

Tannigen (tæ·nidʒen). *Pharm.* [f. TANN(IN + -GEN.]

Tannin (tæ·nin). *Chem.* [a. F. *tannin,* f. *tan* TAN: see -IN.]

TAP.

Tap (tæp), sb.[1] Forms: 5-6 tappan, 5-6 tappe, 6 tapp, 7-8 tapp, 3- tap; also Sc. (it sense 4) b) 5-7 topp (pa. 6, taip, 6-7 topp, 7 top, topt). [Com. Teutonic: OE. *tæppa*, from *tæppe* (*tæ* sb.[1] = MLG., MDu., LG., and Du. *tappen*, MHG., Ger. *zapfen*, ON. *tappe*, Du. *tappe*, all from the cognate sbs. Cf. 2. Dan. *tap*.]

I. To open (a cask, reservoir).

...

Tap (tæp), v.[1] Forms: 3 tappen, 5-6 tappe, 6 tapp, 7-5 tap; also Sc. in sense 4 b) 5-7 topp (pa. 6, talp, 6-7 topt, 7 topt).

TAPADERO.

Tapadero (tāpădērⁿo). Also -dera, tapi. [Sp. *tapadero* cover, lid, mask.] A heavy leather housing for the front...

TAPALPITE.

Tapalpite (tāpa·lpəit). *Min.* [Named 1869 from Sierra of Tapalpa (Mexico): see -ITE[1].] Sulphotelluride of bismuth and silver, found in metallic masses (Chester).

Tapayaxin (tāpāyæ·ksiŋ). [Native Mexican.] The orbicular horned lizard, *Phrynosoma orbiculare*, incorrectly called the *horned frog* or *toad*.

Tape (tēp), sb.[1] Forms: 1 tappe, (3 tappe, 6 tapp) 4- tape. [OE. *tæppe* or *tæppa*, not found; origin unascertained. The lengthening of the vowel from ME. *tape* to *tāpe* is unexplained.]

1. A narrow woven strip of stout linen, cotton, silk, or other textile, used as a string for tying garments, and for other purposes for which flat strings are suited, also for measuring lines, etc.

TAPER.

Taper (tē·pəɹ), sb.[1] Forms: 1 tapor, 3- taper, 4-5 tapre, -ur, -yr, 5-7 tapper; 3- tapre. [OE. *tapor*, -ur; not in the cognate langs.]

Taper (tē·pəɹ), a. Also 7 taper, 4-5 tapere, 4-5 tapre, -ur, -yr, 5-7 tapper; ...

TAPER. 84 TAPESTRY. TAPESTRY. 85 TAPINAGE

Tapering, vbl. sb. [f. TAPER v. + -ING[1].] The action of the verb TAPER in various senses.

Tapering, ppl. a. [-ING[2].] That tapers; taper.

Tapster, obs. form of TAPSTER.

TAPESTRY.

Tapestry (tæ·pestri), sb. Forms: 1 teped, tappet; 3-4 (9) tapit, 4-5 tapyt, 4-6 tapite, -yte, -ite (5), tapytt, -e, (7 tapit), 5-6 tappet, 4- tapet. ...

1. *trans.* To cover, hang, or adorn with, or as with, tapestry.

Tapestry-work = TAPESTRY sb. 1.

TAPINAGE.

Tapinage (tæ·pined3). Obs. Also 4 tappy-, tapenage. [a. OF. *tapinage* place of concealment, f. *tapin*...]

3236

Tarantant.

Tarantara, Tarantarara.

Tarantas, Tarantass.

Tarantass.

Tarantate.

Tarantella.

Tarantism.

Taraxacum.

Tarboggin, var. TOBOGGAN.

Tarboosh.

Tar-box.

Tar-brush.

Taroot.

Tarcay.

Tar-barrel.

Tarbet.

Tardation.

Tardigrade.

Tardily.

Tardiness.

Tardive.

Tarde.

Tardity.

Tardle.

Tardy.

Tare.

Tared.

Tarentine.

Tarentula.

Tarentole, tuia.

Tarer.

Tarette.

Tarf.

Targa.

Targe.

Target.

TARGET.

lever with target on top. **1900** H. M. Wilson *Topogr. Surveying* 91

Target, *sb.* [f. Target *sb.*] ...

Targeted (tā·ɪgetid), *ppl. a.* Furnished with a target or shield, or with something resembling one.

Targeteer (targeti·ɪ), *Obs. exc. Hist.* ...

Targeting (tā·ɪgetiŋ), *vbl. sb.*

†Targeter. *Obs.* In **1** a targeter. [f. Target *sb.* + -er 1.]

Target-shooting ...

Targ *Eccl. Hist.* ...

†Targe, *sb.* [Etym. uncertain.] Jamieson compares Sw. *targa* to tear.] A tatter, a shred.

Targe, *obs. f. Large; var. Targ.*

Target, *sb.*

1 *a. trans.* To protect with or as with a target; to shield. *Obs.*

2 To use (a person) as a target. *Also fig.*

3 *U.S.* To signal the position of (a railway switch, etc.) by means of a target (Target *sb.*¹ 4d).

Targhel (tā·ɪghel), *U.S. colloq.* [f. Tar *sb.* + Heel *sb.*] A nickname for a native or inhabitant of North Carolina, in allusion to use as a principal product of that State. *So attrib.*

Targum (tā·ɪgʌm, tahɪgum). *Also* 6-7 **targûm.** [a. Chaldee (tar'gūm), lit. interpretation: see Dragoman.]

Each of several Aramaic translations, interpretations, or paraphrases of the various divisions of the Old Testament, made after the Babylonian captivity, at first preserved by oral transmission, and committed to writing from about A.D. 100 onwards.

Targumic (tāɪgū·mik), *a.* [f. Targum + -ic.]

Targumist. [f. Targum + -ist.]

Tarheel: see Targhel.

Tariff (tæ·ɪif), *sb.* Forms: 6-8 **terrif,** 8 **terif,** 8-9 **tarif;** 7- **tariff.** [a. It. *tariffa* arithmetical or casting of accounts (Florio), 'a booke of rates for duties' (Baretti), — Sp., Pg. *tarifa*, ad. Arab. *ta'rīf* notification, explanation, definition, article, f. *'arafa* to know; to notify, make known. So F. *tarif.*]

TARIFF.

1. *intr.* To have to do with a tariff. *nonce-use.*

2. *trans.* To subject to a tariff-duty; to fix the price of (something) according to a tariff; to put a price on.

3. A classified list or scale of charges made in any private or public business; as, a hotel tariff, a railroad tariff. *(U.S.)*

Tariff-reform. *gen.* The reform of a tariff, or of existing tariff conditions; *spec.* in recent U.S. politics, 'a reform favouring a general reduction of import duties, but in other senses the opposite' (Cent. Dict. 1891).

Tarin, obs. form of Terrace.

Taring (tē·ɪriŋ), *vbl. sb.* [f. Tare *sb.*³ + -ing¹.] The calculation and abatement of the tare on goods; † abatement for defective goods (*obs.*).

Taris, obs. form of Terrace.

Ta·rish, *a.* [f. Tare *sb.*¹ + -ish¹.]

Tarlatan (tā·ɪlătăn). *Also* 8 tarnatan, 9 tarlatane, tarleton. **1.** F. *tarlatane*, dissimilated form *tarnatane* (1723 in Hatz.-Darm.: cf. quot. 1727-41); prob. of Indian origin.]

Tarm, obs. form of Term; var. Tharm.

Tarmac (tā·ɪmăk). *a.* (also *attrib.*) *slang.*

Tarn (tǎɪn), *sb.* [a. ON. *tjǫrn*, *tjarn*, *tjǫrn* = Swed. dial. *tjärn*, *tärn*, Norw. *tjørn*, *tjǫrn;* of obscure origin.]

Tarnation (taɪnē·ʃən). *U.S.* and dial. **Forms:** 8 tarnation, 9 tarnation. [app. a variant of *darnation*, Damnation *sb.* 3; app. associated with Tarnal.]

Tarnish (tā·ɪniʃ), *v.* [a. F. *terniss-*, extended stem of *ternir* to dull, dim.]

Tarnished (tā·ɪniʃt), *ppl. a.*

Tarnowitzite (Breithaupt 1841): see ibid.] A variety of Aragonite containing about 4 per cent. of carbonate of lead, found at Tarnowitz in Silesia.

Taro (tā·ro, tæ·ro). *Also* 8 tarrow, 9 taro, taroo. [Native Polynesian name, found by Cook in the Sandwich Islands.] A food-plant, Colocasia antiquorum, N.O. Araceæ, cultivated in many varieties (C. esculenta, macrorhiza, etc.) in most tropical countries for its starchy root-stocks.

Taroc (tæ·rǒk). *Also* 7-9 tarock, tarok. **1.** *trans.* in (it. *tarocchi*, of unknown origin. Also Sc. *tarot*: see Tarot.

a. — Tarot. *b.* (also in *pl.*) — Tarot b.

†Tarot (tæ·rot). *Obs.* [a. F. *tarot* (also 16th c. *tarault*, *taraux*), ad. It. *tarocco* (pl. *tarocchi*): see Taroc.]

Tarpaulian, *sb.* and *a. Obs.* **Forms:** 7 tarpauling, tarr pawlin, tarrpauwling, tarpolin, palling, paulin, (-pallion), 7-8 -pawlin, 7-9 -pawling, -pauling, 7- tarpaulin.

Tarpon (tǎ·ɪpǒn). **Forms:** 7 tarpom, 8-om, 9 tarp, 9 tarpon. [So Du. *tarpoen;* ultimate origin not ascertained.] The Jew-fish, *Megalops atlanticus*, a large fish of the herring tribe found in the warmer waters of the western Atlantic.

Tarragon (tæ·răgŏn). **Forms:** also 6 tarchon, 7 targon, (given in 1538-9 as the English for med.L. *tragonia* and *tarchon*: cf. 16th c. F. *targon* (Rabelais, Cotgr. 1611), It. *taracone*, *tarcone* (Florio 1598, 1611), Sp. *taragoncia*, *tagoncia* (Oudin 1607), ad. Arab. *tarkhūn* (in Ibn Beithar, Avicenna, Razī), *altarcon* in Gerard of Cremona, a 1187; according to Arabic lexicographers a foreign word: some think ad. Gr. *δράκων* (1brevic), by an early association, similar to what is found in the 16th c. with the Gr. *δρακόντιον*, *-ωντιον* (Hippocr., Dinsc.)

Tarras, tarras'e, obs. ff. Terrace.

Tarred (tǎɪd), *ppl. a.* [f. Tar *v.* + -ed¹.] Smeared or covered with tar.

Tarriddiddle, variant of Taradiddle.

Tarras, tarrass'e, obs. ff. Terrace.

TARRY.

1. One who tarries or delays; a lingerer, procrastinator; one who stays or remains.

Tarry (tæ·ri), *sb.* [f. Tarry *v.*] **1.** Tarrying; a stay.

†2. The act of tarrying; spending or loss of time; delay, procrastination.

Tarrier (tæ·riǝr). **Forms:** 5 tarrer(e, 6 tarryour, 7-8 terrier. [var. of Terrier² (dog).]

†Tarrier², *sc.* var. of Terrier a.

Tarring (tā·riŋ), *vbl. sb.* [f. Tar *v.* + -ing¹.]

Tarrock (tæ·rǒk). **Forms:** 7 tarock, 8-9 tarrock, 9 tarrok, also tarry. [Of uncertain origin; the ending -ock is app. diminutive, as in *puttock*, etc.] A name applied locally to various sea-birds.

Tarry (tǎ·ri), *a.* [f. Tar *sb.*¹ + -y.] **1.** Consisting or composed of tar; of the nature of tar.

Tarry (tæ·ri), *v.* [ME. *tarien*, *terien*.]

Tarry, obs. form of TARRIES, TERRIER.

Tarrying (tæ·riiŋ), vbl. sb. [-ING.] 1. The action of the verb TARRY, q.v.; delaying, loitering, etc.

2. Abiding, sojourning; also in later Dicts.

Tarrying-iron = see TIRING-IRON.

Tarrysome, a. rare⁻¹. In 6 tariment. [f. TARRY v. + -SOME.]

Tarryour, obs. form of TARRIER 2.

Tarrysome, var. form of TARRIES.

Tars, tarse. Obs. Also 5 tarse.

Tarsied (tā·sid), a. Obs. rare. [ad. It. tarsia.]

Tarsus (tā·səs). [mod. L. a, Gr. ταρσός.] 1. The first or posterior part of the foot : a collective name for the seven small bones of the human ankle.

§ 2. Of or pertaining to the tarsi of the eyelids.

Tarsall, obs. form of TERCEL, hawk.

† **Tarsel**¹. Obs.

† **Tarsel, tarcel.** Obs.

Tarsectomy, -ectopia : see TARSO-.

Tarso-, combining form of TARSUS 2 (Anat.), as in:

Tarso-metatarsal (tā·so,metatā·sal), a. and sb. Comp. Anat.

Tarso-metatarsus (tā·so,meta,tā·səs). Comp. Anat.

Tarsorrhaphy (tā·sorăfi). Surg.

Tarsotomy a., -medio-tarsal

Tarso-tomy (Gr. -τομία cutting).

Tart (tāt), sb.¹ Also 4-6 tarte, 5 taarte.

Tart, a. Also 3 teart.

Tart, v. rare. 1 Obs.

Tartan¹ (tā·tăn). sb.¹ Also 6-7 tartane, tartaine, (6 teartane).

Tartan², Naut. Also 6-7 tartane.

† **Tartan**³, sb.³ rare⁻¹. [f. TARTAN sb.¹]

Tartaned (tā·tănd), a.

Tartan-purry (sc. local) : see quots.

Tartana (tātā·na). Also 7 tartane.

Tartane, var. TARTAN sb.², a long covered carriage.

Tartar¹ (tā·tăr). Also 5 tartre, 7 tarter. [ad. med.L. tartarum.]

Tartar², sb.² Also 7-8 tartar, 7-8 tartare. [f. TARTAR sb.¹]

Tartar³, sb.³ = TARTARUS.

Tartarean (tātēə·riăn), a.

Tartareous (tātēə·ri̯əs), a.¹ [f. mod.L. tartareus.]

Tartareous, a.² Obs. [f. TARTARUS.]

Tartaret, obs. form of TARTERET.

Tartaric (tātæ·rik), a.¹ [f. TARTAR sb.¹]

Tartaric, a.² = TARTAREAN.

Tartaric ... **Tartarin** ... **Tartarize** ... **Tartarized** ... **Tartarum** ... **Tartary** ... **Tartar-root** ... **Tartars** ... **†Tartas** ... **†Tartrarin** ... **†Tartarine** ...

Tartarology ... **Tarten** ... **†Tartareous** ... **Tartarous** ... **Tartarus** ... **tartarus** ... **Tartine** ... **Tartle** ... **†Tartartorial** ... **Tartarine** ...

Tartralic ... **Tartramic** ... **Tartramide** ... **Tartaric** ... **Tartranil** ... **Tartar** ... **Tartrate** ... **tartrate** ... **Tartrazine** ... **Tartronic** ... **Tartrovinic** ... **Tartwhine** ... **Tar-vetch** ... **Tarve**

TAR-WATER. From the precipitation of tartrate of potash...

Tarwhine ... **Tary** ... **Tasco** ... **Tane** ... **Tasco** ...

Task (tǎsk), sb. [f. TASK v. Cf. to tax, etc.] ...

Task (tǎsk), v. ...

Taskable ... **Task-master** ... **Task-mastership** ... **Task-mistress** ... **Tasker** ... **Taskwork** ...

Tasse ... **Tassel** ...

the clasp or fibula through which the cords passed which secured the mantle on the shoulder.]

2. A pendent ornament consisting of a bunch or thick fringe of threads or small cords hanging in a somewhat conical shape from a solid rounded knob or mould, or from a knot formed by their junction with a cord. Frequently attached to a curtain, cushion, walking-cane, umbrella, etc., or forming the pull of a blind-cord or bell-cord.

13.. *Gaw. & Gr. Knt.* 219 A lace..Wyth tryed tasselez þerto tacched in-noghe. c 1440 *Promp. Parv.* 487/1 Tassel, *tassellus.* 1480 *Wardr. Acc. Edw. IV* (1830) 125 For the makyng of xvj laces and xvj tasshels for the garnysshing of divers of the Kinges bookes. 1530 PALSGR. 279/2 Tasself that hangeth at a thyng of sylke or golde, *houppe dorce.* 1590 SPENSER *F. Q.* I. viii. 3 An horne of bugle small, Which hong adowne his side in twisted gold And tasselles gay. 1624 CAPT. SMITH *Virginia* II. 35 All their tailes meete in the toppe of their head like a great Tassell. a 1625 FLETCHER *Nice Valour* II. i, And smile, and wave a chair with comely grace too, Play with our tastle gently. 1706 PHILLIPS (ed. 6), *Tassels of a Coach*, certain Silk-cords fasten'd on each Side the Doors, which serve for a Stay to those that ride in it. 1718 *Free-thinker* No. 44 ¶ 10 A young Damsel..tied a Gold Cord with two large Tossels of Gold to his Sword. 1755 *Connoisseur* No. 97 ¶ 1 The fellow-commoners, noblemen, and other rich students, whom ..the courtesy of the University [of Cambridge] has honoured with a cap adorned with a gold tossel. 1792 in *Hist. Broughton Place Ch. Edin.* (1872) 20 A' their taisels, vain an' gay To mak us stare. a 1815 in G. Rose *Diaries* (1860) II. 438 He put out his hand to pull the bell, but could not catch the tassel. 1849 LAYARD *Nineveh & Rem.* I. iii. 49 A knotted girdle, ending in tassels, encircled the loins. 1886 RUSKIN *Præterita* I. vii. 233 A cushion of crimson velvet.. with gold tassels at the corners.

†**b.** *Univ. slang.* One who wears a cap with a tassel; an undergraduate. Cf. TUFT. *Obs.*

1828 *Sporting Mag.* XXI. 428 A capital front rank of 'tassells'..all eager for a 'slap at a snob'.

3. Anything resembling or suggesting a tassel: **a.** In a tree or plant, a pendent catkin, blossom, flower, or bud; *spec.* the staminate (terminal) inflorescence of the maize-plant (*U.S.*): see also *tassel-hyacinth* in 5.

1646 WINTHROP *New-Eng.* (1826) II. 267 Great harm was done in corn..by a caterpillar...They eat up first the blades of the stalk, then..the tassels, whereupon the ear withered. 1755 *Gentl. Mag.* Sept. 408/2, I found a fine stalk of Indian corn..; I cut off the male tossil as soon as it appeared, and there was produced a large ear, but no good grains upon it. 1824 MISS MITFORD *Village* Ser. I. (1863) 61 In early spring, when the fragrant palms were on the willow, and the yellow tassels on the hazel. a 1835 MRS. HEMANS *Voice of Spring* iii, The larch has hung all his tassels forth. 1863 KINGSLEY *Water-Bab.* i. 15 The bird-cherry with its tassels of snow. 1894 E. EGGLESTON in *Century Mag.* Apr. 850 Our country people, when speaking of the male flower of the maize, preserve the broad vowel of their ancestors: 'tossell' it will remain in spite of the schoolmaster.

†**b.** A tuft; a fringe. *Obs.*

1609 C. BUTLER *Fem. Mon.* i. (1623) B iij, Besides their Soueraigne, the Bees haue also subordinate Gouernours... For difference from the rest they beare for their crest a tuft or tossell, in some coloured yellow, in some murrey, in manner of a plume. 1672 JOSSELYN *New Eng. Rarities* 35 The other is nothing but Bones with Tassels hanging from their Jaws, with which they [whales] suck in their prey.

¶**4.** In med. (Anglo-) Latin, *tassellus* is given by Du Cange as used = *fimbria*, fringe of a cope or chasuble. Dr. Rock, *Church of our Fathers* (II. 32–), explains Du Cange's quots. otherwise, and holds that *tassellus* had the following uses: **a.** The large thin sheet of gold or silver hanging behind on the cope; **b.** Any piece of gold or silver plate fastened to a vestment (copes and chasubles having 'their *tasselli* sparkling with gems, hung all about them'); **c.** The ornaments on the back of episcopal gloves, when not done in embroidery, but made of silver or gold plate. By Dr. Rock himself, and some writers after him, the English word *tassel* has been used in senses b and c.

[c 1188 GERV. CANT. in Dugdale *Monast. Angl.* (1655) I. 21 Duas capas de pallio cum tassellis auro paratis. c 1250 MATT. PARIS *Vitæ Abb. S. Albani* (1639) 55 Capam unam purpuream, morsu et tassellis charissimis redimitam. a 1252 *Visit. Churches St. Paul's* 14 in *Camden Misc.* (1895) IX, Item capa chori crocea cum duobus tassellis brusdatis Majestate et Maria.] 1849 ROCK *Ch. our Fathers* II. 161 *note*, These tassels, as we said before, were thin plates of beaten gold or silver. 1887 *Archæologia* L. II. 448 Upon the 'tassels' of the cope of Richard Ruffus were depicted the martyrdoms of St. Stephen and St. Thomas.

5. *attrib.* and *Comb.*, as *tassel-board, -drop, -maker, -making*; *tassel-hung* adj.; **tassel-cock**, a game-cock which has a tuft of feathers in place of the comb; **tassel-corn**, (*U.S.*) the grain of maize borne abnormally on the 'tassel' (see 3 a); **tassel-fish**, an Australian fish, *Polynemus quadridactylus*, the pectoral fins of which terminate in a number of long threads; **tassel-flower**, (*a*) a tassel-like flower; *spec.* the orange, scarlet, or yellowish blossom of *Emilia sagittata* (*Cacalia coccinea*), N.O. *Compositæ*, or the plant itself; (*b*) a shrub or tree of the genus *Inga* (*Cent. Dict.* 1891); **tassel-grass**, (*a*) a grass or (?) sedge with pendent spicules; (*b*) *Ruppia maritima*, an aquatic herb of which the seed-vessels are borne on clusters of lengthened pedicels; **tassel-hyacinth**, *Muscari comosum*, the stalk and flower of which resemble a tassel; also called *purse-tassel*, *purple tassels* (Miller *Plant-n.* 1884); **tassel-pondweed** = *tassel-grass* (*b*) (ibid.); **tassel-stitch**, an embroidery stitch used in forming a fringe, loops of thread being left, which are afterwards cut; **tassel-tree** = TASSEL-BUSH (*Cent. Dict.* 1891); **tassel-worm**, a grub which feeds on the tassel of the maize-plant.

a 1639 SPOTTISWOOD *Hist. Ch. Scot.* VI. (1677) 407 Every Chair had a *Tassel-boord covered with fine Velvet. 1898 *Pall Mall G.* 3 Feb. 9/1 'Henny' cocks..have won more battles..than any other birds, except it be the '*tassel' cock. 1883 E. L. STURTEVANT in *Science* I. 234/1 (Variability of Maize) *Tassel-corn,—some of the kernels heavily, others slightly husked. 1852 R. S. SURTEES *Sponge's Sp. Tour* (1893) 150 A chased and figured fine gold brooch, with two pendent *tassel-drops. 1898 MORRIS *Austral Eng.*, *Tassel-fish, a thread-fish of Queensland, of the genus *Polynemus*. 1902 J. T. CRITCHELL in *Encycl. Brit.* XXXII. 110/2 Several species of the tassel fish (*Polynemus macrocohoir*), from which isinglass is procured, have been taken by fishermen. 1885 G. ALLEN *Babylon* vi, Do you know the *tassel-flower? 1810 SOUTHEY *Kehama* XIII. xi, *Tassel-grass, whose silvery feathers play O'ertopping the young trees. 1861 MISS PRATT *Flower. Pl.* V. 336 Sea Ruppia or Tassel-grass..has slender, much-branched stems ..and long slender bristly leaves with sheaths. 1850 TENNYSON *In Mem.* cii, The low love-language of the bird In native hazels *tassel-hung. 1902 *Daily Chron.* 9 Sept. 3/6 A number of the *tassel-makers were independently interviewed in their own homes while at work...*Tassel-making is one of the three worst paid of the various home industries open to sweating. 1882 CAULFEILD & SAWARD *Dict. Needlework* 194/2 *Tassel Stitch, a stitch used to make a looped fringe as an edging to Embroideries.

Tassel, torsel (tæ·s'l, tǭ·s'l, tǭ·ɪs'l), *sb.*[2] *Arch.* Also 7–9 **tossel**, 9 **tassal**. [a. OF. *tassel*, mod.F. *tasseau*, = It. *tassello* a bit of stone or wood to stop a hole, :—L. *taxillus* a small die. The form *torsel* app. arises from workmen's lengthening of the vowel in *tossel*.] A short board or 'templet' placed under the end of a beam or other timber where it rests on brickwork or stonework.

1632 in E. B. Jupp *Carpenters' Co.* (1887) 301 The making of all mantletrees tassels and footepaces of timber. 1654 *Ibid.* 316 That no Timber..be laid in Chimneys except the mantle trees Tassells and Discharges. 1667 PRIMATT *City & C. Build.* 82 Allow six foot of Timber for every Chimney, for Mantle-trees and Torsels. 1703 MOXON *Mech. Exerc.* 264 When you lay any Timber on Brick-work, as Torsels for Mantle-Trees to lye on. 1823 P. NICHOLSON *Pract. Build.* 595 *Torsel*, a piece of wood laid into a wall for the end of a timber or beam to rest on. 1842–76 GWILT *Archit.* Gloss., *Tassal, Tassel, Torsel*, or *Tossel*, the plate of timber for the end of a beam or of a joist to rest on.

Tassel (tæ·s'l), *v.* Also 4 **tassil**, 5 **tacel**, 8 **tassel**. [f. TASSEL *sb.*[1]]

1. *trans.* To furnish or adorn with or as with a tassel or tassels.

In *pa. pple.* in *Her.* indicating that the tassel or tassels are of a tincture different from that of the rest of the bearing.

? a 1366 CHAUCER *Rom. Rose* 1079 A robe..With orfrays leyd was everydel,..And with a bend of gold tasseled. c 1386 — *Miller's T.* 65 By hir girdel heeng a purs of lether Tasseled with grene and perled with latoun. 14.. *Sir Beues* (MS. N.) 3777 + 7 Tacellid wiþ rosys off syluyr bryȝt. 1572 BOSSEWELL *Armorie* II. 92 He beareth Argente, a pursse gules, doble tasseled d'azure. 1724 *Lond. Gaz.* No. 6290/2 A Velvet..Cushion edged and tasselled with Gold. 1894 *Blackw. Mag.* Sept. 317/2 The blond sallow tasselled itself with gold.

2. *intr.* Of maize and sugar-cane: To form 'tassels', to flower, bloom. Chiefly *U.S.*

1785 WASHINGTON *Writ.* (1891) XII. 227 It [Indian corn] should be kept clean and well worked..till it shoots and tassels at least. 1881 NICHOLSON *Fr. Sword to Share* xxii. 153 Cane grew..almost everywhere..at altitudes up to 3,000 feet above sea-level, at half that height it ceased to blossom or tassel.

Hence **Ta·sselling, ta·sseling** *vbl. sb.* (also *concr.* work composed of tassels) and *ppl. a.*

1829 *Anniversary, Beatrice* 232 She couches in the pleached bower Which tasselling honeysuckles deck. 1881 NICHOLSON *Fr. Sword to Share* xxix. 222 In November the cane tops will throw out a feathery, dove-coloured blossom, called tasselling. 1908 *Westm. Gaz.* 12 July 7/3 The sides of the stairs..are..finished off with gold tasselling.

Tassel, obs. form of TEASEL, TERCEL.

Ta·sselated, *ppl. a. rare*⁻¹. [f. assumed vb. *tasselate (f. TASSEL *sb.*[1] + -ATE [3]) + -ED [1]: cf. *tessellated, castellated, foliated*, etc.] = TASSELLED.

c 1860 B. HARTE *My Otherself* in *Fiddletown*, etc. (1873) 127 There was no rustle of the tasselated corn.

Tassel-bush (tæ·s'lbuʃ). [f. TASSEL *sb.*[1] + BUSH *sb.*[1]] The common name in America of an evergreen shrub, *Garrya elliptica*, a native of California, Mexico, Cuba, and Jamaica: so called from its elegant long drooping catkins.

1891 in *Cent. Dict.* 1900 *Field* 22 Dec. 972/1 The Tassel Bush..is an evergreen bush from California, the tip of every young growth being now laden with clusters, or bunches of soft-grey tassels or catkins, that give to it a very distinct and ornate appearance.

Tasselet (tæ·sělėt, -ėt). [f. TASSEL *sb.*[1] + -ET.] A diminutive tassel.

1577 HARRISON *England* II. v. (1877) I. 121 Two mantels.. with laces, tasselets, and knops of blue silk.

Tassel-gentle, tassel-hawk: see TERCEL.

Tassell, obs. form of TEASEL, TERCEL.

Tasselled, -eled (tæ·s'ld), *ppl. a.* [f. TASSEL *sb.*[1] or *v.* + -ED.] **a.** Furnished or adorned with or as with a tassel or tassels; of a person, wearing a tassel or tassels. **b.** Formed into, or resembling in some way, a tassel or tassels; of a fern, having divisions like tassels at the apex of each frond.

a. 1611 COTGR., *Houpé*..tufted, or tasselled. c 1633 MILTON *Arcades* 57 Ere the..tasselld horn Shakes the high thicket, haste I all about. 1784 COWPER *Task* II. 749 The tasseled cap and the spruce band. 1808 SKURRAY *Bidcombe Hill* 49 Not long ago, on Cherwell's banks we rov'd, Link'd arm in arm, like other tassell'd youths. 1841–4 EMERSON *Ess.* Ser. I. xi. (1876) 263 You shall still see..the tasselled grass, or the corn-flags.

b. 1882 *Garden* 29 Apr. 301/3 A very elegant Hare's-foot Fern, having the long graceful fronds tasselled at the tips.

Tasseller, -eler (tæ·sělər, tæ·s'lər). [f. TASSEL *v.* + -ER [1]; cf. OF. *taseleor.*]

†**1.** One who makes tassels. *Obs. rare.*

1301 *Rolls of Parlt.* I. 248/2 Matilda la Taselere. *Ibid.* 255/2 Gilbert le Taselere.

2. One who wears a cap with a tassel; †*gold tasseller*, a nobleman who is a member of a university, distinguished by his academic cap having a tassel of gold thread: cf. TASSEL *sb.*[1] 2, quot. 1755.

1846 LANDOR *Citation Shaks.* Wks. II. 285/2 The worst question to any gold tasseller is, 'How do you do?'

Ta·sselly, -ely, *a.* [f. TASSEL *sb.*[1] + -Y.] Characterized by or abounding in tassels.

1611 COTGR., *Houpelu*..lockie, tassellie, tufted. 1901 *Elizabeth & Germ. Gard.* 164 Four little podgy, buttony, tasselly red chairs.

Tasset. *Archæol.* Only in pl. **tassets** (tæ·sėts). [ad. F. *tassette*, in OF. *tassete*: see TASSE *sb.*[1]] In *pl.* = *tasses*: see TASSE *sb.*[1] (App. only in recent archæological or romantic use.)

1834 PLANCHÉ *Brit. Costume* 241 Tassets and cuishes, composed of several plates instead of one, are seen upon the thigh. 1872 LONGF. *Wayside Inn* III. *Charlemagne* 49 His greaves And tassets were of iron. 1876 H. AINSWORTH *Leaguer of Lathom* (1878) 32 Both were accoutred in steel breastplates and tassets.

‖**Tassette** (tæse·t). [Fr. dim. of *tasse*, TASS [2]: see -ET.] A small pointed infusible earthenware cone, used in sets of three to support objects in a kiln or muffle, in place of a stilt or triangle.

1891 in *Cent. Dict.*

Tasshel, obs. form of TASSEL *sb.*[1]

Tassie (tæ·si). *Sc.* [dim. of TASS [2]: see -IE.] A small cup or 'tass'.

17.. *Homely Ballad* (in *Burns' Poems* (1834) II. 229 *note*), Ye'll bring me here a pint of wine, A server and a silver tassie. 1788 BURNS *My Bonie Mary* i. a 1810 in Cromek *Rem. Nithsdale Song* 94 But here's my Jean's health i' the siller-lipped-tassie!

Tassil, -ill, obs. forms of TEASEL, TERCEL.

Tastable: see TASTEABLE.

Taste (tēⁱst), *sb.*[1] Forms: 4–8 **tast**, 4–5 **taast**, 4–6 (*Sc.* -7) **taist**, (6 *Sc.* **test**), 5– **taste**. [a. OF. *tast* touching, touch, = It. *tasto* a feeling, a touch, a trial, a taste (Florio); f. OF. *taster* (mod. F. *tâter*), It. *tastare*: see TASTE *v.* Cf. also OF. *taste*, It. *tasta*, a surgical probe.]

I. †**1.** The sense of touch, feeling (with the hands, etc.); the act of touching, touch. *Obs.*

[1292 BRITTON III. ii. § 13 Et puis soynt chargez qe eles.. enquergent de la femme qe se fet enceynte par tast de soen ventre et de ses mameles.] 13.. *Cursor M.* 542 (Cott.) Þis vnder wynd him gis his aand, þe erth þe tast, to fele and faand. 1422 tr. *Secreta Secret., Priv. Priv.* 208 The taste is a commyn witte, Spraden throgh the body, but hit Shewyth hym most by the handys..; by that witte we knowen hote, colde, dry, moyste, and other Suche thynges. c 1430 *Pilgr. Lyf Manhode* I. lxxii. (1869) 42 At the taast, and at the sighte, at the smellinge, and at the sauouringe, bred and wyn it may seeme.

†**2.** A trying, testing; a trial, test, examination.

1377 LANGL. *P. Pl.* B. XII. 131 Kynde witte cometh of alkynnes siȝtes,..of tastes of treuthe, and of deceytes. 1586–7 Q. ELIZ. in *Four C. Eng. Lett.* (1880) 30 To make tast of the greatest witz amongs my owne, and then of French and last of you. 1605 SHAKS. *Lear* I. ii. 47, I hope for my Brothers iustification, hee wrote this but as an essay, or taste of my Vertue. 1663 *Flagellum, or O. Cromwell* (1672) 155 To appoint a Tast or Recognition of the Government.

†**b.** A trial, an attempt. *Obs. rare*⁻¹.

c 1330 R. BRUNNE *Chron. Wace* (Rolls) 5400 He wende haue taken þe toun in hast, Bot he failled of his tast.

II. †**3.** The act of tasting, or perceiving the flavour of a thing with the organ of taste (sense 4); the fact of being tasted. *Obs.*

13.. *Coer de L.* 3075 When he has a good tast, And eeten weel a good repast. 1340–70 *Alex. & Dind.* 357 Þere-of we taken a tast what time þat vs nedeþ. 1393 LANGL. *P. Pl.* C. I. 228 Tauerners 'a tast for nouht' tolden þe same. 1579 LYLY *Euphues* (Arb.) 176 For before the tast of the Gospel I was worse then a beast. 1592 SHAKS. *Rom. & Jul.* II. vi. 13 The sweetest honey Is loathsome in his owne deliciousnesse, And in the taste confoundes the appetite. 1667 MILTON *P. L.* I. 2 The Fruit Of that Forbidden Tree, whose mortal tast Brought Death into the World, and all our woe. 1766 ENTICK *London* IV. 367 They obtained a grant of..the taste and assize of bread.

b. *transf.* The means of tasting; hence, such a small quantity as admits of being tasted; a very small quantity (esp. of alcoholic drink), a sip.

1530 in W. H. Turner *Select. Rec. Oxford* (1880) 91 He sent for the tast of wyne..dew to him of every hoggshed.

15.. *Aberdeen Reg.* (Jam.), And send one taist of the wyne to the yerll of Rothes. 1723 S. SEWALL *Diary* 4 Apr., My wife sent them a Taste of her Dinner. 1888 'R. BOLDREWOOD' *Robbery under Arms* xxxviii, Bring me a taste of grog, will ye? 1904 in *Eng. Dial. Dict.* [from Scotl., Irel., N. Engl.].

c. *fig.* A slight experience, received or given; a slight show or sample *of* any condition or quality.

1390 GOWER *Conf.* II. 373 Whanne I beclippe hire on the wast, Yit ate leste I stele a tast. 1526 *Pilgr. Perf.* (W. de W. 1531) 234 That is none other thynge but a taste how swete our lord Jesu is. 1586 DAY *Eng. Secretary* I. (1625) A ij b, Socrates in his cradle had no taste of his after-wisedome. c 1595 CAPT. WYATT *R. Dudley's Voy. W. Ind.* (Hakl. Soc.) 40 Most of them havinge some little tast of the Spanish tounge. 1669 PENN *No Cross* xxi. § 39 A soul Mortified to the World, and quickned to some Tasts of a Supernatural Life. 1825 LAMB *Elia* Ser. II. *Superannuated Man*, Where was..the promised rest? Before I had a taste of it, it was banished. 1897 A. MORRISON *Dorrington Deed-box* i, My first taste of grouse-shooting was a complete success.

d. *A taste* (advb.): *colloq.* to a small but perceptible degree; slightly; a little. Cf. BIT *sb.*[2] 5.

1894 HALL CAINE *Manxman* I. v, Aisy! Your legs a taste higher, sir, just to keep the pickle off your trousers. *Ibid.* III. xii, 'Nancy will tidy the room a taste', she said coaxingly.

4. The faculty or sense by which that particular quality of a thing described in 5 is discerned, the organs of which are situated chiefly in the mouth; one of the five bodily senses.

c 1380 WYCLIF *Serm.* Sel. Wks. I. 87 Whan þer tast is freishe, for to juge þe goodnesse, and after whan þei ben drunken and þer taist failiþ, þanne he puttiþ wers wyn. c 1394 *P. Pl. Crede* 537 Þanne haue y tynt all my tast touche and assaie! 1398 TREVISA *Barth. De P. R.* III. xx. (1495) d vj b/2, The taast is a wytte of knowynge sauours. 1587 MASCALL *Govt. Cattle, Horses* (1627) 111 Sometimes a horse will loose his tast, which commeth of sorrow. 1600 SHAKS. *A. Y. L.* II. vii. 166 Second childishnesse, and meere obliuion, Sans teeth, sans eyes, sans taste, sans euery thing. 1680 MORDEN *Geog. Rect., Germany* (1685) 119 Fruits more pleasant to the sight or tast. 1861 HULME tr. *Moquin-Tandon* II. I. 49 Taste is a species of touch of still more delicate character. 1884 *Cornh. Mag.* Dec. 620 Taste..is not equally distributed over the whole surface of the tongue alike.

b. *Out of taste*, not able to distinguish flavours.

a 1541 WYATT *Sonnets* xviii, And if I have, after such bitterness, One drop of sweet, my mouth is out of taste. 1646 JENKYN *Remora* 20 The palat..is put out of taste. 1729 SWIFT *Direct. Servants, Footman* ¶ 28 Your mistress will confess that her mouth is out of taste.

5. That quality or property of a body or substance which is perceived when it is brought into contact with certain organs of the mouth, etc., esp. the tongue; savour, sapidity; the particular sensation excited by anything in this manner.

1382 WYCLIF *Jer.* xlviii. 11 Therfore abod stille his tast in hym, and his smel is not chaungid. c 1400 MAUNDEV. (1839) xxvii. 273 Full gode fissch..of right goode tast. c 1430 LYDG. *Min. Poems* (Percy Soc.) 15 Damysyns wiche withe her taste delyte. 1535 COVERDALE *Wisd.* xvi. 2 A new & straunge taist. 1594 PLAT *Jewell-ho.* II. 11 A far more liuely & penetratiue tast. 1605 TIMME *Quersit.* I. v. 19 Diuers kindes of saltes..haue diuers tastes. 1702 J. PURCELL *Cholick* (1714) 87 The acid Taste of this Recrement, and its coagulating of Milk, are undoubted. 1800 tr. *Lagrange's Chem.* II. 74 Iron..has a styptic taste, very sensible. 1857 MILLER *Elem. Chem.* (1862) III. 161 Sometimes a wine acquires a peculiar flavour known as the 'taste of the cask'.

fig. 14.. HOCCLEVE *Compl. Virgin* 213 Ther-in fynde I a bittir taast: For now the taast I feele & the streynynge Of deeth. 1579 LYLY *Euphues* (Arb.) 176 How comfortable is the feeling and tast of grace. 1605 SHAKS. *Macb.* v. v. 9, I haue almost forgot the taste of Feares. 1720 MRS. MANLEY *Power of Love* (1741) III. 187 All the Favours upon Earth, from the greatest Beauties could have no Taste for Roderigo. 1904 *Daily News* 14 Dec. 5 The poems leave a nasty taste in the mouth; the taste of a snarl and a sneer.

†**b.** Odour, scent, smell. *Obs.*

c 1400 *Destr. Troy* 1668 Þat smelt is & smethe, smellis full swete, With taste for to touche the tabull aboute. ? c 1475 *Sqr. lowe Degre* 850 Frankensence and olibanum That whan ye slepe the taste may come.

III. †**6.** Mental perception of quality; judgement, discriminative faculty. *Obs.* exc. as in 8.

13.. *Cursor M.* 11327 (Cott.) Þis symeon þat had his tast Toched o þe hali gast. a 1425 *Ibid.* 15889 (Trin.) Þe salmes seiþ bi good taast His wonynge shulde be wilde & waast. 1502 ATKYNSON tr. *De Imitatione* I. xxii. 171 Thou hast no spirituall tast. 1692 DRYDEN *St. Euremont's Ess.* 350 If so be they demand of me..more than discretion in Commerce, and a taste in Confidence.

7. The fact or condition of liking or preferring something; inclination, liking *for*; †appreciation.

c 1477 CAXTON *Jason* 72 Therfore wille thou..employ thy corage after the taste of our desires. 1552 *Godly Prayers* in *Liturg. Serv. Q. Eliz.* (1847) 253 That we..may have some taste and feeling for it in our hearts. ? c 1580 T. HACKET *Treas. Amadis* 236 She hath somewhat a regarde to things that are agaynst my owne taste. 1635 N. R. *Camden's Hist. Eliz.* II. 153 From the time that I had any tast of Religion. 1711 ADDISON *Spect.* No. 93 ¶ 13 A Man that has a Taste of Musick, Painting, or Architecture. 1727 POPE, etc. *Art of Sinking* 73 The taste of the bathos is implanted by nature itself in the soul of man. 1728 SWIFT *Intelligencer* No. 3 ¶ 3 Whoever hath a taste for true humour. 1791 MRS. INCHBALD *Simp. Story* III. v. 70 She had acquired a taste for those amusements. 1838 LYTTON *Alice* I. ix, The other girl is more amusing, more to my taste. 1880 L. STEPHEN *Pope* iv. 86 Every opportunity for the indulgence of his favourite tastes.

†**b.** Enjoyment, pleasure, 'relish'. Const. *in, of.*

1604 E. G[RIMSTONE] *D'Acosta's Hist. Indies* III. ix. 150 He found not in himselfe any disposition to goe to any other place, nor to take any taste in any thing. a 1716 BLACKALL *Wks.* (1723) I. 15 The Happiness of a Man's life consists not in the Abundance of the things that he possesses..But in the taste and relish that he has of them.

c. *transf.* The object of one's liking or preference.

1739 G. STONE in *Buccleuch MSS.* (Hist. MSS. Comm.) I. 392 White beauties..are the taste of the Irish nation.

8. The sense of what is appropriate, harmonious, or beautiful; *esp.* discernment and appreciation of the beautiful in nature or art; *spec.* the faculty of perceiving and enjoying what is excellent in art, literature, and the like.

1671 MILTON *P. R.* IV. 347 Sion's songs, to all true tasts excelling Where God is prais'd aright. 1694 CONGREVE *Double Dealer* I. ii, No, no, hang him, he has no Taste. 1712 ADDISON *Spect.* No. 409 ¶ 1 Rules..how we may acquire that fine Taste of Writing, which is so much talked of among the Polite World. 1768 W. GILPIN *Ess. Prints* 160 There is a fine taste in his landskips. 1776 SIR J. REYNOLDS *Disc. Art* (1778) 311, I have mentioned taste in dress, which is certainly one of the lowest subjects to which this word is applied. 1784 J. BARRY in *Lect. Paint.* ii. (1848) 108 The word Taste, as applied to objects of vision,..means.. that quick discerning faculty or power of the mind by which we accurately distinguish the good, bad, or indifferent. a 1834 COLERIDGE *Treat. Method* i. (1849) 16 A fine Musical taste is soon dissatisfied with the Harmonica, or any similar instrument of glass or steel. 1835 URE *Philos. Manuf.* 254 Taste is displayed both in the forms and grouping of the figures, and the disposition of the colours. 1850 W. IRVING *Goldsmith* xxvii. 268 The latter part of the year 1768 had been made memorable in the world of taste by the institution of the Royal Academy of Arts. 1872 MINTO *Eng. Prose Lit.* Introd. 29 The word *taste* in its wider sense is equivalent to artistic sensibility,..in its narrower sense it may be expressed as artistic judgment.

b. Style or manner exhibiting æsthetic discernment; good or bad æsthetic quality; the style or manner favoured in any age or country.

1739 LABELYE *Short Acc. Piers Westm. Br.* 44 The People who design'd and executed London-Bridge, and other Bridges in the same Taste. 1755 *Compl. Lett.-writer* (1759) 227 Her own old-fashioned breast-plate in the taste of the last century. 1819 SCOTT *Ivanhoe* xxviii, A rich habit, which partook more of the Eastern taste than that of Europe. 1826 DISRAELI *Viv. Grey* II. xii, Nothing could be more moderate, or, as Miss Gusset said, 'in better taste'. 1843 BORROW *Bible in Spain* xxxvi. (Pelh. Libr.) 256 It was..built something in the Moorish taste.

IV. 9. *attrib.* and *Comb.*, as *taste-area, -centre, -fibre, -meter*; *taste-pleasing* adj.; **taste-beaker, -bud, -bulb, -goblet**, one of the flask-shaped bodies in the epithelium of the tongue, believed to be organs of taste; **taste-cell**: see quot.; **taste-corpuscle** = *taste-cell*; **taste-cup, -pit**, one of the minute pits found on the epipharynx of an insect, having in the centre a peg, the termination of a nerve; **taste-hair**, one of the setæ or bristles, near the mouth of an insect or other arthropod, supposed to be organs of taste; †**taste-paper**, in the (old) Greats examination at Oxford, the paper in which passages were set from the classical authors for critical and exegetical treatment.

1901 E. B. TITCHENER *Exper. Psychol.* I. iv. 64 Each papilla carries a number of *taste-beakers, clusters of taste-cells and supporting cells, which constitute the specific end-organs of taste. 1883 *Science* I. 232/2 The *taste-bulbs, numbering 700 or more, lying in the papillary wall of the valla. 1888 J. G. M'KENDRICK in *Encycl. Brit.* XXIII. 79/2 The terminal organs of taste consist of peculiar bodies named taste-bulbs or taste-goblets. 1890 BILLINGS *Nat. Med. Dict.* s.v. *Taste*, *Taste-cells*, spindle-shaped or staff-shaped cells in the interior of the taste-bulbs. 1891 *Cent. Dict.*, *Taste-center*, the gustatory nervous center, located by Ferrier in the gyrus uncinatus of the brain. 1898 PACKARD *Text-bk. Entomol.* 45 The structure and armature of the epipharyngeal surface even besides the *taste-pits, *taste-cups, and rods, is very varied. 1899 *Allbutt's Syst. Med.* VI. 793 Whether the *taste-fibres pass by the second or third divisions of the nerve. 1905 *Jrnl. R. Micros. Soc.* Apr. 180 *Taste-hairs, homologous with Kræpelin's taste-hairs in Muscidæ, are found in various orders of insects. 1814 COLERIDGE in Cottle *Remin.* (1837) II. 211 This *taste-meter to the fashionable world, gives a ludicrous portrait of an African belle. 1860 HUGHES *Tom Brown at Oxf.* xxiv, In the *taste paper.., as they compare notes, he seems to have almost struck the bull's eye in his answers. 1898 *Taste-pit [see *taste-cup*]. a 1586 SIDNEY *Arcadia* I. (1622) 8 A place cunningly set with trees of the most *tast-pleasing fruits.

Taste (tēⁱst), *sb.*[2] *U. S. local.* [Origin unascertained.] A kind of narrow thin silk ribbon used for edge-binding: now commonly called taffeta-binding. See also WIRE-*taste*.

1847 in WEBSTER. a 1889 F. A. P. BARNARD in *New Haven* (Conn.) *Palladium* 18 Apr., If..Mrs. S. has any taste she will oblige me by sending me half a yard, no matter of what color, so it be not black.

Taste (tēⁱst), *v.* Forms: 3–5 **tasten**, (3 **tasti**, 4 **tasty**, **taaste**, 4–6 **taast**, 4–8 **tast**, 4–7 **taist**, 6 *Sc.* **test**, 7 **teast**), 4– **taste**. [ME. *tasten*, a. OF. *tast-er* to touch, feel (12th c.), in 13–14th c. also to taste, mod.F. *tâter* to feel, touch, try, taste, = Pr., OSp. *tastar*, It. *tastare* to feel, handle, touch, grope for, try (Florio):—Com. Romanic or late pop.L. *tastare, app. from *taxtāre:—*taxitāre, freq. of *taxāre* to touch, feel, handle (Gellius, etc.): see TAX *v.*]

I. Of touch, feeling, or experience generally.

†**1.** *trans.* To try, examine, or explore by touch; to feel; to handle. *Obs.*

c 1290 *St. Michael* 312 in *S. Eng. Leg.* I. 308 With þat finguer he wole hit tasti ȝif it is a-riȝt i-wrouȝt. c 1330 R. BRUNNE *Chron. Wace* (Rolls) 9011 He tasted his pous,..He seide he knew his medycyn. c 1330 *Amis & Amil.* 1401 Leches..That gun to tasty his wounde. 1390 GOWER *Conf.* III. 315 This noble clerk, with alle haste Began the veines forto taste. 1480 CAXTON *Ovid's Met.* x. vii, She toke hardynes for the derknes, and tasted the waye on the ryght side & lyft. 1525 LD. BERNERS *Froiss.* II. xxxviii. 115 The men of armes entre into the dykes,..and tasted the dyke with their speares, and passed ouer to the fote of the wall. 1648 CRASHAW *Delights Muses, Music's Duel* 112 With a quiv'ring coynesse tasts the strings.

†**b.** *intr.* To feel, touch; to grope. *Obs.*

1377 LANGL. *P. Pl.* B. XVII. 147 Þe fyngres..Bitokneth sothly þe sone..Þat toched and tasted atte techynge of þe paume. c 1450 *Merlin* xxxiii. 681 She be-gan to taste softly till he fill on slepe. 1481 CAXTON *Reynard* xii. (Arb.) 27 Isegrym..crope a lityl in, and tasted here and there, and at laste he sayde..what I seche I fynde not. 1483 — *G. de la Tour* F ij b, He tasted aboute & founde well that the dede was trewe.

†**c.** *trans.* To come into contact with, to touch.

1634 SIR T. HERBERT *Trav.* 18 Such as haue the Scuruy.. so soone as they taste the shore..eat three-leafed-grasse.

†**2.** *trans.* To put to the proof; to try, test. *Obs.*

13.. *Cursor M.* 12934 (Gött.) Þe warlou wili..wold him tast wid sin, To witt if he had part him in. c 1450 LOVELICH *Grail* lii. 603 He lyht Adown..and tasted his harneis In that stede, þat it scholde not faille whanne he hadd nede. 1585–6 SIR T. SHERLEY in *Leycester Corr.* (Camden) 174, I thowght to tast her affectyon unto your lordship. 1615 CHAPMAN *Odyss.* XXI. 211 And he now began To taste the bow. 1670 COTTON *Espernon* II. v. 206 Him he first tasted by Lafin, the same who had made himself a Mediator betwixt the Duke of Espernon and l'Esdiguieres in Provence.

b. *spec.*: see quots.

1711 W. SUTHERLAND *Shipbuild. Assist.* 164 *Tasting of Plank or Timber*, chipping of it with an Addice to try the Defects. c 1850 *Rudim. Navig.* (Weale) 155 *Tasting of plank or timber*, chipping it with an adze, or boring it with a small augur, for the purpose of ascertaining its quality.

†**c.** To attempt, try *to do* something. *Obs. rare.*

c 1330 R. BRUNNE *Chron. Wace* (Rolls) 13834 On many manere ilk oþer tasted Ilk oþer to slo, ilk oþer to wounde. c 1450 *Merlin* xxxii. 649 He caste a-wey his clubbe and tasted to chacche the kynge in his armes.

3. *fig.* To have experience or knowledge of; to experience, feel; to have a slight experience of.

Often (in later use perh. always) *fig.* from 4.

a 1300 *Cursor M.* 18940 Als gaf to þaim þe haligast Alkin wiit to tuche and tast. c 1380 WYCLIF *Serm.* Sel. Wks. I. 126 He shal not taaste þe longe deþ. 1576 FLEMING *Panopl. Epist.* 35 In ciuil commotions all thinges are miserable:..this our present age also hath oftentimes tasted. 1630 *R. Johnson's Kingd. & Commw.* 138 [The Gaules] who from Caesars time till then, had not tasted the force of a forren power. 1693 *Humours Town* A ij b, You have tasted the Pleasures of the Town. 1717 OCKLEY in *Lett. Lit. Men* (Camden) 353, I enjoy more repose here than I have tasted these many years. 1864 BURTON *Scot Abr.* I. iv. 207 John Knox, who was just returned from tasting the tender mercies of France as a galley-slave.

†**b.** To have carnal knowledge of. *Obs.*

1611 SHAKS. *Cymb.* II. iv. 57 If you can mak't apparant That you have tasted her in Bed; my hand, And Ring is yours. a 1639 T. CAREW *Poems* (1651) 32 So shalt thou be despis'd, fair Maid, When by the sated lover tasted. 1752 YOUNG *Brothers* IV. i, What, see, talk, touch, nay taste her!

II. Of the special sense that resides in the tongue and palate.

4. *trans.* To perceive by the sense of taste; to perceive or experience the taste or flavour of.

1340–70 *Alex. & Dind.* 952 In menskinge of mouþ mirþe we hauen, In tendere touchinge of þing, & tastinge of swete. c 1375 *Cursor M.* 23456 (Fairf.) In þis werlde has men liking..squete spiceri to tast [*Cott.* fell] & smelle. c 1430 LYDG. *Min. Poems* 14 Wellys most holsom of savour, For to be tasted of every governour. c 1440 *Promp. Parv.* 487/1 Taastyn, *gusto*. 1535 COVERDALE 2 *Sam.* xix. 35 This daye am I foure score yeare olde. How shulde I..taist what I eate or drynke? 1592 SHAKS. *Rom. & Jul.* I. iii. 30 When it did tast the Worme-wood. 1774 GOLDSM. *Nat. Hist.* (1776) VI. 242 When once it has tasted human flesh, it never desists from haunting those places where it expects the return of its prey. 1909 *Daily Chron.* 17 Nov. 8/4 She said the smells were so bad that they could be tasted as well as smelt.

†**b.** *fig.* To perceive or recognize as by the sense of taste. *Obs.*

1583 BABINGTON *Commandm.* i. 10 Euen a world it is to see how all, as dead, doo tast no sinne in it. 1591 HARINGTON *Orl. Fur.* Pref. ¶ viij b, Three syllabled wordes..which who mislike, may tast lamp oyle with their eares. 1616 B. JONSON *Devil an Ass* I. vi, Nay, then I taste a Trick in 't.

c. *absol.* or *intr.* To experience or distinguish flavours; to have or exercise the sense of taste.

1387 TREVISA *Higden* (Rolls) II. 181 Þey..mowe noþer see ne hire, ne taste, ne smelle. c 1560 A. SCOTT *Poems* (S. T. S.) xxxi. 18 No wit salbe degest, To heir, se, smell, nor test. 1601 SHAKS. *Twel. N.* I. v. 98 O, you are sicke of selfe-loue, Maluolio, and taste with a distemper'd appetite. *Mod.* I have got a very bad cold, and can neither taste nor smell.

5. *transf.* (*trans.*) To perceive by some other sense, esp. smell. Now only *poet.* or *dial.*

1656 EARL MONM. *Advt. fr. Parnass.* 380 Would you have men taste the odoriferousness of those Aromaticks which you ..have brought from the Indies? 1674 RAY *N. C. Words*, To *Tast*; i. e. to smell in the North. 1796 PEGGE *Derbicisms* (E.D.S.), *Taste*, to smell, in the North. See Ray. You commonly ask a person to *taste* your snuff. 1819 KEATS *Isabella* ix, I must taste the blossoms that unfold In its ripe warmth this gracious morning time. 1844 KINGLAKE *Eöthen* ii. (1878) 25 To taste the cold breath of the earliest morn.

6. To try the flavour or quality of by the sense of taste; to put a small quantity of (something) into the mouth in order to ascertain the flavour, etc.; *spec.* to test the quality of by tasting, for trade purposes. Also *absol.*

a 1300 *Cursor M.* 13403 (Cott.) Þai fild a cupp þan son in hast, And gaf it þe architricline to tast. *Ibid.* 16773 (Gött.) Þat bitter drinc..He tasted it, bot noght he dranc. 1388 WYCLIF *Rom.* xi. 16 If a litil part of that that is tastid be hooli, the hool gobet is hooli. 1535 COVERDALE *Job* xxxiv. 3 For like as the mouth tasteth [1382 WYCLIF bi tast demeth] the meates, so the eare proueth & discerneth the wordes. 1552 HULOET, Taste afore or fyrste, *prolibo*. 1604 in *Eng. Gilds* (1870) 435 The ale teaster to teast the ale before they sell it. 1769 COOK *Voy. round World* I. iii. (1773) 44 Having tasted the liquor, they returned it, with strong expressions of disgust. 1837 WHITTOCK, etc. *Bk. Trades* (1842) 441 This system of tasting constitutes the acme of the great Teaman's trade.

b. *intr.* with *of*: see 12 a.

c. *spec.* (*trans.*) To test or certify the wholesomeness of (food provided) by tasting it; also *absol.* to act as taster *to* a person. Also *fig.*

1595 SHAKS. *John* v. vi. 28 How did he take it [poison]? Who did taste to him? 1600 J. PORY tr. *Leo's Africa* Introd. 32 He [the emperor] is tasted vnto, not before, but after he hath eaten and drunke. 1678 DRYDEN *All for Love* I. i. 15 Thou and I, Like Time and Death, marching before our Troops, May taste fate to e'm; Mowe e'm out a passage. 1682 SOUTHERNE *Loyal Brother* I. i, True, I make bold To taste their letters to 'em, as they pass Through my Employment.

d. *fig.* To make trial of as by the sense of taste; to try the quality of. Also with *obj. cl.*, and *absol.* or *intr.* Cf. sense 2.

1382 WYCLIF *Ps.* xxxiii. 9 [xxxiv. 8] Tastith, and seeth, for sweete is the Lord. 1390 GOWER *Conf.* II. 395 Mi fader, nay; bot I have tasted In many a place as I have go, And yit love I nevere on of tho. 1597 MORLEY *Introd. Musicke* Annot., Who hath tasted the firste elements of musicke. 1601 B. JONSON *Poetaster* v. iii, Then come home, And taste a piece of Terence. 1819 KEATS *Isabella* xlix, O turn thee to the very tale, And taste the music of that vision pale. 1896 MRS. CAFFYN *Quaker Grandmother* 294 She waited breathlessly to taste the quality of her mercy.

7. To have or take a taste of (food or drink); to take only as much as is sufficient to try or perceive the taste of, to eat or drink a little; but often by meiosis, simply for 'eat' or 'drink'. Negatively, *not to taste* = not even to taste, not to eat or drink at all. Also *fig.* to get a 'taste' of.

a 1300 *Cursor M.* 12559 (Cott.) Noþer durst þai drinc ne ete, Ne brek þair brede, ne tast þair mes Til he war cummen til þair des. 1382 WYCLIF *Luke* xiv. 24, I seie to ȝou, for noone of tho men that ben clepid, schal taaste my souper. 1596 DALRYMPLE tr. *Leslie's Hist. Scot.* (S. T. S.) I. 69 Of mony things we sal taist a few as we may. 1624 QUARLES *Job* xi. Medit. 35 Wisdom digests, what knowledge did but tast. 1653 WALTON *Angler* i. 2, I often..taste a cup of Ale there. 1700 ASTRY tr. *Saavedra-Faxardo* I. 31 It will suffice therefore for a Prince to tast the Arts and Sciences. 1754 GRAY *Pleasure* 60 She eyes the clear crystalline well [of Pleasure], And tastes it as it goes. 1853 KINGSLEY *Hypatia* x, He had tasted no food since noon the day before.

b. *absol.* or *intr.* ellipt. for 'taste wine or alcoholic drink'; to take a little drink. *Sc.*

1823 GALT *R. Gilhaize* v. (E.D.D.), He pressed my grandfather to taste. 1901 S. MACNAUGHTON *Fortune of Chr. M'Nab* ii, 'Thank you', said Christina, 'I do not taste'. *Mod. Sc.* Will you not taste? Do you never taste?

8. To like the taste of (usually *fig.*); to relish, approve of, enjoy, like, take pleasure in; in earlier use sometimes in neutral sense: to appreciate. Now *arch.* or *dial.*

1605 EARL OF SALISBURY in *Buccleuch MSS.* (Hist. MSS. Comm.) 81 This [proposal] was at first but little tasted by them. a 1617 BAYNE *On Eph. i.* (1634) 244 Many.. taste their pottage, like Esau, better than their birthright. 1624 BEDELL *Lett.* iv. 81 A more sensible proofe how the Pope tastes these Titles. 1751 CHATHAM *Lett. Nephew* ii. 6, I hope you love and taste those authors [Homer and Vergil] particularly. 1768 EARL HARDWICKE *Let.* 17 May, The king seemed to taste the Duke of Grafton, and commended his parts. 1791 BOSWELL *Johnson* 2 Apr. an. 1775, If I wondered at Johnson not tasting the works of Mason and Gray, still more have I wondered at their not tasting his works. 1805 MRS. R. TRENCH in *Rem.* (1862) 170 Mad. de Sévigné, whom for the first time I really taste and admire. 1879 GEO. ELIOT *Theo. Such* i. 10 The work..I am told is much tasted in a Cherokee translation. 1896 'IAN MACLAREN' *Kate Carnegie* 33 The story was much tasted by our guard's admirers.

9. *intr.* Of a substance: To have a taste of a specified or implied kind; to produce a certain taste in the mouth; to have a taste or flavour *of*.

1552 HULOET, Tastynge or castynge an yll taste or sauoure, *virosus*. 1615 G. SANDYS *Trav.* 66 Blacke as soote and tasting not much unlike it. 1653 WALTON *Angler* iii. 73 It looks well, and tastes well. 1655 FULLER *Ch. Hist.* I. ii. § 11 This new Wine, put into old Vessels, did in after-Ages taste of the Caske. 1681 CHETHAM *Angler's Vade-m.* xxxix. § 1 (1689) 253 It will make him to tast very sour. 1729 SWIFT *Direct. Servants, Cook* ¶ 26 If your butter tastes of brass, it is your master's fault. 1871 CALVERLEY *Proverb. Philos.* in *Verses & Transl.* (ed. 4) 95 Let him drink deeply.., nor grumble if it tasteth of the cork. *Mod.* The milk has begun to turn; it tastes rather sour.

b. *fig.* To produce a particular effect upon the mind or feelings; to partake of the nature, character, or quality *of*; to savour *of*.

1559 W. CUNNINGHAM *Cosmogr. Glasse* 5 All other artes (whiche taste of the Mathematicalles). c 1575 J. HOOKER *Life Sir P. Carew* (1857) 19 His behaviour tasting after the French manner. 1613 SHAKS. *Hen. VIII*, III. iii. 89 How tasts it? Is it bitter? 1621 SANDERSON *Serm.* I. 179 This ungodly king Ahab; see how all that come of him, taste of him. 1840 CLOUGH *Dipsychus* Poems (1892) 109 The place, the air Tastes of the nearer north.

†**c.** *trans.* To savour of. *Sc. Obs.*

1596 DALRYMPLE tr. *Leslie's Hist. Scot.* x. 417 Ony thing ..of him said that taisted not Ill talk, haitred, and Invie.

†**10.** To cause a pleasant taste in (the mouth); to affect (the palate) agreeably; hence *fig.* to please, suit, be agreeable to. (Orig. *intr.* with dative obj.; in quot. 1672 with *to*.) *Obs.*

a 1586 SIDNEY *Arcadia* III. (1622) 352 Bitter griefs tastes mee best, pain is my ease. 1624 HEYWOOD *Gunaik.* VIII. 383 When wholesome foode would not tast their mouths, they devised sweet meates to realish their pallats. 1631 — *Maid of West* III. Wks. 1874 II. 299 Call for what wine best tasts you. 1672 MARVELL *Reh. Transp.* I. 184 Nothing less will taste to your palate.

11. To impart a taste or flavour to; to flavour; also *fig.* Now *rare.*

a 1577 GASCOIGNE *Flowers* Wks. (1587) 40 A salad or a sauce, to tast your cates withall. 1598 B. JONSON *Ev. Man in Hum.* I. iv, We will have a bunch of radish and salt to taste our wine. 1904 J. WELLS *J. H. Wilson* xxi. 293 All his teachings were coloured and tasted by the channel through which they ran.

12. Taste of, a construction used in several senses, sometimes simply = taste, sometimes = take a taste of, eat or drink a little of. So *taste on* (now *dial.*), †*taste to* (obs.).

In some cases, as in quots. 1526 in b and c, perhaps a literalism of translation (not found in the Vulgate, Wyclif, or Rhemish N. T.); but see OF 29 a, and cf. *take a taste of.*

a. To make trial of by tasting, to try the taste of; = 6. Also *fig. arch.*

a 1400–50 *Alexander* 2074 Þan pullis him vp þe proude kyng & on þe pepire tastis. c 1491 *Chast. Goddes Chyld.* 11 The bee goth and tasteth of many fair floures. c 1550 CHEKE *Matt.* xxvii. 34 When he had taasted on it [TINDALE therof], he wold not drink. 1604–63 *Inscr. on Ch. Bells* in North *Ch. Bells Linc.* (1882), I sweetly toling men do call to taste on meats that feeds the soule. 1807 SOUTHEY *Espriella's Lett.* II. 196 We tasted of this bread: it was dry, but not unpleasant. 1848 J. H. NEWMAN *Loss & Gain* 154, I taste of every thing, I depend on nothing.

b. To eat or drink only a little of; with negative, not to eat or drink at all; = 7. Also *fig.*

13.. *K. Alis.* 5070 (Bodl. MS.) The kyng..forbed..Þat non ne shulde..Of þe water drynk ne taste. c 1400 *Destr. Troy* 6427 The tydis not to taste of þis triet meite. 1526 TINDALE *Luke* xiv. 24 None of those men which were bidden shall tast of my supper [μου τοῦ δείπνου]. 1591 SHAKS. 1 *Hen. VI*, II. iii. 79, I craue..that we may Taste of your Wine. 1607 TOPSELL *Four-f. Beasts* (1658) 19 Asses are subject to madness when they have tasted to certain herbs growing neer Potnias. 1667 MILTON *P. L.* IX. 651 Of this Tree we may not taste nor touch. 1699 DRYDEN *Epist. to J. Dryden* 61 For age but tastes of pleasures, youth devours. 1765 T. HUTCHINSON *Hist. Mass.* I. ii. 232 They had but tasted of the words..of the gentlemen.

c. To have experience or knowledge of; to feel, experience; = 3.

1526 TINDALE *Matt.* xvi. 28 Some there be a monge them that here stonde, whych shall nott taste of deeth [οὐ μὴ γεύσωνται θανάτου], tyll they shall [etc.]. 1552 LATIMER *Serm. 4th Sund. Epiph.* (1584) 315 b, He himself hath tasted of al trouble. a 1568 G. CAVENDISH *Metr. Vis., Earl of Essex* vi, I ame tastyng on the payn. 1599 MASSINGER, etc. *Old Law* II. ii, So contentedly, You cannot think unless you tasted on't. 1667 MILTON *P. L.* IX. 476 Hope here to taste Of pleasure. 1742 GRAY *Adversity* 6 The Proud are taught to taste of pain. 1832 HT. MARTINEAU *Ireland* v. 75 Wherever the population had tasted of oppression.

†**d.** = 3 b. *Obs.*

1607 TOURNEUR *Rev. Trag.* II. ii, I do embrace this season for the fittest To tast of that yong Lady.

e. See 9, 9 b.

Tasteable, tastable (tēⁱ·stăb'l), *a.* Also 6 **tastible**. [In ME. a. OF. *tastable* having the capacity of feeling, f. *taster* to feel, touch; in mod. Eng. f. TASTE *v.* + -ABLE.]

I. †**1.** Capable of feeling or perceiving by the sense of touch. *Obs. rare*⁻¹.

c 1400 tr. *Secreta Secret., Gov. Lordsh.* 98 Þe wyttys þat er yn þe hondes ys in a touchable & tastable styrngh [F. *li sens qi est en la main est en force touchable e tastable*; L. *palpativa*].

II. **2.** Capable of being tasted. Also *fig.*

1572 J. JONES *Bathes of Bath* II. 18 The fittest instrument, the truest touchestone, of all properties, trying both toucheable and tasteable qualities. 1589 PUTTENHAM *Eng. Poesie* II. i. (Arb.) 78 Things that haue conueniencie by relation, as the visible by light..: the tastible by sauours to the rate: the tangible by his objectes in this or that regard. 1627–77 FELTHAM *Resolves* II. xliv. 245 Pleasures are not truly tastable, but in the solid tracts of Temperance. 1755 MILLER in *Phil. Trans.* XLIX. 163 This juice has no other tasteable quality but that of heating without turning sour. 1829 JAS. MILL *Hum. Mind* (1869) I. 13 We should have no idea of objects as seeable, as hearable, as touchable, or tasteable.

†**3.** Pleasant to the taste; savoury, 'tasty'. *Obs.*

a 1641 BP. MOUNTAGU *Acts & Mon.* vii. (1642) 443 Esseni are those that live the life of Monks, eating no pleasant or tasteable meat at all. 1791 *Gentl. Mag.* Feb. 127/1 The fruit was tasteable.

Tasted (tēⁱ·stėd), *ppl. a.* and *adj.* [f. TASTE *v.* and *sb.*[1] + -ED.]

A. *ppl. a.* [f. TASTE *v.*] Perceived by the taste, etc.: see the verb.

c 1403 ? LYDG. *Crt. Sapience* Proeme vii, As tasted bytternesse All swete thynge maketh be more precyous.

B. *adj.* [f. TASTE *sb.*]

1. Having a specified taste (with adj. or adv.).

1604 JAS. I *Counterbl.* in *Ess. Poesie*, etc. (Arb.) 107 The miraculous omnipotencie of our strong tasted Tobacco. 1607 TOPSELL *Four-f. Beasts* (1658) 208 They are much fatter and better tasted. 1682 WHELER *Journ. Greece* IV. 295 The white..is very well tasted. 1684 BUNYAN *Pilgr.* II. 133 They were very good tasted Fruit. 1707 MORTIMER *Husb.* (1721) II. 297 A pleasant tasted Perry. 1725 DE FOE *Voy. round World* (1840) 328 The water..was very sweet, wholesome, and good tasted. 1812 SOUTHEY in *Q. Rev.* VII. 69 *note*, The milk..is ill tasted. 1836 W. IRVING *Astoria* (1849) 409 Mountain mutton..extremely well tasted.

2. Having taste or critical discernment (of a specified kind).

1802 H. C. ANDREWS *Bot. Rep.* I. 255 The late elegantly tasted Mrs. North.

Tasteful (tēⁱ·stfŭl), *a.* Also 7–8 **tastful.** [f. TASTE *sb.*[1] + -FUL.]

†**1.** Having the capacity of tasting or trying.

1647 CRASHAW *Poems, Flaming Heart* 50 What is't your tasteful spirits do prove In that rare life of her and love?

2. Having an agreeable taste; palatable, toothsome, tasty. Now *rare.*

1611 COTGR., *Savoureux*, sauorie, tastfull, tart, well smacking. 1621 BP. MOUNTAGU *Diatribæ* 358 Stolne waters are sweet,..no Bread so tastefull, as that of the Sanctuarie. 1707 *Curios. in Husb. & Gard.* 217 The tasteful Cider. 1747 *Gentl. Mag.* May 243/2 With Temp'rance came, delightful guest! Health,—tasteful food, and balmy rest. 1887 HISSEY *Holiday on Road* 177 Sheep that live upon such a pasturage should yield a tasteful dish.

†**b.** *fig.* Mentally pleasant or agreeable. *Obs.*

a 1659 OSBORN *Ess.* iii. Wks. (1673) 562 Since nothing is more tasteful to Humanity, than Understanding. a 1701 MAUNDRELL *Let. to Sir C. Hedges* in *Journ. Jerus.* (1732) Pref., An Affectation, which however tastful it may be to the Persons who use it [etc.].

c. Full of taste; highly-flavoured. *rare.*

1881 SALA in *Illustr. Lond. News* 14 May 467/3 Punch is too strong and tasteful with turtle soup.

3. Having or showing good taste, as a person; displaying good taste, as a work of art, etc.

1756 *Connoisseur* No. 120 ¶ 6 These are the poets who favour us with..tasteful compositions. 1816 SINGER *Hist. Cards* 213 They were drawn on the blocks by the tasteful pencil of Stothard. 1849 *N. & Q.* I. 28/2 The tasteful publisher of the 'Aldine Poets'. 1863 LYELL *Antiq. Man* ii. 10 The pottery..is of a more ornamental and tasteful style.

b. Of or pertaining to taste; æsthetic.

1851 J. HAMILTON *Royal Preacher* x. (1858) 134 Conceding ..the same right to exert his tasteful and intellectual faculties when listening to a sermon as when perusing a..book.

Hence **Ta·stefully** *adv.*, in a tasteful manner, with good taste; **Ta·stefulness**, the quality or state of being tasteful (in various senses).

1611 COTGR., *Savoureusement*, sauorily, *tastfully, tastingly, with a good stomacke. 1808 MRS. KEMBLE *Day after Wedding* 3 A Lady's Dressing-room tastefully furnished. 1900 *Westm. Gaz.* 22 Oct. 4/2 The tastefully-arranged gardens which are to be found at many stations on that railway. 1727 BAILEY vol. II, *Tastefulness*, Relishableness, Palatableness. 1844 DICKENS *Mart. Chuz.* ix, Mr. Pecksniff's delight in the tastefulness of the house.

Tasteless (tēⁱ·stlės), *a.* Also 7–8 **tastless.** [f. TASTE *sb.*[1] + -LESS.]

1. Destitute of the sense of taste; unable to taste. Also *fig.* Now *rare.*

1591 SYLVESTER *Du Bartas* I. iv. 148 When wilfully his taste-less Taste delights In things unsavory to sound appetites. a 1631 DONNE *Funeral Elegy* Poems (1654) 219 As aged men are glad Being tastlesse grown, to joy in joyes they had. 1704 CIBBER *Careless Husb.* v. (1705) 60 Won't you think me tastless to the Joy you've given me? 1713 ROWE *Jane Shore* v. i, My tasteless Tongue cleaves to the clammy Roof. 1820 C. R. MATURIN *Melmoth* (1892) III. xxvii. 104 Every thing that could tempt the tasteless palate of age.

2. Without taste or flavour; exciting no sensation of taste; insipid.

1611 FLORIO, *Insaporito*, vnsauorie, tastelesse. 1661–79 BOYLE *Scept. Chem.* IV. Wks. 1772 I. 533 He never was able to make them [chymical oils] tasteless. 1748 *Anson's Voy.* II. xii. 267 Very dry and tasteless food. 1831 J. DAVIES *Manual Mat. Med.* 329 A powder of an orange yellow colour, inodorous, and tasteless.

3. *fig.* Exciting no interest; dull, insipid, uninteresting.

1603 FLORIO *Montaigne* (1634) 143 Enterludes and commedies rejoyce and make us merry, but to players they are tedious and tastelesse. 1781 COWPER *Conversat.* 715 The song of Sion is a tasteless thing, Unless when rising on a joyful wing. 1814 WORDSW. *Excurs.* I. 612 A while on trivial things we held discourse, To me soon tasteless. 1822 LAMB *Elia* Ser. I. *Distant Corr.*, If it [sentiment] have time to cool, it is the most tasteless of all cold meats.

4. Devoid of good taste; of persons, lacking in discrimination, or in critical discernment and appreciation; of things, showing want of good taste.

1676 ETHEREDGE *Man of Mode* III. ii, Nature..puts sophisticate dulness often on the tasteless multitude for true wit and good-humour. 1709 SWIFT in *Lett. Lit. Men* (Camden) 342 Your Lordship is universally admired by this tastless People. 1791 GILPIN *Forest Scenery* II. 75 It not only shews the hand of art; but of the most tastless art. 1843 PRESCOTT *Mexico* I. ii. (1864) 17 As different from their ancestors as are the modern Egyptians from those who built, —I will not say, the tasteless pyramids. 1853 KINGSLEY *Hypatia* vii, The tasteless fashion of an artificial and decaying civilization.

Hence **Ta·stelessly** *adv.*, in a tasteless manner; without taste.

1854 *Tait's Mag.* XXI. 386 Even that comes tastelessly on the ear of the player on the world's stage, unless it is accompanied with a bouquet. 1880 *Daily News* 30 Nov. 3/1 Their houses..are solidly if tastelessly furnished.

Tastelessness (tēⁱ·stlėsnės). [f. prec. + -NESS.]

1. Lack of the sense of taste; *fig.* lack of relish or appreciation. Now *rare.*

1626 DONNE *Serm.* iv. (1640) 38 Our palate dead in a tastlesnesse. 1713 BERKELEY *Guard.* No. 49 ¶ 9 A secret indignation at the tastelessness of mortal men, who, in their race through life, overlook the real enjoyments of it. a 1774 TUCKER *Lt. Nat.* (1834) II. 404 Such austerities and labours of devotion, such a tastelessness of all innocent enjoyments.

2. Absence of taste or flavour; insipidity. Also *fig.*

1600 SURFLET *Countrie Farme* III. lxi. 567 Their sharpnes, sowrenes, tartnes, harshnes, eagernes, sweetenes, and tastlesnes. 1875 H. C. WOOD *Therap.* (1879) 468 On account of its tastelessness, this preparation..is sometimes employed as a purgative for children.

3. Absence or want of æsthetic discernment.

1778 MALONE *Note on Tit. A.* in *Shaks.'s Wks.* VIII. 561 One of their own fraternity, (who cannot well be suspected of asinine tastelessness, or Gothic prepossessions). 1825 *Blackw. Mag.* XVIII. 240 Others assign it to the nonchalance and tastelessness of managers. 1855 DORAN *Hanov. Queens* II. i. 30 Garrick, considering he was a man of taste, displayed great tastelessness on this occasion.

†**Ta·sten**, *v. Obs. rare*⁻¹. [f. TASTE *sb.*[1] + -EN [5].] *trans.* To produce a sensation of taste in.

1579 LODGE *Def. Poetry* 15 The receipt is bitter, therfore I would wysh you first to tasten your mouth with the Sugar of perseuerance.

Taster [1] (tēⁱ·stər). Forms: 4–6 **tastour**, 5 **-ar**, **taastowre**, 6– **taster**. [a. AF. *tastour* = OF. *tasteur*, f. OF. *taster*: see TASTE *v.* Later treated as agent-n. of the Eng. vb.: see -ER [1].]

1. One who tastes, or tries the quality of a thing by tasting; *spec.* one whose office, business, or employment is to test the quality of victuals sold to the public, as ale, wine, tea, etc. by taste; hence in comb. ALE-TASTER, TEA-TASTER, q. v. Also *fig.* In quot. 1596, the mouth.

c 1440 *Promp. Parv.* 487/1 Taastowre, *gustator, ambro.* c 1450 in *Surtees Misc.* (1888) 62 Two ale tastars, yᵉ qwhyche two tastars..schall taste the ale of all common brewers every weke. 1526 *Pilgr. Perf.* (W. de W. 1531) 274 b, To be vynteners, discerners, and tasters of the same. 1596 HARINGTON *Metam. Ajax* (1814) 36 Riding on a great sow and holding before her taster a dirty pudding. 1633 G. HERBERT *Temple, Odour* i, As Amber-greese leaves a rich sent Unto the taster. 1756 C. LUCAS *Ess. Waters* I. 79 Judicious tasters dilute hot liquors. 1854 LOWELL *Jrnl. in Italy* Pr. Wks. 1890 I. 115, I reckon myself a good taster of dialects. 1866 CARLYLE *Remin., E. Irving* (1881) 314, I.. demanded back my poor MS. from Murray, received with it some apologetic palaver (enclosing an opinion from his taster..), and much hope [etc.]. 1905 *Sat. Rev.* 17 June 816/1 On the whole the first literary 'taster' of the MS. was, we think, justified in rejecting Coryat.

b. *transf.* A device which tests as by tasting.

1837 WHEWELL *Hist. Induct. Sc.* (1857) III. 24 Which thus acted as a sort of electric taster.

2. A domestic officer whose duty it is to taste food and drink about to be served to his master, in order to ascertain their quality, or to detect poison.

1387 TREVISA *Higden* (Rolls) VIII. 197 A monk..made a drink of venym,..and drank to þe kyng as it were his tastour. 1580 HOLLYBAND *Treas. Fr. Tong* s.v. *Eschanson*, A taster of meates to kinges or other. 1602 T. FITZHERBERT *Apol.* 31 The Emperour Claudius, poysoned by his taster. 1662 HIBBERT *Body Div.* I. 206 Princes have their tasters before they eat, lest there should be poison in the dish. 1738 SWIFT *Pol. Conversat.* I. 13 What, Miss, Will you be my Taster [of a dish of tea]? 1895 *Westm. Gaz.* 30 Oct. 3/2 Not a morsel or a drop ever passes the Sultan's lips, they say, until he has tried it first on a taster. *fig.* 1640 REYNOLDS *Passions* xvii. 179 Knowledge is Appetites Taster.

3. An implement by which a small portion of anything is taken for tasting.

a. A small shallow cup of silver, often with an embossed or corrugated bottom which reflects the light through the liquor, for tasting wines.

1420 *E. E. Wills* (1882) 46 A tastour of seluer with myn owne merke ymade in þe bottom. 1530 PALSGR. 279/2 Tastour a lytell cuppe to tast wyne, *tasse a gouster le uin.* 1681 *Lond. Gaz.* No. 1665/4 One Silver Brandy Taster, marked with R. H. A. 1704 *Ibid.* No. 4055/4 Two long footed Silver Cups, one Taster. 1858 [see b].

b. An instrument by which a small portion is taken from the interior of a cheese; a skewer for testing the condition of hams.

1784 TWAMLEY *Dairying* 79, I told her Cheese of that countenance always was sweet. I put my taster into one and gave it her to taste. 1811 [see *cheese-taster*, CHEESE *sb.*[1] 7]. 1858 SIMMONDS *Dict. Trade, Taster*,..a scoop for tasting cheese; a skewer for trying hams; a dram cup.

4. A small portion of food, etc., or of anything, for a sample; a taste.

1826 SYD. SMITH *Granby* Wks. 1867 II. 90 It shall be the taster of the cheese, and we are convinced it will sell the whole article. 1891 *Daily News* 28 July 7/2 He went to the defendant's [an ice-cream vendor] stall in London-wall and asked him for a 'taster'. 1899 *Westm. Gaz.* 20 May 2/1 The 'taster', a free gift bestowed of yore in order to retain the..goodwill of regular but temporarily impecunious customers.

‖**Taster** [2] (ta·stər). *Zool.* [G. *taster* feeler, antenna, f. *tasten* to feel, touch.] In certain Hydrozoa, A modified zooid situated on the polypstem, and somewhat resembling the polypites, but having no mouth; a hydrocyst or feeler.

1884 *Stand. Nat. Hist.* I. 100 Alternating with the polypites at intervals along the polypstem are found very curious bodies called tasters, which have a close likeness to the flask-shaped zooids. [1888 ROLLESTON & JACKSON *Anim. Life* 770 *Siphonophora*...The various parts..(1) The polypite or gastrozooid..(2) Hydrocysts or feelers (= Taster of German writers)...These structures are polypites in which the distal or oral extremity is imperforate and usually armed with cnidoblasts. The pedicle is absent or short.]

†**Ta·stesome**, *a. Obs. rare.* [f. TASTE *sb.*[1] + -SOME.] Pleasant to the taste; 'tasty', toothsome.

1598 FLORIO, *Gusteuole*, smacking, tastesome, tasting well.

Tastily (tēⁱ·stĭli), *adv.* [f. TASTY *a.* + -LY [2].] In a tasty manner; tastefully.

1799 R. WARNER *Walk* (1800) 80 The slope..is tastily managed and appropriately ornamented. 1809 PINKNEY *Trav. France* 24 The fruits were in plates very tastily painted in landscape. 1845 M. J. HIGGINS *Ess.* (1875) 216 Tastily but inexpensively dressed.

Tastiness (tēⁱ·stinės). [f. as prec. + -NESS.] The quality or state of being tasty.

1882 HOWELLS in *Longm. Mag.* I. 44 Lexington has escaped the ravages alike of 'tastiness' and of enterprise. 1902 MARY E. MANN *Fields Dulditch* iii. 39 He ain't to comparison in tastiness to th' gage.

Tasting (tēⁱ·stiŋ), *vbl. sb.* [-ING [1].]

1. The action of the verb TASTE. **a.** In a general sense, trying, testing; †esp., in early use, touching, feeling; also the sense of touch (*obs.*).

13.. *K. Alis.* 4031 (Bodl. MS.) It is ywrite þat euery þing Hym self sheweþ in þe tastyng. c 1375 *Sc. Leg. Saints* vi. (*Thomas*) 407 Wittis four,..sycht, herynge, gustyne, tastyne. c 1430 *Pilgr. Lyf Manhode* I. cxxi. (1869) 63 Alle tastinges generalliche is vnderstonde bi the hondes. 1711, 1850 [see TASTE *v.* 2 b].

b. Now, the action of TASTE *v.* II; †also formerly, the faculty or sense, and the quality of a substance so apprehended: = TASTE *sb.*[1] 4, 5 (*obs.*).

1390 GOWER *Conf.* III. 33, I take of love my fiedinge Withoute tastinge or fielinge. 1426 AUDELAY *Poems* 7 Thi heryng, thi seyng, as I the schewe, Thi syȝt, thi smellyng, here be iij. Thi touchyng, thi tastyng, here v. ther be. c 1460 J. RUSSELL *Bk. Nurture* 1199 Credence is vsed, and tastynge, for drede of poysenynge. 1530 PALSGR. 279/2 Tastyng with the mouthe, *gouster.* 1774 GOLDSM. *Nat. Hist.* (1776) II. 183 The sense most nearly allied to smelling is that of tasting. 1841–4 EMERSON *Ess., Exper.* Wks. (Bohn) I. 178 Intellectual tasting of life will not supersede muscular activity. 1898 'IAN MACLAREN' in *Woman at Home* Oct. 56/1 If Thomas takes to tasting [i. e. tippling, drinking] ..it's all over with him.

2. quasi-*concr.* A small portion taken to try the taste; a taste (esp. of spirituous liquor). Also *fig.*

1526 *Pilgr. Perf.* (1531) 49 For they be but tastynges, shadowes, or tokens of the gloryous fruytes to come. 1830 CUNNINGHAM *Brit. Paint.* II. 69 He gave them a tasting of his spirit in two or three sarcastic sentences. 1893 J. SKINNER *Autobiog. Metaphysician* vii. 48 He got a glass from Mr. Reed and another tasting from another neighbour.

3. *attrib.* and *Comb.*, as *tasting power*; **tasting-bone**, a bone put into the broth to give it a taste or flavour; **tasting-knife**, a cheese-taster (see TASTER 3 b); **tasting-order**, an order to visit stores of wine, etc., and to taste or sample them.

1850 MRS. CARLYLE *Let. to Carlyle* 8 Sept., It [Kingsley's *Alton Locke*] seems to me..a mere..broth of *Morning-chronicle-ism*, in which you play the part of the *tasting-bone of Poverty Row. 1757 H. WALPOLE tr. *Hentzner's Trav.* 52 At last came an unmarried Lady..and along with her a married one, bearing a *tasting-knife. 1859 SALA *Gas-light & D.* xiv, Quite gone in liquor and overcome with the *tasting-orders of years. 1599 DAVIES *Immort. Soul* ccxv, Therefore the Soule doth vse the *tasting power.

Ta·sting, *ppl. a.* [-ING [2].] That tastes.

1598 [implied in next]. 1907 *Contemp. Rev.* Oct. Lit. Suppl. 2 The tasting sense is soon ruined.

Ta·stingly, *adv.* [f. prec. + -LY [2].] In a tasting manner.

1598 FLORIO, *Saporitamente*, sauourly, smackingly, tastingly, hungerly. 1894 BARING-GOULD *Kitty Alone* II. 150 The fire..sending the tips of its flames tastingly towards him.

†**Ta·stive**, *a. Obs. rare*⁻¹. [f. TASTE *sb.*[1] or *v.*: see -IVE.] Having the quality of taste; sapid.

1644 DIGBY *Nat. Bodies* xxvii. § 6. 246 The same thinges that yield also tastiue particles.

Tastle, obs. form of TASSEL.

Tasty (tēⁱ·sti), *a.* Now *colloq.* and *dial.* [f. TASTE *sb.*[1] + -Y.]

1. Pleasing to the taste; appetizing, savoury.

1617 HIERON *Wks.* II. 203 Sowre herbs, with which that tastie meat, the paschall lambe..was to be eaten. 1795 in *Spirit Pub. Jrnls.* IV. 220 A tasty bird, that pheasant. 1849 CURZON *Visits Monast.* 144 A famous pie, or pilau, with rice and a tasty sauce. a 1862 BUCKLE *Misc. Wks.* (1872) I. 381 The arts of compounding a pleasant pudding or combining a tasty pie.

b. *fig.* Pleasant, agreeable, attractive.

1796 MRS. M. ROBINSON *Angelina* III. 179 'Here you are, my tasty ones!' exclaimed Sir Edward. 'Why, you played us a trick'. 1821 CLARE *Vill. Minstr.* I. 201 Pausing o'er each tasty flower.

2. Characterized by or displaying good taste; tasteful, elegant. Now *rare.*

1762 GOLDSM. *Cit. World* lxxvii, [The silk] is at once rich, tasty, and quite the thing. 1784 *New Spectator* No. 16. 5 [Ranelagh] This region of taste was visited on Friday evening, by a great number of tasty people indeed. 1813 J. C. HOBHOUSE *Journey* (ed. 2) 501 The head-dress of the younger girls is tasty; their hair falls down their backs in profusion. 1821 COLERIDGE in *Blackw. Mag.* X. 254, I wish I could find a more familiar word than *aesthetic*...To be sure, there is *tasty*; but that has been long ago emasculated for all unworthy uses by milliners, tailors, and..dandies. 1862 THACKERAY *Philip* xxiv, My..waistcoat..is a much more tasty thing than these gaudy ready-made articles.

3. *Comb.*, as *tasty-looking*.

1867 F. FRANCIS *Angling* x. (1880) 375 This is a very tasty-looking fly. 1888 F. COWPER *Capt. of Wight* (1889) 50 Some tasty-looking rolls, fresh butter, and cheese.

Tasul, tasyl, -yll, -ylle, obs. ff. TEASEL.

Tat (tæt), *sb.*[1] *slang.* Also **tatt**. [Origin unascertained.] *pl.* **Tats**: Dice; *esp.* false or loaded dice. **b.** *Comb.* as **tat-box**, a dice-box; **tat-monger**, a sharper who uses false dice. See also TATSMAN.

1688 SHADWELL *Sqr. Alsatia* I, *H.*...Pox o' the Tatts for me! I believe they put the Doctor upon me. *B.* Tatts and Doctor! what's that? *S.* The tools of Sharpers, false dice. *Ibid.*, He was but a Sharper, a tat-monger. a 1700 B. E. *Dict. Cant. Crew*, *Tatts*, false Dice. a 1809 J. PALMER *Like Master* (1811) I. xv. 215 He ransacks every house in St. James's parish, where the tats are at work, to punish those for what he, himself, practised. 1812 J. H. VAUX *Flash Dict.*, *Tatt-box*, a dice-box. 1887 HENLEY *Villon's Straight Tip* ii, Rattle the tats, or mark the spot.

Tāt (tāt), *sb.*[2] *East Ind.* Also **taut**. [Hindī *ṭāṭ* a strip of very thick hemp-canvas, about 10 inches wide, of which several are sewn together to make a mat or screen.] Coarse canvas made from various fibres, esp. jute, and used as sacking.

1820 *Trans. Lit. Soc. Bombay* III. 244 (Y.) Made into coarse cloth taut, by the Brinjaries and people who use pack bullocks, for making bags (gonies) for holding grain, &c. 1858 SIMMONDS *Dict. Trade*, *Tat*, a name in India for cloth made from the fibre of the *Corchorus olitorius*. Hence 1864 in WEBSTER; and in later Dicts.

Tat, tatt, *sb.*[3] *Anglo-Ind.* Short for TATTY *sb.*

1812 MARIA GRAHAM *Jrnl. Resid. India* 125 (Y.) During the hot winds tats (a kind of mat), made of the root of the koosa grass,..are placed against the doors and windows. 1837 *Lett. fr. Madras* (1843) 77, I have a tatt, or thick mat, at my window, which excludes the sun, and men sit outside pouring water on it all day, so that the wind..blows always cooled through the water.

Tat, tatt, *sb.*[4] *Anglo-Ind.* Short for TATTOO *sb.*[3], a native pony of India.

c 1840 in Parker *Bole Ponjis* (1851) II. 215 With its bright brass patent axles, and its little hog maned tatts. 1845 STOCQUELER *Handbk. Brit. India* (1854) 109 The pony (familiarly called *tat*—corruption of the native name for the small animal, *tattoo*). 1891 *Blackw. Mag.* May 684 Cantering his tat up to the door.

Tat, *sb.*[5] *slang.* [Origin uncertain: cf. OE. *tættec* a rag, and TATTY *a.*] A rag.

1851 MAYHEW *Lond. Labour* I. 424/2 I'll tell you about the tat (rag) gatherers; buying rags they call it.

Tat, *sb.*[6] *Sc.* Also (*erron.*) **taut, tawt**. [Origin obscure: cf. TATTY *a.*] (See quot.)

1887 JAMIESON *Suppl.*, *Tat, taut, tawt*, a tangle, matted tuft or lock of wool or hair.

Tat, *sb.*[7], in phr. *tit for tat*: see TIT.

Tat, *v.*[1] [Origin uncertain: ? echoic; cf. *tap, pat.*] *trans.* **a.** To touch lightly, pat, tap. *dial.*

†**b.** A euphemism for To flog. *Obs. slang.*

1607 DEKKER & WEBSTER *Northw. Ho* II. i, Come tit me, come tat me, come throw a kiss at me. 1812 J. H. VAUX *Flash Dict.*, *Tat*, to flog, or scourge. 1847–78 HALLIWELL, *Tat*...(3) To touch gently. *Hants.*

Tat, *v.*[2] Also **tatt**. [Origin unknown: cf. TATTING.] **a.** *intr.* To do tatting. **b.** *trans.* To make by tatting.

[1842: see TATTING.] 1882 MRS. ALEXANDER in *Belgravia* July 104 Winnie produced her tatting, and applied herself to it...At the mention of his mother Laura involuntarily clasped her hands, and Winnie ceased to tatt. 1905 MRS. E. GLYN *Viciss. Evangeline* 123 They knitted ties and crocheted comforters, and one even tatted.

Tat, *v.*[3] *slang.* [f. TAT *sb.*[5]] *intr.* To gather rags.

1851 MAYHEW *Lond. Labour* I. 417/1 He goes tatting and billy-hunting in the country (gathering rags and buying old metal). 1910 *Nottingham Guardian* 2 June, The prisoner ..told the police that he came in possession of the lead when he went round 'tatting'.

Tat, *v.*[4] *Sc.* and *north. dial.* [Goes with TAT *sb.*[6]] *trans.* and *intr.* To tangle, or make tangled or matted: see TAUT *v.*

1829 BROCKETT *N. C. Gloss.* (ed. 2), *Tat*, to mat, to entangle. 1887 in JAMIESON *Suppl.* 1894 *Northumb. Gloss.*, *Tat*, to mat together.

Ta-ta (tă tā·), *int.* A nursery expression for 'Good-bye'; also used playfully by adults.

1837 DICKENS *Pickw.* xxvii, 'Tar, tar, Sammy', replied his father. 1878 F. C. BURNAND *Strapmore* i. 15 Ta-ta, little one *très cher*! Bye-bye. 1891 MRS. WALFORD *Mischief of Monica* III. 171 'Ta-ta'; and the speaker slipped behind backs and vanished.

Tataow, obs. f. TATTOO *v.*[2] **Tatar**: see TARTAR [2]. **Tatarwagge**: see TATTER *sb.*[1] 3. **Tatch, tatche**: see TACHE. **Tatchy**, dial. f. TETCHY.

Tate (tet, tiᵊt), *sb.*[1] *Sc.* and *north. dial.* Forms: 7–9 **tait**, 8 **teat, tet, tett**, 6– **tate**. [Origin obscure; prob. Norse: cf. Icel. *tæta* to tear to shreds, to tease, *tæta* a shred; also, fluff of wool, etc., a particle of anything.]

1. A small tuft or lock of hair, wool, or other fibrous material, consisting of only a few fibres; a small handful of grass, hay, or corn.

1513 DOUGLAS *Æneis* VI. v. 11 Apon his chin feill cannos haris gray, Lyart feltat tatis. 1570 LEVINS *Manip.* 39/14 A Tate, *fibra*. 1618 *Trial Marg. Barclay*, etc. in Scott

Supplement, p. 3873; Corrigenda, p. 4092; Spurious words, p. 4093; Books quoted, p. 4094

deynfully, nor tauntynglye as though you were offended at them. 1607 SHAKS. Cor. I. i. 114 (Fol. 2) The belly..tauntingly replyed To'th'discontented Members. 1646 J. WHITAKER Uzziah 13 [It] was tauntingly spoke of Christ, He saved others, himself he cannot save. 1876 MOZLEY Univ. Serm. v. (1877) 116 The question has often been asked tauntingly—Why has not Christianity done away with war?

So **Tau·ntingness.** rare⁻⁰.

1727 BAILEY vol. II, Tauntingness, a sharp, haughty, biting Reproachfulness. 1731 Ibid., Tauntingness, Raillery.

Taunt ne caunt: see TANT NE QUANT.

Taunton (tǭ·ntən, locally tā·ntən). Name of a town in Somersetshire; hence short for *Taunton cloth*, a woollen cloth formerly made there.

1499 in Somerset Medieval Wills (1901) 379 To William Busshop halfe a packe of Tauntons. 1607 Act 4 Jas. I, c. 2 § 7 Every Broade Cloth..called Tauntons, Bridgwaters, and Dunsters made in the Westerne partes of Somersetsheire.

Tau·ntress. rare. [f. TAUNTER + -ESS.] A female taunter, a taunting woman.

1557 Agst. Vnstedfast Woman in Tottell's Misc. (Arb.) 177 O temerous tauntres, that delightes in toyes..Ianglyng estres, depraueres of swete ioyes.

Tauny, obs. f. TAWNY. **Tauorsay**: see TAV-.

Taupie, variant of TAWPIE.

†**Taur.** Obs. [ad. L. taur-us or OF. tor, taur, thaur, bull.] A bull; the constellation Taurus.

c 1386 CHAUCER Wife's Prol. 613 Myn Ascendent was Taur and Mars ther-Inne. c 1425 WYNTOUN Chron. II. 1269 A taur, þat is a buyl..Scho saw ner by hir on þe greyn.

†**Taure.** Obs. rare⁻¹. Corruption of TOUR, a fringe of hair worn on the forehead, by association with *taurus* bull: cf. BULL-HEAD 3, quot. 1688.

1688 R. HOLME Armoury II. 464/2 Women wear Hair..in Taures when the hair on the forehead is curled and standeth out. Ibid., Bull-heads, when the said curled forehead is much larger than the Taure.

Taurean (tǭrī·ǎn), a. rare. [f. L. taure-us adj. (f. taurus bull) + -AN.] Of or belonging to a bull.

1656 BLOUNT Glossogr., Taurean, Taurine, of or belonging to a bull. 1900 LEWIS & SHORT Lat.-Eng. Dict., Taureus, of a bull or ox,..[taurea] vincla, i.e. taurean bands (a poet. expression to denote glue), Lucr. 6, 1071.

Tauri-, combining form of L. *taurus* bull, in TAURICIDE, etc.; see TAURUS, and cf. TAURO-.

Tau·rian, a. rare⁻¹. [irreg. f. L. taur-us bull + -IAN.] = TAUREAN, TAURINE a.

1882 Harper's Mag. Sept. 563/1 Three days of bull-fighting..with eight taurian victims each day.

Tauric (tǭ·rik), a. [f. Gr. ταῦρος or L. taurus bull + -IC.] Pertaining or relating to, or of the nature of, a bull; taurine.

1816 G. S. FABER Orig. Pagan Idol. I. 406 The tauric Jupiter was the parent of the Cretan Minos. 1818 — Horæ Mosaicæ I. 314 He set up at Bethel two calves of gold in apparent imitation of the tauric Cherubim of the temple. 1882 R. BROWN Law Kosmic Order 43 In the tauric and bovine form.

Tauricide (tǭ·risəid). rare. [f. L. taur-us bull: see TAURI- and -CIDE.] **a.** A bull-slayer; a matador. **b.** The slaughter of a bull.

1845 E. WARBURTON Crescent & Cross I. ix. 169 Cambyses, the tauricide,..and the desert..have left little trouble to the tourist. 1852 Fraser's Mag. XLV. 536 The great tauricide still hesitated. 1882 Pall Mall G. 11 Sept. 2 If you kill him you are guilty of felony or tauricide.

†**Tauricornous,** a. Obs. rare⁻¹. [f. as prec. + L. cornu horn + -OUS.] Having horns like those of a bull.

1646 SIR T. BROWNE Pseud. Ep. v. ix. 247 Their descriptions must be relative, or the Tauricornous picture of the one, perhaps the same with the other. 1656 BLOUNT Glossogr., Tauricornous, horned like a Bul.

Taurid (tǭ·rid). Astron. [f. TAUR-US, after LEONID, PERSEID. In F. taurides pl. (Littré 1877).] In *pl.* A system of meteors which appear to radiate from a point in the constellation Taurus, about the 20th of November.

1888 Cassell's Encycl. Dict., Taurides.

Tauridor, obs. form of TOREADOR.

†**Tauri·ferous,** a. Obs. rare⁻⁰. [f. L. taurifer (f. taurus bull) + -OUS: see TAURI- and -FEROUS.]

1656 BLOUNT Glossogr., Tauriferous, which beareth or nourisheth Buls or neat. 1721 in BAILEY.

Tauriform (tǭ·rifǭm), a. [ad. L. tauriform-is, f. taurus bull: see TAURI- and -FORM.] Having the form of a bull.

1721 BAILEY, Tauriform,..in the Shape of a Bull. 1803 G. S. FABER Cabiri I. 347 Bud-Arc, the tauriform god of the Arc. 1809 E. DAVIES Mythol. Druids 170 The usual residence of the tauriform god. 1877 A. W. WARD in Encycl. Brit. VII. 403/2 The tauriform sun-god whom his worshippers adored with loud cries.

Taurine (tǭ·rain), sb.¹ Chem. Also -in. [f. tauro- in taurocholic + -INE⁵.] A neutral crystallizable substance, $C_2H_7NSO_3$, *amido-ethyl-sulphonic acid*, obtained in 1826 by L. Gmelin from ox-bile, and contained in the bile of most other animals, resulting from the transformation of taurocholic acid under the influence of acids and alkalies.

1845 G. E. DAY tr. Simon's Anim. Chem. I. 47 Taurin forms colourless regular six-sided prisms, terminated by four- or six-sided pyramids. 1868 WATTS Dict. Chem. V. 701 Taurocholic acid..when boiled with water, or with alkalis,..is resolved into taurine and cholic acid. 1869 ROSCOE Elem. Chem. (1871) 438 A peculiar substance termed taurin is obtained by the action of acids on bile.

Taurine (tǭ·rəin), a. (sb.²). [ad. L. taurin-us, f. taurus bull: see -INE¹.] Of, pertaining to, of the nature of, or resembling a bull; bovine.

1613 HEYWOOD Brazen Age I. Wks. 1874 III. 176 Hadst thou not stoopt thy horrid Taurine shape I would haue peece-meale rent..thy tough hide. 1809 E. DAVIES Mythol. Druids 173 The wounding of this bull, who represented the taurine god. 1818 R. P. KNIGHT Symbolic Lang. (1876) 79 The taurine figures of Bacchus and the Rivers have more or less of the original bull. 1876 M. COLLINS Fr. Midnight to M. III. v. 57 Immovable as a taurine statue of Nineveh.

B. sb. A taurine beast, a bull. nonce-use.

1888 Harper's Mag. Apr. 783 Sturdy and stocky as a Jersey bull, and with not a little of that taurine's pugnacity.

Tauriscite (tǭ·risəit). Min. [ad. G. tauriscit (Volger 1855), from the Latin name of its locality, *Pagus Tauriscorum* (Canton Uri, Switzerland): see -ITE¹.] Native ferrous sulphate, like copperas, but occurring in acicular crystals.

1868 DANA Min. 644. 1896 CHESTER Dict. Names Min. 266.

†**Tauri·ze,** v. Obs. nonce-wd. [f. L. taur-us bull + -IZE.] intr. To play the bull, to take the form of a bull.

1727 SOMERVILLE Wife 12 What form great Jove would next devise, And when his godship would again Taurise?

Tauro-, repr. Gr. ταυρο-, combining form of ταῦρος (= L. taurus) bull, occurring in a few words derived from Greek and modern chemical terms, and in rare nonce-formations. **Tauro·latry** [-LATRY], worship of a bull (in quot. with allusion to 'John Bull'). **Tauromo·rphous** a. [Gr. ταυρόμορφος, f. μορφή form], having the form of a bull. **Tauro-se·rpentine** a., relating to a bull and a serpent. See also below.

1901 Speaker 8 June 278/2 Is not *Taurolatry the religion of Englishmen? 1891 Cent. Dict., *Tauromorphous. 1855 BAILEY Mystic 58 As told in mysteries *tauro-serpentine.

Tauroboly (tǭrǫ·bǒli). Gr. Antiq. [ad. L. taurobolium (also in Eng. use), f. Gr. ταυροβόλος striking or slaughtering bulls, f. ταῦρος bull + stem of βολή cast, stroke, wound. So F. taurobole.] The slaughter of a bull or bulls; *spec.* a pagan sacrifice of a bull in honour of Cybele, with its attendant rites, including a bath in bulls' blood; also, the representation of such a slaughter or sacrifice in sculpture, etc.

1700 tr. Danet's Dict. Grk. & Rom. Antiq., Tauropolium, or Tauropolion [sic], Sacrifices of Bulls, which were offered to Cybele,..to render Thanks..for her teaching Men the Art to tame those Animals. 1879 FARRAR St. Paul (1884) I. xviii. 187 note, Such were the taurobolies and kriobolies—hideous blood baths. 1882 [see KRIOBOLY]. 1889 FARRAR Lives Fathers I. ix. 562 He [Julian] washed away the lustral waters of baptism in the reeking horrors of a Tauroboly. 1891 Smith's Dict. Grk. & Rom. Antiq. II. 762/2 A temple of the Magna Mater where these rites of taurobolium were celebrated stood on the Vatican.

Taurochenocholic (tǭro,kīnokǫ·lik), a. Chem. [f. next, by insertion of -cheno- from Gr. χήν goose.] In *taurochenocholic acid*, a sulphuretted acid ($C_{29}H_{49}NSO_3$) found in goose-bile.

1868 WATTS Dict. Chem. V. 700.

Taurocholic (tǭrokǫ·lik), a. Chem. [f. TAURO- + Gr. χολή gall, bile + -IC: cf. CHOLIC.] In *taurocholic acid*, an acid ($C_{26}H_{45}NSO_7$) found in the bile of the ox and of most other animals, mostly together with glycocholic acid. Hence **Tauro·cholate** (tǭrǫ·kolět), a salt of taurocholic acid.

1857 MILLER Elem. Chem. III. xii. § 2. 702 Both of these resinous acids (the glycocholic and the taurocholic) contain nitrogen. The taurocholic acid also contains sulphur. Ibid. 706 The taurocholates of the alkalies are very soluble in water and in alcohol. 1872 THUDICHUM Chem. Phys. 17. 1872 HUXLEY Phys. v. 122 The taurocholate and glycocholate of soda, or bile salts, as they are sometimes called.

Tau·rocoll. rare. Also in L. form **-colla.** [ad. Gr. ταυρόκολλα, f. ταῦρος bull + κόλλα glue.] Glue made from bulls' hides.

1678 PHILLIPS, Taurocolla, a glutinous substance made out of Bulls Hides, and therefore so called, though oft times it is made of the Ears and Feet of fourfooted Creatures. 1753 CHAMBERS Cycl. Supp., Taurocolla, bull-glue, a sort of glue much used among the antients in works that required strength. 1847 WEBSTER, Taurocol. 1882 OGILVIE (Annandale), Taurocoll, Taurocolla.

Tauromachy (tǭrǫ·măki). [ad. Gr. ταυρομαχία, f. ταῦρος bull + μάχη fighting (see -MACHY): so F. tauromachie.] The practice or custom of bull-fighting; also (with *a* and *pl.*) a bull-fight.

1846 THACKERAY Cornhill to Cairo ii, It was not a real Spanish tauromachy—only a theatrical combat. 1846 Times 17 June 5/6 The art of tauromachy has just sustained an irreparable loss by the death of Montes, the Spanish matador. 1892 Cornh. Mag. Sept. 292 In the interests of civilisation and progress, it declares against the tauromachies. 1902 Munsey's Mag. XXVI. 524/2 Under the Bourbons, it [bull-fighting] went out of royal fashion, though it was still practised, and it was restored by Ferdinand VII, who established a college of tauromachy.

So **Tauromachian** (-mēⁱ·kiăn), **Tauromachic** (-mæ·kik) [F. tauromachique] adjs., of or pertaining to tauromachy.

1845 FORD Handbk. Spain I. 146 A tendency to gitanesque and tauro-machian slang. 1846 — Gatherings fr. Spain (1906) 233 The beloved monarch shut up the lecture rooms forthwith, opening..by way of compensation, a tauromachian university. 1887 Daily Tel. 17 June (Cassell), The matador is forbidden by the laws of tauromachic etiquette to attack the bull. 1894 Westm. Gaz. 13 June 2/1 There are about fifteen special tauromachic newspapers..in France.

‖**Taurus** (tǭ·rǒs). [L. taurus bull.]

1. Astron. **a.** The second of the zodiacal constellations, the Bull, in which are included the groups of the Pleiades and Hyades. **b.** Also, the second of the divisions or signs of the Zodiac, into which the sun enters on or near the 21st of April: originally identical with the constellation (cf. CANCER 2). Symbol ♉.

c 1391 CHAUCER Astrol. I. § 21 As aries hath [respect to] thin heued, & taurus thy nekke & thy throte, gemyni thyn armholes & thin armes. 1398 TREVISA Barth. De P. R. VIII. x. (Bodl. MS.), Taurus..is an erþy signe..And he is þe hous of substaunce and of ryches and possessioun of fonging & of ȝeuynge. 1588 SHAKS. Tit. A. IV. iii. 69 See, see, thou hast shot off one of Taurus hornes. 1664 BUTLER Hud. II. III. 904 Some say the Zodiack-Constellations Have long since chang'd their antique Stations Above a Sign, and prove the same In Taurus now, once in the Ram. 1667 MILTON P. L. X. 769 As Bees In spring time, when the Sun with Taurus rides. 1868 LOCKYER Elem. Astron. § 94. 36 In 1861 it was found that a small nebula, discovered in 1856 in Taurus..had disappeared.

†**2.** Zool. An obsolete genus including the common ox (now *Bos taurus*).

Taurylic (tǭri·lik), a. Chem. [f. L. taur-us bull + -YL + -IC.] In *taurylic acid*, a colourless oil (C_7H_8O) obtained together with phenol from human urine and that of cows and horses.

1868 WATTS Dict. Chem. V. 701 Taurylic acid..isomeric with anisol, benzylic alcohol, and cresol—perhaps identical with the latter. 1873 RALFE Phys. Chem. 56 Taurylic acid is a colourless, oily liquid, fluid at 18°.

Tau-staff: see TAU.

Taut, taught (tǭt), a. Forms: α. 3–4 toȝt, -e, 4 toght, touht, towt, -e, (tout); 5 towght, 5–7 (9 dial.) tought (7 toft). β. 5–9 taught. γ. 7–9 tort. δ. 8– taut. [The history of this word is in many points obscure. Though the form *taught* (now spelt *taut*) is known to us only after 1600, there is little doubt that it is the same word as the ME. *toȝt, toght, tought*, used also by Capt. Smith 1612 (and in Forby). The etymology of *toȝt, toght*, is doubtful; but it is generally held to be related in some way to the ablaut-grade *tog-, toȝ-* of OE. *téohan, téon, TEE v.¹, Goth. *tiuhan* to draw. See Note below.]

†**1.** Tense, as a surface; tight, distended, full to distention. Obs.

α. c 1325 Poem Times Edw. II 160 in Pol. Songs (Camden) 331 He maketh his mawe touht off the beste. Ibid. 238 ibid. 334 The best he piketh up him-self, and maketh his mawe touht. c 1380 Sir Ferumb. 4390 Þat ech of hem ne drof forþ on, With pakkes y-charged euerechon, Wyþ harneys y-fillid toȝte. c 1386 CHAUCER Sompn. T. 559 Than shul this cherl with bely stif and toght As any Tabour, hither ben ybrought. c 1450 Songs, Carols, etc. (E.E.T.S.) 118/24 Your brest is so towght, Tyll ye haue well cowght. 1612 CAPT. SMITH Map Virginia 28 They haue a great deepe platter of wood. They couer the mouth thereof with a skin, at each corner they tie a walnut,..with a small rope they twitch them togither till it be so tought and stiffe, that they may beat vpon it as vpon a drumme.

δ. 1878 H. M. STANLEY Dark Cont. I. xvii. 456 Their rounded bodies were as taut as a drumhead.

†**b.** fig. (?) Firm, firmly fixed or settled, clinched. (See also TOUGHT a.)

13.. E. E. Allit. P. A. 521 Gos in-to my vyne, dotz þat ȝe conne. So sayde the lorde & made hit toȝt.

2. Tightly drawn, as by longitudinal tension; stiff, tense, not slack. Chiefly in nautical use.

α. 1604 Peele's Tale Troy 256 Away they fly, their tackling toft [ed. 1589 teft] and tight. a 1825 FORBY Voc. E. Anglia, Taught, tought, tight.

β. a 1625 Nomenclator Navalis (Harl. MS. 2301), We saie sett taught ye shrowdes yᵉ staies or anie other Roape when it is to slack. 1627 CAPT. SMITH Seaman's Gram. ix. 42 Cast of that Boling.., and hale vp taught the other. 1669 STURMY Mariner's Mag. I. ii. 18 Hawl them taught and belaye them. 1793 SMEATON Edystone L. § 259 We..fixed our great tackle to it..and hove all taught. 1816 SCOTT Antiq. viii, Haul taught and belay! c 1820 G. BEATTIE John o' Arnha' 55 (Jam.) Ilk tendon, taght like thairm, was lac'd. 1828 WEBSTER, Taught [pron.] taut, stretched; not slack. 1833 MARRYAT P. Simple xxx. II. 174 The yards carefully squared, and the ropes hauled taught.

γ. a 1687 PETTY Treat. Naval Philos. I. ii, Setting of the Shrowds loose or tort as the Condition of Sailing of the Vessel requires. 1806 W. TAYLOR in Ann. Rev. IV. 773 Tort and smooth threads of flax and hemp. 1847 EMERSON Poems (1857) 99 Yet holds he them with tortest rein.

δ. 1727–41 CHAMBERS Cycl., Taught, or Tau't,..in the sea language, is the same as stiff, or fast. 1796 NELSON in Southey Life (1813) II. vi. 1 My complaint is as if a girth were buckled taut over my breast. 1840 R. H. DANA Bef. Mast xxvii, The land-breeze set in, which brought us upon a taut bowline. 1883 STEVENSON Treas. Isl. v. xxiii, The hawser was as taut as a bowstring.

transf. 1748 SMOLLETT Rod. Rand. xxiv. (1760) I. 191 Many a taught gale of wind has honest Tom Bowling and I weathered together.

b. Tightly or trimly done up; put into good order. Of a person: Neat in appearance.

1870 Daily News 1 Dec., Shops ran up shutters, everything was made taut. 1871 WHITTIER Sisters xii, In the tautest schooner that ever swam He rides at anchor in Annisquam. 1880 CLARK RUSSELL Sailor's Sweetheart vii, By breakfast-time the ship was clean and taut fore and aft. 1881 Scribner's Mag. XXI. 271/1 [She appeared] in Miss B——'s shop, taut and trim. 1887 BESANT The World went i, A fair wind, and the ship taut and trim.

c. fig. Of a person: Strict or severe as to duty.

1833 MARRYAT P. Simple xii, He was considered to be the taughtest (that is, the most active and severe) boatswain in the service. 1851 KINGSTON Pirate Medit. (1860) 4 What sort of a chap is our skipper? He looks like a taut hand.

[Note. For the interchange of *taught, tought*, cf. *aught, ought; naught, nought* (where however *au* is the earlier), and the falling together in sound in mod. Eng. of *bought, sought, wrought, brought, thought* (OE. bohte, sōhte, worhte, brōhte, þōhte) with *caught, distraught, raught, taught* (ME. cahte, distraught, OE. rǣhte, tǣhte, tāhte), where the two sounds remain distinct in Sc. (*bocht, thocht, cauwcht, tauwcht*) and northern Eng. *Toȝt, toght*, has been suggested to be:—an OTeut. *tokto' (from ablaut-grade *tog-*), which is improbable, since no trace of such a form appears in OE. or any of the cognate languages; also, to be a syncopated form of ME. *toȝed*, now *towed* (see TOW v.²); this seems impossible. With more probability it has been viewed as an altered form of ME. *tiȝt*, TIGHT, under the influence of *toȝed*, or more prob. of *toȝen* 'drawn', pa. pple. of TEE v.¹ It is noticeable that *toȝt, touȝt, tought*, occur also in ME. and Sc. as variants of TOUGH a.]

Taut (tat, tāt), v. Sc. Also **tawt, tat.** [Origin obscure: cf. TATTY a.; also TATTER sb.¹] **a.** trans. To tangle or mat together (hair or wool). **b.** intr. To become tangled or matted, as hair or wool. Hence **Tau·ted** (**tautit**) ppl. a., tangled, matted; having the hair tangled.

1782 BURNS Poor Mailie's Elegy vi, She was nae get o' moorland tips, Wi' tawted ket, an' hairy hips. 1786 — Twa Dogs 20 Nae tawted tyke, tho' e'er sae duddie. 1853 J. CRAWFORD in Whistle-Binkie (1890) II. 224 While frae the bairnie's tautit hair The frozen crystals hung. 1882 JAMIESON Supp. s.v. Tat, Dinna taut your hair sa. 1893 STEVENSON Catriona xx, God's truth, it's the tautit laddie!

Taut, var. f. TAT sb.², a coarse Indian cloth.

Taut, taute, obs. ff. *taught*: see TEACH.

Tautaug, variant of TAUTOG.

Tautegorical (tǭtĭgǫ·rikăl), a. nonce-wd. [f. TAUT(O-, after ALLEGORICAL.] (See quot. 1825.) So **Tautegory** (tǭ·tĭgǒri) [after ALLEGORY].

1825 COLERIDGE Aids Refl. 199 The base of Symbols and symbolical expressions; the nature of which as always tautegorical (i.e. expressing the same subject but with a difference) in contra-distinction from metaphors and similitudes, that are always allegorical (i.e. expressing a different subject but with a resemblance). 1825 — in Rem. (1836) II. 352 This part of the mythus in which symbol fades away into allegory but..never ceases wholly to be a symbol or tautegory. 1846 JOWETT in Life & Lett. (1897) I. v. 146 In one word he [Coleridge] had comprised a whole essay, saying that mythology was not allegorical but tautegorical. 1862 STANLEY Jew. Ch. (1863) I. vi. 136 The wilderness, as it intervenes between Egypt and the Land of Promise..is, as Coleridge would have said, not allegorical, but tautegorical, of the events which..we designate by those figures.

Tauten (tǭ·t'n), v. Also 9 **taughten.** [f. TAUT a. + -EN⁵.]

1. trans. To make taut, to or cause to become taut; to tighten.

a 1814 C. DIBDIN Song, Sailor's Jrnl., While taught'ning the forestay, I saw her faint. 1880 CLARK RUSSELL Sailor's Sweetheart III. ii. 57 The warp sang out as we tautened the bight of it. 1885 SHELDON tr. Flaubert's Salammbo xiii. 310 [Catapults] were tautened with levers, pulleys, capstans, or drums. 1903 L. BECKE in Pall Mall G. 28 Mar. 2/2 In another moment or two your line is tautened out.

2. intr. To become taut, as a rope under tension.

1849 Blackw. Mag. LXVI. 732 The dip of the hawser scarce tautening at each strain. 1879 BEERBOHM Patagonia v. 66 The shock, as the lasso tautened, threw his horse on its haunches. 1896 Strand Mag. XII. 350/2 The life-line tautened, and I was soon lifted from my feet.

Hence **Tau·tened** ppl. a., **Tau·tening** vbl. sb.

1840 R. H. DANA Bef. Mast xxiii, Our ship being very good upon a tautened bowline. 1879 Man. Artill. Exerc. 633 Wedges, oak, small..20 Tautening lashings. 1906 E. K. ROBINSON Relig. Nat. 28 The sudden tautening of the muscles.

Tauthrie, obs. f. TAWDRY. **Tautie,** var. TATTY.

Tautly (tǭ·tli), adv. [f. TAUT a. + -LY².] In a taut manner; with tautness.

1882 NARES Seamanship (ed. 6) 182 The bunt..will not allow the parrel to be passed tautly. 1882 O'DONOVAN Merv Oasis I. i. 20 A very thick cable..is drawn as tautly as possible across the stream.

Tautness (tǭ·tnes). [f. as prec. + -NESS.] The state or quality of being taut.

1861 E. S. KENNEDY in Peaks, Passes & Gl. Ser. II. I. 166 The taughtness of the rope unavoidably makes it difficult to retain a foothold. 1889 J. M. DUNCAN Clin. Lect. Dis. Wom. xxix. (ed. 4) 233 There being only a little tautness left on one side.

Tauto- (tǭto), before a vowel properly **taut-**, repr. Gr. ταὐτο-, combining form of ταὐτό, contraction of τὸ αὐτό, the same (cf. AUTO-); occurring in TAUTOLOGY, TAUTOMERISM, and their derivatives; also the following technical words, mostly of rare occurrence. **Tau·toba·ryd,** Math. [irreg. f. Gr. βαρύς heavy], that curve upon which the pressure of a heavy particle moving under gravity is the same at every point (cf. TAUTOCHRONE). **Tautogra·phical** a. [Gr. γραφικός descriptive], presenting the same geographical features throughout, monotonous in form. **Tautohe·dral** a., Cryst. [Gr. ἕδρα base], having the same face or side in common: see quot. **Tautome·tric, Tautome·trical** adjs., Pros. [late Gr. ταὐτόμετρος, f. μέτρον measure], of the same metre; having the same arrangement of syllables in the verse, or occupying the same position metrically. **Tautomo·rphous** a., Cryst. [Gr. μορφή form], applied to a symmetrical form such that corresponding points or faces of it can be brought into congruence by revolution about an axis. **Tau·tonym,** Nat. Hist. [Gr. ταὐτώνυμ-ος a., f. ὄνυμα, ὄνομα name], a scientific name in which the same word is used for genus and species; so **Tautony·mic** a., pertaining to or constituting a tautonym; **Tauto·nymy,** the use of tautonyms. **Tauto,ou·sian** (tautou·sian), **-ious** adjs., Theol. [f. eccl. Gr. ταὐτοούσιος (Epiphanius), f. οὐσία essence], having absolutely the same essence. †**Tauto·pathy** [Gr. ταὐτοπάθεια, f. πάθος suffering], suffering caused by the same thing as was habitually used previously. **Tauto·phony** [med. Gr. ταὐτοφωνία (Eustathius), f. φωνή voice], repetition of the same (vocal) sound; so **Tautopho·nic, -ical** adjs., repeating the same sound. **Tauto·pody,** Pros. [Gr. ταὐτοποδία, f. πούς, ποδ- foot], repetition of the same metrical foot; a double foot or dipody consisting of the same foot repeated twice; so **Tautopo·dic** a., belonging to or constituting a tautopody. **Tautozo·nal** a., Cryst., belonging to or situated in the same zone; hence **Tautozona·lity,** the quality of being tautozonal.

1891 Cent. Dict., *Tautobaryd. 1860 Temple Bar Mag. I. 121 Syria is the most wearying, sun-baked, *tautographical place in the world,..blinding limestone ridges, limestone mule-paths, limestone valleys, limestone everything and everywhere. 1895 STORY-MASKELYNE Crystallogr. iii. § 36 When two zones have a face in common, that is to say when their zone-circles intersect in a pole, they will be spoken of as *tautohedral in that face or pole. 1894 FENNELL in Class. Rev. Feb. 49/1 *Tautometric responsion of single words is as a rule without significance and may sometimes be due to chance. 1892 Athenæum 16 July 92/1 Mr. Bury has either failed to detect, or neglected to notice, ..κεινοῦ σὺν ἀνδρός, v. 9, *tautometrical with ἀνδρὸς φιλεῖν-, v. 20. 1895 STORY-MASKELYNE Crystallogr. vi. § 150 It is not difficult to determine whether in any particular case correlative mero-symmetrical forms are enantiomorphous or *tautomorphous; i.e. cannot be brought into congruence, or can be so brought by revolution round one or more zone-lines. 1901 Ibis Oct. 722 We cannot agree with Señor Berg that everyone ought to call..the Night-Heron *Nycticorax nycticorax*, for we do not ourselves recognise the obligations of the new system of *tautonyms. 1896 Ibid. July 364 This repeating of the specific name seems specially awkward in the cases of the unavoidable *tautonymic names. 1908 Athenæum 18 Mar. 342/1 He concluded with a proposal to get rid of *tautonymy—as in *Trutta trutta, Apus (Apus) apus*, or other comical arrangements—by a plan distinguishing what was legal in the past from what is to be legal in the future. [1678 CUDWORTH Intell. Syst. I. iv. § 36. 611 That the ancient orthodox fathers, who used the word Homoousios against Arius, intended not therein to assert the Son to have one and the same singular or individual essence with the Father, appeareth plainly from their disclaiming and disowning those two words, Tautoousion and Monoousion. Concerning the former of which, Epiphanius thus;..'We affirm not the Son to be Tautoousion, (one and the same substance with the Father) lest this should be taken in any way of compliance with Sabellius'.] Ibid., Athanasius..disclaimeth a monoousian Trinity, as Epiphanius did before a *tautoousian: both of them a Trinity of meer names..they alike distinguishing them from the homoousian Trinity, as a Trinity of real Hypostases or Persons. 1846 WORCESTER, Tautoöusian, *Tautoöusious, having the same identical essence. 1882 OGILVIE, Tautoöusian, same as Tautousian...Tautousian, Tautousious, in theol. having absolutely the same essence. 1652 N. CULVERWELL Treat. I. xvii. (1661) 152 Anacreon..by a most emphatical *Tautopathy, was choak'd with the husk..of a Grape. 1847 WEBSTER, *Tautophonical..*Tautophony. 1881 G. W. MOON Revisers' Eng. xxiv. (1882) 64 They say 'That ye may be sons of your Father which is in heaven: for he maketh his sun to rise'..tautophony, suggestive of a pun. 1898 F. HARRISON in 19th Cent. June 942 If your ear does not hear the false note, the tautophony or the cacophony in the written sentence as you read it. 1891 Cent. Dict., *Tautopodic..*Tautopody. 1878 GURNEY Crystallogr. 21 They are also said to be *tautozonal, by which is meant that they all lie in one and the same zone. 1895 STORY-MASKELYNE Crystallogr. iii. § 36 Two or more poles (or their faces) are said to be tautozonal or heterozonal with a third, according as they lie in the same or different zone-circles (or zones) with it. 1880 L. FLETCHER in Philos. Mag. Feb. 84 The property of *tautozonality is a permanent one.

Tautochrone (tǭ·tǒkroᵘn). Math. [f. TAUTO- + Gr. χρόνος time: cf. F. tautochrone (Dict. Trévoux 1771).] That curve upon which a particle moving under the action of gravity (or any given force) will reach the lowest (or some fixed) point in the same time, from whatever point it starts. So **Tautochronism** (tǭtǫ·krŏniz'm), the property of a tautochrone; **Tauto·chronous** a., having the character of a tautochrone; occupying the same time, isochronous.

a 1774 GOLDSM. Surv. Exp. Philos. (1776) II. 142 The time spent in determining the figure of a tautochrone might have been more usefully employed in this research. 1842 BRANDE Dict. Sc., etc. s.v., Newton and Hermann also determined the tautochrone in a vacuum, when gravity is supposed to be directed towards a given centre. Newton likewise showed that the cycloid is also the tautochrone in a resisting medium, when the resistance is proportional to the velocity. 1842 Exam. Papers 47 (Dubl. Univ. Cal. 1843), Prove that the cycloid is the only plane curve possessing the property of tautochronism. 1846 SMART Suppl., Tautochronous, arriving at the same time; having the property of the tautochrone.

Tautoclin (tǭ·toklin). Min. [ad. Ger. tautoklin (Breithaupt 1830), f. Gr. ταὐτό (TAUTO-) + κλίνειν to bend, incline; so called 'because it has the same rhombohedral angle as dolomite' (Chester).] A greyish-white variety of ANKERITE.

1868 DANA Min. (ed. 5) 685.

Tautog (tǭtǫ·g). Also **tautaug, totaug.** [ad. Narragansett *taut-auog*, pl. of *taut* name of the fish: see quot. 1643.] A labroid fish, *Tautoga americana* (*T. onitis*), also called *black-fish* or *oyster-fish*, abundant on the Atlantic coast of N. America, and esteemed for food.

1643 ROGER WILLIAMS Key to Lang. of America xix. 115 Of Fish and Fishing. Taut-añog. Sheeps-heads. 1828–32 WEBSTER, Tetaug, the name of a fish on the coast of New England; called also black fish. 1848 BARTLETT Dict. Amer., Tautaug. 1851 HAWTHORNE Ho. Sev. Gables xviii, Real turtle, we understand, and salmon, tautog, canvass-backs, pig, English mutton. 1888 G. B. GOODE Amer. Fishes 288 'Tautog' would consequently seem to be a word from the dialect of the Narragansett Indians.

Tautographical, -hedral: see TAUTO-.

†**Tau·tolite.** Min. Obs. [ad. Ger. tautolit (Breithaupt 1826); 'adapted from [Gr.] ταὐτόμετρος of the same measure, referring to a supposed axial relation, and λίθος' (Chester); see TAUTO- and -LITE.] An obsolete synonym of ALLANITE.

1828 Philos. Mag. May 398 The tautolite seems to be related to the chrysolite, as the ceylanite to the spinelle. 1868 DANA Min. (ed. 5) 286 Bucklandite is anhydrous allanite in small black crystals...Tautolite..is probably the same species.

Tautologic (tǭtolǫ·dʒik), a. rare. [f. Gr. ταὐτολογία TAUTOLOGY + -IC: cf. the adv. ταὐτολογικῶς in Eustathius c 1160.] = next, 1.

1828 Blackw. Mag. XXIV. 906 Dr. Johnson..he charges ..with a plethoric and tautologic tympany of sentence. 1858 CARLYLE Fredk. Gt. VII. v. (1872) II. 287 No end of florid inflated tautologic ornamental balderdash.

Tautological (tǭtolǫ·dʒikăl), a. [f. as prec. + -AL: see -ICAL.]

1. Pertaining to, characterized by, involving, or using tautology; repeating the same word, or the same notion in different words.

1620 T. GRANGER Div. Logike 387 Lest thy discourse be tedious, Tautologicall, erroneous. 1670 BLOUNT Law Dict. s.v. Alnager, Measurer, and Alneger, which last, though it be a Tautological expression (Aulnage and Measure, being the same thing denoted in two Languages) yet long usage and custom have brought them to distinct Offices. 1800 in Four C. Eng. Lett. (1880) 355 Now and then, in the career of declamation, he becomes tautological and ineffective. 1869 INGLEBY Introd. Metaph. II. ii. 176 One writer..desperately declares that the Laws of Motion are mere truisms, or tautological judgments.

2. Of an echo: Repeating the same sound several times. ? Obs.

1677 PLOT Oxfordsh. 7 These return syllables and words, the same oftentimes repeated, and may therefore be stiled Tautological Echo's. 1807 JOYCE Sci. Dial. xiii. (1846) 232 Called tautological or babbling echoes.

†**3.** loosely. Of the nature of a repetition, identical (*with*). Obs. rare⁻¹.

1689 G. HARVEY Curing Dis. by Expect. xvi. 125 Compound Waters..tautological the one with the other.

Tautologically (tǭtolǫ·dʒikăli), adv. [f. prec. + -LY².] In a tautological manner, with tautology.

1620 T. GRANGER Div. Logike 292 Handle the same matter (homogeneously, not tautologically). 1820 COLERIDGE Let. C. A. Tulk 17 July (in Pearson's Catal. (1894) 14) At once superfluous and defective, tautologically superfluous in the point of co-equality, and dangerously defective in that of the subordination. 1840 HOOD Up Rhine 61, I join with Dr. Watts' sluggard in wishing tautologically, for 'a little more sleep and a little more slumber'.

So **Tautolo·gicalness** (Bailey 1727 vol. II).

Tautologism (tǭtǫ·lŏdʒiz'm). rare. [f. TAUTOLOGIZE: see -ISM.] The use or practice of tautology; an instance of this. Used by Farrar *spec.* for the combination of two synonymous words or syllables for the sake of precise expression of the meaning, as in Chinese.

1815 Sporting Mag. XLVI. 117 Hard and callous, form a tautologism. 1816 BENTHAM Chrestom. 293 The reproach of tautologism,—incurred..by the observation. 1869 FARRAR Fam. Speech iv. (1873) 122 This chaos [of homonyms in Chinese]..is reduced to order and meaning..partly by what may be called tautologism, i.e. by using a *second* synonym to define the word which is vague; in point of fact, by making two vague words into one definite word.

Tautologist (tǭtǫ·lŏdʒist). [f. as prec. + -IST.] One who practises tautology.

1708 STEELE Funeral I. 14 Oh! that Damn'd Tautologist too—That [Mr.] Puzzle and his Irrevocable Deed! 1727 BAILEY vol. II, Tautologist, one who says the same Things over and over. 1805 W. TAYLOR in Ann. Rev. III. 649 All such literary tautologists are proper objects of epitomization.

Tautologize (tǭtǫ·lŏdʒəiz), v. [f. TAUTOLOGY + -IZE. (The Gr. equivalent was ταὐτολογεῖν.)

Cf. APOLOGIZE.] intr. To repeat the same thing in the same or different words; to use tautology. Also with *it* (quot. 1656).

1607 TOPSELL Serpents (1658) 761 To take occasion to tautologize, or to speak one thing twice. 1615 JACKSON Creed IV. iv. § 1 Even the most acute amongst the schoolmen whiles they seek to clear this doubt do but falter and tautologize. 1656 S. H. Gold. Law 1 We are constrained ..to Tautologize it in repetitions, even to a wearying of our selves and the world with words. ?16.. Plutarch's Mor. IV. 220 (L.) The tautologizing babler, if he be a physitian, certainly is more troublesome than the disease.

Hence **Tauto·logizer,** one who tautologizes; a tautologist.

1657 J. WATTS Vind. Ch. Eng. 241 A vain babler, a tautologizer and a vain repeater.

Tautologous (tǭtǫ·lŏgəs), a. [f. Gr. ταὐτολόγ-ος repeating what has been said (f. ταὐτό the same + -λογος saying, f. λέγειν to say) + -OUS.] = TAUTOLOGICAL 1.

1714 J. FORTESCUE-ALAND Pref. Fortescue's Abs. & Lim. Mon. 67 The County of Devon, in the old way of Speaking.. called the County of Devonshire, which is the constant Expression in old Deeds, and signifies the same thing tho' it be tautologous. 1786 H. TOOKE Purley I. ix. 406, I have been purposely tautologous, that by my indifferent application of the two words *of* and *for*..the smallest..opposition between these prepositions might be done away. 1853 Fraser's Mag. XLVII. 358 The circuitous jargon—the tautologous gabble..of special pleading. 1884 SIR W. B. BRETT in Law Times Rep. 10 May 315/2, I have come to the conclusion..that the Legislature intended in this case to be verbose and tautologous, and to say the same thing twice over.

Hence **Tauto·logously** adv. = TAUTOLOGICALLY.

1865 J. P. COLLIER Bibl. Catal. I. 109 It begins thus tautologously: 'The present plagues that now we fele'. 1904 Westm. Gaz. 22 Oct. 3/2 'Fraud-pilfered'—the indictment is tautologously complete.

Tautology (tǭtǫ·lŏdʒi). [ad. late L. tautologia (c 350 in Mar. Plotin. Sacerd.), a. Gr. ταὐτολογία, f. ταὐτολόγος: see TAUTOLOGOUS; in F. tautologie.] **a.** A repetition of the same statement. **b.** The repetition (esp. in the immediate context) of the same word or phrase, or of the same idea or statement in other words: usually as a fault of style.

1587 FLEMING Contn. Holinshed III. 1553/1 This ambassage is reported in the historie of Scotland, whereunto (for the auoiding of tautologie) we refer the reader. a 1653 GOUGE Comm. Heb. (1655) 99 To shew that there is no tautology, no vain repetition of one and the same thing therein. 1686 GOAD Celest. Bodies I. xii. 56 The Taedium of Tautology is odious to every Pen and Ear. a 1748 WATTS Improv. Mind II. ii. § 4 By securing you from an appearance of tautology, or repeating the same words too often. 1790 WESLEY Wks. (1872) IV. 487 That villanous tautology of lawyers, which is the scandal of our nation. 1869 FARRAR Fam. Speech iv. (1873) 134 One leading syllable thrusting itself with the most obtrusive tautology through a whole sentence.

c. With *a* and *pl.* An instance of this; a tautological phrase or expression; †a repetition *of* something already said (quot. 1599).

1579 FULKE Confut. Sanders 644 It is a foolish tautologie, for you sayed the same immediatly before. 1599 Broughton's Let. ix. 32 Euery later paperwork of yours is but a Tautology of the former. 1698 WANLEY in Lett. Lit. Men (Camden) 258, I called the library a venerable place; the Books sacred reliques of Antiquity, &c.; with half a dozen tautologies. 1844 LD. BROUGHAM Brit. Const. xix. § 1 (1862) 309 Repetitions and tautologies are used.

d. Applied to the repetition of a statement as its own reason, or to the identification of cause and effect.

1659 PEARSON Creed ii. (1839) 157 To assign any thing as the cause or reason of itself, is a great absurdity, and the expression of it a vain tautology. 1662 H. MORE Philos. Writ. Pref. Gen. (1712) 15 The resolution of such Phaenomena as we experience in ourselves..into this vital oneness,..is no vain Tautology, or the mere saying a thing is so because it is so. 1836–7 SIR W. HAMILTON Metaph. (1859) II. xxxix. 377 There is thus conceived an absolute tautology between the effect and its causes. We think the causes to contain all that is contained in the effect; the effect to contain nothing which was not contained in the causes.

e. transf. A mere repetition of acts, incidents, or experiences; in quot. 1650, used for the sending of a thing to its place of origin.

1650 FULLER Pisgah II. v. 128 Some wil object it was a real tautology to bring purples to Tyre, seeing the best of the world were made in that place. 1657 W. DILLINGHAM Contn. Siege of Ostend in Sir F. Vere's Comm., It was so thick stuck with bullets, that the Ordnance could scarcely shoot without a tautologie, and hitting its former bullets. 1687 NORRIS Coll. Misc. (1699) 324 Our whole Life is but a nauseous Tautology. 1863 COWDEN CLARKE Shaks. Char. i. 14 The poet has avoided a dramatic tautology (if I may so use the term) in bringing about the death of two worthy men immediately upon the heels of each other.

Tautomerism (tǭtǫ·mĕriz'm). Chem. [f. Gr. ταὐτο-, TAUTO- + μέρος part, after ISOMERISM; rendering Ger. tautomerie (Laar 1885).] The property exhibited by certain organic compounds of behaving in different reactions as if they possessed two (or more) different constitutions, that is, as if the atoms of the same compound or group were arranged in two (or more) different ways, expressible by different structural formulæ (e.g. the group —CH:C(OH)—, or —CH₂.CO—, in ethyl aceto-acetate). So **Tautomer** (tǭ·tŏmər), any one of the forms of a tautomeric compound in relation to another; **Tautomeric** (tǭtome·rik) a., pertaining to or exhibiting tautomerism; **Tautomery** (tǭtǫ·mĕri) [ad. Ger. tautomerie], = tautomerism.

1885 CONRAD LAAR in Ber. Dtsch. Chem. Ges. XVIII. 652 Um die gegenseitige Beziehung gleichberechtigter Formeln ..kurz bezeichnen zu können, schlage ich hierfür den Ausdruck 'Tautomerie' vor.] 1886 tr. Richter's Organic Chem. (1899) I. 55 Laar..assumes that such compounds consist of a mixture of structural isomerides, in that an easily mobile hydrogen atom oscillates between two positions in equilibrio, and thereby the entire complex becomes mobile. He designates the phenomenon as tautomery. 1890 GOLDSCHMIDT & MEISSLER in Jrnl. Chem. Soc. LVIII. 499 Assuming that in the reactions of tautomeric compounds which take place under the influence of electrolytes, the intramolecular change is brought about by the free ions. 1890 NEF ibid. 983 A discussion of the alleged cases of tautomerism in ethyl succinosuccinate and analogous compounds. 1901 DIXON ibid. LXXIX. 543 Hitherto no isomerism (or tautomerism) has been established amongst mineral derivatives analogous to that subsisting between the normal and *iso*thiocyanates of organic radicles. 1903 Amer. Chem. Jrnl. May XXIX. 406 It [thio-urea] may react with the metal [silver] to form a sulphide, or its tautomer may form an insoluble silver compound. 1904 Ibid. Dec. 606 There are ten possible tautomeric formulas for this phenylacetylurazole, and four possible positions for the acetyl group. 1905 WALKER Chem. Soc. Annual Rep. 9 It is suggested that an absorption band appears wherever there is tautomeric change within the molecule.

Tautometric to **Tautozonal**: see TAUTO-.

Tavarn, obs. form of TAVERN.

†**Tava·sco.** Obs. Variant of TABASCO.

1652 WADSWORTH Chocolate 14 Some doe put into it [chocolate] black Pepper, and also Tauasco.

Tave (tēⁱv), v. Now dial. Also 7 **tauve**, 8–9 **taave**, 9 **teave**. [app. of Norse origin: cf. Norw. dial. *tava* to toil or struggle without much effect, to fumble, be exhausted.] intr. To move the limbs ineffectually, to sprawl; to strike out at random with the arms or legs; to throw oneself about, as a person in a passion, in a fever, etc.; to act violently in any way; to strive, toil, labour, or struggle in work, difficult walking, etc.

c 1350 St. Mary Magd. 401 in Horstm. Altengl. Leg. (1881) 85 Sethin it [the child] swelid and turned & tauyd. 14.. Beryn 2061 Sith yee of hym be sesid, howe evir so yee [?hee] taue, Let hym nevir pas. 1566 DRANT Horace A iv, Where now and then (O just rewarde) in raginge surge sum taves. 1674 RAY N. C. Words 47 To Tave; Lincoln. to rage. 1691 Ibid. 73 Sick People are said to *tave* with the Hands when they catch at any thing. 1681 HICKERINGILL Black Non-Conf. Postscr., Wks. 1716 II. 168 Him that bespoke a Picture of a Horse lying (tauveing) upon his Back. 1790 MRS. WHEELER Westmld. Dial. (1821) 40, I wur sae teerd wie maanderin up an dawn an teaavin ith ling, I laaid me dawn on a bread Scar, an sean fel asleep. 1825 BROCKETT N. C. Words, Taving, irregular motion; picking the bed-clothes in febrile delirium. 1828 Craven Gloss., Tave, to kick with the feet like a distracted person. 1855 ROBINSON Whitby Gloss., To Teeave, to paw and sprawl with the arms and legs. 1891 T. HARDY Tess xii, See how I've got to teave and slave, and your poor weak father with his heart clogged like a dripping-pan.

Tave = *to have*: see T¹ and HAVE v.

†**Tavel,** sb. Obs. Forms: 1 tæfl, tæfel, 3 tævel, tavel. [OE. tæfel fem., = WGer. *tabal, ON. tafl, OHG. zabal, ad. late L. or Com. Romanic tav(o)la:—L. tabula table, board, esp. board to play on, in which sense it was taken app. bef. 400 into WGer. See TABLE.] A die for playing with; also, a game of chance, or the board on which it is played. Also *attrib.* Hence (in OE.) **tæfl-stán**, a piece or 'man' for playing with, a die; (ME.) **tævelbred** = TABLE-BOARD 1, ON. *taflborð*; (OE.) **tæflere**, a player at tavel or with dice.

a 800 Erfurt Gloss. 6 Alea, tefil. c 1000 ÆLFRIC Voc. in Wr.-Wülcker 150/21–5 Alea, tæfel. Aleæ, tæfelstanas. Aleator, tæflere. Pirgus, cyningstan on tæfle. Tessere, uel lepusculæ, feðerscite tæfel. c 1000 in Thorpe Codex Exon. 331/19 Dryhten..dæleð sumum tæfle cræft, bleo-bordes gebregd. Ibid. 345/2 Hy twegen sceolon tæfle ymb sittan ..habban him gomen on borde. c 1205 LAY. 8133 Summen pleoden on tæuelbrede. c 1275 Ibid., Somme pleoide mid tauel.

†**Ta·vel,** v. Obs. [OE. tæflian, f. tæfel, TAVEL sb.] intr. To play at dice.

a 1100 Voc. in Wr.-Wülcker 267/8 Cotizo, ic tæfle. a 1250 Owl & Night. 1666 Riȝt swa me gred þe manne a schame, þat taueleþ & forleost þat gome.

Tavel, early var. of TEVEL v. Obs. or dial.

Tavelett, obs. form of TALLET.

†**Ta·velin.** Obs. Also 5–6 **tavelyn**, 6 **-yng, -ing, tavalyn.** [app. ad. It. *tavolino* 'any little boord, table, tablet' (or some cognate word), dim. from *tavola* 'a table, planke, or flat boorde' (Florio).] Formerly, with furriers, (in *pl.*) app. the boards between which small packages of skins were imported; hence, a small package of skins or certain portions of fur (usually or always four), put up between two boards. (Cf. TIMBER, applied to a package of forty skins between two stout boards of timber (Skene).)

1439 Inv. T. Burgh (Comm. Crt., Lond., Prowet 22), xxx lose tavelyns xv d. 1503 Privy Purse Exp. Eliz. of York (1830) 89, iiij tavelyns of shankes for the coler and fent of the said gowne, ijs. 1505 Acc. Ld. High Treas. Scot. III. 42 Item, for xiiij tavalyns of ermyng to the samyn goun, brocht be the Quenis maister of wardrob; ilk pece ij s. iiij d, summa..vj li. x s. 1545 Rates of Customs C vij b, Tauelynges the hundreth vj s. viij d. 1586 Ibid. E viij, Taueling the c, xiij s. iiij d.

†**Ta·vell.** Silk-weaving. Obs. exc. as Fr. **tavelle** (tave·l). Also 6 **tavel, tavyll, tavil.** [a. F. *tavelle* (in sense 2), app. ad. L. *tabella* tablet.]

†**1.** The bobbin on which silk is wound for use in the shuttle. Obs.

1523 SKELTON Garl. Laurel 791 To weue in the stoule sume were full preste, With slaiis, with tauellis, with hedellis well drest. a 1529 — Agst. Comely Coystrowne 31 Wele sped in spyndels and turnyng of tauellys. 1530 PALSGR. 279/2 Tavell an instrument for a sylke woman to worke with. 1538 ELYOT, Liciatorium, a weauers shyttel, or a sylke womans tauell, wheron sylke or threde beinge wounden, is shot through the web or lome. 1620 THOMAS Lat. Dict. s.v. Liciatorium.

‖**2.** (mod. Fr. **tavelle.**) A large drum or bobbin on which the silk is wound off the cocoons.

1868 Rep. U. S. Commissioner Agric. (1869) 286 These [machines] consisted of, 1st, a series of tavelles to wind, clean, and equalize the threads during their automatic winding off [etc.].

Taver (tēⁱ·vəɹ), sb. Sc. Also 9 **taiver.** [app. of Norse origin: cf. Norw. *tave* clout, rag, any torn piece of stuff, Da. *tave* fibre, filament of tow, wool, etc.] A mere shred or filament; a 'rag' (of meat).

1808 JAMIESON, Taivers, s. pl. tatters; as, boiled to taivers, Fife. 1819 TENNANT Papistry Storm'd (1827) 15 Sorrow gin Paip was boil'd to taivers, And I'd a platefu' o' the bree! 1822 GALT Steam-boat xii. 288 They don't know how to cook yonder..they boil the meat to tavers.

Taver (tēⁱ·vəɹ), v. Sc. Also 9 **taiver.** [freq. of TAVE v.] intr. To wander vaguely or aimlessly; to wander mentally, to talk incoherently as one delirious; to talk idly and foolishly. Hence **Ta·vering** vbl. sb. and ppl. a., wandering, etc.; **Ta·vert** ppl. a., fatigued or exhausted with wandering, or with toil or struggle; incoherent, confused, stupefied, stupid; also **Ta·versome** a., fatiguing, exhausting.

1535 STEWART Cron. Scot. (Rolls) III. 420 Fra hill to hill rynnand as tha war hyrit, In mure and mos so tavert war and tyrit. a 1598 ROLLOCK Serm. Wks. 1849 I. 435 He callis our warkis tavering, going out of the way. Ibid. 436 His actiounis ar taverings, all wandring out of the way. [So ed. 1599; ed. 1616 wauering, wauerings.] 1808–18 JAMIESON, Taiver, to wander;..to rave as mad...Taiversum, tiresome, fatiguing. Taivert. 1822 GALT Sir A. Wylie xxx, Ye wouldna hae me..to sit till I'm tavert?..I fin' the wine rinnin in my head already. 1823 — Entail xviii, I would na trust the hair o' a dog to the judgment o' that tavert bodie, Gibby Omit. 1887 J. SERVICE Dr. Duguid xxii, The taivert tenets of the Antiburgher Kirk.

Tavern (tæ·vəɹn), sb. Forms: 3–7 taverne, (4 tavarn, 5 tawern, 6 taverin, Sc. taveroun), 7– tavern. [a. OF. taverne (1256 in Littré):—L. *taberna* a shed constructed of boards, a hut, booth, stall, shop, workshop, also a tavern or inn (so in earliest French and Eng. examples). Cf. TABERN.]

1. In early use, A public house or tap-room where wine was retailed; a dram-shop; in current use = PUBLIC HOUSE 2 b.

See also humorous use (word-play on name *New Inn Hall*) in quot. 1904.

[1286 Memoranda K. R. 14 & 15 Edw. I 3 b, Tauernes ke sunt en meimes la Meisun ke est assise par entre la Meisun Thomas le Vineter vers le Su.] 1297 R. GLOUC. (Rolls) 4024 Hor ydelnesse hom ssa. bringe to sunne of lecherye, To tauerne & to sleuþe, & to hasardrie. 1303 R. BRUNNE Handl. Synne 1025 Tauerne ys þe deuylys knyfe Hyt sleþ þe, oþer soule or lyfe. 1340 Ayenb. 56 Þe tauerne ys þe scole of þe dyeule huere his deciples studieþ. c 1440 Jacob's Well 147 Þe tauerne is welle of glotonye, for it may be clepyd þe develys scolehous. 1570 B. GOOGE Pop. Kingd. IV. 53 This done, they to the Taverne go, or in the fields they dine. 1593 SHAKS. Rich. II, v. iii. 5 Can no man tell of my vnthriftie Sonne?..Enquire at London, 'mongst the Tauernes there. 1611 COTGR., Tavernier,..a Victualler, of whom (as in our Tauernes of London) one may haue meat, and drink for his money. 1693 Humours Town 108 The Taverns are the Nurseries of Profaneness and Treason. 1710 SWIFT Lett. (1767) III. 14, I dined to-day at a tavern with Stratford. 1785 TRUSLER Mod. Times III. 76 When we reached London.. we put up at one of those taverns called hotels. 1809 KENDALL Trav. III. lxxii. 128 The doctor keeps a public house, or, as the term is, a tavern. 1840 DICKENS Barn. Rudge ii, This tavern would seem to be a house of call for all the gaping idlers of the neighbourhood. 1904 Westm. Gaz. 11 May 1/2 Richard Shute—the only first-class man ever produced by the defunct 'Tavern', as New Inn Hall [Oxford] used to be called.

†**2.** A shop or workshop attached to or under a dwelling-house; often under ground, a cellar. Cf. CELLAR 2, WINE-CELLAR. dial. Obs.

1521 in Test. Ebor. (Surtees) VI. 4 Al my tymber and bordes in the Taverne, except a kilnehouse of x postes that lieth in the laithe and in the gaitehouse. 1566 in S. O. Addy Evolution Eng. House (1905) 96 William Tomson for his taverne stare, iiij d. 1575 Ibid. 95 Payd to ij dykers for casting earth furth of the taverne iiij daies, ij s. viij d. 1583 Will Myles Fox (Somerset Ho.), My Shop with two undershops or Taverins. 1703 THORESBY Let. to Ray (W. Yorksh. Words), Tavern, a cellar. 1905 ADDY (as above) 94–5 In England shops in front of town houses were sometimes known as 'taverns',..and were below the surface of the streets, like cellars...These 'taverns' were entered by stairs.

3. As a rendering of L. *taberna*: see the etymology.

1382 WYCLIF Acts xxviii. 15 Whanne bretheren hadden herd, thei runnen to vs til to the cheping of Appius, and to a place that is clepid Thre tauernes [Vulg. tres Tabernas]. 1611 BIBLE ibid., They came to meet vs as farre as Appii forum, and the three Tauernes.

4. attrib. and Comb. **a.** Attributive, as *tavern-bill, -boy, -bully, -bush* (BUSH sb.¹ 5), *-chair, -discourse, -door, -drawer* (DRAWER sb.¹ 2), *-fellow, -house, -lady, -lantern, -man, -music, -quarrel, -reckoning, -score, -supper, -talk, -wine*, etc. **b.** Objective and obj. gen., as *tavern-frequenter*, †*-ganger, -goer, -haunter, -hunter, -hunting, -keeper, -tracer*. **c.** Instrumental, locative, etc., as *tavern-gotten, -tainted* adjs. **d.** Special combs.: †**tavern-fox**, in phr. *to hunt a tavern-fox*, to get drunk: see FOX sb. 1 d and v. 2; **tavern-token**, a token given in change by a tavern-keeper, which he will again accept in payment; † *to swallow a tavern-token*, to get drunk (obs.).

1611 SHAKS. Cymb. v. iv. 161 You shall..fear no more *Tauerne Bils. 1796 H. HUNTER tr. St.-Pierre's Stud. Nat (1799) III. 286 The appellation of 'good man', so frankly bestowed on him by the *tavern-boy. 1852 THACKERAY Esmond II. i, A *Tavern-bully beaten. 1570 FOXE A. & M. (ed. 2) 1206/1 Seing good wyne nedeth no *tauerne bushe to vtter it. a 1668 DAVENANT News fr. Plymouth Wks. (1673) 2 In the Metropolis,..Where still your Taverne Bush is green and flourishing. 1787 SIR J. HAWKINS Johnson 87, I have heard him assert, that a *tavern-chair was the throne of human felicity. 1660 R. COKE Justice Vind. Pref. 12 The subject of all *tavern-discourses. 1474 Coventry Leet Bk. (E. E. T. S.) 400 Yf he sell any feetiff wyn his *Tauerne durre to be sealed Inne, and he to make a fyne at the kynges wyll. a 1704 T. BROWN Lond. & Lacedem. Oracles Introd., Wks. 1709 III. III. 124 The Oyster-wench in her lawful Occupation at the Tavern-door. 1721 CIBBER Rival Fools I. i, Can't you practise..upon a *Tavern-Drawer, or a Box-keeper at the Play-House? 1899 Month June 613 The roystering joviality of Prince Harry's *tavern-fellow. 1635 J. TAYLOR (Water P.) Old Parr C ij b, Nor did hee ever hunt a *Taverne Fox. 1483 Cath. Angl. 378/2 A *Tawern ganger, attabernio. 1797 T. PARK Sonn. 82 Meeting with some *tavern-goer. 1538 ELYOT, Circumcelliones, *tauerne haunters, or raylers aboute. 1583 GOLDING Calvin on Deut. li. 305 These Tauernhaunters or Alehouse Knightes which counterfeit the preachers. 13.. Cursor M. 28462 (Cott.) Til *tauerne huse my-seluen was wont, And draun men þer-til vnstont. 1553 BECON Reliques of Rome (1563) 28 The aforesayd pope made..a decree, that priestes should be no *tauern-hunters. 1641 MILTON Animadv. xiii. Pr. Wks. (1847) 69/2 Their laziness, their *tavern-hunting, their neglect of all sound literature. 1611 COTGR., Tavernier,..a *Tauerne-keeper. 1779 Mirror No. 46 ¶ 23 Familiar..to the very tavern-keepers of this city. 1763 MRS. F. SHERIDAN Discovery II. i, I don't doubt but he is going to some of his *tavern-ladies. 1664 ETHEREDGE Love in Tub IV. ii, Go with a *Tavern-Lanthorn before me at Noon-day. 1755 JOHNSON, *Tavernman, one who keeps a tavern. 1643 SIR T. BROWNE Relig. Med. II. § 9 That vulgar and *Taverne-Musick. 1820 HAZLITT Lect. Dram. Lit. 30 Marlow was stabbed in a *tavern quarrel. 1714 MANDEVILLE Fab. Bees (1724) I. 19 Those, that remain'd,..when they paid their *Tavern Score, Resolv'd to enter it no more. a 1680 BUTLER Rem., Charac. (1759) II. 439 He is the Whores Jackal,..and at Night has his Share in a *Tavern-Supper. 1760 Cautions to Officers Army 124 Tavern-Suppers are generally expensive. 1609 Ev. Woman in Hum. III. i. in Bullen O. Pl. IV, Urge no more, 'tis *Taverne talke. 1638 FORD Lady's Trial II. ii, You are grown a tavern-talk, Matters for fiddlers' songs. 1598 B. JONSON Ev. Man in Hum. I. iii, Drunk sir? perhaps he swallow'd a *tauerne token, or some such deuise sir. 1604 Meeting Gallants 17 Indeed he had swallowed downe many Tauerne-tokens, and was infected with the plague of drunkennes. 1604 DEKKER Hon. Wh. I. iv, If he have but..a spleene not so big as a taverne token.

Hence (mostly *nonce-wds.*), **Ta·vernize** v. intr., to frequent taverns; **Ta·vernless** a., devoid of taverns or inns; **Ta·vernly** a., smacking of the tavern; **Ta·vernous** a. [after *cavernous*], tavern-like; **Ta·vernry,** tavern-expenses; **Ta·vernwards** adv., towards a tavern.

1851 Fraser's Mag. XLIV. 425 The frequent *tavernising, if we may coin a word, is another peculiarity. Pepys was a giant in this way, and sang and roystered..in the public houses of the day. 1897 'MARK TWAIN' More Tramps Abroad lxxi, The Bishop..was once making a business-progress through the *tavernless velt. 1612 SHELTON Quix. (1746) I. III. ii. 119 So returning him Thanks with *Tavernly Phraze for his large Offers. 1866 LD. HOUGHTON Sp. in Life (1890) I. ii. 73 The low..ill-lit, cavernous, *tavernous gallery. a 1670 SPALDING Troub. Chas. I (1851) II. 102 Thay comptit and reknit for thair *tavernrie with ther mistressis. 1892 Daily News 10 Mar. 2/4 Thirty young fellows..were promptly on the 'double' *tavernwards.

Ta·vern, v. Now rare or Obs. [f. prec. sb., as a rendering of med.L. *tabernāre*, f. *taberna* (common in 14–15th c.).]

†**1.** trans. Of a leaseholder or copyholder: To subdivide his tenement; ?*orig.* to erect a cottage (*taberna*) on his holding, and apportion a piece of land to it. north. Obs.

[1365 Durham Acc. Rolls (Surtees) I. 38 Idem Johannes illud [tenementum] tabernavit sine licencia. Ibid. 42 De Johanne Anderson pro licencia tabernandi unum cotagium. 1402 Charta (Du Cange), Ne scolaribus detur occasio mercandi seu Tabernandi.] 1534 Augm. Off., Convent. Leases, Yorks. No. 888 That the said Thomas and Roger his sonne..shall not taverne the said fermhold nor no parcell therof bot to dwell and remane of the said fermhold apon payn [etc.]. 1551 Richmond Wills (Surtees) 72 If it happ my wife to latt or taverne any parte of said fermehold, (not beyng of habilitie to occupie the same) then I will that Roland my eldest sonne have it. 1575 [see TAVERNING 1]. 1577 Eccl. Proc. Bp. Barnes (Surtees) 18 And doe not let out, lease out, or taverne out, their livings.

2. intr. To frequent taverns; also *to tavern it*.

1580, etc. [see TAVERNING 2]. 1610 Histrio-m. VI. 209 Each..taverns it with drunken suppers still.

†**b.** trans. with *out*: To spend in 'taverning'.

1628 FELTHAM Resolves II. [I.] lvii. 164 When, like Nero, thou should'st Taverne out thy time with Wantons.

Taverner (tæ·vəɹnəɹ). Also 4 **tavernyer, tavarnere,** 5 **tawerner, -yrner, tavernere,** 6 **-ar,** Sc. **-eir,** 7 **-o(u)r;** (5 **taberner**). [a. AF. taverner = OF. tavernier used in senses 1 and 2 below (c 1200 in Godef. Compl.), f. taverne, TAVERN, or:—post-cl. L. *tabernārius* shopkeeper.]

1. One who keeps a tavern; a tavern-keeper. arch.

13.. Sir Beues (A.) 4357 He askede at þe tauarnere, Þat armede folk, what it were. 1340 Ayenb. 44 And zelleþ ontreweliche, ase doþ þise tavernyers þet uelleþ þe mesure myd scome. 1382 WYCLIF Ecclus. xxvi. 28 The tauerner shal not be iustified fro synnes of lippis. 14.. Nom. in Wr.-Wülcker 688/19 Hic tabernarius, taberner. 14.. Lytyll Thanke 19 in Ritson Anc. Songs (1792) 78 They callyd the tawyrner to ffyll þe quarte, And lette note for the coste. 1500–20 DUNBAR Poems xxxiv. 46 (R. MS.) 'Be Godis bluid', quod the taverneir, 'Thair is sic wyne in my selleir As neuir come in this cuntrie'. 1530 PALSGR. 279/2 Tavernar a wyne sellar, tauernier. 1603 HOLLAND Plutarch's Mor. 46 Are you become indeed a Tavernour, Whose father was a woorthy governour? 1720 STRYPE Stow's Surv. II. 194/1 This Company anciently consisted of..The Vinteners, who were the Merchants that imported Wine.., and the Taverners, who kept Taverns for them, and sold it out by Retayl. 1760 J. ADAMS Diary Wks. 1850 II. 85 [He] may..multiply taverns and dram shops, and thereby secure the votes of taverner and retailer. 1868 E. EDWARDS Ralegh I. iv. 66 Under the powers of the assigned patent, [he] considerably increased the number of licensed taverners.

†**2.** One who frequents a tavern or taverns; a tippler. Obs.

1340 Ayenb. 51 Vor alþeruerst he becomþ tauernyer, þanne he playþ ate des. 1579 TWYNE Phisicke agst. Fort. II. xc. 278 b, There is..nothyng more vayne then typplers and Tauerners. 1612 T. TAYLOR Comm. Titus i. 7 (1619) 129 So should I be a swearer? a taverner? a drunkard?

Ta·verning, vbl. sb. Now rare or Obs. [f. TAVERN v. + -ING¹.] The action of the verb TAVERN.

†**1.** See TAVERN v. 1. Obs.

1575 SIR J. FORSTER in St. Papers Eliz., Borders XIX. 81 (P.R.O.) When anye Inhabitant here hath..a Tenement ..scant sufficient for the meinteignaunce of one person, yf he chaunce to dye havinge two sonnes, he devydeth the said Tenement betwixt them bothe, and thus the taverninge of the Queynes lande ys hinderance for kepinge of hors and armor.

2. The action or practice of frequenting taverns.

1580 in Liturg. Serv. Q. Eliz. (Parker Soc.) 574 The Sabboth days..is spent full heathenishly, in taverning, tippling, gaming, playing and beholding of Bear-baiting and Stage plays. 1597–8 BP. HALL Sat. II. i, Or wicked Rablais dronken revellings, To grace the mis-rule of our tavernings. 1654 WHITLOCK Zootomia 503 Another cries out on the ones Taverning (where he would not spend a six pence, he never knew any come to good that did). attrib. 1837 New Monthly Mag. LI. 41 No wonder that, with these taverning habits, Jonson lived poor and died no richer.

3. The keeping of a tavern.

1774 J. WENTWORTH in F. Chase Hist. Dartmouth Coll. (1891) I. 264 Inquiring into the reasons of granting license to Mr. Payne for taverning and retailing.

Tavert, ppl. a.: see TAVER v.

Tavism, variant of TAOISM.

†**Ta·vistock.** Obs. In 6 **Tave-.** A woollen cloth formerly made at the town of Tavistock.

1535–6 Act 27 Hen. VIII, c. 12 § 3 Any clothes called Tavestockes, Westerne doseyns, Friseys, Kendalles, Cottons, and all manner of course clothes made for lyyynges. 1545 Rates of Customs d iij b, vj Tauestockes for a clothe. [1551–2 Act 5 & 6 Edw. VI, c. 6 § 29 Any Clothe or Clothes made in the Towne of Tavestoke in the Countie of Deuon..commenlye called Tavestoke Clothes.]

Tavistockite (tæ·vistǫkəit). Min. [Named by Dana, 1868, from *Tavistock*, a town in Devonshire, where found: see -ITE¹.] 'Hydrous phosphate of aluminum and calcium, found in microscopic acicular crystals' (Chester *Names Min.*).

[1865 A. H. CHURCH in Jrnl. Chem. Soc. 264 Our present mineral is from Tavistock, Devonshire.] 1868 DANA Min. 582 Tavistockite.

†**Tavorsay.** Old Cookery. Obs. [?] A dish of spiced cod's head and liver.

c 1450 Two Cookery-bks. 114 Tauorsay. Nym ye hed of ye codlyng & ye liuere, & pike out ye bones, cast therto goud poudre of piper & gyngiuer, and gif forth.

†**Taw,** sb.¹ Obs. rare. [f. TAW v.¹]

1. Tawed leather; white leather.

c 1562 in J. T. Gilbert Calr. Anc. Rec. Dublin (1891) II. 23 Gloves, purses, whit tawe and suche like wurke apperteyninge to thoccupacion of glover.

2. A thong, whip, lash.

Perh. a different word; app. the sing. of TAWS, TAWSE (which is evidenced much earlier).

1787 GROSE Provinc. Gloss., Taw, a whip. N. 1853 W. WATSON Poems 28 (E.D.D.) The nippy taw Comes whiskin' whiles athort us a'. [1864 WEBSTER, Taw,..(pl.). A whip or instrument of punishment used by a schoolmaster.]

Taw (tǭ), sb.² Also 8 **tau,** 9 **tor.** [Origin unascertained, and order of senses uncertain: perh., like *alley*, ALLY sb.², an abbreviation.]

A large choice or fancy marble, often streaked or variegated, being that with which the player shoots.

1709 STEELE Tatler No. 30 ¶ 1 He is hiding or hoarding his Taws and Marbles. a 1761 CAWTHORN Wit & Learn. Poems (1771) 48 He minded but his top, or taw. 1807, 1833 [see ALLY sb.²]. 1837 DICKENS Pickw. xxxiv, After enquiring, whether he had won any alley tors or commoneys lately. 1843 THACKERAY Irish Sk. Bk. xxiv, Large agate marbles or 'taws'. a 1845 HOOD Clapham Acad. xiv, Five who stoop The marble taw to speed. 1857 HUGHES Tom Brown I. iii, His small private box was full of peg-tops, white marbles (called 'alley-taws' in the Vale), [etc.]. 1876 GRANT Burgh Sch. Scotl. II. v. 179 A still greater favourite is shooting a 'taw', which requires no small dexterity.

b. transf. A game played with such marbles.

1709 STEELE Tatler No. 112 ¶ 3 A Game of Marbles, not unlike our modern Taw. 1784 COWPER Tiroc. 307 To kneel and draw The chalky ring, and knuckle down at taw. 1798 Sporting Mag. XII. 169 At cricket, taw, and prison-bars, He bore away the bell. 1840 THACKERAY Paris Sk.-bk. (1869) 45, I would lay a wager that..their school learning carried them..only to the game of taw.

c. The line from which the players shoot in playing the game. Hence in phrases: see quots.

1740 DYCHE & PARDON s.v. Knuckle, They frequently say, Knuckle down to your taw, or fit your hand exactly in the place where your marble lies. 1854 MISS BAKER Northampt. Gloss. s.v., 'Shoot from taw'. 'You don't stand at taw'..'If you don't do so and so I'll bring you to taw'. 1881 Leicesters. Gloss. s.v., A ring is scratched on the ground, and at some distance from it a straight line called taw. Ibid., We thus get the phrases..'come up to scratch' and 'come up to taw'.

†**Taw,** sb.³ Obs. rare. [Derivation unascertained.] A rootlet, a fibre of a root.

1615 W. LAWSON Country Housew. Gard. (1626) 16 Though they get some hold in the earth with some lesser taw, or tawes, which giue some nourishment to the body of the tree. Ibid. 24 To dresse the roots of trees, to take away the tawes, and tangles, that lap and fret and grow superfluously. 1670 CAPT. J. SMITH Eng. Improv. Reviv'd 58 A Plant by its Roots and Tawes, or Fibres, sucks in the Juice of the Earth. 1765 Museum Rust. V. 117 Its root..is round, and thick set with taws.

Taw (tǭ), v.¹ Forms: 1 tawian, 3 (Orm.) tawwenn, 3–4 tauwen, 4–6 tawe, 6– taw. [OE. *tawian* = MLG., MDu., Du. *touwen*, LG. *tauen*, *töwwen* to prepare (leather), to tan, to curry, OHG. *zawjan, zowjan* (MHG. *zouwen, zöuwen*) to prepare, make, Goth. *taujan* to do, make:—OTeut. *tawðjan and *tawjan; from a stem *taw-, tōw-*, not certainly found in pre-Germanic.]

1. trans. To make ready, prepare, or dress (some raw material) for use, or for further manipulation; e.g. to soften (hides) by beating, to heckle (hemp), etc.; † in early use, to till (land).

a 900 tr. Bæda's Hist. IV. xxix. (1890) 366 Þa bæd se Godes man þæt him man isern geloman mid hwæte ðyder brohte þæt land mid to tawienne. c 1200 ORMIN 15903 All swa summ þe nowwt i ploh þe turrnenn erþe & tawwenn. 1545 Rates of Customs C v, Sylke tawe[d] and died the pounde viii s. 1555 W. WATREMAN Fardle Facions II. ix. 193 He.. taweth the skinne betwixte his handes, vntill it become very souple and soft. 1628 Robin Goodfellow II. (1841) 28 And whilst that they did nimbly spin, The hempe he needs must taw. 1651 BIGGS New Disp. Pref. 7 Being tawed open by wedge after wedge. 1861 Jrnl. Brit. Archæol. Assoc. Mar. 20 A slick-stone for tawing or softening hides by friction.

2. spec. To make (skins) into leather by steeping them, after suitable preparation, in a solution of alum and salt; the product is white and pliant, and is known as *alum, white*, or *Hungarian leather*.

(In early quots. not separable from sense 1.)

a 1225 Ancr. R. 418 Þet heo [ower cloðes] beon unorne & warme, & wel i-wrouhte—uelles wel i-tauwed. a 1300 Sat. People Kildare ix. in E. E. P. (1862) 154 Daþeit þe sotter þat tawiþ ȝure leþir. c 1410 Master of Game (MS. Digby 182) vi, Þe furrure..is not feyre; and also it stynketh euer, but if hit be wele ytawede. 1474 Coventry Leet Bk. (E.E.T.S.) 401 The sise of a whittawer is that he make nor tawe no maner of lether but Shepes lether, Gettes lethir, deris ledur, horse-lethir, or houndes-lether. 1560 Let. in Hakluyt Voy. (1598) I. 307 If you send 100 of them [seal skins] tawed with the haire on, they will bee solde, or else not. 1607 TOPSELL Four-f. Beasts (1658) 45 The hides..being tawed and wrought artificially they make garments of them. 1613 FLETCHER, etc. Captain III. iii, Yes if they taw him as they do whit-leather Upon an iron. 1711 Lond. Gaz. No. 4862/4 Mills..where they shall Tan, Taw or Dress..any such Hides. 1877 KNIGHT Dict. Mech., Tawing, a process of tanning in which mineral agents are substituted for vegetable extracts. 1879 Cassell's Techn. Educ. IV. 88/1 Carefully-prepared goat-skin, tanned, tawed, dyed, and grained.

†**3.** fig. To treat (a person) abusively or with contumely; to vex, torment; to harass, afflict; to abuse, outrage, profane. Obs.

c 893 K. ÆLFRED Oros. IV. i. § 1 Þa þe þær gefongne wæron, hie tawedan mid þære mæstan unieðnesse. c 1000 ÆLFRIC Saints' Lives (1890) II. 102 Forðan ðe he godes templ tawode to bysmore. c 1000 — Hom. II. 486 And se deofol eow tawode þurh his drymen. a 1023 WULFSTAN Hom. xxxiii. (Napier) 162 [Hi] scendað and tawjað to bysmore þæs þegnes cwenan and hwilum his dohtor. 13.. Minor Poems fr. Vernon MS. liv. 76 To a piler I was I-piht, Togget and tauwed al þe niht. 1549 CHALONER Erasm. on Folly G ij, To be briefe, they are not tawed nor plucked asunder with a thousand thousand cares.

b. To whip, flog, thrash. Obs. exc. dial.

1600 HOLLAND Livy VIII. xxviii. 301 He caused him to be stripped naked, and whipping cheare to be presented unto him. The poore stripling thus pitteously tawed and torn, ran

Taw, *v.* form of TAU, TOW.

†**Tawa**, *sb.* [The Maori name.] A tall and handsome forest tree of New Zealand, *Beilschmiedia (Nesodaphne) Tawa*, N.O. *Lauraceæ*, with damson-like fruit; allied to the Tawhai, but distinct from the natives.

†**Tawai**, *v.* to awake: see T.

Taw, *sb.* form of TAU, TOW.

Tawern, -bron, -burn, *Sc. var.* TABORN *Obs.*

Tawhe, tawcht, *obs. Sc.* forms of TALLOW.

Tawhti, *obs. Sc.* f. *told, ta.* t. and pple. of TELL.

Tawd, *obs. Sc.* f. *told, ta.* t. and pple. of TELL.

†**Tawder**, *v.* *Obs.* *nonce-wd.* [. TAWDRY *a.*] *trans.* To deck out in tawdry finery.

Tawdrily (tǫ'drĭli), *adv.* [f. TAWDRY *a.* + -LY²]. In a tawdry manner; with cheap finery.

Tawdriness (tǫ'drĭnes), *sb.* [f. TAWDRY *a.* + -NESS.] The quality of being tawdry.

†**Tawdrum**. *Obs. nonce-wd.* A tawdry decoration.

Tawdry (tǫ'drĭ), *sb.* and *a.*

Tawdry lace. *Obs.* [See T (the letter 7.]

†**Tawer** (tǫ'a). Forms: 4-7 *tawier*, 5-6 *tawyer*, 6 *tawar*, 6 *tawour*.

Tawern, *obs. form* of TAVERN.

Tawing (tǫ'ĭŋ), *vbl. sb.* [f. TAW *v.*²]

Tawhe, tawcht, *obs. Sc.* forms of TALLOW, TAWD, *obs.*

†**Tawdryne**. *Obs.*

†**Tawn**, *sb.* *Obs. rare⁻¹.*

†**Tawne**, *v.* *Obs. rare⁻¹.*

Tawny (tǫ'nĭ), *a.* and *sb.* Forms: *a.* 4-7 *tauny*, 5-*tawny*; also 4 *tawne*, (4-5 *taunde*), (6 *tawney*), 6-7 *tanne*, 5-6 *tanne*, *tany*; 5-7 *tannye*, *tawnee*.

†**Tawny-moor**, sb. *Obs. rare.* f. BLACKMOOR.]

Tawpie, tawpy (tǫ'pĭ), *sb.* and *a. Sc.* and *north.*

†**Tawse, tawes** (tǫz), *sb. pl.* *Chiefly Sc.* Forms: 6 *tawis*, -es, 8 *taws*, 9a. 8-*tawse*.

Tawt, Taut *v.,* Tawte, tawth, *obs. f.* TAUGHT: see TEACH *v.* Tawyer, *var.* TAWER.

Taws, *obs. f.* TAWSE.

Tax (tæks), *sb.* [a. F. *taxe*.]

Tax (tæks), *sb.* [a. OF. *taxer* (13th c. in Littré), ad. L. *taxāre* to censure, charge, tax with a fault; to rate, value, reckon, compute (at so much), assess, valuation of; in med.L. also to impose a tax.]

Taxable (tæ'ksăb'l), *a.* (*sb.*) [f. TAX *sb.* + -ABLE.]

Taxableness (tæ'ksăb'lnes), *sb.* [f. prec. + -NESS.]

Taxably *adv.*, in a taxable manner; in quot. 1906, in relation to taxation.

Taxaceous (tæksē'shŏs), *a.* *Bot.* Belonging to the N.O. *Taxaceæ* (see -ACEOUS), including the yews.

†**Taxage** (tæ'ksĕdʒ). *Obs. rare⁻¹.*

†**Taxation** (tæksē'shŏn). *sb.* [a. AF. *taxacioun* (1216 in Th. Cange), = Taxation.]

Taxaspidean (tæksăspĭ'dēăn), *a.* *Ornith.* [f. mod.L. *taxaspidea*, neut. pl. (f. Gr. τάξις arrangement + ἀσπίς shield.)]

Taxation (tæksē'shŏn), *sb.* Forms: *a.* taxacioun, 5-7 -acion, 6 -atioun; *Sc.* taxatioun, 7 taxation, -tion. *b.* 6- taxation.

Taxative (tæ'ksătĭv), *a. rare.* [ad. med.L. *taxātīvus* (Alcuatus c 1325), f. *taxāt-*, ppl. stem of *taxāre* to TAX: see -ATIVE.]

Taxe, *obs. f.* TAX.

†**Taxed**, *ppl. a.* [f. TAX *v.* + -ED¹.]

†**Taxel**. *Obs.*

Taxer (tæ'ksə(r)). Also 5-6 *-our.* [ad. med.L. *taxātor*, agent-n. from *taxāre* to TAX. So *taxateur* (16th c. in Hatz.-Darm.)]

†**Tax-cart.** *Obs.* = *Taxed cart:* see TAX, 2.

Taxi- (tæ'ksĭ-), Gr. τάξι-, combining form of Gr. τάξις arrangement.

Taxiarch (tæ'ksĭɑːk). *Anc. Gr. Hist.* [ad. Gr. ταξίαρχος, f. τάξι- + ἄρχειν to rule.]

Taxi-cab, taxicab *pl.* ... [Short for TAXIMETER *cab*, and itself shortened to TAXI.] A cab for public hire, fitted with a taximeter; *sp.* an automobile or motor-cab so furnished.

Taxicorn ...

Taxidermal ...

Taxidermic ...

Taxidermist ...

Taxidermize ...

Taxidermy ...

Taxin ...

Taxing ...

Taxinomy ...

Taxis ...

Taxite ...

Taxing ...

Taxinomy ...

Taxonomy ...

Taxon ...

Taxor, -our ...

Taxpayer, tax-payer ...

Taxus ...

Taxwax ...

† Tay, tey, *Obs.* ...

Taxy ...

Taxology ...

Te, ME. assimilated form of THE, THEE, after dentals, etc.; see T 8.

Te, obs. or dial. variant of TO-.

Tea ...

Tayse, var. TEISE sb. and v. *Obs.* TAYT var.

Tea ... 124 ... TEA. TEA. 125 TEACH.

TEACH.

A. Illustration of Forms.

1. *Infin.* ...

2. *Past pple.* ...

3. *Pres. Indic.* ...

4. *Past tense.* ...

B. Signification.

1. To show, etc.

2. To show or point out.

5. *To teach a thing*: To impart or convey the knowledge of; to give instruction or lessons in (a subject); to make known, deliver (a message). With simple obj. or obj. clause.

6. To teach a person a thing ...

7. To teach a person or agent ...

Teachable, variant of TACHE sb.[2]

Teached (tī́ʃt), *ppl. a. Obs. or arch.* — TAUGHT.

Teacher (tī́ʃəɹ), *sb. ... Forms: ... -ure, -our. [TEACH v. + -ER.]**

1. That which teaches or points out; an indicator; the index-finger. *Obs.*

2. One who or that which teaches or instructs; an instructor, esp. in a school.

3. *absol. or intr.* To communicate knowledge; to act as a teacher; to give instruction.

Teachable (tī́ʃəb'l), *a.* [TEACH v. + -ABLE.]

1. Able or apt to teach, *Obs.*

2. Capable of being taught (as a person); apt to receive instruction; docile; tractable.

3. Capable of being taught (as a subject); that may be communicated or imparted by instruction.

Hence **Teachable-ness**.

Teachableness.

The quality or state of being teachable.

Tea-chest. [f. TEA sb. + CHEST sb.[1]]

Teaching, *vbl. sb.* Forms: see the verb. [f. TEACH v. + -ING.[1]]

1. The action of the verb TEACH.

2. The imparting of instruction or knowledge; the occupation or function of a teacher.

Tea-drinker. One who drinks tea, *esp.* one who drinks it habitually or in large quantities.

Tea-drinking, *vbl. sb. & a.* The drinking of tea; a social gathering at which tea is provided (*obs.*); also *attrib.*

Tea-garden. A garden or open-air enclosure, connected with a house of entertainment, where tea and other refreshments are served.

Tea-gardened, *a.*, having a tea-garden ...

Teagle. ...

Tea-gown ...

Teague (tīg), *sb.* ... A nickname for an Irishman.

Tea-growing ...

Teak. A large East Indian tree (*Tectona grandis*, N.O. Verbenaceae), with opposite egg-shaped leaves and panicles of white flowers; the heavy, hard, durable wood.

Teal. A small fresh-water fowl, *Querquedula* or *Anas crecca*, or other species of the ducks.

TEALT.

Tea-leaf. The leaf of the tea-plant; *esp.* in *pl.* the leaves after being infused to make the beverage.

Tea-leaved (tī́-lī́vd), *a.* having leaves like those of the tea-plant; *spec.* applied to a species of willow (*Salix phylicifolia*).

Tealess (tī́les), *a.* [f. TEA sb. + -LESS.] Without tea; not having had one's tea.

Tealt ... *a. Obs.* [Orig. *teald adj.*] ...

TEAM.

Team (tīm), *sb.* ... Forms: 1-4 team, tem, (1-7 theam, theame), 3-6 teme, 4 teome (5-7 them), 4-7 teame, 5 tayme, 6 thame, 7- team. [OE. *tēam* ...]

1. The bringing forth of children; child-bearing. *Obs.* [Cf. MHG. *kint ziehen* to bring forth children, *Ger. viehzucht* cattle breeding.]

2. A family or brood of young animals; now *dial.* applied to a litter of pigs, a brood of ducks.

3. Two or more beasts, or a single beast, along with the vehicle which they draw; a horse and cart, or wagon with two horses (now *dial.*).

III. In Anglo-Saxon Law.

Tealte, Teally, *obs. ff. TILT, TILTH, TETCHY, TEETHILY*.

Teaming, *vbl. sb.* Forms: see the verb. [f. TEAM v. + -ING.[1]]

Supplement, p. 3873; Corrigenda, p. 4092; Spurious words, p. 4093; Books quoted, p. 4094

Teamer. One who drives a team; a teamster.

Teaming, *vbl. sb.*

Teamless, *a.*

Teamster. The driver or owner of a team.

Teamwise, *adv.*

Team, *v.* Also 6 teem.

Tea-maker.

Teaman, tea-man. A merchant who deals in tea; a tea-dealer.

Tea-planter. One who makes it his business to cultivate tea-plants.

Tea-pot. A pot with a lid, spout, and handle, in which tea is made or brought to table.

Teapoy (tī'poi). *Anglo-Ind.* Also **tepoy.**

Tear (tēr). *sb.[1]* Forms: see below.

Tea-plant. The plant from which tea is obtained.

Tea-party.

Tea-plate.

Tea-poy.

Tear (tēā), *sb.[2]*

Tear, *v.[1]*

Tearable (tēə'răb'l), *a.*

Tea-bottle.

Tearage.

Teare, obs. form of TEARE, TIERCE.

Teard, obs. pa. t. and pa. pple. of TEAR[1].

Teare, obs. form of TEAR, TIER.

Tearer (tēə'rər).

Tearful (tīə'fŭl), *a.*

Tearing, *vbl. sb.*

Tearing, *ppl. a.*

Tearing-machine.

Tea-sage = Tea-scrub: see TEA.

Tea-scrub.

Tease (tīz), *v.*

Tearless (tīə'lĕs), *a.*

Tea-rose.

Teart, obs. and dial.

Teary (tīə'ri), *a.*

Tease, v.² *local*. Also teaze. [ad. mod.F. *tiser* (technical) 'to introduce fuel into a melting-furnace' (Littre); to fan a furnace; to stir up for *attiser* = It. *attisare*, Sp., Prov. *atisar* to stir (the fire), f. à- = *ad* to + Lat. *titio* a firebrand.] *trans.* To feed (a furnace fire) with fuel; to attend to (a fire or furnace).

Teased (tīzd), *ppl. a.* [f. TEASE v.¹ + -ED¹.]
1. Having the fibres pulled asunder: see TEASE v.¹ 1. In quot. 1620 *fig.* Also *teased out*.

Tea-ze-hole. [f. TEASE v.² + HOLE sb.]

Teasel, teazle (tī'z'l), *sb.* Forms: 1 tæsl, tæsel. 3-5 tasel, 5 teasyll, 5-7 teasle, 5-7 teasell, 6 teaill, teasell, tayzyll, 6-7 teasle, teaszell, teasel, -ill, 7-8 teazil, 7- teasel, teasle, teasel, 8 teasle. 4-5 -ly, 4-6 -yll, 6 -ollie, teazyll, 5-7 tassel, 6 teazell, -yll, teasayll, 6-7 teasell, 7 tassill, teasle, teasell, 8 teasill. [OE. *tǽsel*, -sil; see TEASE v., HOSE.]

Teasel, teazle, v.¹ *trans.* To raise a smooth nap on (cloth) with or as with teasels; to tease. Also *transf.* Hence **Tea·seling** (teazling) *vbl. sb.*, [also *attrib.*].

Teasel-head.

Teaser (tī'zər), *sb.* [f. TEASE v.¹ + -ER¹.]
1. One who teases, vexes, or puzzles.

Teasing (tī'ziŋ), *vbl. sb.* [f. TEASE v.¹ + -ING¹.]
1. The pulling asunder of the fibres of wool, hair, animal tissue, etc.; see TEASE v.¹

Teaser (tī'zlər), *sb.*

Teaser (tī'zər), *sb.*²

Teasing (tī'ziŋ), *ppl. a.* [f. TEASE v.¹ + -ING².]

Tea·sing, *ppl. a.*

Teasish, Teasy: see TETCHY, TESTY.

Teat (tīt). Forms: 2 titt, titte, 3-5 tytte, 3 giat tit, 4 tete, tette, 4-5 teete, 4-7 teate, tete, 6 tete, 6-8 teate, teate, 8 tutte. [OE. *tit*(t masc., cognate with MDu., MLG. *titte*, LG. *titt*, tite (Du. dial. *tet*); late MHG. *zitze* fem., Ger. *zitze* masc., etc., *zitzmeuz*, and fem. wk. *Tüt* (*tittie*) are two dialectal.]

Tea-table. [f. TEA sb. + TABLE sb. 6.]
1. A table at which tea is taken, or on which tea-things are placed for a meal.

Teatish, Teaty: see TETCHY, TESTY.

Teat-tree.

Tea-taster.

Tea-thing, -time, etc.: see TEA sb. 9.

‡ Techir (tekbīr). Also **tekbir**. [Arab. *takbir* 'to magnify, proclaim the greatness of'; inf. of 2nd form of *kabara* to be great.] See quot. 1708.

Techie, obs. form of TETCHY, TEACHY.

Techie, obs. f. TEACH v.

Techie, Techy, etc., obs. ff. TETCHY, etc.

Technic (te·knik), *a.* and *sb.* L. *technic-us* (Quint.), a. Gr. *τεχνικ-ός* of or pertaining to art, f. *τέχνη* art, craft : see -IC. So F. *technique* (1731 in Hatz.-Darm.)

Technical (te·knikăl), *a.* (*sb.*) [f. Gr. *τεχνικ-ός* (see TECHNIC) + -AL.]

Technicality (teknikæ·liti), *sb.* [f. prec. + -ITY.]

Technically (te·knikăli), *adv.* [f. as prec. + -LY.]

Technician (tekni·ʃăn), *sb.*

Technicist (te·knisist), *sb.*

Technico-, combining form of TECHNIC, as in technical terms.

Technics (te·kniks), *sb. pl.*

Technique (tekni·k), *sb.*

Techno- (te·kno), repr. Gr. *τεχνο-*, combining form of *τέχνη* art, occurring in TECHNOLOGY, etc.

Technologer (tekno·lŏdʒər), *sb.*

Technological (teknolo·dʒikăl), *a.* [f. TECHNOLOGY + -IC + -AL.]

Technologically, *adv.*

Technologist (tekno·lŏdʒist), *sb.*

Technology (tekno·lŏdʒi), *sb.* [ad. Gr. *τεχνολογία* systematic treatment (of grammar, etc.), f. *τέχνη* art, craft : see -LOGY. So F. *technologie* (1812 in Hatz.-Darm.).]
1. A discourse or treatise on an art or arts; the scientific study of the practical or industrial arts.

Tectology (tekto·lŏdʒi), *Biol.* [ad. Ger. *tektologie* (Haeckel), f. *τεκτ-* carpenter, builder (f. ARCHITECT) + -LOGY.]

Tectonic (tekto·nik), *a.* [ad. late L. *tectonic-us*, a. Gr. *τεκτονικ-ός* pertaining to building, f. *τέκτων* carpenter, builder.]

Tectorial (tektō·riăl), *a. Anat.* [f. L. *tectōri-um* a covering, f. *tect-* (see TECTUM) + -AL.]

Tectum (te·ktŏm), *Anat.* [ad. L. *tectum* roof.]

Ted (ted), *v.* Forms: 3-6 tedd, 5-7 tedde, 7 teds, 6- ted. [prob. a. ON. *teðja* to spread dung.]
1. *trans.* To spread out, scatter, or strew abroad (new-mown grass) for drying.

Teenfully, **Teenful**, etc.

Teenfully, adv. Obs. sorrowfully, sadly, lamentably, grievously; harmfully, injuriously; angrily, wrathfully.

Teen, Teen's, obs. ff. TEEN.

Teenty, a. U.S. colloq. From TEENY. Very tiny, delicately small.

Teeny (tī'nī), a.[1] Obs. exc. dial. Characterized by 'teen'; malicious; peevish.

Teeny (tī'nī), a.[2] and colloq. An emphasized form of TINY; esp. in childish use. Also in comb. teeny-tiny; teeny-weeny.

Teer (tī·ɹ), v. Now dial. and techn. Also teer, terre, app. 6. OF. terre, terrer.

Teer, obs. f. TAR, TEAR, TIER.

Teercel, **Teerd**, **Teerus**, **Teers**, obs. ff. TERCEL, TIERD, TERM, TIERCE. **Teery-leery**, etc.

Teese, obs. f. TEASE; var. TEISE sb.[2] Obs.

Teesoo (tī·sū), E. Ind. Also teso, teeso, teeso, tiaao.

Teetee (tī·tī), sb.[1] Also titi. [Native name in Tupi.]

Teetee, obs. f. TEAT.

Teeter (tī·tǝɹ), v. dial. and U.S. Also teeter, teeter-board.

Teeth, pl. of TOOTH sb.

Teeth (tīθ), v. Obs. rare.[1]

Teethe (tīð), v.

Teething (tī·ðiŋ), vbl. sb. [f. TEETHE v. + -ING.]

Teethy (tī·θi), a. dial.

Teety, tetty, a. Now dial. Obs. q[uasi]-teety.

Teg (teg), sb.

Teint, -e, obs. ff. TAINT, TENT, TINT.

Teetotal (tītō·tǎl), a. and sb.

Teetotaller, **-aler**, [as prec. + -ER.[1]]

Teetotally, adv.

Teetotalism (tītō·tǎliz'm), sb.

Teetotalise, -ize (tītō·tǎləiz), v.

Teetotum (tītō·tǒm), sb.

Teind, etc.

Teetotaller, **-aler**, [as prec. + -ER.[1]]

Tegment (te·gment), sb. rare.

Tegmental (tegme·ntǎl), a.

Tegmen (te·gmen), sb. Pl. -mina.

Tegmentum (tegme·ntǒm), sb. Pl. -ta.

Tegmental (tegme·ntǎl), a.

Tegre, obe. form of TIGER.

Teguexin (te·gwǝksin). Zool.

Tegula (te·giǔla), sb. Entom.

Tegular (te·giǔlaɹ), a.

Teguly, adv.

So Te·gulated a.

Tegumen, obs. form of TEGMEN.

Tegument (te·giǔment), sb.

Teichopsia (təikǒ·psiǎ). Path.

Tei, obs. f. TY.

Teian (tī·ǎn), a. See forms of TIE sb., TACHE sb.[1]

Teicher, Sc. and north. f. TEAR sb.[1] and v.

Teil, **Teile** (tīl). Now chiefly Sc. and dial.

Teind (tīnd). Chiefly Sc. and north. Forms: 3-5 tend, -e.

Teind (tīnd), v. Now Sc. and north. Obs. Forms: see TEIND sb.; cf. tithe v.

Teine, obs. bad spelling of TINE.

Teinscope (təi·nǒskoup), sb.

Teint, -e, obs. ff. TAINT, TENT, TINT.

Teinter, pa. f. TENTER, TEINTURE. etc.

Teise, taise sb. Obs. Also 5 teis, toys, tayse.

Teise, taise v. Obs. Also 5 teyse, teas.

Teist (tīst, tī·ist), local.

Tek, **teken**, adv. and prep. Obs.

Teke, teken, adv. and prep. Obs.

Teko, obs. form of TEAK, TICK.

Tel-, repr. Gr. τηλε-.

Tela (tī·lǎ), sb. Anat.

Telamon (te·lǎmǒn), sb. Archit.

Telang- (tǝlang-).

Telangiectasis (tǝlandʒie·ktǎsis). Path. Pl. -ases.

Telangiectatic (tǝlandʒie·ktǎtik), a.

Telar ... *rare*—[f. L. *tēla* web + -ar.] Pertaining to or of the nature of a web. Hence **Te'larly** *adv.*, in the manner of a web. So **Telaration** (tēlə̆rē'ʃən) ..., that spins a web, as a spider.

Telari, telapoon : see TALAPOIN.

Te'lary ...

Telautograph (telǭ'tǫgraf) *sb.* [f. Gr. *τῆλε* afar off + AUTOGRAPH, after *telegraph*.] A telegraphic apparatus by which writing or drawing done with a pen or pencil at the transmitting end is reproduced in facsimile at the receiving end, by means of an electric current conveyed along a wire, and (in the usual form of the instrument) communicating movements to the receiving pen corresponding to those made with the transmitting pen or pencil. Hence **Telautogra'phic** *a.*, pertaining to the telautograph; **Telau'tography**, the use of the telautograph.

Teld, *sb. Obs.* Forms: 1 teld, 1, 4-5 tielde, (3 tield), 4 teild, teuld, 4-5 tilde, 5 tild, -te, telde, ... [OE. *teld*, *geteld* = OLG. *tteld*, OHG. *telto*, Kilian), MLG. *telt*, MHG., ... OHG. *zelt* (mostly *gizelt*), MHG. *zelt* (usually *gezelt*), Ger. *zelt*; ...] A tent, pavilion, covering; hence, a tabernacle, dwelling.

Tele, *v. Obs.* Forms: 1 telan (telan), 2-3 tælen (3 teolen), 3-5 tielen, 3-4 tele. [OE. *téon* *téalan* (Angl. *téian*) ... see TELE 1 *sb.*]

+ Tele, *int. Obs.* Forms: 1 tǣl, 4 tēl, ... snare, trap, ... **Teling** *vbl. sb.*

Telega (tĕlĕ̄'gǎ). Also 6 telenga, **telegga**, **telga**, (telegua). [a. Russ. *telĕga*, ...] A four-wheeled Russian cart, of rough construction, without springs.

Telegony (tĕlĕ'gŏnĭ). [f. Gr. *τῆλε* afar + *-γονια*.] The supposed influence of a previous sire on the progeny of a subsequent sire from the same mother.

Telegram (te'lĭgræm). [f. Gr. *τῆλε*, TELE- + -GRAM, after *telegraph*.] A message sent by telegraph; a telegraphic dispatch or communication.

Telegraph (te'lĭgraf), *sb.* [a. F. *télégraphe*.]
1. An apparatus for transmitting messages to a distance, usually by signs of some kind. ...

Telegram ...

Telegrapher (te'lĭgrafə̆r) ... [f. TELEGRAPH.]

Telegraphic (telĭgra'fĭk), *a.* [f. as prec. + -IC; cf. F. *télégraphique*.]

Telegraphist (te'lĭgrafist, tĕlĕ'grafist). [f. as prec. + -IST.] A person employed, or skilled, in working a telegraph.

Telegraphy (tĕlĕ'grafĭ). [f. as prec. + -Y.]

Teleosaurus (telǐ-ǫsǭ'rǒs). ...

Teleostean (telǐǫ'stǐǎn), *a. and sb.* [f. mod.L. *teleostei* ...] Belonging to or characteristic of the teleost fishes.

Tellable (tel′ab′l), a. [f. TELL v. + -ABLE.] Capable of being told or related; fit to be told; that may be told or is tellable.

Tellar, var. TILLER sb. 3, a young tree.

Tell-box, etc.: see TELL.

Tellen (te′len). [ad. L. tellina a Gr. τελλίνη.] A bivalve of the genus Tellina or family Tellinidae.

Teller (te′lər). Also 4-7 tellere, telar, etc. [f. TELL v. + -ER¹.] One who or that which tells, in various senses.

Tell-, the stem of TELL v. in combination with sbs.

Tellership (te′lərʃip). [f. TELLER + -SHIP.] The office or position of a teller.

Tellicherry (tel′itʃeri). Also attrib. The name of a town on the Malabar coast.

Telligraph. Hist. [ad. mod. (Anglo-)L. telligraphum, irreg. f. L. tellus land + -graph.] A description of the boundaries of land; a charter of lands in which the bounds are described: — TERRIER.

†Tellicet. Obs. [f. L. tellina TELLEN + -ET.]

Telling (te′liŋ), vbl. sb. [f. TELL v. + -ING.] The action of the verb TELL.

Tellinite (tel′inait). Palæont. [ad. mod. L. tellinites + tellina a Gr. τελλίνη + -ITE².] A fossil shell of, or resembling, the genus Tellina; a fossil tellen.

Telluric (teliū′rik), a.² Chem. and Min. [f. TELLURIUM + -IC.] Derived from or containing tellurium.

Tellurium (teliū′riŏm). Chem. [mod. L., f. L. tellus, tellur-em the earth + -IUM, suffix of names of metals.]

Telluride (te′liūraid). Chem. [f. TELLURIUM + -IDE.] A combination of tellurium with an electro-positive element.

Tellurion (teliū′riŏn). [f. L. tellus, tellur-em the earth + -ION.] An apparatus illustrating the effect of the earth's diurnal rotation.

Tellurism (te′liūriz'm). [f. L. tellus, tellur-em the earth + -ISM.]

Tellurite (te′liūrait). Min. Also +tellururet. [f. TELLURIUM + -ITE.]

Tellurize (te′liūraiz), v. [f. TELLURIUM + -IZE.]

Tellurous (te′liūrŏs), a. Chem. Also +tellurious.

Telluretted, Tellureted (te′liūretid), a. Chem.

Tellurian (teliū′riăn), a. and sb. [f. L. tellus, tellur-em the earth + -IAN.] A. adj.

+Te.llurane. Chem. Obs. [f. TELLURIUM + -ANE.]

to alecithal and centrolecithal. **Telophase** (-fās)

Teloteremata. **Teloteropathy, Telepathy.**

Telotrocha (teloʻtroka). Zool. [f. Gr. τέλος end + τροχός wheel.]

Telotrochal, Telotrochous (teloʻtrŏkăl, -kŏs), a.

Telpher (te′lfər), a. and sb. [Syncopated from telephor or telphor < telephore, etc. 1884 in TELPHERAGE.] A. adj.

Telpherage (te′lfəridʒ).

Telphering (te′lfəriŋ).

Telpherage (te'lfərědʒ). [f. as Telpher- + -age.] Transport effected automatically by the aid of electricity; *spec.* a system adapted to the conveyance of minerals and other goods in vessels suspended from a cable, and moved by means of an electric motor supplied with current from an adjacent conductor. Also *attrib.*

Telson (te'lsən). *Zool.* [a. Gr. τέλσων a limit.] The last segment of the abdomen or the median axis in certain crustaceans and arachnidans, as the middle flipper of a lobster's tail, the long sharp spine of the king-crab, or the sting of the scorpion.

Telugu, **Teloogoo** (te'lŭgū), *sb. a.* Also **Teloogoo**, **Telugu**. [Native name of the language, and of a man of the race. Origin and derivation uncertain.] **1.** The language of a Dravidian people or race who speak this language. (See also GENTOO.) **2.** One of the Dravidian people or race who speak this language.

Temenos (te'mĕnos). *Gr. Antiq.* [a. Gr. τέμενος, f. τέμ- stem of τέμνειν to cut off, sever.] A piece of ground surrounding or adjacent to a temple; a sacred enclosure or precinct.

Temerarious (temĕreə'riəs), *a.* Now only *literary.* [f. L. temerāri-us fortuitous, rash (f. temere blindly, rashly (see TEMEROUS) + -ADI-ous): cf. centr-ārius, extr-ārius, necess-ārius) + -OUS.]

Temerity (time'riti). Forms: 5 -yte, 6 -itie, 6-7 -ite. 6-7 timeritie, 7 -ity. [ad. L. temeritās, -tātem, rashness, f. temere adv. by chance, blindly: see -ITY. So F. témérité (15th c. in Godef.).]

Temerous (te'mĕrəs), *a.* Now *rare.* [f. L. temer-āre blind, heedlessly + -OUS.]

Temerously, *adv.* [f. prec. + -LY.]

Temerousness. [f. TEMEROUS + -NESS.]

Temia (tī'miă). *Ornith.* [The native Javanese name of the bird.] (See quots.)

Temin, obs. f. var. TIMMER, TIMBER.

Tomine, **Temmes**, obs. f. TEMSE, TEMSE.

Temnospondylous (temnospo'ndiləs), *a.* *Comp. Anat.* [f. Gr. τέμνειν to cut + σπονδυλ- vertebra + -OUS.]

Temoin, obs. f. TIMON.

Tempe (te'mpī). [L., a Gr. Τέμπη, a. Gr. τ-έμπη.] The proper name of a charming valley in Thessaly, watered by the Peneus, between Mounts Olympus and Ossa.

Temper (te'mpəɹ), *sb.* Forms: 4 tempre, 4-5 tempur, 5-6 tympre, 6- temper. [f. TEMPER v.] **I. 1.** The due or proportionate mixture or combination of elements or qualities. **2.** Proportionate arrangement of parts; regulation, adjustment. **3.** Mental balance or composure. **II.** Applied to mortar or plaster. **III.** Concrete senses, in technical use.

Temper (te'mpəɹ), *v.* Forms: 1 temprian, 3 temprien, 4-7 tempre, 4-6 tempir, -yr, -ur, 6- temper. [OE. temprian (so also in OS. temperon), ad. L.]

Tempera (te'mpĕră). [It.] **1.** Distemper; painting in distemper.

Temperable (te'mpĕrəb'l), *a.* Now *rare.* [f. TEMPER v. + -ABLE.]

Temperal, **-alite**, **-alte**, obs. ff. TEMPORAL, -ALITY.

Temperality, obs. Humorously misused for TEMPORALITY.

Temperament (te'mpĕrəmənt), *sb.* Also 5 temperment. [ad. L. temperāmentum due mixture, f. temperāre to TEMPER: see -MENT.]

Temperamental (tempĕrəme'ntal), *a.* [f. prec. + -AL.]

Temperamentally, *adv.* [f. prec. + -LY.]

Temperance (te'mpĕrəns). [a. AF. temperaunce (F. tempérance), ad. L. temperantia.]

(Dense dictionary text in multiple columns; principal headword entries include: **Temperance**, **Temperate**, **Temperately**, **Temperateness**, **Temperated**, **Temperately**, **Temperature**, **Temperative**, **Temperatured**, **Temperer**, **Tempered**, **Tempering**, **Temperish**, **Temper-pot**, **Temperous**, **Temper-screw**, **Tempest**, **Tempestful**, **Tempest-tossed**, **Tempestial**, **Tempestivity**, **Tempestive**, **Tempestuous**, **Tempestuously**, **Templar***.)*

TEMPLAR.

Hence **Templarism**, the community or body of Templars; **Templarize** v. *Obs.*, of or pertaining to the Templars; the principles of Templars (in *quot.* at the sense, *e.g.* = 'Good Templarism'); **Templarlike** *arb.*, like a Templar.

...

Templar (te'mplar), *sb.* Forms: 1–2 templ, templ (*3 four* templ). 3–temple. Also 4 tempel, -ele, -ile, -ille. (template), 4–6 templl, -yll, -3 yl(e, -ul, 5–6 -ell, -yl, 6–el (5–6 -l, templum); retrieved in ME. by F. *temple* (10th c. in Godef. *Compl.*) ...

...

TEMPLE.

...

TEMPO.

TEMPORALTY.

TEMPORALWARD.

TEMPORIZER.

Temporizing, vbl. sb.

Temporizing, ppl. a.

Tempor-

Temporo- (tempŏrŏ-), before a vowel sometimes tempor-, used in Anat. as combining form of L. temporal temples (of the head), forming adjectives in the sense 'pertaining to the temple or temples (and some other part)', as temporo-alar belonging to the temporal region and the wing.

Tempour, Tempora, obs. ff. TEMPER, TEMPERA.

Tempre, adv. Obs.

† Temprely, adv. Obs.

† Tempurance, obs. form of TEMPERANCE.

Tempt (tem°t), v.

Temptable, a.

Temptability, Temptableness, accessibility to temptation.

Temptation (temptēi·ʃən), sb.

Tempter (te·mptəɹ), sb.

Tempting, vbl. sb.

Tempting, ppl. a.

Temptress (te·mptres), sb.

Temulence (te·miulens), sb.

Temulency (te·miulensi).

Temulent (te·miulĕnt), a. Now rare. [ad. L.

Temulentious.

Temulentive, a.

Temure, Temus, obs. ff. TEMSE, TEMSE.

Ten (ten), a. (sb.) (adv.)

Ten, v. Obs.

Ten, obs. form of TEEN v., TEEN sb.

Tenability [f. next: see -ITY.]

Tenable (te·nǎb'l, tī·n-), a.

Tenableness. [f. TENABLE + -NESS.]

Tenace (tenæs), sb.

Tenacious (tĭnēi·ʃəs), a. Also † -ATIOUS, -ACEOUS.

Tenaciously (tĕnā'shŏsli), adv. [f. prec. + -LY².] In a tenacious manner; with a strong hold; persistently, stubbornly.

Tenaciousness (tĕnā'shŏsnes). [f. as prec. + -NESS.] The quality of being tenacious; tenacity.

Tenacity (tĕnæ'sĭti). [ad. rare L. *tenācitās*, f. *tenāci-*, *tenax*: see TENACIOUS and -ITY.] The quality of being tenacious.

Tenacle (te'nǎk'l). Now rare. [ad. L. *tenaculum* holder: see below.]

Tenaculum (tĕnæ'kiŭlŏm). Pl.-la. [mod. uses of L. *tenaculum* a holder, f. *ten-ēre* to hold.]

Tenaille (tĕnē'l). Forms: 6-8 tenaile, 7 tenal, 8-9 tenaill, 7- tenaille. [F. *tenaille* (tmā'y) forceps (12th c. in Godef. Compl.), ...]

Tenaillon (tĕnæ'lyŏn) Fortif. [F. *tenaillon* (tmā'yŏn) in same sense, f. *tenaille* (see prec.).]

Tenancy (te'nǎnsi). [f. TENANT: see -ANCY; representing med.L. *tenentia* (11th c in Murator. *Antiquitates* IX. (1776) 430), also *tenentia* (1120 in Du Cange).]

Tenant (te'nǎnt), *sb.* Forms: 4-6 tenaunt, -aunte, -ante, Sc. -ande (-ape), 4 (pl. -auns), 5 awnte, 4-7 -aunt, 5-6 tenaunte, 6-7 -ant, -ent(e, 7-8 tenent, 4- tenant. [a. F. *tenant*, -aunt, sb., use of pr. pple. of *tenir*:—L. *tenēre* to hold.]

Tenant (te'nǎnt), *v.* [f. prec. sb.]

Tenanted ppl. a., held by a tenant or occupation.

Tenantable (te'nǎntǎb'l), a. [f. TENANT + -ABLE.]

Tenant at will. *Law.* One who holds at the will or pleasure of the lessor. Also *fig.*

Tenanting: see TENANT v., TENONING.

Tenantism, *nonce-wd.* [f. TENANT *sb.* + -ISM.]

Tenantless (te'nǎntles). a. [as prec. + -LESS.] Without a tenant or tenants; untenanted, unoccupied, empty. *lit.* and *fig.*

Tenant-right. [f. TENANT *sb.* + RIGHT *sb.*]

Tenantry (te'nǎntri). Forms: 4- tenantry, -endry, 5-6 tenentry, 5-.

1. The state or condition of being a tenant; occupancy as a tenant; tenancy; tenantship.

2. Land held of a superior; land let to tenants; also, the profits of such land.

3. Tenants collectively.

Tenantship (te'nǎntship). [f. TENANT *sb.* + -SHIP.]

Tenantry (te'nǎntri), *var.* TENANTRY.

Tenant, obs. variant of TENON.

Tenant(e, -asmus, obs. forms of TENESMUS.

Tena'smon (13th c. in Godef.), *a.* obs. F.; *tenasmus*.

Tenax (te'nǎks, -næks), *a.* and *sb.* [a. L. *tenax* tough: see TENACIOUS.]

Tench (tenʃ). Forms: 4-6 tenche, 5 tench(e, 6 teynche, tenche, 7 tensh, etc. [a. OF. *tenche* (12th c. Picard *tenke* in Godef. Compl.), mod.F. *tanche* (13th c. in Littré):—late L. *tinca*.]

Tenché, *Sc.* obs. var. TENCH.

Tench, *v.* [f. the sb.]

Tend, *sb.¹* [aphetic f. ATTEND *sb.*]

Tend (tend), *v.¹* Also 4-7 tende, 5 tonne. [Aphetic form of ATTEND *v.*]

Tend (tend), *v.²* Forms: 6-7 tende, 6 *Sc.* tend, 4- tend. See also TEND v.¹ [a branch of ATTEND *v.*]

Tend, *v.³* [a. F. *tendre*:—L. *tendere* to stretch, extend, direct intr. *to have a motion*.]

Tendable, *a.* [f. TEND *v.* + -ABLE.]

Tendance (te'ndǎns). Also 8-9 (improperly) *tendence*. [Aphetic form of ATTENDANCE, or sometimes f. TEND *v.¹* + -ANCE.]

Tendancy, obs. rare.⁻¹. [f. TEND *v.¹*] In *b.* (improp.)

Tendant, *a.* and *sb.* Also 4 'aunt, 7 (improp.) -ent. [Aphetic f. ATTENDANT.]

Tendence (te'ndns). Now *rare* and *literary.* Also 7-9 -ance, 6- tendence. [F. *tendence* a. 1374, Oresme, Du Cange, etc.; cf. L. *tendentia* (13th c. in Godef. Compl.).]

Tendency (te'ndnsi). Also 7 (improp.) -ancy. [ad. med.L. *tendentia*, n. of action f. L. *tendĕre* to TEND.]

Tendent (teˈndant). [f. as next +-AL.] Of the nature of, or characterized by having, a tendency; *spec.* *rare*.

Tendential (tendeˈnʃăl), a. [f. as next + -AL.] Of the nature of, or characterized by having, a tendency; *spec.* *rare*.

Tendentious, var. TENDANT.

Tendration (tendreˈiʃən), *rare*. Having a purposed tendency; composed or written with such a tendency or aim.

Tender (teˈndəɹ). sb.1 Also 5 -our. [f. TEND v.1 + -ER.1, or aphetic form of ATTENDER.]

Tender (teˈndəɹ). sb.2 Also 6 tendre, tendour. [f. TENDER v.2]

Tender (teˈndə), a. (adv.) and sb.3 [a. OF. tendre, tendir, Fr. tendre = Pr. tenre, tendre, Sp. tierno, It. tenero, L. tener-um (nom. tener).]

Tender (teˈndə), v.1 3 arch. or dial. [f. TENDER a. : cf. OF. tendre-r.]

Tender (teˈndə), v.2 [a. OF. tendre, F. tendre: — L. tendere.]

Tenderable (teˈndərăb'l), a. [f. TENDER v.2 + -ABLE.] That may be tendered; available for delivery in fulfilment of contract.

Tenderer (teˈndərəɹ), [f. TENDER v.2 + -ER.1] One who tenders or makes a formal offer.

Tenderee (tendəriˈ), [f. TENDER v.2 + -EE.1] One who tenders or tends with; *spec.*

Tenderfoot (teˈndəfut). *U.S.* and *Colonial.* pl. -foots, -feet.

Tender-hearted, a. [f. TENDER a. + HEART + -ED.2] Having a tender heart; easily moved by fear, pity, sorrow, or love.

Tender-heartedness. Hence **Tender-hea˞rtedness**.

Tenderish, a. [f. TENDER a. + -ISH.] Somewhat tender.

Tenderize, *trans.* To make tender: — TENDER v.2

Tenderling (teˈndəɹliŋ). [See -LING.1]

Tenderloin. *U.S.* [f. TENDER a. + LOIN sb.]

Tenderly, a. adv. Obs. rare. As prec.

Tenderness. The quality or state of being tender.

Tendicle. *Obs. rare⁻¹.* [ad. L. tendicula.]

Tendicule. *Surg.* Obs. rare. [ad. L. tendicula, f. tendere to stretch: see -CULE.] Name of an instrument for dilating an opening.

Tendinal (teˈndinăl), a. rare⁻¹. [ad. med.L. tendo, -dinem.]

Tendinous (teˈndinəs), a. [ad. F. tendineux, -euse, ad. med. or mod.L. tendinōsus.]

Tendo (teˈndo). [L.: = TENDON.] Used chiefly in *tendo Achillis*, the great tendon of the heel.

Tendon (teˈndən). Also 6 tenon. [ad. med.L. tendo, tendōn-em.]

Tent (tent), *sb.*[1]

Tent, *sb.*[2]

Tent, *sb.*[3]

Tent, *v.*[1]

Tent, *v.*[2]

Tent, *v.*[3]

Tentable, *a.*

Tentaculated, *a.* *Zool.*

Tentacular, *a.* *Zool.*

Tentaculate, *a.* *Zool.*

Tentacle (te'ntăk'l), *sb.* *Zool.*

Tentaculite (tentæ·kiŭləit), *sb.* *Zool.*

Tentaculiferous, *a.* *Zool.*

Tentaculocyst (tentæ·kiŭlŏsist), *sb.* *Zool.*

Tentaculoid (tentæ·kiŭloid), *a.* *Biol.*

Tentaculum (tentæ·kiŭlŏm), *sb.* *Zool.*

Tentage (te'ntēdȝ), *sb.*

Tentamen (tentē·men), *sb.*

Tentation (tentē·ʃən), *sb.*

Tentative (te'ntătiv), *a.* and *sb.*

Tentatively (te'ntătivli), *adv.*

Tentativeness, *sb.*

Tent-bed.

Tented (te'nted), *ppl. a.*

Tenter (te'ntə̆r), *sb.*[1]

Tenter (te'ntə̆r), *sb.*[2]

Tenter (te'ntə̆r), *v.*[1]

Tenter (te'ntə̆r), *v.*[2]

Tenter (te'ntə̆r), *v.*[3]

Tenter-ground. *Obs.*

Tenter-hook.

Tentful, *a.*

Tenth (tenþ).

Tentering, *vbl. sb.*

Tenterbelly.

Tenter-hooking, *a.*

TENTH.

Tenth. ... in the tenth place.

Tenthly (ˈtenθli), *adv.* [f. TENTH *a.* + -LY²] In the tenth place.

Tent-hook, *obs.* f. TENTER-HOOK.

Tenthredinid, *Entom.* [Latinized form of Gr. τενθρηδών, -δόν-, a kind of wasp ...] ... belonging to the Tenthredinidæ.

Tentible, *a.* [f. TENT *v.*¹ to attend + -IBLE.] Apt to attend, attentive.

Tenticle, *Obs.* [f. TENT *sb.*¹ as if after a L. type *tenticula*.] A small tent.

Tentie, variant of TENTY.

Tentiginous (tentiˈdʒinəs), *a. Obs.* [f. L. *tentīgin-, -tīgo* ...] 1. Excited to lust; itching, lecherous. 2. Provocative of lust; lascivious.

Tentigo (tenˈtaigou), *Obs.* [L. *tentīgo* tension, erection] An attack of priapism, an erection; lecherousness, lust.

Tentile, *a.* Apheti- form of *attentile*, ATTENTIVE, duly qualified, trustworthy.

Tenti·llum, *Zool.* [mod.L., f. L. *tempt-, tent-* stem of *temptāre, tentāre* to feel + dim. suffix]

Tentily (tenˈtili), *adv. Sc. rare.* [As if f. TENTY *a.* + -LY²]

Tenting (tentiŋ), *vbl. sb.*¹ [f. TENT *v.*¹ + -ING¹] 1. *vbl. sb.* Lodging in or in tents; encamping; sojourning. Chiefly *attrib.*

Tenting, *vbl. sb.*² [f. TENT *v.*² + -ING²] Resembling a tent; converging as the sides of a tent.

Tention, *Obs. rare.* Short for INTENTION.

Tentious, *Obs.* var. TENTATIOUS.

Tentive, *a. Obs. exc. dial.* Also 4–5 -iffe ... Short form of ATTENTIVE.

Tentless (tentlǝs), *a.* [f. TENT *sb.* + -LESS.] Without a tent or tents; having no tent.

Tentlet (tentlet), [f. TENT *sb.*¹ + -LET.] A miniature tent.

Tent-maker. 1. One who makes tents.

Tentwise, *adv.* ¹, ²; see TENT *sb.*¹ 3.

TENTWISE.

Tentor (tentōr), [L.] 1. One of the unbranched twigs which stud the retractile tentacle of some Siphonophora.

Tentorial *a.* ... Of or pertaining to the tentorium.

Tentorium (tenˈtōriəm), [L. *tentōrium* ...] a. A tent-like covering; an awning; a canopy.

Tentory, *Obs.* pl. of TENTORY.

Tentour, *Obs. rare.* In quot., rendering *tentorium*.

Tent-peg. One of the (usually wooden) pegs, with a notch at the upper end, to which when stuck in the ground the ropes of a tent are fastened.

Tent-pegging, an Indian cavalry sport in which the player, riding at full speed, tries to transfix and carry off ... the point of his lance.

Tentral, erron. form of TENTRAL.

Tentretane = *to entertain*: see T'.

Tent-stitch. Also *ten-*. [First element uncertain ...] A kind of embroidery or worsted-work.

Tenue (tnü). [Fr. *tenue* deportment, *sb.*]

Tenues (teˈnjuːiz), pl. of TENUIS.

Tenui- (tenjuːi-). Combining form of L. *tenuis* 'thin, narrow, slender'.

Tentuous, *a. Now rare.* [L. *tenu-is* thin + -OUS (cf. *ingenu-ous*).] 1. Thin or slender, narrow.

Tentuous, erron. form of TENTATIOUS.

TENT-WORK.

Tent-work¹. [f. TENT *sb.*¹ + WORK *sb.*]

Tent-stitch = TENT-STITCH.

Tentwort (tentwǝt). Also 6 *taynt-*.

TENURE

Tenty (tenti). [f. *tent*] 1. Thinness of form or size (*muscle*).

Tenue (tnü). [Fr. *tenue* ...] 1. ... Carriage, bearing, deportment; also, costume, 'rig'.

Tenuis (teˈnjuːis). Pl. *tenues*.

Tenuious, *a.* [L. *tenuis* thin + -OUS] ...

Tenuity (tenˈjuːiti). 1. Thinness of form or size (muscle).

Tenure (ˈtenjǝr). Forms: α. 5– tenure, (5 te-...). 1. The action (or fact) of holding a tenement.

Tenure at will.

TENURER.

Tenurial (tenjuːˈriǝl), *a.* [f. med.L. *tenūra* + -AL.] Of, pertaining to, or of the nature of the tenure of land. Hence **Tenu·rially** *adv.*, in respect of tenure.

Tenurage. ... whatever belongs to a tenure or tenures; general conditions of tenure.

Tenurer. [f. TENURE + -ER + ... NT.] one who deals with or treats of tenures.

Tenuto (teˈnuːto), *a. Mus.* [It.]

Tenuty, -ye, *obs.* forms of TENUITY.

Tenzon, variant of TENSON.

Teocalli (tiːǝˈkɑli). Also 7 *teucalli*. [Mexican *teocalli*, f. *teotl* god + *calli* house.]

Teology, Teon, Teone (ǝ, obs. ff. THEOLOGY, TEAM, TEEN, TUNE.

Teopan. [Shortened from Mex. *teopantli* temple, f. *teotl* god + *pantli* wall.] A Mexican temple, a teocalli.

Teosinte (tiːǝˈsinti). Also 7 *teosintl* (Bull. Soc. d'Acclim. 1871, 38). Mex. *teocintli*.

Teothe, Teothing, obs. ff. TITHE *sb.*, TITHING.

Tepa, early form of TEPEE.

Tepal (tiːpǝl). *Bot. rare.* [f. ...]

TEPAT·E

Tepat·e, tepet, *obs.* forms of TIPPET.

Tepee (tiːpiː, tiːˈpiː). Also *teapee, tepie, teepe*. [Sioux or Dakota Indian *tī pī* tent, house, dwelling; *tī* dwelling, *pī* used for.] A tent or wigwam of the American Indians.

Tephramancy (teˈfrǝmǝnsi). [f. Gr. τέφρα ashes + -MANCY.] Divination by ashes.

Tephrite (teˈfrǝit). *Min.* [f. Gr. τεφρός ash-coloured (f. τέφρα ashes) + -ITE.] ... **Tephritic**, *a.* ... **Tephritoid**, a variety of tephrite containing no nepheline.

Tephroite (teˈfrǝuǝit). *Min.* [ad. Ger. *Tephroit* (Breithaupt, 1823), irreg. f. Gr. τεφρός ash-coloured (f. τέφρα ashes) + -ITE.] A silicate of manganese, occurring in crystalline masses of an ashy grey or reddish colour.

Tephromancy = TEPHRAMANCY.

Tephrosia (teˈfrǝuziǝ). [mod.L. f. Gr. τεφρός ash-coloured.]

Tepid (tepid), *a.* Also 5 *teped*, 6 *tepit*. [ad. L. *tepidus*, f. *tepēre* to be warm.] Moderately or slightly warm; lukewarm.

Tepidarium (tepiˈdeǝriǝm). Pl. *-ia.* [L., ...] 6 in anglicized form *tepidarie*.

Tepidity (teˈpiditi). [ad. late or med.L. *tepiditās* (6 in Gellia Christiana II. 186), f. *tepidus* TEPID.] The quality or condition of being tepid.

Tepidly (tepidli), *adv.* In a tepid or lukewarm way.

Tepidness. The quality or state of being tepid.

Tepor (tiːpǝr). *Obs.* Also 7 *-our.* [L. *tepor*.] = TEPIDITY.

Tephillin, -im (teˈfilin, -im). *sb. pl.* [Rabb. Heb. תְּפִלִּין *t'phillīm*, Aramaic *t'phillīn* ...] A name for Jewish phylacteries.

Tephrite (teˈfrǝit). *Min.* ...

TER-.

Ter- (tǝr), comb. form. 1. Prefixed to adjs. and sbs. : = *thrice*, three times.

Terand, -ane, Terandry, obs. ff. TYRANT, -RY.

Teraph (teǝrǝf). Also 7 *-our.* [L. adv. *ter* thrice, three times.]

Teratical (teˈrætikǝl), *a. rare.* [f. Gr. τέρας, τέρατ-] Relating to marvels or prodigies.

Teraglin (tiˈræglin). [Aboriginal name.] A fish of New South Wales, *Otolithus atelodus*, sometimes called Silver Jew-fish.

TERAGLIN.

Teraphim (teǝrǝfim). *sb. pl.* [Heb. תְּרָפִים *t'rāphīm*, pl. (in form sing.) of a word of doubtful origin and meaning ...] ... Small images ... consulted as oracles.

Terapin, obs. form of TERRAPIN.

Terata, pl. of TERAS.

Teratogenesis (teratǝuˈdʒenisis). *Biol.* [f. Gr. τέρας, τέρατ- + GENESIS.]

TER-.

Path. [mod.L., f. Gr. τέρας, *terat-* + -vorovs (see TERATA)]

Teratogeny (terǝˈtɒdʒini). The production of monsters or misshapen organisms.

Teratogenetic (-dʒiˈnetik), **Teratogenic** (-dʒenik) *adjs.*, pertaining to teratogeny; producing monsters.

Teratoid (teǝrǝtɔid), *a.* [Gr. τερατο-ειδής + -OID.]

Teratolite (teˈrætǝlǝit). *Min.* Also erron. **ter-atolite** (*l ...*). [f. Gr. τέρας, *terat-* + λίθος stone.]

Teratological (terǝtǝˈlɒdʒikǝl), *a.* [f. next + -IC.] Of, pertaining to, or characterized by teratology.

Teratologist (terǝˈtɒlǝdʒist). One who deals in stories of marvels or prodigies. b. One versed in teratology (sense 2).

Teratology (terǝˈtɒlǝdʒi). [f. Gr. τέρας, *terat-* marvel, prodigy, monster + -LOGY.] 1. A discourse or narrative concerning prodigies; a marvellous tale, or collection of such tales.

2. *Biol.* The study of monstrosities or abnormal formations in animals or plants.

Teratoma (terǝˈtǝumǝ). *Path.* [mod.L., f. Gr. τέρας, *terat-* + -OMA.] A kind of tumour.

Teratoscopy (terǝˈtɒskǝpi). [f. Gr. τέρας, *terat-* + -σκοπία observation.]

TERCEL

Terbium (tǝbiǝm). *Chem.* [f. the name of *Ytterby* in Sweden: cf. ERBIUM.] One of the rare metallic elements ...

Terce (tǝs). 1. = TIERCE *sb.*

Tercel, tiercel (tǝsǝl, tiǝsǝl). Forms: α. 5 *tercel, tercell* ... [a. OF. *tercel, tercuel, tierchel*, It. *terzuolo*, *terzolo*.] The male of the peregrine falcon.

Tercel jerkin, see *jerkin*.

Tercelet.

Tercel, tiercelet (tûꞏsel, tîꞏ-). Forms: 4-5 ters-, terse-, tarse-, 4-6 tercel, -el, -lel; 4- tercelet. [a. OF. terçelet, tiercelet, f. tiercel (tîꞏ-, also OF. tercel, Tercel), whence later Eng.] — prec.

Tercel-gentle, after Falcon-gentle. The male of the falcon.

Tercellene. Obs. rare—¹. [deriv. of Tercel.]

Tercentenary (tâꞏsenteꞏnäl), a. and sb. [f. Ter- + Centenary, after L. ter centēni three hundred each. For the special use in reference to years cf. Centenary.]

Tercentennial (tâꞏsen·teꞏnïäl), a. and sb. [f. Ter- + Centennial.]

Tercer. Obs. [a. AF. *tercer, *tercier, L. tertiārius.] A third person, f. tercia third; cf. quarteron, quinteron.

Tercine (tâꞏsin). Bot. [—F. tercine (Mirbel 1828), f. L. tertius third.]

Tercio, tertio (tûꞏsiо, tûꞏʃiо). [Sp. tercio (Minsheu), mod.L. tertio.]

Tercel (as above) [cf. Kersey], Tercel, a Third in Musick.

Terebene (teꞏrǐbīn). Chem. [f. L. Tereb(inth) + -ene.]

Terebenthene (terěběnþīn). Chem. [a. F. térébenthène, ad. L. térébinthīna (résina); cf. -ene as in Benzene.]

Terebic (těreꞏbik), a. Chem. [f. Tereb(inth) + -ic.]

Terebilenic (terěbìlěꞏnik), a. Chem. [irreg. f. L. terebinthus.]

Terebinthina a., in terebenic acid, synonym of Terebic acid; see quot. 1868 s.v.

Terebilene (terěbìlēn). Chem. Obs.

Terebinthinate (terěbìꞏnþinět), a. and sb.

Terebinthine (terěbìꞏnþin, -ain), a. and sb.

Terebinth (teꞏrǐbinþ). Forms: 4 therebynte, terebynt, 5-6 therebinthe, 6 terebynte, -bint, -binthe, terbinth, 6- terebinth. [— OF. therebint(e (13th c. in Hatz.-Darm.), tārebyn, -thin, terebinte (Godefroy Compl.),—Sp., It. terebinto; ad. L. terebinth-us (Pliny), a. Gr. τερέβινθος, earlier τέρμινθος and τέρμινθος, prob. a foreign word.]

Terebinthaceous (terěbìnþēiꞏʃæs), a. Bot. Also -taceous. [f. mod.L. Terebinthus, L. terebinthus: see prec. and -aceous.]

Terebic, sb. [deriv.]

Terebenic (terěbēꞏnik), a. Chem.

Terebral (teꞏrěbræl), a. [f. L. terebra + -al.]

Terebrant (teꞏrěbrant), a. (sb.) [ad. L. terebrant-, terebrāns, pr. pple. of terebrāre to bore.]

Terebrate (teꞏrěbrěit), v. [f. ppl. stem of L. terebrāre to bore.]

Terebration (terěbrēiꞏʃän). Now rare or Obs. Also terebaration. [ad. L. terebrātiōn-em.]

Teredo (těrīꞏdo). Pl. teredines (těrīꞏdìnīz), teredos (těrīꞏdoz). [L. teredo, ad. Gr. τερηδών a wood-gnawing worm, f. τείρειν to rub hard, wear away, bore.]

Terek (teꞏrek). [From the name of the river Terek.]

Tereen, obs. form of Tureen.

Terenite (teꞏrěnait). Min. [Named by Emmons 1837, f. Gr. τήρεν tender + -ite.]

Terentian (těreꞏnʃän), a. [ad. L. Terentiān-us, f. Terenti-us Terence.]

Terephthalic (terěfþæꞏlik), a. Chem. [f. Tereb + Phthalic.]

Terephthalamide, an amide of terephthalic acid.

Terepole v. see Terpole.

Teresa. Obs. Also there'se.

Tergal (tûꞏgæl), a. Zool. [f. L. terg-um the back + -al.]

Tergant (tûꞏgant), **tergiant** (tûꞏdʒiänt), a. Her. rare—⁰.

Tergeminate (tûdʒeꞏminět), a. Bot. rare—¹. [f. next + -ate¹.]

Tergeminous (tûdʒeꞏminäs), a. [f. L. tergemin-us + -ous.]

Tergal, Tergite, obs. forms of Target, Tergant.

Tergiversate (tûꞏdʒivèsěit), v. [f. L. tergiversāt-, ppl. stem of tergiversārī.]

Tergiversation (tûdʒivèsēiꞏʃän), sb. [ad. L. tergiversātiōn-em.]

Tergiversator (tûꞏdʒivèsēitèr). [ad. late L. tergiversātor.]

Tergite (tûꞏdʒait). Zool. [f. L. terg-um the back + -ite¹.]

Tergiversatory a., f. prec.

Tergiverse v.

Tergo-, Tergum combining form of L. terg-um the back.

Terin, Terine, obs. forms of Tarin.

Terin (teꞏrin). Obs. [ad. OF. tarin, terin (14th c.).]

Terlis, Terlyst, obs. Sc. forms of Trellis, -ed.

Terlerie, -lery. Obs.

Terlether, obs. Sc. form of Tableather.

Terli terlow see Terlerie.

Terling. Obs. rare.

Term (tûm), sb. Forms: 3-7 terme, (4-5 teerme, 5 tearme), 5-7 tearme, 6-7 tarme, (6, 9 tearm), 4- term. [a. F. terme (12th c.), in OF. also time (or place)—termine, L. terminum limit, boundary; re F. terme.]

Terem, Termless, etc.

Term, sb. — see prec.

Term, v. [In sense 1 a OF. *termer* ... In sense 2 b.]

Termagant (tɜːˈmægənt), *a.* and *sb.*

Termatic (tɜːˈmætɪk), *a. Anat.*

Terminable (ˈtɜːmɪnəb'l), *a.*

Terminal (ˈtɜːmɪnəl), *a.* and *sb.*

Terminate (ˈtɜːmɪneɪt), *ppl. a.*

Terminate (ˈtɜːmɪneɪt), *v.*

Terminately (ˈtɜːmɪnəlɪ), *adv.*

Termination (tɜːmɪˈneɪʃən).

Terminational, *a.*

Terminative, *a.*

Terminator (ˈtɜːmɪneɪtə(r)).

Terminatory, *a.*

Termine, *v.*

Terminer, in oyer and terminer: see OYER.

† Terminer, v. Obs. Also 5 termynour. [a. F. terminer = It. terminare: see TERMINATE v.] One who or that which terminates, ends, or limits. Also one who determines or decides.

† Terminine. Obs. rare⁻¹. [? Error for terminine; or extended form of TERMINE.] Something extended or terminated.

Terminism (tǝˈmɪnɪz'm). [ad. mod. L. terminismus, limit + -ISM. So F. terminisme, G. terminismus.] a. Philos. The doctrine that universals are mere terms or names: = NOMINALISM.

b. Theol. The doctrine (maintained by Reichenberg at Leipzig in the 17th c.) that God has appointed a definite term or limit in the life of each individual, after which the opportunity for salvation is lost.

So **Terminist** (cf. med. L. terminista), one who holds or maintains terminism (in either sense); hence **Terminist** attrib. a.

Terminise (tǝˈmɪnaɪz), v. rare. [f. L. terminus.] To supply with terms; to furnish a nomenclature for.

Terminology (tǝˌmɪnɒˈlɒdʒɪ). Pl. -ies. [ad. G. terminologie, f. med. L. termin-us, limit + -ITION. So F. terminologie, G. terminologie.]

Terminus (tǝˈmɪnǝs). Pl. termini (-aɪ). [L., = end, limit, boundary; also as in sense 2.]

Termon (tǝˈmɒn). Ir. Hist. and Eng.

Termor (tǝˈmʌr). Law. Also 4-ur, 6-7 -our, -er. [a. AF. termer, termour, f. terme TERM.] One who holds lands or tenements for a term of years, or for life.

Term-time. The period during which the law-courts are in session.

Tern (tǝːn). Also 7 tearne. [Cf. Sw. tärna, Norw. and Færo. terno⁻ON. þerna, the tern or sea swallow.]

Termly (tǝːmlɪ), a. Now rare. [f. TERM sb. + -LY¹.]

Ternal (tǝːnal), a. rare. [ad. med. L. ternal-is, f. L. ternus.]

Ternary, terner (tǝːnarɪ). Obs. exc. Hist. [ad. late L. ternari-us: see TERNARY.]

Ternary (tǝːnarɪ), a. and sb. [ad. late L. ternari-us consisting of three, f. tern-i: see TERNAL and -ARY. Cf. F. ternaire (15th c.).]

Ternariant (tǝˈnɛːrɪant). Math. [f. TERNARY + -ant the ending of INVARIANT, etc.]

Ternate (tǝːneɪt), a. [ad. mod. L. ternat-us, f. L. tern-i three, by three: see TERN.]

Ternary (tǝːnarɪ), a. and sb. [ad. late L. ternārius consisting of three, f. tern-i: see TERNAL and -ARY. Cf. F. ternaire (15th c.).]

Ternately (tǝːneɪtlɪ), adv. [f. TERNATE a. + -LY².] In a ternate manner; in threes.

Ternate-pinnate, a. Bot. [f. TERNATE + PINNATE.] Applied to a compound leaf having three pinnate divisions proceeding from a common petiole.

Ternato-pinnate (tǝːnatoˈpɪn-), a. Bot. [f. mod. L. ternātus (after comb. combining forms in -o-) + PINNATE.]

Terne (tǝːn). Also 6- tarn. [Also F. terne.] 1. Gloomy; fierce. Obs. Also † ternard a.

Terne-plate. Also terne-. [prob. f. TERNE a.] Dull, lacking brilliancy, in reference to the dullness of terne-plate, in comparison with tin-plate.]

Ternery (tǝːnarɪ). rare. [f. TERN sb.² + -ERY.] A place where terns congregate to breed.

Ternion (tǝːnɪǝn). [ad. L. ternion-em a company of three, a triad.]

Ternity, ternyte, obs. forms of TRINITY.

Ternstroemiaceous (tǝːnstriːmɪˈeɪʃǝs), a. Bot. [f. mod. L. Ternstroemia + -ACEOUS.]

Terpel: see TERNAR.

Terpene (tǝːpiːn). Chem. [ad. G. terpen (Kekulé 1866), f. terpen-tin turpentine + -ENE.]

Terpilene (tǝːpɪliːn). Chem. Also -ine. [f. as TERPENE + -IL- + -ENE.]

Terpin (tǝːpɪn). Chem. Also -ine. [f. as TERPENE + -IN¹.]

Terpinol (tǝːpɪnɒl). Chem. [f. TERPIN + -OL.]

Terpodion (tǝːpoʊdɪǝn). Mus. Obs. [a. G. terpodion, f. Gr. τέρπειν to delight + ᾠδή song.]

Terrace (tɛrǝs), sb. Also 6-7 terras, -ass, -ace. [ad. OF. terrace, -asse (mod.F. terrasse) = Pr., Sp., Pg. terraza.]

Terra (tɛrǝ). [L. (and It.) terra earth, used, with qualifying adjectives, to form names of medicinal and other earths, bole, and the like.]

Terra-cotta (tɛrǝˈkɒtǝ). Also 8 terra cotta, terracotta. [a. It. terra cotta, i.e. baked earth.]

Terracer (tɛrǝsǝr), one who stands or walks on a terrace.

Terraciform (tɛˈræsɪfɔːm), a. [f. TERRACE + -i- + -FORM.] Having the form of a terrace.

Terracing (tɛrǝsɪŋ), vbl. sb. [f. TERRACE v.] 1. The formation of terraces. b. concr. A terraced structure or formation.

Terracy (tɛrǝsɪ). [f. TERRACE sb. + -Y¹.]

†Terra damnata. Alchemy. Obs. [L., = condemned or finally rejected earth.] = CAPUT MORTUUM I.

†Terra filius (terrā fī̆liŭs). Pl. terrae filii.

1. A person of obscure parentage.

2. Formerly, at the University of Oxford: An orator privileged to make humorous and satirical strictures in a speech at the public 'act'.

†Terra firma (terrā fɜ̄rmă). [L., = 'firm land'; used in several senses.]

1. In 17th c. partly a. L. *terra firma*.

2. Firm or solid land or ground; a continent or mainland, as distinct from portions of land partly or wholly insulated by water.

†3. spec. a. The territories on the Italian mainland which were subject to the state of Venice.

†b. The northern coastal-land of South America (Colombia), as distinguished from the West India Islands.

†4. transf. and catachr. Landed estate; land.

†Terrage. Obs. Also 5 terage. [a. OF. terage.]

1. Land; a territory, country.

2. Old Law. Some kind of payment or duty.

†Terragnol. Obs. rare—. [obs. F. terragnol.]

†Terraillon. Obs. rare—.

Terrain (terē̆n), sb.

Terramara (terămā′ră), sb. Also 8–9 terramare.

†Terran. Obs. rare—.

Terrane (terē̆n), sb.

Terranean, a. rare—.

Terranean, -eous, adjs.

Terrapin (te′răpin), sb. Also form of Terrapen.

Terra sigillata. [mod. L.]

Terraqueous (terē̆′kwi̯ə̆s), a. [f. L. terra earth + AQUEOUS.]

Terraquean, etc.: = TERREPLEIN.

Terraquean, a. rare—.

Terrar, terrer. Obs. exc. Hist.

Terras, terrass. variants of TERRACE.

†Terra Sienna. Obs. Also terra di (da) Sienna.

Terre. [ad. It. terra di Siena, in F. terre de Sienne.] = SIENNA.

†Terra sigillata. [med. L.]

Terremote (te′rēmōt), sb. Obs. Forms: 4–6 terremote. [a. OF. terremote.] An earthquake.

Terremotive (te′rēmō′tiv), a. rare. [f. L.]

†Terrene (terē̆′n), sb. [a. AFr. or OF. terreyn.] = TERRAIN.

Terrene (terē̆′n), a. (adv.)

1. Belonging to the earth or to this world; earthly; worldly, material; temporal.

2. Consisting of earth; earthy.

†Terreplein (te′rēplān), sb.

Terrene, var. Terrine, early f. Tureen.

Terrenely (terē̆′nli), adv. [f. TERRENE + -LY².]

†Terreno (terē̆′nō). Obs. rare—.

†Terrenity (terē̆′niti). Obs.

Terreno (terē̆′nō). [= It. (piano) terreno = L.]

†Terreous, a. Obs. [f. L. terreus.]

Terreplein, sb.: see TERREPLEIN.

Terrestrial (terē̆′striăl), a. and sb.

Terrestrially (terē̆′striăli), adv.

Terrestrialness.

Terrestrious, a. Obs. rare.

†Terrestrian, a. Obs. rare—.

Terrestrify, v. Obs. rare.

Terrestrity, terrestreity. Obs. [ad. med. L. terrestritas.]

Terret (te′ret), sb. Forms: 5–8 tyret, toret, 6 tyrette, 6 yrette, 7 tirret, torret, 9 terret, etc.

Terret, int. Obs. rare—.

Terre-tenant. Law. Also 5–6 tere-, 6–7 tere-, 6–8 ter-.

Terre-verte (tē̆rvert). Also 7–8 terre-vert.

Terribility (te′ribi′liti), sb. rare.

Terrible (te′rib’l), a. (sb. and adv.)

Terribleness.

Terribly (te′ribli), adv.

†Terriblous, a. Obs. nonce-wd. [f. TERRIBLE + -OUS.]

Terricole (te′rikōl), sb. Zool.

Terricolous (terikō̆′ləs), a. Zool.

Terrier (te′riə̆r), sb.[1]

†Terriculament, sb. Obs.

Terrier (te′riə̆r), sb.[2] Law.

Terrify, v.

Terrigenous (teri′dʒinə̆s), a.

†Terrine, sb. Obs.

Terrie, terry. Obs. rare—. [app. a. OF.]

Terrien, a. Obs. Also 5 -yen. OF. *terrien* (11th c.) terrestrial, seignorial (12th c. in Godef. Compl.) 'of terre land + -ien, -IAN: corresp. to a L. type *terrānus*. Earthly, worldly; territorial.

Terrier[2] (te'rɪə). Forms: 5 terrere, ter-ryare, 6 terryer, taryer, terrour, 7 terriar, terrar, tarier, tarriour, 7 terier, 9 (vulgar) tarrier, 6- terrier. [a. F. (chien) *terrier*, also as subst. *terrier* a hunting-dog used to start badgers, etc., from their earth or burrow: see TERRIER[1]: med.L. *terrārius*, f. *terra* earth (see prec.).]

1. A small, active, intelligent variety of dog, which pursues its quarry (the fox, badger, etc.) into its burrow or earth...

Terri-fic (tĕrĭ'fĭk), a. (sb.) [ad. L. *terrific-us* terrifying, f. stem of *terrēre* to frighten: see -FIC. So sb. F. *terrifique* (13th c. in Godef.).]

1. Causing terror, terrifying; fitted to terrify; dreadful, terrible, frightful.

Terri-fically, adv. [f. prec. + -AL.] = TERRIFICALLY; Terri-ficness, the quality of being terrific.

Terrification (te'rĭfĭkeɪʃən). [f. as prec. + -AL.] In the evening we had terrifical ghost stories.

Terrify (te'rĭfəɪ), v. [ad. L. *terrificā-re* to frighten, terrify, f. *terrific-us* TERRIFIC: see -FY.]

Territorial (te'rĭto'rĭəl), a. and sb. [ad. late L. *territōriāl-is*, f. *territōri-um* TERRITORY. Cf. F. *territorial* (18th c. in Hatz.-Darm.).]

Territorialism (-ɪz'm). [f. as prec. + -ISM.]

Territorialist. [f. as prec. + -IST.]

Territoriality (-æ'lĭtɪ). [f. as prec. + -ITY.]

Territorialize. [f. as prec. + -IZE.]

Territorially, adv. [f. as prec. + -LY[2].]

Territoried (te'rĭtorĭd), ppl. a.

Territory (te'rĭtorɪ). Also 5 teri-, terry-. [ad. L. *territōri-um* the land round a town, a domain, district, territory.]

Territour, var. TERRITORY.

Terr-oceanic (te'rōʃɪæ'nɪk), a. *rare−*[1]. [f. *terra* earth + OCEANIC.] Of or belonging to both land and ocean.

Terro-cement. [f. *terre*, taken as combining form of L. *terra* earth.]

† **Terroir.** Obs. *rare*. [a. F. *terroir*, OF. *terrïer* (12th c. in Godef. Compl.) *terrouer* (13th c.).]

Terror (te'rə), sb. Also 4–6 –our, 4–7 terrour. [ME. *terrour*, a. F. *terreur* (14th c.): − L. *terrōr-em*, nom. *terror*, f. *terrēre* to frighten: see –OR[1].]

Terror, v. Obs. or arch. [f. prec. sb.] rare.

Terrorism (te'rɔrɪz'm). [a. F. *terrorisme* (1798 in Dict. Acad., Suppl.), f. L. *terror* dread, TERROR: see –ISM.]

Terrorist (te'rɔrɪst). [a. F. *terroriste*, f. as prec.: see –IST.]

Terrorize (te'rɔrəɪz), v. [f. as prec. + –IZE.]

Terry, sb.[1] = Tenny.

Terry, var. TABY v. Obs. to provoke.

+**Terryce.** Obs. Short (or error) for TERRIER[2].

6. **Comb.** attributive & adj. *terror-drop*, *-fit*, *-gleam*; objective (with *pr. pples.*), as *terror-breathing*, *-piping*, *-inspiring*, *-preaching*, *-striking*, etc., adjs.

Terse-sanctus (tɜː-sæ'ŋktəs).

Terrorless (te'rɔles), a. [f. TERROR + –LESS.]

Terse, a. (and adv.) [ad. L. *ters-us* wiped, brushed; smoothed; clean-cut, sharp-cut; polished, burnished; neat, trim, spruce.]

Tersely, adv. [f. TERSE + –LY[2].]

Terseness (tɜː'snes). [f. TERSE + –NESS.]

Tersion (tɜː'ʃən). Obs. *rare*. [ad. L. type *tersiōn-em*, n. of action from *tergēre* (–*ter-*) to wipe: see STERSE.]

Tersulphuret (tɜːsʌ'lfjurɛt). [f. TER- + SULPHURET.]

Tertia. Now *Hist.*

Tertial (tɜː'ʃəl), a. and sb. Also 6 teryary. [f. L. *terti-us* third + –AL, after *primaries*, *secondaries*.]

Tertian (tɜː'ʃən), a. and sb. Forms: 4 tertiane, 4–6 cian(e, –cyan, 6 –cyon, 7 tar-cian), 8 tercian, 8– tertian. [ME. in *Lanfrac*, ad. L. (*febris*) *tertiāna*.]

Tertiary (tɜː'ʃərɪ), a. and sb. Also 6 terciary. [ad. L. *tertiāri-us* of or belonging to the third, f. *tertius* third.]

Supplement, p. 3873; Corrigenda, p. 4092; Spurious words, p. 4093; Books quoted, p. 4094

Testament.

II. In Christian Latin use of *testamentum*.

Testamentar, *a., Sc. Law.* ...

Testamentarily, *adv. rare.*

Testamentarious, ...

Testamentary, *a.*

Testamentation. *Obs. rare⁻¹.*

† Testamentarine, *a., Sc. Law. rare⁻¹.*

Testamentor.

Testamentarine.

Testate, *a.*

Testate, *v.*

Testation.

Testator.

Testatrix.

Testatum. *Law.*

† Testatur. *a writ formerly issued when a writ of capias...*

Testatur. [L., 'he testifies', from *testārī* to bear witness, etc.]

Teste¹. *Obs. rare.*

Teste² (test'). Also 6 testey, -y, 7 -ee.

Tester² (te'stər). *arch.* Forms: *a.* 6 testour, etc.

Tester³ (te'stər). *arch.* Forms: *a.* 6 testorn.

Testicle (te'stik'l). Also 5 testicule. [ad. L. *testiculus*, dim. of *testis* TESTIS.]

Testicular, *a.*

Testiculate, *a. Bot.*

Testicond, *a. Zool.*

Testicule.

Testify (te'stifəi), *v.* [ad. L. *testificārī*.]

Testificate. *Sc.*

Testification.

Testificator.

Testificatory, *a., Obs. rare⁻¹.*

Testifier.

Testified, *ppl. a.*

Testifier.

Testifying, *vbl. sb.* and *ppl. a.*

Testimonial (testimōu'niăl), *sb.* and *a.*

Testimonialize, *v.*

Testimonialization.

Testimonied, *ppl. a.*

Testimony (te'stiməni), *sb.*

Testimony, *v.*

Testing, *vbl. sb.¹*

Testing, *vbl. sb.²*

Testimonium (testimōu'niŭm). [L., *testi-* ; see -MENT.]

Testis [1]. *Obs.* Pl. **testes** (testē). The Latin word for 'witness': from its legal use (cf. TEST [1]); occasional in English context.

Testis [2]. *Anat.* etymology uncertain.

1. **Testicle** in man and mammals.
 b. in other animals.

Testo (te'sto). *Mus.* [It. *testo* = L. TEXT.] The text or words of a song ; the libretto of an opera.
 b. The text, theme, or subject of a composition.

Teston, testoon (te'stən, testūn). *Obs.* exc. *Hist.* Also 6 testowne, -yon, 6-7 -oin, Sc. -ane [a. F. *teston* (in Godef. Compl.) = It. *testone*, augmentative of *testa* head : see -oon. See TESTER.]

Testor, -orne, -ourn, obs. forms of TESTER.

Testudinal (testiūdi·nal), *a.* [f. L. *testudin-*, *testudo* + -AL.] Pertaining to or resembling a tortoise.

Testudinate (testiūdi·nēt), *a.* [ad. late L. *testūdināt-us*.]
1. Formed like a testudo ; arched, vaulted.
2. Of or pertaining to tortoises.

Testudineal (testiūdi·nēal), *a.* [f. L. *testūdine-us* (see next) + -AL.] Pertaining to or resembling a tortoise.

Testudineous (testūdi·niəs), *a.* [f. L. *testūdine-us* + -OUS.] Of or pertaining to tortoises.

Testudo (testiū·do). Also 7 in anglicized form testudo. [a. L. *testudo*, f. *testa* a pot, shell, etc. : see TEST [2].]

Testy (te'sti). *a.* Forms : 4-5 testif, -yf, 5 testif, 6-7 testiue. β. 5 testi, 6-7 -ie, 6-.

Tetanism (te·təniz'm). [f. TETANUS + -ISM.]

Tetanization (tetənai'zēſən). [n. of action f. next.]

Tetanize (te·tənəiz). *trans.* To produce tetanus or tetanic spasms in. Hence **Te·tanized** *ppl. a.*

Tetanus (te·tənəs). [a. L. *tetanus*, a. Gr. τέτανος spasm.]

Tetany (te·təni). [ad. F. *tétanie*.]

Tetar, obs. form of TETTER.

Tetarto- (tē'tərto), combining form of Gr. τέταρτος fourth (cf. TETRA-), in scientific terms belonging chiefly to crystallography. **Teta·rtohe·dral** *a.* [Gr. ἕδρα base]. **Tetarto·hedral** *a.* **Teta·rtohe·drism**. **Teta·rtohe·dron**.

Tetano- (teʈano), combining form of Gr. τέτανος TETANUS.

Tetano·id *a.* [Gr. -οειδής] resembling tetanus.

(Cf. TOUCHY, which has been associated with this from early in the 17th c.)

Tête de mouton. *Obs.* [Fr., lit. 'sheep's head'.]

Tête de pont. *Obs.* [Fr., 'bridge head'.]

Teter, var. TESTER, TETTER.

Teterrimous (tēte'riməs), *a.* rare. [f. L. *těterrimus*, superl. of *teter* (*tēter*) foul + -OUS.]

Tether (te'ðər), *sb.* [? prec. sb.]
1. A rope or chain used to confine with a tether.

Teth, obs. form of TEETH, TEETHE.

Tethe, Tething, obs. ff. TITHING.

Tethee, obs. form of TEETHY, testy.

Tether (te'ðər), *v.* [f. prec. sb.]

Tête (tēt), *sb.* [Fr.]

Tête-à-tête (tēt-ā-tēt), *adv., sb.*, and *a.*

Tetrabranchus (-brə·kəs), pl. -ii [Gr. βράχιον arm], a monster having four arms

Tetracerous (-se'rəs), *a., Zool.* having four horns.

Tetrachord (te'trəkōrd), *sb.* [a. Gr. τετράχορδ-ον.]

Tetrad (te'trad). [ad. Gr. τετράδ-, τετράς group of four.]

Tetradactyl (tetrəda·ktil), *a.* and *sb.* [Gr. τετρα-δάκτυλος four-fingered.]

Tetragon (te'trəgən). [ad. Gr. τετράγων-ον.]

Tetragonal (tetræ'gənal), *a.*

Tetragram (te'trəgram). [Gr. τετράγραμμος of four letters.]

Tetragynous (tetræ'dʒinəs), *a., Bot.* having four pistils or styles.

Tetrahedron (tetrəhē'drən). [Gr. τετρά-εδρον, f. τετρα- + ἕδρα base, seat.]

Tetrapneumonian (-pnyūmō'niən), *Zool.*, *a.* or pertaining to the *Tetrapneumones*, a division of spiders with two pairs of lung-sacs.

Tetraptote (te'trəptōt), *Gram.* a noun having only four cases.

Tetrapteran (tetræ'pterən), *a.* having four wings.

Tetrarch (te'trārk, tē'trārk). [ad. L. *tetrarcha*, -es, a. Gr. τετράρχης.]

Tetraspore (te'trəspōr), *Bot.* one of four spores.

Tetrastich (te'trəstik). [ad. L. *tetrastichon*, a. Gr. τετράστιχον.]

Tetrastyle (te'trəstəil), *a.* and *sb. Arch.* [ad. Gr. τετράστυλος.]

Tetrasyllable (tetrəsi'lab'l). [ad. L. *tetrasyllabus*.]

Tetrabasic, *a. Chem.* Of a salt: Containing four atoms of hydrogen replaceable by more electropositive elements or radicals.

Tetrachord (teˈtrakǫrd). [ad. Gr. τετράχορδον.] A Greek musical instrument, a lyre or harp with four strings.

Tetrachotomous (tetrakˈǫtomǫs), *a. Zool.* Branching in four ways.

Tetraclade (teˈtraklēd), *a. Zool.*

Tetractinose to **-chronous**: see TETRA-.

Tetracyclic: see TETRA-.

Tetrad (teˈtrad). [ad. Gr. τετράς (τετράδ-).] A group of four, the number four.

Tetradactyl (tetradăkˈtil), *a.* and *sb.* Also **-dactyle**. [ad. Gr. τετραδάκτυλ-ος.] *adj.* Having four fingers or toes.

Tetradactyly (tetradăkˈtili), *Zool.* The condition of having four digits.

Tetradrachm (teˈtradram).

Tetragon (teˈtragǫn). [ad. Gr. τετράγων-ον.] *Geom.* A figure having four angles and four sides; a quadrangle considered as one of the polygons.

Tetragonal (teˈtragonǎl), *a.*

Tetragrammaton (tetragrămˈaton). Pl. **-ta, -s**. [a. Gr. τετραγράμματον (Philo I. 157), neut. of τετραγράμματ-ος, having four letters.] The word of four letters (the Hebrew word YHWH), the name of God.

Tetrahedron (tetrahīˈdrǫn, -heˈdrǫn). Pl. **-a** or **-ons**. [ad. Gr. τετράεδρον, -εδρον.] *Geom.* A solid figure contained by four plane faces; a triangular pyramid.

Tetralogy (tīˈtralǫdʒi). [ad. Gr. τετραλογία.]

Tetrameter (tīˈtramɪtǝr), *a.* and *sb.* *Pros.* [ad. L. tetrametr-us, a. Gr. τετράμετρος.]

Tetramorph (teˈtramǫrf). [ad. Gr. τετράμορφ-ος.]

Tetrapla (teˈtraplǎ). Also **-ae**.

Tetrarch (teˈtrǎrk, tiˈtrǎrk). [ad. L. tetrarch-es, a. Gr. τετράρχης, ruler of a fourth part.]

Tetrarchic (tetrǎrˈkik), *a.*

Tetrarchical ... Now *rare*.

Tetrarchy ...

Tetrasto-o-spherical ...

Tetrasporangium, *Bot.*

Tetraspore ...

Tetrasporous ...

Tetraster ...

Tetrastich ...

Tetrastichous ...

Tetrastigm ...

Tetraxon to **Tetrazonian** ...

Tetrazole ...

Tetrastyle ...

Tetrastylar ...

Tetrasyllable ...

Tetrasyllabic ...

Tetratheism ...

Tetravalent ...

... **Tetrobol** ...

Tetronal, **Tetrazoöld** ...

Tetrosomal, **Tetrazoöld** ...

Tetraxone ...

Tetraxile ...

Tetramin ...

Tetramine ...

Tetrevangelium ...

Tetric, *a.* Obs.

Tetrical ...

Tetraxida, *Chem.*

Tetroxy ...

Tetryl ...

Tetrical ...

Tetrode, *Zool.*

Tetrodon, **tetrodon** ...

Tetrazule ...

Tetronal ...

Tetronymal ...

Tetrose ...

Tetrous ...

Tetter, *v.*

Tetter-berry ...

Tetterous ...

Tetterwort ...

Tetterworm ...

Teuto- ...

Tetoto-latry ...

Teut ...

Teucrin ...

Teuk ...

Tettix ...

Teuton ...

Teutonic ...

Teutonism ...

Teutonize ...

Teutonicism ...

Teutonist ...

Teutonity ...

Teutonically ...

Teutontically ...

Tew, *v.*

Tevel, **tavel** ...

Tewel ...

Tewit ...

Tewly ...

Teuto- ...

Tew, *sb.*

Tewaw ...

Tewer ...

Tewtaw ...

Tewtaw. Also *tewtaw, tewter.*

Tewtaw, *v.* Also *tewtal, tewter.*

Tewyre, corrupt f. TUYERE: cf. TWYER-IRON.

Textale *= to exalt:* see T⁴ and EXALT.

Texan (te'ksăn), *a.* and *sb.* [f. next + -AN.] Of or pertaining to the State of Texas. In some specific names of animals, plants, etc. : e.g.

Texas (te'kSas). The name or one of the United States, formerly a province of Mexico, then for short time an independent republic.

Text (tekst), *sb.* [a. F. *texte,* also a texte, *tyxt*(e, 4-5 *text,* 4-texte; (3-5 *tyxt* also), 4-texte, also ONF. *tiste, tiste* (12th c. in Godef.), F. *texte,* also ONF. *tiste, tiste* (12th c. in Godef.)]

Text, *v.* Now *rare.* [f. TEXT *sb.*]

Textile (te'kstĭl, -təl), *a.* and *sb.* [ad. L. *textil-is* woven, *textile* (sc. *opus*) woven fabric, f. *text-,* ppl. stem of *texĕre* to weave.]

Textman (te'kst,măn).

Texted, *a.* [f. TEXT *sb.* + -ED.]

Text-hand. A fine large hand in writing.

Textor'ian, *a. rare⁻.*

Textour, *Obs. rare,* [a. AF. *textour,* ad. L. *textor.*]

Text-pen. A pen specially suitable for writing text-hand, or for engrossing.

Textrine, *a.* *Obs. rare,* [f. L. *textrin-us* of or pertaining to weaving + -INE.]

Textrix, *Obs. rare.* [L. fem. of *textor* weaver.]

Textual (te'kstiŭăl), *a.* (*sb.*) Also 4-5 *tuel,* [in form *textual,* a. OF. F. *textuel* only 13th c. in Godef), ad. L. type *textuāl-is,* f. *textus* : see TEXT.]

Textualist (te'kstiŭălist). [f. prec. + -IST.]

Textualism (te'kstiŭălĭz'm). [f. prec. + -ISM.]

Textually (te'kstiŭălĭ), *adv.* [f. as prec. + -LY.]

Textuary (te'kstiŭărĭ), *a.* and *sb.* [ad. med. L. *textuāri-us,* f. *textus* TEXT *sb.*]

Textuist (te'kstiŭist). [f. TEXT *sb.* + -IST.]

Textualist (te'kstiŭălist). *a.* and *sb.* [mod.L. *Textulāria,* genus name.]

Textural (te'kstiŭrăl), *a.* [f. L. *textūra* TEXTURE + -AL.]

Texture (te'kstiŭr), *sb.* [ad. L. *textūra* web, structure, f. *text-,* ppl. stem of *texĕre* to weave.]

Texture, *v.* [f. prec. sb.]

Textureless, *a.* [f. prec. + -LESS.]

Textured (te'kstiŭrd), *a.* [f. TEXTURE *sb.* + -ED.]

Texturing, vbl. sb.

Textury, *Obs. rare⁻.* [f. TEXTURE *sb.* + -Y.]

Textus, *sb.* [L. *textus* TEXT.]

Texture-case, a case or cover for this (*Cent. Dict.* 1891).

Teyne, *Obs. rare.* [a. ON. *tein-n* twig.]

Tezkere, tezkere (te'zkĕrĕ). Also 7 *tezkeria,* -caria, 9 -caré, tischera, teskera [Arab.], *sb.*

TH, in words of Old English or Old Norse origin, and in words from Greek, is a consonantal digraph representing a simple sound, or rather (in two tonic words), a pair of simple sounds, *breath* and *voice,* indicated in this dictionary by the OE. letters (*þ*) and (*ð*).

Th-, þh- (ME. *þ-*), a clipped form of *thou.*

Th. an abbreviation of THORIUM, THURSDAY.

Thack (þæk), *sb.* Now *dial.* Forms: 1 *þæc,* 4 *þak, þakke,* 4 *thac,* 5 *thakke,* 6- *thack.*

Thack, *v.* Now *dial.* [OE. *þac*(c)*ian.*]

THACK (þæk), *v.*

Thack (þæk), *sb.*

Thackeray (þækərə)

Thackless, *a.*

Thackster (þækstər)

Thae, *demons. pron. and adj.*

Thairm (þɛəm)

Thain, *obs. form of* THANE.

Thairf, *var.* THARF.

Thak, thakkle, etc.

Thalamencephalon (θæləmɛnˈsɛfælɒn), *Anat.*

Thalamic (θəˈlæmik), *a.*

Thalamiflora (þəˌlæmiˈflɔərə)

Thalamifloral (þəˌlæmiˈflɔərəl), *a. Bot.*

Thalamite (θæləməit), *Gr. Antiq.*

Thalamium (θəˈleimiəm)

Thalamo- (θæləmo)

Thalamus (θæləməs)

Thalassian (θəˈlæsiən)

Thalassic (þəˈlæsik), *a.*

Thalassinian (θæləˈsiniən)

Thalasso- (θəˈlæso)

Thalassoccracy (þælæˈsɒkrəsi)

Thalassocrat (þəˈlæsokræt)

Thalassography (þælæˈsɒɡræfi)

Thale-cress (þeilkrɛs)

Thaler (tɑːlər)

Thalia (θəˈliə)

Thalian (θəˈliən)

Thallic, *a.*

Thalliferous

Thallic

Thallium (þæliəm)

Thalline

Thallious

Thallium

Thallogen (þælodʒən)

Thalloid (þælɔid), *a. Bot.*

Thallome (þæloum), *sb. Bot.*

Thallophyte (þæloufəit), *Bot.*

Thallus (þæləs), *Bot.*

Thalweg

Thames (tɛmz)

Thamnium

Than (ðæn)

Thanage (þeinidʒ)

Thane (þein)

Thanatism

Thanatist

Thanato- (θænæto)

Thanatography

Thanatognomonic

The excellent 'Newgate Calendar'..contains the biographies and *thanatographies of Hayes and his wife. 1841 *Fraser's Mag.* XXV. 270 The deuteroscopic or *thanatomantic faculty of the Germans. 1860 MAYNE *Expos. Lex.*, *Thanatometrum*, ..term by Nasse [of Berlin] for a means of indicating the actual presence of death; a death-measurer: a *thanatometer. 1899 *Syd. Soc. Lex.*, *Thanatometer*, a thermometer capable of being introduced into the stomach to determine whether the depression of temperature is sufficient to be looked on as a sign of death. 1860 MAYNE *Expos. Lex.*, **Thanatophobia*, term for a dread or fear of death: *thanatophoby. 1903 *Alien. & Neurol.* May 170 Pessimism is frequently associated with morbid fear of death (thanatophobia). 1816 W. C. BRYANT (*title*) *Thanatopsis. 1860 MAYNE *Expos. Lex.*, **Thanatotyphus*. 1890 in BILLINGS *Med. Dict.*

Thanatoid (þæ·nătoid), *a. Path.* [f. Gr. θάνατος death + -OID. Cf. Gr. θανατώδης.] (See quot.)

1857 DUNGLISON *Med. Lex.*, *Thanatoid*, resembling death; apparently dead. 1890 in BILLINGS *Nat. Med. Dict.*

Thanatology (þænătǫ·lŏdʒi). *rare.* [f. Gr. θάνατος death + -LOGY. Cf. F. *thanatologie.*] The scientific study of death, its causes and phenomena. So **Thanatolo·gical** *a.*, of or pertaining to thanatology; **Thanato·logist**, a student of or a person versed in thanatology; in quot. 1901 (*nonce-use*), one who studies dead animals.

1842 DUNGLISON *Med. Lex.*, *Thanatology*, a description, or the doctrine, of death. 1862 G. W. BALFOUR tr. *Casper's Forensic Med.* II. Title-p., Thanatological division. 1881 G. R. JESSE in *Athenæum* 9 Apr. 504/1 This sums up the thanatological results of an enormous amount of cruelty in previous experiments. 1901 E. SELOUS *Bird Watching* viii. 224 We have studied animals only to kill them, or killed them in order to study them. Our 'zoologists' have been thanatologists. 1903 MITCHELL tr. *Metchnikoff's Nat. Man* xii. (1904) 298 The scientific study of old age and of death, two branches of science that may be called *gerontology* and *thanatology*.

‖**Thanatophidia** (þænătofi·diă), *sb. pl. Zool.* [f. *thanat-*, THANATO- + OPHIDIA.] A division of *Ophidia*, comprising the venomous snakes. Hence **Thanatophi·dian** *a.*, of or pertaining to the *Thanatophidia*; *sb.* a serpent of this division; **Thanatophidio·logist**, a student of the zoology of the *Thanatophidia*.

1872 FAYRER (*title*) The Thanatophidia of India, being a Description of the Venomous Snakes of the Indian Peninsula. 1884 J. DONNET in *Nature* 27 Mar. 504/1, I believe it to be a generally accepted opinion among thanatophidiologists that, from what is known of the virulent properties of snake-poison, though fatal to man and other living beings, it is innoxious in its effects to serpents of like nature. 1891 *Cent. Dict.*, Thanatophidian *a.* and *sb.*

‖**Thanato·sis.** *Path.* [a. Gr. θανάτωσις a putting to death, f. θανατοῦν to put to death.]

1860 MAYNE *Expos. Lex.*, *Thanatosis*,..term for Mortification. 1890 in BILLINGS *Nat. Med. Dict.*

Thane [1] (þēⁱn). *Hist.* Forms: 1 þegn, þegen, -in, (þeng), 1–2 þén, þeign (6–7 theigne), 2 þening, 2–3 þein (6, 9 thein), 3–4 þ-, theyn(e (6 theyn), 4 thain (8 -e), 4–6 thayn(e, 5– thane. See also THEGN. [OE. *þegn*, *þegen*, *þén*, = OS. *thegan*, OHG. *degan* boy, servant, warrior, hero (MHG., G. *degen*), ON. *þegn* freeman, liegeman:—OTeut. **þegno^z*, orig. child, boy, lad:—pre-Teut. **tek-nó-* (cf. Gr. τέκνον child), f. root *tek*: *tok* to beget.

The regular modern repr. of OE. *þegn*, if the word had lived on in spoken use, would have been *thain* (cf. *fain*, *main*, *rain*), as it actually appears in some writers, chiefly northern, from 1300 to near 1600. But *thain* was in 15–16th c. Sc. written *thane* (in L. *thanus*), and this form, being used by Boece, Holinshed, and Shakspere (in Macbeth), was adopted by Selden, Spelman, and the legal antiquaries and historians of the 17th c. to represent the Anglo-Saxon *þegn*, and became the usual form in Eng. history. Recent historians, as Stubbs, Freeman, and Green, in order to distinguish the Anglo-Saxon use from the Sc. in sense 4, have revived the OE. *þegn* as THEGN, q. v.]

†**1.** A servant, minister, attendant; in OE. often applied to (Christ's) disciples. *Obs.*

a 700 *Epinal Gloss* (O.E.T.) 101 *Adsaeculam* [= *assecula*], thegn. *c* 725 *Corpus Gloss* 77 *Adsaeclum*, þegn. *c* 888 K. ÆLFRED *Boeth.* vii. § 2, ʒif þu þonne hiora þegen beon wilt. *a* 900 tr. *Bæda's Hist.* IV. xxv. [xxiv.] (1890) 346 Þa bæd he [a monk] his þegn..þæt he in þæm huse him stowe ʒegearwode..Þa wundrode se þegn. *c* 950 *Lindisf. Gosp.* Matt. xxiv. 45 Hwa woenes ðu is geleaf-full ðegn & hoga? 971 *Blickl. Hom.* 67 Iohannes, se deora þegn. *Ibid.*, Lazarus þær was ana sittende mid Hælende & mid his þegnum. *c* 1000 *Ags. Gosp.* Matt. xx. 26 Sy he eower þen. *Ibid.* John ii. 9 Þa þenas soðlice wiston þe þæt wæter hlodon. *a* 1175 *Cott. Hom.* 229 An þera twelf Christes þeigne se þe was iudas ʒehaten. *c* 1275 *Death* 177 in *O. E. Misc.* 179 Hwer beoþ þine þeynes þat þe leoue were? 13.. *Cursor M.* 5373 (Cott.) First he was here als our thain [*Gött.* thrall, *Trin.* þral]. 1591 LAMBARDE *Archeion* (1635) E iij, By certaine Messengers, which they tearmed Theignes; that is to say, Ministers, or Servants.

†**2.** A military attendant, follower, or retainer; a soldier. *Obs.*

Beowulf 400 Aras þa se rica ymb hine rinc maniʒ þryðlic þegna heap. *a* 800 CYNEWULF *Elene* 549 (Gr.) Þa cwom þegna heap to þam heremeðle. *c* 893 K. ÆLFRED *Oros.* V. ii. § 3 Ueriatuses þegn þæm obrum to longe æfterfylgende, oþ mon his hors under him ofsceat. *c* 950 *Lindisf. Gosp.* Matt. viii. 9 Ic..hæfo under mec ðeignas [*Vulg.* milites]. *c* 1000 *Ags. Gosp.* ibid., Ic hæbbe þegnas [*c* 1160 *Hatton* þeignes] under me. *c* 1000 ÆLFRIC *Voc.* in Wr.-Wülcker 119/31 *Agaso*, hors þen.

†**b.** *poet.* A warrior, a brave man. Cf. EARL 1 b.

Beowulf 2709 Swylc sceolde secg wesan, þegn æt ðearfe. *c* 893 K. ÆLFRED *Oros.* III. vii. § 2 ʒif ʒe swelce þegnas sint, swelce ʒe wenað þæt ʒe sien, þonne sceoldon ʒe swa lustlice eowre agnu brocu aræfnan. *a* 1272 *Luue Ron* 13 in *O. E. Misc.* 93 Þeos þeines þat weren bolde beoþ aglyden.

3. One who in Anglo-Saxon times held lands of the king or other superior by military service; originally in the fuller designation *cyninges þegn*, 'king's thane, military servant or attendant'; in later times simply *thegn*, as a term of rank, including several grades below that of an *ealdorman* or *eorl* (EARL *sb.* 2) and above that of the *ceorl* or ordinary freeman.

In this sense the name was superseded by *baron* and *knight* in the 12th c., and continued only in historical use, in which it was written *thane* in the 16th c. Recent historians have revived the OE. form as THEGN.

805 *Charter* in *O. E. Texts* 442 Beforan wulfrede arcebiscope..& esne cyninges ðegne. *a* 900 *O. E. Chron.* an. 897, Maniʒe þara selestena cynges þena...Eadulf cynges þegn..& Ecgulf cynges hors þegn. 971 *Blickl. Hom.* 211 Wæs his fæder ærest cyninges þegn, & ða..he wæs cininges þegna aldorman. *c* 1000 ÆLFRIC *Gram.* ix. (Z.) 50 *Optimas*, ðegn. *c* 1000 — *Voc.* in Wr.-Wülcker 155/20 *Primas*, heafodman, *uel* þegn. *Ibid.* 155/23 *Satrapa*, þegn. *c* 1029–60 *Laws Ranks* c. 1 in Liebermann *Gesetze* (1903) 456 Ælc be his mæðe, ʒe eorl ʒe ceorl, ʒe þegen ʒe þeoden. *c* 1050 *Byrhtferth's Handboc* in *Anglia* (1885) VIII. 326 Þegnas & ceorlas habbað landmearke. 1066 *Writ of Eadweard* in Earle *Land-Charters* 342 Eadward cyningc gret Hereman biscop, and Harold eorl, and Godric, and ealle his þeʒenas [L. version *barones*]. *a* 1100 *O. E. Chron.* an. 1086 (Laud MS.) Ealle þa rice men ofer eall Engla land, arce biscopas, & leodbisceopas, abbodas & eorlas, þegnas & cnihtas. *a* 1175 *Cott. Hom.* 231 Mid ærlen and aldren, mid cnihten, mid þeinen. *c* 1300 *Havelok* 2260 Siþen drenges, and siþen thaynes, And siþen knithes, and siþen sweynes. *c* 1325 *Chron. Eng.* (Ritson) 583 Alle the theynes of Walschelonde He made bowe to ys honde. 1570–6 LAMBARDE *Peramb. Kent* (1826) 453 As for *twelf Pindman*, it was given to the Theyn or Gentleman, because his life was valued at Twelve hundreth shillings. 1598 HAKLUYT *Voy.* I. 126 If a Thein so thriued, that he serued the king, and on his message rid in his houshold, if he then had a Thein that followed him..he became an Earle.

1577–87 HOLINSHED *Chron.* I. 190/1 Harold..slue thirtie gentlemen of honor, or thanes (as they called them). 1614 SELDEN *Titles Hon.* 267 The neerest name for Baron was that of Thane, anciently written also Thegn. *c* 1630 RISDON *Surv. Devon* § 284 (1810) 296 The thane was descended of ancient lineage, and such a one as we call gentleman. 1754 HUME *Hist. Eng.* (1761) I. App. i. 96 The nobles were called thanes; and were of two kinds, the king's thanes and lesser thanes. 1809 BAWDWEN *Domesday Bk.* 18 In *Loctusu* (Lofthouse) two Thanes had four carucates to be taxed. 1853 JOS. STEVENSON tr. *O. E. Chron.* an. 1036, Leofric the earl, and almost all the thanes north of the Thames..chose Harold for chief of all England. 1853 — tr. *Florence of Worcester* an. 897, Ecgulf the kings horse-thane. 1875 MAINE *Hist. Inst.* v. 135 There are in the early English laws some traces of a process by which a Ceorl might become Thane. 1888 EARLE *Land-Charters* Introd. 71 These words ..eorl, gesith, thane, knight, squire, gentleman. The last two run abreast.

4. In *Scottish Hist.* A person, ranking with the son of an earl, holding lands of the king; the chief of a clan, who became one of the king's barons.

[1130 *Stat. Alex. II*, c. 2, in *Scot. Statutes* (1844) I. 398 De terris episcoporum abbatum baronum militum et thanorum qui de Rege tenent.] 14.. *transl. of prec.*, Of þe landis of bischopis abbotis barounis knychtis and thaynis þe quhilkis haldis of þe Kyng. 1422 in *Thanes of Cawdor* (Spalding Club) 10 To spouse and til haf to your wife, the douchter of the saide Donald thayne of Caldor. *c* 1425 WYNTOUN *Cron.* VI. xviii. 1904 Lo, ʒonder þe thayne of Crumbaghty! *Ibid.* xix. 2318 Makduf of Fif þe thayne. *c* 1470 HENRY *Wallace* XI. 894 That Erll was cummyn off trew haill nobill blud, Fra the ald thane, quhilk in his tym was gud. 1535 STEWART *Cron. Scot.* (Rolls) II. 637 'The Thane of Glames, gude morne to him', said scho. [1596 DALRYMPLE tr. *Leslie's Hist. Scot.* I. (S.T.S.) 112 *margin*, The first nobils in Scotland war called Thani; thay war of the clan cheif...In ald tymes Dukes war called Thani.] 1605 SHAKS. *Macb.* I. iii. 71 By Sinells death, I know I am Thane of Glamis, But how, of Cawdor? the Thane of Cawdor liues. *Ibid.* v. iii. 50 Doctor, the Thanes flye from me. 1609 SKENE *Reg. Maj.* 73 b, *Item*, the Cro of ane Earles sonne, or of ane Thane, is ane hundreth kye. *Item*, the Cro of the sonne of ane Thane, is thriescore sax kye. 1759 ROBERTSON *Hist. Scot.* I. (1802) I. 229 The ancient Thanes were the equals and the rivals of their prince. 1810 A. BOSWELL *Edinburgh* 260 Hill after hill some cunning clerk shall gain, Then, in a mendicant, behold a Thane!

b. *transf.* to modern persons, in various senses; e. g. a Scottish lord. Often in allusion to Shaks. *Macbeth* v. iii. 50. (See above.)

1750 SHENSTONE *Odes, Rural Elegance* 7 Ye rural thanes that o'er the mossy down Some panting, timorous hare pursue. *a* 1764 LLOYD *Poetry Prof.* Poet. Wks. 1774 I. 39 Hail to the Thane, whose patriot skill Can break all nations to his will. 1839 LD. BROUGHAM *Statesm. Geo. III*, *Dundas* I. 232 He [Pitt] held the proxies of many Scottish Peers in open opposition! Well might his colleague exclaim to the hapless Addington in such unheard-of troubles, 'Doctor, the Thanes fly from us.' 1888 BRYCE *Amer. Commw.* lxiii. II. 455 Sometimes however he is rebuffed by the powers at Washington and then his State thanes fly from him.

5. *Comb.* **Thane-right**, the legal rights and privileges of a thane; **Thane-wer** [OE. *þegnwer*], the wer-gild of a thane (sense 3).

1008 [see THEGNWER]. 1844 LINGARD *Anglo-Sax. Ch.* (1858) II. xii. 234 *note*, His thane-wer, and thane-right in life and in the grave means the same as his worldly goods, and Christian sepulture.

Hence **Tha·ness**, a female thane; a thane's wife.

1807 SCOTT *Surg. Dau.* iii, All the rural thanes and thanesses attended on these occasions. 1849 J. WILSON *Christopher under Canvass* No. 5 The Thaness [Lady Macbeth] is self-stayed.

Thane [2], Sc. form of FANE [1].

1496 *Acc. Ld. High Treas. Scot.* I. 286 Item, for xiij dowbill platis to be thanis to the pailʒounis. 1570 *Satir. Poems Reform.* xxii. 84 Lyke wauering thane, thy proces vane Will brew the bitter gall. 1716 in *Thanes of Cawdor* (Spalding Cl.) 417 Thanes for the horse heads [at a funeral], £80. 1782 OREM *Chanonry Aberdeen* 21 With cross thanes of iron on the top of each of them.

Thane, obs. f. THEN *adv.* [1]; inflexion of THE.

Thanedom (þēⁱ·ndəm). [f. THANE + -DOM.] The domain or jurisdiction of a Scottish thane.

c 1425 WYNTOUN *Cron.* VI. xviii. 1910 In his ʒouth heid Off þai thayndomes þe thayne wes maid. 1579 *Reg. Privy C. Scot.* III. 140 The lordschip and thanedome of Fettarcarne. 1776 PENNANT *Tour Scot.* II. Addit. 13 This thanedom was transferred into the house of the Campbels. 1807 G. CHALMERS *Caledonia* I. III. vii. 426 The titles of Glamis, and Cawdor, were borrowed by Boece from thanedoms of more recent origin. 1837 SKENE *Highlanders Scot.* (1902) II. v. 261 Thanedoms were certainly hereditary in Scotland.

†**Tha·nehede.** *Obs.* [f. THANE [1], in sense 1 'servant' + *-hede*, -HEAD. Essentially an earlier form of next, but unconnected with it in use, being founded on an earlier sense of OE. *þegn*.] Service, servitude; bondage, thraldom.

a 1300 *Cursor M.* 5404 (Cott.) Land and lijth wit bodi we bede, Þat þou vs tak in þin thainhede [*v.rr.* bonde-, bundhede]; In thainhed [*Fairf.* bondehede; *Gött.* & *Trin.* þraldam, -dome] tak our landes all, For sede we mai þam sau wit-all. *Ibid.* 5791, I sal þam [Israel] bring vte of thainhede [*v.rr.* þraldome, thralhede], In-till a land, a wonsun thede. *Ibid.* 6990 In thain-hede ar þai worth to be, Þat wil noght thole, and mai be fre.

Tha·nehood. [f. THANE (senses 3, 4) + -HOOD. Cf. THEGNHOOD.] The condition or rank of a thane.

1897 E. CONYBEARE *Hist. Cambs.* 89 Raised to the Thanehood by their own or their forefathers' merits.

Tha·ne-land. Now *Hist.* (See also THEGNLAND.) Land held by a thane, or by military tenure.

a 1641 SPELMAN *Feuds & Tenures* viii, For better manifestation that Thanelands were subject to no feudal Service, consider, I pray you, the Words of the Saxon passage before mention'd, where it is said that a Thane must have three Hides at least of his..own Land. 1701 *Cowell's Interpr.*, *Thane-Lands*, Lands..granted by Charters of the Saxon Kings to their Thanes. 1809 BAWDWEN *Domesday Bk.* 370 Ulnod holds one oxgang of the same land in thaneland.

Thanen, þanen, -ene, *adv.*: see THENNE.

Thaneship (þēⁱ·nʃip). [f. THANE [1] + -SHIP: cf. OE. *þegnscipe*.] The office or position of a thane: esp. in the Sc. sense. (See also THEGNSHIP.)

1766 STEEVENS *Note Shaks.*, *Macb.* I. iii. 48 The thaneship of Glamis was the ancient inheritance of Macbeth's family. 1844 LINGARD *Anglo-Sax. Ch.* (1858) I. App. 371 These lands ceasing to support an earthly thaneship or service. 1865 KINGSLEY *Herew.* xv, He shall have..a thaneship in East Anglia. 1896 MANLY *Notes on Macbeth* 101 Since Macbeth's accession to the thaneship of Cawdor.

Thanist, -stry, obs. forms of TANIST, -STRY.

Thank (þæŋk), *sb.* Forms: α. 1–4 þanc, (3 ðhanc), 1–5 þank, (3 *Orm.* þannk), 4 thanc (thang), 4–5 þanke, 4–6 thanck(e, 4–7 thanke, (6 thangke), 4– thank. β. 1 thonc, 1–4 þonc, 2 þeonk, 2–5 þonk, (3 þong), 3–5 þonke, 4 þoncke. [OE. *þanc*, *þonc* = OFris. *thonk*, OS. **thank* (MDu. *danc*, D. *dank*), OHG., MHG. *danc* (G. *dank*), ON. *þökk* (:—*þanku* fem.), Sw. *tack*, Da. *tak*, Goth. *þagks*:—OTeut. **þanko^z*, f. ablaut stem *þenk*: *þank*: *þunk*: see THINK. The primary sense was therefore *thought*.]

I. †**1.** = THOUGHT. *Obs.* (See also I-THANK.)

735 BÆDA *Death-song* 2 Naenig uuiurthit thonc snotturra [*or* thoncsnotturra] than him thaarf sie. *a* 900 *Andreas* 557 (Gr.) Saga þances gleaw þeȝn, ȝif þu cunne, hu þæt gewurde be werum tweonum. *c* 1000 *Ags. Ps.* (Th.) lxxxvii[i]. 11 Ne on ðeostrum ne mæg, þances ʒehyʒdum, æniʒ wislicu wundur oncnawan. *c* 1160 *Hatton Gosp.* Matt. xv. 19 Of þare heorte cumeð þa yfele þankes [*c* 1000 ʒeþancas]. *c* 1175 *Lamb. Hom.* 3 Heo urnen on-ʒein him..mid ufele þeonke. *a* 1200 *Moral Ode* 90 He þurhsiheþ uches monnes þonc. *c* 1200 *Trin. Coll. Hom.* 9 We..folʒeð on þonke, and on speche, and on dede, þat him is iqueme. *a* 1225 *Ancr. R.* 222 He..put..a swuc[h] þonc in hire softe heorte. *c* 1300 *Prov. Hending* i. in *Sal. & Sat.*, etc. (1848) 270 Gode þonkes and monie þewes for te teche fele schrewes.

†**2.** Favourable thought or feeling, good will; graciousness, grace, favour. *Obs.*

a 1000 *Cædmon's Gen.* 796 (Gr.) Þis is landa betst, þæt wit þurh uncres hearran þanc habban moston. *c* 1000 *Ags. Ps.* (Th.) ci. 15 [cii. 17] Oft he þearfendra bene þance gehyrde. 1340 *Ave Maria* in *Rel. Ant.* I. 42 Hayl Marie of thonke vol [*Vulg. Luke* i. 28 Ave! gratia plena]. 1609 BIBLE (Douay) *Ecclus.* xii. 1 If thou wilt doe good, know to whom thou doest it, and there shal be much thanke [*Vulg.* gratia multa] in thy good deedes.

†**b.** The genitive case *thanks*, ME. *thankes*, lit. 'of thought', 'of good will', was used adverbially in sense 'willingly, voluntarily', esp. with preceding possessive pronoun, e. g. *his thankes* = with his consent, good will, or approval: so *Godes thankes* = *Deo volente*. Cf. UNTHANKES, unwillingly. *Obs.*

c 888 K. ÆLFRED *Boeth.* xiii, Sæge me nu hwæðer se þin wela [þines] ðances swa diore seo, þe for his aʒenre ʒecynde. 1008 *Charter of Bp. Theodred* in Birch *Cart. Sax.* III. 200 Mines erfes þat ic begiten habbe & ʒet bigete Godes þankes and hise halegen. 1066 *O. E. Chron.* (MS. C.), Tostig ..nam of þam butse karlon sume mid him, sume þances sume unþances. 1154 *Ibid.* an. 1140 (MS. Laud), Hi of Normandi wenden alle fra þe king..., sume here þankes & sume here un þankes. *c* 1175 *Lamb. Hom.* 17 Al swa þu waldest for þe nuste dude þe þines þonkes. *a* 1250 *Owl & Night.* 70 Ek for þe þe sulue mose Hire þonkes wolde þe totose. *c* 1386 CHAUCER *Shipman's T.* 188 Pardee, I wol nat faille yow, my thankes. *c* 1400 MAUNDEV. (Roxb.) xxxi. 140 Þis ile dare na pilgrim come in ne nere it, þaire thankes. *a* 1450 MYRC *Par. Pr.* 891 Koghe þow not þenne by þonkes.

†**3.** Kindly thought or feeling entertained towards any one for favour or services received; grateful thought, gratitude. Rarely in *pl. Obs.*

The sense of 'gratitude, kindly or loving feeling for favour or benefit' must have been developed between that of 'good will, good feeling' generally, and that of 'the expression of gratitude'. But the feeling passes so naturally into its expression that it is not easy to separate them in the quotations, except by the accompanying verbs: *to express one's thanks*, and the archaic *to con thanks*, ought to mean to express one's *feelings of gratitude*; but *to give, offer, return* or *receive thanks*, ought to mean to give or receive *the expression of gratitude*; so *to have thanks*, but this is less clear. In many instances it is impossible to say which is meant; some of the examples given here may belong to 4.

1297 R. GLOUC. (Rolls) 9379 Muche þonc were it vs of god mid him vorto fiʒte. 13.. *Gaw. & Gr. Knt.* 1380 Haue I þryuandely þonk þurh my craft serued? *c* 1374 CHAUCER *Troylus* III. 1728 (1777) Þis encres of hardynesse and myght Com hym of loue, his ladyes thank to wynne. *c* 1400 *Destr. Troy* 12724 The lady..þonkit hym þroly with þonks in hir hert. *c* 1420 *Brut* 343 Þanne þei..went hom ayen yn-to her owne cuntre, with grete loue & moche þanke. 1500–20 DUNBAR *Poems* xvi. 19 Or the gift deliuerit be, The thank is frustrat and expyrd. *a* 1677 BARROW *Wks.* (1687) I. viii. 94 It was a satyrical answer (that of Aristotle)..who being asked..What doth the soonest grow old? replied..Thanks.

4. The expression of gratitude; the grateful acknowledgement of a benefit or favour. †**a.** in sing. *Obs.*

†*Gode þank*, *God-thank* [= L. *Deo gratias*, F. *grâce à Dieu*], thanks (be) to God, thank God.

Beowulf 1779 Þæs siʒ metode þanc, ecean dryhtne, þæs ðe ic on aldre ʒe-bad. *c* 888 K. ÆLFRED *Boeth.* xxxv. § 4 Þa ʒesceafta næren nanes þonces ne nanes weorðscipes wyrðe. *c* 897 — *Gregory's Past. C.* 2 Gode almiehteʒum si ðonc ðætte we nu æniʒne on stal habbað lareowa. *a* 1000 *Cædmon's Gen.* 1116 (Gr.) Him þæs þanc sie. *c* 1375 *Sc. Leg. Saints* xxvi. (*Nycholas*) 324 Thang to al-mychtty god he ȝaulde. *c* 1440 *Promp. Parv.* 490/1 Thanke, *grates*, *graciarum accio*, *gratulamen*. 1483 CAXTON *Gold. Leg.* 195/2 Thanke and glorye to god & honoure to the vyrgyne. 1534 MORE *Treat. Passion* Introd., Wks. 1271/1 Turning to god with lawde and thanke. *a* 1553 UDALL *Royster D.* II. ii, *Doughtie.* He will thank you woman. *Madge.* I will none of his thanke. 1642 ROGERS *Naaman* 385 Is this the thanke which you returne to God?

c 897 K. ÆLFRED *Gregory's Past. C.* 9 Gode ðonc. *Ibid.* i. 27. *c* 1200 *Trin. Coll. Hom.* 11 Unbileue..is aiware aleid and rihte leue arered godeðonc. 1297 R. GLOUC. (Rolls) 2578 Þe King was gode þonk aboue in four batailes. *c* 1300 *Havelok* 2005 Þus wolde þe theues me haue reft, But godþank, he hauenet sure keft.

b. in plural. †Formerly sometimes const. as *sing.*

1340 *Ayenb.* 18 Me..him ne yeldeþ þonkes of his guodes, þet he ous heþ ydo. 1481 CAXTON *Reynard* iv. (Arb.) 8 All hath he but lytyl thanks. 1509 HAWES *Past. Pleas.* iv. (Percy Soc.) 21 At whose encreace there is great thankes rendred. 1538 ELYOT, *Grates*, thankes. 1588 SHAKS. *Tit. A.* I. i. 215 Thankes to men Of Noble mindes, is Honourable Meede. 1592 — *Rom. & Jul.* II. vi. 23 Else is his thanks too much. 1651 HOBBES *Leviath.* II. xxxi. 191 Prayers precede, and Thanks succeed the benefit. 1753 HANWAY *Trav.* (1762) I. II. xvi. 72 Our soldiers were fed luxuriously at the fisheries, for nothing more than thanks. 1805 R. FULTON in *Sinclair's Corr.* (1831) II. 64, I return it to you with my sincere thanks. 1871 R. ELLIS *Catullus* xlix. 4 Thanks superlative unto thee Catullus Renders. 1881 'RITA' *My Lady Coquette* iii, Yolande gives her a smile of thanks.

c. *A thank* (formerly also *a thanks*): an expression of gratitude; a thanking, a thank-you. Now *rare*.

†*To pick* (*get*, *win*) *a thank*: see PICK *v.* [1] 8 b. *Obs.*

13.. *Gaw. & Gr. Knt.* 1984 Vche mon þat he mette, he made hem a þonke, For his seruyse. 1474 CAXTON *Chesse* III. vii. (1883) 139 To thende that they myght haue a thanke & be preysed. 1560 DAUS tr. *Sleidane's Comm.* Pref. 5 b, Verye manye of those wryters seke to pike a thanke. *a* 1577 GASCOIGNE *Herbs*, etc. Wks. (1587) 119 While Pierce the plowman hopes to pick a thank. 1579–1627 [see PICK *v.* [1] 8 b β]. 1601 B. JONSON *Poetaster* IV. vii, Without a thankes, to be sent hence! 1678 R. L'ESTRANGE *Seneca's Mor.* I. xv. (1696) 81 He..contents himself with a bare Thank for a Requital. *a* 1810 TANNAHILL *Poet. Wks.* (1846) 67 With his lordship's thank. 1839 LONGF. *Black Kn.* 47 The children drank, Gave many a courteous thank.

II. Phrases and phraseological uses.

5. *Thanks*: a much abbreviated expression of gratitude for a favour received or recognition of a service; = *I give you my thanks*, *my thanks to you*, or the like. Also *many thanks*, *best thanks*.

1588 SHAKS. *L. L. L.* v. ii. 559 If your Ladiship would say thankes Pompey, I had done. *La.* Great thankes, great Pompey. 1605 — *Macb.* II. i. 30 *Macb.* Good repose the while! *Banq.* Thankes, Sir: the like to you! 1647 PEACHAM *Worth of a Penny* 14 He answers you with Monosyllables, ..Yes, No, That, Thankes, True, &c. 1803 *Forest of Hohenelbe* I. 167 Thanks, Baron, for your good wishes. 1803 PITT in *G. Rose's Diaries* (1860) II. 16 Many thanks for your letter. 1866 E. FITZGERALD *More Lett.* (1901) 82 Don't you dislike the way some People have of saying perpetually '*Thanks!*' instead of 'Thank you'?..It is like cutting Acknowledgment as short as possible...*Thanks* [is] about one of the most hideous monosyllables, even in the English Language. 1870 MISS BRIDGMAN *Rob. Lynne* II. xiv. 299 'Would you like to read the letter, Robert?' 'No, thanks'.

6. *Thanks to*: Thanks be given to, or are due to; hence, Owing to, as a result of, in consequence of. (Often ironical.) So *no thanks* (†*thank*) *to*, no credit to, not by virtue or merit of; not because or by reason of.

1633 EARL MANCH. *Al Mondo* (1636) 115 It is no thankes to a man to pay that willingly, which he must doe of necessitie. 1633 BP. HALL *Medit. & Vows* (1851) 150 It is scarce any thank to me that he prevails. 1647 TRAPP *Comm. Rev.* iii. 4 No thank to the Pastour, who was a mercenary eye-servant. *a* 1687 PETTY *Pol. Arith.* vi. (1691) 99 No thanks to any Laws which have been made to that purpose. 1737 POPE *Hor. Epist.* II. ii. 68 But thanks to Homer) since I live and thrive, Indebted to no Prince or Peer alive. 1813 SCOTT *Rokeby* v. vi, It is a sight but rarely spied, Thanks to man's wrath and woman's pride. 1894 *Westm. Gaz.* 21 Aug. 3/3 The passengers—thanks, I expect, to the bitter cold—behaved more quietly at night than in the morning.

†**7.** *In* (*on*) *thank*, *to thank*, with pleased mind, with pleasure or satisfaction; pleasantly, graciously; with thanks, gratefully. *Obs.*

a 1000 *Andreas* 1114 (Gr.) Hie þa lac hraðe þegon to þance. *a* 1000 *Cædmon's Gen.* 2442 Hie on þanc curon æðelinges est. *a* 1300 *Cursor M.* 15047 (Cott.) Þou tak to thanc þat we þe mak Sli mensking als we mai. *c* 1375 *Sc. Leg. Saints* vi. (*Thomas*) 12 Þat he in grete thank vil take, And als reward hym t[h]ankfully. *c* 1400 *Rom. Rose* 4577 He seyde, 'In thank I shal it take, And high maister eeke thee make'. *c* 1430 *Syr Gener.* (Roxb.) 9803 If I wist to thank ye wold it take, A mariage fayne wold I make. 1513 DOUGLAS *Æneis* VII. v. 153, I grant thine axing, Troiane messinger, And ȝour rewardis ressauis in thank.

8. *To can*, *con*, *cun* (*great*, *little*) *thank*(*s*, to acknowledge or express gratitude, to make known gratitude, to give thanks, to thank. *Obs.* exc. *dial.* See CAN *v.* [1] 10, CON *v.* [1] 4.

†**9.** *To have* (or *get*) *thank*: to be thanked; also, to be thought worthy of thanks, to get the credit *for*, to have the merit or honour *of* (something); hence, contextually, *thank* = thanks due or merited, recompense, reward, credit, merit, and *ironically* discredit, blame. *Obs.*

c 950 *Lindisf. Gosp.* Luke xvii. 9 Ahne ðonc hafeð esne ðæm forðon dyde ða ðe him ʒehaten hæfde? *c* 1000 *Ags. Gosp.* ibid., Hæfð se þeowa æniʒne þanc forþam ðe he dyde þæt [etc.]? *c* 1020 *Rule St. Benet* v. (Logeman) 25 He for swylcere dæde æniʒne ne begitt þanc. *c* 1175 *Lamb. Hom.* 137 Þa ðe doð god for to habben ðer of aʒen in þisse liue, nabbeð heo nenne þonc on eche weorlde. 1297 R. GLOUC. (Rolls) 9915 Þe wrecche luþer giwes..a riche presant..sende þis noble kinge, ac hor þonc was lute. *a* 1300 *Cursor M.* 13841 Þar-for haf he neuer thank! *c* 1320 *Sir Tristr.* 2081 Maister, þank haue ʒe. For þou me þis bode brouʒt Mi robe ȝiue y þe. *c* 1385 CHAUCER *L. G. W.* 452 For who so yeveth a yifte or dooth a grace, Do it by tyme, his thank ys wel the more. *c* 1460 FORTESCUE *Abs. & Lim. Mon.* vii. (1885) 125 Off somme man [h]is highnes shall haue more thanke ffor money then ffor lande. 1483 *Cath. Angl.* 381/2 A Thanke, *meritum*, *emericio*, *emericium*. 1533 BELLENDEN *Livy* II. iv. (S.T.S.) I. 142 Thir twa lawis..war pronuncit allanerlie ..be auctorite of þe said valerius (þat he mycht þarethrow haue þe thank þareof). 1539 BIBLE (Great) *Luke* vi. 32 Yf ye loue them which loue you, what thanke haue ye? [so 1611, 1881; TINDALE, what thanke are ye worthy of? *Rhem.* what thanke is to you?]. 1545 ELYOT *Dict.* s.v. *Ineo*, *Gratiam inire*, to get thanke or frendes with some pleasure done vnto them. 1584 *Mirr. Mag.* 9 It is a work of more thank to preserue health, then to cure Sicknesse. 1600 NASHE *Summers Last Will* Introd., He..must be making himselfe a publike laughing stock, & haue no thanke for his labor. 1633 BP. HALL *Hard Texts*, *N. T.* 4 The thanke of this is Gods, not yours. 1669 R. MONTAGU in *Buccleuch MSS.* (Hist. MSS. Comm.) I. 424 Lord Clarendon would have the thanks and credit of it.

10. *To give thanks* (†*thank*, †*to do thank*(*s*), to express gratitude; *spec.* = 'to give thanks to God'; now esp. of saying grace at a meal. *arch.*

971 *Blickl. Hom.* 39 Don we..Drihtne þancas þe us þa wæstmas sealde. *Ibid.* 191 Þanc ic do, Crist þu goda hyrde. *Ibid.* 217 He..Ælmihtiʒum Gode þære ʒife þanc sæʒde. 1477 EARL RIVERS (Caxton) *Dictes* 1 To gyue therfore synguler louynges & thankes. 1526 TINDALE *Matt.* xxvi. 26 Jesus toke breed, and gave thankes, brake it, and gave it to his disciples. 1596 SHAKS. *Tam. Shr.* IV. i. 162 Will you giue thankes, sweete Kate, or else shall I? 1765 T. HUTCHINSON *Hist. Mass.* I. 262 The general court..gave them thanks for their good services. 1808–18 JAMIESON s.v. *Grace-drink*, After the giving of thanks at the end of a meal. 1831 SCOTT *Ct. Robt.* ix, All gave me fair thanks for the knightly manner of quitting myself towards them, except one.

11. *To return thanks*, to render thanks in return for a benefit or favour. Now chiefly used of the formal or public expression of thanks, or of grace at a meal.

1591–1780 [see RETURN *v.* 20]. 1717 LADY M. W. MONTAGU *Let. to C'tess Mar* 18 Apr., I returned her thanks, and.. took my leave. 1827 *Edin. Weekly Jrnl.* 28 Feb., He begged leave to return thanks for the honour which had been conferred on the Patrons of this excellent Institution. 1849 C. BRONTË *Shirley* vii, 'Let us return thanks', said he; which he did forthwith, and all quitted the table.

III. 12. *attrib.* and *Comb.*, as *thank-receiver*, *thanks-prayer*; †*thank-picking*, *thanks-freighted* adjs.; †**thank-render**, a rendering of thanks, a thanksgiving; **thanks-day**, Thanksgiving Day (*U.S.*); **thanksdoing**, **thanks-living** (*nonce-wds.*, after *thanksgiving*), action or conduct indicative of a thankful spirit. See also THANK-OFFERING, THANKSGIVING, etc.

1633 FORD *Love's Sacr.* IV. i, Edged on by some *thank-picking parasite. 1786 COWPER *Let. to Lady Hesketh* 31 Jan., I will constitute you my *Thank-receiver-general for whatsoever gift I shall receive hereafter. 1548 GEST *Pr. Masse* in Dugdale *Life* (1840) App. I. 98 It is a forged worship and *thankerendre. 1696 W. BATES *Serm. Forgiveness* 123 Let our thanksgiving be joined with *thanksdoing. 1881 SPURGEON *Treas. Dav.* Ps. cxix. 65 We lose ourselves in adoring thanksgiving, and find ourselves again in careful *thanks-living. 1900 *Month* Feb. 133 Passages..which seem to have reference to this primitive *Thanksprayer.

Thank (þæŋk), *v.* Forms: α. 1–2 þancian, 2–3 þankien, 3–5 þanken, 4–6 thanken, 4–7 thanke, thanck, (4 þ-, thanc, 4–5 þanky, thange), 5–thank. β. 1 ðoncian, 2 þonkien, 3–5 þonke(n, (3 þonki, 4 þonkie), 4–6 thonk, (5–6 thong). [OE. *þancian*, *þoncian* = OS. *thankôn* (MDu., Du. *danken*), OHG. *dankôn* (MHG., G. *danken*), ON. *þakka* (Sw. *tacka*, Da. *takke*):—OTeut. **þank-ôjan*, f. **þanko^z* THANK *sb.*]

†**1.** *intr.* To give thanks. *Obs.* exc. as *absol.* of 3.

c 950 *Lindisf. Gosp.* Matt. xxvi. 27, ʒenimmende calic ðoncunco dyde *vel* ðoncade & sealde him. *c* 975 *Rushw. Gosp.* ibid., ʒenom cælic þongade & salde heom. *c* 1000 *Ags. Gosp.* ibid., He ʒenam þone calic þanciende. *c* 1000 ÆLFRIC *Hom.* II. 400 Drihten ðancode ærðan ðe he ða hlafas tobræce. *c* 1290 *St. Brandan* 595 in *S. Eng. Leg.* 236 Iudas þonkede reufolliche. *c* 1500 *Melusine* xxxvi. 247 'Fayre lordes', said Geffray..'that ought to be thanked for' [*indirect passive of* 'one ought to thank for that'].

†**2.** *intr.* in particular constructions. **a.** To give thanks *to* a person (orig. with simple *dative*, at length treated as *accusative*: see 3). *Obs.*

c 888 K. ÆLFRED *Boeth.* v. § 3 Ðonca nu Gode þæt he ðe gefultumade. *a* 1000 *Cædmon's Satan* 536 [Hi] þanceden þeodne, þæt hit þus ʒelomp. *c* 1000 *Ags. Gosp.* Luke xvii. 16 He..feoll to his foten & him þancode. *c* 1175 *Lamb. Hom.* 153, Iþonked wurðe him [Let it be thanked to him]. *a* 1450 *Le Morte Arth.* 1478 On knes Felle thay..And thankyd All to god. 1508 DUNBAR *Gold. Targe* 101 Syne to dame Flora..Thay saluse, and thay thank a thousand syse. 1542 UDALL *Erasm. Apoph.* 145 That persone, to whom onely..thou art bound to thanke.

†**b.** *of* (= on account of, for) a thing (orig. *genitive*): see c. *Obs.*

971 *Blickl. Hom.* 43 Ne sceal he..to lyt þancian heora ælmessan. *Ibid.* 203 Hie..þancudan þæs siʒes ðe hie gefered hæfdon.

†**c.** (combining a and b) to a person (*dative*), *of* a thing (orig. *genitive*), the dative (mostly a pronoun) passing into an accusative: the usual constr. in OE. and early ME.; passing into 3 b. *Obs.*

Beowulf 1397 Se gomela gode þancode..þæs se man gespræc. *a* 1000 *Cædmon's Gen.* 257 (Gr.) He..sceolde his drihtne þancian þæs leanes. *c* 1000 ÆLFRIC *Saints' Lives* (1885) I. 104 Iulianus þa sona þæs þancode Gode. *c* 1175 *Lamb. Hom.* 39 Þet þu luuie þine drihten and him þonkien alles þinges. *c* 1200 *Vices & Virtues* 29 Þanke ðar-of ðine lauerde gode. *c* 1200 *Trin. Coll. Hom.* 197 Iob..þonkede him of þan wowe, alse dude ar of þe wele.

3. *trans.* To give thanks to; to express gratitude or obligation to. (Orig. *intr.* with *dat.*: see 2 a. By 1200 the *dat.* was treated as *acc.*, and might be subject of the passive voice.) Sometimes const. *that*.

c 1200 *Trin. Coll. Hom.* 3 Þanked be ure louerd ihesu crist. 1297 R. GLOUC. (Rolls) 1154 Vaire he þonkede is gode folc. *Ibid.* 9281 Ich þonke ʒou..Þat ʒe me so muche loue ssewep. *a* 1300 *Cursor M.* 3321 (Cott.) Thancand god, til erth he fell. *c* 1350 *Will. Palerne* 2794 Þat we so scaþli ar a-schaped god mowe [we] þonk. 1362 LANGL. *P. Pl.* A. XII. 48, I..þankede hure a þousand syþes. *c* 1420 *Chron. Vilod.* 461 Þey thongedone god and mournedone no more. 1537 WRIOTHESLEY *Chron.* (Camden) I. 67 The maior and aldermen riding about the cittie thancking the people. 1598 SHAKS. *Merry W.* I. i. 293, I had rather walke here (I thanke you). 1648 *Hamilton Papers* (Camden) 250 Powley is returned from London. He brings a most sleevles letter.. which signifyes nothing...Judge if I thanked him. *a* 1796 BURNS *Selkirk Grace*, We hae meat and we can eat, Sae let the Lord be thankit. 1818 SCOTT *Hrt. Midl.* xxxvii, That he has subjects in Scotland, I think he may thank God and his sword. 1841 LANE *Arab. Nts.* I. 114 The young prince kissed his hand and thanked him. 1906 *Outlook* 18 Sept. 346 He who solicits a favour by letter not infrequently concludes with the phrase, 'thanking you in anticipation', which came into vogue some ten years ago.

†**b.** Const. *of* a thing. *Obs.*

The continuation of 2 c; usual in ME.

c 1175 *Lamb. Hom.* 7 ʒif we þonkiet ure drihten alles þinges þe he us sent. *c* 1230 *Hali Meid.* 19 To þonki godd of his grace & of his goddede. *a* 1300 *Cursor M.* 5304 Knele i sal befor þe king, And thank him of his grett menskıng. *c* 1375 *Sc. Leg. Saints* v. (*Johannes*) 644 He..bad I suld..thange ʒou of ʒore gud vyl. *c* 1412 HOCCLEVE *De Reg. Princ.* 1062 God thanke alwey of thyne ese and of thyne smert. *a* 1533 LD. BERNERS *Huon* lxi. 212, I thanke you of your courtesye. *a* 1548 HALL *Chron.*, *Edw. IV* 236 b, The Frenche kyng..thanked the kyng of Englande of his kynde offre.

c. Const. *for* a thing: now usual.

a 1591 H. SMITH *Serm.* (1637) 133 He is not thankfull before God, which thanks him only for his benefits. 1653 HOLCROFT *Procopius* I. 11 He thanckt the man much for his good will. 1715 DE FOE *Fam. Instruct.* I. i. (1841) I. 7 How must I thank him for it? 1764 GOLDSM. *Trav.* 72 And thanks his gods for all the good they gave. 1910 W. H. HUDSON *Introd. Study Lit.* Pref. 6, I have to thank my friend..for the invaluable assistance which..he has again rendered me.

d. *fig.* To make a return to a person in evidence of obligation or gratitude. (In quot. ironical.)

1821 SCOTT *Kenilw.* xxvi, I were like to be thanked with a horse-whip.

e. In the future tense, used to express a request: *I will thank you to do so-and-so*.

1843 THACKERAY *Ravenswing* vi, The page..instantly thanked her to pay his wages. 1852 — *Esmond* III. v, I want to speak with your employer, Mr. Leach. I'll thank ye go fetch him. *Mod.* I will thank you to hand me my field-glass. I will thank you for a glass of water.

f. Phr. *To thank one for nothing*: esp. in (*I*) *Thank you for nothing*, an ironical expression indicating that the speaker thinks he has got or been offered nothing worth thanks.

1703 MOXON *Mech. Exerc.* 60 But perhaps these Pretenders mean the Iron or Steel shall be as soft as Lead, when the Iron or Steel is red-hot: if so, we may thank them for nothing. 1712 ADDISON *Spect.* No. 391 ¶ 3 Jupiter thanked him for nothing. 1754 FOOTE *Knights* I. Wks. 1799 I. 67 Part with Favourite! no, I thank you for nothing. 1848 [see THANK YOU].

g. Ejaculatory phrases, as *thank God* (†*I thank God* (obs.), *God be thanked*, etc.), *thank goodness*, *thank heaven*. *To thank one's* (or *the*) *stars*, to congratulate oneself on one's good fortune: see STAR.

c 1330 R. BRUNNE *Chron.* (1810) 134 Þanked be God of heuen. 1340 *Ayenb.* 196 God be yhered and y-þonked. 1426 *Test. Ebor.* (Surtees) I. 76, I..in gud mynd, thanket be God. *c* 1489 CAXTON *Sonnes of Aymon* xxiv. 530 Hole & sounde, thanked be god. 1530 PALSGR. 754/2, I am one of them, God be thanked! 1599 SHAKS. *Much Ado* III. v. 15 Yes I thank God, I am as honest as any man liuing, that is an old man, and no honester then I. 1796 MME. D'ARBLAY *Camilla* III. 99 Now...I have not the gift of writing, at which, thank God, I have left off repining. 1811 L. M. HAWKINS *C'tess & Gertr.* III. 283, I was all that, thank goodness, as I always say, last grass. 1840 THACKERAY *Shabby-genteel Story* ii, I am here, thank Heaven, quite alone. 1872 [see GOODNESS 5].

1614 B. JONSON *Barth. Fair* Induct., Yet I kept the Stage in Master Tarleton's time, I thanke my starres. 1730 FIELDING *Temple Beau* IV. iii, Sir Harry, you may thank your stars that conducted you to me. 1834 T. HAWKINS *Mem. Ichthyos. & Plesiosauri* 42 But I should..thank the stars and the Cholera that it was no worse.

†**4.** With dative of person (indirect obj.) and accusative of thing (direct obj.): = 3 b or c. *Obs.* (Cf. TELL *v.* 3 (*a*).)

c 1175 *Lamb. Hom.* 5 We ahte to..þonkien hit ure drihten þe hit us lende. *a* 1300 *Cursor M.* 16219 Herod thankes þe þi sand. 1362 LANGL. *P. Pl.* A. VII. 17 We haue no lymes to labore with: vr lord we hit þonken. *c* 1475 *Rauf Coilȝear* 271 Mair the King spak nocht, Bot thankit thame thair deid.

b. With the thing as sole obj.: To return thanks for, express one's gratitude for; to repay. *rare.*

c 1470 ASHBY *Dicta Philos.* 925 A goode man thanketh euery benefete, After the yeuers possibilite. 1818 BYRON *Mazeppa* xx, Charles forgot To thank his tale. 1819 — *Juan* I. cxii, His young lip thank'd it with a grateful kiss. 1867 MORRIS *Jason* XV. 226 And I am well aweary of it now, And of my toil, thanked with hard word and blow.

5. To give the thanks or credit *for* something to; to consider or hold responsible: esp. in ironical use, = to blame.

1560 DAUS tr. *Sleidane's Comm.* 189 Him that brought hym vp, and whome both he and his father may thanke for all theyr good fortune. 1667 MILTON *P. L.* X. 736 Who.. but..will curse My Head..For this we may thank Adam; but his thanks Shall be the execration. 1794 MRS. RADCLIFFE *Myst. Udolpho* xxxi, She might thank herself for what happened. 1885 SIR N. LINDLEY in *Law Rep.* 14 Q.B.Div. 817 If..any mistake was made by the sheriff, the defendant had only himself to thank for it.

Thankee (þæ·ŋki), vulgar colloq. for *thank ye*, THANK YOU. See 'EE.

1824 in *Spirit Pub. Jrnls.* (1825) 302 My friends, the Yankees. For ten such plays, I guess, wouldn't give ten thankees. 1848 DICKENS *Dombey* xl, Thankee my Lady. Lord bless you, my Lady.

Thanker (þæ·ŋkəɹ). [f. THANK *v.* + -ER [1].] One who thanks.

a 1591 H. SMITH *Serm.* (1637) 132 Moe have gone away speeders, then have gone away thankers. 1800 COLERIDGE *Wallenstein* IV. ii. 111 The devil take such thankers! 1844 BROWNING *Colombe's Birthday* II, Stay, Sabyne; let me hasten to make sure Of one true thanker.

Thankful (þæ·ŋkfŭl), *a.* [f. THANK *sb.* + -FUL.]

1. Feeling or expressing thanks or gratitude; prompted by feelings of gratitude; grateful.

971 *Blickl. Hom.* 169 Weorð þancfulle þon Hælende eoweres andleofan. 1500–20 DUNBAR *Poems* lxxvii. 72 Be thankfull to this burgh of Aberdein. 1535 COVERDALE 1 *Sam.* ii. Contents, The thankfull songe of Anna. 1592 SHAKS. *Rom. & Jul.* III. v. 149 Not proud you haue, But thankfull that you haue. 1685 DRYDEN *Thren. August.* 533 Live then, thou great encourager of arts: Live ever in our thankful hearts! 1748 BUTLER *Serm.* Wks. 1874 II. 317 The generality of mankind have cause to be thankful that their station exempts them from so great temptations. 1856 FROUDE *Hist. Eng.* I. v. 430 We have reason to be thankful that the thing, well or ill, was over.

†**b.** Satisfied, content. *Obs.*

a 900 tr. *Bæda's Hist.* v. xxii[i]. (1890) 478 Scottas..wæron þoncfulle heora gemæruum. *c* 1050 *Gloss.* in Wr.-Wülcker 367/18 *Contentus*, ðancful.

c. *fig.* Cf. GRATEFUL *a.* 2 b.

1610 HOLLAND *Camden's Brit.* (1637) 273 The ground..is thankefull to the husbandman, in so much as it doth afford corne to be carried forth.

†**2.** Worthy or deserving of thanks, gratitude, or credit; pleasing, acceptable, grateful, agreeable.

c 1000 in *Anglia* (1890) XIII. 381 We halsiaþ..god þæt þeow þin cyne ure..to þe..þancfull he mæʒe becuman. *c* 1050 *Suppl. Ælfric's Voc.* in Wr.-Wülcker 191/15 *Gratiosus*, ðancful. 1375 BARBOUR *Bruce* v. 278 He had done mony a thankfull deid. 1456 SIR G. HAYE *Law Armis* (S.T.S.) 63 Unrychtwis offerandis ar nocht acceptable na thankfull to his godhede. 1511 HEN. VIII *Let.* in Burton & Raine *Hemingbrough* 380 Wherby ye shall ministre unto us right singler and thankfull pleasure. 1552 HULOET, Thanckefull, *acceptus*. 1596 DALRYMPLE tr. *Leslie's Hist. Scot.* I. (S.T.S.) 130 The name of king was maist grate and thankful to thame al. 1611 TOURNEUR *Ath. Trag.* I. ii, His good successe shall be most thankeful to your trust.

†**b.** *Sc.* Of a payment: Giving satisfaction, satisfactory. *Obs.*

1497 *Acc. Ld. High Treas. Scot.* I. 315, I resauit..for the Erle Marschael his thankfull and reddy payment. 1517 *Caldwell Pap.* (Maitland) I. 61 Alslang and howlang ye said Johnne and his airs mak to me and my airs gud and thankful service. 1612 *Sc. Acts Jas. VI* (1816) IV. 472/1 To mak thame thankfull teynding. 1672 in *Proc. Soc. Ant. Scot.* (1892) XXVI. 194 To make tymeous and thankfull payment.

†**3.** ? Done without reward or payment; gratuitous: cf. next, 3. *Obs. rare.*

c 1380 WYCLIF *Serm.* Sel. Wks. I. 282 Þe fifte manere þat prestis shulden have shulde be þankful traveilinge; for ʒif þei wolen have þank of God, þei shulden here fle symonie, and neiþer sille her preching ne oþer workes þat þei done.

Thankfully (þæ·ŋkfŭli), *adv.* [f. prec. + -LY [2].] In a thankful manner.

1. With thankfulness; with thanks; gratefully.

c 1000 ÆLFRIC *Saints' Lives* (1890) II. 198 Þa ongeat eustachius þæt seo fore-sæde costnung him ða æt wæs and þancfullice hi under feng. *c* 1380 WYCLIF *Serm.* Sel. Wks. I. 130 Siþ Crist suffride þus for synne of his breþeren, þei schulden suffre þancfulli for her owen synne. 1567 *Triall Treas.* (1850) 18, I cannot but thankefully render Such commendations as is requisite to be. 1611 SHAKS. *Cymb.* I. vi. 79 Yet Heauen's bounty towards him might Be vs'd more thankfully. 1725 DE FOE *Voy. round World* (1840) 248 He accepted thankfully all my presents. 1875 JOWETT *Plato* (ed. 2) V. 365 We will desire the one to give their instructions freely, and the others to receive them thankfully.

†**b.** With satisfaction; graciously. *Obs.*

1513 DOUGLAS *Æneis* I. ix. *heading*, How Eneas with all his rowt bedene War thankfullie ressavit of the quene. *a* 1578 LINDESAY (Pitscottie) *Chron. Scot.* (S.T.S.) I. 90 The king grantit the same verray thankfullie. 1597 A. M. tr. *Guillemeau's Fr. Chirurg.* ˆv, Receaue thankfully this my laboure.

†**2.** So as to gratify, please, or satisfy; acceptably, pleasingly; satisfactorily. *Obs.*

c 1375 *Sc. Leg. Saints* iii. (*Andreas*) 877 He liffit sa thankfully to god and mane. 1482 *Exch. Rolls Scotl.* IX. 284 *note*, That ye redily and thankfully content and pay to the said Johne..the said yerely pensioun. 1500 *Ibid.* XI. 266 *note*, That ye cause hir to be thankfullie pait of hir said pension. 1538 ELYOT, *Placabiliter*, thankefully, contentfully. 1576 in *Maitl. Cl. Misc.* (1840) I. 16 The prices tharof salbe thankfullie allowit to ȝow in ȝour comptis.

†**3.** Gratuitously; for thanks alone. *Obs.*

1552 HULOET, Thanckfully, or for nothynge, or without rewarde or deserte, but onelye for gramercye, *gratim*.

Thankfulness (þæ·ŋkfŭlnės). [f. as prec. + -NESS.] The quality or condition of being thankful.

1. Gratefulness, gratitude.

1552 in *Vicary's Anat.* (1888) App. xvi. 291 Whiche thyng, with al due thanckefulnesse, thei receiued at his maiesties handes. 1611 BIBLE *Acts* xxiv. 3 Wee accept it alwayes.. with all thankfulnesse. 1741 RICHARDSON *Pamela* II. 158 O how shall I find Words to express my Thankfulness! 1856 FROUDE *Hist. Eng.* I. v. 361 Such a resolution would probably have been welcomed with passionate thankfulness.

†**b.** Contextually: Thanks. *Obs. rare.*

1647 MAY *Hist. Parl.* I. ix. 104 The Scottish Commissioners ..returned thankfulnesse to the Parliament..for that great sum of 300000*l.*

†**2.** Gratification, satisfaction. *Obs. rare.*

1500 *Reg. Privy Seal Scotl.* I. 70 The hartlie lufe..he has and beris to the said Jonet, and..the thankfulnes done be hir oft tymes to his gud grace.

Thanking (þæ·ŋkiŋ), *vbl. sb. arch.* [f. THANK *v.* + -ING [1].] The action or an act of giving thanks; the expression of gratitude; thanks.

c 893 K. ÆLFRED *Oros.* I. iv. [viii.] § 2 To wundrianne þæt þa Egipti swa lytle þoncunge wiston Iosepe. *c* 950 *Lindisf. Gosp.* John vi. 23 Ðoncunge dedon Drihtne. *c* 1000 ÆLFRIC *Hom.* II. 170 He underfeng ða lac mid ðancunge. 1382 WYCLIF *Matt.* xxvi. 27 He takynge the cuppe, dede thankyngis. *c* 1420–30 *Prymer* (1895) 51 Whanne þei ben holpe, þei moun ʒelde þankyngis to þee in þi chirche. 1508 BP. FISHER 7 *Penit. Ps.* cii. Wks. (1876) 190 Gyuynge thankynges vnto hym. 1611 SHAKS. *Cymb.* v. v. 407 He would haue well becom'd this place, and grac'd The thankings of a King. 1851 MRS. BROWNING *Casa Guidi W.* I. 239 We thank you that ye first unlatched the door, But will not make it inaccessible By thankings on the threshold.

Tha·nkless, *a.* [f. THANK *sb.* + -LESS.]

1. Not moved by or expressing gratitude; unthankful, ungrateful. Also *fig.* of things: Making no return, unresponsive.

1536 LYNDESAY *Answ. Kingis Flyting* 33 Full sair I rew That euer I did Mouth thankles so persew. *c* 1560 A. SCOTT *Poems* (S.T.S.) v. 65. 1598 MARSTON *Sco. Villanie* III. ix, All as thanklesse as ungratefull Thames He slinks away, leauing but reeking steames Of dungy slime behinde. 1637 MILTON *Lycidas* 66 And strictly meditate the thankles Muse. 1792 COWPER *Stanzas Bill Mortality* 1 Thankless for favours from on high. 1865 DICKENS *Mut. Fr.* I. i, How can you be so thankless to your best friend?

2. Of a task, or the like: Which brings no thanks; receiving or deserving no thanks.

a 1547 SURREY *Æneid* II. 125 But whereunto these thanklesse tales in vaine Do I reherse? 1591 SAVILE *Tacitus' Hist.* II. lix. 83 A thancklesse office and displeasing. 1690 NORRIS *Beatitudes* (1694) I. 178 Not only a thankless, but an odious, difficult and hazardous Undertaking. 1868 MISS BRADDON *Dead-Sea Fr.* i, It is but a thankless task to catalogue such a face.

3. Without thanks: unthanked. *rare.*

1638 SIR T. HERBERT *Trav.* (ed. 2) 163 The Ambassador had no patience to digest it, save by equall contempt to.. send him thanklesse back againe. 1897 *Westm. Gaz.* 22 Feb. 2/1 Prince Max comes to the Court of Ferdinand to return, thankless, a picture painted by Ferdinand.

Tha·nklessly, *adv.* [f. prec. + -LY [2].] In a thankless manner; without thanks; unthankfully.

1626 BP. HALL *Contempl.*, *O. T.* xx. ii, The will of God may be done thanklessly. 1881 in Spurgeon *Treas. Dav.* Ps. cxix. 75 Thanklessly receiving the gifts with no thought of the Giver.

Tha·nklessness. [f. as prec. + -NESS.] The quality or condition of being thankless; ungratefulness, unthankfulness.

1583 GOLDING *Calvin on Deut.* vii. 41 Were it not too shamefull a thankelesnesse in vs if we shoulde not bee [etc.]. 1628 WITHER *Brit. Rememb.* IV. 404 Thy thanklesnesse, And such like Sinnes. 1840 J. HUNT *Legend of Florence* I. ii, Friendship ends, In treachery and in thanklessness begun. 18.. PUSEY *Min. Proph.* 273 Thanklessness shuts the door to God's personal mercies to us.

†**Tha·nklewe,** *a. Obs. rare.* [f. THANK *sb.* + -LEWE.] ? Deserving of thanks, thankworthy; or ? grateful, agreeable.

1430 in Sharpe *Lond. & Kingd.* (1895) III. 374 In performing at þis tyme of our prayer ye may do unto us so notable and þanklewe service þat we wol wel considre hit in tyme comyng.

†**Tha·nkly,** *adv. Obs. rare*[−1]. [irreg. f. THANK *sb.* + -LY [2].] Thankfully.

1591 SYLVESTER *Du Bartas* I. iii. 809 He giueth frankly what we thankly spend.

Tha·nk-o:ffering. [f. THANK *sb.* + OFFERING *vbl. sb.*] In the Levitical law, An offering presented as an expression of gratitude to God; hence in ordinary use, An offering or gift made by way of thanks or acknowledgement.

1530 TINDALE *Lev.* vii. 12 Yf he offer to gene thanckes, he shall brynge vnto his thanckofferynge [1560 (*Genev.*) for his thankes offring] swete cakes myngled with oyle. 1539 BIBLE (Great) 2 *Chron.* xxxiii. 16 He..sacrificed theron peace offerynges, & thank offerynges. 1839 THIRLWALL *Greece* VI. xlix. 171 He dedicated the waggon in the citadel, as a thank-offering to the king of the gods. 1888 BURGON *Lives 12 Gd. Men* I. i. 45 He sent at once a thank-offering for distribution among the poor.

†**Tha·nksgive,** *v. Obs. rare*[−1]. [Back-formation from THANKSGIVING.] *trans.* To give thanks for.

a 1638 MEDE *Diatribe* (1642) 55 Irenæus also affirmeth, That our Saviour, by the institution of the Eucharist had confirmed oblations in the New Testament. Namely, to thanksgive or blesse a thing in way to a sacred use, he took to be an offering of it unto God.

Tha·nksgi:ver. [f. as next + GIVER.] One who gives thanks.

1621 AINSWORTH *Annot. Song Sol.* I. 3 Thankesgivings, in Nehem. 12. 31 [are] for companies of thankesgivers. 1690 C. NESSE *O. & N. Test.* I. 71 The life of thanksgiving is the good life of the thanks-giver. 1818 BENTHAM *Ch. Eng.* 123 Exhausted by that same grand effort, the stock of thanksgivers is gone. 1883 J. PARKER *Tyne Chylde* 270 Thankfulness elevates and ennobles the thanksgiver.

Thanksgiving (þæ·ŋks,gi:viŋ). [f. *thanks*, pl. of THANK *sb.* + GIVING *vbl. sb.*]

1. The giving of thanks; the expression of thankfulness or gratitude; *esp.* the act of giving thanks to God.

1533 TINDALE *Supper of Lord* E iv b, One or other Psalme or prayer of thankes giuyng in the mother tongue. 1539 BIBLE (Great) 1 *Tim.* iv. 4 For all the creatures of God are good, and nothing to be refused, yf it be receaued with thankesgeuynge. 1562 WINȜET *Cert. Tract.* iii. Wks. (S.T.S.) I. 29 Gyf sic zeirlie memorial in blythnes and thankisgeifing wes haldin. 1588 SHAKS. *L. L. L.* II. i. 193, I cannot stay thanks-giuing. 1658 *Whole Duty Man* v. § 8 The fifth part of prayer is thanksgiving; that is, the praising and blessing God for all his mercies. 1842 MISS MITFORD in L'Estrange *Life* (1870) III. ix. 159 Think how full of thanksgiving were my prayers last night.

b. A public celebration, with religious services, held as a solemn acknowledgement of Divine favours; also, a day set apart for this purpose; *spec.* in *U.S.*, Thanksgiving Day (see 3 b).

1641 *Nicholas Papers* (Camden) 10 It was resolved that there shalbe on yᵉ 7ᵗʰ of September next a publique thanksgiving for this good accord betweene yᵉ 2 nacions. 1665 MANLEY *Grotius' Low C. Warres* 217 Publick Thanksgivings were Ordered to be given to God for this Victory. 1760 J. ADAMS *Diary* 26 Nov., Night before Thanksgiving. 1869 MRS. STOWE *Oldtown Folks* xxvii, Great as the preparations were for the dinner, everything was so contrived that not a soul in the house should be kept from the morning service of Thanksgiving.

2. An act or expression of thanks; *esp.* a form of words, a prayer or religious service used to render thanks for Divine benefits.

General Thanksgiving, the first of the forms of thanksgiving in the Book of Common Prayer, that for the blessings of life in general. *Great Thanksgiving*, in early and oriental liturgies: see quot. 1708–22.

1535 COVERDALE *Ps.* xxxix. [xl.] 3 He hath put a new songe in my mouth, euen a thankesgeuynge vnto oure God. 1552 *Bk. Com. Prayer* (*heading*), The Thankes geuing of Women after Childe birth. 1662 *Ibid.*, Prayers & Thanksgivings upon several occasions...A General Thanksgiving. 1708–22 J. BINGHAM *Chr. Antiq.* XV. iii. (1845) 770 After this the priest went on with the εὐχαριστία properly so called, that is the great thanksgiving to God for all his mercies, both of creation, providence and redemption. 1849 MACAULAY *Hist. Eng.* ii. I. 185 The ministers selected from that liturgy such prayers and thanksgivings as were likely to be least offensive to the people.

3. *attrib.* and *Comb.*

1641 EVELYN *Diary* Aug., The next Sunday was the thanksgiving sermons perform'd in Col. Goreing's Regiment. 1814 SOUTHEY *Carmen Triumph.* xvi, With one consent, The high thanksgiving strain to heaven is sent,..Glory to God! Deliverance for Mankind! *a* 1859 MACAULAY *Hist. Eng.* xxiii. (1861) V. 17 They had still in their ears the thanksgiving sermons and thanksgiving anthems.

b. Thanksgiving day, a day set apart for public thanksgiving for Divine goodness; *spec.* in the United States, an annual festival religious and social, now appointed by proclamation and held on the last Thursday of November.

The first celebration was held by the Plymouth colony in 1621, in thankfulness for their first harvest in America after a year of struggle and privation, and the usage became general in New England. After the Revolution, it extended to the Middle States, and later to the West; after the Civil War gradually to the South. Its national observance has been annually recommended by the President since 1863.

1674 JOSSELYN *Voy. New Eng.* 214 Towards night I returned to Boston again, the next day being Thanksgiving day, on Fryday the Tenth day we weighed Anchor. 1704 LUTTRELL *Brief Rel.* (1857) V. 460 Sir Christopher Wrenn is erecting a throne in St. Paul's cathedral for her majestie to sitt in on the thanksgiving day. 1714 S. SEWALL *Diary* 25 Nov., Thanksgiving day; very cold. 1844 WHITTIER *Pumpkin* iii, Ah! on Thanksgiving day..When the gray-haired New Englander sees round his board The old broken links of affection restored. 1903 *Daily Chron.* 6 Nov. 5/1 Thanksgiving Day long remained an institution peculiar to New England, but it has been observed annually in New York State since 1817.

†**Tha·nkworth,** *a. Obs.* [f. THANK *sb.* + WORTH *a.*] = next.

? 1426 *Lett. Marg. Anjou & Bp. Beckington* (Camden) 33, I quyte me soo to yow in that matere,..as were thanke worth. 1550 COVERDALE *Spir. Perle* Pref. 1 b, The more daungerous be his sores and sicknes, and the more thancke worth the cure therof. 1627–47 FELTHAM *Resolves* 30 To trust him for an estate when we have the evidences in our iron chest, is easie; and not thankeworth.

Tha·nkworthy, *a.* Also 6–7 thanks-. Worthy of thanks; deserving gratitude or credit.

1387–8 T. USK *Test. Love* Prol. (Skeat) l. 39 Although this booke be lytel thank worthy for the leudnesse in trauail. 1481 SIR H. LUTTRELL in Ellis *Orig. Lett.* Ser. II. I. 86 Wherfore..he ys thankworthy. 1533 J. HEYWOOD *Play Weather* (1903) 1125 Thy labour is ryght myche thankeworthy. 1534 TINDALE 1 *Pet.* ii. 19 For it is thankeworthye yf a man for conscience towarde god endure grefe, sufferinge wrongfully. 1594 CAREW *Huarte's Exam. Wits* xiii. (1596) 202 No lesse thanks-worthie a part of Seruice. 1672 WILKINS *Nat. Relig.* 31 It would not be thank-worthy for a man to believe that which of necessity he must believe. 1891 T. K. CHEYNE *Orig. Psalter* Introd. 17 A faulty but at that time thankworthy book.

Hence **Tha·nkworthily** *adv.*, in a thankworthy manner; **Tha·nkworthiness**, the quality or condition of being thankworthy.

1553 BALE *Gardiner's De vera Obed.* C vij, To exercise our selues godly and *thankeworthyly. 1874 SWINBURNE *Bothwell* I. i. 7 And we that do it, we do it for all men's good, For the main people's love, thankworthily. 1847 WEBSTER, **Thank-worthiness*.

Tha·nk you. [Aphetic for *I thank you*.] A phrase used in courteous acknowledgement of a favour or service. *Thank you for nothing*: see THANK *v.* 3 f. So, rarely, **Thank thee.** Cf. THANKEE.

14.. *Why I can't be a Nun* 159 in *E. E. P.* (1862) 142 'Thanke yow, lady', quod I than. 1616 B. JONSON *Devil an Ass* IV. ii, *Eith.* Thanke you good Madame...Thanke thee, good Eyther-side. 1705 VANBRUGH *Confed.* I. i, Thank you kindly, Mrs. Amlet, thank you kindly. 1738 SWIFT *Pol. Conversat.* ii. 140 No, thank ye, Colonel. 1848 THACKERAY *Van. Fair* xxiv, It's you who want to introduce beggars into my family? Thank you for nothing, Captain. 1862 MISS YONGE *C'tess Kate* ii. 24 She..said something meant for 'No, thank you'; but of which nothing was to be heard but 'q' [*i.e.* —k you]. 1875 JOWETT *Plato* (ed. 2) III. 206 [He] goes about learning of others, to whom he never even says Thank you.

b. as *sb.* (written with hyphen or as one word): An utterance of this phrase.

1887 *Chr. World* 4 Aug. 589 He utters a hearty 'Thank-you!' 1894 *Westm. Gaz.* 21 Aug. 3/3 The majority of passengers retreated from the tables regardless of their running fire of 'thankyous', which were thankyous for nothing. 1900 *Ibid.* 6 Sept. 2/1 We had not said nearly enough 'thank-yous'.

Thank-you-ma'am. *U.S. colloq.* Also **thank'ee-marm.** A hollow or ridge in a road, which causes persons passing over it in a vehicle to nod the head involuntarily, as if in acknowledgement of a favour; *spec.* a ridge or hollow on a hill road serving to throw off descending rain-water.

1849 LONGF. *Kavanagh* xi, We went like the wind over the hollows in the snow;—the driver called them 'thank-you-ma'ams', because they made everybody bow. 1867 O. W. HOLMES *Guard. Angel* xiv, Life's a road that's got a good many thank-you-ma'ams to go bumpin' over, says he. 1897 HOWELLS *Landl. Lion's Head* 192 At one of the thank-you-marms in the road, the sick man stopped, like a weary horse, to breathe.

Thanna(**h**, var. TANA [1], Indian police station.

Thanne, þanne, obs. ff. THAN, THEN.

†**Tha·nnic,** *a. Chem. Obs.* [f. *Thann* (name of a town in the Vosges where Kestner the discoverer lived) + -IC.] In *thannic acid*: see quot.

1853 *Pharmac. Jrnl.* XIII. 110 Racemic acid was..discovered by Kestner,..in the year 1820. It was called thannic acid by its discoverer.

Thape, dial. var. *fape*: see FEABERRY, gooseberry.

‖**Thapsia** (þæ·psiă). *Bot.* Also 4–6 **tapsia**. [L. *thapsia* (*tapsia*), a. Gr. θαψία, said to mean a plant brought from Thapsus.] A genus of umbelliferous perennials, of the tribe *Laserpitieæ*, containing four species, natives of the Mediterranean region. That formerly in medical repute is *T. garganica*, also called Deadly Carrot.

c 1400 *Lanfranc's Cirurgie* 195 Þe place shal be frotid in þe sunne wiþ an oynement of tapsia. *c* 1440 *Pallad. on Husb.* I. 1044 This tapsia, this wermot, and eleure, Cucumber wilde, and euery bitter kynde Of herbe is nought for hem. 1578 LYTE *Dodoens* III. xxiv. 365 The barke of the roote of Thapsia. 1586 *Rates of Custome* E viij, Tapsia the pound xij.d. 1857 DUNGLISON *Med. Lex.*, *Thapsia*...The root operates violently, both upwards and downwards.

b. *attrib.* and *Comb.*, as *thapsia-plaster* (*Cent. Dict.* 1890), *-resin* (see quot.), *-root*.

1890 BILLINGS *Nat. Med. Dict.*, *Thapsia resin*, a soft extract prepared by digesting thapsia-root in hot alcohol.

‖**Thapsus** (þæ·psŏs). *Bot.* Also 4–5 (8) **tapsus**, 8 **thapsos**. [med.L., a. Gr. θάψος a plant used for dyeing yellow (Dioscor.).] An old name of the genus *Verbascum*, esp. of *V. Thapsus*, the great mullein.

a 1387 *Sinon. Barthol.* 41/2 *Tapsus barbastus*, flosmus idem. 1578 LYTE *Dodoens* I. lxxxi. 119 Mulleyn is called ..in Shoppes *Tapsus Barbatus*. 1718 ROWE tr. *Lucan* IX. 1566 The Gummy Larch-Tree and the Thapsos there, Wound-wort and Maiden-weed perfume the Air.

‖**Thar** (tʰār), *sb. Zool.* [Native name.]

1. The native name in Nepāl of a goat-antelope, *Nemorhædus bubalina*, belonging to the same genus as the Goral (*N. goral*).

1833 B. H. HODGSON in *Proc. Zool. Soc.* 10 Sept. 105 As compared with the Ghōrāl, *Antilope Goral*, Hardw...the Thār is a massive beast, twice the size, and has suborbital sinuses, and a mane along the back of the neck and shoulders. *Ibid.* 24 Sept. 111 A cavity also exists in the osseous core of the horns of the Thār Antelope. 1834 *Ibid.* 12 Aug. 86. 1834 *Penny Cycl.* II. 89/2 The Thar (*A. thar*, Hodgson) was described for the first time in a paper by B. H. Hodgson, Esq., British resident in Nepaul...The thar inhabits the central region of Nepaul. 1885 *Cycl. India* III. 885/1 Thar, the forest goat, is the Nepal name of *Nemorhædus bubalina*, called Eimu and Ramu on the Sutlej and Kashmir, and Serow in the hills generally.

2. Also applied to the TEHR, or Himalayan wild goat (*Hemitragus jemlaicus*).

1896 *List Anim. Zool. Soc.* 166 *Hemitragus jemlaicus* (Hodgs.) Thar. 1902 WEBBER *Forests Upper India* vi. 52 *Hemitragus jemlaicus* is a true wild goat, here called 'thar' by the natives...The thar is gregarious. 1902 LYDEKKER in *Encycl. Brit.* XXXIII. 939/1 The discovery of a species of thar (*Hemitragus*) in southern Arabia. 1903 *Spectator* 4 Apr. 527/2 Open and high ground..more suitable for wild sheep, such as the thar.

†**Thar,** *v. Obs.*: see THARF.

Thar (ðar, þar), ME., chiefly northern, form of THERE. Also in compounds, as *ðar abutan*, etc.: see THEREABOUT and other words to THEREWITH.

Thar, thare, obs. ff. THEIR; var. THIR *Obs.*, these; obs. gen. and dat. sing. fem. and gen. pl. of THE; 3 sing. and pl. pres. indic. of THARF *v. Obs.*

Tharandite (tærǣ·ndəit). *Min.* [a. Ger. *tharandit* (Freiesleben, 1817), f. Tharandt in Saxony (where it occurs) + -ITE [1].] A variety of dolomite occurring in greenish yellow crystals, containing a small percentage of ferrous oxide.

1850 ANSTED *Elem. Geol.*, *Min.* etc. § 385. 1868 DANA *Min.* 682 Tharandite, from Tharand, near Dresden, is crystallized, and contains 4 p.c. of Fe.

Tharatour, *Sc.*: see THEREATOUR.

Tharborough, corrupt form of THIRDBOROUGH.

Thar-, tharck-cake: see THARF-CAKE.

Thare, obs. f. TARE *sb.* [1]; also of THERE.

†**Tharf,** *sb. Obs.* Also 1 þearf, ðearf, 2 þerf, 3 (*Orm.*) þarrfe. [f. THARF *v.* Cf. OS. *tharf*, OHG. *darba*, ON. *þorf*.] Need, necessity.

Beowulf 1798 Sele-þegn..se for andrysnum ealle beweotede þeʒnes þearfe. 735 BÆDA *Death-song* 2 Thoncsnotturra than him tharf sie. *c* 1000 *Sax. Leechd.* II. 84 ʒif þearf sie, sele hwilum wyrtdrenc. *c* 1175 *Lamb. Hom.* 9 Nis hit nan þerf þet me her on þisse liue for his saule bidde pater noster. *c* 1200 ORMIN 12247 Onn alle þa þatt haffdenn ned & þarrfe to þin hellpe. *c* 1330 *Arth. & Merl.* 16 And wele ysen, ʒif þai willen, Þat hem no þarf neuer spillen.

Tharf, *a. Obs.* or *dial.* Forms: 1 þeorf, þearf, (ðorof, ðerf), 3 (*Orm.*) þeorrf, 4 þerf, -e, 4–5 therf, 5 tharf, -e. See also THARF-CAKE. [OE. *þeorf* (:—*þerf*), unleavened, unsoured; of milk, sweet; Com. Teut. = OFris. *therf*, *derf*, MDu. *derf* (Kilian has '*derf-brood*, panis azymus'), OHG., MHG. *derp* unleavened, Ger. *derb* solid, compact, rough, coarse, ON. *þjarfr* unleavened, insipid. With sense 2, cf. the mod. Ger. sense of *derb*; app. referring to the solid, heavy, or stiff quality of unleavened bread. Pre-Teut. etymology unknown.]

†**1.** Of bread, etc.: Not prepared with leaven, unleavened. *Obs.* exc. in THARF-CAKE.

c 950 *Lindisf. Gosp.* Matt. xxvi. 17 Ða forma uutedlice doege ðara ðorofra [*Rushw.* ðefra *for* ðerfa] mæta. *c* 1000 ÆLFRIC *Hom.* II. 210 Þeorfe hlafas we bringað Gode to lace. *c* 1000 — *Exod.* xii. 39 Hi..worhton þeorfe heorþbacene hlafas. *c* 1000 ÆLFRIC *Voc.* in Wr.-Wülcker 153/32 *Azimus*, ðeorf. *c* 1200 ORMIN 997 Bræd All þeorrf wiþþutenn berrme. *a* 1300 *Cursor M.* 6079 Wit therf bred and letus wild. 1382 WYCLIF *Gen.* xix. 3 He made a feest, sethede therf breed, and thei eten. — *Mark* xiv. 1 Pask and the feeste of therf looues was aftir the secunde day. *c* 1400 MAUNDEV. (Roxb.) iii. 10 Þai say we erre þat makes þe sacrement of tharf breed. *c* 1425 *Voc.* in Wr.-Wülcker 657/30 *Panis siliginius*, tharfbred. *c* 1440 *Promp. Parv.* 490/2 Therf, wythe owte sowre dowe. 1483 *Cath. Angl.* 381/2 Tharfe, *azimus*.

2. *transf.* Lumpish, stiff, heavy, slow; hence *fig.* reluctant, unwilling, diffident, tardy. *dial.* Hence **Tha·rfish** *a.* in same sense; **Tha·rfly** *adv.*, in a tharf or tharfish manner.

1747 HOOSON *Miner's Dict.*, *Tharf* [is] when a Vein or Pipe alters from its own intrinsical Nature to another, that is more Hask, Barren, and Dry, and more bound up, and stiff. 1828 *Craven Gloss.*, *Tharf*, stark, stiff, metaphorically, backward, unwilling. 1876 *Mid-Yorks. Gloss.*, *Tharf*,.. *Thauf*, diffident; unwilling; reluctant; tardy...Also *tharfish* adj., and *tharfly* adv. 1876 *Whitby Gloss.*, *Tharf*, *Tharfish*, shy, diffident. *Tharfly*, slowly. 'The rain comes nobbut tharfly'. 1894 *Northumbld. Gloss.*, *Tharf*, *Tharfish*, lumpish, heavy-countenanced, forbidding. Applied to substances it means 'sad', heavy, like liver in texture. *Tharfly*, slowly, reluctantly.

†**Tharf, thar,** *v. Obs.* exc. *Sc. dial.* Forms: see below. [A Com. Teutonic verb, belonging to the class of preterite-presents, in which the present tense is an original preterite (cf. CAN, DOW, DARE, etc.): OE. **þurfan*, pres. *þearf*—*þurfon*, pa. *þorfte*, = OFris. **thurva*, *thurf*(*thorf*.)—*thurvon*, OS. *thurban*, *tharf*—*thurbun*, *thorfta*, MDu. *dorven*, *dorfte* (Du. *durven*), ON. *þurfa*, *þarf*—*þurfom*, *þurfta* (Sw. *tarfva*), OHG. *durfan*, *darf*—*durfun*, *dorfta* (MHG. *durfen*, G. *dürfen*), Goth. **þaurban*, *þarf*—*þaurbum*, *þaurfta*:—OTeut. **þarf-*, **þurb-*; corresp. to a pre-Teut. ablaut series **terp-*, **torp-*, **trp-*, which has not been certainly identified. The ME. β-forms had lost the *f* or *v*, app. first in the 2nd sing. present *þearft*, *þeart-tu*, *þer-tu*, leaving a stem *þar-*, *þer-*, *þor-*, *þur-*, which was afterwards often confused with the *dar-*, *dor-*, *dur-* of DARE *v.* [1], so that the latter had forms in *th*, while there are here forms in *d*, esp. in the 2nd and 3rd person singular of the present: see γ. This confusion of *tharf* and *dare* is also found in the cognate languages: see DARE *v.* [1]]

A. Inflexions.

1. *Pres. Indic.* **a.** *1st sing.* 1 þearf.

Beowulf 2007 Ic þæt eall ʒe-wræc swa..[ne] ʒylpan þearf grendeles maʒa. *a* 1000 *Cædmon's Gen.* 2176 (Gr.) Ne þearf ic yrfestol eaforan bytlian.

b. *2nd sing.* α. 1 þearft, 2 þerft, (3 þerf).

Beowulf 1675 Þæt þu him on-drædan ne þearft. *c* 1000 *Sax. Leechd.* II. 180 Ne þearft þu þone wermod to don. *c* 1175 *Lamb. Hom.* 37 Soðliche ne þerft þu bidden namare. *a* 1225 *Leg. Kath.* 1160 Þu wenest ʒet þæt tu wenen ne þerf.

β. 3 þeart, þert, þer(tu), 3–4 þers(tou), 4 þertes(tow), 4–5 tharst, 5 thar, thare.

c 1205 LAY. 14482 Ne þært [*MS.* þræt] þu nauere habben kare of uncuðe leoden. *a* 1225 *Ancr. R.* 136 Ne þer tu nout dreden þe attrie neddre of helle. *c* 1300 *St. Brandan* 626 Ne therstou nothing drede. *c* 1330 R. BRUNNE *Chron. Wace* (Rolls) 4877 Of Kent ne þertestow fle þat cost. 1390 GOWER *Conf.* II. 61 Me semeth that thou tharst noght care. *a* 1450 *Le Morte Arth.* 3285 Othure warke thou thare not wene. *c* 1460 *Towneley Myst.* ii. 293 Thar thou nowther flyte ne chyde.

γ. 3 dert, 4 dars(tou, -tow).

c 1205 LAY. 22923 Ne dert [*c* 1275 þert] þu nauere adrede. *c* 1320 *Cast. Love* 975 Ne darstou on erþe þenchen elles nouht. 1377 LANGL. *P. Pl.* B. XIV. 55 If..so þat þow be sobre..Darstow [*v.rr.* Tharst þow, Thardestow] neuere care for corne, ne lynnen cloth ne wollen.

c. *3rd sing.* α. 1 ðearf, þearf (ðorfæð, -eð), 2 þerf, 3 (*Orm.*) þarrf, 3–4 þarf, 4 tharf

c 888 K. ÆLFRED *Boeth.* xxiv. § 4 Ne ðearf he nanes þinges. *c* 950 *Lindisf. Gosp.* John xiii. 10 Seðe ʒeðuæn is ne ðorfæð [*c* 975 *Rushw.* ðorfeð] þætte aðoa hine. *c* 975 *Rushw. Gosp.* Matt. xxi. 3 Sæcgaþ þæt dryhten heora ðearf. *c* 1175 *Lamb. Hom.* 9 Nu ne þerf na mon his sunne mid wite abuggen. *a* 1250 *Prov. Ælfred* 161 in *O. E. Misc.* 113 Monymon weneþ þat he wene ne þarf longes lyues. *c* 1330 *Amis & Amil.* 935 Tharf the neuer haue of him drede.

β. 3 þerh, 4 (tar), thars, 4–5 þar, thar, þare, thare, there, 5 tharre, tharth, 9 *Sc. dial.* ther.

a 1300 *Cursor M.* 13554 Fra nu thar him namar be ledd. *Ibid.* 19870 (Edin.) Þat to do þare þe nochte lete. 1340 HAMPOLE *Pr. Consc.* 2167 He þat hates þis lyfes lykyng Thar noght drede þe dedes commyng. ? 1370 *Robt. Cicyle* 325 More then thars be an c. folde. *a* 1400–50 *Alexander* 5377 Þe thare bot graunt me to geue quat guds as I craue. 1414 BRAMPTON *Penit. Ps.* (Percy Soc.) 45 Me thar no more but aske and have. *c* 1425 *Cursor M.* 10565 (Laud) For to aske there no man Yf they were glad & ioyfull þan. *c* 1475 Tharth [see B. 2].

γ. 3 derf, 3–4 darf, 4 darh, 4–5 dar, dare.

a 1240 *Ureisun* in *Cott. Hom.* 187 Hwa derf beon unsauuet þe haueþ se mihti salue. 1297 R. GLOUC. (Rolls) 6471 Me ne dar noʒt esse weþer he were kene þo & prout. *a* 1300 *Floriz & Bl.* 315 Ich wene ne darf me axi noʒt. *c* 1320 *Cast. Love* 723 Ne dar he seche non oþer leche. *a* 1327 *Pol. Songs* (Camden) 250 Of gode knyhtes darh him

Supplement, p. 3873; Corrigenda, p. 4092; Spurious words, p. 4093; Books quoted, p. 4094

Tharf-cake.

Tharf, dorm., obs. f. THRALL sb.¹, THRALDOM.

Tharm (þärm). Now dial. Forms: 1 Angl. þearm, þarm, WSax. þearm, þearm; 3 þerm, þarm, 4 þerm, 4 þearm, 5 þaarme, 5–6 þarm; 6–7 dial. therm, 8–9 dial. tharm.

1. An intestine; chiefly in pl., bowels, viscera, entrails; in quot. c 1460 transf.

2. An intestine as cleansed and prepared for some purpose: see quots. Also, in sing., as a substance or material: catgut for fiddle-strings, etc.

3. Signification and use.

† Tharn, v. Obs. Forms: 3 OE þærnen, 4 þarn, 4–5 þarne, 5 þorne. Also þern, þerne, etc.

Tharve, Tharst, Tharth: see THARF v. Obs.

Thas, obs. form of THOSE; obs. abbrev. of it has; obs. pa. t. of THAT. See THES.

That (ðæt), dem. pron., adj., and adv.

† A. Illustration of Forms.

That (ðæt). In OE. inflected for gender, number, and case.

1. In OE. inflected for gender, number, and case.

B. Signification and use.

I. Demonstrative Pronoun. Pl. † THO (obs.), THOSE, q.v.

As simple demonstrative pronoun.

1. Denoting a thing or person pointed out or present, or that has just been mentioned.

2. Used emphatically, instead of repeating a previous word or phrase.

II. Demonstrative Adjective. Pl. as in 1.

1. The simple demonstrative used (as adjective in concord with a sb.), to indicate a thing or person either as being actually pointed out or present, or as having just been mentioned and being thus mentally pointed out.

2. Indicating (from the definite article THE as being *demonstrative*, i.e. pointing out, not merely *definitive*, i.e. distinguishing or singling out).

3. Indicating quality or nature. Const. *that* (conj.), *as*, *with* (simple) inf., inf. (without *as*), rel. pron. (also with ellipsis of the rel. pron.) or rel.: rarely without correlative. Now chiefly arch. (or dial.).

III. Demonstrative Adverb. (Closely related to the adjective use in II. 4.)

To that extent or degree: so much, so. (Qualifying an adj., adv., or ppl. adj.: rarely a vb.) Now only dial. and Sc. (exc. as in b.)

C. Relative Pronoun.

I. Introducing a clause defining or restricting the antecedent, and thus completing its sense.

II. Introducing a clause stating something additional about the antecedent (the sense of the principal clause being complete without the relative clause). Now only *poet.* or *rhet.*, the ordinary equivalents being *who* (obj. *whom*) of persons, and *which* of things.

III. In various special and elliptical constructions.

D. Conjunction.

That (ðæt), *adv.* Now dial. In sense 5 conj. Also 1 þæt, 2–3 þet, 3–5 þat, etc.

I. Introducing a dependent substantive-clause, as subject, object, or other element of the principal clause; or in apposition with a sb. or adj., or in apposition with a sb. therein.

II. Introducing a clause expressing purpose or intended result.

III. Introducing a clause expressing cause or reason.

That.

Thatch (sb.)

Thatch (v.)

Thatched, ppl. a.

Thatcher.

Thatching, vbl. sb.

Thatchless, a.

Thaught, variant of THOUGHT, rower's bench.

Thaumasite (þǭ·măsǝit). Min. [mod. (Nor-

Thaumato-, combining form of Gr.

Thaumaturge (þǭ·mătǝudʒ).

Thaumaturgic, a.

Thaumaturgical, a.

Thaumaturgist.

Thaumaturgus.

Thaumaturgy.

Thaumatrope (þǭ·mătroup).

Thave, variant of THEAVE.

Thavel, variant of THIVEL.

Thaw (þǭ), sb.

Thaw (þǭ), v.

Thawed, ppl. a.

Thawer.

Thawing, vbl. sb.

Thawless, a.

Thawt, variant of THOUGHT, rower's bench.

Thawy, a.

The (ðī, ðǝ).

THE. 258 THE. THE. 259 THE.

THE. 260 THEAL. THEANDRIC. 261 THEATRE

Theatre. (Continued entries, senses c–f.)

c. Dramatic performances as a branch of art, or as an institution; the drama.

d. Dramatic works collectively.

4. A temporary platform, dais, or other raised stage, for any public ceremony.

5. A room or hall fitted with tiers of rising seats facing the platform, lecturer's table, or president's seat, for lectures, scientific demonstrations, etc.

6. *fig.* Something represented as a theatre (in sense 1 or 2) in relation to a course of action performed or a spectacle displayed; *esp.* a place or region where some thing or action is presented to public view (literally or metaphorically).

Hence **Theatre** v., *intr.* to go to the theatre; **Theatredom**, the domain or sphere of things theatrical and persons connected therewith; also, the district in which theatres are situated; **The'atreful**, as many as a theatre will hold; **Theatreless** a., without a theatre or theatrical entertainments; **The'atrewards** adv., towards a theatre; **The'atrewise** adv., in the manner of a theatre.

Theatric (þiæˈtrik), a. (sb.) [ad. late L. theatric-us, ad. Gr. θεατρικός.] = THEATRE.

Theatrical (þiæˈtrikăl), a. (sb.) [f. as prec. + -AL: see prec.]

Theatrically (þiæˈtrikăli), adv. [f. prec. + -LY.]

Theatricalism (þiæˈtrikăliz'm). [f. THEATRICAL + -ISM.]

Theatricality (þiæˌtrikăˈliti). [f. as prec. + -ITY.]

Theatricalize (þiæˈtrikălaiz), v. [f. THEATRICAL + -IZE.]

Theatricals (þiæˈtrikălz), sb. pl.

Theatricism (þiæˈtrisiz'm). [f. THEATRIC + -ISM.]

Theatrics (þiæˈtriks), sb. pl.

Theatrize (þiæˈtraiz), v. [ad. Gr. θεατρίζειν.]

Theatro- (þiˈætro, þiæˈtro), combining form of Gr. θέατρον THEATRE.

Theave, thaive (þiv, þeiv), local.

Theban (þiˈbăn), a. and sb. [ad. L. Thēbān-us.]

Thebe, Thebenine, etc.

Theca (þiˈkă). Pl. thecæ (þiˈsiː). [a. L. theca, Gr. θήκη case, cover.]

Thecal (þiˈkăl), a.

Thecodont (þiˈkodɒnt), a. and sb. Zool.

Thecodontosaurus. Zool.

Theddre, obs. form of THITHER.

Thede. Obs. exc. dial.

Theegloe, theche, obs. forms of THEOLOGY.

Thecophora, thecosoma, etc.

Theck, Sc. variant of THACK, to thatch.

Theclan (þiˈklăn), a. Entom. [f. mod.L. Thecla + -AN.]

Theco-, combining form of Gr. θήκη.

Thee (þiː), pers. pron. Forms: 1 (acc.) þec, (Northumb. Seb. ðech); 1–6 (dat. and acc.) þe; 2–5 þee, 3–5 þe, 4–5 þee, 4–7 thee, (thee 7 dot). *Thee* (þiː) is the objective case of THOU.

Thee (þiː), v. Obs. exc. arch. [Forms: 1 (acc.).]

Theedom, thedom, var. THEEDOM Obs.

Theek, theik (þik), v. Sc. and north. dial.

Theekster, theekster, etc.

Theel. Obs. rare.

Theet, obs. form of THEET.

Theft (þeft). Forms: 1 þiefð, þeofð, þyft, (þiefð), 2–4 þeofðe, þefðe, þefte, & 4 þifte, (4 þyfte, thifte), etc.

1771 *Junius Lett.* lxv. (1820) 328 The thief was taken in the theft. 1909 *Q. Rev.* July 176 His borrowings were not thefts but prolific suggestions.

†**b.** *By theft*, stealthily, furtively, by secret craft. *Obs. rare*^{-1}.

c1470 Henry *Wallace* xi. 592 Thai be thyft hecht to put Wallace doun.

2. *concr.* That which is or has been stolen; the proceeds of thieving. Now *rare*.

962-3 *Laws of Edgar* iv. c. 2 § 2 To ðy þæt..þeof nyte, hwær he þyfþe [*MS. C.* þeofte] befæste. c1175 *Lamb. Hom.* 57 Ne þu naȝest for to stele, Ne nan þefþe for to heole. a1300 *Cursor M.* 6754 Þat he mai yeild again his thift, He sal be saald. 1340 *Ayenb.* 38 Þe þyeues be uelaȝrede byeþ þo þet parteþ of þe þyefþe. 1413 *Pilgr. Sowle* (Caxton 1483) iii. v. 53 The theft which they haue stolen ye haue you self receyued. 1530 Tindale *Exod.* xxii. 4 Yf the thefte [Wyclif, that that he hath stoln] be founde in his hande alyue..he shall restore double. 1665 G. Havers *P. della Valle's Trav. E. I.* 145 We found the theft in his breeches ty'd to his naked flesh. 1864 Kingsley *Rom. & Teut.* x. 284 If a free man be caught thieving,..he replaces the theft, and pays 80 solidi, or dies.

3. *attrib.* and *Comb.*, as *theft-guilty* adj.

1613-16 W. Browne *Brit. Past.* ii. i, What store of houres theft-guilty night had spent. 1907 *Westm. Gaz.* 19 Oct. 9/2 The Police Commissioner..gave it as his opinion that the theft theory was the most probable.

Theft-boot, -bote. *Obs.* exc. *Hist.* Also 3, 6 **thef-**, 6 **theefe-**, 6–7 **theif(e-**. [orig. *thef-bote*, f. *thef*, Thief + *bote*, Boot *sb.*[1] Afterwards altered (app. first by Scottish writers) to *theftbote*: cf. Theftdom, Theftly.

The early form suggests an OE. **þéof-bót*, but this has not been found; the nearest equivalent in the Ags. Laws being *þéof-gyld* in Laws of Æthelred i. c. 1 § 2, iii. c. 4, and of Cnut ii. c. 30 § 1.]

The taking of some payment from a thief to secure him from legal prosecution; either the receiving back by the owner of the stolen goods or of some compensation, or the taking of a bribe by a person who ought to have brought the thief to justice.

Nichols (1865) in *Britton*, in note to quot. 1292, suggests that the word 'originally signified the legal *bote* or composition for theft', and was then 'applied to the illegal compounding of theft, or taking money to maintain or connive at such offenders'. But all our quotations refer to illegal payment, a form of compounding a felony.

α. 1284 *Stat. Wall.* an. 12 Edw. I, c. 4 De Thefbote, hoc est de emenda furti capta sine consideracione Curiæ Domini Regis. 1292 Britton i. xxi. § 11 Et puis soit enquis de ceux qi ount pris thefbote. 1369 *Liber Assisarum* § 5 (1606) 258 b, Et les Iustices disoient q' vn home q' reprist son chattel emblee dun laron ne fuit pas thefbote, eins thefbote fuit proprement ou vn home prist ses chattels dun laron de luy fauourer & mainteiner, et nemy auterment. 1579 *Expos. Termes Law* 177 b/2 *Thefbote*, is when a man taketh any goodes of a theefe to fauour and mainteine him. And not when a man taketh his owne goodes that were stollen from him &c.

β. a1450 *Sc. Acts Robt. I*, c. 9 (1844) I. 109/2 (*heading*) Of þe takyn of thyftbute [*orig.* rechatum de latrone]. 1515 *Sc. Acts Jas. V* (1814) II. 282/2 Gif this complenar..wald concord with the said theif and tak thiftbute and put him fra the Law, in that caice he sall vnderly the Law. 1597 [see next]. 1619 Dalton *Country Just.* cviii. (1630) 288 Some other seeme to take this for theeftboot and so to be punishable..onely by ransome and imprisonment. 1678 Sir G. Mackenzie *Crim. Laws Scot.* i. xx. § i. (1699) 106 Theft-boot is committed by securing a Thief against the punishment due by Law. 1745 *Univ. Spect.* 10 Aug., Yorkshire Tom was committed to Clerkenwell-Bridewell..for Theft-boot, accepting of 17 Guineas and a half, not to prosecute John Ditcher, a notorious Pick-pocket. 1769 Blackstone *Comm.* IV. x. 133 The offence of theftbote, which is where the party robbed not only knows the felon, but also takes his goods again, or other amends, upon agreement not to prosecute. 1814 Scott *Wav.* xv, The Bailie opined that this transaction would amount to theft-boot, or composition of felony. 1885 *Law Times* LXXX. 115/2 The offence of compounding a felony was really the old crime of theft-bote.

The·ftdom. *Sc.* [Altered from **thefdom*, Thiefdom.] The action or practice of stealing; theft; thievery.

1566 *Sc. Acts Jas. I*, c. 154 That nouther Lord of Regalitie, Schiref, Barrone, na vthers sell ony theif, or fyne with him of thiftdome done [*Record ed.* (1814) of thift done]. 1597 Skene *De Verb. Sign.* s.v. *Bote*, Thieft-bote..quhen ony sellis onie thiefe, or finis with him for thieft-dome done, or to be done. 1854 Mrs. Oliphant *Magd. Hepburn* I. 221 Gentle or simple maunna tell me that God's will is for villany and theftdom.

†**The·ftfully,** *adv. Obs. rare.* In 5 **thift-**. [f. Theft + -ful + -ly[2].] By stealth: = Theftly.

c1400 *Sc. Trojan War* ii. 1301 Vlixes..frome Troy is passit thiftfully With all þaim of his company.

Thefthorn, variant of Theve-thorn *Obs.*

The·ftless, *a. rare.* [f. Theft + -less.] **a.** That is not a theft. **b.** Not liable to be stolen.

1696 S. H. *Gold. Law* 68 How punisht he poor Achan for a theftless theft to see to? 1803 Leyden *Scenes Infancy* iv. 361 Teviot's sons..devoid of fear Bind to the rush by night the theftless steer.

†**The·ftly,** *adv. Sc.* and *north. dial. Obs.* [Altered from ME. *þefly*, Thiefly.] By stealth, furtively.

c1400 *Sc. Trojan War* ii. 271 He gyffande thiftely ws till The palladinar at our will. *Ibid.* 623 Bycause þe palladinar was Out of þe temple ȝone thyftly. a1485 *Promp. Parv.* (MS. S), Stelyngly (theftely), *ffurtive, latrocinaliter.* 1498 *Reg. Privy Seal Scot.* I. 23/1, ix catell thiftly tane fra Thomas Sowtar. 1525 *Nottingham Rec.* III. 343 Reyseyvng off oder menys goodes theyftely.

Theftuous (þe·ftiu,əs), *a.* Originally *Sc.* Forms: α. 5 **thiftwis**, 5–6 **thiftuis**, 6 **thiftewus**. β. 6–7 **thifteous**, (7 **thiefteous**, 6 **thiftius**). γ. 6 **thiftuus**, 6–7 **-uous**, 7 **theftous**, 6– **theftuous**. [ME. *thiftwis*, f. Theft + Wise *sb.*: cf. Righteous from *rihtwis*.]

1. Of the nature of theft, thievish.

c1400 [implied in Theftuously]. 1491 *Reg. Privy Seal Scot.* I. 2 For the thiftwis owtputtin and awaytakin of the gudis. 1502 *Ibid.* 117/1 The thiftewus distruction of Johne Mans gudis. 1569 *Reg. Privy Council Scot.* II. 22 In thiftuous maner. 1593 *Sc. Acts Jas. VI* (1814) IV. 43/2 Pairtakaris in thair thifteous and wicked deidis. 1678 Sir G. Mackenzie *Crim. Laws Scot.* i. xx. § 3 (1699) 108 Whoso ever..assists them in their theftous Stealings. 1837 B. H. Hodgson in *Jrnl. Asiat. Soc. Bengal* VI. 367 It is..remarkable..for its theftuous propensities. 1880 Muirhead *Gaius* Digest 506 Theftuous removal of property.

b. *transf.* Furtive, secret, sneaking.

1881 Masson *De Quincey* xi. 138 A theftuous hope to amuse an hour for you after dinner.

2. Of the nature of a thief; given to theft.

1632 Lithgow *Trav.* (1906) 363 The Hungarians have ever beene thiftuous, treacherous and false. 1859 M. Napier *Visct. Dundee* I. p. x, That theftuous animal a cheap book-seller's hack. 1883 *Century Mag.* XXVII. 183 Pettily theftuous, like the English gypsies. 1885 *St. James' Gaz.* 28 Mar. 6/1 No man ever saw the most theftuous sparrow ashamed of himself.

b. *fig.* Said of an animal or vegetable parasite.

1883 H. Drummond *Nat. Law in Spir. W.* (ed. 2) 342 By means of its twining and theftuous roots it [*Sacculina*] imbibes automatically its nourishment ready-prepared from the body of the crab. 1883 R. Turner in *Gd. Words* July 470/2 Some [plants]..living by theftuous practices alone.

Theftuously (þe·ftiu,əsli), *adv.* Chiefly *Sc.* [f. prec. + -ly[2].] In a theftuous manner; by or as by theft; stealthily, secretly.

c1400 *Sc. Trojan War* ii. 1637 Vlixes stall thiftuisly Away, as grauntand him gilty. 1567-8 *Reg. Privy Council Scot.* I. 609 The leid upoun the Cathedrall Kirkis..is thiftuouslie stowin and takin away. 1653 Urquhart *Rabelais* ii. xiv, One little villainous Turkie..rogue came thiefteously to snatch away some of my lardons. 1880 Muirhead *Ulpian* vii. § 2 If a husband have theftuously abstracted anything of his wife's in prospect of divorce. 1882 *Chamb. Jrnl.* XIX. 73 On a late occasion, the tomb of a noble family was theftuously rifled of its contents.

Thefysch, obs. f. Thievish. **Thegh,** obs. f. Though, Thigh. **Thegither,** Sc. f. Together.

Thegn (þēin). *Hist.* A form used by some recent historians to represent the OE. *þegn* (*þegen*, *þén*), Thane[1], in its sense of tenant by military service, and as a term of rank below the *ealdorman* or *eorl* and above the *ceorl*, corresponding in its various grades to the post-conquest *baron* and *knight*.

The purpose of this spelling is to distinguish the Anglo-Saxon from the Scottish use of Thane[1] (sense 4), made familiar by Shakspere.

1848 Lytton *Harold* i. i, A Thegn forfeited his rank if he lost his lands. 1867 Freeman *Norm. Conq.* I. vi. 428 *note*, The signatures are no doubt those of local Thegns. 1874 Stubbs *Const. Hist.* I. vi. 155 Closely connected with the *gesith* is the *thegn*...The thegn seems to be primarily the warrior *gesith*; in this idea Alfred uses the word as translating the *miles* of Bede. But he also appears as a landowner. *Ibid.* 156 The name of thegn covers the whole class which after the Conquest appears under the name of knights, with the same qualification in land and nearly the same obligations. 1890 Gross *Gild Merch.* I. 185 The merchant who made three voyages across the ocean at his own cost became a thegn.

Hence **The·gn-born** *a.*, of noble or gentle birth. **The·gndom,** the position or rank of thegn. **The·gnhood,** the condition or position of a thegn; the order of thegns, thegns collectively. **The·gn-land,** land held by a thegn. **The·gnly,** *a.* and *adv.* [OE. *þegnlic, -lice*], **a.** *adj.* of or pertaining to, or becoming a thegn; **b.** *adv.* in a manner becoming a thegn. **The·gn-right,** the legal rights and privileges of a thegn. **The·gn-ship** [OE. *þegnscipe*], the office, function, or position of a thegn (in various senses). **The·gn-wer** [OE. *þegnwer*], the wer-gild of a thegn. **The·gn-worthy** *a.*: see quot.

?c935 *Dunsæte* c. 5 in Liebermann *Gesetze* (1903) 376 Sy he *ðegenboren, sy he ceorlboren. 1874 Stubbs *Const. Hist.* I. vi. 156 The thegn-born are contrasted with the ceorl-born. 1897 Rampini *Hist. Moray & Nairn* i. 46 The principle of comradeship..underlay English *thegndom. 1867 Freeman *Norm. Conq.* I. iii. 95 The growth of the *Thegnhood was, on the whole, depressing to the Ceorls. 1881 S. R. Gardiner *Introd. Stud. Eng. Hist.* ii. 34 The thegnhood pushed its roots down, as it were, amongst the free classes. a1100 *Charter of Will. II* in *Tabularis Ramesiensi* clxxviii (Du Cange), Si terra de Isham..si vero *Teinlanda tunc fuisse inveniatur. 1628 Coke *On Litt.* 86 In the book of Domesday land holden by knight's service was called *Tainland*. 1876 Digby *Real Prop.* i. § 2 (ed. 2) 13 Tain- or thegn-land. This seems to mean not a particular species of tenure, but land which was as a fact held or owned by a king's thegn. c1000 Ælfric *Hom.* I. 586 Andreas..is ȝerebt *ðegenlic. a1038 *Charter of Eanwene* in Kemble *Cod. Dipl.* IV. 55 Heo..to ðam þeȝnon cwæð: Doð þeȝnlice and wel! Abeodað mine ærende to ðam gemote. 1876 Freeman *Norm. Conq.* V. xxiv. 450 The words of Eanwene, when she bade the Scirgemót of Herefordshire to 'do thegnly and well'. 1897 Maitland *Domesday & Beyond* 53 The men..are usually men of thegnly rank. *Ibid.* 165 Each..will be entitled to a thegnly wergild and swear a thegnly oath. c1000 *Oaths* in Liebermann (1903) 464 Se mæssepreost..bið *þegenrihtes wyrþe. 1872 E. W. Robertson *Hist. Ess.* 118 None could pretend to the privileges of full thegn-right without the possession of at least a township. 959-63 *Laws of Edgar* iii. c. 2 Se dema, se ðe oðrum ou woh ȝedeme..þolize a his *þeȝnscipes. c1000 Ælfric *Saints' Lives* (1890) II. 82 Beoð nu ȝehyrte..and healdað mid ðeȝen-scipe ða halgan Godes æ. 1897 Maitland *Domesday & Beyond* 163 We begin by thinking of thegnship as a relation between two men...Then the thegnship becomes more than a relationship, it becomes a status. 1008 *Laws of Ethelred* V. c. 9 Þæt be sy *þegenweres & þegenrihtes wyrðe. 1874 Stubbs *Const. Hist.* I. vi. 155 The ceorl who has acquired five hides of land,..with other judicial rights, becomes *thegn-worthy; his oath and protection and wergild are those of a thegn.

Thei, þei, obs. f. They, Though.

Theic (þī·ik). [f. mod.L. *the-a* Tea + -ic 3: cf. Theism[2].] One addicted to immoderate tea-drinking, or who suffers from such excess; a tea-drunkard.

1886 *Medical News* (U.S.) XLIX. 305 It is possible to be a 'theic' by profession or a 'theic' by passion. 1899 in *Syd. Soc. Lex.*

Theid, Sc. var. Thede *Obs.* **Theie, theiȝe,** obs. ff. Thigh. **Theif,** obs. f. Thief.

Theiform (þī·ifǭɹm), *a.* [ad. mod.L. *theiform-is*, f. *thea* Tea: see -form.] Resembling the tea-plant.

1846 Worcester, *Theiform*, being in the form of tea. *Everest.* 1860 in Mayne *Expos. Lex.*

Theigh, þeiȝ, þeigh, þeiȝt, obs. ff. Though. **Theight,** obs. f. Tight. **Theign(e,** obs. ff. Thane, Theine *v.* **Theik,** var. Theek, to thatch. **Theil,** var. Thail, tael. **Theim,** obs. ff. Them. **Thein, þein,** obs. f. Thane; var. Thyne *Obs.*, thence.

Theine (þī·ǝin), *sb. Chem.* Also †thei·na. [f. mod.L. *thea* Tea + -ine[5].] A vegetable alkaloid, originally thought to be a principle peculiar to tea, but found to be identical with Caffeine.

1838 T. Thomson *Chem. Org. Bodies* 295 Oudry has..announced that he has discovered in tea a salifiable basis, to which he has given the name of *theina*. 1842 *Penny Cycl.* XXIV. 304/2 Thein, or Theina, the peculiar principle of tea. 1853 Ure *Dict. Arts* II. 834 Theine was obtained from coffee by the same process slightly altered. 1863-72 Watts *Dict. Chem.* I. 707 Oudry.., in 1827, found in tea a crystalline substance, which he called theine. 1881 A. Griffith in *Science Gossip* No. 203. 248 Tea contains from a half to five per cent. of theine.

†**Theine, theign,** *v. Obs.* Forms: 1–2 þeȝnian (1 ðeȝn-), þénian, 2 þeiȝnen, 3 þeinen, þeine(n. [OE. *þegnian*, f. *þegn*, Thane = ON. *þegna*, OHG. *deganôn* :—OTeut. **þegnôjan*, f. **þegno* Thane.] *intr.* To be a servant or minister, to perform the duties of an office. With *dative*: To minister to, wait or attend upon, serve. (a person); hence, quasi-*trans.*

Beowulf 561 Ic him þenode deoran sweorde swa hit ȝedefe wæs. a900 tr. *Bæda's Hist.* iii. xvii. [xxiii.] (1890) 237 Þa he ða moniȝ ȝer..biscophad þeȝnade. 971 *Blickl. Hom.* 33 He wæs soþ God, þe him englas þeȝnedon. c975 *Rushw. Gosp.* Matt. viii. 15 Hiu aras & ðæȝnade heom. c1000 *Ags. Gosp.* ibid., Ða aras heo & þenode him. c1160 *Hatton Gosp.* ibid., Þa aras hyo & þeiȝnede hym. a1175 *Cott. Hom.* 239 Mid al þan þe..laȝelice ber him þenið. c1175 *Lamb. Hom.* 109 Vnwurðe bið þe on elde þet him oðer men þenien. c1205 Lay. 24595 Þeȝ weoren a þusen cnihtes bald..þat þeineden þan kinge. *Ibid.* 24621 A þusend hire eode biuore..to þæinen þere quene. a1225 *St. Marher.* 23 Þeos þreo in an iþeinet of engles. a1250 *Prov. Ælfred* 499 in *O. E. Misc.* 132 Loke þat þu him þeine mid alle þeuues þines.

Hence †**Theining** (þeiȝnung, þening), ministration, service, office.

c888 K. Ælfred *Boeth.* xxxvii. § 1 ȝif him mon þonne awint of þa claþas, & him oftihð þara þenunga & þæs anwealdes. a900 tr. *Bæda's Hist.* ii. xiv. [xvi.] (1890) 144 Næniȝ..hrinan dorste ne ne wolde buton his nedþearflicre þeȝnunge. 971 *Blickl. Hom.* 209 Englas beoð to ðegnunge gæstum fram Gode hider on world sended. c1000 *Ags. Gosp.* Matt. xxvi. 19 Hiȝ ȝe-ȝearwodon him easter-þenunga. a1175 *Cott. Hom.* 233 His water [us werpð] drench and fiscynn his fer manifeald þeninge.

Their (ðē·ɹ), *poss. pron.* Forms: see below. [In existing form *their*, in Ormin *þeȝȝre*, a. ON. *þeir(r)a*, genitive pl. of simple demonst. *sá, sú, þat* (= OE. *se, sēo, þæt*), used in ON. also as pl. of 3 pers. pron. The β-forms *þer, þar, þere*, etc., were prob. due mainly to the unstressed pronunciation of *their, thair*, confused sometimes with that of the adv. *þær, thare*, There; but they may sometimes represent OE. *þéra*, late form of *þára*, gen. pl. of *sé* those, substituted for the same case of the personal pronoun. Cf. Them.]

A. Illustration of Forms.

α. 3 (*Orm.*) **þeȝȝre**, (**teȝȝre**), 4 **þeir(e, þeyr, þayre, þayire, þaier**, 4–5 **þair, þaire**, 5 **þeire**; 4–5 **thaire**, 5 **thayre**, 5–7 **theire, theyr**, 6 **thayr**, (**thier**, 6–7 **yair**), 4– *Sc.* **thair**, 5– **their**.

c1200 Ormin Ded. 84 All þurrh þeȝȝre sinne. *Ibid.* 3933 Þatt teȝȝre genge sholdde ben þurrh hallȝhe sawless ekedd. 1303 R. Brunne *Handl. Synne* 874 Þarefore þat day al holy cherche þeyr seruyse of bere þey werche. 13.. *Cursor M.* 794 (Cott.) Al þaier kin. *Ibid.* 21800 (Edin.) Mani man.. Þate thair [*v.r.* þair] bele hauis getin bare. a1340 Hampole *Psalter* lxxvii. 51 He gaf..þaire trauails til þe locust. c1400 *Destr. Troy* 6738 Menelaus, and Thelamon,..with theire tite batels. c1440 *Pallad. on Husb.* i. 116 Oute of thaire [*v.r.* their] kynde eke seedes wol renewe. 1470-85 Malory *Arthur* vii. xviii. 240 All they felle vpon their knees. 1522 *Rutland Papers* (Camden) 84 To putt all thier stuf of householde in euery office. 1538 Starkey *England* i. iv. 120 To tempur and refrayne thayr malyce. 1549 *Baxter-bks. St. Andrews* (1903) 5 Thomas mortowne To be yair Decane. a1568 *Wyfe of Auchtermuchty* xii, That straik dang baith thair harnis owt. 1630 Sir R. Naunton in *Fortescue Papers* (Camden) 139 Theyr general aunswer to his Majesties commandement. 1641 Best *Farm. Bks.* (Surtees) 126 Holes, of that bignesse that one may thrust in theire neafe.

β. (1 **þæra, þeora**) 4 **þer, þar,** (**þur**), 4–5 **þere**, 4–6 **þare, thar**, 5 **thare**, 5–6 **ther**, 6–8 **there**, 7 **thir** (used by Milton as unstressed form of *their*).

[?a1100 *O. E. Chron.* (Laud MS.) an. 449, On þeora dagum gelaðode Wyrtgeorn Angelcin hider. *Ibid.* an. 1086, Þæt þa godan men niman æfter þeora godnesse.] c1330 R. Brunne *Chron.* (1810) 127 Þe popille him bisouht þer kyng forto be. 13.. *Cursor M.* 476 (Cott.) Þat sithen þar [*v.rr.* þair(e, ber] sted was neuer sene. *Ibid.* 666 Bath he sette in þare [*v.rr.* þair(e, her] fre will. *Ibid.* 13970 Moyse þur lagh þaim broght. c1400 *Destr. Troy* 12467 Trees, thurgh tempestes, tynde hade þere leues. c1450 *Godstow Regr.* 491 Ther heires lawfully I-be-gote of ther bodies. c1460 *Towneley Myst.* ix. 119, I shalle fownd to crak thare crowne. 1513 Douglas *Æneis* iv. ix. 33-4 The ryning fludis thar wattir stop can scho mak, And eik the sternis turne ther cours abak. 1526 There [see B. 1]. 1533 Bellenden *Livy* ii. xix. (S.T.S.) I. 205 Þai obeyit weill eftir to þare capitanis. 1663 Chas. II in Julia Cartwright *Henrietta of Orleans* (1894) 139 They will shew there affections to me. 1671 Milton *P. R.* ii. 235 He ceas'd, and heard thir grant in loud acclaim. 1757 Mrs. Griffith *Lett. Henry & Frances* (1767) I. 56 Rogueries..which, they thought, brought a disgrace on there bruteships.

B. Signification.

1. *Poss. adj.* (orig. *gen. pl.* of *pers. pron.*) Of, belonging, or pertaining to them; also *refl.* of or belonging to themselves.

c1200 Ormin 127 Naffdenn þeȝȝ þurrh þeȝȝre streon Ne sune, child, ne dohhterr. c1330 R. Brunne *Chron. Wace* (Rolls) 1115 Brutus wiþ his folk..wente þer weye. 1340 Hampole *Pr. Consc.* 3884 Prelats..Sal account yhelde..Of þair suggets undir þair powere. 1526 Tindale *Matt.* vi. 5 Vereley I saye vnto you they have there rewarde. 1589 Puttenham *Eng. Poesie* i. vi. (Arb.) 27 Vnder the conduict of Totila and Atila and other their generalles. 1617 Moryson *Itin.* ii. 219 Consider the inward motiues of their crauing mercy. 1640 tr. *Verdere's Rom. of Rom.* I. xviii. 78 With that they tooke their leaves of her. 1774 Goldsm. *Nat. Hist.* (1776) VI. 222 The great agility of these animals prevents their often being taken. 1797 Godwin *Enquirer* i. vi. 41 We must dwell upon their every word. 1847 De Quincey *Orthogr. Mutineers* Wks. 1860 XIV. 105 When..he [Milton] wishes to direct a bright jet of emphasis upon the possessive pronoun *their*, he writes it as we now write it. But when he wishes to take off the accent, he writes it *thir*. [Cf. A. β. 1671.] 1853 M. Arnold *Empedocles* ii. 19 With men thou canst not live; Their thoughts, their ways, their wishes, are not thine. 1858 O. W. Holmes *Aut. Breakf.-t.* iv, Long after the frost and snow have done their worst with the orchards. 1864 Tennyson *Aylmer's F.* 383 These old pheasant-lords..Who had mildew'd in their thousands, doing nothing Since Egbert.

b. *Obj. gen.* Of (for, to) them. (Cf. His B. 2.)

1553 T. Wilson *Rhet.* (1580) 77 For a tyme your grace muche bewailed their lacke. 1579 [see 5]. 1590 Spenser *F. Q.* iii. iii. 43 Shall..quite from off the earth their memory be raste? 1607 Topsell *Four-f. Beasts* (1658) 66 Yet can there not be in any nation a neglect of oxen; and their reverence was so great that, in ancient time [etc]. 1780 Beckford *Biog. Mem.* 108 Humanity pleads strongly for the abridgment of their relation. *Mod.* We mourn their loss.

c. Const. with gen. pl. of *all, both*: *their aller, their bother, beyre* (obs.); also *all their, their both, both their, each of their* (arch.): meaning 'of all, both, or each of them'. See All D. 4, Both 4 b, Bo *a.* c.

a1250 *Owl & Night.* 1584 Þe louerd..Vareþ vt on þare beyre neode. a1300 *Cursor M.* 18766 He stei up in þair aller sight. c1380 Wyclif *Serm.* Sel. Wks. I. 289 Þe fend ..is þer alþer kyng. c1465 *Eng. Chron.* (Camden) 48 Be thair bothe assent. 1559 *Mirr. Mag.* (1563) D v, Lo thus fond hope dyd theyr both lyues abrydge. a1568 [see A. α]. 1589 Puttenham *Eng. Poesie* i. viii. (Arb.) 35 Saying thus in all their hearings. 1654-66 Earl Orrery *Parthen.* (1676) 550 With both their helps I was carried to a Chamber. 1672 Temple *Misc.* i. 64 According to each of their hunger or need. 1874 Swinburne *Bothwell* ii. i, Mine and all their free and sovereign king.

2. Used of a thing with which a number of persons have to do, or which is assumed to be the common possession of a class; e.g. 'These boys know their Greek syntax'. Cf. His *poss. pron.* 1 b.

1785 Burns *Halloween* ii, To burn their nits, an' pou their stocks, An' haud their Halloween. 1905 *Daily Chron.* 2 Sept. 3/1 All those who love their Devon and especially their Dartmoor.

3. Often used in relation to a singular sb. or pronoun denoting a person, after *each, every, either, neither, no one, every one*, etc. Also so used instead of 'his or her', when the gender is inclusive or uncertain. Cf. They *pron.* 2, Them *pron.* 2; Nobody 1 b, Somebody. (Not favoured by grammarians.)

13.. *Cursor M.* 389 (Cott.) Bath ware made sun and mon, Aiþer wit þer ouen light. c1420 *Sir Amadace* (Camden) l, Iche mon in thayre degre. 14.. *Arth. & Merl.* 2440 (Kölbing) Many a Sarazen lost their liffe. 1533 [see Themselves 5]. 1545 Abp. Parker *Let. to Bp. Gardiner* 8 May, Thus was it agreed among us that every president should assemble their companies. 1563 Winȝet *Four Scoir Thre Quest.* liv, A man or woman being lang absent fra thair party. 1642 [see A. α]. 1643 Trapp *Comm. Gen.* xxiv. 22 Each Country hath their fashions, and garnishes. 1749 Fielding *Tom Jones* vii. xiv, Every one in the House were in their Beds. 1771 Goldsm. *Hist. Eng.* III. 241 Every person ..now recovered their liberty. a1845 Syd. Smith *Wks.* (1850) 175 Every human being must do something with their existence. 1848 Thackeray *Van. Fair* xli, A person can't help their birth. 1858 Bagehot *Lit. Studies* (1879) II. 206 Nobody in their senses would describe Gray's 'Elegy' as [etc.]. 1898 G. B. Shaw *Plays* II. *Candida* 86 It's enough to drive anyone out of their senses.

†**4.** After a sb. (usually a proper name), instead of the genitive inflexion. Cf. His *poss. pron.* 4, Her *poss. pron. 3rd pl.* 3. *Obs.* or *rare arch.*

1551 Robinson tr. *More's Utop.* ii. (1895) 172 Vntyll the vtopians their creditours demaunde it. 1600 *Shakspere's Titus A.* (title-p.), As it hath sundry times beene playde by the Right Honourable the Earle of Pembrooke,..and the Lorde Chamberlaine theyr Seruants. 1642 Featley *Dippers Dipt* (1646) 11 These travellers their report, and the testimony of those witnesses. 1642 Drumm. of Hawth. *Skiamachia* Wks. (1711) 193 An answer to the parliament of England their declaration. 1667 Pepys *Diary* 3 Jan., The House of Lords their proceedings in petitioning the King. 1681 R. Burthogge *Argt. for Inf. Bapt.* (1684) 6 From the Children of Believers their being Abraham's Spiritual Seed.

5. Serving as antecedent to a following relative; equivalent to 'of those'. (Now usually avoided.)

1579 Tomson *Calvin's Serm. Tim.* 134/2 Under their obedience whome God hath set ouer us. 1593 in J. Morris *Troubles Cath. Forefathers* Ser. iii. (1877) 124 The chiefest favour must be procured by their means that have spoiled us before. 1655 Fuller *Ch. Hist.* ix. vii. § 14 This prediction ..yet miss'd their meaning, who both first reported, and most believed it.

†**6.** *absol.* = Theirs. Cf. Her *poss. pron. 3rd pers. pl.* 4. *Obs.*

13.. *Cursor M.* 7465 (Cott.) A man o þair gains an of vr. 1592 G. Harvey *Four Lett.* Wks. (Grosart) I. 216, I offer them my hande: and request their. 1618 Wither *Motto* Ciij b, My clothing keeps me full as warm as their [*rime* are]. *Ibid.* C iv, And my esteeme I will not change for their.

Their(e, obs. ff. There, Thir *dem. pron.*, etc. = these.

†**Theirkin,** *a. Obs.* Their kind of, of their kind. (Cf. Thakin, Thiskin.)

13.. *Cursor M.* 12346 (Cott.) Þe leons..Honur him on þairkin wise [*F.* þaire kin; *G.* opon þair wise].

Theirn, a midl. and south. dial. form for Theirs, on the analogy of *ourn, yourn, hisn, hern*. See *Eng. Dial. Dict.*

Theirs (ðē·ɹz), *poss. pron.* Forms: 4–5 **þayres, thayres, þair(e)s, thaires**, 4–6 **þairis, thairis, þeires, theires**, 5 **þers, therys**, 5–6 **theyr(e)s, theyr's**, 6 **therse**, 8–9 **their's**, 5– **theirs** (*Sc.* **thairs**). [In form a double possessive, f. Their + -es (cf. *hers, ours, yours*). Of northern origin.] The form of the possessive pron. Their, used when no sb. follows, i.e. either absolutely or predicatively: That or those belonging to them. (= F. *le, la leur, les leurs*; G. *der, die, das ihrige, die ihrigen*.)

a1300 *Cursor M.* 22578 (Edinb.) Vntil hir channel sal sco [the sea] turne And als til þayres [*Cott.* þairs, *Gött.* þairis, *Trin.* hores, *Laud* heris] ilk a burne. *Ibid.* 14132 A castel was bath his and þairs [*Fairf. & Gött.* þairis, *Trin.* þeires]. 13.. *R. Brunne's Chron. Wace* (Rolls) 11632 (Lamb. MS.) Þer nis no power to þeires liche [*Petyt MS.* non is þer pere ne to þam]. 13.. *E. E. Allit. P.* B. 1527 Heyred hem as hyȝly as heuen wer þayres. 1375 Barbour *Bruce* iii. 745 That thai and thairis..Suld be in all thing at his will. 1425 *Rolls of Parlt.* IV. 296/2 Yat any of the said parties, by yayme or yaires, procede. c1430 *Life St. Kath.* (1884) 27 Folowe our faders lyke as þey blessedly folewede thayres. c1440 *Generydes* 2980 This day is therys, A nother shalbe ourez. 1484 Caxton *Fables of Æsop* v. iii, Telle to them that it is thyn and not theyrs. 1526 Tindale *Matt.* v. 10 Theirs ys the kingdome off heven. 1674 Boyle *Excell. Mech. Hypothesis* 7 [They] have no recourse to any peculiar agency of theirs to account for Eclipses. 1719 De Foe *Crusoe* (1840) II. iii. 50 The island was theirs. 1853 Whewell *Grotius* III. 377 Theirs is the sounder opinion, which hold that such a grant continues. 1855 Tennyson *Charge Light Brigade* ii, Their's not to make reply, Their's not to reason why, Their's but to do and die.

b. *Of theirs*: see Of 44.

c1400 *Laud Troy Bk.* 3521 That he scholde euere be on of thaires. c1400 Love *Bonavent. Mirr.* xxxix. (1908) 197 A frende of theires. 1555 Eden *Decades* 134 A childe of therse. 1564 *Brief Exam.* ** , This gaye booke of theyrs. 1692 Bentley *Boyle Lect.* ii. 63 These Atoms of theirs. 1831 *Society* I. ii. 16 An old acquaintance of theirs.

†**c.** Used instead of Their (*rare*); in 17–18th c. when followed by another possessive, e.g. 'theirs or our country', now 'their country or ours'. *Obs.*

c1200 Ormin 2506 And all onn ane wise fell Till eȝȝþerr þeȝȝress herrte. 1560 *Inchaffray Charters* (S.H.S.) 167 Als fre as..ouris or thairis granitaris or chalmirlanis..Josit brukit or intromettit with. 1562 Turner *Baths* Ded., For theyrs sake that are honest and vertuous men. 1652 Gaule *Magastrom.* 274 The event fell out contrary to theirs, and according to the Apostles prediction. 1667 Marvell *Corr.* lxxviii. Wks. (Grosart) II. 223 Upon the importation.. into theirs or our country. a1774 Goldsm. tr. *Scarron's Com. Romance* (1775) II. 54 He thought it both theirs and his duty to mount immediately.

†**d.** *Maugre theirs*: in spite of them, against their will: see Maugre *prep.* 1 c. *Obs.*

c1330 R. Brunne *Chron. Wace* (Rolls) 12811 Maugre þeires he dide þem go In to þe wode. *Ibid.* 15336. 1375 Barbour *Bruce* x. 118 Magre thairis he it wan. 1480 *Coventry Leet Bk.* 427 Wheder we shall make the people to abide styll here.., magre theirs, or els let hem departe.

Theirself, -selves: see Themselves III.

Theis, *adv.* [Cf. This *adv.* and Dyce.] Thus.

a1828 M. G. Lewis *Jrnl. W. Ind.* (1834) 5 Sea terms.—.. *theis* (*thus*) you are near enough.

Theism[1] (þī·iz'm). [mod. f. Gr. θε-ός god + -ism. Cf. F. *théisme* (Voltaire).] **a.** *gen.* Belief in a deity, or deities, as opposed to *atheism*. **b.** Belief in one god, as opposed to *polytheism* or *pantheism*; = Monotheism. **c.** Belief in the existence of God, with denial of revelation: = Deism. **d.** *esp.* Belief in one God as creator and supreme ruler of the universe, without denial of revelation: in this use distinguished from *deism*.

1678 Cudworth *Intell. Syst.* Pref., Nor indeed out of a meer Partiall Regard to that Cause of Theism neither, which we were engaged in. 1711 Shaftesb. *Charac.* (1737) II. 209, I consider..that to be a settled Christian, it is necessary to be first of all a good theist. For theism can only be oppos'd to polytheism, or atheism. a1774 Tucker *Lt. Nat.* (1834) II. 323 We find the introduction of theism, that is, the doctrine of an intelligent Agent, the Author of nature,.. claimed for Pythagoras. 1841 Elphinstone *Hist. India* I. 163 The theism inculcated by the Védas..has been supplanted by a system of gross polytheism and idolatry. 1877 R. Flint *Theism* i. 18 Theism is the doctrine that the universe owes its existence, and continuance..to the reason and will of a self-existent Being...It is the doctrine that nature has a Creator and Preserver. 1888 F. L. Patton *Syllabus Lect. Theism* 1 (Funk) Theism may be considered religiously [as embracing] polytheism, pantheism, monotheism (theism par excellence).

Theism[2] (þī·iz'm). *Path.* [f. mod.L. *the-a* Tea + -ism.] A morbid condition characterized by headache, sleeplessness, and palpitation of the heart, caused by excessive tea-drinking.

1886 *Science* VIII. 132 It is customary to speak of acute, subacute and chronic 'theism', a form that has no connection with theological matters. 1906 *Daily News* 14 Sept. 6 It is well to keep an eye on 'acute caffeism' and 'chronic theism'.

Theist[1] (þī·ist). [mod. f. Gr. θε-ός god + -ist. Cf. F. *théiste* (Voltaire).] One who holds the doctrine of theism: in earlier use = Deist; in later use, esp. as distinguished from this: see note s.v. Deist.

1662 E. Martin *Five Lett.* 45 To have said my office.. twice a day..among Rebels, Theists, Atheists, Philologers, Wits, Masters of Reason, Puritanes [etc.]. a1679 W. Owtram *Serm.* (1682) A v, What theist was ever known to live according to the principles of natural religion? a1734 North *Exam.* iii. viii. § 11 (1740) 590 He [Oates] did but use the Privilege of a Theist or Freethinker, of which Crew, or worse, he plainly declared himself. 1820 Polwhele in *Lavington's Enthus. Meth. & Papists* Introd. 135 The highly-polished preacher, whose audience are theophilanthropists or theists. 1870 J. H. Newman *Gram. Assent* v. § 2. 120 No one is to be called a Theist, who does not believe in a Personal God.

b *attrib.* and *Comb.*

1711 Hickes *Two Treat. Chr. Priesth.* (1847) I. 267 His atheist-ridden, or theist-ridden..mind. 1755 Amory *Mem.* (1766) II. 107 The writings of the old theist philosophers.

The·ist[2]. *nonce-wd.* [f. mod.L. *thea* Tea: cf. Theism[2].] A person addicted to tea-drinking.

c1818 Shelley in Medwin *Life* (1847) II. 47 [Shelley..was a lover of tea, calling himself..humourously a] Theist.

Theistic (þī,i·stik), *a.* [f. Theist[1] + -ic.]

1. Of or pertaining to theists or theism.

1780 Warton *Sir T. Pope* vi. (ed. 2) 208 From an abhorrence of superstition, he appears to have adopted the most distant extremes of the theistic system. 1875 Voysey *Revised Prayer Bk.* (ed. 2) Pref., This modest attempt to adapt the Liturgy of the venerable Church of England to a purely Theistic worship. 1876 Gladstone in *Contemp. Rev.* June 5 Those who, professedly rejecting all known expressions of dogma, are nevertheless believers in a moral Governor of the Universe...I denominate the Theistic school.

2. Used in the sense: Of or pertaining to a god or gods; divine. *rare.*

1854 Brimley *Ess.*, *Comte's Pos. Philos.* 324 A region of phenomena where Will.., quite apart from all consideration of theistic interference, introduces a disturbing element that baffles the previsions of science. 1878 Gladstone *Prim. Homer* vi. § 2. 66 Zeus..combines, more than any other deity, the human and the theistic quality.

Theistical (þī,i·stikăl), *a.* [f. as prec. + -al: see -ical.] = prec. 1. Hence **Thei·stically** *adv.*, in a theistical manner.

1697 C. Leslie *Short Meth. w. Deists* i. § 11 (1699) 45 *note*, The Theistical Clubb have set this up as a Principle. 1738 Warburton *Div. Legat.* iii. ii. 304 That future State, which, I suppose, the Theistical Philosophers did not believe. 1841 Elphinstone *Hist. India* I. 223 The work of Patanjali..is the text-book of the theistical sect.

Theive, obs. form of Theave, Thieve.

Theivil, Sc. var. Thivel, pot-stick.

Theke (þīk). *Bot.* [ad. Gr. θήκη.] = Theca 2.

1872 Tuckerman *N. Amer. Lichens* 30 [Spores] occurring in eights in the thekes. 1882 *Ibid.* I. Introd. 8 The hymenium, consisting of thekes (thecæ, the spore-bearing organs). 1900 in B. D. Jackson *Gloss. Bot. Terms.*

Theke, obs. form of Theek, Thilk.

Thel, thele, variants of Theal *Obs.*, a board.

†**Thelema·tic,** *a. Obs. rare.* [f. Gr. θεληματ-, stem of θέλημα will + -ic.] Of or pertaining to will or volition; voluntary.

1813-21 Bentham *Ontology* Wks. 1843 VIII. 207/2 Thelematic [motions], those in the production of which volition..is seen to be concerned.

Thelemite (þe·lǐmait). *rare.* [a. F. *thelemite* (Cotgr.), f. Gr. θέλημα will + -ite[1], with reference to the abbey of Thélème in Rabelais, the only law of which was *Fay ce que vouldras*, Do what thou wilt.] (See quots.)

1656 Blount *Glossogr.*, *Thelemite*, a libertine, one that does what he list. 1908 *Nation* 24 Oct. 144/1 We will.. take our oath to observe the Thelemite rule of 'Do what thou wilt', because, as its founder said, 'men that are free, well-born, well-bred, and conversant in honest companies have naturally an instinct and spur that prompts them unto virtuous actions'.

Thelephoroid (þǐle·fǒroid), *a. Bot.* [f. mod.L. *Thelephora* (f. Gr. θηλή a teat + -φορος bearing) + -oid.] Resembling or having the form of the genus *Thelephora* of hymenomycetous fungi. So **Thelepho·reous** *a.*, of or pertaining to this genus.

1860 Mayne *Expos. Lex.*, *Thelephoreus*,..applied by Persoon to a Family..of the *Exosporii Sarcomyci*..: thelephoreous. 1891 *Cent. Dict.*, Thelephoroid.

Thelke, obs. form of Thilk.

†**Thellich,** *a.* and *pron. Obs.* Forms: α. 1 **þyslic, þyllic, þillic, þilic**, 2 **þellic**, 3 **þullich(ii)**, **þulli (ü)**, 4 **þellich**. β. 1 **þylc, þilc**. [OE. *þyllic*, by assimilation from *þyslic* (beside *þuslic, þullic*), f. *þus, þys*, Thus + *-lic*, -ly[1]. See also Thilk.]

A. *adj.* Of this or such a kind; suchlike, such.

Beowulf 2637 ȝif him þyslicu þearf ȝelumpe. a890 tr. *Bæda's Hist.* ii. ix. [xii.] (1890) 130 Se ðe þyslice ȝife & swa micle..forecwiþ. c897 K. Ælfred *Gregory's Past. C.* xliii. 314 Ðyllic fæsten ic ȝeceas. c1000 Ælfric *Saints' Lives* xxxiii. 142 Ac þyllic lif nis na ȝewunelic on ure ceastre. c1000 *Ags. Gosp.* Matt. xviii. 5 Swa hwylc swa anne þyllicne [*v.r.* þilicne, *Hatt. G.* þellicne, *Lindisf.* ðuslic] lytling on minum naman onfehþ, me onfehþ. — Mark vii. 8 Manega oþre þyllice [*v.r.* þylce, *Hatt. G.* þellice] ðing ȝe doð. c1050 *Liber Scintill.* 33 Ac swyþe feawa synd þa þylce ȝebedu habban. *Ibid.* 80 Þes þylc fela spycð. a1225 *Ancr. R.* 8 Þeos & swuche oþre [*MS. C.* þullich oðere] beoð alle ine freo wille to donne. c1230 *Hali Meid.* 9 Þe þohtes þat..leareð þe and eggeð toward þulli þeowdom. a1240 *Sawles Warde* in *Cott. Hom.* 255 Of þulliche nesche wepnen ich mahte carien summes weis. *Ibid.* 265 Sikere ha beoð of al þis of þulli lif, of þulli wit, of þulli luue..ant of þulli blisse. 1340 *Ayenb.* 27 Of þelliche þinges him gledeþ ine his herte.

B. *pron.* [absol. or ellipt. use of the adj.] A thing or things of this, that, or such a kind; such.

a890 tr. *Bæda's Hist.* iii. xvi. [xxii.] (1890) 228 Þyslic wæs seo syn, þe se cyning fore ofslegen wæs. c893 K. Ælfred *Oros.* iv. iv. § 2 Nu Romane him self þyllic writon. a1000 *Egbert's Confess.* c. 15 ȝif..he awiht þylces do. c1000 Ælfric *Colloquy* in Wr.-Wülcker 96/42 Þylces fela, *his similia.* c1000 *Ags. Gosp.* Luke ix. 9 Hwæt is þes be þam ic þilc [*Hatt.* þellic, *Lind.* ðuslico] ȝehyre? a1225 *Leg. Kath.* 849 Low! þullich is al þæt ȝe þencheð to dei for to weorrin me wið. 1340 *Ayenb.* 7 Þe þridde heste is þellich.

Thelphusian (þelfiū·siăn), *a.* (*sb.*) *Zool.* [f. mod.L. *Thelphūsa* + -ian.] Of or pertaining to the genus *Thelphusa* of fresh-water crabs, as *T. fluviatilis*, which burrows in river banks. **b.** *sb.* A crab of this family.

1842 *Penny Cycl.* XXIV. 303/2 *Thelphusa, Thelphusians*, M. Milne Edwards's name for a tribe of brachyurous crustaceans belonging to his family of *Catometopes*. *Ibid.*, Many of the Thelphusians.

Thelyblast (þe·li-, þī·liblæst). *Biol.* [f. Gr. θῆλυς female + -blast.] The female element of a sexual cell. Hence **Thelybla·stic** *a.*

1877 C. S. Minot in *Proc. Boston Soc. Nat. Hist.* XIX. 170 The sexual generation may be called *genoblasts*, the male *arsenoblasts*, the female *thelyblasts* (direction cells, nucleoli of Infusoria and spermatozoa). 1890 Billings *Nat. Med. Dict.*, *Thelyblasts*, term proposed by Minot to include mature ova and sperm-blastophores or seminal mother-cells.

‖**Thelycum** (þī·li-, þe·likǒm). Pl. **thelyca.** [mod.L., ad. Gr. θηλυκόν, neuter of θηλυκός feminine, f. θῆλυ-ς female.] Name for a structure on the ventral surface of the thorax in the female of certain macrurous crustaceans.

1888 C. S. Bate in *Challenger Rep.* XXIV. 244 The ventral plate or thelycum in the female [*Penæus canaliculatus*]. *Ibid.* 245 The peculiar formation of the complementary external female apparatus which I propose to call thelycum.

Thely·genous, *a. Bot.* [f. Gr. θῆλυ-ς female + -gen + -ous.] Producing the female element.

1900 B. D. Jackson *Gloss. Bot. Terms* 270/1 *Thelygenous*, inducing the female element, as thelygenous castration, the production of pistils in the male-flowers of a host by *Ustilago*.

Thelykaryotic (þe·li-, þī·likæri͡ǫ·tik), *a. Biol.* [irreg. f. Gr. θῆλυ-ς female + κάρυον nut, kernel + -otic, after *mitotic*.] Having a female nucleus.

1909 J. W. Jenkinson *Experim. Embryol.* 267 In the two-celled stage one blastomere has a male and a female nucleus, ..while the other has only a female (thelykaryotic).

†**Thelyphtho·ric,** *a. Obs. nonce-wd.* [f. mod. L. *thelyphthora* (M. Madan 1780), f. Gr. θῆλυ-ς female + φθορά corruption: cf. Gr. φθορικός corrupting.] That corrupts or ruins women.

[1780 M. Madan (*title*) Thelyphthora; or, A Treatise on Female Ruin, in its Causes, Effects, Consequences, Prevention, and Remedy.] 1794 Mathias *Purs. Lit.* i. 160 Must I with Madan, bent on gospel truth, In Thelyphthoric lore instruct our youth.

Thelytokous (þǐli·tǒkəs), *a. Zool.* Also *erron.* **thelyotokous** (-ǫ·tǒkəs). [f. Gr. θηλυτόκος bearing females (f. θῆλυ-ς female + -τόκος bearing) + -ous.] Producing only female offspring, as the parthenogenetic females of some species: opposed to *arrenotokous*. So **Thely·toky** (also **thelyo·toky**), the production of females only in parthenogenesis.

1877 Huxley *Anat. Inv. Anim.* vii. 446 The terms arrenotokous and thelytokous have been proposed by Leuckart and Von Siebold to denote those parthenogenetic females which produce male and female young respectively. 1895 D. Sharp *Cambr. Nat. Hist.* V. iv. 141 The result of parthenogenesis in some species is the production of only one sex, which in some Insects is female, in others male; the phenomenon in the former case is called by Taschenberg Thelyotoky, in the latter case Arrhenotoky. *Ibid.* xxii. 498 Thelyotokous parthenogenesis is common in sawflies.

Them (ðem, ðěm), *pers. pron.* Forms: see below. [Three types are found in ME. α. *þeȝȝm*, *þeym*, a. ON. *þeim* 'to those', 'to them', dat. pl. of the demonst. *sá, sú, þat*, the plural of which also supplies that of the 3rd pers. pron. (see They). This came down to the 16th c. in Eng. in the form *theim*, and still exists in north. dial. and in Sc. as *thaim*. β. Northern Eng. *þam*, app. bef. 1300; this appears to represent *þæm, þám*, dat. pl. of OE. *se, sēo, þæt*, pl. *þá* (see That, Tho), found already as accus. in the Rushworth Gospels, where Lindisf. has *hia*, Ags. Gosp. *hiȝ*, Hatton *hyo*, all in the sense 'them'. This came down in Sc. as *thame* to 16th c. γ. The existing form *them*, found in R. Brunne c1330. This may have originated as an unstressed form (ðěm, ðăm) of *þeim* or (?) *þam*, or it may actually have represented the OE. Anglian *þæm* of the Rushworth Gospels.

Although the form from Norse is not known before Ormin, it must have been current in the Danelaw much earlier, since it was only dative in Norse, and must have been taken into OE. as dative, and have shared in the peculiar English change by which the accusative and dative of the pronouns were levelled under the dative form. In the singular *hine*, *him*, instances of this change are seen in the Rushworth Gospel Gloss c975 (see Him 1 d); and it is noteworthy that the same Gloss shows the use of *þæm* as acc., = *hia, hiȝ, hyo*, as mentioned above. This use of *þæm* as pers. pron. may itself have been due to Norse influence, the OE. word being used in the same sense as the Norse *þeim*.

The commoner pron. of 3rd pers. pl. obj. (dat. and acc.) in OE. and ME. was Hem, surviving colloq. and dial. as *'em*.]

A. Illustration of Forms.

α. 2–3 (*Orm.*) **þeȝȝm**, 4–6 **þeym, þeim, theym(e, theim**, 6 **theime**; 4 **þaime, paym**, 4–6 **þaim**, (4 **þaem**, 4–5 **taim**), 4–6 (4– *Sc.*) **thaim**, 4–6 **thaym(e**, 6 **thaime**.

c1200 Ormin 1751 Þatt he þeȝȝm ȝife blisse. *Ibid.* 1768 And hellpe þeȝȝm..To winnenn eche blisse. a1300 *Cursor M.* 47 (Cott.) A saumpul ber be þaem [*Gött.* þaim, *F.* ham, *T.* hem] I say. *Ibid.* 19378 (Edin.) Þai lerid at taim to suffer harde. c1330 R. Brunne *Chron. Wace* 13072 Wawayn.. smot aboute, & made þeym rounn. c1375 *Sc. Leg. Saints* xxvii. (*Machor*) 724 He betwene þaym pes can ma. c1400 tr. *Secreta Secret., Gov. Lordsh.* 58 Worschippe..þayme þat þou seez þat doon to be worschipped. 1523 Ld. Berners *Froiss.* I. clxxxvi. 220 A stryfe fell bytwene theym and they of Parys. 1533 Gau *Richt Vay* (S.T.S.) 3 Thay quhilk red thayme or buyr thaime. 1534 Cromwell in Merriman *Life & Lett.* (1902) I. 374 They..make not so muche for your purpose as ye allege thaim for. 1536 Wriothesley *Chron.* (Camden) I. 43 Great lamentation that the poore people made for theim. 1537 *Adm. Crt. Exemplif.* i. No. 174 Seeing a ship coming somewhat rome with theym. 1565 Allen *Def. Purg.* xv. 272 Sumwhiles by thabasing of theime. 1873 Thaim [see B. 5].

β. 1 **þæm**, 3–4 **þam**, 4–6 **þame** (6 **yame**), 4–7 **thame, tham**.

c975 *Rushw. Gosp.* Matt. xx. 25 Hælend þa ceiȝde þæm [*Lind.* hia, *Ags.* hiȝ, *Hatt.* hyo] to him. 13.. *Cursor M.* 4900 (Cott.) Þe sargantz..Ran and ouertok þam [*Gött.* þaim] þare. *Ibid.* 7120 A redel þam wndo he badd. c1330 R. Brunne *Chron.* (1810) 2 Iuor & Ini were disconfite þat day, Þe Iris & þe Wals with þam fled away. 1357 *Lay Folks Catech.* (MS. T.) 30 That..suld teche thame. *Ibid.* 65 To lere tham. a1400 *Isumbras* 122 For thame es alle my kare. 1513 Douglas *Æneis* xiii. x. 88 Gyf thame happynis careit for to be Tyll ony wther sted. 1577 Holinshed *Chron., Hist. Scot.* I. 371/2 To yame that receyuit thy noble father yᵉ Duke of Longcastell. 1641 in Row *Hist. Kirk* (Wodrow Soc.) p. iii, Being found qualifeit be thame.

γ. 4 **þem**, 4– **them**, (5–6 **theme**).

c1330 R. Brunne *Chron. Wace* (Rolls) 15336 Oure kynde ..Schal do þem bowe, maugre þayres. 13.. *Cursor M.* 13725 (Cott.) Him for to tak bituix þem tua. c1430 Them [see B. 4]. 1482 in *Eng. Hist. Rev.* XXV. 123 If ye wylle not, we bene purveyde of theme yat wylle. 1573 *Satir. Poems Reform.* xl. 21 To theme that was his fais.

B. Signification. **I.** Personal pronoun.

1. As pronoun of the third person plural, objective, direct and indirect (accusative and dative) of They. Also as antecedent pron. followed by relative, or prepositional phrase, and having then a demonstrative function, equivalent to *those* but less emphatic.

a. Direct object or accusative. (= L. *eos, illos*, G. *sie.*)

c975 [see A. β]. c1200 [see A. α]. a1300 *Cursor M.* 1228 He þam for-soke in all þer nedis. *Ibid.* 8118 He beild þam to þaim for to kys. c1330 [see A. γ]. 1470-85 Malory *Arthur* x. lxix. 533 The grene knyghte hath..beten all them of Orkeney. 1474 *Coventry Leet Bk.* 389 To bye theym in þe Croschepyng. 1552 Lyndesay *Monarche* 4822 Unoccupyit thay halde thame in thare neif. 1560 Bible (Genev.) 1 *Sam.* ii. 30 Them that honour me, I wil honour. 1586 T. B. *La Primaud. Fr. Acad.* i. (1589) 383 Have them in great estimation and admiration. 1667 Milton *P. L.* ix. 420 By Fountain or by shadie Rivulet He sought them both. 1864 J. H. Newman *Apol.* iv. (1904) 125/1 Charges..which..I fully believed at the time when I made them.

b. Indirect object or dative. (= L. *eis, illis*, G. *ihnen*.)

c1200 Ormin 1142 Þatt he þeȝȝm..Forrȝæfe þeȝȝre gilltess. a1300 *Cursor M.* 667 Witte and wisdam he þam gaue. 1375 Barbour *Bruce* i. 79 Þis ordynance þaim thocht þe best. c1400 *Rule St. Benet* 20 And by-kenne it taim þat best can serue god & te cuuent. c1500 *Merch. & Son* 269 in Hazl. *E. P. P.* I. 151 The maryage of them ij. ys made. 1523 Ld. Berners *Froiss.* I. ccxli. 353 He sent..and made alyaunces with them thre. 1535 Coverdale *Jer.* xxxv. 2 Geue them wyne to drynke. 1656 Earl Monm. tr. *Boccalini's Advts. fr. Parnass.* i. i. (1674) 2 If their Lord..do but cast an artificial smile them, they take it as..a reward. 1779 *Mirror* No. 23 ℙ 2 To show them what they are to understand. 1812 Crabbe *Tales* xviii, Men..whose pains, Credit, and prudence, brought them constant gains. *Mod.* I give them credit for good intentions.

c. As the object of a preposition.

c1300 *Harrow. Hell* 29 (MS. E) Crist loked þaim vnto. c1340 Hampole *Prose Tr.* 28 Þou will noghte tente to thaym. 1474 Caxton *Chesse* 7 Take not from them that is theyres. 1535 Coverdale *Ps.* xvii[i]. 48 Thou shalt lift me vp from them that ryse agaynst me. 1663 Gerbier *Counsel* f viij, Letters, which the Ægiptians did attribute unto them. 1780 *Mirror* No. 96 ℙ 2 They are neither of them niggardly. 1847 Tennyson *Princess* Concl. 68 Too solemn for the comic touches in them. *Mod.* What will he do with them?

d. Sometimes *indefinitely*, as objective case of They 3. *colloq.* or *dialectal*.

2. Often used for 'him or her', referring to a singular person whose sex is not stated, or to *anybody, nobody, somebody, whoever*, etc. Cf. They 2.

1742 Richardson *Pamela* III. 127 Little did I think..to make a..Complaint against a Person very dear to you,..but dont let them be so proud..as to make them not care how they affront everybody else. 1853 Miss Yonge *Heir of Redclyffe* xliv, Nobody else..has so little to plague them. 1874 Dasent *Half a Life* II. 198 Whenever any one was ill, she brewed them a drink.

3. Used for the nominative *they*. **a.** As antecedent or demonstrative pronoun: = Those. Now only *dial.* or *illiterate*.

c1489 Caxton *Sonnes of Aymon* iii. 78 All the foure brethern, and all theym of theyr companye arayed them selfe. c1530 Ld. Berners *Arth. Lyt. Bryt.* 393 Blessyd be them that hath brought that about. 1581 Marbeck *Bk. of Notes* 150 Such are them to whom yᵉ Lord doth giue his holy spirit. 1632 Lithgow *Trav.* vii. 333 In a moment, them of the Villages came downe on horse and foote. 1873 Murray *Dial. S. Scotl.* 184 Thaim at dyd it. 1891 Barrie *Little Minister* iii, Them as says there's no has me to fecht. a1825 Forby *Voc. E. Anglia* Introd. 141 Them are the women I meant. 1877 L. J. Jennings *Field Paths* iii. 47 Them be my two children. 1901 N. Lloyd *Chronic Loafer* i. 11 Them wasn't our only troubles.

b. As personal pronoun after *than, as*, and in the predicate after the verb *to be*. Common *colloq.*, but considered incorrect grammatically.

1654-66 Earl Orrery *Parthen.* (1676) 708 It was an impossibility that these could be them. 1777 Mickle *Cumnor Hall* xix, How far less blest am I than them! 1845 E. Warburton *Crescent & Cross* I. 331 It was not them we wanted. 1888 'J. S. Winter' *Bootle's Childr.* xiv, It was them told me about her. 1888 'R. Boldrewood' *Robbery under Arms* xxxiv, It was them or us..now. 1901 Theo. W. Wilson *Bacca Queen* xi. 89 Such as them enjoys therselfs.

II. 4. As reflexive pron. = themselves. (= L. *se, sibi*, G. *sich*.)

As direct or indirect obj. of vb. (*arch.*), or obj. of prep.

13.. *Cursor M.* 1713 Þe meke be þam ai tua and tua, Þe wild do be þam-self al-sua. *Ibid.* 15757 (Cott.) Þai fell þaim don vn-to þe grund. 1375 Barbour *Bruce* i. 205 Gyff þat ony man þaim by Had ony thing þat wes worthy. c1430 *Syr Tryam.* 770 The knyghtes gysed them fulle gay, And proved them fulle preste. 1535 Coverdale *Exod.* xxxii. 8 They haue made them a molten calfe. a1550 *Christis Kirke Gr.* xi, To dans thir damysellis thame dicht. 1565 Cooper *Thesaurus*, *Rubricata*,..roset colour that women vse to paynte them. 1794 Mrs. Radcliffe *Myst. Udolpho* lvii, Superior attainments of every sort bring with them duties of superior exertion. 1848 J. H. Newman *Loss & Gain* ii. xx. (1904) 254 What a way those fellows have with them! 1855 Macaulay *Hist. Eng.* xxii. IV. 697 They then bethought them of a new expedient.

III. 5. As demonstr. adj. = Those. Now only *dial.* or *illiterate*.

a. Qualifying an objective (direct or indirect). Also strengthened by adding *there* (*'ere, air*).

1596 H. Clapham *Bible Hist.* 92 To Samaria and them partes. 1598 Barret *Theor. Warres* i. i. 4 The warres and weapons are now altered from them dayes. 1621 Ainsworth *Annot. Pentat.* Gen. xxvii. 6 Foure of them Logs make a Kab. 1726 Cavallier *Mem.* iii. 231 If I had but one of them Hangmen. 1809-12 Mar. Edgeworth *Absentee* xii, I hope, then, the agent will give you encouragement about them mines. 1840 Thackeray *Catherine* vii, It was a rare rise we got out of them chaps. 1878 Mrs. Stowe *Poganuc P.* i, He don't believe in keeping none of them air prayer-book days.

b. Qualifying a nominative.

1607 Topsell *Four-f. Beasts* (1658) 126 Them few [dogs] which be kept must be tyed up in the day time. 1610 Healey *Vives' Comment St. Aug. Citie of God* xii. xvi, Augustine..saith that them times were called eternall. 1778 J. Crank in F. Chase *Hist. Dartmouth* (Mass.) *Coll.* (1891) I. 389 The major part tories, or them sort of creatures called neuters. 1842 S. Lover *Handy Andy* xxviii, Them ribbons of yours cost a trifle, Kitty. 1889 Tennyson *Owd Roä* viii, 'Faithful an' True' them words be i' Scriptur. 1901 M. E. Francis *Fiander's Widow* ii. v. 255 'Them there legs o' yourn should be pretty well stretched by now.'

‖**Thema** (þe·mă, þī·mă). Pl. **themata** (þe·mătă). [mod.L. *thema*, a. Gr. θέμα Theme.]

†**1.** The theme or subject of a declamation or discourse; a position to be maintained or demonstrated; a thesis. *Obs.*

1531 Elyot *Gov.* i. xiv, A case is appoynted to be moted by certayne yonge men, contaynyng some doubtefull controuersie, which is in stede of the heed of a declamation called *thema*. a1734 North *Exam.* i. i. § 8. (1740) 18 His grand *Thema* or Historical Position is, That King Charles II. was a concealed Papist. *Ibid.* ii. § 47. 53 Another of the Author's *Themata* or Positions.

2. The stem-form of a word; = Theme 5.

1615 Bedwell *Arab. Trudg.*, *Alkoran*, the thema is not *Karana*,..as they would make vs beleeue: but *Kara*, which signifieth, to reade. 1883 *Athenæum* 6 Jan. 15/2 Scholars are still divided as to what thema or base to refer certain forms [of Icelandic nouns].

3. *Mus.* = Theme 4.

1801 Busby *Dict. Mus.* 1871 Graeme *Beethoven* ii. (1876) 27 Beethoven..requested a thema for an improvisation.

4. A dissertation or thesis submitted for a degree; cf. Theme 3.

1888 *Athenæum* 28 July 120/3 'The Conflict of East and West in Egypt'..appears to be an enlargement of a *thema* for the doctorate of Columbia College.

Thematic (þǐmæ·tik), *a.* (*sb.*) [ad. Gr. θεματικ-ός, f. θέμα Theme: see -ic.] Of or pertaining to a theme or themes.

1. Of or pertaining to a subject or topic of discourse or writing. *rare.*

1871 tr. *Lange's Comm. Jer.* 104 These introductory verses thus acquire a thematic character.

†**b.** *Logic.* Relating to or connected with the matter or subject of thought. *Obs.*

1697 tr. *Burgersdicius his Logic* i. i. 2 A System of Logical Precepts consists of two Parts, Thematick and Organic. ..The first is that which is imploy'd about Theams, and their various Affections, and second Notions, as about the Matter of the Instruments of Logick.

2. *Mus.* Of, pertaining to, or constituting themes or subjects (see Theme 4); relating to themes and their contrapuntal development. In *thematic catalogue, index, summary*, = containing the opening themes or passages of musical pieces.

1864 *Reader* 21 May 660 A handy thematic summary of the work is given in the 'Orchestra' for last week. 1878 C. F. Pohl in Grove *Dict. Mus.* I. 66/2 The thematic catalogue which Mozart himself had kept of his works. 1906 *Athenæum* 1 Sept. 250/2 The thematic material has been carefully chosen, and its treatment shows thought and skill.

3. *Gram.* Of or pertaining to the theme or stem-form of a word: see Theme 5.

Thematic vowel, a vowel which comes between the root and the inflexions in a verb or sb., as the *e* and *o* in φέρ-ο-μεν, φέρ-ε-τε, the *i, e*, and *a* in OE. *ber-i-þ, ber-e-þ, luf-a-ð*.

1861 Goldstücker *Pāṇini* 257 There must be reasons for this variety of thematic forms which constitute the declension of the same base. 1877 Papillon *Man. Comp. Philol.* viii. (ed. 2) 167 Curtius..explains the vowel in question as a 'thematic vowel', i.e. a suffix to or increase of the stem or 'theme' previous to the reception of the inflections. 1887 Cook *Sievers' O. E. Gram.* 143 The thematic *w* being sometimes retained and sometimes lost. 1888 Kennedy *Revised Lat. Primer* § 148 (1900) 94 Verbs..In which the Verb-Stem was formed by a so-called Thematic vowel added to the root.

B. as *sb.* That part of logic which deals with themes or subjects of thought. 1891 in *Cent. Dict.*

So **Thema·tical** *a.* = *thematic*; **Thema·tically** *adv.*, in a thematic manner; with respect to a theme or themes; †**The·matism** *Obs. nonce-wd.* [ad. Gr. θεματισμός a laying down], a placing, arrangement; **The·matist**, one who composes or writes themes (Ogilvie, 1882).

1890 *Athenæum* 3 May 579/1 The *thematical material in the four movements of the work is..interesting, and..the music is pleasantly unconventional. *Ibid.* 25 Jan. 125/2 Structurally as well as *thematically we note a welcome advance towards clearness. 1729 Shelvocke *Artillery* v. 334 The first then shall be the **Thematism* (from the Greek Word θεματισμός) which signifies the Decorum and Gracefulness of any Pile.

Theme (þīm), *sb.* Forms: α. 4–6 **teme**, (4–5 **teeme**, 5 **teem**, 5–6 **tyme**). β. 4– **theme**, (6–7 **theame**, 6–8 **theam**). [a. OF. **teme* (not in Godef.: but cf. *tesme*, with graphic *s* indicating vowel-length (13th c. in Godef. *Compl.*); also *teume, thieume*); in β conformed to L. *thema*, a. Gr. θέμα proposition, f. θε-, root of τιθέναι to put, set, place, lay down. In 16–17th c. commonly spelt *theam* (þēm). Cf. Antetheme.]

1. The subject of discourse, discussion, conversation, meditation, or composition; a topic.

α. a1300 *Cursor M.* 18495 (Cott.) Bot lenthius yald up his teme Bath to ioseph and to nichodeme. 13.. *E. E. Allit. P.* C. 358 Þe trwe tenor of his teme he tolde on þis wyse. c1380 Wyclif *Serm.* Sel. Wks. I. 306 Crist..toke þe same word for his teme þat Baptist toke whanne he prechide.

β. 13.. *E. E. Allit. P.* A. 943 Þe nwe [Iberusalem] þat lyȝt of godez sonde, Þe apostel in apocalyppce in theme con take. c1386 Chaucer *Pard. Prol.* 5 My theme [teeme, teme, teem, tyme] is alwey oon and euere was Radix malorum est Cupiditas. 1485 Caxton *Paris & V.* Prol., I vndertake this theme, because I haue all my life taken pleasure in the reading of Romances. 1570 Googe *Pop. Kingd.* iv. 44 b, Now to my theame again. a1600 [see These *sb.*]. 1649 Milton *Eikon.* ix, The overworn theme, and stuffing of all his discourses. 1708 *Brit. Apollo* No. 18. 3/2 And Love and Pleasure be my Endless Theam [*rime* name]. 1804 Wellington in Gurw. *Desp.* (1837) III. 81 His Highness's notorious treachery,..the theme of all the public dispatches. 1870 Bryant *Iliad* vi. I. 200 A theme of song for men in time to come.

†**b.** *transf.* A subject treated by action (instead of by discourse, etc.); hence, that which is the cause *of* or *for* specified action, circumstance, or feeling; matter, subject. *Obs.*

1588 Shaks. *Tit. A.* v. ii. 80 See heere he comes, and I must play my theame. 1602 — *Ham.* v. i. 289 *Ham.* Why I will fight with him vppon this Theme...*Qu.* Oh my sonne, what Theame? *Ham.* I lou'd Ophelia [etc.]. 1634 Sir T. Herbert *Trav.* 110 An infallible Theame of endlesse troubles. 1713 Swift *Cadenus & Vanessa* 298 In vain..You form'd this project in your brain.. Nor shall Vanessa be the theme To manage thy abortive scheme. 1806 H. Siddons *Maid, Wife, & Widow* I. 179 His son grew up to man's estate, and gave him farther theme for uneasiness.

†**c.** *Logic.* That which is the subject of thought.

1620 T. Granger *Div. Logike* 1 The externall is euery Theme, or matter propounded, whereof a man discourseth, or may discourse by his reason. 1697 tr. *Burgersdicius his Logic* i. ii. 2 A Theme is whatsoever may be propos'd to the Understanding to be known. Themes are either Simple or Composed. 1725 Watts *Logic* i. ii. § 1 Every object of our idea is called a theme, whether it be a being or not-being; for not-being may be proposed to our..thoughts, as well as that which has a real being.

†**2.** *spec.* The text of a sermon; also, a proposition to be discussed. *Obs.* (or merged in 1).

α. 1362 Langl. *P. Pl.* A. iii. 86 A Sarmoun he made,..And tolde hem þis teeme [*v.r.* teme]. *Ibid.* viii. 122 Thou mihtest preche whon þe luste, *Quoniam literaturam non cognoui* mihte be þy Teeme! c1440 *Promp. Parv.* 488/1 Teme, of a sermone, *thema*. 1513 More *Rich. III*, Wks. 60/2 He toke for his tyme *spuria vitulamina non agent radices altas*. That is to say bastard slippes shal neuer take depe roote. 1530 Palsgr. 281/1 Tyme of a sermonde, *thesme*.

β. 1387 Trevisa *Higden* (Rolls) VIII. 151 (MS. γ) He took a theme [L. *sumpto themate*] of holy writt, and gan to preche. 1432-50 tr. *Higden* ibid., This theme of scripture. c1530 L. Cox *Rhet.* (1899) 44 The theme of Tullyes oracyon or plee for Milo was thys, that he had slayne Clodius laufully. 1560 Daus *Sleidane's Comm.* 367 The deuines had Themes geuen them to discusse and reason vpon. c1566 *Merie Tales of Skelton* S.'s Wks. 1843 I. p. lxi, He dyd take that for hys antethem, the which of late dayes is named a theme, and sayde, *Qui se exaltat* [etc.]. 1594 T. B. *La Primaud. Fr. Acad.* ii. 590 In the ende all woulde be but vanitie, according to Salomons theame, which hee handleth in his booke of the Preacher. 1618 Hales *Rem.*, *Lett. fr. Synod of Dort* ii. 50 He took for his Theme the 122. Psalm.

3. An exercise written on a given subject, *esp.* a school essay; an exercise in translation. Now *rare*.

1545-7 in *Archæologia* XXXIV. 41 After none they [form III] have a theme to be made in Laten. 1581 Pettie *Guazzo's Civ. Conv.* ii. (1586) 59 Like a schoolemaister, which doth dictate or rehearse to his schollers some Theame or Epistle. 1644 Milton *Areop.* (Arb.) 56 The theam of a Grammar lad. 1739 Cibber *Apol.* (1756) I. 7, I remember I was once whipp'd for my theme. 1824 in Grant *Burgh Sch. Scotl.* (1876) ii. iv. 154 The Rector dictated an English theme to be translated into Latin. 1878 Bosw. Smith *Carthage* 263 In Juvenal's time Roman schoolboys declaimed upon it in their weekly themes.

4. *Mus.* The principal melody, plainsong, or *canto fermo* in a contrapuntal piece; hence, any one of the principal melodies or motives in a sonata, symphony, etc.; a subject; also, a simple tune on which variations are constructed.

[1597 Morley *Introd. Mus.* 86 Your plainsong is as it were your theme, and your descant as it were your declamation.] 1674 Playford *Skill Mus.* iii. 2 It was usual with them to have a Tenor as a Theam, to which they were compelled to adapt their other Parts. 1854 *Cherubini's Counterpoint* 63 The subject, or theme of the fugue, should neither be too long nor too short. 1866 Engel *Nat. Mus.* iii. 103 A manifold and clever treatment of the motives of which the theme consists, contributes especially to the oneness and clearness of a musical composition.

5. *Philol.* The inflexional base or stem of a word, consisting of the 'root' with modification or addition; thus in Gr. λείπειν and τέρπειν, the roots are λιπ, τερπ, the present themes or stems λειπ-, τερπ-; in τέκνον, the root is τεκ, the theme τεκνο-.

Formerly applied to the 1 pers. sing. pres. indic. of a verb; later identified with *root* (as in Greek); the modern application began with Curtius.

1530 Palsgr. Introd. 31 The fyrst [conjugation]..hath his thre chefe rotes..his theme, his preterit participle, and his present infynityve ever of many syllables. *Ibid.*, The thyrde [conjugation] hath his theme most commenly in *S*.. as *je voys..je preus..je dis*. 1580 Hollyband *Treas. Fr. Tong*, I call the Theame, speaking to the vnskilfull in the Latine tong, whereby we begin to decline a Verbe. 1615 Bedwell *Index Assurat.* O iij, The theame or roote, as they call it, from whence it [*Koran*] is deriued, is..*Karn'*, to reade. 1741 Watts *Improv. Mind* i. vii. § 6 In reducing the words to their original or theme. 1870 F. A. March *Compar. Gram. Ags.* § 60 The variable final letters of a noun are its case-endings, the rest is its theme. 1875 Whitney *Life Lang.* x. 207 In the derivative theme or base.

6. *Astrol.* The disposition of the heavenly bodies at a particular time, as at the moment of a person's birth. Cf. Horoscope *sb.* 1.

1652 Gaule *Magastrom.* 293 Augustus had..such a confidence in this fatidical præsagition, that he divulged his natalitial theme. 1727-41 Chambers *Cycl.*, *Theme*, among astrologers, denotes the figure they construct when they draw the horoscope; representing the state of the heavens for a certain point, or moment required; *i.e.* the places of the stars, and planets, for that moment. 1775 Ash *Dict.*, *Theme*,..a horoscope in astrology. [1819 Wilson *Dict. Astrol.*, *Thema cœli*, a figure of the heavens.]

7. *Anc. Hist.* Each of the twenty-nine provinces into which the Byzantine empire was divided.

1788 Gibbon *Decl. & F.* xlviii. V. 13 The Anatolian *theme* or province. *Ibid.* liii. 464 An accurate survey of the provinces, the *themes*, as they were then denominated, both of Europe and Asia. 1864 Bryce *Holy Rom. Emp.* ix. (1889) 135 Nicephorus demanded the 'theme' or province of Rome as the price of compliance.

8. *attrib.* and *Comb.*, as *theme-maker*.

a1661 Holyday *Juvenal* To Rdr., Surely thou wilt acknowledge Juvenal to be a poet, but Horace to be some poor theme-maker.

Hence **Theme** *v. trans.*, to furnish with a theme or subject; **The·meless** *a.*, without a theme, having no theme; **The·mer**, one who sets or proposes a theme; **Themester** (þī·mstəɹ), one who labours at a theme (*contemptuous*).

1594 R. Southwell *St. Peters Compl.*, etc. To Rdr., This *theames my heavie penne to plaine in prose. 1641 J. Jackson *True Evang. T.* i. 10 [Points] capable to be spread out so as to theame the Preachers speech. 1840 Galt *Demon of Destiny* vi. 41 The *themeless babble of his idiot child. 1611 Tarlton *Jests* (1844) 28 Such commendations Tarlton got, that hee supt with the bailiffe that night, where my *theamer durst not come, although he were sent for. 1843 *Blackw. Mag.* LIV. 105 Where now, base *themester?

Theme, obs. f. Team (sense 8); also of Them.

Themel, -elle, obs. forms of Thimble.

‖**Themis** (þe·mis, þī·mis). [a. Gr. Θέμις, goddess of law and order, Justice personified.]

1. Name of the ancient Greek goddess of law and justice; hence, Law or Justice personified.

1656 Blount *Glossogr.*, *Themis*, the Godesse of Justice, that gave out Oracles at Bœotia. 1784 Cowper *Task* iii. 257 Such thine, in whom Our British Themis gloried with just cause, Immortal Hale. 1880 J. Payn *Confid. Agent* iv, She found a rival, not in Themis, but in Isabel Thurlow.

2. *Astron.* Name of the twenty-fourth of the Asteroids, discovered 5 April 1853 by De Gasparis.

Themistian (þǐmi·stiăn). *Ch. Hist.* [f. *Themisti-us*, name of the founder of the sect (see quot. 1882–3) + -an.] In plural: A sect of the Monophysites who attributed to Christ imperfect knowledge. Cf. Agnoites.

1874 in Blunt *Dict. Sects, Heresies, &c.* 1882-3 *Schaff's Encycl. Relig. Knowl.* I. 36 The second sect (founded in the sixth century by Themistius, deacon of Alexandria), sometimes called the Themistians. 1883 *Cath. Dict.* (1885) 598/1 The Themistians, or Agnoetæ, held that the human element in Christ before his resurrection was subject to ignorance.

Themselves (ðěmse·lvz), *pron. pl.* Forms: see Them and Self. [The original construction was nom., acc. *hí, héo selfe*, dat. *heom selfum*, whence ME. *hemselve(n*, etc. In 14th c. this was superseded in north. dial. by *þaim self(e, þaim selven*, and in Standard Eng. *themself* was the normal form to c1540, but disappeared c1570. *Themselfs, themselves* appears c1500, and became the standard form c1540. For *theirself, theirselves*, see III.]

I. Emphatic. = Those very persons or things.

1. Standing in apposition with the pronoun *they* (rarely *them*), or with a sb., or adj. used subst.

α. 13.. *Cursor M.* 3708 (Cott.) All þaa þat blisses þe Sal þam-self blessed be. *Ibid.* 8131 (Gött.) Þaim-selue again þai tok þair sty [*Cott.* þamself a-gain tok þai stil, And went þaim þan to ethiopy. c1460 *Towneley Myst.* xxx. 566 Thare neghburs thai demyd Thaym self as it semyd. 1533 More *Apol.* 7 b, They se full well them selfe, that they saye not trew.

γ. 1502 in *Lett. Rich. III & Hen. VII* (Rolls) II. 107 Thei them selves coulde not acertayne us of the tyme. 1555 Eden *Decades* To Rdr. (Arb.) 53 More monstrous then the monsters theim selues. 1561 T. Hoby tr. *Castiglione's Courtyer* ii. (1577) I vij b, Oftentimes to them themselues, they thrust out filthy and most dishonest wordes. 1651 Howell *Venice* 143 Approv'd of by the Popes Breve's themselfs. 1779 *Mirror* No. 54 ℙ 7 You tell us the effects of your feelings, child; but you don't distinguish the feelings themselves. 1810 Crabbe *Borough* ii. 110 Monuments themselves memorials need. 1872 Hardy *Under Greenw. Tree* Pref., Music-paper (which they mostly ruled themselves). 1876 Gladstone *Glean.* (1879) II. 205 Themselves knowing nothing of difficulty, or of obscurity,..they are liable to be intolerant of other men who stumble.

2. Used alone for emphasis as a simple nominative. *arch.*

α. 1512 *Helyas* in Thoms *Prose Rom.* (1828) III. 30 Thiniuries that them self had made. 1549 Coverdale, etc. *Erasm. Par. Rom.* 38 Vnlearned people.., whiche thinke nothing rightful, but that them selfe do.

β. 13.. *Cursor M.* 23517 (Edin.) God..louis þaim als his auen sonis, Mar þan þaim-selwin lof þair dribt [*Cott.* Mare þan þam-seluen luue þai dright].

γ. 1542 Udall *Erasm. Apoph.* 105 Theimselfes by great pielage..dooe growe dayly & encrease in welthe. 1624 Bedell *Lett.* x. 135 Themselues doe vtterly denie it. 1701 Swift *Contests Nobles & Com.* Wks. 1755 II. i. 51 To remember how themselves sate in fear of their persons. 1853 Lynch *Self-Improv.* ii. 44 People's timorousness.. shows how insecurely grounded themselves are.

b. *To be themselves*: to be in their normal condition of mind, body, or behaviour: see Self D. 1.

1698 Lister in *Phil. Trans.* XX. 247 They came so out of their Fits, that they were also well and as much themselves as ever. 1698 Fryer *Acc. E. India & P.* 379 Yet

II. Reflexive: = L. *sibi*, *se*; F. *se*, *soi*; G. *sich*.

3. Adirect refl. (accusative), indirect obj. (dative), or object of a preposition.

III. From the 14th c. there has been a tendency to treat *self* as a sb. (= person, personality), and substitute *their* for *them* (cf. *his self*), HIMSELF IV.)

Themyl , -ylle, obs. (ME.) f. THIMBLE.

Then (ðen), *adv.* (*conj.*, *adj.*, *sb.*) Forms: see below.

B. Signification.

A. Demonstrative adverb of time.

I. At that time. (Referring to a specified time, past or future: opposed to Now 1.)

2. At the time indicated by a relative or other clause (with verb in pres. tense). (Cf. Now 4.)

3. At the moment immediately following the action, etc. just spoken of; upon that, thereupon, directly after that; also in wider application, indicating the action or occurrence next in order of time; next, after that, afterwards, subsequently (often in contrast to *first*).

4. In that case (a series of circumstances); if that be (or were) the fact; if so; when that happens. Often correl. to *if* or *when*. *What then?* (ellipt.), what happens (or would happen) in that case? what of that?

5. (As a particle of inference, often emphasized or enclitic.) That being the case; since that is so; on that account; therefore, consequently, as may be inferred; so. *Now then:* see Now 6.

6. *As relative or conjunction adv. of time.*

7. Preceded by a preposition, as *by*, *since*, *till*, etc. (*by*, etc. that time). (Cf. Now 1.2.)

8. That time; the time referred to (esp. a past time; often contrasted with *now*. Cf. Now 14, 15.

Then-a-days (ðe'nǎdēz), *adv.* rare. [THEN + A-DAYS] In those days, at that time (past) time.

Then after, then-a'fter, adv. Obs. After that, after that time; = THEREAFTER.

So † Then afterward (+ adv. phr. in same sense.)

By then that, by the time; ellipt. *by then* (as relative), by the time: see BY A. 21 c. Now *arch.* or *dial.*

Thenal (ðī'nal), *a. Anat.* [THEN-AR + -AL] Of, pertaining or relating to the thenar.

Thenar (ðī'när). *Anat.* Also † tenar, theoor. [mod.L., a. Gr. θέναρ palm of the hand, sole or flat of the foot. Cf. OHG. *tenar*, MHG. *tener*; F. *thénar* (16th c.).] The ball of muscle at the base of the thumb; the palm of the hand; the sole of the foot.

Thence (ðens), *adv.* Forms: see below.

Thenceforth (ðe'nsfōrþ', ðens-), *adv.* [f. orig. two words: thence and forth adv.]

Thenceforward (ðensfō'rwărd), *adv.* [f. THENCE and FORWARD adv.]

Thenceforwards, adv. Obs. [f. prec. + -ward.]

Thence-from, adv. arc. [An inversion of *from thence*; cf. *hence-from*.] From that place or source; thence.

Thence-out, adv. arc. [f. THENCE + OUT adv.] Out of that place; out from there.

The norward, adv. Obs. [f. THENCE + -WARD] From that direction; thence.

Thenne, penne, obs. forms of THAN, THEN, THENCE.

Thenward, adv.: see under THENNE adv.

Theo-, comb. form of Gr. θεός god.

Theobroma (þiobrō'ma). *Bot.* [mod.L., f. THEO- + Gr. βρῶμα food.]

Theocracy (þiŏ'krăsi). Also † theocraty. [ad. Gr. θεοκρατία, f. θεός god + -κρατία rule.] A form of government in which God (or a deity) is recognized as the king or immediate ruler.

Theo-democracy: see THEO-.

Theocrasy (þiŏ'krăsi). Also † theocrasie, *-cracie*, *-crasy*. [ad. Gr. θεοκρασία, f. θεός god + κρᾶσις a mixing.] A mingling of various deities or divine attributes into one personality; also, a mixture of the worship of different deities.

Theocrat (þī'okræt). [next: see -CRAT. Cf. mod.F. *théocrate* (Littré).]

Theocratic (þiokræ'tik), *a.* [f. Gr. θεοκρατία + -IC: see -CRATIC.]

Theocratical (þiokræ'tikăl), *a.* [f. as prec. + -AL.]

Theocratically, adv. [f. prec. + -LY.]

Theodicy (þiŏ'disi). [ad. F. *théodicée* (Leibniz 1710).]

Theodolite (þiŏ'dŏlait). Forms: 6-7 theodelitus, 7 theodolit, -dolite, -delite. [Origin unknown: see Note below.] A portable surveying instrument.

Theodolitic (þiodŏli'tik), *a.* [f. prec. + -IC.] Pertaining to a theodolite.

Theodom, † -dome, sb. Obs. [OE. *þéodóm* servitude, f. þéow servant + -dóm.]

Theodosian (þiodō'ziăn, -dō'siăn), *a. and sb.*

Theogonal (þī'ŏgŏnăl), *a.* [irreg. f. THEOGONY + -AL.]

Theogonic (þiogŏ'nik), *a.* [f. Gr. θεογονικός, f. θεογονία: see next and -IC.]

Theogonist (þiŏ'gŏnist). [f. THEOGONY + -IST.]

Theogony (þiŏ'gŏni). Also 8-9 *errom. -gony*.

Theolatry (þĭ·lătri), *sb*. [f. Gr. θεο- god + -λατρεία a begetting.] So F. *théogonie*.] The generation of the gods; *esp*. an account or theory, or the belief or study, of the genealogy or birth of the deities of heathen mythology.

Theohuman, **theohumanity**. see THEO-.

Theolatry (þĭ·lătri), *sb*. [f. Gr. θεό god + λατρεία worship.] The worship of a deity or deities; *see* -LATRY. The worship of a deity or deities.

Theolepsy (þĭ·lepsi), *rare*. [f. Gr. θεόληπτος.] Seizure or possession by a deity, inspiration. So **Theoleptic** [Gr. θεοληπτικ-ό–] *adj.*, one possessed or inspired by a deity.

Theolog, obs. form of THEOLOGUE.

Theologal (þĭ·lŏgăl), *a.* and *sb*. [f. *theological* adj. and sb. (14th c. in Hatz.-Darm.), f. Gr. L. *theologal*= theologian: see -AL.]
† **A.** *adj*. in *theologal virtues* [OF. *vertus théologales* (14th c.): see THEOLOGICAL A. 2. *Obs*.

Theologaster (þĭˈlŏgæstər). [a. med. L. *theologaster* (Luther 1518), f. *theolog*= theologian: see -ASTER.] A shallow or paltry theologian; a smatterer or pretender in theology.

Theologate. [ad. med. L. *theologātus*.] A theological college or seminary.

Theologer (þĭˈlŏdʒər). [f. *stem* of Gr.–L. *theolog*-us or Eng. *theolog-y* + -ER: see -LOGER.] One who studies or busies himself with theology; = THEOLOGIAN (but now with less implication of scholarship). In reference to Christianity or other monotheistic religion.

Theologian (þĭˈlŏdʒiăn). Also *5–6 -yen*. [f. *theologie* (see THEOLOGY) + -AN.] One who is versed in theology; a student of theology.

Theologic (þĭˈlŏdʒik), *a.* and *sb*. [ad. F. *théologique* or ad. L. *theologicus*: see -IC.]

Theologician (þĭˌlŏdʒiˈʃən). Now *rare*. Also **-ician**. = THEOLOGIAN.

Theological (þĭˈlŏdʒikăl), *a.* (*sb*.) [ad. med. L. *theologicālis* (Duns Scotus *a* 1308), f. L. *theologicus* (see prec.) + -AL.]

Theologien, obs. form of THEOLOGIAN.

Theologist (þĭˈlŏdʒist). [f. *theolog-y* + -IST.] = THEOLOGIAN.

Theologium (þĭˈlŏdʒiəm). Gr. Antiq. Also **-eion**. [Gr. θεολογεῖον speaking-place.] In the ancient theatre, a small balcony above the stage, from which those impersonating the gods sang their parts.

Theologization, *rare*. Also *6 -acioun*. [f. next, perh. through a med. L. *theologizātio*: see -ATION.] The action of theologizing.

Theologize (þĭˈlŏdʒəiz), *v*. [In sense 1, ad. med. L. *theologizāre* (Albertus Magnus *c* 1250); in Aquinas, Duns Scotus, Wyclif, etc.), f. *theologia* theology: see -IZE. So F. *théologiser* (Godef. Compl.).]

Theologo- (þĭˈlŏgo-), combining form from Gr. θεολογο- = THEOLOGICAL; **-,;** as in *theologico-astronomical*, *-ethical*, *-historical*, *-metaphysical*, *-military*, *-moral*, *-mystical*, *-political* adjs.; also with *sbs*., as in *theologico-politician*.

Theologian (þĭˈlŏdʒiăn). [f. THEOLOGIST or THEOLOGER: see -ISM; cf. F. *théologisme* (1752).] The action or product of theologizing; a theological notion or system; usually in a derogatory sense.

† **Theologoumenon** (þĭˌlŏgəˈmɛnɒn), *sb*. *pl.* **-mena**. [Gr. θεολογούμενον, neut. of pr. pple. pass. of θεολογέω to theologize, f. θεολόγος theologian.] A theological statement or utterance on theology: distinguished from an inspired doctrine or revelation.

Theologue (þĭˈlŏg). Also *5–6 theolog*, *6–9 theolog*. [ad. L. *theolog-us*, a. Gr. θεολόγος one who treats, or gives an account, of the gods: e.g. Hesiod, Orpheus), or of God's words.]

Theology (þĭˈŏlŏdʒi). Forms: see below. [In earliest use, ad. OF. *theologie*, a. L. *theologia*, a. Gr. θεολογία (14th c. in Aristotle), f. θεολόγος: see THEOLOGUE.] 1. The study or science which treats of God, His nature and attributes, and His relations with man and the universe; 'the science of things divine' (Hooker); divinity.

Theomachist (þĭˈɒmăkist), one who fights against the gods, or against God.

Theomachy (þĭˈɒmăki). [Gr. θεομαχία.] A striving or warring against God, opposition to the will of God. **b.** *spec*. See prec.

Theomancy (þĭˈəmænsi). [Gr. θεομαντεία spirit of prophecy, f. θεός god + μαντεία divination: see -MANCY.] A kind of divination: see quots.

Theomania (þĭˌəˈmeiniə). Gr. θεομανία. A form of insanity in which the patient believes himself God or inspired by God.

Theomorphic (þĭˌəˈmɔːfik), *a.* [f. Gr. θεός god + μορφή form + -IC.] Having the form or likeness of God; of or pertaining to theomorphism.

Theomorphism (þĭˌəˈmɔːfiz'm). [f. as prec. + -ISM.] The doctrine that man has the form or likeness of God; **Theomorphise** *v*., to form in the image of God.

Theomythology (þĭˌəmiˈθɒlədʒi). [f. THEO- + MYTHOLOGY. Cf. Gr. θεομυθολογία divine lore, mythology.] A combination of theology and mythology. Hence **Theo-mythologer**.

Theonomy (þĭˈɒnəmi). [f. Gr. θεός God + -νομία, -NOMY, after Ger. *theonomie* (1838 in Heyse).] Administration or government by God; the condition of being ruled or governed by God.

Theopantism, **-pantism**: see THEO-.

Theopaschite (þĭˌəˈpæskəit). *Ch. Hist.* Also *6 -paschit*, *7 -pasit*. [ad. eccl. L. *theopaschīta*, ad. Gr. θεοπασχίτης, f. θεός God + πάσχειν to suffer: see -ITE.] A member of a Monophysite sect of the 6th c., who held that the divine nature of Christ suffered on the Cross.

Theopathy (þĭˈɒpəθi). [f. THEO- + -PATHY, after *pathetic* etc.] Of, pertaining to, or characterized by theopathy; see quot.

Theophagy (þĭˈɒfədʒi), *n*. [f. THEO- + -PHAGY.] God-eating. So **Theo-phagy** (-dʒi), the eating of God (in the mass or communion rite).

Theophany (þĭˈɒfəni). [a. L. *theophania* (400 in Rufinus), a. Gr. θεοφάνεια and θεοφάνια (neut. pl.), f. θεός God + φαίνειν to show: see -PHANY. Cf. TIFFANY.] A manifestation or appearance of God to a god to man.

Theophilanthropist (þĭˌəˌfilænˈθrɒpist). [f. THEO- + PHILANTHROPIST, after F. *théophilanthrope*.]

Theophyllic: see THEO-.

Theor, obs. form of THEORY.

Theorbo (þĭˈɔːbo). Also *7 theorboes*, *7–8 theorbos*. [ad. F. *téorbe*, *tiorbe*, *theorbe* (17th c.), ad. It. *tiorba*.] A large kind of lute with a double neck and two sets of tuning-pegs, the lower holding the melody strings and the upper the bass strings; much in vogue in the 17th century.

Theorboed (-bōd) *ppl. a.*, converted into a theorbo; played on the theorbo.

Theorem (þĭˈərɛm), *sb*. Also *6–7 -eme*. [ad. late L. *theorēma* (Gellius), a. Gr. θεώρημα, *-ματ-*, spectacle, speculation, theory, (in Euclid) a proposition to be proved, f. θεωρεῖν to be a spectator (θεωρός), to look at, inspect. Cf. THEORY.] A universal or general proposition or statement, not self-evident (thus distinguished from an AXIOM), but demonstrable by argument (in the strict sense, by deductive reasoning); a demonstrable theoretical judgement. **b.** *Math.*

Theorematic (þĭˌərɛˈmætik), *a.* [ad. Gr. θεωρηματικός, f. θεώρημα, *-ματ-* THEOREM, after -IC. Cf. *problematic*.] Pertaining to, by means of, or of the nature of a theorem. Also = prec. **Theorema·tical** *a.*, = prec. Hence **Theorema·tically** *adv.*

Theorematist = *theorematist*.

The·orematize, = *theorematize*.

Theoretic (þĭˌəˈrɛtik), *a.* and *sb*. [ad. late L. *theōrēticus*, a. Gr. θεωρητικός, f. θεωρητός that may be seen, f. θεωρεῖν to look at, contemplate, inspect.] **A.** *adj*.

Theoretical (þĭˌəˈrɛtikăl), *a.* (*sb*.) [f. prec. + -AL: see -ICAL.]

Theoretician (þĭˌərɛˈtɪʃ'n). rare. [f. Gr. θεωρητικός + -IAN: see -ICIAN.] One who treats of or deals with the theoretical side of a subject; = THEORIST 2.

Theorist (þĭˈərist), *sb*. [f. THEORY + -IST.] **1.** One who theorizes or forms theories; a speculator.

Theoric (þĭˈɒrik), *sb*. and *a.* *Obs*. or *arch*. Also *4–5 -ik*, *6–7 -ike*, *4–9 -ique*, *5–6 -yk(e*, *-icque*, *-ique*, *6–8 -ick*. [ME. *theorique* in Gower, ad. F. *théorique* (13th c. in Oresme); or med.L. *theorica* (Boeth.), a. Gr. θεωρική.] **A.** *sb*. **1.** Theory.

Theoric.

Theorical, *a.* *Obs.*

Theorist (þī·ŏrist).

Theorism

Theorize (þī·ŏrəiz), *v.*

Theory (þī·ŏri), *sb.*

Theorization

Theosoph

Theosophical

Theosophically, *adv.*

Theosophism

Theosophist

Theosopher

Theosopheme

Theosophy (þĭ·ŏsŏfi), *sb.*

Theosophistical, *a.*

Theosophic

Theosophy (*continued*)

Theotechnal

Theotechny

Theosophize

Theotheca

Theotheology

Theotokos, **Theotokion**

Theow, *sb.* A slave, bondman.

Theow, thew, *v.*

Theowdom, thewdom.

Theow-like, thew-like, *a.*

Theow-man, *sb.*

Therapeutae

Therapeutic (þerăpiū·tik), *sb.*

Therapeutical

Therapeutist

Therapeusis

Therapeutic, *a.*

Theraph, Teraph

Theraphose

Therapeuta

Therapeutic

Therapist

Therapon

Therapy (þe·răpi), *sb.*

There (ðēɐ), *adv.*

Thereology

So **Thereologist**, one skilled in thereology.

Thereon

Thereout

Thereover

Thereright

Thereto

Thereunder

Thereunto

Thereupon

Thereuntofore, adv. Forms:

Thereof

Thereupon

Thereout

Thereto, adv.

Thereunto

Thereup

Therewith

Therewithal

Therewhile

Therewithin

Theridion

Therf, **Therf-cake**

Theriac

Theriacal

Theriacle

Theriaca

Theriodont

Theriomorphic

Thermal

Thermality

Thermo-

Thermantidote

Thermometer

Thermomorphic

Therm

Thermidor

Thermaesthesia

Thermal

Thermality

Supplement, p. 3873; Corrigenda, p. 4092; Spurious words, p. 4093; Books quoted, p. 4094

Thermo-aesthesia to **-chaotic**: see THERMO-.

Thermochemistry.

Thermochemic *adj.*, of or pertaining to thermochemistry; **Thermochemically** *adv.*, by means of or with reference to thermochemistry; **Thermochemist**, one who is skilled in thermochemistry.

Thermochrosy

Also **thermochrose**

Thermochrose (Melloni).

Thermochroic

Thermochrology, the science of thermochrosy.

Thermocline (-current): see THERMO-.

Thermod

Thermolin

Thermodyne (see DYNAMIC), *a.*

Thermodynamic (see DYNAMIC) *a.*

So **Thermodynamical** *adv.*, in same sense; **Thermodynamian**, **Thermodynamist**, one versed in thermodynamics.

Thermodynamics, *sb.*

Thermogeography

Thermo-geographical, *a.*

Thermo-electric, *a.* (*sb.*).

Thermo-electrical *adv.*, in a thermo-electric manner

Thermo-electrometer

Thermo-electricity.

Thermocline

Thermo-electronic

Thermo-electrometer to **-gauge**: see THERMO-.

Thermogen.

So **Thermogenic**

Thermogenesis.

Thermogenetic; **Thermogenous**; **Thermogeny**, thermogenesis.

Thermogram.

Thermograph.

Thermographic (-græfik, *a.*

Thermography

So **Thermographical**

Thermo-hydrology to **-kinematics**: see THERMO-.

Thermolabile

So **Thermolability**, thermolabile quality.

Thermology

Hence **Thermological** *a.*, of or pertaining to thermology.

Thermolysis

Thermo-luminescence, etc.: see THERMO-.

Thermolytic

Thermo-magnetic to **-metamorphism**: see THERMO-.

Thermometer

Hence **Thermometer-trivially** *adv.*, pertaining to or by means of the thermometer or its indications.

Thermometric

Thermometrical

Thermometrically *adv.*, by means of or with involving the use of the thermometer.

Thermometrograph + **GRAPH**.

Thermometry

Thermo-motor

Thermo-multiplier

So **Thermo-multiple** in same sense.

Thermonatrite

Thermo-neutrality, etc.: see THERMO-.

Thermophil + **-PHIL**.

Thermophil-phile (θə̄mŏfil), *a.* and *sb.*

Thermophilic

So **Thermophilous**

Thermophins

Thermone

So **Thermopile** in same sense.

Thermophone

Thermopolion, -ium

Thermo-siphon.

Thermopot, -pote. *Obs. rare*

Thermo-radiometer -regulator: see THERMO-.

Thermos

Thermoscope

Thermostat.

Thermostatic

Thermostatics

So **Thermostatical**

Thermomotic, *a.*

Thermometry

Thermotaxis.

Thermotactic, *a.*

Thermotelephone, etc.: see THERMO-.

Thermotic

So **Thermotical** *a.*, in same sense; **Thermotics** *sb. pl.*, the science of heat.

Thermotropism.

Thermotropic

Thermotype

Thermotypic *a.*, of or pertaining to thermotypes or thermotypy.

Thermotypy, the process or art of making thermotypes.

Theropodous

Thero-, repr. Gr. θηρο-, combining form of θήρ wild beast.

Hence **Theroid** (**Therioid**), *a.*

Therapside

Theriodont

Theromorph

Theromorpha, *sb. pl.*

Theromorphic *a.*

Theromorphous *a.*

Theropsida

Therst(e, obs. f. THIRST.

Therve-cake, var. THARF-CAKE.

Therwe, perwe, obs. form of THROUGH.

Thes, *adv.* (*conj.*). *Obs.* Forms: 1-3 þus,

Theroid

Theology

Hence **Theologic**, **Theologize** *adj.*; **Theologous** *a.*, of or pertaining to theology; a mammalogist.

Theorova

Theology

Thero-

Theromorpha

Theromora

Theromorph

Therst

Thesaurus

Thesaurarial

Thesaurize

Thesaury

The-saury, -aure. *Obs.*

Thesaurus (þĭsōᵊrəs). Pl. **-ri** (-rəi),

These, *sb.*

2. 'treasury' or 'storehouse' of knowledge, as a dictionary, encyclopædia, or the like.

These, *demonstr. pron. and adj.* (*plural*).

Thesaurarial

Thesaurary

Thesaurize

The-saurer, -aurie. *Obs.*

These, *sb.* [a. F. *thèse* (1579 in Godef. Compl.), or ad. med. L. *thesis*.]

These

Thesaurize

THESE

THESIS.

THESMOPHILIST.

THETICAL.

THETICALLY.

296

THEW.

297

THICK.

THICK AND THIN.

Thick and thin, thick-and-thin, *phr.*

Thicken (þik'n), *v.* [f. THICK *a.* + -EN.] To make or become thick or thicker.

Thickener (þik'nə).

Thickening (þik'niŋ), *vbl. sb.*

Thickening, *ppl. a.*

Thicker, *Thick-and-thick Block.*

Thickfold, *a. (adv.).*

Thickly (þik'li), *adv.*

Thick-head. One who or that which has a thick head.

Thick-headed, *a.*

Thickne, variant of THICK-KNEE.

Thickness (þik'nes), *sb.*

Thickening.

Thick-knee (þik'nī).

Thick-leaved (-līvd), **-leafed** (-līft).

Thick-lipped, *a.*

Thick-set, *a.*

Thick-skin.

Thick-skinned, *a.*

Thick-skinned wheat.

Thick-skull. Having a thick skull; hence *fig.* slow or dull of apprehension; dense, dull-witted ; — THICK-SKULLED.

So **Thick-skull**, a thick-skulled person.

Thick-sown, adj. Also **8 thick-sowed.** Sown thickly or with little interval between the seeds.

So **Thick-sow** *v.* (*rare*), to sow thickly.

Thick-witted (stres var.), a. Having 'thick' wits; dull of intellect, stupid.

Thicky, *adv.* dial. in THICK a.

Thief (þîf). *Pl.* **Thieves** (þîvz). Forms: 1 þeóf, þiof, þeof, (þeaf, þeof,) 2 þef *(dat.* þeove), 2-5 þeof; 3 *dat.* þeve, 3-4 þef, 3-6 þeof, þeif, 4 þeef, þief, þyef, þyf, þ-6 thefe, 5-6 thief.

1. One who takes portable property from another without the knowledge or consent of the latter, converting it to his own use; one who steals.

a. *spec.* One who does this by stealth, esp. from the person; one who commits theft or larceny.

So **Thi'ckway**, *adv.* Obs. *rare.* [f. THICK a. + WAY.] In the direction of the thickness.

Thidder, -ir, etc., obs. ff. THITHER.

Thie, obs. form of THIGH.

Thiefdom, thievedom (þîfdəm, þîvdəm).
1. The practice of theft; thieving, robbery, *rare.*
2. The realm or domain of thieves.

Thief-like (þîflaik), a. and adv.
A. *adj.* Resembling a thief; thievish, furtively.
B. *adv.* In a thievish or thief-like manner; by stealth; stealthily, furtively.

†This-ly, *a.* and *adv.* Obs.

Thievery (þîvri), *vbl. sb.* [app. f. THIEVE + -Y.] = THIEVERY.

Thieve (þîv), *v.* Forms: 6- thieve. [OE. þéofian (= þéofan), f. þéof THIEF.]

1. *intr.* To act as a thief; commit theft, steal.

2. *trans.* To steal (a thing).

†3. *Comb.* To practise theft on, rob.

Thieve-friend. *nonce-wd.* A friend of thieves.

Thievery (þîvəri), *sb.* Of uncertain origin; first in Ramsay.

Thieveless (þîvlis), *a.* Sc. Of uncertain origin; first in Ramsay.

Thieving (þîviŋ), *vbl. sb.* [app. f. THIEVE + -ING1.] The act or practice of thieving.

So **Thief-taking** (in quot. *attrib.*).

Thievish (þîviʃ), *a.* Forms: 4-5 thef-, 6 theuish, 6-8 theeu-, 6 theev-, 6-8 theev-, 6-8 thievish. [f. THIEF, thiev- (see note in etym. s.v. + -ISH1.]

1. Infested or frequented by thieves. *Obs.*

2. Inclined or given to thieving; dishonest.

3. Of, pertaining to, or characteristic of a thief or thieves; thief-like; furtive, stealthy.

Hence **Thievishly** *adv.*, **Thievishness.**

Thigger (þigər). Sc. [f. THIG *v.* + -ER1.] One who thigs; a beggar, a mendicant.

Thigging (þigiŋ), *vbl. sb.* [f. THIG *v.* + -ING1.]

Thigh (þai), *sb.* Forms: see below. [OE. þéoh, þioh, þeoh, Anglian þéh = OFris. thiach, neuter, OLG. -thiok, ÔG. *thio (MHG. *dieh*, *diech*, Du. *dij*), ON. *þjó* OHG. *dioh* (MHG. *diech*), -OTeut. *þeuh-*, from Indo-Eur. ablaut-series *teuk-, tauk-, tuk-.]

1. The upper part of the leg, from the hip to the knee (in man).

Thigh-bone. Also **5** *north.* **tho-bane.** The bone of the thigh; the femur; in quot. 1825 an emblem of death : cf. dead.

Thighed (þaid), a. Also 7 thyght. [f. THIGH *sb.* + -ED2.] Having thighs (of a specified kind); often in parasynthetic combinations.

Thight (þait), *a.* Now *dial.* Forms: 4 thyght (Sc.), 5 thygh, thyh, 6 thicht (Sc.), 7 (9 *dial.*) thite, thyte, 7-8 (9 *dial.*) tight, theet, theet. [Found c 1375; the earlier form of the word TIGHT. App. a. ON. *þéttr*, in later ON. *þéttr* tight, water-tight, close in texture, solid (Norw. *tjett*, *tett*, Sw. *tät*, Da. *tæt* tight, compact, close).]

Thilk (þilk), *dem. adj.* and *pron.* Obs. exc. *dial.* Forms: 3-4 þilke, þulke, 4-6 thilke; 4-7 thulke, thylk, thilc; 5 thelk, thilck, 6 thick (9 *dial.*). [orig. a combination of the def. article + ILK (OE. *ylc*, *ilc*), variously reduced.]

Thill (þil), *sb.* [A local term of unknown origin.]

Thill [2] (þil), *sb.* [f. next.] The stratum of fire-clay etc. usually underlying a coal-seam; underclay; the floor or bottom of a seam of coal.

Thiller (þilər), *sb.* Also 5 *dial.* tiller: see also **thill-horse.** [f. THILL [1] + -ER [1].]

Thill-horse (þilhors), *sb.* [f. THILL [1] + HORSE *sb.*] A thill-horse; a shaft-horse or wheeler in a team.

Thilly, *a.* [f. THILL [1] .] Of the nature of thill.

Thimble (þimb'l), *sb.* Forms: 1- þýmel, 5-6 thymelle, -yl (9 *dial.*), thymble, -omb-, -ylle, -yl (9 *dial.*), 5 thombil, thomble, 5- thimble, 6-7 thymbell, thimbell, 6- thimble. [OE. þýmel, f. þúma THUMB *sb.* + -LE, suffix forming names of instruments; cf. *handle*.]

THIMBLE.

plate; thimble-rubber: see quots.; thimble-shift, shifting, the shifting of the pea from one thimble to another by a thimblerigger; also *fig.*; thimble-skein, a skein or axle made in tubular form; thimble-surface, *Ceramics*, a surface of raised dots produced by closely pitting the interior of the mould; thimble-wood: see quot.

Thimbled (ϸimbᵘld), *a.* [f. THIMBLE + -ED².] Having, or furnished with, a thimble; in *thieves' slang*, wearing a watch.

Thimble-eye (ϸimbᵘlˌəi), *sb.* [f. THIMBLE + EYE.] ... *Naut.* See quots. 1867, 1875. b. A fish, the Chub Mackerel, *Scomber colias.* So **Thimble-eyed** *a.*, having eyes like thimbles, as this fish.

Thimbleful (ϸimbᵘlˌful). [f. THIMBLE + -FUL.] As much as a thimble will hold; hence, a small quantity, esp. of wine or spirits; a dram; also *fig.* of something immaterial.

Thimblerig (ϸimbᵘlˌrig), *sb.* [f. THIMBLE + RIG *sb.*] A swindling game usually played with three thimbles (see THIMBLE 3 c) and a pea which is ostensibly placed under one of them...

Thimblerigger, one who practises the trick of the thimblerig; also *transf.* a cheat in a juggling manner or as with sleight of hand. b. *trans.* To manipulate (a matter or thing) in this manner.

So **Thimblerig'ged** (rigd) *ppl. a.*, duped by the game of thimblerig; disturbed or affected by thimblerigging, as a market; — RIGGED *ppl. a.* (b).

Thimblerigging *vbl. sb.* and *ppl. a.*

Thimblerigger'ie (ϸimb'lˌrigan²), [f. THIMBLERIG *sb.* + -ERY.] A professional sharper who cheats by thimblerigging; also *transf.* one who cheats by means of tricks, or juggles with phrases, etc.

Thimbleric ...

Thimbling, *vbl. sb.* [f. prec.] ... see THIMBLE.

Thime, obs. form of THYME.

Thin (ϸin), *a.* (*sb.* and *adv.*) Forms: 1 ϸynne, ϸyn, ϸin, 2-5 ϸunne, 3-6 ϸyn, 2 ϸenne, 4-6 ϸynne, (4 ϸynn), 4-7 ϸynne, (4 ϸyn), 4-6 thin. 6-8 thin. *Comb.* thin, (4-9 thine), 6-9 thin-.

A. *adj.*

I. **1.** Having relatively little extension between opposite surfaces; of little thickness or depth.

THIN.

b. *transf.* and *fig.* Wanting body or substance; unsubstantial; intangible.

c. *spec.* Having little flesh; lean, spare, not fat or plump.

2. Wanting depth or intensity; faint, weak, dim, pale. Formerly of light (*arch.*): in mod. use, of colours, painting, or the like.

3. Of sound. Wanting fullness, volume, or depth; weak and high-pitched; shrill and feeble.

4. Penetrable by light or vision, like a thin veil; *fig.* easily seen through; transparent, flimsy, as a pretext or excuse.

II. Consisting of or characterized by individual constituents or parts placed at relatively large intervals; not thick, dense, or bushy. Opposed to THICK *a.* 4.

b. Of the members of a collective group or class: Not numerous or abundant; scarce, rare, few. Opposed to THICK *a.* 5.

c. Of a place: Sparsely occupied or peopled; with of, sparsely furnished or supplied with.

3. Of a liquid or a pasty substance: Of slight density or consistence; fluid; of air or vapour: not dense; rare, tenuous, subtle.

b. Of a nasty substance: Of slight density, thinness in proportion to length; slender, tenuous, attenuated.

c. Of liquor: Without body; not strong or rich; of low alcoholic strength.

d. Of an assembly or body of people: Scantily furnished with members; thinly attended; not full.

III. As *adverb*: with participles or adjectives, to which *thin* is now joined by a hyphen, or as a single word; forming adjs., usually of obvious meaning, unlimited in number.

THINE.

the distinction between the mission, character, education, and vocation of Christ.

2. *intr.* To become thin or thinner; to become gradually thinner until it disappears, as a layer or stratum. Also *fig.*

b. Chiefly parasynthetic adjectives, as thin-bedded, -blooded, -drained (in sense A. 4.), -cheeked, -faced, -flanked, -gutted, -haired, -leaved, -lipped, -ribbed (-rinned), -soled, -stemmed.

c. *spec.* To lose flesh; to become spare or lean.

3. *trans.* To make thin; to reduce in thickness or depth.

b. *spec.* To diminish the intensity of; to dilute.

Thine (ϸain), *poss. pron.* Forms: 1-4 ϸin, ϸine, ϸyn, 3-4 ϸine, (ϸin), 3-6 thyne, thin, thyn, 4-6 thyne. [OE. ϸin, pers. and poss. adj. and pron., genitive of ϸu THOU.]

THINE.

II. The possessive adjective or pronoun of the second person sing.: Belonging to thee.

2. *Attributively* (= Ger. dein, F. ton). Now *arch.* or *poet.* before a vowel or *h*, or following the *sb.*: otherwise superseded by THY.

3. *Predicatively* (= Ger. der deinige, F. le tien). That which is thine.

4. *Elliptically*, equivalent to THY with a sb. to be supplied from the previous context.

5. *absol.* a. That which is thine; thy property.

b. (*pl.*) Those who are thine; thy people, family, or kindred.

c. *sing.* that (or are) thine; belonging to thee: see *Of* prep. 44.

Thine, obs. form of THYNE adv. (THIN).

Thing (ϸiŋ), *sb.* Forms: 1-5 ϸing, 1-5 ϸing, 3-5 ϸinge, 4-5 ϸyng, ϸynge, (thyngge), 4-6 thyng, 5-6 thynge, thynge, 4 think, 4-5 thyngk(e), Pl. 1-3 ϸing, 3 thinge, ϸing (see below), *Com. Teut.* cf. OFris. *thing, ting*, OS. *thing, thing*, OHG. *ding, thing* (MHG. *dinc*, mod. G. *Ding*), ON. *þing* (Sw., Da., Norw. *ting*), Goth. *þeihs*.

THING.

a story, tale; a part or section of an argument or discourse; a witty saying, a jest (*usu. good thing*).

13. – *Canon* M. 2388 a 371 (Cax.) In alle thinges that he...

14. *gen.* That which is signified, as distinguished from the word, symbol, or idea by which it is represented; the actual being or entity as opposed to a symbol of it. † *In thing*, in reality, really, actually (opposed to *in name* = nominally).

b. A material substance (usually of a specified kind); stuff, material; in mod. use chiefly applied to substances used as food, drink, or medicine.

8. Applied without life or consciousness; an inanimate object, as distinguished from a person or living creature. See also 8.

9. Applied (usually with qualifying word) to a living being or creature; occasionally to a plant.

10. Applied to a person, now only in contempt, reproach, pity, or affection (esp. to a woman or child); formerly also a term of endearment or honour.

11. *spec.* (*pl.*) Articles of apparel; clothes, garments; esp. such as women wear; also, in addition to the indoor dress, outdoor things.

12. The chief, principal, or notable point.

13. An individual work of literature or art; a composition; a writing, piece of music, etc.

IIa. *absol.* and *Comb.*: thing-aspect, -element.

THING. 310 THINK. 311 THINK.

THINK. 312 THINK. 313 THINKING.

living and high thinking are no more. 1885 J. Martineau *Types Eth. Th.* I. I. i. § 3. 159 Thinking is the very essence of mind, as extension is of matter.

b. *pl.* Thoughts; meditations, courses of thought. 1382 Wyclif *Isa.* lxv. 2 A puple..that goth in a wei not good, after ther thenkingus. 1491 Caxton *Vitas Patr.* (W. de W. 1495) II. 192 b/2 So oryson with fastyng casteth out..the foule thoughtes & vayne thynkynges. 1548 Udall *Erasm. Par. Luke* v. 70 The secrete thinkynges of theyr hertes. 1601 Shaks. *All's Well* v. iii. 128, I am wrap'd in dismall thinkings. 1812 Southey *Lett.* (1856) II. 283 Put together all your recollections and memoranda, I will put together my gleanings and thinkings. 1840 Dickens *Old C. Shop* viii, All these sayings and doings and thinkings.. affected him not in the least.

†**c.** *spec.* Imagination, fancy; idle fancy. *rare.* c 1420 *Chron. Vilod.* 1702 Þe sweuene Of þe tweyn appullon þat fellon from þe tre in to þe water in his thenkyng. 1502 *Ord. Crysten Men* (W. de W. 1506) I. iii. 23 These wordes..be not made for no thynge and with thynkynge.

d. With various constructions: see the verb. *There is no thinking*, one cannot or need not think. 1638 Baker tr. *Balzac's Lett.* (vol. II.) 111 There is no thinking therefore to deceive you by a shew of good. 1669 R. Montagu in *Buccleuch MSS.* (Hist. MSS. Comm.) I. 436 Without her ever thinking of it. 1849 Clough *Dipsychus* II. ii. 105 My pleasure of thought is the pleasure of thinking How pleasant it is to have money.

2. The holding of an opinion or opinions; judging, mental viewing; opinion, judgement, belief; phr. *to* († *after, in*) *my thinking* = in my opinion. c 1410 *Master of Game* (Digby MS. 182) Prol. 13 What shalbe in euery sesoun moste durable and, to my thynkynge, ..oftenest most desportfull of all games. 1490 J. Kay tr. *Caoursin's Siege of Rhodes* (1870) ₽ 10 That hyt was jmpossible, after hys thynkyng, to fynde in all the world such instruments of werre. 1597 Shaks. 2 *Hen. IV*, v. v. 114, I heare a Bird so sing, Whose Musicke (to my thinking) pleas'd the King. 1599 Dallam in *Early Voy. Levant* (Hakl. Soc.) 11 In my thinkinge it seemed not to be above 3 myles. c 1775 Burke *Addr. to King* Wks. IX. 177 In.. opposition to the..confirmed sentiments and habits of thinking of an whole people. 1879 B. Taylor *Stud. Germ. Lit.* 143 Frauenlob, the last, and, to my thinking, the poorest of the Minnesingers.

3. *attrib.* and *Comb.*, as *thinking-party, -place, process, -room, -substance*; **thinking-cap** (see Cap *sb.*[1] 9, and cf. *considering-cap*, Considering *vbl. sb.* 2 b); **thinking part** (*Theatr. colloq.*), a part in which the actor has no words to speak, a silent part; **thinking-shop** (*humorous*), a building or institution for study, as a university; **thinking-time, -while**, time to think, a short space of time. 1874 Coues *Birds N. W.* 527 Startled in his retreat while his *thinking-cap is on, he [the bittern] seems dazed, like one suddenly aroused from a deep sleep. 1903 *Daily Chron.* 21 Jan. 5/4 It is satisfactory to know that the Post Office Department has its 'thinking-cap' on. 1898 *Daily News* 12 Mar. 6/3 The great Benefit which is to be given to Nellie Farren next week at Drury Lane...Some of the most famous [actresses] are content with what are humorously called good '*thinking' parts. 1908 *Greenroom Bk.* 667 He made his professional debut in 1867 in a 'thinking part'. 1897 *Q. Rev.* Apr. 348 That remarkable series of reading-parties (or more truly of *thinking-parties). 1883 Jefferies *Story of my Heart* 74 This..was a favourite *thinking-place. 1899 *Allbutt's Syst. Med.* VII. 423 These kinæsthetic images..play only a small part in *thinking processes. 1862 Thoreau *Yankee in Canada* i. (1866) 13 When every house..will have not only its sleeping-rooms, and dining-room, and talking-room or parlor, but its *thinking-room also. 1836–48 B. D. Walsh *Aristoph., Clouds* I. ii, I am come To be a Scholar in the *Thinking-shop. 1890 *Spectator* 19 Apr., It turned Oxford into an aristocratic boarding-school from a democratic thinking-shop. 1884 J. Tait *Mind in Matter* (1892) 99 The etherialised medium of force, which probably connects the brain with the *thinking-substance. 1667 Dryden & Dk. Newcastle *Sir Martin Mar-all* v. i, I'll put you upon something, give me but a *thinking time. *Ibid.* III. i, As a whiff of tobacco ..[used] in the midst of a discourse for a *thinking-while.

Thi·nking, *ppl. a.* [f. as prec. + -ing [2].]

1. That thinks; having, or exercising, the faculty of thought; cogitative. 1678 Dryden & Lee *Œdipus* III. i, A thinking soul is punishment enough. 1709 Steele & Addison *Tatler* No. 111 ₽ 1 What was the proper Employment of a thinking Being? 1800 *Med. Jrnl.* III. 281 According to the laws of the thinking faculty, the understanding and reason. 1864 Bowen *Logic* i. 2 The Thinking or Elaborative faculty,— i. e. the Understanding.

2. Given to thinking; habitually exercising one's mind; having special or well-trained powers of thought; thoughtful, reflective, intellectual. (Cf. Thinker 1 c.) 1681 *Let. to Person of Hon.* in *Select. Harl. Misc.* (1793) 461 To have an account of the sense of the thinking-men about the town concerning it. 1779 *Mirror* No. 16 ₽ 3 Those moments of deeper pensiveness to which every thinking mind is liable. 1837 W. Irving *Capt. Bonneville* III. 225 The senior chief..was a thinking man, and a man of observation.

3. *fig.* Said of very life-like sculpture: cf. Breathing *ppl. a.* b. 1732 M. Green *Grotto* 57 The thinking sculpture helps to raise Deep thoughts, the genii of the place.

Hence **Thi·nkingdom** (*nonce-wd.*), a realm of thinking persons; **Thi·nkingly** *adv.*, in a thinking manner, in the way of thought; with thought, consciously, deliberately; in (one's own) thought or supposition (quot. 1894); **Thi·nkingness**, thinking quality; thoughtfulness, intellectuality; the essence of a thinking being (quot. 1865). 1880 *Q. Rev.* Oct. 415 Christendom..is far enough as yet from having been replaced by the Utopian *Thinkingdom (*Cogitantenthum*), to which one of the modern German apostles of materialism..looks forward. 1847 Webster, **Thinkingly*, by thought. 1887 Mary Linskill *In Exchange for Soul* xlviii, Quite thinkingly he sent the message in his wife's name. 1673 O. Walker *Educ.* v. 43 Contrary to that seriousnes and *thinkingnes requisite to prudence and gallantry of spirit. 1838 *New Monthly Mag.* LIII. 118 All men say..good things of the courage of Englishmen, the chastity of English women, the thinkingness of both sexes. 1865 J. Grote *Explor. Philos.* I. 140, I recognise two manners of existence,..thinkingness and thoughtness.

Thinkling (þi·ŋkˌliŋ). *nonce-wd.* [f. Think *v.*[2] + -ling.] A petty or inferior thinker. 1815 J. Gilchrist *Labyrinth Demolished* 22. 1816 — *Philos. Etym.* 247 A proper Etymological Dictionary, which petty thinklings—quackish pretenders affect to despise.

Thi·nk-so. *nonce-wd.* [The phr. (*I*) *think so* (Think *v.*[2] 9 c) used as a sb.] A mere opinion. 1666 Bunyan *Grace Ab.* § 97 How if all our Faith, and Christ, and Scriptures, should be but a Think-so too? 1675 — *Saved by Grace* Wks. (1692) I. 568/1 He thinks former encouragements were Fancies, Delusions or meer Think-so's. 1887 Hall Caine *Deemster* xxxix, All the dread I had felt hitherto..was no more than a thinkso.

Thin-laid, -leaved, etc.: see Thin *a.* D.

Thinly (þi·nli), *adv.* [f. Thin *a.* + -ly [2].] In a thin manner.

1. With little thickness or depth; with thin clothing. Also *fig.* 13.. *K. Alis.* 5906 (Bodl. MS.) Thynnelich hy beþ y-hatered. 1746 Francis tr. *Hor., Sat.* II. vi. 94 This Morning Air is very bad For them, who go but thinly clad. 1770 *Phil. Trans.* LXI. 334, I covered the bottom with it thinly. 1855 Macaulay *Hist. Eng.* xxi. IV. 570 The scheme of assassination, thus thinly veiled, was communicated to James. 1859 Gullick & Timbs *Paint.* 229 Pictures in oil ..may, of course, be thinly painted throughout.

b. *fig.* Poorly, meagrely. ? *Obs. rare.* 1537 Cromwell in Merriman *Life & Lett.* (1902) II. 75 Your neighbours, without whom..all the rest of you would live full thynnely.

2. With large intervals of space or time; sparsely; not closely or thickly. c 1545 in Dugdale *Monast.* (1821) III. 283, v. acrez di. thinly growyne with olde bechez and some oke. 1667–8 Sir T. Browne *Brampton Urns* Wks. 1835 III. 500 Great ones were but thinly found. a 1727 Newton *Chronol. Amended* i. (1728) 178 He found that country..peopled but thinly. 1827 Hone *Every-day Bk.* II. 106 The market was..thinly attended.

3. In combination with pa. pples. or adjs. used attributively; now usually hyphened. 1757 Dyer *Fleece* I. Wks. (1761) 60 The thinly-scatter'd meal. 1797 Godwin *Enquirer* II. xii. 454 Ten thinly printed pages. 1862 Ansted *Channel Isl.* I. ii. (ed. 2) 26 Thinly-bedded grey rocks. 1890 'R. Boldrewood' *Col. Reformer* (1891) 70 An open, thinly-timbered, well-grassed country. 1902 *Daily Chron.* 25 Jan. 3/2 He makes thinly-veiled love to the young lady.

†**Thi·nmost,** *a. Obs. rare*[−1]. [f. Thin *a.*: see -most.] Thinnest. 1644 Nye *Gunnery* (1670) 83 If this Peece were fortified.. onely so much, as the thinmost part of the metall is.

Thinned (þind), *ppl. a.* [f. Thin *v.*[1] + -ed [1].] Made thin or less thick, in senses of Thin *v.*[1]; reduced in thickness, density, frequency, number, etc. 1710 J. Clarke *Rohault's Nat. Phil.* I. xxvii. (1729) I. 210 The Superficies of the thinned Body, where it is of any one Thickness. 1857 Ld. Dufferin *Lett. High Lat.* xii. (ed. 3) 359 The thinned ranks on board the '*Iron Beard*' are constantly replenished. 1899 *Allbutt's Syst. Med.* VIII. 695 Pigment is irregularly accumulated in the thinned epidermis.

Thi·nner. [agent-n. from Thin *v.*[1]: see -er [1].] One who thins. 1832 *Planting* 63 in *Libr. Usef. Knowl., Husb.* III, Leaving them to press upon each other more severely than vigorous thinners would permit. 1889 *Pall Mall G.* 2 July 2/2 The case of the little turnip-thinners in Saxony.

Thinness (þi·nˌnės). [f. Thin *a.* + -ness.] The quality or condition of being thin.

1. Narrowness of dimension between opposite surfaces; absence of thickness or depth. 1577 B. Googe *Heresbach's Husb.* II. (1586) 80 b, Fulnesse and emptinesse, or thicknesse and thinnes. 1617 Moryson *Itin.* III. 175 Cotton cloth..for thinnesse not vnlike our boulting cloths. 1715 Desaguliers *Fires Impr.* 113 Where you cannot dig in the Back-Wall of a Chimney by reason of its thinness. 1807 Vancouver *Agric. Devon* (1813) 54 The thinness of the seam [of coal]. 1863 Lyell *Antiq. Man* iii. 34 The extreme thinness of the film of matter.

b. Lean or spare habit of body; spareness. 1827–35 Willis *Leper* 65 There, alone, Wasted to ghastly thinness, Helon knelt.

c. *fig.* Deficiency, poverty, meagreness, feebleness; lack of depth or fullness. c 1000 *Sax. Leechd.* I. 134 Hit ʒehælð þa þynnysse þære ʒesihðe. 1623 W. Balcanqual *Serm. St. Maries Spittle* 98 The thinnesse of our Ioy, because we did sowe our teares too thin. 1903 *Daily Chron.* 20 Feb. 3/6 That there was much 'intellectual thinness' among young men.

2. The condition of being thinly arranged, occupied, or attended; want of fullness; sparseness. c 1440 *Promp. Parv.* 491/1 Thynnesse, of wodys, cornys, and oþer lyke, *raritas.* 1573–80 Baret *Alv.* T 166 Thinnesse: seldomnesse, *rarité.* 1690 Locke *Govt.* II. vi. § 74 The Thinness of People gives Families Leave to separate into unpossessed Quarters. 1774 A. Gib *Pres. Truth* II. 40 None of these brethren opened a mouth about the thinness of the meeting. 1826 F. Reynolds *Life & Times* II. 200 Expressing my surprise at the..thinness of the house.

3. Absence or lack of density, consistence, or viscosity; fluidity, tenuity, rarity. c 1000 *Sax. Leechd.* II. 199 Þonne þara metta meltung biþ & þynnes. 1398 Trevisa *Barth. De P. R.* XI. i. (Tollem. MS.), Eyer haþ more þinnesse and clerenesse þan oþer elementis. c 1440 *Promp. Parv.* 491/1 Thynnesse, or thynhede of licurys. 1582 Stanyhurst *Æneis* I. (Arb.) 37 From earthly thicknesse, too thinnesse vannished ayerie. 1684–5 Boyle *Min. Waters* 26 Of the thinness or viscosity of the Mineral Water. a 1854 Caroline B. Southey *Poet. Wks.* (1867) 67 Milk..tempered down To wholesome thinness.

†**Thi·nnify,** *v. Obs. rare*[−1]. [f. Thin *a.* + -ify, -fy.] *trans.* To make thin; = Thin *v.*[1] 5. a 1693 Urquhart's *Rabelais* III. iv. 40 The Heart doth in its left side Ventricle so thinnifie the Blood.

Thi·nning, *vbl. sb.* [f. Thin *v.*[1] + -ing [1].] The action of Thin *v.*[1], in various senses; reduction or decrease in thickness, closeness, number, density, etc. Also with *out, off, away, up*, etc. c 1000 *Sax. Leechd.* II. 260 Læcedomas þa þe þynnunge mæʒen hæbben. 1398 Trevisa *Barth. De P. R.* XIX. xi. (Bodl. MS.), White mater is igendred of thynnynge and spredinge of aier. 1799 J. Robertson *Agric. Perth* 257 Weeded down by various thinnings. 1839 Ure *Dict. Arts* 1269 The thinning up, or quantity of turpentine required to bring it to its proper consistence. 1851 Carpenter *Man. Phys.* (ed. 2) 268 By the thinning-away of its wall at its most projecting part. 1868 *Rep. U. S. Commissioner Agric.* (1869) 423 Upon thinning out, enough plants were cast away to have run at least twelve rows additional.

b. *concr.* usually *pl.* That which is removed in the process of thinning. (Cf. *sweepings.*) 1771 *Usef. Proj.* in *Ann. Reg.* 115/2 Sir John..never receives less than a guinea an acre in thinnings throughout his plantations. 1805 R. W. Dickson *Pract. Agric.* I. Pl. xxx. 110 A fir paling of the horizontal kind, made from the thinning of trees of that kind. 1893 *Jrnl. R. Agric. Soc.* Dec. 826 Thinnings and rubbish should be immediately removed and burnt.

Thi·nning, *ppl. a.* [f. Thin *v.*[1] + -ing [2].] That thins, in various senses of the verb. 1550 Bale *Eng. Votaries* II. 81 To confirme the thynnynge shewe of hypocresye. 1790 Wolcott (P. Pindar) *Rowland for Oliver* 92 Art thou a Doctor? Yes, of thinning skill. 1888 *Pump Court* 31 Oct. 5/2 His gradually thinning hair. 1899 Mackail *Life Morris* II. 154 A mere thinning remnant between two divergent and increasing camps.

Thinnish (þi·niʃ), *a.* [f. Thin *a.* + -ish [1].] Somewhat thin; tending to thinness. 1545 Raynold *Byrth Mankynde* 139 Her vryne shall appeare whyte and thynnyssh. 1780 C. A. Burney in *Mme. D'Arblay's Early Diary* (1889) II. 289 The Masquerade at the Pantheon was rather thinnish. 1827 F. Cooper *Prairie* I. ii. 30 They told us..we should find settlers something thinnish hereaway. 1884 *Century Mag.* XXIX. 138/1 My somewhat slight figure and thinnish legs.

Thinnye, obs. form of Tunny.

Thinocorine (þainǫkǫ·rǝin), *a. Ornith.* [f. mod.L. *Thinocorus* (properly *-ys*), f. Gr. θίς, θῑν- beach, sea-shore + κόρυς lark: see -ine [1].] Of, pertaining to, or characteristic of the *Thinocoridæ* or quail-snipes, a family of South American wading birds, typified by the genus *Thinocorus*. 1885 *Stand. Nat. Hist.* IV. 92 The Thinocorine palate, in which the vomer is connected with the nasal cartilages in a manner recalling that of the Ægithognathæ.

Thinolite (þai·nǫlait). *Min.* [f. Gr. θίς, θῑν- (see prec.) + λίθος stone: see -lite.] 'A variety of calcite, occurring in pseudomorphous crystals, the original mineral being still in doubt' (Chester *Dict. Min.* 1896). 1879 C. King *Geol. 40th Parallel* I. 508 (Chester).

Thin-skinned (-skind: stress var.), *a.*

1. Having a thin skin or rind. 1598 Chapman *Blinde Begger of Alexandria* Wks. 1873 I. 11 Round faces and thinne skinde are happiest still. 1707 Mortimer *Husb.* (1721) II. 155 Chuse the large, round, white, and thin-skinned ones. 1875 Bennett & Dyer *Sachs' Bot.* 539 A stony endocarp surrounding the thin-skinned seed.

2. *fig.* Sensitive to criticism, ridicule, or abuse; easily hurt or offended; touchy. 1680 Baxter *Answ. Stillingfl.* lxxviii. 99, I..never was so thin Skin'd as to be unable to bear a Cholerick breath. 1771 Smollett *Humph. Cl.* 8 June, My apothecary, who is a proud Scotchman, very thin skinned. 1818 Cobbett *Pol. Reg.* XXXIII. 311 The professional gentlemen in Pennsylvania are..extremely thin-skinned, when they are the party attacked. 1894 Froude *Life & Lett. Erasmus* xvii. 328 Erasmus..was thin-skinned as ever.

Hence **Thin-ski·nnedness**, the condition or quality of being thin-skinned; sensitiveness. 1882 Sala *Amer. Revis.* (1883) I. iii. 43 *note*, A very gratifying proof of the diminution of what may be termed 'thin-skinnedness'. 1897 *Spectator* 23 Oct. 552/1 This thin-skinnedness among experienced public men.

Thin-sown (þinˌsōun: stress var.), *a.* Also 7 thin-sowed. Sown or planted thinly; *lit.* said of plants, or a crop; *fig.* scattered at wide intervals, scarce; also, of a field or territory: scantily furnished *with* († *of*). 1589 R. Harvey *Pl. Perc.* (1590) 18 Good deeds, which are now both thin sowne.., and thinner growne. a 1631 Donne *Lett.* (1651) 159 This Countrie is so thin sowed with such persons, as he comes to seek; that he will scarce know, where to find a corn to peck at. 1698 Norris *Pract. Disc.* IV. 60 Very good Men..were always very thin sown. a 1846 in J. Baxter *Libr. Pract. Agric.* (ed. 4) II. 398 In the early stages..the appearance of thick-sown corn is much superior to that of the thin-sown.

Thi·n-spun, *a.* (stress var.) Spun thinly; drawn out in spinning to a slender thread. Also *fig.* 1637 Milton *Lycidas* 76 Comes the blind Fury with th' abhorred shears, And slits the thin spun life. 1642 H. More *Song of Soul* II. iii. IV. ix, Thin-spun reason and exile discourse. 1821 Clare *Vill. Minstr.* I. 93 How thin-spun clouds glide swiftly by. *Ibid.* 120 Nor broken seam, nor thin-spun screen.

Thi·n-walled (-wǭld), *a.* Having thin walls. 1854 Owen *Skel. & Teeth* (1855) 7 The thinnest-walled and widest air-bone of the bird of flight was first solid. 1875 Bennett & Dyer *Sachs' Bot.* 90 Alternate layers of narrow thick-walled and broad thin-walled cork-cells are formed. 1875 Huxley & Martin *Elem. Biol.* (1877) 184 Posteriorly, the oviducts dilate into capacious thin-walled chambers.

Thio- (þaiˌo), also before a vowel **thi-**, repr. Gr. θεῖον sulphur; a formative element in names of things containing or connected with sulphur.

1. in *Chem.* (See also Thiol-, Thion-.) In names of compounds containing sulphur = *sulpho-*.

In systematic nomenclature restricted to those in which one or more atoms of sulphur take the place of one or more of oxygen in the substance designated by the rest of the name; e.g. *thiacetic* acid $C_2H_3O.SH$, from acetic acid $C_2H_3O.OH$, *tri-thiocarbonic* acid H_2CS_3, from carbonic acid H_2CO_3. So *thio-acid, -alcohol, -aldehyde, -ether, -salt*; also *thio-antimo·nic, -antimo·nious, -arse·nic, -arse·nious, -lactic, -phosphoric, -phosphoryl, -stannic, -tungstic*, etc. But many names do not conform exactly to this systematic use.

The following are the chief combinations of *thio-*.

Thia·cetate, a salt of thiacetic acid. **Thiace·tic** *a.*, in *thiacetic acid* ($C_2H_3O.SH$), a colourless liquid boiling at 93° C. **Thi·a·cid** = *thio-acid.* **Thia·ldine** [Ald(ehyde + -ine [5]], a crystalline substance, $NH:2(CHCH_3.S):CHCH_3$, produced by passing hydrogen sulphide into a solution of aldehyde ammonia. **Thi·alol** [Al(cohol + -ol 3], a name for diethyl disulphide, $(C_2H_5)_2S_2$, a colourless oily compound, having an odour like garlic. **Thi·amide,** generic name for substances formed by replacing the oxygen of an amide by sulphur, as *thiacetamide*, $CH_3CS.NH_2$, from acetamide, $CH_3CO.NH_2$. **Thi·amine,** generic name for amines containing the group NHSH, as *ethylthiamine*, $C_2H_5.NHSH$. **Thiazole** [Azo- + -ole, -ol 3], $N\langle{}^{CH.S}_{CH:CH}$, a liquid boiling at 117° C. **Thi·enyl** [contr. of *thiophenyl*, proposed 1883 by V. Meyer], the radical C_4H_3S contained in *thiophene*, C_4H_4S. **Thi·o-acid, thi·-acid,** an acid in which oxygen is replaced by sulphur. **Thio-a·lbumose,** a deutero-albumose containing a large amount of sulphur. **Thio-a·lcohol,** a compound of the nature of an alcohol in which sulphur takes the place of oxygen, as mercaptan, $C_2H_5.SH$, analogous to ethyl alcohol, $C_2H_5.OH$. **Thioca·rbamate,** a salt of thiocarbamic acid. **Thiocarba·mic** *a.*, in *t. acid*, $NH_2.CO.SH$ and $NH_2.CS.OH$: now distinguished as *thiolcarbamic* and *thioncarbamic* acids: see Thiol-, Thion-. **Thioca·rbamide,** $CS(NH_2)_2$ or $HS.C(NH_2):NH$, a crystalline substance melting at 170° C. **Thioca·rbonate,** a salt of thiocarbonic acid. **Thiocarbo·nic** *a.*, in *t. acid*: in derivatives, as *mono-, di-, tri-thiocarbonic acid*: the last, H_2CS_3, is a dark yellow strongly smelling oil, very easily decomposed by heating into CS_2 and H_2S; esters of *dithiocarbonic acid*, H_2COS_2, and of *monothiocarbonic acid*, H_2CO_2S, are known. **Thioca·rbonyl,** the radical $(CS)''$, in which the oxygen of carbonyl $(CO)''$ is replaced by sulphur. **Thioca·rbylamine** = *iso-thiocyanic* acid, CHNS, = C≡N.SH. **Thiocresol** (þaiˌoˌkre·sǫl), a compound with the formula $CH_3:C_6H_4SH$, of which there are three modifications, two crystalline and one liquid. **Thiocy·anate,** a salt of thiocyanic acid. **Thiocya·nic** *a.*, in *t. acid*, N:C.SH = cyanic acid, N:C.OH, in which oxygen is replaced by sulphur; a liquid with a penetrating odour. **Thiocya·nogen,** the radical CNS of thiocyanic acid; in comb. *thiocyano-*. **Thiofo·rmic** *a.*, in *t. acid*, H_2COS, a crystalline substance melting at 120° C. **Thiona·phthene,** a colourless crystalline compound, C_8H_6S, consisting of benzene, C_6H_4, of which two atoms of H are replaced by CH:CH.S. **Thionic** (þaiˌǫ·nik) *a.*, in *t. acids*, group name for the acids represented by the formula $H_2S_nO_6$, where n = 2, 3, 4, 5, and perhaps 6. These acids are called *dithionic, trithionic, tetrathionic, pentathionic*, and *hexathionic* acid. **Thi·onine,** a brownish-black dye, $SC_{12}H_9N_3$, crystallizing in plates, called *phenylene violet*, or *Lauth's v.*, and largely used to stain microscopic objects. **Thionu·rate,** a salt of thionuric acid. **Thionuric** (þaiˌǫnˌiū^ə·rik) *a.* [f. Gr. θεῖον + Uric], in *thionuric acid*, $CO:2(NH.CO):CH.NH.SO_3H$, formed by the action of ammonia and sulphurous acid on alloxan in aqueous solution. **Thi·onyl** [-yl], the radical $(SO)''$: so named in 1857 by Schiff (*Annalen der Chem. und Pharm.* CII. 113). **Thi·ophene,** C_4H_4S, a colourless liquid with an odour like benzene, occurring in benzene from coal-tar to the extent of about 0·5 per cent.; hence **Thiophe·nic** *a.*, in *thiophenic acid*, $C_4H_3S.CO_2H$, derived from thiophene. **Thiophe·nol,** a colourless liquid, C_6H_5SH (= Phenol with S in place of O), with the odour of garlic. **Thi·ophthene** [Na)phthene], a colourless oily compound, $C_6H_4S_2$, obtained by the distillation of citric acid with P_2S_3. **Thi·oreso·rcin,** also **Thioreso·rcinol,** $C_6H_4(SH)_2$, a yellowish-grey substance, used medicinally as a substitute for iodoform. **Thi·osalicy·lic** *a.*, in *t. acid*, $HOC_6H_4CO(SH)$, a brownish-yellow amorphous substance, used in medicine as an antiseptic. **Thio-salt,** a salt of a thio-acid, as a thiosulphate. **Thiosi·namine** [L. *sinapis* mustard + Amine] = *allyl-thio-urea*, $C_3H_5NH.CS.NH_2$, a crystalline substance produced by the action of ammonia on allyl mustard oil. **Thiosu·lphate,** a salt of thiosulphuric acid; formerly called *hyposulphite*. **Thiosulphu·ric** *a.*, in *t. acid*, $H_2S_2O_3$, an acid only known in solution and soon decomposing, the salts of which are stable, and are applied in bleaching and photography; it is sulphuric acid, H_2SO_4, in which one atom of oxygen is replaced by sulphur; formerly called *hyposulphurous* acid. **Thioto·luene** [Toluene] = *methylthiophene*, $C_4H_3(CH_3)S$, a colourless oily compound, found as an impurity in crude toluene; two isomeric forms are known. **Thio-urea** (þaiˌoˌiū·ˌrīă), $CS(NH_2)_2$ or $HS.C(NH_2):NH$ = *thiocarbamide*. **Thioxa·nthone** [Xanthone], $C_{13}H_8OS$, crystallizing in yellow needles. **Thioxene** (þaiˌǫ·ksīn), **Thioxylene** (þaiˌǫksilīn) [named *thioxene* by Victor Meyer (*Ber. Deut. Chem. Ges.* 1884, XVII. 789)] = *dimethylthiophene*, $C_4H_2(CH_3)_2S$, found as an impurity in xylene; there are several isomeric forms.

1854 Kekulé in *Proc. Roy. Soc.* VII. 38 *Thiacetic Acid,—Sulphuretted Acetic Acid—has been obtained by me by acting on monohydrated acetic acid with tersulphide of phosphorus. 1847 Wöhler & Liebig in *Mem. Chem. Soc.* III. 303 A new organic alkali free from oxygen..which we call *thialdine..contracted from θεῖον and aldehyde. 1881 Watts *Dict. Chem.* VIII. 1952 *Thiamides..may be conveniently prepared by the action of phosphorus sulphide ..on amides. 1888 Hantzsch & Weber in *Jrnl. Chem. Soc.* LIV. 256 *Thiazole is the name given to [these] isomeric compounds. 1885 Peter *Ibid.* XLVIII. 141 **Thienylmethylacetoxime* $C_4H_3S.CMe:NOH$..forms a white crystalline mass. 1882 Will *Ibid.* XLII. 1088 *Thiocarbamates...A continuation of the author's researches. 1878 Guareschi *Ibid.* XXXIV. 860 **Thiocarbamide* $CS(NH_2)_2$ [etc.] when oxidised by permanganate likewise yield all their sulphur in the state of sulphuric acid. 1891 *Anthony's Photogr. Bull.* IV. 397 Prof. J. E. Reynolds, who was the original discoverer of the rinsing sulphur urea, now known as *thio-carbamide*. 1883 *Jrnl. Chem. Soc.* XLIV. 405 The use of potassium *thiocarbonate as a remedy against phylloxera. 1887 *Ibid.* LI. 272 The conversion of *thiocarbonyl chloride into thiocarbonyl tetrachloride by the assimilation of two atoms of chlorine takes place at ordinary temperatures. 1877 *Ibid.* XXXII. 869 *Thiocyanates of the acid radicles are prepared by the action of acid chlorides on dry lead thiocyanate. 1877 *Ibid.* XXXII. 423 Action of Nascent *Thiocyanic Acid on Alcohol. 1857 *Ibid.* IX. 285 *Thioformic acid crystallises from formic acid, or from boiling alcohol, in slender needles. 1880 *Ibid.* XXXVII. 593 A qualitative reaction, by which pentathionic acid is clearly distinguished from any other of the *thionic acids. 1839 Thomson *British Ann.* 377 *Thionurate of zinc. *Ibid.*, *Thionuric acid. 1874 Watts *Dict. Chem.* V. 779 Thionuric acid..forms a crystalline mass, consisting of fine needles. *Ibid.* 780 *Thionyl. SO.—The radicle of the sulphurous compounds: e.g. sulphurous chloride, $(SO)''Cl_2$ = chloride of thionyl. 1883 Meyer in *Jrnl. Chem. Soc.* XLIV. 1091 A substance contained in Coal-tar Benzene..to which the author has given the name of **thiophene*. 1899 *Syd. Soc. Lex.*, **Thiophenol*,..phenyl mercaptan. *Ibid.*, **Thioresorcin*,.. a popular substitution of resorcin..Used as a dusting powder. 1853 Ure *Dict. Arts* I. 32 *Thiosinnamine. 1881 Piesse & Stansell in *Jrnl. Chem. Soc.* XL. 207 *Thiosinamine* is an oily substance at 100°, but gradually solidifies when cold. 1873 Watts *Fownes' Chem.* 198 The solution of a *thiosulphate. 1874 *Jrnl. Chem. Soc.* XXVII. 771 The close relation between the thiosulphates and sulphates is shown by the formulæ—$SO_2{}^{SNa}_{ONa}$ and $SO_2{}^{ONa}_{ONa}$. 1873 Watts *Fownes' Chem.* 204 *Thiosulphuric Acid is scarcely known. 1874 *Jrnl. Chem. Soc.* XXVII. 770 On the Constitution of Hyposulphurous (Thiosulphuric) Acid. 1885 *Ibid.* XLVIII. 251 A Simple Method of obtaining *Thiotolene. 1894 Muir & Morley *Watts' Dict. Chem.* IV. 710 Formed by adding Br to an alcoholic or cold aqueous solution of *thio-urea. 1885 *Jrnl. Chem. Soc.* XLVIII. 251 A simple method of obtaining..*thioxylene.

2. In pharmaceutical and other terms.

Thiobacte·ria, name proposed by Migula for sulphur and iron bacteria mostly found in seawater and soils. **Thi·ocamph** [Camph(or], a fluid disinfectant, used for fumigation, formed by the action of sulphur dioxide on camphor. **Thi·ocol** [Guaia)col], a preparation of guaiacol, used in lung diseases. **Thi·oform** [after *chloroform*], trade-name of a basic bismuth di-thiosalicylate, as an antiseptic for wounds. **Thiogenic** *a.* [-gen I + -ic], producing sulphur, *spec.* applied to bacteria which produce free sulphur by the oxidization of sulphuretted hydrogen. **Thio·genol,** trade-name of a solution of sodium sulphonate as a medical wash. **Thi·olin** [L. *linum* flax], trade-name of a dark-green substance prepared from linseed oil by the action of sulphur; hence **Thioli·nic** *acid*. **Thiosa·piol, -sapol** [L. *sapo* soap], **-sa·vonal,** trade-names of soap containing sulphur in chemical combination. ‖ **Thi·othrix** [Gr. θρίξ hair], a genus of sulphur bacteria found in sulphur springs.

1900 A. C. Jones tr. *Fischer's Str. & Funct. Bacteria* 65 The sulphur bacteria, **Thiobacteria*, whose cells are often crammed full of spherical refringent masses of pure sulphur, occur in nature in places where free sulphuretted hydrogen is present. *Ibid.*, Thiobacteria can be found at any time of the year, but are most abundant in the early spring and late autumn. 1899 *Syd. Soc. Lex.*, **Thiocamph*..on exposure evolves sulphur dioxide in steady fumes. *Ibid.*, **Thioform* ..a light yellowish powder, without odour or taste..has.. been introduced into surgery with promising success. 1910 Brickdale *Guide Newer Remedies* 60 A dithiosalicylate ..has been..named Thioform. 1894 Remington *Pract. Pharm.* (ed. 3) 1433 **Thiolin*. Salts of thiosulphonic acid. Salt of thiolinic acid. Sulphonated and sulphurated linseed oil. 1899 *Syd. Soc. Lex.*, Thiolin, thiolinic acid. *Ibid.*, **Thiosapiol*, a sulphuretted soap, containing 10 per cent. of sulphur, obtained by heating sulphur and oleic acid together...A successful application to many skin diseases.

Thiol- (þai·ǫl). *Chem.* [arbitrarily f. Thio-.] A name for the group SH in combination, analogous to hydroxyl, OH.

It indicates the presence of an -SH group (or an -SR group, where R is an alkyl radical), as in *methyl-thiolcarbamate*, $H_2N.CO.SCH_3$, as distinguished from *methyl carbamate*, $H_2N.CO.OCH_3$, and also from *methyl-thioncarbamate*, $H_2N.CS.OCH_3$: see Thion-. Also, in those cases in which *hydroxy-* would mean the presence of an -OH group, *thiol-* indicates the presence of an -SH group; and where *methoxy-, ethoxy-*, etc., would indicate CH_3O-, C_2H_5O-, RO- groups, *methylthiol-, ethylthiol-, R-thiol-*, indicate CH_3S-, C_2H_5S-, RS- groups; thus, the sulphur compound corresponding to *sodium ethoxyacetate* $C_2H_5O.CH_2.CO_2Na$ is *sodium ethylthiolacetate* $C_2H_5S.CH_2.CO_2Na$. Cf. Thion-.

1899 *Jrnl. Chem. Soc.* LXXVI. I. 797 The authors adopt the Geneva nomenclature, *thion* being used to denote compounds containing the group .CS.OR, and *thiol* those containing the group .CO.SR. 1905 *Ibid.* LXXXVIII. I. 626 a-Thiolbutyric acid, $SH.CHEt.CO_2H$, is an oil boiling at 118–122° under 19 mm. pressure.

Thion- (þai·ǫn). *Chem.* [a. Gr. θεῖον sulphur: cf. Thio-.] A name for sulphur taking the place of oxygen in a compound and joined by two bonds to carbon.

e.g. in *methyl thioncarbamate*, $H_2N.CS.OCH_3$, as distinct from methyl carbamate and methyl-thiolcarbamate: see Thiol-. (Certain words beginning with *thion-* do not conform to this system: see Thionic, etc. under Thio-.)

1899 *Jrnl. Chem. Soc.* LXXVI. I. 797 [see Thiol-]. 1904 *Ibid.* LXXXVI. I. 990 The crude ester..is best converted directly into thionoxanilic acid, $NHPh.CS.CO_2H$.

Thir (ðīr, ðǝ̄ɹ), *dem. pron.* and *adj. Sc.* and *north. dial.* Forms: 3?, 4– thir; also 4 (**þeir, þier**), **þer(e, þar(e, there,** 4–5 **þir(e,** 4–7 **ther,** 5 **thire, theire, thair,** (8–9 *north. dial.* **ther, thor, thoor, thur**). [Origin obscure. The introduction of the word app. coincided with the change of *þās* in the north from being plural of *this* to being synonymous with *þā*, pl. of *that*: see These, Those, Tho. The earliest evidence is that of Cursor Mundi and the northern works of 1300–1350, in which *þās* and *þā* appear as plural of *that*, and *thir* in various spellings is the established plural of *this*, = southern *thēs*, midland *thise, these*. Some suggest its adoption from ON. *þeir, þær* 'those', pl. masc. and fem. of the simple demonstrative *sá, sú, þat*, of which the plural was used also as 3rd pers. pron. pl. 'they'. Others have suggested a combination of *þe* with *hēr* 'here', as if = the here, those here. Both suggestions present difficulties. See Note.]

A. *pron.* = These *dem. pron.*

13.. *Cursor M.* 6291 (Cott., Gött.) Þir [*F., Tr.* þes] er þe folk of israel. *Ibid.* 6481 (Cott.) Þir [*F.* þer, *G.* þis, *Tr.* þese] er þe coma[n]mentes ten. *Ibid.* 23053 (Edin., Gött.) Gret lauerdschip sal þir [*Cott.* þar, *F.* ham] be lent. *Ibid.* 23643 (Edin., Gött.) Þir sal worsip al creature. a 1340 Hampole *Psalter* iii. 2 Þere ere leghers, and þai say to bigile þe. 13.. *Evang. Nicod.* 28 in Herrig's *Archiv* LIII. 392 We, whatkyn godes er þire [*rimes* syre, ire, desyre]? c 1450 *St. Cuthbert* (Surtees) 3521 Þir [five onions], he saide, has bene my mete. 1456 Sir G. Haye *Law Arms* (S.T.S.) 85 Of all thir, thare is nane sa gude as..defens of gude rycht. 1552–3 *Reg. Privy Council Scot.* I. 137 Thir ar the artikills of the Lordis. 1637–50 Row *Hist. Kirk* (Wodr. S.) 197 Any one of thir requyrs a wholl man. 1825 Brockett *N. C. Words*, Thur, these. 1828 *Craven Gloss.*, Thur, thir, these.

B. *adj.* = These *dem. adj.*

13.. *Cursor M.* 4085 (Cott.) Þeir [*Gött.* þir, *F.* þes, *T.* þese] breþer, þat i said of are. *Ibid.* 5938 'Yee prai your lauerd', he said, 'þat he Wald do þier frosses [*F.* þere froskis, *G.* þir froskis, *T.* þese frogges] a-wai fra me'. *Ibid.* 19391 Þir [*F.* þer, *Tr.* þese] seuen were Sett be-fore þe aposteles sere. 1340 Hampole *Pr. Consc.* 1682 Als þir clerkes fyndes writen. c 1400 Maundev. (Roxb.) Pref. 2 Þir werldly lordes. c 1420 *Anturs of Arth.* 575 Witturly ther weys [*Douce MS.* þes wighte mene] thayre weppuns thai weld. 1423 Jas. I *Kingis Quair* li, I..said thir versis sevin. c 1440 *Alphabet of Tales* 55 He lukid evur when þir fendis suld com agayn. 1490 *Exch. Rolls Scotl.* X. 663 To quhais knauleg thire our letterris salcum greting. 1553 Kennedy *Compend. Tract.* in *Wodrow Soc. Misc.* (1844) 109 Sen the tyme of the Apostolis to thir our dayis. 1678 *Contract* in *Proc. Soc. Ant. Scot.* (1896) XXX. 21 Both pairties are content that ther present[s] be insert. 1715 *Wodrow Corr.* (1843) II. 33 Thir two men have bred trouble enough. 1790 Burns *Tam o' Shanter* 155 Thir breeks o' mine, my only pair. 1790 Mrs. Wheeler *Westmld. Dial.* Pref. 11 Thor Men hed been at a College, coad Cambridg.

[*Note.* Difficulties of derivation from ON. *þeir, þær* are: (1) The retention of inflexional *-r*, otherwise unexemplified, and the fact that *þei-r* had already been adopted in its pronominal sense as *þeʒʒ, they, thei*, in the north *þai, þay*, and was in full use in Cursor M. and other northern works: see They. Moreover, neither *thir* nor *ther* appears to represent *þei-r* phonetically, as Ormin's *þeʒʒ* and E. Midl. *þei* did. (2) The sense is quite different; the ON. word means 'those' or 'they', distinct from *þesser, -ar* 'these'; while *thir* has been from the beginning emphatically 'these', as distinct from *þā, þās* 'those'. The explanation 'the here', 'those here' suits the sense; but (1) no trace has been found of these in an uncombined form; and (2) the addition of *here* to a demonstrative, common in the midlands and south of England (see Here 1 d), is not known as a northern idiom.]

Thir, obs. unstressed form of Their.

Third (þǝ̄ɹd), *a.* (*adv.*), *sb.* Forms: see below. [OE. *þridda, -e, þird(d)a, -e*, Comm. Teut. and Indo-Eur.; = OFris. *thredda*, OS. *thriddio* (MLG. *drudde, derde*, Du. *derde*), OHG. *dritto* (MHG., G. *dritte*), ON. *þriðe, -i* (Sw. *tredje*, Da. *tredie*), Goth. *þridja*, :—OTeut. **þridjó-*, :—Indo-Eur. **tritjó's*: cf. Gr. τρίτος, L. *tertius*, Skr. *trtī́yas*.

The metathesis of *third* for *thrid* appears already in ONorthumb. c 950, but *thrid* was the prevalent type down to the 16th c.]

A. Illustration of Forms.

α. 1 (3) **þridda,** 2–5 **þridde,** 3 **þride,** 4 **þryd(e, threid, þred,** 4–5 **thrydde, thride, þrid, thridd,** 4–6 **thridde, thryd, thredde,** 4–7 **thred,** 4–6, *Sc.* –8 **thrid,** 5 **thryde, thrudde,** (**tryd**).

a 800 Cynewulf *Christ* 726 Wæs se þridda hlyp. c 1000 *Sax. Leechd.* II. 298 Þridde mæʒen is. c 1200 Ormin Ded. 6 Broþerr min i Godess hus, ȝet o þe þride [*elsewhere* þridde] wise. c 1250 *Gen. & Ex.* 3516 Ðe ðridde moneð in is cumen. a 1300 *Cursor M.* 8471 (Cott.) Þe thride boke efter þa tua. *Ibid.* 16892 To rise þe thrid [*Gött.* thred] dai. *Ibid.* 18646 To þe thrid [*G.* threid] morn. 13.. *E. E. Allit. P.* B. 300 The lolef lapheth watz gendered þe þryd. 1382 Wyclif *Acts* xx. 9 He ledd by sleep fel down fro the thridde stage. c 1450 *Two Cookery-bks.* 113 (Laud MS.) Ye thrudde perty shal be sugar. 1588 A. King tr. *Canisius' Catech.* Kalendar 1 Feb., S. Ignatius bischop of Antioch threid efter S. Peter. 1606 *Sc. Acts Jas. VI* (1816) IV. 279/2 The thrid day of this instant. c 1730 Thrid [see B. I. 1].

β. 1 (*Northumb.*) **ðirda, ðirdda,** 2 **þerdde,** 4 **þirde,** 5–6 **thyrd(e,** 5–7 **thirde,** 6 **theyrd, thurd,** 5– **third.**

c 950 *Lindisf. Gosp.* Luke xii. 38 ʒif on ða ðirdda wacan ʒe-cymeð. a 1200 *Moral Ode* 138 (Lamb. MS.) Nolde he for al middeneard þe þerdde [*v.r.* þridde] [dei] þer abiden. 1393 Langl. *P. Pl.* C. XXII. 264 And matheu þe þirde. 1446 Lydg. *Nightingale Poems* I. 299 Ye that are in the third age Of your lyfe ande passed morow & prime. 1473 Warkw. *Chron.* (Camden) 3 In the thyrde ȝere of the reygne of Kynge Edwarde. 1552 Huloet, Thyrde fayre or market proclaymed.

B. Signification. **I.** *adj.*

As with other ordinals, usually *the third*: see The *def. art.* B. 18.

1. The ordinal numeral corresponding to the cardinal three: last of three; that comes next after the second. **a.** with sb. expressed.

a 800 [see A. α]. 971 *Blickl. Hom.* 15 Þy þriddan dæʒe he of deaþe ariseþ. a 1225 *Ancr. R.* 14 Þe þridde dole. 1340 Hampole *Pr. Consc.* 1664 Here bigynnes þe thred part. 1497 *Naval Acc. Hen. VII* (1896) 141 The thyrde day of Marche. 1533 Bellenden *Livy* III. xi. (S.T.S.) I. 292 To be haldin þe thrid day eftir þe nundinis. 1552 Huloet, Thyrde sillable, *ante penultima*. 1597 A. M. tr. *Guillemeau's Fr. Chirurg.* 30/1 The finger called *Medicus*, or thirde finger. c 1730 Burt *Lett. N. Scotl.* (1818) I. 20 Inquire for such a launde.., where the gentleman stayd, at the thrid stair, that is three stories high. 1847 Helps *Friends in C.* I. vi. 92, I prefer real life..where there is no third volume [as in a novel] to make things straight.

b. Following the names of sovereigns, popes, etc.: cf. Second A. 1 b. 1414 *Rolls of Parlt.* IV. 59/2 Kyng Henry the Thridde. 1550 Bale *K. Johan* (Camden) 42 Pope Innocent the thred. 1735 Johnson *Lobo's Abyssinia, Descr.* v. 73 King John the Third [of Portugal].

c. with sb. understood. c 950 *Lindisf. Gosp.* Matt. xxii. 26 ʒelic ðe æftera..& ðe ðirda [*Rushw.* þridde]. c 1175 *Lamb. Hom.* 133 Ðreo þing.. þet oðer is goddes word and þet ðridde is weldede. a 1300 *Cursor M.* 358 (Cott.) Þe thrid es air, and fir þe ferth. 1382 Wyclif *Dan.* v. 7 Shal be the thrid in my rewme. c 1440 *Gesta Rom.* xv. 51 (Harl. MS.) And so he wrote to the thrid, þat seid she lovid him. 1552–3 *Inv. Ch. Goods, Staffs.* in *Ann. Lichfield* (1863) IV. 70, iij vestements, one of whyte fustian, another of blacke chamblet, & the thryd of blewe sarsynet. 1662 Playford *Skill Mus.* II. (1674) 92 Six strings,..the first ..is called the Treble; the second, the Small Mean; the third, the Great Mean. 1821 Scott *Kenilw.* xxxviii, 'Hush! thou knave!' said a third; 'how know'st thou who may be within hearing?'

d. *Gram.* In *third person*: see Person *sb.* 8. Also in *third declension, conjugation*, and in names of tenses, as *third future, preterite*, where the reference is to a conventional order of enumeration adopted by grammarians. 1530 Palsgr. 93 In verbes of theyr thyrde conjugation I fynde a litell more difficultie. a 1586 Sidney *Arcadia* II. (Sommer) 137 He had..forgotten in speaking of him selfe to vse the third person. 1764 W. Primatt *Accentus Rediv.* 111 Provided they were third persons plural. 1848 J. T. White *Xenophon's Anab.* II. iv. § 5 Notes (1872) 116 Sometimes..the third future is used, instead of the common future, to point out more forcibly all but immediate occurrence of some future action. 1857 Williams *Sanskrit Gram.* § 415 Fortunately..the third preterite occurs but rarely in the better specimens of Hindū composition.

2. Additional to and distinct from two others already known or mentioned. *Third person* (in *Law*) = Third party. †*Third place*, a place which is neutral ground to two persons (*obs.*). c 1290 *Beket* 415 in *S. Eng. Leg.* I. 118 Þat þridde þing ȝeot mest of alle and sonest in wraþþe hem brouȝte. c 1400 *Apol. Loll.* 3 And þe þrid, if he be moost obedient to God and to His lawe. 1579 W. Wilkinson *Confut. Familye of Loue* 17 b, Incorporall and immateriall essences cannot be coupled in the same third matter. 1709 E. Ward tr. *Cervantes* 189 Any thing is easily believ'd that is to the Disreputation of a third Person. 1757 Chesterf. *Lett.* 31 Dec., I could neither visit, nor be visited by, the Ministers of those two Crowns: but we met every day, or dined at third places. 1818 Cruise *Digest* (ed. 2) I. 444 The clause.. extends..to third persons only; not to the persons conveying, or to those to whom lands are conveyed to uses. 1865 Kingsley *Herew.* xvii, Martin Lightfoot..was as a third hand and foot to him all day long. 1878 Stewart & Tait *Unseen Univ.* iv. § 122. 133 There can be no third thing besides body and void. [*Cf.* Tertium quid.]

†**b.** *Third tongue*, a backbiter; a slanderer. Used by Wyclif and Coverdale to render *lingua tertia* of the Vulgate, in LXX. γλῶσσα τρίτη. *Obs.* 1382 Wyclif *Ecclus.* xxviii. 16 The thridde tunge manye men stirede. 1388 *Ibid.* 19 *margin*, The tunge of the preuey bacbiter is clepid the thridde tunge..and the bacbiter him silf hath the thridde tunge, for he, as the thridde, makith debate betwen a man and his neiȝbore. 1535 Coverdale *Ecclus.* xxviii. 14–15 The thirde tonge hath disquieted many one, and dryuen them from one londe to another...The thirde tonge hath cast out many an honest woman, and robbed them of their labours.

3. *Third part* = B. II. 1. Now *rare*: see Part *sb.* 5. a 1300 *Cursor M.* 973 (Cott.) Þe half parte gladli or þe thrid We wil þe giue. 1375 Barbour *Bruce* II. 305 Þe thrid part went to þe forray. 1483 *Cath. Angl.* 385/2 Þe Thryd parte of a halpeny, *trissis*. 1570–6 Lambarde *Peramb. Kent* 228 The Monkes should enioy the whole tongue, and two third partes of the rest of the body. 1611 Bible *Rev.* viii. 8 The third part of the sea became blood.

4. The last of each successive group of three; one in every three, i.e. one third of the whole. *Third penny*: one third of the whole sum; *spec.* (see quot. 1706). *Third sheaf and teind*: see *third and teind*, II. 1. c 1400 Maundev. (Roxb.) xix. 87 Sum..at ilke a thridd passe knelis doune apon þe erthe. 1423 *Cal. Letter Bk. I. Lond.* (1909) 295 Have he, for his labour, the tryd peny that shal be recovered. a 1578 Lindesay (Pitscottie) *Chron. Scot.* (S.T.S.) II. 315 Thair come in be sie sa meikill victuallis that it come downe the thrid penny. 1597 [see Every 1 e (c)]. 1627 *Rep. Parishes Scott.* (Bann. Cl.) 3 Ten landis..payis presentlie the thrid scheiff and teind led. 1706 Phillips (ed. Kersey), *Third-penny*, the third part of Fines and Profits, arising from Law-Processes, which in every County was heretofore allow'd to the Sheriff; the other two Parts being appointed for the King's Use. 1727 Swift *Poisoning E. Curll* Wks. 1755 III. I. 152 You shall have your third share of the Court poems. 1904 [see Quartan A. 1, def.].

b. *Third-day ague*, tertian ague. 1817–18 Cobbett *Resid. U. S.* (1822) 319 You would frighten him into a third-day ague.

5. Combinations, collocations, or phrases with special meaning (some of which may be used *attrib.* or as *adj.*), as *third base, cousin, cousinship, degree, form* (hence *third-former*), *heir, magnitude, person, story, term* (hence *third-termery*): see the sbs.; **third ague,** tertian ague; **third best,** third in point of quality, that is next inferior to the Second best; **third-day,** the Quaker name for Tuesday, as being the third day of the week; **third estate,** the Commons: see Estate *sb.* 6; **third floor,** (*a*) in England, the floor or story of a building separated by two from the ground floor; (*b*) in *Sc., U. S.*, etc., the third story, counting the ground floor as the first; **third hour,** (*a*) among the Jews, the third of the twelve equal divisions of time between morning and evening; the hour between 8 and 9 a.m.; (*b*) in *R.C.Ch.*, the hour of Tierce; **third house,** (*U.S. polit. slang*): see quot.; **third man,** *Cricket*, a fielder placed between point and short slip, but further out; an additional short slip; also, the position occupied by him; **third order:** see Tertiary A. 5; **third penny:** see 4 above; †**third place:** see 2 above; **third point,** *Arch.* = Tierce *point*: see quot.; **third rail,** in some systems of electric railways, an additional rail which conveys the current; **third rime, rhyme,** = Terza rima; **third season man,** = *third year man*; **third staff,** = *third stave*; †**third state,** = *third estate*; **third stave:** see quot.; †**third tongue:** see 2 b above; **third ventricle,** that portion of the central cavity of the brain that lies between the optic thalami; **third year man,** a student who has entered upon the third (often the last) year of a course of study.

1674 N. Fairfax *Bulk & Selv.* 131 In the very fit of a *Third Ague. 1375 Barbour *Bruce* XIII. 321 He was the *thrid best knycht, perfay, That men wist liffand in his day. 1859 *Habits Gd. Soc.* iii. 155, I am wondering whether everybody arranges his wardrobe as our ungrammatical nurses used to do ours, under the heads of 'best, second-best, third-best', and so on. 1902 *Daily News* 31 Jan. 7/3 The *third-cousinships of German Princes. 1677 in Penn *Trav. Holland* (1694) 9 A Monthly Meeting..upon the third *third day of the Month. 1901 *Scotsman* 5 Apr. 6/4 In the *third degree in [Free] Masonry a skull and cross-bones are employed. 1604 in Rymer *Fœdera* XVI. 562/1 Knightes and Burgesses..doe present the Bodie of the *Thirde Estate. 1855 F. B. Wells tr. *Thierry* (*title*), The Formation and Progress of the Tiers État, or Third Estate in France. 1875 Stubbs *Const. Hist.* II. xv. 185 That portion of the third estate which was represented by the knights of the shire. 1908 *Daily Chron.* 14 Aug. 8/6 Immediately after the arrival of the 'third-floor-back lodger a transformation takes place. 1687 Settle *Refl. Dryden* 63 So old a Phrase,..that it has been in twenty *third-Form School-Boys Exercises. 1869 Blackmore *Lorna D.* ii, A *third-former nearly six feet high. c 1400 26 *Pol. Poems* xxvi. 208 Men seyen 'good geten vnrewely, The 'iij^{de} eyre browke hit ne may'. 1484 Caxton *Fables of Avian* xviii, Of the thynge wrongfully and euylle goten, the thyrd heyre shalle neuer be possessour of hit. 1382 Wyclif *Acts* ii. 15 It is the *thridde our of the day. 1706 tr. *Dupin's Eccl. Hist.* 16th C. II. v. 43 Called Tierce, because it began at the Third Hour of the day. 1889 Farmer *Dict. Amer.* s.v. *Lobby*, The lobby is also called the '*Third House'. 1905 *Westm. Gaz.* 13 Feb. 10/1 In the constellation of the Twins, near the *third-magnitude star Mu. 1871 Hoppe, **Third man*, einer der *fielders* im Cricket. 1881 *Standard* 14 June 3/8 The catch that dismissed him was an easy one at third man. 1891 W. G. Grace *Cricket* 260 Third man must ask the bowler whether he should stand rather fine or square. 1629 Wadsworth *Pilgr.* vii. 72 There is besides another Nunnery of the *third Order of St. Francis. 1753 Challoner *Cath. Chr. Instr.* 184 Besides these there are the..Nuns of the third Order of St. Francis. 1908 *Westm. Gaz.* 24 Dec. 6/3 The..version of the Rule of the Third Order found..in the Capistran Convent in the Abruzzi. 1727–41 Chambers *Cycl.*, **Third Point*, or *Tierce-point*, in architecture, the point of section in the vertex of an equilateral triangle. Arches or vaults of the third point..are those consisting of two arches of a circle, meeting in an angle a-top. 1901 *Westm. Gaz.* 23 July 4/3 A new electric railway..built on the '*third rail' system, which is believed to represent a great economy as compared with the overhead system. 1905 *Daily Chron.* 2 Feb. 3/4 Avoiding the dangers which had been experienced with the third-rail system. 1656 H. Phillips *Purch. Patt.* (1676) A iv b, An house of the *third rate. 1820 Byron *Let. to Murray* Wks. (1846) 505/1 You will find ..in *third rhyme (*terza rima*),..Fanny of Rimini. a 1860 Alb. Smith *Lond. Med. Stud.* (1861) 17 His mentor is ready in the shape of a *third-season man. 1667 E. Chamberlayne *Pres. St. Eng.* I. xix. (1684) 322 Of the *Third State, or Commons of England. 1898 Stainer & Barrett *Dict. Mus. Terms*, **Third Stave*, a name given to the stave upon which pedal music is written for the organ. 1679 Moxon *Mech. Exerc.* vii. 130 Your Ground-plot, or second or *third Story. 1890 *Cincinnati Commerc. Gaz.* 30 June, There would be no *third termery in it, as he [Pres. Cleveland] had not two consecutive terms.

II. *sb.*

1. A third part (B. I. 3) *of* anything; any one of three equal parts into which a whole may be divided.

Third and teind, one-third of the produce and one-tenth of the remainder (making two-fifths of the whole) paid as rent.

1382 Wyclif 1 *Macc.* x. 29 Nowe Y assoile ȝou..of tributis, and I forȝeue to ȝou the pricis of salt, and forȝeue crownys, and the thriddis [1388 thridde part] of seed. 1479 *Act. Dom. Conc.* (1839) 32/2 Þat þe schiref..deliuer þe said vmfra & his tennandis ane evinly thrid þarof. 1611 Shaks. *Cymb.* v. iv. 19 Men, Who of their broken Debtors take a third, A sixth, a tenth, letting them thriue againe. 1705 Addison *Italy* 136 No Sentence can stand that is not confirm'd by Two Thirds of this Council. 1799 J. Robertson *Agric. Perth* 139 In most parts of Strathallan, the land is kept in thirds, (i.e.) one third in tillage for three year, and two thirds always grass. 1852 R. F. Burton *Falconry in Vall. Indus* vi. 71 One will require at least a third more breaking than another. 1884 J. Tait in *U. P. Mag.* Apr. 156 The Master was to have the third and teind shorn and set up. 1893 *Law Times* XCIV. 504/1 Whether such a gift..would be divisible into moieties or thirds.

2. *Law.* (Mostly *pl.*) The third of the personal property of a deceased husband allowed to his widow. Also, the third of his real property to which his widow might be legally entitled for her life (*obs.* exc. *Hist.*). Cf. Terce 2. 1396 in *Scott. Antiq.* XIV. 318 Swa mykyl as pertenys to the modyr of the forsaid Erle..be resone of hir thryd. 1540 *Test. Ebor.* (Surtees) VI. 106 She [the wife] to be fullie content with hir thirds. 1596 Bacon *Use of Law* Wks. 1879 I. 585/1 By this course of putting lands into use there were many inconveniences, as..The wife was defrauded of her thirds; the husband of being tenant by courtesy [etc.]. 1609 Skene *Reg. Maj.* I. 113. 1636 in *Crt. & Times Chas. I* (1848) II. 239 Having renounced her jointure and thirds, she may be so utterly undone. 1664 *Early Rec. Groton, Mass.* (1880) 145 Vnto which alienation the wiues of them both doe giue their consent to the giuing vp their thirds. 1709 S. Sewall *Diary* 18 Nov., 30*l.* more to Grace, and 12. to her Brother, to come out of their Mothers Thirds now to be divided. 1767 [see Dower *sb.*[2] 1]. 1864 Thoreau *Maine W.* (1894) 207 There you are never reminded that the wilderness which you are threading is, after all, some villager's familiar wood-lot, some widow's thirds.

†**3.** A third of the proceeds of captures, or of certain fines, forfeitures, etc., of which two thirds were due to the king. *Obs.*

1429 in Rymer *Fœdera* X. 422 Eny Thriddes, or other Gaines of Werre. 1444 in *Coll. Hist. Staff.* (1891) XII. 319 The thrides of the thrides of all maner Prisoners, Prises, and wynynges. 1627 in *Crt. & Times Chas. I* (1848) I. 234 A commission to proceed against recusants for their thirds due to his majesty by law.

4. *Sc. Eccl. Hist.* See quot. 1838. 1573 *Satir. Poems Reform.* xlii. 812 Thir thriddis, I say, but stopping ony, The Kirkis Collectouris suld vptane, Syne vnto the Excheker gane. c 1575 *Balfour's Practicks* (1754) 143 The teindis, landis, maillis, fermis, and dewteis of landis assumit in the thriddis of benefices. 1586 in *Dunfermline Regr.* (Bann. Cl.) 449 The haill prelaceis of our realme ar bund and obleissit to warrand their thridis to ws fra thair awin deidis. 1838 W. Bell *Dict. Law Scot.*, *Thirds*...Before the annexation of the year 1587, the King, in order to prevent the entire abstraction of their provisions from the acting clergy,..assumed into his own hands a third of the revenues of all ecclesiastical benefices, which he intrusted to the Commissioners of Plat, who assigned to the ministers respectively sufficient provisions, and reserved the remainder for the King. [See Plat *sb.*[3] 6.]

†**5.** *pl.* The sum paid by an incoming freshman for the furniture, etc. of his college rooms, usually assessed at two thirds of the amount paid by the preceding tenant. *Obs.* 1687 Wilding in *Collect.* (O. H. S.) I. 255 Reced of my Chum for thirds. 1826 C. Wordsworth *Let.* in *Ann. Early Life* I. 38 Tell my father that I expect he will hear something about 'the thirds' which we pay for furniture, &c. 1853 'C. Bede' *Verdant Green* I. iv, Mr. Filcher then explained the system of thirds, by which the furniture..was to be paid for. 1858 Hogg *Shelley* I. 69 Transferring the.. movables to the successor on payment of thirds, that is, of two-thirds of the price last given.

6. *Mus.* A note three diatonic degrees above or below a given note (both notes being reckoned); also (usually) the interval between this and the given note, equivalent either to two tones (*major third*), or to one tone and one diatonic semitone (*minor third*); also, the harmonic combination of two such notes.

Diminished third, an interval equal to two diatonic semitones, being less by a chromatic semitone than a minor third.

1597 Morley *Introd. Mus.* 70 Which distances make a Concord or consonant Harmony? ..A third, a Fift, a Sixt, and an eight. 1662 Playford *Skill Mus.* I. v. (1674) 20 You will tune from Sol to Mi which is a Third. 1752 tr. *Rameau's Treat. Musick* 34 Those Notes, which are a Third above, are deemed Thirds. 1855 Browning *Toccata of Galuppi's* vii, Those lesser thirds so plaintive. 1855 — *Lovers' Quarrel* xviii, We shall have the word In a minor third There is none but the cuckoo knows. 1884 Parry in Grove *Dict. Mus.* IV. 102 *Third*, one of the most important intervals in modern music...Three forms are met with in modern music—major, minor, and diminished.

7. The third of the subdivisions of any standard measure or dimension which is successively subdivided in a constant ratio; the subdivision next below seconds: see Prime *sb.*[2] 2. †Formerly, in Scotland, a weight of account = the 13,824th part $(1 \div 24^3)$ of a grain (*obs.*). 1594 J. Davis *Seaman's Secr.* (1643) D j b, Euery degree.. doth containe 60 minutes, and euery minute 60 seconds, and euery second 60 thirds, &c. 1604 in Moryson *Itin.* I. (1617) 282 (Table of Scottish Weights of Coins, xx. s. [sterling] = 06 pennyweights, 10 graines, 16 mites, 18 droits, 10 periots, English Weight; 07 deniers, 21 graines, 07 primes, 01 seconds, 09 thirds, 19 fourths, Scottish Weight. 1694 Holder *On Time* ii. 32 To divide..an Hour into 60' (Minutes), a Minute into 60'' (Second Minutes), a Second Minute into 60''' (Thirds). 1840 Lardner *Geom.* 56 This system of division is sometimes carried even further, a second being divided into sixty equal parts called thirds; but it is more usual to express small angles or arcs in decimal parts of a second.

†**b.** In decimal fractions: see quots. *Obs.* 1660 J. Moore *Arith.* 10 Some call their Tenth part Primes, the Hundereth parts Seconds, the 1000 parts Thirds. 1766 Hutton *School Master's Guide* 55 The 1st, 2d, 3d, 4th, &c. places of decimals..are denominated the places of primes, seconds, thirds, and fourths, &c. respectively.

8. *Comm. pl.* Goods of the third degree of quality. 1823 J. Badcock *Dom. Amusem.* 163 Flour or bread,..of the usual London manufacture, as *seconds, thirds*, and *browns*. 1832 G. R. Porter *Porcelain & Gl.* 186 Crown glass is sold, according to its quality, under four different denominations —firsts, seconds, thirds, and fourths. 1888 *Times* (weekly ed.) 14 Sept. 19/1 Fruit should be sorted into bests and seconds and in some cases into thirds. 1903 *Daily Chron.* 21 Apr. 2/6 Cork butter.—Firsts, 86s.; seconds, 80s.; thirds, 78s.

9. Elliptical uses of the adj. passing into sb.

a. *Third of kin* (*Sc.*): one related in the third degree of consanguinity. 1535 Stewart *Cron. Scot.* (Rolls) III. 260 The erle of Arrane, lord of Hammiltoun, Evin thrid and thrid to him [that] weiris the croun. 1569 *Reg. Privy Council Scot.* II. 39 The said Erll and the said umquhile Johnne Suthirland quha wes slane thrid and ferdis of kin [the Earl's father was cousin to John's grandmother]. 1583 *Ibid.* III. 622 Quha and he ar secundes and thriddes of kin. 1892 G. Stewart *Shetland Fireside T.* ix. (ed. 2) 71 Auld Ibbie Bartley, dat wis trids o' kin to my wife's foster midder, an' her oey.

b. Elliptical for third person (in Grammar); third day (of the month); third chapter (of a book of the Bible); third year (of a reign). 1530 Palsgr. Introd. 33 The thyrde syngular [endeth].. most commenly in T. 1536 Cromwell in Merriman *Life & Lett.* (1902) II. 1 From Eltham thridde of Janua[ry]. 1539 Tonstall *Serm. Palm Sund.* (1823) 86 It is written in the thirde of Matthewe. 1747 *Gentl. Mag.* May 247/1 On Sunday the 3d of May. 1857 Williams *Sanskrit Gram.* § 330 It is the only conjugation that rejects the nasal in the 3d. plur.

c. A card of the third size; also *thirds card*: see quots. 1891 *Cent. Dict.* s.v., *Thirds card*, a card 1½ by 3 inches, the size most used for a man's visiting-card. (Eng.). 1892 *Chiswick Press Calendar*, Sizes of Cards..Extra Thirds 3 × 1½. Thirds 3 × 1⅛ in.

d. *Third of exchange*: the last of a set of three bills of exchange of even tenor and date: see Exchange *sb.* 5.

e. Generally, the word omitted being usually obvious from the context; esp. in familiar use. a 1635 Sibbes *Confer. Christ & Mary* (1656) 104 He must be a friend or enemy; there is no third in God. 1859 *Habits Gd. Soc.* (new ed.) 44 In the third [class railway-carriage] he will have to sit next to an odoriferous ploughboy. 1864 Bowen *Logic* iii. 49 The Axiom which is usually called the Law of Excluded Third. 1889 Linskill *Golf* iii. (1895) 15 Odd No. 1. 'Stroke a hole'...Sometimes a 'third' is given, which means the application of Odd No. 1 at every third hole. 1891 *Cent. Dict.*, *Third*...In *base-ball*, same as *third base*. 1900 *Monthly Rev.* I. 46 The Russian peasant who travels third is not accustomed to luxuries. 1903 *Westm. Gaz.* 30 Dec. 11/1 It is of course the Third Preference stock which is directly affected...Some operators are anticipating that the Thirds will get a half per cent. more than for last year. *Mod.* Mr. A. did badly; he only got a third in Greats.

Third, *v.* [f. prec.]

1. *trans.* To divide (anything) into three equal parts; to reduce to one third of the number or bulk. 1455 *Sc. Acts Jas. II* (1814) II. 44/2 Þ^t na man gang away w^t na maner of gudis quhill it be thriddyt, and partyt befor þe chiftane. 1612 *Two Noble K.* I. ii, What man Thirds his owne worth? 1747 Franklin *Lett.* Wks. 1887 II. 97 That celerity doubled, tripled, &c., or halved, thirded, &c. 1874 Furnivall in *10th Rep. Committee E. E. T. S.* 16 Such a course would have halved or thirded the number of our subscribers.

†**b.** To buy or sell (college furniture, etc.) at two thirds of its last selling price: see Third *sb.* 5. *Obs.* 1811 [R. Fenton] *Tour Genealogy* 157 The same..tale..is always worse told by him that tells it last; till like college furniture, too often thirded, it becomes too threadbare for credit.

2. To speak in favour of (a motion, proposition, etc.) as third speaker; to support the seconder. 1656 *Burton's Diary* (1828) I. 90 It has been firsted, seconded, and thirded. 1707 Luttrell *Brief Rel.* (1857) VI. 233 A motion of the lord Wharton, seconded and thirded by the lords Somers and Hallifax. 1893 E. H. Baker in *King's Business* (New Haven, Conn.) 174 That resolution ..was seconded by a theological professor...It was thirded by a pastor in the Episcopal Church.

†**b.** To support or back up in the third place: cf. Second *v.* 2. *Obs.* 1602 Carew *Cornwall* 84 b, The next Captains should forthwith put themselves with their companies into their assigned sea coast townes, whom the adjoyning land-forces were appoynted to second and third.

†**3.** To hoe (turnips), clean (wheat), etc., the third time. *Obs.* 1683 J. Erskine *Jrnl.* 20 Sept. (1893) 17, I was winding and thirding some corn. 18.. *Moor's Suffolk MS.* (Halliw.), 'Ar them there tahnups done woth?' 'No, we are thirding 'em.'

Thi·rdborough, thi·rdborrow. *Obs.* exc. *Hist.* Also 5–6 (7–8) thrid-, 6 thred-, thur-, thar-, 6–7 therd-; 5 -borro, 6 -bourogh(e, -borow(e, 6–7 -barow(e, -barrow, 7 -borrow, -bearer. [In 15th c. *thridborro*, 16th c. *thridborowe*, later *third-borow*; and with both elements variously corrupted. Early evidence of origin scanty; but, as pointed out by Professor Skeat, prob. a ME. corruption of *fridborgh* :—OE. *friðborg* peace-pledge, peace-surety: see Frithborh, Frank-pledge. The corruption may have been due to Norman scribes, but not necessarily so: cf. Th (6). See Note below, and cf. Borrowhead, Borsholder, Headborough.]

Formerly, The head man of a frithborh or frank-pledge; hence, the conservator of peace or peace-officer of a tithing, the petty constable of a township or manor.

? c 1475 *Hunt. Hare* 199 Jac of Bonam he was constabull. ..Hobb Andrw he was thridborro; He bad hom, 'Pesse! God gyff hom sorro! For I may arrest yow best'. 1512 *Act 4 Hen. VIII*, c. 19 § 6 Preceptes to the Constables Hedbouroghes Thirdbouroghes Subconstables Tythingmen Borsalders. 1523 Fitzherb. *Surv.* 20 b, The othe of all maner of Offycers generally...I shall true constable be, trewe thridborowe, trewe reue, trewe frankelege [etc.]..and truely and duely do and kepe all thynges that belongeth to myne offyce to do. 1536 *Act 28 Hen. VIII*, c. 10 § 6 Euery ..Hedborowe, Thredborough, Borsolder, and euery other Lay Officer. 1547 in J. H. Glover *Kingsthorpiana* (1883) 84 If any customery tenant or suter..do rebuke, revyle, or dysobey the constables, thurbarowes, ale-tasters, haywarde, or other officers sworne in doyinge their offyce. 1581 Lambarde *Eiren.* I. iii. (1588) 15 Where each third Borow only hath a Constable, there the officers of the other two Borowes, be called Third-borowes. 1588 Shaks. *L. L. L.* I. i. 185, I my selfe reprehend his owne person, for I am his graces Tharborough. 1596 — *Tam. Shr.* Induct. i. 12 *Host.* I know my remedie, I must go fetch the Head-borough. *Beg.* Third, or fourth, or fift Borough, Ile answere him by Law. 1607 Cowell *Interpr.*, *Thridborow*, is vsed for a constable..which seemeth to be corruptly vsed for the Saxon *freoborh* i. *ingenuus fideiussor*. 1610 Norden *Spec. Brit., Cornw.* (1728) 30 The hundreds haue Constables, Tythinges haue Therd-barows, in some places Hedborows, in some Borowsheds, and in the weste partes a tythingman. a 1625 Sir H. Finch *Law* (1636) 336 The conseruator of peace..is called..In a Tything, a petie Constable, Borsholder, Headborough, Thirdborough, Boroughhead, Tything-man, or Chiefe pledge. 1634–5 *Althorp MS.* in Simpkinson *Washingtons* (1860) App. p. lxix, March 5. To the third bearers of Brington for cryeing and prayseing a baye straye nagg taken up. 1645 *MS. Rec. Court Leet Castle Donington, Leicester.* 25 Apr., They present R. R., J. B., R. W. and T. T. to serve the kinge and the lord of this mannor in the office of Thirdborrow for one whole year which they refused. 1658 Phillips, *Thridborough* or *Thirdborough*, a word used in some old Acts, for a Headborough or Constable. 1755 Johnson, *Thirdborough*,.. an under-constable. 1831 Carlyle *Sart. Res.* III. i, Some prospect of..an honourable Mastership in Cordwainery, and perhaps the post of Thirdborough in his Hundred.

[*Note.* The *fribborh* or *frithborgh* was orig. the 'association of ten men in common responsibility' to prevent crime and breach of the peace. In ME. legal use the word was worn down to *fridborgh, friborg*, and *freoborg*, and, the first element being associated with *freo* 'free', was rendered in Anglo-Fr. *frank plege*, Anglo-L. *francum plegium*. The head man of the frithborh was in the 12th c. called *fridborges heved* or *frithborges heved*, 'head of the frithborh' (*Laws of Edw. Conf.* 20 (or 19), § 3), and was later known as *bor(r)ewhead, head-bor(o)ugh, bor(h)s-holder*, and *burrow-elder* (:—**borh-ealdor*), also in Anglo-L. *plegius capitalis* 'head or chief pledge'. In Fleta I. xlvii. § 10, it is said, 'frithborgh [*printed* frich-] est laudabilis homo astrarius testimonii... per quem omnes iuxta ipsum commorantes firmiori pace sustententur sub stabilitate fideiussionis eius vel alterius per denarium numerum, unde quilibet est quasi plegius alterius'. In this we see the transition of *frithborh* from the association to its individual members, and esp. to the headborough. In certain cases the latter acted with two of his fellows, 'duos de melioribus suorum frithborgorum' (*Laws of Edw.* 20 (or 19), § 3), and this association of three may have contributed to the change of name from *fridborgh* to *thridborgh* and *thirdborough*. The probable connexion of *thridborow* with *freoborh* was suggested by Cowell: see quot. 1607.]

Third class, third-class, *phr.* (*sb.* and *a.*)

1. *sb. phr.* The class next below the second; esp. of railway carriages; also in an examination list; hence, a place in the third class in an examination. 1845 *Bradshaw's Railway Guide* Aug. 5 Fares between London and Brighton..by..third class, 5*s.* *Mod.* Mr. A. got a third class in History.

2. *attrib.* or *adj.* Of or belonging to the class next below the second. 1839 *Bradshaw's Railway Time Table* 19 Oct., Children under seven years of age..for Second Class Carriages [charged] Third Class price. 1840 *Bradshaw's Railway Comp.*, Third class passengers are conveyed by the 6 a.m. and 8 p.m. Down Trains. 1852 R. S. Surtees *Sponge's Sp. Tour* (1893) 76 The introduction of railways, whose worst third-class accommodation is far better than the old coaches' best. 1859 *All Year Round* No. 30. 78 The third-class carriages, as a rule, were the mere seatless and unsheltered cattle-trucks that still linger on the road from London to Greenwich. 1871 M. Collins *Marq. & Merch.* III. iv. 127 The train was third class. 1886 C. E. Pascoe *London of To-day* xix. (ed. 3) 186 The economical traveller will find many a worse resting-place than its third-class carriages provide. 1891 *Cent. Dict.*, *Third-class matter*, in the postal system of the United States, printed matter other than newspapers or periodicals, sent through the mails by the publishers.

3. quasi-*adv.* By a third-class conveyance. 1864 Trevelyan *Compet. Wallah* (1866) 24 Natives almost invariably travel third-class.

†**Thirdel.** *Obs.* Forms: 3 thriddedel, 4 þridde deel, 5 thryddele, 6 thirdle, thirdel. [ME. *thriddedel* :—OE. *þridda dǣl* third part: see Deal *sb.*[1] Cf. Ger. *drittel*.] A third part (*of* anything); = next. 1297 R. Glouc. (Rolls) 283 Þe þriddedel mi kinedom ich ȝiue þe to be mi fere. 1387 Trevisa *Higden* (Rolls) III. 169 Þe quene hadde i-sent hire ȝong sone wiþ þe þridde deel [*MS. β.* thriddel, Caxton thryddele] of heere oost aȝenst Cirus. 1542 Recorde *Gr. Artes* K vj b, There bee tertians (that is to say thirdles) of pypes, of hogges heddes, and of barels. *Ibid.* L iij, Take awaye 2 thyrdeles frome any summe, and you muste needes graunt, that that whyche remayneth, is 1 thyrdele of the summe laste before.

†**Thi·rdendeal.** *Obs.* Forms: 1 **þriddan dǣl;** 4 **þridden-,** 4–5 **thridden-,** 5 **threden-, thredden-, thryden-, thyrdyn-,** 6 **thirdin-, thyrden-,** (**thirding-,** 7 **thurron-**), 6–8 **thirden-;** 4–5 **-del,** 5–7 **-dele,** 6 **-deale, deall,** 7 **-dell,** 7–8 **-deal;** 4–6 (9 *dial.*) **-dale.** [OE. (*þone*) *þriddan dǣl*, accus. case of (*se*) *þridda dǣl* the third part (see Thirdel, Deal *sb.*[1], Dale [2]). Cf. Halfendeal, Farthingdeal.]

1. The third part of anything; a third. c 1000 *Sax. Leechd.* I. 98 Seoþe on wætere to þriddan dæle. *Ibid.* II. 120 Bewyl oþ þriddan dæl. 13.. *Guy Warw.* (A.) 7306+st. 65 Þriddendel his lond haue he schold. 14.. *E. E. Misc.* (Warton Cl.) 72 With the thyrdyndele of gume, and twyse so myche of water. a 1500 in Arnolde *Chron.* (1811) 147 Euery Sonday a soule out of purgatory and the thredden dele of al synnes relesed. 1558 Warde tr. *Alexis' Secr.* I. I. (1580) 37 b, Drinke thereof two thirdendales of a glassefull. 1581 J. Bell *Haddon's Answ. Osor.* 459 b, A thyrdendeale of the Crowne of Thornes is shewed at Paris in the Holy Chappell there.

2. A third of a tun; = Tertian B. 2. 1423 *Rolls of Parlt.* IV. 256/1 Thredendels and hoggeshedes so aftur lesse mesure. 14.. *MS. Cantab.* Ff. 5. 48, lf. 55 b (Hartshorne *Anc. Metr. T.* (1829) 54), Hit holdis a gode thrydendele Ful of wyne euery mele.

3. (See quots.)

†3. *spec.* (*ellipt.*). The type of thirty years (of age, old, etc.).

Thirty-day, *Obs.* A commemoration of a deceased person thirty days after his death.

Thirtyfold, *a.* (*adv.*) [See -FOLD.] Thirty times as great or as much; increased thirty times.

Thirty-one. The name of a game (or games) of cards.

Thirty-two.

1. The abstract number; also, a symbol representing this. So *thirty-one*, *thirty-six*, etc.

2. *The thirties:* the years during which the numbers begin with 30; the fourth decade of a century.

Thirtytwomo (-tǎ·mo). [English reading of the symbol 32mo or XXXIImo, for L. *tricesimo secundo:* cf. *twelvemo, sixteenmo.*] The size of a book, or of a leaf of a book, formed of sheets each folded five times, making thirty-two leaves; hence, a book of this size.

So **Thirtytwomo** (*thirty-sizes*).

This (ðis), *dem. pron.* and *adj.* Pl. THESE, q.v.

A. Forms and Inflexions. (For plural see THESE.)

B. Signification.

I. Demonstrative Pronoun.

II. Demonstrative Adjective.

Thisness (ði·snes). [f. THIS + -NESS: rendering med. (scholastic) L. *hæccēitās.*] The quality of being 'this' (as distinct from anything else): = HÆCCEITY.

Thissel-cook = THROSTLE-COCK.

Thisson (ði·s'n), *adv. dial.* Also 9 this'ne, this'-on, thisn, thisna. *dial.* In this way or manner. Usually *a thisn* or *a thissun*, in this way or manner.

Thister, *pister,* variant of THISTER *Obs.*, dark.

Thistle (ði·s'l), *sb.* Forms: 1 thistil, ðistel, þystel, 4-6 thistel, thystle, 5 thestel, thistle, -tylle, 5-6 thistell, thistyll, thessel, 7 thissel, thisle, 8 chistly, 7 thirsle, 8-9 thrissle, 9 thristle, 9-4 *dial.* thistle, *dial.* thestle. [OE. ðistel, = OHG. *distil* (Ger., ON. ðistill), etc.]

Thistle, *obs.* variant of THIXEL, an adze.

Thistle-down (ði·s'ldaun). [THISTLE *sb.* + DOWN *sb.*] The down or pappus which covers the 'seeds' or achenes of the thistle, and by means of which they are carried along by the wind.

Thistle-finch. *Obs.* = FINCH; cf. G. *distelfink,* OHG. *distilvinko,* Du. *distelvinc.*

Thistly (ði·s'li), *a.* [f. THISTLE + -Y.]

1. Of the nature of or resembling a thistle; spiny, prickly; consisting of or constituted by thistles.

2. Full of, abounding or overgrown with thistles.

Thiswise (ði·swaiz), *adv.* Now rare. [Short for *a this wise.*]

This world, The present world; the present state or stage of existence.

Thither (ði·ðər), *adv.* (*a.*) Forms: see below.

THITHER.

1. To or towards that place (with verb of motion expressed or implied). (Now almost exclusively literary; in ordinary speech superseded by THERE.)

α. 1 þæder, þædær.

Thitherto, adv. variant of THITHER.

1. Up to that time; until then. Now rare.

Thitherward, adv. Now arch. [f. THITHER + -WARD.]

1. Towards that place; in that direction; thither.

Thitherwards, adv. arch. [f. prec.: see -WARDS.]

THIXEL.

Thixel, thixle (þi'ks'l). Now dial. Forms: 4 þixil -el, 5 thyxyl, ba... ell, -ille, -elle (uxxhy), tixil, thyxtyll, -ill, thixtill, 7 thixle, bu... bu... thyx... 9 thixle, thixell.

THLASPI.

† Thlaspi (þlæ'spi). Bot. Also 7 thlaspe, 8 thæ-.thæt-, thliteses.thyt-el. [Burmese]

† Thlipsis (þli'psis). Path. Also 7 thlipsis...

So **† Thlipsencephalus** (þli'psen..fæ'ləs) [Gr.
Thlipsencephalocele...

Thlimmyny, obs. variant of FLUMMERY.

Thnetopsychism (þnītopsəi'kiz'm). [f. eccl.
Gr. θνητοψυχ- maintaining the mortality of the soul...

† Tho, def. art. and adj. (rel. pron.), pl. Obs.

THODE.

tho, (5-6 thoe). [OE. ðá, þá = ON. þau (Norw...

THOFT.

Thoe, var. THO pron., adj., and adv. Obs.

Thoes, pl. of THOS, a canine beast; obs. f. THORE.

Thof(e, obs. f. ON, or dial. f. THOUGH.

Thof, thoft, obs. and dial. ff. THOUGHT; see also THINK f.

THOFT.

Thoft (þɔft). Now north. dial. Forms: 1
þofta, 4 þoufte,... 9 (north. dial.) thaft (Shetl.), f. of
Man taft, taff).

THOLEMODE.

1. A vertical pin or peg in the side of a boat against which in rowing the oar presses as the fulcrum of its action; esp. one of a pair between which the oar works (hence, a rowlock).

Thole (þōl), v. Now north. dial. or arch.

Tholemode, a. and sb. Obs. Forms: 1-4
polemod, polmod, 7 polo-), 3 polebyarde.

THOLEMODELY.

† Tholemodely, adv. Obs.

† Tholemodeness, sb. Obs.

Tholing (þō'liŋ), vbl. sb.

Tholite (þō'ləit), Arch. [f. Gr. θόλος...

Tholobate (þɔ'ləbeit). Arch. [f. Gr. θόλος...

Tholus (þō'ləs). Arch. Pl. tholi (-ai).

St. Thomas', in composition. St. Thomas'
balsam = balsam of TOLU.

THOMSONIANISM.

= CHRISTADELPHIAN, from the name of the founder,
Dr. John Thomas.

Thomble, thome, obs. forms of THUMB.

Thomism (tō'miz'm), [a. F. Thomisme...

Thomist (tō'mist), sb. and a. Eccl. [ad. med. L.
Thomista...

Thomite (tō'məit). rare⁻⁰. [f. THOM-AS +
-ITE.]

Thomsonian (tɔmsō'niən), a. [f. Thomson...

Thomsonite (tɔ'msənəit), [named after
Dr. Thomas Thomson...

Thomsonianism (tɔmsō'niəniz'm), [f. prec.]

THOMSONITE ... believe in the mind cure—Thompsonian.—metallic tractors—Christianlcence? Named, 1820, after it. ... a form of empiric medicine introduced by Samuel Thomson (1769–1843) of Massachusetts. Sweating, lobelia, and capsicum, were the principal agencies relied on.

Thomsonite (tᵊ·msᵊnəit), Min. [Named, 1820, after its discoverer, Dr. Thomas Thomson (1773–1852), professor of chemistry at Glasgow: see -ITE.] A hydrous silicate of aluminium, calcium, and sodium, found often in fibrous radiated masses, which reddish-brown in colour; a COMPTONITE.

Thon (ðᵒn), dem. pron. and a., dial. [app. a comparatively recent alteration of yon, the initial consonant being assimilated to this and that. A suggestion that it arose from miscasting the written y as the compendious form of th, as in yᵉ, yᵗ, yᵘ, yᵃᵗ, yⁱˢ, yᵃⁿʸ, etc., is, in view of the wide popular diffusion of thon and thonder, inadequate.]

Thong (þɒŋ), sb. Forms: α. 1 þwong, þuong, þwang, þwæng, 5 utæong, 1–3 þwang; 4–5 þwang (dial.), 5–6 north., 5–7 thwang; 5–7 thwyng (dial. 7–9 with hw, wh- for þw-) whaing, whang; 4–5 þwong, þuong, þwong, etc.

Thoracic (þᵒ·ræ·sik), a. [ad. L. thoracic-us pertaining to the chest: see -IC.]

Thoracical ... pertaining to the Thoracostraca, a division of crustaceans...

Thorite (þōᵊ·rəit), Min. [a. Swed. thorit (Berzelius, 1828–9), f. Thor (as in thoria, thorium) + -ITE I.]

Thorium (þōᵊ·riᵘm). Chem. [f. THOR, the Norse deity + -ium in other names of metals.]

Thorn (þɔɹn), sb. Forms: 1 þorn (1–2 þorn, 3 þeorn, 5 þorne), 1 þorne, etc.

Thorn (þɔɹn), v. [f. THORN sb.]

Thorned (þɔɹnd), a. [f. THORN sb. + -ED 2.]

Thorn-apple. The common name of Datura Stramonium, N.O. Solanaceæ (see DATURA).

Thorn-back (þɔ·ɹnbæk). Forms: see THORN sb. and BACK sb. 1; also -bagge, 7–bage, bage. Also Thornbuck.

Thorn-broom. ...

Thorn-bush. Any bush that bears thorns; e.g. a hawthorn, a bramble.

Thorn-hedge. A hedge of thorny shrubs; spec. a hedge composed of hawthorn 'sets'. Hence **Thorn-hedged** a., furnished with or enclosed by a thorn-hedge.

Thornily (þɔ·ɹnili), adv. [as next + -LY 2.]

Thorniness (þɔ·ɹninés). [f. THORNY + -NESS.]

Thornish, a. Obs. rare. [f. THORN sb. + -ISH.]

Thornless (þɔ·ɹnlés), a. [f. THORN sb. + -LESS.] Having no thorns; free from thorns; without a thorn.

Thornlet (þɔ·ɹnlét). [f. THORN sb. + -LET.] A diminutive thorn-bush. A minute thorn.

Thornset, a. [f. THORN sb. + SET.]

Thorn-tree. A tree having or bearing thorns.

Thorny (þɔ·ɹni), a. Forms: see THORN sb.; also 1 þyrne. [OE. þyrne, f. THORN sb. + -Y 1.] 1. Abounding in, characterized by, or consisting of thorns or spines; prickly.

THOROUGHBRACE. 336 **THOROUGH-LIGHT.** **THOROUGHLY.** 337 **THORTER.**

Thorter, *adj.* Crossing, lying athwart, transverse.

Thorter-ill, *Sc.* A disease of sheep, characterized by distortion of the neck; loaping-ill.

Thorty, *obs. form of* THIRTY.

Thoru, poru, thorugh, thorw, etc., obs. ff. THOROUGH, THROUGH *adv.*

Thos (þɒs), *n.* [L. *thos*, Gr. θώς.] The golden or black-backed jackal.

Those (ðouz), *dem. pron. and adj.* [-s.] Forms:

Thost(e, obs. form of TUSCAN.

Thou (ðau), *pron.* and *sb.*

Thother (ðˈʌðə(r)). [Combination of THE and OTHER.]

Though (ðou), *adv.* and *conj.* Forms:

Thought (θɔt). Forms: 1–3 þoht, 1–4 þoht, 2–4 þouht, 3–4 þoȝt, 3–5 þouȝt, 6–7 thoght, 5–7 þought, 6 thowght, thought, tho'.

A. Signification.

B. Signification.

I. The action or process of thinking; mental action or activity in general.

II. The particular action of thinking about or calling to mind.

Thoughless, palæ, *adv.* or *conj. Obs.* Nevertheless.

THOUGHT. (first column)

Thoughtful (þ[)ʊˌfŭl), a. [f. THOUGHT[1] + -FUL.] Full of or characterized by thought, in various senses.

Thought, thaught (þ[). Now dial. Also a thought, thous, þ thaws, þ thaus, slowt. Altered from the earlier THOFT, q.v. with change of (f) to (x), (the converse of what occurs in thaft for thaught, ...)

Thought (þ[t), pa. t. and pple. of THINK v.

Thoughtated (þ'ted), a. [f. THOUGHT[1] + 2.]

Thoughtfully (þ'fŭli), adv. [f. prec. + -LY[2].] In a thoughtful manner; with thought or consideration; meditatively, musingly; reflectively; considerately, kindly.

Thoughtfulness. [as prec. + -NESS.] The quality or state of being thoughtful.

THOUGHT-READING. (second column)

† Thoughten, a. Obs. rare[−1]. [irreg. form of THOUGHT.] Having a (specified) thought or belief; thinking.

Thoughtless, a. see THOUGHT[1] + -LESS.] That is without thought, in various senses: the opposite of THOUGHTFUL.

Thought-reading, sb. The reading of another person's thoughts; direct perception by one mind of what is passing in another, independent of ordinary means of expression or communication; a power alleged to be possessed by certain persons or by persons in certain psychic states. Hence allusively. So **Thought-reader,** n. one who practises thought-reading; **Thought-reading** a., that practises thought-reading.

THOUGHTSOME. (third column)

† Thoughtsome, a. Obs. rare. [f. THOUGHT[1] + -SOME.] Addicted to thought; thoughtful.

Thoughty, a. [as prec. + -Y.] Given to thought, thoughtful. a. Heedful, attentive, intent. b. Pensive, melancholy, anxious.

Thoul-whether, adv. Obs. Forms: 1 þeah-hwæþere, 2 peah-, pooh-, þahwhweðre, -wþere, -weðer, 2 þohhwheþþe (Orm.)...

Thoul, e, Thoums, obs. ff. THUMB.

Thousand (þaʊ'zand), sb. and a. Forms: 1-3 þusend, 2-3 -end, (Orm.) þ-and, -und, pousand, 3-4 þusond...

THOUSANDEL. (fourth column)

2. Often used vaguely or hyperbolically for a large number: cf. hundred.

5. Comb. Forming a) attrib. compounds with sb., as thousand-acre, -dollar...

THOUSANDFOLD. 344 THRALL. THRALL. 345 THRASH.

Thousandfold (þaʊ'zandfōld), a., adv., and sb. [OE. þūsendfeald: see THOUSAND and -FOLD.]

Thousandth (þaʊ'zandþ), a. and sb. The ordinal number belonging to the cardinal THOUSAND.

Thousandweight (þaʊ'zandˌweɪt). rare. A weight of a thousand pounds.

Thracian, obs. var. of THRASONICAL.

Thral, obs. form of THRALL.

Thraldom (þrɔ'ldəm). Forms: see next. [ON. þrǣldom-r.]

Thrall (þrɔl). sb. and a. Now arch. or Hist. [Late OE. þrǣl ...]

Thrall, thrawl (þrɔl). sb.[2] Now dial. Also þthrole. [Origin uncertain: ? an application of THRALL sb.[1]]

Thrall, a.[2] Obs. [Etymology obscure.] ? Strenuous, hard, severe.

Thrall, v. arch. [partly ME. þrallen, f. THRALL sb.[1]]

Thralled (þrɔld), ppl. a.

Thralless (þrɔ'lˌles), a. [f. THRALL sb.[1]] One who enthralls.

Thrall-less (þrɔ'lˌles), a. Obs. rare. [f. THRALL sb.[1] + -LESS.] Without a thrall; a bondwoman.

Thralliful, a. Obs. rare[−1]. [f. THRALL sb.[1] + -FUL.] Full of misery or thraldom; cf. THRALL sb.[1] 3.

THRALL / THRASH (fifth–sixth columns)

Thralldom-hood. Obs. [f. THRALL sb.[1] + -HOOD.] = THRALDOM.

Thralship. Obs. [See -SHIP.] Thraldom.

Thraly, Thranes, var. THOLY, THORNESS.

Thranite (þrə'naɪt), a. and sb. In the ancient trireme, a rower in one of the tiers, as generally supposed; the uppermost tier, which had the longest oars...

Thrapple, sb. dial. form of THROPPLE.

Thrash, thresh (þræʃ, þreʃ), v. Forms: 1 þerscan, þrescan...

Thrash, sb. Also **dresh.**

6– **thresh.** dial. (6 tross, drayse, draysche, 8–9 draish, dresh).

Supplement, p. 3873; Corrigenda, p. 4092; Spurious words, p. 4093; Books quoted, p. 4094

THRASH.

Thrash, thresh, *sb.²* Sc. Also 7 thrush.

Thrasher¹, thresher. One who or that which thrashes or threshes.

Thrash, thresh, *sb.¹* (f. prec. vb.)

THRASHING.

Thrashing, threshing (þreˈʃɪŋ), *vbl. sb.*

Thrashing, threshing, *ppl. a.*

Thrashing-floor, threshing-floor.

Thrashing-machine, threshing-machine.

Thrashing-mill, threshing-mill.

Thrasone (þræˈsəʊn), *sb.*

Thrasonical (þræˈsɒnɪkal), *a.*

Thrasonically, *adv.*

Thrasonism, *Obs. rare.*

Thrave, threave (þreɪv), *sb.*

Thraw (þrɔː), *v.*, the earlier form of THROW *v.*

Thraw, northern and Sc. form of THROW *sb.*

Thraward (þrɔˈwərd), *a. Sc. and n. dial.*

Thrawart, *a.*, variant of THRAWARD.

THRAWARDNESS.

Thrawly, *adv. Sc.*

Thrawartly, *adv. Sc.*

Thrawardness, thrawartness, *sb.*

Thrawcrook, variant of THROW-CROOK.

Thrawe, obs. f. THRAVE, THREE, THROW.

Thrawl, obs. f. THRALL, THRAW, THROW.

Thrawn (þrɔːn), *ppl. a.* Sc. Also 6–9 thraw(i)n, 7 thrown.

THREAD.

Thread (þrɛd), *sb.* Forms: 1–3 þræd, 1 þred, 3–5 þred, 4–7 þred, 4–9 (*dial.*) threed, 6–7 thridde, *etc.* 7 threde, threede, 7 thrid, 7– thread.

THREAD.

Thread, *v.*

Threadman. 1799 *Hull Advertiser* 23 Feb. 3/2 A..fire broke out..which entirely consumed nine *thread-mills. 1907 *Daily Chron.* 2 Oct. 6/6 Exciting scenes..in connection with the Paisley thread mill strike. 1864 M. G. Campbell in *Intell. Observ.* No. 33. 155 The *thread-mosses are an interesting and numerous tribe. 1899 *Daily News* 7 Dec. 11/1 Spidery kinds [of chrysanthemums] include the *thread-petalled Mrs. Carter. 1861 Miss Pratt *Flower. Pl.* V. 291 *Thread Rush, or Slender Rush..is remarkable for its thread-like stems. 1721 C. King *Brit. Merch.* I. 285 *Thred Sisters. 1844 Stephens *Bk. Farm* II. 416 The *Chorda filum*, or *thread-tangle. 1877 Knight *Dict. Mech.*, *Thread-waxer, a bowl of heated shoemaker's wax, through which the thread is conducted in sewing-machines for boots, shoes, and leather. 1825 J. Nicholson *Operat. Mechanic* 398 When either of the threads break, the *thread-wire through which it passes falls down. 1753 *World* No. 4. ⁋ 5 'The happiest in the world, madam', returned the *thread-woman. 1856 R. A. Vaughan *Mystics* (1860) II. viii. ix. 97 The deftly-woven *threadwork of the tissues. 1861 Lytton *Str. Story* (1862) II. 185 Pillows edged with the thread-work of Louvain. 1906 *Daily Chron.* 10 May 9/4 Mill girls employed in the thread works joined this organisation. 1888 *Dublin Rev.* July 69 The subject..is *threadworn.

Thread (þred), *v.* Forms: 4–6 **threde**, 6 **threede**, 6–7 **thred**, 7 **threed**, 7– **thread**; also 6– **thrid**. Pa. t. and pple. **threaded**; also 9 (*arch.*) **thrid** (*pa. pple.* **thridden**). [f. Thread *sb.*: independently in various senses.

The spelling *thrid* is still quite common in some of the transf. and fig. uses.]

1. *trans.* To pass one end of a thread through the eye of (a needle) in order to use it in sewing; to furnish (a needle) with a thread; also, to treat (any perforated object) in the same way (as in quot. 1607).

?*a* 1366 Chaucer *Rom. Rose* 99 A sylvre nedle forth I droughe,..And gan this nedle threde anon. 1530 Palsgr. 755/2, I threde a nedell to sowe with, *je enfile.* 1570 Levins *Manip.* 52/27 To Threede, *acum filo inducere.* 1607 Topsell *Four-f. Beasts* (1658) 307 Thread all the other rings with the loose end of the rope. 1676 C. Hatton in *H. Corr.* (Camden) 124 Good for nothing but to sit in ladyes chambers and thred their needles. 1709–10 Steele *Tatler* No. 141 ⁋ 2 The Girl can scarce thread a Needle. 1840 Haliburton *Letter Bag* i. 14 He threaded my needle for me.

b. *transf.* To cause (something) to pass through something else, as a thread through the eye of a needle.

1851 Mantell *Petrifact.* iii. § 7. 341 The graphic simile ..that the Plesiosaurus might be compared to a serpent threaded through the shell of a turtle. 1894 H. Gardener *Unoff. Patriot* 27 Nature built these mountains, and threaded that little river over the stones. 1901 Waterhouse *Conduit Wiring* 3 Size of Conductors which can be threaded through Simplex Conduits. 1908 *Westm. Gaz.* 28 Apr. 5/2 The [foot-]ball was..threaded in and out among the Southampton players.

c. *fig.* To pass through, make a hole through, penetrate, pierce.

1670 Pettus *Fodinæ Reg.* 2 When the Miners by these Shafts or Adits do strike or threed a Vein of any Metal. 1896 *Pall Mall Mag.* May 12 Tom out here will have leave to thrid you with bullets. 1899 B. Capes *Lady of Darkness* xvi, Thridding Ned's brain as they passed with a receding sound like that made by pebbles hopping over ice.

2. To fix (anything) upon a string or wire that passes through it; *esp.* to connect (a number of things) by passing a thread through each, to string together on or as on a thread. Also *fig.*

1633 G. Herbert *Temple, Sunday* v, The Sundaies of mans life, Threded together on times string. 1650 Earl Monm. tr. *Senault's Man bec. Guilty* Ep. Ded., If you will adde Charity enough..to pardon the faults escaped in the Presse, I shall thread it to the rest of my Obligations. *a* 1668 Davenant *Song* Wks. (1673) 321 Thy Teares to Thrid instead of Pearle, On Bracelets of thy Hair. 1705 F. Hauksbee in *Phil. Trans.* XXIV. 2166 Amber..beads, about the bigness of small Nutmegs, and Threaded. 1809 Scott *Let.* 14 Sept., The sight of our beautiful mountains and lakes..[has] set me to threading verses together. 1867 F. Francis *Angling* vii. (1880) 268 Threading the bait upon the hook. 1874 Spurgeon *Treas. David* Ps. ciii. 3 He selects a few of the choicest pearls.., threads them on the string of memory. *Mod.* The girl was threading beads on a string of catgut.

b. To make or embellish with or as with things strung on or fastened together by a thread.

1796 Mrs. M. Robinson *Angelina* I. 230 No blithesome groups, thridding the roseate wreath, Or tripping in fantastic measures by. 1877 S. Lanier *Tampa Robins* 11, I Will ..thrid the heavenly orange-tree With orbits bright of minstrelsy.

3. *fig.* To run or pass like a continuous thread through the whole length or course of; to pervade.

1830 *Examiner* 485/2 The melody which threads the first duet. 1858 *Eclectic Rev.* Ser. vi. III. 413 The burr of which [consonants]..thridding the open music of the vowel-sounds. 1871 Earle *Philol. Eng. Tongue* 259 One spirit and purpose threads the whole, and gives a sort of unity. 1905 *Westm. Gaz.* 13 Oct. 1/3 A haunting mystical vision that always threaded my slumbers.

b. *intr.* for *refl.* To connect itself as by a thread.

a 1848 R. W. Hamilton *Rew. & Punishm.* ii. (1853) 78 It has been seen how thought can thrid with thought, and feeling flow into feeling.

4. *trans.* To make one's way through (a narrow place, a passage presenting difficulties or obstacles, a forest, a crowd, or the like); to pass skilfully through the intricacies or difficulties of. *To thread out*, to pick out and follow, to trace (a path).

1593 Shaks. *Rich. II*, v. v. 17 It is as hard to come, as for a Camell To thred the posterne of a Needles eye. 1607 — *Cor.* iii. i. 127 They would not thred the Gates. *a* 1619 Fletcher *Bonduca* iv. ii, See where he thrids the thickets. 1633 G. Herbert *Temple, Vanitie* i, The fleet Astronomer can bore, And thred the spheres with his quick-piercing Minde. 1751 Smollett *Per. Pic.* xcvi. (1779) IV. 175 A captain of the guards, who..had threaded every station in their community. 1809 Malkin *Gil Blas* i. vi. ⁋ 3, I threaded all the windings of this new labyrinth. 1832 Lytton *Eugene A.* iv. x, Events thicken, and the mare is nearly thridden. 1863 Geo. Eliot *Romola* i, A labyrinth of narrow streets ..rarely threaded by the stranger. 1866 Dora Greenwell *Ess.* 219 A land intersected and thridden by the channels of benevolence.

b. *To thread one's way, course*, etc. in same sense.

1825 Coleridge *Aids Refl.* (1848) I. 323 He..thrids his way through the odorous and flowering thickets into open spots of greenery. 1868 E. Edwards *Ralegh* I. x. 179 He ..proceeded to thread his course amidst the tortuous.. channels. 1887 Bowen *Æneid* ii. 634, I..through foemen and flames, by the goddess's grace Thrid my way.

c. *intr.* = b.

1660 F. Brooke tr. *Le Blanc's Trav.* 5 The other [stream] ..threds through the middle of the Town. 1872 Jenkinson *Guide Eng. Lakes* (1879) 68 Bend to the left..and thread in an up-and-down course amongst the bare, rugged rocks. 1893 Stevenson *Catriona* xi. 119, I..threaded through the midst of it [the wood], and returned to the west selvage. *Ibid.* xxii. 260 We thrid all the way among shoals.

†**d.** *trans.* *To thread the difference*: to trace out or follow the narrow dividing line. *Obs. rare.*

1627 Wren *Serm. at Whitehall* 17 Feb. 15 The Epidemiall prophanation of our times, that will thrid you a difference now betwixt this feare and perfect worship.

5. *intr.* To move in a thread-like course or manner; to flow in a slender stream; to creep, twine, wind.

1611, 1626 [see Threading *vbl. sb.*]. *a* 1879 T. Ormond in *Mod. Sc. Poets* II. 356 Gracefully the ivy green Did round the craprods thread.

6. *trans.* To weave as a thread into the texture of something; to interweave.

1853 Rock *Ch. of Fathers* III. ii. 25 These old 'tropes' ..used to be twined and threaded into the words of the daily service.

b. *passive.* To be penetrated, permeated, or interspersed as with threads.

1861 Dora Greenwell *Poems* 215 The thrice refined gold Was thrid with baser clay. 1875 — *Liber Human.* 108 The elements which, mixed and threaded with whatever imaginable alloy, go to make up man's moral nature. 1891 Zangwill *Bachelor's Club* 21 His tawny hair, too, began to be threaded with silver.

†**7.** To bring on or induce gradually, as by the gentle drawing of a thread or line; to lead on. *Obs.*

1709 Wodrow *Corr.* (1842) I. 48 Our corruptions, and so our desolation for a season, are like to be threaded in gradually upon us. *Ibid.* 61 Provided we be not gradually threaded in to greater encroachments on the Church's rights this way. 1716 *Ibid.* II. 202 We are like to be threaded out of the exercise of our power as to fasts and thanksgivings by the Assembly.

8. To stretch threads across or over; to intersperse with threads so stretched.

1884 *Chr. Commw.* 20 Mar. 536/2 The devil's long lines of temptation, with which the stream of life is so thickly threaded. 1907 *Westm. Gaz.* 25 Feb. 2/3 Heavy spraying.. and threading [fruit-trees]..he has found to be a failure. *Mod.* I am obliged to thread my crocuses and polyanthuses every spring to protect them from destructive birds.

9. To form a screw-thread on; to furnish (a bolt or the like) with a screw-thread.

1858 Simmonds *Dict. Trade* s.v. *Screw*, Threading is effected by a saw which [etc.]. 1877 Knight *Dict. Mech.* 2074/1 Screw-threading machine. 1888 Hasluck *Model Engin. Handybk.* (1900) 46 The extreme end is threaded for a nut, as shown in the section of cylinder. 1893 *Brit. Jrnl. Photogr.* XL. 801 A hole is bored in the neck and threaded, and the valve is screwed..in.

Threadbare (þre·dbɛ̄ə), *a.* Also 5 *Sc.* **thred bar**, (8 **thread-bear**), 5– **thread(-)bare.** [f. Thread *sb.* + Bare *a.*]

1. Of a garment, etc.: Having the nap worn off, leaving bare the threads of the warp and woof; worn to the thread; shabby; worn-out.

1362 Langl. *P. Pl.* A. v. 113 But ȝif a lous couþe lepe I con hit not leue Heo scholde wandre on þat walk hit was so þred-bare. *c* 1386 Chaucer *Prol.* 260 He was nat lyk a Cloystrer With a thredbare cope as is a poure scoler. *c* 1470 Henry *Wallace* vi. 449 Thi ald hud, becaus it is thred bar. 1590 Spenser *F. Q.* i. iv. 28 Thred-bare cote, and cobled shoes, hee ware. 1693 Bowles *Juvenal* v. 193 Will any Freedom here from you be born, Whose Clothes are thread-bare? 1712 Addison *Spect.* No. 42 ⁋ 2 Dresses and Clothes that were thread-bare and decayed. 1824 W. Irving *T. Trav.* I. 196 Wit and coin are always doubted with a thread-bare coat.

2. *fig.* Resembling a threadbare garment; hence, poorly furnished or provided; meagre, scanty, poor, beggarly; contemptible, 'sorry'.

c 1412 Hoccleve *De Reg. Princ.* 1431 Som person is so threde-bare of konnynge. 1462 Marg. Paston in *P. Lett.* II. 83 Yelverton is a good thredbare frend for yow. *c* 1518 Skelton *Magnyf.* 223 Welth and Wyt, I say, be so threde bare worne. *a* 1550 *Fane wald I luve* 19 in *Dunbar's Poems* (S.T.S.) 308 Sum strykis down a threid bair cheik. 1586 Day *Eng. Secretary* i. (1625) 44 With bad attire, and thred-bare dyet, he liued with him a pretty season. 1676 Marvell *Mr. Smirke* 10 What Power they have, they will not wear it thred bare. 1704 Swift *T. Tub* Introd. ⁋ 25 A conscience thread-bare and ragged with perpetual turning. 1864 Pusey *Lect. Daniel* (1876) 438 We should often have had but a threadbare history.

b. *esp.* Having lost its influence, freshness, or force by much use; trite from constant repetition; commonplace, stale, hackneyed.

1598 E. Gilpin *Skial.* (1878) 26 So long he hath vsde cry, *oh rare*, That now that phrase is growne thin & threadbare. 1657 J. Watts *Vind. Ch. Eng.* 107 A trite, a thredbare exception. 1746 Chesterf. *Lett.* (1870) 23 Trite, threadbare jokes of those who set up for wit without having any. 1805 Scott *Let.* 29 Apr., If this quotation be rather threadbare. 1891 Mrs. Oliphant *Jerusalem* i. iv. A strange sermon upon..the fallacy of the hopes of man, which is a threadbare subject.

3. Of persons: Wearing threadbare clothes; shabby, seedy; hence, impecunious, hard up; down-at-heel, out-at-elbows. Now *rare* or *Obs.*

1577 R. Wrighte in Ellis *Orig. Lett.* Ser. ii. III. 75 ..shall not onley be thrid bare but ragged. 1628 Earle *Microcosm., Prison* (Arb.) 82 Onely to be out at elbowes is in fashion here, and a great Indecorum, not to be thredbare. 1678 Shadwell *Timon* i. Wks. 1720 II. 298 Honesty, The foolish, slender, thread-bare, starving thing. 1713 Steele *Englishm.* No. 16. 108 You shall see him..in close Whisper with a thread-bare Philosopher. 1760–72 H. Brooke *Fool of Qual.* (1809) IV. 136 [He] took the thread-bare Longfellow under the arm, and carried him away.

4. *Comb.*, as *threadbare-genteel* (cf. *shabby-genteel*).

1849 Clough *Amours de Voyage* i. 130 Some Threadbare-genteel relations.

Threa·dbareness. [f. prec. + -ness.] The state or quality of being threadbare.

1530 Palsgr. 280/2 Threde bareness, *deureur.* ?*c* 1600 *Distr. Emperor* i. i. in Bullen *O. Pl.* (1884) III. 169 Thou that hast worne thy selfe and a blewe coate To equall thryddbareness. 1771 Mackenzie *Man Feel.* xxi. (1886) His look..spoke of the sleekness of folly and the threadbareness of wisdom. 1870 Lowell *Among my Bks.* Ser. i. (1873) 3 A little threadbareness in the similes.

So **Threadba·rity** *nonce-wd.*, in same sense.

1892 Besant *Ivory Gate* 69 The rags and duds and threadbarity too often enter largely into the picturesque.

Threaded (þre·dèd), *ppl. a.* [f. Thread *v.* (and *sb.*) + -ed.]

1. Furnished with a thread (as a needle); strung on or as on a thread (as beads); interlaced, twined; consisting of or ornamented with threads.

1541 Copland *Guydon's Quest. Chirurg.* L iij, In puttynge threded nedles in to theym [wounds]. 1758 J. S. *Le Dran's Observ. Surg.* (1771) 274, I supported the Compress with a threaded Dossil. 1821 *Sporting Mag.* VIII. 262 She [a mare] had large corns on each foot, one of which was what is termed a threaded corn. 1821 Joanna Baillie *Wallace* lv, Tissue of threaded gems is worn. 1856 Bryant *West Wind* i, And hear the breezes of the West Among the threaded foliage sigh. 1876 Geo. Eliot *Dan. Der.* iv. xxx, Standing with her arms thrust down and her fingers threaded. 1904 Farrer *Gard. Asia* viii. 74 A threaded chain of lanterns.

2. Having or furnished with a screw-thread.

1844 *Civil Eng. & Arch. Jrnl.* VII. 153/2 On approaching the farther or opposite end they are made irregular, commonly called 'drunken threaded'. 1884 C. G. W. Lock *Workshop Receipts* Ser. iii. 288/1 The shank and threaded part of the tap. 1898 *Cycling* 49 Working upon the threaded end of the axle.

3. [f. Thread *sb.*] As the second element in parasynthetic combinations, as *bare-*, *gold-*, *grey-*, *small-threaded.*

1616 J. Deacon *Tobacco Tortured* 66 They make..well bred Gentelmen, but bare thredded Yeomen. 1617 Minsheu *Voc. Hisp. Lat.*, *Arañuelo*,..a small threaded net to catch birds. 1896 *Godey's Mag.* Feb. 211/2 Long opera wraps of gold-threaded brocade.

Threaden (þre·d'n), *a.* Now *arch.* or *dial.* Forms: see Thread *sb.*; (also 5 therdyn). [f. Thread *sb.* + -en⁴.] Composed or made of thread; *spec.* made of linen thread.

c 1400 *Land Troy Bk.* 8351, I ȝeue not a threden lace Of thyn euel wil and thi manace! 1499 *Croscombe Churchw. Acc.* (Som. Rec. Soc.) 23 A therdyn cerchewe. 1590 Lodge *Euphues' Gold. Leg.* 59b, A dozen of new thredden points of medley coulour. 1594 Willobie *Avisa* (1880) 76 Not worth in proofe a threden poynt. 1610 B. Jonson *Alch.* i. i, A thredden cloake. 1688 R. Holme *Armoury* iii. 224/1 They went always covered with Threaden Caps or Hoods. 1756 Warner *Let.* 24 Aug., in Jesse *Selwyn & Contemp.* (1844) IV. 366 Of his threaden sails [he] has made wings to his riches wherewith to fly away. *a* 1825 Forby *Voc. E. Anglia* s.v., Within our memory 'threaden stockings' were an article of Sunday apparel for village servants and apprentices. 1870 Rock *Text. Fabr.* Introd. v. 127 Very old threaden cloths..for liturgical purposes.

Threader (þre·dəɹ). Also 5 **thredere**, 9 **thredder.** [f. Thread *v.* + -er^1.] One who or that which threads; *spec.* **a.** a person employed to keep the shuttles threaded in weaving; **b.** a bodkin for threading tape or ribbon through interstices in a garment or the like; see also quot. 1877.

c 1430 *Pilgr. Lyf Manhode* iv. lviii. (1869) 204 My mooder Charitee was cordere and thredere [Fr. *fillaciere*]. 1877 Knight *Dict. Mech.*, *Threader*, a device for guiding the thread into the eye of a needle. See *Needle-threader.* 1906 *Daily News* 1 Aug. 5/1 He went, at the age of ten, into a lace mill, where he advanced from the position of a 'jacker off' to that of a 'thredder'. 1911 *Ibid.* 3 May 8 Inspection of automatic threaders and inquiring into their adaptability.

Threa·diness. *rare.* [f. Thready + -ness.] The quality of being thready; in quot., stringiness.

c 1425 tr. *Arderne's Treat. Fistula* 82 Arsenic & auripigment bene boþe one,..but auripigment is..more disesy to grynde for his þredinez. 1864 in Webster.

Threa·ding, *vbl. sb.* [f. Thread *v.* + -ing^1.] The action of the verb Thread in various senses; an instance of this.

1611 Cotgr., *Filet d'huyle*, a small drop, or threading of oyle. 1626 Bacon *Sylva* § 293 We see in Liquors, the threading of them in Stillicides. 1852 R. S. Surtees *Sponge's Sp. Tour* (1893) 118 The collar..exhibited all the stitchings and threadings incident to that department of the garment. 1887 E. Gurney *Tertium Quid* II. 45 Accurate thridding of labyrinthine things. 1889 *Pall Mall G.* 25 Nov. 7/1 The machine which does the threading [of screws] is complicated and slow. 1908 R. W. Chambers *Firing Line* xxviii, Another woman awoke to take up the ravelled threadings of her life again.

†**Threa·dish,** *a.* *Obs. rare*$^{-1}$. [f. Thread *sb.* + -ish^1.] Resembling a thread; thread-like.

1578 Lyte *Dodoens* ii. i. 147 The roote is tender & of threddish strings.

Threa·d-lace. Lace made of linen or cotton thread as distinguished from silk lace.

1581 *Acc. Bk. W. Wray* in *Antiquary* XXXII. 117 A grose white thred lace, vs. vjd. 1765 in *Home Counties Mag.* (1902) IV. 226 One of the best thread lace-makers in England. 1821 J. Smyth *Pract. of Customs* 118 No Thread Lace can be imported in a less quantity than 12 yards, unless of the value of £2 per yard or upwards. 1861 Geo. Eliot *Silas M.* i, Great ladies, clothed in silk and thread-lace.

Threadle (þre·d'l), *v. dial.* Also 9 **threddle, thriddle.** [f. Thread *sb.* + -le 3.] = Thread *v.*

1746 Bowlker *Art Angling* (1833) 52 Threadle this gudgeon. 1767 J. Bickerstaffe *Love in City* i. ii, Here threadle my needle. 1881 *Isle of Wight Gloss.*, *Threadle*, to thread; to string. 1887 Bowen *Æneid* ii. 454 A passage adjoined Thriddling the inner palace. 1888 *Berks. Gloss.* s.v., To 'threddle' a needle is to pass thread through the eye of it ready for sewing.

Threadless (þre·dlès), *a.* [f. as prec. + -less.]

1. Without a thread; having no thread; unthreaded.

1822 *Blackw. Mag.* XII. 711 Threadless, knotless, endless, useless mysteries, tragedies, and dramas. 1866 T. Bruce *Summer Queen* 14 Fancy lost in threadless maze Was running to and fro.

2. Having no screw-thread.

1886 *Cyclist* 4 Aug. 1081/1 It [a bicycle]..is made with Clarke's patent threadless spokes.

Threadlet (þre·dlèt). [f. as prec. + -let.] A minute thread; a slender filament.

1882 J. Parker in *Homil. Mag.* (N. Y.) May 459 By what threadlets is he lifted up? 1887 C. L. Morgan *Anim. Biol.* iii. 29 A delicate dark thread, from which minute threadlets pass off.

Thread-like (þre·dləik), *a.* [f. as prec. + -like.] Like a thread; also, like that of a thread.

1774 Mrs. Delany in *Life & Corr.* Ser. ii. (1862) II. 47 A little brassish, copperish, goldish thread-like stuff adhering to a bit of slate or coal. 1814 Southey *Roderick* xvii. 50 The stream's perpetual flow..with its..Dimples and thread-like motions infinite. 1835–6 *Todd's Cycl. Anat.* I. 604/1 Cellular tissue formed of white thread-like filaments. 1901 *Scribner's Mag.* XXIX. 433/2 Ridges over which the white tracks wind, thread-like, toward the hazy rim of mountains.

b. Of the pulse: = Thready 4.

a 1829 in *Good's Study Med.* (1829) II. 612 Difficulty of swallowing; thread-like pulse. 1897 *Allbutt's Syst. Med.* II. 818 The heart's action becomes extremely feeble, and the pulse threadlike and uncountable. *Ibid.* IV. 389 It may be found that a pulsation of thread-like smallness will pass in spite of almost any pressure which the finger can apply.

†**Threa·dmeal,** *adv.* *Obs. rare.* [f. as prec. + -meal.] Thread by thread.

1565 Cooper *Thesaurus*, *Filatim*,..threade meale: threade by threade. *Ibid.* s.v. *Distraho*, *Filatim distrahi*, to be pulled a sunder threadmeale.

Threa·d-needle. Also **thread-the-needle; threadthe(my)needle-eye, my grandmother's, the tailor's needle;** *dial.* **grandy needles.** [f. Thread *v.* + Needle.]

1. A children's game, in which, all joining hands, the player at one end of the string passes between the last two at the other end, the rest following.

1751 *Advent. G. Edwards* 140 (Halliwell) Eight people.. joining hands like children at thread-needle. 1797–1805 S. & Ht. Lee *Canterb. T.* III. 450 Children..playing thread my grandmother's needle. 1825–7 Hone *Every-day Bk.* I. 692 The prettiest sight..was a game at 'Thread my needle', played by about a dozen lasses. 1856 Miss Mulock *J. Halifax* xxv, From top to bottom, the young men and women were running in a long 'Thread-the-needle'.

2. Thread the needle, as *verb phrase*: (*a*) in dancing, denoting the movement in which the lady passes under her partner's arm, their hands being joined; (*b*) to pass in and out in a winding course; (*c*) in shooting; see quot. 1895^2.

1844 Dickens *Christmas Carol* ii, Advance and retire, both hands to your partner, bow and curtsey, corkscrew, thread-the-needle, and back again to your place. 1895 *Daily News* 12 June 7/2 The toiling oarsman..might then have to 'thread the needle' (inshore for the boat, outside for the punt, close astern). 1895 *Funk's Standard Dict.* s.v., *To thread the needle* (*Western U.S.*), to fire a rifle-ball through an auger-hole barely large enough to allow the ball to pass without enlarging the hole.

Threa·d-paper. A strip of thin soft paper folded in creases so as to form separate divisions for different skeins of thread; the paper so folded forming a long and narrow strip.

1761 Sterne *Tr. Shandy* III. xli, What is become of my wife's thread-paper? 1796 Mme. D'Arblay *Camilla* II. 404 [She] had lost the thread-paper from which she was to mend her gown. 1880 *Plain Hints Needlework* 57 It should be cut at each end of the skein and folded securely into a 'thread paper'.

b. *fig.* A person of slender or thin figure.

1824 Miss Mitford *Village* Ser. i. 153 So tall and so limp, bent in the middle—a thread-paper, six feet high! 1833 Marryat *P. Simple* xxix, If the common sailors were ..such little thread-papers as you. 1881 Huxley in *Life* (1900) II. ii. 35, I was a thread paper of a boy myself.

c. *attrib.* Having the attributes of a thread-paper; long and narrow slender, attenuated; limp, feeble, flimsy.

1746–7 Mrs. Delany in *Life & Corr.* (1861) II. 450, I expect soon to see the other extreme of thread-paper heads and no hoops, and from appearing like so many blown bladders, we shall look like so many bodkins stalking about. 1803 *Naval Chron.* X. 510 Bonaparte's thread paper flotilla. 1882 P. Fitzgerald *Recreat. Lit. Man* (1883) 186 [Landing from a Calais steamer] Singers, actresses, ladies of quality, princesses, queens, all reduced to the common thread-paper level. 1884 Stevenson *New Arab. Nts.* 308 She was a thread-paper creature.

Threadworm (þre·dwɔɹm). A worm of thread-like form, as the Guinea worm, Hair-worm, etc.; *esp.* the pin-worm, *Oxyuris* (*Ascaris*) *vermicularis*, parasitic in the human rectum, chiefly in children.

1802 Bingley *Anim. Biog.* (1813) III. 400 The Indian thread-worm, or guinea-worm,..enters the naked feet of the slaves. 1822–34 *Good's Study Med.* (ed. 4) I. 274 The head of the thread-worm is subulate, nodose, and divided into three vesicles. 1879 Wright *Anim. Life* 582 The Thread Worm (*Gordius aquaticus*) is viviparous, and the young differ in form from the mother. 1899 *Allbutt's Syst. Med.* VIII. 512 [Eczema] may follow the irritation of thread worms.

Thready (þre·di), *a.* [f. Thread *sb.* + -y.]

†**1.** Full of or covered with thread. *Obs.*

1594 Willobie *Avisa* 37 b, When thready spindle full was grown. 1757 Dyer *Fleece* iii. 135 The thready shuttle glides along the lines.

2. Of thread-like texture; composed of fine fibres; stringy, fibrous.

c 1425 [implied in Threadiness]. 1715 tr. *Pancirollus' Rerum Mem.* I. i. iv. 12 Its threaddy Substance may be weav'd into a Web. 1750 tr. *Leonardus' Mirr. Stones* 71 Amianton is a stone of a lucid colour, and thready, like feathered alum. 1797 *Encycl. Brit.* (ed. 3) XII. 371/2 The bark [of the mulberry tree]..is rough, thick, thready, and fit for being made into ropes. 1809 tr. *Landt's Descr. Feroe Isl.* (1810) 141 Compact, thready, or radiant zeolite. 1826 Carlyle *Early Lett.* (1886) II. 350 Abundance of grand thready peats.

b. Of liquid: Forming strings; viscid, ropy.

1733 *Ordinary of Newgate* No. 1 Advt., Urine foul, slimy, thready. 1846 G. E. Day tr. *Simon's Anim. Chem.* II. 182 The mucus will become very tough, and almost thready. 1897 *Allbutt's Syst. Med.* IV. 435 [The fluid of a pyonephrosis] is more or less thready and glairy.

c. Of a plant: Bearing thread-like fibres or parts; filamentous, hairy. *rare*$^{-1}$.

1804 Charlotte Smith *Conversations*, etc. II. Notes 204 Thready Yucca, an Aloe, I believe.

d. Having thread-like markings; veined.

1601 Holland *Pliny* (1634) I. 493 Ioyners doe chuse the mistresse threadie grain that is most streight.

e. Threadbare; showing the threads.

1910 *Nation* 15 Jan. 639/2 The envelope fluttered to the thready carpet.

3. Of the nature of, consisting of, or resembling a thread or a mass of loose threads; thread-like, hair-like; of a root: fibrous.

1597 Gerarde *Herbal* i. ii. § 4. 3 The roote is threddie. 1621 T. Granger *Comm. Eccles.* xii. 6. 325 The small and threddie rootes of a tree. 1671 Marten *Voy. Spitzbergen* in *Acc. Sev. Late Voy.* ii. (1694) 92 Her Feathers are thready or hairy. 1698 J. Petiver in *Phil. Trans.* XX. 405 Its Style is thready, and about an Inch long. 1733 W. Ellis *Chiltern & Vale Farm.* 231 Here it will twist and fasten its thready Entanglements to them almost from top to bottom. 1879 G. Macdonald *Sir Gibbie* i, Her black hair..would have revealed a thready glitter of grey. 1882 — *Castle Warlock* xxviii, Many a thready weed.

4. Of the pulse: see quot. 1899.

1753 N. Torriano *Gangr. Sore Throat* 109 A frequent, and very thready Pulse. 1764 *Phil. Trans.* LIV. 239 His pulse was too quick..and withall low and thready. 1860–1 Flor. Nightingale *Nursing* 80 The pulse becomes quick, perhaps 130, and so thready, it is not like a pulse at all, but like a string vibrating just underneath the skin. 1897 *Allbutt's Syst. Med.* III. 621 The pulse becomes small, sharp, wiry or thready. 1899 *Syd. Soc. Lex.*, *Thready pulse*, a small, scarcely perceptible pulse found in the terminal stages of fatal diseases.

5. Of the voice, etc.: Dry and thin; wanting in fullness. (Cf. Thread *sb.* 4 b.)

1860 *All Year Round* No. 41. 344 Incapable of knowing how exceedingly high he is pitching his thready old voice. 1874 Lisle Carr *Jud. Gwynne* I. iii. 92 Sickly pianos and thready harps. 1908 Miss Broughton *Lavinia* (ed. Tauchn.) 235 A fuller sound in the thready voice.

Threap (þrīp), *sb.* Now *Sc.* and *north. dial.* Forms: 3–4 **þrep**, 4–5 **þrepe**, **threp**, 4–6 **threpe**, 6 **threip**, **threype**, 7 **threape**, 8–9 **threep**, 8– **threap.** [f. Threap *v.*]

1. The action of threaping; contradiction, contention, argument, discussion; controversy, dispute; strife, quarrel, contest.

a 1300 *Cursor M.* 13310 (Cott.) Wit-vten threp [*Gött.* ani threpe] or strijf. *Ibid.* 27609 O pride bicums throues o thrett, Hething, threp [*v.r.* þrepe], and athes grett. 13.. *E. E. Allit. P.* B. 350 Enter in þenne..& haf þi wyf with þe, Þy þre sunez with-outen þrep, & her þre wyuez. *c* 1400 *Destr. Troy* 5246 Þai hade no strenght to withstonde þe striff of þe pepull, Þat were þro men in threpe. 1418 26 *Pol. Poems* xiv. 78 Stryf wiþ comons, threp, and thro, To brynge þat in amendement. 1535 Stewart *Cron. Scot.* (Rolls) I. 37 We sall mak threip ȝit or we ar ouirthrawin. 1794 *Har'st Rig* lxi, They stop at last, but still look laith The threap to yield. 1866 Carlyle *Let.* Apr. in Froude *Life in L.* (1884) II. xxviii. 308, I had privately a kind of threap that the brandy should be yours. 1886 *S. W. Linc. Gloss.* s.v., We had a bit of a threap about it.

2. An act of threaping; a contradictive or pertinacious assertion; a hostile charge or accusation.

1538 Cromwell in Merriman *Life & Lett.* (1902) II. 128 To desire to conquer me by shrowde wordes, to vanquishe me by sharpe threpes of scripture. *a* 1699 J. Fraser in *Wodrow Soc. Sel. Biog.* (1847) II. 214 Let us..hear patiently all assertions and threaps. 1742 R. Forbes *Ajax* viii, At threeps I am na' sae perquire, Nor auld-farren as he. 1768 Ross *Helenore* iii. 111, I nae mair sall say this threap about,..That on my side the bargain did na fa'. 1864 Carlyle *Fredk. Gt.* xv. xv. (1872) VI. 119 He had taken a threap that he would have it finished. 1837 Snaith *Fierceheart* vi. 67 The threep was fause, an he..got a thrawn thrapple for a deed he didna dae.

b. Phr. *To keep (to) one's threap.*

1756 Mrs. Calderwood *Jrnl.* (1884) 318 Encouraging her to keep to her threap. 1818 Scott *Br. Lamm.* xxvii, Lady Ashton..will, as Scotchmen say, keep her threep.

†**3.** Reproof, rebuke. (Cf. Threap *v.* 1.) *Obs. rare.*

1636 James *Iter Lanc.* 276, I leaue thy heape Of bloodie crimes to God's revendge and threape.

4. *Comb.* **threap-ground, threap-land(s**, land of disputed ownership, debatable land; *spec.* applied to the Debatable Lands of the Border.

1259 *Registr. Aberdon.* (Maitl.) I. 26 Super quadam terra que dicebatur threpland inter terram de Bondyngton..et terram de Newton. 1449 in Rymer *Fœdera* XI. 245/1 As touching the Landez callid Batable Landez or Threpe Landez in the West Marchez. 1568 in H. Campbell *Love-Lett. Mary Q. Scots* App. (1824) 15 The contraversy yerely arising by occasion of certein grounds upon the frontiers in the east marches, commonly called the threap-land, or debatable. 1825 E. Mackenzie *Hist. Northumbld.* II. 257 A long tract of land..which was formerly Debateable Land, or Threap Ground; but which, in 1552, was divided by agreement between the proper officers of both nations. 1858 Denham *Folk-Lore* 55 (E.D.D.) Part of Wooler Common is still undivided, owing to disputes respecting it. It is called Threap-ground. 1894 Heslop *Northumbld. Gloss.*, *Threap-lands, Threap-ground*,..land the ownership of which is disputed.

Threap (þrīp), *v.* Now *Sc.* and *north. dial.* Forms: 1 **ðreapian**, 3 **þreape**, (*Orm.*) **þreapenn**, 3–5 **þrepe**, 3–7 **threpe**, 4–6 **threppe**, (4–5 *pa. t.* **þrappit**, **þreppit**), 5–6 **threip**, 6 **thraip**, 6–7 **threape**, 6–9 **threep**, 6– **threap.** [OE. *þréapian* to rebuke, reprehend: of uncertain history.]

1. *trans.* To rebuke, reprove, chide, scold, blame.

c 897 K. Ælfred *Gregory's Past. C.* xxi. 165 Ðonne he to suiðe & to ðearllice ðreapian wile his hieremenn. *a* 1300 *E. E. Psalter* xciii[i]. 10 Þat vndretakes genge, noght threpe mon, Þat leres man wisedome to kun? 1582 Stanyhurst *Æneis* iv. (Arb.) 106 Let not mee falslye be threpped. 1682 Shadwell *Lanc. Witches* v. 71 Who threped and threped, and aw to becaw'd me. 1787 Grose *Provinc. Gloss.*, *Threap*, or *Threapen*, to blame, rebuke, reprove, or chide. 1877 *N. W. Linc. Gloss.* s.v., I wen't be threp by a bairn like thoo. 1879 Clough *B. Bresskittle* 14 (E.D.D.) Th' owd lass.. threap'd me foinly.

†**b.** *To threap* (a person) *with kindness* = *to threap kindness upon*: see 4 b. *Obs.*

1567 Jewel *Let. to Harding* in *Def. Apol.* Rrrj b, Yee threape her Maiestie fondely with kindenesse.

2. *intr.* To contend in words; to inveigh *against*; to argue, dispute; to quarrel, bicker, disagree; to wrangle about terms, haggle.

c 1200 Ormin 5744 Acc himm birrþ þreapenn aȝȝ wiþþ skill Onnȝæness alle sinness. 1303 R. Brunne *Handl. Synne* 4352 Whan ȝe aȝens þe prechur þrepe. *Ibid.* 6065 Aȝens mokerers wyl y þrepe. *c* 1400 *Destr. Troy* 2152 Than ..priam..þonket hom þroly, þrappit no lengur. *Ibid.* 12235 He þroly with þrong wil þreppit agayn. *c* 1475 *Rauf Coilyear* 79 Thank me not ouir airlie, for dreid that we threip. 1535 Stewart *Cron. Scot.* (Rolls) III. 454 The erle of Craufurd that same tyme and he,..Begouth to threip quha than that war best peiris. 15.. *Ballad, Take thy old cloak about thee* 67 It's not for a man with a woman to threape Unless he first gave oer the plea. 1755 Johnson, To *Threap*, a country word denoting to argue much or contend. 1847 C. Brontë *J. Eyre* xxix, They were so agreeable with each other—never fell out nor 'threaped'. 1871 [see Threaping *vbl. sb.*]. 1873 Lytton *Parisians* ix. iii, Threap and argue as we may.

†**b.** *intr.* To fight, struggle, strive, contend. *Obs.*

13.. *Gaw. & Gr. Knt.* 504 Bot þenne þe weder of þe worlde wyth wynter hit þrepez. ?*a* 1400 *Morte Arth.* 930 Of the nyghtgale notez the noisez was swette, They threpide wyth the thro-stilles, thre hundreth at ones! *c* 1400 *Destr. Troy* 2003 Þre dayes þroly þai þrappit with stornys. *Ibid.* 10098 Mony thoghtes full þro þrappit in his hert. *Ibid.* 12134 In þronge and in þraldom þrepe with þe werld.

3. *trans.* (usu. with *obj. cl.*) To persist in asserting (something contradicted or doubted); to affirm positively or pertinaciously; to maintain obstinately or aggressively.

c 1386 Chaucer *Can. Yeom. Prol. & T.* 273 Sol gold is and Luna siluer we threpe. *c* 1475 *Rauf Coilyear* 199 Thay threip that I thring doun of the fattest. 1509 Fisher *Wks.* (1876) 299 Some other threpe that he hathe forgoten theym. 1656 Blount *Glossogr.*, *Threpe*,..to affirme positively, or to face one down with confidence; still used in the North. 1728 Ramsay *Cameleon* 26, I say he's blue; He threaps, he's green: now what say you? *a* 1774 Fergusson *Drink Ecl.* Poems (1845) 53 Will ye your breedin' threep ye mongrel loun? 1816 Scott *Antiq.* xxiv, He threeps the castle and lands are his ain as his mother's eldest son. 1887 P. M'Neill *Blawearie* 50 A group o' miners..threepit doon my throat that the grave..was only about four feet deep.

b. *To threap* (a person) *out of*: to move or do (him) out of (something) by persistent assertion.

1677 Gilpin *Demonol.* (1867) 168 Thus are men threaped out of their own persuasions. 1885 J. Hartley *Clock Alm.* 40 (Yorks.) (E.D.D.) Shoo tried to threap me aght on it.

c. with *inf.* To insist on or persist in doing something. *rare*$^{-1}$.

1827 Scott *Surg. Dau.* i, She threeps to keep on a black fause-face, and skirls if we offer to take it away.

4. *To threap* (something) *upon* (a person): †**a.** To impose (an assertion) upon; to lead or try to lead one to believe by persistent assertion. *Obs.*

c 1440 *Alphabet of Tales* 482 When his servandis wolde eatt any gude meate, þai wolde threpe vppon hym at he was seke. 1530 Palsgr. 755/2, I threpe a mater upon one, I beare one in hande that he hath doone or saide a thing a mysse...This terme is..farre northren. He wolde threpe upon me that I have his penne. 1608 Hieron *and Pt. Def. Ministers' Reas. Refusal Subscription* 72 Slaundring the Ministers and threaping one and the same..slaunder vpon them.

†**b.** To impute, attribute, ascribe (something) to a person. *To threap kindness* or *love upon* (also *of*): to attribute kindness, etc. to; to give (one) credit for love or goodwill, to urge to the exercise of kindness. (See also 1 b.) *Obs.*

1559 Bercher *Nobylytye Wymen* (1904) 104 In dede..you threape kindenes vppon me, and surely..I can well a way wᵗʰ yoʳ prayse. 1579 W. Wilkinson *Confut. Familye of Loue* 65 It is but a vayne kyndnes, which Theophilus in this place threapeth on God. 1589 R. Bruce *Serm.* (1843) 129 Thou suld threap kindness of him. 1596 Nashe *Saffron Walden* 152 The baudie rymes he threapes vpon me. *a* 1603 T. Cartwright *Confut. Rhem. N.T.* (1618) 231 You do but threap kindnesse of the Hereticks, as you call them; for they acknowledge no such miracles to be done by your reliques. 1648 J. Beaumont *Psyche* v. ccxxvii, Behold how gross a Ly of Ugliness They on my face have threaped. 1660 Dickson *Writings* (1845) I. 42 If any wilt threap love upon God, they shall not be disappointed. 1730 T. Boston *Serm. Song of Sol.* ii. 17 Wks. 1855 V. 552 It will make men very peremptory for Christ, that they will not take a refusal, to threap kindness on him and special interest in him.

c. To thrust, obtrude, press (something) upon a person; to urge upon him acceptance of or acquiescence in.

1571 Golding *Calvin on Ps.* xv.ii. 3 If Sathan threpe any feare uppon us, it may be kept farre of from enterance. 1690 C. Nesse *O. & N. Test.* I. 68 Araunah had a princely spirit..but generous David threaps upon him fifty shekels. 1816 Scott *Antiq.* xv, Monkbarns had threepit on them to gang in till 't to see the wark o' the monks lang syne. 1869 'Ouida' *Puck* xlii, Look'ee here! These arena goods to threap.

5. *To threap down*: to put down or silence by vehement or pertinacious assertion; also, with double object (sb. and clause), *to threap* (a person) *down* (*that*...): to try to force a statement upon (a person) by strength of assertion or insistent reiteration.

1599 Nashe *Lenten Stuffe* (1871) 51 Bolingbroke,..at his removing..into banishment, as Father Froissart threaps down, was accompanied with forty-thousand men, women, and children weeping. 1674 N. Fairfax *Bulk & Selv.* 83 You may as well threap one down, that a ghost is heavier or lighter, colder or hotter,..whiter or blacker than a body. 1841 R. W. Hamilton *Nugæ Lit.* 340 A man will say of a clamorous talker, he did not convince me, but he threaped me down. 1877 Leigh *Cheshire Gloss.* s.v., He thraped me down it were noine, but I knowed it were a dozen.

Hence **Threa·ping** *vbl. sb.* and *ppl. a.*; **Threa·per**, one who 'threaps' or persistently asserts.

c 897 K. Ælfred *Gregory's Past. C.* xxi. 167 gif him mon to ungemetlice mid ðære ðreapunga oferfylgð. 13.. *E. E. Allit. P.* B. 183 For þeft, & for þrepyng, vnþonk may mon haue. *c* 1400 *Destr. Troy* 10847 A thowsaund full þro, þrepand in wer. *c* 1440 *York Myst.* xl. 105 Thei thraste hym full thraly, þan was þer no threpyng. *c* 1460 *Towneley Myst.* xxviii. 19 Do way youre threpyng! are ye wode? 1785 [W. Hutton] *Bran New Wark* 38 Naa brawling or threaping is heard. 1871 W. Alexander *Johnny Gibb* i, Johnny offered 'sax poun'..after much 'threepin' as his ultimatum. 1871 P. H. Waddell *Ps.* xxxv. 11 Thar raise amang them threepers o' ill. 1899 *Leeds Merc., Suppl.* 18 Feb. (E.D.D.), Ah niver knew sich a threaper as thee.

Threa·pen, *v.* *Obs.* exc. *dial.* [app. f. Threap *v.* + -en^5; but, in sense 1, perh. for *threaten*.]

†**1.** To threaten (*trans.* and *intr.*). *Obs.*

1340 *Ayenb.* 84 Naȝt ne habbeþ more of myȝte aye uirtues kueade mysfalles and zorȝes ne al þet fortune may þreapny and do: more þanne þer byeþ dropen of rayn ine þe ze. *Ibid.* 97. *Ibid.* 162 Hardyesse uor to þolie alle þe kueadnesse þet þe wordle may þreapni. 1559 Bercher *Nobylytye Wymen* (1904) 128 Yf they be threpned [It. *se sono minacciate*] they langwyshe, yf they be cheryshed they be prowde.

2. To blame, rebuke, chide, reprove: = prec. 1.

a 1667 Skinner *Etymologicon* (1671), To Threap or Threapen, *vox agro Linc. usitatissima*, ab AS. *Ðreapian, Redarguere, vel Ðrafian, Urgere.* 1691 Ray *N. C. Words*, *Threap, Threapen*, to blame, rebuke, reprove, chide. 1904 *Eng. Dial. Dict.* (E. Yorks.), *Threapen*, to reprove, rebuke, chide.

Hence **Threa·pening** *vbl. sb.*

1340 *Ayenb.* 65, vij. o're boȝes. Huer-of þe uerste is strif, þe o'er chidinge, þe bridde missiginge, þe uerþe godelinge, þe uifte atwytinge, þe zixte þreapninge, þe zeuende vnonynge arere. *Ibid.* 66 Efterward zuo comeþ þe þreapnynges and beginneþ þe medles and þe werres.

Threat (þret), *sb.* Forms: 1–3 **þreat**, (1 **ðreot(t, ðreatt**), 2 **þreatt**, 3 **þræt**, 3–4 **þrat**, 4 **þret**, **thrett**, 4–5 **þret(e**, **thret(e**, 6 **thrette**, 6– **threat.** [OE. *þréat* masc. (With sense 2 cf. ON. *þraut* fem. struggle, labour, trouble):—OTeut. **þrauto*^{z}, -*ā*, from ablaut-series **þreut-*, *þraut-*, *þrut-* (cf. OE. *þréotan* to trouble, weary, Goth. *us-þriutan* to trouble, threaten, OHG. *ir-driozan*, MHG. *ver-driezen*, Ger. *ver-driessen*, Du. *verdrieten* to trouble, vex; cf. L. *trūdĕre* to press, thrust). Sense 1 has the same form as 2 in OE. and early ME., and is commonly considered the same word; it appears to go back, like 'throng' and 'press (of people)', to the radical sense 'to press'.]

I. †**1.** A throng, press, crowd, multitude of people; a troop, band, body of men. *Obs.*

Beowulf 2406 Se wæs on ðam ðreate þreotteoþa secg. *a* 800 Cynewulf *Elene* 329 Hio..þrungon..on þreate. *c* 950 *Lindisf. Gosp.* Mark iii. 32 gesætt ymb hine ðreat [*c* 975 *Rushw. G.* ðe ðreatt, L. *turba*]. *Ibid.* viii. 2 Ic milsa ofer ðreat [*R.* ðreott]. *c* 1205 Lay. 9791 Riden ut to-some..þritti þusend þe þræt wes þa mare. *Ibid.* 26294 Hit is feole ȝere þat heore þrættes [*c* 1275 þretes] comen here.

II. †**2.** Painful pressure, oppression, compulsion; vexation, torment; affliction, distress, misery; danger, peril. *Obs.*

a 800 Cynewulf *Juliana* 465 Is þeos þrag ful strong, þreat ormæte; ic sceal þinga gehwylc þolian. 971 *Blickl. Hom.* 119 Hie seoþþan ealle worlde wean & ealle þreatas oforhogodan. *c* 1200 *Trin. Coll. Hom.* 61 Listed nu wich þreat dauid setted uppen us bute [we] lesten ure bihese. 13.. *E. E. Allit. P.* B. 55 Þenne þrat moste I þole. *c* 1330 R. Brunne *Chron.* Prol. (1810) p. xcviii, With mykelle wo, In sclaundire, in threte & in thro. 13.. *Minor Poems fr. Vernon MS.* xliv. 36 And þretes—þo beoþ vuele þre, Furst and hunger and þesternesse. *c* 1450 Lovelich *Grail* xiii. 626 They wenden han put him to gret thret.

3. A denunciation to a person of ill to befall him; *esp.* a declaration of hostile determination or of loss, pain, punishment, or damage to be inflicted in retribution for or conditionally upon some course; a menace. Also *fig.* an indication of impending evil.

The radical sense appears to be 'pressure applied to the will by declaration of the harm that will follow non-compliance'. It is thus indirect compulsion.

It is doubtful whether quots. *c* 1000 belong here or to sense 2.

c 1000 Ælfric *Saints' Lives* xxv. 220 Ac mathathias nolde ..godes æ forgægan for his [the king's] gramlican ðreate. *Ibid.* xxviii. 105 Ða hæþenan..beton hine secgan mid swyðlicum þreate hweþer he cristen wære. *c* 1200 *Vices & Virt.* 87 Oðerhwile cumeð maniȝe þohtes of godes þreatt of helle pines. *a* 1250 *Owl & Night.* 58 Ne recche ich nouht of þine þrete. *c* 1325 *Song of Yesterday* 148 in *E. E. P.* (1862) 137 Ȝif þi neiȝebor þe manas Oþer to culle oþer to bete..þou wold drede þi neiȝebores þrete. 1526 *Pilgr. Perf.* (W. de W. 1531) 14 b, Wherby he myght scape the menasses and threttes of god. 1601 Shaks. *Jul. C.* iv. iii. 66 There is no terror Cassius in your threats. 1750 Gray *Elegy* 62 The threats of pain and ruin to despise. 1874 Green *Short Hist.* vii. § 1. 348 He met the hostility of the nobles with a threat which marked his power. 1884 *Manch. Exam.* 19 Feb. 5/4 Clouds full of the threat of rain.

Threat (þret), *v.* *arch.* and *dial.* Forms: see below. [OE. *þréatian* weak vb., pa. t. *þréatode*, f. *þréat*, Threat *sb.*:—OTeut. type **þrautōjan.*]

A. Illustration of Forms.

1. *Pres. stem.* **α.** 1 **þreatian**, 3 **-en**, **-in**, **þretie(n**, **þræten**, **þreat**, 3–5 **þrete**, 5 **þreete**, 5–6 **threte**, 6 **threete**, 6–7 **threate**, 6– **threat.**

c 888 K. Ælfred *Boeth.* xxxvii. § 1 Þa..þreatiað eal moncynn mid hiora þrymme. *a* 1225 *Leg. Kath.* 623 Me ham walde þreatin & leaden unlaheliche. *a* 1225 *Juliana* 13 Nulle ich þe her onont þreate se þu þreate buhe ne leien. *a* 1250 *Owl & Night.* 1609 Me myd stone & lugge þreteþ. 1483 *Cath. Angl.* 385/2 To Threte, *minari.* 1530 Palsgr. 755/2, I threete, or I thretten one to do hym harme, *je menasse.* 1600 Threat [see B. 5].

β. 4–6 **thret**, **thrette**, 4–7 **thrett.**

13.. *Cursor M.* 18247 Nu þai threit [*v.r.* thret] vs sare. *Ibid.* 19181 Þar-for sal we thret þam herd. *c* 1375 *Sc. Leg. Saints* xliii. (*Agatha*) 147 Gyf þe fyre þu threttis me. 1523 Ld. Berners *Froiss.* I. clx. 194 Whan ye be at Parys..ye do thret thenglysshmen. *a* 1533 — *Gold. Bk. M. Aurel.* (1546) Gg iij b, She..thretteth them that be absent.

γ. 3 **þrattien**, **-en.**

c 1205 Lay. 20341 Swiðe heo gunnen þrattien [*c* 1275 þretie] Arður þene king. *Ibid.* 18738 þrattest [see B. 4 a].

2. *Past tense.* **α.** 1 th-, **þreatade**, **-ode**, 2 **-ede**, 3 **þreated**, **þræted**, **þret-**, **þrætt-**, **þrettede**, 4 **þreted**, 5–6 **thretid**, 6– **threated.**

c 725–*c* 1000 [see B. 1]. *c* 1160 [see B. 2]. *c* 1205 Lay. 504 Þe king þræted [*c* 1275 þretede] Brutun. *Ibid.* 27131 Summe þrætteden [*c* 1275 þrettede] heore ueond. *c* 1250 Ðreated [see B. 3]. 13.. *Minor Poems fr. Vernon MS.* liv. 33 Harde þei þreted me in her þouȝt. *c* 1440 Thretid [see B. 3]. *a* 1529 Skelton *Wofully Araid* 13 The Jewis me thretid. 1673 Wood *Life* 14 July (O.H.S.) II. 266, I threated to geld the translator.

β. 3–4 **þrette**, 4 **þret**, 4–5 **thrett**, 4–6 **thret**, **thrette**, 5 **threte**, (**thred**).

c 1250 Ðrette, *c* 1300 Þrette [see B. 5]. 13.. *Cursor M.* 19603 Saulus..thrett [*v.rr.* þrette, þret] All þe cristen. *c* 1330 R. Brunne *Chron.* (1810) 44 Þe corsaynt & þe kirke he threte for to brennyng. *c* 1400 *Laud Troy Bk.* 10493 He chased the Troiens & thret. *c* 1440 *Alphabet of Tales* 81 And þan he thred hur. *c* 1440 *Generydes* 500 She threte hym sore. 1523 Ld. Berners *Froiss.* I. cccl xxxiii. 645 They thret them of London.

γ. 2–4 **þratte**, 4 **þrat**, 5 **thrat(t**, 5–6 **thratte**, 6 **thrate.**

c 1200 Ormin 15514 He þratte stirne wind o sæ & itt wass stille & liþe. 13.. *E. E. Allit. P.* B. 937 Þe aungelez hasted þise oþer & aȝly hem þratten. 13.. *Gaw. & Gr. Knt.* 1980 Fele þryuande þonkkez he þrat hom to haue. *c* 1400 *Laud Troy Bk.* 6907 Thei thrat him alle, that he was tan. 1589 R. Robinson *Gold. Mirr.* (Chetham) 38 Albion Isle he thrate.

3. *Pa. pple.*: 3 **i-ðrat**, 4–5 **þret**, **-tt**, **-tte**, 4–6 **threted**, 7 **threat**, 5– **threated.**

a 1225 *Ancr. R.* 304 Ich was ined [*MS. T.* iðrat] ..13.. *Gaw. & Gr. Knt.* 1725 Þer he watz þreted, & ofte thef called. *a* 1400–50 *Alexander* 707 Þik & þrathly am I þret. 1470–85 Malory *Arthur* x. lxii. 520 Ful sore are we thret. 1472 Sir J. Paston in *P. Lett.* III. 38 That poor woode is soor manashed and thrett. 1631 Threat [see B. 3].

B. Signification.

†**1.** *trans.* To press, urge, try to force or induce; esp. by means of menaces. (With clause or inf.)

c 725 *Corpus Gloss.* (O.E.T.) 1275 *Maceratus*, þreatad. *Ibid.* 2169 *Urguet*, threatade. *a* 900 *O. E. Martyrol.* 18 Apr. 58 Adrianus se caser[e hine] þreatade þæt he Cristes widsoce. *c* 950 *Lindisf. Gosp.* Matt. v. 42 Ðæm nedende vel ðæm ðreatende [*Vulg.* uolenti] huerfa ðec ne acerr. *c* 1000 Ælfric *Hom.* I. 416 Þa cempan..hine ðreatedon þæt he ðære deadan anlicnysse his lac offrian sceolde. *a* 1225 *Ancr. R.* 248 Ne mei he [the devil] buten schulde, þe uord sumhwat of his apeware, & oluhnen, oðer þreatien, þet me bugge þerof. 13.. [see A. 2 γ]. *c* 1470 *Dicta Philos.* 308 Who that wol nat be feire entreted, sholde be foule & rigorously threted. 1501 *Plumpton Corr.* (Camden) 157 Ever they thratte me that I shold go to London. 1638 *Hamilton Papers* (Camden) 4 They..threat privatt men to singe the Covenatt.

†**2.** To rebuke, reprove. *Obs.* Cf. Threap *v.* 1.

a 1000 *Ags. Ps.* (Th.) lxvii. 27 [lxviii. 30] On wuda wildeor wordum þreatast. *c* 1160 *Hatton Gosp.* Luke iv. 35 And he be-wente hine and hyo þreatede. *c* 1200 [see A. 2 α]. *a* 1300 *E. E. Psalter* vi. 1 Lauerd, ne threte me in þi wreþþe.

3. To hold out threats against; = Threaten 2.

a 1000 *Ags. Ps.* (Th.) ix. 29 [x. 8] And þreatað þone earman mid his eaxum. *c* 1205 Lay. 641 He..þreated þene castel þat folc þer inne. *c* 1250 *Gen. & Ex.* 4125 And wið ðis canticle..Ðat ðreated ðo men bitter-like Ðe god ne sal hem luue-like. 1428 in *Surtees Misc.* (1888) 3 Wham he thret with bodily harm. *c* 1440 *Alphabet of Tales* 430 He apperid vnto hym & thretid hym att he was ferd for. *c* 1489 Caxton *Sonnes of Aymon* xvii. 390 It becometh not to suche a knighte as ye be, for to threte me thus. 1526 *Pilgr. Perf.* (W. de W. 1531) 66 He that threteth a childe for his barkyng prouoketh hym to more felnesse. 1631 *Arraignm. Whole Creature* x. § 2. 84 The Apostles..being told that they were threat, and beat for the Name of Christ. 1781 *Hist. Europe* in *Ann. Reg.* 25/2 The Spaniards seemed so great a force..as seemed sufficient..to threat the British fleets and islands with the most imminent danger. 1848 Lytton *Harold* i. iv, Send for me if danger threat thee.

b. With inf. or clause as complement.

a 1330 *Otuel* 736 Hou þei..þratten roulond to die. *c* 1330 R. Brunne *Chron. Wace* (Rolls) 8294 [The Britons] þratte Hengist to wake hys wough. *c* 1440 *Alphabet of Tales* 97 Þe devull come aforn hym with a byrnand stake, and thratt hym þat he sulde þruste itt in at his mouthe. 1461 *Paston Lett.* II. 25 She is thret if that she myght be take, she shuld be slayne. *a* 1517 in G. P. Scrope *Castle Combe* (1852) 295 He..thret hym that he schulde make hyme aper before my lordys grase. 1611 *Coryat's Crudities* Panegyr. Verses, iij, All the Sophists he did threat Their problemes to confound. 1642 J. Eaton *Honey-c. Free Justif.* 475 It would be a foolish part to set it [a kettle] beside the fire, and to charge it to be hot, and to threat it that else it shall be built.

c. *fig.* Said of things; = Threaten 4.

1422 [see Threating *vbl. sb.*]. *c* 1590 Marlowe *Faust.* vii. 18 A sumptuous temple..That threats the stars with her aspiring top. 1634 Milton *Comus* 39 This drear Wood, The nodding horror of whose shady brows Threats the forlorn and wandring Passinger. *a* 1717 Parnell *Bookworm* 70 To see what dangers threat the year. 1800 Coleridge *Piccolom.* i. iii. 46 This tempest, which..threats us from all quarters. 1832 *Fraser's Mag.* IV. 764 The storm which threats kingdoms.

4. To hold forth (something) by way of a threat; = Threaten 3. **a.** with inf. or clause as obj.

c 1205 Lay. 17300 He gon þretien swiðe þat al he wolde heom to-driue. *Ibid.* 18738 Þu..þrattest hine to slænne. *c* 1250 *Lutel Soth Sermun* 82 in *O. E. Misc.* 190 Hire louerd hire dame þreteþ hire to bete. 1375 Barbour *Bruce* iv. 288 Vmbeset With fayis þat to slay hym thret. *c* 1555 Abp. Parker *Ps.* Dij, If the adversaries flocke to-gether, and threate to destroy the house of God. 1633 Bp. Hall *Hard Texts, O. T.* 413 Who is this..that threats to sweep all before him? 1681 Dryden *Abs. & Achit.* 801 If ancient fabricks nod, and threat to fall. 1724 Ramsay *Royal Archers* 25 And dares to threat,..' No man unpunish'd shall provoke my rage.'

b. With sb. or pron. as obj.

c 1386 Chaucer *Parson's T.* ⁋ 572 He threttith moore than he may parfourme. 1526 *Pilgr. Perf.* (1531) 61 What peyne & turment is threte to the wycked & euyll liuers. 1581 Mulcaster *Positions* vi. (1887) 47 Where this case threates harme, there thinning fines the substance. 1594 Shaks. *Rich. III*, v. iii. 205 Euery one did threat To morrowes vengeance on the head of Richard. 1633 Bp. Hall *Hard Texts, N. T.* 17 Let the Tyrants..threat what they please. 1795 Burns *Dumfries Volunteers* i, Does haughty Gaul invasion threat? 1821 Clare *Vill. Minstr.* I. 4 Where black neglect..threats her constant winter cold and chill.

5. *absol.* or *intr.* To offer threats; = Threaten 5.

c 1250 *Gen. & Ex.* 2023 Often ðhe ðrette, often ðhe bad. *c* 1300 *Havelok* 1163 Sho was adrad, for he so þrette. 1390 Gower *Conf.* III. 57 Bot they with proude wordes grete Begunne to manace and threte. *c* 1491 *Chast. Goddes Chyld.* 14 She..spekyth somtyme sharply somtyme she threteth. 1545 Wyatt *Penit. Ps.* vi. 30 That drede of deathe, of deathe that ever lastes, Threateth of right. 1600 Holland *Livy* viii. xxxii. 304 Some were heard to intreat, others to threat. 1605 Shaks. *Macb.* ii. i. 60 Whiles I threat, he liues. 1725 Pope *Odyss.* ii. 231 Threat on, O prince! elude the bridal day, Threat on, till all thy stores in waste decay. 1822 Byron *Werner* ii. ii. 266 Threat'st thou? 1901 Savage-Armstr. *Ball.* 64 (E.D.D.) Whun danger threats, return.

Hence †**Threat** *ppl. a.*, obtained by threats, forced, compulsory.

c 1375 *Cursor M.* 26944 (Fairf.) Wiseli loke þou be shriuin & noȝt wiþ strenght þer-to driuen For þret shrift mai haue na mede. *c* 1375 *Sc. Leg. Saints* xi. (*Symon & Judas*) 338 God wald one na wyse Of ony man haf thret seruice.

Threaten (þre·t'n), *v.* Forms: 1 **þreatnian**, 3 **þret(t)ne(n**, **þretni**, 4–5 **þret(t)en**, 4–6 **threten**, **thretne**, 6 **thretten**, *Sc.* **threiten**, (6–8 **thretn-**), 6– **threaten.** [OE. *þréat-n-ian*, f. *þréat*, Threat *sb.* + -en^5 2.]

†**1.** *trans.* To press, urge, force; = Threat *v.*^{1} 1. Only in OE.

c 1000 Ælfric *Hom.* I. 424 Neadað se decfol eow þæt ge cristene men to his biggengum ðreatniað?

2. To try to influence (a person) by menaces; to utter or hold out a threat against; to declare (usually conditionally) one's intention of inflicting injury upon (in quot. 1816, one's certainty that some specified injury will fall upon); to menace. Const. *with* the thing; also with compl. clause (with finite vb. or inf.).

c 1290 *S. Eng. Leg.* I. 35/41 He þrettnede faste hermogenes. 1297 R. Glouc. (Rolls) 2391 Þe picars were wroþe ek & þretnede him ynou. 1387 Trevisa *Higden* (Rolls) III. 419 Alisaundre þrettneþ þe Iewes. 14.. *Sir Beues* 3341 (MS. N.) He me thretenyd for to slen. [15.. *Ibid.* (Pynson) 3001 He threteneth me to be slayne.] 1474 Caxton *Chesse* ii. v. (1883) 68 A tyrant dide do tormente Anamaximenes & thretenyd hym for to cutte of his tonge. 1526 *Pilgr. Perf.* (W. de W. 1531) 177 b, Traian commaunded hym to speke no more of it, thretnynge hym, that yf he dyd, he sholde lese his heed. 1651 Hobbes *Leviath.* ii. xxxi. 186 Threatning them with Punishment. 1715 De Foe *Fam. Instruct.* i. iv. (1841) I. 83, I won't be threatened neither. 1816 Scott *Old Mort.* xliv, In vain his wife..hung by his skirts, threatening him with death..for meddling with other folks' matters. 1834 *Picture of Liverpool* 39 All classes were threatened to be overwhelmed in one universal ruin.

†**b.** To charge or command with threats of punishment or displeasure; to command sternly or strictly. (Chiefly in biblical versions.) *Obs.*

1382 Wyclif *Mark* viii. 30 And he thretenyde hem, that thei schulden nat seie to ony man of him. 1526 Tindale *Acts* iv. 17 Lett vs threten and chaurge them that they speake hence forth to noo man in this name. 1555 Eden *Decades* 158 They..threatned them to auoyde the lande excepte they woolde bee distroyed euery manne. 1582 N.T. (Rhem.) *Mark* i. 25 And Iesvs threatened him, saying, Hold thy peace, and goe out of the man.

c. *fig.* (chiefly of impersonal agents or objects): To be likely to injure; to be a source of danger to; to endanger actively.

1638 R. Baker tr. *Balzac's Lett.* (vol. II.) 34 Perhaps the tempest that threatens my head will fall but at my feet. 1725 De Foe *Voy. round World* (1840) 302 The wind..blew very hard, threatening us with a storm. 1781 Gibbon *Decl. & F.* xix. II. 139 The Persian monarch, elated by victory, again threatened the peace of Asia. 1835 Thirlwall *Greece* x. I. 381 Where one threatens the existence of another. 1877 Froude *Short Stud.* (1883) IV. i. ii. 23 France and England had been..drawn together by a special danger which threatened Christendom.

3. To hold out or offer (some injury) by way of a threat; to declare one's intention of inflicting. **a.** with infin. or clause as obj.

1297 R. Glouc. (Rolls) 11209 Þe burgeis were þo bolde, & þretnede to nime mo. 1567 *Satir. Poems Reform.* vi. 71 The Propheit threitnit..That war and battell sould his land pas throw. 1649 Bp. Reynolds *Serm. Hosea* iv. 59 God threatneth terribly to shake the earth. 1682 Bunyan *Holy War* 49 They threatned also what men they would be. 1748 *Anson's Voy.* ii. iii. 146 Threatning to murder all who should oppose them. 1855 Macaulay *Hist. Eng.* xxi. IV. 663 He was at last forced to threaten that he would immediately make the whole matter public.

b. with sb. or pron. as obj.

1297 R. Glouc. (Rolls) 9383 Mid word he þretneþ muche & lute deþ in dede. *c* 1450 *R. Gloucester's Chron.* (1724) 483/1 *note* (MS. Coll. Arms), He meketh prout men, and he threteneth werre. 1590 Marlowe *2nd Pt. Tamburl.* v. iii, These cowards..threaten conquest on our sovereign. 1649 Bp. Reynolds *Serm. Hosea* i. 43 They..should unwillingly suffer what he threatneth. 1774 Burke *Corr.* (1844) I. 498 The party that has lost the election threatens a petition. 1844 H. H. Wilson *Brit. India* ii. xii. II. 585 Reluctant to inflict the penalty that had been threatened.

4. *fig.* Of things, conditions: To give ominous indication of (impending evil); to presage, portend.

1611 Shaks. *Wint. T.* iii. iii. 4 The skies looke grimly, And threaten present blusters. 1644 Evelyn *Diary* 22 Oct., Another pendant Towre like that at Pisa, always threatning ruine. 1818–20 E. Thompson tr. *Cullen's Nosol. Method.* (ed. 3) 247 A sense of hunger threatening syncope. 1853 W. C. Baldwin *Afr. Hunting* viii. 339 The weather constantly threatens rain.

intr. (for *pass.*). 1850 D. G. Mitchell *Reveries Bachelor* 175 Hostilities would sometimes threaten between the school and village boys.

b. with infin.: To appear likely *to do* some evil.

1780 *Mirror* No. 81 ⁋ 9, I am sometimes..frightened with dangers that threaten to diminish it [my estate]. 1848 Dickens *Dombey* iv, It threatens to be wet to-night. 1899 'A. Hope' *King's Mirr.* ix, Age had not bent, but it threatened to break him. *Mod.* The new drainage scheme threatens to be an expensive undertaking.

5. *absol.* or *intr.* To utter or use threats; to declare one's intention of injuring or punishing in order to influence. **a.** *lit.* (absol. use of 2 or 3).

1297 R. Glouc. (Rolls) 10308 Nou sir clerc quaþ þe king ȝe mowe þretni ynou. *c* 1450 tr. *De Imitatione* iii. xviii. 86 Þou shalt not þreten euerlastingly. 1602 Shaks. *Ham.* iii. iv. 57 An eye like Mars, to threaten or command. 1774 Goldsm. *Nat. Hist.* (1776) VII. 221 If too closely pursued, they [snakes] hiss and threaten. 1864 in Ellacombe *Ch. Bells Devon*, etc. (1872) 267 Do not threaten,..never let down your dignity by one single word of violence.

b. *fig.* (absol. use of 2 c or 4). To portend evil.

1610 Shaks. *Temp.* v. i. 178 Though the Seas threaten they are mercifull. 1725 Pope *Odyss.* ii. 6 A two-edged faulchion threatened by his side. 1793 Mann in *Lett. Lit. Men* (Camden) 437 Our political horizon blackens and threatens more and more. *Mod.* The weather threatens.

¶**6.** *To threaten kindness* (*upon* a person); app. an altered form of the phrase *to threap kindness*: see Threap *v.* 4 b. *Obs.*

1560 Daus *Sleidane's Comm.* 247 The byshop of Rome sendeth his letters to the Swisses, & threatning vpon them kindnes, for the frenship that had ben betwene them & his predecessours. 1577–87 Holinshed *Chron.* (1807) II. 249 The moonks being overcome with the kings words, threatning kindnesse upon them, fulfilled his request. 1579 Lyly *Euphues* (Arb.) 84 Philautus..threatneth such kindenesse at my handes, and suche curtesie at yours, that he shoulde accompt me his wife before he woe me.

Hence **Threa·tenable** *a.*, that may be threatened.

1841–4 Emerson *Ess., Exper.* Wks. (Bohn) I. 186 The chagrins which the bad heart gives off..take form..and threaten or insult whatever is threatenable and insultable in us.

Threatened (þre·t'nd), *ppl. a.* [f. prec. + -ed^1.]

1. That is the object of a threat; assailed by menaces. Proverb *Threatened men live long.*

1533 Lady Eliz. Wheathill in Mary A. E. Wood *Lett. Roy. & Illustr. Ladies* (1846) II. 91 There is an old saying, —'threatened men live long'. *a* 1642 Sir W. Monson *Naval Tracts* ii. (1704) 287/1 It is an old Saying, That a threaten'd Man eats Bread. 1855 Macaulay *Hist. Eng.* xx. IV. 401 He took his post near Louvain, on the road between the two threatened cities. 1894 *Westm. Gaz.* 27 Nov. 5/3 The best-hated and the most threatened man in Germany.

2. Of evil: Held out or presented as impending.

1567 Golding *Ovid's Met.* vi. (1593) 129 Neptunus standing striking with his long threatned blade Upon the ragged rocke. 1660 South *Interest Deposed* (title-p.) In the threatned and expected Ruin of the Laws. 1794 Mrs. Radcliffe *Myst. Udolpho* xxxi, She determined to brave the threatened vengeance. 1831 Scott *Ct. Robt.* xxiv, The Turks..had resolved to prevent the threatened attack of the crusaders.

Threatener (þre·t'nəɹ). [f. as prec. + -er^1.] One who threatens.

a 1541 Wyatt *Song of Iopas* 46 The starre of Saturne olde, A threat'ner of all liuing things with drought. 1595 Shaks. *John* v. i. 49 Threaten the threatner, and out-face the brow Of bragging horror. 1630 *R. Johnson's Kingd. & Commw.* A ij b, That Enemie and Threatner of our English Nation. 1748 Richardson *Clarissa* (1810) III. ii. 10 Threateners..were seldom to be feared. 1867 Jean Ingelow *Story Doom* vii. 140 A feeble threatener with a foolish threat.

Threatening (þre·t'niŋ), *vbl. sb.* [f. as prec. + -ing^1.] The action of the verb Threaten; menacing; also, an instance of this, a threat.

c 1290 *St. Kenelm* 242 in *S. Eng. Leg.* I. 352 So gret þretningue for him heo made. 1388 Wyclif *Acts* iv. 29 And now, Lord, biholde in to the thretnyngis [1382 thretingis] of hem. 1489 Caxton *Faytes of A.* i. xvi. 46 By thretnyng he shal also fraye hem. *a* 1548 Hall *Chron.*, *Hen. IV* 7 b, The said kyng..menaced theym with sore thretenynges. 1611 Bible *Eph.* vi. 9 Doe the same things vnto them, forbearing threatning. 1719 De Foe *Crusoe* (1840) II. iii. 54 The Spaniards, despising their threatening. 1865–6 H. Phillips *Amer. Paper Curr.* II. 12 The threatenings of war were then only heard at a distance.

Threa·tening, *ppl. a.* [f. as prec. + -ing^2.] That threatens; conveying or indicating a threat or menace; portending some impending evil.

1530 in W. H. Turner *Select. Rec. Oxford* (1880) 83 Gevyng hym many thretenyng and opprobryous words. 1656 Earl Monm. tr. *Boccalini, Pol. Touchstone* (1674) 287 With threatning countenances they said [etc.]. 1724 De Foe *Mem. Cavalier* (1840) 48 If Tilly did but write a threatening letter. 1809 Scott *Anne of G.* xxx, There muster yonder in the west some threatening clouds. 1898 *Allbutt's Syst. Med.* V. 118 The fever is high, and the condition of the patient is threatening.

Threa·teningly, *adv.* [f. prec. + -ly^2.] In a threatening manner; menacingly.

1601 Shaks. *All's Well* ii. iii. 85 The honor sir that flames in your faire eyes, Before I speake too threatningly replies. 1819 Wordsw. '*Departing summer hath assumed*' vii, Woe! woe to Tyrants! from the lyre Broke threateningly. 1857 W. Collins *Dead Secret* v. iii, The booming of the surf sounding threateningly near in..the fog.

So **Threa·teningness.**

1891 Atkinson *Last of Giant Killers* 239 The suddenness of the action, and the threateningness of it.

†**Threa·ter.** *Obs. rare*$^{-0}$. [f. Threat *v.*^{1} + -er^1.] = Threatener.

c 1440 *Promp. Parv.* 492/2 Thretare, *minator.*

Threatful (þre·tfŭl), *a. rare.* [f. Threat *sb.* + -ful.] Full of threats; threatening.

c 1557 Abp. Parker *Ps.* E iij, The thretfull warninges of the judgement. 1611 Speed *Hist. Gt. Brit.* ix. viii. (1623) 582 By their threatfull letters. 1760–72 H. Brooke *Fool of Qual.* (1809) IV. 129 A threatful and agile whirl of his staff. 1878 Farrar *Early Chr.* II. 6 Not the threatful Law of Moses,..but the royal Law, the perfect Law of liberty.

Hence **Threa·tfully** *adv.*, threateningly.

1565 Stapleton tr. *Bede's Hist. Ch. Eng.* 50 S. Austen thretfully proficied, that, if they would not take peace with their brethern, they should receaue..warre from their enemies. 1634 Sir T. Herbert *Trav.* 190 [A] flaming Semiter (threatfully held against him). 1822 Hood *Lycus* vi, The spirits of sin..that..threatfully warr'd with the light.

Threating (þre·tiŋ), *vbl. sb.* *Obs.* or *arch.* [f. Threat *v.*^{1} + -ing^1.] The action of the verb Threat; threatening; a threat.

1046 *O. E. Chron.* (MS. D), On þam ȝeare ȝegaderade Eadward cyng mycele scypferde on Sandwic þurh Magnus þreatunge on Norwegon. *a* 1225 *Ancr. R.* 156 Vre Louerd hefde ifuld him of his þreatunge. 1382 [see quot. 1388 s. v. Threatening *vbl. sb.*]. 1422 tr. *Secreta Secret., Priv. Priv.* 152 Seneca..wriet the hede atte the t[h]retyngis of the Swerde. 1482 *Monk of Evesham* (Arb.) 96 Whenne he herde..this thretyng he was sore aferd. 1562 J. Heywood *Prov. & Epigr.* (1867) 129 Not to wag their beardes in brawlyng and threatyng. 1643 Bp. H. Leslie *Serm. St. Mary's, Oxford* 9 Feb. 4 None of his threatings could fall to the ground.

Threa·ting, *ppl. a.* *Obs.* or *arch.* [f. as prec. + -ing^2.] That threats; threatening, menacing.

13.. *K. Alis.* 930 (Bodl. MS.) Wiþ cryeyng & þretyng wordes. 1483 *Cath. Angl.* 385/2 Threthynge, *minans, minax.* 1510 *Sel. Cas. Crt. Star Chamber* (Selden) 205 With thretyng wordes [they] Caused the Carpynders to leve ther werke. 1641 A. Scott *Journ.* in *Sc. Hist. Soc. Misc.* (1904) 278 The threating danger of the Scottish mist.

Threatless (þre·tlès), *a. rare.* [f. Threat *sb.* + -less.] Devoid of threats; not threatening.

1605 Sylvester *Du Bartas* ii. iii. iv. *Captaines* 201 Threat-lesse their brows, and without braves their voyce.

Threave, variant of Thrave.

Thred(e, thredde, obs. ff. Third, Thread.

Three (þrī), *a.* and *sb.* Forms: see below. [OE. *þrí* (*þríe*), *þrío*, *þréo*, Com. Teut. and Indo-Eur.; = OFris. *thre* m., *thria* f., *thriu*, *thria* n.; OS. *thrie* (*thria*, *threa*) m., *threa* f., *thrua* (*thriu*, *thria*) n. (MLG., LG. *drē*, *drū* n., MDu., Du. *drie*); OHG. *drî*, *drio*, *driu* (MHG. *drîe*, Ger. *drei*); ON. *þrír*, *þrjár*, *þrjú* (Norw., Sw., Da. *tre*); Goth. **þreis*, *þrija*;—OTeut. **þrī*^{z} (:—**þrijiz*), **þrijō*:—Indo-Eur. *treies*, *treja.* Cf. Skr. *trayas*, Zend *θri*, Gr. *τρεῖς*, *τρία*, L. *trēs*, *tria*, Lith. *trỹs*, OSlav. *trĭje*, *trije*, Irish and Welsh *tri*. The masc. has the form of a plural -*i* stem.]

A. Illustration of Forms.

α. *nom.* and *acc.* 1 masc. **þrí**, **þríe**, **þrý** (**þréo**), fem. and neut. **þrío**, **þréo**, (*ONorth.* **ðriu**, **ðria**, **ðréa**); 2–4 **þreo**, 1–5 **þre**, (2 **þru** (?*ū*), 2–3 **þri**, **þro**, 2–4 **þrie**), 4 **þree**, (**tre**), 4–6 **thre** (6 **threy**, **thrie**), 5– **three.**

803 *Charter Cnðred* in *O. E. T.* 442 Þisses londes earan ðrie sulong. *c* 825 *Vesp. Hymns* v. (*O. E. T.* 405), Ðreo foeðan [*ternos stateres*]. *c* 891 *O. E. Chron.* an. 891, Þrie Scottas comon. *c* 950 *Lindisf. Gosp.* Mark viii. 2 Ðrio dogor ge-abidas mec. *Ibid.* ix. 5 Ðrea [*c* 975 *Rushw.* ðria] husa. — Luke xi. 5 Sel me ðreo [*Rushw.* ðria] hlafas. 971 *Blickl. Hom.* 145 Þa þre fæmnan. *c* 1000 Ælfric *Gen.* xl. 12 Þa þreo clystru þæt sind..þri dagas. *c* 1000 *Ags. Gosp.* Matt. xii. 40 Þry dagas and þreo niht. 11.. *Sax. Leechd.* III. 134 Lege þarto þru dæges & þre niht. *a* 1175 *Cott. Hom.* 237 Þri ampres were an mancyn. *c* 1175 *Lamb. Hom.* 73 Þro þing boð þet ech Mon habbe mot. *c* 1200 *Trin. Coll. Hom.* 3 On þesse þre wuken. *Ibid.* 27 Þese þrie þing. *c* 1205 Lay. 53 Þa þre boc. *Ibid.* 391 He ȝef Assaracun..þreo [*c* 1275 þre] castles. *c* 1275 *Ibid.* 16589 Þreo daȝes and þreo niht. 13.. *Cursor M.* 5469 (Cott.) Þar of tre yeir was him wan. *Ibid.* 9192 (Gött.) Þat was vmgang jornays thrie. 1340 *Ayenb.* 88 Þe þri greteste guodes. 1362 Langl. *P. Pl.* A. i. 20 Þreo [1377 B. Þree, 1393 C. Þre] þinges. 1483 *Cath. Angl.* 385/1 Three, *tres & tria.* 1552–3 *Inv. Ch. Goods Staffs.* in *Ann. Lichfield* (1863) IV. 46 Stoles & fannes for threy vestiments. 1596 Thrie [see B. I. 3]. 1600 in *Shaks. Cent. Praise* (Shaks. Soc.) 36 The L. montegle with some thre more.

β. *dative*, 1 **þrim**, **þrym**, **þriim**, **þrém**, 1–3 **þréom** (3 **þrom**); *genitive*, 1 **þríora**, **þréora.**

c 893 K. Ælfred *Oros.* Contents iv. vi, On þriora consula dæge. *Ibid.* iii. ix. § 5 On ðæm þrim ȝearum..on þrim folc ȝefeohtum. *c* 950 *Lindisf. Gosp.* Matt. xxvi 61 Æfter ðrim [*c* 1000 *Ags. Gosp.* þrym; *c* 1160 *Hatt. Gosp.* þrem] dagum. — Mark xv. 29 On ðriim dagum. *c* 1000 *Ags. Gosp.* John ii. 6 Ælc wæs on twegra sestra gemete oððe on þreora. *c* 1100 *O. E. Chron.* an. 1078, Þreom nihton ær Candelmæssan. *c* 1205 Lay. 8059 Þas dæies an þreom [*c* 1275 a þreo] wiken. *Ibid.* 10034 Wið innen þan þrom ȝeren.

B. Signification.

The cardinal number next above two, represented by the symbols 3, III, or iii.

I. as *adj.* **1.** In concord with a sb. expressed.

803–*c* 1000 [see A]. *c* 1175 *Lamb. Hom.* 11 Nu weren þas þreo laȝe ȝe-writen inne þa oðre table breode sunderlipes. *c* 1250 *Gen. & Ex.* 557 Noe and hise ðre sunen. *a* 1300 *Cursor M.* 182 Fiue thosand men..he Fedd wyt fiue laues and fisses thre. *c* 1412 Hoccleve *De Reg. Princ.* 1801 Of thre conclusions moot I cheese one: Or begge, or stele, or sterue. *c* 1460 *Wisdom* 293 in *Macro Plays* 45 Ye haue iij enmyes:..The worlde, þe flesche, & þe fende. 1526 *Pilgr. Perf.* (W. de W. 1531) 1 This treatyse..is..diuyded in to thre bokes. 1753 Challoner *Cath. Chr. Instr.* 9 The three Divine Virtues of Faith, Hope and Charity. 1775 Sheridan *Rivals* iv. ii, Like Cerberus, three Gentlemen at once. 1872 Tyndall *Fragm. Sci.* (1879) I. xii. 358 Rocksalt cleaves in three directions.

b. Standing alone as predicate, or in concord with and following a pronoun, or pronominal adj.

c 1050 *Charter of Eadwine* in Kemble *Cod. Dipl.* IV. 260 Ðise write sinden þre. *c* 1200 Ormin 18657, & tohh þeȝȝ sinndenn alle þre An Godd. 1362 Langl. *P. Pl.* A. ix. 100 As þei þreo assenten. 13.. *Pol. Rel. & L. Poems* 228

Supplement, p. 3873; Corrigenda, p. 4092; Spurious words, p. 4093; Books quoted, p. 4094

Three-quartered. *Obs.*

Threescore (θrīˈskōˈr, θrēˈskoːr), *sb.*

Three-squared, *a. Obs.*

Three-stringed (-strīŋd), *a.* Having three strings : usually of a musical instrument.

Three-tined (-taind), *a.* Having three tines or prongs, three-pronged.

Three-tongued (-tr̥ŋd), *a.* Having three tongues ; also, knowing or using three languages, trilingual.

Three-way, *a.* Having, or connected with, three ways, roads, or channels ; situated where three ways meet.

Three-year, year, *c.*

Three-year-old, *a.* & *sb.*

Threne (θrīn), *sb.*

Threno-, combining form of Gr. θρῆνος lamentation.

Threnetic (θrīˈnetik), *a.*

Threnode (θrīˈnōd, θreˈnǫud), *sb.*

Threnodial (θrīˈnǫudiāl), *a.*

Threnodic (θrīˈnɔdik), *a.*

Threnodist (θrɛˈnǫdist), *sb.*

Threnody (θreˈnǫdi), *sb.*

Threnos (θrīˈnǫs), *sb.*

Thresh, *v.*, the earlier and etymological form of the vb. now also written **Thrash**, *q. v.*

Threshel (threˈʃel), *Obs.*

Threshfold, *obs. var.* **Threshold.**

Threshing, vbl. sb.

Threshold (θreˈʃǫuld), *sb.*

Thresher : see **Thrasher**.

Three-sharp *a.* (With suffix T.) A member of an Irish political organization instituted in 1806.

Thrasher, *var. of* **Thresher**, 2. A.-Amer. bird.

Threptic (θreˈptik), *a. rare*.

Threst, *thrast. Obs.* [f. OE. *þræstan*.]

THRESTING. 360 THRIFT. THRILL. 361 THRILL.

Thresting, vbl. sb.

Thretch, obs. f. **Threat**, **Thretch**, *v. Obs.*

Threte, *sb. Obs.*

Threte, *v. Obs.*

Thretteen, obs. form of **Thirteen**.

Threw, pa. t. of **Throw** *v.*

Thrice (θrəis), *adv.*

Thridace (θriˈdās), *sb.*

Thriddle, var. **Thirdle**.

Thride, *obs. var.* **Third.**

Thrie, thrye, *adv. Obs.*

Thrift (θrift), *sb.* [Origin obscure. Cf. ON. *þrift*.]

Thrift, *v.*

Thriftily (θriˈftili), *adv.*

Thriftiness (θriˈftinɛs), *sb.*

Thriftless (θriˈftlɛs), *a.*

Thrifty (θriˈfti), *a.*

Thrill (θril), *sb.* [OE. *þyrel*, ON. *þverr*.]

Thrillant, *a. Obs.*

Thrillage, *sb. Obs.*

Thrill (θril), *v.*

Thrill, sb. Obs. exc. dial. [f. THRILL v.]

1. Of the action of material bodies.

†Thrill, a. Obs. rare. [a. ON. *þrjól-r*...] Thrilling, piercing.

Thrilled, ppl. a.

†Thrillant, a. Obs. rare. [irreg. f. THRILL v.1 + -ANT.]

Thrill-hole, thrillhód. Obs.

Thriller (þri'lər).

Thrilless, a. rare.

Thrilly, a.

Thrilling, ppl. a.

Thrin, thrinne, a. (sb.) Forms: 1 þrinna, 3–4 þrynne, 3–5 þrinne, 4 þrynne, þrine, þrin. [Late OE. *þrinna*, 4 early ON. *þrinn-*]

†Thrinfald, a. Obs. rare.

Thring, v. Obs. exc. dial. [OE. *þringan*]

A. Illustration of Forms.

Thrinter.

Thrip (þrip), v. Obs. dial. Also 7 threppe.

Thripping, vbl. sb.

†Thrips (þrips). Entom. Often erron. taken as pl., with a false sing. thrip; the analogical Eng. pl. would be *thripses*.

Thripple (þri'p'l), sb. Now local.

†Thripple, v.

Thrive (þraiv), v.

A. Illustration of Forms.

Thriven (þri'v'n), ppl. a.

Thriver (þrai'vər). Now rare.

Thriving, vbl. sb.

Thriving, ppl. a.

Thrivingly, adv.

†Thro, sb.

†Thro, v.

Throat (þrōt), sb.

1. The passage in the anterior part of the neck.

2. Applied to various objects resembling a throat.

Supplement, p. 3873; Corrigenda, p. 4092; Spurious words, p. 4093; Books quoted, p. 4094

THROUGH

Supplement, p. 3873; Corrigenda, p. 4092; Spurious words, p. 4093; Books quoted, p. 4094

deevil. 1884 *Lays & Leg. N. Irel.* 11 If his Riv'rance released him he'd thraw him no more.

b. *intr.* To go counter, to act in opposition; to be at variance or awkward; to exhibit dislike or aversion; to quarrel or contend *with*. *Sc.*

a 1578 Lindesay (Pitscottie) *Chron. Scot.* xxi. iv. (1728) 125 Bishop Forman had..caused the duke to thraw [*so 3 MSS.*; 2 *MSS.* stur(e)] with him till he gave certain Benefices to the Duke to give unto his friends. 1807 Hogg *Laird of Lairistan* xxiii, Jealous of the Stuart race, The English lords begin to thraw. 1824 Mactaggart *Gallovid. Encycl.* (1876) 214 At nature ay to girn and thraw..Is sure a sin infernal. 1888 D. Grant *Scotch Stories* 10 Thraw wi' him, an' he was just as stubborn an' rampageous as a wild ox.

**6. *trans.* To form or fashion by means of a rotary or twisting motion. a. To turn (wood, etc.) in a lathe; to shape (round pottery) on a potter's lathe or 'throwing-wheel'. Now *techn.* or *dial.*

c 1440 *Promp. Parv.* 493/1 Throwyn, or turne vessel of a tre, *torno*. 1570 Levins *Manip.* 45/39 To Thraw or turne, *tornare*. 1604 *Shuttleworths' Acc.* (Chetham Soc.) 159 To the disshe-thrower, ix days throwing disshes and bassenes ..iij*s*. 1674 Ray *N. C. Words*, To *Throw*, to Turn as Turners doe. 1752 *Gentl. Mag.* Aug. 348 Rooms for throwing, turning, and stove drying the ware. 1755 Johnson s. v., Balls thrown in a lathe. 1839 Ure *Dict. Arts*, etc. 1011 Throwing is performed upon a tool called the potter's lathe..The mass of dough to be thrown is weighed out or gauged by an experienced hand. 1900 *Daily News* 25 May 6/2 Further on a potter is 'throwing' pots on his wheel.

b. *Silk Manuf.* To prepare and twist (raw silk) into thread; *spec.* to form into thread by twisting two or more threads or 'singles' in the direction opposite to that of their component filaments.

1455 [implied in Throwster 1]. 1463-4 [implied in Thrown 2]. 1483 *Act 1 Rich. III*, c. 10 § 1 Calle sylk or coleyn silk throwen or wrought. 1670 Blount *Law-Dict.*, *Silk-thrower*,..a Trade, or Mystery, that winds, twists, and spins, or throws silk, thereby fitting it for use. 1796 *Trans. Soc. Arts* XIV. 328, I became convinced that Bengal Silk could be thrown in this country. 1839 Ure *Dict. Arts*, etc. 1105 The raw silk..requires to be regularly wound upon bobbins, doubled, twisted, and reeled in our silk-mills. These processes are called throwing silk, and their proprietors are called silk throwsters. 1877 Knight *Dict. Mech.* s.v. *Thrown Singles*, Silk filaments are twisted to form *singles*. Several of these are combined and twisted together (doubling) forming *dumb singles*. A number of the latter are associated and twisted together (throwing), forming *thrown singles*. 1897 *Daily News* 9 Dec. 10/5 Silk is still 'thrown' at Derby.

c. To make by twisting: cf. Throw-crook.

1896 P. A. Graham *Red Scaur* v. 78 We began to throw straw ropes for them.

†7. To form, fashion, dispose, arrange; = Cast *v.* 45. *Obs. rare.*

c 1320 *Cast. Love* 739 A Trone..Of whit Iuori..Wiþ Cumpas I-þrowen and wiþ gin al I-do. *Ibid.* 807 Þe þreo baylys..Þat wiþ þe cornels byth so feyre I-set, And throwen [*v.r.* I-cast] wiþ cumpas and walled abowte.

II. To project or propel through the air, and connected uses; to cast, fling, hurl, drive, shoot (away from the propelling agent).

8. *trans.* To project (anything) with a force of the nature of a jerk, from the hand or arm, so that it passes through the air or free space; to cast, hurl, fling; *spec.* to cast by a sudden jerk or straightening of the arm, esp. at the level of or over the shoulder (as distinguished from *bowl*, *pitch*, *toss*). Cf. Cast *v.* I.

Now the main sense of the word (= Fr. *jeter*, Ger. *werfen*, L. *jacĕre*, *jactāre*), which is contained or involved in all the later senses and applications; *throw* being the primary, most general, and most proper word for this action.

a 1300 *E. E. Psalter* cxxxix. [cxl.] 11 In fire sal tou thrawe þam swa. *a* 1300 *K. Horn* 1076 Horn þreu him ouer þe brigge. 1387 Trevisa *Higden* (Rolls) V. 9 Ignacius..was i-brouȝt to Rome, and i-þrowe to wylde bestes. 1399 Langl. *Rich. Redeles* iv. 82 Ne had þei striked a strake ..or þe blast come, þey had be throwe ouere þe borde backewarde ichonne. *c* 1440 *Promp. Parv.* 493/1 Throwyn, or castyn, *jacto*. 1513 Douglas *Æneis* xi. vi. 142 Ane lance towartis his aduersar thrawis he. 1530 Palsgr. 756/1, I threwe a potte at his head. 1567 *Satir. Poems Reform.* iii. 174 Jesabell, Quhome throw ane windo suirlie men did thraw. 1651 Hobbes *Leviath.* ii. xxi. 108 When a man throweth his goods into the Sea for feare the ship should sink. 1724 De Foe *Mem. Cavalier* i. 76 I'd throw it [money] all into the Elbe. 1818 Scott *Br. Lamm.* xxiv, He threw the fellow a dollar. *Ibid.* xxxiii, Throwing Craigengelt from him with such violence that he rolled down the steps. 1863 Geo. Eliot *Romola* xx, There were practical jokes of all sorts, from throwing comfits to throwing stones. 1869 *Prov.* [see Glass-house]. *Mod.* Throw me a rope.

b. *absol.* To hurl a missile, a weapon, etc.

13.. *Sir Beues* (A.) 3106 Þow miȝt nouȝt sen ariȝt to þrowe. 1869 *Temple Bar Mag.* VI. 283 Parr threw 109 yards, the soldier only three yards less. 1889 Doyle *M. Clarke* 34 The turnip on a stick at which we used to throw at the fairs.

†c. *trans.* To assail *with* missiles, to pelt. *Obs. rare*[−1].

13.. *K. Alis.* 4702 (Bodl. MS.) Men hem þrew wiþ drytt & dunge [*v.r.* to heom throwe drit and donge].

9. *refl.* To fling or cast oneself; to precipitate oneself; † of a river, to precipitate itself, fall *into* another river, a lake, etc. (*obs.*) Also *fig.*

13.. *Sir Beues* (A.) 2179 Beues in to þe sadel him þrew. 1387 Trevisa *Higden* (Rolls) III. 411 Alisaundre..þrewe hym self into a water þat renneþ þere. 1576 Fleming *Panopl. Epist.* 310 Another throweth himselfe headlong from the topp of an house, and breaketh his necke. *c* 1630 Risdon *Surv. Devon* § 220 (1810) 227 The river Thrushell..throws itself into Lyd. 1714 Addison *Spect.* No. 556 ¶ 6, I..threw myself into an Assembly of Ladies. 1794 Mrs. Radcliffe *Myst. Udolpho* xl, 'This is too—too much!' exclaimed Valancourt,..throwing himself into a chair. 1795 Burke *Corr.* (1844) IV. 324 If you throw yourself into one of the early coaches, you would be here very quickly. 1843 Lever *J. Hinton* xi, He threw himself upon his horse.

b. *To throw oneself upon*: to attack with violence or vigour; to fall upon. (Cf. 28.)

1823 Scott *Quentin D.* iv, He threw himself upon the ragout, and the plate was presently vacant.

10. *trans.* To cast (dice) from the dice-box; to make (a cast) at dice; also *absol.* or *intr.* to cast or throw dice, to play at dice. Also *fig.*

† *To throw at all*: to stake or venture all one has (*obs.*).

1587 Greene *Penelopes Web* Wks. (Grosart) V. 181 Least ..we set our rest on the hazard and so desperately throw at all. 1601 Shaks. *All's Well* ii. iii. 84, I had rather be in this choise, then throw Ames-ace for my life. 1605 — *Lear* i. iv. 136 Set lesse then thou throwest. *a* 1667 Jer. Taylor *Wks.* (1835) I. 533 (Cent.) That great day of expense, in which a man is to throw his last cast for an eternity of joys and sorrows. 1698 *Act 10 Will. III*, c. 23 § 3 Every Person or Persons that..shall play throw or draw at any such Lottery..shall forfeite for every such Offence the Sum of Twenty Pounds. 1720 *Lond. Gaz.* No. 5872/6 The Winning Horse to be thrown for at 40 Guineas by the Contributors. 1848 Thackeray *Van. Fair* xxii, George had thrown the great cast. 1892 *Monthly Packet* May 558 If I should throw doublets, we will share the stakes.

b. To play (a card) out of one's hand; *esp.* to discard.

1748 [see *throw away*, 37 c]. 1879 'Cavendish' *Card Ess.*, etc. 109 Throwing the ace of hearts to the last spade. 1891 *Harper's Mag.* Mar. 603/1 He can therefore safely throw his queen on the ace. 1891 *Field* 28 Nov. 842/3 We should throw four diamonds, and the seven of spades, but do not say it is the proper 'discard'.

c. To cast (a vote): = Cast *v.* 1 f.

1844 W. Phillips in *Life of Garrison* (1889) III. iv. 99 No one can take office, or throw a vote for another to hold office. 1888 Bryce *Amer. Commw.* I. v. 55 *note*, 37 additional presidential votes..all thrown for the Democratic candidate. 1890 *Spectator* 8 Mar., Their usual leaders do not know their thoughts, and until their votes are thrown, can form only guesses as to the way their sympathies are tending.

11. To hurl, project, shoot, as a missile engine does; also of a person using such an engine. Often *absol.* (esp. in reference to distance or direction).

1393 Langl. *P. Pl.* C. xxi. 295 Sette mahon at þe mangonel and mulle-stones þroweþ. *a* 1400-50 *Alexander* 2218 Thre thousand of thra men to thraw with engynes. 1726 Leoni *Alberti's Archit.* I. 69/1 This will baulk the aim of the military engines, and make them throw over the wall. 1880 *Daily Tel.* 23 Dec., Although throwing only a 7lb. projectile, they [guns] are [etc.]. 1890 Clark Russell *Ocean Trag.* II. xviii. 106 That gun'll throw about three quarters of a mile. 1900 Pollok & Thom *Sport Burma* vi. 212, I tried the weapon, and found that both barrels threw considerably to the left.

12. To put forth with a throwing action (a fishing net, line, or bait); to cast, make a cast with. Also *absol.*

1841 Lane *Arab. Nts.* I. ii. 101 And threw his net. 1889 Crommelin & Brown *Violet Vyvian* II. ix. 154 Violet.. learnt to throw a fly. 1891 *Sat. Rev.* 20 June 734/1 Good anglers..can throw to a hairbreadth and not miss.

13. Of the sea or wind: † a. To toss or drive violently about; also, to drive, send, impel (*obs. rare*): b. *esp.* to drive or cast with violence (on rocks or a coast); to cast away, wreck.

1382 Wyclif *Matt.* xiv. 24 Sotheli the boot in the mydil see was throwen [L. *iactabatur*] with wawis. 1423 Jas. I *Kingis Q.* xvii, My feble bote full fast to stere and rowe, ..the wynter nyght I wake, To wayte the wynd that furthward suld me throwe. 1659 D. Pell *Impr. Sea* Proœm. d ij b, They are thrown irrecoverably upon Rocks and Sands. 1879 Minto *Defoe* ix. 142 [He] might have been thrown on a desert island. 1886 Burton *Arab. Nts.* (abr. ed.) I. 126 A billow..threw me with a long cast on dry land.

14. To project (a ray, beam, light) *on*, *upon*, *over*, etc.; to emit (light); to project, cast (a shadow).

1598 B. Jonson *Ev. Man in Hum.* iii. i, To through the least beame of regard upon such a [fellow]. 1600 Fairfax *Tasso* xviii. xv, The morning's lusty queen, Begilding, with the radiant beams she threw, His helm. 1797 Mrs. Radcliffe *Italian* vii, A nun, kneeling..beneath a lamp which threw its rays aslant her head. 1876 Tait *Rec. Adv. Phys. Sc.* ix. (ed. 2) 213 Throwing the spectrum of light..on the screen. 1893 *Harper's Mag.* Jan. 280/2 The great mound ..threw a long shadow westward.

b. In *fig.* phrases, esp. *to throw (a) light on*, to contribute to the elucidation of, to make clearer or plainer; *to throw a lustre over*, to illuminate or render lustrous; also *to throw a shadow, cloud, gloom, over*: see the sbs.

1598 [see prec. sense]. 1769 [see Lustre *sb.*[1] 4]. 1774 Goldsm. *Nat. Hist.* (1776) V. 78 The testimony of a single witness..will throw more light on the subject than the reasonings of an hundred philosophers. 1825 Moore *Sheridan* I. 510 It was in the power of the orator..to throw a lustre over the historian. 1825 T. Hook *Sayings* Ser. ii. *Passion & Princ.* ix. III. 153 Showers of rain..threw a gloom over the gaieties. 1875 Jowett *Plato* (ed. 2) I. p. xviii, Ancient and modern philosophy throw a light upon one another. 1890 Sir A. Kekewich in *Law Times Rep.* LXIII. 684/1 The defendants' evidence does not throw much light on the question.

15. To direct (words, an utterance) *towards*, etc., esp. in hostility or contempt; to hurl, cast; to cause (sound, or *fig.* a gesture) to pass or travel; to waft (a kiss), to cast (a nod).

1580 Sidney *Ps.* xxxi. ix, Those lips..Which..throw their words against the most vpright. 1600 Shaks. *A. Y. L.* i. iii. 3 Not a word? *Ros.* Not one to throw at a dog. *a* 1748 Watts (J.), There is no need to throw words of contempt on such a practice. 1822 Scott *Nigel* i, The poor youth had not a word to throw at a dog. 1831 — *Cast. Dang.* ii, 'Never fear me, Augustine,' said the old man,..throwing a kiss towards the boy. 1844 Mrs. Browning *Drama of Exile* Poems 1850 I. 75 The blessed nightingale which threw Its melancholy music after us. 1892 *Field* 19 Nov. 771/2 The hideous yells that were thrown at him.

b. *To throw the tongue*: see Tongue.

16. *To throw one's eye* or *eyes*, *a glance*, *a look*: to turn or direct one's gaze, to look; *esp.* to look hastily, rapidly, or cursorily; to glance: = Cast *v.* 7.

1590 Spenser *F. Q.* iii. i. 16 Still as she fledd her eye she backward threw. 1779 *Mirror* No. 17 ¶ 1 To throw your eye sometimes upon the inferior ranks of life. 1800 *Char.* in *Asiat. Ann. Reg.* 45/1 The mother lifting up her eyes,.. instantly threw them to the ground. 1885 Fitzpatrick *T. N. Burke* II. 35 Happening to throw his eye over the address delivered..at Boston. 1892 *Longm. Mag.* Jan. 276 Mrs. Duffield..threw inquiring glances across the table.

†17. To give, deliver (blows); also *absol.* or *intr.* to aim blows, strike. (Cf. to '*lay* about him'.) *Obs. rare.*

c 1470 *Golagros & Gaw.* 709 Thai threw in that thrang Stalwart strakis and strang. 1590 Spenser *F. Q.* iii. ix. 16 Then drew he his bright sword, and gan about him throw.

† b. *trans.* ? To deliver a blow at; to strike.

c 1470 Henry *Wallace* iv. 252 That staff he had, hewy and forgyt new, With it Wallace wpon the hede him threw, Quhill bayn and brayn all in to sondyr ȝeid.

18. To perform, execute (a somersault or a leap, in which the body is thrown with force); also *to throw a fit*, to have a fit (*U. S. slang*).

1826 *Examiner* 585/1 Throw a somerset, leap a stick, tumble through a hoop. 1889 Baden-Powell *Pigsticking* viii. 39 Mr. Kingscote threw about three back somersaults. *Ibid.* xiii. 99 Don't be surprised to find your horse unexpectedly 'throwing leps'. 1897 Flandrau *Harvard Episodes* 132, I don't suppose the creature thought I was throwing a fit like that just for exercise.

III. Pregnant uses.

* = *throw down*; ** = *throw off*; *** = *throw out* or *up*.

*19. *trans.* To cause to fall to the ground; to cast down, knock down, prostrate, lay low; *spec.* in *Wrestling*, to bring (one's opponent) to the ground, also with double object, *to throw one a fall*. Cf. *throw down*, 40.

13.. *K. Alis.* 2219 (Bodl. MS.) A riche kyng..smoot tholomewe þat he of his hors hym þrewe. Tholomeu on fote lep, And who hym þrewe he name gode kepe. 1530 Palsgr. 756/1 Wrestell nat with me, for I wyll throwe the on thy backe. *c* 1620 T. Robinson *Mary Magd.* 819 A newe delusion throughes Her pride as lowe as Phlegetonicke maine. 1820 *Sporting Mag.* VI. 177 Tom..throwed his opponent in masterly style. 1824 in *Examiner* 759/1 Cannon, grappling his man, threw him a tremendous fall. 1908 *Brit. Med. Jrnl.* No. 2154. 880 Three years ago [he] was thrown at football and hurt his knee.

b. *fig.* or in *fig.* context: To defeat in a contest; also, to be the cause of defeat to; to give or gain the verdict against in an action at law (*U. S.*): cf. Cast *v.* 14.

1850 Tennyson *In Mem.* cix. 6 Seraphic intellect and force To seize and throw the doubts of man. 1887 in *Lisbon* (Dakota) *Star* 20 May 2/5, 'I am compelled to throw you in the cost', said a justice of the peace. 1888 *Poultry, Pigeons*, etc. 27 July 377 (Prize list) Third..a good black Red, but a little out of feather, which, no doubt, threw her. 1909 W. R. Inge *Faith* xi. (1910) 193 The sceptic cannot throw his opponent if his own feet are in the air.

20. To cause forcibly (a tree or structure) to fall; to bring, knock, break, or cut down; to fell. In *Coal-mining*: see quot. 1881.

1568 Grafton *Chron.* II. 139 Some of them, they threwe to the grounde and consumed with fire. 1878 Jefferies *Gamekeeper at H.* i. 14 In the spring when the oak timber is throwed [*dial. speech*]. *Ibid.* iii. 52 The entire wood is thrown and renovated. 1881 Raymond *Mining Gloss.*, *Throwing*,..the operation of breaking out the spurns, so as to leave the hanging coal unsupported, except by its own cohesion. 1908 *Daily News* 25 Jan. 9 Some 40 telephone wires had to be temporarily cut, in order to enable the [chimney] shaft to be 'thrown'.

b. *spec. To throw an ant-hill*: see quot. and cf. Geld *v.*[1] 3 d. *dial.*

1848 *Jrnl. R. Agric. Soc.* IX. i. 17 Ant-hills..are quickly checked by throwing, or gelding. *Ibid.* 25 [see Geld *v.*[1] 3 d].

**21. Of a horse, etc.: To cause (the rider) to fall off; to unseat, shake off; = *throw off*, 42 a; also in passive *to be thrown* (from a horse or vehicle).

1531 Elyot *Gov.* ii. xiii, The courser..will stere and plonge and endeuour hym selfe to throwe hym. 1623 Massinger *Bondman* ii. ii, This morning, As I rode to take the air, the untutored jade Threw me, and kicked me. 1748 *Anson's Voy.* ii. xii. 265 One of their horses fell down and threw his rider. 1890 J. Payn *Burnt Million* II. xxx. 248 He was thrown from his horse in the steeplechase. 1893 *Field* 4 Mar. 335/3 Had the (bicycle-)rider been thrown or killed.

22. Of a snake, a bird, etc.: To cast (the skin); to moult (feathers). Of a horse: to cast or lose (a shoe).

1590 Shaks. *Mids. N.* ii. i. 255 There the snake throwes her enammel'd skinne. 1765 *Treat. Dom. Pigeons* 41 If your Pigeons..stop in their molting, so that they don't throw their feathers well. 1821 Scott *Kenilw.* ix, To shoe my horse...you may see that he has thrown a forefoot shoe. 1841 J. T. Hewlett *Parish Clerk* I. 168 The post-boy..contrived to 'throw a shoe' [i.e. off his horse].

23. Of domestic animals: To produce as offspring; to give birth to, to drop. Also *absol.*, *to throw true*, to produce offspring true to the parent type. (Cf. also *throw back*, 38 d.)

1845 *Jrnl. R. Agric. Soc.* V. ii. 546 You cannot possibly tell what sort of foal your mare may throw. 1858 *Ibid.* XIX. i. 28 In a breeding sow for a dairy farm..we should have a disposition to throw large farrows and a good supply of milk. 1892 *Pall Mall G.* 16 June 2/3 Each of these [three varieties of the rabbit] has marked and unmistakable characteristics, and each of them, to use the naturalist's phrase, 'throws true'. 1903 *Times* 9 Jan. 5/2 In 1884 she threw a calf to a bison bull.

b. *gen.* To produce: see quots.

1891 *Morning Post* 25 Dec. 6/5 Indian or Ceylon teas.. throw a stronger liquor than the same amount of China tea would in double or treble the time. 1893 *Garden* 27 Aug. 194 Sown early and transplanted a good distance apart, the plants will throw immense heads of flowers.

***24. Of a fountain or pump: To eject or project (water); to discharge; also *absol.* Of a locomotive steam-engine: *to throw fire*, to discharge burning fuel from the funnel. Cf. *throw out*, *up*, senses 44, 48.

1644 Evelyn *Diary* 27 Feb., The fountain of Laocoon is in a large square pool, throwing the water neere 40 feet high. 1697 Dryden *Virg. Georg.* iii. 374 (*orig.* 241) The Waters boil, and belching from below, Black Sands, as from a forceful Engine throw. 1806 O. Gregory *Mech.* (1807) II. 175 A machine by which water is thrown upon fires. 1864 *Jrnl. R. Agric. Soc.* XXV. ii. 293 The pumps..throw daily 60,000 to 70,000 gallons. 1893 *Field* 4 Mar. 332/3 Bad stoking may be..the cause of a locomotive 'throwing fire'.

25. A horse is said to *throw* his feet, when he lifts them well in moving, esp. over rough ground. Also *transf.* (*slang*): see quot. 1900.

1827 Scott *Chron. Canongate* ii, A famous piece of rough upland pasture, for rearing young colts, and teaching them to throw their feet. 1900 J. Flynt *Tramping w. Tramps* iv. 397 *Throw the Feet*, to beg, 'hustle', or do anything that involves much action.

26. To form by throwing up with a spade or shovel; to cast up, raise (a mound, etc.). = *throw up*, 48 d. *rare.*

1843 Marryat *M. Violet* xlii, Nearly all the hills in this part of New York were thrown by human hands.

27. To vomit; cf. *throw up*, 48 b. *Sc.* and *dial.*

18.. Wilson *Tyneside Songs* (1890) 374 He retched an' he threw i' the hight oo his anguish. *Mod. Sc.* 'I no sooner get up but I begin to throw'.

IV. Intransitive senses related to II and III.

28. *intr.* To cast or fling oneself impetuously; to spring, start, leap, rush. *Obs.* exc. as in quots. 1812, 1891, and in sense 48 j.

(Allied in sense to 9, but found earlier, and app. not derived from it.)

c 1205 Lay. 807 Of his horse he þreou [*c* 1275 aþreu]. *Ibid.* 12321 Þa cheorles up þreowen [*c* 1275 vp þreuwen]. 1508 [see *throw out*, 44 o]. 1535 Stewart *Cron. Scot.* (Rolls) II. 192 Out of his wame ane meruelus multitude Of foule serpentis..thair threw. 1812 *Sporting Mag.* XXXIX. 186 Which she [the hare] was prevented doing by all the dogs throwing at her at the same time. 1891 Atkinson *Moorland Par.* 83 The black dog, according to the expression used, 'threw at her'.

†29. *intr.* To fall with violence or force. *Obs.* (Looks like an intrans. or passive of sense 19, but occurs earlier.)

1297 R. Glouc. (Rolls) 6831 Þe king bi an laddre to þe ssip clam an hey & þreu vp to doun in þe se. 1362 Langl. *P. Pl.* A. v. 201 He þrompelde atte þrexwolde and þreuh [*v. rr.* fel, stey] to þe grounde.

V. Figurative and transferred senses.

30. *trans.* To cause to pass, go, or come into some place or position by some action likened to throwing; to put or place with haste, suddenness, or force; e. g. to put (a garment) *on* or *off* hurriedly, hastily, or carelessly.

(Many of these uses come very near the literal sense, and form a transition to the more fig. senses following.)

c 1384 Chaucer *H. Fame* iii. 235 And euery man Of hem ..Had on him throwen a vesture. *a* 1400 *Sir Beues* (E.) 3777+3 Euery knyȝt and hys squyer Fayre queyntyse on hem ganne þrowe For no man scholde hem knowe. 1655 Stanley *Hist. Philos.* iii. (1701) 101/1 He is now coming to Athens, being thrown out of his House by the People. 1711 *Spect.* No. 116 ¶ 6 The Hare immediately threw them [the hounds] above a Mile behind her. 1722 Steele in *Addison's Drummer* Ded., He only spoke it, and I took all the Pains of throwing it upon Paper. 1786 J. Hunter *Treat. Venereal Dis.* vi. iii. § 2 (1810) 509 The quantity of mercury, to be thrown into the constitution..must be proportioned to the violence of the disease. 1799 *Med. Jrnl.* I. 424 No doubt but the father would have suffered equally with the son, had it [poison] not so soon been thrown off the stomach. 1806 Coleridge *Three Graves* xxxiii, Her arms Round Ellen's neck she threw. 1816 J. Dallaway *Stat. & Sculp.* 350 The paludamentum was a vestment.. thrown over the cuirass and fastened over the shoulder with a golden clasp. 1843 R. J. Graves *Syst. Clin. Med.* vii. 84 *note*, I threw some common injection into the tibial arteries. 1859 *Musketry Instr.* 39 Throw the rifle smartly to the front of the right shoulder. 1891 A. Gissing *Moorland Idyll* II. iv. 102 To throw a hand to a drowning man.

b. In figurative uses of various phrases, as *to throw the reins on*, *to throw a veil over*, etc.; *to throw good money after bad*, to incur a further loss in trying to make good a previous one; *to throw oneself* or *be thrown at* (a man), of a woman, to put herself or be put designedly in the way of, so as to invite the attention of; *to throw oneself into the arms of*, to become the wife or mistress of.

c 1611 Chapman *Iliad* i. 214 Throw Reins on thy passions, and serve us. 1825 Scott *Talism.* iv, That modest pride which throws fetters even on love itself. 1831 — *Ct. Robt.* xxxi, To be, without her own consent, thrown, as it were, at the head now of one suitor, now of another. 1833 J. H. Newman *Arians* ii. i. (1876) 147 However plausible may be the veil thus thrown over heterogeneous doctrines, the flimsy artifice is discomposed so soon as [etc.]. 1871 Freeman *Norm. Conq.* IV. xviii. 231 Their wives were throwing themselves into the arms of other men. *a* 1891 Besant in J. M. Dixon *Idiom. Eng. Phr.* 336 As for the girls, Claire, they just throw themselves at a man.

c. With immaterial object (e.g. blame, influence, power, obstacles, etc.).

c 1620 T. Robinson *Mary Magd.* 301 So the bewitchinge oracle yt throughes, About the maidens fancy, strange Deludinge showes. 1697 Dryden *Virg. Georg.* iv. 325 Thro' Heav'n, and Earth, and Ocean's Depth he throws His Influence round. 1728 Pope *Iliad* xiii. 291 On Greece no blame be thrown. 1753 Miss Collier *Art Torment.* ii. ii. (1811) 129 Throw a languidness into your countenance;.. appear so perfectly dejected and low-spirited, that [etc.]. 1856 *Jrnl. R. Agric. Soc.* XVII. ii. 367 The carriage of materials is usually thrown upon the tenant. 1869 W. Longman *Hist. Edw. III*, I. viii. 138 Philip threw every obstacle in the way of reconciliation. 1871 Earle *Philol. Eng. T.* 133 They throw the accent often on the close of a word. 1890 Tout *Hist. Eng. from 1689* 36 Skill in such arts gradually threw real power into the hands of a ring.

d. To put *into* as an addition; to add, incorporate; = *throw in*, 41 b.

1676 Lister in *Ray's Corr.* (1848) 125, I would either put them [observations] out separately,..or throw them into Mr. Willughby's store. 1862 *Temple Bar Mag.* VI. 503 The saddle being thrown into the bargain. *a* 1904 A. Adams *Log Cowboy* vii. 85 Flood's attention once drawn to the brand, he ordered them thrown into our herd.

31. *spec.* a. A person is said to be *thrown into prison*, etc. when roughly or forcibly imprisoned.

1560 Daus tr. *Sleidane's Comm.* 175 The Turke throweth his Ambassadoure in pryson. 1776 *Trial of Nundocomar* 73/1 When Maha Rajah was first thrown into confinement. 1849 Macaulay *Hist. Eng.* v. I. 630 This impostor was thrown into prison for his fraud. 1892 Gardiner *Stud. Hist. Eng.* 285 Richard was carried to London and thrown into the Tower.

b. Troops, succour, supplies, or the like are said to be *thrown* into a besieged place, or a strategic position. Also *refl.*

1617 Moryson *Itin.* ii. 119 The Town had beene carried ..if Sir Francis Vere had not throwne himselfe into it with one thousand sixe hundred English. 1693 *Mem. Cnt. Teckely* ii. 145 A great number of Gentry who had thrown themselves into the place. 1736 Lediard *Life Marlborough* I. 157 The States..threw 12,000 Men into that Place. 1823 *Examiner* 95/2 Provisions had been thrown into Corinth previously to this incursion. 1836 Alison *Hist. Europe* (1849-50) V. xxvii. § 68. 58 He threw six thousand men across the principal arm into a wooded island. 1844 H. H. Wilson *Brit. India* iii. ii. III. 57 A detachment was thrown forward to Ramoo. 1869 T. Hughes *Alfred* ix. 108 He throws himself into a castle or fort called Cynwith.

c. A bridge or arch is said to be *thrown* from one side to another of, or *over*, a river, passage, or space. Also *fig.*

1751 J. Brown *Shaftesb. Charac.* 74 This visionary arch which he hath..thrown over the depths of error. 1793 *Regal Rambler* 74 He proposes to throw a bridge over the Fleet-market. 1819 Scott *Ivanhoe* xlii. *note*, The skill to throw an arch,..or erect a stair. 1849 *Tait's Mag.* XVI. 16/1 A suspension bridge has been thrown over the river.

32. To cause to fall, pass, or come into or out of some condition or relation (or place or thing implying this); properly with the connotation of abruptness, suddenness, or force; to cast, force, drive, plunge, thrust. Usually with *prep.*

1560 Becon *Chr. Knt.* Wks. II. 148 Adam & Eua, whom after thou haddest deceaued through thy lyenge, thou threwest them hedlonge into synne and death. *a* 1652 J. Smith *Sel. Disc.* ix. viii. (1859) 442 God hath never thrown the world from Himself. 1705 in Hearne *Collect.* 28 Sept. (O.H.S.) I. 49 They..threaten'd to..throw me out of my Chaplain's place. 1766 Goldsm. *Vic. W.* xviii, The fatigues I had undergone threw me into a fever. 1809 Malkin *Gil Blas* xii. vii. (Rtldg.) 432 Chance threw me across him, as he came out of a printing-house. 1815 Scott *Guy M.* xviii, I do not suspect his equanimity of being so easily thrown off its balance. 1821 *Examiner* 386/1, I cannot let the land be thrown out of cultivation. 1869 W. Longman *Hist. Edw. III*, I. iv. 63 The Scots were thrown into confusion. 1893 *Nat. Observ.* 7 Oct. 527/1 Recruited by men thrown idle by the selfish policy.

b. To put deftly into a particular form or shape; to express in a specified form (in speech or writing); to convert or change *into* some other form; to turn or translate *into* another language.

1723 Waterland *2nd Vind. Christ's Div.* xxiii. Wks. 1823 III. 408, I have reason to complain of your..not throwing your disjointed materials into a more neat and regular order. 1740 J. Clarke *Educ. Youth* (ed. 3) 177 A Master should be able to throw the Latin..into proper English. 1766 *Compl. Farmer* s. v. *Lucern*, A quarter of an acre; which we threw into fifty-four rows. 1789 Mrs. Piozzi *Journ. France*, etc. I. Pref. 6, I have not thrown my thoughts into the form of private letters. 1824 *Examiner* 362/1 Two dress boxes..were thrown into one. 1892 H. R. Mill *Realm Nat.* xii. 233 The surface..is thrown into a sheet of ridges. 1893 Traill *Soc. Eng.* Introd. 30 Cædmon..throws Scripture into metrical paraphrase.

c. *To throw open* (*apart*, *asunder*): to set open (separate, break asunder) with a sudden or energetic impulse; hence *fig.* to make publicly accessible or available (also *to throw open the gates of*). *To throw open one's doors to*, to receive as a guest, to welcome.

1709-10 Addison *Tatler* No. 116 ¶ 1, I had ordered the Folding-Doors to be thrown open. *c* 1790 Imison *Sch. Art* I. 72 The explosion of the gun-powder will throw asunder the roof. 1827 Roberts *Voy. Centr. Amer.* 235 The depositories were not thrown open. 1830 *Examiner* 408/2 The railway..will be thrown open..in August. 1844 A. B. Welby *Poems* (1867) 46 As the blossom waits the breeze Before it throws the leaves apart. 1850 *Tait's Mag.* XVII. 85/2 Labouring to throw open the gates of commerce. 1885 Mrs. C. Praed *Affinities* vi, He..threw open the shutters. 1890 T. F. Tout *Hist. Eng. from 1689* 192 A University Reform Act..threw open the endowments.

33. *refl. To throw oneself on* or *upon*: to have urgent recourse to (some one) for succour, support, or protection; to commit oneself entirely to (his generosity, mercy, or the like). Also in *pass.* to be made or become dependent upon.

1650 Jer. Taylor *Holy Living* iv. i. 235 In time of temptation be not busie to dispute, but..throw your self upon God. 1801 Charlotte Smith *Lett. Solit. Wand.* I. 87 To throw myself into the protection of my only parent. 1812 *Examiner* 24 Aug. 534/1 They are obliged to throw themselves on the parish for aid. 1830 *Ibid.* 550/1 Thrown upon their own resources. 1877 Miss Yonge *Cameos* Ser. iii. ix. 80 His wife threw herself upon James's mercy. 1891 *Temple Bar Mag.* Apr. 489, I must throw myself upon Ida's indulgence.

34. *To throw oneself into*: to engage in with zeal or earnestness.

1868 in Q. Victoria *Life Highl.* Pref. 7 A mind..throwing itself..into the enjoyment of [etc.]. 1871 Freeman *Hist. Ess.* Ser. i. iv. 113 The faculty of throwing himself with a lively interest into times so alien to our own. 1881 Gardiner & Mullinger *Stud. Eng. Hist.* i. v. 86 England threw herself..into a war of conquest against France. 1888 Burgon *Lives 12 Gd. Men* II. v. 46 He was..prepared to throw himself heart and soul into any project.

b. So *to throw one's soul*, *heart*, *life*, *spirit*, *energy*, *efforts*, etc. *into* a thing or action.

1829 *Examiner* 373/2 She threw her whole soul into her voice. 1868 E. Edwards *Ralegh* I. iii. 43 He continued to throw all his energy into the distasteful duty. 1890 *Field* 8 Nov. 707/3 The Blackheath forwards threw great spirit into their play.

VI. In combination with adverbs.

35. **Throw about.** a. *trans.* See simple senses and About.

1377 Langl. *P. Pl.* B. xx. 163 This sleuthe..a slynge made, And threwe drede of dyspayre a dozein myle aboute. 1719 De Foe *Crusoe* (1840) II. iii. 52 They..threw everything about in such a manner, that the poor men found.. some of their things a mile off. 1885 *Manch. Exam.* 6 May 5/1 A policeman had seen him throwing his arms about.

b. *Naut. absol.* or *intr.* To turn about at once; to go directly upon the other tack; to go about, put about. Also *fig.* Also *to throw round*.

1591 Spenser *M. Hubberd* 80, I..meane for better winde about to throwe. 1757 Capt. Randall in *Naval Chron.* XIV. 98 They threw about, and stood for us again. 1894 *Times* 10 July 11/1 When the vessels next met the American was far enough ahead to throw about on the Britannia's weather bow. 1894 *Daily News* 24 July 8/4 Shortly afterwards Vigilant threw round, and stood in.

36. **Throw aside.** a. *trans.* See simple senses and Aside.

1530 Palsgr. 281/1 Throwyng asyde, disordring, *debaux*. 1695 Telfair *New Confut. Sadd.* (1696) 10 His dog catcht a Fulmard by the way, which Andrew threw aside when he came into the House. 1841 Lane *Arab. Nts.* I. i. 44 When thou atest the date, and threwest aside the stone, it struck my son. *Ibid.* ii. 79 He threw aside the jar. 1857 Miller *Elem. Chem.* (1862) III. 162 When masses of the husk of the grape..are thrown aside, and allowed to ferment.

b. *spec.* To cast aside out of use, or as useless; *fig.* to discard, cease to use.

1827 Clare *Sheph. Cal.* 59 The old beechen bowl..is thrown aside. 1857 Miller *Elem. Chem.* (1862) III. 14 A little of the dried oxide of copper. which is thrown aside. 1880 Fowler *Locke* viii. 128 He throws aside the technical phraseology of the schools.

37. **Throw away.** † a. *trans.* To cast away from oneself; to reject; to refuse to admit or accept. *Obs.*

1382 Wyclif *1 Sam.* xv. 23 Forthi..that thow hast throwen aweye the word of the Lord, the Lord hath throwen awey thee, that thow be not kyng. 1387 Trevisa *Higden* (Rolls) VI. 12 Þrow not awey þat þou hast to forbonde approved.

b. To cast away out of one's hands or possession as useless or unneeded.

1530 Palsgr. 756/2, I throwe awaye, as we do thynges that we care nat for..., *je deguerpis*, *je desjecte*. *a* 1548 Hall *Chron.*, *Edw. IV* 204 b, The Lyncolnshyre men.. threw away their coates, the lighter to runne away, and fled. *a* 1667 Jer. Taylor (J.), He that will throw away a good book because not gilded, is more curious to please his eye than understanding. 1690 Locke *Hum. Und.* i. i. § 5 They will..throw away the Blessings their hands are fill'd with, because they are not big enough to grasp every thing. 1700 Dryden *Charac. Gd. Parson* 37 He melts, and throws his cumbrous cloak away. 1742 *Lond. & Country Brew.* i. (ed. 4) 64 A fresh Cask must be tapped..and the remaining Part of the other throw'd away. 1893 Hodges *Elem. Photogr.* (1907) 101 The used solution..is thrown away.

c. To spend or use without adequate return; to squander, waste; to bestow upon an unworthy object; also, to neglect to take advantage of (an opportunity, etc.); *spec.* at *Cards*, to play (a losing card) when one cannot follow suit, to discard.

1653 Jer. Taylor *Serm. for Year* i. xxii. 294 We are pleased to throw away our time. 1714 *Spect.* No. 624 ¶ 1 Advice..would be but thrown away upon them. 1748 Hoyle *Games Impr.* (1778) 56 Do not trump it, but throw away a losing Card, which makes room for your Partner's Suit. 1761 Gray *Let. to Wharton* 9 May, I had rather Major G. throwed away his money than somebody else. 1798 Wordsw. *We are Seven* xvii, 'Twas throwing words away; for still The little Maid would have her will. 1861 *Temple Bar Mag.* II. 447 The Abbé's prayers will not be thrown away. *Mod.* Do not throw away your chance.

d. *refl. To throw oneself away*: chiefly said of a woman in reference to marriage.

1680 Otway *Orphan* i. i. Where Dilatory Fortune plays the Jilt With the brave noble honest gallant man, To throw her self away on Fools and Knaves. 1891 E. Peacock *N. Brendon* I. 243 She had thrown herself away on one utterly unworthy of her.

38. **Throw back.** a. *trans.* See simple senses and Back *adv.*

a 1822 Shelley *A Juno* Wks. 1888 I. 410 The manner in which the act of throwing back one leg is expressed. 1831 Scott *Cast. Dang.* i, The reflection of the evening sun, sometimes thrown back from pool or stream. 1859 *Habits Gd. Soc.* iii. 148 The frock-coat should be ample and loose, and a tall well-built man may throw it back. 1890 Gerard *Sensitive Plant* (1891) III. iii. xvi. 149 Each tall mirror threw back the image in the other.

b. To put back in time or condition; to delay, make late, throw behind; to retard or check in expected or desired progress; to reduce to a previous or lower condition.

1840 *Jrnl. R. Agric. Soc.* I. iv. 453, I..am not thrown back in getting the land sown. 1850 *Ibid.* XI. ii. 419 Wet weather is what throws sheep back. 1858 *Ibid.* XIX. ii. 294 The loss of that fortnight..throws an incoming tenant back a whole year. 1868 Freeman *Norm. Conq.* II. vii. 114 That..parliamentary life which..the Norman Conquest threw back for many generations.

c. With *upon*: to compel to fall back upon, or recur to; cf. Fall *v.* 81.

1851 J. H. Newman *Cath. in Eng.* Ded., The violence of our enemies has thrown us back upon ourselves and upon each other. 1892 *Chamb. Jrnl.* 4 June 355/2 If there is no comic boy,..we are thrown back upon Checkley.

d. *intr.* To revert to an ancestral type or character not present in recent generations; to exhibit atavism. *colloq.* Also *fig.* (Cf. 23.)

1879 'Cavendish' *Card Ess.*, etc. 63 'Throwing back' more nearly..to the parent games, Poker..is invented. 1887 A. Lang *Myth, Rit. & Relig.* I. 195 Another child may be said in the language of dogbreeders to have 'thrown back'. 1893 *Standard* 22 Apr. 4/3 In politics Lord Derby 'threw back' to the family creed of an earlier generation. 1899 *Allbutt's Syst. Med.* VIII. 279 She 'throws back' to her savage ancestors. 1911 Galsworthy *Patrician* ii. i. 176 He and his ideas throw back to the Middle Ages.

e. *intr.* To go back in date *to*, to have a history reaching back *to*; to hark back, cast back.

1892 *Sat. Rev.* 28 May 635/1 His Metaphysic..begin with Kant, and only 'throws back' to Kant's forerunners. 1892 *Illustr. Sporting & Dram. News* 17 Sept. 39/2 An old hostelry that throws back nobody knows how many centuries..; throwing back three quarters of a century, a hundred men mustered here.

39. **Throw by.** a. *trans.* To put aside with decision; to reject from present use; to discard.

1611 B. Jonson *Catiline* i. i, It can but shew Like one of Ivnoes..disguises..: and will..When things succeed, be throwne by, or let fall. 1674 Flavel *Husb. Spir.* i. 27 My lazy heart throws by the shovel, and cryes, 'Dig I cannot!' 1770 *Hist.* in *Ann. Reg.* 39 Aly Bey..has thrown by the mask, and..boldly mounted the throne. 1825 J. Neal *Bro. Jonathan* III. 187, I took another name. I threw by that of my father.

† b. To dismiss from consideration; to set aside.

1710 S. Palmer *Proverbs* 141 His best actions thrown by and lessen'd by false turns. 1710 Hearne *Collect.* (O.H.S.) III. 36 They are very angry with him, and throw by what he has done as being against the Government.

40. **Throw down** († adown). a. *trans.* See simple senses and Down *adv.*

To throw down a horse, (of a rider) to cause or allow it to fall.

c 1250 *Long Life* 37 in *O. E. Misc.* 158 Weilawei deþ þe schal adun þrowe Þet þu wenest heȝest to steo. *c* 1275 Lay. 2323 Þe cheorles..þa king icnewen and hine adun þreuwe. 1387 Trevisa *Higden* (Rolls) VII. 349 A grym strook of ꝥunynge smoot þe cherche tour..and þrew [*v. r.* þruw] doun þe crucifex,..and þrew doun oure Lady ymage. 1586 Sidney *Arcadia* iii. (1598) 361 After her song with an affected modestie, she threw downe her eye. 1660 F. Brooke tr. *Le Blanc's Trav.* 371 The Mountains..throw down divers Rivers. 1714 *Spect.* No. 558 ¶ 4 Another after a great deal of puffing, threw down his Luggage. 1787 'G. Gambado' *Acad. Horsem.* (1809) 44 Take care never to throw your horse down, it is an unlucky trick.

b. Expressing a symbolic action; as *to throw down one's arms*, to surrender; *to throw down one's brief* (of a barrister), to decline to go on with a case; so *to throw down one's pipe*, etc.

To throw down the Gauntlet *or* Glove: see these words.

1700 S. L. tr. *Fryke's Voy. E. Ind.* 58 Most of them threw down their arms. 1711 Steele *Spect.* No. 49 ¶ 2 Mr. Beaver has thrown down his Pipe. 1833 Disraeli *Cont. Flem.* i. i, I throw down the volume in disgust. 1855 Macaulay *Hist. Eng.* xx. IV. 523 Williams threw down his brief.

c. To cause to fall, to overthrow, demolish (a building, etc.); also *fig.*

c 1330 *Arth. & Merl.* (Kölbing) 9306 Baners & castels adoun y-þrawe. 1340 *Ayenb.* 23 Þe grete wynd, þet þrauþ doun þe greate tours. *c* 1425 *Eng. Conq. Irel.* 18 Thay lay all I-drow a-doune and I-cast to grond. 1528 *Sel. Cas. Star Chamb.* (Selden) II. 19 That the sayd J. M. shuld throwe downe and avoyde the sayde enclosures from the sayd comon grownde. 1530 Palsgr. 756/2, I throwe downe to the grounde, or distroye a thynge. 1645 Evelyn *Diary* 8 Feb., The ruines of a very stately Temple or Theatre..throwne downe by an earthquake. 1713 Addison *Cato* ii. v. 67 Must one rash word..Throw down the merit of my better years? 1766 Fordyce *Serm. Yng. Wom.* (1767) I. vii. 302 The admiration raised..is often..thrown down. 1838 Thirlwall *Greece* III. 101 The Athenians..ordered the Potidæans to throw down the walls of their town on the side of the Peninsula of Pallene.

d. To deposit or cause to be deposited from solution; to precipitate.

1812 Sir H. Davy *Chem. Philos.* 120 Earths, and oxides, are usually thrown down from their solutions in union with water. 1838 T. Thomson *Chem. Org. Bodies* 188 Alcohol throws it down from its aqueous solution. 1864 *Jrnl. R. Agric. Soc.* XXV. ii. 566 Water that contains much lime on boiling throws down a white deposit.

e. *Agric.* (*a*) To plough (land) so as to level it down; opposed to *gather up* (Gather *v.* 16). (*b*) To convert (arable land) into pasture; to lay down to grass. (Cf. Lay *v.* 51 m.)

1844 Stephens *Bk. Farm* I. 477 The mode of ploughing exactly opposite to twice-gathering-up is that of cleaving or throwing down land. 1891 S. C. Scrivener *Our Fields & Cities* 143 It is capable of being applied..to almost any land, including that 'thrown down' to grass.

f. *fig.* To put down with force; to lower in rank or station; to degrade, humiliate; to deject in spirits; also, to destroy the effect of, bring to nought.

c 1450 tr. *De Imitatione* iii. xxi. 89, I am sone þrowen doun with litel aduersite. 1567 *Satir. Poems Reform.* vi. 23 God wil haue the pride of man doune thrawin. 1610 Holland *Camden's Brit.* (1637) 725 Lifting and throwing downe Princes at her pleasure. 1729 G. Adams tr. *Sophocl.*, *Antig.* v. i. II. 65 Fortune raises up, and throws down, makes one fortunate, and another miserable.

g. *slang.* To overcome; to prove too much for; to floor, 'give a fall' to.

1891 *Harry Fludyer* 98 (Farmer), I think I shall floor mine ['exam.'], and Dick's sure to throw his examiners down.

h. *U. S. slang.* To discard, throw off.

Mod. U. S. 'Is she still engaged?' 'Why no, she threw her beau down'.

41. **Throw in.** a. *trans.* See simple senses and In.

13.. *K. Horn* 1176 (Harl. MS.) Þe ryng þat þou yn þrewe. 1679 M. Rusden *Further Discov. Bees* 91 Throwing in a few handsfull of peas. 1730 A. Gordon *Maffei's Amphith.* 303 The Window above that Stair throws the Light in. 1892 *Illustr. Lond. News* 21 May 634/3 He was thrown in with men who..had been intimately acquainted with the Zulu people. *Mod. Cookery Bk.* Throw in a bunch of sweet herbs.

b. To put in as a supplement or addition; to add, esp. to a bargain. Cf. 30 d.

1678 Lady Chaworth in *12th Rep. Hist. MSS. Comm.* App. v. 45 Lord Shrewsbery is like to marry Mr. Chiffens his daughter, who will be first and last made worth 40,000*l.* to him, and they talke as if the King should throw in a Dukedome. 1679 Mrs. Behn *Feign'd Curtizan* iii. i, Cou'd you not..throw in a little Love and Constancy, to inch out that want of Honesty of yours? 1824 *Examiner* 471/2 Additional dialogue and incident should be..thrown in. 1892 *Black & White* 22 Oct. 476/1 [The] story turns..on murder and revenge, with a little love thrown in.

c. To introduce, insert, or interject in the course or process of something; *esp.* to interpose or contribute (a remark); to put in.

1704 Norris *Ideal World* ii. xii. 509 A further reflection which it may be convenient to throw in to this explanatory account to make it more full and entire. 1739 tr. *Algarotti on 'Newton's Theory'* (1742) I. 7, I threw in, from Time to Time, little Digressions to vary the Conversation. 1821 Clare *Vill. Minstr.* II. 85 The old dames..Throw in their hints of man's deluding ways. 1890 Baring-Gould *Urith* xxxi, 'Not a grain', threw in Julian, hotly. 1891 *Harper's Mag.* Dec. 102/1, I wish to throw in a parenthesis.

d. In technical uses (often *absol.*). (*a*) *Fishing.* To make a cast (in quot. *fig.*). (*b*) *Hunting.* To start (hounds) upon the scent. (*c*) *Wrestling* and *Pugilism.* To toss one's hat into the ring as a challenge or acceptance; hence *fig.* to become a candidate, put in *for*. (*d*) *Football* and *Cricket.* Cf. *throw-in* sb. (Throw- 2).

1823 *Mirror* No. 14. I. 213/2 When you launch a good thing, which is only heard by the person next you, wait patiently for a pause, and throw in again. 1844 J. T. Hewlett *Parsons & W.* liv, The hounds were thrown in. 1886 Elworthy *W. Somerset Word-bk.*, *Drow in*, to give or accept a challenge in a wrestling or cudgel-playing match. 1887 Shearman *Athletics & Football* 348 [Association] The halves at the sides too must learn to throw in from touch, for this duty as a rule devolves upon them. 1889 H. Vassall *Rugby Game* 27 There are endless ways of throwing in, and he must practise. 1892 *Field* 8 Oct. 553/3 [He] prefers the glory of winning the Cambridgeshire to throwing in for his chance of the £5000 to-morrow.

e. *To throw in one's lot with*: to enter into association with, so as to share the fortunes of (see Lot *sb.* 1 e); so with *fortune*, *interest*.

1867 [see Lot *sb.* 1 e]. 1870 Rogers *Hist. Gleanings* Ser. ii. 97 He would have thrown in his lot with the Hydes. 1889 Mrs. C. Carr *Marg. Maliphant* III. xxx. 27 On which side do you suppose he would throw in his interest? 1890 *Eng. Illustr. Mag.* Dec. 173 He willingly threw in his fortune with theirs.

† f. *intr.* At the game of hazard: To throw a number the same as the main (Main *sb.*[3] 1: see note there) or which has a certain correspondence with it (see Nick *sb.*[1] 6); to win at hazard. *Obs.*

1880 *Encycl. Brit.* XI. 547/1 The player or 'caster' calls a 'main' (that is, any number from five to nine inclusive). He then throws with two dice. If he 'throws in', or 'nicks', he wins the sum played for from the banker or 'setter'..If the caster 'throws out' by throwing aces, or deuce ace (called crabs), he loses.

42. **Throw off.** a. *trans.* (*lit.* and *fig.*) See simple senses and Off.

1447-8 J. Shillingford *Lett.* 2 Feb. (Camden) 36 How hit was procured and shortly throwen of. 1647 Hammond *Power of Keys* iii. 30 He had thus confidently thrown off these Epistles from being written by Ignatius. 1730 Waterland *Eight Serm.* 115, I was once inclinable to defer the Treating of it some time longer; thinking it most suitable..to throw it off to the last part of what I intend upon this Subject. 1726 Leoni *Alberti's Archit.* I. 15/1 The Covering..shou'd..incline of one side to throw off the Rain. 1747 Franklin *Lett.* Wks. 1840 V. 182 To show that points will throw off as well as draw off the electrical fire. 1790 Mrs. Wheeler *Westmld. Dial.* ii. 65 Bil Watson..flayd Galoway, et it set off a Gallop an thraad him off. 1823 J. Badcock *Dom. Amusem.* 52 A concave glass..will throw the objects off and reduce their size. 1892 *Sat. Rev.* 7 May 542/1 The pumps..were throwing off 7,000 gallons per minute.

b. To rid or free oneself by force from, to get rid of, shake off (a yoke, restraint, burden, etc.); to repudiate or reject the authority of; also, to cast off, disown (an associate).

1618 Bolton *Florus* (1636) 131 The first who threw the yoake off, were the Macedonians. 1681 Dryden *Span. Friar* iii. iii, 'Twould be better yet, Cou'd you provoke him to give you th' occasion, And then to throw him off. 1793 J. Bowles *Real Ground Pres. War w. France* (ed. 5) 75 Throwing off every restraint of honour and principle. 1822 *Examiner* 229/2 The Spanish Colonies..have thrown off the yoke of the mother country. 1879 Dowden *Southey* iii. 64 Unless the disease were thrown off by regular exercise. 1899 *Allbutt's Syst. Med.* VIII. 156 An extraordinary power of throwing off fatigue.

c. To cast off, put off energetically (something put on or assumed, as a garment); to divest oneself of (a quality, character, habit, feeling, etc.); to lay aside quickly or decisively; to discard.

1681 Dryden *Span. Friar* iv. ii, Virtue must be thrown off; 'tis a coarse garment. 1697 J. Lewis *Mem. Dk. Glocester* (1789) 8 To throw off childish toys, saying he was then a man. 1706 E. Ward *Wooden World Diss.* (1708) 41 He throws off his Gown and Hypocrisy together. 1872 C. E. Maurice *S. Langton* i. 52 He throws off his chancellorship at once. 1883 *Manch. Exam.* 28 Sept. 5/3 If he should suddenly throw off his coat in a cold room. 1893 *Nat. Observ.* 7 Oct. 535/2 Monson threw off the pirate and appeared the king's officer.

d. To shake off or divert (a pursuer or competitor in a race); = *throw out*, 44 k; also, to throw off the scent.

1695 Blackmore *Pr. Arth.* i. 354 Reason..stops her pace, Is soon thrown off, and quits th' unequal Chase. 1891 *Blackw. Mag.* CXLIX. 468/1 He wasn't to be thrown off by a false scent. 1892 *Field* 2 Apr. 475/1 A check threw hounds off for a minute. 1893 *Ibid.* 11 Feb. 186/3 The leading hounds are very near him; he cannot throw them off.

e. *Hunting.* To free from the leashes, to start (hounds) in the chase; to let fly (a hawk, etc.). Now *esp. absol.* or *intr.*, of foxhunters or hounds: To begin hunting; hence *fig.* to make a beginning in anything; to begin.

1735 Somerville *Chase* ii. 123 Where..the rank Mead Affords the wand'ring Hares a rich Repast; Throw off thy ready Pack. 1784 Cowper *Wks.* (1837) XV. 150 On Friday..we attended an attempt to throw off a balloon at Mr. Throckmorton's. 1825 Scott *Betrothed* xxiii, Each holding a hawk on his wrist, and anxiously adjusting the mode in which they should throw them off. 1892 *Field* 7 May 664/2 They threw off the hounds, found an otter, and, after two hours, killed. *intr.* 1811 *Sporting Mag.* XXXVII. 88 They [hounds] throw off generally three times a week. 1818 Col. Hawker *Diary* (1893) I. 162, I threw off in the great woods round Cold Henley. 1866 Gladstone in Morley *Life* (1903) II. v. ix. § 5. 156, I had to throw off in my new capacity. 1892 *Field* 26 Nov. 808/1 Many packs would not have thrown off at all on such a morning.

f. To eject, emit, give off, esp. from the body or system; *esp.* to expel or discharge (waste or morbid products); *rarely*, to vomit.

1737 Bracken *Farriery Impr.* (1756) I. 235 These Creatures throw off a vast deal from their Lungs in Respiration. 1747 tr. *Astruc's Fevers* 105 A crisis, or critical depuration of the humours, whereby the peccant matter is thrown off:.. just as we see in the small-pox, measles, &c. 1829 *Examiner* 267/2 When he found anything disagreeing with his stomach, he retired and threw it off. 1846 *Jrnl. R. Agric. Soc.* VII. ii. 308 Plants decompose carbonic acid, and throw off oxygen. 1862 *Temple Bar Mag.* VI. 474 Dense volumes of smoke are thrown off. 1864 *Gd. Words* 102/1 They exude, or throw off from themselves, the spent materials which are excrementitious. 1891 *Harper's Mag.* Aug. 357/1 From all parts of the living body living gemmules are being thrown off.

g. To produce and send forth (as offspring or the like); esp. of a hive of bees: to send forth (a swarm). Cf. 23. Also = *throw out*, 44 d.

1828 *Examiner* 541/2 A swarm of bees thrown off from one of his scapes. 1842 J. Aiton *Domest. Econ.* (1857) 268 The gray rabbit..generally throws off three, four, five, or six litters..by the first of June. 1862 *Temple Bar Mag.* IV. 548 A massive pillar..threw off rough branches of stone. 1892 *Gd. Words* Dec. 816/1 Its territory was small and it threw off many colonies.

h. To produce with speed and facility (a literary or artistic work or sketch); to execute in a ready and spontaneous manner.

1761 *Ramsay's Ever-green* I. 5 *note*, That this Way of throwing off a Verse easily was first introduced by him. 1823 J. Badcock *Dom. Amusem.* p. iv, The new articles.. having been 'thrown off at a heat', stood particularly in want of re-revision. 1850 *Tait's Mag.* XVII. 115/2 Those exquisite works which..Chantrey so frequently threw off in marble. 1893 *Temple Bar Mag.* XCVIII. 518 Having thrown his compositions off at white heat.

i. *Printing.* To print off. (Often with mixture of the literal sense.)

1803 Scott *Let. to Ballantyne* 21 Apr., in *Lockhart*, I have to thank you for the accuracy with which the Minstrelsy is thrown off. Longman and Rees are delighted with the printing. 1873 Spencer *Stud. Sociol.* vi. 126 Its own immense edition is thrown off in a few hours every morning.

j. To deduct from the total; to knock off.

1821 *Examiner* 385/2 An abatement of rent, Mr. S! Why ..last year I threw you off 200*l.* 1845 *P. Parley's Ann.* VI. 299 Perhaps, if you are a good girl, and pay regularly every week, I may throw you off something at the end of the year.

43. **Throw on.** a. *trans.* See simple senses and On. b. To put on (apparel) hastily or carelessly: the opposite of *throw off*, 42 c. c. To put (hounds) on the scent. † d. ? To win (a main) at hazard (*obs.*); cf. *throw in*, *throw out*, 41 f, and 44 m.

c 1374 Chaucer *Compl. Mars* 99 He throwe [*v. rr.* threw(e, throweth] on his helme of huge wyght. 1801 *Sporting Mag.* XVIII. 95 He once won 17,000*l.* at hazard, by throwing on, as it is called, fourteen successive mains. 1825 *Ibid.* XLV. 253 After the usual law, the hounds were thrown on. 1862 *Temple Bar Mag.* VI. 421 He throws on his colour at once, with a very evident freedom of pencil. 1873 J. Richards *Wood-working Factories* 76 Watch persons trying to throw on a belt [upon a pulley]..The one will throw it on instantly.

44. **Throw out.** (See also Out-throw.) a. *trans.* See simple senses and Out; *spec.* of frost, etc.: to force (young plants) out of the ground.

1590 Spenser *F. Q.* i. vi. 6 The pitteous mayden..Does throw out thrilling shriekes, and shrieking cryes. 1600 J. Pory tr. *Leo's Africa* ii. 81 His theeues carcase is throwne out to be deuoured of dogs. 1706 E. Ward *Wooden World Diss.* (1708) 100 He..falls to throwing every Thing out at the Window. 1753 Chambers *Cycl. Supp.* s.v. *Marygold*, The flowers of the common marygold..promote sweat, and are good to throw out the small-pox, or any other eruption. 1830 Lyell *Princ. Geol.* I. 406 [In an earthquake] Cones of sand, six or eight feet in height, were thrown out of the lands near the Runn [of Cutch]. 1840 *Jrnl. R. Agric. Soc.* I. iii. 272 The wheat is usually only thrown out in severe frosts. 1847 *Ibid.* VIII. i. 66 The rolling and treading..prevent the plants being thrown out by alternate frosts and thaws. 1885 J. K. Jerome *On the Stage* 42 To make your voice 'carry', you have to throw it out, instead of letting it crawl out when you open your mouth.

b. To put out forcibly or suddenly from a place, office, or employment; to eject, expel, turn out.

1526 *Pilgr. Perf.* (W. de W. 1531) 18 Whome..god suffreth ..vtterly to be throwen out from the kyngdome of glorye. 1710 Hearne *Collect.* (O.H.S.) II. 348 Ld. Rialton..will be thrown out the next Election. 1780 Warner in Jesse *Selwyn & Contemp.* (1844) IV. 382, I suppose it is not possible to throw Barrow out. 1826 *Examiner* 387/2 General Palmer has been thrown out for Bath.

c. *transf.* and *fig.* To put forth vigorously from within; to emit, radiate (heat or light); to exude; to produce, be the source of; to send out, put forth (buds, shoots, etc.).

1750 tr. *Leonardus' Mirr. Stones* 99 It grows warm, and throws out a heat. 1756 P. Browne *Jamaica* 236 Whereever the trunk or larger branches of this tree are wounded, they throw out a thick resinous gum. 1838 T. Thomson *Chem. Org. Bodies* 995 Plants, when exposed to the light, absorb carbonic acid, decompose it, and throw out again the greatest part of the oxygen. 1845 *Jrnl. R. Agric. Soc.* VI. ii. 580 Artichokes..throwing out stems from 7 to 10 feet in length. 1850 Lynch *Theoph. Trin.* xii. 235 Truth and goodness throw out a vivifying electric agency. 1880 C. R. Markham *Peruv. Bark* xviii. 210 The plants..had begun to bud and throw out young leaves.

d. To cause to project, protrude, stretch out, or extend; *spec.* in Bookbinding, see quot. 1880.

1849 Thackeray *Pendennis* xxii, We'll throw a conservatory out, over the balcony. 1851 *Jrnl. R. Agric. Soc.* XXII. ii. 352 Both ranges throw out spurs. 1880 Zaehnsdorf *Bookbinding* 8 By mounting a map on a guard the size of the page it may be kept laid open on the table beside the book..This is technically called 'throwing out' a map. 1890 R. M. Kettle *Old Hall* ii. ii, The old trees..threw out giant branches.

e. To bring into prominence or relief, to cause to 'stand out'.

1860 Ruskin *Mod. Paint.* V. ix. viii. § 4. 283 The tone of the whole is dark and gray, throwing out the figures in spots of light.

f. *Mil.* To send out (skirmishers, etc.) to a distance from the main body. Also in *fig.* context.

1834-47 J. S. Macaulay *Field Fortif.* (1851) 265 The infantry will..throw out skirmishers, and..push on to support them. 1862 *Temple Bar Mag.* V. 373 Mamma throws out skirmishing parties among likely shops. 1863 Ld. Lytton *Ring Amasis* x, His senses, all on the alert, were throwing out scouts and outposts in every direction. 1893 Forbes-Mitchell *Remin. Gt. Mutiny* 258 We bivouacked on the plain, strong piquets being thrown out.

g. To give utterance or expression to; now *esp.* to put forward tentatively, give (a hint or suggestion); also with obj. clause, to suggest.

1611 Beaumont & Fl. *Maid's Trag.* iv. ii, I have thrown out words That would have fetch'd warm blood upon the cheeks Of guilty men. 1633 Earle *Microcosm.* lxxviii. (Arb.) 103 Not a jest throwne out, but he will make it hitt him. *a* 1763 W. King *Polit. & Lit. Anecd.* (1819) 246 Such an infamous appellation, that I scarce believe the most fiery sectarist among us..would dare to throw out. 1793 *Trial of Fyshe Palmer* 33 He at first threw out that till these were totally abolished we would contend with them. 1869 A. W. Ward tr. *Curtius' Hist. Greece* II. iii. ii. 392 Athens unhesitatingly accepted the challenge thrown out. 1891 *Cornh. Mag.* July 106 The hint of danger which Norbury threw out was the one thing needed.

h. To put forth visibly, display, exhibit; also † *refl.* to express oneself freely; to 'launch out'.

1710 Pope *Lett.* (1735) I. 116, I Resume my old Liberty of throwing out myself upon Paper to you. 1763 J. Brown *Poetry & Mus.* v. 85 His warlike Genius threw itself out, in Subjects that were grand and terrible. 1806 A. Duncan *Nelson* 32 The signal was thrown out for the.. fleet to prepare for action. 1890 Mrs. R. Jocelyn *M.F.H.'s Daugh.* xvii, Belton's horse also threw out signs of distress.

i. To dismiss from acceptance, use, or consideration: to reject; to leave out of a reckoning; in *Écarté*, to discard, 'throw away'.

1618 in Foster *Eng. Factories Ind.* (1906) 48 What I found grose I thrue out or cutt. 1660 Milton *Free Commw.* Wks. (1847) 449/1 To us who have thrown it [monarchy] out, received back again, it cannot but prove pernicious. 1753 Miss Collier *Art Torment.*, *Fable* 233 The letter L.. confined the competitors to the lion, the leopard, the lynx, and the lamb. The lamb, by almost general consent, was instantly thrown out, as knowing nothing of the subjects treated of. 1821 Sir Wm. Scott *Dodson's Rep.* I. 31 Some circumstances stated on behalf of Captain Honeyman, which I may also throw out as immaterial. 1856 Olmsted *Slave States* 241 They..made further clearings in the forest, and 'threw out', to use their own phrase, so much of the land as they had ruined. 1896 *Indianapolis Typogr. Jrnl.* 16 Nov. 407 When the contract expires, this newspaper will throw out its linotype machines.

j. Of a legislative assembly or a grand jury: To reject (a bill, etc.).

1707 *Vulpone* 2 This Proposal..occasion'd very great Debates..and was Scandalously Treated and thrown Out. 1732 Hearne *Diary* 27 Sept., His petition..was thrown out of the house. 1827 *Parl. Deb. Ho. Lords*, The grand jury..whose duty it was to find the bills had thrown them out. 1873 P. V. Smith *Hist. Eng. Inst.* ii. v. 175 The Ballot Bill..was thrown out by the Lords.

k. *Sporting.* To put out of place or order by leaving behind in a chase or race; to distance, outpace.

1713 Addison *Cato* i, A Virtue that has cast me at a Distance, And thrown me out in the Pursuits of Honour. 1807 *Sporting Anecd.* 179 Jack was mounted on a hunter, which he assured me was never yet thrown out. 1823 Scott *Quentin D.* ix, I had been unluckily thrown out, and was riding fast, to be in my place. 1889 W. Westall *Birch Dene* III. xii. 202 More than once he threw them [his pursuers] out by a double.

l. To disturb (a person) from his self-possession, train of thought, normal or equable state of mind, or ordinary course of action (see Out *adv.* 5); = *put out*, Put *v.*[1] 47 f.

1844 J. H. Newman *Lett.* (1891) II. 442 He was surprised and thrown out by finding I did not seem to be what he had fancied. 1891 *Murray's Mag.* Apr. 551 Seeing her there acting the part of a governess..threw him out. 1891 *Field* 28 Nov. 837/3 The visitors kicked off, but the heavy ground at first seemed to throw them out.

† m. *absol.* In the game of hazard, To make a losing cast (see note s. v. Main *sb.*[3] 1). *Obs.*

a 1680 Butler *Satyr Gaming* 80 Although he..crucify his Saviour worse Than those Jew-Troopers that threw out, When they were raffling for his Coat. 1765 Earl March in Jesse *Selwyn & Contemp.* (1843) I. 308, I am very sorry to hear that you are still throwing out [*note*, at hazard] as well as me.

n. *Cricket.* Of a fieldsman: To put (the batsman) 'out' by throwing the ball so as to hit his wicket. So in *Baseball*, to put (a base-runner) 'out' by throwing the ball to a player on or near a base.

1871 Hoppe s.v. *Out*, '*Out*' wird der einzelne Schläger.. wenn ein andrer der *fielders* während des *crossing* den Ball gegen das *wicket* werfen kann (*he is thrown out*). 1892 *Field* 11 June 870/3 Mr. Jackson threw him out from cover-point, when the batsmen were attempting a short run.

o. *intr.* (for *refl.*) † To turn out, throng or press out (*obs.*); to move outwards from a centre; to strike out with hands or feet; to let oneself go; to push out (as a root). Cf. sense 9.

1508 Dunbar *Flyting* 217 Off Edinburgh, the boyis as beis owt thrawis. 15.. *Peblis to the Play* v, Thai out threw Out of the townis untald. 1771 Wollaston in *Phil. Trans.* LXI. 561 The pendulum did not..throw-out so far by about 7′ as it generally did. 1798 J. T. Duckworth in *Naval Chron.* (1799) I. 78 The wind throwing out caused me to anchor. 1798 in *Spirit Pub. Jrnls.* (1799) II. 256 He threw out and kicked a good deal. 1809 Malkin *Gil Blas* iii. iv. ¶ 4 The fear of talking absurdly prevents you from throwing out at all. 1825 J. Nicholson *Operat. Mechanic* 518 The pallet A can throw out till it reach *a*,.. B will throw out as far on the other side. 1855 *Jrnl. R. Agric. Soc.* XVI. i. 176 Such soils turn up as a fine mould.. and the roots can throw out without impediment.

p. *intr.* or *absol.* Of a printing machine: To fail to register.

45. **Throw over.** a. See simple senses and Over.

1857 Hughes *Tom Brown* ii. viii, Jack Raggles is furious, and begins throwing over savagely to the further wicket.

b. To throw overboard (in *fig.* sense); to cast off (a lover, associate, or ally); to abandon.

1836 T. Hook *G. Gurney* II. 186, I was satisfied that Emma had thrown me over. 1874 Stubbs *Const. Hist.* I. vi. 163 *note*, Mr. Freeman..throws over the latter part of Palgrave's theory. 1890 T. F. Tout *Hist. Eng. fr. 1689* 27 They threw over their allies.

Throw round (*Naut.*): = *throw about*, 35 b.

46. **Throw to.** † a. *trans.* To put quickly with something else which is already there. *Obs.*

a 1400-50 *Alexander* 2939 Anoþire boll was him broȝt, & bathe he deuoydid, And ȝit he threw to þe thrid, & thrast in þare-eftir.

b. To close (a door, etc.) with force.

1741 Richardson *Pamela* (1824) I. xv. 26, I made shift to get into it (the chamber), and threw-to the door, and it locked after me. 1892 *Chamb. Jrnl.* 23 July 473/1 The slamming of one of the church doors, as if thrown-to by a draught.

47. **Throw together.** a. *trans.* See simple senses and Together.

1717 Berkeley *Let. to Pope* Wks. 1871 IV. 82 A wonderful variety of hills, vales, ragged rocks, fruitful plains, and barren mountains, all thrown together in a most romantic confusion.

b. To put together hastily or roughly; to combine or collect without much care or finish. (Said in relation to literary work.)

1711 Addison *Spect.* No. 105 ¶ 3 On my retiring to my Lodgings, I could not forbear throwing together such Reflections as occurred to me upon that Subject. 1713 Berkeley *Guard.* No. 88 ¶ 3, I shall throw together some passages relating to this subject. 1748 *Anson's Voy.* iii. ii. 308, I shall..throw together the most interesting particulars..in relation to..Tinian.

c. To bring (persons) casually into contact or association.

1831 *Society* I. 207 They were to meet as old friends, when they were next thrown together in London. 1889 Froude *Two Chiefs Dunboy* xxi. 313 They had been thrown together as children, but had rarely met since.

48. **Throw up.** a. *trans.* See simple senses and Up. † *spec.* To throw open (a gate, etc.) (*obs.*).

To throw up the sponge, to give in, surrender: see Sponge *sb.*, and cf. Chuck *v.*[2] 2 b.

14.. *Sir Beues* (M.) 1655+20 Anon the gates he gan up throwe. *c* 1422 Hoccleve *Jereslaus' Wife* 364 Vp he threew an heuy syk. 1675 Brooks *Gold. Key* Wks. 1867 V. 511 You may throw up your caps at them, and bid them do their worst. 1780 Coxe *Russ. Disc.* 253 The chain of islands here laid down may..be considered as thrown up by some late volcanos. 1797 *Encycl. Brit.* (ed. 3) XVI. 492/2 When the cable is finished, to shorten it two fathoms more, which our workmen call *throwing the turn well up*. 1833 J. Holland *Manuf. Metal* II. vii. 189 The fresh coals..will throw up..a body of thick smoke. 1842 *Jrnl. R. Agric. Soc.* III. ii. 171 Land..thrown up into very narrow ridges. 1850 *Ibid.* I. iv. 381 Milk..throws up less cream in glass than in wood. 1861 *Temple Bar Mag.* III. 221 She hastily threw up the window. 1893 *Argosy* Aug. 116 The seaweeds thrown up on his estate.

b. To discharge by vomiting; to vomit. Also (*slang*) *to throw up one's accounts*, in same sense (cf. Cast *v.* 83 b).

1732 Arbuthnot *Rules of Diet* iii, It is easy to judge of the Cause by the Substances which the Patient throws up. 1763 C. Johnston *Reverie* I. 135 Before he can be on the guard, hitting him a plump in the bread-basket, that shall make him throw up his accounts. 1822-34 *Good's Study Med.* (ed. 4) II. 449 Blood from the stomach..thrown up by vomiting.

c. To raise (the hands, eyes, etc.) quickly or suddenly; *spec.* in *Throw up your hands*, as a command to surrender: cf. *Hands up* (Hand *sb.* 54).

1746 Francis tr. *Hor.*, *Sat.* ii. vii. 54, I throw my Nose up to a savoury Steam. 1821 *Examiner* 524/1 Eternally throwing up their eyes to heaven. 1880 [see Bail *v.*[3] 2]. 1887 I. R. *Lady's Ranche Life Montana* 37 He was suddenly aware of a horse galloping rapidly up behind him, and heard a shout: 'Throw up your hands!' 1890 Fenn *Double Knot* III. i. 19 The woman threw up her hands and reeled. 1891 *Eng. Illustr. Mag.* No. 88. 306 Bail up, throw up your hands now, or I'll shoot every man jack of you.

d. To cast up (a heap or earthwork) with or as with the spade; to erect or construct hastily.

1586 Day *Eng. Secretary* i. (1625) A iij, The gardiner, who first throweth vp his earth on a rude heape. 1709 Steele *Tatler* No. 6 ¶ 10 The Greeks threw up a great Intrenchment to secure their Navy. 1869 Hughes *Alfred the Gt.* vi. 71 They..threw up earthworks, and entrenched themselves there. 1880 R. Mackenzie *19th Cent.* iii. ii. 287 Armed crowds began to appear, and barricades were thrown up.

e. To render prominent or distinct; to cause to 'stand out'; to make noticeable by contrast.

1882 Mrs. Oliphant *Lit. Hist. Eng.* I. 288 A..background to throw up and bring into full relief the figure. 1885 Monkhouse in *Mag. Art* Sept. 474/2 The dado is darker..and throws up the rest effectively. 1891 G. D. Galton *La Fenton* vi, The black folds of her dress throwing up..the marble pallor of her face.

f. *Naut. To throw* (a ship) *up in* (*into*, *on*) *the wind*, to turn the vessel into the wind till she points almost directly to windward; also *absol.* said of the navigator.

1769 Falconer *Dict. Marine* (1789), *Donner vent devant*, to throw a ship up in the wind, or in stays. 1832 Marryat *N. Forster* xlvii, The Windsor Castle was thrown up on the wind. 1833 — *P. Simple* xvi, We threw up in the wind.

speckled breast, found in central and eastern Europe, thrush-tit, a book-name for birds of the genus *Cochoa* or *Xanthocepsy*, inhabiting the Himalayas, China, and Java [...]

Thrush (prɒ̆). [Not known in either sense before the 17th c., though the phonology of the word, with *þ* and *sh*, indicates English origin, and points to an OE. *þrusc.* The only continental cognates appear to be, in sense 1, Sw. and ODa. *torsk*, Da. *trøde*, Sw. dial. *trosk*, which Falk and Torp refer to an ON. *þruskr.* [...]

1. A disease, chiefly of infants, characterized by white vesicular specks on the inside of the mouth and throat, and on the lips and tongue, caused by a para-sitic fungus (*are* *thrush-fungus* in 3) scientifically called *aphtha* or *parasitic stomatitis.* [...]

2. In the horse. An inflammation of the lower surface of the frog of the hoof accompanied with a fetid discharge. [...]

3. *Comb.* : thrush-fungus, the parasitic fungus (*Saccharomyces albicans*, which causes thrush (sense 1); thrush-lichen, thrush-moss, a species of lichen, (*Peltigera aphthosa*, found on moist alpine rocks, and used in Sweden boiled in milk as a cure for thrush (sense 1); thrush-paste, an astringent paste f-r curing thrush in horses (*sense 3*). [...]

Thrush, variant of THRASH, goblin.

Thrush, thrush-nush, *see* THRASH sb.?

Thrush-a-thrush. *dial. form.* Also *thrush*.

Name of some boys' game.

Thrushling, *nonce-wd.* [See -LING.] A young thrush.

Thrusty, *a.* [f. THRUSH²+-Y.] Pertaining to or affected with thrush (sense 1).

Thrust (þrʌst), *sb.* [f. THRUST *v.*] [...]

THRUST. [*388*] **THRUGGE.**

THUGGERY. 389 THUMB.

[The remaining columns consist of dense dictionary entries for THRUST, THRUTCH, THRUTHE, THUCKE, THUD, THUG, THUGGEE, THUGGERY, THUGGERY, THUJA, THULE, THULITE, THUMB, and related forms, in text too small to transcribe reliably.]

THUMB. 390 THUMBING.

THUMBLE. 391 THUMP.

THUMP. 392 THUNDER.

THUNDER. 393 THUNDER.

Ti—Tz.

Ticketless (ti'ketles), *a.* Securing from the 'ticketing room' a penal of Britannia.

Ticketless (ti'ketles), *a.* [f. Ticket + -less.] Having no ticket; without a ticket of admission, a railway ticket, etc.

1862 *Daily News* 6 July, Regulations which keep the ticketless public at a distance.

Ticket of leave. A ticket or document giving leave or permission; an order, a permit (*rare*). Now, in specific use, a licence to be at large after the expiration of part of the sentence, formerly granted to convicts in the Australian colonies; since 1840, the usual colloquial name for an 'order of licence' giving a convict his liberty under certain restrictions before his sentence has expired, the proportion remitted being dependent on his conduct and industry.

1772 *Acc. Workhouses* 1.77 No person presume to go out of the street door without a Ticket of Leave, to return in good order.

Ticket-porter. A member of a body of porters in the City of London who were licensed by the Corporation; orig. called *street-porters*, and distinct from the Tackle-house porter of the twelve great Merchant Companies; in later times the two classes of porters were united in the *Society of the Tackle-house and Ticket Porters*. Now Hist.

2. A (railway) porter who collects tickets.

Tick-hole. [f. Tick sb.3 + Hole sb.] A cavity in nodular stone, usually lined with a crystalline incrustation.

Ticking, vbl. sb.1 Forms: 6-7 tyking, -8 tiking; 8 †tike. [f. Tick v.2 + -ing1.] The material of which bed-ticks are made: see Tick sb.4

Tickle (ti'k'l), sb.1 [Generally held to be derived from Tickle v. 6, and so to go with Tickle sb.3 (see quot. 1908); but some would identify it with Eng. dial. *tickle* 'a rapid shallow place in a river'. In Nova Scotia also *tittle*.] A name given on the coasts of Newfoundland and Labrador to a narrow difficult strait or passage.

Tickle (ti'k'l), sb.2 [f. Tickle v.] An act of tickling, in various senses of the vb.; a touch that tickles; a tickling sensation; a tickled or tickling excited feeling.

Tickle (ti'k'l), sb.3 Forms: see the verb; also 4-5 tikil, -ul, tikel; 4 tekyl, -ol, tykell, 6 tyckyll, 6-7 tickell, 7 dial. tickle. [Goes with Tickle v.: the use of the vb.-stem as adj. is unusual; but cf. Kittle a.]

Tickle (ti'k'l), *a.* affected in any way; not firm or steadfast; loose; susceptible to tickling; ticklish or tingled. *Tickle credit*, ready or facile trust or belief; credulity.

4. Having the quality of tickling, tickly. Obs.

5. Not to be depended upon; uncertain (in fact, action, duration, etc.); unreliable; changeable, inconstant, capricious, fickle, 'tickle'. Now rare.

Tickle (ti'k'l), v.1 [ME. tikelen; an onomatopoeic formation; see Tickle v.2] An intransitive sense.

†1. To be affected or excited by a pleasantly tingling or thrilling sensation; to be titivated or moved with a thrill of pleasure: said of the heart, lungs, blood, spirits, etc., also of the person. Obs.

2. To tingle; to itch; also *fig.* to have an uneasy or impatient desire (usually to do something); to be eager. Now rare.

II. Transitive senses.

3. To touch or stroke lightly with, or as with the finger-tips, a straw, a feather, a hair, or the like; to tease, annoy, or irritate lightly, so as to cause a peculiar uneasy sensation. Also said of the thing.

4. To touch or poke (a person) lightly in a sensitive part so as to excite spasmodic laughter. Also *absol.*

7. To excite, affect, move, also, to vex, irritate, provoke.

Ticklely, adv. Obs. rare.

†Tickly, ticky, adv. Obs. rare. Also 7 tickely, tickly. [f. Tickle v. + -ly2.] In an insecure or unstable manner; ticklishly.

Ticklenburgs (tik'lnbɔɹgz.), sb. Also 7 Ticklenburs, Ticklingburs. [For *Tecklenburg*, from a town and county of this name in Westphalia, noted for its manufacture.] A kind of coarse linen cloth; see quots.

†Tickleness. Obs. [f. Tickle a. + -ness.] The quality or state of being tickle; insecurity, instability; critical situation, precariousness; inconstancy; uncertainty.

Tickler (ti'klɛɹ). [f. Tickle v. + -er1.] One who or that which tickles, in various senses.

Ticklesome (ti'k'lsəm), *a.* [f. Tickle v. + -some.]

Tickle-tail, sb. 1. A loose or wanton woman; cf. Tickle a. 3 b.

Tickling (ti'klɪŋ), vbl. sb. [f. Tickle v. + -ing1.]

Ticklish (ti'klɪʃ), *a.* [f. Tickle v. or v. + -ish1.]

1. Easily tickled; sensitive to tickling.

Ticklishly (ti'klɪʃli), adv. [f. prec. + -ly2.] In a ticklish position or fashion; insecurely, critically, delicately.

Ticklishness (ti'klɪʃnɛs). [f. as prec. + -ness.] The quality of being ticklish: see the adj.

Tickly (ti'kli), *a.* [f. Tickle v. + -y1.] Tickle; = Kittly.

Tickney. Obs. or dial. [From *Ticknal*, name of a place near Derby where this earthenware was made.]

Ticky (ti'ki), *a.* Also dial. ticket, tickey. [Echoic.]

Tick-tack (ti'ktæk). Also 6 Sc. tik tak, 7 dial. tick-a-tack, tic-tac, tic-tic-tac, etc.

1. An imitation of a reduplicated or alternating ticking sound.

Ticky (ti'ki), sb. S. Afr. Also dial. tickie, tickey. [Origin uncertain: see Note.]

Tic, Tic-toe, Tick-toe. = Tick-tack, Tick-tock.

Tid (tid), *a.* 1 local. [app. an alteration of Tit sb.?] Soft, tender, nice.

†Tid, *a.* 2 Obs. A word app. deduced by Bailey from *tid-bit*, but also in independent dialect use.

Tidal (tai'dəl), *a.* [f. Tide sb.II. + -al.]

1. Of, pertaining to, or affected by tides; ebbing and flowing periodically.

Tickelishness. 9 Tidal.

Ticklishness (ti'klɪʃnɛs). [f. as prec. + -ness.] The quality of being ticklish: see the adj.

1896 Allbutt's *Syst. Med.* I. 314 Sphygmographic tracings show a lowering in the height of the tidal and forced waves.

2. *transf.* and *fig.* That "ebbs and flows"; periodic, intermittent, alternating, varying.

Tidal air (*Phys.*), the air passing in and out of the lungs at each ordinary respiration; tidal breathing (*Path.*), respiration in which there are pauses alternating with shorter periods of respiratory activity; periodic respiration.

b. *tidal* adv. in an ordinary breathing so to go inches of what is conveniently called "tidal" air out.

Tidally (tai·dăli), adv. [f. TIDAL + -LY.] In a tidal manner; by the action of the tide.

1879 G. H. DARWIN in *Phil. Trans.* CLXXI. 713 On the Secular Changes in the Elements of the Orbit of a Satellite revolving about a Tidally Distorted Planet.

Tidance, obs. form of TIDINGS.

Tid-bit, an earlier form of TIT-BIT.

† Tidder, v.[1] Obs. Forms: 1 tideran, tydran, tȳdðr(i)an, 3 tuderen. [OE. *tȳdran*, related to *tudd'or* or TUDDER, progeny, offspring.] **a.** *intr.* To be productive or prolific. **b.** *trans.* To produce (offspring), to engender.

† Tidder, v.[2] Obs. rare—[?]

Tiddervale, dial. variant of TITIVATE v.

Tiddle (ti·d'l), v. Obs. exc. dial. or slang. Also 7-9 tittle. The two senses may be distinct words.

1. *trans.* To fondle or indulge to excess; to pet, pamper; to tend carefully, nurse, cherish.

2. *intr.* To potter, trifle, "fiddle"; to fidget, fuss.

Tiddledy, dial. variant of TITTLE-TATTLE and *tiddly* "little."[?]

Tiddler (ti·d'lər), slang. [A diminutive by-form of TICKLE n. to tickle.]

Tiddly (ti·d'li), *a.* slang. Also 4-6 tidely. [f. TIDDLEY.]

Tiddlywink (ti·d'liwiŋk). Also tidley-, tiddley-, tiddle-a-wink. [In sense 1 perh. connected with slang *tiddly* a drink, drunk.]

1. An unlicensed public-house or pawnshop; a small beershop; also *tiddywink*, slang.

2 a. A game played with dominoes.

3. *pl.* Knick-knacks of victuals. slang.

Tiddy (ti·di). [Origin unknown.]

TIDDY. In the game of gleek, the four of trumps.

Tide (təid), *n.* Forms: 1 tíd (týd), týdd, 3-6 tide. Also 4-7 tyd, 4-6 tyde. [OE. *tíd* (MLG., Ld. *tíd, týd*), OFris. *tíd*, MDu., MHG. *tît*, Sw., Da. tid] referred by some to a root *tî-* to extend (whence 2 TIME).

I. Time.

† 1. A portion, extent, or space of time; an age, a period, a time, a while;— TIME *sb.* 1-3. Obs.

2. A more or less definite point or season in the course of the year, of life, etc., usually defined by a prefixed word; as *April-tide*, *June-tide*; *New-Year's-tide*, *summer-tide*, *winter-tide*, etc.; esp. AUTUMN-TIDE, SPRING-TIDE, SUMMER-TIDE, WINTER-TIDE, etc. — TIME *sb.* 13 *b. arch. or poet.*

b. The time of the year; season.

3. A definite time in the day or season.

4. Any definite time in the day or season; as EVENTIDE, MORROW-TIDE, NOON-TIDE, q. v.; *spec.* "at the tenth tide of the day" — HOUR 3. Obs.

5. Each of the seven canonical hours; also, the services recited at these;— HOUR 5. Obs.

6. An anniversary or festival of the church; — TIME 15. Obs.

b. in phrases (chiefly technical); as cross tide, a tide running across the direction of another; **high tide,** (*a*) = HIGH WATER; (*b*) = SPRING TIDE; **low tide** = LOW WATER; leeward, neap, windward tide: *see* LEE, NEAP, etc.; FLOOD-TIDE, SPRING TIDE, HALF-TIDE. Also in fig. uses.

7. The flowing or swelling of the sea, or its alternate rising and falling, twice in each lunar day, due to the attraction of the moon and, in a less degree, of the sun; the alternate inflow and outflow produced by this; — HOUR 3. Obs.

8. Applied to that which is like the tide of the sea in some way; as the spring of flowing, rising or falling, or "turning" at a certain time.

9. *fig.* Applied to that which is like the tide of the sea in some way; as *tide-bore* [Race 16].

10. *spec.* = FLOOD-TIDE. Also *fig.*

11. *transf. fig.* A body of flowing water or other liquid; a stream, a current. *poet. and rhet.*

12. The water of the sea; the sea (esp. when the tide is flowing); poet.

III. Phrases.

† 13. Tide and (or) time: *see time and tide*: etc. Obs.

b. The tide abides for, terrieth (for) no man, stays no man, Tide nor time tarrieth no man: now superseded by *Time and tide wait for no man*. Here tide originally meant "time," but from the 16th c. has usually meant the tide of the sea. Cf. *Time and tide*, in both senses. Obs.

14. (In) double tide, ? as if taking advantage of both the tides in one day; hence to make double tides, to work as hard or as long as possible; so to roar, spin, etc. double tide. Cf. sense 8.

V. Combinations.

15. attrib. Things belonging to 1, as tide-bell, dial. beef provided for a "tide" or feast; tide-serving, tide-time (see 6 b); † tide-wise adv. at times, now and then.

16. In senses belonging to II. a. simple attrib. of the tide, II a, as *tide-bar* [Race 6], -channel, -flow, -flux, -load (Gloss 4); -level, -limit, -line, -mark, -race (Race 26); -reach, run, rush, -stream, -turn, -wash; (b) -dependent on or regulated by the state of the tide, II a, as *tide-coach, harbour*; -fleet, flowed, or covered by the tide, as *tide-hole*, -land, -marsh, -pool, -reef; -generating, -producing, -riding, as *tide-gauge*; (c) instrumental, etc., as *tide-bed, -beat, -bound, -caught*, -worn; -driven, -flooded, -free, -lit, -locked, -ribbed, -tossed, -trapped, -washed, -wave, etc.

b. *transf.* and *fig.*

III. Phrases.

† b. The tide abides for, terrieth (for) no man, stays no man, Tide nor time tarrieth no man: now superseded by *Time and tide wait for no man*. Here tide originally meant "time," but from the 16th c. has usually meant the tide of the sea. Cf. *Time and tide*, in both senses. Obs.

b. Special combinations, as a tide-crack, in polar regions, an ice-crack near the shore caused by the rise and fall of the tide, which breaks the floating ice from the shore ice; tide-current, the current caused in a tidal channel.

by the rise or fall of the tide (Ogilvie, 1882); **tide-day** (see quot.); **tide-duty,** import or export duty levied at a port; **tide-flap,** a tidal valve opening outward at the mouth of a drain or small tidal stream; **tide-house,** a (public) house adjacent to a tidal stream; **tide-lock,** a double lock between tidal water and a canal or the like; a guard-lock; **tide-maker,** that which causes the tides; also, a vessel which is compelled to take advantage of the tide; **tide-plate,** a dial on which the state of the tide is indicated; **tide-register,** a register of the movements of the tide; **tide-rode,** *Naut.* (of *tide-riden*), swung by the tide, as a ship at anchor; opposed to *wind-rode*; **tide-runner,** a fish which moves with the tide (U. S.); **tide-time,** the time at which the tide serves at any place; **tide-way,** the undulation which passes over the surface of the ocean, and causes high or low tide at its highest or lowest point reaches any place; also *fig.*; **tide-weather** (see quot.); **tide-wheel,** a water-wheel turned by the flowing and ebbing of the tide through a narrow channel; **tide-work,** work which can be carried on only during hours when the tide is low, or that is paid for by the tide (cf. 8); also, part of the mechanism of a tide-gauge. See also TIDE-BOAT to TIDEWAY.

Tide (təid), *v.* [f. TIDE *sb.* II.]

1. *trans.* **a.** To carry, as the tide does.

b. To carry (through (an undertaking) (*obs.*); to enable (a person) to surmount (a difficulty, etc.).

2. *intr.* To meet with, experience (good or evil fortune). Obs.

3. To fare; to get on (well or ill). Obs. rare—[?]

4. *trans.* **a.** To flow or surge, as the tide; to flow to and fro; sometimes—"flow" as opposed to "ebb." Also *fig.*

b. To tide over (well or ill). Obs.

Tidement, Obs. rare—[?] [f. TIDE *sb.* + -MENT.]

1. A mill driven by the flux and reflux of the tide acting on a water-wheel.

Tide-mill. [f. TIDE *sb.* 7 + MILL.]

Tide-boat. A boat or small vessel which travels with or by means of the tide.

Tide-rip. [f. TIDE *sb.* + RIP *sb.*[?]]

Tideful (təi·dful), *a.* [f. TIDE *sb.* 3 b, 7 + -FUL.]

Tidesman (təi·dzmăn). Also 8-9 tideman.

† Tide-gate. **† Tide-gate.**[2]

Tide-surveyor. A customs official who supervised the tide-waiters.

Tidegate [? as prec. + GATE *sb.*[1]] A gate through which the water passes into a dock or the like at flood-time, and which it is retained during the ebb.

Tideless (təi·dl˘es), *a.* [f. TIDE *sb.* + -LESS.] Having no tide; unaffected by tides; not washed or covered by a tide. Also *fig.*

Tideless-blooded *a.*, whose blood is unstirred by passion or emotion.

† Tidely, adv. Obs. [f. TIDE *sb.* 4 + -LY.[2]] At each tide; each time the tide serves.

Tidely, obs. f. TIDILY; *var.* TITELY Obs.

Tide-mark. The mark left or reached by the tide at high-water.

Tide-water.

1. Water brought by the flood-tide.

2. U. S. Water affected by the ordinary ebb and flow of the tide; tidal water. Also *attrib.*

Tideway. A channel in which a tidal current runs; also the tidal part of a river; *transf.* a strong current running in such a channel; — *transf.* and *fig.*

Tidend(e, Tider(e, obs. ff. TIDING, THITHER.

Tiderip. [f. TIDE *sb.* + RIP *sb.*[?]]

Tidife, *rare.* Also a tydyfe; tidy(f)e, obscure; *cf.* also TYDIE, and TIDEY bird. (Swainson, after Skinner.) Name of some small bird.

Tidiness. [f. TIDY *a.* + -NESS.]

The quality or condition of being tidy (in various senses: see the adj.); † seasonableness; orderliness.

Tidily (təi·dĭli), adv. Also 4-6 tidely. [f. TIDY *a.* + -LY.[2]] In a tidely, seasonable, fitting manner; suitably, in an orderly manner, skilfully, neatly, etc. — see TIDY.

Tiding, vbl. sb. [f. TIDE *v.* or OE. *tídung* vbl. n.]

1. Sing. † tiding(e, † tidingge, a betiding. Obs.

b. Sing. 3 tithing, 3 tidinge, 4 tything, 4 tithinges, 4-5 typinges, † tidings, -ynges, 5 tithynges, tithinges, tydinges, 6 tidinges, tithings, tidings.

Tidings, *sb. pl.* (orig. and formerly sing.) Forms: see sense 1 below.

Tidement, Obs. rare—[?]

Tiding, vbl. sb. [f. TIDE v.2, or TIDE sb.]

Tiding (tīʹdiŋ), vbl. sb. and ppl. a. Also dial. tidding.

Tidology (taidŏʹlŏdʒi), rare. [irreg. f. TIDE sb. + -(O)LOGY.] The study or science that treats of the tides.

Tidy (taiʹdi), a. (sb., adv.) Forms: 3-5 tidi, 4-5 tide, 4-7 tydy, 5 tyde, (6 tidie), 6 tidie, trydye, 7 tyddie, 7-9 dial. teydey), 4-7 tidy. [ME. f. tīd time, TIDE + -Y. Sw., Du. tīdig (Ger. zeitig); Du. tijdig.]

Tie (tai), sb.1 Forms: 1 téah, tég, téh, téag, 3 teȝe, 4-9 tye, 7 tey, tegh, 6-7 tye, 5- tie. [OE. téah, téag fem., rope.—O.Teut. *taug-, -ō str. fem.]

Tie (tai), v. Inflected tied, tying. Forms:

Tie-beam. Arch. The horizontal beam which connects the feet of a pair of principal rafters.

Tie- combining form.

Tie-and-dye

Tied, ppl. a. [f. TIE v. + -ED.]

Tie-dog, Obs. Forms: see TIE and DOG.

Tiemannite (tīʹmanait), Min. [ad. Ger. Tiemannit, named by Haidinger, 1855, from the discoverer, Tiemann: see -ITE.] Native selenide of mercury.

Tien, obs. f. TINE a. Tiend, obs. f. TEIND.

Tienthe, obs. f. TENTH.

Tier (tiər), sb.1 Also 6-9 tire, (6-8 tyre, 6 teare, 7 teer), 7-9 teer, 8 tear. [prob. a. F. tire, f. tirer to draw.]

Tier (taiʹər), sb.2 One who, or that which, ties.

Tieless (taiʹlɛs), a. Having no neck-tie.

Tier. ...

Tierce, 6–7 tearce, 7 tearse, teirse, teirse, ters, ...

Tierce, obs. form of TEAR and TIRE.

Tierce, 6–7 tearce, ...

Tiercel, Tiercelet: see TERCE, TERCELET.

Tierceron ...

Tierced ...

Tie-up ...

Tieth, obs. form of TITHE, TIGHT.

Tierras ...

Tiers état ...

Tiercel, Tiercelet: see TIERCE, TERCELET.

Tie-wig. Also tye-wig. [Cf. TIE 3.] A wig having the hair gathered together behind and tied with a knot of ribbon.

Tie-wigged ...

Tiff, v.[1]

Tiff, sb.[1] [Origin obscure; perh. onomatopoeic; cf. TIFF v.[2]] 1. Liquor, esp. poor, weak, or 'small' liquor; 'tipple'. ...

Tiffany, sb. 7 tiffanie, –enay, eney, –inie, iny, tiffine, tiffiny, 7–9 tiffeny, 9 tiffney. ...

Tiff, v.[2] ...

Tiffin, sb. ...

Tiffing ...

Tiffle ...

Tiffy ...

Tifty-taffety, a. ...

Tift, sb.[2] ...

Tift, sb.[3] ...

Tift, v. ...

Tig, sb.[1] ...

Tiger (təi·gəʳ), sb. Forms: 1 (pl.) tigras, 2–6 tygre, 4–7 tygre, 4 tigris, 4–7 tyger, 6 tygir, 5c. tegir, tegre, 6–7 tiger, etc. ...

Tig, sb.[2], variant of TYG, a drinking-cup.

Tig, sb.[3] ...

Tig, v.[1] ...

Tig, v.[2] ...

Tigella (təidʒe·la). [mod. L.] ...

Tigelle (təidʒe·l). ...

Tigellate (tidʒelət) ...

TILE (continued)

† **b.** As used in building generally, and including thicker slabs of the shape and quality of bricks; cf. TILE-STONE 1. *Obs.*

c. As used for roofing tiles, fire-places, etc.

2. The material of which tiles or bricks consist, burnt clay.

3. *slang.* A hat.

4. The covering of a roof, roofing. *Obs. rare.*

5. Short for TILE-FISH.

TILE-FISH

A deep-sea fish, *Lopholatilus chamæleonticeps*, found in abundance in 1879 off the coast of New England.

TILE-KILN

A kiln in which tiles are baked.

Tile-maker

A maker of tiles; a workman employed in making tiles.

So **Tile-making**.

† **Tilesman.** *Obs.* [f. TILE + -MAN.] A tile-maker.

Tile-pin. A 'pin' (PIN *sb.*) used for fixing the tiles to the laths of a roof.

Tiler (*tai'laɹ*). Also **2 tyelere, 5 tylare, tylier, tiller, tiller, teyller, teler, 6 tylyare, tiler, 7 tylere, 5–9 tyler.** [f. TILE *sb.* + -ER.]

1. One who covers the roofs of buildings with tiles, a tile-layer; also formerly, a tile-maker.

2. *Freemasonry.* (Usually tyler.) The door-keeper who keeps the uninitiated from intruding upon the secrecy of the lodge or meeting.

Tilery (*tai'ləɹi*). [f. TILE, TILER: see -ERY.] A place where tiles are made; a tile-field or -kiln.

Tilestone (*tai'lstoun*). [f. TILE *sb.* + STONE.]

Tiling (*tai'liŋ*), *vbl. sb.* [f. TILE *v.* and *sb.* + -ING.]

TILL

Till, *sb.* Orig. and chiefly *Sc.* [Origin unascertained.] A stiff clay, more or less impervious to water.

Till, *sb.* A box, case, or closed compartment, contained within or forming part of a larger box, chest, or cabinet.

Till, *sb.* Printing. [Cf. MHG. *ge-tille* (LG. *tulle*, Du. *dille*) a socket in which is ...

Till, *sb.* or *dial.* [f. TILL *v.*]

Till, *v.* Forms: ... [OE. *tilian* (*tillian*).]

1. *intr.* To strive, exert oneself, labour, work.

2. *trans.* To labour, work for or at; cultivate.

3. To take care of or attend to medically; to treat (a patient, or a disease). Const. as in 2. Only *OE.*

4. *trans.* To bestow labour and attention, such as ploughing, harrowing, etc., upon (land) so as to fit it for raising crops; to cultivate.

5. To stretch (a thing) out.

Till, *prep., conj., adv.* Forms: 1, 3–7 til, 4–5 tille, tylle, 4–6 til, tyl, 5 tell, 3 tull, 4 til, 4–7 till. [OE. *til* ...]

A. *prep.* I. Local and dative. Now only *n. dial.* and *Sc.*, where normally used instead of *to* before a vowel or *h.*

1. To *or* up to, in the ordinary local sense of *to.*

B. *conj.* (orig. the prep. governing the demonstrative pron. *that*, in apposition with the following clause).

I. To the time when; up to (the point) when.

II. Of time.

III. = To with the infinitive. Now only *Sc.*

Tillable (*ti'labl*), *a.* [f. TILL *v.* + -ABLE.] Capable of being tilled or cultivated.

TILLAGE

Tillage (*ti'lidʒ*), *sb.* [f. TILL *v.* + -AGE.]

1. The act or operation of tilling or cultivating land so as to fit it for raising crops; cultivation, agriculture, husbandry.

2. The state or condition of being tilled or cultivated. *In tillage,* in or under cultivation.

3. *Tilled* or cultivated land.

Tillaged (-ĕdgd)., brought under tillage.

Tillandsia (tilæ·ndzia). *Bot.* [mod.L. (Linnæus), named after Elias Tillands, a Swedish botanist.] A large genus of herbaceous plants of the pine-apple family (*Bromeliaceæ*), found in tropical and subtropical America and the West Indies, chiefly epiphytic on trees.

Tiller (ti·ləɹ). [var. forms.] Of arch. Forms:— 3-4 tilere, 4 teollare, teiler, tiloer, 4-5 tilier or tilyer, tilyer, 5 tylyar, telear, tillioure, tylyers, 5-6 tyllyar, 6 telere, 7 teiler, tiler. [ME. *tilere*, taking the place of OE. *tillia* (Tiller), f. *tillian*, *till*, v.: *see* -ER¹.] subseq. spelt conformably to the verb.

Tiller, *sb.*¹ Forms:— 3 (4 AF. teiler), 5 teler, 6 tyller, -our, 6-7 tillar, 6- tiller. [a. OF. *telier* (12th cent.), *teillier*, in sense 1 orig. a weaver's beam (*telier de i cxanab*, Godef.), med.L. *télārium*, i. L. *téla* web: *see* -ARY².]

Tiller, *sb.*² Now dial. Forms: 1 [see etym.]; 7- tiller, 8-9 tillar, teller; 7 teiler, *tealgor str. tr.*, also *teigra* wk. tr. [see sense¹], extended forms of *telga* wk. masc. 't sprout.' ; OE. *tiʒeleʒ* term., MLG., LG., Du. *telg*, MHa. *zelch*, *zelg*, ne. *tolch*, *teigra* wk. tr., and ne. MHG. *zelch*, *zelge*, sprout. Not found in Eng. between 1100 and 1660; the phonetic history is obscure. The dial. *tillow* may repr. OE. *telga.*]

Tiller, *sb.*³ Obs. *rare*⁻¹. [app. f. TILL *sb.*¹ + -ER¹; *tiller drawer*.] = TILL *sb.*¹

Tiller, *sb.*⁴ Obs. *rare*⁻¹. [cf. TILL v.⁴]

Tiller, v.¹ [f. TILLER *sb.*²]

Tiller, v.² dial. form of TILLOW.

Tillering, *vbl. sb.*¹ Obs. *rare*. [Implies a *tiller tiller*, from TILLER *sb.*² or -ING¹.]

Tillet † (ti·let). Obs. Forms:— 5 tylet(e, tiltette, 6 tyllet, 7 -tillett, -15, 6- tilt, 9-ot. [app. ad. OF. *teillette* (14th c. in Godef.), dim. of *til*, *tel*; *see* TEIL and *til*.] A kind of coarse cloth, used for wrapping up textile fabrics and (formerly) garments; also for making awning.

Tilleul (tĭlø·l). [Fr., OF. *tillet*, *teillet* (14-15th c. in Godef.), dim. of *til*, *teil*; *see* TEIL and *til*.] A lime or linden-tree.

Tilley, Tilly. *see* TILLEY.

Tilley tree, *Tilly-tree*. [Origin unknown.] An exclamation of pain.

Tilling, *vbl. sb.*¹ [f. TILL v.¹ + -ING¹.] The act of TILL v.¹ ; work done upon land for raising crops; cultivation, tillage.

Tilling, *vbl. sb.*² [f. TILL v.⁴ + -ING¹.] That which cultivates land.

Tilt (tilt), *sb.*¹ Forms:— 5, 6-7 tylt, 6 tylte, 7 tilte. [Collateral form of ME. *tild*, *teld*, *sb.*, pech, influenced by prec.]

Tilt, *sb.*² [prob. f. TILT v.²]

Tilt, *sb.*³ [f. TILT v.¹]

Tilter. [f. TILT v.¹ + -ER¹.]

Tilt-hammer. [f. TILT v.¹ + HAMMER.] A heavy hammer used in forging, fixed on a pivot and acted upon by a cam-wheel or an eccentric.

Tilting, *vbl. sb.*¹ [f. TILT v.¹ + -ING¹.] The action of TILT v.¹

Tilting, *vbl. sb.*² [f. TILT v.² + -ING¹.]

Tilting, ppl. a. [f. TILT v.¹ + -ING².] That tilts, in various senses.

1. Moving unsteadily, rising and falling, swaying up and down. (See also 3.)

Tilt-up, sb. and a. [Uses of phr. to tilt up: see TILT v. and UP.] Something that tilts up.

Tilt-yard (tilt̪yäd). Also attrib. [f. TILT sb.² + YARD.] A yard or enclosed space for tilts and tournaments; a (permanent) tilting-ground.

Timbal, tymbal (tim̄bal). Now Hist. or arch. Also timbul. — mod.F. timbale (1646 in Hatz.-Darm.), It. timballe, Sp. timbal.

†Timariot (tim̄ariŏt). Obs. Also τ ʒy-, -ott, -riote, timarriott, &c.

Timar (tim̄är). Obs. Also ʒ -arr. [Persian (and Turkish.)]

Timber (tim̄bæ₁), sb.¹ Forms: α. 4-6 tymbre, 5, 9 timbre, 6-7 tymber, 7 timir.

1. trans. To build, construct, make (as a house, ship, etc.); spec. (in later use) to build or construct of wood. Obs. or arch. R.

Timberer. [f. TIMBER² + -ER¹.]
1. = TIMBERMAN 2.

Timbering (tim̄bær̆ıŋ), vbl. sb. [f. -ING¹.]
1. The action of the verb TIMBER, in various senses.

Timber-work. Wood suitable for structural purposes. — TIMBER sb.¹ 3.

Timber-work.
1. Work executed in timber; the wooden part of a structure.

2. concr. Building material (esp. of wood); timber-work (in Mining, the timber used to support the sides of a shaft or the roof of a working.

Timbery (tim̄bæri), a. [f. TIMBER sb.¹ + -Y.] Abounding in or characterized by timber.

Timber-yard. An open yard or place where timber is stacked or stored.

Timbre (tim̄bæ₁, tæ̃br), sb.² [a. F. timbre.]
1. The character or quality of a musical sound (distinct from its pitch and intensity).

Timbrel (tim̄brĕl). Now chiefly biblical. Also 6 tymbrell, timbrell, -ille, St. timbrall, 6-7 tymbrel.

Time (taim), sb. Forms: α 2 time, tyma, 2-8 tyme, 4 tym, tima, -e, maa-; 4-6 tyme, tym; 5-6 tyme.
I. A space or extent of time.

TIME.

38

TIME.

TIME.

39

TIME.

TIME.

40

TIME.

TIME.

41

TIME.

† **Timorosity.** *Obs.* Forms: (5 tymoryste) 6-7 timorosity, -itie, tymer-; (tamer-)timorositie, 6-7 timorosity. [as TIMOROUS + -ITY: cf. obs. It. *timorosità* (Florio).] Timorousness, timidity.

Timorosome (formerly sim-timorousome). *Obs.* Now *dial.* Also 7-9 timmer-, timor-, trimer-, timor-. (8 timorof-)... timmor-.

Timorous, *a.* Forms: 4-5 timorus, 6-7 -ouse, 7-8 timerous, 8. (6 temerous.) 6 tymorous, (7 timorous, tim'rous.)

Timorously, *adv.* In a timorous manner: timidly.

Timorousness. The quality or state of being timorous: fearfulness, timidity.

Tin (tin), *sb.* Forms: 1-3 tin, 3-7 tyn, 4-6 tynne, 5 tynne, 5-7 tynn, (6 teene, *Sc.* twne, 8in.), 6-7 tinne, 7 tinn, 5-tin. [OE. *tin* neut.— MLG., MDu. *tin* (LG., EFris. *tin*, OHG., MHG. *zin* (G. *zinn*), ON. (Da. *tin*, Sw. *tenn*).—OT.use. *tin-a* pl.: not known outside Teutonic. Si. *tinne* is from OE.]

Tinamou (tin'amoo). [a. F. *tinamou* (Barrère 1741, Buffon 1771), a. native name in Galibi.] A bird of the genus *Tinamus* (Latham 1790) of family *Tinamidae*, dromognathous birds, native to South and Central America...

Tincal (tin'kal), *sb.* Forms: 6 tincal, 7-8 tinckall, 7 tinkal, 7-8 tinkal; 8- tincal. [ad. Pers. *tinkār*, *tinkal*, whence the Arabic and Altincan.]

Tinchel (tin'shel), *sb.* *Sc.* Forms: 6 tinchill, tynchal, teinchell, 6-7 tinchell, 8-9 tinkell, 9 tinchel, tinkal, tinchal, tinchell. [ad. Gael. *timchioll*]

Tinct, *ppl. a. and poet.* [ad. L. *tinct-us*, pa. pple. tinged; dyed, coloured. Const. as pa. pple.]

Tinct (tinkt), *sb.* Also 6 tinckt. [f. L. *tinct-*: see TINCT and TINCTURE.]

Tinct, *v.* [f. L. *tinct-*, ppl. stem of *tingĕre* to dye, colour.]

Tinction (tink'ʃən), *sb.* *rare.* [ad. L. *tinctiōn-em* a dipping: baptism administered by non-Catholics.]

Tinctorial (tiŋktō'riəl), *a.* [f. L. *tinctōri-us* (Pliny) (*l. tinctor* and *l. dyer*) + -AL.] Of, pertaining to, or used in dyeing: yielding or using dye or colouring matter.

Tincture (tiŋk'tiuə), *sb.* [ad. L. *tinctūra* a dyeing, tinging, f. *tinct-*: see *tingĕre* to dye: see -URE.]

1. *trans.* To impart a tincture or quality to: colour, tinge, imbue.

Tinctured (tiŋk'tiuəd), *ppl. a.* [f. TINCTURE *v.* + -ED.] Imbued with a tincture or colour; having a tincture (esp. of a specified kind): dyed, coloured, stained, tinged.

Tind, *v. Obs.* exc. *dial.* Forms: *a.* (1 tendan), 2-3 tenden, 3-5 tende, 4 (*3rd pers.* tent), *a.* teende, 5 *Sc.* teynd, 4-5 tend. *b.* tynde, 4-5 teende, (6-9 *dial.* teand), 7 *Sc.* tind, 5-6 tyne, 6-7 *Sc.* tyne, 7-9 tin *pa. t.* tynded, tinded, tind, tined, teened.

Tind, *obs. variant of* TIND.

Tindal (ti'ndal). *E. Ind.* [ad. Malayālam *tandal*, Telugu *tandēlu*, also Hindūstānī *tindēl*, chief or head man of a body of men.] *a.* A petty officer among lascars, boatswain's mate; *b.* an overseer of labourers on public works.

Tinder, tinder-.

Tindal, *Obs.* *See* quots.

Tinder (tində·ɹ). *Forms:* α. 1 tyndre, tyndir, 1–7 tynder, 5 -yr, 3- tinder (7 -ar).

Tinder-box.

Tindern, *a. Obs. rare.*

Tinder, *tender, v. Obs. rare*[-1]. [ME. *tendren, t. tendre,* v. form of TINDER *sb.*] *intr.* To become inflamed, glow, burn.

Tindery.

Tindle (ti·nd'l). *dial.*

Tine (tain), *sb.*[1]

Tine (tain), *sb.*[2]

Tine (tain), *sb.*[3] *Obs. exc. dial.*

Tine, tyne (tain), *sb.*[4] *exc. dial.*

Tine, tyne (tain), *v.*[1] Chiefly (now only) *north. dial. and Sc.*

Tine, tyne (tain), *v.*[2]

Tine, variant of TINE (after a dental).

Tinea (ti·nɪ·ă). [L.]

Tinean, *a. and sb.*

Tined (taind), *a.*

Tineman.

Tiner.

Tinet. *See* TINNET.

Tine-tare, Tine-weed.

Tine-worm.

Tin-field, -floor, etc. *See* TIN *sb.*

Tinfoil (ti·nfoil), *sb.*

Tinful (ti·nfŭl). [f. TIN *sb.* + FUL.]

Ting (tiŋ), *sb.*

Ting (tiŋ), *v.*

Ting-a-ling, ting-a-ring = TING *sb.* b.

Tinge (tindʒ), *sb.*

Tinge (tindʒ), *v.*

Tingent.

Tinger.

Tingible, *a.*

Tingle, *sb.*[1]

Tingle, *sb.*[2]

Tinging (tiŋiŋ), *vbl. sb.*

Tingo.

Tinging (tindʒiŋ), *vbl. sb.*

Tin-glass.

Tin-glaze, -glazed.

Tingle (tiŋg'l), *sb.*[1]

Tingle (tiŋg'l), *v.*

Tingle-tangle.

Tingling (tiŋgliŋ), *vbl. sb.*

Tingling (tiŋgliŋ), *ppl. a.*

Tinglingly (tiŋgliŋli), *adv.*

Tinsel, v.² [f. TINSEL sb.³]

1. trans. To make glittering with gold or silver (or imitations thereof) interwoven, brocaded, laid on. Also fig. b. To embellish (pictures, letters, etc.) with gold leaf; to embellish (ceramic ware) with metallic effects (Cent. Dict. Suppl. 1909). Hence **Tinselling** vbl. sb.

2. To give a speciously attractive or showy appearance to; to cover the defects of with or as with tinsel.

Tinselled, ppl. a. Also 6–7 tinceld.

Tinsel-smith (ti'nsəlsmiþ). [f. TIN + SMITH: cf. goldsmith, silversmith, etc.] A worker in tin; a maker of tin utensils; a whitesmith.

Tin-stone. The most commonly occurring form of tin ore; cassiterite, native tin dioxide (peroxide). Also attrib.

Tin-stream. Usually in pl. See quot. 1891, and cf. stream-tin v. b. 1.

Tin-streamer, one who obtains tin from a deposit of sand or gravel by washing; Tin-streaming, the washing of tin from such a deposit.

Tint (tint), sb.¹ [app. altered from the tinct of TINCT, which may already have been so pronounced] but It. tinta tint, hue, may have influenced the technical use in painting.]

1. A colour, hue, usually slight or delicate; esp. any one of the several lighter or deeper shades or varieties, or degrees of intensity, of the same colour.

2. After negative: (Not) a bit, particle, trace.

Tint (tint), v. [f. TINT sb.¹] trans. To impart a tint to; to colour, esp. slightly or with delicate shades; to tinge. Also absol.

Tint-back. A tack, or short light iron nail, coated with tin.

Tintage (ti'ntedʒ). [f. TINT sb.¹ + -AGE.] Tints in the mass; tinting.

Tintamarre (tintămaˑr). Now rare. Forms: 6 tyntamar, 7 tintamare, -mart, tintimare, (tinamar), 7–8 tintamar, (9 -tinta, -marre, tintimar), 7– tintamarre. [a. F. tintamarre...] A confused noise, uproar, clamour, racket, hubbub, clatter.

Tinter (ti'ntəɹ). [f. TINT v. + -ER¹.] One who or that which tints; now esp. an artist

†Tinternel. Obs. Also tyn-. [?] Some form of instrumental music. Hence †Tinternelling a.

†Tint for tant (redupl. form). [A redupl. phrase with antithetic modification of the first member: cf. Mod. altered from taunt for (poor) taunt (TAUNT sb.¹).] Retaliation, retort in kind.

†Tintinnate, v. Obs. rare⁻¹. [f. L. tintinnāre] To ring, as a bell; to tinkle. Hence †Tintinnation Obs. rare⁻¹, a ringing, a tinkling.

Tintinnabula (tintinæ·biŭla), a. [f. L. tintinnăbŭl-um + next ad.] next.

Tintinnabular (tintinæ·biŭlar), a. [f. L. tintinnăbŭl-um + -AR¹.]

Tintinnabulant (tintinæ·biŭlănt), a. [f. as next + -ANT¹.] Ringing or tinkling as a small bell; jingling.

Tintinnabulary (tintinæ·biŭlări), a. rare. [ad. L. tintinnăbŭlum bell: see -ATE² 2.] Bell-shaped.

Tintinnabulation (tintinæbiŭlē·ʃən). [f. as prec. + -ARY¹. Cf. med.L. tintinnăbŭlātus] Of or pertaining to bells or bell-ringing; of the nature of a bell; characterized by bell-ringing.

Tintinnabulous (tintinæ·biŭləs), a. rare. [ad. L. tintinnăbŭl-um bell + -OUS.] Tinkling as a bell.

Tintinnabulum (tintinæ·biŭləm), pl. -a. [L.] A ringing of a bell or bells, bell-ringing; the sound or music so produced.

Tintist (ti'ntist). [f. TINT sb.¹ + -IST 4.] One skilled in tinting, a tinter; one who prefers tinting to colouring.

Tinting (ti'ntiŋ), vbl. sb. [f. TINT v. + -ING¹.] The action of TINT v.; the result of this; tint or tints; colouring. Also attrib.; tinting-tool = TINT sb.³

Tint-less, a. Having no tint or tints.

†Tinto (tinto), sb. Obs. [a. Sp. tinto tint, deep-coloured, in vino tinto 'a blackish wine in Spaine' (Minsheu).] Tent wine: see TENT sb.³

†Tinto (tinto), a. rare. [It.] Tinted; sb. a tint.

Tintometer (tintɔ·mĕtəɹ). [f. TINT sb.¹ + -OMETER.] An apparatus for the exact determination of colour: see quots. and cf. COLORIMETER.

†Tintregh. Obs. Forms: 1 tintrega, 3 tintreo, -he, tintreowe. [OE. tintreg, st. neut., tintrega wk. masc.] Torment, torture, agony. Also fig.

Tinty (ti'nti), a. [f. TINT sb.¹ + -Y¹.] Full of tints; having the tints too prominent or inharmoniously combined. Hence **Tintiness**.

Tin-type (ti'ntaip). Photogr. [f. TIN + -TYPE.] A photograph taken as a positive on a thin plate: cf. FERROTYPE 2. Also attrib.

Tin-typer, a photographer who takes tin-types.

Tin-vat, the tin-bath in galvanizing.

Tin-worm to Tin-work: see TIN sb. 5 and TINE-WORM.

Tiny (təi'ni), a. and sb. Also 6–7 tyny, tynie, teeny. [app. a.] Very small, little, or slight; wee, minute. **b.** sb. A little child; also applied to a small creature or thing generally. **c.** A tiny amount, a very little.

Tip (tip), sb.¹ Forms: 5 typpe, typ, 6 tyyppe, tippe, 5– tip. [ME. tip, typpe...]

1. The slender extremity or top of a thing; esp. the pointed or rounded end of anything long and slender; the top, summit, apex, very end.

b. fig. Utmost point, extremity; highest point, apex, crown, Obs. (Cf. also TIPE 2.)

c. Often name for an anther, or summit of a stamen. Cf. APEX 6 a. Obs.

Tip, sb.² Also 5 typpe. [app. f. TIP v.¹] An act of tipping, a light but distinct impact, blow, stroke, or hit; a noiseless tap; a significant touch.

Tip, sb.³ A small present of money given to an inferior, esp. to a servant or employee of another for a service rendered or expected; a gratuity, a douceur: see TIP v.⁴

Tip, sb.⁴ [f. TIP v.⁴ sense 2 (which occurs c 1700).] A small present of money given to an inferior, esp. to a servant or employee of another for a service rendered or expected; a gratuity, a douceur: see TIP v.⁴

Tip, sb.⁵ [f. TIP v.², esp. senses 1 b, 2, 3.]

1. Skittles. (Cf. TIP v.²)

Tip, v.¹ Also 5 typpe. [app. f. TIP v.¹] An act of tipping, a light but distinct impact, blow, stroke, or hit.

II. The act of tilting and derived uses.

2. An act of tipping up or tilting, or the fact of being tilted; inclination. (Cf. TIP v.² 1.)

Tip, v.² [f. TIP sb.¹]

1. trans. To strike or hit smartly but lightly; to give a slight blow, knock, or touch to; to tap noiselessly.

2. To mis-neel = tip: orig. in circus slang (see quot. 1897); hence, to fail in one's aim or object.

Tip, v.³ [f. TIP sb.¹; a by-form, perh. belong here with the sense 'until the need or necessity arises or this'.]

Tip, v.⁴ [Origin uncertain.]

1. trans. To strike or hit smartly but lightly; to give a slight blow, knock, or touch to.

Tip, v.⁵ To overthrow, knock, or cast down, cause to fall or tumble; to overturn, upset; to throw down (off a support, out of a vehicle, etc.) by effort or accidentally.

2. intr. To step lightly; to walk min-cingly, or on tiptoe; also fig.

II. Intransitive senses.

1. To overthrow, knock, or cast down, cause to fall or tumble; to overturn, upset.

II. Transitive senses.

2. To assume a slanting or sloping position; to incline, tilt; e.g. of a balance; now esp. of a cart, a plank, etc. (usu. with up), to tilt up at one end and down at the other so that anything supported by it is (or may be) thrown off or emptied out.

3. To empty out (a wagon, cart, truck, or the like, or its contents) by tilting it up; to dump.

4. To drink off, 'toss off'; sling and deal.

Tip, v.⁶ Forms: a. 4–7 typpe, 5–6, 9 dial. tipe (tip); infl. 5 typen, 6 typed, 6–9 tipped; ppl. 7–8 tip'd, tipped, 8 tipp'd; 7–9 tipping. [Origin and form-history obscure: known first in type (14th c.), tipe, in literary use as late as 1631 (sense 1), and an inflectional form from Cumberland in Shrgu. and E Anglia.]

Tip, v.⁷ [prob. imitative.]

Tip-cat. [f. TIP v.² + CAT sb.¹] The game of cat or tipcat. Also attrib.

Tip-top, sb., a. and adv. [f. TIP sb.¹ + TOP sb.¹]

1. trans. To furnish with a tip [TIP sb.¹]; to put something on at the tip.

Tipper¹, one who or that which tips.

Tippet, sb. [f. TIP v.² + -ER¹.]

3. Phrase. To tip (or a) wink, to give a wink to a person as a private signal or warning.

Supplement, p. 3873; Corrigenda, p. 4092; Spurious words, p. 4093; Books quoted, p. 4094

Hence **Ti·pto·pness**; **Tip-to·pper**, a 'tip-top' person or thing; in quot. 1822, applied to a glass filled to the very top, a bumper; **Tip-to·pping** [TOPPING ppl. a.], **Ti·ptopping** adv. (*nonce-wds.*) — B.

Tipula (ti'piŭlă). Pl. **tipulæ** (-īī). [L. *tīpula* (incorrectly *tippula*) a water-spider or water-fly.]

Tipulary (ti'piŭlări), a. Belonging or allied to the genus *Tipula* or family *Tipulidæ*; also as *sb.* (a insect); **Tipulary** (ti'piŭlāri) a. —prec. adj.; **Ti·pulid**, **Tipu·lidan**, a. belonging to the family *Tipulidæ*; also as *sb.*; **Tipu·lideous** a. —prec. adj.

Tip-up, *sb.* and a. [f. phr. *tip up*: TIP v.2]

Tir, *sb.* Obs. Also 3 **tyr**. [OE. *tír* glory, honour, cognate with ON. *tírr* str. masc. glory, renown; related to OHG. *ziri*, *siari*, MHG. *sier* adj. costly, splendid, whence OHG. *siarī* fem., MHG. *siere*, Ger. *zier* splendour, beauty, adornment; OE. *tíer*.]

Tirade (tīrē'd), *sb.* [Fr. *tirade* = It. *tirata*, Sp. *tirada*, f. *tirare* to draw: cf. TIRE v.1]

Tire (taiᵊɹ), *sb.4* Forms: 5, 7, 9 **tyre**, (8–9 *dial.*) **tyr.** See also TIER. [Probably the same word as prec., the *tire* being originally (sense 1) the 'attire', 'clothing', or 'accoutrement' of the wheel.]

Tire (taiᵊɹ), *sb.5* Obs. Also 6–7 **tyre**. [ad. F. *tir* sense 'shot', volley', verbal *sb.* from *tirer* to draw.]

Tireless (taiᵊɹles), a.1 [f. TIRE sb.4 + -LESS.] Tireless, fatigue.

Tire (taiᵊɹ), *sb.6* *dial.* and *colloq.* [From TIRE v.3] Tiredness, fatigue.

Tire, tyre, etc. Variant of TEAR sb.2 b, the finest fibre of flax, etc.

Tire, obs. f. TEER n., TIER sb.2, TYRE.

Tireling (tiᵊɹliŋ), *sb.* (a) *dial.* [app. f. TIRE v.3 + -LING: cf. *hireling*, *shaveling*.] A tired person or animal; in quot. *attrib.* or as *adj.*: cf. *hireling* prec, etc.

Tiresome (tiᵊɹsŏm), a. [f. TIRE v.3 + -SOME.] 1. Causing physical fatigue; fatiguing, tiring.
2. Causing weariness; wearisome, tedious.

Hence **Ti·resomely** adv. A tiresomely importunate instinct reminded me that vivacity (at least in me) was displaced. **Ti·resomeness.**

Tiresomeness. [f. prec. + -NESS.] The condition of being tired; weariness. *Obs. rare.*

Tiring (taiᵊɹiŋ), *vbl. sb.1* [f. TIRE v.3 + -ING.] The fitting of a wheel with a tire; the condition or mode of being fitted with tires.

Tiring-house. *Obs. or arch.* Also 6–7 **tyring-**. [f. TIRE v.2] A dressing-room; *esp.* the room or place in which the actors dressed for the stage: = TIRING-ROOM.

Tiring-irons (taiᵊɹiŋ·aiᵊɹnz), *sb. pl.* Also 7–8 **tyring-**, **tarring-**, 8 **tarring-**. [In its current forms 1, *tiring-*, or *pple.* of TIRE v.1 from] A puzzle consisting of a number of rings.

Tiring-room (taiᵊɹiŋ·rūm). [= TIRING vbl. sb.1] A room used for tiring or attiring; *esp.* a dressing-room of a theatre; = TIRING-HOUSE.

Tiring (taiᵊɹiŋ), *vbl. sb.3* Also 6–7 **tyring**. [f. TIRE v.1]

Tirl, v.1 Now chiefly Sc. and north. Forms: 4–7 **tirle**, (*turle*), 7 **tirle**, 8–**tirl**. [Metathetic variant of TRILL v.1 Cf. EFris. *tirreln* to turn about quickly.]
I. 1. *trans.* To turn; to cause to rotate or revolve; to twirl, spin, whirl.
2. *trans.* To pluck (a tense string, etc.) so as to cause vibration.

Tirl, v.2 *Sc.* and *north. dial.* [Apparently related to TIRVE v.1 and TIRR v. in same sense; perh. orig. a freq. *tyrflen*: cf. *whirl* from *hwirf-*.]

Tirl, *sb.1 Sc.* To roll or turn back, *full* or strip off (a garment, the clothes, etc.; the bed-clothes from a person, his back, etc.; the bed-clothes from a bed); the thatch or roof from a building.

Tirl, *sb.2 Sc.* [f. TIRL v.1] 1. Act of tirling (see TIRL v.1 2); loosely, a tap or tapping.

Tirl, *sb.3 Sc.* Also 6 **tyrle**. [Origin uncertain: app. not connected with any sense of TIRL.]

son Muse's Threnodie v. (1774) 133 O how they bend their backs and fingers tirle! 1781 J. Hutton Tour to Caves (ed. 2) Gloss. (E.D.S.), Tirl, v., to turn over, as leaves in a book. 1825 Brockett N. C. Words, Tirl,..to turn over the leaves of a book quickly. 1844 Ayrshire Wreath 155 We had a tough game at tirlin' the trencher. a1869 C. Spence Poems (1898) 72 Soft wind sighing o'er the waste, Tirling the seared leaves. 1894 Northumbld. Gloss. s.v., 'Tirled heels up', suddenly overturned or turned inside out.

† b. ? To cause to move; to circulate; in phrase *tirl on the berry*, ? pass round the wine. Cf. *troll the bowl*. Obs.

1519 Interl. Four Elem. B ij, Make rome, syrs, and let vs be mery, With huffa galand synge tyrll on the bery, And let the wyde worlde wynde. c1537 Thersytes in Four O. Plays (1848) 79 And we shall make merye And synge tyrle on the berye. [a1553 Udall Royster D. ii. iii. (Arb.) 36 Heigh derie derie, Trill on the berie.]

2. intr. To turn over; to rotate in moving or falling; to roll, whirl.

1824 Mactaggart Gallovid. Encycl. s.v. Cankert, Afore she tirl'd owre [= died] my prayers war fervant. 1860 Blackie Lyr. Poems, Jenny Geddes vii, Stool after stool, like rattling hail, came tirling through the air. 1894 Northumbld. Gloss. s.v., Slates are said to 'come tirlin doon' when they are stripped off in a gale.

II. 3. intr. To make a rattling noise by turning or moving something rapidly to and fro or up and down. a. In the phr. *to tirl at* († *upon*) *the pin*, to make such a noise on some part of the gate or door, in order to gain admittance; also *to tirl at the latch, at the sneck*.

An old phrase of ballad poetry, which in the 19th c. was taken up and used by Scott, and others after him. Now generally identified by antiquaries with the use of the appendage called the *risp and ring* (Risp sb.2 2), formerly used for this purpose. (Cf. Tinkle v.1 3, Bob Norice ix, 'When he came to Lord Barnet's castel He tinklet at the ring'.) But in this identification there are difficulties; a *risp* is not a 'pin', nor has it any resemblance to a 'pin', in any known sense of the word; the *pin* of a door was the latch or handle which was 'lifted' or 'turned' to open the door: see quots. under Pin sb.1 1 b; whereas the 'risp' was a fixed appendage which could neither be lifted nor turned, having no connexion with the latch or door-handle. Hence it would seem that 'to tirl at the pin' was to make a noise by moving the latch up and down rapidly. It is possible that the 'risp and ring' was a later device, which came to be erroneously considered as the apparatus by which the 'tirling at the pin' was performed.

[c1500 Songs, Carols, etc. 111 Hogyn cam to bowers dore, He tryld vpon þe pyn for love, Hum, ha, trill go bell..Vp she rose & lett hym yn.] 15.. Ld. Beichan in Ballads & Songs (Percy Soc.) 90 When she came to Lord Beichan's gate, She tirled softly at the pin. ?16.. in Ramsay's Tea-t. Misc. (1762) 324 Ay he tirled at the pin, But answer made she none. ?17.. Pr. Robt. ix. in Minstr. Scot. Bord. (1869) 381 O he has run to Darlinton, And tirled at the pin. 1816 Scott Antiq. xl, There cam..first Pride, then Malice, then Revenge,..then False Witness; and Murder tirl'd at the door-pin, if he camna ben. 1833 M. Scott Tom Cringle xii. (1859) 270, I hear my next door neighbour Madam Adversity tirling at the door pin. 1843 Nicholson Hist. & Trad. T., Brownie o' Blednoch 80 He tirled na lang, but he glided ben Wi' a dreary dreary hum. 1879 Perthshire in Bygone Days ii. v. 300 My Nannie will smile in her sleep and awake When I tirl at the latch of my door. 1895 Crockett Men of Moss-Hags xiii, She tirled fretfully at the pin, the servant-maid opened, and we went within.

b. trans. in *to tirl the sneck*. Sc. rare.

(Cf. the name, Jonnie Tirlsneck, of the beadle in Scott's St. Ronan's Well.)

a1794 Pickering 'Keen blaws the Wind' in Burns' Wks. (1856) IV. 91 The Gaber-lunzie tirls my sneck And shivering tells his waefu' tale. 1892 J. Lumsden Sheep-head & Trotters 44 They..tirl the neebors' snecks Like ouphes this nicht.

4. intr. Said of the sound of rain on a roof. rare.

1886 Stevenson Kidnapped xxvi, When the wind gowls in the chimney and the rain tirls on the roof.

Hence **Ti·rling-pin**, the 'pin' or latch on which persons 'tirled' for admittance: see above, sense 3.

1875 Jas. Grant One of the 600 i, The old Scotch tirling-pin—to be found now nowhere save in Fife—in lieu of bells and knockers. 1878 N. & Q. 5th Ser. IX. 319, I have seen and tirled at an original tirling-pin on the chief entrance door of the vicarage house at Ovingham-on-Tyne. 1894 Northumbld. Gloss. s.v. Tirl, Doors were formerly provided with a long, notched, iron handle on which a loose iron ring was hung. Instead of rousing the house with a knock, the caller tirled the ring up and down the notches of the 'tirling pin', or handle. [But this was the *risp and ring*.]

Tirl(e, tyrl(e, v.4 Sc. Var. of Thirl v.1, 3, Thrill v.1

1825–80 Jamieson, Tirl, Tirle,..to quiver, vibrate, thrill. a1870 Thomson Musings (1881) 120 Tyrants will ne'er care a snuff for your word, Till ance they heart tirl frae the point o' your sword.

Tirleis, -lies, obs. Sc. forms of Trellis.

† **Ti·rler**. Obs. [f. Tirl v.3 + -er 1.] One who tirls; *tirler of square bones*, a thrower of dice, a dicer.

[Cf. c1550 Lusty Juventus D iij, I wyll trill the bones while I haue one grote.] 1609 Holland Amm. Marcell. xxviii. iv. 340 Certaine..who decline the name of Alcatores, i. Dice-players, and therefore are desirous to be called Tesserarij, i. Tirlers of square bones.

† **Ti·rlery**, a. (or ? sb.) Obs. Also tyr-, -liry, -lary. [? Related to Tirl v.3] ? Whirling, flighty, trifling, trumpery: in a few obs. combs.: see quots., and cf. Terlerie.

1546 Bale Eng. Votaries i. (1550) 24 b, Bertha the quene ..then beynge a Frenche woman caused kynge Ethelbert to admit them wyth al theyr tyrlery trashe. c1560 Dr. Doubble Ale 437 in Hazl. E. P. P. III. 321 Farewell and adewe, With a whirlary whewe, And a tirlary typpe; Beware of the whyppe. 1638 Ford Lady's Trial III. i, The best..prove themselves but flirts, and tirliry-pufkins [see Puffkin].

Ti·rlie, ti·rly, sb. and a. Sc. [f. Tirl sb.1, v.3]

A. sb. 1. (See quot.)

1882 Jamieson's Dict., Tirlie, tirly, sb. applied to a waving or ornamental line in scroll-work or carving; also, to the ornament itself.

2. A turnstile.

1824 Mactaggart Gallovid. Encycl., Tirlies, little circular stoppages in pathways which turn round.

B. adj. Full of twirls or whirls, as in **Tirly-toy, Ti·rlie-whi·rlie**, a whirled figure, ornament, or pattern; anything having this form; a whirligig; a musical twirl or turn of the voice: also *attrib*.

a1807 Skinner Misc. Poet. (1809) 183 What can ye be that cou'd employ Your pen in sic a 'tirly-toy'? 17.. Dainty Davie ii. in Herd Coll. (1776) II. 215 It was in and through the window broads, And a' the 'tirlie wirlies o'd; The sweetest kiss that e'er I got. 1742 Forbes Shop Bill x. in Ajax, etc. (1755) 40, I hae to fit the little girl..Wi' mony a bony tirly wirl about the queets [= ankles]. 1816 Scott Antiq. xxi, They hae contrived queer tirlie-wirlie holes, that gang out to the open air, and keep the stair as caller as a kail-blade. 1885 'Strathesk' More Bits xiv. (ed. 2) 274 Matthew Riddell..sang with a great many 'tirlywirlies' and grace-notes the following curling song.

Tirling, Tirling-pin: see Tirl v.3

Tirlist, obs. Sc. form of Trellised.

Tiro, tyro (təiᵊ·ro). Pl. -oes, -os (-oz). Forms: α. 7 tyron, tyrone, pl. 7–9 tyrones (-ōᵘ·nīz). β. 7–9 tyro, 8–9 tiro, pl. 7–8 tyro's, 7- tyros, tyroes, 8- tiroes. [a. L. *tīro*, pl. *tīrōnēs* (in med.L. often spelt *tyro, tyrones*: so in Du Cange), a young soldier, a recruit, a beginner; It. *tirone*, Sp. *tiron*. Commonly spelt *tyro*, after med.L., down to the date of Cowper's *Tirocinium*, 1784, and still so spelt by the majority of writers; in the 17th c. *tyrone* was even written for It. *tirone*, and *tyrones* as plural after L. is found down to 1824. But a plural of English form *tyroes* (cf. *heroes, negroes*) is found in 1672, and *tyros* in 1690; Cowper has *tiroes*.]

A beginner or learner in anything; one who is learning or who has mastered the rudiments only of any branch of knowledge; a novice.

1611 Coryat Crudities 63 Of those punies, those tyrones that are brought up under those threescore, there are no less then a thousand and five hundred. 1647 R. Stapylton Juvenal 109 Exercising and training like the tyrones or young souldiers in Camp Mart. 1656 Blount Glossogr., Tyrone.., a fresh water-souldier; a young beginner in any art or science, a novice. 1670 E. Maynwaring Physician's Repos. 92 They do but qualify you as a Tyro. 1672 Manley Cowell's Interpr. Pref., The Students of the Law be no Tyroes in other Learning; or, at least, ought not to be. 1697 Evelyn Numism. vii. 252 For the Ease and Benefit of Tyros. 1699 Garth Dispens. iii. 31 There stands a Structure on a rising Hill, Where Tyro's take their Freedom out to kill. 1726 Leoni Alberti's Archit. III. 24/1 The Tyroes in the art of Painting. 1784 Cowper Tiroc. 220 The management of tiroes of eighteen Is difficult. 1797 Monthly Mag. III. 240/1 Dr. Travis..was..on entering into this province of theological polemics, a Tiro, compared with his antagonists. 1810 Edin. Rev. XV. 399 The tyro will not complain that it [the word] is obscure. 1824 Scott Redgauntlet let. xiii, A subject upon whilk all the tyrones have been trying their whittles. 1828 Whately in Encycl. Metrop. (1845) I. 287/1 It will..be advisable for a tiro in composition to look over what he has written. 1851 Ruskin Mod. Paint. (ed. 2) I. Pref. 36 The merest tyro in art knows that [etc.]. 1869 Farrar Fam. Speech ii. (1873) 49 The youngest tiro is hardly surprised to learn that *lieu* and *coucher* both spring from one root. 1875 Jowett Plato (ed. 2) IV. 13 It is difficult to acquit Plato..of being a tyro in dialectics, when he overlooks such a distinction. 1880 Swinburne Stud. Shaks. 14 Easily recognisable by the veriest tiro in the school of Shakespeare.

attrib. a1660 Contemp. Hist. Irel. (Ir. Archæol. Soc.) I. 162 Those tyron soldiers and novices in the arte militarie. 1860 Piesse Lab. Chem. Wonders 142 A tyro-chemist in search of the philosopher's stone. 1903 H. G. Hutchinson in Watson Eng. Sport 272 Conveying some information to the tiro golfer. 1905 Daily Chron. 14 July 5/7 Rifle Clubs' Tyro Competition, open to teams of five tyro members.

Tiro-: see also Tyro-.

‖ **Tirocinium** (təirosi·niŏm). Also (less correctly) tyro-. [L. *tīrōcinium* first military service or campaign, young troops, f. *tīro*, Tiro + *-cinium*, as in *latrōcinium* robbery, *vāticinium* prophecy.]

a. First experience of or training in anything; apprenticeship, pupilage, novitiate; hence, inexperience, rawness. b. concr. A band of novices or recruits.

1651 Life Father Sarpi (1676) 89 The Tyrocinium or the young Militia of state in the Commonwealth. 1654 Gayton Pleas. Notes 37 It is the right discipline of Knight-Errantry, to be rudimented in losses at first, and to have the Tyrocinium somewhat tart. 1711 Shaftesb. Charac. (1737) III. v. ii. 274 There the Tyrocinium of Genius's is annually display'd. 1784 Cowper (title) Tirocinium; or, A Review of Schools.

† **Tiro·ciny**. Obs. In 7 tyro-. [ad. L. *tīrōcinium*: see prec.] = prec.

1600 Tourneur Transf. Metam., Ded. Sir C. Heydon 14 Mæcenas, strengthen my Tyrocinie. 1646 G. Buck Rich. III, i. 1 The Linage, Family, Birth, Education, and Tyrociny of King Richard the third. 1663 Waterhouse Fortescutus Illustr. 138 The King incorporated them into the Tyrociny of Nobility. 1670 W. Simpson Hydrol. Ess. 30 Your tyrociny in these abstruse studies plead your excuse.

† **Tiro·logy**. Obs. nonce-wd. [f. Tir-o + -ology.] Properly, the science of tiroes; in quots. used for Elementary knowledge.

1560 Becon Cast. Comfort Wks. II. 106 Some of the papistes..where so euer they finde *Ignis*, take it for Purgatory streyghtwayes. O noble doctors of Tyrology, rather than of Theology. 1563 — Display. Popish Mass ibid. III. 39 But where learned ye this tyrologye? For theologie is it not.

Tiron, tirone, obs. forms of Tiro.

T-iron: see T 3.

Tironian (təirōᵘ·niăn), a. [ad. L. *Tīrōniān-us*, in *notæ Tīrōniānæ* Tironian notes.] Of or pertaining to Tiro, the freedman of Cicero: *Tironian notes*, a system of shorthand in use in ancient Rome, said to have been invented or introduced by Tiro.

1828 Edin. Rev. Dec. 359 Manuscripts written entirely in the Tironian notes are not unfrequent in libraries of the date of the seventh century, as it is supposed. 1887 Daily News 6 Oct. 5/3 One of the earliest examples shown is a psalter in Tironian notes—the shorthand characters..invented by Marcus Tullius Tiro, the freedman of Cicero; it is in Latin—written early in the tenth century.

Tironic, tyronic (təirǫ·nik), a. nonce-wd. [f. L. *tīrōn-*, stem of *tiro*, Tiro + -ic.] Of, pertaining to, or characteristic of a tiro; betraying inexperience; amateurish. So (nonce-wds.) **Ti·-, ty·ronism**, inexperience; **Ti·-, ty·ronist** = Tiro; **Ti·-, ty·ronize** v., intr. to play the tiro, to be a beginner; hence **Ti·-, ty·ronizing** ppl. a.

a1660 Contemp. Hist. Irel. (Ir. Archæol. Soc.) I. 29 As ignorant of martiall discipline, as the most tyronizinge of them all. 1716 M. Davies Athen. Brit. III. 3 They..are fitter for Veterans and Criticks in Closets and Libraries, than for Tyronists and Trivialists in Schools. 1832 Examiner 660/1 The critic,..though modest and professing tyronism, is a good moderator. 1909 Daily Chron. 23 June 3/1 His handling of form and plot is occasionally tyronic, if one may be permitted a word that ought to exist.

† **Tirpei·l**. Obs. Forms: 4 tirpell, -peile, tyrpeyl, -payl, turpel, 5 -pell, -pele. [Metathetic form of OF. *trepeil* uproar, trouble (12th c. in Godef.); according to Diez from OF. *trepeiller* to run hither and thither, f. *treper* to hop, Trip, of German origin: cf. MLG. *trippen* to tread; also mod.F. *trépigner* to stamp.] A broil, encounter, tumult.

c1330 R. Brunne Chron. Wace (Rolls) 1665 Þe Troiens þat had ben yn turpel [v.r. tirpell], At midnight tok þey conseil. Ibid. 15422 Þey [Britons] gadered þem to consail How to venge þat tyrpayl. c1330 — Chron. (1810) 216 Withouten his conseile, or þe kynges wittyng, To maynten þer tirpeile he suore ageyn þe kyng. c1400 Land Troy Bk. 8841 But not-for-thi so it be-fell, That he was hurt at that turpell. Ibid. 18020 Foure hundrid of damyseles That lyued afftir that turpeles.

Tirr (tir, tɔ̄r), v. Sc. and n. dial. Also 6–7 tyr, tyrr, 6–9 tir, 7 tirre, 9 terr. [app. a reduced form of Tirve v.1 in same sense (see quot. 1553 in 1 b), and cf. Sc. *ser'* for *serve*, *turris* for *turves*.]

1. trans. To strip or tear off (a covering, esp. the thatch, slates, or roofing of a house).

1571–5 Diurnal Occurr. (Bann. Cl.) 219 Ane commandement gevin..to tir and tak doun all the tymmer werk of all houssis in Leith Wynd and Sanctmarie Wynd. 1584 Reg. Privy Council Scot. III. 681 [He] tirrit and reft doun the faill and thak of his barnis. 1635 Dickson Pract. Wks. (1845) I. 83 He shall tirr the visorne off your faces. 1670 R. Law Mem. (1817) 33 It tirred the sclates off it. 1777 in Cramond Ann. Banff (1893) II. 97 There is no mending of the slating without tirring the sclates. 1795 A. Wilson Spouter 581 Mony a fierce storm had tirred the thack.

2. To strip (a person) naked; to uncover, unroof (a house, etc.). Also *fig*.

1553 Douglas' Æneis ix. viii. 78 In quhat land lyis thou manglit and schent, Thy fare body and membris tyrryt [ed. Small tyrvit] and rent? 1572–5 Diurnal Occurr. (Bann. Cl.) 307 The laird of Collingtonis hous in Forrestaris Wynd wes half tirrit. 1578–9 Reg. Privy Council Scot. III. 83 Als meikle to say 'Tyr the kirk and theik the queir'. 1590 Reg. Privy Council Scot. IV. 492 Eftir thay wer tirrit to thair sarkis. 1644 Ibid. VIII. 101 They causit thair officers and hangman tirre us mother naked. a1670 Spalding Troub. Chas. I (1850) I. 70 Quhilk the said James espying, fallis to shortlie and tirris the houss. Ibid. (1851) II. 407 Thir cruell Irishis, seing a man weill cled, wold first tyr him and saif the clothis onspoyllit, syne kill the man. 1763 in Lauder & Lauderd. (1902) 86 The west side of the Manse must be tirred and sclated anew. 1808 Jamieson s.v., Tir one to the skin, i.e. strip him naked. 1894 P. H. Hunter J. Inwick xi. (1900) 153 A man..that cares na wha be tirred gin he be theekit. 1901 Dundee Advert. 11 Feb. 6 In a minute or two the whole of the north side of the roof was completely tirred.

b. intr. (for *refl*.) To take off one's clothes; to strip, undress.

1787 W. Taylor Scots Poems 67 Hame I gaed..An' than I tirr'd, an' to my bed. 1825 Jamieson, Tirr,..to undress, to pull off one's clothes. 1891 A. Matthews Poems & Songs 52, I quickly tirr'd doon to the sark.

3. trans. To bare (land) of its surface covering; to pare off (the turf or surface soil) from land; to lay bare (the stone in a quarry) by removing the superincumbent soil and clay. With the thing laid bare, or the covering, as object. Also *absol*.

c1567 Survey Shilbottle in New County Hist. Northumbld. (1899) V. 425 The ground also, by reason of castyng so great numbre of turves, [is] so tyrred and maide baire, that of a greate parte therof groweth no grasse. 1593 Aberdeen Regr. (1848) II. 85 The saidis Inchis ar sa flayne and tirrit, that..thair is na faill to be had thairin. 1808 Jamieson, Tirr,..to pare off the sward by means of a spade..before casting peats. 1867 D. D. Black Hist. Brechin ii. 18 The earth was tirred from the garden on the top of the bank. 1899 Montgomerie-Fleming Notes on Jamieson 169 Tirr, ..to remove the soil and sub-soil from above a bed of sandstone in a quarry.

Hence **Tirr** sb., the soil or sub-soil removed from the bed of a quarry (Montgomerie-Fleming *Notes on Jamieson*, 1899); **Ti·rring** vbl. sb., the stripping off of the incumbent soil, etc.

1794 Statist. Acc. Scot. XIII. 201 These quarries require very little tirring. 1902 Daily Record & Mail 11 Sept. 3 A couple of men had agreed to do some quarry tirring... The tirr suddenly collapsed and a man..was killed.

Tirracke, -iok, -ook, Sc. dial. ff. Tarrock.

1792 Statist. Acc. Scot. V. 189 Redshanks, herons, tirricks. 1822 Scott Pirate x, The querulous cry of the tirracke and kittiewake. 1825 Jamieson, Tirracke, Tirrook.

Tirra-lirra (ti·rä‚li·rä). Also 7 teery-larry, -lerry, -leery, tyra-lyra. Cf. Tiralee. [Echoic. Cf. OF. *turelu, tureluru*, 'a comic or burlesque refrain' (Godefroy), *turelure* a bagpipe, a refrain, F. *turlut* a titlark; and quot. 1889.] A representation of the note of the skylark, or of a similar sound uttered as an exclamation of delight or gaiety.

1611 Shaks. Wint. T. iv. iii. 9 The Larke, that tirra-Lyra chaunts. 1613 W. Browne Brit. Past. i. v, The Larke.. With the shrill chanting of her teery-lerry. 1688 R. Holme Armoury ii. 310/2 The Lark singeth Tyra Lyra. 1832 Tennyson Lady of Shalott iii. iv, 'Tirra lirra', by the river Sang Sir Lancelot. 1889 Grove Dict. Mus. IV. 805/1 Ture-Lure, or Toure-Loure, a very ancient lyrical burden or refrain, probably of Provençal origin. The old English form is 'tirra-lirra'.

Hence † **Tirrili·rring** ppl. a., that sings tirra-lirra; † **Tiry-tiry-leerer**, a lark.

1659 Torriano, Tirilirante lòdola, the Tiriliring lark. 1599 T. M[oufet] Silkwormes 50 Let Tiry-tiry-leerers [marg. larkes] vpward flie.

Tirran, -and, -ane, -ant, obs. Sc. ff. Tyrant.

Tirret, Tirrill, obs. ff. Terret, -it, Tirl sb.1

Tirrit (ti·rit). rare. [perh. illiterate for *terror* (Nares).] A fit of fear or temper; an 'upset', disturbance of one's equanimity.

1597 Shaks. 2 Hen. IV, ii. iv. 220 Here's a goodly tumult: Ile forsweare keeping house, before Ile be in these tirrits, and frights. 1892 Harper's Mag. Feb. 405/2 My lady will have her tirrets.

Tirrivee·, ti·rrivie. Sc. Also tiri-, tiry-, tirry-, tirrie-, tery-, turry-, tira-, tirravee, -vie. [Origin obscure: some suggest a corruption of Tailyevey.] A fit or display of ill temper or passion; an unchecked outburst.

1813 Hogg Queen's Wake 342 note, He suspected his spouse had taken some of her tirravies. 1814 Scott Wav. lxix, A very weel-meaning good-natured man..when he wasna in ane of his tirrivies. 1898 N. Munro in Blackw. Mag. Feb. 184/2 I'm willing to make some allowance for a lover's tirravee. 1910 W. Finlay in Poets Ayrshire 273 When a party ends up in a wild tirivee.

Tirrs, obs. Sc. form of Truss.

‖ **Tirshatha** (tirʃā·þa). [Heb. תרשתא *tirshāthā*, a. OPersian *tarsāta* 'his reverence', in LXX ἀθερσαθά (-αθά), Vulg. *athersatha* (i.e. *hat-tirshāthā*).] The title of an ancient Persian viceroy or prefect: applied in O. T. to Nehemiah.

1382 Wyclif Ezra ii. 63 Athersatha [1388 Attersatha]. — Neh. viii. 9 Athirsata. 1535 Coverdale Ezra ii. 63 Hathirsatha. 1611 Ibid., The Tirshatha. 1890 Hunter After Exile II. ix. 192 He stood forward with all the authority that belonged to him as Tirshatha. 1902 Hastings' Dict. Bible IV. 779 The Tirshatha appears to have been a royal commissioner..invested with the full powers of a satrap or viceroy, and employed on a special mission.

† **Tirve**, v.1 Obs. Forms: 4–6 tirue, tyrue (= -ve), 4 turue (= -ve), (5 terve), 6 tirve, tyrff. [Not in OE.; known from 1300. Identical in meaning with Tirr v. (which seems to be a reduced form of the same word), and Tirl v.2 App. distinct in sense from next; but, formally, **tyrfan* and **tierfan* might both be derived from different grades of a verbal ablaut series **terƀ-, tarƀ-, turƀ-*.

It has also been suggested to represent an OE. **tyrfan*, deriv. of *turf*, Turf, to have originally meant 'to strip the turf off the ground', and to have been extended to stripping the turf or thatch off roofs, the clothes off persons, and the hides off beasts. This is plausible, but is not favoured by the chronology of the senses.]

1. trans. To roll or pull back, or pluck *off* (the covering, clothes, skin, etc. from a person or animal); to strip off (clothes, armour; the thatch, slates, or roof of a house, stack, etc.).

c1300 Havelok (1902) 603 [They] sone..funden, Als he [= they] tirueden of [= off] his serk On his rith shuldre a kyne merk. 13.. E. E. Allit. P. B. 630 He [Abraham] cached to his cobbous & a calf bryngez..bed tyrue of þe hyde. 13.. Gaw. & Gr. Knt. 1921 Syþen þay tan raynarde & tyruen of his cote. a1400–50 Alexander 4114 Tuke out þe tuskis & þe tethe & teruen of þe skinnes. 1513 Douglas Æneis v. v. 32 A habirgeoun..Quhilk he,..with his strang handis .. Tirvit and rent of bald Demoleo.

b. To strip (a person) of his clothes, etc., (an animal) of its skin, (a house) of its roof; to strip naked or bare; to unroof.

[c1300 Havelok 918 Ful wel kan ich cleuen shides, Eles to-turuen of here hides.] c1386 Chaucer Can. Yeom. Prol. & T. 721 (Ellesm.) The deuel out of his skyn Hym terve [other MSS. torne, turne] I pray to god. 1500–20 Dunbar Poems lxxii. 23 Of his claithis thai tirvit him bair. Ibid. 33 In tene, thai tirvit him agane, And till ane pillar thai him band. 1533 Bellenden Livy v. xi. (S.T.S.) II. 187 He gart tirve [v.r. tyrff] þis maister nakit of al his clothis. 1590–1 Reg. Privy Council Scot. IV. 587 The said Naper.. and others..come and tirvit the said complenaris houssis, and tuke of the rigging and thak thairof.

† **Tirve, terve**, v.2 Obs. Forms: 5 tirue (-ve), tyrve, -we, 5–6 terue (-ve), (9 tirvie). [Known c1330 in the comp. Over-terve: app. representing an OE. **tierfan* = OLG. **tęrƀan*, OHG. *zerben*, :—**zarƀjan*, refl. to turn, turn over or about: cf. OE. *tearflian* to roll over and over, wallow. If this is right, the better form is *terve*. (Texts of MSS. printed before 1900 have usually *n* for *u* (= *v*), the word being taken as a variant of *turn*.)]

1. intr. To turn; esp. to turn upside down, topple over, fall down; also *fig*. to turn *to* some course or action.

c1400 Destr. Troy 430 Erthe dymmed by dene, ded men Roose, The gret tempull top terued to ground. c1425 Disp. Mary & Cross xxxvii. in Leg. Rood 207 (MS. Roy.) Truyt and treget to helle schal terve. c1440 Psalmi Penitent. (1894) 45 To trecherie schulde we noght terve [rime kerve]. 1567 Golding Ovid's Met. v. I v b, Ioues ymage..made with crooked welked hornes that inward still doe terue [rime serue]. [1829 W. Tennant Papistry Storm'd (1827) 206 He made him tirvie down and tapple Head-foremost wi' a bang.]

2. trans. To turn; esp. to overturn, overthrow; also *fig*.

c1400 Destr. Troy 1512 How his towne was taken and tiruyt to grounde. Ibid. 4763 The grete toures þai toke, tiruyt the pepull. Ibid. 10197 To take you with tene & tirue you to ground. c1420 Brut 378 Our stakez made hem top ouyr terve, eche on oþer, þat þay lay on hepis. c1422 Hoccleve Min. Poems xxiv. 573 Shee That had him terued with false deceitis.

b. To turn *to* some course or *to do* something.

c1400 Destr. Troy 2943 Throgh whiche treason betydes, & teruys vmqwhile Bolde men to batell and biker with hond.

c. To turn over, up, or down (the edge or hem of a garment). (Cf. Tarf, Turf sb.2)

1482 Caxton Contin. Higden's Polycron. viii. xiii, The yemanry hadde theyr hosen teruen [? terued] or bounden bynethe the knee hauynge longe jackys.

Hence † **Tirving** vbl. sb., turning; concr. a border turned back or up.

c1440 Promp. Parv. 494/2 Tyrf, or tyrvynge [v.r. tyrwynge] vp on an hoode or sleue.

Tirvis, obs. Sc. pl. of Turf sb.

† **Tirwhit, tirwit**, obs. var. Tewhit, lapwing.

1671 in Skinner Etymolog. Hence 1706 in Phillips, etc.

† **Tiry** (təiᵊ·ri), a. Obs. [f. Tire v.1 + -y.] Tired, weary. Hence † **Ti·riness**, tiredness.

1611 Coryat Crudities 37 My horse began to be so tiry that he would not stirre one foote out of the way. 1697 R. Peirce Bath Mem. i. ix. 192 Having a great share of this Tyrie Distemper. Ibid. ii. iii. 295 [She] was not unsensible of her Tyryness and Dispiritedness.

'Tis (tiz), abbreviation of *it is*, formerly common in prose, now poetic or archaic; see also It A. γ.

c1450 Mankind 821 in Macro Plays 30 Alas! tys pety yt schuld be þus. a1566 R. Edwardes Damon & Pithias (1744) 280 Tis a pestens queen. 1598- [see It A. γ].

Tis, ME. assimilated form of This after dentals, etc.: see T 8.

Tisan, tisane, var. Ptisan, barley-water.

Tisar (tizā·r). Glass-manuf. rare. [ad. F. *tisart* opening of a furnace, f. *tiser* to poke, stir, etc.: see Tease v.2] The fireplace or furnace used to heat the annealing arch for plate-glass.

1839 Ure Dict. Arts 587 The carquaise is heated by means of a fire-place of a square form called a *tisar*, which extends along its side.

Tische, -ey, obs. Sc. ff. Tissue. **Tischera**, var. Tezkere. **Tise**, obs. f. Tice v. **Tiseday**, obs. Sc. f. Tuesday. **Tisheldar**, var. Tahsildar. **Tishew, -oo, -ue**, obs. ff. Tissue.

‖ **Tishri** (ti·ʃri), **Tisri** (ti·zri). [ad. late Heb. תשרי *tishrī*, f. Aramaic שרא *sh'rā* to begin.] The Babylonian name of the first month of the Jewish civil year, or the seventh of the ecclesiastical, corresponding to parts of September and October: substituted after the captivity for the earlier name Ethanim.

1833 [see Abib]. 1877 C. Geikie Christ xlix. (1879) 578 The seventh month Tisri, part of our Sep. and Oct. 1904 Daily Chron. 9 Sept. 6/7 To-night marks the advent of Tishri, the most important month in the Jewish calendar. 1904 Jewish Encycl. VIII. 672 Tishri is characterized as the month of the birth of the Patriarchs.

Tisick, tisical, (tiss-), obs. and dial. forms of Phthisic, -al. Hence **Tis(s)icking** a. = Phthisicky; † **Tisickness**, phthisic or asthmatic quality.

1533 Elyot Cast. Helthe (1539) 82 Tisiknesse or shortnesse of breth. a1825 Forby Voc. E. Anglia, Tissick,..a tickling faint cough: called also a 'tissicky cough'. 1888 Doughty Arabia Deserta II. 521 The Sherif visited Beyrût some years ago..for the health of a tisical son. 1890 Blackw. Mag. CXLVIII. 463/2 Snipe bummed and bleated out a tissicking music. 1904 in Eng. Dial. Dict. s.v. Tissick, etc.

† **Tisince**, obs. form of *ptisans*, pl. of Ptisan.

c1623 Lodge Poore Mans Talentt (Hunter. Cl.) 9 The patient..must bee content to drink Tisince, balme water, or the Iuleb of roses.

Tisor, variant of Teaser 2, fireman.

Tisri: see Tishri.

Tissane, obs. var. Ptisan, barley-water, etc.

† **Tissed**, ppl. a. Obs. [ad. F. *tissu*, pa. pple. of OF. *tistre*:—L. *texere* to weave (cf. Textile): see -ed 1.] In phr. *gold tissed, cotton tissed*, modelled on F. *or tissu, coton tissu* (cf. *gold of tisshue*, quot. 1501 s.v. Tissue sb. 1 a).

1585 T. Washington tr. Nicholay's Voy. i. xxi. 27 b, A gowne of cloth of gold tissed [orig. vne robbe de drap d'or figuré]. Ibid. ii. xxii. 60 A fine & long smock of cotton tissed [orig. vne fine & longue chamisolle de cotton tissue].

Tissey, obs. f. Tizzy. **Tissiok**, etc: see Phthisic, Tisick. **Tisso**, var. Tesoo.

† **Tissu**, ppl. a. Obs. rare—1. [a. F. *tissu*, pa. pple.: see Tissue sb.] Woven. (Const. as *pa. pple*.)

1549 Compl. Scot. vii. 69 Ane syde mantil..the quhilk hed bene tissu ande vrocht be thre syndrye fassons of verkmenschips.

Tissual (ti·ʃiu‚ăl, ti·siu‚ăl), a. rare—1. [irreg. f. next + -al, after *virtual*, etc.] Of or pertaining to (living) tissue: see next, 5.

1837 P. Keith Bot. Lex. 343 Plants..exhibiting..indications of such tissual and organic susceptibilities as are proper to their rank in the scale of being.

Tissue (ti·ʃiu, ti·siu), sb. Forms: α. 4–5 tyssu, 4–6 tissewe, 5 tyssew, -eu, -ywe, (pl. -eux), 5–6 tyssue, 5–7 tissu, tissew, 6 tyssewe, tyssewe, 5– tissue. β. 5–6 tisshue, tisshewe, Sc. tusche, (tuscha), 5–8 tishew, 6 tyshew, tysshewe, tysshiew, tushwe, Sc. tischey, -ay, tische, tysche, 7 tishue, tishoo. [a. OF. *tissu* sb., applied to a kind of rich stuff (c1200 in Godef. *Compl.*), from pa. pple. of obs. F. *tître*, OF. *tistre*:—**tissre*:—L. *tex-ĕre* to weave.]

1. a. A rich kind of cloth, often interwoven with gold or silver. Obs. exc. Hist.

? a1366 Chaucer Rom. Rose 1104 The barres were of gold ful fyne, Upon a tyssu of satyne. 1429 in Dugdale Monast. Angl. II. 222 Cum tribus capis choralibus de panno Tyssewys vulgariter nuncupato. 1501 in Calr. Doc. rel. Scotl. (1858) 336 A gown of tawny cloth of gold of tisshue. 1509 Hawes Past. Pleas. xvi. (Percy Soc.) 61 With cloth of tyssue in the rychest maner The walles were hanged. 1513 Bradshaw St. Werburge i. 1647 Fresshely embrodred in ryche tysshewe and fyne. 1543 Grafton Contn. Harding 591 The quene ..clothed in a riche mantell of tissue. 1562 in Feuillerat Revels Q. Eliz. (1908) 114 Cloth of Silver purple tysshiew. 1585 T. Washington tr. Nicholay's Voy. iii. viii. 82 Girded with a large girdle of Tissue, or of silke and golde. 1648 Crashaw Delights Muses Wks. (1904) 160 Something more than Taffata or Tissew can. c1710 Celia Fiennes Diary (1888) 4 Good bed Chambers and well furnished velvet damaske and tissue. 1785 G. A. Bellamy Apology I. 130 A dress for me to play the character of Cl[e]opatra,..the ground of it was silver tissue.

b. Now applied to various rich or fine stuffs of delicate or gauzy texture.

1730 Swift Lady's Dressing-room Wks. 1755 IV. i. 113 Array'd in lace, brocades and tissues. 1769 Public Advertiser 2 June 1/3 Sale of Silks..Brocades, Tissues. 1821 Joanna Baillie Metr. Leg., Wallace liv, Tissue of threaded gems is worn. 1910 Westm. Gaz. 12 Mar. 15/2 Tissues studded with jewels are lightly draped over satin.

† 2. A band or girdle of rich stuff. Obs.

c1374 Chaucer Troylus ii. 590 (639) His helm..That by a tissew heng his bak byhynde. c1430 Pilgr. Lyf Manhode i. xciv. (1869) 51 The scrippe was of greene selk, and heeng bi a greene tissu. c1440 Partonope 6726 That tyssew and bocle..all to peses brak. c1450 Holland Howlat 405 Mony schene scheld With tuscheis of trast silk tichit to the tre. 1488 Acta Dom. Conc. (1839) 98/2 A tuscha of silk siluerit price v merkis. 1503 Acc. Ld. High Treas. Scot. II. 388, xjd elne tisches to mend the bordoring of the Kingis sadill bordorit with tischeis. 1508 Test. Ebor. (Surtees) IV. 274 A gyrdill wt a golde tushwe. 1513 Douglas Æneis i. vii. 136 And quhair hir pap was for the speir cut away Of gold thairon was belt ane riche tischay. Ibid. xii. v. 133 Quhar as the wovin gyrdill or tysche Abufe his navill was beltit, as we se. 1603 Holland Plutarch's Mor. 629 Venus ..cast aside her daintie jewels..and threw away that tissue and lovely girdle of hers.

3. Any woven fabric or stuff. In quot. 1850 *transf*. weaving.

1565 Cooper Thesaurus, Trilix..tissue made of three threads of diuers colours. 1757 Gray Bard i. iii, They.. weave with bloody hands the tissue of thy line. [Cf. ii. i, Weave the warp, and weave the woof The winding-sheet of Edward's race.] a1765 Shenstone Progr. Taste i. 24 Constant wear..turns the tissue into tatters. 1850 Gladstone Homer II. ii. 129 In the arts of tissue and embroidery. 1879 Lubbock Sci. Lect. v. 155 Tissues of woven flax have been found in some of the Swiss lake-villages.

4. *fig*. Something likened to a woven fabric, as being produced by the intertwining of separate elements; an intricate mass or interwoven series, a 'fabric', 'network', 'web' (*of* things abstract, most usually of a bad kind, as absurdities, errors, falsehoods, etc.). Also, the structure or contexture of such a 'fabric'.

1711 Addison Spect. No. 62 ¶ 6 Those little occasional Poems..are nothing else but a Tissue of Epigrams. 1762 Goldsm. Cit. W. xlii, The history of Europe,..a tissue of crimes, follies, and misfortunes. 1793 Jefferson Writ. (1859) IV. 89 The hasty amendments..had so broken the

tissue of the paragraph, as to [etc.]. 1820 W. Irving Sketch Bk. I. 104 The tissue of misrepresentations..woven round us. 1842 Whittier Raphael xvi, The tissue of the Life to be We weave with colors all our own. 1878 Gladstone Prim. Homer 107 He works it..into the tissue of the poems.

5. Biol. The substance, structure, or texture of which an animal or plant body, or any part or organ of it, is composed; esp. any one of the various structures, each consisting of an aggregation of similar cells or modifications of cells, which make up the organism. a. in animals.

The chief forms of tissue in the higher animals are the *epithelial* (incl. *glandular*), *connective* (incl. *cartilaginous* and *osseous*), *muscular*, and *nervous* tissues. (The term is sometimes extended to include the *blood* as a 'fluid tissue'.)

1831 Carlyle Sart. Res. i. i, Every cellular, vascular, muscular Tissue. 1834 J. Forbes Laennec's Dis. Chest (ed. 4) 279 Chronic inflammation..of the pulmonary tissue. 1846 G. E. Day tr. Simon's Anim. Chem. II. 40 Materials ..to supply the place of those that have been removed from the body in consequence of waste of tissue. 1857 Buckle Civiliz. I. xiv. 818 The tissues of the teeth are..analogous to those of other parts. 1861 Hulme tr. Moquin-Tandon ii. i. 41 The organic Tissues are three in number: 1st, cellular tissue; 2nd, muscular tissue; and 3rd, nervous tissue... Some writers admit other organic tissues. 1869 Huxley Phys. i. (ed. 3) 11 Every such constituent of the body, as epidermis, cartilage, or muscle, is called a 'tissue'. 1880 Bastian Brain 28 Nerve tissues are..divided into 'grey' and 'white' matter. 1889 Mivart Truth 149 The arteries, veins and heart are full of a fluid 'tissue'—the blood.

b. in plants.

The various forms of plant tissue may be generally reduced to two classes, typified by *parenchyma* and *prosenchyma*. In the higher plants there are three systems of tissues, the *epidermal, fundamental*, and *fibro-vascular*.

1837 [implied in Tissual]. 1845 Lindley Sch. Bot. x. (1858) 159 Tissue is called Woody Fibre when it is composed of slender tubes placed side by side. 1875 Bennett & Dyer Sachs' Bot. 68 Every aggregate of cells which obeys a common law of growth..may be termed a Tissue. Ibid. 103 The relationship of the three systems of tissue may be observed.. in..foliage-leaves.

c. generally; also *fig*.

1836 Dove Logic Chr. Faith ii. § 2. 114 The new chart must clothe the world with its living tissues. 1858 Lewes Sea-side Stud. 400 Histology is the doctrine of the tissues; and tissues are the webs out of which the organism is fabricated. 1872 Bagehot Physics & Pol. 178 The germ might be foreign, but the tissue was native. 1878 Bell Gegenbaur's Comp. Anat. 16 Conversion of the cells into tissue.

6. Short for Tissue-paper, q.v.

1780–1 Act 21 Geo. III, c. 24 § 2 For every Bundle of Paper made in Great Britain for Printing, called Demy Tissue. For every Bundle of Paper called Crown Tissue. 1797 Nemnich Waaren-Lexicon 30/1 Die Englischen Papiersorten...Crown, single, inferior, double, double inferior, and tissue;..Demy single, inferior, plate, short, tissue, writing [etc.].

(The reference here was prob. to sizes of specially prepared tissue-paper (now spoken of as 'printing paper' and 'printing tissue'), on which designs were printed from copper plates for transference to pottery-ware. This was specially taxed.)

7. Photogr. Paper made in strips coated with a film of gelatine containing a pigment, used in carbon printing.

1873 E. Spon Workshop Receipts Ser. i. 267/1 This carbon tissue consists of a layer of gelatine containing the carbon or other permanent pigment spread on paper. 1878 Abney Photogr. xxiv. 165 Many improvements in the manufacture of the tissue have been made, and the different substances added to the gelatine are only partially known to the public. 1891 Anthony's Photogr. Bull. IV. 80 Tissue can be obtained from London and sensitized as required for use.

8. Collector's name for two species of moth, *Scotosia* (*Triphosa*) *dubitata* and *cervinata*.

1832 Rennie Butterfl. & Moths 128 The Tissue (T[riphosa] dubitata, Stephens)... Wings..brown, shining; first pair having a tinge of purple. Ibid., The Scarce Tissue (T. cervinata, Stephens).

9. attrib. and Comb. a. attrib. Made or consisting of tissue (sense 1); in quot. a1625, dressed in tissue.

1480 Wardr. Acc. Edw. IV in Privy Purse Exp. Eliz. York, etc. (1830) 149 A long gowne of grene velvet upon velvet tisshue cloth of gold. 1570 Foxe A. & M. (ed. 2) 2143/2 The Vicechauncellour hauing on a tyshew cope. a1625 Fletcher Love's Cure i. iii, Smooth City fools or tissew Cavaliers. 1704 Lond. Gaz. No. 3981/4 A rich Silver Tishia Gown. 1708 Brit. Apollo No. 37 2/2 Tishew Sleeves. 1796 Mar. J. Holroyd in Girlhood M. J. H. (1896) 373 Milady wore..a Gold Tissue..Train.

b. Comb., chiefly in sense 5, as *tissue-building* sb. and adj., *-cell, -change, -death, -element, -form, -former, -forming* adj., *-growth, -like* adj., *-product, -system, -transformation*; **tissue-lymph**, lymph derived from the tissues (not directly from the blood); **tissue-secretion**: see quots. 1848, 1861. See also Tissue-paper.

1848 Dana Zooph. iv. 51 Secretions formed within the animal which are mostly calcareous..may be called tissue-secretions. ..These secretions take place from the tissues of the sides and the base of the polyp. 1861 Greene Man. Anim. Kingd., Cœlent. 153 The sclerobasic corallum is by Mr. Dana termed 'foot secretion'; the sclerodermic, 'tissue secretion'. 1866 Odling Anim. Chem. 1 Recent advances in chemistry of tissue-products. 1872 Huxley Phys. vi. 139 Proteids are tissue-formers. 1873 T. H. Green Introd. Pathol. (ed. 2) 24 The increased tissue-change which accompanies acute febrile diseases. Ibid. 88 The pulmonary pigment..may be seen..within the connective tissue-cells. 1875 Bennett & Dyer tr. Sachs' Bot. 78 In this manner arise in the higher plants..systems of tissue-forms, which may be designated simply as Systems of Tissue. 1886 A. Winchell Walks Geol. Field 308 The processes of digestion,..assimilation, and tissue-building. c1890 A. Murdoch Yoshiwara Episode 26 He..wondered..what the soft, flimsy, tissue-like paper was. 1896 Allbutt's Syst. Med. I. 213 It is quite possible that a trace of albumose might thus be formed after tissue-death. 1903 G. Oliver in Lancet 3 Oct. 942/1 Physiologists are divided as to whether tissue lymph is a pressure product..or a secretion.

Ti·ssue, v. Now rare. [f. Tissue sb.] trans. To make into a tissue, to weave; spec. to weave with gold or silver threads, to work or form in tissue; to adorn or cover with tissue (cf. prec. 1 a).

1483 Caxton Gold. Leg. 237/1 A whyte mantel In whiche there were litil ouches and crosses of gold tissued. 1491 — Vitas Patr. (W. de W. 1495) ii. 249/2 To tyssue the sayd roddes & palmes to make mattes. 1547 Harl. MS. 1419 B, lf. 535 b, Clothe of silver tissued withe flowres of golde and silver. 1562 in Feuillerat Revels Q. Eliz. (1908) 114 Gold tysshewed with silver. a1626 Bacon New Atl. (1650) 25 The Charriot was covered with cloth of Gold tissued upon Blew. a1851 Moir Birth Flowers vi, Her vesture seem'd as from the blooms Of all the circling seasons wove,..And tissued with the woof of Love.

b. *fig*.

1637 Wotton in Reliq. (1672) 104 To Countenance any Great action; and then..to Tissue upon it some Pretence or other. 1800 Moore Anacreon xlvi. 14 Cultured field, and winding stream, Are sweetly tissued by his beam. 1905 Athenæum 6 May 558/2 'Dream and Reality' is tissued from a series of such metaphors.

Tissued (ti·ʃiud, ti·siud), ppl. a. [f. prec. vb. (or sb.) + -ed.]

1. Woven; spec. woven with gold or silver thread: see Tissue sb. 1 a and v.

1584 in Feuillerat Revels Q. Eliz. (1908) 365 The pages sute of Oringe tawney tissued vellet. 1619 Rutland MSS. (1905) IV. 516, 19 yardes ½ of tissued grogram at 48s. the yard. 1790 Cowper Mother's Picture 75 Thy vesture's tissu'd flowers. 1879 Farrar St. Paul (1883) 224 He entered the theatre..in an entire robe of tissued silver.

fig. 1629 Milton Ode Nativity 146 Mercy..With radiant feet the tissued clouds down stearing. 1789 E. Darwin Bot. Gard. (1791) II. 52 Long threads of silver light Dart on swift shuttles o'er the tissued night! 1790 Merry Laurel Lib. 7 Where starry Night weaves thick her tissued rays.

2. Dressed or arrayed in 'tissue': see Tissue sb. 1.

?16.. Wharton (Webster 1864), Crested knights and tissued dames.

Ti·ssueless, a. [f. Tissue sb. + -less.] Destitute of tissue (i.e., in quot., of flesh).

1864 Blackmore Clara Vaughan lxxxi, It rang among the skeletons, and rattled their tissueless joints.

Ti·ssue-pa·per. [See quot. 1880, which may be correct; but earlier authority is wanted.] A very thin soft gauze-like unsized paper, used for wrapping delicate articles, for covering engravings or other illustrations in books, as copying-paper, etc.

Various grades are distinguished, as *silver tissue*, specially prepared for wrapping silver ware; *copying tissue*, for copying letters, etc.; *printing tissue*: see Tissue sb. 6.

1777 Henly in Phil. Trans. LXVII. 114 A number of circular pieces of tissue-paper. 1815 J. Smith Panorama Sc. & Art II. 161 The paper must be of that kind called tissue or silver paper. 1854 Phemie Millar 24 Encasing in tissue paper a set of ivory handled knives. 1865 Lowell Wks. (1890) V. 285 Leaping through a hoop with nothing more substantial to resist than tissue-paper. 1880 Birdwood Ind. Arts II. 75 The flimsy paper called tissue-paper was originally made to place between the tissue to prevent its fraying or tarnishing when folded.

Tist, tiste: see Tice v.

Ti·sty-to·sty, int., sb., a. dial. Forms: 6- tisty-tosty, 6 tistitostie, 9 teesty-tosty. [In sense 1 perh. a mere ejaculation. In sense 3 it has been compared with † *tyte tust(e* or † *tussemose* a nosegay: see Tuzzy-muzzy; but current dialect use associates it rather with *toss*, and *tost, tossed*.]

† 1. int. as an ejaculation of triumph or exultation.

1568 Fulwel Like Will to Like C iij, Hey tisty tosty an owle is a bird. c1570 Marr. Wit & Science iv. iv. E j, Mother must I haue his Cote, now mother must [I]? Chal [= I shall] be a liuely lad, with hey tistye tosty.

† 2. sb. A swaggering or blustering fellow (? one who uses the ejaculation). Also *attrib*. or *adj*. Obs.

1598 Florio, Sbrauo, a swash-buckler, a swaggrer, a hackster, a cutter, a tistitostie. Ibid., Squassa pennacchio,..a tisti-tostie-fellow, a swaggrer.

3. sb. A bunch of flowers, a nosegay (*obs*.); in mod. dial., a cowslip-ball: also *tisty-tosty ball*.

1825 Jennings W. Country Gloss., Tresty-tosty, the blossoms of cowslips collected together, tied in a globular form, and used to toss to and fro for an amusement called teesty-tosty...Sometimes called simply a tosty. 1865 Cornh. Mag. July 41 'Blossom-ball'..is evidently formed after the West-country 'cowslip-ball', the 'tisty-tosty ball' of Dorsetshire and Somersetshire, which children yearly make.

b. attrib. or adj. Round like a cowslip-ball; plump and comely.

1888 T. Hardy Wessex Tales (1889) 35 She's a rosy-cheeked, tisty-tosty little body enough.

Tiswin (tis-, tizwi·n). U.S. Also tizwin. [ad. Amer. Sp. *texguino*.] An intoxicating drink made from maize, wheat, or mesquite beans by the American Indians.

1891 J. G. Bourke in Cent. Mag. Mar. 655/1 The Apache intoxicant, 'tizwin'..[is] beer, made from fermented corn. 1911 Webster, Tiswin, tizwin.

Tit (tit), sb.1 dial. (chiefly Sc.) [? f. Tit v.1] A sharp or sudden pull; a tug, jerk, twitch.

1340 Hampole Pr. Consc. 1915 Yf þat tre war tite pulled oute At a titte with al þe rotes oboute. 1581 Satir. Poems Reform. xliii. 75 Sa Fortoun mountit neuer man sa hie,.. Bot with ane tit sho turnis the quheill. 1827 Kinloch Ballad Bk. 63 He gied the tow a clever tit That brocht her out at the lum. 1881 Paul Aberdeen. 111 The craetur' gied a tit, an' afore I kent fat I was about, I was lyin' o' the braid o' my back.

Tit, sb.2 [Goes with Tit v.2]

1. In phr. **tit for tat** [app. a variation of *tip for tap*, known a century earlier: see Tap sb.2, Tip sb.2, and cf. prec. But perh. wholly or partly onomatopœic.] One blow or stroke in return for another; an equivalent given in return (usually in the way of injury, rarely of benefit); retaliation.

The whole phrase is used sometimes as a *sb*., sometimes as *adj*. or *adv*.; also, elliptically or as *interj*.

1556 J. Heywood Spider & F. xxxvii. 26 That is tit for tat in this altricacion. 1586 J. Hooker Hist. Irel. in Holinshed II. 94/1 That they would not sticke to set his seruants at libertie, so he would redeliuer them the youth of the citie, which was nothing else in effect, but tit for tat. 1710 Addison Tatler No. 229 ¶ 3, I was threatened to be answered Weekly Tit for Tat. 1809 J. Quincy in Life 181, I shall..give..what politicians call a Rowland for their Oliver, and what the ladies term tit for tat. 1881 Saintsbury Dryden iv. 80 A fair literary tit-for-tat in return for the Rehearsal. 1891 Daily News 16 July 5/1 Fair Traders, Reciprocity men, or believers in the tit-for-tat plan of dealing with other nations. 1905 H. A. Vachell The Hill viii, Tit for tat. If I do this for you, will you do something for me?

2. A light stroke or tap; a slap: cf. Tip sb.2

1808 Jamieson, Tyt, tit...2. A slight stroke, a tap. 1891 Hartland Gloss. s.v., I'll gi'e 'ee a tit under the yur.

3. Comb.: **tit-tat**, an imitation of the sound of alternating taps or blows; **tit-tat-toe**, the beginning of a formula used in 'picking' or fixing upon a person or thing, hence a children's game; also *tick-tack-toe, tip-tap-toe*.

In quot. a1700 imitating the noise made in toddling.

a1700 B. E. Dict. Cant. Crew, Tit-tat, the aiming of Children to go at first. 1855 Anne Manning O. Chelsea Bun-house xiii. 211, I played at Tit-tat-to with Joe, and posed him with hard riddles. 1909 Daily Chron. 27 July 7/1 Drawing to be diversified by noughts and crosses and 'tit tat toe'.

Tit, sb.3 Also 6 tyt, titte, 6–8 titt, 7 tytt. [app. of onomatopœic origin, as a term for a small animal or object; found also to some extent in Scandinavian and Icel.; cf. Norw. dial. *titta* little girl, *tita* a little fish, trout, sprout, minute growth, little kernel, little ball or marble, Icel. *tittr* a little plug or pin, also, a titmouse (Norw. *tite*): see also Titling, Titmouse, in which *tit* occurs much earlier than by itself.]

I. 1. A name for a horse small of kind, or not full grown; in later use often applied in depreciation or meiosis to any horse; a nag. Now *rare*.

1548 Patten Exped. Scotl. D j, He rode on a trottynge tyt well woorth a couple of shillynges. 1563 Golding Cæsar iv. (1565) 85 But such [beastes] as are bred among them though they be littel tittes & yll shapen, they make..to be very good of labor. 1598 Florio, Bidetto, a little horse, a nagge, a tit, a little doing horse. 1616 Surfl. & Markh. Country Farme 538 If you will let them haue anie Tytt or meane Iade to goe before them, and lead the way. 1706 Phillips (ed. Kersey), Tits, a Country-word, for small Cattel. 1726 Dict. Rust. (ed. 3), Tit, a little Horse, and some call a Horse of a middling Size a double Tit. 1797 Sporting Mag. IX. 338, I keep a curricle and a brace of tits. 1821 Scott Kenilw. xi, I have as good a tit as ever yeoman bestrode. 1894 Astley 50 Years Life II. 186 A very promising tit named Woodstock.

† b. *fig*. of a person, etc. See also 2. Obs.

1706–7 Farquhar Beaux Strat. i. i, As to our Hearts, I grant ye, they are as willing Tits as any within Twenty Degrees. a1734 North Exam. i. iii. § 40 (1740) 145 As the willing Tits of the Party, and weaker Brethren.

2. A girl or young woman: often qualified as *little*: cf. *chit*. (*a*) Usually in depreciation or disapproval: esp. one of loose character, a hussy, a minx. (*b*) Sometimes in affection or admiration, or playful meiosis. (Common in 17th and 18th c.; now *low slang*.)

1599 Middleton Micro-Cynicon Wks. (Bullen) VIII. 122 He hath his tit, and she likewise her gull; Gull he, trull she. 1606 Sir G. Goosecappe iv. ii. in Bullen O. Pl. III. 69 Hang am Tytts I ile pommell my selfe into am. 1606 Choice, Chance, etc. (1881) 66 His Dad a Tinker, and his Dam a Tit. 1693 Humours Town 11 My little Tit..loves the Town, as well as my self. 1787 Beckford Italy (1834) II. 363 A bevy of young tits dressed out in a fantastic, blowzy style..drew their chairs round us [at an assembly in Madrid]. 1837 T. Creevey Papers, etc. (1904) II. 324, I am sure from Lady Tavistock that she thinks the Queen a resolute little tit. 1886 Fenn Master Cerem. vii, She's a pretty little tit.

† b. Rarely applied to a lad or young man. Obs.

1599 Massinger, etc. Old Law iii. ii, Must young court tits Play tomboys' tricks with her, and he [her husband] live?

II. 3. A word used in comb. in the names of various small birds as Titlark, Titling, Titmouse, Tomtit, q.v. Used alone, as a shortened form of Titmouse, applied to a. any bird of the genus *Parus*, and, more widely, any member of the family *Paridæ*; b. With qualification: some birds of other families as the *Bearded tit*: see Titmouse 2 b; *Hill-tit*: see Hill sb. 4 f.

1706 Phillips (ed. Kersey), Tit, or Titmouse, a little Bird.

1802 Marsh Tit [Marsh 4 b]. 1831 Bearded Tit [see reed-pheasant, Reed sb.1 14]. 1843 [see Coal-tit]. 1845 Blue-tit [Blue a. 12 a]. 1851 Bottle-tit [Bottle sb.1 5]. 1859 Tennyson Geraint & Enid 275 Tits, wrens, and all wing'd nothings peck him dead! 1880 A. R. Wallace Isl. Life ii. 20 These are all the European tits, but there are many others. 1906 Westm. Gaz. 14 Apr. 15/2 No longer do bands of tits drift through the woods or along the hedgerows... Strange..that the long tailed tit, the only species of the group that builds its nest in a bush, should be the first to start.

c. attrib. and Comb., as *tit-like* adj.; **tit-babbler**, one of several species of hill-tits, esp. *Trichostoma rostratum*; **tit-pipit**, a name of the Titlark or meadow pipit, *Anthus pratensis*; **tit-warbler**, 'a bird of the subfamily *Pariinæ*' (Swainson).

1893 Newton Dict. Birds 26 The..Babblers, often with a prefix such as Bush-Babbler, Shrike-Babbler, 'Tit-Babbler, ..belong chiefly to the Ethiopian and Indian Regions. 1907 Westm. Gaz. 15 Mar. 4/2 But all the rest are bustling about in their own restless, 'tit-like manner. 1819 G. Samouelle Entomol. Compend. 303 Inhabits the black grouse and 'tit-pippit.

Tit, sb.4 techn. [Of uncertain and possibly diverse origin; in sense 1 perh. related to Tit sb.1 or 2; in sense 2 perh. = Teat.]

1. Nail-making. A loose piece of steel used to jerk the finished nail out of the bore.

1902 Baring-Gould Nebo the Nailer ii, Working in the bore is the 'tit' that..ejects the finished nail. 1912 Let. to Editor, The 'tit' is a small loose plain piece of steel which is placed in the 'bore' for the purpose of ejecting the nail from the bore after the nail is headed.

2. A small core of metal accidentally left by the shifting of the drill point in boring a hole.

1884 F. J. Britten Watch & Clockm. 129 If the centre is missed a tit is formed which gives trouble.

Tit, sb.5 [? Infantile variant of Kit sb.3] Used as a call to a cat.

1828 Craven Gloss., Tit, this, with its adjunct puss, is frequently used for calling a cat. 1837 Dickens Pickw. xvi, 'It must have been the cat, Sarah', said the girl... 'Puss, puss, puss—tit, tit, tit'.

Tit, a. Obs. exc. dial. Editors suggest, in quot. c1400, 'Dear, loved'. In *mod. dial*. Fond: cf. Tid a., Tit-bit.

c1400 Destr. Troy 7106 Þen vnhappely hys hest he hastid to do, Þat angart hym after angardly sore, Turnyt hym to tene & all the tit Rewme. 1854 Miss Baker Northampt. Gloss. s.v., When a person is particularly attentive to, or indulgent to another, it is said, 'He is very tit of her'.

Tit, v.1 dial. (chiefly Sc.) Also 4–5 tyt, 4–6 titte; pa. t. 4 tite, (tyd), 4–5 tit, titt, tyt, 5 tyte, 7- titted (9 -et); pa. pple. 4 tytted, 5 tyt, tytt, 6–7 tit, 7- titted. [Etymology obscure: goes with Tit sb.1; see Note below.]

trans. To pull forcibly, to tug; to snatch. Also *intr*. to pull *at*.

13.. Cursor M. 15303 (Cott.) His fote ful tite he til him tite [Gött. titt], Him schamed it was well sene. Ibid. 15837 (Gött.) And als þai fra þe erd him titt [Trin. pulde] His bodi was all stund. 1375 Barbour Bruce v. 603 He tit the bow out of his hand. c1470 Henry Wallace vi. 143 Ane maid a scrip, and tyt at his lang suorde; 'Hald still thi hand', quod he, 'and spek thi word'. c1470 Henryson Mor. Fab. ix. (Wolf & Fox) xxiv, The wecht thairof neir tit my tuskis out. 1873 J. Ogg Willie Waly, etc. 115 Hoo angry he was when ye tittet his tails. 1896 Barrie Tommy xxiv. 281 She realised that Miss Kitty was titting at her dress.

† b. To pull *up*, esp. in a halter; hence, to hang. Obs.

c1375 Sc. Leg. Saints xl. (Ninian) 983 About his nek þai knyt a rape, & tit hym vpe, & lefit hyme þare. c1470 Henry Wallace vii. 212 Be he entrit, hys hed was in the swar; Tytt to the oauk, hangyt to ded rycht thar. 1500–20 Dunbar Poems xvii. 28 Sum..nevir fra taking can hald thair hand, Quhill he be tit vp to ane tre. 1638 Brathwait Barnabees Jrnl. iii. (1818) 125 A piper being here committed, Guilty found, condemn'd and titted.

† c. To lay hold of forcibly, clutch, seize; ? to pull or drag about. Obs.

c1425 Wyntoun Cron. iv. vii. 1074 His stewart made on hym a schot And tyt [v.r. claucht] hym dourly be þe throte. c1450 Holland Howlat 837 The Golk..tit the Tuchet be the tope, ourtirvit his hed. c1475 Rauf Coilȝear 123 He tyt the King be the nek. Ibid. 432 For to towsill me or tit me, thocht foull be my clais, Or I be dantit on sic wyse, my lyfe salbe lorne.

[Note. The sense agrees with that of Tight v.1, sense 1, but regular Sc. forms of that appear in 14th c. as *ticht, tycht*, and the disappearance of the *ch* would be abnormal. It is unlikely that OE. *tyhtan, tihtan*, should have become **titte* in the language of the Danes in England, in accordance with the treatment of *ht* in ONorse itself.]

Tit, v.2 Now dial. [Goes with Tit sb.2: app. an onomatopœic match to Tat v.1, the lighter vowel expressing lighter action and sound: cf. *tip* and *tap, pit-a-pat*, etc.]

1. trans. and intr. To strike or tap lightly, pat, tip.

(Quot. 1589 appears to be a parody of 'Come tit me, come tat me, Come throw a kiss at me', quoted of date 1607 under Tat v.1 This seems to have been a couplet from an old song, current before 1589.)

1589 [? Lyly] Pappe w. Hatchet B j b, Elderton swore hee had rimes lying a steepe in ale, which shoulde marre all your reasons: there is an olde backer that shall take order for to print them...The first begins, Come tit me, come tat me, come throw a halter at me. 1607 [see Tat v.1]. 1901 G. Douglas Ho. w. Green Shutters v. 42 He's a brother o' —eh..(tit-tit-titting on his brow)—oh, just a brother o' Dru'cken Will Goudie.

2. † *To tit one in the teeth*: to cast in one's teeth, upbraid one *with* (*obs*.); hence *to tit* (simply), to twit, upbraid; *intr*. to scoff or jeer *at*.

1622 Mabbe tr. Aleman's Guzman d'Alf. i. 147 Or that it should be tit in my teeth, that I had beene at the Court, and not seene the King. Ibid. ii. 133 They would vpbraid me therewith..; Titting and flouting at me. 1629 J. M. tr. Fonseca's Devout Contempl. 424 Notwithstanding all this Absalon titted him in the teeth, saying, Is this thy loue to thy friend? 1631 Celestina xii. 146 Doe not tit mee in the teeth with these thy idle memorialls of my Mother. 1891 Hartland Gloss., Tit..to twit or tease. 1904 Eng. Dial. Dict. s.v., To tit a person about anything.

Tit, var. Teat (cf. Titty 3); obs. 3rd sing. pres. of Tide v.1; var. Tite adv.

Titan 1 (təi·tǎn). [a. L. *Tītan, -ānem*, name of the elder brother of Kronos, and ancestor of the Titans; also in poetry his grandson, the Sun-god = Hēlios; a. Gr. Τιτάν, in pl. Τιτᾶνες, the Titans, a race of gods expelled by Zeus out of heaven. So F., Sp. *Titan*, Pg. *Titão*, It. *Titano*, Du., Ger. *Titan*.]

1. Used (chiefly in poetry) as a name for the Sun-god, Sol, or for the sun personified.

1412–20 Lydg. Chron. Troy iii. 5416 Þe dede cors to carien in-to toun Of worþi Hector, whan Titan went doun. 1501 Douglas Pal. Hon. Prol. 33 The assiltrie and goldin chair of price Of Tytan, quhilk at morrow semis reid. 1606 Shaks. Tr. & Cr. v. x. 25 Let Titan rise as early as he dare. 1638 Sir T. Herbert Trav. (ed. 2) 2 The third of April at Titans first blush [ed. 1634 early in the morning] we got sight of Porto Santo. 1708 J. Philips Cyder i. 10 Then wo to Mortals! Titan then exerts His Heat intense, and on our Vitals preys. 1911 Sir E. Ridley in 19th Cent. May 870 Till flaming Titan nigh to either Pole Beheld thy empire.

2. a. Gr. Mythol. In *sing*. The ancestor of the Titans: see etymology above. In *pl*. a family of giants, the children of Uranus (Heaven) and Gæa (Earth), who contended for the sovereignty of heaven and were overthrown by Zeus.

1667 Milton P. L. i. 510 Th' Ionian Gods..Titan Heav'ns first born With his enormous brood, and birthright seis'd By younger Saturn. 1727–41 Chambers Cycl. s.v., This war lasted ten years; but at length the Titans were vanquished; Jupiter remained in peaceable possession of heaven, and the Titans were buried under huge mountains thrown on their heads. 1858 Bushnell Serm. New Life ii. (1869) 19 A race of Titans broken loose from order and warring on God and each other. 1908 G. K. Chesterton Orthodoxy viii. (1909) 258 The Titans did not scale heaven; but they laid waste the world.

b. transf. and allusively, usually denoting a person (mountain, tree, etc.) of gigantic stature or strength, physical or intellectual, a 'giant'; sometimes, one who belongs to the race of 'giants' as distinct from the *Olympians* or 'gods'.

1828 Scott F. M. Perth xxvii, The clan of Titans seemed to be commanded by their appropriate chieftains—..Ben Lawers, and..Ben Mohr. 1829 — Anne of G. vi, The sun was just about to kiss the top of the most gigantic of that race of Titans [the Swiss mountains]. 1838 Emerson Addr., Lit. Ethics Wks. (Bohn) II. 205 Men looked..that nature ..should reimburse itself by a brood of Titans. 1870 Swinburne Ess. & Stud. (1875) 260 The ranks of great men are properly divisible, not into thinkers and workers, but into Titans and Olympians. 1903 J. Stewart Dawn in Dark Cont. i. 22 The weary Titan need not complain too much.

c. Applied descriptively to machines of great size and power; e.g. a dredger, crane, etc.

1876 Daily News 30 Oct. 6/4 A novel kind of dredger is in use, consisting of a centrifugal pump, called a 'Titan', which raises the sand together with a certain proportion of water, and discharges it in the barges. 1894 Times 29 Jan. 14/2 A titan steam crane will be mounted on deck for moving any of the heavy parts for examination or repair. 1911 Encycl. Brit. IV. 479 These sloping blocks are laid by powerful overhanging, block-setting cranes, called Titans, which travel along the completed portion of the breakwater, and lay the blocks in advance.

3. Astron. Name of the sixth and largest of Saturn's eight satellites.

1868 Lockyer Guillemin's Heavens (ed. 3) 252 The diameter of Titan, the largest satellite,..is..more than half the diameter of the Earth. 1878 Newcomb Pop. Astron. iii. iv. 353 The smallest telescope will show Titan.

4. attrib. or as adj.; transf. Titanic, gigantic.

1697 Dryden Æneid vi. 782 The rivals of the Gods, the Titan race. 1851 Mayne Reid Scalp Hunt. i, As though ..hurled from the hands of Titan giants! 1858 N. J. Gannon O'Donoghue, etc., Lines on Late War, Such hands as theirs have more than Titan strength. 1860 Tyndall Glac. i. xx. 139 The Titan obelisk of the Matterhorn. 1860 C. Sangster Hesperus, etc. 53 Titan strength and queenly beauty.

b. attrib. and Comb. (chiefly in sense 2), as *Titan-born, -like* adjs.; also (from 1) † **Titan beam**, a sunbeam.

a1649 Drumm. of Hawth. Poems Wks. (1711) 44 Whilst eagles stare on Titan beams. 1816 Byron Ch. Har. iii. cv, Their steep aim Was, Titan-like, on daring doubts to pile Thoughts which should call down thunder and the flame Of Heaven. 1839 Bailey Festus xxvii. (1852) 467 Thoughts which were once my masters, now I hold In retributive bondage, Titanlike. 1847 Emerson Poems (1857) 45 Titan-born, to hardy natures Cold is genial and dear. 1904 Speaker 28 May 206/2 The Trip-shake and Tumble-tread of Titan-footed Reels.

† **Ti·tan** 2. Obs. rare. [ad. F. *titane*, ad. mod.L. Titanium.] a. Chem. = Titanium. b. Min. = Titanite. Also *attrib*.

1803 in Trans. Roy. Irish Acad. (1806) X. 17 Rutilite. Calcareo-siliceous titan ore of Kirwan. 1828 Webster, Titan, Titanium, a metal of modern discovery. 1882 in Ogilvie (Annandale).

Titanate (təi·tănēᵗt). Chem. [f. Titan-ic a.2 + -ate 4.] A salt of titanic acid.

1839 Ure Dict. Arts 1234 By calcination with nitre, it [titanium]..forms titanate of potassa. 1873 Watts Fownes' Chem. (ed. 11) 429 The titanates have not been much studied.

Hence **Titana·tion**: see quot.

1904 Van Hise in U. S. Geol. Surv., Monogr. XLVII. 205 Titanation is the union of titanic acid with base, or the substitution of titanic acid for another combined acid, in either case producing titanates.

Titanesque (təitǎne·sk), a. [f. Titan 1 + -esque.] Resembling or having the characteristics of the Titans; colossal, gigantic.

1882 Froude Carlyle xx. I. 383 His extraordinary metaphors and flashes of Titanesque humour. 1906 Marie Corelli Treas. Heaven xi, Titanesque human figures with threatening arms outstretched.

Titaness (təi·tǎnės). [f. Titan 1 + -ess.] A female Titan; a giantess. Also *fig*.

1596 Spenser F. Q. vii. vi. 4 So likewise did this Titanesse [Mutability] aspire Rule and dominion to her selfe to gaine. 1649 T. Ford Ludus Fort. 82 We can find no place free from the rule of this Titanesse. 1853 C. Bronte Villette xli, Truth,..O Titaness amongst deities! 1862 B. Taylor Home & Abr. Ser. ii. ii. iv. 90 St. Helene..rises grandly above all the neighboring chains...This Titaness is robed in imperial hues. 1904 Brandes Main Curr. 19th C. Lit. V. xii. 168 In that generation of heaven-storming Titans and Titanesses he appears a peculiarly earth-bound creature.

Titanian (təitēᵊ·niăn), a.1 [f. L. *Tītāni-us* of or belonging to the Titans + -an.] Of, pertaining to, or like the Titans; Titanic. Also (quot. 1614) of the sun-god; solar, sunlike.

1614 Raleigh Hist. World i. (1634) 6 The Moone's bright Globe, and Stars Titanian. 1667 Milton P. L. i. 198 As whom the Fables name of monstrous size, Titanian, or Earth-born. 1685 Cotton tr. Montaigne (1711) I. iv. 27 The Thracians..fall to shooting against Heaven with Titanian madness. 1776 J. Bryant Mythol. III. 76 All these were of the Giant, or Titanian race. 1820 Byron Mar. Fal. iv. i. 83 Titanian fabrics, Which point in Egypt's plains to times that have No other record.

† **Tita·nian**, a.2 Chem. Obs. [f. Titani-um + -an.] Of or pertaining to titanium. (Superseded by Titanic a.2)

1828 in Webster. 1846 in Worcester (citing Ure).

Titanic (təitæ·nik), a.1 [ad. Gr. τιτανικ-ός, f. Τιτᾶν-ες the Titans: see -ic.]

† 1. Of or pertaining to the sun. Obs. rare—0.

1656 Blount Glossogr., Titanic,..of or belonging to the Sun. 1658 in Phillips.

2. Pertaining to, resembling, or characteristic of the Titans of mythology; gigantic, colossal; also, of the nature or character of the Titans.

1709 J. Clarke tr. Grotius' Chr. Relig. v. ix. (1818) 226 note, Some wicked Daemons and (as I may call them) Titanic or Gigantic ones who were rebellious against the true God. 1818 Byron Ch. Har. iv. xlvi, We pass The skeleton of her [Rome's] Titanic form. 1852 Kelly tr. Cambrensis Eversus III. 483 He has assailed heaven itself with titanic audacity. 1858 Carlyle Fredk. Gt. i. i. (1872) I. 6 The figure of Napoleon was titanic.

Tita·nic, a.2 [f. mod.L. Titani-um + -ic 1 b.] Of, pertaining to, or derived from titanium; in Chem. applied to compounds in which titanium has its higher valence, as *titanic oxide* (*t. acid*), a white tasteless powder, TiO_2. In Min., *titanic iron-ore* = Ilmenite; *titanic schorl* = Rutile.

1826 Henry Elem. Chem. II. 701 Method of separating titanic acid from oxide of iron. 1839 Ure Dict. Arts 682 All volcanic rocks contain a greater or less quantity of titanic iron-ore. 1842 Brande Dict. Sc., etc. s.v. Titanium, The peroxide, or titanic acid, exists nearly pure in titanite, or rutilite. 1868 Joynson Metals 87 Bessemer metal containing phosphorus may be dephosphorised by employing titanic pig-iron, in repeated doses, to eliminate the phosphorus. 1894 Bowker in Harper's Mag. Jan. 410 Ilmenite, or titanic iron $(FeTi)_2O_3$..is an ore in which one of the iron molecules of hematite is replaced by the metal titanium.

† **Titanical** (təitæ·nikăl), a. Obs. rare. [f. as Titanic a.1 + -al: see -ical.] = Titanic a.1 2.

1642 H. More Song Soul ii. i. i. xxi, Rash labour, a Titanicall assay To pluck down wisdome from her radiant seat. 1678 Cudworth Intell. Syst. i. ii. § 3. 61 A Gigantical and Titanical Attempt to dethrone the Deity.

Hence **Tita·nically** adv., in a titanic manner.

1816 T. Taylor Pamphleteer VIII. 57 She is bound in body Prometheically and Titanically. 1891 G. Meredith One of our Conq. vi, A more than Titanically audacious balloonist.

Tita·nico-, Chem., combining form of Titanic a.2, esp. in names of double salts, resulting from the combination of a titanic with another salt. **Titanico-hydric** a.: see quot. (now *hydrotitanic*).

1860 Mayne Expos. Lex., Titanico-hydricus..applied by Berzelius to a titanic haloid salt..combined with the hydracid of the same halogenous body..: titanicohydric.

Titaniferous (təitǎni·fĕrəs), a. [f. Titan-ium + -i-ferous.] Containing or yielding titanium.

1828 in Webster (citing Cleaveland). 1829 J. Phillips Geol. Yorks. 105 Magnetic sand (oxydulated titaniferous iron). 1836–41 Brande Chem. (ed. 5) 872 Titaniferous Oxide of Iron, which is more abundant than rutilite, may be used as a source of titanium. 1883 Encycl. Brit. XVI. 426/1 Schorlomite (Ferrotitanite)...Perhaps a titaniferous garnet

Titanious (taitǣˈniǝs), a. rare. [f. TITANI-UM + -OUS.] a. Min. Containing or combined with titanium. † b. Chem. Obs. = TITANOUS.

Titanism (tai'tǎnĭz'm), sb. [f. titanisme (F. d. 1824 in Littré): see -ISM.] The character of a Titan. A revolt against the order of the universe.

Titanite (tai'tǎnǝit). Min. [ad. Ger. titanit (Klaproth, 1795). f. TITAN-IUM + -it, -ITE: named from its containing the metal titanium.]
1. A mineral composed chiefly of calcium titano-silicate, $CaO.TiO_2.SiO_2$, also called sphene.

Titanium (tai'tǣ'nĭǝm), sb. Chem. [mod.L. f. TITAN + -IUM. Named by Klaproth 1795, on the analogy of URANIUM previously named by him.]

Titano- combining form of TITAN or TITANIUM.

Titano-therium [mod.L., f. Gr. θηρίον beast], an extinct genus of ungulates from the Tertiary formation, resembling gigantic rhinoceroses.

Titanous (tai'tǎnǝs), a. [f. TITANI-UM + -OUS.] Containing titanium, spec. in its lower valency state, sesquioxide of titanium, Ti_2O_3; contrasted with TITANIC a.2

†Titanite (tai'tǎnǝit), a. Min. rare. Obs. [f. TITANI + -IC.] = TITANIC a.2

Tit-bit (ti'tˌbit), tid-bit (ti'dˌbit). [In 17th c., tyd bit, tid-bit. f. TID sb. + BIT; later also tit-bit, perh. after compounds of TIT sb.1] A small and delicate or appetizing piece of food; a toothsome morsel, delicacy, bonne bouche.

Tite, obs. pres. 3rd sing. of TIDE v.1; obs. erron. f. TIGHT a.

Titely, titly, adv. Obs. or dial. Forms: a. tidliche, 3 tidlike, 4 titly, 5 tydely. β. 4-5 titili, titly, 6-7 tyt, -tyt, 5-6 titely. 7-4 tijtly, -li. [f. TITE, TIGHT a.1 + -LY 2.] Quickly, smartly; soon. As titely (cf. F. aussitôt), immediately.

†Tith, a., adv. Obs. App. a dial. or colloquial variant of TIGHT a. or TIGHT v.

Titer, var. TITRE; var. of TIGHT v.

Tith (taith), sb.1 Also 4-5 tyth, tithe, 5-6 tythe, 5-7 tyth, 6 toith (thethe), 6-7 tith, tyeth, 7 tith-e, tithe, 3-4 tæðe, 6-8 teithe, teth, theoþe, 4 teoþe, teðe, tethe. [OE. teogoþa, teoþa; see TENTH.]

†Tith (taith), a.1 and sb.2 Forms: a. 1 teogoþa, etc. (see TENTH A. 1 a.), 3 tigeðe, titõe, 4 tyþe, 4-5 tiþe, (5-7 tyth, 6 toith (thiethe), 6-7 tith, tyethe), 4-6 tithe, 5-6 theth. [OE. teogoþa, teoþa.]
A. adj. Tenth. A. Of order: see TENTH A.
B. sb. = a tenth part; specifically TITHE sb. 1.

Tithable (tai'ðǝb'l), a. Also 4-5 tythable, 5-7 tythable, 6-8 tytheable. [f. TITHE v.1 + -ABLE.]
1. Obj. product: Subject to the payment of tithes.
2. Liable to pay tithes. rare.

Tithal (tai'ðǎl), a. rare. [TITHE sb.1 + -AL] cf. Obs. rare. Of, pertaining to, or connected with tithe.

Tithe (taið), sb.1 Forms: a. 1 teoþa, etc. (see TENTH A. 1 a.), 3 tiȝeðe, titõe, 4-5 tiþe, (5-7 tyth), 6 tyethe, 4-6 tithe.
1. A tenth part of the annual produce of agriculture, etc., being a due or payment (orig. in kind) for the support of the priesthood, religious establishments, etc.

Tithe (taið), v.1 [OE. teoþian.]
1. trans. To grant or pay one tenth of (one's goods, earnings, etc.), esp. to the support of the church; to pay tithes on.
2. To take the tenth of; to levy a tithe on.

Tithe-barn. A barn for holding the parson's tithe.

Tithed (taiðd), ppl. a. [f. TITHE v.1 + -ED 1.] Subject to, charged with, or liable for the payment of tithes; taken or paid by way of tithe.

Titheless (tai'ðlǝs), a. [f. TITHE sb.1 + -LESS.] Without tithes; not in receipt of tithes.

†Titheling. Obs. rare. [f. TITHE sb.1 + -LING.] Tenth part, tithe.

Tithely, obs. form of TIGHTLY, TITELY.

Tithe-man. [f. TITHE sb.1 + MAN sb.1]
1. One who pays tithes; a tithed man.
2. = TITHINGMAN 1.

Tithe-pig. A pig due or taken as tithe.

Tithe-proctor. An agent employed to collect a parson's tithes, or one who farmed the tithes.

Tither (tai'ðǝr), sb.1 [f. TITHE v.1 + -ER 1.] One who pays or is liable to pay tithes.

Tithing (tai'ðiŋ), vbl. sb.1 [f. TITHE v.1 + -ING 1.] a. Payment of tithes.

Tithing (tai'ðiŋ), sb.1 [OE. teoþung.]
1. One tenth given to the church.

Tithing-man. A collector of tithes; a tithe-proctor.

Ti-thonian (ti-þōˈniǝn), a. Ancient astron. Pertaining to or characterized by Tithonus.

Tithonic (ti-þoˈnik), a. [f. Gr. Τιθωνός name of Eos (Aurora) + -IC.] Pertaining to or designating those rays of the spectrum.

Tithonography, a photograph produced by the action of 'tithonic' rays on a sensitized surface.

Tithonometer, **Tithonotype**, etc.

Titi (ti'ti). [Native or local name, of various origin.]
1. In U.S., a name given to certain trees of the N.O. Cyrilleæ.
2. A name of Oxydendron arboreum, N.O. Ericaceæ.

Titillate (ti'tĭlēt), v. [f. L. titillāt-, ppl. stem of titillāre to tickle.]
1. trans. To excite or stimulate as by tickling; to tickle agreeably; gratify (the sense of taste, smell, or touch, the imagination, etc.).
2. intr. To tickle.

Titillation (tĭtĭlēˈʃǝn). [ad. L. titillātiōn-em, n. of action f. titillāre to TITILLATE. Cf. F. titillation.]
The action of tickling, or touching lightly so as to tickle.

Titillative (ti'tĭlǝtĭv), a. [f. L. titillāt- (see TITILLATE) + -IVE.] Tending to tickle, having the power of tickling.

Titillator (ti'tĭlētǝr). [agent-n. in L. form f. titillāre: see -OR 2.] One who or that which titillates; a tickler.

Titivate, tittivate (ti'tĭvēt), v. colloq. [L. stem uncertain: perh. f. TIDY + -ivate.] To put into proper order, to smarten up.

Titivil. *Obs.* Forms: 5 Tyti-, Tyty-, Titi-, Tityuillus, -villus, 5-6 Tituille, -villus, Tytyuyllus, 6 titiuil, -ille, -ylle, (Tom Tituile), titti-, tytyuelle, titifull, tytyfylle, titifyl, 7 -ill. Also 2 Tytyuytyr, Tytuillug. [ad. med.L. *Tuti-, Titivillus,* in OF. also *Tutiville.*] of unknown origin. Connexion has been suggested with L. *titivillitium* used once by Plautus, and inferred to mean 'a mere trifle, a bagatelle.'

1. A name for a devil said to collect fragments of words dropped, skipped, or mumbled in the recitation of divine service, and to carry them to hell, to be registered against the offender; hence, a name for a demon or devil in the mystery plays. Also found in France and Germany, 13-15th c.

2. Hence, a term of reprobation: A bad or vile character, a scoundrel, knave, villain. *b. esp.* A tattling tell-tale, mischievous tale-bearer.

†Titiviller. *Obs. rare.* Also 6 *Sc. tutivillae.* [Extended form of prec.] = prec.

Title (təi'tl), *sb.* Forms: 1 titul, 4 tytel, -e, 4-5 titele, (-ell), tityll, 4-6 titil, -ill, (4 tittille), 4-7 tytle, 5 titul, -ille, (tetele), 5-6 tyttyl, tytil, 6 tyttel, -yll, title, (6 tetel), 8 titel, -e; also 6 tyttel, -ile. [ME. *a.* OF. *title* (12th c. in Godef. Compl.) :— L. *titulus* superscription, title; in mod.F. *titre.* — *Titulus* was directly from L. as in the later French *title,* titule. The *i* in OE. and early ME. was prob. short, after L.; also **TITTLE**.]

†1. An inscription placed on or over an object, giving its name or describing it; a legend; sometimes, a placard hung up in a theatre giving the name of the piece, etc. *Obs.*

2. The descriptive heading of each section or subdivision of a book (now only in law-books); the formal heading of a legal document; hence, *a part or division of a book, or of a subject* (*obs.*).

3. The name of a book, a poem, or other (written) composition; an inscription at the beginning of a book, describing or indicating its subject, contents, or nature, and usually also giving the name of the author, compiler, or editor, the name of the publisher, and the place and date of publication; also **TITLE-PAGE.** Also, the designation of a picture or statue.

4. A descriptive or distinctive appellation; a name, denomination, style.

5. An appellation attaching to an individual or family in virtue of rank, function, office, or attainment, or the possession of or association with certain lands, etc.; *esp.* an appellation of honour pertaining to a person of high rank; *also transf.* (*colloq.*) a person of title (quot. 1900).

6. That which justifies or substantiates a claim; a ground of right; hence, an alleged or recognized right. Const. with *inf.*, or *to, of,* the thing claimed.

7. *spec. Law.* Legal right to the possession of property (esp. real property); the evidence of such right.

8. *Assaying,* etc. The expression in carats of the degree of purity of gold (or silver).

9. *Eccl.* Each of the principal or parish churches in Rome, the incumbents of which are cardinal priests; a cardinal church (CARDINAL *a.* 6).

10. *Eccl.* A certificate of presentment to a benefice, or a guarantee of support, required (in ordinary cases) by the bishop from a candidate for ordination.

Title (təi'tl), *v.* [f. prec.] **†1.** To write, set down, or arrange under titles or headings; to make a list of; to set down in writing; to inscribe, record, chronicle. *Obs.*

2. To furnish with a title; to give a (specified) title to (a book or other literary composition); to inscribe the title on (a book or the like); to write the heading or headings to or in (a manuscript or document). Cf. **ENTITLE** *v.* 1.

3. To dedicate (by name); to assign, ascribe.

4. To inscribe as a title. *Obs. rare.* To attach as a label. *Obs. rare.* Cf. **TITLE** *sb.* 1.

5. *Entitle a, a. (Eccl.)*

Titling (tiˈtliŋ). *Obs.* [? f. TITLE *sb.* + -ING.] A small size of dried stockfish.

Titling (tiˈtliŋ). dial. [? f. TIT *sb.* + -LING.] A name for various small birds. b. The hedge-sparrow.

Title-deed (təi'tl,dīd). A deed or document containing or constituting evidence of ownership.

Titlemouse. Obs. var. of **TITMOUSE.**

Titless (tiˈtlǝs), *a.* [f. TITLE *sb.* + -LESS.] Destitute of a title (in various senses of TITLE *sb.*); untitled.

Titling, var. TIDLING v., to fondle; to trifle.

Titmouse (tiˈtmaus). Pl. titmice (-mais).
Forms: a. 4 timouse, 5-6 titmose, titmos, titmouse, 6 tytmose, 6 tytmouse, (6-7 tyti-, titti-); 6-titmouse. [ME. *titmōse,* f. TIT *sb.*[3] + *mōse* tit, a titmouse.] The smallest and one of the commonest of British small birds.

Titoki (tiˈtoki). [Native Maori name.] A New Zealand tree, *Alectryon excelsum,* N.O. Sapindaceæ, producing tough, crooked timber.

Titrate (tiˈtret), v. Chem. [f. TITRE + -ATE.] To ascertain the amount of a constituent in (a mixture, or (less usually) a compound) by volumetric analysis; i.e. by adding to a solution thereof of known proportion, a solution of a reagent of known strength, until a point is reached at which reaction occurs or ceases.

So **Titrated** ppl. a. F. titré: see quot. Also **Titrate** a. rare, titrated.

Titration (titrēˈʃən). [n. of action f. prec.; see -ATION.] The action or process of titrating; volumetric analysis.

Titre (tiˈtǝr), sb. Chem. [a. F. titre: see TITRATE.] The fineness of gold or silver; in Chem. the weight of a solution as determined by titration.

Ti-tree. The cabbage-tree of New Zealand.

Titrimetry (titriˈmǝtri). Chem. [f. F. titre: see TITRATE and -METRY.] = TITRATION. So **Titrimetric** a., of or pertaining to titrimetry.

Titter (tiˈtǝr), v.[1] [app. echoic: cf. Sw. dial. titta to giggle (Rietz); but perh. related to TITTER-TOTTER.] To laugh in a suppressed or covert way (often as a result of nervousness, or in affectation or ridicule); to giggle.

Titter (tiˈtǝr), sb.[1] [f. TITTER v.[1]] The act of tittering; a stifled laugh, a giggle.

Titter, adv. Now only north. dial. Also 3-4 tyttar, 4-5 -er, 7-8 tider. [Comparative of TITE adv., with shortened vowel: cf. rather, latter, utter, etc. Cf. ODa. tidre more quickly, sooner.]

Titter (tiˈtǝr), v.[2] dial. To totter, tremble; to shake.

Titter-totter. 1. intr. To move unsteadily, as if about to fall; to totter, reel; to sway to and fro.

2. intr. To see-saw. See also TITTER-TOTTER.

Titter-totter, sb. = TEETER-TOTTER, a titter-totter; tilter, a see-saw.

Titteration, Tittery-totter.

Titting, var. TITTING vbl. sb.

Tittivate, Titivate.

Tittle (tiˈtl), sb. Forms: 4 tittil, -el, 5 tytyl-, tittle, -ille, tittilla, 5-9 tittle, 6 tittyl, -il, tytle, tittle, (6 tittil,) 6 titel. [ad. L. *titulus:* see TITLE; a parallel form of TITLE sb.]

1. A small stroke or point in writing or printing.

2. fig. The smallest or a very small part of something; a minute amount. Esp. in phrase *jot or tittle.*

Tittle (tiˈtl), v. [f. TITTLE sb.[1]] 1. trans. To furnish with a tittle or vowel-points; having the points inserted, pointed: cf. POINT v.[1] 3 c.

Tittle (tiˈtl), v.[2] Now dial. or colloq. Forms: -7 tittle, 7 tyttle, 9 tittle, tittle. [Of obscure origin; perh. a frequentative of TITE v.] To talk, chatter, prattle; esp. empty or trifling talk.

Tittle-tattle (tiˈtltætl), sb. Also 6 tytel tattyll, 6-8 tittle-/tattle, 7 tittel tattel. [A reduplicated compound of TATTLE sb., expressing repeated alternate action: cf. next.] 1. Talk, chatter, prattle; esp. empty or trifling talk (often of a gossiping kind).

Tittle-tattle, v. To chatter, prate, gossip.

Tittup (tiˈtǝp), sb. Also -up. [app. imitative.] 1. A horse's canter; a hand-gallop; also a curvet.

TITTUP.

2. An impudent or forward woman or girl; a hussy, a minx.

Tittup (ti'təp), v. Also titup. [Goes with TITTUP *sb.*] *intr.* To walk or go with an up-and-down movement; to walk in an affected manner; to mince or prance in one's gait; of a horse or other animal, to canter, gallop easily; also, to prance; hence of a rider, or one driving a vehicle; of a boat, to toss with abrupt jerky movements.

Tittupy (ti'təpi), *a.* Also tittupy. [f. TITTUP *sb.*] Inclined to tittup or tip; unsteady, shaky.

Titty (ti'ti). *sb.* *colloq.* Also tittie. [perh. infantile pronunciation of *tittie*, sister *; associated with TIT *sb.*] A sister; a young woman or girl.

Titty[2]. Also betty, tittie. A dial. and nursery dim. of TEAT, the breast, esp. the mother's breast.

Tittymeg (ti'timeg). *U.S.* Also 8 tittymeg, tittameg, tickomeg; attikimek, attihawemeg.

TITULAR.

Titubancy (ti'tiubánsi). *rare.* [ad. late L. *titubāntia*, f. *titubāre* to TITUBATE.] The condition of being titubant; unsteadiness, tipsiness.

Titubant (ti'tiubant), *a.* *rare.* [ad. L. *titubant-em*, pr. pple. of TITUBATE.] Staggering, reeling, unsteady; *transf.* and *fig.* stammering, rolling, tipsy; uncertain, hesitating, wavering.

Titubate (ti'tiubeit), *v.* *rare.* [f. L. *titubāt-*, ppl. stem of *titubāre* to stagger, reel, totter, stumble; to rock, roll.

Titubation (titiubei'ʃən). *rare.* [ad. L. *titubātiōn-em*, n. of action f. *titubāre* to TITUBATE.]

Titulado (titu'lädo), *sb.* *Obs.* [Sp., pa. pple. of *titular* to give, = L. *titulāre.*]

Titular (ti'tiulər), *a.* and *sb.* [ad. med. or mod.L. *titulāris*, f. *titulus* TITLE.]

TITULARITY.

1. One who bears a title of rank; a titled person.

2. R.C.Ch. (See quot. 1885.)

3. Of, pertaining to, consisting of, or denoted by a title of dignity; also, having a title of rank, titled; bearing, or conferring, the appropriate title.

Titulary (ti'tiulári), *a.* (*sb.*) [ad. F. *titulaire*, as L. *titulāris.*]

Titular-warbler: see TIT *sb.*[3] 2.

†Tityre-tu (ti'tire,tiú'-rítis). *Obs.* Also Titire-

TO.

To, Tytire tu, Tytere-tu, Tittery tu, tittyty. [From L. *Tityre tū*, the first words of Virgil's first eclogue.]

Tivy (ti'vi). *sb.*, *int.* and *v.* *rare.* [See TANTIVY.]

Tixell, obs. form of TRIXEL *dial.*

Tiza, obs. form of TEAZE.

Tjalk (tjálk). [Du. and LG. *tjalk*, a kind of ship, a WFris. *tjalk* (*tjalk*), according to Franck, perh. dim. of *tjal* for *tjal* = OE. *cēol* KEEL.]

TO.

A. *prep.* In ordinary use, before a *sb.*

B. *adv.*, before a *vb.*

Supplement, p. 3873; Corrigenda, p. 4092; Spurious words, p. 4093; Books quoted, p. 4094

TO.

16. With inf. after a dependent interrogative or relative; equivalent to a clause with *may, should*, etc. (Sometimes with ellipsis of *whether* before or in an alternative dependent question.)

V. Peculiar constructions.

†19. *To* was formerly often used with the second of two infinitives when the first was without it, esp. after an auxiliary, with words intervening between the infinitives. (See also note s.v. THAN *conj.* 1.)

20. Occasionally an adverb or advb. phr. (formerly sometimes an object or predicate) is inserted between *to* and the infinitive, forming the construction now usually (but loosely) called 'split infinitive'. (See Onions *Adv. Eng. Syntax* § 177.)

To, *prefix*: the prep. and adv. To used in combination with verbs, sbs., adjs., and advbs. in the sense of motion, direction, or addition to; or as the mark of the infinitive: see in their alphabetical places, TO-DAY, TO-DO, TO-DRAUGHT, TO-GAINST, TOGETHER, TO-MORROW, TO-WHILE, etc. Also the following sbs. verbs:—

To-, *prefix*[2]. *Obs. exc. in rare arch. or dial.* use. [OE. *tó*, ME. *to-* (*æ-*) = OFris. *ti-, te-* (*to-*), OS. *ti-* (*to-*), OHG., &c. *za-, zar-, zur-* (MHG., *zer-, zir-, zür-*, Ger. *zer-*):—WGer. *tiz-*.—OTeut. *-tiz-* = L. *dis-*, a particle expressing separation, asunder, apart, in pieces.]

Toad. [f. prec., after *toad-eat*, etc.] *trans.* To act as a toady to; to toady. Also *intr.*

Toad-eat (*tō͞ud˙īt*), *v. rare.* [Back-formation from TOAD-EATER.] *trans.* To flatter, fawn upon (a person); to toady. Also *intr.* So **Toad-eating** *vbl. sb.* and *ppl. a.*

Toader (*tō͞u˙dəɹ*), *rare.* — TOAD *sb.* 2.

Toadery (*tō͞u˙dəɹi*). [f. TOAD *sb.* + -ERY.] A place where toads are kept or abound.

Toad-fish (*tō͞ud˙fiʃ*). A name applied, from its swollen appearance, to various fishes.

Toad-flax. [f. TOAD *sb.* + FLAX, from the flax-like appearance of the foliage.] A popular name of the European plant *Linaria vulgaris*; hence extended as a generic name to species of *Linaria*, as Ivy-leaved Toad-flax, *L. Cymbalaria*, Purple T., *L. purpurea*. Bastard Toad-flax, name for *Thesium linophyllum*, and the American genus *Comandra*.

Toadstone (*tō͞ud˙stōn*). *local.* [Of uncertain origin; thought by some to be so named from the resemblance of its amygdaloidal spots to those on a toad's skin; by others to be a corruption of Ger. *totes gestein* 'dead rock', reduced perh. to *Toat-stein*.]

Toadstool, **Toad-stool**. Forms: see TOAD and Stool. [f. TOAD *sb.* + Stool, a familiar name; cf. Sc. *paddock-stool*.] A fungus having a round disk-like top and a slender st.lk, a mushroom.

Toadyism (*tō͞u˙diiz'm*). [f. TOADY + -ISM.] The conduct or behaviour of a parasite or sycophant; mean and interested servility.

Toady (*tō͞u˙di*), *sb.* Also 7 *toady*, 9 *toadey*. [f. TOAD *sb.* + -Y[1].]

To and fro, adv. (*sb.*, *a.*) [f. TO adv. + AND + FRO adv., prep., sb., a.] *adv.* To and from some one place, etc.; hence more vaguely: In opposite or different directions alternately; with alternating movement; from side to side; backwards and forwards; hither and thither; up and down.

Toarcian (tǒǎ·sian), *a.* (*sb.*) Geol. [ad. F. *Toarcien*, f. L. *Toarcium*, F. *Thouars*, in western France.] Applied to a series of strata corresponding in position to the Upper Lias of England, which are extensively developed in Central and Southern France.

Toase, Toaser, obs. ff. Toze, Tozer.

Toast (tǒust), *sb.*[1] Cf. OF. *tostée* (13th c.) toast. Sp. *tostada* (=*post.* *tostāta*).

Toast, *sb.*[2] [f. prec.]

Toast, *sb.*[3] A figurative application of Toast *sb.*[1]

Toast, *v.*[1] [f. Toast *sb.*[1]]

Toast, *v.*[2]

Toa·ster ¹ (tǒ·stəz). [f. Toast *v.*[1] + -ER¹.]

Toa·ster ², [f. Toast *sb.*[2] + -ER¹.]

Toast-rack. [f. Toast *sb.*[1] + Rack *sb.*[1]]

Toa·sty (tǒu·sti), *a.* [f. Toast *sb.*[1] + -Y¹.]

Toa·stable, *a. rare.* [f. Toast *v.*[1] + -ABLE.]

Toa·stee, *v.* [f. Toast *v.*[1] + -EE.]

Tobacco (tǒbæ·kǒ). Forms: α. 6-8 tabaco, 6-7 tabacco, 7 tabacho. β. 6-7 tobacho, 6-8 tobaco, 7 tobaccho, tobacho, tobacco, 6 tobaca, 6 erron. tobago, 6-7 towbaco, tobacco, 7 erron. tobago), 6- **tobacco**. [a. Sp. and Pg. *tabaco*.]

Toastmaster.

Tobacco·nist, *sb.* [f. Tobacco + -IST.]

Tobacco-box. 1. A box for holding tobacco, *esp.* a small flat box to be carried in the pocket.

Tobacco-pipe. A pipe for smoking tobacco, made of clay, wood, or other material, of various shapes and sizes.

Tobacco-plant. The plant which yields tobacco.

†**Tobacco-plant.**

Tobacco·y, *adj.* see after TOBACCO.

Tobe (tōb). Also *toob*, *tope*. [a. Arab. *ṯaub* (locally pronounced *tōb*, *tŏb*) a garment.] A length of cotton cloth (*see* quot. 1886), worn as an outer garment by natives of Northern and Central Africa, and in some parts used as currency.

†**To-be**, *v. Obs.*

†**To-bear**, *v. Obs.* [OE. *tóberan*, f. To- ² + *beran*, BEAR *v.*[1]] *trans.* To carry in different directions; to carry off, take away; also *fig.* to separate (persons) in feeling, etc.; to part, sunder, set at variance.

†**To-beat**, *v. Obs.* [OE. *tóbéatan*, f. To- ² + *béatan*, BEAT *v.*[1]]

†**To-bell**, *v. Obs.* Also **to-belle**.

†**To-bell**, *v. Obs.* Also **to-bollen**.

Tobin bronze. An alloy invented by John A. Tobin of U.S. navy, composed mainly of copper, zinc, tin, with some lead.

†**Tobine**, *sb. Obs.*

†**To-blow**, *v. Obs.* Forms: *see* BLOW *v.*[1]

†**To-bollen**, *ppl. a. Obs.* *see* TO-BELL *v.*

Tobogan, Tobog(g)an (tǒbŏ·găn), *sb.* Also **tabagane, ta-, tobognay, tarbog(g)in, toboggin, tobogin, tobougin, tobogan, sabougin, taboggan.** [Adaptation of a Canadian F. word *tabagane*, *tobogan* (in Quebec and Micmac *tobâkun*).]

Tobogan, Tobog(g)an, *v.* [f. prec.] 1. *intr.* To ride on a toboggan or sleigh; *esp.* to 'coast' or slide down a snowy (or other) slope on a toboggan.

Tobogganing (tǒbŏ·gănĭŋ), *vbl. sb.*

Toboggan(n)er, Tobog(g)anist.

To-brast, *v. Obs.* Forms: *see* BRAST *v.*

†**To-braid**, *v. Obs.* [OE. *tóbregdan*, f. To- ² + *bregdan*, BRAID *v.*[1]] *trans.* To wrench apart, pull to pieces, rend; also, to tear asunder.

†**To-break**, *v. Obs.* [OE. *tóbrecan*, f. To- ² + *brecan*, BREAK *v.*]

To-bruise, *v. Obs.* Forms: *see* BRUISE *v.*

†**To-bryt, -brit**, *v. Obs. rare.* Cf. BRIT *v.*

To-burn, *v. Obs.* Forms: *see* BURN *v.*

†**To-bryn**, *v. Obs.*

†**To-bune**, *v. Obs.*

To-burst, *v. Obs.* [OE. *tóberstan*, f. To- ² + *berstan*, BURST *v.*]

Toby. *intr.* To burst asunder, to be shattered.

Toby, *sb.* [The familiar form of the Christian name Tobias, employed in various unconnected senses. (But some of the senses here grouped may have a different origin.)]

Tocher, (*tŏ·χər*), *sb.* Sc. and north. dial.

Tocsin, (*tŏ·ksin*), *sb.*

Tod (*tŏd*), *sb.1*

To-cherless, *a.* Sc. [See -LESS.] Having no tocher or portion, portionless.

To-chew, *v. Obs.*

To-chine, *v. Obs.*

To-come, *v. Obs.*

To come, to-come, *vbl. sb.* and *a.* That which is to come, the future: see COME.

Tocornalite (*tŏkɔ·ʃnălăit*), *Min.*

Tocque, obs. form of TOQUE.

To-crush, *v. Obs.*

Tod (*tŏd*), *sb.2*

To-day (*tŏde·i*), *sb.*

To-dayish, *a.*

Toddle, *v.*

Toddle (*tŏ·d'l*), *sb.*

Toddler (*tŏ·dlər*), *sb.*

Toddy (*tŏ·di*), *sb.*

Todea (*tŏ·dĭă*), *Bot.* [Named in honour of H. J. Tode.]

To-deal, *v. Obs.* [OE. *tōdǽlan*, f. TO-2 + *dǽlan* to DEAL.]

To-draught, *Obs. rare.*

To-draw, *v. Obs.*

To-drive, *v. Obs.* [OE. *tōdrífan*, f. TO-2 + *drífan* to DRIVE.]

Tody (*tŏ·di*), *sb.*

Toe (*tŏu*), *sb.*

To-tear, *v. Obs.*

Toe, *v.*

Supplement, p. 3873; Corrigenda, p. 4092; Spurious words, p. 4093; Books quoted, p. 4094

Togger (tǒ·gɹ). Oxford slang. [f. Toggery.] A boat rowing in the Oxford college races called 'Torpids'; in pl. the Torpids.

Toggery (tǒ·gɹi). slang or colloq. [f. Tog sb.¹ + -ERY.] Garments; clothes collectively.

Toggle (tǒ·g'l), sb. Also 8–9 toggel. [Said to be orig. in nautical use; of obscure etymology, but app. closely related to Toggle v. to catch, hold fast, entangle, and to Tangle v. to catch, and their nasalized form Tangle.] The use of a toggle was originally to catch or hold fast a rope or chain and prevent its slipping.

1. Naut. A short pin passed through a loop or the eye of a rope, or a link of a chain, or through a bolt, to keep it in place, or for the attachment of another line.

Toggle (tǒ·g'l), v.¹ [f. prec. sb.]

1. trans. To secure or make fast by means of a toggle or toggles.

Toggy, tuggy. [? Connected with Tog sb.¹ or the native Bengiss.] A kind of overcoat for the arctic regions.

To-go, obs. var. To-gang, Go.

To-grade v., var. of To-grade¹.

To-grind, v. Obs. rare. [OE. tógrindan.] trans. To grind to dust.

To-grow v., Obs. rare. [f. To-² + Grow.] trans. To grow to or towards (something).

‖Tohu-bohu (tōu·bōu·). Also Tohu va Bohu. [Heb. tōhū wā-bōhū 'emptiness and desolation', in Gen. i. 2, rendered in Bible of 1611 'without form and void'.] That which is empty and formless; chaos; utter confusion.

‖Tohunga (tōu·ŋga). [Maori tōhunga, lit. one skilled in signs and marks, f. tohu sign, omen.] A Maori priest; a native doctor.

Togue (tōg). [Adaptation of Indian name in Maine and New Brunswick.] The great lake trout (Salvelinus namaycush) of North America.

Tog-ul-gher, -ther, obs. ff. Together.

To-hield, v. Obs. [OE. tóhieldan, f. To-² + hieldan, Hield v. Cf. OE. tóheald.] intr. To incline, lean, bend, or fall over.

To-hew, v. Obs. [OE. tóhéawan, f. To-² + héawan, Hew v.] trans. To hew in pieces.

Toil (toil), sb.¹ Forms: 4-7 toyle, (7 toyl, toile). [a. AF. toil, toyl dispute, tumult, f. toiler, Toil v.]

Toil (toil), sb.² Also 6-7 toyle, 6-7 toyl, 7 toile, (7 toil). Usually in pl. [a. F. toile cloth, web, etc.— L. téla web.]

Toil (toil), v. [ME. toilen, to pull, drag, tug about.]

I. 1. intr. To contend in a lawsuit or argument; to dispute, argue; also, to contend in battle; to fight, struggle. Obs.

II. 5. intr. To struggle for some object or for a living; to engage in severe and continuous labour or exertion; to labour arduously. Often in the collocation toil and moil.

To-day, -tear v.: see Tode.

Tole, obs. f. Toll; var. Toyl sb.

Toiled (toild), ppl. a.¹ [f. Toil v. + -ED.] Wearied, tired, fatigued.

Toiled, ppl. a.² [f. Toil sb.² + -ED.] Furnished or enclosed with toils or nets.

Toiler (toi·lɹ). [f. Toil v. + -ER¹.] One who toils, a hard worker.

Toilet (toi·let), sb. Forms: 6 G. toilet, tolat, 7-8 toylett, toylet, 7-9 toilette, (8 twilight). [a. F. toilette, dim. of toile cloth.]

1. A towel or cloth thrown over the shoulders during hair-dressing; also, a shawl.

2. A cloth cover for a dressing-table (formerly often of rich material and workmanship); now usually called a toilet-cover.

3. A dressing-room; in U.S. esp. a dressing-room with bathing facilities; in restricted sense, a bath-room, a lavatory (Funk's Stand. Dict.).

Toilful, a. [f. Toil sb.¹ + -FUL.] Full of toil.

Toilinet, -ette, toilene·tte. Also S-enet, -9 -anotte. [Origin unascertained.] A fancy stuff trade-name; app. f. F. toile linen, cloth.

Toil-worn (toi·lwōɹn), a. [f. Toil sb.¹ + Worn.] Worn by toil; showing marks of toil.

Tois, obs. f. toes, pl. of Toe.

Toise (tois), sb. In 6-7 toyse. [a. F. toise.]

‖Toison d'or (twazɔ̃ dɔr). Also 7 toyson d'or. [F.] A heraldic name for the golden fleece.

Toilous, a. Obs. rare. Also 5 toyl-. [f. Toil sb.¹ + -ous.] Full of toil; toilsome.

Toil-sick, var. Tor-sick v., a New Zealand grass.

Toilsome (toi·lsʌm), a. [f. Toil sb.¹ + -SOME.] Of actions, conditions, etc.: Characterized by or involving toil; laborious, tiring.

Hence **Toi·lsomely** adv., in a toilsome manner, laboriously; **Toi·lsomeness**, laboriousness.

Toi·l-worn, ppl. a. see Toil-worn.

Tokay¹ (tokē·). Also 8 tockay. [Name of a town in Upper Hungary.] (Also Tokay wine.) A rich sweet wine of an aromatic flavour, made near Tokay in Hungary. Also applied in U.S. to a Californian wine made in imitation of this.

‖Tokay² (tō·kē). Also tokee, tockay, tookai, tōkeq, with final q often silent: see GECKO. A species of Gecko, or lizard of the family Geckonidæ, app. G. verticillatus, of Burma, Siam, and the Malay region.

Toke, obs. pa. t. of Take v.

Token (tō·k'n), sb. Forms: 1-2 tácn, tácen, 3-4 takn, tacne, -en, 3-7 token. [Common Teut.: OE. tác(e)n = OFris. tēken, OS. têkan (MLG., MDu., LG. teiken), OHG. zeihhan (MHG., Ger. zeichen), ON. teikn (Sw. tecken), Goth. taikns.]

1. Something serving as a sign or evidence of a fact or statement; a symbol.

Toll ... Also **toll**, 6-7 **towle**, **toul**(e, 6-7 (9 *dial.*) **towl**, 7 **toull**, 7-8 **tole**. [Found in this sense in 13th c.: nothing similar outside Eng. Prob. *orig.* a particular use of Toll v.1 to 'pull': the sense having passed from 'pull the bell-rope', to 'pull the bell', and so to 'make the bell sound by pulling the rope'. The variant forms are exactly the same as in TOLL v.1; but no distinct evidence of the transfer of sense from 'pull' to 'ring' appears in the quots., although these are compatible with it.]

1. *trans.* To cause (a great bell) to sound by pulling the rope, esp. in order to give warning or a signal; to ring (a great bell), *arch.* or *rhet.*

5. *trans.* To announce (a death, etc.) by tolling.

b. *absol.* or *intr.* To ring.

2. *spec.* To cause (a large or deep-toned bell) to give forth a sound repeated at regular intervals by pulling the rope so that the bell swings through a short arc (in contrast to *ringing* it in full swing), or by striking it with a hammer or the like, or pulling the clapper; esp. for summoning a congregation to church, and *transf.* and *fig.* of the occasion of a death (the passing-bell) or funeral.

3. *intr.* To take or collect toll; to exact or levy toll.

Toll-bait. U.S. [f. TOLL v.2 + BAIT sb.] A book containing a register of boats or goods to be sold at a market or fair, and the tolls payable for them; *in the toll-book*, in the market, for sale (*in* quot. 1607 *fig.*); also, a collector's register or assessment-book. Also in comb. **toll-book keeper**.

Tollon, var. TOYON.
Tollsat: see TOLLSAT.
Tollutate, tollutation: see TOLUTATION.

† To'lmen. [Given by Borlase, 1754, as a common name in Cornwall, and explained by him as 'hole of stone', f. *tol* hole + *men* stone.] A form of TOLMEN.

Tolu (to'lū, ǭ). Old Laws. Rare. Also Old Laws. Hence **Tolu'lic**, earlier name of *toluene*.

Tolypeutine (tǫlipiū'tɪn), *a.* and *sb. Zool.* Belonging to the genus *Tolypeutes* of armadillos.

Tolypyrin (tǫlɪpī'rɪn). *Pharm.* The compound ... the homologue of antipyrin.

Toley: var. **Taum**: obs. form of TOLBEEN.

Tom (tǫm), *sb.* Forms: 4–6 tomme, (5 thomme, 6 thom, 6– Tom.

1. With capital T: a familiar shortening of the Christian name *Thomas*; often a generic name for any male representative of the common people ...

2. The knave of trumps in the game of gleek.

3. As the name of some exceptionally large bells, *esp. in great, mighty Tom, Tom of Lincoln, Tom of Christ Church, at Oxford, Tom of Exeter, etc.*

4. Followed by another word denoting or attributing to something (esp. the action or characteristic distinguishing the person to whom it is applied) ...

5. As the first element in a personal name applied allusively, as Tom Astorer (Estenor), Tom Brown, Tom Dingle (see quot.); Tom Farthing, a fool, simpleton; Tom Paper (Naut.), a liar; Tom Tailor, the tailor generically; Tom Tiler, Tyler, any ordinary man; also, a henpecked husband; Tom Towly, a simpleton ...

6. (usually fem.) A long trough formerly used in gold-washing: see quot. 1859. Sometimes applied to the rocker or 'cradle'.

b. *Long Tom:* a long gun ...

8. In names of animals, denoting the male: also **TOM CAT.**

Tom, var. **TAUM**: obs. form of TOOM *sb.*[1]

Tomahawk (tǫ'măhǭk), *sb.* [a. Renápe *N. Amer. Indian of Virginia*) *tămăhák* (given by Capt. J. Smith as *tomahack*) ...

1. The ax of the North American Indians, used as a weapon of war and the chase, and also as a tool and agricultural implement ...

2. attrib. and Comb., as *tomahawk-blow, -critic, -dance, -type* (quot. 1890); also, *tomahawk-improvement*, an "improvement" of a slight character, made to secure a right of pre-emption (Thornton) ...

Tomahawk (tǫ'măhǭk), *v.* [f. prec. sb.]

1. *trans.* To strike, cut, or kill with a tomahawk.

b. *fig.* To attack savagely or mercilessly in speech (more usually in writing): to 'cut up' or demolish in a review or criticism.

c. *transf.* Applied to similar weapons used by savages elsewhere; also *Naut.* a pole-ax used by sailors; in Australia, the usual word for *hatchet.*

Hence **To·mahawking** *vbl. sb.* and *ppl. a.*; also **To·mahawker**, one who tomahawks (lit. and *fig.*).

Toman[2] (tǫ·man). (*erron.* toman.) [Gaelic *toman* hillock, dim. of *tom* hill.] A hillock ...

Tomalley (tǫmæ·lɪ, tǫmǣ·lɪ). Also *tomauly, taumally, tomalline.* [According to J. Davies ...] The 'liver' of the North American lobster, which becomes green when cooked, and is then known as *canvally* sauce.

Tomally *var. form of* TAMAL.

Tomashā (tǫmā·shă), *sb.* [Pers. تماشا *tamāshā*, according to Devic, a Turber ...]

Tomato (tǫmā·tǫ, U.S. -ǣ·tǫ). Forms: 6– tomate; (8 8– tomatas); 9 Sp. tomata; 8 tomatum, 9 -us. Pl. 8 tomatas, 8– tomatoes, 9– tomatos. [In 17th c. *tomate,* a. F. *tomate*, or Sp. and Pg. *tomate* ...]

1. The pulpy edible fruit of a solanaceous plant *Solanum Lycopersicum* or *Lycopersicum esculentum*, a native of tropical America, now cultivated as a garden vegetable in temperate as well as tropical lands.

b. **Tree Tomato,** the shrub *Cyphomandra betacea, N.O. Solanaceæ,* a native of Colombia and Peru, now naturalized in many tropical and subtropical countries; also its fruit.

2. With qualifying words, applied to varieties of this fruit or plant, as *cherry-, currant-tomato,* or to other species resembling it, as *cannibal's tomato, strawberry- or husk-tomato:* see quots.

Tombac (tǫ·mbæk). Forms: 7 tomaga, tambayeke, tumbeck, 7 tombago, tumbak, 9 tombac. Pl. 8 tombacs. [a. F. or It. *tambac* ...]

An alloy, of East Indian origin, of copper and zinc, in various proportions, containing from 80 to 99 per cent. of copper.

Tomb (tūm), *sb.* Forms: see the sb.[1]

1. *trans.* To deposit (a body) in the tomb; to lay in the grave, bury, inter, entomb.

b. *in fig. senses of 'bury'.*

2. *trans.* Anything that is or may become the last resting-place of a corpse.

Tombal (tǫ·mbăl), *a. rare.* [f. TOMB + -AL.] Of or pertaining to a tomb.

Tombalette (tǫmbălē·t). *Min. Obs.* [Named in Ger. *tombasit* by Breithaupt 1838, in allusion to ... Indians colour.] An obsolete synonym of GERSDORFFITE, a sulph-arsenide of nickel.

Tom·bak: see **TOMBAC.**

Tom·bal·le *var.* TUMBREL.

Tombel, -erel, obs. forms of TUMBREL.

Tombic (tǫ·mbik, tǫmbī·k), *a.* [f. TOMB *sb.* + -IC.] Of, pertaining to, or connected with tombs, sepulchral: esp. in reference to the view that the Great Pyramid was a tomb.

Tombless, *a. rare.* [f. TOMB + -LESS.] Having no tomb or sepulchral monument, destitute of a grave: unburied.

Tomb-stone (tǫ·mstǫun), *sb.* [TOMB *sb.* + STONE.]

1. A horizontal stone covering a grave; in early use, the cover of a stone coffin, on the grave itself.

Tombac (tǫ·mbæk). (Obs. forms of TUMBAK.)

Tombolo (tǫ·mbǫlǫ), *a. rare.* [It. *tombolo.*] A kind of lottery resembling *loto.*

Tombon (tǫ·mbǫn), *sb.* Also ad. in F. tome tombe. [Native name.] General African W. Coast name of the fruit of the wine palm, *Raphia vinifera*; also, the native palm wine obtained from it.

Tombs (tūmz), *sb. pl.* The name popularly given to the city prison of New York City.

Tomboy (tǫ·mbǫi). Also 8 in F. form tombe. [TOM + BOY *sb.*]

1. A rude, boisterous, or forward boy.

2. A bold or immodest woman.

3. A girl who behaves like a spirited or boisterous boy; a wild romping girl; a hoyden.

Hence **Tomboyism**, the state or character of a tomboy.

Tombombill (tǫ·mbǫmbil), *sb.* A name for several small fishes. ... the frost-fish (FROST *sb.*[1])

Tom-cod (tǫ·mkǫd), *sb.* Name for several small fishes, ... the tom-cod proper, *Microgadus tomcod,* of the Atlantic coast of North America.

Tomentose (tǫmentǫ·us, tǫ·měntǫus), *a.* [ad. mod. L. *tomentōsus*, f. *tomentum*.] Covered with short, dense matted hairs; pubescent, downy.

Tomentum (tǫmē·ntǫm), *sb.* [L. *tomentum.*]

1. *Bot.* Closely matted pubescence growing on the stems, leaves, or seeds of certain plants.

2. *Anat.* A downy covering or investment; *spec.* the matted vascular network on the surface of the pia mater.

Tom-fool, sb. [f. TOM + FOOL sb.]

Tomfoolery, sb.

Tomial, a. Ornith.

Tomin, tomin.

Tomium, variant of TOMIDINE.

Tomjohn, corruption of TONJON.

Tommy, sb.

Tommy Atkins.

Tom-tom, sb.

Ton, sb.

Ton, sb.

Tonal, a.

Tonality, sb.

Tonalite, sb.

Tondino, sb.

Tondo, sb.

Tone, sb.

Supplement, p. 3873; Corrigenda, p. 4092; Spurious words, p. 4093; Books quoted, p. 4094

TONNAGE. — 134 — TONSOR.

TONSORIAL — 135 — TOO.

Tonnage (continued)

... large scale which the demand would undoubtedly warrant. ...

6. a. Weight in tons. *rare.*

b. Weight of (iron or other heavy merchandise) in the market.

7. Mode of reckoning the ton of cargo for freightage.

8. *attrib.* and *Comb.*, as *tonnage bounty, capacity, ... -dues, -duty, -length, -money, -tax* ; *tonnage annuity,* a government annuity payable out of the proceeds of tonnage duties ; ...

Tonne, obs. form of TON, TUN.

† Tonnean (tɔˈnɪən). [F. *tonneau*, spec. application of *tonneau* cask, tun.]

Tonneau, having a tonneau.

† Tonnel, -ell. *Obs.* [a. OF. *tonnel*, etc.]

+ Tonnel, -ell. *Obs.* ...

Tonnish, see TONISH.

Tonnage, *n.* [f. prec. sb.]

1. *trans.* To impose tonnage upon (see prec. 1) ; hence To'nnaging *vbl. sb.* : in *quot. fig.*

2. To have a tonnage of (so much) ; see prec. 4.

Tonne, obs. form of TON, TUN.

Tonnish, see TONISH.

Tonometer (toˈnɔmɪtə). [f. TONO- + -METER.]

1. *Music.* An instrument for determining the pitch of tones...

2. *Physiol.* An instrument for measuring (*a*) tension of the eyeball in glaucoma, (*b*) intravascular blood-pressure, (*c*) strains within a liquid.

Hence **Tono'metry** (tɔˈnɔmɪtrɪ), *Tono'metric,* the using of a tonometer; measurement of vibrations of sound or of tones.

Tonophant (tɔˈnəfant). [...]

Tonous (tɔˈnəs), *a.* [L. *tonus* TONE + -OUS.] Having a full tone or sound; sonorous.

TONSOR column:

Tonse, obs. form of TUCK.

Tonse, *v.* [L. *tonsus,* ppl. stem of *tondēre* to shear, clip.]

Tonsil (tɔˈnsɪl). [a. F. *tonsille* (17th c.).]

1. Each of two oval lymphoid glands situated one on each side of the fauces between the anterior and posterior arches.

2. Each of the two lobes of the cerebellum ; also called *amygdala.*

Tonsurate, ... To clip or shave off the hair ; to confer the ecclesiastical tonsure.

Tonsil (continued) ... *attrib.* and *Comb.*

Tonsilitic, (-ˈɪtɪk), *a.* ...

Tonsillitis (tɔnsɪˈlaɪtɪs). *Path.* [f. L. *tonsilla* + -ITIS.] Inflammation of the tonsils.

Tonsillotome, etc.

Tonsillotomy, excision of the tonsils.

Tonsilly, ... Affected by the tonsils.

Tonsion, variant of TUNSION, beating.

Tonsor (tɔˈnsɔː). [a. L. *tonsor* barber, agent-n. f. *tondēre* to shear, clip.]

TONSORIAL column:

I. a barber.

Tonsorial (tɔnˈsɔːrɪəl), *a.* ... Of or pertaining to a barber ; often used humorously, as 'a *tonsorial artist*'.

Hence **Tonsuring** *vbl. sb.* and *ppl. a.*

Tonsured (ppl. a.)

1. That has received tonsure ; hence, in orders.

2. Clipped, as a yew or box. *rare.*

Tonsure (tɔˈnʃə). [a. F. *tonsure,* ad. L. *tōnsūra.*]

1. *gen.* The action or process of clipping the hair ...

2. *spec.* The shaving of the head or part of it as a religious practice or rite, esp. as a preparation to entering the priesthood or a monastic order.

b. The part of a priest's or monk's head left bare by shaving the hair.

Tontine (tɔnˈtiːn), *n.* [F. *tontine,* from name of Lorenzo Tonti, a Neapolitan banker, who initiated the scheme in France c 1653.]

1. A financial scheme by which the subscribers to a loan or common fund receive each an annuity during his life, which increases as their number is diminished by death, till the last survivor enjoys the whole income; also applied to the share or right of each subscriber.

2. *attrib.* and *Comb.,* as *tontine-cap, tontine-plate* (see quot.).

Hence **Tontiner** (tɔnˈtiːnə), a shareholder in a tontine.

TOO column:

Tony (tɔˈnɪ), *sb.* slang. Obs. ...

Tony (tɔˈnɪ), *a.* slang. Also 8 **tony.** [f. Tony 1.] ...

Tonyle, Tonyd, obs. ff. TUNICLE, TONGUE.

Tool (tuːl), *sb.* [OE. *tōl.*]

Toom (tuːm), *a.* and *sb.* [ME. *tōm,* a. ON. *tómr.*]

TOO. — 136 — TOOL.

TOOL — 137 — TOOM.

Too (tuː), *adv.* [OE. *tō,* orig. the preposition *tō* TO used as adv.]

1. To that which is expressed or implied; in addition; besides; as well, also, likewise.

2. In a higher degree than is allowable, fitting, or desirable; in excess; more than enough; beyond what is proper.

Too-too, ... excessively, extravagantly.

Toot, obs. form of TUT.

Tooart, Also **tewart, tuart.** The-tree name in Australia. A West Australian tree, *Eucalyptus gomphocephala,* which furnishes a very hard heavy durable timber used in ship-building.

Tooth, ...

Tooching, obs. form of TOUCHING.

Toodle, *v.* [echoic.] To hum or sing in a low tone (as to a baby).

Toodle-loo-dle, ... an imitation of the sound of a pipe or flute.

Tool (continued)

Tool, *v.* [f. TOOL *sb.*]

1. To work on or shape with a tool ...

2. *Bookbinding.* To impress an ornamental design upon (the binding of a book) with a special tool (see prec. 1 d). Most usually in *pa. pple.*

b. *intr.* To work with a tool; to tool.

Tooling (tuːˈlɪŋ), *vbl. sb.* [f. TOOL *sb.* and *v.* + -ING 1.]

1. Provision of tools; tools collectively. *Obs.*

2. The action of the verb TOOL; workmanship performed with some special tool ; also the dressing of stone with a broad chisel ; also, elaborate ornamental carving in stone or wood.

b. *Bookbinding.* The impressing of ornamental designs upon the covers of books by means of heated tools or stamps; also applied to the design so formed: either with gilding (*gold-* or *gilt-tooling*) or without it (*blind-tooling*).

Tooler (tuːˈlə). [f. TOOL *v.* + -ER 1.] A broad chisel used by stone-masons for random tooling; a drove.

Tooless, *a.* [f. TOOL *sb.* + -LESS.] Having no tools; destitute of tools.

Toolman (tuːlmən), *sb.* [f. TOOL *sb.* + MAN *sb.*] A man who makes or uses tools.

Toolsee, -si, ... variant form of TULSI.

Toom (tuːm), *a.* and *sb.* Sc. [a. ON. *tómr.*] Empty.

Toom, *v.* Sc. [a. ON. *tóma.*] To empty.

Toom, a. *Sc.* and *north. dial.* [f. Toom v.]

I. 1. *trans.* To empty (a vessel, receptacle, etc.).

2. To empty by drinking, to drink off the contents of.

3. To empty out, discharge, pour out (water, the contents of a vessel, etc.).

Toomacogooroo, variant of TUMATA-KURU.

Toomble, obs. form of TUMBLE.

†**Toomhead**. *Obs. rare.* [f. TOOM a. + -HEAD.] Emptiness, vanity. Over toomhead, uselessly, to no purpose.

Too-tely, adv. *Sc.* and *north. dial.* [f. TOOM a.1 and a. + -LY.]

1. In a leisurely way; somewhat slowly; without haste.

2. *fig.* Idly, without occupation. *Obs.*

3. Emptily, vainly, to no purpose.

4. With empty saddle.

Toompe, obs. form of TUMP.

†**Toomsome**, a. *Obs. rare.* [f. TOOM a. + -SOME.] Leisurely, free from haste.

†**Toon**, *sun* (obs.). *Sc. Ind.*

2. *slang.* The devil, *Linc.* (Hallw.)

Toot (tūt), *sb.*1 [Anglicized form of the Maori name *tutu.*] A shrub or small tree, *Coriaria ruscifolia*, of New Zealand.

Toot (tūt), *sb.*2 Now *dial.* Forms: 1 tótian, 3-4 tōten, 4-7 tote, toote, 5- toot.

2. Of a wind-instrument: To give forth its characteristic sound; to sound.

3. Of an animal: To make a sound likened to that of a horn, etc.; to trumpet as an elephant, bray as an ass; *spec.* of grouse, to 'call'.

Toot (tūt), *sb.*3 Now *dial.*

II. *trans.* 4. To cause (a horn, etc.) to sound by blowing it.

5. To sound (notes, a tune, etc.) on a horn, pipe, or the like.

6. To call out aloud, to trumpet abroad.

Too-ting *ppl. a.*, that toots, as a horn, siren, etc.

Toot, tout (tūt), *sb.*3 *Sc.* and *U.S.* [In *Sc. tout* (tūt), in Anglicized spelling *toot.* Of obscure origin.]

1. *intr.* To drink copiously; to take a large draught. (Jam.)

2. *trans.* To empty the vessel from which one drinks, to drink its whole contents. (Jam.) Const. *off, out, up.*

3. *intr.* To go or sit; to make a night of it. *U.S.*

Toot (tūt), *sb.*4 Also 6 tute, 6-7 toote, 6 towt, 6, 9 *Sc.* tuith.

Tootanag, obs. form of TUTENAG.

Too-ter1 (tū·tə·ɹ). [f. TOOT v.1 + -ER.]

1. One who gazes; a watchman; a prier or peeper.

2. Something that projects, in quot., a prominent nose.

Too-ter2 (tū·tə·ɹ). [f. TOOT v.2 + -ER.]

1. One who toots, or plays a wind-instrument; a trumpeter or piper.

Tooth (tūþ), *sb.* Also 6 tute, toothe; *pl.* teeth, 1-4 teþ, tēþ. [OE. tōþ (:—*tanþ-), pl. tēþ.]

Tooth (tūþ), *v.* [f. TOOTH *sb.*]

o. In expressions referring to speech (now *esp.* with teeth).

II. *transf.* A projecting part or point resembling an animal's tooth.

Toother. [f. TOOTH v. + -ER.] One who makes the teeth of saws; a machine for doing this.

III. *Phrases.*

4. In the teeth, in (one's) teeth. In direct (local) opposition or attack; *in the teeth of*, in direct opposition to, so as to face or confront, straight against.

5. In the teeth of, in presence of, in the face of; usually implying hostility or danger; threateningly confronted by.

II. *Various phrases.*

Tooth-and-nail (orig. *with tooth and nail*), adv.: *in the teeth of* (obs.), *to throw in* (one's) *teeth*: to reproach, upbraid, or censure with; to bring up in reproach against.

Tooth-brush. A small brush with a long handle, used for cleansing the teeth.

Too-thachy, a. (colloq.), affected with toothache. So **Too-th-aching**, aching of the teeth.

Tooth (tūþ), *poet.* *sb.*, *v.* (-ēd), a.; *pl.* teeth.

Tooth-bill (tū·þ·bil), *n.* *Ornith.* So BILLED.] Having one or more tooth-like projections on the edge of the bill; dentirostral or serratirostral.

Toothbill. a. tooth-billed pigeon.

Tooth-comb. A small brush, 1 with long handle, used for cleansing the teeth.

Too-thbrushy a. *nonce-wd.*, resembling a tooth-brush; bristly.

Tooth-drawer. One who 'draws' or extracts teeth; a dentist.

Toothache (tū·þ·ēk). Forms: *see* TOOTH *sb.* and v. + -ACHE. An ache or continuous pain in a tooth or the teeth. (As a malady, commonly *the tooth ache* down to 17th c.)

Tooth-fee. [Literal rendering of ON. *tann-fé*, f. *tann*, tann- tooth + *fé* money.] A gift to an infant on cutting its first tooth, a custom mentioned in Old Norse, and first observed in Iceland (Vigfusson). Also *toot-tooth-gift*, *-money*, *-piece*.

Toothful (tū'θfŭl), a. [f. Tooth sb. + -ful.] *lit.* As much as would fill a tooth; a small mouthful, esp. of liquor.

Toothful (tū'θfŭl), a. [f. Tooth sb. + -ful 1.]
† 1. Pleasant to the taste = Toothsome. *Obs.*
† 2. Destitute of teeth. *rare*.

Tooth-hill (tū'thil). Also 4 tote, 4-5 tute, 6-8 tooth-hill. Preserved in many forms *tout-, tote-, tot-, tut-* in place-names. [ME. *tōt-hill* (Tout sb.1 + -hill.] A natural or artificial hill or mound used for a look-out place; a prominent hill; — Toot sb.1 1. (In quot. 1250 a place-name.)

Toothily (tū'þile), *adv.* [f. Toothy + -ly.] In a toothy manner.

Toothing (tū'þiŋ), *vbl. sb.* [f. Tooth sb. or v. 1 + -ing 1.]
1. Development or 'cutting' of the teeth, dentition = Teething vbl. sb. 1. *Obs. or rare.*
2. A structure or formation (natural or artificial) consisting of teeth or tooth-like projections; such teeth collectively; dentation, serration.
3. *spec.* in Building. Bricks or stones left projecting from a wall to form a bond for additional work to be built on; the bond or attachment thus formed; the construction of this. Also *fig.*
4. *attrib.* and *Comb.*, as *toothing-plane*, a plane having two rows of teeth; *toothing-stone*, one of the stones forming toothing.

Toothless (tū'þlès), a. [f. Tooth sb. + -less.]
1. Having no teeth; destitute of teeth.
2. *transf.* Destitute of tooth-like formations or projections; not jagged or serrated.
3. *fig.* Destitute of keenness or 'edge'; not biting or corrosive; also *fig.*

Tooth-picker. = prec. 1. *Obs.*

Toothlet (tū'þlèt). [f. Tooth sb. + -let.] A small tooth or tooth-like projection; a denticle.

Toothpick (tū'þpik). Forms: see Tooth sb.; also 5-6 -pike, 6 -picke. [See Pick sb.1 4.] An instrument for picking the teeth, usually a pointed quill or small piece of wood; sometimes of gold, silver, or other material.

Toothsome (tū'þsŭm), a. [See -some 1.]
1. Pleasant to the taste, savoury, palatable; *cf.* Tooth sb. 7 a.
2. *attrib.* as *toothing-glass*, *looking-glass*; *tooting-hill* = *tooting-hill*; so *tooting-hole*, *peep-hole*; *tooting-place*, *-tower*, etc.

6. attrib. and Comb. **a.** attrib. or **a.** adj., **+ (a)** in reference to the use of the toothpick as an idle occupation; **(b)** denoting objects of narrow and pointed shape.

Toothy (tū'þi), a. [f. Tooth sb. + -y 1.]
1. Having numerous, large, or prominent teeth.
2. One who picks the teeth; *in* first quot. use of a bird which was fabled to pick the teeth of the crocodile; in second quot. with allusion to this.

Tooth-picking, a. Picking the teeth; *fig.* careless, nonchalant; cf. Toothpick 6 a (a).

Tooth-powder. A powder, usually in the form of a paste, for cleansing the teeth.

Tooth-sheet, *sb.* = Toothpick.

Tootle (tū'tl), v. [freq. f. Toot v.2 + -le 1.]

Tootmout or **toot-mot**, 1. The bait or charm of any enticement; cf. Tout v.

Top (top), sb.1 [OE. top (topp) Com. WGer. and Com. Teut.] 1. A tuft, crest, or summit or crown of the head; the hair of the head. *Obs. exc. dial.*

Topman, see Topman.

Toot-net (tū'tnet). *Sc. local.* [Toot sb.1 + Net.] A large fishing net anchored (Jam.), which it is watched in order to be drawn in when the fish enter it.

Top (top), sb.2 [OE. (*topp*) Com. WGer. app.]
1. The highest or uppermost part or point.

Toot-too (tū'tū'). v. [Echoic: usually deprecative.] *intr.* To make an instrument or vocal sound resembling these syllables. Hence Toot-tooing sb.

8. In various applications. a. In Gem-cutting: see quot.
11. In various technical applications:
a. **TOP.** 144 **TOP.** **TOP.** 145 **TOP.**

Tope, sb.[1] ... [Etymology not ascertained.] A small species of shark, *Galeus canis* ...

Tope, sb.[2] *East Indies.* [ad. Tamil *tōppu*, Telugu *tōpa*.] A clump, grove, or plantation of trees; in Upper India, chiefly of fruit-trees ...

Tope, sb.[3] *East Indies.* [Hind. (Panjābī) *ṭōp.*] An ancient structure, in the form of a dome or tumulus of masonry, for the preservation of relics or in commemoration of some fact ...

Tope, sb.[4] [Known from 1669; of obscure origin.] Synonymous with TOP sb.

Tope, v.[1] Now only *literary* or *arch.* [Known 1654; origin obscure.] Synonymous with the earlier TOP v.[3] ...

Tope, v.[2] Now only *literary* or *arch.* 1. *trans.* To drink, *esp.* to drink copiously and habitually.

Hence **Toping** vbl. sb. (also *attrib.*) and ppl. *a.*

Tope, int. Obs. [See Note below.] ...

Toper (tō·paɹ). Now chiefly *literary.* [f. TOPE v.[2] + -ER[1].]

Top-full (tǫ·pfᵁl), a. Now *rare.* Also *erron.* topful. [f. TOP sb.[1] + FULL a.]

Topet, **Topeus**, obs. ff. TOPPET, TOPAZ.

Top-ful, *a. Obs. rare*⁻¹. = TOP-FULL.

Topgallant (tǫpgæ·lǝnt, tǫ·pgæ·lǝnt), sb. and a. Also †-galand.

Topmast, and thus in a loftier position than the original top-castle or top.

Topi[1], **tophe** (tǫʊ·fī). Now *rare.* [ad. L. *tōpha.*] = TOPHUS.

Top-ha·t, *colloq.* A man's silk or beaver hat with high cylindrical crown; a tall or high hat.

Top-heavy (tǫ·phe·vi), a. Disproportionately heavy at the top; having the upper part so heavy ...

Toph[1] (tǫf). [Heb. תֹּף *tōph.*] A musical instrument of music, of the nature of a timbrel or tabret.

Tophaceous, see -ACEOUS.

Tophaike (tǫfǫi·k). [ad. vulgar Turkish *tüfek* ...] A (Turkish) musket.

Toy-ha·mper [f. TOP sb.[1] + HAMPER sb.[2].]

Toph[2] (tǫf). [Heb. תֹּפֶת *tōpheth.*]

Tophet (tō·fet). Also †-feth, 4-9 tophethe. [Heb. תֹּפֶת *tōpheth.*]

Tophus (tō·fǝs). [a. L. *tōphus*, var. of *tōfus.*]

Topi[2], **toppee** (tǫ·pī). *East Ind.* [a. Hind. *ṭopī* hat.]

Topia (tō·piǎ). [L. *topia.*] The white *sombrero* solah topee ...

Topi-, **topee-wallah** (tǫpī-ǫlǎ), also **-wala** [a. Hindī *ṭopīwālā*, one who wears a hat, i.e. a European, because he wears a hat.]

Topia, obs. variant of TOPAZ.

Topiarian (tǫʊpiǝ·riǎn), a. = next.

Topiary (tō·piǎri), a. and sb. [ad. L. *topiārius.*] 1. *a.* Of or pertaining to ornamental gardening.

Topian (tō·piǎn), a. [f. L. *topia* + -AN.]

Topic (tǫ·pik), sb. and a. [ad. L. *Topica.*]

Topical (tǫ·pikǎl), a. (sb.) [f. TOPIC + -AL.]

Topically (tǫ·pikǎli), adv. [f. prec. + -LY[2].]

Topinambou (tǫpinæ·mbū). [F. *Topinambou.*]

Topism, **Topist**, etc.

Toplet, rare. [f. TOP sb.[1] + -LET.]

Topmost (tǫ·pmǝst, -moʊst). [f. TOP sb.[1] + -MOST.]

Topoman, obs. f. TOPMAN.

Topography (tǫpǫ·grǎfi). [ad. L. *topographia.*]

Top-maker, **-making**: see TOP sb.[1] + MAN sb.[1]

Topman (tǫ·pmǎn). [f. TOP sb.[1] + MAN sb.[1]]

Topmast (tǫ·pmast, -mǝst). A smaller mast fixed on the top of a lower mast ...

Topographer (tǫpǫ·grǎfǝɹ). [f. as TOPOGRAPHY + -ER[1].]

Topographic (tǫpǫgræ·fik), a. = TOPOGRAPHICAL.

Topographical ... **Topographic** ... **Topographically** ... **Topographist** ... **Topographize** ... **Topographometric** ... **Topography** ... **Toponomy** ... **Toponym** ... **Toponymy** ...

Topophone ... **Topound** ... **Top-over-terve** ... **Topped** ... **Topper** ... **Top-piece** ... **Topping** ... **Toppingly** ...

Topple ... **Toppling** ... **Topsail** ... **Top-sawyer** ... **Topset** ... **Topsy-turve** ... **Topsoil** ... **Topsman** ... **Topside** ... **Top-stone** ... **Topsy-turvy** ... **Toque** ...

THACKERAY *Ravenswing* iv, Her hats, toques..marabouts, and other fallals. 1881 MISS BRADDON *Asph.* xxvii, Her neat travelling-gown of darkest olive cashmere, and coquettish little olive-green toque. 1903 *N. & Q.* 9th Ser. XI. 366/1 The term 'bonnet', as applied to the costume of ladies, may be taken to mean either bonnets or tocques, but not hats.
attrib. 1884 *West. Daily Press* 29 May 3/7 The toque hat is too comfortable, too convenient, and too becoming to be lightly laid aside.

2. *Toque monkey*, also simply *toque*: the bonnet-monkey or bonnet-macaque, *Macacus pileatus*, a native of Ceylon (see BONNET *sb.* 10).
1840 *Cuvier's Anim. Kingd.* 59 The Bonneted Macaque (*Macacus sinicus*) and the Toque (*M. radiatus*) have the hairs on the top of the head disposed as radii. 1882 OGILVIE (Annandale), *Toque*..2. A name given to the bonnet-macaque. 1883 *List Anim. Zool. Soc.* 16 *Macacus pileatus* (Shaw), Toque Monkey. 1892 *Pall Mall G.* 28 Sept. 3/1 The Guinea baboons and the toque monkeys.

To-queme, Toquher: see QUEME *sb.*, TOCHER.

Tor (tǭɹ), *sb.* Forms: 1, 6– torr, 4–7 torre, 4– tor. [Occurs as an element in topographical names in early West Saxon charters; also, as a local term for a topographical feature from OE. onward. Generally held to be Celtic; but, though frequent in place-names in Cornwall, Devon, etc., not recorded as a 'common noun' in Cornish or Breton. In Welsh the nearest word is app. *tŵr* (= tûr), OW. *twrr* 'heap, pile' (rare in place-names, but cf. *Mynydd Twrr*, old name of Holyhead Mountain, Rhŷs). Prob. cognate with Gaelic *tòrr* 'hill of an abrupt or conical form, lofty hill, eminence, mound, grave, heap of ruins' (Macleod and Dewar), primarily 'heap, pile', cf. *tòrr* vb. 'to heap up, pile up, bury', Ir. *torraim* 'I heap up', and the deriv. Gael. *torran* 'little hill, knoll, hillock', Ir. *torrán* 'heap, pile, hillock'. Cf. also quot. 1905.]

1. A high rock; a pile of rocks, *gen.* on the top of a hill; a rocky peak; a hill. In proper names of eminences or rocks in Cornwall, Devon, Peak of Derbyshire; also sporadically in some other counties, e.g. *Glastonbury Tor*, in Somerset.
847 *Grant by K. Æthelwulf* in Birch *Cart. Sax.* II. 34 Ærest on merce cumb [in Dorset], ðonne on grenan pytt, ðonne on ðone torr æt merce cumbes æwielme. a 1000 *Boeth. Metr.* v. 17 Oð him [a brook] oninnan felð muntes mægenstan..atrendiod of ðæm torre [in *Prose* vi, Micel stan wealwiende of þam heohan munte]. a 1400–50 *Alexander* 4863 So hedous & so hoge hillis þam beforn, Cloȝes at was cloude he [cloud-high] clynterand torres, Rochis & rogh stanes, rokkis vnfaire. 1539 POLLARD in *Lett. Suppress. Monast.* (Camden) 261 The late abbott of Glastonberye..was drawyn thorowe the towne apon a hurdyll to the hyll callyd the Torre, wheare he was putto execucion. a 1552 LELAND *Itin.* (1711) II. 38 Camallate, sumtyme a famose Toun or Castelle, apon a very Torre or Hille, wunderfully enstrengthenid of nature. 1610 NORDEN *Spec. Brit., Cornw.* (1728) 38 Mount St. Michaells, a steepe and most craggie torr. c 1630 RISDON *Surv. Devon* (1810) 6 A chain of hills..whose tops and torrs are in the winter often covered with a white cap. 1681 COTTON *Wond. Peake* (1702) 42 Tor in that Country-Jargons uncouth sense, Expressing any Craggy Eminence. 1806 GOUGH *Camden's Brit.* II. 423/2 Matlock great Torr is 140 yards perpendicular. 1894 BARING-GOULD *Kitty Alone* II. 169 Tors rise to the height of from twelve to fifteen hundred feet. 1905 *Eng. Dial. Dict.* s.v. *Torr*, In E. Cornw. 'Tor' means a pile of rocks, and is never used for a hill, or the top of a hill, unless the hill or top is so very rocky that the whole may be considered one pile of rocks. 1913 *Let. to Editor*, A high hill in Haslingden, Lancashire, is simply called 'The Tor'.

b. Locally in Scotland, applied to an artificial mound; a burial mound.
1794 BUCHANAN *Def. Scott. Highl.* 142 What are the Torrs ..but burrying hills? 1845 *Statist. Acc. Scot.* VI. 887 Its name [Torrance] was taken from an artificial mound of earth, still known by the name of the Tor, which is situated a quarter of a mile from the present house of Torrance.

†**2.** ? A heavy mass of cloud. *Obs.*
(But the sense 'rock mass' seems also possible.)
13.. *E. E. Allit. P.* A. 874 A hue fro heuen I herde þoo, Lyk flodez fele laden, runnen on resse, & as þunder þrowez in torrez blo. *Ibid.* B. 951 Torres, þat þe þik þunder þrast þirled hem ofte.

3. *attrib.* **Tor ouzel**, local name of a bird, the ring ouzel, *Turdus torquatus.*
1770 G. WHITE *Selborne* xxxi. (1789) 84 [The ring ousels] breed in great abundance all over the Peak of Derby, and are called there *Tor-ousels.* 1885 SWAINSON *Provinc. Names Birds* 8 Ring Ouzel (*Turdus torquatus*)..Tor ouzel (Devon). Rock, or crag ouzel (Craven).

†**Tor**, *a. Obs.* Forms: 3–5 tor, 4 toor, 4–5 toore, 5 tore, toure. See also TERE *a.* [The Old Norse and OE. adverbial particle *tor-* 'hardly, with difficulty, ill-', used esp. with verbal adjs. as in ON. *tor-fengr* hard to get, *tor-næmr* hard to learn, *tor-synn* hard to see, *tor-talinn* pple., counted with difficulty, *tor-tryggr* hard of belief; also OE. *tor-cyrre* hard to turn or convert, *tor-beglte* hard to get. In ME., esp. in those parts in which the Norse influence was strong, this particle was treated as a separate word, in the sense 'hard, difficult, ill', and was used esp. with the infinitive, as *tor* (*for*) *to tell, tor for to ken*; the former of these was a favourite phrase of the alliterative poets. In some instances, as already in Ormin, *tor* alone was used attributively. ON. and OE. *tor-* were cognate with OHG. *zur-*, Gothic *tuz-*, Gr. δυσ-, Skr. *dus-*, hard, evil, ill-: with the ON. and OE. words cf. Gr. δυσαής ill-blowing, δύσβρωτος hard to eat, δυσμαθής difficult to learn. Senses 2 and 3 appear to be the same word, but the change of sense is remarkable.]

1. Difficult, hard, toilsome; irksome, tedious; = TERE *a.*
c 1200 ORMIN 6350 Harrd & strang & tor & hefiȝ lif to ledenn. a 1225 *Ancr. R.* 108 (MS. T.) Ho is gruccbere, & ful itohen: dangeruse & tor for to paien. *Ibid.* 254 An honful ȝerden arn tor to breken [*v.r.* beoð erueð forte breken]. 13.. *Cursor M.* 14085 (Cott.) O þair gladnes war tor to tell. c 1350 *Will. Palerne* 5066 It were toor forto telle treuli al þe soþe. c 1400 *Destr. Troy* 644 But this tyme is so tore & we no tome haue.

2. Strong, sturdy. (? Hard to conquer.)
a 1400–50 *Alexander* 5500 Ser Tarbyn, a tulke with many toore thousandis. c 1400 *Destr. Troy* 330 Grete toures full toure all þe toune vmbe. *Ibid.* 1035 Of the tidiest of Tesaile, tore men of strenght. *Ibid.* 1131 Telamon, þat is a tore kyng. *Ibid.* 6156 Dissyrus..Of all the Troiens to tell torest in armys.

3. In vague or loose uses: **a.** Full, replete; **b.** Great, violent, excessive.
c 1400 *Destr. Troy* 3348 Trowe ye not Troy is tore of all godis, As plaintiouse in yche place as þe prouynse of Achaia? *Ibid.* 13723 Þis proud in hir yre..Bad hym turne vnto tessail in a tore hast.

Tor, erron. spelling of TAW *sb.*², a marble; obs. pa. t. of TEAR *v.*¹

†**To-ra·ce, to-ra·nce, to-ra·se**, *v. Obs.* Forms: 3–4 to-raunoen, -rancen, -rassen; 3–5 -racen, -rasen. [ME. *to-racen*, etc., f. TO-² + RACE *v.*³, RANCH *v.*², RASE *v.*¹] *trans.* To hack, slash, cut, or tear to pieces.
1297 R. GLOUC. (Rolls) 524 He was al to ranced pecemele in a stounde, Ech lime fram oþer, among þe rockes, ar he com to gronde. *Ibid.* 4412 Hor king..Wiþ woundes to Raunced so þat he moste nede deye. 13.. *Gaw. & Gr. Knt.* 1168 What wylde so at-waped wyȝes þat schotten Watz al to-raced & rent, at þe resayt. c 1386 CHAUCER *Clerk's T.* 516 Burieth this litel body in som place, That beestes ne no briddes it to-race. a 1400–50 *Alexander* 2088 Þai haue bedid of oure hathils..Bet doun oure bachelers, my banir to-rased. c 1450 *Mirour Saluacioun* 4370 With breres and with sharpe thornes thaire bodyes alto racyng.

†**To-ra·g**, *v. Obs.* [ME., f. TO-² + RAG *v.*¹] *trans.* To tear the clothes of, to make very ragged.
c 1430 *Pilgr. Lyf Manhode* iii. xxii. (1869) 148 That is thilke that hath thus to ragged me and to clowted me. a 1550 *Friar & Boy* 266 in Hazl. *E. P. P.* III. 72 All to ragged and to rente, And torne on euery syde.

‖**Torah** (tǭ·rā). Forms: 6, 9 thora, 7 tora, 7, 9 thorah, 9 torah. [Heb. תּוֹרָה *tōrāh* 'direction, instruction, doctrine, law', f. ירה *yārāh* 'to throw', in Hiphil 'to show, direct, instruct'.] The teaching or instruction, and judicial decisions, given by the ancient Hebrew priests as a revelation of the divine will; the Mosaic or Jewish law; hence, a name for the five books of the law, the Pentateuch.
1577 tr. *Bullinger's Decades* i. (1592) 9 The lawe of Moses, which is in deede the lawe of God, and is most properly called Thora, as it were the guide and rule of faith. 1842 BONAR & M'CHEYNE *Narr. Mission to Jews* iv. (1843) 215 The [Samaritan] priest agreed to shew us the copy of the Torah, or five books of Moses..so famed for its antiquity. 1875 M. ARNOLD *God & Bible* iv. 188 Thus the Pentateuch, or five books of Moses, stood alone as the 'Thora'. 1890 P. H. HUNTER *After the Exile* xiv. 273 The word Torah.. signifies doctrine, instruction. This wider sense is lost in the usual translation by νόμος or law.

‖**Toran** (tǭ·rǎn). [Hindi *tōran*:—Skr. *toraṇa* arched portal.] A sacred Buddhist gateway, of wood or stone, consisting of a pair of uprights with one or more (often three) cross-pieces; sometimes elaborately carved.
1886 E. C. ROBINS *Temple of Solomon* (1887) 27 A design ..based on the Japanese and Indian *toran*, like those forming gateways to the Great Tope at Sanchi.

To-rance, to-rase, by-forms of TO-RACE *v.*

†**To-ra·t**, *v. Obs. rare*⁻¹. [f. TO-² + RAT *v.*³] *trans.* To break up, scatter.
? a 1400 *Morte Arth.* 2235 Thane þe Romayns..alle torattys oure mene with theire riste horsses.

Torbanite (tǭ·ɹbǎnəit). *Min.* [f. *Torbane Hill* in Linlithgowshire, where found: see -ITE¹ 2 b.] A deep brown shale, allied to cannel coal: also called **Torbane Hill mineral** or *Boghead coal*; valuable for the production of petroleum and gas, and famous as the subject of a great lawsuit hinging upon the dispute whether or not it was legally 'coal'.
1858 GREG & LETTSOM *Man. Mineral.* 16 Torbanite... Boghead mineral. Boghead coal. c 1865 LETHEBY in *Circ. Sc.* I. 139/2 Mr. James Young..has..been engaged in producing an oil..from a shale known as the Torbanehill mineral. 1867 W. W. SMYTH *Coal & Coal-mining* 18 It is by no means easy..to draw a distinct line of demarcation between cannel and the black basses, bats, or crisp shales, which occur in the coal measures...And between all these and the torbanite, or 'Boghead mineral', there exists a relationship which makes the difference only one of degree.

Torbant, obs. form of TURBAN.

Torbel, torble, obs. ff. TROUBLE *sb.* and *v.*

Torbernite (tǭ·ɹbəɹnəit). *Min.* Also torberite. [ad. Ger. *torbernit* (Werner 1792), orig. *torberit*, f. *Torbernus*, latinized form of the name of the chemist Torber Bergmann: see -ITE¹.] A native phosphate of uranium and copper, found in bright green tabular crystals; also called *copper-uranite*, and (erroneously) *chalcolite*.
1852 BROOKE & MILLER *Phillips' Introd. Min.* 517 Torberite.—Uranite (in part)..is found in attached crystals, massive, and investing other minerals, in veins in slate and in granite. 1868 DANA *Min.* 585 Torbernite.

Torbith, obs. form of TURBIT.

Torc: see TORQUE¹.

Torcas, obs. f. TURQUOISE. **Torcasse**, var. TURKIS, -E *v. Obs.*, to distort, transform.

Torce, variant of TORSE¹, *Her.*, wreath.

†**To·rcenous**, *a. Obs. rare*⁻¹. *erron.* toroencious. [a. AF. *torcenous*, OF. *torçonos* (also *torçonereus*), f. *torçon*, *torcion* extortion, *torçoneor* extortioner.] Extortionate, exacting.
[1292 BRITTON i. xxii. § 13 Et ausi de totes torcenouses prises fetes par nos ministres. 1314–15 *Rolls of Parlt.* I. 292/2 Dont il prient qe tiel torcenouse demaunde soit oste.] 1387–8 T. USK *Test. Love* i. vi. (Skeat) l. 131 The gouernementes..of your citee, left in the handes of torcencious citezins, shal bring in pestilence and distruccion to you.

Torch (tǭɹtʃ), *sb.* Forms: 3–6 torche, (4 torge, thorche, 5 tourche, 6 tortche, towrge, *pl.* torchesse), 6– torch. [ME. a. OF. *torche* = Pr. *torcha*, according to Diez:—late pop.L. **torca*, from stem **tork-* of *torquēre* to twist; cf. also It. *torcia* (Veronese, and Venetian *torzo*), Sp. *antorcha*, earlier *entorcha*, Pg. *tocha* 'torch'. The primary sense is taken to have been 'a twist', 'something twisted', torches having been made of twisted tow dipped in pitch, or the like. Cf. also TORTIS.
(The derivation of the Eng. from F. *torche* is certain, but the etymology of the latter, and of the Romanic forms as a whole, is still in dispute: see Diez s.v. *Torciare*, Gröber *Archiv f. Lat. Lexicog.* VI. 128, Körting *Lat. Rom. Wbch.* 1901 s.v. *Tortica* 9616.)]

1. A light to be carried in the hand, consisting of a stick of resinous wood, or of twisted hemp or similar material soaked with tallow, resin, or other inflammable substance. Also applied to a lamp carried on a pole or similar appliance.
c 1290 *S. Eng. Leg.* I. 467/187 With-oute liȝht of torche. c 1330 *Assump. Virg.* 598 (B.M. MS.) Loke þat ȝe haue candele Torches boþe faire & fele. 13.. *Sir Beues* (A.) 1659 Þar inne he seȝ torges [*v.r.* torches] i-liȝt. 1377 LANGL. *P. Pl.* B. xvii. 203 To a torche or a tapre þe trinitee is lykned; As wex and a weke were twyned togideres, And þanne a fyre flaumende forth oute of bothe. 1483 *Cath. Angl.* 390/1 A Torche, *torticius, torchia.* 1546–7 in Swayne *Sarum Churchw. Acc.* (1896) 274, viij lb. of waxe to make twoo torches agaynst Alholloutyde. 1555 in *Shropsh. Par. Documents* (1903) 56 Peyde towrd byying of ii towrges. 1606 SHAKS. *Tr. & Cr.* v. i. 92 Follow his Torch, he goes to Chalcas Tent. 1721 BAILEY, *A Torch*..a Staff of Deal on which Wax-Candles are stuck, to be lighted on several Occasions. 1821 SCOTT *Kenilw.* xxx, Onward came the cavalcade, illuminated by two hundred thick waxen torches. 1906 *Daily Chron.* 14 July 5 The ordinary tarred-rope torch.

b. *fig.* or *allusively*. Something figured as a source of illumination, enlightenment, or guidance, or of heat or 'conflagration'.
1621 BURTON *Anat. Mel.* iii. ii. vi. i. (1651) 545, I light my Candle from their Torches. 1664 JASZ-BERENYI (*title*) A new Torch to the Latine Tongue. 1775 SHERIDAN *Rivals* Epil., The torch of love. 1878 BOSW. SMITH *Carthage* 19 The torch of Greek learning and civilisation was to be extinguished.

2. *transf.* **a.** A spike composed of spikelets; also *fig.* said of a red or flame-coloured flower.
1578 LYTE *Dodoens* i. lxiii. 91 Of this kinde, there is founde an other, the Spikes, eares, or torches wherof, are very dubble,..in steede of the little knappes or heades, it bringeth forth a number of other smal torches, wherof eche one is lyke to the spike or torch of great Plantayne. 1862 B. TAYLOR *Poet's Jrnl.* ii. *Lost May*, And burns in meadow-grass the phlox His torch of purple fire.

b. (Usually in *pl.* **Torches.**) The Great Mullein, *Verbascum Thapsus* (or other species): from its tall spike of yellow flowers (or, according to some, from the use of its thick woolly leaves and stalks as material for torches).
1552 COOPER *Elyot's Dict.*, *Blattaria*, an herbe called Moleyne, or a kinde of Moleine called Torche. 1578 LYTE *Dodoens* i. lxxxi. 120 Mulleyn is called..in English also.. Hig[h]taper, Torches, and Longworte. [Cf. 118 The whole top with his pleasant yellow floures sheweth like to a waxe Candell or taper cunningly wrought.] 1657 W. COLES *Adam in Eden* cxii, Called of the Latines *Candela Regia* and *Candelaria*, because the elder age used the stalks dipped in Suet to burn...In English also some call it Torches. 1861 MISS PRATT *Flower. Pl.* IV. 135 Its tall tapering spike of light yellow flowers..suggested..the old names of High Taper..and Torches.

†**c.** Applied to a species of cactus or cactaceous plant: prob. = TORCH-THISTLE. *Obs.*
1597 GERARDE *Herbal* 1015 The torch or thornie Euphorbium..called of the Indians *Vragua*..a torch, taper, or waxe candle, whereupon..in Latine of those that understoode the Indian toong, *Cereus*, or a torch. 1666 J. DAVIES *Hist. Caribby Isles* 62 The Plant..some of the European Inhabitants of these Islands call the Torch: it is a kind of great Thistle.

3. *attrib.* and *Comb.*, as *torch-blaze, -brand, -carrier, -flame, -glare, -stick, -waving, -wick*; *torch-like* adj. and adv., *-lit* adj.; also, **torch-blade**, the Great Mullein (= 2 b); **torch-course** = *torch-race*; **torch-dance**, a dance in which some of the performers carry lighted torches; **torch-fish**, a deep-sea fish, *Linophryne lucifer*, having a luminous bulb upon the first dorsal spine, above the eye; **torch-fishing**, fishing by torch-light at night (also called *torching*: see TORCH *v.*¹ 3); **torch-flower**, any bright red or yellow flower resembling or suggesting a torch, e.g. the *torch-lily*; †**torch-herb**, the great mullein; **torch-holder**, one who or that which holds a torch; *spec.* a device for supporting a torch; also, a gas-bracket or the like imitating this; **torch-lily**, the liliaceous genus *Tritoma*, having spikes of bright scarlet flowers; also called 'red-hot poker'; **torch-man**, a man who carries a torch, a torch-bearer; also *fig.*; **torch-pine**, *Pinus rigida* of N. America; = *pitch-pine*; **torch-plant** = TORCH-THISTLE; **torch-race**, in *Gr. Antiq.*, a race held at certain festivals, in which the runners carried lighted torches, and (in some cases) passed them on to other runners posted at certain points: = LAMPADEDROMY; **torch-staff** (*pl.* -staves), a staff upon which a torch is carried; †**torch-tree**, rendering L. *tæda*, a resinous species of pine, the wood of which was used for torches; also *Ixora parviflora*, an East Indian shrub with showy flowers. See also TORCH-BEARER, etc.
1861 MRS. LANKESTER *Wild Flowers* 102 Great Mullein, ..*Torch-blade', or 'King's Taper'. 1818 MILMAN *Samor* 317 A *torchblaze, meet to search Earth's utmost. 1825 SCOTT *Talism.* iii, I am Theodorick of Engaddi—I am the *torch-brand of the desert—I am the flail of the infidels. 1864 TREVELYAN *Compet. Wallah* (1866) 220 The other half are listening to a disquisition of the *torch-carrier. 1839 T. MITCHELL *Aristoph., Frogs* 124 *note*, From.. Pausanias we learn that three *torch-courses were held in the Ceramicus. 1907 *Discovery* Oct. 122 The *Torch-fish... On the upper jaw..there is a larger ovate bulb supported on a tentacle...It possesses powerful phosphorescent properties, the light being under the control of the fish. This is the 'torch'. 1840 BROWNING *Sordello* i. 80 Like a *torch-flame turned By the wind. 1849 [W. M. CALL] *Reverberations* i. 59 The *Torch-flower burning by the river. 1905 in *Daily Chron.* 28 Dec. 3/2 It is now ablaze with the red torch flowers of an aloe. 1908 L. BINYON in *Academy* 14 Mar. 553/1 He stands on high in the *torch-glare. 1598 FLORIO, *Lunaria*, the herbe called *torch herbe or woolblade. 1874 tr. *Hugo's Ninety-Three* iii. i. xix, They stuck an iron *torch-holder into the wall. 1579 J. JONES *Preserv. Bodie & Soule* i. xl. 87 [Comets] Swordlike, hornelike, *torchlike. 1897 *Daily News* 25 June 2/6 Meanwhile our [Jubilee] bonfires [on Skiddaw]..burned torch-like downwards with a grand bead of flame. 1884 MILLER *Plant-n.*, *Torch-lily, the genus *Tritoma*. 1842 SIR A. DE VERE *Song Faith* 186 The *torch-lit gloom of Auchen's aisle. a 1618 SYLVESTER *Mayden's Blush* 364 The sacred *Torch-man (to that end imploy'd). 1856 J. M. KAYE *Sir J. Malcolm* I. vii. 162 The bearers or torchmen who ran by his side. a 1845 HOOD *Incendiary Song* xviii, Burn all *torch-parading elves! 1890 *Cent. Dict.* s.v. *Pine*, *Pitch-pine*, (*a*) in America, *Pinus rigida*...Also called **torch-pine*. 1696 *Phil. Trans.* XIX. 296 The Dildoe-tree is the same with the Cereus or *Torch-Plant. 1812 C. DUNSTER tr. *Aristoph., Frogs* i. ii. *note*, In [Ceramicus] was situated the academy, where the *torch-race was held. 1875 JOWETT *Plato* (ed. 2) III. 12 The promise of an equestrian torch-race in the evening. 1599 SHAKS. *Hen. V*, iv. ii. 46 The Horsemen sit like fixed Candlesticks, With *Torch-staues in their hands. 1601 HOLLAND *Pliny* xvi. x. I. 462 A sixt sort..of these trees..is properly called Teda (i. the *Torch-tree): the same yeeldeth more plentie of moisture and liquor than the rest. 1862 BALFOUR *Timber Trees Asia* (ed. 2) 135 *Ixora parviflora*:..Torch Tree..A small tree..more used for torches than for any other purpose, as it burns very readily and clearly. 1706 PHILLIPS (ed. Kersey), **Torch-weed*, a kind of Herb. 1444 *Compota Domest.* (Abbotsf. 1836) 18 In vij petris di...huiusmodi *torchweke emptis.

Torch (tǭɹtʃ), *v.*¹ [f. TORCH *sb.*]
1. *trans.* To furnish, or light, with a torch or torches. (See TORCHED, and cf. TORCHER¹ 1.)
2. *intr.* To flare like a torch; to rise like smoke from a torch. *dial.*
1847–78 HALLIWELL s.v., Recently heard at Boyton,.. 'Law! how them clouds torch up, we shall ha rain'.
3. To catch fish, etc., by torch-light. *U.S.*
1887 *Fisheries of U.S.* Sect. v. II. 502 Another method, known as 'torching',..is practiced principally by negroes. Having provided themselves with torches they visit the sandy shores at night and catch the terrapins as they come upon the beach to spawn.

Torch (tǭɹtʃ), *v.*² [a. F. *torcher* to wipe, daub, rough-cast, build or plaster with clay mixed with chopped straw, etc., f. *torche* twisted straw, etc. (the same word originally as *torche* TORCH *sb.*).] *trans.* In *plastering*, To point the inside joints of slating laid on lath with lime hair mortar.
a 1850 [Remembered in use by workmen in Oxford]. 1851 [implied in TORCHER²]. 1882 in OGILVIE (Annandale). 1895 *Jrnl. R. Inst. Brit. Archit.* 14 Mar. 351 The roof should be torched—not bedded.
Hence **To·rching** *vbl. sb.*, pointing or daubing of this kind: see also TORCHER².

Torch, var. of TROCH, -E, tine of stag's horn.

Torch-bearer (tǭ·ɹtʃ,bēˑɹəɹ). One who carries a torch. Also *fig.*
1538 ELYOT, *Facularii*, torche bearers. 1596 SHAKS. *Merch. V.* ii. vi. 40 Descend, for you must be my torch-bearer. 1624 BEDELL *Lett.* xi. 140 As if all that are made Priests among you were Psalmists, Sextons, Readers, Exorcists, Torch-bearers, Subdeacons, and Deacons before. 1814 SCOTT *Ld. of Isles* ii. xxii, Twelve sandall'd monks, who reliques bore, With many a torch-bearer before. 1847 GROTE *Greece* ii. xxxii. IV. 272 The enterprising mariners who inhabited it had been the torch-bearers of Grecian geographical discovery in the west. 1853 DALE tr. *Baldeschi's Ceremonial* 189 The Torch-bearers having genuflected, consign their torches to the first they meet in choir.
So **To·rch-bea:ring** *sb.* and *a.*
1721 STRYPE *Eccl. Mem.* III. xxi. 175 There he saw torch-bearing in day-light, at mass. 1881 RUSKIN *Bible of Amiens* ii. 88 No torch-bearing maid of battle, like Clotilde.

Torched (tǭɹtʃt, *poet.* tǭ·ɹtʃėd), *a.* [f. TORCH *sb.* or *v.*¹ + -ED.] Furnished with a torch or torches; lighted with torches.
1819 KEATS *Isabella* xiv, In torched mines and noisy factories. 1901 *Harper's Mag.* CII. 774/1 Whirling six-foot sticks, torched at each end, in circles of fire.

Torcher¹ (tǭ·ɹtʃəɹ). [f. TORCH *v.*¹ + -ER¹.]
†**1.** One who gives light, as by carrying a torch. *Obs. rare*⁻¹.
1601 SHAKS. *All's Well* ii. i. 165 Ere twice the horses of the sunne shall bring Their fiery torcher his diurnall ring.
2. One who fishes by torch-light: see TORCH *v.*¹ 3. *U.S.* 1891 in *Cent. Dict.*

To·rcher². [f. TORCH *v.*² + -ER¹.] A workman employed in torching.
1851 TURNER *Dom. Archit.* I. 25 The wages of workmen.. as..mud-plasterers, torchers, excavators, and barrow-men.

‖**Torchère** (torʃę̄r). [Fr., f. *torche* TORCH.] A tall ornamental candlestick or lamp-stand.
1910 *Sale Catal.*, Boudoir and Bed-room Furniture, Louis XVI. carved console table,..pair Adam torchères.

†**To·rchet**. *Obs.* Also 5–6 -ett(e. [= OF. *torchete*, dim. of *torche*: in med.L. *torchetta* (1420 in Du Cange).] A small torch; also *fig.*
1470–1 *Mem. Ripon* (Surtees) III. 214 Nec r. de aliquo proficuo proveniente de torcheis sive torchettis consimili modo oblatis ad corpora mortuorum. 1497 in W. M. Williams *Ann. Founders' Co.* (1867) 48 Paid to the Wax-chandler for ij torchets weynt iij quarters, vj d. 1535 in *Rep. Hist. MSS. Comm., Var. Coll.* IV. 218 That then the said torches and torchettes to be in a redynes, light with convenyent berers. 1604 in *Househ. Ord.* (1790) 305 Mortores, Torchetts, Torches, Quarriours, Waxelights, Sizes, and Pricketts. 1614 GORGES *Lucan* vi. 429 Where Leos sparkling torchets are In enterchange with Cancers starre.

Torchless (tǭ·ɹtʃlės), *a.* [f. TORCH *sb.* + -LESS.] Without a torch; not lighted by a torch.
1814 BYRON *Lara* ii. xii, Consenting Night Guides with her star their dim and torchless flight. 1901 tr. *Hugo's Notre-Dame* (ed. Nelson) 388 Showing the interior of the Church..torchless and voiceless.

To·rch-li:ght. The light of a torch; illumination by a torch or torches.
c 1425 *Brut* ccxliii. 367 He was brouȝt to London on an hors beere, with myche torche lyghte. 1470–85 MALORY *Arthur* xvii. ii. 691 The mayde..armed hym by torche lyght. 1555 *Coventry Leet Bk.* 813 Euery of them to haue a man weyting vppon hym with torche-light. 1619 MIDDLETON *Love & Antiq.* Wks. (Bullen) VII. 329 His lordship returns by torchlight to his own house. 1726 POPE *Odyss.* xviii. 401 The shining baldness of his head survey, It aids our torch-light. 1855 MACAULAY *Hist. Eng.* xvi. III. 629 He made a final inspection of his forces by torchlight.
fig. 1847 WHITTIER *Lost Statesman* 25 Yet firmer hands shall Freedom's torchlights trim.
b. The time when torches are lighted; dusk.
a 1656 BP. HALL *Hard Meas.* Rem. Wks. (1660) 47 It now grew to be Torch-light. 1798 SOPH. LEE *Canterb. T., Yng. Lady's T.* II. 323, I faintly recollect, that it was torch-light.
c. *attrib.* Performed or carried on by torch-light.
1876 BANCROFT *Hist. U.S.* III. xix. 521 In the evening, a torch-light procession. 1884 *West. Morn. News* 15 Sept. 5/4 Lord Fife gave a torchlight ball at Mar Lodge.

‖**Torchon** (torʃoṅ). [F., f. *torcher* to wipe.] The French word for a duster or dish-cloth: used *attrib.* in **torchon board**, a board covered with *torchon paper*, used in water-colour drawing; **torchon lace** (also abbreviated *torchon*, pl. *-ons*), a coarse bobbin lace, of loose texture; **torchon mat**, a picture-frame mat (MAT *sb.*² 3) made of torchon paper; **torchon paper**, a kind of paper with a rough surface, used for water-colour drawing and for picture-frame mats.
1879 MRS. A. E. JAMES *Ind. Househ. Managem.* 10 But laces certainly would not, not even the 'Torchon' now so much in vogue: the very first wash they are torn, look ragged and unsightly. 1891 *Times* 1 Oct. 9/3 Operations in torchon and cheap Maltese laces are still on a small scale. 1908 *Athenæum* 16 Feb. 198/3 From Russian lace to torchon is not a wide step, but the latter is superior, shading off..into Maltese.

Torch-thistle (tǭ·ɹtʃ,þis'l). A name for a columnar cactus of the genus *Cereus*.
1731–3 MILLER *Gard. Dict.* s.v. *Cereus*, The Torch-Thistle. Call'd Cereus, because it is, as it were, a kind of taper or torch..because when these plants have been cut down and dry'd upon the ground, they dip them into oil, and burn them as torches. *Ibid.* s.v. *Greenhouse*, Euphorbiums, Torch-Thistles, and other tender succulent Plants. 1753 HOGARTH *Anal. Beauty* viii. 44 The indian-fig or torch-thistle,..as well as all that tribe of uncouth shaped exotics. 1884 MILLER *Plant-n.* 177 *Cereus*, Torch-thistle.

Torchwood, torch-wood (tǭ·ɹtʃ,wud).
1. (*torch-wood*) Resinous wood of which torches are made.
1601 HOLLAND *Pliny* xxiv. vii. II. 184 As for Tæda or Torch-wood, if it be sodden in vinegre, it maketh a singular collution for to wash the teeth withall when they ake. 1603 — *Plutarch's Mor.* 685 Trees tha. yeeld torch-wood and pitch, as pines, cone trees, and such like. 1842 BONAR & M'CHEYNE *Narr. Miss. to Jews* vi. (1843) 343 The Jews [there] are much employed in gathering and selling torch-wood.
2. (*Torchwood*) Name for several plants. **a.** A tree of the genus *Amyris*, N.O. *Rutaceæ*, having resinous wood, as *A. sylvatica* and *A. balsamifera*, of West Indies and Florida. **b.** A West Indian shrub, *Casearia* (*Thiodia*) *serrata*, N.O. *Samydaceæ*. **c.** A species of cactus, *Cereus heptagonus*.
1866 *Treas. Bot.*, Torchwood, *Cereus heptagonus*: also *Thiodia serrata*. Torchwood, Mountain, *Amyris balsamifera*. 1880 *Libr. Univ. Knowl.* (N.Y.) VI. 65 There are [in Florida] splendid flowering magnolias,..palmette, mangrove, torchwood.

Torchwort (tǭ·ɹtʃwɒɹt). [f. TORCH *sb.* + WORT.] The Mullein: = TORCH *sb.* 2 b, *torch-herb*.
1642 H. MORE *Song of Soul* i. ii. lix, At either end of this well raised sod A stately stalk shot up of Torchwort high.

Torchy (tǭ·ɹtʃi), *a. rare.* [f. TORCH *sb.* + -Y.] Full of torches; in which torches are used.
1629 F. LENTON *Gallant's Whirligigg* 16 All his spangled rare perfum'd attires, Which once so glistred in the Torchy Fryers, Must to the Broakers to compound his debt.

Torcion, Torcious: see TORSION, TORTIOUS.

‖**Torcular** (tǭ·ɹkiulǎɹ), *sb.* [L., a press for wine or oil; also an oil-cellar.]
1. *Anat.* (in full *torcular Herophili*) = *Press of Herophilus*: see PRESS *sb.*¹ 11 b.
1657 *Physical Dict.*, *Torcular*, a press. 1693 tr. *Blancard's Phys. Dict.* (ed. 2), *Torcular Herophili*, that place where the four Cavities of the thick Skin of the Brain [*Dura Mater*] are joyned. 1840 G. V. ELLIS *Anat.* 56 Its opening into the torcular Herophili is sometimes double. 1879 *St. George's Hosp. Rep.* IX. 152 A pus-laden clot extending to the neighbourhood of the torcular.
2. *Surg.* A TOURNIQUET.
1727–41 CHAMBERS *Cycl.*, *Torcular*, among chirurgions, a contrivance for stopping bleedings in amputations. 1860 MAYNE *Expos. Lex.*, *Torcular*..applied to the tourniquet.

To·rcular, *a.* [ad. L. *torculārius*, f. *torcular*: see prec. (In 2 arbitrary f. *torques*: see TORQUE¹.)]
1. *Anat.* Pertaining to or connected with the *torcular Herophili*: see prec. 1.
1656 BLOUNT *Glossogr.* s.v. *Vein*, *Torcular vein* (*vena torcularia*), the second branch of the outward throat vein. 1899 *Allbutt's Syst. Med.* VII. 602 Never plug the torcular end of the sinus if it can possibly be helped.
†**2.** Twisted, spiral, torqued. *Obs. rare*⁻¹.
1661 LOVELL *Hist. Anim. & Min.* Introd., The Turbinate have a torcular shell, out of the middest whereof commeth the head with two hornes.
So †**Torcula·rious**, *a. Obs. rare*⁻⁰. (See quots.)
1656 BLOUNT *Glossogr.*, *Torcularious*,..of, or belonging to a Presse that squieseth grapes. 1658 PHILLIPS, *Torcularious*, belonging to a Vine presse.

Tord, torde, obs. ff. TOWARD, TURD.

Tore (tōɹ), *sb.*¹ *Sc.* Also 6, 9 tor, 7 torre, 8 torr. [Origin uncertain: Welsh *torr* belly, bulge, boss, knob, has been compared.]
†**1.** An ornamental knob upon a piece of furniture, as a chair or a cradle. *Obs.*
1560 ROLLAND *Seven Sages* 56 Betuix thame twa, the Creddill ouir thay cast, With boddum vp, and on the Toris it stude ..That the four Toris sauit the Childis face. a 1572 KNOX *Hist. Ref.* iv. Wks. 1848 II. 404 The Quene..wes placeit in the chyre, baifing twa faithfull supportis, the Maister of Maxwell upoun the ane tor, and Secretour Lethingtoun on the uther tor of the chyre. a 1825 *Balankin* xi. in Child *Ballads* iv. (1886) 323/2 Till all the tores of the cradle wi the red blood down ran.
2. The pommel of a saddle. *rare* or *Obs.*
a 1671 SIR A. BALFOUR *Lett.* ii. (1700) 33 To Carry one.. in a Carpet Bag..tyed to the Tore of my Saddle. 1751 in Burton *Crim. Trials Scot.* (1852) I. 62 Placing her body across the horse upon the torr or forepart of the saddle. 1828 *Thomas o' Yonderdale* in Whitelaw *Scot. Ball.* (1874) 147/1 On the tor o' her saddle A courtly bird did sweetly sing.

Tore (tōᵊɹ), *sb.*² [a. F. *tore*, ad. L. *torus*.]
1. *Arch.* See quot. 1704; = TORUS 1.
1664 EVELYN tr. *Freart's Archit.*, etc. i. vii. 24 He thinks fit to deck the Tore's with I know not what delicate foliages. 1704 J. HARRIS *Lex. Techn.* I, *Tore*, and *Torus*..is that round Ring which encompasses in the Column, between the Plinth, and the List. This is the third Member of the Base of a Column. 1723 CHAMBERS tr. *Le Clerc's Treat. Archit.* I. 66 The preceding Orders..have two Tores. 1850 INKERSLEY *Roman. & Pointed Archit. in France* 182 A central tore flanked by a smaller parallel one.
2. *Geom.* = TORUS 4.
1867 TAIT *Quaternions* ix. § 322 An immediate proof of the very singular property of the ring (or tore) discovered by Villarceau. 1890 EAGLES *Descript. Geom.* 248 This surface is known as a tore or anchor ring.

Tore (tōᵊɹ), *sb.*³ *local.* Also toar (*Eng. Dial. Dict.*). [Origin unascertained.] Long coarse grass remaining in the field in winter or spring. Also *attrib.*
1707 MORTIMER *Husb.* (1721) I. 234 Which you must proportion according to the quantity of Rowen or Tore that you have upon the Ground; The more Tore you have, the less quantity of Hay will do. *Ibid.*, When your Tore is

quite eaten up, which it will commonly be about February, you must house your Milch-Cows, that you give Hay to in your Cow-house all Night. 1766 *Compl. Farmer*, *Tore*, rowen, or winter-grass. 1836 SIR G. HEAD *Home Tour* 253, I found fields over-run with coarse tore grass, in many parts blotchy and covered with thistles. 1904 in *Eng. Dial. Dict.* from Kent, Sussex, Surrey, Hampshire.

Tore, pa. t. and obs. and dial. pa. pple. of TEAR *v.*¹

Tore, *a. Obs.*: see TOR *a.*

‖**Toreador** (tǫriădōᵊɹ). Also 8 tauridore, tawridore, 8–9 torreadore, 9 torreador, tauridor, (tauréador). [Sp. *toreador* 'a bull-baiter' (Minsheu), mod.Sp. 'a bull-fighter on horseback'; so in Fr. The forms in *taur-* agree with earlier Fr. *tauréador* and with L. *taurus*.] One who engages in a (Spanish) bull-fight, esp. on horse-back; a bull-fighter.
1618 T. LORKIN in *Crt. & Times Jas. I* (1848) II. 82 The Conde de Cantilliana, that excellent Toreador, hath stolen away the wife of a Procurador de Corte. 1797 *Encycl. Brit.* (ed. 3) III. 771/1 When the price of the horses and bulls, and the wages of the Torreadores, have been paid. 1823 BYRON *Age of Bronze* vii, Up! up again! undaunted Tauridor! 1825 T. HOOK *Sayings* Ser. ii. *Passion & Princ.* xii. III. 263 As the Matador puts the finishing stroke to the ..victim of the lighter efforts of the Picadores and Torreadores who have preceded him. 1884 *Pall Mall G.* 3 June 3/2 The entertainment commenced with a flourish of trumpets as the tauréadors, five in number, marched in, bowed to the public, and ranged themselves.
¶ **b.** Erroneously used for 'bull-fight'. *Obs.*
1728 ? DE FOE *Capt. Carleton's Mem.* 304 A Diversion less to be complained of than their Tauridores; because attended with less Cruelty to the Beast, as well as Danger to the Spectator.
c. *attrib.*: esp. in fancy names of styles of women's hats or dresses.
1892 *Daily News* 14 Nov. 6/3 The Zouave is as great a favourite as it has been for some seasons, and though it varies in form—being sometimes a bolero, sometimes a toreador, and sometimes a cross between an Eton jacket and a Zouave. 1899 *Westm. Gaz.* 5 Oct. 3/2 The toreador toque is another very popular species just now—a toque, or really a hat, of rounded crown and rounded brim that is always much tilted to one side by a broad bandeau.

†**To-rea·ve**, *v.*¹ *Obs.* [f. TO-² + ME. *reve*, REAVE *v.*¹] **a.** *intr.* To commit robbery or plunder. **b.** *trans.* To rob, plunder, deprive by violence *of*.
13.. *Minor Poems fr. Vernon MS.* xxxvii. 515 Wel wynnen he may, But Robbe ne to-reue Nouþer niht ne day. 1393 LANGL. *P. Pl.* C. iv. 203 Religion hue [Law] al to-reueþ. 1563 *Mirr. Mag.* ii. Induct. R j b, We sawe.. pale death..to reve her of her breath.

†**To-reave**, *v.*² *Obs. rare.* Also 5 torafe. [f. TO-² + REAVE *v.*²] *trans.* To break, shiver, or tear in pieces.
a 1400 *Sir Beues* (E.) 2753+87 Hys helme, was al toreuyd, To gedere he ffastnyd on hys heuyd. c 1400 *Destr. Troy* 7629 Þe grym windes..al to rafet & rent all the riche clothes.

Torel, -elle, obs. forms of TOURELLE.

†**To·rely**, *adv. Obs.* [f. *tore*, TOR *a.* + -LY².] Stoutly, sturdily.
c 1400 *Destr. Troy* 8015 The Troiens, on the tothir syde torely withstode.

Toren, obs. f. *torn*, pa. pple. of TEAR *v.*¹

†**To-re·nd**, *v. Obs.* [OE. *torendan*, f. TO-² + *rendan* to REND. So OFris. *to-, te-renda.*] *trans.* To rend in pieces.
c 950 *Lindisf. Gosp.* Mark xiv. 63 Se heh ðonne sacerd torende woedo his. a 1000 *Ags. Ps.* (Th.) cxxiii[i]. 7 Grin bið on sadan grame torænded. a 1225 *Ancr. R.* 362 He.. þet to-tereð his olde kurtel, & to-rendeð þe olde pilche of his deadliche uelle. c 1330 R. BRUNNE *Chron. Wace* (Rolls) 2145 Lym fro lym hym al to-rent. 1388 WYCLIF *Matt.* xxvii. 51 The veil of the temple was to-rent in twey parties. — *Acts* xiv. 13 Whanne the apostlis..herden this, thei to-renten her cootis. 1430–40 LYDG. *Bochas* viii. xiii, Hir clothes to rent, bedewed with weepynge. 1596 DANETT tr. *Comines* (1614) 266 Their nauie all to rent and torne. 1631 WEEVER *Anc. Fun. Mon.* 306 He..plucked the other out of his place, and all to rent his casule, Chimer, and Rochet.
Hence †**To-re·nt** *ppl. a.*, †**To-re·nding** *vbl. sb.*
1388 WYCLIF *Isa.* xxxvi. 22 Eliachym..and Sobna..entriden with to-rent clothis to Ezechie. — *Nahum* iii. 1 Wo to the citee of bloodis, al of leesyng, ful of to-reendyng [*dilaceratione*].

†**To-re·nt**, *v. Obs.* [f. TO-² + RENT *v.*²] = TO-REND.
c 1410 *Master of Game* (MS. Digby 182) x, She altorenteth hem with hyr tethe. 1526 TINDALE *Matt.* vii. 6 Lest..the other tourne agayne and all to rent you. 1608 DOD & CLEAVER *Expos. Prov.* ix–x. 21 Christ saith, that hogs will all to rent them that so offer to feede them.

†**To-reo·se**, *v. Obs.* [OE. *to-hrēosan*, f. TO-² + *hrēosan*, REOSE (where see Forms).] *intr.* To fall to pieces, fall into ruins; to decay.
a 900 tr. *Bæda's Hist.* i. xi. [xiii.] (1890) 48 Monige oðre ceastre tohrorene wæron. a 1023 WULFSTAN *Hom.* xlix. (Napier) 263 Þonne bið..þa lichaman tohrorene and to duste ȝewordene. c 1205 LAY. 9245 Al heo gunnen toreosen. *Ibid.* 9426 Þus Port-chæstre to-ræs [c 1275 to-reos].

‖**Torero** (torē·ro). Also 8 tauriro. [Sp.] A (Spanish) bull-fighter (on foot). Cf. TOREADOR.
1728 ? DE FOE *Capt. Carleton's Mem.* 264 So that the poor Creature may be said to fight, not only with the Tauriro (or Bull-hunter..) but with the whole Multitude in the lower Class at least. *Ibid.* 267 The Tauriroes are very well paid. 1832 MACGILLIVRAY tr. *Humboldt's Trav.* xix. 287 They observe the manners of the crocodile as the torero studies those of the bull.

†**To-re·se**, *v.*¹ *Obs.* [ME. *to-ræsen, -reasen, -resen*, f. TO-² + *ræsen*, OE. *ræsan* to rush, RESE *v.*¹] *intr.* To make a violent assault or attack.
c 1205 LAY. 18682 Ofte heo to-ræsden [c 1275 hii to-resde]. *Ibid.* 26813 Bruttes heom to-ræsden. *Ibid.* 26964 Romleoden ræsden to [c 1275 to-reasde].

†**To-re·se**, *v.*² *Obs.* [ME. *to-rusien, to-rese*, f. TO-² + RESE *v.*²] *intr.* To shake, to quake; to be shaken to pieces.
c 1205 LAY. 15946 Þe eorðe gon to rusien & þi wal toreosen. c 1275 *Ibid.*, Þe eorþe gan to-cwakie and þin wal to-rese. a 1225 *Juliana* 58 Swa þat hit al to resde [*v.r.* to reasde].

†**Toret**, ? *pa. pple. Obs.* Of doubtful meaning.
13.. *Gaw. & Gr. Knt.* 960 Hir frount folden in sylk.. Toret & treieted with tryflez aboute.

Toret, -ett(e, obs. forms of TORRET, TURRET.

Toreumatography (torūmătǫ·grăfi). *rare*⁻⁰. [ad. med.L. *toreumatographia*, f. Gr. τόρευμα(τ-, embossed work, etc. (f. τορεύειν: see TOREUTIC) + -GRAPHY.] Description of the toreutic art, or of works done in it: see TOREUTIC. So **Toreumato·logy**, *rare*, the science or study of toreutics.
1727–41 CHAMBERS *Cycl.*, *Toreumatography*, a Greek term, signifying the knowledge, or rather description, of ancient sculptures, and basso-relievo's...The invention of *toreumatographia* is owing to Phidias, and its perfection to Polycletes. 1842 BRANDE *Dict. Sc.* etc., *Toreumatology*..signifies either the science or art of sculpture, or a description of ancient and modern sculpture and bas-relief. 1846 WORCESTER, *Toreumatography*, *Toreumatology* [cites *Brande*].

‖**Toreutes** (torū·tīz). [a. Gr. τορευτής, f. τορεύειν: see next.] A worker in toreutics; an artist in metal or ivory.
1840 tr. *C. O. Müller's Hist. Lit. Greece* xiii. § 15 *note*, Anacreon's advice to the toreutes, who is to make him a cup. 1847 LEITCH tr. *C. O. Müller's Anc. Art* § 85 *note*, The designation of toreutes hovers between cælator or enchaser and artist in gold and ivory. *Ibid.* § 173 The work of the toreutes..was especially prized in Etruria.

Toreutic (torū·tik), *a.* and *sb.* [ad. Gr. τορευτικός, f. τορεύειν to work in relief, etc.]
A. *adj.* Of or pertaining to toreutics (see B.); chiefly in phr. *toreutic art* = toreutics; also, of figures, etc., executed according to the toreutic art; of an artist, working in toreutics.
1837 *Antiq. Athens* 38 The Minerva of the Parthenon, also by Phidias, wrought in ivory and gold, the noblest example of the *toreutic* art. 1854 GANTILLON tr. *Propertius, Elegies* 87 *note*, *Mys.*—A toreutic artist who lived B.C. 444. 1874 *Edin. Rev.* July 187 The best toreutic representations of children are those of the Flemish artist du Quesnoy. 1910 D. G. HOGARTH in *Encycl. Brit.* I. 248/2 The..free sculpture and toreutic handiwork of Crete.
B. *sb.* [rendering Gr. τορευτική (sc. τέχνη) toreutic art: the Romanized form *toreuticē* occurs in 17th c. Eng. use]. Chiefly in pl. **Toreutics**: The art, esp. the ancient art, of working in metal or ivory, including embossing, work in relief, chasing, etc.
[1662 EVELYN *Chalcogr.* (1769) 16 Then the *toreuticē*..for I can only name them briefly.] 1847 LEITCH tr. *C. O. Müller's Anc. Art* § 85 This species of work..is reckoned as a branch of toreutics, by which is meant sculpture in metals..and also this combination of metal with other materials. 1900 *Year's Work Class. Stud.* 45 Pernice continues his notes on toreutic.

Torey (tōᵊ·ri), *a. nonce-wd.* [for *tory*, f. TORE *sb.*³ + -Y.] Of the nature of or consisting of 'tore' or coarse grass.
1893 *Blackw. Mag.* Mar. 392 The bleached torey grass of a sheltered hillside suits him.

Torf, obs. form of TURF.

Torfaceous (tǫɹfēⁱ·ʃəs), *a. Bot. rare.* [f. assumed mod.L. *torfa* TURF + -ACEOUS.] 'Growing in bogs or mosses' (*Treas. Bot.* 1866).

†**Torfer**. *Obs.* Forms: 4 torfere, (-phere), -fir, 4–5 -fer, -fare, 5 torfor, tourfer, torfoyr, *Sc.* torfeir. [Northern ME., a. ON. *tor-fǽra* fem., or *torfǽri* neut. (mod.Norw. *torføre*), a difficult or dangerous passage, f. *torfǽrr* adj. hard or difficult to pass, f. *tor-* TOR *a.* + *fǿr*, pret. stem of *fara* to go.] Hardship, trouble, distress; harm, mischief, injury.
13.. *Cursor M.* 6498 (Cott.) Þat he sal hald vs hale and fere, And warn vs fra ilkin tor-fere [*Fairf.* alkin torfere]. *Ibid.* 20002 Ful mani torfer [*Trin.* mony turment] sufferd þai. c 1325 *Metr. Hom.* (1862) 158 For than pin we our bodye, With torfir and with martyrye. ? a 1400 *Morte Arth.* 1956 That schalle turne the to tene and torfere for ever. a 1400–50 *Alexander* 3729 Quat tene & torfare may tide & tent to þine ende. c 1440 *York Myst.* xl. 174 Suche torfoyr and torment of-telle herde I neuere. c 1470 *Golagros & Gaw.* 876 Ye sall nane torfeir betyde, I tak vpone hand.

Torfle (tǭ·ɹf'l), *v. dial.* Also 7–9 -fell, 9 -fil. [Origin unascertained. Cf. TORPLE.] *intr.* To founder, go lame (? *obs.*); to decline in health, pine away, languish; *fig.* to lose interest in or draw back from an undertaking.
(Hogg's use of the word is vague.)
1575–6 *Durham Depos.* (Surtees) 285 This deponent..had an ox that torfled. 1818 HOGG *Brownie of B.*, etc. II. 149 It was reportit, that there was to be seen every morning at two a clock, a naked woman torfelling on the Alemoor loch, wi' her hands tied behind her back, and a heavy stane at her neck. 1820 — *Bridal of Polmood* viii, I..fleechyt Eleesabett nooie to let us torfell in the waretyme of owir raik [in the springtime of our life's journey]. 1825 — *Q. Hynde* i. 439 She saw him swathed in bloody red, And torfell'd on the monster's head. 1876 [see TORPLE 2].

To·rgant, *a. Her.* Also targant. [app. an erroneous form of *torquent*, L. *torquent-em*, or for TORQUED.] = TORQUED 2.
c 1828 BERRY *Encycl. Her.* I. Gloss., *Targant, Torgant*, or *Torqued*, bending and rebending, like the letter S. 1890 ELVIN *Dict. Her.*, *Targant*, see Torqued.

‖**Torgoch** (tǭ·ɹgǫχ). Also 7 torcoch; (*erron.*) 7 torcoth, 8 torgotch. [Welsh *torgoch*, f. *tor* belly + *coch* red.] The red-bellied char, a variety of the common char, found in the Welsh lakes.
1611 SPEED *Theat. Gt. Brit.* (1614) 123/2 In the poole Lin-Peris, there is a kinde of fish called there Torcoch, having a red belly, no where else seene. 1756 in *Gentl. Mag.* XXVI. 616/2 Torgotch, or Red-belly, which distinguishes the female. 1787 BEST *Angling* (ed. 2) 4 The English fishes that we have in our ponds, rivers, &c. are as follow: Umbla minor, Gesn. The Red Charr, or Welch Torgoch.

†**Torht**, *a. Obs.* [OE. *torht* bright, splendid, illustrious.] Bright, clear.
a 1000 *Phœnix* 96 Æþelast tungla...Torht tacen godes. 12.. *Prayer to our Lady* 20 in *OE. Misc.* 193 Mi brune her is iwit bicume..& mi to[r]hte rude iturnd al in-to oðre debe.

Tori, pl. of TORUS.

Toric (tǭ·rik), *a.* [f. TOR-US + -IC.] Of or pertaining to a torus (see TORUS 4); having the form of a torus or a portion of one.
1900 *Buck's Handbk. Med. Sc.* I. 595 A concave spherical combined with a convex toric surface.

Torify: see TORYFY.

Toriness, toryness (tōᵊ·rinės). *nonce-wd.* [f. TORY *a.* + -NESS.] Tory quality or condition.
1890 *Sat. Rev.* 12 Apr. 425/1 Mr. Gladstone deplored the Toriness of Hertfordshire.

Torism, obs. form of TORYISM.

†**To-ri·t**, *v. Obs.* [ME., f. TO-² + *ritten*, RIT *v.*¹] *trans.* To cut or tear asunder.
13.. *Orfeo* (Auchinleck MS.) 43 Hir riche robe hye al to rett [*Ashm. MS.* to-rytte] And was remeyd out of hir witt.

†**To-ri·ve**, *v. Obs.* [ME., f. TO-² + RIVE *v.*¹]
1. *trans.* To rive or tear asunder; to split open, cleave. Also *fig.*
c 1300 *Havelok* 1953 Hwo haues the thus ille maked. Thus to-riuen, and al mad naked? 13.. *K. Alis.* 6216 (Bodl. MS.) Schippes..Ful ycharged of her clay, Þat men clepeþ Butumay, Þat water non ne may to Ryue Ne irne ne steel ne metal to dryue. 13.. *E. E. Allit. P.* A. 1196 Þer-for my ioye watz sone to-riuen. *Ibid.* C. 379 His ryche robe he to rof of his rigge naked. 13.. *Sir Beues* (A.) 2159 Þat hors.. His rakenteis he al te-rof. c 1400 *Destr. Troy* 1234 The king..the rod all-to roofe right to his honde. 1470–85 MALORY *Arthur* i. xxviii. 75 The shyp..was al to ryuen.
2. *intr.* To burst asunder; to split, cleave, splinter, shiver.
c 1275 LAY. 7844 Mani sip al to-rof. c 1330 R. BRUNNE *Chron.* (1810) 170 Þat schip salle alle toryue. 1390 GOWER *Conf.* III. 296 The mast tobrak, the Seil torof. c 1440 *York Myst.* xiii. 153 Was neuer wight sa wa, for ruthe I all to ryff. c 1470 HENRY *Wallace* ii. 52 The tre to raiff & fruschit euiredeille. 1470–85 MALORY *Arthur* viii. xxxviii. 330 A wynde drofe hem..vpon this yle of seruage..and there the Barget all to rofe.

Tork, variant of TORQUE¹.

Torkes, var. TURKIS *v. Obs.*, to distort, alter.

Tormaline, Tormarith, obs. ff. TOURMALINE, TURMERIC.

Torment (tǭ·ɹmĕnt), *sb.* Forms: 3–6 turment, (4 -te), tourment, (5–6 -te), 3– torment, (*pl.* 3–4 -menz, -mens). (Also β. 5 tornament, tourne-, turna-, turnement, 6 tornement.) [ME. a. OF. *tor-, tourment*, ONF. *turment* (11th c.) = It., Sp., Pg. *tormento*:—L. *torment-um* (:—**torqu(e)mentum* something operated by twisting, f. *torquēre* to twist). In sense 5, a. F. *tourmente* fem. from L. *tormenta* neut. pl., which became fem. sing. in Romanic, sometimes with final *-e* in ME. The β-forms show confusion with TOURNAMENT.]
†**1.** An engine of war worked by torsion, for hurling stones, darts, or other missiles. *Obs.*
1382 WYCLIF 1 *Macc.* vi. 51 And ordeynede there balistis, and engynes, and dartis, or castyngis, of fyr, and tourmentis for to cast stoons and dartis. 1398 TREVISA *Barth. De P. R.* xviii. ix. (Bodl. MS.), Regulus þe Emperoure slowe an addre..þat was xx. fote longe wiþ alblastes and tormentes. 1531 ELYOT *Gov.* i. viii, All turmentes of warre, whiche we cal ordinance. [1866 J. B. ROSE tr. *Ovid's Met.* 229 Like the bolt from the tormentum cast, Smiting the wall.]
2. An instrument of torture, as the rack, wheel, or strappado (*rare* or *doubtful*); hence, the infliction of torture by such an instrument as a form of punishment, a means of extracting information, etc.; torture inflicted or suffered.
c 1290 *S. Eng. Leg.* I. 84/33 Heo bad ore louerd..þat he ire ȝeue þere Studefaste bi-leue..And in hire tormenz treowe heorte. c 1300 *Seyn Julian* 49 Þe more turment þat hi hire dude þe bet hi hire paide. 1340 *Ayenb.* 166 We redeþ of zaynte Agase, þet mid greate blisse hi yede to torment alsuo ase hi yede to feste. c 1384 CHAUCER *H. Fame* i. 445 And euery turment eke in helle Saugh he. 1413 *Sat. agst. Lollards* 113 in *Pol. Poems* (Rolls) II. 246 And namly James among hem alle, For he twyes had turnement. 1483 CAXTON *Gold. Leg.* 289/2 He dyde doo strayne and payne them in the torment of Eculee. 1494 FABYAN *Chron.* iv. lxviii. 46 [Mexencius] pursued ye Christen with all kynde of turment. 1550–1 *Acts Privy Counc.* (1891) III. 230 Order shalbe given that he may be sent up hither to be put to tornement. 1610 SHAKS. *Temp.* i. ii. 289 It was a torment To lay upon the damn'd. 1668 CULPEPPER & COLE *Barthol. Anat.* iv. ii. 161 That torment which the Italians call *Tratta de corda*, the Strappado. 1709 J. JOHNSON *Clergym. Vade M.* ii. 169 Those who had done sacrifice thro' the violence of torment in time of persecution. 1725 POPE *Odyss.* ix. 454 They swift let fall The pointed torment on his visual ball.
b. *spec.* The punishment of hell.
1852 MRS. STOWE *Uncle Tom's C.* xviii, 'I knows I'm gwine to torment', said the woman, sullenly.
3. A state of great suffering, bodily or mental; agony; severe pain felt or endured.
c 1290 *Beket* 434 in *S. Eng. Leg.* I. 119 So þat þe preost was i-brouȝt In tormenz bi þe meste. 13.. *Guy Warw.* (A.) 325 Thus ne lay in grete turment, Til þat þe fest was al to-went. c 1386 CHAUCER *Knt.'s T.* 440 That doubleth al my torment [*v.r.* turment] and my wo. c 1489 CAXTON *Sonnes of Aymon* i. 34 Ye haue broughte me in grete sorowe and tournement irrecouerable. 1500–20 DUNBAR *Poems* lxxvi. 6 A schoirt torment for infineit glaidnes. 1590 SPENSER *F. Q.* i. x. 28 In which his torment often was so great, That like a Lyon he would cry and rore. 1732 POPE *Let. to Swift* 5 Dec., In acute torment by the inflammation in his bowels and breast. 1861 KINGSLEY *Lett.* (1878) II. 134 The feeling of being always behind-hand ..is second only in torment to that of debt.
†**b.** *spec.* A griping or wringing pain in the bowels: = TORMINA. *Obs.*
1578 LYTE *Dodoens* ii. xcii. 273 The seede of Ameos is very good against the griping payne and torment of the belly. c 1610 *Women Saints* 112 She..endured moste sharpe payne and torment of stomacke. 1688 R. HOLME *Armoury* ii. 172/1 Swelling and Torment in the Belly [of Cows] ..if not speedily helped, is Death to the Beast.
4. An action, circumstance, or condition which causes extreme pain or suffering of body or mind; a source of pain, trouble, or anguish, or in weakened sense, of worry or annoyance.
1599 SHAKS. *Much Ado* ii. iii. 130 No, and sweares she neuer will, that's her torment. 1611 B. JONSON *Catiline* v. vi, Why, death's the end of evils, and a rest Rather than torment. 1789 MRS. PIOZZI *Journ. France* II. 364 Want of language, our still recurring torment. 1825 T. HOOK *Sayings* Ser. ii. *Passion & Princ.* vii. III. 102 The conviction that he had made himself absurd..was his torment. 1841 HELPS *Ess.*, *Aids Contentm.* (1842) 13 A habit of mistrust is the torment of some people.
b. Applied to a person who causes trouble. Cf. PLAGUE *sb.* 2 c.
1784 COWPER *Task* iv. 632 That instant he [a recruit] becomes the serjeant's care, His pupil, and his torment, and his jest. 1873 'OUIDA' *Pascarèl* I. 32 They were the pride and torment of Mariuccia's life. 1881 'RITA' *Lady Coquette* i, Will you be quiet, you torment.
c. In jocular use: An instrument of irritation or annoyance: = TORMENTOR 3 f. (In quot. *attrib.*)
1882 *Daily News* 30 May 2/1 The Vale of Health was.. the most frequented spot of all,..the 'torment' and squirt fun rather too buoyant.
5. A violent storm; a tempest, tornado. *Obs.* (exc. in Fr. form *tourmente*).
a 1300 *Fragm. Pop. Sc.* (Wright) 184 For þeras the weder is, þer is turment strong Of wynd, of water, and of fur. c 1330 R. BRUNNE *Chron.* (1810) 148 In to þe se of Spayn wer dryuen in a torment. 1471 CAXTON *Recuyell* (Sommer) 540 Ther roose so a grete torment in the see [*orig.* si grant tormente leva de vent]. 1530 PALSGR. 282/1 Torment a storme on the see, *tourmente, tempeste*. 1604 E. G[RIMSTONE] *D'Acosta's Hist. Indies* iii. xxvi. 199 Vpon the coast of Peru, there be no torments from heauen, as thunder and lightning. [1847 G. B. CHEEVER *Wand. Pilgr.* xii. 90 The fury of these tourmentes is inconceivable. 1909 *Blackw. Mag.* Sept. 341/1, I reached it..in a more than usually objectionable tourmente of snow.]
6. *attrib.* and *Comb.*, as *torment-house, robe*.
1649 J. E[LLISTON] tr. *Behmen's Epist.* v. 62 Being in the torment-house of the stars. 1846 T. AIRD *Poet. Wks.* (1856) 240 With torment-pointed threatenings. 1890 E. HATCH *Fields of Light* 55 Saints who were wafted to the skies In the torment robe of flame.

Torment (tǫɹme·nt), *v.* Forms: see prec. sb.; also 5 *pa. pple.* (*contr.*) tor-, turment. [a. OF. *tor-, turmenter* (12th c.), *tourmenter*, f. *tor-, turment* sb.: cf. med.L. *tormentāre*, f. *tormentum*, Pr. *turmentar*, Sp. *tormentar*, It. *tormentare*.]
1. *trans.* To put to torment or torture; to inflict torture upon.
c 1290 *St. Edmund* 181 in *S. Eng. Leg.* I. 436 Fiet and hondene þat neren nouȝt i-tormentede with þat here Necke and face and al is heued. c 1300 *St. Brandan* 595 Oure maister ous hath i-turmented so grisliche allonge niȝt. 1382 WYCLIF *Rev.* xiv. 10 This..shal be tourmentid [1388 turmentid] with fijr and brunston. c 1440 *Alphabet of Tales* 177 When a devull had turment horrebly a man þat he was in. 1475 *Bk. Noblesse* (Roxb.) 66 They turmentid hym in prison in the most cruelle wise to dethe. 1560 DAUS tr. *Sleidane's Comm.* 168 To moue the Frenche kynge, that innocente persones be not tormented, for Religion. 1651 HOBBES *Leviath.* iii. xxxviii. 238 For what offences..men are to be Eternally tormented.
2. To afflict or vex with great suffering or misery, physical or mental; to pain, distress, plague.
1297 R. GLOUC. (Rolls) 4920+36 Seynt Petur to hym come, as þe slep hym toke, & tormented hym sore ynou. 1382 WYCLIF *Acts* v. 33 Whanne thei herden thes thingis, thei weren turmentid, and thouȝten for to sle hem. c 1480 *Chron. Vilod.* 2302 Þo whyche was wᵗ sekenesse so tourmentyd. a 1450 *Knt. de la Tour* (1906) 41 The pepille that were.. oute of her mynde and turmented. 1514 BARCLAY *Cyt. & Uplondyshm.* (Percy Soc.) 6 Whan the northe wynde.. Hath brought cold wynter pore wretches to turment. a 1548 HALL *Chron.*, *Rich. III* 28 b, What ys he..that wil not..be moued & tormented with pitie and mercie? 1713 STEELE *Englishm.* No. 48. 308 Great Evils..torment the Life of Man. 1804 *Med. Jrnl.* XII. 143 A disease which had tormented me for sixteen years. 1856 [see TORMENTING *ppl. a.*].

b. In lighter sense: To tease or worry excessively; to trouble, 'plague'.
1718 LADY M. W. MONTAGU *Let. to Abbé Conti* 19 May, We are tormenting our brains with some scheme of politics. 1862 MAURICE *Mor. & Met. Philos.* IV. vii. § 44. 373 He tormented the Rabbins with questions.
†**3.** To throw into agitation; to toss, disturb, shake up, or stir physically. *Obs.* (exc. as a Gallicism).
1491 CAXTON *Vitas Patr.* (W. de W. 1495) ii. 246 Lyke.. raymentes when the foller fulleth them & tourmenteth them often vnder his fete. a 1533 LD. BERNERS *Huon* xlvi. 156 The shyppe was so sore tormentyd, that the shyppe brast all to peces. 1667 MILTON *P. L.* vi. 243 That warr..then soaring on main wing Tormented all the Air; all Air seemed then Conflicting Fire. 1784 COWPER *Task* ii. 101 The fixed and rooted earth, Tormented into billows, heaves and swells. 1822 [see TORMENTED *ppl. a.*]. 1908 *Academy* 27 June 927/2 After madame had 'tormented' the ingredients—the salad was a dish from fairyland.
b. *fig.* To twist, distort (sense, style, etc.).
1647 HAMMOND *Power of Keys* iii. 26 Sure this is to pervert and torment the sense. a 1680 BUTLER *Rem.* (1759) I. 230 And pay 'em for tormenting Texts. 1895 *Daily News* 18 Oct. 4/7 In Mr. Pater we had a writer of singular natural gifts, who..ended by embroiling and tormenting his style.
Hence **Torme·nted** *ppl. a.* (whence **Torme·ntedly** *adv.*); also **Torme·ntable** *a.*, capable of being tormented, susceptible of torment; †**Tormenta·tion** *Obs.*, tormenting, torment; †**Torme·ntative**, †**Torme·ntive** *adjs. Obs.*, that torments, tormenting.
1876 EMERSON *Ess.*, *Circles* Wks. (Bohn) II. 263 The great man is not convulsible or *tormentable. 1789 A. C. BOWER *Diaries & Corr.* (1903) 53, I shall have no more *Tormentations. 1654 GAYTON *Pleas. Notes* iii. viii. 124 From Furies, and things worse *tormentative. 1552 HULOET, *Tourmented, *cruciatus, excruciatus*. 1686 HORNECK *Crucif. Jesus* v. 72 A fiery serpent..a symbol of God's presence and power to heal the tormented Israelites. 1808 G. EDWARDS *Pract. Plan* iii. 16 Evils, which our tormented imaginations apprehend. 1822 SCOTT *Pirate* vii, More than once, large fragments..gave way before him, and thundered down into the tormented ocean. 1891 *Longm. Mag.* Mar. 531 She was going to break out *tormentedly, pleadingly: 'For God's sake tell me!' 1653 F. G. tr. *Scudery's Artamenes* viii. i. (1655) IV. 3 His presence is so *tormentive unto me.

†**To·rmentful**, *a. Obs.* [f. TORMENT *sb.* + -FUL.] Full of, or fraught with torment.
1596 R. L[INCHE] *Diella* (1877) 30 My most tormentfull case. 1647 TRAPP *Comm. Matt.* vi. 31 Carefulness is a tormentful plodding upon businesses. a 1694 TILLOTSON *Wks.* (1717) II. 199 In what Nature soever they [malice, envy, revenge] are, they are as vexatious and tormentful to it self, as they are troublesome and mischievous to others.

Tormentil (tǭ·ɹmĕntil). Forms: 5 tormentille, -ylle, 6 -yll, 6–8 -ill, -ile, (8 tormentle), 6– tormentil; 5 turmentylle, 5–6 -ill, 6 -yll. [= F. *tormentille* (1314 in Hatz.-Darm.), ad. med.L. *tormentilla*, in form dim. of *tormentum*: see TORMENT *sb.* Reason of name obscure: cf. quot. 1616; according to others from its being used to relieve the gripes, L. *tormina*.] A low-growing herb, *Potentilla Tormentilla* (*Tormentilla repens*), N.O. *Rosaceæ*, of trailing habit, common on heaths and dry pastures, bearing small four-petalled yellow flowers, and having strongly astringent roots; in use from early times in medicine, and in tanning. Also called *septfoil*.
[a 1387 *Sinon. Barthol.* (Anecd. Oxon.) 42/1 Tormentilla pilos, pentafilon non habet ullos.] a 1400–50 *Stockh. Med. MS.* 6 Water of turmentill. 1530 PALSGR. 284/1 Turmentyll an herbe, *tourmentine*. 1578 LYTE *Dodoens* i. lvii. 83 Tormentill is much like vnto Sinckefoyle. 1610 FLETCHER *Faithf. Sheph.* ii. i, This Tormentil, whose vertue is to part All deadly killing poyson from the heart. 1616 SURFL. & MARKH. *Country Farme* 204 Called Tormentill, because the powder or decoction of the root doth appease the rage and torment of the teeth. 1698 M. MARTIN *Voy. St. Kilda* (1749) 56 Their Leather is tanned with the roots of Tormentil. 1906 *Daily Chron.* 4 May 6/7 Tormentil and potentil, names fulfilled of pleasure, Set the world in tune again with the May Day measure.
b. *attrib.*, as *tormentil-root*.
1712 tr. *Pomet's Hist. Drugs* I. 43 The best Tormentil Roots come from grassy, wet Places about the Alps and Pyrenees. 1811 A. T. THOMSON *Lond. Disp.* (1818) 400 Tormentil root is a powerful astringent.
So †**To·rmentine** [from F.] in same sense.
14.. *Nom.* in Wr.-Wülcker 713/6 *Hec tormentilla*, tormentyne [cf. 1530 PALSGR. above].

Torme·nting, *vbl. sb.* [f. TORMENT *v.* + -ING¹.] The action of the verb TORMENT; torturing, vexing; an instance of this.
c 1290 *S. Eng. Leg.* I. 12/389 His soule wende to þe Joye of heouene After is tormentingue. 1382 WYCLIF *Isa.* xiii. 8 Tormentingus and sorewes thei shul holde. 1535 COVERDALE *Wisd.* ii. 19 Let vs examen him with despitefull rebuke and tormentinge, that we maye knowe his dignite & proue his pacience. 1633 P. FLETCHER *Elisa* ii. iv, So sat she, as when speechlesse griefs tormenting Locks up the heart. 1884 *Athenæum* 6 Dec. 732/2 [They] suffer from no fancied ills and self-conscious tormentings.

Torme·nting, *ppl. a.* [f. as prec. + -ING².] That torments, in various senses of the verb.
1575 [implied in TORMENTINGLY]. 1594 SHAKS. *Rich. III*, i. iii. 226 While some tormenting Dreame Affrights thee. 1637 PRYNNE *Passages Star Chamb.* in *Harl. Misc.* (1809) IV. 234 Let me be put to the tormentingest death they can devise. 1667 MILTON *P. L.* iv. 505 Sight hateful, sight tormenting! 1780 *Mirror* No. 74 ᴾ 9 Haunted with the most tormenting thoughts. 1856 KANE *Arct. Expl.* II. viii. 87 The eruption, a tormenting and anomalous symptom.
Hence **Torme·ntingly** *adv.*; **Torme·ntingness**.
1575 GASCOIGNE *Dan Barthol. of Bathe* Wks. 1907 I. 105 He bounst and bet his head tormentingly. 1727 BAILEY vol. II, *Tormentingness*, tormenting Quality or Faculty. 1857 *Chamb. Jrnl.* VII. 397 Visits were tormentingly delayed.

†**Tormenti·se**. *Obs.* Torment, torture.
c 1386 CHAUCER *Monk's T.* 527 But nathelees this Seneca the wise Chees in a Bath to dye in this manere Rather than han any oother tormentise.

Tormentor (tǫɹme·ntəɹ). Also 5–9 -er. [ME. and AF. *tormentour* = OF. *tor-, tourmenteur*, earlier *-teour, -teor* (c 1150 in Godef.):—L. type **tormentātōr-em*, agent-n. from *tormentāre* to TORMENT.] One who or that which torments.
1. An officer who inflicts torture or cruelty; an official torturer; an executioner. Also *transf.*
c 1290 *St. Edmund* 43 in *S. Eng. Leg.* I. 298 His luþere tormentores þat beoten him so sore. a 1350 *St. Andrew* 171 in Horstm. *Altengl. Leg.* (1881) 6 Þe turmentours.. Toke his bodi with bitter brayde, Vnto þe cros þai gun it bend. 1382 WYCLIF *Matt.* xviii. 34 His lord wroth, tok hym to tourmentours [1388 turmentouris; 1582 (Rhem.) tormenters; 1611 tormentors], til that he paiede al the dette. 1483 CAXTON *Gold. Leg.* 185 b/2 The tormentour as he had smyten of his heed both his eyen sterte out of his heed. 1513 MORE *Rich. III* (1883) 79 He that playeth the sowdayne is percase a sowter. Yet if one should..calle him by his owne name.., one of his tormentors might hap to breake his [= one's] head. 1581 PETTIE *Guazzo's Civ. Conv.* i. (1586) 25 Such, who..are holden for infamous, as Sergeants, Hangmen, Tormentours. 1895 RIDER HAGGARD *Hrt. of World* xxv, That your souls be handed over to the tormentors of the under-world.
2. One who or that which persistently inflicts intense pain, suffering, vexation, or annoyance.
In quot. 1642 *humorously*: = TEASER¹ 2.
1553 BECON *Reliques of Rome* (1563) 199 They dissent both in the tormentours and in the tormentes of the soules. 1593 SHAKS. *Rich. II*, ii. i. 136 These words hereafter, thy tormentors bee. 1642 MILTON *Apol. Smect.* Pref., Wks. 1851 III. 274 Certainly this tormentor of Semicolons is as good at dismembring and slitting sentences. 1712 ADDISON *Spect.* No. 447 ᴾ 10 They will naturally become their own Tormentors. 1751 *Affecting Narr. of Wager* 84 The Prospect of that horridest Tormenter, Famine, [was] continually before our Eyes. 1846 J. BAXTER *Libr. Pract. Agric.* (ed. 4) I. 419 A host of tormentors, in the shape of flies,..persecuting the poor animal. 1897 'OUIDA' *Massarenes* viii, The person whose instructress and tormentor she was.
3. An instrument that torments in some way.
†**a.** Some device for catching fleas. *Obs.* **b.** *pl.* A long-handled fork used for taking the meat from the coppers on board ship; also, *Sc.* 'an implement on which to toast bannocks, etc.' (*E.D.D.*); in quot. 1866 (*sing.*), a piercing implement carried by excise officers. **c.** A wheel-harrow of which each tine is a small share or hoe, for breaking up stiff soil. **d.** *pl.* A slang name for riding-spurs. **e.** *Theatre.* (See quots.) **f.** A device used to annoy at pleasure-fairs: cf. TICKLER 2 b, SCRATCH-BACK 2. *colloq.*
a. 1609 HEYWOOD *Rape of Lucrece*, *Cries of Rome* Wks. 1874 V. 254 Buy a very fine Mouse-trap, or a tormentor for your Fleaes. 1614 B. JONSON *Barth. Fair* ii. iv. a 1619 FLETCHER *Bonduca* ii. iii, *Daughter.* Are they not our Tormentors? *Car.* Tormentors? flea-traps! 1622 J. TAYLOR (Water P.) *Trav. Twelve-pence* (1635) B vij b, Of MowseTraps, and tormentors to kill Fleas. **b.** 1706 E. WARD *Wooden World Diss.* (1708) 84 He [a sea-cook] is never without a Pair of Tormentors in his Hand. 1823 GALT *Gilhaize* I. ii. 22 Toasting an oaten bannock on a pair of tormentors. 1866 FITZPATRICK *Sham Sqr.* 18 Sham made a violent pass at Peck with his tormentor. 1898 F. T. BULLEN *Cruise Cachalot* 186 The cook uncovered his coppers, plunged his tormentors therein, and produced such a succession of ugly corpses of fowls as I had never seen before. **c.** 1807 VANCOUVER *Agric. Devon* (1813) 121 Scarifiers, scufflers, shims, and broad-shares of various constructions,..called under the general name of tormentors. 1882 JAGO *Cornw. Gloss.*, *Tormentor*, an agricultural implement for breaking up the clods of a ploughed field. **d.** 1875 WHYTE MELVILLE *Riding Recoll.* iv. (1879) 59 Fordham..wholly repudiates 'the tormentors', arguing that they only make a horse shorten his stride, and 'shut up'. **e.** 1886 *Stage Gossip* 70 The 'tormentor' is the name for a door, placed in the R. I. E. and L. I. E., and which prevents anybody from obtaining a view of the performance from either of the entrances named, and also prevents the actor being seen by the 'house'—these doors are annoying at times. 1893 *N. York Herald* 25 Dec. 26/2 (Funk) The first wing has been known to the stage as 'tormentor' wing from time whereof memory of man runneth not to the contrary. 1898 *Westm. Gaz.* 12 Jan. 9/3 A strip of white bunting is waved by a master of the ceremonies from a wooden hutch in the 'tormentor' wing. **f.** 1891 in *Cent. Dict.* 1903 FARMER & HENLEY *Slang Dict.*, *Tormentor*..3 (common), a back-scratcher.

†**Torme·ntous**, *a. Obs. rare.* [f. L. *torment-um* TORMENT + -OUS: cf. OF. *tormentos*.] Of tormenting nature; torturing. Hence †**Torme·ntously** *adv.*
1583 STOCKER *Civ. Warres Lowe C.* ii. 47 His body being trysed vp into the ayre with a tormentous [*printed* tormentrous] Engine, they bynd to his feete instruments of Yron. 1657 THORNLEY tr. *Longus' Daphnis & Chloe* 195 Astylus was not to learn that Love was a tormentous fire. 1669 *Address Hopeful Yng. Gentry Eng.* 87 Why so tormentously [do they] rend their weary throats?
So †**Torme·ntuous** *a.* [ad. late L. *tormentuōsus*.]

TORMENTRESS.

Tormentress (tǫˑmĕntrĕs), *sb.* AF. *tormentrice*, fem. of *tormentour* TORMENTOR. A female tormentor.

Tormentry. Now rare. [f. TORMENT + -RY.] †1. A company or body of tormentors or executioners. *Obs.* [Cf. *Jewry*, *yeomanry*.] †2. The infliction or suffering of torture or torment, as by executioners or fiends. *Obs.*

3. Tormenting feeling; severe suffering, pain, or vexation. Now rare.

Hence **Tormentry** *a., pl. Path.* [L. *tormina* gripes, griping of the bowels, pl. of *tormen*, *f. torquere* to twist.] 1. *Anat.* griping or wringing pains in the bowels; gripes. Also *fig.*

Hence **Tor·minal**, **Tor·minous** *adjs.*, of the nature of or characterized by tormina; affected with tormina.

Tormit, tinal, form of TURNIP.

Tormodont (tǫˑmǫdǫnt), *a. Ornith.* [f. Gr. τόρμο·ς hole, socket + ὀδούς, ὀδόντ- tooth.] Of a tooth or teeth: Set each in a separate socket or alveolus, as in certain fossil birds; of a bird: having socketed teeth.

Tormoyl, obs. form of TURMOIL.

Torn (tǫin), *ppl. a.* [pa. pple. of TEAR *v.*1], *v.* for Forms.] Rent or riven by being violently rended; wearing torn garments.

Hence **Tor·minal** *a.*, of or characterized by tormina; affected with tormina.

Tornada (tǫinæ·da), *sb. pl. Path. Also 7 tornathe.* Anglicized form of TORNADE.

†Torna·de. *Obs. rare. Also 7 tornathe.* Anglicized form of TORNADE.

Tornadic (tǫinæ·dik), *a.* [f. next + -IC.] Of, pertaining to, or of the nature of a tornado.

Tornado (tǫinēˑdō). Forms: (6-7 tornado), 7- tornado; also 7 turnado, 7 tornatho, tornada, 8 tournado). See also TORNADE. 1. A violent storm of wind or thunder.

Tornal, var. TORNUS.

Tornaria (tǫinēˑria), *sb. Zool.* [mod.L., f. L. *tornus* a turner's wheel.] The larval form of species of the Sea-acorn, *Balanoglossus*. Hence **Torna·rian** *a.*, of or pertaining to a tornaria.

†Tornati, *a. Obs. rare.* [See *quot.*] Tossed, or made with a wheel.

Torne·y, obs. form of TOURNEY, TURN.

Torne, obs. f. TORN, TOURN, TURN.

Torose (tǫirōs·), *a. Nat. Hist.* [ad. L. *torōsus*, f. *torus* TORUS.] Bulging, swollen, protuberant; esp. of an approximately cylindrical body swollen here and there.

Torosity (tǫirǫˑsiti), *sb. rare.* torose condition.

Torous (tǫˑrəs), *a. [L. torōs-us TOROSE.* as if through f. *torōsus* see -OUS.] = TOROSE.

Tor-ousel: see TOR-SEL.

†Torpedinal (tǫipēˑdinăl), *a. Obs. rare.* [f. *torpēdin-em*, TORPEDO + -AL.] Of or pertaining to the torpedo or electric ray.

Torpedineer (tǫipēdĭniǝ·), *sb. rare.* [a. pr. *-KER* : cf. *engineer.*] One who is engaged in the management of marine torpedoes.

Torpedinidæ (tǫipēdĭnĭˑdē), *sb. pl. Zool.* [mod.L., f. *torpēdin-em*, see TORPEDO + -IDÆ.] A family of fishes of which the torpedo or electric ray belongs to the *Torpedinoidea* or *Torpedinidæ* considered as a group distinct from the true rays and the skate-fishes.

Torpedinous (tǫipēˑdinəs), *a. rare.* [Obs.] Having the quality of a torpedo; benumbing, paralysing; also *fig.*

Torpedo (tǫipīˑdō), *sb.* 6-ido. Pl. -oes. [a. L. *torpēdo* stiffness, numbness, also the cramp-fish or electric ray, f. *torpēre* to be stiff or numb. — Sp., Pg. *torpedo*. Cf. F. *torpille.*] 1. A flat fish of the genus *Torpedo* or family

TORPEDO BOAT.

Torpe·do boat. A vessel carrying one or more torpedoes; now a small, fast war-ship from which torpedoes are discharged. Hence **Torpedoboat** *v.* (*nonce-wd.*), *trans.* to furnish or arm with torpedo boats.

Torpefy (tǫˑpifai), *v. rare.* [ad. L. *torpe-facĕre*, f. *torpēre* to be numb + *facĕre* to make.] *trans.* To render torpid, benumb, deaden, paralyse. Also *fig.* Hence **Tor·pefying** *ppl. a.*

Torpent (tǫˑpənt), *a.* and *sb. rare.* [ad. L. *torpent-em*, pr. pple. of *torpēre* to be sluggish.]

Torpescent (tǫipĕˑsənt), *a. rare.* [ad. L. *torpēscent-em*, pr. pple. of *torpēscĕre* inceptive of *torpēre* to be numb.] Becoming torpid; becoming numb. Hence **Torpe·scence** *sb.*

Torpid (tǫˑpid), *a.* [ad. L. *torpidus*, f. *torpēre* to be numb.] 1. Benumbed; deprived or devoid of the power of motion or feeling; in which activity, animation, or development is suspended; dormant.

Torpidity (tǫipiˑditi), *sb.* [f. prec. + -ITY.] The condition or quality of being torpid; torpor, sluggishness, numbness.

Torpitude (tǫˑpitiud), *sb. rare.* [Irregularly for *torpitude*, f. L. *torpēre* + -TUDE: the L. form, if existent, would be *torpitudo*: cf. *consuētūdo*, *habitūdo*.] Torpidity.

Torque (tǫik), *sb.* [a. F. *torque*, *-orem*, f. *torquēre* to twist.] 1. A collar, necklace, bracelet, or similar ornament consisting of a twisted narrow band or strip, usually of precious metal, worn especially by the ancient Gauls and Britons.

Torque (tǫik), *sb.* [a. L. *torquēre*, *-orem*, *f. torquēre* to twist.] *Physics.* The twisting or rotary force in a piece of mechanism (as a measurable quantity); the moment of a system of forces producing rotation.

Torqued (tǫikt), *ppl. a.* [f. TORQUE *sb.* + -ED.] 1. Twisted, convoluted; formed like a torque.

Torquate (tǫˑkwēt), *a.* [ad. L. *torquātus* adorned with or wearing a *torque*: see TORQUE and -ATE.] Having a ring-like mark, formed by hairs or feathers of special colour or texture, round the neck; collared.

Torrent (tǫˑrənt), *sb.* [a. F. *torrent* (1100 in Godef. Compl.), ad. L. *torrent-em* burning, boiling, rushing, impetuous, pr. pple. of *torrēre* to scorch, burn; also as a torrent.] 1. A stream of water flowing with great swiftness and impetuosity, whether from the steepness of its course, or from being temporarily flooded.

Torret, **turret**, *sb. Obs.* Forms: 4-5 toret, 5 torret, touret, 5-6 torrett, 6 turrett, 5-8 turret, 6 (9) turret. [ME. *toret*, *touret*, a. OF. *touret*.] 1. A ring or the like, often moving on a swivel, whereby an object can be attached to a chain.

Torricellian (tǫrriˈseliǎn), *a.* [f. the name of *Torricelli*, an Italian physicist (1607–1642) + -AN.] Of or belonging to Torricelli.

Torrid (tǫˈrid), *a.* Also 7 *erron.* torred. [ad. L. *torrid-us*, f. *torrēre* to dry with heat.]

Torsel, *var.* TASSEL 2.

Torsi, *pl.* of TORSO.

Torsibility. [f. *torsible* (f. L. *tors-*, ppl. stem) + -ITY.] Capability of being twisted; esp. in reference to degree or amount.

Torsile (tǫˈrsail, -il), *a.* [f. L. *torsilis*, f. *tors-*, ppl. stem.] Of the nature of torsion.

Torsion (tǫˈrʃǎn). Also 4 *torsion*, 6 *-syon*, 7 *tortion*. [a. F. *torsion* (1314 in Littré, in sense 1 below), ad. late L. *torsiōn-em* (Vulg.), by-form of *tortiōn-em*, n. of action from L. *torquēre*, *tort-um* to twist, wring.]

Torsional (tǫˈrʃǎnal), *a.* [f. prec. + -AL.] Of, pertaining or relating to, or caused by or resulting from torsion.

Torsive (tǫˈrsiv), *a.* [f. prec. + -IVE.] Twisted spirally; contorted.

Torsk (tǫsk). Also locally *tusk*, *tosk*, *tusker*. [a. Norw. *torsk*, Da. *torsk*.]

Torso (tǫˈrsou), *sb.* *Pl.* torsos, torsi. [It. *torso* stalk, stump (= OF. *trons*), ad. L. *thyrsus* stalk, stem (of a plant), a. Gr. θύρσος the THYRSUS (q.v.)]

Torsooclusion (tǭrsǒkluˈʒǎn). *Surg.* [f. med.L. *tors-us* twisted + OCCLUSION.]

Tort (tǫrt), *sb.* Also 4–6 *torte*, 5–6? *tort* (6 th c. in Hatz.-Darm.), 7 *tort*. [a. F. *tort*, = Pr. *tort*, *tuerto*, It. *torto*, med.L. *tortum*, wrong, injustice.]

Tortile (tǫˈrtil, -ail), *a.* [ad. L. *tortilis*, f. *tort-*, ppl. stem of *torquēre* to twist, wring.]

Tortilla (tǫrtiˈlja). [Sp. dim. of *torta* cake.] In Mexico, a thin round cake of maize-flour, baked on a flat plate of iron, earthenware, etc.

Tortility (tǫrtiˈliti). *rare*. [ad. L. type *tortilitas*, f. *tortilis* TORTILE.]

Tortilly (tǫˈrtili), *a.* *Her.* [ad. F. *tortillé* twisted, (in heraldry) wreathed, pa. pple. of *tortiller* to twist.]

Tortis (tǫˈrtis). *Obs.* Forms: 1 Gloss., Twentill 4 French, *torse*, *torteau*, etc. [a. OF. *tortis* wreathed.]

Tortion (tǫˈrʃǎn), *Obs.* or *arch.* [ad. L. *tortiōn-em* wrenching, torment; see TORSION.]

Tortious (tǫˈrʃǎs), *a.* Also 4–6 torcious, 6 *tort-*. [An abnormal formation on TORT, as if from *tort* + *-ous*: cf. righteous, wrongous, etc.]

Tortoise (tǫˈrtǫs, -tis). Forms: see below. [Found in 15th c. forms *tortuca*, *tortuce*, *tortuge*, *tortu*, etc.]

Tortive (tǫˈrtiv), *a.* *rare*. [ad. L. *tortiv-us*, f. *tort-*, ppl. stem of *torquēre* to twist: see -IVE.] Twisting, twisted, tortuous.

Tortle, obs. form of TURTLE.

Tortoise-shell (tǫˈrtǫsʃel), *collog.* tǫˈrtǫˈʃel). 1. The shell, esp. the upper shell, of carapace, of a tortoise, consisting of large scales covering the dermal skeleton.

Tortor. *Obs.* Also 6–7 *-our(e*. [L., agent-n. from *torquēre*, *tort-um* to twist, torture.] A torturer, tormentor; an executioner.

Tortricid (tǫˈrtrisid), *a.* and *sb.* [f. med.L. *Tortricidæ* (L. TORTRIX: see -ID 1), a. *Tortrix*, *-ricis*, *fem.* of TORTOR.]

Tortrix (tǫˈrtriks). *Pl.* tortrices (-aiˈsēz). [mod.L. *tortrix*, *-icem*, *fem.* of TORTOR, *tort* taken in the literal sense 'twister', in reference to the leaf-rolling habits of the larva.]

Tortu, *tortue*, *tortuo*, *tortue*, sbs. forms of TORTOISE.

Torturable (tǫˈrtiǔrǎb'l), *a.* *rare*. [f. TORTURE v. + -ABLE.] Capable of being tortured.

Torture (tǫˈrtiǔr, -tjǔr), *sb.* Also 6–7 tortour, tortor. [a. F. *torture* (12–13th c. in Hatz.-Darm.), ad. L. *tortūra* twisting, torment, torture.]

Torture, *v.* [f. prec. sb.] 1. *trans.* To inflict torture upon, subject to torture, put to the torture.

Torture. ... One who that which inflicts or causes torture; a tormentor; *spec.* one who executes judicial torture.

Torturesome (-səm), *a. rare.* [f. Torture *sb.* + -some.] Characterized by, or causing torture; extremely painful or distressing.

Torturing, *vbl. sb.* [f. Torture *v.* + -ing.] The action of the verb Torture; infliction of torment; torturing; *fig.* wresting, perversion.

Torturing, *ppl. a.* [f. as prec. + -ing.]

Torturing-stock (*sense-vol.*), one upon whom torture is inflicted.

Torturous (-tiəs), *a.* [f. Torture *sb.* + -ous.]

Tortus, -tose, obs. forms of Tortoise.

Tortys, tortyse: see Tortis.

Torula (tɒˈrūlă). *Mod.* pl. **-læ** (-lī), dim. (with change of gender) of Torus (sense 1): cf. F. *torule* masc.] 1. A small rounded swelling or bulge.

Torulaceous (-ˈeiʃəs), *a.* [f. prec. + -aceous.] *Bot.* Belonging to the order *Torulaceæ* of fungi.

Toruliform (-fɔːm), *a. Nat. Hist.* [f. Torula + -i- + -form.]

Torulose (-ləʊs), *a., a Nat. Hist.* [f. Torula + -ose (after L. type *torulōsus*): cf. mod.F. *toruleux.*]

Torulus (-ləs). *Entom.* Pl. **toruli** (-lī).

Torus (tɔːˈrəs). Pl. **tori** (tɔːˈraɪ).

Tory (tɔːˈrɪ), *sb.* and *a.* Also 5, 7 torterous.

A. *sb.* In the 17th c., one of the dispossessed Irish, who became outlaws, subsisting by plundering and killing the English settlers and soldiers...

To-rush, *v. Obs.* [f. To-[2] + rushen, f. To-[2] + rushen.] *trans.* To dash in pieces.

Torve (tɔːv), *a. rare.* [ad. L. torv-us grim, frowning: cf. obs. F. *torve* (Cotgr.), Sp., Pg., It. *torvo.*] Stern in aspect; grim, fierce-looking.

Torvid (-vid), *a.* same sense.

Torvity [ad. L. *torvitā-s* frowning, fierceness of aspect.]

Torvous (-vəs), *a.* [f. as prec. + -ous.]

Torvoid, Torvity, Torvous: see after Torve.

Tory (tɔːˈrɪ), *sb.* and *a.* [Anglicized spelling of Irish *tóraidhe,* orig. (?later) pursuer, implied in the derivative *tóraidheacht* pursuit...

b. with various qualifications, as...

Tory (tɔːˈrɪ), *sb.* and *a.* Also 5, 7 torterous.

Tory. 1. Used advb. in phr. *to talk, vote Tory.*

2. *Comb., as Tory-Radical sb.* and *adj.; Tory-Irish, -leaning, -ridden, -voiced adj.*

Toryish (tɔːˈrɪɪʃ), *a.* [f. Tory *sb.* + -ish.]

Toryism (tɔːˈrɪɪz'm). Also **7-8 Toriism.** [f. as prec. + -ism.] The principles, practices, and methods of Tories; *spec. a.* those of the British Tory party; Conservatism.

Toryfy, torify (tɔːˈrɪfaɪ), *v. humorous.* [f. Tory *sb.* + -fy.]

Torying (tɔːˈrɪɪŋ), *vbl. sb.*

Toryship (tɔːˈrɪʃɪp). [f. Tory *sb.* + -ship.]

Tosaphoth (təˈsɑːfəθ). Also **tosafoth.** [Heb.]

Tosh, *sb.[1] slang.* Some kind of fire-wood, or a form in which it was sold in 14th to 16th c.

Tosca (tɒsˈkă). Also **tosco, tosk.** [Sp. *tosco, lena, of tosca coarse.*] *Bot.* A soft dark-brown limestone occurring embedded and sometimes stratified in the surface formation of the Pampas.

Toscan, obs. or alien form of Tuscan.

To-scatter, *v. Obs.* [ME. *to-scater-en,* f. To-[2] + scatter *v.*] *trans.* To scatter abroad; disperse.

Tosh, *sb.[2] slang.* Nonsense; bosh; rubbish.

Tosh, *v.[1] slang.* [Origin not ascertained.]

Hence Toshy (tɒˈʃɪ) *a. slang,* trashy, rubbishy.

Tosh, *v.[2]* [Origin not ascertained.] 1. Neat, clean, tidy, trim.

2. Agreeable, comfortable; friendly, intimate.

B. *as adv.* ... *Tashly* (see below).

To-same, to-samen, *adv. Obs.* Forms: 1 tosomne, tosamon, 7-3 to somne, (*Orm.*) tosamenn, 2-4 to same, 3 to somen, 3-4 samen, 4 to samne. [OE. *tōsamne, tōsomne,* f. To-[2] + samen together. Cf. OFris. *to samine,* OS. *tō samne,* tosamne (MDu. *te-samen,* Du. *zamen*), OHG. *zisamane, zi tsamane* (MHG. *zesamene,* Ger. *zusammen*).]

Tosh-er (tɒˈʃə). *slang.* A Thames waterman... whose purloins copper sheathing from the bottoms of vessels in the river or from the docks.

To-shred, *v. Obs.* [OE. *tosceádan,* f. To-[2] + sceádan v.] *trans.* To separate, disperse.

To-shear, *v. Obs.* [OE. *tosceran.*] *trans.* To shear asunder.

Toshy, see Tosh *v.[1]*

To-shiver, *v. Obs.* [f. To-[2] + Shiver v.] *trans.* To shiver to pieces.

To-shatter, *v. Obs.* [f. To-[2] + Shatter v.] *trans.* To shatter to small pieces.

To-shoot, to-she-te, *v. Obs.* [OE. *to-sceótan,* f. To-[2] + sceótan v.] *trans.* To shoot asunder, scatter.

Tosh-ive, *v. Obs.* To shiver.

Toss, *sb.* [f. Toss *v.*] 1. The act of tossing, pitching, throwing, or hurling; a throw, a pitch.

Toss, *v.* Forms: see Toss *v.* and Toce. [App. of obscure origin.]

To-spread, *v. Obs.* Forms: see Spread *v.* [OE. *tōspreádan,* f. To-[2] + spreádan v.]

To-sprout, *v. Obs.* intr. To sprout, shoot.

To-spring, *v. Obs.*

To-squat, *v. Obs.*

Toss, *v.* 1. *trans.* To throw, pitch, cast, fling, or hurl.

Toss, *sb.*² *dial.* [A variant of Tass¹.] A heap, stack; — Tass².

Toss (tǫs), *v.* Pa. t. and pple. tossed (tǫst), also 6– tost.

I. *trans.* 1. To throw, pitch, or fling about, here and there, or to and fro: expressing the action of wind or wave, or the light, careless, or disdainful action of a person, on something easily moved.

†b. *fig.* A chance where the probability either way is equal; an even chance. *collog.*

2. To throw up; to jerk up.

3. To shake, shake up, stir up.

†b. To fling (hay, wood, etc.) about; to loosen the mass. *Obs.*, exc. as in 1.

3. To shake, shake up, stir up.

†b. To fling (hay, wood, etc.) about; to loosen the mass. *Obs.*, exc. as in 1.

II. *intr.* †5. To be in constant agitation or distraction; to be disquieted in mind or circumstances. *Obs.*

6. a. *for refl.* 7. To throw, or impel by hitting (a ball, etc.): to and fro between them: *cf. to toss from pillar to post* (Pillar *sb.* 11). Often *fig.* or in *fig.* context.

8. *egh.* Of two players: To throw, or impel by hitting (a ball, etc.): to and fro between them.

III. *trans.* * To throw in a specified direction.

7. To throw, cast, pitch, fling, hurl (without any notion of agitation).

11. To lift, jerk, or throw up (the head, etc.) with a sudden, impatient, or spirited movement.

12. *Toss off.* a. To drink off with energetic action. b. To dispose of in an offhand manner.

13. *Toss out.* See prec. senses and Out; in quot., to dress smartly, 'trick out'.

14. *Toss up.* a. See prec. senses and Up.

Tossed (tǫst), *ppl. a.* Also **tost**. [f. Toss *v.* + -ED.] Thrown about, hurled this way and that; disordered; disturbed, troubled: see the vb.

Tosser (tǫ'sǝr). 1. One who or that which tosses. Also *with adv.*

†To-swell, *v. Obs.* [OE. *tōswellan*, f. To- ² + *swellen*, Swell *v.* So OHG. *zisuuellan*, MHG. *zerswellen*.] To swell out; also *fig.* to be puffed up, as with an emotion. Chiefly in pa. pple.

Tossicate, variant of Tosticate.

To-ssing, *vbl. sb.* [-ing ¹.] The action of Toss *v.* in various senses. Also *with adv.*

To'ssing, *ppl. a.* [f. Toss *v.* + -ing ².] That tosses: see the vb.

†Tost. See Toss, Tossed.

†Tostament, *Obs. rare.* [f. Toss *v.* + -ment.] The action of tossing or fact of being tossed.

Tosspot (tǫ'spǫt), *sb.* [f. *tos* s + pot, Toss *v.* + pot.] One accustomed to toss off his pot of drink; a heavy drinker; a toper, drunkard.

Toss, a. Comb., as *tost-like adv.*

To'ssy, a. *rare.* Hence **To'ssily** *adv.* Contemptuous, pert. Hence **To'ssily** *adv.*

†Tost, *v.* Corruption of Toss *v.*

Tot (tǫt), *sb.*¹ *collog.* [f. Tot *sb.*²] *trans.* To add together and bring out the total of; to sum up.

Tot, *sb.*² [Not recorded before 1725.] ? playful shortening of *totter* or *tottle*. Connexion with Tor *sb.*¹ ('tiny child') uncertain.

Total (tǫ'tǎl), *a.* and *sb.* [a. F. *total* (14th c. in Hatz.-Darm.) = Sp., Pg. *total*, It. *totale*, ad. Schol.L. *tōtāl-is* (in Bernard 1130), f. L. *tōt-us* entire: see -AL.]

To-tal, *v.* [f. Total *sb.*] 1. *trans.* To reach the total of, amount to.

Totality (tǫtæ'liti), *sb.* [ad. schol.L. *tōtālitās* (= 1141 in Hugo de S. Victor, also in Albertus Magnus, Aquinas, Duns Scotus), f. *tōtālis* (14th c. in Hatz.-Darm.).]

To-talize, *v.* [f. Total *sb.* + -IZE.]

Totalizer (tǫ'tǎlaizǝr). 1. One who totalizes; in *spec.* use = TOTALIZATOR.

Totally (tǫ'tǎli), *adv.* [f. TOTAL *a.* + -LY ².] In a total manner or degree; wholly, completely, entirely, altogether.

Totalizator (tǫ'tǎlaizeitǝr). [f. *totalize* + -ATOR.] A machine or apparatus for registering and showing the total of operations, measurements, etc.

Totalizator (tǫ'tǎlaizeitǝr). That which totalizes; in *spec.* = TOTALIZATOR.

Totanine (tǫ'tǎnin), *sb.* A large New Zealand coniferous tree, *Podocarpus Totara*, producing light, durable, tough timber of a dark red colour.

Totara (tǫ'tǎrǎ), *sb.* Also totarra.

†Tote, *v.*¹ *Obs.* Forms: = Tout *v.*¹

Tote (tǫut), *v.*² *orig. U.S. collog.* Also **toat**. [In current use 1676–7; origin unascertained.]

Tote (tǫut), *sb.*¹ Also 9 goat. *dial.* form of Toot *v.*³ to project, stick out.

Totalize (in Eden). Hence **Totalizing** *vbl. sb.* and *ppl. a.*; *totalizing* machine, a totalizator.

Tote (tǫut), *sb.*² Also 9 tote. [Short for *total* or L.] 1. The total amount, number, or sum. Mostly in pleonastic phrase *the whole tote*.

To-tear, *v. Obs.* Forms: = TEAR *v.*¹ *trans.* To tear to pieces.

†To-te-ran, *v. Obs.* [OE. *tō-teran*, f. To- ² + *teran*, TEAR *v.*¹ So MHG. *zerren*.] *trans.* To tear to pieces.

Totem (tǫu'tem), *sb.* [From Ojibway, or some kindred Algonkin dialect. Mentioned (apparently) in 1609 by Lescarbot as *aoutem*; in Acadia by Henry 1776. Cooper 1826, Catlin 1841 as *totem*, by Rev. P. Jones (a native Ojibway) as *toodaim* or *dodaim*.]

Totemic (tǫte'mik), *a.* [f. prec. + -IC.] Of, pertaining to, or of the nature of a totem or totems; characterized by having totems.

Totemically, *adv.* in reference to totems or totemism; after the manner of a totem.

Totemism (tōu'tĕmiz'm). [f. TOTEM + -ISM.]
The use of totems, with the clan division, and the social, marriage, and religious customs connected with it.

Totemist. [f. TOTEM + -IST.]
1. One who belongs to a totem clan, or has a totem.

2. One who is versed in the history of totemism.

So **Totemistic** a., of, pertaining to, or characterized by totemism.

Totemite. [f. TOTEM + -ITE[1].]

Tother, Tother (tŏ'ðər), pron. and a.
1. The other (of two): often opposed to tone.

Totient (tōu'ʃent). Math. [irreg., f. L. totiēs, totiens, f. tot so many, after QUOTIENT.] The number of numbers (including unity) less than and prime to a given number.

Toties quoties (tōu'ʃiēz kwō'ʃiēz), adv.

Totle, Tottam: see TOTTLE v.[1], TOTTENHAM.

Toto (tōu'tǒ), abl. sing. masc. and neut. of L. tōtus all, whole.

Totle, totoo (16th c.), i. e. too too: see TOO.

To-torn a. Obs. [ME. to-torn, pa. pple. of to-tear v.]

To-torve, To-tose, To-tray, etc.: see TO-.

Tot-quot. [L. tot quot as much or as many as (there may be).]

Totter (tŏ'tər), sb.[1] Also 3-5 toter, 6 totre. [f. TOTTER v.]

Totter (tŏ'tər), sb.[2] Now dial. [Aphetic f. or var. of TATTER sb.]

Totter (tŏ'tər), v. Also 3-5 toter, 6 totre. [Of uncertain origin.]
1. A swing: a board suspended by two ropes, on which a person sits and is swung to and fro.
2. intr. To rock, be unsteady.
3. attrib. and Comb.

Tottered (tŏ'tərd), ppl. a. Obs. [Orig. a variant of TATTERED.]

Totterer. [f. TOTTER v. + -ER[1].]

Tottering, vbl. sb. [f. TOTTER v. + -ING[1].]

Totting, e. obs. form of TITHING sb.

To-threat, To-thrust: see TO-.
To-throw v.[1] Obs. Forms: see THROW v.[1]

Totting (tŏ'tiŋ), vbl. sb.[2]
To-thwite, v. Obs.

Totipalmate (tōutipæ'lmeit), a. Ornith.

Totipotent (tōutipōu'tent), a. Biol. [f. L. tōti-(see prec.) + POTENT.] Capable of developing into or producing any organism.

Totipotentiality (tōtipōtenʃiæ'liti), [f. prec.]

Totipresence, a. Obs. nonce-wd. [f. L. tōti- all, whole + PRESENCE.] Present throughout the whole of space.

Totipresent, a. Obs. nonce-wd. [= prec. + -ENT.] Present throughout the whole of space.

Totitive: see TOTIENT.

Tottle, Potnam: see TOTTLE, TOTTENHAM.

Toto, Totum: see TOTTLE.

Toto- combining form of L. tōtus whole.

To-tread, v. Obs. [OE. totredan, f. TO- + tredan]
To-tug, v.

To-trenching and **To-tousle,** etc.

Totter (tŏ'tər), sb. + I Totter-totter.

Tottenham (tŏ'tn̩əm). In 6 Potnam. + Tottenham in turned French, a proverb used in reference to any unlikely or remarkable change.

Totter (tŏ'tər), sb.

Totter-grass, Totter-head, etc.

To-torve, To-tose, To-tray: see TO-.

Tot-quot. [L. tot quot as much or as many as.]

Totter, sb.[2]

Tottering, vbl. sb.
The action of the verb TOTTER; oscillation, wavering, shaking as if about to fall.

Tottering, ppl. a.
That totters; moving unsteadily; apt to tip or topple; shaky; crazy; also fig. shaky in intellect.

Totteringly, adv. [f. prec. + -LY[2].]

Tottering, sb. Also, in various senses of the verb.

Totterishly, adv.

Totterishness.

Tottery (tŏ'təri), a. [f. TOTTER v. + -Y.]
Given to tottering; shaky; unsteady.

Tottle, v.[1] Obs. [f. TOTTER v. + -LE.]

Tottle, v.[2] Obs. Familiar diminutive of TOTTER v.

Tottle, variant of TOTAL.

Tottling, sb.: see TOT sb.[3], v.[1] and 2.

Tottle (tŏ'tl), sb. [f. tot- in TOTTER v.]

Tottle (tŏ'tl), v.[3] Also 8-9 totle. Chiefly dial.
1. intr. To move and bubble, as a boiling liquid.
2. intr. To move unsteadily and with short tottering steps; to toddle.

Totty-grass: see TOTTER sb.

Tot-wheel. Obs.

Totty (tŏ'ti), a.[1] Obs. Also tottie, totie.
Affectedly diminutive of TOT sb.[1]; a tiny tot or little child. Also as adj. Tiny, wee.

Totty (tŏ'ti), a.[2] Now dial. Forms: 4-6 toty, 6 totye, 6-7 totty. [app. f. tot-, as in totter v. + -Y.] Unsteady, shaky, tottery; dizzy, dazed; tipsy, fuddled.

Totty, variant of TOTTER v.

Toty, var. TOTTY a.[2]

Toucan (tū'kən). Also 8 tocan, 9 toucano, etc. [a. Brazilian, Tupi tucana, Guarani tuca, tucã (in nasal), the native name, prob. from its cry or call; but other suggestions have been offered.]
A Neotropical bird of the genus *Rhamphastos*, or, in a wider use, of the family *Rhamphastidæ*.

Touch (tōtʃ), sb. Forms: 4 tuche, 5 towche, 6 tuch, Sc. tuiche. [ME. tuche, touche, a. OF. tuche, touche, f. the vb.]
1. The action or an act of touching (with the hand, finger, or other part of the body); exercise of the faculty of feeling upon a material object.

2. The sense of touch.

b. The sensation caused by touching something (considered as an attribute of the thing); tactile quality, feel.

3. The action or process of testing the quality of gold or silver by rubbing it upon a touchstone.

4. A touchstone. (See touchstone.)

5. An attribute of the performer: Capacity, skill, or style of playing; now esp. in reference to the action of the fingers upon the keys of a keyboard instrument.

6. Mus. or manner of touching or handling a musical instrument, so as to bring out its tones; now esp. the manner of striking the keys of a keyboard instrument so as to produce special varieties of tone or effect.

7. An act of touching a surface with the proper tool in painting, drawing, writing, carving, etc.; a stroke or dash of a brush, pencil, pen, chisel, or the like; hence, a stroke or dash of colour added in drawing or painting.

8. Capacity of the brush, pencil, pen, or other instrument; artistic skill or faculty.

9. Bell-ringing. Any series of changes less than a peal.

10. An act of touching or musical sounding.

Touchable (tʌ·tʃăb'l), a. [f. TOUCH v. + -ABLE.] Capable of being touched; tangible.

Touch and go, sb. and adj. phr. (Also with hyphens.) [The vbl. phrase touch and go (TOUCH v. 26) used as sb. or adj.]

Touched (tʌtʃt), ppl. a. [f. TOUCH v. + -ED.] In various senses corresponding to those of TOUCH v.

Touch-hole. [f. TOUCH- in touch-powder + HOLE.] A small tubular hole in the breech of a fire-arm, through which the charge is ignited; the vent.

Touchily (tʌ·tʃili), adv. [f. TOUCHY + -LY.]

Touchiness (tʌ·tʃiněs). [f. as prec. + -NESS.] The quality of being touchy.

Touching (tʌ·tʃiŋ), vbl. sb. [f. TOUCH v. + -ING.] The action of the verb TOUCH.

Touching (tʌ·tʃiŋ), ppl. a. [f. TOUCH v. + -ING.] Forms: see TOUCH v.

Touching, prep. Now somewhat arch. Forms: see TOUCH v.

Touch-line. [f. TOUCH sb. or v. + LINE sb.]

Touch-me-not, sb. [phrase used as sb.]

Touch-needle. [f. TOUCH sb. 6.]

Touchwood (tʌ·tʃwud). [f. TOUCH-.] Wood of any kind, esp. in such a state as to catch fire readily, and which can be used as tinder.

Tough (tʌf), a. (adv., sb.) Forms: a. 1 tóh, 3 tou3, 3–5 tou3, tow3, 3–6 tow, 4 tooh, towh, towe, 4–7 togh, towe, 5 tou3e, tough.

Touchy (tʌ·tʃi), a. [f. TOUCH v. + -Y.] Easily moved to anger; apt to take offence on slight cause; highly sensitive in temper or disposition; irascible, irritable, testy, tetchy.

Tou3 (tig). [a. F. touq, ad. Turk. tugh tail of a horse.]

Toughen (tʌ·f'n), v. [f. TOUGH a. + -EN.]

Toughish (tʌ·fiʃ), a. [f. TOUGH a. + -ISH.] Somewhat tough.

Toughly (tʌ·fli), adv. [f. TOUGH a. + -LY.] In a tough manner (in various senses of TOUGH).

Toughness (tʌ·fněs). [f. TOUGH a. + -NESS.] The state or quality of being tough, in various senses of the adjective.

Tought, -e, obs. ff. TAUT, TOUGH. **Toughy**, dial. var. TOFFEE. **Touk**, var. TUCK. **Touk-e-up**, dial. var. TUCK.

Toupé, tupé, tuppee, 6 towpe. A curl or artificial lock of hair on the top of the head, esp. as a crowning feature of a periwig.

Toupet (tupp, tū·pe, tū·pet), sb. [a. F. toupet.]

Toupi (tū·pi), obs. form of TUPI.

Toupie, toupée, -ie, obs. ff. TOUPEE.

Toupinambou, obs. form of TOPINAMBOU.

Tour (tūǝr), sb. [a. F. tour, towr, turn, a turn, winding, circuit, compass, etc.] A turn, a round; an excursion or journey including the visiting of a number of places in a circuit or sequence; often qualified, as cycling, walking, wedding tour, etc.

Toupeted, ppl. a. [f. TOUPEE + -ED.]

Toup, toupe, obs. forms of TUP.

Toupee (tū·pi, tū·pe). Now rare. Also 8

Touting (tou'tiŋ), vbl. sb.[1] [f. Tout v.[3] + -ING.] The action of Tout v.[3]

Touting, ppl. a.[1] in *touting-hen*: see Toot, Tout v.[3]

Toutsayne, early form of Tutsan.

Touzaunt, Touzie: see Toward, Tousle.

† Tovet. *Obs. local.* Forms: 6 tovett, vett, 7 talvett, tovit(t, 7–8 tot(f)et, 7–9 tovet; also 9 tavort, tobit, totet, totfet (*Eng. Dial. Dict.*). [A local word of Kent; evidently the same as *tolfet* (see Toll ME 2 b).] A measure of two pecks or half a bushel.

**Tovore, variant of Tofore Obs., before.

Tow (tō, *Sc.* tru, tou), sb.[1] Forms: 4–7 towe, 5 tuwe, 6–9 (7–8 tow), 5–9 tawe, 5– tow. [Known only from late *OE. tōw* (*WGer.* *tou*).]

(main text continues in dense columns)

Tow (tau), sb.[2] Forms: 5 toughe, 7 towen, 4–9 tog(h)e, 4–8 towe, (6 tough, tough), 6–7 togh, 6 taw, 6–7 towe, 5–9 tow. [OE. *togen* to draw or pull by force, to drag.]

Tow, sb.[3] [f. Tow sb.[1]] Pottery manuf.

Towage (tou'ēdʒ). [f. Tow v.[1] + -AGE.]
1. The charge or payment for towing a vessel.
2. The action or process of towing or being towed.

Towai (tou'wai). Also **tawhai**. [Native Maori name.]

Towan (tou'an). *Cornw.* Also **towin**, **tewen**, **tuan**, **tŷn**. [Cornish *towan*, Welsh *tywyn* in same sense.]

Towaille, -aille, -ale, -all, obs. ff. Towel.

Town, obs. Sc. form of Tower sb.[1],[3]

Toward (tou'(w)ǎd, tō'ǎd), *a.* and *adv.* Forms:

Toward (tou'ǎd, tō'ǎd), *prep.* (*adv.*). Forms: 1–2 toward, 2 toward, 3 toward, 2–4 to-ward, 4–6 to-, 5 toward, toward.

Towardly (tou'ǎdli, tō'ǎdli), *a.* [f. Toward a. + -LY.] Cf. OE. *toweardlīc*, in time to come, in the future.

Towardliness (see next). Now *dial. or arch.* [f. Towardly a. + -NESS.] The quality or character of being 'towardly.'

Towardness (tou'ǎdnes, tō'ǎdnes). Now *Obs. or arch.* [f. as prec. + -NESS.] The quality or condition of being 'toward.'

Towards (tou'(w)ǎdz, tō'ǎdz), *prep.* and *adv.* [OE. *tōweardes*.]

To-watch, *v.* Cf. Watch. To keep watch.

Towbery, -bury: see Tolbooth.

To-waste, To-wave, To-wawe: see To- pref.

Towaylle, -aylle, obs. ff. Towel.

Towcher, obs. form of Toucher.

Towd, obs. form of Toad, Towed.

Towel (tou'el), sb. Forms: see below. [ME. *towaille*, *-alle*, etc., a. OF. *touaille* (= Pr. *toalha*, Cat. *tovalla*, Sp. *toalla*), etc.]

a. *dial.* At Oxford and Cambridge: The civic community or body of citizens or townsmen as distinct from members of the university; esp. in phr. *town and gown*...

8. *U.S.* A geographical division for local or state government. **a.** A division of a county, which may contain one or more villages or towns (in areal sense)...

7. *fig. and transf. (from* a). **a.** Something analogous to a town as being the home of many people.

8. Phrases. (See also *a.*) **a.** *To come* (*or go*) *to town*, to make one's appearance, arrive, come in; **+** *to come to stay*, to become common (*obs.*).

9. *attrib.* and *Comb.* **a.** Simple attrib. passing into adj. use (now usually without hyphen): Of, pertaining to, or characteristic of the town...

10. Special combs. **+** *town-adjutant*, formerly, a garrison officer, ranking as lieutenant, charged with certain routine duties; cf. **TOWN-MAJOR**...

11. Combinations with *town's*, as *townschildren*, *town's-folk*, *town's-man*, *town's people*, etc.

Town-born, *a.* Born in or of the town.

Town-bound to-**church**: see TOWN 9, 10.

Town-clerk. The clerk or secretary to the corporation of a town...

Town-cress, *Obs.* Town Cress or CRESS. [OE. *tūncerse*, f. *tūn* enclosure, TOWN + *cerse*, *cresse* CRESS.] Garden Cress (*Lepidium sativum*).

Town-clock to-**councillor**: see TOWN 9, 10.

Town-crier to-**-dike**: see TOWN 9, 10.

Town-ditch. *Now Hist.* The ditch or moat surrounding a walled town.

Town-drummer: see TOWN 9.

Town-dweller. One who dwells in a town; a townsman.

Town, v. *rare*. (Only in *pa. pple.* Towned.) **1.** *trans.* **a.** To furnish with a town. **b.** To make into or constitute (a community) a town.

Towne, obs. form of TUN, TOWN.

Town book. Also 6 *St.* townis buk. A book in which the records of a town are kept.

Tow-net (*tōu*net), *sb.* [f. TOW *sb.*[1] or *v.*[1] + NET *sb.*[1].] A drag-net or dredge used for the collection of natural specimens. Hence **Tow-net-ting**, to drag with a tow-net; *intr.* to use a tow-net; whence **Tow-netter** *(tow-netting)* ...

Town-father: see TOWN 9.

Townful (*toun-ful*). [f. TOWN *sb.* + -FUL.] As many as a town contains or will contain.

Town-gate[1]. The gate of a walled town.

Town-gate[2]. *Sc.* and *north. dial.* Also 6-7 gait(e). The main street of a town or village.

Town-green to-**guard**: see TOWN 9, 10.

Town-hall. A large hall used for the transaction of the public business of a town, the holding of a court of justice, assemblies, entertainments, etc.

Town-head, -herd: see TOWN 10, 9.

Town-ho. *Obs.* Also 8 townson (see quots.)

Town-house, town house. 1. A municipal building containing the public offices, court-house, and Town Hall, and in some continental towns the official residence of the chief magistrate. Cf. F. *hôtel de ville*; Ger. *stadthaus*.

Towning (*toun-ing*), *vbl. sb.* [f. TOWN *v.* + -ING[1].] **1.** Of or pertaining to a town; living, situated, or existing in a town; urban. *Obs.*

Town-husband: see TOWN 10.

Townify (*toun-i-fai*), *v.* [f. TOWN + -(I)FY.] *trans.* To render town-like, or characteristic of the town. Hence **Townified** *ppl. a.*

Towniness: see TOWNY.

Town-land. 1. ... **b.** *collect.* Land belonging to or held by a town.

Townliness, *collog.* Townly quality or condition.

Town-ling. A small town; a townlet.

Townly (*toun-li*), *a.* [f. TOWN + -LY[1].] Pertaining to, or characteristic of the town; having the manners or habits of town-dwellers.

Town-major. A major of a town-guard, as formerly in Edinburgh.

Town-man. A man of the town; a townsman.

Town-master. ...

Town-meeting. *spec.* in U.S. A legal meeting of the qualified voters of a town for the transaction of public business, having certain powers of local government.

Town-mill to-**place**: see TOWN 9, 10.

Townness. *Obs.* ...

Town-planning, n. The preparation and construction of plans in accordance with which the growth and extension of a town is to be regulated...

Town-plat to-**pump**: see TOWN 9, 10.

Townred, Obs. *rare.* ...

Town-reeve to-**row**: see TOWN 9b, 10.

Town-scape, *nonce-wd.* [f. TOWN *sb.*, after *landscape*.] A picture or view of a town.

Township (*toun-ship*). [OE. *tūnscipe* (see TOWN) + -scipe, -SHIP. Cf. for sense, *landscape*.] ... 1. In OE., the inhabitants or population of a *tūn* or village collectively; the community or dwelling in and occupying a *tūn* (sense 2). *Obs.*

2. The inhabitants of a particular manor, parish, or division of a hundred, as a community. Now chiefly *Hist.*

4. *Sc.* A farm held in joint tenancy.

5. In *Canada* and *U.S.* A county having certain corporate powers of local administration...

6. In *Australia*, A site laid out prospectively for a town, meanwhile often consisting of a few 'shanties' grouped around a railway station, store, hotel, post office, or the like; a village or hamlet.

out to farmers, for loss of sheep by dogs..three hundred and ninety-eight dollars. 1888 Bryce *Amer. Commw.* II. II. xlviii. 235 *note*, Any county desiring to forsake township organization may do so by a vote of the electors. 1904 *Daily Chron.* 19 Oct. 8/3 A simple and traditional dramatisation of some scene in early English township life. 1910 W. L. Mathieson *Awakening Scot.* vi. 276 The type of agriculture..is still that of the township farm.

Town-side, -site, etc.: see Town 10.

Townsman (tau·nzmăn). Forms: see Town. [f. *town's*, genitive of Town + Man sb.1]

†1. OE. (*túnesman*). One who lives in a *tún*; a villager, a villein. *Obs.*

962–3 *Laws of Edgar* iv. c. 13 And ic wille, þæt tunesmen and heora hyrdas habban þas ylcan smeagunge on minum cucum orfe and on minra þegena, ealswa hy habbað on heora agenum. 1028–60 *Laws Northumbld. Priests* c. 59 ʒif hwilc tunesman ænigne pænig forhele oððe forhæbbe, ʒilde se landrica þone pæniʒ and nime ænne oxan æt ðam men.

2. A man who lives in a town or city; a citizen: esp. as distinguished from a countryman, a stranger, a soldier of the garrison, or other such.

1433 in *Hist. Sudbury* (1896) 125 A Supplicacon of the Maior and Tonsmen of Sudbury to the B. of Norwich. 1519 *Coventry Leet Bk.* 666 Iff eny fforener or Townesman fforstall eny Corne within the libertie of this Cetie of Couentre or it com into the markett. 1577 tr. *Bullinger's Decades* (1592) 144 Of the countrie men as well as of the townesmen. 1615 G. Sandys *Trav.* 6 Here a garrison is kept; supplyed by the townesmen. 1745 *De Foe's Eng. Tradesman* xxvi. (1841) I. 265 She being a good honest townsman's daughter. 1749 *Little Cornard (Suff.) Overseers' Acc.* (MS.), Paid to Sarah Flower by the order of the Townes men that She Laid out. 1863 H. Cox *Instit.* III. ix. 727 The whole body of resident trading townsmen.

b. A man of one's own or the same town; a fellow-townsman. Usually after *possessive*. Cf. Countryman 2.

1601 A. Dent *Pathway to Heaven* (1617) 18 For me thinks you go too far, you goe beyond your learning in this, that you condemne good neighbours, and good Townesmen. 1715–20 Pope *Iliad* xviii. 578 There, in the forum swarm a numerous train, The subject of debate, a townsman slain. 1838 Thirlwall *Greece* II. xv. 258 A citizen of Abdera advised his townsmen to offer a solemn thanksgiving to the gods.

c. An ordinary citizen or resident of a university town as distinguished from a *gownsman* or member of the university; cf. Town sb. 5 d.

1768 Wilkes *Corr.* (1805) III. 254 Only another proof that the townsmen of Oxford have always hated the university. 1823 Lamb *Elia* Ser. II. *Poor Relations*, The distance between the gownsmen and the townsmen, as they are called ..is carried to an excess that [etc.]. 1889 Jessopp *Coming of Friars* vi. 273 The townsmen under great provocation had seized three of the gownsmen.

3. *New England.* = Selectman.

1656 in T. Dwight *Trav. New Eng.* (1821) I. 343 [In 1656] town's-men [(or select-men) were chosen]. 1696–1715 *Maryland Laws* iv. (1723) 11 Any Action..arising between the Townsmen or Freemen of the said Town. *a* 1817 T. Dwight *Trav. New Eng.* (1821) I. 243 At this meeting the inhabitants choose, not exceeding seven men, inhabitants, able, discreet and of good conversation, to be Select-men, or Townsmen, to take care of the order, and prudential affairs of the town.

Townspeople (tau·nzˌpīːp'l). Also 7 townes people. [f. as prec. + People. Orig. two words; now written as one.] People or inhabitants of a town or towns; townsmen and townswomen; townsfolk. (Usually const. as *pl.*)

1648 Cromwell *Let.* 23 Nov., And without money the stubborn towns-people will not trust them for the worth of a penny. 1691 in *Somerset & Dorset N. & Q.* June (1905) 263 Many died as also many Townes people of yᵉ same distemper. 1833 Marryat *P. Simple* xxi, We had no parole, and but little communication with the townspeople. 1849 Macaulay *Hist. Eng.* v. I. 575 The town's people repaired to the cliffs and gazed long and anxiously. 1872 Bagehot *Physics & Pol.* iv. 132 The place was crowded and a whole townspeople looking on.

b. People inhabiting the same town; fellow-townsmen. (Usually after *possessive*.)

1823 *Examiner* 761/1 They are townspeople, we believe, the native place of both being..Edinburgh. 1870 Emerson *Soc. & Solit.* iii. 45 Not by his friends or his townspeople or his contemporaries.

Town-stocks, Townswoman: see Town 9, 11.

Tow·n-ta·lk. The common talk or gossip of the people of a town; the subject or matter of such talk or gossip.

1654–5 Cromwell *Speech to Parl.* 22 *Jan.* 23 If it be not folly in Me to listen to Town-talk, such things have been proposed. 1667 Pepys *Diary* 26 Apr., All the town-talk is now-a-days of her extravagancies. 1694 Congreve *Double-Dealer* III. i, You'll ruin me if you take such public Notice of it, it will be a Town-Talk. 1712 Swift *Jrnl. to Stella* 26 Mar., The news of the French desiring a cessation of arms..was but town talk. 1848 Thackeray *Van. Fair* lv, It was town-talk for at least three days. 1867 Aug. J. E. Wilson *Vashti* xii, Why should she taboo society, and make herself the town-talk?

Town-tallow to **-wait**: see Town 9, 10.

Tow·n-wa·ll. The wall of a fortified town.

c 1400 *Destr. Troy* 10746 The troiens in toures, & on toun walles, Laidon spies specially. 1480 *Coventry Leet Bk.* 447 Employe hit to oder reparacions of þe seid town wall. 1548 Udall, etc. *Erasm. Par. Acts* ix. 36 They..by nyght let hym downe by a corde of the towne walles, in a basket. 1649 Milton *Eikon.* viii. Wks. (1847) 294/1 The king much incensed proclaims him traitor before the town walls. 1843 *Penny Cycl.* XXVII. 456/1 The town-wall of Worms.

Townward (tau·nwǫ̈ɹd), *adv.* (*a.*) [f. Town sb. + -ward.] Towards or in the direction of the town. (Originally *to the townward*.)

1434 *Indenture Fotheringhey* in Dugdale *Monast.* (1846) VI. 1414/2 A dore yn the west side..to the town-ward. 1633 T. Stafford *Pac. Hib.* II. xii. (1821) 362 The Irish.. beat the Spaniards from their ground to the Towneward. 1808 Scott *Marm.* III. xxxi, He heard..The foot-tramp of a flying steed, Come town-ward rushing on. 1846 Longf. in *Life* (1891) II. 52 A beautiful pile of granite.. looking townward and seaward.

b. *adj.* Going or directed toward the town.

1806 J. Grahame *Birds Scot.* 35 Follow his townward steps. 1833 L. Ritchie *Wand. by Loire* 184 Ditches..still remain on the townward side. 1864 Longf. in *Life* (1891) III. 34 Walking..along the accustomed townward walk,.. I met the East Wind. 1893 *Chicago Advance* 27 July, Evidence of the townward drift of the people.

c. *Comb.*

1870 Morris *Earthly Par.* III. iv. 288 In a fair-hung townward-looking bower.

Townwards, *adv.* [-wards.] = prec.

1895 P. Hemingway *Out of Egypt* II. 175, I stood watching a vessel in the harbour, that stared townwards with a hundred unblinking eyes. 1908 *Daily Chron.* 15 Feb. 7/5 A West London [cycling] club, recently returning..townwards, through Brentford.

Town-watch to **-woman**: see Town 9, 10.

Towny (tau·ni), *a.* and *sb.* *colloq.* Also -ey, -ie. [f. Town sb. + -y.]

A. *adj.* Of, pertaining to, or characteristic of the town; townish.

1837 *New Monthly Mag.* L. 248 His acquired habits were of the town, towny. 1857 E. M. Whitty *Friends in Bohemia* I. 211 Are you not weary of this towney life? 1908 *Treasury* Feb. 507 A house so towny and stylish, compared with our farm homesteads.

B. *sb.* 1. A town-bred man; *spec.* a Londoner.

1828 P. Cunningham *N. S. Wales* (ed. 3) II. 223 If we could not say we had committed as many [robberies] as these townies, they would look upon us with contempt. *Ibid.* 230 Many surgeons find that by putting all the old townies into double irons whenever robberies begin to prevail, a cessation soon takes place.

2. *U.S. university slang.* A townsman as distinct from a member of the university; cf. Townee.

1853 *Yale Lit. Mag.* XIX. 2 (Thornton) The genus by the German students denominated 'Philistines', by the Cantabs ignominiously called 'Snobs', and which custom here has named 'Townies'. 1869 W. T. Washburne *Fair Harvard* 54 (ibid.) One beholds the conscious 'towney' on his evening promenade.

3. A fellow-townsman or townswoman. *slang.*

1865 *Morn. Star* 18 July, She is a 'towny' (of the same town) of mine, and I want to see her safe home. 1869 *Routledge's Ev. Boy's Ann.* 347 Then you and me's 'towneys' it seems. 1892 Stevenson & Osbourne *Wrecker* xii, A townie of mine was lost down this way, in a coal-ship.

To-wond(e, pa. t. of To-wend *v.* *Obs.*

†**To-worth,** *v.* *Obs. rare.* [ME. *to-wurðen*, f. To-2 + *wurðen*:—OE. *weorðan* to become.] *intr.* To come to nought; to perish.

c 1205 Lay. 20744 For betere us is on londe Mid monscipe to liggen þene we þus here For hungere to-wurðen.

To-wowe, -writhe, -wry: see To- *pref.*2 1.

Tow-path (tōu·paþ). [f. Tow *v.*1 + Path.] A path by the side of a canal or navigable river for use in towing; = *towing-path* (Towing *vbl. sb.*1 b).

1846 Worcester, *Tow-path*, a narrow path travelled by horses in dragging boats along a canal. *Baldwin.* 1882 R. Mackenzie *America* 305 He had begun life on the tow-path as a driver of mules. 1910 *Blackw. Mag.* May 634/1 The towpath was knee-deep in water.

Tow-pung, ?error or misprint for *tom-pung*, orig. form of Pung sb.2, q. v., quot. 1851.

Towrd, Towres, Towret, -ette, obs. forms of Toward, Tours, Turret.

Tow-rope (tōu·rōup). [f. Tow *v.*1 + Rope sb.1] A rope (hawser, cable, or the like) used in towing.

1743 Bulkeley & Cummins *Voy. S. Seas* 119 We called to them to take hold of a Towe-Rope, but they refused. 1801 Jefferson *Writ.* (ed. Ford) VIII. 75 You will follow the bark of liberty only by the help of a tow-rope. 1865 Dickens *Mut. Fr.* III. viii, The tow-rope was slackened by a turn of the stream.

Hence **Tow·-ro·ping,** in railway-shunting, the drawing of a vehicle by an engine on a parallel line of rails by means of a rope connecting the two. An illegal practice. See Propping *vbl. sb.* 3 for quots.

Tow-row (tau·rau·), *sb.* and *a.* [Reduplicated or extended form of Row sb.2; orig. *dial.*]

A. *sb.* An uproar, hubbub, noisy disturbance, din.

1877 *Holderness Gloss.*, *Tow-row*, a confusion, or noisy disturbance. 1886 Stevenson *Kidnapped* iv, A blinding flash,..and hard upon the heels of it, a great tow-row of thunder. 1894 Crockett *Raiders* (ed. 3) 15 Then..came a great towrow of laughter. 1894 Max Pemberton *Sea-Wolves* xxii, For a long space they kept up the tow-row and the din.

†B. *adj.* Intoxicated (? 'drunk and disorderly'). *slang.* *Obs.*

1709 Steele & Swift *Tatler* No. 71 ⁋ 8 He that drinks till he stares, is no more Tow-Row, but Honest.

So **Tow-row** *v.*, *intr.* a. to make a tow-row; b. *dial.* (see quot. 1854). Hence **Tow-rowing** *vbl. sb.*

1840 Thackeray *Barber Cox* Mar., Directly the tow-rowing began, off went Trumpeter like a thunder-bolt. 1854 Miss Baker *Northampt. Gloss.*, *Tow-rowing*, cleaning out dirty and disorderly places. 'I've been tow-rowing about all day among the dust'. 1899 Mrs. E. Kennard *Morals Midlands* xxvii. 240 The hounds were tow-rowing all round the covert.

Towrpyke, a winding stair: see Turnpike.

†**Tow·ry-low·ry.** *dial.* (Cf. Tirra-lirra.)

1632 Brome *North. Lasse* I. ii, And then towry, lowry, faith, my noble Governor, and I. 1878 *Cumberld. Gloss.*, *Towry lowry*, all in disorder.

Towsell, obs. form of Tolsel, tolzey.

Towser (tau·zəɹ), *sb.* Also 7 towzer, touzer, 9 touser. [f. Touse *v.* + -er1; with senses c, d, e cf. *thumper*, *whopper*, etc.] One who or that which touses. a. (with capital T). A common name for a large dog, such as was used to bait bears or bulls; also *transf.* of a person.

1678 Otway *Friendship in F.* IV. i, Fresh Game; that great Towser has started it already. 1681 *Trial S. Colledge* 59 Mr. Char...it was the Pictures of the Tantivies and the Towzer [Roger L'Estrange]. 1681 T. Flatman *Heraclitus Ridens* No. 30 (1713) I. 197 *Earn.* What Papers? Did he mean the Towzers, and the Gallows, and the Broom, for which he was so famous? 1682 N. N. (*title*) The Heu and Cry: or, a Relation of the Travels of the Devil and Towzer, Through all the Earthly Territorys, and the Infernal Region. 1684 Otway *Atheist* III. i, Never was seen so termagant a Towzer. 1696 tr. *Du Mont's Voy. Levant* 257 Poor Towzer was condemn'd to be Cudgel'd to Death. 1881 A. McLachlan in *Mod. Sc. Poets* II. 261 Ahint him Towser wags his tail.

†b. The five of trumps in the game of gleek. *Obs.*

1680 Cotton *Compl. Gamester* vi. (ed. 2) 65 The fifth [is called] Towser, the sixth Tumbler, which if in hand Towser is five and Tumbler six, and so double if turn'd up. 1688 R. Holme *Armoury* III. xvi. (Roxb.) 73/2 Towser, is the fifth of the trumps.

†c. A large ship. *Obs.* d. A large coarse apron. *dial.* e. A rough or energetic person. *dial.*

c. 1690 *Pagan Prince* xxix. 81 Now the Belgians, having lost..some three or four more of their biggest Towzers, made all the Sail they could to their own Coasts. d. 1865 R. Hunt *Pop. Rom. W. Eng.* Ser. II. 244 The Touser is a large apron or wrapper to come quite round and keep the under-garments clean. 1882 Jago *Cornw. Gloss.*, *Touser*, a large coarse apron for kitchen use. e. 1901 E. Phillpotts *Striking Hours* 222 A wonnerful bowerly maid her was, an' a towser for work, an' 'mazin' even-tempered tu. 1901 R. M. F. Watson *Closeburn* xiii. 221 A certain big, uncouth, unhallowed 'towser' named Tibbie Murdoch.

Hence **Tow·ser, -zer** *v.* (*nonce-wd.*), *trans.* to worry as a dog does.

c 1680 Hickeringill *Hist. Whiggism* I. Wks. 1716 I. 37 If they get a piece of a Text by the end..they do so tear it, and towze it, and towzer it..that they lose themselves.

Towst, Towsy: see Toust, Tousy.

Towster (tōu·stəɹ). *nonce-wd.* [f. Tow *v.*1 + -ster.] = Tower sb.2

1885 Warren & Cleverly *Wand. 'Beetle'* 24 The towsters came to a halt.

†**Towtaw·,** *v.* *Obs. rare*—1. [f. Tow sb.1 + Taw *v.*1] *trans.* To scutch (flax). Cf. Tow *v.*3

1649 Blithe *Eng. Improv. Impr.* (1653) 260 Kilne-drying it, then breaking and towtawing it, then hetchelling and dressing it up.

Towtch, obs. form of Touch.

Towy (tōu·i), *a.* [f. Tow sb.1 + -y.] Like or of the nature of tow.

1601 Holland *Pliny* xix. i. II. 4 You shall know by the skin or rind thereof if it be loose and readie to depart from the towie substance of the stem. 1673 Grew *Anat. Trunks* I. ii. § 30 The Lignous and Towy Parts of all Plants are Tubulary. 1858 *Sat. Rev.* 21 Aug. 184/2 Painted..with bullet eyes, vermilion cheeks, towy locks, and pudgy limbs. 1881 *Gard. Chron.* XVI. 654/3 Its leaves .. produce a soft towy herbage.

Towylle, obs. form of Towel.

†**Towyth,** obs. erroneous form of Thought.

c 1430 *Hymns Virg.* 121 We be sorry þatt we dede agayn þi wille Or with towyth or with dede.

Towze, Towzer: see Touse, Towser.

†**Towze-match.** *Obs. rare.* [? f. Touse *v.* 4 + Match sb.2 2 b.] 'Match' made of 'toused' or teased hemp or other fibrous material.

1627 Capt. Smith *Seaman's Gram.* ii. 13 Okum is old Ropes torne in peeces like Towze Match, or Hurds of Flax. 1630 — *Trav. & Adv.* v. 8 Over that a strong Searcloth, then over all a good thicknesse of Towze-match well tempered with oyle of Linseed.

Tox (tǫks), *sb.* *Zool.* [ad. Gr. τόξον Toxon 1.] A sponge-spicule having the form of a double curved rod, like a Cupid's bow; = Toxaspire.

1909 in *Cent. Dict. Supp.*

†**Tox,** *v.* *Obs.* ? *slang.* Short for *intoxicate*. Hence †**Toxed, toxt,** †**To·xing** *ppl. adjs.*

1635 Heywood *Philocothon.* i. 3 When their more sober consciences can Iustifie against their toxed Insolence. *Ibid.* iv. 20 Addicted to strong and toxing drinkes. 1637 — *Dial.* iv. Wks. 1874 VI. 191 Braines well toxt with wine.

Tox-1, combining form, repr. Toxi- or Toxo-2 before a vowel. ‖**Toxæmia** (tǫksī·miă), also anglicized **toxemy** [Gr. αἷμα blood, after *anæmia*, etc.], a morbid condition of the blood caused by a toxin; blood-poisoning; hence **Toxæmic** (-ī·mik) *a.*, pertaining to or affected with toxæmia. **Toxalbumin** (-ælbiū·min), also -en, a poisonous or pathogenic albumin or protein produced by bacteria; a protein toxin; hence **Toxalbu·mic** *a.*, pertaining to or caused by a toxalbumin; so

Toxa·lbumose, a poisonous albumose. **To·xamine** (-āmǝin), a poisonous amine. **Toxanæmia** (-ănī·miă), anæmia caused by the action of a poison, usually a ptomaine.

1860 Mayne *Expos. Lex.*, *Toxæmia*,..a contaminated state of the blood, as in syphilis; poisoned blood; toxemy. 1881 *Trans. Obstet. Soc. Lond.* XXII. 283 There was a dangerous state of toxæmia. 1876 Bristowe *The. & Pract. Med.* (1878) 124 Which so often..cause *toxæmic symptoms. 1899 *Allbutt's Syst. Med.* VIII. 418 The post-febrile insanities are divisible into two classes—the purely anæmic, and the toxæmic. 1902 *Buck's Handbk. Med. Sc.* V. 33 As the effects of other chemical or *toxalbumic poisons manifest themselves as a psychosis. 1890 *Pall Mall G.* 26 Apr. 6/3 *Toxalbumen is said to be the excretion of a bacillus of diphtheria. 1892 *Pop. Sc. Monthly* XLI. 633 It neutralizes the potent toxalbumin of tetanus in test-tube cultures. 1896 *Allbutt's Syst. Med.* I. 767 Brieger and Fränkel then described a proteid poison which they obtained from cultures of the tetanus bacilli and named tox-albumin. 1902 R. Muir in *Encycl. Brit.* XXVI. 64/2 Such a powder gives a proteid reaction, and is no doubt largely composed of albumoses, hence the name *toxalbumoses has been applied. 1897 *Allbutt's Syst. Med.* III. 735 Certain specimens of cheese contain a *toxamine, termed by its discoverer, Professor Vaughan, 'tyrotoxicon'. 1891 *Cent. Dict.*, *Toxanemia*, *Toxanæmia*. 1899 *Syd. Soc. Lex.*, *Toxanæmia*, *Toxanemia*, anæmia caused by the actions of ptomaines.

Tox-2: see Toxo-1.

Toxarch (tǫ·ksaɹk). *Anc. Gr. Hist.* [ad. Gr. τόξαρχος 'lord of the bow', captain of the archers, f. τόξον bow + -αρχος ruler.] The title of the captain of the city-guard of mercenaries at Athens.

1828 [G. C. Lewis] tr. *Böckh's Publ. Econ. Athens* I. 278 The public slaves who composed the city-guard..are generally called bow-men (τοξόται), or, from the native country of the majority, Scythians... Their officers had the name of Toxarchs (τόξαρχοι).

Toxaspire (tǫ·ksăspəiəɹ). *Zool.* [irreg. (for **toxospire*) f. Gr. τόξο-ν bow + σπεῖρα coil, Spire.] In sponges, a form of microsclere or flesh-spicule: see quots. Hence **Toxaspi·ral** *a.*, pertaining to or of the form of a toxaspire.

1887 Sollas in *Encycl. Brit.* XXII. 417/2 A turn and a part of a turn of a spiral of somewhat higher pitch than that of a sigmaspire gives the *toxaspire*. 1888 — in *Challenger Rep.* XXV. p. lxii, *Toxaspire*.—A spiral rod in which the twist a little exceeds a single revolution. The pitch of the spiral is usually great and the spicule consequently appears bow-shaped when viewed laterally.

Toxi- (tǫksi), combining form arbitrarily repr. Toxic or Toxin, in recent scientific words, chiefly pathological. **Toxidermic** (-dǭ·ɹmik) *a.* [Gr. δέρμα skin], pertaining to skin-disease produced by a poison: cf. *toxicodermitis* in Toxico-. **Toxi·ferous** *a.* = *toxophorous* in Toxo-2. **Toxignomic** (-gnǫ·mik) *a.* [Gr. γνώμη judgement, opinion], enabling one to diagnose the action of a toxin. ‖**Toxihæ·mia** [Gr. αἷμα blood] = *toxæmia*: see Tox-1. **Toxi-infe·ctious, -infe·ctive** *adjs.*, involving or characterized by infection due to a toxin. ‖**Toxiphagus** (-i·făgǒs), pl. **-phagi** (-fădʒəi) [Gr. -φάγος eating], one who eats poisons: cf. *toxicophagous* in Toxico-. ‖**Toxipho·bia** [-phobia], fear of being poisoned, as a form of insanity or monomania; hence **Toxipho·biac,** one affected with toxiphobia. **Toxipho·ric** (-fǫ·rik) *a.* = *toxophoric*: see Toxo-2. **Toxiresin** (-re·zin), name of a poisonous substance obtained from digitalis by the action of acids.

1899 *Allbutt's Syst. Med.* VIII. 587 A pilo-sebaceous folliculitis of..microbic or *toxidermic character. 1899 *Syd. Soc. Lex.*, *Toxiferous*, carrying or conveying poison. 1890 Billings *Med. Dict.*, *Toxihæmia*, Toxæmia. 1907 *Jrnl. Med. Research* Dec. 352 The statement of Dide, who asserts that there is a diminution in alexin in patients suffering from the '*toxi-infectious' forms of insanity. 1897 *Allbutt's Syst. Med.* III. 749 Microbic agency which sets up *toxi-infective processes. 1875 H. C. Wood *Therap.* (1879) 377 The *toxiphagi are asserted to be remarkably long-lived people. 1876 C. A. Cameron in *Dublin Jrnl. Med. Sc.* Feb. 98, I propose to apply the term *toxiphobia to a species of monomania..those labouring under which believe that persistent attempts are being made to poison them. Of the sixty-three *toxiphobiacs, only two were obviously insane. 1902 G. M. Sternberg in *Science* 24 Oct. 665/1 The atom-groups which..Ehrlich calls the '*toxiphoric side chain'. 1890 Billings *Med. Dict.*, *Toxiresin*, a product of the action of acids upon digitoxin; a powerful cardiac poison. 1899 *Syd. Soc. Lex.*, Toxiresin.

Toxic (tǫ·ksik), *a.* (*sb.*) [f. med.L. *toxic-us* poisoned, imbued with poison, f. Toxic-um. So F. *toxique* 'poison' (1762 in *Dict. Trévoux*).]

1. Of the nature of a poison; poisonous.

1664 Evelyn *Sylva* 65 The toxic quality was certainly in the liquor.., not in the nature of the wood; which yet he [Pliny] affirms is cur'd of that Venenous quality by driving a brazen wedge into the body of it. 1674 Blount *Glossogr.*, *Toxic*, venenous, poisonous. 1876 T. Bryant *Pract. Surg.* I. ii. 53 Poisoning..due to the introduction into the torrent of the circulation of toxic substances. 1899 *Allbutt's Syst. Med.* VII. 815 The urine is normally toxic, and incessantly takes from the blood its toxicity.

2. Caused or produced by a poison; due to poisoning.

1872 *Contemp. Rev.* XX. 751 Whether it be the toxic condition of the blood. 1874 Maudsley *Respons. in Ment. Dis.* iii. 79 The peculiar disorders of the physical and mental functions..to which he gave the name of Toxic Insanity. 1899 *Allbutt's Syst. Med.* VIII. 310 Toxic insanity depends on poisons either derived from without or generated within the body.

b. Of intoxication, intoxicated; tipsy. *humorous.*

1899 Mary Kingsley *W. Afr. Stud.* i. 2 A toxic state where a man can't see the holes through a ladder.

B. *sb.* A toxic substance, a poison.

1890 *Spectator* 6 Dec., M. Pasteur..pointing out..that the lymph is really a 'toxic' or poison, of terrible energy and unknown effects. 1904 *Westm. Gaz.* 15 June 2/1 Alkaloids and toxics, such as chloral, emit the N-rays freely.

Toxical (tǫ·ksikăl), *a.* [f. as prec. + -al: see -ical.] Of toxic nature or character.

1607 Topsell *Four-f. Beasts* (1658) 199 Goats bloud sod with marrow may be taken against all toxical poison. 1650 Charleton *Paradoxes* 65 Why the blood of a Bull is toxicall and poysonous. 1855 Wharton & Stillé *Med. Jurispr.* § 496. 378 The production of toxical effects. 1863 *N. Syd. Soc. Year-bk. Med.* 444 Symptoms of the toxical action of the drug. 1884 *Manch. Exam.* 29 Dec. 6/5 Tobacco smoke ..contains a second toxical principle called colidine.

Hence **To·xically** *adv.*, poisonously; in quot., in relation to toxicology.

1887 A. M. Brown *Anim. Alkal.* 39 This base is toxically interesting.

Toxicant (tǫ·ksikănt), *a.* and *sb.* *rare.* [f. pr. pple. of med.L. *toxicāre* to poison: see -ant.] a. *adj.* Acting as a poison; poisonous, toxic. b. *sb.* A poisonous substance, a poison.

1882 Ogilvie (Annandale), *Toxicant*,..a poison of a stimulating, narcotic, anæsthetic nature, especially such as seriously affects the health when habitually indulged in. *Dr. Richardson.* 1891 *Cent. Dict.*, *Toxicant* adj. 1892 *Illustr. Lond. News* 13 Aug. 211/3 Coffee (that favourite vehicle of the deadlier toxicants in the East).

†**To·xicate,** *ppl. a.* *Obs.* Also 5 toxicat, 6 tocksicate. [f. med.L. *toxicāt-us*, pa. pple. of L. *toxicāre* to smear with poison: see next.] Charged or infected with poison; poisoned; poisonous.

c 1470 Henryson *Mor. Fab.* III. (*Cock & Fox*) xxx, Flatteraris..With fals mening, and mynd maist toxicate. *c* 1475 *Partenay* 1429 The king..With toxicat uenym replete was certain. 1581 J. Studley *Seneca's Hercules Œtæus* 199 b, So yet my wits be tocksicate, although my feare be gone.

†**To·xicate,** *v.* *Obs.* [f. ppl. stem of med.L. *toxicāre* to poison (in John of Salisbury, *c* 1150), f. L. *toxic-um* poison: see Toxicum.] *trans.* To poison. Hence †**To·xicating** *vbl. sb.*

1635 Heywood *Hierarch.* viii. 518 Which Feuer shakes him,..And a strange Megrim toxicates his head. 1653 Chisenhale *Cath. Hist.* 12 Each morning to bite on Rue, which..secures her against the toxicating of that venomous Basilisk.

Toxication (tǫksikēi·ʃən). [n. of action f. med.L. *toxicāre*: see prec.] Poisoning: esp. by toxic substances produced by disease-germs.

1821 Coleridge in *Blackw. Mag.* X. 243, I..know of no reason, why to these *toxications* (especially when taken through the skin, and to the cataleptic state produced by them,) we should not attribute the poor wretches' own belief of their guilt. 1860 in Mayne *Expos. Lex.* 1887 A. M. Brown *Anim. Alkal.* 127 The patients so affected have all the appearance of toxication, and by the poisonous alkaloids—that is, the vital alkaloids or leucomaines.

Toxicity (tǫksi·sĭti). [f. Toxic + -ity.] Toxic or poisonous quality, esp. in relation to its degree or strength.

1881 *Nature* 3 Nov. 24/2 On the comparative toxicity of different metals, by M. Richet... He named the limit of toxicity the quantity of poison per litre of water, allowing a fish to live more than forty-eight hours. 1881 *Pharmaceut. Jrnl.* 26 Nov. 439/2 Neither would there appear to be any relation between toxicity and chemical function, for although potassium and sodium are nearly allied.., the former is—at least in respect to fish—twenty-four times more poisonous than sodium. 1898 P. Manson *Trop. Diseases* xvii. 283 The microbes were increased in toxicity to a definite point.

Toxico- (tǫ·ksiko), before a vowel **toxic-**, repr. Gr. τοξικόν in sense 'poison' (see Toxicum), but chiefly used as combining form of Toxic, in scientific terms, mostly pathological. ‖**Toxicæ·mia, -e·mia** [Gr. αἷμα blood] = *toxæmia*: see Tox-. ‖**Toxicoderma** (-dǭ·ɹmă), **-dermati·tis, -dermi·tis** [Gr. δέρμα skin: see -itis], inflammation of the skin caused by an irritant poison. **Toxicogenic** (-dʒe·nik) *a.* [-*genic*: cf. -gen, -geny], producing or generating poison. ‖**Toxicohæ·mia,** also anglicized **-hemy** [Gr. αἷμα blood] = *toxæmia*: see Tox-. ‖**Toxicoma·nia** [Mania], a morbid craving for poisons. **Toxicophagous** (-ǫ·făgəs) *a.* [Gr. -φάγος eating], addicted to eating poisonous substances; so **Toxicophagy** (-ǫ·fădʒi), the habit of eating poisonous substances. **Toxicophobia** (-fōu·biă) = *toxiphobia*: see Toxi-. **To·xicotrauma·tic** (-trǭmæ·tik) *a.* [Gr. τραυματικός, f. τραῦμα wound], pertaining to a poisoned wound. See also Toxicodendron, Toxicology, etc.

1857 Dunglison *Med. Lex.*, *Toxicæmia*, Toxicohæmia. 1890 Billings *Med. Dict.*, *Toxicoderma* or *Toxicodermatitis*... *Toxicodermitis*, dermatitis caused by a poison. 1899 *Syd. Soc. Lex.*, *Toxicogenic*,..as a toxicogenic micro-organism. 1902 *Buck's Handbk. Med. Sc.* IV. 184 A relatively small number of bacteria are capable of making poisonous products, and to these..the term *toxicogenic* may be applied. 1871 Yule *Marco Polo* III. xxv. (1903) II. 392 *note*, The famous *toxicophagous Sultan Mahmūd Begara (1459–1511). 1899 *Allbutt's Syst. Med.* VI. 657 Oppenheim attributes the latter..to a *toxico-traumatic cause.

‖**Toxicodendron** (tǫ·ksikoˌde·ndrǫn). *Bot.* [mod.L. (Tournefort, 1700, in sense a), f. Gr. τοξικόν (see Toxicum) + δένδρον tree.]

a. A former genus, now reckoned as a species of *Rhus* or sumac (*R. Toxicodendron*), a N. American shrub, also called *poison-ivy* (see Poison sb. 5 b). b. A synonym of *Hyænanche*, a S. African genus of euphorbiaceous trees or shrubs with poisonous fruit, used for killing noxious animals, whence the local names *Wolveboon* (i. e. Wolf's-bane) and Hyena-poison.

1721 W. Sherard in *Phil. Trans.* XXXI. 147 The Poyson-Tree...Tis a species of Toxicodendron, tho' not nam'd by Dr. Tournefort in his Institutions. 1755 *Gentl. Mag.* Sept. 395/1 Experiments made on staining of linen with the juice of Toxicodendron. 1758 Ellis in *Phil. Trans.* L. 445 He still insists on it, that these two Toxicodendrons are the same. 1801 Mason *Suppl. to Johnson*, *Toxicodendron*, a North-American plant. 1888 *Nicholson's Dict. Gard.* IV. 63 *Toxicodendron* Syn. *Hyænanche*.

Hence **To·xicode·ndric** *a.*, *Chem.* applied to an acid derived from *Rhus Toxicodendron* and other species, subsequently found to be identical with acetic acid; **To·xicode·ndrol** [-ol 3], *Chem.* a non-volatile oil constituting the poisonous principle of *Rhus Toxicodendron* and other species.

1865 J. M. Maisch in *Proc. Amer. Pharm. Assoc.* 172 A new organic acid, for which I propose the name of *Toxicodendric acid*. 1876 Duhring *Dis. Skin* 325 The poison is an exceedingly volatile acid,—toxicodendric acid. 1898 *U. S. Dept. Agric., Bot.* Bulletin No. 20. 37 The poison is in reality a non-volatile oil. In January, 1895, Dr. Franz Pfaff ..announced this discovery. The oil has since been purified and named toxicodendrol.

To·xicoid, *a.* [f. Gr. τοξικόν (Toxicum) + -oid.] Resembling poison.

1891 *Cent. Dict.* cites Dunglison. 1899 in *Syd. Soc. Lex.*

Toxicology (tǫksikǫ·lŏdʒi). [= F. *toxicologie* (1812 in Hatz.-Darm.), f. Gr. τοξικόν taken in sense 'poison' (see Toxicum) and -logy.] The science of poisons; that department of pathology or medicine which deals with the nature and effects of poisons. So **To·xicolo·gical** *a.*, belonging or relating to toxicology (sometimes erron. used for *toxical*). Thence **To·xicolo·gically** *adv.*, in relation to toxicology; **Toxico·logist,** a person versed in toxicology, one who studies poisons.

1839 *Blackw. Mag.* XLV. 59 To guess whether the *toxicological agent..was a mineral, a vegetable, or an animal poison. 1842 Brande *Dict. Sc.*, etc. s. v. *Toxicology*, We have elsewhere..referred to their toxicological history. *c* 1865 J. Wylde in *Circ. Sc.* I. 320/2 In toxicological analyses. 1882 Springmuhl in *Standard* 23 Mar. 2/2 It differs *toxicologically and constitutionally from pure Aconitine. 1829–32 R. Christison *Treat. Poison* xiii. (ed. 2) 387 The rule laid down by almost all modern *toxicologists. 1897 *Allbutt's Syst. Med.* II. 876. 1799 Hooper *Med. Dict.*, *Toxicology*,..a dissertation on poisons. 1853 W. Gregory *Inorg. Chem.* (ed. 3) 230 The reader is referred to the works on toxicology and legal medicine.

‖**Toxicosis** (tǫksikōu·sis). *Path.* Pl. **-oses** (-ōu·sīz). [mod.L., f. as prec. + -osis.] A disease or morbid condition produced by the action of a poison.

1857 Dunglison *Med. Lex.*, *Toxicoses*, a family of diseases ..caused by the reception of poisons into the system.

‖**To·xicum.** Pl. **-a.** [L. *toxicum* 'poison', orig. 'poison for arrows', ad. Gr. τοξικὸν φάρμακον poison (φάρμακον) for smearing arrows (τοξικός, -όν, f. τόξα pl. arrows, transf. fr. τόξον bow). Τοξικόν = 'of or pertaining to the bow', and had originally nothing to do with poison. But the effect of using τοξικόν, *toxicum* as short for the Gr. phrase was to transfer the sense 'poison' from φάρμακον to *toxicum*, first as 'poison for arrows' and at length as 'poison' generally, = L. *venēnum*.] Poison: cf. Toxic *sb.*

1601 Holland *Pliny* xxix. iv. II. 355 It is generally thought, that for the venome called Toxicum, there is not a better counterpoyson than dogs bloud. 1657 *Physical Dict.*, *Toxicum*, a venom or poyson wherewith arrows are poysoned. 1669 W. Simpson *Hydrol. Chym.* 78 The vital spirits stand amazed as if smitten with a thunder-clap from the uterine toxicum. 1693 tr. *Blancard's Phys. Dict.* (ed. 2), *Toxica*, poysonous Medicaments, wherewith Barbarians use to anoint their Arrows. 1704 in J. Harris *Lex. Techn.* I.

Toxidermic to **Toxi-infective**: see Toxi-.

To·xifer. *Zool.* [ad. mod.L. *Toxifera* (Gray), f. Gr. τόξα arrows (or τόξευμα arrow, dart) + L. *-fer* bearing.] A mollusc of the sub-order *Toxifera*. (Cf. Toxoglossate.)

1853 J. E. Gray in *Ann. & Mag. Nat. Hist.* Ser. II. XII. 177 The subulate barbed teeth are implanted by a distinct root into the substance of the tube...The structure and organization of the mouth are so unlike that of the other *Proboscidifera* and *Rostrifera*, where the teeth are placed on a lingual ribbon and used to rasp the food..that I am inclined to form the *Cones* into a third sub-order, which may be called *Toxifera*. 1861 P. P. Carpenter in *Rep. Smithsonian Instit.* 1860, 193 So far as known, the teeth and proboscis are like those of other Toxifers. 1863 — in *Proc. Zool. Soc.* 23 June 347 Species belonging to different families of Proboscidifers and Toxifers.

Toxin (tǫ·ksin). Also *erron.* -ine. [f. Tox-ic + -in 1.] A specific poison, usually of an albu-

minous nature, esp. one produced by a microbe, which causes a particular disease when present in the system of a human or animal body.

1886 E. R. Lankester *Advancem. Science* (1890) 168 In other cases the toxin and the vaccin seem almost certainly to be distinct. 1891 *Lancet* 3 Oct. 792 In a few cases..the introduction of the toxines secreted by the bacilli sufficed to set up a commencement of the process in the joints characteristic of rheumatism. 1904 *Brit. Med. Jrnl.* 10 Sept. 557 The union of toxin and antitoxin is dissociable. 1905 G. A. Reid *Princ. Heredity* ii. 21 Toxins, extremely complex chemical compounds, are defensive weapons which protect the organisms producing them from their enemies, the phagocytes of the blood and tissues.

b. *attrib.* and *Comb.*

1896 *Allbutt's Syst. Med.* I. 893 In order to produce an immunity all that is required is to render the body toxin-proof. 1902 *Encycl. Brit.* XXVI. 66/2 In the development of toxin-immunity the doses, small at first, are gradually increased. 1903 *Brit. Med. Jrnl.* 4 Apr. 784 No proof is afforded..of a separate toxophore group in the toxin molecule. 1904 *Ibid.* 10 Sept. 576 The chemical interpretation of toxin-antitoxin antagonism.

Hence ‖**Toxinæmia** (-ī·miă) [Gr. αἷμα blood], the presence of a toxin in the blood: cf. *toxæmia* (Tox-1), *toxicæmia* (Toxico-).

1900 *Buck's Handbk. Med. Sc.* I. 284 Various toxæmic conditions..and the different toxinæmias induced by the infectious diseases—diphtheria and typhoid or typhus fever.

Toxin, rare obs. spelling of Tocsin.

Toxiphagus to **Toxiresin**: see Toxi-.

To·xity, abbreviated form of Toxicity.

1887 A. M. Brown *Anim. Alkal.* 103 Previous alkaline saturation of the material did not revive its toxity. 1894 *Westm. Gaz.* 11 Oct. 2/1 By multiplying the intensity of the toxity of the bacillus.

‖**Toxius** (tǫ·ksiǒs). *Zool.* Pl. **toxii** (-iˌəi). [mod.L., f. Gr. τόξον bow.] A form of sponge-spicule: see quot.

1886 *Proc. Zool. Soc.* 21 Dec. 562 Sponges..Flesh-Spicules...6. Toxius. Curved in the centre, the two ends in a straight line, thus ⌒.

Toxo-1 (tǫkso), before a vowel **tox-**, combining form repr. Gr. τόξον bow, in Toxocampid, Toxodon, Toxology, Toxophilite, etc., q. v.

Toxo-2, used as combining form of Toxin (cf. Toxi-) or instead of Toxico-, in recent scientific terms, chiefly of pathology or physiological chemistry. **Toxo-infe·ctious** *a.*, involving infection by a toxin: = *toxi-infectious* (Toxi-). **Toxope·ptone,** (*a*) a poisonous substance, of the nature of a peptone, found in cultures of cholera bacillus (*Cent. Dict. Suppl.*); (*b*) = Peptotoxin. **To·xophil** (-fil) *a.* [Gr. -φιλος loving], having affinity for a toxin. **To·xophore** (-fōəɹ), **Toxophoric** (-fǫ·rik), **Toxophorous** (-ǫ·fŏrəs) *adjs.* [Gr. -φορος bearing, carrying], poison-bearing; applied to a particular group of atoms in the molecule of a toxin to which its toxic properties are due. **Toxophylaxin** (-filæ·ksin) [Gr. φύλαξ guard, protector], **Toxosozin** (-sōu·zin) [Gr. σώζειν to save], names for defensive proteins or antitoxins (see quots.). **Toxoprotein** (-prōu·tiˌin), a toxic protein, or mixture of a toxin and a protein.

1907 *Med. Record* 17 Aug. 279 The original cause of the lack of coagulation may be *toxoinfectious, or due to marked congestion. 1896 *Allbutt's Syst. Med.* I. 526 Scholl, growing the vibrio, in eggs, obtained a *toxo-peptone. 1902 Vaughan & Novy *Cellular Toxins* (ed. 4) 182 The body cells must possess *toxophil side chains. By this we mean that..there are groups of atoms which may combine with bacterial toxins. 1900 *Lancet* 18 Aug. 528/1 The *toxophore group of the toxin molecule being much less stable than the haptophore group was much more easily destroyed. 1903 *Brit. Med. Jrnl.* 21 Mar. 654 The other atomic group is toxophore, namely, is the cause of the specific toxic action. 1902 *Ibid.* 29 Mar. 785 The toxin molecule..must possess a second group which he [Ehrlich] calls the *toxophoric group. 1904 *Ibid.* 10 Sept. 574 Although the toxophoric group may be similar, the haptophor is dissimilar. 1902 *Encycl. Brit.* XXVI. 65/1 In the molecule of toxin there are at least two chief atom groups—one, the 'haptophorous', by which the toxin molecule is attached to the cell protoplasm; and the other the '*toxophorous', which has a ferment-like action on the living molecule, producing a disturbance which results in the toxic symptoms. 1899 *Syd. Soc. Lex.*, *Toxophylaxin*, a defensive proteid produced in the body of an animal which has acquired immunity for a given infectious disease, and which has the power of rendering inert the toxic products of the pathogenic micro-organisms to which the condition was due. 1896 *Allbutt's Syst. Med.* I. 523 The *toxo-proteins in reality are mixtures of albuminous, proteid, or albuminoid bodies with the true toxins. 1899 *Syd. Soc. Lex.*, *Toxosozin*, a defensive proteid found in the body of a normal animal which has the power of protecting itself to a greater or less degree against micro-organisms and their products.

Toxocampid (tǫksokæ·mpid), *sb.* and *a.* *Entom.* [ad. mod.L. *Toxocampidæ*, f. *Toxocampa*, f. Gr. τόξον bow + κάμπη caterpillar.] a. *sb.* A Noctuine moth of the family *Toxocampidæ*, typified by the genus *Toxocampa*, having bow-shaped marks on the fore wings, e. g. *Toxocampa Pastinum*, the black-neck. b. *adj.* Belonging to or having the characters of the family *Toxocampidæ*.

Toxodon (tǫ·ksŏdǫn). *Palæont.* [mod.L. (Owen, 1837), f. Gr. τόξον bow + ὀδούς, ὀδοντ- tooth: see quot. 1849.] A genus of large extinct quadrupeds, having strongly curved molar teeth, whose remains are found in Pleistocene deposits in S. America. Hence **To·xodont,** *adj.* belonging to or having the characters of the order *Toxodonta*, typified by this genus; *sb.* a quadruped of this order.

1837 Owen in *Proc. Geol. Soc.* II. 542 So far as dental characters have weight, the *Toxodon* must be referred to the rodent order. 1839 G. Roberts *Dict. Geol.*, *Toxodon*, ..a gigantic quadruped approaching, in character, to the pachydermata. 1849 *Sk. Nat. Hist.*, *Mammalia* III. 115 The molar teeth also were rootless, and curved, whence the name toxodon. 1859 Darwin *Orig. Spec.* xi. (1878) 294 Remains of Mastodon, Megatherium, Toxodon and other extinct monsters.

To·xoglo·ssate, *a.* *Zool.* [f. mod.L. *Toxoglossa* (Troschel, 1848), f. Gr. τόξα arrows, darts + γλῶσσα tongue (not from τοξικόν poison): see -ate 2 2.] Having the characters of the *Toxoglossa* of Troschel, a group of gastropod molluscs; the same as Gray's *Toxifera*.

[1848 Troschel in Wilfmann & Ruthe's *Handbch. d. Zoologie* (ed. 3).] 1853 J. E. Gray in *Ann. & Mag. Nat. Hist.* Ser. II. XI. 270 [following Troschel] Sub-order *Rostrifera*...Section 2. *Toxoglossa*, lingual membrane with two series of subulate, elongate, often barbed lateral teeth. 1891 *Cent. Dict.* s.v., A toxoglossate gastropod. [1913 Prof. G. C. Bourne in *Let.*, I am pretty sure that Troschel compared the teeth to arrows..when he described and classified 3 families as *Toxoglossa*... As a matter of fact all the *Toxoglossa* have a poison-gland, but this was a later discovery.]

Toxoid (tǫ·ksoid). [f. Tox(in (cf. Tox-1) + -oid.] A modification or transformation product of a toxin, in which the toxophoric group of atoms is lost, and which has therefore no toxic effect, but retains affinity for the antitoxin. Also *attrib.*

1900 *Lancet* 18 Aug. 528/1 Very sensitive animals such as mice and guinea-pigs might..be easily and rapidly immunised against tetanus by means of toxoids only. 1902 *Brit. Med. Jrnl.* 29 Mar. 785 The modified toxin consists of a molecule with a haptophoric but no toxophoric group and is called 'toxoid'. 1903 *Ibid.* 21 Mar. 654 The toxoids may again be subdivided into three groups, according to their affinity for the antitoxin, which may obviously be either greater (protoxoid), equal (syntoxoid), or less than (epitoxoid) that of the toxin. 1904 *Ibid.* 10 Sept. 577 They were however able to produce toxoid formation in this constituent.

Toxology (tǫksǫ·lŏdʒi). *nonce-wd.* [f. Gr. τόξον bow + -logy.] *prop.* The study of the bow, i. e. archery; in quot. humorously used for 'archery'.

1843 *Fraser's Mag.* XXVII. 401 He is reluctant to..run the risk of exposing his well-varnished cab as a pleasing target for the poles of the loitering omnibuses, the drivers of which latter have obtained a well-earned fame for their dexterity in this..department of toxology.

Toxon 1 (tǫ·ksǫn). *Zool.* [a. Gr. τόξον bow.] A bow-shaped sponge spicule. Cf. Tox *sb.*

1894 *Jrnl. Marine Zool.* Feb. 40 A second and slender form of spicule, bow-shaped (toxon) can also be made out.

To·xon 2. *Path. Chem.* [f. Tox(in + -*on*, -one.] (See quotation.)

1900 *Lancet* 18 Aug. 528/1 Löffler's diphtheria bacillus produced substances of two kinds—toxins and toxons...The action of the toxons was different from, and weaker than, that of the toxins. 1904 *Brit. Med. Jrnl.* 10 Sept. 567 The diphtheria poison is not a single substance, but consists of two chief components, toxin and toxon.

Hence **To·xonoid,** a modification of a toxon, in which the toxic properties are lost. (Cf. Toxoid.)

1904 *Brit. Med. Jrnl.* 10 Sept. 573 Ehrlich explained the peculiarity that the 'toxon' has acute killing properties, by the assumption of two different kinds of toxon, thus introducing the conception of a new body—the toxonoid.

Toxopeptone, Toxophil: see Toxo-2.

Toxophilite (tǫksǫ·filəit). [app. f. *Toxophil-us* (imaginary proper name invented by Ascham, and hence title of his book (1545), intended to mean 'lover of the bow' (f. Gr. τόξον bow + φίλος lover), for which the regular Gr. formation would have been *φιλότοξος: see -phil, Philo-) + -ite1: *quasi* 'a follower of Toxophilus'.] A lover or devotee of archery, an archer.

1813 J. C. Hobhouse *Journey* (ed. 2) 929 Memorials of the distance to which some of the Sultans, and other distinguished Toxophilites, have shot their arrows. 1845 Thackeray *Leg. Rhine* viii, His Grace..gives an archery meeting once a year, and prizes for which we toxophilites muster strong. 1868 Miss Braddon *Dead Sea Fr.* xxi, A triumphant display of his genius as a toxophilite.

b. *attrib.* Of or pertaining to archers or archery.

1794 *Sporting Mag.* III. 206 That the Toxophilite Society shall not exceed the number of one hundred and sixty subscribing members. 1845 Thackeray *Leg. Rhine* viii, All his new toxophilite friends. 1848 — *Van. Fair* iii, To wear Lincoln Green toxophilite hats and feathers.

Hence (*nonce-wds.*) **Toxophilitic** (-i·tik) *a.*, pertaining or relating to archers or archery; **Toxo·philitism, Toxo·philism, Toxo·phily,** the practice of, or addiction to, archery.

1887 *All Year Round* 29 Sept. 185 The spirit of *toxophilism is essentially different from..the spirit of the age. 1857 *Chamb. Jrnl.* VII. 141 The *toxophilitic proficiency of William Tell. 1840 T. Hook in *New Monthly Mag.* LX. 152 Dressed in green, with hats, and feathers, and quivers, and all the paraphernalia of *toxophilitism. 1887 *Field* 16 July 103/1 Amongst the votaries of *toxophily.

Toxophore to **Toxosozin**: see Toxo-2.

Toxt: see Tox *v.*

Toy (toi), *sb.* Forms: ?4, 6–7 toye, 6– toy; *Pl.* 6–7 toyes, toies, 6– toys. [*Toy* sb. and vb. (formerly *toye*) have been in common use since *c* 1530, when both are given by Palsgr., and used by Skelton and Tindale. But a single instance of *toye* sb., apparently the same word, occurs in Robert of Brunne. It is difficult to conceive how such a word in use *c* 1300 should thus disappear for two centuries, and then should all at once burst into view with a wide sense-development. The etymology is equally problematic, and, in spite of current conjectures, must still be considered unascertained: see Note below.]

I. Abstract senses, meaning action, act, notion, feeling.

†1. Amorous sport, dallying, toying; with *pl.*, an act or piece of amorous sport, a light caress.

[1303 R. Brunne *Handl. Synne* 7891 Whedyr hyt be yn a womman handlyng, Or yn any oþer lusty þyng;..Amendeþ ʒow, pur charyte, And makeþ nat a-mys þe toye [*so all MSS.*], Þat þe fende of ʒou hane Ioye.] 1565 Cooper *Thesaurus* s.v. *Amo*: *Amatoriæ leuitates*, Louers toyes. 1590 Spenser *F. Q.* II. vi. 37 A foe of folly and immodest toy. 1594 — *Epithal.* 365 For greedy pleasure, carelesse of your toyes, Thinks more upon her paradise of joyes, Then what ye do. 1594 Willobie *Avisa* xlvii. iii, These toyes in tyme will make her yielde. 1667 Milton *P. L.* ix. 1034 So said he, and forbore not glance or toy, Of amorous intent, well understood Of Eve. 1668 Etherege *She Would if She Could* II. ii, Her toy was such, that every touch Would make a lover madder. 1707 Ward *Hud. Rediv.* II. ii. 8 (Farmer) Kisses, Love-Toys, and am'rous Prattle.

†2. A sportive or frisky movement; a piece of fun, amusement, or entertainment; a fantastic act or practice; an antic, a trick. *Obs.*

a 1500 Medwall *Nature* I. 786 (Brandl), Though I say yt a praty boy..He maketh me laugh wyth many a toy, The vrchyn ys so mad. *Ibid.* 1001 He that wold lordshyp enioy And playe euer styll the old boy Me semeth he doth but make a toy. 1530 Tindale *Answ. More* Wks. (1572) 249/1 We heare but voyces with out signification,..& wonder at disguisings & toyes wherof we know no meanyng. *c* 1555 Harpsfield *Divorce Hen. VIII* (Camden) 291 Neither was there ever any bearwards Jackanapes that made more pastime and toys to the people, than this. 1561 Hollybush *Hom. Apoth.* 9 Somtyme croweth he like a cocke, somtyme barketh he like a dogge, and many such foolish toyes vseth he. *c* 1575 *Perfect Bk. Kepinge Sparhawkes* (1886) 15 Lest she get a toye of flinginge her head. 1616 R. C. *Times' Whistle* v. 1948 Are apish tricks and toies, which vse to bring Men in dirision, sportes to breed delight? 1777 *Horæ Subsec.* 437 (E.D.D.) He hath taken a toy to scratch his head, when he is speaking to a gentleman.

3. A fantastic or trifling speech or piece of writing; a frivolous or mocking speech; a foolish or idle tale; a funny story or remark, a jest, joke, pun; a light or facetious composition. *arch.*

1542 Udall *Erasm. Apoph.* I. *Diogenes* § 79 Nothyng but a toye, in daliyng with the affinitee and similitude of woordes. 1553 T. Wilson *Rhet.* (1580) A iv, Suche as seeke the greatest praise for writyng of Bookes, should doe beste.. to write foolishe toyes, for then the moste parte would best esteme them. 1577 Breton *Flourish on Fancie* (Grosart) 11/2 Toyes of straung deuise, With stories of olde Robin Hood. 1590 Shaks. *Mids. N.* v. i. 3, I neuer may beleeue These anticke fables, nor these Fairy toyes. 1621 Molle *Camerar. Liv. Libr.* III. xx. 215 They gaue credit to all these foolish toies. 1719 D'Urfey *Pills* (1872) I. 126 Fye George, she crys, these Words are but Toys.

arch. 1821 Scott *Kenilw.* xvi, Think of what that arch-knave Shakspeare says—a plague on him, his toys come into my head when I should think of other matters. 1905 R. Garnett *Shakespeare* 104 She hath heard A little toy of thine, a comedy ('Tis called, I think, The Taming of a Shrew).

b. †(*a*) A light, frivolous, or lively tune. *Obs.* (*b*) A particular turn or phrase of melody in a bird's song: see quot. 1851.

1591 Greene *Art Conny Catch.* III. (1592) 19 In the time of ceissing betweene the seuerall toyes and fancies hee plaied. 1641 Sanderson *Serm.*, *Ad Aulam* xiii. (1660) II. 267 One would have a grave Pavane, another a nimbler Galliard, a third some striking toy or Jigg. 1851 Mayhew *Lond. Labour* (1861) III. 14 There are four-and-twenty changes in a linnet's song... It sings 'toys', as we call them.

†4. A foolish or idle fancy; a fantastic notion, odd conceit; a whim, crotchet, caprice. *Obs.*

c 1530 H. Rhodes *Bk. Nurture* 330 in *Babees Bk.* (1868) 80 Cast not thyne eyes to ne yet fro, as thou werte full of toyes. 1555 W. Watreman *Fardle Facions* II. x. 225 This people [Tartarres] hath many superstitious toyes. 1563 B. Googe *Eglogs* vii. (Arb.) 59 But yf a toye com in your Brayne, your mynde is altered quyght. 1591 Florio *2nd Fruites* 161 Euen as the toy takes me in the head. 1642 Rogers *Naaman* 98 So deadly doth this conceit and toy of his owne braine worke with him. 1668 R. L'Estrange *Vis. Quev.* (1708) 101 Yet when the Toy took them, they'd make now and then a Sally. 1699 — *Fables* II. vii. (1715) II. 5 A New Marry'd Couple had a Toy took them in their Heads, so soon as ever the Office was over, to Shrift one another before they came together.

†b. *spec.* A foolish or unreasoning dislike or aversion: esp. in phr. *to take* (*a*) *toy* (in quot. 1612 = to take fright, start, shy) *at* something. *Obs.*

a 1593 Marlowe *Hero & Leander* v. Wks. (Rtldg.) 304/2 [To hear this] Made the well-spoken nymph take such a toy, That down she sunk. 1612 *Two Noble K.* v. iv. 79 The hot horse, hot as fire, Took Toy at this. 1647 Sanderson *Serm.*, *Ad Aulam* xiv. (1660) II. 277 Common friends many times ..take toy at a trifle,..and pick quarrels to desert us. 1697 J. Sergeant *Solid Philos.* 308 Thence they take a Toy at Metaphysics, and pretend it insuperably hard and mysterious

II. Concrete senses.

(Sense 5 is also often *abstract*, connecting I and II; the connexion of 10 with the other senses is doubtful.)

5. *gen.* A thing of little or no value or importance, a trifle; a foolish or senseless affair, a piece of nonsense; *pl.* trumpery, rubbish. (In mod. use regarded as *fig.* from next sense.)

1530 Palsgr. 281/2 Toy a tryfell, *truffe*, *friuolle*. 1538 Elyot, *Abydena*, trifles, thinges of smalle estimation, wanton toyes, thynges vnseemely for menne to vse. 1587 Harrison *England* II. vi. (1877) I. 165 To stand vpon such toies would spend much time. 1605 Shaks. *Macb.* II. iii. 98 From this instant, There's nothing serious in Mortalitie: All is but Toyes. 1631 Gouge *God's Arrows* I. § 29. 44 Of Popish toyes to pacifie God. 1664 H. More *Myst. Iniq.*, *Apol.* 554 If they leave not off their animosities and asperities of mind about toys and trifles. 1719 Watts *Hymn*, '*Come, holy Spirit, Heavenly Dove*' ii, Look, how we grovel here below, Fond of these earthly Toys. 1848 Thackeray *Van. Fair* ix, But a title and a coach and four are toys more precious than happiness in Vanity Fair.

6. A material object for children or others to play with (often an imitation of some familiar object); a plaything; also, something contrived for amusement rather than for practical use (esp. in phrase *a mere toy*). In quot. *a* 1586 *playing toy*. Now the leading sense, to which the others are referred.

a 1586 Sidney *Arcadia* iv. Wks. 1725 II. 771 There was never poor scholar, that having instead of his book some playing toy about him, did more suddenly cast it from him. 1598 Barckley *Felic. Man* (1631) 152 The rattles and toyes which children use to play with. *a* 1656 Bp. Hall *Occas. Medit.* (1851) 111 We cry for every toy, even that which may most hurt us. 1672 R. Wild *Poet. Licent.* 29 We all know Popes-head-Alley trades in Toyes, Our Merchants come not thither, but our Boys. 1781 Cowper *Hope* 128 Men deal with life as children with their play, Who first misuse, then cast their toys away. 1881 Stevenson *Virg. Puerisque*, *Child's Play* (1905) 157 Lead soldiers, dolls, all toys, in short, are in the same category. 1893 J. A. Hodges *Elem. Photogr.* (1907) 14 The very low-priced sets [of photographic apparatus]..are generally mere toys.

fig. 1893 Liddon, etc. *Life Pusey* I. xvi. 363 He handles it with the delight that a new mental toy inspires in most men at a certain time of life.

7. A small article of little intrinsic value, but prized as an ornament or curiosity; 'a petty commodity' (J.), a knick-knack, trinket, gewgaw; hence (often in allusion to 6) applied to anything small, flimsy, or inferior of its kind (now chiefly *attrib.*: see 11 b).

1596 Shaks. *Tam. Shr.* iv. iii. 67 Heere is the cap...Why 'tis a cockle or a walnut-shell, A knacke, a toy, a tricke, a babies cap. 1624 Capt. Smith *Virginia* I. 3 We presented him with diuers toyes, which he kindly accepted. *c* 1630 Hales *Serm. John xviii. 36* Rem. (1673) 154 So like one another, that one of them must wear a toy in his cap, that so the spectators may distinguish them. 1711 in *10th Rep. Hist. MSS. Comm.* App. v. 139 A weak town, haveing noe outward works, but a toy of a pallisade before a litle part of the wall. 1712 Arbuthnot *John Bull* III. i, Ladies, hung about with toys and trinkets. 1768 *Tom Thumb's Folio* I. 4 His Father was greatly disconcerted at having such a little tiney Toy of a Child. 1888 Black *Houseboat* xi, Perched on the top of a hill was a conspicuous toy of a church.

b. Applied technically to small steel articles, as hammers, pincers, buckles, button-hooks, nails, etc. More fully 'steel toys' (? i.e. steel petty things).

1833 J. Holland *Manuf. Metal* II. 319 Heavy Steel Toys. By this not very appropriate description the Birmingham manufacturers refer to a class of articles...To enumerate all the 'toys' of this class would be to transcribe a large list of miscellaneous cheap and useful wares, from a joiner's hammer to a shoemaker's tack. The pincers of the last-named workman, and the edged nippers..in use for breaking up loaf-sugar, are both of them well-known specimens.

c. *Thieves' slang.* A watch; *toy and tackle*, a watch and chain. Cf. *toy-getter* (see 11 d).

1877 Horsley *Jottings fr. Jail* i. (1887) 17 He was very tricky at getting a poge or a toy, but he would not touch toys because we was afraid of being turned over.

8. *fig.* Applied to a person: a. (from 5) slightingly or contemptuously; in quot. 1822 affectionately = pet, darling (cf. 7); b. (from 6) as being used as a plaything or for sport.

1598 Shaks. *Merry W.* v. v. 46 Elues, list your names: Silence, you aiery toyes. 1616 B. Jonson *Devil an Ass* iv. vii, I ha' sworne to ha' him by the eares: I feare The toy, wi' not do me right. 1681 Dryden *Span. Friar* iv. ii, O, Vertue! Vertue!..That men should leave thee for that Toy, a Woman? 1821 Byron *Mar. Fal.* I. ii, Thou idle, gilded, and degraded toy. 1822 T. Mitchell *Aristoph.* II. 171 Why, Xanthias, my toy, Why, what ails the poor boy! 1883 Stepniak in *Contemp. Rev.* Sept. 317 A Russian..being a mere toy in the hands of the commonest policeman. 1888 Stevenson *Black Arrow* 46 This toy..that's not fit for wounds or warfare.

9. Applied to a diminutive breed or variety of animals. a. Short for *toy dog*: see 11 c.

1877 *Field* 24 Feb. 214/2 In toys no great change has taken place, except that..pugs, Italian greyhounds, and toy terriers are on the decline. 1899 *Pall Mall G.* 3 Oct. 9/1 Ladies' toys were in strong force...Sporting dogs were not numerous. 1903 *Daily Chron.* 25 May 5/2 The 'chiens de luxe', or Toys, are in a roomy and well-warmed 'pavilion' by themselves.

b. Any dwarf variety of tame pigeon.

1909 *Cent. Dict. Suppl.* s.v., The toys resemble the tumblers in general build and are among pigeons what bantams are among fowl.

10. *Sc.* A close cap or head-dress, of linen or wool, with flaps coming down to the shoulders, formerly worn by women of the lower classes in Scotland. ? *Obs.* Also *toy-mutch* (11 d). [In this sense perh. = Du. *tooi* attire, dress: see Note below.]

(The *English* quots. 1611, 1612, are placed here as perh. suggesting the origin; but they may belong to 7.)

[1611 Shaks. *Wint. T.* iv. iv. 326 Any Silke, any Thred, any Toyes for your head? 1612 *Two Noble K.* I. iii, On my head no toy But was her pattern.] 1724 Ramsay *Tea-t. Misc.* (1762) 2 Their toys and mutches were sae clean, They glanced in our ladses' een. 1793 *Statist. Acc. Scot.* IX. 325 The tenants wives wore toys of linen of the coarsest kind, upon their heads, when they went to church, fairs or market. 1816 Scott *Old Mort.* xxxix, The face of Alison ..now presented itself, enveloped in a 'toy'. 1824 — *Redgauntlet* Let. iv, An elderly woman, in a grey stuff gown, with a check apron and 'toy'. 1900 H. G. Graham *Soc. Life Scot. in 18th C.* v. vi. (1901) 181 Farmers' wives and daughters with 'toys' or head-covering of coarse linen.

III. 11. *attrib.* and *Comb.* a. *attrib.* That is a toy (in sense 6): applied to small models or imitations of ordinary objects used as playthings, as *toy boat*, *cannon*, *dog*, *engine*, *horse*, *house*, *man*, *train*, *trumpet*, *woman*, etc.

1836 [Miss Maitland] *Lett. fr. Madras* iv. (1843) 25 Cape Town is just like the Dutch toy-towns. *a* 1860 Alb. Smith *Lond. Med. Stud.* (1861) 13 A stethescope—a curious instrument, something like a sixpenny toy-trumpet with its top knocked off. 1880 Mrs. F. D. Bridges *Jrnl. Lady's Trav. round World* xviii. (1883) 298 One never quite gets over the impression of being amongst dolls and living in a toy-house.. in Japan. 1888 Hasluck *Model Engin. Handybk.* iii. (1900) 24 The most simple form of toy-engine is that illustrated below. 1897 *Edin. Rev.* Oct. 480 The babies had toy-animals on wheels.

b. *transf.* and *fig.* Applied to things of diminutive size, flimsy construction, or petty character, as if intended for sport or diversion rather than serious use.

1821 Scott *Kenilw.* xli, You go not to your gew-gaw toy-house yonder; you will sleep to-night in better security. 1855 Ht. Martineau *Autobiog.* I. 437 My surprise at the smallness and toy-character of Abbotsford was extreme. 1895 Miss Braddon in *Westm. Gaz.* 6 Nov. 1/3 A very popular writer may launch three of these toy-pinnaces in a year. 1897 Gladstone *E. Crisis* 5 The Concert of Europe included toy-demonstrations, which might be made under the condition that they should not pass into reality. 1909 *Daily Chron.* 19 Feb. 3/2 Ruritania was something more than the first toy-kingdom of our modern stage.

c. Applied to an animal, esp. a dog of a diminutive breed or variety, kept as a pet, e.g. a *toy spaniel* or *terrier*.

1863 *Sat. Rev.* 28 Mar. 408/1 These very large dogs are not much more useful than the very small ones which are called, with perfect aptness, toy dogs. 1872 B. Clayton *Dogs* 20 A Toy Terrier was exhibited which weighed only six ounces. 1889 G. Stables *Dog Owners' Kennel Comp.* vi. § 10. 66 There are several other kinds of Toy Terriers.. but I need only mention..the Toy Black and Tan and the Toy Blue or Slate colour.

d. *Comb.*: attrib. (of or for toys), as *toy-box*, *-cupboard*, *-fair*, *-land*, *-manufacture*, *-trade*; objective and obj. gen., as *toy-maker*, *-making*, *-turner*; instrumental, similative, etc., as *toy-bewitched*, *-like*, *-sized* adjs.; also **toy-block,** one of a set of wooden or papier-mâché blocks, usually with letters or designs, for children to play with; **toy-getter** (*Thieves' slang*), a watch-stealer; so *toy-getting*; †**toy-headed** *a.*, having 'toys' or odd fancies in the head, crotchety; **toy-line** = *toy-railway*; **toy-mutch,** *Sc.* = sense 10; †**toy-pate,** a head full of 'toys', crotchets, or frivolities (cf. *toy-headed*); **toy-railway,** (*a*) a model of a railway, with its engine, train, etc.; (*b*) *pop.*, a small narrow-gauge railway, often orig. constructed for the use of slate-works or the like, but subseq. carrying tourists or other passengers; also *toy-line*; **toy-service,** a church-service at which toys are brought as an offering for sick or poor children; **toy-woman,** a woman who keeps a toy-shop. See also Toyman, -shop, -wort.

1794 Coleridge *Relig. Musings* vii, We become An anarchy of Spirits. *Toy-bewitched. 1891 *Cent. Dict.*, *Toy-block*, one of a set of small blocks,..forming a plaything for children. 1865 (*title*) Aunt Louisa's *Toy Books. 1831 Carlyle *Sart. Res.* II. vi, He descries lying far below, embosomed among its groves and green natural bulwarks, and all diminished to a *toybox, the fair Town. 1900 *Westm. Gaz.* 11 Dec. 12/1 The season for the ransacking of *toy-cupboards. 1908 *Westm. Gaz.* 29 Oct. 1/2 The order.. that there shall be no *toy-fairs in London this Christmas-tide deprives the City of..one of its sights. 1896 A. Morrison *Child of the Jago* 102 Dicky knew the small man for a good *toy-getter. 1633 T. Adams *Exp. 2 Peter* ii. 1 It sticks upon the stomach of some *toy-headed professors. 1908 *Daily Chron.* 5 Nov. 7/5 No one realises unless he penetrates into *Toyland how much whimsical humour, how much scientific skill and craftsman's ingenuity are devoted to the invention of the playthings for the festive season. 1818 Scott *Hrt. Midl.* i, The gay glancing of the equipage, its diminished and *toy-like appearance at a distance. 1883 *Manch. Exam.* 26 Nov. 5/3 The Swiss lake steamers are..too toy-like to ensure their passengers against reasonably probable risks. 1878 Jenkinson *Guide N. Wales* 271 Leaving the Cambrian train at Mynffordd Junction, the traveller walks up a path to the *toy line, and enters one of the little carriages. 1859 *Habits of Gd. Society* v. (new ed.) 194 Worth all the amusements which a *toy-maker could dream of. 1858 Carlyle *Fredk. Gt.* IX. iii. (1872) III. 87 *Toy-manufactures of those simple people. 1742 Forbes *Dominie Depos'd* II. i, The *toy-mutch maun then gae on, Nae mair bare-hair'd. 1693 Penn *Maxims* lx. Wks. 1726 I. 847 He never deals but in substantial Ware, and leaves the rest for the *Toy-Pates (or Shops) of the World. 1892 Baddeley *Guide N. Wales* (ed. 4) 165 *heading*, Portmadoc to Ffestiniog by the '*Toy' Railway. *Ibid.*, No orthodox tourist visits Wales without taking a turn..on the 'Toy' railway. 190. *Guide to Lynton, Lynmouth*, etc. Introd. 19 *heading*, Barnstaple to Lynton by the Toy Railway. 1889 *Standard* 1 Feb., '*Toy Services' which are becoming very popular in some of our churches. 1895 Clive Holland *Jap. Wife* (ed. 11) 27 *Toy-sized cups of tea. 1757 W. Thompson *R. N. Advoc.* 41 Our Sons of War are to be served after our Sons of *Toy-Trade. 1893 A. N. Palmer *Hist. Wrexham* IV. 11, I find mentioned..one *toy-turner. 1827 Scott *Diary* 2 Oct., in *Lockhart*, An old lady, who proved a *toy woman in Edinburgh.

[*Note.* Eduard Müller suggested the identity of *toy* with Du. *tooi*, late MDu. *tôi*, 16th c., 'attire, ornament, finery, dress', which suits the form, but hardly the sense (exc. ? in 10 or 7). Others have thought of Du. *tuig* 'harness, horse-trappings', in pl. 'sails, rigging, implements, tools; stuff, lumber, refuse, trash'; in Kilian 1599 *tuygh*, dial. *tuych*, *tugh*, 'arms, implements, armaments, impedimenta, ornaments', = Ger. *zeug* 'apparatus, tools, gear, furniture, stuff, trash, etc.', LG. *tüg*, *tüüg*, MLG. *tüch*, *tüg*. But, if the sense-development shown above is historically correct, it is difficult to see in either of these suggestions, the origin of the English word. It is indeed true that Du. *speeltuig*, Ger. *spielzeug*, and Da. *legetøi*, mean 'play-tool or implement, plaything, toy', and that Sidney in 1586 used 'playing toy', which might conceivably be a rendering of one of these compounds; but this would still leave the earlier English history unexplained.]

Toy, *v.* [Goes with Toy *sb.*, q. v.]

1. *intr.* To act idly or without seriousness; to trifle, 'play', deal carelessly (*with* a person or thing); also † to make sport, mock (*obs.*).

a 1529 Skelton *Bouge of Courte* 290 It was no tyme with him to jape nor toye. 1530 Palsgr. 758/2, I toye, or tryfell with one, I deale nat substancyally with hym, *je me truffe*. 1549–62 Sternhold & H. *Ps.* xxxv. 16 Yea abject slaves at me did toy with mocks and cheekes ful stout. 1563 *Homilies* II. *Inform. H. Script.* I. (1859) 373 It is a shame that christian men should be so light headed, to toy as ruffians do with such manner of speeches. 1576 Dering *Expos. Heb.* v. 4–6. Cc iij, They must haue oyle, candels.. wine and water,..trifled and toyed with all. 1653 W. Ramesey *Astrol. Restored* 19, I fear I do toy in recording these vain Objections. 1868 Dixon *Spir. Wives* I. vii. 75 He toyed with astrology, and had fitful dreams of enjoying the elixir of life. 1888 Bryce *Amer. Commw.* II. lxxxi. 296 [Class issues] are usually toyed with by both parties alike.

b. So *to toy it*.

1657 J. Sergeant *Schism Dispach't* 379 Thus Dr. H. toyes it with his Readers. *Ibid.* 574 Let them not toy it now.

2. To sport amorously; to dally, flirt. Usually const. *with*. (Cf. Toy *sb.* 1.)

15.. *Song Bachelor's Life* 7 (Ritson) If he [the married man] be merie and toy with any, His wife will frowne, and words geve manye. 1566 in *Daily News* 10 Sept. (1897) 6/7 That none toy with the maids, on paine of 4d. 1592 Shaks. *Ven. & Ad.* 106 And for my sake [he] hath learnd to sport, and daunce, To toy, to wanton, dallie, smile, and iest. *c* 1613 Middleton *No Wit like Woman's* v. i, Not toy, nor bill, and imitate house-pigeons. 1727 Gay *Begg. Op.* I. viii, O Polly you might have toy'd and kist. 1811 W. R. Spencer *Poems* 73 Whilst he and Psyche toy'd together.

fig. 1793 Wordsw. *Descr. Sketches* 52 To where the Alps, ascending white in air, Toy with the Sun, and glitter from afar. 1842 H. Rogers *Ess.* I. i. 4 He had in early life toyed a little with the muses.

3. To play, sport, amuse oneself; to move sportively, play or frisk about.

1530 Palsgr. 758/2, I toye, I playe with one, *je me joue*. 1590 Spenser *F. Q.* II. ix. 35 But other some could not abide to toy; All pleasaunce was to them griefe and annoy. 1678 Cudworth *Intell. Syst.* I. v. § 44. 674 The senseless atoms, playing and toying up and down without any care or thought. 1827 Pollok *Course T.* v. 1007 The hare, unscared Sported and toyed familiar with his dog. 1836 O. W. Holmes *Poetry* ii. 18 Pale dreamers, whose fantastic lay Toys with smooth trifles like a child at play. 1848 Kingsley *Saint's Trag.* II. iv. 63, I have toyed too long..down the stream of life.

b. *Toy with*: to play with (a material object), to handle or finger idly; hence, to work idly or carelessly with or at.

1822 W. Irving *Braceb. Hall* xxvi. (1845) 121 The gallant general took his station..at her side, and toyed with her elegantly ornamented work-bag. 1840 Dickens *Barn. Rudge* lxiv, The fire was seen sporting and toying with the door. 1879 E. Garrett *House by Works* I. 115 Mrs. Pendlebury looked down, and toyed with her rings.

4. *trans.* (with adv.) To spend or waste in toying; to bring by toying (into or out of some condition).

1575 Abp. Parker *Corr.* (Parker Soc.) 474, I toy out my time, partly with copying books. 1685 J. Scott *Chr. Life* II. 134 So fools and fleers on, till he hath toyed and laughed himself out of all sense of Religion. 1749 Johnson *Irene* I. i, He toys his hours away.

To-yans, to-ʒanes: see To-gains.

Toydom (toi·dəm). *nonce-wd.* [f. Toy *sb.* + -dom.] a. The condition of being or resembling a toy. b. The realm or domain of toys.

1882 M. A. Barker in *Macm. Mag.* XLVI. 68/1 The tan sail of a canoe or whiter sheet of a fishing boat..dwarfed into toydom whenever they come near the great war ship. 1905 *Times* 7 Jan. 11/2 At the Crystal Palace..side-shows are numerous, and toydom there is most attractive.

To-year (tŭˌyīə·ɹ), *adv.* Now *dial.* Forms: see Year. [f. To *prep.* A. 7 + Year: cf. *to-day*, *to-night*.] This year.

Tracer. ... Tracing. ... Tracingly. ... Traceried. ... Tracery. ... Trachea. ... Tracheal. ...

Trachelate. ... Tracheliped. ... Trachelo-. ... Trachean. ... Tracheate. ... Trachenchyma. ... Tracheo-oesophageal. ... Tracheophone. ... Trachea. ...

Trachy-. ... Trachyte. ... Trachytic. ... Trachytoid. ... Tracing. ... Track. ...

Track. ... Track-chart. Track-cleaner. Track-hound. Track-layer. Track-scale. ... Track (verb).

Track ... (entry column)

Track-boat ...

Trackage (ˈtrækedʒ), *sb.* [f. TRACK + -AGE.]

Tracker ...

Track. *v.* ...

Trackless (ˈtræklɛs), *a.* [f. TRACK *sb.* + -LESS.]

Track-road ...

Track-walking: see TRACKWAY.

Trackway ...

Tract-boat ... variant of TRACK-BOAT.

Track-rail ...

Track-schuyt, -scoot, -scout, -skuit, anglicized forms of TREKSCHUIT.

Track-shoe ... -walking: see TRACK *sb.*

Trackway. [f. TRACK *sb.* + WAY.]

Track-work: see TRACK *sb.* 13.

Tract (trækt), *sb.*[1]

Tract, *sb.*[2] R.C.Ch.

Tract, *sb.*[3]

Tract, *v.*[1]

Tract, *v.*[2] *Obs.*

Tractability (træktəˈbiliti), *sb.*

Tractable (ˈtræktəb'l), *a.*

Tractableness ...

Tractably, *adv.*

Tractal, *a.* *Obs.* *rare*[-1].

Tractarian (træktɛˈərian), *sb.* and *a.*

Tractarianism ...

Tractate (ˈtrækteit), *sb.*

Tractation (trækˈteiʃən), *Obs.*

Tractator (trækˈteitor), *Obs.*

Tractatrix (trækˈteitriks). Pl. **-trices**.

Tractatule (ˈtræktətiul), *rare*[-1].

Tractellum (trækˈtɛləm), *Biol.* Pl. **tractella**.

Tractable (2), etc.

Tract-boat, obs. form of TRACK-BOAT.

Tractile (ˈtræktil, -ail), *a.* *rare*.

Tractility (trækˈtiliti), ...

Traction (ˈtrækʃən), *sb.*

Traction-engine. ...

Tractional, *a.*

Tractitious, *a.* *Obs.*

Tractive (ˈtræktiv), *a.*

Tractless, *a.* *Obs. or arch. rare*. [f. TRACT + -LESS.]

Tractlet (ˈtræktlɛt), *sb.* [f. TRACT + -LET.]

Tractor (ˈtræktər). [Late or med.L.]

Tractorize (ˈtræktəraiz), *v.*

Tractorizing, *sb.*

Tractory (træ'ktŏri), a. and sb. rare. [ad. L. tractōri-us of or for drawing, f. tract-, ppl. stem of trahĕre to draw: see -ORY.]

1. a. adj. Serving for traction; tractive. Obs.

B. sb. 1. Old name for some part of a plough: see quot. Obs.

2. Ca. Illit. = TRACTATION (b.) Obs.

3. Geom. = TRACTRIX.

Tractrix (træ'ktriks), a. and sb. rare. [ad. L. tractrīx-īcis or for drawing, f. tract-, ppl. stem of trahĕre to draw: see -TRIX.]

[Tractrix (træ'ktriks), Geom. Tr. tractrice** (-iks). [mod.L. (Huygens) fem. of tractor: see TRACTOR, and cf. DIRECTRIX.] A curve such that the intercept on the tangent between its point of contact and a fixed straight line is constant.

2. [Tracture Obs. rare—. [ad. med.L. tractūra (Du Cange), f. tract-, ppl. stem of trahĕre to draw: see -URE.] Drawing, attraction, enticement.

Tractus (træ'ktŏs). R. C. Ch. [med.L. tractus, a spec. use of L. tractus 'drawing, drawing out', lit. trahĕre 'to draw': 'quia trahendo, id est tractim, canitur': see Du Cange s.v.] = TRACT sb.²

Tractye, obs. form of TREACLE.

Tradable, var. TRADEABLE.

Trade (trēd), sb. Forms: 4–6 Sc., 7 trod, 4–7 S. traid, 5 trade, 6 traide, trawde, thrade,⁷ 7 traide, 5 Sc.– trade. [a. MLG. trade (ablaut) fem., track (Schiller & Lübben), LG. traïe (traam) fem. (Bremisch Wtb.); also WFlem. tra (–traat) walk, march, course (De Bo).]

I. 1. A course, way, path; with possessive or of: the course trodden by a person, or followed by a ship, etc.;

2. The track or trail of a man or beast; footprints;

3. Course, way, or manner of life; course of action; mode of procedure; method.

c. A regular or habitual course of action; a practice or habit of doing something.

6. The trade: those engaged in the particular business or industry concerned or in question; spec. the publishers and booksellers; now more commonly, those engaged in the liquor trade.

b. Any one of the corporations of craftsmen (usually seven in number) in a Scottish burgh, each of which formerly elected one or more members to the town-council.

11. 7. a. sb. Passage to and fro; coming and going.

12. Abbreviation of TRADE-WIND; chiefly pl.

13. attrib. and Comb. a. attrib., as trade-body, -cask, -company (COMPANY sb. 8), trade-protection, etc.

14. attrib. and Comb.

Trade (trēd), v. Forms: see prec.

Trade-mark. A mark (now, one secured by legal registration) used by a manufacturer or trader to distinguish his goods from those of others.

Traded (trē'dĕd), ppl. a. and a. [f. TRADE sb. and sb.+-ED.]

Trade-road, board, etc.: see TRADE 14, 15.

Tradescantia (trædĕskæ'ntia). Bot. [mod. (Linnæus), named after John Tradescant (the elder), a 17th c. naturalist.] A. American genus of perennial herbs (N.O. Commelynaceæ).

Tradesfolk (trē'dzfōk). pl. [f. TRADE sb. + FOLK.] People in trade; tradespeople. a. Artisans.

Tradesman (trē'dzmǎn). Pl. -men. [f. TRADE sb.'s MAN sb.]

1. One who is skilled in and follows one of the industrial arts; an artificer, artisan, a craftsman.

Tradeswoman. Pl. -women. [f. as prec. + WOMAN.] A woman engaged in trade, or in a particular trade or calling.

Trade-union, trades-union. [f. TRADE or pl. trades + UNION.] An association of the workers in any trade or in allied trades for the protection and furtherance of their interests in regard to wages, hours, and conditions of labour, and for the provision, from their common funds, of pecuniary assistance to the members during sickness, unemployment, etc.

Trade-wind, **Trade-way,** etc.: see TRADE 15.

Tradition (trǎdi'ʃŏn), sb. Also 4–6 -icion, 5 -ision, -isyoun, 7 -ioun.

1. The action or handing over (something material) to another; delivery, transfer.

Traditional (trădi·ʃǝnal), a. (sb.) [f. Tradition + -al; or ad. F. traditionnel, also med.L. trāditiōnālis.] Belonging to, consisting in, or of the nature of tradition; handed down by or derived from tradition.

Traditionalism. [ad. F. traditionalisme, or f. prec. + -ism.]

Traditionalist. [f. Traditional + -ist.] An adherent of traditionalism; one who upholds the authority of tradition.

Traditionism.

Traditionist.

Traditionally (trădi·ʃǝnali), adv. [f. prec. + -ly.] In a traditional manner; by, in the way of, or according to tradition.

So **Traditioned** (-ʃǝnd), a. rare⁻¹, having tradition of a kind specified by the prefixed word.

Traditionless, a. rare. [f. as prec. + -less.] Having no traditions.

Traditionary (trădi·ʃǝnari), a. (sb.) [f. Tradition + -ary: cf. additionary. (In mod.L. trāditiōnārius.)]

Traditive (træ·ditiv), a. [ad. F. traditif, -ive (13th c.) traditional, f. L. tradit-, ppl. stem of trādĕre to hand over, deliver: see -ive.]

Traditor (træ·ditŏr), sb. [L. trāditor deliverer, giver up, betrayer, agent-n. from trādĕre to hand over, deliver.]

Traditory a. Obs. rare⁻¹. [ad. L. trāditōrius.]

Traducement (trădiū·sment). [f. prec. + -ment.] The act or action of traducing; defamation, calumny.

Traducent (trădiū·sent), a. rare. [ad. L. trādūcent-em.] Traducing, slanderous.

Traducer (trădiū·sǝr). One who traduces.

Traducian (trădiū·sian), sb. (and a.) [ad. late L. trādūciān-us, -ĭ pl., f. trādux, -ŭc-em a layer or shoot for propagation.]

Traducianism (trădiū·sianiz'm). [f. prec. + -ism.]

Traducianist.

Traducible (trădiū·sib'l), a. Obs. rare⁻¹. [f. producible.] Capable of being 'traduced' or transmitted; transmissible.

Traduct, v. Obs. [f. L. trāduct-, ppl. stem of trādūcĕre to Traduce.]

Traduction (trădœ·kʃǝn). [a. OF. traduction (13th c. in Hatz.-Darm.), or ad. L. trāductiōn-em 'leading across, transference, leading in triumph, public exposure'.]

Traductive (trădœ·ktiv), a. [f. L. trāduct-ppl. stem (see above) + -ive.]

Trady (trǣ·di), a. colloq. [f. Trade sb. + -y.]

Trafalgar (trăfæ·lgɑr, træ·falgăr). Name of a cape on the S. coast of Spain, famed for a great victory of the British fleet over the combined fleets of France and Spain on 21 Oct. 1805, in which Admiral Nelson was killed.

Traffic (træ·fik), sb. Forms: 4- traffike, 6 traffyk(e, -ique, -icque, etc.) 6-7 traffick, -ike, (7- traffique), traffike, 7- traffic. [a. F. trafique (1441 in Godef.), traffique (fem.) mod.F. trafic (m.), trafique (1549-74); Prov. trafic, trafiz; It. traffico (14th c.) traffico; Sp. tráfico, tráfago, Pg. tráfego; cf. Med.Gr. τραφικόν.]

Traffic, v. Forms: see prec. [a. F. traffiquer, trafiquer (1542 in Godef.), It. trafficare, Sp. traficar, trafagar, Pg. traficar.]

Hence **Trafficked** (-ikt), **trafficking** vbl. sb., **Traffickless** a.

TRAFFICABLE. | 230 | TRAGEDY. | TRAGEDY. | 231 | TRAGICAL.

Trafficable (træˈfikăb'l), *a.* [f. TRAFFIC *vb.*]

Trafficked (træˈfikt), *ppl. a.* [f. TRAFFIC *vb.*]

Trafficker (træˈfikəɹ). [f. TRAFFIC *v.* + -ER¹.]

Traffic Tra'fficking *vbl. sb.* and *ppl. a.*

Trafin, -e, obs. forms of TREPHINE.

Tragacanth (træˈgăkanθ). Also 6 traga-chant, 7 tragant, 8 trequant, -anth; *see also* ADRAGANT, DRAGANT, DRAGON². [ad. F. *tragacanthe* (16th c.) = It., Sp. *tragacanta*, ad. L. *tragacantha* (Pliny), a. Gr. τραγάκανθα goat's-thorn, shrub, f. τράγος he-goat + ἄκανθα thorn.

Trage-comedy, obs. form of TRAGI-COMEDY.

Tragal (træˈgăl), *a. Anat.* [f. TRAG- + -AL.] Pertaining to or situated upon the tragus.

† Tragalism. *Spanish Hist.* Obs.

† Tragaline, *a. Obs. rare.* [f. L. *tragædia* + -AC] an anomalous formation for 'tragedic.'

† Trage-dial, *a. Obs. rare.* [f. as prec. + -AL.]

Tragedian (trăˈḡˈdiăn). Also 4-5 tragedyen, -ien, (tragedion), 7-8 tragoedian. [ME., orig. a. OF. *tragedien* (1372 in Hatz.-Darm.), later and mod.F. *tragédien*, f. *tragedie* TRAGEDY : see -AN.]

† Tragedious, *a. Obs. rare.* [f. L. *tragædia* + -AC] Befitting tragedy; tragic in style.

2. A stage-player who performs in tragedy; a tragic actor.

Tragedienne (trəgēdɪˈen). [Fr., fem. of TRAGEDIEN.] A female tragedian or actor of tragedy : a tragic actress.

† Tragedietta (trădʒidɪˈetă). [In form an It. dim. of *tragedia* : see -ETTA : cf. *comedietta*.] A slight or short tragedy; a dramatic sketch of tragic character.

Tragedise (trădʒˈidəiz), *v.* [f. TRAGEDY + -ISE: cf. *harmon-ise*, etc.]

Tragedy (trăˈdʒĭdi). Forms: 4-6 tragedye, (5 tragedie, tregedie), 4-7 tragedie, -idie, (tregedi), 5-6 tragedi, -ide, 6 tragedie, (trigēde, -idy), 5-present TRAGEDY. [a. OF. *tragedie* (14th c. in Godef.), ad. L. *tragædia*, a. Gr. τραγῳδία, app. goat-song, f. τράγος goat + ᾠδή, ᾠδή ode, song.

† Tragic (træˈdʒik), *a.* Also 6 -icke. [ad. L. *tragicus*, a. Gr. τραγικός, f. τράγος goat.]

Tragical (træˈdʒikăl), *a.* [f. prec. + -AL.]

Tragicality | 232 | TRAHYSH. | TRAIK. | 233 | TRAIL.

Tragically (træˈdʒikăli), *adv.* [f. as prec. + -LY².]

Tragicalness. [f. as prec. + -NESS.]

Tragicness. [f. TRAGIC + -NESS.]

Tragicomedy (trădʒiˈkɒmidi). Also 6 tragi-comoedie. [ad. L. *tragicomœdia*, f. *tragi-* TRAGIC + *comœdia* COMEDY.]

Tragi-comic (trădʒiˈkɒmik), *a.* [f. TRAGI- + COMIC.]

Tragi-comical (-ăl), *a.* [f. prec. + -AL.]

Tragopan (træˈgŏpæn). *Ornith.* [a. L. *tragopan* (Pliny xxxvii), name of a reputed bird in Ethiopia (perh. the horned vulture); f. Gr. τράγος goat + Πάν Pan.]

Tragopogon (trægoˈpōgon). *Bot.* [a. Gr. τραγοπώγων, goat's beard.]

† Tragus (træˈgŭs), *Anat.* Pl. **Tragi** (træˈdʒəi). [a. L., a. Gr. τράγος the part of the ear in front of the hole, named on account of the bunch of hairs which it bears.]

Traheen (traˈhiːn). *Anglo-Irish.* [ad. Ir. *troighthín* (Dinen), *troighín* (O'Reilly), a little foot or sole.]

† Trahent, *a.* and *sb. Obs. rare.* [L. *tra-hent-em*, pr. pple. of *trahěre* to draw.]

Trahysh, var. TRAISE *v. Obs.*, to betray.

Traise, Traict, obs. forms of TRAIT, TREAT.

Traictise, obs. form of TREATISE.

Traid(e, obs. f. TRAY. **Traifoyle,** obs. f. TREFOIL.

Traie : see TRAY. **Traik** (trēk), *sb.* Sc.

Traik, *v. Sc.* Also 6 traike, 6-9 traick.

Traikit, traikt, ppl. a. of TRAIK.

Trail (trēl), *sb.* [related to TRAIL *v.*]

Trail (trēl), *v.* Forms: 4 traile, 5 trayle, -yll, 6- trail.

I. Something that trails or hangs trailing.

II. Something trailed or made by trailing.

III. Action of trailing.

IV. Comb.

Trail, *sb.* and *v.* Entries covering trail-plate-eye, trail, trailing, trailaster, trailbaston, trailer, etc.

Entries covering trailingly, trailless, trail-net, traily, trailye, train, etc.

terous, -turuae, traytrous, tretroua,6-9 trayter-, tretterous, 6- traitorous. &c.

Traitorously, *adv.* Forms: see prec.: also 4 traytroures-, traytrourisle, traitourly, 5 traytroly, 5-6 -torisly, appr. f. Traitorous. &c. + -LY [.

Traitorousness. [f. prec. + -NESS.] The quality of being traitorous.

Traitory, *Obs.* Forms: 4 traitre, 4-7 -terie, 4-5 -torie, 4-7 -tery, 5-6 tory, traytrie, 4-5 -torye, 5-6 -tery (6, 5 -treierie, -tourie, 4-6 -toury), 6-torye, -torie, 5 treytori, 5-6 -tory. [f. TRAITOR + -Y (f. *senstry, maistry*; cf. OF. *traiterie, -tour*, treachery; treason.

Traitory, *adv.* Forms: 4 traitre, 4-2 -tere, 4-9 -tourie, 4-7 -torie, 5-6 -torye, traytrie, 4-5 -torye, 5-tire, 5-treitorie. &c.

Traits(traits). *Obs.* Forms: 4 traitores, -eresse, (6 -eres), 4-7 traytoresse.

Trajectile (trădʒe'ktil, -ail), *a. and sb. rare.*

Trajection (trădʒe'kʃɔn). [ad. L. *trajectiōn-em* a crossing over, transportation, n. of action f. *trajicere* to throw or convey across: see TRAJECT.]

Trajectitious.

Trajection.

Trajectitious (trădʒekti'ʃəs), *a. rare.*

Trajectory (trădʒe'ktəri), *sb. and a.*

Trajet (træʒ, trædʒet). *Obs.*

Tralatitious (trălăti'ʃəs), *a. Also 9 -icious.*

Trail, Traleis, obs. ff. TRAIL, TRELLIS.

Traliant, *v. Obs. rare.*

Tram, Tralucency, Tralucent = TRANS-.

Tram (træm), *sb.[1]*

Tram, *sb.[2]* [Short for TRAMMEL *sb.[1]*]

Tram (træm), *v.[1]*

Tram, Tramline, etc.

Trammel (træ'mel). *sb.[1]*

Trammel, *v.*

Trammeller.

Trammelled, -eled (-ld), *ppl. a.*

Trammelling, -ing, *vbl. sb.*

Trammel-net.

Trammer (træ'mar).

Tramontane (trămɔ'ntein, træmɔntei'n), *a. and sb.*

† **Tramontation.** *Obs. nonce-wd.* [n. of action f. L. *tramontare* to pass over the hill.] Setting (of the sun).

† **Tramount,** v. *Obs.* [app. f. L. *trā-, trans-* beyond + *mors*, *mortem* death, *mortuus* dead.] A putrefying carcase; a corpse.

Tramosericeous, a. Entom. [f. mod.L. *tramosericus*, f. L. *trāma* TRAM sb.² : see SERICEOUS.] Having a satiny lustre, as the elytra of certain beetles.

Tramp, sb.¹ [f. TRAMP v.]

1. An act of tramping; a heavy or forcible tread, a stamp; hence, an injury to the foot of a horse caused by its setting one foot on another: cf. TREAD sb.

2. The measured and continuous tread of a body of persons or animals; hence, the sound of heavy footfalls.

† **Tramp,** sb.² *Obs.* [prob. f. L. *trib-, trans-*]

Tramp, v. [ME. *trampe-n* = Ger., LG. *trampen* (whence Da. *trampe*, Swed., Norw. *trampa*), of same grade of *tremp*, *tramp*, *trump* to tread]

1. *intr.* To tread or walk with a firm, heavy, resonant step; to stamp.

2. *intr.* To tread heavily or with force (*on* or *upon* something); to stamp (*upon*).

3. *trans.* To press or compress by treading; to tread or trample upon.

Tramper (*trampər*). [f. TRAMP v.¹ +-ER¹.]

1. One who tramps, a stamping person.

Tramp-plate. [TRAM sb.² + PLATE sb.¹.] One of the flat or flanged iron plates used in forming early tramways (in mines or above ground), instead of the wooden or stone 'rail' previously used.

Trampling, vbl. sb. [f. TRAMPLE v. + -ING¹.]

Trampoline, **Trampolin.** stilts: cf. *trampolero* 'to go on stilts at high startops' (Florio, 1598).] A performance on stilts.

Trampoose (*trampū·z*), v. *U.S. slang.* Also **tramboose, -pouse, -pouse.** [app. a capricious extension of TRAMP v.¹: cf. *vamoose*, *namjouse*.] *intr.* To tramp; trudge.

Tram-road (*træm·rōud*). [f. TRAM sb.² + ROAD.] A way for mining districts, a road having 'trams' or beams of wood, lengths of stone, or later, iron plates or 'rails' laid in two parallel lines.

Tramway (*træm·wēi*). [f. TRAM sb.² + WAY.]

1. A track of parallel rails (originally flat plates of wood, afterwards lengths of stone or plates of iron), forming wheel-tracks in a tram-road.

Tramscon, obs. form of TRANSOM.

2. An unconscious or insensible condition; a swoon, a faint; in *mod. use*, a state characterized by a more or less prolonged suspension of consciousness and inertness to stimulus; a cataleptic or hypnotic condition.

Trance, v. [a. OF. *transir*, f. L. *transīre* to pass away; to die]

Tranced (*trǎnst*, *poet.* *trǎn·sed*), *ppl. a.* [f. TRANCE v.]

Trancedly, adv.

Trancate, obs. form of TRUNCATE.

Tranchant, a. Also 6 **tranchaunt.** [F.]

Tranche (*trǎnʃ*), sb. Also 7-8 **tranche.** [F., a slice, f. *trancher* to cut: see TRENCH.]

TrancheR. [a. F. *tranche* (*trǎnʃ*), f. *trancher* to cut: see TRENCH.]

Tranché (*trǎnʃē*), a. Also 7-8 **tranche.** [F., *tranché*, pa. pple. of *trancher* to cut: see PARTY a.]

Trankum. *Obs.* Also **trancum.** [f. TRINKET.]

Trangam. *Obs.* Also 7 **trangame, 7-8 trankey.** For a pearl-diver's net, or perh. its adjectival use.

Trangle (*træ·ŋg'l*). *Her.* Also F. *trangle* (Cotgr. 1611), var. of *tringle* or TRINGLE.

Trank (træŋk). [f. *trank*.] An oblong piece of kid or other skin from which a glove is to be cut.

Trankum. *Obs.* Also **trancum.** [Alteration of TRINKET, as in the reduplicated *trinkum-trankum*; perh. influenced by TRANGAM.]

Tranquil (træ·ŋkwil), a. Also F. **tranquille.** [a. F. *tranquille* (16th c.), ad. L. *tranquillus.*]

1. Free from agitation or disturbance; calm, quiet, peaceful, serene; still, undisturbed.

Tranquille.

†**Tranquille**, a. Obs. rare. Used of F. *tranquille* = pres. *tranquil*. Cf. L. *tranquillus* peace, quiet-ness.

Tranquilize, var. TRANQUILLIZE.

†**Tranquillate**, v. Obs. rare⁻¹. [f. L. *tranquillāt-* pa. ppl. stem of *tranquillāre*.] To render tranquil; to calm, soothe.

Tranquillity (træŋkwi'lĭti). Also 4-7 -ite, 6 -itee, 4-7 -itie. [ad. F. *tranquillité* (13th c. in Hatz.-Darm.), ad. L. *tranquillitās* (- tāt-), f. *tranquillus*: see -ITY.] The quality or state of being tranquil; freedom from disturbance or agitation; serenity, calmness; quietness, peaceful-ness.

Tranquillization (træŋkwilīzē'ʃən). [f. next + -ATION.] The act or action of tranquillizing.

Tranquillize (træŋkwilăiz), v. Also 8-9 -illise. [f. TRANQUIL + -IZE, or F. *tranquilliser* (16th c. in Hatz.-Darm).]

1. *trans.* To render tranquil; to calm, soothe.

b. *intr.* To become tranquil or quiet.

Tranquillizer (træŋkwilăizə̆). The action or agent which tranquillizes.

†**Tranquilly** (træŋkwi'li), adv. Obs. rare⁻¹. In a tranquil style or manner.

Tranquilly (træ'ŋkwili), adv. In a tranquil manner; calmly, quietly.

Tranquilness. rare. [f. TRANQUIL + -NESS.] Tranquillity.

Trans-, pref. The Latin preposition *trans*, used in comb., (1) with verbs, and their derived sbs. and adjs., e.g. *transire* to go across, *transitio*, *transitus*, *transitor*, *transitōrius*; (2) with adjs. derived from sbs. (more strictly with sb. adjectival suffix).

Transaccidentation.

Transaccidentation (trænsæksidentē'ʃən). Theol. [ad. Schol. L. *transaccidentātiō* (Duns Scotus: the attribution to P. Lombardus in Marbeck is a mistake due to confounding commentary with text).] A transubstantiation in which the substance alone is changed.

Transact (trænsæ'kt, -zæ'kt), v. [ad. L. *transact-*, pa. ppl. stem of *transigere* to drive through, ac-complish, f. TRANS- + *agere* to drive, do, act.]

1. *intr.* To carry through negotiations; to have dealings, do business; to treat; also, to manage or settle affairs. Now rare.

2. *trans.* To carry on, perform (an action, etc.); to manage (an affair); now esp. to carry on, conduct, do (business).

Transaction (trænsæ'kʃən, -zæ'-). [ad. L. *transactiōn-em*, n. of action f. *transigere*: see prec. Cf. F. *transaction* (13th c. in Codef. Compl.).]

1. A Roman and Civil Law. The adjustment of a dispute between parties by mutual concession; compromise.

2. The action of transacting or fact of being transacted (the carrying on or completion of an action or course of action).

Transactional (trænsæ'kʃənal, -zæ'-), a. [f. prec. + -AL; or F. *transactionnel* (Littré).] Of, pertaining to, or involving a transaction.

Transactionally, adv. By means, or by way of a transaction; practically.

Transactioneer, nonce-wd. [f. as prec. + -EER.] One who is concerned or has to do with transactions.

Transactor (trænsæ'ktər, -zæ'-). [a. L. *transactor*, agent-n. f. *transigere*: see TRANSACT.] One who transacts; a negotiator or intermediary; a manager, conductor, performer, doer.

Transalpine (trænsæ'lpăin, -zæ'-), a. (sb.) [ad. L. *trānsalpīnus* beyond or across the Alps, f. TRANS- + *alpīnus* Alpine, f. *Alpēs* the Alps.]

1. That is situated beyond the Alps.

Transalpinely.

Transalpinely, adv. (cf. sense 1.) In a transalpine way.

†**Transanimate**, v. Obs. rare. [Back-formation from next: see -ATE.] *trans.* To transfer the soul of (a person) from one body to another.

Transanimation. Now rare. [ad. med.L. *transanimātiō-em* (in Jerome Epistle 124. 4).]

Transboard, v. rare. [f. TRANS- + BOARD sb.] *trans.* To tranship.

Transborder, a. [f. TRANS- + BORDER sb.] Lying or living beyond a (or the) border; occupying territory outside the border.

Transcend (trænse'nd), v. [ad. L. *transcend-ĕre* to climb over or beyond, surpass, excel, exceed, f. TRANS- + *scandĕre* to climb.]

1. *trans.* To go beyond in some respect, quality, or degree; to go above, surpass, excel, exceed.

2. To pass or extend beyond or above (a non-physical limit); to go beyond the limits of (some-thing immaterial); to exceed.

Transcendence (trænse'ndəns). [ad. med.L. *transcendentia*, f. L. *transcendent-em* TRANSCEND-ENT : see -ENCE. C f. F. *transcendence* (18th c.).]

1. The action or fact of transcending, surmount-ing, or rising above; surpassing excellency or eminence, exceeding greatness.

Transcendency (trænse'ndənsi). Also -ant. [ad. med.L. *transcendentia*, f. *transcendent-em* : see prec. + -ENCY.] = TRANSCENDENCE 1.

Transcendent (trænse'ndənt), a. and sb. Also -ant. [ad. L. *transcendent-em*, pr. pple. of *trans-cendĕre* to TRANSCEND. For the spelling with -ant cf. F. *transcendant* (14-15th c. in Hatz.-Darm.), also *ascendant*, descendant.]

1. Surpassing or excelling others of its kind; going beyond the ordinary limits; pre-eminent; superior or supreme; extraordinary. Also loosely, great, striking or good; cf. 'excellent'.

Transcendental (trænsende'ntal), a. [ad. med.L. *transcendentāl-is* (c1305, Wyclif Mate-ria et Forma (1902) 243), f. as prec. + -AL.]

1. Of transcendent quality or nature; surpassing; excelling; exalted. = TRANSCENDENT a. 1.

1829 CARLYLE *Misc.* (1857) II. 74 The Idealist boasts that his Philosophy is Transcendental. 1842 EMERSON *Transcendentalist* Wks. (Bohn) II. 283 It is well known..that the Idealism of the present day acquired the name of Transcendental, from the use of that term by Immanuel Kant, of Konigsberg. 1872 MINTO *Eng. Prose Lit.* II. ix. 596 German transcendental philosophy. 1878 DOWDEN *Stud. Lit.* 47 The transcendental thinker [holds] that the mind contributes of its own stores ideas or forms of thought not derived from experience.

d. By Schelling 'transcendental philosophy' was used for the philosophy of mind as distinguished from that of nature.

1903 ADAMSON *Developm. Mod. Philos.* I. 265 Philosophy of nature and philosophy of mind or transcendental philosophy are therefore at once parallel and complementary.

3. In uses derived from the philosophical sense: **a.** Beyond the limits of ordinary experience, extraordinary.

1831 CARLYLE *Sart. Res.* II. v. (1858) 87 Sometimes it is even when your anxiety becomes transcendental, that the soul first feels herself able to transcend it. 1837 — *Fr. Rev.* III. I. i, Very frightful it is when a Nation..becomes transcendental. 1856 EMERSON *Eng. Traits* Wks. (Bohn) II. 104 This mental materialism makes the value of English transcendental genius. 1863 GEO. ELIOT *Romola* xxxix, That bust of Plato had been long used to look down on conviviality of a more transcendental sort. 1868 NETTLESHIP *Ess. Browning's Poetry* i. 34 Views..which, while less transcendental..are perhaps of more practical value.

b. Super-rational, superhuman, supernatural.

1826 SCOTT *Woodst.* xiv, The dexterity with which he threw his transcendental and fanatical notions, like a sort of veil, over the darker visions excited by remorse. 1841 MYERS *Cath. Th.* IV. xvi. 265 A revelation which may justly be termed Transcendental—wholly incapable of being explained, but yet not incapable of being believed. 1850 WHIPPLE *Ess. & Rev.* (ed. 3) I. 228 It [poetry] thus transcends the sphere of the senses, and is, in a measure, transcendental. 1858 KINGSLEY *Lett.* (1878) II. 67 Below all natural phenomena, we come to a transcendental—in plain English, a miraculous ground. 1903 F. W. H. MYERS *Human Personality* I. p. xv, Transcendental vision, or the perception of beings regarded as on another plane of existence.

c. *Vaguely*, Abstract, metaphysical, *a priori*.

1835 I. TAYLOR *Spir. Despot.* v. 212 Abstract and transcendental notions of an intolerant kind. 1840 THACKERAY *Paris Sk.-bk.* xv. (1872) 172 Having watched the Germans with their..mysterious transcendental talk. 1847 EMERSON *Repr. Men, Plato* Wks. (Bohn) I. 295 If he made transcendental distinctions, he fortified himself by drawing all his illustrations from sources disdained by orators and polite conversers. 1851 CARLYLE *Sterling* I. xv, To such length can transcendental moonshine, cast by some morbidly radiating Coleridge into the chaos of a fermenting life, act magically there. 1853 MAX MÜLLER *Chips* (1880) I. iii. 66 The exhausting atmosphere of transcendental ideas in which they [Hindus] lived. 1856 *N. Brit. Rev.* XXVI. 173 Proofs..that the most abstract and apparently transcendental truths in physical science will sooner or later add their tribute to supply human wants, and alleviate human sufferings. 1875 JOWETT *Plato* (ed. 2) I. 77 An unmeaning and transcendental conception. 1901 *Edin. Rev.* Apr. 427 He [Mill] rejected all transcendental conceptions.

d. Applied to the movement of thought in New England of which Emerson was the principal figure: see TRANSCENDENTALISM 1 b.

1844 DICKENS *Mart. Chuz.* xxxiv, Two literary ladies present their compliments to the mother of the modern Gracchi...It may be another bond of union..to observe, that the two L.L.'s are Transcendental. 1887 CABOT *Memoirs of Emerson* I. vii. 249 [In the Boston or New England Transcendentalism] the transcendental was whatever lay beyond the stock notions and traditional beliefs to which adherence was expected because they were generally accepted by sensible persons.

4. *Math.* Not capable of being produced by (a finite number of) the ordinary algebraical operations of addition, multiplication, involution, or their inverse operations; expressible in terms of the variable only in the form of an infinite series.

The typical transcendental functions are $\sin x$, e^x, $\log x$.

1706 PHILLIPS (ed. Kersey), *Transcendental Curves*,..are such Curves, as when their Nature or Property comes to be express'd by an Equation, one of the Variable or flowing Quantities there, denotes a Curve or crooked Line. 1811 HUTTON *Course of Mathematics* III. ix. 188 Transcendental or mechanical curves, are such as cannot be..expressed by a pure algebraical equation. Thus, $y = \log x$, $y = A . \sin x$, ..$y = A^x$, are equations to transcendental curves. 1843 *Penny Cycl.* XXV. 120 The roots of equations of the fifth and higher degrees are..transcendental: there is no mode of expression except by infinite series. 1879 CAYLEY in *Encycl. Brit.* IX. 818/2 The so-called circular functions..the exponential function..the logarithmic function..are all of them transcendental functions. 1882 GLAISHER *Ibid.* XIV. 773/1 The small group of transcendental functions, consisting only of the circular functions..$\sin x$, $\cos x$, &c.,..e^x, and $\log x$. 1902 *Encycl. Brit.* XXXI. 287/2 There are numbers..which cannot be defined by any combination of a finite number of equations with rational integral coefficients. Such numbers are said to be *transcendental*.

B. *sb.* [the adj. used *absol.*] A transcendental conception, term, or quantity.

1668 WILKINS *Real Char.* II. i. 24 The right ordering of these Transcendentals is a business of no small difficulty; because there is so little assistance or help to be had for it in the Common Systems. 1711 HICKES *Two Treat. Chr. Priesth.* (1847) II. 165 Generical terms come so near to the nature of transcendentals, that they are seldom capable of..exact definition. 1726 SWIFT *Gulliver* II. vii, As to ideas, entities, abstractions, and transcendentals, I could never drive the least conception into their heads. 1843 *Penny Cycl.* XXV. 120 The expression of the old transcendentals as recognised functions, and the writing of them accordingly, as $\log x$, $\sin x$, $\cos x$, &c.

Transcendentalism (trɒnsendeˑntăliz'm). [f. prec. + -ISM. Cf. F. *transcendantalisme* (Littré).]

1. Transcendental philosophy; a system of this; applied to that taught by Kant and other philosophers; also, to the idealism of Schelling.

1803 *Edin. Rev.* Jan. 265 The theory of transcendentalism may therefore be a better dogmatism than others. 1817 T. L. PEACOCK *Melincourt* III. 40 He has thus discovered the difference between objective and subjective reality and this point of view is transcendentalism. 1851 CARLYLE *Sterling* I. viii. (1872) 46 He was thought to hold..alone in England, the key of German and other Transcendentalisms. 1866 DK. ARGYLL *Reign Law* ii. (ed. 4) 117 What is transcendentalism but the tendency to trace up all things to the relation in which they stand to abstract Ideas? 1878 DOWDEN *Studies in Lit.* 58 Transcendentalism, seeking the supernatural everywhere, loses sight of it as such.

b. The religio-philosophical teaching of the New England school of thought represented by Emerson and others: see quot. 1911.

1842 EMERSON *Lect., Transcendentalist* Wks. (Bohn) II. 279 What is popularly called Transcendentalism among us, is Idealism. 1876 *N. Amer. Rev.* CXXIII. 468 Boston and its immediate neighborhood..really made up the kingdom ruled by Transcendentalism. 1887 CABOT *Emerson* I. vii. 248 The Boston or New England Transcendentalism had, as Dr. Hedge says, no very direct connection with the transcendental philosophy of Germany, the philosophy of Kant and his successors. 1911 *Encycl. Brit.* XXVII. 172/2 (*Transcendentalism*) The most famous example of the pseudo-philosophic use of the term is for a movement of thought which was prominent in the New England states from..1830 to 1850. Its use originated in the Transcendental Club (1836) founded by Emerson, Frederic Henry Hedge, and others. The movement had several aspects: philosophical, theological, social, economic.

2. Exalted character, thought, or language; also, that which is extravagant, vague, or visionary in philosophy or language; idealism.

1831 CARLYLE *Sart. Res.* I. iii. (1858) 8 If through the high, silent, meditative Transcendentalism of our Friend we detected any practical tendency whatever, it was at most Political. 1837 THACKERAY *Carlyle's Fr. Rev.* Wks. 1900 XIII. 249 It teems with sound, hearty philosophy (besides certain transcendentalisms which we do not pretend to understand). 1859 SMILES *Self-Help* xi. (1860) 287 Nor did the lofty transcendentalism of his books by any means palliate the acted meannesses of his life. 1871 W. H. MILLER *Cult. Pleasure* Pref. (1872) 10 It is time, indeed, that the whole subject of happiness should be dragged down from the regions of transcendentalism.., and be made, if possible, to take its place in the highways and byeways of every-day life.

3. The quality or character of transcendent excellence; transcendency. *rare.*

1840 CARLYLE *Heroes* iii. (1872) 80 Dante and Shakespeare.. dwell apart...In the general feeling of the world, a certain transcendentalism, a glory as of complete perfection, invests these two.

Transcendentalist (trɒnsendeˑntălist). [f. as prec. + -IST. Cf. mod.F. *transcendantaliste* (Littré).] An adherent of some form of transcendentalism. Also *attrib.*

1803 *Edin. Rev.* Jan. 267 We will admit to the transcendentalist his solitary noumenon, and its separate functions. 1829 CARLYLE *Misc.* (1857) II. 75 To a Transcendentalist, Matter has an existence, but only as a Phenomenon. 1840 *Boston Q. Rev.* 270 The men who are affected by it [the new movement] are called by their opponents, Transcendentalists. 1876 LOWELL *Among my Bks.* Ser. II. 32 Transcendentalist as he was by nature, so much so as to be in danger of lapsing into an oriental mysticism. 1879 R. H. HUTTON in *W. Bagehot's Lit. Stud.* Pref. Mem. 28 A thorough transcendentalist, by which I mean one who could never doubt that there was a real foundation of the universe distinct from the outward show of its superficial qualities, and that the substance is never exhaustively expressed in these qualities. 1882 *Athenæum* 17 June 767/1 Miss Peabody..was prominent in the old transcendentalist movement.

Hence **Transcendentaliˑstic** *a.*, of, pertaining to, or of the nature of transcendentalism; belonging to or held by transcendentalists.

1892 *Monist* II. 265 If a philosophy denies the existence of transcendentalistic thought-entities or of any such things in themselves, which serve as cement to combine the *disjecta membra* of their world conception, it is generally declared to lead straight on to nihilism.

Traˑnscendentaˑlity. *rare.* [f. as prec. + -ITY: cf. Ger. *transcendentalität* (D. Jenisch in *Kant Briefwechsel* 1902, III. 75).] Transcendental quality. (In quot. 1880 *humorous.*)

a 1846 SALISBURY cited in WORCESTER. 1880 W. S. GILBERT *Patience* I. 7 There is a transcendentality of delirium—an acute accentuation of supremest ecstacy.

Transcendentalize (trɒnsendeˑntăloiz), *v.* [f. as prec. + -IZE.] *trans.* **a.** To render transcendent. **b.** To render transcendental; to idealize. Hence **Transcendeˑntalized** *ppl. a.*

1846 MOZLEY *Ess.* (1878) I. 233 The magnanimity, generosity, ardour, and refinement of ordinary virtue were transcendentalised in him. 1866 LIDDON *Bampt. Lect.* viii. (1875) 450 Nor is it to transcendentalize Him into an abstraction which mocks us when we attempt to grasp it as an unsubstantial phantom. 1875 *Contemp. Rev.* Nov. 996 How often even they are found seeking to transcendentalize their own religion, to escape from its old dogmas, and efface its ancient discipline! 1881 *Contemp. Rev.* Mar. 380 Some transcendentalized form of tolerance. 1883 *Century Mag.* XXIX. 200/2 The Venetian gondola, refined, transcendentalized.

Transcendeˑntally, *adv.* [f. as prec. + -LY[2].] In a transcendental manner or degree; according to a transcendental system.

1803 *Edin. Rev.* Jan. 277 Of moral duty it may be said, in like manner, that transcendentally it cannot exist. [1842 MRS. BROWNING *Bk. Poets* Poems 1890 V. 241 Some have discovered that he [Shakspere] individualized, and some that he generalized, and some that he subtilized—almost transcendentally.] 1877 E. CAIRD *Philos. Kant* II. iii. 244 We hold that space and time are transcendentally ideal, i.e. that they have no objective validity..apart from the constitution of the sensibility through which they are apprehended.

¶ **b.** *erron.* = TRANSCENDENTLY.

1870 *Eng. Mech.* 11 Mar. 636/2 The diamond, so transcendentally beautiful.

‖ **Transcendentia** (trɒnsendeˑnʃiă), *sb. pl. Obs. rare*[−1]. [L., neut. pl. of *transcendens* TRANSCENDENT.] Transcendent traits or qualities.

1674 JOSSELYN *Voy. New Eng.* 89 There are certain transcendentia in every creature, which are the indelible characters of God, and which discover God.

Transcendently (trɒnseˑndĕntli), *adv.* [f. TRANSCENDENT *a.* + -LY[2].] In a transcendent manner or degree; so as to transcend; surpassingly, supremely, pre-eminently.

1623 GOUGE *Serm. Extent God's Provid.* § 1 He saith not simply, you are as good; but transcendently, more worth. 1638 SIR T. HERBERT *Trav.* (ed. 2) 85 His genius [is] so transcendently efflated with pride and ambition, that he beholds his equals with disdaine and anger. 1712 ADDISON *Spect.* No. 543 ¶ 1 It was the work of a Being transcendently wise and powerful. 1871 MORLEY *Crit. Misc., Carlyle* (1904) I. 164 The transcendently firm and clear-eyed intelligence of Goethe. 1907 *Verney Mem.* I. 71 Reserved for some transcendently important occasion.

Transceˑndentness. *rare.* [f. as prec. + -NESS.] The quality or character of being transcendent: = TRANSCENDENCY.

1625 BP. MOUNTAGU *App. Cæsar* viii. 75 Why are you enraged against me, if I cannot attaine the measure of your transcendentnesse, but confesse my disability and imperfection? 1730 [see TRANSCENDINGNESS]. 1874 PUSEY *Lent. Serm.* 308 [S. Paul] piles up words upon words to utter as he may, that which is unutterable; the transcendentness of the might of the grace of God to usward.

† **Transceˑndiary.** *Obs. nonce-wd.* [? irreg. after *incendiary*, f. L. *transcend-ĕre* to TRANSCEND: see -ARY.] A transcendent person or thing; in quot., an eminent quality.

1654 FULLER *Two Serm.* 60 Some grand Vices..infected the transcendiaries of their highest atchievements.

† **Transceˑndible,** *a. Obs. rare.* [f. as TRANSCEND + -IBLE.] Capable of being transcended or surmounted.

1684–94 tr. *Plutarch's Mor.* (1874) II. 220 It appears that Romulus slew his brother, because he attempted to leap over a sacred and inaccessible place, and to render it transcendible and profane.

Transcending (trɒnseˑndiŋ), *ppl. a.* [f. TRANSCEND *v.* + -ING[2].] That transcends; surpassing; supereminent; transcendent.

a 1529 [implied in TRANSCENDINGLY]. 1598 [see TRANSCENDENT A. 1]. 1641 *Vind. Smectymnuus* xiii. 113 A building of that transcending loftiness. 1713 DERHAM *Phys.-Theol.* IV. xii. 216 Man..being endowed with the transcending Faculty of Reason. 1852 MRS. JAMESON *Leg. Madonna* 196 An angel..might well prostrate himself as witness of the transcending miracle.

Hence **Transceˑndingly** *adv.*, transcendently; **Transceˑndingness**, transcendence.

a 1529 SKELTON *Replyc.* Wks. 1862 II. 232 Excellently enformed and transcendingly sped in moche high connyng. 1730 BAILEY (folio), *Transcendentness*, Transcendingness, Surpassingness. 1817 A. BONAR *Serm.* II. xx. 443 How transcendingly glorious does he appear! 1874 PUSEY *Lent. Serm.* 306 'That the transcendingness of the power', they say, 'may be of God, and not from us'.

Transcension (trɒnseˑnʃən). *rare.* [ad. med.L. *transcensiōn-em* (*c* 380 Jerome Ezech. Homil. XI. 1), n. of action from *transcend-ĕre* (ppl. stem *transcens-*) to TRANSCEND.] A passing beyond or above, transcendence.

c 1611 CHAPMAN *Hymne to Venus* 487 My muse, affecting first, thy fame to raise; Shall make transcension now, to others praise. 1886 *American* XII. 152 He laid great stress on miracles and all transcensions of law.

† **Transceˑnt.** *Obs. rare.* [f. TRANSCEND, after *ascent, descent.*] The act of passing over or crossing.

1621 G. SANDYS *Ovid's Met.* IX. ii. (1626) 177 Nor seekes the smoothest wayes: Nor by declining his transcent delayes.

† **Transˌchaˑnge,** *v. Obs.* [f. TRANS- 2 + CHANGE *v.*: cf. obs. F. *transchangement* (Cotgr.).] *trans.* To transform; to transmute.

a 1598 ROLLOCK *Serm.* Wks. 1849 I. 398 Be schining it culd never sa transchange ane creature. *a* 1636 FITZ-GEFFRAY *Holy Transport.* (1881) 197 O Tygers into humane shape transchang'd. 1662 J. CHANDLER *Van Helmont's Oriat.* To Rdr., The which colour hath transchanged thee into black darkness; thou being a white and red Virgin.

† **Transˌchaˑngeative,** *a. Obs. rare.* [irreg. f. prec. + -ATIVE; cf. *talkative.*] Having the faculty of changing or tendency to change.

1662 J. CHANDLER *Van Helmont's Oriat.* 157 The objects of taste sitting immediately in some body, cannot by reason of their corporeal thickness, form a transchangeative Image. *Ibid.* 244 The transchangeative virtue of the Archeus.

Trans-chaˑnnel, *a.* [TRANS- 3, 8.] (Passing) across a channel, esp. across the English or Irish Channel; crossing the Channel.

1894 *Westm. Gaz.* 7 June 7/1 Trans-channel cycling. 1901 *Daily Chron.* 6 Sept. 6/2 The Admiralty Pier [at Dover] from which the trans-Channel passenger traffic is now conducted. 1909 *Westm. Gaz.* 12 July 7/1 The monoplane.. would not be ready to make the actual trans-Channel flight.

Transchour, obs. form of TRENCHER.

† **Transˌclouˑt**, *v. Obs. nonce-wd.* [f. TRANS- 2 + CLOUT *sb.*[1] 4 b.] *trans.* To transform or disfigure with clouts or mis-shapen clothing.

1647 WARD *Simp. Cobler* 25 Those women..disfigure themselves with such garbes, as not onely dismantles their native lovely lustre, but transclouts them into gant bar-geese.

† **Traˑnsˌcolate,** *v. Obs. rare.* [f. ppl. stem of mod.L. **transcōlāre* (after *percōlāre* to PERCOLATE), or obs. F. *transcouler* (Cotgr.) from same source + -ATE[3].] *trans.* To cause (liquid) to pass through a porous substance or medium; to strain, filter; = PERCOLATE *v.* 1. Hence † **Traˑnscolating** *ppl. a.*

1615 CROOKE *Body of Man* 416 The vrine is transcolated through the flesh of the kidneis. 1661 LOVELL *Hist. Anim. & Min.* 315 The kidnies..are to draw, seperate, and transcolate whatever is serous and aqueous in the vessels, both veines and arteries. 1684 tr. *Bonet's Merc. Compit.* III. 93 Fortis transcolates the juices through Sand. 1817 PETTIGREW *Mem. Lettsom* III. 303 By transcolation, or by passing through the transcolating pores of all the solids.

† **Transˌcolaˑtion.** *Obs.* [f. as prec. + -ATION. Cf. obs. F. *transcoulation* (Cotgr.).] The process of transcolating; straining, filtration; = PERCOLATION a.

1634 T. JOHNSON *Parey's Chirurg.* IX. i. (1678) 216 That solution of Continuity..which is generated by sweating out and transcolation, [termed] Diapedesis. 1662 STILLINGFL. *Orig. Sacr.* III. iv. § 6 Meer transcolation may by degrees take away that which the Chymists call the fixed salt. 1702 W. COWPER in *Phil. Trans.* XXIII. 1185 In Bruises when the Blood is extravassated, it goes off either by Transcolation or else causes an Abscess. 1817 [see TRANSCOLATING].

† **Transˌcoˑlorate,** *v. Obs. rare.* [f. TRANS- 2 + COLORATE *v.*] = TRANSCOLOUR. Hence † **Transcoˑlorated** *ppl. a.*, transcoloured.

1813 J. BADCOCK *Dom. Amusem.* 43 The Transcolourated Writing.

Transˌcoloraˑtion, -colouraˑtion. Now *rare* or *Obs.* [f. TRANS- + COLORATION.] The action or process of transcolouring; change of colour.

1664 POWER *Exp. Philos.* I. 74 Experiments in the Extraction, Commixtion, and Transcoloration of Tinctures. *c* 1790 IMISON *Sch. Art* II. 94 Among the most pleasing as well as surprizing phenomena of nature [are] the transcolourations produced by chemistry. 1827 *Blackw. Mag.* XXI. 781 True, through all transformations, and transfigurations, and transcolorations, to their original..forms, figures, and colours.

† **Transˌcoˑlour,** *v. Obs. rare.* [f. TRANS- 2 + COLOUR *v.*: cf. It. *transcolorare* 'to discolour or chaunge colour' (Florio).] *trans.* To change the colour of; to cause to change colour.

1664 POWER *Exp. Philos.* I. 75 By its acidity is transcoloured into English Beer. 1669 COKAINE *Poems* 47 Do not believe I counterfeit, who think Verses in your praise would transcolour Inke. 1837 C. LOFFT *Self-formation* II. 262, I was never so transcoloured.

Trans-coˑndyloid, *a. Surg.* [f. TRANS- 5 + CONDYLE: cf. *condyloid.*] Traversing or cutting across the condyles.

1885 *Buck's Handbk. Med. Sc.* I. 169/2 Hence this [Dr. W. Stokes'] amputation is generally known as the supracondyloid amputation, that of Carden being known as the trans-condyloid operation. 1899 *Syd. Soc. Lex.*, *Trans-condyloid amputation of thigh*, Carden's operation.

Trans-coˑnscious, *a. rare*[−1]. [TRANS- 4.] That is beyond or outside of consciousness or cognition.

1865 MASSON *Rec. Brit. Philos.* ii. 96 He recognised the ideas of three supra-sensuous or trans-conscious objects—God, the Soul, and the World.

Traˑns-contineˑntal, *a.* [f. TRANS- 3 + CONTINENTAL. Cf. mod.F. *transcontinental* (Littré).] That extends or passes across a continent; also, of or pertaining to the farther side of a continent.

1869 J. A. POOR (*title*) Transcontinental Railway [from Atlantic to Pacific in U. S.]. 1876 J. A. ALLEN *Amer. Bison* (1877) 465 The great trans-continental emigrant route by way of the South Pass. 1883 W. J. SMITH in *19th Cent.* Nov. 841 The transcontinental railway which Queensland is about to construct. 1898 *Westm. Gaz.* 27 Sept. 6/1 Mr. R. L. J—, the well-known Trans-Continental cyclist, arrived safely in Khiva on the 5th inst.

† **Transˌcoˑrporate,** *v. Obs. rare.* [f. late L. *transcorporāre* (*a* 200 Irenæus): see -ATE[3], and cf. med.L. *transcorporātus* (Du Cange).]

1. *trans.* To change into a different body or substance; to transubstantiate.

1570 FOXE *A. & M.* (ed. 2) 1314/1 Notwithstandyng that ye substance of bread and wyne was nowe banished out of the Sacrament, and vtterly transcorporated into the substance of Christes very body and bloud: yet was not this body eleuated..nor adored..till the dayes of Pope Honorius the 3.

2. *intr.* To migrate from one body to another; to transmigrate. Hence † **Transcoˑrporating** *ppl. a.*, holding the doctrine of transmigration. Cf. TRANSINCORPORATION, and med.L. *transcorporatio.*

1658 SIR T. BROWNE *Hydriot.* iv. 34 The Pythagorians and transcorporating Philosophers, who were to be often buried, held great care of their enterment.

Transˌcoˑrtical, *a. Anat.* and *Path.* [TRANS- 5.] Crossing the cortex of the brain; in quot., caused by a lesion involving a cross-section of the cerebral cortex.

1900 *Brit. Med. Jrnl.* 5 May 1104 This phenomenon the author considered analogous to the motor disturbances in the shape of aphasia which has been termed transcortical motor aphasia. 1901 *Lancet* 20 Apr. 1126.

Transˌcreaˑte, *v. nonce-wd.* [TRANS- 2.] *trans.* To create by or in the way of transmission.

1834 COLERIDGE in *Lit. Rem.* (1839) IV. 166 Not the qualities merely, but the root of the qualities is transcreated. How else could it be a birth,—a creation?

Tranˌscriˑbble, *v. rare.* [f. TRANS- + SCRIBBLE *v.*, after *transcribe.*] *trans.* To transcribe carelessly or hastily. So **Transcriˑbbler,** a careless or hasty transcriber.

1746 GRAY *Let. to Wharton* in W. Mason *Mem.* (1807) II. 37 He [Aristotle] has suffered vastly from the transcribblers, as all authors of great brevity necessarily must. 1750 COVENTRY *Pompey Litt.* II. xii, He..once in a quarter of a year, took the pains to transcribble a sermon out of various authors. 1821 BYRON *Let. to Moore* 19 Sept., Such licentiousness of Verb and Noun as may tend to 'disparage my parts of speech' by the carelessness of the transcribblers.

Transcribe (trɒnˌskrəiˑb), *v.* Also 7 transcribe. [ad. L. *transcrībĕre*, f. *trans*, TRANS- + *scrībĕre* to write.]

1. *trans.* To make a copy of (something) in writing; to copy out from an original; to write (a copy). Also *absol.*

1552 HULOET, Transcribe, *transcribo*. 1611 COTGR., *Transcrire*, to transcribe, to write or copie out. 1621 ELSING *Debates Ho. Lords* (Camden) 101 He coulde not tell whether all was transcrybed by his clerke. 1655 *Nicholas Papers* (Camden) II. 238 The enclosed leters..which I have desired your sonne for your beter satisfaction to transscribe. 1732 BERKELEY *Alciphr.* VI. § 3 The primitive Christians were careful to transcribe copies of the gospels. 1837 LOCKHART *Scott* I. v. 134 The Writer's Apprentice receives a certain allowance in money for every page he transcribes. 1850 MACAULAY in *Life & Lett.* (1913) II. xii. 256 Tomorrow I shall begin to transcribe again and to polish.

b. Less exactly: To copy or reproduce the matter or statements of (a writing or book) without regard to the wording; to quote, cite. Now *rare.*

a 1633 AUSTIN *Medit.* (1635) 221 A Tradition (which I find not in Abdias, Bishop of Babylon; nor in any of the common Legends that I thinke were almost all transcribed from him). 1646 SIR T. BROWNE *Pseud. Ep.* II. i. 50 Solinus who transcribed Plinie..hath in this point dissented from him. 1676 RAY *Corr.* (1848) 122 All which..makes me suspect he transcribed what he hath out of some writer, either Dutch, French, or Italian. 1726 POPE *Odyss.* V. Notes 285, I have sometimes used Madam Dacier as she has done others, in transcribing some of her Remarks without particularizing them. 1747 WESLEY *Prim. Physick* (1762) p. xviii, A few plain, easy rules. Chiefly transcribed from Dr. Cheyne. 1850 SCORESBY *Cheever's Whalem. Adv.* vi. (1858) 76 Which we have not room to transcribe here.

2. To write out in other characters, to transliterate; to write out (a shorthand account) in ordinary 'long-hand'; formerly also, to translate or render accurately in another language.

1639 T. C[ARY] (*title*) The Mirrour which Flatters not.. Transcrib'd into English from the French [of La Serre],..And devoted to the well-disposed Readers. 1669 tr. *Beguinus' Tyroc. Chym.* To Rdr., It becomes every man, about to transcribe, or render the Works of another in his own native Tongue, neither to add any thing of his own, nor to omit of the Author's. 1724 A. COLLINS *Gr. Chr. Relig.* 138 All the books..were transcrib'd, as is usually suppos'd, out of the Hebrew into the Chaldee Character. 1875 RENOUF *Egypt. Gram.* 1 The omitted vowels are conventionally transcribed by the letter *e*. 1877 BROWNING (*title*) The Agamemnon of Æschylus transcribed by Robert Browning.

b. *Mus.* To adapt (a composition) for a voice or instrument other than that for which it was originally written. 1891 in *Cent. Dict.*

† **3.** *fig.* To copy or imitate (a person, his qualities, actions, etc.); to reproduce. *Obs.*

1647 CRASHAW *Poems* 106 Thou and the lovely hopes that smile in thee Are ta'en out, and transcribed by thy great mother! 1664 EVELYN tr. *Freart's Archit.* Ep. Ded. 5 As many of those Illustrious Persons as by their large and magnificent Structures transcribe your Royal Example. 1709 WATTS *Hymn 'My dear Redeemer'* ii, Such love, and meekness so divine, I would transcribe, and make them mine. *a* 1729 ROGERS (J.), If we imitate their repentance as we transcribe their faults.

† **4.** To attribute or ascribe *to* another by transference. *Obs.*

1561 T. NORTON *Calvin's Inst.* IV. xiv. (1634) 634 *margin*. Sacraments..be meanes whereby faith groweth, yet so that no power proper unto God be transcribed from him unto them. 1610 R. ABBOTT *Old Way* 15 The Papists..who haue transcribed the authority of Religion to mortall Men, to Doctors, and Fathers, and Councels. 1651 C. CARTWRIGHT *Cert. Relig.* II. 34 As he used to transcribe to the Father whatsoever divine power was in him, so the Apostle doth not improperly transferre to the Father that which was Christs most proper work.

5. *Roman Law.* To transfer, assign, make over *to* another; = L. *transcribere*: cf. TRANSCRIPTION 4. 1880 [see *transcribed* below].

Hence **Transcribed** (-skrəiˑbd) *ppl. a.*; **Transcriˑbing** *vbl. sb.* and *ppl. a.*

1700 P. LORRAIN in *Pepys' Diary*, etc. (1879) VI. 229 The transcribing of the Appendix. 1709 STEELE *Tatler* No. 19 ¶ 2 Small Quill-men and Transcribing Clerks. 1880 MUIRHEAD *Gaius* III. § 128 A literal obligation is created by transcribed entries; and these are made in two ways,—either from thing to person, or from person to person.

Transcriber (trɒnˌskrəiˑbəɹ). [f. TRANSCRIBE + -ER[1].] One who transcribes; a copyist or copier, as distinct from an original writer.

1610 HOLLAND *Camden's Brit.* (1637), The carelesse negligence of transcribers. 1654 FULLER *Ephemeris* Pref. 3, I.. who have no commission to be an Authour, but a Transcriber. 1791 *Gentl. Mag.* Jan. 21/1 The dull transcribers of printed sermons. 1841 D'ISRAELI *Amen. Lit.* (1867) 218 Spurious writings..ascribed by ignorant transcribers to some ancient sage.

Transcript (trɑˑnˌskript), *sb.* (*a.*) Forms: α. 3–4 **transcrit,** (3 **traunscrit**), 5 **transcrite,** (6 **tancrete**). β. 5–7 **transcripte,** (6 **-scrypt**), 5– **transcript.** [a. OF. *transcrit* (AF. also *transescrit, transecrit*) copy of a document, etc. (1221 in Godef.):—L. *transcript-um*, sb. use of pa. pples. of F. *transcrire*, and L. *transcrībĕre* to TRANSCRIBE. In 15th c. assimilated to the L. form *transcriptum* (evidenced from *c* 1200, in English use). A worn-down F. form *tancrist, tanscrit* (13th c. in Godef.), appears to be represented in 16th c. Eng. by *tancrete* (Skelton): see B.]

1. A written copy; also *transf.* a printed reproduction of this; *spec.* in *Law*, a copy of a legal record.

α. *c* 1290 *Beket* 551 in *S. Eng. Leg.* I. 122 Of ower olde lawes transcrit ȝe me take. *Ibid.* 553 Þe king him let a traunscrit take of his custumes echon. 1454 *Rolls of Parlt.* V. 248/1 That a transcrite of this same Act..be sent unto our seid Tresorer. 1522 [see B.].

β. 1467 *Mann. & Househ. Exp. Eng.* (Roxb.) 402 Item, for a transcripte of the offyce of Gorge, ij. s. 1481 *Coventry Leet Bk.* 493 A transcript of which lettre hereaftur ensueth. 1538 FITZHERB. *Just. Peas* 187 The clerke of the petit bagge to certify the transcrypt of every suche offyce. 1611 SPEED *Hist. Gt. Brit.* IX. viii. § 54 The Archbishop and other Barons, are so cunningly named in the Popes Transcript, as if [etc.]. 1642 CHAS. I *Answ. Declar. both Ho.* 1 July 56 That which now remains being but a Transcript of a Transcript. 1788 GIBBON *Decl. & F.* xliv. (1869) II. 637 Authentic transcripts were multiplied by the pens of notaries and scribes. 1803 in Gurw. *Wellington's Desp.* (1837) II. 117 *note*, The note that I addressed to him.., a transcript of which is contained in the enclosure. 1875 SCRIVENER *Lect. Text N. Test.* 15 The successive transcripts between the sacred autograph and the document before us.

b. A verbal or close translation or rendering. ? *nonce-use.* Cf. TRANSCRIBE *v.* 2.

1871 BROWNING (*title*) Balaustion's Adventure: including a transcript from Euripides.

2. *transf.* and *fig.* A copy, imitation, reproduction; a representation, rendering, interpretation.

1646 J. GREGORY *Notes & Obs.* Pref. (1650) 1 The Lesser worlds or men are but the Transcripts of the Greater, as Children and Bookes the Copies of themselves. 1647 CLARENDON *Hist. Reb.* I. § 53 Some Transcripts of such Expressions..he met with amongst the People. 1657 TRAPP *Comm. Job* iv. 3 Let our lives be a true transcript of our Sermons. 1711 ADDISON *Spect.* No. 166 ¶ 1 Words are the Transcript of those Ideas which are in the Mind of Man, and ..Writing or Printing are the Transcript of Words. 1781 COWPER *Expost.* 198 They only..Received the transcript of the eternal mind. 1860 WESTCOTT *Introd. Study Gosp.* vii. (ed. 5) 367 The Gospel of St. Mark is essentially a transcript from life. 1869 MCLAREN *Serm.* Ser. II. iii. (1875) 42 The artist that is satisfied with his transcript of his ideal will not grow any more.

B. *ppl. a.* Transcribed, copied.

c 1450 *Godstow Reg.* 102 A Transcripte charter of philippe Basset I-made to the mynchons of Godestowe. 1522 SKELTON *Why not to Court* 417 It shall be as he wyll Stop at law tancrete, An abstract or a concrete.

† **Tranˌscriˑpt,** *v. Obs. rare.* [f. L. *transcript-*, ppl. stem of *transcrībĕre* to TRANSCRIBE.] *trans.* = TRANSCRIBE. Hence † **Transcriˑpting** *vbl. sb.*

1592 G. HARVEY *Pierce's Super.* Wks. (Grosart) II. 123, I haue lost more labour then the transcripting of this Censure. 1609 *Sir T. Smith's Commw. Eng.* To Rdr. 2 Corruption of coppies, happening..by the often transscripting. 1633 T. STAFFORD *Pac. Hib.* III. xiii. (1821) 623 A Letter from Sir Robert Cecill unto the Lord Deputie, and the same transcripted..unto the President.

Transcription (trɒnˌskriˑpʃən). [ad. L. *transcriptiōn-em*, n. of action f. *transcrībĕre* to transcribe, or a. F. *transcription* (16th c. in Godef. *Compl.*).]

1. The action or process of transcribing or copying. Also *fig.*

1598 FLORIO, *Trascrittione*, a transcription, a writing, or copying out. 1610 HEALEY *St. Aug. Citie of God* 548 The error was committed in the transcription of the copy from Ptolomies library. 1664 H. MORE *Myst. Iniq.* 93 By a diligent comparing of Copies upon every transcription. 1762 J. KENNEDY *Compl. Syst. Astronom. Chronol.* ad fin., Evidence which no transcription can corrupt. *a* 1848 R. W. HAMILTON *Rew. & Punishm.* i. (1853) 43 We might take the Decalogue and trace its transcription upon the soul of man. 1858 J. H. NEWMAN *Hist. Sk.* (1873) III. IV. xi. 426 Manual labour..applied to the transcription and multiplication of books..was a method of instruction.

b. Transliteration.

1869 FARRAR *Fam. Speech* i. (1873) 10 He succeeded in demonstrating the law of transcription, and for the first time reading these names in their proper form. *Ibid.* 24 The transcription into Russian letters.

2. The product of this process; a transcript; a copy.

1650 *Vind. Hammond's Addr.* § 88 Besides this transcription, there is but one passage.., to which he thinkes fit to make reply. 1657 RUMSEY *Org. Salutis* Ep. Ded. (1659) 11 Most medicinal Books are usually but bare transcriptions from former Writers. 1696 PHILLIPS (ed. 5), *Transcription*, a Writing copied, or transcribed. 1882–3 *Schaff's Encycl. Relig. Knowl.* I. 116/2 A transcription of the work, made in the beginning of the third century.

3. *Mus.* The arrangement, or (less properly) modification, of a composition for some voice or instrument other than that for which it was originally written; an instance of this, a transcribed piece.

1864 in WEBSTER. 1878 E. J. HOPKINS in Grove *Dict. Mus.* I. 21/1 Variations or adaptations like the popular 'Transcriptions' of the present day. 1885 *Athenæum* 26 Dec. 851/1 To the musicianly ear the term 'transcription' has generally an unpleasant sound, because it frequently bears reference to some uncalled-for distortion of a composer's original idea.

4. *Roman Law.* A transfer, assignment (of a debt or obligation); = L. *transcriptio*.

1677 OWEN *Justif.* Wks. 1851 V. 170 This he [Paul] did by the transcription of both the debts of Onesimus to himself. 1880 MUIRHEAD *Gaius* III. § 129 There is transcription from thing to person when, for example, I enter to your debit a sum you already owe me by reason of a purchase, a conduction, or a partnership.

Hence **Transcriˑptional** *a.*, of, pertaining to, or of the nature of transcription; **Transcriˑptionally** *adv.*, on transcriptional grounds.

1881 WESTCOTT & HORT *Grk. N. T.* Introd. § 29 Transcriptional Probability is not directly..concerned with the relative excellence of rival readings, but merely with the relative fitness of each for explaining the existence of the others. 1905 J. R. HARRIS in *Expositor* Sept. 166 Traces of such transcriptional errors. 1907 H. S. CRONIN in *Eng. Hist. Rev.* Apr. 294 Both Latin versions must have had some transcriptional history. 1911 K. LAKE *Earlier Ep. St. Paul* 419 The omission is transcriptionally slightly the more probable reading.

Transcriptitious (trɒnˌskriptiˑʃəs), *a. rare.* [f. L. *transcript-*, ppl. stem of *transcrībĕre* to TRANSCRIBE + -ITIOUS[1]. Cf. late L. *transcripticius, -itius* belonging to a transfer or assignment.] Derived from or arising out of transcription; of the nature or character of a transcript.

1655–87 H. MORE *App. Antid.* (1712) 181 That there is no such Idea of God..as we have describ'd, neither Innate, nor Acquisititious, or Transcriptitious; because it involves in it the Notion of a Spirit. 1802–12 BENTHAM *Ration. Judic. Evid.* (1827) II. 436 Preappointed evidence may be distinguished into original and transcriptitious. *Ibid.* III. 396 Evidence..termed transcriptitious or transcriptural.

Transcriptive (trɒnˌskriˑptiv), *a.* [f. as prec. + -IVE; cf. *descriptive*, etc.]

1. Having the quality or habit of transcribing; given, devoted, or tending to transcription.

1646 SIR T. BROWNE *Pseud. Ep.* I. viii. 29 Although excellent and usefull Authors, yet being either transcriptive, or following the common relations of things, their accounts are not to be swallowed at large. *Ibid.* 33 He is to be embraced..as a transcriptive relator. 1823 BYRON *Let.* in *Eng. Stud.* (1897) XXXIII. 453, I sent to Mrs. S—— a few Scenes more of the drama begun for her transcriptive leisure. 1888 CAVE *Inspir. O. Test.* viii. 455 Transcriptive Inspiration..moves the writers to write.

2. *Rom. Law.* Transferring obligation: cf. TRANSCRIPTION 4.

1875 POSTE *Gaius* III. § 131. 11 Transcriptive entries differ from mere entries of a person as debtor to cash.

Hence **Tranˌscriˑptively** *adv. rare*, in a transcriptive manner; by way of transcription.

1646 SIR T. BROWNE *Pseud. Ep.* I. vi. 21 Authors write often dubiously...Not a few transcriptively,..meerely transcribing almost all they have written.

† **Tranˌscriˑptor.** *Obs. rare.* [a. L. type **transcriptor*, agent-n. from *transcrībĕre* to TRANSCRIBE: cf. rare F. *transcripteur* (Littré).] = TRANSCRIBER.

1617 MORYSON *Itin.* II. 29 The Transcriptor fifty three shillings foure pence. 1811 in *2nd Rep. Rec. Irel.* 141 A Transcript of the Process..lodged with the Transcriptor and Foreign Apposer, previously to passing his Accounts for the year of his Sheriffalty.

Tranˌscriˑptural, *a.* [f. L. *transcript-us* transcribed, after *scriptural.*] = TRANSCRIPTIONAL.

1802–12 BENTHAM *Ration. Judic. Evid.* (1827) III. 223 Chains of written evidence in the form of transcriptural evidence. *Ibid.* V. IX. VI. ii. 516 Whether, provisionally at least, inferior evidence may not be employed..: transcriptural, for instance, instead of original. 1863 WESTCOTT in *Smith's Dict. Bible* II. 517/2 *note*, Two characteristic transcriptural errors occur in the passage.

† **Tranˌscriˑve,** *v. Obs. rare.* [f. TRANS- + SCRIVE *v.* (Cf. F. *transcriv-*, stem of *transcrire* :—L. *transcribĕre*.)] = TRANSCRIBE.

1665 in *Maitland Cl. Misc.* (1840) II. 524 For transcryveing a paper in a fine hand sent to London.

† **Transˌcuˑr,** *v. Obs. rare.* [ad. L. *transcurrĕre* to run across. Cf. OF. *transcourir* (12th–15th c. in Godef.).] *trans.* and *intr.* To run across or over; to run or rove to and fro.

1528 LYNDESAY *Dreme* 777 Tygris, Ganges, Ewphrates, and Nyle, Quhilk, in the est, Transcurris mony ane myle. 1626 BACON *Sylva* § 720 It is caused by the Fixing of the Minde upon one Object..whereby it doth not spatiate and transcurre, as it useth.

† **Transˌcuˑrrence.** *Obs. rare.* [f. as next: see -ENCE.] A running or passing over rapidly.

1656 BLOUNT *Glossogr.*, *Transcurrence*.., a running over, a passing over quickly. 1658 in PHILLIPS.

Transcurrent (trɒnsˌkʌˑrĕnt), *a.* [ad. L. *transcurrent-em*, pr. pple. of *transcurr-ĕre.*]

† **1.** Running or passing across, over, or through.

1608 HIERON *Defence* III. 56 The honoring of a consecrated creature,..with an honor passant, or transcurrent, from and through it to the Creator. 1664 POWER *Exp. Philos.* III. 169 All the Circles of the Armillary Sphære are really.. inhærent in the Earth, by virtue of the transcurrent Atoms.

2. *Entom.* Extending or running transversely.

1826 KIRBY & SP. *Entomol.* IV. 340 Transcurrent...When a postfrænum is at first adnate to the sides of the postscutellum, and then diverges across the pannel to the base of the wings.

† **Transˌcuˑrsion.** *Obs.* [ad. late L. *transcursiōn-em*, n. of action f. *transcurrĕre* to run across.]

1. The action of running or passing across or through; a going or moving through, transition, penetration; also, a journey or passage through a country, across the sea, etc.

1624 WOTTON *Archit.* in *Reliq.* (1651) 307 Such notes as I have taken in my forraigne transcursions or abodes. 1626 BACON *Sylva* X. Pref., In a Living Creature..the Sense, and the Affects of any one Part of the Body, instantly make a Transcursion thorowout the whole Body. 1653 H. MORE *Antid. Ath.* II. xii. § 17 (1712) 84 To wonder at the transcursion of Comets. 1655 FULLER *Ch. Hist.* X. vi. § 6 The transcursion of Italians hither, added much to the discovery of the Papal abominations. 1665 HOOKE *Microgr.* xxxv. 166 To impede, for the greatest part, the transcursion of the Air.

2. *fig.* A running through a subject in discourse.

1641 H. L'ESTRANGE *God's Sabbath* 55 Not to expatiate too farre in collaterall transcursions. 1657 HOWELL *Londinop.* 41 Having made a short transcursion through the Government of the City of London.

3. Passage, lapse (of time).

1622 MABBE tr. *Aleman's Guzman d'Alf.* II. 44 Wisedome is the Daughter of Experience, which is gotten by the transcursion of Time. *Ibid.* 288 Nor was transcursion of time needfull in this case.

† **Transˌcuˑrsive,** *a. Obs. rare.* [f. L. *transcurs-*, ppl. stem of *transcurr-ĕre* + -IVE.] Characterized by running rapidly over a subject; cursory.

1599 NASHE *Lenten Stuffe* (1871) 8 In this transcursive reportory, without some observant glance, I may not overpass the gallant beauty of their haver. 1614 JACKSON *Creed* III. To Rdr. 5 b, To sift more of their arguments, then in these short transcursiue disputes I could.

† **Transˌcuˑrsory,** *a. Obs. rare.* [f. as prec. + -ORY[2]: cf. *cursory*, and late L. *transcursōri-us.*] = prec. Hence † **Transcuˑrsorily** *adv. Obs. rare.*

1727 EARBERY tr. *Burnet's St. Dead* (1728) I. 238, I shall therefore just take a transcursory View of his Arguments. *Ibid.* II. 117, I have transcursorily taken a view of the Doctor's Notions.

Transcurvaˑtion. [TRANS- 6.] Transverse or lateral curvature (of the spine).

1822–34 *Good's Study Med.* (ed. 4) III. 263 This species offers us the four following varieties..γ Lateralis. Tetanic transcurvation.

Transdialect (trɒnsdəiˑălekt, -z-), *v. rare.* [f. TRANS- + DIALECT.] *trans.* To translate from one dialect into another.

1698 C. BOYLE *Bentley's Dissert.* (ed. 2) 52 If some Copyer ..thought that Ocellus's Physics would look better out of Doric, than in it, and therefore transdialected 'em. 1776 BURNEY *Hist. Mus.* I. 331 The poems under the name of Orpheus were written in the Doric dialect, but have since been trans-dialected, or modernised. 1830 J. DOUGLAS *Truths Relig.* (1832) 361 The book of Job appears to be the original Arabic of Job and his friends transdialected and amplified by Moses.

† **Transdiˑgnify,** *v. Obs. rare.* [TRANS- 2.] *trans.* To transfer from one dignity or rank to another.

1655 J. SERGEANT *Schism Disarm'd* 212 The Popes Universal Power must be supposed to be transdignifi'd into a private Patriarchate.

Transdiurnal (trɒnsdəiˌɜ̄ˑınăl, -z-), *a. nonce-wd.* [TRANS- 3.] That is beyond the confines of day.

1848 LOWELL *Fable for Critics* 504 C[arlyle] shows you how every-day matters unite With the dim transdiurnal recesses of night,—While E[merson] in a plain, preternatural way, Makes mysteries matters of mere every day.

Transduction (trɒnsˌdʌˑkʃən). *rare.* [ad. L. *transductiōn-em* (usually *trāductiōnem*), n. of action f. *tra(ns)dūcĕre*: see TRADUCE.] The action of leading or bringing across.

1656 BLOUNT *Glossogr.*, *Transduction*, a leading over, a removing from one place to another. *a* 1816 BENTHAM *Offic. Apt. Maximized, Introd. View* (1830) 19 In lieu of *adduction*, as the purpose requires, will be subjoined *abduction*, *transduction*,..and so forth.

‖ **Transduˑctor.** *Anat.* [L. agent-n. from *tra(ns)dūcĕre*: see prec.] That which draws across: applied to a muscle of the great toe.

[1890 BILLINGS *Med. Dict.*, Transductor hallucis.] 1899 *Syd. Soc. Lex.*, *Transductor*, syn. of *Transversus pedis.*

Transe, obs. form of TRANCE.

† **Transearth** (trɒnsˌɜ̄ˑıþ, -z-), *v. Obs. rare.* [f. TRANS- 2 + EARTH *sb.* or *v.*] *trans.* To move from one soil to another; to transplant.

1628 FELTHAM *Resolves* II. [I.] xix. 60 Fruites of hotter Countries, trans-earth'd in colder Climates.

† **Transeate** (trɑˑnsiˌeit), *v. Obs. rare*[−1]. [erron. f. L. *transe-o* I pass over (as if **transe-āre*) + -ATE[3].] *intr.* To pass over or across.

1657 TOMLINSON *Renou's Disp.* 221 The vinous parts of the wine transeating into vinegar.

Transect (trɒnseˑkt), *v.* Also 9 **transsect.** [f. TRAN(S- + *sect-*, ppl. stem of L. *secāre* to cut: see SECT *v.*[2]] *trans.* To cut across; to divide by passing across; in *Anat.* to dissect transversely. Hence **Transeˑcted** *ppl. a.*

1634 SIR T. HERBERT *Trav.* 161 Who with a Sword of a hundred Cubits length, cut off at one blow ten thousand Christians heads, and transected Taurus. 1846 DANA *Zooph.* (1848) 711 The concentric layers in these transsected knobs. 1861 E. T. HOLLAND *Iceland* in *Peaks, Passes*, etc. Ser. II. I. 8 The plain of Thing-vellir..is transected by numerous longitudinal crevasses in the lava. 1888 *Amer. Jrnl. Psychol.* May 488 The transsected sheaths of the tubules. 1890 O. CRAWFURD *Round Calendar in Port.* 178 The river Douro that transects the northern provinces of Portugal from east to west.

So **Transection** (trɒnseˑkʃən) [cf. SECTION], the action of transecting; a transverse section.

1899 *Allbutt's Syst. Med.* VI. 518 Transection of the spinal cord above the lumbar enlargement depresses the knee-jerk for a time.

Transelement (trɒnsˌeˑlĭment), *v.* [ad. med.L. *transelementāre*, f. TRANS- + L. *element-um* ELEMENT.] *trans.* To change or transmute the elements of. Hence **Transˌeˑlementing** *vbl. sb.*

1567 JEWEL *Def. Apol. Ch. Eng.* II. 238 For, as he saith, wee are Transelemented, or transnatured, and changed into Christe, euen so,..wee saie, The Breade is Transelemented, or changed into Christes Body. 1583 FOXE *A. & M.* 1379/2 [Chrysostom] hath these same playne words, transelemented, and transformed. 1656 S. HOLLAND *Zara* (1719) 33 For that he remained for a time as one transelemented. 1812–29 COLERIDGE in *Lit. Rem.* (1838) III. 94 That the body of our Lord was not transelemented or transnatured by the *pleroma* indwelling, we are positively assured by Scripture. 1855 PUSEY *Doctr. Real Presence* Note Q. 186 The Divine gifts were amnesty of evils, removal of sin, transelementing of nature. 1878 GLADSTONE *Glean.* (1879) III. 264 The old monotheism was (so to speak) transelemented, and caricatured, into the gorgeous but gross and motley religion of the Greek and Italian peninsulas.

So † **Transˌelemeˑntate** [med.L. *transelementātus*] *ppl. a.*, transelemented; **Transˌelemeˑntate** *v.* = *transelement.*

1579 FULKE *Heskins' Parl.* 296 The bread & wine are transelementated into the vertue of his flesh & bloud. 1583 FOXE *A. & M.* 1382/1 The bread (sayth [Chrysostom]) is transelementate, and transmuted into an other substaunce then it was before. 1899 W. R. INGE *Chr. Mysticism* vii. 257 *note*, The last-named [Theophylact] goes on to say that 'we are in the same way transelementated into Christ'.

Transˌelementaˑtion. [n. of action from med.L. *transelementāre*: see above, and quot. 1896.] The action or process of changing the elements of something.

1550 HOOPER *Serm. Jonas* vi. Siij, The transelementacion and alteracion of the breade, no place of ye scripture commaundeth vs to beleue. 1624 F. WHITE *Repl. Fisher* 421 In Transubstantiation the matter is destroyed, and the quantitie and accidents remaine, and in Transelementation the matter remaineth, and the essentiall and accidentall formes are altered. 1654 JER. TAYLOR *Real Pres.* xii. ¶ 5 The name of Transelementation, which Theophylact did use, seems to approach nearer to signify the propriety of this mysterie, because it signifies a change even of the first elements. 1706 tr. *Dupin's Eccl. Hist. 16th C.* II. v. 53 If any one is offended with the new Term *Transubstantiation*, he will find that the Ancients used the terms *Conversion*, *Transmutation*, *Transformation*, *Transelementation.* 1855 PUSEY *Doctr. Real Presence* Note Q. 223 Through what the transelementation of our nature from mortal to immortal takes place. 1896 R. F. CLARKE in *Month* Feb. 207 A conversion (μεταβολή), a transmutation (μεταποίησις), a transelementation (μεταστοιχείωσις).

† **Transˌeˑminent,** *a. Obs. rare.* [f. TRANS- 4 + EMINENT.] Eminent beyond others; pre-eminent, supereminent. So † **Transˌeˑminency,** pre-eminence: † **Transˌeˑminently** *adv.*, pre-eminently.

1642 *Answ. Observ. agst. King* 19 What State businesses soever are fairely carried,..redound transeminently and really to the glory of the Crowne. 1660 BURNEY Κέρδ. Δῶρον (1661) 3 This is the transeminencie of the Persons, and they have the Illustrious Character of Kings. *Ibid.* 22 Our Soveraign Lord.., who hath Reigned in all ages, in the persons transeminent.

Transempirical (trɒnsˌempiˑrikăl), *a. rare.* [TRANS- 4.] Pertaining to things beyond the range of experiential knowledge; metempirical.

1906 W. JAMES in *Jrnl. Philos., Psychol.*, etc. 20 Dec. 712 A conclusion supposed to flow from the intrinsic absurdity of transempirical objects.

Transept (trɑˑnsept). Forms: 6 **transsept,** 7 **-scept,** 8– **transept.** [First found in 16th c., ad. med. or mod. (Anglo-)L. **transseptum*, f. TRANS- + SEPTUM, prop. *sæptum* hedge, fence, enclosure, f. *sæpīre* to hedge in, fence in, enclose. (Early history and actual origin unascertained.) Hence mod.F. *transept* (introd. 1828). The Anglo-L. *transeptum* is often used by Leland, and in one instance Englished as *transsept*; but the word was rare before 1700.] The transverse part of a cruciform church considered apart from the nave; also, each of the two subdivisions or arms of this (the *north* and *south transepts*).

1538–42 LELAND *Itin.* (1907) I. II. 131 It stode in the midle of the transeptum of the chirch. *Ibid.* III. 239 One Sir John Scylley a knight and his wyfe sumtyme dwellyng in that paroche [Crideton] be buried in the north part of the transsept [*ed.* 1711 transept] of this [church]. *Ibid.* 287 In Transepto Eccl. in Merid. parte. *Ibid.* 292 An exceding goodly Chapel in Transepto of Bishop Stillington and King. 1692 WOOD *Ath. Oxon.*, *Fasti* 821 His body was buried in the south Transcept or large south Isle joyning to the Choir of St. Peter's Church in Westminster. 1782 WARTON *Hist. Kiddington* 8 The pediment of the southern Transept is pinnacled, not inelegantly, with a flourished Cross. 1815 J. SMITH *Panorama Sc. & Art* I. 130 The part running north and south is called the cross or transept. 1870 F. R. WILSON *Ch. Lindisf.* 79 The chancel roof,..like those of the nave and transepts, is open-timbered.

b. *attrib.* and *Comb.*, as *transept aisle, chapel.*

1890 C. H. MOORE *Gothic Archit.* iii. 160 Where there are no transept aisles..there are..no vertical divisions in the façade [end of transept]. 1900 *Yorkshire Archæological Jrnl.* XV. 281 The vaults of the presbytery and transept-chapels.

Transeptal (trɒnseˑptăl), *a.* [f. prec. + -AL.] Of, pertaining to, or of the nature of a transept. Hence **Transeˑptally** *adv.*, in the manner of a transept.

1846 *Ecclesiologist* V. 152 A parclose..screening off the north transeptal chapel. 1856 *Ibid.* XVII. 88 A spacious narthex with the prescribed chapels..opening into it transeptally. 1884 *Ch. Times* XXII. 86 Exeter is noteworthy for its transeptal or 'paddle-box' towers. 1886 WILLIS & CLARK *Cambridge* III. 261 The chapel is to the west of the hall, and has a transeptal antechapel.

Trans-equatoˑrial, *a.* [TRANS- 3: cf. *equatorial.*] Situated on the other side of the equator; also crossing the equator.

1900 *Jrnl. R. Geog. Soc.* Apr. 381 The Southern, Australian, or trans-equatorial land of our hemisphere.

Transˌesseˑntiate, *v. rare.* [f. TRANS- 1 + ESSENTIATE *v.*] *trans.* To change from one essence or being into another. Hence **Transˌesseˑntiating** *vbl. sb.* So **Transˌesseˑntiate** *ppl. a.* [ESSENTIATE *ppl. a.*], changed into another essence. (Const. as pa. pple.)

1675 PENN *Eng. Pres. Interests Consid.* Wks. 1782 III. 220 Here is no transessentiating or transubstantiating of being, from people to representative. 1839–52 BAILEY *Festus* xxxv. 534 Curse transessentiate into blessing!

Transetorious, -tory, etc., obs. ff. TRANSITORIOUS, TRANSITORY, etc.

† **Tranˌseˑxion.** *Obs. rare.* [irreg. f. TRANS- + L. *sex-us* SEX + -ION, after *connexion*, etc.] Change of sex.

1646 SIR T. BROWNE *Pseud. Ep.* III. xvii. 147 Not only Mankinde, but many other Animals, may suffer this transexion, we will not deny, or hold it at all impossible. *Ibid.* 148 Surely it much impeacheth this iterated transexion of Hares, if that be true which Cardan and other Physitians affirm, that Transmutation of sex is only so in opinion.

Transfashion (trɑnsfæˑʃən), *v.* [TRANS- 2.] *trans.* To alter or change the fashion of, to transform.

1601 DEACON & WALKER *Spirits & Divels* 134 He transmuted, transfashioned, transfigured, transformed, or metamorphozed himself into an angel. 1619 W. SCLATER *Exp. 1 Thess.* (1630) 305 To see..our people so Cameleon-like transfashioned into [etc.]. 1855 PUSEY *Doctr. Real Presence* Note Q. 233 God shall 'transfashion (μετασχηματίσει) our vile bodies, to be made like unto His glorious Body'.

Transfeature (trɑnsfīˑtiūı), *v.* [TRANS- 2.] *trans.* To change the features of.

1875 DORA GREENWELL *Liber Hum.* 33 Outward nature itself is transfigured and transfeatured to their view.

Transfeminate (trɒnsfeˑmineit), *v. rare.* [f. TRANS- + L. *femina*: cf. EFFEMINATE *v.*] *trans.* See quot. 1656. Hence **Transfeˑminated** *ppl. a.*

1646 SIR T. BROWNE *Pseud. Ep.* III. xvii. 148 These transfeminated persons were really men at first, although succeeding years produced the manifesto or evidence of their virilities. 1656 BLOUNT *Glossogr.*, *Transfeminate*.., to turn from woman to man, or from one sex to another. 1898 G. MEREDITH *Odes Fr. Hist.* 39 With a breath he blew them out, to beat their wings The way of such transfeminated things.

Transfer (trɑˑnsfəı), *sb.* [f. TRANSFER *v.*]

1. *Law.* Conveyance from one person to another of property, *spec.* of shares or stock.

1674 *Court Bks. Roy. Afr. Co.* (P.R.O.), [Form of acceptance] I do accept of —— his transfer of £— abovesaid the day and year abovewritten. 1693 *Act 5 Will. & Mary* c. 7. § 47 The Fee for examining..a Tickett or Tally in order to make a true Assignement or Transfer..shall..be One penny. 1694 *Bank of Eng. Charter* 27 July, There shall be constantly kept..a Register, or Book or Books, wherein all Assignments and Transfers shall be entered. 1727 SWIFT *What passed in Lond.* Wks. 1755 III. I. 189 All the Thursday morning was taken up in private transfers. 1766 BLACKSTONE *Comm.* II. i. 9 The reciprocal transfer of property by sale, grant, or conveyance. 1788 JEFFERSON *Writ.* (1859) II. 367 Observations on the transfer of our domestic debt to foreigners. 1817 JAS. MILL *Brit. India* II. IV. i. 5 The office in which are effected the transfers of the Company's stock and annuities. 1836 J. GILBERT *Chr. Atonem.* vii. (1852) 204 The lowest case of legal transfer is that of a debt.

2. *gen.* The act of transferring or fact of being transferred; conveyance or removal from one place, person, etc. to another; transference; transmission.

1785 BURKE *Corr.* (1844) III. 33 To remonstrate against the transfer of an immense sum of public money from the national service. 1811 J. ADAMS *Wks.* (1856) X. 3, I wait with patience for a transfer to another scene. 1843 LYTTON *Last Bar.* I. iii, An amply sufficient cause for the transfer of his allegiance. 1870 JEVONS *Elem. Logic* iv. 32 Equivocal words have become so by a transfer of meaning. 1877 KNIGHT *Dict. Mech.* 1334/2 The third lithographic method is by transfer...The work is not drawn or engraved upon the stone direct, but is placed there in a completed condition from some source furnishing it. 1907 *Trans. Devon Assoc.* 50 The transfer of the county See to Exeter.

b. *Naut.* In tacking: The distance traversed at right angles to the line of advance.

1889 *Cent. Dict.* s.v. *Advance* 12, In naval tactics, the distance made by a ship under way, in the direction of her course, after the helm has been put to one side and kept there; opposed to *transfer*, the distance made at right angles to the original course.

3. A thing (*rarely*, a person) that is transferred; *spec.* writing, drawing, or a design, conveyed from one surface to another in lithography, photography, and the like.

1839 *Trans. Royal Soc.* IV. 133 Twenty-three specimens of photographs, made by Sir John Herschel, accompany this paper..copies of engravings and drawings, some reverse, or first transfers; and others second transfers or re-reversed pictures. 1864 WEBSTER, *Transfer*..a soldier removed from one troop, or body of troops, and placed in another. 1877 KNIGHT *Dict. Mech.*, *Transfer*, an impression taken on paper, cloth, etc., and then laid upon an object and caused to adhere thereto by pressure. 1880 *Print. Trades Jrnl.* XXXI. 38 A transfer paper is prepared.., on which the transfer to be preserved is pulled. 1883 *Hardwich's Photogr. Chem.* 311 If a mat surface be desired, the transfer should be stripped from the glass before it is quite dry.

4. A means or place of transfer. Chiefly U.S. *spec.* **a.** *U.S. Post Office.* A telegraphic money-order. **b.** On a railway, etc.:

(*a*) A place at which trains or cars are transferred to a ferry for water transport; also, a ferry by which trains or cars are transported. (*b*) A siding connecting tracks at a crossing or on different levels (Webster 1911). (*c*) A transfer-ticket (*Cent. Dict.*). (*d*) The conveyance of passengers and luggage from one railway station to another, when these are not contiguous; hence *transfer-company*, a company which undertakes such conveyance between stations.

c. *Archery.* A sheet to which all scores are transferred from the target-papers.

1909 *Cent. Dict. Suppl.* s.v., The transfers are the official record from which the prize-list is made up.

5. *attrib.* and *Comb.*, as *transfer-boat, -clerk, -company* (4 b), *-deed, -department, -form, office, -process, rate*; **transfer-book,** a register of transfers of property, esp. that of its shares or stock, kept by a joint-stock company; **transfer-day,** at the Bank of England, a day for the register of transfers of bank-stock; **transfer-elevator,** a crane for transferring cargo from one vessel to another; **transfer-fee,** that charged by a joint-stock company for registering a transfer; **transfer-gilding,** in ceramics, transfer of a pattern in gold, as from paper to unglazed ware; **transfer-ink,** ink used in lithography; **transfer-jar,** a jar used in the collection of gases over liquid; **transfer-lathe**: see quot.; **transfer-lithography**: see sense 3; **transfer-paper,** paper used in making transfers in lithography and other processes; **transfer-press,** in engraving, a transferring machine; **transfer-printing,** a process by which designs are printed on fictile and other ware (so **transfer-printed** adj.); also printing by means of lithography; **transfer-station** (*U.S.*), a point at which transfer-tickets are given, and passengers transferred from one car to another (*Cent. Dict. Supp.*); **transfer-table** (*U.S.*), a railway traverse-table; **transfer-ticket,** a ticket entitling a passenger to change from a conveyance to one on another line or route without re-booking or further payment; a through ticket; **transfer-work,** designs made by transferring or transfer-printing.

1888 *Daily News* 10 Dec. 6/8 The *transfer boat Maryland was conveying a section of a train from Washington to Boston across the Haarlem River, at midnight. 1694 J. HOUGHTON *Collect. Improv. Husb. & Trade* V. No. 102 (13 July) The Seller goes to the Clerk of the Company.. appointed to keep a Book of Alienations, called a *Transferr Book, and there he transferrs the Shares he has sold to the Buyer. 1701 *Lond. Gaz.* No. 3737/4 The Transfer Books of the Bank will be shut up from Monday the 13th Instant to Friday the 10th of October next, in order to a Dividend. 1746 FIELDING *True Patriot* No. 10 The cash, transfer books, &c. removed to the tower, from the Bank. 1834 [S. SMITH] *Lett. J. Downing* xxvi. (1835) 170 What the Treasury calls contingent drafts, and *transfer checks, and Treasury warrants. 1899 *Westm. Gaz.* 7 Sept. 7/1 It is nothing.. for a *transfer clerk to wait for forty-five minutes at the Associated office. 1909 ELIZ. L. BANKS *Myst. Fras. Farrington* 159 These trunks had been delivered by a responsible *Transfer Company's waggon. 1771 *App. Chron.* in *Ann. Reg.* 209/2 He recollected it was not *transfer-day. 1884 KNIGHT *Dict. Mech.* Suppl., **Transfer-elevator*, an elevator or crane for hoisting from one vessel into another. 1832 BABBAGE *Econ. Manuf.* xi. (ed. 3) 78 A single copy might be printed off with *transfer ink. 1827 FARADAY *Chem. Manip.* xv. (1842) 322 Capped or *transfer jars are such as, being open above, have a cap cemented upon them, the latter being surmounted by a stop-cock. *Ibid.* xxiv. 627 Fill a transfer jar..with water..over the trough. 1877 KNIGHT *Dict. Mech.*, **Transfer-lathe*, for..reducing large designs in relief to proportions suitable for coin. 1897 *Westm. Gaz.* 5 Apr. 7/3 To the average man the difference between 'lithography' and '*transfer-lithography' matters little. 1693 *Act 5 Will. & Mary* c. 7. § 54 The *Transfer Office above mentioned shall bee continued. 1858 SIMMONDS *Dict. Trade*, **Transfer-paper*, prepared paper used by lithographers; thin, unsized paper for taking copies of letters with a copying-press. 1878 ABNEY *Photogr.* (1881) 171 A piece of transfer paper (which is paper coated with gelatine subsequently rendered insoluble in water by alum or other such body) is placed in water of about 60° C., and softened. 1877 KNIGHT *Dict. Mech.*, **Transfer-press*. 1865 *Athenæum* 25 Nov. 733/1 *Transfer-printing in pottery. 1905 *Daily Chron.* 24 Aug. 3/2 The single invention in porcelain decoration at our credit in the eighteenth century was transfer-printing. 1877 KNIGHT *Dict. Mech.* 2368/2 Jacob Perkins, of Massachusetts, the inventor of the *transfer-process. 1861 *Massachusetts Stat.* 199 § 2 *Transfer ticket.

Transfer (trɑnsfɜ̄ˑı), *v.* Also 5–7 **-ferre,** 7 **-ferr.** Inflected **transfeˑrred,** etc. [a. F. *transférer* (3rd s. *transfère*) (14th c. in Littré), or its source, L. *transfer-re*, f. TRANS- + *ferre* to bear, carry, bring.]

1. *trans.* To convey or take from one place, person, etc. to another; to transmit, transport; to give or hand over from one to another.

1382 WYCLIF *Ezek.* xlviii. 14 Nether the first fruytis of the lond shuln be transferrid [*gloss* or born ouer, 1388 translatid], for thei ben halewid to the Lord. *c* 1425 *St. Christina* xxxvii. in *Anglia* VIII. 133/25 Þe biggynge of the abbeye was transferred to a better place. *c* 1430 *Art of Nombryng* 9 Put a cifre þer and transferre the article towarde the lift hande. 1516 in *Acts Parlt. Scott.* (1875) XII. 36/2 It is thocht..that þe said governoure..suld transfer himselff to uthir cuntreis. 1624 GODWIN *Moses & Aaron* (1641) 158 The moderne Jewes doe transferre the fault upon certaine proselyte Ægyptians who came forth with them. 1655 STANLEY *Hist. Philos.* II. (1701) 73/1 He first transferr'd Natural Philosophy out of Ionia to Athens. 1703 MOXON *Mech. Exerc.* 316 Divide one of these nine equal parts into two equal parts, and transfer that distance to the other eight equal parts. 1771 GOLDSM. *Hist. Eng.* II. 357 Campegio.. shortly after transferred the cause before the court of Rome. 1783 BURKE *Rep. Affairs Ind.* Wks. XI. 42 If the court of directors should disapprove of his being transferred to Bengal. 1809 R. LANGFORD *Introd. Trade* 86 For transferring £5690 Reduced Stock into the Four per Cents. 1818 in Willis & Clark *Cambridge* (1886) I. 573 Transferring three or four of the trees to another site. 1844 LD. BROUGHAM *Brit. Const.* vii. (1862) 94 The people's power being transferred to the representative body. 1860 TYNDALL *Glac.* I. xxii. 151, I transferred my scrip to his shoulders, and led the way.

b. *fig.* esp. in Sematology: see quots.

1586 A. DAY *Eng. Secretary* II. (1625) 77 *Metaphora*, which is, when a word from the proper or right signification is transferred to another neere vnto the meaning. 1883 MURRAY *Eng. Dict.* Gen. Explan. p. xxi, As the primitive sense [of words] has been..transferred boldly to figurative and analogical uses.

c. *intr.* for *refl.* or *pass.*

1646 G. DANIEL *Upon Virgil* 32 Wks. 1878 I. 22 But Wee.. averre Soules are not lost, or Dye, but doe transfer. 1901 *Daily Chron.* 24 Oct. 3/4 He transferred later to the 19th Hussars, in which regiment he served in the Soudan campaign. 1911 WEBSTER, *Transfer*, to change from one car, line, or the like, to another for continuing one's journey on a transfer.

2. *Law.* To convey or make over (title, right, or property) by deed or legal process.

1598 FLORIO, s.v. *Trascriuere*, To transfer or giue ouer his right to another. 1651 HOBBES *Leviath.* I. xiv. 67 My right is not transferred, but remaineth till I transferre it by some other Act. 1671 *Court Bks. Roy. African Co.* 19 Dec. (P.R.O.), I do transfer £500 of my subscription in the new joint stock of the Royal Company to the Rt. Hon. George Lord Berkeley. 1694 J. HOUGHTON *Collect. Improv. Husb. & Trade* V. No. 102 [*Form*] 'I A. B. do hereby sell, assign, and transferr unto C. D. Ten Shares in the Joynt-Stock.. with all the present and future Profits thereof'. 1771 *Junius Lett.* lxvii. (1797) II. 235 To this son-in-law..you meant to transfer the..property. 1818 CRUISE *Digest* (ed. 2) IV. 65 A grant only transfers what the grantor may lawfully give. 1878 JEVONS *Prim. Pol. Econ.* 14 Sometimes things can be literally handed over, like a watch or a book; sometimes they can be transferred by a written deed.

3. To convey (a drawing or design) from one surface to another, esp. (*a*) to a lithographic stone, to earthenware, glass, etc., by means of transfer-paper; (*b*) to a new back or ground, as an embroidered pattern, etc.

1839 URE *Dict. Arts* 1017 This [roll of flannel] is used as a burnisher, one end of it being rested against the shoulder, and the other end being rubbed upon the paper; by which means it transfers all the engraved traces to the biscuit. 1860 *Ibid.* (ed. 5) III. 501 There are two distinct methods of printing in use for china and earthenware; one is transferred on the bisque..and the other is transferred on the glaze. The first is called 'press printing', and the latter 'bat printing'. 1877 KNIGHT *Dict. Mech.* 2611/2 In engraving, a tracing may be made in pencil and transferred to the ground by running through the plate-press. An impression from a plate or stone may also be transferred to a stone.

Hence **Transferred** (-fɜ̄ˑıd) *ppl. a.*, conveyed from one person, place, sense, etc. to another.

1863 H. ALLON *Mem. J. Sherman* 279, 102 members were added in 1839 and 63 in 1840, including transferred members. 1883 MURRAY *Dict.* Gen. Explan. p. xxi, The word was first taken into English..in a figurative, transferred, or specialized use. 1886 J. EBSWORTH *Roxb. Ball.* VI. 165 As a transferred ballad, Dulcina was entered to John White and Thomas Langley, in the Registers of the Stationers' Company.

Transferable (trɑnsfɜ̄ˑrăb'l), *a.* [f. prec. + -ABLE: cf. *preferable, referable.* See also TRANSFERRABLE.] Capable of being transferred or legally made over to another; *spec.* of bills, drafts, cheques, etc.: assignable in the course of business from one person to another; negotiable.

Transferee.
Transferent.
Transference.
Transfer.
Transferor.
Transferrable.
Transferral.
Transferrer.
Transferring.
Transferography.

Transfiguration.
Transfigurable.
Transfigurate.
Transfiguratus.
Transfigurative.
Transfigure.
Transfigured.
Transfiguredly.

Transfix.
Transfixation.
Transfixed.
Transfixion.
Transfluent.
Transfluvial.
Transfluxion.

Transforate.
Transforation.
Transform.
Transformable.
Transformableness.
Transformant.
Transformate.
Transformation.

Transformational.
Transformationist.
Transformative.
Transformer.
Transformism.
Transformist.
Transformmingly.

Transfrete.
Transfretation.
Transfuge.
Transfund.
Transfunde.
Transfusable.
Transfuse.
Transfusible.
Transfusion.

Transfrontal.
Trans-frontier.
Transfusive.
Transfusive.

Transgredient.
Transgress.
Transgressible.
Transgression.

Supplement, p. 3873; Corrigenda, p. 4092; Spurious words, p. 4093; Books quoted, p. 4094

my charge. 1651 HOBBES *Leviath.* II. xxvi. 148 Punishments ordained beforehand for their transgression. 1722 DE FOE *Relig. Courtsh.* I. ii. (1840) 67 The children shall not be punished for the father's transgression. 1824 L. MURRAY *Eng. Gram.* I. 491 The transgression of this rule makes what are called harsh or forced metaphors.

b. The action of passing over or beyond. (Only as the etymological sense of the word.)

1623 COCKERAM, *Transgression*, a passing or going ouer. 1643 BURROUGHES *Exp. Hosea* (1652) 238 Sin is called by the name of Transgression..that is going beyond their bounds, going over the hedge. 1857 MAURICE *Ep. St. John* iii. 47, I call it transgression; that is, the passing over a boundary which was marked out for me. 1907 ILLINGWORTH *Doctr. Trinity* x. 190 Sin is always transgression, the overstepping of due bounds, the refusal to be limited.

2. *Geol.* The spread of the sea over the land along a subsiding shore-line, producing an overlap by deposition of new strata upon old.

1882 GEIKIE in *Nature* 13 July 242/2 In a section 'Upon Abrasion and Transgression', the author insists upon the paramount influence of the sea as an agent in planing down the surface of the land. 1903 CLAYPOLE in *Amer. Geol.* Aug. 91 The depression in southern Ohio, where the outcrop of the Corniferous limestone and the Corniferous-Hamilton is concealed by the transgression of the shale.

Hence **Transgre·ssional** *a.*, of or pertaining to transgression; of the nature of a transgression.

1690–1 LD. ROCHESTER *Let.* in Burnet *Own Times* (1823) VI. 284 Forgive this transgressional rapture, and receive my thanks..for your kind letter.

Transgressive (trɒnsgre·siv, -z-), *a.* [f. L. *transgress-*, ppl. stem (see TRANSGRESS) + -IVE. Cf. late L. *transgressivus*.]

1. Having the character or quality of transgressing. **a.** Involving transgression; sinful.

1646 SIR T. BROWNE *Pseud. Ep.* I. x. 37 Adam..from the transgressive infirmities of himselfe might have erred alone, as well as the Angels before him. 1797 *Hist.* in *Ann. Reg.* 57/1 The powers assumed..were explicitly termed unconstitutional, and transgressive of the authority lodged in them by the laws.

b. Passing beyond some limit.

1735 H. BROOKE *Univ. Beauty* III. 30 Where the Solar Heat, and searching Air Transgressive, pierce our actuated Sphere.

†**2.** *Music.* ? Not coming in regular sequence; or ? Overlapping (cf. CONJUNCT B. 6). *Obs.*

1760 STILES *Anc. Gk. Mus.* in *Phil. Trans.* LI. 704 Systems were there considered as differing in respect, first, to magnitude; secondly, to genus; thirdly, to the being consonant or dissonant; fourthly, to the being rational or irrational; fifthly, to the being sequent or transgressive.

3. *Geol.* Overlapping: cf. TRANSGRESSION 2. (So Fr. *transgressif* (Littré).)

1854 [implied in TRANSGRESSIVELY]. 1860 MAYNE *Expos. Lex.*, *Transgressivus*,..applied to a couch or bed that becomes deposited on others of different natures and different levels by rising over them, so that it is necessarily more or less inclined: transgressive.

Hence **Transgre·ssively** *adv.*, in a transgressive manner; *spec.* in *Geol.* † (*a*) unconformably; (*b*) so as to overlap the formation next below it.

1847 WEBSTER, *Transgressively*,. by transgressing. 1854 MURCHISON *Siluria* viii. 169 The Silurian series overlap transgressively or unconformably the edges of the subjacent sandstone. 1879 GEIKIE in *Encycl. Brit.* X. 371/2 Upraised Lower Silurian rocks, upon the upturned and denuded edges of which the Carboniferous Limestone lies transgressively.

Transgressor (trɒnsgre·sɒɹ, -z-). Also 4–7 -our, 6 -er. [a. AF. *transgressour* = F. *transgresseur* (14th c. in Hatz.-Darm.), a. late L. *transgressōr-em*, agent-n. from *transgredi* to TRANSGRESS.] One who transgresses; a law-breaker; a sinner.

1377 LANGL. *P. Pl.* B. I. 96 And taken *trangressores* [*v.r.* transgressouris] and tyen hem faste. 1432–50 tr. *Higden* (Rolls) III. 263 He..did chide the transgressores of the lawes. 1463–4 *Rolls of Parlt.* V. 502/2 To committe the transgressours..to the next Gaole. 1526 TINDALE *Jas.* ii. 9 Ye commit synne, and are rebuked off the lawe as transgressours. — 11 Thou arte a transgresser off the lawe. 1638 *Penit. Conf.* viii. (1657) 235 His Conscience arraigneth him. as a Transgressor. 1667 MILTON *P. L.* XI. 164 Such title should belonge To me transgressour, who for thee ordaind A help, became thy snare. 1875 JOWETT *Plato* (ed. 2) V. 100 Whoever shall transgress the strains by law established is a transgressor of the laws.

Transhape, variant of TRANS-SHAPE.

†**Transhaw**, *a.* or *adv. Obs. rare.* Meaning and origin uncertain: perh. 'exposed' to the blast, opposed to 'borrow' sheltered from the blast.

1665 D. DUDLEY *Metallum Martis* (1854) 31 How to mend their Natures, by finning or setting the finery, lesse transhaw more borrow, which are terms of art, and by altering and pitching the works. *Ibid.*, If the work be set transhaw and transiring from the blast, the Iron is more coldshare, lesse Fined.

Tranship (trɒn,ʃi·p), *less commonly* **transship** (trɒns,ʃi·p), *v.* [f. TRANS- + SHIP *v.*]

1. *trans.* To transfer from one ship to another; also *transf.*, from one railway train or other conveyance to another. Also *absol.*

1792 LD. MACARTNEY *Jrnl.* in Barrow *Life* (1807) II. 180 All the baggage and presents [were] put on board the large junks, to be transshipped into smaller ones. 1797 — *Emb. to China* II. i. 4 In order to tranship them. 1802 C. ROBINSON *Adm. Cas.* III. 247 He is not bound..either to tranship or to repair. 1813 WELLINGTON *Let.* 26 June in Gurw. *Desp.* (1839) X. 461, I am afraid it will be necessary to tranship the ordnance &c. into smaller vessels. 1846 ADDISON *On Contracts* II. ii. § 4 (1883) 494 If the vessel becomes disabled ..the master is bound to tranship and forward the cargo, if he has the means of transhipment at hand. 1876 CALLIS *Cutlery* 181 It was the practice of German manufacturers.. to..transship them without allowing them to land. 1900 *Blackw. Mag.* Oct. 559/1 He didn't give them time to tranship enough provisions.

2. *intr.* Of a passenger: To change from one ship or other conveyance to another.

1879 ATCHERLEY *Boërland* 264 At East London..we transhipped into the steamship *African*. 1892 E. REEVES *Homeward Bound* 87 After going a mile or two we stopped, got out, and transhipped into another train. 1892 *Daily News* 18 Oct. 5/6 Passengers going by her had not to tranship either at Hong Kong or Shanghai. 1895 RAMSAY *Paul the Trav.* 283 He [Paul] had to transship in Troas.

3. *Comb.* in which *tra·nship* is app. = *transhipment*: as **tranship-shed**, a shed at a railway joint station for the transference of goods from one railway to another; **tranship-train**, a train running in connexion with a steamer into which the passengers tranship; **tranship-van**: see quot.

1903 *Westm. Gaz.* 14 Jan. 5/1 We have 'tranship', or road-vans, specially appointed to work on branches and at stations where there is not the heavy traffic. These take goods from a certain starting-point to be delivered at a number of roadside stations. 1903 *Ibid.* 21 Feb. 7/1 Inviting seven English and Scotch companies to co-operate in the matter of a tranship shed at Carlisle. 1904 *Daily News* 22 Oct. 9 When near the new station at Talacre the engine of a heavy tranship train jumped an obstruction... The guard of the disabled tranship hurried Chesterwards.

Hence **Transhi·pping** *vbl. sb.* (also *attrib.*).

1801 SIR WM. SCOTT in C. Robinson *Adm. Cas.* III. 259 If he [the master] had not the means of transhipping. 1816 TUCKEY *Narr. Exped. R. Zaire* iii. (1818) 88 The transhipping the stores..being finished. 1840 *Evid. Hull Docks Comm.* 121 The transhipping of them, either by rafts or small vessels. 1892 *Nation* (N.Y.) 1 Sept. 155/1 A better transshipping point.

Transhi·pment, trans-shi·pment. [f. TRANS- + SHIPMENT, or f. prec. + -MENT.] The action or process of transhipping or changing from one ship or other conveyance to another.

1796 VAUGHAN *Examination* 13 Landing a ship's cargo.. with as few intermediate trans-shipments as possible. 1813 WELLINGTON in Gurw. *Desp.* (1839) XI. 218, I am obliged to go through the details of all the orders for the transhipment. 1846 WARBURTON *Hochelaga* I. 259 The frequent locks and trans-shipment of the cargo must ever be a great embarrassment. 1856 *Farmer's Mag.* Nov. 424 The inconvenience of two transshipments, one at each end of the Erie Canal. 1885 LD. BLACKBURN in *Law Rep.* 10 App. Cas. 419 The cost of transhipment or reshipment, as the case may be. 1899 *Statesman* (Calcutta) 27 Sept., There exists communication by train from Siliguri to Gyabari with one transhipment. *attrib.* 1892 *Pall Mall G.* 24 Nov. 2/1, I refer especially to the transhipment trade. 1899 *Westm. Gaz.* 20 Dec. 9/1 Heavy dock charges [etc.] have lost the port the bulk of the transhipment business.

Transhuman (trɒns,hiū·măn, -z-), *a. rare.* [f. TRANS- 4 + HUMAN; after It. *trasumanar* in Dante.] Beyond the human; superhuman. So **Transhu·manate** [It. Dante *trasumanar*, Florio *tra(n)shumanare*], **Transhu·manize** *vbs.*, *trans.* to make transhuman; **Transhumana·tion** [Florio *tra(n)s-(h)umanatione*], a making or becoming transhuman.

1812 CARY *Dante, Parad.* I. 68 Words may not tell of that transhuman change [*orig.* I. 70 trasumanar significar per verba Non si poria]. 1841 GALLENGA *Italy* I. (1848) I. 135 Dante's contact with God was trans-humanating. 1847 *Oxf. to Rome* (ed. 2) 215 A transhumanation takes place. 1872 LOWELL *Dante* Prose Wks. 1890 IV. 168 Souls..transhumanized to the divine abstraction of pure contemplation. 1885 A. J. BUTLER *Parad. of Dante* I. 70 To signify in words transhumanation were impossible. 1892 NORTON *Dante's Parad.* I. 4 Transhumanizing cannot be signified in words.

Transience (trɒ·nsiĕns, -z-; trɒ·nʃĕns, -ʒ-). [f. as TRANSIENT: see -ENCE.]

1. The action or fact of soon passing away; also, the condition or state of being transient, transiency.

1745 BROOKE *An Anthem* iv, Here, from time and transience won, Beauty has her charms resign'd. *a* 1822 SHELLEY *Ess. & Lett.* (1852) I. 184 A being..whose 'thoughts wander through eternity', disclaiming alliance with transience and decay. 1849 *Tait's Mag.* XVI. 8 Shadows..glide away, in transience fleet. 1875 JOWETT *Plato* (ed. 2) III. 126 Regarding the transience of pleasure as a proof of its unreality. 1905 *Westm. Gaz.* 22 Apr. 12/3 Any other explanation of the transience of French Protestantism.

2. The state or quality of being 'transient' in sense 2; = TRANSCENDENCE 1 b.

1882–3 *Schaff's Encycl. Relig. Knowl.* I. 370 [Calvinism] emphasizes at once the transience of God beyond, and the immanence of God within, the world.

Transiency (trɒ·nsiĕnsi, -z-; trɒ·nʃĕnsi, -ʒ-). [f. as prec.: see -ENCY.]

1. The quality or condition of being transient; brevity of existence; transitoriness.

1652 GAULE *Magastrom.* 96 How is it possible there should either be any..observation on the artists and art, in a transiency so imperceptible? 1805 W. TAYLOR in Robberds *Mem.* (1843) II. 98 A more eager popularity, like that of the 'Minstrel's Lay', would be symptomatic of transiency. 1812 COLERIDGE in *Lit. Rem.* (1836) I. 381 From their minuteness and transiency not calculated to stiffen or inflate the individual. 1831 *Blackw. Mag.* XXIX. 522 They try to perpetuate the transiency of emotions. 1905 F. YOUNG *Sands of Pleasure* I. v, Vaguely conscious of the transiency and instability of material life.

2. A transient thing or being. *rare.*

1866 CARLYLE *Edw. Irving* 318 Poor sickly transiencies that we are, coveting we know not what! 1881 PALGRAVE *Vis. Eng.* 200 On the trivialest transiencies fix'd, or plucking for fruit Dead-sea Apples and ashes of sin, more brute than the brute.

Transient (trɒ·nsiĕnt, -z-; trɒ·nʃĕnt, -ʒ-), *a.* (*sb.*) Also 7 *erron.* **transeant**, **-scient**; 7–9 (chiefly in sense 2) **transeunt**. [f. L. *transiens* (in oblique cases *transeunt-*, whence the form *transeunt*), pr. pple. of L. *transīre*, f. *trans* across + *īre* to go.]

1. Passing by or away with time; not durable or permanent; temporary, transitory; *esp.* passing away quickly or soon, brief, momentary, fleeting.

1607 *Schol. Disc. agst. Antichr.* I. i. 17 Whose parts are transeant and aereall, and presently vanishing. 1612 STURTEVANT *Metallica* v. 56 Instruments and means are said to be Transient, when in respect of their vse, they serue but once. 1659 PEARSON *Creed* (1839) 380 It containeth two distinct parts; one transient, the other permanent. 1662 J. DAVIES tr. *Mandelslo's Trav.* 261 They are transient showers soon over. 1713 BERKELEY *Guardian* No. 70 ¶ 8 The transient enjoyments of this life. 1813 SIR H. DAVY *Agric. Chem.* (1814) 282 This manure is transient in its effects, and does not last for more than a single crop. 1873 HAMERTON *Intell. Life* IV. v. (1875) 166 The few and transient hours that we can call our own.

2. Passing out or operating beyond itself; transitive; opposed to *immanent*. (Often spelt *transeunt* for distinction from sense 1.)

1613 PURCHAS *Pilgrimage* I. i. 4 The workes of God, which are either inward and immanent, or outward and transient. 1625 GILL *Sacr. Philos.* I. 98 You may observe a difference of actions, of which some are immanent, or indwelling in the doer..: some againe are transeunt, or passing from the doer upon that which is done. *a* 1677 HALE *Prim. Orig. Man.* 35 Those two great transeunt or emanant acts or works, the works of Creation and Providence. 1836–7 SIR W. HAMILTON *Metaph.* (1870) II. xxv. 118 An act of the mind going out of itself, in other words, a transeunt act. 1847 DE QUINCEY *Milton v. Southey & Landor* Wks. XII. 177 In metaphysical language, the moral of an epos or a drama should be immanent, not transient. 1890 *Athenæum* 8 Nov. 631/1 Volitionally reactive rediintegration with its two stages, immanent and transeunt action.

3. Passing or flowing through; passing from one thing or person to another. Now *rare.*

1619 DENISON *Heav. Banq.* 341 If the worship at our receiuing did determine in the Sacrament, or were transient by it to God. 1644 [H. PARKER] *Jus Pop.* 57 They lurke between scripture and reason, and remain in a kind of transcient posture. 1671 GREW *Anat. Plants* I. (1682) 7 A Filtre to the transient Sap. *a* 1703 BURKITT *On N. T.* 1 Thess. ii. (1818) 16 Hereditary, and..transient from one generation to another. 1847 TENNYSON *Princess* v. 37 Away we stole, and transient in a trice From what was left of faded woman-slough To sheathing splendours..issued in the sun.

4. Passing through a place without staying in it, or staying only for a short time; in quot. 1731 of birds, migratory; *spec.* (*U.S. colloq.*) applied to a guest at a hotel, etc. (often *ellipt.* as *sb.*: see B. 2).

1685 BAXTER *Paraphr. N. T.*, *Mark* (1701) Introd., Whether this Mark was Bishop of Alexandria, or only a transient Evangelist there a while, is an Historical Controversie. 1713 SWIFT *Cadenus & Vanessa* 768 Love, hitherto a transient guest, Ne'er held possession of his breast. 1731 SIR J. CLERK in *Mem. W. Stukeley* (Surtees) I. 247 There are many transient fowls that come into Britain at certain seasons. 1740 W. DOUGLASS *Disc. Curr. Brit. Plant. Amer.* 3 The Author is not a transient Person, who from Humour or Caprice..may expose the Province. 1788 *Massachusetts Spy* 11 Dec. 3/2 A transient jockey came to the house of Mr. Jonathan Hubbey, and agreed to purchase a horse of him. 1822 MONTGOMERY *Hymn, 'This stone to Thee in faith we lay'* v, But will, indeed, Jehovah deign Here to abide, no transient guest?

5. *Mus.* Introduced in passing, as a note, chord, etc. not belonging to the harmony, or to the key, of the passage; passing.

1801 in BUSBY *Dict. Mus.* 1838 G. F. GRAHAM *Mus. Comp.* 29/2 Passing notes, changing notes, transient notes, etc. 1878 F. TAYLOR in Grove *Dict. Mus.* I. 75/1 A so-called 'auxiliary note' (sometimes 'transient' or 'changing' note).

B. *sb.*

1. A transient thing or being; something passing or transitory, not permanent.

1652 SPARKE *Prim. Devot.* (1663) 279 If we (meanwhile) but rise from graves of sin And transients (which the most are buried in). 1661 GLANVILL *Van. Dogm.* 81 A kind of stop or arrest, by the benefit of which the Soul might have a glance of the fugitive Transient. *a* 1674 TRAHERNE *Poet. Wks.* (1903) 18. 1860 BOYD *Recr. Country Parson* ii. 27 These gray transients have changed to shivering skeletons.

2. *U.S. colloq.* A person who passes through a place, or stays in it only for a short time; *spec.* a 'transient guest' at a hotel or boarding-house.

1880 MRS. ROLLINS *New Eng. Bygones* (1883) 84 My grandmother held these transients in low esteem. 1893 KATE SANBORN *S. California* 20 On an open, sunny site, and ..frequented by 'transients' and business men of moderate means. 1894 *Outing* (U.S.) XXIV. 260/1 Summer residents, transients, and all, had turned out early.

Tra·nsiently (see prec.), *adv.* [f. prec. + -LY [2].] In a transient manner; in passing through; briefly, momentarily; hastily.

1641 R. YOUNGE *Counterpoyson* 398, I have transiently found (in making up the Index) some literall mistakes, points misplaced, &c. 1649 J. H. *Motion to Parl. Adv. Learn.* 25 Some ends which I have transiently..glanced at. 1684 BAXTER *Parish Congreg.* 20 They might occasionally Communicate in our Parishes transiently. 1748 RICHARDSON *Clarissa* VI. xlvi. 69, I thought, transiently thought, that the tea..had an odd taste. 1806 SCOTT *Woodst.* iii. A smile passed transiently over his clouded brow. 1900 *Speaker* 29 Dec. 336/2 Not only transiently, but permanently declining.

Tra·nsientness. [f. as prec. + -NESS.] The quality or state of being transient; transience.

1667 *Decay Chr. Piety* x. ¶ 1 As they resemble the wind in fury.., so they might do also in transientness. 1698 NORRIS *Pract. Disc.* IV. 368 The Pleasure of this Life is..in regard of its Transientness, like the Pleasure of a Dream. 1907 *Edin. Rev.* July 177 Suzanne..could not believe in the transientness of [Gibbon's affections].

Transierd: see TRANSIRE *v. Obs.*

Trans,i·liac, *a. Anat.* [f. TRANS- 5 + L. *ilium*: cf. ILIAC.] Lying across the ilium; extending transversely from one iliac bone to the other.

1891 in *Cent. Dict.*

Transilience (trɒnsi·liĕns). *rare.* [f. as next: see -ENCE.] A leaping from one thing to another, an abrupt transition: *spec.* in *Min.* abrupt transition of one mineral or rock into another.

1657 REEVE *God's Plea* 204 Man may haue..his diffluences, redundances,..and transiliences of speech. 1811 PINKERTON *Petralogy* II. 169 Rocks of black trap, surmounted by porphyry of the same base, the transilience being clear and palpable. 1830 HERSCHEL *Stud. Nat. Phil.* 330 Transferred by contact, or by sudden and violent transilience of the interval of separation..under the form of sparks and flashes.

So † **Transi·liency** [see -ENCY], the quality of being transilient; less correctly = prec. *Obs. rare*[−1].

1661 GLANVILL *Van. Dogm.* xii. 114 By an unadvised transiliency leaping from the effect to its remotest cause.

Transilient (trɒnsi·liĕnt), *a.* [ad. L. *tran(s)silient-em*, pr. pple. of *tran(s)silīre* to leap across, skip over, omit, f. *trans* across + *salīre* to leap.] Leaping or passing from one thing or condition to another; in *Min.* said of one rock substance passing abruptly into another.

Transilient fibres, nerve-fibres passing from one convolution of the brain to another not immediately adjacent (*Syd. Soc. Lex.* 1899).

1811 PINKERTON *Petralogy* I. p. v, The Transilient Rocks, an interesting series, in which one substance..passes into another, as granite into porphyry, trap into wacken. *Ibid.* 550 British rocks are often anomalous, or transilient, and can scarcely be reduced to precise denominations.

†**Transili·tion.** *Obs. rare*[−1]. [ad. late L. *transilītiōn-em* (Augustine), n. of action f. *transilīre*: see prec.] The action of leaping over or 'skipping'; omission of intermediate numbers.

1582 T. WATSON *Centurie of Loue* lxxx, Founded by transilition or ouer skipping of number by rule and order, as from 1 to 3, 5, 7, and 9. *Ibid.* [see TRANSPOSITION 2].

Transilluminate (trɒns,ilʹū·mineɪt), *v.* [f. TRANS- + ILLUMINATE *v.*] *trans.* To cause light to pass through; *spec.* in *Med.* to throw a strong light through (an organ or part) to discover the presence or cause of disease. So **Transillumina·tion**, the action or process of transilluminating.

1890 *Lancet* 1 Mar. 480/2 It [a tooth] was translucent by electric transillumination, showing that the pulp was living. 1900 *Ibid.* 25 Aug. 617/1 If in a darkened room the electric lamp used for transilluminating the frontal sinus was placed against the thyroid cartilage. 1901 *Ibid.* 11 May 1328/2 Transillumination is often used to find out if the antrum is diseased. 1912 KEITH *Human Body* i. 20 It may have occurred, however, to the onlooker that, since we can trans-illuminate the human body [*i.e.* with Röntgen-rays], it is no longer necessary to dissect it.

Trans-impre·ssion. *rare*[−1]. [TRANS- 1.] An impression transferred or taken over (*from* something).

1812–29 COLERIDGE in *Lit. Rem.* (1838) III. 152 The very words, 'conception', 'comprehension', and all in all languages that answer to them, suppose this trans-impression from the mind.

Trans,incorpora·tion. [TRANS- 1.] Passage from one body to another; transmigration of the soul.

1810 W. TAYLOR in *Monthly Mag.* XXX. 47 The doctrine of the trans-incorporation of souls, or of their migration through successive human bodies, was taught..by a Jewish rabbi. 1843 ROBBERDS *Mem. W. Taylor* II. iv. 305 Its contents are full of curious information, more particularly those on the transincorporation of souls.

Trans,i·nsular, *a.* [f. TRANS- 3 + L. *insula* island: cf. *insular.*]

1. Crossing or going across an, or the, island.

1895 *Buffalo Current Hist.* (N.Y.) V. 404 When the colony [Newfoundland] would have to work its transinsular railway system. 1900 *Engineering Mag.* XIX. 684 Any trans-insular railroad project is chimerical.

2. *Anat.* Applied to a fissure of the brain that crosses the insula or island of Reil, and divides it into a cephalic and a caudal region.

1889 *Buck's Handbk. Med. Sc.* VIII. 160/1 Normal, human subfissures are..the transinsular and others crossing the surface of the insula.

‖ **Transire** (trɒns,əi·rɪ), *sb. Law.* [L. *transīre* to go across, pass over, f. *trans* across + *īre* to go.] A warrant issued by the custom-house, permitting the passage of merchandise.

1599 NASHE *Lenten Stuffe* (1871) 70 They would grant him his coquet, or *Transire*. 1656 in *Misc. Sc. Burgh Rec. Soc.* 30 Receiving moneys for writeing bills, cocquetts, and transires. 1662 *Order Ho. Com. as to Customs* (1663) 9 A Transire or Let-passe from Port to Port in England. 1750 *Act* 23 *Geo. II*, c 29 § 2 No officer of his Majesty's customs shall sign or grant any cocquet, sufferance, transire, let-pass, warrant, or certificate..for exporting..such bar iron. 1888 *Act* 51 & 52 *Vict.* c. 24 § 5 (*a*) Any port..at which her transire is to be obtained.

† **Transire** (trɒns,əi·ɹ), *v. Obs. rare.* Also 6 **transier.** [irreg. f. L. *transīre* (see prec.), the inf. form being taken instead of the ppl. stem *transit-* (TRANSIT *v.*).] *intr.* To go or pass across; in quot. 1665, ? to lie transversely.

1592 WYRLEY *Armorie* 121 Pretended iorney if they onward hould, Transierd they were, as it was to me tould. 1665 D. DUDLEY *Mettallum Martis* (1854) 31 If the werk be set transhaw and transiring from the blast.

Trans,i·schiac (-i·skiæk), *a. Anat.* [f. TRANS- 5 + L. *ischiac-us*, f. *ischi-um*: see ISCHIUM, and -AC.] Extending transversely from one ischial bone to the other.

1891 in *Cent. Dict.* 1899 in *Syd. Soc. Lex.*

Trans-i·sthmian, *a.* [f. TRANS- 3 + ISTHMUS: cf. *isthmian.*] Crossing or extending across an isthmus, esp. the Isthmus of Panama.

1885 GROVER CLEVELAND *Ann. Message to Congress U. S. A.* Dec., Our interests in any transisthmian route which may be opened. 1908 *Q. Rev.* Oct. 674 The Key to any possible trans-isthmian canal.

Transit (trɒ·nsit, -z-), *sb.* Also 5 **trancyte**, 5–7 **transite.** [ad. L. *transit-us* (-ū stem), verbal sb. from *transīre* to cross, f. *trans* across + *īre* to go. So It. *transito*, whence Fr. *transit* (17th c.).]

1. The action or fact of passing across or through; passage or journey from one place or point to another. Often in phrase *in transit*, L. *in transitu*.

c 1440 *Gesta Rom.* ii. 12 (Add. MS.) Above oure hede there is a transite of men [*Harl.* passage and goyng of peple]. 1716 M. DAVIES *Athen. Brit.* II. 171 Henry..of Huntington.., who writ ten Books *Historiæ Anglorum*, from the Transit and Introit of the Saxons hither, to the Year 1153. 1766 W. DIGBY in Jesse *Selwyn & Contemp.* (1843) II. 12, I lay at Gloucester in my transit. 1833 RITCHIE *Wand. Loire* 27 Sometimes..the transit from Nantes to Orleans takes two months! 1841 CATLIN *N. Amer. Ind.* xlvi. II. 87, I..made a transit across the prairies. 1853 KANE *Grinnell Exp.* vii. (1856) 50 Of the voyages to Lancaster Sound..the transit of the middle ice is the essential feature. 1877 BLACK *Green Past.* xxxii, In our rapid transit from place to place.

† **b.** *concr.* A way for passing, a passage.

c 1440 *Promp. Parv.* 499/2 Trancyte, where menn walke, *transitus*.

c. The passage or carriage of persons or goods from one place to another.

1800 COLQUHOUN *Comm. Thames* viii. 259 Property.. stationary on the Quays or in transit on the River. 1855 MACAULAY *Hist. Eng.* xiii. III. 254 While he governed, no prohibition..impeded the transit of commodities from any part of the island to any other. 1866 ROGERS *Agric. & Prices* I. xx. 504 The cost of carriage. Occasionally..this is charged in the value given, the transit being..undertaken frequently by common carriers. 1870 YEATS *Nat. Hist. Comm.* 62 The means of transit are so bad, that much good corn is left to rot upon the ground.

d. *transf.* A place at which a river may be crossed; a crossing. *rare.*

1852 GROTE *Greece* II. lxix. IX. 39 A..flourishing town, a centre of commerce enriched by the important ford or transit of the river Euphrates close to it.

2. *fig.* (in various senses.) A passing across; a transition or change; *esp.* the passage from this life to the next by death.

1657 W. MORICE *Coena quasi Κοινὴ*, Diat. v. 237 There can be no such transite from one kinde of action to another. 1765 H. WALPOLE *Otranto* iii. (1798) 50 To pray for her happy transit to a better life. 1810 KNOX & JEBB *Corr.* II. 19 The transit from autumn to winter. 1823 SCOTT *Quentin D.* vi, Speak a word of comfort to him ere he make his transit, Trois-Eschelles. 1859 HOLLAND *Gold F.* xv. 182 Old men..whose work of life is..done, and who may in peace.. sit down and wait their mysterious transit. 1871 EARLE *Philol. Eng. Tongue* § 270 This verb made an early transit to the weak form.

3. *Astrol.* The passage of a planet across some special point or region of the zodiac.

[1621 BURTON *Anat. Mel.* I. ii. I. iv, If ♄, by his revolution, or *transitus*, shall offend any of those radicall promissors in his geniture.] 1671 SALMON *Syn. Med.* I. xxix. 61 In Directions and Transits three things are to be considered; first the Significator, secondly the Promissor; thirdly the sign and house in which they happen. 1819 J. WILSON *Dict. Astrol.* s.v., The transits of the ☽ are said to cause all the daily passing events of a man's life, as she transits the △, ✱, □, ☍, or ☌, of any particular house.

4. *Astron.* **a.** The passage of an inferior planet (Mercury or Venus) across the sun's disk, or of a satellite or its shadow across the disk of a planet; formerly also applied to an occultation of a star or planet by the moon, or of a star by a planet.

1669 FLAMSTEAD in *Phil. Trans.* IV. 1110 Let me desire those, who have fit..Instruments, to observe this Transit. 1704 J. HARRIS *Lex. Techn.* I, *Transit*, in *Astronomy*, signifies the passing of any Planet just by or under any Fixt Star; or of the Moon in particular, covering or moving close by any other Planet. 1769 M. CUTLER in *Life*, etc. (1888) I. 20 The 3d of this month happened the Transit of Venus over the sun's disk. 1769 COOK *Voy. r. World* I. xiii. (1773) 137 On Thursday the 1st of June, the Saturday following being the day of the Transit, I dispatched Mr. Gore in the long-boat to Imao. 1829 *Chapters Phys. Sc.* 398 The transits of Mercury and Venus are really eclipses of the sun. 1868 LOCKYER *Guillemin's Heavens* III. II. i. (ed. 3) 478 The value of the Sun's distance at present received has been deduced from the transits of Venus in 1761 and 1769. 1910 *Whitaker's Almanack* 88 Only Satellite IV [of Jupiter] will be visible at 2.30 a.m. February 24—Satellite II. being in transit, Satellite III. occulted, and Satellite I. eclipsed.

transf. 1859 in *Merc. Marine Mag.* (1860) VII. 65 The Shoal first seen was in transit with Embleton Island, bearing N.E. ¾ E.

b. The passage of a star or other celestial body across the meridian at its culmination.

1812 WOODHOUSE *Astron.* viii. 48 Two successive transits of a star over the meridian. 1834 MRS. SOMERVILLE *Connex. Phys. Sc.* vii. 61 While observing transits of the fixed stars across the meridian at Cayenne.

c. Short for *transit-circle*, *-compass*, *-instrument*, or *-theodolite*: see 5. *colloq.*

1843 *Penny Cycl.* XXV. 122/1 Transit, or Transit Instrument. *Ibid.* 122/2 Such an account of the transit as will enable any one to use it with tolerable success. 1879 NEWCOMB & HOLDEN *Astron.* 74 The meridian transit instrument, or briefly the 'transit'. 1897 *Edin. Rev.* July 66 The institution, furnished only with a transit when he took it in charge.

5. *attrib.* and *Comb.*, usually in relation to the conveyance of goods and passengers, as *transit-company*, *-depot*, *-road*, *-room*, *-time*, *-traffic*, *-way*; also **transit-circle**, an astronomical instrument consisting of a telescope carrying a large graduated circle, by which the right ascension and declination of a star may be determined by observation of it in transit (sense 4 b); a meridian-circle; **transit-clock**, a clock used in conjunction with a transit-instrument; **transit-compass**, an instrument, resembling a theodolite, used in surveying for the measurement of horizontal angles; **transit-duty**, a duty paid on goods passing through a country; **transit-instrument**, an astronomical telescope mounted on a fixed east-and-west axis, by which the time of the passage of a celestial body across the meridian may be determined; usually applied to one without a circle (cf. *transit-circle*); **transit-pass**, a warrant to pass through a country without payment of duty; **transit-theodolite** = *transit-compass*; **transit-trade**, trade arising out of the passage of foreign goods through a country.

1843 *Penny Cycl.* XXV. 133/1 A *transit circle may be made to answer both purposes. 1897 *Edin. Rev.* July 68 In 1851 a new transit circle, of great optical power and enormous mechanical stability, superseded Troughton's masterpiece of 1812. 1843 *Penny Cycl.* XXV. 130/1 To have a second clock called a journeyman, which strikes loudly and speaks as it were for the *transit clock. 1845 R. BROWN in *Mem.* ii. (1866) 28 We got into one of the *Transit Company's vans. 1887 MOLONEY *Forestry W. Afr.* 248 The Public Works Department of each Colony offers a ready *transit-depot for such contributions. 1776 ADAM SMITH *W. N.* v. ii. II. 515 In some small states duties..are imposed upon goods carried across the territory..from one foreign country to another. These are in some countries called *transit-duties. 1809 *State Papers* in *Ann. Reg.* 697/1 The transit duties on the goods thus imported or exported. 1812 WOODHOUSE *Astron.* vi. 32 It may be used as a *transit instrument: that is, the presence of a star on the meridian may be ascertained by it. 1889 *Pall Mall Gaz.* 2 Sept. 7/3 Less..than it cost foreigners to bring it to Pakhio under *transit-pass. 1861 J. NICHOL in *Mem.* (1896) 37 As regular as the *transit-room clock. 1862 *Catal. Internat. Exhib.* II. XIII. 3 A first-rate 6-inch *transit theodolite,..with vertical and horizontal circles. 1803 *Edin. Rev.* III. 243 Those..nations whose wealth has been promoted by the *transit trade. 1852 CONYBEARE & H. *St. Paul* (1862) II. xxiii. 329 The Valley of the Nile was the channel of an active transit trade in spices, dyes, jewels, and perfumes. 1903 *Expositor* May 335 Jerusalem had no natural command of the *transit-traffic. 1904 *Q. Rev.* Oct. 341 The trade-winds..contribute greatly to the salubrity and comfort of this *transit-way.

Transit (trɒ·nsit, -z-), *v.* [f. L. *transit-*, ppl. stem of *transīre*: see prec. Cf. L. *transitāre*, freq. of *transīre* (instanced in pr. pple. *transitāns* Cic.). In earlier use stressed *transi·te*.]

1. *intr.* To pass through or over; to pass away.

c 1440 *Gesta Rom.* xc. 415 The porter is the worlde; and right as by the porter so by the worlde we may transite. 1595 CHAPMAN *Ovid's Banq. Sence* (1639) 11 As Intellects themselves transite to each intelligible qualitie. 1775 'JOEL COLLIER' (Alex. Bicknell) *Mus. Trav.* (ed. 2) 68, I then transited to the gentleman himself. 1797–1803 FOSTER in *Life & Corr.* (1846) I. 173 The comets of the mind; they transit off. 1803 *Ibid.* 196, I have transited into another person. 1852 N. L. WALKER *Life in Spirit* xiii. (1853) 212 One or two transit off from our Divinity Halls annually.

2. *trans.* To pass across or through (something); to traverse, cross. Also *fig.*

1674 JEAKE *Arith.* (1696) 249, I have..transited Decimals and Astronomicals, and shall now apply myself to overlook Logarithmes. 1890 *Pall Mall Gaz.* 10 Mar. 3/1 Another line which would transit Germany, Russia,..Afghanistan, and India.

3. *Astrol.* To pass across (a sign, 'house', or special point, of the zodiac). Also *absol.* or *intr.*

1647 LILLY *Chr. Astrol.* lxvii. 409 When the unfortunate Anareta transits the degree ascending. 1686 GOAD *Celest. Bodies* III. ii. 403 Feavers..do annoy us, when the Heavenly Bodies Transit, or take up Station in such Parts of the Zodiack. 1819 J. WILSON *Dict. Astrol.* s.v. *Transits*, If the lord of the 8th..transit the cusp of the horoscope, it threatens death.

4. *Astron.* To pass across (the disk of a celestial body, the meridian of a place, or the field of view of a telescope). Also *absol.* or *intr.*

In quot. 1686 of the moon, to occult (a star or planet).

1686 GOAD *Celest. Bodies* I. xii. 49 The ☽ transiting ♀ that Night raised the Tides. 1755 B. MARTIN *Mag. Arts & Sc.* I. 45 In the Years 1753, 1786, 1799, in the Month of April, he [Mercury] will transit the Sun's Disk. 1833 HERSCHEL *Astron.* viii. 256 Rendering the planet invisible, unless..where it transits the sun's disc and appears on it as a black spot. 1870 PROCTOR *Other Worlds* viii. (ed. 2) 184 The markings seen on the third satellite, when transiting Jupiter's disc. 1878 LOCKYER *Stargazing* 354 The value of the divisions of the micrometer screw having been previously determined by allowing an equatorial star to transit.

Transitable (trɒ·nsităb'l), *a. rare.* [f. as prec. + -ABLE.] Capable of being passed across or over; affording means of transit.

1843 *Blackw. Mag.* LIV. 660 The river Chagre..is the nearest transitable point to Panama. 1866 RUSKIN in Spielmann *Life* (1900) 50 If you think it at all curable or transit-able, I'll advance her 20 pounds without interest. 1897 *Jrnl. R. Geog. Soc.* July 63 The efforts..made to open a transitable road to [the valley of the Rio Grande de Terraba] from the north..have proven futile.

‖ **Transita·rium.** *Obs. rare.* [mod.L., f. TRANSIT *sb.* 4 a; cf. *planetarium.*] An apparatus for illustrating the transit of a planet.

1761 *Brit. Mag.* II. 668 Earl Ferrers..presented to the [Royal] Society..a transitarium invented by his lordship for giving an ocular demonstration of the principles relating to the theory of that planet [Venus].

† **Transita·tion.** *Obs. rare.* [n. of action f. L. *transitāre*: see TRANSIT *v.* and -ATION.] The action of passing; passage. (In quots. *humorous.*)

1600–9 ROWLANDS *Knave of Clubs* 37 As on the way I Itinerated, A Rurall person I Obuiated, Interogating times Transitation. 1605 VERSTEGAN *Dec. Intell.* vii. 205.

Tra·nsiter. *rare.* [f. TRANSIT *sb.* or *v.* + -ER [1].] Name for a form of the apparatus usually called a 'recording micrometer', and attached to the eye-end of a transit telescope.

1902 *Science* (U.S.) 2 May 693/2 The actual arrangement in use at the Philadelphia Observatory, called for brevity a 'transiter'...The transiter seemed to furnish all the necessary facilities of motion and of recording, and..permitted elimination of all errors excepting that of bisection.

Transition (trɒnsi·ʒən, -si·ʃən, -zi·ʃən). [ad. L. *transitiōn-em*, n. of action f. *transīre*, *transit-* (see TRANSIT *v.*). Cf. F. *transition* (13–14th c. in Hatz.-Darm.).

(The first and prevailing pronunciation, contrary to the general analogy of words in *-tion*, is app. due (as suggested by Walker) to a desire to avoid the collocation of the two similar (voiceless) sibilants *s* and *ʃ*.)]

1. A passing or passage from one condition, action, or (rarely) place, to another; change.

1551 GARDINER *Explication, Of Transubstantiation* 123 In the mysterie of Christes person, there is no transition of the deitie into the humanite, or humanite into the deitie. 1621 G. SANDYS *Ovid's Met.* VI. (1626) 109 The vast sky painted with a mightie Bowe: Where, though a thousand seuerall colours shine, No eye their close transition can define. 1751 JOHNSON *Rambler* No. 172 ¶ 7 A quick transition from poverty to abundance can seldom be made with safety. 1851 HAWTHORNE *Ho. Sev. Gables* xvii, Transition being so facile, what can be any man's inducement to tarry in one spot? 1862 SIR H. HOLLAND *Ess.* I. 1 We are living in an age of transition. 1899 STALKER *Christology of Jesus* v. 186 Death was..only a stage of transition to a higher form of life.

2. Passage in thought, speech, or writing from one subject to another.

1592 tr. *Junius on Rev.* vii. 1 This first verse is a transition. 1674 MILTON *P. L.* (ed. 2) XII. 5 Heer the Archangel paus'd..Then with transition sweet new Speech resumes. 1724 WATTS *Logic* IV. ii. vii. § 3 Acquaint yourself with all the proper..forms of transition from one part of a discourse to another. 1798 EDGEWORTH *Pract. Educ.* (1811) I. 115 The transition of attention from one subject to another. 1875 JOWETT *Plato* (ed. 2) V. 15 The Timaeus..one of his [Plato's] most finished works, is full of abrupt transitions.

3. *Mus.* † **a.** The passing from one note to another by means of a passing-note (*obs.*). **b.** The passing from one key to another, modulation; *spec.* a passing or brief modulation; also, modulation into a remote key.

1667 C. SIMPSON *Compend. Mus.* 88 A Note is somtimes broken to make a Transition by degrees to some other Concord. These Transitions or Breakings are commonly express'd in Quavers or Crochets. 1877 STAINER *Harmony* xii. § 150 A transition is the rapid passing through any key, without remaining sufficiently long in it to establish a modulation. 1889 PROUT *Harmony* x. (ed. 3) 101 Some writers use the term 'Transition', when the modulation is to a remote or unrelated key.

4. The passage from an earlier to a later stage of development or formation. **a.** *Geol.* Formerly *spec.* applied *attrib.* to certain early stratified rocks believed to contain the oldest remains of living organisms; now classified as Silurian: see quot. 1813.

1813 BAKEWELL *Introd. Geol.* (1815) 9 The lowest of the secondary rocks have..been called by the German geologists transition rocks, from the supposition that they were formed when the world was passing from an uninhabitable to a habitable state. 1815 W. PHILLIPS *Outl. Min. & Geol.* (1818) 116 To primitive rocks succeeds another class, which Werner denominates *Transition* rocks. 1823 BUCKLAND *Reliq. Diluv.* 117 It lies in a bed of transition limestone. 1834–5 J. PHILLIPS *Geol.* in *Encycl. Metrop.* VI. 593/2 On the East side of the transition ranges of the Wrekin and Wenlock Edge lies the coalfield of Coalbrook Dale. 1839 MURCHISON *Silur. Syst.* I. xxxiv. 452 It also presents certain beds of transition between the limestone and the Old Red Sandstone. 1855 J. PHILLIPS *Man. Geol.* 104 The two parts connected by a transition band (upper caradoc). 1885 GEIKIE *Text-bk. Geol.* VI. II. ii. § 1. 658 Murchison was the first to discover that the so-called 'Transition Rocks' or 'Grauwacke' of early geological literature were capable of subdivision into distinct formations..he gave them the name of Silurian.

b. *Arch.* Change from an earlier style to a later; a style of intermediate or mixed character.

1835 R. WILLIS *Archit. Mid. Ages* i. 9 These may be called Imitation Specimens, to distinguish them from regular Transitions. 1842–76 GWILT *Archit.* Gloss., *Transition*, a term used to denote the passing from one period of a style to another, exhibiting features peculiar to both, some of which have not quite been given up, and some of which were beginning to be introduced. 1874 PARKER *Goth. Archit.* I. iii. 39 The remainder of the eleventh century may be considered as a period of transition.

c. *Philol.* The historical passage of language from one well-defined stage to another; e.g. from Old English or Anglo-Saxon to Middle English; or from Middle English to Modern English; hence applied to the interval occupied by this, and to the intermediate or transitional stage or form of the language during this interval.

1873–4 SWEET *Hist. Eng. Sounds* 160 We have..two periods of transition, one in which *nama* and *name* exist side by side, and another in which final *e* is beginning to drop...The former, commonly called Semi-Saxon.., is characterized by many far-reaching changes. I propose..to call the first the *Transition* period *par excellence*, distinguishing the two, when necessary, as first and second *Transition*, the more important one being generally called simply *Transition* or *Transition-English*. *Ibid.* 38 In the Transition period.. we are confronted by [a] curious and apparently inexplicable phenomenon. 1878 MURRAY *Eng. Lang.* in *Encycl. Brit.* VIII. 391/2 Transition Old English, or 'Semi-Saxon' 1120 to 1200..Transition Middle English 1400 to 1485...Many writers carry the Transition Old English down to 1250. *Ibid.* 397/2 The change of the language during the second period of Transition. *Ibid.* 402 Chronological Chart [has] Old English Transition 1123–1200. Middle English Transition, 1400–1485.

5. *attrib.*, as *transition form*, *species*, *stage*, *state*, etc.: see also 4 a and c. Often equivalent to TRANSITIONAL.

1805–17 R. JAMESON *Char. Min.* (ed. 3) 126 All the crystals that lie between two principal crystals, and form the transition of one into the other, constitute what is called a transition-suite. 1826 KIRBY & SP. *Entomol.* (1828) III. xxix. 161 Groups..connected by certain transition species. 1843 R. J. GRAVES *Syst. Clin. Med.* xxvii. 343 The most obstinate form [of the disease] generally selects such transition spots or intermediate tissues. 1853 J. SMITH *Treat. Mus.* 33 Transition or passing notes. 1856 FROUDE *Hist. Eng.* I. ii. 86 Wolsey..holding a middle place between an English statesman and a catholic of the old order, was essentially a transition minister. 1865 TYLOR *Early Hist. Man.* vii. 188 A very good example of this interesting transition work. 1884 J. TAIT *Mind in Matter* (1892) 50 The transition-stages set forth by revolutionists.

Transitional (trɒnsi·ʒənăl, -si·ʃ-, -zi·ʃ-), *a.* (*sb.*) [f. prec. + -AL.] Of or pertaining to transition; characterized by or involving transition; intermediate.

c 1810 COLERIDGE in *Lit. Rem.* (1838) III. 262 The Jewish Rabbis..represented the Millennium as the preparative and transitional state to perfect spiritualization. 1859 DARWIN *Orig. Spec.* vi. (1860) 172 By this theory innumerable transitional forms must have existed. 1867 A. J. ELLIS *E. E. Pronunc.* I. i. 30 Shakspere and Milton are transitional between Spenser and Dryden. 1867 FREEMAN *Norm. Conq.* I. i. 3 At a transitional period in the world's development. 1874 PARKER *Goth. Archit.* I. iii. 58 The arches are transitional, two being round and two pointed.

b. *Transitional case* in grammar, a case in some languages expressing motion toward.

1890 A. S. GATSCHET *Gram. Klamath Lang.* 484 Transitional case in -na...This locative case-suffix..corresponds to our *to*, *toward*, *into*, *in*.

B. *ellipt.* as *sb.* (in quot. for *transitional cell*: cf. quot. 1904 s.v. MONONUCLEAR).

1904 *Brit. Med. Jrnl.* 10 Sept. 583 They [mononuclear white blood cells] become transformed in the blood (according to Ehrlich) into the transitionals.

Hence **Transi·tionally** *adv.*, **Transi·tionalness.**

1874 RUSKIN *Fors Clav.* xliv. 164 This plate of mine, melted down, after being transitionally serviceable to the burglar, will enter again into the same functions among the silver of the world. 1896 *Scot. Leader* 1 Jan. 7 A deep sense of the transitionalness of conclusions which were once thought to be for all time.

Transitionary (trɒnsi·ʒənări, -si·ʃ-, -zi·ʃ-), *a.* [f. as prec. + -ARY [1].] = TRANSITIONAL.

1685 H. MORE *Paralip. Prophet.* xxi. 181 This third Introductory Vision is a kind of Transitionary Introduction to the Opened Book-Prophecy. 1827 *Examiner* 630/2 The rapid, elastic, transitionary style of this actor. 1858 BUCKLE *Civiliz.* (1864) I. viii. 472 The transitionary state which France began to enter. 1900 *Literature* 14 July 28/1 The Induction..is essentially of a transitionary character.

Transi·tionist. *rare*[−1]. [f. as prec. + -IST.] One who supports transition; in quot. *attrib.*

1856 E. G. K. BROWNE *Tractarian Movem.* (1861) 438 The advanced guard of the Transitionist party.

† **Transi·tious,** *a. Obs. rare*[−0]. [f. TRANSITION + -OUS.] Transitional. Hence † **Transi·tiously** *adv.* (*obs. rare*[−1]), transitionally, by transitions.

1652 URQUHART *Jewel* Wks. (1834) 292 Speeches extending a matter..auxetically, digressively, transitiously.

Transitival (trɒnsitəi·văl, -z-), *a. Gram. rare.* [f. TRANSITIVE + -AL: cf. *adjectival*, *genitival*, etc.] = TRANSITIVE 2.

1871 EARLE *Philol. Eng. T.* § 270 This was a new and quite different verb, and should have had the transitival use.

Transitive (trɒ·nsitiv, -z-), *a.* (*sb.*) [ad. late L. *transitīvus* (Priscian), f. *transit-* (see TRANSIT) + *-īvus*, -IVE; in F. *transitif* (16th c.). With sense 1 cf. OF. *transitif* transient (13th c. in Godef.).]

† **1.** Passing or liable to pass into another condition, changeable, changeful; passing away, transient, transitory. *Obs. rare.*

1560 ROLLAND *Crt. Venus* I. 67 Thair waillit weid..Sa gay it was,..Sa wariant to sicht and transitiue. 1625 BRATHWAIT *Five Senses* 296 What availes it thee now to enjoy the transitive honours of this life? 1845 [implied in TRANSITIVENESS].

2. *Gram.* Of verbs and their construction: Expressing an action which passes over to an object; taking a direct object to complete the sense.

1571 [implied in TRANSITIVELY a]. 1590 STOCKWOOD *Rules Constr.* 64 A verbe transitiue..is such..as passeth ouer his signification into some other thing, as when I say, 'I loue God'. 1673 O. WALKER *Educ.* 153 Others are transient, when the Agent and Patient are divers, and are expressed by Verbs transitives, as striking, heating [etc.]. 1845 STODDART *Gram.* in *Encycl. Metrop.* (1847) I. 48/1 Verbs transitive and intransitive are, in other words, active and neuter; for the verb active is considered as passing over from the agent to the object, whilst the neuter is considered as not passing over.

b. as *sb.* A transitive verb.

1612 BRINSLEY *Lud. Lit.* 129 That other rule for the Acusatiue after the Verbe, is of Transitiues, whose action passeth into another thing.

3. *Philos.* Passing out of itself; passing over to or affecting something else; operating beyond itself; = TRANSIENT 2. (Opposed to *immanent.*)

1613 PURCHAS *Pilgrimage* I. i. 5 For all the proprieties of God are infinite, as they are immanent in himselfe, yet in their transitiue and forren effectes are stinted and limited to the modell and state of the creature. 1626 BACON *Sylva* § 70 Cold is Active and Transitive into Bodies Adjacent, as well as Heat. 1785 REID *Intell. Powers* II. xiv. (1803) I. 306 Logicians distinguish two kinds of operations of the mind; the first kind produces no effect without the mind, the last does. The first they call immanent acts; the second transitive. 1893 FAIRBAIRN *Christ in Mod. Theol.* II. II. iii. 441 It is of the essence of both to be transitive. Love regards an object whose good it desires; righteousness is the conduct which fulfils the desire of love.

4. Characterized by or involving transition, in various senses: that has something passing through it (*obs.*); that itself passes through stages; that forms a transition (real, or in thought) between two stages, positions, or conditions; that is in an intermediate stage or position; transitional; intermediate; transformational. Now *rare* or *Obs.*

1660 JER. TAYLOR *Duct. Dubit.* II. ii. rule vi. § 7 An image that is understood to be an image can never be made an idol; or if it can it must be by having the worship of God pass'd thorough it to God;..by being the analogical, the improper, the transitive, the relative (or what shall I call it) object of Divine worship. 1811 PINKERTON *Petralogy* I. 73 This transitive grunstein occurs in the Hartz. 1836 I. TAYLOR *Phys. Thr. Another Life* xii. (1847) 166 The preparations that are made by any of the transitive species of animals..for their approaching metamorphosis. 1854 F. BAKEWELL *Geol.* 5 The lower portion, resting on the crystalline rocks, being called the transitive series. 1860 MAYNE *Expos. Lex.*, *Transitivus*, applied by Werner to rocks or soils that present..the vestiges of organised bodies;..as forming the transition of soils from the first class to those of the third, with which they are nearly related: transitive. 1865 GROTE *Plato* I. xvii. 494 The transitive process, above described, represents the successive stages by which every adult mind has been gradually built up from infancy.

5. Of the application of words: Transferred. *rare.* ? *Obs.*

1810 D. STEWART *Philos. Ess.* II. i. 226 The greater part of the transitive or derivative applications of words depend on casual and unaccountable caprices of the feelings or of the fancy.

6. *Math.* In the theory of groups: see quots.

1890 *Cent. Dict.* s.v. *Group*, A group is called doubly, triply, or n times transitive if any set of 2, 3, n elements can be brought to any places. 1902 *Encycl. Brit.* XXIX. 121/1 If it is possible to find an operation S of the group such that O.S is any assigned one of the set of objects, the group is called *transitive* in respect of this set of objects. When this is not possible, the group is called *intransitive* in respect of the set.

Transitively (trɒ·nsitivli, -z-), *adv.* [f. prec. + -LY [2].] In a transitive manner; in the way of transition. **a.** *Gram.* In a transitive sense or construction; with a direct object.

1571 GOLDING *Calvin on Ps.* vii. 7. 20 The woord might also be taken transityvely for too settle or stablish David in his ryght. *a* 1638 MEDE *Wks.* (1672) 676 To construe the words transitively. 1737 WATERLAND *Doctr. Eucharist* v. 115 Εὐλογεῖν is taken transitively in this very Case by the Apostle. *Mod.* Many verbs in English can be used both transitively and intransitively.

b. (See senses 3 and 4 of TRANSITIVE.)

1656 JEANES *Fulness Christ* 32 The divine properties are communicated to the humanity, not transitively, but intransitively. 1660 JER. TAYLOR *Duct. Dubit.* II. ii. rule vi. § 4 Vasquez..thinks it lawful to give Divine worship relatively or transitively to a man. 1822 T. TAYLOR *Apuleius* 310 It will always perceive intellectually, without transition, or transitively. 1855 PUSEY *Doctr. Real Presence* Note Q. 257 The bread still remains in its own substance; yet so that the whole proposition should be understood, not as actually, but transitively. 'This is my Body', i.e. passes into the body, or from this becomes the body.

Tra·nsitiveness. [f. as prec. + -NESS.] The quality or state of being transitive; in quot., transitoriness.

1845 J. H. NEWMAN *Ess. Developm.* 71 A belief in the transitiveness of worldly goods.

Transiti·vity. [f. late L. *transitīv-us* TRANSITIVE + -ITY.] = prec.: see TRANSITIVE 6.

1891 *Cent. Dict.*, *Transitivity*, the character of being transitive, as a group.

Transitorily (trɒ·nsitərili, -z-), *adv.* [f. TRANSITORY + -LY [2].] In a transitory manner; in passing through; temporarily, briefly, transiently.

1611 COTGR., *Casuellement*,..vncertainly, transitorily. 1612 DONNE *Lett.* (1651) 92, I make account to be in London, transitorily, about the end of August. 1762 KAMES *Elem. Crit.* III. xix. 24 The mind is transitorily amused with the new object. 1847 *Illustr. Lond. News* 10 July 29/1 A flash of lightning now and then illuminated the entire panorama, but too transitorily to catch any of its features. 1899 CAGNEY tr. *Jaksch's Clin. Diagn.* vii. (ed. 4) 394 In acute lead-poisoning..large quantities of albumen are often transitorily present in the urine.

Tra·nsitoriness. [f. as prec. + -NESS.] The quality or condition of being transitory.

1590 NASHE *Pasquil's Apol.* I. D ij, In respect of the transitorinesse of worldly kingdoms. 1670 CLARENDON *Contempl. Ps.* Tracts (1727) 685 The vanity of this world, of the unsteadiness and transitoriness of all things in it. 1756 JOHNSON *Let.* 15 Apr. in Boswell, The uncertainty of fortune,.. the transitoriness of beauty. 1852 LEWIS *Observ. & Reason. in Pol.* I. 221 Written memorials are distinguished by permanence and solidity, as contrasted with the fugacity and transitoriness of oral tradition. 1899 INGE *Chr. Mysticism* i. 23 We may regard the spiritual world as endless duration opposed to transitoriness.

† **Transito·rious,** *a. Obs.* [f. late L. *transitōri-us* (see next) + -OUS.] = TRANSITORY.

1492 RYMAN *Poems* lxxxv. 1 in *Archiv Stud. neu. Spr.* LXXXIX. 255 This worlde is mutabilite That transitorious is. 1502 ATKYNSON tr. *De Imitatione* I. i. 154 Coruptible ryches, transetorious honours. 1550 BALE *Image Both Ch.* D vj b, Departynge from thys transitoryous lyfe. *a* 1598 ROLLOCK *Wks.* (Wodrow Soc.) II. 4 The creatures of God in themselves are but transitorious shadows.

Transitory (trɒ·nsitəri, -z-), *a.* (*sb.*) Also 4–5 **transitore**, 4–7 **-itorie**, 5 **-etorie**, **-itoire**, (**trancitorie**), 5–6 **transetory**, **-ytory(e**, **-itorye**, 6 *Sc.* **-itoir.** [ad. F. *transitoire* (12th c. in Godef. *Compl.*), ad. post-Aug.L. *transitōrius* having or allowing a passage through, in Chr.L. transient, passing, f. *transit-*: see TRANSIT *v.* and -ORY [2].]

1. Having the quality of passing away; not lasting; fleeting, momentary, brief; transient.

c 1374 CHAUCER *Troylus* III. 778 (827) Now yf he wot þat Ioye is transitorie [*v.r.* trancitorie]. *c* 1375 *Sc. Leg. Saints* ii. (*Paulus*) 219 Þat eftire þis lyfe transitore Euire-lestand lyfe is me before. 1481 CAXTON *Myrr.* I. iv. 13 This world is not but a vayn thinge and transitoire. 1543–4 *Act* 35 *Hen. VIII*, c. 1 § 6 This Realme, after the Kinges transitorie lief,..shoulde be destitute of a laufull governour. *a* 1633 AUSTIN *Medit.* (1635) 279 So they are as transitorie as a Shepheards Tent. *Ibid.* 280 Like Things of that transitory nature, they begin to weare away. 1654 H. L'ESTRANGE *Chas. I* (1655) 3 That adventure..gave him also a transitory view of that excellent Lady. 1712 SWIFT *Wonderful Prophecy* (*heading*), This vain and transitory world will shortly be brought to its final dissolution. 1859 KINGSLEY *Misc.* (1860) II. 75 All the Continental Nations look upon our present peace as but transitory, momentary.

† **2.** Having a passage-way, allowing passage through. *Obs. rare.*

1613 GODWIN *Rom. Antiq.* (1625) 9 It had the name of *Forum Transitorium*, the transitorie Forum, because there was *Transitus*, *id est*, a way or passage through it into three seuerall market places.

b. Of the nature of a passage or transition; transitional. *rare.*

1592 tr. *Junius on Rev.* xix. 1 This chapter hath..two parts, one transitory or of passage unto the things that follow. 1906 *Rep. Vice-reg. Comm. Poor Law Ref. Ireland* I. 31 The transitory period between the old and new systems.

3. *Law. Transitory action*, an action in which the venue might be laid in any county.

1665 EVER *Tryals per Pais* x. 133 The Jurors of one County may finde any transitory thing done in another County. 1708 *Termes de la Ley* 419 An Action of Trespass for Battery, is transitory and not local. 1768 BLACKSTONE *Comm.* III. xxiii. 384 Actions transitory follow the person of the defendant, territorial suits must be discussed in the territorial tribunal. 1848 WHARTON *Law Lex.* 390/1 Personal actions are for the most part transitory, i.e., their cause of action may be supposed to take place anywhere.

† **4.** (app.) Trifling, of little moment. *Obs.*

1672 DRYDEN *Assignation* II. ii, You may scape with the loss of a Leg, or an Arm, or some such transitory Limb. 1673 — *Amboyna* II. i, Remember, no transitory sum, three hundred quadruples in your own country gold.

B. *sb.* † **1.** A transitory or fleeting thing. (Chiefly in *pl.*) *Obs.*

1649 ROBERTS *Clavis Bibl.* 367 A comfortable transitory enjoyment of transitories. 1654 WHITLOCK *Zootomia* 15 He that too closely imbraceth Transitories, is much the worse for them. 1665 GLANVILL *Scepsis Sci.* 50 This fleeting Transitory our Life.

† **2. a.** The transverse limb of the cross-staff (CROSS-STAFF 2). **b.** A transit-instrument. *Obs.*

(In sense a, Bourne has also *transvastory* and *transversary*.)

1574 BOURNE *Regiment for Sea* vi. (1577) 26 To take the heigth of the Sunne, to knowe the Altitude of the Pole aboue the Horizon, doo this...Put the Transitorie [ed. 1580, lf. 29 Transuastorie; ed. 1631, lf. 29 Transuersary] vpon the long staffe, then sette the end of the long staffe close at the corner of your eye [etc.]. [1578 — *Treas. Trav.* I. ix. 17 Concernyng the making of a Crosse staffe..you shal make an other short staff, called a Transuastorie, of two foote long, and in the very myddle of it you shall make a square hole.] *Ibid.* x. 18 b, If that the distaunce be further then the Transitorie wyl take, and the wal too shorte: then remoue the Plattes or wynges of the Transitorie to the markes, sixe ynches from both the endes of the Transitorie. 1751 *Phil. Trans.* XLVII. xxii. 159, I had several times seen Venus on the meridian with a three-foot transitory.

‖ **Transitu** (trɒ·nsitiū), in L. phr. *in transitu*: see ‖ IN 19; also as adj. in *transitu business*, etc.

1858 HOMANS *Cycl. Comm.* 452/1 The large increase of *transitu* business between the principal southern ports and the markets of Europe. *Ibid.* 453/1 Parties who operate in *transitu* cotton.

† **Tra·nsiture.** *Obs. rare.* [f. L. type *transitūra: see TRANSIT and -URE.] Passing; passage.

1578 BANISTER *Hist. Man* I. 17 It yeeldeth ample scope.. to the transiture of meate and drinke. *Ibid.* 20 Two Processes..with larger holes for the transiture [*printed* -turie] of the Veyne, and Arterie vnto the Scull.

† **Tra·nsive,** *a. Obs. rare.* [f. *transe*, TRANCE *sb.*[1] + -IVE.] Of the nature of a trance; of or pertaining to a trance.

1609 ARMIN *Maids of More-Cl.* (1880) 103 My mother's fast asleepe, and I awake, am in a transiue maze. 1609 — *Ital. Taylor* (1880) 149 These transiue apparitions dealt, As madmen in their fits.

† **Transje·ction.** *Obs. rare*[−0]. [n. of action f. L. *transjicĕre*, the uncontracted form of *trāicĕre*: see TRAJECT.] = TRAJECTION.

1656 BLOUNT *Glossogr.*, *Transjection*, a casting over, or thorow, an overthrowing.

Transkei (trɒns,kəi·), *sb.* (*a.*) [f. TRANS- 7 + *Kei*, a river of S. Africa.] A territory situated across the river Kei, which falls into the Indian Ocean, *c* 28° 20′ E., and was from 1847 to 1877 the boundary between Kafirland or Caffraria and Cape Colony, of which the Transkei territory now forms a part. Also *attrib.* or as *adj.* Hence **Trans,kei·an** *a.*

1879 *Whitaker's Almanack* 257/1 The area [of Cape Colony], including Basutoland and Transkei, 222,308 square miles. *Ibid.* 259/2 The Transkeian territories stretch from the Kei to Natal. 1898 *Ibid.* 515 (Cape Colony) The Transkei territories. *Ibid.*, (Principal events) Incorporation of all the Transkeian territories, except part of Pondoland, with the Colony, completed 1885; annexation of Pondoland 1894. 1899 *Daily News* 20 Oct. 7/1 The Pondos and the other Transkei tribes are not absolutely to be relied on. 1911 J. LENNOX *Missions S. Afr.* 81 A question of a much more difficult nature has exercised the Kafrarian and Transkeian Churches.

Trans,la·de, *v.* [TRANS- 2.] *trans.* To transfer the lading of one ship or carriage to another. Hence **Transla·ding** *vbl. sb.*

1881 *Daily News* 17 Mar. 5/3 A question of transit and the terminal charges for lading, unlading, and translading.

Translatable (trɒns,lēi·tăb'l), *a.* [f. TRANSLATE *v.* + -ABLE.] Capable of being translated.

1745 H. WALPOLE *Corr.* (1846) II. 15, I..without having recourse to the Countess's translatable periods, am pleased with his company. 1830 MACKINTOSH *Eth. Philos.* Wks. 1846 I. 88 Modes of expression scarcely translatable into the only technical language in which that mind is wont to think. 1870 EMERSON *Soc. & Solit.* viii. 164 What is really best in any book is translatable.

Hence **Translatabi·lity, Transla·tableness.**

1867 LUDLOW *Fleeing to Tarshish* 115 To carry on his cogitations for him, with their accustomed wondrous translatability by the imagination. 1882 *Athenæum* 4 Mar. 278/1 We own to a certain scepticism as to La Fontaine's translatableness. 1911 MUNRO *Fundamentals* 31 The Translatability of Scripture.

† **Trans,la·te,** *a.* and *sb. Obs.* Also 7 -at. [ad. L. *translāt-us*, *-a*, *-um*, pa. pple.: see next.]

A. *adj.* Translated (see next); in quot. 1589, transferred in meaning, metaphorical.

1589 RIDER *Bibl. Schol.* Direct. for Rdr., First I place the proper Latine word vnder the figure of 1: then the figuratiue or translate vnder the figure of 2.

B. *sb.* Something translated; a translation. [Cf. L. *translātum* sb., OF. *translat* 13th c.]

1585–6 EARL LEYCESTER *Corr.* (Camden) 467, I sent to the register of the states for the act.., the translate whereof I send your honour hearein. 1619 CARLETON in *Eng. & Germ.* (Camden) 85 Divers lettres..I have made transcripts of some, and translats of others. 1655 *Chym. Med. & Chyrurg. Addr.*, *Table*, A Translate of the Eleventh Chapter. 1668 *Lond. Gaz.* No. 254/4 The prohibitions made against the vending or reading any of the late Translates of the New Testament into French. 1803 COLLINS in Gurwood *Wellington's Desp.* (1837) III. 133 *note*, I..enclose a copy and translate of a note I..received from the Berai Rajah.

Translate (trɒns,lēi·t), *v.* Also 4 (*Sc.*), 6 **translat**, 5–6 **traunslate**, 6 *Sc.* **translait.** Pa. t. and pple. **translated**; also 4–6 **translate**, (*pa. pple.*) **translat.** [Prob. first used in *translat(e* pa. pple., ad. L. *translāt-us*, pa. pple. of *transferre* to TRANSFER. The pa. pple. soon became *translat-ed*, and *translate* the verb stem (see -ATE suffix 3). But the verb may also immediately repr. F. *translater* (12th c. in Godef.). Cf. also med.L. *translātāre* (11th c. in Du Cange).]

I. 1. *trans.* To bear, convey, or remove from one person, place or condition to another; to transfer, transport; *spec.* to remove a bishop from one see to another, or a bishop's seat from one place to another, and, in Scotland, a minister from one pastoral charge to another; also, to remove the dead body or remains of a saint, or, by extension, a hero or great man, from one place to another.

a 1300 *Cursor M.* 9162 (Cott.) Helias was in þat square, Translated in a golden chiare. *Ibid.* 9220 Þe Iues now er put o state And þair kingrik translate. *c* 1330 R. BRUNNE *Chron.* (1810) 203 Þis is þe same Hubert, þat we saw of nam, Þat translate S. Gilbert in þe hous of Sempyngham. *c* 1380 WYCLIF *Sel. Wks.* II. 318 We witen þat we ben translatid fro deþ to lyf. 1433 LYDG. *St. Fremund* 819 The Bysshop.. Translatyd hym to Dunstaple. 1432–50 tr. *Higden* (Rolls) II. 77 The seete of the metropolitan of alle Wales, whiche was translate afterwarde to Meneuia. 1517 TORKINGTON *Pilgr.* (1884) 49 Hys body was translat to Rome. 1529 S. FISH *Supplic. Beggars* (Arb.) 13 Then shall not youre.. power, crowne, dignitie..be translated from you. 1579 LYLY *Euphues* (Arb.) 41 Plante and translate the crabbe tree, where..it please you, and it wyll neuer beare sweete Apple. 1613 PURCHAS *Pilgrimage* (1614) 106 Hee translated the highest seat both of spirituall and Temporall Regiment to Jerusalem. 1625 in Willis & Clark *Cambridge* (1886) II. 445 He translated yᵉ Vestrie. 1651 N. BACON *Disc. Govt. Eng.* II. xxviii. (1739) 131 This Headship was translated to the King. 1663 WOOD *Life* (O. H. S.) I. 472 After he had taken in another class of six there, he translated himself to the house of Arthur Tylliard an apothecary. *c* 1683 BURNET *Orig. Mem.* in *Own Time* (1902) I. Suppl. 67 Morley, made at first bishop of Worcester, and soon after..translated to Winchester. 1794 J. HUTTON *Philos. Light*, etc. 47 Heat is translated among bodies in a certain manner, and electricity in another. 1865 *Pall Mall G.* 11 Apr. 4 A discussion has arisen on the question whether the Charterhouse School ought or ought not to be translated into the country. 1869 FREEMAN *Norm. Conq.* III. xv. § 5. 518 The body of Harold, first buried under the cairn by Hastings, was afterwards translated to his own minster at Waltham. 1904 R. SMALL *Hist. U. P. Congregat.* I. 503 In 1829..the Synod at his own request, and without a vote, refused to translate.

b. To carry or convey to heaven without death; also, in later use, said of the death of the righteous.

1382 WYCLIF *Heb.* xi. 5 Bi feith Enok is translatid, that he schulde not se deeth; and he was not founden, for the Lord translatide him. 1387 TREVISA *Higden* (Rolls) II. 213 And so schulde þe body..be translated and chaunged in þe blisse of heuene wiþ oute deienge and deeþ. 1535 COVERDALE *Wisd.* iv. 10 He pleased God,..so that where as he lyued amonge synners, he translated him. 1708 *Lond. Gaz.* No. 3809/1 That after a long and happy Enjoyment of this your Earthly Crown, you may be translated to one Immortal. 1798 COLERIDGE *Fears in Solitude* 121 As if the wretch, Who fell in battle..Passed off to Heaven, translated and not killed. 1848 MRS. JAMESON *Sacr. & Leg. Art* (1850) 331 She was ninety years of age when the Lord translated her. 1904 JEBB in *Proc. Brit. Acad.* 3 Here, and here alone, the Hyperborean land is an Elysium to which mortals are translated without dying.

c. *Med.* To remove the seat of (a disease) from one person, or part of the body, to another. Now *rare* or *Obs.*

1732 ARBUTHNOT *Aliments* etc. 366 To translate the Morbifick Matter upon the Extremities of the Body. 1754 J. BARTLET *Farriery* (ed. 2) 105 The humours frequently settle, or are translated to the lungs, and other bowels. 1769 E. BANCROFT *Guiana* 394 The patient is either relieved, or the disease translated on the extremities. 1826 SOUTHEY in *Q. Rev.* XXXIV. 330 He could..cure a carbuncle..by making upon it the sign of a cross, and translate swellings from his pupil's arm to his own.

d. *Physics.* To move (a body) from one point or place to another without rotation: cf. TRANSLATION 1 f.

II. 2. To turn from one language into another; 'to change into another language retaining the sense' (J.); to render; also, to express in other words, to paraphrase. (The chief current sense.)

a 1300 *Cursor M.* 232 Þis ilk bok it es translate In to Inglis tong to rede. *c* 1350 *Will. Palerne* 167 For he of frensche þis fayre tale ferst dede translate. *c* 1385 CHAUCER *L. G. W.* 329 (*Balade*) Thow hast translatid the romauns of the rose. 1477 EARL RIVERS (Caxton) *Dictes* 2 It was translated out of latyn in to frenshe. 1589 PUTTENHAM *Eng. Poesie* I. xxxi. (Arb.) 75 Doctour Phaer one that.. excellently well translated into English verse Heroicall certaine bookes of Virgils Æneidos. 1689–90 TEMPLE *Ess. Poetry* Wks. 1731 I. 241 The first Change of Poetry was made by translating it into Prose. 1693 DRYDEN *Disc. Orig. & Progr. Satire* Ess. (ed. Ker) II. 92 'Tis only for a poet to translate a poem. 1776 JOHNSON 11 Apr., in *Boswell*, Poetry..cannot be translated; and, therefore, it is the poets that preserve languages. 1850 WHIPPLE *Ess. & Rev.* (ed. 3) I. 300 If the phrase, realizing the ideal, were translated into the phrase, actualizing the real, much ambiguity might be avoided. 1874 GREEN *Short Hist.* vii. § 1. 342 Retiring to Hamburg Tyndale translated the Gospels and Epistles.

b. *absol.* To practise translation; to make a version from one language or form of words into another; also *intr.* for *pass.*, of a language, speech, or writing: To bear or admit of translation.

c 1440 *Pallad. on Husb.* I. 735 Yet as myn auctor spak so wold I speke Sith I translate, and looth am from hym breke. 1576 FLEMING *Panopl. Epist.* 253 If you translate out of the Latine speach, into the Greeke. 1690 LOCKE *Hum. Und.* III. iv. § 9 This is to translate, and not to define, when we change two words of the same signification one for another. 1731 FIELDING *Author's Farce* II. v, The rogue had a trick of translating out of the shops as well as the languages. 1812 SOUTHEY *Omniana* II. 30 Claudian throughout would translate better than any of the ancients. 1827 — *Lett.* (1856) IV. 64 The Welsh, I suspect, is not a language which translates well. 1831 MACAULAY *Ess.*, *Johnson* (1887) 194 Sometimes Johnson translated aloud.

† **c.** To use in a metaphorical or transferred sense: see *translated*, quot. 1553, and cf. TRANSLATE *a.*, TRANSLATION 4. *Obs.*

3. *fig.* To interpret, explain: to expound the significance of (conduct, gestures, etc.); also, to express (one thing in terms of another).

Translating (trɑːnsleɪtɪŋ), vbl. sb. [f. TRANSLATE v. + -ING[1].] The action of the vb. TRANSLATE; translation, in various senses.

Translation (trɑːnsleɪʃən), sb. [a. OF. translation (11th c. in Godef. Compl.), or ad. L. translatiōn-em a transporting, translation, n. of action f. transla-t-, ppl. stem of transferre to TRANSFER.] The action of translating (or its result).

I. 1. Transference; removal or conveyance from one person, place, or condition to another.

Iliad stood very high in his estimation.

III. 4. To change in form, appearance, or substance; to transmute; to transform, alter; spec. in industrial use: of a tailor, to renovate, turn out down (a garment); of a cobbler, to make new boots from the remains of (old ones).

Translative (trɑːnsleɪtɪv), a. [ad. L. translātīv-us.] 1. pertaining to transfer or translation (see TRANSLATE and -IVE); cf. F. translatif (14th c.) in legal use.] Involving or of the nature of translation (in various senses).

To replace (letters or characters of one language) by those of another used to represent the same sounds; to write (a word, etc.) in the characters of another alphabet. Hence **Translit'erated** ppl. a.

Translit'eration (trɑːnslɪtəreɪʃən). [f. as prec. + -ATION.] The action or process of transliterating; the rendering of the letters or characters of one alphabet in those of another.

Transliterator (trɑːnslɪtəreɪtər). [f. as TRANSLITERATE + -OR.] One who transliterates.

Translatory (trɑːnslətəri, trɑːnsleɪtəri), a. [f. prec.: see -ORY[2].]

Translatress (trɑːnsleɪtrɛs). [f. TRANSLATOR + -ESS.] A female translator.

Translatrix (trɑːnsleɪtrɪks). [fem., in L. form, of TRANSLATOR: see -TRIX.]

Translation (trɑːnsleɪʃən), sb.

Translatitious (trɑːnslətɪʃəs), a. Obs. [f. L. translātītius, -tīus transferred, carried from one person or place to another, metaphorical, f. translāt-: see TRANSLATE v. and -ITIOUS.]

Translucent (trɑːnsluːsənt), a.

Translucency (trɑːnsluːsənsi). [f. TRANSLUCENT: see -ENCY.]

Translucid (trɑːnsluːsɪd), a.

Translucidity (trɑːnslusɪdɪti). [ad. F. translucidité.]

Translunary (trɑːnslunəri), a.

Transmarine (trɑːnsməriːn), a.

Transmedian (trɑːnsmiːdiən), a. Anat. and Zool.

Transmental (trɑːnsmɛntəl), a.

Transmental'ity (trɑːnsmɛntælɪti).

Transmigrate (trɑːnsmaɪgreɪt), v.

Transmigration (trɑːnsmaɪgreɪʃən).

Transmigrant (trɑːnsmaɪgrənt), a. and sb.

Transmigratory (trɑːnsmaɪgrətəri), a.

Transmigrative (trɑːnsmaɪgreɪtɪv), a.

Transmissibility (trɑːnsmɪsɪbɪlɪti).

Transmissible (trɑːnsmɪsɪbəl), a.

Transmission (trɑːnsmɪʃən).

Transmissive (trɑːnsmɪsɪv), a.

| TRANSMISSIVELY. | 270 | TRANSMOVE. | TRANSMUE. | 271 | TRANSMUTED. |

| TRANSMUTER. | 272 | TRANSOM. | TRANSOMED. | 273 | TRANSPARENTLY. |

Transposable (trᴀnspōuˈzăbˈl), a. [f. Transpose v. + -able.] Capable of being transposed; interchangeable. Hence **Transposabiˈlity**.

Transpose (trᴀnspōuˈz), v. [a. F. transposer (14th c. in Hatz.-Darm.), f. Trans- + poser to place : see Pose, Compose.]

1. trans. To change (one thing) to or into another; to transmute, transmute, convert. Obs.

2. To change (a writing or book) into another language, style of composition, or mode of expression; to translate; to transfer; to adapt. Obs.

3. To change the purport, application, or use of; to apply or use otherwise; to give a different direction to; in bad sense, to corrupt, pervert; to misapply, abuse. Obs.

4. To remove from one place or time to another; to transfer, shift (lit. and fig.: now rare exc. as in 5); † to transplant (obs.).

5. To alter the order (of a set or series of things), or the position (of a thing) in a series; to put each (of two or more things) in the place of the other or others, to interchange; spec. to alter the order of letters in a word or of words in a sentence. (Now the ordinary sense.)

Transposer (trᴀnspōuˈzᴀɹ). [f. prec. + -er¹.] One who transposes: esp. in sense 7.

Transpositive (trᴀnspɒˈzĭtiv), a. [f. Transpose v., after positive, etc. Cf. L. transpositīvē (18th c.), and rare L. transpositīva (Quintil.).]

Transpositor, rare⁻¹. [agent-n. in L. form from transpos'd (see Transpose) : cf. F. transpositeur (1835 Dict. Acad.) and Positor.] One who transposes; a transposer.

Transpository (a. rare⁻¹) = Transpositive.

Transpour, v. Obs. rare. [Trans- 2.] trans. To pour from one to another; transfuse.

Transprint, v. [f. Trans- 2 + Print.] trans. To reprint from another book, etc. Hence **Transpriˈnting** vbl. sb.

Transproˈcess. Anat. [Trans- 6.] A transverse process of a vertebra; a diapophysis.

Transprose, v. Orig. a nonce-word, to match Transverse v.², q.v. trans. To turn into prose : to translate or render in prose. (Chiefly humorous.)

Transpulmonary, a. [f. Trans- 5 + L. pulmo, pulmōn-em lung.] Acting or operated through the lungs : said of the respiration in birds, in which the lungs are connected with large air-sacs, into and out of which the air passes through the lungs.

Transquantity, v. [f. Trans- 4 + Quantity.] trans. To change from one quantity to another.

Transrational, a. [Trans- 4.] Going beyond or surpassing what is rational.

Transreal, a. [Trans- 4.] Beyond the real; outside the world of reality.

Transregionate, ppl. a. [ad. L. transregiōnāt-us, f. trans- + regiōn-em region + -ate².] Transferred to or inhabiting another region.

Transrhenane (trᴀnsrēˈnēn), a. [ad. L. transrhēnānus adj. and sb., f. trans- across + Rhēnus the Rhine. Cf. F. transrhénan, ane (in Littré).] That is across or beyond the Rhine; hence, German as opposed to Roman or to French.

Transubstantiate (trᴀnsʊbstæˈnʃieit), v. Also trans-. [f. ppl. stem of med.L. transubstantiāre (Du Cange), f. trans- + substantia substance. Cf. F. transsubstantier (14th c. in Godef. Compl.).]

Transubstantial, a. [f. Trans- 4 + Substance + -ing-, repr. med.L. transubstantiālis.]

Transubstantiation (trᴀnsʊbstæˌnʃieiˈʃən), sb. Also trans-. [ad. med.L. transubstantiātiōn-em (Du Cange), f. transubstantiāt-, ppl. stem of transubstantiāre : see next.]

Transubstantiationalist. 280 **Transumption.** **Transumptive.** 281 **Transverse.**

Transubstantiator (trᴀnsʊbstæˈnʃieitᴀɹ). [agent-n. in L. form, from med.L. transubstantiāre : see Transubstantiate v.]

Translade, v. Obs. rare⁻¹. [ad. med.L. translād-ere, f. trans- + lādere : cf. L. translātus : see Translate.]

Transude (trᴀnsiūˈd), v. Also trans-. [a. F. transuder, f. L. trans- through + sūdāre to sweat. Cf. F. transsuder.]

Transudation (trᴀnsiudeiˈʃən). [a. F. transudation, or ad. med.L. type transudātiōn-em, n. of action from transudāre : see Transude v.]

Transudatory, a. [f. ppl. stem of med.L. transudāre : see next and -ory².] Having the quality of transuding; characterized by transudation.

Transude (trᴀnsiūˈd), sb. Also trans-. [f. Transude v.]

Transume (trᴀnsiūˈm), v. Obs. exc. Hist. Also 5–7 transumpt. [ad. L. transūm-ere, f. trans- + sūm-ere to take.]

Transumpt, ppl. a. Obs. [ad. L. transumpt-us, pa. pple. of transūmere.]

Transumption (trᴀnsʌmˈpʃən). [ad. late L. transumptiōn-em, n. of action f. transūmere : see Transume v.]

Transumptive, a. Obs. or arch. [ad. L. transumptīv-us (Quintilian), f. transumpt- ppl. stem : see prec. and -ive. Cf. OF. transsumptif (Godef.).]

Transvasate, v. Obs. rare. [ad. med.L. transvasāt-, ppl. stem of transvasāre, f. trans- + vas vessel.]

Transvasation. [n. of action from prec. : see -ation.]

Transvection (trᴀnsveˈkʃən). [ad. L. transvectiōn-em, n. of action from transveh-ere (-vect-), f. trans- + vehere to carry.]

Transversalis (trᴀnsvᴀɹseiˈlis). Anat. [med. and mod.L. : see prec.] A transverse muscle; one of the several muscles called transversalis.

Transversality (trᴀnsvᴀɹsæˈlĭti). [f. Transversal + -ity.] The condition or state of being transversal.

Transversant, a. [ad. L. transversant-em.]

Transvert (trᴀnsvᴀɹt), v. Obs. rare. [ad. L. transvert-ere, f. trans- across + vertere to turn : cf. Transverse.]

Transverse (trᴀnsvᴀɹs), a. and sb. [ad. L. transvers-us turned or directed across, pa. pple. of transvertere : see Transvert.]

Transverse.

1. Lying across; situated or lying crosswise or athwart; *esp.* situated or extending across the breadth of something; *spec.* at right angles (opp. to *longitudinal*). Also *const. to.*

2. By transverse [L. *per transversum*], in a transverse position, crosswise; athwart.

C. *adv.* In a transverse direction or position; transversely.

1. *Her.* Crossing the escutcheon from one side to the opposite one.

2. In a bivalve shell: Of greater breadth than length or height; having the longer diameter transverse to the hinge.

d. In special collocations:—**Transverse artery**, *Anat.* one of the small branches given off at nearly right angles from the larger; **transverse axis**, (*a*) an axis transverse to the main axis, as in a crystal; (*b*) *Geom.* the axis passing through the foci of a conic section (in an ellipse, the major axis); see AXIS¹; **transverse bone,** *Zool.* in some reptiles, a bone connecting the pterygoid and maxilla; **transverse colon,** *Anat.* (see COLON²); **transverse fissure,** *Anat.* (*a*) the cleft between the hemispheres of the brain into which the pia mater extends to form the velum interpositum and choroid plexuses; (*b*) a short transverse cleft on the lower surface of the left lobe of the liver; **transverse ligament,** part of the cotyloid ligament; **transverse nerve,** one of the transverse muscles or bar-magnets so that its poles are at the sides, not at the ends; **transverse magnetism,** the magnetisation at right angles to the length of a magnetised bar; **transverse muscle,** one of various muscles extending across some other part; **transverse strain,** a simple net-work of veins connecting the two inferior petrosal sinuses; **transverse suture,** the suture between the frontal and facial bones; **transverse vein,** *Anat.* any one of the several short veins of the wings of an insect, connecting two longitudinal ones.

2. Something that is transverse; *esp.* a transverse part or member.

3. In combination with other adjs. (*Entom.*): **transverse-nodial,** -**medial** adj. = **TRANSVERSO-CUBITAL, -MEDIAL**; **transverse-quadrate,** -**quadrate** with the transverse diameter the longest. Also *tr. Comb. s Anim. Kingd.*

Transverse, v.

1. Something that is transverse; *esp.*

Transversely, adv.

Transverseness, rare.

Transversion. [n. of action f. **TRANSVERT** v.]

Transverse, v.

Transversion.

Transverter.

Transvert, v. *Obs. rare.*

Transvert, v. *Obs. rare.*

Transverti'ble, a.

Transvolve, v. *Obs. rare.*

Transwaft, v. *intr.* To float across through air or water.

b. *trans.* To convey or carry across a river or sea.

Transwaftage [cf. WAFTAGE], a conveying or floating across.

Trat, sb.

Trant, v.

Trant, v.¹ *rare.* Now *dial.* Also 6 traunt.

Tranter.

Trap, sb.¹

Trap, sb.² *Sc.* Also 8 trantlin, -lim.

Trap, sb.³

Trap, sb.⁴

Trap, sb.⁵

Trap, sb.⁶ *Min.* Also 8 trapp.

Trap, v.¹

Trap, v.²

Trap, v.³

Trap-ball.

Trap-brilliant.

Trap-cut, ppl. a.

Trap-door.

Trapes, trapse, v.

Trapes, sb.

Trapesing, traipsing, vbl. sb.

Trapesing, traipsing, ppl. a.

Trapeze (trăpī·z), sb.

Trapezate (trĕ·pĭzeit), a.

Trapezial (trăpī·zĭǎl), a.

Trapezian (trăpī·zĭǎn), a.

Trapezist (trăpī·zist).

Trapezium (trăpī·zĭŭm), sb.

Trapezohedron, erron. f. TRAPEZOHEDRON.

Trapezo-, combining form of TRAPEZIUM.

Trapezist (trăpī·zist).

Trapezium (trăpī·zĭŭm).

Trapezius (trăpī·zĭŭs), Anat.

Trapezohedron (trăpī·zŏhī·drŏn).

Trapezoid (trăpī·zoid), sb. and a.

Trapezoidal (trăpĭzoi·dǎl), a.

Trapfall (trăp·fǫl), sb.

Trapferous (trăpī·fĕrǎs), a.

Trapish (trăp·ish), a.

Trap-net. see TRAP sb.

Trappan (trăpæ·n), sb.

Trappan (trăpæ·n), v.

Trapped (trăpt), ppl. a.

Trapper (trăp·ǝr), sb.

Trapping (trăp·ĭŋ), vbl. sb.

Trapping, ppl. a.

Trappist (trăp·ist), sb.

Trappistine (trăp·istin), -ine.

Trappoid (trăp·oid), a.

Trappose (trăpǭ·s), a.

Trappous (trăp·ǝs), a.

Trappy (trăp·i), a.

Trapse, Trapsing: see TRAPES.

Trap (trăp), v.

Trapstick (trăp·stik), sb.

Tra-ra (träră·), int. and sb.

Tras, Trase, Trash, obs. ff. TRACE, TRASH.

Trash (trăsh), sb.[1]

Trash, sb.[2]

Trash, v.[1]

Trash-cord: see TRASH sb.[1]

Trashery (trăsh·ǝri).

Trash-nail. Obs.

Trashily (trăsh·ili), adv.

Trashiness (trăsh·inĕs).

Trashtrie (trăsh·tri), Sc.

Trashy (trăsh·i), a.

Traskite (träs·kǝit), Ch. Hist.

Trason, v. Venery. Obs.

Tra-sh-mire dial.

Trass (trăs).

Trat, Trate: see TROT.

Trature, -uruse, obs. ff. TRAITOR.

Travail (træ·vĕl), sb.

Travail (træ·vĕl), v.

Travale, Travel: see TRAVAIL.

Trauchle (trǫ·x'l), v. Sc.

Traught, Traul, obs. ff. THOUGH, TRAWL.

Trauma (trǫ·mǎ), Path.

Traumatic (trǫmæ·tik), a. and sb.

Traumatism (trǭ·mǎtizm), Path.

Traumatize (trǭ·mǎtǝiz), v. Path.

Traumato- (trǭ·mǎtŏ), repr. Gr. τραῦμα-, τραυματ- combining form.

Traumatropism (trǭmătropĭz'm). *Biol.* [Short for *traumatotropism*, f. Gr. τραῦμα wound, after *geotropism*, *heliotropism*, etc.] A peculiar growth or curvature of an organism (esp. a plant) resulting from a wound. So **Traumatropic** *a.*, of, pertaining to, or of the nature of traumatropism.

Travail (træ'veɪl), *sb.*[1] Forms: α before 1600 usually written α, 6 Sc. *other* α. 6 3-7 *travail*, -ayl, 4-6 -ayll, -aile, -aile, 4-7 -aill, -aile, -ayle, 5-6 -aylle; 4 travaill, 4-7 -aill, -aile, -ayle, 5 (6-8 -ayll), -ale, 4 travaill, -walje, -aille, -ayle, 5 (trewaill), 4-9 trauayll, 8 trauaylle, 4-7 -aill, -6, 5-6-oill, -ille, -yll; 5 trawaill, 5-8 travel, (7 travel); 5-6 Sc. trawell, 8 -OF. *travail* suffering or painful effort, trouble (13th c. in Godef. Compl.)

Travoy-roads ... These 'travoy-roads'—the name comes from the French *travois*—have to be cleared by the swampers. *Ibid.*

Traw, trawe: see THROW *sb.*[1], TRAVE *sb.* TROW *v.*, THUR. **Trawalle, -al, -el, -ell, etc.** obs. Sc. spellings of TRAVAIL, TRAVEL. **Trawethe, obs.** f. TROTH.

Trawl (trọl), *sb.* Also 7 trall, (troul, 8-9 trowl). [Origin and age obscure. If quot. 1481-90 belongs here, *trawalle* might be related to rare MDu. *traghel* drag-net (in *Teuthonista* 1475), referred by Verwijs and Verdam ult. to L. *tragula* drag-net. But the MS reading is indistinct, and some would read *tramelle* (TRAMMEL *sb.*[1]).

I. 1. A strong net or bag dragged along the bottom of fishing-banks; a drag-net ; = TRAWL-NET 1; that now often distinguished as the *beam-trawl*, developing in the modern form in quot. 1880. ...

2. *intr.* To fish with a net the edge of which is dragged along the bottom of the sea to catch the fish living there, esp. flat-fish ; to fish with a trawl-net or in a trawler.

Trawl-net. [f. TRAWL *sb.* or *v.* + NET *sb.*[1].] A fishing-net used in trawling ; esp. = TRAWL *sb.* 1.

Trawler (trọ·ləɹ). [f. TRAWL *v.* + -ER[1].] **1.** One who trawls ; one who fishes with a trawl or trawl-net ; (also) a ship or vessel for trawl-fishing.

Trawling (trọ·liŋ), *vbl. sb.* [f. TRAWL *v.* + -ING.] Fishing with a trawl or trawl-net ; also, the action of TRAWL *v.* in other applications.

Trawley, variant of TROLLEY.

Trawth, trawpe, obs. forms of TROTH.

Tray (tré), *sb.*[1] Forms: 1 trega, 4 treȝe, 3 treȝe, 3-4 treie, 4 trei, treye, 4-7 traie, 4-5 tray, tray 7 treye, 5-6 traye, 8 tr. tra. [OE. *trega* (wk. masc.) trouble, pain—OTeut. *traga* (wk. masc.).]

†Tray, *sb.*[2] Forms : 1 †treȝ, 4 treȝe, 3 treȝe, 4-6 traye. [OE. *trēg*, *trīg.*] A flat board or vessel with a raised rim, or of a shallow box without a lid, made of wood, metal, or other material, of various sizes and shapes (round, oval, quadrilateral with rounded corners, etc.) ; now used for carrying plates, dishes, glasses, small vessels, cards, etc., for containing and exhibiting small articles, as jewellery, natural history specimens, etc. ...

Tray, *sb.*[3] *Venery.* Also tres. [The same word as TRAY three, in dice, cards, etc.: re-spelt after BAY *sb.*[6] Believed to go back in ult. use to 18th c. at least.] The third branch of a stag's horn.

Traythly, *adv.* TROTH. *rare.* Etymology and history uncertain.

Traytice, -yse, var. TRETIS *a.* OBS. **Tray-trip, var.** TRAY-TRIP *sb.* **Traywes, obs.** f. TROW. **Treas, obs.** form of TRACE *sb.*[1]

†Treacher (tre·tʃəɹ). *Obs.* Forms : 3 trichour, 4 trechour, -oure, 4 trecheour, -our, -oure 6 trycher ; 4 trichor, treachour, 4 trechour, treochour, 4-(5) treochour, 5 -ure ; 6 trechor, (trachour, trachour) 4-5 trecher, 6 treacher. [a. OF. *trichere*, *trecheor*, nom. of *tricheor*, *trecheor*. ...] A deceiver, cheat ; one who deceives by trickery ; *sometimes*, a traitor.

†Treacherize, -ise, *v. Obs. rare*[-1]. [f. TREACHER + -IZE.] *intr.* To act in a treacherous manner ; to play the deceiver or traitor.

†Treacherly, *adv. Obs. rare*[-1]. [f. TREACHER + -LY[2].] In a treacherous or traitorous manner.

Treachery (tre·tʃəɹi). Forms : 3-4 tricherie, -ri, trycherye, (3 tricherige), 3-4 tricherye, (4 tricheorie, trioohori, 5 tricherie, -ory, 6 tretcherie) ; 4-7 trecherie, -ery, 4-5 trecchery, -ie, 5 trechory, -ury, tretchery, 6 -orie, (5-6 trechery), 6- treachery, (7 treacherie), 6 -ery. [a. OF. *trecherie* (11th c. in Godef.) ...]

Treacle (trī·k'l), *sb.* Forms: 4-5 tryacle, -7 triacle, 5 tryacell, -cul, -kylle, -kell, 6 tri-, trakele, tryckell, 7 triackle, -akole ; 6-5 triacle, -ticle, 4-7 treacle ; ... [ME. *triacle*, a. OF. *triacle*, 6 *theriacle*, beside *triacle* (-tacle), triacle (15th c.)— ...]

Treacle clover. *Herb. Obs.* A name given to ...

Treacle mustard. ...

Tread (tred), *sb.* Forms: 3 (pl.) treden, tredden ; pe. treddle, (5-6 tred, 6-7 trede, 5 trade, pr. staal, tread, 6 Early ME. *trede* (pl. treden), f. stem of OE. *tredan* to TREAD. ...

Tread (tred), *v.* Pa. t. trod (trọd), arch. trode (trōd). Pa. pple. trodden (trọd'n), arch. trod. [OE. *tredan* ...]

TREAD.

B. Signification.

1. *trans.* To step upon; to pace or walk on (the ground, etc.); to walk in (a place); hence, to go about in (a place, etc.).

2. To step or walk upon or along; to follow, pursue (a path, track, or road), *lit.* and *fig.*

3. *intr.* To walk, go; to set down the feet in walking; to step. Also *said* of the foot.

4. *intr.* To step on (something in one's way); to put the foot down upon accidentally or intentionally, *esp.* so as to press upon.

5. *trans.* To tread the stage (the boards), to act upon the stage, to follow the profession of an actor (also *fig.* to write stage-plays).

6. *trans.* To copulate.

7. *trans.* To press (something) downwards with the foot or feet in treading or pedalling.

8. Of the male bird: To copulate with (the hen). Also *absol.*

Treader (tre·dǝɹ). [f. TREAD v. + -ER¹.]

1. One who or that which treads, in various senses.

2. — TREADLE *sb.* 2. *rare.*

3. *trans.* To thresh (corn) by trampling it on a threshing-floor.

Treading (tre·dɪŋ), *vbl. sb.* [-ING¹.]

1. The action of the verb TREAD in various senses.

2. *trans.* To press (grapes) by working a treadle.

Treadle (tre·d'l). Forms: 1 tredel; 5 tredel, -yl, -ylle, 6-9 treaddle, (8 -il,) 7 tredle, (tredelle, 8-9 treadle, (8 -el,) 7 trydle, triddle (also 9 dial.)

1. A step or stair. *Obs. rare.*

2. A lever or pedal worked by the foot in machines and mechanical contrivances, usually to produce reciprocating (as *orig.* in the loom) or rotary motion.

3. The umbilical cord of the bird's egg.

Treadmill (tre·dmɪl), *sb.* [f. TREAD v. + MILL *sb.*] A horizontal cylinder made to revolve by the weight of persons treading on boards arranged as steps around its periphery.

Treadle-wheel, *sb.* = TREADMILL; tread-wheel.

Tread-softly, U.S., the spurge-nettle.

Tread-wheel, *sb.* A wheel turned for the tread of persons or animals to put in motion machinery.

Treasurableness. TREASURABLENESS.

Treason (trīˈz'n). Forms: 3-4 treison, 5-6 treyson; 3-5 (*Sc.* -6) trayson, -one, 4 (*Sc.* -6) -oun; 4-5 treson, -oune; 4 tresone.

Treasonable (trīˈz'nǝb'l), *a.* [f. TREASON *sb.* + -ABLE.] Of the nature of treason; characteristic of or involving treason; perfidious, treacherous.

Treasonableness, *sb.*

Treasonably, *adv.*

Treason-felony, *sb.*

Treasonful, *a.*

Treasonish, *a.*

Treasonous (trīˈz'nǝs), *a.*

Treasonry, *sb.*

Treasony, *sb.*

Treasurable (tre·ʒʊɹǝb'l), *a.*

Treasure (tre·ʒǝɹ), *sb.* Forms: 2-6 tresor, 3-6 -our, 4-6 -ore, -oure, 5 -owre, -er, 3-6 -ure, 5 treysour, treasour, 6- treasure.

1. Wealth or riches stored or accumulated, *esp.* in the form of precious metals; gold or silver coin; hence in general, money, riches, wealth.

Treasure found, = TREASURE-TROVE *b.*

Treasure-house, *sb.* a house, building, or chamber in which treasure is kept; a treasury.

Treasurer (tre·ʒǝɹǝɹ). [In 13-14th c. treasorer, -a. ONF. and AF. tresorer = OF. tresorier, f. tresor TREASURE, after late L. thesaurārius (whence Fr. thésaurier, etc.); whence It. tesoriere, Sp. tesorero.]

1. One who has officially the charge of treasure; *orig.* a person entrusted with the receipt, care, and disbursement of the revenues of a king, noble, or other dignitary, of a state, city, or church; now, one who is responsible for the funds of a public body, or of any corporation, association, society, or club.

b. **Lord High Treasurer** of England, of Great Britain, also called **Lord Treasurer**, **High Treasurer**, **Treasurer of the Exchequer**.

c. **Lord High Treasurer** of Scotland.

d. **United States.** An officer of the Treasury Department, who receives and keeps the moneys, disbursing them only when authorized by the Secretary of the Treasury and duly recorded and countersigned.

Treasurership (tre·zŭrafīp). [f. prec. + -SHIP.] The office of treasurer.

Treasure-trove (tre·zŭrtrōuv). [Orig. two words in A.F. *tresor trové* treasure found, founde, found ; in 16th c. with the Fr. form anglicized treasure trovey, trove, trouvé.]

Treasurous, a. Obs. rare. [f. TREASURE sb. + -OUS.] Full of or of the nature of treasure ; treasonous.

Treasury (tre·zŭri), sb. Forms : 3-5 tresorye, 3-6 -orie, 4-5 -oury(e, 4-6 -ory, 6 -owri, 7 -ury ; 3-5 thesaurie, 5 thesaurye ; 4-6 tresory, 5-7 treasorie, 6-7 -urie, 6-Sc treasurie. [ME. a. OF. *tresorie* (11th c. in Godef.), f. OF. *tresor*, TREASURE (after med.L. *thesauraria*: see TREASURY) + -ie, -Y.]

Treasury-ship. [f. prec. + -SHIP.] = TREASURERSHIP.

Treat (trīt), sb.[1] Forms : 3-5 trett, trete, treyte), 5-6 (9 Sc.) trett, 6 Sc. trett, 6-7 trayte, 6-8 treat, 7 treate. [In early use a. OF. *tret, trait*, or other deriv. f. TREAT v. ; in 17-18 f. TREAT v. or other deriv. of the same stem.]

Treat (trīt), v. Forms : 2-7 trete, treten, 3-6 tret, 4-6 trette, treatte, 5-6 trayte, trect, treet, 6 Sc. treit, trett, 6-7 Sc. treat, 6-7 treate. [Early ME. *trete*, a. OF. *traitier* (12th c. in Godef.), F. *traiter* :—L. *tractāre* TRACTATE.]

Treater (trī·tĕr). [f. TREAT v. + -ER[1].] One who treats, in various senses.

Treating (trī·tiŋ), vbl. sb. [f. TREAT v. + -ING[1].] The action of the verb TREAT.

Treatise (trī·tis, -iz), sb. Forms : 4-5 tretis, -ys, -ise, 4 -ee, -esse, -yse, -ice, 5 -ice, -yee, 4-7 tretise, 5-6 treatise, -yse ; 6 tratise, traictise, treatise. [a. AF. *tretis*, *tretiz* (= OF. *traitis*, *treitis*) :— L. type *tractātum*, f. *tractāre* : see TREAT v.]

Treaty (trī·ti), sb. Forms : 4-5 tretee, 4-6 trete, tretey, 3 treatee, 4-6 tretie, -ye, 5-6 treatie, 5-7 treaty, 6-7 -ie, 6 treaty, treytie, 6-7 treaty ; *-l. tractātum* TRACTATE.]

Treatable (trī·tăb'l), a. Forms : 4-7 tretable, (5 tretable, tretabill, -yble, 6-7 -ible), 5-7 treatable. [ME. *tretable*, a. f. *tractable* (13th c. in Godef.)]

Treating-house, a house of entertainment or refreshment.

Treatment (trī·tmĕnt). Also 6 treat-, 7 treit-. [f. TREAT v. + -MENT. Cf. F. *traitement* (1258 in Hatz.-Darm.).]

'conventio publica', or 'foedus', from the end of the 17th century. In the language of modern diplomacy the term 'treaty' is restricted to the more important international agreements, especially to those which are the work of a congress, while agreements dealing with subordinate questions are described by the more general term 'convention'.

†**4.** Entreaty, persuasion, request. *Obs.*

c 1450 *Mirour Saluacioun* 3972 A wise womman..whilk turned the prince ire to pece thorgh hire tretee. c 1470 *Golagros & Gaw.* 1083 For ony trety may tyde..I wil noght turn myn entent. c 1470 HENRYSON *Mor. Fab.* II. (*Town & C. Mouse*) xxiv, With fair tretie yit scho gart hir ryse And to the burde thay went. 1606 SHAKS. *Ant. & Cl.* III. xi. 62 Now I must To the young man send humble Treaties, dodge And palter in the shifts of lownes. 1649 DAVENANT *Love & Hon.* II. i, The gentle Treaties, Sir, of love are fit For hours more happy.

†**5.** Treatment, usage; behaviour. *Obs. rare.*

1630 B. JONSON *New Inn* I. i, *Host.* They call me Good-stock. *Lov.* Sir, and you confess it, Both in your language, treaty, and your bearing. 1654 tr. *Martini's Conq. China* 118 To partake of his sweet treaty, rather than of his cruelty. *Ibid.* 217 They were to expect no better Treaty from this Tyrants hands.

6. *attrib.* and *Comb.*, as *treaty-ally*, *-breaker*, *-money*, *-right*, *skill*, *-stipulation*; *treaty-breaking*, *-making* sbs. and adjs.; *treaty-bound*, *-sealed* adjs.; **treaty coast, shore**, a coast on or along which some foreign nation has certain rights guaranteed by treaty; **treaty-port**, a port opened to foreign commerce by a treaty (esp. applied to certain ports in China, Japan, and Korea, in relation to commerce with European nations).

1904 *Daily Chron.* 1 Feb. 5/1 It would ill beseem King Edward, the *treaty-ally of the Mikado, to pay a visit to the Tsar. 1908 *Westm. Gaz.* 29 Feb. 3/1 The French are *treaty-bound to keep the open door. 1706 PRIOR *Ode to Queen* xx, Thus the Royal *Treaty-Breaker said. 1723 BLACKMORE *Alfred* x. 359 At his Tribunal let them be arraign'd Who *Treaty-breaking Principles maintain'd. 1909 *Daily Chron.* 7 July 3/1 Any delay in that grant would have led to an accusation of treaty-breaking. 1899 *Westm. Gaz.* 26 June 7/1 The whole *treaty coast is in a most excited state. c 1500 *Melusine* xxviii. 214 For to fulfyll..that he had promysed at *traytee makynge of the peas. 1856 KANE *Arct. Expl.* I. xvii. 210 They did not return: I had read enough of treaty-makings not to expect them too confidently. 1796 WASHINGTON *Let. to U. S. Ho. Repr.* 30 Mar., The *treaty-making power. 1763 SCRAFTON *Indostan* iii. (1770) 102 Demanded security for the payment of the remainder of the *treaty-money. 1881 J. HATTON *New Ceylon* iv. 114 With the *treaty ports of China and with Hong Kong we exchange annually upwards of twenty million pounds' worth of goods. 1901 *Westm. Gaz.* 4 Jan. 2/2 The extinction of the rights clearly possessed by France on the *Treaty Shore [of Newfoundland]. 1742 BLAIR *Grave* 500 Now vain their *Treaty-Skill! Death scorns to treat.

Hence (*nonce-wds.*) **Trea·ty** *v.*, *intr.* to make a treaty; *trans.* (with advb. extension), to bring or get (into some specified condition) by a treaty; **Trea·tyist**, one who frames or is bound by a treaty; **Trea·tyless** *a.*, having no treaty.

1862 CARLYLE *Fredk. Gt.* XIV. ii. (1873) V. 152 In spite of treatyings innumerable. 1888 *Glasgow Even. Citizen* 3 Sept. 2/5 China must feel..irritated in having her people 'treatied' out of America and our Colonies. 1888 *Voice* (N. Y.) 26 Apr., A yearly addition of 150,000,000,000,000 of young codfish to vex future treatyists. 1892 *Nation* (N. Y.) 25 Aug. 137/3 There the negotiations hang, leaving these two high-protection countries in almost as helpless and ridiculous a plight as unhappy and treatyless England.

†**Treave**, obs. var. THRAVE, THREAVE *sb.* and *v.*

1768 *Case of Jeffry Ruffle* 2 When cut down, the whole ought to be put into treaves of an equal size, and every tenth treave set out for the tythes. *Ibid.*, He tythed it at the times he gathered in his corn for treaving or loading, by separating and setting out every tenth sheaf.

†**Trebant**, obs. variant of TRABANT.

1712 *Lond. Gaz.* No. 4967/1 His Majesty [at Vienna]..was on Horseback, preceded..by the Trebants, who are a sort of Yeomen of the Guards.

Trebget, -got, obs. forms of TREBUCHET.

Treble (tre·b'l), *sb.* Forms: see next. [a. OF. *treble*, sb. use of TREBLE *a.*]

I. 1. Anything threefold; a sum or quantity three times as great as another; the product of a sum or magnitude multiplied by three.

[1324–5 *Rolls of Parlt.* I. 416/1 Que amounteront a treble & quatreble de lour coustages.] c 1430 *Art Nombryng* xi. (E.E.T.S.) 17 Thow most trebille the digit, and that triplat is to be put vnder the 3rd next figure towarde the right honde, And the vnder-trebille vnder the trebille. 1463 *Rolls of Parlt.* V. 502/2 Forfeiture..of the treble of his seid wages. 1475 *Ibid.* VI. 121/2 Uppon peyn of forfeiture of the treble of somoche as he so hath receyved or taken. 1799 WILSON in *Phil. Trans.* LXXXIX. 302 The equation of the halves, or quarters, or doubles, trebles, &c. of those functions.

2. In technical and elliptical uses. **a.** A triple barrier; an obstacle consisting of three successive fences.

1569 STOCKER tr. *Diod. Sic.* III. xi. 120/2 Hys Campe which he with a treble of wood and earth fortified. 1895 *Daily News* 1 May 7/5 The fences..On one side of the ring..are arranged in a 'treble', just far enough apart to give room between for a horse to pull himself together for each effort.

b. *Paper-making* and *Printing.* A frame on which hand-made paper or printed sheets are hung to dry.

1727–41 CHAMBERS *Cycl.* s.v. *Paper*, Carried up into the loft, and hung six or seven sheets together upon lines fastened to a thing called a Tribble, each tribble containing thirty lines ten or twelve foot long. 1766 C. LEADBETTER *Royal Gauger* II. xiv. (ed. 6) 371 The Sheets of Paper, taken from between the Felts, are laid one upon the other till the next Day and then are hung up, on Lines called Trebles, in the Drying-House. 1896 *Daily News* 23 Mar. 8/4 If time be no object, the sheets are hung on 'trebles' (the towel-horse is the domestic equivalent) in an ordinary room.

c. A kind of step-dance; the measure of or music for this. *dial.*

1805 G. McINDOE *Poems* 18 We'll sen' for fiddling Alic, and the piper he'll play treple. 1895 D. D. DIXON *Whittingham Vale* v. 67 A variety of step-dancing such as the 'treble', the single and double 'shuffle', the 'cut' [etc.].

d. *Whist.* A game (at short whist) in which one side scores five and the other none, counting three points to the winners.

1870 HARDY & WARE *Mod. Hoyle* 30 If one side scores five while the adversaries have made not one point, the winning side makes a treble. 1876 A. C. WALKER *Correct Card* (1880) Gloss., *Treble*, scoring five before your adversary scores one.

e. *pl.* A quality or grade of small coal.

1901 *Scotsman* 15 Oct. 4/8 There are four bush washers..one for trebles.

f. A method of crocheting in which three loops of thread are carried on the hook; also a line or chain of crochet work done by this method.

1882 CAULFEILD & SAWARD *Dict. Needlework* 127/2 s.v. *Crochet, Treble Stitch, Raised.*—Work three rows of Ribbed Stitch. Fourth row—work 2 Ribbed Stitches, and make a Treble for next, putting the hook into the stitch underneath it of the first row, work 2 Trebles in this way [etc.]. c 1900 THÉRÈSE DE DILLMONT *Encycl. Needlework, Crochet* 304 Trebles are little columns or bars made of loops or stitches.. They are of different kinds; the half or short treble, the plain or ordinary treble [etc.].

3. One of three things or persons that are exact counterparts. *nonce-use* after DOUBLE *sb.* 2 b.

1898 *Westm. Gaz.* 29 June 1/2 There are many 'doubles' in the House of Commons. There seem..to be in that assembly at least two groups of trebles.

II. 4. *Music.* The highest part in harmonized musical composition; the soprano part. Cf. TREBLE *a.* 2. [The musical use is supposed to have arisen from the fact that in early contrapuntal music the chief melody or *cantus firmus* was given to the tenor (TENOR *sb.* 4 a), the voice parts added above being the *discantus* or alto, and the *treble* (? third part) or soprano; but the history is somewhat obscure, esp. as *triplex*, *triplus* meant 'threefold' and not 'third', and in OF. *treble* was applied to a trio.]

c 1330 R. BRUNNE *Chron. Wace* (Rolls) 11263 Þo clerkes þat best couþe synge, Wyþ treble, mene, & burdoun. c 1430 LYDG. *Min. Poems* (Percy Soc.) 54 Thi [nasal] organys so hihe begynne to syng ther messe, With treble meene and tenor discordyng as I gesse. 1500–20 DUNBAR *Poems* xxxii. 19 All to small To sic ane tribbill to hald ane bace. 1567 *Trial Treas.* Biv, I will sing the trouble with all my harte. 1626 BACON *Sylva* § 109 In one of the lower Strings of a Lute, there soundeth not the Sound of the Treble,..but only the Sound of the Base. 1782 BURNEY *Hist. Music* (1789) II. v. 456 The third and Triplum the highest or treble, of which term this was the origin. 1884 H. C. DEACON in Grove *Dict. Mus.* IV. 165 *Treble*..has been said to be a corruption of Triplum, a third part superadded to the Altus and Bassus. *fig.* 1532 MORE *Confut. Tindale* II. i. 95 His false translacyon wyth theyr farther false construccion, they thought sholde be the basse and the tenour wheruppon they wold synge the trouble wyth mych false descant. 1577 B. GOOGE *Heresbach's Husb.* III. (1586) 112 The grasiers trade the treble and the tillers occupation the base. 1638–56 COWLEY *Davideis* I. 458 Water and Air he for the Tenor chose, Earth made the Base, the Treble Flame arose. 1892 *Daily News* 16 Sept. 3/3 The dark tone of the ground..acts as bass to the treble of the silk.

5. A treble voice; also, a singer having a treble voice; one who sings the treble part.

? c 1475 *Sqr. lowe Degre* 782 Than shall ye go to your evensong, With tenours and trebles among. 1658 MARVELL *Poems, Music's Empire* 10 And Virgin Trebles wed the manly Base. 1719 D'URFEY *Pills* (1872) I. 7 The ravishing trebles delight every ear. 1801 STRUTT *Sports & Past.* IV. i. 254 Two celebrated trebles;..who occasionally made twenty shillings a day by ballad-singing.

b. *transf.* A high-pitched or shrill voice, sound, or note.

1600 SHAKS. *A. Y. L.* II. vii. 162 His bigge manly voice, Turning againe toward childish trebble, pipes And whistles in his sound. 1647 H. MORE *Poems, Cupid's Conflict* vi, How well agreed the Brooks low muttering Base, With the birds trebbles. 1827 DISRAELI *Viv. Grey* VI. iii, 'So please your Serene Highness, I am here!' answered a very thin treble. 1855 TENNYSON *Brook* 40, I chatter over stony ways, In little sharps and trebles.

6. The string of treble pitch in a musical instrument; also, the chanter of a bagpipe.

1562 J. HEYWOOD *Prov. & Epigr.* (1867) 186 Which string ..wouldst thou..harpe on? Not the base.., Nor the treble. 1623 LISLE *Ælfric on O. & N. Test.* Ded. xxxviii, What sports they now deuise With Treble and Drone, and Bonfiers, and Bels. 1682 DRYDEN *MacFl.* 46 At thy well-sharpened thumb,..The treble squeaks for fear, the basses roar.

†**7.** A musical instrument of treble pitch, as a violin. *Obs.*

1634 *MS. Archd. Oxon, Berks.* c. 74 lf. 230 He plaied uppon a trebble in the house of Francis Iennings uppon a Sondaie. 1670 EACHARD *Cont. Clergy* 62 People..presently phansi'd the Moon, Mercury, and Venus to be a kind of violins or trebles to Jupiter and Saturn. 1710 in E. W. Dunbar *Soc. Life in Moray* (1865) 15, I can play on the Treble and Gambo, Viol, &c.

b. = *treble bell*: see TREBLE *a.* 2 b.

1598–9 in Swayne *Sarum Churchw. Acc.* (1896) 147, ij newe gudgins for yᵉ Treble and nailes, 3s. 6d. 1652–3 *Ibid.* 227 The Sexton shall ring the Treable at 5 a Clocke in the Morning. a 1658 FORD, etc. *Witch Edmonton* II. i, Double Bells!..Trebles: buy me Trebles, all Trebles: for our purpose is to be in the Altitudes.

8. *attrib.* and *Comb.*, as **treble bob**: BOB *sb.*5; **treble-ringer**, the ringer of the treble bell in a peal.

1872 Treble bob royal [see BOB *sb.*5]. 1899 *Westm. Gaz.* 31 Oct. 10/1 For sixty-seven years..Bunce was the treble ringer.

Treble (tre·b'l), *a.* and *adv.* Also 4–8 **trebble**, 6 **-il**; 5 **trebel, -yl(le, -ille, -ull**, 6 **treaboll**, 6–7 **-ble**, 7 *Sc.* **treeble**; 5 **tribull**, 5–6 *Sc.* **trib(b)ill**, 5–7 **trible**, 7–8 (9 *dial.*) **tribble**; 5 **tryble, -ylle**; (6 **trouble**). [a. OF. *treble*, *trebble*, *treuble*, etc. (12th c. in Godef.):—pop.L. *triplus* for L. *triplex*. See also prec.]

A. *adj.* **1.** Consisting of three members, things, or sets combined; threefold; made of three thicknesses or layers of material; = TRIPLE *a.* 1.

c 1374 CHAUCER *Boeth.* IV. metr. vii. 115 (Camb. MS.) He drowh cerberus the hownd of helle by his treble cheyne. 1413 *Pilgr. Sowle* (Caxton) I. xxv. (1859) 30 Byndyng with double and treble boundes. a 1673 J. CARYL in Spurgeon *Treas. Dav.* Ps. cxl. 3 Serpents are..said to have a treble tongue, because, moving their tongue so fast, they seem to have three tongues. 1697 DRYDEN *Æneid* X. 1112 Thro' treble Plates it went Of solid Brass. 1781 GIBBON *Decl. & F.* xviii. II. 107 A treble inclosure of brick walls was defended by a deep ditch. 1832 R. & J. LANDER *Exped. Niger* II. xii. 183 They had formed themselves into a large treble circle. 1907 C. HILL-TOUT *Brit. N. Amer., Far West* vii. 130 A kind of shirt of double or treble elk-hide.

b. Of actions, conditions, etc.: Of threefold character or application; existing or occurring in three ways or relations; of three kinds.

1390 GOWER *Conf.* III. 159 Thus thei worchen treble sinne, That ben flatours aboute a king. c 1450 *Mirour Saluacioun* 1529 The feend thoght crist to tempt be treble vice. 1571 GOLDING *Calvin on Ps.* lx. 6 The greate men were dubble and trebble traytours. 1694 F. BRAGGE *Disc. Parables* vii. 238 It would be a double and treble charity; 'twould provide for the happiness of both body and soul. 1818 SCOTT *Br. Lamm.* xii, It was attended with a treble difficulty. 1886 F. HARRISON *Choice Bks.* iii. 49 Every part and episode has its double and treble meaning.

c. Three times as much or as many; of three times the number or amount; triple.

1423 *Rolls of Parlt.* IV. 257/2 Uppon peine de inprisonement..and trible dammages to the partie greved. 1489 *Barbour's Bruce* XVIII. 30 (Edin. MS.) Schir Eduard..said, that he suld fecht that day, Thouch tribill and quatribill war thai. 1563 W. COTHE in *15th Rep. Hist. MSS. Comm.* App. II. 32 It is not treble the company we have here, that is able to defend it. 1664 M. FELL in *Extr. S. P. rel. Friends* II. (1911) 187 People had theire goods distreaned trible the vallue of their fines. 1788 JEFFERSON *Writ.* (1859) II. 526 It sells..for treble the price of common whale oil. 1835 URE *Philos. Manuf.* 156 The roller A, moving with a treble surface velocity.

2. *Mus.* Of, pertaining to, or suited to the highest part in harmonized musical composition.

Treble voice: a voice ranging from about middle C to a twelfth or two octaves above it; a soprano voice. *Treble clef*: the G clef when placed (as usually) upon the second line of the stave.

c 1440 *Promp. Parv.* 501/1 Treblesonge (*K.* treble of orgene songe, *S.* trebyl songe), *precentus*. *Ibid.*, Trebyl syngare. 1530 PALSGR. 286/1 Wayte treble, *bussine*. 1674 PLAYFORD *Skill Mus.* 43 Increasing of the Voice in the Treble Part.. doth oftentimes become harsh. 1678 PHILLIPS (ed. 4), *Treble*, the highest part in Musick, called in Latin *Altus*. 1801 BUSBY *Dict. Mus.* Introd. 23 The Treble-cliff is used for the first or shrillest class, both of voice and instruments. 1876 STAINER & BARRETT *Dict. Mus. Terms* (1898) s.v., The treble or soprano voice is the most flexible of all vocal registers.

b. Hence in the names of musical instruments (or strings) of the highest pitch. Cf. *bass*, *tenor*.

Treble bell: the smallest bell of a peal.

1530 PALSGR. 282/2 Treble stryng of an instrument, *chanterelle*. 1595–6 in Swayne *Sarum Churchw. Acc.* (1896) 145 A Rope for yᵉ Treabell bell, 2s. 5d. 1597 SHAKS. *2 Hen. IV*, III. ii. 351 The Case of a Treble Hoeboy was a Mansion for him. 1674 PLAYFORD *Skill Mus.* 109 The Treble-Violin is a cheerful and spritely Instrument. 1872 ELLACOMBE *Ch. Bells Devon*, etc. 235 In 1718, two treble bells were added to the peal of S. Bride's.

c. High-pitched; high or sharp in tone; shrill.

1562 J. HEYWOOD *Prov. & Epigr.* (1867) 110 In hir treble voyce, she fell so to cacklyng. 1602 MARSTON *Ant. & Mel.* III. Wks. 1856 I. 35 What treble minikin squeaks here? 1727 GAY *Fables* xlvi. 15 A village cur,..Imagined that his treble throat Was blest with music's sweetest note. 1860 GEO. ELIOT *Mill on Fl.* III. vi, Bob spoke with a sharp and rather treble volubility.

†**d.** ? Upper. *Obs. rare.*

1551 *Gray's N. Y. Gift* iii. in Furniv. *Ball. fr. MSS.* I. 418 Yet at this presence—ye shall vnderstand—The popest be Ranke, and on the treble hand: Som comfford the have; I cannot tell howe.

3. Special collocations. *Treble bar*, *treble gold stripe*, collectors' names for various moths: see quots. *Treble hook*, a fish-hook consisting of three single hooks fastened back to back. †*Treble letter*, a letter consisting of three sheets formerly charged triple postage (*obs.*). *Treble lock*, a lock operating by three turns of the key. *Treble star*, three stars so near (really or visually) as not to be separately visible without a telescope. †*Treble time* (*obs.*), triple time. See also in 2.

1832 RENNIE *Conspect. Butterfl. & Moths* 201 The Tawny *Treble Bar (*Argyromiges trifasciella*, Curtis)..Wings..with three somewhat straight, equidistant, brown bands. *Ibid.*, The *Treble Gold Stripe (*Argyromiges tristigella*, Stephens). Wings..tawny-brown, with a straight silvery-golden band before, and a second in the middle. 1867 SMYTH *Sailor's Word-bk.*, *Treble-block, one fitted with three sheaves or rollers. 1895 *Outing* (U.S.) XXVII. 222/2 Attached to each line were a sinker and a *treble hook, i.e., three hooks soldered together at such angles that when a fish has once gorged the thing, disgorgement is almost an impossibility. 1753 *Scots Mag.* July 328/2 The rates of double letters, are always double; of *treble letters, treble. 1805 *Act 45 Geo. III*, c. 11 § 1 For every single letter one penny; for every double letter twopence; for every treble letter or other letter under an ounce in weight three-pence. 1661 BAXTER *Mor. Prognost.* II. xxi. 50 There shall be a *Treble-Lock upon the Door of the Ministry. 1782 HERSCHEL in *Phil. Trans.* LXXII. 100 The beautiful *treble star in Monoceros's right fore-foot. 1686 PLOT *Staffordsh.* ix. 371 Seven bells rung together in peal...Their number excludes them, from ever being brought, either into common or *treble-time.

B. *adv.* **1.** In three ranks or rows, threefold; to three times the extent; three times over; trebly.

13.. *K. Alis.* 6606 In hire mouth buth teth treble set. 1552 HULOET, Treble, *tripliciter*. 1563 A. NEVELL in B. Googe *Eglogs*, etc. (Arb.) 87 All these conclude him blest..And trible blest agayne. 1622 FLETCHER *Beggar's Bush* V. i, And I'll deserve it treble. 1675 WOOD *Life* 18 Sept. (O.H.S.) II. 322 Piers was double or treble paid by Dr. Fell. 1708 *Constit. Watermen's Co.* lvii, Every person offending therein, shall forfeit..treble as much as he or they respectively shall demand.

2. In a high-pitched tone; shrilly.

1811 [implied in *treble-skirling*: see C. 2].

C. Combinations.

1. The adj. in combination. **a.** with sbs., as **treble-coursing**, the division of an air-current in a mine into three courses or channels; **treble-seam** (*Cricket slang*), a leathern cricket-ball stitched with three seams; **treble-tree**, an arrangement of swingle-trees for three horses abreast.

1897 *Globe* 9 July 1/5 The old bowler..declared there was a lot of human nature in a *treble-seam. 1877 KNIGHT *Dict. Mech.*, *Treble-tree, a whiffletree for three horses. An equalizer.

b. Parasynthetic combs. forming adjs., as *treble-barrelled*, *-breathed*, *-caped*, *-headed*, *-mailed*, *-piled*, *-rampired*, *-seated*, *-sinewed*; **treble-voiced**, having a treble or soprano voice.

1784 *New Spectator* No. 1. 4 The ladies have assumed the *treble-caped great coat and belt. 1805 *Med. Jrnl.* XIV. 92 How our *treble-headed Pithon is to be augmented and increased. 1876 GEO. ELIOT *Dan. Der.* xxxvi, Gnawed by a double, a treble-headed grief. 1611 COTGR., *Tremaillé*, *treble-mailed. 1821 SCOTT *Kenilw.* xxiv, Velvet, single, double, *treble-piled. 1649 G. DANIEL *Trinarch., Hen. IV*, cxvii, As the wings of long-lost Day Breakes *treble-Rampired Clouds. 1808 BENTHAM *Sc. Reform* 36 The permanent substitution of *treble-seated..to single-seated judicature. 1606 SHAKS. *Ant. & Cl.* III. xiii. 178, I will be *trebble-sinewed, hearted, breath'd. 1552 HULOET, *Treble voyced, or shyll tuned, *acutus, a, um*.

c. With sbs., forming adjectives or attributive phrases, as *treble-cylinder*, *treble-shovel*; **treble-bite, treble-wedge-fast**, systems of breech-action in hand-guns.

1892 GREENER *Breech-Loader* 22 With an efficient holding-down bolt, engaging with it as in the *treble-bite breech-action. 1877 KNIGHT *Dict. Mech.*, *Treble-cylinder Steam-engine*, an engine having a pair of large cylinders for the continuation of the expansion, one at each side of the small cylinder. *Ibid.*, *Treble-Shovel Plow*, one having three shares. A form of cultivator. 1881 GREENER *Gun* 174 Our patent *treble-wedge-fast action, with either hammerless or back-action locks and low hammers.

2. The adv. in comb. **a.** with pples., forming adjectives, as *treble-brandished*, *-damned*, *-refined*, *-ribbed*, *-riveted*, *-twisted*, etc.; **treble-dated**, living three times as long (as man); (in sense B. 2) *treble-skirling*. **b.** with vbs., as *treble-man*, *-shot*.

1877 TENNYSON *Harold* I. i, Yon grimly-glaring, *treble-brandish'd scourge. 1834 COLERIDGE *Lett., to J. Gillman* (1895) 730 If he be not a *treble-damned liar. 1601 SHAKS. *Phœnix & T.* 17 Thou *treble-dated crow,..'Mongst our mourners shalt thou go. 1805 PIKE *Sources Mississ.* (1810) 31 We were obliged to take on but one sled at a time and *treble man it. 1694 SALMON *Bate's Dispens.* II. vi. (1713) 604/2 With its equal Weight of *trebble-refined Sugar. 1896 *Daily News* 14 Nov. 6/6 Besides deed-boxes, there were other receptacles..some *treble-ribbed with iron or copper. 1662 GERBIER *Princ.* 18 Casements *treble riveted, to keep out Wind and Rain. 1874 THEARLE *Naval Archit.* 131 For treble-riveted butt straps, nineteen diameters in breadth are required by Lloyd's. 1884 H. COLLINGWOOD *Under Meteor Flag* 74 Request Mr. Flinn to *treble-shot his larboard broadside. 1811 W. TENNANT *Anster Concert* xiii, High o'er the tenor sounded shrill The *treble-skirling women. 1867 BAKER *Nile Tribut.* ii. (1872) 32 A powerful hook, fitted upon *treble-twisted wire.

Treble (tre·b'l), *v.* [f. prec. Cf. OF. *trebler* (13th c. in Godef.).]

1. *trans.* To make three times as many or as great; to increase threefold; to multiply by three.

a 1325 *MS. Rawl. B.* 520 lf. 32 Ʒif þe contreie..ne ansuuerez noȝt..þe peine sal ben itrebbled. c 1430 *Art of Nombryng* xi. (E.E.T.S.) 17 Thow most trebille the digit. 1596 SHAKS. *Merch. V.* III. ii. 302 Double sixe thousand, and then treble that. 1666 SANCROFT *Lex Ignea* 28 His Insolence doubles and trebles the Vexation. 1720 *Lond. Gaz.* No. 5833/2 Which trebles the Duty..payable by the Exporter. 1885 DUNCKLEY in *Manch. Exam.* 20 July 6/1 During the present century the population has just about trebled itself.

b. To fold in three thicknesses; to make in three layers.

1598 HAKLUYT *Voy.* I. 62 Caparisons for their horses made of leather artificially doubled or trebled vpon their bodies. 1638 SIR T. HERBERT *Trav.* (ed. 2) 316 A Cambolin of pure lawn..trebled on and about their naked shoulders.

c. To be three times as many or as much as.

1615 G. SANDYS *Trav.* 115 Madein, A coyne of siluer that trebles the Asper for value. 1842 BORROW *Bible in Spain* xxxiv. (Pelh. Libr.) 250 A body of the Carlists,..whose numbers more than trebled his own.

2. *intr.* (for *refl.*) To grow to three times the number, amount, or size; to become threefold.

1625 FLETCHER *Noble Gent.* II. i, Now I see your Fathers honours Trebling upon you. 1797–8 WELLINGTON in Owen *Desp.* (1877) 777 It has more than trebled since the peace of '83. 1815 SIMOND *Tour Gt. Brit.* I. 170 The rent of land has trebled in the last fifty years. 1882 PEBODY *Eng. Journalism* xix. 145 Mr. Levy reduced the price of the paper...The circulation doubled, trebled, quadrupled.

†**3.** *intr.* To emit a high-pitched or shrill sound; also, to sing the treble part to (const. *upon*) the lower parts or plain-song in a harmonized composition (in quots. *fig.*). *Obs.*

c 1425 *Cast. Persev.* 1900 in *Macro Plays* 134, I here trumpys trebelen al of tene. a 1591 H. SMITH *Wks.* (1866) I. 458 A nightingale..when she is in a pleasant vein, quavers and capers, and trebles upon it. 1606 S. GARDINER *Bk. Angling* 103 The singster of Israel hath..giuen vs the Notes wee must alwayes treble vppon.

†**b.** *trans.* To utter in a high-pitched or shrill tone. *Obs. rare*[−1].

1616 CHAPMAN *Homer's Hymn to Hermes* 645 He outrageously (when I accus'd him) trebled his reply.

Hence **Tre·bled** *ppl. a.*, made treble, threefold.

? c 1400 LYDG. *Æsop's Fab.* i. 23 With trebled [*v. r.* treble] laudis yeve to the trynité. 1653 R. SANDERS *Physiogn.*, *Moles*, etc. 38 Divide the trebled number into two. a 1711 KEN *Preparatives* Wks. 1721 IV. 43 While I by trebled Zeal and Tears Strive to retrieve my careless Years.

†**Tre·blefold**, *a.* and *adv.* *Obs.* [f. TREBLE + -FOLD.] **a.** *adj.* Three times as great or numerous; threefold. **b.** *adv.* Three times as much, thrice over.

1387–8 T. USK *Test. Love* I. iii. (Skeat) l. 152 Treble folde so mokell muste I suffer, ere tyme come of myne ease. 1561 T. HOBY tr. *Castiglione's Courtyer* I. (1577) C vij, They speake accompanying euery worde with certaine treblefolde sighes. 1587 Q. ELIZ. in H.-Campbell *Love Lett. Mary Q. Scots* App. (1824) 62 God reward thee trebblefold in the double for the most troublesome charge so well discharged.

Tre·bleness. *rare.* [f. TREBLE *a.* + -NESS.]

†**1.** Treble quality (of sounds); high pitch.

1626 BACON *Sylva* § 183 The Just and Measured Proportion of the Aire Percussed, towards the Basenesse or Treblenesse of Tones, is one of the greatest Secrets in the Contemplation of Sounds.

2. The quality of being threefold.

1888 in *Cassell's Encycl. Dict.*

†**Trebler**, a treble-singer: see TRIBLER.

Treblett, erron. form of TRIBLET.

Trebling (tre·bliŋ), *vbl. sb.* [f. TREBLE *v.* + -ING[1].] The action of the verb TREBLE.

1. Increasing threefold; multiplication by three.

1591 PERCIVALL *Sp. Dict.*, *Trasdobladura*, trebling, *triplicatio*. 1694 *Phil. Trans.* XVIII. 70 The doubling, trebling, quadrupling, &c. of Rations is performed by squaring, cubing, biquadrating, &c. of the terms.

2. *Naut.* See quots.

1856 KANE *Arct. Expl.* I. xxxi. 423 The outside trebling or oak sheathing. 1867 SMYTH *Sailor's Word-bk.*, *Trebling*, planking thrice around a whaler's bows in order the more effectually to withstand the pressure of the ice.

Trebly (tre·bli), *adv.* [f. TREBLE *a.* + -LY[2].]

1. In a threefold degree or manner; triply.

1590 SPENSER *F. Q.* I. xi. 22 Trebly augmented was his furious mood. 1629 WADSWORTH *Pilgr.* v. 47 She was left destitute, the..Iesuites being trebly paid. 1697 DRYDEN *Æneid* X. 1113 Linnen trebly rowl'd. 1814 SCOTT *Ld. of Isles* III. vii, Wicket and gate were trebly barr'd, By beam and bolt and chain. 1850 TENNYSON *In Mem.* cii. 16 This hath made them trebly dear.

†**2.** In a treble or high-pitched tone. *Obs. rare*[−1].

1679 in *Verney Mem.* (1907) II. 330 A Mercy, wᶜʰ makes mee merrily & Trebly sing, Gaudiamus and Haleluia.

Trebuchet (tre·büʃet, ‖trebüʃe). Forms: α. 4 **trepejette, trepget**, 4–5 **-eget**, 5 **trepgett(e, trip-, trypgette**, 6 **trepegett, -gete, trepa-**; β. 4–5 **tri-, tre-, treybochet**; 5 **trebget** (*err.* **-got**); 6 **trabu-**, 7 **trebuschet**, (8–9 **trebucket**), 8– **trebuchet**. [In I, a. OF. *trebuchet*, also *trebuket*, *-busket*, *trabuchet* (12th c. in Godef.) siege-engine, bird-trap, mod.F. *trébuchet* trap, balance (= Prov. *trabuquet*, Sp. *trabuquete*, It. *trabocchetto*, med.L. *trā-*, *trēbuchētum*, Du Cange), f. OF. *tre-*, *tres-*, *trabucher* (11th c.) to overturn, overthrow, stumble, fall, in med.L. *trābuchāre*: see TRABUCH. The early α-forms (trepedʒet, etc.) are imitations of OF. *trebuchet* (trebütʃe·t). The word was obsolete in the 16th c.; from 18th c. historical and antiquarian. Sense 3 is from mod.Fr. In II, an application, in England, of med.L. *trēbuchētum* (see above), to the device known popularly from c 1200 as *cuck-stool*, *cucking-stool*. The Latin form remained app. as a legal term, rendered *trebuchet* in 17th c. by the legal antiquaries. Cf. 1611 COTGR., *Trebuchet*, a pitfall for birds; a pit, with a trap doore, for wild beasts; also, a paire of gold weights; also, an old-fashioned Engine of wood, from which great, and battering stones were most violently throwne.]

I. 1. A mediæval military engine for casting heavy missiles. *Hist.*

Described as consisting of a pivoted lever with a sling at one extremity, which was strained back against a heavy counterpoise, and then suddenly released. Cf. CATAPULT 1.

[1224 *Close Roll* 8 *Hen. III*, m. 4 Facias usque Doura maeremium ad trubechetum nostrum faciendum. — 9 *Hen. III*, m. 24, viij. Roellas ereas quas fieri fecistis at trubechettum nostrum. 1377 *Rolls of Parlt.* III. 10/2 Un trebuchet outre ascun mesure qe l'en avoit unqes veeu.] α. 13.. *Coer de L.* 5227 With trepeiettes they slungen alsoo. 1388 WYCLIF 1 *Macc.* vi. 20 Thei maden arblastis, [*gloss*] ether trepeiettis, that is, an instrument for to caste schaftis, and stoonys. c 1400 [see MANGONEL]. c 1420 *Brut* 428 The Kynge..leid therto his grete Gounnys, Trepgettis and Engenys, and bete adowne the wallis. 1520 *Caxton's Chron. Eng.* VII. 145/1 Gonnes, Engynnes, and trypgettes [1482 trip-]. 1599 THYNNE *Animadv.* (1875) 41 'Trepegett' yoᵘ expounde 'a Ramme to batter walles'. But the trepegete was the same that the mogonell. [1896 *Eng. Hist. Rev.* Apr. 357 Eustace the monk was taken, and Stephen of Winchelsea..gave him his choice of having his head cut off on the trapget or the bulwarks [rather of being hurled from the trapget or having his head cut off on the bulwarks].] β. a 1400–50 *Alexander* 1296 With traumes & with tribochetis þe tild to asaile. c 1400 *Siege of Troy* 838 in *Archiv neu. Spr.* LXXII. 33 An hundrid gynnys þer were vpset, Of Maungeneles and Treybochet. c 1440 *Promp. Parv.* 501/1 Trebget, for werre (*S.* trepgette), *trabucetum*. 1795 SOUTHEY *Joan of Arc* VIII. 198 Who kneeling by the trebucbet, Charged its long sling with death. 1825 SCOTT *Betrothed* viii, 'Well driven, trebuchet—well flown, quarrel!' cried the monk. 1885 C. W. C. OMAN *Art of War* 57 The feeble siege-artillery of the day, perrieres, catapults, trebuchets, and so forth.

†**2.** A trap or gin to catch small birds or beasts. *Obs. rare.* (So in Fr. from 14th c.)

1362 LANGL. *P. Pl.* A. XII. 86 Þou tomblest wiþ a trepget ȝif þou my tras folwe. c 1440 *Promp. Parv.* 501/1 Trebget [*pr.* -got], sly instrument to take brydys or beestys (*S.* trepgette), *tendicule*.

3. A small delicately poised balance or pair of scales; an assay balance; a tilting scale. (So Fr.)

1550 *Reg. Mag. Sig. Scot.* 105/1 Par de lie trabuschettis 15 sol. 1613 BP. FORBES *Comm. Rev.* xviii. § 6. 191 It is a hard thing to fall into the hands of the Lord: before whom all Nations are but as the droppe of a Bucket, or as the dust of a Trebuschet. 1871 M. C. LEA *Photogr.* 420 The French pattern of 'trebuchet', or tilting scale, now largely manufactured here. 1877 KNIGHT *Dict. Mech.*, *Trebucket*.

II. 4. An instrument of punishment, = CUCKING-STOOL, q. v.

[c 1200 *Chron. of Jocelin de Brakelond* (Camden) 38 Levaverunt homines de Illegga quoddam trebuchet, ad faciendam justiciam pro falsis mensuris panis vel bladi mensurandi. ? 1266–7 *Judicium Pillorie* in *Stat. Realm* (1870) I. 201/1 Paciatur judicium corporis, scilicet, Pistor Collistrigium, et Braciatrix trebuchetum vel castigatorium. c 1440 *Promp. Parv.* 107/1 Cukstole, for flyterys,..*turbuscetum*, *cadurca*. 1500 *Ortus Vocab.*, *Terbichetum*, a cokstole.] c 1640 J. SMYTH *Hundred of Berkeley* (1885) 143 Cucking stool and other Judicials, Collistrigia et trebuchets. 1667 E. CHAMBERLAYNE *Pres. St. Eng.* I. (1684) 48 Scolding women are to be set in a Trebuchet, commonly called a Cuckingstool..placed over some deep water into which they are let down and plunged under water thrice. 1769 BLACKSTONE *Comm.* IV. xiii. 169 A common scold,..if convicted, shall be sentenced to be placed in a certain engine of correction called the trebucket, castigatory, or cucking stool. 1867 *Cornh. Mag.* Jan. 38 A homely provision made for the punishment of mere bad language in the bridle and trebuchet or ducking-stool.

†**Trebuke**, variant of TRABUCH.

c 1482 J. KAY tr. *Caoursin's Siege of Rhodes* (1870) P ii A man of Grece,..counseyled the Lord Mayster and the Rhodyans to make and ordeygne an engyne called Trebuke lyke a slynge, which was grete hye and myghty, and casted grete and many stones into the hoste of the Turkes.

†**Trebuler**, *a.* *Obs.* [f. *Trēbula*, name of a place: cf. *Trēbulāna vina* (Pliny).] ? Of Trebula.

1606 S. GARDINER *Bk. Angling* ix. 158 The trebuler sort [of vines] that are thrust to the wall, that neuer growe high, or ouerdreepe others little.

Trebuttar, obs. form of TRIBUTARY.

Treoche: see TRECHE *v.*

Trecher, -erie, -erous, -our, etc., obs. forms of TREACHER, -EROUS, -ERY, etc.

†**Trecentene**, *a.* *Obs. rare*[−0]. [f. L. *trecentēnī* three hundred each.] (See quotation.)

1656 BLOUNT *Glossogr.*, *Trecentene*, pertaining to three hundred.

‖**Trecento** (tre,tʃe·nto). [It., lit. 'three hundred', short for *mil trecento* 1300; cf. CINQUECENTO.] The fourteenth century (13..), as a period of Italian art, architecture, etc.; also *attrib.*

1841 W. SPALDING *Italy & It. Isl.* II. 215 The vigour and expressiveness of the *trecento*. 1873 'OUIDA' *Pascarèl* I. 9 The beautiful *trecento* windows were filled with eager faces. 1878 VILLARI *Machiavelli* (1898) I. III. viii. 149 The literature of the Trecento may be considered as exclusively Tuscan. 1899 *Westm. Gaz.* 17 Mar. 3/1 They treat..of the *trecento* painters, of Giovanni Bellini and the early Venetians.

Hence **Trece·ntist**, ‖**Trecenti·sta** (It., pl. -isti), an Italian artist, author, etc., of the 14th c.

1821 BYRON *Juan* III. lxxxvi, In Italy he'd ape the 'Trecentisti'. 1883 C. C. PERKINS *Ital. Sculpt.* Introd. 23 The character of his work is so different from that of any other Italian trecentist.

†**Treche, trich**, *v.* *Obs.* Also 3 **tricche**, 5 **trecche**. [a. OF. *trichier*, *trechier* (3rd s. pres. *triche*, *treche*), to deceive, cheat, in Picard *trikier*, *trike*), mod.F. *tricher*, Prov. *trichar*, *triquar*, It. *treccare*. Ulterior origin uncertain: supposed by Diez to be from a German dialect (cf. also Mackel *Germ. elemente in franz.* 104); but others think from a late L. **triccāre* for L. *trīcārī* to trifle, shuffle, play tricks, f. *trīcæ* trifles, quirks, wiles, tricks (see Storm in *Romania* V. 172).

For the family of words belonging to this vb. see TREACHER to TREACHERY, also TRICHARD, and (more remotely) TRICK and its derivatives.]

trans. To deceive, cheat, betray, play false with.

c 1230 *Hali Meid.* 9 Nu þu sest þat ha habbeð itricchet te as treitres. a 1327 *Pol. Songs* (Camden) 69 Richard, thah thou be ever trichard, trichen shalt thou never more. c 1425 *Cast. Persev.* 253 in *Macro Plays* 84 Þese iij are nobyl, trewly I trowe, Mankynde to tenyn, & trecchyn a tyde.

Treche, var. TRESCHE *Obs.* **Trecher, -ercus, -ery**, etc., obs. ff. TREACHER, -EROUS, -ERY.

†**Trechet**, *v.* *Obs. rare.* [deriv. of TRECHE *v.* perh. error for *trecher*).] *trans.* To deceive, cheat, play false with. Hence †**Trechetting** *vbl. sb.* (See also TREACHETOUR.)

c 1330 R. BRUNNE *Chron.* (1810) 313 Þe[i] sent ageyn & said to kyng, 'it was no haunte Of certeyn sette & laid, to trechet þer conaunte. *Ibid.* 164 Whan he with trechettyng bi nyght away so ran, Wenes he our men Inglisse for to tretcher [*MS.* trecther] so?

Trechmannite (tre·kmănəit). *Min.* [? f. surname *Trechmann* + -ITE[1].] A rare mineral occurring in red rhombohedral crystals in the dolomite of the Binnenthal. It is prob. a sulpharsenite of silver.

1909 in *Cent. Dict. Suppl.*

Trechometer (trekǫ·mĭtəɹ). [a. F. *trechomètre*, f. Gr. τρέχ-ειν to run: see -METER.] An instrument which records the distance run by a vehicle.

1858 SIMMONDS *Dict. Trade*, *Trechometer*, a French machine for reckoning distances, specially adapted for vehicles.

Trechor, -our, -ory, -ur, -ure, -ury: see TREACHER, TREACHERY. **Trechoure**, obs. f. TRESSURE. **Treck-** in *treckschuit*, etc.: see TREK-.

Trecker: see TRIGGER.

Trecther, scribal error for *tretcher* (cf. TREACHER): see TRECHET *v.* **Tred**, obs. f. TREAD.

Tredding: see TRADING *vbl. sb.* (quot. 1654).

Treddle (tre·d'l). Now *dial.* Forms: α. 1 **tyrdel**, 5 **-dyl**, 6 **-dell, -dle, tirdil, turdyll**, 6–7 **terdle**, 7 **tir-, turdle**; β. 5 **tredel(e, triddil, tridel, trydelle**, 7–9 **truddle**, 6– **treddle**; γ. 6 **treatle**. See also TRATTLE *sb.*[2] [ME. *tyrdyl*, etc. (whence by metathesis *tridil*, *treddle*), = OE. *tyrdel*, dim. of *tord*, TURD: see -EL *suffix*[1].]

A pellet of sheep's or goat's dung: usually in *pl.*

α. c 1000 *Sax. Leechd.* II. 72 ȝenim gate tyrdlu. *Ibid.* 214 Haran tyrdlu. c 1440 *Promp. Parv.* 494/2 Tyrdyl, schepys donge. 1530 PALSGR. 281/2 Tyrdell. *Ibid.* 284/1 Turdyll shepes donge, *fient de brebis*. 1552 HULOET, Tyrdles of gootes or shepe, *rudus*, *eris*. 1563 HYLL *Art Garden.* (1593) 107 If you take the seeds of euery colour of Gilliflours and put them altogither into a thin small reed, or terdle of a sheep or goat. 1647 HEXHAM I, Sheeps dung or tirdles. 1671 SKINNER *Etymol. Ling. Angl.*, The Treddles *vel* Truddles, q. d. Turdles. β. c 1410 *Master of Game* xi. (1904) 40 Men clepen þe steppes or þe marckes of þe Otere..and his fumes tredeles or spraintes. 14.. *MS. Lincoln Med.* lf. 291 (Halliw.) The triddils of an hare. 1483 *Cath. Angl.* 393/2 A Trydelle, *ruder*. 1577 B. GOOGE *Heresbach's Husb.* II. (1586) 55 b, Taking a Treddle of Sheepe, or Goates doung. 1601 HOLLAND *Pliny* XIX. xii. II. 33 The round treddles of a Goat. 1736 W. ELLIS *New Exper. Husb.* 25 Price for the neat Treddle, clear of all Hay, Straw, Flaff, or other Mixture. 1905 in *Eng. Dial. Dict.* from Lincoln, Herts, Kent, Surrey.

Treddle, variant of TREADLE.

Treddling (tre·dliŋ), *sb. dial.* In 5 **tirdelyng**; 9 also (*pl.*) **trid(d)lings, treddlins**. [f. TREDDLE + -ING[1].] Treddles of sheep, etc. in the mass.

c 1440 LYDG. *Hors, Shepe & G.* 381 Of the sheepe..To the lond gret profite doth his tirdelyng [*v. r.* tyrtelyng]. 1828 *Craven Gloss.*, *Tridlins*, excrement of sheep. 1869 *Lonsdale Gloss.*, Treddlin's, Triddlin's. 1876 *Whitby Gloss.*, Triddlings.

†**Tre·decile**, *a.* or *sb.* *Astrol.* *Obs.* Also -il. [ad. mod.L. *tredecil-is*, f. L. *trēs* three + *dec-em* ten; cf. *quartile*, *sextile*.] Denoting an aspect, introduced by Kepler, in which the planets are $\frac{3}{10}$ of a circle, i.e. 108°, apart. Cf. DECILE.

1647 LILLY *Chr. Astrol.* iii. 32 Of late one Kepler, a learned man, hath added some new ones as follow..A Tredecile..consisting of 108 degrees. 1674 JEAKE *Arith.* (1696) 11 Aspects...Sesquiquintil or Tredecil. 1727–41 CHAMBERS *Cycl.*, *Aspect*, To the five ancient aspects, the modern writers have added several more; as decile,..tredecile,..[etc.]. 1819 J. WILSON *Compl. Dict. Astrol.* 101 The new aspects invented by Kepler are mostly produced by subdividing the others..The Tredecile, of 108°, is a quintile and half, or three deciles..Those arising from a division of the Δ or ✱ by 5 were [thought by Kepler to be] good; thus..the tredecile, being a quintile and a half, is good.

†**Tre·decuple**, *a.* *Obs. rare.* [f. L. *tredecim* thirteen, after *decuple*.] Thirteen times as great.

1570 BILLINGSLEY *Euclid* XVI. xxix. 453 To proue that an octohedron geuen, is tredecuple sesquialter to a trilater equilater pyramis inscribed in it.

Tredel, obs. form of TREADLE, TREDDLE.

Tredge, obs. form of TRUDGE.

Tredrille, tredille (tredri·l, -di·l). Also 8 **tresdille**, 9 **tradrille**. [f. QUADRILLE by substitution of *tre-* three for *qua(d-)*.] A card-game played by three persons, usually with thirty cards.

1764 H. WALPOLE *Let. to Earl Hertford* 8 June, Lady Albemarle was at tredille. 1767 LADY MARY COKE *Jrnl.* 2 May, The Duchess, Lady Blunt and I play'd at tresdille. 1769 *Ibid.* 15 June, I play'd at tredrille..with Madame de Viry and a French Officer for a shilling a fish. 1816 SINGER *Hist. Cards* 266 *Tredrille*, a modification of Quadrille which might be played by three persons..It was considered as very inferior to the game Quadrille played by four. 1821 LAMB *Elia* Ser. I. *Mrs. Battle's Opinions on Whist*, To explain to me how far it [ombre] agreed with, and in what points it would be found to differ from, tradrille. 1825 MRS. SHERWOOD *Bitter Sweet* II. 5 A hand at tredille or three-handed whist. 1860 T. L. PEACOCK *Gryll Gr.* xxiii, Quadrille is played with forty cards: tredrille usually with thirty: sometimes, as in Pope's Ombre, with twenty seven.

Tree (trī), *sb.* Forms: see below. [OE. *trēow*, *trīow*, OE., ME. *trēo*, etc. = OFris. *trē* (NFris. *trē*, *trê*), OS. *trio*, *treo*, *trew-* (MDu. in comb. *-tere*, *-tære*, Kilian); ON. *tré* (Da. *træ*, Sw. *trä* timber, *träd* tree); Goth. *triu*, gen. *triw-is* wood (wanting in OHG. and now also obsolete in LG. and Du.):—OTeut. **trewo-*, cognate with Skr. *dru* tree, wood, *dāru* wood, log, and with Gr. δρῦς oak, δόρυ spear; OSlav. *drievo* (from *dervo*) tree, wood, *drūva* pl. wood, Russ. *de·revo*, *drevo* tree, wood, Serv. *drvo* tree, *drva* wood, Czech *drva*, Pol. *drwa* wood; Lith. *dervà* pine-wood; also with OIr. *daur*, Welsh *derwen* oak. The modern Eng. *tree* is a regular repr. of OE. *trēo*, ME. *treo*; *trē* is the form in the Bestiary of c 1220; but the final prevalence of this over the other ME. forms *treow*, *trew*, *trow*, *trau*, was prob. assisted by its coincidence with Norse *tré*; *trē*, *tree* are the northern forms from *Cursor Mundi* onward. For form-history cf. KNEE.]

A. Illustration of Forms and Inflexions.

1. *Sing. nom.* 1 **triow**, (*late*) **tryw**, 1–2 **treow, treu**, (1) 3 **trew**, (1)–4 **treo**, 3–6 **tre**, 3– **tree**; 4 (*Kent.* **trau, tra(u)w**); **trough**; 5 *Sc.* **trey**, 6–7 **trie**. *dat.* 1 **treowe, trēo**, 2 **treuwe, trewe**, 4 **trow(e, trauwe**. [The development of OE. nom. acc. sing. was OTeut. **trewo*", **rewa*, *trew*, *trēu*, *trēo*, then with *w* from oblique cases (*trewes*, *treowes*, etc.), *trēow*, (*triow*).]

c 890 tr. *Bæda's Hist.* II. xi. [xiv.] (1890) 138 He..of treo [*v. r.* treowe] cirican ȝetimbrode. c 897 K. ÆLFRED *Gregory's Past. C.* xlv. 338 Ælc triow [*v. r.* treow] man sceal ceorfan. c 1000 *Ags. Gosp.* Matt. iii. 10 Ælc treow [*MS. B.* tryw, *Lind.* treu] þe godne wæstm ne bringð. c 1200 *Vices & Virt.* 27 Ðe treu of paradise. c 1200 *Trin. Coll. Hom.* 107 Of coren of eorðe, and of treuwe. c 1220 *Bestiary* 674 Ðus fel adam ðurȝ a tre, Vre firste fader, ðat fele we. c 1250 *Gen. & Ex.* 3301 A funden trew ðor-inne dede Moyses. a 1300 *Cursor M.* 657 (Cott.) Þis tree ys done in my friþe. 1340 *Ayenb.* 28 Ne in gerse, ne in busse, ne in trauwe. *Ibid.* 95 Þet trau of lyue. *Ibid.* 202 Þys traw wext and profiteþ. 13.. *K. Alis.* 6829 Alle tho That scholde with him to the trough go. 1393 LANGL. *P. Pl.* C. XXI. 200 Yf þei touchede þe treo and of þe frut eten. c 1530 R. HILLES *Common-Pl. Bk.* (1858) 140 Sone crokyth the tre that crokyed wyll be. 1535 STEWART *Cron. Scot.* (Rolls) II. 687 With the speir that wes of suir trie, He hit the king richt in at the e. 1573 TUSSER *Husb.* (1878) 109 Let Iuie be killed, Else trée will be spilled. a 1584 MONTGOMERIE *Ch. & Slae* 341 The trie sa hich of growth.

2. *Pl. nom.* α. 1 **trēo, treow, triowu, treowu, -a**, 1–2 **treowe**; 2 **trowen**, 2–4 **treon**, 3–6 **trēn**, 4 (**troen**), **trene**, 4–7 (–9 *dial.*) **treen**, 5 **trenne**, 5–6 **treene**. β. 2 **treos**, 2–3 (*Orm.*) **trewwes**, 2, 4 **trewes**, 2–5 **tres**, 3 **troues**, 3–4 **trouwes**, 3–5 **treus**, 4 **trews, trowes, traues, trawes**, 4–6 **treis**, 5 **trese**, 6 **treys**, *Sc.* **treyis**, 6–7 **tries**, 4– **trees**. [The development of OE. nom. acc. pl. was WGer. *trewu*, *trēu*, *trēo*; then again with *w* (from oblique cases), *trēow*, *treowu* (*-a*). The pl. *trēo* occurs in Vesp. Ps. and Lind. Gosp.]

c 825 *Vesp. Ps.* cxlviii. 9 Treo westemberu and alle cederbeamas. c 890 tr. *Bæda's Hist.* I. i. (1890) 26 Hit is weliȝ þis ealond on wæstmum & on treowum. c 897 K. ÆLFRED *Gregory's Past. C.* xl. 292 Sumu treowu he watrade. a 1000 *Epist. Alex. ad Aristot.* in Cockayne *Narrat.* 27 Eac þær wæron obre treow. *Ibid.* 28 Ða halgan triow-swiðe wepen. c 1000 ÆLFRIC *Hom.* II. 588 Deorwurðe stanas, oþþe treowa. c 1175 *Lamb. Hom.* 5 Heo stiȝen uppe on þe godes cunnes treowe. *Ibid.* 41 He him sceawede heȝe treon. c 1200 ORMIN Introd. 13 Full gode treos inoȝhe. *Ibid.* 15468 Off gresess, & off tres. c 1200 *Trin. Coll. Hom.* 25 Gres and trowen. *Ibid.* 37 Hwile uppen trewes. c 1250 *Gen. & Ex.* 3305 Then [*i. e.* ten] and sexti palme tren. c 1275 LAY. 511 Alle hi solde hongie vppe heȝe troues. a 1300 *Cursor M.* 545 (Cott.) It grouues tres [*Fairf.* trees] and gress. 13.. *Ibid.* 651 (Gött.) Of treis ..here es gode wone. ? a 1300 *XI Pains of Hell* 33 Per beoþ bernynde treon. a 1325 *MS. Rawl. B.* 520 lf. 32 b, Þis statut ne portenez noȝt to grete hokes ne to oþere grete troen. a 1325 *Prose Psalter* xcv[i]. 12 Þan shul alle þe trews of þe wodes gladen. 13.. *K. Alis.* 6763 Þou shalt fynde trowes two. 1340 *Ayenb.* 25 Þe greatte traues. *Ibid.* 95 Uol of guode trawes. 1387 TREVISA *Higden* (Rolls) III. 445 Where þou knowe nouȝt þe treen [*v.r.* tren]. a 1400 *Pistill of Susan* 90 Turtils troned on trene. c 1400 Trees [see B. 1]. c 1400 *Ywaine & Gaw.* 2965 He loked in bitwix the trese. 1422 tr. *Secreta Secret., Priv. Priv.* 239 With lewys of trenne. *Ibid.* 243 The humours of tren and herbis. c 1430 LYDG. *Min. Poems* (Percy Soc.) 17 Twoo grene treene there grewe uprighte. a 1450 MYRC *Festial* i. 3 Treus and herbys. 1562–3 in Willis & Clark *Cambridge* (1886) II. 568, x greate tries at xxviijᵈ the trie. 1563 *Mirr. Mag. Induct.* 2 With blustring blastes had al ybared the treen. 1565 *Satir. Poems Reform.* i. 45 Wynter windes..that doth I-bayre the tren. 1570 *Ibid.* xv. 50 All greinis and plesand treis [*rime* eyis]. 1596 DALRYMPLE tr. *Leslie's Hist. Scot.* VII. (S.T.S.) II. 17 Aple tries, and orchardis. 1600 FAIRFAX *Tasso* III. lxxv, The shadie tops of shaking treene. 1635, 1771, 1861 Trees [see B. 1]. 1843 E. JONES *Poems, Sens. & Event* 38 Vast interbranching treen.

B. Signification.

1. A perennial plant having a self-supporting woody main stem or *trunk* (which usually develops woody branches at some distance from the ground), and growing to a considerable height and size. (Usually distinguished from a *bush* or *shrub* by size and manner of growth; but cf. b.)

c 825, c 890, c 897 [see A. 2]. c 1000 ÆLFRIC *Gen.* iii. 6 Þæt treow wæs god to etanne. c 1175 *Lamb. Hom.* 109 Iliche þan treo þe bereð lef and blosman. c 1290 *St. Brendan* 41 in *S. Eng. Leg.* I. 221 Of treon and herbes, þikke i-noVȝ. 1377 LANGL. *P. Pl.* B. XV. 327 A forest..ful of faire trees. 1398 TREVISA *Barth. De P. R.* XVII. i. (Tollem. MS.), A tre haþ..þe rynde, bowes, twigges, leues, blosmes, floures and frute. c 1400 *Destr. Troy* 12467 Trees thurgh tempestes tynde hade þere leues. 1481 CAXTON *Reynard* xii. (Arb.) 28 He brake a rodde of a tree. c 1530 R. HILLES *Common-Pl. Bk.* (1858) 140 Hyt ys a febyll tre thet fallyth at the fyrst strok. 1600 FAIRFAX *Tasso* VII. i, Through forrests thicke among the shadie treene. 1635 LAUD *Diary* 1 Dec., Many elm leaves yet upon the trees. 1771 *Junius Lett.* lvii. (1820) 298 He or his deputy were authorised to cut down..trees. 1861 BENTLEY *Man. Bot.* 540 Cunoniaceæ..Nearly allied to Saxifragaceæ, but differing from them in being trees or shrubs.

b. Extended to include bushes or shrubs of erect growth and having a single stem; and even some perennial herbaceous plants which grow to a great height, as the banana and plantain.

c 1340– [see ROSE-TREE]. c 1532 [see GOOSEBERRY 7]. 1640 [see PLANTAIN[3] 4]. 1649 [see CURRANT 4]. 1697 [see BANANA 1]. 1765 [see RASPBERRY 4]. 1855 BROWNING *Women & Roses* i, I dream of a red-rose tree. 1858 HOGG *Veg. Kingd.* 790 As a food, the Plantain is wholesome and agreeable. A tree generally contains three or four clusters.

c. Applied *fig.* or allusively to a person.

1594 SHAKS. *Rich. III*, III. vii. 167 The Royall Tree hath left vs Royall Fruit. 1807 WORDSW. *Force of Prayer* xiii, He was a tree that stood alone, And proudly did its branches wave.

2. The substance of the trunk and boughs of a tree; wood (esp. as a material of which things are made); timber. *Obs.* or *arch.*

To go between the bark and the tree: see BARK *sb.*[1] 6.

c 890 tr. *Bæda's Hist.* II. xi. [xiv.] (1890) 138 He þær hrædeȝeweorce of treo cirican ȝetimbrode. c 1122 *O. E. Chron.* an. 626 (Laud MS.) Þær he ær het ȝetimbrian cyrican of treowe. c 1290 *S. Eng. Leg.* I. 91/154 In one cheste of treo. ? c 1366 in Arnolde *Chron.* (1811) 138 Affixed wᵗ nayles of irne or of tree. c 1440 *Partonope* 407 A brygge of stone and not of tree. c 1500 *Whole Prophecie of Scotland* 1603 (in Murray *Thomas of Erceldoune* Introd. p. xxxv), At Aberladie he shall light With hempen halters and hors of tree. 1531 ELYOT *Gov.* III. xvii, Eatyng his meate in a dissh of tree. 1638 JUNIUS *Paint. Ancients* 124 A horse made of maple tree. 1896 KIPLING *Seven Seas, Sea-Wife* iv, To ride the horse of tree [a ship].

3. A piece of wood; a stem or branch of a tree, or a portion of one, either in its natural state, or more usually (now always) shaped for some purpose. **a.** A pole, post, stake, beam, wooden bar, etc.; *esp.* (now only) one forming part of some structure, as a vehicle, plough, ship, etc.; usually as the second element in combinations, as AXLE-TREE, CHESS-TREE, CROSS-TREE, DOOR-TREE, DRAUGHT-TREE, ROOF-TREE, SWINGLE-TREE, etc.

971 *Blickl. Hom.* 187 Ond þa æfter þon het Neron ȝewyrcean myceIne tor of treowum & of myclum beamum. c 1200 ORMIN 15835 Þatt temmple þatt wass wrohht Off trewwess & off staness. a 1300 *Cursor M.* 12399 (Cott.) Þe knaue þat þis timber fett..ouer scort he broght a tre. 1375 BARBOUR *Bruce* XIII. 238 Schetis..Thai festnyt in steid of baneris Apon lang treis and on speris. 1523 FITZHERB. *Husb.* § 3 The ploughe-beame is the longe tree aboue. *Ibid.* § 4 The sharbeame is the tree vnderneth, wherevpon the share is set. 1642 in J. Watson *Jedburgh Abbey* (1894) 85 Thrie scoir singill tries, threttie double tries, two hundred daills to be scaffolding and centries. 1787 *MS. Deed*, Such trees and pipes as are now laid for conveying water from the said spring. 1848 KINGSLEY *Night Bird* 4 All night I heard a singing bird Upon the topmast tree. 1887 *Suppl. to Jamieson* s.v., A straight piece of rough timber used as a pole, lever, prop, or stay, is called a *tree*; as, a dyer's-*tree*, a raising-*tree* or lever for moving a mill-stone.

b. A stick, *esp.* a staff, cudgel: cf. PLANT *sb.*[1] 1 b. *Obs.* exc. *Sc.*

c 893 K. ÆLFRED *Oros.* IV. i. § 6 Hie namon treowu, & slogon on oþerne ende monige scearpe isene næglas. c 1205 LAY. 25978 His fur he beten agon & muchele treowen leide on. a 1225 *Ancr. R.* 402 'Louerd', cweð heo to Elie, 'lo! ich geder two treon'. 14.. *Emaré* 365 She was wax lene as a tre. c 1470 HENRY *Wallace* II. 97 A huntyn staff in till his hand he bar; Thar with he smat on Willgham Wallace thair. Bot for his tre litill songhe he maid. 1588 *Reg. Privy Council Scot.* Ser. I. IV. 270 The said Robert Lekky..maliciouslie straik and dang thame with rungis and treis. c 1680 *Songs of Scotl.* (1893) 43, I am a puir silly auld man, And hirplin' ower a tree. 17.. *Gude Wallace* x. in Aytoun *Ballads Scot.* (1858) I. 56 He's gane to the West-muir wood, And there he pull'd a trusty tree.

4. a. The cross on which Christ was crucified, the holy rood. *arch.* and *poet.*

a 1000 *Rood* 25 (Gr.) Hwæðre ic..beheold hreowceariȝ hælendes treow. c 1275 *On Serving Christ* 30 in *O. E. Misc.* 91 As he for monkunnes neodes don wes on þe treo. 1382 WYCLIF *Acts* v. 30 The God of oure fadris reyside Jhesu, whom ȝe slowen, hangynge in a tree [TINDALE, and hanged on tree]. — 1 *Pet.* ii. 24 He..suffride, [*gloss*] or bar, oure synnes in his body on the tree. 1460 CAPGRAVE *Chron.* (Rolls) 106 A nayle, with whech oure Lord was nayled to the tre. 1596 R. COTTON *Armor of Proofe* xiv, Christ,.. who did our sinnes and foes to tree fast binde. 1635 PAGITT *Christianogr.* III. (1636) 52 Helena the Empresse found the Crosse, and adored the King, but not the Tree. 1707 WATTS *Hymn*, '*Alas! and did my Saviour bleed?*' iii, Was it for crimes that I had done He groan'd upon the tree? 1820 T. KELLY *Hymn*, '*We sing the praise of Him who died*' ii, He bears our sins upon the tree.

b. A gallows. Also †*dry tree*, *Tyburn tree*.

c 1425 *Cast. Persev.* 177 in *Macro Plays* 82 Pyncecras, Parys, & longe Pygmayne, And euery toun in Trage, euyn to þe dreye tre. 1500–20 DUNBAR *Poems* xvii. 28 Sum..nevir fra taking can hald thair hand, Quhill he be tit vp to ane tre. a 1533 LD. BERNERS *Huon* xviii. 49 Not lettynge for fere of any deth, though it be to go to the dry tre. 1535 COVERDALE *Esther* vi. 4 To hange Mardocheus on ye tre yᵗ he had prepared for him. 1609 B. JONSON *Masque of Queens* ad init., From the dungeon, from the tree That they die on, here are we [witches]! a 1704 T. BROWN *Satire on Quack* Wks. 1730 I. 62 Though it was thy luck to cheat the fatal tree. 1818 SCOTT *Hrt. Midl.* iv, The area of the Grassmarket.. in the centre of which arose the fatal tree, tall, black, and ominous, from which dangled the deadly halter. 1847 KINGSLEY *Outlaw* x, And when I'm taen and hangit,.. ye'll steal me frae the tree.

5. The wooden shaft of a spear, handle of an implement, etc.; hence, a spear, lance (in phr. *to break a tree*). Now *dial.*

? a 1366 CHAUCER *Rom. Rose* 948 Ten brode arowis hilde he there,..But iren was ther noon ne stelle, For al was golde, ..Outake the fetheres & the tree. c 1400 *Laud Troy Bk.* 12607 He was wounded with a spere..Hede & tre lefft bothe In him. a 1600 MONTGOMERIE *Misc. Poems* xlix. 24 We dout not bot they [thy knights] dar..be bold to brek a tre. 1611 COTGR., *Abrier d'Arbeleste*, the tree of a Crossebow. 1765 *Museum Rust.* III. 240 The person should have a spade.. about four inches broad, and eighteen inches long in the bit, ..with a tree in it of three feet six inches long. 1881 *Leicester Gloss.*, *Tree*, a wooden handle or stail.

†**b.** A wooden structure; applied *poet.* or *rhet.* to a ship; in quot. 1513 to the wooden horse at the siege of Troy. *Obs.*

1382 WYCLIF *Wisd.* xiv. 1 Another thenkende to seilen,.. the tree berende hym. 1513 DOUGLAS *Æneis* II. i. 60 In this tree ar Grekis closit. 1535 COVERDALE *Wisd.* x. 4 Whan yᵉ water destroyed yᵉ whole worlde, wysdome preserued the righteous thorow a poore tre. 1594 MARLOWE & NASHE *Dido* IV. iv, Here's Aeneas' tackling, oars, and sails...Oh, cursed tree, hadst thou but wit or sense, To measure how I prize Aeneas' love.

c. A wooden vessel; barrel, cask, 'the wood'. *Sc.*

1513 *Acc. Ld. High Treas. Scot.* IV. 487 Item to bir in aile, full to seywart xxiiij last and a barrell,..ilk barrell contenand xij gallonis, price of the galloune xx d; summa of the last with the tree..xiij li. viij s. 1532 *Ibid.* VI. 156, xij ½ barrellis of aill, ilk barrell contenand v gallonis...Item, for xij treis to put the samyn intill, for ilk tree xviij d. 1656 TUCKER *Rep. Revenues Scot.* (Bann. Cl.) 10 The Scots use noe certaine vessells, but such as by a generall terme they call Trees,..some holding more or lesse gallons the tree. a 1814 RAMSAY *Scotl. & Scotsmen in 18th C.* viii. (1888) II. 78 The scourging a nine-gallon tree..consisted in drawing the spigot of a barrel of ale, and never quitting it..till it was drunk out.

d. The framework of a saddle: = SADDLE-TREE, q. v. for earlier quots.

1535 STEWART *Cron. Scot.* (Rolls) III. 300 Ane hors he fand..Without saidill, curpall, tre, or brydill. 1592 GREENE *Art Conny Catch.* II. (1592) 5 His saddle is made without any tree. 1665 SIR T. HERBERT *Trav.* (1677) 314 Saddles of the better sort are usually of Velvet;..the trees are curiously painted. 1737 BRACKEN *Farriery Impr.* (1756) I. 328 If the Saddle be too narrow in the Tree. 1862 *Catal. Internat. Exhib., Brit.* II. No. 4721 Elliptical spring-seat saddle, and tree showing action of spring.

e. A block upon which a boot is shaped or stretched: = *boot-tree* (BOOT *sb.*[3] 8).

1541 *Knaresborough Wills* (Surtees) I. 35, ij paire of boytte treys. 1596 NASHE *Saffron Walden* 17 Rayse thy conceipt on the trees, or..new corke it at the heeles, before it should thus walke bare-foote. 1766 [see *boot-tree*, BOOT *sb.*[3] 8]. 1839 THACKERAY *Fatal Boots* Nov., As I was polishing on the trees a pair of boots. 1891 KIPLING *Light that Failed* viii, As Dick..busied himself among the former's boots and trees.

6. Something resembling a tree with its branches.

a. A diagram or table of a family, indicating its original ancestor as the root, and the various branches of descendants; in full, *family* or *genealogical tree*. Also *fig.* a family, race, stock. (*b*) *Porphyrian tree* (*Logic*): see PORPHYRIAN.

1297 R. GLOUC. (Rolls) 7255 Þo smot uerst þis tre aȝen to is kunde more [*i. e.* natural root]. a 1300 *Cursor M.* 1625 (Cott.) Bot first a tre,..I sal sette hire [*v.r.* here] of adam kin. 1693 STEPNEY in *Dryden's Juvenal* viii. 11 Vain are their Hopes, who fancy to inherit By Trees of Pedigrees, or Fame, or Merit. 1762–71 H. WALPOLE *Vertue's Anecd. Paint.* (1786) V. 305 Two genealogic trees. 1825 T. HOOK *Sayings* Ser. II. *Doubts & F.* v, A more honourable tree does not flourish in the archives of heraldry than ours. 1858 M. ARNOLD *Merope* 865 So dies the last shoot of our royal tree!

b. Any structure or figure, natural or artificial, of branched form.

spec. (*a*) (tr. *arbor* in med.L. phrases). An arborescent mass of crystals forming from a solution, as of silver (DIANA'S *tree*), of lead (SATURN'S *tree*), etc. (*b*) Applied to the spinal nervous system, consisting of the spinal cord and the nerves branching out from it. (*c*) A branched respiratory organ in Holothurians. (*d*) A worked design of tree-like form. (*e*) *Math.* A figure or diagram consisting of branching lines.

1706– [see DIANA 2]. 1843 R. J. GRAVES *Syst. Clin. Med.* xxx. 396 A certain portion of the extreme branches of the nervous tree. 1844 Lead-tree [see LEAD *sb.*[1] 12]. 1857 CAYLEY *Math. Papers* (1890) III. 242 On the Theory of the analytical Forms called Trees. 1865–8 WATTS *Dict. Chem.* III. 478 By the electro-chemical action of zinc in a solution of acetate of lead, it is deposited in an arborescent form, known under the name of *Saturn's Tree*. 1870 ROLLESTON *Anim. Life* Introd. 145 In the Holothurioidea these coeca take a great development, and are known as the 'lungs' or 'respiratory trees'. *Ibid.* 149 The left respiratory tree. 1879 *Unif. Reg.* in *Navy List* July (1882) 497/1 Tree of trimming braid at top of back.

7. Phrases. *At the top of the tree*, in the highest position: see TOP *sb.*[1] 14. *Up a tree* (*colloq.*, orig. *U.S.*), debarred from escape, like a hunted animal driven to take refuge in a tree; entrapped; in an awkward position, in a difficulty or 'fix'. *One cannot see the wood for the trees*: see WOOD *sb.*

1774 FOOTE *Cozeners* I. (1778) 16 Master Moses is an absolute Proteus; in every elegance, at the top of the tree. 1782– [see TOP *sb.*[1] 14]. 1825 J. NEAL *Bro. Jonathan* II. 103 If I didn't—I'm up a tree—that's a fact. 1839 THACKERAY *Major Gahagan* v, I had her in my power—up a tree, as the Americans say. 1857 HUGHES *Tom Brown* I. vii, 'What a pull', said he, 'that it's lie-in-bed, for I shall be as lame as a tree, I think'.

b. Phrases with *of*. *Tree of Buddha*, or *of wisdom* = BO-TREE. *Tree of chastity* = AGNUS CASTUS (*Treas. Bot.*); also called *chaste-tree* (CHASTE *a.* 9). *Tree of Diana*: see DIANA 2, and cf. 6 b (*a*) above. *Tree of heaven* = AILANTO. *Tree of Jesse*: see JESSE. *Tree of knowledge*, (*a*) loosely used as = next; (*b*) a figurative or symbolic expression for knowledge in general, comprising all its 'branches'. *Tree of the knowledge of good and evil*: see Gen. ii. 9, etc. *Tree of liberty*, a tree (or a pole) planted in celebration of a revolution or victory securing liberty (chiefly in reference to the French Revolution); also *fig.* *Tree of life*, (*a*) a tree symbolic of life or immortality, esp. that in the narrative of the garden of Eden (Gen. ii. 9, etc.); also *fig.*; (*b*) a shrub of the genus *Thuya*; = ARBOR VITÆ 1; (*c*) *Anat.* = ARBOR VITÆ 2. *Tree of mercy*, in mediæval legend, the allegorical tree which yielded the oil of mercy, and was at length to bear Christ for the healing of mankind. *Tree of Paradise*, the plantain (*Musa paradisiaca*). *Tree of Porphyry* (*Logic*): = PORPHYRIAN *tree*. *Tree of the universe*, the mythical ash-tree or *Yggdrasil* of Scandinavian mythology. *Tree of wisdom* = *tree of Buddha*.

c 1820 *Philos. Recreat.* 131 A curious Chemical Experiment, called the Tree of *Diana. *Note*, This is the modern silver tree. 1849 [see DIANA 2]. 1845 Tree of *heaven [see AILANTO]. 1898 *Daily News* 31 May 5/3 Some handsome specimens of tropical trees—the tree of heaven and the tulip tree. 1535 COVERDALE *Gen.* ii. 9 The tre of life in the myddest of the garden, and the tre of *knowlege of good and euell. 1848 LOWELL *Fable for Critics* 766 Their backs he salutes With the whole tree of knowledge torn up by the roots. 1765 *Universal Mag.* XXXVII. 376/2 (*Amer.*) Known by the name of the Tree of *Liberty ever since the memorable 14th of August. 1837 CARLYLE *Fr. Rev.* II. I. xii, A Tree of Liberty sixty feet high; and Phrygian Cap on it, of size enormous. 1890 LECKY *Hist. Eng.* xxvii. VII. 207 Trees of liberty had been planted in Antrim, and bonfires lit in consequence of French victories. 1382 WYCLIF *Gen.* ii. 9 The tree of *lijf in the mydle of paradys. 1599 DAVIES *Immort. Soul* XXXI. vii. (1714) 109 But Truth, which is eternal, feeds the Mind: The Tree of Life, which will not let her die. 1712 J. PETIVER in *Phil. Trans.* XXVII. 423 American Tree of Life. 1760 J. LEE *Introd. Bot.* App. 317 Tree of Life, *Thuya*. 1913 R. C. MACLAGAN *Our Ancestors* viii. 121 There was another locality for the Tree of Life. c 1375 *Canticum de Creatione* 620 in Horstmann *Altengl. Leg.* (1878) 132 And to þe tre of *mercy blyf Where out renneþ oyle of lyf His angel wil doun sende. *Ibid.* 695 To haue mercy on Adam,..And hem senden his angel fro hy To ȝeuen hem of þe tre of mercy Oyle, to helen him wyth. 1567 MAPLET *Gr. Forest* 63 The tree of *Paradise saith Cardane, is of short life, for the second yeare his bodie drieth vp and waxeth barraine: It beareth fruit like a cluster of Grapes, but in bignesse of an Apple. 1910 *Encycl. Brit.* IV. 739/1 The sacred Bo tree or tree of *wisdom.

8. *attrib.* or as *adj.* (in sense 2). Made or formed of 'tree', wooden: = TREEN *a.* 1. *Obs.* exc. *dial.*

c 1375 *Cursor M.* 12389 (Fairf.) Tree [*v.rr.* treen, trein] beddis coude he make. *Ibid.* 21048 Of tree wandis golde he wroȝt. 1402–3 *Durham Acc. Rolls* (Surtees) 217, j stane-trogh et j tre trogh. 1480 CAXTON *Chron. Eng.* IV. (1520) 37/1 In olde tyme the consecracyon..was made in tree vessell. 1587–8 *Burgh Rec. Edinb.* (1882) IV. 515 To caus mak ane pair of trey buits. 1599 *Lanc. Wills* (Chetham Soc.) III. 10 All other tree vessell whatsoever. 1640 R. BAILLIE *Canterb. Self-Convict.* 77 Their very tree-shoone. 1750 in *Cloud of Witnesses* (1778) App. 361 A cripple with a tree leg. 1881 *Leicester Gloss.* s.v., A 'tree leg' is a wooden leg.

9. *attrib.* and *Comb.* **a.** General attrib. (= 'of a tree or trees'), as *tree-avenue*, *-bark*, *-belt*, *-bole*, *-bough*, *-branch*, *-foliage*, *-foot*, *-fruit*, *-group*, *-life*, *-lore*, *-nursery*, *-root*, *-seed*, *-shadow*, *-soul*, *-stem*, *-stump*, *-trunk*, *-twig*, etc. **b.** Objective and obj. gen., as *tree-enchanter*, *-fancier*, *-feller*, *-lopper*, *-planter*; *tree-boring*, *-chopping*, *-climbing*, *-daubing*, *-felling*, *-growing*, *-haunting*, *-inhabiting*, *-lopping*, *-loving*, *-planting*, *-smearing* sbs. and adjs. **c.** Instrumental, as *tree-bordered*, *-clad*, *-covered*, *-crowned*, *-dotted*, *-fringed*, *-garnished*, *-girt*, *-lined*, *-planted*, *-set*, *-shaded*, *-skirted*, etc. adjs. **d.** Locative, as *tree-dweller*; *tree-dwelling*, *-feeding*, *-living*. **e.** Similative, etc., as *tree-great*, *-like* adjs.

1910 HADDON *Races of Man* 74 Men still wear the *tree-bark loincloth and the women a tree-bark wrapper. 1836–48 B. D. WALSH *Aristoph., Clouds* I. iv, Fly to the tops of the *tree-clad mountains! 1894 *Pop. Sci. Monthly* June 69 Such is the name of the *tree-dweller. 1908 SIR H. JOHNSTON *Grenfell & Congo* II. xxi. 507 These *tree-dwelling Pygmies. 1865 KINGSLEY *Herew.* xxx, Swaffham, Quy, and Waterbeach, and the rest of the *tree-embowered hamlets which fringed the fen. 1788 COWPER *Mrs. Throckmorton's Bullfinch* xi, The *tree-enchanter Orpheus. 1853 *Zoologist* II. 4035 Instances of *tree-feeding species. 1849 J. FORBES *Physic. Holiday* i, They..indulge in farming, gardening, *tree-felling. 1855 KINGSLEY *Heroes* III. (1868) 32 Round the *tree-foot was coiled the dragon. 1704 J. PITTS *Acc. Mohammetans* 66 They have but little *Tree-Fruit. 1601 WEEVER *Mirr. Mart.* E vij, *Tree-garnisht Cambriaes loftie mountaines. 1812 W. TENNANT *Anster F.* II. xxxiv, All the *tree-girt country-seats. 1904 SPENCER & GILLEN *North. Tribes Central Australia* xvii. 527 A visit to the *tree grave. 1600 FAIRFAX *Tasso* XI. xxxvii, With dreadfull hornes of iron tought *tree-great. 1871 DARWIN *Desc. Man* II. xvi. (1890) 489 *Tree-haunting birds. 1898 *Saga-Bk. Viking Club* Jan. 122 The *tree-life of Western Greenland. 1630 R. *Johnson's Kingd. & Commw.* 7 The hollow trunks of most *tree-like canes being full of water. 1776 WITHERING *Brit. Plants* (1796) II. 316 Stem tree-like. 1844 MRS. BROWNING *Lost Bower* iii, A little wood..As it climbeth..Sideway from the *tree-locked valley. 1589 FLEMING *Virg. Bucol. & Georg.* 3 The *treelopper..Shall chaunt and sing. 1885–94 R. BRIDGES *Eros & Psyche*, *Aug.* xiv, The great hill-haunting and *tree-loving Pan. 1905 A. R. WALLACE *Life* II. 153 The gardens, the greenhouses, the *tree-nursery. 1864 H. WOODWARD in *Intell. Observer* V. 181 Piece of a Vase ornamented with a *tree pattern. 1825 COBBETT *Rur. Rides* (1885) II. 227 Experienced *tree-planters. c 1440 *Alphabet of Tales* 488 He sett hym down at a *tre-rute in þe son to comfurth hym. 1870 MORRIS *Earthly Par.* III. IV. 385 Like to a *tree-set garden. 1854 H. MILLER *Sch. & Schm.* xxiii. (1858) 499 A *tree-skirted glade. 1871 KINGSLEY *At Last* xi, We were aware, between the tree-stems, of a green misty gulf. 1857 T. MOORE *Handbk. Brit. Ferns* (ed. 3) 56 A decaying mossy *tree-stump. 1894 H. NISBET *Bush Girl's Rom.* 200 There..sat the chief ..with his back against a *tree-trunk. 1914 MUNRO *Prehist. Britain* viii. 185 Only two or three..tree-trunk coffins have been found in Britain.

10. Special Combs. **a.** in names of plants, usually denoting species or varieties that grow to the stature or in the form of a tree, sometimes those that grow on trees; as *tree amaranthus*, *cabbage*, *carnation*, CELANDINE, *crane's-bill*, *fuchsia*, HOUSELEEK, MALLOW, *melon*, MIGNONETTE, ONION, *pea*, PEONY, POPPY, PRIMROSE, *rhododendron*, TOMATO, VIOLET, WILLOW, WORMWOOD; **tree aloe**, *Aloë dichotoma*; **tree azalea**, *Azalea* (*Rhododendron*) *arborescens*; **tree-beard**, (*a*) *Tillandsia usneoides*; (*b*) the lichen *Usnea barbata*; **tree cactus**, a tall-growing cactus, as the saguaro; **tree clover**, *Melilotus alba*; **tree cotton**, *Gossypium arboreum*; **tree cranberry** = CRANBERRY-*tree*; **tree germander**, *Teucrium fruticans* (Miller *Plant-n.*); **tree golden-rod** = GOLDEN-ROD *tree*; **tree-hair**: see quots.; **tree heath**, *Erica arborea*; **tree lily**, (*a*) a plant of the genus *Vellozia* (N.O. *Amaryllidaceæ*), comprising arborescent species found in Brazil and S. Africa, with lily-like flowers; (*b*) a name for the genus *Dracæna* (N.O. *Liliaceæ*); **tree lotus**, the nettle-tree, *Celtis australis*; = LOTE-TREE a; **tree lungwort**, (*a*) a lichen, *Sticta pulmonaria*, = LUNGWORT 5; (*b*) a boraginaceous plant, *Mertensia virginica* (cf. LUNGWORT 3 b); **tree lupine**, *Lupinus arboreus* of California; **tree medick**: see quot.; **tree nettle** = NETTLE-TREE 2; **tree onion**: see ONION 2; **tree orchid**, **orchis**, an orchid growing on trees, as those of the genus *Epidendrum*; **tree poke**, *Phytolacca dioica*; **tree purslane** = PURSLANE-*tree* (*b*); **tree sorrel**, *Rumex Lunaria*; **tree-tobacco**: see quot. (See also TREE-CREEPER 2, -FERN, -MOSS, -TREFOIL.)

1786 ABERCROMBIE *Gard. Assist.* 115 India pink, mignonette,..*tree-amaranthus. 1884 MILLER *Plant-n.*, *Azalea arborescens*, Smooth Azalea, *Tree Azalea. 1861 BENTLEY *Man. Bot.* 675 *Tillandsia usneoides* is commonly called *Tree-beard or Old Man's Beard, from the..mass of dark coloured fibres, which hang from the trees in South America. 1829 *Glover's Hist. Derby* I. 199 The ten-thousand-headed cabbage, or *tree cabbage. 1884 *De Candolle's Orig. Cultiv. Plants* 406 Upper Egypt,..where we know the *tree-cotton to be wild. 1868 B. J. LOSSING *Hudson* 35 Here and there among the rocks..the *tree-cranberry appeared. 1712 J. PETIVER in *Phil. Trans.* XXVII. 420 Hermans round-leaved Cape *Tree Cranes-bill. 1597 GERARDE *Herbal* II. cciii. 532 Of *Tree Germander. 1866 *Treas. Bot.* 1161 *Tree-hair*, a name sometimes given to the dark wiry pendulous entangled masses of a lichen, *Cornicularia jubata*,..not uncommon on trees in sub-alpine woods. *Ibid.* 1197 The species [of *Usnea*]..are often called Tree Moss or Tree Hair. 1777 HUNTER in *Phil. Trans.* LXVIII. 40 The *erica ar-*

herbs or 'Tree-heath, a native of Spain and Portugal. **1907** *Gentl. Mag.* July 36/2 The big tree-heaths begin about 2500 ft.

b. in names of animals living in or on or frequenting trees, as *tree-ant*, *-bee*, *-beetle*, *-boa*, *-chafer*, *-cuckoo*, *-falcon*, *-kangaroo*, *-leech*, *-linnet* (Sc. *-lintie*), *-martin*, *-partridge*, *-pipit*, *-shrike*, *-slug*, *-squirrel*, *-swallow*, *-swift*, *-warp*, *-wren*; *-asp*, a venomous species of the genus *Dendraspis*; *tree-boar* (*U.S. local*), a name for the raccoon; *tree-bug*, any one of various hemipterous insects which feed upon the juices of trees and shrubs; *tree-butterfly*, a butterfly that lives among trees, as those of the S. African genus *Charaxes*; ...

wax, any kind of wax produced from a tree, as Chinese wax, Japan wax; tree-wool, a woolly substance obtained from a tree, as pine-wool (PINE *sb.*[2] 7); †tree-worship (*obs.*), work in wood, carpentry; as †tree-workers, a carpenter; tree-worship, worship rendered to trees or to the spirits supposed to inhabit them; so tree-worshipper, tree-worshipping.

Tree, v. [f. prec. sb.]

†1. *intr.* To grow into a tree, attain the size of a tree. *Obs. rare*[-1].

b. *intr.* To take a tree-like or branching form, as a deposit from a solution under the influence of an electric current.

2. *trans.* To drive into or up a tree; to cause to take refuge in a tree, as a hunted animal, or a man pursued by a wild beast.

Treeful (trī'ful), *sb. rare.* [f. TREE *sb.* + -FUL 2.] A quantity or number that fills or crowds a tree.

Treeful (trī'ful), *a. rare.* [f. TREE *sb.* + -FUL 1.] Full of trees; abounding in trees.

Tree-goose, *sb.* exc. *Hist.* A name for the barnacle-goose, formerly believed to be produced from the fruit of the barnacle (cirriped).

Treehood (trī'hud), *sb. rare.* [f. TREE *sb.* + -HOOD.] The state of a (full-grown) tree.

Treeify (trī'ifai), *v. nonce-wd.* [f. as prec. + -FY.] *trans.* To make or change into a tree.

Treeless (trī'les), *a.* [f. TREE *sb.* + -LESS.] Destitute of trees; containing no trees.

Tree-angle, *obs.* form of TRIANGLE.

Tree-creeper.
A name for various birds which creep on the trunks and branches of trees; *esp.* the common European *Certhia familiaris*, or other species of the family *Certhiidæ*; also, a bird of the South American family *Dendrocolaptidæ*. Cf. CREEPER 3.

Treenail, trenail (trī'nēl, tren'l), *sb. rare.* [f. TREE *sb.* + NAIL *sb.*] Forms: 3-4 trenayle, 6 treenaile, 7 tree nail, trenel, 8 treenail, 9 trennel, trunnel, (7-8 trundle), 9 trennail. Also 3-6 NAIL *sb.*

A pin or peg of hard wood used in fastening timbers together, *esp.* in shipbuilding and other work where the materials are exposed to the action of water.

Treen, treene, *obs.* or *dial.* *pl.* of TREE.

tree trefoil. The shrub *Medicago arborea*, also called tree-medick (TREE *sb.* 10 a); the *κύτισος*, *cytisus* of the ancients.

Treeward (trī'wəd), *a. nonce-wd.* [f. TREE *sb.* + -WARD.] Toward a tree or trees. So **Treewards** *adv.*

Tree-worm, *sb.* [f. TREE *sb.* + WORM *sb.*] The teredo or ship-worm.

†2. A set or rosette of three leaves; the first three leaves of a young plant. *Obs. rare*[-1].

3. An ornamental figure representing or resembling a trifoliate leaf; *spec.* in *Arch.* an ornament with an opening divided by cusps so as to present or suggest the figure of a three-lobed leaf. (Cf. QUATREFOIL, QUATREFOIL.)

Tregar, *sb.* *Obs.* Also *Sc.* 4 tryget, 6 tragete, trigit, (†tregget). [a. ? contr. (11th c. in Godef.) *tresget* (15th c. *traget*) enchantment, magic, vb. *tresgeter* = TRANSJECTOR.] Juggling, trickery, deceit.

Tregetour (tredʒ'itər), *sb.* *Obs.* Also a trogetour, 4-6 tregetoure, 5 tregytoure, -itour, -atour, 6 tregettour. [a. OF. *tregetour*, *tresgeteour*, agent-n. of *tresgeter*: see above.]

Treget (tredʒ'et), *sb.* *Obs.* Also *Sc.* 4 tryget, 6 traget, (†tregget). Juggling, trickery.

Trellis (trel'is), *sb.* S. Afr. (1900) (1907) [The elephants] turned their faces to the northward, and trekked steadily along ...

Trellis (trel'is), *sb.* Forms: 4-6 trelis, -ys, -yse, 4-6 trellice, -ys, 6-7 trelles, treillis, 6 treleis, treillisse, trellesse, 7 trellice, 7-9 trellice, 8 trellis. *Pl.* trellises. Also -ice, -es. ...

+*līcium* a thread of the warp; said of strong woven fabrics (cf. TREILLIS). OF. had also a rarer form *treslis*, showing an early confusion of the prefix with OF. *tres-* :—L. *trans-*: so Pr. *treslitz*, It. *traliccio*, med.L. *trans-*, *trās-*, *trālicium*, a stout woven fabric. The application of the word to things woven of iron wire, gold, withes, etc. app. brought the sense into contact with OF. *treille*, Pr. *treilla*, *trelha*, med.L. *trelia*, *trillia*, etc. (see TRAIL *sb.*[2]), and resulted in the later F. form *treillis* and the later signification 'lattice, grille'. Some of the 16th c. Scottish forms are difficult to distinguish from the pl. of *treilʒe*, TRAILYE.]

1. A structure of light bars of wood or metal crossing each other at intervals and fastened where they cross, with open square spaces between; used as a screen in window openings or the like; a window, gate, screen, etc. so constructed; a lattice; a grating. Now *rare*.

a 1400-50 Treles [implied in TRELLIS *v.* 1]. 1422 Trelys [see *trellis-window* in 3]. *c* 1440 *Promp. Parv.* 501/2 Trelys, of a wyndow, or oþer lyke (or grate..), *cancellus*. 1450-1 *Durham Acc. Rolls* (Surtees) 240 Et in ij Trelis emp. pro fenestra cove, vij d. 1498-9 *Ibid.* 101 Pro iij fenistris voc. trelez pro Scaccario Cellerarii et le Sethynghous. 1513-14 *Ibid.* 663 Pro ij trelesez ad ustrinum, vj d. 1531-2 *Durham Househ. Bk.* (Surtees) 74 Et Roberto Kyrver pro factura le treylsys 8 d. 1532-3 *Ibid.* 163 Pro factura le treyllesys. 1535 COVERDALE *Judg.* v. 28 His mother..cried piteously thorow the trallace. — *Prov.* vii. 6 Out of the wyndowe of my house I loked thorow the trelies. 1549 *Aberdeen Regr.* (1844) I. 271 Conuikit..for the strublance of Duncane Freser and ryving of his tirleise of his vyndok. 1553-4 *Burgh Rec. Edinb.* (1871) II. 285 Payit for ane tyrleis of irne to the portell of the counsal hous dure. 1582-8 *Hist. James VI* (1825) 46 Upoun the wyndo thairof, he..cuttit a small hole of the blak cloth that coverit the traleis. 1634 SIR T. HERBERT *Trav.* 49 The Windowes [at Gombroon]..in stead of Glasse vse wooden trellizes or casements. 1641 R. BAILLIE *Lett.* (Bann. Cl.) I. 316 (*Trial of Strafford*) At the back of the throne, there was two roomes on the two sydes; in the one did Duke de Vanden..and other French nobles sitt; in the other, the King, the Queen [etc.]; the tirlies, that made them to be secret, the King brake doun with his own hands; so they satt in the eye of all. 1768 STERNE *Sent. Journ.* (1775) II. 86 (*Passport, Hotel Paris*) The bird..attempting his deliverance, and thrusting his head through the trellis, pressed his breast against it, as if impatient. 1886 SHELDON *Flaubert's Salammbô* 21 Darting..glances through the golden trellisses into the silent apartments.

†**b.** An enclosure of lattice-work, a grating.

c 1500 *Melusine* lii. 329 Whan they that were in the traylles of yron herd it. 1555-6 *Burgh Rec. Edinb.* (1871) II. 364 Item, coft vij jestis to be ane tirleis to the deid banis at the south kirk dur. *Ibid.*, Item to Hennislie to cast the deid banis in the west tirleis iij s. 1593 *Rites of Durham* (Surtees 1903) 37 Yᵉ highte of yᵉ said trellesse was striken full of iron pikes..to thentent yᵗ none should clyme ouer it.

c. Short for *trellis-door* or *-gate*: see 3. *Sc.*

?*c* 1800 *State, Fraser of Fraserfield* 194 (Jam.) At or near the westmost pole—there is a tirlass, at which a single person may enter.

d. *Her.* The figure of a trellis used as a charge. *In trellis*, with the pieces of which the charge is composed crossing and nailed at the joints, not interlacing.

1823 SCOTT *Quentin D.* xxiii, Sable, a musion passant Or, oppressed with a trellis gules, cloué of the second. 1882 CUSSANS *Her.* vii. (ed. 3) 120 Portcullis: An iron gate formed of bars armed at the base, and bolted in trellis. 1889 [see TRELLISED 2 b].

2. A similar framework used as a support upon which fruit-trees or climbing plants are trained.

1513 DOUGLAS *Æneis* XII. Prol. 100 The wyne grapis ȝing Endlang the treilȝeis [ed. 1553 trailzeys] dyd on twystis hing. 1725 *Bradley's Fam. Dict.* s.v. *Pomegranate*, He must..take Care to plash all the Branches..against a Trellis made on purpose. 1766 *Compl. Farmer* s.v., Some persons ..erect trellises against their walls, extending from the inside of one pier to the nearest inside of the next. 1818 SHELLEY *Let. to Mrs. Shelley* 20 Aug., The vines are..trailed on low trellisses of reeds. 1850 *Beck's Florist* Feb. 59, I always fix the trellis on the pot at the time of potting.

fig. 1861 S. WILBERFORCE *Let.* in *Life* (1881) II. xiii. 454 The earthly love becomes the trellice, up which the heavenly love creeps. 1894 H. DRUMMOND *Ascent Man* 193 Language formed the trellis on which Mind climbed upward.

3. *attrib.* and *Comb.*, as *trellis-border*, *-door*, *-frame*, *-gate*, *-grating*, *-hut*, *-lace*, *-pattern*; *trellis-covered*, *-shaded*, *-woven* adjs.; **trellis-window**, a window furnished with a trellis; see also quot. 1913. See also TRELLIS-WORK.

1897 *Daily News* 12 Apr. 7/7 A pair of beakers, with baskets and sprays of flowers in *trellis borders. 1867 LADY HERBERT *Cradle L.* i. 14 The ladies..were conducted by black eunuchs through *trellis-covered walks. 1756 MRS. CALDERWOOD in *Coltness Collect.* (Maitl. Cl.) 219 They's chapells!..and a fine dressed-up Virgin in every one of them, and a *tirless door to let her be seen! 1897 R. N. BAIN tr. *Jókai's Pretty Michal* xxxii. 251 At the stroke of two, she was already in the shop below, the trellis-door of which, leading to the street, was closed. 1766 *Compl. Farmer* s.v. *Trellis*, For peach, nectarine, and apricot trees..the squares of the *trellis frame should not exceed three or four inches. 1697 in *Mem. Alloa* (1874) 66 To put on a *tirlace gate, with lock and key thereto. 1825 JAMIESON (1882), *Tirless-yett*, a turnstile. 1876 B. CHAMPNEYS in Willis & Clark *Cambridge* (1886) III. 238 *Trellis gratings fitted with adjustable valves. 1825 HONE *Every-day Bk.* I. 289 This saint lived in a *trellis hut. 1874 H. H. COLE *Catal. Ind. Art S. Kens. Mus.* 173 Bracelet. *Trellis pattern of plain and green glass beads. 1422 *Searchers Verdicts* in *Surtees Misc.* (1888) 16 The *trelys wyndowe at the somer hall. *a* 1651 CALDERWOOD *Hist. Kirk* (1843) II. 11 So Bothwellhauche shott at him with a hacquebutt, through a tirleis window. 1913 EDEN *Anc. Glass* 51 The branches of the tree or vine seemed to run in and out of a trellis, a circumstance which has given name to such windows—trellis windows. 1751 G. WEST *Education* xvii, Labyrinths involv'd and *trellice-woven bow'rs.

Trellis (tre·lis), *v.* Forms: see prec. [Almost always in pa. pple. *trellised* (tre·list), f. prec. + -ED. Cf. F. *treillisé* (14th c. in Godef. *Compl.*).]

1. *trans.* To furnish with a trellis or with lattice-work; to enclose in a trellis or grating.

a 1400-50 *Alexander* 3343 Þe thrid [step] of a Topas a-tyred & trelest & grauen. *c* 1470 HENRY *Wallace* XI. 197 A fell lyoun..With in a barrace,..Terlyst in yrn. 1593 *Rites of Durham* (Surtees 1903) 37 Aboue yᵉ said dor, it was likewaies trellesed almoste to yᵉ hight of yᵉ valt aboue. 1634 SIR T. HERBERT *Trav.* 61 Windowes trellized very curiously. 1816 GALT *Life B. West* 92 Near a pile of ruins fringed and trellised with ivy. 1883 'VERNON LEE' in *Mag. Art* Nov. 3/1 Two villages, with..paved lanes trellised with grapes. *fig.* 1873 E. BRENNAN *Witch of Nemi* etc. 224 Some love that trelliseth the heart.

2. *intr.* To make a trellis. *rare.*

c 1520 *Mem. Ripon* (Surtees) III. 202 Will'mo Caruer trelyssyng et carvyng per j diem, 6*d*.

3. *trans.* To train (a plant) upon a trellis; to support on or as on a trellis. Also *fig.*

1818 SHELLEY *Jrnl.* 26 Mar., The vines..are trellissed upon ..stakes. 1849 RUSKIN *Sev. Lamps* iv. § 34. 125 The living flowers..which..the French and Italian peasantry often trellis with exquisite taste about their casements. 1873 E. BRENNAN *Witch of Nemi* 5 A virgin round the summers of whose years Love trellissed joys to warp consuming fears.

Trellised (tre·list), *ppl. a.* [f. TRELLIS *sb.*[2] or *v.* + -ED.]

1. Furnished with a trellis or trellis-work; formed of trellis-work; trained upon a trellis.

1472 *Durham Acc. Rolls* (Surtees) 94 Pro iiij Trillest-wyndous empt. pro coquina. 1513 DOUGLAS *Æneis* III. iii. 10 The full mone..In throw the tirlist wyndo schane by nycht. 1656 BLOUNT *Glossogr.*, *Trellised*, crosse-barred, latticed, grated, with wood. 1814 SOUTHEY *Roderick* XVI. 28 Their trelliced vines. 1844 LEVER *T. Burke* xxvii, The trellised walls covered with honeysuckles and wild roses. 1889 S. LANGDON *Appeal to Serpent* ii. 42 Assisting the tendrils of a beautiful passion-flower to grasp the next highest bar of a trellised arch.

2. Shaped or arranged like a trellis; having a pattern or markings resembling a trellis.

1664 POWER *Exp. Philos.* I. 5 The Common Fly..The like foraminulous perforations or trelliced eyes are in all Flyes. 1822 J. PARKINSON *Outl. Oryctol.* 40 Ramifications..disposed in a trellised form. 1828 TYTLER *Hist. Scot.* (1864) I. 320 [The armour of David earl of Huntingdon] is of the species called by the contemporary Norman writers the 'trellissed', and consists of a cloth coat, or vest,..intersected by broad straps of leather, laid on so as to cross each other, but to leave intervening squares of the cloth, in the middle of which is a round knob or stud of steel. 1835-6 *Todd's Cycl. Anat.* I. 712/1 These striæ, ridges and furrows, may cross one another, and the shell is then trellised. *a* 1873 LYTTON *Ken. Chillingly* II. ix, Its..trellised [wall-]paper.

b. *Her.* = LATTICED 2 c.

1889 ELVIN *Dict. Her.*, *Treille* or *Trillise*, a Lattice, or Trellis, a pattern resembling fretty, but always nailed at each intersection; also termed Trellised cloué. 1894 in *Parker's Gloss. Her.* 586.

Trellising (tre·lisiŋ), *vbl. sb.* [f. TRELLIS *v.* + -ING[1].]

1. The action of TRELLIS *v.*; the making of, or furnishing with, a trellis.

1474-5 *Durham Acc. Rolls* (Surtees) 95 Operantibus circa le trilessyng et facturam..fenestrarum.

2. *concr.* Trellis-work, a trellis.

1860 *All Year Round* No. 41. 341 A gallery, latticed like a dairy window, behind which birdcage trellising women were admitted. 1913 MRS. WHARTON *Custom of Country* I. ix, Under the leafless trellising of a wistaria arbour.

Tre·llis-work. [f. TRELLIS *sb.*[2] + WORK *sb.*] Wood or metal work consisting of light cross-bars; = TRELLIS *sb.*[2] 1. Also, anything resembling this in structure or pattern. Also *attrib.*

1712 J. JAMES tr. *Le Blond's Gardening* 74 Cabinets of Trellis-work altogether plain. 1739 GRAY *Let. to West* 21 Nov., Trellis-works covered with vines. 1814 WORDSW. *White Doe* IV. 49 Shades Of trellis-work in long arcades. 1822-34 *Good's Study Med.* (ed. 4) IV. 99 The corpus spongiosum as well as the corpora cavernosa [of the penis] are divided into cells or trellis-work by an infinite number of fine membranous plates. 1878 STUBBS *Const. Hist.* III. xviii. 214 The two kings met, with a grating of trellis-work between them, on the bridge of Pecquigny. 1898 *Westm. Gaz.* 10 Mar. 3/2 A very charming blouse..is that with a trellis-work. 1898 *Daily News* 5 Sept. 5/1 The tomb..was whitewashed all over and surrounded by a trelliswork fence. 1908 [MISS FOWLER] *Betw. Trent & Ancholme* 10 A Clematis Montana, surrounding the trellis-work frame.

Trematode (tre·mătōᵘd), *a.* and *sb.* *Zool.* [ad. mod.L. *Trēmatōda* neut. pl., a. Gr. τρηματώδης having holes, perforated, f. τρῆμα hole, orifice.]

A. *adj.* Belonging to the class or order *Trematoda* or *Trematoidea* of parasitic worms, found in the bodies of various animals, having a flattish or cylindrical form, with skin often perforated by pores, and usually furnished with adhesive suckers; the flukes (FLUKE *sb.*[1] 2) are typical examples.

In Cuvier's classification the *Trematoda* constituted the second family of parenchymatous entozoa, containing besides the flukes some animals not now reckoned as trematodes.

1836-9 *Todd's Cycl. Anat.* II. 121/1 The Trematode Order ..includes only two species infesting the human body. 1864 *Reader* 3 Dec. 712/1 He had discovered upon the angel-fish (*Squatina angelus*) a trematode worm of very singular organization, which will constitute a new genus. 1867 J. HOGG *Microsc.* II. iii. 567 One of the most remarkable of the Trematode helminths is Bilharzia haematobia of Cobbold. 1876 *Beneden's Anim. Parasites* Introd., Cestode and trematode worms.

B. *sb.* A trematode worm.

1876 tr. *Wagner's Gen. Pathol.* 120 Trematodes are parasitic solitary flat-worms with inarticulate leaf-shaped bodies. 1904 *Brit. Med. Jrnl.* 17 Sept. 663 Sections of a minute adult trematode. 1905 *Q. Rev.* Apr. 488 The pearls in our fresh water mussel were formed by the larvae of a fluke (a trematode).

So **Tre·matoid** *a.* and *sb.*

1882 OGILVIE (Annandale), Trematode, Trematoid, *a.* 1891 *Cent. Dict.*, Trematoid, *a.* and *n.*

†**Tre·mblable,** *a.* *Obs. rare.* [f. TREMBLE *v.* + -ABLE; cf. OF. *tremblable* (Godef.).] Fitted to cause trembling or fear; **a.** Demanding reverential fear; **b.** Causing dread or horror; dreadful.

1560 DAUS tr. *Sleidane's Comm.* 318 That the Canon of the Masse..be spoken softlye, to the intente those tremblable misteries maye retaine theyr auncient dignities. 1609 G. BENSON *Serm.*, etc. 72 Which is tremblable and monstrous, there be some, who, when God smites them, they fly vnto a witch or an Inchauntresse, and call for succour. 1651 R. WITTIE tr. *Primrose's Pop. Err.* II. vi. 93 In this Country the Consumption is an evill so ordinary and tremblable.

Tremble (tre·mb'l), *sb.* Forms: see the verb. [f. TREMBLE *v.*]

1. An act or the action of trembling; a fit or state of trembling; a tremor; a vibration.

1609 BIBLE (Douay) 2 *Esdras* xv. 37 They shal shake..and tremble shal take them. 1677 *Phil. Trans.* XII. 836 (According to him) Sound may be caused by the tremble of solid bodies without the presence of gross Air. 1719, 1760-72 [see b]. 1775 ASH, *Tremble* (s. *colloquial*, from the verb), a tremor. 1848 DICKENS *Dombey* xxvii, A terrible tremble crept over her whole frame. 1884 T. WOOLNER *Silenus* I. II. 21 Sitting beside the reeds He saw a tremble shivering thro' their leaves. 1894 'IAN MACLAREN' *Bonnie Brier Bush, Cunning Sp. Drumtochty* (1895) 185 He micht gie a bit trimmil.

b. In colloq. phrases (*all*) *in*, *all of a tremble*, *on* or *upon the tremble*, trembling, esp. with agitation or excitement.

1719 MISS HOWE in *Lett. C'tess Suffolk* (1824) I. 39 Mama has invited me to stay here,..which put me in such a tremble that I am hardly recovered. 1760-72 H. BROOKE *Fool of Qual.* (1809) II. 151, I am already all of a tremble. 1800 LAMB *Let. to Manning*, I am still on the tremble, for I do not know where we could go. 1818 COLERIDGE in *Lit. Rem.* (1836) I. 206 Why should I be in such a tremble all the while he talked? 1830 *Chron.* in *Ann. Reg.* 35/2 He seemed all of a totter and tremble.

c. Tremulousness or unsteadiness (of the voice) caused by emotion.

1779 *Mirror* No. 54 ¶ 13 There is a melting tremble in her voice, which..is inimitably beautiful and affecting. 1848 DICKENS *Dombey* xxxiii, A deep impassioned earnestness.. that made the very tremble in her voice a part of her firmness.

2. *pl.* *The trembles*: Any disease or condition characterized by an involuntary shaking, as ague or palsy (esp. in sheep); the tremor due to mercurialism, delirium tremens, etc.; the 'shakes'; in N. Amer., milk-sickness (MILK *sb.* 10).

1812 J. WALKER *Ess. Nat. Hist.* 525 Ovis in pascuis montosis morbo obnoxia est, hactenus insanabili,..the Trembles. 1848 A. S. TAYLOR *Poisons* xxxiii. 561 The disease produced by the use of the flesh or milk of animals fed in these districts, is known under the name of milk-sickness, or *trembles*. 1860 MAYNE *Expos. Lex.*, *Trembles*, a popular term for the disorder mercurial tremor. 1864 HAWTHORNE *S. Felton* (1883) 321 A hardness of hearing, and a dimness of sight, and the trembles. 1865 DICKENS *Mut. Fr.* IV. viii, What are popularly called 'the trembles' being in full force upon him. 1887 *Buck's Handbk. Med. Sc.* V. 9/1 The flesh of an animal suffering from trembles..would also produce the disease [milk-sickness].

3. The American aspen, *Populus tremuloides*.

1749 in *Rep. Comm. Ho. Comm.* II. 246/2 (Hudson's Bay Co.) The Beavers chiefest Food is, the Poplar or Tremble. 1770 J. R. FORSTER tr. *Kalm's Trav. N. Amer.* (1772) II. 356 They likewise make use of those which grow on the asp-tree or tremble.

†**Tremble,** *a.* *Obs. rare*[−1]. [ad. L. *tremulus*, after next.] Trembling.

1568 TURNER *Herbal* III. 81 To be geuen..vnto them that haue the palsey, or any num or tremble member.

Tremble (tre·mb'l), *v.* Forms: α. 4-5 tremle, -el, -yl, (4 trenle, *Sc.* tremal), 5 -ylle, -ul, trymmel, 5-6 *Sc.* tri-, trymle, 6 *Sc.* trimm-, trymm-, -le, -yll, etc., trumle, 9 *Sc.* trimmil; β. 4-6 trem-, (trim-, trym-), -bel, -byl, etc., (6 trumbill), 4- tremble. [a. F. *trembler* (11th c. in Godef. *Compl.*):—pop. and med.L. *tremulāre* (Du Cange), by which the early *tremel*, *-le*, *-yl* form may have been influenced, f. L. *tremul-us* tremulous, f. *tremĕre* to tremble, quake, shake. Cf Prov. *tremblar*, Sp. *temblar*, It. *tremolare*.]

1. *intr.* Of persons (less commonly of animals), or of the body or a limb: To shake involuntarily as with fear or other emotion, cold, or weakness; to quake, quiver, shiver.

1303 R. BRUNNE *Handl. Synne* 9390 Hys herte began to tremle and colde. 13.. *St. Cristofer* 629 in Horstm.

Altengl. Leg. (1881) 461 For ferde he tremlide ylka bone. *c* 1375 *Sc. Leg. Saints* xvi. (*Magdalena*) 877 He tremaland, as he mocht. *Ibid.* xxxiii. (*George*) 257 Fast tremeland. 1412-20 LYDG. *Chron. Troy* III. 5425, I..þat..Fele myn hond boþe tremble and quake. 1413 *Pilgr. Sowle* (Caxton 1483) I. xv. 11, I tremble as doth a leef vpon a tree. *c* 1475 *Rauf Coilȝear* 458 Trewlie that tenefull [a tiger] was trimland than. 1514 BARCLAY *Cyt. & Uplondyshm.* (Percy Soc.) 6 We tremble naked, and dye almost for colde. 1598 SYLVESTER *Du Bartas* II. i. III. *Furies* 204 At every word they trimbled then for aw. *a* 1668 DAVENANT *Siege* II. i, I tremble like a tender Lamb, In a cold Winter night. 1681 FLAVEL *Meth. Grace* ix. 192 The bird that has been delivered out of the tallons of the hawk, trembles afterward at the noise of his bells. 1797 MRS. RADCLIFFE *Italian* i, He trembled with anxiety. 1820 W. IRVING *Sketch Bk.* I. 51, I felt Leslie's hand tremble on my arm. *a* 1850 ROSSETTI *Dante & Circ.* I. (1874) 94 Gives me full oft a fear that trembleth: So that I call on Death. *Ibid.* 167 Ah! Ballad, unto thy dear offices I do commend my soul, thus trembling.

b. *fig.* and *rhet.* To be affected with dread or apprehension, or with any feeling that is accompanied by trembling. Const. *at*, *for*, *to do* something.

c 1400 *Apol. Loll.* 55 W[h]o is þe formar and original cause.. of þis þus gret iuel, I drede ungly to sey, tremel and quake. 1552 LYNDESAY *Monarche* 6018, I trimyll tyll heir tell The terribyll Turmentyng of hell. 1562 WINȜET *Last Blast* Wks. (S.T.S.) I. 40 We exhorte ȝow..to feir and trimble at the feirfull exemplis of deid. 1717 LADY M. W. MONTAGU *Let. to C'tess Bristol* 1 Apr., The Grand Signior, with all his absolute power, trembles at a janissary's frown. 1766 GRAY *Kingsgate* 6 Earl Goodwin trembled for his neighbouring sand. 1778 COWPER *Hymn*, '*What various hindrances we meet*' iii, Satan trembles when he sees The weakest saint upon his knees. 1815 SHELLEY *Dæmon* 282 While human tongues Tremble to speak. 1911 MARETT *Anthropol.* ii. 43 Then man presumably killed game..on top of the Wealden dome, how many years ago one trembles to think.

2. Of things: To be agitated or affected with vibratory motion; to shake, quake, quiver.

c 1374 CHAUCER *Boeth.* I. met. i. 1 (Camb. MS.) The slake skyn trembleth of myn emptyd body. *c* 1375 *Cursor M.* 24413 (Fairf.) Þe erþe be-gan to tremble & quake. 1484 CAXTON *Fables of Æsop* IV. xiv, Whan the toune is taken..the Country aboute..ouȝt to tremble and shake. 1555 EDEN *Decades* 322 The poynt of the needle styll respected the northe..sauynge that it sumwhat trembeled and declyned a lyttle. 1697 DRYDEN *Æneid* x. 418 They run their ships aground: the vessels knock,..and tremble with the shock. 1827 CARLYLE *Misc., Richter* (1869) 20 Then began the Aeolian Harp of the Creation to tremble and to sound. 1908 [MISS FOWLER] *Betw. Trent & Ancholme* 39 A little Harebell trembling in the breeze.

b. Said of the tremulous or vibratory motion or effect of light, sound, speech, etc.

c 1400 [see TREMBLING *vbl. sb.*]. *c* 1440 *Partonope* 5790 Wyth voys tremelyng. *a* 1628, 1634 [see TREMBLING *ppl. a.*]. 1708 POPE *Ode St. Cecilia* 17 In broken air, trembling, the wild music floats. *Ibid.* 114 Yet ev'n in death..Eurydice still trembled on his tongue. 1737 — *Imit. Hor.* II. vi. 189 Tell how the Moon-beam trembling falls. 1821 SHELLEY *Epipsych.* 548 Where the pebble-paven shore..Trembles and sparkles as with ecstasy. 1842 TENNYSON *Vision of Sin* 17 Low voluptuous music winding trembled.

c. *fig.*

1819 SHELLEY *Fragm., Questions* 8 A dream, Part of which comes true, and part Beats and trembles in the heart. *a* 1862 BUCKLE *Civiliz.* (1869) III. iii. 121 The liberties of Scotland..were trembling in the balance.

†**3.** *trans.* To regard with trembling or dread; to tremble at. (Cf. L. *tremĕre*.) *Obs. rare.*

1382 WYCLIF *Isa.* lxvi. 2 To whom..shall I beholde, but to my porelet [Vulg. *pauperculum*] and contrit in spirit, and tremblende [*trementem*] my wrdis? 1450-1530 *Myrr. our Ladye* 185 Thy mother, whome the companyes of helles tremel and drede. 1565 T. STAPLETON *Fortr. Faith* 104 That whiche..the deuil, aboue al thinges, trembleth.

4. To cause to tremble or shake.

1591 SPENSER *Virg. Gnat* 616 Either Scipion..To whom the ruin'd walls of Carthage vow'd, Trembling their forces, sound their praises lowd. 1649 G. DANIEL *Trinarch., Hen. V*, xxv, The Palsey of the common Earth, Trembles my Quill. 1651 W. DURHAM *Maran-atha* (1652) 11 It was much that a prisoner should so soon tremble his Judge. 1746 TANSUR *New Mus. Gram.* 23 A Shake, or Trilloe..is to shake, tremble, or warble your Voice, or Instrument. 1818 KEATS *Endym.* I. 468 Thou art as a dove Trembling its closed eyes. 1850 MRS. BROWNING *Woman's Shortcomings* ii, She trembles her fan.

5. *intr.* To pass tremulously. Chiefly *poet.*

1730-46 THOMSON *Autumn* 151 Soon as the morning trembles o'er the sky And unperceived unfolds the spreading day. 1795 COLERIDGE *Eolian Harp* 46 Organic Harps..That tremble into thought. *a* 1817 T. DWIGHT *Trav. New Eng.* etc. (1821) II. 413 With a snail-like progress..we trembled through this part of our way. 1842 TENNYSON *Talking Oak* 161 A teardrop trembled from its source. 1864 LOWELL *Fireside Trav.* 295 On the dial of time the shadow has not yet trembled over the line that marks the beginning of the first century.

6. *trans.* *Tremble out*: To utter tremulously or falteringly.

1868 ADAH I. MENKEN *Infelicia* 35 And trembling out prayers, and waiting to die.

Hence **Tre·mbled** *ppl. a.*, made to tremble.

1819 KEATS *Ode to Psyche* 11 The whispering roof Of leaves and trembled blossoms.

Tremblement (tre·mb'lmĕnt). [a. F. *tremblement* (15th c. in Godef.), f. *trembler* to TREMBLE: see -MENT.]

1. The action or condition of trembling (*lit.* and *fig.*); vibration, agitation; also, an instance of this, a tremor.

1677 GALE *Crt. Gentiles* II. IV. 147 It is..vapors within the bowels of the earth, raised up by subterraneous fires that cause Earthquakes and Tremblements. 1844 MRS. BROWNING *Lost Bower* iv. The wood..Thrills in leafy tremblement. 1867 JEAN INGELOW *Christ's Resurrect.* xvii, The waiting world doth quake with mortal tremblement.

2. A cause of trembling; a terror. *rare.*

1677 GALE *Crt. Gentiles* II. IV. 131 Some read it thus, 'Ephraim was a tremblement to him that heard him', i.e. so long as he kept close to God he was formidable to al his enemies. 1895 *Daily News* 27 May 8/3 Italian villains, pirate marquises, and almost every possible tremblement—fierce wars and faithful loves—do moralise his song.

Trembler (tre·mblər). [f. TREMBLE *v.* + -ER[1]: cf. F. *trembleur*.] One who or that which trembles.

1. One who trembles, esp. with fear; a timorous or terrified person.

1552 HULOET, Trembler, *tremulus*, *i.* *a* 1660 HAMMOND *Serm. Matt.* xi. 30 Wks. 1684 IV. 479 Those base submissions, that the covetous Mammonist or cowardly trembler drudges under. 1770 GOLDSM. *Des. Vill.* 199 Well had the boding tremblers learned to trace The day's disasters in his morning face. 1878 SEELEY *Stein* II. 531 A frightened trembler and maker of obeisances.

†**2.** A name given to those whose devotional exercises were accompanied by trembling, quaking, or shaking; *spec.* a Quaker. *Obs.* or *Hist.*

[1678 R. BARCLAY *Apol. Quakers* xi. § 8 (1736) 359 Sometimes the Power of God will break forth;..every individual will be strongly exercised, as in a Day of Battle; and thereby Trembling and a Motion of Body will be upon most, if not upon all:..And from this, the name of Quakers, i.e. Tremblers, was first Reproachfully cast upon us.] 1689 R. WARE *Foxes & Firebrands* III. 108 These Sectaries..be as follows: 1 Independents..17 Quakers, or Tremblers. 1706 E. WARD *Hud. Rediv.* XV. 21 Of these quaint primitive Dissemblers, In old queen Bess's Days call'd Tremblers. *a* 1741 CHALKLEY *Wks.* (1766) 101, I was one called a Quaker, or Trembler. 1820 tr. *Trav. Cosmo III* (1821) 447 The sect of the Tremblers or Quakers was begun by James Naylor.

3. *transf.* Applied to **a.** a fish which gives an electric shock, as the electric eel of Africa; **b.** a bird or other animal which keeps up a shaking motion of the tail or body.

1832 LYELL *Princ. Geol.* II. 106 The trembler, or *Silurus electricus* [belongs] to the rivers of Africa. 1867 SCLATER & SALVIN *Exotic Ornithol.* Pl. x, *Cinclocerthia ruficauda*, (Red-tailed Trembler). 1911 WEBSTER, *Trembler*, any of certain West Indian birds of the genera *Cinclocerthia* and *Rhamphocinclus*, of the family *Mimidæ*.

4. *Electr.* A vibrating spring blade which alternately makes and breaks the circuit in an induction coil.

1877 *Telegr. Jrnl.* 15 Nov. 280/1 M. Trouvé, Paris, has made some improvements in the contact-breaker or trembler of induction coils. *Ibid.*, Vibrating stem of the trembler. 1903 *Motor. Ann.* 80 Troubles..caused through the petrol, float-jet, or tremblers not having been understood by the motorist. 1907 *Daily News* 10 Apr. 6 Next the trembler in the coil stuck, and the engine stopped.

5. *attrib.* (in sense 4), as *trembler-blade*, *-coil*; **trembler-bell**, an electric bell rung by a hammer attached to a trembler; also called *trembling bell*.

1884 in *Jrnl. Franklin Inst.* (1886) CXXI. Supp. 69 Audible signals are given..on board the locomotive by a *trembler bell. 1905 PREECE & SIVEWRIGHT *Telegraphy* (new ed.) 254 There are many forms of these trembler bells, but the principle in all is alike. 1904 in *Westm. Gaz.* 28 May 5/3 The *trembler blade which governs the spark, and is in its turn controlled by the movement of the motor. 1908 *Ibid.* 6 Feb. 4/2 The ignition is effected by high-tension magneto and accumulator with *trembler-coil and self-starting switch.

‖**Trembleuse** (trānblöz), *a.* or *sb. attrib.* [F., fem. of *trembleur* trembler; cf. Littré, '*Trembleuse*, tasse retenue dans sa soucoupe par une sorte de galerie'.] In *trembleuse cup*, a cup having a saucer with a 'well', into which it fits so as to be kept from falling off.

1883 *Daily News* 26 June 3/1 Sale of..china..a gros bleu trembleuse cup and saucer, exotic birds, 95*l*. 1893 *Auction Catal. Porcelain Cassiobury Park* 5 Old Sèvres Porcelain. 20. A Trembleuse Cup, Cover and Saucer. 1894 *Times* 16 June 7/6 A trembleuse cup and saucer, with landscape and trophies in medallions on white and gold ground.

Trembling (tre·mbliŋ), *vbl. sb.* [f. TREMBLE *v.* + -ING[1].] The action of the verb TREMBLE in various senses; in quot. 1902, *spec.* ague in sheep (see TREMBLE *sb.* 2).

1303 R. BRUNNE *Handl. Synne* 4912 Ȝyf he lerne gylerye Fals wurde and feynt trenlyng [*v.r.* tremlynge]. 1382 WYCLIF *Eph.* vi. 5 Seruauntis, obeysche ȝe to fleishly lordis with drede and tremblyng, in symplenesse of ȝoure herte, as to Crist. *c* 1400 *Song Roland* 54 Trymlinge of tabers And tymbring soft. *c* 1440 *Promp. Parv.* 501/2 Tremelynge, or qwakynge, *tremor*. 1526 *Pilgr. Perf.* (W. de W. 1531) 112 b, Transformynge our gesture or countenaunce, as in tremblynge. 1647 H. MORE *Song of Soul* II. App. iv, All my spirits move with pleasant trembeling. 1693 LUTTRELL *Brief Rel.* (1857) III. 25 A ship from Jamaica brings that the earth there had some tremblings again. 1809-10 COLERIDGE *Friend* (1865) 2 At the sound of the word trembling came upon me. 1902 N. MUNRO in *Blackw. Mag.* Nov. 602/2 Sheep had been lost by the trembling.

b. *attrib.*, as *trembling fit*; †**trembling-stop**, a tremolo organ-stop.

1659 LEAK *Waterwks.* 34 The Systemes and Measures of the Organ Pipes,..also of the manner of the Registers,.. the Trembling stop, &c. 1856 KANE *Arct. Explor.* I. xvi. 191 Men..were seized with trembling-fits and short breath.

Tre·mbling, *ppl. a.* [f. as prec. + -ING[2].] That trembles, in various senses of the verb.

a 1400-50 *Alexander* 4914 (Ashm. MS.) Þe testre trased full of trones with trimballand wingis. 1526 *Pilgr. Perf.* (W. de W. 1531) 257 With tremblynge herte and holy fere, thynkyng hym selfe vnworthy to touche that moost holy body. *c* 1614 SIR W. MURE *Dido & Æneas* I. 269 A contrare blast Doth force his saile against the trembling mast. *a* 1628 SIR J. BEAUMONT *Bosworth F.* 66 Which like a twinkling Star, with trembling Light Sends radiant Lustre through the darksome Air. 1634 SIR T. HERBERT *Trav.* 207 The lookers on incessantly warble out soft trembling Musique. 1797 MRS. RADCLIFFE *Italian* xi, It was delivered in..low and trembling accents. 1877 FROUDE *Short Stud.* (1883) IV. I. x. 122 [He] let in the trembling wretches who had been shut out.

b. *transf.* Characterized or accompanied by trembling.

c 1430 LYDG. *Min. Poems, Pater Noster*, Atwyxe dred and tremblyng reuerence Astoned I am. 1613 SHAKS. *Hen. VIII*, I. ii. 95 Sixt part of each? A trembling contribution. 1794 BLAKE *Songs Exper., Little Boy Lost* 10 In trembling zeal he seized his hair. 1818 SCOTT *Br. Lamm.* xxxv, To the butler's trembling entreaties..he at first returned no answer.

c. In specific applications: **trembling aixies** or **exies** (cf. ACCESS 10), the ague (*Sc.*); **trembling beef**, some dish of boiled beef (?*obs.*); cf. *trembling-piece*; **trembling bog**, bog-land formed over water or soft mud, which shakes at every tread, a quaking bog; so *trembling prairie*, in Louisiana, U.S.A.; **trembling-chair**: see quot.; **trembling eel**, the gymnotus; **trembling-grass**, quaking-grass (*Briza media*); **trembling-ill**, the ague in sheep (*Sc.*); **trembling palsy**, paralysis characterized by trembling of the extremities or the head (*Syd. Soc. Lex.*, 1899); **trembling-piece** [F. *pièce tremblante*], a joint of beef so interlarded with fat as to quiver; **trembling-poplar**, the Aspen, *Populus tremula*, also the N. American *P. tremuloides*.

1808-18 JAMIESON, *Trembling Fevers*, the ague, Ang. *Trembling Aixes [*ed.* 1825 Exies]. 1818 SCOTT *Br. Lamm.* xi, The cookmaid in the trembling exies. 1806 A. HUNTER *Culina* (ed. 3) 238 *Trembling Beef. Take a brisket of beef, and boil it gently [etc.]. 1697 DRYDEN *Virg. Georg.* III. 653 He lives on standing Lakes, and *trembling Bogs. 1899 *Syd. Soc. Lex.*, **Trembling chair*, a vibrating chair used in the treatment of paralysis. 1807 JOYCE *Sci. Dialogues* xvi. (1846) 397 (*Electricity*) In Firmin's 'Natural History of Surinam' is some account of the *trembling eel. 1853 G. JOHNSTON *Bot. E. Bord.* 216 *Briza media*, *Trembling-grass: Quaking-grass. 1833 WILSON *Fr. & Eng. Dict.* s.v. *Tremblant*, *Trembling-piece. 1861 MISS PRATT *Flower. Pl.* V. 120 (Aspen, or **Trembling Poplar*)..is a middle-sized tree.

Tremblingly (tre·mbliŋli), *adv.* [f. prec. + -LY[2].] In a trembling manner; tremulously; with trembling; so as to tremble.

1552 HULOET, Tremblyngly, *trepidanter*. 1581 A. HALL *Iliad* x. 183 He stoode so tremblingly, That one full wel might heare his teeth togither so to shake. 1617 COLLINS *Def. Bp. Ely* I. i. 95 Tremblingly we referre them to the heauenly censure. 1771 MME. D'ARBLAY *Early Diary* 3 July, That..agonizing sensibility which is tremblingly alive to each emotion of sorrow. 1863 W. PHILLIPS *Speeches* viii. 217 Tremblingly anxious to save Garrison's life.

Tre·mblingness. *rare*[−0]. [f. as prec. + -NESS.] The state of trembling; tremulousness.

1727 BAILEY vol. II, *Tremulousness*, tremblingness.

Trembly (tre·mbli), *a.* *colloq.* [f. TREMBLE *v.* or *sb.* + -Y[1].] Full of trembling; tremulous.

1848 LOWELL *Fable for Critics* (1865) 223 A single anemone trembly and rathe. 1848 DICKENS *Dombey* i, So trembly and shaky from head to foot. 1879 O. W. HOLMES *Archbishop & Gil Blas* 21 Is your voice a little trembly?

†**Tre·mebund,** *a.* *Sc.* *Obs.* [ad. L. *tremebundus* trembling, f. *tremĕre* to tremble.] Inclined to tremble; timorous, timid.

c 1560 A. SCOTT *Poems* (S.T.S.) xxvi. 56 Thay [women].. ar of nature tremebund.

†**Tremefa·ction.** *Obs. rare.* [ad. late L. *tremefaction-em*, n. of action f. *tremefacĕre* to cause to tremble.] Shaking, trembling. So †**Tremefacting** *ppl. a.*, that shakes or trembles.

1597 A. M. tr. *Guillemeau's Fr. Chirurg.* 28/2 The Chyrurgiane must, without anye tremefactione, vse the same [lancet]. 1599 — tr. *Gabelhouer's Bk. Physicke* 197/2 The braynes of a Hare..will prævent the tremefactione both of handes and feete. *Ibid.* 207/2 Croockede, and tremefactinge loynctes.

Tremefy (tre·mĭfəi), *v.* *rare*[−1]. [ad. L. *tremefacĕre* (see prec.), with -FY, prop. repr. L. *-ficāre*: cf. *satisfy*.] *trans.* To cause to tremble.

1832 J. WILSON in *Blackw. Mag.* XXXI. 424 A nod that tremefies Olympus.

Tremel, obs. form of TREMBLE.

‖**Tremella** (trĭme·lă). *Bot.* [mod.L. (Dillenius 1741), dim. from *tremulus*, *-ula* shaking, shivering.] A genus of amorphous hymenomycetous fungi consisting of tremulous gelatinous substance, typical of the N.O. *Tremellaceæ* or *Tremellineæ*, most species of which grow on decayed wood, but a few on the ground.

Tremella Auricula is known as Earth-jelly, *T. albida* as Fairy Bullet. *T. mesenterica* is conspicuous in dead hedges in winter from its orange tint.

1760 J. LEE *Introd. Bot.* Table i, Tremella, Cryptogamia, Algæ. 1778 LIGHTFOOT *Flora Scot.* II. 901 *Tremella purpurea*...Little red-knobb'd Tremella. 1786 THOMPSON in *Phil. Trans.* LXXVII. 124 Any thing resembling tremella

or that kind of green matter, or water moss, which forms upon the bottom and sides of the vessel.

Hence **Tremellaceous** (tremĕlē¹·ʃəs) *a.* *Bot.*, pertaining to the *Tremellaceæ* or *Tremellineæ*; **Treme·lliform** *a.* *Bot.*, of the form of the thallus in *Tremella* (Webster, 1911); **Treme·llin** *Chem.* [cf. F. *trémelline* (Littré)], (see quot. 1868); **Tre·melline** *a.* *Bot.*, pertaining to the genus *Tremella* or N.O. *Tremellineæ* (*Funk's Stand. Dict.*, 1895); **Tremelli·neous** *a.* *Bot.* = *tremellaceous*; **Tre·melloid** *a.* *Bot.*, resembling *Tremella* in form or substance; **Tre·mellose** *a.* *Bot.*, shaking, like *Tremella*, tremulous.

1860 MAYNE *Expos. Lex.*, *Tremellin. 1868 WATTS *Dict. Chem.* V. 878 *Tr[emella] mesenterica* was found by Brandes to contain, in the dry state,..5 pts. of a peculiar crystallisable resinous body, called tremellin. 1860 MAYNE *Expos. Lex.*, *Tremelloides*,..applied to a lichen, the membranous, delicate, and almost transparent expansions of which resemble those of the *Tremella*: *tremelloid. 1874 COOKE *Fungi* 72 Anomalous as it may at first sight appear to include these tremelloid forms with the dust-like fungi. 1887 W. PHILLIPS *Brit. Discomycetes* 333 *Calloria luteo-rubella*. ..Somewhat tremelloid. *Ibid.* 22 *Leotia lubrica*...Gregarious, somewhat cæspitose, *tremellose. *Ibid.* 420 *Tremellose*, shaking like jelly, of a jelly-like consistence.

†**Treme·nd,** *a.* *Obs. rare.* [ad. L. *tremend-us*: see next.] = TREMENDOUS.

1581 MARBECK *Bk. Notes* 346 Earthquakes, Thunderings and Lightenings, be tokens and tastes of Gods most treme[n]d and dreadfull power. 1650 TRAPP *Comm. Deut.* x. 8 That sacred and tremend function of the ministery.

Tremendous (trĭme·ndəs), *a.* Also 7-8 tremenduous. [f. L. *tremend-us* 'that is to be trembled at, fearful, dreadful, frightful, terrible', gerundive of *tremĕre* to tremble, tremble at: see -OUS. The by-form in *-uous* was shaped after adjs. from L. adjs. in *-uus*, as *conspicuous*.]

1. Such as to excite trembling, or awe; awful; 'dreadful; horrible; astonishingly terrible' (J.).

1632 LITHGOW *Trav.* x. 460 Hee, after many tremenduous threatnings, commanded the Scriuan to draw vp a Warrant. 1657-83 EVELYN *Hist. Relig.* viii. (1850) II. 17 Not blaspheming the tremendous name of God. 1661 BLOUNT *Glossogr.* (ed. 2), *Tremendous*...greatly to be feared. 1689 T. PLUNKET *Char. Gd. Commander* 44 But the tremenduos Tetragrammaton Will not, not always be a looker on. 1742 YOUNG *Nt. Th.* IV. 9 Black-boding man Receives, not suffers death's tremendous blow. 1796 J. MOSER *Hermit of Caucasus* I. 166 Rocks, torrents, and all the variety of tremendous scenery. 1803 JANE PORTER *Thaddeus* ix, The air..was rendered livid and tremendous by long spires of fire. 1871 MACDUFF *Mem. Patmos* xi. 147 The Day, the Great day.. of His wrath...Now, to what does this tremendous description refer?

b. *absol.* That which is tremendous. *nonce-use.*

1742 YOUNG *Nt. Th.* v. 691 What heart of flesh Would trifle with tremendous? dare extremes? Yawn o'er the fate of infinite?

2. Hyperbolically, or as a mere intensive: Such as to excite wonder on account of its magnitude or violence; astounding; extraordinarily great; immense. (Cf. the similar use of *awful*, *frightful*, *terrible*, etc.) *colloq.*

1812 SOUTHEY *Ess.* (1832) I. 111 During the last forty years, a tremendous change has been going on. 1845 FORD *Handbk. Spain* I. 16 They..drive at a tremendous pace. 1866 G. MACDONALD *Ann. Q. Neighb.* vi, A tremendous splash reached my ears from the pond. 1882 FLOYER *Unexpl. Baluchistan* 91 He..evidently determined to smother his feelings in a tremendous dinner.

b. Extraordinary in respect of some quality indicated in context. *slang.*

1831 *Ch. Patronage Reporter* Jan. 26 Owing..latterly to the tremendous state of the weather. 1847 HELPS *Friends in C.* I. vii. 117 Over-managing people..are tremendous to live with. 1866 GEO. ELIOT *F. Holt* ii, This young Debarry is a tremendous fellow at the classics.

Tremendously (trĭme·ndəsli), *adv.* [f. prec. + -LY[2].] In a tremendous manner or degree; dreadfully; hence *colloq.* as a hyperbolical intensive: Exceedingly, extremely, excessively, very greatly.

1680 BAXTER *Cath. Commun.* (1684) 36 And Peter oft, and once tremendously..rebuk't by Christ. 1731 BAILEY, *Tremendously*, dreadingly. 1776 PENNANT *Zool.* (ed. 4) I. 177 White Owl: This species..will often scream most tremendously. 1817 SOUTHEY *Ess.* (1832) II. 43 The game was of the same kind, though the stake differed tremendously in magnitude. 1863 W. C. BALDWIN *Afr. Hunting* ix. 394 If he should have gone, I shall have some tremendously hard work for nothing. 1904 *Yorks. Post* 9 Sept. 4/3 How tremendously costly a thing naval 'supremacy' has become.

Tremendousness (trĭme·ndəsnĕs). [f. as prec. + -NESS.] The quality of being tremendous.

1727 BAILEY vol. II, *Tremendousness*,..tremendous Quality, Worthiness to be feared or dreaded. 1851 H. MELVILLE *Whale* xli, The pre-eminent tremendousness of the great Sperm Whale. 1894 *Chicago Advance* 3 May, It is good.. to recognize the tremendousness of death. 1906 *19th Cent.* June 974 Æschylus overpowers us with his tremendousness.

‖**Tremie** (trĕ·mi). *Engin.* [F. *trémie*, OF. *tremuie*, *-uye* (mill-)hopper (*c* 1300 in Godef. *Compl.*) = It. *tramoggia*:—L. *trimodia* a three-peck measure, f. *tri-* three + *modius* peck.] A movable tube, widening at its upper end into a hopper, for depositing concrete under water.

1905 *Engineering Rec.* (N.Y.) 14 Jan. 53 Up to a height of 6 ft. below low water level, the concrete was deposited under water by means of a tremie. 1911 *Min. Proc. Inst. Civ. Engin.* CLXXXV. 9 The deposition of concrete..by means of tremies operated from scows.

‖**Tremis** (trī·mis). *Rom. Antiq.* [L., f. *trēs* three, after *sēmis* half an as.] A Roman gold coin of the later emperors, the third part of an *as aureus*.

1706 PHILLIPS (ed. Kersey), *Tremissis*, or *Golden Triens*, a Roman Gold Coin worth five Shillings Sterling. 1756 NUGENT *Montesquieu's Spir. Laws* (1758) II. XXII. ii. 72 The sou of two tremises [F. *deux tremisses*] answered to an ox of twelve months.

Tremle, obs. form of TREMBLE.

‖**Tremocto·pus.** *Zool.* [mod.L., f. Gr. τρῆμα hole, pore + OCTOPUS.] A subgenus of Octopus having two large aquiferous pores on the back of the head.

1851 WOODWARD *Mollusca* I. 65 Between the branchiæ are two rows of brown or violet spots, like the pigment cells of the tremoctopus. 1878 BELL *Gegenbaur's Comp. Anat.* 327 Sometimes over a few of the arms only (4 in Tremoctopus), or over them all.

Tremogram (tre·mŏgræm). [f. Gr. τρέμειν to tremble, quiver + -GRAM.] **a.** A tracing recording involuntary muscular motion. **b.** An irregularity characterizing a person's handwriting: see quot. 1907. So **Tre·mograph** [-GRAPH], an instrument for recording involuntary muscular tremor.

1899 *Syd. Soc. Lex.*, *Tremogram*, the tracing of tremor made by means of the Tremograph. 1904 G. S. HALL *Adolescence* I. iii. 145 The tremograph, a thimble attached to a pivoted lever moving freely in all directions, showed that children could not hold the index-finger still for half a minute. 1907 P. FRAZER in *Jrnl. Franklin Inst.* Apr. 268 The curious marginal irregularities which accompany and seem to a certain degree to characterize the handwriting of each writer, which I have called 'tremograms'.

‖**Tremolando** (tremola·ndo). *Mus.* Also tremulando. [It., pr. pple. of *tremolare* to shake, quaver, warble (Florio).] **a.** *adj.* (or *attrib.*) Tremulous, shaking. **b.** *adv.* In a tremulous or quivering manner; with a tremolo; used to indicate that a note or passage is to be thus rendered. **c.** *ellipt.* as *sb.* = TREMOLO 1, 2.

1852 SEIDEL *Organ* 24 Another absurd..contrivance is the tremulando, a register which..was to indicate the sobbing, sighing, and trembling of men. 1854 J. SCHUBERT *Mus. Hand-bk.* (ed. 4), *Tremolant*, a stop in german organs producing a tremolando effect. 1876-98 STAINER & BARRETT *Dict. Mus. Terms*, *Tremolando*,..(1) A chord or note played or bowed with great rapidity so as to produce a quivering effect. (2) Vibration of the voice in singing, arising from nervousness or a bad production; or used for the purpose of producing a special effect. *Ibid.*, *Tremolant*,..a fan-wheel by rotating in front of the wind chest causes a *tremolando*. 1887 *Athenæum* 26 Nov. 720/1 The violins accompany *tremolando* in descending thirds.

Tremolant (tre·mŏlănt). [a. G. *tremolant*, ad. It. *tremolante*, TREMULANT.] = TREMOLO 2.

1854 [see prec.]. 1876-98 STAINER & BARRETT *Dict. Mus. Terms*, *Tremolant*, or *Tremulant*, an organ and harmonium stop which causes the air as it proceeds to the pipes or reeds to pass through a valve having a moveable top...The up and down movement of the top of the valve gives a vibratory movement to the air which similarly affects the sound produced.

Tremolite (tre·mŏləit). *Min.* [Named 1796, f. *Tremola*, in Switzerland, where found + -ITE[1].] A white or grey (sometimes transparent) variety of AMPHIBOLE, composed of magnesia and lime, with little or no iron, occurring in fibrous masses or thin-bladed crystals. Also called *grammatite*.

1799 KIRWAN *Geol. Ess.* 219 Not far from St. Gothard, it is found mixed with tremolite, and stratified. 1807 T. THOMSON *Chem.* (ed. 3) II. 476 *Tremolite*...is a compound of silica and lime, or perhaps rather carbonate of lime. 1834-5 J. PHILLIPS *Geol.* in *Encycl. Metrop.* VI. 563/1 That [*sc.* marble] of Glen Tilt, characterized by its accompanying tremolites, lies in a quartzose mica slate. 1849 DANA *Geol.* xvii. (1850) 631 Acicular crystals of white hornblende or tremolite.

Hence **Tremoli·tic** *a.*, of the nature of, or containing tremolite, as *tremolitic marble*.

1879 DANA *Man. Geol.* (ed. 3) 70 Granular Limestone.. Varieties.—a. Statuary Marble;..Tremolitic; contains bladed crystallizations of..tremolite.

‖**Tremolo** (tre·mŏlo). *Mus.* In 8 tremola; also 9 tremulo. [It. *tremolo* adj. trembling, shaking, quavering:—L. *tremul-us* TREMULOUS.]

1. A tremulous or vibrating effect produced on certain musical instruments or in the human voice in singing, esp. to express intensity of emotion: cf. VIBRATO.

[1724 *Short Explic. For. Wds. in Mus. Bks.*, *Tremola*, to Tremble, a particular Grace in Musick.] 1801 BUSBY *Dict. Mus.*, *Tremolo*, *Tremolante*, or *Tremente*, a word intimating that the notes are to be drawn out with a tremulous motion. 1865 MISS BRADDON *Sir Jasper* xvii, The trickling arpeggios and treble tremulos of a modern nocturne were all-sufficient. 1884 H. C. DEACON in Grove *Dict. Mus.* IV. 166/2 The instrumental tremolo is more nearly allied to the vocal vibrato. Indeed, what is called 'vibrato' on bowed instruments is what would be 'tremolo' in vocal music.

attrib. 1896 *Godey's Mag.* Feb. 195/1 Some cheap melodramatic stuff with *tremolo* shudders in the orchestra.

b. *transf.* and *fig.*

1877 LOCKHART *Mine is Thine* xviii, Her back still turned and a tremolo in her voice. 1897 *Daily News* 23 Nov. 6/2 He [a writer] executes so many tremolos and elaborate modulations on his theme.

2. A mechanical contrivance in an organ by which such an effect is produced; a tremulant. Also *tremolo stop*.

1867 AUG. J. E. WILSON *Vashti* xi, The..overwhelming pathos of the tones affected Dr. Grey much as the tremolo stop in some organ-overture in a dimly-lighted cathedral. 1869 M. J. MATTHEWS in *Eng. Mech.* 31 Dec. 385/3 A sixth is the 'tremolo', the least valuable of the lot.

Tremor (tre·mǝɹ, trī·mǝɹ). Also 4-9 -our, 5 -oure. [ME. *tremour*, a. OF. *tremor*, *-our* fear, terror (13th c. in Godef.), also a trembling or quivering (15th c.):—L. *tremor*, *-ōrem*, f. *tremĕre* to tremble. In 17th c. reintroduced in L. form *tremor*.]

†**1.** Terror. *Obs.*

c 1374 CHAUCER *Troylus* v. 255 Swich a tremor [*v.r.* tremour] fele a-boute his herte That of þe feer his body sholde quake. 1490 CAXTON *Eneydos* xv. 60 To solace and dysporte thy self euermore wyth the thondre and weddrynges, for to gyue unto vs tremoure and feere. *Ibid.* xxii. 81 Horrible dremes & cruel, comen to-fore her in hir mynde that tormente her in tremoure merueyllous.

2. Involuntary agitation of the body or limbs, resulting from physical infirmity or from fear or other strong emotion; trembling: see quot. 1866.

[1611 SHAKS. *Wint. T.* I. ii. 110, I haue *Tremor Cordis* on me: my heart daunces.] 1615 CROOKE *Body of Man* 401 The disease called Tremor, or the shaking palsie. 1762-71 H. WALPOLE *Vertue's Anecd. Paint.* (1786) IV. 154 His lips are contracted by tremor. 1807 *Med. Jrnl.* XVII. 428 An approach to syncope, accompanied with more or less of universal tremor, and spasmodic twitchings, are said to have occurred. 1866 A. FLINT *Princ. Med.* (1880) 815 Tremor, that is, alternate contraction and relaxation of muscles in rapid succession, is a symptom of certain lesions of the nervous centres.

b. With *a* and *pl.* An instance of this; a fit of trembling.

1616 BULLOKAR *Eng. Expos.*, *Tremour*, a trembling. 1731 ARBUTHNOT *Aliments* v. (1735) 146 By its styptick and stimulating Quality it [tea] affects the Nerves..occasioning Tremors. 1813 J. THOMSON *Lect. Inflam.* 97 A tremor of the hands is often lessened or removed, for a while, by a dram, or some strong wine. 1871 R. ELLIS *Catullus* lxiv. 305 To a tremor of age their gray infirmity rocking.

c. *fig.* A nervous thrill caused by emotion or excitement; also, a state of tremulous agitation or excitement.

1754 RICHARDSON *Grandison* IV. vii. 51 He ceased speaking. I was in tremors. 1814 SCOTT *Ld. of Isles* VI. ii, The tremors that unbidden rise. 1838 DICKENS *Nich. Nick.* xxviii, He went about all day in a tremor of delight. 1866 G. MACDONALD *Ann. Q. Neighb.* xii, [She] drew herself up very haughtily..to hide her tremor.

3. A tremulous or vibratory movement caused by some external impulse; a vibration, shaking, quivering. *Earth-tremor*, an earthquake.

1635 HEYWOOD *Hierarch.* IX. 570 One of these Tremors lasted forty dayes, When six and twenty tow'rs and castles fell. 1656 BLOUNT *Glossogr.*, *Tremor*, quaking, trembling, shaking, great fear, also an earthquake. 1728 PEMBERTON *Newton's Philos.* 270 Motion consequent upon the tremors of the air, excited by the vibrations of sonorous bodies. 1830 LYELL *Princ. Geol.* I. 324 All countries are liable to slight tremors..when some great crisis of subterranean movement agitates an adjoining volcanic region. 1853 KANE *Grinnell Exp.* xxix. (1856) 250 The peculiar tremor of a cotton-factory. 1878 HUXLEY *Physiogr.* 187 Waves or tremors may be propagated in all directions through the solid ground.

4. A tremble or quaver in the voice; a tremulous sound or note.

1797 MRS. RADCLIFFE *Italian* ii, The tremor of his voice.. heightened its eloquence. 1838 LYTTON *Calderon* ii, There seemed a touch of true feeling in the tremor of his rich sweet voice. 1866 G. MACDONALD *Ann. Q. Neighb.* xxxi, There was a tremor in the old lady's voice more of disappointment and hurt than of anger.

5. *attrib.*, as **tremor disk**, the telescopic image of a star, as apparently enlarged by the vibration of the telescope and of the atmosphere; **tremor storm**, a prolonged series of earth-tremors.

1889 MILNE in *Nature* 31 Oct. 658/1 At certain seasons tremor storms are very marked. 1905 H. F. NEWALL in *Athenæum* 29 Apr. 534/1 On the general design of spectographs for equatorials of large aperture, considered from the point of view of 'tremor discs'.

Hence **Tre·morful** *a.* *dial.*, **Tre·morous** *a.* *rare*, full of tremor; tremulous.

1901 'ZACK' *Tales Dunstable Weir* 39 'I'll not go nigh the maid', Martin cried, sort of tremorful. 1907 F. THOMPSON *New Poems, Orient Ode* 28 The tremorous nurse of joy.

Tremorless (tre·mǝɹlĕs), *a.* [f. TREMOR + -LESS.] Without tremor or excitement; untrembling, unshaken. Also *fig.*

1869 *Contemp. Rev.* XI. 43 A suicide, whose words, written just before he committed the act, prove his lucid and tremorless sanity. 1882 *Fraser's Mag.* XXV. 415 An albatross blown along by its outstretched tremorless wings. 1898 R. PRIMROSE in *Brit. Weekly* 6 Oct. 411/1 Brave men..with tremorless souls the worst can face.

Hence **Tre·morlessly** *adv.*, without tremor; without a ripple.

1890 CLARK RUSSELL *Ocean Trag.* III. xxxii. 187 The sea ..tremorlessly circling the island.

†**Tremp,** *v.* *Obs. rare.* [a. F. *tremp-er*: see TRAMP *v.*[2]] *trans.* To mix, temper.

1480 CAXTON *Ovid's Met.* x. vii, She gaf hym a dranke, tremped wᵗ herbes & wyne.

Trempe, var. TRAMP *sb.*[2], temper. *Obs.*

Tremulant (tre·miŭlănt), *a.* and *sb.* Also erron. -ent. [ad. *tremulānt-em*, pr. pple. of late L. *tremulāre* to TREMBLE; in B. 2 repr. It. *tremolante* in same sense.]

A. *adj.* Tremulous; trembling.

1837 CARLYLE *Fr. Rev.* I. v. ii, Hapless De Brézé; doomed to survive long ages, in men's memory, in this faint way, with tremulent white rod. 1884 *Pall Mall G.* 8 July 4/2 The Queen of the Opera can sing clean and firm, and with a touch of tremulant emotion, only just when and where it is wanted. 1899 *Allbutt's Syst. Med.* VI. 516 The muscular contractions which execute willed movements are themselves found..to be often slightly tremulant.

B. *sb.* *Mus.* **1.** = TREMOLO 2.

1862 *Catal. Internat. Exhib., Brit.* II. No. 3411, 9. Tremulant to swell. 1876 HILES *Catech. Organ* iii. (1878) 20 A Tremulant is a contrivance that gives to the tone of any department of an Organ to which it may be applied, a waving, or undulating effect. 1903 *Westm. Gaz.* 26 Mar. 8/1 The largest organ in the world is being built..for the St. Louis Exhibition of 1904...There are to be ninety-nine mechanical appliances, thirty-six couplers, five tremulants, and forty-eight adjustable pistons.

2. = TREMOLO 1.

1884 *Pall Mall G.* 30 Apr. 4/1 We strongly recommend Mesdames Durand and Laterner to subdue the tremulant in their voices.

Tremulate (tre·miŭlĕit), *v.* *rare.* [f. late L. *tremulāre* to tremble (Quicherat *Addenda*): see -ATE[3] 5, 6.]

1. *intr.* To tremble, vibrate; to palpitate, quiver.

1749 ABP. RHYS *Tour Spain & Port.* (1760) 92 Tender Limbs, that tremulate and wanton in the air. 1768 [W. DONALDSON] *Life Sir B. Sapskull* I. xiv. 137 His heart flutter'd! and the whole man was tremulating with affection! 1813 T. BUSBY *Lucretius* II. IV. Comm. 34 The auditory nerve tremulates, and the brain is agitated.

2. *trans.* To cause to tremble or vibrate.

1764 GRAINGER *Sugar Cane* III. 205 The faint breeze oft flags on listless wings, Nor tremulates the cocos airiest arch. 1813 T. BUSBY *Lucretius* I. III. Comm. 8 No musician is provided..to tremulate the strings. *Ibid.* II. VI. Comm. 8 [The winds] tremulate whatever substances they encounter.

Hence **Tre·mulated, Tre·mulating** *ppl. adjs.*

1813 T. BUSBY *Lucretius* I. II. 467 Those colours which.. Impress the tremulating nerves of sight. *Ibid.* II. IV. Comm. 27 Certain pulsations communicated to the air, by the tremulating organs of the voice. *Ibid.* 28 Substituting for his philosophy of vocal atoms, that of a tremulated medium.

Tremulation (tremiŭlē¹·ʃən). [n. of action f. TREMULATE: see -ATION.] The action or condition of trembling; an instance of this, a trembling.

1651 WITTIE *Primrose's Pop. Err.* III. xiii. 173 Hence do palsies, tremulations, and other evils arise. 1665 HOOKE *Microgr.* lviii. 219, I have often taken notice of the tremulation of the Trees and Bushes. 1718 *Entertainer* No. 9. 67 Before most violent Eruptions of Mount Etna,..they feel Convulsions and Tremulations in the Earth thereabout. 1880 H. A. A. NICHOLLS in *Nature* 19 Feb. 373/2 The resistance to the volcanic force was too small to cause much tremulation.

Tremulous (tre·miŭləs), *a.* [f. L. *tremul-us* trembling, quivering, shaking (f. *trem-ĕre* to tremble, shake) + -OUS.]

1. Of persons, their limbs, etc.: Characterized or affected by trembling or quivering from nervous agitation or weakness, of mental or physical origin; hence, fearful, timorous.

1611 SPEED *Hist. Gt. Brit.* IX. viii. (1623) 569 The Monkes [being] very tremulous to enter matter of new intrications. 1667 *Decay Chr. Piety* xi. 310 The tender tremulous Christian, 'tis easie to discern how much he must be distracted and amaz'd by them. 1714 R. FIDDES *Pract. Disc.* I. 310, I shall appear to be of an abject and tremulous spirit. 1784 COWPER *Task* II. 729 His voice unstrung Grew tremulous. 1897 R. HICHENS *Londoners* (1902) 101 She gained the purple drawing-room on rather tremulous feet.

b. Said of writing, a line, or the like, done by a tremulous hand; hence, finely wavy.

2. Of things: Characterized by trembling or vibration; vibratory; easily caused to vibrate or tremble.

1616 CHAPMAN *Homer's Hymns, To Mother of Gods* 4 That doth with Cymball sounds, delight her life; and tremulous diuisions of the Fife. 1664 POWER *Exp. Philos.* I. 21 In my long Telescope I can some days see a tremulous Motion and Agitation of rowling fumes, and strong Atoms in the air. 1774 GOLDSM. *Nat. Hist.* (1776) VI. 265 A tremulous motion which this animal [torpedo] is found to possess. 1815 J. SMITH *Panorama Sc. & Art* II. 497 Gelatine, or jelly,..has a soft tremulous consistence. 1860 FARRAR *Orig. Lang.* i. 6 The tremulous ripple on the surface of the sea.

b. Ready to vibrate in response *to* some influence; also *fig.* tremblingly sensitive or responsive.

1794 G. ADAMS *Nat. & Exp. Philos.* IV. xlix. 349 Columns of marble or porphyry are tremulous to thunder explosions, and to certain tones of an organ. 1867 H. MACMILLAN *Bible Teach.* i. (1870) 3 He is tremulous..to all the influences of the hour and scene.

†**3.** Affecting the organs of taste with a trembling or quivering sensation. *Obs. rare.*

1675 GREW *Disc. Tasts Plants* i. § 15 Tasts are either Still, as usually; or may be called Tremulous, as the Heat produced by *Pyrethrum*. 1707 *Curios. in Husb. & Gard.* 39 Grew..finds in Plants sixteen sorts of Tastes...16. Tremulous, as the Root of wild Pellitory.

4. Characterized by use of the tremolo in singing. (*nonce-use.*)

1884 *Pall Mall G.* 26 July 4/1 He quivered and shook himself all to pieces with the tremulous fever now so fashionable. 1887 *Daily News* 25 July 4/8 The tremulous vocalists one after the other failed to win popular favour.

Tremulously (tre·miŭləsli), *adv.* [f. prec. + -LY[2].] In a tremulous manner; tremblingly.

1730-6 BAILEY (folio), *Tremulously*, with trembling, tremblingly. 1757 W. WILKIE *Epigon.* v. 127 Their lofty spires..O'er the pale ashes tremulously glow. 1811 SHELLEY *Let.* in Dowden *Life* (1886) I. iv. 167 Once I was tremulously alive to tones and scenes. 1886 *Manch. Exam.* 9 Jan. 5/1 The great Protestant and industrial interests stand tremulously on the watch.

Tremulousness (tre·miŭləsnĕs). [f. as prec. + -NESS.] The state or quality of being tremulous.

1727 BAILEY vol. II, *Tremulousness*, tremblingness. 1755 JOHNSON, *Trill*, quaver; tremulousness of musick. 1817 J. EVANS *Excurs. Windsor*, etc. 74 His whole manner evidently marked by a nervous tremulousness. 1857 H. SPENCER in *Fraser's Mag.* Oct. 401/2 This tremulousness of voice is very effectively used by some vocalists.

Tremyl, -ylle, obs. forms of TREMBLE.

Tren, Trenail: see TREE, TREEN, TREENAIL.

Trench (trenᵗʃ), *sb.* Also 4-7 trenche, (6 trenshe, *Sc.* treinch, trinch, -e, trynsch(e, trinsch(e, 7 trintch). See also TRANCHE. [a. OF. *trenche* (1288 in Godef.), later OF. and mod.F. *tranche*, an act of cutting, a cut, a gash; a ditch or trench; a slice, etc., verbal sb. from OF. *trenchier*, F. *trancher* to cut, TRENCH *v.* See also TRANCHE. Many of the Eng. senses, wanting or obs. in mod.F., are supplied by *tranchée*.]

†**1.** A path or track cut through a wood or forest; an alley; a hollow walk. *Obs.*

c 1386 CHAUCER *Sqr.'s T.* 384 And in a trench [*v.r.* trenche] forth in the park gooth she. *c* 1420 LYDG. *Thebes* I. in *Chaucer's Wks.* (1561) 358/2 As thei rengen the trenches by and by Thei heard a noise. 1575 TURBERV. *Venerie* 98 By this word Trench is vnderstoode euery small way, not so commonly vsed...So is there also a difference betweene a Trench and a path. For trenches as I say, be wayes and walkes in a woode or Forest.

2. A long and narrow hollow cut out of the ground, a cutting; a ditch, fosse; a deep furrow. Also *fig.*

1489 CAXTON *Faytes of A.* I. ix. 23 To lepen ouer trenchis or dyches. 1553 EDEN *Treat. Newe Ind.* (Arb.) 13 They moued neare vnto the trenche or ditche of the castell. 1677 YARRANTON *Eng. Improv.* 192 The River Dee must be carried in a large Cut or Trench through the lands..as far as Flint Castle, and then dropt by a large Cut, into the Deep Water below the Brewhouse. 1782 MISS BURNEY *Cecilia* VII. vi, How deep a trench of real misery do you sink, in order to raise this pile of fancied happiness! 1842 TENNYSON *Audley Court* 41 Be shot for sixpence in a battle-field, And shovell'd up into some bloody trench. 1911 J. WARD *Roman Era in Brit.* viii. 140 A single trench disclosed broken pottery and charcoal.

3. *Mil.* An excavation of this kind, the earth from which is thrown up in front as a parapet, serving either to cover or to oppose the advance of a besieging force. Chiefly in *plural*. **a.** More particularly applied to the ditch or excavation.

c 1500 *Three Kings Sons* 42 That ther might be made grete trenches, that ther might be grete nombre of people hid theryn. 1513 DOUGLAS *Æneis* XI. xvii. 104 Thai..delvys trynschis all the wallis abowt. *a* 1548 HALL *Chron., Hen. V*, 74 b, They without made mynes, cast trenches and shot gunnes daily at the walles. 1623 MASSINGER *Bondman* II. i, There are trenches too..In which to stand all night to the knees in water In gallants breeds the tooth-ache. 1879 *Cassell's Techn. Educ.* II. 103/2 When this excavation is behind the mound it is called a trench.

b. *pl.* Including both the excavation and the mound or embankment: see quot. 1828. *To mount*, *relieve the trenches*: see quot. 1706. *To open trenches*: see OPEN *v.* 4 b, quot. 1853.

1585 T. WASHINGTON tr. *Nicholay's Voy.* I. xvii. 20 [They] did in the meane space diligently aduaunce their trenches and approaches for planting of their ordinance. 1607 SHAKS. *Cor.* I. vi. 12, I saw our party to their Trenches driuen. *a* 1674 CLARENDON *Hist. Reb.* XIII. § 22 Cromwell knew them too well to fear them..when there were no Trenches..to keep him from them. 1706 PHILLIPS (ed. Kersey) s.v., Trenches are Works..either cut into the Ground..or else raised above it when rocky, with Bavins, Wooll-packs, Bags or Baskets filled with Earth. *Ibid.*, *To Mount the Trenches*, is to go upon Duty in them. *To Relieve the Trenches*, is to relieve those that have been upon Duty there. 1777 WATSON *Philip II* (1839) 95 By the advice of Dragut he resolved to extend his trenches and batteries, on the side next to the town. 1828 J. M. SPEARMAN *Brit. Gunner* (ed. 2) 397 Trenches. A general term for all the approaches at a siege. 1848 LYTTON *Harold* VII. iii, On the other side of the trenches were marching against them their own countrymen.

†**c.** Sometimes more particularly applied to the rampart, mound, or embankment. *Obs.*

1536 BELLENDEN *Cron. Scot.* (1821) I. 160 To bring treis to fill the fowseis,..otheris maid sindry instrumentis to breke down thair trinschis. 1560 DAUS tr. *Sleidane's Comm.* 259 To bring yᵉ pioners to cast down their trenches. 1617 MORYSON *Itin.* II. 169 It was resolued that the ditches.. should bee deepned, and the trenches highthned. 1678 tr. *Gaya's Art of War* II. 113 A Trench, a casting up of Earth by way of Parapet, with a Ditch or Foss on the side of the Enemy. 1693 in *Macfarlane's Geog. Collect.* (S.H.S.) II. 218 Ane ruinous tour surrounded with ane trintch of stone and earth. 1726 LEONI *Alberti's Archit.* II. 100/1 Severus threw up a trench a hundred and twenty two miles long.

d. *fig.* or *transf.*

1601 R. JOHNSON *Kingd. & Commw.* (1603) 23 The sea, which to the inhabitants is a deep trench against hostile inuasions. 1677 GILPIN *Demonol.* (1867) 299 A soul that is within the trenches of present peace. 1723 MANDEVILLE *Fab. Bees* (1725) I. 66 Seducers..don't make their Attacks at Noon-day, but cut their Trenches at Night.

4. *transf.* Something resembling a trench. **a.** A cut, scar, furrow, or deep wrinkle in the face.

1588 SHAKS. *Tit. A.* v. ii. 23 Witnesse these Trenches made by griefe and care. 1823 SCOTT *Quentin D.* vii, 'Thou name ladies' love, with such a trench in thy visage!' said Guthrie. 1830 GODWIN *Cloudesley* II. xii. 185 Without trench or wrinkle, in his honest countenance.

b. *Anat.* and *Zool.* A cavity, pit, fossa.

1615 CROOKE *Body of Man* 392 That cauity which is commonly called..the Trench or Spoone of the heart. 1631 WIDDOWES *Nat. Philos.* 62 From the trench of the veynes hang downeward white, narrow veynes. 1634 T. JOHNSON tr. *Parey's Chirurg.* III. i. (1678) 54 The trench of the heart which..the Latines [called] *scrobiculus cordis*. 1846 DANA *Zooph.* (1848) 257 Bottom of trench convoluto-porous. *Ibid.* Gloss., *Trench* (Fossa), a meandering cell in the Meandrine Corals.

†**5.** A slice. Cf. TRANCHE. *Obs. rare.*

1558 WARDE tr. *Alexis' Secr.* (1559) 70 Take..sixe Lemons cut in trenches.

†**6.** A trencher. *Obs. rare.*

(Perh. only in pl. *trenches* for *trenchers*.)

1602 in *Collect. Archæol.* (1863) II. 105 Pottes and cruses xxx..Trenches viij dossen.

†**7.** = TRENCHEFIL, TRANCHEFIL (in both senses).

a. 1611 COTGR., *Trenchefile*,..the trench, or trenching of a Crossebow string; that part thereof whereinto the neb of the arrow entreth.

b. 1607 TOPSELL *Four-f. Beasts* (1658) 231 The Indians were wont to use no bridles..but only..putting a long round trench through his [the horse's] mouth, to the edge whereof they fasten the rains, wherewith all they guide the beast. 1614 MARKHAM *Cheap Husb.* I. ii. (1668) 16 Now and then drawing the trench to and fro in his Mouth. 1639 T. DE GRAY *Compl. Horsem.* 345 Tye it to his snaffle, trench, or bit. *c* 1720 W. GIBSON *Farrier's Dispens.* IX. iii. (1734) 201.

†**8.** A griping or colic in the horse; also, a kind of worm infesting the horse. [= F. *tranchée*; cf. Cotgr., '*Trenchée*..., a fretting, wringing, or griping in the bellie..; the wormes, or bellie-ache.'] *Obs.*

1578 LYTE *Dodoens* II. lxxiv. 246 It cureth the trenches or gryping payne in the small of the bellie or bowels. 1587 MASCALL *Govt. Cattle, Horses* (1596) 133.

9. *attrib.* and *Comb.*, as *trench-cutting*, *-digger*, *-digging*, *-fighting*, *-guard*, *-lines*, *-work*; *trench-encircled*, *-like* adjs.; **trench-brace**, an extensible screw-brace or strut used to prevent the caving in of the side walls or to support the sheet-piling of a trench; **trench-cart** *Mil.*, a narrow hand-cart on which ammunition can be carried through the trenches; **trench-cavalier** *Mil.*, a high parapet constructed by the besiegers upon the glacis to command and enfilade the covered way of the fortress; **trench-drain**, **trench-elm**: see quots.; **trench-kitchen** *Mil.*, a field-kitchen where the fire is made in a small trench; **trenchman**, a labourer who opens trenches for pipe-laying; †**trench-master**, an officer in charge of the construction of trenches; **trench-planting**: see quot. 1905; †**trench-sergeant**, cf. *trench-master*. See also TRENCH-PLOUGH.

1877 KNIGHT *Dict. Mech.*, *Trench-cart. 1834-47 J. S. MACAULAY *Field Fortif.* (1851) 234 A return is then made to the trench, and the whole of the end of each is converted into a *trench cavalier. 1853 STOCQUELER *Milit. Encycl.* 254/2 At the angle of the glacis, high breastworks, called trench cavaliers, are formed, to allow a plunging fire..to be directed into the covered-way. 1876 'OUIDA' *Winter City* vi, Palestrina often saw its lord..plan *trench-cuttings to arrest the winter-swollen brooks. 1770 LANGHORNE *Plutarch* (1851) II. 1045/2 Making excursions to harass the *trench-diggers. 1846 *J. Baxter's Libr. Pract. Agric.* (ed. 4) I. 153, I have often had fine crops [of carrots] upon poor soils by *trench-digging the land to the depth of twenty inches. 1805 R. W. DICKSON *Pract. Agric.* II. 923 *Trench Drain.— A deep ditch, or drain, which meets the trenches for the purpose of taking the water away speedily after the irrigation is performed. 1676 M. COOK *Forest-trees* xi. 50 The best sort [of Elm] is that which..shoots with a shoot not much less than a Sallow when it is lopped: it is called by some the *Trench-Elm, by others the Marsh-Elm. 1881 W. CORY *Lett. & Jrnls.* (1897) 468 A few bits of *trench-fighting. 1903 O. CAUSTON in *Cornh. Mag.* Feb. 202 The long white *trench-graves on the summit move one more, perhaps, than any others in South Africa. 1849 JAS. GRANT *Kirkaldy of Gr.* xxviii, He drove the *trench-guards down the Lawn-market in disorder. 1900 *Westm. Gaz.* 19 Jan. 2/1 The *trench kitchen is more generally used in South Africa. 1908 *Blackw. Mag.* Apr. 502/1 A treble tier of *trench lines. 1577-87 HOLINSHED *Chron.* III. 1133/2 Edward Chamberleine esquier capteine of the pioners, sir Richard Leigh *trenchmaster. 1617 MORYSON *Itin.* II. 148 Captain Josias Bodley, Trench-Master. 1830 *Planting* 35 (Libr. Usef. Knowl.) Slit-planting..holing or pitting..*trench-planting ..furrow-planting. 1905 *Terms Forestry* (U.S. Dep. Agric., Bulletin lxi.), *Trench planting*, a method of planting on dry ground, in which the seeds or young trees are set in trenches. *Syn.*: pit planting. 1755 *Mem. Capt. P. Drake* II. iii. 73 He would make me *Trench-Sergeant...In this Duty I was to attend in the Trenches twice a Day,..to have under my Command a Detachment of thirty unarmed Men ..to gather the Pick-axes, Shovels, Wheel-Barrows, etc. that should be left or scattered by the Workmen. 1884 *Mil. Engineering* (ed. 3) I. II. 29 Fig. 1..represents this arrangement in a parallel executed by common *trench-work, and Fig. 2 in one constructed by flying trench-work.

Trench (trenᵗʃ), *v.* Forms: see the sb. [a. OF. *trenchier* (11th c. in Godef. *Compl.*), F. *trancher* to cut, hew, slice, etc. = Prov. *trencar*, *trinquar*, Catal. *trencar*, Sp., Pg. *trincar*; cf. It. *trinciare*. These Romanic forms are held to represent a popular L. **trincāre*, altered from L. *truncāre* to cut or lop off, f. *truncus* the trunk of a tree: cf. TRUNCHEON. Our sense 1 is directly

Trench. ...

Trenchancy (tre'nʃǎnsi), *sb.* ...

Trenchant (tre'nʃǎnt), *a.* (*sb.*) ...

Trenchantly, *adv.* ...

Trenchantness. ...

†Trenchefer, trenchefil. ...

†Trenchepain. ...

Trencher (tre'nʃǎr). ...

†Trencher-chaplain. *Obs.* ...

†Trencher-fly. *Obs.* ...

Trencher-friend. ...

†Trenchering. *Obs. rare.* ...

Trencherless, *a.* ...

Trencher-man. ...

Trench-plough, -plow. ...

Trenchmore. ...

Trenchment. *Obs. rare.* ...

Trenching, *vbl. sb.* ...

Trench-let. ...

Trenchman. ...

Trend, *sb.* ...

Trend, *v.* ...

Trende. *Obs. rare.* ...

Trending, *vbl. sb.* ...

†Trendled, *a.* ...

Trendle. ...

Trenne, Trennel. ...

Trenton. *Geol.* ...

Trent, *obs. f.* TRUE. ...

Trent, *sb.* ...

Trental. ...

Trentine, *a.* ...

Trepan, *sb.* ...

Trepan, trapan ...

Trepan. **Trepanation.** **Trepang.** **Trepanner.** **Trepan'ner.** **Trepans, pass.** **Trephine.** **Trephination.** **Trepid.** **Trepidant.** **Trepidate.** **Trepidation.** **Trephined.** **Trepidatory.** **Trepidity.** **Trepidous.** **Tresaiel.** **Trespass.**

Trespasable. **Trespass.** **Trespassement.** **Trespasser.** **Trespassing.** **Tress.** **Tressed.** **Tressel.** **Tressette.** **Tressure.** **Tressed.** **Trest.** **Trestle.**

Trestle. [ME. *trestel*, *trestle*, a. OF. *trestel* (mod.F. *tréteau*) :— L. *transtillum*, dim. of *transtrum* cross-beam.]

5. *transf.* and *fig.* esp. (*pl.*) applied to the legs.

b. *Obs.*

8. *attrib.* and *Comb.*: trestle-bed, a portable or movable bed supported upon trestles, as used in a hospital tent, etc.; trestle-board, a board laid upon trestles to form a table; trestle-bridge, a bridge supported upon trestles or trestlework (see *4*); † trestle-cloth; † trestle-foot; † trestle-table, a table made of a movable board or boards laid upon trestles; trestle-work, a framework composed of a series of trestles (of wood or iron) fastened together, for supporting a bridge or viaduct, esp. on a railway.

Hence **Trestle** v. *trans.*, to place upon trestles; **Trestled** (trest'ld) a., provided with or supported upon trestles; **Trestlewise** *adv.*, in the manner of a trestle (in quot. *fig.*); **Trestling**, a structure of trestles, trestlework.

Trestle-tree. *Naut.* Forms: see TRESTLE.

Trestle-work (trest'l-w3·k). [f. TRESTLE + WORK.]

Hence **Tresun**, obs. form of TREASON.

Tret (tret), *sb.* *Comm.* *Obs. exc. Hist.* [Known *c* 1500: origin and history obscure.]

† Tret, a. *Obs. rare*⁻¹. [App. a shortened form of TRETIS.]

Tret, Tretabili, -ble, **Tretar**, obs. ff. TREAT, TREATABLE, TREATER.

† Tretis, a. *Obs.* Forms: *tretys*, *tretis*, -ise, -es, *traytise*, -yse. [a. OF. *tretis*, *tretice*, -*ice*, -*iz* (in Godef.) ...] Well-proportioned, neat, graceful, handsome.

† Treve. *Obs. rare.* Also 3 **trieue** (for trieve), † **treue** (for treve). [a. L. *trēo*, OF. also *trive* (13th c. in Godef.)...] 1. A true; a truce.

Tretour, (-owre), -ourous, obs. ff. TRAITOR, TRAITOROUS. **Tretifolle**, -y, trettifolle, obs. ff. TREACLE, -Y, etc. **Trettle**, **Trettil**, obs. ff. TREAT, TREATY, TRETTLE, obs. f. TRATTLE sb.

† Treunt, v. *Obs. rare.* [Etymol. obscure: has some likeness to TRUANT.] *intr.*? To depart.

Treuage, **truage**. *Obs.* Forms: 3-6 **truage**, 4-5 **trowage**, 4-5 **trewage**, 4-5 **treuage**, 5 **truwage**. [a. OF. *treuage* (13th c. in Godef.), tribute, f. OF. *treu*, *trew* (Roland, 11th c.) :— L. *tribūtum*.] **Tribute.**

† Trevally. *Obs. or dial.* Forms: † trevall, (travalline), travally, † vale, travally, -vala, travalley, -vale. [Supposed to be an alteration ...]

† Trevally. Also -valley, -valli, -valla, travalley, -vale.

Of CAVALLY. A name applied in Australasia to several sea-fishes, mostly of the family *Carangidæ* or Horse-Mackerels.

† Tret, *sb.* **Treat**, *v.*

† Treve. *Obs. rare.* Also 3 **trieue** (for trieve), † **treue** (for treve). [a. L. *trēo*, older *trēud* (Roland, 11th c.) : see TREWAGE. Tribute. *Bring to treve*, to subject to tribute, make tributary.

Trevess, obs. form of TRAVERSE, TRAVIS sb.

† Trevet (tre·vit). *Obs.* Also **trevat**, **trivat**, **trevette** (*Cent. Dict.* 1891). [Derivation unascertained.] An instrument with a sharp blade formerly used for cutting the loops which form the pile of velvet, Wilton carpets, etc., when hand-woven.

Treveth, **treveth**, obs. ff. TRIVET. **Trevethick**, obs. f. TRIVET. **Trewbat**, obs. ff. TRULY, TRIUMPH. **Trewhle**, -hle, obs. ff. TRULY. TRIUMPH.

Trevis, **trevisse**, obs. ff. TRAVERSE, TRAVIS. **Trewp(e**, trewthe, obs. ff. TRUTH. **Trewvesse**, **Travis**, **Trevet**, obs. f. TRIVET. **Tre·vice†** var. TRAVIS. **Treviss**, **Travis**, obs. f. TRIVET.

† Trew. *Sc. Obs.* [a. *treu*, obs. sing. of TREWS: TRUCE.] To protect by a truce.

Trew, obs. ff. TREE, TREW v., TRUCE, TRUE.

Trewage, **truage**. *Obs.* Forms: 3-6 **truage**, 4-5 **trowage**, 4-5 **trewage**, 4. OF. *treuage* (13th c. in Godef.), tribute, f. OF. *treu*, *trew* (Roland, 11th c.) :— L. *tribūtum* ...

Trewagher *Obs.* One subject to tribute, a tributary. (Cf. *Aunager.*)

† Trewall. *Obs.* var. TRIVAL.

Trewaille, **Trewant**, obs. ff. TRAVAIL, TRUANT. **Trewberry**, obs. f. STRAWBERRY.

† Trewe. *Obs.* Also 5 **treow**, 6 **trewis** (8-9 *trule*). [ad. Irish *triu*, Gael. *triubhas*, sb. sing. ad. Eng. TROUSE (singular, with pl. *trouses*) ...] **Trews** (trūz), *sb. pl.* Also 6 trewis (8-9 *truis*). Close-fitting trousers, or breeches combined with stockings, formerly worn by Irishmen and Scottish Highlanders, and still by certain Scottish regiments.

Trewellyng, obs. f. TRAVELLING.

Trews, **trewis**, **trewyse**, obs. f. TRUCE.

Trewsman. A wearer of trews; a Highlander.

Trews, **trewins**, **trewyoo**, -ys, obs. ff. TRUCE. **Trewp(e**, trewthe, obs. ff. TRUTH.

Trey (trē), *sb.* Forms: 4-7 **treye**, 6-9 **tray**, 7 **trie**, 5- **trey**. [a. OF. and AF. *treis*, *trei*, 6 *trois*, dial. *tray* :— Prov. *treis*, nom. *trei*, Sp. *tres*, ...]

3. *Comb.* **trey-ace**, a throw that turns up trey with one die and ace with the other; so **trey-deuce**; **trey-point** = sense 1; † **trey-table**, f. **trey-trace** (?).

Trey, **tray**, v. : app. f. TREY *sb.*] To divide or deal (a pack of cards) into three heaps in order to separate the suits (in the order of which new cards are or were packed), before shuffling in the usual way.

† Treygobet. *Obs.* [Evidently, *trey go bet* = three go better: cf. *bygobet* (BIT 2): but origin unknown.] Name of an old game at dice.

Tri- (troi, accr. tri), *prefix*, a. L. *tri-* and Gr. *τρι-*, *τρία*, repr. the combining form of L. *trēs* three, neut. *tria*, also Gr. *τρεῖς*, *τρία* ... Forming adjs. (and derived sbs. and advbs.) with the senses:

I. Having, characterized by, or consisting of (rarely, belonging or relating to) three (of the things denoted by the second element).

Triad (troi·æd). Also 6-7 **triade**. [L. L. *triad-*, *triad-em* ...]

I. A union of three.

II. 1. *Chem.* An element or radical having a combining capacity equal to three hydrogen atoms ...

Triacid (troi·æsid), a. *Chem.* [TRI- + ACID.]

Triaconta-, comb. form of Gr. *τριάκοντα* thirty.

Triad (troi·æd). Also 6-7 *adv.* TRI-, *triad-*.

Tri- *prefix.* L. L. (*Continued from preceding page.*)

Tridynamous (troidi·næmos) *Bot.* [after DIDYNAMOUS, TETRADYNAMOUS] having six stamens of which three are longer than the others.

Triable (troi·ab'l), a¹. [a. AF. *triable*, f. as TRI 1 + -ABLE.] That may be tried.

Triad (troi·æd). Also 6-7 **triade**.

Triad.

Cf. F. *triade* (1564 in Hatz.-Darm.).]

1 A group or set of three (persons, things, words, attributes, etc.); three collectively or in connexion.

b. The number three (in Pythagorean philosophy).

2. Specific uses. **a.** Applied to the Trinity.

Triadic (traɪˈædɪk), *a.* [f. TRIAD + -IC.] Of, pertaining to, or constituting a triad; consisting of triads.

Triadist.

Triadisphorus.

Triakis- (traɪˈækɪs).

Trial (traɪəl), *sb.*[1] Also < Sc. triel, 6-7 *St.* tryal[l], 6-7 tri-, tryall, 7-8 (9 *dial.*) tryal. [< AF. *trial*, *triel*, f. *trier* to TRY, instanced in 16th c., but not in mod. F.]

1. *Law.* The examination and determination of a cause by a judicial tribunal; determination of the guilt or innocence of an accused person by a court.

2. The determination of a person's guilt or innocence, the judgement of the accuser and accused.

3. The action of testing or putting to the proof the fitness, truth, strength, or other quality of anything; test, probation.

Trialism (traɪəlɪz'm). [f. as prec. + -ISM, after *dualism*.]

1. The doctrine of the threefold constitution of man, as body, soul, and spirit, or other three separate essences.

2. A union of three states or countries.

Triality (traɪˈælɪtɪ). *rare.* [f. as prec., after *duality*, *plurality*.]

1. The holding of three benefices at once. *Obs.*

2. The condition or quality of being threefold.

Trialogue (traɪˈæləg). [Erroneous formation on supposed analogy of *dialogue*, the first syllable of this being mistaken for the prefix DI- ²= two. Cf. med.L. *trialogus* (Wyclif).] A dialogue or colloquy between three persons.

Triamide.

Triamine (traɪˈæmiːn). *Chem.* [f. TRI- 5 a + AMINE.] A carbon compound containing three amidogen or amino-groups (NH₂), but excluding the amides, in which the amidogen may be viewed as replacing acid hydroxyl groups.

Triandrian, Triandrous.

Triandria (traɪˈændrɪə). *Bot.* [mod.L. (Linnæus 1735.)]

Triangle (traɪˈæŋg'l). *Bot.* [mod.L.]

a. *Astron.* The constellation *Triangulum*, or *Aries*, characterized by three stars in the position of the angular points of an isosceles triangle.

b. *Naut.*

Triangle (traɪˈæŋg'l), *sb.* [ad. (through OF. *triangle*) L. *triangulum*, neut. of *triangulus* three-cornered, f. TRI- + *angulus* ANGLE.]

1. *Geom.* A plane figure having three angles and three sides; a plane rectilineal figure bounded by three straight lines.

Triangled (traɪˈæŋg'ld), *a.* Also **3-angled**, etc. [f. prec. + -ED².] Three-cornered, triangular. *Obs.*

Trianglewise (traɪˈæŋg'lwaɪz), *adv. Obs.* [f. TRIANGLE *sb.* + -WISE.] In the manner of a triangle; triangularly.

Triangular (traɪˈæŋgjʊlər), *a.* [ad. late L. *triangulāris*, f. L. *triangulum* TRIANGLE: see -AR¹. Cf. OF. *triangulaire* (13th c. in Godef.).]

1. Having, or arranged in, the form of a triangle; having three sides and angles; three-cornered, three-sided.

Triangularity (traɪˌæŋgjʊˈlærɪtɪ).

Triangularly (traɪˈæŋgjʊlərlɪ), *adv.*

Triangulate (traɪˈæŋgjʊleɪt), *v.* [ad. mod.L. *triangulāt-*, ppl. stem of med.L. *triangulāre* to make triangular.]

Triangulate (traɪˈæŋgjʊlət), *ppl. a.* [ad. mod.L. *triangulātus*, TRI-ANGULATE *v.*, in terms of Nat. Hist. denoting a combination of this with another form.]

Triangulated (traɪˈæŋgjʊleɪtɪd), *ppl. a.*

Triangulation (traɪˌæŋgjʊˈleɪʃən). [ad. mod.L. *triangulātiōn-* (Abelard, &c.), n. of action from *triangulāre* to TRIANGULATE. So F. *triangulation* (1835 in Dict. Acad.).]

Triangulo- (traɪˈæŋgjʊlo), used in combination.

Trianguloid. *Phil. Trans.* XXIX. 183 A series of Fractions..whose Numerator is a given Number and Denominators are triangular or pyramidal or triangulo-triangular Numbers, &c.

Trianguli, Obs. form of TRIANGLE.

Triangular-ous (traiˈæŋgjuˌləs), a. Obs. rare. [f. L. *triangul-us* + -OUS.] Resembling a triangle; of somewhat triangular form.

Trianisal (traiˈænisˌæl). Obs. rare three. [f. L. *trianisal-*] Occurring every three years; lasting for three years; = TRIENNIAL

Triannual, a. Obs. Occurring thrice a year.

Triantelope (traiˈæntəˌləup). *Australia.* Also triantelupe. Popular corruption of TARANTULA, applied to a large spider of the genus *Voconia.*

Triantheous = see TRI- 1.

Triapsal, a. [f. TRI- + L. *aps-is, apsid-em* APSE + -AL] Having three apses. Also **Triapsidal**.

Triarch (traiˈɑːk), *sb.* Obs. [ad. Gr. τριαρχία, f. τρι- three + ἀρχή rule.] 1. The ruler of one of three divisions of a country or territory.

Triarchate (traiˈɑːkət). [f. as prec. + -ATE.]

Triarchy (traiˈɑːki). [f. TRI- + Gr. -αρχία government, and ad. Gr. τριαρχία triumvirate.]

Triassic (traiˈæsik), a. *Geol.* [f. TRIAS + -IC.] Of belonging to the Trias; *Triassic system* = TRIAS 2.

Triasso-, combining form, Tri- body.

Triatic (traiˈætik), a. *Naut.* [Origin obscure.]

Triatomic (traiˈætɒmik), a. *Chem.* [f. TRI- + ATOM + -IC.]

Tribadism (ˈtribədiz'm). [f. TRIBAD- + -ISM.]

Tribasic (traiˈbeisik), a. *Chem.* [f. Gr. τρι- THREE + BASIC.]

Tribasilar: see TRI- 1.

Tribrill, tribrillo, obs. var. TREBLE.

Tribber: see TRI- 1.

Tribe (traib), *sb.* Forms: a. 3 *pl.* tribus, 4-6 tribu, (*pl.* -us), 5 trybu-s. β. 4-6 trybe, (7 *Sc.* tryb), 4- tribe. [a. L. *tribus.*]

Tribeless, a. [f. TRIBE *sb.* + -LESS.] Belonging to no tribe.

Triblet (ˈtriblet). Also prec. + -LET.]

Tribe-man = see TRIBESMAN.

Tribesman (ˈtraibzmən). [f. TRIBE'S, genitive of TRIBE *sb.* + MAN *sb.*]

Tribler, tribble, app. obs. for *trebler,* a treble-singer.

Tribromhydrin (traibrɒmˈhaidrin). *Chem.*

Triblet (ˈtriblet).

Triboluminescence (tribəˌljuːmiˈnɛs'ns). [f. Gr. τρίβος rubbing + LUMINESCENCE.] The quality of emitting light under friction or violent pressure.

Tribometer (traiˈbɒmitə). [f. Gr. τρίβος + -METER.] An instrument for estimating sliding friction.

Tribophosphorescence.

Triboelectric.

Tribrach (ˈtraibræk, ˈtrib-). *Prosody.*

Tribrach (ˈtraibræk). [f. TRI- + Gr. βραχύ-arm.]

Tribrachial.

Tribulation (tribjuˈleiʃən). Also 4-6 tribulacioun, 4-5 tribulacyon.

Tribuloid (ˈtribjuˌlɔid). a. *Bot.* [f. mod.L.]

Tribuna (triˈbjuːnə). [It. and mod.L. *tribuna* TRIBUNE *sb.*]

Tribunal (traiˈbjuːn'l, tri-). *sb.* [a. F. *tribunal* or ad. L. *tribunal*.]

Tribunalled, *ppl. a.* [f. TRIBUNAL + -ED.]

Tribunate (ˈtribjuˌnət, -neit). [ad. L. *tribunat-us.*]

Tribune (ˈtribjuːn, tri-). *sb.* 1. [ad. L. *tribun-us.*]

Tribuneship.

Tribunitial, -ial (tribjuˈniʃəl), a. [f. L. *tribunici-us* + -AL.]

Tribunitian, -ician (tribjuˈniʃən), a.

Tribunitive, a. rare.

Tributary (ˈtribjuˌtəri), a. and *sb.* [ad. L. *tributari-us.*]

Tribute (ˈtribjuːt).

Tri-bladed, -blastic: see TRI- 1 c, a.

TRIBUTE.

Tribute (tri·biūt), *sb.* ...

Tribute (tri·biūt), *v.* [f. prec. *sb.*] ...

Tribute-money. ...

Tributer, tributee (tri·biŭtar). ...

Tributorious, *a. rare.* ...

Tributory, *a.* and *sb. Obs.* ...

Tributyrin. *Chem.* ...

Tricalcium ...

Tricalcic, *a. Chem.* ...

TRICALCIUM.

Tricapsular (traikæ·psiŭlăr), *a. Nat. Hist.* ...

Tri-car or Tricaudate: see Tri- 4 C, 1 a.

Tricarbon (trai·kāɹbŏn), *a. Chem.* ...

Trichory, -ori. *Obs. rare.* [f. forms of TREACHERY.]

Trice, *sb.* *Obs. rare.* ...

Trice (trais), *sb.[2].* ...

Trice (trais), *v.[1].* ...

TRICAPSULAR.

-trice, *suffix,* ...

Triceps (trai·seps), *a.* and *sb.* ...

Tricennary (trise·nări), *a.* ...

Tricennial (trise·nial), *a.* and *sb.* ...

Tricentenary, Tricentennial. ...

Tricerium: see Tricerion.

Triceratops (traise·rătŏps). *Palæont.* ...

Tricollary: see Tri-.

Tricenary (tri·sĕnări), *a.* ...

Tricenarious, *a.* ...

Trich- : see Tricho-.

TRICHI.

Trichi (trai·kai). ...

Trichiniasis ...

TRICHIASIS.

Trichiasis (triki·ăsis). *Path.* ...

Trichidium (triki·diŭm). *Bot.* Pl. -ia. ...

Trichina (tri·kinə, trikai·nə). *Zool.* Pl. -æ. ...

Trichite (tri·kəit, trai·-), *a.* ...

Trichitic (triki·tik), *a.* ...

Trichiuriform, *a.* ...

Trichloro-, trichlor- (trai·klōro-). *Chem.* ...

Trichloride (trai·klōrəid). *Chem.* ...

Trichobranchia ...

344 TRICHO-.

Trichæanthe- ...

Trichangia ...

Trichoblast ...

Trichocyst ...

Trichogen ...

Trichogyne ...

Trichoid ...

Trichoma ...

TRICHO-. 345

Trichoptera ...

Trichology. The study of the structure, functions, and diseases of the hair. ...

Trichoma (tri·kŏmə). *Path.* Pl. tricho·mata. ...

Trichomanes (trikŏ·mănīz). *Bot.* ...

Trichord (trai·kōɹd). ...

TRICHOTOMY.

Trichotomic (trike·, traikŏ·tŏmik), *a.* ...

Trichotomism (traikŏ·tŏmiz'm). ...

Trichotomize (traikŏ·tŏmaiz), *v.* ...

Trichotomous (traikŏ·tŏmas), *a.* ...

Trichotomy (traikŏ·tŏmi). ...

| TRICHROIC | 346 | TRICK. | TRICK. 347 | TRICKIFY. |

Trichroic (trai·kro·ik), a. [f. Gr. τρίχρωο-ς three-coloured + -IC: cf. DICHROIC.] Having or showing three colours; spec. of crystals, exhibiting three different colours when viewed in three different directions.

Trichroism (trai·kro·iz'm). [f. as prec. + -ISM.] C. f. *trichroisme.] The property of being trichroic; spec. a. Cryst.: see prec.

Trichromatic (traikroumæ·tik), a. [f. Gr. τρι-, Tri- + χρωματ- CHROMATIC.] Having three colours; trichroic; spec. a. Optics. Having or relating to the three fundamental colour-sensations (red, green, violet) of normal vision. b. Applied to lithographic printing in three colours.

Trichromic (traikro·mik), a. [f. DICHROMIC.] Three-coloured; three-colour; = TRICHROMATIC.

So **Trichro·matism**, the quality of being trichromatic.

Trichromism (trai·kro·miz'm), rare. [f. prec.] = TRICHROMATISM.

Trichrome (trai·kro·m), a. [as prec. + -ONE.] Three-coloured.

Tricipital (traisi·pital), a. rare⁻⁰. [f. L. triceps, -cipit-em three-headed.]

Tricircular (traisö·kiŭlaĭ), a. Geom. [f. TRI- + CIRCULAR.]

Trick (trik), sb. [First in 16th c.]

Trick (trik), v. [f. TRICK sb.]

Tricked (trikt), ppl. a.

Tricker (trikar). See TRIGGER.

Trickery (tri·kari). [f. TRICK v. or sb. + -ERY.]

Trickily (tri·kili), adv. [f. TRICKY + -LY².]

Trickiness (tri·kinès). [f. TRICKY + -NESS.]

Tricking (tri·kiŋ), vbl. sb. [f. TRICK v. + -ING¹.]

Trickish (tri·kiʃ), a. [f. TRICK sb. + -ISH.]

Trickle (tri·k'l), v. [Forms: 4-6 trekel, (4 Sc. trygle, 4-5 trikle, trekil, 6 Sc. trigle, ill), 5 trekyl, 5, 6 trikill, ol, -ell, 6 tryckel, (tricole, trycole, 7 trukle), 6- trickle.]

Trickle (tri·k'l), sb. [f. TRICKLE v. + -LY².]

Trickling, vbl. sb.

Trickment, rare. [f. TRICK v. + -MENT.]

Tricksiness (tri·ksinès). [f. TRICKSY + -NESS.]

Trickster (tri·kstaĭ). [f. TRICK sb. or v. + -STER.]

Tricksy (tri·ksi), a. [f. TRICKS, pl. of TRICK sb. + -Y.]

Trickily, adv.

Trick-track. See TIC-TAC.

Tricky (tri·ki), a. [f. TRICK sb. + -Y.]

Tricolic, a.

Tricolor, tricolour (trai·kŭlaĭ). [a. F. tricolore.]

Triconsonantal, a.

Semitic languages. Hence **Triconsona·ntalism**, triconsonantal formation. So **Triconsona·ntic** *a.*

1863 *Smith's Bible Dict.* III. 1539/1 It is more than probable that the triconsonantal has been evolved out of a biconsonantal root. *Ibid.*, The bisyllabism [of the Hebrew verb] is in reality triconsonantalism, the vowels not forming any part of the essence of the root. 1869 FARRAR *Fam. Speech* iii. (1873) 88 The root of the Semitic verb is always triliteral, or rather triconsonantic.

Tricorn (trəi·kǭɹn), *a.* and *sb.* Also (as or after Fr.) **tricorne**. [ad. F. *tricorne* or L. *tricornis* three-horned, f. *tri-*, TRI- + L. *cornū* horn.]

A. *adj.* Three-horned; having three horns or horn-like projections; *spec.* applied to a cocked hat with the brim turned up on three sides.

1844 HOBLYN *Dict. Med. Terms*, *Tricorne*, ..a term applied to each lateral ventricle of the brain, from its three-horned shape. 1864 M. J. HIGGINS *Ess.* (1875) 201 With their tricorn hats they looked very much like Knaves of Spades. 1883 A. WALLIS in *N. & Q.* 6th Ser. VIII. 363/1 A white bob-wig surmounted by a tricorne hat completes the ordinary costume of a gentleman living in the second Georgian period. 1909 *Daily Graphic* LXXX. 13/1 An ermine tricorne hat.

B. *sb.*

1. An (imaginary) creature with three horns.

1760 *Impostors Detected* III. viii. II. 78 These creatures were distinguished..by a lump on their heads,..supported by three small protuberances; from whence they were called Tri-corns. 1823 [see BICORN]. 1895 F. E. HULME *Nat. Hist. Lore & Leg.* 147 What can have..suggested the idea of such a very unpleasant tricorn, it is impossible to say.

2. A tricorn hat: see A.

1876 G. MEREDITH *Beauch. Career* ii, A shocking bad, bald, brown-rubbed old *tricorne*. 1903 J. CONRAD & HUEFFER *Romance* v. i, He wore a large and shadowy tricorn.

So † **Trico·rnous** *a.* (*obs. rare*⁻⁰), three-horned. 1656 in BLOUNT *Glossogr.*

Tri-cornered, -cornigerous, -cornute, etc.: see TRI- 1 c, 1.

Tricorporal (trəikǭ·ɹpŏrăl), *a.* [f. TRI- + L. *corpus, corpor-* body + -AL: cf. *corporal.*] Having three bodies; three-bodied. So **Trico·rporate**, **Trico·rporated** *adjs.* in same sense, *spec.* in *Her.*: see quots.; also **Trico·rporous** *a.* (*rare*⁻⁰).

1730–6 BAILEY (folio), **Tricorporal*, that hath three bodies. 1822 T. TAYLOR *Apuleius* III. 59 Coequal to the destruction of the tricorporal Geryon, or the three-headed Cerberus. 1731 BAILEY vol. II, **Tricorporate, Tricorporous*, that hath three bodies. *c* 1828 BERRY *Encycl. Her.* I. Gloss., *Tricorporate* is said when the bodies of three beasts are represented issuing from the dexter, sinister, and base points of the escocheon, and meeting conjoined to one head in the centre point. 1572 BOSSEWELL *Armorie* II. 42 *Tricorporated. 1610 GUILLIM *Heraldry* III. xv. (1611) 141 A Tricorporated Lion issuing out of the three corners of the Escocheon all meeting vnder one head. 1727 BAILEY vol. II, **Tricorporous.*

Tricoryphean, -costate: see TRI- 1.

Tri·cosane, tri-i·cosane. *Chem.* [f. Gr. τρία three + εἴκοσι twenty + -ANE.] A hydrocarbon belonging to the paraffin series, containing 23 atoms of carbon.

1894 MUIR & MORLEY *Watts' Dict. Chem.* IV. 793 *n*-Tricosane $C_{23}H_{48}$ (melting point 48°C.)...Obtained also by fractional distillation of paraffin oil from brown coal...Glittering plates. 1902 *Jrnl. Chem. Soc.* LXXXII. I. 734 Pennsylvania Petroleum..furnished a small proportion of a solid tricosane, $C_{23}H_{48}$, which melts at 45°.

† **Tricot**¹. *Obs. rare*⁻¹. [Allied to OF. *tricotage* chicanery, trickery (Godef. *Compl.*), *tricotement* chicane (*c* 1400 in Godef.), *tricoterie* 'cousenage, cheating, trecherie, deceit, in the following of a suit, &c.' (Cotgr.), which imply a vb. **tricoter* to cozen, cheat, and perh. a sb. **tricot*; but these do not appear in this sense, unless they are fig. uses of *tricoter* to knit, *tricot* knitting.] Trickery, fraud.

c 1430 *Pilgr. Lyf Manhode* III. xxvi. (1869) 150 The oother hand..is cleped..tricot..and disceyuaunce.

Tricot² (trīko). [F. *tricot* knitting, knitted work, f. *tricoter* to knit; of uncertain origin.] Knitting; knitted work or fabric; a woollen fabric, knitted by hand, or by machinery in imitation of hand-knitting; also, name of a woollen fabric (see quot. 1904). Also short for *tricot-stitch*.

1872 BROWNING *Fifine* iii, The human beauty..Tricot fines down if fat, padding plumps up if lean. 1882 CAULFEILD & SAWARD *Dict. Needlework* 128/2 Make a Foundation chain and work a row of Tricot. 1893 A. ZIMMERN tr. *Blümner's Home Life Anc. Grks.* xii. 440 The costume and the tricots, as well as the grotesque masks, are worthy of notice. 1898 *Daily News* 5 Mar. 6/4 A mourning walking dress in woollen tricot. 1904 *Woollen Draper's Terms* in *Tailor & Cutter* 4 Aug. 480/1 *Tricots*, a woollen fabric, with diagonals running straight across the piece, and something like cassimere handle.

b. *attrib.*, as *tricot-stitch, tricot-work.*

1880 *B'ham Weekly Post* 2 Oct. 1/5, I have an interminable piece of trico work in hand, which has been my resource for several years. 1882 CAULFEILD & SAWARD *Dict. Needlework* 128/1 *Tricot stitch*...The easiest of crochet stitches, but only suitable for straight work; it is usually worked with Berlin or fleecy wool, and a wooden hook, and is suitable for couvrepieds, counterpanes, muffatees, mufflers, and other warm articles.

† **Tricotee**, *sb. Obs.* Also 7 **trick-a-tee**, 8 **tricotes**. [a. F. *tricotets*, also *tricotée* (Lamonnoye in Littré), f. *tricoter* to dance in a lively manner: origin uncertain.] A lively kind of old dance. Hence † **Tricotee** *v.* (with *it*), to dance this. *Obs.*

1659 *Lady Alimony* I. ii. A iij b, A Monkey dancing his Trick-a-tee on a Rope. 1664 COTTON *Scarron.* IV. (1741) 120 Poor Dido..tho' oppressed with Woe and Care, cut Capers, and Tricotee'd it barefoot. 1667 FLECKNOE *Damoiselles à la Mode* IV. ii. 80 The dancing Bears shall dance the Tricotees with him for a wager. *a* 1701 SEDLEY *Grumbler* II. i, Will you have a minuet, Sir?..What then? (here he names half a dozen dances) The trocanny, tricotez, rigadon?

Tricotyledonous: see TRI- 1.

Tricquet, variant of TRIQUET *Obs.*

Tricrotic (trəikrǫ·tik), *a. Physiol.* [f. TRI-, after DICROTIC; cf. Gr. τρίκροτος rowed with triple stroke, as a trireme.] Of the pulse or a sphygmographic tracing: Having or showing three undulations for each beat of the heart. *Tricrotic wave*, the third of such undulations. So **Tri·crotism**, tricrotic condition; **Tri·crotous** *a.* = *tricrotic.*

1876 tr. *Wagner's Gen. Pathol.* (ed. 6) 630 The pulse of aged persons is tricrotic. 1877 ROBERTS *Handbk. Med.* (ed. 3) II. 21 This form of pulsation is sometimes called tricrotous. 1890 BILLINGS, *Tricrotic wave*, the third curve of the sphygmogram. 1891 *Cent. Dict.*, Tricrotism. 1913 DORLAND *Med. Dict.* s.v. *Pulse*, *Tricrotic pulse*, one that is marked by three abnormally distinct sphygmographic waves to the pulse-beat.

Tricrunodal, -crural: see TRI- 1.

Tric-trac (tri·k,træ·k). Also 7– **trick-track**. [a. F. *tric-trac*, † *trique-trac* (16th c. in Littré; cf. also *jeux de triquetacts*, Godef. *Compl.*); so called from the clicking sound made by the pieces in playing the game: F. *tric-trac*, an echoic word (15th c.), applied to various clicking noises.] An old variety of backgammon: = TICK-TACK 2.

[1653 URQUHART *Rabelais* II. vii. 41 The trictrac of the knocking Friars.] 1687 SEDLEY *Bellamira* IV. i, I lost three sets at back-gammon, and a tout at trick-track. 1690 R. DAVIES *Jrnl.* (Camden) 78, I taught them to play grand tric-trac. 1788 *Gentl. Mag.* Dec. 1071/1 One of the kinds of trictrac used in Europe. 1852 THACKERAY *Esmond* I. iv, He loved to play at cards and tric-trac with him. 1897 DOWDEN *Fr. Lit.* V. i. 336 The destiny of nations is satirically viewed as a vulgar game of trick-track.

attrib. 1800 MAR. EDGEWORTH *Belinda* xxx, There's Mrs. Delacour leading Miss Portman off into the trictrac cabinet. 1819 LAMB *Let. to Miss Wordsworth* 25 Nov., In the trick-track board, where the hits are figured.

Tricube, Tricurvate: see TRI- 4 a, 2.

Tricuspid (trəikʊ·spid), *a.* (*sb.*) [ad. L. *tricuspis, -cuspid-em* three-pointed, f. *tri-*, TRI- + *cuspis* point: cf. F. *tricuspide* (Littré).] Having three cusps or points. **a. Tricuspid valve** or **valves** (*Anat.*): the valve consisting of three triangular segments (or, as otherwise regarded, the set of three triangular valves) which guards the opening from the right auricle into the right ventricle of the heart. Also *absol.* or as *sb.*; hence *attrib.*, as *tricuspid murmur, obstruction, opening, regurgitation*, etc.

1670 *Phil. Trans.* V. 2097 We did also observe two Ventricles with the tricuspid [and] sigmoid-valves. 1834 J. FORBES *Laennec's Dis. Chest* (ed. 4) 547 In hypertrophy of the right ventricle..the thickening..is always a little greater in the vicinity of the tricuspid valves. 1872 HUXLEY *Physiol.* ii. 36 On the right side there are..three of these broad pointed membranes, whence the whole apparatus is called the tricuspid valve. 1877 ROBERTS *Handbk. Med.* (ed. 3) II. 10 Said to accompany tricuspid obstruction. *Ibid.* 43 Tricuspid Regurgitation. 1898 *Allbutt's Syst. Med.* V. 786 Valvular incompetence..at the tricuspid opening. *Ibid.* 869 We may notice occasionally..a tricuspid systolic murmur.

b. Of various structures, as a tooth, leaf, etc.: also *absol.* or as *sb.* a tricuspid tooth.

1849 *Florist* 212 There is something very striking..about their tricuspid petals, and quaint, lively markings. 1856 WOODWARD *Mollusca* III. 449 The central teeth are..tricuspid in Loligo. 1881 J. ANDERSON *Scot. in Early Chr. T.* iii. 130 In the West Highland crosses they are..terminated by a peculiar conventional, tricuspid leaf.

So **Tricu·spidal, Tricu·spidate, Tricu·spidated** *adjs.* in same sense.

1822–34 *Good's Study Med.* (ed. 4) I. 520 The *tricuspidal valve, with the..sigmoid valve of the pulmonary artery..never exhibit bony deposits. 1852 SALMON *Higher Plane Curves* vi. (1879) 253 The quartic is tricuspidal. 1752 J. HILL *Hist. Anim.* 11 The Brachionus, with..a *tricuspidate tail. 1881 BAKER in *Jrnl. Linn. Soc.* XVIII. 280 Stigma capitate, obscurely tricuspidate. 1822 J. PARKINSON *Outl. Oryctol.* 197 An inequivalved..shell; *tricuspidated at the base. *Ibid.* 275 Teeth of cartilaginous fishes..triangular, conical, single pointed, tricuspidated, tridentated.

Tricu·ssate, *a. Bot.* [irreg. f. DECUSSATE, with substitution of TRI- for *de-*.] (See quot.)

1900 B. D. JACKSON *Gloss. Bot. Terms*, *Tricussate*, used for whorls of three leaves each, the leaves of each whorl alternating with those above and below.

Tricyanate, Tricyanide: see TRI- 5 a.

Tricycle (trəi·sik'l), *sb.* [a. F. *tricycle*, used in sense 1 in 1827; in sense 2 in Dict. Acad. 1878; f. TRI- + Gr. κύκλος circle, wheel: cf. BICYCLE.]

†1. A three-wheeled coach or omnibus drawn by two horses, formerly used in Paris. *Obs.*

1828 *Chron.* in *Ann. Reg.* 185/1 Tricycles.—Christmas-day was rendered memorable to the Parisians by the starting of this new species of carriage...The tricycle is a kind of coach, mounted on three wheels; it is drawn by two horses only.

2. A velocipede with three wheels (now usually one in front and one on each side behind), driven by treadles actuated by the feet, or (*motor tricycle*) by a small motor attached.

1868 *London Society* Nov. 411 The tricycle, or three-wheeled Velocipede, is easier to guide and safer to use than the bicycle. 1881 *Philad. Record* No. 3459. 2 M. Trouve riding at ease through the streets of Paris upon a tricycle driven by stored-up electricity. 1896 Motor tricycle [see MOTOR A. 5]. 1902 *Encycl. Brit.* XXVII. 325 As far back as 1883 or 1884 the whole of Europe had been covered by women on tricycles.

attrib. and *Comb.* 1885 *Graphic* 21 Feb. 186/1 An Englishman..tricycle-riding the country. 1896 *Daily News* 28 May 3/2 Infantry bring up a tricycle Maxim gun.

Hence **Tri·cycle** *v.*, *intr.* to ride a tricycle (whence **Tri·cycling** *vbl. sb.* and *ppl. a.*); **Tri·cycler, Tri·cyclist**, one who rides a tricycle; **Tricy·cular** *a.* [irreg. after *vehicular*; cf. BICYCULAR], pertaining to tricycles.

1883 *Sat. Rev.* 28 July 107/2 The modern heroine..rides, boats, *tricycles, and plays lawn-tennis. 1902 *19th Cent.* Nov. 764, I was tricycling homeward one evening. 1881 *Daily News* 18 July 5/5 Some member of Parliament should take the matter up, so as to relieve the steam *tricyclers from the restriction. 1888 J. & E. R. PENNELL *Sent. Journ.* 180 A meeting of tricyclers was not an every-day occurrence in their town. 1882 *Standard* 15 May 2/8 *Tricycling divisions of bicycle clubs. 1882 RICHARDSON in *Gd. Words* 177 Mr. Browning called my attention to *tricycling as a healthful recreation. 1878 *Prospectus Bicycle Touring Club*, Any amateur Bicyclist or *Tricyclist—lady or gentleman—is eligible for election to the Bicycle Touring Club. 1887 *Times* 9 Apr. 5/5 The tricyclists were formed into the main column. 1870 *Belgravia* Feb. 444 The latest contrivance in that way comes more under the *tricycular head.

Tricyclic (trəisi·klik, -səi·klik), *a.* [f. Gr. τρι-, TRI- + κύκλος circle + -IC.]

1. *Bot.* Arranged in three whorls.

1900 in B. D. JACKSON *Gloss. Bot. Terms.*

2. *Chem.* Of a carbon compound: Having three rings or closed chains of atoms in its structural formula; e.g. phenanthrene. (Ger. *tricyklisch.*)

1891 *Jrnl. Chem. Soc.* LX. 1258 The two best known tricyclic compounds, anthracene and phenanthrene.

‖**Tridacna** (trəi-, tridæ·knă). *Zool.* [mod.L. (Da Costa 1776), f. Gr. τρίδακν-ος eaten at three bites, f. τρι-, TRI- + δάκν-ειν to bite.] A genus of bivalve molluscs, including the *Tridacna gigas* or Giant Clam, the largest bivalve shell known. Also *attrib.*

1776 DA COSTA *Conchol.* 294 A Tridacna, the Bason Conch or Clamp. 1860 WRAXALL *Life in Sea* xiv. 299 The giant Tridacna, which is five feet broad, forms entire submarine banks. 1904 *Athenæum* 24 Sept. 419/1 In graves at Rubiana were found rings of tridacna shell and other objects of the same material carved in a fretwork design.

So † **Tridacnan** *a. Obs. rare*⁻⁰.

1623 COCKERAM, *Tridacnan*, any thing that is so big that must be cut in three pieces, or morsels, ere it can be eat.

Tridactyl (trəidæ·ktil), *a.* Also **-yle**. [ad. Gr. τριδάκτυλ-ος, f. τρι-, TRI- + δάκτυλος finger, digit.] Having three fingers or toes.

1812 SHAW *Gen. Zool.* VIII. 104 Tridactyle Kingfisher. 1822 J. PARKINSON *Outl. Oryctol.* 321 The feet of this animal were tridactyle. 1877 LE CONTE *Elem. Geol.* I. (1879) 431 Only three functional toes on the hind foot, which therefore formed a tridactyl track. 1912 *Return Brit. Museum* 179 A tridactyl Reptilian foot-print.

Trida·ctylous, *a.* [f. as prec. + -OUS.]

1. = prec.

1828 in WEBSTER. 1851 MANTELL *Petrifact.* i. § 3. 65 The foot-tracks are, for the most part, tridactylous (three-toed). 1856–8 W. CLARK *Van der Hoeven's Zool.* II. 379 Feet tridactylous, palmate, with hallux none.

† 2. *Chem.* Applied to a compound of an atom of one element with 3 atoms of another, as SO_3. *Obs.*

1865 MANSFIELD *Salts* 483 The simple molecule Sn...does not imitate the molecule Sb. in forming tridactylous compounds either with O. or with H.

Tridaily: see TRI- 3.

Triddil, Triddle: see TREADLE, TREDDLE.

‖ **Tride** (‖trīd, trəid), *a.* ? *Obs.* [F. *tride* 'terme de manège, vif, serré' (Littré), a. Eng. *tread* in sense 'gait, pace'.] (See quots.)

1727 BAILEY vol. II, *Tride* (with Horsemen), short and swift. *Tride-pace*, is a going of short and thick Motions, tho' united and uneasy. *Tride-career*, a fast Gallop that has its Times and Motions short and nimble. To work Tride..upon Volts, is to mark his Time with his Haunches short and ready. [Also in later Dicts. and Cyclopædias.]

Tride, obs. f. *tried*, pa. t. and pple. of TRY *v.*

Tridecane (trəi·dĭkēn). *Chem.* [f. Gr. τρία three + δέκα ten + -ANE.] A colourless liquid hydrocarbon of the paraffin series, containing 13 atoms of carbon; its melting point is −6°C. and boiling point 234°C.

1894 MUIR & MORLEY *Watts' Dict. Chem.* IV. 793 Tridecane, $C_{13}H_{28}$. 1902 *Jrnl. Chem. Soc.* LXXXII. I. 733 Hydrocarbons in Pennsylvania Petroleum...Tridecane [etc.].

So **Tridecyl** (trəi·dĭsil) [-YL], the radical ($C_{13}H_{27}$) contained in tridecane. Hence **Tridecy·lic** *a.* in *tridecylic acid*, $C_{13}H_{26}O_2$; also called **Trideco·ic** or **Tridecato·ic** *acid.*

1868 WATTS *Dict. Chem.* V. 880 Tridecyl. 1880 *Jrnl. Chem. Soc.* XXXVIII. 34 Tridecylic, Pentadecoic, [etc.] Acids..The discovery of tridecoic and pentadecoic acids makes the list of fatty acids complete as far as stearic acid. 1913 THORPE *Dict. App. Chem.* (ed. 2) V. 529 Tridecatoic or Tridecylic Acid..crystallises in thin plates; m. p. 40·5°.

† **Tri,dece·nnary**, *a. Obs. rare*⁻¹. [An irregular formation from L. *tredecim* thirteen.] Intended to mean: Of or pertaining to the number thirteen. (By the form, it ought to mean 'Of thirteen years'.)

1783 ROBERTSON *Hist. Amer.* (ed. 4) III. 385 Computed..first by what he calls a tridecennary progression of days from one to thirteen,..and then by a septenary progression of days from one to seven, making in all twenty.

Tri·decila·teral, *a. rare.* [irreg. f. L. *tredecim* thirteen + LATERAL.] Thirteen-sided.

1882 VINES *Sachs' Bot.* 205 The shoot itself may be said to be tri-, quadri-, quinqui-, octo-, trideci-lateral, &c.

Tridecile, Tridel: see TREDECILE, TREDDLE.

Trident (trəi·dĕnt), *sb.* (*a.*) [ad. L. *tridens, trident-em*, f. *tri-* three + *dens, dent-em* tooth. Cf. F. *trident* (13–14th c. in Godef. *Compl.*).]

1. An instrument or weapon with three prongs.

a. *esp.* A three-pronged fish-spear or sceptre as the attribute of the sea-god Poseidon or Neptune, also figured as borne by Britannia.

1599 NASHE *Lenten Stuffe* (1871) 18 In the swing of his trident he constituted two lord admirals ouer the whole navy of England. 1607 SHAKS. *Cor.* III. i. 256 He would not flatter Neptune for his Trident, Or Ioue, for 's power to Thunder. 1612 DEKKER *Lond. Triumph.* Wks. 1873 III. 241 In his hand he holds a siluer Trident, or Three-forked Mace. 1697 DRYDEN *Æneid* I. 208 The God himself with ready trident stands, And opes the deep, and spreads the moving sands. 1849 JAMES *Woodman* vii, Some serrated at the edges like Neptune's trident. 1898 RAWLINGS *Brit. Coinage* 113 In 1797 we have the first English regal copper penny...Britannia seated to right, the union shield at her side, a palm branch in her right hand and a trident in her left.

b. A three-pronged spear used by the *retiarius* in ancient Roman gladiatorial combats.

1693 STEPNEY in Dryden *Juvenal* viii. (1697) 209 As Retiarius he Attacks his Foe; First waves his Trident ready for the throw, Next casts his Net. 1891 FARRAR *Darkn. & Dawn* xxxix, He flung down net and dagger and trident, and, retreating to the barrier, stood there with folded arms.

c. *fig.* or in *fig.* context.

1638 R. BAKER tr. *Balzac's Lett.* (vol. II.) 202 The Syllogisme, which by the saying of a Grecian is the Trident and Mace of Philosophie, is in your Writings all painted and perfumed. 1698 CONGREVE *Birth of Muse* 109 To Worlds remote, she [Britannia] wide extends her Reign, And wields the Trident of the stormy Main. 1804 A. DUNCAN (*title*) The British Trident; or, Register of Naval Actions. 1812 WELLESLEY *Parl. Deb.* 30 Nov., To concede the points..would be to throw into her hands the trident of the main.

2. *transf.* Applied to something resembling a trident in shape or configuration, as a three-pronged fork, a piece of land with three promontories.

1730 SWIFT *Let. to Gay* 10 Nov., Tell her Grace, that the ill management of forks is not to be help'd when they are only bidential..her Grace hath cost me thirty pounds to provide Tridents for fear of offending her. 1869 TOZER *Highl. Turkey* I. 101 The two other peninsulas, which form the trident of Chalcidice.

3. *Geom.* Name of a plane cubic curve of a form suggesting a three-pronged weapon; also *trident curve*. Also called *Cartesian parabola* (PARABOLA b).

1710 J. HARRIS *Lex. Techn.* II, *Trident* is a Name given by Sir Is. Newton to that kind of Parabola, by which D'Cartes constructed Equations of six Dimensions. 1795 HUTTON *Math. Dict.* II. 191 Cartesian Parabola..$xy = ax^3+bx^2+cx+d$..being Newton's 66th species of lines of the 3d order, and called by him a *Trident*. 1864 CAYLEY *Math. Papers* V. 364 The Trident Curve.

4. *attrib.* and *Comb.*, as *trident-bearer, -swayer, tooth*; *trident-armed, -bearing, -shaped* adjs.

1866 J. CONINGTON *Æneid* I. 226 He, *trident-armed, each dull weight heaves. 1749 G. WEST *Odes Pindar* I. Antistr. v, Invocating oft the name Of the *Trident-bearing God. Strait the *Trident-bearer came. 1871 KINGSLEY *At Last* xiv, A curious *trident-shaped stand..on the horns of which garlands of flowers are hung as offerings. 1904 C. LANIER *Sonn.* in *Daily Chron.* 21 Apr. 3/2 *Trident-swayer of emotion's trembling sea! 1901 G. MEREDITH tr. *Iliad*, *Reading of Life* 128 The God drives deep his *trident teeth.

B. as *adj.* Having three prongs or forks; tridental. Also *fig.*

1589 GREENE *Menaphon* (Arb.) 24 Neptune..with his trident mace. 1648 EARL WESTMORELAND *Otia Sacra* (1879) 97 A Trident mischief that doth wound, Requires a Treble Patience to afford Relief. 1864 [see 3 above]. 1910 *Expositor* Aug. 139 He is represented..hurling the trident lightning and with a huge club.

Tridental (trəide·ntăl), *a.*¹ [f. as prec. + -AL.]

† 1. Bearing a trident. *Obs. rare.*

1635 QUARLES *Embl.* I. ii. iv, The white-mouth'd Water now usurpes the Shore, And scornes the pow'r of her trydentall Guide.

2. Of, pertaining to, or of the nature of a trident; three-pronged, trifurcate.

1648 GAGE *West Ind.* vii. 20 Catching one with a tridentall iron Fork. 1791 COWPER *Iliad* v. 458 The bold Son of Amphytrion with tridental shaft Her bosom pierced. 1843 R. H. HORNE *Orion* III. iii. 166 Now had Poseidon with tridental spear Torn up the smitten sea. 1892 *Graphic* 28 May 637/2 These picturesque tridental bays have contributed backgrounds to many of the artist's pictures.

Tride·ntal, *a.*² *rare*⁻⁰. = TRIDENTINE. Hence **Tride·ntally** *adv.*, in accordance with the Tridentine decrees.

1842 G. S. FABER *Prov. Lett.* (1844) II. 49 A very possible advance, from the fourth century, to the yet more fully instructed, because tridentally instructed, sixteenth.

Tridentate (trəide·ntĕt), *a. Bot.* and *Zool.* [f. TRI- + L. *dentāt-us* toothed: see -ATE² 2.] Having three teeth or tooth-like processes; three-pronged, three-pointed.

1760 J. LEE *Introd. Bot.* II. xxii. (1765) 124 Corolla..either ..tridentate; or quinquedentate. 1852 DANA *Crust.* I. 662 The only species..have the front of the carapax deeply tridentate. 1856–8 W. CLARK *Van der Hoeven's Zool.* I. 313 Tarsi with tridentate claws.

So † **Tride·ntated** *a. Obs.* in same sense.

1752 J. HILL *Hist. Anim.* 35 The grey Fly..with tridentated marks on the abdomen. 1822 J. PARKINSON *Outl. Oryctol.* 275 Numerous teeth of cartilaginous fishes..triangular,..tricuspidated, tridentated.

Tridented, *a.* [f. as TRIDENT + -ED.]

1. (trəide·ntĕd). Three-toothed, three-pronged; = TRIDENTATE.

1620 QUARLES *Jonah* Sect. vi. F ij, Neptune..Held his tridented Mace vpon the South. 1816 *Encycl. Perthensis* V. 639/2 The pappus [is] monophyllous and tridented.

2. (trəi·dĕntĕd). Having or furnished with a trident.

1624 QUARLES *Sion's Elegies* iii. 12 Tridented Neptune. 1866 J. B. ROSE tr. *Ovid's Met.* VIII. 236 Unto Neptune tridented I prayed.

† **Tride·ntifer**. *Obs. rare.* [a. L. *tridentifer*, f. as TRIDENT + *-fer* bearing.] He who bears a trident; the wielder of the trident; Neptune.

1600 TOURNEUR *Transf. Metamorph.* xl, Is that great gift Tridentifer presents, To make faire passage for his foule intents?

So **Tridenti·ferous** *a.*, trident-bearing.

1656 in BLOUNT *Glossogr.* 1727 in BAILEY vol. II.

Tridentine (tri·dĕntəin, trəide·ntəin), *a.* and *sb.* [ad. med.L. *Tridentīn-us*, f. *Tridentum* the city of Trent.] **A.** *adj.* Of or pertaining to the city of Trent in Tyrol, or to the Council of the Roman Catholic Church held there (1545–63).

1561 BARLOW in H. N. Birt *Eliz. Relig. Settlement* x. (1908) 424 Thomas Stapleton and Edward Goddeshalfe..as it is bruited were the last summer at Tridentine Council. *a* 1711 KEN *Hymnarium* Poet. Wks. 1721 II. 134 The Faith Nicene he spake exact, But when to that the Tridentine he tack'd, This a new Gospel is. 1849 SIR J. STEPHEN *Eccl. Biogr.* (1850) I. 475 The most promising quarrel which had arisen in the Church since the close of the Tridentine Council. 1901 BP. GORE *Body of Christ* iv. § 4 (1907) 257 When they [Protestants] rejected the Tridentine doctrine of the Melchizedekian priesthood.

B. *sb.* One who accepts and conforms to the decrees of the Council of Trent; an orthodox Roman Catholic.

a 1836 R. H. FROUDE *Rem.* (1838) I. 434 [In answer to the statement that] the Romanists were Schismatics in England, but Catholics abroad, [Froude replied] No, they are wretched Tridentines every where. *a* 1882 *Dublin Rev.* (Ogilvie), Anglicans have styled Catholics of the present day Tridentines.

So **Tri·dentize** *v. rare, intr.* to conform to the Tridentine decrees.

1826 G. S. FABER *Diffic. Romanism* (1853) 110 [It] is evident to common sense, and will readily be admitted by the tridentising Romanist.

Tri deri·vative. *Chem. rare.* [TRI- 5 c.] A derivative containing three substituted atoms of radicals of the same kind; a tri-substitution product.

1875 *Jrnl. Chem. Soc.* XXVIII. 567 Contributions to our knowledge of the Connection between the Bi- and Tri-derivatives of Benzene. 1891 *Cent. Dict.* s.v., Trichloracetic acid is a triderivative of acetic acid.

Tridge, dial. and obs. form of TRUDGE *v.*

Tridiametral, -diapason, -digital, etc.: see TRI- 1, 4 a.

Tri-dimensional (trəi,dime·nʃənăl), *a.* [f. TRI- 1 a + DIMENSIONAL.] Having or exhibiting three dimensions, as a solid body. Hence **Tri-dimensiona·lity**, the condition or quality of being of three dimensions (in quot. 1894 loosely used).

1875 CAYLEY in *Phil. Trans.* CLXV. 678 Theorem C, in the particular case of *tridimensional space. 1894 *Nation* (N.Y.) 23 Aug. 145/1 The tridimensional graphs of Wislicenus. 1906 *Athenæum* 19 May 612/3 An ingenious series of star charts..which when looked at through red and green spectacles exhibit the stars as appearing in tri-dimensional space. 1894 *Nation* (N.Y.) 13 Sept. 192/2 There are three fundamental color-sensations..; but there is nothing corresponding to this *tri-dimensionality in the vibrations themselves. 1901 TITCHENER *Exper. Psychol.* I. ix. 138 The two figures will approach each other, and at last will overlap...At the moment of complete overlapping, the cone stands out with an almost startling tridimensionality.

Triding: see TRITHING.

Tridiurnal (trəi,dəi,ɜ̄·ɹnăl), *a.* [f. TRI- 3 + DIURNAL.] **a.** Comprising three days. **b.** Occurring three times a day.

a. 1828 J. STERLING *Ess.*, etc. (1848) II. 45 Various minor periods,..monthly, weekly, tridiurnal, and daily. **b.** 1884 *Athenæum* 10 May 602/1 He..commenced to make tridiurnal meteorological observations and to issue a daily weather report.

Tri-dodecahedral: see TRI- 2 b.

‖**Tri-domi·nium.** [In form mod.L., f. TRI- + L. *dominium* lordship, rule, DOMINION.] The joint rule of three powers or states: applied to that of Gt. Britain, Germany, and United States in Samoa.

1899 *Westm. Gaz.* 1 Mar. 2/3 Herr von Bülow..is reported to have said with regard to Samoa that the Tri-dominium had failed. 1900 *Edin. Rev.* Apr. 499 The break up of the unworkable tridominium..has been satisfactory to all parties.

Tridrachm (trəi·dræm). *Gr. Antiq.* [ad. Gr. τρίδραχμον, f. τρι-, TRI- + δραχμή DRACHM.] A silver coin of ancient Greece, of the value of three drachms: see DRACHM 1.

1771 RAPER in *Phil. Trans.* LXI. 469 Their larger Coins above the Drachm were, the Didrachm, the Tridrachm, and the Tetradrachm. 1827 ROBINSON *Archæol. Græca* V. xxvi. (ed. 2) 550, 3 dr[achmæ] or tridrachm, 1/11½. 1842 *Smith's Dict. Grk. & Rom. Antiq.* s.v. *Drachma*, Among those [silver coins] now preserved, the tetradrachm is commonly found; but we possess no specimens of the tridrachm, and only a few of the didrachm.

Triduan (trəi·diu,ăn), *a.* Also 7 **-ane**. [ad. L. *trīduān-us*, f. *triduum*: see below and -AN.] Lasting for three days (in quot. 1600 *transf.*); also, occurring every third day.

1597 J. KING *On Jonas* (1618) 299 The triduan rest of Christ in the graue, must bee vnderstood by the figure *synecdoche*, a part put for the whole. 1600 W. WATSON *Decacordon* (1602) 48 To raise a triduane Lazarus from death to life againe. 1658 PHILLIPS, *Triduan*, (Lat.) continuing three dayes. 1755 JOHNSON, *Triduan*, 1. Lasting three days. 2. Happening every third day.

‖ **Triduo** (trī·duo). *R.C.Ch.* [It. and Sp. *triduo*:—L. *triduum*: see below.] A three days' prayer or festal celebration.

1848 MANNING *Jrnl.* in *Life* (1895) I. xix. 402 Then was sung the *Veni Creator* (a triduo for the Roman State at this time). 1869 *Life of Marg. M. Hallahan* (1870) 473 We are meditating a great Triduo to our Holy Mother. 1871 *Echo* 28 Feb., The Cardinal Vicar is at present occupied in getting up triduos for the tercentenary of the Battle of Lepanto.

‖ **Triduum** (trəi·diu,ɒ̆m). [L. *triduum*, prop. neut. of **triduus* adj. (sc. *spatium*), f. *tri-*, TRI- + *diēs* day.] **a.** A period of three days; *esp.* in *R.C.Ch.* the last three days of Lent. **b.** = TRIDUO.

1883 SCHAFF *Hist. Church* II. xi. lxxi. 525 The mysterious triduum between the crucifixion and the resurrection. 1885 *Pall Mall G.* 7 Nov. 7/2 Yesterday there commenced at the Church of the Servite Fathers..a Triduum to celebrate an event of interest in the early history of our Royal family. 1910 *Universe* 3 June 9/1 A solemn Triduum in honour of the feast of Corpus Christi was preached in St. Mary's Cathedral, Edinburgh.

Tridymite (tri·dimait). *Min.* [ad. Ger. *tridymit* (vom Rath 1866), f. Gr. τρίδυμος threefold, f. τρι-, TRI- + -δυμ-ος, as in δίδυμος twin; named in allusion to its compound forms consisting of three individual crystals.] A crystallized form of silica, occurring in small hexagonal tables, found in trachyte and other igneous rocks.

1868 DANA *Min.* (ed. 5) 805 Tridymite occurs in small hexagonal tables, colorless and transparent, which are usually compound, and mostly of three individuals. 1888 RUTLEY *Rock-Forming Min.* 130 Tridymite is essentially a volcanic mineral.

Tridynamous: see TRI- 1.

Trie, Trielie, early forms of TRY *a.*, TRYLY.

Trie, obs. form of TREE, TRY *v.*

Tried (trəid), *ppl. a.* [f. TRY *v.* + -ED¹.]

1. Separated from the dross or refuse; of metals: purified, refined; of fat: rendered, clarified; of an egg-yolk: separated from the white; of flour, etc.: sifted, bolted, fine. Mostly *Obs.*

Tried out, said of a whale the blubber of which has been cut off, melted down, and run into casks.

13.. *K. Alis.* 828 (Bodl. MS.) Riche rede Itried golde. 13.. *Coer de L.* 6342 Tryyd sylvyr and tresore fyn. 1382 WYCLIF *Ex.* xvi. 31 The taast of it as of tryed floure with hony. *c* 1430 *Two Cookery-bks.* 51 Take fayre y-tryid ȝolkys Raw, & Sugre, an pouder Gyngere. 1611 COTGR., *Argerite*, the (Siluer-coloured) foame of tried lead. 1627 CAPT. SMITH *Seaman's Gram.* xv. 75 Legs of Mutton..with tried sewet or butter. 1639 T. DE GRAY *Compl. Horsem.* 304 Take..of old tryed hogs grease one pound.

† 2. Chosen, select, choice; excellent. *Obs.*

13.. *E. E. Allit. P.* B. 1317 He trussed hem in his tresorye in a tryed place. 1362 LANGL. *P. Pl.* A. I. 126 Treuþe is tresour triedest on eorþe. *c* 1400 *Destr. Troy* 1840 Fro Priam, full prist,..That in Troy truly is a triet kyng. *Ibid.* 10842 A tryet ost Of grekes..were gedrit. 1581 A. HALL *Iliad* v. 97 Dame Juno of the tryed horsse in hand doth take the raynes.

† **b.** As *sb.* Distinguished one. *Obs.*

c 1400 *Destr. Troy* 13791 To the toumbe of þat tried truly ho yode.

3. Proved or tested by experience or examination.

c 1412 HOCCLEVE *De Reg. Princ.* 2007 Deth hath but smal consideracioun Vnto þe vertuous,..No more..Than to a vicious maistir losel tried. *c* 1440 *Promp. Parv.* 502/2 Tryyd,..*probatus, examinatus.* 1508 KENNEDIE *Flyting w. Dunbar* 513 Cankrit Caym, tryit trowane, Tutiuillus. 1583 STUBBES *Anat. Abus.* II. (1882) 100 Choose foorth certeine persons of a tried conuersation. 1604 G[RIMSTONE] *D'Acosta's Hist. Indies* II. vii. 95 It is approoved by many tryed experiences. 1724 DE FOE *Mem. Cavalier* (1840) 277 He [was] an old tried soldier. 1760 R. BROWN *Compl. Farmer* II. 17 My design is..to promote tried experiments. 1841 W. SPALDING *Italy* III. 82 Public men of tried abilities.

Hence † **Tri·edly** *adv. Obs.*, in a tried manner; choicely; experiencedly.

c 1400 *Destr. Troy* 3054 Hir tethe þat tryetly were set, Alse qwyte & qwem as any qwalle bon. *Ibid.* 10583 Þai tild vp a toure, triedly wroght. 14.. *Langland's P. Pl.* B. Prol. 14, I seigh a toure on a toft trielich [*MS. O.* triedliche] ymaked. 1549 COVERDALE, etc. *Erasm. Par.* 1 *Peter* iv. 12 That thing..whyche wente long ago before in the triedly proued prophetes. 1557 *Tottell's Misc.* (Arb.) 141 So triedly did he treade..That fortune found no place to geue him once a check.

Triedral, obs. variant of TRIHEDRAL.

Tri-elementary: see TRI- 1.

† **Tri,e·nnal**, *a.* and *sb. Obs. rare.* Also 4 **tri-, tryenal(e, -ennal(e, -el, trinel.** [ad. med.L. *triennāl-e* (sc. *officium*), neuter of *triennālis* of three years: cf. F. *triennal* (16th c.).]

A. *adj.* = TRIENNIAL. *rare*⁻⁰.

1611 COTGR., *Triennal*, triennall, of three yeares.

B. *sb.* A dispensation or indulgence for three years. (In 14th c. a disyllable = *trī·nal*.)

1362 LANGL. *P. Pl.* A. VIII. 157 [I] diuinede þat Dowel Indulgence passede, Bienals and Trienals and Busschopes lettres. *Ibid.* 166 Bote trustene to Trienals [B. VII. 170 triennales; C. X. 330 triennels] treuly me þinkeþ Is not so syker for þe soule sertes, as do-wel. *c* 1380 WYCLIF *Sel. Wks.* III. 400 Biggynge of beneficis, of indulgensis and trinels, pardouns, and veyne privileges.

Triennial (trəi,e·niăl), *a.* and *sb.* Also 7 **tryenniall, triennuall**, 8 **trienial.** [f. L. *trienni-s* of three years, *trienni-um* a space of three years (f. *tri-*, TRI- + *annus* year) + -AL. Cf. prec.]

A. *adj.* 1. Existing or lasting for three years, 'three-years'; changed every three years.

Triennial Act (*Eng. Hist.*), an act of 1640, limiting the duration of parliament to three years; also the name given to an act of 1694, following an earlier one of Charles II, providing against any longer intermissions of parliament than three years. Cf. sense 2.

1640 *Jrnls. Ho. Comm.* II. 83 Amendments..to the Bill of Triennial Parliaments. 1643 PRYNNE *Sov. Power of Parl.* II. 25 The Admiralls Patents (which anciently were..but annuall or Trienuall at most). *c* 1645 HOWELL *Lett.* (1650) I. 70 My friends, whom I so much long to see after this triennial separation. 1701 *Lond. Gaz.* No. 3756/9 Whenever the Dissolution of this Present..Parliament shall happen, either by Virtue of the Triennial Act, or Prerogative Royal. 1807 HORSLEY *Serm.* (1812) II. 316 We, in the writings of the evangelists have a complete summary of his [Christ's] triennial preaching. 1863 H. COX *Instit.* I. vi. 35 The Triennial Act of William III limited the duration of Parliament to three years at the furthest.

2. Recurring every three years.

1642 HOWELL *For. Trav.* (Arb.) 77 If these Lights grow dim, there is a Trienniall Snuffer for them. 1663 BLAIR *Autobiog.* v. (1848) 77 Primate Usher's triennial visitation. 1782 T. WARTON *Hist. Kiddington* 8 To the bishop for Procurations, on account of his triennial visitation. 1821 MISS MITFORD in L'Estrange *Life* (1870) II. vi. 140 We have been very gay..with our triennial theatricals. 1872 YEATS *Growth Comm.* 182 There was a triennial change of officers.

B. *sb.* 1. A period of three years; a triennium.

1661 *Sir H. Vane's Politics* 13 During our Principality, which breathed out many Triennials. 1892 *Min. Nat. Counc. Congr. Ch.* (U.S.) 143 No other triennial in the history of the society has a tithe of the work in the way of..printed appeals.

2. An event recurring every three years; *spec.* the visitation of his diocese by a bishop every three years.

1640 *Archdeaconry of Essex Minutes* 29 July (MS.) We were this day inhibited for the Bp's. of London's tryenniall, by Gilson. 1724 BP. DOWNES in *Nicolson's Epist. Corr.* 576 The expence of the Triennial may leave your pocket empty.

Hence **Triennia·lity** [cf. F. *triennalité*], the condition of being triennial.

1806 W. TAYLOR in *Ann. Rev.* IV. 240 The parliament..produced fewer great men during its trienniality, than since the prolongation. 1817 BENTHAM *Parl. Reform* Introd. (1818) 283 Moderate reform insists at stopping at the stage indicated by the word trienniality.

Triennially (trəi,e·niăli), *adv.* [f. TRIENNIAL *a.* + -LY².] Every three years; once in three years.

1689 in *6th Coll. Papers rel. Pres. Juncture* 25 The Parliament to be chosen Triennially, and to meet Annually. 1727 BAILEY vol. II, Triennially. 1806 W. TAYLOR in *Ann. Rev.* IV. 714 It appears that the tithe ought to be levied triennially. 1881 *Chamb. Jrnl.* No. 914. 419/1 The gorgeous festival given..triennially at the Crystal Palace.

† **Trie·nniated**, *a. Obs. rare.* [f. L. *trienni-um* (see below) + -ATE + -ED.] Made triennial. (In quot., as the second element of a compound.)

1661 *Sir H. Vane's Politics* 8 By obliging sundry eminent Chieftans of our long-trienniated Assembly.

‖ **Triennium** (trəi,e·niɒ̆m). [L., prop. neuter of **triennius* adj. (sc. *spatium*), f. *tri-*, TRI- + *ann-us* year.] A space or period of three years.

1847 BUNSEN *Church of Future* v. 119 The first theological examination follows upon the academical triennium. 1876 BOURNE *Life Locke* I. ii. 52 He adopted the less usual course of shortening his triennium by two terms. 1894 *Nation* (N.Y.) 14 June 444/1 Just home from his triennium in Germany.

‖ **Triens** (trəi·enz). Pl. **trientes** (trəi,e·ntīz). [L., = third part.] The third part of anything; *spec.* in *Rom. Antiq.* a copper coin worth one-third of the as; also in later times, a gold coin, one-third of the aureus: cf. next.

1601 HOLLAND *Pliny* xxxiv. xiii. II. 513 The Servilij..have among them a certaine peece of brasse coine called a Triens (*i.* the third part of a Romane Asse) which they doe keepe and feed with silver and gold...I will set downe..the verie words of old Messala: The house (quoth he) of the Servilij hath a certaine sacred Trient. 1693 tr. *Blancard's Phys. Dict.* (ed. 2), *Triens*, the third part of a physical Pound. 1706 PHILLIPS (ed. Kersey), *Triens* (Lat.), the third part of the Roman Pound, or Coin call'd *As*, weighing four Ounces: Or the third of any entire Thing divisible into twelve Parts.

† **Trient**. *Obs.* [ad. L. *triens, trient-em* third part.] **a.** The ancient Roman copper coin called *triens*: see prec. **b.** An angle of 120°, comprising one-third of the circumference of a circle; in *Astrol.* = TRINE B. 2 (also *adj.* = TRINE A. 2).

1563 HYLL *Art Garden.* (1593) 24 When they are asunder 120 degrees, which is called a triangle, Trygon, or Trient aspect. 1601 [see TRIENS]. 1657 TOMLINSON *Renou's Disp.* 160* Three ounces..or at most a trient, that is four ounces. 1657 *Physical Dict.*, *Trient*, a third part. 1673 WALLIS in Rigaud *Corr. Sci. Men* (1841) II. 570 If the angle be more than a trient, and less than two trients, whose subtendant ..I suppose to be the chord of a trient increased by one of the arches.

† **Trie·ntal**, *a.* and *sb. Obs. rare.* [ad. L. *trientālis*, f. *triens, trient-em*: see TRIENT and -AL.]

A. *adj.* Pertaining to or constituting a third part (e.g. ⅓ of a foot in length, of a pound in weight, etc.).

1656 BLOUNT *Glossogr.*, *Triental* (*trientalis*), of or being four inches broad or ounces in weight. 1891 *Cent. Dict.*, *Triental*, *a.* of the value of a triens; of or pertaining to the triens, or third part.

B. *sb.* An ancient Roman drinking-vessel containing one-third of a *sextarius*.

1656 BLOUNT *Glossogr.*, *Triental* (Lat.), a vessel containing the third part of *Sextarius*, half our Pint. 1789 MADAN tr. *Persius* III. (1795) 91 But a trembling comes on whilst at his wine, and the warm triental He shakes out of his hands.

Triequal: see TRI- 2.

Trier (trəi·əɹ). Forms: 4–5 **triour**, 5 **tryoure**, 6 **trior, tryar**, 7 **triar**, 6– **trier, tryer**; in senses 2 and 4, also 6–8 **triour**, 7 **tryor**, 8–9 **trior.** [f. TRY *v.* + -ER¹; in the early form *triour*, a. AF. **triour* (-OUR) in legal use. Cf. F. *trieur*.]

1. One who examines and determines a cause or question; one who examines judicially; a judge.

c 1330 R. BRUNNE *Chron.* (1810) 250 Þe triours alle þat caste, & put þer saw tille on. 1472 *Coventry Leet Bk.* 382 These persons folowyng be ordeyned & chosen to be triours within þis Cite to determyn variances betwixt parties within þis Cite as touchyng metes & bondes & Gutters & such oþer. *a* 1586 SIDNEY *Arcadia* III. Wks. 1724 II. 693 The almighty powers, whom I invoke as triers of mine innocency, and witnesses of my well-meaning. 1645 *Ordinance* in Neal *Hist. Purit.* (1736) III. 293 That certain persons be appointed Triers..to determine the validity of Elections. 1659–60 *Free Parl.-Letany* iii, From Vow-breakers & King-tryers—Libera nos, Domine! 1809 JEFFERSON *Writings* (1830) IV. 128 The testimony..is the more grateful, as proceeding from eye-witnesses and observers, from triers of the vicinage. 1821 SCOTT *Kenilw.* xi, To get old Gaffer Pinniewinks, the trier of witches,..to comprehend Wayland Smith. 1821–30 LD. COCKBURN *Mem.* ii. (1874) 101 A dexterous and practical trier of ordinary cases. 1885 DIXON *Hist. Ch. Eng.* III. 377 The bishop himself was to be the chief trier.

2. *pl.* Two persons appointed by a court of law to determine whether a challenge made to the panel of jurors, or to any of them, is well founded.

[*a* 1377 *Rolls of Parlt.* II. 400/1 Sur quele chose furent esleuz Triours par la Court, qe disoient qe le Viscounte fust eidaunt et bien voillant a la partie du dit Evesqe.] 1521 in W. H. Turner *Sel. Rec. Oxford* (1880) 4 He commawnded the ij tryarse in the King's name to tell Hullys parte owt of the dore [of the gildhall]. *c* 1570 *Pride & Lowl.* (1841) 18 Ye shall have triers two or three, That shall judge of their [jurymen's] indifferencie. 1665 EVER *Tryals per Pais* ix. 128 When any challenge is made to the Polls, two tryors shall be appointed by the Court, and if they try one indifferent, and he be sworn, then he and the two tryors shall try another. 1768 BLACKSTONE *Comm.* III. xxiii. 363. 1863 H. COX *Instit.* II. iii. 354 Two triers appointed by the Court.

3. *Hist. pl.* A committee appointed by the King to determine to which court petitions should be referred, and if necessary, to report them to the parliament. The practice was disused in 1886.

[1332 *Rolls of Parlt.* II. 68/1. 1485 *Ibid.* VI. 268/1 Et sount assignez Triours des Petitiones de Gascoigne, et d'autres Terres et Paiis de par dela, et des Isles [names follow].] 1844 T. E. MAY *Treat. Parl.* xix. 301 Receivers and triers of petitions were appointed...The triers were committees of prelates, peers, and judges [etc.]..By them the petitions were examined...The functions of receivers and triers of petitions have long since given way to the immediate authority of Parliament at large. 1878 STUBBS *Const. Hist.* § 757 III. xx. 452 As soon as the opening speech of the chancellor was ended, the names of the receivers and triers of petitions were read by the clerk of the crown. The receivers were clerks or masters in chancery; the triers were selected by the king from the list of the lords spiritual, the lords temporal, and the justices. [1886 *Jrnls. Ho. Lords* CXVIII. 19/2 Les Triours des Petitions, etc. as in 1485.]

4. *pl.* Members of the House of Lords sitting as a jury at the trial of a peer for treason or felony. In full, *lords triers.*

1539 *Act* 31 *Hen. VIII*, c. 10. § 9 Peres that shalbe called hereafter to be triours of suche treasons. 1596 WARNER *Alb. Eng.* x. lvi. (1612) 246 These Noble Tryers, iustly then examining the Cause. 1676 C. HATTON in *Hatton Corr.* (Camden) 134 Ther were 31 Lords tryers present. 1794 BURKE *Rep. Lords' Jrnls.* Wks. 1842 II. 607 A course of precedents, in a legal court, composed of a peer for judge, and peers for triers. 1831 MACKINTOSH *Hist. Eng.* II. vii. 198 Queen Anne and her brother Rochford were tried..before the duke of Norfolk,..assisted by twenty-six 'lords triers', who in some degree performed the functions of jurors in this tribunal. 1849 MACAULAY *Hist. Eng.* vi. II. 39 The high steward was sole judge of the law; and the lords triers formed merely a jury to pronounce on the question of fact. Jeffreys was appointed high steward. 1855 *Ibid.* xviii. IV. 158 The Lords insisted that every peer should be entitled to be a Trier. The Commons were with difficulty induced to consent that the number of Triers should never be less than thirty six.

5. *Church Hist.* One of a body of commissioners appointed in 1654 'for the approbation of all public preachers and lecturers before their admission to benefices'. Also *transf.*

1655 *Clarke Pap.* (Camden) III. 53 His Highnesse..left Mr. Cordwell, the minister, to be concluded by the Tryers of London. 1657 [see EJECTOR 1]. 1664 BUTLER *Hud.* II. ii. 813 And do they not as Triers sit To judge what Officers are fit? *a* 1691 BAXTER in *Reliq.* (1696) 72. 1691 WOOD *Ath. Oxon.* I. 861 Afterwards he enjoyed two livings successively without examination by the Tryers. 1808 W. WILSON *Hist. Dissent. Ch.* I. 471 The Commissioners were in all thirty-eight..and were commonly known by the name of Tryers. 1862 VAUGHAN *Nonconformity* 186 The number of ministers ejected by the Triers was considerable.

6. An umpire in sports or games. Now *dial.*

1607 MARKHAM *Caval.* III. (1617) 79 These Tryers are certaine indifferent Gentlemen, chosen by both the parties that make the match, who are to see that there be faire play, and that the Articles be fully performed on both parties. 1747 J. RELPH *Poems* 16 At spworts, if I was trier. 1826 *Sporting Mag.* XVIII. 321 A trier, or stickler as he is commonly called, is an umpire. 1888 ELWORTHY *W. Somerset Word-bk.*, *Trier*, the umpire at a wrestling, cudgel-playing, or any other match.

7. One who or that which tests or proves something; a prover; a tester or test.

a 1483 *Liber Niger Edw. IV* in *Househ. Ord.* (1790) 75 This seyde sergeaunt, or the yoman tryoure, or the groome tryoure,..dayly to be redye in the hall. 1538 ELYOT, *Spectatores*, beholders, triers of money. *a* 1541 WYATT *Poet. Wks.* (1861) 169 Of good and bad the tryers are these twain. 1552 HULOET, Tryers, *comprobatores.* 1607 SHAKS. *Cor.* IV. i. 4 You were vs'd To say, Extreamities was the trier of spirits. 1610 BP. CARLETON *Jurisd.* Pref., When it was examined by vnskilfull and deceitfull triars,..taking vpon them to be triars of truth. 1712 BUDGELL *Spect.* No. 307 ¶ 7 There should be certain Triers or Examiners..to inspect the Genius of every particular Boy. 1760 *Cautions to Officers of Army* 162 There was formerly in the Army, particularly in Queen Ann's Time, a Sett of Officers in most Corps, who were called Provers, or Tryers; these upon a young Officer's joining the Regiment,..without any Cause picked a Quarrel with him: when, if the young Man acquitted himself with Honour, and escaped with Life, he passed the Rest of his Time quietly enough. 1796 CAPT. BOWEN in *Naval Chron.* XXIII. 368, I ordered one gun to be fired, as a trier of her intention. 1817–18 COBBETT *Resid. U. S.* (1822) 98 They are the best of triers. Whatever they prefer is sure to be the richest thing within their reach. 1869 SPURGEON *Treas. Dav.* Ps. lxxiii. 21 God is frequently called..the Trier of the hearts and reins.

8. One who (or that which) tries out or separates (metal, honey, grain, oil, etc.) from impurities.

1523 LD. BERNERS *Froiss.* I. ccccii. 699 They set but lytell by the manassyng of a sonne of a tryer of hony. *a* 1637 B. JONSON *Eupheme's Mind* vii, Disdaining any tryer, 'Tis got where it can try the fire. 1725 *Phil. Trans.* XXXIII. 262 The Triers, that open them [whales] when dead,..never observed any Grass, Fish, or any other Sort of Food in the right or Whalebone Whale. 1869 *Lonsdale Gloss.*, *Trier*, a corn-screen.

† 9. One who finds *out* or tries to find out by search or examination. *Obs.*

1547–64 BAULDWIN *Mor. Philos.* (Palfr.) 65 Law is the finder & trier out of truth. 1563 FOXE *A. & M.* 1297/1 Mayster Thomas Bilney..a trier out of Sathans subtleties.

b. *spec.* (See quot.)

1778 *Eng. Gazetteer* (ed. 2) s.v. *Youle*, Youle, York, E. Rid. ..Here are a sort of people, called triers, who with a long piece of iron search into the soft boggy ground hereabouts for subterraneous trees.

10. One who tries or attempts to do something; in *Cricket slang*, a player who perseveres in trying to win.

1891 in *Cent. Dict.* 1897 *Daily News* 28 July 11/5 He trusted they would remember that even when the eleven did badly they were always tryers. 1903 *Daily Chron.* 24 Feb. 3/2 Mr. Bernard Capes may be described, in the language of the cricket-field, as 'a great try-er'.

11. **a.** Something devised to try or test quality. **b.** Something that is trying or difficult, or that tries one's patience or mettle.

1797 *Encycl. Brit.* (ed. 3) VIII. 238/1 Though the common powder-triers may show powder to be better than it really is, they can never make it appear to be worse than it is. 1893 *Field* 11 Feb. 187/2 The district being a trier, many and various were the mishaps. 1901 *U. S. Dept. Agric., Year-bk.* 237 These samples are drawn by means of a 'trier', or clover-seed sampler, which is thrust through the bag, allowing the seed to run out at the open end of the trier.

12. *Trier on*, one who 'tries on' garments in order to test the fit; *spec.* an assistant to a clothier or dressmaker who helps customers to try on garments, or who displays their style by wearing them (= MODEL *sb.* 11 b).

1895 *Blackw. Mag.* Apr. 557 The girl bethought herself of the 'tryer-on' [*cf. above* 'a young woman, discharging in perfection her function of wearing clothes so skilfully as to tempt buyers with them']. 1900 *Westm. Gaz.* 12 Jan. 5/3 The 'tryers-on'..had spent nearly four hours in hard work.

Trierarch (trəi·ĕrāɹk). *Gr. Hist.* Also 7 **-arck**, 9 **-arc.** [ad. L. *triērarch-us*, or its Gr. source τριήραρχος, -άρχης, f. τριήρης trireme + -αρχος ruling, ruler. Cf. F. *triérarque* (Oresme, 14th c.).] **a.** The commander of a trireme. **b.** A citizen who, singly or in conjunction with others, was charged with the duty of fitting out a trireme or galley for the public service.

1656 BLOUNT *Glossogr.*, *Trierarck*.., the mr. of a Ship or Galley. 1697 POTTER *Antiq. Greece* I. xxvi. (1715) 158 The

Trierarchs, and Overseers of the Navy. 1734 tr. *Rollin's Anc. Hist.* XIII. vii. (1827) V. 290 The..Trierarchs..were appointed to fit out the galleys in time of war.

Trierarchal (trəi·ĕrāɹkăl), *a.* [f. as prec. + -AL.] Of or pertaining to a trierarch or trierarchs. So **Triera·rchic, -ical** *adjs.* [Gr. τριηραρχικός].

1837 WHEELWRIGHT tr. *Aristophanes* II. 127 The city had been full of martial tumult and trierarchal clamour. 1853 GROTE *Greece* II. lxxxvii. XI. 381 Demosthenes belonged to a trierarchic family. 1866 FELTON *Anc. & Mod. Gr.* I. II. xii. 502 The fitting out of war-ships, called the trierarchic liturgy. 1891 *Athenæum* 25 July 128/1 The law of Periander in 357 B.C...placing 1,200 citizens in the trierarchical symmories.

Trierarchy (trəi·ĕrāɹki). [ad. Gr. τριηραρχία, f. τριήραρχος TRIERARCH.] The position or office of a trierarch; the equipment and maintenance of a trireme or other vessel, as a public service or 'liturgy'; the system by which a fleet was thus maintained. **b.** 'The trierarchs collectively' (Ogilvie, 1882).

1837 BULWER *Athens* II. 462 Extraordinary liturgies—such as the Trierarchy or equipment of ships which entailed also the obligation of personal service on those by whom the triremes were fitted out. 1839 THIRLWALL *Greece* VI. xlv. 51 The citizens who were liable to the charges of the trierarchy. 1850 GROTE *Greece* II. lv. VII. 47 As a rich young man, also, choregy and trierarchy became incumbent upon him. 1869 A. W. WARD tr. *Curtius' Hist. Greece* II. III. iii. 477 The trierarchy, i.e. the obligation incumbent upon the citizens to make the ships belonging to the state ready for sea, to hire crews, etc.

Triet, obs. form of TRIED.

Trieteric (trəi,ĭte·rik), *a.* and *sb. Antiq.* [ad. Gr. τριετηρικός, L. *trietēricus*, f. τριετηρίς a festival celebrated every third, i.e. alternate, year, f. τρι- three + ἔτος year.]

A. *adj.* Taking place every alternate year, as the festivals of Bacchus and other divinities.

1656 BLOUNT *Glossogr.*, *Trieterick*.., that is every third year. 1847 LEITCH tr. *C. O. Müller's Anc. Art* § 390 The Mænads at the trieteric festival on Mount Parnassus thought they descried the satyrs and heard their music. 1852 GROTE *Greece* II. lxxv. IX. 477 *note*, The Isthmian games were trieteric, that is celebrated in every alternate year. 1911 *Athenæum* 15 Apr. 493/3 Dr. Farnell has..a theory of 'trieteric' agricultural rites.

B. *sb.* (also *pl.*) A festival, esp. of Bacchus, celebrated every alternate year.

1592 R. D. *Hypnerotomachia* 90b, As in the daunce called Thiasus, in the trieteric [*pr.* -ie; *orig.* Trieterici] of Bacchus. 1627 MAY *Lucan* V. 86 To whome in mixed sacrifice The Theban wiues at Delphos solemnize Their trieterickes.

So † **Tri,ete·rical, Tri,ete·rican** *adjs. Obs.* = A.

1646 J. GREGORY *Notes & Obs.* xxi. 106 The trietericall sports,..that is the mysteries of Bacchus. 1775 ASH *Suppl.*, *Trieterican*, belonging to the trieterica.

Triethyl (trəi,e·þil). *Chem.* [f. TRI- 5 + ETHYL.] **a.** A formative denoting the presence of three ethyl groups, C_2H_5, in a compound, as **triethylbi·smuthine**, $Bi(C_2H_5)_3$, **triethyl phosphine**, $P(C_2H_5)_3$; see also *Triethylamine* below. **b.** *spec.* denoting the substitution of three ethyl groups for three hydrogen atoms in the substance designated by the rest of the name; e.g. **trie·thylbe·nzene**, $C_6H_3(C_2H_5)_3$, in which three ethyl groups take the place of three H atoms in benzene, C_6H_6; so **trie·thylme·thane**, $CH(C_2H_5)_3$, from methane, CH_4; **trie·thylca·rbinol**, $C(C_2H_5)_3OH$; **trie·thylu·rea**, $CONH(C_2H_5)N(C_2H_5)_2$. Also used attrib., as *triethyl phosphate*, $(C_2H_5)_3PO_4$. Hence **Triethy·lic** *a.* = triethyl *attrib.*

1858 FOWNES *Elem. Chem.* (ed. 7) 615 Triethylstibine $SbAe_3$. 1873 — *Chem.* 587 Triethylic borate is formed by the action of boron trichloride on alcohol. 1868 WATTS *Dict. Chem.* V. 880 Triethylglycerin or Triethylin..is a liquid having a pleasant ethereal odour. 1889 MUIR & MORLEY *Watts' Dict. Chem.* II. 306 Tri-ethyl-phosphine. ..Colourless mobile liquid. Its odour is very penetrating but not disagreeable.

Hence **Triethylamine** (trəi,e·þilămain), the tertiary amine of ethyl, $N(C_2H_5)_3$, in which the three hydrogen atoms of ammonia, NH_3, are replaced by three ethyl groups; formerly also called *Triethyl ammonia* and *Triethylia*.

1850 DAUBENY *Atom. The.* viii. (ed. 2) 242 Triethylamine, consisting of 3 atoms of ethyle replacing 3 of hydrogen. 1857 MILLER *Elem. Chem.* III. 211 Triethylia..is also a soluble, volatile, and powerful base. 1858 FOWNES *Elem. Chem.* (ed. 7) 595 Triethylamine, Triethyl-ammonia...is a colourless, powerfully-alkaline liquid, boiling at 91° C.

Trieues, -eux, -ewis, obs. ff. TREVE, TRUCE.

Triexoctoedron, var. TRI-HEXOCTAHEDRON.

Tri-faced: see TRI- 1 c.

Trifacial (trəifē̆·ʃăl), *a. Anat.* [f. TRI- + FACIAL.] A name for the fifth pair of cranial nerves (also called TRIGEMINAL), which divide into three branches supplying the face and some adjacent parts. Also *transf.* pertaining to or affecting the trifacial nerves.

1840 G. ELLIS *Anat.* 82 Branches of..the first, second, or third divisions of the fifth or trifacial nerve. 1842 E. WILSON *Anat. Vade M.* (ed. 2) 407 The Trifacial Nerve is analogous to the spinal nerves in its origin by two roots. 1863 J. DEAN *Gray Subst. Medulla Obl.* etc. II. i, I have not been able to discover any connection between these columns and the trifacial or auditory roots. 1899 *Allbutt's Syst. Med.* VI. 662 A carious tooth may set up a trifacial neuralgia.

† **Tri·fallow**, *v. Obs.* Also 8 **try-, tre-**; see also THRY-FALLOW. [app. altered from the earlier *three-, thry-fallow*, after TWIFALLOW, or under the influence of TRI- prefix as in *tri-weekly, triennial*, etc.] *trans.* To plough (land) a third time in the course of its lying fallow. Also *absol.*

[1573, 1641: see THRY-FALLOW.] 1610 W. FOLKINGHAM *Art of Survey* I. ii. 43 Orders and seasons for fallowing, twifallowing, trifallowing and seed-furre. 1681 WORLIDGE *Dict. Rust.* s.v. *Fallow*, Thus may you fallow, twifallow, and trifallow; that is once, twice, or thrice plough it before the seed-time. 1707 MORTIMER *Husb.* (1721) I. 53 About the latter end of July or beginning of August, is the time of Try-fallowing, or last plowing before they sow their Rye or Wheat. 1766 *Complete Farmer*, *To Trefallow*, to plough land the third time before sowing.

Trifarious (trəifē̆·riəs), *a. rare.* [f. L. *trifāri-us* (compared by some with Gr. τριφάσιος in same sense) + -OUS.]

1. Of three sorts; facing three ways.

1656 BLOUNT *Glossogr.*, *Trifarous* (*trifarius*), of three manner of wayes. *c* 1800 BP. MILNER in Husenbeth *Life* (1862) 39 No longer prate on huge Briareus, On monstrous triple bodied Geryon; For I have seen a real trifarious Protesting—Catholic—Presbyterian!

2. *Bot.* Arranged in three rows.

1846 WORCESTER, *Trifarious*,..in three rows. 1857 BERKELEY *Cryptog. Bot.* § 565 Leaves trifarious, the third row smaller than the others.

Trifasciated, -faucian: see TRI- 1.

† **Tri·ferous**, *a. Obs. rare.* [f. L. *trifer* (f. TRI- + *-fer* bearing) + -OUS.] Thrice-bearing; bearing fruit or flowers thrice a year.

1656 BLOUNT *Glossogr.*, *Triferous* (*trifer*), that brings forth fruit thrice a year. *a* 1682 SIR T. BROWNE *Tracts* 70 Some are biferous and triferous which bear twice or thrice in the year.

Trifet, obs. form of TRIVET.

† **Triff-traff**. *Obs.* In 6 **tryfetrafe.** [app. a reduplicated form of TRAFFE baggage: cf. *trish-trash*, redupl. from *trash*. But it may also be associated with *riff-raff*.] Trumpery, trash, rubbish; = RIFF-RAFF¹ 2.

1547 *Bk. Marchauntes* b j b, Of brotherhodes, inuentions, tradicions, deceptions, lawes and wythout nombre of such tryfetrafe, wherby they can meruelously well drawe money to them.

Trifid (trəi·fid), *a.* [ad. L. *trifid-us*, f. *tri-*, TRI- + *fid-*, stem of *findĕre* to split.] Split or divided into three by deep clefts or notches; three-cleft; *esp.* in *Bot.* and *Zool.*

1753 CHAMBERS *Cycl. Supp.* s.v. *Leaf*. 1760 J. LEE *Introd. Bot.* II. ix. (1765) 93 Such as have Trifid Corollæ. 1769 PENNANT *Brit. Zool.* III. 320 The tail is naturally bifid, but in many is trifid. 1872 MIVART *Elem. Anat.* ii. 50 In the Howling Monkeys we find a trifid spine. 1895 *Pop. Sci. Monthly* Sept. 692 As far back as 1800 Pliny Moody had observed trifid markings upon sandstones.

b. *gen.* Divided into three parts, or of the nature of such division; tripartite. *rare.*

1871 EARLE *Philol. Eng. Tongue* viii. 417 In that chapter the third section assumed a trifid form. 1902 *Sat. Rev.* 6 Dec. 711/2 The old trifid division of mammals.

Trifilar to Triflagellate: see TRI- 1.

Trifle (trəi·f'l), *sb.* Forms: *α.* 3–5 **trufle**, (3–4 **truyfle**), 4 **trufel, truffe**, (**trewful**), 4–5 **truful**, 5 **-fulle, truffulle, truffille.** *β.* 4 **trofle, trofil**, 4–5 **trofel**, (5 **trowful**). *γ.* 4 **tryffel**, 4–5 **trifil(e, -ful**, (4 **tryuol, trefle**, 4–5 **-fele**), 4–6 **tryfel, -fyl, -fle**, 4–7 (8 *Sc.*) **triffle**, 5 **tryfil, trifelle, triffol**, 5–6 **tryfell(e**, 6 **-fille, -full(e, -fyll(e, (tryefull)**, **trifill, -fulle, triffelle, trifill(e**, 7 **triffel, tryffel, -le**, 4– **trifle.** [ME. *trufle*, etc., a. OF. *trufle* (13th c. in Godef.), *treufle, truffle* (1370), parallel forms of *trufe, truffe*, 'moquerie, tromperie' (1265 in Godef.), = It. *truffa*, 'a cozening, cheating, conicatching' (Florio), Pr., obs. Sp. and Pg. *trufa*, 'a gibe, a iesting or ieering' (Minsheu); of uncertain origin. The phonology of the word in English presents difficulties; but *trufle*, with *ü*, would give later *tryfle, triffle*; and *u* sometimes varied dialectally with *o*, as in the ME. *trofel*. The short *ĭ* indicated by *ff* in *tryffel, triffol, triffle*, appears from the 14th to the 18th c.; but *trifle* with single *f* is ambiguous, and does not show when *trĭfle* became *trīfle*.

For the ulterior etymology, Diez was inclined to identify F. *truffe, trufle* with *truffe*, Pr. *trufa* (Littré), a TRUFFLE, a subterranean edible fungus. But it is app. only in F. (and Prov.) that the two words have the same form, and no connexion of sense has been ascertained: see TRUFFLE.]

† 1. A false or idle tale, told (*a*) to deceive, cheat, or befool, (*b*) to divert or amuse; a lying story, a fable, a fiction; a jest or joke; a foolish, trivial, or nonsensical saying. *Obs.*

The shades of sense cannot always be distinguished.

α. *a* 1225 *Ancr. R.* 106 Þeos ant oðre trufles þet he bitrufleð monie men mide. 1297 R. GLOUC. (Rolls) 8613 Wanne me sede him of suche wondres..to trufle [*v.rr.* trifle, tryffel] he it wende. 1340 *Ayenb.* 58 Þe bourdes and þe trufles uol of uelþe and of leazinges. 1390 GOWER *Conf.* III. 344 Mi Sone, unto the trouthe wende..And lete all othre truffles [*v.rr.* trifles, triffles] be. 1393 LANGL. *P. Pl.* C. XXI. 151 Hit is trufle [*v.rr.* tryfle, triful, trewful] þat þou tellest. *c* 1440 *York Myst.* V. 125 Allas! þat I..trowed þe trufuls þat þou me saide. *Ibid.* xxxi. 300 But telle vs nowe some truffillis betwene vs twoo. 1483 *Cath. Angl.* 395/2 Truffillis, *nuge, gerra.*

β. 13.. *Cursor M.* 253 (Cott.) To wast þair liif, in trofel and truandis. *Ibid.* 27623 (Cott. Galba) Of pride cume-..sang of trofils [*Cott.* truful] or lesing. 1340 HAMPOLE *Pr. Consc.* 183 Many has lykyng trofels to here. *c* 1400 *Rule St. Benet* 1735 Tales of trofils þai sal non tel.

γ. 1303 R. BRUNNE *Handl. Synne* 5031 Þys yche tale ys no tryfyl, For hyt ys wryte yn þe bybyl. 13.. *Gaw. & Gr. Knt.* 108 Talkkande bifore þe hyȝe table of trifles ful hende. 1377 LANGL. *P. Pl.* B. XVIII. 147 It is but a trufle [*v.rr.* tryfule, truyfle] þat þow tellest. *c* 1380 WYCLIF *Wks.* (1880) 442 Iapis & gabbingis or oþere tryuolis. *c* 1440 *Generydes* 4664 These are butt triffolys and delayes. 14.. *Voc.* in Wr.-Wülcker 617/42 *Trufa*, a trefele. *c* 1440 *Promp. Parv.* 502/2 Tryfle, *trufa.* *c* 1518 SKELTON *Magnyf.* 1142, I am yet as full of game As euer I was, and as full of tryfyls [*rime* nyfyls]. 1548 UDALL, etc. *Erasm. Par. Matt.* xv. 67 The Phariseis teache and obserue supersticiously these folysh tryfles. 1681 W. ROBERTSON *Phraseol. Gen.* (1693) 1258 Nifles and trifles; vain tales of Robin Hood; *aniles fabulæ.*

2. Hence, A matter of little value or importance; 'a thing of no moment' (J.); a trivial, paltry, or insignificant affair.

c 1290 *S. Eng. Leg.* I. 412/345 Þare-fore mot ech holi man ..tuyrne is herte to some truyfle. 1340 *Ayenb.* 142 Þer treteþ he of his greate quereles hueruore alle oþre niedes him þingþ trufles. *c* 1380 WYCLIF *Sel. Wks.* II. 185 Worldli goodis, fame of þe world, and oþer trifilis. 1513 MORE *Rich. III* (1883) 48 Leneth mi lord thi master so muche to such trifles? 1585 *Reg. Privy Council Scot.* IV. 32 The materis..wer bot triffillis in respect of uthiris of greitar importance. 1604 SHAKS. *Oth.* III. iii. 322 Trifles light as ayre, Are to the iealious, confirmations strong As proofes of holy Writ. 1706 E. WARD *Wooden World Diss.* (1708) 33 He's a mighty exact Man about Trifles. 1758 JOHNSON *Idler* No. 23 ¶ 7 There is scarcely any man without some favourite trifle which he values above greater attainments. 1833 HT. MARTINEAU *Brooke Farm* ix. 110 Some trifles went wrong in the cottage. 1882 PEBODY *Eng. Journalism* xxii. 176 A Society journal, dealing..with the trifles of the day.

b. Without article. *rare.*

1768 TUCKER *Lt. Nat.* (1834) I. 219 The advantage of virtue over vice and trifle does not lie in the very act, but in the consequences. *Ibid.* 620 As well in matters of trifle as of moment.

† **c.** *transf.* A worthless person; a trifler. *Obs.*

c 1475 *Pict. Voc.* in Wr.-Wülcker 806/21 *Hic nugigerulus*, a trifelle. *a* 1625 FLETCHER *Love's Cure* III. iv, *Syav.* Pray wear these trifles. *Clara*...You are a trifle, wear your self, sir, out. 1675 TRAHERNE *Chr. Ethics* 392 You will look as like a trifle, a knave, or a fool, as one of them; and be as very a mad man. *a* 1716 SOUTH *Serm.* (1744) XI. 18 It shews him to be a fop, a trifle and a mere picture.

3. *concr.* A small article of little intrinsic value; a toy, trinket, bauble, knick-knack.

1375 *Will of Eliz. Lister* (Somerset Ho.), A goun et vnum trufle sșelf egged. *a* 1400–50 *Alexander* 1894 Þe trufils þat ȝe to me sent, þe herne-pan, þe hand-ball, þe hatt made of twiggis. 1530 PALSGR. 283/1 Tryfell, a knacke, *friuolle.* 1630 *R. Johnson's Kingd. & Commw.* 196 Divers sorts of Linnen-cloth, with innumerable other small trifles. 1719 DE FOE *Crusoe* I. 44 To purchase..for Trifles, such as Beads, Toys, Knives, Scissars, Hatchets, Bits of Glass, and the like; not only Gold Dust,..Elephants Teeth, &c. but Negroes. 1756 MRS. CALDERWOOD in *Coltness Collect.* (Maitl. Cl.) 148 If you buy a triffle..then they are very civill. 1912 *Daily Graphic* 31 Dec. 13/2 These elegant trifles [hat-pins] are made in a variety of graceful designs.

4. A literary work, piece of music, etc., light or trivial in style; a slight or facetious composition; a bagatelle. Often used in meiosis.

1579 LYLY *Euphues* (Arb.) 106 If Lucilla reade this trifle, shee will straight proclaime Euphues for a traytour. 1665 BOYLE *Occas. Refl.*, *Disc. Occas. Medit.* (1848) 1 The Trifles of this kind, your Commands make me trouble you with. *a* 1704 T. BROWN *1st Sat. Persius* 66 Read his trifles, and scarce in one line You'll find him guilty of the least design. 1751 EARL OF ORRERY *Remarks Swift* vi. (1752) 47 Poems to Stella, and trifles to Dr. Sheridan, fill up a great part of that period. 1837 KEITH *Bot. Lex.* 2 Anacreon, in one of his little trifles in honour of drinking, makes the very trees of the forest drink. 1884 W. C. SMITH *Kildrostan* 47 A little song—A trifle..Which I had writ for Mairi once to sing.

5. A small sum of money, or a sum treated as of no moment; a slight 'consideration'.

c 1595 CAPT. WYATT *R. Dudley's Voy. W. Ind.* (Hakl. Soc.) 39 The Captaine præsentinge him with a trifle from our Generall, hee [etc.]. 1615 G. SANDYS *Trav.* 116 Giving a trifle for oile, about midnight we departed. 1746 FRANCIS tr. *Hor. Sat.* II. iii. 214 'What will it cost? Nay, hold!'—'A very trifle.'—'Sir, I will be told.'—'Three pence.' 1762–71 H. WALPOLE *Vertue's Anecd. Paint.* (1786) II. 157 Some not suiting the places, were brought back, and sold for a trifle after the death of my father. 1818 SCOTT *Let.* 30 Apr. in Lockhart *Life* (1837) IV. ix. 138, I could bet a trifle the doors, &c. will arrive the very day I set out.

b. An insignificant quantity or amount.

1722 DE FOE *Plague* (1884) 132 Here is fifty thousand.., within a Trifle. 1911 BEVERIDGE *North Uist* v. 63 Nor can it ever have afforded more than a mere trifle of arable soil.

c. *A trifle* (advb.): To a trifling or slight extent; in a small degree, a little; somewhat, rather.

1859 READE *Love me Little* xi, The bank itself was small and grave and a trifle dingy. 1860 G. MEREDITH *E. Harrington* xi, The chairman welcomed them a trifle snubbingly. 1887 JESSOPP *Arcady* vii. 214 Jehu is a trifle below middle height. 1892 *Speaker* 3 Sept. 291/2 We may inquire, perhaps, if it be not a trifle arrogant.

6. † **a.** A dish composed of cream boiled with various ingredients. *Obs.* **b.** A light confection of

Trig, sb.

Trifle, sb.

Trifle, v.

Triflingly, adv.

Triflingness.

Trifluor-, **Trifluoro-**.

Trifoliate, **Trifolium**.

Trifold, a.

Trifoliolate, **Trifoliolate** leaflet.

Trifoly.

Trifora.

Triforium.

Triform.

Trig, sb.

Trig, a.

Trig, v.

Trigamous, a.

Trigamy.

Trigastric.

Trigeminal.

Trigeminous.

Trigeminy.

Trigenic, a.

Trigental.

Triger.

Trigesimal.

Trigger, sb.

Trigintal.

Triglandular.

Triglochid.

Triglot.

Triglyceride.

Triglyph.

Triglyphical.

TRILOGIST

Some Sicilian examples exhibit the triglyphed frieze.

Trigones: see under Tato 2.

Trigon (trəi·gǒn). Also **7 trygon**, 7–8 tri-gone. [a. L. *trigōn-um*, ad. Gr. τρίγωνον triangle, neuter of τρίγωνος, f. τρι-, TRI-+γωνία angle, -cornered.]

1. A figure having three angles and three sides; a triangle.

2. *Astrol.* A set of three signs of the zodiac, distant 120° from each other, as if at the angles of an equilateral triangle. (Also *fig.* or *allusively*.)

3. *Mus.* A triangular instrument used in surveying; also, one used in dialling.

Trigonate (tri·gǒnĕt), *a.* *Zool.* [as prec. + -ATE] — prec. adj. 1 and 2.

Trigone (trigǒn, trigō·nĕ), *Anat.* [ad. F. *trigone*, ad. L. *trigōn-um* TRIGON.]

Trigonal (tri·gǒnăl), *a.* [ad. L. *trigōn-us* + -AL.]
1. Pertaining or relating to, a trigon or triangle; of the form of a triangle, having three angles, triangular.
2. *Bot.* & *Anat.* Having three angles.

Trigonally (tri·gǒnăli), *adv.* [f. prec. + -LY.]

Trigonometric (trigǒnǒmĕ·trik), *a.* [f. TRIGONOMETRY: see -METRIC.] — next.

Trigonometrical (trigǒnǒmĕ·trikăl), *a.* [f. as prec. + -ICAL.] — prec.

Trigonometrically (-kăli), *adv.* [f. prec. + -LY.]

Trigonometry (trigǒnǒ·mĕtri). [ad. mod.L. *trigōnometria* (B. Pitiscus 1595), f. Gr. τρίγωνο-ν + -μετρία measurement. So Fr. *trigonométrie*.]

Trigonous (tri·gǒnŭs), *a.* [f. L. *trigōn-us* + -OUS.]

Trigram (trəi·grăm). [f. Gr. τρι-, TRI- + γράμμα letter.]

Tri-hexahedral: see TRI- 2 b.

Tri-hexoctahedron. *Geom.* *Obs.*

Trihedral (trəihī·drăl), *a.* *Geom.* [f. TRI- + -HEDRAL.]

Trihemimeris (trəihĕmi·mĕris). *Anc. Pros.*

Trill (tril), *v.* Now *dial.* or *arch.*

TRILL 361

Trilobal (trəilō·băl), *a.* = TRILOBATE.

Trilobate (trəilō·bĕt), *a.* [f. TRI- + LOBATE.]

Trilobed (trəi·lōbd), *a.* = prec.

Trilobite (trəi·lŏbəit). [ad. mod.L. *Trilobites* (Walch, 1771), f. Gr. τρι-, TRI- + λοβός lobe.]

Trilogical (trəilǒ·dʒikăl), *a.* = TRILOGY.

Trilogist (tri·lŏdʒist). [f. TRILOGY + -IST.]

Trilogue (trai'lɒg). [f. TRI- + Gr. λόγος word, discourse.] A group of three words or sayings (cf. next. 3.), as the Welsh triads.

Trilogy (tri'lŏdʒi). [ad. Gr. τριλογία (see def. 1), f. τρι-, TRI- + λόγος discourse: see -LOGY. Cf. F. trilogie.]

1. Gr. Antiq. A series of three tragedies (originally connected in subject), performed at Athens at the festival of Dionysus.

2. Any series or group of three related dramatic or other literary works.

3. transf. and fig. A group of three related utterances, sayings, subjects, etc.

So **Trilogical** a.

Trilophodont to **Triluminous**: see TRI- 2.

Trim, trim sb. Also 6-7 trym, trimme, 7-8 trimm. [f. TRIM v.]

I. Nautical senses.

II. General senses.

Trim, a. (and adv.) Forms: 6- trim; also 6 Sc. trime, trym, trymmes, tryme; 6-7 trimme, 7 trimm, trimm. [History obscure.

So **Trima**-, **Trime**- in comb.

Trim, v. Infl. trimmed, -ing. Forms: 1 trymman, trymian, treman; 4 trymy, trymme, tryme, (treme), 5-7 trimme, 6- trim, (7 trime). [The existing senses of this verb begin early in the 16th c. ...]

Trimachy (trī'məki). rare⁻. [f. Gr. τρι-, TRI- + -μαχία, μάχη fight, battle, combat.]

Trimacular (traimæ'kiŭlăr). a. Nat. Hist. [f. TRI- + L. macula spot + -AR¹.] Having or marked with three spots. So **Trima'culate** a. [mod.L. trimaculāt-us], **Trima'culated** a.

Trimble (tri'm'b'l). sb. [ad. F. trimère sb. (Cotgr., 1611), ad. L. trimestris adj., L. TRI- + mensis month.]

Trimble-trumble, -tramble. [First element imitative.]

Tri'meltoat. Sc. 6-7 trymie. [First element uncertain.]

Trimelic, **Trimellic** (traimeli'k). a. Chem.

Trimellitic (trimeli'tik). a. Chem.

Trimembral (traime'mbrăl). a. [f. TRI- + L. membr-um member + -AL¹.]

Trimer (trai'mer). Chem. [ad. mod.L. trimer-us ad. Gr. τρίμερ-ης having three parts...]

Trimeran, **Trimerous** a.

So **Trimeran** (trimeran). sb. [f. mod.L. Trimera.]

Trimester (traime'stər). [ad. F. trimestre sb. (Cotgr., 1611), ad. L. trimestr-is adj. of three months.]

Trimestral (traime'străl), **Trimestrial** (-strĭăl) adjs. [f. L. trimestri-s + -AL¹.]

Trimeter (tri'mĭtər). [ad. L. trimetr-us, ad. Gr. τρίμετρ-ος of three measures.]

Trimethyl (traime'θil). Chem.

Trimethylamine, **Trimethylene**, **Trimethylic**.

Trimetric (traime'trik). a. [f. TRI- + Gr. μέτρ-ον measure.]

Trimetrical (traime'trikăl). a.

Trimly (tri'mli), adv. [f. TRIM a. + -LY².]

Trimly, a. rare. [f. TRIM a. + -LY¹.]

Trimmer (tri'mər). [f. TRIM v. + -ER¹.]

Trimming (tri'miŋ), vbl. sb. [f. TRIM v. + -ING¹.]

Trimming, ppl. a. [f. as prec. + -ING².]

Trimness (tri'mnes). [f. TRIM a. + -NESS.]

Trimoda necessitas. Old Eng. Hist.

Trimnet: see under TRIMBOAT.

Trimonth'ly, a.

Trimorph.

Trimorphic, a.

Trimsaie: see TRICKSY a. 1.

Trim-tram (trim,træm).

Trimtailment: see TRIMONTANE.

Trin (trin).

Trinacriform, a.

Trinal (trai'nal), a.

Trinary (trai'nări), a. and sb.

Trindle (tri'nd'l), sb.

Trindle, v.

Trindle-bed, -tail: see TRUNDLE-BED, -TAIL.

Trine (train), a. and sb.

Trine, v.¹

Trine, v.²

Tring (trig). Ornith. rare.

Tringa (Linn.).

Tringle (tri'ng'l).

Trinidado (trinidā·do). Obs. or arch.

Trinitarian (trinitēⁱ·riăn), a. and sb.

Trinitrate (trainai·trĕt). Chem.

Trinitrin. Chem.

Trinitro- (trainai·tro), a formative element.

Trinity (tri'niti).

Trinunity, variant of TRINUNITY.

Trink, sb.¹ Obs.

Trink, sb.²

Trinker. Obs.

Trinket, sb.¹

Trinket, sb.²

Trinket, sb.³

Trinket, v.¹

Trinketer. Obs.

Trinketing, vbl. sb.

Trinketry (triŋ'krĕtri). [f. TRINKET sb.[1] + -RY.] Trinkets collectively; articles of personal decoration or of ornament viewed as trinkets or toys. Also *fig.*

Trinkets, *a. colloq. rare.* [f. TRINKET sb.[1] + -Y.] Of the nature of a trinket or things of little importance; trivial, paltry.

†Trinkle, *Obs. rare.* app. perversion of TRINKET or TRINKLE.

Trinking: see under TRINKER.

Trinkle (triŋ'k'l), *v.*[1] *Sc.* and *dial.* Also **5-6** *trynkyl,* **6, 8-9** *trinkle,* **thrinkle.** [app. a nasalized modification of TRICKLE *v.*]

1. *intr.* To trickle, to flow or fall drop by drop. Also *fig.* Hence **Tri'nkling** *ppl. a.*

2. *trans.* To cause to trickle; to shed (tears). Hence **Tri'nkle** *sb.* = TRICKLE *sb.*[1]

Trinkle, *v.*[2] *dial.* [Altered f. TINGLE, TINKLE.]

1. To tinkle, make a tinkling sound.

Trinkle, *v.*[3] *Obs.* Also **5, 8-9** *trinkle,* *krynkel,* **6** *dial.* **5, 8-9** *trinkle,* *obs.,* intrigue (*quirk*) : — TRINKET *v.*

Trinkelment, Trinketment. *Now dial.* Also **6** trentill-**tintilment.** [Irregularly f. TRINKET sb.[1] *or* **6** *tryncle* trinket (1474 in Godef.).] Adornment; in *pl.* 'trinkets, knick-knacks' (E.D.D.).

Trinklet (triŋ'klĕt). *rare.* Also **6** *triklet.* [app. an alteration of TRINKET sb.[1], after diminutives in -LET; cf. *giglet.*]

1. ? A woman decked out with 'trinkets' or finery. *Obs. rare*[−1].

†Trinket *sb.*[3], **5.**

Trinomial (troino'mi*a*l), *a.* and *sb.* [Formed with TRI- after BINOMIAL, *q. v.*

A. *adj.* **1.** *Math.* Consisting of three terms, as an algebraical expression.

2. *Nat. Hist.* Consisting of three terms, the first being that of the genus, the second that of the species, the third that of the subspecies or variety, instead of the two former only; involving or characterized by three terms, as a system of nomenclature.

B. *sb.* **1.** *Math.* An expression consisting of three terms connected by + or −.

2. *Nat. Hist.* The name of a subspecies or variety when composed of three terms (the names of the genus, species, and subspecies or variety).

Trinomialism, the trinomial system of nomenclature, or the use of trinomial names (as **A. 2**).

Trinomiality, the quality or character of being trinomial; **Trino'mially** *adv.,* in a trinomial manner; by the use of trinomial names.

Trinominal (troino'minăl), *a.* and *sb.* [= TRINOMINAL NOMINAL.] Having three names (cf. in *Nat. Hist.* = TRINOMIAL A. 2).

Trinominalism (troinymi'n*a*l), *sb.* Also in L. form **triobolus.** [ad. Gr. τριώβολον, f. τρι-, TRI- + ὀβολός OBOL.] An ancient Greek coin of the value of three obols, or a drachma.

Trinomy[1], *Math. rare.* [formed with TRI- after BINOMY.] = TRINOMIAL B. 1.

Trinomy[2] (tri'nomi), *rare.* **1, 6.** TRI- + Gr. -νομία, -NOMY.] Worth, law, rule, or arrangement.

Triobol (troi'ybŏl), a threefold law, rule, or arrangement.

Trinucleate: see TRI-.

Triobolary (also -ulary) *a.* in same sense. Hence **Trinucleate,** see TRI-.

Trio-bolary (also -ulary) *a.* in same sense.

Triobol (troi'ybŏl, troi'ŏbʱl). Also in L. form **triobolus.** [ad. Gr. τριώβολον, f. τρι-, TRI- + ...

Trinquetrile (tri'trinŭel), *a.* [f. Gr. τρι-, + τετρα-, τετρ- + ...

Trinundine (troinu'ndin). *Obs.*

Triobolar (troio'bŏlăr), *a.* Also in L. form **triobolaris.** [ad. L. triobolāris, f. τρι-, TRI- + ...

Trion (troi'ŏn). *Zool.* [ad. Gr. τρίων, f. τρι-, TRI- + ...

Trional (troi'ŏnăl). *Pharm.* [Trio- s + -ONAL, ...

Trionychoid (troini'koid), *a.*

Trip (trip). *sb.*[1] Also **5** *tryp,* **5-7** *trippe, 7-8* trippe, 7-8 trypppe. [f. TRIP *v.*]

I. 1. The action or an act of tripping or moving lightly and quickly; a light, lively movement of the feet; tripping gait or tread; *fig.* ...

2. A short voyage or journey; a 'run.' ...

3. A short voyage or journey; a 'run.' ...

Tripartite.

2. Made in three corresponding parts or copies, as an INDENTURE (q.v.) drawn up between three persons or parties, each of whom preserves one of the copies.

3. Engaged in or concluded between three parties.

4. *Her.* Applied to the field when divided into three parts of different tinctures : = TIERCE.

5. Consisting of three parts or divisions, as a member or organ of an animal or plant.

b. *Bot.* : *spec.* of a leaf, etc., Divided into three segments nearly to the base. (Abbrev. *3-partite*.)

6. *Math.* Involving three sets of variables.

B. † a. A tripartite indenture (see 2). *Obs.*

b. A book, document, or treatise in three parts.

† **Tripartite,** v. *Obs. rare.* [f. as prec.] *trans.* To divide into three parts, or among three persons.

Tripartited, *ppl. a. Obs. rare.* [f. prec. + -ED.] Divided into or composed of three parts; made between three parties : = TRIPARTITE 2.

Tripartitely, *adv.* [f. TRIPARTITE *a.* + -LY.] In a tripartite manner; in or into three parts.

Tripartition (traipɑː·tiʃən). [f. L. *tripartitus*: see TRIPARTITE *a.* and -TION.] Division into three corresponding parts or copies.

Tripe (traip). Also § -*y.* trippe, 5-6 trippe, 6 trype, 5-8 trype. [a. OF. *tripe*, entrails of an animal (13th c. in Hatz.-Darm.) ...]

1. The first or second stomach of a ruminant, esp. of the ox, prepared as food ; formerly including also the entrails of swine and fish.

† **Tripe.²** *Obs.* Forms : 5-6 trype, 6 tryp, 7 traype, 7-8 tripe. [a. OF. *tripe* (13th c. in Godef. *Compl.*; cf. also *triperie* 1175).]

1. A tripe of roche (trip də rɒʃ). [F. 'rock tripe', from the appearance of the thallus.] A name originally given in Canada to various edible lichens of the genera *Gyrophora* and *Umbilicaria*.

b. Applied opprobriously or contemptuously to a person; also *bag of tripe*.

2. The intestines, bowels, guts, as members of the body ; hence, the paunch or belly including the stomach. *In pl.* Commonly *in pl.*

3. *transf.* and *fig.* (in various applications.)

Tripenny, var. TRIPOLI (polishing powder).

Tripe·nnate, *a. Bot. rare.* [L. TRI- + PENNATE.] = TRIPINNATE.

Tripedite (traipe·dait), *Chem.* [Named by Fischer, 1902, f. TRI- + TEP(ONE + -IDE).] A compound containing the residues of three amino-acids.

Triphane (trai·fən), *Min.* [a. F. *triphane* (Haüy, 1801), f. Gr. *τριφανής* appearing threefold] = SPODUMENE.

Triphthong (tri·fθɒŋ). Also § *triphthonge,* *triphthong,* 9 *triphthongue.* [f. TRI- after DIPHTHONG.] A combination of three vowel sounds in a single syllable.

Triphyline, -lite (tri·filin, -ləit). *Min.* [a. Gr. *τριφυλία* (as if) *τρίφυλος*: see TRIPLE + -INE.]

Tripe-personal.

Tri-personal (trai,pɜː·sənăl), *a. Theol.* [f. TRI- + PERSONAL *a.*] Consisting of or existing in three persons : said of the Godhead.

Triperson·alism.

Tripersonalism, the doctrine or theory of three persons in the Godhead.

Tripery (trai·pəri), *n.* [f. TRIPE + -ERY.] A place where tripe is prepared or sold.

† **Triped** (trai·ped), *a. Obs. rare,* made into three parts.

Tripetalous (traipe·tăləs), *a. Bot.* [TRI- + *petalum* PETAL + -OUS.] Having, or consisting of, three petals.

Triphony (tri·fəni), *Mus.* [ad. med.L. *triphōnia* (see below).] In early medieval music, Diaphony in three voices.

Triple (tri·p'l). Also *§ triphthonge.*

Tripe-hammer, [TRIP + HAMMER.] A massive machine-hammer operated by a tripping device.

Triphylite, see TRIPHYLINE.

Triphyllous (trifi·ləs), *a. Bot.* [Gr. *τρίφυλλος* (as φύλλον leaf) + -OUS.] Having or consisting of three leaves.

Triphysite (tri·fisəit), *a.* [f. TRI- + Gr. φύσις nature + -ITE.] = MONOPHYSITE.

† **Triplous,** *a. Obs. rare⁻¹.* [f. L. *tri-* three + *pli-* or hair + -OUS.] Having three (anal) hairs.

Tripinnately, *adv.* In a tripinnate manner.

Triple (tri·p'l). Forms : 6 *tryple,* (*treeple*,) *triphyll,* 7-8 (*C.S.*) *tripple,* 6- *triple.* [a. F. *triple* (16th c. in Godef. *Compl.*), or ad. L. *triplus* threefold, *Gr. τριπλοῦς.*]

Triplicate.

Triplication (triplikei·ʃən). [ad. L. *triplicātiōn-em*, n. of action from *triplicāre*: see TRIPLICATE.] The action or process of making threefold, or multiplying by three; also, the result of this.

Triplicative (tri·plikĕitiv), a. [f. L. *triplicāt-*, ppl. stem of *triplicāre* to TRIPLICATE + -IVE.] Having the quality of tripling.

Triplicity (tripli·sĭti). [ad. late L. *triplicĭtāt-em*, f. L. *triplex*, *-icem*: see TRIPLEX and -ITY. Cf. F. *triplicité* (14–15th c. in Hatz.-Darm.).]

Triplicostate, -form, -nerved: see TRIPLI-.

Tripling (tri·pliŋ), *vbl. sb.* [f. TRIPLE *v.* + -ING 1.] The action of the verb TRIPLE.

Triplite (tri·plait). *Min.* [f. Gr. τριπλόος triple + -ITE 1.]

Triplo- (triple), before a vowel *tripl-*, combining form repr.

Triploid (tri·ploid). *Surg. rare.* [f. Gr. τριπλόος: see prec. and -OID.]

Triplum (tri·plŏm). [med.L. *triplum*, neut. of *triplus* triple.]

So **Triply** (tri·pli), *adv.*

Triplumbic, a. *Chem.* [f. TRI- 5 + L. *plumb-um* lead + -IC.]

Trip·madam, *v. Herb.* Also 7 **trip-madame.** [app. a. F. *trippe-madame*, according to Hatz.-Darm., an alteration of the earlier *trique-madame*, TRICK-MADAM.]

Tripod (trai·pŏd), *sb.* and *a.* Also 7 *tripod*, 7-8 *tripode*. [ad. L. *tripod-*, *tripūs*, a. Gr. τρίπους, τρίπος three-footed, *sb.* a three-footed vessel.]

Tripodal (tri·pŏdăl), a. [f. L. *tripod-*, *tripūs* (see prec.) + -AL.]

Tripody (tri·pŏdi). *Pros.* [f. TRI-, after TRIPODY.]

Tripoli (tri·pŏli). [= F. *tripoli* (16th c. in Godef. Compl.)]

Tripolitan, *sb.* and *a.* [f. as TRIPOLI + -AN.]

Tripolite (tri·pŏlait). *Min.* [f. TRIPOLI + -ITE 1.]

Tripos (trai·pŏs). [Latinized form of *tripus*: see TRIPOD.]

Trippant (tri·pănt), a. *Her.* [a. OF. *trippant*, pres. pple. of *tripper* to TRIP.] = TRIPPING.

Trippet¹ (tri·pĕt). Forms: 4-5 *trippet*, *tryppet*, 6 *tryppyt*, *trippett*, 9 *dial.* -et, 7- **trippet.** [Of obscure origin; cf. TRIP *sb.*]

Trippet² (tri·pĕt). *Now north. dial.* Also 6 -ett, *trippett*, 7-9 *tripet*. [Cf. OF. *trepied*, *tripie*, *tripier* (13th c. in Godef. Compl.), and TRIVET.]

Tripper (tri·pəɹ). [f. TRIP *v.* + -ER 1.] One who or that which trips.

Tripping (tri·piŋ), *vbl. sb.* [f. TRIP *v.* + -ING 1.] The action of the verb TRIP in various senses.

Tripping, *ppl. a.* [f. TRIP *v.* + -ING 2.]

Tripling (tri·pliŋ), *sb.* and *ppl. a.*; also **Tri·pping,** a verb-noun.

Tripping, *ppl. a.* [as prec. + -ING 1.] That trips, in various senses.

1. Moving quickly and lightly; light-footed, nimble.

2. Stumbling, erring, sinning.

So **Trippingly**, *adv.*

Trippingness.

Trippist (tri·pist), a. *colloq. rare.* [f. TRIP *sb.* + -IST.]

Tripple (tri·p'l). *sb. Africa.* [f. TRIPPLE *v.*]

Tripple, *v.* [Du. *triple* slow triple-pace; prob. a. LDu. *triple* to tread.]

Trippse-homerous, -prostyle: see TRI- 1 a.

Tripsis (tri·psis). [a. Gr. τρῖψις rubbing.]

Tripsome (tri·psʌm), a. [f. TRIP *sb.* + -SOME 1.] Characterized by tripping; nimble.

Tript, variant of *tripped* (see TRIP 2.)

Tripterous (tri·ptərəs), a. [f. Gr. τρί- three + πτερόν wing.]

Triptote (tri·ptōt), *sb.* and *a. Gram.* Also 7-8 *triptot*. [ad. L. *triptota*, pl., nouns that have only three case-endings.]

Triptych (tri·ptik). *sb.* Also triptic. [f. Gr. τρίπτυχος of three folds, τρί- three + πτυχή a fold.]

Triptyque (triptī·k), *sb.* [Fr.]

Tripudiary (tripiū·diări), a. *rare.* [f. L. *tripudium*: see below.]

Tripudiate (tripiū·dieit), *v. rare.* [f. L. *tripudiāt-*, ppl. stem of *tripudiāre* to dance.]

Tripudist (tri·pudist).

Tripudium (tripiū·diəm). *Rom. Antiq.* [L.]

Tripunctal, a.

Triquetra (traikwē·tra). *sb. Archæol.* Also 7-8 *triquet*. [ad. L. *triquetra*, fem. of *triquetrus* three-cornered.]

Triquetral (traikwē·trăl), a. [f. L. *triquetr-us*: see next.]

Triquetric, a. rare⁻¹. [f. L. *triquetr-us* + -IC.]

Triquetrous (traikwē·trəs), a. [f. L. *triquetr-us* three-cornered, triangular + -OUS.]

Triquetrum (traikwē·trəm). [L.]

Triradial (trairei·diăl), a. [f. TRI- + L. *radius* ray: see RADIAL and -AL.]

Triradiate (trairei·di-ĕt), a. (*sb.*) [f. TRI- + RADIATE.]

Tris-, prefix, repr. Gr. τρίς thrice (which occurs as prefix, repr. L. *ter*- in numerous Gr. compounds, chiefly adjs.).

Trisaccharide (traisæ·kărəid). *Chem.* [f. TRI- + SACCHARIDE.]

Trisacramentarian (n.)

Trisagion (trisæ·giŏn, -gĭŏn). Also 4-9 in Latin form *trisagion*. [a. Gr. (τὸ) τρισάγιον.]

Trisect (traise·kt), *v.* [f. TRI- + L. *sect-*, ppl. stem of *secāre* to cut, after BISECT.] *trans.* To divide into three equal parts.

Trisection (traise·kʃən). [f. prec.: see -ION.]

Trisector (traise·ktəɹ). [f. TRISECT *v.* + -OR.]

Triserial (traisī·riăl), a. [f. TRI- + L. *series* + -AL.]

Trisilicate (traisi·likĕt). *Chem.* and *Min.* [f. TRI- + SILICATE.]

Triskele (tri·skēl). Also in quasi-Gr. form **triskelion** (triske·liŏn), error, -trion, and **triskeles.** [f. Gr. τρίσκελ-ής three-legged.]

Trismegistic (trismegi·stik), a.

Trismus (tri·smʌs). *Path.* [mod.L., a. Gr. τρισμός gnashing, grinding.]

Trisoctahedron (triso·ktæhē·drŏn). *Geom.* [f. Gr. τρίς thrice + OCTAHEDRON.]

Supplement, p. 3873; Corrigenda, p. 4092; Spurious words, p. 4093; Books quoted, p. 4094

Tritylodontoid (trī-tī-lŏ-dŏn'toid), a. and sb. [f. mod.L. *Tritylodon*, -*ont*- (f. Gr. τρι- TRI- + τύλος knob + ὀδούς, ὀδόντ- tooth) + -OID.] a. adj. Resembling the genus *Tritylodon*, or belonging to the family *Tritylodontidæ*, of extinct monotreme mammals, found in the Triassic and Jurassic formations, and characterized by tritubercular molar teeth. b. sb. A member of this family.

Trium-feminate, *nonce-wd.* [f. L. *trium*, gen. pl. of *tres* or *tria* three + *femina* female, woman + -ATE¹, after TRIUMVIRATE.] A group of three women associated in government.

Triumph (trī'ŭmf), sb. Forms: 4-7 triumphe, tryumphe, (5 treyumphe, triumphe, triumphoe, 6 trumpe, tryumphe, tryoumfe, 6-7 tryumph, 6 triumpf. [ME. = OF. *triumphe* (13th c.), F. *triomphe* = Prov. *triomfe*, Sp. *triumfo*, Pg. *triumfo*, It. *triumfo*, ad. L. *triumphus*, earlier *triumpus* (older form *triumpus*): cf. Gr. θρίαμβος hymn to Bacchus.]

1. Rom. Hist.
The entrance of a victorious commander with his army and spoils in solemn procession into Rome, permission for which was granted by the senate in honour of an important achievement in war. Also *transf.*

TRIUMPHAL.

Triumphal (trī-ŭmf'al), a. (sb.) [ad. L. *triumphālis*, f. *triumphus* TRIUMPH. Cf. OF. *triumphal* (*triomphal*, 13th c. in Godef. Compl.), F. *triomphal*: see -AL.]

1. Of, pertaining to, or of the nature of a triumph; celebrating or commemorating a triumph or victory.

Triumphant (trī-ŭm'fant), a. [ad. L. *triumphant*-em, pres. pple. of *triumphāre* to TRIUMPH, or = F. *triumphant*, triomphant (14th c.): see -ANT.]

TRIUMPHANCY.

Triumphancy (trī-ŭm'fansi). [f. TRIUMPHANT: see -ANCY.] The state or quality of being triumphant.

Triumphator (trai-umfei'tor). [a. L. *triumphātor*, agent-n. f. *triumphāre* to TRIUMPH.] A conqueror; spec. a Roman general who was granted a triumph.

Triumpher (trai'ŭmfar). [f. TRIUMPH + -ER¹.] One who triumphs.

Triumviral (trai-ŭm'viral), a. [ad. L. *triumvirālis*, f. *triumvir* TRIUMVIR.] Of or pertaining to a triumvir or a triumvirate.

Triumvirate (trai-ŭm'viret), sb. [ad. L. *triumvirātus*, f. *triumvir*: see TRIUMVIR and -ATE¹.]

Triumvir (trai-ŭm'vir). [a. L. *triumvir*.] Also pl. -*viri*.

Triunal (trai-yū'nal), a. *poet. rare.* [f. as next + -AL.] = TRIUNE.

Triune (trai'yūn, ai·ai), a. (sb.) [f. L. *tri-* TRI- + *unus* one: the name Triune the mystic four Triune God adorn.]

Triunity (trai-yū'niti), sb. [f. TRI- after BI-UNITY. The quality of being three in one.

Trivalve (trai'vælv), sb. and a. Nat. Hist. [f. TRI- + VALVE, after *bivalve*.]

Triverbial, a. rare. [ad. L. *triverbium*.]

Trivet (triv'et). Forms: 1 trefet, 5 trevid, trevet, trefet, -d, 5-6 trevette, 5-9 trevet, 6 trevett, treyvette, trivette, tryvette, 6-7 trivet, trevet, 7 triffet, -9 dial. treevet, 6-9 trivet. [OE. *trefet*, prob. ad. L. *tripēs*, *triped*- three-footed.]

Trivial (triv'ial), a. (sb.) [ad. L. *triviālis*, f. *trivium*: see TRIVIUM) + -AL.]

TRIVIALISM.

Trivialism (triv'iǎliz'm). rare. [f. prec. + -ISM.] Trivial character; triviality; something of trivial import; a triviality.

Triviality (triviæl'iti). [f. TRIVIAL + -ITY. Cf. F. *trivialité*.]

Trivially (triv'iǎli), adv. [f. TRIVIAL + -LY².] In a trivial manner.

TROCHALOPOD.

Trochal (trŏk'al), a. [f. Gr. τροχός wheel + -AL.] Zool. Resembling a wheel; rotiform: as the *trochal apparatus*, disk, or organ of the Rotifera.

Trochalopod (trŏk'ălŏpŏd), sb. (a.) Zool. [ad. mod.L. *Trochalopoda*, neut. pl.]

Trochalopodous, adj. running, rolling + πούς, foot.] A member of the *Trochalopoda*, a group of heteropterous insects in which the posterior coxæ have a rotary motion. b. *adj.* Belonging to the *Trochalopoda*. Also **Trochalopodous** Heteroptera are round. 1909 Cent. Dict.

Trochanter (trōkæ·ntəɹ). *Anat.* and *Zool.* [a. F. *trochanter* (Paré, 16th c.), a. Gr. τροχαντήρ (in sense 1), f. τρέχειν to run.]

1. A protuberance or process in the upper part of the thigh-bone, serving for the attachment of certain muscles; usually, as in man, two in number, *the great trochanter* (L. *major*) for the external rotator muscles, and *the lesser trochanter* (L. *minor*) for the ilio-psoas muscle.

2. *Entom.* The second joint of an insect's leg, next to the coxa (coxa 2); originally consisting of two joints (cf. Thigh).

Trochantin (trōkæ·ntin). *Anat.* and *Zool.* a. = F. *trochantin*, L. *trochanter* (see above).] a. The lesser trochanter. b. *Entom.* The proximal joint of the trochanter (Trochanter 2) when two-jointed. Hence **Trochantinerian**, a. (F. *trochantinien*), pertaining to the trochantin.

Trochar, -art, variants of Trocar.

Troche, obs. f. Trough.

Troche (trōk, trō·tʃi). *Pharm.* Also 6 troach, 7 troch. [ad. 7 troch, in Dicts. erron. torch. a. OF. *troche* (13th c. in Godef.) cluster, mass, also in sense 2 below; in Twety *dez de Venerie* (a 1327) in sense 1, with which cf. OF. *trocheure* (14th c. in Godef. Compl.), F. *trochure*. Cf. also Trock, Troching.]

1. A cluster of three or more tines at the summit of a deer's horn; distinguished from a *fourche* (f. 4 fork) of two tines.

Trochee (trōkī), *Pros.* Also in Gr.-Lat. form 6 trochæus, 6–7 (9) trochæus. [ad. L. *trochæus*, ad. Gr. τροχαῖος, prop. adj. (sc. πούς) running, tripping, f. τρόχος a running course, f. τρέχειν to run.] A metrical foot consisting of a long followed by a short syllable; in accentual verse, of an accented followed by an unaccented syllable. Also called Choree.

Trochisk (trō·kisk). *Obs.* Forms: 5 troois, 6 cysoe, -oyake, -cisquo, 6–7 -ciske, -chiske, -chisco, -chisque, -chis, 7 -cisk, -chisc(k, -chist, 7–8 -chiste(i); also, in L. form 6 *trochiscus*. [a. F. *trochisque* (*trocisque*, *trocisse*, 1425 in Godef. Compl.) = it. *trochisco*, Sp. *trochisk*; ad. L. *trochiscus*, Gr. τροχίσκος, dim. of τρόχος wheel, small globe, pill, lozenge, dim. of τρόχος wheel.] A medicated tablet or disk; a (round or ovate) pastille or lozenge.

Trochite (trō·kaɪt). *Palæont.* Now *Obs.* [ad. mod.L. *trochītes*, f. Gr. τρόχος wheel: see -ITE.] A name for the detached wheel-like joints of encrinites; = Entrochite, Entrochus.

Troll (trōl). *sb.²* Also 6 trowell, 7 trole, trowl, trowle, 7–9 trowl. [partly a. ONorse and Swed. *troll*, Da. *trold*, a. ONorse and Swed. *troll*, Da. *trolla* to charm, bewitch, ON. *trolldómr* witchcraft.] (Adopted in English from Scandinavian in the middle of the 19th cent.; but it survived from Norse (in *troll*), it had survived from Norse dialect formerly spoken there.)

In Scandinavian mythology, One of a race of supernatural beings formerly conceived as giants, now in Denmark and Sweden, as dwarfs or imps, supposed to inhabit caves or subterranean dwellings.

Trolly, variant of TROLLEY.

Troll-lolly, int. [Cf. TROLLOLL.]

Trollope. See TROLLOP.

Tro'mba. Obs. rare⁻¹. Mus.

Trombash, var. TROMBASH.

Trommel (tṛǫ'mĕl, -'l). Mining. U.S.

Trommeter. An instrument for measuring.

Trombone (tṛǫmbǭ'n). [ad. It. trombone.] A large wind-instrument of the trumpet kind.

Trombone, variant of TROMBE. var. TROMPE.

Trompe, obs. form of TRUMPET, sb.

Trompe. Obs. rare⁻¹. [a. OF. trompe.]

Trompet, -er, pl. obs. forms of TRUMPET, etc.

Trope (trǭp). Also trombe, tromp.

Tromquot, -ro, obs. ff. or var. TRUMPER.

Tron, variant of TROLLEY.

Trone. See TRON.

Tronage (trǭ'nĕdʒ). [a. AF. tronage, f. OF. trone TRON : see -AGE.]

Troop (trūp). Forms 6 troupe, (troppe), 7–9 troop.

Trooper (trū'pǝɹ). [f. TROOP sb. + -ER ¹.]

Trooping (trū'piŋ), vbl. sb. [-ING ¹] 1. The action of TROOP v.

Troostite (trū'stǝit). [Named after Prof. G. Troost of Nashville, Tennessee: see -ITE ¹.]

Trope (trǭp), sb. [ad. L. tropus, a. Gr. τρόπος turning.]

you alter the word, you destroy the Figure. 1837 MACAULAY *Ess., Bacon* (1887) 428 Irony is one of the four primary tropes. 1876 GLADSTONE *Homeric Synchr.* 262 To treat as a poetical trope this idea of kings as god-born or god-reared. 1888 BRYCE *Amer. C.* III. cxi. 597 [American] rhetoric is Rhodian rather than Attic, overloaded with tropes and figures.

attrib. 1799 HAN. MORE *Fem. Educ.* (ed. 4) I. x. 221 By this negligence in the just application of words, we shall be.. much misled by these trope and figure ladies.

†2. In Gregorian Music, A short distinctive cadence at the close of a melody. *Obs.*

1603 HOLLAND *Plutarch's Mor.* 1358 To let passe therefore the five positures of the Tetrachords, as also the first five tones, tropes, changes, notes or harmonies. 1605 BACON *Adv. Learn.* II. v. § 3 Is not the trope of music, to avoid or slide from the close or cadence, common with the trope of rhetoric of deceiving expectation? 1626 — *Sylva* § 113.

†3. [= Gr. τροπή.] The 'turning' of the sun at the tropic; also = TROPIC A. 2. *Obs. rare.*

1677 GALE *Crt. Gentiles* II. IV. 258 The Sun has..its annual Tropes and Vicissitudes, what they call Solstices, whereby it is nearer to or remoter from us. 1735 H. BROOKE *Univ. Beauty* IV. 169 Now 'thwart the trope, or zone antartic steer.

†4. *Logic.* = MOOD *sb.*^{2} 1. *Obs. rare.*

1656 STANLEY *Hist. Philos.* VIII. (1701) 315/1 Of Moods or Tropes there are two kinds, one of Indemonstrables,..the other of Demonstrables.

5. In the Western Church, A phrase, sentence, or verse introduced as an embellishment into some part of the text of the mass or of the breviary office that is sung by the choir.

(Tropes were discontinued at the revision of the missal under Pope Pius V in the 16th cent.)

1846 MASKELL *Mon. Rit.* I. p. xxxvii, The Tropes..were ..sung either before or after the Introit and Hymns in the service of the Mass. 1853 ROCK *Ch. of Fathers* IV. xi. 21 A.. practice..had..grown up..in the north and western quarters of Christendom..of weaving certain pious sentences, called by the Romans 'festive praises', by the Franks 'tropes', between the words of the psalm in the introit at mass. 1894 W. H. FRERE *Winchester Troper* p. ix, 'Trope'..is the regular word to describe additions to the Introit, Offertory and Communion, and is also more rarely found in connection with the Ite missa est or Benedicamus at the close of Mass.

6. In the Moravian Church, One of the three divisions forming the 'Unity of the Brethren'.

[1780 B. LA TROBE tr. *Cranz's Hist. Brethren* 355 In.. 1749..the administration of the Reformed tropus in the Unity of the Brethren was tendered to, and accepted by, the Bishop of Sodor and Man, Thomas Wilson.] 1809 BOGUE & BENNET *Hist. Dissenters* (1833) II. i. 64 The three different classes of persons who compose the Unity, bear among the brethren the name of tropes or tropuses.

7. In Greek Philosophy: see quots.

1866 FERRIER *Grk. Philos.* I. xv. 467 Of these tropes or Sceptical arguments Sextus enumerates ten. 1910 R. D. HICKS *Stoic & Epicurean* 376 Ænesidemus undertook to arrange the whole material at the disposal of the Sceptic in his contention against the dogmatic position under ten heads or tropes. The word trope properly denotes procedure; the ten tropes were intended to contain the means of refuting dogmatism in all possible forms, and to provide directions for stating every line of available argument which could lead to negative conclusions and paralyse assent.

8. *Geom.* The reciprocal of a node on a curve or surface; in different cases, a multiple tangent or tangent plane, or a plane or developable surface touching the given surface in a particular way.

1869 CAYLEY *Math. Papers* VI. 330 Using 'trope' as the reciprocal term to node. 1875 [see TROPAL].

Tropee, obs. form of TROPHY.

Tropeic (tropīˑik), *a. Ichth.* [f. Gr. τρόπις keel + -IC.] Applied to the ventral fold in certain sharks.

1895 in *Funk's Stand. Dict.*

Tropeine (trōuˑpīˌəin). *Chem.* [Arbitrarily altered from TROPINE.] Generic name for the esters or compound ethers of tropine.

1883 *Science* I. 401/2 A series of derivatives, called by the author tropeines, results from the action of various organic acids with hydrochloric acid upon tropine. 1895 in *Funk's Stand. Dict.*

†**Tropel.** *Obs. rare.* Also (*pl.*) 5 **troplys**, 7 **trowples.** [a. OF. *tropele* (*a* 1200 in Godef.), dim. f. OF. *trope* TROOP: see -EL^2.] A small troop or company.

1375 BARBOUR *Bruce* XIII. 275 Thai scalit in tropellis [*v.rr.* troplys, trowples] ser. *c* 1400 *Laud Troy Bk.* 5577 Paris come thenne with his tropel, With alle his knyghtes hardi and fel.

Troper (trōuˑpəɹ). *Eccl.* (now only *Hist.*) Also 5 **tropere, tropoure, tropure,** 8 **tropar.** [OE. *tropere*, ad. med.L. *troperium* (see TROPARY); cf. OF. *tropier, troper* (12th c. in Godef.).] A book containing tropes (TROPE 5); also, a book containing sequences; a sequencer.

a 1073 *Charter Bp. Leofric* in Thorpe *Charters* 430, II. fulle sangbec..& I. tropere & II. salteras. *a* 1400–50 *Alexander* 1568 With tablis & t[r]opoures. *c* 1400 *Laud Troy Bk.* 9369 The Bible ne no Missale,..The Grael ne the Tropere. *c* 1475 *Pict. Voc.* in Wr.-Wülcker 755/3 *Hoc troparium*, tropere. *a* 1746 LEWIS in Gutch *Coll. Cur.* II. 169 A Tropery, or book of Sequences. It was called in English a T[r]oper. 1894 W. H. FRERE *Winchester Troper* p. vi, The Tropers practically represent the sum total of musical advance between the ninth and the twelfth century.

Tropery: see TROPARY.

†**Trophæˑal,** *a. Obs.* [f. L. *trophæ-um* TROPHY + -AL.] Pertaining to or adorned with trophies.

1646 J. GREGORY *Notes & Obs.* (1650) 163 He stiled himself thus Augustus Cæsar Octavianus Trophaeall. 1660 *Charac. Italy* 6 Her streets of old did shine with triumphing Cæsars and Consuls in their trophæal Chariots.

Trophæum: see TROPÆUM.

Trophal (trōuˑfăl), *a. Zool.* [f. TROPH-I + -AL.] Pertaining to or forming the trophi.

1902 D. SHARP in *Encycl. Brit.* XXIX. 500/1 The appendages of the posterior three, or trophal, segments become the parts of the mouth.

Trophe, -ee, obs. forms of TROPHY.

Trophesy (trǫˑfĭsi). *Path.* [irreg. f. Gr. τροφή nourishment, with ending app. after *dropsy, palsy.*] 'Defective nutrition due to disorder of the trophic nerves' (Dorland *Med. Dict.* 1900–13). Hence **Trophesial** (trofīˑʃiăl, -ziăl) *a.*, pertaining to trophesy; in quot. 1899, pertaining to nutrition: = TROPHIC.

1883 E. C. MANN *Psychol. Med.* 349 (Cent. Dict.) Excessive thought, with mental anxiety,..is much more exhausting, and therefore more commonly followed by trophesies. 1891 *Cent. Dict.*, Trophesial. 1899 *Allbutt's Syst. Med.* VIII. 408 A morbid cerebral condition impairing psychical and trophesial function. *Ibid.* 409 The trophesial function of the cortex.

‖**Trophi** (trōuˑfəi), *sb. pl. Zool.* [mod.L., pl. of *trophus*, a. Gr. τροφός feeder, f. τρέφειν to nourish.] A collective name for the mouth-parts in insects, as organs for seizing and preparing the food. Also applied to the parts of the pharynx in rotifers, having a similar function.

1826 KIRBY & SP. *Entomol.* xxxiii. III. 355 *Trophi*, the different instruments or organs contained in the mouth, or closing it, and employed in manducation or deglutition. They include the *Labrum, Labium, Mandibulæ, Maxillæ, Lingua*, and *Pharynx*. 1833 LYELL *Princ. Geol.* III. 277 The antennæ, tarsi and trophi are generally very obscure or distorted. 1888 ROLLESTON & JACKSON *Anim. Life* 633 Class Rotifera...The mouth leads into an oesophagus, followed..usually directly by a muscular pharynx or mastax containing the chitinous jaw-apparatus or 'trophi'...The shape of the 'trophi' is variable.

Trophic (trǫˑfik), *a.* (*sb.*) *Biol.* [ad. Gr. τροφικός, f. τροφή nourishment: see -IC. Cf. F. *trophique.*] Of or pertaining to nutrition; *spec.* of certain nerves and nerve-centres, Concerned with or regulating the nutrition of the tissues.

1873 A. FLINT *Physiol. Man, Nervous Syst.* ii. 80 Centres attached to the sensory system of nerves, which have, as far as we know, a purely trophic influence over the nerves. 1875 H. C. WOOD *Therap.* (1879) 559 Nerves which preside over nutrition,—the so-called trophic nerves. 1894 *Lancet* 3 Nov. 1030 The large amount of wasting of the muscles.. might suggest the possibility of a trophic lesion. 1899 *Allbutt's Syst. Med.* VII. 124 Another affection of the lower limbs, possibly trophic,..is rupture of the tendo Achillis.

B. *sb.* Something that promotes nutrition.

1893 E. S. D'ODIARDI *Med. Electricity* 54 The second class is composed of trophics, or nutrients, *i.e.*, promoters of nutrition.

So **Troˑphical** *a.* (*rare*) = *trophic* adj.; hence **Troˑphically** *adv.*, in relation to nutrition.

1857 DUNGLISON *Med. Lex.*, *Trophical Nerves*, the organic nerves, or nerves of the sympathetic system. 1900 *Lancet* 23 June 1779/2 This..implies continuity of the protoplasm of one neurone with another, but trophically and genetically the two are independent.

Trophied (trōuˑfid), *a.* Also 8 **trophy'd.** [f. TROPHY *sb.* or *v.* + -ED.]

1. Adorned with a trophy or trophies. Also *fig.*

1622 DRAYTON *Poly-olb.* xxx. 150 From whose stone-trophied head, it [the echo] on to Wendrosse went. 1718 ROWE tr. *Lucan* VIII. 1122 The Name that wont the trophy'd Arch to grace. 1798 S. ROGERS *Epist. Friend* 200 Thro' trophied tombs of heroes and of kings. 1844 H. G. ROBINSON *Odes Horace* I. xii, The peaceful reign Of Numa, or the proudly trophied state Of Tarquin. 1905 CAPT. GLASFURD *Rifle Ind. Jungle* 387 That mighty head shall be accorded the post of honour on already well-trophied walls.

2. Formed into or constituting a trophy.

a 1843 SOUTHEY *Comm.-pl. Bk.* IV. 55/1 The trophied armour damp gleaming to the central fire. 1887 *Daily News* 16 May 5/7 The Exchange was..tastefully decorated, each window..having its trophied flags and shield.

Trophilegic (trǫfileˑdʒik), *a. Biol.* [irreg. f. Gr. τροφή nourishment + L. *legĕre* to gather, to collect + -IC. (Perhaps suggested by L. *frūgilĕgus* fruit-gathering.)] Collecting nutriment.

1898 *Nature* 3 Nov. 15/1 The trophilegic action of the fronds [of ferns], in connection with which certain arrangements have been observed, destined to facilitate the passage of water to the roots.

Trophism (trǫˑfiz'm). *Phys.* [f. Gr. τροφή nourishment + -ISM.] The process of nutrition of the tissues; 'direct trophic influence' (Dorland *Med. Dict.* 1900–13).

1878 A. HAMILTON *Nerv. Dis.* 444 Various depraved conditions of sensibility, motility, and trophism may follow.

Tropho- (trǫˑfo), combining form repr. Gr. τροφή nourishment, f. τρέφειν to nourish: entering into various technical terms, chiefly of biology and allied sciences. **Troˑphoblast** [-BLAST], a layer of cells external to the embryo, having the function of supplying it with nourishment; also applied by some to the morbid growth in cancer, as held to be an abnormal development of the same tissue; hence **Trophoblaˑstic** *a.*, relating to or consisting of trophoblast. **Trophocaˑlyx** [CALYX], a cup-shaped body from which the placenta is developed in certain mammals, as bats and moles. **Troˑphocyte** (-səit) [-CYTE], each of a set of cells forming one of the constituents of the fatty tissue in adult insects. **Troˑphodisc, -disk,** a disk-shaped body from which the placenta is developed in certain mammals, as rabbits. ‖**Tropholecithus** (-leˑsiþǫs) [mod.L., f. Gr. λέκιθος yolk], the nutritive yolk of an ovum; hence **Tropholeˑcithal** *a.* **Trophoˑlogy** [-LOGY], that department of physiology which deals with nutrition. ‖**Trophoneˑma** (pl. -neˑmata) [mod.L., f. Gr. νῆμα thread], each of the glandular villi of the uterus in certain viviparous fishes, which supply nutriment to the embryos. ‖**Troˑphoneurosis** (-ūəˑsis), pl. **-oses** (-ūəˑsīz) [NEUROSIS], any one of a class of functional disorders due to derangement of the trophic action of the nerves; hence **Trophoneurotic** (-ǫˑtik) *a.*, pertaining to or of the nature of trophoneurosis. **Trophoˑpathy** [Gr. -πάθεια suffering], any derangement of nutrition, esp. of a tissue. **Troˑphophore** (-fōəɹ) [ad. Gr. τροφοφόρος bringing nourishment], any one of the wandering amœboid nutritive cells in a sponge which give rise to gemmules or embryos. **Trophophoric** (-fǫˑrik) *a.* [f. as prec. + -IC], having the function of supplying provisions. **Trophophorous** (-ǫˑfŏrəs) *a.* [f. as prec. + -OUS], pertaining to or of the nature of a trophophore. **Troˑphoplasm** (-plæz'm), Nägeli's term for that portion of the protoplasm of a germ or cell which is supposed to furnish nutriment to the *idioplasm*; hence **Trophoplaˑsmic** *a.*, pertaining to or of the nature of trophoplasm. **Troˑphoplast**, Meyer's term for a specialized granule of protoplasm in a vegetable cell: = PLASTID 2. **Troˑphopoˑllen** [cf. *trophosperm* below], a proposed name for the partition of the loculus of an anther. **Troˑphosome** (-sōum) [Gr. σῶμα body], the aggregate of nutritive zooids of a hydrozoan (distinguished from *gonosome*); hence **Trophosoˑmal** *a.* **Troˑphosperm** [ad. F. *trophosperme* (Richard, *a* 1819), f. Gr. σπέρμα seed], a proposed name for the placenta of a seed-vessel. **Troˑphosphere,** a spherical body (consisting of the *trophoblast* and the *trophospongia*) from which the placenta is developed in certain mammals, as hedgehogs. ‖**Trophospongia** (-spǫˑndʒiă) [mod.L. (Hubrecht), f. Gr. σπογγιά sponge], a compact layer of cells between the trophoblast and the decidual tissue; hence **Trophospoˑngial, -ian** *adjs.* ‖**Trophotaˑxis** [mod.L.: cf. TAXIS 6], = *trophotropism.* **Trophotroˑpic** *a.*, pertaining to or exhibiting trophotropism. **Trophoˑtropism** [Gr. -τροπος turning: after *heliotropism*, etc.], reaction of an organism or cell to the stimulus of a source or supply of food by movement towards or away from it (*positive* or *negative t.*). **Trophozoite** (-zōuˑəit) [Gr. ζῷον animal: cf. -ITE^1 3], a sporozoon (endoparasitic protozoon) in its growing stage, when it is absorbing nutriment from its host. **Trophozooid** (-zōuˑǫid), a nutritive zooid of any colonial organism, as a hydrozoan.

1889 HUBRECHT in *Q. Jrnl. Microsc. Sci.* Dec. 299 This striking difference between somatic mesoblast and *trophoblast becomes still more accentuated in the next developmental phases. *Ibid.* 385 If we agree..to designate the outer layer alone as trophoblast, the outer layer plus a thin layer of somatic mesoblast without blood-vessels as diplotrophoblast [etc.]. 1907 *Contemp. Rev.* Sept. 411 A cancer is 'irresponsible trophoblast'. 1889 HUBRECHT (as above) 301 Mesoblastic warts, ridges, and outgrowths being soon surrounded on three sides by the *trophoblastic proliferation. 1907 *Contemp. Rev.* Sept. 410 The trophoblastic theory of cancer. 1889 HUBRECHT (as above) 359 The *trophocalyx (as this specialized region may conveniently be called, both in the bat and the mole, per analogiam with the trophosphere of the hedgehog and the trophodisc of the rabbit). 1904 *Jrnl. Roy. Microsc. Soc.* Oct. 527 Imaginal Adipose Tissue in Muscidæ.—Ch. Pérez has made a study of this tissue, which consists of two kinds of elements—*trophocytes and œnocytes. 1889 HUBRECHT (as above) 323 Corresponding regions of the rabbit might be indicated by the name of *trophodisc, that of the bat and mole of trophocalyx. 1891 *Cent. Dict.*, *Tropholecithal. 1879 tr. *Haeckel's Evol. Man* I. viii. 216 The nutritive yolk (*vitellus nutritivus*, or *tropholecithus*)..is a mere appendage of the true egg-cell, and contains hoarded food-substance,..so that it forms a sort of storehouse for the embryo in the course of its evolution. 1890 BILLINGS *Med. Dict.*, **Trophology*, science of nutrition. 1891 *Proc. Roy. Soc.* 19 Mar. 363 We propose to term the villiform structures of the uterine mucous membrane in Selachians, which essentially secrete nutriment, **trophonemata*. *Ibid.* 365 Transverse sections of a trophonema shew [etc.]. 1857 DUNGLISON *Med. Lex.*, **Trophoneuroses*, morbid conditions of the process of nutrition, owing to modified nervous influence. 1876 tr. *Wagner's Gen. Pathol.* 292 Many forms of disease rarely occurring, but..highly characteristic and very evident to the senses, tropho-neuroses. 1896 *Allbutt's Syst. Med.* I. 179 Facial hemi-atrophy and scleroderma from their distribution would suggest a trophoneurosis. 1891 *Cent. Dict.*, *Trophoneurotic. 1897 *Allbutt's Syst. Med.* II. 47 The so-called 'varieties' or 'forms' of leprosy..(2) the *smooth* (also called 'anæsthetic', 'non-tuberculated', 'tropho-neurotic', etc.). 1890 *Lancet* 8 Mar. 535 The belief of the writers that *trophopathy..has more to do with the cause of the so-called incurable diseases than the profession gives credit to. 1890 BILLINGS *Med. Dict.*, *Trophopathies*, disorders of nutrition. 1891 *Cent. Dict.*, *Trophophore, *Trophophorous. 1892 LD. LYTTON *King Poppy* I. 67 *note*, Official ranks, civil, military, and *trophophoric. 1893 tr. *Weismann's Germ-Plasm* I. i. 38, I shall..call the vital substance of the cell the 'formative plasm' or morphoplasm (Nägeli's '*trophoplasm'), in contrast to the idioplasm. [1899 *Allbutt's Syst. Med.* VI. 718 [The axis cylinder] is a prolongation of the achromatic amorphous substance, called also trophoplasma.] 1903 *Bot. Gaz.* May 340 Everything seems to point to the ooplasm as *trophoplasmic in character. 1885 GOODALE *Physiol. Bot.* (1892) 287 General Term.. *Trophoplast. Special Terms..anaplast, autoplast, chromoplast. 1889 *Science* 22 Nov. 355/1 The nucleus and other granules (the trophoplasts) within the cell...Each protoplast possesses the organs necessary for continuous transmission; the nucleus for new nuclei, the trophoplasts for new granules of all kinds. 1832 LINDLEY *Introd. Bot.* I. ii. 126 That part of the anther..which is called..the *trophopollen by Turpin. 1870 NICHOLSON *Man. Zool.* 26 The individual Campanularia consists of a series of nutritive zooids, collectively called the '*trophosome'. 1888 ROLLESTON & JACKSON *Anim. Life* 245 The Sea-fir..forms a fixed colony or *hydrosoma*...The hydrosome consists of a number of *hydranths* or nutritive zooids collectively forming the *trophosome* and connected to one another by a branching *cænosarc*. 1819 LINDLEY tr. *Richard's Observ. Fruits & Seeds* 6, I substitute the name of **Trophosperm* for that of *Placenta*, which botanists have given to the internal part of the pericarp, on which the seeds are immediately attached. 1889 HUBRECHT (as above) 322 These two together [the trophoblast and the trophospongia], forming in Erinaceus a sphere which is shut off from the uterus lumen by the fusion of the lips of the decidua reflexa, should be indicated by the name of *trophosphere. *Ibid.*, It is to this cell-mass of which we have just traced the maternal origin, that I propose to give the name of *trophospongia. *Ibid.* 326 The topography of the *trophospongian region. 1897 C. B. DAVENPORT *Exper. Morphol.* I. § 3. 39 Chemotaxis is, therefore, in some cases, a response to the stimulus afforded by substances which can be employed by the organism as food; under which circumstances it can be called '*Trophotaxis'. 1891 *Cent. Dict.*, *Trophotropic. 1887 GARNSEY & BALFOUR tr. *De Bary's Fungi*, etc. ix. 449 *Trophotropism.—Vegetating plasmodia spread out on surfaces which yield little or no nutriment move towards bodies which contain nutrient substances as soon as they are offered to them. 1906 *Lancet* 27 Oct. 1161/2 The problem of digestion is intimately related to.. 'trophotropism', both positive and negative. 1900–13 DORLAND *Med. Dict.* (ed. 7), *Trophozoite. 1909 *Cent. Dict. Suppl.*, Trophozoite. 1888 W. A. HERDMAN in *Encycl. Brit.* XXIII. 615/2 Nutritive forms (*trophozooids) which remain permanently attached to the nurse, and serve to provide it with food.

Trophonian (trofōuˑniăn), *a.* [f. L. *Trophōnius*, Gr. Τροφώνιος, proper name (see below) + -AN.] Pertaining to Trophonius, the mythical builder of the original temple of Apollo at Delphi, who after his death was worshipped as a god, and had an oracle in a cave in Bœotia, which was said to affect those who entered with such awe that they never smiled again: hence *allusively*.

1792 in Morse *Amer. Geog.* (1794) I. 398 Two young ladies ..who had heroism enough to make the trophonian [*mispr.* trophimium] tour with us. 1796 BURKE *Regic. Peace* i. Wks. VIII. 103 There is great danger that they who enter smiling into this Trophonian cave, will come out of it sad and serious conspirators. 1896 GOSSE in *Contemp. Rev.* Jan. 87 His face had the solemn Trophonian pallor, the look of the man who has seen death in the cave.

Trophy (trōuˑfi), *sb.* Forms: 6–7 **trophe, -ee, -ey, -æ,** (6 **-æe**), 7 **-ea, -ie, -ye,** (**tropee, -æe**), 7– **trophy.** See also TROPÆUM. [a. F. *trophée* (15th c. in Hatz.-Darm.), ad. post-cl.L. *trophæum*, cl.L. *tropæum*, ad. Gr. τρόπαιον, neut. of τροπαῖος, f. τροπή turning, putting to flight, defeat.]

1. *Gr.* and *Rom. Antiq.* A structure erected (originally on the field of battle, later in any public place) as a memorial of a victory in war, consisting of arms or other spoils taken from the enemy, hung upon a tree, pillar, etc. and dedicated to some divinity. Hence applied to similar monuments or memorials in later times.

1550 T. NICHOLS *Thucydides* I. 36 The Athenians dyd make and set vp their Trophe or signe of victorye, pretending to haue had the better. 1638 JUNIUS *Paint. Ancients* 145 Religion..hindering the Rhodians to deface this monument, because dedicated tropæes might not be removed. 1697 DRYDEN *Æneid* VII. 254 Around the posts hung helmets, darts, and spears, And captive chariots, axes, shields, and bars, And broken beaks of ships, the trophies of their wars. 1700 PRIOR *Carmen Seculare* 369 Let every Sacred Pillar bear Trophies of Arms, and Monuments of War. 1776 GIBBON *Decl. & F.* ii. (1788) I. 45 Alexander erected the Macedonian trophies on the banks of the Hyphasis. *a* 1854 H. REED *Lect. Eng. Hist.* iv. (1855) 146 The banners of the ships of Spain hung out as trophies from the battlements of the Cathedral of St. Paul. 1881 JOWETT *Thucyd.* I. 159 The Athenians..raised a trophy on the place from which they had just sailed out to their victory.

b. *transf.* A painted or carved figure of such a memorial; by extension, an ornamental or symbolic group of any objects, or a representation of such a group in decorative art.

1634 SIR T. HERBERT *Trav.* 64 The Trophies of his Ormus Victory..painted in Gold..wherein are set downe..the assaults and massacres of the Ormusians. 1688 *Lond. Gaz.* No. 2363/4 A Steel Sword, the Hilt cut with Trophies, the Trophies black, the Ground inlaid with Gold. 1716 LADY M. W. MONTAGU *Let. to C'tess Mar* 14 Sept., Near the Empress was a gilded trophy wreathed with flowers. 1753 CHAMBERS *Cycl. Supp.*, *Trophy*, in architecture, an ornament which represents the trunk of a tree, charged.. with arms or military weapons. 1848 THACKERAY *Bk. Snobs* xxvi, His gorget, sash, and sabre of the Horse Marines, with his boot-hooks underneath in a trophy.

2. a. *transf.* Anything taken in war, or in hunting, etc.; a spoil, prize: esp. if kept or displayed as a memorial. Also *fig.*

1513 DOUGLAS *Æneis* XI. iv. 75 For all the Tuscane menȝe ..Greyt trophe and rich spulȝe hyddir bringis. 1599 B. JONSON *Cynthia's Rev.* I. ii, That trophæe of selfe-loue, and spoile of nature. 1612 DRAYTON *Poly-olb.* iv. 317 For a Trophy brought the Giants coat away, Made of the beards of Kings. 1681 FLAVEL *Right. Man's Ref.* x. 244 They are.. not left as a prey and trophy to their enemy. 1788 GIBBON *Decl. & F.* lxiii. (1846) III. 580 A defeat and a wound were the only trophies of his expedition. 1810 SCOTT *Lady of L.* I. xxvii, All around, the walls to grace, Hung trophies of the fight or chase. 1860 MAURY *Phys. Geog. Sea* (Low) xiv. § 586 It was upon this plateau that Brooke's sounding apparatus brought up its first trophies from the bottom of the sea. 1895 J. G. MILLAIS *Breath fr. Veldt* (1899) 322 Sable antelope, the heads of which are, to my thinking, the finest trophies that Africa produces.

b. *fig.* Anything serving as a token or evidence of victory, valour, power, skill, etc.; a monument, memorial.

1569 SPENSER *Vis. Bellay* xi, She raisde a Trophee ouer all the worlde. 1644 MILTON *Areop.* (Arb.) 31 Whereof this whole Discourse..will be a certaine testimony, if not a Trophey. 1661 SECRETARY NICHOLAS *Let.* 18 Nov. in *Remembrancia* (London, Town Clerk's Office), The officers of the Trained Bands of the City had been put to great expense and charges in providing themselves with trophies and other necessaries. 1675 TRAHERNE *Chr. Ethics* 397 Hands, hearts, and souls, our victories, And spoils, and trophies, our own joyes! 1750 GRAY *Elegy* 38 If Mem'ry o'er their Tomb no Trophies raise. 1847 EMERSON *Poems, Ode to Beauty* 89 The leafy dell, the city mart, Equal trophies of thine art. 1871 MACDUFF *Mem. Patmos* xxi. 292 The triumphs and trophies of intellect.

3. *attrib.* and *Comb.*, as *trophy-badge, -bearer, decoration* (see 1 b), *flag, -hunter, -hunting, -work*; **trophy-cress** = *trophywort*; **trophy-lock,** 'a lock of hair cut from the head of a slain enemy, used to adorn a weapon or shield' (*Cent. Dict.* 1891); **trophy-money, trophy-tax,** a tax formerly levied in each county, now only in the City of London, for incidental expenses connected with the militia: see quot. 1727–41, and cf. quot. 1661 in 2 b; **trophywort,** a book-name for the genus TROPÆOLUM.

1891 WESTERMARCK *Hist. Human Marr.* (1894) 172 Many ornaments are really nothing but *trophy-badges. 1614 T. WHITE *Martyrd. St. George* C iij b, Thou..the..name dost gaine Of *Trophee-bearer. 1888 *Cassell's Encycl. Dict.*, **Trophy-cress*, the genus Tropæolum. 1891 *Cent. Dict.* s.v. *Decoration*, **Trophy decoration*, decoration by means of groups of arms, musical instruments, scrolls, tools of painting and sculpture, and the like, or what may by extension be called trophies, especially in Italian decorative art. 1663 BUTLER *Hud.* I. II. 1121 The Squire in State..bore The *Trophee-Fiddle and the Case. 1898 G. MEREDITH *Odes Fr. Hist.* 78 To clasp his *trophy flag, and call him Saint. 1909 *Westm. Gaz.* 16 Apr. 3/3 He interweaves..many little incidents that would escape the notice of the mere *trophy-hunter. 1899 W. H. FURNESS *Folk Lore Borneo* 15 That savage love of *trophy-hunting which seems inborn in mankind. 1664 in J. Croft *Excerpta Ant.* (1797) 21 Item, paid for *Trophye Money, 3*l* 8*s.* 8*d.* 1727–41 CHAMBERS *Cycl.*, *Trophy money*, a duty paid annually..towards providing harness, drums, colours, etc., for the militia. 1766 ENTICK *London* IV. 29 In 1682 a suit was commenced with the college..for trophy-money. 1897 *Outing* (U.S.) XXX. 227/1 The occasional sailor has no chance in the *trophy races. 1901 *Daily Chron.* 24 July 5/2 The '*Trophy Tax', or, to give it its full designation, the Trophy Tax Militia Rate..is peculiar to the City of London, and is a relic of the old train-band system. 1708 *New View Lond.* II. 491/2 A neat white marble monument, enricht with *Trophy work, an Urn, Cherub and Palm branches. 1866 *Treas. Bot.*, *Trophywort, *Tropæolum.*

Hence **Troˑphyless** *a.*, without a trophy.

1897 *19th Cent.* May 703 The disappointment at returning trophyless.

Troˑphy, *v.* [f. prec. sb.] *trans.* (chiefly *pass.*) †a. To transform into a trophy. *Obs. rare*$^{-1}$. b. To bestow a trophy upon, celebrate with a trophy. c. To adorn with a trophy or trophies; also *fig.* (See also TROPHIED.)

1599 B. JONSON *Cynthia's Rev.* v. xi, And so, swolne Niobe..was trophæed into stone. 1631 HEYWOOD and *Pt. Fair Maid of W.* I. i, If it prove as I have fashiond it, I shall be trophide ever. 1632 — *1st Pt. Iron Age* IV. Wks. 1874 III. 328 You beare your selfe more equall then you ought, With one so trophy'd. 1806 MOORE *Epist.* ix. 159 Heroes, trophied high In ancient fame. 1816 BYRON *Ch. Har.* III. xvii, Is the spot mark'd with no colossal bust? Nor column trophied for triumphal show? 1825 CAMPBELL *Poems, Stanzas Spanish Patriots* i, Looking on your graves, though trophied not, As holier hallow'd ground than priests could make the spot! 1847 R. W. HAMILTON *Disq. Sabbath* ii. (1848) 55 The Sabbath of the old covenant..descends to us trophied with holy illustrations.

Tropic (trǫˑpik), *sb.* and *a.*^{1} Forms: 4 **tropik,** 6 **-yeque(-we), -yk(e,** 6–7 **-ike, -ique, -icke,** 6–8 **-ick,** 7– **tropic.** [ad. L. *tropicus*, a. Gr. τροπικός pertaining to the 'turning' of the sun at the solstice, tropical (hence as sb. (sc. κύκλος circle) the tropic); also, of the nature of a trope, figurative, f. τροπή turning. Cf. F. *tropique* (16th c.).] A. *sb.*

I. 1. *Astr.* †a. Each of the two solstitial points, the most northerly and southerly points of the ecliptic, at which the sun reaches his greatest distance north or south of the equator, and 'turns' or begins to move towards it again; also (*loosely*), each of the two signs (Cancer and Capricorn) at the beginning of which these points occur. *Obs.*

In quot. 1662 erroneously extended to include the equinoctial points.

c 1391 CHAUCER *Astrol.* I. § 17 This signe of cancre is cleped the tropik of Somer, of *tropos*, þat is to seyn Agaynward, for thanne by-gynneth the sonne to passe fro vs-ward. 1579 E. K. *Gloss. Spenser's Sheph. Cal.* Nov. 15 The sonne draweth low..toward his Tropick or returne. 1615 G. SANDYS *Trav.* 98 The Sunne performing his course in the winter Tropick. 1662 STANLEY *Hist. Chaldaic Philos.* (1701) 17/2 In Aries is the Spring Tropick, in Capricorn the Winter, in Cancer the Summer, in Libra the Autumnal.

b. Each of two circles of the celestial sphere (*tropic of* CANCER and *tropic of* CAPRICORN), parallel to the equinoctial or celestial equator, and distant about 23° 28′ north and south of it, touching the ecliptic at the solstitial points.

1503 *Kalender of Sheph.* I ij, The other two [cercles] ar namyt tropycqwes, the oon of sommer the other of wynter. 1555 EDEN *Decades* 183 The soonne..remaynynge continually betwene the two tropykes of Cancer and Capricorne. 1561 — tr. *Cortes' Arte Navig.* I. xv. 16 The Estiuall or sommer Tropyke. 1607 TOPSELL *Four-f. Beasts* (1658) 112 Other by the Dogs, do understand the two Tropicks, which are (as it were) the two porters of the Sun for the South and North. 1625 N. CARPENTER *Geog. Del.* I. vi. (1635) 144 The Tropicks are Parallels bounding the Suns greatest declination. 1658 WALLER *On Cromwell's Death* 21 Under the Tropick is our Language spoke. 1837 WHEWELL *Hist. Induct. Sc.* (1857) I. 114 Where the sun's path touches the tropics. 1868 LOCKYER *Elem. Astron.* iii. (1879) 65 At 23½° on either side of the equator are the Tropics.

c. *fig.* Turning-point; limit, boundary. (In quot. 1635 otherwise used: cf. 2 c.)

1635 QUARLES *Embl.* III. vii. (1718) 155 Our equinoctial hearts can never lie Secure, beneath the tropicks of that eye. *a* 1639 WOTTON *Charac. Kings Eng.* in *Reliq.* (1651) 166 States have their Conversions and Periods as well as Naturall Bodies, and we were come to our Tropique. 1670 EACHARD *Cont. Clergy* 54 It was a zodiacal mercy!..for Christ keeps within the tropicks; He goes not out of the pale of the church. 1844 N. PATERSON *Manse Garden* 63 Let rest and fatigue be your tropics and you will travel with unabated vigour over the undulating line of your ecliptic.

2. *Geog.* Each of two parallels of latitude on the earth's surface (corresponding to the celestial circles, 1 b, and called likewise *tropic of Cancer* and *tropic of Capricorn*), distant about 23° 28′ north and south of the equator, being the boundaries of the torrid zone.

1527 R. THORNE in Hakluyt *Voy.* (1589) 252 From the Tropickes to both the Poles. 1604 E. G[RIMSTONE] *D'Acosta's Hist. Indies* II. iv. 87 In Regions which lie without the Tropicks. *c* 1645 HOWELL *Lett.* (1688) III. 409 Our late Navigators..who use to cross the Equator and Tropiques so often. 1711 ADDISON *Spect.* No. 170 ¶ 13 It is a Misfortune for a Woman to be born between the Tropicks. *a* 1780 WATSON *Philip III* (1839) 175 Countries..on this side of the northern tropic. 1878 HUXLEY *Physiogr.* xx. 356 The boundaries of these zones are called tropics.

b. *pl.* With *def. art.*: The region between (and about) these parallels; the torrid zone and parts immediately adjacent.

1837 W. IRVING *Capt. Bonneville* III. 145 The Mississippi; whose rapid current traverses a succession of latitudes..in a few days..almost from the frozen regions to the tropics. 1854 EMERSON *Lett. & Soc. Aims, Resources* Wks. (Bohn) III. 203 The tropics are one vast garden. 1880 HAUGHTON *Phys. Geog.* iii. 130 The warm waters of the tropics are carried, bodily, into the temperate zone.

Comb. 1887 *Daily News* 7 Nov. 3/1 That pulmonary disease..generally..fatal to the tropic-born anthropoids.

c. *fig.* in allusion to the excessive heat or luxuriant growth of the tropics.

1641 J. JACKSON *True Evang. T.* I. 38 The sixt Persecution..did so scorch within the Tropicks of the Church, that many thousands suffered. 1893 *N. Y. New-Church Messenger* 19 Apr. 244 Mastodon-affections..swarming through the tropics of his soul.

II. †3. *pl.* [tr. L. *tropicī* (Athanasius, etc.).] Name for a sect who interpreted Scripture, or certain passages of Scripture, metaphorically. (Cf. TROPIST.) *Obs.*

1585–7 T. ROGERS *39 Art.* v. (1633) 23 Some affirme the holy Ghost to be but a meere creature, as did Arius,..the Tropickes, [etc.].

†4. *pl.* Tropical or metaphorical uses of words; tropes. *Obs.*

1697 tr. *Burgersdicius his Logic* I. xxvi. 104 The Change of the Word, from its proper Signification, as in the Tropicks.

B. *adj.*

I. 1. *Astr.* Connected with the sun's 'turning back' towards the equator at the solstices; pertaining to the tropics, or to either tropic (in sense A. 1 a or b): = TROPICAL 1. *Tropic circle* or *line* = A. 1 b; *tropic point* = A. 1 a. Now *rare* or *Obs.*

1551 RECORDE *Cast. Knowl.* (1556) 24 These other two cycles..are called the two Tropike cycles after the greeke deriuation. 1616 *Marlowe's Faust.* vi. Wks. (Rtldg.) 117/2 He views the clouds, the planets, and the stars, The tropic Zones. 1667 MILTON *P. L.* x. 675 Som say the Sun Was bid turn Reines from th' Equinoctial Rode..Up to the Tropic Crab. 1667 DRYDEN *Sir Martin Mar-all* v. i, I have seen your hurricanos and your calentures, and your ecliptics

and your tropic lines. 1701 *Stanley's Hist. Philos.* Biog. b], Stanley..thinks his Gnomon did only note the Tropick and Equinoctial Points.

†b. *fig.* or *allusively.* Of or pertaining to turning (in quot., in allusion to *Jas.* i. 17). *Obs.*

1677 GALE *Crt. Gentiles* II. IV. 258 It casts various shadows and causeth varietie of Seasons,..such is the ἀποσκίασμα or tropic shadow of the sun. But now the immutable God admits no such tropic shadows or variations.

2. *Geog.* Belonging to the tropics (in sense A. 2 or 2 b): = TROPICAL 2.

1799 WORDSW. *Ruth* vii, No dolphin ever was so gay Upon the tropic sea. 1806 MAURICE *Fall of Mogul* II. iv. 53 Relentless as the tropic whirlwind's rage. 1855 KINGSLEY *Westw. Ho!* xxv, The rapid tropic vegetation has reclaimed its old domains. 1875 BENNETT & DYER *Sachs' Bot.* 832 The vital conditions of all plants growing at a great elevation and in Arctic countries must be different from those growing in the lowlands of the Tropic and Temperate zones.

b. *fig.* = TROPICAL 2 c.

[1802 WORDSW. *Sonn.*, '*We had a female Passenger*' 10 Yet still her [a negro's] eyes retained their tropic fire.] 1887 *Daily News* 29 June 5/2 Spring completely lost its way..and it was winter,..till this tropic time came upon us unawares.

3. a. **Tropic bird,** any bird of the family *Phaethontidæ*, comprising sea-birds resembling terns, widely found in tropical regions, and characterized by webbed feet, rapid flight, and varied coloration.

1681 GREW *Musæum* I. IV. iii. 74 The Tropick Bird. So called because said never to be seen but between the Tropicks. 1756 P. BROWNE *Jamaica* 482 The Tropic Bird..breeds on the most desolate rocks and lonely places and is seldom seen near any inhabited shores. 1825 WATERTON *Wand. S. Amer.* II. (1903) 64 Sometimes..the tropic bird comes near enough to let you have a fair view of the long feathers in his tail. 1896 NEWTON *Dict. Birds* 990 The Yellow-billed Tropic-bird, *P[haethon] flavirostris*. *Ibid.* 991 The Red-tailed Tropic-bird, *P. rubricauda* or *phœnicurus*.

b. **Tropic crow**: see quot.

1781 LATHAM *Synopsis Birds* I. I. 331 Tropic [1800 SHAW, Tropical] Crow. Length twelve inches and a half..From O-wy-hee..in the South Seas.

c. **Tropic grape,** the gulf-weed: = SEA-GRAPE 6.

1850 MISS PRATT *Comm. Things Sea-side* II. 111 The Sea-grape is an olive-green weed, with long slender leaves, and berries about as large as a pea, from which it derived its name of Tropic Grape. 1852 TH. ROSS *Humboldt's Trav.* I. iii. 129 To the north of the Cape Verd Islands we met with great masses of floating seaweeds. They were the tropic grape (*Fucus natans*), which grows..only from the equator to the fortieth degree of north and south latitude.

II. 4. *Biol.* [Properly the second element of GEOTROPIC, HELIOTROPIC, etc. used as an inclusive or generic term (cf. TROPISM).] Pertaining to, consisting in, or exhibiting tropism.

1903 T. H. MORGAN *Evol. & Adapt.* xi. 399 Another instinct, that appears to be due to a tropic response, is the definite time of day at which some marine animals deposit their eggs.

Troˑpic, *a.*^{2} *Chem.* [Arbitrarily formed from ATROPIC: cf. TROPINE.] In *tropic acid*, an acid forming a constituent of atropine.

1881 WATTS *Dict. Chem.* VIII. 2062 *Tropic acid*, $C^9H^{10}O^3 = CH^2(OH).CH(C^6H^5).CO^2H$. This acid, one of the proximate constituents of atropine, has lately been prepared synthetically from atropic acid. 1882 *Nature* 2 Feb. 315/1 By decomposing atropine he obtained tropic acid and tropine, and by recombining these products he again formed atropine.

Tropical (trǫˑpikăl), *a.* [f. as TROPIC *a.*^{1} + -AL. Cf. mod.F. *tropical.*]

1. *Astr.* Pertaining or relating to the tropics, or either tropic (in sense A. 1 a or b). Chiefly in *tropical year*, the interval between two successive passages of the sun through the same 'tropic' or solstitial point (or, equivalently, through the same equinoctial point); the natural year of the seasons, as reckoned from one (winter or summer) solstice or (vernal or autumnal) equinox to the next. So *tropical month*, the time taken by the moon in passing from either tropic (or either equinoctial point) to the same again.

1527 R. THORNE in Hakluyt *Voy.* (1589) 252 The quantitie of the earth vnder the Equinoctiall to both the Tropicall lines. 1594 BLUNDEVIL *Exerc.* III. I. xxxviii. (1636) 353 The Astronomicall yeere is either Tropicall or Syderall. 1662 STANLEY *Hist. Chaldaic Philos.* (1701) 17/2 Tropical [signs] are those to which when the Sun cometh he turneth back. 1715 tr. *Gregory's Astron.* (1726) I. 408 The Tropical Year is that space of time wherein the same Seasons of the Year return again. 1812 WOODHOUSE *Astron.* xxxi. 305 The tropical revolution of the Moon, or the revolution with respect to the equinoxes. 1834 *Nat. Philos.* III. *Astron.* i. 41/1 (Usef. Knowl. Soc.) The year from equinox to equinox is called the equinoctial year, or sometimes the tropical year. 1868 LOCKYER *Elem. Astron.* v. (1879) 203 The tropical month is the revolution of the moon with respect to the moveable equinox.

2. *Geog.* Pertaining to, occurring in, or inhabiting the tropics; belonging to the torrid zone.

1698 FROGER *Voy.* 3 At three o'clock in the morning we passed the tropick of Cancer;..and in the afternoon performed the ceremonies of Tropical baptism or duckings, which are commonly us'd by mariners in those places. 1699 DAMPIER *Voy.* II. I. ii. 33 Many reasons..beside the accidental ones from the make of the particular Countries, Tropical Winds, or the like. *a* 1700 SALMON (J.), The pine-apple is one of the tropical fruits. 1788 GIBBON *Decl. & F.* l. (1846) V. 2 The face of the desert..is scorched by the direct and intense rays of a tropical sun. 1851 CARPENTER *Man. Phys.* (ed. 2) 67 The highest temperature which the soil usually possesses in tropical climates, is about 126°. 1862 DANA *Man. Geol.* 615 Coral formations are most abundant in the tropical Pacific. 1880 HAUGHTON *Phys. Geog.* vi. 272 The second and third of the sub-orders are confined to the tropical forests of South America.

b. *Path.* Applied to diseases to which one is liable in tropical regions.

1828 WEBSTER, *Tropical*, 2. Incident to the tropics; as, tropical diseases. 1843 R. J. GRAVES *Syst. Clin. Med.* xi. 118 [Salivation] has been also very extensively recommended by army and navy surgeons, in the treatment of tropical fevers. 1893 A. DAVIDSON *Hygiene & Dis. Warm Climates* xvii. 613 Tropical Liver. 1905 *Daily Chron.* 9 Oct. 5/3 The notorious disease known in Germany as 'tropencholer', or tropical frenzy.

c. *fig.* Like the climate or growth of the tropics; very hot, ardent, or luxuriant.

1834 *Tait's Mag.* I. 383/1 Home he came, after an absence of fifty years, in a hissing hot fit of tropical rage. 1850 S. DOBELL *Roman* vi. Poet. Wks. (1875) 85 My fierce and tropical fancy, Hot with swift pulses. 1880 'OUIDA' *Moths* I. 174 We Russians have a passion for tropical houses. *Mod.* The heat was perfectly tropical.

3. *Zool.* (transf. from 1 or 2.) Used to describe the position of certain spines in the skeleton of some radiolarians: see quot.

1888 ROLLESTON & JACKSON *Anim. Life* 874 *note*, Imagine a globe with an axis of rotation, and five circles inscribed on it, an equatorial, two tropical and two polar. The twenty spines lie four in each of these circles, the equatorial and polar spines in the same meridian lines,..the tropical in meridian lines exactly intermediate.

4. Pertaining to, involving, or of the nature of a trope or tropes; metaphorical, figurative.

1567 MAPLET *Gr. Forest* 97 To sende ouer Owles to Athens. In Tropicall sense, ment of such as bestow largely vpon them that haue no neede. 1620 T. GRANGER *Div. Logike* 19 Whether the words bee plaine, and proper, or tropicall, and figuratiue. 1646 SIR T. BROWNE *Pseud. Ep.* III. iii. 111 A strict and literall acception of a loose and tropicall expression. 1725 WATTS *Logic* I. iv. § 7 They are used in a figurative or tropical Sense, when they are made to signify some things, which only bear either a Reference or a Resemblance to the primary Ideas of them. 1819 G. S. FABER *Dispensations* (1823) II. II. v. 190 The great sheet let down from heaven was as perfect a tropical hieroglyphic as any invented by the ingenuity of Moses. 1862 H. SPENCER *First Princ.* xv. (1875) 349 These [writings] had been partially differentiated into the kuriological or imitative, and the tropical or symbolic.

5. *Math.* ? Relating to the number of values of a function corresponding to one value of the variable.

1887 CAYLEY *Math. Papers* XII. 433 We wish to know whether *u* is a monotropic function of *z*. It will not be so if we have a tropical point,..such that [etc.].

Tropicalian (trǫpikēˑliăn), *a. Zoogeog.* [f. mod.L. *Tropicalia* (f. Gr. τροπικός tropic + ἅλς sea) + -AN.] Belonging to the marine region called *Tropicalia*, comprising the seas between the isocrymes of 68° Fahr. on each side of the equator.

1888 *Proc. Biol. Soc. Washington* II. 34 (Cass. Supp.) Generic and specific modifications of the Arctalian and Tropicalian realms.

Tropicalize (trǫˑpikăləiz), *v.* [f. TROPICAL + -IZE.] *trans.* To make tropical; to give a tropical character to. Hence **Troˑpicalized** *ppl. a.*

1885 LADY BRASSEY *The Trades* 125 Vegetation not unlike a patch of British fern suddenly transferred to a temperature of about fifty degrees above what it is accustomed to,—and thus, as it were 'tropicalised'. 1888 *Harper's Mag.* Sept. 616 The architecture is a tropicalized Swiss style.

Tropically (trǫˑpikăli), *adv.* [f. as prec. + -LY^2.] In a tropical manner.

1. In the way of a trope; metaphorically, figuratively.

1564 J. RASTELL *Confut. Jewell's Serm.* 140 The body of Christ is, onlye figuratiuelye,..tropicallie, imaginatiuelie, in the Sacrament. 1602 SHAKS. *Ham.* III. ii. 247 *King.* What do you call the Play? *Ham.* The Mouse-trap: Marry how? Tropically. 1646 SIR T. BROWNE *Pseud. Ep.* III. iii. 111 Spanish Mares, whose swiftnesse [is] tropically expressed from their generation by the wind. *a* 1703 BURKITT *On N. T.* Gal. v. 24 The work of mortification (called here tropically, a crucifixion). 1809 W. IRVING *Knickerb.* v. ix. (1849) 302 It is tropically observed by honest old Socrates, that heaven infuses into some men..a portion of intellectual gold. 1879 R. T. SMITH *St. Basil* 91 There are multitudes of expressions applied in Scripture to God, which we agree are to be tropically taken.

2. In a way characteristic of the tropics; with tropical heat, luxuriance, or violence.

1852 HAWTHORNE *Blithedale Rom.* xvii. (1885) 173 The sunshine lay tropically there. 1886 *Pall Mall G.* 10 June 9/1 The rain..continues, although not quite so tropically. 1896 *Academy* 11 July 27/1 Hume's tropically coloured account of what..he called 'the Irish rebellion'.

Tropicopolitan (trǫˑpikoˌpǫˑlităn), *a. Nat. Hist.* [f. TROPIC, after COSMOPOLITAN.] Belonging to or inhabiting the whole of the tropics, or tropical regions generally.

1878 P. L. SCLATER in *19th Cent.* Dec. 1050 'Tropicopolitan' forms, by which I mean tropical forms that are found in the tropics of both hemispheres. 1879 A. R. WALLACE *ibid.* Feb. 254 The tropical land..which afforded the passage of the tropicopolitan forms from one continent to the other. 1895 C. DIXON in *Fortn. Rev.* Apr. 652 We have many tropicopolitan families that are confined absolutely to the great equatorial zone round the entire earth.

Tropidial (tropiˑdiăl), *a. Zool.* [f. Gr. τρόπις, τροπιδ- keel + -IAL.] Pertaining to the *tropis* or keel of a C-shaped sponge-spicule.

1887 SOLLAS in *Encycl. Brit.* XXII. 418/1 (*Sponges*) The pterocymba is subject to considerable modifications;..the pteres may be lamellar or ungual; additional lamellæ (tropidial pteres) may be produced by a lateral outgrowth of the keel.

Tropidine (trǫˑpidəin). *Chem.* [Arbitrary formation from TROPINE.] A colourless oily alkaloid obtained from tropine by the action of acids. So **Tropiˑlidine,** a liquid hydrocarbon, C_7H_8, obtained by the dry distillation of tropine with quicklime (Webster, 1911).

1883 *Science* 11 May 401/2 When distilled with soda-lime, tropine is decomposed, giving methylamine and tropilidine (C_7H_8); and, when treated with fuming hydrochloric acid, a volatile base, tropidine ($C_8H_{13}N$), is formed. 1890 BILLINGS *Med. Dict.*, *Tropidine*, $C_8H_{13}N$, a liquid basic substance obtained from tropine by heating with strong hydrochloric acid in a sealed tube.

Tropidosternal (trǫpidoˌstɜˑɹnăl), *a. Ornith.* [f. mod.L. *Tropidosternī* pl. (f. Gr. τρόπις, -ιδ- keel + στέρνον, L. *sternum* breast-bone) + -AL.] Belonging to the division *Tropidosterni* (= *Carinatæ*) of birds; having a keeled breast-bone.

In recent Dicts.

Tropilidine: see TROPIDINE.

Tropine (trōuˑpəin). *Chem.* [Arbitrarily formed from ATROPINE.] An alkaloid forming a constituent of atropine.

1881 WATTS *Dict. Chem.* VIII. 2062 *Tropine*, $C^8H^{15}NO$. This base, which Kraut obtained, together with atropic acid, by the action of baryta-water on atropine, may also be extracted..from the residues of the preparation of atropine.

Troping (trōuˑpiŋ). [f. TROPE + -ING^1.] a. Figurative or metaphorical speech or conversation. b. The composition or use of tropes (sense 5).

1678 DRYDEN *Kind Keeper* v. i, Will you leave your Troping, and let me pass? 1907 J. M. MANLY in *Mod. Philol.* IV. 593 It was an age of troping. Tropes—that is, insertions in the authorized liturgy—were composed by the hundreds, and of all conceivable varieties.

‖**Tropis** (trōuˑpis). *Zool.* Pl. **tropides** (trǫˑpidīz). [mod.L., a. Gr. τρόπις keel.] The 'keel' or middle part of a *cymba* or C-shaped sponge-spicule, between the *proræ* or 'prows'.

1887 SOLLAS in *Encycl. Brit.* XXII. 417/2 (*Sponges*) A truly C-shaped spicule...The back of the 'C' is the keel or *tropis*; the points are the prows or *proræ*.

Tropism (trǫˑpiz'm). *Biol.* [The second element of HELIOTROPISM, GEOTROPISM, etc., used as an inclusive or generic term.] The turning of an organism, or a part of one, in a particular direction (either in the way of growth, bending, or locomotion) in response to some special external stimulus, as that of light (*phototropism, heliotropism*), heat (*thermotropism*), gravity (*geotropism*), etc.

1899 C. B. DAVENPORT *Morphology* II. 480 All cases of true tropism are cases of response to stimuli: such are chemotropism, hydrotropism, thigmotropism, traumatropism, rheotropism, geotropism, electrotropism, phototropism and thermotropism. 1909 J. W. JENKINSON *Experim. Embryol.* 273 The outgrowth and anastomoses of nerves, glands, ducts, the concrescence of layers may be tropisms of various sorts.

Tropist (trōuˑpist). *rare*$^{-0}$. [f. as TROPE + -IST; cf. F. *tropiste* (Calvin, 1560).] a. A member of a sect who interpreted Scripture or some passage of Scripture in the way of trope or metaphor: see TROPIC *sb.* 3. b. One who deals in tropes or metaphors.

1727–41 CHAMBERS *Cycl.*, *Tropists*, or *Tropici*, the name of a sect...The reason of the name tropist was that they explained the scripture altogether by tropes and figures of speech...The Romanists also give the appellation tropists to those of the reformed religion, in regard of their construing the words of the eucharist figuratively. 1775 ASH, *Tropist*, one who deals in tropes, one who explains the scriptures by tropes and figures.

Tropistic (tropiˑstik), *a. Biol.* [f. TROPISM: see -ISTIC.] Pertaining to or constituting tropism. Hence **Tropiˑstically** *adv.* [see -ICALLY], in the way of tropism.

1910 F. KEEBLE *Plant-Anim.* ii. 41 We may use the term tropistic to describe the reactions of both fixed and free organisms to directive stimuli. *Ibid.* 52 Responding tropistically to unilateral light.

Trople, variant of TROPEL *Obs.*

Tropo-, combining form repr. Gr. τρόπος turning, etc. (see TROPE), occurring in a few modern technical terms. **Tropometer** (trǫpǫˑmĭtəɹ) [-METER], an instrument for measuring the angle of turning or torsion of some part of the body, as the eye-ball or a long bone. **Tropophil** (trǫˑpofil), **Tropophilous** (tropǫˑfiləs) *adjs.* [Gr. -φιλος loving], applied to a plant adapted to a climate which is alternately moist and dry (or cold, the physiological effect of cold being similar to that of dryness); so **Tropophyte** (trǫˑpofəit) [Gr. φυτόν plant], a tropophilous plant; whence **Tropophytic** (-fiˑtik) *a.* **Tropostereoscope** (trǫpoˌsteˑrĭoskōup), a stereoscope with an arrangement for rotating the figures so as to bring them into some required position, in experiments on vision.

1881 *Athenæum* 11 June 787/1 The *tropometer, an instrument for measuring the angle of torsion of the humerus. 1902 I. B. BALFOUR in *Encycl. Brit.* XXV. 439/2 Parasitism ..occurs in..*tropophil woods of temperate regions, and alpine slopes. 1900 B. D. JACKSON *Gloss. Bot. Terms*, **Tropophilous*,..loving change of condition, as Tropophytes. 1903 tr. *Schimper's Plant-Geog.* I. i. 21 The vegetation of districts with climates alternately damp and dry or cold, is alternately of a hygrophilous and of a xerophilous character; it is therefore tropophilous. 1900 B. D. JACKSON *Gloss. Bot. Terms*, **Tropophyte*. 1903 tr. *Schimper's Plant-Geog.* I. i. 3 It appears..necessary to place in a third category all plants whose conditions of life are, according to the season of the year, alternately those of hygrophytes or of xerophytes. All such plants, including..the great majority of the plants composing the Central European flora, should be termed tropophytes. *Ibid.*, There are hygrophytic, xerophytic, and *tropophytic climates. 1901 TITCHENER *Exper. Psychol.* I. II. 272 Ludwig's *tropostereoscope..is..a refined form of the tube stereoscope.

†**Troˑpologeˑtically,** *adv. Obs. rare*$^{-1}$. [Extended form of TROPOLOGICALLY, after *apologetically.*] = TROPOLOGICALLY, TROPICALLY 1.

1652 URQUHART *Jewel* Wks. (1834) 292, I could have enlarged this discourse..tropologetically, by metonymical, ironical, metaphorical and synecdochical instruments of elocution.

Tropologic (trǫpolǫˑdʒik), *a.* [ad. late L. *tropologicus* (Jerome, *a* 400), = late Gr. τροπολογικός (*c* 1160), f. τρόπος trope: see -LOGIC. Cf. F. *tropologique* (Godef. *Compl.*).] = next (in either sense).

c 1380 WYCLIF *Sel. Wks.* II. 277 Þe þridde witt is tropologik, þat bitokeneþ witt of vertues. 1388 — *Gen. Prol. Bks. Proph.* 226 Moral ether tropologik [vndurstondyng of scripture] techith what we owen to do to fle vices, and kepe vertues. 1677 GALE *Crt. Gentiles* II. III. 153 These mystic Divines glorie in their Tropologic, Anagogic and Allegoric explication of Scripture: Neither is there any so plain, literal, or historic, but they have some tropologic or mystic sense for it. 1884 *Expositor* Jan. 45 The three traditional divisions of the mystic sense into allegoric, tropologic or moral, and anagogic or spiritual.

Tropological (trǫpolǫˑdʒikăl), *a.* [f. as prec. + -AL.] Belonging to or involving tropology.

1. Metaphorical, figurative: = TROPICAL 4.

1555 EDEN *Decades* 44 *margin*, Here nedeth sum tropologicall interpretour. 1621 BURTON *Anat. Mel.* III. iv. I. iii. (1628) 607 Tropological, allegorical expositions, to salve all appearances. 1862 NEALE *Hymns East. Ch.* 24 The ingenuity of some tropological applications.

2. Applied to a secondary sense or interpretation of Scripture, relating or applied to conduct or morals.

1528 TINDALE *Obed. Chr. Man* 129 They devide ye scripture in to iiij senses, ye literall, tropologicall, allegoricall, anagogicall. 1607 R. C[AREW] tr. *Estienne's World of Wonders* 255 To reduce all they haue to say, to certaine Allegoricall, Anagogicall, and Tropologicall senses. 1734 WATERLAND *Doctr. Trinity* vii. § 6. 438 Such a kind of Exercise I take many of those Allegorical Comments (Those especially of the Tropological kind) to have been. 1882–3 *Schaff's Encycl. Relig. Knowl.* I. 784 The moral, or tropological [sense of Scripture] teaches what to do.

Tropoloˑgically, *adv.* [f. prec. + -LY^2.] In a tropological manner (in either sense of the adj.).

1549 CHALONER *Erasm. Praise Folly* N iv b, Moralisyng the same bothe Allegorically, Tropologically, and Anegogically. 1678 CUDWORTH *Intell. Syst.* I. iv. § 32. 512 This was the General opinion concerning the Greekish Fables, that some of them were Physically, and some Tropologically Allegorical. 1730 WATERLAND *Script. Vind.* Pref. 18 The Law about the Sabbath..may be supposed..tropologically to denote the Rest of the Soul and its Cessation from Sin. 1888 SCHAFF *Hist. Chr. Ch.* VI. I. xxxii. 139 Jerusalem means..allegorically the good, tropologically virtue, anagogically reward.

Tropologize (trǫpǫˑlŏdʒəiz), *v. rare*$^{-1}$. [f. as TROPOLOGY + -IZE.] *trans.* To convert by a trope or metaphor; to use in a tropological sense.

1678 CUDWORTH *Intell. Syst.* I. iv. § 33. 520 If Athena or Minerva be tropologized into Prudence, then let the Pagans show what substantial essence it hath, or that it really subsists according to their tropology.

Tropology (trǫpǫˑlŏdʒi). [ad. late L. *tropologia* (Jerome, *a* 400), a. late Gr. τροπολογία (Justin Martyr, *a* 160), f. τρόπος trope: see -LOGY. Cf. F. *tropologie* (*a* 1300 in Godef. *Compl.*).]

1. 'A speaking by tropes' (Blount, 1656); the use of metaphor in speech or writing; figurative discourse.

1519 HORMAN *Vulg.* 98 b, The figuris of construction and locucion: and specially allygoris: and tropologies: & anagogies. 1613 PURCHAS *Pilgrimage* (1614) 88 Those, that by Allegories and Tropologies peruert and obscure the Historie of their Gods. 1678 [see TROPOLOGIZE]. 1873 F. HALL *Mod. Eng.* vi. 170 But, whether due to tropology, or to whatever other cause, multivocals, as conducing to brevity and expressiveness, are unwisely condemned, or deprecated, except where they entail ambiguity.

2. A moral discourse; a secondary sense or interpretation of Scripture relating to morals (cf. TROPOLOGICAL 2).

1583 FULKE *Defence* 47, I can not, following both the storie, and the tropologie or doctrine of maners, comprehend both briefly. 1706 PHILLIPS (ed. Kersey), *Tropology*,..a Moral Discourse tending to the Reformation of Manners. 1896 LINA ECKENSTEIN *Woman under Monast.* 113 The four-square pattern of ecclesiastical usage, namely according to the letter, allegory, tropology and anagogy.

3. A treatise on tropes or figures of speech.

a 1667 JER. TAYLOR *Serm.* Wks. 1831 IV. 160 Vocabularies, tropologies, and expositions of words and phrases. 1768 J. BROWN (*title*), Sacred Tropology.

Tropometer to **Tropostereoscope**: see TROPO-.

†**Troque** (trōuk). *Obs. rare.* [ad. L. *trochus*, a. Gr. τροχός: see TROCHE^2, TROCHUS.] A hoop: = TROCHUS 1.

1743 FRANCIS tr. *Hor., Odes* III. xxiv. 58 More skill'd in.. The whirling troque, or law-forbidden dice. 1746 — *Art Poetry* 515 The bounding Ball, round Quoit, or whirling Troque.

Tros, tross, trosse: see TRUSS. **Trossers**: see TROUSERS. **Trost, Trosty,** obs. ff. TRUST, TRUSTY. **Trostell, -yle,** obs. ff. TRESTLE.

Trot (trǫt), *sb.*^{1} Also 3–7 **trott,** 5–6 **trotte,** 5–7 **trote.** [a. F. *trot* (12th c. in Godef. *Compl.*), verbal sb. of *trotter* to TROT.]

I. 1. A gait of a quadruped, originally of a horse, between walking and running, in which the legs move in diagonal pairs almost together, so that in a slow trot there is always one foot at least on the ground, but in a fast trot one pair leaves the ground before the other reaches it, all four feet being thus momentarily off the ground at once; hence applied to a similar gait of a man (or other biped), between a walk and a run.

a 1300 *Cursor M.* 15872 (Cott.) His [Christ's] hend þai band and ledd him forth, A-trott and noght þe pas [2 *MSS.* a-pas, a pas]. 13.. *E. E. Allit. P.* B. 976 Trynande ay a hyȝe trot þat torne neuer dorsten. *c* 1386 CHAUCER *Can. Yeom. Prol. & T.* 22 His hat heeng at his bak doun by a laas For he hadde riden moore than trot [*v.rr.* trote, trotte] or paas. *c* 1425 *Cast. Persev.* 3100 in *Macro Plays* 169 Now dagge we hens a dogge trot. *a* 1547 SURREY *Æneid* IV. 957 Redouble gan her nurse Her steppes, forth on an aged womans trot. 1590 BARWICK *Disc. Weapons* 9 b, They retired a soft trote: their enemies..made after them with more speed. 1638 SIR T. HERBERT *Trav.* (ed. 2) 35 Our Chariot drawn by 2 Buffolls who by practise are nimble in their trot. 1737 BRACKEN *Farriery Impr.* (1757) II. Index s.v., A good Trot may be judged of by the Ear. 1755 JOHNSON, *Trot*, the jolting high pace of a horse. 1780 *Mirror* No. 92 A smart young man..passed by in his carriage at a brisk trot. 1818 SCOTT *Rob Roy* v, His [a fox's] drooping brush, his soiled appearance, and jaded trot, proclaimed his fate impending. 1835 ALISON *Hist. Europe* (1849–50) V. xxviii. § 43. 124 The pontoons arrived at a quick trot, from Dietikon. 1845 FORD *Handbk. Spain* I. 52 Their pace is the peculiar '*paso Castellano*', which is something more than a walk and less than a trot.

†b. An action of trotting; a journey or expedition on horseback. *Obs.*

a 1670 SPALDING *Troub. Chas. I* (1850) I. 186 The barronis ..rydis fra Turreff to New Abirdein,..Thay plunder the laird of Kermok...The covenanteris, heiring of this trot of Turref..began to hyde thair goodis. 1676 COTTON *Angler* II. ii. 22 I'le make as bold with your meat; for the Trot has got me a good stomach.

c. The sound of a horse, etc., trotting.

1858 CAPERN *Ball. & Songs* (1859) 138 The lime-team's trot, And milkmaid's carol...Are the chief sounds. 1882 'OUIDA' *In Maremma* I. 6 The trot of the chargers and the clash of the steel had passed into silence.

d. *transf.* and *fig. On the trot*, continually moving without intervals for rest; on the go.

a 1625 FLETCHER & MASS. *Custom of Country* IV. iv, Nor am I able to endure it longer,..I am at my trot already. 1646 JENKYN *Remora* 28 Shall we go a dull Asses trot heavenward? 1697 DRYDEN *Virg.* Ded. (1721) I. 20 The Virtuoso's Saddle, which will be sure to amble, when the World is upon the hardest Trott. 1822 W. IRVING *Braceb. Hall* (1823) I. xiv. 103 One of those who eat and growl, and keep the waiter on the trot. 1892 G. MEREDITH *Poet. Wks.* (1912) 454 Away on the trot of thy servitude start.

2. A trotting-race. *rare.*

1891 *Auckland Star* 1 Oct. 8/6 Spring Meeting...Handicap Maiden Trot, of 40 sovs; second horse to receive 5 sovs from stakes...Selling Trot...Pony Trot Handicap. 1893 *Scott. Leader* 12 June 1 Grand Handicap Trot—First, £10; Second, £3; Third, £2.

3. †*Irish trot* (obs.), *Turkey trot*, names of dances. Also †*shake a trot* (Sc. obs.).

1549 *Compl. Scot.* vi. 66 In the fyrst, thai dancit al cristyn mennis dance, the northt of scotland, huntis vp,..schaik a trot. 1652 *News fr. Lowe-Countr.* 7 The Scottish Jigg, the Irish Trot.

4. A toddling child; also, a small or young animal. *colloq.* Hence **Troˑttie,** a little toddling child.

1854 THACKERAY *Newcomes* x, Ethel romped with the little children—the rosy little trots—and took them on her knees, and told them a thousand stories. 1895 SKELTON *Table-Talk* iv. 72 Black, hairy little trots..with their big bills and their big feet. 1905 *Contemp. Rev.* July 62 A practising school is maintained, partly of grave little trots from outside and partly of little boarders.

5. *U.S.* A literal translation of a text used by students; a 'crib'. Cf. HORSE *sb.* 13, PONY *sb.* 3. (*College slang.*)

1891 in *Cent. Dict.*

II. 6. *Fishing.* (Perhaps a different word: cf. TRAT.) A long-line lightly anchored or buoyed, with baited hooks hung by short lines or snoods a few feet apart; a trawl-line; also called a *trot-line*; also, each of the short lines attached to this.

1858 [see *trot-line* in 7]. 1883 *Fisheries Exhib. Catal.* 10 Floating Trots and Spillers. 1884 *St. James's Gaz.* 18 Jan. 6/2 A 'trot' is a line some twenty yards long. 1886 R. C. LESLIE *Sea-painter's Log* x. 199 Much longer lines than the trots just described are used for flounders.

III. 7. *attrib.* and *Comb.* **trot-line** = sense 6; **trot-rope,** a rope securely pegged down at each end, on which runs a sliding ring to which a horse is tethered, enabling him to graze a strip the length of the rope (*Cent. Dict. Suppl.* 1909).

1858 in A. E. Lee *Hist. Columbus, Ohio* (1892) I. 146 Father went down to the river to examine a trotline.

Trot (trǫt), *sb.*^{2} Forms: α. 4 **trate,** 4–6 **trat, tratte**; β. 6 **trott, trotte, trote,** (8 **trout**), 6– **trot.** [AF. *trote* occurs twice in Gower's French *Mirour de l'Omme*, ll. 8713 and 17900 ('la viele trote q'est jolie'), but the ME. instances have all *trat(e, tratte*, and the word has not been found in Continental French either as *trote* or *tratte*, so that the derivation is uncertain. It can hardly be connected with TROT *sb.*^{1}, or with OF. *baudetrot*, BAWDSTROT.] An old woman; usually disparaging: an old beldame, a hag.

α. *c* 1350 *Will. Palerne* 4769 Þat þo two trattes þat William wold haue traysted. *c* 1380 *Sir Ferumb.* 1370 Þan ful doun þat olde trate in-to þe salte see. *c* 1460 *Towneley Myst.* xvi. 394 Gett out of thise wonys! ye trattys, all at onys. 1513 DOUGLAS *Æneis* IV. xi. 114 Thus said Dido; and the tother, with that, Hichit on furth with slaw pase lyke ane trat. 1570 LEVINS *Manip.* 37/14 A tratte, *anus*.

β. 1530 PALSGR. 642/1 Se yonder olde trot howe she mumbleth, *auises ceste vielle* [etc.]. 1596 SHAKS. *Tam. Shr.* I. ii. 79 Marrie him to a Puppet or an Aglet babie, or an old trot with ne're a tooth in her head. 1598 DRAYTON *Heroic. Ep.* xiii. 105 And call me, Beldam, Gib, Witch, Night-mare, Trot, With all despight that may a Woman spot. 1654 WHITLOCK *Zootomia* 78 An old Trot (that boasted of her Giftishnesse in Waterology). 1719 D'URFEY *Pills* V. 74 You are...A fulsome Trot and good for nought. *a* 1845 HOOD *Forget-me-nots* ii, Some strange, neglectful, gossiping old Trot. 1906 E. V. LUCAS *Listener's Lure* (1910) 282 Miss Graham got an old trot after a good deal of messing about.

Trot (trǫt), *v.* Forms: see TROT *sb.*^{1}; also 5 **trot.** [ME. a. OF. *troter* (12th c. in Hatz.-Darm.), F. *trotter* (Prov., Sp., Pg. *trotar*, It. *trottare*) to TROT. A med.L. deriv. *trottare* appears *c* 1150 in Thesaurus of Thomas.]

I. 1. *intr.* Of a horse, and occasionally other quadrupeds: To go at the gait called the trot (see TROT *sb.*^{1} 1). Also said of a man.

To trot all (see ALL C. 4), *altogether* (ALTOGETHER B. 2), *high* (HIGH *adv.* 1 b), *large* (LARGE B. 6), *rough* (ROUGH *adv.* 1), *short* (SHORT C. 4); *to trot out*, to trot with extended action (opposed to *trot short*).

1362 LANGL. *P. Pl.* A. II. 135 Fauuel fette forþ Foles of þe beste, And sette..fals on a sysoures backe þat softly trotted. *c* 1386 CHAUCER *Merch. T.* 294 No man fynden shal Noon in this world, that trotteth [*v. r.* (*Petw. MS.*) treteþ] hool in al Ne man ne beest. *c* 1410 *Master of Game* (MS. Digby 182) iv, Somtyme þei [roe-deer] trotteth and goth a paas. 14.. *Beryn* 939 As hors þat evir trottid...It were hard to make hym aftir to ambill well. *c* 1450 *Merlin* 279 A Curroure trottynge on foote. 1553 T. WILSON *Rhet.* 61 Trotte sire and trotte damme, how should the fole amble? *c* 1566 *Merie Tales of Skelton* in *S.'s Wks.* (1843) I. p. lx, Hee was a litell olde fellowe, and woulde lye as fast as a horse woulde trotte. 1633 MARMION *Antiquary* I, You'll hardly find..beast that trots sound of all four: There will be some defect. 1674 *Lond. Gaz.* No. 882/4 A light gray Mare about fourteen hands high, five years old, trots altogether. 1675 *Ibid.* No. 959/4 A Brown Bay Nag,..Trots all. 1676 *Ibid.* No. 1107/4 Gray Mare,..trots rough. 1677 *Ibid.* No. 1222/4 A Sorrel Chesnut Gelding..., paces little, but trotteth high. 1706 Trot out [see SHORT C. 4]. 1856 MISS MULOCK *J. Halifax* ii, He took me on his back..and fairly trotted with me down the garden-walk. 1859 GEO. ELIOT *A. Bede* I. i, Gyp with his basket, trotting at his master's heels. 1883 H. CRAIG in *Harper's Mag.* Aug. 346/1 She trotted a mile in the unparalleled time of 2.10¼. 1897 *Daily Chron.* 23 Aug. 8/2, I trotted down the wicket very slowly.

b. *transf.* Of a rider, etc., or of a vehicle.

c 1386 CHAUCER *Wife's Prol.* 838 Amble, or trotte [*v. r.* trote], or pees, or go sit doun, Thou lettest oure disport. *a* 1450 *Le Morte Arth.* 3339 Arthur with knyghtis fully xiiij..With helme, sheld, And hauberke shene; Ryght so they trotted vppon þe grownde. 1599 SHAKS. *Hen. V*, III. vii. 86, I will trot to morrow a mile. *c* 1682 CLAVERHOUSE in *15th Rep. Hist. MSS. Comm.* App. VIII. 270 The smith at Menegaff,..after whom the forces has troted so often. 1688 R. HOLME *Armoury* III. xix. (Roxb.) 186/2 Words of command about wheelings of Horsmen...Trot large, and wheele to the left. 1807 CRABBE *Par. Reg.* I. 487 Who trots to market on a steed so fine. 1833 *Regul. Instr. Cavalry* I. 66 '*Trot Out*'—Increase gradually to the trot of manœuvre, 8½ miles per hour. When steady, '*Trot Short*'—Collect the horses to the school pace again. 1833 T. HOOK *Parson's Dau.* I. iii, At Windsor..a royal coach may be often seen trotting about the town. 1913 *Times* 14 May 6/2 The Brigade was an imposing picture as it trotted past the King.

c. *transf.* and *fig.*

c 1430 *Pilgr. Lyf Manhode* III. xl. (1869) 157 Alwey j muste make the chyn trotte, and the throte gaape. 1600 SHAKS. *A. Y. L.* III. ii. 331 Time..trots hard with a yong maid, between the contract of her marriage, and the day it is solemnizd. 1612 DEKKER *If it be not good* Wks. 1873 III. 275 Vncle write that. *Oct.* Fast as my pen can trot. 1671 R. MACWARD *True Nonconf.* 273 Your loftie Pindarick.. doth trote more rudely, and lamely, then our hobling meeter. *a* 1758 RAMSAY *Generous Gentl.* iii, She lean'd upon a flow'ry brae, By which a burnie trotted. 1852 THACKERAY *Esmond* II. xi, We college poets trot..on very easy nags. 1893 SALTUS *Madam Sapphira* 31 A woman is never led astray. She trots, or gallops or bolts astray, but never is she led.

†d. In the alliterative phrases *trot and tremble, tremble and trot. Obs. rare.*

c 1425 *Cast. Persev.* 459 in *Macro Plays* 91 Now I sytte in my semly sale; I trotte & tremle in my trew trone. *c* 1485 *Digby Myst.* (1882) III. 555 A! how I tremyl and trott for ȝese tydynges!

TROT.

2. *intr.* To go or move quickly; to go briskly or busily; to bustle; to run. Also *refl.*, and with *it.* Now *colloq.*, implying short, quick motion in a limited area. (Cf. Trot *v.* 1.)

3. *trans.* To trot (something) (*rare*).
b. To make, describe, or execute by trotting; to go through at a trot. c. To follow, traverse (a path) as if by trotting (*rare*). *Obs.*

4. *trans.* To cause to trot; to lead or ride at the trot.
b. *To trot out*: To lead out and show off the paces of (a horse); hence *fig.* to bring forward (a person, an opinion, etc.) for or as for inspection or approval; to exhibit, show off. *colloq.*

Trotvale, -nale. *Obs. rare.* Also trotovale, trotynale. [Derivation unascertained.]

TROTH.

Troth (trō). *sb.* Forms: 1-5 treuthe, 3-7 trowthe, 3 (*Orm.*) trowwthe, 4-5 troughe, 4 truthe, 4-6 trowth, 5 trouth, (trowith, -yth, 5-6 trouth.
b. Faith, trust, confidence. (Cf. Truth 3 a.)
Troth, *v. Obs. or arch.* [f. Troth *sb.*]
Trot-let: *nonce-wd.* [f. Trot + -let.] A diminutive trot.
Trottee (trŏt). *nonce-wd.* [f. Trot *v.* + -ee.]

Trotter (trŏtər). [f. Trot *v.* + -er.]
Trotting (trŏtɪŋ), *vbl. sb.* [f. Trot *v.* + -ing.]
Trotting, *ppl. a.* [f. as prec. + -ing.]
Trottoir (trŏtwar). [F.] A paved footway.

TROTTOIRED.

Hence **Trottoired** *a.*, furnished with a trottoir.
Trou, Trouage, Trouant: *see* Trow, Trew- age, Truant.
Troubadour (trū‿bədŭr). *sb.* [a. F. *troubadour* (16th c. in Godef. *Compl.*), ad. Prov. *trobador* — Cat. *trobador*, Sp., Pg. *trovador*, It. *trovatore*, agent-n. f. Prov. *trobar*, Sp., Pg. *trovar*, It. *trovare*, F. *trouver* to find, invent, compose in verse; cf. Trouvère.]

Trou-blable, *a. Obs. rare⁻¹.*
Trou-blance. *Obs.*

TROUBLE.

Trouble (trŏb'l). *sb.* Forms: 3-7 truble, (3 trubuil), 4-6 troble, -el, (-il), -yl, -ul, trouble, 5 (truble, trobull), 5-6 torbul, trouble, (troubel), trowbel, (-ill, -yll, -ull), 4-trouble. β. 4-6 turble, -el, -il, 5 torble, 6 tourbel.

Trouble (trŏb'l), *v.* Forms: *see* Trouble *sb.* [ME. a. OF. *trobler, torbler, tourbler, turbler* (11-14th c.), F. *troubler* = late L. *turbulāre.*]

TROUBLE.

droune. 1509 Payne Royll Marr. 95 Like perilous Caribeis.
Hence **Trou-bleness**, troubledness, turbidity.

Trouble (trŏb'l), *v.* Forms: *see* Trouble *sb.* [ME. a. OF. *trobler, torbler, tourbler, turbler* (11-14th c.), F. *troubler* = late L. *turbulāre.*]

TROUBLESOME.

stormy; of water, wine, etc., stirred up so as to disperse the sediment, made thick or muddy, turbid.
Troublement (trŏb'lment). *Obs. rare⁻¹.*
Troubler (trŏb'lər). [f. Trouble *v.* + -er.]
Troublesome (trŏb'lsəm), *a.* Forms: *see* Trouble *sb.* [f. Trouble *sb.* + -some.] Full of, characterized by, or causing trouble.

Supplement, p. 3873; Corrigenda, p. 4092; Spurious words, p. 4093; Books quoted, p. 4094

Troublesomely (trŭb'lsŏmli), adv. [f. prec. +-ly2.] In a troublesome manner; confusedly. Obs.

Troublesomeness (trŭb'lsŏmnes). [f. as prec. +-ness.] The quality or condition of being troublesome.

Troubling (trŭb'liŋ), vbl. sb. [f. TROUBLE v. +-ING1.] The action of the verb TROUBLE, or an instance of this (in various senses).

Troublous (trŭb'lŏs), a. [f. TROUBLE sb. or v. +-ous.]

Trough (trǫf), sb. Forms: 1-2 trog, troh, 4 trowȝ, trouȝ, 4-6 trowe, 4-7 (8-9 dial.) trow, 5-6 trogh, troghe, &c. trough (in 9 dial.), 5-7 troughe, trowghe, &c., 9 troff, trough. [OE. trog (troh).]

Trough-ing (trǫfiŋ), vbl. sb. [f. TROUGH sb. +-ING1.]

Trounce (trauns), sb. [Of obscure origin; usually compared with OF. troncher, Cotgr. tromcir, troncier to cut, cut off a piece from, retrench, truncate.]

Trounce (trauns), v. [f. prec. sb.]

Trouncer (traunsǝr). [f. TROUNCE v.1 +-ER1.]

Trouncing (traunsiŋ), vbl. sb. [f. TROUNCE v.1 +-ING1.]

Troupe (trūp). [F. (16th c.) = OF. trope (13th c.): see TROOP sb.]

Trousers (trauzǝrz), sb. pl. Forms: 7-8 trossers, trowzers, trowsers, 7- trousers, a. [f. TROUSE sb.]

Trousered (-ǝrd) a., wearing or dressed in trousers.

Trout (traut), sb.1 Forms: 1 truht, 3 trout, 4 trouȝt(e, troȝte, 4-5 trote, trowte, 4-7 troute, 7- trout. [OE. truht.]

Trout, sb.² dial. Also 5 scout. [Of uncertain origin.] pl. (See quot. 1691.)

Trout, v. Obs., to become, or to be coagulate.

Trout, obs. form of TROAT.

Trouter (trɑuˈtəɹ). [f. TROUT sb.¹ + -ER¹.] One who fishes for trout; a trout-fisher.

Trouthe, obs. form of TROTH, TROUGH.

Troutiness. [f. TROUTY a. + -NESS.] The condition or quality of being 'trouty'; speckled-ness, spottiness.

Trouting (trɑuˈtɪŋ), vbl. sb. [f. TROUT sb.² + -ING¹.] Fishing for trout; trout-fishing.

Troutlet (trɑuˈtlɛt). [As prec. + -LET.] A little or tiny trout. Also attrib.

Troutling (trɑuˈtlɪŋ). [As prec. + -LING¹.]

Trouty (trɑuˈtɪ), a. [f. TROUT sb.² + -Y¹.] Full of, abounding in, or containing trout.

Trouvaille (truvaˈj). [F., f. trouver to find.] A lucky find; a windfall.

Trouvère (truvɛˈɹ, -ɛˈ), trouveur (truvɜˈɹ). [OF. trovere, -eur, trouvère (): f. trover, trouver, to find.] One of a school of poets who flourished in Northern France from the 11th to the 14th c., whose works are chiefly epic in character.

Trove (trəʊv), sb. Short for treasure-trove.

Trover (trəʊˈvəɹ). Law. [subst. use of OF. trover (11th c.), F. trouver (see prec. inf., to find.]

Trovy, int. Obs. [? a. OF. trové, pa. pple. of trover, F. trouver to find.] ? A call in hawking.

Trow (trəʊ, trɒʊ), sb.¹ Now dial. [? = Swed. troll: see TROLL sb.¹] ? = TROLL sb.¹

Trow (trəʊ, trɒʊ), sb.² Orkney and Shetl. [= Swed. troll: see TROLL sb.¹] = TROLL sb.¹

Trow (trəʊ), sb.³ dial. variant of Trough.

Trow (trəʊ), v.¹ [OE. trēow(i)an, trīewan (tr-), etc.]

†Trow, v.²

Trowable, a. Obs. [f. TROW v. + -ABLE.]

Trowan, -ande, -ane, etc., obs. ff. TRUANT.

Trowandise, yse, etc., var. TRUANDISE Obs.

Trowel (trɑuˈɛl), sb. Forms: 4-5 trowelle, 4-7 truel, 5 trowylle, 7 trewel, 5-8 trowell, 6-4 trullo, 5 trowle, 7 troull, trowle. [ad. OF. truel (13th c.), F. truelle (14th c.), ad. vulgar or late L. truella (1163 in Du Cange), for cl. L. trulla, dim. of trua stirring-spoon, skimmer, ladle, whence the monosyllabic trual.]

Trowelled, ppl. a.; trowelled stucco, stucco of the best description intended to be painted.

Trow maddam, var. TROLL-MADAM Obs.

Trower (trəʊˈəɹ), sb.¹ [f. TROW v.¹ + -ER¹.] A believer.

Trowet, obs. form of THREE; obs. f. TRUCE.

Trowett, Trowte, obs. forms of TROAT, TROTH.

Trowie (trɒuˈɪ), a. Orkney and Shetl.

Trowing (trɒuˈɪŋ), vbl. sb. Obs. or arch. [f. TROW v.¹ + -ING¹.]

Trojan, -en,·e: see TROJAN. Hence **Trojanly** adv.

Troll, obs. f. TROLL.

Trolly sb.

Trowl(e, obs. ff. TROLL, TROWEL.

Trowly, adv. Obs. form of TRULY.

Trowman (trəʊˈmæn), sb. [f. TROW sb.² + MAN sb.¹] The master or captain of a 'trow'.

Trows, Trowsnecowen, Trowple, Trowse, Trowth**: see THROE, TRUNCHEON, TROPEL, TROUSERS, TRUTH.

Troy¹ (trɔɪ), sb.¹ The name of an ancient city in Asia Minor, besieged and taken by the Greeks.

Troy² (trɔɪ), sb.² [= OF. troie, 3 troie, 5-7 troys; also Sc. 5-7 trois, 6 troise, troys, (troo).] The received opinion is that it took its name from a weight used at the fair of Troyes in France.

Truancy (trɑ̄ˈansɪ). [f. TRUANT: see -ANCY.] The action, or an act, of playing truant; truant conduct or practice.

†Truandal. Obs. [OF. truandaille, truand, assemblage of beggars.] ? Beggars; camp-followers.

Truandise. Obs. Forms: 3 truw-, 4 treu-, trewandise, -ise, trewand, 6-5 san, 5 trewandise, trowandise, -aundyse, -entyse, truaundise, trwandyse, -aundise, 5-6 trewandise, -yse, 6 truantise. [a. OF. tru-andise (13th c. in Godef.), f. truand TRUANT (q.v.) + -ice, suffix -ISE: see -ISE²]

Truant (trɑ̄ˈant), sb. and a. Forms: a. 3 truant, 4 -ent, (6 -aunt), 4 truaunt, 6 truant, 5 truwaunt(e, (trewant), truaund, 6 -sande, 6-ande, (trewnt), 6-7 trewant, 6 -ant, truent, 6 trowent, trwant), 5 trewand, 8-9 truand, 4 dial. 8-9 truant, 9 troan. See also TRIVANT. [ME. a. OF. truant (12th c. in Godef.), (now only) as b. -Prob. from a Celtic source (Thuneysen): cf. Welsh truan wretched, wretch, Gael. truaghan wretched creature.]

†Truant, v. Forms: a. 5 truant, 5-7 trewant, 6-7 truant. [f. the vagabond or rogue.]

Truantism (trɑ̄ˈantɪz'm). [f. TRUANT sb.¹ + -ISM.] The practice of a truant; truancy.

Truantly (trɑ̄ˈantlɪ), a. and adv. Now rare. [f. as prec. + -LY¹, ²]

Truantship. [f. TRUANT sb. + -SHIP.] = TRUANTCY.

Truce (trɜ̄s), sb. Forms: a. sing. 4 trewe, 4-5 trewe, 5 trwe. B. pl. 3 trewes, trewe, 4 trewes, 4-6 trewes, 5 trowes, truwes, -ys, trewwa, trwys, truz, 5-6 trewes, 4-5 trowse, 6 trewce, truse, 7-9 truce. [ME. sing. trewe, trewes.]

Truceless (trɜ̄sˈlɛs), a. [f. TRUCE sb. + -LESS.]

Truchman (trɜ̄ˈtʃmæn). Forms: 5 tourche-man, 5-6 truch-, trough-, trudge-, 6-7 trucheman, 6 truchman; also med.L. truchmannus. [ad. Arabic tarjumān interpreter.]

Trucidation, obs. form of DRAGOMAN.

Truce-breaker, -breaking, -bearer.

Truchsess.

Supplement, p. 3873; Corrigenda, p. 4092; Spurious words, p. 4093; Books quoted, p. 4094.

Truch'manry. *Obs.*, the office or function of an interpreter; cf. † **Truch uspire** *nonce-wd.*, a spirit acting as interpreter or messenger; † **Truch uswoman** *Obs.* [cl. *Mussulwoman*], a female interpreter.

Truciation (trŭ'ădi͞eʹšən), *n.* [ad. L. *truciātiōn-em, n.* of action, f. *truciāre* to cut to pieces, kill cruelly, slaughter.] A cruel killing or murdering; in late *humorous* slaughter.

Truck (trŏk), *sb.*[1] Also 6–7 **trucke**, 8–9 *Sc.* **troke**, **trock**. [a. F. *troque*, f. *troq, troc, troc* (16th c.), AF. *truke* (13–), f. *troquer*: see TRUCK *v.*[1]]

1. The action or practice of trucking; trading by exchange of commodities; (*often* in *attrib.* use) barter.

2. The payment of wages otherwise than in money; the system or practice of such payment, the *truck system* (see 1); in quots. 1879, 1911, goods supplied in lieu of wages.

3. 'Traffic', intercourse, communication, dealings.

4. *U.S. Market-garden produce*; hence as a general term for culinary vegetables.

5. Small articles of a miscellaneous character; sundries; stuff; chiefly in depreciative use: odds and ends; things of little value; trash, rubbish.

6. Commodities for barter. *Obs.*

Truck (trŏk), *sb.*[2] Also 7 **truke**. [app. deriv. of TRUCKLE, a. AF. *trocle*, or identified with TRUCK *sb.*[1] in certain senses.]

1. A small solid wooden wheel or roller; *spec. Naut.* one of those on which the carriages of ships' guns were formerly mounted.

2. *Naut.* A circular or square cap of wood fixed on the head of a mast or flag-staff, usually with small holes or sheaves for halliards, etc.

3. One of the small wooden blocks through which the rope of a parrel is threaded to prevent its being frayed against the mast.

4. A wheeled vehicle for carrying heavy weights; variously applied.

Truck (trŏk), *v.*[1] Forms: 3 **trukie**, 5 **trukke**, 6–7 **trucke**, (7 **truque**, 8 *Sc.* **troak**, 8–9 *Sc.* **troke**, **trock**, 9 *Sc.* **troque**, 8–*dial.* **truck**. [ME. *trukie, trukken* (Cotgr.), Norman-French form of OF. *troquer, troquer,* med. L. *trocāre* (1257) in Cartulary, Hatz.-Darm.], F. *troquer* to barter, exchange, Pg. *trocar*, It. *truccare* (Florio, 1598); of unknown origin: see suggestions in Diez.]

1. *trans.* To give in exchange (*for* something else); to exchange (one thing) *for* another; also, to exchange (a thing) *with* (a person: see *absol.*).

Truck (trŏk), *v.*[2] [f. TRUCK *sb.*[2] or *v.*[2]

1. *trans.* To put on or into a truck; to convey by means of, or truck or trucks.

2. To carry about (or sell) by means of a truck.

3. To barter away (something unworthy); to hawk, peddle.

Truckage[1] (trŏ'kĕdʒ). [f. TRUCK *sb.*[2] or *v.*[2] + -AGE.] Conveyance by truck or trucks, or the cost of this; also, supply of trucks collectively (cf. TONNAGE *sb.*).

Truckage[2] (trŏ'kĕdʒ). [f. TRUCK *v.*[1] + -AGE.] The action of trucking; exchange, barter.

Trucker[1] (trŏ'kɛɹ). [f. TRUCK *v.*[1] + -ER.] One who trucks or barters; a barterer, bargainer.

Trucker[2]. [f. TRUCK *sb.*[2] + -ER.] A labourer who uses a truck.

Trucking[1] (trŏ'kĭŋ), *vbl. sb.*[1] [f. TRUCK *v.*[1] + -ING.] The action of TRUCK *v.*[1]; exchanging, bartering, trafficking, bargaining; dealings, intercourse.

Truck, *v.*[2] [f. TRUCK *sb.*[2]]

Truckle (trŏ'k'l), *sb.* Forms: 5 **trokel**, ill, **trookyll**, **trok'l**, 7 **troklye**, 5–6 **trokell**, 7 **troukle**, 6 **trokle**, **truckill**, 7 **trukel**, **truckle**, **trickle** (*dial.*) 7– **truckle**. [a. AF. *trocle* = OF. *trocle*: see TROCHLEA.]

1. A small wheel with a groove in its circumference round which a cord passes; a pulley, a sheave.

2. A small roller or wheel placed under or attached to a heavy object to facilitate moving it; a castor on a piece of furniture. *Now dial.*

3. Short for TRUCKLE-BED.

4. A low-wheeled car; a truck. Chiefly in Irish use.

5. A small barrel-shaped cheese. *dial.*

Truckle (trŏ'k'l), *v.* Also 8 *Sc.* **trookle**. [f. TRUCKLE *sb.*]

1. *intr.* To sleep in a truckle-bed. Const. *under* (*beneath*) the person occupying the high bed, or the high bed itself. Also *fig.*

2. *fig.* To take a subordinate or inferior position; to be subservient; to submit; to give precedence. Const. *to* a person.

Truckle-bed. [f. TRUCKLE *sb.*[2] + BED.] A low bed running on truckles or castors, usually pushed beneath a high or 'standing' bed when not in use; a trundle-bed. *To* TRUCKLE *v.* 1.

Truckler (trŏ'klɛɹ). [f. TRUCKLE *v.* + -ER.] One who truckles (in sense 2 of the verb).

Truckling (trŏ'klĭŋ), *vbl. sb.* [f. TRUCKLE *v.* + -ING.] The action of the verb TRUCKLE.

Truckling, *ppl. a.* [f. TRUCKLE *v.* + -ING.]

Trucks: *see* TRUCK *sb.* and *v.*

Truckle-cheese, *a truck-like car*, *-cheese* (5).

Truculency (trŭ-kͅ, turkiu̇lēnsi), *a.* [as prec.] The quality of being truculent.

Truculent (trŭ'kiu̇lent), *a.* [ad. L. *truculentus*, f. *truc-* (*truc-em*) fierce, savage; cf. obs. F. *truculent* (Cotgr. 1611).]

1. Characterized by or exhibiting ferocity of cruelty; fierce, cruel, savage, barbarous.

2. Of speech or writing: Violent; rude; scathing; savage; harsh.

Truculently, *adv.* In a truculent manner; savagely.

Truculous, *a. Obs. rare*[-1]. Truculent; savagely fierce.

Truddle, obs. form of TREADLE.

Trudge (trŏdʒ), *v.* Also 6 **tredge**, 6–7 (8–9 *dial.*) **tridge**, 7 **truge**. [Of obscure origin. Skeat suggests F. *trucher* to beg from laziness (in Oudin, 16th c.), but this does not agree.]

1. *intr.* To walk laboriously, wearily, or without spirit, but steadily and persistently; 'to jog on'; to march heavily or ('J.). Sometimes merely an undignified equivalent of 'walk', 'go on foot'.

2. *trans.* To traverse on foot.

Trudge (trŏdʒ), *sb.* [f. TRUDGE *v.*[1]] A person who trudges; a trudger.

Trudgeon, *n.*[1]: see TRUDGE *v.*[1]

Trudge-man (trŏdʒ-mæn), variant of TRUCHMAN.

Trudgeon (trŏ'dʒʌn), *sb.* [app. arbitrary f. the surname *Trudgen*.] One who swims with a toddling child.

Trudger[1]: see after TRUDGE *v.*[1], TRUDGEON.

True (trū̇), *a.* (*sb.*, *adv.*). Forms: 1 (3) **trēowe**, **trȳwe**, 1–4 **trewe**, 3 **treowe**, 3–4 **trīewe**, 3–7 **treowe**, 5 **trwe**, 3–4 **trou**, **trow** (5 **trow**), 6 *Sc.* **trew**, 4–7 **trewe**, 4– **true** (3 *Orm.* **trow**).

1. Of persons: Steadfast in adherence to a commander or friend, to a principle or cause, or to one's plighted word; faithful, loyal, constant, trusty.

2. Of one's word or speech: Honest, sincere, veracious.

3. Consistent with fact; agreeing with the reality; representing the thing as it really is.

4. Accurately placed, fitted, or shaped; exact in position or form, as an instrument, a part of mechanism, or the like.

5. Real, genuine; rightly answering to the description.

Trumper.

† Trumper.

Trumpery (trʊ'mpəri), *sb.*

Trumpet (trʊ'mpet), *sb.*

Trumpet, *v.*

Trumpeted

Trumpeter (trʊ'mpetər).

Trumpeting (trʊ'mpetiŋ), *vbl. sb.*

Trumpetless

Trumpet-tongue to **Trumpetry**: see after **Trumpet** *sb.*

†Trumpettier. *Obs.*

Truncage (trʊ'ŋkedʒ), *Hist.*

Truncal (trʊ'ŋkal).

Truncate (trʊ'ŋkeit), *v.*

Truncate, *ppl. a.*

Truncated (trʊ'ŋketid), *ppl. a.*

Truncately (trʊ'ŋketli), *adv.*

Truncation (trʊŋke'iʃən).

Truncato- (trʊŋke'to), combining form of L. *truncatus*.

Truncator (trʊŋke'itər), *rare*.

†Truncature.

Truncel.

†Trunch, *sb.* and *a.* *Obs.*

Trunch, *v.*

Truncheon (trʊ'nʃən), *sb.*

Truncheon, *v.*

Truncheoner, Truncheonist

†Truncheoned, *ppl. a.*

Truncheoneer

Truncheonry.

Truncus (trʊ'ŋkəs).

Trundle. nerve. b. *Zool.* The trunk or body of an animal, without the head, limbs, and tail; in *Entom.* the thorax. c. *Bot.* The trunk or stem of a tree.

1. Something that trundles or is trundled.

2. A device consisting of two disks turning on an axle, and connected by a series of parallel staves cylindrically arranged, which engage with the teeth of a cog-wheel; a lantern-wheel.

3. Also, each of the staves of this device.

4. A low trestle or carriage on small wheels.

5. An act of trundling or rolling; an impulse that causes something to roll.

6. *Agr.* A going away or away; a course; departure; in *Cricket* a bowler.

III. 7. *attrib.* and *Comb.* (in some cases directly from the vb.): **trundle-head**, **-tail**.

Trundle, *v.* Forms: see prec.

Trunk.

Trunked, *ppl. a.*

Trunk-fish.

Trunk-hose.

Trunkful.

Trunk-maker.

Trunking, *vbl. sb.*

Trunnel, *-ell*, variants of TREENAIL.

Trunnion.

Truss.

TRY.

testing his qualifications.—[TRIAL sb.¹ 6, TRIER 5. Obs. or Hist.

Trygon (trī·gŏn). [L. trȳgōn (Pliny), a Gr. τρυγών a dove, also the fish.] A fish with a sharp spine in its tail, a sting-ray.

Trygon, Tryhumphe, obs. ff. TRIGON, TRIUMPH.

Trying (trəi·iŋ), vbl. sb. [f. TRY v. + -ING¹.] The action of the verb TRY, in various senses.

Trypanosoma (tripănǒ·sŏ·mǎ). Zool. [mod.L. f. Gr. τρύπανον borer + σῶμα body.] A genus of parasitic protozoa, species of which are parasitic in the blood of man and other animals, causing specific diseases, such as sleeping-sickness; an infusorian of this genus.

Trypanosomatic, Trypanosomiasis, Trypanosome.

Tryssail (trəi·səl, trəis'l). Naut.

Trypsin (tri·psin). Physiol. Chem. [app. for *tripsin, f. Gr. τρῖψις rubbing.]

Tryptic, Tryptophan, Trypsinogen.

Tryst (traist), sb. Orig. and chiefly Sc. [f.

Tryst (traist), v.

Trysting (trəi·stiŋ), vbl. sb.

Tryster, Trystie.

Tsetse (tse·tse). Also 9 tzetze. [S. African name.] A dipterous insect (Glossina morsitans) of the family Tabanidæ.

Tsamba, Tsar, Tsarevitch, Tsing, Tsuga.

Tuan, Tuart, Tuath, Tuatara.

Tub (tʌb), sb. Forms: 4-7 tubbe, 5-6 tobbe, 5-7 tub; also 6 tobe. A vessel of wood, usually circular, formed of staves and hoops of cylindrical or slightly concave form, with a flat bottom.

tub (continued) ... Turman, Tub-preacher, Tub-thumper, etc.

Tub (tɒb), v. ...

Tubage (tiū·bedʒ), ... [F. tubage (Littré).]

Tubal (tiū·bal), a. [L. tub-us TUBE + -AL.]

Tubation ...

Tubba ... Also **tooba**. [Arab. (in Koran xiii. 28) طوبى ṭūbah]

Tuba (tiū·ba). Also **tooba**. [Arab.]

Tubber[1] (tɒ·bər). ... Also **tooba**.

Tubber[2], local. Also **tubble**.

Tubbiness (tɒ·bines). [f. TUBBY + -NESS.] Tubby quality or condition.

Tubbing (tɒ·biŋ), vbl. sb. [f. TUB v. or sb.] The action of TUB v.

Tubbish (tɒ·biʃ), a. [f. TUB sb. + -ISH.] Somewhat tubby; resembling a tub.

Tubboo (tɒ·bū). Also **tubba**. [native word in W. Africa.]

Tubble see **Tubbal**.

Tubby (tɒ·bi), a. [f. TUB sb. + -Y.] Resembling or suggesting a tub.

Tube (tiūb), sb. [a. F. tube (1460 in Godef. Compl.), ad. L. tub-us.] I. Artificial.

Tube (continued), v.

Tubed (tiūbd), ppl. a. [f. TUBE v. or sb. + -ED.]

Tubeless, a., having no tube or tubes.

Tube-worm ...

Tuber[1] (tiū·bər), sb. [ad. L. tuber (1489 in Littré).]

Tuber[2], Obs. Pl. **tuberes**. [L. tuber masc.]

Tuber[3], Obs. [the tree?] A kind of apple, or the tree on which it grows.

Tuber[4] (tiū·bər). [a. L. tuber neut., a hump, swelling, pl. tubera.]

Tuberaceous (tiūbərēɪ·ʃəs), a., Bot. [f. mod.L. Tuberāceī (tribe), etc.]

Tuberant ...

Tuberated (tiū·bərēɪted), a. [f. L. tuberāt-um TUBER² + -ATE.]

Tuberation (tiūbərēɪ·ʃən). rare⁻¹. [f. prec. + -ATION.]

Tuberose, sb.

Tuberose, a.

Tuberosity ...

Tuberous ...

Tuberculo-, combining form of mod.L. tuberculum TUBERCLE.

Tubercular (tiūbəɹ·kiʊləɹ), a.

Tubercularize ...

Tubercule (tiū·bəɹkiūl), = TUBERCLE.

Tuberculate (tiūbəɹ·kiūlēt, -lət), a.

Tuberculated (tiūbəɹ·kiūlēted), a.

Tuberculation (tiūbəɹkiūlēɪ·ʃən), sb.

Tubercule ...

Tuberculiferous (tiūbəɹkiūli·fərəs), a.

Tuberculiform ...

Tuberculin (tiūbəɹ·kiūlin), sb.

Tubercule ...

Tuberculo-, combining form of TUBERCLE.

culoci·dia [-IN [1]], an albumose obtained from tuberculin, used as a tuberculicide. ‖ **Tube·rculode·rma** [Gr. δέρμα skin], tuberculosis of the skin (*Cent. Dict. Suppl.* 1909). **Tube·rculo-fi·broid** *a.*, 'characterized by tubercle that has undergone a fibroid degeneration' (Dorland). **Tube·rculo-opso·nic** *a.*, relating to the opsonin of the tubercle-bacillus. **Tube·rculopho·bia** [-PHOBIA], a morbid dread of tuberculosis. **Tube·rculopla·smin**, a solution of the protoplasm of tubercle-bacilli. **Tube·rculosecto·rial** *a.*, *Zool.* [SECTORIAL *a.*[2]], applied to a type of molar teeth having high conical tubercles or cusps adapted for cutting. **Tube·rculo-squa·mous** *a.* [SQUAMOUS], characterized by tubercles and scales. **Tube·rculothe·rapy** [Gr. θεραπεία nurture, medical treatment], 'treatment of tuberculous patients by feeding with the raw flesh of animals affected by tuberculosis' (Dorland). **Tube·rculoto·xin**, 'any toxin of the tubercle bacillus' (*ibid.*). **Tube·rculotro·pic** *a.* [? after *heliotropic*, etc.: cf. TROPIC *a.*[1] 4], having the property of combining chemically with the tubercle-bacillus.

c 1900 *Buck's Handbk. Med. Sc.* I. 461 *Tuberculocide. 1891 *Pall Mall G.* 23 July 5/1 An experiment..on twelve more or less tuberculous persons with the so-called *tuberculocidin, which is a modification of Professor Koch's remedy, invented by Professor Klebs, of Zurich. 1895 *Buck's Handbk. Med. Sc.* IX. 903/1 Tuberculin yields about two and a half per cent. of tuberculocidin. 1898 *Allbutt's Syst. Med.* V. 255 Sir A. Clark..describes two main forms [of pneumoconiosis] as..the *tuberculo-fibroid and fibro-tuberculous. 1907 *Med. Record* 14 Dec. 987 In one of these [cases] the *tuberculo-opsonic index was from normal to 0·7 below normal. 1901 *Lancet* 27 July 192/1 *Tuberculophobia must not be produced, the patient must not be made a pariah. c 1900 *Buck's Handbk. Med. Sc.* I. 692 *Tuberculoplasmin. 1893 *Proc. Zool. Soc.* 28 Feb. 197 The..*tuberculo-sectorial type of inferior molars. 1879 *St. George's Hosp. Rep.* IX. 592 Rupial sore; *tuberculo-squamous eruption. 1909 *Cent. Dict. Suppl.*, *Tuberculotropic.

Tuberculoid (tiubə̄·ɹkiŭloid), *a. Zool.* [f. L. *tübercul-um* TUBERCLE + -OID.] = TUBERCULIFORM.
1891 in *Cent. Dict.*

Tuberculome (tiubə̄·ɹkiŭlōᵘm). *Path.* [ad. mod.L. *tüberculōma*, f. *tübercul-um* TUBERCLE, after *sarcoma*, etc.] A tumour or abscess caused by the tubercle-bacillus.
1903 *Nature* 5 Mar. 431/2 If the tuberculous abscess or tuberculome is not too large, a cure may be effected by a simple washing with an antiseptic liquid.

Tuberculose (tiubə̄·ɹkiŭlōᵘs), *a.* [f. L. type **tüberculōs-us*, f. *tübercul-um* TUBERCLE: see -OSE.] = TUBERCULOUS 2, TUBERCULATE.
1752 J. HILL *Hist. Anim.* 249 The green Turdus..is a very beautiful fish;..it is not unfrequently..almost entire black, and sometimes spotted or tuberculose. 1854 WOODWARD *Mollusca* II. 191 Doris Bilamellata:..Back elevated, tuberculose. 1900 in B. D. JACKSON *Gloss. Bot. Terms*.

Tuberculosed (tiubə̄·ɹkiŭlōᵘzd), *a. Path.* [f. TUBERCULOS-IS + -ED [2].] Affected with tuberculosis; rendered tuberculous.
1886 *Med. News* 25 Aug. 216 We must distinguish those forms in which the tuberculosed lymphatic glands are separated in chains. 1897 *Daily News* 22 Apr. 3/1 Methods.. for dealing with tuberculosed meat. 1899 H. STUART *Locks & Loch Fishing* I. iv. 34 They contained the bacilli of consumption, and were, in a word, tuberculosed or consumptive fish.

‖ **Tuberculosis** (tiubəɹkiŭlōᵘ·sis). *Path.* [mod.L., f. *tübercul-um* TUBERCLE: see -OSIS.] *Originally*, Any disease characterized by the formation of tubercles; now, since the discovery by Koch in 1882 of the tubercle-bacillus, *spec.* restricted to disease caused by this bacillus in any of the bodily tissues; examples are pulmonary consumption or phthisis (tuberculosis of the lungs), and scrofula (tuberculosis of the lymphatic glands). Also *attrib.*
1860 TANNER *Pregnancy* ii. 48 Many females with a tendency to tuberculosis having a copious watery catamenial flow. 1873 T. H. GREEN *Introd. Pathol.* (ed. 2) 203 Acute tuberculosis is..a general infective disease,..characterized.. by..numerous minute nodular lesions..in the various organs and tissues. 1877 ROBERTS *Handbk. Med.* (ed. 3) I. 267 Looking upon tuberculosis as a constitutional disease, it has almost universally been regarded as having a hereditary origin. *attrib.* 1898 *Westm. Gaz.* 13 June 10/1 The provision of sanatoria for poor tuberculosis patients. 1899 Q. VICTORIA in *Daily News* 27 May 7/6, I beg your Excellency to express in my name to the Lung Tuberculosis Congress my best thanks for the good wishes tendered to me. 1913 *Times* 6 Aug. 8/4 Milk containing tuberculosis bacilli.

Tuberculo-so-, combining form of L. type **tüberculōsus* TUBERCULOUS, in combination with an adj. of form, as *tuberculoso-subramose*.
1846 DANA *Zooph.* (1848) 497 Either convoluted-foliate, or tuberculoso-subramose.

Tuberculous (tiubə̄·ɹkiŭləs), *a.* [ad. L. type **tüberculōs-us*, f. *tübercul-um* TUBERCLE: see -OUS; cf. F. *tuberculeux* (1812 in Hatz.-Darm.).]
1. *Path.* Pertaining to or produced by tubercles; consisting or of the nature of tubercles; affected with tubercles.
1747 tr. *Astruc's Fevers* 129 Though the..tuberculous ulcers may seem to be healed, yet they frequently return.
a 1834 R. CARSWELL *Pathol. Anat.*, *Tubercle* (1838) a iv b, I have never found these [scrofulous] glands..exempt from the presence of tuberculous matter. 1897 [see TUBERCULAR 2].

b. Since 1882, almost always used *spec.* in reference to the tubercle-bacillus or to tuberculosis, and thus technically distinguished from *tubercular* in the general sense: see TUBERCULAR 2, 2 b.
1891 *Dublin Rev.* Jan. 162 The new remedy can only act on living tuberculous tissue. 1897 *Allbutt's Syst. Med.* II. 17 Guinea-pigs inoculated subcutaneously..by virulent tuberculous material. 1899 *Ibid.* VII. 466 Tuberculous meningitis is an acute disease depending on the invasion of the cerebral pia mater by the tubercle bacillus. 1903 *Times* 7 Mar. 15/2 The eating of tuberculous pork. 1913 *Ibid.* 13 Aug. 3/2 A steady increase in the use of hospitals for the tuberculous sick.

2. *Nat. Hist.* Full of or covered with tubercles; tuberculate, tubercular. (Now disused.)
1828 WEBSTER, *Tubercular*, *Tuberculous*,..full of knobs or pimples. 1833 *Penny Cycl.* I. 114/2 The three first molars are pointed and trenchant, and the other four tuberculous. 1846 DANA *Zooph.* (1848) 502 Surface tuberculous, with the tubercles subconical.

‖ **Tuberculum** (tiubə̄·ɹkiŭlə̆m). Pl. **tubercula**. [L. dim. of *tüber*, TUBER [2].] = TUBERCLE (in various senses).
1693 tr. *Blancard's Phys. Dict.* (ed. 2), *Tubercula*, the same that *Phymata*. 1721 BAILEY, *Tubercula*, (among Surgeons) little Swellings or Pushes. 1857 DUNGLISON *Med. Lex.*, *Tuberculum Cinereum*, 'Ash-coloured tubercle', a mass of cineritious substance at the top of the calamus scriptorius [in the medulla oblongata]. 1872 NICHOLSON *Palæont.* 350 The ribs have distinct capitula and tubercula.

Tuberiferous (tiūbəri·fĕrəs), *a. Bot.* [f. L. *tüber*, TUBER [2] + -I)FEROUS.] Producing or bearing tubers.
1846 WORCESTER cites GRAY. 1847 W. E. STEELE *Field Bot.* 174 *Melanthew*. Mostly bulbiferous or tuberiferous plants, possessing highly poisonous, acrid, and narcotic properties. 1881 BENTHAM in *Jrnl. Linn. Soc.* XVIII. 347 Their rhizome is..more or less tuberiferous.

Tuberiform (tiū·bərifǭɹm), *a. Nat. Hist.* and *Path.* [f. L. type **tüberiform-is*: see TUBER [2] and -FORM.] Having the form of a tuber; also characterized, as a disease, by growths of this form.
1822 J. PARKINSON *Outl. Oryctol.* 61* A free, carnose, tuberiform polypifer. 1834 COOPER *Good's Study Med.* (ed. 4) II. 555 *note*, Tuberiform melanosis. 1854 JONES & SIEV. *Pathol. Anat.* (1874) 141 A globular tumour, with a smooth or somewhat tuberiform surface. 1899 *Allbutt's Syst. Med.* VI. 106 Another variety [of malignant pleural growth] is the tuberiform.

Tuberin (tiū·bərin). *Org. Chem.* [f. TUBER [2] + -IN [1].] A globulin occurring in potato-tubers.
1900 C. F. LANGWORTHY in *Year-bk. U. S. Dept. Agric.* 340 The potato contains two proteids, a globulin, to which the name 'tuberin' is given, and a proteose.

Tuberless (tiū·bəɹlės), *a.* [f. as prec. + -LESS.] Destitute of tubers; not bearing tubers.
1851 *B'ham & Midl. Gard. Mag.* Dec. 217 Finding..that the plant [*Tropæolum Deckerianum*] was tuberless, I came to the conclusion that it must be an annual.

Tu·bero-, combining form of TUBER [2], as in **tu·bero-cy·stic**, having or forming a tuberous cyst.
1879 *St. George's Hosp. Rep.* IX. 433 Tubero-cystic tumour of the ovary.

† **Tuberon, -e** [ad. Pg. *tubarão*], obs. forms of TIBURON, a large shark.
[1521 PETER MARTYR *De nuper repertis insulis* 9 Piscis vorax qui Tuberon vocatur.] 1555, 1579 [see TIBURON]. 1599 NASHE *Lenten Stuffe* (1871) 76 A shark or tuberon, that lay gaping for the flying fish. 1665 SIR T. HERBERT *Trav.* (1677) 6 When..men swim in the bearing Ocean, the greedy Hayen called Tuberon or Shark..pursue them. 1784–5 *Chron.* in *Ann. Reg.* 241/1 The dog-fish, or tuberone of Josselyn, never exceeds three feet and a half in length.

Tuberose (tiū·bərōᵘs, *often incorrectly* tiū·b,rōᵘz), *sb.* Also 7 **tuberuse, -euse, (tuber-rose)**. [ad. L. *tüberōsa*, the specific name of the plant (see below), fem. of *tüberōsus* (see next); corrupted by popular etymology into a disyllable, as if f. *tube* + *rose*, and so most commonly pronounced. (In the obs. forms *tuberuse, -euse*, a. F. *tubéreuse*, ad. L. *tüberōsa*.)] A liliaceous plant, *Polianthes tuberosa*, with creamy white, funnel-shaped, very fragrant flowers, and a tuberous root; a native of the East Indies, cultivated in southern Europe and the southern U.S., and in northern parts as a green-house plant.
1664 EVELYN *Kal. Hort.* 200 Now take out your Indian Tuberoses, parting the Off-sets. *Ibid.* 208 Tuber-rose. 1691 *Lond. Gaz.* No. 2654/4 There are lately brought from Italy several Orange and Limon Trees,..Onions of Tubereuse. a 1718 PRIOR *Solomon* I. 80 The smelling Tub'rose and Junquele declare, The stronger Impulse of an Evening Air. a 1763 SHENSTONE *Ode to Sir R. Lyttelton* xiii, So would some tuberose delight, That struck the pilgrim's wondering sight. 1820 SHELLEY *Sensit. Plant* I. x, The jessamine faint, and the sweet tuberose. 1873 MRS. H. KING *Disciples, Ugo Bassi* II. (1877) 66 In the cool shadow heaps of tuberose Lay by the fountains in the market-place.

b. A perfume extracted from the flowers of this.
1682 MRS. BEHN *City Heiress* 22 Sprinkle my Handkercher with Tuberose. 1867 AUG. J. E. WILSON *Vashti* xix, Stooping to pick it [a handkerchief] up, he inhaled the delicate, tenacious perfume of tube-rose.

Tuberose (tiū·bərōᵘs), *a.* [ad. L. *tüberōs-us*, f. *tüber*, TUBER [2]: see -OSE [1].] = TUBEROUS.
1704 [see TUBER [2] 1 b]. 1796 KIRWAN *Elem. Min.* (ed. 2) II. 259 Indurated [Calx of Arsenic]...Found Massive, or Stalactitic with a tuberose or botryoidal surface. 1815 J. SMITH *Panorama Sc. & Art* II. 670 A tuberose root, as exemplified in the turnip and carrot. 1878 H. M. STANLEY *Dark Cont.* I. xv. 381 The tuberose muscles of the flanks. 1898 SIR P. MANSON *Trop. Diseases* xxxvii. 574 Vincent.. found it [i.e. the parasite of mycetoma] in the unbroken tuberose swellings under the skin. *Comb.* 1806 GALPINE *Brit. Bot.* § 77 *Symphytum*..*tuberosum*, tuberose-rooted.

Tuberosity (tiūbərǫ·sĭti). [a. F. *tubérosité* (Paré, c 1550), f. late L. *tüberōsitās*, f. *tüberōs-us* TUBEROSE + -ITY.]
1. The quality or condition of being tuberous; bulging; gibbosity. Now *rare* or *Obs.*
1541 R. COPLAND *Guydon's Quest. Chirurg.* Q iv b, Hardnes and tuberosyte of the ioyntes outwarde. 1610 GUILLIM *Heraldry* II. vi. 63 A bow, which being bent hath a moderate bowing voide of excess of tuberositie.
2. *concr.* A tuberous formation or part; a swelling, protuberance, prominence. a. *Anat.* and *Zool.*: *esp.* a large irregular projection of a bone, usually serving for attachment of a muscle.
1611 COTGR., *Condyle*, the tuberiositie, out-swelling, roundnesse, or knots, of the thigh, knee, ankle, elbow, or knuckle-bones. 1741 MONRO *Anat.* (ed. 3) 134 The internal posterior Part of the Tuberosity and Alveoli of the Teeth. 1852 TH. ROSS *Humboldt's Trav.* I. i. 27 The brownish tuberosities of its body. 1870 ROLLESTON *Anim. Life* 13 The great triangular tuberosity of the humerus.
b. *generally.* A swelling, a swollen mass.
1611 COTGR., *Tuberositez*, tuberosities, swellings;..knobs; knots. 1831 CARLYLE *Sart. Res.* I. v, Whether he flow gracefully out in folded mantles;..swell-out in starched ruffs, buckram stuffings, and monstrous tuberosities; or [etc.]. *Ibid.* III. vi, I sojourned in that monstrous tuberosity of Civilised Life, the Capital of England.

Tuberous (tiū·bərəs), *a.* [ad. F. *tubéreux*, *-euse* (Paré, c 1550), ad. L. *tüberōsus*, f. *tüber*, TUBER [2]: see -OUS.]
1. *Anat.*, *Zool.*, etc. Of the form of, or constituting, a tuber or rounded projection; covered with such projections; knobbed, knobby. Now *rare.*
1650 BULWER *Anthropomet.* iii. 63 This forehead is..neither globous nor tuberous as the forehead of women. 1678 RAY *Willughby's Ornith.* II. xv. § 2. 182 A broad circle of naked, tuberous, white flesh compasses the Eyes, as in the Carriers. 1804 SHAW *Gen. Zool.* V. 208 Tuberous Carp...Carp with thirteen rays in the anal fin, and slightly tuberous body.
2. *Path.* Affected with tubers or morbid swellings; of the nature of such a swelling; characterized, as a disease, by such swellings.
1656 BLOUNT *Glossogr.*, *Tuberous*, full of bunches, swellings, wennes or knots. 1762 R. GUY *Pract. Obs. Cancers* 150 The tuberous Vessels were rather fuller than ordinary. 1834 COOPER *Good's Study Med.* (ed. 4) I. 353 The origin of vascular tuberous growths. 1900 J. HUTCHINSON in *Arch. Surg.* XI. 73 His face was covered with tuberous acne.
3. *Bot.* a. Of the nature of a tuber; chiefly in *tuberous root*, (*a*) a tuber, or an underground stem bearing tubers (see TUBER [2] 1); (*b*) more strictly, a true root (usually one of a cluster) thickened so as to resemble a tuber, but bearing no buds; as in the lesser celandine and the dahlia.
1668 Tuberous roots [see TUBER [2] 1]. 1730 MARTYN in *Phil. Trans.* XXXVI. 385 Their Roots are either bulbous, tuberous, or consisting of thick, fleshy Fibres. 1776 WITHERING *Brit. Plants* (1796) IV. 346 *Peziza tuberosa*...Stem growing at the base to a blackish fungous tuberous substance. 1807 J. E. SMITH *Phys. Bot.* 140 The knobs of genuine tuberous roots, like the potatoe, are studded with them [buds]. 1872 OLIVER *Elem. Bot.* I. vii. 66 When the branches or fibres of a root become thickened in this way, as..in the Garden Dahlia, the root is said to be tuberous.
b. Of a plant: Producing or bearing tubers; tuberous-rooted.
1664 EVELYN *Kal. Hort.* Sept. (1729) 218 Tuberous Indian Jacinth. 1786 ABERCROMBIE *Gard. Assist.* 51 Bulbous and tuberous irises. 1861 MISS PRATT *Flower. Pl.* IV. 55 Tuberous Comfrey. *Ibid.* VI. 56 Tuberous Fox-tail.
4. *Comb.* **Tuberous-rooted** *a.*, having a tuberous root (in either sense: see 3 a).
1731 MORTIMER *Husb.* II. 226 Irises are both bulbous and tuberous Rooted. 1808 KNIGHT in *Phil. Trans.* XCIX. 174 Such tuberous rooted plants as the potatoe. 1914 *Daily Mail* 31 Jan. 9/2 The planting of tuberous-rooted anemones and ranunculuses.
Hence **Tu·berously** *adv.*; **Tu·berousness.**
1681 GREW *Musæum* III. I. i. 255 The tuberousness of the Bone in some places. 1847–9 *Todd's Cycl. Anat.* IV. 133/2 This disease produces..irregular tuberousness of the hand. a 1891 *Bull. of Ill. State Laboratory* II. 28 (Cent. D.) Tuberously.

Tubful (tʊ·bfŭl). [f. TUB *sb.* + -FUL.] As much as a tub will hold.
1788 LD. AUCKLAND *Corr.* etc. (1861) II. 71 We have a large tubful brought to us every morning. 1812 SIR J. SINCLAIR *Syst. Husb. Scot.* II. 72 The rain is pouring on in tubfuls. 1894 J. MENZIES *Our Town* xx. 211 A gudewife had come to her door with a tubful of soapsuds.

Tubi- (tiūbi), combining form of L. *tubus* TUBE, in modern scientific terms, chiefly zoological. **Tubicolar** (tiubi·kŏlăɹ), **Tubicolous** (tiubi·kŏləs) *adjs.* [mod.L. *tubicola*, f. *colĕre* to cultivate, inhabit], inhabiting a tube; applied to annelids and rotifers that secrete tubular cases, spiders that spin tubular webs (cf. *tubitelar*), and molluscs with shelly tubes (cf. TUBE-*shell*, *tubivalve*); so **Tubicole** (tiū·bikōᵘl) *a.* = prec.; *sb.* a tubicolar annelid

or mollusc. **Tu·bicorn** [L. *cornū* horn], *sb.* a hollow-horned ruminant; *adj.* hollow-horned, as a ruminant; also **Tubico·rnous** *a.* **Tubifacient** (-fēⁱ·ʃĕnt) *a.* [L. *facient-em* making], making a tube for habitation, as a tubicolous annelid, etc. **Tu·bifer** [L. *-fer* bearing], an animal bearing a tube, as a tubicolous annelid; so **Tubi·ferous** (-fĕrəs) *a.*, bearing a tube or tubes. **Tubiflorous** (-flōᵊ·rəs) *a.*, *Bot.* [L. *flōs*, *flōr-* flower], having tubular flowers or florets, as the division *Tubifloræ* of composite plants (= TUBULIFLOROUS). **Tu·biform** *a.*, having the form of a tube; tube-shaped, tubular. **Tubilingual** (-li·ŋgwăl) *a.* [L. *lingua* tongue], belonging to the division *Tubilingues* of passerine birds, having long extensile tubular tongues used for sucking up honey. **Tubinarial** (-nēᵊ·riăl), **Tubinarine** (-nēᵊ·rəin) *adjs.* [L. *nāris* nostril], belonging to the order *Tubinārēs* (Illiger, 1811) of water-birds, comprising the albatrosses and petrels, having nostrils of tubular form. **Tubiparous** (tiubi·părəs) *a.* [-PAROUS], producing a tube; applied to certain glands in tubicolous annelids, supposed to secrete the substance which forms the tube. **Tu·bipore** (-pōᵊɹ) *sb.*, a member of the genus *Tubipora*, family *Tubiporidæ*, or order *Tubiporaceæ*, of alcyonarians (the organ-pipe corals), in which each polyp has a tubular corallet opening by a pore; *adj.* belonging to or having the characters of this genus, family, or order; in quot., containing or formed of fossil tubipores; so **Tu:biporacean** (-porēⁱ·ʃiăn), **-poraceous** (-porēⁱ·ʃəs) *adjs.*, belonging to the order *Tubiporaceæ*; **Tubi·porid**, a coral of the family *Tubiporidæ*; **Tubi·porite** [-ITE [1] 2 a], a fossil tubipore; **Tubi·poroid** *a.* [-OID], resembling or allied to the genus *Tubipora*; **Tubi·porous** *a.* = *tubipore* adj. **Tubitelar** (-tī·lăɹ) *a.* [L. *tēla* web], belonging to the division *Tubitelæ* or *Tubitelariæ* of spiders, which spin tubular webs; so **Tu:bitelarian** (-tĭlēᵊ·riăn) *a.* = prec.; *sb.* a spider of this division (*Cent. Dict.* 1891). **Tu·bivalve**, *sb.* a bivalve mollusc having a shelly tube in addition to the valves of the shell; a tube-shell; *adj.* having such a tube.

1835–6 *Todd's Cycl. Anat.* I. 619/1 A common marine *tubicolar worm. 1877 HUXLEY *Anat. Inv. Anim.* v. 238 The tubicolar Annelids possess neither proboscis nor teeth. 1842 BRANDE *Dict. Sc.* etc., **Tubicoles*, *Tubicola*, the name of an order of Annelidans, comprehending those which live in tubes..; also the name of a family of..Mollusks, including those which have a tubular calcareous sheath in addition to the two shelly valves. 1864 WEBSTER, *Tubicole*... one of an order of annelides most of which live in shelly tubes. 1891 *Cent. Dict.*, Tubicole, *a.* and *n.* 1870 H. SPENCER *Princ. Psychol.* (ed. 2) I. I. i. 6 The *tubicolous Annelids. 1881 E. R. LANKESTER in *Jrnl. Microsc. Sc.* Jan. 123 The proximal region of the stomach..was infested by a remarkable little free swimming, yet tubicolous Rotifer. 1842 BRANDE *Dict. Sc.* etc., **Tubicorns*, *Tubicornia*,.. Ruminants comprehending those in which the horns are composed of a horny axis covered with a horny sheath. 1891 *Cent. Dict.*, *Tubicorn*,..*a.* hollow-horned, as a ruminant. 1864 WEBSTER, *Tubicornous. 1891 *Cent. Dict.*, *Tubifacient. 1899 in *Syd. Soc. Lex.* 1842 BRANDE *Dict. Sc.* etc., **Tubifers*, *Tubifera*, the name given by Lamarck to an order of the class *Polypi*,..whose surface is..covered with retractile hollow tubes. 1860 MAYNE *Expos. Lex.*, *Tubiferus*,..bearing tubes: *tubiferous. 1888 ROLLESTON & JACKSON *Anim. Life* 246 A Cyclostomatous Polyzoan,.. which with its aggregated calcareous cells presents an appearance not unlike that of a small *tubiflorous flower belonging to a plant of the order *Compositæ*. 1745 NEEDHAM *Microsc. Disc.* Introd. 6 The Barnacle..a small *tubiform Animal,..adhering in Clusters to Rocks. 1880 GÜNTHER *Fishes* 57 A pair of small tubiform bones, the turbinals. 1891 *Cent. Dict.*, *Tubilingual. 1882 W. A. FORBES in *Rep. Challenger Exped.*, *Zool.* IV. 64 One branch of this stock has since become greatly modified in the *Tubinarial direction. 1895 *Funk's Stand. Dict.*, *Tubinarine. 1890 *Q. Jrnl. Microsc. Sc.* June 186 *note*, Such thoracic nephridia in other sedentary annelids have been called '*tubiparous glands' by Claparède and others. 1800 HATCHETT in *Phil. Trans.* XC. 333 In the interstices of the *Tubipore. 1846 DANA *Zooph.* iv. (1848) 68 In the Tubipores, the polyps form, by their secretions, parallel tubes. 1876 PAGE *Adv. Text-bk. Geol.* xviii. 353 The tubipore cherts and flints of the mountain limestone. 1895 *Funk's Stand. Dict.*, *Tubiporid. 1828 WEBSTER, **Tubiporite*. 1895 *Funk's Stand. Dict.*, *Tubiporoid. 1848 SMART, **Tubiporous*, pertaining to, or resembling tubipores. 1882 OGILVIE, **Tubivalve*, an annelid [*sic*: *read* mollusc] of the order Tubicolidæ. 1891 *Cent. Dict.*, Tubivalve *n.* and *a.*

† **Tubi·cinate**, *v. Obs. rare*⁻⁰. [f. med.L. *tubicināt-*, ppl. stem of *tubicināre*, f. L. *tubicen* trumpeter, f. *tuba* trumpet + *canĕre* to sing, play.] (See quot.) So † **Tubicina·tion** (*obs. rare*⁻⁰).
1656 BLOUNT *Glossogr.*, *Tubicinate*.., to sound the Trumpet. 1658 PHILLIPS, *Tubicination*,..a sounding of a Trumpet, Pipe, or Cornet.

Tubing (tiū·biŋ), *vbl. sb.* [f. TUBE *v.* or *sb.* + -ING [1].] The action of furnishing with a tube or tubes; also *concr.* tubes collectively, or as a material; a length or piece of tube. Also *attrib.*
1845 I. FARRELL *Archimedean Railw.* 8 This rail is made of iron tubing. 1854 J. SCOFFERN in *Orr's Circ. Sc.*, *Chem.* 350 India-rubber tubing can be obtained. 1881 RAYMOND *Mining Gloss.*, *Tubing*, lining a deep bore-hole by driving down iron tubes. 1886 J. BARROWMAN *Sc. Mining Terms* 69 *Tubing*, sheet-iron lining of a bore-hole. 1909 *Installation News* III. 112/1 Any carpenter could locate the weak spots in tubing work.

Tubman, tub-man (tʊ·bmæ̆n). [f. TUB *sb.* + MAN *sb.* [1]]
† 1. = TUB-PREACHER. *Obs.*
1642 P. BLAND *Royall Position* 9 No Conventicling Tubman should have made my words his text. a 1643 LD. FALKLAND, etc. *Infallibility* (1646) 97 The meanest Seducer may doe mischiefe, as we finde by the effects of the Tubmen. 1651 JANE Εἰκὼν Ἀκλαστος 213 Tubmen whose prayers not only want salt, but are besmeared with prophanes.
2. † a. ? A maker of tubs, a cooper. *Obs.* b. At Christ's Hospital, formerly, one who had charge of the latrine tubs; now, a lavatory attendant.
1677 (*title*) A Caution to Married Couples..how a man having beat his wife, murthered a Tub-man that endeavoured to stop him from killing her. 1723 *Lond. Gaz.* No. 6196/7 John Thumwood,..Tub-man. c 1865 *Skit Christ's Hospital*, Has she a round of butter'd toast to give to tubman Joe?
3. A barrister in the Court of Exchequer whose place was beside the tub used as a measure of capacity in excise cases; the position conferred the right of precedence in motions, except over the 'postman' and in Crown business. Cf. POSTMAN [3]. *Obs.* exc. *Hist.*
1768 BLACKSTONE *Comm.* III. iii. 28 *note*, In the court of exchequer two of the most experienced barristers called the *post*-man and the *tub*-man..have also a precedence in motions. 1841 MEESON & WELSBY *Rep.* VII. 188 The Attorney-General moved in this case. The Postman and Tubman claimed pre-audience; but upon the Attorney-General's stating that it was the Queen's business in which he moved, the Court decided that he was entitled to be heard before the Postman and Tubman. 1882 *Daily News* 15 Dec. 2/1 With the appointment of Mr. Anstie as a Queen's Counsel, the ancient office of tubman to the Exchequer disappears. 1886 [see POSTMAN [3]].

† **Tu·bnell**. *Obs. rare*⁻¹. [app. irreg. dim. of TUB *sb.*, or arbitrary alteration of TURNEL.] A small tub.
1688 R. HOLME *Armoury* III. xiv. (Roxb.) 18/1 This conteineing half a Barrell of water or something lesse, is called a Tub; if lesse a Tubnell, that is vulgarly a Turnell.

Tubo- (tiūbo), used in certain cases as combining form of L. *tubus* TUBE (instead of the usual Latin form TUBI-: see -O) in several terms of zoology, anatomy, etc. a. *Zool.* in adjs. denoting a combination of tubular with some other form, as *tu:bo-labe·llate*, *-na·riform*. b. *Anat.*, etc. in terms relating to the Fallopian (rarely, the Eustachian) tube in connexion with some other part; chiefly adjs., as *tu:bo-abdo·minal* (pertaining to or occurring in the Fallopian tube and the abdomen), *-ligame·ntous*, *-ova·rian*, *-peritone·al*, *-u·terine*, *-vagi·nal*; *tu:bo-ty·mpanal* (pertaining to the Eustachian tube and the tympanum); rarely sbs., as *tu:bo-ovario·tomy* (excision of the Fallopian tube and ovary).
1846 DANA *Zooph.* (1848) 432 The nariform calicle is tubular at base—tubo-nariform. *Ibid.* 444 Corallum having the calicles tubo-labellate. 1857 BULLOCK *Cazeaux' Midwif.* 245 Tubo-ovarian Pregnancy. *Ibid.* 246 Tubo-abdominal Pregnancy. 1889 J. M. DUNCAN *Lect. Dis. Women* viii. (ed. 4) 243 An interstitial pregnancy may become tubo-uterine. 1900–13 DORLAND *Med. Dict.*, *Tuboligamentous*, pertaining to an oviduct and a broad ligament. *Tubo-ovarial*, *tubo-ovarian*,..*Tubo-ovariotomy*,..*Tubeperitoneal*, *Tubotympanal*,..*Tubovaginal*.

Tu·b-prea:cher. [See TUB *sb.* 4.] One who preaches from a 'tub' (TUB *sb.* 4); a dissenting preacher or minister (*contemptuous*). So **Tu·b-prea:ching** *sb.* and *a.*
1643 *xiv Art. of Treason exhib. I. Pennington* 5 Stephan Evans, alias Prince of Morocco, Knight of the Burning Pestle, Salter, and Tub-preacher, on Snow Hill. 1661 J. DAVIES *Civ. Warres* xxxii. 52 Tub-Preachings and Conventicle-Lectures were listened to as to Oracles. a 1670 HACKET *Abp. Williams* II. (1693) 165 Your lawful Ministers..to whom ..you do not resort,..but to Tub-preachers in Conventicles. 1719 D'URFEY *Pills* IV. 14 The Tub-preaching Saint was so zealous a Blade. 1899 S. R. GARDINER *Cromwell* 48 Those who looked down with scorn on the vagaries of the tub-preacher.

† **Tu·b-brugge.** *Obs. rare.* Also 3 **tobrugge**, 4 **tuybrugge**. [The second part is the ME. *brugge*, BRIDGE; the first is uncertain; perh. a deriv. of OE. *togian* or *tēon* to draw (see TOW *v.* [1], TEE *v.* [1]): cf. Ger. *zugbrücke*, MHG. *zogebrucke*, drawbridge.] A drawbridge.
1297 R. GLOUC. (Rolls) 11257 Þe castel brugge..he barnde fram þen ende To þe tobrugge [*v.r.* tuybrugge] along. *Ibid.* 11595 Þe tu brugge [*v.r.* tun brugge] hii drowe vp.

† **Tu·bster.** *Obs.* [f. TUB *sb.* + -STER.] A tub-preacher. (*Contemptuous*.)
1681 T. FLATMAN *Heraclitus Ridens* No. 45 (1713) II. 34 A certain Dissenting Tubster, who told his Audience, he would..divide the Observations he should make from his Text, into forty eight Particulars. 1682 *Ibid.* No. 82. 248 Why, if we should lay down,..the Tubsters would appoint a solemn Day of Thanksgiving among themselves. 1700 T. BROWN *Amusem. Ser. & Com.* 121 He, says the Tubster, that would be Rich.., must play the Thief or the Cheat.

Tu·b-thu:mper.
1. A speaker or preacher who for emphasis thumps the pulpit; a violent or declamatory preacher or orator; a ranter.
1662 H. FOULIS *Hist. Plots Pretended Saints* 80 Tub-thumpers, a sort of people more antick in their Devotions than Don Buscos Fencing-Master. 1720–1 *Lett. fr. Mist's Jrnl.* (1722) II. 225 An honest Presbyterian Tub-thumper, who has lost his Voice with bawling to his Flock. 1864 *Athenæum* 27 Aug. 267/3 Preachers, humorous tub-thumpers. 1908 *Daily Chron.* 3 Nov. 5/7 It would reduce the M.P... to the position of a Temperance tub-thumper.
2. A cooper. *humorous dial.*
1872 HARTLEY *Yorks. Ditties* Ser. I. 98 At last au set up as tub-thumper. 1880 L. J. JENNINGS *Rambles* 110 'A tub-thumper?'..'Ay Mister—what you call a cooper.'
So **Tu·b-thu:mping** *sb.* and *a.*
1883 *Contemp. Rev.* Aug. 253 Very modest gifts, belonging to what may be called the tub-thumping school of oratory. 1894 *Westm. Gaz.* 22 Aug. 1/2 What we demand is not a display of tub-thumping at the fag-end of a Session,..but a deliberate plan of campaign, carefully thought out and doggedly pursued. 1909 *Times* 21 Mar., A democratic election, with all its tub-thumping and unreasoning passion and sheer noise.

Tubular (tiū·biŭlăɹ), *a.* [f. L. *tubul-us* a small tube, a pipe + -AR; cf. F. *tubulaire* (1771 in *Dict. Trévoux*).]
1. Having the form of a tube or pipe; constituting or consisting of a tube; cylindrical, hollow, and open at one or both ends; tube-shaped.
Tubular bridge, a bridge formed of a great tube or hollow beam, usually of wrought iron, through which the roadway passes.
1673 GREW *Anat. Trunks* I. iv. § 15 The Pins being also conceived to be Tubular. 1827 FARADAY *Chem. Manip.* xvi. (1842) 405 These tubular vessels may be supported with facility..upon the table across two or three pieces of glass. 1850 E. CLARK (*title*) The Britannia and Conway Tubular Bridges. 1875 YEATS *Techn. Hist. Comm.* 243 The idea of tubular bricks is not new, for they were used by the Romans.
b. *Bot.*: *esp.* applied to a flower or floret consisting mainly of a tube, with small or inconspicuous limb; *spec.* to such florets in a composite flower (opp. to LIGULATE).
1776 J. LEE *Introd. Bot.* Explan. Terms 396 *Tubulosa*, Florets that are all tubular and equal. 1807 J. E. SMITH *Phys. Bot.* 457 Flowers..with united tubular anthers. 1877–84 F. E. HULME *Wild Fl.* p. vii, Primrose,—Calyx tubular, five-toothed. 1880 GRAY *Struct. Bot.* vi. § 5 (ed. 6) 248 *Tubular*..strictly..denotes a gamophyllous perianth with limb inconspicuous..as in Trumpet Honeysuckle.
c. *Zool.* and *Anat.*
1794 SULLIVAN *View Nat.* II. 175 Those of the coral class, of a ramified and tubular form. 1808 BINGLEY *Anim. Biog.* (1813) I. 46 The tongue..in several [insects]..is fleshy and tubular. 1872 COUES *N. Amer. Birds* 29 Rounded nostrils may have a raised border or rim; when this is prolonged they are called tubular.
2. Relating to, or performed by means of, a tube.
a 1716 R. COTES *Lect.* (1738) A vj, Experiments for the most part tubular.
3. Constructed with or consisting of a number of tubes; as a *tubular boiler* (see also TUBULOUS 2 b and cf. *tubular-flued*).
1804 TROUGHTON in *Nicholson's Philos. Jrnl.* Dec. 225 (*title*) Description of a Tubular Pendulum. *Ibid.* 228 The first pendulum which I made of the tubular kind, had only three steel wires, and one tube above the bob. 1819 *Pantologia* s. v. *Pendulum*, We may date the invention of the tubular pendulum..about the year 1775. 1825 J. NICHOLSON *Operat. Mechanic* 517 Troughton's tubular-pendulum ..is constructed of an exterior tube of brass,..within which is another tube, and five brass wires in its belly. 1858 SIMMONDS *Dict. Trade*, *Tubular-boiler*, a boiler consisting of tubes. 1862 *Catal. Internat. Exhib.*, *Brit.* II. No. 6132 Metallic tubular bedsteads. 1877 KNIGHT *Dict. Mech.*, *Tubular Boiler*, a name properly applicable to a steam-boiler in which the water circulates in pipes,..the fire encircling them.
4. a. *Path.* (See quot.) ? *Obs.*
1822–7 GOOD *Study Med.* (1829) I. 287 Diarrhœa Tubularis. Tubular Looseness. The dejections consisting more or less of membrane-like tubes, whitish, viscous, and inodorous. *Ibid.* V. 49 Tubular diarrhœa.
b. *Phys.* and *Path.* Applied to a high-pitched respiratory murmur, like the sound made by blowing through a tube, heard normally over the trachea and bronchial tubes, and in diseased conditions over the lung.
1834 J. FORBES *Laennec's Dis. Chest* (ed. 4) 119 The stethoscope detected..no other respiratory sound, but that of a dry respiration, evidently tubular or bronchial. 1898 *Allbutt's Syst. Med.* V. 205 The breath-sounds are tubular or cavernous—the term 'tubular' is used here as synonymous with bronchial.
5. *Comb.*, as *tubular-shaped*; *esp.* in *Bot.* with another adj., denoting a combination of tubular with another form, as *tubular-campanulate*, *-urceolate*; **tubular-flued**, having tubular flues.
1815 J. SMITH *Panorama Sc. & Art* II. 825 In a proper cylindrical, almost tubular-shaped vessel, two feet high. 1840 *Encycl. Brit.* (ed. 7) XX. 674/2 These tubular-flued boilers are at the present day extensively used. 1847 W. E. STEELE *Field Bot.* 118 [*Erica*] *Mediterranea*. Cor[olla] tubular-urceolate. 1870 HOOKER *Stud. Flora* 379 Polygonatum...Perianth tubular-campanulate.
Hence **Tubularity** (-æ·rĭti), the quality of being tubular, tubular form of structure; **Tu·bularly** *adv.*, in a tubular manner, so as to form a tube.
1746 DA COSTA in *Phil. Trans.* XLIV. 402 Such different Effects as Solidity and Tubularity. 1856 R. SHIELD *Pract. Hints Moths & Butterfl.* 74 In tubularly rolled leaves of honeysuckle we shall find the larvæ. 1890 *Manch. Exam.* 20 June, The special advantage of tubularity in bells seems

to be that they are only heard in the immediate neighbourhood.

Tubularian (tiūbiŭlēᵊ·riăn), *a.* and *sb. Zool.* [f. mod.L. *Tubulāria* (in Linnæus, 1755, f. *tubulus* TUBULE) + -AN.] a. *adj.* Belonging to the Linnæan genus *Tubularia*, the group *Tubulariæ*, or the family *Tubulariidæ*, of gymnoblastic Hydrozoa, in which the polyps are of tubular form, protected by a perisarc, with naked hydranths. b. *sb.* A tubularian hydroid. Also **Tubularidan** (-æ·ridăn) *a.* and *sb.* in same sense (*Cent. Dict.* 1891).
1859 *Todd's Cycl. Anat.* V. 296/2 In the Tubularian Polyp the canal is modified. 1864 WEBSTER, *Tubularian*,..one of a family of polypoid acalephs, having simple or branched horny tubes, and terminating above in polyp-like extremities. 1883 *Science* I. 196/2 The Anthomedusæ (e.g., *Margelis*), from the tubularian hydroids. 1888 ROLLESTON & JACKSON *Anim. Life* 247 A Campanularian differs from a Tubularian in three important respects.

Tubulary (tiū·biŭlări), *sb. Zool.* [ad. mod.L. *Tubulāria*: see prec.] † a. ? A tubular species of coral. *Obs.* b. = TUBULARIAN *sb.*
1708 *Phil. Trans.* XXVI. 79 *Tubularia*, The Tubulary, or Lesser Pipe-shell. [1753 CHAMBERS *Cycl. Supp.*, *Tubularia Fossilis*,..a species of coral found very often fossile in Germany and Italy, and composed of a great number of tubes.] 1876 *Beneden's Anim. Parasites* iv. 84 The tubulary observed by Gwyn Jeffreys..perhaps belongs to the same species.

† **Tu·bulary**, *a. Obs.* [f. as TUBULAR: see -ARY [2].] = TUBULAR.
1673 *Phil. Trans.* VIII. 6133 Lignous, consisting of Tubulary vessels. 1673 GREW *Anat. Trunks* I. iv. § 10 Sometimes the Pith is hollow or Tubulary. 1754 ELLIS in *Phil. Trans.* XLVIII. 506 That genus of corallines which I have called tubulary.

Tubulate (tiū·biŭlĕt), *a. Nat. Hist.* [ad. L. *tubulāt-us*, f. *tubul-us* TUBULE: see -ATE [2].] Formed into or like a tube; tubular.
1753 CHAMBERS *Cycl. Supp.* App. s. v. *Petal*, The tubulate bell-fashioned flowers. 1760 J. LEE *Introd. Bot.* II. xxii. (1765) 124 Syngenesia...Characters of the Florets...Corolla ..is either *tubulate*..; *ligulate* [etc.]. 1846 DANA *Zooph.* (1848) 151 A few tubulate pores over the surface. 1872 NICHOLSON *Palæont.* 74 The group of the Tubulate Corals is now much reduced in numbers.

Tubulate (tiū·biŭleⁱt), *v.* [f. as prec.: see -ATE [3]; cf. *tubulation*.] *trans.* a. To form into a tube. b. 'To furnish with a tube' (*Cent. D.* 1891).
1802 W. TAYLOR in *Monthly Mag.* XIII. 207 A wooden cullender..the orifices of which have in the center a wire or skewer, which tubulates the extruded dough [macaroni].

Tubulated (tiū·biŭleⁱtĕd), *a.* [f. L. *tubulāt-us* TUBULATE *a.* + -ED [1].]
1. Furnished with a tube; *esp.* of a retort or receiver: Having a short tube with a stopper (*tubulature* or *tubulure*), through which substances can be introduced.
1663 BOYLE *Usef. Exp. Nat. Philos.* II. v. vii. 173 This kind of Vessel is inferior to those tubulated Retorts. 1758 REID tr. *Macquer's Chym.* I. 176 Some retorts are also made with an opening on their upper side, like that of tubulated glass alembics,..closed..with a glass stopple. 1831 BREWSTER *Nat. Magic* xii. (1833) 343 To expose nitrate of ammonia in a tubulated glass retort to the heat of an Argand's lamp.
2. Formed into, or like, a tube; longitudinally perforated; tubular.
1713 DERHAM *Phys. Theol.* IX. i. 437 The Teeth are tubulated, for the Conveyance..of the Poyson into the Wound. 1753 CHAMBERS *Cycl. Supp.* s. v. *Tubulated Flower*, The tubulated floscules generally compose the disk [of *Compositæ*], and the ligulated ones the radius of the compound flowers. 1774 PRINGLE *Torpedo* 28 Those singular tubulated organs of the torpedo consist..of many bodies of a prismatic form. 1859 SEMPLE *Diphtheria* 96 Some slender and tubulated fragments of false membranes, mixed with mucus, were expelled.
So **Tubulation** (-ēⁱ·ʃən) [ad. L. *tubulātiōn-em*, n. of action f. *tubul-us*, TUBULE, as if from **tubulāre*], the process of making or becoming tubular; **Tubulature** (tiū·biŭlătiŭɹ) [see -URE], the tube of a tubulated retort: = TUBULURE.
1656 BLOUNT *Glossogr.*, *Tubilation* [*ed.* 1674 *Tubulation*] (*tubulatio*), a making hollow like pipes. 1827 FARADAY *Chem. Manip.* vii. (1842) 201 The tubulature is safest when it is not much thicker than the retort at the part where they join, but should thicken upwards. 1855 *Q. Jrnl. Chem. Soc.* VII. 98 The liquid..was placed in a retort with a thermometer in the tubulature. 1866 *Reader* No. 163. 154/1 Pseudopodial tubulation.

Tubule (tiū·biŭl). [ad. L. *tubul-us*, dim. of *tubus* TUBE; cf. F. *tubule* (Cotgr.).] A small tube; a minute tubular structure in an animal or plant body, as the *Malpighian* or *uriniferous tubules* of the kidney, the *dentinal tubules* of the teeth, etc.
1677 tr. *Groeneveldt's Treat. Stone* 19 The stone growing in the tubule or pelvis of the kidney. 1699 J. WOODWARD in *Phil. Trans.* XXI. 211 Reduced to single Corpuscles, all fit to enter the Tubules and Vessels of Plants. 1867 J. HOGG *Microsc.* II. i. 333 Contrivances to enable the tubules of the woody tissues to discharge their contents. 1869 HUXLEY *Phys.* xii. 322 The chief constituent of a tooth is dentine... It presents innumerable, minute, parallel, wavy tubules... The wider ends of these tubules open into the pulp cavity.
Hence **Tu·bulet** [-ET], a minute tubule.
1826 KIRBY & SP. *Entomol.* III. xxxiii. 363 *Tubulus* (the Tubulet), The tube or retractile base of the *Rostellum*. *Siphunculus* (the Siphuncle), the real instrument of suction, which when unemployed is retracted within the tubulet.

Tubuli- (tiū·biŭli), combining form of mod.L. *tubulus* TUBULE, in several scientific terms. **Tu:bulibra·nch** (-bræŋk), **Tu:bulibra·nchian** *Zool.*, *sb.* a member of the *Tubulibranchiata*, branchiate gastropod molluscs with tubular shells, in Cuvier's classification; *adj.* = next. **Tu:bulibra·nchiate**, *adj.* belonging to the *Tubulibranchiata*; *sb.* = prec. **Tu·bulico:le**, *Zool.* [L. *-cola* inhabitant], *sb.* a member of the *Tubulicolæ* in Cuvier's classification, a tubularian; *adj.* inhabiting a tubule; belonging to the *Tubulicolæ*. **Tu:bulide·ntate** *a.*, *Zool.* [L. *dentātus* toothed], belonging to the *Tubulidentāta*, a group of edentates having compound teeth traversed by parallel vertical tubules. **Tubuli·ferous** *a.*, *Nat. Hist.* [-FEROUS], bearing tubules; *spec.* having a tubular ovipositor, as the females of certain insects. **Tu:buliflo·ral, -flo·rous** *adjs.*, *Bot.* [L. *flōs*, *flōr-em* flower], belonging to the division *Tubulifloræ* of Composite plants, having either all the florets, or those of the disk, tubular. **Tu·bulifo:rm** *a.*, having the form of a tubule, tubular. **Tu·bulipo:re**, *Zool.* [L. *porus* PORE], a polyzoan of the genus *Tubulipora* or family *Tubuliporidæ*, having tubular calcareous calicles; also **Tubuli·porid** (*Funk's Stand. Dict.* 1895). **Tubuli·poroid** *a.* [see -OID], resembling, or having the characters of, the family *Tubuliporidæ* (*Cent. Dict.* 1891).
1855 T. WILLIAMS in *Ann. & Mag. Nat. Hist.* Ser. II. XVI. 408 The two preceding *Tubulibranchs. *Ibid.* 407 The *Tubulibranchiate genera. 1842 BRANDE *Dict. Sc.* etc., *Tubulibranchians...**Tubulicoles*, a name applied by Cuvier to a family of Polypes. 1822 J. PARKINSON *Outl. Oryctol.* 40 With *tubuliferous lobes. 1852 *Zoologist* X. 3405 They were certainly tubuliferous and not merely membranous appendages. 1881 M. T. MASTERS in *Jrnl. Bot.* XI. 39 The *Tubulifloral division of the Composites. 1891 *Cent. Dict.*, *Tubuliflorous. 1796 KIRWAN *Elem. Min.* (ed. 2) I. 30 **Tubuliform*, slender cylinders. 1877 HUXLEY *Anat. Inv. Anim.* vii. 381 Glands..divisible into five different kinds (aciniform, ampullate, aggregate, tubuliform, and tuberous). 1864 WEBSTER, *Tubulipore.

† **Tu·bulite.** *Obs.* [ad. mod.L. *tubulītēs*, introduced by Gesner, *Tractat. Physic. de Petrificatis*, 1758.] A fossil or petrifaction of a tube or tubular shell occupied by an animal.
Gesner specified the tubular shell of the ship-worm, a lamellibranch mollusc, the coiled tube of a *Serpula*, the tubular shell of a *Dentalium*, all then regarded as 'worms'. But as these were the shells of different animals, the word was not permanently used.
1799 KIRWAN *Geol. Ess.* 236 Common marlites..frequently [contain] shells, or petrifactions, ammonites, pectinites, tubulites. 1834 BOASE *Primary Geol.* 372 Those secondary strata, which contain tubulites and similar fossils.

Tubulo- (tiū·biŭlo), used as combining form of mod.L. *tubulus* TUBULE, instead of the usual TUBULI-, either before a word of Greek derivation, or in adverbial relation to an adj. (see -O); occurring in a few recent scientific terms. **Tu:bulocy·st** (-sist), 'any cystic dilatation of an obsolete canal or functionless duct' (Dorland *Med. Dict.* 1900–13). **Tu:bulode·rmoid**, 'a dermoid tumor due to the persistence of a fetal tube' (*ibid.*). **Tu:bulo-race·mose** (-ræsĭmōᵘs) *a.*, 'both tubular and racemose, as, a *tubuloracemose* gland' (*ibid.*). **Tu:bulosa·ccular** *a.*, 'both tubular and saccular' (*ibid.*). **Tu:bulostri·ate** *a.*, 'having the surface striated with hollow ribs, as some brachiopod and molluscan shells' (*Cent. Dict. Suppl.* 1909).
c 1900 *Buck's Handbk. Med. Sc.* VII. 10 Tubulosaccular.

Tubulose (tiū·biŭlōᵘs), *a.* [ad. mod.L. *tubulōs-us*, f. L. *tubulus* TUBULE.]
1. = next, 1. Now *rare.*
1713 J. PETIVER in *Phil. Trans.* XXVIII. 203 Small tubulose Scarlet Flowers. 1752 J. HILL *Hist. Anim.* 268 The Trigla, with a bifid rostrum, and tubulose nostrils. 1826 KIRBY & SP. *Entomol.* IV. xlvi. 312 Tongue..Tubulose... When it..is long and tubular, and capable of inflation.
2. *Palæont.* Belonging to the *Tubulosa*, a group of palæozoic corals characterized by tubular thecæ.
1891 in *Cent. Dict.*

Tubulous (tiū·biŭləs), *a.* [ad. mod.L. *tubulōs-us*; cf. F. *tubuleux* (1771 in *Dict. Trévoux*).]
1. Having the form of a tube; = TUBULAR 1.
1664 POWER *Exp. Philos.* I. 4 The stings in all Bees are hollow and tubulous. 1755 *Gentl. Mag.* Jan. 8/2 The flower is red and tubulous. 1826 SAMOUELLE *Direct. Collect. Insects & Crust.* 23 A very short tubulous haustellum.
2. Containing or composed of tubes: = TUBULAR 3. a. *Bot.* (See quot.) *rare*⁻⁰.
1864 WEBSTER, *Tubulose*, *Tubulous*..2. Containing small tubes; composed wholly of tubulous florets; as, a tubulous compound flower.
b. Of a steam boiler: Having either fire-tubes or water-tubes.
1860 *Illustr. Lond. News* 5 May 422/3 Safety-boilers (Tubulous)..are now made with water fire-box. 1892 *Spectator* 19 Mar. 386/1 The tubulous boiler [for ships]..is growing in favour both in France and America.
Hence **Tu·bulously** *adv.*, in a tubulous form; **Tu·bulousness** (Bailey, 1727, vol. II).
1818 T. NUTTALL *Genera N. Amer. Plants* II. 80 Spatha tubulously cucullate.

Tubulure (tiū·biŭliŭɹ). [a. F. *tubulure* (Baumé, 1773), f. L. *tubul-us* TUBULE: see -URE.] A short tube, or projecting opening for the insertion of a tube, in a retort or receiver. (Cf. TUBULATED 1.)
1800 tr. *Lagrange's Chem.* I. 55 Put iron filings into a jar with two tubulures,..pour into the jar through the second tubulure diluted sulphuric acid. *Ibid.* 85 Fit to one of the tubulures of the bottle another tube. 1863 TYNDALL *Heat* i. 24 This glass bulb has three tubulures. 1883 R. HALDANE *Workshop Receipts* Ser. II. 46/1 The water enters the apparatus by the tubulure.

‖ **Tubulus** (tiū·biŭlŏs). Pl. **tubuli** (-əi). [dim. of L. *tubus* TUBE.]
1. = TUBULE; in *Entom.* a tubular ovipositor.
[1681 tr. *Willis' Rem. Med. Wks.* Vocab., *Tubuli*, small little pipes, the veins and very small arteries, or little hollow parts of the bowels so called. 1704 J. HARRIS *Lex. Techn.* I, *Tubuli Lactiferi*, certain Lactiferous..Pipes..through which [the milk] flows to the Nipples.] 1826 KIRBY & SP. *Entomol.* III. xxxiii. 390 *Tubulus*. A tubular ovipositor, consisting of several pieces often retractile within each other, like the tubes of a telescope. 1878 T. BRYANT *Pract. Surg.* I. 565 The tubuli serving to convey nutrition from the pulp to the periphery.
2. = TUBULURE.
c 1900 *Buck's Handbk. Med. Sc.* IV. 784 A small tubulated receiver, from the *tubulus* of which a tube..is in air-tight communication.

Tuca(n: see TUSA. **Tucan**, var. TOUCAN.
Tucatuca, -tucu: see TUCUTUCU.

† **Tucet.** *Obs. rare*⁻¹. [ad. L. *tūcētum*, *tucc-ētum* 'a kind of sausage or haggis' (Lewis and Short); cf. It. *tocchetti* 'minced meate, shread, sliced, or cut in collops' (Florio 1598), dim. f. *tocco* piece, scrap, collop.] A collop; a small piece of meat.
1653 JER. TAYLOR *Serm. for Year* I. xvi. 212 The pulse and the leeks, Lavinian sausages, and the Cisalpine tucets or gobbets of condited bulls flesh [cf. *Schol. Persii* (Du Cange) Tucetum, bubula condita apud Gallos Cisalpinos condimentis crassis oblita et macerata].

Tuch, obs. f. TUSH *int.*
† **Tuch, tuche**, obs. ff. TOUCH (in quots. in sense 6 of TOUCH *sb.*, touchstone).
1591 HARINGTON *Orl. Fur.* XLII. lxviii, The Porch was all of Porpherie and Tuch. a 1647 HABINGTON *Surv. Worc.* in *Worc. Hist. Soc. Proc.* II. 410 Noble monuments..formed of Tuche, Marble, Alabaster and Rauns.
Tuchet, Sc. var. TEWHIT, the lapwing.
Tucht, obs. Sc. f. TOUGH. **Tucia**: see TUTTY.

Tuck (tʊk), *sb.* [1] Forms: 4–7 **tucke**, 9 *Sc.* **towk**, 6– **tuck**. [f. TUCK *v.* [1], in various senses.]
1. A fold or pleat in drapery; † in quot. 1613, a plait of the hair (*obs.*); now *spec.* a flattened fold (or one of several parallel folds) in a garment, secured by stitching, either to shorten the article or for ornamentation.
1387–8 T. USK *Test. Love* I. v. (Skeat) l. 132 That no iangling may greue the lest tucke of thy hemmes. 1591 PERCIVALL *Sp. Dict.*, *Alforza de vestido*, a plaite in a garment, a tucke. 1613 CHAPMAN *Maske Inns Court* A iv, Her tresses in tucks, braided with siluer. 1824 MACTAGGART *Gallovid. Encycl.*, *Towk*, a take up in ladies' clothing. 1861 *Gloucestershire Chron.* 21 Sept., 'What do you do when you have outgrown your clothes?' 'You throw them aside, don't you?' 'Oh, no', replied the little girl, 'we let out the tucks'. 1882 CAULFEILD & SAWARD *Dict. Needlework*, *Tucks*..are parallel folds of material, lying..on any article of dress,..either for shortening a garment, or for the purpose of ornamentation.
2. The gathering of the ends of the bottom planks of a ship under the stern; that part of the hull where the bottom planks are collected and terminated by the *tuck-rail* (see 8).
a 1625 *Nomenclator Navalis* (Harl. MS. 2301), *Ye Tuck*, the word is significant for it is (as you would saie) the verie gathering vp of the Ships quarter, vnder water. a 1687 PETTY *Treat. Naval Philos.* I. i, The..Stern-post, and Dead-rising up the Tuck. 1709 *Lond. Gaz.* No. 4510/7 The Hoy Burthen 9 or 10 Tun,..Moon shap'd in her Sleir, with a square Tuck. 1833 MARRYAT *P. Simple* xxvii, He's built like a Dutch schuyt, great breadth of beam, and very square tuck. c 1850 *Rudim. Navig.* (Weale) 157 The *tuck*, the aft-part of the ship where the ends of the planks of the bottom are terminated by the tuck-rail.
3. *Fishing.* Short for TUCK-NET.
1602 CAREW *Cornwall* 1. 30 The Tucke..is narrower meashed, and..with a long bunt in the midst. 1865 COUCH *Fishes Brit. Islands* IV. 91 To take up the fish [pilchards]..the principal sean is left undisturbed, while the volyer passes within the enclosure and lays its sean, termed the Tuck, round the former on the inner side; and then the latter is drawn together so as gradually to contract the space and raise the fish to the surface.
4. A pluck, twitch, pull, tug; in quot. 1648 referring to the 'tucking' of freshmen at Oxford: see TUCK *v.* [1] 4 b. Now only *dial.*
1648 WOOD *Life* 15 Feb. (O.H.S.) I. 139 Nothing was given him but salted drink..with tucks to boot. 1805 A. SCOTT *Poems* 105 (Jam.) Whan thou had fairly pass'd the clips, An' a' the taylor's tukes an' nips. 1887 *Suppl. to Jamieson*, *Took*, *touk*, *towk*, a tug, pluck, pull: 'He gied her sleeve a bit took'.
5. The thrusting in of the ends or edges of anything so as to secure them in position. Also with *in.*
1852 MRS. STOWE *Uncle Tom's C.* xiii, She ever and anon came to the bedside, and smoothed and arranged something about the bed-clothes, and gave a tuck here and there. 1865 DICKENS *Mut. Fr.* III. ii, The sentinel smartly giving his

rolled shirt-sleeves an extra tuck on the shoulders. 1900 *Daily Mail* 5 Feb. 7/1 The guimpe or tiny tuck-in chemisette.
b. A flap on one cover of a book, which folds over and is tucked in a band or the like on the other cover, serving to keep the book closed.
1880 *Print. Trades Jrnl.* No. 32. 30 A double tuck, rendering a clasp of any description unnecessary. 1893 [see *tuck-cover* in 8].
6. *slang.* Usually *tuck-out* (also *tuck-in*): A hearty meal; esp. in school use, a feast of delicacies, a 'blow-out'.
1823 in *Spirit Pub. Jrnls.* 232 He, being inclined for a tuck out, repaired where he was likely to meet with oysters. 1836 E. HOWARD *R. Reefer* xxxviii, Tell my steward to give them a good tuck-out and a glass of grog. 1844 J. T. HEWLETT *Parsons & W.* xv, We meant to save all our money for the tuck. 1856 F. E. PAGET *Owlet Owlst.* 172, I was at the dessert; and a jolly good tuck I had, besides. 1886 T. HARDY *Mayor Casterbr.* ix, We will have a solid, staunch tuck-in.
b. Food, eatables; *esp.* delicacies, as sweet-stuff, pastry, jam, etc. (*school slang*). Cf. TUCKER *sb.* 6.
1857 HUGHES *Tom Brown* II. v, The Slogger looks rather sodden, as if he didn't take much exercise and ate too much tuck. 1860 TYLOR *Anahuac* viii. (1861) 210 Ten or twelve of these little bowls on the table, each with a different kind of 'tuck' in it. 1899 E. PHILLPOTTS *Human Boy* IV. ii. 93 [He spoke] regretfully, as though he was being robbed of tuck.
c. A hearty appetite for food. *dial.*
1838 HOLLOWAY *Dict. Provincialisms* s. v., 'He has a pretty good Tuck of his own', means that a man is a great eater. *Hants. Sussex.* 1847–78 HALLIWELL, *Tuck* (1) to eat. Also, an appetite.
7. Phrases. † a. *Ducks and tucks* (of uncertain meaning). *Obs.*
1598 BARCKLEY *Felic. Man* (1631) 621 Covet not to win estimation..by..Frierly ducks, and such like Italian and Spanish tricks and tuckes. 1609 SIR E. HOBY *Let. to T. H[iggons]* 106 *margin*, Leaue your ducks and your tuckes, and your apish toies, and serue God in spirit and truth.
b. *Nip and tuck*: see NIP *sb.* [1] 6.
8. *attrib.* and *Comb.* (some f. the verb-stem): **tuck-basket**, a basket used in dipping the fish from the tuck-net; **tuck-boat**, in seine-fishing, a boat which carries the tuck-net; **tuck-cover** (see 5 b); **tuck-creaser**, **tuck-folder**, an attachment in a sewing-machine which marks the line of, or folds down, the next tuck in readiness for stitching (Knight *Dict. Mech.* 1877); † **tuck-hole**, a hole in a ploughshare by means of which it is hooked to the beam (cf. TUCK *v.* [1] 8, quot. 1733); **tuck-hunter**, one in search of a feast; **tuck-joint**, a joint in tuck-pointing (see TUCK-POINT); **tuck-marker** = *tuck-creaser*; **tuck-plate**, in an iron ship, a curved plate of the hull at the point where the stern-post is bolted to the transom-frame: cf. sense 2; **tuck-rail**: see quot.; **tuck-seine** = TUCK-NET. Also TUCK-MILL, -NET, -POINT, -SHOP.
1883 *Fisheries Exhib. Catal.* (ed. 4) 127 *Tuck basket for taking fish out of seine. 1855 J. R. LEIFCHILD *Cornwall Mines* 15 The '*tuck' boat then makes the inner circuit of the 'seine', the smaller net being dropped overboard as she goes. 1893 *Westm. Gaz.* 24 June 7/2 With *tuck cover (like pocket-book), and flap and pencil. 1805 R. W. DICKSON *Pract. Agric.* I. Pl. v. 40 Heel to *tuck hole of share—2 ft. 6¼ in...Tuck hole to point of share—8¼ in. 1840 A. BUNN *Stage* I. xii. 295 Nothing can stop the mouth of a *tuck-hunter. 1879 *Cassell's Techn. Educ.* IV. 226 Rough arches ..finished off with..a '*tuck joint'. This consists in marking the divisions by a neatly raised line of fine white plaster. 1877 KNIGHT *Dict. Mech.*, **Tuck-marker*, ..also known as a tuck-creaser, for making a crease on goods as a guide for width in making the next fold. c 1850 *Rudim. Navig.* (Weale) 157 **Tuck-rail*, the rail which..forms a rabbet for the purpose of caulking the butt ends of the planks of the bottom [see sense 2]. 1825 *Encycl. Lond.* XX. 435/1 [In pilchard fishing] three boats belong to each sean; the first and largest is called the sean-boat...The next boat is called the vollier (follower).., and carries another sean, called the *tuck-sean, which is about 100 fathoms long, and 18 deep...The third boat is called the lurker. 1874 [see SEINE *sb.* [1] β].

Tuck (tʊk), *sb.* [2] *arch.* and *dial.* Chiefly *Sc.* (tʊk). Forms: 5 **tuk**, 6 **tuicke**, 6–9 **touk**, 8 **tuke**, 8–9 **took**, 6– **tuck**. [f. TUCK *v.* [2]: cf. Pr. *toco*, It. *tocco* 'a stroke or knock, also a stroke of a bell or clocke', f. *toccare* 'to touch, hit, to smite, strike' (Florio).]
† 1. A blast of a trumpet. *Obs. rare*⁻¹.
c 1400 *Destr. Troy* 7107 With the tuk of a trump, ail his tore knightes He assemblit full sone.
2. A blow, a stroke, a tap; esp. in *tuck of drum.*
a 1500 *Battle of Harlaw* xv. in *Sel. Coll. Sc. Ballads* (1790) III. 17 With trumpets and with tuicke of drum. 1513 DOUGLAS *Æneis* VIII. iv. 119 Hercules it smyttis wyth a mychty touk Apon the richt half, for to mak it jouk. 1640–1 *Kirkcudbr. War-Comm. Min. Bk.* (1855) 23 Within eight days efter intimatioune be maid thairof, aither at the severall merkat croces, or by touk of drume, or by advertisement. 1710 RUDDIMAN *Douglas' Æneis* Gloss., *Touk*, stroak, blow, ..a touch, pull; as *to take a touk of any thing*, i.e. have a touch at it. 1761 in *St. Andrews Citizen* 21 Mar. (1903), Published through the city by took of drum. 1818 SCOTT *Hrt Midl.* xii, An open convocating of the king's lieges.. by touk of drum. 1892 *N. W. Devon Gloss.*, *Tuck*, a blow.
b. *fig.* or allusively.
1825 CARLYLE *Schiller* App. (1845) 259 Schubart was happy to evacuate Munich without tuck of drum. 1878 STEVENSON *Inland Voy.* 85 Wherever death..sounds his own potent tuck upon the cannons.
† 3. (?) A kiss. *Obs. rare.*
1611 COTGR., *Bouquer*, to take, or giue a tucke, or kisse.

Tuck (tʊk), *sb.* [3] *arch.* Forms: 6 **toke, tocke, touke**, *Sc.* **towk**, 6–7 **tucke**, (7 **took, touk, tuke**), 7– **tuck**. [app. ad. F. *estoc* in same sense, in OF. and Norm. dial. *étoc* = Pr. *estoc*, It. *stocco*, ad. Ger. *stock* stick.] A slender, pointed, straight, thrusting sword; a rapier. Also *transf.* and *fig.*
1508 *Acc. Ld. High Treas. Scot.* IV. 122 Item for gilting and grathing of the lang towk,..iiij li. 1525 *Rutland MSS.* (1905) IV. 267 For the delyverance of a toke to my Lorde, xxd. c 1526 *Harl. MS.* 4217 lf. 10 A longe Tocke iij square, the hafte of siluer. 1553 *Will of H. Cornish* (MS.), A gilte saddell..a touke, a dagger, stirropes spurres and a handgoune. 1566 DRANT *Horace*, *Sat.* I. A j b, The Tucke, the targe, the sheilde. 1625 DARCIE *Hist. Eliz.* III. 223 To fight..in Duels, with a Rapier called a Tucke, onely for the thrust. 1647–8 COTTERELL *Davila's Hist. Fr.* (1678) 25 Running him into the Visor with his Tuck. 1683 SIR J. TURNER *Pallas Armata* 176 Long Rapiers and Touks. 1688 R. HOLME *Armoury* III. 91/2 A Tuck [is] a four square Blade. a 1699 LADY HALKETT *Autobiog.* (1875) 63 Run through the body with a tuke. 1707 J. STEVENS tr. *Quevedo's Com. Wks.* (1709) 176 My Sword..was a stiff Tuck. 1770 LANGHORNE *Plutarch* (1879) II. 880/1 He appeared with a tuck, such as is used by robbers. 1826 SCOTT *Woodst.* i, He wore..a tuck, as it was then called, or rapier. 1885 *Harper's Mag.* Mar. 656/1 The..'tuck' or 'rapier' has been refined into the *épée* or duelling sword.
b. *attrib.* and *Comb.*, as *tuck-sheath*; **tuck-cane**, a cane in which a tuck or rapier is carried, serving as a sheath; a sword-cane; **tuck-fish**: see quot.; **tuck-stick** = *tuck-cane.*
1700 S. L. tr. *Fryke's Voy. E. Ind.* 160, I had a *tuck Cane in my hand. 1785 TRUSLER *Mod. Times* II. 18, I.. never went out afterwards, but with a tuck cane and a brace of pistols loaded. 1681 GREW *Musæum* I. v. i. 86 The Head of the *Tuck-Fish...The Snout is not so flat as in the Rapier-fish, but thicker and rounder, more like a Tuck, from whence I take leave to name it. 1506–7 *Acc. Ld. High Treas. Scot.* III. 250 Tua *towk schethis. 1765 *Lond. Chron.* 19 Dec. 588 The master run the apprentice through the body with a *tuck-stick, which killed him.

Tuck (tʊk), *v.* [1] Forms: α. 1 **túcian, túcizan**; 3–5 **tuke**, 4 **touke**, 5 **tuck**, 5–6 **toke**, 7 *Sc.* **towk**. β. 5 **tokke**, 5–6 **tukke, tuk**, 6–7 **tucke**, 5– **tuck**. [The forms of this verb fall into two distinct groups; the development of the senses also offers difficulties. The α-forms (with long vowel or diphthong) belong to senses 1 and 2 and the earlier quots. under 3; the β-forms (with short vowel) to the rest of sense 3 and all the other senses, beginning in 14th c. in senses 4, 7, and occurring in 15th c. in sense 6 (and in one or two later instances in sense 2). The latter appear to correspond to MLG. *tucken*, *tocken* to draw, pull sharply or forcibly, MDu. *tocken*, *tucken*, OHG. *zocchōn*, *zucchen* to move or remove with a jerk, snatch away, pluck, pull, mod.Ger. *zucken* to jerk, tuck, tug, *das schwert zücken*, to draw the sword. The shortening of the *ū* in OE. *túcian*, early ME. *tuke*, etc. to *u* (*ʊ*) in *tuck* is notable, but is paralleled by that of OE. *súcan* to SUCK; cf. also DUCK *v.* from ME. *dūke(n)*.]
† 1. *trans.* To afflict by way of punishment; to punish, chastise; to ill-treat, torment. *Obs.*
c 888 K. ÆLFRED *Boeth.* xxxviii. § 7 Lustlice hi woldon lætan þa rican hi tucian æfter hiora agnum willan. a 1000 *Boeth. Metr.* xxiv. 60 Unrihtwise eorðan cyningas..Þe þis werige folc wyrst tuciað. c 1000 ÆLFRIC *Judg.* xv. 8 He.. heora fela ofslol, and to sceame tucode. c 1000 — *Saints' Lives* xxiii. 715 Swingan and to ealre sorge tucigan. c 1200 *Trin. Coll. Hom.* 21 His heued [was] beled mid þornene crune and on fele wise [he was] rewliche tuked. a 1225 *Ancr. R.* 366 He..was..so scheomeliche ituked. c 1230 *Hali Meid.* 17 Leccherie..tukeð hire [maidenhood] al to wundre & þreat to don hire schome.
† b. *intr. Obs.*
a 1250 *Owl & Night.* 63 Þu tukest wroþe & vuele Hwar þu myht ouer smale vowele.
† 2. *fig.* To reprove, check, rebuke, find fault with; to upbraid, reproach. *Obs.*
In quot. 1584 with *up* (but sense doubtful).
a 1225 *Leg. Kath.* 550 Ha tukeð ure godes to balewe & to bismere. a 1225 *Ancr. R.* 316 Þet is tocne of hatunge þet men tukeð to wundre þet þing þet me hateð swuðe. 1584 B. R. tr. *Herodotus* II. 99 The vassals hauing ended their speeche, Protheus turned hymselfe to Alexander, and tucked hym vp with thys rounde tale. 1600 in *Maitland Club Misc.* (1843) III. 102 Towking outragious countenance. 1616 *Orkney Witch Trial* in Rogers *Soc. Life Scot.* (1886) III. 298 She haid tuckit him and given him mony injurious wordis. 1651 R. BAILLIE *Lett. & Jrnls.* (1841) III. 163 His brother Adam Wilson towks him, calling him a fool and bidding him desist.
3. To dress or finish (cloth) after it comes from the weaver, esp. to stretch on tenters; cf. TUCKER *sb.* 1; also *intr.* to work as a tucker. Now *local.*
α. [1273: implied in TUCKER *sb.* 1.] 1377 LANGL. *P. Pl.* B. xv. 447 Cloth þat cometh fro þe weuyng is nouȝt comly to were, Tyl it is fulled vnder fote or in fullyng stokkes, Wasshen wel with water and with taseles cracched, Ytouked, and ytented. 1459 in *10th Rep. Hist. MSS. Comm.* App. v. 300 It was ordayned that no woman sholde touke in no manere place aforstrete within the saide citie. 1467–8 *Rolls of Parlt.* V. 621/2 Yef..the seid Cloth [were] toked and fulled within this your Reame, your Highnes should have the Custume and Awnage for the same. 1513–14 *Act* 5 *Hen. VIII*, c. 2 Noo person make noo such Clothys..to sell without that be he whan he is rawe redy to be tokyd of the brede of a yerde and half quarter.
β. 1621 in Harding *Hist. Tiverton* (1817) II. 181 Not.. white weavers or tuckers that make white kersies, but.. such as weave and tuck upon coloured mixed kerseys. 1780 A. YOUNG *Tour Irel.* II. 34 A mill for milling, tucking, &c. broad cloths. 1837 WHITTOCK, etc. *Bk. Trades* (1842) 255 After the process of fulling and dyeing, the dressed cloths are..pricked on the tenter hooks and stretched to their utmost bearing...This is considered as *tucking*, in the west of England. 1882 JAGO *Cornw. Gloss.*, *Tucking*, working in a fulling-mill.
4. † To tug at; to snatch, pluck, pull; to gather (herbs, fruit, etc.) (*obs.*); now *spec.* to pluck or pull the loose hay from the sides of (a new rick) (*dial.*).
13.. *K. Alis.* 2305 (Bodl. MS.), Als he hit [his weapon] tukked [*v.r.* toggid] out to habbe, Philot hym ȝaf anothere dabbe. 1625 T. GODWIN *Moses & Aaron* III. iii. 125 They held it vnlawfull, to roste an apple, to tucke an herbe, to climbe a tree, to kill or catch a flea. 1658 tr. *Porta's Nat. Magic* IV. xi. 136 You must tuck them off the Tree with your hand. *Ibid.* [see TUCKER *sb.* 2]. 1794 P. FOOT *Agric. Middlesex* 57 The hay-farmer pays great attention to have the stack well tucked and thatched. 1888 ELWORTHY *W. Somerset Word-bk.* s.v., Now, Bob, don't bethink thy vingers, tuck'n in tight, mind—i.e. pull it out until you get to the solid mass.
† b. See quot. 1647. *Obs.*
c 1640 SHAFTESB. in *Remin. Oxford* (O.H.S.) 37, I caused that ill custom of tucking freshmen [at Oxford] to be left off. 1647 WOOD *Life* Dec. (O.H.S.) I. 134 If any of the freshmen came off dull, or not cleverly, some of the forward or pragmatical seniors would 'tuck' them, that is, set the nail of their thumb to their chin, just under the lower lipp, and by the help of their other fingers under the chin, they would give him a mark, which sometimes would produce blood.
5. *Fishing.* To take the fish from (the seine) by means of a *tuck-net*; also with the fish as object.
1786 *Act 26 Geo. III*, c. 26 § 11 (Cod fishing) It shall not be lawful..to use..any Sean or Net..for the Purpose of catching Cod Fish by hauling such Sean or Net on Shore, or tucking such Sean or Net into any Boat or Boats, the Scale or Mesh of which said Sean or Net shall be less in Dimension than Four Inches. 1857 *Morning Chron.* 28 Aug. (Cassell's), 185 hogsheads [of pilchards] were tucked on Sunday. 1866 *Standard* 3 Oct. 3/4 All these [i.e. seines] have enclosed fish, which are being tucked, and many thousands of hogsheads are expected to be landed. 1879 *Encycl. Brit.* IX. 254/2 'Tucking' the fish..is performed with the tuck-sean,..and as it is hauled in, the foot of the bunt is raised so as to bring the fish to the surface, whence they are dipped out in large baskets and put into attendant boats to be carried on shore.
6. To pull or gather up in a fold or folds; to fold or turn up; *esp.* to gird up (a garment, etc.). Usually const. *up.*
c 1440 *Promp. Parv.* 504/2 Tukkyn vp, or stykkyn vp (*K.* tuckyn or stychyn up clothis),..*suffarcino*. 1513 DOUGLAS *Æneis* v. x. 21 Thair haris all war tukkit wp on thar croun. 1523 FITZHERB. *Husb.* § 151 Theyr cotes be so syde [=long] that they be fayne to tucke them vp whan they ryde. 1590 SPENSER *F. Q.* III. ix. 21 Her well-plighted frock, which she did won To tucke about her short when she did ryde. 1687 A. LOVELL tr. *Thevenot's Trav.* I. 156 They are tuck'd aside, that the Diamonds may not be covered. 1756 MRS. CALDERWOOD in *Coltness Collect.* (Maitl. Cl.) 218 All the Capucines..were marching in sixes and sevens with their gowns tucked up, great fat carles. 1835–6 *Todd's Cycl. Anat.* I. 479/1 The intestines are.. tucked up into folds and sacs. 1840 DICKENS *Old C. Shop* iii, He tucked up his sleeves and squared his elbows. 1880 'OUIDA' *Moths* I. 77 The stout north countrywoman tucked up her petticoats, and began to climb up the steep path with a will. 1885 *Cornh. Mag.* Mar. 283 Priests sitting with their legs tucked up tailor-wise, in the attitude of Buddha.
b. To put a tuck or tucks in; to shorten or ornament with tucks.
1626 *Vestry Bks.* (Surtees) 181 Item for tuckeinge up the surples, xij d. 1709 [see TUCKED *ppl. a.* 1]. 1873 ELIZ. PHELPS *Trotty's Wedding Tour* 126 She tucked the pantalets, darned the stockings.
7. To pull or gather up and confine the loose garments of; to gird (a person) *up.* Chiefly in *pa. pple.* Now *rare.*
c 1385 CHAUCER *L. G. W.* 982 (*Dido*) Saw ȝe..Onye of myne susteryn..I-tukkid [*v.r.* Itucked] vp with arwis in hire cas? c 1386 — *Sompn. T.* 29 With scrippe and tipped staf, ytukked [*v.rr.* tucked, tukked, tokked] hye In euery hous, he gan to poure and prye. c 1440 *Generydes* 4397 Tokkyd vppe she [the queen] was well fro the grounde. c 1450 in Aungier *Syon* (1840) 342 Some of the brethren tukke the mynysters..in the begynnyng of masse, and also tuk the confessour whan he taketh the cope aboute the ende of the same masse. 1483 CAXTON *Gold. Leg.* 160/2 A pylgrym tucked and made redy for to goo hastely ouer see. 1558 PHAER *Æneid* I. Bj, Tukt she was that naked was her knee. 1566 DRANT *Horace*, *Sat.* viii. D viij b, Bare foote, hyr lockes about her heade, ytuckde in pukishe frocke. 1787 [see TUCKED *ppl. a.* 1]. a 1801 BLOOMFIELD *Rural T.*, *Rich. & Kate* xi, Who, snug tuck't up, walk'd slow behind. 1841 ORDERSON *Creol.* ix. 96 She was..'tucked up', in the indecorous manner of those days.
b. To shorten or short-coat (an infant). Usually with *up. dial.*
1888 ELWORTHY *W. Somerset Word-bk.* s.v., I was a-frightened to zee the cheel a-tuck'd up a'ready. 1901 E. PHILLPOTTS *Striking Hours* 135 Afore I was tucked-up, or, as you might say, 'short-coated', her went..down to Cornwall. a 1905 in *Eng. Dial. Dict.* s.v., Tuck it in May, Tuck it away.
c. *fig.* To cramp or hamper by lack of space, time, or means. See also TUCKED *ppl. a.* 2 c.
1886 *Field* 13 Feb. 179/3 They [fox-hunters] have been

Supplement, p. 3873; Corrigenda, p. 4092; Spurious words, p. 4093; Books quoted, p. 4094

Tuftedness ... **Tufter** ... **Tuft-hunter** ... **Tufty** ...

Tug ... **Tugger** ... **Tugging** ...

Tuilyie, tulyie, tulie, tuilzie.

Tuition ... **Tuitional** ... **Tuitive** ... **Tuism** ...

Tulip ... **Tulip-tree** ... **Tulip-wood** ...

Tulwar. Also **talwar.** [Hindī]

Tuly, *a.* *Obs.* Forms: 4 tuli, tuly, tuely, twily, 4–5 tewly, 5 toly. [app. a. OF. *tuly*, *tulé* red colour, f. *Toulouse*, the city.]

Tumbester, *Obs.* Also 4–5 tombester(e, tombestere, 5 -istere. [Feminine of OE. *tumbere* tumbler, dancer, acrobat: see **-STER**. Cf. OF. *tumberesse*, *tumeresse* (f. *tombeur* to fall), in same sense (13th c. Godef.).] A female tumbler or dancer. *See also* TUMBLESTER.

Tumble (tŏ·mb'l), *sb.* [f. next.] An act of tumbling; the condition of being tumbled.

1. An act of acrobatic tumbling; an acrobatic feat. *rare.*

2. An accidental fall; also, the falling of a stream.

3. Tumbled condition; disorder, confusion, disturbance; a confused or tangled heap.

4. In phrase ROUGH-AND-TUMBLE.

Tumble (tŏ·mb'l), *v.* Also 4–6 tumbil, 4–7 tomble, 5 towmble, tumbell, -bill (also 6 Sc.), 5–6 tombell, 6 toumble; 4 tumblen, etc. [ME. *tumbel*, etc. = MLG., LG., mod.Ger. (*tummeln*), Du. *tuimelen*, etc.; frequent. f. the stem in OE. *tumbian*.]

I. *intr.* To fall; *esp.* to fall in a helpless manner, from stumbling or violence; to be precipitated, fall headlong; also said of a stream falling in a cataract.

II. 3. *intr.* To fall in a helpless manner, from stumbling or violence; to be precipitated, fall headlong.

III. *intr.* Of the sides of a ship: To incline or slope inwards above the point of extreme breadth; to contract above the point of extreme breadth. Opposed to FLARE *v.* Also *transf.*

Tumbler (tŏ·mbləɹ), *sb.* [f. TUMBLE *v.* + -ER[1].]

1. One who performs feats of agility and strength; somersaults, leaps, and gymnastics; an acrobat.

2. *Carpentry.* See quot.

Tumble-, the vb.-stem in combination.

Tumbled (tŏ·mb'ld), *ppl. a.* [f. TUMBLE *v.* + -ED[1].]

Tumblerful (tŏ·mbləɹful). [f. TUMBLER *sb.* + -FUL.] The quantity that fills a tumbler.

Tumbling (tŏ·mbliŋ), *ppl. a.* [f. TUMBLE *v.* + -ING[2].]

Tumbling-, the vbl. and ppl. adj. in combinations and special collocations, as *tumbling-boy*, *girl*, *-ground*, *lass*, *-trick*; also *tumbling-barrel* = *tumbling-bay*; *tumbling-box*, an outfall from a river, canal, or reservoir.

Tumbling (tŏ·mbliŋ), *vbl. sb.* [f. TUMBLE *v.* + -ING[1].]

Tumblification (tŏ·mblifik[ē]·ʃən). *humorous.* [irreg. f. TUMBLE *v.* + -FICATION.] Tumbling, falling, or tossing; the pitching and rolling.

Tumbly (tŏ·mbli), *a. rare.* [f. TUMBLE *v.* + -Y.] Tending to tumble down, ruinous.

Tumboorn, var. TAMBOURA, musical instrument.

Tumbrel, tumbril (tŏ·mbrel, -il). Forms: 4 tomberel, 4–5 tumberell, tumrelle, 5 tomberel, tomerel, tumrel, 5–7 tumbrell, 6 -brill, 6–8 -brell, 7 -bril, 6–7 timbrell, 6–7 timberel, 7– tumbrel, tumbril. [a. OF. *tomberel*, *tumberel* (Du Cange), -*ellus* OF. *tumbel*, *tomberel*, *tumberel*, etc. f. *tomber* to fall, tumble.]

Tumefy (tiū·mifai), *v.* [ad. F. *tuméfier* (16th c. in Godef. Compl.), f. L. *tumefacere*.]

Tumefaction (tiūmif[a]·kʃən). [ad. F. *tuméfaction* (16th c.).]

Tumefied (tiū·mifaid), *ppl. a.* [f. prec. + -ED[1].]

Tumefy (tiū·mifai), *v.* [ad. F. *tuméfier*.]

Tumefying ... **Tumulose** ... **Tumult** ... **Tumultuous**

Tumefying, *vbl. sb.* ... to cause to swell; see -FY, and cf. *stupefy, rubefy.*

Tummel, to make to swell, or puff up.

Tumid (tiū'mid), *a.* Also 6 -yde. [ad. L. *tumid-us, f. tumēre* to swell: see -ID[1].]

1. Swollen; characterized by swelling. Morbidly affected with swelling, as a part of the body.

2. *fig.* esp. of language or literary style: 'Swelling', inflated, turgid, bombastic.

Hence **Tu·midly** *adv.*, in a tumid manner (*lit.* and *fig.*); **Tu·midness**, tumidity.

Tumidity (tiūmi'diti), [ad. late L. *tumiditās*, f. *tumidus* TUMID.] The quality or condition of being tumid; swollenness.

Tumly, **Tumidy**, swelling. *Obs.*

Tumour, tumor (tiū'mǎɹ). [a. L. *tumor*, f. *tumēre* to swell.]

1. The action, or an act, of swelling; distension, increase of bulk; swelling. *Obs.*

2. *concr.* A part rising above or projecting beyond the general level or surface; a swollen part or object; a swelling. *Now rare or Obs. exc. as in* 3.

3. An abnormal or morbid swelling or enlargement in any part of the body of an animal or plant; an excrescence; a tumefaction. Now usually in restricted sense: see 3 b.

4. *fig.* = TUMIDITY 2.

Tumoured, tumored (tiū·mǎɹd) *a., obs.*, affected with tumour or swelling (*lit. and fig.*) const. *as adj. or sb. ppl.*

Tump (tʌmp), *sb. local.* Also 6 tumpe, 7 toompe, toomp. [Not found before end of 16th c.; chiefly a western and w. midl. word; see *Eng. Dial. Dict.*; origin obscure.]

Tump, *v. local.* [f. prec. *sb.*] To make a 'tump' or mound about the root of a tree. Also, to store roots in a tump (*E.D.D.*).

Tumulate ... **Tumulation** ...

Tumulose, -ous, *a., obs. rare⁻⁰*. [ad. L. *tumulōsus*.]

Tump-line, *local U.S.* [Origin obscure: cf. TUMP *v.*]

Tum-tum ... **Tumult** ...

Tumulary, *a., obs. rare⁻⁰*.

Tumular (tiū·mĭlǎɹ), *a.* [L. *tumulus*-us (see TUMULUS) + -AR[1].] Pertaining to or consisting of a mound or tumulus.

Tumulate (tiū·miŭleit), *v. rare.* [f. ppl. stem of L. *tumulāre* to bury, f. *tumulus*: see TUMULUS and -ATE[3].] To bury in a tumulus.

Tumultuarily (tiŭmʌ·ltiŭărili), *adv.* [f. TUMULTUARY + -LY[2].] In a tumultuary manner.

Tumult (tiū·mʌlt), *sb.* [a. F. *tumulte* or ad. L. *tumultus*, f. root of *tumēre* to swell.]

1. Commotion of a multitude, usually with confused speech or uproar; public disturbance; disorderly or riotous proceeding.

2. *gen.* Commotion, agitation, disturbance.

3. Disposed to, marked by, or of the nature of a tumultuary people.

Tumultuary (tiŭmʌ·ltiŭări), *a.*

Tumultuate ...

Tumultuation ...

Tumultuous (tiŭmʌ·ltiŭǎs), *a.* Also 6-7 -ous.

1. Full of tumult or disturbance; marked by confusion and uproar; disorderly and noisy and clamorous; turbulent.

2. Making a tumult or commotion; acting in a disorderly and noisy way; turbulent, riotous.

Tumultuously *adv.* [f. prec. + -LY[2].] In a tumultuous manner; with tumult or commotion; with confusion and uproar; riotously.

Tumultuousness. The quality or state of being tumultuous or disturbed.

Tumulus (tiū·miŭlǎs), *sb.* Pl. tumuli (-lai). [L. *tumulus*, f. *tumēre* to swell.] An ancient sepulchral mound, a barrow.

Tumyde, obs. form of TUMID.

Tun (tʌn), *sb.* Forms: 1 tunne, 4 tonne, 4-5 tonne, 4-6 tunne, 4, 7-8 tunn, 5-6 towne, 5-7 tone, 5*c.* twne, 6-7 toone. Also 3-7 tonne, tons, 5-8 ton, 6 toon. See also TON.

1. A large cask or barrel, usually for liquids, wine, ale, or beer; or for various substances.

Tun, *v.* [f. TUN *sb.*]

1. *trans.* To put into or store in a tun or tuns. Often with *up*, more rarely *in*; also *absol.*

Tun-bellied, *a.* Having a belly like a tun; big-bellied.

Tun-belly, a belly like a tun, a big round belly.

Tuna[1] (tū·na). Also 7-8 -tunke. [ad. Welsh *tune*; see TUNE.]

Tuna[2] (tū·na). Also 7-8 tunke. [Sp., f. *tunal.*] A grove or thicket of tunas; cf. TUNA[1].

Tuna[3] (tū·na). [Maori name.] The common eel of New Zealand.

Tunableness, tune- (tiū·nǎb'lnes). [f. prec. + -NESS.] The quality of being tunable; tunefulness, harmoniousness, sweetness of sound.

Tunably, tuneably (tiū·nǎbli), *adv.* [f. as prec. + -LY[2].] In a tunable manner; tunefully, musically, harmoniously.

Tund (tʌnd), *v. Obs.* Also 7-8 tunke. [ad. L. *tundĕre* to beat.] To beat.

Tunder, **-dyr**, obs. or dial. ff. TINDER.

Tun-dish, tundish (tʌ·ndiʃ). Now *local.* [f. TUN *sb.* + DISH *sb.*] A shallow vessel with a tube at the bottom fitting into the bung-hole of a tun or cask, forming a kind of funnel used in brewing; hence *gen.* a funnel.

Tun-dun ... **Tundun**: see TURNDUN.

Tune (tiūn), *sb.* Forms: (4 tun), 4- tune, 5 toyn, 6 *sc.* tuin, twne, 6-7 towne, toyne, 6 *sc.* tuin, toine, toone, tune; *sc.* also TOON *v.* [A peculiar phonetic variant of TONE *sb.*]

1. Tuneful, musical, melodious, harmonious, sweet-sounding; *arch.* & TUNABLE, musical instruments, the singing voice, etc.

2. A rhythmical succession of musical tones produced (or composed) in an orderly sequence; an air, melody; esp. a simple air or melody.

Supplement, p. 3873; Corrigenda, p. 4092; Spurious words, p. 4093; Books quoted, p. 4094.

3431

Tune (tiūn), *sb.*

1. *†* a. To adjust the tones of (a musical instrument) to a standard of pitch; to bring into condition for producing the required sounds correctly; to put in tune.

b. *fig.* in phr. in tune, out of tune, in or out of order or proper condition; in or out of harmony with some person or thing. (See also 4, and Cf. TONE *sb.*)

2. a. To adapt the tone of; to attune.

b. To adjust the voice, song, etc.; to a particular tone, or to the expression of a particular feeling or subject.

3. a. *trans.* To adapt, put into accordance, or make responsive, in respect of some physical quality or condition.

b. *trans.* To set (a machine, etc.) in order for accurate working; to adjust.

4. *† Tune* (sb.), earlier form of *tune*, TINE *v.*[1]

5. To bring into accord or harmony; to attune.

Tuneable, etc.: see TUNABLE, etc.

Tuned (tiūnd, *poet.* tiū·nĕd), *ppl. a.* [f. TUNE *v.* + -ED[1].]

1. Full of 'tune' or musical sound; musical.

2. Producing or yielding musical sounds; making melody; performing or skilled in music; musical.

3. Retaining or adapted to music.

Tuneless (tiū·nlĕs), *a.* [f. as prec. + -LESS.]

1. Having no sweetness of tone; untuneful, unmusical, unmelodious, harsh-sounding.

II. With adverbs.

6. **Tune in.** *intr.* To strike into a chorus; to interpose in a conversation.

7. **Tune off.** *intr.* To get out of 'tune' or adjustment.

8. **Tune up.** *trans.* and *intr.* To raise one's voice (in song or otherwise); to sing out (cf. 2.)

Tuner (tiū·nǝɹ). [f. as prec. + -ER[1].] One who or that which tunes.

1. One who produces or utters musical sounds; a player or singer.

2. One who puts a particular (vocal) tone to something.

Tuneful (tiū·nfŭl), *a.* [f. as prec. + -FUL.]

1. Full of 'tune' or musical sound; musical, tuneful.

Tunesome (tiū·nsǝm), *a. rare*[-1]. [f. TUNE *sb.* + -SOME.] Having 'tune' or melody; tuneful.

Tunful: see TUNEFUL.

Tungate (tʊ·ŋgeit), *sb. Chem.* [f. TUNGST(IC + -ATE[2].] A salt of tungstic acid.

Tung-oil: see WOOD-OIL.

Tung-tongue: see TONGUE.

Tungsten (tʊ·ŋstĕn), *sb. Chem.* [= Sw. tungsten, f. tung heavy + sten stone.]

Tungstenite (tʊ·ŋstĕnǝit), *Min.* [f. TUNGSTEN + -ITE[1].]

Tungstic (tʊ·ŋstik), *a. Chem.* [f. TUNGST(EN + -IC.]

Tungstite (tʊ·ŋstǝit), *Min.* [f. TUNGST(EN + -ITE[1].]

Tunic (tiū·nik). Forms: 1 tunece (tonica), 1-2 tunice, 3 tunike, 5-7 tunick, tunike, tunique (also 9 as Fr.), 5- tunic. [ad. L. tunica (whence also Fr., Sp., Pg. túnica, It. tonica, tonaca, tunica, OE. tunece, OHG. zúnihha).]

I. A garment resembling a shirt or gown, worn by both sexes among the Greeks and Romans; in OE. and mediæval times, a body-garment or coat over which a loose mantle or cloak was worn.

2. In modern costume. A close, usually plain body-coat; now *spec.* that forming part of the uniform of soldiers and policemen.

b. A garment worn by women, consisting of a bodice and an upper skirt, belted or drawn in of fitted to the waist, worn over and displaying a longer skirt.

3. *Bot.* = TUNICLE *sb.* 2.

4. *Eccl.* = TUNICLE 1. *Obs.*

4. *transf. Anat.* A membranous sheath enveloping or lining an organ of the body; a 'coat'.

b. The integument of a part or organ in a plant; *spec. in Bot.* any loose membranous skin not formed from the epidermis; also, each layer or coating of a tunicate bulb.

5. *attrib.* and *Comb.*

Tunica (tiū·nika), *Anat.* [L., TUNIC.] A kind of animal cellulose.

Tunicate (tiū·nikeit), *a.* and *sb.* [ad. L. *tunicātus.*]

A. *adj.* Having or enclosed in a tunic or covering: *spec.* having or consisting of a series of concentric layers, as a bulb; *Entom.* sheathed in or issuing from one another, as the joints of an antenna.

B. *sb.* A member of the *Tunicata;* a tunicated mollusc.

Tunicated (tiū·nikeitĕd), *ppl. a.* [f. prec. + -ED[1].]

Tunicin (tiū·nisin), *Chem.* [f. TUNIC + -IN[1].]

† Tunicate (tiū·nikeit), *v. Obs. rare*[-1]. [f. L. *tunicāt-,* ppl. stem of *tunicāre* to clothe with a tunic, cover with a tunic, peel, etc.; f. *tunica* TUNIC.]

Tunicle (tiū·nik'l). Forms: 1 *tunece,* 4-6 *tunycle,* 5-6 *tunicle,* 6- *tunicle.* [ad. L. *tunicula,* dim. of *tunica* TUNIC.]

1. A vestment resembling the dalmatic, worn by subdeacons over the alb (and also by bishops under the alb and the dalmatic) at celebrations of the Eucharist.

2. *Eccl.* A vestment resembling the dalmatic, worn by subdeacons over the alb.

3. *transf.* A membranous sheath; a covering, integument.

Tunicle (tiū·nik'l): also *fig.* a wrapping, covering.

† Tunicated (tiū·nikeitĕd), *ppl. a. Obs. rare.*

Tuning (tiū·niŋ), *vbl. sb.* [f. TUNE *v.* + -ING[1].]

The action of the verb TUNE.

1. The action or process of putting an instrument in tune; a system according to which this is done.

Tuning-fork.

A small steel instrument (invented in 1711 by John Shore) consisting of a stem with two stout flat prongs which on being struck give a musical note of constant pitch, thus serving as a standard for tuning musical instruments and in acoustical investigations, etc.

tuning-fork (tiū·niŋ-fȯɹk), *sb.*

Tunique, obs. and Fr. form of TUNIC.

Tunist (tiū·nist), *rare.* [f. TUNE *v.* + -IST.]

Tunk: see TUNG, TUNK.

Tun-moot, *Hist.* [repr. OE. *tūngemōt,* f. TUN + *gemōt* meeting: see MOOT[1].] A public meeting of the town or village community.

Tunnage (tʊ·nedʒ), obs. form of TONNAGE.

Tunnel (tʊ·nel), *sb.* Forms: 7 *tonnel,* 6 tunnel, 7-9 *tonel,* 7- tunnel. [a. OF. *tonnel* (now Fr. *tonneau*), dim. of *tonne* TUN.]

1. *†* a. The flue or funnel of a chimney. *Obs.*

b. A funnel-shaped conductor. *Obs.*

c. A pipe or tube in general. *Now rare.*

2. An underground passage; a road-way excavated under ground, esp. under a hill or mountain, or beneath the bed of a river.

3. *transf.* The burrow of an animal.

4. A subterranean passage; a road-way excavated under ground.

Tunnel, *v.* [f. prec.]

Tunnelled, -eled (tʊ·neld), *ppl. a.* [f. TUNNEL *v.* + -ED[1].]

1. Formed like a pipe or funnel; tubular.

2. Perforated with a tunnel.

3. Furnished with tunnels.

Tunneller, -eler (tʊ·nelǝɹ). [f. TUNNEL *v.* + -ER[1].]

1. One who catches birds with a tunnel-net. *? Obs.*

2. One who excavates a tunnel; a maker of tunnels.

Tunnelling, -ling (tŏ·nĕliŋ), vbl. sb. [f. TUNNEL v. (and sb.) + -ING1.]
I. The use of a tunnel-net to catch birds.
2. The work or process of making a tunnel, excavation of, or by a tunnel.
3. attrib.

†Tunner. Obs. sc. dial. Forms: 4 tonour, 5 -owre, tunnowre, 6 tuner. [f.]
1. An instrument for tunning liquor; a funnel.
2. One who tuns liquor.

Tunnery, a place in which liquor is tunned.

Tunnified (tŏ·nifəid), ppl. a. humorous nonce-wd.

Tunning (tŏ·niŋ), vbl. sb. [f. TUN v. + -ING1.]
The action of the verb TUN.
1. Putting into or storing in a tun or tuns. Also with adj.
2. Characterized by 'tune' or 'melody'; melodious; sometimes depreciative.
Hence **Tuniness.**

Tun (tŭʌn), vb. Also tuney.
Tunny (tŭʌni), colloq. Also tuney.

†Tunsion. Obs. rare. [ad. L.]

†Tunster. sc. Obs. rare. [f. TUN + -STER.]

Tun (tŭp), sb. Forms: 4 tupe, 6 Sc. toupe, 4-6 tuppe, (6 toupe, tupp), 6-9 Sc.and north.dial. tup (tŭp), keep, teap, toop.

Tup (tŭp), v.
1. trans. Of the ram: To copulate with (the ewe); also transf.
2. intr. Of the ewe: To admit the ram. b. Of the ram: To copulate. Also transf.
3. trans. and north.dial. To furnish with horns like a ram's.

Tupaia (tupɑ̄i·a), sb. [mod.L. ad. Malay tupai.] Zool.

†Tupak-grass (tū·pak-gras). [f. the Maori name + GRASS sb.1.] A New Zealand grassy sedge, Carex appressa.

†Tupaiki. [Maori.] A small tree of New Zealand, Coriaria ruscifolia.

Tupelo (tū·pĭlo). Also 8 tupelow, 9 tupe-loo, tupola, [N. Amer. Ind.] Native name of trees of the North American genus Nyssa (N.O. Alangiaceæ or Nyssaceæ), large trees growing in swamps or on river-banks.

Tupi (tū·pi). Also 8 Tupy. [Brazilian.] A native language widely spoken in Brazil, which has yielded various names of animals, plants, etc.

Tupik (tū·pik). Also topek. [Eskimo of Alaska.] A hut or tent of skins used by Eskimo as a summer residence.

†Tupinambou. [mod.L., said to have been coined by Lamarck, after L. TUPI.] A genus of South American lizards.

Tuppence, obs. var. TWOPENCE.
Tupperian, -n, and ad. A. adj. Of, belonging to, or in the style of Martin F. Tupper's Proverbial Philosophy.

†Tupsee. E. Indies. Also tupsy, tupsey. [Hind.] tapsi.

Tupsi-tupsy (tŏ·psi·tŏ·psi).

Turanian (tiurǣ·niăn). A. adj.

†Turabura. [Native name in Guiana.] A small tree of Brazil and Guiana, Humirium floribundum.

Turb (tŏ̄b). Obs. exc. Hist. Forms: 4-6 turbe, 5-6, 9 tourbe, 7-9 turb. f. L., f. tourbe.

Turban (tŏ̄·băn), sb. [ad. Pers. dulbend.]
1. A member of any of the races speaking the 'Turanian or Ural-Altaic languages:
2. Applied loosely to a group or supposed 'family' of languages.

Turbit (tŏ̄·bit), sb. [a. Canadian Fr., f. F. toque, TOQUE.] A knitted stocking-cap tapered and closed at both ends.

Turb (tŏ̄b). A. sb. A member of any of the races speaking the 'Turanian or Ural-Altaic languages:

Turban (tŏ̄·băn), sb. [ad. Pers. dulbend.] I. 1. A head-dress of Moslem origin worn by men of Eastern nations, consisting of a cap round which is wound a long piece of linen, cotton, or silk.

Turban, sb.
I. 2. Cookery.
b. A head-dress made to resemble or suggest the oriental turban, worn by ladies in Europe and America.
3. Zool. A species of echino-derms, esp. the genus Cidaris.

Turbaned (tŏ̄·bănd), a.

Turbary (tŏ̄·bări). Forms: 4-6 turbarye, (5 -brye), 6 (6 tu·)rberie), 8 turbery, 6- turbary, [a. AF. turberie (Britton), med.L. turbaria, turbiaria (Kilian).]

Turban, sb.

TURBARY. 472

Turbation (tŏ̄bēi·ʃən). Obs. [ad. L. turbation-em.]

Turbid (tŏ̄·bid), a. [ad. L. turbid-us full of confusion or disorder; troubled, muddy; perplexed, violent, etc.]
I. Of liquid: Thick or opaque with suspended matter; not clear; cloudy, muddy.

Turbidity (tŏ̄bi·dĭti). [ad. L.] The quality or condition of being turbid; thickness of a fluid; cloudiness, etc.

Turbidly (tŏ̄·bidli), adv. In a turbid or troubled manner.

Turbid-ness.

Turbinaceous (tŏ̄binēi·ʃəs), a. rare. [f. L.]

Turbinal (tŏ̄·binăl). [ad. med.L. turbinalis (Albertus Magnus, c.1255), f. L. turbin-.]

Turbinate (tŏ̄·binət), a. [ad. L. turbinatus.]

Turbinated (tŏ̄·binēitĕd), ppl. a.

Turbine (tŏ̄·bin, -bəin). sb. [a. F. turbine, ad. L. turbin-em, turbo spinning-top, whirlwind.]

TURBATION. 473 **TURBINE.**

2. Law. In full common of turbary: The right to cut turf or peat for fuel on a common or on another person's land.

Turbat, -batt. obs. ff. TURBAN, TURBOT.

†Turbation (tŏ̄bēi·ʃən). Obs. [ad. L. turbation-em, f. turbare to disturb.] Confusion, disorder, etc.

Turbeh (tŭ·rbe). Also turbe. [Turkish, Arab. turba tomb, sepulchre.] A small mosque-like building erected over the tomb of a Moslem.

Turbellaria (tŏ̄belēə·ria). [mod.L.] Chem.

Turbellarian (tŏ̄belēə·riăn), a. and sb. [f. L. turbella, dim. of turba crowd.]

Turbidus, obs. var. TURBID.

Turbith, var. TURPETH.

Turbinaceous.

Turbine (tŏ̄·bin, -bəin). sb. [a. F. turbine, ad. L. turbin-em, turbo spinning-top, whirlwind.]
1. Top-shaped, top-like; spec. in Nat. Hist. whorled.

Turbinate (tŏ̄·binət), a. [ad. L. turbinat-us.]

Turbination (tŏ̄binēi·ʃən). [f. L.]

Turbine (tŏ̄·bin, -bəin). sb. [a. F. turbine, ad. L. turbin-em, turbo spinning-top, whirlwind.]
1. Originally applied to a wheel revolving on a vertical axis, and driven by a stream of water falling into its interior, and escaping by pipes, channels, or apertures so arranged as to press on the periphery of the wheel, and cause.

Turfless, a. [f. TURF sb.¹ + -LESS.] Devoid of turf, bare.

Turfy (tɜ·ɹfɪ), a. Forms: see TURF sb.¹

1. Covered with or consisting of turf; grassy; turfen; in quot. 1733, of arable land; full of weeds and roots, not 'clean.'

2. Of the nature or characteristic of turf or peat; peaty.

3. Pertaining to or characteristic of the turf; suggestive of horse-racing; horsy.

Hence **Turfiness**, turfy character, horsiness.

†Turgeman, obs. f. TRUCHMAN, an interpreter; cf. METURGEMAN.

†Turgenous, a. The action or becoming swollen.

†Turgency, Obs. [ad. med. or mod.L. turgentia.]

Turgent (tɜ·ɹdʒent), a. Now rare or Obs.

1. Physically swelling or swollen; distended, turgid.

2. fig. An inflated or bombastic style of language.

Turgesce (tɜɹdʒe·s), v. [ad. L. turgescĕre.]

Turgescence (tɜɹdʒe·sens). [ad. med. or mod.L. turgescentia.]

1. The action or condition of swelling up; the fact or state of being swollen.

2. fig. Progressive swelling or increase.

Turgescency (tɜɹdʒe·sensɪ). [ad. mod.L. turgescentia.]

Turgescent (tɜɹdʒe·sent), a. [ad. L. turgescent-em; see prec. and -ENT.]

Turgescible (tɜɹdʒe·sɪb'l), a. [f. L. turgesc-ĕre : see above and -IBLE.] Capable of swelling up.

Turgid (tɜ·ɹdʒɪd), a. [ad. L. turgid-us swollen, inflated, f. turgēre to swell : see -ID.]

1. Swollen, distended, inflated.

2. fig. Inflation of language; grandiloquence, pompous, bombastic.

Turgidity (tɜɹdʒi·dɪtɪ). [f. L. turgid-us (see prec.) + -ITY.]

Turgidly (tɜ·ɹdʒɪdlɪ), adv. In a turgid manner; in turgid style or language.

Turgidness. [f. as prec. + -NESS.] The quality of being turgid; = TURGIDITY.

Turgite (tɜ·ɹgəit). Min. [Named by Hermann 1845, from the Turgĭnsk mine, Ural Mtns., where found : see -ITE.] A hydrous sesquioxide of iron, allied to limonite but containing less water.

Turgor (tɜ·ɹgɔɹ). [a. L. turgor, f. turgēre.]

Turgy. Cf. TURDION.

Turion (tiū·ɹiɒn). Bot. [= F. turion (16th c.), ad. L. turio, turionem, formerly also in Eng. use.]

Turk (tɜɹk). Also 4–7 Turke, 5 turque, 7 Turc; 9'Toork (sense 1.) – F. Turc, turc Ital. turco, turquo, It., Sp., Pg. Turco, med. L. Turcus, -a, Byz. Gr. Τοῦρκος, Pers. (and Arab.) تُرك turk. A national name of unknown origin.

1. A member of the dominant race of the Ottoman empire; in earlier times, a Seljuk; since 1300, an Osmanli or Osmanic, a descendant of the Osmanlis or other Turks.

2. transf. Applied to any one having qualities attributed to the Turks; a cruel, rigorous, or tyrannical man; any one behaving as a barbarian or savage; one who treats his wife harshly; a bad-tempered or unmanageable man.

3. Often, with alliterative qualification, terrible Turk.

†Turk, sb.² [Etymology uncertain. Taken by bleac as a deriv. of F. torquer to twist, to writhe, wreath, wind in, wrap about.] A turkey.

†Turken (tɜ·ɹken), v. Also 6 turquen. [Etymology uncertain.]

Turkess(e, -ais, Obs. Forms: 6 korkoase, 7 turkeise, turquesse, turkis(s turkise, turoase, turches.

Turkess(e, ... dently related to TURKISM, and, like that verb, referred in some to F. torquer, ad. L. torquēre to twist.

Turkey (tɜ·ɹkɪ). Also 5 torkey, 6–8 Turkie, 6–8 Turky, (6, 7 Turkey, Turquey, Turkeye, 7, 7 Turkye). [= F. Turquie; orig. med. Germ-a·vo, Germānia. Germania; cf. Indus, India.]

1. The land of the Turks, 'Turkey in Asia' and 'Turkey in Europe'; commonly sometimes Türkestan or Tartary.

Turkey² (tɜ·ɹkɪ). Also 6–7 turkie, 6–8 turky, (7 turkye.) [Short for TURKEY-COCK, -HEN, app. applied orig. to the Guineafowl, a native of Africa, with which the American turkey was at first confounded : see TURKEY-COCK.]

†1. The Guinea-fowl. Obs.

2. In current use: A well-known large gallinaceous bird of the Linnæan genus Meleagris, the species of which are all American, M. gallopavo, which was found domesticated in Mexico at the discovery of that country in 1518, and was soon after introduced into Europe, and is now valued as a table fowl in all civilised lands.

3. U.S. and Canada. Allusively, in colloquial or dialect phrases, etc.

Turkey-cock, **-hen.** ... They are also the of large water-fowl, with red heads (more than turkey vultures).

Turkey carpet. A carpet manufactured in or imported from Turkey, or of a style in imitation of this; made in one piece of richly-coloured wools, without any imitative surface, of close texture, and with a deep thick pile, so as to resemble velvet.

Turkey-cock (tɜ·ɹkɪkɒk). Also 6–7 Turkie-cock(e. [f. TURKEY¹ + COCK sb.] In the 16th c. synonymous with Guinea-cock or Guinea-fowl, an African bird known to the ancients (the μελεαγρίς of Aristotle, meleagris of Varro and Pliny), the American bird being at first identified with or treated as a species of this.

Turkey-hen. [Cf. TURKEY-COCK.]

Turkey red [TURKEY.] A brilliant and permanent red colour produced on cotton goods, essentially a madder red in combination with oil or fat, with an aluminous mordant. Also called *Adrianople* or *Levant red*. Also *attrib*.

b. Cotton cloth of this colour.

Turkey, Turkese, *a*. Obs.

Turkey stone. [TURKEY.]

Turkey wheat. The cereal Maize, called also *Guinea corn* and *Indian corn*.

Turkey work [TURKEY.] Turkish tapestry work, or an imitation of this. Also *attrib*. Hence **Turkey-worked** *a*.

Turki (tu·rki), *a*. (*sb*.)

Turkic (tu·rkik), *a*. [f. TURK¹ + -IC.]

Turkicize, *v*.

Turkification, a rendering Turkish.

Turkify, *v*. Obs.

Turkis, turkes, -esse (tu·rkis).

Turkish (tu·rkiʃ), *a*. and *sb*. [f. TURK¹ + -ISH¹.]

b. B. *sb*. The Turkish or Turk's language.

Turkise, *v*. Obs.

Turkish bath.

2. In special collocations.

Turkise (tu·rkəiz), *v*. rare.

+ **Turkish**, *v*. Obs.

Turkism (tu·rkiz'm), *sb*.

Turkissh, obs. f. TURQUOISE.

Turkize, var. TURKISE v. Obs.

Turkle, obs. form of TURTLE.

Turkoman (tu·rkəmæn). Also TURCOMAN. Obs.

Turk's cap. [TURK¹.]

Turm (tûrm). [a. OF. *turme*, *torme* (= It. in Godef.), ad. L. *turma* a troop, squadron.]

Turk's-head grass, *Lagurus ovatus*.

Turmagant, **Turmalin(e**, **Turmat**. = TERMAGANT, TOURMALINE, TURRET.

+ **Turmatur**. Obs. rare.

Turmerol (tû·rmərol). Chem. [f. TURMER-IC + -OL.]

Turmoil (tû·rmoil), *sb*. Forms: see TURMOIL *v*.

Turmoil (tû·rmoil), *v*. Also 6 four-, 6–7 -moile, -moyle, 7 -moyl.

Turmoiler.

Turmoiling, *ppl. a.*

+ **Turmoilous**, *a*. Obs. rare.

Turmoly, obs. f. TURMOIL *v*.

Turmulë, obs. f. TURMOIL.

Turmut, dial. var. TURNIP.

Turn (tûrn), *sb*. Forms: also 3–7 turne, 4–6 torn, turne, 5 tourn, tourne, 5–7 tourne. [partly a. AF. *turn*, *torn*, OF. *torn*, *tour*, F. *tour*: see TOUR *sb*.]

Turn (tûrn), *v*. Forms: 1 *tyrnan*, *tirnan*, *tiernan*, etc.

Supplement, p. 3873; Corrigenda, p. 4092; Spurious words, p. 4093; Books quoted, p. 4094

78. Turn out of. (See simple senses and Out *adv.*)

a. *trans.* To drive, send, or put out of (a place); to dismiss from (a position or office), formerly or peremptorily; to expel or eject from; formerly more widely, to put or take out of in any way; *fig.* to bring out, deliver from; to dissuade from.

b. *intr.* To get out of, leave, quit. (Cf. 71 o, p.)

77. Turn over. (See simple senses and Over *adv.*) *trans.* a. To turn (something) from its position so as one side, or from one side to the other, or upside down; to invert, reverse; to knock over, overturn, upset; *refl.* (now *rare*) = below. Cf. senses 7, 10, and Over *adv.* 4, c.

b. To change to the opposite opinion, state of mind, etc.; *esp.* to change from a friendly to a hostile attitude; with *on* or *upon*, to assail suddenly, esp. in words (cf. 33).

c. To reverse (a leaf, or the successive leaves of a book) in order to read (or write) on further; to read or search through, peruse (a book) by doing this. Cf. 11 b.

To turn over a new leaf (*fig.*): see Leaf sb. 7 b.

d. To cause to revolve or rotate (cf. 1); also, to cause to face in all directions successively.

e. *fig.* To agitate or revolve in the mind, go through and examine mentally, consider and re-consider; cf. 8.

f. To turn over to another (a person) or another (a place); to another ship (cf. TURN-OVER sb. 2); in quot. 1632², to convert to a different use.

79. Turn to. a. *intr.* To apply oneself to some task or occupation; to set to work. Cf. 38 c.

b. To betake oneself; hence, to till.

c. To turn the handle or tap of (a lamp or gas-jet) so as to raise the wick, or increase the flow of gas.

80. Turn up. (See simple senses and Up *adv.*)

a. *trans.* To direct or bend upwards (also *fig.*).

b. To fold over, fold up, form by a turning or folding.

Turn-, combining form or attrib.

81. With adverbs, as *turned-back*, *-down*, *-in*, *-out*, *-up*: see TURN v. VIII.

Turndun, **tundun**. [Native Australian of the Kurnai tribe in Gippsland.]

Turnable (tɔ̄·nǎb'l), a. *rare.* [f. TURN v. + -ABLE.] That may be turned.

Turnabout (tɔ̄·nǎbaut), sb. [f. the verbal phr. *turn about* (TURN v. 65).]

Turnbroach, erroneous f. TURNBROACH.

Turn-buckle. [f. TURN v. + BUCKLE sb.]

Turn-down, sb. and a. [f. the verbal phr. *turn down* (TURN v. 7 d).]

Turned (tɔ̄nd), *ppl. a.* [f. TURN v. + -ED¹.]

Turnel (tɔ̄·nĕl), sb. *exc. dial.* Also 6 -ylle, 6-7 -il, 6-7 -nil, 7 tournell, 7-9 turnil. [Derivative of TURN v.]

Turner (tɔ̄·nǎu). *Hist.* Also 7 turno(u)r.

Turneraceous (tɔ̄nerē·ʃʏs), a. [f. mod.L.]

TURNERAD. · 498 · TURNING. · TURNING. · 499 · TURNIP.

TURNIP. · 500 · TURNIP. · TURNIX. · 501 · TURNPIKE.

Turnerad — pertaining to the *Turneraceæ*, a small order of tropical herbs and undershrubs, mainly American and African, having yellowish or blue axillary flowers and alternate leaves.

Turnerian, a.

Turnerite (tˈə̄·nəˌrəit), *Min.* [f. the name of C. H. Turner + -ITE.] A variety of monazite, occurring in yellow or brown crystals.

Turnery (tˈə̄·nəri). Also 7 -*tourn*-. [f. TURN *v.* + -ERY.]
1. The art of the turner; the fashioning of objects or designs by means of a lathe.
2. Collectively: Turner's work; objects fashioned on the lathe; turnery ware.
3. *attrib.* and *Comb.*, as turnery-room, -ware, -warehouse, -work.

Turnesol, obs. form of TURNSOLE.

Turnet. *Obs. rare.* [var. of, or error for, *turret* TORRET; cf. obs. F. *tournet* 'a small turning-ruddle, or ring, in the mouth of a Bit' (Cotgr.).] = TORRET *c*.

Turney, dial. var. TORNEY, attorney.
Turney, obs. f. TOURNEY *sb.* and *v.*
Turneys, obs. f. TOURNOIS.

†Turgiddy, *a.* and *sb. Obs. rare.* [f. TURN *v.* to rotate + GIDDY *a.* Cf. TURN-SICK *a.*] *a. adj.* Giddy as from turning round; dizzy; affected with vertigo. *b. sb.* Giddiness, dizziness. Hence **†Turgi·ddiness** *Obs. rare* = b.

†Turngiddiness *Obs. rare* = b.

†Turngree, sb. Chiefly *Sc. Obs.* [f. TURN *v.* + GREE *sb.*] A winding stair, as in a turret, etc.

Turnicine (tˈə̄·nisin), *a.* *Ornith.* [f. mod.L. *Turnic-*, *Turnix*, + -INE[1].] Belonging to the *Turnicidæ*, a family of birds of which the turnix is the type.

Turning (tˈə̄·niŋ), *vbl. sb.* [f. TURN *v.* + -ING[1].] The action of the verb TURN, in various senses (also concretely).
1. Movement about an axis or centre; rotation, revolution.
2. The action of shaping or working something on a lathe; the art of shaping things by means of a lathe; the work of a turner.
3. Shaping, moulding, fashioning (of literary work, etc.).
4. The action, or an act, of changing posture or direction by moving as on a pivot; movement so as to face or point in a different, or in some particular, direction. Also *fig.*
5. Reversal of movement or course; †return, going back (*obs.*).

Turning, *ppl. a.* [f. as prec. + -ING[2].] That turns, in various senses of the verb.
1. That moves round, or so as to face another way; rotating, revolving, etc. (See also 7.)
2. Changing direction of movement or course; winding, sinuous; branching off, as a road or path.
3. Reversing its course; beginning to go back.
4. Changing, changeful, variable. *Obs. or rare.*
5. With adverb (cf. TURN *v.* VIII), as *turning-up*.
6. In combinations or special collocations: *turning-box*, a kind of tun-tub; *turning-bridge* = TURN-BRIDGE; †*turning-platform* = TURN-TABLE[1]; *turning-plough*, -*turn-plough* (see TURN[1]); †*turning-stile* = TURNSTILE; *turning-table* = TURN-TABLE[1]; *turning-wheel*, (a) a turnstile or similar device; (b) an apparatus consisting of a rapidly revolving wheel.

Turning-lathe, sb. [f. TURNING *vbl. sb.* + POINT *sb.*]
1. *lit.* A point at which something turns, or changes its direction of motion, etc.; *spec.* a maximum or minimum point on a graph, where it begins to tend downwards or upwards.
2. *fig.* Near what may be the highest point of its course, where its spacious stream is divided.

Turning-point. [f. TURNING *vbl. sb.* + POINT *sb.*]

Turning-evil, sb. [f. TURNING *vbl. sb.* + EVIL *sb.* 7.] = TURN-SICK *sb.* 2.

Turnip (tˈə̄·nip), sb. Also 6-7 turnepe, (-eppe, -op), 6-9 turnep, (7 turnepp, turnup, turneap, turnoop); *dial.* turmit, -at, turmuts, turneat, etc. [The first syllable is of obscure origin; in 16–17th c. *turnepe*, in 10–19th c. *turnep*, from c. 1784 *turnip*, the second element being NEEP, *nepe*, or *nep*, OE. *næp*: L. *napus* 'turnip'.]
1. (a) The fleshy, globular or spheroidal root of a biennial cruciferous plant, *Brassica Rapa*, var. *depressa*, having toothed, somewhat hairy leaves, and yellow flowers, cultivated from ancient times as a culinary vegetable, and for feeding sheep and cattle; also, the plant itself, of which the young shoots (*turnip-tops*) are frequently boiled as greens.
 (b) The spheroidal root itself. *Obs. rare.*
2. *slang.* A large watch of old-fashioned make.

Turnix (tˈə̄·niks), *Ornith.* [Bonna-terre, 1790), *app.* shortened from L. *coturnix* quail.] A genus of quail-like birds (also called *Hemipodius*; see HEMIPOD); the bush-quail.

Turnkey (tˈə̄·nˌki), sb. and a. [f. TURN *v.* + KEY *sb.*]
1. One who has charge of the keys of a prison; a jailer, *esp.* a subordinate; also *transf.*
2. A tooth-key; an instrument for extracting teeth.

Turn-out (tˈə̄·nˌaut), sb. and a. [f. the verbal phr. *turn out* (TURN *v.* 75).]
1. A turning out or getting out (of bed, etc.); hence, a call to duty, *esp.* during one's period of rest; *Mil.* a signal to the troops.
2. A withdrawal of workmen from their place of employment by common consent; a strike.
3. An apparatus or arrangement on a rail- or tram-way; also, in a narrow road, a part wider than the rest, or a short side road, to enable vehicles to pass one another.

Turn-over (tˈə̄·nˌəʊvə(r)), sb. and a. [f. the verbal phr. *turn over* (TURN *v.* 77).]
1. The action of turning over, in various senses: *see* quots. *spec.* in *Polit. slang*: a transference of votes from one party to another.
2. The amount of business done in a given time; also, the amount of goods produced and disposed of by a manufacturer; also, the 'turning over' of the capital involved in a business, etc., the net profit derived from a business in a given time.

Turnpike (tˈə̄·nˌpaik), sb. and a. [f. TURN *v.* + PIKE *sb.*]
1. *a.* A spiked barrier fixed in or across a road or passage, as a defence against sudden attack, esp. of men on horseback.

Iron. 1711 *Milit. & Sea Dict.* (ed. 4), *Chevaux de Frise*,..the same as Turnpikes,..one being the French, the other the English Name, yet both indifferently now used in England, and the French rather the most. 1716 PERRY *St. Russia* 47 The Czar having disposed his Army behind a Line of Chevaux de Frize, or Turn-pikes shod with Iron,..maintain'd so regular and strong a fire, that [etc.]. 1724 DE FOE *Mem. Cavalier* I. 108 Coming up to the Turn-pike, I found it defended by 200 Musqueteers.

†**b.** *transf.* and *fig.* in various applications. *Obs.*

a 1616 BEAUMONT *Antiplatonic* v, Love stormes his lips, and takes the fortresse in, For all the bristled turn-pikes of his chin. 1641 G. H. *Wit's Recreat.* X vj, He hath such subtile turnes and nookes, Such turne-pegs, mazes, tenter-hookes. 1661 FELTHAM *Resolves* II. xxix. (ed. 8) 241 It makes a man a Turn-pike, that will be sure to prick you, which side soever you come on. 1661 K. W. *Conf. Charac.*, *Covetous Usurer* (1860) 74 That Fryday face of his, whose rowsey whiskers and brischy turn-pikes make him resemble some shaggy meteor, or some borish Turk. 1665 HOOKE *Microgr.* I. 205 Each of these legs were bestuck..with multitudes of small hairs, or (if we respect the proportion they bore to the bigness of the leg) turnpikes. 1679 V. ALSOP *Melius Inquir.* I. i. 77 He that..shall thrust other men upon the turn-pikes of sin, and force them to act against their light.

†**2.** A horizontal cross of timber turning on a vertical pin, set up to exclude horse-traffic from a foot-way; a turnstile. *Obs.*

1547 in J. R. Boyle *Hedon* (1875) App. 125 For makynge on hoppe to the tornepyke, iiij.d. 1600 W. KEMP *Nine Days' Wonder* D j, The Cittizens [of Norwich] had caused all the turne-pikes to be taken vp..that I might not be hindred. 1626 B. JONSON *Staple of N.* III. i, I moue vpon my axell, like a turne-pike. 1684–5 in Willis & Clark *Cambridge* (1886) II. 642 Painting the barrs and Turnepikes in the entrance to the New walke. 1755 JOHNSON, *Turnpike*,..a cross of two bars armed with pikes at the end, and turning on a pin, fixed to hinder horses from entering.

†**3.** A barrier across a water-course or stream; a water-gate, allowing the water to flow, but obstructing cattle; also, a lock on a navigable stream. Also *turnpike-lock* (see 9). *Obs.*

1623–4 *Act 21 Jas. I*, c. 32 § 1 To open prepare or make all Weares and Lockes or Turnepickes fitt for the said Passage. *Ibid.*, To make and erect any Wharfes Lockes or Turnepickes or Pennes for Water. 1677 PLOT *Oxfordsh.* 233 Where the declivity of the Channel, and fall of water is so great, that few barges could live in the passage of them, there we have Turn-pikes. 1708 *Act 1 Anne* St. II. c. 11 § 2 Altering the said Wharfs Sluces Wears Sasses Locks Turnpikes or Pens for Water or Passages. 1751 *Act 24 Geo. II*, c. 8 § 2 Tenants or Occupiers of all Locks, Weirs, Bucks, Winches, Turnpikes, Dams, Flood-Gates.

4. A barrier (orig. of the nature of a turnpike in sense 2, later a gate or gates) placed across a road to stop passage till the toll is paid; a toll-gate. Cf. TURNSTILE. Now chiefly *Hist.*

a 1678 [see b]. 1695–6 *Act 7 & 8 Will. III*, c. 9 § 4 The Place for collecting the said Toll to be in some convenient Place upon the said Highway..by setting up a Turnpike or otherwise. 1705 *Lond. Gaz.* No. 4125/4 Whoever..gives Notice to Mr. John Baker, Keeper of the Turn-Pipe [*sic*] aforesaid,..shall have a Guinea Reward. 1723 MANDEVILLE *Fab. Bees* (1725) I. 363 A poor Traveller that at every Ten Miles end is stop'd by a Turnpike. 1771 SMOLLETT *Humph. Cl.* 26 June, Considering the tax we pay for turnpikes, the roads of this country constitute a most intolerable grievance. 1806 *Chron.* 23 Feb., in *Ann. Reg.* (1808) 375/2 Close to Oxford-street turnpike. 1829 *Chapters Phys. Sc.* 58 The weighing-machine is formed of a combination of levers..and is commonly used at turnpikes in weighing waggons, to ascertain that they are not loaded beyond what is allowed by law to the breadth of their wheels. 1845 MCCULLOCH *Taxation* Introd. (1852) 33 Turnpikes being erected only on the principal roads, the old plan for keeping up cross or parish roads [by statute labour, or at the cost of the parish] was not affected by their institution. 1885 *Act 48 & 49 Vict.* c. 37 § 5 The provisions now in force respecting turnpikes and tolls [etc.]..shall continue in force until Parliament otherwise provides.

b. *transf.* and *fig.*

a 1678 MARVELL *Growth Popery* 11 It will suffer no man to pass without paying at their Turn-pikes. 1730 FIELDING *Rape upon Rape* II. ii. 16 The Laws are Turnpikes, only made to stop People who walk on Foot. 1745 *Season. Adv. Protest.* 38 A Tax to the Priests, for suffering them to pass the Turnpike of Purgatory. 1765 FOOTE *Commissary* II. i, He capers through a whole region of turnpegs. 1807 OPIE in *Lect. Paint.* ii. (1848) 271 The possessors..had..been often denied the usual road to eminence:..they defrauded the turnpike, and conducted their silent march another way.

c. *dial.* A wire snare set by a poacher across a hare's or rabbit's run.

1879 JEFFERIES *Amateur Poacher* ii. 29 The blacksmith started the idea of putting up a 'turnpike',—i.e. a wire.

5. Elliptical for TURNPIKE ROAD; also *fig.*

1748 DE FOE *Tour Gt. Brit.* II. 178 The Road is by this means so continually torn, that it is one of the worst Turnpikes round about London. 1755 *Demi-Rep* 10 You may ride the turnpike to her heart. 1796 BURKE *Regic. Peace* i. Wks. VIII. 124 There is a Minister from Denmark at Paris...We sent through this turnpike to demand a passport. 1802 *Debates in U. S. Congress* 25 Feb. (1850) 759 As plain as a turnpike. 1861 GEO. ELIOT *Silas M.* i, [Raveloe] was nestled in a snug well-wooded hollow, quite an hour's journey on horseback from any turnpike. 1875 W. MCILWRAITH *Guide Wigtownshire* 77 Here the turnpike winds along a terrace hewn from the hillside.

b. Short for *turnpike trust* (see 9) or the like.

1728 VANBR. & CIB. *Prov. Husb.* I. i, He won't sit long enough to give his Vote for a Turn-pike. 1773 *Observ. State Poor* 105 The roads of our nation are its standing opprobrium, the complaint and the jest of foreigners. The few, which under the direction of turnpikes, are justly exempted from this general censure or ridicule, only serve to facilitate the conveyance of provision to the capital.

†**6.** A turn-table on a railway. *Obs.*

1793 SMEATON *Edystone L.* § 167 *note*, The carriage being turned a quarter round upon the Turnpike, or Turnrail.

7. *U.S.* A small cake used to raise bread: see quots. ? *local.*

1850 SUSAN WARNER *Wide, Wide World* xiv, I am scalding this meal with it to make turnpikes. 1850 *Knickerbocker Mag.* (N. Y.) July 83 (Thornton) Some little yellow cakes, called turnpikes, and used, I believe, for some purpose or other in baking bread.

II. 8. *Sc.* A staircase which winds round a central axis; a spiral or winding stair; later applied to other forms of staircase: cf. *turnpike stair*, *staircase* in 9.

1501 DOUGLAS *Pal. Hon.* III. xvii, A palice..with mony royall towris,...Pinnakillis, fyellis, turnpekkis mony one, Gilt birneist torris,..Skarsment, reprise, corbell, and battellingis. 1516 *Acc. Ld. High Treas. Scot.* V. 78 For the makin of ane turnpek in the palis of the Abbay Halyrudhous. 1546 LYNDESAY in *St. Papers Hen. VIII*, V. 560 Normond Leslie and his cumpanye met hym [Cdl. Beaton] in þe turnpyk þer off, and slew hym. 1552 *Acc. Ld. High Treas. Scot.* X. 91 Item, foure lokkis put in the ȝett, ȝard ȝett, and durris of the tway turnpykis of my lord governouris lugeing of the Kirk of Feild,..iij li. *c* 1590 J. STEWART *Poems* (S.T.S.) II. 53/93 Butt and ben he bends from bour to bour, Vp turnpyks, turats, And from tour to tour. 1600 *Gowrie Conspir.* in *Harl. Misc.* (Malh.) II. 343 The Earle of Gowrie and his seruants made them for another way vp a quyet turnpyke, which..was onlie then left open, as appeared for that purpose. 1643 in A. Maxwell *Hist. Old Dundee* (1884) 213 [The Council] concludit that the turne-pyk upon the steeple be presently repaired. 1730 *Mem. Capt. Creichton* in *Swift's Wks.* (1869) 534/2 Steele suddenly opening the door, fired a blunderbuss down at the two dragoons as they were coming up the stairs; but the bullets, grazing against the side of the turnpike, only wounded and did not kill them. 1818 SCOTT *Rob Roy* xxii, The turnkey, who..led me up a 'turnpike' (so the Scotch call a winding stair). 1899 CROCKETT *Black Douglas* (1900) 106 He was upon the last step of the turnpike and at the entrance of the corridor.

III. 9. *attrib.* and *Comb.* (chiefly in sense 4), as *turnpike act, bridge, -house, -keeper, -man, -people, -system, trust*; in sense 8, as *turnpike foot, head, stair, staircase*; also **turnpike cake**: see sense 7; **turnpike-free** *a.*, free from tolls for passage; **turnpike gate**, †(*a*) a gate or door at the foot of a turnpike stair (*Sc.*); †(*b*) = sense 1; (*c*) = sense 4; †**turnpike-lock** = sense 3; **turnpike meeting**, a meeting of a turnpike trust; **turnpike sailor**, a beggar in the guise of a distressed sailor. See also TURNPIKE ROAD.

1794 DONALDSON *Agric. Carse of Gowrie* 32 Making another application to parliament, and in a short time a *turnpike act was procured, in which these, and other particular roads in the county, were included. 1841 *Penny Cycl.* XX. 29/1 The inefficiency of the system of maintenance by parish and statute labour was proved before the passing of the first Turnpike Act in 1653. 1903 *Law Rep.* 1 K. B. 407 A bicycle is not a carriage for the purposes of a turnpike Act. 1840 *Act 3 & 4 Vict.* c. 88 § 1 That no Toll shall be demanded or taken on any *Turnpike..Bridge for any Horse, or Police Van, Carriage or Cart,..in the Service of the Police. 1850 SUSAN WARNER *Wide, Wide World* xiv, Cakes, child, cakes!—*turnpike cakes—what I raise the bread with. 1565 in Hay Fleming *Reform. in Scot.* (1910) Append. M. 610 In the chalmer at the *turne pyk fuit. 1903 J. K. JEROME *Tea T. Talk* (ed. Tauchn.) 112 The world's highroads run *turnpike-free from pole to pole. 1513 *Acc. Ld. High Treas. Scot.* IV. 526 To the..smyth for viij score of square hedit nalis to the *turnepyk yett of the nethir toure. 1688 R. HOLME *Armoury* III. xvi. (Roxb.) 88/1 A Turne pike...Some terme it a Turnepike Gate. 1806 *Chron.* 19 Feb., in *Ann. Reg.* (1808) 371/2 A boy riding on a cart, drove against a turnpike-gate. 1840 DICKENS *Barn. Rudge* iii, The horse stopped until the turnpike gate was opened. 1889 GRETTON *Memory's Harkb.* 115 The wheelers..knocked against the turnpike-gate-post in passing through. 1623 *Reg. Mag. Sig. Scot.* 151/1 Infra *lie turnpyke* ejusdem cameram *lie* *turnpyke-heid*, occidentalem..et mediam cameram. 1774 NICHOLSON in *Phil. Trans.* LXIV. 351 These appearances continued till I reached the *turnpike-house. 1806 *Chron.* 15 May, in *Ann. Reg.* (1808) 405/1 The toll-table, against the turnpike house, at Whalley. 1863 DICKENS *Uncomm. Trav.* xxii, The Turnpike-house was all overgrown with ivy; and the Turnpike-keeper, unable to get a living out of the tolls, plied the trade of a cobbler. 1738 *Gentl. Mag.* May 247/2 From the Respect he was treated with by the *Turnpike-keeper, I perceived..that he was..some Person of Distinction. 1771 *Act 11 Geo. III*, c. 45 § 8 Making *Turnpike Locks on the Sides of the present Locks. 1769 EARL MARCH in Jesse *Selwyn & Contemp.* (1843) II. 366, I wrote you a note with a pencil upon the road, which a *turnpike-man promised to send to you. 1782 COWPER *Gilpin* 119 In a trice the turnpike-men Their gates wide open threw. 1876 BLACKMORE *Cripps* xxxii, He would rather have a row with three turnpike-men than presume to speak to a gentleman. 1764 FOOTE *Mayor of G.* I. i, After twenty years attendance at *turnpike-meetings. 1858 DICKENS *Holly Tree Inn* i, Even *turnpike people have children. 1851 MAYHEW *Lond. Labour* I. 415/2, I became a *turnpike sailor,..and went out as one of the Shallow Brigade. 1884 CLARK RUSSELL in *Longm. Mag.* III. 563 The roadway was filled with a crowd of grimy fellows, turnpike sailors, loafing scarecrows. 1730 *Mem. Capt. Creichton* in *Swift's Wks.* (1869) 534/1 The dragoons..went up a pair of *turnpike stairs. 1779 ARNOT *Hist. Edin.* 246 *note*, A turnpike stair is the term used..over all Scotland, to denote a stair, of which the steps are built in a spiral form, like a screen winding round the same axis. 1805 FORSYTH *Beauties Scotl.* II. 309 A small turnpike-stair, built in the wall. 1818 SCOTT *Hrt. Midl.* xxvi, A half-circular turret,..bartizan'd on the top, served as a case for a narrow turnpike-stair. 1888 STEVENSON *Black Arrow* IV. iv, The authors..had clattered down a turnpike stair and decamped. 1800 W. F. BAYLAY *Northern Tour* 267 (MS.) A beautiful *turnpike staircase here..the roof of it winding like a snail cap. 1801 *Farmer's Mag.* Apr. 158 The defective principles, adopted when the *turnpike system was first introduced, are completely avoided. 1895 *Westm. Gaz.* 28 Oct., The last of the turnpike system. ..The turnpike gates, which will enjoy the honour of thus being last in the field, belong to that portion of the Shrewsbury and Holyhead-road which traverses the island of Anglesea, the trust for which was continued by a special Act of Parliament until November 1, 1895. 1843 *Penny Cycl.* XXV. 429/1 *Turnpike trusts. Turnpike-roads are..highways placed..under the management of trustees or commissioners.

Hence **Tu·rnpike** *v.*, *trans.* to erect turnpikes on (a road); to make into a turnpike road; **Tu·rnpiker**, one who frequents the turnpike or turnpike road; hence (*a*) a foot-traveller; (*b*) = *turnpike sailor* (see 9 above).

1806 WEBSTER, *Turnpike*,..to form or erect a turnpike. 1825 *Amer. St. Papers, Post-office* (1834) 137 The road from Elkton to Staunton has been turnpiked. 1903 H. T. CROFTON *Old Moss Side* 6 The lane was but little altered even after Acts are passed in 1749 and 1793 for turnpiking and improving it. 1812 *Boston Gaz.* 27 Aug. (Thornton), The heroes, who were to have mounted the heights of Abram, are yet in the garb of *turnpikers, unaccoutred and undisciplined. 1896 CLARK RUSSELL *What Cheer!* xi. 189 When it came to lee shores and frightful cliffs resounding the thunder of the tempest of the Atlantic..the turnpikers bent their backs and pulled with a will.

Tu·rnpike road. A road on which turnpikes are or were erected for the collection of tolls; hence, a main road or highway, formerly maintained by a toll levied on cattle and wheeled vehicles. Also *fig.*

1745 WESLEY *Wks.* (1830) I. 485 Turnpike roads were not known in that part of England till some years after. 1776 ADAM SMITH *W. N.* I. xi. I. (1869) I. 156 Some of the counties in the neighbourhood of London petitioned the Parliament against the extension of the turnpike roads into the remoter counties. 1845 MCCULLOCH *Taxation* Introd. (1852) 33 It was not..till after the peace of Paris, in 1763, that turnpike-roads began to be extended to all parts of the kingdom. *Ibid.* II. x. 377 It has..been proposed to abolish tolls, as being essentially partial and unfair, and to raise a fund for constructing and repairing turnpike roads by a tax on property assessed and collected in the same way..as the rate for cross and parish roads. 1875 W. S. HAYWARD *Love agst. World* 16 After an hour's ride, by cross-country lanes and by-paths, they struck into the turnpike road.

Turn-rice, -rise, var. TURNWREST.

Turn-serving (tə̄·ɹnsə̄ɹviŋ), *sb.* and *a.* [f. TURN *sb.* 30 + SERVING *vbl. sb.* and *ppl. a.*] **a.** *sb.* The action or practice of serving one's own turn; the promotion of one's private interest; self-seeking; an instance of this. **b.** *adj.* That serves its own turn; promoting one's own ends. So †**Tu·rn-served** *a.*, that has served his own turn (*obs.*); **Tu·rn-server**, one whose motive is his own interest. Cf. TIME-SERVER, etc.

1613 CHAPMAN *Masque Inns of Court* Plays 1873 III. 109 The sight of an attendant for reward is abominable in the eyes of a *turne-seru'd Politician. 1611 SPEED *Hist. Gt. Brit.* IX. xvi. (1623) 839 A deceitfull man, a *turn-server. 1710 *Answ. to Bp. of Oxford's Sp.* 18 The Memory of all Time and Turn-Servers will be forgotten. 1611 SPEED *Hist. Gt. Brit.* IX. xi. § 62 His name was abased to all sorts of *turne-seruings. 1616 BACON *Let. to Sir G. Villiers* 12 Aug., Though now, since Choice goeth better both in Church and Common-wealth, yet Money, and Turn-Serving, and Cunning Canvises, and Importunity, prevail too much. 1584 POWEL *Lloyd's Cambria* 278 Let people take heede how they build upon *turne-seruing freendship. 1842 G. S. FABER *Prov. Lett.* (1844) II. 189 A mere temporary and turn-serving appeal to Antiquity.

Turn-sick (tə̄·ɹnsik), *a.* and *sb.* *Obs.* exc. *dial.* Also 5–6 **-seke**, 6 **-sycke**, **-sicke**. [f. TURN *v.* + SICK *a.*]

†**A.** *adj.* Affected with vertigo; giddy; dizzy.

c 1440 *Promp. Parv.* 507/1 Turnseke, *vertiginosus*. 1534 WHITINTON *Tullyes Offices* I. (1540) 49 We here tell of Lysander of Lacedemony, a turnesycke person and a man that myght abyde all paynes. 1626 BACON *Sylva* § 795 If a Man see another turn swiftly, and long; Or if he look upon Wheels that turne, Himselfe waxeth Turne-sick. 1657 J. WATTS *Dipper Sprinkled* 6 Running round in a ring until you be turn-sick and giddy-headed.

fig. *a* 1603 T. CARTWRIGHT *Confut. Rhem. N. T.* (1618) 179 You are fallen out with your selues, and turne-sick with the maze of your own inuentions. *Ibid.* 382 These turnesick Iesuites make their note cleane contrary to the text. *a* 1617 BAYNE *On Eph.* (1658) 104 An escape of a turn sick brain blinded with wilfulness. 1664 J. C. *Praxis Lat. Syntax* 130 Divers teachers, so giddy turn-sick.

†**b.** *Turn-sick giddiness*, vertigo. *Obs.*

1577 B. GOOGE *Heresbach's Husb.* IV. (1586) 192 The water of this hearbe..helpeth the turnesicke giddinesse of the heade.

B. *sb.* †**1. a.** Vertigo, swimming in the head; also, staggers in the horse. *Obs.*

c 1450 in *Vicary's Anat.* (1888) App. ix. 229 Be-hynde þe eres er twa vayns þat er gude to be opynd for turnseke and for scall, & alsso for euyll sight. 1565 BLUNDEVIL *Horsemanship* IV. xvi. (1580) 8 In the ventricles or celles of the braine..do breede the turnesicke, or staggers. 1592 in *Vicary's Anat.* (1888) App. ix. 228 If thowe lett blode of thoo, His syght shall neuer fale, And heles of torne-seke, and of scale.

2. A disease caused by an encysted worm in the brain of the sheep; the gid or sturdy. *dial.* Cf. TURN *sb.* 3.

1834 YOUATT *Cattle* 294 The sheep is subject to a disease

strangely termed *turnsick*, in which the animal goes round and round. 1837 — *Sheep* 391 The turnsick is not so frequent as it used to be thirty or forty years ago. 1844 STEPHENS *Bk. Farm* III. 877 There is a disease in sheep called sturdy or turnsick. 1870 ROLLESTON *Anim. Life* 136 The cause of the disease commonly known as the 'sturdy', 'gid', 'staggers', or 'turn-sick'.

Hence †**Turnsickness** = B. 1. *Obs.*

1559 MORWYNG *Evonym.* 137 The headache, fallinge sicknesse, swindle or turnsicknes.

†**Turnsilver.** *Obs. rare*⁻¹. [?f. TURN *sb.* or *v.* + SILVER *sb.*] A local payment of uncertain nature.

1578 in Whellan *Hist. Cumb. & Westm.* (1860) 208/2 [From the inquisition taken in 1578, we learn the following particulars...The tenants of Ulterside pay yearly]..for cornage, 4 s. 6 d.; for seawake, 7 d.; for turnsilver, 1 s. 3 d.

Turnsole (tə̄·ɹnsōl). Forms: 4 **turnisoll**, 4–8 **turnesole**, (5–6 **turne-**, 7 **turnsoyle**, **turn(e)-soil(e)**, 6 **turnesoll**, **-sell**, **-sall**, **-saule**, **turnsale**, **-sowell**, **tornsole**, **-sell**, **-salle**, **tornesall(e**, **-sol(e**, **-solt**, **tournesoll**, **-sole**, **-soule**, 6–7 **turnsall**, 7 **-soll**, **-soule**, 7–8 **turnesol**, 8 **tournsol**, 6–9 **turnsol**, 5– **turnsole**. [a. F. *tournesol* (14th c. in Littré), prob. ad. older Prov. *tournasol* (now *tournosol*) = Sp. and Pg. *tornasol*, It. *tornasole*, f. Romanic *tornare* to TURN + L. *sōl* the sun.

In F., as in Eng., first recorded as the name of the colouring matter derived from one of the plants bearing the name. In mod. Sp., Pg., and It. chiefly used in sense 2 b.]

1. A violet-blue or purple colouring matter, obtained from the plant *Crozophora tinctoria* (see 2 a), formerly much used for colouring jellies, confectionery, wines, etc., and later as a pigment. (See also quots. 1712 and 1830.)

Coarse linen rags are steeped in the juice, and then dried and exposed in vats over an ammoniacal mixture; hence the designation †*turnsole in rags* = F. *tournesol en drapeau*.

1375 *Exch. Rolls Scotl.* II. 507 Computat per empcionem de iij libris alkynet, j libra de turnisoll, et j libra de savndre. 1392 *Earl Derby's Exp.* (Camden) 154 Pro iij lb. turnesole ad xiiij d. *c* 1440 *Anc. Cookery* in *Househ. Ord.* (1790) 437 Colour hit with turnesole, or with ynde, or with alkenet, or saunders, or saffron. 1513 *Bk. Keruynge* in *Babees Bk.* (1868) 268 Tornsole is holsome for reed wyne colourynge. 1573 *Art of Limming* 4 To make azure and bize sadder, take good blewe tournesoll and wet it in gumme water. 1606 PEACHAM *Art of Drawing* I. xxiii. (1612) 86 The sorts of Red are these, Vermilion. Synaper lake...Red lead. Roset. Turnsoile [etc.]. *Ibid.* 88 Turnesoile is made of old linnen ragges died:..it is good to shadow carnations, and all yealowes. 1615 MARKHAM *Eng. Housew.* II. ii. 70 If you will haue [the jelly] coloured, then put in a little Tournesall. 1616–61 HOLYDAY *Persius* 308 The armorists indeed slight your common purple made of grocer's turnesol, a mixture of vermilion and blew bysse, or cynnaber, or the colour of violets. 1688 [see 2 a]. 1712 tr. *Pomet's Hist. Drugs* v. 93/2 Tornesol or Turnsole in Rags, is made of Linnen Cloth dyed at Constantinople, with Cocheneal and some Acids. The Cotton Turnsole, call'd Portugal or Spanish Wool, is made from Cotton that is..dyed in Spain or Portugal with Mestich Cochineal. Both Sorts are made use of to colour Liquors, Fruits and Gellies. There is another Kind of Turnsole that is made with Rags dipp'd in a red Tincture, prepar'd with the Juice of the Berry, and a little acid Liquor. 1783 *Phil. Trans.* LXXIII. 39 Acids possess the property of changing the juice of turnsol, or infusion of litmus, red. 1830 LINDLEY *Nat. Syst. Bot.* 103 The preparation called Turnsol,..chiefly obtained from Crozophora (Croton) tinctoria, is to be procured equally abundantly from many other plants of the order [Euphorbiaceæ]. 1866 *Treas. Bot.* 352/1 C[rozophora] *tinctoria*..is cultivated in the South of France for the sake of a dye which is obtained from it. This dye is called Turnsole, and is obtained by grinding the plants..to a pulp in a mill, when they yield about half their weight of a dark green coloured juice, which becomes purple by exposure to the air or under the influence of ammonia.

fig. 1599 *Broughton's Let.* xi. 38 Coloured with the Turnsalue of your Phantasticall braine.

b. *transf.* = LITMUS.

So F. *tournesol* and *tournesol en pain*.

1839 URE *Dict. Arts* 53 The lichen which produces archil is subjected to another preparation, to make turnsole (litmus). This article is made in Holland. 1842 BRANDE *Dict. Sc.* etc. 671/1 *Litmus*..a blue pigment obtained from the lichen *Rocella*..it is often called *turnsol*, and yields the dye called *archil*.

2. A plant of which the flowers or leaves turn so as to follow the sun; a heliotrope. **a.** An annual euphorbiaceous plant, *Crozophora tinctoria*, the *Small Tornesol* of Lyte's Herbal, found wild by the Mediterranean, and cultivated in the south of France for its colouring juice (see 1).

In earlier botanical use called *Croton tinctorium* (or *-ius*), *Ricinoides* (Tournefort), and (after Pliny) *Heliotropium tricoccum*.

1578 LYTE *Dodoens* I. xli. 61 With the seede of the smal Tornesoll..they die and stayne old linnen cloutes and ragges into a purple colour,..wherewithall in this countrey men vse to colour gellies, wynes, fine Confections, and Comfitres. 1688 R. HOLME *Armoury* II. 91/1 Turnsole, at the leaves comes forth three berries..which have within them a juice, or moisture of a purple colour of which that Turn-sole is made; sold by the Drugists. 1728 CHAMBERS *Cycl.*, *Tornesol*, *Tournesol*, or *Turnsol*, called also *Heliotrope*, and *Sunflower*, and by the Botanists *Ricinoides*. *Ibid.*, The *tournsol* being no Plant of their [i.e. Dutch] Growth. 1756 C. LUCAS *Ess. Waters* I. 21 Blews obtained from..archil, tournsol, &c. have their colors exalted or preserved by alcalies.

b. The plant *Heliotropium europæum*, the *Great Tornesol* of Lyte's Herbal; sometimes used by modern botanists as a name for the genus *Heliotropium*.

1578 LYTE *Dodoens* I. xli. 60 The great Tornesol hath straight round stalkes, couered with a white bearie cotton... The floures be white, at the toppe of the stalke, growing thicke togither in rewes. 1603 B. JONSON *Jas. I's Entertainm.* Wks. (Rtldg.) 528/2 Agrypnia, or Vigilance, in yellow,..her chaplet of Heliotropium, or turnsole. 1707 *Curios. in Husb. & Gard.* 142 The Famous Plant, call'd Heliotrope, Turn-Sole, or Sun-Flower. 1731 MILLER *Gard. Dict.* s.v. *Heliotropium*, The great Turnsole of Dioscorides. *Ibid.*, Blue American Turnsole, with Clary Leaves. *a* 1832 BENTHAM *Deontol.* i. (1834) I. 20 Let the moralist regard the great Deontological law, as steadily as the Turnsole looks upon the sun. 1866 *Treas. Bot.* 576/2 The Heliotrope or Turnsole, is a large genus of *Ehretiaceæ*...They are herbs or undershrubs found chiefly in tropical and subtropical regions, but a few species reach Europe, and one, *H[eliotropium] europæum*, is distributed over..southern and central Europe. 1887 MOLONEY *Forestry W. Afr.* 388 Indian Turnsole (*Heliotropium indicum*, L.).—Small annual.

c. Formerly applied to the Sunflower; also to the Sun-spurge or Wartwort, *Euphorbia helioscopia*.

1725 *Family Dict.* s.v. *Sunflower*, It's named *Turn-Sol* by the Italians and French. *Ibid.*, Between which [trees], at three Foot distance one from the other, our Turn-Sols may be planted. 1804 MALKIN *Scen. etc. S. Wales* 606 Turnsoles,..though beautiful, are never planted on graves, because they are not sweet-scented. 1863–79 PRIOR *Pop. Names Brit. Plants*, *Turnsole* or *Tornsole*, a name erroneously given in some old works to the wartwort.

3. *attrib.*, as *turnsole paper, rag, tincture.*

1733 SHAW *Chem. Lect.* xi. (1755) 210 We put four Ounces of what is commonly called Turnsol Rags into an earthen Vessel. 1753 *Chambers' Cycl.* Supp. s.v. *Turnesol*, The plant that afforded the Turnesol colour. *Ibid.*, The true Turnesol plant here described. 1797 PEARSON in *Phil. Trans.* LXXXVIII. 35 It reddened turnsole paper and tincture. 1836 J. M. GULLY *Magendie's Formul.* (ed. 2) 191 The solution in question reddened turnsol paper.

Turnspit (tə̄·ɹnspit). [f. TURN *v.* + SPIT *sb.*; cf. TURNBROACH.]

1. A dog kept to turn the roasting-spit by running within a kind of tread-wheel connected with it; a *turnspit dog*. Also *fig.*

1576 FLEMING tr. *Caius' Dogs* (1880) 35 A certaine dogge ..when any meate is to bee roasted they go into a wheele.. turning rounde about with the waight of their bodies...Whom the popular sort herevpon call Turnespets. *a* 1619 FLETCHER *Mad Lover* III. ii, Get thee to school again, and talk of turnspits. 1793 [E. D. CLARKE] *Tour S. Eng.* iv. 215 Dogs are universally used, in this part of the world, as turnspits. 1801 COL. G. HANGER *Life* II. 246 These turnspits, who, in the metaphysical wheel, turn the spit of conjecture. 1863 JESSE in Chambers *Bk. Days* 8 Apr. I. 490/1 His two turnspits..were long-bodied, crook-legged, and ugly dogs.

2. A boy or man whose office was to turn the spit. Also used as a term of contempt.

1607 *Puritan* I. ii. 3 As hot as a turn-spit. 1683 *Roxb. Ball.* (1885) V. 455 Fat Turnspit Frank,..Whom we despise, in time may rise to be Jester to King Perkin. 1723 SWIFT *French Dog* Wks. 1755 IV. I. 36 A turn-spit in the royal kitchen. 1802–12 BENTHAM *Ration. Judic. Evid.* (1827) II. 139 The King's turnspit used to be a member of parliament. 1809 MALKIN *Gil Blas* II. i. ¶ 3 Leonarda..passed for a very decent plain cook; but a mere turnspit to dame Jacintha. 1869 BLACKMORE *Lorna D.* v, All good people..knowing his kitchen range to be cold, no longer would play turnspit.

3. A roasting-jack. *rare.*

1606 CHAPMAN *Gent. Usher* III. i, Euen as in a turne-spit calld a Iacke..the great wheeles, Turning but softly, make the lesse to whirre. 1858 SIMMONDS *Dict. Trade*, *Turnspit*, a clock-work machine for cooking.

4. *attrib.*, as *turnspit-boy, cur, dog, -jack, terrier.*

1820 SCOTT *Monast.* xiv, A little dirty *turnspit-boy. 1603 HARSNET *Pop. Impost.* xxii. 145 Moved..as a Wheele is by a *turnspit curre, that is put into it. 1625 N. CARPENTER *Geog. Del.* I. iv. (1635) 81 *Turne-spit-dogs labouring in their wheeles. *a* 1704 T. BROWN *Laconics* Wks. 1711 IV. 14 Seeing one of the Turn-spit Dogs bask himself in the Sun. 1845 YOUATT *Dog* ii. 18 Colonel Sykes says..among the pariahs is frequently found the turnspit-dog. 1674 PETTY *Disc. Dupl. Proportion* 39 In any good *Turnspit-Jack,..a quadruple weight makes double Velocity. 1857 HUGHES *Tom Brown* I. iii, Toby the *turnspit terrier.

Turnstile (tə̄·ɹnstəil). [f. TURN *v.* + STILE *sb.*] A gateway formed of four radiating arms of timber or iron at right angles to each other, revolving horizontally on a fixed vertical post, set up in a passage or entrance, originally to exclude any but foot-passengers; now often to prevent the passage of more than one person at a time at a place where fees, fares, or tickets are collected, or where it is desired to count those passing.

a 1643 CARTWRIGHT *Lady Errant* I. v, Double forked Like a turn-stile, or some such engin. 1650 B. *Discolliminium* 48, I can devise none fitter then Weather-cocks and a Turne-stile. 1716 GAY *Trivia* III. 108 Where twirling turnstiles intercept the way, The thwarting passenger shall force them round. 1818 LEIGH *New Pict. Lond.* 313 The kind of iron turn-stiles, which admit of only one person passing at a time. 1861 *All Year Round* 29 June 324 The railway station is full, the voluminous gowns are jamming up the ticket collectors' turnstiles. 1890 *Spectator* 31 May 756 Sixty thousand passed the turnstiles of the Zoological Gardens.

fig. 1852 JERDAN *Autobiog.* II. xxi. 206 Bills..were frequently only turnstiles opening into paths of difficulty.

b. *attrib.*

1688 R. HOLME *Armoury* III. 336/2 A Turning Hatch, or Turnstyle gate. 1877 KNIGHT *Dict. Mech.* s.v., A turnstile counter for omnibuses and cars is described in English patent No. 2189, of 1854. *Turnstile-register*,..for registering the number of persons who pass through a turnstile. 1896 *Daily News* 21 Aug. 3/5 Turnstile attendant at the Crystal Palace.

Turnstone (tə̄·ɹnstōn). [f. TURN *v.* + STONE *sb.*] A limicoline bird (*Strepsilas interpres*) of about the size of the snipe, widely distributed in the Old and New Worlds, which turns over stones to get at the crustacea and other small animals to be found under them.

1674 RAY *Words, Water Fowl* 91 The Turn-stone:..Cinclus Turneri. This bird we observed on the coast of Cornwall: it is lesser then a Plover, and somewhat bigger then a Black-bird. 1678 RAY *Willughby's Ornith.* III. v. 311 The Turn-stone, or Sea-Dottrel. 1731 MORTIMER in *Phil. Trans.* XXXVII. 176 The Turn-Stone or Sea-Dottrel..is a Native both of England and America. 1802 MONTAGU *Ornith. Dict.* s.v., The Turnstone is subject to great variety in respect to the markings about the head and neck. 1862 ANSTED *Channel Isl.* 207 The turnstone is found about the neighbourhood of Herm throughout the year. 1904 *Blackw. Mag.* Feb. 250/2 The turnstones..breed in Alaska.

Turn-table (tə̄·ɹntēib'l). [f. TURN *v.* + TABLE *sb.*]

1. On a railway: A revolving platform turning on a central pivot, laid with rails connecting with adjacent tracks, for turning railway vehicles; a turn-plate.

1835 *Massachusetts Stat.* 4 Apr., To unite any rail-road or rail-roads..by turn-tables or otherwise. 1838 N. WOOD *Railroads* (ed. 3) 186 On each of these lines..circular turn-tables are placed, upon which the carriages are run. 1854 *John Bull* 2 Sept. 558/1 An engine having been accidentally put in motion while on the turn table, ran over a side wall, and rested on end in the street below.

2. A revolving platform, table, stand, or disk of various kinds: see quots.; *spec.* (*a*) a rotating disk on which microscope slides are held for tracing the circular cement cells in which specimens are placed for examination; (*b*) see quot. 1889; (*c*) a turning device allowing a photographic camera to rotate on the stand or tripod; (*d*) a rotating plate-glass show stand used in shop-windows (*Funk's Stand. Dict.* 1895).

1865 *Morn. Star* 2 Sept., The burial board..determined on placing a stand, or what is called a 'turn-table', in the church, and also one in the chapel [for use at funerals]. 1867 J. HOGG *Microsc.* I. iii. 254 The little box contains:—Shadbolts turn-table, brass table [etc.]. 1887 T. A. TROLLOPE *What I remember* II. xv. 279 His food..is passed in to him by a little turntable made in the wall. 1889 WELCH *Text Bk. Naval Archit.* v. 79 The four heavy guns are carried on revolving turntables in two fixed armoured redoubts or barbettes. 1892 *Photogr. Ann.* II. p. cxci, A special form of Turntable is fixed to the Camera, to which the legs may be quickly attached...The centre of the Turntable is cut away.

3. *attrib.*, as *turn-table ladder, stack.*

1893 *Nation* (N. Y.) 13 July 28/3 At the Columbian Fair there is a turn-table stack of official publications. 1912 *Times* 19 Dec. 12/6 A horsed escape, a fire engine, a turn-table ladder, and ten men turned out from the Theobald's-road fire station.

Tu·rn-tail, *sb.* and *a.* [f. the verbal phr. *turn tail* (TURN *v.* 59).]

A. *sb.* **1.** One who turns tail; one who abandons or forsakes his former associates or principles; also, a coward. Now *rare.*

1621 BRATHWAIT *Nat. Embassie*, etc. (1877) 301 Thou art the rich mans claw-backe,..Go turne-taile go. *a* 1650 SPALDING *Troub. Chas. I* (1850) I. 206 Mony covenanteris proveit turne-taillis throw plane feir, and cam most willinglie into him. 1819 LINGARD *Hist. Eng.* I. xix. III. 136 *note*, Under the penalty of culvertage (culvert, a turn-tail) that is perpetual slavery.

†**2.** A variety of domestic pigeon. *Obs.*

1741 *Compl. Fam.-Piece* III. 512 The Croppers are valuable for their Sweil...The Turn-tails for their turning them up almost to their Back.

B. *adj.* That turns tail.

1861 GEO. ELIOT *Silas M.* vi, I aren't a turn-tail cur.

Turn-up (tə̄·ɹn,ʌp), *sb.* and *a.* [f. the verbal phr. *turn up* (TURN *v.* 80).]

A. *sb.* †**1.** See quot., and cf. *turn up*, TURN *v.* 80***. *Obs. rare*⁻¹.

1612 *Benvenuto's Passenger* I. iv. 315 They are whores, harlots, trulls, baggages, bayards, turne-vps, curtesanes.

2. The turned up part of anything, esp. of a garment.

1688 R. HOLME *Armoury* IV. iv. (Roxb.) 295/2 A pilgrims hat of St. James,..on the turne-vp, two staves in salter debrused with an Escalop shell Or. *Ibid.* v. 307/1, I haue obserued that sleeues both in coates and crests haue had their Turn-vps of diuerse fashions. 1764 FOOTE *Patron* I. 5 He found the turn-up of her nose too exactly resemble the bust of the princess Popæa. 1901 *Daily Record* 21 Dec. 4 They..have velvet collars, narrow turn-ups at the cuffs, and are well shaped to the waist. 1902 ELIZ. L. BANKS *News-paper Girl* 230 A hat..that'd suit you to a T! It's exactly made for you, turn-up on the side and all!

3. The turning up of a particular card or die in games of chance; the card or die turned up; hence *fig.*, a mere chance, a 'toss-up'; a result which is purely a matter of chance; also, an unexpected appearance or phenomenon.

1810 *Sporting Mag.* XXXVI. 265 He..recorded turns up of all the chances. 1820 W. IRVING *Sketch Bk.*, *Stratford* (1865) 327 It is often a turn-up of a die, in the gambling freaks of fate, whether a natural genius shall turn out a

great rogue or a great poet. 1844 J. T. HEWLETT *Parsons & W.* vi, What the 'turn-up' would be I knew no more than a card-player, who has just had the pack cut to him. 1870 HARDY & WARE *Mod. Hoyle*, *Cribbage* 79 If the turn up should also be of the same suit, you count one extra. 1884 J. BURROUGHS in *Century Mag.* XXVII. 926 The type of men of which Emerson and Carlyle are the most pronounced ..examples..are comparatively a new turn-up in literature.

b. *spec.* in Racing: see quot. 1873.

1873 *Slang Dict.*, *Turn up*,..an unexpected slice of luck. Among sporting men bookmakers are said to have a turn up when an unbacked horse wins. 1895 *Westm. Gaz.* 10 Sept. 7/2 With such a moderate field nobody will be surprised if the result is a 'turn-up' as astonishing as was the victory of Throstle last year. 1900 *Ibid.* 15 May 8/1 The Jubilee Handicap on Saturday ended in a tremendous turn-up for the fielders.

4. A boxing contest; hence, *loosely*, a fight, a set-to, esp. with the fists; also, a tussle, struggle; a disturbance, row.

1820 *Sporting Mag.* XXXVI. 195 The next amusement was a turn-up betwixt Crib and Richman. 1827 SCOTT *Two Drovers* ii, We must have a turn-up, or we shall be the talk of the countryside...Come, stand forward like a man. *c* 1874 G. H. KINGSLEY *Sport & Trav.* vi. (1900) 160 Campbell, however, had a turn-up with a grizzly. 1891 SARAH J. DUNCAN *Amer. Girl in Lond.* 78 The why and the wherefore of all this turn-up.

B. *attrib.* or *adj.* That is turned up, or turns up, in various senses.

1685 *Lond. Gaz.* No. 2032/4 A small Spaniel Lap Dog.., with..a short turn-up Nose. *c* 1690 *Roxb. Ball.* (1895) VIII. 17 Turn-up stockings they constantly wear. 1767 in *Daily Chron.* 19 Nov. (1908) 4/7 You may sit in their Royal presence, not in pews, but in turn-up seats on the side of them. 1800 *Hull Advertiser* 19 Apr. 3/2 An infant..was smothered..with the bed-clothes of a turn-up bedstead. 1809 MALKIN *Gil Blas* XI. ii. (Rtldg.) 397 The sharp-pointed, turn-up chin of a pantaloon. 1821 LAMB *Elia* Ser. I. *Mrs. Battle on Whist*, She would not take advantage of the turn-up knave. 1848 RICKMAN *Archit.* 211 Stalls with turn-up seats and benches. 1874 BURNAND *My Time* xix. 166 It was neatly furnished, with a small table, a turn-up bedstead, etc. 1909 *Daily Graphic* 20 Oct. 13/1 The hat with the turn-up brim.

†**Turnway**¹. *Rhet.* *Obs. rare*⁻¹. [f. TURN *v.* + WAY *adv.* away, after Gr. ἀποστροφή.] = APOSTROPHE¹ 1.

1589 PUTTENHAM *Eng. Poesie* III. xix. (Arb.) 245 When we haue runne a long race in our tale..we do sodainly flye out and either speake or exclaime at some other person or thing, and therefore the Greekes call such figure (as we do) the turnway or turnetale.

Turnway² (tə̄·ɹnwēi). [f. TURN *sb.* + WAY *sb.*] A system or method of turns; in quot. *attrib.*

1897 WEBB *Indust. Democ.* I. II. ix. 437 The 'turnway' societies of the Thames watermen, for regulating the 'turns', or order in which the men plying at any particular 'stairs' serve the passengers who present themselves.

Turnwrest (tə̄·ɹnrest), *a.* (*sb.*) Also 8–9 **turnwrist**, **-rise**, 9 **-rice**. [f. TURN- + WREST *sb.* (See also REEST *sb.*)] *Turnwrest plough*, a plough in which the mould-board may be shifted from one side to the other at the end of each furrow, so that the furrow-slice is always thrown the same way; a one-way plough.

In the 18th cent. freq. called the *Kentish plough*.

1653 BLITHE *Eng. Improv. Impr.* II xxix. (ed. 3) 203 There is another double Wheeled-plough, & it is called the Turn wrest plough, which of all ploughs that ever I saw, surpasseth for weight and clumsiness. 1766 *Museum Rust.* VI. 129 He had made one, which he called a turn-rise plough. 1794 A. PRINGLE *Agric. Westmorland* 34 The turnwrist plough is about to be introduced into the county. 1812 SIR J. SINCLAIR *Syst. Husb. Scot.* I. 136 A plough with a shifting mould-board, usually called a turn-wrest plough, admits of ploughing both backwards and forwards. 1846 DAVIS in *Jrnl. R. Agric. Soc.* VII. II. 526 This I accomplished with a monster turn-rice plough made for the purpose. 1856 MORTON *Cyclop. Agric.* II. 628–30 (Various forms described). 1884 *W. Sussex Gaz.* 25 Sept., Strong turnwrist, round, snap, and strike furrow ploughs.

transf. 1844 STEPHENS *Bk. Farm* II. 624 The mountain turn-wrist snow-plough.

b. *ellipt.* as *sb.* Also *attrib.*

1778 [W. MARSHALL] *Minutes Agric.* 25 Oct. an. 1775, A Turn-wrist is obviously preferable to a fixed-wrist, for cross-plowing. 1846 CLARKE in *Jrnl. R. Agric. Soc.* VII. II. 512 The old Kentish turn-wrest. 1908 *Westm. Gaz.* 7 Nov. 7/2 In the North Kent Agricultural Association's ploughing match..the variety of ploughs to be seen was surprising. The old wooden turnrise type was well to the fore.

†**Turny** (tə̄·ɹni), *a.* *Obs. rare.* [f. TURN *sb.* 3 + -Y.] Of an ox, etc.: Affected with the turn.

1651 *Manch. Crt. Leet Rec.* (1887) IV. 51 Thomas Peele [presented] for sellinge a leane turney beast.

†**Turon.** *Obs. rare.* [ad. med.L. *Turonia* or *Turonī*: see next.] The city of Tours; used *attrib.* = next, b.

Freq. in Trevisa's *Higden* as the name of the city.

1568 GRAFTON *Chron.* II. 136 He..solde him his title that he had in Normandy, Gascoyne and Guyan...Taking for the same title three hundreth thousande of small Turon money.

†**Turoneis, Turoneys**, *sb.* and *a.* *Obs.* [ad. med.L. *Turonensis* (f. *Turonēs*, later *Turonī*, *Turonii*, a people of ancient Gaul, whence Tours on the Loire took its name), with ending assimilated to OF. *torneis* (F. *tournois* TOURNOIS *a.*).] **a.** *sb.* *pl.* The people or citizens of Tours. **b.** *adj.* Of or pertaining to Tours; = TOURNOIS.

The sing. form *Turoney* employed by Trevisa is irregular. Both Trevisa and the anonymous translator of Higden also employ the Latin ending *-ens(e*.

1387 TREVISA *Higden* (Rolls) VI. 259 He sette and pighte a lettre of gold of þe wight of an hondred pound of Turoneys [*v.rr.* Turoneyes, -eies]. *Ibid.*, He schal not spende at his comeucement passynge þre þowsand of grootes turonens [*v.r.* turoneies]. Þe groot turoney is somwhat lasse worþy þan an Englische groote, flor..I have i-fonge in chaunge enlevene grotes turoneys for a duket...But þere is double manere of money of turoneis [*v.r.* turoneies], more and lasse [etc.].

Turonian (tiurōᵘ·niān), *a.* *Geol.* [= F. *turonien*, f. L. *Turonēs*: see prec. and -IAN.] Denoting a subdivision of the Cretaceous or Chalk period and series of strata, answering to the 'Lower White Chalk without flints' of English geologists.

1850 ANSTED *Elem. Geol.*, *Min.* etc., Index, Turonian formation. [*Ibid.* § 792 These beds are represented in France by the lower members of the 'Terrain turonien', which exhibit nearly the same peculiarities as in England, though to a somewhat greater extent.] 1885 GEIKIE *Text Bk. Geol.* VI. II. iii. § 2 (ed. 2) 820 The Cretaceous system of Europe has been subdivided as follows:—Upper..Danian, Senonian, Turonian, Cenomanian, Gault. Lower..Neocomian.

†**Turow**, ? var. of *thorow*, THROUGH *sb.*¹ 2.

1533 in Weaver *Wells Wills* (1890) 139 To be buryd in holy turow.

Turpel, -pele, -pell, var. TIRPEIL *Obs.*

Turpentine (tə̄·ɹpĕntəin), *sb.* Forms: *α.* 5–6 **terebentine**, **-yne** (see also TEREBINTHINE); *β.* 4–5 **terb-**, 5 **turbentyne**; *γ.* 5–6 **terpentin**, **turpentyne**, 6 **-tyn**, 7 **terpentine**, 6– **turpentine**; *δ.* 5 **turmyntyne**, 6 **termenteyne**. [In 14–15th c. *terebentyne*, *terbentyne*, a. OF. *tere-*, *terbentine*, ad. L. *terbentina* or *terebinthina* (*rēsīna*): see TEREBINTHINA, -INE. Already *a* 1400, OF. had *tourbentine* (in R. Estienne 1550, *turbentine*); so Eng. *turbentyn* and *turpentine*. The 15–16th c. variant *termenteyne* curiously approaches the earlier Gr. τερμινθίνη (ῥητίνη) terebinthine resin, turpentine.]

1. A term applied originally (as in Gr. and Lat.) to the semifluid resin of the terebinth tree, *Pistacia Terebinthus* (Chian or Cyprian turpentine); now chiefly to the various oleoresins which exude from coniferous trees, consisting of more or less viscid solutions of resin in a volatile oil.

α. [1398 TREVISA *Barth. De P. R.* XVII. clxiv. (Bodl. MS.) lf. 222/1 Therebintus..is a tre þat sweteþ rosine..and þe rosine þereof hatte Therebentina.] *c* 1425 tr. *Arderne's Treat. Fistula* 31 Putte to of terebentyne als moche as sufficeþ.. moue it strongly wiþ a spature vnto þat þe terebentyne be dronken in. 1541 R. COPLAND *Guydon's Formul.* X j b, Fomentacyon with oyle and terebentyne medled & warmed. 1597 A. M. tr. *Guillemeau's Fr. Chirurg.* 42 b/2 Made of Oyle of Egges and of Venetiane Terebentine.

β. 1322 in *Wardr. Acc. 16 Edw. II* 23/20 Terbentyn 7ᵈ þe lb. *c* 1400 MAUNDEV. (1839) v. 51 A gome, þat men clepen Turbentyne. *c* 1425 tr. *Arderne's Treat. Fistula* 32 Terbentyne. 1460–70 *Bk. Quintessence* II. 25 Wiþ frank-encense, mirre, and rosyn, terbentyn and rewe.

γ. *c* 1400 MAUNDEV. (Roxb.) vii. 26 A maner of gumme, þat es called Turpentyne. 1576 BAKER *Jewell of Health* 128 Turpentine, which is a lycour dystilled and gotten of the Fyrre tree. 1580 HOLLYBAND *Treas. Fr. Tong*, *Terebinthine*, turpentyne. 1601 HOLLAND *Pliny* XV. xii. I. 465 In Syria they use to plucke the barke from the Terebinth, yea, and they pill the boughs and roots too for Terpentine. 1673 GREW *Anat. Trunks* I. ii. § 18 Out of these Vessels all the clear Turpentine, that drops from the Tree, doth issue. 1718 QUINCY *Compl. Disp.* 125 Common Turpentine..is procured from the Larch-Tree. 1813 SIR H. DAVY *Agric. Chem.* iii. (1814) 97 When a portion of the bark is removed from a fir tree in Spring a matter exudes which is called turpentine. 1875 H. C. WOOD *Therap.* (1879) 131 Turpentine is remarkable for having the property of absorbing oxygen and converting it into ozone.

δ. 1448–9 in Willis & Clark *Cambridge* (1886) I. 403, j lb et di. de Turmyntyne. 1502 ARNOLDE *Chron.* 35/2 Kark of termenteyne, xij d.

b. With qualification, indicating different varieties. See quot. 1831.

1577 FRAMPTON *Joyful News* 45 Adde therto three Ounces of Venise Turpentine. 1634 PEACHAM *Gentl. Exerc.* I. xxvii. 98 Temper it with Spanish Turpentine. 1728 CHAMBERS *Cycl.* s.v. [Various kinds described.] 1744 BERKELEY *Siris* § 20 The Strasburgh turpentine..is procured from the knots of the silver fir. *Ibid.*, Venice turpentine, which is got by piercing the larch tree. 1831 J. DAVIES *Manual Mat. Med.* 191 The principal kinds of turpentine are—the American Turpentine, furnished abundantly by the *Pinus palustris*, Lin., *P. australis*, Michaux, a tree growing principally in the southern states; the Common Turpentine, *Terebinthina communis*, obtained from the *Pinus sylvestris* and *P. rubra*, Lin.;..the Bordeaux Turpentine, *Terebinthina picea*, from the *P. maritima*, Lin., Bordeaux pine: the Strasbourg Turpentine, *Terebinthina abietina*, from the *P. picea*,..silver fir tree; the Venice Turpentine, *Terebinthina laricea*, from..*P. larix*, Lin., white larch; and..Canada or Fir Balsam, *Terebinthina canadensis*,..furnished by the *P. balsamea*, American silver fir. *c* 1865 LETHEBY in *Circ. Sc.* I. 106/1 The oleo-resin is imported into this country under the names of common turpentine, Bordeaux t..., Strasburg t..., and Venice t.

c. *pl.* Varieties of turpentine.

1605 TIMME *Quersit.* III. 184 After one manner, hony,.. after another, turpentines and gummes (as mastic, euphorb[i]um, styrax, and such like)..are to be distilled. 1718 QUINCY *Compl. Disp.* 7 Of Turpentines, Gums, and all of that Tribe. 1843 *Penny Cycl.* XXV. 432/1 As turpentines have a very disagreeable taste, it is customary to form them into pills or boluses. 1874 GARROD & BAXTER *Mat. Med.* (1880) 366 Canada balsam resembles the other turpentines in its action, but it is not often given as a medicine.

d. = *Oil of turpentine*: see 3. *To talk turpentine* (colloq.), to discuss painting.

1876 BRISTOWE *The. & Pract. Med.* (1878) 607 Among the remedies..recommended [for scurvy] are perchloride of iron, acetate of lead, arsenic, digitalis, turpentine. 1891 KIPLING *Light that Failed* vii. 118, I was told that all the world was interested in my work, and everybody at Kami's talked turpentine.

2. †**a.** The fruit of the terebinth tree. *Obs.* **b.** A terebinth tree; = TEREBINTHINE B. 1, TURPENTINE TREE 1. Also, any tree that yields turpentine, as the larch.

1562 TURNER *Herbal* II. 115 The fruite [of Sumach] is lyke vnto small clusters of grapes of the bignes of a turpentine. 1577 B. GOOGE *Heresbach's Husb.* (1586) 72 b, The cherie refuseth not the companie of the Peach, nor the Turpentine, nor they his. 1601 CHESTER *Love's Mart.* (N. Shaks. Soc.) 96 The Turpentine that sweet iuyce doth deplore. 1615 G. SANDYS *Trav.* 90 Cypresse trees and Turpentine, with divers others. 1885 'WANDERER' *Beauteous Terrorist* 29 There 'mid giant turpentines Groups of climbing, clustering vines. 1898 MORRIS *Austral Eng.*, *Turpentine, Brush*, name given to two trees—*Metrosideros leptopetala*,..and *Rhodamnia trinervia*,..both N. O. *Myrtaceæ*.

3. Oil of turpentine (also vulgarly known as *spirit of t.*), a volatile oil, contained in the wood, bark, leaves, and other parts of coniferous trees, and usually prepared by distilling crude turpentine. There are many varieties according to the source, which, though all having the same formula, $C_{10}H_{16}$, vary in their physical and, more especially, their optical properties.

1597 A. M. tr. *Guillemeau's Fr. Chirurg.* 30/2 Hott oyle of Terpentin. 1660 BOYLE *New Exp. Phys. Mech.* xxiv. 188 Common Oyl or Spirit (for in the Shops..the same Liquor is promiscuously call'd by either name) of Turpentine. 1728 CHAMBERS *Cycl.* s.v. *Turpentine*, What is commonly sold under the name of Oil of Turpentine, or Etherial Oil. is only a Distillation of the Rosin called Galipot, fresh from the Tree. 1791 HAMILTON tr. *Berthollet's Dyeing* I. I. I. i. 6 The oil of turpentine..has a considerable refracting power. 1859 GULLICK & TIMBS *Paint.* 208 The rectified oil, improperly called Spirit of turpentine, is now most commonly employed. Its great use among house painters, under the cant name of 'turps', is to thin and assist the drying of oil paints. 1875 H. C. WOOD *Therap.* (1879) 501 Oil of turpentine is never employed to increase the flow of urine.

4. *attrib.* and *Comb.*, as *turpentine ball, business, clyster, distiller, epithem, fomentation, liniment, odour, pill, smell, stupe, varnish*; 'pertaining to the production of turpentine or the cultivation of turpentine trees', as *turpentine camp, district, farm, farmer, orchard, region, wood*; instrumental, as *turpentine-anointed, -filled* adjs.; **turpentine bucket**: see quot.; **turpentine camphor**, a name sometimes given to the solid mono-hydrochlorate, sometimes to the solid hydrates of turpentine oil; **turpentine gall-nut**, an excrescence formed by the puncture of an insect on the branches of the terebinth-tree; **turpentine gum**, American THUS (*sb.*) (*Cent. Dict. Supp.* 1909); **turpentine hack**, a tool for hacking the bark of pine trees, to cause the turpentine to exude (Knight *Dict. Mech.* 1877); **turpentine moth**, a leaf-roller moth of the genus *Retinia*, of which the larvæ bore into the twigs of conifers (*Cent. Dict.* 1891); **turpentine oil** = *oil of turpentine*; **turpentine ointment**, an ointment of which turpentine oil is a principal ingredient (*ibid.*); †**turpentine rod**, a rod of a terebinth tree; **turpentine shrub**, a name of the Prairie Burdock, *Silphium terebinthinaceum*, a tall herbaceous plant with bright yellow flowers, a native of North America cultivated in European gardens since 1765 (*Cassell's Encycl. Dict.* 1888); **Turpentine State** (U.S.): see quot.; **turpentine still**, an apparatus for distilling turpentine from pine wood or spirit from turpentine (Knight *Dict. Mech.* 1877); **turpentine vessel**, in a coniferous tree, one of the tubes formed in the interstices of tissue, into which turpentine or like secretion naturally drains during the growth of the plant; **turpentine weed** = *turpentine shrub*. See also TURPENTINE TREE.

1861 KNIGHT *Pop. Hist. Eng.* VII. xvii. 309 Robespierre ..sets fire to the *turpentine-anointed images. 1844 A. PAGE *Suppl. to Kirby's Suffolk Trav.* 141 A *turpentine ball.. which they set on fire. 1877 KNIGHT *Dict. Mech.*, *Turpentine-bucket*, a cup or vessel to catch crude turpentine as it exudes from the tree. 1856 OLMSTED *Slave States* 338 There are very large forests of [*Pinus Palustris*] in North and South Carolina, Georgia, and Alabama; and the *turpentine business is carried on..in all these States. 1901 *Westm. Gaz.* 16 Mar. 4/1 A *turpentine camp in Baldwin County, Alabama. 1857 MILLER *Elem. Chem.* III. 452 *Turpentine camphor..($C_{20}H_{16}$, 4 HCl). 1694 SALMON *Bate's Dispens.* III. viii. (1713) 708/2 *Enema Terebinthinatum*, A *Turpentine Clyster. 1858 SIMMONDS *Dict. Trade*, *Turpentine and Tar Distiller*, a refiner of these substances. 1901 *Westm. Gaz.* 4 May 5/2 The *turpentine district along the St. John's River has been completely wiped out. 1843 R. J. GRAVES *Syst. Clin. Med.* x. 107 *note*, A warm *turpentine epithem should be placed upon this region. 1867 H. LATHAM *Black & White* 124 The paths which lead among the *turpentine farms. 1856 OLMSTED *Slave States* 350 The majority of what I have termed *turpentine-farmers—..the small proprietors of the long-leafed pine forest land. 1887 FENN *Dick o' the Fens* ii, They were the roots of *turpentine-filled pines. 1879 *St. George's Hosp. Rep.* IX. 319 Great tenderness over the lower half of the abdomen. *Turpentine fomentations were applied. 1860 MAYNE *Expos. Lex.*, *Turpentine Liniment*,..a preparation ..of yellow basilicon ointment diluted with turpentine. 1830 LINDLEY *Nat. Syst. Bot.* 127 A copious flow of limpid oil of a pungent *turpentine odour. 1868 WATTS *Dict. Chem.* V. 920 The diversities of character exhibited by *turpentine-oils..relate chiefly to the specific gravity, boiling-point, and optical rotatory power. 1884 C. S. SARGENT *Rep. Forests N. Amer.* 518 Their owners oftener..employing them [negroes in N. Carolina] in *turpentine orchards than in the cotton-fields. 1622 DEKKER & MASSINGER *Virgin Mart.* III. Wks. 1873 IV. 52 One gave me *turpentine pils. 1856 OLMSTED *Slave States* 325, I was now..in the *Turpentine region of North Carolina. 1632 LITHGOW *Trav.* (1906) 230 A *Turpentine rod brought from Jordan and given to King James. 1887 MOLONEY *Forestry W. Afr.* 372 The plant has a strong *turpentine smell. 1859 BARTLETT *Dict. Amer.*, *Turpentine State*, the State of North Carolina, so called from the quantity of turpentine obtained from its pine forests. 1877 ROBERTS *Handbk. Med.* (ed. 3) I. 130 Occasionally *turpentine-stupes or sinapisms are needed in order to give relief. 1815 J. SMITH *Panorama Sc. & Art* II. 791 It dries as well as any other *turpentine-varnish, and when dry it appears to be as durable as any other solution of copal. 1868 WATTS *Dict. Chem.* V. 925 *Turpentine-varnishes*, solutions of resins in oil of turpentine. 1673–4 GREW *Anat. Trunks* I. ii. § 20 The..*Turpentine-Vessels of Pine are likewise remarkably bigger..than the Milk-Vessels themselves. 1861 BENTLEY *Man. Bot.* 55 In the Coniferæ they.. have..been termed turpentine vessels. 1866 *Treas. Bot.* 1059/1 The plant [*Silphium laciniatum*] is also known as the..*Turpentine-weed. 1885 F. WHYMPER in *Girl's Own Paper* Jan. 171/1 The compass plant—..known, also, as the ..turpentine weed—is a vigorous perennial. 1892 *Pall Mall G.* 15 Nov. 2/3 The Florida convicts..were mostly put to work in the *turpentine woods.

Tu·rpentine, *v.* [f. prec. sb.] *trans.* To treat, rub, or smear with turpentine or turpentine oil. Hence **Tu·rpentined** *ppl. a.* So **Tu·rpentining** *vbl. sb.*, the process of obtaining crude turpentine from living pine-trees (*Cent. Dict. Supp.* 1909).

1759 *N. Jersey Archives* XX. 374 Stolen..A Battoe.. painted with Spanish Brown in the Inside, and the Outsides turpentined. 1789 WOLCOTT (P. Pindar) *Subj. for Painters* 110 Fir'd like turpentin'd poor roasting rats. 1836 DICKENS *Sk. Boz*, *Old Lady*, The table-covers are never taken off, except when the leaves are turpentined and bees'-waxed. 1893 *Spons' Mechanics' Own Bk.* (ed. 4) 433 Put in others with the second marbling colour, also on a turpentined feather.

Tu·rpentine tree.

1. *orig.* The Terebinth, *Pistacia Terebinthus* (N. O. *Anacardiaceæ*), the source of Chian or Cyprian turpentine.

1562 TURNER *Herbal* II. 20 Amongest other rosynes, it of ye turpentinetre is best. *Ibid.* 151, I call it Turpentine tre, because Turpentine cometh oute of it. 1615 G. SANDYS *Trav.* 176 Some two miles from the City..there groweth a Turpentine-tree yet flourishing. 1726 LEONI *Alberti's Archit.* II. 6/2 The Turpentine-tree near Hebron, which was reported to have stood from the creation of the world to the days of Josephus. 1728 BRADLEY *Dict. Bot.* s.v. *Terebinthus*, The Broader-leav'd Turpentine-Tree. *Ibid.*, The Narrow-leav'd Turpentine-Tree. 1869 H. SNOW *Theocritus, Epigr.* i. Notes (1873) 214 The terebinth or turpentine-tree (*Pistachia Terebinthus*), is often mentioned in the Bible, under the names of oak or terebinth.

2. Any tree yielding turpentine, esp. species of pine and fir, as the Larch, *Abies Larix*, which yields Venice turpentine; *Bursera gummifera* (N. O. *Amyridaceæ*), of the West Indies; in Australia, species of *Eucalyptus*, *Syncarpia*, and *Tristania*; in New Zealand, the Tarata (Morris).

1726 LEONI *Alberti's Archit.* I. 26/2, I do not know any Wood that is to be preferr'd to the Larch, or Turpentine Tree. 1818 OXLEY *Jrnls. Two Exped. N. S. Wales* (1820) 331 The timber was chiefly..stringy bark, turpentine tree, and forest oak. 1866 *Treas. Bot.*, Turpentine-tree, *Pistacia Terebinthus*; also *Bursera gummifera*. —, Australian, *Tristania albicans*. 1889 J. H. MAIDEN *Usef. Native Plants Australia* 493 *Eucalyptus microcorys*..North of Port Jackson it bears the name of 'Turpentine Tree', and 'Forest Mahogany'. *Ibid.* 523 *Eucalyptus Stuartiana*.. frequently called 'Turpentine Tree', or 'Peppermint Tree'.

Turpentinic (-ti·nik), *a.* *Chem.* [f. TURPENTINE *sb.* + -IC.] In *turpentinic acid*, a synonym of TEREBIC *acid*.

1868 WATTS *Dict. Chem.* V. 724 Discovered by Bromeis, who called it turpentinic acid.

Tu·rpentinous, *a.* *rare.* [f. TURPENTINE *sb.* + -OUS.] Of the nature of turpentine.

1909 *Eng. Rev.* Jan. 311 Powder 'em and get a little tar and turpentinous smell in..woodpacking for hot baths.

Tu·rpentiny, *a.* [f. as prec. + -Y.] Containing turpentine; having the smell or other properties of turpentine; smeared with turpentine.

1735 *Dict. Polygraph.* I. S ij, The best wood for this purpose,..provided it be not turpentiny. 1866 *Treas. Bot.* 718/2 Manna of Briançon, a turpentiny saccharine exudation from the larch. 1894 DU MAURIER *Trilby* III. (1901) 44/2 Clasping his painty turpentiny hand. 1906 *Macm. Mag.* Sept. 800, I should have..got my fingers all sticky and turpentiney.

Turpeth, turbith (tə̄·ɹpĕþ, -biþ). Forms: *α.* 5 **turbyte**, 5–8 **-bit**, 6 **torbith**, **turbythe**, *pl.* **-bithes**, 7–9 **turbeth**, 6– **turbith**; *β.* 7– **turpith**,

-peth. [a. OF. *turbit*, *-ith*, *turpet* (F. *turbith*) or ad. med.L. *turbith(um*, *turpethum*, *turpetum*, ad. Pers. and Arab. تربد *turbid*, *-bed*, whence also Pg., Sp. *turbit*. *Turbith* was the preponderant Eng. form to the 18th c., till assimilated to med.L. *turpethum*.]

1. A cathartic drug prepared from the root of East Indian jalap, *Ipomœa Turpethum*, an Indian and Australian plant; also, the plant itself, or its root.

†*Garganic Turbith*: see quot. 1760.

α. *c* 1400 *Lanfranc's Cirurg.* 180 He mote ofte purge fleume with turbit. 1460–70 *Bk. Quintessence* 16 Þo laxatyues þat purgen flewme & viscous humouris, as a litil of euforbie, or turbit, or sambucy. 1545 *Rates of Custom-ho.* C vj b, Torbith the pounde, xij d. 1567 MAPLET *Gr. Forest* 63 Tvrbit whose Leafe is like the Laurell, groweth in Ægypt ..It is giuen to purge fleume. 1652 CULPEPPER *Eng. Physic.* (1809) 261 For choler, rhubarb; for phlegm, turbith; for watery humours, scammony. 1760 J. LEE *Introd. Bot.* App. 330 Garganic Turbith, *Thapsia*. *Ibid.*, Indian Turbith, or of the Shops, *Convolvulus*. 1785 MARTYN *Rousseau's Bot.* xvi. (1794) 185 This genus contains several remarkable plants; as..Turpethum or Turbith.

β. 1658 ROWLAND *Moufet's Theat. Ins.* 1119 The Turpeth drives them from their nests. 1758 J. S. *Le Dran's Observ. Surg.* (1771) A a iv b, Turpeth, Hermodactyles, Polypody of the Oak. 1905 H. D. ROLLESTON *Dis. Liver* 262 Turpeth, the Ipomœa turpethum of the Colonial and Indian Pharmacopœias, is recommended in 20 grain doses.

b. *Montpellier Turpeth*, common name for *Globularia alypum*, the decoction of the leaves of which acts as an active but gentle purgative.

1860 in MAYNE *Expos. Lex.*

2. *Turpeth* or *turbith mineral* (MINERAL *a.* 4): basic sulphate of mercury ($HgSO_4 . 2HgO$), obtained as a lemon-yellow powder from the normal sulphate by washing with hot water.

It has emetic, cathartic, and sternutatory properties, but is no longer used internally.

α. 1616 BULLOKAR *Eng. Expos.*, *Turbith minerall*, a certaine red powder..which is vsed against the French disease. 1669 W. SIMPSON *Hydrol. Chym.* 60 Dissolving quicksilver in oyl of vitriol, according to what is done in making turbith mineral. 1685 BOYLE *Eng. Notion Nat.* vi. 233 A patient, who..could not be brought to salivate, neither by the gentler ways, nor by turbith-mineral and other harsher medicines. 1758 REID tr. *Macquer's Chym.* I. 402 Wash this yellow matter in five or six warm waters, and it will be what is called in medicine Turbith mineral; that is, a combination of the Vitriolic Acid with Mercury, five or six grains whereof is a violent purgative, and also an emetick; qualities which it possesses in common with the vegetable Turbith, whose name it hath therefore taken. 1849 D. CAMPBELL *Inorg. Chem.* 236 This yellow powder is a subsulphate [of mercury] ($3HgO . SO_3$), and is known as turbeth mineral. 1874 GARROD & BAXTER *Mat. Med.* (1880) 110 The yellow subsulphate above mentioned, under the name of Turbith Mineral, has been employed as an errhine.

β. 1716 M. DAVIES *Athen. Brit.* II. 352 Turpith Mineral, made of Hydrargyry and Oil of Vitriol. 1815 J. SMITH *Panorama Sc. & Art* II. 795 King's yellow, turpith mineral, and Dutch pink, all form very bright yellows. 1868 WATTS *Dict. Chem.* V. 925 *Turpeth* or *turbith mineral*, an old name for basic mercuric sulphate, $HgSO_4 . 2HgO$. 1899 *Allbutt's Syst. Med.* VIII. 516 Native mercurous sulphate (turpeth mineral) is much used in France.

†**3.** *ellipt.* = prec. sense. *Obs.*

Black turpeth: see quot. 1895.

α. 1658 PHILLIPS, *Turbith*,..a red Mineral, which being beaten to powder, is used in physick. 1675 *Phil. Trans.* X. 299 Mercury..having been..reduced into water, turbith and ashes. 1707 *Curios. in Husb. & Gard.* 325 Olaus..tormented some Quicksilver..into Water, Turbith and Ashes.

β. 1678 PHILLIPS (ed. 4), *Turpith*, a Chymical preparation of Mercury, and the Oyl of Vitriol, whereby the Mercury is precipitated into a sweetnesse. 1800 *Phil. Trans.* XC. 215 Not only the pure red oxide, but the red nitrous oxide, and turpeth, may be substituted. 1895 *Funk's Standard Dict.* s.v., *Black turpeth*, black mercurous acid: old name.

4. *attrib.*, as *t. plant, root, vomit.*

1773 T. PERCIVAL *Ess.* II. 163 The powerful effects of Turpeth vomits in white swellings of the joints. 1860 MAYNE *Expos. Lex.*, *Turbeth Plant*, common name for the *Convolvulus turpethum*. 1868 WATTS *Dict. Chem.* V. 925 *Turpeth* or *turbith root*.

Turpethic (təɹpe·þik), *a.* *Chem.* [f. mod.L. *turpeth-um* TURPETH + -IC.] Of or pertaining to turpeth or turbith; in *turpethic acid*, $C_{34}H_{60}O_{18}$, produced by the action of bases on turpethin. So **Turpethin** (tə̄·ɹpĕþin), *Chem.* [see -IN¹], a brownish-yellow purgative resin, $C_{34}H_{56}O_{16}$, obtained from turpeth- or turbith-root; **Turpetho·lic** *a.*, in *turpetholic acid*, $C_{16}H_{32}O_4$, a derivative of turpethin, crystallizing in a mass of slender microscopic needles having an irritant taste; hence **Turpe·tholate**, a salt of turpetholic acid.

1868 WATTS *Dict. Chem.* V. 926 When turpethin is dissolved in warm baryta-water, the baryta removed [etc.], turpethic acid remains as an amorphous yellowish mass. *Ibid.*, Under the influence of mineral acids, it [turpethin] is re-dissolved into glucose and turpetholic acid. *Ibid.*, Turpetholate of Sodium, $C_{16}H_{31}NaO_4$.

Turpeyl, var. TIRPEIL *Obs.*, fear.

Turph, -y, obs. ff. TURF, TURFY.

Tu·rpid, *a.* *rare.* [irreg. f. L. *turp-is* ugly, unsightly, foul, disgraceful + -ID, after *torpid*, etc.] Base, filthy, worthless. Hence **Tu·rpidly** *adv.*

1623 COCKERAM, *Turpid*, filthy. 1866 J. R. ROSE tr. *Virg. Georg.* II. 60 But fruit degenerates,—its flavour lost, The turpid grapes are left to birds or frost. 1867 — *Æneid* 44 Smitten with turpid fear. 1866 — tr. *Ovid's Fasti* VI. 623 The female crew..Turned turpidly and fled.

†**Tu·rpie**, *a.* *Obs. rare.* [f. L. *turpi-s* ugly, foul; in quot. after the L. phrase *turpe lucrum* (see FILTHY *a.* 4 b).] Filthy.

1632 NASHE *Quaternio* 90 How the nostrils savour nothing more than turpie lucre.

Tu·rpify, *v.* *rare.* [ad. L. *turpificāre* (recorded only in pa. pple. *turpificātus*) to make filthy, foul, or bad, f. L. *turpi-s* + *-ficāre*: see prec. and -FY.] *trans.* To make foul or filthy; to befoul, besmirch.

a 1586 SIDNEY *Wanstead Play* Wks. (1629) 620 O [that] a woman..should thus turpifie the reputation of my doctrine, with the superscription of a foole.

†**Turpin.** *Obs. rare.* A fanciful name for, or appellation of, the hare.

a 1325 *Names of Hare* in *Rel. Ant.* I. 133 He shal saien on oreisoun In þe worshipe of þe hare..The scotewine, the skikart, The turpin, the tirart.

†**Turpin**, obs. abbreviated f. TURPENTINE.

1688 R. HOLME *Armoury* II. 80/1 The Turpin, or Turpentine Tree [hath] the leaves smooth, four on a side.

Turpinite (tə̄·ɹpinəit). [a. F. *turpinite*, f. Turpin, name of the inventor + -ITE¹.] An explosive, used in making shells.

1895 *Daily Chron.* 6 Dec. 6/1 'Turpinite', a comprehensive word coined in honour of a string of episodes bearing upon the new methods of putting a stop to war by the prospective destruction of all cities.

Turpith: see TURPETH.

Turpitude (tə̄·ɹpitiūd). Also 5 **turpytude.** [a. F. *turpitude* (*a* 1417 in Godef. *Compl.*), or directly ad. L. *turpitūdo*, f. *turpi-s* base: see -TUDE.]

1. Base or shameful character; baseness, vileness; depravity, wickedness.

1490 CAXTON *Eneydos* xxii. 83 In sygne of vengaunce of the dethe of hys fader, And turpytude dyshonest of clytemnestra his moder. 1589 PUTTENHAM *Eng. Poesie* III. xxiv. (Arb.) 295 All maner of conceites that stirre vp any vehement passion in a man, doo it by some turpitude or euill and vndecency that is in them. 1606 SHAKS. *Ant. & Cl.* IV. vi. 33 How would'st thou haue payed My better seruice, when my turpitude Thou dost so Crowne with Gold. 1659 HAMMOND *On Ps.* cxix. 137–8 Paraphr. 609 Those which have a natural turpitude and indispensable sinfulnesse in them! *a* 1711 KEN *Preparatives* Poet. Wks. 1721 III. 25 Some for their Turpitude had Shame, And Terrors of infernal Flame. 1794 LD. AUCKLAND *Corr.* (1862) III. 261 Indignation and horror at the infatuated turpitude of some of the allied powers. 1849 MACAULAY *Hist. Eng.* iii. I. 402 The artists corrupted the spectators, and the spectators the artists, till the turpitude of the drama became such as must astonish all who are not aware that extreme relaxation is the natural effect of extreme restraint. 1879 *Temple Bar Mag.* Oct. 172 A career great from the historical importance of the period.. but inglorious and almost without a parallel in recent times for moral turpitude and unscrupulous self-seeking.

b. With *a* and *pl.* An instance of this.

1597 J. PAYNE *Royal Exch.* 28 Every Christian ought.. to lament to se suche turpitudes. 1607 COKE *Charge at Norwich Assizes* 5 Partialitie in a Judge is a Turpitude, which doth soyle and stayne all the Actions done by him. 1810 BENTHAM *Packing* (1821) 71 A picture in which all deformities and turpitudes are plaistered over with the most brilliant colours. 1833 CHALMERS *Const. Man* (1835) I. iii. 157 Temptation to a turpitude or a crime. 1913 *19th Cent.* Aug. 393 The minor offences and turpitudes which are condemned in the court of conscience.

†**c.** Rendering L. *turpitudo* of the Vulgate: 'nakedness'; 'shame'. *Obs. rare.*

1570 FOXE *A. & M.* 157/2 The holy lawe of God forbiddeth to reueale the turpitude of thy blood or kyndred. *Ibid.*, Thou shalt not reueale the turpitude of thy father.

†**2.** in *lit.* sense: Foulness, offensiveness, unsightliness. *Obs. rare.*

1684 tr. *Bonet's Merc. Compit.* XIX. 719 This Medicin helps notably any cutaneous turpitude whatsoever.

Turple, var. TORPLE.

Turps (tə̄ɹps). [Colloq. (workmen's or painters') abbreviation of TURPENTINE; the final *-s* appears to be collective.] Oil of turpentine.

1823 P. NICHOLSON *Pract. Build.* 411 Oil of Turpentine, or Turps, is made from the resin of that name, which is obtained from all larch and fir-trees. 1867 F. FRANCIS *Angling* xiv. (1880) 506 Cut up some white indiarubber..dissolve it in turps. 1894 *Brit. Jrnl. Photogr.* XLI. 5 Not soluble in either benzole, turps, or xylol.

Turque, obs. f. TURK. **Turquen**, var. TURKEN *v.* *Obs.* **Turques**, var. TURKIS *v.* *Obs.*

†**Turque·sque.** *Obs. rare.* [a. obs. F. *turquesque* (= It. *turchesco*) Turkish.] *pl.* ? Turkish cloths or carpets.

1594 BLUNDEVIL *Exerc.* V. IV. (1597) 259 b, The chiefe marchandizes that come from this countrie [Turkey] to other Prouinces are..Veluets, Damaske, Grograins, Turquesques and Wood.

†**Turquet**¹. *Obs. rare*⁻¹. [app. f. *Turque*, TURK + -ET; cf. F. *turquet* 'petit chien, d'origine turque, à nez camus et à poil ras' (16–17th c. in Hatz.-Darm.). But *Turquets* may be a misprint for *Turques*.] A player dressed up to resemble a Turk.

1625 BACON *Ess.*, *Masques* (Arb.) 540 Anti-masques..haue been commonly of Fooles, Satyres, Baboones, Wilde-Men, Antiques, Beasts, Sprites, Witches, Ethiopes, Pigmies, Turquets,..and the like.

†**Turquet**². *Obs. rare*⁻¹. [a. F. *turquet*, now = maize, but given by Cotgr. as a var. of *turguet* spelt.] ? Spelt.

†Turquin, a. Obs. rare. [a. F. turquin (= Sp. and Pg. turqui), ad. It. turchino (med.L. turchinus): f. Turco Turk.] Different senses are assigned for the use of the adj. to designate 'blue.' In sense 1 the meaning of 'Turkish' may be perceived.

1. A dark-green pumpkin.

2. A bluish-grey or slate-coloured marble.

Turquoise (tɜː́kɔɪz, tɜ́-kɔɪz, -kwɔɪz). Forms: see below. [In 15–16th turkeis, -keys, a. OF. turquoise, -quaise, later turquoyse, fem. of turqueis, -quais, turqueis adj. Turkish, in full pierre turqueise; a 'Turkish stone' (cf. Marco Polo c. xxiv 'pierres qui s'appellent turqueises').] ...

Turret (tʊ́rɛt), sb.[1] Forms: 4 turret, ...

1. A small tower forming part of a larger structure; esp. a rounded addition to an angle of a building, sometimes commencing at some height above the ground, and freq. containing a spiral staircase.

b. A low flat armour-plated tower, commonly cylindrical or conical, on a ship of war or a fort, made to contain a gun and gunners, and usually to revolve horizontally.

Turr, sc. form of TURF.

†Turrel. Obs. [Derivation uncertain]

Turret, sb.[1]

Turreted (tʊ́rɛtɪd), a. [f. TURRET sb.[1] + -ED.]

1. Furnished with or having a turret or turrets.

2. Furnished with something resembling a turret.

Turret-back. [TURTLE sb.[1]]

Turtle (tɜ́tl), sb.[1] [OE. turtla masc., turtle fem. (Du. tortel masc.) either ad. L. turtur TURTLE-dove, or ...]

1. A turtle-dove.

Turtle, sb.[2] [Often mentioned or alluded to as a feature of civic banquets.]

1. Any of various species of sea- or fresh-water tortoise.

TURTLE-BACK. [TURTLE sb.[1]]

1. An arched structure over the deck of a steamer at the bow and often also at the stern, to protect it from damage by a heavy sea.

Turtle-dove (tɜ́tl̩dʌv). Forms: see TURTLE sb.[1] and DOVE.

1. A dove of the genus Turtur, esp. the common European species T. communis, noted for its plaintive cooing, and for the affection of the mates.

Turtler (tɜ́tlə(r)). [f. TURTLE sb.[2] + -ER.]

Turtling (tɜ́tlɪŋ), vbl. sb. [f. TURTLE sb.[2] + -ING.]

Turtlet (tɜ́tlɛt). [dim. of TURTLE sb.[1]]

Turtle (tɜ́tl), v. [f. TURTLE sb.[2]]

Turional (tjʊəri'ɒunăl), a. rare⁻¹. [f. L. turio, -ōnem] ...

Turricular (tɜrɪ́kjʊlə(r)), a. rare⁻¹. [f. L. turricula (see prec.) + -AR.] Having the form or resembling a turret.

Turriculated (tɜrɪ́kjʊleɪtɪd), ppl. a. [f. prec. + -ATE + -ED.]

Turriferous (tɜrɪ́fərəs), a. rare⁻¹. [f. L. turrifer (f. turris tower) + -OUS.] Bearing or supporting a tower.

Turriform (tʊ́rɪfɔːm), a. rare⁻¹. [f. L. turri-s + -FORM.] Having the form of a tower; tower-shaped.

Turrigerous (tɜrɪ́dʒərəs), a. rare⁻¹. [f. L. turriger, turris tower) + -OUS.] Carrying a tower or castle.

Turrilite (tʊ́rɪlaɪt). Palæont. [a. mod.L. Turrilites (Lamarck, 1801), f. L. turri- tower.] A fossil cephalopod belonging or allied to the genus Turrilites, allied to the ammonites, but having a long spiral (turreted) shell, found in the Cretaceous formations.

Turrited (tʊ́rɪtɪd), a. [f. L. turritus + -ED.]

Turrilitoid (tɜrɪ́lɪtɔɪd), a.

Turtivary. Obs. Forms: 1, 4–5 turtur.

Tush (tʌʃ), sb.[1] Also 4 tusche, 5 tusshe. Forms: a. 1 tusc, 4 tosche, (5 tousche), 7–9 tush; β. 1 túsc, 4–5 tosch.

Tusk (tʌsk), sb.[1]

TUTOR.

3. One employed in the supervision and instruction of a youth in a private household. Also, one engaged to travel abroad with one or more pupils, a *travelling* or *foreign tutor*.

b. A master charged with the special supervision of a particular boy.

6. *transf.* the name of an instruction book in any subject.

Tutor (tiū̆·tŏɹ), v. [f. TUTOR *sb.*]

1. *trans.* To act the part of a tutor towards; to give special or individual instruction to; to teach, instruct (*in* a subject).

b. With extension : To get (a quality or the like) *out of* or *by* instruction or discipline.

2. To instruct under discipline ; to subject to discipline, control, or correction ; to school ; also to admonish or reprove.

3. To instruct (a person) in a course of action, to tell (one) what to do or say ; often in sinister sense : to sophisticate or tamper with (a witness or his evidence).

4. To take care or charge of. *Obs. rare.*

Hence **Tutoring** *vbl. sb.*, Tu·toring *vbl. sb.*

Tutorage (tiū̆·tŏɹėdȝ). Also 7 tutridge, tutorage. [f. TUTOR *sb.* + -AGE.]

1. The office, authority, or action of a tutor or guardian ; tutorship, guardianship, custody ; tutorial control, direction, or supervision ; instruction.

b. A master's place as tutor.

Tutorate (tiū̆·tŏɹ¡t). *rare.* [L. *tūtōri-us* (see prec.) + -ATE¹ : cf. *professoriate*.] A body of tutors ; the tutorial staff of a college.

Tutorhood (tiū̆·tŏɹhud). *rare.* [f. TUTOR *sb.* + -HOOD.] The condition or office of a tutor, tutorship ; also, ↑ a society or body of tutors.

Tutorial (tiū̆tōˑɹi̯ăl), *a.* and *sb.* [f. L. *tūtōrius* (f. *tūtor* TUTOR) + -AL.]

1. *Rom.* and *Sc. Law.* Of or pertaining to a legal guardian ; cf. TUTOR 2 b.

2. Of or pertaining to a teacher or instructor ; *esp.* pertaining to a college tutor.

Hence **Tuto·rially** *adv.*, in a tutorial manner ; as or by a tutor ; by way of tuition.

Tutoress (tiū̆·tŏɹės). Also 7 tutoresse. [f. TUTOR *sb.* + -ESS.] A female tutor.

Tutoriate (tiū̆tōˑɹi̯ėt). *rare.* = TUTORATE.

Tutorism. [f. as prec. + -ISM.] The sphere or duty of a tutor.

Tutorize (tiū̆·tŏɹaiz), v. [f. TUTOR *sb.* + -IZE.] *trans.* To be tutor to ; to instruct as a tutor.

Tu·torism. [as prec. + -ISM.] The sphere or duty of a tutor.

Hence **Tu·torizing** *vbl. sb.*, tutoring, tuition.

Tutoress. A female tutor.

Tutorless (tiū̆·tŏɹlės), *a.* [as prec. + -LESS.] Without a tutor.

Tutorly (tiū̆·tŏɹli), *a.* *rare.* [f. as prec. + -LY¹.] Befitting or pertaining to a tutor ; like a tutor ; didactical, pedagogic.

Tutorship (tiū̆·tŏɹʃip). [f. as prec. + -SHIP.] 1. The office of guardian or protector ; guardianship. *Obs.*

2. The position or office of an instructor or teacher.

Tutorix (tiū̆·tŏɹiks). *rare.* [f. L. *tūtrix*, fem. of *tūtor* TUTOR. Cf. prec. and TUTRESS, TUTORESS.] A female tutor. A female guardian. In a instructress, a governess.

Tutory (tiū̆·tŏɹi), *sb.* *rare.* [f. as prec. + -Y.] 1. Guardianship, charge, protection ; *spec.* the custody of a ward. *Obs. exc. in Law.*

2. Tutorship.

Tutress (tiū̆·tɹės). Also 6–7 tutresse, 7 tutouresse, 8–9 tutrees. [ad. OF. *tutresse*, f. *tutor* : see TUTOR.] A female tutor.

Tutrix (tiū̆·tɹiks). Also 6–7 tutrice. [ad. L. *tūtrīx*, fem. of *tūtor* TUTOR.] A female guardian. In Law, an instructress, a governess.

Tutsan (tʊ·tsăn). Also 4 tutesane, 4–5 tutsane, etc. [a. OF. *toute-saine*, lit. 'all-wholesome'.] A species of St. John's wort.

Tutty (tʌ·ti), *sb.*¹ Forms: 4–7 tuttie, 6–8 tutie, 5–8 tutye, tuttye ; 8– tutti. [a. F. *tutie*, ad. med.L. *tutia*, a. Arab. *tūtiyā* oxide of zinc.]

Twaddle (twɔ·d'l), *v.* [var. of TWATTLE.]

1. *intr.* To utter twaddle ; to talk or write in a silly, empty, or trashy style.

2. *trans.* To utter as a twaddle, in a trashy and prosy way.

Twaddler (twɔ·dlăɹ). [f. TWADDLE *v.* + -ER¹.] One who talks or writes twaddle.

Twaddling (twɔ·dlĭŋ), *ppl. a.* [f. TWADDLE *v.* + -ING².] 1. Having the character of twaddle ; empty and prosy.

Twaddly (twɔ·dli), *a.* [f. TWADDLE *sb.* + -Y.] Characterized by, or of the nature of, twaddle.

Twain (twēn), *numeral a.* and *sb.* *arch.* Forms: 1 twegen, tuegen, 1–2 twæᵹen, twegen, etc. [OE. *twēᵹen*, masc.] Two ; a couple.

Twait, twaite (twēt), *local.* Forms: 7 tweat, thwait, twoart, thwaite, twaite. [Origin not ascertained.] A European species of shad, *Alosa finta*.

| TWANG. | 518 | TWANG. | TWANGDILLO. | 519 | TWATTLER |

Twang (twæŋ), sb.¹ Also 6 twange, twangue.

Twang, sb.²

Twang, v.¹

Twang, v.²

Twangdillo. Obs. rare. Also twangdillow.

Twangle, v.

Twangle (twæŋ'g'l), sb.

Twanging, ppl. a.

Twanging, vbl. sb.

Twangle, v.

Twangy, a.

Twankay (twæ·ŋke). Also twanky.

†**Twattle.** Obs. rare.

Twattle (twɒ·t'l), sb.

Twattle, v.

Twattling, ppl. a.

Twatter, v.

Twat (twɒt), sb.

Twit, v.

Twitch, etc.

| TWATTLING. | 520 | TWEAKER. | TWEDDLE. | 521 | TWEEZER-CASE |

Twattling, vbl. sb.

Twattling, ppl. a.

Tway, numeral a. Now arch. Forms: see below.

Twayblade. Also 8 twyblade.

Tweag, tweague, obs. or dial. ff. Twig v.

Tweak (twiː̆k), sb.

Tweak (twiː̆k), v.

Tweaker.

Tweddle (twē·d'l), v.

Tweddle, var. Twiddle v.²

Twee (twiː), sb.

Tweed (twiː̆d), sb.

Tweedle (twiː̆·d'l), v.

Tweedle-dee v.

Tween, †tween (twiː̆n), prep. Forms: see below.

Tweer, var. Tuyere, Twire.

Tweese, obs. pl. of tweeze, Tweezers.

Tweese, v.

Tweese. Obs. Also pl. tweeses, twines; rare in sing.

Tweezer, sb.

Tweezer, v.

Tweezer-case. Obs.

Tweezers, sb. pl. Also 7 tweezes.

TWEEZERS.

Tweezers (twī·zəz), sb. Also 7 twizers, twisers, tweezurs. [An extended form of *tweezes*, pl. of TWEEZE (cf. TROUSE sb.[2] and TROUSERS). See also TWEEZER. v.[1]]

1. A set or case of small instruments. As a *pair* (= set) of *tweezers*. Obs. exc. Hist.

2. Small pincers or nippers (orig. as included in the case of a tweezer) used for plucking out hairs from the face or for grasping minute objects. Also *a pair of tweezers*.

Tweel, twele, obs. ff. TWAY. **Tweich**, obs. Sc. form of TOUCH. **Tweien**, twein, tweine, obs. ff. TWAIN. **Tweies**, tweis, obs. ff. TWICE.

Tweif, twelfe, twels, obs. ff. TWELVE.

Twelfth (twelfθ), *a.* and *sb.* [OE. *twelfta*, m. *OFris. twelfta, twelfta* (WFris. *toalfte, -de*), MDu. *twalf-t(t)e, twelf-t(t)e*. etc.] ...

A. *adj.*

1. The ordinal numeral corresponding to the cardinal TWELVE; last of twelve, that comes next after the eleventh. In concord with a sb. expressed.

B. *sb.*

1. A twelfth part : see A. 2.

+2. A twelfth part of rents or movables granted or levied by way of tax. Obs.

+3. Mus. **a.** A note twelve diatonic degrees above or below a given note (both notes being counted); the octave of a fifth; hence (usually) the interval, or consonance, between two such notes. **b.** An organ-stop sounding a twelfth above the normal pitch. Obs.

Twelfthtide. Obs. Forms : 6 twelfe tyde, 6-7 twelftide, tweelftide (to 7 also with hyphen), 6-8twelftyde, [Twelfthtide occurs app. only in modernized editions.] Twelfth-tide (cf. Twelfth-night): the season including Twelfth-night and Twelfth-day; the season of Epiphany; formerly the concluding part of the Christmas festivities. (Cf. the *twelve days* s. v. TWELVE.)

Twelfth-eve. Obs. The eve of Twelfth-day; Twelfth-night.

Twelfthly (twelfθli), *adv.* [f. TWELFTH + -LY.] In the twelfth place ; as the twelfth in a series.

Twelfth-night. Forms : see TWELFTH and NIGHT. The evening before Twelfth-day, formerly observed as a time of merry-making. Also *attrib.*

Twelfth-day. Forms : see TWELFTH and DAY. The twelfth day of Christmas; the day of the Epiphany, twelve days after Christmas.

Twelve (twelv), *numeral a.* and *sb.* Forms : see below ; ...

I. *adj.* [I]. The cardinal number composed of ten and two; represented by the symbols 12 or XII.

II. *sb.* (with plural *twelves*).

TWELVEFOLD.

Twelvefold (twe·lvfould), *a.* and *adv.* [f. TWELVE + -FOLD. Cf. OE. *twelf-feald* adj.]

Twelvemo (twe·lvmo), English reading of the abbreviation *12mo* or *xiimo* for DUODECIMO. Also *attrib.*

Twelvemonth (twe·lvmɒnθ). Forms : see TWELVE and MONTH ; also 4 twelfmoth ; β. 4 tuelmonath, -month, 5 twelvemonth, 4 twelmonth, 5 -monyth, twolmonthe, 5-6 twel-monethe, 5-6 monthe, -mond(e (6 -mote) ; γ. 5 twelvmonth, 6 twelfmoneth, 6-7 twelvemoneth.

Twelvepence (twe·lvpēns). **a.** A sum of money equal to twelve pennies ; a shilling. **b.** A coin of this value, a shilling (obs.).

Twelvepenny (twe·lvpēni), *a.* (*sb.*). Also formerly *twelve-penny-worth* (obs.).

TWENTIETH.

Twentieth (twe·ntiiθ), *a.* and *sb.* Forms : see below.

A. *adj.*

1. The ordinal numeral corresponding to the cardinal TWENTY; last of twenty; next after the nineteenth. In concord with a sb. expressed.

B. *sb.*

1. A twentieth part : see A. 2.

TWENTY.

Twenty (twe·nti), *numeral a.* and *sb.* Forms : 1 twentig, (tuentig, tuoentig), 2-6 twentie, 3 twenty, 3 (Orm.) twennti3, 3-6 tuenti, 4 tuenty, 5 tuwenti, 5-6 twenti, twynty...

I. *adj.* [I]. The cardinal number composed of twice ten; represented by the symbols 20 or XX (formerly sometimes *xx* with a point over it).

A. *adj.* [I]. In concord with a sb. expressed (or in OE. in plural form with implied sb.).

II. *sb.*

Twenty-eight. [TWENTY A. 1 b.]
Twenty-five. [TWENTY A. 1 b.]
Twentyfold (twentifōld), a., adv. and n. [TWENTY + -FOLD. Cf. OE. twentigfeald.]
Twenty-four. [TWENTY A. 1 b.]
Twentyfour.mo.
Twenty-one. Mus. [TWENTY A. 1 b.]
Twentysome. nonce-wd. Obs.
Twere, variant of TWERE.
Twey, tweye use TWAY, TWIN.
Twey- = TWI-.
Twi-, (twī-), vwl. pref. [OE. twi- = OFris. twi-, MLG. twe-, OHG. zwi-, zwī-, zwē-, etc.]
Twibill, twybill (twī-bil, -t wī̆bl), arch. and dial. Forms: 1 twibille, 4 twybil, -byle, etc.
Twice (twais), adv. (sb.), a. Forms: 1 twiwa, 3 (Orm.) twizzess, twizess, 4 twiges, twies, etc.
Twice-born, a. 1. Born twice: esp. in classical mythology as an epithet of Bacchus.

Twice-laid, a. 1. Counted or reckoned twice; twice as much, twice (in amount). 2. Named or related twice.
Twice-told, a. (adv.)
Twicer (twai'sər), colloq. or slang. [f. TWICE.]
Twiddle (twi'd'l), v. [See TWEEDLE v.; cf. TWIRL.]
Twiddle, sb.
Twiddling (twi'dliŋ), vbl. sb.
Twiddling string.
Twiddly a.
Twig (twig), sb.1 Forms: 1-2, 4-7 twigge (1 twigge, twiȝ), 4-6 twygge, etc.
Twig, sb.2
Twig, v.1 slang or colloq. To watch; to look at; to inspect.
Twig, v.2 slang or colloq. [Origin unascertained.]
Twigged (twigd), a. [f. TWIG sb.1 or v.1]
Twiggen (twi'g'n), a. arch. [f. TWIG sb.1]
Twifallow, twy-, v. Obs. [f. TWI- + FALLOW v.2]
Twifold, twyfold, a. adv. and n. arch.
Twifoldly, adv.
Twig-bottle.
Twine, sb.
Twine, v.
Twofold use TWOFOLD.
Twoodle.
Twoo, various forms.

‑EN.] a. Made of twigs or wickerwork; also, having a wickerwork covering. b. Arising from burning twigs or brushwood.

Twigger (twi'gər), *sb.* [f. TWIG *v.*[2] + -ER[1].]

1. Like a twig; slender, as a shoot or branch; also, *a* made of twigs or wickerwork (*obs.*).

†Twiggy, variant of QUINSY *adj.*

†Twight, *obs.* pa. t. and pple. of TWITCH *v.*

Twiggle (twi'g'l), *v.* Forms: 5 twylyght, -lyghte, twye lyghte, 6 twie light, twylyght, St. twa licht, lycht, 6-8 twylight, 6- twilight.

Twilight (twai'lait), *sb.* (*a.*)

1. The light diffused by the reflection of the sun's rays from the atmosphere before sunrise, and after sunset; the period during which this prevails between daylight and darkness.

†Twi'leke, var. *fancy-leke* : see TWAY *4. Obs.*

Twilit, twilight, obs. f. TOILET.

2. *transf.* A dim light resembling twilight; partial illumination.

3. *fig.* An intermediate condition or period; a condition before or after full development.

Twilight, *v. trans.*, to light imperfectly or dimly; *†twilighted a.,* partly illuminated; **Twilighting,** *vbl. sb.*

Twilit (twi'lit), *ppl. a.* [pa. pple. of TWI-LIGHT *v.*] Lit by or as by twilight.

Twill (twil), *tweel* (twil), *sb.*[1] Forms: *a.* 4 twyle, 6 twile; *5-7* twyll (6 twyell), *4-6* twylle (6 tweylle, tyll), *5-* twill (6 twill, 7 twilt, quill, 7 tweel. [Northern and Sc. forms of TWILLY *sb.*[1], with normal change of the final -e, and (esp. in Sc.) lengthening of original *i* to *ī* in the unstressed syllable; cf. *will,* *wull.*]

Twill, (twil), *v.* trans., to produce diagonal ridges on the surface of the cloth.

Twilled (twild), *ppl. a.* Woven with a twill, having diagonal lines or ridges on the surface.

†Twilly (twi'li), *sb.* Forms: *see TWILLY sb.*[1] *ME. twillen; OFris. twillia, LG. twillen.* A twilled fabric or texture; also, the process of producing this. Also, *attrib.*, twilling-bar, a device in the twilling-machine; twilling-hook, one of the hooks for lifting the warp-threads in a twilling-machine.

Twillock, obs. var. WILLOCK.

†Twilly (twi'li), *sb.*[2] Also twilley, twylly, twyelle, twyle 7 twylie, 7 twelye, twylly-c. [OE. twili = OFrig. *twili;* *OHG. zwilih. The Germanic form of Latin bilix.]

Twilt, obs. var. QUILT *sb.*; cf. TWILL *sb.*[2]

†Twilly (twi'li), *sb.*[2] Also twilley [Altered f. *willy,* WILLOW *sb.*] A willowing machine: = DEVIL *sb.* 4; also called twilly-devil. Hence **Twilly** *v. trans.,* to willow.

Twill (twil), *v.*[1] [f. TWILL *sb.*[1] or TWEEL *sb.*] *trans.* and *intr.* to produce diagonal ridges on the surface of the cloth.

Twin (twin), *a.* and *sb.* Forms: *1 adj.* twinn, *3-6* getwinnas, 3 twinnes, 1 twynne, *3-7* twinne, 4 twine, *5-6* twyne, *4-7* twynn, *5-7* twynne, 6 twynn, 7 twin. [OE. *twinn* adj. (rare), *getwinn adj, sb.*

A *adj.*

1. Consisting of two; twofold, double. (*exc.* as in 4.)

Twin (twin), *sb.* and *a.*[2] *Sb.* Also *4* ty-wele, twyle, 7 twyele; *5* twelye, 6 twyley,[7] twylly(-e. [OE. *twili* = OFrig. *twili;* etc.] Also attrib., twill, *or* bilix from our *twi-* OF. TWILLY. *The ME. var. twile* is parallel to *thrile,* the reduced form of *thrili,* and is the source of the northern Twill. *sb.* adj. Twilled.

Twin (twin), *v.*[1] Forms: see prec.; cf. also TWINE[2] [ME. *twinnen,* f. TWIN *a.*] For the development of the senses cf. TWIN *a.*

1. *trans.* To put asunder (*properly* two things or persons, or one *from* the other); to separate, dissever, disunite, sunder, sever, part, divide; †to deliver, set free; *fig.* to distinguish.

Twin-faced, *a.* [TWIN *sb.* II] a. twofold, with two faces or elements in close connexion; **twinhood,** Twi'n-ism, Twi'n-ness = TWINSHIP. †*Twi'nly,* characteristic of or befitting a twin (*brother or sister).

Twin-born, *a.* Born at the same birth, as two children or animals, or one of such. See also TWIN-BROTHER, -SISTER.

Twinity, [after *trinity*], a group of two in intimate union; *twin so* (one.); †*Twi'nly a.,* characteristic of or befitting a twin (brother or sister).

Twin, *v.*[2] [f. TWIN *a.* and *sb.*]

1. To bring forth two children or young at a birth; to bear twins.

2. *intr.* To grow or be disposed in pairs; to twine, twin, wind.

3. *refl.* To couple or to join, combine, unite; to be parallel or equal, to agree.

Twinge (twind'd'z), *v.* Also *5-6* twinche, twynge, *5-6* twenge, 6 twindge. [OE. *twengan* to pinch:—OTeut. *twangjan.*]

1. *trans.* To pinch, tweak, nip.

2. To affect with a sharp local physical pain.

3. *fig.* To affect with a twinge or sharp touch of mental pain.

Twinge, *sb.* [f. prec.]

1. A pinch, nip, tweak; a twitch.

2. A sharp sudden physical pain; esp. a local, momentary, darting pain.

3. *fig.* A sharp sudden access of mental pain.

Twinkle (twi'ng'kl), *v.*[1] Forms: *1* twinclian, *3-6* twinkle, 5-6 twynkle, 6 twyncle. [OE. *twinclian,* frequentative of obs. *twincan* to wink.]

1. *intr.* Of the eyes: To wink, blink; to open and shut the eyelids rapidly; to be half-closed.

2. Of a light or bright object: To shine with a light now bright, now faint; to shine with a quivering, intermittent, or tremulous gleam.

Twinkle, *sb.* [f. prec.]

1. A wink or blink of the eye.

2. A gleam or sparkle of the eye.

3. The action or an act of twinkling; a gleam.

Twine (twain), *sb.* [OE. *twīn* = MLG., MDu. *twīn* (Du. *twijn*), neut.]

1. Thread or string composed of two or more yarns or strands twisted together; now *spec.,* strong thread, made of two, three, or more strands of hemp, cotton, or other fibre, used for sewing coarse materials (as canvas or sacking), tying packages, netting, and the like; with *a* and *pl.* a piece of such thread.

Twine (twain), *v.* Forms: *1* twīnan, *3-7* twyne, *4-7* twine. [OE. *twīnan;* cf. ON. *tvinna.*]

1. *trans.* To twist, twine, wind.

Twinge, *sb.* see TWINGE.

Twine. ... hold a ball of twine on a counter. 1817 COLERIDGE *Biog. Lit.* 8a Lane, black, 'twine-like hair. ...

†Twine, *sb.* ... [app. f. TWI-after TRINE (cf. *twinity*, s.v. TWIN *a.* and *sb.*).] Division, separation, disunion. ...

Twine, *app.* an error for TURNY.

Twine (twəin), *v.* ... Forms: 4-7 twyne, 4 (9 *dial.*) twyne, 4-5 twyn, 6-7 twine. Pa. t. and *pa. pple.* twined; also *pa. t.* & *5 twan*, *6 twon.* ...

1. *trans.* 1. To twist (two or more strands of filaments) together ...

2. To cause (one thing) to encircle or embrace another; to twist, wreathe, clasp, or wrap (a thing) in or into another with a twisting or sinuous movement (also *fig.*). ...

3. To enfold, wreathe, or encircle (one thing) *with* another; also of a plant, wreath, etc.; to clasp, encircle, enwrap. Also *fig.* ...

4. To turn (something) *about*, *away*, *round*, etc.; to twist or wring. Now *dial.* ...

5. To bend, bow, or sink with wriggle, squirm. Now *dial.* ...

6. To contort the body; to writhe, wriggle, squirm. Now *dial.* ...

7. To proceed or proceed in a winding manner; to bend, incline circuitously; to wind (about, round), meander; of a serpent, etc. to crawl sinuously (also *refl.*). ...

8. To contort the body; to writhe, wriggle, squirm. Now *dial.* ...

Twine, *v.²* Sc. [Later form of TWIN *v.¹*, prob. by misunderstanding of ambiguous spellings under the influence of TWINE *v.¹*] *intr.* and *trans.* To separate, part, etc. = TWIN *v.¹* in various uses. ...

Twined (twəind), *ppl. a.* [f. TWINE *v.* + -ED¹.] That has been twined, in various senses of the verb; twisted, plaited, curled, coiled, wreathed, etc. ...

Twiner (twəi'nər). [f. TWINE *v.* + -ER¹.] 1. One who or that which twines; *esp.* one who or a machine which twines or spins thread; also a rope-maker. ...

b. A plant of twining habit. ...

†Twine-hand. Obs. [TWINE *sb.³*] A twisted or double-spun thread; also *collect.*, cord, twine. ...

Twing, *sb.* Now *dial.* Also 7 twyng. [Of obscure origin.] ... A small red spider. ...

† Twing, *v.* Now *dial.* Also 7 twynge. [? var. of TWINGE *v.*] *trans.* To affect (the body or mind) with a twinge or sharp pain; to prick (the conscience). ...

Twinge (twind), *v.* Forms: 6 twynge, 6-7 twindge, (twing), 7- twinge. [OE. *twengan* ...] ...

1. *trans.* To pinch, tweak, twitch. Also *intr.* ...

2. To affect with a twinge; to give a pang or pangs to. ...

Twinge (twind), *sb.¹* [f. prec.] 1. An act of tweaking or pinching; a tweak or pinch. Also *fig.* ...

2. A sharp mental pain; a pang of shame, remorse, sorrow, or the like; a prick of conscience; in quot. *attrib.* ...

Twinger (twin'dʒər), one who or that which twinges. ...

Twinge, *v.²* Obs. *rare.* [Perh. intended as a fig. use of prec., but prob. originating in some misunderstanding of earlier glosses. ...] ...

Twingle (twi'ŋgl), *v.* *rare.* Now *dial.* [Prob. frequentative; ...] *intr.* To twist, twine, wriggle, writhe. ...

Twingle-twangle (twi'ŋgltwæŋgl). [Reduplication of TWANGLE.] A representation of the continuous sounds of a harp or the like. Also *attrib.* ...

Twing twang (twi'ŋtwæŋ). [Reduplication of TWANG.] A representation of the sound of the harp, or other such instrument. ...

Twining (twəi'niŋ), *vbl. sb.* [f. TWINE *v.¹* + -ING¹.] The action or habit of TWINE *v.¹*; twisting, spinning, winding, embracing, writhing. ...

Twining (twəi'niŋ), *ppl. a.* [f. as prec. + -ING².] That twines, in various senses; twisting, coiling, writhing, etc.; *spec.* of a plant growing spirally round a support. ...

Twink (twiŋk), *sb.* Also 7 twincke. 1. A wink of the eye; *transf.* the time taken by this; a twinkling; now always in phrase *in a twink*; formerly *all*, *in* (also *of a*) twink *of an eye*; *also with (a or the) twink of an eye-lash*; ... cf. BEDSTAFF. ...

b. *intr.* To experience a twinge or smart. ...

Twink (twiŋk), *sb.²* Obs. rare. [Echoic; cf. TINK, TWANK.] ... The note of the chaffinch. ...

Twink, *v.* Now dial. [Of obscure origin.] To chastise. ...

Twinkle (twiŋ'k'l), *sb.* Forms: see TWINKLE *v.¹* [f. TWINKLE *v.¹*] 1. A winking of the eye; a wink, blink; also, a momentary glance (cf. quot. 1593, of the mind); cf. BLINK *sb.* 2, 7 (*fig.*). ...

b. *transf.* A slight tremulous movement; a twitch, a flicker, a quiver. ...

2. The time it takes to wink; = TWINKLING *vbl. sb.¹* 3; now only in phrase *in a twinkle*, *in the twinkle of an eye*. ...

3. An intermittent or tremulous shining; a sparkle, a scintillation; also, a faint or momentary gleam; a glimmer. ...

b. *transf.* and *fig.* ...

Twinkle (twiŋ'k'l), *v.¹* Forms: 1 twinclian, 4 twinkel, twynkle, twynkele, (4 -kil, 6 -kell, twinkel), 4-5 twinkle, 6-8 twinckle, (twinggle), 4- twinkle. [OE. *twinclian*, freq. of *twincan* ...] ...

1. *intr.* To shine with rapidly intermittent light; to emit tremulous radiance; to sparkle; to glitter; †to shine dim, to flicker (*obs.*). ...

2. *trans.* To guide or light to some place by twinkling. ...

Twinkled (twiŋ'k'ld), *ppl. a.* [f. TWINKLE *v.¹* + -ED¹.] One who or that which twinkles.

Twinkle, *v.²* (*trans.*) ...

Twinkledom (twiŋ'k'ldəm). An imitation of the sound of the guitar. ...

Twinkler (twiŋ'klər). [f. TWINKLE *v.¹* + -ER¹.] One who or that which twinkles. ...

Twinkling (twiŋ'kliŋ), *vbl. sb.¹* [f. TWINKLE *v.¹* + -ING¹.] 1. The action of TWINKLE *v.¹* 1. The act of shining with a tremulous or faint radiance; scintillation; glimmering. Also *transf.* ...

2. *transf.* Appearing and disappearing with rapid alternation; producing an effect as of tremulous light by rapid vibratory movement; tremulous, fluttering, quivering. Also *fig.* ...

3. The action or an act of winking; nictitation; also *fig.* ...

4. In *a twinkling* (of an eye), *etc.* = *in the twinkling of an eye* (in quot. 1300 *of a mind*), *as prec.*: instantly. ...

Twinkly (twiŋ'kli), *a.* [f. TWINKLE *v.¹* + -Y.] Characterized by twinkling. ...

Twinklingly (twiŋ'kliŋli), *adv.* [f. prec. + -LY².] In a twinkling manner; by alternate appearances and disappearances. ...

Twinling (twi'nliŋ). Now *dial.* [f. TWIN *sb.* + -LING¹.] A twin lamb. ...

Twinned (twind), *ppl. a.* [f. TWIN *v.* + -ED¹.] 1. Born two at one birth; twin. ...

2. United; paired, coupled, matched. ...

Twinning (twi'niŋ), *vbl. sb.¹* [f. TWIN *v.¹* + -ING¹.] 1. Production of two children or young at a birth; bearing of twins. ...

Twinning (twi'niŋ), *ppl. a.* rare. [f. TWIN *v.* + -ING².] Characterized by twinning. ...

Twinny (twi'ni), *a.* rare. [f. TWIN *sb.* + -Y.] Resembling, or in the nature of, or resembling, twins.

†Twinter, Obs. rare. [f. TWIN *v.¹* 4, after ONLEFT.] Twofold, double. ...

Twinship (twi'nʃip). [f. TWIN *sb.* + -SHIP.] The condition of being twin, or a relation of a twin or twins. ...

Twin-sister. [Also as two words.] [TWIN *a.* 3.] A sister born at the same birth, as one of twins. Also *fig.* (Cf. TWIN-BROTHER.) ...

Hence **Twin-sisterhood**, the relation of twin sisters. ...

Twinter (twi'ntər), *sb.* and *a.* Chiefly *north.* and *Sc.* Forms: 5-6 twynter, (5 twyntour, 6 twinter, twyntyr, tynter, twenter), 6-7 twinter, twintter, (also 6 twinter, quinter). [f. TWI- + WINTER *sb.*] ...

†Twire, *sb.¹* Obs. [? related to TWIRE *v.¹*] A glance, a leer. ...

Twire, *v.¹* ... [Of obscure origin, but corresponding in form to MHG. *zwieren* (now Bavarian dial.) to blink, to peer. ...] 1. *intr.* To look narrowly or covertly; to peer, to pry; to peep. Also *fig.*, of light, etc. ...

Twire, *v.²* Obs. rare⁻¹. [? var. of TWIRL.] ... to twirl, to twist. ...

†Twire-pipe. Obs. rare. [?] 1. App. a contemptuous name for a musical pipe. ...

2. *transf.* A tippler or drunkard. ...

Twirk, var. of QUIRK. ...

Twirl (twǝːl), sb. Also 6, 8 twirle, 7 twerle.

Twirl (twǝːl), v.

Twirl-bast, -wind, -whirlwind, twirl-mop a mop, that twirls a mop.

Twirler (twǝːlǝr).

Twirligig, Twirligigging.

Twirlwind.

Twisel, twisnel.

Twirly.

Twit. Obs.

Twist (twist), sb.1 Forms: 4-6 twyst, -e, 4-7 twiste, (5 twest, tweste, 5-6 twys, 6 twyste, Sc. tuist), 4- twist.

Twist, sb.2 Forms: 4-6 twyst, 4-7 twiste, twyste.

Twist, v. Forms: 3-6 twyste, (4 twyst, twiste), 4- twist.

Twister (twistǝr).

Twistable (twistǝb'l), a.

Twisted, ppl. a.

Column 1 (p. 542)

Twister (twɪstə(r)). Now *dial.* [f. TWIST v. + -ER[1].]

† **1.** *trans.* and *intr.* To twist, spin thread.

2. *intr.* To wind, meander. *dial.*

Hence **Twistering** *ppl. a.*, winding, twisting; also † **twisterer** *Obs.*, a twister or spinner.

Twistical (twɪstikăl), *a.* *colloq.* [irreg. f. TWIST + -ICAL.] Somewhat twisted or crooked; *fig.* not straight or plain in character; morally or mentally tortuous.

Twistification (twistifkēɪ·ʃən), *nonce-wd.* [f. as prec.: see -FICATION.] A twisting, a twisted object or part.

Hence **Twistering** *ppl. a.*, a winding, twisting; also **twisterer** *Obs.*

Twisting (twɪstɪŋ), *vbl. sb.* [f. TWIST v. + -ING[1].] The action of the verb TWIST.

† **1.** Pruning, clipping.

2. The spinning of thread, etc.; twining, wreathing, plaiting; also *with in* (in quot. 1813 *fig.* the swearing in of a Luddite), and *attrib.*

3. Wringing, screwing; spiral turning; contortion, distortion, *fig.* perversion or wresting of sense; *slang*, a scolding; a trouncing.

† **4.** Tortuous course; intricate winding; turning this way and that; *fig.* evasion, prevarication; also turning aside, or about; rotation.

Column 2 (p. 542)

Twit (twɪt), *v.* Forms: *a.* 6 twyte, (twhyte), 6–7 (9 *dial.*) twite, (twight). *B.* 6– twit, (7 twitt, twytt). 6 *aphetic* form of ATWITE, q. v.]

1. *trans.* To blame, find fault with, censure, reproach, upbraid (a person), esp. in a light or annoying way; to cast an imputation upon; to taunt.

b. *Const.* most usually *with*; also *about* (rare), *for, of* (now *rare* or obs.), *on*; † also *with* clause or infin. (*obs. rare*).

† **2.** *absol.* or *intr.* To cast in one's teeth. *Obs. rare.*

Twit, *sb.*[1] Also 6 twyte. [f. TWIT v.] An act of twitting; a (light) censure or reproach; a taunt.

Twit, *sb.*[2]

Twit, *int.* and *sb.*[3] Also 6 twyte.

Column 3 (p. 543)

Twitch (twɪtʃ), *sb.*[1] [f. TWITCH v.[1]]

1. *trans.* To give a sudden abrupt pull at; to pluck; to jerk; to pluck (a person) *by* some part of the body or dress; also, to pluck (the strings of a musical instrument, etc.)

2. *intr.* To be pulled or jerked sharply or forcibly; to give a sharp pull or jerk (*at* something); to tug. Also *fig.*

3. *trans.* To draw tight by means of a cord or the like; to tie, fasten, secure tightly or firmly. Also with the cord as object. Now *dial.*

4. *intr.* (With various advs. and preps.) To pull, draw, or take suddenly or with a jerk; to pull sharply or forcibly; to pluck, snatch. To *twitch up* (the strings of an instrument), to sound by plucking.

5. *intr.* To move quickly or irregularly (*obs. rare*); now always in reference to involuntary bodily movements: to move in a jerky, spasmodic, or convulsive manner; to jerk, jump, start. Also *refl.* (const. *into*).

6. *trans.* To match by way of robbery or theft.

Column 1 (p. 544)

Twitch (twɪtʃ), *v.*[1] [Alteration of quitch, QUETCH v., perhaps partly after *twit*.] *intr.* To move, stir.

Twitch, *v.*[2] *Obs. rare.* [Alteration of *quitch* q. v.]

Twitching *vbl. sb.*[1]: see TWITCH *v.*[1]

Twitching *vbl. sb.*[2], *Obs.*: see TWITCH *v.*[2]

Twitchy (twɪtʃi), *a.*[1] [f. TWITCH *v.*[1] + -Y[1].] Characterized by twitching; having a tendency to twitch; also, nervous, fidgety, restless.

Twitchel [1] *dial.* [f. TWITCH *v.*[1] or *sb.*[1] A narrow passage between walls or hedges.

Twitchel [2] *dial.* [f. TWITCH *v.*[2] A wooden lever with a loop of rope fastened to one end.

Hence **Twitchelled** *a.*, noosed, held in a noose.

Twitchet (twɪtʃet). [f. TWITCH *v.*[1] + -ET[1].] One who or that which twitches.

1. An instrument for plucking or pinching something.

Twitty (twɪtɪ), *a.* [f. TWIT *v.* + -Y[1].] Full of or irritated with twitch; made of twitch.

Twitten (twɪt'n). *Sussex dial.* Also *twitting.*

Column 2 (p. 544)

Twite (twəɪt). Also dial. form of TWIT *v.*

Twithe, obs. Sc. form of TOOTH.

Twitter, *sb.*[1] [f. TWITTER *v.*[1] + -ER[1].]

Twitter, *sb.*[2]

Twitter, *sb.*[3] Now *dial.* [f. TWIT *v.* + -ER[1].]

Twitter, *sb.*[4] *rare.* [f. TWIT *v.* + -ER[1].] One who twits; a tale-bearer.

Twitter-bone, *rare.* [var. of *quitter-bone*, QUITTER *sb.*[4]] A suppurating tumour on a horse's foot. Hence **Twitter-boned** *a.*, affected with a twitter-bone.

Twitter (twɪtə(r)), *v.*[1] [imit.] To chirp, twitter. Also *transf.* of a person.

† **Twitterer** (twɪtərə(r)). [f. TWITTER *v.*[1] + -ER[1].]

Twittering (twɪtərɪŋ), *vbl. sb.* [f. TWITTER *v.*[1] + -ING[1].]

Twittering, *ppl. a.* [as prec.]

Twitter-light, *obs.* [var. of TWILIGHT.] Twilight.

Column 3 (p. 545)

Twitterly, *a.* *rare*[-1]. [f. TWITTER *sb.*[1] or *v.*[1] + -LY[1].]

Twitter (twɪtə(r)), *v.*[2] + -Y.] Apt to twitter or tremble; feeble, shaky; also *fig.*

Twitter, *v.*[3] Now *dial.* [f. TWIT *v.* + -ER[3].]

Twitting (twɪtɪŋ), *vbl. sb.* [f. TWIT *v.* + -ING[1].] The action of TWIT *v.*; taunting.

Twitting, *ppl. a.* [f. TWIT *v.* + -ING[2].]

† **Twixen**, (twɪks'n) *prep. Obs.* [Cf. BETWIXEN.]

† **Twizzled**, *a.* *Obs. rare*[-1]. [Perh. a survival of OE. *twisled* ; but cf. TWIZZLE *v.*]

Twizzle (twɪz'l), *sb.* Chiefly *dial.* [Cf. next.]

1. A twist or turn; a change of direction.

2. A spinning-machine, the eye of a flyer.

Twizzle, *v.* [imit.: cf. next.] An imitative formation suggested by TWIST *v.*; cf. TWIDDLE *v.*

1. *intr.* To rotate rapidly, spin, twirl.

Twizzen, variant of TWEEZE.

Two (tū), *numeral a.*, *sb.* (*adv.*) Forms: see next.

Twofold, variant of TWAIN.

Twizzle, variant of TWEEZE.

Two (tū), *numeral a.*, *sb.* (*adv.*)

Two-faced ...

Two-foot ...

Two-footed ...

Twofold ...

Two-forked ...

Two-hand ...

Two-handed ...

Two-headed ...

Two-leaf ...

Two-leaved ...

Two-legged ...

Twolf ...

Twoling ...

Twoll, twolne ...

Twoses ...

Twoops ...

Two-part ...

Twopence ...

(Oxford English Dictionary columns — entries including Twopenny, Twopenny halfpenny, Two-pile, Two-sided, Twound, Two-way, Two-year-old, Twy-, Twybill, Twyvete, Twyvel, Twyvere, Tychonian, Tychonic, Tycoon, Tyddy, Tydie, Tye, Tyg, Tyee, Tyke, Tyle, Tylopod, Tyler, Tylerism, Tyllole, Tylylene, Tylose, Tylosis, Tylote, Tylotic, Tylotis, Tympan, Tympana, Tympani, Tympanic, and related forms.)

vividly depicted on the tympanic background, and the saviour upon the cross in connexion with it.

† Tympanical, a. *Obs. rare.* [f. as prec. + -ICAL.] = TYMPANITIC.

† Tympanichord. *Anat.* [ad. L. *tympanichordus* (Cuvier), f. TYMPANUM + Gr. χορδή CHORD *sb.*] The chorda tympani, a branch of the facial nerve which traverses the mucous membrane of the tympanum. Hence **Tympanichoˈrdal** a., pertaining to the tympanichord.

Tympanicity (timpəˈnisiti). [f. TYMPANIC + -ITY.] The condition of being tympanic, or affected with tympanism.

Tympaniform (tiˈmpaniform), a. *Nat. Hist.* [ad. F. *tympaniforme* (Cuvier), f. TYMPANUM + -FORM.] Having the form of a drum, or (usually) of a drum-head; stretched like a drum-head: *spec.* applied to certain membranes in the bronchi of birds.

Tympanism (tiˈmpəniz'm). [cf. Gr. τυμπανισμός a beating of drums, *δωνπμανισμός* also a cudgelling: see TYMPANIZE and -ISM. So F. *tympanisme*.]

Tympaniˈtes (timpəˈnaitiz), *Path.* [Late L. *tympanītes*, a. Gr. τυμπανίτης (Galen), f. τύμπανον drum: cf. ATHETES. So F. *tympanite*, F. *tympanitis* (Ol. *timpanides*), It. *tispanida*.]

Tympaˈnitic, a. *Path.* [ad. L. *tympanīticus*, a. Gr. τυμπανιτικός (Galen): see prec. and -IC.]

Tympaˈnitis. [mod.L. f. Gr. τύμπανον drum + -ITIS.]

Tympanˈoid, a. *Nat. Hist.* [ad. Gr. *tympanoīd-* + -OID.]

† Tympanous, a. *Obs.* [f. TYMPANUM or TYMPAN-Y + -OUS.]

† Tympanize, v. *Obs.* [ad. Gr. τυμπανίζειν to beat a drum, f. τύμπανον TYMPAN: cf. F. *tympaniser*.]

Tympanum (tiˈmpǎnŏm). Pl. **tympana.** [L. *tympanum* drum, wheel for raising weights, face of pediment, etc., a. Gr. τύμπανον, f. root of τύπτειν to strike, beat.]

Tympany (tiˈmpǎni). Also 6 *tympanye*, 6-7 *tym-*, *timpanie*, *timpany*. [ad. med.L. *tympanium*, a. Gr. τυμπανίας, f. τύμπανον, f. τύπτειν: cf. TYMPANUM.]

Type (taip), *sb.* Also 6-7 *type*. [ad. F *type* (16th c. in Littré) or L. *typus*, a. Gr. τύπος blow, impression, figure, type, f. the root of τύπτειν to beat, strike.]

Type (taip), *v.* Also 6-7 *type*. [ad. F *type* sb.]

Typewrite (taiˈprəˈtər). [f. TYPE *sb.* + WRITER.]

Typewriter (taiˈprəitər). A writing-machine having types for the letters of the alphabet, figures, and punctuation-marks, arranged on separate rods (or on the periphery of a wheel) that on each key of the machine is impressed the corresponding character is imprinted in line on a moving sheet.

Typha (taifə). *Bot.* [mod.L. (Tournefort), a. Gr. τύφη.] A genus of aquatic herbs (type of the N.O. *Typhaceæ*), containing the common cat's-tail or reed-mace (*T. latifolia*).

Supplement, p. 3873; Corrigenda, p. 4092; Spurious words, p. 4093; Books quoted, p. 4094

Tyrannize ...

Tyranner ...

Tyranness ...

Tyrannial ...

Tyrannic ...

Tyrannical ...

Tyrannicide ...

Tyrannicidal ...

Tyrannish ...

Tyrannize ...

Tyrannoid ...

Tyrannous ...

Tyrannously ...

Tyrannousness ...

Tyranny (tirǎ·ni). *sb.* ...

Tyrant (tai·rănt), *sb.* ...

Tyrant *v.* ...

Tyrantlike ...

Tyrantly ...

Tyrantry. ...

Tyrantship (tai·răntʃip). *rare.* ...

Tyranty ...

Tyre ...

Tyre, tyer ...

Tyrian (tai·riǎn), *a.* and *sb.* ...

Tyrite (tai·rəit). *Min.* ...

Tyro, Tyrocinium, etc.: see TIRO, etc.

Tyrogenous ...

Tyroglyphid ...

Tyroid ...

Tyrolean ...

Tyrolese ...

Tyrolienne ...

Tyroleucin ...

Tyrolite ...

Tyroma ...

Tyromancy ...

Tyronic, -ism, -ist, -ise: see TIRONIC.

Tyrosin, -sine ...

Tyrosinase ...

Tyrite ...

Tyrosis (təirōu·sis). *Path.*, etc. ...

Tyrotoxicon (tairoto·ksikŏn). *Chem.* ...

Tyrotoxicosis ...

Tyrrhene (tiˑrīn, tirīˑn), *a.* and *sb.* ...

Tyrrhenian (tirīˑniǎn), *a.* and *sb.* ...

Tysonite ...

Tythe, Tything: see TITHE, TITHING.

Tzar, Tzarina, etc.: see CZAR, TSAR.

Tzigane (tsigāˑn), *sb.* and *a.* ...

Tzirid, obs. f. JERID, wooden javelin.

Supplement, p. 3873; Corrigenda, p. 4092; Spurious words, p. 4093; Books quoted, p. 4094

U.

U (yū), the 21st letter of the modern English, the 20th of the ancient Roman alphabet, is in the latter identical in form and origin with V (q.v.), the same symbol being employed both as a vowel and a consonant. In Latin MSS. written in capitals the form U is retained; but in small MSS, of which the earliest specimens belong to the third or fourth century, the modified form U appears, and is continued in the later half-uncial (the c 500) and minuscule MSS. (from the eighth century) as U.

†U·berant, a. Obs. rare. [ad. L. ūberant-, pres. pple. of ūberāre, f. ūber rich, plentiful.] Abundant, copious.

†U·berate, v.¹ Obs.— Also ub-. [f. ppl. stem of L. ūberāre: cf. prec.] (See quot.)

Uberous (yū·bərəs), a. Now rare. [f. L. ūber rich, full, fruitful, abundant, etc. + -ous, or ad. med.L. ūberōsus.] Plentiful.

Uberty (yū·bərti). Now rare. Also ū-, vberte, uberte(e ; ? vbertie. [a. OF. ubertè ? f. L. ūbertā-, -tās: cf. prec. and -TY.] Rich growth, fruitfulness, fertility; copiousness, abundance.

Ubiety (yū·bəti). [ad. mod.L. ubiētās, f. L. ubi where : cf. quiddity, quality from quā-, quālis.] Condition in respect of place or location; local relationship; whereness.

Ubiquarian (yūbikwē·riən), sb. and a. Also ubiquerian. [f. L. ubique wherever, anywhere, everywhere.]

Ubiquist (yū·bikwist). [ad. mod.F. ubiquiste, Sp. and It. ubiquista.]

Ubiquitarian (yūbikwitē·riən), sb. and a. = Ubiquitary sb. and a.

Ubiquitary (yūbi·kwitări), sb. and a. [ad. mod.L. ubiquitārius, f. L. ubique everywhere: see -ary.]

Ubiquitous (yūbi·kwitəs), a. [f. L. ubique everywhere: see -ous.]

Ubi (yū·bi). L. ubi where. So Sp. ubi place, position.

†Ubi·quiter. Sc. Obs. rare. [f. prec. and -ER.]

Ubiquitism (yūbi·kwitiz'm). [f. Ubiquit-ary + -ism.]

†Ubi·quity. Obs.— [cf. prec. and Ubiquit-ous.]

'Ud, abbrev. form of would WILL v.

Udal (yū·dal). Forms: a. 6 outhale, 6-7 outhell, owthell, 7 owthall ; 7 uthall, -ail, 6-7 udall, uddal, -ail. [Orkney and Shetland form of Norw. odal, odel, ON. óðal ODAL.]

Udaler (yū·dalər). Also 6 udaller, udlar, 9 udaller. [f. prec. + -ER.]

†U·ddery, a. Obs.— [f. UDDER + -Y.] Soft as the flesh of an udder.

Udder (ö·dər). Forms: a. 1 úder, 3-6 udder; a. 1 ûdir, 6 udyr, uddyr.

U·dderful, a. [f. UDDER + -FUL.]

U·dderless, a. Having an udder.

U·dderless, a. unsuckled, motherless.

†U·ddery, a. Obs.—

Uein, Ueir, Uell, southern ME. varr. FAIN adv., FAIR a., FELL n., WELL sb. etc.

Ufen, var. of ūfan above: see Uf.

Ug (ög), v. Now Obs. exc. dial. [a. ON. ugg-a to fear, dread.]

Ug (ög), sb. Obs. exc. dial. [f. prec.]

Ugging, vbl. sb.

UGGLE

† Uggle, v. Obs. [f. the stem of UGG v. and mod.Norw. uggall (Ross).]

Uglesome (ɔ′g′lsəm), a. Now rare. Also 6–7 ugly-, 5 ugglesome. [f. UGLY + -SOME.] Fearful, horrible, gruesome.

Ugly (ɔ′g′li), sb. rare. [f. UGLY a.]

Ugh (uh, ʌx), int. and a. [Imitative.]
1. A representation of an inarticulate sound of the nature of a hollow cough; a sound or utterance of this nature.
2. An interjection expressive of disgust.

Ugh′o, obs. forms of YEW.

Ughin, var. of dial. AGIN prep.

† Ughten. Obs. Forms: 1 uhtan, 3 uhhtenn, 4 ухен, ughtens. See also UGHTIDE.

Ugliness (ɔ′g′linɛs).

Uglify (ɔ′g′lifai), v. [ad. L. UGLY + -FY + -T] trans. To make ugly or repulsive in appearance; to disfigure.

UGLY

Ugly (ɔ′g′li), a., adv., and sb. Forms (ɔ′g′li), 4–5 vg-, ugli, 4–5 ugly (4–7 vgly, 5 igly, Sc. wgly, 5, 7 vgaly), 4–7 vglye, 6–7 ugy, ugle (6 Sc. wg-); 4 uggeli, 5–6 vgely, ougly, ougely, 6–7 vgly, ougly.

Uglily, adv. rare.

Uglilook, a.

-ULAR

-ular, suffix, representing L. -ulāris (whence also F. -ulaire, Sp. and Pg. -ular).

ULCER

Ulcer (ɔ′lsər), sb. Also 5–7 vlcer, 6 vlcere, 6 ulcre. [ad. F. ulcere.]

Ulcerate (ɔ′lsəreit), v.

Ulcerated (ɔ′lsəreitɛd), ppl. a.

Ulcerating, ppl. a.

Ulceration (ɔlsəreiˈʃən).

Ulcerative (ɔ′lsərətiv), a.

Ulcerous (ɔ′lsərəs), a.

Ugric

Ugric (ū′grik), a. and sb.

Ugrian (ū′griən), a. and sb.

Uhlan (ū′lɑn), sb. Also 8 ulan; 8 houlan, 9 hulan.

Ukase (yūkē′z). Also 8 oukaze, ukause, 9 oukass.

Ukrainian (yūkrē′niən), a. and sb.

Ulander (ū′-), sb.

tubercles and the formation of an ulcerous excavation. 1897 *Allbutt's Syst. Med.* III. 886 In some instances the foreign bodies had escaped from the appendix through the ulcerous openings they had made in its walls.

fig. 1601 [? MARSTON] *Pasquil & Kath.* v. 20 Why, now the vlcerous swelling of my hate Is broken forth. 1602 MARSTON *Antonio's Rev.* IV. iii, The polluting filth Of ulcerous sinne.

2. Afflicted with an ulcer or ulcers; exhibiting ulceration.

1599 B. JONSON *Ev. Man out of Hum., The Stage* 73 Euery seruile imitating spirit..striues to fling His vlc'rous body in the Thespian spring, And streight leaps forth a Poet. 1600 R. CAWDREY *Treasurie* 266 Scuruie, Scabbie, and vlcerous persons. 1605 SHAKS. *Mach.* IV. iii. 151 Strangely visited people All swolne and Vlcerous..he cures. 1662 HIBBERT *Body Divinity* I. 313 They observed..whether the bowels were of an unnatural colour, or ulcerous. 1899 *Allbutt's Syst. Med.* VI. 105 Cavities resulting from their destruction present irregular, anfractuous, ragged and ulcerous walls.

absol. 1889 H. M. STANLEY in *Stanley & Africa* xvii. (1890) 392 Assiduously dressing and trimming up the ulcerous ready for the march to Zanzibar.

b. *fig.* (Cf. ULCERATED *ppl. a.* 1 b.)

1611 SPEED *Hist. Gt. Brit.* IX. xvi. § 20 A weauer (the Bailiffe of the Towne) was the vlcerous head, to which that corruption gathered. 1643 MILTON *Divorce* II. iii. Wks. 1851 IV. 65 Did God for this come down..to patch up an ulcerous and rott'n commonwealth with strict and stern injunctions? 1660 T. M. *C. Walker's Hist. Independ.* IV. 22 Belching forth the scandalous language of their ulcerous tongues to incense the People. 1879 H. GEORGE *Progr. & Pov.* x. v. (1881) 494 A just man would crush with his foot such an ulcerous ant-hill!

3. Developed in, proceeding from, ulcers.

1660 O. SEDGWICK in Spurgeon *Treas. David* Ps. xix. 12 Methinks sin is..like evil and ulcerous humours. 1718 QUINCY *Compl. Disp.* 121 Ulcerous Exudations, which by their loose situations are easily carried along with the Medicine. 1844 G. S. FABER *Eight Dissert.* (1845) II. 311 By reason of some colouring ulcerous matter, the skin of the sufferer would pass through the different successive shades of dark red and lead colour and complete black.

4. Characteristic of, appropriate to, ulcers.

1642 in Rushw. *Hist. Coll.* (1692) III. I. 218, I cannot but admire how this..Body of Judicature should swell up into such a vast and ulcerous dimension. *c* 1720 W. GIBSON *Farrier's Dispens.* III. xiv. (1721) 268/2 To dry up watry Corruptions, which create an ulcerous Disposition in the Legs. 1842 TENNYSON *St. Sim. Styl.* 13 Thrice ten years, Thrice multiplied by superhuman pangs,..In coughs,..ulcerous throes and cramps. 1896 *Allbutt's Syst. Med.* I. 127 The development of ulcerous conditions when the process affects free surfaces.

5. = ULCERATED *ppl. a.* 3.

1751 FOTHERGILL (*title*), Account of the Ulcerous Sore Throat. 1761 *Phil. Trans.* LII. 264 His disorder has been a malignant or ulcerous sore throat. 1859 SEMPLE *Diphtheria* 84 Severe and obstinate ulcerous inflammations of the skin and mucous tissue. 1889 DUNCAN *Clin. Lect. Dis. Women* (ed. 4) xxii. 189 A disease exactly resembling the acute ulcerous stomatitis of children.

Hence **U·lcerously** *adv.*; **U·lcerousness.**

1727 BAILEY (vol. II), *Ulcerousness*, ulcerous State, Condition, or Quality. 1847 WEBSTER, *Ulcerously.*

U·lcery, *a.* *rare*[−1]. [f. ULCER *sb.*] Of the nature of an ulcer.

1611 COTGR., *Mammelons*, be certaine little, red, hard, vlcerie, and teat-like swellings, which break out of the skin of the head.

Ulche, ME. variant of EACH *a.*

U·lcuscle. *rare*[−1]. [ad. L. *ulcusculum*, dim. of *ulcus* ULCER *sb.*] A small ulcer.

1794 E. DARWIN *Zoon.* I. 400 The specific medicines..act only by increasing the absorption of the matter in the ulcuscles of those diseases.

So **Ulcu·scule.** (Webster, 1847.)

Ulde, -ere, -est, ME. ff. ELD, -ER, -EST.

† **Uldron,** variant of *oldron* OLERON *Obs.*

1590 *Admir. Crt. Exemplifications* 3, No. 167, Serten packes of canvas namyd uldrons of Methernek.

Ule, obs. var. OIL *sb.*[1]; obs. f. OWL *sb.*, YULE.

-ule, *suffix*, representing the Latin diminutive ending *-ulus, -ula, -ulum* (whence also F. *-ule*, Sp. and Pg. *-ulo, -ula*, It. *-ulo, -ula, -olo, -ola*), as in *globulus* globule, *glandula* glandule, *grānulum* granule. Among words now current with this ending a certain number correspond to actual Latin forms, as *capsule, cellule, ferule, macule, nodule, pustule, spherule, valvule*; others are of modern formation, as *anguillule.* Only a few of these were in use before the 17th century. Some examples, as *angule, circule, scrupule*, failed to establish themselves against the earlier forms of French origin in *-le*; others, as *formule*, have given way to the purely Latin form. In some cases both forms exist in scientific use, as *ligule* and *ligula, macule* and *macula, valvule* and *valvula*; in some the Latin form is commonly or exclusively employed, as *lingula, tabula.*

‖ **Ulema** (ūlĕmā·, ū·lĕmă, *u-*, yulī·mă). Also 7 **ulemi,** 9 **oulema, ublema, oolama, ulama.** [a. Arab. (also Turk. and Pers.) علما *ʿulemā*, pl. of عالم *ʿālim* knowing, learned, f. *ʿalama* to know. Hence also Sp. *Ulema*, Pg. *Ulemas*, F. *Uléma.*]

1. *pl.* or *collect.* Those who have had special training in the knowledge of Mohammedan religion and law, and are regarded by Moslems as the authorities on these matters; *spec.* the body of Mohammedan doctors under the headship of the Sheik-ul-islam, which exercises great political influence in the Turkish empire.

1688 *Lond. Gaz.* No. 2313/2 The next day was a great Consultation held with the Ulemi or Interpreters of their Law. 1768 SIR J. PORTER *Observ. Turks* Pref. (1771) 30 They have the Ulema..composed of all the members of the church or law; a body of men..who stand as an intermediate order between the prince and people. 1803 *Edin. Rev.* II. 292 Russia, and imperial Rome, had its prætorian guards. Turkey has its *uhlema.* 1848 LAYARD *Nineveh* (1849) I. Introd. p. xxiv, The ulema having at length pronounced that these figures were the idols of the infidels, the Mohammedans..destroyed them. 1892 TENNYSON *Akbar's Dream* 45 But our Ulama..Are like wild brutes new-caged.

attrib. 1847 MRS. A. KERR tr. *Ranke's Hist. Servia* v. 89 The establishment of the influence of some great Ulema families which had become almost hereditary. 1888 *Encycl. Brit.* XXIII. 654/2 The juridical and spiritual precepts of the Koran and its 'ulemā interpreters.

2. A Mohammedan doctor or divine.

a 1843 in Southey *Comm.-pl. Bk.* Ser. II. (1849) 350 A great part of the oulemas and of the people in office delayed not to partake of this luxury. 1848 W. H. KELLY tr. *L. Blanc's Hist. Ten Y.* I. 260 The divan was rescued from the mystic domination of the ulemas. 1882 *Macm. Mag.* XLVI. 474 The army was accompanied by a number of moullas and ulemas.

-ulent, *suffix*, ad. L. *-ulentus* employed to form adjs., usually with the force of 'abounding in', 'full of' (some thing or quality), as *fraudulentus* fraudulent, *opulentus* opulent, *truculentus* truculent, etc. (Variant forms of the suffix are *-olentus*, as in *vinolentus* vinolent, *violentus* violent, and *-ilentus* as in *gracilentus* slender, *pestilentus* pestilent.) A considerable number of the formations occurring in Latin have been adopted in English, and a few have been added either from mediæval or modern Latin, or by direct formation on Latin stems, as *cinerulent, flatulent, herbulent, nidorulent, torpulent.*

‖ **Ulex** (yū·leks). *Bot.* [mod.L. (Linnæus, 1737), a. L. *ulex* (Pliny) a shrub resembling rosemary.] A genus of thorny papilionaceous shrubs belonging to the order *Leguminosæ*; a plant belonging to this genus, esp. *Ulex Europæus* the common furze, gorse, or whin.

1753 *Chambers' Cycl.* Suppl. s.v. 1755 *Dict. Arts & Sci.*, *Ulex*, in botany, a genus..of plants, with a papilionaceous flower; and an oblong turgid pod for its fruit. 1859 DARWIN *Orig. Spec.* xiii. (1860) 432 The embryonic leaves of the ulex or furze..are pinnate or divided like the ordinary leaves of the leguminosæ.

Ulexine (yū·leksəin). *Med.* [f. prec. + -INE.] An alkaloid prepared from the seeds of gorse.

1887 *Brit. Med. Jrnl.* 21 May 1144/2 The value..of kavaine and ulexine as local anæsthetics. 1888 F. H. LESCHER *Recent Mat. Medica* (ed. 3) 88 Ulexine..discovered by A. W. Gerrard. A powerful organic base, soluble in water, insoluble in ether.

Ulexite (yū·leksəit). *Chem.* [See quot. 1867.] (See quots. and BOROCALCITE.)

1867 BRANDE & COX *Dict. Sci.*, etc. III. 892/2 *Ulexite*, a name given to native borate of lime (Hayesine), after Ulex, by whom it was analysed. 1875 *Ure's Dict. Arts* (ed. 7) III. 1050 *Ulexite*, a native borate of lime and soda, known also as Boronatrocalcite. It occurs at Iquique, in Peru; and in the Province of Tarapaca.

Uley, obs. Sc. variant of OIL *sb.*

Ulican, variant of ULLAGONE.

‖ **Ulicon** (ū·likɒn). Also **ulikon, eulachon, ulken**; and OOLAKAN, -CHAN, etc. [Native name in British Columbia.] A small fish of the north-western parts of North America, ascending the rivers in immense numbers to spawn; the candle-fish.

1807 P. GASS *Jrnl.* 187 In the afternoon some of the natives came to visit us, and brought some of the small fish, which they call Ulken...At noon our fishermen returned with some ulken and sturgeon. 1880 *Libr. Univ. Knowl.* (N.Y.) I. 205 All the early navigators and explorers..have spoken of the immense numbers of salmon, cod, halibut, mullet, ulicon, etc. 1885 SIMMONDS *Animal Food Resources* ix. 318 The ulikon or oulachan (*Thaleichthys pacificus*, Gerard)..has long been an ichthyological curiosity...It is a small silvery fish, averaging about fourteen inches long, and in general appearance much resembling a smelt.

Ulie, obs. Sc. variant of OIL *sb.*

Uli·ginal, *a.* *Bot.* [f. L. *ūlīgin-* (see next) + -AL.] Growing in moist or wet ground.

1863 J. G. BAKER *N. Yorksh. Stud. Bot.*, etc. 181 Aboriginal species characteristically paludal, uliginal, ericetal, and sylvestral.

Uligino·se, *a.* *rare.* [ad. L. *ūlīginōs-us* full of moisture, f. *ūlīgin-*, *ūlīgo* moisture, marshiness. Cf. It., Sp., Pg. *uliginoso*, F. *uligineux.*]

1. = ULIGINOUS *a.* 2 b. *rare*[−1].

c 1440 *Pallad. on Husb.* x. 29 This moone in lond vliginose or lene,..In thicked lond also, is to demene, When day and nyght yliche longe is holde.

2. *Bot.* = ULIGINAL *a.*

1866 *Treas. Bot.*, *Uliginose*, growing in swampy places.

Uliginous (yuli·dʒinəs), *a.* [f. as prec., or directly f. L. *ūlīgin-* + -OUS. Cf. F. *uligineux* (of soil or plants).]

1. Of a watery, slimy, or oozy nature.

1576 NEWTON *Lemnie's Complex.* II. iii. 109 b, For it is a certayne vliginous moystishnes and superfluous excrement, which ought rather to be sent out and purged. 1610 W. FOLKINGHAM *Art of Survey* I. x. 24 It reuiues the radicall and vliginous humour. *a* 1656 USSHER *Ann.* VI. (1658) 240 One Proxenus..found a spring of a fatty, and uliginous, or oily liquor. 1669 *Phil. Trans.* IV. 1132 The Birch and Alder feed more kindly on a thin uliginous moisture. *a* 1728 WOODWARD *Fossils* (1729) I. 118 The uliginous lacteous Matter,..in the Coral Fishings upon the Coast of Italy, was only a Collection of the Corallin Particles thus sustained in the Sea Water.

2. Of places: Soaked with water or moisture; water-logged, plashy, swampy.

1610 W. FOLKINGHAM *Art of Survey* I. x. 33 Their vliginous and soaked Mosses doe recompence their meane ayre with vnctious Turffes. 1680 VENNER *Via Recta* i. 20 Contrary to this is that which is of a laxe and open substance, such as is commonly growen in low and vliginous places. 1664 EVELYN *Sylva* xv. 32 The water-galls, and uliginous parts of Forests that hardly bear any grass, do many times spontaneously produce it in abundance. 1699 — *Acetaria* (1729) 155 Those who live in marshes and uliginous Places like the Hundreds of Essex. 1867 SMYTH *Sailor's Word-bk.* 705 *Uliginous channels*, those connecting the branches of rivers, by cuts through the soil.

b. Similarly of soil.

1650 CHARLETON tr. *Van Helmont's Paradoxes* 15 If..they are..buried in a muddy uliginous earth; when they begin to putrifie, they then operate upon..the Patient. 1802 R. HALL *Bot.* 192 *Uliginous Soil*,..spongy, filled with putrid water.

† **3.** Of air: Damp, moist. *Obs. rare.*

1661 EVELYN *Fumifugium* Misc. Writ. (1805) I. 217 The impure and uliginous [air], as that which proceeds from stagnated places, is..the most vile and pestilent. 1697 R. PEIRCE *Bath Mem.* 85 He liv'd near the Fenns, to which Uliginous Air, was ascrib'd the beginning of his Illness.

† **Ulipy.** *Sc. Obs.* Also **vly-.** [Prob. ad. older Du. or Flem. **oliepij(e*, f. *olie* oil + *pij(e* PEE *sb.*[1] Cf. the equivalent WFlem. *oliebaai.*] ? An oilskin coat or jacket.

1529 *Acc. Ld. High Treas. Scot.* V. 369 For ane coit of ulipy in all uncostis. *a* 1568 in *Bannatyne MS.* fol. 158 b, His clais is oft in wanting and sic is his gyis, He thrawis and he puttis fast at his vly pyis.

Ulk, ME. var. ILK *adjs.*; obs. Sc. f. WEEK.

Ulken, obs. var. ULICON. **Ulklie,** obs. Sc. f. WEEKLY. **'Ull,** dial. f. WILL *v.*

Ullage (ʊ·ledʒ), *sb.* Forms: 5 **oylage, vlage,** 6 *Sc.* **vlege,** 8– **ullage.** [ad. AF. *ulliage*, OF. *ouillage, eullage* (*heulliage*), *œillage* (also Anglo-L. *oliagium, oyll-, ull-, ulagium*), Pr. *ulhage, oulhage*, f. OF. *ouiller, eullier, oiller, œiller* (Anglo-L. *oillare*), Pr. *ulha, oulha*, to fill up (a barrel). Forms with initial *a-* are also given by Godefroy, viz. *aouillage* and *aouillier, aoillier, aeullier*, etc. (1295–).]

1. The amount of wine or other liquor by which a cask or bottle falls short of being quite full (originally the quantity required to make good the loss by leakage or absorption).

[1297 *Chanc. Misc.* (P.R.O.) Bd. 2 No. 15 (5), Tradidi etiam eidem vnam pipam pro oliagio prædictorum doleorum. 1329 *Exchequer Rolls Scotl.* (1878) I. 224 De ij doliis et j pipa vini...Et in vlagio..j et dimidium. *a* 1377 *Rolls of Parlt.* II. 384 Item par Adam le Ken pur ulliage es Vins mesme l'an 1 ton' 1 pip'.]

1444 *Compota Domest.* (Abbotsf. Cl. 1836) 26 In vlage et lecage per tempus predictum, [84] lagene [bere]. 1481–90 *Howard Househ. Bks.* (Roxb.) 288 Paid for iiij. galons wyne, iij. qrtes, for oylage for the ton wyne, iij. s. ij. d. 1565 *Burgh Rec. Edinb.* (1875) III. 211 The twa of wyne at this present..xvj crownis of the sone;..item, of fraucht xvj crownis; item, for vlege vj li. 1706 PHILLIPS (ed. Kersey), *Ullage of a Cask*, is what such a Vessel wants of being full. 1749 W. YEO *Ullaging & Inching* 3 As often as these Lines are used for determining the Ullages of Casks. 1755 *Dict. Arts & Sci.* s.v., The ullage of a vessel, whose axis is parallel to the horizon, may be found thus. 1833 LOUDON *Encycl. Archit.* § 1324 It is usually tunned into hogsheads of a hundred gallons each, leaving a few gallons ullage. 1835 MARRYAT *Olla Podr.* III. 297 *Moonshine*), I held the bottle up to the candle to ascertain the ullage. 1885 W. ECOCKES in *Civilian* 3 Jan. 141/2 A work..comprising tables of ullages of casks, whose bung diameters range from 15 to 40 inches.

b. *On ullage*, (in a vessel) not completely full.

1863 T. G. SHAW *Wine, Vine & Cellar* xi. 302 It is injurious to Rhenish wine to be left on ullage. 1880 *Act* 43 & 44 *Vic.* c. 24 § 43 The casks in which spirits are removed may be either full or..on ullage. 1883 *Times* 17 Nov. 10 The wines should not remain long on ullage.

2. a. (See quots.)

1832 S. ROOSE *Ullaging* 5 By knowing the vacuity, and subtracting it from the whole content, leaves the Ullage or the quantity of liquor then in the cask. 1867 SMYTH *Sailor's Word-bk.* 705 *Ullage*, the remainder in a cask or package which has leaked or been partially used. 1883 *Encycl. Brit.* XVI. 18/2 The quantity of liquor contained in a cask partially filled and the capacity of the portion which is empty are termed respectively the wet and dry ullage.

b. *slang.* (See quots.)

1874 *Slang Dict.* 332 *Ullages*, the wine of all sorts left in the bottoms of glasses at a public dinner. 1889 *Pall Mall G.* 21 Aug. 2/1 'Pray what is "ullage"?' 'The washings out of casks, sir,' replied my friend.

3. *transf.* **a.** Liquid that has oozed through a substance.

1824 T. HOGG *Carnation* 30 Upon this stratum or bed of dung..the ullage occasioned from time to time by the rains will all be received.

b. The waste of metal in engraving.

1860 *Cornh. Mag.* I. 272 In graving deep, tiny spirals of gold and silver curl away from the trenchant tool, and there is precious ullage in chasing and burnishing—spirals and ullage worth money in the market.

c. *Naut.* (See quots.)

1901 *Daily Chron.* 23 May 5/1 The mass of her crew will all too probably be 'ullage'—to use the naval term for a preponderance of undesirables. 1904 KIPLING *Traffics & Discov.* 113 'You're a disgrace to the Service, and your boat's offal.' 'Awful?' I said. 'No—offal—tripes—swipes—ullage.'

4. *attrib.*, as *ullage bottle, cask, contents.*

1743 BULKELEY & CUMMINS *Voy. S. Seas* 46 This Morning found the Store Tent robbed of Brandy; filled up all the ullage Casks. 1784 J. BOYDELL (*title*), The Ullage Cask Gauger; comprised in a series of Tables..whereby the Ullage Contents of any Cask..is at one view known. 1812 J. SMYTH *Pract. of Customs* (1821) 363 The ullage cask..must be re-gauged, as must all casks entered for exportation. *Ibid.* 409 Landing Ullage Contents. 1864 *Daily Tel.* 4 June, There is scarcely a ship..in which the examining officer's attention is not called to ullage casks. 1889 *Pall Mall G.* 19 Jan. 7 It might have been made by putting two ullage bottles into one.

U·llage, *v.* [f. prec.]

1. *trans.* To calculate the amount of ullage in (a cask).

1749 W. YEO (*title*), The Method of Ullaging and Inching all sorts of Casks and other Utensils used by Common Brewers, Victuallers, Distillers, &c. 1832 S. ROOSE *Ullaging* 11 To Ullage a Cask in the form of the frustum of a Cone.

2. a. To draw or tap to a slight extent. **b.** To fill up again (an ullaged cask, etc.).

1881 *Standard* 3 Oct. 2/1 There..a cask of some rare vintage was 'ullaged,' with a biscuit and cheese accompaniment. 1888 *Wine, Sp. & Beer* 8 Mar. 186/1 To stir in some pure olive oil..and then flood the oil out by ullaging.

Hence **U·llaging** *vbl. sb.*

1749 W. YEO *Ullaging & Inching* p. iii, That part of it [*sc.* gauging] which relates to the Ullaging of Casks. 1832 S. ROOSE *Ullaging* 5 The Ullaging of a Cask is to find how much liquor there is in it, when it is not full.

U·llaged, *ppl. a.* [f. prec. or the sb. + -ED. Cf. *unullaged* (1646).]

1. Of a cask or bottle: Short of contents.

1549 in R. G. Marsden *Sel. Pleas Crt. Admir.* (Selden Soc.) II. 59 One hundreth and fyftie tonnes of wyne full and ullagid. 1867 SMYTH *Sailor's Word-bk.* 705 *Ullaged* is used for damaged, short of contents. 1908 ATTON & HOLLAND *King's Customs* 195 A demijohn or two in the captain's locker, and an ullaged anker in the forecastle.

2. Of wine: Affected in quality by the presence of ullage.

1907 *Sat. Rev.* 29 June 815/1 Without..the clash of personalities the story is like a bottle of ullaged wine.

3. *transf.* Of inferior quality; refuse.

1892 *Spectator* 9 Jan. 41/1 If you have to feed ten men on twopence, you must buy ullaged flour.

U·llager. [f. ULLAGE *v.*] One who ascertains the amount of ullage.

1885 W. ECOCKES (*title*), The Ullager's Pocket Gem, comprising tables for finding the ullages of casks.

‖ **Ullagone,** *sb.* and *int.* *Anglo-Irish.* Also **ullagoane, ullaghone, ul(l)agon, hullagone, ullagawn, ulican.** [ad. Ir. Gael. *olagón, ologón, olagán*, of imitative origin.] A cry of lamentation, a wail; *spec.* a funeral lament. Also as *int.*

1828 T. C. CROKER *Fairy Leg. & Tradit. S. Irel.* II. 191, I heard the dismallest ullagoane in the world, enough to break any one's heart. *Ibid.* 236 Oh ullagone, ullagone! this is a wide world. 1845 MRS. S. C. HALL *Whiteboy* v, A scream—loud and long—as of a woman in bitter trouble; it was, in fact, a 'keen', a regular 'ullagawn'. 1901 W. BARRY *Wizard's Knot* 219 (E.D.D.), It was a dirge, an ulagón, over Cathal, and his ruined walls.

Hence ‖ **Ullagone** *v. intr.*, to wail or lament loudly.

1828 T. C. CROKER *Fairy Leg. & Tradit. S. Irel.* II. 76 Then the poor woman began to cry and ullagoane so finely that it would do any one good to hear her.

Ulle, obs. Sc. var. OIL *sb.*

Ullmannite (ʊ·lmănəit). *Min.* [From the name of Prof. J. C. *Ullmann* + -ITE[1]; in sense b named by J. Fröbel in 1850.] (See quots.)

† **a.** 1839 *Penny Cycl.* XIV. 382/1 Phosphate of Manganese and Iron: Ullmannite...Occurs at Limoges in France.

b. 1868 WATTS *Dict. Chem.* V. 936 *Ullmanite*, antimonial or antimonio-arsenical nickel-glance. 1875 *Ure's Dict. Arts* (ed. 7) III. 1050 *Ullmannite*, an antimonio-sulphide of nickel, occasionally containing arsenic. It occurs at Freusberg, in Nassau.

Ully, obs. Sc. variant of OIL *sb.*

Ulmaceous, *a.* *Bot.* [f. mod.L. *Ulmace-æ*, an order of plants including the elm, f. L. *ulm-us* ULME.] (See quot.)

1849 CRAIG, *Ulmaceous*, pertaining to the elm; belonging to the order Ulmaceæ.

Ulmate (ʊ·lmĕt). *Chem.* [f. ULM-IC *a.*: see -ATE[4]. So F. *ulmate*, Pg. *ulmato.*] A salt produced by the action of ulmic acid.

1836 BRANDE *Man. Chem.* 924 A brown liquid is obtained (ulmate of potassa), from which acids throw down ulmin. 1843 *Penny Cycl.* XXV. 491/1 When cold, the product, which contains ulmate of potash, is dissolved in water.

Ulme. *Obs.* or *dial.* [ad. L. *ulm-us* elm. Cf. G. *ulme*, Du. *olm.*] An elm-tree. (Cf. ULM-TREE.)

The forms *olm, holm, wim*, are recorded as surviving in northern English and southern Scottish dialects in the latter part of the 19th cent.

1567 DRANT *Horace, Epist.* I. vii. D vj, Our cittizen is now a Corridon. He trimmes his ulmes. 1698 J. FRYER *Acc. E. India & P.* 295 A Catalogue of Plants growing at Spahaun...Sycamore. Ivy...Poplar. Ulmes. Willows.

Ulmic (ʊ·lmik), *a.* *Chem.* [f. L. *ulm-us* elm, after ULMIN. Cf. F. *ulmique*, Pg. *ulmico.*] *Ulmic acid*: **a.** = ULMIN 1.

A distinction between ulmic acid and ulmin or ulmine has been made by various chemists, but without agreement in the precise application of the terms.

1831 T. THOMSON *Chem. Inorg. Bodies* II. 105 Ulmic acid appears to be a vegetable substance of very great importance..obtained from the exudation of the elm by dissolving the exudation in water and precipitating the ulmic acid. 1836 BRANDE *Man. Chem.* 923 As it [*sc.* ulmin] combines with bases, Boullay terms it *ulmic acid*... He represents ulmin, or ulmic acid, as a compound [etc.]. 1868 WATTS *Dict. Chem.* V. 936 The name 'ulmic acid', or 'ulmin', was given by Klaproth to a gummy substance contained in the black alkaline excrescences on the stems of unhealthy trees, especially of elms.

b. = ULMIN 2.

1843 *Penny Cycl.* XXV. 491/1 Ulmic acid plays an important part in manures and soils, and what is called moss-water owes its peculiar properties to its presence. 1868 WATTS *Dict. Chem.* V. 936 The ammoniacal solution..deposits brown or black gelatinous flocks of ulmic acid.

Ulmin (ʊ·lmin). *Chem.* Also **ulmine.** [f. L. *ulm-us* elm + -IN: named by Thomson. Cf. F. *ulmine*, Pg. *ulmina.*]

1. A substance which exudes spontaneously from the inner bark of the elm and some other trees; *spec.* the final stage of this as a distinct chemical principle.

α. 1813 T. THOMSON *Syst. Chem.* (1817) IV. 48 Ulmin..was first noticed in 1804, by Klaproth, who found it in a spontaneous exudation from the elm. 1819 BRANDE *Chem.* 366 Ulmin is of a dark brown colour, with scarcely any taste or smell...The exudation from the elm is generally combined with carbonate of potassa, and is therefore readily soluble in water. 1842 *Penny Cycl.* XXII. 26/1 Simaruba is the bark of the root of the Simaruba amara...Its chief constituents are..ulmin, mucilage, and some salts.

β. 1838 TUPPER *Proverb. Philos.* Notes 219 With reference to the elm, I would remark, that no use has yet been discovered in the principle called 'ulmine'. 1853 ROYLE *Mat. Med.* (ed. 2) 632 It [the bark of Elm] contains Tannin..and a peculiar mucilaginous or gummy principle, called Ulmine.

2. A dark-brown or black product resulting from the decay of wood or vegetable matter, or artificially obtained by the action of powerful chemical agents on sugar and some other substances.

α. 1843 *Penny Cycl.* XXV. 491/1 Ulmin, or ulmic acid, may be artificially obtained..by the following process. 1857 MILLER *Elem. Chem.*, *Org.* 54 If the solution [of sugar] be kept boiling for some hours,..a certain quantity of formic acid, and of a brown sparingly soluble substance termed *ulmin*, are produced. 1868 WATTS *Dict. Chem.* V. 936 Ulmin is also the name of a brown pigment, produced by the action of strong acids or alkalis on various organic bodies.

β. 1848 FOWNES *Chem.* (ed. 2) 371 *note*, This [substance] is generally called ulmic or humic acid, and its origin ascribed to the reaction of the alkali on the ulmine or humus of the soil. 1861 GESNER *Coal, Petrol.*, etc. (1865) 128 The decay of wood is produced by oxidation, and ulmine is the result.

U·lmous, *a.* *Chem.* [f. as prec. + -OUS.] Partaking of the character of ulmin.

1868 WATTS *Dict. Chem.* V. 936 Ulmous or Humous Substances.

† **Ulm-tree.** *Obs. rare.* [f. L. *ulm-us* elm + TREE *sb.* Cf. ULME and MHG. *ulmboum*, Du. *olmboom.*] An elm-tree.

c 1000 ÆLFRIC *Gloss.* in Wr.-Wülcker 138 *Ulmus*, ulmtreow. 1382 WYCLIF *Isaiah* xli. 19, I shal sette in desert fyrr tree, and vlm tree, and box togidere.

‖ **Ulna** (ʊ·lnă). *Anat.* [L. *ulna* (hence also It., Pg. *ulna*), related to Gr. ὠλένη and OE. *eln* ELL[1] (cf. ELBOW *sb.*).]

1. The large inner bone of the fore-arm, extending from the elbow to the wrist.

1541 R. COPLAND *Guydon's Quest. Chirurg.* G j b, The arme..is deuyded in thre great partyes. One is called vlna, the other lytel arme. *Ibid.* G ij, Howe many bones are in yᵉ fyrste parte of the great hande that is named vlna or adiutor? 1646 SIR T. BROWNE *Pseud. Ep.* IV. iv. 184 The other or lower division of the artery descendeth by the ulna. 1693 tr. *Blancard's Phys. Dict.* (ed. 2), *Ulna*,..the greater Bone, betwixt the Arm and the Wrist, which is jointed upward with the Shoulder. 1726 MONRO *Anat. Bones* (1741) 252 At the superior Extremity of the Ulna are two Processes. 1728 CHAMBERS *Cycl.* s.v., The Ulna lies on the inside of the Fore-Arm, reaching from the Elbow to the Wrist. 1803 *Med. Jrnl.* X. 358 The head of this bone was separated from the surrounding parts, as well as its union with the ulna. 1825 T. HOOK *Sayings* Ser. II. *Doubts and F.* i, Who conceived that some desperate injury had been done to her Ladyship's radius or ulna. 1881 *Med. Temp. Jrnl.* XLVI. 86 There was discharge from incisions both at the back and front of the hand and over the lower part of the ulna.

2. The corresponding bone of the foreleg in quadrupeds, and of the wing in birds.

1831 YOUATT *Horse* xiii. 236 The long and front bone, called the *radius*, is nearly straight...The short and hinder bone is called the *ulna.* 1839 *Penny Cycl.* XIV. 69/1 In the ruminants generally the ulna is scarcely more than an appendage to the radius. 1879 E. P. WRIGHT *Anim. Life* 57 The fore-arm [in bats] consists of a rudimentary ulna, and a long, curved radius. 1884 COUES *N. Amer. Birds* 107 The enlarged proximal extremity of the ulna is called the olecranon, or 'head of the elbow'.

3. *Palæont.* and *Ichthyol.* (See quots.)

(*a*) 1839 G. ROBERTS *Dict. Geol.*, *Ulna*..., the bone or plate which, together with the radius, forms the first row, after the humerus, in the *front* paddles of an ichthyosaurus and plesiosaurus.

(*b*) *a* 1843 *Encycl. Metrop.* (1845) VII. 303/1 Between the lower edge of the spoke-bone and the upper edge of the ulna or cubit. 1854 OWEN *Orr's Circ. Sci.*, *Org. Nat.* I. 175 Of the two flat bones connecting the fin with the coracoid, the upper one is the 'ulna'.

U·lnad, *adv.* [f. prec. + -AD.] Toward the ulnar aspect of the forearm.

1803 BARCLAY *New Anat. Nomencl.* 166 Ulnad will signify towards the ulnar aspect. 1808 — *Muscular Motions* 384 When it is rolled radiad or ulnad, the power of the one will be necessarily increased proportionally as that of the other is diminished.

Ulnage (ʊ·lnėdʒ). *Obs.* exc. *Hist.* [ad. med.L. *ulnagium* (14th c.), f. L. *ulna* after OF. *aulnage* ALNAGE.]

1. = ALNAGE 1.

1447 *Ord. Exchequer* 35. c. 62 (6) A v b, For euerye foreyn accompte of sheryffes and vlnage. 1454 *Rolls of Parlt.* V. 247 The Fermours of the Ulnage in the Counte of Somers[et] yerely. 1495 *Act* 11 *Hen. VII*, c. 62 § 1 The fermour of Ulnage in the Citie of Coventre.

2. = ALNAGE 2.

1450 in *Archæol.* (1770) I. 92 The issues and profits coming of the ulnage and subsidue of wollen clothes. 1450 *Rolls of Parlt.* V. 186/1 To be taken of the Subsidie and ulnage of Clothes. 1545 *Lanc. Wills* (Chetham Soc.) II. 61 My lease wyche I have of the ulnage and subsidie within the countie palatyne of Lancast[er].

Ulnager (ʊ·lnėdʒəɹ). *Hist.* [f. prec. + -ER[1].] = ALNAGER.

1750 in *10th Rep. Hist. MSS. Comm.* (1885) App. I. 304 [Prosecuting his suit for the recovery of the patent office of] Ulnager [in Dublin]. 1832 *Rolls Parlt.* VII. 953/1 Office of Ulnager of Worsteds. 1867 BRANDE & COX *Dict. Sci.*, etc. III. 893/2 These officers were called *alnagers* or *ulnagers*, and the accounts rendered by them to the exchequer are still preserved.

Ulnar (ʊ·lnăɹ), *a.* and *sb.* *Anat.* [f. ULN-A + -AR. So F. *ulnaire*, Pg. *ulnar*, Sp. *ulnario.*]

1. Pertaining to the ulna, in various senses: **a.** In *ulnar artery, nerve, vein*, etc.

1741 MONRO *Anat. Nerves* (ed. 3) 70 The ulnar Nerve is in the Palm of the Hand. 1800 *Phil. Trans.* XC. 103 The median proceeding along the arm, with the large blood-vessels, and giving off two branches of communication with the ulnar nerve. 1813 J. THOMSON *Lect. Inflam.* 267 As the brachial [artery] is sometimes observed to be divided..into radial and ulnar arteries. 1840 E. WILSON *Anat. Vade Mecum* vi. 318 The posterior ulnar vein. 1870 ROLLESTON *Anim. Life* 9 The ulnar sesamoid bone, or 'os pisiforme', is not reckoned as a carpal bone. 1885 *Buck's Handbk. Med. Sci.* I. 313/2 The ulnar nerve is placed to the inner side of the artery in the wrist.

b. With other sbs.

1803 [see ULNAD *adv.*]. 1808 BARCLAY *Muscular Motions* p. xx, An aspect..towards the side on which the ulna is situated [is] *ulnar.* 1846 BRITTAN tr. *Malgaigne's Man. Oper. Surg.* 6 During the operation the ulnar border of the left hand should be pressed on the skin behind the right. 1854 OWEN in *Orr's Circ. Sci.*, *Org. Nat.* I. 190 The ulnar portion of the bone developes a short..olecranon. 1872 HUMPHRY *Myology* 185 Towards the ulnar side of the hand these tendons are usually absent.

2. *absol.* as *sb.* The ulnar nerve.

1899 *Allbutt's Syst. Med.* VIII. 9 The physician then examines the nerve-trunks of both limbs simultaneously by means of gentle pressure on the ulnars behind the olecranons.

Ulno- (ʊ·lno), combining form (on Greek types) of ULNA, occurring in a few technical terms, as *ulnocarpal, -metacarpal, -radial.*

a 1843 *Encycl. Metrop.* (1845) VII. 327/2 In the Penguins, the Ulno-carpal bone..is largely developed.

Ulode·ndroid, *a.* *rare*[−1]. [f. mod.L. *Ulodendr-on* (see def.), f. Gr. οὖλος crisp, curly + δένδρον tree.] Of or connected with *Ulodendron*, a genus of extinct fossil plants.

1900 *Nature* 15 Nov. 53/2 The nature of the large scars on the well-known Ulodendroid branches.

Uloid (yū·loid), *a.* and *sb.* *Path.* [f. Gr. οὐλή scar + -OID.] **a.** *adj.* Having the appearance of a scar or cicatrix. **b.** *sb.* A scar-like spot or mark on the skin.

1901 DORLAND *Med. Dict.* (ed. 2).

-ulose, a compound adjectival suffix representing L. *-ulōsus*, formed by the addition of *-ōsus* (see -OSE) to stems in *-ul-us, -a, -um*, as *angulōsus* from *angulus*, *fābulōsus* from *fābula*, *perīculōsus* from *perīculum.* Such formations are rare in earlier Latin, but a considerable number are employed by post-Augustan writers, as Pliny, Columella, etc. Among the English examples which have their source in classical or post-classical forms are *angulose, calculose, fabulose, fistulose, glandulose, nebulose, pustulose, ramulose, sabulose, vermiculose.* On the analogy of these, various others have been introduced, as *flosculose, globulose, granulose, scrofulose, siliculose, tubulose, tumulose.* These forms are parallel to a certain number of

those in -ULOUS, being as a rule either obsolete variants of these, or introduced later in order to convey the distinction commonly observed between the endings -OSE and -OUS.

Ulotrichan (yulǫ·trikăn). [Cf. next.] A person belonging to the crisp-haired division of mankind.

1888 *Cassell's Encycl. Dict.*

Ulotrichous (yulǫ·trikəs), *a.* Also **oulo-.** [f. mod.L. *Ulotrichi* (see def.), f. Gr. οὖλος crisp, curly + -τριχος -haired, f. τριχ-, θρίξ hair. Cf. F. *ulotrique*, Pg. *ulotrico.*] Of or belonging to the *Ulotrichi*, the division of mankind (in Bory de St. Vincent's classification) having crisp or woolly hair.

1857 MAYNE *Expos. Lex.* 847/2 Oulotrichous. 1884 *Imp. Dict.* 1909 A. C. HADDON *Races of Man* 3 These three varieties [of hair, *i.e.* straight, wavy, and woolly] are now termed leiotrichous, cymotrichous, and ulotrichous.

-ulous, a compound adjectival suffix representing the two Latin endings *-ulōsus* and *-ulus.* In the former case there are frequently variants in *-ulose*, which in modern use are as a rule more specific in meaning. To this class belong *angulous, calculous, fabulous, fistulous*, etc. (see -ULOSE); also *crapulous, meticulous, populous, scrupulous*, etc. The number of purely modern formations is not large. To the group which corresponds to Latin forms in *-ulus* belong *bibulous, credulous, emulous, garrulous, pendulous, sedulous, stridulous, tremulous.* In a very few instances both forms occur in Latin, as *querulus*, rarely *querulōsus*, querulous; *rīdiculus*, rarely *rīdiculōsus*, ridiculous.

† **Ulpic.** *Obs. rare.* In 5 **vlpike.** [ad. L. *ulpicum.*] A kind of leek.

c 1440 *Pallad. on Husb.* II. 224 Al the route Of rucul serue hit like this, cool also, Garlec, vlpike ek sowe hem now bo too. *Ibid.* IV. 166, XII. 71.

Ulster (ʊ·lstəɹ). [The name of the most northerly of the four provinces of Ireland.

The name occurs in ME. (14–15th cent.) as *Ulster* (also *Hulster*) and in the fuller form *Ulvester* (in Sc. also as *Ullister, Ulsister*, and *Ulcister*), = AF. (*a* 1225) *Ulvestre* (*Hulv-*), Anglo-L. (*c* 1200) *Ulvestera, -tira, -tria*, corresponding to ON. *Ulfastir*, a variant of the more usual *Ulaztir, Ulaðstir* (also *Ulaþsir*), the first element of which is the Irish *Ulaidh* (gen. *Uladh*), men of Ulster. The origin of the suffix, which also appears in Leinster and Munster (Ir. Gael. *Laighean, Mumha*), is not clear, but it may represent Ir. *tír* land.]

1. *pl.* Ulstermen (forming a regiment). *rare.*

1649 CROMWELL *Let.* 19 Dec. (Carlyle), Being informed that..Lieutenant-general Ferral with his Ulsters was to march out of Waterford,..I ordered Colonel Zanchy..to march..to the relief of our friends. *Ibid.*, The Ulsters..made indeed for the time a good resistance.

2. The king-of-arms for Ireland.

1552 EDWARD VI *Jrnl.* in *Lit. Rem.* (Roxburghe Cl.) II. 395, [February] 2. Ther was a king of armes made for Irland, whose name was Ulster, and his province was al Irland. 1627 CHAS. I in *State Papers, Ireland* (1900) 223 You shall also see Ulster (who is the Chief Herald) countenanced in a herald's commission of visitation of various places in Ireland. 1712 *Lond. Gaz.* No. 4970/2 Coat of his Arms carried by Ulster King of Arms. 1857 *Lit. Rem. Edw. VI* (Roxb. Cl.) II. 395 *n.*, The arms given to the office of Ulster were, Argent, St. George's cross, and on a chief gules a lion between a harp and portcullis, all or. 1880 *Encycl. Brit.* XI. 688/1 In Ireland also there is but one king-at-arms, Ulster.

3. A long, loose overcoat of frieze or other rough cloth, frequently with a waist-belt.

The 'Ulster Overcoat' was introduced by J. G. M'Gee & Co. of Belfast in 1867; the abbreviated name has been in common use from 1879.

1878 H. S. LEIGH *Town Garland* 87 When the Ulster descends from its home on the hook, And the warmth-giving wrappers return from the wash. 1879 MISS BRADDON *Cloven Foot* xii. 110 Celia running home..with all her wedding finery smothered under a waterproof Ulster. 1888 RIDER HAGGARD *Col. Quaritch* III. xi. 169 He put on a pair of shooting-boots, an old coat, and an ulster.

attrib. 1878 *Era Almanack* 35 The ulster epidemic was raging even at this time. 1879 E. O'DONOVAN *Merv Oasis* xvi. (1883) 174 Over my shoulders was a drenched leopard skin, beneath which could be seen my travel-stained, much-worn ulster overcoat. 1880 *Cassell's Family Mag.* 122 The ulster muff is of a rectangular shape.

4. *attrib.* Used to designate the custom prevalent in Ulster by which a tenant has certain rights of occupancy, disposal, or compensation, in regard to land held by him; usually *Ulster tenant-right.*

1870 *Act* 33–34 *Victoria* c. 46 § 1 The usages prevalent in the province of Ulster, which are known as, and in this Act intended to be included under, the denomination of the Ulster tenant-right custom, are hereby declared to be legal. 1878 [see TENANT-RIGHT]. 1879 H. GEORGE *Progr. & Pov.* VI. i. (1881) 291 If what is known as the Ulster tenant right were extended to the whole of Great Britain, it would be but to carve out of the estate of the landlord, an estate for the tenant. 1882 M. ARNOLD *Irish Ess.*, etc. 28 It has been suggested..by the Ulster custom of compensating them [*sc.* tenants] for their improvements, and letting them sell the value which by their improvements they had added to the property.

b. *Ulsterman*, a native or inhabitant of Ulster.

In recent use also *Ulsterite.* Cf. ULTONIAN.

1845 CARLYLE *Cromwell* I. 497 'Lieutenant-General Ferral with his Ulsters;' *note*, Ulster-men. 1868 (*title*), Modern Ireland: its Vital Questions, Secret Societies, and Government: by an Ulsterman.

Hence (from sense 3) **U·lstered** *a.*, wearing an ulster. **Ulstere·tte,** a small or light ulster. **U·lstering,** material suitable for ulsters.

1880 MISS BROUGHTON *Second Thoughts* I. v. 62 A few 'ulstered, comforted men, stamping up and down, waiting for the night mail. 1889 SKRINE *Mem. Thring* 201 The group of flannelled and ulstered players. 1887 J. ASHBY STERRY *Lazy Minstrel* (1892) 171 My smart 'ulsterette, e'en a poet might sing, 'Tis white corduroy, with a rose-coloured lining! 1888 *Cambridge* (Mass.) *Tribune* 24 Nov., These 'Inverness' overcoats are close-fitting, and when worn without the cape have the appearance of an ulsterette. 1888 *Myra's Jrnl.* 1 Nov. 656/1 Patterns of Cloths, Homespuns, and 'Ulsterings for ladies' and children's jackets and ulsters. 1890 *Textile News* 20 June (List Manufacturers), Fancy meltons, ulsterings, costumes, coatings, &c.

Ult., abbrev. of ULTIMO.

1750 DUNCOMBE in *Lett. Eminent Persons* (1772) II. 170, I have read yours of the 30th ult. with great pleasure. 1767 J. GARDEN *Elegant Epist.* (1790) 730/1, I am..favoured with your's of the 25th ult. 1798 *York Courant* 1 Oct. 2/5 On Saturday the first ult a new peal of six bells..was opened. 1815 *Sporting Mag.* XLV. 354 On the 3d ult. they fell in with a fox.

† **Ultagh, -ogh.** *Anglo-Irish.* *Obs.* Also **Ultock.** [a. Ir. Gael. *Ultach*, f. *Ult-*, stem of OIr. *Ulaid* (d. pl. *Ultaib*, a. pl. *Ultu*) men of Ulster.] An Ulsterman.

1649 in *Contemp. Hist. Irel.* (Ir. Archæol. Soc.) II. 335 Those under the command of George Monro, part whereof were formerly his own, and part were of Owen O'Neals Ultoghs. 1652–3 *Ibid.* III. 370 Created Earle of Tyrone, by the Ultaghes. 1690 J. MACKENZIE *Siege London-Derry* 48 'Great numbers of Women and Boys (which the Ultoghs always carry along with them, when they expect spoil).

attrib. 1688 in Somers *Tracts* (1814) XI. 451 How often do we now hear the Ultock Irish boast of their merit.

Ulterior (ɒltī·riəɹ), *a.* and *sb.* [a. L. *ulterior* further, more distant, comp. of **ulter* (cf. *ultrā, ultrō* advs.) that is beyond. Hence also It. *ulteriore*, Sp. and Pg. *ulterior*, F. *ultérieur* (16th c.).]

A. *adj.* **1.** Lying beyond that which is immediate or present; coming at a subsequent point or stage; further, future.

1646 SIR T. BROWNE *Pseud. Ep.* II. i. 49 If the prescription of time, and numerositie of assertors, were a sufficient demonstration, we might sit downe herein, as an unquestionable truth; nor should there need *ulterior* disquisition. 1661 BOYLE *Style of Script.* 211 The Ulterior Accomplishment of that Part of it [*sc.* Scripture], which once Promis'd God's People, that Kings should be its Nursing Fathers. 1816 A. KNOX *Rem.* (1834) I. 54 These changes were meant by Providence to subserve ulterior movements. 1827 JARMAN *Powell's Devises* II. 75 The principle which confers upon him the ulterior interest in the lands directed to be sold would seem to exclude him in the converse case. 1856 FROUDE *Hist. Eng.* (1858) I. iv. 336 The request was only preparatory to ulterior measures. 1884 *Manch. Exam.* 10 May 5/4 The attitude and disposition of those Powers, as bearing upon their ulterior action, necessarily enter into the question.

b. *spec.* Lying beyond what is openly stated, avowed, or evident; intentionally kept in the background or concealed.

1735 BOLINGBROKE *Study Hist.* viii. (1752) II. 98 By reserving still a right of making ulterior demands, they reduced the Carthaginians at last to the necessity of abandoning their city, or of continuing the war. 1825 T. HOOK *Sayings* Ser. II. *Man of Many Fr.* (Colburn) 86 Without any knowledge of her uncle's ulterior intentions on the subject. 1856 *N. Brit. Rev.* XXVI. 197 There is no reason for suspecting him of ulterior designs of a deeper and more treacherous dye. 1877 FROUDE *Short Stud.* (1883) IV. I. iii. 30 He was ..the most unlikely..to have adopted a course so marked without some ulterior purpose.

2. Lying on the further side of a point or boundary; more remote in position.

1721 BAILEY, *Ulterior*, on the farther Side. 1798 *Phil. Trans.* LXXXVIII. 167 This scale..containing three parallel lines engraven thereon, on the exterior and ulterior of which are three divisions. 1817 CHALMERS *Astron. Disc.* iii. (1852) 63 To shoot afar into those ulterior regions which are beyond the limits of our astronomy. 1864 BAILEY *Festus* (ed. 7) 120 The thunderous bars Of Heaven's ulterior orb.

B. *sb.* A further aim or end.

1843 CHALMERS in Hanna *Mem.* (1852) IV. xviii. 351 This will open..a bright and beautiful ulterior, to which every eye should be directed.

Hence **Ulterio·rity,** an ulterior thing or matter.

1814 PARR *Let. to S. Butler* 1 Apr., Wks. 1828 VII. 363, I shall say something about the ulteriorities, and you must sympathise and co-operate with me.

Ulte·riorly, *adv.* [f. ULTERIOR *a.* + -LY[2].] At (or to) a further stage or point; subsequently; afterwards.

1818 BENTHAM *Ch. Eng.*, *Catech. Exam.* 209 The future probable Bell-taught and ulteriorly teachable Parish School-boy. 1833 CARLYLE *Misc. Ess.*, *Diderot* (1888) 32 Nor do the generality, on either side, yet see whither ulteriorly it is tending. 1854 J. S. C. ABBOTT *Napoleon* (1855) II. xxxv. 663 Beneath its lofty dome, where the massive tomb of Napoleon was ulteriorly to be erected, a magnificent cenotaph was reared.

Ultimacy (ʊ·ltimăsi). [f. ULTIM-ATE *a.*: see -ACY.] The quality or state of being ultimate.

1842 SIR W. HAMILTON *Diss.* in *Reid's Wks.* II. 760 The simplicity, ultimacy, and incomprehensibility of our original apprehensions. *a* 1848 W. A. BUTLER *Hist. Anc. Philos.* (1856) I. 161 The ultimacy of the laws of motion has been lately made the subject of disquisition. 1893 FAIRBAIRN *Christ in Mod. Theol.* II. II. iii. 430 As to the ultimacy of the will Calvin is explicit.

Ultimata, pl. of ULTIMATUM *sb.*

Ultimate (ʊ·ltimĕt), *a.* and *sb.* [ad. late L. *ultimāt-us*, pa. pple. of *ultimāre* to be at the end, f. *ultimus* last, final: see ULTIME *a.*]

A. *adj.* **1.** Of ends, designs, etc.: Lying beyond all others; forming the final aim or object.

1654 JER. TAYLOR *Real Pres.* i. 10 The faithful and pious communicants receive the ultimate end of his presence, that is, spiritual blessings. 1664 POWER *Exp. Philos.* I. 67 In the obtainment of which he hath come to the ultimate design of his endeavours. 1675 BAXTER *Cath. Theol.* I. I. 61 God is this ultimate End of man,..to which all are means. *a* 1721 PRIOR *Dial. Dead* iii. Wks. 1907 II. 258 The beginning, Progress, and Ultimate end of Thought. 1758 JOHNSON *Idler* No. 1 P3 To be idle is the ultimate purpose of the busy. 1782 PRIESTLEY *Corrupt. Chr.* I. Pref. p. xiii, If my proper and ultimate object be considered. 1847 G. HARRIS *Life Ld. Hardwicke* I. iv. 354 A far higher and nobler reward is their ultimate aim. *a* 1871 GROTE *Eth. Fragm.* iv. (1876) 72 They would..esteem different agents in proportion as they tended to assist these same ultimate purposes. 1892 H. LANE *Differ. Rheum. Dis.* (ed. 2) vi. 119 The ultimate goal of all our investigations and observations.

2. Coming at the end of a process, course of action, etc., or as the last in a succession or series; arrived at as a final result or in the last resort.

1660 R. COKE *Justice Vind.* 8, I am content with Aristotle's definition of the will,..That it is the ultimate resolution, end, or determination of counsel. 1671 MILTON *P. R.* III. 210 My harbour and my ultimate repose, The end I would attain, my final good. 1755 YOUNG *Centaur* ii. Wks. 1757 IV. 159 All agree, that several goods being proposed for our ultimate enjoyment, it is impossible in our nature not to chuse the best. 1785 PALEY *Mor. Philos.* VI. xii. (1818) II. 426 Containing that which in peace and war is equally unjustifiable—ultimate and gratuitous mischief. 1827 FARADAY *Chem. Manip.* ii. (1842) 30 The oscillations..will be found to be quick, and the beam will soon take its ultimate state of rest. 1841 MIALL in *Nonconf.* I. 2 Ultimate success will require union, patience, persevering energy. 1860 RUSKIN *Unto this Last* (1862) 8 No man ever knew, or can know, what will be the ultimate result to himself, or to others, of any given line of conduct. 1890 H. LANE *Differ. Rheum. Dis.* 5 Not to exhaust the subject, nor even to lead the way to the ultimate hope of eradicating the source and origin of the evil.

b. Of resolves, etc.: Final, determinate, absolute.

1687 MIÈGE *Gt. Fr. Dict.* II. s.v., This is the ultimate Resolution. 1779 J. MOORE *View Soc. France* (1789) I. i. 4, I have now formed an ultimate resolution against gaming. 1786 JEFFERSON *Writ.* (1859) I. 570 An ultimate opinion should not be formed till we see Mr. Randall. 1803 in Gurw. *Wellington's Desp.* (1837) II. 138 *note*, I consented to wait till then for their ultimate decision.

c. Putting an end to further continuance, development, or action; final, decisive.

1755 JOHNSON, *End*,..ultimate state; final doom. 1782 COWPER *Hope* 640 Nature opposes..This riving stroke, this ultimate divorce. 1803 MALTHUS *Popul.* (1817) I. 17 The ultimate check to population appears then to be a want of food. 1827 POLLOK *Course T.* VI. 365 Some disaster great and ultimate. 1838 PRESCOTT *Ferd. & Is.* Introd. ii. I. 79 To protect the subject from the oppressions of the crown and its officers, over all which cases it possessed original and ultimate jurisdiction. 1870 MOZLEY *Univ. Serm.* iii. (1877) 60 The natural philosopher is practically assured from the concurrence of data before him, of a result, before the ultimate test is got.

d. Forming a final stage, point, or limit; beyond which there is no advance or progress.

1794 G. ADAMS *Nat. & Exp. Philos.* I. v. 204, I informed them that the creatures [larvæ] before us were not in their ultimate state, but were the produce of the bee-fly. 1815 J. SMITH *Panorama Sci. & Art* II. 34 This salt..causes the hair to contract itself, until it has attained the ultimate limit of its contraction. 1869 RANKINE *Mach. & Millwork* 497 The ultimate shearing strength, or modulus of resistance to shearing. 1878 B. TAYLOR *Deukalion* III. v. 127 Why should I conceal The ultimate barrier where I needs must pause?

3. Beyond which no advance can be made by investigation or analysis; forming a limit or final stage in respect of nature or quality; fundamental or elemental.

1659 PEARSON *Creed* ii. 147 We must acknowledge that the actuall giving of salvation to us, is the ultimate and conclusive ground of the title *Saviour.* 1681 *Ess. Peace & Truth Ch.* 9 Man therefore is justly defined to be a Rational Religious Creature, therein consisting the formal ultimate difference from a Brute. 1739 HUME *Hum. Nat.* Introd. (1874) I. 308 Any hypothesis, that pretends to discover the ultimate original qualities of human nature. 1749 HARTLEY *Observ. Man* II. 32 Since God is the ultimate Author of all Motion, we must suppose him to be immaterial. 1792 N. CHIPMAN *Rep.* (1871) 53 The King was, in view of the law, the ultimate owner of all lands within his dominions. 1808 JEBB in *Knox & Jebb's Corr.* (1834) I. 453 There are ultimate truths, far above human ken. 1836 J. GILBERT *Chr. Atonem.* iv. (1852) 113 The ultimate law of moral agents must be the will of God. 1850 M'COSH *Div. Govt.* III. i. (1874) 295 In the inquiry into virtue and vice, we come back to ultimate principles, on which all morality rests. 1880 SAYCE *Introd. Sci. Lang.* (1890) I. 113 The sentence, in short, is..the ultimate starting-point of all our linguistic inquiries.

b. Of material things, *esp.* of the component particles of matter.

1808 BARCLAY *Muscular Motions* 273 These fibres, composed of the fibres that are called *ultimate*, are seldom seen extending from the one extremity of a muscle to the other. 1815 J. SMITH *Panorama Sci. & Art* II. 303 All that can be affirmed of the state in which the ultimate particles of matter exist, is only the result of conjecture. 1836–41 BRANDE *Chem.* (ed. 5) 1053 Although the ultimate principles of vegetable substances are few in number. 1857 MILLER *Elem. Chem.*, *Org.* 11 To determine the relative proportion in which each of the ultimate elements exists. 1871 TYNDALL

Fragm. Sci. (1879) II. vi. 81 This formative power,..ready to..build the ultimate particles of matter into definite shapes.

transf. 1831 T. P. JONES *New Convers. Chem.* xxviii. 282 When we decompose them [*sc.* proximate principles], to ascertain how much they contain of each of the simple bodies, the operation is called *ultimate analysis.* 1857 MILLER *Elem. Chem.*, *Org.* 6 The determination of the proportions..furnishes an illustration of what is meant by *ultimate* organic analysis.

c. *Math.* *Ultimate ratio*, the final limiting ratio between two variable quantities which simultaneously approach definite fixed values or limits. (Correl. to *prime ratio*: see PRIME *a.* 9 d.)

1729 A. MOTTE tr. *Newton's Principia* I. 46 The ultimate ratio of the arc, chord, and tangent, any one to any other, is the ratio of equality. 1749 HARTLEY *Observ. Man* II. 32 According to the mathematical Doctrine of ultimate Ratios, not even an infinite Series..could remove it. 1818 VINCE *Fluxions* (ed. 5) 16 The ingenious..Author of the *Analyst* ..went upon the term *ultimate* ratio, assuming equality where it was never intended. 1842 BRANDE *Dict. Sci.*, etc. 974/2 They are called prime ratios, or ultimate ratios, according as the ratios of the variables are considered as receding from, or approaching to, the ratios of the limits.

4. Not followed by another; last. *rare*[−1].

1728 MORGAN *Algiers* II. iv. 292 Returning home, he bad farewel to the fluid Element; this being his ultimate Expedition.

5. Forming a result or conclusion of a character different from the starting-point or present state; eventual, resultant.

1777 PRIESTLEY *Disc. Philos. Necess.* Ded. p. ix, All seeming discord is real harmony, and all apparent evil, ultimate good. 1795 BURKE *Th. Scarcity* Wks. 1842 II. 253 The quiet of the town is purchased by the ruin of the country, and the ultimate wretchedness of both. 1832 HT. MARTINEAU *Homes Abroad* ix. 127 One yields temporary benefit to a few at the expense of ultimate injury to the many. 1874 GREEN *Short Hist.* iv. § 1. 161 Neither trick nor conquest could shake the firm faith of the Celt in the ultimate victory of his race.

6. Final, last; occurring in, or falling on, the last syllable of a word.

1837 G. PHILLIPS *Syriac Gram.* 28 If the ultimate syllable be perfect without the terminating consonant. 1862 MARSH *Lect. Eng. Lang.* 380 The great frequency of ultimate and penultimate accentuation.

7. Most remote in space or position. *rare*[−1].

1848 JOHNSTON in *Proc. Berw. Nat. Club* II. 297 The ultimate [joint] armed with a long curved..claw.

B. *sb.* **1.** The final point or result; the end or conclusion; the last step.

1681 RYCAUT tr. *Gracian's Critick* 113 Ordinary Toyes, applauded by a Castilian, for but being his own, with praises as might befit the ultimate of all Perfection. 1718 J. FOX *Wanderer* 72, I..once hoped I might attain to the very Ultimate of what you propos'd by Sunday last. 1728 ELIZA HEYWOOD tr. *Mme. de Gomez's Belle A.* (1732) II. 2 Thelamont,..having now obtain'd the ultimate of his Desires, appear'd more bright and gay than ever. 1794 HUTTON *Philos. Light*, etc. 211 A proper fulminating composition, which seems to be the ultimate to which we may proceed. 1880 SHELLEY *Ess. & Lett.* (1852) II. 225, I shall write to you the ultimates of my Commission in my next letter. 1852 BAILEY *Festus* (ed. 5) 534 Ends and beginnings mingle at the last; All ultimates are foreordained. 1890 BOOTH *Darkest Eng.* II. vi. 230 They carried their principles of freedom and license to the logical ultimate.

2. The point at which investigation or analysis stops; a final or fundamental fact or principle.

1709 MRS. MANLEY *Secret Mem.* (1720) IV. 101 It was not her Fault that she became not Mistress of the great Secret, the Ultimate of Chymistry. 1774 J. BRYANT *Mythol.* I. p. xii, The Deluge..was esteemed..the ultimate of Gentile history. *Ibid.* II. 267 The ancient Poet..spoke of him as the father of mankind. In short he was the ultimate, to which Grecian history referred. 1841 *Blackw. Mag.* XLIX. 151 Mind seems as it were to be getting loose upon space. It reposes upon no religious ultimates. 1862 H. SPENCER *First Princ.* II. iii. § 50 (1875) 169 We come down then finally to Force, as the ultimate of ultimates. 1856 E. P. WHIPPLE *Character & Characteristic Men* 268 If he calls his notion Law and makes law an ultimate, beyond which the human reason cannot go.

Ultimate (ʊ·ltimēᵗt), *v.*[1] [f. prec. or L. *ultimāt-*, ppl. stem of *ultimāre* (cf. It. *ultimare*, Sp. and Pg. *ultimar* to finish).]

1. *trans.* To carry to an end; to complete.

1849 E. H. SEARS *Regeneration* III. i. (1859) 131 Works are filled and vitalized by that angelic benevolence which is not complete until clothed and ultimated in action. 1866 BESSIE R. PARKES *Vignettes* 399 My parents had seen my education ultimated in practical life. 1881 E. S. HOLDEN *Sir W. Herschel* 53 His researches on the construction of the heavens would have been made; those were in his brain, and must have been ultimated.

refl. 1860 EMERSON *Cond. Life* viii. 169 It is the soundness of the bones that ultimates itself in a peach-bloom complexion. 1880 HOWELLS *Undisc. Country* iii. 50 A ferment of the kind he speaks of in the world of spirits would be more apt to ultimate itself here in the mind than in the stomach. 1885 L. OLIPHANT *Sympneumata* 14 The moral forces which ultimate themselves dynamically in the actions of men.

2. *intr.* To result finally; to end (*in* something).

c 1834 A. H. STEPHENS in Johnston & Browne *Life* (1878) 95 How the thing will ultimate I cannot tell. 1868 L. OLIPHANT *Let.* in *Life* (1891) viii. II. 41 We have no place here for those who like to meditate, unless the meditation ultimates in useful work. 1887 *Pop. Sci. Monthly* Aug. 564/2 Believing that they..must ultimate..in an increase of egoism.

U·ltimate, *v.*[2] *rare.* [Back-formation from ULTIMATUM *sb.*] *trans.* = ULTIMATUM *v.*

1892 *Black & White* 30 Jan. 135/2 President Harrison has at last 'ultimated' Chili, as the Americans will probably soon be saying. 1898 *Pall Mall G.* 28 Sept. 2 At last the four Powers are going to ultimate the Sultan about the Turkish troops in Crete.

Ultimately (ʊ·ltimĕtli), *adv.* [f. ULTIMATE *a.* + -LY[2].]

1. In the last resort; when carried to the natural or logical conclusion; fundamentally.

1660 R. COKE *Justice Vind.* Pref. 13 If I could not ultimately resolve the Dictates of my Reason as a Christian, into plain places of Scripture. 1690 LOCKE *Hum. Und.* II. i. § 2 In one word, From Experience: in that, all our Knowledge is founded; and from that it ultimately derives it self. ? 1743 in *10th Rep. Hist. MSS. Comm.* App. I. 279 To which nevertheless their Immunities must ultimately resort. 1775 JOHNSON *Tax. no Tyr.* 23 All government is ultimately and essentially absolute. 1776 GIBBON *Decl. & F.* vi. (1782) I. 185 The young emperor, on whose personal qualities the happiness or misery of the Roman world must ultimately depend. 1835 NEWMAN *Par. Serm.* (1837) I. iv. 64 What will it ultimately profit a man to profess without understanding? 1866 CRUMP *Banking* v. 131 Credit given to the holder of a bill by the person ultimately liable is considered equivalent to payment. 1869 MOZLEY *Univ. Serm.* i. (1877) 18 Every kingdom ultimately depends on moral influence and not on physical force.

2. In the end; at the last: **a.** As the conclusion or final stage of a process, course of action, etc.

1755 JOHNSON, *Finally*, 1. Ultimately; lastly; in conclusion. [Quoting Milton *Samson A.* 1296.] 1794 MATTHIAS *Purs. Lit.* (1798) 306 All passions submit ultimately..to the inability of gratifying them. 1796 MME. D'ARBLAY *Camilla* IX. iii, The heart-breaking event to which it had ultimately led. 1818 MRS. SHELLEY *Frankenst.* iii, I doubted not that I should ultimately succeed. 1839 JAMES *Louis XIV*, III. 235 It became daily apparent to all parties that war must ultimately be the result. 1860 HOLLAND *Miss Gilbert* ii. 19 It was supposed by the gossips of the village that Dr. Gilbert would ultimately marry Aunt Catharine. 1878 LECKY *Eng. in 18th C.* I. iii. 452 It is of the nature of a constitution so formed as ours..ultimately to work well.

b. As a point in a series, or in time.

1818 CRUISE *Digest* (ed. 2) II. 430 A feoffment was made to the use of the feoffor for his life..and ultimately to the use of himself and his heirs for ever. 1827 FARADAY *Chem. Manip.* ii. (1842) 37 It economises time to have the smaller weights arranged in order..and ultimately the large weights. 1880 TROLLOPE *Duke's Children* I. iii. 35 Frank's mother..would sometimes surmise..that the entire property must ultimately come to him. 1884 THOMPSON *Tumours of Bladder* 33 He..suffered much for a long time; ultimately there was some improvement.

3. In a final or conclusive manner; definitely.

1785 JEFFERSON *Corr.* Wks. 1859 I. 342 These questions, however, cannot be decided, ultimately, at this day. 1793 — *Writ.* (1830) IV. 479 It had no right to dismember or alienate any portion of territory once ultimately consolidated with us. 1798 S. & HT. LEE *Canterb. T.* II. 206 Yet nothing but a favourable judgment from the civilians in England could ultimately relieve [his] mind.

U·ltimateness. [f. as prec. + -NESS.] The quality of being ultimate; finality.

1884 *Century Mag.* XXVIII. 636 To have in it a certain completeness, ultimateness, and sacredness.

Ultima Thule: see THULE.

Ultimation (ɒltimēⁱ·ʃən). [f. L. *ultimāt-*, *ultimāre*: see ULTIMATE *v.*[1] Cf. It. *ultimazione.*] The action or process of bringing to an ultimate result; final issue or development.

1791 H. WALPOLE *Let. to Miss Berry* 23 June, As this must take its passage..early to-morrow morning,..I shall perhaps not know the ultimation, but you probably will before you receive this. 1805 EUGENIA DE ACTON *Nuns of Desert* I. 117 The ultimation of their meditated kindness, was only to bestow upon her an indisputable right to the title of a penitent. 1858 SEARS *Athan.* III. ii. 258 The words *heaven* and *hell*, as they are used in popular speech, describe the complete ultimations of good and evil. 1883 L. OLIPHANT *Altiora Peto* II. 65 When a sufficient number have..attained a sufficient development for the ultimation of new results.

So **U·ltimatisa·tion.** *rare.*

1885 L. OLIPHANT *Sympneumata* 117 Because of this abnormal ultimatisation of organisms in this subsurface world.

U·ltimative, *adj.* *rare*[−1]. [f. as prec.] That tends to produce some final result.

1885 L. OLIPHANT *Sympneumata* 239 The ultimative or operative region of earthly manhood.

Ultimatum (ɒltimēⁱ·tɒm), *sb.* Pl. **-ata** (-ēⁱ·tă). [ad. late L. *ultimātum*, neut. sing. of *ultimātus*, pa. pple. of *ultimāre*: see ULTIMATE *v.*[1] So in F., It., Pg., G., Du., etc.]

1. In diplomacy, the final terms presented by one power (or group of powers) to another, the rejection of which may lead to the severing of diplomatic relations, and eventually to a declaration of war.

sing. 1731 *Gentl. Mag.* Jan. 39/1 There are privately handed about here Copies of the *Ultimatum* (or last Proposals) of the Allies of Seville, as transmitted hither from Paris. 1759 SMOLLETT *Hist. Eng.* VIII. (ed. 3) IX. 143 He delivered to the mediator an ultimatum, importing, That he adhered to the treaties of Westphalia and Nimeguen. 1784–5 *Ann. Reg.*, *Hist. Europe* 107/1 A new statement of the emperor's claims and demands, described as his *ultimatum*, was presented to the Dutch ministers. 1832 tr. *Sismondi's Ital. Rep.* xiii. 287 Charles still insisted on disgraceful conditions, which his secretary read as his ultimatum. 1876 BANCROFT *Hist. U.S.* VI. lviii. 48 Fitzherbert ..reflected that peace with the United States would be the best means of forcing France and Spain to declare their ultimatum.

pl. 1773 *Ann. Reg.*, *Hist. Europe* 40/1 The delegates were also appointed..to receive the ultimata of the three powers. 1796 HAMILTON *Wks.* (1886) VII. 121 In general, where more had been obtained by a treaty than the *ultimata* prescribed to the negotiator, it would be inexpedient to publish those *ultimata.* 1859 L. OLIPHANT *China & Japan* I. 98 Mr. Wade..proceeded..to Canton, and delivered the *ultimata* of the French and English plenipotentiaries. 1883 *Harper's Mag.* April 676/1 *note*, Different ultimata had been adopted with respect to the boundaries.

b. *transf.* A final condition or stipulation; one's last word on a matter.

1733 SWIFT *Let. to Pope* 31 Mar., But, there must be some stipulations for my riding, with other necessary postulatums, and ultimatums. 1787 M. CUTLER in *Life*, etc. (1888) I. 299 We therefore begged leave to state to the Board the terms on which we were ready to close the contract, and that those terms must be our *Ultimatum.* 1813 *Examiner* 11 Jan. 23/1 His Lordship would require, as the ultimatum, ..that a competent portion of the natives shall perform duty under British Officers. 1848 DICKENS *Dombey* xl, I have stated my *ultimatum*, Madam. 1869 TROLLOPE *He knew*, etc. xxxvii. (1878) 207 The official shrugged his shoulders and signified that his ultimatum had been pronounced.

2. The final point, extreme limit; an ultimate end or aim.

1748 RICHARDSON *Clarissa* (1768) III. 53 That single pressure..delighted me more than ever I was delighted with the *Ultimatum* with any other woman. 1793 R. WILLETT in *Archaeologia* XI. 106 The size of our ships seems now to have reached nearly its ultimatum. 1804 JEBB *Corr.* (1834) I. 153 And now I will tell you an ultimatum, which I would far prefer,..the librarianship of Armagh. 1804 EUGENIA DE ACTON *Tale without Title* II. 26 Their ultimatum was obtained, and they were considered as persons of consequence.

b. Const. *of.*

1770 *Monthly Rev.* 502 This surely is the *ultimatum* of astronomical precision. 1790 *Bystander* 308 The ultimatum of earthly enjoyment was to give him invitations to their houses. 1802 MRS. E. PARSONS *Myst. Visit* I. 132 To be married was still the ultimatum of her wishes. 1812 SHELLEY *Proposals* Pr. Wks. 1888 I. 280 The attainment of the good which I propose as the ultimatum of philanthropic exertion. 1856 KANE *Arct. Expl.* I. x. 114 At last we came to the Esquimaux ultimatum of simplicity,—raw meat and a fur bag. 1888 J. ELLIS *New Chr.* ii. 51 If..all chemical and mechanical changes, or effects, are but the ultimatum of spiritual causes.

c. Final lot or destiny. *rare*[−1].

1861 G. MOORE *Lost Tribes* iv. 84 To trace the meaning of God's handwriting concerning the origin and ultimatum of our race.

† **3.** *slang.* The hinder parts; the buttocks. *Obs.*

1823 C. WESTMACOTT *Points of Misery* iii. 31 Old Brummagem and the fat lady being thrown head downwards, formed an excellent step-ladder with their *ultimatums* for the purpose. 1824 in *Spirit Pub. Jrnls.* (1825) 38 He..at the same time felt his spinal extremities and his ultimatum covered by a shower of slimy material of a very offensive odour. 1825 C. WESTMACOTT *Eng. Spy* I. 165 As for the inexpressibles they hung round his *ultimatum* like petticoat trousers.

4. A primary element, beyond which analysis becomes impossible; something fundamental.

1858 O. W. HOLMES *Aut. Breakf.-t.* i. (1859) 10 No men can have satisfactory relations with each other until they have agreed on certain *ultimata* of belief not to be disturbed in ordinary conversation. 1867 H. MACMILLAN *Bible Teach.* i. 22 The truth is, that all our scientific investigations will never conduct us to the ultimatum—the commencement of matter. 1868 BAIN *Ment. & Mor. Sci.*, *Ethics* II. 498 Sensible Perception,..whereby we perceive that the triangle before us is a geometrical ultimatum.

5. Furthest destination; most distant point (to be) reached.

1862 CARLYLE *Fredk. Gt.* XI. ii. III. 44 Almost to the coast of the Baltic; their ultimatum there a place called Köslin.

Hence **Ultima·tum** *v. trans.*, to present with an ultimatum. (Cf. ULTIMATE *v.*[2])

1897 *Pall Mall G.* 23 Sept. 2 General Woodford never ultimatumed the fiery untamed Duke of Tetuan.

† **Ultime,** *a.* *Obs.* Also **ultim.** [ad. L. *ultimus*, superl. of **ulter*: cf. ULTERIOR. So It., Sp., Pg. *ultimo*, OF. *ultime.*] Ultimate, final.

1626 BACON *Nat. Hist.* § 59 Whereby the true and Ultime Operations of Heat are not attained. 1654 H. L'ESTRANGE *Chas. I* (1655) 103 Nothing was wanting now to the perfecting of this League, but the ultime and compleating act, the solemn confirmation by Oath. 1659 — *Alliance Div. Off.* 295 The perficient and ultim act of marriage.

Ultimity (ɒlti·miti). Now *rare.* [f. as prec. + -ITY. Cf. med.L. *ultimitas.*]

1. The final point or ultimate development of an action or thing; the last stage.

1613 BACON *Let. to Jas. I*, Wks. 1868 XI. x. 369 That those tragical arguments and (as the schoolmen call them) ultimities of persuasions which were used last Parliament should for ever be abolished. 1626 — *Sylva* § 838 The Degrees of Alteration, of one Body into another, from Crudity to Perfect Concoction; which is the ultimity of that Action, or Processe. *a* 1706 EVELYN *Hist. Relig.* (1850) I. 77 [The Almighty] knows all that does not actually exist, even the ultimities of what can or may be.

2. An ultimate principle or fact.

1898 *Expositor* June 453 In everything appertaining to origins and causes, to ultimities and universalities.

† **Ultimo,** *sb.* *Obs.*[−1] [? a. It., Sp., or Pg. *ultimo*: see ULTIME *a.*] = ULTIMUM.

1622 in Foster *Eng. Factories Ind.* (1908) II. 11 Which is as farr as the Nabobs perwanna importes, and is the ultimo of there and our owne expectacions.

‖ **Ultimo** (ʊ·ltimo), *a.* and *adv.* [L. *ultimō* (sc. *diē* or *mense*), abl. sing. masc. of *ultimus* last. So in G., Du., Sw., etc.]

†1. On the last day (of a specified month). *Obs.*

2. Of last month. (Abbreviated **Ult.** and **Ulto.**)

†Ultimum. *Obs.* [L., neut. sing. of *ultimus*.] The final point or limit.

†Ultion. *Obs. rare.* Also **6** *Sc.* **vltioun.** [ad. L. *ultiōn-em*, noun of action f. the stem of *ulcīscī* to avenge. So OF. *ultion*, It. *ulzione*.] Vengeance, revenge, avengement.

Ultonian, *a.* and *sb.* [f. med. L. *Ultonia* Ulster, f. OIr. *Ulu, Ulaid* : see **Ultagh**.]

A. *adj.* Of or belonging to Ulster.

B. *sb.* An inhabitant or native of Ulster.

Ultra (*ø·ltrǎ*), *sb.*, *a.*, and *adv.* [Independent use of **Ultra**, orig. as an abbreviation of F. *ultra-royaliste*, and sep. mainly due to Lady Morgan. Cf. F. *ultra sb.* (in senses B. 1 and 2.)]

A. *adj.* Ultra-royalist.

2. Exceeding ordinary, proper, or reasonable limits; going beyond what is usual or right; extreme, excessive.

3. Of persons : Holding extreme views in politics or other matters of opinion.

B. *sb.* **1.** An ultra-royalist (*F.*)

Ultra-, *prefix*, representing L. *ultrā* beyond, employed as a prefix in the post-classical *ultrāmundānus* ultramundane, and the later *ultrā-*.

1. Signifying 'beyond, spatially beyond or on the other side of' : **a.** With sbs., as *ultra*-equinoctial (pl.), those who live beyond the equinox.

b. With adjs., as *ultra*-Gangetic, *-Martian, median, -terrene, -terrestrial, -zodiacal*.

2. Signifying 'beyond, surpassing, or transcending the limits of' (the specified concept), as *ultra*-human, *-incarnatic, -natural, -pecuniary*, etc.

Ultra-. Sept. 127 Science itself not unfrequently derives motive power from an ultra-scientific source.

2. One who holds extreme views, particularly in religion or politics.

3. One who goes to the extreme of fashion.

Ultra- *prefix*

1. In the pl. *ultra vires* (*vai·rīz*), beyond the power or legal authority (of a person, etc. ; also used with ellipse of *for*).

2. Lying beyond. (Cf. **Ultra-** C.)

Ultra- (*ø·ltrǎ*)

accordingly...took an early occasion to associate the ultra-revolutionary party with the foreign enemies of the republic.

b. In some special terms, as *ultra*-basic, *-brachy-cephalic, -dolichocephalic, -elliptic*.

With sb. in the same sense : **b.** Denoting persons.

Ultra-crepida·rian, *a.* and *sb.* [f. the Latin phrase *ultrā crepidam* 'beyond the sole' in allusion to the reply given by Pliny (*Hist. Nat.* XXXV. x. § 36) to the cobbler.]

a. *adj.* Going beyond one's proper province.

b. *sb.* One who ventures beyond his scope ; an ignorant or presumptuous critic.

Ultra-crepida·rianism.

So Ultracrepida·te, *v. intr.*, to venture beyond one's scope. **Ultra-crepida·tion**, *-cre·pidaing*, the action or fact of criticising ignorantly.

Ultra·dian. *a.* [f. the L. phrase *ultrā diem* 'beyond a day'.] Going beyond mere faith ; blindly credulous. Also **Ultrā·dianism.**

Ultra·geous, *a. rare.* [f. **Ultra** *a.* or *sb.*, after *outrageous*.] Violently extreme.

Ultraism (*ø·ltrǎ·iz'm*). [f. **Ultra** *sb.* + **-ism**.]

So Ultra·ist, **Ultra·istic.**

Ultramontanism (*ø·ltrǎmo·ntǎniz'm*). [ad. F. *ultramontanisme* (18th c.), = Sp., Pg. *ultramontanismo* : see prec. and **-ism**.]

Ultramontanist [Cf. prec. and **-ist**.]

1. An adherent of ultramontane principles and doctrines ; a supporter of the absolute supremacy of the Pope.

2. **= Ultramontane** B. 1. *rare.*

Ultramontanize, *v.* [Cf. prec. and **-ize**.]

Ultramontanizing, *vbl. sb.* [Cf. prec. and **-ing**.] The process of making ultramontane in character.

Ultramundane (*ø·ltrǎmo·ndén*), *a.* and *sb.* [ad. late L. *ultrāmundānus*, f. *ultrā* beyond + *mundus* the world.] Lying beyond or outside of the world ; or belonging to things beyond the limits of the solar system.

Ultroneously, *adv.* [f. prec. + **-ly²**.] Of one's own accord ; spontaneously, voluntarily.

Ultroneous, *a.* [f. L. *ultrōneus* + **-ous**.] Voluntary actions ; spontaneity.

Ultroneousness, *rare.* [f. as prec. + **-ness**.]

Ulva (*ø·lvǎ*). *Bot.* [mod.L. *Ulva* : see prec.] Resembling or belonging to the *Ulvaceæ*.

†Ulve, *v.* *Obs.* **= Ulva** and **-ore**.

Uly(**e**, obs. Sc. variants of **Oil** *sb.*, **Oily** *a.*

Ulysses (*ʒ·lise·z*). [ad. L. *Ulysses* (also *Ulixes*), ad. Gr. Ὀδυσσεύς *Odysseus*, king of Ithaca and hero of the Odyssey.]

† Ulitable, *a.* *Obs.*

Ulitant [ad. L. *ululant-*, pr. pple. of *ululāre* : see next.]

1. Having the character of ululation.

2. Ululating, howling.

Ululate (*ʒ·liulét*), *v.* [f. L. *ululāt-*, ppl. stem of *ululāre* (freq. in imitative origin, f. the base *ul-*) ; cf. imitative origin.]

Ululation (*ʒliulē·ʃən*, *ʒʒ·li-*). [ad. L. *ululātiōn-, -ōnem* : see prec. So OF. *ululation*.]

1. A howl or wail ; a cry of lamentation.

2. The action of howling or ululating.

† Ulumbination. *Obs.*

† Ulvative, *v.* Wailing, lamenting.

Ulvatory, *a.* *Obs.*

Ultroneous, *a.*

Um (*ø·m*), *int.* [Imitative. Cf. **Hum** *int.*]

1. Used to indicate hesitating or inarticulate utterance on the part of a speaker.

2. Used to indicate hesitation or doubt in replying to another.

Uma, obs. var. of **Ha, Hum** prec.

Umb-, var. of **Umbe-** *prefix*.

Umbe-, *prefix*, app. ad. ON. *umb-* (earlier form of *um-*), corresponding to MLG. and MHG. *umb-*, OE. *ymb-*, *emb-* : see **Umbe-**.

Umbe, *prep.* [= **Umbe-** *prefix*.] Around, about.

Umbe throwe, **= Umbewhile** *adv.*

† Umbe, *prep.* and *adv.* *Obs.* Forms : 1-2 *ymbe*, 3 *umbe*, *umb*. [OE. *ymbe*, *umb-* : see **Umbe-** *prefix*.]

1. Around, about.

2. About, concerning.

and represent a kind of umbones. **1712** Gell *Pompeiana* ...

3. *a.* **Conch.** The point at which a univalve shell, of each valve of a bivalve shell, is most protuberant... from the bottom.

b. *Bot.* The knob or prominence in the centre of the pileus of a fungus.

c. *Ent.* (See quot.)

d. *Zool.* One of the perforated ambulacral plates of echinoderms.

4. *Path.* A central patch in an efflorescence or other affection of the skin.

5. *attrib.* (See first quot.)

d. *Zool.* One of the perforated ambulacral plates of echinoderms.

Umbo, Umbos, variants of UMBOTH *Sc. Obs.*

Umbonal (*vmbōnǎl*), *a.* [f. L. *umbo* UMBO + -AL.] Of, belonging to, situated near, the umbo; of the nature of an umbo.

Umbonate (*vmˈbōneit*), *a. Bot.* Furnished with, rising up in, an umbo or boss. Chiefly *Bot.*

Umbonulate, *a. Bot.* [ad. mod.L. *umbonulāt-us*, f. *umbonulus* dim. of L. *umbo*.]

Umboth, Orth and UmbH. *Obs.* Also 6 *umbuth*, *umbod*, *umbous*, -bots, 9 *umbith*. [a. ON. *umboð* (Norw. *umbod*, Sw. and Da. *ombud*)...

Umborial *rare*. [f. L. *umbōn-em*.]

Umbra ¹ (*vmbrǎ*). Pl. *umbræ* (*vmbríː*), [L. *umbra* shade, shadow, UMBER *sb.* ¹] †1 *L. ombra, dusty, ticket.

†2. The shade of a deceased person; a phantom or ghost. Also *fig.*

3. An uninvited guest accompanying one who is invited.

4. *Astr.* The shadow cast by the earth or moon as visible in an eclipse ; now *spec.* that portion in which the shadow is complete, as contrasted with the *penumbra*.

b. In sun-spots : the nucleus.

Umbra ² (*vmbrǎ*). *Ichth.* [L. = the grayling.]

1. The grayling = UMBER *sb.*²

2. A marine fish of the genus *Umbrina*, the *Mediterranean species U. cirrhosa.*

Umbra, Umbre, *v. Obs. rare.* [Alteration of EMBRACE *v.*, by substitution of U.] *trans.* To surround; to obtain.

Umbracious, *a. rare* [f. L. *umbra*, after SPACIOUS, etc.]

Umbracle (*vmˈbrǎk'l*). *Obs.* Also 6 *Sc. vmbrakill, -kle.* [L. *umbrāculum*, shady place, etc., dim. of *umbra* UMBRA.]

Umbraculiform [f. *umbracul-um* + -(I)FORM.] Shade of shadow ; a shady place.

Umbrage (*vmˈbrēdʒ*), *sb.* Also 7-9 *ombrage.* [a. F. *umbrage*, *ombrage*, Pr. *umbratge* ... L. *umbrāticum, -icus*, f. *umbra* shadow.]

†1. Shade, shadow. *Obs.*

†**b.** Shadow, semblance ; a colour or false excuse for. *Obs.*

2. Shade or shadow cast by trees or the like.

†**3.** A shadowy appearance or indication, a semblance, outline, or faint representation, a glimmering or trace; of something. Now *rare.* (Common in 17th *c.*)

4. Shade, protection, screen. *Obs.*

†**5.** Shelter, protection, screen. *Obs.*

6. *a.* A reason or ground for suspicion, an opinion.

†**b.** A suspicion, hint, inkling, or slight idea, of a matter. *Obs.*

7. *a.* The feeling of being offended by some word or action ; the fact of taking offence ; resentment ; displeasure.

b. In the phr. *to give* (. .) *umbrage*, to be in disfavour, etc.

†**8.** Displeasure, annoyance, offence, resentment. *Obs.*

†**b.** In the phr. *under the umbrage of* a person or persons.

Umbrage, *v.* [f. prec.]

†**1.** *trans.* To shade or shadow ; to overshadow, put in the shade.

†**b.** *fig.* To shroud, veil, hide.

†**2.** To give a pretext or ground for. *Obs.*

Umbrageous (*vmˈbrēidʒəs*), *a.* Also 6-8 *umbragious*, 7, 9 *ombrageous* (7-ious). [ad. F. *ombrageux* (OF. *also -ous*), f. *ombrage* (see UMBRAGE *sb.*) ; directly f. UMBRAGE *sb.* + -OUS.]

1. *a.* Forming or affording shade; shady.

b. Abounding in shade; shaded by trees or the like; overshadowed.

2. Of persons : Suspicious; jealous; apt or disposed to take offence.

b. Caused by thick foliage.

Umbral, *a.* [f. UMBRA ¹ + -AL.]

1. *Algebra.* Based on the use of umbræ in notation ; consisting of umbræ.

2. Pertaining to the umbra of sun-spots or eclipses.

Umbrate, *v. Obs.* Forms: 4 *vmbreyde, -breyde*, 5 *vmbrāyd*, 5-6 *vmbrayde, 5-6 vm-brayde (6 -bryde)*, 5 *vmbrayed, -brayd, -brede*; 3 *vmbrayd(e, -bruide.* [After the influence of verbs in Um-.] *trans.* To upbraid, reproach.

Umbrate, *a. Obs. rare* [ad. L. *umbrāt-us*, pa. pple. of *umbrāre* to shade : see UMBRATILE.]

Umbrated, *a. Her.* Also 7 *umbreted.* Faintly shadowed.

Umbratic, *a. rare* [ad. L. *umbrāticus*.]

Umbratical, *a. Obs. rare* [f. prec.] Of or pertaining to the shade; shadowy.

Umbratile, *a.* [ad. L. *umbrātilis*, f. *umbra* shade, shadow.]

†**1.** Shadowy, foreshadowing.

2. Confined to the shade or to retirement ; retired, secluded.

Umbratilous, *a. Obs. rare.* [ad. L. type *um-brātil-is*, *umbratile.*] So L. *umbra-brātiosus*]

Umbration. *Obs. rare.* [ad. L. type *umbrātion-em*, n. of action f. *umbrāre* : see UMBRATE.]

†1. *Her.* A faintly outlined figure = ADUMBRATION.

2. A shadowy indication or faint representation (of something).

Umbre, var. UMBER *sb.* and *v.*; UMBRE *Obs.* form of UMBER.

Umbrel, *sb. Obs.* Also 6 *-ell, 7 *umbril.* Also 6-8 [corruption of UMBRERE.]

Umbrella (*vmˈbrelǎ*). Also 7 *ombrella*, 8 *-brello*, 7-8 *umbrello*, 8 *umbrella*, 8 *umbrello*, 7-8 *ombrella*, 1 *umbrella* shade. [ad. It. *umbrella*, *ombrella*, dim. of *ombra* shade, shadow, L. *umbra.*]

1. = UMBELLA 1.

2. *a.* A portable screen or shade, usually circular in form and supported on a central stick or staff, used in hot countries as a protection for the head or person against the sun.

b. In some Oriental and African countries used as a symbol of rank or state.

3. A structure resembling in shape an outspread umbrella, or serving for protection against something.

b. Anything which temporarily or permanently has the form of an umbrella.

4. A broad-brimmed hat.

5. *Zool.* The gelatinous disk or bell-shaped structure of a jelly-fish.

6. *Conch.* A limpet-like gastropod of the genus *Umbrella*; also the part of the shell resembling an umbrella.

Umbrella. ... **Umbrellaed**, *ppl. a.* ... **Umbrella-tree.** ... **Umbrella-like**, *a.* ... **Umbrella-man.** ... **Umbrian**, *sb. and a.*

Umbro-, *combining form.* ... **Umbrose**, *a.* ... **Umbrosity.** ... **Umbrous**, *a.* ... **Umbrel.** ... **Umbel.** ... **Umble.** ... **Umbles.**

Umpire, *sb. and v.* ... **Umpirage.** ... **Umpiress.** ... **Umpiring.** ... **Umpirism.**

Umset. ... **Umsiege.** ... **Umstand.** ... **Umstride.** ... **Umstroke.** ... **Umthink.**

Un-, *prefix.*

Unamiability. Unamiableness.

Unamiable, a.

Unamiableness.

Unamiably, adv.

Unamused, ppl. a.

Unamusing, ppl. a.

Unamusingly, adv.

Unana, Sc.

Unamazed, ppl. a.

Unanalysable, a.

Unanalysed, ppl. a.

Unanchor, v.

Unanchored, ppl. a.

Unane led, a.

Unanimity.

Unanimous, a.

Unanimously, adv.

Unanimousness.

Unanimate, a.

Unanimated, ppl. a.

Unanimatedly, adv.

Unanimated, a.

Unanimity.

Unanime, a.

Unanimely, adv.

Unanimistic, a.

Unanimousness.

Unanimous, a.

Unanswerable, a.

Unanswerableness.

Unanswerably, adv.

Unanswered, ppl. a.

Unanticipated, ppl. a.

Unanticipating, ppl. a.

Unanxious, a.

Unapologetic, a.

Unapostatized, ppl. a.

Unapostolic, a.

Unappalled, ppl. a.

Unapparelled, ppl. a.

Unappeased, ppl. a.

Unappalled, ppl. a.

Unapparel, v.

Unapparelled, ppl. a.

Unappealable, a.

Unappealing, ppl. a.

Unapparent, a.

Unappeasable, a.

Unappeasably, adv.

Unappeased, ppl. a.

Unapplausive, a.

Unappliable, a.

Unapplicable, a.

Unapplied, ppl. a.

Unappointed, ppl. a.

Unapposed, ppl. a.

Unappreciable, a.

Unappreciated, ppl. a.

Unappreciating, ppl. a.

Unappreciative, a.

Unapprehended, ppl. a.

Unapprehending, ppl. a.

Unapprehensible, a.

Unapprehensive, a.

Unapprehensively, adv.

Unapprehensiveness.

Unapprised, ppl. a.

Unapproachable, a.

Unapproached, ppl. a.

Unappropriate, a.

Unappropriated, ppl. a.

Unapproved, ppl. a.

Unapproven, a., Sc.

Unapt, a.

that the Vale may have Vegetables analogous to our Grass, Shrubs, and Trees. 1785 T. Balguy Disc. 5 Unaccustomed to suffer harm, we are unapt to suspect it. 1828 Scott F. M. Perth viii, You may have thought me unapt to be moved by light complaints. 1874 Micklethwaite Mod. Par. Churches 241 Men of little creative power, but not unapt to take up ideas suggested to them.

c. Without const.: Unready, backward.

1849 Mill Ess. (1859) II. 401 Lord Brougham has condescended to bestow upon these unapt scholars his view of some of the essential requisites of a popular Constitution.

†Una·pt, *v. Obs.* [f. prec., or Un-2 6 a + Apt *a.*] *trans.* To render unapt.

1593 Nashe Christ's T. (1613) 156 Our full platters..vnapt vs to any exercise of Christianitie. 1628 R. Hobart Edw. II, cccxvii, Let not..false surmises Unapt their meanes, and crosse their owne devises. 1641 Exam. Abstr. Answ. agst. Votes Bps. in Parl. 77 It puts them out of their Calling, unapts them for the proper worke of it.

†Una·ptitude. *Obs.-1* [Un-1 12 and 5 b.] Inaptitude. (Const. *of* = for.)

1545 Raynald Byrth Mankynde 144 Most communely the vnaptitude of conception (in women hauynge ther helth) springeth of the superfluyte of cold & moyst humours.

Una·ptly, *adv.* [Un-1 11 and 5 b.] Inaptly.

1548 Udall, etc. Erasm. Par. Luke Pref., Why than should the ghospell seme to be vnaptely sent vnto those which are handlers and louers of the ghospell? 1579 W. Wilkinson Confut. Fam. Love 20 Yet are these places by him very vnskilfully cited and vnaptly to the purpose. c 1643 Ld. Herbert Autobiog. (1824) 56 It may be not unaptly called the paying our debts with another Man's money. 1659 Gentl. Calling 57 In this respect therefore I may not unaptly apply that Exhortation which the Apostle makes in another. 1748 Smollett R. Random xxxiii, This composition was, by the sailors, not unaptly stiled Necessity. 1798 S. & Ht. Lee Canterb. T. II. 101 Dennis, my silver-headed foster-father, may not unaptly personate my real one. 1852 Mrs. Stowe Uncle Tom's C. xi, Mr. Wilson's mind was one of those that may not unaptly be represented by a bale of cotton. 1866 Felton Anc. & Mod. Gr. I. 168 A soft, yet spicy vivacity, in which it has been not unaptly compared to the Castillian.

Una·ptness. [Un-1 12 and 5 b.] Inaptitude.

1557 Act 4 & 5 Phil. & Mary c. 3 § 1 The same Disability and Unaptness notwithstanding, the same unable and unmeet Persons..have been also released. 1595 Daniel Civ. Wars iv. xviii, And languishing luxuriousnes had spred Feeble vnaptnes ouer all the land. 1605 Verstegan Dec. Intell. ix. 291 The trees grow but low..by reason of the vnaptnesse of the soyle. 1652 W. Hartley Inf. Bapt. 12 The prohibition hath peculiar relation to the unaptness of the sacrificers. 1676 Phil. Trans. II. 739 That seminal root..hindred by the unaptness of the place. 1710 Norris Chr. Prud. ii. 98 He often fails as to his Means, as well as to his End, I don't mean as to their unaptness.

b. Const. *for, to* (with sb. or inf.).

1548 Elyot, Prosedanium, a disease which happeneth to..beastes, whiche is vnaptenesse to generacion through to muche labour. 1600 W. Watson Decacordon (1602) 165 M. Blackwels simplicitie and vnaptnesse to gouerne. 1654 Nicholas Papers (Camden) II. 55 The naturall unaptness hee has for that exercise. 1670 Clarendon Contempl. Ps. Tracts (1727) 729 An unaptness to be confident of what they see and feel. a 1688 W. Clagett 17 Serm. (1699) 216 There will be laziness and slothfulness, and unaptness for instruction. 1860 Rawlinson Herodotus ix. lxx. IV 442 note, A general unaptness for the mechanical arts?

Unaraced: see Unraced *ppl. a. Obs.*

Unarbitrariness. (Un-1 12.) 1825 Coleridge in Lit. Rem. (1836) II. 359 The coincidences would bring the truth, the unarbitrariness, of the preceding exposition as near to demonstration as can rationally be required. **Una·rbitrary,** *a.* (Un-1 7.) 1793 Holcroft tr. Lavater's Physiog. iv. 35 If unarbitrary Nature patched up countenances like arbitrary Art. **Una·rbitrated,** *ppl. a.* (Un-1 8.) 1821 Shelley Let. to T. L. Peacock 10 Aug., All these [animals] ..walk about the house, which every now and then resounds with their unarbitrated quarrels.

Unarch (ʊnā·ɹtʃ), *v.* [Un-2 3.] *trans.* and *intr.* To uncurve; to straighten.

1598 Florio, Disarcare, to vnbend, to vnarche. 1885 Jefferies Open Air (1890) 234 His flexible back bends and undulates, arches and unarches, rises and falls as a wave rises and rolls on.

Unarchdea·con, *v.* (Un-2 6 b.) 1555 Philpot Exam. 100 In dede M[aster] D[octor] ye haue among you vnarchediaconed me as nowe.

Una·rched, *a.* [Un-1 9.]

1. Not covered over with an arch.

1658 Osborne Adv. Son (1896) 132 [A] tomb also hinders the variety of such contingent Resurrections as unarched Bodies enjoy.

2. Not provided with arches.

1832 Froude in Rem. (1838) I. 297 The awkwardness of mixing up arched and unarched architecture is thus entirely avoided.

Unarchite·ctural, *a.* [Un-1 7.]

1. Not in accordance with the principles of architecture.

1849 Ruskin Sev. Lamps ii. § 18. 47 It is lawful to paint either pictures or patterns...But it is not less true, that such practices are essentially unarchitectural. 1862 E. Falkener Ephesus i. iv. 49 The old style of building, which, from its irregularity and unarchitectural character, resembled that still used in Eastern climates. 1873 Mrs. Whitney Other Girls xxxi, An odd rambling wing...slanting off at a wholly unarchitectural angle from the main house.

2. Not skilled in architecture.

1884 Pall Mall G. 18 July 11/1 It is difficult from the mere text of this report for the unarchitectural reader to get a clear notion of what is proposed.

Una·rguable, *a.* (Un-1 7 b and 5 b.) 1881 Times 11 May 6/5 The President said that point was wholly unarguable. 1885 Law Times LXXIX. 244/1 The case for the first mortgagee would have been absolutely unarguable.

Una·rgued, *ppl. a.* (Un-1 8.)

1616 B. Jonson Epigr. i. cx, He wrote with the same spirit that he fought; Not that his work lived in the hands of foes, Unargued then. 1628 Bp. Hall Old Relig. Ded. ¶ vj, No corner of truth hath lyen vnsearcht, nor vnargued. 1667 Milton P. L. iv. 636 To whom thus Eve.. My Author and Disposer, what thou bidst Unargu'd I obey; so God ordains. 1777 Howard Prisons Eng. (1780) 152 The orders given by the commissary of the marines enchanged with the care of prisoners are to be strictly complied with unargued and undisputed.

Unargume·ntative, *a.* (Un-1 7.)

1722 Lett. fr. Mist's Jrnl. I. Pref. p. ii, The most impudent and unargumentative weekly Paper the Town was ever infested with. 1837 G. S. Faber Prim. Doctr. Justif. v. 235 The doctrine would not have been a whit the worse, had the..unargumentative curses been omitted. 1870 J. H. Newman Gram. Assent i. v. 119 The inward voice of that solemn Monitor, personal, peremptory, unargumentative.

Hence **Unargume·ntatively** *adv.*

1840 G. S. Faber Prim. Doctr. Regen. 66 Just as if the writers unargumentatively thought, that no one..could ever doubt its propriety.

Unari·sen, *ppl. a.* (Un-1 8 b.) 1865 Swinburne Hesperia 74 Now that the white skies thrill with a moon unarisen. 1894 Woman's Signal 5 Apr. 224/2 A working principle.. as yet unarisen in the public mind. **Unaristocra·tic,** *a.* (Un-1 7.) 1841 in Monypenny Disraeli (1912) II. 123 We do not know the latest appointments; but up to the latest, except Gladstone, there is not one single untitled or unaristocratic individual. 1863 Sat. Rev. 7 Feb. 183/2 Stung at times into unaristocratic ebullitions of rather helpless spleen. **Unarithme·tic,** *a. Obs.-1* (Un-1 7.) 1789 H. Walpole Let. to Mrs. H. More 4 Nov., My head is as unmechanic as it is un-arithmetic, un-geometric, un-metaphysic, un-commercial. **Unarithme·tical,** *a.* (Un-1 7.) 1671 Crowne Juliana i, Five times ten hundred crowns: most monstrous, prodigious, gigantique, pedantique, unarithmetical sum. 1858 Miss Mulock Th. about Wom. vi. 156 Unarithmetical ladies, who have always reckoned their accounts by sixpences. **Una·rk,** *v.* (Un-2 5.) 161. J. Davies Sco. Folly cclxxxv, Till thou be left vpon Th' Armenian mount of safety, ioy and rest; Where when thou art thou maist thyselfe vn-arke.

Una·rm, *v.* Also 4–5 onarm (4 oun-), 4–7 unarme (5 *Sc.* wnarm). [Un-2 4.]

1. *trans.* To relieve (a person) of armour; to assist in putting off armour.

13.. Sir Beues (A.) 1081 King Ermin..clepede is douȝter & saide: 'Iosian, þe faire maide, Vn-arme Beues, he wer at mete.' c 1386 Chaucer Sqr.'s T. 173 This knyght is to his chambre lad anoon, And is vnarmed, and vn to mete yset. 1470–85 Malory Arthur vii. xviii. 241 The mayden Lynet..vnarmed hym and serched his woundes. c 1489 Caxton Sonnes of Aymon xv. 337 He made hym to be vnarmed, and made his wounde to be wrapped. 1568 Grafton Chron. II. 232 Assoone as the King was vnarmed, he..went vp to the Castell to salute the Countesse of Sarisbury. 1573 in Feuillerat Revels Q. Eliz. (1908) 202 [To] Roger Tyndall..for his seruauntes Attendaunces to arme & vnarme the children in the play. 1606 Shaks. Tr. & Cr. iii. i. 163 Sweet Hellen, I must woe you, To helpe vnarme our Hector...You shall..disarme great Hector. 1720 Mrs. Manley Power of Love (1741) 337 [He] commanded the Conqueror should be unarm'd and set before his Face, to receive the Reward due to his Valour.

absol. 1606 Shaks. Ant. & Cl. iv. xiv. 35 Vnarme Eros, the long dayes taske is done, And we must sleepe.

b. *refl.* To free or strip (oneself) of armour. (Also with *head* as obj.)

13.. Guy Warw. (A.) 5506 Otus to his pauiloun he ȝede, & vnarmed him of his wede. c 1400 Land Troy Bk. 10241 Vn-Arme the at my prayere. c 1430 Pilgr. Lyf Manhode i. cxxxiv. (1869) 70 Allas, whi woldest thou euere vnarme thee? c 1477 Caxton Jason 7 b, The lousters vnarmed them, And put hem in fayr araye. a 1533 Ld. Berners Huon lix. 206 They vnarmyd them, and went to dyner. 1581 A. Hall Iliad iv. 66 He soft vnarmes him, and his scarfe, and Curet off doth take. 1609 Heywood Brit. Troy xiii. lxxxv, King Priam by Antenors mouth desires To unarme him streight and to the Courte returne. 1684 — Gunaik. v. 246 When with the slaughter of his enemies tyred He doff'd his cushes, and unarm'd his head. 1719 D'Urfey Pills I. 175 The Great Mars of the Battle unarms him and plays. 1823 Scott Quentin D. xxxvi, Go, tell no man to unarm himself; and let them shoot, in case of necessity.

absol. c 1450 Merlin xxvii. 555 Elizer was besy to serue sir Gawein..and helped him to vn-arme. 1606 Shaks. Tr. & Cr. i. i. 1 Call here my Varlet, I vnarme againe. Ibid. v. iii. 3 Vnarme, vnarme, and doe not fight to day. a 1625 Fletcher Hum. Lieut. iii. vi, Will ye unarm, and yield your selves his prisoners?

†2. To deprive of arms or armour; to disarm.

1560 Daus tr. Sleidane's Comm. 101 To send their ayde agaynst the Turke..were to unarme them selves and to cut their owne senewes. 1569 J. Sanford tr. Agrippa's Van. Artes 125 b, To kill them, to take them, to unarme them, to spoile them. a 1618 Raleigh Maxims St. in Rem. (1661) 43 To unarm his people of weapons, money, and all means, whereby they may resist his power. 1635 Pagitt Christianogr. i. ii. (1636) 48 The Turke usually in his Conquests unarmeth the Christians. 1654 Earl Monm. tr. Bentivoglio's Wars Flanders 106 A Brigade of the Spanish foot forthwith entered the Town, and unarmed every one therein.

†b. *transf.* and *fig. Obs.*

1568 Grafton Chron. II. 757 If deuision and dissencion of their friendes had not vnarmed them, and left them destitute. 1646 Sir T. Browne Pseud. Ep. 385 Galen.. would not leave unto the world too subtile a Theory of Poisons; unarming thereby the malice of venemous spirits. a 1668 Davenant Epithal. Wks. (1673) 312 So an excessive purity of Love Unarmes you to invite offence.

†3. To empty or strip of arms. *Obs.*

1560 Daus tr. Sleidane's Comm. 405 By unarmyng the armaries, and openyng the waye to confiscation. 1636 G. Sandys Paraphr., Ps. xlvi, He breaks their Bowes, unarmes their Quivers, The bloody Speare in pieces shivers. 1665 Manley Grotius' Low C. Wars 209 The Queen..Commands by her Letter, the Lord Admirall Howard..that he should unarm and discharge the best of her Ships.

†4. To disarm, render harmless. *Obs.-1*

1700 Dryden Ovid's Met. viii. Meleager 120 No blood he drew; Dian unarm'd the Javelin as it flew.

Una·rmed, *ppl. a.* Also 3 uniarmed, 5 *Sc.* unermyt, onarmed. [Un-1 8.]

1. Not armed; having no armour or weapons.

1297 R. Glouc. (Rolls) 11274 Vn iarmed out he wende to be barons wel stille. c 1330 Arth. & Merl. 6947 (Kölbing), Vnarmed were þe paiens alle, Our folk hem gun to talle. 1387 Trevisa Higden (Rolls) I. 353 Þey fiȝteþ vnarmed, naked in body. 1412–20 Lydg. Chron. Troy iii. 1719 Cruelly þei had his hede of smet, For he vnarmyd al at meschef stood. 1456 Sir G. Haye Law Arms (S.T.S.) 113 A man that is outhir unarmyt, or evill armyt may nocht hald felde in bataill place. a 1533 Ld. Berners Huon lxvii. 230 All his company were vnarmed, & all the other .xl. were clene armed. 1579 W. Wilkinson Confut. Fam. Love Ep. Ded. *iij, Neither are able many of them being vnarmed to withstand the enemy. 1632 W. Lithgow Trav. iii. 89, I neuer could see a Greeke come forth of his house vnarmed. 1671 Milton P. R. iv. 626 He all unarm'd Shall chase thee with the terror of his voice. 1748 Anson's Voy. ii. vi. 200 He came down unarmed to a centinel of ours. 1794 S. Williams Vermont 170 An unarmed defenceless stranger. 1839 Thirlwall Greece VI. 223 The Thracians were keeping very negligent guard, and, in imagined security, were mostly unarmed. 1882 De Windt Equator 69 The remainder of the tribe were unarmed, as it is made a strict rule in Sarawak that..all arms..shall be left behind.

absol. 1590 Barwick Disc. Weapons 10 b, The musket.. will kill the armed of proofe at ten skore yardes,..and the vnarmed at thirty skore.

transf. 1634 Milton Comus 582 Th' unarmed weakness of one Virgin Alone, and helpless! 1827 Pollok Course T. ix. 965 Sin's dark tactics, such as boyish man, Unarmed by strength divine, could ill withstand.

2. Of animals, etc.: Not fitted for attack; not furnished with horns, teeth, or the like.

1398 Trevisa Barth. De P. R. xviii. lxxx. (Bodl. MS.), The schepe..is a nesche beeste and bereþ wolle & is vnarmed & plesinge in herte. 1649 Lovelace Lucasta Poems (1904) 95 A Falcon..Unarm'd of Wings and Scaly Oare. 1804 Shaw Gen. Zool. V. i. 14 Unarmed Silure, Silurus Inermis. 1834 McMurtrie Cuvier's Anim. Kingd. 495 Furcularia...The body is unarmed. 1855 Orr's Circ. Sci., Inorg. Nat. 108 Reptiles..whose two tusks, in an otherwise unarmed jaw, strikingly distinguish them from any of their contemporaries. 1869 Tanner Clin. Med. (ed. 2) 309 The unarmed or beef tape-worm,..as its name implies, is unfurnished with hooks around its head.

3. Of plants: Destitute of prickles, spines, or thorns.

1676 Grew Anat. Flowers ii. App. § 11 The Top is Thorny, as in Furz; or Vnarmed. Vnarmed, either produced, that is, poynted, or at least, Roundish. 1793 Martyn Lang. Bot., Inerme folium, an unarmed leaf. 1845 Steele Field Bot. 218 Bracts of invol linear-lanceolate, almost unarmed. 1855 Miss Pratt Flower. Pl. II. 298 Unarmed Hornwort. Fruit without either spines or tubercles. 1870 Hooker Stud. Flora 107 Prunus communis,..Sub-sp. domestica;..branches straight unarmed.

4. Of things: Not provided with anything that assists or strengthens.

1693 Dryden Juvenal x. 310 The same foulness does to Age belong, The self same Palsie,..And Gums unarm'd to mumble Meat in vain. a 1721 Prior Journ. to Copt-Hall 12, I mount, and great as Hudibrass, With unarm'd kick urge on my horse. 1860 Tyndall Glac. i. xxvii. 200 Pattens ..sank less deeply than the unarmed feet. 1860 Emerson Cond. Life v. 156 In Siberia, a late traveller found men who could see the satellites of Jupiter with their unarmed eye.

†5. Of a magnet: Not provided with an armature. *Obs.*

1662 J. Bargrave Pope Alex. VII (1867) 120 Two large loadstones, one armed with steel...The other..is unarmed. 1730 Phil. Trans. XXXVI. 325, I placed the Pole of the upper Armour about 4 or 5 Inches from the Top of the unarmed Bar. 1777 Ibid. LXVII. 135 A fine, smooth, unarmed load-stone.

Hence **Una·rmedness.**

1684 H. More Answer 208 This Lamblike condition of it is chiefly represented in this present Vision, its seeming harmlesness and unarmedness.

Una·rmoured, *a.* [Un-1 9.]

1. Of vessels: Not armour-clad.

1869 Sir E. Reed Our Iron-Clad Ships iv. 73 When we pass from unarmoured to armoured ships, the contrast is still more striking. 1879 Cassell's Techn. Educ. IV. 61/1 In the unarmoured iron ships recently built for the navy tie-plates have been entirely dispensed with.

2. Of persons: Not protected by armour.

1873 Morris Love is Enough 18 Barehanded, unarmoured, he handled the spear-shaft. 1892 Tennyson Foresters iv, And walkest [thou] here Unarmour'd? all these walks are Robin Hood's And sometimes perilous.

Unarou·sed, *ppl. a.* (Un-1 8.) 1855 Singleton Virgil II. 207 Burns Unaroused and moveless hitherto Ausonia. **Unarrai·gnable,** *a.* (Un-1 7 b.) 1886 Swinburne Misc. 52 Work unarraignable alike by fair means or foul. **Unarrai·gned,** *ppl. a.* (Un-1 8.) 1595 Daniel Civ. Wars iii. xxii, Neuer shall this poore breath of mine consent That he..Should here be iudged vnheard, and vnaraignd. 1858 Merivale Hist. Rom. Emp. iii. (1865) VI. 256 He did not venture to command his execution, unarraigned and unconvicted. **Unarra·nged,** *ppl. a.* (Un-1 8.) [1775 Ash.] 1791 Boswell Johnson an. 1737, The disjecta membra scattered throughout, and as yet unarranged. 1840 Carlyle Heroes v. (1904) 160 How many powerful forces are seen working in a wasteful, chaotic, altogether unarranged manner. 1897 Pullen Burry Blotted Out 51 Death is an unsurveyed land, an unarranged science.

†Unarray·, *v. Obs.* [Un-2 4.] *trans.* To deprive of array; *esp.* to undress, disrobe.

14.. Chaucer's Sqr.'s T. 173 (Camb. MS.), This knyght ..is on-arayed [other MSS. vnarmed] & to mete i-set. a 1483 Liber Niger in S. Pegge Cur. Misc. (1782) 79 Two [Esquires of the Body] to be attendant on the King's person to array and unarray him. 1483 Cath. Angl. 12/1 To vn Aray, exornare, & cetera; vbi to dysaray. 1590 Stockwood Eng. Accidence 65 This verbe exuo, of araying, or rather indeed of vnaraying, hath two accusative cases. 1602 Lambarde Dict. Angl. Topogr. (1730) 69 She forth-with unarrayed her selfe, untrussed her Heare.

Unarray·ed, *ppl. a.* [Un-1 8.]

1. Not arrayed or put in order.

c 1340 Hampole Prose Tr. 28 If þou..latis þame spill for defaute of kepynge—unarayede, unkepide,..thou pleses Hym noghte. 1390 Gower Conf. III. 275, I sih also The noble peple of Irahel Dispers as schep upon an hell, Withoute a kepere unarraied. c 1400 Brut 13 Whan Humbar saw hem come, he was sore adrad, forasmyche as his men wist it not, & also þey were vnarrayed. 1727 Bailey (vol. II), Unarrayed, not ranged in Order of Battle.

2. Not dressed; unclothed; unarmed.

c 1380 Sir Ferumb. 821 Duke Roland þan was sore amayed, So wern þe doþþepers,..for þay wern oun-araid. c 1440 York Myst. xxiv. 6 We will bere witnesse..How we hir raysed all vnarayed,..Wher sche was with hir leman taide. a 1450 Knt. de la Tour (1906) 153 There shall now be sheued you of the good ladyes that were vnaraied, duellynge in Rome. 1611 Cotgr., Desabillé, vncloathed, vndressed, vnarrayed. 1665 Dryden Ind. Emp. i. i, As if this Infant World, yet unarray'd, Naked and bare, in Nature's Lap were laid. 1685 — Thren. August. 54 Half unarray'd he ran to his Relief, So hasty and so artless was his Grief. 1839 Bailey Festus 187 Thou art as the cloudless moon, Undimmed and unarrayed; No robe hast thou.

Unarre·stable, *a.* (Un-1 7 b), **-ably,** *adv.* (Un-1 11). 1855 Prince Albert Sp. in B'ham 22 Nov., The former is an unarrestable movement towards the fountain of truth. 1884 E. Abbott Flatland 75, I could feel him slowly and unarrestably slipping from my contact.

Unarre·sted, *ppl. a.* [Un-1 8. Cf. MDu. ongearresteert.]

1. Not arrested or apprehended.

c 1400 Beryn 2188, I woll..assay, yf I may, in eny maner wise, Ascapen vnarestid more in suche maner wise. 1498, 1531 [see Unattached ppl. a. 1]. 1533 More Apol. 259 b, By thys pacyfyers good deuyse, heretykes maye go unarrested. 1611 Cotgr., Descalengé, vnarrested, vnapprehended. 1891 E. Kinglake Australian at Home 77 The wife of a certain unarrested absconder was observed to have command of plenty of money.

2. Not stopped or checked.

1733 Tull Horse-Hoeing Husb. xiv. 199 The under Stratum must be the richer for receiving what the upper Stratum lets pass Unarrested. 1859 Tennent Ceylon II. vii. v. 197 The temples of Kandy..are dilapidated edifices, apparently perishing from unarrested decay. 1869 G. Lawson Dis. Eye (1874) 79 If the disease be unarrested by treatment, the whole pupillary margin becomes sealed to the lens capsule.

Unarri·ved, *ppl. a.* [Un-1 8.]

1. Not yet arrived (at a place, or in time).

1666 in Foster Eng. Factories India (1909) III. 155 The shipps expected and unarrived. 1742 Young Nt. Th. ix. 294 These, as two monarchs, on their borders meet, (Monarchs of all elaps'd, or unarriv'd!)

b. That has not yet attained success.

1902 Academy 25 Jan. 76/2 Liverpool offers great possibilities to the unarrived novelist.

2. Not yet arrived *at*; unattained.

1669 [see Unaimed ppl. a.].

Una·rrogant, *a.* (Un-1 7.) 1831 D. E. Williams Sir T. Lawrence I. 12 He had an unarrogant self-possession which few men enjoy. **Una·rrogating,** *ppl. a.* (Un-1 10.) 1748 Melmoth Fitzosborne Lett. (1763) 349 Whoever pursues his speculations with this humble unarrogating temper of mind [etc.]. 1864 E. Sargent Peculiar I. 152 The quiet unarrogating air of one whose nobility is a part of his nature.

†Una·rted, *a. Obs.* [Un-1 9.]

1. Ignorant of the arts; unskilled.

1603 Florio Montaigne i. li. 166 They are..rude, simple, and unarted in the combate of talking. 1606 Warner Alb. Engl. xiv. To Rdr., Shunne Eares vnarted, rude, precise. 1699 Cibber Xerxes ii, I am unarted, Sir, in any grace of speech To stir the soul! My words are plain and honest.

2. Unartificial; plain.

1628 Feltham Resolves ii. xcix. 291 Wise Innocence, friends like, and good Vnarted-meat, kind neighbourhood.

Una·rtful, *a.* [Un-1 7.]

1. Not artificial or contrived; artless.

1669 Dryden & Davenant Tempest iii. (1670) 31 I'm sure unartful truth lies open In her mind, as Crystal streams their sandy bottom shew. 1693 Congreve in Dryden's Juvenal xi. (1697) 291 A chearful Sweetness in his Looks he has, And Innocence unartful in his Face. 1713 Guard. No. 127 Crt. Venus 70 Unartful Tears, and hectick Looks, that show With silent Eloquence the Lover's Woe. 1763 Falconer Fond Lover 14 Since all her thoughts by sense refined, Unartful truth express. 1820 W. Tooke tr. Lucian I. 147 Much less can it be affirmed, that it (sc. sponging) is an unartful art. 1899 Venral in A. C. Brown Life E. W. Benson (1900) I. 219 The same delightful and unartful arts were displayed.

b. Free from artifice or cunning.

1703 Rowe Fair Penit. ii. ii. 596 This Son, if Fame mistakes not, Is more hot, More open, and unartful.

2. Displaying no technical skill; inartistic.

1675 Cocker Morals 49 Rashness draws crooked and unartful Lines. 1703 Savage Lett. Antients ix. 32 Beneath this humble Roof he stood, and this plain unartful Floor supported him. 1712 Blackmore Creation iii. 179 So full of faults is all the unartful frame. 1759 Goldsm. Bee No. 5. 90 To have almost every personage on the scene almost of the same character..was unartful in the poet to the last degree. 1883 Pall Mall G. 24 Nov. 4/2 Prose which borrows in a manner pleasant enough in result, and by no means unartful, the more obvious and seductive attractions of verse.

b. Of persons: Unskilful, maladroit. *rare.*

1683 Mrs. Behn Yng. King ii. iii, I am a man, whose martial disposition Renders unartful in my language. 1709 Mrs. Manley Secret Mem. (1720) IV. 88 A swift and sure Contempt succeeds upon what-ever the unartful Husband shall happen to do after.

Hence **Una·rtfully** *adv.*

1724 Swift Drapier's Lett. iii. Wks. 1841 II. 17/2 The report, which, although it be not unartfully drawn,..yet there was no great skill required to detect the many mistakes..in it. 1726 — Gulliver iv. ii, Matts of straw, not unartfully made. 1793 Minstrel III. 137, I discovered a door, not unartfully concealed by some rude chiseling in the rock. 1840 Thackeray Pict. Rhapsody 116 This plan has been not unartfully contrived.

Unarti·culate, *a.* [Un-1 7 and 5 b.]

†1. = Inarticulate *a.* 2. *Obs.*

1603 J. Davies (Heref.) Microcosmos Wks. (Grosart) I. 12/2 No Beast..But in his voice (though vnarticulate) Salutes these times. 1611 Cotgr., Sphinge, the..Sphinx..; his vnarticulate voice like that of a hastie speaker.

2. = Inarticulate *a.* 1.

1855 Pusey Doctr. Real Presence Note 440 The one..is upright, articulate,..but the other..is round, unarticulate, inanimate.

Unarti·culated, *ppl. a.* [Un-1 8. Cf. G. unarticulirt, Sw. oarticulerad.]

1. Not articulated or distinct.

a 1700 Ken Hymnarium Poet. Wks. 1721 II. 25 God from the Moment we draw breath,..Our words, when unarticulated, hears. 1823 Lamb Let. Old Gentl. Misc. Wks. (1871) 451 That unarticulated language, which was before the written tongue. 1840 Willis Loiterings II. 139 The touching attitudes and utter abandonment of all around to their unarticulated devotions.

2. Not jointed; not fitted together.

1861 Hulme tr. Moquin-Tandon ii. vii. xiii. 399 The egg encloses a short unarticulated embryo. a 1894 C. H. Pearson in Stebbing Life (1900) 77 A cupboard full of unarticulated human bones.

Unartifi·cial, *a.* [Un-1 7 and 5 b.]

1. Not displaying special art or skill; unskilful, inartistic, clumsy. Now *rare* or *Obs.*

1591 Harington Orl. Fur. Pref., If I shold confesse..that my verse is vnartificiall, the stile rude, the phrase barbarous. 1597 Morley Introd. Mus. 80 It is an vnartificiall kinde of descanting in the middle of a lesson, to let the plainsong sing alone. 1602 Campion Art Eng. Poesie Ded., The vulgar and vnartificiall custome of riming. 1702 S. Parker tr. Cicero's De Finibus iii. 154 The Common-Places and suggestions of your Advocates for Pleasure are, at best, but very Shallow and Unartificial. 1790 Burke Fr. Rev. 275 They have levelled and crushed together all the orders which they found, even under the coarse unartificial arrangement of the monarchy. 1825 Bentham Ration. Reward 204 Art and science, on the one hand, and unartificial practice and unscientific knowledge, on the other.

2. Not artificial; simple, natural.

1603 Florio Montaigne iii. xii. 628 It representeth in an vn-artificiall boldnesse, and infantine securitie, the pure impression and first ignorance of nature. 1656 Earl Monm. tr. Boccalini's Advts. fr. Parnass. i. lxxvii. (1674) 100 Men who live in sincerity,..with an undisguised and unartificial goodness. 1799 Monthly Rev. XXX. 345 Example arising from a natural unartificial developement of incidents.

Unartifi·cially, *adv.* [f. prec.] †Inartistically, unskilfully.

1591 Harington Orl. Fur. Pref., And yet for Ariostos tales that many thinke vnartificially brought in, Homer him selfe hath the like. 1598 Hakluyt Voy. I. 484 The barrel is rudely and vnartificially made. 1622 Peacham Compl. Gent. x. (1634) 89 Hee goeth unartificially to worke even in the very beginning. 1670 Milton Hist. Eng. iii. Wks. 1851 V. 102 The material being only Turf, and by the rude multitude unartificially built up,..avail'd them little. 1706 Stevens Span. Dict. i, Inhabilmente, unhandily, unartificially, unskilfully, ignorantly.

Unarti·stic, *a.* (Un-1 7 and 5 b.) 1854 Grace Greenwood Haps & Mishaps 68 It certainly strikes the unartistic as a most unsuitable alliance. 1865 Athenæum No. 1955. 520/3 A vague unartistic tale. **Una·rtistlike,** *a.* and *adv.* (Un-1 7 c and 11 b.) 1654 Gayton Pleas. Notes iii. iii. 81 It was very improper, and unartist-like done in Sancho, to permit him to sleep. 1757 Grose Voy. E. Indies 173 Their naval, like their other architecture, has always something clumsy, unfinished, and unartist-like in it. 1837 Lytton Athens II. 115 The elaborate description of this work [a bridge] given by Herodotus proves it to have been no clumsy or unartistlike performance.

†U·nary. *Obs.-1* [f. L. ūn-us one.] A unit.

1576 Fleming tr. Caius' Dogs (1880) 36 This countrey was cleerely discharged of rauenyng wolfes, & none at all left, no, not to the least number, or the beginnyng of a number, which is an Vnari.

Unasce·ndable, *a.* (Un-1 7 b.) 1615 G. Sandys Trav. 171 He..confined the Royall progeny within high and vnascendable mountaines. 1628 Feltham Resolves ii. [1.] xxix. 90 A Hill almost vn-ascendable. 1801 Southey Thalaba xii. xvi, The depth was unascendable. **Unasce·nded,** *ppl. a.* (Un-1 8.) 1821 Shelley Adonais xlvi, It was for thee yon kingless sphere has long Swung blind in unascended majesty. 1861 F. W. Jacomb in Peaks, Passes & Glaciers Ser. ii. I. 315 Removing a mountain from the unascended list. **Unasce·ndible,** *a.* (Un-1 7.) 1801 Southey Thalaba vii. iv, The heights precipitous, Impending crags, rocks unascendible. **Unascertai·nable,** *a.* (Un-1 7 b.) 1802–12 Bentham Ration. Judic. Evid. (1827) V. 237 It is only..to an amount altogether precarious and unascertainable, that it does away the mischief. 1876 A. S. Murray Mythol. 14 By keeping constantly before the mind a sense of the unascertainable and infinite powers of nature.

Unascertai·ned, *ppl. a.* [Un-1 8.] **†a.** Not certified or apprised. *Obs.* **b.** Not ascertained or known.

1668 in Foster Eng. Factories India (1909) III. 193 What is become of Beale, whether living or dead, we are yett unascertained. 1751 Harris Hermes ii. i. (1765) 217 The Article (A) leaves the Individual itself unascertained, whereas the Article (The) ascertains the Individual also. 1784 Cook Third Voy. vi. iv. III. 269 The only part of the Russian empire that now remains unascertained. 1815 J. Smith Panorama Sci. & Art II. 319 The standard temperatures desired, remained unascertained till the time of Newton. 1879 St. George's Hosp. Rep. IX. 127 An unascertained quantity of oxalic acid and white precipitate.

†Unascri·ed, *ppl. a. Obs.-1* [Un-1 8.] Undescried, unobserved.

a 1548 Hall Chron., Hen. VIII, 32 So that alwaies it was forsene that..the Frenchemen shoulde not come on them sodainly vnaskryed.

Unasha·med, *ppl. a.* (Un-1 8.)

Hence, in recent use, *unashamedly* adv., *-ness*.

1600 Fairfax Tasso v. lxxi, This foolish crew of louers, vnashamed,..Ran forward still, in this disordred sort. 1619 H. Hutton Follie's Anat. (Percy Soc.) 24 See this incarnate monster of her sex Play the virago, unashamde, perplext. 1827 Pollok Course T. viii. 782 Lust of wealth and power Inordinate, and lewdness unashamed. 1855 Browning Two in Campagna vii, Let us, O my dove, Let us be unashamed of soul. 1887 Lowell Democracy, etc. 200 Coleridge's words have the unashamed nakedness of Scripture.

Una·sinous, *a.* [f. L. ūn-us one + asinus ass, after *unanimous*.] Agreeing in stupidity.

1656 Hobbes Six Lessons vi. ad fin., Go your wayes you uncivil Ecclesiasticks,..De-doctors of Morality, unasinous collegues [etc.].

Una·sk, *v.* (Un-2 3.) 1843 Geo. Eliot in Cross Life (1885) I. 120, I cannot desire that you should unask violin and Flute, unless a postponement would be..as agreeable to you and them. **Una·skable,** *a.* (Un-1 7 b.) 1854 Ferrier Inst. Metaph. ix. xxxv. 498 The truths which it has reached renders that question absurd. It is unanswerable, because it is unaskable.

Una·sked, *ppl. a.* Also 6, 9 *dial.*, unaxed. [Un-1 8, 8 c.]

1. Without being asked; not requested or invited; uninvited.

a 1225 Ancr. R. 336 Þe hwule þet tu const siggen out (in shrift), seie al unasked. 1456 Sir G. Haye Law Arms (S. T. S.) 139 Gyf a knycht..had gevyn a coursour to the Provost of Paris unaskit. 1582 Stanyhurst Æneis ii. (Arb.) 55 In gentil manner thus he soone discoursed, vnasked. 1628 J. Taylor (Water P.) Penniless Pilgr. Wks. (1630) 123/1 Master Taylor, at the Sarazen's head, Vnask'd (vnpaid for) me both lodg'd and fed. 1697 Dryden Virg. Past. iii. 100 Fair Amyntas comes unask'd to me, And offers love. 1710 Prior Examiner, To Earl Godolphin 10 Unask'd you offer, and unseen you give. 1746 Francis tr. Hor., Sat. i. iii. 3 Sing they can never at a friend's request, Yet chant it forth, unask'd, from morn till night. 1820 Crabbe Borough xviii. 56 He shows the shipping;.. He makes (unask'd) their ports and business known. 1879 Meredith Egoist xxiv, She went to the music-rack and gave the song unasked.

†b. Left uninvited. *Sc. Obs.*

c 1730 Burt Lett. N. Scot. (1754) II. 204, I have several times been unasked to eat.

2. Not asked for; not made the subject of a request.

1456 Sir G. Haye Law Arms (S. T. S.) 96 Quhat thingis ..has sauf condyt be privilege unaskit at the princis. 1529 S. Fish Supplic. Beggars (1871) 8 There was giuen theim ynough vnaxed. 1592 Shaks. Ven. & Ad. 102 Yet hath he ..begg'd for that which thou unask'd shalt have. 1618 J. Taylor (Water P.) Penniless Pilgr. Wks. (1630) 123/2, I thought it no good manners to refuse, But thank'd him for his kinde vnasked gift. 1658 Osborne Jas. I, 53 The Scots, by whom nothing was unasked, and to whom nothing was denied. 1712 Addison Spect. No. 357 ¶ 10 Adam..expostulates with his Creator for having given him an unasked Existence. 1751 Warburton Pope's Wks. IX. 247 note, To the issue of that unasked and unsought compliment these words allude. 1819 Scott Leg. Montrose x, He delivered his unasked opinion as follows. 1870 Morris Earthly Par. II. iii. 426 Indeed I thought That news of ill unasked would soon be brought.

b. Similarly with *for*.

1714 Mandeville Fab. Bees (1733) II. 117 The unask'd-for bounty and downright generosity of his benefactor. 1861 Lady Lyttelton Let. 15 Dec., The Queen..sent me an account on the 10th (unasked for..) through Lady Augusta Bruce. 1876 T. Hardy Ethelberta xxxvi, An unasked-for concession to their cause.

Una·sking, *ppl. a.* (Un-1 10.)

1722 Wollaston Relig. Nat. v. 116 That he..should have many things granted him, which are not given to the careless, obdurate, unasking part of mankind. 1799 in Spirit Pub. Jrnls. III. 271 Laid under contribution to the unasking necessities of the pupil of Mercury. 1876 Lanier Clover 97 This cool, unasking Ox Comes browsing o'er my hills and vales of Time.

b. In ppl. use: Without asking for. (Un-1 5 d.)

1754 Shebbeare Matrimony (1766) I. 225 Unasking more, he implored only the Continuation of Health to himself and Family.

†Unaspe·cted, *ppl. a. Obs.-1* [Un-1 8: cf. Aspect *v.* 1.] Unsuspected, unexpected.

1578 Florio 1st Fruites 86 The forreyne knyfe doothe disbarke it [sc. a tree], the bee of unaspected causes dooth consume it.

†Unaspe·ctive, *a. Obs.-1* [Un-1 7 + Aspect *v.*] Unregardful.

1661 Feltham Resolves ii. lxxiv. 348 In which the Holy Ghost is not wholly unaspective to the custome that was used among men.

†Unaspie·d, *ppl. a. Obs.* = Unespied *ppl. a.*

c 1400 Destr. Troy 1426 Of a sparke unaspied, spred vnder askys, May feston vp fyre to mony freike sorow. 1508 Dunbar Tua Mariit Wemen 427 That I may spy, vnaspyit, a space me beside.

Una·spirated, *ppl. a.* (Un-1 8. Cf. G. unaspirirt.) [1775 Ash.] 1793 Parr Combe's Horace Wks. 1828 III. 33 Lambin gives ἄωτος for the Æolic verb unaspirated. 1867 Pall Mall G. 26 Aug. 3/1 Mr. and Mrs. Williamson's unaspirated piety might have been spared with advantage.

Unaspi·ring, *ppl. a.* (Un-1 10.)

a 1729 J. Rogers Serm. (1736) 173 An easy unaspiring Temper which rests satisfy'd with its present Share of the Bounties of Providence. 1806 R. Mant Poems, To Bp. Durham i. 2 She loves..To cheer with unaspiring lay The dear domestic shade. 1852 Ld. Cockburn Jeffrey I. 103 The unaspiring life, I believe, has the least positive wretchedness.

Hence **Unaspi·ringness.**

1681 Whole Duty Nations 64 The Humility, Modesty, and unaspiringness of Christianity. 1861 Mill Repr. Govt. iii. 64 Inactivity, unaspiringness, absence of desire, are a more fatal hindrance to improvement than any misdirection of energy.

Una·ss, *v.* (Un-2 5.) 1654 Gayton Pleas. Notes iv. iii. 184 Gines Passamont..With Sancho's Asse unto a Fare was packing: The quick-eyed Bore had spied him, and unass'd him.

Unassai·lable, *a.* [Un-1 7 b.]

1. Not assailable; not open to assault or attack. Also *fig.*

1596 Spenser F. Q. v. ix. 5 Thereto both his owne wylie wit (she sayd), And eke the fastnesse of his dwelling place, Both vnassaylable, gaue him great ayde. 1601 Shaks. Jul. C. iii. i. 69, I do know but One That vnassayleable holds on his Ranke, Vnshak'd of Motion. 1825 J. Neal Bro. Jonathan III. 121 He was always the same,..alike unassailable —inscrutable. 1841 Elphinstone Hist. Ind. I. 543 The chief had occupied an unassailable position, but was drawn out by a pretended flight. 1871 Macduff Mem. Patmos xii. 167 They have a..heritage of tribulation: but their spiritual safety is unassailable.

2. Not open to adverse criticism.

1830 Mackintosh Progr. Eth. Philos. Wks. 1846 I. 120 In both cases he occupies the unassailable ground of an appeal to consciousness. 1884 Manch. Exam. 27 Sept. 4/6 The President's address..does not actually lead us to any unassailable conclusions.

Hence **Unassai·lableness; -ably** *adv.*

Also, in recent use, *unassailability*.

1870 Pall Mall G. 20 Oct. 3 America possesses over us the advantages of distance and unassailableness. 1876 Bancroft Hist. U. S. VI. xxxvii. 184 The two oceans, between which the republic has unassailably intrenched itself.

Unassai·led, *ppl. a.* (Un-1 8.)

a 1586 Sidney Arcadia iii. vii. (1912) 385 The quietnesse of his unassailed senses. 1593 Shaks. 2 Hen. VI, vi. ii. 18 It greeues my soule to leaue thee vnassail'd. 1634 Milton Comus 220 The Supreme good..Would send a glistring Guardian if need were To keep my life and honour unassail'd. 1735 Thomson Liberty iii. 456 Unarm'd he stray'd, unguarded, unassail'd. 1819 Scott Ivanhoe xliv, If unassailed, we depart assailing no one. 1887 Moloney Forestry W. Africa 194 Nevertheless the trade in jute holds its own unassailed.

Unassa·ssinated, *ppl. a.* (Un-1 8.) 1842 Poe Marie Roget Wks. 1865 I. 227 If starting from the living Marie, we find her, yet find her unassassinated.

Unassau·ltable, *a.* (Un-1 7 b.)

1571 Golding Calvin on Ps. xlviii. 11 A Citie very wel fortified and unassaultable. 1580 Bentley Mon. Matrones 334 When I bethinke me what a tower of strength..and unassaultable habitation thou hast euer beene. 1611 Speed Hist. Gt. Brit. ix. xxiii. 114 A breach made in the wall, not farre from the Water-gate, but yet vnassaultable, the English within so maintained the defence. 1653 A. Wilson Jas. I, 216 It is a great disadvantage for living Bodies to fight against dead Walls, being so high, and unassaultable. a 1711 Ken Christophil Poet. Wks. 1721 I. 516 O Realm of undisturb'd repose, Thrones unassaultable by Woes!

Unassau·lted, *ppl. a.* (Un-1 8.)

1611 Speed Hist. Gt. Brit. v. vi. § 17. 37 The German Saxons..neuer left their attempts vnassaulted till they set the glorious diademe thereof vpon their owne heads. 1655 Moufet & Bennet Health's Improv. (1746) 207 He..left no fair Woman unassaulted. a 1711 Ken Psyche Poet. Wks. 1721 IV. 209 That I secure may grow, When unassaulted by my Foe. 1758 Johnson Idler No. 20 ¶ 11 The commanders ..durst not leave the place unassaulted.

Unassay·ed, *ppl. a.* (Un-1 8.)

c 1374 Chaucer Boeth. ii. pr. iv. (1868) 42 Alwey to euery man þere is..somwhat þat vnassaied he ne wot not, or elles he dredeþ þat he haþ as-aied. c 1403 Lydg. Temple Glas 1249 For vn-assaied men may no trouþe preue. 1513 Douglas Æneid viii. iv. 58 Na maner of wickitnes nor dissait Mycht be, that he ne durst nocht tak on hand, Ne onassait leif. 1560 Daus tr. Sleidane's Comm. 105 b, Who leaveth no waye unassayed to accomplyshe his ambition. 1617 Moryson Itin. i. 275 These good fellowes leave nothing unassaied, in the wished discovery of these fraudes. 1649 Milton Eikon. xi. Wks. 1851 III. 427 To be ridd of these mortifying Propositions he leaves no tyrannical evasion unassaid. 1708 Philips Cyder i. 362 They sedulously think To meliorate thy Stock; no Way, or Rule Be unassay'd. 1784 Cowper Task iii. 451 To raise the prickly and green-coated gourd, ..is an art..at this moment unassay'd in song. 1912 Lady Burghclere Life Dk. Ormonde I. x. 317 He could not afford to leave unassayed any issue that promised escape.

Unasse·nting, *ppl. a.* (Un-1 10.) 1836 Sir H. Taylor Statesman xiii. 88 Otherwise the hand, if an unassenting one, will carry an advantage over the head. 1883 Miss Betham-Edwards Disarmed xx, Arthura smiled, a sad, unassenting smile. **Unasse·rted,** *ppl. a.* (Un-1 8.) [1775 Ash.] 1856 Lever Martins of Cro' M. lxv, He is now back here once more; come to insist upon his long unasserted rights. **Unasse·rtive,** *a.* (Un-1 7.) 1861 Dickens Gt. Expect. lvii, He would sit and talk to me..in the old unassertive protecting way. 1880 Ch. Q. Rev. Apr. 140 Unanxious and unassertive, where certainty fails it.

†Unasse·rved, *ppl. a. Obs. rare.* [Un-1 8.] **a.** Unserved. **b.** Undeserved.

c 1400 Beryn 56 'Graunt mercy, gentil Sir!' quod she, 'þat yee been vnaservid'. c 1400 R. Gloucester's Chron. 1256 (MS. Digby 205), I haue holde him on his londe and my mede þer of is That he me wolde dryue awey and unasserued j wis.

Unassi·duous, *a.* (Un-1 7.) 1776 Bentham On Govt. Wks. 1843 I. 295 All these leading points,..with as many points of detail subservient to each as a meditation not unassiduous has suggested.

Unassi·gnable, *a.* (Un-1 7 b.)

Hence, in recent use, *unassignability*.

1674 N. Fairfax Bulk & Selv. 62, I see this roomthiness in the whole, must as well have unassignable parts or such as cannot be laid out. 1780 T. Twining in R. Twining Recreat. & Stud. (1882) 76 In gracing, he does the most beautiful, most unassignable..things I ever heard. 1780 Bentham Princ. Legisl. xii. § 15 Such party may be either an assignable individual..or else a multitude of unassignable individuals. 1883 Sir E. E. Kay in Weekly Notes 15 Dec. 212/1 A vested reversionary interest subject to a life interest in leasehold property..[is] not an unassignable possibility.

Unassi·gned, *ppl. a.* (Un-1 8.)

1495 Cov. Leet Bk. 565 Yf..eny persone vnassigned take vppon hym to ruyde contrarie to þis ordenaunce, they to lese at euery defalt x s. 1812 Woodhouse Astron. xvii. 161 Effects with unassigned causes. 1870 Swinburne Ess. & Stud. (1875) 341 Many sketches by hands unknown...Also unassigned, is a vigorous drawing of a monk's head.

Unassi·milable, *a.* (Un-1 7 b and 5 b.) 1873 E. H. Clarke Sex in Educ. 23 Our girls revel in those unassimilable abominations. 1880 Athenæum 4 Mar. 286/1 America is being invaded by Socialist Germans..and unassimilable Chinese. **Unassi·milatable,** *a.* (Un-1 7 b.) 1858 J. H. Bennet Nutrition iv. 89 The kidneys..[remove] from the circulating fluid effete unassimilatable nutritive elements.

Unassi·milated, *ppl. a.* (Un-1 8. Cf. G. unassimilirt.)

1748 Hartley Observ. Man i. iii. § 6. 393 It circulates with the Fluids in an unassimilated State. 1811 Abernethy Surg. Wks. (1827) II. 201 Much unassimilated matter being conveyed into the blood with the chyle. 1866 Whipple Char. & Charac. Men 11 Unassimilated knowledge—knowledge that does not form part of the mind, but is attached to it.

Unassi·milating, *ppl. a.* (Un-1 10.) 1796 Mme. D'Arblay Camilla i. i, [Fortune's] most rapid vicissitudes, her most unassimilating eccentricities, are..distanced by the wilder wonders of the Heart of man. **Unassi·stant,** *a.* (Un-1 7.) 1796 Plain Sense (ed. 2) III. 203 To suffer..her most strenuous protector, thus to depart unassistant to her wants,..pressed..heavily on her mind.

Unassi·sted, *ppl. a.* (Un-1 8.)

Hence, in recent use, *unassistedly* adv.

1614 Gorges Lucan v. 179 Cæsar..As vnassisted now he stands: And almost left to his owne sword. 1705 Clarke Disc. Attributes ii. xiii, Many of them not discoverable by bare Reason unassisted with Revelation. 1751 Earl Orrery Remarks Swift (1752) 120 The pure instincts of brutes, unassisted by any knowledge of letters. 1820 Scott Monast. ii, In case of assault, the proprietor would have to rely upon his own unassisted strength. 1849 Ruskin Sev. Lamps ii. § 7. 33 The pillars would be, if unassisted, too slight for the weight.

b. *spec.* Of the eye or sight: Unaided, naked.

1661 Boyle Certain Physiol. Ess. (1669) 196 Notwithstanding the unassisted Eye can discern no such matter. 1707 Curios. in Husb. & Gard. 27 A naked and unassisted Eye. 1781 Cowper Retirem. 56 Contrivance intricate, express'd with ease, Where unassisted sight no beauty sees. 1794 G. Adams Nat. & Exp. Philos. I. i. 28 Microscopical observations that discover animals, thousands of which could scarce form a particle perceptible to the unassisted sense. 1865 Mrs. L. L. Clarke Common Seaweeds ii. 42 How could we with the unassisted eye see aught that is lovely in those dark purple or olive-brown tufts?

Unassi·sting, *ppl. a.* (Un-1 10.) 1694 Dryden Love Triumph. iv. i, They stretch their unassisting Hands in vain, But none will plunge into the raging Main, To save the sinking Passenger from Death. 1716 Pope Iliad v. 395 Nor Sthenelus, with unassisting hands, Remain'd unheedful of his lord's commands.

Unassi·zed, *ppl. a.* [Un-1 8.] †Not brought up to the proper assize; under weight.

1616 Southampton Court Leet Rec. (1907) iii. 512 We have ..from each of them..taken some smale quantities of there howseholde vnassized bread.

Unasso·ciable, *a.* (Un-1 7 b.) 1816 J. Gilchrist Philos. Etym. 215 Not to mention the unassociable, repellent natures of their tastes and styles. 1829 Jas. Mill Hum. Mind (1869) I. 98 There is therefore a further condition required to render two ideas unassociable. **Unasso·ciably,** *adv.* (Un-1 11.) 1892 Pater Marius II. 72 The immemorial waterfall, plunging down so unassociably among those human habitations.

†Unasso·ciate, *ppl. a. Obs.* [Un-1 8 b.] = next. (Const. *of* = with.)

1545 Raynald Byrth Mankynde 17 Nether is there any notable vaine vnassotiat of an artyre. Ibid. 33 None of this vaynes run to the matrice or otherwhere, vnassosiat of an Artyre.

Unasso·ciated, *ppl. a.* (Un-1 8.)

1709 Shaftesb. Charac. (1711) II. 313 Even on the supposal, that there was ever such a Condition or State of Men, when as yet they were unassociated, unacquainted. 1790 Hamilton Wks. (1886) VII. 48 The accommodation..of unassociated persons and families who may emigrate thither. 1839 De la Beche Rep. Geol. Cornwall, etc. x. 286 The manganese ores of North Devon are, however, unassociated with trappean rocks. 1897 Westm. Gaz. 17 Mar. 2/2 In this case the unassociated schools were better off than the associated.

Unassoi·led, *a.* [Un-1 8.]

1. Not assoiled; not absolved from sin.

c 1440 Alph. Tales 16 He was wrothe þat his monke died vnasoylid. a 1513 Fabyan Chron. vii. 335 This Frederyke dyed vnassoylyd. 1844 Mrs. Browning Lost Bower xxxix, Unassoiled by Ave Marys Which the passing pilgrim prays. 1868 Lowell Heartsease & Rue 71 The unclean bird Hooting to unassoiled shapes as they pass.

†2. Not settled; undecided. *Obs. rare.*

1387 Trevisa Higden (Rolls) VII. 451 Þe pope..now..leveþ þe stryf al unassoiled [L. indeterminatum]. a 1513 Fabyan Chron. vii. ccxxviii. 257 The pope gaue suche a defuse sentence in this mater yt he lefte ye stryfe vndetermyned & vnassoyled.

Unasso·rted, *ppl. a.* (Un-1 8. Cf. G. unassortirt.) [1775 Ash.] 1865 Gladstone Farew. Addr. Edin. Univ. 24 They were no longer a chaotic assemblage of unassorted or even conflicting units. 1877 Raymond Statist. Mines & Mining 253 Assays, unassorted, from $210 to $300.

Unassua·geable, *a.* (Un-1 7 b.)

1611 Florio, Inplacabile, vnasswageable. 1802–12 Bentham Ration. Judic. Evid. Wks. 1843 VII. 436 No mischief is so unassuageable as that which employs for its instrument a mass of corrupted language. 1817 Shelley Address Pr. Wks. 1888 I. 374 A calamity..such as the English nation ought to mourn with an unassuageable grief. 1884 G. Macdonald Unspoken Serm. Ser. ii. 39 The unassuageable rest of repulsion with which he regards such conditions.

Unassua·ged, *ppl. a.* (Un-1 8.)

1654 R. Baker tr. Balzac's Lett. (vol. II) i. 119 There is no..pain unaswaged by his words before it be expelled by his wit. 1784 Cowper Task vi. 463 The pangs Of hunger unassuag'd. 1799 Campbell Pleas. Hope ii. 434 That spark ..shall beam on Joy's interminable years, Unveiled by darkness, unassuaged by tears. 1815 Wordsw. Artegal & Elidure 35 Till she, in jealous fury unassuaged, Had slain his paramour. 1892 Pall Mall G. 11 Oct. 2/3 The unassuaged agony of the animal.

Unassu·med, *ppl. a.* (Un-1 8.) [1775 Ash.] 1828 Hazlitt Table T. xviii, The true, unassumed equality of greatness.

Unassu·ming, *ppl. a.* [Un-1 10.] Free from assumption; unpretentious: **a.** Of persons.

1726 Thomson Winter 772 See now the cause, Why unassuming worth in secret liv'd, And dy'd, neglected. 1780 Mirror No. 90, In his manners simple and unassuming. 1839 Dickens Nickleby xviii, A very unassuming young woman. 1860 Calverley Verses & Transl. (ed. 2) 49 Once, an unassuming Freshman Through these wilds I wandered on.

b. Of character or manners.

1796 Mme. D'Arblay Camilla IV. 401 His character [was] unassuming. 1797 S. & Ht. Lee Canterb. T. (1799) I. 369 The unassuming and simple dignity of Lothaire. 1803 Southey in Ann Rev. II. 570 A gentleman of unassuming talents. 1875 Jowett Plato (ed. 2) II. 392 He walks about on the sea shore in an unassuming way.

c. Of things.

1805 Wordsw. Prelude xiii. 46 The unassuming things that hold A silent station in this beauteous world. 1838 Lytton Alice i. v, The expensive, yet unassuming robe de soie. 1896 Mrs. Caffyn Quaker Grandmother 146 Stooping to hit at the blackened unassuming remains of a dock.

Hence **Unassu·mingness.**

Also, in recent use, *unassumingly* adv.

1768 Woman of Honor I. 48 An unassumingness, which was the result of most perfect modesty. 1799 Southey in Robberds Mem. W. Taylor (1843) I. 303 Davy is a surprising young man, and one who, by his unassumingness,..soon conciliates our affections. 1830 James Darnley xxi, A sort of unassumingness, which seemed to hold his own high qualities as light, silenced much envy. 1876 Mrs. Whitney Sights & Insights xii. 124 That unassumingness which is conscious of nothing to assume.

†Unassu·re, *a. Obs.-1* [Cf. Unassured and Sure *a.*] Unreliable.

1531 in Ellis Orig. Lett. Ser. iii. II. 216, I..wyll prove myself, though the powrest,..yet not the vnassurest or vntrustiest of your frends.

†Unassu·re, *v. Obs.-1* [Un-2 3.] *trans.* To cancel the assurance of.

1643 Caryl Sacr. Covt. 20 When at any time ye can..be resolved that these are insufficient grounds of making a Covenant,..ye may goe, and un-assure the Covenant which ye make this day.

Unassu·red, *ppl. a.* [Un-1 8.]

1. Not assured or safe; insecure.

c 1430 Lydg. Min. Poems (Percy Soc.) 76 Riche with wysshis, pore of possessioune; Stable unassured, assured eke unstable. 1596 Spenser Hymn of Love 263 The doubts, the daungers, the delayes,..The fayned friends, the unassured foes. 1611 Cotgr., Desassurer, to disassure;..to make vnsetled, vnassured. 1647 N. Bacon Disc. Govt. Eng. i. xlv. 117 In the middest of his strong and conquering army he held himselfe unassured. 1896 Daily News 29 Oct. 6/5 The confusion..superinduced by unassured peace.

2. Not certain or sure (*of* something).

a 1529 Skelton Replyc. 93 Your selfe thus ye discured As clerkes vnassured, With ignorance obscured. 1577 tr. Bullinger's Decades (1592) 504 The sentence definitive is suspended or else it is otherwise ghessed at by humane and vnassured suspition. 1646 Sir T. Browne Pseud. Ep. 194 To invent or assign a cause, when we remain unsatisfied or unassured of the effect. 1651 Hobbes Leviath. ii. xxvii. 156 When men are by any accident unassured they have slept, [dreams] seem to be reall Visions. 1736 Thomson Liberty v. 718 As thick to view these varied Wonders rose, Shook all my soul with transport, unassur'd, The Vision broke. 1776 M. Morgann Ess. Dram. Char. Falstaff (1777) 12 Their ill-gotten..gold feels loose in their unassured grasp.

3. Not self-possessed or confident; not sure of oneself or of one's safety.

1607 Lisander & Cal. v. 81 A troubled countenance and an unassured voice. 1697 Collier Ess. Mor. Subj. ii. (1709) 153 He that is Embarrassed in his Liberty, is apt to be unassur'd in his Actions. 1713 Guard. No. 32 ¶ 8 He moved towards her with an easie but unassured air. 1760–78 H. Brooke Fool of Qual. (1809) IV. 73 [They] stood yet awhile, pale, astonished, and unassured. 1822–2 Wordsw. Eccl. Sonn. iii. xxxvii. 8 Had we, like them, endured Sore stress of apprehension,..From month to month trembling and unassured. 1825 Scott Betrothed xxvii, Lady Eveline approached his bedside with unassured steps, fearing she knew not what.

4. Not insured against loss or damage.

1828–32 Webster s.v.

Hence **Unassu·redly** *adv.*, **Unassu·redness.**

1648 Hexham ii, Ongewisselick, Vncertainly, or Vnassuredly. 1660 Ingelo Bentiv. & Ur. i. (1682) 130 Incredulous Philosophers, of whose vitious lives I cannot but think their unassuredness in this matter to have been a great cause.

Unasto·nished, *ppl. a.* (Un-1 8.)

1533 Bellenden Livy v. xxi. (S.T.S.) II. 220 Fabius..past sturdelie throw all þe stationis and watche of Inemyis vnastonist be ony of þare wourdis or terrouris. c 1605 Rowley Birth Merl. iv. i, Mother speak freely and unastonished; That which you dared to act, dread not to name. 1621 Sandys Ovid's Met. viii. 267 She..vnlocks a posterne doore: Then past the foe (bold by her merit made), Vnto the King not vn-astonisht, said. 1828 Carlyle Misc. (1857) I. 224 Cool, unastonished, holding his equal rank from Nature herself. 1891 Const. MacEwen 3 Women in 1 Boat 117 Xenia rose slowly, indifferently, and quite unastonished from her lounge.

†Unastrai·ned, *ppl. a. Obs.-1* In 5 *Sc.* vnastrenȝet. [Un-1 8.] Unconstrained.

c 1375 Sc. Leg. Saints iii. (Andrew) 341 He tholit þar cne for to hynge, vnastrenȝet, bot of fre will.

Unastrono·mical, *a.* (Un-1 7.) a 1849 Poe Eureka Wks. 1865 II. 127 The difficulty, if not impossibility, of presenting..to the unastronomical, a picture at all comprehensible. 1887 Ruskin Præterita II. 391 This—unastronomical readers will please to note—being one of the leaden influences on me of the planet Saturn.

Unat, variant of Unnait *a. Obs.*

Unathle·tic, *a.* (Un-1 7.) 1759 H. Walpole Let. to Mann 13 Sept., With your unathletic constitution I think you will have a greater weight of glory to represent than you can bear. 1888 Daily News 25 Aug. 5/2 The absence of nerves in the unathletic Chinaman.

Unato·nable, *a.* Also -eable. [Un-1 7 b.]

†1. Unaccordable. *Obs.-1*

1645 Milton Tetrach. Wks. 1851 IV. 267 He who sees not this argument how plainly it serves to divorce any untunable, or unattonable matrimony, sees little.

2. Irreconcilable.

1683 Howe Union among Prot. Wks. 1724 II. 243 If such men were capable of being reason'd with..I would ask them, 'What, are you altogether unatoneable? Will nothing divert you from this pursuit?' 1830 W. Taylor Hist. Surv. Germ. Poetry I. 213 How the waves rush, the thunders roar, and the voice of winds tells of this unatonable vengeance. 1853 Ruskin Stones Ven. ii. viii. § 45. 372 The great unatoneable division between the disciple and the adversary.

3. That cannot be atoned for or expiated.

1689 Apol. Fail. Walker's Acc. 19 The unattoneable Guilt of retarding the Conveyance of those Arms and Ammunition. 1881 W. Collins Black Robe i. x, I have committed the one unatonable and unpardonable sin.

Unato·ned, *ppl. a.* [Un-1 8, 8 c.]

1. Not atoned for or expiated. Also with *for*.

(a) 1727 Thomson Britannia 60 And his guilty stores, Won by the ravage of a butcher'd world, Yet unatton'd, sunk in the swallowing deep. 1771 Mrs. Griffith Hist. Lady Barton III. 220 There is a hope beyond the grave, and nought but vice, unatoned by penitence and piety, need ever urge despair! 1811 Scott Don Roderick ii. xlix, Nor unatoned, where freedom's foes prevail, Remain'd their savage waste. 1837 Lytton Athens II. 7 Time past on, the injury was unatoned, the remembrance remained.

(b) 1753 Richardson Grandison (1781) V. x. 50, I acquainted her with his former fault, unatoned for as it was. 1856 Lever Martins of Cro' M. 279 The great fact remained unatoned for—his family, his own connexions, 'had done nothing for him'. 1876 Bancroft Hist. U.S. III. i. 316 They cherished a deep sense of the wrongs unatoned for and unavenged.

†2. Unreconciled. *Obs.-1*

1730 T. Boston View Covt. Grace (1734) 167 That Spirit they could not have from an unattoned God.

Unato·ning, *ppl. a.* (Un-1 10.) 1838 Lytton Alice xi. iv, What hand could dare to send a criminal..so black with crime, unatoning, unrepentant, and unprepared, before the judgment seat of the All-Just?

Unatta·ch, *v.* [Un-2 4 b.] *trans.* To free from attachment.

1671 F. Philipps Reg. Necess. 246 When it is and hath been not unusual for the Judges..to free or unattach goods attached in the City of Lond.

Unatta·chable, *a.* (Un-1 7 b.) 1843 in Life A. Fonblanque (1874) 257 There is no temple, and there is to be no temple, and the unattached and unattachable gates are mere lumber.

Unatta·ched, *ppl. a.* Also 5–6 *Sc.* -attechit. [Un-1 8.]

†1. Not arrested or seized. *Obs.*

1498 Reg. Privy Seal Scot. I. 34/2 All his men..to be une-sumond, une-attechit, une-arrestit, in his or thairis persoun or gudis. 1531 Ibid. II. 134/2 The saidis personis ..to be unattechit, unarrestit,..and untrublit. 1639 R. Junius Sin Stigm. 368 He that is pursued, will cry, Stop Theife, that by this meanes he may escape unattached.

2. Not attached or united (*to* something).

In the first set of quots. used with reference to physical attachment or connexion.

(a) 1822 J. Parkinson Outl. Oryctol. 96 Mr. Mantell.. ascertained it to have been an unattached animal, and without a column. 1861 H. Macmillan Footn. fr. Page Nat. 46 It [the bog-moss] has no roots whatever, but floats unattached in an upright position in the water. 1878 Abney Photogr. 100 Bromide of silver with unattached atoms of metallic silver, is formed.

(b) a 1821 V. Knox Spir. Despotism § 34 True patriotism and true philosophy, unattached to names of particular men, or even to parties. 1844 Disraeli Coningsby viii. vi, Her eye soon glanced over the page, unattached by its contents. 1865 'Mrs. Alexander' At Bay iii, 'Pray do not trouble yourself,' returned Doering hastily, 'I can exist for half an hour in an unattached condition'.

3. Of persons: Not attached to, or definitely associated with, a particular body, institution, sphere of work, etc.: **a.** Of military officers: Not attached to a particular regiment or company.

1796 List Officers Army 13 Thomas Nesbitt,..Capt. of Foot, unattached. 1806 Ibid. 17 Late Unattached Officers. 1826 Gentl. Mag. I. 638 Promotions..J. Haverfield, from unattached full pay. 1835 Marryat Olla Podr. vii, He was put on full pay unattached. 1852 Burn Naval & Milit. Dict. s.v. Disponibilité, To place on the unattached list. 1859 J. Lang Wand. India 363 As a General of Division, he had been unattached, and had never done a single day's duty. 1876 Voyle & Stevenson Milit. Dict. 445/1 Unattached list, in the British army, officers not attached to regiments.

b. Of clergy: Not attached to a particular diocese or church.

1865 Pusey Truth Eng. Ch. 285 note, Lord Westbury has ..declared him in fact an unattached Bishop. 1902 R. Bagot Donna Diana v. 43 One of the unattached priests to be met with by hundreds in the streets of Rome.

c. Of students: Not attached to any college; non-collegiate. Also *transf.* and *sb.*

1870–1 Ann. Rep. Deleg. Stud. not attached 16 A Grocers' Company's Exhibitioner and Unattached Student in the University of Oxford. Ibid. 4 The amount of intellectual life and industry developed by the Unattached system. 1897 Escott Soc. Transform. Vict. Age xiv. 184 The Davis scholarship in Chinese was for the fifth time won a few years ago by an unattached.

d. In miscellaneous uses.

1888 'R. Boldrewood' Robbery under Arms xl, We must get you in the police force..or make you an inspector, unattached. 1893 Joyce Short Hist. Irel. 70 The oldest.. passed out of the organization altogether, and became an ordinary unattached member of the tribe. 1899 Daily News 26 June 8/4 Reporters attached to no particular journal have dashed up with news.., though the importance of the unattached men has waned.

4. Not engaged or married. Also *absol.*

1874 Lisle Carr J. Gwynne II. vii. 184 You lovers have such a provoking way of showing your immense superiority to us unattached creatures. 1897 Westm. Gaz. 9 Dec. 10/1 We are absolutely out of single young ladies just now, and ..they specially invited some charming 'unattached' from Johannesburg.

b. Not belonging to any family, owner, etc.

1888 Pall Mall G. 12 Oct. 11/2 That would bring to decent places the unattached children. 1898 Tit-Bits 26 Feb. 420/2, 40000 cats,..of which half are 'unattached', and live largely on refuse.

c. Not assigned to any special group.

1899 Allbutt's Syst. Med. VIII. 855 The Microsporon Audouini is as yet 'unattached'.

Unatta·ckable, *a.* [Un-1 7 b.]

1. Not liable or open to assault.

1805 Ld. Grenville in Dk. Buckingham Mem. Geo. III, (1855) III. 457, I am confident that Toulon is absolutely unattackable with such a force as you speak of. 1862 Carlyle Fredk. Gt. xiii. xii. (1872) V. 122 Height which he judged unattackable, and on the side of which he pitches his camp accordingly.

2. Not susceptible to the effects of detrimental or dissolvent agencies.

1881 Nature XXIV. 249/1 The oxides formed on the surface may preserve it by their very presence, furnishing a sort of unattackable varnish. 1882 U.S. Rep. Prec. Met. 649 To make some of the particles of gold wholly unattackable by mercury.

Hence **Unatta·ckably** *adv.*

1865 Carlyle Fredk. Gt. xviii. xiii. (1872) VIII. 56 So unattackably strong was this position at Klein Kamin.

Unatta·cked, *ppl. a.* (Un-1 8.)

1663 Cowley Cutter Coleman-St. Pref. ad fin., There are others..who think it a sign of weakness or stupidity to let anything pass by them unattaqued. 1693 Mem. Ct. Teckely ii. 145 It having not been imagin'd that the Turks would leave behind them Comorra and Raab unattack'd. 1772 Burke Sp. Acts Uniformity Wks. 1812 V. 325 However, as none of them wholly abandon that post, it will not be safe to leave it behind me unattacked. 1828 Lytton Pelham III. iii, I am undisturbed and unattacked in the enjoyments best suited to my taste. 1878 Abney Photogr. 28 Treat all these residues with nitric acid, and they will all be found to remain unattacked by it.

Unattainabi·lity. (Un-1 12 and next.) 1850 Carlyle Latter Day Pamphlets, Jesuitism 29 Moral evil is unattainability of Pig's-wash; moral good, attainability of ditto.

Unattai·nable, *a.* and *sb.* [Un-1 7 b and 12.]

A. *adj.* That cannot be attained or reached.

1662 Bp. Hopkins Serm., Funeral (1685) 52 Those thirty or forty years, which were judged by thee in thy childhood an unattainable age. 1690 Locke Hum. Und. ii. xxi. § 40 The will..cannot, at any time, be moved towards what is judged, at that time, unattainable. 1736 Pope Let. to Swift 25 Mar., A View of the useful and therefore attainable, and of the un-useful and therefore un-attainable, Arts. 1771 Junius' Lett. lxiii. (1788) 334 This, though a wicked purpose, is neither absurd nor unattainable. 1809 Edin. Rev. XIV. 283 The great body of the people never yet engaged eagerly in the pursuit of an unattainable object. 1860 Ruskin Unto this Last (1862) 80 Though absolute justice be unattainable, as much justice as we need for all practical use is attainable.

B. *sb.* **1.** An unattainable thing. *rare.*

1661 Glanvill Van. Dogm. 112 Temperamentum ad pondus, may well be reckon'd among the three Philosophical unattainables. 1786 Cowper Let. to Lady Hesketh 10 Apr., Range and jack [in a kitchen] are not unattainables; they may be easily supplied.

2. With *the*: That which is not attainable.

1857 Maurice Ep. St. John xx. 340 In one sense I can admit that man is always striving after the unattainable. 1880 Miss Braddon Mt. Royal I. iii. 101 All women sigh for the unattainable.

Hence **Unattai·nableness; -ably** *adv.*

1690 Locke Hum. Und. ii. xx. § 11 Despair is the thought of the unattainableness of any Good. 1863 Hawthorne Our Old Home (1879) 371 A strange repulsion and unattainableness in the very spell that made her beautiful. 1894 Hall Caine Manxman iii. xxv, She would be with him always;..the more reproachfully and unattainably, because she would be the wife of another man.

Unattai·ned, *a.* and *sb.* [Un-1 8.]

†1. Untouched, unaffected. *Obs.-1*

1613 Sir A. Sherley Trav. Persia 136 Any of those bring extrinsicke danger, or intrinsicke errours, from both which you must liue free and vnattained.

2. Not attained or reached.

1671 Clarendon Dial. Tracts (1727) 326 The art of Logick..is rarely unattained there by any who spend their time there with any application. 1774 Goldsmith Nat. Hist. (1776) II. 92 When the mind reflects with regret upon some good unattained or lost. 1794 Mrs. Radcliffe Myst. Udolpho xxvi, Unless the crime..was instigated merely by resentment,..its object must be unattained till the niece was also dead. 1868 Morris Earthly Par. (1870) I. ii. 585 Days once bright, With foolish hopes of unattained delight.

b. *sb.* With *the*: That which is not attained.

1854 Longf. Epimetheus xii, Thou makest each mystery clearer, And the unattained seems nearer. 1870 Whittier My Triumph vii, I better know than all How little I have gained, How vast the unattained.

Unattai·ning, *a.* (Un-1 10.) 1831 Carlyle Sart. Res. ii. iv, No mortal's endeavour or attainment will..content the as yet unendeavouring, unattaining young gentleman.

Unattai·nt, *a.* [Un-1 7: cf. next.]

1. = Unattainted *ppl. a.* 2.

1649 G. Daniel Trinarch., Rich. II, cclxxv, These, by a Publicke Act, stand vnattaint. Ibid., Hen. IV, xxii, The rest who fell Confederates with them, are vn-attaint.

2. = Unattainted *ppl. a.* 1.

1850 S. Dobell Roman ii, Unattaint, Perchance the Arethusan blood of Rome Hath coursed the conduits of a tyrant's veins. 1896 E. Fitzgerald Salaman (1909) 59 From Darkness came to Light a Child, Of Carnal Composition unattaint.

Unattai·nted, *ppl. a.* [Un-1 8.]

1. Unstained, unspotted; free from blemish.

1592 Shaks. Rom. & Jul. i. ii. 90 With vnattainted eye, Compare her face with some that I shall show. 1600 W. Watson Decacordon (1602) 274 [The catholics] liue in sorrow, heauiness, and suspition had of their vnattainted loyalties in generall, for some priuate offences in speciall. 1641 Milton Reformation ii. Wks. 1851 III. 54 To..ingage the unattainted Honour of English Knighthood..for so unworthy a purpose. 1716 Swift Misc. Poems, To Earl of Oxford 8 Virtue repuls't, yet knows not to repine; But shall with unattainted Honour shine. 1845 Hirst Com. Monmouth, etc. 44 That bears on high in knightly fight An unattainted crest.

2. Not attainted in law.

1794 W. Hutchinson Hist. Cumbld. I. 378 Whereupon it was adjudged that the title remained unattainted. 1821 Byron Two Foscari i. i, Wouldst thou have His state descend to his children, as it must, If he die unattainted?

Unatte·mpered, *ppl. a.* (Un-1 8.) [1775 Ash.] 1884 Wylie Hist. Protestantism ..ii. i. I. 411/1 Nor have their souls remained untempered by the grandeurs amid which they daily move. **Unatte·mptable,** *a.* (Un-1 7 b.) 1656 Cromwell Let. 28 April (Carlyle), Whether Cadiz itself be unattemptable. 1865 Carlyle Fredk. Gt. xx. v. (1872) IX. 94 Hopes there were of getting back Dresden itself; but that, on closer view, proved unattemptable.

Unatte·mpted, *ppl. a.* [Un-1 8.]

1. Not attempted or tried.

a 1548 Hall Chron., Hen. VI, 105 b, Thei..assauted the walles, and left no thyng vnattempted, whiche might bee to theim, any aduantage. a 1586 Sidney Arcadia ii. xv. (1912) 250 Leaving no meanes unattempted of destroying his son. 1655 Nicholas Papers (Camden) II. 191 Yet no meanes shall bee vnattempted to discharge my duty. 1667 Milton P. L. i. 16 Things unattempted yet in Prose or Rhime. 1734 Col. Rec. Pennsylv. III. 561 That we might leave no means unattempted for the Relief of these..Men. 1744 Akenside Pleas. Imag. i. 606 To adorn This unattempted theme. 1826 Bentham Chrestom. 239 The imperfection, so long as the work has any use, will not afford any sufficient reason for leaving it unattempted. 1846 Mrs. A. Marsh Father Darcy II. xiii. 230 Whatever the work left unattempted at home [etc.].

2. Upon, or against, which no attempt has been made.

1595 Shaks. John ii. i. 591 My hand, as vnattempted yet, Like a poore begger, raileth on the rich. 1687 Shadwell Juvenal 372 While flourishing Troy Yet unattempted, did full peace enjoy. a 1704 T. Brown Walks round London, Westm.-Abby (1709) 48 The Thief stole the Head and left the Trunk unattempted.

Unatte·mpting, *ppl. a.* [Un-1 5 a and 10.] **†a.** Not attempting. *Sc. Obs.* **b.** Unenterprising.

1585 Reg. Privy Council Scot. III. 759 That thay contene thameselffis, in peceable and quiet maner at this tyme, unattempting ony..revenge aganis ony Englishman. 1730 Waterland Script. Vind. Pref. 23 Many have been too forward and enterprizing in that way..; and many also have been too cautious and unattempting.

Unatte·ndance. [Un-1 12.] †Inattention.

c 1449 Pecock Repr. iv. ix. 470 Al tho lay persoonys..y bi-seche for to attende into these thingis,..whos vnattendaunce hath causid ful myche yuel.

Unatte·nded, *ppl. a.* [Un-1 8.]

1. Not attended or waited upon; unaccompanied.

1603 Drayton Bar. Wars v. xxiv, Car'd for of none, nor look'd on, vnattended, Sadly returning, with a heauie

† **Unba·shed**, *ppl. a. Obs.*—¹ [Un-¹.] = Un-ABASHED *ppl. a.*

Unba·utiful, *a.* [Un-¹ 7.]

Unba·tful, *a.* [Un-¹ 8.]

Unba·tted, *a.* [Un-¹ 8.]

Unba·warded, *ppl. a.*

Unba·y, *v.* [Un-² 5.]

† **Unba·zaled**, *ppl. a. Obs.*—¹

Unbe, *v.*¹ [Un-¹ 14.] *intr.* To lack being: to be unbeing.

Unbe, *v.*² [Un-² 5.] *trans.* To deprive of being; to make non-existent.

Unbea·med, *ppl. a.* [Un-¹ 8.]

Unbe·aring, *ppl. a.* [Un-¹ 10. Cf. OHG.]

Unbea·ten, *ppl. a.* [Un-¹ 8 b.]

Unbe·dewed, *ppl. a.* [Un-¹ 8.]

† **Unbe·come**, *v. Obs.*

† **Unbe·comely**, *a. Obs.* Forms: 3 unbicome-lich, -cumeliche, 4 cnebycomeliche.

Unbeco·ming, *ppl. a.* [Un-¹ 10 and 9 d.]

Unbe·fitting, *ppl. a.*

Unbefo·re, *adv.* [Un-¹ 11.]

Unbe·gotten (also -get), *ppl. a. Obs.*

Unbe·gun, *ppl. a.*

Unbe·d, *v.* [Un-² 5.]

Unbe·dded, *ppl. a.*

Unbe·ginning, *ppl. a.* [Un-¹ 10.] Having no beginning.

Unbeho·lden, *ppl. a.* [Un-¹ 8 b.]

† **Unbeho·lding**, *ppl. a. Obs.*

Unbeho·vable, *a. Obs. rare.* [Un-¹.]

† **Unbeho·veful**, *a. Obs.*

† **Unbeho·vely**, *a. Obs.*

Unbe·ing, *vbl. sb.*

Unbe·ing, *ppl. a.*

Unbeke·nd, -kent, *a.* Sc. and north.

Unbeknow·n, *ppl. a.*

Unbeknow·nst, *a.*

Unbelee·ved.

Unbelie·f. [Un-¹ 12.]

Unbelie·vable, *a.* Also 6 unbeleue(a)ble.

Unbelie·ve, *v.* [Un-² 4.]

† **Unbelie·ved**, *ppl. a. Obs.*

Unbelie·ver. [Un-¹ 12: see next.]

Unbelie·ving, *ppl. a.* [Un-¹ 10.]

Unbelie·vingly, *adv.*; †-beliuvingness.

Unbelo·ved, *ppl. a.*

Unbe·lt, *v.* [Un-² 4.]

Unbe·nd, *v.* [Un-² 3, 5.]

Unbe·nded, *ppl. a.*

Unbe·nder, *rare*—¹.

Unbe·nding, *ppl. a.* [Un-¹ and 3.]

Unbene·ficed, *ppl. a.* [Un-¹ 8.]

Unbene·fited, *ppl. a.*

Unbeni·ghted, *ppl. a.*

Unbeni·gn, *a.* [Un-¹ 7.]

Unbeni·ghtmed.

Unblinkingly, *adv.* [Un-¹ 11.]

Unbliss. [Un-¹ 12. So OE. *unbliss.*]

Unblissful, *a.* [Un-¹ 7.] Unhappy; destitute of bliss.

† Unbli'the, *a.* [OE. *unblíðe* (f. un- Un-¹ 7 + blíðe Blithe *a.*)]

Unbloody, *a.* [Un-¹ 7. So OE. *unblódig* (once). — Du. *onbloedig*, G. *unblutig*, ON. *úblóðigr*, Sw. *oblodig.*]

Unblown, *ppl. a.*¹ [Un-¹ 8 b, 8 c + Blown *ppl. a.*²]

Unblown, *ppl. a.*² [Un-¹ 7.]

Unblushing, *ppl. a.* [Un-¹ 10.]

Unblu'nted, *ppl. a.* [Un-¹ 8.]

Unbo'astful, *a.* [Un-¹ 7.]

Hence Unbo'dding.

Unboa'sting, *ppl. a.* [Un-¹ 7.]

Unboastfully, *adv.*

Unbo'dy, *v.* [Un-² 4.]

Unbli'nd, *v.* [Un-² 1 b.]

Unbli'ndfold, *v.*

Unbli'nded, *ppl. a.* [Un-¹ 8.]

Unbli'nking, *ppl. a.* [Un-¹ 8.]

Unbo'den, *ppl. a.* Obs. exc. dial. [Un-¹ 8 b.]

Unblo'ck, *v.* [Un-² 2.]

Unbloo'ded, *ppl. a.* [Un-¹ 8.]

Unblo'odied, *ppl. a.* [Un-¹ 8.]

Unblo'tted, *ppl. a.* [Un-¹ 8.]

Unblo'odily, *adv.*

Unblo'wn-up, *ppl. a.*

Unbo'died, *a.* and *ppl. a.* [Un-¹ 9 and Un-² 8.]

Unboi'led, *ppl. a.* [Un-¹ 8.]

Unblu'sh, *v.*

Unbo'lting, *vbl. sb.*

Unbo'lted, *ppl. a.* [Un-¹ 8 and Un-² 8.]

Unbo'ne, *v.* [Un-² 4.]

Unbo'ned, *ppl. a.*

Unbo'ning, *vbl. sb.*

Unbo'nneted, *ppl. a.* [Un-¹ 8.]

Unbo'ok, *v.* [Un-² 2.]

Unbo'okish, *a.* [Un-¹ 7.]

Unbo'oted, *ppl. a.* [Un-¹ 8.]

Unbo'ot, *v.* [Un-² 4.]

Unbo'rdered, *ppl. a.* [Un-¹ 8.]

Unbo'red, *ppl. a.* [Un-¹ 8.]

Unbo'rn, *ppl. a.* [OE. *unboren* (Un-¹ 8 b), *unboren*, MDu. *onboren* (Du. *ongeboren*), OHG. *ungaboran* (G. *ungeboren*), ON. *úborinn*.]

Unbo'rrowed, *ppl. a.* [Un-¹ 8. Cf. also Du.]

Unbo'som, *v.* [Un-² 4 and 7.]

Unbo'somer.

Unbo'ttle, *v.* [Un-² 2.]

Unbo'ttom, *v.* [Un-² 4 and 7.]

Unbo'ttomed, *ppl. a.* [Un-¹ 8. Cf. also Du.]

Unbought, *ppl. a.* [Un-¹ 8 c.]

Unbou'nd, *ppl. a.* Forms: (see Bind *v.*) [Un-¹ 8 b. Cf. MDu. and Du. *ongebonden*, MHG., G. *ungebunden*, NFris. *ünbinjen*, ON. and Icel. *úbundinn*.]

Unbound, *pa. pple.* of Unbind *v.*

Unbou'ndable, *a.* [Un-¹ 7 b.]

Unbo'wable, *a.* Obs. [Un-¹ 7 b.]

| UNBOWDLERIZED. | 69 | UNBRANCHED. | 70 | UNBRIDLED. |

| UNBRIDLEDLY. | 71 | UNBROUGHT. | 72 | UNBURDENSOMENESS. |

Supplement, p. 3873; Corrigenda, p. 4092; Spurious words, p. 4093; Books quoted, p. 4094

Unbur·ial. Unbur·ied. Unbur·row. Unbur·then. Unbur·thensome. Unbu·ry. Unbur·rushed.

Unbu·st. Unbu·sied. Unbu·skin. Unbu·sk. Unbu·som. Unbu·sted.

Unbu·ttered. Unbu·tton. Unbu·ttoned.

Unbu·xom. Unbu·xomly. Unbu·xomness. Unbu·xomhead.

Unca·im. Unca·lled. Unca·mp. Unca·ndid. Unca·nker. Unca·nny.

Unca·nonic. Unca·nonical. Unca·nonically. Unca·nonize. Uncano·nical·ity. Unca·p. Unca·pable. Unca·per. Unca·ping. Uncapa·bility. Uncapa·citate.

Uncared-for. Uncaredly. Uncareful. Unca·rnate. Uncarnate. Uncarpeted. Unca·rt. Uncarved. Uncase. Uncash·able. Uncasketed. Unca·sque. Uncastrated.

2. Not mutilated or expurgated. 1737 Chesterf. *Lett.*, About the middle of the king's Reign, an uncastrated Copy did arise.

Uncastrated, ppl. a.

Uncate, a.

Uncatechised, ppl. a. Not formally instructed or examined in religion. Also attrib.

Uncatholic, a. Not catholic or universal, in an ecclesiastical sense; also *sport*, not Roman-Catholic.

Uncatholicize, v.

Uncaught, ppl. a.

Uncausable, a.

Uncaused, ppl. a.

Unce, obs. f. OUNCE.

Unc'le, sb. One who is not a Catholic.

Uncaused, ppl. a.

Uncealed, ppl. a.

Uncertained, ppl. a. *Obs.*

Uncertainly, adv.

1. In an uncertain or variable manner; at random, by chance or accident.

2. Not certainly known or knowable; a doubtful point.

Uncertainness.

Uncertainty.

Uncertificated, ppl. a.

Uncertified, ppl. a. Not made certain.

Uncessable, a. *Obs.* = INCESSABLE.

Uncessant, a. *Obs.* = INCESSANT.

Unchalkable, a.

Unchalked, ppl. a.

Unchallengeable, a.

Unchallengeableness.

Unchallenged, ppl. a.

Unchambered, ppl. a.

Unchanceable, a.

Unchancy, a. Chiefly *Sc.*

Unchanged, ppl. a.

Unchangingly, adv.

Unchangeable, a.

Unchariot, v.

Uncharitable. [Un.¹ 7 b and 4 b.] Not charitable; lacking in charity.

Uncharitableness. [prec. + -ness.] The quality or character of being uncharitable.

Uncharitably, adv. [Un.¹ 5 c.] In an uncharitable manner; without charity.

Uncharity. [Un.¹ 9.]

Uncharm, v. [Un.² 3.]

Uncharmed, ppl. a. [Un.¹ 8.]

Uncharming, ppl. a. [Un.¹ 10.]

Uncharnel, v. [Un.² 5 c, 6.]

Unchary, a. [Un.¹ 7.]

Unchaste, a. [Un.¹ 7.] Not chaste; lacking chastity.

Unchastely, adv. [Un.¹ 5.]

Unchasteness. [Un.¹ 9.]

Unchastened, ppl. a. [Un.¹ 8.]

Unchastised, ppl. a. [Un.¹ 8.]

Unchastity. [Un.¹ 9.]

Uncheck, v. [Un.² 5.]

Uncheckable, a. [Un.¹ 7.]

Unchecked, ppl. a. [Un.¹ 8.]

Uncheerful, a. [Un.¹ 7.]

Uncheerfulness. [prec. + -ness.]

Unchild, v. [Un.² 6 b.]

Unchildlike, a. [Un.¹ 7.]

Unchilled, ppl. a. [Un.¹ 8.]

Unchivalrous, a. [Un.¹ 7.]

Unchoke, v. [Un.² 6.]

Unchosen, ppl. a. [Un.¹ 8.]

Unchristen, v. [Un.² 6 b.]

Unchristened, ppl. a. [Un.¹ 8. Cf. MSw. okristnad and Unkristned pl. a.]

Unchristian, a. [Un.¹ 6 b. Cf. Du. onchristen.]

Unchristianity. [Un.¹ 9.]

Unchristianize, v. [Un.² 4 b.]

Unchristianized, ppl. a. [Un.¹ 8.]

Unchristianly, a. and adv. [Un.¹ 7, 11.]

Unchristianlike, a. [Un.¹ 7.]

Unchristianness. [Un.¹ 9.]

Unchristened, ppl. a.

Unchurch, v. [Un.² 4, 6 b.]

Unchurching, vbl. sb.

Unchronicled, ppl. a. [Un.¹ 8.]

Unchronological, a.

Unchurchlike, a. [Un.¹ 7.]

Uncia. [L. uncia.]

Uncial, a. and sb.

Uncially, adv.

Unciary, a.

Uncinate, a. [ad. L. uncinātus.]

Uncircumcised, ppl. a.

Hence **Uncircumcisedness.**

Uncircumci·sion.

Uncircumscri·bable, a.

Uncircumscribed, ppl. a.

Uncircumscript, a.

Uncircumspect, a.

Uncircumspection.

Uncircumstantial, a.

Unci·ty, v.

Unci·vil, a.

Unci·vilizable, a.

Uncivilisa·tion.

Unci·vilize, v.

Unci·vilized, ppl. a.

Unci·villy, adv.

Unci·vilness.

Unclack, v.

Un·cked, a. Obs.⁻¹

Unklad, ppl. a.

Unkla·sped, ppl. a.

Unclaim·ed, ppl. a.

Unclaim·able, a.

Unclam·p, v.

Uncla·rified, ppl. a.

Uncla·sp, v.

Uncla·ssed, ppl. a.

Uncla·ssified, ppl. a.

Uncla·y, v.

Un·cle, sb.

Hence Uncle·ship vbl. sb.

Uncle-in-law, the husband of one's aunt.

Uncle, v.

Uncleansed, ppl. a.

Unclean, a.

Unclea·n·ly, a.

Unclean·liness.

Unclean·ness.

Uncleansable, a.

Unclea·nse, v.

Unclea·nsed, ppl. a.

Uncleared, ppl. a.

Uncle·rgyable, a.

Uncle·rgy, v.

Uncle·rical, a.

Uncli·mbable, a.

Unclinch, v.

Uncling, v.

Unclever, a.

Unclew, v.

Uncli·mb, v.

† Uncommo·dious, *a. Obs.*

So **† Uncommo·diously** *adv.*

Uncommon, *a.* (and *adv.*)

Uncommu·nicated, *ppl. a.*

Uncommu·nicating, *ppl. a.*

Uncommu·nicative, *a.*

Hence **Uncommu·nicativeness**.

Uncommuta·tiveness.

Uncommu·ted, *ppl. a.*

Uncompact, *a.*

Uncompa·cted, *ppl. a.*

Uncompa·nionable, *a.*

† Uncompa·nion, *a. Obs.*

Uncompa·nied, *ppl. a.*

Uncompa·nionable, *a.*

Uncompa·ny, *v.*

Uncompa·nioned, *ppl. a.*

Uncomparable, *a.*

Uncompa·ssionate, *a.*

Uncompa·ssionated, *ppl. a.*

Uncompa·ssionately, *adv.*

Uncompassionately ... **-ness**

Uncompe·lled, *ppl. a.*

Uncompe·nsable, *a.*

Uncompe·nsated, *ppl. a.*

Uncompe·tence.

Uncompe·tent, *a.*

Uncompi·led, *ppl. a.*

Uncompla·cency.

Uncompla·ining, *ppl. a.*

Uncompla·isant, *a.*

Uncomple·te, *a.*

Uncomple·ted, *ppl. a.*

Uncomple·x, *a.*

Uncompli·ant, *a.*

Uncompli·mentary, *a.*

Uncompli·mented, *ppl. a.*

Uncompo·sable, *a.*

Uncompo·sed, *ppl. a.*

Uncompo·und, *a.*

Uncompo·unded, *ppl. a.*

Uncomprehe·nded, *ppl. a.*

Uncomprehe·nding, *ppl. a.*

Uncomprehe·nsible, *a.*

Uncomprehe·nsive, *a.*

Uncompre·ssed, *ppl. a.*

Uncompri·sed, *ppl. a.*

Uncompro·mised, *ppl. a.*

Uncompro·mising, *ppl. a.*

Hence **Uncompro·misingly** *adv.*; **-ness**.

Uncompt, *a.*

Uncomptable, *a.*

Unconce·aled, *ppl. a.*

Unconcei·vable, *a.*

Unconcei·ved, *ppl. a.*

Unconce·ntred, *ppl. a.*

Unconce·rn, *v.*

Unconce·rn, *sb.*

Unconce·rned, *ppl. a.*

Unconce·rnedly, *adv.*

Unconce·rnedness.

Unconce·rning, *ppl. a.*

Unconce·rnment.

Unconce·rnness.

Unconcludent, *a.*

Unconcludible, *a.*

Unconclu·ding, *ppl. a.*

Unconclu·sive, *a.*

Unconco·cted, *ppl. a.*

Unconco·ction.

Unconco·rrupt, *a.*

Unconclu·ded, *ppl. a.*

Uncondensable, *a.*

Uncondensed, *ppl. a.*

Uncondescending, *ppl. a.*

Uncondi·tional, *a.*

Uncondi·tionally, *adv.*

Uncondi·tionate, *a.*

Uncondi·tionated, *ppl. a.*

Uncondi·tioned, *ppl. a.*

Uncondi·tionedness.

Uncondo·led, *ppl. a.*

Uncondu·cive, *a.*

Unconducted, *ppl. a.*

Unconfess

Unconfessed, ppl. a. Also 6 Sc. wconnfessyt, 7–8 unconfest. [Un-1 8.]

Unconfident, a. [Un-1 7 and 5 b.]

Unconfidential, a. [Un-1 7.]

Unconfiding, ppl. a. [Un-1 10.]

Unconfine, a.

Hence Unconfinedly adv. ; **Unconfinedness.**

Unconfined, ppl. a. [Un-1 8.] Released from confinement.

Unconfirmed, ppl. a. [Un-1 8 and 5 b.]

Unconform, v. [Un-2 and Un-1 7.]

+ Unconform, a. [Un-1 7 and 5 b.]

Unconformability. [Un-1 11. Cf. next.]

Unconformable, a. [Un-1 7 b and 5 b.]

Unconformity, adv.

Unconformist. Obs. [Un-1 12 and 5 b.]

Unconformity. [Un-1 11.] Geol.

Unconformed, ppl. a. [Un-1 8.]

Unconforming, ppl. a. [Un-1 10.]

So Unconformedly adv.

Hence Unconformedly adv.

Unconfound, v. [Un-2 3.] trans. To free from confusion.

Unconfounded, ppl. a. [Un-1 8.]

Unconfused, ppl. a. [Un-1 8 and 5 b.]

Unconfusedly, adv.

Uncongealable, a. [Un-1 7 b.]

Uncongeal, v. [Un-2 3 and 7.] trans. and intr.

Uncongealed, ppl. a. [Un-1 8.]

Uncongenial, a. [Un-1 7 and 5 b.]

Unconjugal, a. [Un-1 7.]

Unconjunctive, a. [Un-1 7.]

Unconnected, ppl. a. [Un-1 8 and 5 b.]

Unconnectedly, adv.

Unconnectedness. [f. as prec.]

Unconquerable, a. [Un-1 7 b and 5 b.]

Unconquered, ppl. a. [Un-1 8 and 5 b.]

Unconquerableness. [f. prec. + -NESS.]

Unconquerably, adv.

Unconquered, ppl. a.

Unconquerable, a.

Unconscienced, a.

Unconsciencely, adv.

+ Unconscientious, a.

Unconscientious, a. [Un-1 7.]

Unconscientiously, adv. [f. prec. + -LY.]

Unconscionable, a. [Un-1 7 and 5 b.]

Unconscionableness. [f. prec.]

Unconscionably, adv.

Unconscious, a. [Un-1 7 and 5 b.]

Unconsciously, adv. [Un-1 10.]

Unconsciousness. [f. as prec.]

Unconsecrate, v. [Un-2 3.] trans. To render unconsecrate ; to desecrate or profane.

Unconsecrate, ppl. a. [Un-1 8.]

Unconsecrated, ppl. a. [Un-1 8 and 8 c.]

Unconsentaneous, a. [Un-1 7.]

Unconsenting, ppl. a. [Un-1 10.]

Unconsequential, a. [Un-1 7 and 5 b.]

Unconsidered, ppl. a. [Un-1 8 and 5 b.]

Unconsidering, ppl. a. [Un-1 10.]

Unconsistent, a. Obs.

Unconsolable, a. [Un-1 7 b: cf. Consolable.]

Unconsolably, adv.

Unconsolidated, ppl. a. [Un-1 8.]

Unconsonant, a. [Un-1 7.] = Inconsonant.

Unconspicuous, a. [Un-1 7 and 5 b.]

Unconstancy. [Un-1 12 and 5 b.]

+ Unconstancy. = Inconstancy.

+ Unconstant, a. Obs.

+ Unconstantly, adv. Obs. [f. prec. + Inconstancy.]

Supplement, p. 3873; Corrigenda, p. 4092; Spurious words, p. 4093; Books quoted, p. 4094

UNCRITICALLY

Uncritically, adv. ... In an uncritical manner; not in accordance with critical methods.

Hence Uncritically adv.

Uncrop, v. [Un-².]

Uncropped, ppl. a. [Un-¹ 8 b.] 1. Of flowers, etc. : Not cut or plucked; not eaten by cattle.
2. Not cropped or cut; left uncut.
3. Of land : Not used for cropping.

Uncross, v. [Un-² 5.] 1. trans. To take out of, change back from, a crossed position.
2. intr. To become free from crossing.

Uncrossable, a. [Un-¹ 7 b.]

Uncrossed, ppl. a. [Un-¹ 8.] 1. Not swearing or thwarted by a cross.
2. Not obliterated or cancelled. (See CROSS v. 4.)
3. fig. Not thwarted or opposed.

Uncrown, v. [Un-² 3.]

Uncrowded, ppl. a. [Un-¹ 8.]

Uncrown, v. [Un-² 3.]

UNCTION

Uncrushed, ppl. a. [Un-¹ 8.]

Uncrystallizable, a. [Un-¹ 7 b.]

Uncrystallized, ppl. a.

Unct, v. Chiefly Sc. Obs. Also 5-6 vnt-, 5 ynte. [f. L. unct-, ppl. stem of ungĕre, un-gĕre to smear, etc.] trans. To anoint, oil.

Unction (ɐ'ŋkʃən). Forms : 4-5 vnccioun, 5 vnccio(u)n, 6 oynt-, 5 vnction, 7 vncion, 6- unction. [ad. L. unction-, unctiōn-em, n. of action f. ungĕre to anoint : see UNCT v. So F. onction (13th c.), It. unzione, Sp. uncion, Pg. unção.]
1. The action of anointing with oil as a religious or symbolic rite; esp. as a religious ceremony.

U'nctuose, obs. var. UNCTUOUS a.

UNCTIONAL

Unctional, a. [f. UNCTION + -AL.] Of or pertaining to unction; religious.

U'nctionless, a. [f. as prec.] Devoid of spiritual unction.

Unction, v. [ad. L. unctiōnāre.]

†Unctious, obs. var. UNCTUOUS a.

Unctuosity (ɐŋktiuˈɒsɪti). Also 4-7 vnc-tuous, 6 onctuous; 5, 7 vnctuos-, 7 unc-tuosite-aci, f. L. unctuōsus unctuous; f. unct-, stem of ungĕre to anoint.]
1. The nature or quality of an unguent or ointment; oily, greasy.

Unctuous (ɐˈŋktiuəs). Also 4-7 vnc-tuous, 6 onctuous; 5, 7 vnctuos-. [ad. med.L. unctuōsus, f. L. unct- stem of ungĕre to anoint. So F. onctueux, It. unctuoso, Sp. unctuoso.]
1. Of the nature or quality of an unguent or oint-ment; oily, greasy.

UNCULLED

†Unctuous, obs. var. UNCTUOUS a.

U'nctuous sucker : (see quot.).

UNCULPABLE

†Unculpable, a. Obs. [Un-¹ 5 b.] Not culpable or blameworthy; free from fault or blame.

Uncultivable, a. [Un-¹ 7 b.]

Uncultivated, ppl. a. [Un-¹ 8 b, 5 b.]
1. Of land : Not cultivated or tilled.

Uncultivation, a.

Hence Uncultivability.

Unculture, sb. [Un-¹ 9 b.] Lack of culture.

Uncultured, ppl. a. [Un-¹ 8 b.]

UNCURABLE

Uncurable, a. [Un-¹ 7 b and 5 b.] Not curable or healable; incurable.

Uncurableness. [f. prec.]

Uncurbable, a. [Un-¹ 7 b.]

Uncurbed, ppl. a. [Un-¹ 8.]
1. Not curbed; unchecked, unrestrained.

Uncured, ppl. a. [Un-¹ 8.]
1. Not healed or restored to health; not remedied.

Uncurious, a. [Un-¹ 5 b.]

Uncurl, v. [Un-² 3.]

Uncurrent, a. [Un-¹ 5 b.]

UNCURABLENESS

Uncustomed, ppl. a. [Un-¹ 8.]

Uncurtained, ppl. a. [Un-¹ 8.]

UNCUSTOMARY

Uncustomary, a. [Un-¹ 5 b.] Not according to custom; unusual, unwonted.

Undefaced, ppl. a. [Un-¹ 8.]

Undefalcated, ppl. a. [Un-¹ 8.]

Undefending, vbl. sb. irreg. of next. Obs.

Undefaned, ppl. a. [Un-¹ 8.]

Undefatigable, a. Obs. [Un-¹ 7 b and 5 b.]

Undefaulting, ppl. a. [Un-¹ 10.]

Undefaxed, ppl. a. [Un-¹ 8.]

Undefeasible, a. Obs. Also rare.

Undefeated, ppl. a. [Un-¹ 8.]

Undefecated, ppl. a. [Un-¹ 8.]

Undefended, ppl. a. [Un-¹ 8.]

Undefied, ppl. a. [Un-¹ 8.]

Undefiled, ppl. a. [Un-¹ 8.]

Undefinable, a. [Un-¹ 7.]

Undefinably, adv. [prec.]

Undefine, v. [Un-² 6 b.]

Undefined, ppl. a. [Un-¹ 8.]

Undeflorable, a. [Un-¹ 7.]

Undeflowered, ppl. a. [Un-¹ 8.]

Undeformed, ppl. a. [Un-¹ 8.]

Undefoiled, ppl. a. [Un-¹ 8.]

Undefoiling, ppl. a. [Un-¹ 10.]

Undelightful, a. [Un-¹ 7.]

Undelighting, ppl. a. [Un-¹ 10.]

Undelayed, ppl. a. [Un-¹ 8 + Delay v.]

Undelaying, ppl. a. [Un-¹ 10.]

Undelectable, a. [Un-¹ 7.]

Undelegated, ppl. a. [Un-¹ 8.]

Undeliberate, a. [Un-¹ 7 and 5 b.]

Undeliberating, ppl. a. [Un-¹ 10.]

Undeliberated, ppl. a. [Un-¹ 8 + Deliver v.¹]

Undelivered, ppl. a. [Un-¹ 8 + Deliver v.¹]

Undeluded, ppl. a.

Undelusive, a.

Undemanded, ppl. a.

Undemised, ppl. a.

Undemocratic, a. [Un-¹ 7.]

Undemolished, ppl. a.

Undemonstrated, ppl. a.

Undeniable, a. [Un-¹ 7 b and 5 b.]

Undeniably, adv. [prec.]

Undenied, ppl. a. Also ⁷ -denayed. [Un-¹ 8.]

Undenominational, a. [Un-¹ 7 b.]

Undepending, ppl. a. [Un-¹ 10.]

Undependable, a. [Un-¹ 7.]

Undepraved, ppl. a. [Un-¹ 8.]

Undepravedness, sb.

Undepreciated, ppl. a. [Un-¹ 8.]

Undepressed, ppl. a. [Un-¹ 8.]

Under, prep., adv., and sb. [A Com. Teut.: OE. under, = OS., OFris., Du. onder, OHG. untar, MHG., Ger. unter, ON. undir, Goth. undar.]

Undercoat. [UNDER-1 5 a, c.]
1. A coat worn beneath another.
2. A woman's underskirt; a petticoat.
3. The under layer of hair or down in certain long-haired animals.

Under-collector. [UNDER-1 6 a.]

Under-colour, ppl. a.

Under-coloured, ppl. a. [UNDER-1 10 a.]

Under-condition.

Under-conduit.

Under-constable.

Underconstumble, v.

Under-cook. [UNDER-1 6 a.]

Undercover, v.

Under-covert.

Undercraft.

Undercreep, v.

Under-crust.

Undercry.

Undercurrent, sb. and a. [UNDER-1 9 and 6 b.]

Undercut, v.

Undercut, ppl. a.

Undercutter.

Undercutting, vbl. sb.

Under-dark, a.

Underdraw, v.

Under-estimate, sb.

Under-estimate, v.

Underfeel, v.

Under-fiend.

Underfill, v.

Underfind, v.

Under-fired, ppl. a.

Under-flame, v.

Underfoot, v.

Underflow, v.

Underfall, sb.

Underfo, v.

Under-farmer.

Underfed, ppl. a.

Underfeed, v.

Underfong, v.

Underfoot, adv.

Under-foot, sb.

Under-frame.

Under-gardener.

Under-garment.

Undergird, v.

Undergo, v.

Church from undergoing the same fate? 1832 Ht. Martineau *Weal & Woe* ix. 124 His fine spirit was broken by the anxieties he had undergone. 1887 P. McNeill *Blawearie* 121 Soon all speculation anent the punishment we had to undergo was at an end.

absol. 1842 Tennyson *Godiva* 10 She Did more, and underwent, and overcame.

†b. To bear, sustain (a burden, etc.). *Obs.*

c 1460 *Oseney Reg.* 162 All charges to þe saide tithis longyng we..schalle bere and schall vndergoo for euer. *a* 1618 J. Davies *Witte's Pilgr.* II. xvii, Though Atlas on him Heau'n impose, He that huge Burden, staidly undergoes! 1696 H. Phillips *Purch. Patt.* (1676) B 4 b, There may be an equality in the loss and charges, that so the burden may be the more easily undergone by both parties.

6. a. To subject or submit oneself, to be subjected, to (a law, inspection, examination, etc.).

a 1300 *Cursor M.* 9114 It semes wel..þat he wan merci of his mis..for þe scrift he vnder-yede. *c* 1315 Shoreham v. 152 Ope þe heȝe eȝtynde day He onder-ȝede þe gywen lay, And was ycircumcysed. *a* 1425 *Cursor M.* 12755 (Trin.), In watir baptized he alle þo þat wolde bapteme vndir go. 1594 Carew *Tasso* (1881) 18 They all agree to vnder go his lawes. *a* 1704 T. Brown *Two Oxford Scholars* Wks. 1730 I. 4, I must undergo an Examination. 1721 Strype *Eccl. Mem.* II. xxvi. 215 The Book of Public and Common Prayer, which about this time underwent a diligent inspection and reformation, by some of the bishops. 1817 Jas. Mill *Brit. India* II. v. v. 479 The danger to which this event might expose the expedition..underwent deliberation in the Council. 1844 H. H. Wilson *Brit. India* I. 547 On the 1st July several clauses again underwent examination.

b. To come or fall under, to experience; to have imposed on one.

1599 Shaks. *Much Ado* v. ii. 57 Claudio vndergoes my challenge, and either I must shortly heare from him, or I will subscribe him a coward. *a* 1641 Bp. Mountagu *Acts & Mon.* (1642) 22 Those Elders, who..had seen and undergone the wars of Canaan. 1650 Earl Monm. tr. *Senault's Man bec. Guilty* 145, I foresee I cannot condemn this Action without under-going the jealousie of such. 1668 Hale *Rolle's Abridgm.* Pref. 2 It is a Posthumous work, which never underwent the last Hand or Pensil of the judicious Author. 1717 Lady M. W. Montagu *Let. to Miss S. Chiswell* 1 Apr., Every year thousands undergo this operation. 1774 Pennant *Tour Scotl. in 1772* 96 The castle has undergone its different sieges. 1827 D. Johnson *Ind. Field Sports* 155 The Hindoos every morning..undergo ablution. 1840 Dickens *Old C. Shop* xvi, It wouldn't do to let 'em see the present company undergoing repair. 1873 C. M. Davies *Unorth. London* (1876) 81, I made up my mind to undergo a Sunday morning service at one of these churches.

c. To experience, pass through (a change or alteration).

1634 Milton *Comus* 841 She reviv'd And underwent a quick immortal change. 1711 Hearne *Collect.* (O.H.S.) III. 225, I know not what Alterations the Stone may have underwent. 1765 *Museum Rust.* IV. 339 After this has undergone a strong fermentation. 1825 J. Neal *Bro. Jonathan* I. 23 Seeing the error of his ways he had undergone a conversion. 1844 H. H. Wilson *Brit. India* III. 116 The situation of the British forces..had undergone a rapid improvement. 1884 L. J. Jennings *Croker Papers* I. iv. 115 His views underwent a very thorough change in course of time.

†d. To partake of, enjoy. *Obs. rare.*

1603 Shaks. *Meas. for M.* I. i. 24 If any in Vienna be of worth To vndergoe such ample grace, and honour, It is Lord Angelo. 1604 — *Ham.* I. iv. 34 (Q 2), His vertues els be they..As infinite as man may vndergoe, Shall in the generall censure take corruption From that particular fault.

†7. To expose oneself to (risk). *Obs.*—1

c 1315 Shoreham I. 288 Ȝet gret peryl hy vndergoþe þat cristneþ twyes enne.

8. To take in hand; to undertake. Now *rare.*

1601 Shaks. *Jul. C.* I. iii. 123, I haue mou'd already Some certaine of the Noblest minded Romans To vnder-goe, with me, an Enterprize. 1605 Sylvester *Du Bartas* III. ii. *Law* 291 Make me no excuse On thy..unworthinesse To under-goe so great a Businesse. 1655 Stanley *Hist. Philos.* I. 108 Since him a perfect Agent we may call, Who first considers what he undergoes. 1739 Tull *Horse-Hoeing Husb.* (1740) 252 [They] gave me such an Embarras, that if I had foreseen, I would not have underwent. 1817 Jas. Mill *Brit. India* II. v. viii. 670 Responsibility, thus limited, he had no objection to undergo.

†b. To perform or discharge (an employment, office, etc.). *Obs.* (Common in 17th c.)

1609 Daniel *Civ. Wars* IV. xvii. 91 Having the chiefest actions undergone Both foreign and domestical of late. 1631 May tr. *Barclay's Mirr. Mindes* II. 38 Few they are..able to undergoe perpetuall employment, and not confounded with the different face of businesse. 1667 Pepys *Diary* 11 Sept., [He is] a very young man to undergo that place. 1726 Ayliffe *Parergon* 266 It has been a Question among the Doctors, Whether an Executor may be compelled to undergo this Office?

†9. To go under or by, to bear (a name). *Obs.*

1605 *Gunpowder Plot* in *Harl. Misc.* (Malh.) III. 26 Mr. Fawkes underwent the name of Mr. Percy's man. 1809 Malkin *Gil Blas* VII. xiv. ¶ 6 A large ape, which underwent the name of Cupid.

Hence U·ndergo·ing *ppl. a.*

1610 Shaks. *Temp.* I. ii. 159, I haue..Vnder my burthen groan'd, which rais'd in me An vndergoing stomacke.

U·nder-god. (Under- 6 a. Cf. Du. *ondergod*, G. *untergott*, Sw. *undergud.*)

1583 Golding *Calvin on Deut.* xiv. 270 As soone as we fall to bringing in of vndergoddes we forsake the liuing God. 1593 Nashe *Christ's T.* 20 The High-priest (the vnder-god of your Cittie). 1605 A. Wotton *Answ. Popish Pamph.* 47 You Papists..make our Sauiour, as it were an vnder God. 1712 Blackmore *Creation* v. 235 Of his own Substance does he Parts convey, Whose Motive Force the Under-Gods obey. 1891 F. W. Newman *Early Hist. Cdl. Newman* 20 This Power is an under-god...If we have no awe for this under-god, why [etc.].

Undergo·er. *rare.* [f. Undergo *v.*]

1. One who endures or is subjected.

1601 Sir W. Cornwallis *Ess.* II. xxxviii. A a 7 b, Dracoes lawes [were] very good for the behoulders, whatsoeuer they were for the vndergoers.

2. ? An assailant.

1612 R. Daborne *Christian turn'd Turke* 869 All religious lawes Must suffer violence, your wife be exposed Vnto all vndergoers.

Undergo·ing, *vbl. sb.* [f. Undergo *v.*]

1. The action of the verb, in various senses.

c 1380 *E. E. Psalter* xl. 10 [see Undergangine *vbl. sb.*]. *c* 1440 *Promp. Parv.* 511 Vndergoynge, *submeatus.* 1608 D. T[uvill] *Ess. Pol. & Mor.* 119 The prayse of hauing well conducted the course of one, is a bayte, which drawes them on to the vnder-going of another. 1612 W. Sclater *Christian's Strength* 9 What avails it..whether on the right hand, or on the left; by overgoing or undergoing; we be deprived of salvation? 1645 Bp. Hall *Rem. Discontents* Pref. 4 A meek undergoing of those sufferings. 1712 Berkeley *Pass. Obed.* Wks. 1871 III. 136 The undergoing an execution is worse than the hazard of a battle.

2. = Holing *vbl. sb.* 2.

1883 Gresley *Gloss. Coal-m.* 135.

Under-go·re, *v.* (Under-1 4 a.) *c* 1611 Chapman *Iliad* xiv. 408 The dart did undergore His eye-lid, by his eye's dear roots, and out the apple fell. **U·nder-go·verness.** (Under-1 6 a.) 1669 E. Chamberlayne *Pres. St. Eng.* I. 317 Governess, Lady Francis Villiers, 400*l.* Under-governess, Mrs. Mary Kilbert, 150*l.* 1688 *Lond. Gaz.* No. 2355/4 The Lady Marchioness of Powis was Sworn by the Lord Chamberlain.., Lady Governess of their Majesties Children; And the Lady Strickland Under-governess. **U·nder-go·vernor.** (Under-1 6 a.) 1579 J. Stubbes *Gaping Gulf* D j b, By referring you to the proconsulates of Rome vnder that Empire: to the vndergouernors in the former monarchies. 1587 Golding *De Mornay* iii. 29 To be short, hee setteth downe some Gods as principall, some as meane, and othersome as vndergouernours. **U·ndergown.** (Under-1 5 a.) 1819 Scott *Ivanhoe* iv, Her dress was an under-gown and kirtle of pale sea-green silk.

Undergra·d, abbrev. of Undergraduate.

1827 *Brasenose Ale* 16 Why, Undergrads, dine ye so early? 1853 'C. Bede' *Verdant Green* vii. 63 The temporary sojourn that any undergrad has been forced to make there. 1884 Ornsby *Mem. J. R. Hope-Scott* I. 34 A brilliant Oxford undergrad of nineteen.

U·ndergrade, *a.* [Under-2.] (See quot.)

1884 Knight *Dict. Mech.* Suppl. 911/1 *Undergrade*, a term as applied to bridges synonymous with *deck* bridge in which the track is above the truss.

Undergra·duate, *sb.* and *a.* [Under-2.]

Also formerly written *under-graduate* and (rarely) *under graduate.*

A. *sb.* 1. A student in a university who has not yet taken a degree, and thus is still below the academical standing of a graduate.

1630 Laud *Wks.* (1854) V. 29, I think fourteen years is little enough for a bachelor of arts or undergraduate abroad. *a* 1670 Hacket *Abp. Williams* I. (1692) 20 He was an assiduous overseer and interlocutor at the afternoon disputations of the under graduates. 1721 Amherst *Terræ Filius* No. 33, The Thesis pitch'd upon by the excluding doctors for the undergraduates to moralize upon. 1850 Kingsley *A. Locke* I. xiii. 199 They have no influence over the rest of the under-graduates. 1882 Miss Braddon *Mt. Royal* I. i. 18 The traditionary college misdemeanours handed down from generation to generation of undergraduates.

2. *fig.* One imperfectly instructed, or as yet inexpert (*in* something).

a 1659 Osborne *Charac.* Wks. (1673) 624 Which is but the single and wild Opinion of some under-graduates in the Arts of Liveing. 1693 *Humours Town* 97 Thus far I myself have proceeded (that am yet an Under-graduate) in this admirable Science. 1748 Richardson *Clarissa* VII. lxxviii. 238 Now-and-then flitted in..subordinate sinners, under-graduates, younger than some of the chosen phalanx. 1795 Vancouver *Agric. Essex* 110 Here the under graduates in iniquity commence their career with deer stealing. 1832 *Edin. Rev.* LVI. 163 That Mr. Johnson..is still an under-graduate in modern German, will..be sufficiently apparent. 1897 P. Warung *Tales Old Régime* 88 The Three who were undergraduates [in crime] muttered assent to the spokesman of the Three graduates.

B. *adj.* †1. Of lower degree; of inferior importance. *Obs.*

1654 H. L'Estrange *Chas. I* (1655) 119 Sir Giles Allington fell also under censure for a sin of grand, though undergraduate abomination. 1659 — *Alliance Div. Off.* 437 It is ..to be supposed that in this consecration set forms were used, considering withal that they were assigned to undergraduate concernments.

2. Having the standing of an undergraduate; that is an undergraduate. Also *fig.*

1685 in *Roxb. Ball.* (1885) V. 602 See here the minor Undergraduate Tool Takes his degree i' th' Doctor's flogging school. 1687 W. Sherwin in *Magd. Coll.* (O.H.S.) 216 There was a Cloth laid in the Hall for the undergraduate Fellow.

3. Of or belonging to an undergraduate; characteristic of undergraduates.

1854 Faber *Growth in Holiness* xix. (1872) 387 There is something undergraduate about this levity. 1889 Gretton *Memory's Harkb.* 241 In my undergraduate days, one Ash Wednesday, there came down..a tornado of the tropics.

4. Consisting of undergraduates.

1868 M. Pattison *Academ. Org.* iv. 109 The discipline of the undergraduate body is usually administered by the vicegerent.

Hence **Undergra·duatedom,** the body of undergraduates.

1893 *Westm. Gaz.* 1 Mar. 3/3 He became an absentee, so as to remove the voice of undergraduatedom from the jurisdiction of the University.

Undergra·duateship. [f. Undergraduate *sb.* 1.] The condition or status of an undergraduate.

1815 Whewell in Todhunter *Acc. Writ.* (1876) II. 12 Behold the end of my undergraduateship is at hand. 1850 Thackeray *Pendennis* lxx, Time, I think, has..rendered him a more accomplished rascal than he was during your undergraduateship. 1885 *Q. Rev.* Jan. 12 Mansel was rewarded for his laborious undergraduateship with a 'double-first'.

U·ndergrass. (Under-1 5 c.) 1838 Mrs. Browning *Seraphim* I. 144 The yew-tree bows its melancholy head, And all the undergrasses kills and seres.

†Undergri·nd, *v. Obs.* [Under *adv.*] *trans.* To grind by pressing on (something placed below).

1598 Sylvester *Du Bartas* II. i. III. *Furies* 731 Like falling Towers o'rturned by the winde, That break themselves on that they under-grinde. 1608 *Ibid.* iv. IV. *Decay* 847 As with his weight, a hollow Rocky-Hill..Shivers it selfe on stones it under-grindes.

Under-groa·n, *v.* (Under-1 4 a.) *c* 1611 Chapman *Iliad* II. 693 Earth under-groaned their high-raised feet.

†Undergro·pe, *v. Obs.* [Under-1 8 a.] *trans.* To search into, to investigate; to learn.

?*a* 1412 Lydg. *Two Merch.* 351 And whan his freend the sothe gan vndirgrope Of this myscheef. 1412–20 — *Chron. Troy* IV. 4644 But he anon..Gan vndergrope, pleinly, what þei ment. 1447 Bokenham *Seyntys* (Roxb.) 28 The secunde yer of the forseyd pope, As be cronycolers I vndyrgrope, Fel a ful greuous dissencyoun. 1678 Littleton *Lat. Dict.*, *Subtento*, to assay or try underhand, to under-grope.

Undergrou·nd, *adv.* [Under-2.]

Also written *under-ground* and *under ground.*

1. Below the surface of the ground.

1571 [see Ground *sb.* 8]. 1598 Florio, *Sotteraneo*, of or pertaining to things vnderground. *c* 1615 Sylvester *Job Triumphant* III. 273 Mines and veinlings (vnder ground) Whence Silver's fetcht. 1684 T. Burnet *Theory Earth* I. 259 The..passage of the paradisiacal rivers under-ground or under-sea, from one continent into another. 1728 Chambers *Cycl.* s.v. *River*, Some Rivers bury themselves under Ground in the middle of their Course. 1780 Coxe *Russ. Disc.* 68 Their dwellings underground are similar to those of the Kamtchadals. 1850 Thackeray *Pendennis* xlvi, He..wished that lady..underground rather than there. 1876 Huxley *Physiography* 31 The laws which regulate the flow of water underground.

Comb. *c* 1720 C. Place in *Mem. W. Stukeley* (Surtees) I. 157 The old Giants are represented to us as underground-livers all of them. 1857 Henfrey *Bot.* § 634 They are Truffles, or underground-fruiting Fungi.

b. Governed by *from.* (Cf. From *prep.* 15 a.)

1612 *Two Noble K.* Prol. 18 How will it shake the bones of that good man, And make him cry from under ground. 1697 Dryden *Virg. Georg.* III. 820 Tisiphone, let loose from under Ground. 1872 Tennyson *Gareth & Lynette* 1386 Then sprang the happier day from underground.

2. *fig.* In secrecy or concealment; in a hidden or obscure manner.

1632 *Star Chamb. Cases* (Camden) 104 If he had medled with St. Austin and the Fathers, and not medled so much with these workes underground, he might have knowen the difference betweene the Church of Rome and us. 1679 *Animadv. Sp. Fire Jesuits* 16 Since they may still work under-ground, and not be discovered. 1709 Shaftesb. *Charac.* (1711) II. 269 Supplanting and Undermining may, in other Cases, be fair War: But in Philosophical Disputes, 'tis not allowable to work underground. 1820 Hazlitt *Lect. Dram. Lit.* 308 [Jeremy Taylor] does not dig his way underground, but slides upon ice. 1875 J. H. Newman *Let.* 29 Oct., The pains and achievements of an editor are emphatically underground and out of sight.

U·nderground, *a.* and *sb.* [f. prec.]

Also occas. written *under-ground.*

A. *adj.* = Subterranean *a.*

1. a. Found below the surface of the ground.

1610 Holland *Camden's Brit.* 745 Vnder-ground trees, or which haue lien a long time buried there. 1673 Ray *Journ. Low C.* 6 In Friesland..there are great numbers of these under-ground Trees found.

b. Growing, living, or developed underground.

1757 *Phil. Trans.* L. 404 A compressed pod of the..Underground-Pea. 1807 Southey *Lett.* (1856) I. 417 Some Jerusalem or under-ground artichokes. 1842 Loudon *Suburban Hort.* 113 The most injurious of all underground larvæ. *Ibid.* 279 Tubers, or underground stems. 1875 Bennett & Dyer tr. *Sachs' Bot.* 673 The buds on underground rhizomes.

c. Dwelling underground or in the underworld.

1833 Keightley *Fairy Mythol.* I. 314 A treasure which the underground-people must redeem at any price. 1866–7 Baring-Gould *Myths Mid. Ages* (1872) 216 The underground folk seek union with human beings.

2. Situated below the surface of the ground.

1611 Cotgr., *Hypogee*, a vault, celler, or such like vnderground roome. 1664 Ingelo *Bentiv. & Ur.* II. vi. 172 An under-ground Temple consecrated to Melancholy. 1665–6 *Phil. Trans.* I. 109 The Divine Structure of the under-ground World. 1774 Goldsm. *Nat. Hist.* VII. 353 The Mole-Cricket..at night..ventures from its under-ground habitation. 1823 P. Nicholson *Pract. Build.* 353 If a projected building is to have cellars, or under-ground kitchens. 1846 Mrs. A. Marsh *Father Darcy* II. i. 8 One of those long underground passages, used for communication between the different houses. 1878 Huxley *Physiogr.* 31 After slowly trickling through a long dark underground course.

b. In fig. context. (Cf. 4.)

1675 Owen *Indwelling Sin* vi. (1732) 51 It will increase ..until it..makes it self an underground-passage, by some secret Lust that shall give a full Vent unto it. 1822 De Quincey *Confess.* 48 The stream of London charity flows in a channel..noiseless and underground.

c. *Underground railroad, railway,* (*a*) a railway running under the surface of the ground, esp. beneath the streets and buildings of a city; (*b*) *U.S.* The secret system by which slaves were enabled to escape to the Free States and Canada. (Also *u. line.*)

(*a*) 1834–6 P. Barlow in *Encycl. Metrop.* (1845) VIII. 240/1 The under-ground Railways..in Newcastle, and its immediate vicinity. 1885 C. E. Pascoe *London of To-day* xiii. 137 The stuffy underground railway journey to Baker Street. (*b*) 1852 Mrs. B. Stowe *Uncle Tom's C.* viii. 43 Till the gal's been carried on the underground line up to Sandusky or so. 1856 — *Dred* II. xxx. 318 An indefinite yet very energetic institution, known as the *underground railroad.* 1875 *N. Amer. Rev.* CXX. 67 More fugitives than ever came from the slave states, and the underground railroad was in fuller activity than before.

3. Carried on, taking place, underground.

1709 T. Robinson *Nat. Hist. Westmorela.* Pref. A vj, The Inspection of Under-ground Projects of several Kinds. 1795 Earl Dundonald *Connex. Agric. w. Chem.* 171 The clay.. may be wrought by shafting and under-ground mining. 1831 T. Hope *Ess. Orig. Man* II. 73 The earth worm,..to whom a body dense and rigid..would only impede his underground progress. 1872 Yeats *Techn. Hist. Comm.* 218 The abandonment of ridges will render underground drainage even more necessary.

b. Worn while underground.

1827 *Q. Rev.* XXXVI. 89 As soon as the men come to grass they repair to the engine-house, where they generally leave their underground clothes to dry. 1888 F. Hume *Mme. Midas* I. v, They arrayed themselves in underground garments.

c. Working, having control, underground.

1852 *Eng. & Foreign Mining Gloss.* (1860) 60 *Overman*, an underground overlooker. 1871 *Daily News* 21 Sept., The underlookers, and the underground manager [of the colliery]. 1879 Miss Jackson *Shropshire Word-bk.* 348 *Reeve*, the underground overlooker of the pits.

d. Adapted for use underground.

1884 Knight *Dict. Mech.* Suppl. 911/1 Stevens's underground engine.

4. *fig.* Hidden, concealed, secret.

1677 Gilpin *Demonol.* (1867) 250 This is their help, that some secret underground hopes which they espy not, do revive, at least sometimes. 1848 Keble *Serm.* Pref. p. xlv, There may be an unseen, underground unity. 1886 Gurney, etc. *Phantasms of Living* I. 538 We have already had numerous..instances of what may be called 'underground telepathy'.

b. Not open or public; concealed from or avoiding general notice.

1820 J. W. Croker *Diary* 12 Apr. in *C. Papers*, Brougham ..I believe has been for some time in underground communication with Carlton House. 1883 tr. *Kravchinsky's Underground Russia* 49 The inner life of Underground Russia.

B. *sb.* 1. The region below the earth; the lower regions or underworld.

1590 T. Watson *Poems* (Arb.) 159 That..they may lament with guosts of vnder-ground. 1592 Kyd *Sp. Trag.* I. vi. 1 Come we for this from depth of vnder ground? *a* 1618 Sylvester *Job Triumph.* III. 278 Beyond the bounds of Darkness Man hath pry'd And th' excellence of underground descry'd. 1887 *Scribner's Mag.* II. 449 The open spaces of the underground may..be divided into several distinct classes.

b. An underground space or passage.

1594 Kyd *Cornelia* II. i. 377 Those seas..Returne to springs by vnder-grounds. *c* 1611 Chapman *Iliad* xv. 176 This Jupiter, and I, And Pluto, God of under-grounds. 1884 *Daily News* 24 Sept. 3/2 The financial success..had not been such as to encourage costly exploration in unknown underground.

2. a. Underlying ground or soil; subsoil.

So Du. *ondergrond*, G. *untergrund.*

1822 Sir J. Sinclair *Syst. Husb. Scot.* I. 231 A dry, free soil, on a sound under-ground or bottom. 1897 *Allbutt's Syst. Med.* III. 10 The underground of houses in certain localities being infiltrated with the virus [of rheumatic fever].

b. Ground lying at a lower level or below trees.

1842 *Proc. Berw. Nat. Club* II. 7 Rushes and..marsh thistles filled up the under ground. 1878 Mrs. Oliphant *Primrose P.* II. 124 The mossy underground beneath the firs.

3. An underground railway.

1887 Doyle *Study in Scarlet* (1892) 78 A third class carriage on the Underground.

Hence **U·ndergrou·nder, -grou·ndling.**

Also *underground* v., to place or lay under ground (1891 *Cent. Dict.*).

1868 *Once a Week* 18 Jan. 66/1 The Metropolitan railway (the undergroundlings). 1882 *Belgravia* July 67 That the aëronauts had the advantage of the undergrounders.

U·nder-grove. (Under-1 5 b, 5 d.)

1731 J. Trapp tr. *Virg., Eclogues* I. 35 But that above all other Citys tow'rs, As the tall Cypress o'er the Under-Grove. 1798 Wordsw. '*A Whirlblast*' 6, I sat within an undergrove Of tallest hollies. 1820 Keats *Isabella* xiii, Though Dido silent is in under-grove. *a* 1851 Moir *Birth of Flowers* xiii, The undergrove Glow'd bright with rhododendron flowers.

Undergrowe, obs. var. Undergrown.

Undergrow·ing, *ppl. a.* [Under-1 4 a, 8 a.]

Undergrowing should prob. be read in the gloss. (*a* 1400) in *Rel. Ant.* I. 6 *Frutex*, undirglowyng.

†1. Arising, occurring. *Obs.*—1

a 1440 *Found. St. Bartholomew's* (E. E. T. S.) 16 But dyuerse vndirgrowynge ympedymentys, and, at the last, lettyng the Article of deith, that he wold had fulfillid he myght nat.

2. Growing beneath trees, etc.; growing up from below.

1598 *Sidney's Arcadia* III. 349 Sitting her downe vnder one of them, and making a posie of the fayre vndergrowing flowers. 1616 W. Browne *Brit. Past.* II. i. 17 On his legs Like fetters hang the vnder growing Segs.

U·ndergrowl. (Under-1 9 b.) *c* 1848 J. Keegan *Leg. & Poems* (1907) 180 'Och, you thief of the world!' cried the woman, in a kind of under growl. 1895 Meredith *Amazing Marriage* xxxii. The shaking of her gown and the snarl in the undergrowl sounded insatiate.

Undergrow·n, *ppl. a.* [Under-1 4 a, 10 a.]

1. Imperfectly grown or developed.

c 1386 Chaucer *Prol.* 156 She hadde a fair forheed. It was almoost a spanne brood I trowe, For hardily she was nat vndergrowe.

†2. Showing signs of puberty. *Obs.*

1601 Holland *Pliny* I. 345 As well men as women-kind,.. when they are come to fourteene years of age, and be undergrowne. 1609 — *Amm. Marcell.* xxvi. iii. 287 He had put forth a sonne of his, scarce undergrowne, unto a Sorcerer.

3. Furnished with an undergrowth.

1895 *Westm. Gaz.* 14 Aug. 3/1 A thicket of thorn trees, undergrown with long dried-up grass.

U·ndergrowth. [Under-1 5 d, 10 b.]

1. A growth of plants or shrubs under trees or other tall vegetation; brushwood, underwood.

1600 Surflet *Countrie Farme* VI. x. 744 There must good regard be taken euery where, what plants of branches or vndergrowth are dead. 1667 Milton *P. L.* IV. 175 The undergrowth Of shrubs and tangling bushes. 1794 Vancouver *Agric. Cambridge* 117 In this parish is found some very good woodland..; the undergrowth is cut once in fourteen years. 1822 Shelley tr. *Calderon's Mag. Prodig.* I. 3 This intricate wild wilderness of trees..and undergrowth of odorous plants. 1884 Q. Victoria *More Leaves* 308 The tangled undergrowth of fern, &c. is almost like a jungle.

b. The shorter stems of certain cultivated plants.

1765 *Museum Rust.* IV. 457 What is commonly called under-growth [of flax], may be neglected as useless. 1865 *Pall Mall G.* 3 July 5/2 Much of what farmers call the under-growths or under-stems of wheat are not coming into ear at all.

2. A growth of (shorter and finer) hair or wool underlying the outer fur or fleece.

1641 Best *Farm. Bks.* (Surtees) 20 Such sheepe as have their wooll thus risen, have, without question, a goode undergrowth. 1879 *Encycl. Brit.* X. 709/1 This undergrowth [of the Cashmere goat]..is beautifully soft and silky.

3. The condition of being undergrown or undersized; imperfect growth.

1891 *Lancet* 14 Mar. 624/2 Cases of heart disease,..of undergrowth, and underdevelopment.

U·nder-gua·rdian. (Under-1 6 a.) 1554 *Dial. on Laws Eng.* II. xlii. 135 The sherif shal make such vndergardeins for the which they will aunswere. 1611 Cotgr., *Soubcurateur*, an vnder Gardian. **U·nder-ha·bit.** (Under-1 5 a.) 1771 *Ann. Reg., Chron.* App. 216/2 The Knights companions in the full habit of the order,..the Knights elect in the underhabits of their order.

†Under-ha·le, *v. Obs.*—1 [Under-1 4 a.] *trans.* To under-run.

1615 *Admiralty Court of Oyer & Terminer* 76 No. 10, Underhale the cable.

U·nder-ha·mmer. [Under-1 5 b.] In a pianoforte: (see quot. 1860).

1840 [see Hopper1 9]. 1845 G. Dodd *Brit. Manuf.* IV. 160 The key acts on the 'grasshopper', and the 'grasshopper' on the 'under-hammer'. 1860 Rimbault *Pianoforte* 396 *Under-hammer*, a hinged lever..to which the hopper is adjusted; used in upright pianofortes.

Underha·nd, *adv.* [Under-2. Cf. MDu. *onderhande(n)* by degrees, slowly; Du. *onderhandsch* secret, private; Da. *underhaanden* secretly, privately.]

†1. a. In (or into) subjection; under rule or command. *Obs.*

a 900 *Daniel* 71 Hie..gelæddon..Israela cyn on eastwegas ..under hand..hæðenum deman. *a* 1000 in Thorpe *Laws* (1840) II. 218 *note*, Æghwæðer ȝa bisceope underhand. *a* 1300 *Cursor M.* 6442 Þis ilk folk was vntelland, þat moyses had vnder hand. *Ibid.* 7057 Labdon þan had þam vnder-hand, Was ouerman aght yeir þat land.

†b. In (one's) possession or power. *Obs.*

a 1200 in Kemble *Codex Dipl.* (1846) IV. 268 Ðat lond ðat Berric hauede under hande. *c* 1200 in Thorpe *Dipl. Angl. Sax.* (1865) 581 Alle þinge þe hi under honde habben buten þat lond. 1297 R. Glouc. (Rolls) 2984 Þo he adde þe luþer king agag vnder honde, He let him hewe to peces.

†c. In hand; in course of doing. *Obs.*

c 1400 *Ywaine & Gaw.* 3478 This batayl wil he undertake, And he haves yit in other land Ful felle dedes underhand. 1693 *Mem. Ct. Teckely* IV. 26 Which made the People have a suspicion that there was a Design under hand, but it could not be discovered.

†2. a. *Archery.* (Meaning uncertain.) *Obs. rare.*

1545 Ascham *Toxoph.* II. (Arb.) 126 Those that be lytle brested and big toward the hede..be fit for them whiche shote vnder hande. *Ibid.* 164 A byg brested shafte [is bad] for hym that shoteth vnder hande..: a little brested shafte for him yat shoteth aboue ye hande. 1?15.. *Robin Hoode & Qu. Kath.* xxix. (Percy MS.), Loxly puld forth a broad arrowe, He shott it vnder hand.

b. (See quot. 1834.)

1721 S. Sewall *Diary* 18 Nov., Went to the Funeral... The Sight was awfull to see the Father, and then the daughter underhand by four. 1834 Mrs. Bray *Warleigh* xx, The coffin..was borne 'underhand', as it is called in Devonshire, that is, carried by bearers, about a foot from the ground, by napkins passed through the coffin-rings.

c. (See quot.)

1771 Luckombe *Hist. Print.* 502 The Light and Easy, or Heavy and Hard Running in of the Carriage. Thus.., the Press goes light and easy under Hand, or it goes heavy or hard under Hand. 1688 Jacobi *Printers' Vocab.* s.v.

d. With the hand held below; *spec.* in *Cricket* (see Underhand *a.* 1 c).

1816 in Box *Cricket* (1868) 77 The ball must be bowled.. and delivered underhand with the hand below the elbow. 1885 *Graphic* 14 Feb. 166/1 He..drew out a pair of steel handcuffs, which he..threw up and caught underhand in the air.

3. In a secret, covert, or stealthy manner; by secret means; quietly or unobtrusively.

Common from *c* 1580; formerly often written as two words (β), or with hyphen (γ).

α. 1538 Elyot, *Suppilo*, to steale vnderhand [1545 vnder hande] or craftily. 1580 Campion in Allen *Martyrdom* (1908) 22 Neither can I tell who altered his determination saving God, to whom vnderhand I then humbly praied. 1615 G. Sandys *Trav.* 215 The rest being put to the sword, saue those that were vnderhand saued by the Sidonians. 1654 Gataker *Disc. Apol.* 44 Being underhand backed and fed with money by two Tenants. 1684 W. Hedges *Diary* (Hakl. Soc.) I. 148 He told me that Mr. Richard Frenchfeild was, underhand, a great favorer of ye Interlopers. 1733 Neal *Hist. Purit.* II. 605 His Majesty was underhand preparing for war. 1792 Burke *Corr.* (1844) III. 375, I should not be surprised if he did all he could, underhand, to lessen you in the opinion..of those who employ you. 1814 Scott *Wav.* lxiv, Bailie Macwheeble provided Janet underhand with meal for their maintenance. 1894 Stevenson & L. Osbourne *Ebb Tide* vii, Approaching that island underhand like eavesdroppers and thieves.

β. 1545 [see α]. 1577 Holinshed *Chron.* II. 305/1 The same Stigand was an helper vnder hande for king William to atteyne the Crowne. 1611 Tourneur *Ath. Trag.* III. iii, He does it under hand, out of a reseru'd disposition to doe thee good without ostentation. 1653 H. Cogan tr. *Pinto's Trav.* x. 31 He..used the interposure of a Man born in the country, who under hand went to the fishermen. 1726 Cavallier *Mem.* I. 103 Commonly we liv'd by the Assistance of our Friends, who under Hand supplied us in our Marches, with Bread and other Necessaries.

γ. 1583 Bowes & Davison in *B.'s Corr.* (Surtees) 336 He laboureth under-hand to work a peace between the duke and Gowrie. 1639 S. Du Verger tr. *Camus' Admir. Events* 221 Meane time he under-hand advertises Appollinaire to go always well accompanied. 1683 *Lond. Gaz.* No. 1807/3 They begin very much to suspect that..he does under-hand encourage the Turks to the War. 1705 tr. *Bosman's Guinea* 362 These Gentlemen..agree under-hand with those who sell the Slaves. 1748 *Anson's Voy.* II. iii. 148 In appearance to acquiesce in this resolution, whilst he endeavoured underhand to give it all the obstruction he could. 1818 Scott *Br. Lamm.* xx, That friend..was labouring hard under-hand to consolidate a band of patriots.

†4. = Underfoot *adv.* 3. *Obs.*—1

1617 Moryson *Itin.* III. 55 If he bring his Horse thither, those that are to buy him, are such crafty knaues,..as he shall be forced to sell his Horse vnder hand.

U·nderhand, *a.* and *sb.* [f. prec.]

A. *adj.* (In predicative use *underhand.*)

1. †a. *Archery.* Used in shooting 'under hand'. (Cf. Underhand *adv.* 2 a.)

1545 Ascham *Toxoph.* II. (Arb.) 126 Thus the vnderhande [shaft] must haue a small breste, to go cleane awaye oute of the bowe.

b. Made with the hands kept below the level of the body.

1705 tr. *Bosman's Guinea* 129 Paddling the Water with an under-hand stroke.

c. *Cricket.* Of bowling: Performed with the hand held under the ball and lower than the shoulder or (formerly) the elbow. (Cf. Underarm *a.* 1 and Underhand *adv.* 2 d.)

1850 'Bat' *Cricket Man.* 33 By the underhand method of bowling, the ball..went directly to the wicket. 1867 *Lillywhite's Cricketers' Comp.* 8 Underhand bowling is almost extinct. 1905 *F. Sugg's Cricket Annual* 47 It is very essential that he should cultivate the under-hand throw.

d. Using underhand bowling.

1848 W. N. Hutchinson *Dog-breaking* ii. 13 Similar to the swing of an under-hand bowler at cricket. 1851 Lillywhite *Guide to Cricketers* 68 He is a capital under-hand bowler and a dangerous bat.

2. Secret, clandestine, surreptitious. Also *absol.*

1592 Nashe *P. Penilesse* G ij b, All under-hand cloaking of bad actions with Common-wealth pretences. 1621 Elsing *Debates Ho. Lords* App. (Camden) 149 It was ordered ..that..the sollicitor should goe with the officer, whoe had the warrant, and showld searche all underhand workers' howsses. 1649 *Nicholas Papers* (Camden) 139 The former endeavouring by underhand treaties to undermyne him. 1678 Wanley *Wond. Lit. World* v. ii. § 59. 471/1 Manuel..was an underhand enemy to the Western Christians, and an open enemy to the Turks. 1712 Addison *Spect.* No. 550 ¶ 1 Several indirect and underhand Practices. 1823 Scott *Quentin D.* i, These turbulent cities..never failed to find underhand countenance at the Court of Louis. 1868 Freeman *Norm. Conq.* (1877) II. ix. 366 Their influence must have been exercised in a purely underhand way. 1892 Stevenson & L. Osbourne *Wrecker* x, A new element of the uncertain, the underhand, perhaps even the dangerous.

b. Of persons: Not straightforward.

1842 J. H. Newman *Lett.* (1891) II. 393, I am often accused of being underhand and uncandid. 1858 Lytton *What will He do?* I. xvi. You could not mean to be sly and underhand.

3. Not open or obvious; unobtrusive; quiet.

1600 Shaks. *A. Y. L.* I. i. 142, I had my selfe notice of my Brothers purpose heerein, and haue by vnder-hand meanes laboured to disswade him from it. 1656 Earl Monm. tr. *Boccalini's Advts. fr. Parnass.* I. xxxviii. (1674) 51 By this handsom under-hand dealing, I have reduced the formerly ruinous..State..into the condition that now it is. 1824 Miss Ferrier *Inher.* xxiv, For, as she observed, in an underhand way, there was no disputing with a man who held the key of the post-bag. 1856 Ruskin *Mod. Paint.* IV. v. iv. § 14 The most subtle moves of a game of chess,..which are, in dim, underhand, wonderful way, bringing out their foreseen and inevitable result.

4. Held in, manipulated by, the hand.

1706 Baynard in Sir J. Floyer *Hot & Cold Bath* II. 274 He went..with Crutches, and was in six or eight times Bathing so much reliev'd as to walk with an underhand Stick. 1786 Abercrombie *Gard. Assist.* 136 Ridge out melons in underhand glasses.

5. *Mining.* Worked from above downwards.

1877 Raymond *Statist. Mines & M.* 226 Fifteen men were engaged in underhand stoping from the top of winze No. 3.

B. *sb.* 1. An underhand ball; underhand bowling.

1866 Le Fanu *All in Dark* I. xxxiii. 282 He handles the willow pretty well, and would treat you to a tolerably straight, well pitched slow underhand. 1885 Finch-Hatton *Advance Australia!* 328 All display a precocious talent for round-hand bowling, very different to the sneaking underhand affected by the uneducated youth of Great Britain.

2. A position of inferiority.

1886 Stevenson *Kidnapped* xii, I paid the less attention to this, for I knew it was usually said by those who have the underhand.

Underha·nded, *adv.* and *a.* [f. prec.]

A. *adv.* 1. = Underhand *adv.* 3.

1825 Cobbett *Rur. Rides* (1830) I. 342 The Quakers have been urging it on, underhanded. 1857 Dickens *Little Dorrit* II. xx, You are reproaching me, under-handed, with having nobody but you to look to.

2. (Cf. Underhand *a.* 1 c.)

c 1822 *Laws of Cricket* in *Q. Rev.* (1884) CLVIII. 471 The ball must be delivered underhanded, not thrown or jerked.

B. *adj.* (In attributive use *u·nderha·nded.*)

1. = Underhand *a.* 2.

1806 [implied in Underhandedly *adv.*]. 1853 Dickens *Bleak House* xxxvii, Under-handed charges against John Jarndyce. 1865 — *Mut. Fr.* I. ix, Dark deep underhanded plotting. 1884 *Harper's Mag.* Feb. 395/2 Life seemed to go on in an underhanded, secret way.

b. = Underhand *a.* 2 b.

1865 Dickens *Mut. Fr.* II. vii, That's an underhanded mind, Sir. 1899 Mrs. F. H. Burnett *Willoughby Claim* vi, You confounded, sneaking, underhanded little thief!

2. Short of 'hands'; undermanned.

1834 Coleridge *Table-t.* 4 Jan., If that country could be brought to maintain a million more of inhabitants, Norway might defy the world:..but it is much under-handed now. 1858 Froude *Hist. Eng.* III. 143 He was still underhanded, and entreated assistance. 1874 S. Wilberforce *Ess.* II. 97 The clergy are utterly underhanded.

3. *dial.* Undersized.

1856 P. Thompson *Hist. Boston* 728 A little, underhanded fellow. 1868– in Yks. and Cumb. glossaries.

4. Placed or printed below.

1884 *American* VIII. 347 Many of the caricatures were originally published in connection with the 'poem', which is underhanded.

Hence **U·nderha·ndedly** *adv.*; **-ha·ndedness.**

1806 *Feltham's Resolves* I. 106 To applaud virtue would procure us far more honour, than underhandedly seeking to disparage her. 1884 Tennyson *Becket* Prol., All left-handedness and under-handedness. 1886 *Athenæum* 11 Sept. 335/1 A great deal of indirectness—not to say underhandedness. 1891 H. C. Halliday *Someone must Suffer* III. xii. 213 You had acted underhandedly and deceived him.

†Underha·nding, *vbl. sb. Obs.* [Under-2.] The action of taking in hand.

1639 T. de Gray *Expert Farrier* To Rdr., Thou wilt be much bettered and enabled in thy underhanding.

U·nderhang, *sb.* (Under-1 4 d. Cf. Underhanging *vbl. sb.*)

1903 *Smart Set* IX. 8/2 He was a short man,..with the underhang of jaw which tells of indomitable perseverance.

†Underha·ng, *v. Obs.*—1 [Under-1 4 a.] *trans.* To hang, suspend.

1603 Holland *Plutarch's Mor.* 1064 This saying of Antisthenes,..that a man is to be provided either of wit to understand, or else of a with to under-hang himselfe.

U·nderha·nging, *vbl. sb.* [Under-1 4 a. Cf. Underhung *ppl. a.*] Projection, protrusion (of the lower jaw).

1842 Youatt *Dog* iv. (1845) 99 A second cross considerably lessens the underhanging of the lower jaw. 1876 T. Bryant *Pract. Surg.* (ed. 2) I. 545 In some cases complete underhanging of the jaw is present.

U·nderha·nging, *ppl. a.* [Cf. prec.] Having a prominent lower jaw.

1865 Mrs. Craik *Christian's Mistake* ii. 41 Her full-lipped, underhanging mouth.

U·nder-ha·ngman. (Under-1 6 a.) 1611 Shaks. *Cymb.* II. iii. 135 Thou wert dignified enough..to be stil'd The vnder Hangman of his Kingdome.

†Under-hat. *Obs.*—1 [Under *prep.*] Some gambling game.

1609 *Maldon* (Essex) *Documents* Bundle 210, No. 3, They went to plaie at a game with shillings and testers called vnder hatt.

U·nderhead. [Under-1 6 a.]

1. A subordinate official.

1599 Lewkenor *Contarini's Commw. Venice* 163 These heads & vnderheads are all elected by lot. 1876 *Whitby Gloss.* 205/2 *Underheeads*, minor officials.

†2. A person of inferior intelligence. *Obs.*

1643 Sir T. Browne *Relig. Med.* I. § 55 Wiser discretions ..offend without a pardon; whereas under heads may stumble without dishonour. 1686 W. de Britaine *Hum. Prud.* xix. 86, I find by experience, that under Heads and narrow Souls by Industry..work Wonders.

So **†U·nder-hea·ded** *a.*, of inferior intellect or parts. *Obs.*—1

1646 *Crashaw's Steps to Temple* Pref. A 4 It were prophane but to mention here..those under-headed Poets, Retainers to seven shares and a halfe.

†Underhea·r, *v. Obs.* [Under-1 8 a, after obs. It. *sottoudire* (cf. L. *subaudire*).] To overhear.

– *c* 1570 *The Bugbears* v. ii. 4, I wold not that the maydes ..In theis so waightie matters shold hap to vnderhear vs. [1598 Florio, *Sottoudire*.., to vnderheare, or as we say to ouerheare.]

†Underheave: see Under-1 2.

U·nderhea·ven. (Under-1 5 b.)

1598 Chapman *Contn. Marlowe's Hero & Leander* v. 173 The yellow issue of the skie Came trooping forth, jelous of

crueltie To their bright fellowes of this vnder heauen. 1719 Oldisworth *Callipædia* I. 117 When from the Azure Summit awful Jove Beheld this Under-heav'n and World of Love.

†Underhei·ld, *a. Obs.*—1 [Under-1 7; the second element is related to Hield *v.*] Subject.

a 1300 *Cursor M.* 907 And þou, womman,..sal be to man vnder-heild, To him þi buxumnes to yeild.

U·nderhelp. (Under-1 6 b.) 1579 Tomson *Calvin's Serm. Tim.* 927/2 If we say I haue a wise teacher,..all this is but an vnder help.

Underhew·, *v. rare.* [Under-1 4 a and 8 c.]

1. *trans.* To undercut, undermine.

1523 Ld. Berners *Froiss.* I. 675 They..myned and vnder hewed the walles. [1611 Florio, *Settotagliare*, to vnder-cut or hew.]

2. *U.S.* To hew (timber) in such a manner that it contains less than the proper number of cubic feet.

1847 Webster (citing S. S. Haldeman).

Underhid, *ppl. a.* (Under-1 4 a.)

1387–8 T. Usk *Test. Love* I. vi. (Skeat) l. 72 The underhidde malice and the rancour of purposing envye.

U·nder-hill. *rare.* [Under-1 6 b.]

1. A lower hill.

1687 Norris *Coll. Misc.* (1699) 52 Say sacred Mount, what meant thy Trance, And you small under-hills, why did you skip and dance?

2. *attrib.* (Meaning uncertain.)

a 1722 Lisle *Husb.* (1757) 332 He had lost many a pound by not buying coarse or under-hill hay at the first hand of the year for their ewes.

U·nderhi·ve, *v.* [Under-1 10 a.] *trans.* To place (bees) in too small a hive.

1634 C. Butler *Fem. Mon.* 86 The Bees may doo wel enough in a middle-sized Hive: for beeing under-hived, they will cast soomwhat the sooner. 1707 Mortimer *Husb.* 207 Rather under-hive a Swarm, than over-hive them.

U·nderhold, *sb.* [Under-1 5 b.] The hold obtained by a wrestler who gets his arms below those of his opponent. 1895 *Funk's Stand. Dict.*

†Underho·ld, *v. Obs.*—1 [Under-1 8 d.] *intr.* To hold land by a sub-tenure.

1594 R. Ashley tr. *Loys le Roy* 55 b, The Gentlemen in France possesse, in high, base, and meane iustice,..Principalities, and Peereships patrimoniall: with vassells holding, and vnderholding of them, bound by faith, and homage.

So **†U·nderho·lder,** a subtenant. *Obs.*

1605 Camden *Rem.* 94 Noted..as men of least account, and as all, or most vnderholders specified in that Booke.

Underho·le, *v.* [Under-1 4 a.] *trans.* or *intr.* To undermine; *spec.* (in coal-mining), to undercut. Also **Underho·ling** *vbl. sb.*

1398 Trevisa *Barth. De P. R.* XIII. xix. (Bodl. MS), Vnder hoolinge and vnder crepinge and wastinge vnder brymmes..is icleped Alluuio. 1891 *Cent. Dict.* (as U.S. mining-term).

Under-honest, *a.* (Under-1 10 c.)

1606 Shaks. *Tr. & Cr.* II. iii. 133 You shall not sinne, If you doe say, we thinke him ouer proud, And vnder honest.

U·nderho·rsed, *a.* (Under-1 10 a.)

1860 *Cornh. Mag.* Dec. 689 Why won't he get something able to carry him?..It's the stupidest thing in the world to be under-horsed. 1887 *Illustr. Lond. News* 24 Sept. 360/2 That such an institution [sc. the fire-brigade]..should..be underhorsed and undermanned.

U·nder-ho·rsing, *vbl. sb.* (Under-1 10 b.) 1839 Lever *H. Lorrequer* xiv. 108 The dreadful state of the roads,..the frequency of accidents latterly from under-horsing, &c.

U·nder-hou·semaid. (Under-1 6 a.)

1796 Mme. D'Arblay *Camilla* III. 44 Nanny, the under house-maid, now joining them. 1862 Mrs. Craik *Mistress & Maid* xxii, The only face..that she was honestly glad to see..was the under-housemaid. 1896 Mrs. Caffyn *Quaker Grandmother* 131 She returned sadly and fell on the under-housemaid.

Underhu·ng, *ppl. a.* (In attrib. use *u·nderhung.*) [Under-1 4 a.]

1. Having the lower jaw projecting beyond the upper, or coming unusually far forward.

1683 *Lond. Gaz.* No. 1800/4 Lost.., a red fallow Colour'd dun Bull-Bitch,..with a black Muzle under-hung. 1774 Goldsm. *Nat. Hist.* II. v. 91 Those whose upper and under row of teeth are equally prominent, and strike directly against each other, are what the painters call under-hung. *c* 1815 Jane Austen *Persuas.* xv, He..must lament his being very much under-hung, a defect which time seemed to have increased. 1861 Hughes *Tom Brown at Oxf.* ii, [He] had got the trick which many underhung men have of compressing his upper lip.

b. Projecting beyond the upper jaw.

1809 Malkin *Gil Blas* XI. iv. ¶ 4 Wagging his under-hung jaw in a paroxysm of humour-stricken ecstasy. 1868 Darwin *Anim. & Pl.* I. i. 38 Bull-dogs..after two or three generations..lose the under-hung character of their lower jaws. 1899 *Allbutt's Syst. Med.* VIII. 235 The jaw heavy and sometimes underhung.

2. *Mech.* Suspended on an underlying support; *spec.* of a sliding-door which moves on a rail placed below it. (Opposed to Overhung *ppl. a.* 3.)

1855 D. K. Clark *Railway Mach.* I. 207/1 Engine. Cylinders underhung, castings in two pieces bolted together.

Underi·ded, *ppl. a.* (Un-1 8.) 1603 Knolles *Hist. Turks* (1621) 37 The Turkes attending vpon the Sultan could not walke in the streets vnderided. 1611 Florio, *Inderiso*, vnderided, not mocked.

†Unde·ringness. *Obs.* [Un-1 10, 12: see Dere *v.*] Harmlessness, innocence.

a 1300 *E. E. Psalter* xxv. 11 In min underandnesse gane am I. *Ibid.* xl. 13, etc.

U·nder-i·nstrument. (Under-1 6 b.) 1673 [R. Leigh] *Transp. Reh.* 70 Those who were but accessaries and under-instruments of our late troubles.

Underi·vable, *a.* [Un-1 7 b.]

1. That cannot be derived (*from* a source).

1640 Torriano (*title*), The Italian Tutor, With an Alphabet of primative and originall Italian words, underiveable from the Latin. 1884 tr. *Lotze's Logic* 24 Red and yellow seem to be still more essentially different and underivable one from the other.

†2. Not transferable. *Obs.*—1

1643 Prynne *Sov. Power Parl.* III. 78 Whose personall Prerogatives..being incommunicable, underivable to any other, and peculiar to himselfe alone, he can transferre no such protection to others.

Underi·vative, *a.* (Un-1 7 + Derivative *a.* 2.) 1656 Jeanes *Fuln. Christ* 116 The fulnesse agreeable to Christ, as God, is underivative, without a cause. 1856 Dove *Logic Chr. Faith* 258 Truths which are original and underivative.

Underi·ved, *ppl. a.* [Un-1 8.] Not derived or drawn *from* a source; primary, original.

c 1630 Sanderson *Serm.* (1681) II. 307 Because of the eternity of His own being, and that from Himself, and underived from any other. 1660 R. Coke *Justice Vind.* 5 If it be absolute and underived, then how can it be rational? 1719 Waterland *Vind. Christ's Div.* 219 To be able to distinguish between a delegated, and a supreme underived Power. 1799 Kirwan *Geol. Ess.* 485 It must have had calcareous earth underived from shell fish. 1850 McCosh *Div. Govt.* III. i. 289 Suppose that man had been a self-existent underived being like God. 1860 Pusey *Min. Proph.* 408 Life specially belongs to God, since He alone is Underived Life.

b. Of words. (See Derive *v.* 10 b.)

1668 Wilkins *Real Char.* 303 That kind of word..is stiled an Adverb; which may be distinguished into Derived and Vnderived. 1827 *Q. Rev.* XXXV. 191 This not more useful than abused verb,..underived as it is from any parent or adjunct dialect. 1841 Latham *Eng. Lang.* 261 All, in respect to Verbs in general, which the Etymologist has to determine, is whether they be Derived or Underived.

Hence **Underi·vedly** *adv.*; **Underi·vedness.**

1644 Br. Maxwell *Prerog. Chr. Kings* i. 19 It is underivedly, primarily, and natively in the Communitie. 1850 F. W. Newman *Phases* ii. 51 This derivation of the Son and Spirit and the underivedness of the Father alone. 1886 *Mind* Jan. 39 What is that subjective necessity..? It is..not its underivedness in any one's mind, not its priority in time.

U·nder-jaw. [Under-1 5 b.] The lower jaw or mandible.

1687 A. Lovell tr. *Thevenot's Trav.* I. 22 Mahomet the second having taken Constantinople,..beat off the under jaw of one of those heads. 1762 Sterne *Tr. Shandy* v. xxxviii, Touching his under-jaw with the thumb. 1774 Goldsm. *Nat. Hist.* II. v. 91 The under jaw in a Chinese face falls greatly more backward than with us. 1802 Paley *Nat. Theol.* xii. § 2. 238 The retired under jaw of a swine. 1868 *Rep. U. S. Commissioner Agric.* (1869) 329 [The female trout] has a less-projecting under-jaw.

Underjawed, *ppl. a.* (Stress var.) [f. prec.] Having a protruding lower jaw; underhung.

1772 Lady Mary Coke *Jrnl.* 25 Jan., He is under jaw'd and his chin advances a considerable way. 1822 Shaw *Gen. Zool.* II. 475 Under-Jawed Mysticete. 1864 *Realm* 2 Mar. 1 Her mouth, which, slightly underjawed, loses in softness what it gains in piquancy.

U·nder-jo·bbing, *ppl. a.* (Under-1 6 b.) Doing subordinate work. 1697 Bentley *Phal.* (1699) 329 Some under-jobbing Assistant, of a low sordid Spirit.

U·nderkeel. *U.S.* ? *Obs.* [Under-1 5 b, with obscure second element.] 'A cut on the under side' of an animal's ear as a mark of ownership.

1783 *Maryland Jrnl.* 4 Feb. (Thornton), A crop in [a cow's] left ear, and an underkeel in her right. 1784 *Ibid.* 27 Jan., The right ear a crop and slit, the left a slit and underkeel.

†Underkee·p, *v. Obs.* [Under-1 4 a.] *trans.* To keep under or in subjection.

1590 Spenser *F. Q.* III. vii. 33 He lightly lept Vpon the beast, that with great cruelty Rored, and raged to be vnderkept. 1591 — *Tears Muses* 77 Learned Impes..They vnderkeep, and with their spredding armes Doo beat their buds.

U·nderkee·per. [Under-1 6 a.]

1. An assistant keeper of a forest, park, etc.; an under-gamekeeper.

1502 *Privy Purse Exp. Eliz. York* (1830) 29 To the undrekeper of Swalowfeld for the bringing of iij bukkes. 1589 in *Essex Rev.* (1906) XV. 65 [Another deer was] given away by the underkeeper to his freends. 1622 Ld. E. Mountagu in *Buccleuch MSS.* (Hist. MSS. Comm.) I. 257 The Forest of Rockingham..where Sir Francis Fane is under-keeper. 1682 *Secr. Serv. Money Chas. & Jas.* (Camden) 58 Henry Lowin, underkeeper of New Lodge Walk within Waltham Forrest. 1826 Scott *Woodst.* xxxii, The horses are at the underkeeper's hut. 1891 C. James *Rom. Rigmarole* 172 One of the under-keepers carried a little bamboo arrangement.

2. A subordinate custodian or warder.

1598 Florio, *Sotto custode*, an vnder-keeper. 1612 Sir T. Bodley in Macray *Ann. Bodleian* (1880) 408 Ye keeper of the vniversitie Library, with his vnderkeeper. 1637 *Documents agst. Prynne* (Camden) 69 The Keeper or Under-Keeper of the Castle of Lancaster. 1679 *Hist. Jetzer* 37 He waited till the Under-keeper [of the jail] came in. 1710 *Douglas' Æneis* Pref., Under-Keeper of the Advocates Library. 1760–72 H. Brooke *Fool of Qual.* (1809) II. 119 Sir, said the underkeeper [of the jail], there are few men now at liberty, near so wealthy as this gentleman.

†U·nder-kind. *Obs.* [Under-1 6 b.] A subspecies; an inferior or lower kind.

1571 Golding *Calvin on Ps.* lxxii. 1 It is expedient to descende from the general kynd to the underkynd. 1587 — *De Mornay* 15 We reduce the particulars to an vnderkind, the vnderkinds to an vpperkind. 1671 Dryden *Even. Love* I. i, I would use the like an under kind of Chymist, to blow the coals.

U·nder-king. [Under-1 6 a. Cf. Du. *onderkoning*, G. *unterkonig*, ON. *undirkonungr* (Sw. *underkonung*, Da. *-konge*).] A prince or ruler subordinate to a chief king.

c 950 *Lindisf. Gosp.* Matt. x. 18 Hia ȝesellas forðon iuih in ȝemotum..& to under-cyningum..fore meh. *c* 1060 *O. E. Chron.* (MS. C) an. 1056, Swa þæt Griffin swor aðas þæt he wolde beon Eadwarde kinge hold underkingc. *c* 1175 *12th Cent. Hom.* (1909) 22 Underkyng is ihaten þe under þam casere rixað. *c* 1205 Lay. 31340 Cadwalan..nom him to rede ..þat he aȝain wolde..and bi-teche Penda, þe wes his underkinge, folc and his ferde. 1387 Trevisa *Higden* (Rolls) VI. 275 He put out Egbertus þe sone of Alcmundus þe underkyng. *a* 1513 Fabyan *Chron.* v. cxl. 125 This kyngedome,..and the kynges therof, namyd vnder-kynges. 1587 Golding *De Mornay* viii. 110 From the great Monarks we come to the Kings of seuerall Nations, and from them to vnderkings of Prouinces. 1867 Freeman *Norm. Conq.* I. ii. 26 Each having its own Ealdorman or Under-King, though united under one supreme chief. 1874 Green *Short Hist.* i. § 3 (1882) 18 The under-kings of Essex and East-Anglia received the creed of their overlord.

U·nder-ki·ngdom. (Under-1 6 b.)

1581 Sidney *Apol. Poetrie* (Arb.) 63 Where you shal haue Asia of the one side, and Affrick of the other, and so many other vnder-kingdoms. 1859 Tennyson *Merlin & V.* 581 Thro' all the hundred under-Kingdoms that he sway'd. 1877 Freeman *Norm. Conq.* I. App. 774 Cnut, like Charles, established a system of under-kingdoms.

U·nder-la·bourer. (Under-1 6 a.)

a 1667 Jer. Taylor *Serm.* Wks. 1831 IV. 140 You are the ministers of Christ's priesthood, under-labourers in the great work of mediation and intercession. 1690 Locke *Hum. Und.* To Rdr., 'Tis Ambition enough to be employed as an Under-Labourer in clearing the Ground a little. 1704 Norris *Ideal World* II. vii. 350 The proper office of this agent intellect, to serve as an under-labourer to that which is patient. 1836 Keble *Serm.* viii. (1848) 219 We, indeed, as Priests of the second order, are but under-labourers in that most holy cause.

Underlai·d, *ppl. a.* (Stress var.) [Under-1 4 a. Cf. Underlay *v.*]

1. Laid or placed under or below.

a 1100 in Napier *O. E. Gloss.* I. 3518 *Suppositis..torribus*, of under ledum..brandum. 1552 Huloet, Vnder layed, *suffundatus.* 1598 Florio, *Sottondato*, vnderlaide or laid vnder. 1647 Hexham I.

2. Furnished with an under layer or support; strengthened from below; fitted or supplied underneath (*with* something). Chiefly *fig.*

c 1530 *Hickscorner* D iv, Therwith can you cloute me a payre of botes?..I wolde haue them well vnderlayd and easlye. 1618 Bp. Hall *Contempl.*, *O. T.* XII. viii, That mans faith is well underlaid, that upholds it selfe by the Omnipotency of God. 1650 Trapp *Comm. Deut.* iii. 6 Surely, every man in his best estate, or when best underlaid, is altogether vanity. 1658 J. Harrington *Oceana* 91 If a Common-wealth have been introduced at once,..you are certain to find her underlay'd with this as the main foundation. 1712 Budgell *Spect.* No. 379 ¶ 12 The Floor of the Vault was all loose, and underlaid with several Springs. 1820 Shelley *Witch Atl.* liii, They framed the imperial tent..Of woven exhalations, underlaid With lambent lightning-fire.

b. Const. *by* (what underlies).

1850 Ansted *Elem. Geol., Min.*, etc. § 906 Seams of coal ..underlaid by a seam or bed of fire-clay. 1893 Sir H. Howorth *Glacial Nightmare* II. 463 That the coal-beds.. are overlaid by drift I have no doubt; that they are also underlaid by it seems to be most doubtful.

3. *Printing.* Of type, etc.: Raised by means of an underlay.

1771 Luckombe *Hist. Print.* 362 These Underlaid Words standing higher than the rest of the Matter. 1880 *Scribner's Mag.* May 42/2 This addition to the plate springs it up in every part underlaid, so that the surface fairly meets the inking rollers.

†4. Of a horse: ? Strong-limbed. *Obs.*

1674 *Lond. Gaz.* No. 892/4 A strong underlaid Brown Bay Nag. *Ibid.* No. 909/4 A truss well underlaid Horse.

U·nder-land. (Under-1 5 b, c.) 1874 Holland *Mistr. Manse* v, Down in to wonderland—Down to the under-land Go, oh go! 1877 A. Dobson *Prov. Porcelain, To Greek Girl*, From under-lands of Memory.

Underla·p, *v.* [Under-1 4 a.] To extend some way beneath. Hence **Underla·pping** *ppl. a.*

1867 Dk. Argyll *Reign of Law* iii. 141 The feathers of a bird's wing are made to underlap each other. *c* 1900 *Buck's Handbk. Med. Sci.* IV. 680 (Cent. Suppl.), The margin of the underlapping side is sutured to the deep surface of the overlapping side.

U·nder-la·wyer. (Under-1 6 a.) 1638 T. Nabbes *Covent Garden* I. ii, What's his profession? An under-Lawyer, an Attourney.

U·nderlay, *sb.* [Under-1 4 d.]

†1. (See quot.) *Obs.*

1589 Puttenham *Eng. Poesie* III. xix. (Arb.) 211 Ye haue another sort of repetition...The Greeks call him *Epizeuxis*, the Latines *Subiunctio*, we may call him the *underlay.*

2. a. A piece added to the sole of a shoe.

1612 *Pasquil's Night-cap* (1877) 25 She could line her shoes with vnder-laies, So cunningly, that few the fault did spie.

b. = Eke *sb.*1 2 b.

1641 Best *Farm. Bks.* (Surtees) 63 They will or within a monethes space worke downe to the bottome of the hive, and then must yow give them an underlay. There is in an underlay usually five wreathes, viz., one for the hive to stand within, and fower belowe; yow are to puttein an underlay two spelles.

c. A piece inserted as a prop or support, esp. so as to make one part level with another.

1683 Moxon *Mech. Exerc., Printing* ii. ¶ 1 Presses [should] have..an even Horizontal Floor to stand on, That when the Presses are set up their Feet shall need no Underlays. *Ibid.* xxiv. ¶ 1 The aforesaid Battens will also keep these Underlays from working out.

d. *Printing.* A piece of paper or cardboard placed under type, cuts, or plates, to raise these to the required level.

1683 Moxon *Mech. Exerc., Printing* xxiv. 291 He tries

thicker or thinner Vnder-lays till he have evened the Vnderlay with the Face of the Letter. 1688 Holme *Armoury* III. 118/2 Underlays, are small slips of Scabbord put under letters. 1824 J. Johnson *Typogr.* II. xv. 521 They will be found to sink a little from the repeated impressions, consequently the cuts will require an additional underlay. 1880 *Scribner's Mag.* May 43/1 He puts a proper underlay under every cut..that contains much black surface, and fairly braces it to resist hard impression.

3. *Mining.* = Dip *sb.* 5, Hade *sb.*2 (See quots. 1831–55, and cf. Underlie *sb.*)

1831–3 *Encycl. Metrop.* (1845) VIII. 203/1 The underlay of a lode is a term used to denote the direction of its inclination with regard to the horizon. 1855 [J. R. Leifchild] *Cornwall* 101 The dip of a lode..being its inclination from a perpendicular line, or its underlay. 1880 C. C. Adley *Rep. to Pioneer Mining Co., Lim.* 2 Oct. 1 A small shaft will also be sunk,..following the underlay of the lode.

attrib. 1850 Weale *Dict. Terms*, *Underlay shaft*, a shaft sunk on the course of a lode. 1882 *U. S. Rep. Prec. Met.* 461 The mine is entered by an underlay or inclined shaft 150 feet deep.

Underlay·, *v.* [OE. *underlecgan* (see Under-1 4 a and Lay *v.*), = MDu. and Du. *onderleggen*, MHG. *underlegen* (G. *unter-*), MSw. *undirlaggia* (Sw. *underlägga*), MDa. and Da. *underlægge.*]

1. *trans.* To support by placing something beneath; to furnish *with* something laid below. Also *fig.*

c 897 K. Ælfred *Gregory's Past C.* xix. 143 Ðonne ðu se elnboga underled mid pyle & se hnecca mid bolstre. *c* 1000 Ælfric *Hom.* II. 144 Þa bæd he hi anre sylle, þæt he mihte þæt hus on ða sæ healfe mid hære underlecgan. *c* 1250 *Gen. & Ex.* 3383 He is under-leiden wið an ston, Til sunne him seilede in ðe west. 1555 Eden *Decades* (Arb.) 327 They vnderlaye them with grasse. 1577 B. Googe *Heresbach's Husb.* II. (1586) 60 They vse to set the heads vnderlaying them with a Tileshard. 1658 A. Fox *Würtz' Surg.* II. xiv. 110 You ought not to stitch any wounded Finger,..but underlay it with little splinters. 1679 Moxon *Mech. Exerc.* ix. 157 If the Board be too thin, they underlay that Board upon every Joyst with a Chip. 1726 Leoni *Alberti's Archit.* II. 10b, Another way of making the weight slip along..is by underlaying it cross-ways with Rollers. 1851 *Athenæum* Oct. 1049/1 Their project of underlaying the sea with electric wires.

b. To furnish with a lining or backing.

1502 *Acc. Ld. High Treas. Scot.* II. 302 Franch tanne to be ane cote to Jacob..v quartaris doun ostad to underlay the bordoring of it.

†c. To furnish (shoes) with additional solingpieces or heel-plates. Also in fig. context. *Obs.*

c 1530 [see Underlaid *ppl. a.* 2]. 1583 Stubbes *Anat. Abus.* II. F 4, If the sooles be naught (as they be indeede) yet must they be vnderlaied with other peeces of leather, to make them seeme thicke. 1587 Turberv. *Epit.* 190 b, The heeles they vnderlay With clouting clamps of steele. 1632 Holland *Cyrupædia* 181 The Medes use..such a kind of shooes, as they might underlay closely and out of sight. 1661 K. W. *Conf. Charac.* To Rdr. (1860) 1 Should I, like an vnthrifty cobler, haue vnderlayed the rotten soles of these now worn out buskings, with the new and costly leather of applause. 1682 W. Robertson *Phraseol. Gen.* 1272 To underlay a shoe, *suppingere.*

fig. 1592 Nashe *Four Lett. Confut.* 7 Then wil I bind my selfe prentise to a Cobler, and fresh vnderlay all those writings of mine that haue trodde awrie. 1603 Dekker *Wonderfull Yeare* E 3 b, Being a pollitike cobler, and remembring what peece of work he was to vnderlay. ?1622 Fletcher *Love's Cure* v. iii, Our souls have trode awry in all mens sight, We'll underlay 'em, till they go upright.

d. *Printing.* To place paper or cardboard under (type, etc.) in order to raise to the required level for printing.

1683 Moxon *Mech. Exerc., Printing* xxiv. 291 If any Wooden Letters..are too Low, (as they generally be) he Vnder-lays them. 1880 *Scribner's Mag.* May 42/2 The pressman underlays the plate, by pasting on its under side bits of paper of suitable size. 1888 Jacobi *Printers' Vocab.*, *Underlay*, the process of making-ready under type or cuts.

2. To place (something) beneath.

c 1000 Ælfric *Gram.* xxviii. (Z.) 167 *Subpono*, ic underlecge. *c* 1440 *Promp. Parv.* 511/1 Vnderleyyn, *idem quod* underputtyn. 1573 Twyne *Æneid* XII. Nn j, A tower stronge..the prince..had built alone, And choules [? *read* roules] had vnderlayd [L. *subdiderat que rotas*]. 1683 Moxon *Mech. Exerc., Printing* xxii. ¶ 10 If a Page be too big for his Grasp, he underlays the Slice of a Galley.

b. To put underground, to bury.

Used punningly with allusion to sense 1 c.

1639 *Conceits, Clinches*, etc. (1860) 40 If any aske why this same stone was made? (Know) for a cobler newly underlayd Here for his overboasting.

†3. To make subject; to submit. *Obs.*

a 1300 *E. E. Psalter* viii. 7 Þou vnderlaide [L. *subjecisti*] alle þinges Vnder his fete. *a* 1300 *Cursor M.* 18266 Sin þou be king o blis werraid And sua bi-self has vnder-laid. 1382 Wyclif *Jer.* xxvii. 12 Vnderleith [L. *subjicite*] ȝoure neckus vnder the ȝoc of the king of Babyloyne.

4. To lie under or beneath; = Underlie *v.* 3.

1591 Spenser *Virg. Gnat* 99 Ne cares he if the..glistering of golde, which vnderlayes The summer beames, doe blinde his gazing eye. 1611 Cotgr., *Hausse*, the vnderlaying of a shooe, or peece of leather that vnderlayes it. 1799 Kirwan *Geol. Ess.* 178 In the south of France it occurs reposing on granite, and underlaying basalt. *Ibid.*, In the Altaischan mountains it sometimes underlays argillite. 1826 E. Irving *Babylon* II. vii. 227 Our brethren and friends, who still underlay the curse. 1861 Dasent *Burnt Njal* I. Introd. p. xxviii, [The right of duel] underlaid all their early legislation.

5. *intr. Mining.* To slope, incline from the perpendicular; = Underlie *v.* 5.

1728 *Phil. Trans.* XXXV. 403 The Sides of the Load.. constantly underlay either to the North or South. 1802 J. Mawe *Min. Derby* Gloss. s.v., When a vein *hades*, or inclines from a perpendicular line, it is said to underlay. 1855

[J. R. Leifchild] *Cornwall* 101 A lode which underlays towards the north.

Underlay·er1. [f. prec. Cf. Du. *onderlegger*, G. *unterleger.*]

†1. An underlying part or thing; a base or support. *Obs.*

In quot. 1609 applied allusively to a woman.

a 1592 Greene & Lodge *Looking Gl.* I. ii. 255 The Nutmeg ..is, saith one Ballad,..an vnderlayer to the braines. 1609 *Ev. Woman in Hum.* I. i, Ist not some vnderlayer, some she Cammell that will beare as much of her belly, as three beastes on their backe? 1702 Boyer *Dict. Royal* II, Underlayer,..(a piece of Wood to shore up any thing,) *une Etaye, un Étançon.* 1775 Ash, *Underlayer*.., that which is laid under to bear up any thing.

†2. A cobbler. *Obs.*—1

1692 R. L'Estrange *Fables* I. cccci. 373 How many Underlayers,..when they could not live upon their Trade, have rais'd themselves from Cobbling to Fluxing?

3. *Mining.* 'A perpendicular shaft sunk to cut the lode at any required depth.'

1850 Weale *Dict. Terms.*

U·nderlay·er2. [Under-1 5 b.] A lower layer; a substratum.

1896 *Daily News* 15 Dec. 2/2 The carpets are of heavy velvet pile on an underlayer of elastic felt and cork. 1904 W. P. Ker *Dark Ages* 108 Rodulphus represents the permanent underlayer of medieval absurdity above which Gerbert rises so eminently.

Underlay·ing, *vbl. sb.* [f. Underlay *v.*] The action of the verb, or the result of this.

1611 [see Underlay *v.* 4]. 1648 Hexham II, *Onderstel van pilerrnen*, the Vnderlaying or the Ground-worke of pillars. 1683 Moxon *Mech. Exerc., Printing* xxiv. ¶ 1, I am loath to name the Vnder-laying of the Feet, because at the best it is but a Botch, and Subjects the whole Press to an unstable position. 1802 J. Mawe *Min. Derby* Gloss., *Hade*, the underlaying or inclination of the vein. 1882 Southward *Pract. Printing* (1884) 429 In underlaying we put a piece of paper..under the type.

U·nderleaf. [Under-1 5 b.]

1. A variety of cider-apple. Also *attrib.*

1707 Mortimer *Husb.* 540 The Underleaf..is a very plentiful bearer, hath a Rhenish Wine flavour. *Ibid.* 575 The best sorts for Cyder are found to be..the Olive Underleaf Apple [etc.]. 1786 Abercrombie *Arrangem.* p. xi. in *Gard. Assist.*, Apples valued principally for Cyder..[include] Underleaf.

2. The under surface of a leaf.

1873 Tristram *Moab* xviii. 353 The charm of the silvery [poplar] underleaf twinkling in the breeze.

U·nder-lease, *sb.* [Under-1 6 b.] A lease granted by a lessee; a sub-lease.

1702 Boyer *Dict. Royal* I, *Soubail*,..an under-lease. 1730 *Act 4 Geo. II*, c. 28 § 6 Those Leases cannot by Law be renewed without a Surrender of all the Under-Leases. 1803 *Act 43 Geo. III*, c. 75 § 4 It may be for the Benefit of such Persons that Leases, or Under-Leases, should be made of such Estates. 1839 *Penny Cycl.* XIII. 378/2 Where the property is transferred for a part of the original term only, the transfer is called an under-lease, and the under-lessee is not liable to the original lessor. 1885 *Law Times* 7 Mar. 335/2 The underlease contained a covenant that if the underlessee..should..assign the underlease [etc.].

Underlea·se, *v.* [Under-1 8 d.] *trans.* To sublet by an underlease. Also *absol.*

1819 Rees *Cycl.* XXXV. s.v. *Tenure*, The takers having the liberty..to under-lease to other tenants. 1885 *Law Times* LXXIX. 233/1 A large plot of ground is leased for a term of 999 years. A part of this is underleased for 990 years.

U·nder-lea·ther. (Under-1 5 b. Cf. MDu. *onderleder*, G. *unterleder*, Sw. *underläder.*)

1569 *Wills & Inv. N. C.* (Surtees, 1835) 307 Eleuen dakers of vnderleathers xxvj *l*, ij daker of soles x *l*, vij dakers of ouerlethers xvj *l* x *s.* 1611 Cotgr., *La solette d'un esperon*, the vnder leather of a spurre. 1845 G. Dodd *Brit. Manuf.* IV. 100 The shoes may have scarcely any 'under-leathers' to keep the 'uppers' together.

U·nder-le·gate. (Under-1 6 a.)

1426 Lydg. *De Guil. Pilgr.* 2752 Seyn Peter..Hath mad yow..Hys vnderlegatys, ther to stonde, To kepe the passage.

†U·nderle·gged, *a. Obs.*—1 [Under-1 10 a.] = Underlimbed *a.*

1681 *Lond. Gaz.* No. 1566/4 A Brown Bay Gelding,..his neather-lip a little falling, and under-Legg'd behind.

†Underlegger. *Obs.* [Under-1 5 b + *legger* Ledger *sb.*] Some kind of oar.

1405 *For. Acc.* 39 last membr., ij orys vocat' underleggers. 1406 *Exch. Acc.* 44/9 Remi vocati underleggers.

U·nderlessee·. (Under-1 6 a.)

1730 *Act 4 Geo. II*, c. 28 § 6 The Under-Lessees shall hold and enjoy the Messuages. 1839, 1885 [see Underlease *sb.*].

Underle·t, *ppl. a.* [Under-1 4 a.] Let in or inserted beneath.

1884 *Harper's Mag.* Aug. 347/2 Window-curtains of pale greenish-white satin, with underlet appliqués of other pale-hued silks.

Underle·t, *v.* [Under-1 8 c, d.]

1. *trans.* To let at an amount or rental below the true or full value.

1677 Capell in *Essex Papers* (Camden) II. 128 Ormond.. abusing King in underletting the excise to the value of 300,000 lbs. per annum. 1751 Johnson *Rambler* No. 103 ¶ 14 He..knows how much one man's cellar is robbed by his butler, and the land of another underlet by his Steward. 1791 *Rep. Comm. Thames-Isis Navig.* 24 The Two Pound Locks, Tolls, &c. at Ifley and Sandford..were previously much under-let. 1868 Rogers *Pol. Econ.* xiii. 181 Agricultural land in England is rather under than over let. 1874 Green *Short Hist.* vi. § 5 (1876) 320 The land indeed had been greatly underlet.

2. To let to a sub-tenant; to sublet.

U̇nder·lid. The lower lid of the eye.

Underlie·, v. [OE. *underlicgan* f. Under-1 + *licgan* Lie v.]

Underlie·, sb. Mining.

Underlie·, v.² [OE. *underlicgan*.]

Underlier. [f. Underlie v.]

Underlift.

U̇nder·linen.

Underling, sb. and a. Forms: *under·lyng*, *vnder·lyng*.

Underling, v. Mining. [f. Underlie.]

U̇nder·line, sb.

Underline·, v.

Underli·ment.

Underli·ne, v.¹

U̇nder·ling.

U̇nder·live.

Underly·ing, vbl. sb. Mining.

Underly·ing, ppl. a. [Under-1 d.]

U̇nder·look, v.

U̇nder·looker.

Undern. Forms: 1–5, 9 *undern* (2 *undærn*-), 3 *vn-*.

U̇nder·meaning. [Under-1 10 a.]

U̇nder·measure, v. [Under-1 10 a.] trans.

U̇nder·meated, ppl. a. [Under-1 10 a.]

Under-mentioned, ppl. a. [Under-adv. 2 b.]

Underme·nable, a. [Under-1 4 + Cf. next.]

Undermine·, v. Forms: 2–4 *undermyne*, 5 *-mine*, 7 *-mine* (also 4–6 *vnder-*, 4–5 *vndyr-*). [Under-1 4 a + Mine v. Cf. Du. *undermineren*, older Da. *underminere*; Du. etc. MD. *underminneren*.]

Undermining, ppl. a. [f. as prec.]

U̇nder·miner.

U̇nder·minister, sb. Under-1 6 b.] An underling, subordinate, assistant.

U̇nder-mi·nister, v. [Under-1 16 b.] Sub-ordinate service or office.

U̇nder-mi·nistery. [Under-1 16 b.]

Under-moral, a.

Undermo·ney. [Under-1 4 a.] trans.

Undermo·ral.

Undermo·st, a. and adv. [Under adv. + -MOST.]

U̇nder·mow, v. Obs. [Under-1 4.]

Under·serve, v. [UNDER-¹ 8 a, 10 a. Cf.
-servable.]
†1. To be subservient (to). Obs.
2. To serve insufficiently.

U·nder-serve, [UNDER-¹ 6 b.] Service of
an inferior kind; subordinate service.

U·nderset, v. [UNDER-¹ 4 a, etc. Cf. MDu.
onterstellen (Du. -setten), MDu. understellen, MHG.
understetzen (G. -setzen); MDu. ondersetelle.]
1. trans. To support or strengthen by means of
something (esp. of the nature of a post or prop)
placed beneath; to prop up.
2. Mining. To underset.
3. To set or place (a thing) under something else.

U·nderset, sb. [UNDERSETTLE. Obs. rare.
†1. sb. v. Undersetting.
2. Mining. A mining vein or ore.

U·ndersheriff. Forms: (see SHERIFF.)
[UNDER-¹ 6 a: cf. SHERIFF 2.] A deputy sheriff.

U·ndershot, (ppl.) a. (and sb.) [UNDER-¹ 4 a.]
1. Driven by water passing below.

Undershrub. [UNDER-¹ 5 d.] A small or
low-growing shrub; spec. in Bot., a plant having
a shrubby base.

U·ndershut, ppl. a. [UNDER-¹ 4 a, 10 a.]
†1. Imperfectly shut. Obs.
2. Rare.

Under·skin·ker. Obs. [UNDER-¹ 6 a.]
(Skinker 1.)

Under·skirt. [UNDER-¹ 5 c.] A skirt
worn under another, a petticoat; spec. a foundation over which drapery or an overskirt is disposed.

Under·sleeve. [UNDER-¹ 5 c.] A sleeve,
esp. one of light material, worn below another.

Under·soil. [UNDER-¹ 5 b.] Subsoil.

Under·song. [UNDER-¹ 5 b.]
1. A burden or accompaniment to a song.
2. An undertone or subdued song or strain, esp.

Under·sorcerer.
Under·sort. [UNDER-² 1.]
Under·soul. [UNDER-¹ 6 b.]
U·nderspar. [UNDER-¹ 10 a.]
U·nderspend. [UNDER-¹ 10 a.]

Understairs. [UNDER-¹ 10 a.]

U·nderstand, sb. Obs. rare. [f. the vb.]
Understand, v. Forms: (see STAND v.)

UNDERSTAND. 147 UNDERSTAND. 148 UNDERSTANDING.

Understa·ndable, a. Also 5 understand-
able. [UNDERSTAND v. + -ABLE.]

Understa·nder. [f. as prec. + -ER.]
One who understands.

Understa·nding, vbl. sb. [-ING¹.]

| UNDERSTANDING. | 149 | UNDERSTREW. | UNDERSTRIFE. | 150 | UNDERTAKE. |

The following represents a page from the Oxford English Dictionary with entries for words beginning with "under-". The text is extremely dense and set in very small type across multiple columns.

Headword entries visible include:

Understanding.

†**3.** Signification, meaning, sense. *Obs.*

†**b.** Reference or application (*to something*). *Obs.*

4. Intelligence, information. *Obs.*

5. Comprehension of something. *Obs.*

6. A good (or right) understanding, amicable or friendly relations (between persons).

b. A particular arrangement or agreement of an informal but more or less explicit nature.

Understanding-ly, *adv.* In a comprehending or intelligent manner; with understanding.

Understate, *v.* [UNDER-¹ 10 a.] *trans.* To state below what is correct or warrantable. Also *intr.*

Understatement. [UNDER-¹ 10 b.]

Understating, *vbl. sb.*

Understep, *v.*

Understrapper. [f. UNDER-¹ 16 a + STRAP *v.*]

Understra'pping, *sb.*

Understrew, *v.* [UNDER-¹ 4 a.] *trans.* To strew or spread beneath; *fig.* to cast under foot.

Under-steward. *Obs.*

†**Understri'pe**, *v.* *Obs.*—¹ [UNDER-¹ 4 a: see STRIPE.] *trans.* To prop up, support.

Understrike, *v.* [UNDER-¹ 10 a: cf. next.] *Obs.*

Understri'ke, *sb.* Also **under-stroke.**

Understrife, *sb.* [UNDER-¹ 5 c.]

Understrike, *v.*

Understudy, *sb.* [f. next.] An actor or actress who studies a superior performer's part in order to be able to take it if required; also, the study of a part for this purpose. Also *transf.*

Understudy, *v.* [UNDER-¹ 7.]

Understumble, *v.* *collog.* [Alteration of UNDERSTAND *v.*, after STUMBLE *v.*, CL CUMBER-UNDERSTAND *v.*]

Undersubscri'be, *v.* [UNDER-¹ 4 a.]

Undersu'ction, *sb.*

Under-surface. [UNDER-¹ 6 a.]

Under-take, *v.*

Understanding.

Headword entries on lower half include:

†**Underta'kement.** An undertaking. *Obs.*

†**Underta'keant.** *Obs. rare.*

Undertaker. (ʌndəteɪkər.) [f. UNDERTAKE *v.*]

1. One who aids or assists.

2. Taken in hand; enterprised.

Undertaking, *vbl. sb.* [UNDER-¹ -ING¹.]

Undertaking, *ppl. a.* Now *rare.*

Under-tenant. [UNDER-¹ 6 a.]

Undertenure.

†**Underthew**, *v.* [UNDER-¹ 7: cf. THEW.]

b. [UNDER-¹ 10 a.]

Under-thought. (UNDER-¹.)

Underthrow, *v.*

†**Underthraw**, *v.* *Obs.*

Underthra'st, *ppl. a.* [UNDER-¹ 10 c.]

†**Underto'ne**, *v.*

Undertone, *sb.* [UNDER-¹ 5 c.] A subdued tone.

Under-took, past tense of UNDERTAKE.

Under-tow. [UNDER-¹ 5 c.]

Under-trade, *v.* [UNDER-¹ 10 a.]

†**Under-traverse.** [UNDER-¹ 5 b: see TRAVERSE *sb.* 16 B.]

Undertread, *v.* [UNDER-¹ 4 c, CL MDE.]

Undertri'st, *ppl. a.*

Undertriple, *v.*

Supplement, p. 3873; Corrigenda, p. 4092; Spurious words, p. 4093; Books quoted, p. 4094

Undertrodden. Downtrodden.

Undertu·rn, v. [Underturn v.]

Undertu·rn. [Under-1 4, 7.]

Undertwig.

Undervalu·e, v. [Under-1 10 a.]

Undervaluation. [Under-1 10 b.]

Undervalue, sb. [Under-1 10 b.]

Undervaluer.

Underva·luing, vbl. sb.

Underva·luing, ppl. a.

Undervicar.

Underview. [Under-1 a.]

Underviewer.

Under·vived.

Undervoice.

Underwalk, v.

Underwarden. [Under-1 a.]

Underware. [Under-1 4.]

Underwarm, sb.

Underwarm, v.

Underwarming, vbl. sb.

Underwave.

Underwear. [Under-1 5 a.]

Underwear, v.

Underwei·ghing, vbl. sb.

Underweight, sb. [Under-1 10 b.]

Underweight, v.

Underwind, v. [Under-1 5 b and Under-2.]

Underwing. [Under-1 5 b and Under-2.]

Underwit. [Under-1 6 a.]

Underwi·tch.

Underwood. [Under-1 5 d. Cf. MSw. undervid.]

Under-witted, ppl. a. [Under-1 10 a.]

Underwork, sb.

Underwork, v. [Under-1 8 a, 8 b, 10 a.]

Underworker. [Under-1 6 a.]

Underworking, vbl. sb. [Under-1 9 a.]

Underworking, ppl. a. [Under-1 8 a.]

Underworkman. [Under-1 6 a.]

Underworld. [Under-1 5 b, c. Cf. ON. undorverold, Ù, underworld.]

Underwork.

Underwrite, v.1 [Under-1 8 a.]

Underwrite, v.1 [Under-1 8 a.]

Underwriter.

Underwriting, vbl. sb.

Underyoke, v. [Under-1 2.]

Undescribed, ppl. a. [Un-1 8.]

Undescriptive, a. [Un-1 7.]

Undescrye, v.

Undesecrated.

Undesert, sb. [Un-1 12 and 5 b.]

Undeserve, v. [Un-1 4.]

Undeserved, ppl. a. [Un-1 8 d.]

Undeserver. [Un-1 8.]

Undeserving, ppl. a. [Un-1 10.]

Undeservingly, adv. [Un-1 11.]

Undeservedness. [Un-1 12.]

Undesign, v.

Undesigned, ppl. a. [Un-1 8.]

Undesignedness. [f. Undesigned ppl. a.]

Undesigning, ppl. a.

Undesirable, a. [Un-1 7.]

Undesire, v.

Undesired, ppl. a.

Undesirous, a.

Undesiring, ppl. a.

Undesirably, adv.

Undesperate, a.

Undespairing, ppl. a.

Undocile, a. ... Not docile; unteachable.

Undo, v. ¹ [Un- 5.] *trans.* To take (a ship) out of a dock; sometimes *spec.*, to launch.

Undocked, *ppl. a.* ... Not docked; ... of animals, with the tail not docked.

Undoer. ... One who or that which undoes. ... A destroyer, wrecker, ruiner. ... A seducer.

Undoing, *vbl. sb.* ... The action of opening, unfastening, taking apart, loosening, etc. ... The action of bringing to nought; destroying, or ruining; the fact of being so dealt with; the state of being undone; also (with *a*), an instance of this.

Undo'er, *rare*⁻¹. ... One who does not act or perform.

Undoing, *ppl. a.* [f. UNDO v.] Ruinous, destructive.

Undo'ne, *ppl. a.* ¹ [Un-¹ 8 c.] Brought to decay or ruin; ruined, destroyed. ... Undressed; in undone state. ... Unfastened, untied, detached, etc. ... About the nature of which no doubt is entertained.

Undo'ne, *ppl. a.* ² [Un-¹ 8.] Not done; unaccomplished, uneffected. ... Not done away, not removed. ... Not yet done.

Undrawn, *ppl. a.* ... Not drawn.

Undress, **undress**, *sb.* [Un-¹ 12.] Partial or incomplete dress; dress of a kind not ordinarily worn in public; dishabille. Also (*esp.* of men), informal or ordinary dress, as distinct from that worn on ceremonial or special occasions.

Undress, *v.* [Un-² 2.] To divest of clothing.

Undressed, *ppl. a.* [Un-¹ 8, 8 c.] Not dressed by trimming, putting in order, or preparing in some way.

Undressing, *vbl. sb.* [Un-² 2.] The action of taking off (one's own or another's) clothes.

Undulate, *v.* [ad. L. type *undulāt-*, f. *undula* little wave.] To move or cause to move in waves or with a wave-like motion.

Undulate, *ppl. a.* and *a.* [ad. L. *undulātus*, f. *undula*.] Wavy; moving after the manner of waves; rising and falling like waves. ... Furnished with wave-like markings.

Undulate

Undulation

Undulatory

Undulated, **Undulate** ppl. a.

Undulately, adv.

Undulating ppl. a.

Unduly, adv.

Undulationist

Undulature

Unduloid

Undulous

Unduteous

Unduthful

Undutiful

Undutifully, adv.

Undying

Undumpish

Undurable

Undure, v.

Undust, v.

Undusted ppl. a.

Unearth, v.

Unearthed ppl. a.

Unearthly

Unease, sb.

Uneaseful

Uneasily, adv.

Uneasiness

Uneasy, a.

Uneat, v.

Uneatable

Uneatableness

Uneaten ppl. a.

Uneath, a.

Uneath, adv.

Unebriate

Uneclipsed ppl. a.

Unedible

Unedifying, a.

Uneducated ppl. a.

Unelated

Uneffaced ppl. a.

Uneffaceable

Uneffaced, ppl. a. [Un-1 8.]

Uneffected, ppl. a. [Un-1 8.]

Uneffectible, a. [Un-1 7.]

Uneffectual, a. [Un-1 7 and 5 b.]

Uneffectuous, a. [Common 1 1550–1660.]

Uneffeminate, a. [Un-1 7 and 5 b.]

Unegal, a. Obs. [Un-1 7 b 1 and 5. cf. WF. inégal, inegal, and UNEQUAL a.] Unequal.

Unegally adv. [Un-1 7 and 5 b.]

Uneglected, ppl. a. [Un-1 8.]

Unelaborate, a. (Un-1 7 and 5 b.)

Unelastic, a. [Un-1 7.]

Hence **Unelasticity.** (Webster, 1847.)

Unelated, ppl. a. [Un-1 8.]

Unelbowed, ppl. a. [Un-1 8.]

Unelected, ppl. a. [Un-1 8.]

Unelectrified, ppl. a. [Un-1 8.]

Unelectrify, v. [Un-2 3.]

Unelegant, a. Obs. [Un-1 7.]

Unelegantly adv. Obs.

Unelemented, ppl. a. [Un-1 8.]

Unelevated, ppl. a. [Un-1 8.]

Uneligible, a. Obs. [Un-1 7.]

Uneloquent, a. (Un-1 7.)

Uneloquently adv. (Un-1 1; cf. prec.)

Unembarrassed, ppl. a. [Un-1 8.]

Unembarrassedly, adv. (Un-1 11; cf. prec.)

Unembattled, ppl. a. [Un-1 8.]

Unembellished, ppl. a. [Un-1 8.]

Unembodied, ppl. a. [Un-1 8.]

Unembowelled, vbl. sb. [Un-1 8.]

Unembroidered, ppl. a. [Un-1 8.]

Unemendable, a. [Un-1 7.]

Unemphatic, a. and attrib. [Un-1 7.]

Unemphatical, a. (Worcester, 1846.)

Unemphatically, adv. (Un-1 11.)

Unemployable, a. and sb. Also 7 b.

Unemployed, ppl. a. and sb. Also 7 unim-. [Un-1 8.]

Unemployment, sb. (Un-1 7.)

Unempowered, ppl. a. [Un-1 8.]

Unemptiable, a. [Un-1 7.]

Unemptied, ppl. a. [Un-1 8.]

Unemulous, a. [Un-1 7.]

Unenamelled, ppl. a. [Un-1 8.]

Unenchanted, ppl. a. [Un-1 8.]

Unenclosed, ppl. a. Also 7 unin-. [Un-1 8.]

Unencompassed, ppl. a. [Un-1 8.]

Unencountered, ppl. a. Also 7 unin-. [Un-1 8.]

Unencumbered, ppl. a. Also 8 unin-. [Un-1 8.]

Hence **Unencumberedness.**

Unencumbering, ppl. a. [Un-1 7.]

Unendamaged, ppl. a. [Un-1 8.]

Unendangered, ppl. a. [Un-1 8.]

Unendeared, ppl. a. [Un-1 8.]

Unending, ppl. a. [Un-1 7.] Endless.

Unendowed, ppl. a. [Un-1 8.]

Unendurable, a. (and sb.) Also 7 unin-. [Un-1 7.]

Unendurably, adv.

Unenervated, ppl. a. [Un-1 8.]

Unenforced, ppl. a. Also 7 unin-. [Un-1 8.]

Unenfranchised, ppl. a. [Un-1 8.]

Unengaged, ppl. a. Also 7–9 unin-. [Un-1 8.]

Unenjoyable, a. [Un-1 7.]

Unenjoyed, ppl. a. [Un-1 8.]

Unenjoying, ppl. a. [Un-1 7.]

Unenlarged, ppl. a. [Un-1 8.]

Unenlightened, ppl. a. Also 7 unin-. [Un-1 8.]

Unenslaved, ppl. a. [Un-1 8.]

Unentangle, v. [Un-2 3.]

Unentangled, ppl. a. Also 7–8 unin-. [Un-1 8.]

Unenterprising, ppl. a. [Un-1 7.]

Unentertained, ppl. a. Also 8 unin-. [Un-1 8.]

Unentertaining, ppl. a. [Un-1 7.]

Hence **Unentertainingly** adv.

Unenthralled, ppl. a. Also 7 unin-. [Un-1 8.]

Unentitled, ppl. a. [Un-1 8.]

Unenthusiastic, a. [Un-1 7.]

Unenvied, ppl. a. Also 7 unin-. [Un-1 8.]

Unenviable, a. [Un-1 7.]

Unenvious, a. [Un-1 7.]

Unenvying, ppl. a. [Un-1 7.]

Unepiscopal, a. [Un-1 7.]

Unequable, a. [Un-1 7.]

Unequal, a. and adv. [Un-1 7 and 5 b: cf. the earlier UNEGAL (UNEQUALL) and INEQUAL.]

Unequal, sb. [Un-1 7, 2; cf. next.]

Unequalable, *ppl. a.* (Un-¹ 8.)

Unequalled, *ppl. a.* (Un-¹ 8.)

Unequally, *adv.* [Un-¹ 11: cf. *Unequal a.*]

Unequalness. (Un-¹ 12: cf. *Unequal a.*)

Unequitable, *a. Obs.*

Uneq̄uitably, *adv.*

Unequity. (Un-¹ 12.)

Unequivocal, *a.* (Un-¹ 7 b.)

Unequivocally, *adv.* (Un-¹ 7 b and 5 b.)

Unerrable, *a. Obs.* (Un-¹ 7 b and 5 b.)

Unerrableness. (Un-¹ 8.)

Unerring, *ppl. a.* (Un-¹ 7.)

Unerringly, *adv.*

Unerringness. (Un-¹ 12.)

Unessayed, *ppl. a. Obs.* (Un-¹ 8.)

Unessence, *v.* (Un-² 4.)

Unessential, *a.* and *sb.* (Un-¹ 7 and 5.)

Unessentially, *adv.*

Unestablished, *ppl. a.* (Un-¹ 8 and 5 b.)

Unevangelical, *a.* (Un-¹ 7.)

Uneven, *a.* [OE. *unefen*, *-efn*, *-efne*.]

Uneven, *adv.* [OE. *unefne* (f. *unefen*): see *Uneven a.*]

Unevenly, *adv.* [OE. *unefenlíce*.]

Unevenness.

Uneventful, *a.* (Un-¹ 7.)

Unevitable, *a. Obs.* — INEVITABLE *a.*

Unevolved, *ppl. a.* (Un-¹ 8.)

Unexact, *a.* (Un-¹ 7 and 5 b.) = INEXACT *a.*

Unexaggerated, *ppl. a.* (Un-¹ 8.)

Unexamined, *ppl. a.* (Un-¹ 8.)

Unexampled, *ppl. a.* (Un-¹ 8.)

Unexceptable, *a. Obs.*

Unexcepted, *ppl. a.* (Un-¹ 8.)

Unexcepting, *ppl. a.* (Un-¹ 10.)

Unexceptionable, *a.*

Unexceptionableness. (Un-¹ 12.)

Unexceptionably, *adv.*

Unexceptional, *a.* 1. c.

Unexceptionally, *adv.*

Unexcitable, *a.* (Un-¹ 7 b.)

Unexcited, *ppl. a.* (Un-¹ 8.)

Unexciting, *ppl. a.* (Un-¹ 10.)

Unexclusive, *a.* (Un-¹ 7.)

Unexecuted, *ppl. a.* (Un-¹ 8.)

Unexemplary, *a.* (Un-¹ 7.)

Unexemplified, *ppl. a.* (Un-¹ 8.)

Unexempt, *a.* (Un-¹ 7.)

Unexercisable, *a.* (Un-¹ 7 b.)

Unexercise, *v.* (Un-² 8.)

Unexercised, *ppl. a.* (Un-¹ 8.)

Unexerted, *ppl. a.* (Un-¹ 8 b.)

Unexhausted, *ppl. a.* (Un-¹ 8.)
I. Not emptied or drained of contents.
2. Not used up, expended, or brought to an end.

Unexhaustible, *a.* Also 7 -*able*. (Un-¹ 7, 7 b, 5 b.) = INEXHAUSTIBLE 2.

Unexhausted, *ppl. a.*

Unexistent, *a.* (Un-¹ 7 b.)

Unexisting, *ppl. a.* (Un-¹ 10.)

† **Unexorable**, *a. Obs.* (Un-¹ 7 b and 5 b.) = INEXORABLE 1.

Unexorcised, *ppl. a.* (Un-¹ 8.)

Unexpanded, *ppl. a.* (Un-¹ 8.)

Unexpectable, *a.* (Un-¹ 7 b and 5 b.)

Unexpectant, *a.* (Un-¹ 7.)

Unexpectation, *sb.* (Un-¹ 12 and 5 b.)

Unexpected, *ppl. a.* (Un-¹ 8 and 5 b.)
b. With adjs. or advs.

Unexpectedness. (Un-¹ 12 and 5 b.)

† **Unexpedient**, *a.* (Un-¹ 7 and 5 b.) = INEXPEDIENT 2.

† **Unexpensive**, *a.* (Un-¹ 7 and 5 b.) = INEXPENSIVE 2.

Unexpensive, *a.* (Un-¹ 7 and 5 b.) = INEXPENSIVE 2.

† **Unexperience**, *sb. Obs.* (Un-¹ 12 and 5 b.) = INEXPERIENCE.

Unexperienced, *ppl. a.* (Un-¹ 8 and 5 b.)
1. Not furnished with, or taught by, experience; not skilled or trained in this way.
b. Not known or felt by experience.

Unexperienced. (Un-¹ 8 and 5 b.)

Unexpert, *a. Obs.* (Un-¹ 7 and 5 b.)

Unexpertly, *adv.* (Un-¹ 11.)

Unexplicated, *ppl. a.* (Un-¹ 8.)

Unexplicit, *a.* (Un-¹ 7, 11, 5 b.)

Unexplorable, *a.* (Un-¹ 7 b.)

Unexplored, *ppl. a.* (Un-¹ 8.)

† **Unexpressible**, *a. Obs.* (Un-¹ 7 b and 5 b.)

Unexpugnable, *a. Obs.* (Un-¹ 7 b.)

Unextended, *ppl. a.* (Un-¹ 8 and 5 b.)

Unextinguishable, *a.* (Un-¹ 7 b and 5 b.) = INEXTINGUISHABLE 1.

Unextinguished, *ppl. a.* (Un-¹ 8 and 5 b.)
Not extinguished, quenched, or put out.

Unextirpated, *ppl. a.* (Un-¹ 8.)

Unextraordinary, *a.* (Un-¹ 7.)

† **Unextricable**, *a. Obs.* (Un-¹ 7 b and 5 b.)

Uneyed, *ppl. a.* (Un-¹ 8.)

Unfaded, *ppl. a.* (Un-¹ 8.)

Unfadable, *a.* (Un-¹ 7 b.)

Unfading, *ppl. a.* (Un-¹ 10.)
b. In figurative use.

Unfadingly, *adv.* (Un-¹ 11.)

Unfailable, *a. Obs.* (Un-¹ 7 b.)

Unfailing, *ppl. a.* (and *adv.*) (Un-¹ 10.)
1. Not failing or giving way.
2. Not liable to fail.

Unfailingly, *adv.* (Un-¹ 11.)

Unfair, *a.* (Un-¹ 7.)

Unfairly, *adv.* (Un-¹ 11.)

Unfairness. (Un-¹ 12.)

Unfaith, *sb.* (Un-² 2 and 5 b.)

Unfaithful, *a.* (Un-¹ 7.)

Unfaithfully, *adv.* (Un-¹ 11.)

Unfaithfulness. (Un-¹ 12.)

† **Unfallible**, *a.* (Un-¹ 7 and 5 b.) = INFALLIBLE.

Unfallen, *ppl. a.* (Un-¹ 8.)

Unfamiliar, *a.* (Un-¹ 7.)

Unfamiliarity. (Un-¹ 12.)

Unfamous, *a.* (Un-¹ 7 and 5 b.)

† **Unfanatical**, *a.* (Un-¹ 7 and 5 b.)

Unfancied, ppl. a. (Un-8.)

Unfanciable, a. (Un-7.)

Unfashionable, a. (Un-7.)

Unfashionableness.

Unfashionably, adv.

Unfashioned, ppl. a. (Un-8.)

Unfast, a. (Un-1.)

Unfasten, v. (Un-2 a, b.)

Unfastidious, a. (Un-7.)

Unfathered, a. (Un-1, 2.)

Unfatherly, a. (Un-7.)

Unfathomable, a.

Unfathomableness.

Unfathomably, adv.

Unfathomed, ppl. a. (Un-8.)

Unfatigable, a. (Un-7 b and 5 b.)

Unfatigued, ppl. a. (Un-8.)

Unfatiguing, ppl. a.

Unfavourable, a.

Unfavourableness.

Unfavourably, adv.

Unfavoured, ppl. a. (Un-8.)

Unfavouring, ppl. a.

Unfawning, ppl. a. (Un-8.)

Unfaulty, a. (Un-7.)

Unfeared, ppl. a. (Un-8.)

Unfearful, a. (Un-7.)

Unfearfully, adv.

Unfeasible, a.

Unfeasibleness.

Unfeasted, ppl. a. (Un-8.)

Unfeastly, a. (Un-7.)

Unfeather, v. (Un-4 and 7.)

Unfeathered, ppl. a. (Un-8.)

Unfed, ppl. a. (Un-8.)

Unfederal, a. (Un-7.)

Unfee'd, ppl. a. (Un-8.)

Unfeeble, v. (Un-2.)

Unfeeling, ppl. a. (Un-1, 8.)

Unfeelingly, adv.

Unfeelingness.

Unfeignable, a.

Unfeigned, ppl. a. (and adv.)

Unfeignedly, adv. (Un-1.)

Unfeignedness.

Unfeigning, ppl. a.

Unfelicitous, a.

Unfeigningly, adv.

Unfeirie, a.

Unfele, a.

Unfeline, a. (Un-7.)

Unfellable, a. (Un-7.)

Unfellowed, ppl. a. (Un-8.)

Unfelt, ppl. a. (Un-8.)

Unfeltered, ppl. a.

Unfeminine, a. (Un-7.)

Unfemininely, adv.

Unfence, v. (Un-3, 4.)

Unfenced, ppl. a. (Un-8.)

Unfermented, ppl. a. (Un-8.)

Unfertile, a. (Un-7.)

Unfestival, a. (Un-7.)

Unfettered, ppl. a.

Unfight, v. (Un-3 cf. 5 w.)

Unfighting, ppl. a. [Un- 10.]

Unfigured (ppl. a.) [Un- 8 and 9.]

Unfiled, ppl. a. Obs. exc. dial. [Un- 8 and 9; File 2 b.]

Unfiled, ppl. a. [Un- 8 a; File 1.]

Unfilial, a.

Unfilled, ppl. a.

Unfiltered, ppl. a.

Unfine, a.

Unfined, ppl. a.

Unfingered, ppl. a.

Unfinished, ppl. a. [Un- 8.]

Unfired, ppl. a.

Unfit, a. and sb.

Unfit, v. [Un- 7 and 6.]

Unfit, ppl. a. [Un- 8.]

Unfitly, adv.

Unfitness.

Unfitted, ppl. a. [Un- 8.]

Unfitting, ppl. a.

Unfittingly, adv.

Unfix, v. [Un- 2.]

Unfixed, ppl. a.

Unflatteringly adv.

Unfleshed, ppl. a.

Unfledged, ppl. a.

Unfleshed, v.

Unfledge, v. [Un- 4.]

Unflinching, ppl. a.

Unflinchingly, adv.

Unfold, v. [Un- 5 and 2.]

Unfolded, ppl. a.

Unfolder.

Unfolding, ppl. a.

Unfoldment.

Unfollowed, ppl. a.

Unfool, v.

Unfoolish, a.

Unforbidden, ppl. a.

Unforcible, a.

Unforced, ppl. a.

Unforeseeable, a.

Unget-at-able, a.

Ungettable, a.

Ungho·stly, a.

Unghostly, adv. rare⁻¹.

Ungird'ed, ppl. a.

Ungird, v.

Ungi·rded, ppl. a.

Ungi·rdled, ppl. a.

Ungi·rt, ppl. a.

Ungi·rth, v.

Ungla·d, a.

Ungi·rthed, ppl. a.

Ungi·rt, ppl. a.

Ungi·ve, v.

Ungi·ven, ppl. a.

Ungla·d, a.

Ungla·ded, ppl. a.

Ungla·dness.

Ungla·ciated, ppl. a.

Ungla·zed, ppl. a.

U·ngle.

Unglo·ried, ppl. a.

Ungla·ddened, ppl. a.

Ungla·dly, adv.

Ungla·ndly, a.

Ungla·ss, v.

Ungla·zed, ppl. a.

**Unglo·ri
ous**, a.

Unglo·riously, adv.

Unglo·ve, v.

Unglo·ved, ppl. a.

Unglu·e, v.

Unglu·ed, ppl. a.

Unglu·ing, vbl. sb.

Ungo·d, v.

Ungo·ddess.

Ungo·dlike, a.

Ungo·dlily, adv.

Ungo·dliness.

Ungo·dly, a.

Ungo·dly, adv.

Ungo·dward, adv.

Ungo·od, a.

Ungo·re, v.

Ungo·red, ppl. a.

Ungo·rged, ppl. a.

Ungo·rgeous, a.

Ungo·spel-like, a.

Ungo·t, v.

Ungo·tten, ppl. a.

Ungo·ut, v.

Ungo·verned, ppl. a.

Ungo·vernable, a.

Ungo·vernableness.

Ungo·vernably, adv.

Ungo·wn, v.

Ungo·wned, ppl. a.

Ungra·ced, ppl. a.

Ungra·ceful, a.

Ungra·cefully, adv.

Ungra·cefulness.

Ungra·cious, a.

Ungra·ciously, adv.

Ungra·ciousness.

Ungra·dated, ppl. a.

Ungra·ded, ppl. a.

Ungra·duated, ppl. a.

Ungra·ft, v.

Ungra·fted, ppl. a.

Ungra·in, v.

Ungra·ined, ppl. a.

Ungra·ith, v.

Ungrai·thed, ppl. a. Obs. exc. dial.

Ungra·ithly, adv. Obs.

Ungra·mmar, sb.

Ungramma·tic, a.

Ungramma·tical, a.

Ungramma·tically, adv.

Ungra·nt, v.

Ungra·ntable, a.

Ungra·pple, v.

Ungra·sp, v.

Ungra·spable, a.

Ungra·teful, a.

Ungra·tefully, adv.

Ungra·tefulness.

Ungra·tified, ppl. a.

Ungra·tifying, ppl. a.

Ungra·ve, v.

Ungra·vely, adv.

Ungra·zed, ppl. a.

Ungra·ze, v.

Un-Gree·k, sb. and a.

Ungree·dy, a.

Ungree·n, a.

Ungree·nable, a.

Ungree·ted, ppl. a.

Ungree·nedly, adv.

Ungree·nedness.

Ungre·tli, adv.

Ungrie·ved, ppl. a.

Ungrie·ving, ppl. a.

Ungroo·ved, ppl. a.

Ungro·tch, v.

Ungru·dging, ppl. a.

Ungru·dgingly, adv.

Ungru·dged, ppl. a.

Ungrou·nd, ppl. a.

Ungrou·nded, ppl. a.

Ungrou·ndedly, adv.

Ungrou·ndedness.

Ungrou·nable, a.

Ungru·ding.

Ungro·wn, ppl. a.

Ungu·al, a. and sb.

Ungu·ent, sb.

Unguenta·rian, rare.

Unguenta·rium.

Unguenta·ry, sb. and a.

Ungue·ntous, a. rare.

Unguentous, a.

Unguicula, sb.

Unguicular, a.

Unguiculate, ppl. a.

Unguiferous, a.

Unguiform, a.

Unguiligrade, ppl. a.

Ungui·nal, a.

Ungui·nous, a.

Unguis, sb.

Ungula, sb.

Ungulate, a. and sb.

Ungulite.

Ungua·rdedly, adv.

Ungua·rdedness.

Ungua·rd, v.

Ungua·rded, ppl. a.

Ungui·lty, a.

Ungui·ltily, adv.

Ungui·ded, ppl. a.

Ungui·dable, a.

Ungui·le, sb. and v.

Ungui·led, ppl. a.

Ungui·ltiness.

Unha·bit, v.

Unha·bitable, a.

Unha·bited, ppl. a. and sb.

Unhabituated, ppl. a.

Unha·ckled, ppl. a.

Unha·ckneyed, ppl. a. [Un-¹ 8.]

Unhai·led, ppl. a. [Un-¹ 8.]

Unhail, a. See UNHALE a.

Unhalainim, tho. See var. Un-² 4.

Unha·llow, v. [Un-² 4.]

Unha·llowed, ppl. a. [O.E. unhálgod (and ungehálgod), f. Un-¹ 8 + HALLOWED ppl. a.]

Unhand, v. [Un-² 4 b.]

Unha·ncuffed, ppl. a. (Arb.)

Unha·ndsome, a.

Unha·ndsomely, adv. [Un-¹ 11.]

Unha·ndsomeness.

Unha·ndy, a. [Un-¹ 7.]

Unha·ndiness.

Unha·ndled, ppl. a. [Un-¹ 8.]

Unha·ng, v. [Un-² 4.]

Unha·nging, vbl. sb. [Un-² 5.]

Unha·ping, vbl. sb.

Unha·p, sb. [Un-¹ 12. Cf. ON.]

Unha·ppily, adv.

Unha·ppiness.

Unha·ppy, a. [Un-¹ 7.]

Unha·rbour, v. [Un-² 4.]

Unha·rboured, ppl. a. [Un-¹ 8.]

Unhard, a. Obs.

Unha·rden, v. [Un-² 4 b.]

Unha·rdened, ppl. a. [Un-¹ 8.]

Unha·rdiness.

Unha·rdy, a. [Un-¹ 7.]

Unha·rdily, adv.

Unha·rm, v.

Unharmo·nious, a. [Un-¹ 7.]

Unharmo·niously, adv.

Unha·rmed, ppl. a. [Un-¹ 8.]

Unha·rness, v.

Unha·rnessed, ppl. a. [Un-¹ 8.]

Unha·rrowed, ppl. a.

Unha·sp, v. [Un-² 4 b.]

Unha·tched, ppl. a.

Unha·tted, ppl. a.

Unha·ting, ppl. a.

Unhaunted, ppl. a.

Unha·ving, vbl. sb. [Un-¹ 12.]

Unhazarded, ppl. a. [Un-1 8.]

Unhazardous, a. [Un-1 7.]

Unhead, v. [Un-2 5.]
1. *trans.* To behead.
2. To deprive or divest of a head, top, or end.

Unheaded, a. [Un-1 9.] Destitute of a head, in various senses.

†**Unheal.** [OE. *unhǣlu*, -o, -o OHG. *unheili*, -heilī fem. Cf. HEAL sb.] Want of health or soundness; infirmity, trouble, misfortune.

Unheal, var. UNHELE v.

Unhealable, a. [Un-1 7 b.] Incapable of being healed; incurable.

Unhealed, ppl. a. [Un-1 8 b.]

Unhealful, a. [Un-1 8.] Cf. NF. *unhelful*, MHG. *ungeheil*, -heilf fem. Cf. MDu. (rare) and Du. *onheil*, MLG. *unheil*, OHG. *unhail*, *unheil* (also MHG., G.), Goth. *unhails* neut.] Want of health or soundness; infirmity, trouble, misfortune.

Unheal, var. UNHELE v.

Unhealsome, a. Now rare. [Un-1 7.]
The spelling with *a* is erron. 1575-6 due to the Dutch origin of the translations (after Du. *unsin*).

Unhealthful, a. [Un-1 7.]
1. Unhealthy; diseased, morbid. Also *absol.*
2. Of places, climate, etc.: Prejudicial or hurtful to health; insalubrious; unwholesome.

Unhealthfulness.

Unhealthsome, a. [Un-2 7.]

Unhealthy, a. [Un-1 7.]
1. Of persons, etc.: Not possessed of good health; weak or sickly in health. b. *Path.* Not in a sound or healthy condition; diseased, morbid. Also *absol.*
2. Not caused or apprehended by the sense of hearing; not heard.
3. Not heard of; unknown, new, strange.
4. Not listened to.
5. Of persons: Not heard in self-defence or entreaty; not listened to.
6. More usually *with of.*

Unhearsed, ppl. a. [Un-1 8.]

Unheart, v. [Un-2 5.]

Unhearted, ppl. a.

Unhearty, a.

Unheatable, a.

Unheated, ppl. a.

Unheaven, v. [Un-2 5.]

Unheavenly, a.

Unheavy, a.

Unhedged, ppl. a. [Un-1 8 & 9.]

Unheed, v.

Unheeded, ppl. a.

Unheedful, a. [Un-1 7.] Heedless.

Unheedily, adv. [Un-1 11.] Heedlessly.

Unheeding, ppl. a.
1. Not giving heed; heedless, inattentive.

Unheedy, a.

Unhele, v. [OE. *unhelian*, +*bre*, etc.; cf. OHG. *inthelen*.]

Unhelm, v.
1. *trans.* To divest (oneself or another) of a helmet.

Unhelmed, ppl. a.

Unhelmeted, ppl. a.

Unhelp, v.

Unhelped, ppl. a.

Unhelpful, a. [Un-1 7.]
1. Unable to help; not affording help.

Unhelpfully, adv.

Unhelping, ppl. a.

Unhelped, ppl. a.

Unhelmed, ppl. a. [Un-2 5.]
1. Uncombed, unrestrained.
2. Not furnished with a helm or helmet.

Unhelved, a., sb., and adv. [Un-1 8.]
1. Of persons: Discourteous, impolite; ungentle, rude, rough.

Unhemmed, ppl. a.

Unheralded, ppl. a. [Un-1 8.]

Unherd, v.
1. *trans.* To disperse or separate (cattle, etc.) from a herd.

Unhinged, ppl. a. [f. prec.]
1. Thrown into confusion; unsettled, disordered.

Unhinge, v. [Un-2 5.]
1. *trans.* To take (a door, etc.) off the hinges; to remove the hinges from; to open in this way.
2. To make unhidden; to lay open; to disclose, reveal.

Unhinging, vbl. sb.

Unhingement.

Unhinted, ppl. a. [Un-1 8.]

Unhip, v.

Unhired, ppl. a.

Unhistoric, a. [Un-1 7.]

Unhistorical, a. [Un-1 7.]
1. Not in accordance with history.

Unhistorically, adv.

Unhistoried, ppl. a.

Unhit, v.

Unhitch, v. [Un-2 5.]
1. *trans.* To detach (from a practice).

Unhive, v.

Unhoard, v. [Un-2 5.] *trans.* To take or bring out of a hoard.

Unhoarded, ppl. a.

Unholiness.

Unholily, adv. [Un-1 7.]

Unholy, a. [Un-1 7.]
1. Not holy.

Unholpen, ppl. a. Now *arch.* [Un-1 8 b. Cf. MDu. *ongeholpen*, MLG. *ungeholfen*; Sw. *ohulpen*.] Unhelped (by or by means of a helper).

Unholy, *a.* (and *adv.*) [OE. *unhálig* (f. UN-¹ 7 + *hálig* HOLY *a.*).]

Unholily, *adv.*

Unholiness.

Unholy, *v.*

Unhomogeneous, *a.*

Unhome.

Unhonest, *a.*

Unhonesty.

Unhonoured, *ppl. a.*

Unhood, *v.*

Unhooded, *ppl. a.*

Unhonour, *v.*

Unhonourable, *a.*

Unhonoured, *ppl. a.*

Unhook, *v.*

Unhooker.

Unhooked, *ppl. a.*

Unhoop, *v.*

Unhope.

Unhoped, *ppl. a.*

Unhopeful, *a.*

Unhopefully, *adv.*

Unhoping, *ppl. a.*

Unhorse, *v.*

Unhorsed, *ppl. a.*

Unhospitable, *a.*

Unhospitableness.

Unhospital.

Unhoused, *ppl. a.*

Unhouse, *v.*

Unhousel'd, *ppl. a.*

Unhousewife.

Unhulled, *ppl. a.*

Unhuman, *a.*

Unhumanize, *v.*

Unhumanized, *ppl. a.*

Unhumbled, *ppl. a.*

Unhung, *ppl. a.*

Unhurt, *a.*

Unhurted, *ppl. a.*

Unhurtful, *a.*

Unhurtfulness.

Unhurting, *ppl. a.*

Unhusbanded, *ppl. a.*

Unhusk, *v.*

Unhusked, *ppl. a.*

Uni-, repr. L. *úni-* combining form of *únus* one, single, forming the first element in a number of words with the sense 'having, composed or consisting of, characterized by etc., one thing specified by the second element'.

Uniaxal, *a.*

Uniaxial, *a.*

Unibranchiate, *a.*

Unicameral, *a.*

Unicapsular, *a.*

Unicellular, *a.*

Unicity.

Unicolor, *a.*

Unicolorate, *a.*

Unicolorous, *a.*

Unicolour, *a.*

Unicorn.

Unideal, *a.*

Unidentate, *a.*

Unidimensional, *a.*

Unidirectional, *a.*

Unidle, *a.*

Uniflorous, *a.*

Unifoliate, *a.*

Unifoliolate, *a.*

Uniform, *a.* and *sb.*

Uniformal, *a.*

Uniformity.

Uniformly, *adv.*

Uniformness.

Unify, *v.*

Unigenital, *a.*

Unigeniture.

Unijugate, *a.*

Unilabiate, *a.*

Unilateral, *a.*

Unilinear, *a.*

Unilingual, *a.*

Uniliteral, *a.*

Unilobed, *a.*

Unilobular, *a.*

Unilocular, *a.*

Unimaginable, *a.*

while the other bears the device. 1846 DANA *Zooph.* iv. (1848) 65 A species, which usually has polyps only on one surface,—*unifacial. 1881 CARPENTER *Microscope* (ed. 6) xi. § 419 Their simple *uniflagellate Monad (*Monas Dallingeri*). 1860 MAYNE *Expos. Lex.* 1310 *Uniflorus*, Bot., having or bearing one flower: *uniflorate. 1845–50 MRS. LINCOLN *Lect. Bot.* App. 27 Pl. VII, Scape naked, *uni-flowered. Flower drooping, spathaceous. 1849 CRAIG s.v., *Unifoliate. 1881 *Jrnl. Linn. Soc.* XVIII. 291 These apparently unifoliate stems are long petioles. 1866 *Treas. Bot.* 1191/2 *Unifoliate*, **Unifoliolate*, when a compound leaf consists of one leaflet only; as in the orange-tree. 1872 OLIVER *Elem. Bot.* II. 130 Common Barberry,..with fascicled unifoliolate leaves. 1875 BENNETT & DYER tr. *Sachs' Bot.* 823 As in Duchesne's unifoliolate Strawberry. 1891 *Geol. Jrnl.* XLVII. 6 The structure of the zoœcia and of the dorsal surface is the same as in those with shorter nodes, so that we seem to have a series from the *uniglobular. 1887 W. PHILLIPS *Brit. Discomycetes* 13 Sporidia elliptic, obtuse, *uniguttulate. 1849 BALFOUR *Man. Bot.* 79 When a pinnate leaf has one pair of leaflets, it is **unijugate*. 1861 BENTLEY *Man. Bot.* 168 The leaflets..are arranged along the sides of the rachis or common petiole in pairs, and according to their number, the leaf is said to be unijugate or one-paired,.. bijugate, etc. 1875 BENNETT & DYER tr. *Sachs' Bot.* 315 A vein..is formed from the base towards the apex, dividing the *unilamellar lamina into right and left halves. 1876 VAN DUYN tr. *Wagner's Gen. Pathol.* 466 In epithelial regeneration with *unilaminar epithelium. 1851 SYLVESTER in *Lond.* etc. *Phil. Mag.* Feb. 128 Accordingly this may be termed *unilinear-intersection contact, or more briefly, unilinear contact. 1870 ROLLESTON *Anim. Life* 29 Both the liver and the pulmonary organs [of the common ringed snake] are *unilobar, the left lung being merely represented by a rudimentary structure. 1839–47 *Todd's Cycl. Anat.* III. 310/1 In the Potoroo the left lung is *unilobate. 1851 G. F. RICHARDSON *Geol.* 286 In the strata anterior to the lias, almost all the fishes had heterocercal or *unilobed tails. 1897 *Allbutt's Syst. Med.* IV. 170 In a less common variety [of cirrhosis of the liver] a finer network of new fibrous tissue tends to surround individual lobules (*unilobular). 1859 *Todd's Cycl. Anat.* V. [134]/1 The germinal vesicle is *unimacular in general in the small-yolked ova. 1802–12 BENTHAM *Ration. Judic. Evid.* (1827) III. 438 Constitutive of so many modifications or species of unoriginal evidence, we have *unimedial, bimedial, trimedial and so forth: in a word, multimedial evidence. 1865 BRANDE & COX *Dict. Sci.*, etc. II. 378/1 The determinant formed from the coefficients.. is called the modulus of transformation, and when D is equal to unity the transformations are said to be **unimodular*. 1816 T. L. PEACOCK *Headlong Hall* ix, These thousand images, indeed, were but one; and yet the one was a thousand, a sort of *uni-multiplex phantasma. 1835 KIRBY *Hab. & Inst. Anim.* I. viii. 237 The second [order of molluscans] is *Unimuscular, having only one such [attaching] muscle with one impression. 1875 BLAKE *Zool.* 241 If there be but one muscular impression on a valve, then it belongs to monomyary or unimuscular bivalve. 1866 *Treas. Bot.* 1191/2 **Uninervate*,..one-ribbed. 1891 *Nature* XLIII. 454/1 The linear, *uninerved leaves characteristic of the..genus *Asterophyllites*. 1904 *Brit. Med. Jrnl.* 17 Dec. 1644 A chapter is devoted to this subject [i.e. polysomatous terata] under the subheadings of *uniovular twins. 1857 A. GRAY *First Less. Bot.* (1866) 235 **Uniovulate*, having only one ovule. 1845 *Encycl. Metrop.* XXV. 2 This genus [Squilla] belongs to the *Unipeltate family of the Stomapodous order. 1887 SOLLAS in *Encycl. Brit.* XXII. 416/2 Monaxon *Uniradiate Type (stylus).—By the suppression of one of the rays of an oxea, an acuate spicule or stylus results. 1828–32 WEBSTER (citing *Encyc.*), **Uniradiated*, having one ray. 1888 ROLLESTON & JACKSON *Anim. Life* 532 The first antenna is primitively *uniramose. 1890 *Microsc. Sci.* XXX. 100 Six pairs of (thoracic) appendages.., of which the first are long, slender, and uniramose. 1877 HUXLEY *Anat. Inv. Anim.* vi. 283 Entirely destitute of appendages, except a shorter anterior, *uniramous..pair of oar-like organs. 1866 *Treas. Bot.* 1192/1 **Uniseptate*, having but one septum or partition. 1875 COOKE *Fungi* 40 In other..species they [i.e. spores] are uniseptate. 1856 *Putnam's Mag.* Oct. 390/2 Besides, in England a bar-maid was highly respectable. How precious must she be in this *uni-sexed fair! [= California]. 1885 L. OLIPHANT *Sympneumata* 286 The wise and sanguine..infer, both from the suffering and the capacities of present human nature, a future of new order in a *uni-societary world. 1900 *Proc. Zool. Soc.* 20 Feb. 138 Skeleton forming a rather regular reticulum of *unispiculate fibres. 1828 STARK *Elem. Nat. Hist.* II. 168 The Shrimp. Thorax behind, and on each side of the rostrum *unispinose. 1852 DANA *Crust.* I. 414 Emargination uni-spinose. 1819 SAMOUELLE *Entomol. Compend.* 181 Thorax with a gibbous protuberance, *unisulcate above. 1853 URE *Dict. Arts* I. 626 According to this improved plan of working, the wire of communication.. may be considered as a public word road, or an omnitelegraphic way; whereas, in contradistinction, the conductor, as heretofore used, may be considered a private word road, or a *unitelegraphic way. 1889 *Amer. Nat.* XXIII. 597 Microcampana is not the only *unitentacular Medusa found in the prolific waters of our Pacific coast. 1816 R. JAMESON *Char. Min.* (ed. 2) 212 A crystal is named..*Uniternary, when there is one by one row, the other by three rows. 1852 DANA *Crust.* I. 122 Post-medial region with a small tubercle; intestinal *uni-tuberculate. 1856 W. CLARK *Van der Hoeven's Zool.* I. 303 *Gyropus Nitzsch.*—Tarsi *uniunguiculate. 1876 DOUSE *Grimm's Law* App. 206 Our own familiarity with *univocalized consonants.

b. Prefixed to a sb. and forming a compound used attrib., as *uni-direction, -face, -rhyme, -soil*.

1778 [W. H. MARSHALL] *Minutes Agric., Digest* 18 A Unisoil Farm requires fewer Implements than a Polysoil Farm. 1859 E. WILLIAMS in *Cambrian Jrnl.* March 12 Four-lined unirhyme stanzas, of five or six syllables in a line. 1888 BOTTONE *Electr. Instr. Making* (ed. 2) 103 The uni-direction current machine. 1897 W. C. HAZLITT *Suppl. Coinage Europ. Continent* 17 A silver uniface bracteate of Otho I. 1900 *Engineering Mag.* XIX. 740 In some instances the engines are only uni-direction.

2. Forming sbs., as **Unia·xifer**. **U·nicell** *Bot.*, a unicellular plant (Jackson *Gloss. Bot. Terms*, 1900). **Unipe·ltate** (see quot.). **Unisty·list** [L. *stylus*] (see quot.). †**U·nitrine** [L. *trīn-us*], a unity in trinity. *Obs.* **Unitri·nity**, unity in trinity. **U·nitrope** (see quot.).

1869 *Student* II. 12 They [*sc.* polymerous leaves] will be *uniaxifers, biaxifers, etc.; multiaxifers, according as their meriphylls [= the space between two nodes of a leaf] are arranged along a single axis, or an axis ramified two, three, or more times. 1842 BRANDE *Dict. Sci.*, etc. 1275 *Unipeltates, [Cuvier's] *Unipeltata*, the name of a family of Stomapodous Crustaceans, comprehending those in which the carapace is composed of a single shield-like plate. *a* 1849 POE *Marginalia* cxlii, He is as thorough a *unistylist as Cardinal Chigi, who boasted that he wrote with the same pen for half a century. 1605 TIMME *Quersit.* II. ii. 108 It hath pleased the omnipotent Creator to manifest & showe himselfe a *Unitrine or Triune. 1775 ADAIR *Amer. Ind.* 127 Her belief of the *uni-trinity, and tri-unity of the deity. 1910 A. B. BASSET *Treat. Geom. Surfaces* 25 The reciprocal polar of a unode is called a *unitrope.

†**Uniable**, *a.* *Obs.*$^{-1}$ (Meaning obscure.)

a 1450 *Ten Comm. of Love* (MS. Fairfax 16, fol. 185 b), Consider that my conning is disable To write to you the figure vniable.

†**U·nial**, *a.* *Obs.*$^{-1}$ [f. UNI- + -AL. Cf. OF. *uniel, unial* in Godef. *Compl.*] United into one.

1613 SHERLEY *Trav. Persia* 4 Those Countries, limitting vpon the King of Spaines vniall parts.

Uniat, Uniate (yū·niæt, -ēt). [ad. Russ. униятъ *uniyat*, f. унія *uniya* union (spec. the united Greek and Roman Catholic Churches), f. L. *ūni-*, *ūnus* one.] A Russian, Polish, or other member of that part of the Greek Church which, while retaining its own liturgy, acknowledges the supremacy of the Pope and is in communion with the Roman Catholic Church; a United Greek.

1833 R. PINKERTON *Russia* 82 The inroads of the Uniats among the members of the Greek Church. 1863 EDWARDS *Polish Captivity* II. 61 As a Uniate he acknowledges the authority of the Pope. 1883 BERESF. HOPE *Worship & Order* 127 The restoration of the uniates to Eastern communion.

b. *attrib.* or as *adj.* Of, adhering or pertaining to, or denominating the United Greek Church.

1855 *Pict. Chr. Heroism* 37 The Greek-uniat curé of Jansff. 1885 *Ch. Quarterly Rev.* Apr. 162 In Russia, the once powerful Uniat Church has declined. 1905 *Times* 22 Sept. 7 The much persecuted Uniate or Greek Catholic creed.

Uniaxal (yūni,æ·ksăl), *a.* [f. UNI- 1 + AXAL *a.*] = UNIAXIAL *a.* Hence **Unia·xally** *adv.*

1829 *Nat. Philos., Polaris. Light* vii. 24 (L. U. K.), The whole system of rings will appear to be like the uniaxal system. 1866 B. STEWART *Heat* § 43 Crystals that are optically uniaxal. 1881 GLAZEBROOK in *Phil. Trans.* CLXXIII. 595 The Surface of a Uniaxal Crystal.

Uniaxial (yūni,æ·ksiăl), *a.* [f. UNI- 1 + AXIAL *a.*]

1. *Optics* and *Crystall.* Having one optical axis.

1827–8 HERSCHEL in *Encycl. Metrop.* (1845) IV. 520 When the two axes coalesce, or the crystal becomes uniaxial, the lemniscates become circles. *a* 1853 PEREIRA *Polarized Light* (1854) 176 The crystal possesses the singular property of being uniaxial for violet light and biaxial for red. 1888 RUTLEY *Rock-Forming Min.* 37 Uniaxial crystals.

2. *Bot.* and *Zool.* = MONAXIAL *a.*

1879 ROSSITER *Dict. Sci., Uniaxial development*: in all vertebrate animals, some molluscs and annulosa; in some of exogens, endogens, algæ, and fungi.

Uniber, error or mispr. for UMBER *sb.*^{1} 4.

1824 MEYRICK *Ant. Armour* II. 99 The war helmet..shews the intermediate form of the uniber. 1844 JAMES *Agincourt* I. 77 Shields, and pallets and unibers.

†**Unible**, *a.* *Obs. rare.* [ad. med.L. *ūnibilis* (Dief.), f. L. *ūnire* to UNITE. So Sp. and Pr. *unible*, It. *unibile*.] Capable of being united; unitable.

1559 UDALL tr. *Geminus' Anat.* 3/1 A father, by whose grace we haue receaued a nature..vnible to the glorified bodie of his sonne Christ. 1683 BAXTER *Dying Thoughts* 22 Either Souls are partible substances or not. If not partible, how are they unible?

Unic, obs. f. UNIQUE *a.* and *sb.*

†**Unical**, *a.* *Obs. rare.* [f. L. *ūnic-us* UNIQUE *a.* + -AL.] Forming or consisting of one only; alone of its kind, unique.

1598 SYLVESTER *Du Bartas* II. i. II. *Impost.* 651 A body.. differing little from th' One unicall,..the onely-beeing Beeing. 1650 CHARLETON *Paradoxes* Prol. 26 The form or Essence of Verity, is unicall, single, and devoid of all Alterity.

Hence †**Unically** *adv.*, entirely, undividedly.

1689 G. HARVEY *Curing Dis. by Expect.* v. 33 If..your confidence is so unically fixed on the Virtues of Steel.

Unica·meral, *a.* [f. UNI- 1 + CAMERAL *a.*] Having, consisting of, or characterized by one legislative chamber.

1853 F. LIEBER *Civil Liberty & Self-Govt.* xxiv. 242 As a feature of Gallican liberty, must be mentioned here the unicameral system. 1890 *Century Mag.* Feb. 506/1 Georgia, Pennsylvania and New Hampshire abandoned the unicameral system after a short trial of it. 1894 MORLEY in *Daily News* 28 June 7/4 There is very little chance of our being ..what is called unicameral.

Hence **Unica·meralist**, an advocate of a unicameral system. Also **Unica·merist**.

1888 EARL OF PEMBROKE in *Univ. Rev.* I. 101 The ideal of the unicamerists seems to me to be quite out of the region of practical politics. 1893 *Westm. Gaz.* 14 Feb. 1/3 Of course, I, as a Democrat, do not care for the two Chambers, I am a unicameralist.

Unica·psular, *a.* *Bot.* [ad. mod.L. *ūnicapsulār-is* (whence F. *unicapsulaire*): see UNI- and CAPSULAR *a.*] Of a pericarp: Having a single capsule. Of a plant: Characterized by a pericarp of this kind.

Also *Zool.* = MONOCYTTARIAN *a.* (*Cent. Dict.* 1891).

1720 P. BLAIR *Bot. Ess.* ii. 52 Therefore Papaver is only an Unicapsular Plant. 1760 LEE *Botany* I. xv. 38 In respect to external Division, the Pericarpium is either..Unicapsular, ..as in Lychnis [etc.]. 1793 MARTYN *Lang. Bot.* s.v., A Unicapsular pericarp.

U·nicelled, *a.* [UNI- 1.] Unicellular. 1877 LE CONTE *Elem. Geol.* (1879) 154 The beautiful siliceous shells of diatoms (uni-celled plants).

Unicellular (yūni,se·liŭlăɹ), *a.* (and *sb.*). *Biol.* [ad. mod.L. *ūnicellulār-is* (whence also F. *unicellulaire*): see UNI- and CELLULAR *a.*]

1. Composed or consisting of, having, a single cell; said esp. of the organisms belonging to the primary divisions of the animal and vegetable kingdoms.

Also in recent use as *sb.*

1858 CARPENTER *Veg. Phys.* § 35 The minute unicellular plants, known by the name of Diatomaceæ. 1875 DARWIN *Insectiv. Pl.* xiv. 329 All the leaves contained unicellular and other Algæ. 1892 MIVART *Ess. & Crit.* II. 437 The distinction between unicellular and multicellular animals.

2. Characterized by the formation or presence of a single cell or cells.

1863 DANA *Man. Geol.* 747 Plants in passing from the unicellular state by growth lose in power. 1892 J. TAIT *Mind in Matter* (ed. 3) 58 In the animal world colonies are the next approach of unicellular to multicellular organisation.

Unicellula·rity. [a. F. *unicellularité*, or f. prec. + -ITY.] Unicellular condition or formation.

1896 G. W. FIELD tr. *Hertwig's Zool.* 21 The unicellularity of the lowest animals.

Unicist (yū·nisist). [f. L. *ūnic-us* one + -IST.]

1. A believer in the unicity of the Godhead.

1807 COLERIDGE in *Lit. Rem.* (1839) IV. 291 As understood by the modern Unicists. 1832 — *Table-t.* 4 Apr., The schoolmen would perhaps have called you Unicists: but your proper name is Psilanthropists.

2. *Med.* An advocate or adherent of the theory of unicity. Also *attrib.*

1890 BILLINGS *Nat. Med. Dict.* II. 720. 1901 J. EWING in *Jrnl. Exper. Med.* V. 483 Inclined to accept the unicist theory.

Unicity (yūni·siti). [ad. med.L. **ūnicitās* (whence F. *unicité*, It. *unicità*, Sp. *unicidad*), or f. L. *ūnic-us* one, unique: see -ITY.]

1. The fact of being or consisting of one in number or kind; oneness.

1691 J. HOWE *Wks.* (1834) 147/2 The most unquestionable unity or unicity of the Godhead. 1694 R. BURTHOGGE *Reason & Nat. Spirits* 166 Composition is Unity, but simplicity is Unicity. 1817 COLERIDGE '*Blessed are ye that sow*' 55 For Unity or Unition, and indistinguishable Unicity or Oneness, are incompatible terms. 1849 ALFORD *Grk. Testament* I. 608 The καινότης of this commandment consists in its simplicity and (so to speak) unicity. 1880 C. I. BLACK *Proselytes of Ishmael* 301 What our so-called Unitarians teach is..the Unicity of the Godhead.

b. *Med.* The theory that syphilis is caused by only one kind of venereal virus.

1861 BUMSTEAD *Ven. Dis.* 349 Some explanation..of what was called by its discoverer [Ricord] the 'unicity' of syphilis.

2. The fact or quality of being unique; unique nature or character.

1859 *Todd's Cycl. Anat.* V. 106/1 Bernard then goes on to prove, by the method of elimination, the unicity and propriety of this property of the pancreatic secretion. 1887 SAINTSBURY *Hist. Elizab. Lit.* 91 Which..gives The Faerie Queene its unique unicity, if such a conceit may be pardoned.

Unick, obs. f. UNIQUE *a.*

U·nicode. [UNI- 2.] A telegraphic code in which one word or set of letters represents a sentence or phrase; a telegram or message in this.

1886 '*Unicode*': *The Universal Telegraphic Phrase-Book* Pref. p. iii, The 'Unicode' aims at..a low price. *Ibid.* p. v, The 'Unicode' word 'Obumbro'. 1897 *Westm. Gaz.* 20 Jan. 6/3 [He] gave evidence as to sending a unicode to both [persons]. 1899 *Daily News* 23 Dec. 5/3 The dispatch of messages in 'Unicode'.

Unico·lor, *a.* [L.; cf. F. *unicolore*.] Of a single uniform colour. Chiefly *Nat. Hist.*

1781 PENNANT *Hist. Quadrup.* II. 482 Unicolor Shrew of an uniform dusky cinereous color. 1811 SHAW *Gen. Zool.* VIII. 538 Unicolor Lory, *Psittacus unicolor*.

Unico·lorate, *a.* *rare.* [f. L. *ūnicolor* + -ATE^2.] Unicoloured, unicolorous.

1657 TOMLINSON *Renou's Disp.* 302 Its flowers like Pease-bloom, but lesser, unicolorate and purpureous. 1826 KIRBY & SP. *Entomol.* IV. xlvi. 291 Unicolorate (*Unicolor*), when a surface is of one colour. 1837 RICHARDSON *Fauna Bor.-Amer.* IV. 14 Cymindis Unicolor. Unicolorate Cymindis.

Unicolorous (yūnikʌ·lərəs), *a.* Also 7, 9 unicolourous. [f. L. *ūnicolor* + -OUS.] Having only one colour; uniform in colour. Chiefly *Ent.*

1657 TOMLINSON *Renou's Disp.* 197 Two unicolourous juices mixed together. 1843 HUMPHREYS *Brit. Moths* II. 66 The wings rounded, destitute of markings, and unicolorous. 1894 *Naturalist* 226 All unicolorous black, instead of having the typical red elytra.

Unico·lour, *a.* [Cf. UNICOLOR.] = prec.

1860 *Proc. Zool. Soc.* 51 The fur of all parts of the body.. is unicolour, and of a lightish cinnamon-brown.

Unico·loured, *a.* [UNI- 1.] Unicolorous.

1811 PINKERTON *Petral.* II. 121 Others are spotted in infinite variety; and others, though rarely, are unicoloured. 1821 MEYRICK & C. H. SMITH *Costume Orig. Inhab.* 24 The uni-coloured robe of sky-blue. 1890 *Sat. Rev.* 5 Apr. 413/2 The uni-coloured thread that runs throughout my motley history.

Unicorn (yū·nikǫɹn). Forms: 3–7 uni-, 4–6 uny-, 4–7 vni-, vnycorne (6 inny-, ine-; *Sc.* 5 iny-, owni-, 6 wnicorne); 4–5 vny-, 4–6 vni-, 5 unycorn, 5– unicorn (5–6 vnykorn, 6 vnykhorn). [a. AF., OF. (mod.F.) *unicorne* (= Pg. *unicorne*, Pg. and Sp. *unicornio*, It. *unicorno*), or directly ad. their source L. *ūnicorn-*, *ūnicornis* having one horn (also in late Lat. as sb.), f. *ūn-us* UNI- + *cornu* horn. Cf. late L. *ūnicornuus*, med.L. *unicornus*, -(*i*)*um* sbs., from the same source.

The word was corrupted in OF. to *licorne* (the usual form in mod.F.), *lincorne*, etc., It. *liocorno*, Pg. (*a*)*licorne*, etc.]

I. 1. A fabulous and legendary animal usually regarded as having the body of a horse with a single horn projecting from its forehead (cf. 2 *note*); the monoceros of the ancients.

The unicorn has at various times been identified or confused with the rhinoceros, with various species of antelope, or with other animals having a horn (or horns) or horn-like projection from the head. According to Pliny (*Nat. Hist.* VIII. xxi. § 31) it had a body resembling that of a horse, the head of a deer, the feet of an elephant, and the tail of a lion, with one black horn projecting 'two cubits' from the middle of the forehead.

The horn of this animal was reputed to possess medicinal or magical properties, esp. as an antidote to or preventive of poison: see UNICORN'S HORN.

a 1225 *Ancr. R.* 120 Mon wroð is wulf, oðer leun, oðer unicorne. 13.. *K. Alis.* 6710 (Bodl. MS.), Ȝitt þou shalt habbe sex hundreþ Rinoceros..And two hundreþ vnicornes. *c* 1315 SHOREHAM *Poems* v. 113 Of hyre barme hyt was god game, Þer-inne þe vnicorn weks tame Þat er þan was so wylde. 1387 TREVISA *Higden* (Rolls) I. 159 Þere beeþ also ..vnycornes [L. *rhinoceros*], camels, pardes [etc.]. 1423 JAS. I *Kingis Q.* clv, The lufare vnicorne, That voidis venym with his euoure horne. *c* 1511 *1st Eng. Bk. Amer.* (Arb.) p. xxxiii/2 These vnicornes slee many Lyons, and the Lyon sleeth the vnicorne with subtylnes. 1590 SPENSER *F. Q.* II. v. 10 Like as a Lyon, whose imperiall powre A prowd rebellious Vnicorne defies. 1609 DEKKER *Gull's Horn-bk.* ii. 12 The Unicorne, whose horne is worth halfe a City. 1657 TRAPP *Comm. Job* xxxix. 9 This is the..Unicorn... A very fierce and strong creature it is; and now adayes very rare, but anciently more common. 1735 JOHNSON *Lobo's Abyssinia, Descr.* ii. 51 In the Province of Agaus, has been seen the Unicorn, that Beast so much talk'd of, and so little known. 1801 *Monthly Rev.* XXXV. 351 On the probability of the existence of an Unicorn. 1843 DE QUINCEY *Ceylon* Wks. 1859 XII. 8 The whole traditionary character of the unicorn as the antagonist..of the lion. 1895 J. G. MILLAIS *Breath fr. Veldt* 133 Any one who has seen a wild sable antelope galloping cannot fail to be struck by its resemblance to the unicorn.

b. Used in ME. versions of the OT. to render the Vulgate *ūnicornis* or *rhīnocerōs* (Gr. μονόκερως) as translations of Heb. ראם *r'ēm* (also רים *rēym*), and retained in various later versions (but translated by 'wild-ox' in the Revised Bible). See REEM.

a 1300 *E. E. Psalter* xxi. 22 (xxii. 21), Sauf me fra mouth of lioun es, And fra hornes of vnicornes mi mekenes. [Also versions *a* 1340–1611.] 1382 WYCLIF *Numb.* xxiii. 22 Whos strengthe is lijk to an vnycorn. [Also versions 1388–1611.] *c* 1580 SIDNEY *Psalms* XXII. xiii, Show to heare me, By aiding, when fierce Vnicornes come neere me. 1639 SIR W. MURE *Ps.* xxii, Wks. (S.T.S.) II. 89 From the hornes of vnicornes Thine eare (Lord) found I have. 1696 TATE & BRADY *Ps.* xxix. 6 They..leap, like Hinds that bounding go, Or Unicorns in youthful play.

c. In fig. or allusive use.

In quot. 1607 = 'a cuckold'.

1509 BARCLAY *Shyp of Folys* 212 [Let] James of Scotlande.. haue the forwarde, haue ye no disdayne Nor indignation, for neuer kynge was borne, That of ought of warre can shewe the vnycorne. 1592 G. HARVEY *Four Lett.* 52 The only Vnicorne of the Muses. 1607 DEKKER *Northw. Hoe* IV. F j b, Fetherstone..it seemes makes her husband a vnicorne. 1826 GALT *Last of Lairds* vi. 53 Bridle the unicorn o' your impatience.

†d. Horn reputed to be that of the unicorn prepared as an embellishment or ornament. *Obs.*

a 1533 LD. BERNERS *Gold. Bk. M. Aurel.* (1559) Y ij b, It was of wood Libanus, and round about garnished with unicorne. 1599 PEELE *David & Bethsabe* H ij, Shee that in chaines of pearle and vnicorne, Leads at her traine the ancient golden world.

2. A figure, picture, or representation of this animal, esp. in *Her.* either as a charge or more usually as a supporter of the Royal Arms of Great Britain (or Scotland).

Usually depicted heraldically as having the head, neck, and body of a horse, the legs of a deer and the tail of a lion, with a straight and spirally twisted horn growing out of the forehead.

c 1400 *Emaré* 164 The fayr mayden her by-forn Was portrayed an vnykorn, Wyth hys horn so hye. 1488 *Acc. Ld. High Treas. Scot.* I. 85 A couering..browdin with thrissillis and a vnicorne. 1549 in Gage *Hengrave* (1822) 127, iij cuppes with a cover chased, with unicorns on the top. 1610 GUILLIM *Heraldry* VI. vii. 280 Supported by a Lion.. and an Vnicorne Luna, gorged with a Crowne. 1766 in Seton *Law Her. Scotland* (1863) 442 His Majesty's royal coat-of-arms supported on the right side by a unicorn with an imperial crown over the head. 1789 MRS. PIOZZI *Journ. France*, etc. II. 221 The family crest, a unicorn, made in white marble. 1813 *Gentl. Mag.* LXXXIII. 37/2 With supporters (lion and unicorn) of the Royal arms. 1875 W. MCILWRAITH *Guide Wigtownshire* 55 Here is an escutcheon bearing two unicorns and a lion rampant and the crown.

3. *Sc.* The specific designation of one of the pursuivants of the court of the Lyon King of Arms. See PURSUIVANT 1.

1445 *Exchequer Rolls Scot.* V. 204 Quia Unicorn signifer regis illam terram habuit ex concessione regis. 1473–4 *Acc. Ld. High Treas. Scot.* I. 52 Item gevin to Vnicorne herald, ..to his expensis, x li. 1546 *Ibid.* IX. 33 To Petir Thomson, alias Unicorne pursevant. 1636 *Reg. Privy Council Scot.* Ser. II. VI. 605 The deceased George Wast, Unicorn pursuivant. 1662 *Ibid.* Ser. III. I. 259 Leyes..was charged by William Malcolm, Unicorn pursuivant, to compear this day. 1742 NISBET *Syst. Heraldry* II. IV. xvi. 171 As for Pursevants, they are also for most Part locally denominate, Unicorn only excepted. 1863 SETON *Law Her. Scotland* 38 As in the case of the Heralds, the Pursuivants are also six in number, and bear the names of Kintyre, Dingwall, Carrick, Bute, Ormond, and Unicorn.

4. A Scottish gold coin current in the 15th and 16th centuries at the value of 18 shillings Scots; so called from the figure of the unicorn stamped upon its obverse. Also *half unicorn*. Now *Hist.*

1487 *Exchequer Rolls Scot.* IX. 549 In denariis aureis vocatis unicornys. 1500–20 DUNBAR *Poems* lxvi. 78 Vpon the heid of it is hecht Bayth unicornis, and crownis of wecht. 1538 *Aberd. Reg.* XVI. (Jam.), Ane vnicorn gud & sufficient gold. 1845 LINDSAY *Coinage Scot.* 137 The Unicorns generally weigh about fifty-eight grains,..the half Unicorns in proportion. 1887 E. BURNS *Coinage Scotl.* II. 151 The coinages of unicorns that took place under James V.

†b. Used *attrib.* as the designation of a weight, equivalent to about one-eighth of an ounce troy.

1506 *Extr. Aberdeen Reg.* (1844) I. 434 Ane corss of gold, weyand half ane unce, and half ane unicorn weicht. 1560 *St. Giles Charters* (1859) p. xlvii, Foure vnce, ane half, and ane vnicorne weicht of gold.

5. *Astr.* A southern constellation lying between Canis Minor and Canis Major.

This constellation was noted by Hevelius in his *Prodromus Astron.* (1690) pp. 118, 294, under the name of *Monoceros*.

1771 *Encycl. Brit.* I. 487/2 Hevelius's Constellations made out of the unformed Stars [include]..*Monocerus*, The Unicorn. 1868 LOCKYER *Guillemin's Heavens* (ed. 3) 382 The northern half of the Milky Way extends..to the Unicorn at the altitude of and near the belt of Orion.

6. A carriage, coach, etc., drawn by three horses, two abreast and one leader; now usually, a team of three horses so arranged. (Cf. 11 b.)

1785 GROSE *Dict. Vulgar T.*, *Unicorn*, a coach drawn by three horses. 1800 MAR. EDGEWORTH *Belinda* xvi, She drove in her unicorn to Oakly-park. 1866 FREEMAN in *Life & Lett.* (1895) I. 342, I would put on the children's pony..in front of my two, so as to make an unicorn. 1889 *Evening News* 28 Aug 3/2 Their demands of 24*s.* for a single horse, 28*s.* for a pair, and 30*s.* for a 'unicorn'.

transf. 1860 R. F. BURTON *Centr. Afr.* xiii. II. 38 We crossed as usual on a 'unicorn' of negroids, the upper part of the body supported by two men, and the feet resting upon the shoulders of a third. 1887 *Cyclists' Tour. Cl. Gaz.* May 215/1 The unicorn..is made up of a[n]..ordinary bicycle front-wheel coupled to a..sociable.

b. Quasi-*adv.*

1859 *Habits of Gd. Society* v. 200 You will seldom be called upon to drive tandem, unicorn, or four in hand. 1863 MISS BRADDON *Aurora Floyd* v, There were more lofty accomplishments than driving unicorn or shooting..game.

II. †7. The one-horned rhinoceros. *Obs.*

1398 TREVISA *Barth. De P. R.* XIV. ix. (Bodl. MS.), [In] þat londe [*sc.* Ethiopia] beþ..þe rynocerota þat is þe vnicorne, a beste wiþ oon horne. *a* 1700 EVELYN *Diary* 22 Oct. 1684, I went..to see the Rhinoceros, or Unicorn, being the first that I suppose was ever brought into England.

8. As the name of a fish, shell, etc., having a projecting horn or horn-like process, or regarded as resembling the fabulous unicorn in some other respect. Cf. MONOCEROS 2 and 4.

A few examples other than those illustrated here are recorded in American Dicts. from 1891 onwards.

†a. (See quot.) *Obs.*

1668 CHARLETON *Onomast.* 123 *Monoceros Clusii*, the little Vnicorn, or Sawfish.

b. The narwhal or sea-unicorn.

Named also *unicorn-fish, -whale*, and abbrev. UNIE.

1694 *Marten's Voy. Spitzbergen* in *Acc. Sev. Late Voy.* II. 126 The Unicorn is but seldom seen in these parts. 1745 tr. *Egede's Descr. Greenland* 76 Among the different Kinds of Whales, some reckon the Unicorn, as they commonly call him,..but his right Name is Nar-Whale. 1823 W. SCORESBY *Jrnl.* 39 Here we saw a considerable number of 'unicorns' (narwals).

c. A unicorn-shell. (See 11.)

c 1711 PETIVER *Gazophyl.* VI. liii, Grass girdled Indian Unicorn, Cat. 263. A beautiful Shell and rarely met with.

9. *Zool.* A species having one horn.

1822 J. PARKINSON *Outl. Oryctol.* 312 There appear to be three existing species of rhinoceroses:—1. That of India: a unicorn;..—2. That of the Cape: a bicorn.

III. 10. *attrib.* and *Comb.*, as *unicorn bone* (i.e. horn), *horse, -ivory*; *-crested, -like* adjs.

1477 EARL RIVERS (Caxton) *Dictes* D iv, Ther is summe contre that a litil yuory or vnycorne bone is bought for a grete somme of gold. 1838 *Penny Cycl.* XII. 306/1 The ..Onager, figured..with a unicorn-like horn in the midst of its forehead. 1843 *Ibid.* XXVI. 3 Strabo..refers to Unicorn horses with the heads of deer. 1853 R. S. SURTEES *Sponge's Sp. Tour* xlix, The unicorn-crested gates, with tea-caddy looking lodges. 1856 KANE *Arct. Expl.* II. xiv. 141 The natives carried no arms but the long knife and their unicorn-ivory lances.

11. Special combs., chiefly in the names of animals, birds, fishes, plants, etc., which are characterized by a long projecting horn-like process or spine regarded as resembling the horn of the unicorn: **unicorn acanthurus** (see quot. and UNICORN-FISH *c*); **unicorn auk** (see quot.); **unicorn-bird**, the horned screamer, *Palamedea cornuta*; **unicorn file-fish** (see quot.); †**unicorn guard** *Fencing*, a guard in which the sword is advanced well to the front of the fencer; **unicorn hawk** (-**moth**), **hornbill** (see quots.); **unicorn-moth**, the North American moth, *Cœlodasys unicornis*; **unicorn narwhal**, = sense 8 b; **unicorn-plant** *U.S.*, a name for various North American plants, esp. *Martynia proboscidea*, the capsule of which terminates in two horn-like spines; **unicorn-root** *U.S.* (see quots.); **unicorn-shell**, a marine gasteropod having a horn-like lip projecting from the shell, now esp. one belonging to the genus *Monoceros*; **unicorn whale**, = sense 8 b.

1803 SHAW *Gen. Zool.* IV. 374 *Unicorn Acanthurus. *Acanthurus Unicornis.* .. From the front proceeds a strong, conical, horn-shaped process. 1884 COUES *North Amer. Birds* 805 *Ceratorhina monocerata.* *Unicorn Auk. Horn-bill Auk. 1681 GREW *Musæum* I. § iv. ii. 65 The *Unicorne Bird [is]..Horned on his Forehead (with some likeness) as the Unicorne is pictur'd. 1863 BATES *Nat. Amazon* I. 277 The Curicáca..was soon joined by a unicorn bird..; whose harsh screams [etc.]. 1804 SHAW *Gen. Zool.* V. II. 399 *Unicorn File-fish. *Balistes Monoceros*... Immediately over the head..is a very strong..spine of considerable length. 1617 J. SWETNAM *Sch. Sci. Defence* 126 An other very sure and dangerous guard at the Backe-sword, called the *Vnicorne guard, or the fore-hand guard. 1711 WYLDE *Eng. Master Defence* 23 The Medium Unicorn or Center Guard, is made thus. 1832 J. RENNIE *Consp. Butterfl. & M.* 24 The *Unicorn Hawk (*Sphinx Convolvuli*, Linnæus) appears in September. 1834 T. BROWN *Butterflies & Moths* I. 96 Two fine males of the *Sphinx Convolvuli* (Unicorn Hawk-moth). 1811 SHAW *Gen. Zool.* VIII. 11 *Unicorn Hornbill. [*Buceros Monoceros*.]..The casque is prolonged in front into a kind of horn. 1891 *Cent. Dict.* s.v., Larva of *Unicorn-moth. 1813 BINGLEY *Anim. Biog.* (ed. 4) II. 1 The *Unicorn Narwal, or Sea Unicorn. 1796 MORSE *Amer. Geog.* I. 189 *Unicorn [plant] (*Aletris farinosa*). 1845–50 MRS. LINCOLN *Lect. Bot.* II. 110/1 *Helonias diœcia*, scape leafy...Unicorn plant. 1847 DARLINGTON *Amer. Weeds*, etc. (1860) 222 *M. proboscidea*..Long-beaked Martynia. Unicorn Plant. 1891 H. HERMAN *His Angel* 6 Woodbine, unicorn plant, and wild currant surged all about it. 1846 A. WOOD *Class-bk. Bot.* (1850) 559 *Helonias dioica*, Ph. (*Veratrum luteum.* Linn.) *Unicorn Root. 1847 WEBSTER, *Unicorn-root*, a popular name of two plants, viz. *Chamælirium Carolinianum* [= *Helonias dioica*], to which this name was first applied, and *Aletris farinosa*..; both used in medicine. 1891 *Cent. Dict.*, *Unicorn-root*, the blazing star, *Aletris farinosa*. *c* 1711 PETIVER *Gazophyl.* VI. lv, A *Unicorn Shell with Bugle Twirls. *Ibid.* VIII. lxxv, Small Unicorn-shell, with rugged Twirls and Waves between. 1888 *Cassell's Encycl. Dict.*, *Monoceros*,..Unicorn-shell; a genus of prosobranchiate gasteropods..peculiar to the west coast of America. 1668 CHARLETON *Onomast.* 168 *Balæna Monoceros, Vnicornu Marinum*,.. the *Vnicorn Whale. 1694 *Acc. Sev. Late Voy.* p. xix, The Monoceros or Unicorn Whale. 1858 BAIRD *Cycl. Nat. Sci.* 199/1 The.. unicorn whale, *Monodon Monoceros*, has no teeth in the lower jaw.

b. Attrib. in sense 6, as *unicorn carman, fashion, omnibus* (attrib.), *team*.

1856 MORTON *Cycl. Agric.* II. 726 A unicorn team is two abreast and one in front. 1877 'C. BEDE' *Figaro at Hastings* 47 Some [wagonettes] with four horses, some with three (unicorn fashion). 1884 'R. BOLDREWOOD' *Melb. Mem.* i. 14 Frank Liardet is driving his unicorn omnibus team from the lonely beach. 1898 *Westm. Gaz.* 6 Sept. 1/3 A 'unicorn carman'..means 'one who drives three horses'.

†12. Passing into *adj.* Made a unicorn or cuckold (cf. sense 1 c above). *Obs.*$^{-1}$

1603 DEKKER *Wonderfull Yeare* E 4 The vnicorne cobler being ouer head and eares in sleepe.

Unicorn-fish. [Cf. UNICORN 8 b.] The narwhal or sea-unicorn, *Monodon monoceros*.

1688 R. HOLME *Armory* IV. vii. (Roxb.) 324/1 For his Supporters he beareth a vnicorne fish, Argent, the fish or taile part, Azure: Horne, Hoofes, and finns, Or. 1752 J. HILL *Hist. Anim.* 314 Monodon. The Unicorn-fish, or Narwal. 1773 *Gentl. Mag.* XLIII. 220 The Jackulator Fish, the Unicorn Fish, the Trumpet Fish. 1812 J. WALKER *Ess. Nat. Hist.* 327 *Monodon Monoceros.* Linn...Scot. Unicorn Fish. 1860 WRAXALL *Life in Sea* i. 12 The Narwhal, or Unicorn-fish, attains a length of twenty or twenty-five feet.

b. (See quots.)

1876 GOODE *Fishes of Bermudas* 17 The Bahama Unicorn-Fish is *Alutera scripta*. 1900 *Nature* 21 June 182/2 An example of the rare unicorn-fish (*Lophotes cepedianus*) from the Cape of Good Hope.

c. One or other of various fishes belonging to the genus *Acanthurus*. (Webster, 1911.)

Unico·rnic, *a.* *rare.* [f. prec. + -IC.] Resembling, having the form of, a unicorn.

1881 R. BROWN *Unicorn* 14 A unicornic animal frequently appears in archaic art. 1885 — in *Academy* 28 Nov. 363/2 The familiar conventional unicornic representation.

Unico·rnous, *a.* *rare.* [f. L. *ūnicorn-is* (see UNICORN) + -OUS.] Having but one horn.

1646 SIR T. BROWNE *Pseud. Ep.* V. xix. 261 The Rhinoceros, the Indian Asse, and the Unicornous Beetles. [Hence in Blount, Phillips, Bailey, etc.]

Unicorn's horn. Also †**unicorn horn.** [See UNICORN 1.]

1. A horn regarded as or alleged to be obtained from the legendary unicorn, but in reality that of the rhinoceros, narwhal, or other animal, freq. mounted or made into a drinking cup and employed as a preventive of or charm against poison.

α. 1451 *Lincoln Diocese Doc.* (1914) 51 A ryng of vnicorn horne. 1555 *Reg. Gild Co. Chr. York* (1872) 207, I give to Sir Thomas Chaloner, knyghte, my unicorn horne. *c* 1650 *Invent. Goods Chas. I* in Pegge *Curalia* (1806) IV. 122 An unicorn horn.

β. 1549 THOMAS *Hist. Italie* 80 b, Two fayre vnicornes hornes. 1564 BULLEYN *Dial. agst. Pest.* 74 A pece of a Unicornes horne, good against poison. 1603 LODGE *Treat. Plague* Wks. (Hunter. Cl.) IV. 61 The horne of that beast which..the simple sorte [call] vnicornes horne. 1687 *Lond. Gaz.* No. 2227/4 There will be exposed to Sale..considerable quantities of Drugs, Colours, and Unicorns Horns. 1728 CHAMBERS *Cycl.* s.v., What ordinarily passes among us for Unicorn's Horn,..we are assured by Pereyra..to be the Tooth of a large Fish of the Whale Kind. 1838 PRESCOTT *Ferd. & Is.* I. vii. 383 He is said to have kept a reputed unicorn's horn always on his table.

b. Narwhal's horn.

1856 KANE *Arct. Expl.* I. 412 A shaft of unicorn's horn.

†2. The material of this powdered or prepared as a drug and used medicinally, esp. as an antidote against poison. *Obs.*

1590 E. WEBBE *Trav.* (Arb.) 35 Some lewde Gunners ..gaue me poyson in drinke..; his Phisition..gaue me speadely Unicorns horne to drinke. 1631 JORDEN *Nat. Bathes* vii. (1632) 44 This volatill salt. is commonly very Diaphoreticke: & this it is which makes our..supposed Vnicornes horne to be in such esteeme. 1698 *New Descr. Moscovy* 21 Likewise some use the Powder to Antedote Poison, as the Vnicorns horne; this I hold to be the same with the Morse.

3. *Bot.* (See quot.)

1864 *Chambers's Encycl.* VI. 393 The root of *Helonias dioica* is used. as an anthelmintic...The plant..is called Starwort and Blazing Star, also Unicorn's Horn. [Cf. *unicorn-plant, -root* s.v. UNICORN 11.]

‖**Unicum** (yū·nikʌm). [L., neut. sing. of *ūnicus* UNIQUE *a.* So in G. and Du.] A unique example, specimen, or thing.

1885 *Daily Tel.* 14 July 5/3 Some picture, work of art, or old book, which is represented to him as being a 'unicum'. 1892 MRS. J. P. MORGAN tr. *Rubinstein's Conv. on Music* 26 The symphony in G minor (this *unicum* of symphonic-lyric).

Unicursal (yūnikʌ·ɹsăl), *a.* and *sb.* *Math.* [f. UNI- 1 + L. *cursus* course: see -AL.] **a.** *adj.* Having, traversing, or being on one course or path. **b.** *sb.* A unicursal curve.

1866 CAYLEY in *Proc. London Math. Soc.* April, A unicursal curve is nothing else than a curve with a deficiency D = 0. 1871 — *Math. Papers* (1895) VIII. 388 On the Transformation of Unicursal Surfaces. 1873 G. SALMON *Higher Plane Curves* ii. 29 If the coordinates can be expressed as rational functions of a parameter the curve has the maximum number of double points. Curves of this sort are called unicursal curves.

Hence **Unicursa·lity**; **Unicu·rsally** *adv.*

1887 *Amer. Jrnl. Math.* X. 24 In the unicursality-equation a cusp plays the role of an ordinary double-point. 1892 W. W. R. BALL *Math. Recreat.* 124 A figure is described unicursally when the whole of it is traversed in one route.

Unicycle (yū·nisəik'l). *U.S.* [f. UNI- 2 + CYCLE, after *bicycle, tricycle*.] A vehicle or conveyance having only one wheel; esp. a monocycle used by acrobats or for gymnastic displays.

1869 *The Velocipede* (N.Y.) April 76 Hemmings' Unicycle or 'Flying Yankee Velocipede'. 1884 KNIGHT *Dict. Mech.* Suppl. 913/1 *Unicycle*, a one-wheeled vehicle for propulsion by foot-power.

Hence **U·nicyclist**, one who rides a unicycle.

1881 *Sells Bros. Show-Bill*, Celebrated Russian Bicyclists, Unicyclists, and Roller Skaters.

Unide·aed, *a.* Also **unidea'd.** [UN-^{1} 9.] Not furnished with an idea.

1752 JOHNSON in *Boswell* (1904) I. 166 Leaving his social friends, to go and sit with a set of wretched un-idea'd girls. 1822 SCOTT *Peveril* xxvii, A silly scrupulous unidea'd Puritan. 1888 *Jrnl. Educ.* May 242 The un-idea'd vulgarity of the lower middle classes.

Unide·al, *a.* [UN-^{1} 7.]

†1. Of sounds or words: Expressing or conveying no idea. *Obs.*

1751 JOHNSON *Rambler* No. 184 ⁋ 12 However we amuse ourselves with unideal sounds. 1792 W. ROBERTS *Looker-On* No. 23 (1794) I. 324 A language..rich in the unideal terms of a raving philosophy.

†2. Destitute of, lacking in, ideas. *Obs.*

1751 JOHNSON *Rambler* No. 135 ⁋ 9 A short relief from the tediousness of unideal vacancy. 1801 *Phil. Trans.* XCI. 91 Un-ideal operations conducted without principle, purpose, or regularity.

3. Having or following no ideal.

1760 D. WEBB *Beauties of Painting* iv. 68 Those servile and unideal painters. 1856 EMERSON *Eng. Traits, Lit.* Wks. (Bohn) II. 113 The scholars have become un-ideal. They parry earnest speech with banter and levity. 1867 F. HARRISON *Choice of Bks.* (1886) 110 To be fierce is to be unideal, to be unideal is to be sanguinary.

4. Not marked by idealism; having no ideal character or features, etc.

1846 RUSKIN *Mod. Paint.* II. III. xiii. § 2 Unideal works of art,.represent actual existing things. 1873 SPENCER *Stud. Sociol.* ix. (1877) 222 Instead of our practice being unideal, the ideas which guide it verge on the romantic. 1877 L. MORRIS *Epic Hades* III. 276 The bare And unideal aspect of the fields Which Spring not yet had kissed.

Unide·alism, -ist. (UN-^{1} 12.)

Also, in recent use, *unidealistic* adj.

1870 J. GROTE *Exam. Utilit. Phil.* xvii. 273 Utilitarianism may be..either of an idealist or unidealist type. 1888 W. S. LILLY *Right & Wrong* (1890) iv. 121 The singular unidealism..of the English mind in respect of eternal and divine things.

Unide·ntified, *ppl. a.* (UN-^{1} 8.)

1860 R. NOEL in *Vac. Tour.* 467 The site of a town or village unidentified presented itself within incredibly short distances. 1867 LATHAM *Black & White* 68 Of these graves 138,901 will be nameless and unidentified.

Uni·dioma·tic, *a.* (UN-^{1} 7.)

a 1822 SHELLEY *Pr. Wks.* (1888) I. 395 The clear, and exact, but unidiomatic phrases of their native language. 1855 PUSEY *Doctr. Real Presence* 153 The interpretation of Bellarmin is inconsistent and unidiomatic. 1891 DRIVER *Introd. Lit. O. Test.* 445 An author who..translated the Aramaic idiom..into unidiomatic Hebrew.

Uni·dle, *a.* [UN-^{1} 7.] Busy, industrious.

a 1586 SIDNEY *Astr. & Stella* Sonn. xxvi (Qo.^{3}), For me, I doe Nature vnydle know. 1604 MARSTON *Malcontent* v. iii, Is he not a pretty dapper unydle gallant?

†**Unido·latrize**, *v.* *Obs.*$^{-1}$ (UN-^{2} 6 c.) 1659 FULLER *App. Inj. Innoc.* I. 55 The Animadvertor..endeavouring to un-idolatrize the Brittains as much as he could. **Unido·latrous**, *a.* (UN-^{1} 7.) 1841 WISEMAN *Remarks on Lett. Palmer* 6 To substitute an idolatrous, for an unidolatrous, worship. 1881 *19th Cent.* No. 49. 502 The two religions ..were both nominally monotheistic, and both unidolatrous.

Unie (yū·ni), abbrev. of UNICORN 8 b.

1874 A. H. MARKHAM *Whaling Cruise Baffin's B.* 137 A couple of narwhals, or as they are called by the whalers, 'unies' (unicorn abbreviated). 1878 — *Gt. Frozen Sea* v. 67 Another source of amusement..was chasing 'unies'.

Unie, *v.*: see UNY *v.*

Unific (yūni·fik), *a.* [ad. L. type *ūnificus*: see UNI- and -FIC.] That unifies or unites; producing unity.

1788 T. TAYLOR *Proclus* I. 118 A power collective of divisible natures, and unific of such as are multiplied. 1841 *Fraser's Mag.* XXIII. 130 The centre of unific power is the invisible. 1861 *Q. Rev.* CX. 394 That so-called unific principle..by which we are impelled to reduce all that we see and hear to unity. 1877 FARRAR *Days of Youth* xi. 105 The unific rectitude of a manly life.

Unification (yūnifikē·ʃən). [f. UNIFY *v.* (see -ATION), or a. F. *unification*, It. *unificazione*.] The action or process of unifying or uniting; reduction to unity or to a uniform system; the result of this.

Unificationist, sb. and a., has had some slight currency in recent use (1909–).

1851 GALLENGA *Italy* II. i. 25 The unification of Italy would thus be gradual and pacific. 1865 LECKY *Ration.* I. 231 A process of transformation or unification of religious ideas. 1880 E. KIRKE *Garfield* 46 The recent movement for the unification and preservation of nations.

So **U·nificator**, a unifier.

1870 *Contemp. Rev.* XV. 400 The people..proclaimed them in anticipation the 'unificators' of Italy.

Unified (yū·nifəid), *ppl. a.* [f. UNIFY *v.* + -ED^1.] That is or has been made into one from separate parts; united, combined, consolidated.

1862 F. HALL *Hindu Philos. Syst.* 178 The residual part..he is to consider as unified. 1882 *Standard* 30 Dec. 2/2 The Unified Debt fell about 18*l.* 1883 *Fortn. Rev.* July 107 After the whole metropolis is under a unified authority.

b. Used absolutely or as *sb.*

1883 *Pall Mall G.* 30 Nov. 5/2 Egyptian Unifieds continued to rise yesterday. 1884 *Academy* 2 Aug. 74/1 Unification is pleasant to the unifier only, not to the unified.

Unifier (yū·nifəi,əɹ). [f. as prec. + -ER.] One who or that which unifies or unites; one who advocates unification in administration.

1867 SPENCER *First Princ.* II. iii. § 51 (ed. 2) 171 The derivative data needed by Philosophy as the unifier of Science. 1881 *Echo* 2 Feb. 1/6 The Great Victor Emmanuel, the liberator and unifier of Italy.

Unifilar (yūnifəi·lăɹ), *a.* [f. UNI- 1 + L. *fīl-us* thread: see -AR^1.] Of a magnetometer or other magnetic instrument: Having or suspended by a single thread or fibre.

1856 KANE *Arct. Expl.* I. xiv. 153 We had a good unifilar [magnetometer]. 1873 J. C. MAXWELL *Electr. & Magn.* II. 119 The Unifilar Declinometer. 1879 THOMSON & TAIT *Nat. Phil.* I. I. § 435 In the unifilar torsion-balance.

Uniflo·ral, *a.* [UNI- 1.] = UNIFLOROUS *a.*

1849 CRAIG. 1861 BENTLEY *Man. Bot.* 212 A series of single-flowered axes (unifloral) arranged in the form of a raceme.

Uniflorous (yūniflō·rəs), *a.* *Bot.* [f. mod.L. *ūniflōr-us* (f. L. *ūn-us* UNI- + *flōr-*, *flōs* flower) + -OUS. Cf. F. *uniflore* (1753), Pg. *unifloro*.] Having or bearing only one flower.

1760 [see MULTIFLOROUS *a.*]. 1800 *Asiatic Ann. Reg.* 299/1 The hermaphrodite calyx is sometimes biflorous,.. sometimes uniflorous. 1881 *Jrnl. Linn. Soc.* XVIII. 353 Distinguished..by its unifoliate uniflorous stem.

†**U·nifoil.** *Obs.*$^{-0}$ [f. UNI- + FOIL *sb.*^{1}] The plant one-blade, *Smilacina bifolia*.

1688 R. HOLME *Armoury* II. 58/1 He beareth Argent, an Unifoile Vert...Vnifoile or Vnfall. This is an Herb that never hath more then one leaf from a Root,..it is also called one blade. [Hence in Berry *Encycl. Her.* (*c* 1828), Elvin (1889), and in some recent Dicts. as a bearing in Heraldry.]

Uniform (yū·nifǫɹm), *sb.* [f. the adj. Cf. F., It., Sp., and Pg. *uniforme*, Du., G., Sw., and Da. *uniform* in sense 2.]

†I. 1. *In uniform*, in one body or flock. *Obs.*

1623 LISLE *Ælfric on O. & N. Test.* Ded. p. ix, Our sheepe shall feare no Wolfe, or suddaine storme; But goe and come all safe in vniforme.

II. 2. A distinctive dress of uniform cut, materials, and colour worn by all the members of a particular naval, military, or other force to which it is recognized as properly belonging and peculiar.

1748 in *Jrnl. Archæol. Soc.* (1847) II. 79 That no commission-officer or midshipmen do presume to wear any other uniform than what properly belongs to his rank. 1760 *Cautions & Adv. to Officers of Army* 123 You are..to consider what is to be furnished out of this last Sum, and that is your Regimentals or Uniform. 1802 JAMES *Milit. Dict.* s.v., Scarlet is the national uniform of the British army. *Ibid.*, Generally speaking each [corps] has an uniform within itself, yet this uniform, strictly considered, is a regimental. 1837 DICKENS *Pickw.* iv, Colonel Bulder, in full military uniform, on horseback. 1879 *Cassell's Techn. Educ.* III. 363 Insisting that none shall fight who do not wear the uniform of one of the armies engaged.

fig. 1768–74 TUCKER *Lt. Nat.* (1834) II. 121 Passion so commonly marches under the colours and in the uniform of reason,..that [etc.].

b. A distinctive uniform dress worn by the members of any civilian body or association of persons.

1837 DICKENS *Pickw.* ii, The proposed uniform, sir, of the Pickwick Club. 1885 'MRS. ALEXANDER' *At Bay* i, A good-looking boy in the polytechnique uniform. 1897 HALL CAINE *Christian* x, The girls were nearly all nurses, and they wore their nurse's uniform.

c. A single suit of this kind. †Also *pl.*, the separate garments composing this.

1783 *Ann. Reg., Chron.* 193/2 Such flag officers, however, as were provided with the uniforms were permitted to wear the same. 1814 SCOTT *Wav.* xvii, He had laid aside the Highland dress for the time, to put on an old blue and red uniform. 1834 MARRYAT *P. Simple* xxxviii, That is the reason why my uniforms are so shabby. I spoilt them then.

†3. A person wearing a uniform. *Obs.*$^{-1}$

1786 MME. D'ARBLAY *Diary* Oct., I opened the eating-room door,..but saw to my surprise a party of uniforms.

4. *attrib.* **a.** In the sense 'pertaining to, forming (part of) a uniform', as *uniform case, clothes, coat*.

In some instances not clearly distinguishable from the adj. Cf. UNIFORM *a.* 2 c.

1807 P. GASS *Jrnl.* 188 We got a canoe from the natives, for which we gave an officer's uniform coat. 1825 in J. A. Heraud *Voy. Midshipm.* (1837) x. 179 Buy your..uniform clothes (two jackets and one coat) in London. 1852 THACKERAY *Esmond* II. xiii, An officer in a green uniform coat. 1889 HISSEY *Tour in Phaeton* 399 We pack our personal belongings in tin uniform cases.

b. In the sense 'wearing uniform; uniformed'.

1895 *Westm. Gaz.* 1 Jan. 4/3 Several uniform policemen watched the prosecutor and prisoners.

Uniform (yū·nifǫɹm), *a.* Also 6 vnifourme, 6–8 uniforme. [a. F. *uniforme* (14th c. in Godef., = It., Sp., Pg. *uniforme*), or ad. L. *ūniformis*: see UNI- and FORM.]

I. Of things in respect of their own qualities or constitution.

1. Of one form, character, or kind; having, maintaining, occurring in or under, the same form always; that is or remains the same in different places, at different times, or under varying circumstances; exhibiting no difference, diversity, or variation.

1540 PALSGR. *Acolastus* A ij, One selfe and vniforme maner of teachynge of all those Grammaticalle ensygnementes. 1555 WATREMAN *Fardle Facions* I. v. 72 The ordre of Mariage emong the Egiptians is not vniforme. 1601 HOLLAND *Pliny* I. 161 This impression, that maketh either the foresaid uniforme likenesse, or confusion and varietie. 1662 *Extr. St. Papers Friends* Ser. II. (1911) 150 Wee would be glad that all our Subjects could be brought to agree in a uniforme Worship of God. 1710 PRIDEAUX *Orig. Tithes* ii. 127 From whence else should they have such a Uniform Usage but by a Uniform Tradition from them? 1780 BENTHAM *Princ. Legisl.* xiv. § 1 It is lost time to seek for an uniform base of agreement upon so essential an object. 1818 SCOTT *Br. Lamm.* xi, According to a uniform custom in remote places in Scotland. 1869 F. W. NEWMAN *Misc.* 224 A uniform franchise through the whole federation would have followed. 1891 *Law Times* XCII. 124/1 In Ireland the practice in this respect..was not uniform.

absol. 1606 SYLVESTER *Du Bartas* II. iv. II. *Magnif.* 1335 Cause of all Causes, Ocean of all Good,..The Uni-form, which gives all forms their Beeing.

b. Of persons (or personifications), their disposition, etc. Hence, exhibiting or preserving uniformity or consistency in respect of conduct or opinion; consistent.

1551 CRANMER *Answ. to Gardiner* I. 14 The churche of Rome..sheweth her selfe alway vniforme and consonaunt, to confound all the doctrine of Christe. 1647 H. MORE *Phil. Poems* II. lxxii, If he will his own fortunes overturn It cannot well be holp, we must be uniform. 1692 DRYDEN *St. Euremont's Ess.* 339 There is a man so uniform as to have nothing of Inequality and contrariety in his Actions. 1748 RICHARDSON *Clarissa* i. I. 3 Every-body pities you. So steady so uniform in your conduct. 1799 WELLINGTON in Gurw. *Desp.* (1834) I. 16 Of this uniform disposition abundant proofs have been afforded by each of the allies. 1822 SCOTT *Peveril* xlviii, For Buckingham's sins,..he is the regular and uniform sponsor.

†c. Of consent: Unanimous. *Obs.*

1559 in Strype *Ann. Ref.* viii. (1709) 116 We..have with one uniform consent set forth this short declaration. 1620 BRENT tr. *Sarpi's Counc. Trent* VIII. 745 An vniforme consent of Doctors.

d. Of clothing or dress: Of the same pattern, colour, and material amongst a number or body of persons.

Merging into an attrib. use of UNIFORM *sb.* (sense 4).

1746 in *Jrnl. Archæol. Soc.* (1847) II. 77 That a uniform dress is useful and necessary for the commissioned officers. 1768 *Ann. Reg., Chron.* 63/1 The lappels and cuffs of the military uniform frocks, appointed to be worn by the lieutenants of his Majesty's fleet. 1783 *Ibid.* 193/2 The uniform clothing..worn by the flag officers. 1890 *Harper's Mag.* Feb. 333 The practice of clothing soldiers, by regiments, in one uniform dress.

2. Having or presenting the same appearance or aspect; exhibiting no, or little, diversity in respect of form, design, or dimensions; hence, having a plain, unbroken, or undiversified surface or exterior.

In the 17th–18th centuries freq. of buildings, etc.

a 1550 LELAND *Itin.* (1768) I. 107 The Church of S. Mary is excellent, newe, and uniforme yn work. 1621 in Kempe *Losely MSS.* (1836) 456 The church of St. Treguse ys..a very good one, were it uniforme. 1632 MASSINGER & FIELD *Fatal Dowry* III. i, All else about you, cap-a-pie, So uniform in spite of handsomeness, Shews such a bold contempt of comeliness. 1696 WHISTON *Theory of Earth* II. 115 Every such state of external Nature was even, uniform, and regular. 1723 CHAMBERS tr. *Le Clerc's Treat. Arch.* I. 59 Columns..ought not to have any Flutings; for ..plain uniform Columns carry..a better appearance. 1756 NUGENT *Gr. Tour, Netherl.* I. 299 The street called La Rue Royale, is one of the longest, straightest, and most uniform in Europe. 1784 COWPER *Task* VI. 178 All this uniform, uncolour'd scene, Shall be dismantled of its fleecy load. 1859 DARWIN *Orig. Spec.* iii. 73 The face of nature remains uniform for long periods of time. 1884 BOWER & SCOTT *De Bary's Phaner.* 110 The thickening mass is either uniform or pitted.

As *adv.* 1630 *R. Johnson's Kingd. & Commw.* 132 Paris.. is the greater, the uniformer built, and stronglier situate.

†b. *Bot.* Of flowers: (see quots.). *Obs.*

1693 *Phil. Trans.* XVII. 929 Such as have a Uniform Flower, as Senna, or such as have a difform or Papilionaceous Flower. 1704 J. HARRIS *Lex. Techn.* I, *Uniform Flowers* of Plants, the Botanists call such as are all round of the same Figure; or whose fore and back part, and whose right and left parts are exactly alike.

c. Of material things or colour.

In this group the sense sometimes becomes narrowed down to 'not mixed or blended'.

1756 BURKE *On the Sublime & Beautiful* III. xxvii, Nor ..is the power of black as black, or of white as white, so strong as when each stands uniform and distinguished. 1764 HARMER *Observ.* iv. § 27. 192 This mingled wine stands in opposition to new wine, which is, to the eye, an uniform liquor. 1823 SCOTT *Quentin D.* ii, His jerkin, hose, and cloak, were of a dark uniform colour. 1845 *Florist's Jrnl.* 261 Few gardens could boast an uniform luxuriant green among the plants. *c* 1860 FARADAY *Forces Nat.* 67 This piece of glass..being perfectly uniform in its internal structure.

3. Of motion, dimensions, etc.: Free from fluctuation or variation in respect of quantity or amount.

1559 W. CUNNINGHAM *Cosmogr. Glasse* 10 The sterres kepe one vniforme distance in mouing. 1597 HOOKER *Eccl. Pol.* v. lxix. § 2 The heauens..keepe in their motions vniforme celeritie. 1656 tr. *Hobbes' Elem. Philos.* III. xv. 156 Uniform [motion] is that by which equal Lines are alwayes transmitted in equal times. 1764 *Museum Rust.* IV. 58 We should find it in an uniform progression of encrease. 1796 WITHERING *Brit. Plants* (ed. 3) III. 879 Branches of a uniform breadth. 1860 MAURY *Phys. Geog.* (Low) xxii. § 883 The flow of heat from the sun is held to be uniform. 1879 THOMSON & TAIT *Nat. Phil.* I. I. § 20 Velocity..may be uniform, *i.e.* the same at every instant; or it may be variable.

II. Of things of the same class in respect of each other, or of one thing in relation to another or others of the same class.

4. Of the same form, character, or kind as another or others; agreeing or according with one another, conforming to one standard, rule, or pattern; alike, similar.

1548 W. THOMAS in Strype *Eccl. Mem.* (1721) II. App. v. 71 So because we have no neighbour of uniform religion, I determine we can find no friend, whose amity is to be trusted. 1594 HOOKER *Eccl. Pol.* IV. xiii. § 2 The only doubt is about the manner of their unity; how far churches are bound to be uniform in their ceremonies. 1637 SALTONSTALL *Eusebius' Constantine* 77 Thus the Emperours Edict discovered the Dens and uniforme Cages of these Heretickes. 1660 R. COKE *Power & Subj.* 222 The ceremonies of Edward's Reformation were more uniform than before. 1702 *Engl. Theophrast.* 263 Things Past, Present, and to Come, are strangely Uniform and of a Colour. 1762 KAMES *Elem. Crit.* (1833) 481 When two figures are composed of similar parts, they are said to be uniform. 1794 MRS. RADCLIFFE *Myst. Udolpho* xvi, My answers on the subject have been uniform. 1867 SMILES *Huguenots Eng.* i. 6 The copies sold having been compared with each other, were found to be exactly uniform. 1878 BRISTOWE *Th. & Pract. Med.* (ed. 2) 534 The symptoms of rupture of the heart are far from uniform.

†b. Of buildings. *Obs.*

1549 W. THOMAS *Hist. Italy* 207 Buildynges on bothe sides so fayre and vniforme. 1617 MORYSON *Itin.* III. 66 The houses are most of bricke,..and so vniforme, as if they had all beene built at a time, and by the same workemen. 1684 BURNET tr. *More's Utopia* 73 Their Buildings are good, and are so uniform, that a whole side of a Street looks like one House. 1700 in Picton *L'pool Munic. Rec.* (1883) I. 291 Yᵉ buildings be handsome & uniform.

†c. Of persons. *Obs.*

In quot. referring to Matt. xxii. 11–13.

a 1626 BP. ANDREWES *Pattern Cath. Doctr.* (1630) 210 He that was not uniforme was punished.

†d. In agreement with, accordant *to*, something.

a 1586 SIDNEY *Arcadia* II. xii, So divers be the Elements disposed In this weake worke, that it can never be Made uniforme to any state reposed. 1669 in Willis & Clark *Cambridge* (1886) II. 557 Three outward dore cases shalbe arched..with freestone vniforme to the windowes. 1702 H. DODWELL *Apol.* § 19, I have shewn it agreeable to the severest Reasoning..to make his Death uniform to the rest of his Life.

Uniform (yū·nifǫɹm), *v.* [f. the adj. or sb. Cf. Sp. and Pg. *uniformar*, It. *uniformarsi*.]

1. *trans.* To make conformable *to*.

In a parody of pedantic language.

a 1586 SIDNEY *Wanstead Play* in *Arcadia* (1629) 622 Thus must I vniform my speech to your obtuse conceptions.

2. To make or render (a number of persons or things) uniform or alike; to bring or reduce to uniformity.

In later quots. with suggestion of sense 3.

c 1681 HICKERINGILL *Trimmer* iii. Wks. 1716 I. 372 We'll uniform you all, and make you all alike. 1708 T. WARD *Eng. Ref.* I. (1710) 64 To..Uniform the Multitude In Prayer, and joyn the jarring crowd. 1870 LOWELL *Study Wind.* (1871) 258 The more than Protean travesties which words underwent before they were uniformed by Johnson and Walker. 1887 *Harper's Mag.* July 280 It is a human device to uniform people into friends and enemies.

3. To dress in, put into, uniform. Cf. UNIFORMED *a.*, UNIFORMING *vbl. sb.*

1894 *Outing* XXIV. 78/2 Hull persisted in uniforming the militia after his own sweet will.

†**Unifo·rmable**, *a.* *Obs. rare.* [f. L. *ūniformis* UNIFORM *a.* + -ABLE.] Uniform.

1632 LITHGOW *Trav.* X. 474 Vniformable no; some of your Priests giue the Sacrament onely in Bread..; some in Wine without Bread, and some in both. 1653 BLITHE *Eng. Improver Impr.* 155 As easie..to cast or lot out thy Wood into an Artificial uniformable plot, as to do it rudely or confusedly.

Unifo·rmal, *a.* [f. as prec. + -AL.] Uniform, in various senses.

1573 [implied in next]. 1598 FLORIO, *Simbolo*,..an vniformall consent of sundry opinions. *a* 1608 DEE *Relat. Spir.* I. (1659) 4 All things shall be brought into an uniformal order. 1645 HERRICK *Descr. Woman* 11 Her comly nose with vniformall grace Like purest white stands in the middle place. 1848 BAILEY *Festus* (ed. 3) 206 One arrayed in white And one in uniformal black. 1888 D. MAGUIRE *Art Massage* ii. (ed. 4) 18 A uniformal friction on those parts of the body which are irregularly formed.

Hence **Unifo·rmally** *adv. rare.*

1573 BARET *Alv.* s.v. *C*, [The letter C] shoulde haue his proper sownd and euer to keepe the same vniformally in speaking, nor waueringly. 1603 FLORIO *Montaigne* III. ii. 491, I will present my selfe..every where vniformallie. 1624 GATAKER *Transubst.* 48 These being..uniformally recounted by three Evangelists.

Uniformaliza·tion. [f. next + -ATION.] The action of making or fact of being made uniform.

1805 *Ann. Rev.* III. 255 The uniformalization of tenures.

Unifo·rmalize, *v.* *rare.* [f. UNIFORMAL *a.* + -IZE.] *trans.* To make uniform; to reduce to a uniform system.

1805 *Ann. Rev.* III. 294 It is desirable to uniformalize the circulating medium of both countries. 1830 W. TAYLOR *Hist. Surv. Germ. Poetry* I. 161 By uniformalizing coins, weights, and measures.

Uniforma·tion. *rare.* [f. UNIFORM *a.* + -ATION.] The action of making uniform; reduction to uniformity.

1895 *Dublin Rev.* April 335 Not through the blunting, checking, or uniformation of thinking.

U·niformed, *a.* [f. UNIFORM *sb.* 2 + -ED.] Dressed in or wearing uniform. (Freq. *c* 1880–.)

1813 LADY LYTTELTON *Corr.* 12 Dec., Wednesday we dine at Count Romanzoff's—full-dressed, long-trained, uniformed. 1840 GEN. P. THOMPSON *Exerc.* (1842) V. 53 A uniformed agent of the law. 1895 MEREDITH *Amazing Marriage* xliii, A foreign army or tag-rag of uniformed rascals.

fig. and *transf.* 1864 LOWELL *Fireside Trav.* 154 We.. come out uniformed..with habits of thinking and doing cut on one pattern. 1892 *Nation* (N.Y.) 3 Mar. 176/1 The book is handsomely uniformed in Confederate gray.

Unifo·rming, *vbl. sb.* [f. UNIFORM *v.*]

1. The action of making or fact of being made uniform in some respect. *rare*$^{-1}$.

1700–1 GOUGH *Hist. Myddle* (1875) 115 The Twelvth Peiw ..Was a supernumerary Peiw at the uniforming of the seates.

2. The action of clothing in or providing with uniform or a uniform dress.

1891 *Harper's Mag.* March 647/1 In the uniforming of a community set apart for an unworldly purpose. 1897 *Daily News* 4 May 9/2 The uniforming of troops.

Uniformist (yū·nifǫɹmist). [f. UNIFORM *a.* + -IST.] An advocate of or believer in uniformity or a uniform system, esp. in respect of religious doctrine or observance.

1885 R. W. DIXON *Hist. Ch. Eng.* III. 465 He was..as staunch a Uniformist now, as..he had been a Nonconformist. 1891 *Athenæum* 15 Aug. 214/3 A strict uniformist with regard to the phonetics of Latin.

Uniformitarian (yū:nifǫɹmitē·riăn), *sb.* and *adj.* [f. UNIFORMIT-Y + -*arian*.]

A. *sb.* 1. *Geol.* One who maintains or accepts the theory that geological processes and phenomena have always been and still are due to causes or forces operating continuously and with uniformity. (Opposed to CATASTROPHIST or CONVULSIONIST.)

1840 WHEWELL *Philos. Induct. Sciences* I. p. xxxvi, The Catastrophist constructs Theories, the Uniformitarian demolishes them. 1860 HUXLEY *Darwiniana* Coll. Ess. 1893 II. 65 The most philosophical uniformitarian of the present day. 1891 SIR R. BALL *Ice Age* 173 It places the ice-sheet ..at the disposal of the geological uniformitarian.

2. An advocate of uniformity; a uniformist. *rare.*

1890 GILDERSLEEVE *Ess. & Stud.* 214 The Procrustean work of a miserable uniformitarian.

B. *adj.* 1. *Geol.* Of or pertaining to, characteristic of or held by, uniformitarians.

1840 WHEWELL *Philos. Induct. Sci.* II. 135 The uniformitarian doctrine on this subject rests on most unstable foundations. 1869 HUXLEY in *Scientific Opinion* 21 April 464/3 The influence of uniformitarian views has been..favourable to the progress of sound geology. 1884 H. SPENCER in *Contemp. Rev.* July 25 The leading expositor of the uniformitarian theory in Geology.

b. In accordance with the theory of the uniformitarians; proceeding from geological uniformity.

1869 HUXLEY in *Scientific Opinion* April 487/1 All these irregular..catastrophes would be the result of an absolutely uniformitarian action.

c. Of persons: Holding or adhering to the theory or doctrines of the uniformitarians.

1864 BOWEN *Logic* ix. 301 The speculations of those whom Dr. Whewell calls the uniformitarian school of geologists. 1895 *Q. Rev.* April 386 The most influential uniformitarian geologist of our age.

2. Of or pertaining to, advocating or practising, uniformity in something.

1897 *Daily News* 12 July 6/3 The Puritanism of the intolerant, uniformitarian Presbyterians.

Uniformitarianism (yū:nifǫɹmitē·riăniz'm). *Geol.* [f. prec. + -ISM.] The principles or doctrines held by the uniformitarian school of geologists; the theory of uniformity of action in the forces and processes of inorganic nature. (Opposed to CATASTROPHISM or CONVULSIONISM.)

1865 T. MARSDEN *Sacr. Steps Creation* 113 One is induced to ask, whether Uniformitarianism be mere Proselytism in the garb of Philosophy. 1894 *Nature* 26 July 290/1 The natural though exaggerated reaction into scientific uniformitarianism.

Uniformity (yūnifǫ·ɹmiti). Forms: 5 vniformite, 6 -ete, 6–7 -itie, 7 -ity, uniformitie, 7– -ity. [a. F. *uniformité* (14th c., = It. *uniformità*, Sp. *uniformidad*, Pg. *-dade*), or ad. L. *ūniformitāt-*, *ūniformitās*, f. *ūniformis* UNIFORM *a.*: see -ITY. So also Du. *uniformiteit*, G. *uniformität*.] The quality of being uniform.

1. The fact or condition of having the same form or character as another or others; conformity amongst several things, parts, etc., to one form or character.

1432–50 tr. *Higden* (Rolls) III. 215 Zenon, whiche put euery synne to be of vniformite, so that he scholde synne as moche that did steyle chaffe as the man stelenge golde. 1513 DOUGLAS *Æneid* IX. iv. 39 To thir tua was a will in vnite, A lust, and mynd in vniformete. 1611 CORYAT *Crudities* 23 Such is the vniformity of almost al the houses of the same streete..that they are made alike both in proportion of workmanship and matter. 1614 RALEIGH *Hist. World* II. 543 The consent of those that have written thereof, being nothing neare to uniformity. 1630 *R. Johnson's Kingd. & Commw.* 132 Its attributes of a Winding river, and the five Bridges, sorting forsooth to uniformitie of streets. 1701 NORRIS *Ideal World* I. ii. 50 Whence should arise this specific uniformity in the natures of man,..if not that they are all cast in one mould? 1756 BURKE *Subl. & B.* II. ix, Succession and uniformity of parts are what constitute the artificial infinite. 1815 J. SMITH *Panorama Sci. & Art* II. 601 Various differences in the depth, extent, or want of uniformity of the gravelly or clayey strata. 1854 *Poultry Chron.* II. 149/1 Quality, purity, beauty of plumage, and uniformity [in fowls].

b. Conformity to (or compliance with) one standard of opinion, practice, or procedure, esp. in respect of religion or religious observance.

Act of Uniformity, in *Eng. Hist.*, one or other of three Acts regulating public worship, passed in 1549 (21 Jan.), 1559, and 1662 respectively, which prescribed the use and acceptance of the Books of Common Prayer published in those years; esp. the Act (13 & 14 Charles II, c. 4) passed 19 May 1662, which also required the 'assent and consent' of the clergy to everything contained in the Book of Common Prayer; etc.

1549 *Act 2 & 3 Edw. VI*, c. 1 (*title*), An Acte for the Unyformytie of Service and Admynistracion of the Sacramentes throughout the Realme. 1552 ABP. HAMILTON *Catech.* Pref., To keip vniformitie and concord in setting furth to ye people the doctrine. 1611 BIBLE *Transl. Pref.* ⁋ 13 When the father of their Church..findeth so great fault with them for their oddes and iarring; we hope the children haue no great cause to vaunt of their vniformitie. 1651 BAXTER *Inf. Bapt.* 147 His treatise against Uniformity. 1670 in Somers *Tracts* I. 21 All Uniformity (or Colour of it) was distasteful to the Independents. 1708 J. CHAMBERLAYNE *St. Gt. Brit.* I. III. i. (1710) 155 He must carry with him.. Letters Testimonial..from..Three..Reverend Divines, who ..can give a good Account of his Vertue, Uniformity, and Learning. 1830 D'ISRAELI *Chas. I*, III. v. 63 Lord Bacon considered that uniformity in religion was absolutely necessary. 1871 C. DAVIES *Metric Syst.* III. 79 Its adoption was therefore a great and important advance toward uniformity.

Comb. 1647 *Case Kingd.* 10 Till Vniformity-mongers be pointed at as the only Enemies of a State.

c. With *a* or *an*.

1560 DAUS tr. *Sleidane's Comm.* 125 b, Therfore is an vniformitie to be sought for, that maye be grounded vpon the sure foundation of Scripture. 1641 MILTON *Reform.* II. 17 This distinction of honour will bring forth a seemly and graceful uniformity over all the kingdom. 1705 NELSON *Fest. & Fasts* i. (ed. 3) 19 The great Council of Nice ordained there should be a constant uniformity in this Case. 1874 GREEN *Short Hist.* iii. § 3. 125 An uniformity of weights and measures was ordered to be enforced throughout the realm.

2. The condition of having, occurring in, or maintaining only one form or character; resemblance to or agreement with itself at all times or on all occasions; regularity in action or occurrence. Freq. const. *of*.

1577 HARRISON *England* II. iii. (1877) I. 73 For vniformitie of building, orderlie compaction, and regiment, the towne of Cambridge exceedeth that of Oxford..by manie a fold. 1739 BUTLER *Serm.* Wks. 1874 II. 217 There is a wonderful uniformity in the conduct of Providence. 1802 PALEY *Nat. Theol.* xxv. 482 Of the unity of the Deity, the proof is, the uniformity of plan observable in the universe. 1863 KINGLAKE *Crimea* I. 64 That branch of industry which seeks to give uniformity and mechanic action to bodies of men. 1875 JOWETT *Plato* (ed. 2) IV. 415 Genius is of all

Supplement, p. 3873; Corrigenda, p. 4092; Spurious words, p. 4093; Books quoted, p. 4094

Uniformize ... **Unilateral** ... **Uniliteral** ... **Unilluminated** ... **Unimaginative** ... **Unimpeachably**

Unimpeached ... **Unimportant** ... **Unimpressive** ... **Unincarnate** ... **Unincorporate** ... **Unindexed** ... **Unindifferent** ... **Unindustrious** ... **Uninfected** ... **Uninfluenced** ... **Uninfluential**

1657 J. WATTS *Vind. Ch. Eng.* 48 But an Union, one such text, I mean, in all the Bible.

7. That which is united or combined into one; a body formed by uniting one thing to another or others, or several things together; a combination or compound.

1660 JER. TAYLOR *Worthy Commun.* Introd. 10 My purpose is..to gather together into an union al these several portions of truth. 1696 STANHOPE *Chr. Pattern* (1711) 2 What is a man the better for entring into the sublime mysteries of the Trinity, and being able to dispute nicely upon that adorable Union? 1807 J. E. SMITH *Phys. Bot.* 212 Carbonic acid gas, (which was formerly called fixed air, and is an union of oxygen and carbon).

b. A number, group, or body of persons or states joined or associated together for some common purpose or action; an association, league, or society; in later use esp. = TRADE-UNION.

(*a*) 1660 JER. TAYLOR *Ductor* III. iv. rule x. § 11 He is not to be reckoned as a Brother, or a relative in our religious friendship and union. 1736 BUTLER *Anal.* I. iii. 83 To separate from their adversaries, and to form an union among themselves. 1762 FALCONER *Shipwr.* II. 409 [The] sagacious statesman..darts around his penetrating eyes, Where Dangers grow and hostile unions rise. 1832 GEN. P. THOMPSON *Exerc.* (1842) II. 236 Once more to the Political Unions,.. don't endure it [*sc.* slavery]; but hold together like burrs. 1903 *Science* (N.Y.) 5 June 892/2 The International Union of the American Republics, popularly known as the Pan-American Union.

(*b*) 1833 *2nd Rep. Factory Com.* D 2. 39 Our spinners..said they had no fault to find..,but the union obliged them to turn out. 1848 MRS. GASKELL *M. Barton* viii, Block-printers is going to strike; they'n getten a bang-up Union, as won't let 'em be put upon. 1878 JEVONS *Prim. Pol. Econ.* 65 It is certain that the increase of wages is not confined to those trades which have unions.

c. *spec.* A number of states or provinces united together or incorporated into one legislative confederacy; a confederation or federation; esp. the United States of America.

Sometimes in American use restricted to the Northern States which adhered to the Union in contradistinction to the eleven Southern States whose attempted secession from it led to the Civil War of 1861–5.

1775 JEFFERSON *Let.* Writ. 1892 I. 491 So as to bring the Canadians into our Union. 1792 BELKNAP *Hist. New Hampsh.* III. 257 An important branch of the American union. 1817 J. BRADBURY *Trav. Amer.* 277 The separation of the States west of the Alleghanies from the Union. 1865 LOWELL *Wks.* (1890) V. 258 The South will come back to the Union. 1909 in R. H. Brand *Union of S. Africa* 142 The words 'the Union' shall be taken to mean the Union of South Africa as constituted under this Act.

d. A number of parishes united or incorporated together under one Board of Guardians for the administration of the poor laws; an area or sub-district so formed and administered.

1834 *Act 4–5 Will. IV*, c. 76 § 26 Such Parishes shall thereupon be deemed a Union for such Purpose. 1837 MCCULLOCH *Acc. Brit. Empire* II. 630 The operation of Gilbert's Act in the unions formed under it. 1862 GLADSTONE *Sp.* in *Times* 29 Dec. 9/5 The bulk of the cotton manufacture was carried on in a region comprised within 27 Unions.

e. A textile fabric composed of two or more different materials woven together, esp. one containing cotton and linen, or cotton and some other material as wool, silk, or jute. Freq. *pl.*, kinds or varieties of goods or fabrics so woven, union-cloths.

1844 G. DODD *Textile Manuf.* v. 167 A mixture of flax and cotton called 'union'. 1851 MAYHEW *Lond. Labour* I. 378/1 Then we had an Irish linen, an imitation, you know, a kind of 'Union', which we call double twist. 1893 *Photogr. Ann.* 284 Two or three yards of 'union', or white window blind material.

pl. 1851 MAYHEW *Lond. Labour* I. 376/2 Linen of good quality used to be extensively hawked, but from 1820 to 1825, or later,..the hawkers got to deal in an inferior quality, 'unions' (a mixture of linen and cotton) glazed and stiffened. 1879 *Cassell's Techn. Educ.* IV. 387/2 A real Scotch carpet is all wool, but fabrics similar in appearance are made with cotton warps and worsted wefts, in which case they are called 'unions'. 1890 *Textile News* 20 Oct. (List Manufacturers), Manufacturer of black and coloured unions.

8. *Brewing.* One of a series of casks or vats used in the Union or Burton system of cleansing beer.

1876 *Encycl. Brit.* IV. 275/2 When beer is cleansed..it is necessary to keep the casks or Unions full to the bung. 1897 W. J. SYKES *Brewing* 448 When a set of unions are cleansed, the swan-necks are first removed.

III. 9. That which unites or connects one thing to another; *techn.*, a device for connecting the ends of pipes or tubes, or for attaching a pipe to some other part; a coupling, pipe-coupling.

1850 [see *union joint* in sense 12]. 1863 *Appleby's Handbk. Mach. & Iron Work* 59 Wrought-iron Wrenches for Hose Unions. 1864 *Riddel & Co.'s Catal.*, Steam and Valve Cocks, Brass Unions. 1889 *Daily News* 11 Feb. 4/7 Makers of cocks, taps, unions, and bar fittings are fairly busy.

IV. 10. In elliptical senses. a. = UNION-FLAG or UNION-JACK, either as (*a*) a separate flag (also † *Great union*), or (*b*) as inserted in the upper inner canton of the ensign; freq. in phr. *union down* or *downwards*, indicating an inverted position, with the union as if in the lower inner canton, when the flag is hoisted or flown on a vessel as a signal of distress or mourning.

(*a*) 1769 FALCONER *Dict. Marine* (1780) s.v. *Jack*, In the British Navy the jack is..a small union flag..; but in merchant-ships this union is bordered with a red field. 1812 *Ann. Reg., Gen. Hist.* 110 The proud old British Union floated triumphantly over it. 1849 C. STURT *Exped. Centr. Australia* I. 20 Some young ladies of the colony..had worked a silken union to present to Mr. Eyre. 1865 *N. & Q.* 18 Feb. 136/1 His majesty is depicted stepping from a barge with the Union hoisted at the stern.

(*b*) 1804 *Naval Chron.* XII. 144 The colours..were hoisted Union downwards. 1830 CAMPBELL *Dict. Mil. Sci.* s.v. *Colours*, The Red Cross of St. George in a White Field, with the Union in the Upper Canton. 1883 *Harper's Mag.* Jan. 321/1 The American flag..was by mistake hoisted 'union down'.

b. Short for *Union House*, *workhouse* (sense 12).

1843 NEALE *Ball. & Songs for People* 16 We never built the unions Wherein they starve the poor. 1874 T. HARDY *Far fr. Mad. Crowd* xxx, I wonder sometimes if I am doomed to die in the Union.

c. (With capital.) The name at various Universities (orig. at Oxford and Cambridge) of a general club and debating society usually open to all members, or all undergraduates, of the University; also, the buildings or offices of such.

Originally short for *Union Society* or *Union Club*. Also used attrib., as *Union audience, rhetoric, speech*.

1835 *Rep. Committee Oxford Union Soc.* 2 The Treasurer of the Union. 1853 THACKERAY *Eng. Hum., Congreve* (1858) 58 Before the passing of the Reform Bill, there existed at Cambridge a certain debating club, called the 'Union'. 1883 *Oxford Univ. Mag.* 24 Jan. 7/1 No more eloquent speech has been heard in the Union during the last three years. 1891 *Cal. St. Andrews Univ.* 315 The scheme for instituting a Students' Union in the University of St. Andrews. *Ibid.* 316 The general management of the Union.

V. Attrib. and comb., passing into adj.

11. a. In senses 4 b and 7 c, with the sense 'of or belonging to, promoting or advocating, adhering to or supporting (a particular) legislative union', as (*a*) *Union arms, colours, -maker, parliament*; esp. (*b*) in American use (see 7 c note), as *Union banner, league, man, planter*, etc.

(*a*) 1707 *Lond. Gaz.* No. 4374/1 On Two opposite Corners were the Union Arms. *Ibid.*, The Norton Galley hoisted the Union Colours. 1771 SMOLLETT *Humph. Cl.* To Phillips 8 Aug., During a sitting of the union parliament [at Edinburgh, 1707]. 1811 *Gen. Reg. & Orders of Army* 13 The first Standard, Guidon, or Colour of Regiments, which is the Union Colour. 1846 A. AMOS *Gt. Oyer of Poison.* 4 The union-maker, King James.

(*b*) 1863 BRIGHT *Sp. Amer.* 26 Mar. 127 Not Union planters only, but Secession planters began to bring in the produce. 1863 HAWTHORNE *Our Old Home* (1883) I. 23 The latest is now a gallant power under the Union banner. 1872 DE VERE *Americanisms* 280 The Union-men..or Federals..fought for the Union against rebellion. *Ibid.* 289 Loyal Leagues, as well as Union Leagues, were formed all over the country.

b. In general and miscellaneous use, as *union-band, canopy, vowel*, etc.

1723 E. FENTON *Mariamne* III. vi, Such as good spirits are suppos'd to sing O'er saints, while death dissolves the union-band. 1785 [R. GRAVES] *Eugenius* II. xxxi. 188 A great many variegated roses..called union roses (as they unite the party distinctions of York and Lancaster). 1824 T. FENBY *Mulberry Tree* iii, The tree, Which love's union-canopy made. 1879 WHITNEY *Sanskrit Gram.* 78 All the simple vowels come to assume in certain cases the aspect of union-vowels, or insertions between root or stem and ending of inflection or of derivation.

c. In sense 7 b, as *Union-jobber, -smashing* vbl. sb.

1841 *Penny Cycl.* XXI. 411/1 The many dishonest abstractions of their [Pension Societies'] funds, of which the mere Union jobbers are so often guilty. 1897 *Westm. Gaz.* 30 Aug. 1/3 A general policy of union-smashing.

d. In sense 7 e, as *union cloth, cord* (*braid*), *damask, diaper, goods*, etc.; also (of garments), 'made of union cloth or fabric'.

1862 *Catal. Internat. Exhib., Brit.* II. No. 3995, Woollen and union cloths. 1867 *Ure's Dict. Arts* (ed. 6) III. 971 *Union goods*, cloths of a mixed character, as of flax and jute, or cotton and jute. 1868 *Chambers' Encycl.* X. 268/1 Many of the names used in the all-wool class are retained in this [*sc.* fabrics composed of wool and cotton], with the addition of the word 'union', as union merino, union shalloon, union damask, &c. 1882 CAULFEILD & SAWARD *Dict. Needlew.* 507 *Union cord*, a round white cord, made for stay-laces,..composed of both linen and cotton thread. *Ibid.*, Union Cord Braid, Union Diaper. 1896 *Godey's Mag.* Feb. 218/2 Union undergarments of silk or wool.

e. In senses 7 d, 10 b, as *union boy, man*.

1846 (*title*), The Union and Parish Officer's Pocket Almanac and Guide. 1859 J. H. STEGGALL *Hist. Suffolk Man* i. 29, I was worse than any union boy with his hair polled. 1871 'M. LEGRAND' *Cambr. Freshm.* 303 He's out o' the Union. ..The Union men break the stones on the roads.

12. Special combs.: **union bow** *Archery*, a bow made of two or more pieces united together; a backed or back bow (*Cent. Dict.* 1891); **union-grass**, one or other of the grasses belonging to the genus *Uniola* (ibid.); **Union House**, the poorhouse or workhouse of a Poor Law union (cf. senses 7 d and 10 b, and *Union workhouse*); **union-joint** (see quots. and sense 9); **union nut**, (*a*) a nut used with a screw to unite one part to another; (*b*) the Australian timber-tree *Boristoa sapindiformis*, or its wood; **union pear** (see quot.); **union-pump** (see quot.); **union-room** *Brewing*, the room containing the unions or cleansing vats; **union-rustic**, a British night-moth, *Apamea connexa* (*Encycl. Dict.* 1888); **union screw** (see quot. and *union joint*); † **union suit**, ? a set of mirrors; **union system** *Brewing* (see quots. and sense 8); **Union workhouse**, = *Union House*. See also UNION FLAG, JACK.

1847 ALB. SMITH *Chr. Tadpole* xlvi, 'Anything new at the *Union House to-day, Mr. Mole?' 1893 *Daily News* 10 April 5/4 The Prince's inscription in the Dunmow Union House visitors' book. 1850 WEALE *Dict. Terms* 493 *Union screws or joints*,..the brass unions for connecting the elastic bore-pipe of the tender to the feed-pipe of the [locomotive] engine. 1867 J. HOGG *Microsc.* I. ii. 107 A finer [adjustment] is secured by a well made union-joint. 1836 *Civil Eng. & Arch. Jrnl.* I. 133/1 It..is attached to a ferrule by a *union nut and screw, and can be as easily removed. 1889 MAIDEN *Useful Pl.* 387 *Boristoa sapindiformis*, 'Union Nut.' 1731 MILLER *Gard. Dict.* 6 U. The *Union Pear; otherwise call'd Dr. Uvedale's St. Germain. This is a very large long Pear, of a deep green Colour. 1860 J. HOGG *Fruit Man.* 217. 1875 KNIGHT *Dict. Mech.* 2681/2 *Union-pump*,..one in which the engine and pump are united in the same frame. 1886 'BICKERDYKE' *Cur. Ale & Beer* 339 The *union-room..[at Allsopp's] contains 1,424 unions, which can cleanse 230,688 gallons at one time. 1850 WEALE *Dict. Terms* 494 The feed-pipe is likewise attached to the lower end of the pump by a large *union screw. 1714 *Lond. Gaz.* No. 5214/3 All sorts of Coach Glasses, Chimney Glasses, Sconces, Dressing Glasses, *Union Suits, Dressing Boxes, swinging Glasses [etc.]. 1876 *Encycl. Brit.* IV. 275/2 There are three modes of cleansing—..2d, by running the beer into casks, and then allowing the yeast to work out through the bung holes; and 3d, on what is called the *Union, or Burton system, which is the second plan with some improvements. 1886 'BICKERDYKE' *Cur. Ale & Beer* 333 When the fermentation has almost ceased, the beer is put into smaller vessels ..and the froth either works over the side or is skimmed off or, as in the 'union' system at Burton, works up through pipes. 1851 KINGSLEY *Yeast* xii, As he went on, talking wildly to himself, he passed the *Union Workhouse. 1863 FAWCETT *Pol. Econ.* IV. iv. 581 The inmates of the union-workhouse are subject to certain restraints.

Hence **U·nional** *a.*, of or pertaining to union or a union (esp. of countries); **U·nioned** *a.*, joined in union; **U·nioner** *U.S.*, an adherent of the Union during the American Civil War.

1889 *Scott. Leader* 18 Apr. 6 If the Unionist has destroyed both the national and *unional sentiment in the Irish. 1905 *Q. Rev.* July 273 The Unional flag had been hauled down. 1787 J. BARLOW *Vision of Columbus* VI. 191 Great Washington arose in view, And *union'd flags his stately steps pursue. 1880 TOURGEE *Fool's Err.* vii. 31 The old *Unioner's report in regard to the doughty colonel.

U·nion, *sb.*[2] Now *arch.* Also 4 **vniune.** [ad. L. *ūniōn-em*, *ūnio* UNIO: cf. ONION *sb.* 7.

So called (acc. to Pliny *Nat. Hist.* IX. xxxv. § 56) because no two are exactly alike.]

A pearl of large size, good quality, and great value, esp. one which is supposed to occur singly.

Freq. in 17th c., esp. in allusion to or echoes of the story related of Cleopatra: see Pliny *loc. cit.* § 59. The following early instance is prob. of AF. origin: *c* 1305 *Land Cokayne* 89 Per is saphir and vniune, Carbuncle and astiune.

1592 *Soliman & Pers.* II. i, Then they play, and when she hath lost her gold, Erastus pointed to her chaine, and then she said: I, were it Cleopatraes vnion. 1599 HAKLUYT *Voy.* II. 5 Precious unions and costly spyces. 1635 HEYWOOD *Hierarchy* VII. 419 A Pendant Vnion to adorne her Eare, Rarer no Queene was euer seene to weare. 1694 MOTTEUX *Rabelais* IV. iv. 19 Between whose Septenary Links.. Rubies, Emeralds,..and Unions were alternatively set in. *a* 1700 EVELYN *Diary* 21 Feb. 1645, The other Union, that Cleopatra was about to dissolve and drink up.

fig. *a* 1672 P. STERRY *Posth. Wks.* (*c* 1680) II. 227 Pearls are called Unions, because they are ever found alone: a Saint's Pearl is his Union for a contrary Reason, because he is never found alone in his Spiritual Being or Beauty.

b. *attrib.* with *pearl*. Also *transf.*

1656 BLOUNT *Glossogr.* s.v., Union Pearls..are the best sort of Pearl. [Hence in Phillips, Bailey, etc.] 1885 R. F. BURTON *Arab. Nts.* (1887) III. 67 This damsel, the mistress of moons, the union pearl.

† **U·nion**, *v.* *Obs. rare.* Also 5 **unyon.** [f. UNION *sb.*[1]] *trans.* To unite.

a 1470 HARDING *Chron.* CCXLI. *heading*, The kynges tytle to all his londes, briefely reported, with a monicion to vnion Scotlande and Englande. 1475 *Bk. Noblesse* (Roxb.) 23 The countee of Mayne by Maryage was unyoned to the erledom of Angew.

Union flag. [UNION *sb.*[1] 4 b, 7 c.] a. The national flag or ensign, formerly of Great Britain, in later use (from 1801) of the United Kingdom of Great Britain and Ireland, formed by combining the crosses of St. George, St. Andrew, and St. Patrick, retaining the blue ground of the banner of St. Andrew. See UNION JACK, and UNION *sb.*[1] 10 a.

This flag was introduced to symbolize the union of the crowns of England and Scotland and was formed by surmounting the cross saltire of St. Andrew by the cross of St. George; the cross saltire of St. Patrick was added on the union of the parliaments of Great Britain and Ireland, when the whole flag was blazoned by Royal Proclamation (*Lond. Gaz.* 1 Jan. 1801), as follows: Azure, the Crosses saltires of St. Andrew and St. Patrick Quarterly per Saltire, counterchanged Argent and Gules; the latter fimbriated of the Second, surmounted by the Cross of St. George of the Third, fimbriated as the Saltire.

1634 in Rymer *Fœdera* (1732) XIX. 549/1 None shall from henceforth presume to carry the Union Flag in the main Top or other part of their Ships, that is Saint George his Cross and Saint Andrews Cross joined together,..but that the same Union Flag be still reserved as an Ornament proper for our own Ships, and Ships in our immediate Service and Pay, and none other. 1681 in *English Hist. Rev.* Jan. (1911) 50 [An article forbidding] privateers to wear our Union flagg and jack. 1696 *Lond. Gaz.* No. 3190/3 Leaving the Command of the Fleet with my Lord Berkeley, who..has put up the Union Flag on Board the Britannia. 1724 C. JOHNSON *Hist. Pirates* 153 One of

them struck the Union Flag on the Top of the Castle. 1769 [see UNION[1] 10 a]. 1829 MARRYAT *F. Mildmay* viii, A union flag is displayed at the mizen peak. 1844 *Regul. & Ord. Army* 48 The Union Flag or Jack being the distinctive flag or mark of an Admiral of the Fleet, when displayed at the main-top-gallant-mast-head. 1865 *N. & Q.* 11 March 208/2 The incorporation of the red saltier of St. Patrick into the Union Flag.

b. The flag of the federated colonies or provinces of the American Union.

1776 *Pennsylv. Even. Post* 28 May 266/2 The Union Flag of the American States waved upon the Capitol.

Unionic (yūniǫ·nik), *a.* [f. UNION *sb.*[1] + -IC.] Of or pertaining to, characteristic of, a Union or University Union Society; frequenting or debating at the Union.

1855 *Househ. Words* 30 June 521, I breakfasted with jovial undergraduates...I heard old talk..of Unionic speakers eloquent. 1865 *Pall Mall G.* 13 April 10/1 The characteristics of Unionic eloquence. 1884 J. PAYN *Lit. Recoll.* 54 In Mr. Lewis's classification of his fellow-students, it was that of 'the Unionic Cantab.'

Unionid (yū·niǫnid). *Zool.* [a. mod. L. *Unionid-æ* (see def.), f. L. *unio* UNIO: see -ID[3].] A member of the *Unionidæ*, a large family of bivalve molluscs typified by the genus *Unio* of freshwater mussels; a unio.

1861 P. P. CARPENTER in *Rep. Smithsonian Instit.* 1860, 263 The extreme forms of the Unionids.

Unio·niform, *a.* *Zool.* [f. mod.L. *Unio* UNIO: see -(I)FORM.] Belonging to or resembling the *Unionidæ*; unionoid.

1868 R. TATE *App. to Woodward's Mollusca* 71 *Anthracosia* differs from *Unio*, to which genus the majority of the Unioniform shells have been referred.

Unionism (yū·nyəniz'm). [f. UNION *sb.*[1] + -ISM.] The principle or policy of union; combination in union as a system of social organization; advocacy of this. Cf. TRADE(S)-UNIONISM.

1845 MIALL in *Nonconf.* V. 173 The gravest objections against congregational unionism. 1869 J. STIRLING *Trade Unionism* 21 To the unionist himself, the results of Unionism are no less hurtful. 1884 *Brit. Alm. & Comp.* 67 The growth of unionism among farm labourers.

b. *U.S.* Advocacy of, attachment or adherence to, a legislative union between states.

1864 LOWELL *McClellan or Lincoln?* Pr. Wks. 1890 V. 157 The somewhat light Unionism of Mr. Pendleton. 1865 — *Reconstruct.* Ibid. 222 We do not mean to say that there is any very large amount of even latent Unionism at the South. 1883 *American* VI. 92 The obstinate Unionism of the mountaineer farmers.

c. Loyalty to or advocacy of the principles, views, or programme of the Unionist party of Great Britain and Ireland; the political tenets characteristic of a Unionist.

1886 *Sat. Rev.* 5 June 763/2 Unionism has to deal with an enemy perfectly unscrupulous. 1889 MRS. BUXTON in O'Brien *Life Parnell* (1898) I. 220 We talked a little about Home Rule and the future of Ireland—my Unionism getting very shaky.

Unionist (yū·nyənist), *sb.* and *a.* [f. as prec. + -IST. Cf. F. *unioniste*.]

A. *sb.* 1. An adherent of or believer in unionism as a political principle or system of organization; esp. one who advocates or supports the formation or maintenance of some particular legislative union.

Usually with initial capital in particularized sense.

1799 *Monthly Rev.* XXX. 357 [Duigenan] is particularly severe in his criticisms on Lord Minto, a Brother Unionist. 1851 GALLENGA *Italy* 41 Nothing..has been more fatal to the cause of Italian federation than a departure from the views of the Unionists. 1887 MAHAFFY & GILMAN *Alexander's Empire* XXX. 286 There was a large nationalist party ..violently opposed to the unionists,..constantly asserting the right of every Greek state to legislate for itself. 1890 HATTON *By Order of Czar* II. i, [He] was above all things an Imperial Unionist, and would defend to the death the merest scrap of soil over which the flag had ever floated.

b. *U.S.* A supporter or advocate of the Federal Union of the United States of America; esp. one who during the Civil War of 1861–5 was opposed to Secession.

1830 D. WEBSTER *1st Sp. on Foot's Res.* Wks. 1851 III. 259, I am a unionist, and, in this sense, a national republican. 1862 MOTLEY *Corr.* (1889) II. 94 The anti-slavery men became the Unionists, the slaveholders the Destructionists. 1883 *American* VII. 149 A Texas 'Unionist' is going to sue the United States for the value of his slaves.

c. *British Politics.* A member of the political party which advocated or supported maintenance of the parliamentary Union between Great Britain and Ireland; an opponent of Home Rule.

This party was formed in 1886 by the coalition of the Conservatives with those Liberals (Liberal Unionists: see LIBERAL *a.* 5) who were opposed to Gladstonian Home Rule. While the chief tenet of this party was the maintenance of the Union, its general policy and principles gradually became identified with those of the Conservative party.

1886 LD. R. CHURCHILL *Sp. at Manch.* 3 March, Do you not think that such a party might be formed which might combine all that is best of the politics of the Tory, the Whig, or the Liberal?..Might we not call it the party of the Union? Members of that party might be known as Unionists. 1886 in *Pall Mall G.* 6 July 14/1 The opinion ..that..the Liberal Unionists are coming to signal grief... The Unionists have, indeed, pulled the chestnuts out of the fire for Lord Salisbury. 1893 *Times* 25 Apr. 11/1 A representative company of British Unionists to meet the Unionists of Ireland.

2. A member of a trade-union; a TRADE-UNIONIST.

1834 *John Bull* 13 July 219/1 The cases on the Crown side were principally Unionists, charged with administering unlawful oaths. 1854 H. MILLER *Sch. & Schm.* xv. 327 The life of my friend was..pitched on a..higher tone than that of most of his brother unionists. 1879 T. H. S. ESCOTT *England* I. 282 The charges of conspiracy and violence brought against unionists and unionism.

3. One who desires or advocates the union of churches or congregations. Cf. REUNIONIST.

1852 NEWLAND *Lect. Tractar.* 165 We are Tractarians or Unionists or whatever you may please to call us. 1866 G. TALBOT in E. Purcell *Life A. P. de Lisle* (1900) I. xv. 408, I think that the sympathy of the Unionists for the Greek Schism is a proof of want of sincerity. 1869 *Union Review* 311 The Unionist, whether he be a Roman or an Anglican.

B. *attrib.* passing into *adj.* 1. Of or pertaining to, advocating or supporting, a legislative union, esp. that between Great Britain and Ireland.

1816 SCOTT *Bl. Dwarf* xii, The Unionist courtiers, that have bought and sold old Scotland. 1848 DAUNT *Recoll. O'Connell* I. ii. 16, I spoke in reply to a Unionist effusion of Emerson Tennent's. 1863 DICEY *Federal St.* II. 187 The *Atlantic Monthly*..is..staunchly Unionist, and more or less anti-slavery. 1888 A. J. BALFOUR in *Times* 2 Oct. 10/1 The union of the Unionist party.

b. Of or belonging to the Unionists or Unionist Party. (Cf. A. 1 c.)

1886 *Pall Mall G.* 3 July 4/1 The utter failure of the Unionist attack..at Stockton. 1890 RIDER HAGGARD *Beatrice* xviii, He knew the head Unionist whip very well. 1897 H. TENNYSON *Tennyson* II. 412 The large Unionist meetings throughout Great Britain.

2. Of or belonging to trade-unionism or trade-unionists.

1879 H. SPENCER *Data of Ethics* xii. § 78. 211 The unionist principle that the better workers must not discredit the worse by exceeding them in efficiency. 1884 *Pall Mall G.* 11 Sept. 3/1 The success of the unionist movement.

Unioni·stic, *a.* [f. UNIONIST *sb.* + -IC.] Of or relating to, characteristic of, unionists; advocating, promoting, or favourable to union or unionism.

1860 WORCESTER (citing Schaff). 1867 LD. ACTON *Lett.* (1906) 346 The Bishop of Mentz..has written a pamphlet decidedly unionistic. 1882–3 *Schaff's Encycl. Relig. Knowl.* II. 1683 When the unionistic measures of Bucer were being discussed. 1884 *American* VIII. 6 For this reason the simply unionistic feeling burned in the northwest.

U·nionite. *Min.* [Named by Silliman from its locality, *Unionville*, Pennsylvania.] = ZOISITE.

1849 B. SILLIMAN in *Amer. Jrnl. Sci. & Arts* Ser. II. VIII. 384 Unionite..in general appearance..somewhat resembles scapolite or spodumene. 1855 *Orr's Circ. Sci., Geol.*, etc. 321 Antitomus Felspar, Soda Spodumene, Unionite.

Unionize (yū·nyənəiz), *v.* [f. UNION *sb.*[1] + -IZE.]

a. *trans.* To form into a union. *rare*[−1].

1841 R. OASTLER *Fleet Papers* I. No. 23. 182 The breaking up of the old local, domestic, family system of self-government, by unionizing and centralizing society.

b. *esp.* To bring under trade-union rules or principles; to cause (persons) to become members of a trade-union.

Freq. since *c* 1900. Hence (in journalistic use) *Unionization*, *Unionized* ppl. a., *Unionizing* vbl. sb.

1890 *Columbus* (Ohio) *Dispatch* 18 Nov., It has been decided by the Trades Council to take radical measures.. to unionize all work in the building trades. 1903 *Liberty Review* July 16 The servants have been unionised under the rules of the..Federation.

Union Jack. [f. UNION *sb.*[1] + JACK *sb.*[3]] Originally and properly, a small British union flag flown as the jack of a ship; in later and more general use extended to any size or adaptation of the union flag (even when not used as a jack), and regarded as the national ensign. See UNION FLAG a and UNION *sb.*[1] 10 a.

Written either with capitals or small initials.

1674 *Lond. Gaz.* No. 924/1 To Charge..His Subjects.., That from henceforth they do not presume to wear His Majesties Jack (commonly called, The Union Jack) in any of their Ships or Vessels, without particular Warrant. 1694, 1702 [see JACK *sb.*[3]]. 1801 *Union Magazine* Jan. 52 The Royal Union standard was hoisted on the Tower;..the Union Jack on the Parade. 1822 *Admiralty Order* in *Lond. Gaz.* No. 17871. 1893/1 We..authorize all His Majesty's subjects to hoist the Union Jack at the top-mast-head.., or at the fore-top-mast-head.., as a signal for a pilot. 1883 MRS. BISHOP *Golden Chersonese* 222 Everything was 'ship-shape',..a union jack over the desk, from which the liturgy was read, and a tiger-skin [etc.].

b. A figure or representation of this. Also *attrib.*

1848 ALBERT SMITH *Chr. Tadpole* xxiv. 220 Quite unexpectedly they all produced union-jack pocket-handkerchiefs, at the same moment. 1856 MISS YONGE *Daisy Chain* I. xiv, Harry used to write his name all over his-sea—and draw union-jacks on it. 1886 *Pall Mall G.* 3 July 4/1 In Sunderland the Liberals have all taken to wear Union Jacks in their buttonholes.

Hence (with reference to the use of the union jack as a national flag) **Union Ja·ckery**, **Union Ja·ckist**, **Ja·ckite**. *nonce-words*.

1886 *Pall Mall G.* 3 July 4/1 At Nottingham,..the Tory party is locally known as the Union Jackists. 1896 *Spectator* 7 March 342 The national outbursts of 'Union-Jackery' in the courts and music-halls. 1901 *Daily Chron.* 2 Dec. 10/2 Men who no doubt call themselves patriotic Union-Jackites and Big Englanders.

U·nionoid, *a.* and *sb.* *Zool.* [f. mod.L. *Union-* UNIO.] a. *adj.* Of or belonging to the *Unionidæ*; unioniform. b. *sb.* A unionid (*Cent. Dict.* 1891).

1879 H. A. NICHOLSON *Palæont.* (ed. 2) I. 492 Unionoid Bivalves, with thick shells.

Union pipes, *sb. pl.* [? ad. Ir. *píob uilleann*, f. *píob* pipe + *uilleann*, gen. sing. of *uille* elbow.] A form of bagpipes in which the wind-bag is inflated by bellows worked by the elbow; Irish bagpipes.

1851–61 MAYHEW *Lond. Labour* III. 163/1 The union pipes are the old Irish pipes improved. 1877 R. BELL *Early Ballads*, etc. 441 We first heard it sung in Malhamdale, Yorkshire, by..an old Dales'-minstrel, who accompanied himself on the union-pipes.

Unipa·rient, *a.* [See UNI- and PARIENT *a.*] = next 1.

1822–7 GOOD *Study Med.* (1829) V. 227 [These signs] belong as frequently to the uniparient as to the multiparient, and hence are unentitled to attention. 1859 *Todd's Cycl. Anat.* V. 560/2 In Man, although generally uniparient, two or more follicles may..become matured about the same time.

Uniparous (yūni·pärəs), *a.* [f. mod.L. *ūniparus* (whence F. *unipare*, It. *uniparo*, Sp. *uníparo*): see UNI- and -PAROUS.]

1. Bearing or producing one at a birth; characterized by this kind of parturition.

1646 SIR T. BROWNE *Pseud. Ep.* VI. vi. 298 For animals multifidous..there are but two that are uniparous, that is, Men and Elephants. 1662 PETTY *Treat. Taxes & Contrib.* xii. 58 'Tis also the second choice out of the young of multiparous Cattle taken in *specie*,..or else a Composition in Money for the Uniparous. 1744 MONRO *Compar. Anat.* 37 Those of the uniparous Kind have them placed between the posterior Extremities. 1787 *Phil. Trans.* LXXVII. 358 The females of the human species, though most commonly uniparous. 1839–47 *Todd's Cycl. Anat.* III. 315 The oviducts are shorter..in the uniparous Kangaroo,..than in the multiparous Opossums. 1856 GRINDON *Life* iv. (1875) 41 Rousseau ingeniously urges..that woman is a uniparous animal. 1859 OWEN *Lect. Classif. Mammalia* 56 The mastodons, megatheria,..and diprotodons, are uniparous.

2. *Bot.* Of a cyme: Having only one axis or branch; developing a single axis at each branching.

1839 LINDLEY *Introd. Bot.* (ed. 3) 160 [An] axis of uniparous, that is one-peduncled, cymes. 1878 M. T. MASTERS *Henfrey's Bot.* 318 The inflorescence..is probably a uniparous scorpioid cyme. 1887 BENTLEY *Man. Bot.* (ed. 5) 215 The terms *helicoid* and *scorpioid* are thus used by us indifferently to indicate the same form of *unilateral, monochasial*, or *uniparous cyme*.

Unipartite (yūnipā·ɹtəit), *a.* *Math.* [See UNI- and PARTITE *a.*] Consisting of or involving a single part.

1870 CAYLEY *Math. Papers* (1893) VI. 464 The quantic is unipartite, bipartite, tripartite, etc., according as the number of sets [of variables] is one, two, three, etc. 1890 *Nature* 20 Feb. 380/2 In the theory of the single system [of equations] the conceptions and symbolism..are based upon the properties of single integral numbers and their partitions into single integral parts. In this sense the former theory may be regarded as being unipartite.

Uniped (yū·niped), *sb.* and *a.* Also -**pede** (-pīd). [f. UNI- + L. *ped-*, *pēs* foot.]

A. *sb.* A person having only one foot (or leg); a one-footed creature.

1801 SOUTHEY *Thalaba* iv. 218 *note*, There is said to be a nation of one legged men, and one of these unipeds is represented in a print, lying on his back, under the shade of his own great foot. 1846 *Blackw. Mag.* LX. 227 To wake up ten minutes afterwards an unsuffering uniped. 1863 C. M. SMITH *Dead Lock* 248 In all diseases of the toes..the liabilities of the uniped are but as five to ten compared with those of his two-legged brethren.

fig. 1897 *Contemp. Rev.* Oct. 536 The greater sort will escape one-sidedness by inventing some outlet for themselves, but the average will present us with an endless variety of quaint queer unipeds.

B. *adj.* Having only one foot (or leg); one-footed.

1835 KIRBY *Hab. & Inst. Anim.* II. 125 [These] Molluscans ..are the only instance of a *unipede* structure in creation. 1866 R. CHAMBERS *Ess.* Ser. II. 206 An auctioneer..who.. sells off pots and pans, and small uniped tables.

Unipe·rsonal, *a.* [See UNI- and PERSONAL *a.* Cf. F. *unipersonnel* (in sense 2), Pg. *unipessoal*.]

1. Consisting of a single person or individual.

c 1810 COLERIDGE in *Lit. Rem.* (1838) III. 220 If there be a functionary of divine institution, synodical or unipersonal, who with the name of the 'Church' has the right [etc.].

b. Having, or existing as, one person.

Cf. TRI-PERSONAL *a.* and PERSON 7 a.

1869 *Contemp. Rev.* XII. 450 The God of the Bible is neither unipersonal nor tripersonal in that sense of person. 1901 R. C. MOBERLY *Atonem. & Person.* viii. 172 [Not] one of them [*sc.* analogies]..go far towards enabling uni-personal man to enter into the consciousness of Tri-personality.

2. *Gram.* Of a verb: = IMPERSONAL *a.* 1. *rare.*

1860 WORCESTER (citing Wells). [Hence in Webster (1864) and later Dicts.]

Hence **Unipe·rsonalist**, a believer in the unipersonality of the Deity (1846 Worcester, citing Faber); **Unipersona·lity**, existence in one person.

1859 J. MARTINEAU *Ess. & Addr.* (1891) II. 389 If we set up as our essential a doctrine, like that of the Unipersonality of God. 1884 — in *Life* (1902) II. viii. 70.

Unipe·talous, *a.* *Bot.* *rare*[−1]. [ad. mod.L. *unipetal-us* (whence F. *unipétale*): see UNI- and PETALOUS *a.*] (See quot.)

1849 J. H. BALFOUR *Man. Bot.* 178 A corolla rarely consists of one petal, and when this occurs..it depends on the abortion or non-development of others. Such a corolla is *unipetalous*..., a term quite distinct from monopetalous.

Uni·phonous, *a.* *rare*[−1]. [f. UNI- 1, after MONO-, POLYPHONOUS *adjs.*] Producing only one kind of note.

1832 *Westm. Rev.* Nov. (Cassell's), That uniphonous instrument the drum.

Unipla·nar, *a.* [See UNI- and PLANAR *a.*]

1. *Geom.* Having or characterized by coincident planes. *Uniplanar node* (or *point*), a form of node or conical point in which the tangent cone has become a pair of coincident planes; a unode.

1866 BRANDE & COX *Dict. Sci.*, etc. II. 675 When this cone breaks up into two planes, the node is termed a biplanar node, and, when these planes coincide, a uniplanar node. 1869 [see UNIPLANE]. 1889 *Cent. Dict.* s.v. *Dyadic*, *Uniplanar diadic*, a planar diadic in which the plane of the antecedents coincides with that of the consequents.

2. *Mech.* Of motion: Lying or taking place in, confined to, one plane; of or pertaining to such motion.

1882 MINCHIN (*title*), Uniplanar Kinematics of Solids and Fluids. *Ibid.* 1 By uniplanar motion, or one-plane motion, is understood in the following pages motion which takes place in one plane or parallel to one plane.

U·niplane, *a.* and *sb.* [UNI-.] a. *adj.* Forming or lying in one plane. b. *sb.* (See quot. 1869.)

1843 *Civil Eng. & Arch. Jrnl.* VI. 218/2 A pneumatic machine for casting, and a uniplane machine for composing. 1869 CAYLEY *Math. Papers* (1893) VI. 361 U..is a uniplanar node, where the quadric cone becomes a coincident plane-pair; say, the plane is the uniplane.

U·niplicate, *a.* *rare*[−0]. [f. UNI- 1, after MULTIPLICATE *a.*] Having but one fold.

1840 SMART; and in later Dicts.

Unipo·lar, *a.* (and *sb.*). [See UNI- and POLAR *a.* Cf. F. *unipolaire*.]

1. *Electr.* Produced by, proceeding from, one magnetic pole; exhibiting one kind of polarity.

1812 SIR H. DAVY *Chem. Philos.* 168 There are substances that are imperfect conductors which are capable of receiving only one kind of electricity..and which M. Ehrman..has named unipolar bodies. 1873 J. C. MAXWELL *Electr. & Magn.* II. 7 The property produced by magnetism in transparent bodies of twisting the plane of polarization of the incident light, is, like magnetism itself, a unipolar property. 1881 *Nature* XXIII. 616 To illustrate unipolar conductivity. *Ibid.* XXIV. 570 Whether it be not possible entirely to separate one from the other, and to produce what may be called a unipolar discharge. 1888 *Encycl. Brit.* XXIII. 330/1 The so-called 'unipolar' induction supposed to be due to the rotation of the earth.

b. Of apparatus: Having, or operating by means of, one magnetic pole. Also *ellipt.*

1876 *Nature* XIV. 263/2 A unipolar magnetic needle. *Ibid.*, The space through which a subsidiary magnet must be moved in order to restore the unipolar to its original position. 1883 *Daily News* 10 Sept. 2/2 The remarkable machine of Messrs. Siemens and Halske, called the unipolar machine. 1884 *Health Exhib. Catal.* 79/2 A true unipolar continuous current dynamo.

2. *Biol.* Of nerve-cells: Having one pole or fibrous prolongation; connected to the nerve-fibre by a single fibrous process.

1859 *Todd's Cycl. Anat.* V. 436/2 Those [ganglionic corpuscles] from which one tube proceeds are termed unipolar. 1873 A. FLINT *Physiol. Man, Nerv. Syst.* i. 46 Unipolar cells exist in some of the lower orders of animals. 1880 BASTIAN *Brain* ii. 48 Unipolar nerve cells..are alleged to exist in the ganglia on the spinal nerves and elsewhere.

b. (See quot.)

1878 F. J. BELL tr. *Gegenbaur's Comp. Anat.* 597 If the rete remains broken up, then it is known as a diffuse, unipolar, or monocentric rete mirabile.

Hence **Unipola·rity**, the condition or character of being unipolar. (Cf. F. *unipolarité*.)

1888 *Philos. Mag.* Ser. v. XXVI. 129 We do not believe that Ohm ever observed the phenomenon of unipolarity in strong sulphuric acid with [etc.].

Uni·porous, *a.* [UNI- 1. Cf. POLYPOROUS *a.*] (See quot.)

1888 DAWSON *Geol. Hist. Plants* 160 Wood-cells elsewhere called discigerous tissue, and to which I applied the terms uniporous and multiporous.

† **Unipre·sence.** *Obs.*[−1] [f. UNI- + PRESENCE, after OMNIPRESENCE.] The fact, on the part of a number, of being present in one place. So † **Unipre·sent** *a.* *Obs.*[−1]

1619 LUSHINGTON *Recant. Serm.* (1659) 77 The unipresence, or local union of body; 'in one place'. *Ibid.* 96 They were unanimous and unipresent.

Unique (yūnī·k), *a.* and *sb.* Also 7 **unick(e**, 7–8 **unic.** [a. F. *unique* († *unic* masc.), ad. L. *ūnic-us* (whence also Sp., Pg., It. *unico*) single, sole, alone of its kind, f. *ūnus* one. In early use also directly ad. L. *ūnicus*, and stressed on the first syllable.]

Regarded by Todd (1818) as 'an affected and useless term of modern times'.

A. *adj.* 1. Of which there is only one; one and no other; single, sole, solitary.

1622 DOLMAN *La Primaud. Fr. Acad.* (1618) III. 639 Engendring one eternitie, and by an alone vnique action never disturbed, his linage full of understanding. *c* 1645 HOWELL *Lett.* II. xliv, He hath lost..his unic Son in the very flower of his age. 1677 GALE *Crt. Gentiles* IV. I. ii. 53 Divines, who make..right Reason the unic Criterion or Rule of moral Virtue.

1818 TODD, *Unique*, adj.,..sole;..without another of the same kind known to exist. 1861 PALEY *Æschylus, Prometh.* (ed. 2) 39 The student will notice the unique example of στεγνωθεῖα. 1873 HAMERTON *Intell. Life* III. iii. 87 A man ..who made Latin scholarship his unique intellectual purpose. 1882 FARRAR *Early Chr.* II. 476 St. John instantly leaves the subject..to which he has made this unique and passing allusion.

2. That is or forms the only one of its kind; having no like or equal; standing alone in comparison with others, freq. by reason of superior excellence; unequalled, unparalleled, unrivalled.

In this sense readopted from French at the end of the 18th c. and regarded as a foreign word down to the middle of the 19th, from which date it has been in very common use, with a tendency to take the wider meaning of 'uncommon, unusual, remarkable'.

The usage in the comparative and superlative, and with advs. as *absolutely, most, quite, thoroughly, totally*, etc., has been objected to as tautological.

1618 W. BARCLAY *Well at King-horne* A vij, This is a soueraigne and vnicke remedie for that disease in Women. 1794 R. J. SULIVAN *View Nat.* I. 3 A concentrated, and an unique aggregation of almost all the wonders of the natural world. 1809 R. K. PORTER *Trav. Sk. Russia & Sweden* (1813) I. xxv. 285 As it was thoroughly *unique*, I cannot forbear presenting you with so singular a curiosity. 1842 J. P. COLLIER *Armin's Nest Ninn.* Introd., A relic.. not only *unique* in itself, but unprecedented in its kind. 1866 LIDDON *Bamp. Lect.* v. (1867) 368 [Christ's] relationship to the Father..is absolutely unique. 1871 B. TAYLOR *Faust* (1875) II. II. i. 84 A thing so totally unique The great collectors would go far to seek. 1885 *Harper's Mag.* April 703/1 When..these summer guests found themselves defrauded of their uniquest recreations.

b. Of persons.

1808 FOSTER *Contrib. Eclectic Rev.* (1844) I. 233 [Sir T. More] is a person so *unique* in the records of statesmen, that [etc.]. 1871 BLACKIE *Four Phases* 15 Such a unique mortal.. no man can describe. 1885 MABEL COLLINS *Prettiest Woman* xi, He believed this woman whom he loved to be unique.

c. *absol.* with *the*: (see quots.).

1767 *Phil. Trans.* LVIII. 26 All these are examples of the *unique*; that is, of quantities in a state that is..exclusive of all others. 1849 C. BRONTË *Shirley* xxiii, She felt that Rose Yorke was a peculiar child—one of the unique.

† 3. Formed or consisting of one or a single thing. *Obs.*[−1]

a 1631 DONNE *Lett.* (1651) 163 A Mathematique point, which is the most indivisible and unique thing which art can present.

B. *sb.* 1. A thing of which there is only one example, copy, or specimen; esp., in early use, a coin or medal of this class.

1714 R. THORESBY *Diary* 23 June, My Lord showed me some unics and other valuable curiosities. 1730 A. GORDON *Maffei's Amphith.* 47 It..may be an Unic, for what we know as yet. 1774 *Gentl. Mag.* XLIV. 8 A coin, which I have reason to think is a Unic. 1826 DISRAELI *V. Grey* II. viii, Mr. Vivian Grey had promised his Lordship, who was a collector of medals, an unique which had never yet been heard of. 1872 O. W. HOLMES *Poet Breakf.-t.* iii. 89 A unique, sir, and there is a pleasure in exclusive possession.

† b. Something of which only one is possessed by a person or persons. *Obs. rare.*

1783 H. WALPOLE *Let. to C'tess Upper Ossory* 20 June, Lady Pembroke having lent them a servant besides their own unique. 1806 SURR *Winter in Lond.* III. 170 This Belcher girdle was not old; but being an *unique*, it had been..constantly in use.

2. A thing, fact, or circumstance which by reason of exceptional or special qualities stands alone and is without equal or parallel in its kind.

1768 *Phil. Trans.* LVIII. 215 When I presented this map to the Academy..it was looked upon as an Unique. 1781 *Gentl. Mag.* LI. 280/2 The dedication [of a volume of Sermons] being an *unique* in its kind. 1794 PALEY *Evid.* II. ix. iii. ad fin., The propagation of Christianity..is an *unique* in the history of the species. 1835 *Tait's Mag.* II. 651 It is.. an *unique* in English biography. 1838 DE QUINCEY *Lamb* Wks. 1858 IX. 156 Of Lamb's writings..some were so memorably beautiful as to be uniques in their class. 1844 *N. Brit. Rev.* I. 124 A conflict, that stands out from all shadow of parallelism—a wild originality—a terrible unique.

b. A person of this class.

1758 *Case of Authors Stated* 14 He presumes, that he, this *Unic*, must therefore appear in the same stupendous Magnitude to every body else. 1782 COWPER *Let.* Nov., Wks. (1876) 121 He is a man much to my taste, and quite an unique in this country. 1802 MRS. E. PARSONS *Myst. Visit* IV. 145, I trust that he though very good, is not an unique. 1813 *Examiner* 22 Feb. 122/2 Those..charms of manner, which constitute an *unique*. 1866 ALGER *Solit. Nat. & Man* II. 65 The peculiar endowment in which he so far surpasses others as to be an insulated unique.

Uni·quely, *adv.* [f. prec. + -LY[2].]

1. Exclusively, solely; only.

1820 T. MITCHELL *Aristoph.* I. 13 It is a picture uniquely Creek, to have a person of his rank in life giving such a debtor and creditor account of his intellectual pleasures as Dicæopolis does. 1893 SALTUS *Mme. Sapphira* 182 She had married him uniquely to go into society. 1893 *Nation* (N.Y.) 28 Sept. 220/1 That distinction he can still boast to be his uniquely.

b. By itself alone; separately.

1885 LEUDESDORF *Cremona's Proj. Geom.* 43 Therefore D_1 must coincide with D', since the three points $A'B'C'$ determine uniquely the fourth point which forms with them a harmonic range.

2. To a unique degree or extent; so as to be unique; singularly, especially, pre-eminently.

1846 DARWIN in *Life & Lett.* (1887) I. 345, I sent you a uniquely laudatory epistle. 1881 H. W. NICHOLSON *From Sword to Share* vii. 41 The climate is simply and uniquely perfect. 1886 W. J. TUCKER *E. Europe* 310 The uniquely-shaped and quaintly-coloured furniture.

Uni·queness. [f. as prec. + -NESS.] The fact or condition of being unique or unequalled; unique quality or character; an instance of this; a unique fact or circumstance.

1820 COLERIDGE *Lett., Convers.*, &c. I. 152 The contra-distinction between the Shakespearian and the Greek Drama, and its still remaining uniqueness. 1874 H. R. REYNOLDS *John Bapt.* i. § 1. 4 So a great man loses something of his sublimity and uniqueness as we come close to him. 1880 BERTHA THOMAS *Violin-Player* II. x. 231 The novelty, the uniqueness of the scene. 1897 D. W. FORREST *Christ of Hist. & Exper.* v. 205 The uniquenesses of Christ are manifold and indubitable.

Uni·quity. [Irreg. f. UNIQUE *a.* + -ITY, prob. after *antiquity*.] = prec. (Cf. UNICITY 2.)

Also, in recent use (1917), = a unique book.

1789 H. WALPOLE *Let.* 20 July, As rarities, a collector would give ten times more for them: and *uniquity* will make them valued more than the charming poetry. 1793 — *Let.* 17 Sept., I lament that the summer is over; not because of its uniquity, but because you two made it so delightful to me. 1862 B. TAYLOR *Home & Abr.* Ser. II. 399 The originality, the uniquity, of the place. 1886 E. RANDOLPH *Mostly Fools* II. i. 16 The idea..is unique, and uniquity, if I may permit myself the expression, is what we must aim at. 1898 *Atlantic Monthly* LXXXII. 495/1 The lateness..of the bird's appearance, together with what a certain scholarly friend of mine would have called his 'uniquity'.

Unireme (yū·nirīm). [f. UNI- + L. *rēm-us* oar, after *bi-, quadri-, trireme*, etc.] An ancient vessel or galley having one bank of oars.

1699 J. POTTER *Antiq. Greece* III. xiv. II. 135 [A ship] betwixt an Vnireme, and Bireme, consisting of a Bank, and a half. 1799 CHARNOCK in *Naval Chron.* I. 134 The Uniremes ..had only one row of oars. 1900 *Athenæum* 18 Aug. 221/3 The thing shown is meant for a unireme.

Un-I·rish, *a.* (UN-[1] 7.) 1842 LOVER *Handy Andy* ix, The youth endeavoured to become un-Irish in everything. 1854 GRACE GREENWOOD *Haps & Mishaps* 108 An awkward effort at enjoyment and amusement, un-Irish and lamentable in the extreme. **Un-I·rishly**, *adv.* (UN-[1] 11.) 1830 MOORE *Mem.* (1854) VI. 135 They wisely and un-Irishly chose the money.

† **Unirked**, *ppl. a.* *Sc. Obs.* (UN-[1] 8.)

1513 DOUGLAS *Æneid* XIII. xi. 35 The Eneadanis all of his menge Ithandly and onyrkyt luifflit haue I. 1533 BELLENDEN *Livy* IV. xiv. (S.T.S.) II. 99 Horsmen..fresche and vnirkit of lauboure.

Uni·ron, *v.* (UN-[2] 4 and 4 b.)

1611 FLORIO, *Disferrare*, to vniron, to vnshooe a horse. *Ibid.*, *Sferrare*, to vniron, to free or deliuer from out irons or bondes. [1863 SALA *Captain Dangerous* II. i. 18 Captain Handsell had me unironed.]

Uni·roned, *ppl. a.* (UN-[1] 8.)

c 1430 *Pilgr. Lyf Manhode* I. cviii. (1869) 57 A burdoun yrened weyeth more than thilke that is vnyrened. 1788 HOLCROFT tr. *Baron Trenck* (1886) II. 21, I was thus left four days in peace, unironed. 1880 *New Virgin.* I. 57 Unironed shirts and coats.

Unirra·diated, *ppl. a.* (UN-[1] 8.) 1806 SYMMONS *Life of Milton* 544 (Jod.), A mind not unirradiated with the golden visions of fancy. 1816 COLERIDGE *Lay Serm.* (Bohn) 342 The understanding..unirradiated by the reason and the spirit. **Unirrigated**, *ppl. a.* (UN-[1] 8.) 1876 BROWNING *Poets Croisic* 83 Our Academic clodpoles must be dense Indeed to stand unirrigated still. 1883 *Standard* 31 Aug. 4/6 The unirrigated tracts between the head waters of the.. rivers. **Unirritant**, *a.* (UN-[1] 7.) 1822–7 GOOD *Study Med.* (1829) V. 120 We should employ the unirritant tonics. **Unirritated**, *ppl. a.* (UN-[1] 8.) 1649 EARL MONM. tr. *Senault's Use Passions* (1671) 83 Bulls..do little unirritated. 1793 T. BEDDOES *Lett. Darwin* 71, I do not understand why in an irritable state of the body, the iris should be unirritated. **Unirritatedly**, *adv.* (UN-[1] 11.) 1869 BROWNING *Lett.* Ser. II. (1907) I. 34 Yours unirritatedly, R. B.

Uni·rritating, *ppl. a.* (UN-[1] 10.)

Also *unirritatingly* (Webster, 1847).

1797 ABERNETHY *Surg. Ess.* 98 The abscess at last became ..un-irritating to the constitution. 1839–47 *Todd's Cycl. Anat.* III. 613/2 The smooth and unirritating condition of the inner surface of the deserted shell. 1896 MRS. CAFFYN *Quaker Grandmother* 20 Sin is a chastener that conduces to unirritating niceness.

† **Unirroo·ted**, *ppl. a.* *Obs.* [f. UN-[1] 8 c + *y-rooted*, pa. pple. of ROOT *v.*[2] Cf. UNROOTED *ppl. a.*] Not rooted out or eradicated.

1600 TOURNEUR *Transf. Metam.* lviii, Not hable to endure His heart should knowledge of such harme immure An houre, and th' wrong rest vnirrooted out.

Uniserial (yūnisi·riăl), *a.* Chiefly *Bot.*, *Zool.*, etc. [See UNI- and SERIAL *a.*] Arranged in, consisting of, one series or row; characterized by this kind of form or arrangement.

1839 *Proc. Berw. Nat. Club* I. 198 Suckers uniserial. 1859 *Todd's Cycl. Anat.* V. 290/1 In those genera in which these processes form a single line the gills are said to be uniserial. 1872 H. A. NICHOLSON *Palæont.* 325 The teeth are conical and uniserial.

Uniseriate (yūnisī·riět), *a.* *Bot.* and *Zool.* [See UNI- and SERIATE *a.*] = prec.

1846 DANA *Zooph.* (1848) 215 With cellules interruptedly uniseriate, and occasionally biseriate. 1872 H. C. WOOD *Fresh-w. Algæ* 68 Cells uni-seriate. 1887 W. PHILLIPS *Brit. Discomycetes* 243 Sporidia uniseriate.

Hence **Unise·riately** *adv.*

1848 DANA *Zoo.* 133 Upper margin uniseriately tuberculate.

Unisexual (yūnise·ksiuăl), *a.* [ad. mod.L. *unisexual-is* (F. *unisexuel* (1812), Pg. *unisexual*): see UNI- and SEXUAL *a.*]

1. Of one sex; having the essential generative or

reproductive organs of one or other sex developed or present in individuals: a. *Bot.* Of flowers: In which either the stamens or pistils are absent or suppressed. Also, of plants: Characterized by flowers of this kind; = DICLINOUS *a.*

1802 R. HALL *Elem. Bot.* 193 *Unisexual*,..having one sex. 1828 STARK *Elem. Nat. Hist.* II. 461 The last three classes [of plants]..have the flowers thus disposed, and are hence named unisexual. 1839 LINDLEY *Sch. Bot.* 16 In particular species the stamens are found in one flower, and the pistil in another..; such plants are called unisexual. 1854 S. THOMSON *Wild Fl.* 62 These unisexual blossoms being either the production of the same individual plant, or of separate individuals of the same species. 1872 OLIVER *Elem. Bot.* II. 169 Burnet Sanguisorb,..with..unisexual flowers.

Comb. 1877 *Nature* 26 April 548/1 A unisexual-flowering plant.

b. *Zool.* Of animals or their organs.

In *Ent.* of certain agamic broods of *Aphides*: consisting of the female sex only (*Cent. Dict.* 1891).

1830 R. KNOX *Béclard's Anat.* 29 The organs of generation present all the varieties, unisexual, without copulation, hermaphrodite [etc.]. 1861 HULME tr. *Moquin-Tandon* II. I. 47 In a great number of animals the sexes are separated and placed on distinct individuals: these are said to be unisexual. 1877 DARWIN *Forms of Fl.* Introd. 2 The males and females of ordinary unisexual animals.

2. Pertaining or restricted to one sex; *U.S.* esp. of colleges or schools.

1885 L. OLIPHANT *Sympneumata* 182 The relationship of person which would maintain in a painful activity the currents of the decaying unisexual layers of either frame. 1886 *Century Mag.* June 326/1 One final provincialism of the mind there is, which a unisexual college certainly never would have any power to eradicate. 1904 *Daily Chron.* 14 Oct. 6 The present unjust system of unisexual punishments.

Hence **Unise·xually** *adv.*

1891 *Cent. Dict.* s.v., Animals unisexually developed. 1902 *Nature* 10 Jan. 252/1 Not that spontaneous variations are always inherited unisexually.

Unisexua·lity. *Bot.* and *Zool.* [f. prec. + -ITY.] The state or condition of being unisexual.

1830 LINDLEY *Nat. Syst. Bot.* 155 The unisexuality of the flowers of both genera. 1877 HUXLEY *Anat. Inv. Anim.* i. 67 There is some reason to suspect..that unisexuality is the result of the abortion of the organs of the other sex, in males and females respectively. 1898 *Pop. Sci. Monthly* July 298 Asexuality passes through bisexuality into unisexuality.

Unisi·licate. *Min.* [UNI- 2.] (See quot. from Dana.) Also *attrib.*

1879 RUTLEY *Stud. Rocks* x. 140 In chemical composition the garnets are essentially unisilicates of different sesquioxides and protoxides. 1879 DANA *Man. Min.* (ed. 3) 242 In the Unisilicates, one molecule of silicon is combined with two of an element in the protoxide state..; or with two-thirds of a molecule in the sesquioxide state. *Ibid.*, Among the species referred to the Unisilicates there are some that vary from the unisilicate ratio.

Unisolated, *ppl. a.* (UN-[1] 8.) 1886 *Jrnl. R. Microsc. Soc.* VI. 47 The unisolated hyoid muscles of the frog.

Unison (yū·nisən, -zən), *sb.* and *a.* Also 6 **unisonne, vnisone, unizon** (**vnisson**), 7 **unisone.** [a. OF. *unison* (Oresme), later and mod.F. *unisson* (16th c.), or ad. late L. *unison-us* (whence It., Sp., and Pg. *unisono* (also as *sb.*), It. † *unissono*, Sp. *unison*) of the same sound as something else, f. L. *ūni-* UNI- and *sonus* SOUND *sb.*[3]]

The apparently early example in the *York Mystery Plays* XXV. 262 is probably a scribal error for 'vrysoune' (= orison).

A. *sb.* 1. *Mus.* and *Acoustics.* a. A sound or note of the same pitch as another; also loosely, a note taken as a starting-point from which intervals are reckoned. Now *rare*, or taken as *transf.* from b.

1574 F. KETT. *A. Le Roy's Instr. Lute* 17 You must..haue recourse to an other stryng, that maketh the vnisson with that. 1609 DOULAND *Ornithoparcus' Microl.* 17 An Vnison is..a Voyce so qualified, that it neither tendeth to depth nor to height. 1660 BOYLE *New Experiments Phys. Mech.* 211 A string tun'd (as Musicians speak..) to an Unison with it. 1694 HOLDER *Harmony* iv. 54 By Unison is meant, sometimes the Habitude or Ration of Equality of two Notes compared together, being of the very same Tune. Sometimes (as here) for the given single Note to which the Distance, or the Rations of other Intervals are compared. 1728 CHAMBERS *Cycl.* s.v. *Interval*, Unisons, 'tis plain, cannot possibly have any Variety. 1881 *Nature* XXIV. 358 When the higher note has reached a point about half-way between unison and the octave note.

transf. 1677 *Phil. Trans.* XVIII. 840 Not the whole of that other string doth thus tremble, but the several parts severally, according as they are Unisons to the whole.

fig. 1760–72 H. BROOKE *Fool of Qual.* (1792) I. 181 The muscles of Harry's expressive countenance, like an equally-tuned instrument, uttered unisons to every word he heard.

b. Identity in pitch of two or more sounds or notes; the agreement or consonance of the sounds of two or more bodies vibrating at equal rates; the relation of two notes of the same pitch reckoned as one of the musical 'intervals'.

1575 GASCOIGNE *Weedes* Wks. 1907 I. 381 At Musickes sacred sounde, my fansies eft begonne, In concordes, discordes, notes and cliffes, in tunes of unisonne. 1596 BATHE *Brief Introd. Skill of Song* C, A concord is diuided into an Vnizon, Third, Fift, Sixt [etc.]. 1626 BACON *Sylva* § 103 The Diapason or Eight in Music is the sweetest Concord; insomuch as it is in effect an Unison. 1694 [see a]. 1728 CHAMBERS *Cycl.* s.v. *Octave*, The most simple Perception the Soul can have of true Sounds, is that of Unison. 1749 J. MASON *Numbers in Poet. Comp.* 21 Those [metrical] Feet..are in Proportion of the Unison in Musick...And they are said to answer to the Unison. 1806 CALLCOTT *Mus. Gram.* II. i. 90 The Unison,..although it cannot properly be reckoned an Interval, is always considered as such. 1873 BANISTER *Music* § 103 Two, or more, perfect 5ths, perfect 8ves, or perfect unisons, are forbidden between the same two parts. 1896 W. G. WOOLCOMBE *Pract. Work Physics* III. Pref., The nearest approach to unison between two musical notes.

c. A combination of melodies at the same pitch (or, loosely, one or more octaves apart) in different parts, i.e. performed by different voices or instruments. Also in fig. context.

In quot. 1730 used loosely for each of such melodies (in this case on different sets of strings of the same instrument: cf. *unison string* in 5).

[1724 *Short Explic. For. Wds. in Mus. Bks.*, *Unissono*, a Unison...This word is also used when in Symphonies of Songs Two Violins both play the same Thing, or the Violin and Song, or the Bass and Song, &c.] 1730 in *Abridgm. Specif. Patents, Music* (1871) 1 A new invented harpsichord upon which (having only two sets of strings) may be performed either one or two unisons, or two unisons & one octave together. 1795 MASON *Ch. Music* i. 82 Every ear felt the stupendous effect both of unison and harmony. 1799 KOLLMANN *Ess. Mus. Composition* iii. 18 In Unisons, or passages where all instruments play the same melody, though in different Octaves. 1855 PUSEY *Doctr. Real Presence* 721 When the Holy Spirit..swept over the discordant strings of human tongues and thoughts..and blended all their varying notes into one holy unison of truth. 1869 OUSELEY *Counterp.* xiv. 83 When the number of parts exceeds four, unisons may be used.

d. In the phrase *in* (..) *unison* (in sense b or c).

1616 W. BROWNE *Brit. Past.* II. ii. 546 Not suffering her shrill waters, as they run, Tun'd with a whistling gale in unison. 1749 J. MASON *Numbers in Poet. Comp.* 21 Two Strings of equal Length (supposing their respective Tensions and Thickness to be equal) being put in Motion, will be in Unison, or give exactly one and the same Sound. 1765 STERNE *Tr. Shandy* VII. xliii, The nymphs joined in unison, and their swains an octave below them. 1795 MASON *Ch. Music* iii. 208 What old Calvin meant to be sung in unison, they chose should be performed in counterpoint, or in four parts. 1856 MRS. C. CLARKE tr. *Berlioz' Instrument.* 32 To violoncellos..is ordinarily given the part of the double bass, which they double in the octave above or in unison. 1873 HALE *In His Name* vi. 58 As the three voices, in strict unison, closed the little song.

transf. 1828 SCOTT *F. M. Perth* xxvii, The cry from the numberless boats..rose in wild unison up to the Tom-an-Lonach. 1876 HOLLAND *Seven Oaks* xi. 149 'Not at all,' was responded almost in unison.

e. *ellipt.* for 'unison string' (see 5).

1820 *Q. Mus. Mag.* II. 306 He tried the octaves, and found them..all flat..; the unisons, generally speaking, were in tune. 1889 [see *unison-tuning* in 5].

2. A single unvaried tone; a monotone. ? *Obs.*

1609 DOULAND *Ornithoparcus' Microl.* 26 The prayers.. are read in an Vnison. 1742 POPE *Dunc.* IV. 612 Lost was the Nation's Sense, nor could be found, While the long solemn Unison [*sc.* a yawn] went round.

3. A union or combination of concordant sounds; a united and unanimous declaration or utterance.

1806 WORDSW. '*Loud is the Vale*' 3 A mighty unison of streams! Of all her Voices, One! 1871 PALGRAVE *Lyr. Poems* 135 That cry has been heard By a nation's unison swelled.

4. *fig.* a. Something perfectly agreeing or consonant with another; an utterance or expression of perfect agreement or assent; something that responds sympathetically as a string tuned to a corresponding note. Now *rare* or *Obs.*

1650 BULWER *Anthropomet.* 63 A forehead which keeps its natural magnitude is one of the Unisons of the face. 1658 GURNALL *Chr. in Arm.* II. 205 Adam indeed had such a righteousnesse made to his hand, his heart and the Law were unisons. 1702 C. MATHER *Magn. Chr.* III. III. (1852) 539 He thought that ministers and market-men were not unisons. 1796 ELIZA HAMILTON *Lett. Hindoo Rajah* (1811) II. 218 The tender sigh..in vibrating on the ears of Miss Ardent, seemed to touch some pleasant unison, that overspread her countenance with a smile. 1812 COLERIDGE in *Lit. Rem.* (1836) I. 375 To make the intellectual faith a fair analogon or unison of the vital faith.

b. Exact or perfect agreement, concord, or harmony; harmonious combination or union.

1654 WHITLOCK *Zootomia* 454 Physitians..are at Discord the best, but at Unisons the worst; for they do all so disagree [etc.]. 1674 PLAYFORD *Skill Mus.* A 5, Friendship the Vnison of well tun'd Hearts. 1744 THOMSON *Summer* (ed. 5) 1375 Social Friends, Attun'd to happy Unison of Soul,.. Now call'd abroad enjoy the falling Day. 1796 MME. D'ARBLAY *Camilla* I. 4 This exemplary couple was bound to each other by the most perfect unison of character. 1819 KEATS *Vis. Hyperion* I. 418 Nor could my eyes And ears act with that unison of sense Which marries sweet sound with the grace of form. 1858 SEARS *Athan.* ix. 77 Thence life and health spread through our animal frames, restoring them to a unison with divine laws. 1871 FARRAR *Witn. Hist.* v. 183 That beautiful unison of noble manhood, stainless womanhood, joyous infancy, and uncontaminated youth.

† c. *At unison* (also *at..unisons*), = next. *Obs.*

1665 GLANVILL *Scepsis Sci.* xiii. 76 Reason and Faith are at perfect Unisons. 1772 *Test Filial Duty* II. 173 The sensations of friendship have not enough of fire in them, to warm the heart into that proper temperature, requisite to render it at unison with the delirium of lovers. *Ibid.* 238 Set all my affections at unison.

d. *In unison*, in agreement or harmony, concordant, consonant, harmonious. Freq. *in unison with*.

1780 COWPER *Parrot* 36 Each character in ev'ry part Sustain'd with so much grace and art, And both in unison. 1782 V. KNOX *Ess.* xxviii. P 8 It is the more tranquil style which is most frequently in unison with our minds. 1815 JANE AUSTEN *Emma* xli, It was all in unison; words, conduct, discretion and indiscretion told the same story. 1836 W. IRVING *Astoria* I. 287 A mode of redress perfectly in unison with the character of the man. 1860 PUSEY *Min. Proph.* 26 Dumb inanimate nature seems to rejoice and to be in unison with our sense of joy. 1879 FARRAR *St. Paul* I. 312 When such allies were in unison..it was easy to strike a deadly blow at the Nazarenes.

5. *attrib.*: **unison stop**, (*a*) in an organ, a stop of the same pitch as the diapasons; (*b*) in a harpsichord (see quot. 1896); **unison string**, in a pianoforte or other instrument, a string tuned to the same pitch as another (or, loosely, to a pitch an octave higher); **unison tune**, a tune to be sung in unison, as distinct from harmony or 'parts'; **unison-tuning**, the tuning of strings (of a pianoforte, etc.) in unison.

1840 *Penny Cycl.* XVI. 493/1 Trumpet and Oboe stops, being what are called *unison stops,..take their lengths from the open diapason. 1896 A. J. HIPKINS *Pianoforte* 122 *Unison Stop*, properly the second foundation register in a harpsichord; the shorter of the unison strings in a double keyboard one, and sounding on the lower keyboard only. 1665 BOYLE *Effects Motion* vii. 80 A certain impulse of Air, made by one of the *Unison-strings of a musical Instrument, may suffice to produce a visible motion in another. 1732 BERKELEY *Alciphr.* III. § 4, I feel an affection in my soul, like the trembling of one lute, upon striking the unison strings of another. 1896 [see *unison stop* above]. 1869 *Pall Mall G.* 7 July 12/2 Mr. John Goss, Mr. E. J. Hopkins, and Mr. J. Baptiste Calkin have composed *unison tunes for this volume. 1889 BRINSMEAD *Hist. Pianoforte* 186 The same plan as that for learning the *unison-tuning may be adopted for the octave, but care must be taken that the unison of the note is tuned afterwards.

B. *adj.* † 1. Sounding at once or together. *Obs.*[−1]

1582 STANYHURST *Æneis* III. (Arb.) 73 Thus God Apollo cryed; but wee with an vnison outcrye..demaunded, what place God Phœbus apointed.

† b. *fig.* United and consenting, as the pronouncement of a number of persons; expressing complete agreement; unanimous, concordant, consonant, harmonious. *Obs.*

1650 W. CHARLETON *Paradoxes* Prol. f 4 b, By the unisone vote of the multitude. 1651 H. L'ESTRANGE *Answ. Mrq. Worcester* 51 Is the Church of Rome so unison, so all of a piece, as to afford no jarres? *a* 1662 HEYLYN *Laud* II. (1671) 447 The first branch [of a Bill] was carried in the Negative by..an Unison-consent in the Lords then present. 1760–2 GOLDSM. *Cit. W.* XXX, I only beg you'll endeavour to make your souls unison with mine.

† c. Concordant or consonant *to* something. *Obs.*

1710 R. WARD *Life H. More* 234 Some Circumstances.., or Particulars of his Writings, are not so unison to my Slower Faculties. 1760–72 H. BROOKE *Fool of Qual.* (1792) V. 10 This doctrine sounded unison to the secret feelings of our young Englishman.

† d. Like-sounding; equivalent. *Obs.*[−1]

1759 STERNE *Tr. Shandy* I. xix, Tristram!—Melancholy dissyllable of sound! which, to his ears, was unison to Nincompoop.

2. *Mus.* and *Acoustics.* Identical in pitch; singing, sounding, etc., in unison; unisonal, unisonous. Now *rare* or *Obs.*

1614 JACKSON *Creed* III. xviii. § 4 As a string, though untouched, and unable to begin motion of itself, will yet raise it selfe to an vnison voice. 1622 PEACHAM *Compl. Gent.* xi. 104 Two Lutes of equall size being laid vpon a Table, and tuned Vnison, or alike in..any..string: the one stricken, the other untouched shall answer it. 1667 MILTON *P. L.* VII. 599 All sounds on Fret by String or Golden Wire Temper'd soft Tunings, intermixt with Voice Choral or Unison. 1694 HOLDER *Harmony* iv. 51 The Unison Concord..is no Space or Interval, but an Identity of Tune. 1721 A. MALCOLM *Treat. Mus.* 580 When Two Voices sing together one Song, 'tis more agreeable that they be 8ve than unison with one another, in every Note. 1893 S. GEE *Auscult. & Percussion* (ed. 4) I. iii. 60 A unison vibration, convibration, or consonance of the wall is required to the production of tone.

Unisonal (yuni·sǫnăl), *a.* *Mus.* [f. prec. + -AL.] = UNISONOUS *a.* 1.

1728 R. NORTH *Mem. Music* (1846) 66 All was plain-song, that is counterpoint unisonall. 1865 *Reader* 19 Aug. 214 The unisonal female-voice choruses. 1882 *Amer. Missionary* Mar. 70 Their general style is recitative and chorus, though a few are pure solos or unisonal measures. 1898 *Record* 4 Nov. 1084/2 In spite of one's own loving reverence for unisonal singing.

Hence **Uni·sonally** *adv.*, in unison.

1882 *Standard* 20 Feb., A passage of broken quavers.. given out unisonally by the full orchestra. 1887 *Ch. Times* 4 March (Cassell's), Tenors and basses burst in unisonally.

Uni·sonance. *rare.* [ad. L. type *unisonantia (whence Sp. and Pg. *unisonancia*), f. med.L. *unison-us*: see UNISON.] Agreement or identity of sounds (see quots.).

1728 CHAMBERS *Cycl.* s.v. *Concord*, Unisonance, then, being the Relation of Equality between the Tunes of two Sounds, all Unisons are Concords, and in the first Degree. *Ibid.* s.v. *Unison*, What constitutes Unisonance, is the Equality of the Number of Vibrations of the two sonorous Bodies in equal Times. [Hence in Webster (1828–32), etc.]

Unisonant (yuni·sǫnănt), *a.* [f. L. *ūni-* UNI- + *sonant-*, *sonans* (see SONANT *a.*), after *dissonant*, etc. Cf. F. *unissonant*.] Of the same pitch or sound; unisonal, unisonous. Also in fig. context.

1801 BUSBY *Dict. Mus.*, *Unisonus*, or *Unisonant*, an epithet applied to those sounds which are..in unison with each other. 1834 MRS. SOMERVILLE *Connex. Phys. Sci.* xvii. (1836) 168 If two bottles be..tuned by filling them with such a quantity of water as will render them unisonant with two tuning-forks which differ in pitch. 1886 LINSKILL *Haven under Hill* II. ix. 115 The mystic, moving, unisonant harmony that was stirring and breaking upon her own soul.

† Unisone·ity. [f. as next + -(I)TY.] A state of agreement or concord ; unanimity.

Unison·ous (yūni·sǒnəs), a. [f. late L. *unison·us* (UNISON) + -OUS.]

1. *Mus.* Of the same pitch for the different voices or instruments ; composed, performed, or rendered in unison or in octaves, and not in parts ; intonal.

† Unisou·nd. *Obs. rare.* [Alteration of UNISON 2b : see UNI- and SOUND *sb.*1]

† Uniscou·nding, *ppl. a. Obs.*1 [See UNI-.] Having only one sound.

Unit·sound, *ppl. a.* (Jn.-3.)

Unit (yū·nit), *sb.* (and *a.*). Also 6-8 **unite**. [f. L. *ūn-us* one ; the ending was probably suggested by *digit* and *comput·a*(e.]

1. *Mus.* Of the same pitch for the different voices or instruments.

2. Exhibiting agreement, concord, or sameness of character or nature ; concordant.

3. *Math.* A single magnitude or number regarded as an undivided whole and as the ultimate base of all number ; *spec.* in *Arithmetic*, the least whole number ; the numeral 'one', represented by the figure 1.

4. *Physics.* A determinate quantity.

† b. Without article : = UNITY 1 b. *Obs.*

Uni·son·ous, *a.* [f. late L. *unison·us*.]

Unitable (yūnei·tǎb'l), *a.* [f. UNITE *v.* + -ABLE.] That can be united ; capable of union.

4. A substance adopted as a standard by which the specific gravity of various bodies is estimated.

† Uni·tage. *Obs.*—1 [f. UNITE + -AGE.] The action of uniting ; union.

Unital (yūni·tǎl), *a.* [f. UNIT or UNITY + -AL.] That unites ; causing or producing unity or union ; of the nature of a unit ; unitary.

Unitarian (yūnitē·riǎn), *sb.* and *a.* [Partly in theol. use, f. mod.L. *unitari·-us* (1651 : f. L. *ūnitās* UNITY) + -AN, partly f. UNIT + -ARIAN.] So f. *unitarien* a. and sb. Cf. UNITARY *a.*]

A. *sb.* 1. *Theol.* One who affirms the unipersonality of the Godhead, especially as opposed to orthodox Trinitarian ; *spec.* a member or adherent of a Christian religious body or sect holding this doctrine.

Unitarianism (yūnitē·riǎni·z'm). [f. prec. + -ISM. So f. *unitarianisme*.]

1. *Theol.* Belief in or affirmation of the unity of God ; *esp.* the tenets, principles, or views of the Unitarians ; Unitarian doctrine or beliefs.

Unitarianize, *v.* [f. as prec. + -IZE.] *intr.* To become Unitarian. Hence **Unitarianized** *ppl. a.*

Unitarist. [UNITAR-Y + -IST.] An advocate of a unitary system of government ; *spec.* a supporter of the unity of Italy.

Unitary (yū·nitǎri), *a.* [f. UNIT *sb.* or UNITY + -ARY.] Cf. F. *unitaire* sb. and a., It. *unitario*.

1. Crystallography. (See quot.)

2. Of or pertaining to, characterized by, based upon, or directed towards, unity.

Unite (yūnei·t), *v.* [ad. L. *ūnīt*-, ppl. stem of *ūnīre* : see UNITE *v.*1]

1. *trans.* To combine or join (one or more things) *to* or *with* another or others, to bring or put together.

b. *Philos.* Of being or personality.

2. Of persons : Accepting, professing, or advocating the doctrines of Unitarianism ; belonging to a religious body or sect of Unitarians.

Unite, *pa. pple.* and *ppl. a. Obs.* [ad. late L. *ūnītus*, pa. pple. of *ūnīre*.]

exhibit (qualities, etc.) in union or combination ; to combine (features usually regarded as distinct).

4. *intr.* Of persons, personifications, states, etc. : To enter into association, alliance, combination, or union ; to join together or *with* others for some common purpose ; to combine or some action or to something ; to act in concert or agreement.

5. To form one material whole or body ; to become one ; to be joined together, or *to* or *with* others ; to combine physically ; to coalesce ; *spec.* in *Chem.*, to combine by chemical affinity or attraction.

d. *Hortem.* (See quot. and cf. 1 e above.)

Uni·ted, *ppl. a.* [f. prec.]

1. Put or joined together ; combined, made one. (Cf. also sense 4.)

2. Of, belonging to, or produced by two or more persons, agents, or things in union or combination ; conjoint, joint.

3. United Kingdom, the kingdom of Great Britain (after the union with Ireland in 1801) of Great Britain and Ireland. Abbrev. *U.K.*

Unite·dly, *adv.* [f. prec.] In a united, combined, or joint manner ; together ; with agreement or concurrence ; conjointly.

Unite·dness. [f. as prec.] The fact or condition of being united ; union.

Uniter (yūnei·tǎr). [f. UNITE *v.*1 + -ER1.] One who, or that which, unites ; a uniting or combining force or principle.

Unitism. *rare.*—1 [f. UNIT *sb.* + -ISM.] Monism.

Unitive (yū·nitiv), *a.* [ad. late L. *ūnītīvus*, f. *ūnīt*-.] Having the power of uniting, or tending to union.

Unitable (yūnei·tǎb'l), *a.* [f. UNITE *v.* + -ABLE.] That can be united.

Unit-idea. The proper name or distinctive title of a confederacy, federation, or union of States.

1. The kingdom or republic of Holland. = the United Provinces (UNITED *ppl. a.* 4). Also *attrib.*

2. The English colonies in the United States of North America or regarded as distinctly American. *Ta talk United State*, to use strong language, to express oneself forcibly.

Uniting (yūnei·tiŋ), *vbl. sb.* [f. UNITE *v.*1 + -ING1.] The action of the verb ; union ; an instance of this.

Uniting, *ppl. a.* [f. as prec.] That unites or joins.

Unition (yūni·shǒn). [ad. med.L. *ūnītiōn-em*, n. of action f. *ūnīre.*] Union ; conjunction, junction.

Unity (yū·niti). Forms : 4-6 **vnite, vnyte,** 5 **wnyte,** 6 **unitie, unytie,** etc., 4 **vnité,** 5-7 **vnitie, vnite, vnyte, vnytye,** 7 **vnity,** etc. [a. OF. *unité* (1119), mod.F. *unité* = Prov. *unitat*, Sp., Pg. *unidad*, It. *unità*, ad. L. *ūnitātem*, f. *ūnus* one.]

I. **1.** The quality, or condition of being one in mind, feeling, opinion, purpose, or action ; harmonious agreement between the various parties or sections (of the Church, a state, etc.) concerned ; concord or harmony amongst several persons or between two or more.

II. 3. The quality or condition of being one in mind, feeling, opinion, purpose, or action.

UNITY. 241 UNIVERSAL.

UNIVERSAL. 242 UNIVERSAL.

UNIVERSAL. 243 UNIVERSALITY.

UNIVERSALITY. 244 UNIVERSALITY.

Universarian. *rare.* One who belongs to the universe in respect of knowledge (see quot.).

Universary, *sb.* and *a.* [= L. *universāri-um* UNIVERSE *sb.*]
†A. *sb.* The whole body or number of something. *Obs.*⁻¹
B. *adj.* Of or pertaining to, open to, all.
Universe (yū̆nivərs). Also 5 vniuerse, 6 -uers, 7 vniuers, 8 -verse, etc.

Universitarian, *sb.* and *a.* [f. as next + -ARIAN.] Of or pertaining to, characteristic of, obtaining in, a university.
Hence **Universita'rianism,** the educational method or system characteristic of or prevailing in a university; advocacy of university education.

University, *a. rare.* [L. UNIVERSIT-Y + -ART_] Of the nature of, having the character of, a university.

Universitas. *Scots Law.* [L.: see next.] The whole (of an estate or inheritance).

University (yūnivə̄'siti), *sb.* Forms: 6 vniuersite, 5 -versite, 5-6 -uersitee, 4-5 vnyuer-site(e, 5-6 -uerey·te(e; 5-7 vniuersitie (5, 7-8 uni-), 6-7yo, vnyuersyte, -tie, 7 vniuersity, 7-8 vniversity, 6-7 universitie, &c. [ad. L. *ūniversitās*, *-tāt-em*.]

I. 1. The whole body of teachers and scholars engaged, at a particular place, in giving and receiving instruction in the higher branches of learning.

2. *Law.* (See quot. 1832.)

†3. Your university, the collective whole of the members of a body, group, or company of persons specifically addressed in some formal or official document. *Obs.*

†4. A body or company of persons associated together for some purpose. *Obs.*

†b. A body or class of persons regarded collectively; esp. an aggregation of persons forming a corporate body or society, a corporation. *Obs.*

†5. Extension to the whole (of something); —UNIVERSALITY 1. *Obs. rare.*

II. †5. Extension to the whole (of something).

Universit'y, to provide or endow with a University; University-bred, etc., having to do with a University; University-man, one educated at a University; University-town, -training, etc.

‡ Univocacy (yūni'vo̅kăsi). *Logic.* [f. post-cl. L. *ūnivoc-us*: see UNIVOCAL + -ACY.] Univocal quality; oneness or sameness of character.

Univocal, *a.* and *sb.* [f. post-cl. L. *ūnivoc-us* + -AL.]
A. *adj.* Of symptoms, signs, etc.: Indicative of, signifying, or denoting one thing; certain or unmistakable in significance. Chiefly *Med. Obs.*

†Univocalness. *Obs.*⁻¹ [-NESS.] —UNIVOCA-TION.

†Univo'cate, *v.* [ad. late L. *ūnivocāt-*, ppl. stem of *ūnivocāre*.] *trans.* To call by the same name.

Univoca'tion. *rare.* [ad. L. *ūnivocātiōn-em*.] Oneness or identity of name or meaning.

Univocity, *sb. rare.* [f. L. *ūnivoc-us* + -ITY.] The quality of being univocal; univocal character.

†Univo'ltime, or *-lind.* [a. F. *une-volume.*] *sb.* One of a breed of silkworms which produces a single brood in a year.

Univoque, *a. Obs.*⁻¹ [—UNIVOCAL.] —UNIVOCAL 2.

Univoyage, *sb.* —In 6 vnivyage. [a. F. *univoyage*: see UNIVOCAL.]

Uniware, for UNAWARE and UNWARE. Unaware, unawares; esp. *in phr. on* unaware *or* at unaware.

Uniwares, *adv.* —In 3 vnjewares. [As prec. + -s.] Cf. UNAWARES, UNWARES.] Unawares.

†Unja'cobitize, *v.* *trans.* To detach from Jacobite principles.

Unja'ded, *ppl. a.* [UN-¹ 8.]

Unja'gged, *ppl. a.* [UN-¹ 8.]

Unja'rring, *ppl. a.* [UN-¹ 8.]

Unjealous, *a.* [UN-¹ 7.]

Unjealoused, *ppl. a.* [UN-² 3.]

Unjoin, *v.* Now *rare.* [UN-² 3.]
1. *trans.* To detach from being joined; to disjoin, sever, separate.
2. *intr.* To separate the parts (of); to take apart. Also *fig.*, to undo.

Unjoint, *v.* [UN-² 9.]
1. *tr.* Lacking the connexion or cohesion; unconnected, incoherent.
2. Not furnished with, or connected by, joints.

Unjointing, *vbl. sb.* [f. UNJOINT *v.*] The action of disjointing or dislocating.

Unjoy, *v.* [UN-² 7.]

Unjoy'ful, *a.* [UN-¹ 7 b.]

Unjoyous, *a.* [UN-¹ 7.]

Unjoin't, *v.* [UN-² 3.]
1. *trans.* To sever the joints (of); to disjoint, dislocate.

Unjudge, *v.* [UN-² 7 b.]
1. *trans.* To reverse the judgement of; to deprive of the office of judge.
2. Improper; incorrect. *Obs.*
†3. Not brought to judgement.

Unjudged, *ppl. a.* [UN-¹ 8.]

Unjudging, *ppl. a.* [UN-¹ 10.]

Unjudicial, *a.* [UN-¹ 7 b.]

Unjudicially, *adv.* [UN-¹ 7; f. prec.]

Unjoy·fully, *adv.* [f. UNJOYFUL + -LY².]

Unjust, *a.* [UN-¹ 7 b.]
1. a. Of persons: Not acting justly or fairly; not observing the principles of justice or fair dealing. Also *const.* †*a.*
2. Not upright or free from wrong-doing; faithless, dishonest. Also *const.* †*of* or *to. Now rare.*
3. Improper; incorrect.
†4. Unsuitable; unreasonable; unlawful. *Obs.*

Unjusti'ce. *Obs. exc. dial.*
I. Injustice; wrong.
2. An unjust act or thing.

Unjust'ly, *adv.* [UN-¹ 11.]
1. In an unjust manner; contrary to the principles of justice.
2. Not rightly or correctly. *Obs.*

Unjustness. [UN-¹ 12.]

Unjustifiable, *a.* [UN-¹ 7, 5 b.]
Hence **Unjustifiableness**, **Unjustifiably**, *adv.*

Unjust'ify, *v.* [UN-² 6 c.]

Unjusti'fied, *ppl. a.* [UN-¹ 8.]
†1. Not brought to justice; not punished or executed.
2. Not justified from a charge of justification.

Unkaimed, -kamed: see UNCOMBED.

Unkaird(ness, dial. vart. UNKIRD(NESS.

Unked, *a.* (*adv.*), variant of UNKEMMED.

Unke'mpt, *a.* [UN-¹ 8.]
1. Not made known or revealed; unknown, unfamiliar, strange.

Unkempt, *ppl. a.* [UN-¹ 8.]
1. Not combed (esp. of the hair).
2. Rough or untidy in appearance; unpolished, rude.
Hence **Unke'mptness.**

Unkenned, *ppl. a.* [UN-¹ 8.]
1. Not known or recognized; unknown, unfamiliar.

Unked: see UNCKED *a.*

Unkennel, *v.* [UN-² 2 b.]
1. *trans.* To dislodge (a fox) from its hole; to drive out.
2. To bring out, force out.

Unkennelled *ppl. a.*; **Unkennelling** *vbl. sb.*

Unksuer'e, obs. variants of UNCOVER.

Unke, unki v. [Un-⁴ 4 b.] *trans.* To ungag.

Unkey, v. [Un-² 5 c., Key c.]

† Unket, *a.* Chiefly *north.* and *Sc.* [Un-⁵ 8 b.]
1. Undirected, unguarded.
2. Unknown. (Cf. UNKENNED *ppl. a.*)

Unke ye, *ppl. a.* Also 4 unrith, unkepide, 1 (Sc. 4) unkepit; etc. [Un-¹ 8, 8 b.]
1. Not attended to; not tended or looked after; neglected.
2. Not observed or kept; disregarded.

† Unker, *pron.* [Un-, *uncer* (gen. of *wē* two)]

† Unker, *pron.* dual. [OE. *uncer* (cf. prec.) – OS. *unka*, ON. *okkarr*.] Belonging to us two.

† Unkid, var. UNKED *a.* (various senses).

† Unketh, var. UNKER; UNKOUTH.

Unkind, *a.* (*sb.*) [Un-¹ 7.] Cf OE. *uncynde*, *ungecynde*.
1. Strange, foreign. *Obs.*
2. a. Of the nature or climate: Not mild or pleasant; ungenial. Now *dial.* or *arch.*
3. b. Physically unnatural; contrary to the usual course of nature. *Obs.*
4. a. Of actions: Contrary to nature, unnatural; wicked. *Obs.*
5. Unnaturally cruel, severe, or hostile. *Obs.*
6. Lacking in kindness or kindly feeling; acting harshly or ungently to others. Also *absol.*

† Unkind, *v.* [Un-² 6, 8 b.] *trans.* To make unkind; to deprive of natural feeling.

† Unkindful, *a.* [Un-¹ 7.] Cf UNKINDLY *a.*
Unkindfully, *adv.*

Unkindhead, *sb.* [Un-¹ 8.] Unnatural conduct; ingratitude; baseness.

Unkindhearted, *a.* [Un-¹ 9.]

Unkindliness, *sb.* [Un-¹ 9.]

Unkindly, *a.* [repr. OE. *ungecyndelic*.]
1. a. With unnatural immorality or impropriety. *Obs.*
2. Morally unnatural; unnaturally wicked or vile. *Obs.*
3. b. Unnatural in respect of relations or dealings with others. *Obs.*
4. Contrary to right feeling or conduct; improperly; ungratefully. *Obs.*
5. Badly, unsuccessfully.

Unkindly, *adv.* [repr. OE. *ungecyndelice*; or in later use Un-¹ 11 + KINDLY *adv.*]
1. a. With unnatural immorality or impropriety. *Obs.*
2. Uncharitableness; niggardliness. *Obs.*
3. Ingratitude, unthankfulness. *Obs.*

Unkindness, *sb.* [Un-¹ 9.]
1. Unnatural conduct; absence of natural affection or consideration for others. *Obs.*
2. b. Lacking natural affection. b. Cruel, unkind.
3. The fact of being unkind; unkind action or treatment.

Unkindred, *ppl. a.* (and *a.*)

Unking, *v.* [Un-² 6 b. Cf. MDu. *ontkoningen*, Du. *ontkoningen*, G. *entkönigen*.] *trans.* To deprive of the position of king; to depose from sovereignty.

Unkinglike, *a.* Also *-ly*.

Unkingly, *a.* [Un-¹ 7.]
1. Not befitting a king. 2. Not invested with kingship.

Unkinglike, *a.*

Unkiss, v. [Un-² 5.]

Unkissed, *ppl. a.* Also 4-7 unkist, etc.

Unkist, *a.* [Un-² 3.] Obs.

Unknight, *v.* [Un-² 6 b.] *trans.* To deprive of knighthood; to depose from the rank of knight.

Unknightlike, *a.*

Unknightly, *a.* [Un-¹ 8.] Not raised to the rank of knight; not invested with knighthood.

Unknightliness, *sb.*

Unknightly, *adv.*

Uknit, v. [OE. *unwryttan* (Un-⁴ 4 b).]
1. *trans.* To untie or undo (a knot or something tied).
2. In figurative contexts (with *knot* or *bind*).

Unknot, v. [Un-⁴ 4 b.]

Unknotted, *ppl. a.*

Unknow, *v.* [Un-³ 3.]
1. *trans.* Not to know (something); to fail to recognize or perceive. Also *absol.*
2. To disjoint, disunite; to dissolve, destroy; to relax or weaken. Also *absol.*

Unknow, *v.²* [Un-³ 3 a.] *trans.* To cease to know, to forget (what one has known). Also *absol.*

Unknowable, *a.* and *sb.* [Un-¹ 7 b.]

Hence Unknowableness.

Unknowing, *ppl. a.* [Un-¹ 10, 5 d.]
1. Not knowing; not possessed of knowledge; unaware, ignorant.
2. *trans.* Not to know (something); to fail to recognize or perceive.

Unknowing, *vbl. sb.* [Un-¹ 11 + prec.]

Unknowingly, *adv.* [Un-¹ 11 + prec.]

Unknowledge, *sb.* [Un-¹ 12.] Unacknowledgment.

Unknowledged, *ppl. a.* [Un-¹ 8.]

Unknown, *ppl. a.* (and *sb.*) [Un-¹ 8. Cf. OE. *uncnāwen*.] *adj.* 1. Of places.

[Oxford English Dictionary text, top register of entries including **Unknown**, **Unknowable**, **Unknowably**, **Unknowing**, **Unknowledge**, **Unknowledged**, **Unknown**, **Unknownly**, **Unknownness**, **Unla-belled**, **Unlaborious**, **Unlaboured**, **Unla-boured**, **Unlaburned**, **Unla-boring**, **Unlace**, **Unlaced**, **Unlacing**, **Unlade**, **Unladed**, **Unladen**, **Unlading**, **Unladen**, **Unlaid**, **Unlanguaged**, **Unlatch**, **Unlatticed**, etc.]

[Oxford English Dictionary text, lower register of entries including **Unlaudable**, **Unlaudably**, **Unlaugh**, **Unlaughter-mild**, **Unlaw**, **Unlawful**, **Unlawfulness**, **Unlawed**, **Unlay**, **Unlead**, **Unleaded**, **Unleaf**, **Unleal**, **Unleally**, **Unleanness**, **Unlearn**, **Unlearned**, **Unlearnedly**, **Unlearnedness**, **Unlease**, **Unleased**, **Unleashed**, **Unleavened**, **Unleavenedness**, **Unled**, **Unleful**, **Unlefully**, **Unleesome**, etc.]

vnleifsum actis, Ar rent and rewin apone the ractis. 1600 Hamilton in Cath. Tractates (S.T.S.) 235 How mony young wemen..hes murtherit the fruict of thair auin wombes, some be vnlisome drinkis. 1864 Latto Tam. Bodkin x. 92 The loons that had received the unleisum stoutherie. Ibid. xvii. 170 The unleisome possession o' the game.

So **Unlee·somely** adv. ? Obs.

c 1400 Sc. Trojan War II. 1103 [To] lat of hyr virgynite The closoures vnlefsomely [L. illicite] To be broken. 1528 Lyndesay Dreme 230 Vnleifsumlie thay vsit propertie. a 1578 Lindesay (Pitscottie) Chron. Scot. (S.T.S.) II. 207 Putting hand in the quenis grace vnlesomelie..but athir law or ressoune.

Unlee·ze, v. dial. [Un-² 9 + leeze to arrange (threads).] trans. To unravel. 1889 H. Johnston Glenbuckie iv, The hank she had left me to unleeze was truly a tangled one. **Unle·ft**, ppl. a. (Un-¹ 8 b.) c 1611 Chapman Iliad II. 615 Yet were his men unleft Without a chief. 1634 Ford Perk. Warbeck v. iii, Your father..Would blush on your behalf, and wish his country Unleft. 1659 Nicholas Papers (Camden) IV. 179 All malladies and goutes vnleft behynde at Bathe. **Unle·g**, v. (Un-² 4.) 1598 Florio, Sgambare, to vnleg. 1654 Gayton Pleas. Notes III. v. 100 That is to say, with three hard words, un-mule, un-leg and un-able, Alanso Lopez. **Unlegacied**, ppl. a. (Un-¹ 8.) 1556 Wills & Inv. N. C. (Surtees, 1835) 149, I will that my said sonne..shall have..of my goods..on hundreth pounds and the rest vnlegased to be parted betwix barbare and hym. 1846 Worcester (citing Q. Rev.). **Unle·gal**, a. (Un-¹ 7, 5 b.) 1643 Prynne Open. Gt. Seal 29 The unlegall wilfull absence of the..Lord Keeper from the Parliament. a 1810 Tannahill Poems (1846) 68 Selfish, mean, unlegal deeds. 1899 Westm. Gaz. 10 July 3/1 The illegal—or let us say the unlegal—interference of the English Government. **Unle·galized**, ppl. a. (Un-¹ 8.) 1830 Bentham Offic. Apt. Maximized, Further Extr. Const. Codex (1830) 23 Accustomed, though unlegalized profit in every shape. 1860 Froude Hist. Eng. VI. 267 He hated lies—legalized or unlegalized. **Unle·gally**, adv. (Un-¹ 11.) 1888 Pall Mall G. 3 April 3/1 If such a delicate matter as extradition were left to be dealt with unlegally.

Unle·gate, v. [Un-² 6 b.] trans. To deprive of the office of legate.

a 1548 Hall Chron., Hen. VI, 111 Sone after, the bishop of Rome..vnlegated hym, and set another in his stede. 1651 N. Bacon Disc. Govt. Eng. II. xvii. 150 The Cardinall is Un-Legated, and that Power conferred upon the Arch-Bishop of Canterbury.

†**Unlegated**, ppl. a. Obs. [Un-¹ 8.] Not left by will. 1562-3 N. C. Wills (Surtees) II. 38 My goodes unlegated I doe give to my brother. **Unle·gged**, a. (Un-¹ 9.) 1608 Topsell Serpents 609 This monster..nor man nor dragon is,..But man unlegged, and snake unheaded. †**Unle·gible**, a. [Un-¹ 7, 5 b.] Illegible. 1611 Speed Hist. Gt. Brit. x. i. § 57. 892/2 The letter was..somewhat vnlegible. 1655 Earl Orrery Parthen. I. vi. 150 Perceiveing my joy in my Face, it inflam'd his to such a degree, that for a good while his choller was unleagible in any thing else. 1671 Wood Life (O.H.S.) II. 226 The base and unlegible hand of the translator. **Unle·gislative**, a. (Un-¹ 7.) 1791 Bentham Panopt. II. Postscr. 165 More unlegislative minuteness, more unthrifty fixation. †**Unlegi·timate**, a. Obs. [Un-¹ 7, 5 b.] Illegitimate. 1655 Earl Orrery Parthen. I. vii. 347 Shee persever'd in a Passion which tended to..a more vnlegitimate end. †**Unlegi·timate**, ppl. a. Sc. Obs. [Un-¹ 8 b.] Not legitimated. 1516 Reg. Mag. Sig. Scot. 23/1 Borne bastard and unlegittimate be ony mariage. †**Unlegi·timate**, v. Obs. [Un-² 6 a.] trans. To make illegitimate. 1606 Marston Parasit. II. C 4 b, I will vnlegittimate the issue.

Unlei·sured, a. (Un-¹ 9.)

a 1586 Sidney Arcadia II. xxv, But her vnleasured thoughtes ran not ouer the ten first wordes. 1644 Milton Areop. (Arb.) 56 Unlesse he carry all his considerat diligence..to the hasty view of an unleasur'd licencer.

Hence **Unlei·suredness**.

1661 Boyle Style of Script. To Rdr., The Unleisurednesse, and Rellish of the Unsettlednesse of the Wandering Author.

†**Unle·ke**, v. Obs. [Un-² 3 + leke (cf. leke, ME. pa. t. of Louk v.¹).] trans. To unlock (a door). c 1380 Sir Ferumbras 1264 Floripe hure drow to anoþer part, & þar an doute ounlekes þat drow to þe putte ward, & doun in the pyt sche strekes. †**Unle·ngth**. Obs.⁻¹ [Un-¹ 3, 12.] Shortness. a 1250 Owl & Night. 752 Hwy atwitestu me myne vnstrengþe & myne vngrete & myn vnlengþe. **Unle·nt**, ppl. a. (Un-¹ 8 b.) [1775 Ash.] 1887 Daily News 11 June 2/1 Much depends..upon the amount of the unlent surplus of money.

Unlered: see Unleared ppl. a.

Unless (ɒnle·s), prep. phr., prep., conj., and sb. Forms: α. 5 of lasse, oo lesse, o less, oless(e, Sc. oles, 9 Sc. aless. β. 5 vpon less. γ. 5 in lasse, yn las, 5 in less (9 dial. inless), 6 inlesse. δ. 5 on lasse, 5–6 onlesse, 6 oon-, onelee, -les, 5–7 onles, 9 dial. onless. ε. 5 vnlasse, 6–7 vn-, unlesse, 6 vnles, 6- unless. [f. Less a. 7, with the preps. of, in, upon, and on; the last of these by want of stress has been assimilated in form to the prefix Un-¹. Cf. Less conj., also Unleast, Unlest.]

†**1.** prep. phr. On a less or lower condition, requirement, footing, etc., than (what is specified).

With preceding negative, expressed or implied.

c 1400 Maundev. (1919) xxi. 122 But þat may not be vpon less þan wee mowe falle toward heuene. Ibid. (Roxb.) xxv. 118 [see Less a. 7 c]. 1475 Rolls of Parlt. VI. 127/1 His Land, which many persones..fere to take..olesse then they myght be made verrey sure of payment. a 1500 in C. Trice-Martin Chanc. Proc. 15th C. (1904) 5 Robert wil not suffre hym to be laten to baile on lasse than he will make..a generall acquytaunce.

2. Except, if..not: †**a.** With retention of than (cf. prec.), but without a negative. Obs.

1431 Acts Privy Counc. IV. 96 It shulde be entendede unto, namely, olesse þan before þe men can se..þe meenes..of ferþer conduyt of þe werre. c 1449 Pecock Repr. III. xvi. 386 Alle hise successouris ben..excludid for euer, in lasse thanne the same good be 3ouun a3en. 1467 in Eng. Gilds (1870) 408 Vppon peyn of euery man so failynge, vnlesse then be haue a sufficient depute, of xl. d. 1530 Tindale Gen., Prol. Use Script. A v, Inlesse then we entend to be ydle disputers, and braulers aboute vayne wordes.

†**b.** Followed by that. Obs.

1440 in Wars Eng. in France (1864) II. 458 The kyng conceyueth wele that onlesse that it like him to tendre the said duc he [etc.]. 1470–85 Malory Arthur I. x. 47 Onlesse that our kyng haue more chyualry,..he shal be ouercome. 1529 Wolsey in Cavendish Life (1825) II. 261 Onles that yow..do helpe & releve me therin. 1534 in Leadam Star Chamber Cases (Selden) II. 211 [They] cowde not..sell so myche..onelez that they wold sell so reasonable a pennyworthe. 1596 Spenser F. Q. vi. iii. 39 Ne would I gladly combate with mine host,..Vnlesse that I were thereunto enforst.

c. With omission of conjunction before the subordinate clause, and thus passing into conj. (Cf. 4.)

1509 Fisher Serm. Wks. (1876) 277 There is no man..oneles he haue it by reuelacyon that knoweth certaynly [etc.]. 1542 Lam. & Piteous Treat. in Harl. Misc. (1745) IV. 505/2 It was a verey daungerous and ieoperdous Thinge,..inlesse they had been..weryd by longe Soiouryinge. 1563 Mirr. Mag., Blacksmith lxviii, For one [talent] is to much, onles it be well spent. 1607 in Eng. Gilds (1870) 442 Margory Davies..wold not remove her habitacion onles she might haue a way..to passe [etc.]. 1662 Stillingfl. Orig. Sacræ II. iii. § 5 Will God condemn them for that, which it was impossible they should have, unless God gave it them? 1710 Swift Jrnl. to Stella 8 Oct., I was at a loss to-day for a dinner, unless I would have gone a great way. 1752 Young Brothers I. i, Dominion, and the princess, both are lost, Unless you gain the king. 1820 Southey Wesley II. 211 No person was admitted to this rank, unless he were thought competent by the preachers of the circuit. 1877 Ruskin Fors Clav. lxxx. VII. 234, I am never angry with anybody unless they deserve it.

d. Followed by a prepositional or participial clause without verb, or by when, where, etc.

1548–9 (Mar.) Bk. Com. Prayer, Offices, Bapt. Priv. Ho., [That] the people..defer not the Baptisme of infantes..onlesse vp on a greate & reasonable cause. 1610 Fletcher Faithful Sheph. v. v, [Let] not wine, Unless in sacrifice, or rites divine, Be ever known of Shepherd. 1681 Dryden Abs. & Achit. I. 590 Nor ever was he known,..[to] Curse, unless against the Government. 1721 Bradley Philos. Acc. Wks. Nat. 77 We had no Frost or Snow.., unless in the most Inland Parts. 1749 Fielding Tom Jones xvii. ix, Jones passed above twenty-four melancholy hours by himself, unless when relieved by the company of Partridge. 1789 Charlotte Smith Ethelinde (1814) II. 147 But I dare not shew them, unless to you. 1818 Scott Rob Roy v, A beautiful horse, jet black, unless where he was flecked by spots of..foam. 1897 Mary Kingsley W. Africa 439 They never wear clothes unless compelled to.

3. prep. **a.** Except, but.

1531–2 Act 23 Hen. VIII, c. 1 That no suertye be taken onles suche as maye dyspende..yerly..xxvi.s. viii.d. 1563 Hill Art Garden. II. lxiv. (1574) 132 The floures..ought then to be gathered..vnlesse the Lilly..and Rose. 1600 Heywood If you know not me Wks. 1874 I. 205 All forbeare this place, vnlesse the Princess. 1683 D. A. Art Converse 117 They say nothing unless a meer yes sir or no Madam. 1709 T. Robinson Nat. Hist. Westmorld. viii. 53 Inconsistent..with the Nature of Lead, Copper, Coal, or any other Mineral, unless Iron. 1796 Morse Amer. Geog. II. 33 Unless the Swedish part,..the Laplanders can be said to be under no regular government. 1886 Pall Mall G. 4 Aug. 1/2 He did not believe that he would ever obtain anything..unless a species of elevated poor-law system of government.

†**b.** Without; but for. Obs.

1536 St. Papers Hen. VIII (1830) I. 469 Soo that, unles the most infinite mercy of God, both bodyes and soules shuld perishe togither. 1796 Mrs. J. West Gossip's Story I. 190 You instilled into my infant soul principles, which, unless my own fault, must insure my present and future happiness.

†**4.** conj. **a.** Lest. Obs.

1508 Fisher 7 Penit. Ps. cii. Wks. (1876) 142, I fere..oneles I shall fall agayne amonge those theues. 1543 Becon Invect. agst. Swearing E iiij b, I feare vnlesse we shall be redy..to runne hedlong into hell fyre. a 1592 Greene Alphonsus I. i, Presume not, villaine, further tor to go, Vnles you do at length the same repent.

†**b.** But that. Obs.⁻¹

1608 in Harl. Misc. (1744) I. 181 A Flea shall not frisk forth, unless they comment upon her.

5. sb. An utterance or instance of the word; a reservation, proviso.

1861 Dickens in Pall Mall G. 24 Sept. (1891) 3/2 Let us have no unlesses, sir. 1904 Hichens Woman with Fan vii, There's very often an unless hanging about, like a man at a street corner.

Unle·ssened, ppl. a. (Un-¹ 8.) 1736 Butler Anal. I. i. 31 This active power..remains unlessened. 1842 J. B. Fraser Allee Neemroo II. 99 His uneasiness remained unlessened and unaltered. 1891 C. M. J. Mitford's Lett. & Remin. 163 His love for me remained unlessened.

Unle·ssoned, ppl. a. (Un-¹ 8.)

c 1550 Walker Dice-Play D v b, Pety figgers, and vnlessoned laddes. 1596 Shaks. Merch. V. III. ii. 161 An vnlessoned girle, vnschool'd, vnpractiz'd. 1807 J. Barlow Columb. v. 673 To Fame's hard school the warm disciples came, To learn sage Liberty's unlesson'd lore. 1882 Century Mag. XXIV. 658/1 That unlessoned insight which comes of loving them.

†**Unle·st**, obs. var. Unless. (Cf. Unleast.)

1535 in Lett. Suppress. Monast. (Camden) 91 The dean wolde not resigne unto hym, unleste he wolde leffe hym other possessions. 1583 Stubbes Anat. Abus. II. C 8 b, May subiects..rise against their prince? No, at no hand, vnlest they will purchase to themselues eternall damnation. 1599 Thynne Animadv. (1875) 19 Difference of armes semethe a difference of famelyes, vnleste you canne prove that..they altered their armes vppone somme iuste occasione.

Unle·t, ppl. a. Also 5 unlate, 6 unletton. (Un-¹ 8 b; cf. Let ppl. a.)

1453 Paston Lett. Suppl. (1901) 49, I know not oon rode unlate, but alle ocupyed to your profyghte. 1537 in Lett. Suppress. Monast. (Camden) 163 The house..wiche was unlet at the tyme of owre repare thether. 1545 Act 37 Hen. VIII, c. 12 § 16 Hawles of Craftes.., soo long as they bee keapte unletton. 1769 Gray in Corr. G. & Nicholls (1843) 93, I believe all that are unlet will be cheap as the time approaches. 1866 Geo. Eliot F. Holt ii, Having three farms unlet. 1885 Law Times 28 Mar. 384/2 In the present day, when unlet land is becoming so common.

Unle·ttable, a. (Un-¹ 7 b.)

In frequent use from c 1895.

1882 Ch. Times XX. 21, I fear to find myself with a[n]..unlettable glebe on my hands. 1893 Dk. Argyll Unseen Found. Soc. x. 305 Farms which have been unlettable.

†**Unle·tted**, ppl. a. [Un-¹ 8. Cf. MLG. ungeletted, etc.] Unhindered.

a 1500 Chaucer's Dreme 1831 A bird song full low and softely,..Unletted of every wight. a 1553 Becon Jewel of Joy Wks. 1564 II. 35 The holye scripture requireth of us..an vnletted perseueraunce in the vaye of Godlines.

†**Unle·tten**, ppl. a. Sc. Obs. [Un-¹ 8 b.] Not let or allowed.

1574 Sc. Acts Jas. VI (1814) III. 87 That all..vagaboundis..be committit in ward in the commoun presoun;..thair to be kepit vnlettin to libertie,..quhill thay [etc.].

Unle·ttered, a. [Un-¹ 9. Cf. MDu. ongelettert, Du. ongeletterd.]

1. Not instructed in letters; not possessed of book-learning.

c 1340 Hampole Prose Tr. 32 Anoþer mane..unletterede may noght so redyly hafe at his hand Haly Writt. 1387 Trevisa Higden (Rolls) VII. 181 A man forsoþe..þat was unlettred, but ful myghty in money. c 1440 Alph. Tales 468 When þe abbott Pambo was vnletterd, he went vnto a man þat was letterd [etc.]. 1544 Leland N. Y. Gift in Itin. (1768) I. p. xix, The Italians..counte..al other nations to be barbarus and onletterid saving their owne. 1593 [see Unlectured ppl. a.]. 1624 Gataker Transubst. 156 As children or unlettered persons, when they looke on bookes, know not the power of the letter. 1642 Milton Apol. Smect. 36 Such a lost construction, as no man either letter'd or unletter'd will be able to piece up. 1747 Wesley Prim. Physick (1762) p. xxiv, Easy to be applied by plain unlettered Men. 1781 Cowper Conversat. 12 As alphabets in ivory employ..the yet unletter'd boy. 1817 Chalmers Disc. Chr. Revel. ii. 86 The mind of an ordinary and unlettered peasant. 1867 Augusta Wilson Vashti xxv, Sturdy but unlettered mechanics.

absol. 1751 Johnson Rambler No. 180 ⁋ 2 The unlettered and unenlightened. 1812 G. Chalmers Dom. Econ. Gt. Brit. Pref. 14 That the learned are sometimes too confident, and the unlettered always too credulous. 1861 Stanley East. Ch. viii. (1869) 273 Sacred pictures..are the Bibles of the unlettered.

b. Pertaining to, characterized by, ignorance of letters.

1588 Shaks. L. L. L. IV. ii. 18 After his..vnpolished, vneducated,..or rather, vnlettered..fashion. 1697 Collier Ess. Mor. Subj. II. (1703) 99 Books..give a more universal insight into things, than can be learned from unlettered observation. 1763 J. Brown Poetry & Music iv. 36 Savages..in their present unlettered State of Ignorance and Simplicity. 1807 G. Chalmers Caledonia I. III. vii. 423 An upright stone still forms the unlettered memorial of his odious end. 1880 Hazlitt Lect. Dram. Lit. 186 They were learned men in an unlettered age. a 1864 Hawthorne Amer. Note-bks. (1879) I. 142 His conversation has much strong, unlettered sense.

2. Not expressed in, or marked with, letters.

1633 P. Fletcher Poet. Misc., Asclepiads 1 Unletter'd Word, which never eare could heare. 1782 [T. Maurice] Verbeia 37 This unlettered tomb is in a mutilated state.

Hence †**Unle·tteredly** adv., **Unle·tteredness**.

c 1440 Promp. Parv. 366/1 On-letterydly, illiterate. 1653 E. Waterhouse Apol. Learn. 120 Ignorance and unletterednesse ill becomes any man who bears the Image of God. 1890 Br. Hobhouse Churchw. Acc. (Somerset) p. xxiii, The entire unletteredness of the community.

Unleueful, variant of Unleeful a. Obs.

†**Unle·vable**, a. Obs. [Un-¹ 7 b.] Unbelieving, incredulous. 1382 Wyclif Ecclus. xvi. 29 Be thou not vnleeuable to the wrd of hym. 14.. Voc. in Wr.-Wülcker 589/23 Incredulus, unlefable. †**Unle·veful**, a. Obs.⁻¹ [Un-¹ 7: cf. Unbelieffful a. and OE. ungeléafful.] = prec. 1382 Wyclif Ecclus. xxiii. 33 In the lawe of the heȝest she was vnleeueful.

Unle·vel, a. (Un-¹ 7; cf. Illevel a.)

1571 Digges Pantom. I. xii. D iij b, How vneuen or vnleuell so euer the ground bee. 1644 Quarles Sheph. Orac. iii, All things were unlevell, And rude disorder crept into our State. 1683 Moxon Mech. Exerc., Printing xxiv. 338 The small un-level lying of every Sheet..makes each Sheet incline to the lowest side of the Heap. 1771 Ann. Reg., Usef. Projects 109/2 That unlevel pastures may be ploughed down without any injury. 1817–8 Cobbett Resid. U. S. (1822) 286 A place situated..upon high and unlevel lands. 1873 E. Spon Workshop Receipts Ser. I. 36/1 Should the cloth have got unlevel.

Unle·vel, v. [Un-² 6 a.] trans. To make uneven; to divest of levelness.

a 1586 Sidney Arcadia III. xi, [The] place..was so plaine, as there was scarcely any bush, or hillock, either to unleveil, or shadowe it. 1624 Quarles Div. Poems, Job xix. 10 His Lunatick affections doe vnleuell, What Heauen created by iust Waight and Measure. 1648 Herrick Hesper., To the Fever 8 Come thou not neere that Filme so finely spred, Where no one piece is yet unlevelled. 1703 [R. Neve] City & C. Purchaser 189 There are as many places that seem to be unlevel'd, as there are level'd. 1834 Southey Doctor xlvi. (1862) 109 In 1723 the church floor and church-yard, which had both been unlevelled by Death's levelling course, were levelled anew.

Unle·velled, ppl. a. [Un-¹ 8.] Not made level; not reduced to a level condition.

1622 Drayton Poly-olb. xxiii. 184 Where Cheshire..with Lancashire doth lie Along th' unlevel'd shores. 1730 Tickell Kensington Garden 30 Where all unlevell'd the gay Garden lies. 1854 Dora Greenwood Haps & Mishaps Tour Eur. 30 The grandeur of its yet unlevelled walls and towers.

†**Unleventhe**, obs. variant of Eleventh a.

13.. Coer de L. 2455 The unleventhe day they saylyd in tempest.

Unle·vied, ppl. a. (Un-¹ 8.)

1450 Rolls of Parlt. V. 211/1 The Subsidie..is yit unlevied and unpaied. 1540 Act 32 Hen. VIII, c. 5 The residue of the said dett..remayning unlevied or unreceyvid by the said former execution. 1569 Lanc. Wills (Chetham Soc. 1884) 31 Fyve hundrethe marks..or so muche therof as shalbe then unlevyed. 1634 Ir. Act 10 Chas. I, Sess. III. c. 7 § 2 [=quot. 1540]. 1864 Morn. Star 2 Feb., Arrears of unlevied poor rates.

Unle·vigated, ppl. a. (Un-¹ 8.) 1768 R. Dossie Elaboratory 290 The cinnabar should be procured..in an unlevigated state. †**Unle·ving**, ppl. a. Obs. [Un-¹ 10.] Unbelieving. a 1300 Cursor M. 20852 Þe apostlis þat all wide war spred,..til our lagh þe vnleuand led. 1382 Wyclif Isa. xxi. 2 [He] that vnleeuende [1388 vnfeithful] is, vnfeithfully doth.

†**Unlew·ty**. Obs. [Un-¹ 12.] Disloyalty.

a 1300 Cursor M. 7135 Þat was mikel vnleute, To tell hir husband priuete. 13.. Gaw. & Gr. Knt. 2499 Þat he laȝt for his vnleute at þe leudes hondes, for blame. 1456 Sir G. Haye Law Arms (S.T.S.) 25 The thrid part of the sternis was obumbrit with mirknes of unleautee. a 1470 Harding Chron. cxiii. xiv, Through theyr vnlewtee [the Scots] Crowned Girryke a Dane.

Unli·able, a. (Un-¹ 7 b.)

1624 Quarles Div. Poems, Job xvi. 32 How can I.., Vnliable to danger, flatter any? 1664 H. More Myst. Iniq. Pref. 1 margin, This Idea..is..unliable to any uncivil construction. 1679 Puller Moderat. Ch. Eng. v. 88 No where judging of them as unliable to error. 1710 Norris Chr. Prud. vii. 297 Things that..are not so unliable to Disorder and abuse.

Unli·bbed, ppl. a. (Un-¹ 8.) 1607 Topsell Four-f. Beasts 324 They vse to geld them in March..: afterward being well nourished, they [sc. gelded horses] are no lesse strong..then other vnlibbed. **Unli·beral**, a. rare—°. (Un-¹ 7.) 1570 Levins Manip. 15 Vnliberall, illiberalis. 1611 Florio, Inliberale, vnliberall, sparing. **Unli·beralized**, ppl. a. (Un-¹ 8 a c.) 1793 J. Williams Mem. W. Hastings 40 Are there any so unliberalized as to insist, that..the calumniated should only be allowed a passport to Peace from Death? **Unli·berated**, ppl. a. (Un-¹ 8.) 1837 Penny Cycl. VIII. 411/1 The removal of pressure upon the nerves, produced by the advancing and unliberated tooth. 1865 Reader 14 Oct. 438/2 The irregular weapons of a still unliberated press. **Unlibi·dinous**, a. (Un-¹ 7.) 1667 Milton P. L. v. 449 But in those hearts Love unlibidinous reign'd.

Unli·censed, ppl. a. [Un-¹ 8.]

1. Of persons, etc.: **a.** Not authorized by a formal license to carry on some occupation, industry, etc.

1634 in 10th Rep. Hist. MSS. Commission App. IV. 426, 100 unlicensed alehowses. 1643 [see 2 a]. 1746 Francis tr. Horace, Epist. II. i. 154 A doubtful Drug unlicens'd Doctors fear. 1845 McCulloch Taxation II. x, A fine..rigorously exacted from unlicensed dealers. 1855 Macaulay Hist. Eng. xx. IV. 417 With great difficulty and after long search the most important of all the unlicensed presses was discovered.

b. Not furnished with authority, sanction, or formal permission to do something.

1608 Shaks. Per. I. iii. 17 Why, as it were unlicens'd of your loves, He would depart, I'll give some light unto you. 1685 Baxter Paraphr. N. T. To Rdr. A 3 b, The Papists restraint of the Laity unlicensed, from reading it translated in a known Tongue. 1725 Pope Odyss. XIII. 175 To warn the thoughtless self-confiding train No more unlicens'd thus to brave the main. 1795 Southey Joan of Arc IV. 414 Did she upon thy parting steps bestow Her free-will blessing, or hast thou set forth..unlicensed and unblest?

2. a. Of books, etc.: Published without licence.

1643 Order in Milton's Areop. (Arb.) 27 All unlicensed Printing Presses, and all Presses any way imployed in the printing of scandalous or unlicensed Papers. 1644 Milton Areop. (Arb.) 53 All scandalous and unlicenc't books. 1647 (title), An Ordinance against unlicensed or scandalous Pamphlets.

b. Not authorized or sanctioned.

1649 Jer. Taylor Apol. Liturgy § 135 Many such cases will occurre in..unlicenc'd prayers. a 1704 T. Brown Dial. Dead, Reas. Oaths Wks. 1720 IV. 184 Is any..of the good People of Doctors Commons [turned] to unlicens'd Marriages? 1728 Pope Dunciad IV. 228 For Attic Phrase in Plato let them seek, I poach in Suidas for unlicens'd Greek. 1819 Scott Leg. Montrose Introd., No less would our sexton..have held it an unlicensed intrusion. 1856 Froude Hist. Eng. II. 193 The clergy had promised to abstain..from unlicensed legislation.

3. Free from requiring a licence.

1644 Milton (title), Areopagitica: a Speech..For the Liberty of Vnlicenc'd Printing, To the Parlament of England. 1863 H. Cox Instit. I. ix. 146 This Act was kept in force..until 1694, when..it expired. The liberty of unlicensed printing dates from that period.

4. Unregulated, lawless. rare⁻¹.

1828 Tytler Hist. Scot. I. 183 This prelate..with much personal risk, owing to the unlicensed state of the country,..travelled with his suit..as far as Kirkcudbright.

Unlice·ntious, ppl. a. (Un-¹ 7.) 1768–74 Tucker Lt. Nat. (1834) II. 415 The exercise of sober, unlicentious freedom of thought. **Unli·chened**, ppl. a. (Un-¹ 8.) 1843 Ruskin Mod. Paint. I. 239 Unlichened, dead, desolated rock. **Unli·ckable**, a. (Un-¹ 7 b.) 1845 D'Israeli Sybil v. vii, One of the most unlicked and unlickable cubs that ever entered society.

Unli·cked, ppl. a. [Un-¹ 8. Cf. Du. ongelikt, G. ungeleckt.]

1. Not licked into shape. (See Lick v. 4.) Chiefly fig., esp. with cub (or whelp).

1593 Shaks. 3 Hen. VI, III. ii. 161 Like to..an vn-lick'd Beare-whelpe, That carryes no impression like the Damme. c 1618 Moryson Itin. IV. (1903) 1 Being drawne to the writing hereof..out of a naturall affection to give all the members to this my unlicked whelpe. 1687 Dryden Hind & P. I. 36 The bloody Bear, an Independent beast, Unlick'd to form, in groans her hate express'd. 1687 [see Cub sb. 3]. 1728 Vanbr. & Cib. Prov. Husb. II. i, The Son is an unlick'd Whelp, about sixteen. ? 1795 Coleridge After a Walk bef. Supper 30 A little ape with huge she-bear..: An unlicked mass the one—the other An antic huge. 1845 [see prec.]. 1871 Besant & Rice Ready-money Mort. x, You know, Polly, what an unlicked cub I was when I married you.

b. fig. Not reduced to form or order; unfinished, unpolished, rude or crude.

1661 Boyle Style of Script. 185 Confus'd Notions, and Abortive or Unlick'd Conceptions. 1682 Dryden Abs. & Achit. II. 502 But thou in Clumsy verse, unlickt, unpointed, Hast shamefully defi'd the Lord's Anointed. 1758 Wesley Wks. (1872) II. 457, I rode back..to put the society there (an unlicked mass) into some form. 1773 Mme. D'Arblay Early Diary Oct., I saw..the appearance of unlicked nature in all his motions. 1835 Lamb Elia II. Pref., My late friend's writings..are..a sort of unlicked, incondite things.

2. Not licked.

1861 L. L. Noble Icebergs 296 Poor Pussy,..a creature of backbone and ribs, coated with fur unlicked and scorched. 1895 R. W. Chambers King in Yellow, Str. Four Winds i, [The cat's] purple tongue travelled over every unlicked spot..[of] the saucer.

Unli·d, v. Also 3 unlide. [Un-² 4. Cf. OE. unhlidian.] trans. To remove the lid from; to uncover.

a 1250 Ancr. R. 58 note (Trin. MS.), Þe dom is ful grureful & strong o þe þet unliden ham þe put. 1693 R. Lyde Retaking a Ship 17, I answered, alle abau, for I don't want your help, and then they..unlid the Scuttle and went down. 1821 Clare Vill. Minstr. I. 116 The pitmen often..'neath many a loosen'd block, Unlid coffins in the rock. 1853 C. Bronte Villette xiii, Not a paper but was glanced over, not a little box but was unlidded.

Unli·dded, ppl. a. [Un-¹ 8.] Not furnished or covered with a lid.

1819 Keats Song Four Faeries 86 My bare unlidded eyes. 1868 Browning Ring & Bk. III. 1366 If, with the midday blaze of truth above, The unlidded eye of God awake. 1897 Mary Kingsley W. Africa 208 These pots..are unglazed, unlidded bowls.

†**Unlie·f**, a. Obs. [OE. unléof (Un-¹ 7), = MDu. (Du.) onlief, OHG. unliup, unleub, MHG. unliep (G. unlieb), ON. úljúfr, Goth. unliubs.] Not dear or valued; disliked, distasteful, unpleasant.

c 1200 Trin. Coll. Hom. 189 Ðe lichame..and þe gost..fliten and winnen bitwenen hem, þat al þat is on unlef and unqueme, hit is þat oðer iqueme. c 1400 Destr. Troy 2049 Therfore saintes to seche and to sere halowes,..it ledis vnto laithnes and vnlefe werkes. 1430–40 Lydg. Bochas I. i. (1544) a Theyr..unware mischief..It was to them ful uncouth and unlefe. ? a 1500 Chester Pl. (Shaks. Soc.) I. 42 To all men thou shalbe unleffe,..And over all sette at naughte. 1513 Douglas Æneid XII. xiii. 48 Sustenand thus..euery stres, baith le-um and unleif. a 1596 Sir T. Chaloner in Harington's Nugæ Ant. (1804) II. 379 Nat so unleef, that I shold wysh To be thy Trojan wyfe.

Unli·felike, a. (Un-¹ 7 c.) 1818 Hogg Brownie of Bodsbeck II. iv. 75, I see the chaps are living, an' no that unlife-like, as a body may say. 1881 Athenæum 19 Nov. 664/3 The Highland characters of his present story are not unlifelike. **Unli·ftable**, a. (Un-¹ 7 b.) [1775 Ash.] 1818 Art Preserv. Feet 93 Facts..not of sufficient importance to form the basis of a huge unliftable quarto. 1854 Ferrier Inst. Metaph. 59 Suppose he were to call the liftable, the unliftable, the imponderable without any qualification. **Unli·fted**, ppl. a. (Un-¹ 8.) [1775 Ash.] 1815 Byron Destr. Sennacherib v, The tents were all silent,..The lances unlifted. 1882 Ainger Lamb v. 94 The cloud of domestic anxiety was still unlifted. **Unli·fting**, ppl. a. (Un-¹ 10.) 1845 Mrs. Norton Child of Islands 131 Veiling dear eyes..With an unlifting veil. **Unli·gable**, a. rare⁻¹. (Un-¹ 7 b.) Incapable of being bound. 1653 R. Baillie Dissuas. Vind. (1655) 70 Remember what you assert of unligable Proteus.

Unli·ght, a.¹ [Un-¹ 7 + Light a.¹ Cf. ON. úlettr (MSw. olätter), MHG. unlihte.] Not light (in weight or feeling); heavy.

c 1320 Sir Tristr. 419 He toke his lod vnliȝt. Ibid. 1039 A launce vn-liȝt. c 1440 Ipomydon 472 He..takith bys lawe with hert vnlyght. 1480–1 J. Watton Spec. Xristiani 40 A temple..With walles and pylers here onlyght.

Unli·ght, a.² rare—°. [Un-¹ 7 + Light a.²] Not bright or clear; dark, obscure. 1570 Levins Manip. 119 Vnlight, obscurus.

Unli·ght, v. Now s.w. dial. [Un-² 9. Cf. dial. onlight (1825–).] intr. To alight, dismount.

1623 Cockeram I, Degresse, to vnlight from a Horse. 1796 Mrs. M. Robinson Angelina II. 174 I'm sure you hadn't no companion when you unlighted. 1847 Halliwell, 1886—in Glouc., Som., and Devon glossaries, etc.

†**Unli·ght**, ppl. a.¹ Obs.⁻¹ [Un-¹ 8 b + Light v.¹ 6.] Not dismounted. c 1400 Destr. Troy 3445 He raght to the reynes of þe riche qwene,..And led hir vnlight into a large halle. †**Unli·ght**, ppl. a.² Obs. [Un-¹ 8 b.] = next 1. a 1500 Three 15th Cent. Chron. (Camden) 104 The torches unlight met hym at the steyre foote.., and so went byfore hym unlyght to the chirche. 1591 Sylvester Du Bartas I. ii. 670 As lighted Candles doe th' unlight inflame.

Unli·ghted, ppl. a. [Un-¹ 8.]

1. Not lighted; not set on fire; unkindled.

169. Ad Populum Phaleræ ii, Ask him but whence unlighted Candles came? 1718 Prior Solomon III. 708 The sacred Wood, which on the Altar lay, Untouch'd, unlighted glows. 1863 Thornbury True as Steel III. 16 The cannonier, rising, unlighted linstock in hand. 1883 D. C. Murray Hearts xxxiv, With his unlighted pipe between his teeth.

2. Not lighted up or illuminated; not furnished with light. Also fig.

[1775 Ash, Unlighted,..not directed by light.] 1825 T. Hook Sayings Ser. II. III. 102 The countenance of..Fanny; was the only one unlighted by smiles and happiness. 1855 Arnold Balder Dead II. 213 Ye..gave me nine unlighted realms to rule. 1886 C. E. Pascoe London of To-day (ed. 3) 254 A cell..unlighted except by the door.

Unli·ghtened, ppl. a. [Un-¹ 8.]

†**1.** Unenlightened. Obs.

1587 Golding De Mornay xxii. 389 Princes vnlightened by God, are so desirous of vainglorie. 1627 Hakewill Apol. 35 Onely this part of [Christendom]..remaines..vnlightned, in the darkenes of ignorance.

2. Not lighted up; unbrightened; † unlighted.

1637–50 Row Hist. Kirk (Maitland Cl.) I. 113 A glorious altar sett vp, with two unlightned candles, and two basins. 1659 W. Chamberlayne Pharonnida III. ii. 19 Whilst she did remain Unlightened with a beam of comfort. 1852 Bailey Festus (ed. 4) 42 Some seem to live, Whose hearts are like those unlightened stars Of the first darkness. 1896 Westm. Gaz. 2 May 2/2 Sombre gloom, unlightened save for the red staves of the inverted halberds.

Unli·ghtsome, a. (Un-¹ 7.)

1592 R. D. Hypnerotomachia 17 This dark vnlightsome place. 1594 Chapman Shadow of Night 30 When vnlightsome, vast, and indigest, The formelesse matter of this world did lye. 1667 Milton P. L. VII. 355 Of Celestial Bodies first the Sun A mightie Spheare he fram'd, unlightsom first. 1686 J. S[ergeant] Hist. Monast. Convent. 167 The place of Election is very unlightsom, as having but a few Lights.

Unli·gnified, ppl. a. (Un-¹ 8.)

1875 Bennett & Dyer tr. Sachs' Bot. 100 An unlignified gelatinous thickening-mass. 1878 Masters Henfrey's Elem. Bot. (ed. 3) 414 The cell-walls consist of unlignified cellulose.

Unli·ke, a. and sb. Forms: 3–4 un-, vnlich, 4 -liche (-lichy, 5 onliche), -leche; 3 unnlic, 4 vnlic, -lijc, 4–5 vnlyk, 5–6 vnlyke (6 -leke), 3- unlike. [ME. unlich(e, unlik(e (Un-¹ 7), corresponding to OE. ungelic Unliche a. Cf. OFris. (NFris.) unlik, obs. Du. onlijk, MLG. (LG.) unlik, ON. úlíkr (Icel. ólíkur, MSw. oliker, olika, Sw. olik, olika, MDa. ulig, ulige, Da. and Norw. ulig, Norw. ulik).]

1. Not like or resembling, different from, dissimilar to (some other person or thing).

c 1200 Ormin 16859 Forr all þatt follc let tatt he wass Unnlic all oþerr lede. a 1225 Juliana 14 Ich am iweddet to an..þe is unlich him. 1390 Gower Conf. III. 64 He was unlich alle othre there. 1553 Ascham Germany ⁋ 14 He thought it his most honor to be vnlykest such for his gentlenes, which were misliked..for their crueltie. 1596 Shaks. Merch. V. II. ix. 56 How much [thou art] vnlike my hopes and my deseruings! 1634 Sir T. Herbert Trav. 183 [The banana] giues a most delicious..rellish, not much vnlike our choicest Peares. 1676 Glanvill Ess. vi. 30 Those, whose Genius and Ways are so unlike him. 1725 Pope Odyss. IX. 221 A form enormous! far unlike the race Of human birth, in stature. 1750 tr. Leonardus' Mirr. Stones 112 Some jaspers are not much unlike red porphyry. 1829 Jas. Mill Hum. Mind (1869) II. 252 As unlike to any of those..as the sensation of white is unlike the sensations of the seven prismatic colours. 1875 Jowett Plato (ed. 2) I. 401 The philosopher has notions of good and evil unlike those of other men.

b. Const. to; also (quot. 1873) from.

1340–70 Alex. & Dind. 271 Oure lif & oure lawe vnlich is to 3oure. c 1400 Rom. Rose 6360 Vnlyk is my word to my dede. c 1450 Myrr. our Ladye 224 How vnlyke worldely worshyp is vnto gostly ioye. 1531 Elyot Gov. II. xiv, This maner of flatery is mooste unlyke to that whiche is comunely used. 1556 Olde Antichrist 116 b, Two beades..farre unlyke the one to the other. 1670 Baxter Cure Ch. Div. 238 You would shew your selves much..unliker to Satan the accuser. 1825 Scott Betrothed xiv, Their very saints are unlike to the saints of any Christian country. 1873 Pater Stud. Hist. Renaiss. 80 They were of a spirit as unlike as possible from that of Lorenzo. 1876 Gladstone Glean. (1879) II. 271 He was very unlike to any other man.

2. Not like each other; different, dissimilar.

c 1250 Gen. & Ex. 1726 Ðoȝ him boren ðes ones bles Vnlike manije and likeles. c 1380 Antechrist in Todd Three Treat. Wyclif (1851) 150 Loke Cristis copborde, and hers; and þei ben ful unlichy. 1565 Stapleton tr. Bede's Hist. Ch. Eng. 25 b, The parties there wer farre vnleke of condition. 1605 Bacon Adv. Learn. II. xxiii. § 29 The unlikest in the worlde; the one being fierce..; the other solemn. 1641 Milton Ch. Govt. I. iv. 13 There can be no possible imitation of Lording over their brethren in regard of their persons altogether unlike. 1704 J. Harris Lex. Techn. I. s.v., Unlike Quantities and Signs in Algebra. 1807 Crabbe Par. Reg. II. 283 How fair these names, how much unlike they look. 1842 Francis Dict. Arts, Unlike quantities, in algebra, are such as are expressed by different letters, or different roots or powers of the same letter. 1869 Gretton Memory's Harkb. 125 We may take together two other Judges,..as unlike as the baker and the innate gentleman.

absol. 1831 Carlyle Sart. Res. II. v, This approximation of the Like and Unlike. Ibid., In this case of the Like-Unlike.

b. sb. pl. Dissimilar things or persons.

1612 W. Sclater Sick Souls Salve 1 He amplifies it in a comparison of unlikes. a 1626 — Comm. Malachy (1650) 66 It is handled in a plenary comparison of unlikes. 1857 J. Pulsford Quiet Hours 43 Like can reach like, and act upon it, in a way that unlikes cannot.

3. †**a.** Differing from others of the kind; incomparable; unusual. Obs.

1390 Gower Conf. II. 275 Bot certes such usure unliche It falleth more unto the riche. 14.. R. Gloucester's Chron. (MS. Digby 205) fol. 26 He was in his lyue euer ryȝt ;yche Of richesse before al oþer he was vnliche.

b. Differing from, dissimilar to, the thing or person in question. Also absol.

c 1374 Chaucer Boeth. IV. vi. (1868) 138 Ne it ne is nat an vnlyke miracle to hem þat ne knowen it nat. 1542 Udall Erasm. Apoph. 5 Nor a muche vnlyke aunswere dyd Wylliam, late archebishop of Canterbury,..gyue vnto me. 1595 Daniel Civ. Warr v. lxxxii, He saw prepard, against his side, Both vnlike fortune, and vnequall force. 1667 Milton P. L. VI. 517 Part hidd'n veins digg'd up (nor hath this Earth Entrails unlike) of Mineral and Stone. 1847 Helps Friends in C. Ser. I. I. ix. 166 Not only like likes like, but unlike likes unlike. 1865 Swinburne Atalanta 620 A god Faultless; whom I that love not, being unlike, Fear, and give honour. 1877 E. R. Conder Bas. Faith ii. 81 Awaiting the presence of unlike atoms to call them forth in turn.

c. sb. A person differing from another or others.

13.. Sir Beues (A.) 1009 Her is..min vnliche, Brademond king, þat is so riche. [Cf. Uniliche sb.]

1875 Jowett Plato (ed. 2) III. 219 The just does not desire more than his like but more than his unlike. 1896 Pop. Sci. Monthly Feb. 494 As long as it remains a stranger and an unlike.

4. Presenting points of difference or dissimilarity; not uniform or even; unequal.

c 1375 Cursor M. 7917 (Fairf.), Þer was wonande þat was vn-like ij men a pouer and a rike. 1387 Trevisa Higden (Rolls) VI. 289 Þere was unleche noumbre of array of knyȝtes, for aȝenst an hondred..come a þowsand. 1535 Coverdale Ecclus. xxvi. 7 Whan an vnlike pare of oxen must drawe together. c 1550 H. Lloyd Treasury of Health b 5 If the water do appeare vnlike of substance. 1642 J. Eaton Honey-c. Free Justif. 261 That unlike likenesse betweene Adam and Christ, which the Apostle speaks of, Rom. 5. 1645 Milton Tetrach. 9 Where the different sexe in most resembling unlikenes, and most unlike resemblance, cannot but please best.

5. Unlikely, improbable. Now dial. or arch.

a. With subordinate clause.

c 1400 Destr. Troy. 565 The perlouse pointtes þat passe you behoues, Hit is vnlike any lede with his liffe pas. 1400–20 Clanvowe Cuckow & Night. ix, Hit is vnlyk for to be That eny herte shulde slepy be [etc.]. 1535 Cromwell in Merriman Life & Lett. (1902) I. 413 It is not vnlike but that the saide Duke hathe ben deceyued. 1577 Hanmer Anc. Eccl. Hist. (1663) 235 Neither is it unlike, but that these circumstances might be. 1610 Healey St. Aug. Citie of God, Vives' Comm. VIII. xi. 317 It is vnlike that so sharpe a wit..found not the difference and multitude of things. 1729 T. Innes Crit. Essay (1879) 230 In process of time..it is not unlike there might come..new colonies from Spain. 1795 Southey Joan of Arc III. 401 Whether so [it is] not unlike Heaven might vouchsafe its gracious miracle. a 1905 in Eng. Dial. Dict. (Yks., Warw.).

b. With inf.

1400–20 [see a]. 1538 Henry VIII in Wyatt's Wks. (1816) II. 498 Unjust..demands, and unlike to proceed out of a willing heart to conclude. 1584 R. Scot Discov. Witchcr. III. xviii. 54 Being through age unlike to live one whole yeare. 1626 in Rushw. Hist. Coll. (1659) I. 286 He thought the Match very unlike to be effected. 1655 Earl Orrery Parthen. I. I. 26 This Arabian was not altogether unlike to escape unpunished. 1665 Boyle Occas. Refl. I. iii. 168 Blessings, that I do not so much as know of, and which consequently I am very unlike particularly to acknowledge.

†**c.** Without likelihood of something. Obs.⁻¹

1559 Mirr. Mag., Fall R. Tresilian xiv, Thus all went to wracke vnlyke of remedie.

Unli·ke, adv. Forms: 4–5 vnliche, 4 onlyche; 4–7 vnlike (5 -lyk, 6 -lyke), 7, 9 unlike. [Un-¹ 11 b. Cf. Uniliche adv.]

†**1. a.** Unevenly, unequally; in a higher or lower degree. Obs.

a 1300 Fragm. Seven Sins 55 in E.E.P. (1862) 20 Worldis wel fallith vnliche, and noȝt euch man ilich. 1390 Gower Conf. III. 89 Theologie in such a wise Of hih science and hih aprise Above alle othre stant unlike. c 1425 Wyntoun Cron. VIII. xvi. 2594 Na man..euer couþ tell..A maire commendable memore, As þai did of þis pure kinrik, In þat batall bodin vnlik.

†**b.** Incomparably. Obs.

14.. R. Gloucester's Chron. (MS. Digby 205) fol. 10 b, Cloten hadde most riȝte to þis kyngeryche But þe opere were strenger & rycher vnliche [v.r. onlyche]. c 1425 Cursor M. 5325 (Trin.), Þe kyng lete write lettres 3are To gider alle..Þe beste in þat londe vnliche.

2. †**a.** Differently, diversely. Also const. to.

1526 Pilgr. Perf. (W. de W. 1531) 5 Whiche the Romaynes vsed, but vnlyke to vs. 1552 Huloet, Vnlyke or in a diuers fashyon, dissimiliter. 1595 in Cath. Rec. Soc. Publ. V. 350 Some tyme yt pleaseth God to reveale his wille..by dreames, as He did to Joseph, Pharo, and others, and here not unlike to His designed martyr.

b. In a manner differing from (that of a specified person).

1593 Shaks. 2 Hen. VI, I. i. 189 Oft haue I seene the haughty Cardinall..demeane himselfe Vnlike the Ruler of a Common-weale. 1619 Sir A. Gorges tr. Bacon's De Sap. Vet. 82 This Loue..directing his pace..by that which it perceaues neerest, not vnlike blind men that goe by feeling. 1634 Sir T. Herbert Trav. 14 A little haire before, bauld else-where, not vnlike occasion. 1818 Scott Br. Lamm. xxi, The Master has treated me unlike a gentleman. 1841 W. Spalding Italy & It. Isl. II. 387 They stand apart from all the others, because, unlike these, they applied [etc.].

†**3.** Improbably; unlikely. Obs.

a 1548 Hall Chron., Hen. V. 67 b, Some say that he was therto stirred..by the dolphyn (and not vnlike). 1596 Spenser F. Q. v. v. 38 And, though (vnlike) they should for euer last, Yet in my truthes assurance I rest fixed fast.

†**Unli·ke**, v.¹ Obs. rare. [Un-¹ 14.] **a.** intr. To become displeased. **b.** trans. To displease.

c 1275 Lay. 3366 Leir king was wel ipaid and eft onlikede. c 1380 Wyclif Sel. Wks. II. 267 He haþ sorwe of þe synne, bi resoun þat it unlikiþ God.

Unli·ke, v.² rare. [Un-² 7.] intr. To give up liking; to cease to like.

1761 Mrs. F. Sheridan Sidney Bidulph I. 183 My heart is not in a disposition to love... I cannot compel it to like and unlike, and like anew at pleasure.

Unli·k(e)able, a. (Un-¹ 7 b.) 1841 L. Hunt Seer II. (1864) 1 Without trying to render it unlikeable from its inferiority. 1888 Athenæum 31 March 396/1 There are touches about her that..make her unlikable.

Unli·ked, ppl. a. (Un-¹ 8, 8 c.)

1561 B. Googe Palingenius' Zodiac Life I. A j b, Not worse vnliked now shal I be, yf that thou wylt me blesse. 1620 Bp. Hall Hon. Marr. Clergy I. xxvii. (1628) 769 That more vnliked epistle which Ignatius wrote to Saint John. 1641 (title), An Aprovd Answer to the partiall and unlikt of Lord Digbies Speech to the Bill of Attainder.

Unli·kelihood. [Un-¹ 12. Cf. Unlikely a., and MDa. uligelighed.]

†**1.** Unlikeness, dissimilarity, discrepancy. Obs.

1483 Caxton Gold. Leg. 273/1, I fond myself right fer fro the in a Regyon of unlykelyhode [L. dissimilitudinis]. 1550 Thomas Ital. Dict., Disaguaglianza, vnseemelinesse, vnlikelyhoode, or the difference that is betwene the comparison of one thyng to an other. 1564 Brief Exam. 20 b, Euery man..may see a great vnlikelyhood betwixt those tymes and ours. 1613 Purchas Pilgrimage (1614) 573 By which likenesse in name great confusion and vnlikelihoods haue happened in Historie.

2. The state or fact of being unlikely; improbability.

1548 Udall, etc. Erasm. Par. John xix. 109 So muche vnlikelyhoode was it, that the felowship of punishement should defyle hym. 1598 R. Bernard tr. Terence, Andria II. ii, Hauing gathered by sundrie signes and coniectures the vnlikelihood of the marriage. 1646 Earl Monm. tr. Biondi's Civil Wars IX. 199 By the Unlikelyhood and Impossibility that he should escape the hands of a Crafty..Uncle. 1695 J. Edwards Perfect. Script. 238 There was no unlikelihood of the thing. 1767 Mrs. Delany Life & Corr. Ser. II. (1862) I. 116 Knowing the unlikelihood of your being to return to us. 1794 Paley Evid. II. viii, The extreme unlikelihood that such men should engage in such a measure. 1860 Miss Yonge Stokesley Secr. xii, The exceeding unlikelihood of a girl like Elizabeth committing..a theft. 1877 Freeman Norm. Conq. I. vi. 462 Statements which have no inherent unlikelihood in them.

b. With a and pl. An improbable occurrence, fact, statement, etc.

a 1550 Leland Itin. (1769) II. 35 Dyvers Brethren dyed.., and by a great vnlykelihod al the Landes descendid to..the Yonggest of the Brethren. 1561 Daus tr. Bullinger on Apoc. (1573) 2, I will shew the lykelyhodes and the vnlykelyhodes. 1647 Jer. Taylor Lib. Proph. ii. 41 The rarest mixture..of unlikelihoods that I have observed. 1682 Luttrell Brief Rel. (1857) I. 188 By the severall contradictions and unlikelyhoods in his evidence. 1738 G. Lillo Marina III. ii, What strange unlikelihood assaults my mind! 1824 Southey Roderick XII. 14, I will believe that we have days in store Of hope,..Yea, maugre all unlikelihoods,..of peace. 1862 Lever Barrington xv, He hesitated how to measure an unlikelyhood.

Unli·keliness. [Un-¹ 12. Cf. prec. and next.]

†**1.** Unsuitableness. Obs.

c 1374 Chaucer Troylus I. 16 For I þat god of loues seruantz serue Ne dar to loue for myn vnliklynesse.

†**2.** Unseemliness, unbecomingness. Obs.

1456 Sir G. Haye Law Arms (S.T.S.) 130 Nevertheles and he saw..him mak grete repaire till his hous, and unlyklynes, he mycht mak him..exhortacioun to nocht mak sik unlikly repaire. 1685 H. More Paralip. Prophet. xxxiv. 306 What unlikeliness or Indecorum is it, that Proclamation be made who he is, that shall..[open] the Book?

†**3.** Dissimilarity, discrepancy. Obs.

1561 T. Norton Calvin's Inst. II. 143 It shall be sufficient that we wey the wordes of one of them, to attain the meaning of them both. Albeit, there is some vnlikelinesse betwene them. 1604 T. Wright Passions v. iv. 189 Likelinesse or vnlikelinesse are also relatives, and consequently belong to this same predicament. c 1620 Bp. Hall Contempl., N. T. II. ii, Neither was there more unlikelinesse in their disposition and cariage, than similitude in their function. 1730 Bailey (fol.), Dissimilitude, unlikeliness.

4. Unlikelihood, improbability.

1614 Raleigh Hist. World III. vii. § 4. 82 Whether Themistocles perceiued much vnlikelinesse of good successe [etc.]. 1690 Locke Human Understanding IV. xv. § 2. 332 There being degrees herein, from the very neighbourhood of Certainty and Evidence, quite down to Improbability and Unlikeliness. 1841 Gen. P. Thompson Exerc. (1842) VI. 160 The unlikeliness that he should get what he asked for. 1881 Saintsbury Dryden 72 The unlikeliness of his ever having been a very fervent Roundhead.

Unli·kely, a. (and sb.). [Un-¹ 7. Cf. ON. úlikligr (Icel. ólíklegur, MSw. olikliker, Sw. olíklig, MDa. uligelig, Norw. ulikleg).]

1. Not likely to occur or come to pass; improbable in respect of occurrence.

1375 Barbour Bruce IX. 670 He oft full vnlikly thing Brocht rycht weill to full gud ending. 1488 Cely Papers (Camden) 169 They of Bruges sayth all schall be well schorttly but hytt ys onlyckly. 1513 Douglas Æneid XI. viii. 119 Tyme..Reducit hes full mony onlikly thing To bettir fyne than was thair begynning. a 1533 Ld. Berners Gold. Bk. M. Aurel. xxxvi. (1536) R ii, The more yll they vtter, the more vnlykely is the redres therof ageyn. c 1580 Bugbears I. ii. 121 Why is it a thing vnpossyble or vnlikelie that sprites wil deall withe gold? 1642 D. Rogers Naaman 200 Thus Papists conceive it an unlikelyer thing, that [etc.]. 1692 Bentley Boyle Lect. 218 Which makes it..more improbable, that they should interfere..even in the last and unlikeliest instance. 1861 Paley Æschylus (ed. 2) Supplices 979 note, However, κάμψα is an unlikely crasis.

b. Not likely to be true or correct; improbable in respect of fact.

1592 Shaks. Ven. & Ad. 989 The one doth flatter thee in thoughts unlikely, In likely thoughts the other kills thee quickly. 1613 Purchas Pilgrimage (1614) 595 Josephus and Eusebius thinke them to bee the Israelites, which is vnlikely. 1673 Dryden Marr. à la Mode III. i, They tell, for news, such unlikely stories! 1712 J. James tr. Le Blond's Gardening 141 An Opinion very unlikely, to believe Trees have their Male and Female. 1780 Mirror No. 73. If this..be the effect of habit, which is not unlikely. 1871 Freeman Norm. Conq. IV. xviii. 231 The presence of Matilda..at such a time is in itself unlikely.

c. Not likely, in various implications.

1535 Coverdale Ecclus. xi. 6 Many tyrauntes haue bene fayne to syt downe vpon the earth, & ye vnlickly hath worne ye crowne. 1593 Sidney's Arcadia IV. ⁋ 1 That by unlikeliest meanes greatest matters may come to conclusion. 1622 Donne Serm. 25 A farre vnlikelier sort of people, then any of these. 1656 Cowley Davideis IV. 828 Nor would ill Fate that meant me to surprise, Come cloath'd in so unlikely a Disguise. 1694 Atterbury Serm. Isaiah lx. 22 14 This..was an Unlikely way of gaining Proselytes. 1749 Lavington Enthus. Meth. & Papists II. (1754) 129 He cures Diseases..with unlikely Remedies. 1774 G. White Selborne lxi, A succession [of swifts] still haunts the same unlikely roofs. 1847 C. Bronte J. Eyre xxxiv, That a poor lad was come, at that unlikely time, to fetch Mr. Rivers. 1855 A. J. Morris Words for Heart & Life iii. 52 God is in the habit of employing unlikely instruments. 1898 'Merriman' Roden's Corner ii, Cases where brilliant men have failed and unlikely ones have covered themselves with..glory.

Comb. 1858 Faber Spir. Confer. (1870) 131 Those vices of which the unlikeliest-looking souls are often the likeliest to be guilty.

d. sb. An unlikely person.

1867 Latham Black & White 98 He goes round with his..papers, dealing one to each passenger likely or unlikely (because the unlikelies would be offended if omitted).

2. With complement: **a.** With to and inf. (active or passive).

1395 Purvey Remonstr. (1851) 84 The nouelteez of this Innocent Len vnlicli to be sothe. 1412–20 Lydg. Chron. Troy IV. 23 Vnlikly [it was] euere vs to han had victorie. c 1450 Mirk's Festial 140 Ierusalem..was þe strengest cyte yn al þe world, and vnlykly forto haue ben wonon. 1611 Florio, Inaccadeuole, vnlikely to chance or befall. 1658 Osborne Adv. Son Wks. (1673) 112 The not unlikeliest to know Truth. 1711 Steele Spect. No. 143 ⁋ 1 It will be much more unlikely for us to be well-pleased. 1764 Museum Rust. IV. 11 Salt-petre Bay, which is not unlikely to have been so denominated from salt-petre there. 1842 Loudon Suburban Hort. 377 They are the most unlikely to become fruit-buds. 1890 'R. Boldrewood' Col. Reformer (1891) 216 He was as unlikely as Grahame to take..to the improvement of the common people.

b. With that and clause.

1412–20 Lydg. Chron. Troy IV. 3243 For now, allas! vnlikly is þat we Shal euere wynne..þis cite. 1722 Wollaston Relig. Nat. v. (1724) 82 Make him understand how unlikely a thing it is, that they should be placed there only to adorn..a canopy over our heads. 1855 Orr's Circ. Sci., Inorg. Nat. 226 It is not unlikely that the gas thus formed occupies the place of water. 1884 Thompson Tumours of Bladder 55 It is not unlikely that some of these may be congenital.

†**3.** Unsuitable, unsuited; not fit or proper. Obs.

c 1386 Chaucer Merch. T. 936 That whan I considere youre beautee, And ther with al the vnlikly elde of me, I may nat certes..Forbere to been out of youre compaignye. c 1440 Capgrave Life St. Kath. III. 782 His clothis to his woordis arn ful onlykly. 1470–85 Malory Arthur II. viii. 84 Thou art a boystous man and an vnlykely to telle of suche dedes. 1571 Southampton Court Leet Rec. (1905) I. 77 Such as arre..unlyklye and unmeete men to serve for that poorpose. 1588 Nottingham Rec. IV. 221 Yt ys an onlykelye house for suche one to dwelle there.

b. Unseemly, unbecoming; not acceptable or agreeable; objectionable, distasteful. Obs. exc. dial.

1456 [see Unlikeliness 2]. c 1470 Henry Wallace II. 263 On a caar wnlikly thai him cast. a 1586 Sidney Arcadia II. ii. (1912) 153 For a very unlikely envie she hath stumbled upon, against the Princesses..beautie. 1590 Serpent of Devis. B j/2 The most unlikely person and the most wretch that in any countrye might be found. 1725 Ramsay Gentle Sheph. I. i. 24 Yet I am tall, and as weel built as thee, Nor mair unlikely to a lass's eye. 1889 N. W. Linc. Gloss. 586 Unlikely, bad, displeasing.

†**c.** Unpromising; poor in quality or condition.

1560 Rolland Seven Sages 46 This auld tre..fra the 3oung takis all substance and air;..Sa the 3oung plant is sa vnliklie maid. a 1648 Ld. Herbert Hen. VIII (1683) 522 That Forests..should be driven once in the year, and unlikely Tits in them to be killed.

Unli·kely, adv. [Un-¹ 11: cf. prec. and MSw. olikliika.] Improbably.

c 1449 Pecock Repr. III. xiii. 361 The oon bifore seid epistle putt and ascryued vnlikeli to Constantyn. 1641 Milton Ch. Govt. I. vii. 40 [He] may fall not unlikely sometimes..into an uncouth opinion. 1716 Pope Lett. (1737) I. 146 The pleasures..must undoubtedly be of a nobler kind, and (not unlikely) may proceed from the discoveries each shall communicate to another, of God and of nature. 1830 Southey in Corr. w. C. Bowles (1882) 199 This provides also (most unlikely) in case of his half-craziness again becoming whole-craziness. 1867 Freeman Norm. Conq. I. v. 298 The church..may, not unlikely, have been raised..to commemorate the event.

†**Unli·ken**, v. Obs. [Un-² 6 a. Cf. MDu. ontliken.] trans. To dissemble. 1382 Wyclif 1 Kings xiv. 5 Whanne she was comen yn, and hadde vnliknd hire self to be that she was. **Unli·kenable**, a. (Un-¹ 7 b.) 1845 Bailey Festus (ed. 2) 46 The earth..Is not so like the unlikenable One As thou.

Unli·keness. [Un-¹ 12.]

†**1.** Strangeness. Obs.

c 1230 Hali Meid. 13, I þis world þat is icleopet lond of unlicnesse. a 1380 St. Augustin 224 in Horstm. Altengl. Leg. (1878) 65/2, I fond fro þe þat fer I was, As in a kyngdam of vnlikenes.

2. The quality of being unlike; want of likeness or resemblance; dissimilarity.

c 1380 Wyclif Serm. Sel. Wks. II. 227 For noo drede licknesse of breþeren causiþ love among hem, and unliknesse is cause of discord. 1398 Trevisa Barth. De P. R. II. xii. (1495) c j/1 No violence of tyrannye bendyth theym to oppresse..the nether angellis. Therfore Denys sayth that they vse theyr lordshypp wyth vnlyknesse of tyrannye. 1533 More Debell. Salem Wks. 998/2 The causes that he laieth of dyssimilitude & vnlikenes, be twene the witnesses. 1548 Udall Erasmus Par. Matt. v. 37 The unlikenes of manners declareth and argueth a bastarde. 1634 Canne Necess. Separ. (1849) 89 Mark..what they speak here, touching their likeness and unlikeness with the papists. 1645 Milton Tetrach. 9 Where the different sexe in most resembling unlikenes, and most unlike resemblance cannot but please best. 1709 Brit. Apollo II. Supernum. No. 1. 2/1 We meet with some Characters of Unlikeness in this Similitude. 1772 Wesley Jrnl. 11 Feb. (1827) III. 440 For..unlikeness to all the world beside,..the writer is without a rival! 1846 Trench Mirac. xxv. (1862) 359 There are..points of unlikeness in the two miracles. 1853 Kingsley Hypatia xxi, It was..strange in its utter unlikeness to any teaching..which he had ever heard before. 1875 Whitney Life Lang. ix. 173 We know of no other way in which this likeness in unlikeness can be brought about.

b. With a and pl. An instance of dissimilarity or want of resemblance.

1662 South Serm. (1679) 116 As great an unlikeness, as between St. Pauls a Cathedral, and St. Pauls a Stable. 1667 Phil. Trans. II. 611 These two unlikenesses I mention together. 1718 Freethinker No. 155 (1733) 240 Such Unlikenesses as, by their Subtility, escape the Observation of Judgments less acute. 1746 W. Horsley Fool (1748) I. 33 They are the Beau and the Belle; and, if I may be understood in thus speaking, are a similar Unlikeness. 1828 Southey Epist. to A. Cunningham 370, I recognise all these unlikenesses, Spurious abominations though they be. 1879 Sir G. Campbell Black & White 22 The likenesses are much more numerous and much more prominent than the unlikenesses.

3. A bad or poor likeness.

1729 T. Cooke Tales, &c. 127 His ample Shield..On which th' Unlikeness of the Greek appears. 1843 Longf. in Life (1891) II. 4 In the next number is an un-likeness of me,..in a morning-gown.

†**Unli·kening**, ppl. a. Obs.⁻¹ [Un-¹ 10.] Differing. c 1430 Pilgr. Lyf Manhode I. cxxxii. (1869) 70 These ben thinges gretliche unliknynge and discordinge.

Unli·king, vbl. sb. [Un-¹ 13.] Want of liking; dislike; † dissatisfaction.

1398 Trevisa Barth. De P. R. v. xxxvi. (Bodl. MS.), Þe making of þe hert..is þe..wel of meuyng and liking [and] of alle vnliking. c 1400 Cato's Morals in Cursor M. App. iv. 242 Quen þou has of þi þing þorou hap vnliking,..behalde þou on oþer men. 1876 Mrs. Whitney Sights & Ins. II. xxiii. 512 A gradual liking that was at first almost unliking. 1886 D. C. Murray First Person Sing. xxv, Angela had..a genuine unliking for O'Rourke.

†**Unli·king**, ppl. a. Obs. [Un-¹ 10.] Unpleasant, disagreeable.

1393 Langl. P. Pl. C. VIII. 23 Ich hadde leuere..lacke men, and lykne hem in vnlykynge manere, Þan al þat euere Marc made. a 1470 H. Parker Dives & Pauper (W. de W. 1496) XII. v. 213/1 Yf one corde..in the harpe be broke..all the songe..shall be unlykynge to all that here it. ? a 1500 Chester Pl. (Shaks. Soc.) I. 83 Lorde, I muste doe thy byddinge, Though yt be to me unlikinge. c 1520 Skelton Magnyf. 1958, I am lowsy and vnlykynge and full of scurffe. 1570 Levins Manip. 137 Vnliking, displicitus.

Unli·mb, v. [Un-² 4.] trans. To dismember. 1694 Motteux Rabelais IV. liii. 208 Batter 'em, burst 'em, quarter 'em, unlimb 'em,..these wicked Heretics. 1869 J. Conington Horace, Sat. (1874) 17 Still The bard remains, unlimb him as you will. **Unli·mber**, a. (Un-¹ 7.) a 1639 Wotton Charac. F. di Medici in Reliq. (1651) 364 To which temper more septentrionall unlimber Nations have not yet bent themselves.

Unli·mber, v. [Un-² 5.]

1. Mil. To free (a gun) from the limber, by detaching and withdrawing this, preparatory to bringing the gun into action.

1802 James Milit. Dict. s.v. Limber, A two-wheel carriage..taken off..; which is called unlimbering the guns. 1839 F. A. Griffiths Artill. Man. 93 Square can only be formed when..both guns and waggons are unlimbered. 1879 C. R. Low Jrnl. General Abbott ii. 146 Abbott..unlimbered the 24-pounder howitzer.

fig. 1864 Trevelyan Compet. Wallah (1866) 272 Then are the 'English name', and the 'development of the resources of India', unlimbered, and trundled out to overawe the..magistrates.

b. absol. To perform the operation of detaching and withdrawing the limber.

1828 Spearman Brit. Gunner (ed. 2) 177 Unlimbering, or Coming into Action. 1875 Clery Min. Tact. xi. 136 A H. A. battery..unlimbered and came into action.

transf. 1888 Harper's Mag. Sept. 555/1 A travelling band which [was]..in the second-class car, and which good-naturedly unlimbered at the stations.

2. To detach and withdraw the front-wheels of (a boat-carriage).

1853 Douglas Milit. Bridges (ed. 3) 92 To launch the bateau, the carriage is placed with the pole towards the river, and unlimbered: by this means an inclined plane is formed.

Unli·me, v. [Un-² 3. Cf. Flem. ontlijmen 'deglutinare' (Kilian), G. entleimen.]

†**1.** trans. To detach, dissever. Obs.⁻¹

1225 Ancr. R. 256 Þet he wot ful wel: & for þi he is umbe..uorte unlimen ou mid wreððe. [1648 Hexham II, Ontlijmen, to Vnglue, or to Vnlime.]

2. To free (dressed hides) from lime.

1885 Harper's Mag. Jan. 275/2 This washing in warm water is a preparation for 'drenching', the first process of unliming. 1888 Pop. Sci. Monthly Dec. 287 The process of unliming hides and skins.

Unli·med, ppl. a. [Un-¹ 8. Cf. Du. ongelijmd, G. ungeleimt.]

1. Not smeared or clogged with bird-lime. In quots. fig.

1622 S. Ward Christ All in All (1627) 36 Christ, whom hee longed to bee with, and would now with vnlimed and vnentangled wings flye vnto. a 1672 Sterry Freed. Will (1675) 137 It keeps these wings unlimed..by the filth or guilt of fleshly lusts.

2. Not dressed or treated with lime.

1756 F. Home Exper. Bleaching 215 This makes limed cloth easily distinguishable from unlimed. 1801 Farmer's Mag. Nov. 478 As the grain must have lain in the ground for two years, and none was observed in the unlimed part.

Unli·mitable, a. [Un-¹ 7 b, 5 b.] Incapable of being limited; illimitable.

In frequent use from c 1610 to c 1650.

1604 Marston Malcontent I. vi, O vnlimitable impudencie! 1690 Locke Govt. I. ii. (1694) 9 An Absolute, Arbitrary, Unlimited, and Unlimitable Power. 1716 M. Davies Athen. Brit. III. Diss. Drama 33 In talking so much..of other People's unlimitable Liberty of Thinking and Worshipping.

Unli·mited, ppl. a. [Un-¹ 8.]

1. Not limited or restricted in amount, extent, or degree: **a.** Of power or authority, a rule, etc.

c 1445 Pecock Donet 129 Which gouernaunce in it silf is vnlimited and vnassigned to eny special tyme. a 1586 Sidney Arcadia III. i. (1912) 355 It must be an unlimited Monarchy. Ibid. xx. 472, I know thy power is not unlimited. 1644 Hunton Vind. Treat. Monarchy v. 45 That the Power of the Monarch in this Frame is not unlimited. 1690 [see prec.]. 1717 Lady M. W. Montagu Let. to C'tess of Bristol 1 April, The unlimited power of these fellows. 1777 Cook Third Voyage II. xi. (1784) I. 406 The power of the king is unlimited. a 1850 Calhoun Wks. (1874) III. 234 Money is not only the sinew of war, but of politics, over which..it exercises almost unlimited control. Ibid. VI. 133 A government of unlimited powers.

b. In other applications.

a 1586 Sidney Arcadia III. iv. (1912) 371 All such, whom..youth-like mindes did fill with unlimited desires. 1602 Marston Antonio's Rev. III. ii, The curse of Heaven raines In plagues unlimited through all his daies. 1647 Clarendon Hist. Reb. I. § 18 The expences of the Court..[were] vast, and unlimited by the old good rules of economy. a 1704 T. Brown Praise Drunken. Wks. 1730 I. 35 Their highest excellency consists in having their will unlimited by any superior power. 1782 Priestley Corrupt. Chr. I. II. 158 The absolute and unlimited declarations of the divine mercy. 1846 Mrs. Marsh Father Darcy II. 149 My confidence in his talents and energy is unlimited. 1878 Jevons Prim. Pol. Econ. 19 We never want an unlimited quantity of anything.

transf. 1837 Carlyle Fr. Rev. III. II. vi, So violent..are the Limited Patriots and the Unlimited.

2. Not limited in number.

1665 Sir T. Herbert Trav. (1677) 308 Four Wives the Law tolerates, Concubines are unlimited.

3. Math. (See quots.)

1704 J. Harris Lex. Techn. I. s.v., Unlimited Problem..is such a Problem in Mathematicks, as is capable of Infinite Solutions. 1843 Penny Cycl. XXVI. 31/1 Unlimited,..is frequently used by mathematical writers, in the same manner as Indefinite, to avoid the entrance of the word Infinite. It is also used to describe a problem which may have an infinite number of answers, and which is called an unlimited problem.

Unli·mitedly, adv. [Un-¹ 11: cf. prec.] Without limitation.

1611 Florio, Sterminatamente,..infinitely, vnlimitedly. a 1639 W. Whateley Prototypes II. xxvi. (1640) 81 It is an easie thing for inferiours to obey their Governours..a little too unlimitedly. a 1680 Corbet Non-conf. Plea (1683) 19 The said promise must be understood either unlimitedly, or with limitation. a 1716 Blackall Wks. (1723) I. 226 If this had been express'd as universally and unlimitedly. 1796 Burney Mem. Metastasio I. 238 A great..prince, who deigns to be so unlimitedly my protector. 1836 New Monthly Mag. XLVIII. 409 His Grace is unlimitedly hospitable. 1891 Meredith One of our Conq. III. xix. 171 He feels the publishers pouring their gallons through it unlimitedly.

Unli·mitedness. [Un-¹ 12.] The fact of being unlimited; absence of limitation.

1641 Falkland in Marriott Life & Times (1908) 204 This unlimitednesse and independence is onely in spirituall things. a 1664 M. Frank Serm. (1672) 421 The unlimitednesse of His power. 1710 A. B. Answ. to Argts. in Bp. Oxford's Sp. Resistance 13 The unlimitedness of our Obedience. 1796 Lamb Lett. (1888) I. 41 Omnipresence is an attribute the very essence of which is unlimitedness. 1904 A. C. Fraser Biog. Philos. ii. 60 It was impossible to believe either space or time limited: it was equally impossible to understand their unlimitedness.

Unli·ne, v.¹ [Un-² 4.]

1. trans. To divest (a garment, etc.) of lining.

1606 J. Davies (Heref.) Bien Venu Wks. (Grosart) I. 6/2 Two Kings thus met, make Kingdomes richly thriue, Though it vnlines their Purse with wearing much. 1611 Cotgr., Desdoubler, to vnlyne; or take the lynings out of a garment.

2. intr. To separate as a lining.

1848 Lindley Introd. Bot. (ed. 4) I. 331 They all pass out of each other (désemboitent); they all unline.

Unli·ne, v.² (Un-² 4 b + Line v.³)

1598 Marston Sco. Villanie I. iv, To morrow doth Luxurio promise me, He will vnline himselfe from bitchery.

Unli·neal, a. (Un-¹ 7.)

1593 Nashe Strange Newes H 4. The vnlineall vsurper of judgement from all his true owners. 1605 Shaks. Macb. III. i. 63 They..put a barren Scepter in my Gripe, Thence to be wrencht with an vnlineall Hand. 1832 [R. Cattermole] Beckett, etc. 170 The Men of England..From her last Despot wrung The sceptre,..to grace A wiser nor unlineal race. 1884 N. & Q. 6 Oct. 264 The ancient manor house..has long since passed into unlineal hands.

Unli·ned, ppl. a.¹ [Un-¹ 8 + Line v.¹] Not furnished with a lining.

In very frequent use from c 1890.

1521 in Test. Ebor. (Surtees) VI. 4 My unlynded gowne. a 1599 Spenser F. Q. VII. vii. 29 Dight In a thin silken cassock coloured greene, That was vnlyned all. 1630 J. Taylor (Water P.) Trav. Wks. III. 89/1 The men..are clad in thin buckerom, vnlined. 1655 tr. Sorel's Com. Hist. Francion XI. 19 Although it was not unfashionable to have a Cloak unlined as was theirs. 1861 Eng. Wom. Dom. Mag. III. 118/2 Stiff muslin petticoats..are very suitable for wearing with..unlined silk dresses. 1878 March. Dufferin Canad. Jrnl. (1891) 408 Our A.D.C.'s unlined suit of tussore silk.

Unli·ned, ppl. a.² [Un-¹ 8 + Line v.² Cf. Du. ongelijnd.] Not marked with lines.

1865 Mrs. Whitney Gayworthys I. 6 Round fair face, unlined by any perplexity. 1885 Whittier Pr. Wks. (1889) II. 316 The faces represented are not so unlined and ruddy.

Unli·ngering, ppl. a. (Un-¹ 10.) 1849 De Quincey English Mail Coach Wks. 1862 IV. 322 By the word 'sudden' [Cæsar] means 'unlingering'. 1887 Bowen Æneid I. 655 Armed with his royal mission the chief unlingering speeds.

Unli·ning, vbl. sb. [Un-² 13.] (See quots.)

1848 Lindley Introd. Bot. (ed. 4) I. 332 Here we have a succession of true unlinings; but in Crucifers..the large stamens offer an example of simple unlining in the full meaning of the word, since they present a separation into two parts only. 1862 M. C. Cooke Man. Bot. Terms 87 Unlining, a separation of parts originally united.

Unli·nk, v. [Un-² 4 b.]

1. trans. **a.** To undo the links of (a chain, etc.). Also refl., fig., and in fig. context.

1600 Shaks. A. Y. L. IV. iii. 112 About his necke A greene and guilded snake had wreath'd it selfe..: but sodainly Seeing Orlando, it vnlink'd it selfe. 1635 Quarles Embl. v. ix. 7, I cannot mount till thou unlink my chaine. a 1670 Rust Disc. Truth (1682) 185 It will unlink and break that chain and method of Gods Decrees. 1822–56 De Quincey Confess. (1862) 154 Those fatally tortuous paths of which the windings can never be unlinked. 1890 Talmage From Manger to Throne 639 The chain of the most tremendous natural law is unlinked.

b. To detach, set free, by undoing or unfastening a link or chain. Also refl., absol., and fig.

1655 R. Crab in Harl. Misc. (1809) IV. 483 Those that will not unlink themselves from the world. a 1680 Charnock Attrib. God (1834) II. 395 He doth..correct those actions, that unlink the mutual assistance between man and man. 1688 R. Holme Armoury III. xix. (Roxb.) 153/1 March to your horses. Vnlink your horses. Fasten your links. 1796 Instr. & Reg. Cavalry (1813) 235 The men move up to their horses, and unlink. Ibid., Unlink Horses! 1802 J. Baillie 2nd Pt. Ethwald IV. iii, (Stage direction. The chiefs instantly let go hands...) Her. Ha! have I then so suddenly unlink'd you? 1849 H. Mayo Pop. Superst. (1851) 79 The attention..is unlinked from the other faculties.

2. intr. To lose connexion; to part; to become relaxed.

1641 Milton Ch. Govt. I. v. 15 To make a King a type, we say is an abusive and unskilful speech..Therefore your typical chaine of King and Priest must unlink. 1786 W. Gilpin in Mrs. Delany's Life & Corr. (1862) III. 372 We travelled amicably, arm in arm,..we had not one occasion to unlink. 1866 H. Siddons Maid, Wife, & Widow III. 44 He felt her arms unlink, and saw that a convulsive fit had put an end to all her recollections.

Unli·nked, ppl. a. [Un-¹ 8.] Not linked, connected, or united.

1813 Shelley Q. Mab VI. 170 Whilst, to the eye of shipwrecked mariner,..All seems unlinked contingency and chance. a 1857 R. A. Vaughan Mystics (1860) II. VIII. ii. 37 So his life is a series of starts; his actions..unlinked, unharmonized.

Unli·quefied, ppl. a. (Un-¹ 8.) 1705 Addison Italy 237 These huge unwieldy Lumps [of lava]..remain'd in the melted Matter rigid and unliquify'd. 1857 Spencer Progress (1864) 285 Yet the gas remained unliquified!

Unli·quid, a. [Un-¹ 7.]

1. (See Liquid a. 1.)

1547 Boorde Brev. Health cxcvi. 68 b, Take gargarices lyquide and unliquyde. 1611 Cotgr. s.v. Pot, Small vessels wherein..liquors, and sometimes vnliquid things, are kept.

2. (See Liquid a. 6.)

1818 Colebrooke Obligations 195 Though evidently due, it is unliquid, so long as the precise amount of it is unascertained. 1865 Carlyle Fredk. Gt. VI. vi. (1873) II. 188 [She] had left considerable properties;..but all was rather in an unliquid state, not so much as her Will was to be had.

Unli·quidate, a. [Un-¹ 7.] = next. 1818 Colebrooke Obligations 194 Unliquidate damages for non-performance of an agreement.

Unli·quidated, ppl. a. [Un-¹ 8.]

1. Not cleared off or paid.

1765 Ann. Reg., Chron. 155/1 They will likewise forfeit all pretensions on their unliquidated papers. 1788 Cowper Let. Wks. 1837 XV. 206 The accounts of a large estate unliquidated many years. 1812 G. Chalmers Dom. Econ. Gt. Brit. 180 Every war leaves many unliquidated claims. 1883 Fortn. Rev. July 104 There will still remain a considerable debt unliquidated.

2. Not made clear or distinct; indefinite.

1730 Bentham Princ. Legisl. iii. § 10 The best ideas..of such pains..are altogether unliquidated in point of quality. 1818 — Ch. Eng., Catech. Exam. 254 An unliquidated number of instances.

Unli·quidating, ppl. a. (Un-¹ 10.) 1824 Byron Juan XVI. xcix, The Sinking Fund's unfathomable sea, That most unliquidating liquid, leaves The debt unsunk. **Unli·quored**, ppl. a. (Un-¹ 8.) 1642 Milton Apol. Smect. 10, I doubt me whether the very sobernesse of such a one, like an

Unmate, early ME. variant of UNMEET *a.*

Unmate'd, *ppl. a.* [Un-1 8 b.]

Unmaterial, *a.* [Un-1 7.] Immaterial.

Unmaternal, *a.* [Un-1 7.]

Unmathematical, *a.* [Un-1 7.]

Unmatriculated, *ppl. a.* [Un-1 8 b.]

Unmatrimonial, *a.* [Un-1 7.]

Unmatronlike, *a.* [Un-1 7.]

Unmatured, *ppl. a.* [Un-1 8 b.]

Unmaturity.

Unmeaning, *ppl. a.* [Un-1 10.]

1. a. Of features, etc.: Expressionless, vacant, unintelligent.

Unmeant, *ppl. a.* [Un-1 8.]

Unmeasurable, *a.*, *sb.*, and *adv.* Obs. [Un-1 7 b, 8, 12, and 11.]

Unmeasurably, *adv.* [Un-1 11.]

Unmeasured, *ppl. a.* [Un-1 8.]

Unmeasuredly, *adv.* [Un-1 11.]

Unmeated, *ppl. a.* Obs. [Un-1 8.]

Unmechanic, *a.* [Un-1 7.]

Unmechanical, *a.* [Un-1 7.]

Unmechanized, *ppl. a.* [Un-1 8 b.]

Unmeddled, *ppl. a.* [Un-1 8.]

Unmeddling, *ppl. a.* [Un-1 10.]

Unmediated, *ppl. a.* [Un-1 8 b.]

Unmedicinal, *a.* [Un-1 7.]

Unmeditated, *ppl. a.* [Un-1 8 b.]

Unmeditative, *a.* [Un-1 7.]

Unmeek, *a.* [Un-1 7.]

Unmeet, *a.* (and *adv.*) [Un-1 7, OE. unʒemēte.]

Unmeetly, *adv.* [Un-1 11.]

Unmeetness.

Unmelodious, *a.* [Un-1 7.]

Unmelted, *ppl. a.* [Un-1 8.]

Unmember, *v.* [Un-2 4.]

Unmemorable, *a.* [Un-1 7 b.]

Unmemorial, *a.* Obs. [Un-1 7.]

Unmenaced, *ppl. a.* [Un-1 8 b.]

Unmended, *ppl. a.* [Un-1 8.]

Unmenged, *ppl. a.* [Un-1 8 + MANG v.]

Unmentionable, *a.* and *sb.* [Un-1 7 b.]

Unmentioned, *ppl. a.* [Un-1 8 b.]

Unmercenary, *a.* [Un-1 7.]

Unmerchantable, *a.* [Un-1 7 b.]

Unmerciful, *a.* [Un-1 7 c.]

Unmercifully, *adv.* [Un-1 11.]

Unmercifulness.

Unmerciless, *a.* [Un-1 5 a.]

Unmercy. [Un-1 12.]

Unmerged, *ppl. a.* [Un-1 8.]

Unmeritable, *a.* Obs. [Un-1 7.]

Unmerited, *ppl. a.* [Un-1 8 b.]

Unmeritedly, *adv.* [Un-1 11.]

Unmeriting, *ppl. a.* [Un-1 10.]

Unmerry, *a.* [OE. unmyrie.]

Unmetalled, *ppl. a.* [Un-1 8.]

Unmetaphysical, *a.* [Un-1 7.]

Unmeted, *ppl. a.* [Un-1 8 d.]

Unmethodical, *a.* [Un-1 7.]

Unmethodised, *ppl. a.* [Un-1 8.]

Unmewed, *ppl. a.* [Un-1 8.]

Unmild, *a.* [OE. unmilde.]

Unmilitary, *a.* [Un-1 7.]

Unmilked, ppl. a. ...

Unmind, v. ...

† Unminding, vbl. sb. ...

Unmindful, a. ...

Unminister, v. ...

Unministered, ppl. a. ...

Unmistered, ppl. a. ...

Unministerial, a. ...

Unminted, ppl. a. ...

Unmistaking, ppl. a. ...

Unmira culous, a. ...

Unmistakable, a. ...

Unmistakably, adv. ...

Unmixed, ppl. a. ...

Unmixable, a. ...

Unmix'dly, adv. ...

Unmodifiable, a. ...

Unmodified, ppl. a. ...

Unmodish, a. ...

Unmodulated, ppl. a. ...

Unmoist, a. ...

Unmoisten'd, ppl. a. ...

Unmoor, v. ...

Unmolested, ppl. a. ...

Unmolesting, ppl. a. ...

Unmolten, ppl. a. ...

Unmoderate, a. ...

Unmorality. ...

Unmoralize, v. ...

Unmoralized, ppl. a. ...

Unmortal, a. ...

Unmortgage, v. ...

Unmoor regard ...

Unmorti cate, v. ...

Unmortified, ppl. a. ...

Unmotherly, a. ...

Unmoulded, ppl. a. ...

Unmount, v. ...

Unmountable, a. ...

Unmounted, ppl. a. ...

Unmov able, a. ...

Unmovableness. ...

Unmovably, adv. ...

Unmoved, ppl. a. ...

Unmoving, ppl. a. ...

Unmurmuring, ppl. a. ...

Unmutilated, ppl. a. ...

Unmuffle, v. ...

Unmurmured ...

Unmusical, a. ...

Unnail, v. ...

Unobli'ging, ppl. a.

Unobnoxious, a. 1. Not exposed or liable to something. Also *ellipt.* 2. Not objectionable or offensive.

Unobscured, ppl. a.

Unobservable, a. Incapable of being observed; imperceptible.

Unobservance.

Unobservant, a.

Unobserved, ppl. a. Not observed; unperceived, unnoticed.

Unobserving, ppl. a.

Unobstructed, ppl. a.

Unobstru'ctive, a.

Unobtainable, a.

Unobtru'ded, ppl. a.

Unobtru'sive, a.

Unobtru'sively, adv.

Unobtrusiveness.

Unoccupied, ppl. a. 1. Not occupied or engaged in some work or pursuit; idle.

Unode.

Unoffended, ppl. a.

Unoffending, ppl. a.

Unoffensive, a.

Unofficered, ppl. a.

Unofficial, a. and sb. 1. Of things: Not having an official character or stamp. 2. Of persons: Not holding an official position.

Unofficially, adv.

Unofficious, a.

Unoil'ed, ppl. a.

Unoperative, a.

Unopposed, ppl. a.

Unoppressive, a.

Unorder, v. 1. Not to order; to leave unarranged.

Unordered, ppl. a. 1. Not ordered or commanded. 2. Not arranged or regulated.

Unorderly, a.

Unordinariness.

Unordinarily, adv.

Unordinary, a.

Unordinate, a.

Unordinately, adv.

Unorganic, a.

Unorganical, a.

Unorganized, ppl. a.

Unoriental, a.

Unoriginal, a.

Unoriginated, ppl. a.

Unoriginatedness.

Unorigination.

Unoriginative, a.

Unornamental, a.

Unornamented, ppl. a.

Unostentatious, a.

Unostentatiously, adv.

Unoutspeakable, a. Unutterable.

Unoven.

Unoverthrown, ppl. a.

Unowed, ppl. a.

Unowned, ppl. a. 1. Not possessed as property; destitute of an owner or possessor.

Unpacify, v.

Unpacified, ppl. a.

Unpacifiable, a.

Unpack, v.

Unpacked, ppl. a.

Unpacker.

Unpaid, ppl. a.

Unpained, ppl. a.

[This page is a facsimile column from the Oxford English Dictionary. The body text is set in extremely small, dense type across multiple columns and is largely illegible at this resolution. The principal headwords and running headers are transcribed below.]

Unpainful, a. — **Unpaintable**, a. — **Unpainted**, ppl. a. — **Unpaired**, ppl. a. — **Unpalatable**, a. — **Unpale**, v. — **Unpaled**, ppl. a. — **Unpalisaded**, ppl. a. — **Unpalled**, ppl. a. — **Unpalliated**, ppl. a. — **Unpalpable**, a. — **Unpar**, v. — **Unparadise**, v. — **Unparagoned**, ppl. a. — **Unparalleled**, ppl. a. — **Unpardonable**, a. — **Unpardoned**, ppl. a. — **Unpared**, ppl. a. — **Unparliamentary**, a. — **Unparted**, ppl. a. — **Unpartial**, a. — **Unparticipate**, v. — **Unpassing**, ppl. a.

Unpassionate, a. — **Unpassioned**, ppl. a. — **Unpaste**, v. — **Unpatience**, — **Unpatient**, a. — **Unpatiently**, adv. — **Unpatriotic**, a. — **Unpatriotically**, adv. — **Unpave**, v. — **Unpaved**, ppl. a. — **Unpay**, v. — **Unpayable**, a. — **Unpaying**, ppl. a. — **Unpeace**, v. — **Unpeaceable**, a. — **Unpeaceful**, a. — **Unpeg**, v. — **Unpen**, v. — **Unpensioning**, ppl. a. — **Unpeople**, v. — **Unpeopled**, ppl. a. — **Unperceivable**, a. — **Unperceived**, ppl. a.

[Dictionary text in multiple columns — densely set Oxford English Dictionary entries. Headwords visible in this section include:]

Unpleasantly, adv.
Unpleasantness.
Unpleasing, ppl. a.
Unpleasingly, adv.
Unpleasingness.
Unpleasurable.
Unpleated, ppl. a.
Unpledged, ppl. a.
Unplenished, ppl. a.
Unpliable.
Unpliant.
Unpliancy.
Unplough, v.
Unploughed, ppl. a.
Unplucked, ppl. a.
Unplug, v.
Unplumb, v.
Unplumbed, ppl. a.
Unplume, v.
Unplumed, ppl. a.
Unplummed.
Unpoetic, a.
Unpoetical, a.
Unpoetically, adv.
Unpoint, v.
Unpointed, ppl. a.
Unpoise, v.
Unpoised, ppl. a.
Unpolarized, ppl. a.
Unpolicied.
Unpolish, v.
Unpolished, ppl. a.
Unpolishable.
Unpolite, a.
Unpoliteness.
Unpolitic, a.
Unpolitical, a.

[Lower half — further OED entries. Headwords visible include:]

Unpoliticly, adv.
Unpolled, ppl. a.
Unpollute, v.
Unpolluted, ppl. a.
Unpoor.
Unpopular, a.
Unpopularise, v.
Unpopularity.
Unpopulate, v.
Unpopulous.
Unportable.
Unportioned.
Unportmanteaued, ppl. a.
Unpose, v.
Unposed, ppl. a.
Unpositive.
Unpossess, v.
Unpossessed, ppl. a.
Unpowdered, ppl. a.
Unpowered.
Unpractical, a.
Unpractically, adv.
Unpracticalness.
Unpracticableness.
Unpracticed, ppl. a.
Unpractisable.
Unpractise, v.
Unpractised, ppl. a.
Unpray, v.
Unprayed, ppl. a.
Unpraying.
Unpreach, v.
Unpreaching.
Unprecedented, ppl. a.
Unprecise, a.
Unprecious.
Unprecipitated, ppl. a.
Unprecise.
Unpredicable.
Unpredictable.
Unprefigurable.
Unpreferred, ppl. a.
Unpregnable.
Unpreguant.
Unprejudicate, v.
Unprejudiced, ppl. a.

UNQUESTIONEDLY. 305 UNRAILED. UNRAINY. 306 UNREAD.

Unque·stioning, ppl. a.

Unqui·ck, a. rare.

Unqui·cken, ppl. a.

Unqui·et, a.

Unqui·et, v.

Unqui·etly, adv.

Unqui·etness.

Unquiet·ude.

Unqui·red, ppl. a.

Unqui·rtable, a.

Unquo·d, obs. variant of UNKED a.

Unqua·te, obs. form of UNQUIET.

Unquo·ted, ppl. a.

Unquo·th, obs. or dial. var. UNCOUTH a.

Unra·te, v.

Unra·ked, ppl. a.

Unra·ilable, a.

Unra·iled, ppl. a.

Unrai·ny, a.

Unrai·sed, ppl. a.

Unra·ke, v.

Unra·ked, ppl. a.

Unra·ncoured, ppl. a.

Unra·nged, ppl. a.

Unrank, a.

Unra·nk, v.

Unra·nsacked, ppl. a.

Unra·nsomed, ppl. a.

Unra·table, a.

Unra·te, v.

Unra·ted, ppl. a.

Unra·tional, a.

Unra·vel, v.

Unra·velled, ppl. a.

Unra·veller.

Unra·velling, vbl. sb.

Unra·velment.

Unra·velable, a.

Unra·ved, ppl. a.

Unra·ching, ppl. a.

Unrea·ched, ppl. a.

Unrea·ding, ppl. a.

Unread, v.

Unra·zored, ppl. a.

Unra·vishable, a.

Unra·vished, ppl. a.

Unra·y, v.

UNREAD. 307 UNREASON. UNREASONABILITY. 308 UNRECEDING.

Unread, ppl. a.

Unrea·dable, a.

Unrea·dably, adv.

Unrea·dableness, **Unrea·dableness**.

Unrea·dily, adv.

Unrea·diness.

Unrea·ding, ppl. a.

Unrea·dy, a.

Unrea·dy, v.

Unrea·dily, adv.

Unrea·l, a.

Unrea·lity.

Unrea·lisable, a.

Unrea·lise, v.

Unrea·lised, ppl. a.

Unrea·ligned, ppl. a.

Unrea·son, sb.

Unrea·son, v.

Unrea·soned, ppl. a.

Unrea·soning, ppl. a.

Unrea·sonable, a.

Unrea·sonableness.

Unrea·sonably, adv.

Unrea·ching, ppl. a.

Unrea·soning, ppl. a.

Unrea·ve, v.

Unre·bated, ppl. a.

Unrebu·ffable, a.

Unrebu·ked, ppl. a.

Unrebu·ttable, a.

Unrebu·tted, ppl. a.

Unrece·ding, ppl. a.

Unresolvable, a.
Unresolve, v.
Unresolved, ppl. a.
Unresolvedly, adv.
Unresoluteness, [f. prec.]

Unresounding, ppl. a.
Unrespect, sb.
Unrespect, ppl. a.
Unrespectable, a.
Unrespected, ppl. a.
Unrespective, a.
Unrespectfulness.
Unrespite, v.
Unrespited, ppl. a.
Unrespiting, ppl. a.
Unrest, sb.
Unrest, v.
Unresting, ppl. a.
Unrestingly, adv.
Unrestingness.

Unrespirable, a.
Unrespited, a.
Unresponsible, a.
Unresponsive, a.
Unrest, sb.

Unrested, ppl. a.
Unrestful, a.
Unrestfully, adv.
Unrestfulness.
Unresting, vbl. sb.
Unrestored, ppl. a.
Unrestraint.

Unrestable, a.
Unrestrainable, a.
Unrestrainably, adv.
Unrestrained, ppl. a.
Unrestrainedly, adv.
Unrestrainedness.
Unrestricted, ppl. a.
Unreturnable, a.
Unreturnably, adv.

Unreturned, ppl. a.
Unreturning, ppl. a.
Unrevealed, ppl. a.
Unreveled.
Unrevenged, ppl. a.
Unreverence, sb.
Unreverenced, ppl. a.
Unreverend, a.
Unreverendly, adv.
Unreverent, a.
Unreverently, adv.

Unrevivable, a.
Unrevived, ppl. a.
Unrevocable, a.
Unrevocably, adv.
Unrevoked, ppl. a.
Unrewarded, ppl. a.
Unrewarding, ppl. a.
Unrhetorical, a.
Unrhymed, ppl. a.
Unrhythmic, a.
Unrhythmical, a.
Unribbed, ppl. a.
Unrich, a.
Unrid, ppl. a.
Unriddable, a.

Unrideably, adv.
Unridely, adv.
Unridiculed, ppl. a.
Unriddle, v.
Unriddler.
Unridden, ppl. a.
Unride, v.
Unridged, ppl. a.
Unrig, v.
Unrigged, ppl. a.

Unright, a.
Unright, adv.
Unright, sb.
Unright, v.
Unrightful, a.

†**Unright**, *a.* Obs.

†**Unright**, *v.1* Obs.

Unright, *v.2*

Unrighteous, *a.*

I. Not righteous or upright; unjust, wicked.

Unrighteously, *adv.*

Unrighteousness.

Unrightful, *a.*

Unrightfully, *adv.*

Unrightfulness.

Unrightly, *adv.*

Unrightwise, *a.* Obs.

Unrip, *v.* [Un-2 + Rip v.]

1. *trans.* To strip (a house or roof) of tiles, slates, etc.

2. To lay open, slit up, or detach, by ripping.

Unripe, *a.* [OE. unrípe.]

1. Immature; not arrived at full development.

2. Immature; not arrived at full development.

3. Of fruit, etc.: Not matured or grown.

Unripely, *adv.*

Unripened, *ppl. a.*

Unripeness.

Unripped, *ppl. a.*

Unripping, *vbl. sb.*

Unrippling, *ppl. a.*

†**Unrid**, *v.* trans.

†**Unriddance.**

Unriddle, *v.*

Unridden, *ppl. a.*

Unrivalled, *a.*

Unriven, *ppl. a.*

Unrobe, *v.* To divest of a robe.

Unrobed, *ppl. a.*

Unrocked, *ppl. a.*

Unrobbed, *ppl. a.*

Unro.

Unrobed, *ppl. a.*

Unroll, *v.*

Unrolled, *ppl. a.*

Unroll, *v.*

Unrolled, *ppl. a.*

Unrolling, *ppl. a.*

Un-Roman, *a.*

Unromanized, *ppl. a.*

Unromantic, *a.*

Unroof, *v.*

Unroofed, *ppl. a.*

Unroom.

Unroost, *v.*

Unroot, *v.*

Unrooted, *ppl. a.*

Unrough, *a.*

Unroughened.

Unround, *v.*

Unrounded, *ppl. a.*

Unrove, *v.*

Unroused, *ppl. a.*

Unroyal, *a.*

Unroyally, *adv.*

Unrude, *a.*

Unruddered.

Unrude.

Unruffle, *v.*

Unruffled, *ppl. a.*

Unruffling, *ppl. a.*

Unrufe.

Unrug.

Unruinable.

Unruined, *ppl. a.*

Unrule, *sb.*

Unruled, *ppl. a.*

Unruleable.

Unruliness.

Unruly, *a.* (and *sb.*)

Unrumpled, *ppl. a.*

Unrun, *ppl. a.*

Unrung, *ppl. a.* [Un-¹ 8 b + Ring v.²] Not sounded by ringing.

Unrung, *ppl. a.²* — Unringed (of a pig).

Unruly, *ppl. a.³* [Un-¹ 7.]

Unruliment.

Unruly, *a.*

Unruly Man.

Unrusted, *ppl. a.*

Unruth. Now *arch.*

Unruthfully, *adv.*

Unsacerdotal, *a.* [Un-¹ 7.]

Unsacramental, *a.*

Unsacred, *ppl. a.*

Unsacrificed, *ppl. a.* [Un-¹ 8.]

Unsad, *a.* [Un-¹ 7. Cf. OE. *unsǽd* unsated (= ON. *ósaðr*).]

Unsaddle, *v.* [Un-² 4, 5. Cf. older Du. *ontsadelen* (Da. *ontsadelen*), OHG. *intsatalôn* (MHG. *entsatelen*, G. *entsatteln*).]

Unsadness.

Unsafe, *a.* [Un-¹ 7.]

Unsafely, *adv.* [Un-¹ 11.]

Unsafeness.

Unsafety. [Un-¹ 12, 5 b.]

Unsaid, *ppl. a.* [OE. *unsǽd* (Un-¹ 8 b).]

Unsaid, *ppl. a.²*

Unsailable, *ppl. a.* [Un-¹ 7 b, 12.]

Unsailed, *ppl. a.*

Unsained, *ppl. a.* [Un-¹ 8.]

Unsaint, *v.*

Unsaint, *sb.*

Unsainted, *ppl. a.²* [Un-¹ 8.]

Unsalable, *ppl. a.* [Un-¹ 7 b and 5.]

Unsaleableness.

Unsanctioned, *ppl. a.* [Un-¹ 8.]

Unsanctity.

Unsandalled, *ppl. a.*

Unsanguine, *a.* [Un-¹ 7.]

Unsanguineous.

Unsanitary, *a.* [Un-¹ 7 and 5 b.]

Unsatiable, *a.* [Un-¹ 7 b and 5 b.]

Unsatiably, *adv.*

Unsatiate, *a.*

Unsatiated, *ppl. a.* [Un-¹ 8 and 5 b.]

Unsatisfaction. Absence of satisfaction.

Unsatisfactorily, *adv.*

Unsatisfactoriness.

Unsatisfactory, *a.* [Un-¹ 11 and 5 b.]

Unsatisfiable, *a.* [Un-¹ 7 b.]

Unsatisfied, *ppl. a.* [Un-¹ 8 and 5 b.]

Unsatisfiedness.

Unsatisfying, *ppl. a.* [Un-¹ 10.]

Unsatisfyingly, *adv.*

Unsaturated, *ppl. a.*

Unsaturation.

Unsaved, *ppl. a.* [Un-¹ 8.]

Unsavory, *a.* variant of UNSAVOURY.

Unsavoured, *ppl. a.* [Un-¹ 8.]

Unsavoured, *ppl. a.²* [Un-¹ 10.]

Unsavouredly, *adv.*

Unsavoriness.

Unsavoury, *a.* [Un-¹ 7.]

Unsavourily, *adv.* [Un-¹ 11.]

Unsay, *v.* [Un-² 12. Cf. OE. *onsecgan* (once), *tósecgan*, OHG. *intsagen*.]

Unscalable, *ppl. a.* [Un-¹ 9 + Scale *sb.*]

Unscaled, *ppl. a.* [Un-¹ 8 + Scale *sb.²*]

Unscaled, *ppl. a.²* [Un-² 9 + Scale *sb.²*]

Unscandalous, *a.*

Unscaly, *a.*

Unscanned, *ppl. a.* [Un-¹ 8.]

Unscarred, *ppl. a.*

Unscathed, *ppl. a.*

Unscannable, a. ...

Unscanned, ppl. a. ...

Unscarred, ppl. a. ...

Unscared, ppl. a. ...

Unscathed, ppl. a. ...

Unscholarly, a. ...

Unscholastic, a. ...

Unschool, v. ...

Unschooled, ppl. a. ...

Unscience. ...

Unscientific, a. ...

Unscoured, ppl. a. ...

Unscourged, ppl. a. ...

Unscraped, ppl. a. ...

Unscreen, v. ...

Unscreened, ppl. a. ...

Unscrew, v. ...

Unscrewed, ppl. a. ...

Unscripted, a. ...

Unscriptural, a. ...

Unscrupulous, a. ...

Unseal, v. ...

Unsealed, ppl. a. ...

Unseam, v. ...

Unsearchable, a. ...

Unsearchableness. ...

Unsearched, ppl. a. ...

Unseared, ppl. a. ...

Unseasonable, a. ...

Unseasonableness. ...

Unseasonably, adv. ...

Unseasoned, ppl. a. ...

Unseaworthy, a. ...

Unsecond, v. ...

Unseconded, ppl. a. ...

Unsecret, a. ...

Unsectarian, a. and n. ...

Unsecular, a. ...

Unsecularize, v. ...

Unsecure, a. ...

Unseduced, ppl. a. ...

Unsee, v. ...

Unseeable, a. ...

Unseeded, ppl. a. ...

Unseeing, ppl. a. ...

Unseeming, ppl. a. ...

Unseemingly, ppl. a. ...

1619 A. Newman *Pleas. Vis.* (1840) 13 Euen some of.. tender age Vnseemingly can vaunt how they will..carouse. 1656 *Eirenikon* 28 Love.. Unseemingly doth not itself behave. 1897 *Westm. Gaz.* 23 Dec. 2/3 That ophthalmia is unseemingly rife still is proved by [etc.].

† Unsee·mlily, *adv. Obs.* [Un-1 11.] = Unseemly *adv.*

1483 *Cath. Angl.* 329/2 Vn Semelily, *indecenter, inconuenienter.* a 1661 Holyday *Juvenal* (1673) 177 Such [gifts] as thou..dost unseemlily receive at the same times.

Unsee·mliness. [f. next, or Un-1 12.]

1. The quality of being unseemly in respect of action, conduct, etc.

c 1380 Wyclif *Sel. Wks.* III. 43 Unsemelynes schulde not be in Cristes Chirche. 1549 Udall, etc. *Erasm. Par. 2 Thess.* iii. 11 b, Getting their liuyng with their owne handes, rather than to be greuouse vnto other with shamles crauinges & vnsemelines. 1577 tr. *Bullinger's Decades* 510/2 What vnseemelinesse soeuer is committed against God and his Church. 1678 Wanley *Wond. Lit. World* v. i. § 82. 466/2 The Emperour did expostulate the unseemliness of the deed with him. 1829 Lytton *Devereux* i. xiii, I saw the unseemliness of fighting with my preceptor, and a priest. 1871 Jowett *Plato* IV. 170 His virtue being such, that he never ..fell into any great unseemliness.

2. The quality of being unseemly in appearance; uncomeliness.

1597 A. M. tr. *Guillemeau's Fr. Chirurg.* 23/1 The cleavinge in the lippes is such an vnseemlines and deformitye. 1603 G. Owen *Pembrokeshire* (1892) 44 Parchinge of the sunne, and starveinge with cold is a cheefe cause of the vnseemelynes of the comon people of the countrey. 1846 Landor *Imag. Conv.*, Wks. I. 195 *Johnson.* It makes an unseemly appearance in the type. *Tooke.* The unseemliness is not equal to the absurdity.

Unsee·mly, *a.* (and *sb.*). [Un-1 7. Cf. ON. *úsǽmilig-r* (Icel. *ósæmilegur*, Da. *usømmelig*, Norw. *usømeleg*, etc.).]

1. Unbecoming, unfitting; indecent.

a 1310 in Wright *Lyric P.* viii. 31 Ofte in song y have hem set, that is unsemly ther hit syt. 1338 R. Brunne *Chron.* (1810) 171 Þei did a foule trespas, it was vnsemly þing. a 1400–50 *Alexander* 99 For soth it is vnsemely slike sawis of a prynce. c 1440 *Promp. Parv.* 367/1 On-semely, *indecens, inconveniens.* 1542 Hen. VIII *Declar. Scots* A iv, With that vnsemely dissimulation, we were not a lytell moued. 1597 Hooker *Eccl. Pol.* v. xlviii. § 4 Things in themselues vnholie or vnseemly we may not aske. 1645 Ussher *Body Div.* 218 That no unseemely behaviour proceed from us. 1692 E. Walker tr. *Epictetus' Mor.* l, Nor would they anything unseemly say. 1738 Waterland *Chr. Sacr. Expl.* Appendix i. 6 An unseemly Reflection upon.. The Sacrifices of God. 1791 Cowper *Odyss.* xvii. 243 A squalid beggar..in unseemly garb attir'd. 1824 Dibdin *Libr. Comp.* 616 Shall..all editions be passed over in a sort of unseemly silence? 1855 Macaulay *Hist. Eng.* xvii. IV. 39 The news..threw him into a passion..which hurried him into many foolish and unseemly actions. 1871 Freeman *Norm. Conq.* xviii. IV. 155 To offer to William..an insult as unseemly as it was senseless.

absol. 1880 *Sat. Rev.* 7 Aug. 162/2 Partaking not a little of the unwise as well as of the unseemly.

b. Const. *for* († *of, to*) and with inf.

a 1300 *Body & Soul* in *Map's Poems* (Camden) 335 Thou art unsemly for to se, uncomli for to cussen suwete. c 1375 *Sc. Leg. Saints* xxi. (*Clement*) 659 Sayand, vnsemly ware to se cristine man begare to be. c 1445 Pecock *Donet* 139 Ful vnseemely and vntreuli it is to seie þat [etc.]. 1551 Recorde *Pathw. to Knowl.* i. Def., It shall not be vnsemely to call all suche shapes, formes and figures [etc.]. 1581 Mulcaster *Positions* ii. 5 It is a thing not vnseemely for me to deale in. 1583 Stubbes *Anat. Abus.* i. P vij, How vnhonest soeuer, or vnseemly of christian eares his argument be. a 1598 Rollock *1 Thess.* (1606) 183 Any thing, that is vnsetting, or vnseemlie to this Christian calling. 1667 Milton *P. L.* x. 155 Unseemly to beare rule, which was thy part.., had'st thou known thy self aright. 1843 Lytton *Last Bar.* viii. vii, Unseemly it may be for one of your quality..to quit this place with me.

c. *sb.* An unseemly thing.

1654 Whitlock *Zootomia* Pref. A 7 The Candid Interpreter of modest Endeavours, not Exacter of Impossibles, or unseemlies.

2. Uncomely, unhandsome.

c 1340 Hampole *Pr. Consc.* 5023 Þair bodys sal alle unsemely be, And foul, and ugly, opon to se. 1390 Gower *Conf.* I. 96 Which of alle kinde Of wommen is thunsemlieste. 1393 Langl. *P. Pl.* C. ii. 55 The dupe dale and durke vnsemely to see to. c 1400 *Pilgr. Sowle* (Caxton) iv. xxxviii. (1859) 63 He found..an old vnsemely one. I ne can nought calle hyr lady. a 1513 Fabyan *Chron.* vi. cxciv. 198 The Erle..prayed his wyfe..yt she wold..make her selfe as fowle and as vnsemely as she coude. 1581 Pettie *Guazzo's Civ. Conv.* ii. (1586) 114 A man of unseemlie personage. 1683 Moxon *Mech. Exerc., Printing* xvii. ¶ 2 Their Faces stand closer or wider assunder, which is unseemly, when the Letter comes to be Printed. 1684 J. S. *Profit & Pleas. United* 138 If you buy your Bees, Observe they be..Smooth and Shining; Rejecting the Rough and unsemly Ones. 1838 *Civil Eng. & Arch. Jrnl.* I. 394/2 Making the vessel frightfully crank and most unseemly to look at. 1843 James *Forest Days* ii, In other respects he was not an unseemly man. 1870 Dickens *E. Drood* i, He lies, dressed, across a large unseemly bed.

Unsee·mly, *adv.* [Un-1 11. Cf. ON. *úsǽmiliga* (Icel. *ósæmi-*).] In an unseemly or unbecoming manner.

c 1375 *Cursor M.* 24504 (Fairf.), On him mi heued I shoke & saide, vn-semeli, leue sone, artow graide! ? a 1400 *Morte Arth.* 1044 The syghte had he rechice, How vn-semly that sott satt sowpande hym one. c 1449 Pecock *Repr.* ii. x. 207 Ellis it wolde folewe that ther yn thei diden vnaccordingli and vnsemeli. 1591 Drayton *Harmonie of Ch., Song of Annah* 8 Nor yet vnseemly speak such things, so proud and arrogant. 1610 Holland *Camden's Brit.* 297 English women..rode very unseemely astride, like as men doe. a 1641 Bp. Mountagu *Acts & Mon.* (1642) 293 In which action hee..demeaned himself..unseemly for a King. 1725 Pope *Odyss.* i. 292 Yon' jovial Troop..Unseemly flown with insolence and wine. 1871 B. Taylor *Faust* (1875) I. xii. 143 Ah, thought I, in my conduct has he read it,—Something immodest or unseemly free?

Unsee·n, *ppl. a.* and *sb.* [Un-1 8 b, 12. Cf. OE. *ungesewen*, MDu. *ongesien* (Du. *ongezien*), OHG. *ungesëhan* (MHG. *ungesëhen*, G. *-gesehen*), NFris. *unseen*; ON. and Icel. *úsénn, ósénn.*]

1. Not seen; not apprehended by sight; unperceived, invisible.

α. a 1225 *Leg. Kath.* 1784 For he halt in his hond..alle ischepene þing, sehene & unsehene. a 1225 *Ancr. R.* 312 Þet wit & wered us euer wið þe unseiene [*v.r.* unsehene] gostes. c 1375 *Cursor M.* 566 (Fairf.), Saule..has vnderstandynge clene of þinge sayde and vnseyne. 1390 Gower *Conf.* II. 247 If a man wol ben unsein, Withinne his hond hold clos the Ston, And he mai invisible gon. c 1440 *Jacob's Well* 263 No counseyl may be hyd in þe vnseyn & vnknowyn.

β. a 1300 *Cursor M.* 566 Saul..has als vnderstanding clene O thing it seis and of vnsene. 1387–8 T. Usk *Test. Love* i. Prol. (Skeat) l. 57 Wherthrough..arn the unsene privitees of god made to us sightful and knowing. c 1470 Henry *Wallace* x. 626 Off the out watch thus chapyt thai vnseyn. 1500–20 Dunbar *Poems* lxxxv. 39 Haile, schene. vnseyne with carnale eyne! 1590 Spenser *F.Q.* ii. i. 1 Himselfe he frees by secret meanes vnseene. 1644 Digby *Nat. Bodies* xix. § 8 When by meanes of an vnseene haire, they [*sc.* jugglers] draw light bodies to them. 1681 Cotton *Wond. Peak* 59 When a..Ship..Suddenly strikes upon some unseen Rock. 1750 Gray *Elegy* 55 Full many a flower is born to blush unseen. 1798 S. & Ht. Lee *Canterb. T.* II. 27 [He] saw her there, and was not himself unseen. 1855 Tennyson *Maud* i. iv. v, Do we move ourselves, or are moved by an unseen hand..? 1867 H. Macmillan *Bible Teach.* Pref. p. xii, The work of the world is carried on by the unseen force of steam.

absol. 1829 Carlyle *Misc.* (1840) II. 226 The veil and mysterious Garment of the Unseen. 1841 Myers *Cath. Th.* iii. xxxiv. 125 Concerning the Unseen..no device..can preclude the possibility of Doubt.

b. Const. *of* (= by). Also *absol.*

a 1586 Sidney *De Mornay* Wks. 1923 III. 305 Looke up to that same only King..Who..unseene of any mortall wight, Beholdeth all things. 1623 Bp. Hall *Contempl., O.T.* xviii. iv, What an idlenesse it is for foolish hypocrites to hope they can dance in a net, unseen of heaven! c 1800 R. Cumberland *John De Lancaster* (1809) II. 161 Davis.. had entered the room, unseen of young Owen. 1802 J. Baillie *1st Pt. Ethwald* iv. iii, Through the dank and through the dry, Through th' unseen of mortal eye.

2. Not seen previously or hitherto; *esp.* † unfamiliar, strange, unknown.

a 1300 *St. Marher.* 10 Þa seh ha hwer set an unsehen unwiht,..blaccre þen euer eni blamon. a 1300 *Cursor M.* 5946 Þe frosse deid all vp be-dene, Þe hepes o þam war gret vn-sene Þat men gadird on þe grund. *Ibid.* 9091 Þat scrift was soruful and vn-sene,..þai salamon yod vnder. a 1400–50 *Alexander* 2536 Be þis ser Philip son..of feȝtand folk Had semblid ane vnsene sowme. 1435 Misyn *Fire of Love* 69 Bot in treuth in me is cumne an vnsein Ioy. 1549 Coverdale, etc. *Erasm. Par. Rom.* 25 If it be an vnsene and a hiddeous presumpcion, that the clay should with the potter pratle. 1592 R. D. *Hypnerotomachia* 55 A Diamond..of a huge and unseene bignes. 1604 E. G[rimstone] *D'Acosta's Hist. Indies* vii. xxiii. 565 A bird as bigge as a Crane,..but of a strange and vnseene form. 1667 Milton *P. L.* xii. 361 A Starr Unseen before in Heav'n. 1725 Berkeley *Proposal*, etc. Wks. 1871 III. 230 Unseen countries and after ages may feel the effects of his bounty.

b. Of passages for translation: Not previously read. Hence as *sb.*, an unprepared passage.

1879 C. S. Jerram *Anglice Reddenda* Pref., An exercise book in 'unseen', that is, unprepared translations. 1882 *Athenæum* 30 Dec. 897/2 A proposal..to substitute 'unseens' for 'set books' in..examinations. 1892 J. Edgar (*title*), Latin Unseens. *Ibid.* 23 A specimen unseen from Livy. 1897 E. S. Smith (*title*), Greek Unseens in Prose and Verse.

† 3. Unskilled, inexperienced. *Obs.*

1606 Holland *Sueton.* 254 Neither was he unseene in Musick. 1653 W. Ramesey *Astrol. Restored* 279 Somewhat difficult to those who are as yet altogether unseen therein. 1682 T. Flatman *Heraclitus Ridens* No. 63 (1713) II. 142 For any Man now to wonder at it, would but shew him very much unseen in the English History.

† Unsee·nly, *adv. Obs.*—1 [Un-1 11; cf. *unseȝenlike* s.v. Un-1 3.] Invisibly. 1398 Trevisa *Barth. De P. R.* viii. xxvii. (Bodl. MS.), Þe vertu of liȝt worcheþ vnseynlich [L. *invisibiliter*] feling and meuynge in beestes.

Unsegmented, *ppl. a.* (Un-1 8.)

1848 *Proc. Berw. Nat. Club* II. 297 Body ovate, ventricose, ..even and unsegmented. 1875 Huxley & Martin *Elem. Biol.* 206 Its posterior unsegmented part..nearly as long as the segmented part.

Unsei·zable, *a.* (Un-1 7 b.)

1862 R. H. Patterson *Ess. Hist. & Art* 44 Beauty,.. beaming forth like an essence, felt but unseizable, in the wide sunny landscape. 1885 Meredith *Diana* xiii, She swam above them in a cocoon of her spinning, sylphidine, unseizable.

† Unsei·ze, *v. Obs.* [Un-2 3.]

1. *trans.* To detach from something held or that holds; *spec.* in hawking.

1575 Turberv. *Faulconrie* 95 When she hath fedde, take it from hir and vnseaze hir. 1622 Mabbe tr. *Aleman's Guzman d'Alf.* i. To Vulgar, Who is hee that can be so happy as to..unseaze himselfe from thy griping talons? 1635 Quarles *Embl.* i. xii. 1 Be thy lips skrew'd so fast To th' earth's full breast? For shame, for shame unseise thee. *Ibid.* 3 Unseise thy lips. 1728 Chambers *Cycl.* s.v. *Falcon*, To which if she come well. and hastly seize it, let her cast two or three bits thereon. That done, unseize, take her off the Lure.

2. To let go, take one's hands off.

1663 Tuke *Adv. 5 Hours* i. 8 He, at the stroke, unseas'd me, and gave back.

Unsei·zed, *ppl. a.* (Un-1 8.)

a 1400–50 *Alexander* 5334, I sall surely þe saue vnsesid of þe berbrens. 1681 Dryden *Abs. & Achit.* i. 258 If unseiz'd, she glides away like wind; And leaves repenting Folly far behind. a 1700 Evelyn *Diary* 6 Sept. 1666, Watching at all places contiguous to unseised houses. 1818 Keats *Endym.* ii. 464 He was..content to see An unseiz'd heaven dying at his feet. 1895 *Nat. Conne. Congregat. Ch.* (U.S.) 177 The unseized opportunities of this..mission field.

† Unsel, *a.* and *sb. Sc.* and *north. Obs.* Also 6 vnsall, -sale, -sell, 7 ouncel. [var. of Unsele *a.*]

1. *adj.* Unlucky, wretched; wicked.

c 1375 *Sc. Leg. Saints* xv. 40 Gais furth, I send ȝou, I ȝou tel, as lammys amang wolfis vnsel. 1500–20 Dunbar *Poems* xiv. 79 Off Sathanis senȝie syne sic ane vnsall menȝie ..was nevir hard nor sene. a 1583 Montgomerie *Flyting* 87 (Tullib. MS.), Arpit angrie Ettercoip, and auld vnsell aip. a 1614 J. Melvill *Diary* (Wodrow Soc.) 49, I haiff dreamed an unsell dream.

b. As *adv.* Wickedly, vilely.

a 1583 Polwart *Flyting w. Montgomerie* 622 (Tullib. MS.), He was ane fals schismatik, notorlie namit; Baith hurdome, & homeceid, vnsell he vsit.

2. *sb.* A vile or worthless person; a wretch. *Kittie unsel* (Sc.): see Kitty1 1.

155. Lyndesay *Play* 2038 (Bann. MS.), Quhat sayis thow, cairle, art thow Gud Counsale? Swyth, pass the hence, vnhappy vnsale. a 1583 Montgomerie *Flyting* 282 There ane elf on ane ape ane vnsell begat. 1677 Nicolson in *Trans. Royal Soc. Lit.* IX. 321 Unsell, wretched fellow. 1691 Ray *N. Co. Words* (ed. 2) 150 *Unsel*, Nomen..opprobriosum. 1825 Jamieson s.v., In Dumfries-shire, *Scoury unsell* is a contemptuous designation applied to a child, by one who is in bad humour. 1894 *Northumb. Gloss.* 757.

b. The Evil One. *rare.*

c 1669 Garbutt *One Come from Dead* (1675) 27 He is right the Devils Child, the Ouncels Elfe. *Ibid.* 26.

† Unse·lde, *adv. Obs.* [OE. *unseldan* (un- Un-1 11 b + *seldan*: see Seld *adv.*), = Du. *onzelden*, G. *unselten*, ON. *úsjaldan*.] = next.

Only in phr. with *oft*: cf. ON. *oft ósjaldan*.

a 950 *Laws Edw. & Guthrum* Prol. in Thorpe *Ags. Laws* I. 166 Þa witan eac..oft & unseldan þæt seolfe ȝeniwodon. c 967 *Canons of Edgar* ibid. II. 278 Mislice men agyltað oft & unseldon þurh deofles scyfe. c 1320 *Sir Tristr.* 2313 Oft and vnselde Of triamour tok he pray.

Unse·ldom, *adv.* [Un-1 11 b. Cf. prec.] *Not unseldom* (misused for), not rarely, not infrequently.

Du. *niet onzelden* is similarly used.

1658 W. Burton *Itin. Anton.* 204 It is a thing not unseldome seen. 1686 Parr *Life of Usher* 83 Gaming..too often administred to Passion,..and not unseldom to Duelling. a 1836 Mrs. Sherwood *Nun* ii, They not unseldom spent the afternoon under the cedar-trees. 1860 Trench *Deficiencies Eng. Dict.* 64 Johnson..quotes, not altogether unseldom .., Hacket's Life of Archbp. Williams. 1882 *Athenæum* 23 Sept. 401/2 A style which was generally diffuse, and not unseldom obscure.

† Unse·le, *sb. Obs.* Forms: 1 unsæl, 2–3 un-, vnsel, 4–5 vnsell, -sele; 4 vncel(e, 5 vnceyll(e. [OE. *unsǽl* (*un-* Un-1 12 + *sǽl* Sele *sb.*) = ON. and Icel. *úsæla, ósæla* unhappiness.]

1. Unhappiness, misery; misfortune, ill-luck.

a 1023 Wulfstan *Hom.* (1883) 236 Þa deoflu..wæron on miclum unsælum, and þa englas wæron on swiðe micelre blisse. c 1205 Lay. 30541 Unsel him wes on mode. a 1250 *Owl & Night.* 1263 Ich wolde Þer hi wel vnderstonde scholde Þat sum vnsel heom is ihende. c 1275 *xi Pains Hell* 90 in *O. E. Misc.* 149 Snaken..dreyeþ heom in-to a wel Þer heo bolyeþ al vn-sel. 1338 R. Brunne *Chron.* (1810) 278 Þe Scottis I telle for sottis, & wrecchis vnwar, Unsele dyntis to dele þam drouh to Dunbar. 13.. *Guy Warw.* (A.) 1267 Of an vnsele y may ȝou telle, & ȝe wil a stounde duelle. a 1400 *Hymns Virgin* (1867) 106 Þat þou..help to sauen hem from vncele, So þat here soules beo not schent. c 1400 *Laud Troy Bk.* 5985 Ector thanne with mochel vnsele Graunted his askyng. c 1460 *Towneley Myst.* xii. 3 Here is mekyll vnceyll, and long has it last.

b. Unseemly matter. *rare*—1.

a 1400 *Minor Poems fr. Vernon MS.* 503/377 Bi beore onswere þei wuste ful wel Þat þei hedde spoken muchel vncel.

2. An improper time.

c 1200 *Trin. Coll. Hom.* 13 Ȝef man haueð to done mid his rihte spuse on unsele oðer an untime þan man faste sal.

† Unse·le, *a. Obs.* [OE. *unsǽle* (Un-1 7), = ON. and Icel. *ú-, ósæll* (Sw. *osäll*, Da. *ussel*), unhappy, wretched, Goth. *unsēls* evil, wicked. Cf. Sele *sb.*]

a. Unlucky, bad. b. Unfortunate, wretched.

c 1050 *Voc.* in Wr.-Wülcker 421 *Improbus*, unsæle, ȝemah. a 1200 *Moral Ode* 199 Nere namon elles ded ne sec ne nan unsele. c 1275 Lay. 27868 Þe king was onseale þat he euere boht wiþ Arthur to fihte. c 1300 *Prov. Hendyng* in *Rel. Ant.* I. 113 Holde ich no mon for vnsele Oþer whyle þah he fele Sum þyng þat him smerte. 13.. *Cursor M.* 6149 (Gött.), Þaim he did þair asking haue, For to reue þat folk vn-sele.

Hence † Unse·l(e)ly *adv. Obs.*—1

c 1275 Lay. 7022 Suþþen was his sone king, Þat onselliche lifuede.

Unsele·ct, *a.* (Un-1 7.)

1826 Miss Mitford *Village* Ser. ii. 256 A prodigious bundle of autographs, particularly unselect. 1867 P. Fitzgerald *75 Brooke St.* ii. xiii, Select, even in their unselect way. 1882 *Athenæum* 2 Sept. 299/1 The modern Jew as he lives and moves among the unselect.

Unsele·cting, *ppl. a.* (Un-1 10.) [1828–32 Webster.] 1895 *Daily News* 11 June 4/7 Realists try to look at life with the unselecting eyes of the camera.

Unse·lf, *sb.* (Un-1 12.)

1822 Coleridge *Lett., Convers.*, etc. II. 116 There was neither self nor unself in the flash..of pleasurable sensation. 1893 J. Pulsford *Loyalty to Christ* II. 367 Let us examine ..whether His spirit of unself, or the spirit of self and of the world, be the more in us.

Unse·lf, *v.* (Un-2 6 b, 8.) Also **Unse·lfed** *ppl. a.*, **Unse·lfing** *vbl. sb.*

1654 Whitlock *Zootomia* 265 Canst thou afford lying, Dissembling, and servile unselfing thy free born Minde, or Body? 1668 H. More *Div. Dial.* II. 28 God himself, who is that pure, free, and perfectly-unselfed Love. 1765 J. Brown *Chr. Jrnl.* 286 O to be unearthed, unselfed, that I may be like him! 1806 Surr *Winter in Lond.* III. 121, I cannot unself or unsex myself sufficiently to write in the narrative form; it must be I—I—I, and all about me—me—me. 1856 Faber *Creator & Creature* (1886) 55 Holiness is an unselfing of ourselves. 1868 Browning *Ring & Bk.* vii. 707 The grotesque intrigue To make me and my friend unself ourselves. 1890 J. Pulsford *Loyalty to Christ* I. 39 His unutterable sympathy..and His utterly unselfed character.

Unselfcha·nging *ppl. a.*, **-delicious** *a.*, † **-i·nterested** *ppl. a.*, **-know·ing** *ppl. a.*, **-like** *a.*, **-ness**, **-reflecting**, **-va·luing** *ppl. adjs.*, **-wi·lledness.** (Un-1 7, 7 b, 8, 10, 12; cf. Self 1 e, 1 f.)

1591 Sylvester *Du Bartas* i. ii. 212 The World's owne Matter is the waxen Lump, which, *un-self-changing, takes all kind of stamp. *Ibid.* iii. 1057 Such were not yerst Cincinnatus, Fabricius, Serranus, Curius, who *vn-self-delicious,.. With ploughs triumphant plough'd the Roman lands. 1664 H. More *Exp. 7 Epist.* viii. 134 Thou art a lover of unity, *un-self-interessed, a foe to no body. 1685 — *Paralip. Prophet.* l. 465 That full, free, and absolute unself-interessed Good. 1649 Milton *Eikon.* ix. 78 He twitts them with his Acts of grace; proud, and *unself-knowing words in the mouth of any King. 1598 Sylvester *Du Bartas* ii. ii. iv. *Columnes* 195 All Solids else (cast in the Aire) reflect *Unself-like-forms: but in a Globe each tract seems still the same. 1886 G. Macdonald *What's Mine's Mine* xx, He would have attracted attention anywhere, if only from his look of quiet **unselfness*. 1668 H. More *Div. Dial.* II. 69 Like an *un-self-reflecting and an *un-self-valuing childe. 1684 — *Answer* 241 The Wheels and living Creatures being ..acted by the spirit, does not signifie an Earthly state in them, but..an *Unselfwilledness.

Unselfco·nscious, *a.* (Un-1 7.)

1866 G. Macdonald *Ann. Q. Neighb.* xxviii, Instances of quiet unselfconscious faith. 1884 Ruskin *Fors Clav.* xcvi. 286 One who has in some signal..unself-conscious way done her duty. 1899 S. Brooke *Eng. Lit.* 146 This poem..belongs to the joyous, unself-conscious time.

So **Unselfco·nsciousness.**

Also, in recent use (1903–), *unselfconsciously*.

1838 J. Sterling *Ess.*, etc. (1848) I. 199 One other great form of poetry..in which self-consciousness projects itself into external figures, and appears as unself-consciousness. 1894 Lucy H. M. Soulsby *Home Rule* 32 It may be urged that theatricals teach unself-consciousness, but this form of unself-consciousness is worth very little.

Unse·lfish, *a.* (Un-1 7. Cf. Da. *uselvisk*, Sw. *osjälfvisk*.)

1698 J. Norris *Pract. Disc.* IV. 289 That Noble and Generous, disinteressed and unselvish Kind of Love. 1714 H. Grove *Spectator* No. 588 ¶ 2 Notwithstanding which, the Inclination is nevertheless unselfish. 1834 T. Keble in *Tracts for Times* No. 43. 14 St. Paul, that most heroic, and (if there were such a word,) that most *unselfish* of men. 1851 Longf. *Gold. Leg.* Epil. 10 Rise up..And scatter with unselfish hands Thy freshness on the barren sands. 1880 McCarthy *Own Times* xl. III. 224 One of the most unselfish men that ever lived.

Hence **Unse·lfishly** *adv.*, **Unse·lfishness.**

1812 Coleridge *Lit. Rem.* (1836) I. 351 The unselfishness of self-love in the hopes and fears of religion. 1850 Lynch *Theoph. Trinal* v. 77 A most womanly unselfishness. 1862 Shirley (J. Skelton) *Nugæ Crit.* v. 218 A cause, whose success demanded perfect union and unselfishness. *Ibid.* x. 435 Steady, sagacious, moderate, never unselfishly imprudent. 1863 'Ouida' *Held in Bondage* I. 185 None will ever love you more unselfishly than I.

Unse·lfished, *ppl. a.* [Un-2 8.] Deprived of selfish qualities; rendered unselfish. 1643 W. Greenhill *Axe at Root* A iv, The Axe is at the root of our Tree, we hope your spirits are all unselvished, that none are now unpublique. **† Unse·lfly,** *adv.* (Un-1 11.) 1605 Sylvester *Du Bartas* ii. iii. iii. *Law* 253 All Beings Be not (or else un-selfly be) But, from my Being, all their Being gather. **Unse·lling,** *ppl. a.* (Un-1 10; cf. Selling *ppl. a.* 1.) a 1704 T. Brown *Dial. Dead* Wks. 1711 IV. 98 As a Bookseller hates an unselling Author. 1720 *Humourist* 124 As you may see in certain unselling Dialogues of the Art of Poetry.

† Unse·lth. *Obs.* [OE. *unsǽlþ* (*un-* Un-1 12; also *ungesǽlþ*, see Un-1 3), = OHG. *unsâlida, unsâlda, unsâlitha* (MHG. *unsælde*, MLG. *unsâlde*, etc.).] Unhappiness, infelicity, misery.

c 888 K. Ælfred *Boeth.* x, Þæt is seo mæste unsælð on þys andweardan life. c 1000 *Ags. Ps.* (Thorpe) xiii. 7 Hie wilniað ealle mægne oþera manna unsælþa. a 1200 *Moral Ode* 374 Nis þer sorewe ne sor, ne neure nan vn-sealþe. c 1250 *Gen. & Ex.* 3026 Ðo wex vn-selðe on hem wel hard. c 1315 Shoreham i. 823 Na more ne greueþ hyt ihesus..Þaȝ eny best deuoured hyt, Oþer eny oþer onselþe. c 1425 *Eng. Conq. Ireland* 50 Euery selth hath wnselth at þe end.

Unsembly, obs. var. Unseemly *a.*

† Unse·minared, *ppl. a. Obs.*—1 [Un-2 8.] Deprived of virility. 1606 Shaks. *Ant. & Cl.* i. v. 11 'Tis well for thee, That being vnseminar'd, thy freer thoughts May not flye forth of Egypt.

† Unse·ne, *a. Obs. rare.* [Un-1 7 + Sene *a.* Cf. OE. *ungesǽne* and ON. *úsýnn.*] Invisible; not obvious.

c 1200 *Trin. Coll. Hom.* 47 On ure belendes lichame wiðuten sene, þe holie saule wiðinne unsene. c 1250 *Gen. & Ex.* 2878 Ic..swanc and michel sorwe dreȝ; Ȝet ist vnsene hu ic it bi-teȝ?

† Unse·nsably, *adv.* [Un-1 11.] = Unsensibly *adv.* 1. a 1395 Hylton *Scala Perf.* ii. xxiv. (MS. Bodl. 592), Not in bodili liknesse but vnsensabli bi preuie hid presence of his goostli myȝt. **† Unse·nsate,** *a. Obs.*—1 [Un-1 7, 5 b.] Insensate. 1561 Eden *Arte Nauig.* Pref., Yf they be lyuely members and not wythered or otherwyse vnsensate by reason of dead fleshe.

Unsensa·tional, *a.* (Un-1 7.)

Also, in recent use, *unsensationalism, -ally* adv.

1865 *Pall Mall G.* 8 Aug. 11 The name of a French novel, quiet and unsensational. 1881 'Rita' *My Lady Coquette* xxii, Altogether life is very drowsy and unsensational.

Unse·nse, *v.* [Un-2 6 b.] *trans.* To deprive of sense; *esp.* to render insensible.

1611 Florio, *Disensato*, sencelesse, vnsensed, out of reason. 1793 *Minstrel* I. 185, I was a little unsensed by my sudden souse into the stream. a 1809 T. Paine *Farmer's Dog* Poems (1834) 163 And get such mischief by the hit As should unsense him of his wit. 1851 Borrow *Lavengro* I. 331 One blow given with the proper play of his athletic arm, will unsense a giant. 1895 *Educat. Rev.* Sept. 158 The mind has been unsensed or dematerialized.

Unse·nsed, *ppl. a.* (Un-1 8.)

1667 Jer. Taylor *Dissuas. Popery* ii. i. § 2. 75 They tell you the Scripture is but a dead letter, Unsensed Characters, words without sense, or unsensed. 1675 R. Fleming *Short Acc. Doctr. Rom. Ch.* 6 They have no..authentick record to prove their Religion, but what is a Mass of dead unsensed Characters. 1734 Waterland *Imp. Doct. Holy Trinity* i. 18 We do not mean unsensed Characters, or empty Sounds. 1876 Mrs. Whitney *Sights & Ins.* vi, They were like apparitions shining out of the unsensed. 1897 F. Thompson *New Poems* 22 The incredible excess of unsensed sweet, And mystic wall of strange felicity.

† Unsensibi·lity. (Un-1 12, 5 b. Cf. next.)

1551 Robinson tr. *More's Utopia* ii. (1895) 204 For to be wythowte greyffe, not hauinge health, that they call vnsensybylyte and not pleasure. a 1650 May *Satyr. Puppy* (1657) 13 A passionate Man is..nor Man nor Beast: for he wants the sence of the one, and in some kinde the vnsensibilitie of the other.

Unse·nsible, *a. Obs.* exc. *dial.* or as *nonce-wd.* [Un-1 7, 5 b.]

1. = Insensible *a.* 1.

c 1380 Wyclif *Serm.* Sel. Wks. II. 55 It was bigynnyng of tyme unsensible to mannis witt. *Ibid.* 148 Þei trowen to sensible wordis, and oþer signes þat men maken, but unsensible wordis of Goddis Sone..þei trowen litil or nouȝt. c 1400 *Apol. Loll.* 100 To a-wowe is, a resonable creature to obey him to his souereyn, to kep sum hard þing þat is sensible, or vns[ens]ible. 1534 More *Treat. Passion* Wks. 1335/2 Vnder anye of the twoo outwarde sensible Sacramentes..the whole inwarde vnsensyble Sacramente..is..fullye conteyned. 1581 E. Campion in *Confer.* iii. (1584) Q j b, That you say vnsensible, it is true, if you meane the spirituall grace, which is not subiect to sense. 1587 Golding *De Mornay* xv. 285 To extend reason from..things sensible to things vnsensible,..from bodily to spirituall. 1656 M. Casaubon *Enthus.* To Rdr., Neither do I think so meanly of any truth, that can be reduced to any reality, whether sensible or unsensible.

b. = Insensible *a.* 1 b.

1545 Raynald *Byrth Mankynde* Y vj, The blud the whiche daylye and hourely, by vnsensyble swettinge euaporatith. a 1586 Sidney *Arcadia* i. xiii, It being set upon such an unsensible rising of the ground, as you are come to a prety height before almost you perceive that you ascend. 1614 Brerewood *Lang. & Relig.* 12 For which reason, the corruption of speech growing upon them, by little and little, the change hath been unsensible. 1633 Prynne *Histrio-m.* 957 No man becomes extreamely vitious on a sudden, but by unsensible gradations.

c. Imperceptible by reason of minuteness.

1551 Recorde *Pathw. Knowl.* i. Def., A Poynt..is named of Geometricians that small and vnsensible shape, whiche hath in it no partes. 1571 Digges *Pantom.* i. xv. E ij, The angle..groweth so acute, and vnsensible, that great errour ensueth the least mistakyng. 1602 Fulbecke *Pandectes* 9 The present time is so small and unsensible, that it is almost of no continuance.

2. = Insensible *a.* 2.

1555 Eden *Decades* (Arb.) 53 If the greefes of them bee to thee vnsensible by reason of thy..longe sickenes.

3. = Insensible *a.* 3 a.

c 1532 Tindale *Answ. More* Wks. (1572) 279/1 [Christ] dyed not to purchase such honour vnto vnsensible thinges, that [etc.]. c 1555 Harpsfield *Divorce Hen. VIII* (Camden) 252 Unless he be as unsensible as a man that will put and hold his finger in the hot fire and say the fire burneth not. 1583 Melbancke *Philotimus* S ij, The two vnsensible pictures. 1611 Cotgr., *Cal*, a thicke, and vnsensible skin, or brawnie hardnesse of skin. 1627 *Lisander & Cal.* i. 11 The secret places of Calista's affection, which were not marble, nor of any unsensible matter. 1677 W. Hubbard *Narrative* Postscr. 10 This unsensible and hardhearted Monster answered, he liked it very well.

b. = Insensible *a.* 3 b, 3 c.

1568 Turner *Herbal* iii. 50 Rasis in his Simples writeth that the Methel maketh num or vnsensible. a 1616 Beaum. & Fl. *Wit without M.* ii. iv, Your Land has lain long bedrid, and unsensible. 1632 J. Hayward tr. *Biondi's Eromena* 191 Her often swounding kept her alive by making her become unsensible of the sharpenesse of the paine which shee felt. 1669 Worlidge *Syst. Agric.* 160 When the doors are shut..they [*sc.* bees] are dark, and unsensible of so small a heat. 1891 in G. L. Gower *Surrey Words* (1893) 44, I was unsensible for loss of blood.

4. = Insensible *a.* 4 a.

(*a*) 1610 Heywood *Gold. Age* iv. i, Vnsensible of loue, or amorous pitty. 1621 G. Sandys *Ovid's Met.* viii. (1626) 167 They the time beguile with speech: Vnsensible of stay. 1692 South *Serm.* (1697) I. 498, I mean not, that he is unsensible of the good it self, but that..he is wholly unsensible ..of the Benignity of him that does it. a 1804 in Miss Betham *Biog. Dict. Celebrated Women* 452 She thought herself..too unsensible of our Lord's love to her.

(*b*) 1663 Gerbier *Counsel* a ij, It would doubtlesse make me pass for uncensible, how your Majesty..inherited that same clemency. 1664 Ingelo *Bentiv. & Ur.* v. 39 One not altogether unsensible that he hath over-charg'd his Vocation with burthensome Cares. 1719 W. Wood *Surv. Trade* 224, I am not unsensible, how very disadvantagious it is for us [etc.]. 1735 J. Price *Stone-Br. Thames* 16, I am not unsensible that it may be suggested [etc.].

b. = Insensible *a.* 4 b.

1619 J. King *Serm.* 2, I thinke there is none so unsensible that is not moved hereat. 1650 O. Sedgwick *Christ the Life* 26 Dull and unsensible men; of such did one long since complain, That [etc.]. 1676 Etherege *Man of Mode* ii. i, *Town.* Methinks you speak very feelingly, Brother. *Old Bell.* I am but Five and Fifty, Sister, you know, an Age not altogether unsensible! a 1699 J. Kirkton *Hist. Ch. Scot.* (1817) 65 Many a sober man was tempted to exceed, lest he should be condemned as unnatural, disloyal, unsensible.

5. = Insensible *a.* 5.

1560 Pilkington *Expos. Aggeus* Dd ij, Lyke vnreasonable beastes and vnsensyble. 1565 Stapleton *Fortr. Faith* 136* What is now more reuiled of vnsensible protestants then the shauen crowne of reuerent priesthood? a 1586 Sidney *Arcadia* i. iv, He found some of his aunswers..not unsensible. 1814 [Mary Brunton] *Discipline* xxii. III. 26 The poor lad was not so unsensible, but he knew to do his bidding. 1861 Geo. Eliot *Silas M.* xiv, When the drink's out of 'em, they aren't unsensible.

6. Not showing good or sound sense.

a 1586 Sidney *Arcadia* iii. xix, For nothing can be more unsensible, then to thinke what one doth, & to forget the end why it is done. 1858 Bagehot *Lit. Stud.* (1879) II. 154 The strongest unsensible feeling in Scott was perhaps his Jacobitism.

† Unse·nsibleness. *Obs.* [Un-1 12 and 5 b. Cf. prec.] Insensibility.

a 1568 Coverdale *Bk. Death* xxxvii. (1579) 171 That is a very blockish vnsensiblenesse of wilde madde barbarous people. 1571 Golding *Calvin on Ps.* xxviii. 5 Through stubbornnesse [they] harden themselues vntoo vnsensiblenesse. 1603 Florio *Montaigne* ii. xii, I commend not that vnsensiblenesse, which is neither possible nor to be desired. 1676 I. Mather *K. Philip's War* (1862) 94 Our great unsensibleness of the Displeasure of the Lord, in suffering these abominations to be perpetuated. 1730 Bailey (fol.), *Indolency*, unsensibleness of Pain or Grief.

† Unse·nsibly, *adv. Obs.* [Un-1 11, 5 b.]

1. = Insensibly *adv.* 1.

1627 Abp. Abbot in Rushw. *Hist. Coll.* (1659) I. 444 So being unsensibly hatched, it came flying into the World. 1679 C. Nesse *Antichrist* 213 It stole into the world..unsensibly, and at unawares.

b. Unknowingly, unconsciously.

1698 J. Jones *Ovid's Ibis* 127 Though unsensibly she shed bitter tears for her transgression.

2. = Insensibly *adv.* 2.

1565 Jewel *Reply Harding* 217 That after so many wordes ..ye shoulde be founde so nakedly, and so vnsensibly to deceiue the people. 1596 Spenser *State Irel.* Wks. (Globe) 622/2 The later [statute]..is soe unsensibly contryved that it scarce carryeth any reason in it.

† Unse·nsical, *a. Obs.*—1 [Un-1 7.] Nonsensical. 1692 S. Johnson *Argument* 18 His Unsensical Apothegm, 'No Bishop, no King'.

Unse·nsitive, *ppl. a.* (Un-1 7 and 5 b.)

Also, in recent use (1895–), *unsensitiveness*.

1610 Healey *St. Aug. Citie of God* 283 One [soul] liuing in all bodies vnsensitiue, onely hauing life. 1816 *Monthly Mag.* XLI. 209 But figures never affect the feelings; numerical calculations go on in an unsensitive part of the mind. 1838 Mill *Diss. & Disc.* (1859) I. 323 In a world which, for any but the unsensitive, is not a place of contentment. 1881 P. Brooks *Candle of Lord* 273 Some knowledge which the life in its best health was too hard and unsensitive to take.

Unse·nsitized, *ppl. a.* (Un-1 8 a c.) 1889 *Anthony's Photogr. Bull.* II. 53 An unsensitized piece..will soon cause discoloration on any sensitized paper placed against it. **† Unse·nsive,** *a. Obs.*—1 [Un-1 7.] Not perceptible by the senses. 1616 J. Lane *Contn. Sqr.'s T.* x. 284 Feare bears it knowne, thoughe (ofte) no man knoes how, Yea ofte b' vnsensive meanes (as clerkes avowe). **Unse·nsual,** *a.* (Un-1 7.) 1850 Lynch *Theoph. Trinal* v. 76 Wisdom hath a pure unsensual love. 1866 *Sat. Rev.* 3 Mar. 255/2 It is true, that..Plato dwells prominently on the anti-sensual, or at least on the unsensual, side of love.

Unse·nsualize, *v.* (Un-2 6 c.)

1792 W. Roberts *Looker-on* No. 29 (1794) I. 410 Love is so unsensualized and sublimed above passion, that it has forgotten its old retreats. 1796 Coleridge *Destiny of Nations* 80 For Fancy is the power That first unsensualises the dark mind, Giving it new delights. a 1849 H. Coleridge *Ess.* (1851) II. 147 Certain divines who thought to unsensualize mankind by making the body as disgusting as possible. 1889 *Spectator* 7 Sept., An almost Pharisaic observance of the rites and ceremonies which unsensualised them.

Unse·nsuous, *a.* (Un-1 7.) 1850 Mrs. Browning *Sonn., H. S. Boyd* 12 Till Sensuous and Unsensuous seemed one thing, Viewed from one level. 1856 R. A. Vaughan *Mystics* I. 270 The higher calm of unsensuous, imageless contemplation.

Unse·nt, *ppl. a.* Also 8 *Sc.* unsenn. [Un-1 8 b and 8 c. Cf. ON. *úsent* (Da. *usendt*).]

1. Not sent for, unsummoned. (Cf. b.)

c 1530 *Crt. of Love* 174 Of your free will ye should have come unsent. 1717 Ramsay *Elegy Lucky Wood* ii, Death, wha came unsenn To Lucky Wood.

b. With *for* expressed.

1501 *Plumpton Corr.* (Camden) 157 If I wold come up unsent for. 1598 Dallington *Meth. Trav.* X 3 b, They take one of a suddaine, comming vnlooked for and vnsent for. a 1641 Bp. Mountagu *Acts & Mon.* (1642) 298 Herod, unsent for, went to visit him. 1673 Wycherley *Gentl. Dancing-Master* v, We Fiddlers, Sir, often come unsent for. 1717 De Foe *Mem. Ch. Scot.* ii. 36 But Mr. Andrew Melvin..went unsent for. 1753 Richardson *Grandison* (1781) IV. xiv. 104 That no third person, unsent for, can be welcome.

2. Not sent or dispatched.

In recent use esp. of letters or telegrams.

c 1590 Crowley *Inform. & Petit.* iv b, The same Spirits..

wytnesseth wyth my conscience that I renne not vnsent. c 1586 Sidney *Arcadia* i. vi. He armed himselfe, and those few of his servants he had left unsent. 1608 Dod & Cleaver *Expos. Prov.* xi–xii. 122 That we goe not unsent. 1647 Jer. Taylor *Lib. Proph.* vi. 124 More able men may be unsent then sent. 1841 *Fraser's Mag.* Jan. 111/2 Ye came ra here unsent, and ye maun perform your errand. 1855 Kingsley *Westw. Ho!* xxvii, Her strange affection for the English was not unsent by Heaven.

b. With advs. or preps.

1549 Paget in Froude *Hist. Eng.* (1860) V. 182 Send for all the council that be remaining unsent abroad. 1606 Bp. Hall *Heaven upon Earth* xiii. Wks. (1625) 83 Thy heauenly Physician,..vnsent to, sends thee a soueraigne remedie. 1656 in Picton *L'pool Munic. Rec.* (1883) I. 176 Whylst they stay at home unsent away.

Unse·ntenced, *ppl. a.* (Un-1 8.)

1526 *Customs of Pale* in *Archæol.* (1893) LIII. 373 The king's iudicate officers..shall..suffer no accion to departe unsentenced before them. 1613 *Two Noble K.* v. i. 163, I could doombe neither; that which perish'd should Goe too't unsentenc'd. 1661 Heylin *Hist. Ref.* Q. Mary (1670) 6 The King..privately marryeth her within few days after his return, the divorce being yet unsentenced betwixt him and the Queen. 1822 Beddoes *Brides' Trag.* iv. ii, Some vengeance will fall on us in the night If he remain unsentenced. 1862 Shirley (J. Skelton) *Nugæ Crit.* 140 To leave them rather unsentenced and in hope to the mercy.. which alone can fully extenuate..their guilt. 1896 *Harper's Mag.* April 672/2 The secular judge..forgot his duty, and Joan went to her death unsentenced.

Unsente·ntious, *a.* [1775 Ash.] 1846 Worcester (citing *Qu. Rev.*).

Unse·ntient, *ppl. a.* (Un-1 7 and 5 b.)

1768–74 Tucker *Lt. Nat.* (1834) I. 315 We may admit a sentient composed of unsentient parts. *Ibid.* 583 An eternal First Cause, whether intelligent or unsentient. 1835 J. Young *Lect. Intell. Philos.* xlviii. 485 There could be no sensation in an unsentient being. 1864 Bowen *Logic* xiii. 422 Only in the sentient mind, and not in the unsentient matter of the body.

Unsentime·ntal, *a.* (Un-1 7.)

1810 Scott in *Lockhart* (1839) III. 328 The despair.. gave me a most unsentimental horror for sentimental letters. 1853 C. Brontë *Villette* xxi, Never man had a more unsentimental mother than mine. 1898 Haddon *Stud. Man* xiv. 409 An unsentimental survival of this pretty custom.

Hence **Unsentimenta·lity**; **-me·ntalize** *v.*; **-me·ntally** *adv.*

1824 Hook *Sayings & Doings* III. 168 Gaieties..calculated ..to enliven and unsentimentalize the mind. *Ibid.* Ser. ii. I. 28 The impropriety and unsentimentality of her behaviour. *Ibid.* xiv. III. 300 She was..most unsentimentally employed in swallowing a very hearty supper. 1837 Lewis *Lett.* (1870) 84 For the sake of..unsentimentalizing the cause of the Catholic clergy. 1847 L. Hunt *Men, Women, & B.* II. ii. 25 The unsentimentalizing effects of the gallantry of the court of Charles II.

Unse·ntinelled, *ppl. a.* (Un-1 8.) 1817 *Edin. Rev.* XXVIII. 87 The old castle..was ungarrisoned and unsentinelled. 1859 *All Year Round* No. 36. 219 A huge gateway, not unsentinelled.

† Unse·parable, *a. Obs.* (Un-1 7 b and 5 b.)

1398 Trevisa *Barth. de P. R.* xvi. v. (Bodl. MS.), Þe onynge is vnseperable so þat þei mowe not afterward be parted atwynne. 1532 More *Confut. Tindale* Wks. 495/1 Was himself..companion to saynt Poule, & that so continuall and so vnseperable, yt..he neuer departed from him? 1561 T. Hoby tr. *Castiglione's Courtyer* iv. Xx iij b, This is the beawtye vnseperable from the high bountye. 1587 Golding *De Mornay* v. 67 Fire..hath in it both heate and brightnesse vnseparable. 1645 Milton *Divorce* (ed. 2) i. i. 7 The first institution will be objected to have ordain'd marriage unseperable. 1697 Jeremy Collier *Ess. Mor. Subj.* i. 5 Self-love..is an unseparable Passion of humane nature. 1737 *Gentl. Mag.* VII. 24/2 Placed between two Words joyned together in unseparable Concord.

Hence **Unse·parableness.**

1587 Fenner *Def. Ministers* 116 Hee maketh the case of both alike in regarde of the propertie and vnseparablenes of the bande.

† Unse·parably, *adv. Obs.* (Un-1 11 and 5 b.)

1532 More *Confut. Tindale* Wks. 514/2 And with them the godhead vnseperably ioyned. 1586 W. Webbe *Eng. Poetrie* (Arb.) 80 Thys verse is alwayes vnseperably adioyned vnto the Hexameter. 1622 Callis *Stat. Sewers* (1647) 14 A pretty difference, where the act to be done is unseparably tied to ones person, and where not. 1698 S. Clarke *Script. Justif.* iv. 18 That Pardon is unseparably join'd with Justification.

† Unse·parate, *ppl. a. Obs.* (Un-1 8 b, 5 b; cf. next.) Hence **† Unse·parateness.** *Obs.*—1

1553 *Short Catech.* in *Liturgies*, etc. (Parker Soc.) 513 True faith and works *unseparate. 1563 Foxe *A. & M.* 540 As heat followeth euer with the fire vnseparate there from. 1591 Jas. I. *Lepanto, Chorus Angel.* 11 Our onlie one vnseparate, And yet in persons three. 1668 H. More *Div. Dial.* I. 121 Then Rest and Unseparateness of parts are all one,..and *Unseparateness and Union all one.

Unse·parated, *ppl. a.* (Un-1 8.)

1545 Coverdale *Def. Certain Chr. Man* E iiij b, Therfore will we discerne these thre thinges,..but so that they remayne vnseparated. 1577 tr. *Bullinger's Decades* iii. vi. 373/1 He being one and the same Christ vnseperated. 1620 Quarles *Medit.* i, Three speciall Attributes of God .., all Vnseparated From Gods pure Essence. a 1671 Ld. Fairfax *Mem.* (1699) 99 The two Houses of Parliament.., so great an Authority which was then unseparated from the Royal interest. 1725 Pope *Odyss.* x. 585 To whom Persephone, entire and whole, Gave to retain th' unseparated soul. 1860 Farrar *Orig. Lang.* ii. 44 The field and the snow were unseparated. 1893 Tuckey *Amphioxus* 104 The unseparated mesoblast fold.

† Unse·parately, *adv. Obs. rare.* [Un-1 11, 5 b.] Inseparably. 1580 Hollyband *Treas. Fr. Tong, Indissolublement*, vnseparately. 1593 Nashe *Christ's T.* A ij, She thought the Lord vnseparately tyde to his Temple. **Unse·ptate,** *a. Bot.* (Un-1 7.) 1900 Jackson *Gloss. Bot. Terms* 283 *Unseptate*,..applied to a plant which has not partitioning divisions. **Unse·ptated,** *a. Bot.* (Un-1 8 a *b.*) 1899 J. R. Green *Soluble Ferments* xx. 325 A fungus which developes a much-branched unseptated mycelium. **Unse·pulchre,** *v.* (Un-2 5.) 1856 in *Oxford Ess.* 217 As his ploughshare unsepulchred the 'empty helmets and the mighty bones' of the buried foemen.

Unse·pulchred, *ppl. a.* (Un-1 8.)

c 1611 Chapman *Iliad* xxii. 306 Dead, vndeplor'd, Vnsepulcherd; he lies at fleete. 1624 Quarles *Sion's Elegies* ii. 21 Unsepulchred ly my murthred people lye. 1795 Southey *Joan of Arc* ix. 42 For bills of human slain, unsepulchred, Steam pestilence. 1816 Byron *Ch. Har.* iii. lxiii, The Stygian coast Unsepulchred they roam'd, and shriek'd each wandering ghost. 1862 Grattan *Beaten Paths* I. 142 To discover the unsepulchred, uncoffined, and uncerecloathed tailor, standing stiff against the chapel wall.

Unse·pultured, *ppl. a.* (Un-1 8.) [1847 Webster.] 1862 R. H. Patterson *Ess. Hist. & Art* 269 Some unsepultured one, who had departed to join the troop of shivering ghosts. 1897 Gomme *C. Macfarlane's Camp of Refuge* Introd. p. lxv, The cause that so many men were slaughtered and lay unsepultured. **† Unseque·ster,** *v. Obs.* (Un-2 3.) 1664 Kath. Philips *Poems* 146 By a flame from thy blest Genius lent..Unsequester our Fancies, and create A Worth that may upon thy Glories wait. **Unseque·stered,** *ppl. a.* (Un-1 8.) 1654 Whitlock *Zootomia* 149 Which if impartially compared,..our Librarys might be repreived, and our Colledges unsequestred. 1655 Fuller *Ch. Hist.* xi. iii. § 6 His unsequestred Spirit so supported him, that [etc.]. **Unsere·ne,** *a.* (Un-1 7.) 1664 Ingelo *Bentiv. & Ur.* v. 124 How unserene are all the Joyes..upon Earth! 1829 Lamb in *The Gem* 26 The sad orbs..blinded through unserene drops for her dead lord.

Unse·rious, *a.* (Un-1 7.)

1655 Earl Orrery *Parthen.* ii. v. 493 To speake any thing unserious. 1673 Flavel *Saint Indeed* 199 Frothy, vain and unserious persons. 1755 Wesley *Wks.* (1872) II. 326 Any one who behaved in a light or unserious manner. 1860 Hawthorne *Fr. & It. Note-bks.* (1871) II. 357 A plaything, a trifle, an unserious affair.

Hence **Unse·riousness.**

1680 H. Dodwell *Two Lett.* (1691) To Rdr. § 9 The lives and unseriousness of some of our conformable Clergy.

Unse·rrated, *ppl. a.* (Un-1 8.) 1840 *Cuvier's Anim. Kingd.* 79 The edge of the long inferior incisors is unserrated.

Unse·rved, *ppl. a.* [Un-1 8.]

1. Not served or furnished with something; not attended to.

c 1350 *Leg. Rood* (1871) 85 Sen sekenes es sent to þe þir men sall noght vnserued be, Þai sall haue nayles or þai ga. 1433 *Rolls of Parlt.* IV. 439/1 Yf I should paye hem, youre Household, Chambre and Warderope..shuld be unservid and unpaide. 1542 Udall *Erasm. Apoph.* 302 Onely Phocion was remainyng unserved by reason that the poison had been all consumed by the others. a 1585 Montgomerie *Cherry & Slae* 1083 Who came uncald, unserv'd shuld sit. a 1600 Deloney *Jack of Newberie* iv, Well, looke there be not one hog vnserued. 1624 *Essex his Ghost* 16 His people I hope will turne your golden..Coates into Coates of Male, ..rather then your Soueraigne..shall bee vnserued. 1786 R. Heathcote *Sylva* (1786) 256 His boy therefore sent away unserved a customer. 1804 R. Anderson *Cumbld. Ball.* 79 The witch weyfe begg'd in our back seyde, But went unsarra'd away. 1832 Ht. Martineau *Each & All* iii. 33 Conscience awakes..to the cry of unserved humanity. 1899 *Daily News* 3 Nov. 7/6 Several of their unserved guns were shelled vigorously.

b. *spec.* Not attended to by a priest or incumbent. (See Serve *v.* 14.)

The app. early instance in Wyclif's *De Ecclesia* is prob. an error for 'unlerned', the reading of MS. Bodl. 788.

1562 in Strype *Ann. Ref.* (1709) I. xxxi. 312 So that the people be not unserved or defrauded of a reasonable minister. 1587 Holinshed *Chron.* (ed. 2) III. 1142/1 Where through died manie..priests, so that a great number of parishes were vnserued. 1643 Baker *Chron.*, *Q. Mary* 106 This yeer.. was great mortality, and specially of Priests, so as many Churches were unserved. 1765 Blackstone *Comm.* I. 466 It permits an infant to present a clerk..rather than..suffer the church to be unserved till he comes of age.

2. Not worshipped, regarded, or observed.

1387 Trevisa *Higden* (Rolls) II. 85 Þese feyned goddes.. beeþ i-serued in Chestre..Þan is Pluto not vnserued, god of helle. 1390 Gower *Conf.* I. 355 The cherche is brent, the priest is slain,..The lawe is lore and god unserved. c 1450 *Mirk's Festial* 267 Mony seyntys-dayes we leuen yn þe ȝere vnserued; for þay ben so many þat we may not serue hom all. 1532 More *Confut. Tindale* Wks. 495/2 Nor saint Paule..meaneth not yet they shall leaue the sacramentes vnserued which God hath taught.

3. *Law.* a. Of writs, summonses, etc.: Not served upon a person.

1465 *Paston Lett.* II. 201 The shyrf sayd playnly that he.. derst not serve it [*sc.* a writ]..and so it ys yet unservyd. 1476 *Acta Auditorum* (1839) 49/2 Þe persons of þe inqueste allegeit before þe lordis þat þe said breve wes vnseruit. 1908 *Daily Chron.* 10 Jan. 3/5 The constabulary were withdrawn, and the processes remained unserved.

† b. *Sc.* Not returned as heir. *Obs.*

1490 *Acta Dom. Conc.* (1839) 125/2 Patrik and William.. sall nocht fortify þe partij þat beis one seruit be that inquest.

4. Not served up.

1871 Ruskin *Fors Clav.* iii, The waiter then and there packed his knapsack and departed,..leaving my dinner unserved.

5. With *for*: For which service has not been done.

1555 *Inv. Ch. Goods* (Surtees) 157, xij li bequeithed..to the finding of a prieste there for iij yeares.., whereof remayned unserved for at the tyme.., xiijs. iiijd.

† Unse·rviable, *a. Obs.*—1 [Un-1 7 b.] Unserviceable. 1544 Betham *Precepts War* i. xcii. E vj b, They [*sc.* gunners] be vnseruyable, and can do no good. **† Unse·rvice.** *Obs.* (Un-1 4 b, 12.) 1611 Florio, *Disseruitu*, vnseruice, disseruice. 1624 Massinger *Parl. Love* i. v, Where you tax us for unservice, lady, I never knew a soldier yet that could Arrive into your favour.

Unse·rviceable, *a.* [Un-1 7 b and 5 b.]

1. Of things: Not capable of being employed for their proper purpose.

1535 *Wardr. Kath. Arragon* 33 in *Camden Misc.* III, The thurde [chair] is broken and unservesable. 1590 Spenser *F. Q.* i. xi. 25 The beast..his late wounded wing vnseruiceable found. 1600 in *St. Papers, Dom.* (1869) 437 The others [= signets] having become unserviceable from long use. 1663 Boyle *Usef. Exp. Nat. Philos.* ii. App. 328 Besides a not despicable quantity of terrestrial and unserviceable matter. 1690 Locke *Hum. Und.* iii. iii. § 17 The supposition ..is so..unserviceable to any part of our knowledge. 1713 Berkeley *Guard.* No. 35, His intellectuals, I observed, were grown unserviceable by too little use. 1737 tr. *Le Comte's Mem. & Remarks China* Pref., They might not be unserviceable to those who might..take up such a design. 1801 *Farmer's Mag.* Aug. 339 The horse I hire..may be in any degree serviceable or unserviceable. 1830 H. N. Coleridge *Grk. Poets* 1 A perusal of these Introductions may not be unserviceable to many well educated readers. 1857 Dickens *Dorrit* i. xxxii, What with her flapping cap, and..her unserviceable eye.

b. *spec.* Of ships, guns, etc.

1610 Holland *Camden's Brit.* 35 The ships..so shaken with the tempest, that they became altogether unserviceable. 1618 in *Essex Rev.* (1908) XVII. 102 The moderne use doth altogether exclude the caliver as unserviceable. 1707 *Lond. Gaz.* No. 4362/2, 10 Ships were destroyed.., and several others rendred wholly unserviceable. 1748 *Anson's Voy.* ii. iv. 165 Three four pounders, which were altogether unserviceable. 1811 *Regul. & Orders Army* 91 The disposal of Unserviceable Arms. 1865 Cameron *Malayan India* 246 It is not that the forts are ungarrisoned,..but that they are unserviceable. 1876 Voyle & Stevenson *Milit. Dict.* 446/2 *Unserviceable*, the term is applied..to all stores which are no longer of use, being either obsolete or worn out.

2. Of persons: Unable to be of service; not rendering service or help; useless.

1598 Hakluyt *Voy.* I. 240 You haue too much liuing, and are vnseruiceable to your prince, lesse will serue you. 1614 W. B. *Philosophers Banquet* (ed. 2) 121 One that would be vnseruiceable to him, and vnprofitable to the Commonwealth. 1655 *Nicholas Papers* (Camden) II. 217, I did long since tell you that poore man would be made onseruiceable to you. 1856 Kane *Arct. Expl.* II. i. 13 Our sick are about the same;..McGary and Riley unserviceable. 1865 Dickens *Mut. Fr.* iii. ii, I am an unserviceable friend of hers.

b. *spec.* Not capable of rendering military (or naval) service.

1596 Spenser *State Irel.* Wks. (Globe) 653/2 The rebels.. will turne away all theyr rascall people, whom they thinke unserviceable. 1601 Shaks. *All's Well* iv. iii. 152 Fiue or sixe thousand, but very weake and vnseruiceable: the troopes are all scattered. 1681 Luttrell *Brief Rel.* (1857) I. 151 Poor souldiers rendred unserviceable by age, wounds, &c. 1786 Burke *Art. agst. W. Hastings* Wks. 1842 II. 191 The country troops..would be ill-disciplined and unserviceable, if not worse. 1834 Marryat *P. Simple* I. 124 Some of them were retained, but most of them sent on shore as unserviceable. 1881 Jowett *Thucyd.* I. 146 The Plataeans had already conveyed to Athens their wives,..with the rest of their unserviceable population.

transf. 1867 Smyth *Sailor's Word-bk.* 707 *Unserviceable ticket*; this is made out in the same manner, and requires the same notations, as a sick-ticket.

3. Marked by disinclination to be of service.

1614 Raleigh *Hist. World* v. vi. 657 Such men of note.. as had any way discouered an vnseruiceable disposition towards the Romans.

4. Prejudicial, disadvantageous.

1698 Norris *Pract. Disc.* IV. 386 To reform his Temper, which I'm afraid is more unserviceable to Religion than any Hypothesis of mine can be.

Hence **Unserviceabi·lity.**

1884 *Cyclists' Tour. Cl. Gaz.* Nov. 335/1 The unserviceability of the new substitute.

Unse·rviceableness. (Un-1 12; cf. prec.)

1611 Cotgr., *Inutilité*,..vnseruiceablenesse. 1640 Sanderson *Serm.* (1681) II. 173 The unserviceableness of any thing to edification. 1683 Pepys *Diary at Tangier* in *Life*, etc. (1841) I. 452 The unserviceableness of the Mole by reason of those winds. a 1832 Bentham *Draught of Code* Wks. 1843 IV. 399 How many bad and unserviceable ones have, by this very unserviceableness, become popular! 1864 Miss Yonge *Trial* II. 20 The unserviceableness of his maimed arm.

Unse·rviceably, *adv.* (Un-1 11.)

1611 Cotgr., *Inutilement*,..vnseruiceably. 1661 Beveridge *Priv. Th.* (1709) 156 What is the reason, I have hitherto liv'd so unserviceably to God? 1695 Woodward *Nat. Hist. Earth* i. 48 It..does not enlarge the Dimensions of the Globe, or..lye idly and unserviceably there.

Unse·rvicelike, *a.* (Un-1 7 c.) 1614 Andrewes *Serm. on Easter Day* 29 They see how vnseruicelike our seruice is.

Unse·rvile, *a.* (Un-1 7.)

1701 Collier *M. Aurel.* iv. xlix. 61 Does the present Accident hinder your being Honest..and Unservile? 1773 Mrs. Grant *Lett. fr. Mount.* (1807) I. ii. 19 We are charmed with..unservile courtesy in the lower class. 1847 Carlyle in Froude *Life in Lond.* (1884) I. 409 Reporters to the daily papers, whose industry is the humblest of all real or unservile kinds in literature. 1866 Eliza Meteyard *Wedgwood* II. 273 Wedgwood's exquisite yet unservile copies of antique art.

Unse·t, *v.* [Un-2 3, 7. Cf. OE. *unsettan* (once), to take down.]

1. *trans.* To put out of place or position; to undo the setting of.

1602 Marston *Ant. & Mel.* iii. Wks. 1856 I. 37 O, you spoyle my ruffe, unset my haire. 1611 Cotgr., *Desplanter*, ..to vnplant, vnset, remoue. 1761 Gray *Lett.* (1900) II. 204 The man was sent for: he unset it; it was a paste not worth 40 shillings. 1775 Mrs. Delany in *Life & Corr.* Ser. ii. (1862) II. 105 There is some hazard in unsetting enamel for fear of chipping the edges. 1836 Marryat *Midsh. Easy* xxxii, How could he put the young men to fresh tortures by removing splints and unsetting limbs? 1884 *Law Times* 1 Nov. 8/1 On the morning in question Dawson had unset the gun.

2. *intr.* To get out of place or position.

1703 Thoresby *Let. to Ray*, *Spelk*, a wooden splinter tied on, to keep a broken bone from bending or unsetting again.

Unse·t, *ppl. a.* [Un-1 8 b, 8 c. Cf. Du. *ongezet* in sense 1.]

† 1. Of time or place: Not previously appointed or arranged. *Obs.*

Chiefly in phr. *at unset steven*: see Steven *sb.*2 2.

c 1386 [see Steven *sb.*2 2]. 1430–40 Lydg. *Bochas* ii. xxi. (1494) h iiij/1 At the vnset houre their falsnesse he wyll quyte. 1476 *Paston Lett.* III. 162 The Duke toke grete corage to goo..to conquer them, butt the[y] berded hym att an onsett place. 1543–a 1600 [see Steven *sb.*2 2]. a 1600 Montgomerie *Misc. Poems* v. 47 For man may meit at unset stevin, Thoght montanis nevir meitis.

† b. Of events: Not predetermined; unfixed, uncertain. *Obs.*

1550 Baldwin *Mor. Philos.* P vi, But yf that the chaunce of thynges be vnset, It is folly to feare that we knowe we maye let. 1559 *Mirr. Mag.*, *O. Glendour* xxvii, Of things to cum the haps be so vnset That none but fooles may warrant of them make.

† 2. Not seated at table. *Obs.*—1

c 1475 *Rauf Coilȝear* 148 'Gang begin the buird,' said the Coilȝear. 'That war vnsemand, forsuith, and thy self vnset.'

3. Not assigned or allocated (*to* one); unlet.

1480 *Acta Dom. Conc.* (1839) 70/2 Land..baldin of our souuerain lorde and fre vnset for termes or for male. 1523 *Lincoln Wills* (L. Rec. Soc.) V. 120, I will that..all myne inward stuf that was myne owne unset to my wyf remayne to..my daughters. 1580–1 *Reg. Privy Council Scot.* III. 358 To warrand the same unsett, sauld, assignit, or disponit to utheris. 1736 in Picton *L'pool Munic. Rec.* (1886) II. 165 There are some few back seats yet unsett. 1825–9 Mrs. Sherwood *Lady of Manor* I. viii. 334 During the absence of Lord T—, the family-mansion had remained untenanted, the houses of servants and dependents unset.

4. With advs. Not set *down, forth, out, up*, etc.

c 1445 Pecock *Donet* 138 Þese ij..forbodis of avoutrye.., whi ben not þei stillid and vnsett forþ expressely? 1530 Palsgr. Introd. p. v, I have..assayde..that there shulde fewe wordes..worde for worde be unsetforthe. 1547 *Act 1 Edw. VI*, c. 6 § 1 The same poore persons..be now unoccupied and unset aworke. 1594 Hooker *Eccl. Pol.* iii. xi. § 8 They vrge that God left nothing in his word vndescribed, ..nothing vnset-downe. 1629 Hobbes *Thucyd.* 75 The Athenians..recriminated the Megareans, for hauing tilled holy ground, and vnset-out with bounds. 1639 *Knaresb. Wills* (Surtees) II. 168 One new stand bed unsett upp.

5. † a. *Unset leek*, a (young) leek not transplanted. *Obs.*

1530 Palsgr. 249/2 Onsetleke, *porret*. 1563 Hyll *Art Garden.* (1593) 118 If you desire onlie to haue vnset Leekes. 1601 Holland *Pliny* II. 424 Ashes for to be drunke with the juice of unset leeks in cold water. 1611 Cotgr., *Porrette*, Maidens Leeke, bladed Leeke, vnset Leeke.

b. Not planted.

1573 Tusser *Husb.* (1878) 75 Set..yoong bay and his berie. Or set their stone, vnset leaue out none. 1577 Harrison *England* iii. viii. (1878) ii. 57 Notwithstanding that they haue remained there vnset by the space of fortie dais and more: yet some [saffron heads]..haue brought foorth two or three floures a peece. 1597 Gerarde *Herbal* i. i. 2 Common Medow grasse groweth of it selfe, vnset or vnsowen, euery where. 1653 Blithe *Eng. Improver Impr.* 169 Shouldst thou be occasioned..to keep thy sets longer unset, be thou sure thou get their Roots into the ground.

c. Not furnished with plants.

c 1600 Shaks. *Sonn.* xvi, Many maiden gardens yet vnset, With vertuous wish would beare your liuing flowers.

6. Not placed in a setting; unmounted.

1561 T. Hoby tr. *Castiglione's Courtyer* ii. R i b, A iewell that vnsett seemeth faire. c 1592 Bacon *Conf. Pleasure* (1870) 15 If these rich peeces be so faire vnsett, what are they sett? 1684 *Lond. Gaz.* No. 1906/4 An Emerald unset, ..having a narrow Bizel. 1702 *Ibid.* No. 3811/4 Lost.., a large Diamond-drop,..unset. 1884 *West. Daily Press* 20 June 7/5 Necklets of unset amethysts,..and other stones. 1891 *Science-Gossip* XXVII. 36/1 Lack of uniformity in unset specimens.

7. Not composed or arranged.

1631 Brathwait *Whimzies, Traveller* 93 Not an irregular haire about him, nor an unset looke to attend him, nor an uncomposed cringe to accoutre him. 1821 Lamb *Elia* i. *Ears*, Those unconnected, unset sounds are nothing to the measured malice of music.

8. Not surgically set.

a 1661 Fuller *Worthies, General* i. (1662) 6 An unset bone is better then a bone..ill set.

9. Of the sun: Not gone beneath the horizon.

1860 W. W. Reade *Liberty Hall* I. ix. 158 Though very pretty she was only a moon with the sun unset, for [etc.].

† Unse·te, *a.* Also unseete. *Obs.* [Un-1 7. Cf. Sete *a.* and Unsetty *a.*]

1. Unbecoming, improper; bad.

a 1310 in Wright *Lyric P.* viii. 31 For-thi on molde y waxe mot, that y sawes have seid un-sete. *Ibid.* xv. 49 Gabbes, les, ant luthere lore, sunnes bueth un-sete. c 1325 *Body & Soul* in *Map's Poems* (Camden) 342 A! thou foule flesch, unseete, Ful of falsnesse.

2. Unpleasant; painful.

a 1310 in Wright *Lyric P.* iv. 23 That I telle a povre play, that furst is feir ant seththe un-sete. c 1320 *Sir Tristr.* 1238 His bon brast vnder skinne, His sorwe was vnsete.

3. Unwholesome. (Cf. Unsetty *a.*)

13.. in *Archiv Stud. neu. Spr.* LXXXI. 319 Þe watures bitter and vnseete were ymad boþe gode and swete. 1387 Trevisa *Higden* IV. 11 His frendes trowede þat unsete mete þat he hadde i-ete at soper was cause of his siknesse.

4. Of persons: Ill-disposed · dissatisfied or discontented.

a 1310 in Wright *Lyric P.* xii. 43 This mon that Matheu ȝef A peny that wes so bref; this frely folk unsete, ȝet be ȝyrnden more.

Unsett, var. of Unset *v. Obs.*

Unse·tting, *ppl. a.* [Un-1 10.]

† 1. Unbecoming, unfitting. *Obs.*

1567 Drant *Horace, Ep.* B ij, I will tell them..what doth becom, and what unsetting is. a 1598 Rollock *1 Thess.* (1606) 183 Any thing that is vnsetting, or vnseemlie to this Christian calling.

2. Not going beneath the horizon.

1607 *Merry Devil Edmonton* iii. ii. 101 Thou bright vnsetting star..! 1810 Crabbe *T. of Hall* xix. 543 Some spoke of wonders they before had seen, When on their travels..: How they beheld for months th' unsetting sun. 1844 Lowell *Prometheus* 230, I Shall be a power and a memory,..a light Unsetting as the pole-star. 1869 McLaren *Serm.* Ser. ii. viii. 132 The full light of the unsetting Sun.

fig. 1838 Mrs. Browning *An Island* xxvii, The undim Unsetting Godlight.

Unse·ttle, *v.* [Un-2 3 and 7.]

1. *trans.* To undo from a fixed position; to unfix, unfasten, loosen.

1598 Florio, *Discasciare*,..to make loose the teeth, to dismount artillerie, to vnsettle anything. [1755 Johnson, *To Unsettle*, v. a., to move from a place.] 1818 Keats *Endymion* iv. 414 He..strives in vain to unsettle and wield A Jovian thunderbolt.

2. To force out of a settled condition; to deprive of fixity or quiet: a. a state of things, institutions, etc.

1651 Hobbes *Leviath.* ii. xxvii. 154 Such as..take upon them..to unsettle the Lawes with their publique discourse. 1679 Alsop *Melius Inq.* i. i. 91 To set Religion upon its proper Basis, and unsettle it from the feeble foundations upon which former Ages had erected it! a 1700 Evelyn *Diary* 21 April, 1695, Never were so many private Bills pass'd for unsettling estates. 1704 Atterbury *On 1 Tim.* ii. 7 Those Mighty Events, that fix, or unsettle the Peace of the World. 1803 Wordsw. '*England! the time is come*' 4 Old things have been unsettled. 1849 Macaulay *Hist. Eng.* i. I. 71 This theory, though intended to strengthen the foundations of government, altogether unsettles them. 1884 *Leeds Merc.* 15 Nov. 6/4 Such a struggle..must unsettle all the institutions of the country.

b. beliefs, thoughts, the mind, etc.

1644 Milton *Divorce* (ed. 2) i. viii. 19 They should but seek..to unsettle our constancie with timorous and softning suggestions. 1662 Stillingfl. *Orig. Sacr.* iii. i. § 2 When men bent their wits to unsettle the Beleef of such things as tended to Religion. 1671 in *Verney Mem.* (1907) II. 354 My thoughts are unsettled. 1759 Sarah Fielding *C'tess of Dellwyn* II. 261 His Father had unsettled his Resolution. 1794 Mrs. Radcliffe *Myst. Udolpho* xlvii, The long struggle which Agnes suffered..at length unsettled her reason. 1816 Scott *Bl. Dwarf* xviii, The shock was even sufficient to unsettle his wits. 1839 Dickens *Nickleby* iv, None of those ill-judged comings home twice a year that unsettle children's minds so. 1885 *Spectator* 25 July 971/2 That his mind had been unsettled by his peril.

c. persons (in respect of beliefs, etc.).

1833 Coleridge *Table Talk* (1884) 225 What is the spirit which seems to move and unsettle every other man..at this time? 1851 Helps *Comp. Solit.* xii. 236 Provided they do not, as they would say, unsettle their neighbours. 1880 R. G. White *Every-Day Eng.* 140 A phonetic printing of those two words would unsettle all these people.

3. *intr.* To become unsettled.

1605 Shaks. *Lear* iii. iv. 167 His wits begin t' vnsettle. 1624 Sanderson *Serm.* I. 102 The house cannot but unsettle apace, and without speedy repairs fall to the ground. 1543 Milton *Divorce* 8 Their wild affections unsetling at will have been as so many divorces to teach them experience. a 1859 De Quincey *Posth. Wks.* (1891) I. 14 He gazes, and slowly under the blazing scenery of his brain the scenery of his eye unsettles.

4. *trans.* To clear of settlers.

1895 *Advance* (Chicago) 11 Apr. 991/1 Probably no [other] section of our country has ever been un-settled so rapidly.

Hence **Unse·ttling** *vbl. sb.* and *ppl. a.*

Also, in recent use (1901), *unsettler*.

1665 Boyle *Occas. Refl.* i. vii, Troublesome and unsettling Employments. 1775 Ash, *Disconcerting*, p. a... unsettling, discomposing. 1828 Miss Mitford *Village* Ser. iii. 70 The unsettling, and the journey, and the settling again,..fairly killed her. 1866 *Cornh. Mag.* XIII. 437 Christianity..must have raised among the believers in the Law very unsettling questions much akin to these. 1894 H. Gardener *Unoff. Patriot* 10 The unsettling times which brought Methodism..into the ranks of established things.

Unse·ttleable, *a.* (Un-1 7 b.) 1864 Carlyle *Fredk. Gt.* xvi. iii. IV. 276 All details being, in the interim, either got settled, or got flung into corners as unsettleable.

Unse·ttled, *ppl. a.* [Un-1 8, or f. Unsettle *v.*]

1. Not peaceful, tranquil, or orderly; disturbed; not (yet) quietly or firmly established.

1592 Sylvester *Du Bartas* i. ii. 424 Of winged Clouds the wide inconstant House, Th' unsettled Kingdome of swift Æolus. 1699 *Nicholas Papers* (Camden) IV. 265 The new and unsettled Government in England. 1697 Dryden *Æneis* i. 791 My cruel fate, And doubts attending an unsettled state, Force me to guard my coast from foreign foes. 1759 Sterne *Tr. Shandy* i. xi, But the two extremes are more common, and in a greater degree in this unsettled island. 1800 Mrs. Hervey *Mourtray Fam.* I. 41 The hurry and unsettled state which..had attended their first arrival in the country. 1826 Scott *Woodst.* v, The times were dangerous and unsettled. 1876 Bancroft *Hist. U.S.* I. vi. 171 A report of a committee concerning the unsettled government of Virginia.

b. Of weather, etc.: Changeable, variable.

1707 Mortimer *Husb.* 587 If unsettled or moist Weather happen at the time of its working. 1773 Cook *Voy.* (1777) I. 59 The wind continued unsettled. 1803 Mary Charlton *Wife & Mistress* IV. 114 His health, which was yet very unsettled. 1879 Froude *Cæsar* xvi. 255 The weather was too unsettled for his fleet..to join him.

Comb. 1788 J. White *Jrnl. Voy. N.S. Wales* (1790) 105 Strong breezes, with unsettled-looking weather.

c. That has not yet settled down; still in a state of flux or motion.

1691 J. Harrington *Introd.* in *Wood's Ath. Oxon.* II. a i b, The Graces of Measure and numbers..are not to be expected in a rude and unsettled Language. 1845 J. Phillips *Geol.* in *Encycl. Metrop.* VI. 552/1 [Remains of plants] might be long suspended in the unsettled water, and be transported along with the finer matter. 1894 Mrs. Dyan *Man's Keeping* (1899) 100 The dust flying in unsettled clouds about him.

2. Not settled in a particular place or position.

1594 Hooker *Eccl. Pol.* ii. vi. § 3 To set himselfe in an house of cedar trees, and to behold the arke of the Lord's couenant vnsetled. 1729 T. Innes *Crit. Ess.* (1879) 284 The Francs..appear in history as a people unsettled, roving up and down. 1761 Churchill *Rosciad* 988 Next follows Sheridan—a doubtful name, As yet unsettled in the rank of Fame. 1782 Martyn *Geog. Mag.* i. iii. I. 205 A considerable encampment of these unsettled Arabs. 1807 J. Barlow *Columb.* ii. 212 These tribes have forester'd the fruitful zone, Their seats unsettled, and their name unknown. 1863 Boyd *Graver Th. Country Parson* vii. 106 They were a race of hunters; unsettled, cruel and deceitful. 1896 *Harper's Mag.* XXIII. 26/1, I am a single woman, unsettled as yet.

b. *Path.* Not confined to a definite part or spot.

1793 Abernethy *Surg. Ess.* 18 He was..teized with unsettled rheumatic pains. 1819 Lady Morgan *Autobiog.* (1859) 267 A severe illness, arising..from unsettled gout.

3. Not settled or staid in character; of a restless or turbulent disposition.

1594 *Selimus* 823 Resolue to venture it, Fortune doth fauour euery bold assay, And t'were a trick of an vnsetled wit Because [etc.]. 1595 Shaks. *John* ii. i. 66 All th' vnsetled humors of the Land, Rash, inconsiderate, fiery voluntaries. 1607 *Puritan* i. iv. 31 Many desprate, vnsetled souldiours. 1675 Han. Woolley *Gentlewom. Comp.* 38 These unstaid dimensions argue unsettled dispositions. 1803 *Censor* 1 July 84, I am sorry you seem so unsettled; I now..advise you to settle in service. 1837 Ht. Martineau *Soc. Amer.* II. 63 Young people, who might be 'unsettled'; that is, not sufficiently subservient. *Ibid.* III. 136 Too many of them are unsettled, reckless, slovenly.

b. Marked by absence of regularity, uniformity, staidness, or tranquillity.

c 1714 Pope *Lett.* (1735) I. 150 What is commonly called an unsettled Life (and what you with too much unjust Severity call a Vagabond Life). 1787 Burns *Let. to Jas. Smith* 11 June, Should I stay, in an unsettled state, at home, I would only dissipate my little fortune. 1824 Miss L. M. Hawkins *Annaline* I. 307 High compassion called forth at her unsettled and forlorn condition. 1825 Lamb *Mr. Liston* Wks. 1908 I. 315 The orthography varying, according to the unsettled usage of the times. 1830 *Forrester* II. 270, I have already told you..of the unsettled life I led, after the loss of my mother.

c. Unsteady; unquiet.

1794 Mrs. Radcliffe *Myst. Udolpho* xxviii, She..then viewed the face with a long unsettled gaze. 1810 Southey *Kehama* xv. xii, How often did she..from unsettled slumber start, and bear The Winds that moan above!

4. Undetermined, unresolved.

1593 Marlowe *Lucan* i. 264 Now light had quite dissolu'd the mysty night, And Cæsars mind vnsetled musing stood. 1600 Hakluyt *Voy.* III. 667 The Spaniard is not so simple, vnsetled & vncertaine in his determinations, as..to make our papers his Bulwarks. 1618 Gainsford *Hist. P. Warbeck* P 27 Such humility..won the hearts of many as yet unsettled unto him. 1671 Milton *P. R.* iv. 326 Uncertain and unsettl'd [he] still remain, Deep verst in books and shallow in himself. a 1768 Secker *Serm.* (1770) IV. 2 What the prophet Elijah said to the Israelites belongs equally to all of this unsettled Character: How long halt ye between two Opinions? 1823 Mrs. Hemans *Siege of Valencia* v, Ere yet th' unsettled heart hath closed its long Impatient conflicts. 1897 Mary Kingsley *W. Africa* 360 The chiefs came in an unsettled state of mind, and showed at first much opposition to the conclusion of a treaty.

5. Of the mind: Unbalanced, disturbed.

1611 Shaks. *Temp.* v. i. 59 A solemne Ayre, and the best comforter To an vnsetled fancie. 1693 *Dryden's Juvenal* xiv. (1697) 353 It shews a manifest unsettled Brain. 1751 Johnson *Rambler* No. 141 ¶ 2 A combination of circumstances acting when his imagination was unoccupied, and his judgment unsettled. 1779 *Mirror* No. 17, Such violent procedure might have effects too dreadful upon a brain which..is already much unsettled. 1807 Crabbe *Par. Reg.* iii. 180 Accounts perplex'd,..My mind unsettled, and my will unmade. 1825 Scott *Betrothed* xxvii, Is his brain unsettled,..or is there some dreadful mystery in these broken words?

b. Of persons: Mentally affected.

1611 Shaks. *Wint. T.* i. ii. 325 Do'st thinke I am so muddy, so vnsetled, To appoint my selfe in this vexation? 1768 Sterne *Sent. Journ.*, *Maria*, She said, she was unsettl'd much at that time. 1823 S. Rogers *Italy, Foscari* 121 Unnerved, and now unsettled in his mind. 1879 *Cassell's Techn. Educ.* IV. 107/1 A failure so annoyed him, that he became unsettled,..and at length died by his own hand.

6. a. Not assigned by will.

1671 Shadwell *Humourists* iii, Your Estate, by being unsettled, may come to be divided among the Lawyers, after I have killed you. 1800 Mrs. Hervey *Mourtray Fam.* II. 232 You shall not..command a sixpence of my fortune, which I shall keep unsettled, as a check upon you.

b. Undischarged, unpaid.

1811 *Regul. & Orders Army* 214 The Nature of the Claims of any Man which remain unsettled. 1816 '*Quiz*' *Grand Master* ii. 53 Here parcels of unsettl'd bills.

c. Not determined or fixed; not freed from doubt or uncertainty; undecided.

1844 J. S. Mill (*title*), Essays on Some Unsettled Questions of Political Economy. 1857 Ruskin *Pol. Econ. Art* ii. § 65, I haven't made up my mind about the number yet,

Supplement, p. 3873; Corrigenda, p. 4092; Spurious words, p. 4093; Books quoted, p. 4094

Well 181 For on dedly synne vnschreuyn, þou schalt be dampnyd. *c* 1450 *Mirk's Festial* 100 He may do..mony venyall synnys vnshryuen. 1813 Hogg *Queen's Wake* 287 Sires, in dread of sins unshriven. 1850 S. Dobell *Roman* i. 9 Thoughts, which..would have gone..down to hell, unblest, unshriven. 1858 [see Unpriested].

Unshrou·d, *v.*1 [Un-2 5, 3.]

1. *trans.* To strip of a shroud; *fig.* to uncover, lay bare, expose. Also **Unshrou·ding** *vbl. sb.*

1594 Southwell *M. Magd. Funeral Teares* 27 b, Yea, would he haue bin so venturous, as to haue stayed the vnshrowding of the corse? 1633 P. Fletcher *Purple Isl.* xii. xxv, At length the piercing Sunne his team unshrouds, And with his arrows th' idle fogge doth chase. 1653 A. Wilson *Inconstant Ladie* v. iii, Vnshroud thyselfe thou night-rauen. *a* 1773 Fergusson *Poems* (1879) 177 Turn, fair Amanda! cheer your swain, Unshroud him from his veil of woe. 1791 E. Darwin *Bot. Gard.* ii. 133 Now the broad Sun his golden orb unshrouds. 1821 Scott *Kenilw.* viii, Unshrouding the dark lantern, which had hitherto only emitted an indistinct glimmer. 1824 Campbell *Dream* 26 Methought I beheld two hands a space Slow unshroud a spectre's face.

2. To open out.

1846 *New Monthly Mag.* Dec. 488 Without..unshrouding the folds of my mantle, I stalked towards the sofa.

Unshrou·d, *v.*2 [Un-2 4.] *trans.* To strip (a vessel) of shrouds or ropes.

1584 Hudson *Judith* ii. (1608) 36 The quiet see..growes.., And lastly beates the banks, and ships vnshrouds.

Unshrou·ded, *ppl. a.* [Un-1 8.] Not wrapped in, or covered with, a shroud. Also *fig.*

1410 Healey *St. Aug. Citie of God* 384 So be thy face unshrouded And thy pure hornes unclouded! 1742 Blair *Grave* 152 There's not a Dungeon-Slave, that's bury'd In the High-way, unshrouded and uncoffin'd, But..sleeps as sound as He. 1799 Sheridan *Pizarro* iii. ii, He will..open ..his unshrouded eyes, and bless me with his last look. 1823 Praed *Troubadour* i. 516 They walked upon the earth, Unshrouded, in a ghastly mirth. 1855 Singleton *Virgil* II. 266 Had Cytherea not a token deigned From the unshrouded Sky.

Unshru·bbed, *a.* (Un-1 9.) 1610 Shaks. *Temp.* iv. i. 81 Who..with each end of thy blew bowe do'st crowne My boskie acres, and my vnshrubd downe. **Unshru·nken,** *ppl. a.* (Un-1 8 b.) 1862 Lytton *Str. Story* II. 39 With enough of vigour for years to come..in the unshrunken muscle of his limbs. 1897 *Allbutt's Syst. Med.* IV. 475 When the skin is cut into..it remains unshrunken. **Unshu·ffled,** *ppl. a.* (Un-1 8.) [1775 Ash.] 1901 *Munsey's Mag.* XXIV. 871/2 Playing with unshuffled cards.

Unshu·nnable, *a.* (Un-1 7 b.)

1604 Shaks. *Oth.* iii. iii. 275 'Tis destiny vnshunnable, like death. 1839 F. Barham tr. *Grotius' Adamus Exul* v. 47 Deadly rage, And the black hurricane of thick despair Urge on the unshunnable doom. 1890 Furness *Variorum Shaks.* VIII. Pref. p. vii, It makes no difference whether the unshunnable outcry is in French, or German, or English.

Unshu·nned, *ppl. a.* (Un-1 8.) 1603 Shaks. *Meas. for M.* iii. ii. 63 An vnshun'd consequence, it must be so. 1648 Hexham ii, *Ongemijdt,* Vnshunned, or Vn-avoided. **Unshu·nning,** *ppl. a.* [Un-1 10.] †Unavoidable. 1593 Q. Eliz. *Boeth.* v. pr. i. 50 Order it self that goes on with an vnshonning [L. *inevitabili*] turne. **Unshu·nted,** *ppl. a.* (Un-1 8.) 1873 F. Jenkin *Electr. & Magn.* xvi. § 3 The sensibility..of the unshunted galvanometer.

Unshu·t, *v.* [Un-2 3, 7. Cf. OE. *unscyttan.*]

1. *trans.* To open or unlock (a door, etc.); †to undo (a lock). Now *rare.*

13.. *Coer de L.* 4212 On schal dwelle the clos withinne, The gate to unschette and unpynne, And stylly to unschette the lok. *c* 1315 Shoreham i. 2228 Nou, lord, þat coudest maky open þet no man coude ounschette. 1370–80 *Visions of St. Paul* 198 in *O. E. Misc.* 228 He opened þe Mouþ of þat put, Hit stonk foule w30n hit was vn-schut. *c* 1412 Hoccleve *De Reg. Princ.* 679 My purs I wole vnschete. 1470–85 Malory *Arthur* xi. iii. 574 Anone as he had vnshet the wyndowe. *c* 1475 *Mankind* 52 in *Macro Plays* 3 On-schett yowur lokke, & take an halpenye. 1530 Palsgr. 768/2, I unshote, I open, *je defferme.* *Ibid.,* Unshote the doore. [Cf. 285/2 Unshittyng, *defferment.*] 1611 Cotgr., *Defferner,* to open; to vnshut, or vndoe a thing shut. 1873 Browning *Red Cott. Nt.-cap* 274 Compare such paragon With any scarabæus of the brood That..keeps wing in wingcase;.. the couple yonder..never bade unshut from sheath the gauze.

absol. *c* 1430 Lydg. *Min. Poems* 52 Off Abyssi this Aungel bar the keyes, Callid *Clauis Dauid* to shettyn and vnshette.

fig. *c* 1412 Hoccleve *De Reg. Princ.* 1573 Thre causes ben, which I þe wole vnschete And open a-non, whi þou schalt with hire dele. 1513 Douglas *Æneid* xii. Prol. 121 Gymp gerraflouris thar royn levys vnschet. 1589 Fleming *Virg. Georg.* ii. 24, I enter..on things of old and ancient praise,.. being bold t'vnshut or open holie springs.

b. *intr.* To become open.

1390 Gower *Conf.* II. 102 Ther is no dore, which mai charke, Wherof an yhe scholde unschette. *a* 1400 *Stockholm Med. MS.* ii. 390 in *Anglia* XVIII. 317 Ley þem on neuer so strong a lok, It schal onschetyn & onstlok. 1649 G. Daniel *Trinarch., Hen. V,* cxxix, Wee..need not feare an Asse's Load Of Solar Earth, can force the Gates vnshutt.

2. *dial.* To unharness (a horse).

1817 in Burne *Folk-Lore* (1883) 611 His team's unshut, his whip's laid up. 1841 Hartshorne *Salop. Ant. Gloss.,* *Unshut,* to unlink, or ungear horses. 1879 *Shropshire Word-bk.* 310.

Unshu·t, *ppl. a.* [f. prec. or Un-1 8 b.]

1. Opened, unclosed; not closed or shut.

c 1384 Chaucer *H. Fame* iii. 1953 And be day..Been al the dores opened wide And be nyght echon vnshet. 1426 Lydg. *De Guil. Pilgr.* 23403 The gate..Of the castel stood vnshet. 1491 Caxton *Vitas Patr.* (W. de W. 1495) ii. 259/2 An hous the whiche byfore outwarde is moche ornate..but behynde all unshytte &..ruynous. ?1606 Rowlands *Terrible Battell* (Hunterian Cl.) 36 From eare to eare thou hast a mouth vnshut. 1691 E. Taylor *Behmen's Theos. Philos.* 331 Whereby we ascend into his Arms, the unshut Light-World. 1849 M. Arnold *Forsaken Merman* 44 Where great whales come sailing by, Sail and sail, with unshut eye. *a* 1851 Moir *Poems, Tombless Man* iii, And, in the midst,.. An unshut gateway.

2. Not shut *up.*

1610 Bp. Hall *Apol. agst. Brownists* lv. 134 The plague.. of sinne vnshut vp and vncouered.

Unshu·tter, *v.* (Un-2 4.)

1861 Hughes *Tom Brown at Oxf.* xvii, He unshuttered the little lattice window of the room on the ground-floor. [Also in recent use (1901–).]

Unshu·ttered, *ppl. a.* (Un-1 8.)

1845 James *Arrah Neil* II. iii. 39 From an open door, or unshuttered window, the lights..served also for the benefit of the passenger. 1883 'Ouida' *Wanda* I. 58 She seated herself here by the unshuttered casement.

Unshy·, *a.* (Un-1 7.) 1748 Richardson *Clarissa* II. 45 It would be doing Mr. Solmes a spight, to wish him such a shy, un-shy girl. 1841 Lady Lyttelton *Let.* 29 July, I was thinking how totally unshy I was! **Unshy·ly,** *adv.* (Un-1 11.) 1814 Lady Lyttelton *Let.* 12 Sept., Pretty [German school-] girls of all ages answering very unshyly.

Unsib, *sb.*: see Un-1 3 (s.v. *unisibbe*).

†**Unsi·b,** *a. Obs.* [Un-1 7. Cf. OE. *ungesib,* OHG. *unsibbi, -sippi* (MHG. *unsippe*), Goth. *unsibjis.*] Not related, not of kin. In quots. *absol.*

c 1200 Ormin 2474 And 3hot [= she it] forrhall wiþþ alle menn Wiþþ sibbe & wiþþ unnsibbe. 1303 R. Brunne *Handl. Synne* 1198 To holy land, 3yf þou haue hyt hette; Syb, ne vnsyb, may hyt lette.

Unsi·ck, *a.* (Un-1 7. Cf. older Du. *onziek,* ON. *úsjúkr,* MSw. *osiuker,* MDa. *usjug.*)

a 1500 *Chaucer's Dreme* 1205 And I..Up rose..Hole and vnsicke, right wele at ease. *c* 1540 Copland *Hye Way to Spyttel Ho.* 198 Bedrid folke, and suche as can not crave,.. But not every unseke stoborne knave. 1594 Daniel *Cleopatra* K 4 b, What comforts vnsicke Eloquence can sound, And yet all fayles vs in the poynt of trying.

Unsi·cker, *a. Obs.* exc. *Sc.* [Un-1 7. Cf. NFris. *unseker,* MDu. *onseker* (Du. *onzeker*), MLG. *unseker,* OHG. *unsichûre* (MHG. and G. *unsicher*), MDa. *usekker,* Da. *usikker,* Sw. *osäker.*] Uncertain; unsafe; insecure.

a 1225 *Ancr. R.* 144 Deað þet we beoð siker of & unsiker hwonne. *c* 1325 *Metr. Hom.* 83 Gode ensaumpil may thai lere, Unsikir of thaim self to be. *c* 1330 R. Brunne *Chron. Wace* (Rolls) 9636 Bot þer hap was al vnsyker; For synne of Octa..Didé al his felawes & hym be lorn. 1387 Trevisa *Higden* (Rolls) VIII. 327 Þe buldyng uppon..unsiker grounde bygynneþ to slyde. *c* 1412 Hoccleve *De Reg. Princ.* 41 Thus vnsikir of my smal lyflode. 1470–85 Malory *Arthur* xvii. xxiii. 724 Galahad prayed yow to remembre of this vnsyker world. 1533 Bellenden *Livy* iv. v. (S.T.S.) II. 66 He had levir returne to rome with sikkir victorie þan vnsikkir pece of wolchis. *a* 1578 Lindesay (Pitscottie) *Chron. Scot.* (S.T.S.) I. 33 It was vnsickir to comit his lyfe and honoure in the binding up of bandis witht the Earle of Douglas. 1796 Burns *To Colonel de Peyster* iii, Dame Life,..Oh! flickering, feeble, and unsicker I've found her still. 1819 W. Tennant *Papistry Storm'd* (1827) 5 Thou.. flaff't thy wings, and in a crack Flew frae th' unsicker stance!

Hence **Unsi·ckerness,** uncertainty. Also **Unsi·ckerly,** unsafely, insecurely.

c 1340 Hampole *Pr. Consc.* 9049 Alle þe sykernes þat had Enooc and Ely..War noght bot als unsykernes. 1387 Trevisa *Higden* (Rolls) III. 287 Þou schalt haue..unsikernes..of þy children ende. ? *a* 1400 *Morte Arth.* 966 Thow saynned the vnsekyrly to seke to these mountez. *c* 1440 *Jacob's Well* 221 A-forn me I se vnsykernes to wyth-stonde feendys þat temptyn me. *a* 1568 in *Bannatyne MS.* (Hunterian Cl.) 201/55 With wrechitnes wofull away thow wendis; The deid certane, the hour vnsickirnes.

Unsi·ckled, *ppl. a.* (Un-1 8.) 1820 Shelley *Let. Mar. Gisborne* 278 The surface of the unsickled corn Trembles not in the slumbering air. **Unsie·ge,** *v.* (Un-2 4 b.) 1592 Sylvester *Tri. Faith* iii. xi, Hee..Whom Heav'nly arms, from Assur did unsiege; The most religious, matchlesse Ezechias. 1594 *Zepheria* xxv, Let not disdayne thy soule vnsanctifie,..Vnsieging where it seekes to fortifie With deadly frownes the canons of the brow.

Unsi·fted, *ppl. a.* [Un-1 8. Cf. Du. *ongezift.*]

1. Not passed through a sieve; unstrained.

1589 Cogan *Haven Health* (ed. 2) iv. 25 When meale wholly vnsifted..is made into Bread. 1628 May *Virg. Georg.* i. 5 The ground one yeare at rest; forget not than.. to hearten it againe..with unsifted ashes. 1784 Cowper *Task* vi. 108 Swallowing..The total grist unsifted, husks and all. 1870 Tyndall *Fragm. Sci.* (1871) 138 Pure unsifted solar light is white.

2. Unexamined, unscrutinized.

1620 Quarles *Div. Poems, Feast for Wormes* ix. ix, No crime unsifted, no sinne unpresented, Can lurke unseene. 1826 Southey *Lett.* (1856) IV. 38 There must be abundant matter of unsifted information in our public collections. 1858 Gladstone *Homer* I. 219 A poet who, as to facts, was at the mercy of unsifted information. 1882 Pusey *Paroch. & Cathedr. Serm.* i. 3 The unsifted, unexamined conscience of a sinner.

3. Untried, inexperienced.

1602 Shaks. *Ham.* i. iii. 102 You speake like a greene Girle, Vnsifted in such perillous Circumstance.

Unsi·ghed, *ppl. a.* (Un-1 8, 8 c.)

1814 Wordsw. *Laodamia* 100 The past unsighed for, and the future sure. 1898 R. W. Seton Watson *Scotland for Ever* 38 Queen Elizabeth..sank, unsighed for, to a gilded grave.

Unsi·ghing, *ppl. a.* (Un-1 10.) *a* 1743 Ld. Hervey *Epist.* i. 65 The change I cou'd unsighing see. 1822 Byron *Juan* viii. lxvii, The solitudes Of this unsighing people of the woods. 1838 Mrs. Browning *Vanities* v, Those ye love are not unsighing.

Unsi·ght, *sb.* [Un-1 12.] Lack of sight or seeing.

c 1412 Hoccleve *De Reg. Princ.* 5002 The ymages..Maken folke þenke on god..Whan þe ymages þei be-holden & seen; Were oft vnsyte [*v.r.* vnsight] of hem causith restreyntes Of þoughtes gode. 1898 Hardy *Wessex Poems* 163 In vain do I urge my unsight To conceive my lost prize.

Unsi·ght, *v.* [Un-2 6 b.]

1. *trans.* To deprive of sight. *rare.*

1615 Chapman *Odyss.* ix. 595 Their full bags so sore, With being vnemptied; but their shepheard more, With being vnsighted. 1638 N. Whiting *Il Insonio Insonnadado* 468 His armed brow fell down; and lighting right His antlers did the marching god unsight.

2. In *pa. ppl.* Of a coursing dog: Deprived of a sight of the hare.

1825 *Sporting Mag.* XVI. 268/2 If one or both dogs be unsighted, owing to the hare running through bushes or a live hedge,..the course shall be deemed to end there. 1876 *Coursing Calendar* 124 Miss Alice on a strong inside led Handicraft, who threw her head up as though unsighted.

†**Unsi·ght,** *ppl. a.*1 *Obs.* [? var. of Unsighted *ppl. a.* 1.] Only in phr. *unsight, unseen,* without inspection or examination.

?1622 Middleton & Rowley *Old Law* iii. i, Take that at hazard, sir..Unsight, unseen, I take 3. to one. 1632 Brome *North. Lasse* ii. i, I would I had his Neece unsight and unseen I faith for her monies sake. 1710 Palmer *Proverbs* 352 A generous mind..gives unsight and unseen, and trusts the Divine Goodness for the return. 1764 Chesterf. *Lett.* (1774) II. 479 He tells you true as to Comtesse Cosel's diamonds, which certainly nobody will buy here unsight unseen, as they call it. 1790 Cowper *Private Corr.* (1824) II. 217 My very best compliments attend Mrs. Hill, whom I love, unsight unseen, as they say. 1810 *Splendid Follies* I. 167 So you don't dance with me?.. Bernard, I find, is to enjoy that felicity, unsight unseen.

Unsi·ght, *ppl. a.*2 [Un-1 8 b.] Unsighed for. *a* 1618 Sylvester *Elegiac Epistle* 8 What Sea..Could..drown a Sidney's Name..so quickly,..So vn-bewayled, so vn-sigh't, vnsung? **Unsi·ghtable,** *a.* (Un-1 7 b.) *a* 1420 *Wycliffite Bible* 1 Tim. i. 17 To the kyng of worldis, vndeedly and invisyble [*MS. Magd. Coll. Cambr.* vnsi3table]. 1893 Leveson-Gower *Surrey Words* 44 Trees..very unsightable from anywhere.

Unsi·ghted, *ppl. a.* [Un-1 8.]

1. Unexamined; unperceived, unseen.

1584 *Reg. Privy Council Scot.* III. 687 To subscrive.. letters presentit be thame,..unsichtit first and fund ressounable be the officiaris of his estait. *a* 1642 Suckling *'When, Dearest'* i, Beauties that from worth arise, Are like the grace of Dieties, Still present with us, though unsighted. 1898 Meredith *Poems, Day Dau. Hades* ix, Sights that made the unsighted appear.

2. Not furnished with a sight.

1891 *Cent. Dict.* s.v., An unsighted gun.

†**Unsi·ghtful,** *a.,* **-fully,** *adv. Obs.*—1 [Un-1 7, 11.] Invisible; invisibly. *c* 1375 *Sc. Leg. Saints* l. (*Catharine*) 369 A god..wnsichtfull and sichtfull bedene. *Ibid.* xxxvi. (*John Baptist*) 331 Þat quha hofine is..resawis þan þe haly gaste vnsichtfully. †**Unsi·ghtily,** *adv. Obs.*—0 [Un-1 11.] Invisibly. *c* 1440 *Promp. Parv.* 367/1 On-syghtyly, *invisibiliter.*

Unsi·ghtliness. (Un-1 12; cf. next.)

1611 Florio, *Sparutezza,*..vnhandsomnesse, ill-fauorednesse, vnsightlinesse. 1647 Trapp *Comm. Matt.* xiii. 54 The unsightlinesse of his person. 1648 Milton *Observ. Peace Ormond* Wks. 1851 IV. 559 The unsightliness of such a Ceremony. 1676 Wiseman *Surgery* i. xiv. 66 If the unsightliness and pain be in the Legs. 1845 Ford *Handbk. Spain* 122 Time has healed the wounds of our ecclesiastical ruins, but in Spain they remain in all the unsightliness of recent onslaught. 1874 Micklethwaite *Mod. Par. Churches* 35 The argument from their unsightliness is of no value.

Unsi·ghtly, *a.* [Un-1 7. Cf. MDu. *onsicht(e)lijc, -lic* (Du. †*onzichtelijk*), invisible, ugly, MLG. *unsichtlik,* MHG. *unsihtlîch, -lich* invisible.] Unpleasing to the eye; unhandsome, ugly.

In first quot. perhaps = 'unable to see'.

a 1425 *Cursor M.* 6706 (Trin.), Who so smiteþ out his þralles eȝe And makeþ him vnsiȝtiliȝe [*Gött.* vnsihti for to sie; *Cott.* vn-mighti for-to seie]. 1548 Udall *Erasm. Par. Luke* xviii. 139 Beeyng a slouenly felowe and vnsightly in his geare. 1594 T. B. *La Primaud. Fr. Acad.* ii. 59 The face woulde bee euill fauoured and vnsightly, if it were hairy. 1634 Milton *Comus* 629 A small unsightly root, But of divine effect. 1673 [R. Leigh] *Transp. Reh.* 82 They..betray their breeding by..an unsightly bow. 1757 W. Wilkie *Epigon.* vi. 162 Now the place Unsightly shrubs o'erspread. 1784 Cowper *Task* ii. 588 There..it compresses hard The..most unsightly bones. 1855 Prescott *Philip II,* i. iii. I. 34 The unsightly trophies of the heads and limbs of numerous victims. 1892 Stevenson *Across the Plains* vi, You can never have dwelt in a country more unsightly than that part of Caithness.

b. Applied to immaterial things.

1605 Shaks. *Lear* ii. iv. 159 Good Sir, no more: these are vnsightly tricks. 1644 Milton *Areop.* (Arb.) 76 Truth,.. whose first appearance to our eyes..is more unsightly and unplausible than many errors. 1787 Cowper *Poet's N. Year's Gift* 8 To wish thee fairer is no need,..or more freed From temper-flaws unsightly. 1810 Wordsw. *Ess. Epitaphs* p 6 The unsightly manner in which our monuments are crowded together.

†**Unsi·ghtly,** *adv. Obs.*—1 [Un-1 11.] In an unsightly manner.

1726 Leoni *Alberti's Archit.* I. 5/1 No Building..can be placed more unsightly or inconveniently, than in a Valley.

†**Unsi·ghty,** *a. Obs.* [Un-1 7. Cf. MDu. *onsichtich* (obs. Du. *onzichtig*), MLG. *unsichtich,* MHG. *unsihtic, -ec* (older G. *unsichtig*) invisible.]

a. Unsightly. b. Invisible.

13.. *Cursor M.* 6706 (Gött.), Qua-so smytes vte his thrales eye, And mas him vnsihti for to sie. *c* 1440 *Promp. Parv.* 367/1 On-syghty, *invisibilis.*

Unsi·gnable, *a.* (Un-1 7 b.) 1802 Canning *Let.* in *Diaries Ld. Malmesbury* (1844) IV. 96, I commit the paper to your discretion. If signable people should fall in your way, or if unsignable,..use it. **Unsi·gnalized,** *ppl. a.* (Un-1 8 a c.) [1775 Ash.] 1810 Coleridge *Friend* 314 A newly-invested Knight appearing with his blank unsignalized Shield. **Unsi·gnalled,** *ppl. a.* (Un-1 8.) 1868 Geo. Eliot *Sp. Gipsy* 81 In haste He rushed unsignalled through the corridor. 1874 Blackie *Self-Cult.* 40 An unsignalled railway train. **Unsi·gnatured,** *ppl. a.* (Un-1 8.) 1807 Brydges *Censura Lit.* III. 342 Such notes..as appear unsignatured at the bottom of the page. 1877 Blackie *Wise Men* 338 Blind inorganic hinderment, mere man Unsignatured, uncharactered.

Unsi·gned, *ppl. a.* (Un-1 8.)

1598 Chapman *Hero & Leander* iii. 148 She..Tolde him how poore was substance without rites, Like bils vnsignd. 1694 *Lond. Gaz.* No. 3017/4 All such Adventurers that took out any Tickets..(either signed or unsigned). 1740 *Col. Rec. Pennsylv.* IV. 417 Bills..unsign'd by either [the Governor or the Secretary]. 1753 *Scots Mag.* Jan. 47/2 Three unsigned letters were..put into the post-office. 1812 Combe *Syntax, Picturesque* xxv, On the wing there upwards sprung A flight of Dockets, who were join'd By dire Certificates unsign'd. 1885 'Mrs. Alexander' *At Bay* viii, These lines were unsigned, and might be meant for any one, as there was no address.

Unsi·gneted, *ppl. a.* (Un-1 8.) 1585 *Reg. Privy Council Scot.* IV. 15 Be vertew of the saidis letters purchest be him unsignetit. †**Unsigni·ficancy.** *Obs.* [Un-1 12, 5 b. Cf. next.] Insignificance. 1659 Heylin *Animadv.* in Fuller *App. Inj. Innoc.* (1840) 501 But we shall see..that the activity of the next Convocation will make amends for the silence and unsignificancy of this. 1685 in *15th Rep. Hist. MSS. Comm.* App. VIII. 133 The unsignificancie of the militia.

†**Unsigni·ficant,** *a. Obs.* [Un-1 7 and 5 b. Cf. Unsignifying.] Not significant, unmeaning; insignificant. (Freq. *c* 1635–*c* 1665.)

1603 Holland *Plutarch's Mor.* 643 Yet will they..participate with them in a kinde of voice, not altogether inarticulate and unsignificant. 1630 *R. Johnson's Kingd. & Commw.* 82 The Duke..is but a voice unsignificant; for the Senate carrieth the sword. 1673 R. Allestree *Ladies Calling* i. 123 She..is like..to give but an unsignificant attendance at it.

Hence †**Unsigni·ficantly** *adv. Obs.*

1644 Milton *Areop.* (Arb.) 74 The Temple of Janus.. might now not unsignificantly be set open. *a* 1662 Heylin *Laud* (1668) 5 Which words had been impertinently, and unsignificantly used.

Unsigni·ficative, *a.* (Un-1 7, 5 b.) 1664 H. More *Myst. Iniq.* 227 They are not unsignificative of that Wisdom that is said to be more quick and moving then any motion. **Unsi·gnified,** *ppl. a.* (Un-1 8.) [1775 Ash.] 1809 Buckminster in *Biogr. Mem.* (1831) 17 As to the..most important charge in the review, that of unsignified alterations.

Unsi·gnifying, *ppl. a.* (Un-1 10.)

1665 J. Sergeant *Sure Footing* Ep. Ded., They carry the war out of the bounds of Science..and transfer it to a kind of Spatium Imaginarium of Fancy and unsignifying sounds. *a* 1680 Glanvill in *Disc.,* etc. (1681) 407 Such a Faith as this is that which St. James writes so earnestly against, as dead, and unsignifying (of it self alone) to the purpose of Justification. 1727 De Foe *Syst. Magic* i. iii. (1840) 65 Muttering over them some unsignifying significations. 1884 *Encycl. Brit.* XVII. 86/1 A tune is named generally after some place, as 'York',..or by some other unsignifying word.

†**Unsile,** *v. Sc.* [Un-2 3 + Sile *v.*3] = Unseel *v.*

1628 Sir W. Mure *Spirit. Hymn* 229 He doth vnsyle the eyes alone Of soules sincere. 1629 — *True Crucifixe* 32 The Serpent offring..to vnsile his sight.

Unsi·lenceable, *a.* (Un-1 7 b.)

1678 *Lively Oracles* iii. § 70. 279 How sadly will conscience then revenge all its stifled admonitions by an unsilenceable clamor. 1875 M. Arnold *God & Bible* iii. 131 The great, standing, unsilenceable, unshaken witness. 1884 *Harper's Mag.* Mar. 524/2 The winds moaned with unsilenceable grief.

Unsi·lenced, *ppl. a.* (Un-1 8.)

1615 Chapman *Odyss.* Ep. Ded. xlvi, Singing their praises in unsilenced story. 1828 Miss Mitford *Village* Ser. iii. 294 One, however, of his adversaries..still remained unsilenced. 1865 Mrs. Whitney *Gayworthys* xix, This unsilenced having 'If' of fruitless regret.

Unsi·lent, *a.* [Un-1 7.] ?Causing a noise, notorious. 1597 Q. Eliz. in Nichols *Progr.* (1805) III. B 7, More at this time we will not write of this unsilent subiecte. **Unsili·cified,** *ppl. a.* (Un-1 8.) 1877 Huxley *Anat. Inv. Anim.* iii. 117 Siliceous spicula, the majority of which..contain a fine central canal filled with an unsilicified substance.

Unsilly, variant of Unseely *a. Obs.*

Unsi·lvered, *ppl. a.* (Un-1 8.)

1772 *Phil. Trans.* LXII. 100 The back-horizon-glass was silvered,..the upper part being left unsilvered. *a* 1853 Pereira *Polarized Light* (1854) 113 This combination of Fresnel's rhomb and an unsilvered glass. 1895 *Outing* XXVI. 397/1 The mirror..has a small unsilvered spot in the centre.

Unsi·milar, *a.* (Un-1 7.)

Rarely used without preceding negative.

1768 Tucker *Lt. of Nat.* (1834) I. 274 It is not unsimilar to a declaration of St. Paul's. 1804 Eugenia de Acton *Tale without Title* II. 161 This speech, which..was seriously made upon an occasion not unsimilar, raised a laugh. 1863 Mrs. Oliphant *Salem Chapel* ii, They..[were] much of an age, and not unsimilar in worldly means.

Unsi·mple, *a.* (Un-1 7. Cf. MDu. *onsimpel.*)

1541 Copland *Galyen's Terap.* A ij b, For to a symple dysease a symple healynge is due, and to a composed dysease a healynge vnsymple. *a* 1750 A. Hill *Wks.* (1753) II. 274 Every thing is..unsimple, that has foreign and unnatural annexions. 1797 Lamb *Let. to Coleridge* 13 Feb., I wonder you do not perceave..something unsimple and artificial in the expression, 'voiced a sad tale'. 1862 H. Aidé *Carr of Carrl.* II. 230 The very unsimple manners of the English lady (they could hardly be called affected, they were so much a part of herself).

Unsimpli·city. (Un-1 12.) 1855 Kingsley *Westw. Ho!* iv, In his simple unsimplicity, and cunning foolishness. **Unsi·mulated,** *ppl. a.* (Un-1 8.) 1840 De Quincey *Style* Wks. 1858 XI. 171 Ebullitions of absolute unsimulated feeling. 1894 A. K. H. Boyd *St. Andrews* 126 To which the driver replied, with unsimulated heartiness.

Unsi·n, *v.* [Un-2 4 b, 6 b.]

1. *trans.* To annul (a sin) by subsequent action.

1628 Feltham *Resolves* ii. lxxxix. 257 When a sinne is past, griefe may lessen it, but not vnsinne it. 1670 Clarendon *Contempl. Ps.* Tracts (1727) 593 They who..observe the other injunction of the prophet..have unsinned their former sins. 1705 J. Dunton *Life & Errors* 405, I can't Un-Sin the Errours of my past Life. 1868 Browning *Ring & Bk.* iv. 285 The proper process of unsinning sin Is to begin well-doing somehow else.

2. To free (a person) from being a sinner.

c 1629 Donne *Serm.* (1640) 645 *Expeccabis*; and if in our language, that were a word in use, it might be translated, 'Thou shalt un-sin me', that is, look upon me as a man that had never sinned.

3. To maintain or prove to be no sin; to divest of the character of a sin.

1682 Southerne *Loyal Brother* v. i, Gifted Rogues, That ..zealously, upon a fit of Conscience, Sin or Unsin Rebellion to the Croud. *a* 1715 South *Serm.* IV. 123 He who defends it [*sc.* a sin], utterly denies its Guilt, and (as I may so speak) absolutely unsins it.

Unsince·re, *a.* [Un-1 7 and 5 b.]

1. = Insincere *a.* 1: a. Of actions, etc.

1577 tr. *Bullinger's Decades* 566/1 The consideration of the vnsincere feare of God. 1646 Hammond *Death-bed Repent.* 62 Sure there is such a thing as unsincere resolution. 1683 Temple *Mem.* Wks. 1720 I. 410 To act an unsincere Part either in Friendship or in Love. 1718 *Freethinker* No. 83, An affected, unsincere Humility towards God.

b. Of persons. Also *absol.*

1617 Hieron *Wks.* 1620 II. 155 Judas [was] an apostle, yet what careth God for him, being vnsincere? 1664 H. More *Myst. Iniq.* xxii. 85, I cannot pronounce any thing in the behalf of the unsincere, but that Hell it self is their portion. 1700 Congreve *Way of World* i. C 1 b, What, I warrant he's unsincere, or 'tis some such Trifle. *c* 1742 Shenstone *Song, 'On ev'ry tree'* v, My friends..Might well demand one tender tear; For when was Damon unsincere?

†2. = Insincere *a.* 2. *Obs.*

1664 Boyle *Exper. touching Colours* 197 The Light of a Candle..made unsincere, and..Ting'd with a Yellow Colour. 1666 Dryden *Ann. Mirab.* ccix, But ah! how unsincere are all our Joys! 1725 Pope *Odyssey* iv. 1060 O why, Penelope, this causeless fear, To render sleep's soft blessings unsincere?

Hence **Unsince·reness.**

1683 Temple *Mem.* Wks. 1720 I. 435 When the Dutch should grow more impatient of the Slowness or Unsincereness of their Allies Proceedings in the General Treaty.

Unsince·rely, *adv.* (Un-1 11, 5 b.) *c* 1555 Harpsfield *Divorce Hen. VIII* (Camden) 65 The adversaries, that..have so unfaithfully and unsincerely demeaned themselves. 1684 *Pennsylv. Arch.* I. 91 As unsincerely all along as I have been dealt with.

†**Unsince·rity.** *Obs.* [Un-1 12 and 5 b.]

1. Impurity; admixture. Cf. Insincerity 1.

1668 Boyle *Physiol. Ess.* 108 A Spirit of Sea-Salt may without any unsincerity be so prepar'd, as to dissolve the body of crude Gold.

2. Lack of sincerity; = Insincerity 2.

1646 Hammond *Tracts* 42 An argument of the unsincerity of that contrition. 1692 Norris *Two Treat. Div. Light* i. 67 See the Inconsistency and Unsincerity of this Writer! 1707 *Reflex. upon Ridicule* (1717) II. 189 All this opens a prospect to the Bottom of their Hearts, and manifests their Unsincerity.

Unsi·new, *v.* [Un-2 6 b and 4.]

1. *trans.* To weaken the sinews of; to render weak or feeble; to enervate.

1598 Florio, *Snervare,* to vnsinew, to weaken ones bodie. 1639 Fuller *Holy War* v. xv. 255 It is not so much the climate, as bad and unwholesome diet,..which unsineweth those Northern nations when they come into the South. 1645 Wither *Vox Pacif.* 119 This imprudencie will..Your bones unsinnew, and your joynts untie. 1693 Dryden *Persius* vi. 89 Now Toys and Trifles from their Athens come, And Dates and Pepper have unsinnew'd Rome. 1845 *Blackw. Mag.* LVII. 781 Death unsinews the hand that held her against the world.

b. *fig.* To weaken, enfeeble.

1599 Daniel *Musoph.* Wks. (1602) B iiij b, This skill.. Vnsinewes all your powres, vnmans you quite. 1609 G. Benson *Serm. 7 May* 57 The want of this knowledge vnsinewes the powers of a man. 1697 Dryden *Æneis* Ded. p 84 The affected purity of the French has unsinewed their heroic verse. 1744 Akenside *Epistle to Curio* 160 What spells unsinew'd thy determin'd soul? 1866 Lytton *Lost Tales Miletus, Secret Way* 16 The hold Of a strong phantasy, which, night and day,..unsinews life.

2. (See quot.)

1753 *Chambers' Cycl.* Suppl. s.v. *Sinew,* To unsinew a horse,..is to cut the two tendons on the side of the head, about five inches under the eyes.

Unsi·newed, *ppl. a.* [f. prec. or Un-1 8.] Not furnished with sinews; not sinewy or strong; weakened in sinews, enfeebled.

1541 R. Copland *Guydon's Form.* S iij, The seconde intencyon is accomplysshed by hote yron in vnsynewed places..and by corosyues, in meane places. 1615 Daniel *Hymen's Tri.* ii. i, Those vnsinewed amorous heardsmen. 1678 Dryden *All for Love* i. i, Can any Roman see and know him now,..Unbent, unsinew'd, made a woman's toy? 1863 W. Lancaster *Præterita* 116 Old brand, art sham'd with my unsinew'd gripe? 1872 R. W. Buchanan *St. A..* ii. v, As each Saint sank unsinew'd, In his arm-chair be continued: 'Goodman Jones' [etc.].

b. *fig.* (Cf. prec. 1 b.)

1602 Shaks. *Ham.* iv. vii. 10 O for two speciall Reasons, Which may to you (perhaps) seeme much vnsinnowed, And yet to me they are strong. 1643 *Lanc. Tracts Civil War* (Chetham Soc.) 169 From him I must expect an unsinewed and faithles agreement. 1683 Dryden (& Soame) tr. *Boileau's Art Poetry* iii. 189 Without these Ornaments before our Eyes, Th' unsinew'd Poem languishes. 1746 Francis tr. *Horace, Sat.* ii. i. 3 My Lines are weak, unsinew'd, others say.

Unsi·newy, *a.* (Un-1 7 and 5 b.)

1622 J. Hayward *David's Tears* To Rdr. A 8 Some other form-lesse vnsinewie writings. 1641 Earl Monm. tr. *Biondi's Civil Warr* Ep. Ded., I doe not praise the soft unsinnowy goodnesse of Henry the sixth. *a* 1658 Cleveland *Poems, Agst. Ale* iv, May Bards that drink thee, write a small, Unsubstanc'd Line pedantical, Unsinewy, ænigmatical.

Unsi·nful, *a.* (Un-1 7.)

1598 Florio, *Impeccabile,* that cannot sin,..vnsinfull. 1681 Baxter *Answ. Dodwell* iii. 22 They may command any unsinful thing, and excommunicate him that doth not obey. 1767 Cowper *Lett.* (1863) 94 They who are his servants here, shall pay him an unsinful obedience for ever. 1893 A. Whyte *Bunyan Char.* Ser. i. i. 6 Our Lord made His own unselfish and unsinful will to bow to silence and to praise before the holy will of His Father.

Hence **Unsi·nfulness.**

1598 Florio, *Impeccabilita,* vnsinfulnes, puritie. 1681 Baxter *Answ. Dodwell* iii. 22 One that knoweth the unsinfulness of all things in the world that are such.

Unsi·nfully, *adv.* (Un-1 11. Cf. prec.)

c 1400 *Apol. Loll.* 15 No creature mai do iustli,..perfitly, vnsinfully,..ani þing, not but if God wirk þat þing bi him. 1627 Sanderson *Serm.* I. 265 He did it unwittingly, and therefore..unsinfully, as to that species of sin. 1862 T. A. Trollope *Marietta* I. ii. 30 No usance could be unsinfully received.

Unsi·ng, *v.* (Un-2 3.) 1701 De Foe *True-born Eng.* ii. 242 They soon their New Deliverer Despise;..Unsing their Thanks, and pull their Trophies down. 1876 H. Gardner *Sunflowers, Rose Garden* 21 A thought once thought is never unthought, Or a melody sung unsung! **Unsi·ngable,** *a.* (Un-1 7 b.) 1882 *Athenæum* 4 Feb. 153/2 The lyrics throughout the volume are as unlike songs—as 'unsingable' and unlyrical—as ever.

Unsi·nged, *ppl. a.* [Un-1 8. Cf. Du. *ongezengd.*] Not singed; untouched by fire.

1599 [see Unseared]. 1646 Sir T. Browne *Pseud. Ep.* vii. x. 358 He was cast into a Cauldron of burning oyle, and came out againe unsinged. 1697 Dryden *Æneis* xi. 1158 By thee protected, with our naked soles, Through flames unsinged we march. 1737 Earl Orrery *Let. to Swift* 15 Mar., Let the thunder burst where it will, so that you are safe, and unsinged. 1755 Doddridge *'Let Jacob'* iv, Then let the fires their rage display,..Unburnt, unsinged, He leads them through. 1834 T. Moore in Walpole *Life Ld. J. Russell* (1889) I. 203 You at least come safe and unsinged out of the furnace. *a* 1850 Bryant *Medit. Rhode Isl. Coal* 54 That men might to thy inner caves retire, And there, unsinged, abide the day of fire.

Unsi·ngled, *ppl. a.* (Un-1 8.) 1697 Dryden *Æneis* iv. 221 The Stags, a trembling Train In Herds unsingl'd, scour the dusty Plain. **Unsi·ngleness.** (Un-1 12.) *a* 1658 Durham *Comm. Rev.* (1660) 189 Sinfull defects, and unsinglenesse and want of zeal.

Unsinkabi·lity. (Un-1 12. Cf. next.)

1865 *Times* 11 Mar. 8/6 He, too, puts speed first of all.., and armour-plating or 'unsinkability' nowhere. 1891 *Naut. Mag.* Mar. 236 The unsinkability of cargo-carrying vessels.

Unsi·nkable, *a.* (Un-1 7 b.)

Also, in recent use (1912), *unsinkableness.*

1655 Mrq. Worcester *Cent. Inv.* Index p. ij, An unsinkable Ship. 1861 *Times* 10 July, Unsinkable Iron Ships. 1883 *Fisheries Exhib. Catal.* 62 Unsinkable Suits for Fishermen.

Unsi·nking, *ppl. a.* (Un-1 10.)

Also, in recent use (1920), *unsinkingly.*

1705 Addison *Italy* 191 All the dewy Strand Lyes cover'd with a smooth, unsinking Sand. 1816 J. Wilson *City of Plague* i. iii. 38 Let me walk the waves of this wild world Through faith unsinking. 1821 Byron *Cain* iii. i. 529 Oh! thou..whose unsinking Blood darkens earth and heaven! 1823 Mrs. Hemans *Siege Valencia* ii. 429 Enough of woe.. For man to bear, unsinking.

Unsi·nnable, *a.* (Un-1 7 b.) 1570 Foxe *A. & M.* (ed. 2) 2059/2 By that power or authority he is not become vnsinneable. 1612 R. Sheldon *Serm. St. Martin's* 57 It was impeccable, vnsinneable, and not capable of any the lest spot of sinne. **Unsi·nning,** *vbl. sb.* (See Unsin *v.* 2.) *c* 1629 Donne *Serm.* (1640) 645 It is only this expeccation, this unsinning, this taking away of sins formerly committed, that restores me. 1681 J. Scott *Chr. Life* i. iv. 471 Till by an actual unsinning and Revocation of the Facts, we have totally cross'd and discharged them.

Unsi·nning, *ppl. a.* (Un-1 10.)

c 1375 *Sc. Leg. Saints* xvi. (*Magdalene*) 34 Mare Ioy is With angelis..Of a synful, pennance dowand, Þane nyne & nynte vnsynnand. 1642 Milton *Apol. Smect.* 23 To expell quite the unsinning predominance of his anger. *a* 1680 Charnock *Attrib. God* (1834) II. 652 Above the unsinning angels, and perfectly renewed spirits in glory. 1705 Stanhope *Paraphr.* II. 392 That First Covenant..promised Immortality to unsinning Obedience. 1760–72 H. Brooke *Fool of Qual.* (1809) III. 31 In compassion to Adam, and.. to his yet unsinning progeny. 1837 Lytton *Athens* II. 567 Great Jove! a grateful spectacle—if thus May it be said unsinning. 1872 Bushnell *Serm. Living Subjects* 419 He chooses this most passive, most unsinning, unoffending creature.

Unsi·phon, *v.* [Un-2 5, 7.] *trans.* To deprive of the function of a siphon. Hence **Unsi·phoned** *ppl. a.*

1878 J. A. Russell *Sanitary Houses* 19 Traps may be unsiphoned by a body of water coming down the soil pipe,.. making suction behind it. 1884 E. F. Willoughby *Hygiene* v. 194 This simple..preventative of unsyphoning is..little appreciated. 1894 *Times* 20 Feb. 3/6 The unsyphoned traps ..of the waterclosets.

Unsi·ster, *v.* (Un-2 6 b.) 1875 Tennyson *Q. Mary* *.* i, There will be plenty to sunder and unsister them again. **Unsi·stered,** *ppl. a.* (Un-1 8.) 1738 G. Lillo *Marina* ii. i, I vow'd..That all unsister'd shou'd this heir of mine

Remain till she were marry'd. 1860 O. W. Holmes *Prof. Breakf.-t.* x, A lonely and unsistered creature. **Unsi·sterliness.** (Un-1 12.) 1748 Richardson *Clarissa* I. 296 Don't let me be surprized at your seeming unsisterliness. 1879 Stevenson *Edinburgh* iv. 16 Never did four walls look down upon an uglier spectacle than these sisters rivalling in unsisterliness.

Unsi·sterly, *a.* (Un-1 7. Cf. Du. *onzusterlijk,* Sw. *osysterlig.*)

1747 Richardson *Clarissa* (1811) I. 96 Your Bell's unsisterly behaviour. *c* 1815 Jane Austen *Persuas.* vi, Mary was not so repulsive and unsisterly as Elizabeth. 1860 W. S. Hayward *Beautiful Demon* 103 You wrong me, Regina. It is cruel, it is unsisterly of you.

†**Unsi·sting,** *ppl. a.* (Of doubtful meaning.) 1603 Shaks. *Meas. for M.* iv. ii. 92 That spirit's possest with hast, That wounds th' vnsisting [*Fol.* 4 insisting] Posterne with these strokes. **Unsi·tten,** *ppl. a.* (Un-1 8 b. Cf. Sit *v.* 31 b.) 1611 A. Standish *Commons Compl.* 20 If they finde any [wild ducks] egges therein that be vnsitten.

†**Unsi·tting,** *ppl. a. Obs.* [Un-1 10.] Unbecoming, unfitting. (Common *c* 1390–1550.)

Freq. in later eds. misread or misprinted as *unfitting*: cf. the note to Unfitting.

c 1380 Chaucer *Troylus* ii. 307 Were it þyng þat me þoughte vnsittynge To yow nold I no suche tales brynge. 1390 Gower *Conf.* III. 143 It were an unsittende thing. *c* 1412 Hoccleve *De Reg. Princ.* 2361 Þat vn-to hygh degre, Vnsittynge is to swere in any wise. 1456 T. Beckington *Corr.* (Rolls) II. 144 The unsittyng, unleful, and unlawful quarell. 1533 More *Apol.* xii. Wks. 872/1 The priestes agaynste laye people..haue vsed..to speake vnsyttyng woordes. 1567 Turberv. *Epit.,* etc. 91 Vlysses wiues renowne Unsitting is for hir whose loue endureth but a stowne. 1585 Holinshed *Descr. Scotl.* Ded., It is much vnsitting for him that professeth Diuinitie, to applie his time any otherwise.

Hence †**Unsi·ttingly** *adv. Obs.*

c 1412 Hoccleve *De Reg. Princ.* 2349 As he þat custumably Clappith and iangfith..Moot othir while speke vnsittyngly. *Ibid.* 3639 Fresche apparaile and herte leccherous Unsittynly ben in a Prince ioynt. 1476 *Paston Lett.* III. 153 It was nott thowght..that I dalt onkyndly or onsyttyngly, but that I was moor onresonably dalte with.

Unsi·zeable, *a.* [Un-1 7 b.]

†1. Unequal in size; not of the proper or exact size. *Obs.*

1653 Blithe *Eng. Improver Impr.* 197 Make your Horses and Oxen as equall as you can possibly; if they be unsizeable, your highest draw up your lowest, and your lowest draw down the highest. 1678 Moxon *Mech. Exerc.* v. 78 [Do not let] the edge of your Hatchet cut too deep into the stuff, lest you..spoil your stuff by making it unsizeable. 1704 *Lond. Gaz.* No. 3888/3 The 35 Tun of unsizeable and crackt Brass Ordance. 1716 B. Church *Hist. Philip's War* (1867) ii. 26 Bullets..so unsizeable that some of them were forc'd to make slugs while they were ingag'd.

2. Of excessive size; too large or bulky. *Obs.*

1698 Fryer *Acc. E. India & P.* 9 An unsizeable Sword to their Backs. *Ibid.* 162, I was made at by an unsizable Snake. 1710 *Tatler* No. 241 p 3, I am not without hopes, that by this method I shall bring some unsizable friends of mine into shape and breadth. 1736 T. Prince *Chron. Hist. New Eng.* I. 250 If I now proceed to the End of this Second Section, it will make the First Volume too unsizeable.

fig. 1755 Pitt in *Anecd.* (1810) I. xii. 202 This unsizable project, impracticable and desperate as it is,..will..bring bankruptcy upon Great Britain. 1759 Franklin *Ess.* Wks. 1840 III. 529 And who or what are these proprietaries? In the province, unsizable subjects and unsufficient lords.

3. Not grown to a proper size; immature.

1746 R. Griffiths *Ess. Conservacy Thames* 52 [They] annually destroy infinite Numbers of unsizeable Smelts. 1759 *Act 33 Geo. II,* c. 27 § 13 Any Spawn, Fry, or Brood of Fish, or any unsizeable Fish, or any Fish out of Season. 1833 J. Cornish in *Rep. Sel. Comm. Brit. Channel Fisheries* 148 Millions of young and unsizeable fish. 1887 *Field* 24 Dec. 953/2 The keepers are..instructed to..prosecute the possessors of unsizeable pike.

Hence **Unsi·zeableness.**

1746 *Lond. Mag.* 324 Diversity of Weapons.., Unsizeableness of the Men, and Want of..Discipline in their Officers.

Unsi·zed, *ppl. a.*1 [Un-1 8 + Size *v.*1]

†1. = Unassized. *Obs.*—1

1613 *Southampton Court Leet Rec.* (1907) iii. 469 Having made view of vnsissed bread in the markett [and] findinge.. howshold Loaves of no assize.

2. Not made of an exact size or fit; not formed or sorted into sizes.

1700 Congreve *Way of World* iv. I 3, I must have been let out and piec'd in the sides like an unsiz'd Camlet. 1857 *Local Act* 20 & 21 *Vict.* c. 141 Sched. (C), Slates..Unsized Rag, Half Rag, Queen or sized Rag. 1877 Raymond *Statist. Mines & Mining* 426 Several tests made in concentrating unsized ore.

Unsi·zed, *ppl. a.*2 [Un-1 8 + Size *v.*2] Not treated with size.

1794 Kirwan *Elem. Min.* (ed. 2) I. 461 Filtres formed of unsized paper. 1827 Faraday *Chem. Manip.* ix. 235 The thinner varieties of unsized paper, or white blotting-paper. 1888 Jacobi *Printers' Vocab.,* *Unsized paper,* paper made entirely without size, and consequently very absorbent and adapted for plate printing.

Unske·tchable, *a.* (Un-1 7 b.) 1851 Curtis *Nile Notes* 213 Sundry veiled spectres were sketching the unsketchable.

Unski·lful, *a.* [Un-1 7.]

†1. Unreasonable. *Obs.*

c 1330 *Lay Folks' Catech.* (L.) 1342 Glotony..is an vnskylful lykyng or loue in tast or tastynge of mete or drynke. 1377 Langl. *P. Pl.* B. xiii. 277 Of vnboxome speche,..of scoffyng and of vnskilful beryinge. *c* 1400 *Pilgr. Sowle* (Caxton) i. xxx. (1859) 34 They shold serue theyr creatour.. with resonable werkes doyng, and vnskylful werkes forbering. *c* 1491 *Chast. Goddes Chyld.* (Caxton) 25 Her rest was full short by cause it was unskillfull and also unlefull.

†b. Undiscerning; unwise, foolish. *Obs. rare.*

c 1374 Chaucer *Troylus* i. 790, I may not endure þat þow dwelle In so vnskilful [*v.r.* onskylful] an opynyoun. *c* 1449 Pecock *Repr.* iii. xix. 413 But that this seiyng is vnskilful may be schewid thus. 1568 Grafton *Chron.* II. 30 Robert Losaunge that..by the gift of a thousand pound to the King, was made Bishop of Thetforde, repented him after, and bewayled that vnskilfull deede.

†2. a. Ignorant of propriety. *Obs.*—1

c 1475 *Rauf Coilyear* 159 Schir, thow art vnskilfull,..Thow byrd to haue nurtour aneuch, and thow hes nane.

†b. Ignorant *of* something. Also with inf. or dependent clause. *Obs.*

a 1547 Surrey *Æneis* ii. 493 Striken with dred, vnskilfull of the place. 1573 Tusser *Husb.* (1878) 106 Ill huswife vnskilful to make hir owne chees. 1600 Holland *Livy* xxii. xxxi. 451 They fell unadvisedly into an ambush, and being unskilfull of the countrie,..they were soon enclosed among many. 1667 Milton *P. L.* xi. 32 Unskilful with what words to pray, let mee Interpret for him.

3. Lacking in skill; inexpert.

1565 Golding *Cæsar* 32 The whyche pollicie, though it hadde taken place agaynst sauage and vnskylfull people, yet was not Ariouistus so folysh to loke that it should preuaile against oure army too. 1573 Tusser *Husb.* (1878) 15 The father an vnthrift, what hope to the sonne? The ruler vnskilfull, how quickly vndonne? 1617 Moryson *Itin.* ii. 49 At his first entering the gouernment, when he was yet vnskilfull in the affaires of that State. 1639 in *Verney Mem.* (1907) I. 183 Ther was never soe Rawe, soe unskillfull and soe unwilling an Army brought to fight. 1709 Berkeley *Th. Vision* § 12 Those unskilful in optics. 1765 *Museum Rust.* IV. 460 This operation is nice, and may prove dangerous in unskilful hands. 1840 Thackeray *Shabby-genteel Story* vi, He was not unskilful at this kind of exercise. 1867 M. E. G. Duff in *N. Brit. Rev.* XLVII. 484 The attempts of the foreign evangelizers may often be unskilful enough.

absol. 1565 Cooper *Thesaurus, Imperitum vulgus,* the ignorant, rude, or vnskilfull. *c* 1580 [see Void *v.* 11]. 1612 B. Jonson *Alch.* To Rdr., It is onely the disease of the vnskilfull to thinke rude things greater then polish'd. 1726 Leoni *Alberti's Archit.* III. 12 b, It hardly happens..that what delights the Judges, shou'd at the same time strike the Unskilful. 1762 Falconer *Shipwr.* ii. 251 The gallant boatswain..Prompt to direct the unskilful still appears.

transf. 1687 P. Ayres *To Dryden* 15 Could my unskilful pen augment his fame.

b. Displaying lack of skill; clumsy.

a 1586 Sidney *Arcadia* i. ix, No more..then..the diligent Pilot in a daungerous tempest doth attend the unskilful words of a passinger. 1614 Latham *Falconry* ii. vii. 94 Such Hawkes haue beene euilly ordered, and continued in vncleane and vnskilfull keeping. 1651 Hobbes *Leviath.* iii. xxxii. 195 When it seemeth so, the fault is either in our unskilfull Interpretation, or erroneous Ratiocination. 1737 Glover *Leonidas* iii. 250 Assyria's sons Their brazen helms display, th' unskilful work Of rude Barbarians. 1798 Lamb *R. Gray* xiii, His wounds by unskilful treatment had been brought to a dangerous crisis. 1831 James *Phil. Augustus* I. vii, De Coucy..took the instrument, over the strings of which he threw his hand, in a bold but not unskilful manner.

Unski·lfully, *adv.* [Un-1 11.]

†1. Unreasonably; without good reason; to an unreasonable extent. *Obs.*

1338 R. Brunne *Chron.* (1810) 152 Þe kyng..said he was redy, þe testament to fulfille of kyng William, & þat his men fulle ille vnskilfully nam. 1387 Trevisa *Higden* (Rolls) IV. 433 3if it is good to lyve, it is sacrelegy to forsake it unskilfulliche. *c* 1400 Love *Bonavent. Mirr.* (1908) 147 We haue ensaumple that we schulle not lette to do gode werkes for occasioun of sclaundre vnskilfully taken of othere. *a* 1470 H. Parker *Dives & Pauper* (W. de W. 1496) iv. xxv. 192/2 We sholde loue all men..with drede to offende them unskylfully.

†2. Without discernment; foolishly; ignorantly.

1340–70 *Alex. & Dind.* 871 For almus-dede do 3e non as 3e demen alle, But skarsete & skaþe vn-skilfully fonden. 1390 Gower *Conf.* III. 251 Tarquinus made unskilfully A werre..Ayein a toun with walles stronge. *c* 1460 G. Ashby *Dicta Philos.* 1211 He wol..euery thinge determen wilfully, Ayenste Reason, & eke vnskilfully. 1565 Cooper *Thesaurus* s.v. *Inscienter,* Thei sayde he did vnskilfully. 1603 Shaks. *Meas. for M.* iii. ii. 156 Therefore you speake vnskilfully: or, if your knowledge bee more, it is much darkned in your malice.

3. In an unskilful manner; inexpertly.

1565 Cooper *Thesaurus, Imperite,* vnexpertly, vnskilfully, vnlearnedly. 1664 H. More *Myst. Iniq.* 496 Upon which Grotius doth freely and not unskilfully comment after this manner. 1685 Boyle *Enq. Notion Nat.* vii. 266 To clear all those unskilfully framed axioms and phrases, I found to be so intricate a task [etc.]. 1735 Johnson *Lobo's Abyssinia, Voy.* v. 29 One [of the muskets] being unskilfully charged too high, flew out of the Soldier's Hand. 1768–74 Tucker *Lt. of Nat.* (1834) II. 381 That it is highly blasphemous..to imagine that God should have contrived His order of second causes so unskilfully. 1848 Miss Mitford in L'Estrange *Life* (1870) III. xii. 213 The story is very unskilfully told, with an entire want of dramatic power. 1885 *Law Times Rep.* LIII. 305/2 The defendant..negligently and unskilfully navigated..the said vessel.

Unski·lfulness. [Un-1 12.] The quality of being unskilful; inexpertness, †ignorance.

c 1410 *Lanterne Lizt* 115 God forbediþ þe vnleful takyng of oþir mennes goodis & so..refreyneþ þe vnskilfulnes of mannes dede. 1544 Betham *Precepts* i. ccii, Theyr vnskylfulnesse is the great destruction of the whole hoste, when they knowe not howe for to kepe theyr arraye. 1576 Fleming *Panopl. Epist.* ¶ iiij, In consideration of the gatherers vnskilfulnesse. 1613 Purchas *Pilgrimage* (1614) 309 They double their numbers at foure, as we doe at ten, through vnskilfulnesse in nombring. 1691 Hartcliffe *Virtues* 231 Hence we are obliged not to impose upon any Man's ignorance or unskilfulness. 1748 *Anson's Voyage* ii. x. 242 The indolence and unskilfulness of the Spanish sailors. 1776 Gibbon *Decl. & F.* vi. (1782) I. 193 The siege..was protracted to the tenth year..by the unskilfulness of the besiegers. 1828 Lytton *Pelham* III. xi, Tyrrell, who believed he should readily recruit himself by my unskilfulness in the game, fell easily into the snare. 1869 Dk. Argyle *Primeval Man* iii. 100 This..may be due to the unskilfulness of early art.

Unski·ll. [Un-1 12 and 4 b. Cf. ON. and Icel. *úskil, óskil* (Norw. dial. *uskil,* etc., MSw. *oskiäl,* etc., Sw. *oskäl,* MDa. *uskæl,* Da. *uskel,* in sense 1 or 1 b).]

†1. Improper or foolish conduct; folly; wrongdoing; wrong. *Obs.*

c 1175 *Lamb. Hom.* 65 Lauerd forȝef us ure unskile, and alswa we alle oðre wile. *c* 1275 *XI Pains Hell* 58 in *O. E. Misc.* 148 [He] þat..nolde leten his fleyssez wil, Ac folewede al þat wes vnskil. *c* 1300 *Cursor M.* 201 How Iuus wit þer gret vnschill Wend his vprisyng to dill. 1303 R. Brunne *Handl. Synne* 8798 3yf þou dedyst euer þat vnlawe,..Þou hast synned yn moche vnskyl. *c* 1420 *Sir Amadace* (Camden) lxvii, I wille do the no vnskille, Thou schalt dele hit atte thi wille, The godus that here now is. *a* 1500 *Ratis Raving* i. 1033 Bot always serf byme elyk,. Bot gif he do the al wnskill.

†b. Want of reason; unreasonableness. *Obs.*

c 1380 Wyclif *Sel. Wks.* II. 415 If we taken hede to þingis þat touchen þis staat, we moun fynde fulli unskil in ech of hem. *a* 1500 *Ratis Raving* i. 1269 It louis weill to leif be wyll, And callis resone oft vnskill.

†2. *With unskill*: a. Wrongly, wrongfully, improperly. (Also with *at.*) *Obs.*

c 1200 Ormin 427 Swa we don itt wiþþ unnskill Þatt itt ma33 anngrenn obre. *c* 1250 *Gen. & Ex.* 3506 Ne slo ðu no3t wið hond ne wil, Ne rend, ne beat no3t wið vn-skil. *c* 1330 R. Brunne *Chron. Wace* (Rolls) 12643 3if y ha lore hit at vnskyle, Y schal hit wynne eft when God wyle. *c* 1330 *King of Tars* 712 So long i wis hit is agon, I have ilived in prison of ston, With wrong and muchel unskille.

†b. Unreasonably, excessively. (Also with *till, to.*) *Obs.*

c 1220 *Bestiary* 433 He bit us don ure bukes wille, eten and drinken wið unskil. *a* 1300 *Cursor M.* 26991 Hop es god at hald wit houe, Bot til [*Fairf.* to] vnskil noght worth a glone. 13.. *Guy Warw.* 514 After þe hete me comeþ a chele, Þat me greueþ wiþ vn-skele.

3. Lack of skill; inexpertness; †ignorance (*of* something). Now *arch.*

1565 Martial in Harding *Answ. to M. Iuelle's Challenge* A 3 b, Where the faultes of the printers be infinite for the vnskill of the language. 1576 Lambarde *Peramb. Kent* 293 I..doe preferre plaine vnskill and ignorance, before vaine lying and presumptuous arrogance. 1598 Sylvester *Du Bartas* ii. i. i. *Eden* 276 That even light Thrrhon's wavering fantasies Reave him the skill his un-skill to agnize. 1611 Florio, *Inarte,* vnartnesse, ignorance, vnskill. 1905 J. Brierley *Eternal Relig.* 200 Hence more and more the idea will prevail that ignorance, unskill in things,..is in itself a kind of lower morality.

Unski·lled, *ppl. a.* [Un-1 8.]

1. Not skilled or expert *in* something; ignorant *of*; untrained or unable *to.*

1581 T. Howell *Devises* H iv, Thus harte to faine vnskilde, in being whole is broke. 1612 Drayton *Poly-olb.* iv. 174 In fing'ring some unskill'd, but only us'd to sing Unto the other's harp. 1693 Dryden *Persius* iii. 63 Down goes the Wretch at once, unskill'd to swim. 1717 Pope *Iliad* ix. 568 Thy youth as then in sage debates unskill'd. 1725 — *Odyss.* iv. 1021 Thus he [spoke], unskill'd of what the Fates provide! 1791 Cowper *Iliad* v. 77 Unskill'd to spell aright The oracles predictive of the woe. 1823 Mrs. Hemans *Vespers of Palermo* iii. v, If in this unskill'd, you stand alone Amidst our court of pleasure. 1863 H. Cox *Instit.* i. viii. 123 The members of the committee are usually unskilled in the rules of evidence.

b. Without const.

1693 Prior *To C'tess of Exeter* 3 Unskill'd and young, yet something still I writ, Of Ca'ndish Beauty join'd to Cecil's Wit. *a* 1749 A. Hill *Epilogue* 20 The world's wide stage..Sees some act nobly, others play unskill'd. 1818 Shelley *Rosal. & Helen* 1066 An unskilled hand..had the marble warmed With that pathetic life. 1856 Kane *Arct. Expl.* II. 94 Butter..melted from salt beef;..the unskilled might call it tallow. 1871 Jowett *Plato* I. 154 None of us unskilled individuals can..become physicians.

c. *spec.* Not skilled in some handicraft; devoid of technical training.

1851 Mayhew *London Labour* II. 323/1 With unskilled labourers it is otherwise. 1856 Froude *Hist. Eng.* I. 4 Any able-bodied unskilled labourer earns as soon as he has arrived at man's estate.

2. Not involving or requiring skill; displaying lack of skill.

1833 Ht. Martineau *Tale of Tyne* i. 8 All works of tillage have been mixed up together under the name of unskilled labour. 1849 G. Ticknor *Span. Lit.* I. 109 If their unskilled verses were preserved at all. 1869 Froude *Short Stud.* (1871) 337 Take the lowest and most unskilled labour of all, that of the peasant in the field.

†**Unski·lly,** *adv.* [Un-1 11.] Unskilfully. 1648 Hexham ii, *Hoetelen,* to doe a thing unskilly,..to Bungle. 1658 tr. *Usher's Ann.* 142 Which Artemon the Engineer, Ephorus the Historian doth unskilly confound with Artemon Periphoreus.

†**Unski·lwise,** *a. Obs.* [Un-1 7.]

1. Irrational; not endowed with reason.

c 1340 Hampole *Pr. Consc.* 166 Þat man þat..lyves als an unscylwys best, Þat nother has skil, witt, ne mynde. ? *a* 1375 *Relig. Pieces fr. Thornton MS.* 63 For þou..gafe hym lordechipe and powere Abowen all oþer vnskillwise creatures sere.

2. Unreasonable, excessive.

a 1340 Hampole *Psalter* lxxxv. 10, I..ioy in þe witonten vnscilwis sikirnes. *a* 1350 *St. Barthol.* 367 in Horstm. *Altengl. Leg.* (1881) 123 Þai gaf him many unskilwis scorn. 1357 *Lay Folks Catech.* (T.) 493 Glotony..is ane unskilwise likyng, or loue, In taste, or in takyng of mete and of drynk.

So †**Unski·lwisely** *adv. Obs.*

a 1300 *Cursor M.* 19149 Es it..resun þat we Calanged for

ur gode dede be? Vn-skilwisli þan can yee blam. *a* 1340 Hampole *Psalter* xxxv. 7 Men, þat lifis rightwisly, and..ill men, þat lifis vnscilwisly.

Unski·mmed, *ppl. a.* (Un-1 8.)

1634 T. Johnson *Parey's Chirurg. Wks.* xxiv. vi. 891 A certaine thinne skinne..like unto that..over vnscimmed milke. 1687 Montague & Prior *Hind & P. Transv.* 12 He..could not on a sudden Knead up with unskim'd Milk this Reas'ning Pudding. *a* 1722 Lisle *Husb.* (1757) 275 They wean them with unskimmed cow's-milk. 1858 Flint *Milch Cows* 309 Sweet milk cheese is made of the unskimmed milk. 1894 *Westm. Gaz.* 20 April 8/1 The milk..is very often skimmed, and the skimmed milk mixed with unskimmed.

Unski·n, *v.* [Un-2 4.] *trans.* To divest of skin; to flay. Also *fig.*

1598 Florio, *Discotennare,* to flea, to vnskin. *a* 1652 Brome *New Acad.* iv. ii, I'le..not only unmask, but unskin her face too. 1655 Moufet & Bennet *Health's Improv.* xxx. 278 Flaying and unskinning themselves as it were of reasons robe.

Unski·nned, *ppl. a.*1 [Un-2 8, or f. prec.] Stripped of the skin.

1607 Markham *Cavel.* vii. 63 Then casting that powder vpon any vnskinde part, it will presently bring on the skinne againe. 1790 J. Williams *Shrove Tues.* 24 Deal out contumely with dread.., Nor make that ulcerous that's scarce unskinn'd.

Unski·nned, *ppl. a.*2 [Un-1 8.] Not having the skin taken off.

[1775 Ash.] 1882 J. F. S. Gordon *Prov. Moray* I. 36 Unskinned peas boiled into a soup were also a favourite dish. 1899 *Daily News* 7 June 8/3 They threw the unskinned animal on the embers.

Unski·rmished, *ppl. a.* (Un-1 8 c.) 1627 Drayton *Agincourt* 24 And more then this, his Iourneyes to foreslowe He scarce one day vnskirmish'd with doth goe. **Unski·rted,** *ppl. a.* (Un-1 8.) [1775 Ash.] 1886 *Col. & Ind. Exhib., Catal. Exhibits N.S. Wales* (ed. 2) 93 Wool,..Six unskirted fleeces off prize ewes.

Unsla·ck, *a.* (Un-1 7. Cf. OE. *unslæc, unslæc.*) 1622 Wither *Philarete* O 7 b, Thy ioynts are yet nimble, thy sinnewes vnslacke.

Unsla·cked, *ppl. a.* [Un-1 8.]

1. Unslackened, unrelaxed.

1593 Nashe *Christ's T.* 24 b, God is mooued and mollified with often, and vnslacked intercessions. 1848 Aird *Herod. & Azala* i. i, Still their [*sc.* lions'] fronts were racked With lust of blood, their forms were still unslacked.

2. Of lime: (see Slacked *ppl. a.* 2).

1656 Earl Monm. tr. *Boccalini's Advts. fr. Parnass.* i. xxi. (1674) 22 Tyrannies are laid with..the unslackt Lime of..injustice. 1703 Moxon *Mech. Exerc.* 286 Unslackt or Quick Lime. 1760 Brown *Compl. Farmer* ii. 17 Unslacked lime beat to powder. 1808 *Phil. Trans.* XCVIII. 346 They ..were in the highly caustic or unslacked state. *c* 1860 H. Stuart *Seaman's Catech.* 63 Neither should unslacked lime..be allowed below.

3. Of thirst, etc.: Not slacked.

1798 Coleridge *Anc. Mar.* iii. iv, With throat unslack'd [1805 unslaked], with black lips bak'd Ne could we laugh, ne wail.

Unsla·ckened, *ppl. a.* (Un-1 8.)

1770 Glover *Leonidas* (ed. 5) vi. 418 They well may keep the field, Who with unslaken'd [1772 unslacken'd] nerves endur'd that day. 1844 Mrs. Browning *Sonn., Patience* 7 Ocean girds Unslackened the dry land. 1870 *Daily News* 23 Apr., He drove down a narrow road..followed by the waggon and horses with unslackened speed. 1890 'R. Boldrewood' *Miner's Right* xlii, Still the quartz-crushing machine..went thundering on..unchecked, unslackened.

Unsla·ckening, *ppl. a.* (Un-1 10.)

1768–74 Tucker *Lt. Nat.* (1834) I. 628 To turn his steps into the way that..unslackening prudence would have led. 1793 W. Roberts *Looker-on* No. 85 (1794) III. 371 After an unslackening course of..fasting, mortification, and watchfulness. 1836 Keble in *Lyra Apost.* (1849) 18 Faster each hour, on Time's unslackening gale, The dreaming world drives on. 1848 Mill *Pol. Econ.* i. xi. § 1 There is no obstacle to an increase of production..of unslackening rapidity.

Unslai·n, *ppl. a.* [Un-1 8 b. Cf. ON. and Icel. *úsleginn* in sense 2, MSw. *oslaghin* in sense 1, Sw. *oslagen* in sense 3.]

1. Not put to death; not killed.

c 1250 *Gen. & Ex.* 1332 Ðe wurð abraham fri3ti fa3en, for ysaac bi-leaf un-sla3en. 13.. *Gaw. & Gr. Knt.* 1858 My3[t] he haf slypped to be vn-slayn, þe sle3t were noble. *c* 1400 *Laud Troy Bk.* 18250 Prest, ne clerk,..Leffte the Gregais non vn-sclayn. 1470–85 Malory *Arthur* x. lix. 515, I shalle be with yow by that day yf I be vnslayne or vnmaymed. *a* 1533 Ld. Berners *Gold. Bk. M. Aurel.* ii. (1535) 101 b, They leaue no cattayle vnslayne, no gardeyne vnrobbed. 1555 Phaer *Æneid* iii. (1558) F iiij, Saue of Troy this last remayne, The leauinges of Achilles wyld and Grekes abiectes onslayne. 1633 T. Stafford *Pac. Hib.* i. ix. (1821) 117 The rest which were unslaine, returned into the Castle. *a* 1661 Holyday *Juvenal* (1673) 187 To Ceres's son-in-law few kings descend Unslain. 1715 Tickell *Iliad* i. 112 Nor does the god complain Of vows withheld or hecatombs unslain.

fig. *c* 1412 Hoccleve *De Reg. Princ.* 1972 O deth!..his hy vertu astertith Vnslayn fro þe. 1674 R. Godfrey *Inj. & Ab. Physic* 8 Spurious Mercurial [remedies], and ill-made Antimonial ones, that..have the Mercury unslain. 1779 Cowper *Olney Hymns* lvii, One sin, unslain, within my breast, Would make that heav'n as dark as hell.

†2. Uncut, unmown. *Obs.*

c 1440 *Pallad. on Husb.* i. 239 Lupyne and ficchis slayn.. are as doongyng, londis boote. And let hem drie vnslayn, and vp they drinke The londis iuce.

†**Unslake,** obs. var. Unslaked *ppl. a.*

1660 Sharrock *Vegetables* 19 Unto the ashes of every hill [*sc.* heap] you must put a peck of unslake Lime.

Unsla·k(e)able, *a.* (Un-1 7 b.) 1820 C. R. Maturin *Melmoth* xxviii. IV. 262 An unslakeable appetite for the restored splendours of her former state. 1872 C. King *Mountain. Sierra Nev.* i. 21 In a few miles, the unslakable desert has drunk it dry.

Unsla·ked, *ppl. a.* [Un-1 8.]

1. Of lime: Unslacked.

1598 Florio, *Calce vergine,* vnslaked lyme. 1651 French *Distill.* i. 4 Take unslaked Lime, and Linseed Oil, mix them well together. 1669 Sturmy *Mariner's Mag.* v. xii. 67 Plaster ..four parts, of Unslak'd Lime one part. 1816 Scott *Old Mort.* xxi, Would ye build a wall with unslaked mortar? 1837 J. T. Smith *Vicat's Mortars* 79 Those hydraulic mixtures, which are used unslaked, and ground previous to mixture. 1889 *Science-Gossip* XXV. 151/1 The leaves are.. chewed with a little unslaked lime.

2. Unrelaxed.

c 1625 Fletcher *Chances* ii. ii, A likely man, a man Made up like Hercules, unslak'd with service.

3. Of thirst, etc. (See Slake *v.*1 10.)

1692 Dryden *Don Sebastian* iii. i, Her desires new rous'd, And yet unslak'd, will kindle in her fansy. 1805 [see Unslacked 3]. 1818 Byron *Ch. Har.* iv. cxxiv, We gasp away ..; unfound the boon, unslaked the thirst. 1874 Farrar *Christ* 36 Stung by remorse, yet still unslaked with murder.

Unsla·ndered, *ppl. a.* (Un-1 8.) 1621 Sanderson *Serm.* I. 24 If seldom truth scape unslandered, marvel not: the reasons are evident. 1648 Hexham ii, *Ongelastert,* Vnslaundered, or Vncalumniated.

Unsla·te, *v.* (Un-2 4.) Also *fig.*

1598 Florio, *Scoppare,* to vntile, to vnslate. 1637 Saltonstall *Eusebius' Constantine* 70 Some of the Chappels by his command were unslated. 1648 Herrick *Hesper., To the Detracter,* A fellon take it, or some Whit-flaw come For to unslate, or to untile that thumb! 1795 Coleridge *Lines at Shurton Bars* 39 Where stands one solitary pile Unslated by the blast. 1872 Brierley *Cotters of Mossburn* xxiii, He's gone clean off his head. Unslated.

Unslau·ghtered, *ppl. a.* (Un-1 8.)

1719 Young *Par. Job* 230 Hov'ring o'er Th' unslaughter'd host, [the eagle] enjoys the promis'd gore. *a* 1800 Cowper *Odyss.* (ed. 2) xi. 463 The woful end Of other Grecians,.. Who 'scap'd, indeed, unslaughter'd from the field of Ilium. 1827 Southey *Hist. Penins. War* II. 553 The few mules and horses which remained unslaughtered. 1870 *Eng. Gilds* 354 *margin,* Having..goats, sheep, or swine, and selling them unslaughtered.

Unsla·ve, *v.* (Un-2 4 b. Cf. Du. *ontslaven.*)

a 1618 Sylvester *Maiden's Blush* 1641 I'll give you all the golden good I have,..your Brother to un-slave. 1633 P. Fletcher *Poet. Misc., A vow* 25 Thou freest Servant, from this yoke unslave me. 1719 D'Urfey *Pills* VI. 210 Suppose a Man does all he can, To unslave himself from a scolding Wife. 1729 Swift *Let.* 31 Oct., I— C—, who doth his duty of a good governor in unslaving this kingdom as much as he can.

†**Unslaw(e,** obs. varr. Unslain *ppl. a.*

a 1400 in *Eng. Gilds* (1870) 354 þulke, þat..byggeth get, shep, swyn, & a-3en selleþ vn-shlawe [*sic*]. *c* 1430 *Syr Gener.* (Roxb.) 8139 Thei that gate in, and wer vnslaw, The gates thei shet.

†**Unslea·kable,** *a. Obs.*—1 [Un-1 7 b.] Unquenchable. *c* 1400 *Apol. Loll.* 75, I schal brenne þe chaffe wiþ fire vnsleckable.

†**Unslea·ked,** *ppl. a. Obs.* [Un-1 8.] = next.

1525 *Grete Herbal* cxix. (1529) H j, Lyme, whan it is vnsleked. 1594 Plat *Jewell-ho.* 55 Fill a sheepes gut with small vnsleakt limestones. 1615 G. Sandys *Trav.* 69 A composition of Rusma..and vnsleakt lime.

Unsle·cked, *ppl. a.* [Un-1 8. Cf. MSw. *osläkt,* Sw. *osläckt.*] = Unslacked *ppl. a.* 2.

Frequent *c* 1570–*c* 1600.

c 1386 Chaucer *Can. Yeom. Prol. & T.* 806 Vnslekked lym, Chalk, and gleyre of an ey. 1563 T. Gale *Antidot.* ii. 53 Take vnslecked Lime, and quench it in water. 1607 Topsell *Four-f. Beasts* 365 Take..so much vnslect lime as will make that hony thicke like paast.

Unslee·k, *a.* (Un-1 7.) 1859 Tennyson *Elaine* 811 Then she that saw him lying unsleek, unshorn,..Utter'd a little tender dolorous cry. **Unslee·p,** *v.* (Un-2 3.) 1555 *Inst. Gentleman* iiij b, Slepe once passed cannot be vnslept againe. †**Unslee·piness.** *Obs.* [Un-1 12.] Sleeplessness. 1540 R. Jonas *Byrth Mankynde* 70 b, Agaynste vnslepynesse, that is, when the chylde..wanteth his due and naturall reste. †**Unslee·ping,** *vbl. sb. Obs.* [Un-1 13.] Lack of sleep. *a* 1425 tr. *Arderne's Treat. Fistula,* etc. 56 Brennyng with greuous prikkyng, and smertyng, and vnslepyng. *Ibid.* 72 If þat þe thenasmon last long, it bringeþ to..vnslepyng and feblenes of vertu.

Unslee·ping, *ppl. a.* (Un-1 10.)

1667 Milton *P. L.* v. 644 The unsleeping eyes of God. 1744 Thomson *Autumn* 415 She sits Conceal'd, with folded Ears; unsleeping Eyes. 1777 Potter *Æschylus, Prom. Bd.* 7 The joyless station of this rock Unsleeping, unreclining, shalt thou keep. 1805 Southey *Madoc in Wales* iii. 195 The unsleeping eye Of justice. 1863 Ld. Lytton *Ring Amasis* II. 293 Dear heart! Again you have passed a whole night long unsleeping.

fig. *a* 1613 Overbury *A Wife,* etc. (1614) H 2, Policie is the vnsleeping night of reason. 1796 Coleridge *Destiny of Nations* 106 Whose unheard name..Unsleeping Silence guards. 1802–12 Bentham *Ration. Judic. Evid.* (1827) I. 428 Unerring and unsleeping steadiness. 1841 Elphinstone *Hist. Ind.* II. 520 The unsleeping suspicions of Aurangzib were stirred up.

Hence **Unslee·pingly** *adv.*

1877 *Daily News* 16 Jan. 4/5 Our pressure must be friendly, but very firm and unsleepingly watchful.

Unslee·ve, *v.* (Un-2 4 b, 5.) 1598 Florio, *Dimanicare,* to vnhandle, to vnhafte, to vnsleeue. *Ibid., Smanicare,* to unsleaue. *a* 1824 *Gonzanga* iv. vii. in *New Brit. Theatre* III. 143 Unsleeve thy arm, that I may kiss a mark, stamped there indelible by nature's finger.

Unsle·pt, *ppl. a.* [Un-1 8 b, c.]

1. Not having slept.

a 1500 *Chaucer's Dreme* 1836 An aged knight..With visage ..pale, as man longe unslept. 1500–20 Dunbar *Poems* lxxviii. 9 The sentence lay full evill till find, Vnsleipit in my heid behind. 1876 J. Grant *One of the '600'* i. 10 My poor mother, pale, anxious, and unslept,..stole softly into my room. 1894 Froude *Life & Lett. Erasmus* 230, I hurry on board unsupped and unslept.

2. Not slept *in*; not slept *off.*

1821 Byron *Sardanap.* i. ii, Is this moment A fitting one for the resumption of Thy yet unslept-off revels? 1864 Miss Yonge *Trial* I. 289 She had..found..never before, Mr. Ward's bed unslept in. 1880 Mrs. Parr *Adam & Eve* xxxv. 476 The untasted food, the unslept-in bed.

†**Unsli·ckt,** var. Unsleaked or Unslecked *ppl. adjs.*

1573 *Arte of Limming* C iv, Vnslickt lyme. Poulder of white bones. 1605 Timme *Quersit.* iii. 180 Take unslickt lime: let it lye in spring water.

Unsli·ding, *ppl. a.* (Un-1 10.) 1806 O. Gregory *Treat. Mechanics* I. 101 Let E be the unsliding body, which acts in the direction EK.

Unsli·ng, *v.* [Un-2 3, 4 b.] *trans.* To detach from a sling; to free from being slung or suspended.

(*a*) 1630 Capt. J. Smith *True Trav.* xx. 40 Many of them were got to the top to unsling the maine saile. 1783 in *Naval Chron.* (1802) VIII. 364 [We] unslung our lower yards. 1815 Burney *Falconer's Marine Dict.* 603/2 *To unsling* is to take off the slings from boats, butts, buoys, yards, etc. 1839 F. A. Griffiths *Artill. Man.* 187, [No.] 7..slings, and unslings the gun, and lashes it to the pry pole.

(*b*) 1688 Holme *Armoury* iii. xix. (Roxb.) 153/1 Vnsling your musket. 1798 *Naval Chron.* XXV. 200 An Arab.. unslung his carbine. 1818 Scott *Rob Roy* xxx, He..commanded his soldiers to unsling their firelocks. 1838 James *Robber* iii, Lord Harold unslung his sword, and gave it to one of the servants. 1865 Visct. Milton & W. B. Cheadle *N.-W. Passage by Land* vii. 101 He unslings his pack, and sets to work to construct a..wooden trap.

Unsli·p, *v.* [Un-2 3, 4 b.]

1. *trans.* To let slip, set free.

1611 Florio, *Sguinzagliare,* to vncouple, to vnslip, to let goe as Spaniels. 1801 Surr *Splendid Misery* III. 215 'Tis not the sudden impulse of a fleeting passion that has unslipped from caution's trammel a rebellious tongue. 1846 Whittier *To Southern Statesman* 6 When thy eager hand With game afoot, unslipped the hungry pack To hunt down Freedom in her chosen land.

2. To slip back.

1892 Zangwill *Bow Mystery* 125 [He] went downstairs, [and] unslipped the bolt of the big lock.

Unsli·pping, *ppl. a.* (Un-1 10.)

1606 Shaks. *Ant. & Cl.* ii. ii. 129 To hold you in perpetuall amitie, To make you Brothers, and to knit your hearts With an vn-slipping knot. 1822 Ainslie *Land of Burns* 71 The unslipping bauns o' matrimony.

†**Unsli·ssed,** *ppl. a. Obs.* [Un-1 8, after obs. Du. *ongeslist.*] Unslacked. 1597 A. M. tr. *Guillemeau's Fr. Chirurg.* 26 b/2 Like vn-slissed lime. 1599 [see Sliss *v.*]. **Unsli·t,** *ppl. a.* (Un-1 8 b.) 1679 Moxon *Mech. Exerc.* ix. 164 Bauk, a peece of Fir unslit, from four to ten Inches square. **Unslo·ckenable,** *a. Sc.* [Un-1 7 b.] Unquenchable. *c* 1520 M. Nisbet *Luke* iii. 17 The caffis he sal birne with fire vnsloknabile. 1856 H. S. Riddell *Matt.* iii. 12 He will burn up the caff wi' unslockenable fire.

Unslo·ckened, *ppl. a. north.* and *Sc.* [Un-1 8.] Unextinguished.

1434 Misyn *Mending Life* 126 O mery lufe, stronge, rauischand, byrnand,..vnslokynd, þat all my saull brynge to þi seruis. 1435 — *Fire of Love* 97 Þis lufe to fyre vnslokynd I lykyn. 1596 Dalrymple tr. *Leslie's Hist. Scot.* (S.T.S.) II. 164 Not willing to leiue ane spunk vnsloknet,[he] receiuet in fauour the Erle of Angus. 1896 Crockett *Grey Man* xxxiii, There burned a still and unslockened fire in her eye.

Unslo·ken, *ppl. a.* *rare*—1. [Cf. prec.] = Unslaked *ppl. a.* 3. 1871 Swinburne *Songs bef. Sunrise, Tenebræ* 23 A slow song beaten and broken, As it were from the dust and the dead, As of spirits athirst unsloken.

Unslo·t, *v. north.* and *Sc.* [Un-2 3.] *trans.* To unfasten (a door).

1819 W. Tennant *Papistry Storm'd* (1827) 46 Thus said, Don Andrew..Unslot his yett, and out gaed whiddin'. 1855 [Robinson] *Whitby Gloss.* s.v., To *Unslot* or *Unsteck,* to unlatch, to open.

Unslo·thful, *a.* (Un-1 7.) 1648 Hexham ii, *Ontraegh,* vnslothfull, vigilent. 1887 E. Johnson *Antiq. Mater.* 251 Your unslothful love unto the glory of God. **Unslo·thfulness.** (Un-1 12.) 1700 Ray *Persuas. Holy Life* Add., Unslothfulness in Labour, if I may make such a Word, is the means to preserve health.

†**Unslow·,** *a. Obs.* [OE. *unsláw* (Un-1 7).] Not slow; active, quick, swift.

In *Beowulf* 2564 the emendation *unslaw* has been suggested for the MS. reading *unglaw.*

c 1000 Ælfric *Saints' Lives* xxv. 375 Hi slogon þa togædere unslawe mid wæpnum. *a* 1023 Wulfstan *Hom.* x. (1883) 72 Se ðe wære full slaw, weorðe se unslaw to cyrican. 1382 Wyclif *Prov.* vi. 11 If forsothe vnslo3 thou shul be, shal come as a welle thi rip. *c* 1400 *Destr. Troy* 908 The dragon ..gird him agayne with a grym noyse: Mony slecynges vnslogh throughe hys slote yode. 1483 *Cath. Angl.* 343/2 Vn Slawe, *ubi* wyghte.

Unslui·ce, *v.* [Un-1 4 b, 5.]

1. *trans.* To let out as from a sluice; to allow to flow.

1611 Florio, *Schiuso,*..vnshut, vnlockt, vnsclused. 1648 Herrick *Hesper., Sailing fr. Julia,* Forbeare (In my short absence) to unsluce a teare. *a* 1711 Ken *Hymns Evang.* Poet. Wks. 1721 I. 237 Unsluce his Blood, till now undrein'd. 1787 *Generous Attachment* I. 167 Enough to unsluice the water from any female eye. 1826 J. Montgomery *Chron. Angels* Wks. 1841 IV. 309 Angels, with healing virtue in their wings,..unsluice earth's bosom-springs.

2. To furnish with an outlet.

1652 Benlowes *Theoph.* iii. xcv, Here did she seal her lips, unsluice her eyes To flowing rhet'ric. 1700 Dryden *Ovid's Met., Mel. & Atalanta* 365 Now lofty Calidon in Ruines lies; All Ages, all Degrees unsluice their Eyes. 1721 Young *Revenge* ii. ad fin., I must unsluice my overburthen'd heart And let it flow.

Supplement, p. 3873; Corrigenda, p. 4092; Spurious words, p. 4093; Books quoted, p. 4094

Unslumbering, ppl. a.

Unsly, a. (adv.). Obs.

Unsmart, a. (Un-1.)

Unsmartness.

Unsmelled, ppl. a. (Un-1 8 a, c.)

Unsmelling, ppl. a. (Un-1 10.)

Unsmiling, ppl. a.

Unsmirched, ppl. a. (Un-1 8 b.)

Unsmoking, vbl. n.

Unsmitten, ppl. a.

Unsmoked, ppl. a. (Un-1 8 b.)

Unsmoote, a. (Un-1 7.)

Unsmokeable, a. (Un-1 10.)

Unsmoky, a. (Un-1 7.)

Unsober, a. (Un-1 7 b.)

Unsobriety.

Unsnare, v. (Un-2 3 and 7.)

Unsnarl, v. (Un-2 3.)

Unsnubbable, a. (Un-1 7 b.)

Unsnuffed, ppl. a. (Un-1 8.)

Unsoaked, ppl. a. (Un-1 8.)

Unsociability.

Unsociable, a.

Unsociableness.

Unsociably, adv.

Unsocial, a. (Un-1 7.)

Unsocket, v. (Un-2 5.)

Unsodden, ppl. a.

Unsoft, a.

Unsoftened, ppl. a. (Un-1 8.)

Unsoiled, ppl. a. (Un-1 8 b.)

Unsold, ppl. a.

Unsoldier, v.

Unsoldierlike, a.

Unsoldierly, a.

Unsolemn, a.

Unsolemnized, ppl. a.

Unsolicited, ppl. a.

Unsolicitous, a.

Unsolid, a. (Un-1 7, 5 b.)

Unsoluble, a. (Un-1 7 b and 5 b.)

Unsolvable, a. (Un-1 7 b.)

Unsolved, ppl. a. (Un-1 8.)

Unsome, a.

Unsonsy, a. (Un-1 7.)

Unsophisticate, a.

Unsophisticated, ppl. a.

Unsophistication.

Unsorrowed, ppl. a.

Unsorted, ppl. a.

Unsought, ppl. a. (Un-1 8 b, c.)

Unsoul, v.

Unsound, a. (Un-1 7.)

Unsoundable, a.

Unsounded, ppl. a.

Unstrip, v. Now dial. and rare. [Un-2.]

Unstript, ppl. a. [Un-1 8.] Not stripped; not removed by stripping.

Unstruck, ppl. a. [Un-1 8.]

Unstrung, ppl. a. [Unstring v.]

1. Having the string(s) relaxed or removed: a. Of a harp, etc.

Unstudied, ppl. a.; also absol.

Unstuff, v. [Un-3, 4.]

Unstuffed, ppl. a. Not stuffed; unfurnished.

Unstung, ppl. a. [Un-1 8.] Not stung.

Unsturdy, a.

Unsubdued, ppl. a. [Un-1 8.]

Unsubject, a. [Un-1 7.]

Unsubjected, ppl. a. [Un-1 8.]

Unsubmitting, ppl. a. [Un-1 10.]

Unsubordinate, a.

Unsubstantiality. [f. prec.] The quality of being unsubstantial.

Unsubstantiate, a. [Un-1 2.] Not substantiated.

Unsubstantiated, ppl. a. [Un-1 8.]

Unsubstantial, a. [Un-1 7 b.]

Unsuccess, sb. [Un-1 12 and 5 b.] Lack of success, failure; an instance of this.

Unsuccessful, a. [Un-1 7 and 5 b.] Not attended by, not meeting or attaining, success.

Unsufferable, a. and adv. Now rare or Obs. [Un-1 7 b, 11 b, 5 b.]

Unsufferableness.

Unsuffering, ppl. a.

Unsuited, ppl. a. [Un-1 8.]

Unsuggestive, a. [Un-1 7.]

Unsuit, v. Obs. [Un-1 14.]

Unsullied, ppl. a. [Un-1 8.]

Unsuitability. [Un-1 5 b.]

Unsuitable, a. [Un-1 7 b.]

Unsullenness.

Unsummed, ppl. a. [Un-1 8.]

Unsummoned, ppl. a. [Un-1 8.]

Unsun, v. [Un-18 1.]

Unsunned, ppl. a. [Un-1 8.]

Unsuperable, a. Obs. [Un-1 7 and 5 b.]

Unsupervised, ppl. a. [Un-1 8.]

Unsupplanted, ppl. a. [Un-1 8.]

Unsuppliable, a. [Un-1 7 b.]

Unsupplied, ppl. a. [Un-1 8.]

Unsupportable, a. [Un-1 7 b and 5 b.]

Unsupported, ppl. a. [Un-1 8.]

Supplement, p. 3873; Corrigenda, p. 4092; Spurious words, p. 4093; Books quoted, p. 4094.

3547

Unta·lkative. (Un- 1 b.)

Unta·me. *v.* Cf. *In. Obs.*

Unta·me. *a.* (Un- 1 b.)

Unta·meable. (Un- 1 b.)

Unta·med, *ppl. a.* (Un- 1 8 a.)

Hence **Unta·medly** *adv.*, **Unta·medness.**

Unta·mpered, *ppl. a.* (Un- 1 8 c.)

Hence **Unta·mpered** *ppl. a.*

Unta·ngible, *a.* (Un- 1 7 b.)

Unta·ngle, *v.* (Un- 2 4 b.)

Unta·nned, *ppl. a.* (Un- 1 8 c.)

Unta·ped, *ppl. a.* (Un- 1 8 b.)

Unta·rnished, *ppl. a.* (Un- 1 8 c.)

Unta·sted, *ppl. a.* (Un- 1 8 b.)

Unta·ught, *ppl. a.* (Un- 1 8 + Taw 2 ?)

Unta·x, *v.* (Un- 2 4 b.) *trans.*

Unta·xable, *a.* (Un- 1 7 b and 5 b.)

Unta·xed, *ppl. a.* (Un- 1 8.)

Untea·rable, *a.* (Un- 1 7 b.)

Untea·ch, *v.* (Un- 2.)

Hence **Untea·ching** *vbl. sb.*

Untea·chable, *a.* (Un- 1 7 b.)

Hence **Untea·chableness.**

Untech·nical, *a.* (Un- 1 7.)

Unte·mperate, *a. Obs.* (Un- 1 7, 5 b.)

Unte·mperate, *a. Obs.*

Unte·mperately, *adv. Obs.* (Un- 1 12.)

Hence **Unte·mperateness** *Obs.*

Untempered, *ppl. a.* (Un- 1 8. Cf. MDu. *ongetempert*, Du. *ongetemperd*, MHG. *ungetemperet*.)

Untenableness, *sb.*

Unte·nable, *a.* (Un- 1 7 b and 5 b.)

Unte·nant, *v.* (Un- 2 4.)

Hence **Unte·nanting** *vbl. sb.*

Unte·nanted, *ppl. a.* (Un- 1 8.)

Unte·mpting, *ppl. a.* (Un- 1 8.)

Unte·nanted, *ppl. a.* (Un- 1.)

Unte·nded, *ppl. a.* (Un- 1 8 + Tend v. 1)

Unte·nder, *a.* (Un- 1 7.)

Unte·nderly, *adv.* (Un- 1 12.)

Unte·nderness.

Unte·nible, *a.* (Un- 1 7 b.)

Unte·rrified, *ppl. a.* (Un- 1 8.)

Unterri·fying, *ppl. a.*

Unte·state, *a.* (Un- 1 7, 5 b.) Intestate.

Unte·nder, *ppl. a.* (Un- 1.) Not offered.

Unte·nderly, *adv.* (Un- 1 7.)

Untha·nked, *ppl. a.* (Un- 1 8.)

Untha·nkful, *a.* (Un- 1 7. Cf. OE. *unþancful*, OHG. *undancful*.)

Untha·nkfully *adv.*, **Untha·nkfulness.**

Unthatch, *v.* (Un- 2 4.) *trans.* To strip of thatch.

UNTHATCHED. 369 UNTHOUGHT.

UNTHOUGHT. 370 UNTHRIFTY.

UNTHRILLED. 371 UNTIE.

UNTIED. 372 UNTIL.

Supplement, p. 3873; Corrigenda, p. 4092; Spurious words, p. 4093; Books quoted, p. 4094

Unto-asted, *ppl. a.* [Un-1.] *Obs.*

Unto-ld, *ppl. a.* [Un-1 8 b.] Not counted or reckoned; not narrated.

Unto-ne, *v.* [Un-6 b.] *trans.* To deprive of tone.

Unto-ned, *ppl. a.* [Un-1 8.]

Untongue, *v.* [Un-2.] *trans.* To deprive of (the use of) the tongue; to render speechless.

Untongued, *ppl. a.* [Un-1 8 + Tongued *ppl. a.*]

Unto-oth, *ppl. a.* [Un-1 8.] Destitute of a tongue; tongueless.

Untongue-tied, *ppl. a.* [Un-1 8.]

Untonsured, *ppl. a.* [Un-1 8.]

Unto-othsome, *a.* [Un-1 7.]
1. *fig.* Unpalatable, disagreeable.
2. Unpleasant to the taste.

Unto-othed, (*ppl.*) *a.* [Un-1 9, Un-2 8.] Cf. G.G. *ungezähnt.*] Not having, deprived of, teeth.

Untop, *v.* [Un-2 4. Cf. Top *v.*1] *trans.*

Unto-mb, *v.* [Un-2 5.] *trans.* To disentomb.

Untormented, *ppl. a.* [Un-1 8 b.]

Unto-rn, *ppl. a.* [Un-1 8 b.] Not torn or lacerated.

Unto-uched, (*ppl.*) *a.* [Un-1 8.]

Untou-ching, *ppl. a.* [Un-1 5 d, 10.]

Unto-ward, *a.* [Un-1 7.]

Unto-wardliness. [Un-1 12. Cf. next.]

Unto-wardly, *a.* Now *rare.* [Un-1 7.]

Unto-wardness. [Un-1 8.]

Unto-wed, *ppl. a.* [Un-1 8 b.]

Unto-ward, *adv.* [Cf. Toward *prep.* and *adv.*]

Untrace-able, *a.* Now *rare.* [Un-1 7.]

Untra-ced, *ppl. a.* [Un-1 8 and 9.]

Untra-cked, *ppl. a.* [Un-1 8 and 9.]

Untrai-ned, *ppl. a.* [Un-1 8.]

Untra-mmelled, *ppl. a.* [Un-1 8.]

Untra-mpled, *ppl. a.* [Un-1 8.]

Untra-nquil, *a.* [Un-1 7.]

Untra-nsferable, *a.* [Un-1 7 b.]

Untransferred, *ppl. a.* [Un-1 8.]

Untransfo-rmable, *a.* [Un-1 7 b, 5 b.]

Untra-nsformed, *ppl. a.* [Un-1 8.]

Untranspa-rent, *a.* [Un-1 7.]

Untra-nslatable, *a.* [Un-1 7 b, 5 b.]

Untransla-ted, *ppl. a.* [Un-1 8.] Not turned into another language.

Untra-nsported, *ppl. a.* [Un-1 8.]

Untransposed, ppl. a. (Un-1 8.)

Untransubstantiated, ppl. a. (Un-1 8.)

Untrapped, ppl. a. (Un-1 8.) Of a snare or drain: Not fitted with a trap.

Untravailable, a. (Un-1 7 b.)

Untravelled, a. (Un-1 8.)
1. That has not travelled.
2. Not travelled over or through.

Untraversed, a. (Un-1 8.)

Untreasured, ppl. a. (Un-1 8.)

Untreatable, a. (Un-1 7 b.)

Untreated, ppl. a. (Un-1 8 and 8 c.)

Untrembling, ppl. a. (Un-1 10.)

Untremulous, a. (Un-1 7.)

Untrenched, a. (Un-1 8 and 8 c.) a. Not entrenched. b. Not trenched by digging. c. Not encroached upon.

Untrimmable, a. (Un-1 7 b.)

Untrimmed, ppl. a. (Un-1 8.)

Untrod, ppl. a. (Un-1 8 b.) Not trodden or stepped on; untraversed. Also in fig. context.

Untrodden, ppl. a. (Un-1 8 b.) Not trodden or stepped on; untraversed.

Untroubled, ppl. a. (Un-1 8.)
1. Not subjected to trouble or disquiet.
2. Not troubled, disturbed, or agitated.
3. Not interfered with.

Untrue, a. and adv. (OE. untréowe, untrýwe.)

Untruly, adv. (OE. untréowlíce.)

Untrim, v. (Un-2 4 and 4 ontrom. [OE. trum strong].) a. Weak, ailing, ill.

Untrimmed, ppl. a. (Un-1 8.)

Untrue, v. (Un-2 2.)
1. trans. To free from a spot or burden.
2. To undo or unmake (a pack, etc.); to remove or free from some burdening.

Untruss, v. (Un-2.)

Untrust, pa. t. (Un-1 8 b.)

Untrustful, a. (Un-1 7.)

Untrusting, ppl. a. (Un-1 10.)

Untrustiness. (Un-1 12.)

Untrustworthiness. (Un-1 12.)

Untrustworthy, a. (Un-1 7.)

Untrusty, a. (Un-1 7 b.)

Untruth. (OE. untréowþ.)
1. Unfaithfulness; lack of fidelity, loyalty, or honesty.
2. Unfaithful in another. Obs.

Untumultuous, a. (Un-1 7.)

Untunable, a. (Un-1 7 b.)

Untuneful, a. (Un-1 7.)

Untuning, ppl. a. (Un-1 10.)

Untupped, ppl. a. (Un-1 8.)

Unturned, ppl. a. (Un-1 8.)

Untutored, ppl. a. (Un-1 8.)

Unwaveringly, adv.

Unwax, v.[1] Obs.[1] To grow or become less; to decrease. Also fig.

Unwax, v.[2] [Un-.[5]] trans. To deprive of wax; to remove the wax from.

†**Unwayed**, a. Obs.
1. Not provided with ways or roads.
2. Of horses: Not accustomed to ways or roads; hence, restive, intractable.

Unwea'kened, ppl. a. [Un-.[8].]

Unwea'lthy, a. [Un-.[7].]

Unwea'riable, a. [Un-.[7 b.]] Incapable of being or becoming wearied or tired; indefatigable, unremitting.

Unwea'riableness.

Unwea'riably, adv.

Unwea'ried, ppl. a. [Un-.[8].]

Unwea'riedly, adv.

Unwea'riedness.

Unwea'rily, adv.

Unwea'riness.

Unwea'ring, vbl. sb.

Unwea'rying, ppl. a. [Un-.[10].]
1. That does not grow or become wearisome; unremitting, untiring.
2. Not causing or producing weariness.

Unwea'ryingly, adv.

Unwea'ther, Obs.

Unwea'thered, ppl. a. [Un-.[8].]

Unwea've, v. [Un-.[3].]

Unwea'ved, ppl. a. [Un-.[8].]

Unweb, v. [Un-.[3].]

Unwe'dded, ppl. a. [Un-.[8].]

Unwe'dgeable, a. [Un-.[7 b.]] Incapable of being split by wedges; uncleavable.

Unweed, v. [Un-.[3].]

Unwee'ded, ppl. a. [Un-.[8].]

Unwee'ting, adv. Now arch.

Unwee'tingly, adv.

Unwe'ighable, a.

Unweighed, ppl. a. [Un-.[8].]

UNWEIGHING. 395 **UNWHITEWASHED.** 396 **UNWIELDINESS.**

Unwei'ghing, ppl. a. [Un-.[10].]

Unwel'come, a. [Un-.[7].]

Unwel'comed, ppl. a. [Un-.[8].]

Unwel'comely, adv.

Unwel'comeness.

Unwell, a. [Un-.[7].]

Unwe'mmed, ppl. a. [OE. unwemmed.]

Unwhi'te, a. [Un-.[7].]

Unwhi'tened, ppl. a.

Unwhi'tewashed, ppl. a.

†**Unwhole**, a.[1] Obs.
1. Not in good health; unsound, unhealthy; diseased, infirm, sick.
2. Of food, etc.: Not suited with taste; tasteless.

Unwholesome, a.
1. Not conducive to physical health.
2. Not favourable to or promoting good health.

Unwholesomely, adv.

Unwholesomeness.

Unwi'eld, a. Now arch. In a unwelde, unwield, impotence.

Unwi'eldily, adv.

Unwi'eldiness.
1. The quality of being incontrollable or unrestrainable.
2. The state or quality of being unwholesome or unfit for, food, etc.
3. Awkwardness or clumsiness in respect of bulk, build, or movement; esp. awkward corpulence; clumsy size or vastness.
4. The condition or character of being difficult to guide, direct, or control by reason of size.

Unwie'ldly, a. [In early use f. UNWIELD sb. + -LY¹; later a variant of UNWIELDY sb.]

† Unwie'ldly, adv.

† Unwie'ldsome, a.

Unwieldy (ɒnwīˈldi), a. Forms: 5–7 unweldy, 6 ‑yn, 6–7 ‑ie, 5–7 unweeldy, 5 ‑weldi, 6 ‑ie, 6–7 unweeldy, 6–7 un‑weildie, 7 ‑ie, 6–7 unwieldy, Sc. ‑wyldy. (Also 5–7 yn, 5–6 on‑.) 7, 5 + WIELDY a. Cf. the early UNWIELDY a.

† Unwill, v. [Un-² b.]

† Unwill, sb. [Un-¹ b.]

Unwill'ed, ppl. a. [Un-¹ 8 + WILL sb.¹]

Unwilling, ppl. a. [Un-¹ 10.]

Unwillingly, adv.

Unwillingness.

Unwind (ɒnwaiˈnd), v. [Un-² 4 + WIND sb.] trans.

Unwinding, ppl. a. [Un-² 1.]

Unwinged, ppl. a.

Unwinking, ppl. a.

† Unwinly, adv.

Unwinning, ppl. a. rare. [Un-¹ 10.]

Unwinnowed, ppl. a. [Un-¹ 8. Cf. Un‑WINNOWED.]

† Unwinter, v.

Unwiped, ppl. a. [Un-¹ 8 & C.]

Unwire, v.

Unwisdom. [OE. unwísdóm (Un-¹ 12).]

Unwise, a. [OE. unwís (Un-¹ 7.)]

Unwisely, adv. [OE. unwíslíce (Un-¹ 11.]

Unwiseness.

Unwish, v. [Un-² 3.]

Unwished, ppl. a. [Un-¹ 8 & b.]

Unwished-for, ppl. a.

† Unwist, ppl. a. & sb.

Unwistful, a.

Unwithdrawing, ppl. a.

Unwithered, ppl. a. [Un-¹ 8.]

Unwithering, ppl. a.

Unwithhe'ld, ppl. a. [Un-¹ 8 b.] Not withheld or withstood; unopposed; also, not successfully opposed.

Unwi'thstanding, vbl. sb.

Unwi'thstood, ppl. a. [Un-¹ 8 b.] Not withstood or hindered; unopposed; also, not successfully opposed.

Unwi'thstanding, ppl. a.

Unwi'tingly, adv.

Unwi'tnessed, ppl. a.

Unwi'ttily, adv. [f. Unwitty a., or Un-³ 11.] In an ignorant, unwise, or foolish manner; unwittily.

Unwi'tting, ppl. a.

Unwi'ttingly, adv. [f. prec. + -ly², or Un-³ 11.]

Unwi'ttingness.

Unwi'tty, a.

Unwi've, v.

Unwi'ved, ppl. a.

Unwo'man, v. [Un-² 6 b.]

Unwo'maned, ppl. a.

Unwo'maning, vbl. sb.

Unwo'manish, a.

Unwo'manize, v.

Unwo'manized, ppl. a.

Unwo'manlike, a.

Unwo'manliness.

Unwo'manly, a.

Unwo'manly, adv.

Unwo'nt, a.

Unwo'nted, ppl. a.

Unwo'ntedly, adv.

Unwo'ntedness.

Unwo'nted, ppl. a.

Unwo'rded, ppl. a.

Unwo'rdy, a.

Unwo'rkable, a. [Un-¹ 7 b.] Incapable of being worked; unalterable.

Unwo'rkableness.

Unwo'rker.

Unwo'rking, ppl. a.

Unwo'rkmanlike, a.

Unwo'rkmanly, a.

Unwo'rkmanly, adv.

Unwo'rld, sb.

Unwo'rlded, ppl. a.

Unwo'rldliness.

Unwo'rldly, a.

Unwo'rried, ppl. a.

Unwo'rship, sb.¹

Unwo'rship, sb.²

Unwo'rship, v.

Unwo'rn, ppl. a. [Un-¹ 8 b, c.]

Unwo'rshipful, a.

Unwo'rshipfully, adv.

Unwo'rshipped, ppl. a.

Unwo'rth, sb. [OE. unweorð.]

Unwo'rth, a.

Unwo'rthily, adv.

Unwo'rthiness.

Unwo'rthy, a.

UPBRAID

| UPBRAIDED. | 421 | UPBURST. | UP-BY. | 422 | UPDRAW. |

Upbraiding, ppl. a. [f. UPBRAID v. + -ING[2].] Reproachful, reproving.

Upbraidingly, adv. [f. prec.] In an upbraiding manner; with reproach or reproof.

†Upbray, sb. Obs. [Cf. next.] An upbraiding; reproach.

Upbray, v. Obs. [Erroneous back-formation on upbrayd, obs. pa. t. of UPBRAID.]

Upbreak, sb. A breaking-up or dissolution.

Upbrought, pa. pple. [f. UP- 5. Cf. UPBRING v. 2.]

Upbringing, vbl. sb. The action of building. Obs.

Upbroken, pa. pple. [f. UP- 5.]

†Upbray, v. Obs.

Upheaval, sb. The action of raising, or fact of being raised, above the original level, esp. by volcanic action.

| UPDRAWN. | 428 | UPGROWTH. | UPHALE. | 424 | UPHILL. |

Updraw, v.

Updried, pa. pple. and ppl. a.

Upfurled, ppl. a.

Upgang, sb.

Upgather, v.

Up-gradient.

Upgrow, v.

Upgrowing, vbl. sb.

Upgrowth.

Uphand, a.

Upheap, v.

Uphill, sb., a., and adv.

UPHILL.

Uphill, adv., prep., a., and sb.

Uphill'ward, adv. and a.

Uphoard, v.

Uphold, v.

UPHOLDER.

Upholder, sb.

Uphold, sb.

UPHOLDING.

Upholding, vbl. sb.

Upholster, v.

Upholster, sb.

Upholsterer, sb.

Upholsteress.

Upholstering, vbl. sb. and ppl. a.

Upholsterous, a.

Upholstery.

Uphove, var. UPHEAVE.

Uphung, pa. pple.

Uphroe, var. EUPHROE.

UPKEEP.

Upkeep, sb.

UPKEEPING. 427 UPLAY. UPLEAP. 428 UPMAKE.

Upkeeping, vbl. sb.

Upkey-kindle, v.

Upla id, a.

Upturned, ppl. a.

Upland, sb. and a.

Uplander, sb.

Uplandish, a.

Uplay, v.

Upleap, vbl. sb.

Upleap, v.

Uplift, sb.

Uplift, v.

Uplifted, ppl. a.

Uplift able, a.

Uplifter, sb.

Uplight.

Uplock, v.

Uplook, v.

Uploper.

Upmake, sb.

Upmake, v.

Upmaking, vbl. sb. [Up-.]

1. Sc. The action of making up, in various senses.

2. Shipbuilding. (See quot. 1846.)

Upmanship, pbl. sb. Sc. (Up-.)

1. That makes up or for a defect or lack.

2. Seeking acquaintance or intimacy.

Upmost, a. Also Sc. 6 vpmest, 6-9 uppmaist. [Up a:d- + -MOST.]

1. Of local position outside of, but in contact with or close to, a surface.

Up'ness. The quality of being elevated or raised.

Upu'm, n. Obs. [Ur-4. Cf. OFris. opinia, opnema (WFri. opnimme), OHG. upnimen (MLG. upnemen MHG. ofnemen (G.)) trans. To take up.

Hence **Upuning** vbl. sb. Obs.

Upo', prep. Now chiefly Sc. and north. dial. [Up-6.]

Upon (ɒpɒ'n), prep. Forms: α. 2- upon (4-5, 7 up on, 6 Sc. uppon), 4-7 vpon (5-6 vp on, 4, 5 Sc. vppone, Sc. 6 wppone, 6-7 wpon), 3-6 vppon (4 oupon, opan), 4-5 oppon. β. 3-6, 5-7 Sc. appon, approne, 8, 6 poun, 8-9 'pon. See also Upo'. [Early ME. upon, uppon, etc., f. Up adv. + On prep.; distinct from late OE. uppan, uppon 'up on'.]

b. Immediately after; following on.

c. As soon as. Obs.

8. Denoting physical arrangement, order, etc.

b. Denoting state or condition. Obs.

9. Indicating a state of activity or existence.

10. a. Occupied with; engaged in; employed upon.

b. Denoting the basis or reason of reliance, trust, etc.

11. Indicating the basis or reason of reliance, trust, etc.

b. According to; in agreement or accordance with; on the model of.

Supplement, p. 3873; Corrigenda, p. 4092; Spurious words, p. 4093; Books quoted, p. 4094

Kynge..losyde his gonnys of his ordynaunce uppone them. c1500 *Melusine* lix. 360 Be ye he that wyl take the trybute vpon my Fortresse? 1533 *Acc. Ld. High Treas. Scot.* VI. 156 To Johne Drummondis childer wirkand upoune the hagbute stokkis. 1585 T. WASHINGTON tr. *Nicholay's Voy.* i. xviii. 21 We will not leaue the following on vpon our purpose. 1633 MARMION *Fine Companion* i. iii. (1875) 114 They can doe no more good upon me, than a young pittifull Lover upon a mistress that has the sullens. 1656 EARL MONM. tr. *Boccalini's Advts. fr. Parnass.* ii. v. 206 He..had made their places he conferred upon men void of counsel. 1680 *Laws Nevis* iii. (1740) 6 If the said Offenders are not able to pay..then to be compelled to work it out upon the Forts. 1737 WHISTON *Josephus, Antiq.* xvi. iv. § 3 The father may have a suspicion upon all his sons. 1796 *Ann. Reg., St. Papers* 297 The constitution..is sacredly obligatory upon all. 1805 tr. *Lafontaine's Hermann & Emilia* I. 261 Nothing is more detestable than to offer one's self upon a young man. 1850 ROBERTSON *Serm.* Ser. iii. (1857) 7 Persecution is that which affixes penalties upon views held, instead of upon life led. 1896 *Peterson Mag.* Jan. 102/2 The intruded-upon young lady turned her back upon him.

b. Denoting the object of regard, desire, etc.; = ON *prep.* 20 b.

See also DOTE *v.*1 3, EAGER *a.* 6, KEEN *a.* 6 b, MAD *a.* 4, RUN *v.* 70 b, SET *v.* 37.

c1330 R. BRUNNE *Chron. Wace* (Rolls) 7604 Opon þat meyden he wax al mad. 1382 WYCLIF *Psalm* xxxix. [xl.] 17 Ful out ioȝe thei, and glade vpon me, alle that sechen thee. c1449 PECOCK *Repr.* ii. xx. 267 He schal haue miche gretter affeccioun vpon the seid freend. 1470-85 MALORY *Arthur* x. lvi. 518 Louers..soo mad and soo soted vpon wymmen. a1578 LINDESAY (Pitscottie) *Chron. Scot.* (S.T.S.) I. 167 The king..was covatous wpoun money. 1598 BARCKLEY *Felic. Man* i. 51 A young man..that was..enamoured vpon an Image of marble. 1614 BP. HALL *Recoll. Treat.* 982 In this case, Moses should have beene..cast downe..; yet how hot is hee uppon justice. 1711 ADDISON *Spect.* No. 106 ¶ 3 When he is pleasant upon any of them, all his Family are in good Humour. 1843 *Fraser's Mag.* XXVIII. 619 O'Connell is bent upon the disruption of the British empire.

†**c.** Among (a number of sharers, etc.). *Obs.*

1492 in *10th Rep. Hist. MSS. Comm.* App. V. 323 Distributers of the same upon the commynes. 1526 TINDALE *Rom.* xv. 26 To make a certayne distribucion apon the poore sanctes. 1598 DALLINGTON *Meth. Trav.* K 3, Hee diuideth the Lands vpon his horsemen, to each his portion.

d. Indicating the person by whom a cheque, draft, order, etc., is payable, or the bank on which it is drawn; = ON *prep.* 20 c.

See also CHEQUE *sb.* 3, DRAUGHT *sb.* 35, DRAW *v.* 65.

1660 *Nicholas Papers* (Camden) IV. 226 Mr. Fox hauing giuen mee a note upon Mr. Shaw to pay me my allowance. a1722 FOUNTAINHALL *Decis.* (1759) I. 12 The bill upon his wife for £200. 1722 DE FOE *Col. Jack* (1840) 216 He shows me a bill upon me, drawn by my wife. 1798 in *Ushaw Mag.* Dec. (1913) 287 An order upon Mr. Wright for £12 as the price of the book sent you. 1843 *Blackw. Mag.* LIV. 736 It may be quite as well..to draw upon the bank.

21. Indicating a person or thing towards whom or which hostile or adverse action or language is directed; against; = ON *prep.* 21.

See also (*a*) BLOW *v.* 30, COMPLAIN *v.* 6 b, CRY *v.* 21 b, DESIGN *sb.* 1 b, LIE *v.*2 1 b, PEACH *v.* 2, RAGE *v.* 2 b, RAIL *v.*4 1 b, STEAL *v.* 5 e; (*b*) GO *v.* 66 a, MAKE *v.* 81, SEEK *v.* 17.

(*a*) c1200 ORMIN 415 Þatt fand mann nan þing uppon hemm To wreȝenn, ne to tælenn. a1225 *Leg. Kath.* 2204 Þa Porphire iseh feole. Þet me seide hit upon,..dreien to deaðe. c1275 *Passion Our Lord* 241 in *O.E. Misc.* 44 A ueole kunne wise hi lowen him vp-on. c1430 LYDG. *Hors, Shepe & G.* 151 He cryethe affter peasse, compleynnythe vppon þe werres sore. c1440 *Alph. Tales* 12 Þis abbatis..forgaff þaim all þai had saide vppon hur. 1560 DAUS tr. *Sleidane's Comm.* 10 He declareth howe grevously he is complained upon unto the Duke. 1642 LAUD *Diary* 2 Dec., They were sufficiently railed upon in the streets. 1651 H. MORE *Second Lash* in *Enthus. Tri.*, etc. (1656) 253, I now forgive thee heartily for all thy abuses upon me. a1715 BURNET *Own Time* iii. (1900) II. 84 The court carried every question.., though with..a protestation made upon every step that was carried. 1737 WHISTON *Josephus, Hist.* v. xiii. § 1 He also jested upon him. 1753 MISS COLLIER *Art Torment.* ii. ii. (1811) 130 Nor need you be apprehensive of the others telling tales upon you. 1851 F. TEMPLE *Serm.* 274 The unhappy man who has not courage to tell upon himself. 1891 *Law Times* XC. 441/2 The judges..must accept criticism upon their order.

(*b*) c1200 ORMIN 7155 Forr þatt he wennde þatt tatt folle Uppoun himm cumenn wære..for to niþþrenn himm. c1230 *Hali Meid.* 17 Leccherie..secheð earst upon hire, nebbe to nebbe. c1300 *Havelok* 65 Was non so bold.. Þat durste upon his menie bringhe Hunger. 13.. *K. Alis.* 4875 (Laud MS.), Euermore hij beþ werrende, And vpon oþer conquerrende. c1385 CHAUCER *Monk's T.* 537 The peple roos vp-on hym on a nyght. 1393 LANGL. *P. Pl.* C. vii. 106 Ich am wratthe,..wol gladliche smyte Boþe with ston and with staf, and stele vp-on myn enemy. c1450 *Merlin* ii. 21 The hethen assembled a grete oste vpon hem. 1475 *Bk. Noblesse* (Roxb.) 5 They bring assailours uppon this lande. 1518 in Leadam *Star Chamber Cases* (Selden) II. 137 Afterwardes they sought vpon hym at hys boothe with ij clubbys. 1535 COVERDALE 1 *Esdras* i. 27, I am not sent ..to fight agaynst ye, for my warre is upon Euphrates. 1608 *Yorksh. Trag.* vii. 17 It shall be my charge To raise the towne vpon him.

(*c*) 1476 *Acta Auditorum* (1839) 55/2 Elene Tulloch..wes marijt þe tim þat ȝe said det wes recouerit apon hir. 1482 *Cely Papers* (Camden) 85 To see the hurtes and harms he dyd yow uppon your goodes. 1598 BARRET *Theor. Warres* 28 He is to haue great care that his soldiers grow not licencious vpon their poore hosts. 1647 in *Crawford Proclam.* (1910) II. 55/1 Robberies committed by the tories and rebels upon the protestants. 1678 WANLEY *Wond. Lit. World* v. i. § 98 Encroachments upon his Dominions. 1748 *Anson's Voy.* ii. v. 176 The most eligible situation on that coast for cruising upon the enemy. 1754 A. MURPHY *Gray's-Inn Journal* No. 102 ¶ 2 A Design upon one another's Pockets..was introductory of another Crime. 1772 in *Eng. Hist. Rev.* Jan. (1915) 30 He places a number of..sepoys upon them and their families. 1883 *Harper's Mag.* Aug. 448/2 The disadvantages are..unreliability in stays.., hardness upon helms.

b. On or against (a person), by way of vengeance or the like.

a1300 *Cursor M.* 5862 Þat suerd apon hus tak na wrak. c1400 *Pilgr. Sowle* (Caxton, 1483) iii. viii. 55 They alwey hauen sought vengeaunce.., to be wroken vppon tho that ought haue mysliked them. 1470-85 MALORY *Arthur* x. lv. 506 Soone we shold haue ben reuenged vpon the fals knyghtes. 1526- [see REVENGE *v.* 1-2]. 1535 COVERDALE *Isaiah* i. 23, I must ease me of myne enemies, and a venge me vpon them. 1595 *Locrine* ii. v. 86 Reuenge my death vpon his traiterous head. 1860 HOOK *Lives Abps.* I. vii. 377 Edwy had the power to avenge himself upon Dunstan.

ellipt. c1485 *Digby Myst.* (1882) i. 322 A shamefull deth I aske vpon herowde. 1535 COVERDALE *Ps.* lviii. 10 God letteth me se my desyre vpon myne enemies.

c. So as to close in or confine.

1382 WYCLIF 2 *Kings* iv. 5 The woman wente, and closede the dore vpon hir silf and vpon hir children. 1535 COVERDALE *Num.* xvi. 33 They wente downe quycke in to the hell ..And the earth closed vpon them. — *Ps.* lxix. 15 That.. the pitte shut not hir mouth vpon me. 1633 T. ADAMS *Exp.* 2 *Pet.* ii. 5 The Lord..himselfe shut the doore of the Arke upon Noah. 1701 PRIDEAUX *Direct. Ch.-wardens* (1712) 10 If they shall meet..with the Doors lock'd, barred, or bolted upon them. 1844 DICKENS *Mart. Chuz.* xlviii, Softly turning the key upon him as they went out.

22. With respect or regard to; in reference to; touching, concerning; as to; = ON *prep.* 22.

See also AGREE *v.* 10 b, COMPLIMENT *v.* 3, CONCLUDE *v.* 13, CONSULT *v.* 1, INSIST *v.* 3, LOT *sb.* 1, MATTER *sb.* 25 c, PRIDE *v.* 4, TREAT *v.* 2 a, VALUE *v.* 6.

1382 WYCLIF *Ecclus.* xxii. 11 A litil weep vp on the deade, for he restede. 1390 GOWER *Conf.* I. 110, I finde upon Surquiderie, How that..Be olde daies was a King [etc.]. c1400 *Contin. Brut* 321 In þe whiche parlement was treted..how he myȝte best oppon his wrong be avenged. 1439 *Cases bef. King's Council* (Selden) 105 The Kyngis counsaillours examined the persones..upon the ryot. 1484 *Surtees Misc.* (1888) 43 Surmising none othere upon hyme. 1515 in Leadam *Star Chamber Cases* (Selden) II. 85 Two seuerall Writtes..to theym directed to enquere and examyn vpon certen Interrogatoriez. 1584 COGAN *Haven Health* xc. 81 If you will not be at cost vpon spices, you may make a verie sweete water thus. 1609 BIBLE (Douay) 1 *Kings* xxx. 6 The soule of everie man was bitterly affected upon their sonnes, and daughters. 1680 MOXON *Mech. Exerc.* xiii. 227 Having such good Success upon Brass, I improv'd the Invention so, as to make it serve for Wood also. 1710 STEELE *Tatler* No. 150 ¶ 4, I could name Two, who..fell out and parted Beds upon the boiling of a Leg of Mutton. 1760 *Impostors Detected* iii. vii, [She] was not in the least vain or proud upon the encomiums..from every mouth. 1826 *Art of Brewing* (ed. 2) 9 Opinions and practices..completely at variance upon the subject of mashing. 1843 *Blackw. Mag.* LIV. 209, I shall set you at ease..upon that point. 1885 SIR H. C. LOPES in *Law Reports* 14 Q.B.D. 921 This case raises a novel point upon which there is no authority.

b. Denoting the object to or towards which mental activity is directed; = ON *prep.* 22 b.

See also CONSIDER *v.* 11 b, MEDITATE *v.* 4 b, MIN *v.*2 3 b, MIND *sb.*1 7 (quot. 1589), PUT *v.* 27 c, REFLECT *v.* 12, REMEMBER *v.* 4 c, RUN *v.* 70 c, STUDY *v.* 1, 2, THINK *v.*2 3 b, TREAT *v.* 2.

a1300 *Sarmun* xxxvi. in *E. E. P.* (1862) 5 And þench þos wordis her ispoke; for-ȝite ham noȝt ac þench apan. a1300 *Cursor M.* 112 In hir wirschip wald I bigyn A lastand warc apon to myn. 1390 GOWER *Conf.* I. 14 To studie upon the worldes lore Sufficeth now withoute more. a1400 *Isumbras* 427 Sir Ysambrace hym umbithoghte Appone a horse that coles broghte. c1450 *Merlin* iii. 49 The moste remembraunce that I shall haue, shall be vpon yow, and on yowre nedes. 1463 *Bury Wills* (Camden) 34 A remembraunce to thinke vpon me. 1582 N. T. (Rhem.) *Matt.* vii. 28 The multitude were in admiration vpon his doctrine. 1611 BIBLE 1 *Tim.* iv. 15 Meditate vpon these things. 1655 EARL ORRERY *Parthen.* i. viii. 418 Did you reflect upon it with an vnprejudicate opinion. 1719 DE FOE *Crusoe* i. (Globe) 226, I ask'd him what it was he study'd upon. *Ibid.* ii. (Globe) 379 But now the Admiration was turn'd upon another question. 1871 W. ALEXANDER *Johnny Gibb* xlvi, It has a closin'-in heid-piece concern that min's me..upon a mutch that my wife hed ance. 1899 W. J. LOCKE *White Dove* 3 S— was at last able to reflect upon the entire unexpectedness of his presence.

c. Denoting the subject of speech or writing; = ON *prep.* 22 c.

Freq. with verbs, as *rave, talk, write*; AMPLIFY *v.* 7 b, CRITICIZE *v.* 1 b, DISTINGUISH *v.* 8 c, SPEAK *v.* 15.

(*a*) a1390 *Wycliffite Bible* (1850) IV. 303 An other [prologue] vpon Romayns. 1390 GOWER *Conf.* II. 65 Laodomie his lusti wif..Upon a thing wherof sche dradde A lettre ..sende him. 1525 LD. BERNERS *Froiss.* II. Preface, My Preface vpon the fyrst volume of this cronycle. 1533 FRITH *Answ. More* E iij b, The mynde and exposition of the olde Doctours vpon the wordes of Chrystes maundye. 1557 *Tottel's Misc.* (Arb.) 113 Vpon the deceas of W. Ch. 1605 SHAKS. *Macb.* ii. i. 23 We would spend it in some words vpon that Businesse. 1697 DE FOE *Ess. Projects* Pref., I wou'd not adventure to appear in Print upon that Subject. 1709 STEELE *Tatler* No. 114 ¶ 1 Our Discourse chanced to be upon the Subject of Death. 1758 BOSWELL *Lett.* (1924) 6 From 1 to 2, [I] attend a college upon Roman Antiquities. 1801 *Farmer's Mag.* Jan. 66 A series of animadversions..published upon it in a provincial paper. 1824 BYRON *Juan* xvi. xlvii, She..Made epigrams..Upon her friends. 1893 STEVENSON *Catriona* xii, He engaged the goodwife..with some compliments upon the rizzoring of our haddocks.

†(*b*) 1483 CAXTON *G. de la Tour* 107 Now I shalle telle yow upon this matere of a good lady. 1528 in Roy *Rede me*, etc. (Arb.) 152 Austyne sayeth vppon the psalter, ye clergy occupyeth the secular lordshyppe secularly. 1574 R. BRISTOW *Treatise* 47 Vpon these two, Christ..and his Church, ronneth al the Scriptures. 1581 FULKE in *Confer.* iii. (1583) Q ij b I wil not vouchsafe to replie vpon this answere. 1605 CAMDEN *Rem.* 143 But he repaied him with this re-allusion vppon the name. 1710 STEELE *Tatler* No. 14 ¶ 1 My Design of observing upon Things. 1748 RICHARDSON *Clarissa* (1811) I. 185, I..am the less solicitous..to amplify upon the contents of either.

(*c*) 1481 in Blades *W. Caxton* (1882) 231 The polytyque book..whiche that Tullius wrote vpon the disputacons [etc.]. c1600 W. FOWLER *Wks.* (S.T.S.) 9 A Fvneral Sonet, written vpon the death of..Elizabeth Dowglas. 1709 ADDISON *Tatler* No. 163 ¶ 3 The Sonnet..was written upon a Lady. 1776 JOHNSON in *Boswell* (1904) I. 647 A man who has never been engaged in trade himself may undoubtedly write well upon trade. 1791 'G. GAMBADO' *Ann. Horsem.* (1809) 55 Had they spent as much time in riding upon turnips, as they have in writing upon them.

III. In other senses.

†**23.** From (a person or persons), esp. by means of hostile attack; = ON *prep.* 23. *Obs.* (Cf. 21.)

Const. with verbs, as *make, nim, recover, take, win*; also CONQUER *v.* 2 b, GAIN *v.*2 4.

1338 R. BRUNNE *Chron.* (1810) 22 Uppon Saynt Edmunde Northfolk he nam. 1387 TREVISA *Higden* (Rolls) VI. 291 Egbertus..took Chestre uppon þe Britouns. 1412-20 LYDG. *Chron. Troy* iii. 3423 Troyens han wonne a-geyn her londe Vp-on Grekis. 1483 in *Acta Dom. Conc.* II. Introd. 114 Quhilk some was recoverit be..Dure apone the said Schir Johne. a1533 LD. BERNERS *Huon* 527 A ryche shyp, the whiche was wonne vpon the sowdans men. 1568 GRAFTON *Chron.* II. 194 They wanne dayly and yerely vpon the sayd Turkes, so that they had..much of the landes. 1643 PRYNNE *Doom Cowardice & Treach.* 6 At last by such forcible assaults the said Towne was taken upon the said Robert. 1654 BRAMHALL *Just Vind.* i. (1661) 2 Whatsoever the Popes of Rome gained upon us. 1660 *Nicholas Papers* (Camden) IV. 187 The prizes made by the Ostenders upon the Kings subjects. 1742 LEONI *Palladio's Archit.* II. 66 The Spoils made upon Pyrrhus King of Epirus.

†**24.** In respect of; = ON *prep.* 24. *Obs.*

a1310 in Wright *Lyric P.* v. 26 He is blosme opon bleo brihtest under bis. 13.. *Cursor M.* 2034 (Gött.), He lis here vte, cum se þu sal, Naked apon his limes all.

25. On (a musical instrument).

c1384 CHAUCER *H. Fame* iii. 110 Ther herd I pleyen vpon an harpe..Orpheus ful craftely. 1524 *Reg. Privy Seal Scot.* I. 499/1 Playing apoun organis in the Kingis chapell. 1552 in Feuillerat *Revels Edw. VI* (1914) 89, I haue provided one to plaie vppon a kettell drom. 1621 BRATHWAIT *Nat. Embassie* Ded., Able to play vpon an oaten pipe. 1683 KENNETT tr. *Erasm. on Folly* 68 No more skill..than a Pig playing upon the Organs. 1709 MRS. MANLEY *Secret Mem.* I. 149 A great many of 'em..can toot, toot, toot, it upon a Pipe. 1804-6 SYD. SMITH *Mor. Philos.* (1850) 175 Any air..performed upon such an instrument as the bagpipe. 1842 TENNYSON *Locksley Hall* 2 When you want me, sound upon the bugle-horn. 1876 GRANT *Burgh Sch. Scot.* ii. 380 Discoursing laments upon the Bagpipes.

26. Denoting advance from or improvement on some standard, etc.

See also IMPROVE *v.* 8, IMPROVEMENT 6 b, REFINE *v.* 10.

1662 EVELYN *Chalcogr.* 50 Which afterwards Sebastian Serli refining upon composed the better part of that excellent book of his. 1711 ADDISON *Spect.* No. 44 ¶ 6 The French have therefore refin'd too much upon Horace's Rule. 1782 PRIESTLEY *Corrupt. Chr.* I. iii. 301 An improvement was made upon this doctrine. 1843 *Blackw. Mag.* LIV. 197 Mr. Collins has improved greatly upon his last year's exhibition. 1859 GLADSTONE *Glean.* (1879) II. 171 If he continues to advance upon himself as he has advanced heretofore.

†**Upo·n**, *adv.* *Obs.* [Ellipt. use of prec.]

1. a. On it; on or upon the surface.

1307 *York Memo. Bk.* (Surtees) I. 181 Lether with the here apon. 1382 WYCLIF *Ecclus.* xxxiii. 6 An hors courser ..vnder eche man vpon sittende neȝeth. 1547 in Feuillerat *Revels Edw. VI* (1914) 13 Changeable Taffita stripyd vpon with blewe golde dornix. 1567 in *Rep. Hist. MSS. Comm.* (1907) IV. 90 A clothe of blacke and reid wroughte with goulde vpon. 1596 SHAKS. *Merch. V.* ii. vii. 57 A coyne that beares the figure of an Angell Stampt in gold, but that's insculpt vpon.

b. On one's person, as an article of apparel.

a1366 CHAUCER *Rom. Rose* 364 A chapelet, so semly oon, Ne werede neuer mayde vpon. c1386 — *Friar's T.* 84 He [*sc.* a gay yeoman] hadde vp-on a courtepy of grene. 1390 GOWER *Conf.* II. 246 And sche..hir scherte dede upon And caste on hire a mantel clos. 1446 LYDG. *Two Nightingale P.* ii. 123 Whan Crist Ihesu was for mankynd dede And had vpon a garnement ful newe. 1513 BRADSHAW *St. Werburge* i. 1301 His gloues, his gyrdell, the kynge had vpon. 1611 BIBLE 2 *Cor.* v. 2 Desiring to be clothed vpon with our house, which is from heauen. [1643 CARYL *Expos. Job* 1885 Those bodies of Saints..shall be cloathed upon with a house which is from Heaven.]

2. Into or to a position on a surface or object; so as to be put or placed on the thing in question.

1382 WYCLIF *Num.* xvii. 2 Of echon the name thow shalt vpon write [L. *superscribes*] to his ȝerde. c1400 *Lanfranc's Cirurgie* 219 Make it abrood upon a cloob & leie it vpon hoot. c1440 *Pallad. on Husb.* vii. 106 Do donge vppon and vmbe on euery side. 1534 TINDALE *Luke* xx. 18 But on whosoever it faul vpon, it wyll grynde him to powder.

b. In a direction towards something indicated or specified.

c1400 *Apol. Loll.* 2 Þer for, if we wil, we mai calle bischoppis, locars up on. 1593-1611 [see LOOK *v.* 46].

3. On or upon that (in time or order); thereafter, thereupon. Esp. coupled with *anon, near, soon.*

See also HEREUPON, THEREUPON, WHEREUPON *advs.*

14.. *Lydgate's Bochas* v. 2898 Afftir whos deth anon vpon [*MS. Harl. 1245* vpon anoon] suyng, To Euergetes..She was ageyn ioyned in mariage. c1440 *Generydes* 1926 Thanne came the prince of Cesare sone vppon. *Ibid.* 6632 Kyng auferius fell seke anon vppon. 1523 FITZHERB. *Husb.* § 12 So that they be sowen ere the begynnynge of Marche, or sone vpon. 1602 SHAKS. *Ham.* i. ii. 179 *Ham.* I thinke it was to see my Mothers Wedding. *Hor.* Indeed my Lord, it followed hard vpon. 1603 — *Meas. for M.* iv. vi. 14 The.. Citizens Haue hent the gates, and very neere vpon The Duke is entring. 1606 — *Tr. & Cr.* iv. iii. 3 It is great morning, and the houre prefixt..Comes fast vpon.

4. By way of addition, increase, etc.

a1485 FORTESCUE *Wks.* (1869) 487 Why will God put uppon newe turments ovir the travaile of ther labour?

†**Upon**, obs. var. OPEN *a.* (Cf. UPEN *a.*)

13.. *E. E. Allit. P.* B. 453 Þenne wafte he vpon his wyndowe. 14.. *Sir Beues* (E.) 87/1691 Anon þe gate he vpon look.

†**Uponland**, *adv.* *Obs.* Also 3-4 vp o londe, 5 *Sc.* upolande; 5-6 vp of land, and UPALAND. [f. *uppe* UP *adv.*2 + ON *prep.* 1 b (O *prep.*1) + LAND *sb.* Cf. UPLAND *adv.*1] In the country, as opposed to the town.

α. a900 in Thorpe *Anc. Laws* (1840) I. 118 Be ciepe-monna fore uppe on londe. c1386 CHAUCER *Prol.* 702 A poure person dwellynge vp on lond. 1430-40 LYDG. *Bochas* Prol. 84 Folkis that duellyn vp-on lande. c1480 HENRYSON *Twa Mice* i, The vther [mouse] wynnit vponland. — *Sheep & Dog* xviii, Ane schireff stout, Quhilk..dytis all the pure men vpon land [1568 *Bann. MS.* vp of land].

β. c1300 *Havelok* 763 Gode paniers..to beren fish inne, Vp o-londe to selle and fonge. 14.. *Burgh Laws Scotland* xxxiv, It is for to wyt that men upolande may borow thair pundis thryis.

γ. c1440 *Alph. Tales* 173 On a tyme he was lugid on a night in a howse vp of land. 1568 [see α. above].

b. *John Uponland*, a rustic. (Cf. UPALAND b.)

a1568 in *Bannatyne MS.* (Hunter. Club) 269/26 This said Johne vponland.

†**Uponlandis**, obs. Sc. var. UPLANDS *a.*

c1480 HENRYSON *Fables* heading (Harl. MS.), The Taill of the vponlandis Mous and the burges Mous.

†**Uponon(e**, *adv.* *Obs. rare.* Also uponan. [f. UPON *prep.* + ONE *pron.* 30 f.] = ANON *adv.* 4.

c1400 *Destr. Troy* 2418, I onswaret hym esely euyn vponon. *Ibid.* 6712 Polidamas..can fight, With his Enmeis full egurly, euer vpon-one.

†**Uppe**, *v.* *Obs.* Forms: 1 yppan, 2 ippen, 3 uppen. [OE. *yppan* (also *geyppan*), f. *upp* UP *adv.*1, giving southern ME. *üppen*, midland *ippen*. Cf. ON. *yppa* (MDa. *yppe*), and OHG. *ûffan* (MHG. *ûffen, ûfen*, obs. G. *aufen*).] *trans.* To display or make manifest; to bring to notice; to make known.

c897 K. ÆLFRED *Gregory's Past. C.* lix. 451 Ðæt we hit ..forðy yppen ðæt mon God herige. c900 tr. *Baeda's Hist.* iv. xxv. (1890) 352 Se Godes mon..ba unrotnesse his heortan ..ypte & cyðde. a1000 *Colloq. Ælfric* in Wr.-Wülcker 102 Ic ne deor yppan þe digla ure. c1200 *Trin. Coll. Hom.* 165 Here wombe is here crist, and all iuele forbisne hie ippen of hem seluen. a1225 *Ancr. R.* 146 Hercneð nu..hu hit is to uppen & ȝelpen of god dede. *Ibid.*, Ancre þet was iwuned ..wel uorte wurchen, & seoððen..uppede hit & scheawede.

Uppen: see UP *prep.*1

U·ppen, *v.* *E. Angl.* ? *Obs.* [f. UP *adv.*1 + -EN 5. Cf. UPPE *v.*] *trans.* To bring up, mention, disclose.

1565 GOLDING *Ovid's Met.* iii. 344 When that after mickle talke..Joves name was upned. 1567 *Ibid.* xii. 179 Every wyght Delyghts too uppen oftentymes..The perills and the narrow brunts. 1583 — *Calvin on Deut.* xxi. 125/2 It woulde not haue booted at all to haue vppened neuer so many thinges by parcellmeale. 1823 E. MOOR *Suffolk Words* 460 Yeow didnt uppen it did ye?

Up-pe·nt, *pa. pple.* (UP- 5.) 1600 FAIRFAX *Tasso* x. xlii, With this siege, if we be long vp pent, Famine I doubt. 1614 GORGES *Lucan* i. 18 A proud Courser..in the stable close vp-pent. 1870 A. O'SHAUGHNESSY *Poems, Neglected Harp* 15 These wondrous melodies up-pent And languishing in me.

U·pper, *sb.* [From next.]

1. That part of a boot or shoe above the sole and welt. Usu. pl.

1845 J. COULTER *Adv. in Pacific* ix. 112 My shoes were.. only held together by passing straps of goat-skin under the soles, over the uppers. 1862 *Catal. Internat. Exhib., Brit.* II. No. 4769, Grained leather; machine-closed uppers. 1880 *Times* 21 Sept. 4/4 Forcing the needle through the outer sole, the edge of the upper, and the insole.

attrib. 1875 KNIGHT *Dict. Mech.*, *Upper-machines*,..those for cutting out or preparing the uppers of boots or shoes.

b. *U.S.* A cloth gaiter for wearing above the shoe over the ankle (*Cent. Dict.* 1891).

c. *On one's uppers*, in poor or reduced circumstances; having hard luck. *colloq.* (orig. *U.S.*).

1891 *Cent. Dict.* s.v. 1901 *Munsey's Mag.* XXV. 432/1 The rumor whirled about the Street that Greener was in difficulties. Financial ghouls..said..'Greener is on his uppers'. 1905 R. MARSH *Spoiler of Men* xxv. 227 'I'm on my uppers..I want money.' 'So do we all.'

2. An upper jaw, dental plate, tooth, etc.

1878 C. HUNTER *Mech. Dentistry* 79 In the case of edentulous or nearly edentulous uppers or lowers. 1900 *Hutchinson's Arch. Surg.* XI. 222 On the backs of both uppers.. there are now peculiar changes. 1904 F. P. DUNNE in *Westm. Gaz.* 14 Oct. 1/3 He [*sc.* a child] has two uppers an' four lowers.

3. *U.S.* A log or piece of sawed lumber of superior grade.

1877 *Lumberman's Gazette* 24 May, The finest stock of uppers to be found in the country.

Upper (ʌ·pəɹ), *a.* Also 4-6 **vpper**, 5-7 **vper**; 6 **hoper**. [f. UP *a.* + -ER 3. Cf. MDu. *upper* (Du. and Flem. *opper*), LG. *upper, üpper*, MSw., Norw. *yppare*, older Da. *yppere*, better.] Comparative of UP *a.*, and signifying 'higher', 'over', 'loftier', 'top' (in contrast to *lower, nether, under*). In some senses replacing the earlier UVER, OVER *adjs.*

I. 1. Occupying, comprising or consisting of, rising or more elevated ground (and usu. further in the interior). Freq. in proper names of districts, etc.

13.. *K. Alis.* 5691 (Laud MS.), Þe kyng þennes went forþ.. in to ynde in þe norþ, Þat is ycleped..þe vpper ynde. 1526 TINDALE *Acts* xix. 1 Paul passed thorow the vpper costes and cam to Ephesus. 1598 GRENEWEY *Tacitus, Ann.* xii. vii. (1622) 163 About the same time vpper Germany quaked with feare. 1601 SHAKS. *Jul. C.* v. i. 3 You said the Enemy would..keepe the Hilles and vpper Regions. a1660 *Contemp. Hist. Irel.* (Ir. Archæol. Soc.) I. 160 Either to Vper Ormond or the countie of Clare. a1676 HALE *Prim. Orig. Man.* (1677) 219 If Inundations prevailed in Greece and those upper Countries, Egypt..could not easily escape them. 1728 CHAMBERS *Cycl.* s.v. *Nimbis*, The Nimbis is seen on the Medals..of the upper Empire. 1791 GEO. III in *Ann. Reg., St. Papers* 124* His majesty thinks..that.. his province of Quebec..should be divided into two separate provinces, to be called the province of Upper Canada, and the province of Lower Canada. 1849 EASTWICK *Dry Leaves* 22 My vessel being an Upper Sindh boat. 1863 LYELL *Antiq. Man* 43 For the river to bring down from the upper country so large a quantity of earthy matter. 1864- [see WARD *sb.*2 20].

b. Of peoples: Occupying a higher or more inland district.

1617 MORYSON in C. L. Falkiner *Illustr. Irish Hist.* (1904) 215 The Iberni, called the upper Irish, inhabiting about Beer-haven and Baltimore. c1790 *Encycl. Brit.* (ed. 3) V. 484/1 The Lower and Upper Cossacks,..and a part of the Don Cossacks.

c. Situated in, located on, a higher or loftier position, high ground, etc.; more elevated or lofty; higher in altitude.

Freq. in the proper names of hamlets, villages, etc.

1467 *Rolls of Parlt.* V. 586/2 Landes and Tenementes in Netherburneham, Upperburneham, West Wode. 1509 HAWES *Past. Pleas.* xxxii. (Percy Soc.) 159 After this, dame Correccion..first..led me to the upper ward. 1611 BIBLE *Joshua* xv. 19 He gaue her the vpper springs, and the nether springs. 1687 MIÈGE *Gt. Fr. Dict.* ii. s.v., The Upper Region of the Air. 1708 WATTS *Poems* (1743) ii. 160 Around the golden Streets they rove, And bless the Mansions of the upper Skies. 1778 *Encycl. Brit.* (ed. 2) III. 1604/2 The bason [of the lock] being filled with water by an upper sluice to the level of the waters above, a vessel may ascend thro' the upper gate. *Ibid.* 1605/1 So that the water in the lock may rise to a level with the water in the upper canal. 1796 MME. D'ARBLAY *Camilla* V. 296 [She] thought herself in the upper regions, where happiness..consisted of perpetual admiration. 1819 SHELLEY *Peter Bell 3rd* ii. vii, Each had an upper stream of thought. 1857 HAWTHORNE *Eng. Note-bks.* (1870) II. 414 Those misty upper-depths seemed almost to be hung with clouds. 1862 J. BROWN *Minchmoor* (1864) 11 You can get a glimpse of the upper woods of Abbotsford. 1873 GEIKIE *Phys. Geog.* § 89 [These] clouds.. are driven along by upper currents of air. 1883 *Good Words* Aug. 529/2 Those plants and animals which live in the 'upper littoral'.

fig. 1647 N. BACON *Disc. Govt. Eng.* i. lvii. 166 To make him yet more bold, he had the upper ground of the heire.

d. Occupying or forming (part of) the higher or highest portion or division of a building.

1522-3 *Rec. St. Mary at Hill* 317 A chest in the vpper vestry. 1557 BIBLE (Genev.) *Acts* i. 13 They went vp into an vpper chamber. 1597 J. PAYNE *Royal Exch.* 15 The thrid sort be retaylers in the vpper shopps. 1611 FLORIO, *Soprastanza*, an vpper-lodging. 1665 in *Verney Mem.* (1907) II. 247 A lower and an upper chamber. 1764 HARMER *Observ.* iii. § 1. 89 An upper-story, which is flat on the top. 1779 *Mirror* No. 9, Some of the upper boxes were filled with ladies. 1846 MRS. A. MARSH *Father Darcy* II. xiv. 254 He used to lie..upon the floor of his little upper room.

fig. 1647 TRAPP *Comm.* 2 *Cor.* v. 1 In the wonderful frame of man's body the bones are the timber work, the head the upper-lodging. 1699- [see STORY *sb.*2 1 c]. 1796 [see GARRET *sb.*1 3]. 1870 BREWER *Dict. Phrase & Fable* 924/1 'Ill-furnished in the upper story'; a head without brains. 1877 *Holderness Gloss.* 152/1 He's a bit wake (weak) iv his upper-garret.

Comb. 1697 DRYDEN *Æneis* Ded. e 3 b, Our Upper-Gallery Audience in a Play-House.

2. With partitive terms, esp. *end, part, side.*

Occas. hyphened or as one word, as †*upperhand, upperside.*

1484 CAXTON *Fables of Æsop* v. vii, He to whome men purposen to doo somme euylle tourn, syth men holden hym at auauntage, men muste putte hym self at the vpper side of hym. c1489 — *Blanchardyn* xlvi. 178 The noble mayden ..ryght fyersli..began to loke vpon hym, drawyng herselfe to the vpperhande of hym. 1526 *Pilgr. Perf.* (W. de W. 1531) 3 b, The vpper parte of this foresayd ymage. 1568 *Freiris Berwik* 22 The towne,..the castell and the land, The he wallis vpoun the vpper hand. 1570 BILLINGSLEY *Euclid* xi. xxix. 341 Lines..which ioyne together the angles of the vpper and nether bases. a1600 in *Child Ballads* II. 245 2 A grave, a grave,..to put these lovers in; But lay my lady on the upper hand. 1674 HOOKE *Animadv.* 52 The upper side thereof must be plained exactly smooth and flat. 1731 P. MILLER *Gard. Dict.* s.v. *Melo*, The Upperside of the Hotbeds where your early Melons..are planted. 1769 FALCONER *Dict. Marine* (1780), *Down-haul*,..a rope..tied to the upper-corner of the sail. 1778 MISS BURNEY *Evelina* xxi, Driving us to the upper end of Piccadilly. 1805 R. JAMESON *Char. Min.* (1816) 204 When..[the crystal] has upon its upper and under parts, faces that alternate with each other. 1868 *Rep. U.S. Commissioner Agric.* (1869) 360 The well and the opening in the upper side [of the road]. 1886 J. BARROWMAN *Sc. Mining Terms* 69 The upper portion of a [coal] seam.

b. Of surfaces. †*Upperface*, = SUPERFICIES.

1583 STUBBES *Anat. Abus.* ii. B 3, Then came there fire.. and consumed them all, from the vpper face of the earth. 1594 BLUNDEVIL *Exerc.* iii. (1597) 128 b, Superficies or vpperface, is that which onely hath length and breadth. 1596 *Edward III*, i. ii. 152 Where the vpper turfe of earth doth boast His..party colloured cost, Delue there. 1611 COTGR., *Rez*,..the superficies, or vpper face of a plaine, or leuell peece of ground. 1728 BRADLEY *Dict. Bot.* s.v. *Marrubium*, Leaves..smooth and woolly underneath.., but somewhat.. rugged on the Upperside. 1733 TULL *Horse-hoeing Husb.* 404 The Upper-surface of the Fore-end of the Beam. 1826 KIRBY & SP. *Entomol.* III. 364 *Facies*,..the upper surface of the head. 1884 COUES *Key N. Amer. Birds* 110 The upper and under surfaces of the wing.

3. a. That forms the higher of a pair of corresponding things or sets. Also occas. = uppermost.

Upper-case, Printing (quots. 1683-): see CASE *sb.*2 9.

c1460 [*upper crust*: see 12 a]. 1524 *State Papers Hen. VIII*, II. 117 He shall endevour hymself to cause the Kynges subjectes..to have the upper berdes to be shaven. 1530 TINDALE *Deut.* xxiv. 6 No man shall take the nether or the vpper milstone to pledge. 1533 *MS. Rawl. D.* 776 fol. 157 b, The vpper fflowryng of the same wharffe. 1609 BIBLE (Douay) *Exod.* xii. 22 Sprinkle the uppertransome of the doore therwith. *Ibid.* 23 The bloud on the uppersil, and on both the postes. 1611 COTGR. s.v. *Espée*, The vpper boords of a Vine-presse. 1683 MOXON *Mech. Exerc., Printing* ii. § 3. 19 The Whole Vpper-Case is divided into Ninety eight square Boxes. 1726 SWIFT *Gulliver* ii. vii, I first mounted to the upper step of the ladder [= a movable pair of stairs]. 1833 LOUDON *Encycl. Archit.* § 691 The two upper branches or rails of the trunk, or upright piece. 1852 SEIDEL *Organ* 37 A couple of bellows..consist first of an upper and under board. 1867 SMYTH *Sailor's Word-bk.* 708 *Upper masts*, the top-mast, topgallant-mast, and royal-mast. 1873 *Routledge's Yng. Gentl. Mag.* July 503/1 An upper-iron being screwed on to the lower one to turn the shaving back a little.

fig. 1788 *New London Mag.* 264 One blow well told to the upper tire (the head), tells better than three below.

Comb. 1738 CHAMBERS *Cycl.* s.v. *Letter*, Printers distinguish their letters into capital..or upper-case letters,..and.. small, or under-case letters. 1771 LUCKOMBE *Hist. Print.* 261 [These letters] are not reckoned..among Upper-case Sorts.

b. *spec.* in *Anat.*, etc. (Cf. SUPERIOR *a.* 11.)

1546 [see 16 a]. 1548 VICARY *Anat.* v. (1577) F ij b, The bones or bony partes, fyrste of the Cheekes be two;..of the vpper Mandibile, two. 1610 HEALEY *St. Aug. Citie of God* 335 [The] crocodile..moueth his vpper chappe. 1646 SIR T. BROWNE *Pseud. Ep.* 108 It conveyeth it into the duodenum or upper gut, thence into the lower bowells. 1728 CHAMBERS *Cycl.* s.v. *Maxillæ*, The..Upper Jaw, is immoveable in Man. 1774 GOLDSM. *Nat. Hist.* V. 274 The upper chap [of the parrot], as well as the lower, are both moveable. 1826 KIRBY & SP. *Entomol.* III. xxxiii. 374 The Upper or Primary Wings. 1838 *Penny Cycl.* X. 141/2 When the upper lid [of the eye] is raised. 1850 J. F. COOPER *Ways of Hour* I. 104 His front upper teeth were all gone. 1884 COUES *N. Amer. Birds* 110 The upper Primary coverts, or coverts of the primaries.

Comb. 1879 RUSKIN *St. Mark's Rest* Suppl. ii. 20 The man's thigh and upper-arm bones. 1896 *Godey's Mag.* April 430/1 His upper-limb muscles.

c. *Upper bench*, the name during the exile of Charles II of the KING'S BENCH. Now *Hist.*

1649 *Acts Interregnum* (1911) II. 108 Three or more of the Justices of the upper Bench. 1651 in *Kitchin's Jurisdictions* (1653) 579 The most Vsual Writs which have been used in the Kings Bench, and are most like to continue in that Court, now called the Vpper-Bench. a1675 WHITELOCKE *Mem.* (1682) 375 Voted [on 12 Feb. 1649] that the Kings-Bench Court should be called the Upper Bench.

d. *Orange Upperwing*, a European noctuid moth, *Hoporina croceago.*

1832 RENNIE *Brit. Butterfl. & Moths* 85 The Orange Upperwing..appears in September;..first pair [of wings] golden orange..; second pair white. 1869 E. NEWMAN *Brit. Moths* 373/1.

4. †**a.** *Upper-stock*: (see STOCK *sb.*1 40). Usu. pl.

1535 in *Archaeologia* IX. 251 A paire of upper stockis of purple veluette,..also..a newe paire of nether stockis. 1548 *Nottingham Rec.* III. 220 One peyr blacke hoys, the upper stokes blake velvet. c1570 *Pride & Lowl.* (1841) 19 His upper stockes of sylken grogerane. 1606 G. W[OODCOCKE] *Hist. Ivstine* xxxviii. 118 He conueyed a dagger in the vpperstock of his hose. [1821 SCOTT *Kenilw.* xxxi, His upper stocks of white velvet, lined with cloth of silver.]

b. That covers or clothes an upper part of the body, esp. the chest or shoulders. (Cf. 5 a.)

Freq. from 1579 to 1625 in *upper body.*

1579 *Aldeburgh Rec.* in *N. & Q.* 12th Ser. VII. 328/2 An upper bodye and lyninge and a neckercher for hir. 1587 in *Antiquary* (1896) XXXII. 76 For an upper body and lace, xxiij d. 1625 FLETCHER *Fair Maid* ii. ii, Nothing but her vpper bodies. 1871 S. MATEER *Land of Charity* xxi. 278 A cloth or scarf laid over the shoulder, called the 'upper cloth,' as worn by the Súdra women. 1895 C. SILVESTER HORNE *Story of L. M. S.* 298 In 1858, the 'upper cloth' riots broke out again.

5. a. Of garments, etc.: Worn above or outside another; outer, exterior; = OVER *a.* 1 b. (Cf. 4 b.)

1526 TYNDALE *John* xiii. 4 Iesus..layde a syde hys vpper garments. 1547 in Feuillerat *Revels Edw. VI* (1914) 10 Thupper & nether Baces & thunder sleves of clothe of golde. 1598 FLORIO, *Sourafodro*, a false vpper scabbard. 1611 —, *Soprabenda*, an vpper scarfe. 1615 SANDYS *Trav.* 14 Their arme-pits: from whence the skirts flow loosely, fringed below; the vpper shorter than the neather. 1645 RUTHERFORD *Tri. Faith* 305 Christ clothed with love,..and yet his upper garment is vengeance. 1686 *Lond. Gaz.* No. 2193/4 A brown coloured upper Coat. 1759 JOHNSON *Rasselas* xxxviii, When my upper vest was taken off. 1778 CLARA REEVE *Old English Baron* 84 You may take off her upper garments, and any thing of value. 1796 *Grose's Dict. Vulgar T.* (ed. 3), *Upper Benjamin*, a great coat. 1812 J. H. VAUX *Flash Dict.*, *Upper-Ben, Upper-Benjamin, Upper-Tog*, a great coat. 1819 SCOTT *Ivanhoe* ii, The upper dress of this personage resembled that of his companion in shape. 1850 THACKERAY *Pendennis* iii, A white upper-coat ornamented with cheese-plate buttons.

fig. a1634 CHAPMAN *Bussy d'Ambois* v. (1641) 65 Note what he wants? He wants his upper weed, He wants his life, and body.

Comb. 1840 THACKERAY *Pict. Rhapsody* Wks. 1899 XIII. 350 A hideous dress, with upper-Benjamin buttons.

b. Furthest removed from the door or entrance; innermost. Usually with *end* (cf. 2).

1590 SPENSER *F. Q.* ii. ix. 27 Thence she them brought into a stately Hall..At th' upper end there sate..a comely personage. a1613 OVERBURY *Newes* Misc. Wks. (1890) 191 The best company makes the upper end of the table, and not the salt-cellar. 1667 MILTON *P. L.* x. 446 His high Throne..at th' upper end Was plac't in regal lustre. 1711 STEELE *Spect.* No. 129 ¶ 1 We were now arrived at the Upper-end of the Gallery. 1819 SCOTT *Ivanhoe* iii, The walls of this upper end of the hall.

fig. a1672 WILKINS *Nat. Relig.* 331 So only those at the upper end of the world are capable of being counted rich. 1714 R. FIDDES *Pract. Disc.* ii. 157 Sometimes the most profligate sinners are seated at the upper end of the world.

6. a. Said of the surface of the earth and things upon it, in contrast to the under or nether regions.

1667 MILTON *P. L.* x. 422 For those Appointed to sit there, had left thir charge, Flown to the upper World. 1679 C. NESSE *Antichrist* Ded., You may improve this upper-ground whereon you stand. 1697 DRYDEN *Virg. Georg.* iv. 699 The lovely Bride In safety goes,..Longing the common Light again to share, And draw the vital breath of upper Air. 1815 WORDSW. *Artegal & Elidure* 53 Of Arthur,—who, to upper light restored,..Shall lift his country's fame above the polar star! 1822 BYRON *Vis. Judgem.* xii, He's dead— and upper earth with him has done: He's buried. 1887 BROWNING *Apollo & Fates* 10 *The Fates.* (Below. Darkness.)..We..Deal to each mortal his dole of light On earth —the upper, the glad, the bright.

Comb. 1862 SMILES *Engineers* III. 9 The upper-ground workmen employed at the coal-pits.

b. Constituting or forming a stratum, layer, bed, etc., lying nearer the earth's surface or formed later in time; *spec.* of stratifications of more recent formation than another of that character and name.

See also 12 b, GREENSAND 1, OOLITE 2-3, SILURIAN *a.* 2 b.

1696 WHISTON *The. Earth* 77 Our upper strata..being generally factitious, or acquir'd at the Universal Deluge. 1733 TULL *Horse-Hoeing Husb.* 251 The..Hills whereof the Upper-Stratum (or Staple) is Mould. c1775 in *Encycl. Brit.* (ed. 2) IV. 2526/1 If a ditch..penetrate through the upper stratum of clay. 1839 MURCHISON *Silur. Syst.* xlv. 605 The Ludlow and Wenlock Formations, or Upper Silurian Rocks. 1852 SEDGWICK in *London Lit. Gazette* 338/3 A part of my Upper Cambrian series. 1873 DAWSON *Earth & Man* iv. 56 The Lower Silurian is the Upper Cambrian of Sedgwick. 1873 E. HULL *Coal-fields Gt. Brit.* (ed. 3) 192 The strata overlying the 'Upper-foot', or 'Bullion-coal'. 1886 J. BARROWMAN *Sc. Mining Terms* 69 *Upper-leaf*, the upper portion of a seam which is separated by a parting into two portions.

fig. 1859 G. MEREDITH *R. Feverel* xix, Tossed into the upper stratum of civilized life. 1877, 1890 [see STRATUM 6].

Comb. 1865 LUBBOCK *Preh. Times* 299 The height at which the upper-level gravels stand above the present water-line. 1890 *Science-Gossip* XXVI. 146 The upper limestone masses.

7. Occurring or taking place in, directed towards, a higher or the highest position. *Upper cut*, in Pugilism (see quot. 1897).

1607 TOPSELL *Four-f. Beasts* 402 An vpper attaint or ouerreach vpon the backe sinnew of the shanke. 1728 CHAMBERS *Cycl.* s.v. *Attaint*, The Farriers distinguish upper Attaints, given by the Toe of the Hind-foot upon the sinew of the Fore-leg,—And nether Attaints. 1815 J. SMITH *Panorama Sci. & Art* II. 135 The further admission of steam to that side during the upper stroke [of the piston]. 1856 *Sat. Rev.* II. 658/2 Resorting to means of defence against which cross-buttocks and upper-cuts..will do very little good indeed. 1867 SMYTH *Sailor's Word-bk.* 708 *Upper transit*, the passage of a circumpolar star over the meridian above the pole. 1897 *Encycl. Sport* I. 139 *Upper cut*,..a counter, delivered upwards with either hand, when an opponent leads off or rushes in with his head down.

II. 8. Occupying a higher (or the highest) position, station, or rank; superior in authority, place, etc.

1477 *Extr. Aberd. Reg.* (1844) I. 36 That Alexander..be continevit vpper and principale maister of wark. 1526 TINDALE *Acts* xxii. 26 The vnder captayne..went to the vpper captayne, and tolde hym. 1561 in *Maitl. Club Misc.* III. 209 We hawe command of ye vppir poweris to put the same in executione. 1647 *Bury Wills* (Camden) 195 At the disposing of..God, whoe is the onely supreme and vpper Lord of all. 1710 STEELE *Tatler* No. 180 ¶ 4 The Abatement which they suffer when paid, by the Extortion of Upper Servants. 1771 LUCKOMBE *Hist. Print.* 86 He was upper-warden of the Stationer's Company. 1836-9 DICKENS *Sk. Boz, Gt. Winglebury Duel*, I am the upper-boots..; the other man's my man, as..does odd jobs. 1847 C. BRONTE *J. Eyre* v, One of the upper teachers..installed herself at the top of one table. 1862 TROLLOPE *Orley F.* II. 248, 'I was housemaid at Orley Farm.' 'Were you upper or under there?'

b. Higher or highest in respect of influence, wealth, office, or dignity; wealthy, aristocratic, influential.

Freq. since c1890, esp. with *class* (cf. CLASS *sb.* 2).

1825 J. WILSON in *Blackw. Mag.* March 373, I wad aiblins introduce the upper ranks intil the wark. 1837 CARLYLE *Fr. Rev.* i. vii. ii, The best-informed Upper-Circles. 1839 — *Chartism* v, The oppressing or neglecting upper classes. 1844- [see 18]. 1856 EMERSON *Eng. Traits, Universities*, These seminaries are finishing schools for the upper classes, and not for the poor.

Comb. 1837 CARLYLE *Fr. Rev.* ii. v. ix, The riband-cockade, as a symptom of Feuillant Upper-class temper. 1890 *Spectator* 3 May, The upper-class Arabs and Turks. 1897 MARY KINGSLEY *W. Africa* 318 This aristocracy has sub-divisions, the M'pongwe of Gaboon are the upper-circle tribe.

absol. 1898 G. MEREDITH *Odes Fr. Hist.* 12 They, the triumphant tenant towering upper, were under; They, violators of home, dared hope an inviolate home.

9. Consisting of or including more advanced studies or more proficient students; having a higher place or standing in studies or learning.

1629 WADSWORTH *Pilgr.* iii. 15 The Students of the three vnder schooles, go vp to those of the vpper. 1740 J. CLARKE *Educ. Youth* (ed. 3) 209 The Boys of the upper Classes may be admitted. 1749 FIELDING *Tom Jones* ii. iii, His scholars were divided into two classes, in the upper of which was a young gentleman [etc.]. 1857 HUGHES *Tom Brown* i. viii, Three unhappy fellows..whom the Doctor and the master of the form were always endeavouring to hoist into the Upper school. 1897 FLANDRAU *Harvard Episodes* 202 If they happened to be upper classmen.

10. a. Of a higher, better, more excellent, or more comprehensive quality; superior.

a1586 SIDNEY *De Mornay* ii. ¶ 1 We reduce the particulars too an vnderkind, the vnderkinds to an vpperkind, and the vpperkind to a most generall. As for example, we reduce all particular humane persons vnder the terme of man. 1587 GOLDING *Ibid.* x. 163 If the mixture of the Elements cannot make the forme whereby the vpperkyndes differ from one another, as the sencelesse things from the things that haue sence. 1831 CARLYLE *Sart. Res.* ii. ix, Here, then, as I lay in that Centre of Indifference; cast, doubtless by benignant upper Influence, into a healing sleep [etc.]. 1895 MARIE CORELLI *Sorrows Satan* iv, [Genius] is..an 'upper' thing, beyond earthly smells and savours.

†**b.** *Upper fortune*, the upper hand (cf. 14).

1613 FLETCHER *Honest Man's Fort.* i. ii, Since You have the upper fortune of him, 'twill Be some dishonor to you to bear your self With any pride or glory over him.

11. Constituting or producing a higher tone, note, or notes.

1843 *Penny Cycl.* XXVI. 418/2 The upper or female voice part of the scale. *Ibid.* 419/1 The extreme upper notes of the falsetto. 1880 *Grove's Dict. Music* II. 654/1 The difficulty of hearing the upper partial tones. 1895 *Funk's Stand. Dict.*, *Upper keyboard*, the right-hand side of the keyboard. 1896 A. J. HIPKINS *Pianoforte* 122 *Upper Partial*, any partial or simple division of a compound vibrating string that is above the first, or Fundamental.

III. Special collocations.

12. Upper crust: a. The top crust of a loaf. Also *transf.* †**b.** The exterior or surface layer of the earth. **c.** *slang.* The human head; a hat. **d.** *dial.* (See quot.) **e.** (See quot. 1848.) Chiefly *U.S. colloq.* (also *attrib.*).

a. c1460 J. RUSSELL *Bk. Nurture* 342 Kutt þe vpper crust [of the loaf] for youre souerayne. 1542 BOORDE *Dyetary* xi. (1870) 261 Wherfore chyp the vpper crust of your breade. 1591 A. W. *Bk. Cookrye* 20 b, Put therto a peece of vpper crust of white bread. 1768 W. DONALDSON *Life B. Sapskull* II. 108 The upper-crust of that building [the Mansion-house] is thought too heavy for the simple ingredients of an aldermanic pasty. 1823 J. BADCOCK *Dom. Amusem.* 32 Alum throws up a flowery paleness upon the whole upper crust. 1868 FURNIVALL *Babees Bk.* 271 *margin*, The upper crust of a fine loaf.

b. 1555 EDEN *Decades* 234 An other kynde of Rubies.. found in the mountaynes in the vpper crust or floure of the earth. 1669 WORLIDGE *Syst. Agric.* (1681) 230 It..doth not bury the upper-crust of the ground so deep as usually is done by digging. 1696 WHISTON *The. Earth* 53 Such an Upper Crust or Shell of Earth on the face of the Abyss. 1762 MILLS *Syst. Pract. Husb.* I. 39 When the upper crust of the earth is removed, all that can be seen, or dug, is marle.

c. 1826 *Sporting Mag.* XVIII. 253 Tom completely tinkered his antagonist's upper-crust. 1832 EGAN *Bk. Sports* (Farmer), Sam's nob had been in pepper alley, and his upper crust was rather changed. 1851 *Household Words* II. 320/1 A highly-polished Parisian upper-crust..smashed under the weight of a carter's slouch.

d. 1854 MISS BAKER *Northampt. Gloss.* 371 'Mrs. Upper Crust,' a fictitious designation for any female who assumes unauthorised superiority.

e. 1836 HALIBURTON *Clockm.* xxviii, It was none o' your skim-milk parties, but superfine uppercrust real jam. 1843 — *Sam Slick in Eng.* xxiv, I want you to see Peel,..Macaulay, old Joe, and so on. These men are all upper crust here. 1848 BARTLETT *Dict. Amer.* 370 *Upper crust*, the aristocracy, the higher circles. 1850 J. F. COOPER *Ways of Hour* vi. I. 186 Those families..are our upper crust—not upper ten thousand, as the newspapers call it, but upper hundred. 1898 *Daily News* 14 Feb. 2/7, 53 magistrates, 46 of whom belonged to what..[is] sometimes called 'the upper crust'.

13. Upper deck, the highest continuous deck of a ship. (Orig. the higher of two decks, in contrast to the *lower*.)

1591 RALEIGH *Last Fight Revenge* B 3, Sir Richard..was neuer so wounded as that hee forsooke the vpper decke. 1598 FLORIO *Dict.* To Rdr. 9, I was but one to sit at sterne, to pricke my carde, to watch vpon the vpper decke. 1626 CAPT. SMITH *Accidence Yng. Seamen* 10 The vpper Decke should be layd with so many beames as are fitting with knees to bind them. a1687 PETTY *Treat. Naval Philos.* i. i, The Hull under the said upper Deck is divided into the Cavity or Hold [etc.]. 1758 J. BLAKE *Plan Mar. Syst.* 2 It is proposed, that..guns run out on the upper deck only. 1769 FALCONER *Dict. Marine* (1780) s.v. *Deep-waisted*, To leave a vacant space, called the waist, on the middle of the upper-deck. 1846 A. YOUNG *Naut. Dict.* 98 That part of the upper-deck which is between the forecastle and poop..is termed the Main-deck. 1889 E. C. STEDMAN in *Life W. Sharp* (1910) ix. 155 You looked down upon its members from the Servia's upper-deck.

fig. a1613 OVERBURY *Characters, Saylor* Wks. (1890) 75 Nothing but hunger and hard rockes can convert him, and then but his upper decke neither; for his hold neither feares nor hopes.

attrib. 1709 *Lond. Gaz.* No. 4521/3 Upon whom we fired ..our Upper-deck..Guns. 1892 E. REEVES *Homeward Bound* 129 To give third-class passengers a little breathing upper-deck space.

14. Upper hand: a. The mastery, control, or advantage (*of*, or *over*, a person, people, etc.); predominance, rule, or dominion. Usu. const. with verbs, as *attain, gain, get, have, obtain.* Cf. the earlier OVER-HAND *sb.*, UVER-HAND. (Freq. c1560-c1600.) **b.** A person or party in power or authority. **c.** The place of authority or honour; preference, precedence. (Usu. with *give* or *take*.)

a. 1481 TIPTOFT *Tulle of Old Age* (Caxton) g viij b, Marcus Attilius..had the vppirhande and victorye of the men of cartage. 1535 COVERDALE *Ps.* ix. 19 Vp Lorde, let not man haue the vpper hande. 1576 GASCOIGNE *Steele Gl.* (Arb.) 64 Downe goeth al, where they [*sc.* soldiers] get vpper hand. a1616 BEAUM. & FL. *Little Fr. Lawyer* i. i, I have seen fools, and fighters, chain'd together, And the Fighters had the upper hand, and whipt first, The poor Sots laughing at 'em. 1690 SOMERS *Vind. Proc. Late Parlt.* 10 The Jacobites, and the Malecontents..might perhaps get the upper hand, if not prevented in time. 1742 YOUNG *Nt. Th.* iii. 479 Where ev'ry ranger of the wilds, perhaps Each reptile, justly claims our upper hand. 1743 POCOCKE *Descr. East* I. 177 When the Greeks got the upper hand,..they treated them with great rigour. 1838 DICKENS *O. Twist* xv, I've got the upper-hand over you. 1861 LD. BROUGHAM *Brit. Const.* xiii. 195 They blindly followed the dictates of the faction which had the upper-hand. 1865 MRS. CARLYLE *Lett.* (1883) III. 303, I decided to take the upper hand with her, and keep it.

transf. (of things). 1535 COVERDALE *Wisdom* x. 5 Whan wickednes had gotten ye vpper-hande, so yt the nacions were puft vp with pryde. 1546 BP. GARDINER *Detect. Devil's Sophistrie* 16 Whiles the bely hath the vpperhande amonge a greate many. 1579 G. HARVEY *Letter-bk.* (Camden) 87 Summer gettith the upperhande of wynter, and wynter agayne of summer. 1622 PEACHAM *Compl. Gent.* xv. 186 Hereby the minde getteth the dominion and vpperhand. 1712 POPE *Spect.* No. 408 ¶ 3 If a Man suffers them [*sc.* the passions] to get the upper hand. 1796 MME. D'ARBLAY *Camilla* I. 289 Sir Hugh..said it never broke out from him but by accident, which..should never get the upper hand again. 1873 MRS. OLIPHANT *Innocent* III. 160 The natural honesty to which he had appealed gained the upper hand. 1885 *Manch. Exam.* 29 June 5/1 The worst tendencies of the party will gain the upper hand.

b. 1548 HALL *Chron., Hen. VI*, 126 The poore inhabitauntes ..were..compelled to yeilde and rendre theimselfes, to the more power, and vpper hande. 1606 *Sir G. Goosecappe* i. iv, One of these painted communities, that are rauisht with Coaches, and vpper hands.

c. 1580-3 GREENE *Mamillia* Wks. (Grosart) II. 49 If by chaunce the Vestal virgins walkt abroad, the Senators would giue them the vpper hand. 1598 HAKLUYT *Voy.* I. 68 They ..gaue vs and Duke Ieroslaus the vpper hand, when we were abroad in their companie. 1662 J. DAVIES tr. *Olearius' Voy. Ambass.* 9 The *Priestaf* gave the Ambassadours the upper Hand, and conducted them to the Inn. 1663 PEPYS *Diary* 25 Jan., A late dispute between my Lord Chesterfield ..and Mr. Edward Montagu..who should have the precedence in taking the Queen's upper-hand abroad out of the house. 1715 *Lond. Gaz.* No. 5329/1 The Empress..gave the upper Hand to the [Dowager] Empress Amalia. 1746 FRANCIS tr. *Hor., Sat.* ii. v. 26 Yet wait upon him, at his least command, And always bid him take the upper hand. 1809 MALKIN *Gil Blas* vii. ii. ¶ 9 [At] the second table..the whole household..insisted on giving me the upper hand.

fig. 1594 SHAKS. *Rich. III*, iv. iv. 37 If ancient sorrow be most reuerent, Giue mine the benefit of signeurie, And let my greefes frowne on the vpper hand.

d. *adv.* (See quots., and cf. UNDERHAND *adv.* 2 c.)

1771 LUCKOMBE *Hist. Print.* 333 The Nut and Spindle, and the Toe of the Spindle, are all to be well oiled; that they may all perform their several offices the easier..; both Upper and Under hand. 1808 STOWER *Printer's Gram.* 530 When the spindle goes soft and easy,..it goes well upper hand or above hand. 1888 JACOBI *Printers' Vocab.* s.v.

e. Hence **Upperhandism**. *nonce-word.* [-ISM 2 b.]

1845 E. B. BARRETT *Lett. to R. Browning* (1899) I. 26 The curious thing in this world is not the stupidity, but the upperhandism of the stupidity.

15. Upper house, a higher house of deliberation or legislation, esp. the House of Lords.

1532-3 *Act 24 Hen. VIII*, c. 12 § 4 The Spirituall Prelatez and other Abbottes and Priours of the upper House assembled..in the Convocacion. a1577 SIR T. SMITH *Commonw. Eng.* ii. ii. (1584) 38 Besides the Chauncelor, there is one in the vpper house who is called Clarke of the Parliament. 1640 YORKE *Union Hon.* 66 Which was concluded in the upperhouse of Parliament. a1670 HACKET *Abp. Williams* ii. (1693) 180 The Bishops..intended that this Petition.. should be preferred to the King..in the Upper House of Parliament. 1708 J. CHAMBERLAYNE *St. Gt. Brit.* ii. (1710) 481 A List of the Members of the Upper-House of Convocation. 1728 CHAMBERS *Cycl.* s.v. *Convocation*, Things are first usually propos'd in the upper House; then communicated to the lower. 1818 BENTHAM *Ch. Eng.* p. x, The Lower House was indeed untaxable. But the Upper House ..taxed themselves. 1849 MACAULAY *Hist. Eng.* iii. I. 325 The abolition of the monasteries deprived the Church..of her predominance in the upper house of parliament. 1859 W. SWAINSON *New Zealand* xi. 289 The Legislative Council, or Upper House. 1885 LOWE *Bismarck* I. 293 The Lower Chamber would not yield an inch to the Crown and the Upper House.

attrib. 1610 BOLTON *Elem. Armories* 150 Or should I not doe wrong to Campes, and Parliaments, robbing souldiers, and vpper-house men of their colour?

16. Upper leather: a. Leather forming the upper of a boot or shoe; also, = UPPER *sb.* 1. **b.** Sheet-leather suitable or prepared for such.

a. 1528 ROY *Rede me* (Arb.) 82 *Jef.* To mangill their good shues so, Me thynketh it but folisshnes. *Wat.* They cutt but the vpper ledder. 1603-4 *Act 1 Jas. I*, c. 22 § 23 The upper Leather of any Shooes, Startups, &c. 1708 OCKLEY *Saracens* I. 142 Those who had strong Boots on,..had the Soals torn off from the Upper-Leathers. 1759 *Phil. Trans.* LI. 39 With that shoe struck off, and its upper-leather torn. 1841 *Penny Cycl.* XXI. 410/2 The lasting or tacking of the upper-leather to the in-sole. 1846 THACKERAY *Laman Blanchard* Wks. 1899 XIII. 467 Persons who..polish their upper-leathers as well as they can. 1872 T. HARDY *Under Greenw. Tree* ii. ii, The upper-leather of a Wellington-boot.

fig. 1647 N. WARD *Simple Cobler* (title-p.), Willing to help 'mend his Native Country, lamentably tattered, both in the upper-Leather and sole.

b. 1629 *Leather* 12 The..strongest, which might..serue both for sooling leather and vpper leather. *Ibid.* 15 The Market is full of excellent Leather (strong Backes, and good vpper Leathers). 1885 *Harper's Mag.* Jan. 278/1 Upper-leather..is sold by the foot or pound.

17. Upper lip: a. The lip on the upper side of the mouth; the superior lip of a person, animal, or insect. **b.** The higher of the two edges of an organ-pipe mouth. **c.** *Bot.* The superior or upper division of a bilabiate corolla or calyx. **d.** *spec.* (See UNDERLIP 1 b.)

a. 1546 J. HEYWOOD *Prov.* (1867) 77 He can yll pype, that lacth his vpper lyp. 1596 SPENSER *State Irel.* Wks. (Globe) 635/1 That noe man shall weare his bearde but onely on the upper lipp like muschachoes. 1611 BIBLE *Lev.* xiii. 45 The leper..shall put a couering vpon his vpper lip. 1670 MILTON *Hist. Eng.* vi. 304 The English then useing to let grow on their upper-lip large Mustachio's. 1704 *Dict. Rust.* s.v. *Rules buying Horses*, If his Upper-Lip will not reach his Nether. 1748 RICHARDSON *Clarissa* VI. 387 Which made John's upper-lip..rise to his nose. 1758 J. S. tr. *Le Dran's Observ. Surg.* (1771) 42 It possessed the whole Upper-Lip. 1815 *Massachusetts Spy* 14 June 4/4, I kept a stiff upper lip, and bought license to sell my goods. 1826 KIRBY & SP. *Entomol.* III. xxxiii. 355 *Labrum* (the Upper-lip), a usually moveable organ; which..is situate between the Mandibulæ. 1833- [see LIP *sb.* 2, STIFF *a.* 11]. 1836 YARRELL *Brit. Fishes* I. 378 [The loach] with four barbules or cirri.. on the upper lip in the front. 1849 C. BRONTE *Shirley* xxiii, He had the shorter nose and longer upper-lip of his sister.

b. 1728 CHAMBERS *Cycl.* s.v. *Organ*, Over this Aperture is the Mouth..; whose upper Lip.., being level, cuts the Wind as it comes out at the Aperture. 1852 SEIDEL *Organ* 78 The upper lip..forming, together with the under lip, the mouth of the pipe. 1875 KNIGHT *Dict. Mech.* 1709/2 The lower edge of the leaf is termed the upper lip.

c. 1731 MILLER *Gard. Dict.*, *Salvia*..hath a labiated Flower, consisting of one Leaf, whose Upper-lip is sometimes arched. 1793 MARTIN *Lang. Bot.*, *Galea* (an helmet), the upper lip of a ringent corolla. 1796 WITHERING *Brit. Plants* (ed. 3) III. 555 *Digitalis purpurea*...Segments of the calyx egg-shaped, acute:..upper lip nearly entire. 1807 J. E. SMITH *Phys. Bot.* 434 *Ajuga* [has] scarcely any upper lip at all.

18. Upper ten, the upper classes; the aristocracy. *colloq.* Orig. (U.S.) *upper ten thousand.*

(*a*) 1844 N. P. WILLIS in *Even. Mirror* (N.Y.) 11 Nov. 2/1 At present there is no distinction among the upper ten thousand of the city. 1861 LEVER *One of Them* xix. 149 The Peerage,..the bulky volume that records the alliances and the ages of the 'upper ten thousand'. 1871 *Punch* 15 May 187/2 There was no grievance on the part of the 'upper ten thousand'.

(*b*) 1848 BARTLETT *Dict. Amer.* 370 *The upper ten thousand*, and contracted, *the upper ten*,..the upper circles of our large cities. 1860 W. H. RUSSELL *Diary in India* I. 119 Petty jealousy and 'caste' reigned in the Residency; the 'upper ten' with stoical grandeur would die the 'upper ten'. 1886 C. E. PASCOE *Lond. of To-day* xxxii. (ed. 3) 294 Clubs of some note..patronized by the 'upper ten'. [1890 RIDER HAGGARD *Beatrice* xi, Plenty of carriages, and other needful things, including of course the *entrée* to the upper celestial ten.]

transf. 1879 JEFFERIES *Wild Life* 160 Neither is he [*sc.* the robin] a favourite with the upper class of cottagers—for there is an 'upper ten' even among cottagers.

b. Hence **Upper-tendom**, = prec. Chiefly *U.S.*

1855 *Doesticks* xvi. 131, I did go to a ball for the benefit of the poor—a two-dollar commingling of upper-tendom with lower-twentydom. 1863 N. HAWTHORNE *Our Old Home* II. 199 All the girls, whether daughters of the uppertendom, the mediocrity, the cottage, or the kennel. 1887 [W. F. RAE] *Miss Bayle's Romance* I. 253 This countess belongs to the real upper tendom.

19. Upper works: a. That part of a vessel which is above water-level when it is ready or laden for a voyage; = DEAD-WORK 1. (Also †*upper work.*) **b.** The higher portion of a structure. **c.** *slang.* The head; the mental capacity.

a. 1591 RALEIGH *Last Fight Revenge* B 3 b, The mastes all beaten ouer board,..her vpper worke altogither rased. 1627 CAPT. SMITH *Seaman's Gram.* xi. 52 She is brought in narrow to her vpper workes. 1693 *Lond. Gaz.* No. 2865/1 The French Man of War..who fought the Berkeley Castle ..being very leaky,..and all her upper Work torn to pieces. 1745 P. THOMAS *Jrnl. Anson's Voy.* 270 To caulk the Ship's Upper-Works and Decks. 1769 FALCONER *Dict. Marine* (s.v.), Upper-work. 1798 NELSON in Nicolas *Disp.* (1845) III. 106 The Sérieuse was set on fire to burn her upper works which were above water. c1850 *Rudim. Navig.* (Weale) 157 *Upper works*,..all that part which may be considered as separated from the bottom by the main wale. 1898 KIPLING *Fleet in Being* i. 7 The battleships overtook us, their white upperworks showing like icebergs as they topped the sea-line.

fig. 1751 SMOLLETT *P. Pickle* vi, I'd have you take care of your upper works; for if once you are made fast to her poop, egad, she'll..make every beam in your body crack with straining.

b. 1791 SMEATON *Edystone L.* § 60 The object was to repair or restore the Upper Works.

c. 1809 MALKIN *Gil Blas* iii. iii. ¶ 12 Arsenia and Florimonde are not strong in their upper works; but then they have a facility in their vocation which is more than all the wit in the world. 1818 *Sporting Mag.* July 167 Neate gave Oliver..a..hit on his mouth, that his *upper works* were in a complete state of *chaos*. 1860 J. P. KAY-SHUTTLEWORTH *Scarsdale* II. 299 Oi'm i' gradely fettle..i' th' upper warks.

U·pper, *adv.* Now *rare.* [f. UP *adv.*1 or *adv.*2 + -ER 3.] To or in a loftier place or position; higher, further up.

c1384 CHAUCER *H. Fame* ii. 884 With this word, vpper to sore He gan. c1391 — *Astrol.* ii. § 12 As the sonne clymbith vppere & vppere. c1550 CHEKE *Matt.* xxiii. 12 Whosoever abaseth himself schal be set vpper. a1552 LELAND *Itin.* (1711) III. 6 A litle Foreland about a Mile upper then Kenor on Severn. 1901 *Punch* 21 Sept. 224/1 We go up, up, up, and upper, upper,..skirting..precipices.

†**Upper-bodying**, *vbl. sb.* *Obs.* (See UPPER *a.* 4 b.) 1502 *Priv. Purse Exp. Eliz. York* (1830) 22 For upper bodyeng sleving and lynyng of a gowne.

Upper crust: see UPPER *a.* 12.

Upper-cut, *v.* (See UPPER *a.* 7.) 1850 in *Mem. T. Sayers* (1858) 21 Sayers..hit short at Collins with his left, who upper-cut him sharply, and slipped down. 1898 A. M. BINSTEAD *Pink 'Un & Pelican* 237 She wouldn't 'old her tongue the other night, an' so..I uppercuts her with the right.

U·pperest, *a.* Now *rare.* Also 4 **uppurest**, 4-5 **uppereste**, 5 **-ist**; 6 **upperst**. [A superlative formed on UPPER *a.* Cf. MDu. *upperst* (Du. and Flem. *opperst*), LG. *upperst, üpperst*, Sw. and older Da. *ypperst*, Norw. *ypparst, yppast* best, choicest.] Most high in situation, position, or rank; uppermost, highest, loftiest; †outermost.

In modern use rare for *uppermost.*

13.. *K. Alis.* 7063 (MS. Linc.), Þeose seresys..Vppurest folk buþ of ynde. c1374 CHAUCER *Boeth.* i. pr. i. 2 (Camb. MS.), By whiche degrees men myhten clymbyn fro the nethereste lettre to the vppereste. 1387-8 T. USK *Test. Love* i. x. (Skeat) l. 32 We men, that..holden the upperest degree, under god, of benigne thinges. 1483 CAXTON *Gold. Leg.* 62 b/1 Moyses..made hym upperist bysshop for his fader Aaron. *Ibid.* 76 b/1 She wente up in the upperist cubicle of the hows. a1548 HALL *Chron., Hen. VIII*, 2 b, His grace ware in his vpperst apparell, a robe of Crimosyn Veluet.

1874 M. COLLINS *Frances* III. 212 An American of the very upperest five hundred. 1880 W. MORRIS in Mackail *Life* (1899) II. 15 Above the Round House, on what might be called the upperest Thames.

b. *absol.* The uppermost or highest point.

1484 CAXTON *Fables of Æsop* iii. iii, He that..is atte vpperest of the whele of fortune, may wel falle doune.

†**U·pperest**, *adv.* *Obs. rare.* In 5 up(p)rest. [f. UPPER *adv.*] In the highest place or position.

1481 *Cely Papers* (Camden) 71, vij packes..lying be afte the maste, j pack lyeth upprest. *Ibid.* 72 A few broken felles and pesys..lyeth uprest nexte the maste.

Upper-flapped, *a.* (UPPER *a.* 3 a.) 1850 'H. HIEOVER' *Pract. Horsemanship* 107 The Shaftoed upper-flapped, and stuffed lower-flapped saddle.

Upper hand(ism): see UPPER *a.* 14 (also 2).

Upper leather, lip: see UPPER *a.* 16, 17.

U·ppermore, *adv.* and *a.* Now *dial.* Also 5 **vppyr-, vppermare, vpher more**, 6 *Sc.* **vppermair, -mer, vppirmer**, 7 **vppermore**, 9 *north. dial.* **uppermer**. [f. UPPER *adv.* and *a.* + -MORE. Cf. older Da. *yppermere.*]

A. *adv.* Higher locally; further up; at or to a greater altitude. (In later use *Sc.*)

c1400 MAUNDEV. (Roxb.) xiv. 63 Vppermare amanges þe mountaynes es a faire citee. c1410 *Master of Game* (MS. Digby 182) xxi, Þat þe flewe be iii. or iiii. fyngres vppermore þanne þe heed. 1435 MISYN *Fire of Love* i. x. 20 Bettyr it is..þat criste..to vs say, 'frende, cum vppyrmare'. 1501 DOUGLAS *Pal. Hon.* iii. v, Weil I considderit na vppermair I micht, And to discend sa hiddeous was the hicht, I durst not auenture. 1596 DALRYMPLE tr. *Leslie's Hist. Scot.* (S.T.S.) I. 30 Abone or vppirmer, vpon Leuin, is the toune. 1616 *Barbour's Bruce* (Hart) ii. 440 To that word they assented all, And from them walloped vppermere.

B. *adj.* That is the more elevated (of two); higher, upper.

c1400 MAUNDEV. (Roxb.) xx. 90 Bathe þe emisperies, þe vppermare and þe nedermare. a1425 tr. *Arderne's Treat. Fistula*, etc. 44 After þat þe vppermore iuncture of þe bone of þe fynger was drawen out. 1869- in north. dialect use (*Eng. Dial. Dict.*).

U·ppermost, *adv.*, *a.*, and *sb.* Also 5 **wpwr-, wppwrmwste**, 6 *Anglo-Ir.* **uppermuste**; 5 **wpwr-**, 6 **vp(p)ermoste** (6 **vppermooste**), 5-7 **vper-**, 6-7 **vppermost**. [f. as prec. + -MOST.]

A. *adv.* **1.** In or to the highest, upmost, or most elevated position or place.

1481 *Cely Papers* (Camden) 74 A packe lyes wpwrmwste apon Dawlttons behynde the maste. *Ibid.* 75 Thay ly behynde the maste wpwrmoste. 1617 J. TAYLOR (Water P.) *Observ. & Trav. fr. London to Hamburgh* E 1 b, A good featherbed vndermost,..and another featherbed vppermost. 1622 SIR R. HAWKINS *Observ. Voy. S. Sea* 3 With a storme ..shee was turned topse-turvie, her Kele vppermost. 1668 BP. HOPKINS *Serm., Vanity* (1685) 76 His hand turns all things here about like so many wheels;..the same part is now uppermost, and anon lowermost. 1712 ADDISON *Spect.* No. 281 ¶ 11, I..shall therefore only take Notice of what lay first and uppermost. 1747 WESLEY *Prim. Physick* (1762) 55 Lie with that Ear uppermost. 1814 SCOTT *Diary* 7 Aug. in *Lockhart*, This man being uppermost on the cord, ..called out to his brother who was next to him. 1842 LOUDON *Suburban Hort.* 263 Care must be taken that the upper end of the cutting..be kept uppermost. 1860 TYNDALL *Glac.* i. xvi. 118 In making this effort the spike of my axe turned uppermost.

fig. 1866 G. MACDONALD *Ann. Q. Neighb.* vii. (1878) 117 If the wine hadn't got uppermost.

b. In the first or foremost place in respect of precedence, station, rank, or the like.

1526 TINDALE *Matt.* xxiii. 6 They..love to sytt vppermooste at feastes. 1530 PALSGR. 713/2, I set hyest, or upper moste in a companye. 15.. *Bk. Precedence* i. 14 All Dukes daughters shall goe all-one with a nother, soe that alwayes the Eldest Dukes Daughter go vpermost. 1628 [see C. 1 b]. 1850 J. F. COOPER *Ways of Hour* I. 317 It is the people today;..some prince to-morrow; and by the end of the week we may have..a Robespierre uppermost.

c. *fig.* In the chief place or predominancy.

1805 WORDSW. *Prelude* ix. 389 We..saw..generous love.. Uppermost in the midst of fiercest strife. 1850 ROBERTSON *Serm.* Ser. iii. (1857) 125 A mourning in which self is ever uppermost. 1885 'M. RUTHERFORD' *Deliv.* i. 11 Every now and then, when the subject was uppermost.

2. Foremost in, most prominently in or into, the mind, thoughts, conversation, etc.

In frequent use from c1830.

1693 *Humours Town* 54 Perpetual Chat on whatever comes uppermost. 1719 DE FOE *Crusoe* ii. (Globe) 316 It was uppermost in all my Thoughts. 1723 *Pres. St. Russia* II. 151 It was always my Way to say what came uppermost. 1802-12 BENTHAM *Ration. Judic. Evid.* Wks. 1843 VII. 172 Any one word that comes uppermost is sufficient. 1848 THACKERAY *Van. Fair* xli, Ever since she had left them she had not ceased to keep them uppermost in her thoughts. 1860 TROLLOPE *Framley Parsonage* xxvi, To speak out what came uppermost to her tongue.

B. *adj.* **1.** Occupying the highest position or place; loftiest, topmost, highest in place; furthest up (on a river, etc.).

c1500 *Melusine* lix. 358 He yede vp to the vpermost stage of the donjon. 1526 TINDALE *Luke* xi. 43 Ye love the vppermost seates in the sinagoges. a1548 HALL *Chron., Hen. VIII*, 226 b, One of the officers demaunded his vpper garment for his fee, meanyng his goune, and he [*sc.* Sir Thomas More]..tooke him his cappe, saiyng it was the vppermoste garment that he had. 1623 BINGHAM *Xenophon* 133 Xenophon..encamped in the vppermost village neere the mountaines. 1657 HOBBES *Absurd. Geom.* 3 Perhaps you mean that the uppermost quantitie 0 + 1 is equal to the uppermost quantity 1. 1702 *Post Man* 8-11 Aug. 2/1 Inquire at the uppermost House..in the said Buildings. 1764 *Museum Rust.* IV. 19, I preserve only two of the new shoots, the uppermost and its opposite. 1844 KINGLAKE *Eothen* x, The golden juice ascended from..the cellar to the uppermost brains of the friars. 1886 J. A. BROWN in *Q. Jrnl. Geol. Soc.* May 196 There had been a manufactory of Palæolithic implements on this uppermost floor. 1896 A. STERRY *Tale Thames* (1903) 43/1 One the most attractive portions of what may be called the Uppermost Thames.

b. Outermost; most external.

a1548 [implied in quot. under 1 above]. 1560 *First Bk. Discipl.* (1621) 48 The uppermost claith, corps-present; clerk maile, the Pasche-offering. 1567 MAPLET *Gr. Forest* 69 The Adder..casteth off yearely his uppermost skin or coate. 1861 J. R. GREENE *Man. Anim. Kingd., Cœlent.* 103 An expanded bulb, above which are disposed..the various appendages... Of these the hydrocysts are uppermost, or external.

†**2.** Maximum, utmost. *Obs.*—1

1579 in *10th Rep. Hist. MSS. Comm.* App. V. 430 If any [person]..steallinge of any..wares, do..restore the thing or thinges so taken or the uppermuste vallue thereof.

3. Highest in respect of rank, importance, precedence, etc.; chiefest, first.

1680 WALTON in Aubrey *Lives* (1898) II. 15 He was in.. the vpermost fforme in Westminster scole. 1699 BENTLEY *Phal.* 188 The Thought [was] so very obvious and uppermost. 1780 WARNER in Jesse *Selwyn & Contemp.* (1844) IV. 398 In the Westminster [election] struggle Rodney is to-day got uppermost. 1876 MISS YONGE *Womankind* xii, This entire seclusion from all means of reaching the poor..is seldom found in the uppermost classes. 1885 *Manch. Exam.* 6 Apr. 5/2 The weather is, in view of the approaching holiday, the uppermost subject of concern.

b. Having the chief power, control, or authority; predominant, supreme; most influential.

1691 WOOD *Ath. Oxon.* I. 887 In the time of the rebellion he sided with those that were uppermost. 1693 *Humours Town* 42 The Violence of those that are uppermost. 1732 BERKELEY *Alciphr.* ii. § 21 Where heavy heads are lowest, and men of genius uppermost. 1818 SCOTT *Br. Lamm.* xxvii, Uniform adherents to the party who are uppermost. 1855 MACAULAY *Hist. Eng.* xiv. III. 445 The politician whose practice was always to be on the side which was uppermost.

C. *sb.* †**1.** The highest part or portion. *Obs.*

1484 CAXTON *Fables of Æsop* v. xiii, Yf an Egle were at the vppermost of the heuen. 1613-39 I. JONES in Leoni *Palladio's Archit.* (1742) II. 49 The uppermost of the highest Cornice, is of large Tyles. 1646 J. GREGORY *Notes & Obs.* 11 For so they call Τὰ μετέωρα τῶν οἰκημάτων, the uppermosts of their Houses.

b. The highest place or position.

1628 R. H. *J. Owen's Epigr.* ii. liv. 11 Let me set alwayes vppermost at boord, The vppermost in bed I'le you affoord.

†**2.** That which is highest, most predominant, etc. *Obs.*

1687 *Good Advice* 60 It is certain that two predominant Religions, would be two Uppermosts at once. a1753 BP. BERKELEY in Fraser *Life* (1871) 477 Wt judgement would he make of uppermost and lowermost who had always seen through an inverting glass?

†**3.** The upper hand; superiority or dominion.

1718 *Entertainer* No. 43. 302 If ever they get the Uppermost, after their long Struggles for Superiority.

†**Upperplus**. *Obs.*—1 [f. UPPER *a.*, substituted for *sur-* in *surplus.*] Surplus, balance.

1578 *Surrey & Kent Sewers Comm.* (1909) 286 To sell the same and satisfye the chardge and make restitucion of the vpperplus.

†**Upper-stocked**, *a.* *Obs.* (See UPPER *a.* 4 a.) 1535 in *Archaeologia* IX. 250 Two paire of hoose,..the one paire upperstocked with yalowe damaske.

Upper ten, works: see UPPER *a.* 18, 19.

Up-pi·led, *pa. pple.* and *ppl. a.* (UP- 5.)

1600 FAIRFAX *Tasso* xix. xxx. 342 There vnderneath th' vnburied hils vppilde Of bodies dead, the liuing buried lie. 1742 COLLINS *Ode Poet. Char.* 55 High on some cliff, to heav'n up-pil'd. 1796 COLERIDGE *To Yng. Friend* 2 A green mountain variously up-piled. 1818 KEATS *Endym.* ii. 288 He cannot see.., up-pil'd, The cloudy rack slow journeying in the west. 1855 SINGLETON *Virgil* I. 88 Thrice the Sire in ruins laid The up-piled mountains with his flash. 1873

Upping, sb.[1] Obs.

Upping, vbl. sb.[2] [Up v.]

Uppish (ŭ·piʃ).

Upping-block, -stock, -stone, etc., in upping-block.

Uppon, var. Upon prep.

Up-pu·ther, v. Sc. Obs. [Up 8.]

Up-putting, vbl. sb. [Up 7.]

Upraise, sb. [Up- 4.]

Up·raise, v. [Up- 4.]

Up·raising, vbl. sb.

Up·raisal. [Up- 4.]

Uprean. Sc. Obs.

Upraise, v. [Up- 4.]

Upraised, ppl. a. [Up- 5 of prec.]

Upraising, vbl. sb. [Up- 7.]

Upraisement.

Uprear, v. [Up- 4.]

Upreared, ppl. a. [Up- 5.]

Uprest, var. Unrest.

Upright (ŭ·prəit), a. (adv. and sb.)

Upright (ŭprəi·t), adv.

Upright, sb. [Up- 2.]

Upright, v.

Uprighten, v.

Uprightly, adv.

Uprightness.

Uprighteous, a. Obs.

Uprighteousness.

Uprights. [Up- 2.]

Uprisal. [Up- 2.]

Uprise, v. [Up- 4. Cf. ON.]

Uprise, sb. [Up- 2.]

Uprise, v.

Uprising, vbl. sb. [Up- 7.]

Uprising, ppl. a.

Uprist, sb.

Uprive, v.

Up-river (ˈʌprɪvər), adv., a., and sb.

b. Leading or directed towards the source of a river.

2. S. E. WHITE *Blazed Trail* xix, The man from up-river came up.

Uproar (ˈʌprɔər, sb.) Also 6 uprore (6, 7 up-rore (9), uroare. [ad. Du. *oproer* or MLG. *upror* (MHG. *ûfruor*, G. *aufruhr*), f. *op-*, *up-* UP- 2 + *roer*, *rôr* ROAR sb.2 Cf. also WFris. *oproer*, *opruor*, Da. *oprør*, Norw. *uppror*, Sw. *up(p)rör*. In sense 1 associated with ROAR sb.2]

1. An insurrection or rising of the populace; a serious tumult, commotion, or outbreak of disorder among the people or a body of persons. Also *without article*.

2. Loud outcry or vociferation; noise of shouting or tumult.

b. With article (*an* or *the*) and in pl.

3. *fig.* Disordered, mkempt.

Uproarious, a. Also **-ness**.

Uproll, v. 1. *trans.* To roll up.

Uproot (ʌpˈruːt), v. [UP- 1.]

Upseek, v. Obs.-1 [UP- 4.]

Upset (ʌpˈsɛt), v. [UP- 4.]

1. To set up, erected, raised up, etc.

2. To force back the end of a (metal bar, etc.) by hammering or beating up, when heated.

3. Overturned, capsized.

b. To cause to be overturned, capsized.

Upsetter. [UP- 6.] Cf. UPSET v.]

Upshoot, sb. [UP- 2.] Obs. exc. dial.

Upshot, sb. Also 6 *upshut.* [UP- 4. Cf. WFris. *opsjitte*, Du. *opscheiten*, G. *aufschiessen*.]

Upside, sb. [UP- 2.]

Upside down, adv., a., and sb.

Upside-downism. [f. prec.]

Upsides, adv. [UP- 2.]

Upspring, v. Obs.

Upspring, sb. [UP- 2.]

Upspurner. Obs.-1 [UP- 8 + SPURN v. Cf. SPURNER 1 sb.]

Upstair, adv. and a. [Up prep.[1], 7.]

Upstairs, adv., sb., and a. [Up prep.[1], 7.]

Upstand, sb. An upstanding thing; an upright structure or part.

Upstand, v. [OE. *úpstandan*, MHG. *upstân* (G. *aufstehen*), MSw. *upstanda*, *op-st(e)* (Sw. *uppstå*), MDu. *opstanden*, *opsta* (Du. *opstaa*).]

Upstanding, pres. pple. [Up 6.]

Upstanding, ppl. a. [Up 6.]

Upstaring, pres. pple. [Up 6.]

Upstart, sb. and a. [U 3.]

Upstart, v. [Up 4.]

Upstate, a. U.S. [Up prep.[1] 7.]

Upstay, v. [Up 1.]

Upsteaming, pres. pple. and ppl. a. [Up 6 b.]

Upstir, v. Now dial. [Up 1.]

Up-stroke, sb. [Up 2 + STROKE sb.[1]]

Upstirring, vbl. sb. [Up 7.]

Upstirring, ppl. a. [Up 6.]

Upstoop, v. [Up 1.]

Upstraight, a. [Up 5.]

Upstream, adv. (sb.) Also up stream, upstream. [Up prep.[2] 6.]

Upstretch, v. [Up 6 b.]

Upstretched, ppl. a. [Up 6 b.]

Upstriving, pres. pple. and ppl. a. [Up 6 b.]

Upswell, v. Cf. MDu. *opwellen* (Du. *opwellen*), MLG. *upwellen*, MHG. *ūfwellen* (G. *aufschwellen*).

Upsy Friese. [Up, and OE. *upstige* (Cott. *upsti*, *úpsti* *vpsti* of past disposition.)

Upsy, adv.-vb. Obs.⁻¹ [f. *upsy* + TAIL v. II.]

Upsy, sb. Obs. [Cf. next and OE. *upstige*, OHG. *ûfstîc*, ON. *upp-stíga*.] Ascension (of Christ).

Uptails, phr. and sb. Cf. UPSY-TAIL.

Uptake, sb. [Up 4.]

Uptake, v. [Up 4 Cf. ON. and Icel. *upptak* neut., *upptaka* fem.]

Upthrow, sb. [Up 4 + THROW sb.[1]]

Upthrow, v. [Up 4. Cf. THROW v. 8.]

Upthrust, sb. [Up 2.]

Upthrust, v. [Up 4.]

Uptie, v. [Up 1.]

Uptie, sb. Naut. Obs. Forms: 4-5 upteye, vpteigh, vptyegh, vptighe, 5 vptie (hyptie).

Up-town, adv. sb., and a. (Also without hyphen.) [Up prep.[1]]

Uptorn, ppl. a. [Up 5. Cf. UP-TEAR v.]

Uptrain, v. [Up 1.]

Uptrained, ppl. a. [Up 6.]

Upturn, sb. [Up 2.]

Up-turn, v. [Up 4.]

Up-turned, ppl. a. [Up 6 b.]

Up-turning, pres. pple. and ppl. a. [Up 6.]

Upward, adv. [OE. *upweard*, etc.]

Upward, a. [OE. *upweard*, etc.]

Upwards, adv. [f. prec. + -s.]

Upwake, v. rare. [Up 4. Cf. MDu., op-, MLG. *upwaken*, Du. *opwaken*, G. *aufwachen*.]

Upward, sb. [f. UPWARD a. or adv.]

URANOSCOPY ... was by Artedi considered as not generically distinct from the Uranoscopus. ...

Uranoscopy, rare. Also *ourano-* [ad. mod.L. *Gr. ouranoskopia*] ... (See quots.)

Urano'so- occurring in a few chemical terms, as *uranoso-ammonic-potassic-, -uranic.*

Uranous (yū'rănəs), a. Chem. [f. URAN-IUM +-OUS.] ... 1. Formed from or related to the lower oxide of uranium.

Uranous-oxide ...

2. Of or pertaining to, typical of, uranium.

Uran-outang con. f. ORANG-OUTANG.

Uranus (yū'rănŏs). Astr. [L. *Uranus*, a. Gr *Ouranos* husband of Gea (Earth) and father of Cronos (Saturn).] ...

Urany (yū'răni). ... A radical (UO₂) held to exist in many compounds of uranium.

Urari (ūrā'rī) ... Also *urary, urare* ; *urari, oorara.* (See CURARE, and cf. URALI, OORALI, WOORALI.) [See quots. 1839, 1866.]

Urao (ūrā'ō). Min. [Native name. So F. *urao*.] = TRONA.

Ura·ster, [a. mod.L. *uraster* (Agassiz).] The common star-fish, *Asterias rubens.*

Urate·mia. Path. [mod.L. f. URATE + Gr. *aima* blood.] A morbid condition due to accumulation of urates in the blood. Cf. URÆMIA.

Ura·ic (ūre·ik), a. Chem. Also *urat.* [f. URATE.] ...

Uric, a. [f. prec. + -IC 1 b.] Of or pertaining to, containing or consisting of, a urate or urates. *Uratic diathesis:* (see quot. 1885).

Ura·to·sis. Path. [as prec. + -OSIS.] A morbid condition of health resulting from the deposit of urates in the tissues or fluids of the body.

Tu·raught, Anglo-Irish. Obs. Also *uiraght.*

Urban (ə·rbăn), a. and sb. [ad. L. *urbān-us* (whence U·, Sp, Pg, *urbano*), f. *urb-s* city. Rare before the 19th cent.; cf. prec.]

1. Of, pertaining to or characteristic of, occurring or taking place in, a city or town.

2. Having the manners, refinement, or polish regarded as characteristic of a town ; courteous, civil ; also, blandly polite, suave.

Hence **Urba·nely** adv., **Urba·neness** (Bailey, 1721).

Urbanist. [f. the Papal name *Urban* (see defs.) + -IST 2.] An adherent of Pope Urban VI (1378–89), the opponent of anti-pope Clement VII. rare.

Urbanity (ə·rbǣ·nĭti). [ad. F. *urbanité* (13–14th c.), or ad. L. *urbānitāt-em*, *urbānitās*, f. *urbān-us* URBAN. Cf. It. *urbanità*, Sp. *urbanidad*, Pg. *urbanidade.*]

1. The character or quality of being urbane; courtesy, refinement, or elegance of manner; refined or bland politeness or civility.

Urban·ization. [f. next + -ATION.] The process of investing with an urban character; the condition of being urbanized.

Urbanize (ə·rbănaiz), v. [f. URBAN or URBAN A + -IZE, or (in sense 1) ad. F. *urbaniser* (1873). Cf. Pg. *urbanizar* in sense 1.]

1. *trans.* To render urbane or civil; to make more refined or polished.

2. To make of an urban character; to convert or transform into a city.

Hence **Urbanized** ppl. a.

Urbania, a. rare—¹. [f. L. URBANA or URBAN A + -IAN.] = prec.

Urban-us. ... Pertaining to based or founded on, the register of landed property.

U·ret ...

Urceolar, a. Bot. [L. *urceolāri-s*, f. *urceolus* URCEOLUS.] = URCEOLATE 1.

Urceolate (ə·rsĭolĕt), a. [ad. mod.L. *urceolāt-us*, f. L. *urceolus* URCEOLUS.]

U·rceole. Obs.—¹. [a. OF. *urcel* (12th c.), or med.L. *urcell-us* (Dief.), = L. *urceolus* URCEOLUS. A little pitcher.

Urchin (ə·rtʃin). Forms: 4 *urcheon, 4–5 vrchoun, 5 nurchon, norchon*, 5–6 *urchone*, 5 *vrchone*, vrchowne, 6–7, 8–9 *dial. urchon*, 6–7 *vrchon*, 5–7 *urchin*, etc. [a. ONF. *herichon, herichun*, etc.]

1. A hedgehog.

2. Applied allusively to persons (see prec.).

3. One who is deformed in body; a hunchback.

4. A goblin or elf.

U·rchiness. Applied to a literary production. Obs. rare.

U·rchin-like. a. and adv.

Urd. [Hindustani (Pers.), ult. *urdū* camp (cf. Turki *ordu*, etc. : see HORDE sb.), ellipt. for *zabān-i-urdū* 'language of the camp'.]

Urdee, a. Her. Also 7 *urde, 9 urdé.* Of obscure origin : possibly due to a misreading and misunderstanding of F. *vuidée* in the phrase *croix aiguisée et vidée.*

Urdu. [= Hindustani.]

U·re (ū̇ə·r), sb.¹ Obs. [a. AF. *eure*, = OF. *ueure, euvre, ovre* (13th cent.; F. *œuvre*), ad. L. *opera* OPERA 1.]

1. In *ure*: In or into use, practice, or performance. Often with *bring*, *come*, *have*, and esp. *put* (freq. c 1510–c 1630). Also rarely with *into*.

Ure, sb.² Obs. [var. of EURE v.¹] Intr. To have good fortune.

Ure, sb.³ Obs. [var. of URE sb.¹]

Ure, v. Obs. [f. URE sb.¹]

Ure (ū̇ə·r). Also 7 *ewer, ure.* [a. ON. *úr* drizzling rain.]

1. A damp mist.

2. An atmospheric haze, esp. of a coloured nature. Freq. *dry ure.*

Urea (ū̇ə·rī·ǎ). Chem. [ad. (with Latinized ending) F. *urée* (1803), f. Gr. *ouron* urine, or the verb *ourein.* Cf. It., Sp., Pg. *urea.*]

A soluble crystalline compound, forming an organic constituent of the urine in mammalia, birds, and some reptiles, and also found in the blood, milk, etc. ; carbamide, CO(NH₂)₂.

Ureal (ū̇ə·rĭǎl), a. [f. UREA + -AL.] Of or pertaining to, of the nature of, urea ; characterized by excessive urea.

Urechin. ... A kind of sea-urchin.

Uredineal, a. Bot. [f. mod.L. *Uredine-æ* pl. of *Uredo*.] ... Pertaining or belonging to the Uredines.

Uredo (ūrī·dō). Bot. [L. *ūrēdō* a blight, blast, itch, f. *ūr-ĕre* to burn.]

1. A form of blight, or BRAND sb.

2. A species or genus of fungi.

Uredospore. Bot. [f. prec. + SPORE.]

Ure·ox (ū̇ə·rŏks). [ad. MHG. *úr-ochse* (G. *auerochs*, *aurochs* AUROCHS).] = URUS.

U·ret. Chem. ... [ad. F. *-uret.*]

-uret, suffix, repr. F. *-ure*, L. *-ūra* (whence the Romanic forms) ... A terminal denoting a combination of an element with some other body or substance.

hydroguret, telluret, etc. It is now largely replaced by -IDE, q.v.

The French school of chemists in 1787 proposed the suffix *-urētum, -orētum*, in mod.L. terms (as *phosphorētum, sulphurētum*); but in F. words they preferred the suffix *-ure* (1787 De Morveau, etc. *Méthode de Nomenclature Chimique* 207, 231, etc.).

† **U·retary**, *a.* and *sb. Obs. rare.* Also 7 uritary. [ad. F. *uretaire* (16th c.), f. *uretère*: see next.] **a.** *adj.* Of, pertaining to, or constituting the ureters. **b.** *sb.* = URETER.

1578 BANISTER *Hist. Man* v. 75 b, The extreme endes of the vretarie vessels, which both giue passage to the vrine discendyng into the bleddar. 1650 EARL MONM. tr. *Senault's Man bec. Guilty* IV. v. 213 That which Divine Justice shews in the sicknesses of the earthly Monarches when by a grain of sand he stops the uritaries [F. *vretaires*].

Ureter (yurī·təɹ). *Anat.* Also 6–7 vretere, vreter, 7 uriter. [a. medical L. *ūrētēr*, a. Gr. οὐρητήρ, f. οὐρεῖν to make water. Cf. F. *uretère* (1541), It. and Pg. *uretere*, Sp. *urétere*.] Either of the fibro-muscular tubes or vessels which convey the urine from the pelvis of the kidney to the bladder; a urinary duct.

1578 BANISTER *Hist. Man* v. 78 b, From this veyne springeth a vessell called *Vreter*. 1591 JAS. I *Poet. Exerc., Furies* 862 A Stone, which stops..The sliddrie vreter, carier of Salt vrine. 1615 CROOKE *Body of Man* (1631) 190 The paine of the Stone is..acute when it mooueth into or toward the Vreter. 1725 *Fam. Dict.* s.v. *Stone*, To make use of his Probe, and to thrust it [*sc.* the stone] thro' the Ureter into the Bladder. 1800 *Med. Jrnl.* IV. 392 On the left side of the bladder, near the termination of the ureter. 1835–6 *Todd's Cycl. Anat.* I. 348/1 The ureter [in birds]..has the same structure as in the mammalia. 1875 HUXLEY & MARTIN *Elem. Biol.* 198 The duct [of the frog]—ureter (female) or genito-urinary canal (male)—running..to the cloaca. 1893 *Brit. Med. Jrnl.* 7 Jan. 11/2 A calculus impacted in the lower end of the ureter.

attrib. 1601 HOLLAND *Pliny* II. 72 The juice of Mallows ..enlargeth the Vretere conduits. 1898 *Brit. Med. Jrnl.* 5 Nov. 1412/2 The ureter catheters..must be used with aseptic precautions.

b. More usually in pl.

1578 BANISTER *Hist. Man* v. 83 b, Two other passages.. deducyng Urine from the reynes, and called Vreteres. 1594 T. B. *La Primaud. Fr. Acad.* II. 372 Two other passages, called vreteres or vrine pipes. 1615 HART *Anat. Ur.* I. ii. 30 They shew forth the disposition..of the kidneyes, vreters, or vrine-pipes, and the bladder. 1653 H. MORE *Conject. Cabbal.* 156 Fishes, and..birds,..are both also destitute of Vreters. 1707 FLOYER *Physic. Pulse-Watch* 346 This shews the Constitution of the Veins and Ureters, by which we may understand the phlegmatic Temper. 1755 *Gentl. Mag.* XXV. 416 The ureters..are situated near the seminal vessels on each side of the spine. 1808 BARCLAY *Muscular Motions* 556 The urine..is propelled by the successive muscular action of the ureters into the bladder. 1848 CARPENTER *Anim. Phys.* 282 In all Mammalia, and in others, we find the ureters..dilated at their lower extremity into a bladder. 1876 *Clin. Soc. Trans.* IX. 26 Both ureters were full of thick yellow pus.

Ureteral, *a. Anat.* [f. prec. + -AL.] Of or pertaining to, affecting or connected with, a ureter.

1883 DUNCAN *Clin. Lect. Dis. Women* (ed. 2) x. 76 The similar condition of the urine in hysteria..and in ureteral fistula. 1894 *Ann. Surgery* Sept. 267 The treatment of the ureteral wound.

Uretere·ctomy. *Surg.* [f. as prec. + Gr. ἐκτομή: see -TOMY.] Surgical removal of a ureter.

1893 *Brit. Med. Jrnl. Epit.* 1 Apr. 49/3 Ureterectomy. Reynier..reports a case in which he removed the whole of one ureter. 1897 *Allbutt's Syst. Med.* IV. 437 Ureterectomy for diseases of Ureter.

Ureteric (yūəritэ·rik), *a.* [f. as prec. + -IC. Cf. F. *urétérique*.] Pertaining to, affecting, or occurring in a ureter or the ureters.

1822 GOOD *Study Med.* IV. 444 Ureteric stoppage of urine. 1890 BILLINGS *Med. Dict.* s.v., Superior,..middle,..and inferior ureteric arteries. *Ibid.*, Ureteric calculus,..Ureteric fold.

Ureteritis (yurītĕrəi·tis). *Path.* [f. as prec. + -ITIS. Cf. F. *urétérite*, It. *ureterite*.] Inflammation of a ureter.

1823 CRABB *Dict. Technol.* II. s.v. c1840 *Encycl. Metrop.* VII. 653/2 Ureteritis and cystitis rarely co-exist with diseases of other parts. 1889 *Buck's Handbk. Med. Sci.* VIII. 560/2 A simple uncomplicated ureteritis probably never occurs. 1898 *Lancet* 1 Jan. 17/2 If the ureter is found to be..in a condition of tuberculous ureteritis.

Uretero- (yurī·tĕro), combining form of URETER, occurring in various surgical and medical terms, as **uretero-cystoneostomy, -cystostomy, -enterostomy, -lithotomy, -stomy, -tomy** *sbs.*; **uretero-genital, -uterine, -vaginal, -vesical** *adjs.*

Many other instances occur in recent Dicts., etc., as *ureterodialysis, -lith, -lithic, -lysis, -nephrectomy, -plasty, -pyelitis, -pyosis, -rrhaphy, -stenosis, -ureteral.*

1893 *Medical Press* 15 Nov. 503/2 *Uretero-Cystoneostomy,..that [operation] of placing a severed ureter in communication direct with the bladder. 1903 *Med. Record* 13 June 958 (Cent. Suppl.), *Ureterocystostomy. 1893 *Brit. Med. Jrnl. Epit.* 4 Mar. 34/1 Any attempt at *uretero-enterostomy would..be contraindicated in cases of atonic or relaxed condition of the lower orifice of the ureter. 1887 *Lancet* 3 Sept. 496/1 (*heading*), *Uretero-genital fistulæ. 1893 *Brit. Med. Jrnl.* 7 Jan. 11/2 Case III. *Uretero-Lithotomy...The patient was placed in the lithotomy position [etc.]. 1901 *Lancet* 6 April 1034/1 The operations of ureterotomy and lumbar *ureterostomy. 1885 *Ibid.* 14 Feb. 296/2 Removal of the calculus impacted in the ureter by intra-peritoneal *ureterotomy is feasible. 1894 *Ann. Surgery* Sept. 289 This case was one in which *uretero-ureterostomy might have been performed with advantage. 1887 *Lancet* 3 Sept. 496/2 Conditions similar to those which give rise to *uretero-uterine fistulæ. *Ibid.*, *Uretero-vaginal fistulæ. 1893 *Brit. Med. Jrnl. Epit.* 4 March 34/1 The *uretero-vesicle [*sic*] sphincter..is only relaxed to give issue from time to time to a jet of urine.

Urethane (yure·þēⁱn). *Chem.* Also -an. [a. F. *uréthane*: see UR-EA and ETHANE.] Ethyl carbamate; valued as an anæsthetic.

1838 T. THOMSON *Chem. Org. Bodies* 600 The specific gravity of the vapour of urethan. 1844 FOWNES *Man. Chem.* 386 Urethane is a white, solid, crystallizable body, fusible below 212°. 1885 *Lancet* 19 Dec. 1167/2 He had slept comfortably by the aid of urethan.

Urethra (yurī·þrā). *Anat.* [a. late L. *ūrēthra* (whence F. *urèthre, urètre*, It., Sp., Pg. *uretra*, Pg. *urethra*), a. Gr. οὐρήθρα, f. οὐρεῖν to urinate.] The membranous tube or canal through which the urine is discharged from the bladder.

1634 JOHNSON tr. *Paré's Wks.* XIX. i. 723 There bee some who have the Urethra or passage of the yard obstructed by budding caruncles. 1638 A. REID *Anat. Body of Man* 215 There is no conspicuous passage, by the which the seed passeth into the urethra. 1682 T. GIBSON *Anat.* XIX. (1684) 127 In Men it [*sc.* the neck of the bladder] is longer and narrower, and..opens into the Urethra. 1732 ARBUTHNOT *Rules of Diet* iv. (1736) 428 In the Urethra, or Passage of the Urine from the Bladder. c1790 *Encycl. Brit.* (ed. 3) V. 271/2 The urethra..terminates in the podex. 1840 G. V. ELLIS *Anat.* 584 The urethra..reaches from the bladder to the extremity of the penis in the male, or to the vulva in the female. 1880 *Lancet* 24 Jan. 119/1 The urethræ of men differ in calibre. 1884 W. PYE *Surg. Handicraft* 465 Normal urethras differ greatly in their calibre.

attrib. and *Comb.* 1875 KNIGHT *Dict. Mech.* 2684/2 *Urethra-cutter*.., an instrument for enlarging the urethral canal..in case of stricture. *Ibid.*, *Urethra-syringe*,..a syringe with a long nozzle.

Urethra-, combining form of URETHRA (cf. URETHRO-), occurring in a few terms, as **ure·thragraph, -tome, urethra·meter** (see quots.).

1875 KNIGHT *Dict. Mech.* 2684/2 *Urethratome*,..a knife for dividing strictures of the urethra. 1883 G. HERSCHEL in *Lancet* 2 June 943/1 The instrument which I have devised, and to which I propose to give the name of *urethragraph. *Ibid.*, Every surgeon who..habitually makes use of the *urethrameter. 1885 *Brit. Med. Jrnl.* 11 July 54/2 Having found out the number, situations, and sizes of the contractions [of the urethra]..by the urethrameter.

Urethral (yurī·þrăl), *a.* [ad. mod.L. *ūrēthrāl-is*, or f. URETHR-A + -AL. Cf. F. *uréthral*, Pg. *urethral, uretral*.]

1. *Anat.* Of or pertaining to the urethra; constituting the urethra.

1835–6 OWEN in *Todd's Cycl. Anat.* I. 354/1 There is no true urethral canal [in birds]. *Ibid.* 355/2 Prostatic or other urethral glands. 1857 SIR H. THOMPSON *Dis. Prostate* (1861) 16 The urethral mucous membrane. 1884 — *Tumours of Bladder* 25 For which purpose the small urethral incision suffices.

2. *Path.* Affecting or occurring in the urethra; resulting from operating on the urethra.

In frequent use since c1875.

1843 R. J. GRAVES *Syst. Clin. Med.* xxv. 309 The running and urethral inflammation. 1845 *Encycl. Metrop.* VII. 600/2 Urethral hæmorrhage is a flux of blood from the urethra. 1884 W. PYE *Surg. Handicraft* 466 This urethral fever, or urethral shivering,..is generally transient.

3. Adapted for, used in, operating on the urethra.

1852 *Lancet* 7 Feb. 144/1 The prompt removal of strictures of the urinary canal with the urethral guide and tubes. 1861 ERICHSEN *Surg.* (ed. 3) 1028 Urethral lithotrite. 1884 KNIGHT *Dict. Mech.* Suppl. 263/2 The urethral divulsor for obliterating strictures. *Ibid.* 551/2 Urethral forceps... Urethral scoop.

Urethra·lgia. *Path.* [f. URETHR-A + Gr. ἄλγος pain.] A painful affection of the uretha.

1859 *New Syd. Soc. Yearbk.* 195 A case of urethralgia.. yielded to frictions of chloroform liniment.

Urethre·ctomy. *Surg.* [f. URETHR-A + Gr. ἐκτομή: see -TOMY.] Surgical removal of the urethra or part of it.

1893 *Medical Press* 29 March 324/1 Urethrectomy as a method for radical treatment of rupture of the urethra, fistula, or organic stricture. 1898 *Brit. Med. Jrnl.* 11 June 1556/1 A case of urethrectomy for impermeable stricture with retention of urine.

Urethritis (yūəriþrəi·tis). *Path.* [f. URETHR-A + -ITIS. Cf. F. *uréthrite*.] Inflammation of the urethra.

1823 CRABB *Dict. Technol.* II. s.v. 1843 R. J. GRAVES *Syst. Clin. Med.* xxvii. 347 The extension of urethritis sympathetically or by metastasis. 1888 *Lancet* 14 Jan. 58/1 The condition commonly known as chronic granular urethritis.

Hence **Urethri·tic** (-i·tik), *a.* **a.** Arising from, due to, urethritis. **b.** Affected with urethritis.

a. 1860 MAYNE *Expos. Lex.* 1313 Urethritic or gonorrhœal prostatitis. **b.** 1891 *Cent. Dict.*

Urethro- (yurī·þro), combining form of URETHRA, occurring in various surgical and pathological terms, as **urethrocele, -gram, -graph, -meter, -plasty, -rrhaphy, -scope, -scopy, -stenosis, -stomy, -tome, -tomy** *sbs.*; **urethro-genital, -metric, -plastic, -rectal, -scopic, -sexual, -vaginal, -vesical** *adjs.*

Various other terms appear in recent or special Dicts., as *urethrobulbar, -cystitis, -penile, -perineal, -phraxis, -plastic, -scopical, -spasm, -tomic*, etc. (Cf. F. *uréthroplastie, -rrhagie, -rrhaphie, -rrhée, -scope, -scopie, -tome, -tomie.*)

1873 *Lancet* 7 June 811/2 Such a *urethrocele proved extremely inconvenient to a married lady. 1885 *Buck's Handbk. Med. Sci.* I. 519/1 Urethrocele..affects the posterior wall a few millimetres above the orifice. 1840 G. V. ELLIS *Anat.* 452 The *urethro-genital portion of the perinæal space. 1893 *Medical Press* 8 Feb. 144/1 The Urethrometer.—B shows the mechanism which takes a *urethrogram by the pencil points A writing on a sliding slip of paper. 1884 G. HERSCHEL in *Lancet* 5 April 608/1 A technical description of my *urethrograph. 1884 ERICHSEN *Surg.* (ed. 8) II. 1092 For the purpose of measuring these slight strictures, Otis, of New York, has invented an instrument which he calls the *'urethrometer'. 1895 *Arnold & Sons' Surg. Instrument Catal.* 572 Urethrometer (Mac Munn's), automatic. 1884 KNIGHT *Dict. Mech.* Suppl. 916/2 *Urethrometric Sound*, an olivary sound in a canula. 1856 *Lancet* 4 Oct. 378/2 Delpech ..performed a *urethroplastic operation. 1845 *Ibid.* 25 Jan. 83/2(*heading*), *Urethro-plasty. 1861 ERICHSEN *Surg.* (ed. 3) 1095 Urethroplasty may in such cases be advantageously practised. 1857 *Lancet* 5 Sept. 247/2 Followed by the formation of a *urethro-rectal fistula. 1883 *Holmes' Syst. Surg.* (ed. 3) III. 682 *Urethrography is performed by refreshing the edges of the fistula [etc.]. 1893 *Lancet* 13 May 1135/2 The above cases of circular urethrorraphy. 1868 *Ibid.* 12 Dec. 768/2 A very simple *urethroscope. 1886 *Buck's Handbk. Med. Sci.* II. 659 The Urethroscope in position. 1895 *Arnold & Sons' Surg. Instrument Catal.* 573 *Urethroscopic Tube (Otis's). 1899 *Brit. Med. Jrnl.* 2 Dec. 1544 Urethroscopic examination showed the presence of a simple gonorrhœa. 1890 BILLINGS *Med. Dict.* II. 725 *Urethroscopy. 1901 *Lancet* 31 Aug. 590/1 The illumination..by a source of light from the outside, reflected into the tube, is as old as urethroscopy itself. 1835–6 OWEN in *Todd's Cycl. Anat.* I. 348/1 The same segment of the cloaca..is therefore termed the *urethro-sexual cavity. 1841 *Penny Cycl.* XXI. 161/1 The urethro-sexual canal. 1848 DUNGLISON *Med. Dict.* (ed. 7) 874 *Urethrostenosis*, stricture of the urethra. 1900 R. HARRISON *Vasectomy* 44 Remote results of structural lesions in urethro-stenosis. 1900 *Brit. Med. Jrnl. Epit.* 28 April 66/2 Perineal *Urethrostomy:..In this operation, the first stage of which is an ordinary external urethrotomy, the exposed urethra is cut across. 1849 CRAIG s.v., *Urethrotome. 1860 *Lancet* 21 July 58/2 Two cases of stricture of the urethra successfully treated by the urethrotome dilator. 1874 *Ibid.* 13 June 830/2 Along this the tunneled eye of the urethrotome is threaded. 1848 DUNGLISON *Med. Dict.* (ed. 7) 874 *Urethrotomy. 1852 *Lancet* 28 Aug. 204/2 Who invented urethrotomy on a grooved staff as a cure for stricture? 1867 *Biennial Retrospect* (New Syd. Soc. XXXII) 321 Internal urethrotomy is more prompt in execution. 1853 ERICHSEN *Surg.* 864 *Urethro-vaginal fistulæ are..of most common occurrence. 1885 *Buck's Handbk. Med. Sci.* I. 519/1 The whole thickness of the urethro-vaginal wall. 1873 *Lancet* 15 Nov. 699/2 *Urethro-vesical calculus.

Urethylane (yure·þilēⁱn). *Chem.* [f. UR-EA: see ETHYL and -ANE 2 b.] Methyl-urethane; methyl carbamate.

1844 FOWNES *Man. Chem.* 417 It yields with dry ammonia a solid crystallizable substance, called urethylane. 1852 WATTS tr. *Gmelin's Handbk. Chem.* VII. 292 Urethylane crystallizes in tables derived from an oblique rhombic prism. 1863 *Watts' Dict. Chem.* I. 751 Carbamate of Methyl. Urethylane.

Ure·tic, *a.* (and *sb.*). [ad. late L. *ūrētic-us*, a. Gr. οὐρητικός, f. οὐρεῖν to urinate. Cf. obs. F. *uretique* (1581), *ourétique*.] † **a.** *Uretic acid*, phosphoric acid (1857 Mayne *Expos. Lex.* 847/1). *Obs.* **b.** Diuretic (1849 Craig; hence in later Dicts.).

Ure·tte. [f. UR-INE *sb.* + -ETTE.] (See quot.)

1840 J. BUEL *Farmer's Comp.* 72 Urette is animal urine, absorbed and rendered dry by mixture with calcareous earth.

Urge (ɒ̄ɹdʒ), *sb.* [f. next.] The action of urging or fact of being urged or prompted; an impelling motive, force, pressure, etc.

In frequent use from c1910.

a1618 SYLVESTER *Forgive us our Trespasses* xxvii, O may it please thy heavenly grace,..That we may pray without all urge; Forgive us, Lord, our debts. 1884 WHITMAN *Leaves of Grass* 324 O I am sure they really came from Thee, The urge, the ardor, the unconquerable will. 1886 R. W. GILDER *Lyrics, Recognition* i, Creation,..With swift, concentric, never ceasing urge, Resolving gradual to one disk of fire. 1914 J. L. PATON *J. B. Paton* xviii. 317 Every good deed is bound to grow. There is an inward urge that forces it upwards.

Urge (ɒ̄ɹdʒ), *v.* Also 6 urdge. [ad. L. *urgē-re* to press, drive, compel, etc. (whence It. *urgere*, Sp. and Pg. *urgir*).]

I. 1. *trans.* To bring forward, present, or press upon the attention (a fact, reason, argument, etc.) in an earnest or urgent manner; to plead with or by way of argument or excuse; to allege, affirm, or state, esp. in justification, extenuation, or defence.

In frequent use from c1685.

1560 DAUS tr. *Sleidane's Comm.* 315 b, The Emperour.. aunswered him plainly that he could not..praise the same decree, and still vrged his promesse and couenaunt. 1565 CALFHILL *Answ. Martiall* 155 Ye vrge a miracle, for euery ..splinter of the Crosse, inasmuch as a Church..was preserued from burning by it. 1596 *Edw. III*, II. i. 447, A spatious field of reasons could I vrge. 1655 FULLER *Ch. Hist.* I. 8 This..were an argument (as K. James did once pleasantly urge it) to prove our Old stile before the New. a1695 J. SCOTT *Chr. Life* II. Wks. 1718 I. 419 The Apostle urges our having a compassionate High Priest in Heaven to intercede for us. 1713 BERKELEY *Hylas & Phil.* II. Wks. 1871 I. 314, I am at a loss what more to urge. 1784 COWPER *Task* VI. 56 The few.., seeking grace t'improve the prize they hold, Would urge a wiser suit than asking more. 1798 S. & HT. LEE *Canterb. T.* II. 164 [He] urged his weak health, as rendering it necessary he should travel very leisurely. 1816 J. SCOTT *Paris Revisit.* (ed. 3) 321 Canova appeared as a claimant in behalf of Rome, which had only her venerable name to urge. 1855 *Poultry Chron.* III. 242/2 The most fastidious can urge no objection. 1864 D. G. MITCHELL *Sev. Stor.* 279 The Count urged the scandal which would grow out of such a measure.

b. Const. *on, upon*; *to*, etc.; also *against*.

1593 SHAKS. *Rich. II*, II. i. 299 Vrge doubts to them yt feare. 1607 — *Cor.* IV. vii. 19 He knowes not What I can vrge against him. 1654 BRAMHALL *Just Vind.* iii. 35 Yet three things are urged against it. 1667 MILTON *P. L.* VI. 622 The terms we sent were terms of weight,..and full of force urg'd home. 1749 FIELDING *Tom Jones* VII. xv, So far from being an Advocate for the present Prisoner, she urged his Guilt to his Officer. 1841 A. COMBE *Physiol. Digestion* (ed. 3) 304, I shall..urge upon him the necessity of rendering our knowledge more complete. 1872 TENNYSON *Gareth & Lynette* 1313 Lancelot on him urged All the devisings of their chivalry.

c. With clause as object, either introduced by *that* or directly quoted.

(*a*) 1560 DAUS tr. *Sleidane's Comm.* 227 The French men ..especially vrged that the Scotes myght be comprised in the peace. 1596 DRAYTON *Legends* i. 352 Further to urge what she before had said. 1638 JUNIUS *Paint. Ancients* 2 Wee doe therein urge somewhat further, that [etc.]. 1672 H. STUBBE *Justif. Dutch War* 24 The Queen urged, that ..she was to be Arbitress. 1817 JAS. MILL *Brit. India* II. IV. v. 217 It was urged..that the servants..ought not to be deprived of such precious advantages. 1885 'MRS. ALEXANDER' *At Bay* ix, I urged that the disappearance of the.. money..would tell against him.

(*b*) 1689 PRIOR *Epistle to Fleetwood Shephard* 78 So Atoms dancing round the Center, They urge, made all Things at a Venture. a1743 OZELL tr. *Brantome's Sp. Rhodom.* (1744) 67 M. de Lansac urged, It was absolutely necessary. a1792 SIR J. REYNOLDS *Journ. Flanders & Holland* Wks. 1797 II. 124 There is lightness, airiness, and facility in Rubens, his advocates will urge. 1838 DICKENS *Nickleby* vi, 'Father,' urged the maiden [to the monk],.. 'our daily alms have been distributed.' 1865 — *Mut. Fr.* III. i, 'Don't break out, Lammle,' urged Fledgeby, in a submissive tone. 1884 tr. *Lotze's Logic* 424 We are left after all, it will be urged,..walled in within the all-embracing delusions of those ideas.

2. To advocate or advise earnestly (some course of action, etc.); to press with importunity, claim or demand pressingly.

1595 SHAKS. *John* IV. ii. 204 Why vrgest thou so oft yong Arthurs death? 1596 WARNER *Alb. Eng.* IX. xlvi. (1602) 217 Then proudly pricke the mounted Sers, the Harrolds..vrging fees to gentellize their name. 1601 SHAKS. *Jul. C.* IV. iii. 261, I should not vrge thy duty past thy might. 1661 *Reg. Privy Council Scot.* I. 5 The Lord Chancellour..is to urge of them the oath of supremacie. 1682 DRYDEN *Medal* 187 What vengeance will they urge, Whose Ordures neither Plague nor Fire can purge. 1805 *Med. Jrnl.* XIV. 206, I thought it my duty to urge the operation. 1816 SCOTT *Old Mort.* xxxiii, He hath ever urged peace with the malignants. 1831 JAMES *Phil. Augustus* II. v, The many, which were all eager to urge a course that..he would have been the first to follow, but [etc.].

b. With impersonal subject.

1592 KYD *Sp. Trag.* III. i. 61 Embassadour, What news hath vrg'd this sodain entrance? *Ibid.* IV. iv. 87, I see your lookes vrge instance of these wordes. 1605 SHAKS. *Lear* V. i. 52 The Enemy's in view, draw vp your powers;..your hast Is now vrg'd on you. 1667 MILTON *P. L.* IX. 250 For solitude somtimes is best societie, And short retirement urges sweet returne. 1872 GEO. ELIOT *Middlem.* lxxxvi, A past error may urge a grand retrieval.

II. 3. To entreat or plead with (a person) pertinaciously; to importune, press, or ply with arguments or strong persuasion; to prompt, solicit, or request earnestly. Also, with impersonal subject: To incite or impel strongly.

1568 BIBLE (Bishops') *Luke* xi. 53 The lawyers and the pharisees began to vrge hym vehemently, and to prouoke hym to speake many thynges. 1586 DAY *Eng. Secretorie* II. (1625) 25 To vrge me as you doe, may but breed that which neither of vs may returne pleasing. 1595 SHAKS. *John* II. i. 475, I see a yeelding in the lookes of France;..vrge them while their soules Are capable of this ambition. 1640 HABINGTON *Queen of Arragon* II. 366, I urg'd Them with the memory of their former deedes. 1667 MILTON *P. L.* IX. 588 Hunger and thirst at once,..quick'nd at the scent Of that alluring fruit, urg'd me so keene. 1692 DRYDEN *St. Euremont's Ess.* 24 Urged with an apprehension of their ruine, [they] abandoned themselves to the Conduct of Xantippus. 1717 POPE *Iliad* X. 135 Strong necessity our toils demands,..and urges all our hands. 1814 J. AUSTEN *Mansf. Park* xv, Do not urge her, madam... It is not fair to urge her in this manner. 1847 HELPS *Friends in C.* I. v. 83 Men ..cannot be moved in masses as of old. At one time chivalry urged all men—then the Church. 1853 J. H. NEWMAN *Hist. Sk.* (1873) I. 183 The barbarian..moves when he is urged by appetite.

b. Const. *to* with inf.; also with advs. (as *on, onward*) and preps.

(*a*) 1565 COOPER *Thesaurus* s.v. *Insto*, Vrge me not, or presse me not to judge. 1613 SHAKS. *Hen. VIII*, IV. ii. 157 Vrge the King To do me this last right. 1671 MILTON *Samson* 1677 A spirit of phrenzie..Who..urg'd them on with mad desire To call in hast for their destroyer. 1753–4 RICHARDSON *Grandison* II. xxiii. 167 Should she engage without waiting for his consent; as she was urged to do, by Letters. 1816 SCOTT *Bl. Dwarf* xviii, His patriotism urged him to serve his country abroad. 1891 FARRAR *Darkn. & Dawn* xxix, Seneca..urged the Emperor to summon him into his presence.

(*b*) 1600 *1st Pt. Sir J. Oldcastle* IV. ii. 9 Pardon, my Lord; my conscience vrg'd me to it. 1776 PAINE *Com. Sense* 9 Hunger in the mean time would urge him from his work. 1791 COWPER *Iliad* V. 904 Venus..and the Archer..have urged, themselves, to this The frantic Mars. 1832 LYTTON *Eugene A.* I. v, They urge us onward, yet present no limit to our progress. 1846 MRS. A. MARSH *Father Darcy* II. iv. 98 He was not urging others to a course in which he never intended to venture himself. 1871 *Leisure Hour* 480/1 Two guineas paid to..his clerk, to urge him on with the works.

† **c.** To charge strongly *with* something. Also with *that* and clause. *Obs.*

1599 THYNNE *Animadv.* (1875) 54 Speakinge to his wyfe, he urgethe her that she cannott denye yt. 1628 SIR W. MURE *Spir. Hymne* 144 Thou of our innocence the ground, for vs, with guilt was vrgde. 1689 WOOD *Life* (O.H.S.) III. 310 Speed's daughter told the bishop of it and the bishop urg'd him with it. 1703 ROWE *Fair Penit.* v. i, Thou com'st to urge me with the wrongs I ha' done thee.

4. a. To serve or act as a constraining influence on (something); to bear pressingly on; to spur, actuate, or constrain.

1576 FLEMING *Panopl. Epist.* 62 More I may say to you, then any mans mynde is urged to accomplishe. 1592 KYD *Sp. Trag.* III. iv. 14 A guiltie conscience, vrged with the thought Of former euils, easily cannot erre. *Ibid.* IV. iv. 145 But loue of him..Did vrge her resolution to be such. 1633 BP. HALL *Hard Texts, O.T.* 620 Yee have extreamely urged the patience of the Lord. 1823 SCOTT *Quentin D.* ii, I..will pay fitting respect to your age, if you do not urge my patience with mockery. 1843 NEALE *Hymns for Sick* 23 Give me when those last trials urge Thy Very Flesh and Blood. 1878 *Masque Poets* 42, I was wrong to urge your will And wrong to mar your life.

† **b.** To treat (a mineral, etc.) with great heat.

1758 REID tr. *Macquer's Chym.* I. 69 If the calx of Tin be urged by a strong fire. 1828–32 WEBSTER s.v., To urge an ore with intense heat.

III. 5. To hasten or press forward (a proceeding, enterprise, etc.); to prosecute with effort, energy, or vigour; to push forward.

1565 COOPER *Thesaurus* s.v. *Insto, Instabit huic loco*,..He shall vrge this, or be earnest in this. 1583 STUBBES *Anat. Abus.* I. H 4, [It] bringeth death before nature vrge it,..or age require it. 1598 HAKLUYT *Voy.* I. 145 Swandepolcus.. affirming that himselfe neuer prospered so long as he vrged warre against them. 1667 BOYLE *Orig. Formes & Qual.* 430 This Substance..will..(if the Distillation have been urg'd far enough) [be] brittle. 1684 EARL ROSCOM. *Ess. Transl. Verse* 238 Urge your Success, deserve a lasting Name. 1697 DRYDEN *Æneis* V. 273 The Crew of Mnestheus,..with elated Minds, Urge their Success. *Ibid.* VII. 660 While Turnus urges thus his Enterprise. 1713 ADDISON *Cato* III. v, Why wilt thou urge the fate Of wretched men? 1781 COWPER *Table-T.* 214 The peasants urge their harvest. 1789 E. DARWIN *Bot. Gard.* II. 79 When..wither'd Famine urged the work of death. 1855 PRESCOTT *Philip II*, I. viii. I. 239 Henry obstinately urged his fate, and compelled the count ..to take the saddle. 1855 MACAULAY *Hist. Eng.* xii. III. 213 The bills which the Commons were urging forward. 1885 *Daily Tel.* 11 Sept. (Encycl. Dict.), Urging the carriage, and eyeing with pleasure all the horrors of war.

transf. 1857 RUSKIN *Pol. Econ. Art* 110 Every kind deed ..in relieving distress..would..open and urge, in a thousand unforeseen directions, the sluices of commerce and the springs of industry.

6. To press forcibly in some direction; to force or impel forward or onward; to drive. Also with preps. or advs., as *against, away, down, through*.

1594 KYD *Cornelia* V. 188 Now we of our side vrge them to retreate, And nowe before them we retyre as fast. 1634 SIR T. HERBERT *Trav.* 87 The first walke is set with pipes of Lead and Brasse, through which the water is vrged. 1693 T. CREECH *Juvenal* XIII. 93 Rivers chang'd to Blood Roul wond'rous Waves, or urge a Milky Flood. 1742 POPE *Dunc.* IV. 592 From Stage to Stage the licens'd Earl may run,..The Senator at Cricket urge the Ball. 1791 COWPER *Iliad* V. 70 For Menelaus..the spear urged through his breast. 1813 BYRON *Corsair* III. xv, The blue waves sport around the stern they urge. 1827 FARADAY *Chem. Manip.* xvi. 395 The latter [*sc.* air] being urged away from the tube by a force proportionate [etc.]. 1862 CALVERLEY *Verses & Tr.* 16 Still I see you..Urge, towards the table's centre,..the squail.

transf. 1737 POPE *Imit. Hor., Ep.* II. ii. 253 Heir urges heir, like wave impelling wave. 1821 SHELLEY *Adonais* xxi, As long as skies are blue,..Evening must usher night, night urge the morrow.

fig. 1870 BRYANT *Iliad* II. I. 77 The fates Decreed their early death and urged them on.

b. To cause to move, hasten, or gather speed; to accelerate the pace of; to speed up. Usu. with advs. (as *forward, on*) or preps.

a1721 PRIOR *Journey to Copt-Hall* 12, I mount, and..With unarm'd kick urge on my horse. 1760 FAWKES tr. *Anacreon, Ode* lix. 8 With tighten'd Rein, I'll urge thee round the dusty Plain. 1821 SHELLEY *Epithalamion* 20 Nay, return, Vesper! urge thy lazy car! 1846 MRS. A. MARSH *Father Darcy* II. xix. 317 Their wearied horses..gave evidence of the fierce desperation with which they had been urged forward. 1902 VIOLET JACOB *Sheep-Stealers* x, Coachmen were urging their horses up to the door.

refl. 1805 BINGLEY *Anim. Biog.* (ed. 2) II. 159 [Birds] urge themselves forward in the air by means of wings.

c. To press or pursue (one's flight, way, the chase); to hasten or accelerate (one's pace, etc.).

1697 DRYDEN *Virg. Georg.* III. 75 High Epidaurus urges on my speed, Fam'd for his hills, and for his horses' breed. 1703 POPE *Thebais* 558 Hapless Tydeus..Thro' the thick deserts headlong urg'd his flight. 1735 SOMERVILLE *Chase* III. 543 He..up the Breeze Urges his Course with eager Violence. a1763 SHENSTONE *Elegies* XVI. 94 Led by their beams I urg'd the pleasing chase. 1801 M. G. LEWIS *Tales of Wonder, Sir Hengist* ii, Sir Hengist urged his courser's pace. 1804 W. L. BOWLES *Spir. Discov.* IV. 579 With De Quiros to the South Still urge thy way. 1840 THIRLWALL *Greece* VII. 61 He had several motives to urge his progress. 1854 H. MILLER *Sch. & Schm.* xvi. 340, I should have to urge my way through the works of our best writers.

7. a. To stimulate to expression or action; to provoke or excite; to increase or intensify.

1594 *1st Pt. Contention* (1843) 24 Forbeare ambitious Prelate to vrge my griefe. 1594 KYD *Cornelia* I. 166 The wrath of heauen (though vrg'd) we see is slow In punishing the euils we haue done. 1616 W. BROWNE *Brit. Past.* II. iv. 516 Anger and pitty, in his manly brest, Urge, yet restraine his teares. 1800 tr. *Lagrange's Chem.* I. 401 Then urge the fire gradually, bring the crucible to a white heat. 1820 SHELLEY *Prometh. Unb.* I. 42 While from their loud abysses howling throng The genii of the storm, urging the rage Of whirlwind. 1839 URE *Dict. Arts* 1124 The heat having been briskly urged for a short time. 1865 J. M. NEALE *Hymns on Paradise* 28 All his spite my Tempter urges.

b. To provoke to anger; to irritate or annoy. Also with clause (quot. 1593). Now *dial.*

1593 LODGE *Will. Longbeard* E 3 This is it that urgeth me that I fall into his hands. 1655 [see URGING *ppl. a.* 1 b]. 1876– in dialect use (*Eng. Dial. Dict.* s.v. *Urge v.*¹ 2).

8. To ply vigorously; to use, work, or employ briskly or diligently.

1697 DRYDEN *Æneis* V. 301 Both urge their Oars. a1760 I. H. BROWNE *Fireside Poems* (1768) 126, I urge the gay flask With a set of old friends. 1820 SHELLEY *Fragm. Satire on Sat.* 25 Follow his flight with winged words, and urge The strokes of the inexorable scourge.

IV. *intr.* **9.** To press by inquiry or statement; to adduce or bring forward arguments, allegations, etc. Also const. *to* with inf.

1592 *Soliman & Pers.* III. i. 73 Erastus, ile not yet vrge to know the cause That brought thee hether. 1613 SHAKS. *Hen. VIII*, V. iii. 48, I doe beseech your Lordships, That.. my Accusers..may stand forth face to face, And freely vrge against me. 1804 *Something Odd* I. 130 When she had no company at home, he would urge to go and seek it abroad. 1818 SHELLEY *Julian* 616, I urged and questioned still, she told me how All happened.

b. To press solicitously, make a strong claim, *for* something.

1607 SHAKS. *Timon* III. ii. 13 One of his men..vrg'd extreamly for't [*sc.* money], and shewed what necessity belong'd too't. 1660 SHARROCK *Vegetables* 67 Infinite storyes of strange conjunctions which urge earnestly for credit. 1726 SWIFT *Serm. Martyrd. K. Chas.* Wks. 1765 XV. 134 That wicked faction.., not content with all those marks of his justice.., urged still for more. 1753–4 RICHARDSON *Grandison* II. ix. 60 He again urged for her hand, and for a private marriage. 1769 GOLDSM. *Hist. Rome* I. 183 The tribunes..began once more to urge for the removal.

† **c.** To strive *for* (mastery). *Obs.*⁻¹

1691 tr. *Emilianne's Frauds Rom. Monks* (ed. 3) 302 His lovely Countenance, where the Lilly and the Rose did urge for Mastery.

10. To press, push, or hasten on. Esp. with advs., as *along, on, onward, upward*.

1605–8 DONNE *To Sir H. Goodyere* 8 A Palace..decayes: But hee which dwels there, is not so; for hee Strives to urge upward, and his fortune raise. 1653 MILTON *Psalm* vii. 21 Rise Jehovah in thine ire, Rouze thy self amidst the rage Of my foes that urge like fire. 1692 PRIOR *Ode, Imit. Horace* v. 31 Darius flies, young Ammon urges on. 1712 STEELE *Spect.* No. 374 ¶1 Those behind him, if he does not urge on, will tread him down. 1821 CLARE *Vill. Minstr.* II. 27 Thou hast heard the thorn's in flower, And childhood's bliss is urging on. 1857 SUSANNA WINKWORTH tr. *Life Tauler* ix. 247 Through all this he shall urge onward, till [etc.]. 1907 *Westm. Gaz.* 19 Oct. 3/1 A woman.., moaning inarticulately, urges wearily along.

11. To act as an impelling or prompting motive, stimulus, or force; to incite or stimulate; to exercise pressure or constraint.

1645 WALLER *Poems* 142 Let Brutes..that cannot think, So far as drought and Nature urges, drinke. 1656 SMITH *Pract. Physick* 147 Since two things do urge, either Malignity or the Feaver; if that urge, most Antidotes are necessary. a1660 *Contemp. Hist. Irel.* (Ir. Archæol. Soc.) I. 157 Therefore thriued your precept may vrge, but your example is not souldierlike. 1667 MILTON *P. L.* I. 66 Hope never comes That comes to all; but torture without end Still urges. 1698 FRYER *Acc. E. India & P.* 172 The present Occasions urging, and [they] being willing to blind themselves. 1716 POPE *Iliad* VI. 453 The combat urges, and my soul's on fire. 1752 HUME *Pol. Disc.* viii. 138 Necessity calls, fear urges, reason exhorts. 1791 COWPER *Iliad* V. 848 The time Urges, and need appears that we ourselves Now call to mind the fury of our might. 1805–6 CARY *Dante's Inf.* IV. 21 Our length of way Urges to haste.

† **b.** To be of weight or importance. *Obs.*

1654 Z. COKE *Logick* 145 A Syllogism leading to absurdity, much urgeth in disputing.

Hence **Urged** (ɒ̄ɹdʒd) *ppl. a.*

1595 DANIEL *Civ. Wars* IV. lxxxiv, Whilst looking onely on the vrged crime Vnto the farther drift they take no heed. c1611 CHAPMAN *Iliad* XVI. 264 Remember you express Your late-urged virtue. 1628 FELTHAM *Resolves* II. lxv. 186 Gifts are the greatest Vsurie; because a two-fold retribution is an vrged effect, that a Noble nature prompts vs to. 1786 BURNS *On W. Chalmers* ii, I am nae stranger to..his warm-urged wishes. 1883 DUNCAN *Clin. Lect. Dis. Women* (ed. 2) ii. 8 And such urged passing [of uterine bougie] induces spasms.

Urgence (ɒ̄·ɹdʒĕns). [a. F. *urgence* (1572), or f. URGENT *a.*: see -ENCE.]

1. Earnest or pressing solicitation; importunity; = URGENCY 2.

c1592 MARLOWE *Jew of Malta* Prol., This all that he intends, (And that too, at the vrgence of some friends). 1624 HEYWOOD *Gunaik.* II. 100 His urgence overcame the silence of the Oracle. 1634 — *Maidenh. well lost* I. C 2, At my vrgence He promis't you a parley. 1879 HOWELLS *L. Aroostook* 166 She tried to remember at his urgence, something of her childhood. *Ibid.* 219 'Oh I give you the right,' he cried with passionate urgence. 1893 F. ADAMS *Egypt* 255 At the united urgence of France and England.., [he] resigned.

2. Urgent need; pressing necessity or importance; = URGENCY 1.

c1605 BODLEY in *Trecentale Bodleianum* (1913) 44 The Keeper may sometimes, vpon Vrgence of buisnesse,..desire a dispensation for his personal absence from his charge. 1610 HEYWOOD *Gold. Age* IV. i, Urgence calls me hence To an enforced absence. 1639 DAVENPORT *New Trick* I. i, His businesse craves dispatch, And is of serious urgence.

3. Quickness, expedition, haste.

1612 J. COTTA *Dang. Pract. Physic* I. viii. 60 Drunkennesse, whose ordinarily knowne effects are..in some imaginations..quicke and readie, in some with as apparent vrgence, yet senselesse. 1868 GEO. ELIOT *Sp. Gipsy* 72 Late despatches sent With urgence by the Count of Bavien. 1869 BLACKMORE *Lorna D.* x, We found good reason for the urgence and melancholy of the duck-birds.

4. Impelling force; = URGENCY 5.

1874 S. LANIER *Poems, Corn* 13 Expirations strong Throb from young hickories..With stress and urgence bold of prisoned spring. 1876 GEO. ELIOT *Dan. Der.* V. xxxvi, A shrinking finally overcome by the urgence of poverty. 1876 DOWDEN *Poems* 2 The lapsing waters tell The urgence uncontrollable Which makes the trouble of their breast.

Urgency (ɒ̄·ɹdʒĕnsi). [f. next (see -ENCY), or ad. late L. *urgentia*. Cf. It. *urgenza*, Sp. and Pg. *urgencia*, and prec.]

I. 1. The state, condition, or fact of being urgent; pressing importance; imperativeness.

1540 *Act 32 Hen. VIII*, c. 48 § 6 If the importaunce or urgency of the cause..so require. 1594 HOOKER *Eccl. Pol.* I. viii. § 8 Only in case of so great vrgency. 1644 *Impeachm. Dk. Buckhm.* (Camden) 129 Alleadgeing the urgency of the present service. 1686 tr. *Chardin's Trav. Persia* 63, I told him the Urgency of my Occasions. 1793 JEFFERSON *Writ.* (1859) IV. 96 The ascertaining of this point becomes a matter of present urgency. 1797 MRS. RADCLIFFE *Italian* xi, The urgency of your circumstances. 1833 I. TAYLOR *Fanat.* i. 7 There are..motives..of far greater force, and these..have a peculiar urgency in reference to the present moment. 1866 GEO. ELIOT *F. Holt* xxv, I will not wait for the urgency of necessity. 1877 ERICHSEN *Surg.* I. 13 The four cases of extreme surgical urgency.

b. *spec.* (See quot. 1884.)

1883 MAY *Treat. Parlt.* (ed. 9) 383 By the aid of these rules of urgency, a serious political crisis had been overcome. 1884 *Imp. Dict.* IV. 529 In parliament, *urgency* is when, by a vote of three to one in a house of not less than 300 members, a measure is declared urgent in the interest of the state.

2. Pressure by importunity or entreaty; urgent solicitation; insistence.

1611 COTGR., *Importunite*, importunitie, vrgencie, earnestnesse. 1735 SWIFT *Gulliver's Let. to Simpson* ¶1 By your great and frequent urgency, you prevailed on me to [etc.]. 1782 MISS BURNEY *Cecilia* VII. iv, This confession..was torn from her by..[Delville's] impetuous urgency. 1828 LYTTON *Pelham* III. x, In spite of all the urgency and entreaties of my letters for a reply. 1882 T. MOZLEY *Remin. Oriel College*, etc. I. Introd. 4 At his encouragement and urgency I stood for a Fellowship.

3. Stress *of* wind, weather, etc.

1660 BURNEY Κέρδ. Δῶρον (1661) 12 There was never any tender nightingale so preserved in the urgencie of the weather. 1859 W. M. THOMSON *Land & Book* I. 66 Neither heavy weights.., nor the importunate urgency of the wind, can sway it [*sc.* a palm-tree] aside from perfect uprightness.

4. Persistence, eagerness. *rare*⁻¹.

a1677 BARROW *Serm.* XVI. Wks. 1686 III. 184 And why with less expedition or urgency should we persue the certain means of our present security?

5. Impelling or prompting force or quality.

1816 SCOTT *Antiq.* xxxvi, What she has told you..from no apparent impulse but the urgency of conscience. 1858 J. MARTINEAU *Stud. Chr.* 281 The urgency of desire and devotion. 1863 GEO. ELIOT *Romola* II. xxx, The new urgency of this habitual thought brought a new suggestion.

II. 6. An urgent need or situation.

1647 MAY *Hist. Parl.* II. i. 11 Collections through the Kingdom being too slow for such an urgency. 1695 LOCKE *Further Consid. Value Money* 58 The accidental difference ..is sometimes (but rarely) two pence in five shillings, or somewhat more in great urgencies. 1820 KEATS *Isabella* xxix, With sudden speed,..Because of some great urgency and need In their affairs. 1832 *Rolls of Parlt.* Index 467/2 Agrees to respite the Levy..for Two Years,..unless any Urgency should arise.

7. A driving or constraining impulse or motive.

1664 H. MORE *Myst. Iniq.* xx. 76 Pinched betwixt the sense of poverty and quick urgencies of Devotion. 1822 GOOD *Study Med.* I. 343 The patient..will still perhaps be tormented with..a perpetual urgency to expulsion. c1830 CHALMERS *Lect. Romans* lxix. (1840) 346 Evil might ensue from unbridled and unreasonable urgencies of talk upon this subject. 1883 D. C. MURRAY *Hearts* viii, A superstitious reverence for his guest's genius, and its various urgencies.

8. *pl.* Earnest representations or entreaties; importunities.

1823 JEFFERSON *Writ.* (1830) IV. 376 We..met, and after the urgencies of each on the other, I consented to undertake the task. 1877 'H. A. PAGE' *De Quincey* xvii. II. 40 Books ..to be returned, in answer to the urgencies of librarians. 1883 MISS BROUGHTON *Belinda* III. v, Belinda,..despite the warm urgencies of the..strangers, retires in favour of her visitors.

III. 9. *attrib.*, as *urgency order, pledge, rate.*

1883 MAY *Treat. Parlt.* (ed. 9) 383 It became necessary to revive the urgency resolution of the 3rd February 1881. 1890 *Lunacy Act* § 11 In cases of urgency where it is expedient..that the alleged lunatic should be forthwith placed under care and treatment, he may be received and detained ..upon an urgency order. 1891 *Pall Mall G.* 7 April 5/2 It is said Mrs. Cathcart is confined under an urgency order. 1898 MORLEY in *Daily News* 14 Feb. 3/7 The Press agencies ..paid what is called an urgency rate—that is about, I think, twenty or thirty times higher than the ordinary Press rate. 1906 R. WHITEING *Ring in the New* 47 Taking in urgency pledges after the closing of the pawn-shops.

Urgent (ɒ̄·ɹdʒĕnt), *a.* [a. F. *urgent* (14th c.), a. L. *urgent-, urgens*, pres. pple. of *urgēre* to URGE. Cf. It., Sp., Pg. *urgente*.]

I. 1. Pressing, impelling; demanding or calling for prompt action; marked or characterized by urgency. (Freq. from c1800.)

In earliest use with *cause* or *necessity*.

1496 *Rolls of Parlt.* VI. 515/1 Towarde the..mayntenaunce of the Armye aforsaid, and urgent causes concernyng the same. 1526 *Pilgr. Perf.* (W. de W. 1531) 162 b, But onely whan cause vrgent, & very necessite compelleth. 1558 BP. WATSON *Sev. Sacram.* xix. 119 Where the Sacrament is excluded by vrgent necessitye. a1586 SIDNEY *Arcadia* III. iv, The more I stirre about urgent affaires. 1604 THORNBOROUGH *Discourse* (title-p.), The euident vtilitie and vrgent necessitie of the desired happie Vnion. 1660 MILTON *Free Commw.* Wks. 1851 V. 451 To the retarding..oft times of thir Counsels or urgentest occasions. 1676–7 MARVELL *Corr.* Wks. (Grosart) II. 521 The true remedy of the urgent condition of this poore Nation. 1712 SWIFT *Jrnl. to Stella* 25 Feb., I have no urgent business upon my hands. 1755 YOUNG *Centaur* vi. Wks. 1757 IV. 282 With only this additional, and still more urgent,..motive for reformation. 1772 W. BUCHAN *Dom. Med.* (ed. 2) 278 Unless these symptoms are urgent, it is safer to let it alone. 1816 J. SCOTT *Paris Revisit.* (ed. 3) 117 They were soon forced to separate to attend to their respective urgent duties. 1843 R. J. GRAVES *Syst. Clin. Med.* xx. 239 What may be done by simple means in relieving an urgent disease. 1866 ROGERS *Agric. & Prices* I. xxi. 528 The necessity not being so urgent as it is now.

b. Of commands, messages, etc., by which a matter is strongly pressed upon a person's attention.

1611 BIBLE *Dan.* iii. 22 The Kings commandement was vrgent. 1779 *Mirror* No. 32, The remonstrances of his man of business, aided by very urgent requests from me. 1816 BENTHAM *Chrestom.* 262 Other objects, for the illustration of which the demand..is accordingly still more urgent. 1856 STANLEY *Sinai & Pal.* iv. 205 This summons was as urgent as words can describe. 1883 O. W. HOLMES *Pages fr. Old Vol. Life* 63 A second telegraphic message..so direct and urgent that I should be sure of an answer to it. 1886 BARING-GOULD *Court Royal* xxxviii, 'Papa,' said Lady Grace in urgent tones.

2. Of a feeling, etc.: That constrains, impels, or prompts. Also const. *of*.

1559 *Reg. St. Andrews Kirk Session* (S.H.S.) I. 18 Giue thei be vexed and urnet with ustioun and urgent appetites of the flesche. 1566 DRANT *Hor., Sat.* II. i. E vij b, Yf I haue suche vrgent luste, and lykyng to indite. 1641 MILTON *Ch. Govt.* I. vii, The miseries of Ireland are urgent of a speedy redress. 1748 G. WHITE *Serm.* (MS.), If people will not follow nature in her most urgent affections, and importunate Requests. 1873 MORLEY *Rousseau* (1905) II. 34 When men are beginning to feel the urgent spirit of a new time.

3. Of persons: Pressingly solicitous; importunate, insistent. Also with preps., as *for, in, on*, † *unto*.

1548 ELYOT, *Premo*,..*premere*,..to be vrgent or instante vpon. 1565 COOPER *Thesaurus* s.v. *Premo*, I was not more vrgent or instant on any pointe, then, &c. a1593 MARLOWE & NASHE *Dido* III. i, All these..Haue been most vrgent suiters for my loue. 1611 BIBLE *Exod.* xii. 33 The Egyptians were vrgent vpon the people that they might send them out of the land in haste. 1698 COLLIER *Immor. Stage* 107 Oedipus is..Urgent for an account of Particulars. 1732 LEDIARD *Sethos* II. x. 355 The officers of his fleet were urgent in offering their services. 1778 MISS BURNEY *Evelina* ii, The advice and entreaties of all his friends, among whom I was myself the most urgent. 1820 W. IRVING *Sketch Bk.* II. 149 His family have been very urgent for him to make an expedition to Margate. 1883 *Law Times* 20 Oct. 408/1 The public and the Profession were alike urgent in calling for sweeping reforms.

b. Eagerly desirous *to* do something.

1753–4 RICHARDSON *Grandison* II. xxviii. 227, I never knew him to be so very urgent to know my heart. 1798 S. & HT. LEE *Canterb. T.* II. 181 [It] made him..urgent to set out for England. 1826 GALT *Last of Lairds* xxxiv. 302 Mr. Loopy..had been calling, urgent to see me. 1846 MRS. A. MARSH *Father Darcy* II. 243 He is very urgent to see him.

II. 4. Impelling, pressing, or bearing onwards.

1546 *Yorks. Chantry Surv.* (Surtees) 209 When as the waters of Rothere and Downe are so urgent, that the curate of Rotherham cannot to them repayre. 1876 R. BRIDGES *Growth of Love* v, Her launched passion when she sings Wins on the hearing like a shapen prow Borne by the mastery of its urgent wings. 1879 — *A Passer-by* i, Whither, O splendid ship, thy white sails crowding, Leaning across the bosom of the urgent West.

† **5.** Oppressive; severe; heavy. *Obs.*

1545 BRINKLOW *Compl.* ii. 10 b, An vrgent dammage to the common welth. 1600 HAKLUYT *Voy.* III. 49 During the two houres of those two dayes the heat is very vrgent. 1606 SHAKS. *Ant. & Cl.* I. ii. 187 Not alone The death of Fuluia, with more vrgent touches, Do strongly speake to vs. a1699 J. BEAUMONT *Psyche* III. 147 Which Jesus seeing, He upon him threw The urgent yoak of an express Injunction.

† **6.** Of time: Pressing; passing quickly. *Obs.*

1611 SHAKS. *Wint. T.* I. ii. 465 Please your Highnesse To take the vrgent houre. 1791 COWPER *Iliad* I. 74 But time is urgent; haste we to consult Priest, prophet, or interpreter of dreams.

Hence **U·rgentness**, urgency. *rare.*

1598 BARRET *Theor. Warres* II. i. 25 The vrgentnesse of the cause doeth deepely require it. 1727 BAILEY (vol. II), *Pressingness*, Urgentness.

Urgently, *adv.* [-LY².] In an urgent manner.

1548 UDALL, etc. *Erasm. Par. John* xix. 108 b, Therfore the Jewes called more vrgently vpon the matter. 1611 COTGR., *Importunément*, importunately, vrgently, earnestly. 1789 in C. F. Jenkins *Tortola* (1923) 90, I thank thee for thy kind advice thou hast so urgently given me. 1840 THIRLWALL *Greece* VII. 303 His attention..was urgently claimed by the danger which now threatened him. 1871 A. MEADOWS *Man. Midwifery* iii. (ed. 2) 361 Prompt action is urgently necessary.

Urger (ɒ̄·ɹdʒəɹ). [f. URGE *v.* + -ER¹.]

1. One who urges or incites. Also with *on*.

1598 FLORIO, *Scongiuratore*, a conspirer, a coniurer, an vrger. 1605 W. BRADSHAW *Eng. Puritanism* v. 29 They hould that such an ooth (on the vrgers part) is most damnable. 1659 F. OSBORN *Misc. Ess.*, etc. 149, I confesse Necessity cannot onely abate the Edge of these Reasons; but turne their Poynts against the Urger. 1704 D'URFEY *Heir Adopted* lxx, 'Twas past all Bounds before, And needed not an urger on. 1753 RICHARDSON *Grandison* (1781) II. xxix. 276 If the urger suspects not the fitness of his addresses. 1837 B. D. WALSH *Aristoph., Knights* IV. i, The urgers-on of nimble steeds. 1892 *Temple Bar Mag.* Dec. 496 Scott..was the tempter and urger in a ruinous policy. 1903 T. HARDY *Dynasts* I. VI. iii, The Eternal Urger, pressing change on change.

2. An instigator or advocate, an earnest supporter or presenter, *of* something. Now *rare.*

In frequent use c1620–c1670.

1575 *Brieff Disc. Troub. Franckford* 215 From whose.. pennes, the vrgers of theis [letters] receiued first the light off the gospell. 1632 LE GRYS tr. *Velleius Paterc.* 39 Marcus Cato, the perpetuall urger of the destruction thereof. 1640 in Rushw. *Hist. Coll.* (1692) I. 114 The Author and Urger of some Particular Changes. 1678 CUDWORTH *Intell. Syst.* 209 The Urgers of the forementioned Objection. 1847 COVENTRY DICK in Brown *Horæ Subs.* (1882) 406 Nought detains the urger of these pleas, But dinners.

Urging, *vbl. sb.* [f. as prec. + -ING¹.] The action of the verb; an instance of this.

1590 SHAKS. *Com. Err.* V. i. 359 Her vrging of her wracke at sea. 1615 HIERON *Wks.* I. 606 It is by such vrgings as this, which..it pleaseth Him to make effectuall. 1651 HOBBES *Leviath.* II. xxv. 133 [It] is manifest enough, by the long and vehement urging. 1721 BAILEY, *Importunity*, an eager pressing or urging. 1838 LYTTON *Alice* X. iv, After repeated conferences and urgings. 1876 GEO. ELIOT *Dan. Der.* xlv, A painful urging of something vague and difficult. 1897 RHOSCOMYL *White Rose Arno* 82 One whose vigorous urgings to immediate action had [etc.].

U·rging, *ppl. a.* [f. as prec. + -ING².]

1. That serves as a motive or impelling cause; that constrains, or actuates; inciting, spurring, stimulating, strongly prompting; compelling.

1612 SELDEN *Illustr. Drayton's Poly-olb.* VI. 106 If it be the same with *Lyra*, as some think, although urging reason and authority are to the contrary. 1668 OWEN *Indwell. Sin* ii. 16 It is..an inbred, working, impelling, urging Law. 1678 DRYDEN *Limberham* I. i, How stand thy Affections to her, thou lusty Rogue? *Wood.* All o'fire: A most urging Creature! 1723 *Pres. St. Russia* II. 273 Causes..weighty and urging enough for Russia to begin a War. 1728 SWIFT *Let. to Abp. of Dublin* ¶22 We shall..sacrifice all honesty to the present urging advantage. 1802 WOLCOT (P. Pindar) *Isl. Innocence* 63 The sportive fry,..leaping oft as urging hunger calls, Meet the dropp'd crumb. 1870 TYNDALL *Fragm. Sci.* (1871) 322 It is a useful urging force.

b. *dial.* Of words: Taunting, irritating.

1655 *N. Riding Rec.* (1887) V. 191 A Sumersides yeoman [tried] for giving scandallous, urginge and provoking words.

c. Strongly operative or active.

1658 SIR T. BROWNE *Hydriot.* iii. 43 How slender a masse will remain upon an open and urging Fire of the carnall composition.

† **2.** Characterized by urgency; urgent. *Obs.*

1647 COTTERELL *Davila's Hist. Fr.* I. 49 It would be very easie, this urging necessity once past, to moderate..the.. power of the Duke of Guise. 1683 HOWE *Union among Prot.* Wks. 1863 IV. 261 The case was at that time urging and important. 1683 KENNETT *Erasm. on Folly* 150 If at any time some urging occasions require them to become entangled in secular affairs.

Hence **U·rgingly** *adv.*

1893 *Temple Bar* XCVII. 524 She instinctively and urgingly clasped her hands to a faster tune.

Urgo·nian, *a. Geol.* [ad. F. *Urgonien* (D'Orbigny, 1852), f. *Orgon* (see def.).] Forming or belonging to a series of massive limestones of the Lower Cretaceous system as developed at Orgon in the Durance valley.

1856 *Quart. Jrnl. Geol. Soc.* XII. 69 M. d'Orbigny's Urgonian series, or upper division of the Neocomian group. 1888 DAWSON *Geol. Hist. Plants* 282 These beds are regarded as Lower Cretaceous (Urgonian).

-uria (yūə·riă), a second element in Latin form (cf. DYSURIA, ISCHURIA), derived from Gr. -ουρία, employed in various pathological terms denoting morbid conditions of the urine, as *albuminuria, glycosuria, hæmatinuria, hæmaturia, hæmoglobinuria, oxaluria, planuria, polyuria, pyuria.*

Urial, variant of OORIAL.

Uric (yūə·rik), *a. Chem.* Also 8–9 ouric. [a. F. *urique*, f. *ur-ine* URINE *sb.*¹: see -IC 1 b.]

1. *Uric oxide*: (see quot. 1860).

1797 PEARSON in *Phil. Trans.* LXXXVIII. 37 It will be necessary to give a name to this urinary animal oxide...I trust that philological critics will find the name ouric or uric oxide perfectly appropriate. 1803 FESSENDEN *Poet. Petition* 12 Such a man..May view this uric oxyd's basis, And tell exactly what the case is. 1844 *Lancet* 19 Oct. 129/1 It is clear that uric oxide differs from uric acid simply in containing two atoms less of oxygen. 1860 MAYNE *Expos. Lex.* 1314 *Uric Oxide*,..a substance constituting a very rare ingredient in vesical calculi, and otherwise termed urous oxide, and xanthic oxide.

2. *Uric acid*, a crystallizable acid, $C_5H_4N_4O_3$, found in the urine of man, certain animals, reptiles, and birds, being produced in the metabolism of nitrogenous bodies, and excreted by the kidneys.

1800 tr. *Lagrange's Chem.* II. 404 To separate the uric acid from the latter salts. 1803– [see LITHIC *a.* 1]. 1826 HENRY *Elem. Chem.* II. 467 It is in those organs..that a new acid, the uric, is generated. 1872 HUXLEY *Physiol.* v. 106 Urea and uric acid are both composed of the elements carbon, hydrogen, oxygen, and nitrogen.

ellipt. (and *attrib.*). 1822 GOOD *Study Med.* IV. 508 The uric calculi..are of a yellowish or reddish-brown colour. 1846 G. E. DAY tr. *Simon's Anim. Chem.* II. 460 One minute calculus passed at the same time with others of pure uric, had a nucleus of oxalate of lime.

b. *attrib.* and *Comb.*, as *uric acid calculus, diathesis, -excreting, excretion, gravel*, etc.

1819 *Rees' Cycl.* XXXVII. 3 X/2 Lithic or Uric Acid Calculus. 1843 *Penny Cycl.* XXVI. 52/1 Uric Acid Crystals. 1845 *Encycl. Metrop.* VII. 552 A gouty or rheumatic state of the constitution, or uric acid diathesis. 1864 GARROD *Mat. Med.* (ed. 2) 108 In cases of uric acid gravel. 1866 ODLING *Anim. Chem.* 128 The uric acid group of compounds. 1880 *Encycl. Brit.* XI. 7/2 The uric-acid-excreting function of the kidneys.

c. Uric-acidæmia, = URICÆMIA; **uric-acidity**, the condition of containing an excess of uric acid.

1893 *Brit. Med. Jrnl.* Suppl. 26 Aug. 33 Nervous conditions depending upon *uric acidæmia. 1897 *Lancet* 15 May 1338/2 Symptoms..which would seem to depend upon uricacidæmia. 1893 A. S. ECCLES *Sciatica* 30 The *uric-acidity of the blood and tissues.

Uricæmia (yūərisī·miă). *Path.* Also uric-hæmia. [mod.L., f. *uric-us* URIC *a.* + Gr. αἷμ-α blood.] = LITHÆMIA.

1867 A. FLINT *Princ. Med.* 84 An excess of uric acid (in the form of urates) in the blood constituting a condition differing from uræmia; it is desirable to distinguish it by a name... I would propose *uricæmia*. 1900 *Lancet* 25 Aug. 572/1 The relation of urichæmia to the different symptoms of the malady.

Hence **Uricæ·mic** *a.*, = LITHÆMIC *a.*

1900 *Lancet* 25 Aug. 571/2 These urichæmic states in no degree determine gout, renal function being adequate.

Uriconian (yūərikōu·niăn), *a. Geol.* [f. *Uriconi-um*, name of Roman town at Wroxeter, + -AN.] Consisting of, pertaining to, a series of volcanic rocks such as constitute the Wrekin in Shropshire.

1886 C. CALLAWAY in *Q. Jrnl. Geol. Soc.* XLII. 481 In the Uriconian series itself I had found conglomerates full of rounded pieces of granitoid and gneissic rocks. *Ibid.* 483 The Charlton conglomerates are of Uriconian age. 1893 GEIKIE *Text Bk. Geol.* (ed. 3) 710 The Uriconian volcanic group..is probably pre-Cambrian.

U·ride. *Chem.* [f. UR-IC *a.* + -IDE.] A compound of uric acid with another element, or with a radical. Also *attrib.*

1887 A. M. BROWN *Anim. Alkaloids* 68 A body apparently of the uride family. *Ibid.* 90 He had obtained from normal urines a uride, allantoine.

Uridro·sis. *Path.* [mod.L., f. Gr. οὖρ-ον URINE *sb.*¹ + ἱδρόω I sweat: see -OSIS.] A morbid excretion of certain urinary constituents in the perspiration; urinous sweating.

1857 DUNGLISON *Med. Dict.* 947. 1860 MAYNE s.v. 1899 *Allbutt's Syst. Med.* VIII. 736 Uridrosis. A minute amount of urea is normally present in sweat.

-urient (yūə·riĕnt), *suffix*, ad. L. *-ūrient-*, pres. pple. stem of desiderative verbs, occurring first in a few direct adoptions from L., as *parturient* (1592), † *micturient* (1654), *esurient* (a1672), and hence occas. added to L. stems to form adjs. with the meaning 'desiring, characterized by a desire, (to do something)', as in † *novaturient* (1679), *nupturient*, † *vomiturient* (1666).

1878 *Eagle Mag.* (St. John's Coll. Camb.) X. 81 The vapid concourse of dangling men and nupturient maids.

‖ **Urim** (yūə·rim). [a. Heb. אורים *ūrīm*, pl. intens., referred to אור *ōr* 'light', pl. אורים *ōrīm*, and by some taken as = lights, φωτισμοί 'illuminations' (Symmachus).]

1. Certain objects, the nature of which is not known, worn in or upon the 'breast-plate' of the Jewish high-priest, by means of which the will of Jehovah was held to be declared.

Used chiefly in the collocation *Urim and Thummim* (once *Thummim and Urim*), occurring five times in the O. T. In the earlier English versions rendered after the Vulgate *doctrina et veritas* (from the LXX δήλωσις καὶ ἀλήθεια), whence Wyclif 'doctryne [l.v. techyng] and trewthe'; Coverdale has 'light and perfectnesse', following Luther's *licht und recht*, but in the 'Great' Bible of 1539 and in later versions the words are left untranslated.

(*a*) 1537 BIBLE (Matthew's) *Num.* xxvii. 21 Eleazar ye preast..shal aske councell for him after the iudgement of Urim before the Lorde. *Ibid.* 1 *Sam.* xxviii. 6 Nether by dreame nor by Urim nor yet by prophetes. 1598 SYLVESTER *Du Bartas* II. ii. *Babylon* 400 That never Vrim, Dream, or Vision sung Their Oracles, but all in Isaak's tongue. 1641 MILTON *Ch. Govt.* I. v, The Priests..had the Oracle of Urim to consult with. 1659 J. HARRINGTON *Lawgiving* II. ii. 38 When God was enquired of by Urim, he gave his Oracle by the shining of certain stones or jewels in the breastplate of the high priest. 1737 WHISTON *Josephus, Antiq.* III. viii. § 9 *note*, The very last instance of any thing like the prophetic Urim among the Jewish nation.

(*b*) 1537 BIBLE (Matthew's) *Exod.* xxviii. 30 Thou shalt put in the brestlappe of iudgement vrim and Thumin. 1560 BIBLE (Genev.) *Deut.* xxxiii. 8 Let thy Thummim and thine Vrim be wt thine holy one. 1595 W. CLERKE *Polimanteia* I 4, Concerning the reuelation done by Vrim and Thummim. 1613 PURCHAS *Pilgrimage* (1614) 198 Lord, doe it for [Aaron] the Priest, with Vrim and Thummim. 1671 MILTON *P. R.* III. 14 Thy Counsel would be as the Oracle Urim and Thummim, those oraculous gems On Aaron's breast. a1763 SHENSTONE *Ess. Men & Mann.* Wks. 1768 II. 229 An illiterate stupid preacher discoursing upon Urim and Thummim, and beating the pulpit cushion. 1768–74 TUCKER *Lt. Nat.* (1834) II. 343 In the course of the Levitical law,..answers by urim and thummim..gradually ceased. 1874 GEO. ELIOT *Coll. Breakf.-P.* 144 An oracular gem in price beyond Urim and Thummim lost to Israel. 1877 C. GEIKIE *Christ* I. 393 'The.. prophet', who should bring back the lost Urim and Thummim.

b. *transf.* and *fig.*

1618 BP. HALL *Contempl., N. T.* I. i. How little were the Jews better for this, when they had lost the Urim and Thummim, sincerity of doctrine and manners! a1652 J. SMITH *Sel. Disc.* v. 134 Whenever we look upon our own soul... we shall find an Urim and Thummim there, by which we may ask counsel of God himself. a1670 HACKET *Abp. Williams* I. (1693) 164 Conscience and Honour, the Urim and Thummim, with which the Noblest..should consult in all things. 1760–72 H. BROOKE *Fool of Qual.* (1792) III. 19 Every mechanic professed, like Aaron, to carry a Urim and Thummim about him. 1825 J. NEAL *Bro. Jonathan* II. 193 He stood and spoke..like one to whom old age is..the sign of wisdom and power—the urim and thumim of survivorship. 1851 KINGSLEY *Yeast* x, The heart..enshrines the priceless pearl of womanhood,..the 'Urim and Thummim', before which gross man can only inquire and adore. a1886 W. B. ROBERTSON *Dream Foolish Virgin* (1898) 17 And stars repeat it.., The Urim and the Thummim on the breastplate of the night.

2. *Mormon Ch.* (See quots.)

1843 H. CASWALL *Proph. of 19th Cent.* v. 77 The mystic Urim and Thummim, which appeared in the form of two transparent stones, set in the rim of a bow, like a pair of spectacles, and fastened to a golden breastplate. 1864 *Chambers's Encycl.* VI. 569/2 Along with the records was found a curious instrument, called by Smith 'Urim and Thummin'... By means of these stone spectacles [etc.].

U·rinable, *a. rare*⁻¹. [f. URINE *v.* + -ABLE.] Capable of being excreted in the urine.

c1900 *Buck's Handbk. Med. Sci.* III. 543 (*Cent. Suppl.*).

Urinæ·mia. *U.S. Path.* Also -emia. [mod.L.: see URINE *sb.* and cf. URÆMIA.] A morbid condition due to retention in the blood of certain constituents normally eliminated in the urine.

1860 R. FOWLER *Med. Voc.* s.v. 1871 HAMMOND *Dis. Nervous Syst.* 46 Epilepsy, urinæmia, stomachal vertigo.

Urinal (yūə·rinăl), *sb.* Forms: 3–7 vrinal, 4–6 -all(e, 4–5 vrynal, 4–6 -all(e, 6–7 urinall (6 -alle, 7 -ell), 7– urinal; 5 orinal, orynal; also 3 vrnal, 6 vrnall. [a. OF. *urinal* (12th c.; also *orinal*, pl. *orignaulx*), a. L. *ūrīnal*, f. *ūrīna* URINE *sb.*¹ Cf. Pr. *urinal*, Pg. *ur-, ourinol*, It. *orinale*, Pr. and Sp. *orinal*.]

† **1.** A glass vessel or phial employed to receive urine for medical examination or inspection. *Obs.*

c1275 LAY. 17724 He nam his vrinal [c1205 glæs-fat] anon, an þe king meh þar on; one wile after þan þe vrnal an honde he nam. 13.. *Seuyn Sages* (W.) 1049 The yonge man..taketh an vrinal for to sen. c1386 CHAUCER *Pard. Prol.* 19 Thyne vrynals and thy Iurdones. c1440 *Promp. Parv.* 370/1 Orynal, or vrynal, *urinale*. 1495 *Nottingham Rec.* III. 284, ij vrinalles, price iiij d. 1548 RECORDE *Urin. Physick* iv. 14 b, The Vrinall..shulde be of pure clere glasse, not thyck, nor greene in colour. 1596 NASHE *Saffron Walden* R 3 b, Then shee neuer need to haue her water cast in an vrinall for the greene sicknes. 1642 FULLER *Holy & Prof. St.* II. ii. 53 Reasons drawn from the urine alone are as brittle as the urinall. 1685 BOYLE *Effects of Motion* Suppl. 142 Thin Vessels of Glass, especially Urinals, to be diligently made clean with Sand. 1737 *Phil. Trans.* XLI. 707 The *Capillamenta*, whilst in the Urinal, and till the Urine was decanted. 1757 *Keysler's Trav.* IV. 19 While her maid is stirring a medicine in a spoon, and the physician looking into the urinal. 1858 THUDICHUM *Urine* 19 In some hospitals the ancient urinal is still in use.

fig. c1645 HOWELL *Lett.* (1650) II. 2 When I found those letters..which he sends as urinals up and down the world, to look into his water for discovery of the crazie condition of his body. 1663 SIR G. MACKENZIE *Religious Stoic* 19 There ye shall know by the Urinal of his eyes, and the water standing therein, what convulsion-fits his soul suffers.

transf. 1688 HOLME *Armoury* III. xiv. (Roxb.) 10/2 He beareth Argent, a vrinall Azure.

† **2.** *Alchemy.* (See quot. 1738.) *Obs.*

c1386 CHAUCER *Can. Yeom. T.* 73 Sondry vessels maad of erthe and glas, Oure vrynals and our descensories. 1550 MORWYNG *Evonym.* 1 Men call it a receiver or a urinall. *Ibid.* 212 If ij urinals be set together. 1584 R. SCOT *Discov. Witchcr.* XII. xvii. (1886) 212 Take a glasse viall full of bolie water... On the mouth of the viall or urinall, two olive leaves must be laid. 1667 BOYLE *Orig. Forms & Qual.* 298, I took two parcels of Gold,..and having cast each of these in a distinct Urinal,..I caus'd [etc.]. 1738 CHAMBERS *Cycl.*, *Urinal*, in chemistry, is an oblong glass vessel, used for making solutions.

3. A chamber-pot.

c1475 *Cath. Angl.* 405/1 (A.), An Vrynalle, *vrinaria,..vbi* Jordane. 1519 HORMAN *Vulg.* 168 b, Se that I lacke nat by my beddis syde a chayer of easement:..and an vrnall bye. 1542 UDALL *Erasm. Apoph.* 212 b, His groome whose dayly office it was to geue vnto hym his urinall in his chaumbre. 1622 MABBE tr. *Aleman's Guzman d'Alf.* I. 232 Not finding any of his Pages there, he..tooke the Vrinall himselfe, which stood at his beds head. 1642 MILTON *Apol. Smect.* 13 Some Politicians..lyable to a night-walking cudgeller, or the emptying of a Urinall. 1695 CONGREVE *Love for L.* II. iii, [To] warm your Bed, and..set the Candle and your Tobacco-Box, and your Urinal by you. 1739 R. BULL tr. *Dedekindus' Grobianus* p. viii, He finds Occasion to inspect the Urinal and the Bed-pan. a1774 GOLDSM. tr. *Scarron's Com. Romance* (1775) I. 35 Pray reach me the chamber-pot, quoth Rancour...The other..took up the urinal, and gave it to Rancour. 1822 GOOD *Study Med.* IV. 540 Forming red sand on the surface, as it probably would otherwise have done in the bladder or the urinal. 1875 H. C. WOOD *Therap.* (1879) 342 The use of chloral to keep free from odor the urinals of paraplegics.

transf. a1700 B. E. *Dict. Cant. Crew*, *Urinal of the Planets*, Ireland,..because of its frequent and great Rains.

4. A vessel or reservoir with conductor worn on the person for incontinence of urine.

1855 OGILVIE *Suppl.* 1895 *Arnold & Sons' Catal. Surg. Instrum.* 707 Urinals for Invalids, Travellers, etc. The best quality of Urinals are all made of specially prepared Ætherized India-rubber. 1899 *Allbutt's Syst. Med.* VIII. 244 The wearing of indiarubber urinals, and other means of avoiding 'accidents'.

5. A building, erection, or enclosure for accommodating persons when requiring to pass urine.

1851 J. H. STIRLING in A. H. Stirling *Life* (1912) vi. 106, I had put my back to one of the urinals. 1869 E. A. PARKES *Pract. Hygiene* (ed. 3) 319 Earthen-ware or slate urinals should be used, with water running through them. 1898 G. B. SHAW *Plays* II. *Candida* 29 A vast district..well served with ugly iron urinals.

6. *attrib.* and *Comb.*, as *urinal-glass* (= sense 1), *-like, metal*; † **urinal cherry** (see quot. 1629); † **urinal monger**, † **quack**, † **shaker**, a quack doctor who diagnoses by inspecting the urine.

1611 COTGR., *Vrinaire*,..vrinall-like. 1629 PARKINSON *Parad.* 572 The Vrinall Cherrie..is long and round, like vnto an Vrinall. 1641 COWLEY *Guardian* II. v, That damn'd Urinal-monger..has not so much physick as would cure the toothach. 1651 FRENCH *Distill.* I. 37 Put upon it another urinall-glasse inverted. a1652 BROME *Queenes Exch.* IV. E 4 b/2 He thinks my skull's made but of urinal mettal. 1663 COWLEY *Cutter Coleman St.* II. viii, *Wor.* He's a kind of Grave-maker, *Cut.* A Urinal Shaker. 1763 J. CLUBBE *Physiognomy* 7 How came this art into reputation?..By the same means that Urinal Quacks and Conjurors have had a run here. 1881 *Instr. Census Clerks* (1885) 99 Urinal Cleaner, Attendant, &c.

Urinal, *a.* ? *Obs.* [a. F. *urinal* (16th c.), ad. late L. *ūrīnāl-is*, f. *ūrīna* URINE *sb.*¹]

1. a. Of or pertaining to, consisting or characteristic of, urine.

1541 R. COPLAND *Guydon's Quest. Chirurg.* I iv, Wherby receyueth the bladder the superfluite vrynal of the kydnees? 1653 URQUHART *Rabelais* I. xxxvi, The pisse of that Urinal flood ran glib away. 1703 T. H. (*title*), Compleat Treatises of Urines, shewing the right Method of Urinal Prognostication. 1743 *Lond. & Country Brew.* IV. (ed. 2) 285 Though it be of an Urinal Taste.

b. Marked by immoderate discharge of urine.

1822 GOOD *Study Med.* IV. 459 Both [kinds of diabetes] were named indifferently diabetes,..urinary diarrhœa, urinal dropsy, and..water-flux.

2. = URINARY *a.* 1.

1615 CROOKE *Body of Man* (1631) 212 The Pipe or Canale of the yarde which in greeke they call οὐρήθρα, the vrinal pipe. 1620 VENNER *Via Recta* vii. 154 They..purge the reines, and vrinall passages. a1651 *Recorde's Urin. Physick* To Rdr. A 2 b, The Urine..returneth back again in the veines, to the liver and urinall vessels. 1803 *Med. Jrnl.* X. 512 The effects of..cantharides to the urinal system.

† **U·rinalist.** *Obs.* [f. URINAL *sb.*] A urinologist.

1631 DEKKER *Match me in London* III, I..bid him..To keepe my health from falling, which I felt Tottering.., but my Vrinalist..left no Artery Vnstretcht vpon the Tenters.

Urina·lysis. *U.S. Med.* [Irreg. f. L. *ūrīn-a* URINE *sb.*¹ + ANALYSIS.] = URANALYSIS.

1889 *Buck's Handbk. Med. Sci.* VII. 416/1 Processes to be found in large works on urinalysis. 1897 *Columbus* (Ohio) *Dispatch* 18 June 5/2 He..was familiar with the term urinalysis.

U·rinant, *a. Her.* [ad. L. *ūrīnant-, ūrīnans*, pres. pple. of *ūrīnārī* to dive.] Borne with the head downward, and the tail erect.

1688 HOLME *Armoury* II. xiv. 327/1 He beareth Gules, a Dolphin reversed, Argent; (or else a Dolphin with the tail erected;) but more properly a Dolphin Urinant. c1828 BERRY *Encycl. Her.* I. Gloss., *Diving*, or *Urinant*, is said of a dolphin or other fish, borne with the head downwards. 1863 BOUTELL *Her. Hist. & Pop.* xi. 67 A fish is..urinant when its head is in base.

U·rinary, *sb.* ? *Obs.* [ad. med.L. *ūrīnāri-um*, f. L. *ūrīnāre* to URINE. Cf. F. *urinoir*.] † **a.** (See first quot.) *Obs.*⁻⁰ **b.** = URINAL *sb.* 5.

1828–32 WEBSTER, *Urinary, Urinarium*,..a reservoir or place for the reception of urine, &c., for manure. 1836 J. M. GULLY *Magendie's Formul.* (ed. 2) 135 The chloruret of lime may also be..used in the disinfection of water-closets, urinaries,..hospital-wards, &c.

Urinary (yūə·rinări), *a.* [ad. med.L. **ūrīnāri-us* (whence It., Sp., Pg. *urinario*, It. *orinario*, F. *urinaire*), f. *ūrīna* URINE *sb.*¹]

1. Affording passage to, effecting or assisting in the secretion and discharge of, urine.

1578 BANISTER *Hist. Man* v. 83 The begynnyng of the Urinarie passage. 1600 SURFLET *Countrie Farme* II. xxvi. 235 The decoction..casteth out grauell contained in the vrinarie vessels. 1625 HART *Anat. Ur.* II. i. 52 A stoppage of the Liuer, kidneyes, and the vrinarie vessels. 1688 [see 3 a]. 1728 CHAMBERS *Cycl.* s.v. *Bladder*, From whence it takes various Denominations, as Urinary-Bladder, Gall-Bladder, &c. 1732 ARBUTHNOT *Rules of Diet* in *Aliments*, etc. I. 358 Everything which drives the Blood into the Urinary Canals. 1794 G. ADAMS *Nat. & Exp. Philos.* I. xi. 488 The alkaline solution..is apt..to prove irritating to the urinary passages. 1843 *Penny Cycl.* XXVI. 50/1 Indicating..the state of the urinary system. 1864 GARROD *Mat. Med.* (ed. 2) 93 It is desirable to keep uric acid in solution during its transit through the urinary organs. 1877 ROSENTHAL *Muscles & Nerves* (1881) 98 The urinary duct, in which each drop of urine leaving the kidneys produces a wave which propagates itself..to the urinary bladder.

2. Of the nature of urine; excreted as urine.

1646 SIR T. BROWNE *Pseud. Ep.* V. v. 239 Whereby it [*sc.* the bladder] dischargeth the waterish and urinary part of its aliment. 1822 GOOD *Study Med.* IV. 500 The urinary secretion in a state of health is one of the most compound fluids of the animal system. 1872 HUXLEY *Physiol.* v. 105 The urinary fluid flows..into the bladder. 1874 GARROD & BAXTER *Mat. Med.* (ed. 4) 129 Citrate of potash sits easily upon the stomach, and..slightly increases the urinary water.

† **b.** = URINOUS *a.* 1. *Obs.*⁻¹

1819 *Rees' Cycl.* XXXVII. s.v., Some urinary salts crystallize when precipitated.

3. a. Adapted for using on the urinary passage.

b. Adapted for receiving or containing urine.

4. a. Liquid or formed in the urinary organs or bladder; excreted in the urine.

Urinate (yū'rĭneĭt), v. [f. ppl. stem of *ūrīnāre* to pass water, f. L. *ūrīna* URINE *sb.*]

1. *intr.* To discharge urine; to make water; to micturate.

† Urinate, *ppl. a.* Obs.—¹ [f. L. *ūrīnāt-*, ppl. stem of *ūrīnārī* (see quot.).] *intr.* (See quot.)

Urination (yūrĭneĭ'ʃən), *sb.* [ad. med.L. *ūrīnātiōn-*, n. of action f. L. *ūrīnāre* to URINATE. Cf. F. *urination*.] The action of passing water; micturition.

† Urinative, *a.* Obs.—¹ [ad. med.L. type *ūrīnātīvus* (cf. It. *urinativo*), f. *ūrīnāre* to URINATE.] Provoking or stimulating urination.

† Urinator. Obs. [a. L. *ūrīnātor,* agent-noun f. *ūrīnārī* to dive.] One who dives under water; a diver.

Urine (yū'rĭn), *sb.* [a. F. *urine* (12th c.), ad. L. *ūrīna.*] Forms: *a.* 4–5 vryne, 4–6 vryn, 4–7 vrine, 4–5 vrisyne, 4–6 vryne; *β.* 4–6 vrin, 6 vrin'. *γ.* 4–7 vrina, 5 vreyna; *δ.* 5 urien, 6 uren, 6–7 vrin, 7 urin.

1. The excrementitious fluid secreted from the blood by the kidneys in man and the higher animals, stored in the bladder, and voided at intervals through the urethra; = WATER *sb.* 18.

† Urinal, *sb.* Obs. [f. URINE + -AL.] Urinal; containing an urn (of liquid measure).

† Urine, *v.* Obs. [f. URINE *sb.*] *intr.* To pass or make water; to urinate.

† b. [Partly f. the L. *ūrīnārī* to pass urine; urination. Obs. *rare.*

Urino- (yū'rĭnŏ), combining form f. L. *ūrīn-a* URINE *sb.*, in various terms, as urino-genitary, urinogenital. Also var. OBS.

Urinometer (yūrĭnɒ'mĭtǝr), *sb.* [f. prec. + -METER. Cf. F. *urinomètre.*] An instrument for determining the specific gravity or weight of urine.

Urinous (yū'rĭnǝs), *a.* [ad. mod.L. *urinōsus* (whence It. and Pg. *urinoso,* It. and Sp. *orinoso*), f. L. *urina* URINE *sb.* Cf. prec., F. *urineux.*]

1. Possessing or partaking of the essential properties of urine.

Urino'se, *a.* Obs.—¹ [ad. mod.L. *ūrīnōs-us:* see prec.] = URINOUS.

Urlod, *ppl. a.* *north. dial.* [f. prec. + -ED.] Stunted in growth; dwarfed, thwartish, ill-thriven.

† Urling. Obs. [a. dial. variant of WIRLING.]

† Urling'e, *north. dial.* variant of WIRLING.

Urn (ʉrn), *sb.* Also 4 urn (6 Sc. wrn), 4–7 urne, 5 vrn, 7 urne (6 Sc. wrne).

1. An earthenware or metal vessel or vase of a rounded or ovaloid form and with a circular base, used by various peoples esp. in former times (notably by the Romans and Greeks) to preserve the ashes of the dead.

b. The source of a stream, river, etc.; a spring or fountain.

Uro- (yū'rŏ), combining form of Gr. οὖρο-urine, used in many terms of physiological chemistry, etc., which denote esp. (a) pigments present in or derived from urine, as *urocyanin, -cyanogen, -melanin, -phæin; (b) morbid conditions of the urine (or urinary organs), as *urocystitis, -hæmia;* etc.

Urochrome (-krōm). *Chem.* [f. URO-¹ + Gr. χρῶμα CHROME. Hence F. *urochrome.*] A yellow, amorphous pigment found in the urine.

Urology. [f. URO-¹ + Gr. -λογία: cf. F. *urologie.*]

Uroscopy (yūrɒ'skǝpĭ), *sb.* [ad. mod.L. *ūroscopia,* f. URO-¹ + -SCOPY.]

Ursicide. [f. L. *ursi,* urs-us bear + -CIDE] The killing of bears.

wanted to use her by degrees to live without meat. 1873– in dialect use (*Eng. Dial. Dict.*). 1877 Mrs. Lear tr. *Fenelon's Spiritual Lett.* 240 So as to wean you like a child, and use you to dry bread instead of milk.

refl. c 1305 *St. Edmund Conf.* 44 in *E. E. P.* (1862) 72 So longe hi hem vsede þerto. a 1450 *Knt. de la Tour* (1868) 9 For suche lyff as ye wille contynue, use you to in youre youthe. a 1568 Ascham *Scholem.* II. (Arb.) 88 For translating, vse you your selfe..to chose out some Epistle..of Tullie. a 1568 in *Bannatyne MS.* (Hunter. Cl.) 195 In yowtheid vse the to temprance. 1615 tr. *De Montfort's Surv. E. Indies* 39 Those who have us'd themselves to Tobacco. 1697 Dryden *Virg. Georg.* I. 63 Use thyself betimes to hear and grant our Pray'rs. 1719 De Foe *Crusoe* I. (Globe) 211 Using himself to them [*sc.* garments], at length he took to them very well. 1753 L. M. *Accompl. Woman* II. 213 We may use ourselves to fear as well as to be bold. a 1818 M. G. Lewis *Jrnl. W. Ind.* (1834) 296 Mithridates used himself to poisons. a 1850 Keble *Lett.* (1870) 104 Using themselves when they wake in the night to rise and say the fifty-first Psalm.

c. More usu. in pa. pple. (Const. *to* or †*of*.)

c 1480 Henryson *Fables, Two Mice* 58 To tender meit my stomok is ay vsit. 1483 Caxton *G. de la Tour* e iv b, So were the seuen Cytees brenned..by cause that they were moche vsed of the fylthe and ordure of lechery. 1526 *Pilgr. Perf.* (W. de W. 1531) 94 b, Wherby man..be accustomed & vsed to chose..yᵉ thynge that is of lesse goodnes. 1555 Eden *Decades* I. x. (Arb.) 104 Such as haue byn vsed to owr breade made of wheate. 1607 Topsell *Four-f. Beasts* 80 It is requisite that they bee alwaie vsed to hand. c 1645 Howell *Lett.* (1678) 48 This City was us'd to fetch all those Spices. 1682 Lister *Godartius Of Insects* 54 The Catterpillar..as soon as it perceives any thing it is not us't to. 1720 Mandeville *Free Thoughts* (1729) 276 St. Poinct..was used to ask, whether the farce..was ready to be acted. 1796 Mme. D'Arblay *Camilla* IV. 329 I'm not used to be used in this manner! 1833 Disraeli *Cont. Fleming* VI. vi, The friar smiled, and was evidently used to this raillery. 1850 Thackeray *Pendennis* li, A person..used to making sacrifices. 1888 'J. S. Winter' *Bootle's Childr.* xi, Which..had stirred Terry's heart just as it had been used to stir it years and years ago.

V. *intr.* **19.** To do a thing customarily; to be in the habit of so acting or doing; to be wont to do. (Chiefly in clauses introduced by *as*, and now only literary.) **a.** Of persons.

c 1380 Wyclif *Sel. Wks.* III. 434 And so shulde perish makyng of prests and doyng of sacraments, as holy Chirche usiþ. c 1400 Maundev. (1839) v. 40 Clothed in..the Sarazines guyse, and as the Sarazines usen. 1473 *Reg. Cupar Abbey* I. 182 Tha sal tak iijˣˣ of fuderis of petis quhar thai oysit befor. 1533 in Leadam *Star Chamber Cases* (Selden) II. 205 The boucher..grevyd shall signifie..the name..of any such person..that so vsith. 1596 Spenser *State Irel.* Wks. (Globe) 645/1 To manure and husband it as good farmors use. 1616 J. Lane *Contn. Sqr.'s T.* x. 388 This familiar Dove twixt yond twoe kinges went boldlie to and fro, as vsen frendes. 1663 Butler *Hud.* I. i. 632 We should, as learned Poets use, Invoke the Assistance of some Muse. 1720 Ozell *Vertot's Rom. Rep.* (1740) II. XII. 237 In the sight of all the Citizens, as the Censors use, when they [etc.]. 1748 *Earthquake Peru* ii. 161 To kill animals in the same Manner as they always had used. 1791 Smeaton *Edystone L.* § 267 We had got up our stones..as we had used from the beginning. 1816 Wordsw. '*A little onward*' 30 To push forth His arms, as swimmers use, and plunge..into the 'abrupt abyss'. 1852 T. L. Peacock *Misc.* Wks. 1875 III. 364 First, as the truly pious always use, Approach with prayer. 1875 Browning *Aristoph. Apol.* 365 Die at good old age as grand men use.

†**b.** Of things. *Obs. rare.*

1656 tr. *T. White's Peripat. Inst.* 152 It varies its figure with every motion as fire uses. 1676 *Phil. Trans.* XI. 773 In the same manner as the trunk of the lymphaticks uses.

20. With *to* and inf.: To be accustomed or wont *to* do something.

In very frequent use from c 1400, but now only in pa. t. *used to*, with pronunc. (yūˑst tu, yūˑstŭ).

a. 1303 R. Brunne *Handl. Synne* 691 For ryche men vse comunly Sweryn [*v.r.* to swere] grete obys grysly. *Ibid.* 2661. c 1385 Chaucer *L. G. W.* 787 *Thisbe*, For olde payenys that Idolys heryed Vsedyn tho in feldys to ben beryed. c 1386 — *Reeve's T.* 20 A theef he was,..a sly, and vsaunt [*v.r.* usand] for to stele. c 1440 *Gesta Rom.* v. 12 His modir vsith euery day gretly to sorowe. 1464 *Rolls of Parlt.* V. 563/2 Dyvers persones have gretely used to shippe woll..oute of this Reame. 1542 Udall *Erasm. Apoph.* 43 Such as the beggerye philosophiers..usen to weare. 1550 *Southampton Court Leet Rec.* (1905) I. 14 Thomas Casberd hathe vsid to sett his carte in the streate. 1596 Spenser *F. Q.* v. viii. 17 Her name Mercilla most men vse to call. 1612 Webster *White Devil* I. ii. 202 Your silke-worme useth to fast every third day. 1625 J. King *David's Strait* 15 As we vse to maligne a Bayliue. 1670 Milton *Hist. Eng.* VI. 304 The English then useing to let grow on their upper-lip large Mustachio's. 1728 Gay *Begg. Op.* II. iv, You are not so fond of me, Jenny, as you use [*sic*] to be. 1767 *Woman of Fashion* II. 26 How did we all use to admire her! 1837 Lockhart *Scott* I. iv. 122 He used to get all the copies of these ballads he could. 1884 W. C. Smith *Kildrostan* 53 You used to be a leal, true-hearted girl.

Comb. 1883 J. W. Riley *Poems Here at Home* (1893) 21 There lies a land, long lost to me, The land of Used-to-be.

β. c 1375 *Lay-Folks Mass-Bk.* (MS. B) 401 A litel belle men oyse to ryng. c 1425 Wyntoun *Cron.* I. 1265 Tebany þai oysse to calle In to Grece þe Thebis all. c 1470 Henry *Wallace* v. 760 Now thow sall feyll how I oys to lat blude.

b. Predicated of things.

In frequent use from c 1620 to c 1675.

1445 in *Anglia* XXVIII. 267 Al goddesses..Haue ioyned her dauncys within thi breste, which vsid hem to receive. 1547 *Homilies* I. *Salvation* III. ꝑ 7 Therfore scripture vseth to saie, that faithe without woorkes dooth iustifie. 1586 J. Chilton in Hakluyt *Voy.* (1589) 588 Where the ships vse to ride, made fast to ye said wal, with their cables. 1609 Holland *Amm. Marcell.* 333 What time folkes minds..use to be dull and dead. 1662 Stillingfl. *Orig. Sacræ* I. i. § 6 Jewels do not use to lie upon the surface of the earth.

1684 *Contempl. St. Man* II. ix. (1699) 231 Temporal Felicity uses often to end in Eternal Misery. 1726 Leoni *Designs* 5 b, In that Season of the Year when the Water uses to be lowest. 1778 *Hist. Eliza Warwick* I. 260 Alas! his absence ..did not use thus to affect me! 1810 Scott *Lady L.* I. xxi, Yet seemed that tone..Less used to sue than to command. 1839 Fr. A. Kemble *Resid. in Georgia* (1863) 245 It is now ..the rule, though it used not to be so formerly. 1884 F. M. Crawford *Rom. Singer* I. 35 They used to be only a baiocco apiece.

†**c.** In passive construction. *Obs.*

1523 Fitzherb. *Husb.* § 132 If a tree be heeded, and vsed to be lopped and cropped. 1607 Shaks. *Cor.* III. iii. 25 He hath bene vs'd Euer to conquer. a 1648 Ld. Herbert *Hen. VIII* (1683) 399 As concerning Annates used to be paid. a 1706 Evelyn *Hist. Relig.* (1850) I. 402 Nor were they used of old to be read in churches. 1737 Waterland *Eucharist* 393 Prayer was then used to be offered up for that Purpose. 1788 *London Mag.* 399 The Tuilleries, where boats were used to be found.

21. †**a.** To act, conduct oneself or one's affairs, in a particular or specified manner. *Obs. rare.*

a 1325 *Prose Psalter* lxxvi. 12 Y shal þenchen in alle þyne werkes, and y shal vse [L. *exercebor*] in alle þy fundynges. c 1375 *Cursor M.* 24931 (Fairf.), Bot now men vsis on oþer wise, þer is mare of hir seruise. 1523 Ld. Berners *Froiss.* I. xv. 15 Kyng Edward..and yᵉ quene his mother..vsed moche after yᵉ counsell of syr Thomas Wage. 1579 Tomson *Calvin's Serm. Tim.* 181/1 And therfore we haue to vse of our selues modestly.

b. *Sc.* To accustom oneself, become accustomed or habituated, get used, *to* something.

1836 Carlyle *Let.* in *Atlantic Monthly* Sept. (1898) 295/1 'You will use, you will use,' and get hefted to the place, as all creatures do. 1842 Mrs. Carlyle *Lett.* (1883) I. 158 If I do not use to the noise. 1894 Crockett *Raiders* 284 So soon does one use to the sight.

22. To go frequently, to resort or repair customarily, to a place or person; to frequent or haunt a place. Freq. with advs. (as *thither*, *where*), or with preps. (esp. in earlier use with *to*). Latterly *dial.* (Eng. Dial. Dict. s.v.) and *U.S.*

(*a*) c 1470 Henry *Wallace* I. 209 Into the toun he wsyt everilk day. *Ibid.* II. 290 He wsyt offt to that religious place. 1590 in *Cath. Rec. Soc. Publ.* V. 181 [They] be good witnesses ..howe many severall persons have vsed to the saienge of masses. 1599 Sir R. Wrothe in Ellis *Orig. Lett.* Ser. II. III. 181 Sertaine lewde fellowes..doe frequente and use aboute Layton heath. 1602 Breton *Mother's Blessing* Wks. (Grosart) I. 6/1 Presumptuous fooles, and infidell Iewes, Emong the Nobler sort should neuer vse. a 1613 Overbury *Characters, Ord. Widdow*, Shee uses to cunning women to know how many husbands she shall have. 1653 Holcroft *Procopius, Pers. Wars* II. 51 Then shall you by our Country have the conveniencie of using to Roman Seas. 1663 *Extr. St. Papers Friends* Ser. II. (1911) 168 When he is in London he vseth frequently at Mr. Lawries howse. 1834 J. Hall *Kentucky* II. 40 'But you seem acquainted with these woods.' 'Yes, I use about here some.' 1884 'M. Twain' *Huckleberry Finn* vi, If he didn't quit using around there she would make trouble for him.

(*b*) 1470–85 Malory *Arthur* XVIII. xxii. 765, I am a gentilwoman that vseth here in this forest huntynge. 1592 in J. Morris *Troub. Cath. Forefathers* Ser. II. (1875) 54 Cotton did use thither divers times. 1596 Spenser *F. Q.* VI. Prol. ii, Conduct me well In these strange waies, where neuer foote did vse. a 1700 B. E. *Dict. Cant. Crew, Flash-ken*, a House where Thieves use. 1848 Bartlett *Dict. Amer.* 372, I can see where the deer used. 1851 Mayhew *Lond. Labour* II. 475/2 The master of the hotel or the gents that uses there.

transf. 1591 Sylvester *Ivry* 370 Even as a Galley, in smooth Sea subdues The tallest Ship that in the Streights doth use. 1637 Milton *Lycidas* 136 Ye valleys low where the milde whispers use, Of shades and wanton winds.

†**b.** To inhabit, reside, or dwell in or at a place.

a 1585 Montgomerie *Cherrie & Slae* 97 Musis that vsis At fountaine Helicon. 1610 Fletcher *Faithf. Sheph.* III. i. I will give thee for thy food, No Fish that useth in the mud. 1628 May *Virg. Georg.* III. 93 Snakes that use within the house for shade, Securely lurk. 1707 Sloane *Jamaica* I. p. xviii, This is known by the places where they [*sc.* fish] use.

†**c.** To associate (or cohabit) *with* a person. *Obs.*

1382 Wyclif *John* iv. 9 Iewis vsen not with Samaritans. 1559 Bercher *Nobylytye Wymen* (Roxb.) 141 The daughters of Lot, which vsed carnallye with their ffather. 1566 Sternhold & H. *Ps.* xxvi. 4, I do not lust to haunt or vse, with men whose deeds are vayne.

†**23.** To make use *of* some thing. *Obs.*

c 1500 *Melusine* xx. 110 As long that ye shall vse of feythfulnes. 1542 Udall *Erasm. Apoph.* 44 For in the same solemnitees men usen of a custom. 1704 N. N. tr. *Boccalini's Advts. fr. Parnass.* II. 171 He us'd of all the Rhetorick he had, to praise that Vice.

†**b.** Similarly with *with*. *Obs. rare.*

a 1400–50 *Alexander* 3594 Olyfauntis.., As ilkane vsyd with in ynde vmquile with to fiȝte. 1502 *Ord. Crysten Men* (W. de W. 1506) IV. xxi. Xvj, He ought iustely to vse with his puyssaunce and not in abusynge.

Used (yūzd), *ppl. a.* [f. Use *v.* + -ed¹.]

I. †**1.** Customarily employed, experienced, or met with; accustomed, usual, wonted. *Obs.*

c 1374 Chaucer *Boeth.* I. met. v. (1868) 22 Þe euesterre esperus ..comeþ eft aȝeynes hir vsed cours. c 1440 Capgrave *St. Kath.* IV. 1719 These too natures in oure lord ihesu were.. coupled to-geder ageyn vsed kynde. 1445 in Willis & Clark *Cambridge* (1886) I. 343 Thei shall ocupye with all maner of cariagez..the vsed way within the ground. 1449 Pecock *Repr.* v. ii. 489 These now had and vsid religious in the chirche. 1480 *Wardr. Acc. Edw. IV* (1830) 150 A pane of scarlet furrid with used ermyns. 1579 E. K. *Spenser's Sheph. Cal.* Gen. Argt. ꝑ 2 To call them by the vsed and best knowen name. 1650 Howell *Giraffi's Rev. Naples* I. 2 Forcing him [*sc.* Gensericus] to bid a us'd farewell to fair Italie. 1655 Moufet & Bennet *Health's Improv.* xxix. 272, I perswade strong and indifferent stomachs to continue their used Diet.

b. That is or has been made use of; utilized.

1594– [see Well-used]. 1758 B. Franklin *Poor Richard* (1890) 270 The used Key is always bright. 1864 E. A. Parkes *Pract. Hygiene* 157 The used surfaces of the teeth begin to bear a square mark. 1885 J. W. Palmer *Bric-à-Brac* 27 Papering a room with used stamps.

2. †**a.** Established by usage; customary. *Obs.*

c 1450 tr. *De Imitatione* III. xiii. 81 The olde used custom wol wiþstonde, but it shal be ouercomen by a better custom. 1603 Florio *Montaigne* II. xv. 358 An auncient custome, and vsed cerimony.

b. *Used and wont*, that is usual or customary; according to use and custom. *Sc.*

1510 *Reg. Privy Seal Scotl.* I. 315/2 Payand thairfor ȝerelie four pundis thre s. usuale money,..with all maner of dewiteis usit and wount. 1562 *Reg. Cupar Abbey* I. 362 Item, to the convent..for ane part of thair sustentatioun vsit and wont. 1609 Skene *Reg. Maj.* II. Table 63 Bot the fourt heire sall make service vsed and wont. 1718 in *Nairne Peerage Evidence* (1874) 34 With the rights rents and services..used and wont. 1814 Scott *Wav.* l, [He] claimed permission to perform..the service used and wont. 1864 *Jedburgh Council Rec.* 31 Oct. (MS.), With all ceremonies used and wont.

3. Experienced (*in* something); expert. Latterly *Sc.*

c 1425 *Eng. Conq. Irrland* 23 Throgh kynde of Fraunce, we ben wsyd in wepyn. c 1470 Henry *Wallace* III. 379 For thai war wicht, and weill wsyt in wer. 1786 Burns *Epist. to J. Rankine* ix, Some auld us'd hands had taen a note, That [etc.]. 1824 Scott *St. Ronan's* iii, Dick..was an auld used hand.

II. Used up. 4. *U. S.* Discussed thoroughly; talked of, or written about, critically.

1839 Mrs. Kirkland *A New Home* xxxv. 237 After tea the poor Brents were completely 'used up', to borrow a phrase much in vogue with us, and the next day I was.. asked..if I had heard that Mr. and Mrs. Brent were going to 'part'. 1848 Poe *J. R. Lowell* Wks. 1895 VIII. 5 The various criticisms, in which we have been amused (rather ill-naturedly) at seeing Mr. Lowell 'used up'.

5. *slang* or *colloq.* Thoroughly exhausted by physical exertion or hardship; tired out, 'done up'.

1840 R. H. Dana *Bef. Mast* xxviii, [He was] barefooted..; 'cleaned out' to the last real, and completely 'used up'. 1850 Smedley *F. Fairlegh* xlvii, Why, the perspiration is pouring down your face,—you look regularly used-up. 1888 J. C. Harris *Free Joe*, etc. 226 It was a five-mile excursion; and he returned, as Mrs. Haley expressed it, 'a used-up man'.

b. Knocked up by excess.

1890 Gunter *Miss Nobody* xiii, My heavens! what a head I have accumulated over night!..I wonder if Avonmere is used up likewise?

6. Worn out, debilitated, rendered useless, as with hard work, age, dissipation, etc.

1848 Dickens *Dombey* x, A smoke-dried, sunburnt, used-up, invalided old dog of a Major, Sir. 1862 Calverley *Poems* 57 What is coffee, but a noxious berry, Born to keep used-up Londoners awake? 1863 W. C. Baldwin *Afr. Hunting* vi. 214 An old used-up brute [*sc.* horse]. 1871 Eleanor Grove tr. *Ebers' Egypt. Princess* I. Preface (Tauchn.) p. xv, In days when a used-up man of the world, like Antony, could desire in his will that [etc.].

transf. 1852 C. B. Mansfield *Paraguay*, etc. (1856) 369 The more respectable people here..have a sort of used-up look, which is not inviting. 1853 Dickens *Bleak Ho.* liii, The cousin..yawns, 'Vayli'—being the used-up for 'very likely'. 1871 Earle *Philol. English Tongue* § 106 The extreme oddity of our sound of *U* comes out under a used-up or languid utterance. 1875 J. Grant *One of the '600'* iii, The used-up bearing of those..who affect to act as if.. life itself was a bore.

b. Emotionally exhausted; blasé.

1845 C. J. Mathews *Used Up* I. i. 8 Here I am, at thirty-three, completely blazé—a man literally 'used up!' 1853 Mrs. Gaskell *Ruth* xxiii, He was pleased to feel jealous again. He had been really afraid he was too much 'used-up' for such sensations.

7. Reduced, exhausted, or consumed by using; rendered unserviceable by use.

1855 Delamer *Kitchen Garden* 179 In short, make a general clearance of used-up things [in a garden]. 1881 Sharp *Asp. Poetry* 132 The accumulations of used-up verbiage, which had so long choked the sources of inspiration. 1896 *Allbutt's Syst. Med.* I. 312 The contaminated or used-up air.

Hence †**U·sedly** *adv.*, commonly; **U·sedness**. Also **Used-upness**. *nonce-use*.

1561 T. Norton *Calvin's Inst.* IV. 81 But it was..vsedly the custome..to shorten their iourney. 1680 Baxter *Answ. Stillingfl.* xxxiii. 48 If Usefulness and Usedness..may afford us a Prognostick. 1871 Mrs. Whitney *Real Folks* xiii, You would notice instantly the consummate usedness to the world. 1891 'L. Keith' *Halletts* II. 220 There was a good deal of used-upness about Spenceley, though..the world had still certain points open to his combativeness.

Usee·. *U. S.* [f. Use *v.* + -ee¹.] 'A person for whose use a suit is brought in the name of another' (*Cent. Dict.*, 1891).

Use-fruyt, Sc. var. Usufruit *Obs.*

Useful (yūˑsfŭl), *a.* and *sb.* [f. Use *sb.* + -ful.] Implied in the one early instance (1483) of *usefulness*, but app. not current till c 1600; cf. Useless *a.*

1. Of persons: Having the ability or qualities to bring about good, advantage, benefit, etc.; helpful for any purpose; serviceable. Also of animals (cf. 2).

1595 Shaks. *John* v. ii. 81, I am too high-borne to be propertied,..Or [a] vsefull seruing-man. 1646 *Verney Mem.* (1907) I. 343 Women were never soe usefull as now. 1671 Milton *Samson* 564 Now blind, disheartn'd,..quell'd, To

what can I be useful? ?a 1700 *Tak your Auld Cloak about ye* ii. in Ramsay *Evergreen*, My Cromie is a useful cow. 1708 J. C. *Compl. Collier* (1845) 19 Especially when such an Adventurer is so useful to the Publick. 1776 Gibbon *Decl. & F.* ii. (1782) I. 49 If he had any opportunity of rendering himself either useful or agreeable. 1831 Sir J. Sinclair *Corr.* II. 349 Baron Itzenplitz..wishes [to see] his children.. useful for their country. 1861 Whyte Melville *Market Harb.* ix, Useful horses;..and seem pretty fit to go. *Ibid.*, Very like hunters: remarkably useful horses indeed! 1887 Ruskin *Præterita* II. 422 [He] was benevolently useful, as a landlord should be, in his county.

b. *Theatr.* (See quot.)

1824 W. Irving *T. Trav.* II. (1848) 187, I was enrolled among the number of what are called *useful men*; those who enact soldiers, senators, and Banquo's shadowy line.

2. Of things, actions, etc.: Having the character or quality to be of use or utility; suitable for use; advantageous, profitable, beneficial.

1606 Shaks. *Ant. & Cl.* IV. xiv. 80 With a wound I must be cur'd. Draw that thy honest Sword, which thou hast worne Most vsefull for thy Country. 1634 Sir T. Herbert *Trav.* 183 Food no lesse pleasant and vsefull to Kine. 1644 Milton *Educ.* 99 The usefullest points of grammar. 1669 Sturmy *Mariner's Mag.* II. x. 76 How to make a most useful Instrument of the Stars. c 1737 Swift *Corr.* (1913) V. 435, I cannot doubt of your being willing to encourage all useful inventions. 1752 Hume *Pol. Disc.* iv. 67 Every thing useful to the life of man, arises from the ground. 1780 *Mirror* No. 80, They..publish useful information to mankind. 1846 Landor *Imag. Conv.* Wks. I. 197/2 We are not always to consider in our disquisitions what is pleasantest, but sometimes what is usefullest. 1871 Jowett *Plato* IV. 309 Exercises..useful both in peace and war. 1875 R. F. Martin tr. *Havrez's Winding Mach.* 8 We thus see that.. the useful load exceeds the half of the total load. 1890 'R. Boldrewood' *Col. Reformer* (1891) 337 A steady reader in her own line, which she denominated 'useful'.

absol. 1802 C. Findlater *View Agric. Peebles* 55 Admirers of the curious, as much as of the useful, in farming. 1818 J. Foster *Contrib. Eclectic Rev.* (1844) I. 482 The useful was to him the *summum bonum*. 1836–8 [see Useless 1]. 1892 Zangwill *Bow Mystery* 157 A man who has always preached the Useful day and night.

b. *sb.* A useful article. *rare*⁻¹.

1662 Petty *Taxes* 21 Metals, cloth, linen, leather, and other usefuls.

Hence **U·sefullish** *a.*, somewhat useful. *rare*⁻¹.

1848 Carlyle in Froude *Life in London* (1884) I. 421, I seem to them a desperate half mad, if usefullish fireman.

U·sefully, *adv.* [f. prec. + -ly².] In a useful manner; so as to be of use; to a useful end; beneficially, profitably, serviceably.

1634 Massinger *Very Woman* III. ii, Serve usefully, Serve all with diligence. 1656 Cowley *Davideis* III. 281 How the kind Sun usefully comes and goes. 1711 Steele *Spect.* No. 145 ꝑ 2 You cannot employ yourself more usefully. 1781 Gibbon *Decl. & F.* xxx. III. 175 Whose arms would have been more usefully employed to maintain the Roman limits. 1807 G. Chalmers *Caledonia* I. III. v. § 3. 357 The notices of topography come in here, usefully, to illustrate the obscurity of history. 1868 Kinglake *Crimea* III. 244 It was hardly one which could be usefully submitted to a numerous assembly.

U·sefulness. [f. as prec. + -ness.]

†**1.** The advantage or benefit *of* (a place). *Obs.*⁻¹

1483 Duke Gloucs. in R. Davies *Extr. Munic. Rec. York* (1843) 147 For the wele and usefullnes of þe realme.

2. The state or condition of being useful or serviceable; utility, serviceableness.

1617 Woodall *Surg. Mate* (1639) B 3 b, The goodnesse and usefulnesse thereof, for the preserving of mens lives. 1662 Stillingfl. *Orig. Sacræ* III. i. § 16 The peculiar usefulness of the several parts of mans body. 1749 Berkeley *Word to Wise* Wks. 1871 III. 437 We are all agreed about the usefulness of meat, drink, and clothes. 1760 'Portia' *Polite Lady* x. 28 The usefulness and importance of all the different parts of education. 1835 *Penny Cycl.* IV. 398/1 *Bill of Exchange*, a well-known mercantile instrument, of great and extensive usefulness. 1860 Ruskin *Unto this Last* (1862) 125 In accurate terms, usefulness is value in the hands of the valiant. 1871 Jowett *Plato* IV. 19 The preliminary sciences..are to be studied partly with a view to their practical usefulness.

b. With pl.: A good, benefit, or advantage. *rare.*

1664 H. More *Exp. 7 Epist.* Pref. c iv b, And these..are main Usefulnesses discoverable in the Interpretation. 1668 — *Div. Dial.* I. To Rdr. a j b, The particular Vsefulnesses of the Creation.

Usel, obs. variant of Isel (ashes, etc.).

Useless (yūˑslės), *a.* [f. Use *sb.* + -less.]

1. Of things, actions, etc.: Destitute of useful qualities; serving no good end or profitable purpose; not answering or promoting the proposed or desired end; unserviceable, ineffectual, inutile.

In frequent use from c 1650.

1593 Shaks. *Lucr.* 859 The aged man..like still-pining Tantalus..sits, And useless barns the harvest of his wits. a 1623 Fletcher *Love's Cure* I. i, Let your deeds Make answer to me: useless are all words Till you have writ performance with your swords. 1645 Stapylton tr. *Musæus* C 3 b, The giddy Seas their uselesse drinke bestow'd. 1697 Dryden *Virg. Georg.* III. 833 Useless to the Currier were their Hides. 1729 T. Innes *Crit. Essay* (1879) 56 An useless as well as an endless discussion. *Ibid.* 206 It became quite useless towards supporting Buchanan's schemes. 1776 Gibbon *Decl. & F.* ii. (1782) I. 55 According to the useless rhetoric of that age. 1825 Scott *Betrothed* xvii, He..fell.. ere Raoul could afford him his support, useless as that might have proved. 1855 Macaulay *Hist. Eng.* xix. IV. 271 The six thousand waggons which had accompanied the French army were useless. 1890 *Retrospect Med.* CII. 177 Physicians, almost without exception, give nearly useless doses of arsenic.

absol. 1836–7 Sir W. Hamilton *Metaph.* i. (1859) I. 4 What is a utilitarian? Simply one who prefers the Useful to the Useless. 1838 *Penny Cycl.* XI. 345/2 To distinguish good from evil, the useful from the useless.

b. For which there is no present use.

1745 *Transl. & Paraphr.* 50 They'll lay the useless Trumpet by, and study War no more.

2. Of persons: Destitute of competence or capacity; of inadequate or insufficient ability; inefficient.

1670 Covel in *Early Voy. Levant* (Hakl. Soc.) 135 With great courage..[he] turn'd upon the Rogues, who were uselesse, and thought they had him safe. 1710 W. King *Heathen Gods & Heroes* vi. (1722) 12 [Prometheus] brought Men out from the Caves where they liv'd useless, and like Beasts. 1783 Burke *Rep. Aff. India* Wks. 1842 II. 52 That Mr. Hastings..had recalled a useless officer. 1810 Crabbe *Borough* xx. 331, I lost my sight, and my employment gone, Useless I live. 1840 Thirlwall *Greece* VII. 180 He..sent the baggage and all his useless people to Melitæe. 1855 Longf. *Hiaw.* x. 29 Bring not here a useless woman.

U·selessly, *adv.* [f. prec. + -ly².] In a useless or fruitless manner; ineffectually; †so as to become of no use.

1615 G. Sandys *Trav.* III. 151 The grasse wast-high, vnmowed, vneaten, and vselessly withering. 1690 Locke *Hum. Und.* II. i. § 15 To be so idlely and uselesly employ'd. 1765 *Museum Rust.* IV. 371, I would not so uselesly misapply ..your time. 1774 Pennant *Tour Scotl. in 1772*, 272 My money had been so uselessly laid out. 1831 Scott *Cast. Dang.* vi, You have been long, and I hope not uselessly, my pupil. 1880 McCarthy *Own Times* lxvi. IV. 506 He had thrown away his life uselessly in a quarrel.

U·selessness. [f. as prec. + -ness.] The quality of being useless; futility, inutility.

1690 Locke *Hum. Und.* III. iv. § 10 Another Peripatetick definition..which..betrays its Uselessness and Insignificancy. 1733–4 Bp. Berkeley in Fraser *Life* (1871) vi. 217 The impropriety and uselessness of..going to Cloyne. a 1768 Secker *Serm.* (1771) VI. 69 The Revelation of St. John is accused of Obscurity, and consequently of Uselessness. 1845 James *Arrah Neil* v, The uselessness of remonstrance or opposition. 1889 S. Langdon *Appeal to Serpent* i. 23 These vast monuments of laborious uselessness.

†**U·sell**, *a. Obs.* [a. ON. *ú-sæll* unhappy (MSw. *usal*, Sw. *usel*, Da. *ussel*, miserable, pitiful), f. *ú-* Un-¹ + *sæll* happy.] Wretched, miserable. Hence †**U·selldom**, wretchedness. *Obs.*⁻¹

c 1200 Ormin 891 Forr baþe leddenn usell lif I metess & i claþess. *Ibid.* 3668 Unnorne & wrecche & usell child Inn ure mennisscnesse. *Ibid.* 3708 To libbenn her onn eorþe Full wrecchelike inn useldom Off metess & off claþess.

†**Use-man**. *Obs. rare.* [f. Use *sb.* 5, 16 d.]

1. A usurer.

1633 Heywood *Eng. Trav.* III. i, If I can aswell put off my Vse-man This Day, I shall be maister of the field.

2. (See quot. and Use *sb.* 16 d.)

a 1716 South *Serm.* (1717) V. 34 To give those Doctrine and Vse-men, those Pulpit-Engineers their due.

U·se-money. Now *dial.* [f. Use *sb.* 5 b.] = Interest *sb.* 10. Also *fig.*

1616 Healey *Theophrastus* 66 When he coms to his debtors for his vsemony. 1626 Middleton *Anything for Quiet Life* I. i, Never did any man thrive that purchased with use-money. 1656 Trapp *Comm.* (ed. 2) *Matt.* v. 26 All that wicked men suffer here is but a paying the use-money required for that dreadful debt, that must be paid at last. 1700 T. Brown *Amusem. Ser. & Com.* 29 There sneaks a Hunger-starv'd Usurer in quest of a Crasie Citizen for Use and Continuance-Money. 1849– in dialect use (Durham, Cumbld., Yks., Lincs., Somerset). 1874 T. Hardy *Far fr. Mad. Crowd* viii, When the use-money is gied away to the second-best poor folk.

User¹ (yūˑzəɹ). Also 6 *Sc.* usar. [f. Use *v.* + -er¹. Cf. OF. *useur*.]

1. One who has or makes use of a thing; one who uses or employs anything.

c 1400 Love *Bonavent. Mirr.* (1908) 70 So ofte þe maker and þe vsere offendeth god. a 1425 tr. *Arderne's Treat. Fistula*, etc. 8 Þe forseid [counsels]..shal giffe a gracious going to þe vser to þe hiȝte of worship. 1467 in *Eng. Gilds* (1870) 387 That it be so stopped by the doers or vsers therof. 1579 Northbrooke *Dicing* (1843) 177 God graunt that..the magistrates..may..set sharpe punishment for the vsers and teachers thereof. c 1600 Shaks. *Sonn.* ix, But beauties waste hath in the world an end, And kept vnvsde the vser so destroyes it. 1626 Donne *Serm.* (1640) 675 As he [*sc.* God] sees him a good or bad user of his graces. 1683 Tryon *Way to Health* 223 These Superfluities..are become as it were Essential to the Nature of the Users. 1711 *Countrey-Man's Lett. Curat.* 58 What tho' all our Reformers had been users and readers of the English Service? 1738 Warburton *Div. Legat.* I. 84 The utmost Consumption may be made..without Injury to the User. 1846 Greener *Sci. Gunnery* p. vii, The safety of the user of guns. 1846 Mozley *Ess.* (1878) I. 251 He is a user of Puritanism. 1862 *Cornh. Mag.* VI. 608 A moderate user of tobacco. 1876 Whitney *Language & its Study* iii. 74 It seeks..to save time and labour to the users of language.

†**2.** *Sc.* One who puts a writ, etc., in force or execution. *Obs.*

1576 in *Excheq. Rolls Scotl.* XX. 504 David Fowlar,.. usar of the said precept, declarit that he deliverit [it]..to John Kellie. 1609 Skene *Reg. Maj.*, *Forme of Proces* 122 The wreit or evident is declared to be fals:..And the vser thereof, is punished capitallie. c 1630 Sir T. Hope *Minor Practicks* (1734) 242 If the King..give a Letter of Regress; ..when the Order of Redemption is used and declared, the User of the Redemption is immediately seased, upon the Sight of the Regress.

†**3.** A usurer. *Obs.*⁻¹

1566 Drant *Horace, Sat.* I. ii. A viij b, What soeuer cums by vsers skylle, to get, and gender more.

4. *north. dial.* A useful animal.

1828 Carr *Craven Gloss.* s.v., A cow is said to be a good *user*, when she yields abundance of milk, &c. 1863 Mrs. Toogood *Yorks. Dial.* (MS.).

U·ser². *Law.* [a. F. *user* to Use, or inferred from Non-user. Cf. the earlier Abuser², Disuser.] Continued use, exercise, or enjoyment of a right, etc.; presumptive right arising from use.

1835 Crompton, Meeson & Roscoe *Rep. Cases* I. 418 *marg.*, No right having been acquired by user or length of possession. 1858 Ld. St. Leonards *Handy-bk. Prop. Law* xxv. 191 That there should be an user proved every year during the period. 1888 *Pall Mall G.* 29 Feb. 1/1 An open space in which the public has an uninterrupted right of user for purposes of public meeting.

transf. 1875 Blackmore *Alice Lorraine* II. xvi. 207 A crust of mud, as if some underground duct were anxious to maintain user of its right of way.

attrib. 1897 *Westm. Gaz.* 16 June 4/2 In which [judgement] there was only one slight reference to the user question.

Userer, **-y**, etc., obs. varr. Usurer, Usury.

Ush, *sb. Sc.* Also 5–6 vsche, 5 wsche. [See next and Ish *sb.*]

†**1.** = Ish *sb.* 1, Egress *sb.* 1. *Obs.*

1429 *15th Rep. Hist. MSS. Comm.* App. VIII. 10 [He] sall haf fre vsche and entre in to the said castell. 1534 *Munim. de Melros* (Bann. Cl.) 628 To be haldin..in houssis, ..pastouris, lesouris, fre vsche and entray.

†**2.** = Ish *sb.* 2, Issue *sb.* 2.

1463 *Extr. Aberd. Reg.* (1844) I. 23 To fynd the childe of the brok of his gudis to the vsche of fyue yeris. 1472 *Rental Bk. Cupar-Angus* (1879) I. 164 The sade John Sperk entrand at the vsche of his [*sc.* Cant's] tak. 1489 *Sc. Acts, Jas. IV* (1814) II. 215 Þat a proclamacioune be maid at the vsche of this parliament.

†**3.** A fine or amerciament; = Issue *sb.* 7 b. *Obs.*

1417 *Reg. Aberdon.* (Maitland Cl.) I. 215 Þe kyrk..is in possession of þe tend penny of all wardis, relefis, and mariagis, vscheis of courtis, eschetis.

4. = Issue *sb.* 9. *rare.*

a 1900 *Caithness Words* (E.D.D.), *Ush*, the entrails of a slaughtered animal.

Ush, *v.*¹ *Sc.* (†and *north.*). Also 5 vssh(e, 5–6 wsch, 6 vsche, 7, 9 ushe. [var. of Ish *v.*¹]

†**1.** *intr.* To issue, come *out* (or *forth*). *Obs.*

c 1420 *Avow. Arth.* lxiv, On a day we vsshet oute. c 1470 Henry *Wallace* v. 1050 Thai..wsched furth upon the secund day. *Ibid.* VIII. 116 Erll Patrik wschyt, for bid him wald he nocht. ?1550 *Freiris Berwik* 130 (*Maitland MS.*), He had ane preuie postroun..That he micht vsche [*Bann.* ische] quhen [that] him list vnknawin. a 1578 Lindesay (Pitscottie) *Chron. Scot.* (S.T.S.) II. 11 Certaine of the castell men wschit out. a 1614 J. Melvill *Diary* (Wodrow Soc.) 273 Hendrie Hamilton ushes out of a hous, where he lay in wait for bloode.

†**b.** To go or come *in*; = Enter *v.* 1. *Obs.*

a 1400 *Sir Degrev.* 1078 (1062), Þey vschen in with banere, v. hunderyd knyȝtus.

†**2.** *trans.* To clear (a place) of people; to expel or drive out (occupants). *Obs.*

a 1578 Lindesay (Pitscottie) *Chron. Scot.* (S.T.S.) II. 83 [They] dang out the portar ffrome the ȝett and wschit all the rest of the place. a 1614 J. Melvill *Diary* (Wodrow Soc.) 317 The King, taking me asyde, caussit ushe the Cabinet. a 1639 Spottiswood *Hist. Ch. Scot.* VI. (1655) 374 Presently the roomes were ushed, and the Earl with his company went forth. 1685 *Acts of Sederunt* (1790) 163 The Lords..recommends to the Ordinary..to order the house to be ushed and cleared.

b. To empty, cleanse.

1887 *Suppl. Jamieson* 257/1 To ushe the belly.

Ush, *v.*² *dial.* or *colloq.* [Back-formation from Usher *sb.*]

1. *trans.* To guide, escort, or lead.

a 1824 in C. K. Sharpe *Ballad Bk.* (1824) 11 Three valets,.. To beir my tail up frae the dirt, And ush me throw the toun.

2. *intr.* To act the usher. (Usher *sb.* 1 d.) *U.S.*

1910 *Harper's Mag.* Mar. 613/1 Man alive, you've crossed half a continent to 'ush' at that wedding!

Usher (vˑʃəɹ), *sb.* Forms: 4–5 vsscher, usscher, uscher, 5 vschere, vshure, 6 vscher; 4–5 vssher (5 -ere), 4–6 ussher (5 -ere), 6 vsher, 5– usher (7 ushier); 4 oyschere, 5 oischer; *Sc.* 5 isscheare, 5–6 ischar, 6 ischair, -ear, 7 isher. [a. AF. *usser* (12th c.), OF. *ussier*, *uissier*, *uscier*, var. of *huisier*, etc., Huisher *sb.* Cf. Ostiar(y).]

1. An official or servant who has charge of the door and admits people to a hall, chamber, etc.; a door-keeper; in later use esp. an officer in a court of justice, or an attendant who conducts people to seats in a church, public hall, or place of amusement.

c 1386 Chaucer *Sqr.'s T.* 293 The vsshers and the squiers been ygoon, The spices and the wyn is come anoon. a 1400–50 *Boke of Curtasye* 30 in *Babees Bk.* 300 Whille marshalle or vssher come fro þe dore, And bydde the sitte, or to borde the lede. c 1400 *Northern Passion* (H.) 617 Saint iohn spak to vsscher þan. c 1410 *Sir Cleges* 287 The vsscher at the hall dore was Wyth a staffe stondynge. a 1470 H. Parker *Dives & Pauper* (W. de W. 1496) VI. xi. 249/1 She dyd hyr offyce, for she was usshere and keper at the dore. 1525 Ld. Berners *Froiss.* II. xcvi. 110 b/1 Than the squyer..called the vssher to open the dore. c 1610 in [T. Maude] *Verbeia or Wharfdale* (1782) App. 43 The Usher's Wordes of Directions. First,..he must go before them thro' the hall [etc.]. 1677 *Govt. Venice* 121 He disposes of the little Offices about the Palace, as the Ushers and others. 1694 E. Chamberlayne *Pres. St. England* I. III. 681 Chelsea College...There are several other..Servants, as..Sexton, Usher, Porters [etc.]. 1728 Chambers *Cycl.* (1738) s.v., The ushers of the inquisition ..think themselves highly honoured, by only looking to the doors of the sacred tribunal. 1799 *Report Comm. Courts of Justice* 29 Usher of the Court. *Ibid.* 31 The Court of

King's Bench..[Officers include] Usher and Cryer. Deputy Cryers. Deputy Ushers. 1868 Dickens *Let.* 3 Jan., He met one of the 'ushers' (who show people to their seats) coming in with Kelly. 1898 A. M. Binstead *Pink 'Un & Pelican* 181 Like the legal gent.., asked to define the duties of the ushers in the law courts.

b. *fig.*, *transf.*, and in fig. context.

c 1380 Wyclif *Sel. Wks.* II. 163 Crist..haþ resoun of many þingis; for he is dore, he is ussher. 1387 Trevisa *Higden* v. xvii. (MS. Cott. Tib. D. VII.) fol. 188 Seþþe..so meny..prieuleges..were ygrauntet to petur y dare noȝt wiþsygge [so] grete and soche an oyschere and porter. 1573 Tusser *Husb.* (1878) 20 Make eie to be vsher, good vsage to haue, make bolt to be porter. 1594 *Zepheria* v. B 3, Feare, Centinell of sad discretion,..Cares Vsher, Tenant to his owne oppression. 1630 Prynne *Anti-Armin.* 258 Arminianisme is but a Bridge, an Vsher vnto grosse Popery. 1638 T. Whitaker *Blood of Grape* 4 As if Satiation were the Usher of diseases. 1709 Steele & Swift *Tatler* No. 67 ꝑ 10 In this chamber of Fame..no historians are to be admitted at any of these tables; because they..are to be made use of as ushers to the assemblies. 1878 Stewart & Tait *Unseen Univ.* i. § 5. 27 Being the usher of souls in their passage to the future state.

c. Const. *of* (the hall, chamber, etc.).

a 1400–50 *Bk. Curtasye* 432 in *Babees Bk.*, Speke I wylle a lytulle qwyle Of vssher of chambur, with-outen gyle. [Description of his duties follows.] ?1436 *Pol., Rel., & L. Poems* (1903) 13, I was put to þe Soudenys house & was made vssher of halle. 1480 *Acta Dom. Conc.* (1839) 49/1 Sir Johne of Culquhone..vschare in þe tyme of oure souerane lordis chawmer durre. 1503 *Acc. Ld. High Treas. Scot.* II. 311 John Knox ischar of the hall. 1538 Elyot, *Admissionales*, vshers of the chambre. 1623 Cockeram II, An Vsher of a Hall, *atrict*. 1728 Chambers *Cycl.* (1738) s.v., In the French Court there are two ushers of the ante-chamber, or hall where the king dines in public.

fig. a 1500 *Assemb. Ladies* in Skeat *Chaucerian Pieces* (1897) 383, I am..Of her [*sc.* Loyalty's] chambre her ussher. 1501 Douglas *Pal. Hon.* III. lviii, Humanitie and trew Relatioun Bene ischaris of his chalmer.

d. *U. S.* One who performs the functions of an usher (sense 1) at a wedding.

1895 *Outing* (U.S.) XXVII. 181 He sent the young lady a beautiful Colport cup and saucer,..at the same time breathing a prayer that Elliott would not ask him to be usher.

2. An officer at court, in a dignitary's household, etc., whose duty it is on occasion to walk or go before a person of high rank; also, a chamberlain. *Usher of the Black Rod, Green Rod*: (see Black Rod, and quot. 1869).

1518 H. Watson *Hist. Oliver of Castile* (Roxb.) N 2 b, There came dyuers kynges and heraualdes of armes, and after came the Vsshers. 1553 *Rutland Papers* (Camden) 118 The Duke of Northfolke..claymethe to be highe vssher the daye of the coronacion. 1641 *Sc. Acts Chas. I* (1870) V. 332/1 Commandit..to goe befoir the king as Ischear with ane rod in his hand. 1678 Phillips (ed. 4) s.v., Usher of the Black-rod. 1689 *Breviate St. Scot.* 10 The Second Great Heritable Offices in the Kingdom, are The Lord High Constable,..The Heritable Usher. 1718 Echard *Hist. Eng.* III. 622 The Usher of the Black-Rod commanded their Attendance in the House of Lords. 1721 Ramsay *Poems* I. List of Subscribers, Usher of the Green Rod, and daily Waiter to his Majesty. 1850 Marsden *Early Purit.* 402 The king sent down the usher of the House of Lords with a message. 1869 Cussans *Her.* 235 The Officers attached to this Noble Order [of the Knights of the Thistle] are: The Dean;..and the Usher of the Green Rod.

fig. 1641 Milton *Reformation* 2 Faith needing not..the Senses, to be either the Vshers, or Interpreters, of heavenly Mysteries. 1673 A. Walker *Leez Lachrymans* 18 When he is pleased to send this usher of the Black-Rod, Death,..a white-staffe is too weak to make Resistance.

transf. 1577 B. Googe *Heresbach's Husbandry* III. 116 A Colt..passeth bridges, not tarriing for an vsher, nor fearing the Ise. 1606 Shaks. *Ant. & Cl.* III. vi. 44 The wife of Anttony Should haue an Army for an Vsher. 1626 T. H[awkins] *Caussin's Holy Crt.* 37 Anciently Pearles were called Vshers, because they made way for Ladyes, who were attyred with them. 1726 Pope *Odyssey* XVII. 251 The good old proverb how this pair fulfill! One rogue is usher to another still. 1763 Churchill *The Ghost* IV. 37 A downright Usher to admit New-Comers to the Court of Wit.

†**b.** A male attendant on a lady. *Obs.*

1621 Fletcher *Wild-G. Chase* III. i, If she want an Usher; such an implement; One that is throughly pac'd; a clean made Gentleman; Can hold a hanging up. 1649 Davenant *Love & Honour* I. i, Consumptive Ushers that are decay'd In their Ladies service. 1664 Butler *Hud.* II. i. 96 She call'd for Hood And Usher, Implements which Ladies wear. 1749 Smollett *Gil Blas* I. xvi, A lady who..was squired by an old usher [F. *écuyer*], and a little black moor carried her train. 1809 Malkin *Gil Blas* I. xvi. ꝑ 2 She released her sweet hand from the custody of the usher [F. *écuyer*].

3. One who precedes or arrives before another, esp. a higher dignitary or personage; a precursor. Also *transf.* Cf. Harbinger *sb.* 3.

1548 Udall *Erasm. Par. Matt.* iii. 28 By his ussher and messenger John. c 1550 N. Smyth tr. *Herodian* III. 40 b, He had certayne Usshers going before him, whiche commaunded euerye man to auoyde the stretes. 1641 J. Jackson *True Evang. T.* II. 151 That other lesson..[Christ] suffered his Ushers that went before him to teach. 1847 Emerson *Initial Love* 75 Heralds high before him [*sc.* Cupid] run, He has ushers many a one.

b. *transf.* That which precedes or gives intimation of the approach or advent of a person or thing.

c 1586 C'tess Pembroke *Ps.* L. i, God comes,..His guarde huge stormes, hot flames his ushers goe. 1599 Sir J. Davies *Hymne of Astræa* 5 Early, chearfull, mounting Larke, Lights gentle Vsher. 1633 P. Fletcher *Elisa* I. xxviii, Ah death!..Thou one meals fast, usher to endlesse feasting. 1640 J. Gower *Ovid's Festiv.* II. 32 In comes the Lecher bold;.. His groping hands his warie ushers were. 1645 Stapylton tr. *Musæus* C j b, Leander..Expecting the sad Torch, and to be led By that bright Vsher to his private bed.

fig. a 1586 Sidney *Arcadia* II. xxvii, Stretching out his hand, and making vehement countenances the ushers to his speches. 1597 Hooker *Eccl. Pol.* v. lxxii. § 18 Fasts haue beene set as Vshers of festiuall dayes. 1607 Shaks. *Cor.* II. i. 173 [Stage direction] A shout, and flourish. *Volum.* These are the Vshers of Martius. 1632 tr. *Bruel's Praxis Med.* 58 Troublesome dreames are vshers to this disease. c 1670 M. Bruce *Gd. News in Evil Times*, etc. (1708) 26 They make the Sabbath, as it were, Mr. Usher to their Visiting of Christ.

c. *Ent.* A species of moth.

1819 Samouelle *Entomol. Compend.* 360 *Geometra leucophearia*, The Spring Usher. *Ibid.*, [G.] *nigricaria*, The dark-bordered Usher. 1832 Rennie *Brit. Butterfl. & Moths* 102 The Spring Usher (*Anisopteryx leucophearia*, Stephens) appears in oak woods the end of February. *Ibid.*, The Wall Usher (*A. Æscularia*).

4. An assistant to a schoolmaster or head-teacher; an under-master, assistant-master. Now *rare.* Also in fig. context.

1512 *Nottingham Rec.* (1885) III. 453 To..establisshe one free schole of one Schole Maister and one Vssher. 1561 in H. B. Wilson *Hist. Merchant-Taylors' Sch.* (1814) 15 Yff both the maister and the usshers be sick at once (as God defend) then let the schoole cease for that while. 1581 J. Bell *Haddon's Answ. to Osorius* 259 b, Who hath made you usher I pray you, or prepositour of Ciceroes schoole? 1632 D. Lupton *London & Country carbonadoed* 119 Country Vshers..are vnder the Head-maister, equall with the chiefe Schollers, and aboue the lesser boyes. 1653 Baxter *Worc. Petit. Def.* 6 We are but Ushers, and Christ is the ..chief Master of the School. 1669 E. Chamberlayne *Pres. St. Eng.* II. 483 This Colledge consists of a Master.., a Chaplain,..a Master and Usher to instruct 44 Scholars. 1687 Wood *Life* (O.H.S.) III. 247 His being usher to a Presbyterian scholemaster. 1711 Hearne *Collect.* (O.H.S.) III. 205 Tollet is made IIᵈ Master, he being before a chief Usher. 1791 Boswell *Johnson* an. 1732, He accepted of an offer.. as usher in the school of Market-Bosworth. 1818 Scott *Hrt. Midl.* xxvii, Conning over a few pages of Horace or Juvenal with his usher. c 1868 in Hughes *Tom Brown* (ed. 6) Pref., Persecution..he can't stop; no more could all the ushers in the world. 1876 *Scheme C.C. 8 governing Foundation Thetford School Hosp.* 6 From the same date..the present usher of the said School shall cease to hold his office as such Usher.

†**b.** *transf.* A teacher or preceptor acting under another. *Obs.*

1533 More *Confut. Tindale* Wks. 585/2 Oure sauiour.. sent him [*sc.* Judas] forth..for one of hys vsshers to teache in his owne time. 1577 Hanmer *Anc. Eccl. Hist.* vi. xiv. 105 He ordained Heraclas..his fellowe helper, and Usher,.. committing vnto him the instruction of the inferiour sort. 1613 Purchas *Pilgrimage* I. iv. 16 Nature was his Schoole master; or if you will rather, Gods Usher.

c. = Provost *sb.* 8.

1545 [see Provost *sb.* 8]. 1699 Boyer I, *Prevost de sale d'armes*, the Provost, or Usher of a Fencing-School. 1765 Angelo *Sch. Fencing* 52 When an usher..has finished his apprenticeship under an able master,..he is obliged to fence with several masters.

†**5.** *Usher of the coins, Change*, or *Exchange*, an officer of the Mint. *Obs.*

1485 *Cal. Patent Rolls* (1914) 49 [The] countroller,.. clerk and ussher of the coynes. 1485 *Rolls of Parlt.* VI. 365/2 The Office of Usher of the Exchaunge of oure said Soveraigne Lord, within his Towre [of London].

6. *attrib.* and *Comb.*, as *usher life*, *-like*.

1580 Fulke *Martiall Confut.* iv. 164 An other foolish brable and vsherlike construing, he maketh of Cyprians words. 1873 W. Cory *Lett. & Jrnls.* (1897) 341 The eight years I had then gone through of usher life.

Hence **U·sherdom**, the office or status of an usher; **U·sheress**, a female usher; **Ushe·rian**, of or pertaining to an usher or ushers; **U·sherism**, conduct or comportment characteristic of ushers.

1846 Worcester (citing *Qu. Rev.*), *Usherdom. 1905 A. C. Benson *Upton Lett.* 106 The ugly slough of usherdom. 1879 *Ch. Times* 5 Sept., An appointment..as an 'usheress' in a big establishment. 1826 Disraeli *V. Grey* I. iv, Certain powers were..delegated to..beings called Ushers...The 'usherian rule had, however, always been comparatively light at Burnsley Vicarage. 1869 Ellis *E. E. Pronunc.* I. vi. 625 That kind of pedantic self-sufficiency which is the true growth of half-enlightened ignorance, and may be termed 'usherism'.

Usher (vˑʃəɹ), *v.* [f. prec. Cf. Huisher *v.*]

1. *trans.* To act as usher to (a person or persons); to admit ceremoniously; to conduct, attend, or introduce with ceremony *from*, *to* or *unto* or esp. *into* (a place), etc.; to announce, introduce, or bring *in* as an usher.

In frequent use from c 1820. In group (*b*) with advs.

(*a*) 1596 Warner *Alb. Eng.* XII. lxxv. 312 Vnto their Lodging Stafford did the Ladies Vsher then. 1632 J. Hayward tr. *Biondi's Eromena* A 3 b, Excuse my boldnesse in ushering her Excellencie..into so excellent a presence. 1725 Pope *Odyss.* XVII. 447 My Lords! this stranger..The good Eumæus usher'd to your court. 1773 *Cook's Voy S. Pole* II. ii. (1777) I. 202 An old gentleman came along-side, who..was some king or great man. He was accordingly, ushered on board. 1821 Scott *Kenilw.* xiv, The hall..to which Tressilian was ushered by one of the Earl's attendants. 1844 Disraeli *Coningsby* III. iii, Whose gracious lot it was to usher them from the apartment. 1891 Farrar *Darkn. & Dawn* xxv, The tribune ushered her into the Emperor's chamber.

(*b*) 1749 Fielding *Tom Jones* XIV. x, He..ushered his visitant up stairs. 1760 in Doran *Mann. & Manners* (1876) II. 63 For which purpose I set forth in a Coach and Six, and ushered him in. 1835 Dickens *Sk. Boz, Parish* i, Simmons bows assent, and ushers the woman out. 1853 C. Brontë *Villette* xli, Ushering me in, he shut the door behind us.

b. Predicated of things. Also *transf.*

1613 T. Scot *Tongue-Combat* 63 This brauerie..vshers them into the company of best princes. 1697 Luttrell *Brief Rel.* (1857) IV. 311 Boats having mett them with divers sorts of musick to usher them into that harbour. 1807–8 W. Irving *Salmag.* (1824) 169 The piece opens with a gentle *andante affetuoso*, which ushers you into the Assembly-room.

c. *fig.*, *transf.*, and in fig. context.

1594 [Southwell] *Mary Magd. Funeral Tears* 69 b, As desire is euer vshered by hope, and waited on by feare. 1612 Drayton *Poly-olb.* iii. 3 Yet the blushing dawn out of the chearful east Is ushering forth the day. 1623 Cockeram III, *Nusculus*, a friendly fish to the Whale, it vshers him from rocks, shelues, and shores. a 1661 Fuller *Worthies*, *Leic.* II. (1662) 130 Sir Tho. Lake may be said to have ushered him [*sc.* Villiers] to the English Court. 1715 Rowe *Lady Jane Gray* IV. i, As if his traitor father's haggard ghost, And Somerset,..had usher'd him to ruin. 1749 Fielding *Tom Jones* IV. i, [The hero] is generally ushered on the Stage by a large Troop of..Scene-shifters. 1790 Burke *Fr. Rev.* 6 That mode of signature to which you have thrown open the folding-doors of your presence chamber, and have ushered into your National Assembly. 1806 J. Beresford *Miseries Hum. Life* (ed. 4) II. xiii, A furious wind which ushers the dust into your eyes. 1867 H. Macmillan *Bible Teach.* vi. 109 A new class of objects is now ushered upon the scene. 1891 Farrar *Darkn. & Dawn* lxvi, Those whom we ushered into the reader's presence at the beginning of this book.

refl. 1812 *Ann. Reg., Chron.* 47 This singular person ushered himself into public notice in London, by [etc.].

d. *absol.* To act as or after the manner of an usher. Also *fig.*

1612 Donne *Progresse of Soule, 2nd Anniversary* 156 Yet Death must usher, and unlocke the doore. Thinke further on thy selfe, my Soule. 1657 F. Cockin *Div. Blossomes* 4 For to insinuate into his will, And usher, thorough his Judgment to 's Affection..That he may give to Thee all due subjection.

2. To precede, escort, or go before (a dignitary) ceremonially as an usher.

1612 in *10th Rep. Hist. MSS. Comm.* App. I. 599 All his equippage was ushered by certaine officers in ritche coates. 1665 Brathwait *Comment Two Tales* (1901) 47 If I at any time use him for the Squire of my Body, or to Usher me in the streets. 1676 *Office Clerk of Assize* E vij, His Bayliffs, with their white wands in their hands, do usher the Justices from the Court, to the place where they dine. a 1700 Evelyn *Diary* 23 April 1667, His Majesty went to Chappell with the Knights of the Garter.., usher'd by the Heraulds.

†**b.** To precede (a person, esp. of higher rank) as a forerunner or harbinger. Also in fig. context.

1629 Gaule *Pract. The.* A 5, You shall see your Sauiour at once Vshered, Afforded, Humbled, and Exalted: Vshered by his Prophets, afforded in his Person. 1639 Fuller *Holy War* III. vi. 118 [Richard I] set forth [to the Crusade] with many of our nation, which either ushered or followed him. 1646 G. H[ils] *Odes of Casimire* Pref., Juno and Venus ushered by chaste love Through..Flora's banks here move.

c. *fig.* and *transf.*

1599 T. Storer *Life & D. Wolsey* H j b, Who follow'd me, but Fortune was at hand, To follow him? or, if she went before, To vsher him? 1602 Marston *Ant. & Mel.* III. E 2, Gastly amazement..Shall hurry on before, and vsher vs. 1609 B. Jonson *Sil. Wom.* IV. i, Nor will it bee out of your gaine to make loue to her too, so shee follow, not vsher, her ladies pleasure. 1621 Brathwait *Nat. Embassie*, etc. (1877) 203 My friends..Wish'd that all good successe might vsher mee. a 1668 Davenant *Play House to let* III. i, Wilt thou now guided be By that bright Star which ushers me.

d. To precede, come or happen immediately before, in order of time; to lead up to. (Cf. 7 c.)

1607 *Merry Devil Edmonton* I. ii. 55 In and feed, And let that vsher a more serious deed. c 1611 Chapman *Iliad* v. 864 Pitchy tempests threat, Usher'd with horrid gusts of wind. 1616 B. Jonson *Epigrams* ci, Some better sallade Vshring the mutton. 1647 Clarendon *Hist. Reb.* VII. § 282 Such an application to Court as usually ushered those promotions. 1821 Shelley *Adonais* xxi, Evening must usher night, night urge the morrow. 1821 Byron *Sardanap.* v. i, The day at last has broken. What a night Hath usher'd it!

†**3.** To wait at (a banquet) as an usher. *Obs.*⁻¹

1602 Dekker *Satirom.* K 3 b, Euen thus the Mercury of Heauen Vshers th' ambrosiate banquet of the Gods.

4. To introduce (something uttered); to preface. (Cf. 7 e.)

1635 A. Stafford *Fem. Glory* 55 She made two pawses usher her answer. 1637 C. Dow *Answ. to H. Burton* 159 Divine offices..must not bee curtall'd..by..any new-devised formes of praier, either ushering, or following them. 1717 Pope *Eloisa to Abelard* 3 Oh name for ever sad!..Still breath'd in sighs, still usher'd with a tear.

†**5.** To lead, conduct, or direct (a thing) to some point. *Obs. rare.*

1668 Culpepper & Cole tr. *Barthol. Anatomy* II. x. 120 The External [membrane]..sticks close to the intermediate Ligaments.., and ushers along the recurrent Nerves. 1791 Cowper *Iliad* II. 649 Skill In ushering to its mark the rapid lance.

6. To introduce or bring *into* the world.

1679 C. Nesse *Antichrist* 6 Harbingers..to usher him into the world. 1713 Steele *Englishm.* No. I. 5 The Jest ..is ushered into the World by the loudest Laughter. 1756 H. Johnson in J. Duncombe *Lett.* (1773) III. 38 You have done a great favour to the world in ushering so noble..a work into it. 1835 Marryat *J. Faithful* i, It was about a year after the loss.., that I was ushered into the world. 1855 Brewster *Newton* II. xviii. 172 The theory he ushered into the world.

transf. 1835 Marryat *J. Faithful* v, I am very nearly ushered into the next World.

7. To usher in: (see also 1). **a.** To bring in (a banquet, meat, etc.) with ceremony.

1613 Heywood *Silver Age* II. i, Vsher me in a costly banquet straight To entertaine my Lord. 1706 E. Ward *Wooden World Diss.* (1708) 94 The Captain's Bell calls him to usher in the Apple-dumplins. 1829 S. H. Cassan *Lives Bps. Bath & Wells* 262 The meat was ushered in.

b. To inaugurate or bring in (a period of time).

c 1600 Shaks. *Sonn.* cxxxii, That full Starre that vshers in

the Eauen. 1656 S. Winter *Serm.* 147 That so he might usher in the eternitie of the world. 1698 Fryer *Acc. E. India & P.* 276 The Morning being ushered in with..Music. 1781 Cowper *Hope* 717 If chance..A tempest usher in the dreaded morn. 1791 Smeaton *Edystone L.* § 306 The year 1762 was ushered in with stormy weather. 1827 Longf. *Life* (1891) I. viii. 121 The day was 'ushered in', as the newspapers say, by the firing of cannon. 1850 Tennyson *In Mem.* lxxii, Dim dawn,..Who usherest in the dolorous hour With thy quick tears. 1872 Yeats *Techn. Hist. Comm.* 298 The French Revolution ushered in a new era of taste.

c. = sense 2 d.

1641 Maisterton *Serm.* 18 An anteambulo to usher in a thousand pains. 1663 South *Serm.* (1717) V. 89 Every Fast portended some Villany, as still a Famine ushers in a Plague. 1695 J. Edwards *Perfect. Script.* 424 The Lord, who was to be usher'd in by Elijah the prophet. 1707 *Curios. in Husb. & Gard.* 44 Flowers..appear only to usher in the Fruit, or the Seed; afterwards they fade. 1712 Addison *Spect.* No. 363 ꝑ 18 That vision of Lewdness and Luxury which usher in the Flood. a 1721 Prior *Many Daughters have done well* 10 How welcome did that light appear Which usher'd in a form all Heav'nly fair.

d. To mark the introduction, beginning, or occurrence of (an event, etc.); to introduce.

1646 J. Hall *Horæ Vac.* 8 They generally usher in uproares in the State. 1650 R. Stapylton *Strada's Low C. Wars* VII. 49 These punishments seemed only to usher in the Death of the two Counts. 1697 Dampier *Voy.* (1729) I. 394 A convenient place to usher in a Commerce with the neighbouring country. 1784 Cowper *Task* IV. 23 But oh th' important budget! usher'd in With..heart-shaking music. 1801 *Med. Jrnl.* V. 231 Increased heats..already described as ushering in the hæmorrhage. 1843 R. J. Graves *Syst. Clin. Med.* x. 106 The symptoms..bear a very strong analogy to those which usher in typhus. 1870 Freeman *Norm. Conq.* (ed. 2) I. 738 The event of 1018..was ushered in by a comet.

e. = sense 4.

1662 Stillingfl. *Orig. Sacr.* II. vi. § 5 Their deliverance by Cyrus..he ushers..in with this preface that [etc.]. 1673 *True Worship of God* 8 These Sacrifices not only accompanying their Confessions..; but their Hymns and Doxologies also,..to usher them in with more acceptance. 1699 Bentley *Phal.* 222 He would have usher'd the Word in with some kind of introduction. 1757 Gray *Let.* Poems (1775) 252 All that ushers in the incantation from 'Try we yet..', I am delighted with. a 1763 W. King *Lit. & Polit. Anecd.* (1819) 154 He was..so unfortunate as to usher in his criticisms with [etc.]. 1814 Chalmers *Evid. Chr. Revel.* II. ii, The quotation is..ushered in by the general words, 'As it is written'.

Hence **U·shering** *ppl. a.*

1628 [A. Leighton] *Appeal to Parliament* 145 Why breaketh out the fearfull wrath of God..among us, but because of Baal-peor his ushering Ceremonies..? 1634 Milton *Comus* 279 Could that [*sc.* darkness] divide you from neer-ushering guides? 1820 Clare *Rural Life* (ed. 3) 32 That rural call..All noises now to silence lulls, In soft and ushering sounds.

†**U·sherage**. *Obs. rare.* [f. prec. + -age.] The act of ushering or introducing; insertion.

1661 Hickeringill *Jamaica* 28 [An interstice] admitting not so much as the intermedium or usherage of a twig. 1662 — *Apol. Distressed Innoc.* Wks. 1716 I. 298 If the usherage of Sanctity cannot hand in their black deformities of Rapine.

†**U·sherance**. *Obs.* [f. as prec. + -ance.] The action of introducing or bringing in; introduction.

1711 Shaftesb. *Charac.* III. 190 Our Author's First Letter ..occasion'd the revival of this abortive Piece, and gave Usherance to its Companions.

U·sherer. [f. Usher *v.* + -er¹.] One who or that which ushers in; an usher or harbinger. Also with *in*. Occas. *fig.*

1598 Marston *Scourge of Villanie* II. v. E 4 b, Codrus my well-fac'd Ladies taile-bearer, (He that some-times play'th Flauias usherer). 1640 Reynolds *Passions* xxxv. 424 The Usherers in, or Attendants and followers on the Grave, Age, Infirmity, Sicknesse. c 1645 Howell *Lett.* IV. xxix. (1890) 607 True spiritual Pride, the usherer-in of all Confusions. 1824 Galt *Rothelan* II. III. ii. 16 The Past is usherer to the Future. 1892 Walt Whitman in *Harper's Mag.* April 709/2 Thee [*sc.* Death], envoy, usherer, guide at last of all.

U·shering, *vbl. sb.* [f. as prec. + -ing¹.] The action of the verb, in various senses. Also with *in*.

1588 Shaks. *L. L. L.* v. ii. 328 Nay he can sing A meane most meanly, and in Vshering Mend him who can. a 1613 Overbury *Characters, A Fine Gentleman*, Afterwards he maintaines himselfe an implement of houshold, by carving and ushering. a 1693 Urquhart's *Rabelais* III. xxx. 247 At the ushering in [F. *l'apport*] of the Second Service, Panurge..[made] a low Reverence. 1850 O. Winslow *Inner Life* x. 273 The ushering in of that great event. 1851 Gallenga *Italy* I. 21 The ushering in of a new political phasis. 1866 Trollope *Claverings* ii, Even though he had earned that money by 'ushering' for the last two years.

U·sherless, *a.* [f. Usher *sb.* + -less.] Lacking an usher, herald, or harbinger. In earlier use *fig.*

1598 Sylvester *Du Bartas* II. i. IV. *Handy-crafts* 88 Where Usher-lesse, both day and night, the..windes enter and goe forth. 1604 Marston *Malcontent* IV. v. G j, There Vsherlesse the ayre comes in and out. 1815 Milman *Fazio* 80 Who art thou thus usherless and unbidden Scarest my privacy? 1883 J. Payn *Thicker than Water* II. xxix. 217 On the great staircase he met Mrs. Sotheran coming up usherless.

U·sherment. *rare*⁻¹. [f. Usher *v.* + -ment.] The fact of being prefaced, introduced, or ushered in.

1887 Saintsbury *Hist. Elizab. Lit.* ii. 46 These last..do not come in with the somewhat ostentatious usherment and harbingery, which for instance laid the even more splendid bursts of Jeremy Taylor open to the sharp sarcasm of South.

U·shership. [f. Usher *sb.* + -ship.]

1. The office or functions of an usher.

1580 Fulke *Martiall Confut.* iv. 165 Yᵉ Priestes are appointed to vse those signes, which if Martials Vshership will not admit, [etc.]. 1631 T. Powell *Tom of all Trades* 44 To leape into instantly, and immediately out of a Ladies vshership. 1740 Ld. Harrington in *10th Rep. Hist. MSS. Comm.* App. I. 275 The Ushership of the Exchequer. 1788 Cowper *Let.* Wks. 1836 VI. 201 When I was under his ushership at Westminster. 1825 T. Hook *Sayings* Ser. II. III. 93 To assume the ushership of the black rod at Montgomery Place. 1881 *Daily News* 1 Aug. 5/3 In Algeria.. his years of ushership had been the most wretched of his life.

2. A post or position as a (school-) usher.

1825 Hone *Every-day Bk.* I. 79 The son..being put to school, obtained successive usherships. 1880 R. K. Dent *Old & New Birmingham* 79 Johnson having found the drudgery of an ushership..too irksome for him.

Ushewe, obs. f. Issue *sb.*

†**Ushing**, var. Ishing *vbl. sb. Obs.* (Cf. Ush *v.*¹)

1375 Barbour *Bruce* VI. 363 (E.), Hys wyt schawyt hym the strait entre off the furd, and the uschyng alsua.

‖**Usine** (üzin, yuziˑn). [F. *usine* factory, (in early use) water-mill.] A factory; esp. in later use, a West Indian sugar factory.

In first quot. the word is misapplied.

1798 W. Eton *Turk. Empire* 216 Their furnaces are of *usine*, which is particularly adapted to the casting of iron. 1858 Simmonds *Dict. Trade* 396 *Usine*, a glass-house; an iron-work. 1878 *Times* 10 May 4/3 Furnaces and vast usines. 1888 *Daily News* 13 April 5/4 Of these usines, or crushing factories, there are already several in Trinidad, St. Lucia, and British Guiana.

Using (yūˑziŋ), *vbl. sb.* [f. Use *v.* + -ing¹.]

1. The action of making use of something, or the fact of being used.

a 1340 Hampole *Psalter* liv. 2, I am made sary in myn vsynge. 1387–8 T. Usk *Test. Love* III. vi. l. 60 They han as wel dyvers aptes and dyvers maner usinges. c 1400 *Cursor M.* 29369 (Cott. Galba), Þat oþer [case] es of..portere, in vsyng of þaire awin mistere. 1422 Yonge tr. *Secreta Secret.* 247 Vsynge of honementys aftyr the tyme and complexcione. c 1445 Pecock *Donet* 50 Mesurable and resonable vsing of worldly goodis. 1526 *Pilgr. Perf.* (W. de W. 1531) 45 In iust commutacion & vsyng of these thynges. 1560 Bible (Genev.) *Col.* ii. 22 Which all perishe with the vsyng of them. 1656 Earl Monm. tr. *Boccalini's Advts. fr. Parnass.* II. lii. (1674) 202 The using of the same severities which Augustus.. practised. 1690 Locke *Hum. Und.* III. x. § 2 The using of Words, without clear and distinct Ideas. 1705 *Lond. Gaz.* No. 4114/4 A fine Coach lined with Velvet, little the worse for using. 1774 Goldsm. *Nat. Hist.* III. 315 His teeth wear, like those of most other animals, by using. 1826 *Art of Brewing* (ed. 2) 94 The twelve principal houses have..disclaimed the using of any material in their Beer, except malt and hops. 1893 C. C. King in *Social Eng.* I. 43 Of..arrowheads as missile weapons there are none that seem worth the using.

†**b.** The celebration of the Eucharist. *Obs.*

1452 *Paston Lett.* I. 237 The seid servaunts..knelyng to see the usyng of the Masse. 1454 *Ibid.* 280. c 1500 *Langforde's Meditacyons* in Wickham Legg *Tracts on Mass* (1904) 18 From the sacryng vnto the vsing be done, you may remember..the Passyon and deith of our sauyour.

c. The action of accustoming *to* something.

1702 *Eng. Theophrast.* 212 It goes a great way towards Felicity, the using of our selves to other Peoples Follies.

2. Manner of usage or employment.

1388 Wyclif *Rom.*, Prol., Thei weren brouȝt in to the lawe and profetis, that is, in to cerymonyes..acordynge with the cerymonyes, which vsyng is contrarie now to the treuthe.. of Cristis gospel. 1553 T. Wilson *Rhet.* 114 b, iii. The placing of these Images, is like vnto wordes written. iiii. The vtteraunce and vsing of them, is like vnto readynge. 1669 in *Buccleuch MSS.* (Hist. MSS. Comm.) I. 32 Extolling the King of England's using of people. 1726 Leoni *Alberti's Archit.* I. 62 b/2 For the right using of these benefits, the Fathers may provide by Laws and Statutes. 1827 Keble *Chr. Y.*, *Palm Sunday* v, As in this bad world below Noblest things find vilest using.

3. *Using-up*, consumption or exhaustion *of* a commodity, etc.

1863 Jas. Sanderson *Agric. Berw. & Roxb.* 32 The using-up of the manure is the preferable mode. 1889 Hamerton *French & English* I. i. 14 The decline caused by industrialism and the rapid using-up of life in large cities.

4. Special Comb.: **using-file**, a file affixed to the work-bench (instead of being held in the hand), for having the work rubbed upon it; **using-ground** *U.S.*, the haunt of wild-fowl; †**using stone** (see quot. 1688).

1683 Moxon *Mech. Exerc.*, *Printing* xii. ꝑ 2 The Using-File..is about nine or ten Inches long, and three or four Inches broad..The two broad sides must be exactly flat and straight. 1688 Holme *Armoury* III. 303/1 The using File..; the teeth not half so rough as the common File. *Ibid.* 382/1 The Using Stone [of jewellers]..is a flat smooth Stone shooting out into two angles or points on each side. 1893 *Harper's Mag.* Oct. 681/2 The 'using-grounds' of the coveys are generally known or suspected by the farmer.

U·sitate, *a.* [ad. L. *ūsitāt-us*, pa. pple. of *ūsitārī* to use often.] **a.** Customary, usual. **b.** Much used *of* (= by).

1885 Dixon *Hist. Ch. Eng.* xx. III. 462 The usitate dignities of rural deans and archdeacons. 1890 *Sat. Rev.* 27 Sept. 383/1 A form of punishment usitate of French novelists.

U·sitative, *a. rare*⁻¹. [f. as prec. + -ive.] That denotes customary action.

1849 Alford *Gk. Testament* I. 19 Not the usitative aorist, but declarative of the definite past εὐδοκία of the Father in Him.

†**Usker**. *Obs. rare*⁻¹. [a. Irish *usgar*.] An ornament or jewel. In quot. *collect.*

1536–7 *Act 28 Hen. VIII*, in Bolton *Stat. Irel.* (1621) 130 That also no woman vse or weare any kyrtell, or cote.. couched ne layd with vsker, after the Irish fashion.

Usle, obs. var. Isel (ashes, etc.).

U·snate. *Chem.* [f. Usn-ic + -ate¹ 1 c.] A salt produced by a combination of usnic acid with a base.

1866 Watts tr. *Gmelin's Handbk. Chem.* XVII. 50–51 Usnate of Ammonia,..Usnate of Potash,..Usnate of Soda, ..Usnate of Baryta,..Usnate of Copper. 1868 *Watts' Dict. Chem.* V. 970 The usnates of the alkali-metals are soluble in water.

‖**Usnea** (vˑsnĭ,ă). Pl. usneas, usneæ. [med.L. (12th cent.), ad. Arab. and Pers. اشنة *ushnah* moss. Hence F. *usnée* (1530).] A genus of gymnocarpous lichens, typical of the family *Usneidæ*; a species or plant of this.

1597 Gerarde *Herbal* III. clvi. 1369 *Muscus quernus*;..the Arabians and the Apothecaries call it *Vsnea*. 1693 tr. *Blancard's Phys. Dict.* (ed. 2), *Usnea*, Moss which grows upon Bones or Trees. 1706 Phillips (ed. Kersey), *Usnea*, a kind of green Moss..which is us'd in Physick. 1753 *Chambers' Cycl.* Suppl., *Usnea*,..of this genus of plants there are nineteen known species: 1. The stringy-tree moss, or common *Usnea* of the shops. *Ibid.*, 19. The smallest of all the *Usneas*..grows on the barks of old trees. 1857 M. J. Berkeley *Introd. Crypt. Bot.* 417 *Usneæ*, finally, when well-grown, are perhaps the most beautiful of Lichens. 1857 Thoreau *Maine W.* ii. (1867) 155 The spruce still grows shaggy with usnea. 1861 H. Macmillan *Footn. fr. Page Nat.* 109 So late as the seventeenth century, some of the filamentous lichens were sold in the shops of barbers and perfumers under the name of Usnea.

attrib. 1878 H. M. Stanley *Dark Cont.* II. vii. 204 From many of the branches depended the Usneæ moss in graceful and delicate fringes.

U·snic, *a. Chem.* Also usneic. [f. Usn-ea + -ic 1 b.] *Usnic acid*, carbusnic acid: usnin.

1847 W. Gregory *Handbk. Org. Chem.* (ed. 2) 502 Usnic Acid..is found in many lichens,..and in many species of *Usnea* [etc.]. 1848 Fownes *Elem. Chem.* (ed. 2) 514 The *Usnea barbata* and several other lichens contain usneic acid. 1861–7 [see Usnin].

Usnin (vˑsnin). *Chem.* Also -ine. [f. Usn-ea + -in¹.] Usnic acid.

1861 H. Macmillan *Footn. fr. Page Nat.* 82 Alpine lichens generally are more or less of a brown or black colour. This peculiarity seems to be owing to the presence of usnine or usnic acid. 1867 Brande & Cox *Dict. Sci.*, etc. III. 912/2 Usnin or Usnic Acid..forms yellow crystals, which with great difficulty are fused like a resin.

‖**Uso**. *Obs.* [It. or Sp. *uso*.] = Usance 5, 5 b.

1704 *Lond. Gaz.* No. 3992/4 Two first Bills of Exchange, ..payable to Jean Voordagh or Order, at 2 uso 8 days. 1740 W. Douglass *Disc. Curr. Brit. Plant. Amer.* 4, Notes of Hand payable in Silver at certain Uso's or Periods.

†**U·sque**. *Sc. Obs.* Also 8 usquæ, husque, usky (cf. Whisky *sb.*¹). Short for next.

1728 Ramsay *Friends in Ireland* 10 Drinking roundly rum and claret, Ale and usquæ. c 1730 Burt *Lett. N. Scotl.* (1754) I. 188 This drink [common ale] is of itself apt to give a Diarrhea, and therefore..they interlace it with Brandy or Usky. 1739 A. Nicol *Poems* 76 Good ale and Usque ga'd about In Healths.

attrib. c 1730 Burt *Lett. N. Scotl.* (1754) II. 83 My Merchants..mov'd the Usky Vessels before 'em. *Ibid.* 84 The Usky Men were my Companions.

Usquebaugh (vˑskwĭbǭ). Forms: α. 6 vskebeaghe, 7 vsque-ba'he, vskebah (uskkiba), 7–9 usquebah (7 usquabah), 7 vsquebach; 7 vsque-, 7– usquebagh, 7 vsce-, usce-, uskabagh; 6 vscough-, 7– usquebaugh. β. 7 vsque-, usque-, husquo-, uskebath. γ. (Chiefly *Sc.*) 6 iskie-bae, 7 usquebay, 8–9 usquebae (8 usquabae). [a. Irish and Sc. Gaelic *uisge beatha* (*uisci-betha* in Ann. Loch Cé, an. 1405), lit. 'water of life' (cf. Aqua-vitæ), f. *uisge* water, and *beatha* life. The latter word is differently pronounced in Irish and Scottish Gaelic, approximately (bā) and (bē). Cf. Whisky(bae.)] = Whisky *sb.*¹

With α-forms, in very freq. use from c 1610.

α. 1581 Derricke *Image Ireland* F ij, She filles them then with Vskebeaghe. 1600 Sir R. Cecil *Lett.* (Camden) 33 Remember..the Lord Threasurer with a couple of pugges or some vscough baugh. 1610 Beaum. & Fl. *Scornf. Lady* II. i, A bottle of Usquebaugh. 1658 Rowland tr. *Moufet's Theat. Ins.* 913 The Irish prepare a distilled Oenomeli made with Honey, Wine and some herbs, which they cal Vsquebach. 1682 *Lond. Gaz.* No. 1776/4 There is right Irish Usquebagh to be sold..at the Rein-Deer in Tuttle-street,.. By one from Ireland. 1706–7 Farquhar *Beaux' Strat.* I. i, An honest Gentleman that came this way from Ireland, made her a Present of a dozen bottles of Usquebaugh. 1762 Foote *Orators* III. 61 Usquebaugh..is an exhilirator of the bowels, and a stomatic to the head. 1818 Hazlitt *English Poets* vii. 260 The last long precious draught of his favourite usquebaugh. 1882 Miss Braddon *Mt.-Royal* I. iv. 118, I wonder whether she had a strong brogue, and a sneaking fondness for usquebaugh.

attrib. 1630 Randolph *Aristippus* 24 Are you there you Vsquebaugh Rascall, with your Metheglin iuyce?

β. 1621 S. Ward *Life of Faith* 33 Vsing it [*sc.* faith] as Vsquebath and strong Waters for swones and heart qualmes onely. 1681 T. Dineley *Jrnl. Tour Irel.* in *Trans. Kilkenny Archaeol. Soc.* Ser. II. II. 25 As thou did not want Usquebath Oat cakes,..How is it then that thou diedst? 1713 Tyldesley *Diary* (1873) 117 Hee gave us two drames of uskebath.

γ. 1583 *Leg. Bp. St. Androis* 1062 And George Gipsones iskie bae Had all the wyte he womit sae. a 1689 W. Cleland *Poems* (1697) 12 A Tupe Horn fil'd with Vsquebay. 1715 Ramsay *Christ's Kirk Gr.* II. viii, Another gill Of usquebae. 1791 Burns *Tam O'Shanter* 108 Wi' usquabae, we'll face the devil! 1819 Scott *Leg. Montrose* iv, A flask of usquebæ, designed for the refreshment of Lord Menteith. 1840 R. Bremner *Excurs. Denmark*, etc. II. 211 Morning drinkers of usquebae.

| USTEROSIS. | 477 | USUALLY. | USUARY. | 478 | USURE. |

Ussay, ussche, ussoho, ussen, obs. Sc. varr. Issue *sb*. **Us self**, *see* Self A. 3–4. **Us**-sell, obs. or dial. var. Ouzel. **Usshe**, obs. form of Usher, *sb.* **Usselbe**, Ussu, etc., obs. var. Issue *sb.* **Uste**, obs. Sc. var. Host *sb.* 3, 2.

Ustel-, Ustiliagineous, etc.: *see* Hustlement.

† **Usteosis**, obs. var. Hysterosis.

Ustiliago Worthies. Bedford. i. (1662) 321 Meat time fast named) as in Under-Shrell.

Ustilagi'neous (ⁿstilǣgi'nĭŏs), *a*., *Bot*. [f. mod.L. Ustilagine-us (brand fungi) ...

Ustila'go (ⁿstilēʹgō), *Bot*. [L. mod.L., *Ustilago* (util·ēgĭna), *a*., *Bot*. [f. mod.L., Ustilago + -ous.]

Ustion (ⁿsʹtʃən), *sb*.

1. The action of burning, or fact of being burnt.

2. The action of searing; cauterization.

U'stive, obs. rare.

† **Usto'rious**, *a*., *Obs*.

U'stulate, *a*. [ad. L. *ūstulāt-*, ppl. stem of *ūstulāre* to burn.]

Ustulate (*ūstiʹleʹt*), *v*.

Ustulation (*ūstiʹleʹ-ʃən*), *sb*. [ad. med.L. *ūstulātiōn-*, *ūstulātiō*, noun of action f. L. *ūstulāre* to burn.]

1. The action of burning or fact of being burnt; *spec*. in later use, torrefaction, roasting.

† Usage, obs. var. Usage *sb.*

Usual (yūʹʒuǎl, -ĭwǎl), *a*. (*sb*.) [a. OF. *usual*, (*usuel*), *= Pr. uzual* ...]

Usually (yūʹʒuǎli, -ĭwǎli), *adv*. [f. prec. + -ly.]

1. In a usual or wonted manner; according to customary, established, or frequent usage; commonly, customarily, ordinarily; as a rule.

† **b.** *Habitually close* or *near*, *Obs*.

Usufruct (yūʹzĭŭfrŭkt), *sb*. [a. late L. *ūsu-fruct-us* (whence Sp. and Pg. *usufructo*, It. *usu-frutto*, F. *usufruit*) ...]

1. *Law*. The right of temporary possession, use, or enjoyment of the advantages of something belonging to another, so far as may be had without causing damage or prejudice to this. Also *transf*.

Usufructuary (yūzĭŭfrŭʹktĭwǎri), *a*. and *sb*. [ad. late L. *ūsufructuāri-us* ...]

† 2. In a regular manner; regularly. *Obs. rare.*

Usuary (yūʹzĭwǎri), *a. Roman Law*. [ad. L. *ūsuāri-us*, f. *ūsus* Use *sb.*]

Usu-capient, pres. pple. stem of *ūsū-capĕre*: *see* Usu-caption.

Usu-caption (yūzĭŭkæʹpʃən). *Roman Law*. [ad. L. *ūsū-capiōn-*, *ūsū-capiō* ...]

Usucapt (yūʹzĭŭkæpt), *v*. *Roman Law*. [ad. L. *ūsū-capt-*, past pple. stem of *ūsū-capĕre*: *see* Usu-caption.] *trans*. To acquire ownership of or title to (a property, etc.) by usucaption. Also *absol*.

Usuca'ptable, *-ible adj.*, capable of being held by usucaption; **Usuca'ptor**, *= Usufruptor*.

Usuca'ption (yūzĭŭkæʹpʃən), *Roman Law*. [a. OF. *usucaption*, *-cion*, or med.L. *ūsūcaptiō*, ...]

Usufruct (yūʹzĭŭfrŭkt), *sb*. [a. late L. *ūsū-fruct-* (whence Sp. and Pg. *usufructo*, It. *usu-fructo*) ...]

Usufructuary, *a*. and *sb*.: *see* prec.

† 2. Holding or enjoying an office, etc., by usufruct. *Obs.*

Usury (yūʹʒuri), *sb*. *Obs*. Also 4–5 **vsure**, 5 **vser**, and **vsury** (also AF. and F.), and L. *ūsūra* (whence It., Sp., Pg. *usura*, F. *usure*), n. of action f. *ūs-*: *see* Usury *sb.*]

1. The act or practice of lending money at interest.

† Usura'rious, *a*., *Obs. rare*. [f. L. *ūsūrāri-us* (whence It., Sp., Pg. *usurario*, F. *usuraire*), ...]

Usura'tion ...

Usu'ry (yūʹʒuri), *a*. *Obs. rare*. [ad. L. *ūsūrāri-us* ...]

† Usurario'us, *a*. ...

| USURER. | 479 | USURP. | USURP. | 480 | USURPATION. |

Usurer (yūʹʒŭrǎr), *sb*. Forms: α. 3–7 **vsurer**, 4–5 **-ere**, 5, Sc. 6 **-ar**; 5 **usurere**, 6 **-er**, 6–7 **usures** (6 **usar-**). [a. AF. *usurer*, altered ...]

1. One who lends money at interest; a money-lender; in later use one who charges an excessive rate of interest.

b. Characteristic of a usurer.

Hence U'suriously *adv*.

† U'surous, *a*. [f. Usure *sb.* + -ous.] = Usurious *a*.

† U'surer, *Obs*. [a. OF. *usurier*, ad. med.L. *ūsūrārius*.] A usurer.

U'suring, *ppl. a*. *Obs*. Also 6 **usering**.

1. Of persons: Practising or given to usury; usurious.

U'surous, *a*.

Usury (yūʹʒuri), *sb*. [a. OF. *usurer* (14th c.), ad. L. *ūsūrāre* (whence It. *usurare*, Pr., Sp., Pg. *usurar*) to seize for use, to use, employ.]

1. *Law*. To appropriate wrongfully to oneself (a right, prerogative, etc.). Also const. *against*, *upon*.

† 2. To take on oneself unwarrantably; to assume, arrogate.

Usurp (yūzŭʹrp), *v*. [ad. F. *usurper* (14th c.), or ad. L. *ūsūrpāre* to seize for use, ...]

Ag. *and transf.* 1849 Shaks. *Meas. for M.* iii. ii. 9 To...

1. *trans*. To seize or obtain possession of (territory, land, etc.) in an unjust or illegal manner; to assume unjust rule, dominion, or authority over, or appropriate wrongfully. Also const. *on* (= *against*), *over*.

2. To seize or obtain possession of (territory, land, etc.) in an unjust or illegal manner; to assume unjust rule, dominion, or authority over, or appropriate wrongfully.

c. To take (a word or words) into use; to borrow or appropriate from another language, source, etc.

3. To exercise, practise, or inflict (injury, cruelty, etc.); to put into act, impose. Occas. const. *on, towards*. Also *transf. Obs. rare.*

4. To supplant, oust, or turn out (a person); † to deprive (one) of possession. Also *refl. rare*.

5. To exercise, practise, or inflict (injury, cruelty, etc.).

6. To seize, intrude or lay hold upon (land, property, etc.) without right or just cause; to assume authority or domination over, to become superior to.

7. To supplant, oust, or turn out (a person); † to deprive (one) of possession. Also *refl. rare*.

† 8. To take or hold possession of (something belonging to another or others) by sleight or force; to appropriate by ruse or violence; to steal.

† 9. To usurp on or upon. To practise usurpation upon; to commit illegal seizure or action against (a person or persons).

b. To intrude (oneself) improperly or without just cause into (some dignified or important office, position, etc.); to assume or arrogate to oneself (political power, rule, authority, etc.) by force.

10. To take possession of a thing by usurpation; to become participator of. *Obs.*

11. † *intr.* To claim or make pretensions; to assume or attempt arrogantly, *to be or do* something. *Obs.*

† 7. To take or hold possession of (something belonging to another or others) by sleight or force; to appropriate by ruse or violence.

8. To act or play the usurper; to rule or exercise authority as a usurper. Also *const. against. Now rare.*

Hence U'surpedly *adv. Obs.*

Usurpation (yūzŭʹrpeʹʃən), *sb*. [a. OF. and AF. *usurpation* (F. *usurpation*), ad. L. *ūsūrpātiōn-, ūsūrpātiō*, n. of action f. *ūsūrpāre*: *see* Usurp *v*. + -ation.]

1. Claim or assertion that is unwarranted or unauthorized; unjustified assumption, arrogation, or pretension.

2. The action of usurping, illegally seizing, or wrongfully occupying some place or property belonging to a person or persons.

† b. *transf*. Physical encroachment on sea or land. *rare*.

Usurpatory (yūzŭʹrpǎtŏri), *a*. *Obs. rare*. Characterized by, based upon, usurpation; of unwarranted encroachment.

Supplement, p. 3873; Corrigenda, p. 4092; Spurious words, p. 4093; Books quoted, p. 4094

Usurpative.

Usurpatory.

Usurpatrix.

Usurpature.

Usurped, *ppl. a.*

Usurper.

Usurping, *vbl. sb.*

Usurping, *ppl. a.*

Usurpingly, *adv.*

Usurpious.

Usurpment.

Usurpor.

Usurpously, *adv.*

Usurpress.

Usury.

Usurship.

Ut.

Ut-brogen, ME. var. OUTDRAW v.

Ut-bworwe, etc. obs. ff. OUTBORROW.

Ute, v. Obs.

Uten, var. OTON obs. Obs.

Uteran, etc. var. OTTER.

Utermost, var. UTTERMOST.

Utward.

Utas, sb.

Utensil.

Utensile, sb.

Utensils, pl. Obs.

Utensilment.

Uter.

Ut-rage, obs. form of OUTRAGE sb.

Uterine, adj.

Uterine, a.

Utero-, comb. form of L. *uterus*.

Uterus.

Upwite, sb.

Utible, a.

Utilitarian, sb. and a.

Utilitarianism.

Utility.

Utilizable, a.

Utilization.

Utilize, v.

Utilizer.

1873 Dawson *Earth & Man* xv. 380 Man was..to be..a care-taker and utiliser..of the things given to him. 1883 *Standard* 21 Nov. 5/3 Not a man of science, but only a utiliser of scientific results. 1884 *Health Exhib. Catal.* 66/1 Register Stove fitted with the Oxford Heat Utilizers.

‖**U·tinam.** *Obs.* [L. *utinam* oh that! would that!, f. *uti* (*ut* conj.) + *nam* indeed.] An earnest wish or fervent desire.

1643 Sir T. Browne *Relig. Med.* § 24 'Tis not a melancholy *Utinam* of mine owne, but the desires of better heads. 1646 — *Pseud. Ep.* I. x. 38 Nor can the will which hath a power to runne into velleities..have any *utinam* of this. 1718 *Entertainer* No. 9. 56 Our Religion is pure and undefiled... A Glance or a *Utinam*, in Christianity, are Criminal.

†**U·ting,** *vbl. sb. Obs.* [Later var. of *yowting*, *yeoting*, Yoting *vbl. sb.*] The action of steeping grain in the process of brewing. Only attrib. in *uting-fat*, *-room*, *-vat*.

1610 R. Vaughan *Water-Workes* E 4, Vting-rooms, Garnars, Matting-roomes [etc.]. *Ibid.* K 3, The water from my Vting-vats will doe the like. 1702 *Act 1 Anne* Stat. 2, c. 3 § 3 All Cisterns Uting-Fats Utensils and other Vessels. 1720 *Lond. Gaz.* No. 5864/3 Corn..steeped in any Cistern or Uting-Fat. 1800 *Act 41 Geo. III*, c. 6, Every Maltster..should wet or steep his Barley..in the Cistern, [or] Uting-fat.

Utis, variant of Utas.

†**U·tlagary.** *Obs.* [a. AF. *utlagarie*, *-erie*: see Outlawry.] = Outlawry 1.

1440 *Paston Lett.* I. 41 As the seide utlagare was certyfyed. 1567 *Lanc. Wills* (Chetham Soc.) II. 82, I have byn divers tymes wrongfullye sued and brought to the poynt of utlagari. 1642 tr. *Perkins Prof. Bk.* i. § 27. 12 Attainder of Felony..by utlagery, by verdict and by confession. 1660 *Act 12 Chas. II*, c. 12 ¶ 12 Any person..whose Conviction, Utlagary or Attainder is by this Act discharged.

Utlagh(e, -laȝe, -lahe, -law(e, obs. ff. Outlaw. **Utlarie, -y**(e, **-lawry**(e, obs. ff. Outlawry. **Utleden,** var. Outlead *v. Obs.*

†**Utlega·tion.** *Obs.*⁻¹ [ad. med.L. *utlagātion-*, n. of action f. *utlagāre*: see Outlaw *v.*] The legal process by which a person was outlawed. (Cf. Outlawry 1.)

1678 Butler *Hud.* III. i. 1521 When to a Legal Utlegation You turn your Excommunication.

Utlepe, -leph, -lete, obs. ff. Outleap *sb.*, etc.

†**Utmer, utmore,** *a. Obs. rare.* [f. *utm-est* Utmost *a.*, with comparative ending: see -more, and cf. Outmer *a.*] = Outer *a.* 1.

1382 Wyclif *Ezek.* xlvi. 21 That thei bere not out in to the vtmer house [1388 to the outermere halle]. — *Matt.* xxii. 13 Sende ȝee hym into vttermore [*v.r.* vtmore, vtmer] derknessis. *Ibid.* viii. 12.

Utmost (ʊ·tmōᵘst, ʊ·tmǝst), *a.* and *sb.* Forms: α. 1 ute-, utmest (*Northumb.* wut-), 3 ute-, 4 ut-, 5, 6 *Sc.* vtmest; 5 *north.* and *Sc.* vtmast, *Sc.* 6 vt-, 9 utmaist; 4–7 vt-, 5–6 vtte-, 7– utmost (6 vtmoste, vtmoost). β. 3–4 otemost, 4–5 ottemoste; 4 ot-, ottemeste. [OE. *útemest*, *útmest* (rare, and chiefly northern, variants of the usual *ýte-*, *ýtmest*), a double superlative (cf. Foremost, Inmost) from *úte* or *út* Oute, Out *advs.* + *-m-est*: see -most. Cf. the later Outmost *a.*

In Layamon 11023 *utemæste* prob. represents OE. *ýtemeste*. The ME. forms with *ote-*, *otte-*, *ot-* seem to imply an earlier *ūte-* with shortened vowel (as in Icel. *útan* from *út*). The shortening in *utmost* may be partly due to the double consonant, and partly to the influence of Utter *a.*]

I. 1. a. Situated farthest from the centre; occupying, lying at, or dwelling in the extreme bound or bounds; most external or remote in position or location; outermost, uttermost; Outmost *a.* 1.

α. *c* 950 *Lindisf. Gosp.* Matt. xxii. 13 Sendas hine in ðiostrum ðæm utmestum. *c* 1100 *Ælfred's Boeth.* xix. (Bodl. MS.), Þeah hit nu ȝebyriȝe þæt ða utemestan ðioda eowerne naman up ahebban. *c* 1330 *Sir Orfeo* 357 (Auchinleck MS.), Al þe vtmast wal Was..schine as cristal. *c* 1400 *Destr. Troy* 5487 Beyten is out in the orient the vtmast syde. *c* 1425 Wyntoun *Cron.* III. i. 8 Ane of his tais with The vtmast endis be þe lith Quyt wes smyttyn of þaim. *c* 1450 *Godstow Reg.* 106 His ende vttemost toward the tenement of the forsaid Vincente Menge. 1526 Tindale *Matt.* viii. 12 The children of the Kingdom shalbe cast out in to the vtmoost derckness. 1590 Spenser *F. Q.* II. x. 12 Corineus had that Prouince vtmost west To him assigned. 1618 Lawson *New Orchard* (1623) 46 We admit without the fence, of Walnuts in most plaine places, Trees middle-most, and..Elmes vtmost. 1660 Barrow *Euclid* I. prop. 21 The utmost points of one side of a triangle. 1697 Dryden *Æneis* IX. 221 Where the foes their utmost guards advance. 1729 T. Innes *Crit. Ess.* (1879) 63 The utmost extremities of the north of Britain. 1798 S. & Ht. Lee *Canterb. T.* II. 326 The utmost limit of creation! 1820 Shelley *Prometh. Unb.* IV. 372 It..doth pass Into the utmost leaves and delicatest flowers. 1859 Tennyson *Elaine* 525 Knights of utmost North and West. 1877 Ruskin *St. Mark's Rest* iv. (1894) 50 The entire tablet varied to its utmost edge.

fig. 1667 South *Serm.* (1715) II. 24 Which surely must reach the utmost Thoughts of any Atheist whatsoever.

β. 1297 R. Glouc. (Rolls) 11433 Þe castel hii assailede,.. & brake þe otemoste wal. 1387 Trevisa *Higden* (Rolls) I. 303 In þe vttermeste (MS. α. otmeste) ende of all þe erþe. *a* 1390 *Wycliffite Bible* Num. xxii 36 (MS. Bodl. 959), [A] toun..sette in ye otemost coostys of Arnon. 1398 Trevisa *Barth. De P. R.* xv. clv. (Bodl. MS.), Þe ottemoste norþe.. of Germania. *c* 1450 *M. E. Med. Bk.* (Heinrich) 93 Pile þe barke þe ottemoste [*v.r.* ottemoste rynde] awey.

†**b.** Of garments: Outermost; exterior. *Obs.*

1553 *Respublica* 1774 Doe of your vtmoste robes eche one. 1584 T. Hudson *Du Bartas' Judith* IV. (1611) 47 Her vtmost robe was colour blew Cœlest.

c. Furthest extended; greatest in extent, length, measure, etc.

1709 Felton *Diss. Classics* (1718) 12 To put forth Your Hand to the utmost Stretch, and reach whatever You aspire at. 1746 Francis tr. *Horace*, *Epist.* I. xvi. 108 Death is.. That utmost Course, where human Sorrow ends. 1791 Cowper *Odyss.* XI. 454 A night of utmost length. 1844 Kinglake *Eothen* xvii, All the whole earth that I could reach with my utmost sight and keenest listening was still.

2. That is of the greatest or highest degree; of the largest amount, number, etc.; extreme.

Somewhat rare before 1590; in freq. use since 1710.

a 1325 *Prose Psalter* lvii. 6 God shal defoulen her teþe..; our Lord shal breke þe uttemast [*Dublin MS.* ottermast] iuels of þe wicked. *c* 1375 *Sc. Leg. Saints* xii. (*Mathias*) 113 Scho let hym wyt þe vtmast thinge, þat he wes but a fundlynge. 1482 *Monk of Evesham* xxii. (Arb.) 53 He was takyn..to the vtmest peynys and ponissement of dethe. 1526 *Pilgr. Perf.* (W. de W. 1531) 2 b, The vttemost perfeccyon that man may attayne to. 1586 Marlowe *1st Pt. Tamburl.* II. iii, With amitie we yeeld Our vtmost seruice to the faire Cosroe. 1610 *Chester's Triumph* B 4, What e're our more then strained vtmost-All Can possibly performe, performe we shall. 1628 May *Virg. Georg.* III. 84 Her temptations make Two stubborne Bulls..with their Hornes to try their utmost deedes. 1667 Milton *P. L.* I. 103 His utmost power with adverse power oppos'd In dubious Battel. 1704 Evelyn *Diary* 7 Sept., This day was celebrated the thanksgiving..with the utmost pomp and splendour. 1782 Miss Burney *Cecilia* v. iv, Her mind was now in a state of the utmost confusion. 1805 Wordsw. *Waggoner* II. 73 The utmost anger of the sky. 1833 Ht. Martineau *Brooke Farm* iii. 35 The utmost profit of a cow. 1876 Geo. Eliot *Dan. Der.* I. vii, His antigropelos, the utmost approach he possessed to a hunting equipment.

3. Latest in order or time; last, final. Now *rare.*

c 1460 *Towneley Myst.* xxv. 248 Mary, me mynnys, thi moder hight, the vtmast ende of all thy kyn. 1526 Tindale *Matt.* v. 26 Till thou have payed the vtmost [1611 vttermost] farthing. 1590 Spenser *F. Q.* II. i. 49 In these sad words she spent her vtmost breath. 1591 — *Ruins of Time* 45 From their first vntill their vtmost date. 1642 Milton *Apol. Smect.* 41 Many wise men have miscarried in praising great designe before the utmost event. 1670–1 Marvell *Corr.* Wks. (Grosart) II. 367 Censure..against those who, after an utmost day set, shall persist to absent themselves. 1672 Dryden *Conq. Granada* II. i, 'Till I have found the last and utmost Foe. 1691 Swift *Ode Athenian Society* xi, When the sad melancholy muse Stays but to catch his utmost breath. 1772 Priestley *Inst. Relig.* (1782) I. 82 They prolong life to the utmost term of nature. 1809–12 Mar. Edgeworth *Absentee* iv, He would use it [*sc.* the power] to obtain the utmost penny of his debt. 1818 Byron *Juan* I. lxxx, I..hear these freedoms form the utmost list Of all o'er which such love may be a ranger. 1856 Kane *Arct. Expl.* I. xv. 171 Grating it down nicely,..and adding the utmost oil as a lubricant.

II. *absol.* and as *sb.*

In *Lindisf. Gosp.* Mark v. 23 *in utmestum* is used to render the L. *in extremis* (= at the point of death).

4. That which is most outward, distant, or remote; the farthest part, district, limit, etc., *of* an extent or area. Now only *arch.*

c 825 *Vesp. Psalter* cxxxviii. 9 In ðem utmestan sæs. *a* 950 *Ritual Dunelm.* (Surtees) 55 Oð to vtmeste eardes. 1382 Wyclif *Job* xxxvi. 30 The vtmost of the se he shal couere. 1382 — *Acts* i. 8 ȝe schulen be witnessis to me..to the vtmeste [*v.r.* vttermest] of erthe. 1614 W. B. *Philosopher's Banquet* (ed. 2) 43 The vtmost of the taile is poyson. 1615 G. Sandys *Trav.* 177 A City..on the utmost of the ridge of a hill. 1887 Morris *Odyssey* XI. 13 At last unto the utmost of the Ocean-stream we came.

†**b.** *sb. pl.* Remotest parts *of* the earth, etc. *rare.*

1382 Wyclif *Ps.* cxxxiv. 7 Bringende out cloudis fro the vtmostis [*v.r.* vttermostis] of the erthe. 1382 — *Isaiah* vii. 18 The fleȝe, that is in the vtmostes [*v.r.* vttermostis] of the flodus of Egipt.

5. That which is greatest or of the highest degree; the most or greatest possible or attainable in respect *of* force, skill, etc.; the utmost point, extreme limit or degree, *of* something.

1472 *Cov. Leet Bk.* 377 Thei..seid thei wold abyde with the Maire..to the vtmost of herr goodes in that mater. 1526 Tindale *Acts* xxiv. 22 When Lisias..is come, I will know the vtmost of youre matters. 1594 *1st Pt. Contention* C 4, To morrow we will ride to London, And trie the vtmost of these Treasons forth. 1596 Spenser *F. Q.* VI. i. 38 Thinking the vtmost of their force to trie. 1622 Mabbe tr. *Aleman's Guzman d'Alf.* II. 346 The Painter..shew'd therein the vtmost of his skill. 1667 Earl Orrery *St. Lett.* (1742) 331 The utmost I aimed at..was to tell your grace what others told me. 1752 Hume *Ess. & Treat.* (1777) I. 95 The utmost we have to boast of are a few essays. 1764 Reid *Inquiry* i. 75 The utmost which the human faculties can attain. 1805 J. Spaulding *Universalism* 129 That the damned suffer the utmost of their desert. 1838 Thirlwall *Greece* V. 153 Thebes had accomplished the utmost she could now reasonably aim at. 1855 Bain *Senses & Int.* I. ii. § 23 The utmost that can be said in the present state of our knowledge.

b. With possessive adjs.: The highest, greatest, or best of one's ability, power, etc.; the very most. Freq. with *do*.

c 1611 Chapman *Iliad* II. 119 Comethen,..and fly to our loved home; for now, nor ever, shall Our utmost take in broad-wayed Troy. 1646 Gaule *Cases Consc.* 118 Their utmost is but to produce a..false species of things. 1660 South *Serm.* (1715) IV. 23 Nor will it suffice..to rally up all one's little Utmost into one Discourse. 1690 Locke *Hum. Und.* IV. xix. § 15 A Man, having..done his utmost to inform himself in all Particulars,..may [etc.]. 1708 Addison *Pres. State of War* 26 Let us perform our utmost,..and we shall overwhelm 'em. 1785 Burns *To Rev. John M'Math* xvi, [One who] to his utmost would befriend Ought that belang'd ye. 1818 Cobbett *Pol. Reg.* XXXIII. 633 Will you do your utmost to obtain justice? 1856 Miss Yonge *Daisy Chain* I. xviii, His work, after he goes to Oxford, will be doing his very utmost—and you know what an utmost that is. 1887 P. MNeill *Blawearie* 136 It taxed to its utmost the ingenuity of the rival wooers.

c. As *sb.* An extreme amount, degree, or limit.

1856 [see prec. sense]. 1863 Jean Ingelow *Poems* 24 Forever yawns before our eyes An utmost—that is veiled.

6. The end, finish, or issue *of* something.

1603 Shaks. *Meas. for M.* II. i. 36 See that Claudio Be executed;..let him be prepar'd, For that's the vtmost of his pilgrimage. 1666 Boyle *Orig. Forms & Qual.* 264 An Accident robb'd me of my Glasse, before I could see the utmost of the Event. 1674 [see Uttermost *a.* 6].

7. *To the utmost*, to the extreme or uttermost degree, extent, capacity, or limit. Also const. *of* (one's power, etc.).

c 1450 *Mirk's Festial* I. 91 Gracyously he woll þat a man be demed wyth mercy and not to þe vtmast here. 1526 Tindale *1 Thess.* ii. 16 For the wrath off God is come on them, even to the vtmost. 1613 Shaks. *Hen. VIII*, v. iii. 146 Some of ye..Would trye him to the vtmost, had ye meane. 1685 Boyle *Enq. Notion Nat.* vii. 266, I grew weary before I had prosecuted it to the utmost. 1738 Wesley *Ps.* v. vi, Thy wrath on the rebellious Race Shall to the utmost come. 1756 C. Lucas *Ess. Waters* III. 307 Let us pursue our enquiries to the utmost. 1834 Ht. Martineau *Demerara* iv. 46 He was sure to..torment the animal to the utmost. 1860 Motley *Netherl.* II. l. 59 He would keep his pledge to the utmost. 1873 F. Hall in *Scribner's Monthly* VI. 465 The sages..have certainly consulted his comfort to the utmost.

(*b*) 1596 *Edward III*, IV. v. 86 That same man..keepes it [*sc.* his word] to the vtmost of his power. 1659 *Nicholas Papers* (Camden) IV. 147, I shall to the vttmost of my power constantly endeavour to doe him right. 1729 Law *Serious C.* vi. 90 So sure is it, that we are to do them to the utmost of our power. 1802 Mrs. E. Parsons *Myst. Visit* II. 245 The good woman..fortunately succeeded to the utmost of her wish. 1875 Manning *Mission H. Ghost* xli. 346 Let us to the utmost of our power, submit our will to the will of God.

8. *At the utmost* (†*at utmost*), at the very most in respect of time, quantity, etc. Cf. Most *a.* 6.

1619 in Foster *Eng. Factories India* (1906) I. 143, 15 dayes stay there, or 20 at uttmost. 1643 Trapp *Comm. Gen.* xi. 7 [He] beautified it, or, at utmost, inlarged it. 1722 Whiston *The. Earth* III. iii. 247 The Modern Age of Men at the utmost is not 80. 1753 *Chambers' Cycl.* Suppl. *App.* s.v. *Vultur*, The head..has, at the utmost, only a downy matter on it. 1818 Cruise *Digest* (ed. 2) II. 418 At the utmost it was in the discretion of the Court.

Hence †**U·tmostness.** *nonce-use.*

1674 N. Fairfax *Bulk & Selv.* 7 With all that earnestness of threatning, that may beget in man the utmostness of dread.

Utnemis: see Outneme *a.* and *adv.*

Utnume(nn, **-liȝ:** see Outnumen(ly.

†**Utole,** var. Out-toll *Sc. Obs.* (Cf. Out-penny.)

1742 in Kilkerran *Decisions Crt. Sessions 1738–52* (1775) 50; The resignation of an annual-rent out of a tenement in Aberdeen in the year 1720, being made with the symbol of a penny utole.

Utopia (yutōᵘ·piă). [mod.L. (More, 1516), f. Gr. οὐ not + τόπ-ος a place: see -ia¹, and cf. Eutopia. Hence It., Sp., Pg. *Utopia*, F. *Utopie*.]

1. An imaginary island, depicted by Sir Thomas More as enjoying a perfect social, legal, and political system.

1551 (*title*), A fruteful and pleasaunt Worke of the beste state of a publyque weale, and of the newe yle called Utopia; written in Latine by Syr Thomas More knyght [publ. 1516], and translated into Englyshe by Raphe Robynson. 1570 Foxe *Bk. Martyrs* (ed. 2) 1156/2, I do not..thinke, that.. there is any such fourth place of Purgatory at all (vnles it be in M. Mores Vtopia). 1607 A. Brewer *Lingua* II. vi, I remember in the Country of Utopia, they use no other kind of artillery. 1625 Bacon *Ess.*, *Usury* (Arb.) 544 So as that Opinion must be sent to Vtopia. 1685 Crowne *Sir C. Nice* I. Dram. Wks. 1874 III. 270 He will find it is a dream fit for nothing but Utopia. 1692 Bentley *Boyle Lect.* 66 Once upon a time,..in the land of Utopia, there was a dialogue between an oak and a cedar. 1725 [Mrs. E. Haywood] (*title*), Memoirs of a certain Island adjacent to the Kingdom of Utopia. 1751 J. Brown *Shaftesb. Charac.* 65 But of this infallible race I know none, except the inhabitants of Utopia. 1818 [see Cacotopia]. 1837 Macaulay *Ess.*, *Lord Bacon* (1897) 402 An acre in Middlesex is better than a principality in Utopia. 1895 Lupton *More's Utopia* 115 Plate, Reduced facsimile of the woodcut of the Island of Utopia.

transf. 1802–12 Bentham *Ration. Judic. Evid.* Wks. 1843 VI. 206 The law is an Utopia—a country that receives no visits, but [etc.].

b. *transf.* Any imaginary, indefinitely-remote region, country, or locality.

1610 Th. Th[orpe] *Healey's St. Augustine's City of God* Ded., Then [in translating Hall's *Mundus Alter et Idem*, he treated] of a deuised Country scarse on earth, now of a desired Citie sure in heauen; then of Vtopia, now of Eutopia. 1646 Sir T. Browne *Pseud. Ep.* III. xii. 132 Some say it liveth in Æthiopia, others in Arabia, some..in Utopia, for such must that be which is described by Lactantius. 1684 J. P. tr. *J. Ludolphus' Hist. Ethiopia* (ed. 2) 46 Ignorant where this River rises,..whether in Asia, in Africa, or in Utopia. *a* 1779 Warburton *Div. Legat.* II. § 4 Wks. 1788 I. 206 A fabulous relation of a voyage to the imaginary island of Panchæa, a kind of ancient Utopia.

2. A place, state, or condition ideally perfect in respect of politics, laws, customs, and conditions.

1613 Purchas *Pilgrimage* (1614) 708 The reports of this his voyage savour more of an Vtopia, and Plato's Commonwealth, then of true Historie. 1642 Chas. I in Rushw. *Hist. Coll.* (1692) I. 727 That new Vtopia of Religion and Government into which they endeavour to transform this Kingdom. 1691 Norris *Pract. Disc.* 177 To contemplate all this not..as an uncertain Reversion, or imaginary Vtopia, but as a state that will shortly and certainly be. 1738

Warburton *Div. Legat.* I. 272 No romantic impracticable Utopia. 1760–72 H. Brooke *Fool of Qual.* (1792) II. 113 But the law-suits..will not permit me to go in search of my Utopia. 1818 Shelley *Julian* 179 'Aye, if we were not weak—and we aspire How vainly to be strong!' said Maddalo: 'You talk Utopia.' 1871 Morley *Condorcet* in *Crit. Misc.* Ser. I. 78 To find adequate gratification in the artificial construction of hypothetical utopias. 1883 *Manch. Exam.* 22 Nov. 5/2 Ingenious speculators who hope to reach Utopia by the nationalisation of the land.

b. An impossibly ideal scheme, esp. for social improvement.

a 1734 North *Lives* II. 364 Young men, for want of experience,..create Utopias in their own imagination, and calculate according to their present fancy. 1843 Marryat *M. Violet* xliii, These are not the wild utopias of a heated imagination. 1869 Lecky *Europ. Mor.* I. 180 Averse to all enthusiasm, mysticism, utopias, and superstition.

3. *Comb.*, as *Utopia-maker*, *-monger*.

1821 *Edin. Rev.* XXXV. 380 The fantastic brain of some Utopia-monger. 1901 Glover *Life & Lett. in 4th C.* 362 The general satire,..no doubt a fling at the Utopia-makers.

Hence **Uto·pia-ize** *v. intr.*, to conceive or form impossibly ideal schemes. *nonce-word.*

1853 Mrs. Gore *Dean's Daughter* III. 57 A Virginia Hargreave, born to Utopia-ise over a Bostonian tea-table, concerning triumphs to be achieved.

Utopian (yutōᵘ·piăn), *a.* and *sb.* [ad. mod.L. *Utopian-us* (More, 1516): see prec. and -an.]

A. *adj.* **1.** Of or belonging to the imaginary island of Utopia or its people.

1551 Robinson *More's Utopia* Ep. (1895) 1 This boke of the vtopian commen wealth. 1556 *More's Utopia* Printer to Rdr. (Arb.) 168 The Vtopian Alphabete. 1622 J. Taylor (Water P.) *Sir G. Nonsence* Wks. (1630) Aa j b, He..began to declare in the Vtopian speech, what I haue here..Translated. 1633 Rowley *Match at Midn.* v. I 1 b, Two Vtopian Trunks, full of gold and Iewels. 1681 (*title*), A Pleasant Battle between two Lap-dogs of the Utopian Court. 1808 Cayley tr. *More's Utopia* II. 7 That I should anticipate him in what belongs to the Utopian Commonwealth. 1895 Lupton *More's Utopia* 117 On this and other repellent features of the Utopian character, as drawn by More.

†**b.** Having no known location; existing nowhere. *Obs. rare.*

1609 in Capt. Smith *Wks.* (Arb.) 637 It hath beene to the Spaniards more fearefull then an Vtopian Purgatory. 1678 Cudworth *Intell. Syst.* 60 They must be imagined to subsist in certain intermundane spaces and Utopian regions without the world. 1689 Swift *Ode to Sir W. Temple* i, Search out this Utopian ground, Virtue's *terra incognita*.

†**c.** Having no assigned diocese or sphere of work. *Obs.*⁻¹

1709 Bingham *Antiq.* IV. vi, The Nullatenenses of latter Ages, as Panormitan calls Titular and Utopian Bishops.

2. Possessing or regarded as having impossibly or extravagantly ideal conditions in respect of politics, customs, social organization, etc.

In this and next sense occas. with small letter.

1613 Purchas *Pilgrimage* (1614) 520 Yea, no Vtopian State comparable to theirs. 1647 *Mercurius Anti-pragmaticus* No. 6. 4 They are like to wander forty yeeres..ere they arrive in their Utopian Paradise. 1651 C. Walker *Hist.* III. 14 To these..they entrust the Administration of this Utopian Commonwealth. 1768 Tucker *Lt. Nat.* (1834) II. 302 The introduction of an Utopian state. 1782 H. Walpole *Vertue's Anecd. Paint.* IV. 284 When he was laying out so magnificent, charitable, and philosophic an Utopian villa. 1855 Kingsley *Westw. Ho!* xix, When we have babbled together of Utopian governments in days which are now dreams to me. 1856 H. Rogers *Ess.* II. viii. 380 Considered as a possible political structure..Plato's 'Republic' deserves to be considered the most Utopian that ever entered the mind of man.

b. Involving, based or founded on, imaginary or chimerical perfection; impossibly ideal, visionary.

1621 Burton *Anat. Mel.* To Rdr. 58 Vtopian parity is a thing to be wished for rather then effected. 1643 Prynne *Sov. Power Parl.* App. 1 A new Utopian absolute Royall Prerogative..not bottomed on the Lawes of God or the Realm. 1646 J. Cook *Vind. Law* 28 Thats but a Vtopian consideration, a possibility which never comes into Act. 1659 Br. Walton *Consid. Considered* 72 This, I doubt, will prove an Utopian conceit. 1762 Kaimes *Elem. Crit.* ii. (1774) I. 35 For confuting such Utopian systems without the fatigue of reasoning. 1798 Ferriar *Illustr. Sterne* iii. 59 He indulges himself in an Utopian sketch of a perfect government. 1806 H. Siddons *Maid, Wife, & W.* III. 6 The sentiments which inspired me may be laughed at as Utopian. 1849 C. Brontë *Shirley* ix, Marriage! I cannot bear the word: it sounds so silly and utopian. 1877 Burroughs *Taxation* 22 They have regarded any attempt to practise absolute equality as Utopian.

3. Of persons: That belongs to or dwells in a Utopia. *rare*⁻¹.

1630 J. Taylor (Water P.) *Jack a Lent* Wks. (1630) 113/2 As Nymshag an ancient Vtopian Philosopher declares.

b. That conceives, proposes, or advocates impracticably ideal projects or schemes for social welfare, etc.; believing in or aiming at the perfecting of polity or social conditions.

1597–8 Donne *Let. to Sir H. Wotton* 46 If men..Durst looke for themselves..They would like strangers greet themselves, seeing than Utopian youth, growne old Italian. 1661 Cowley *Cromwell* Wks. 1906 II. 373 You are..a Theoretical Common-wealths-man, an Utopian Dreamer. 1680 Butler *Characters* (1908) 24 A Republican is a civil Fanatic, an Utopian Senator. 1691 Baxter *Nat. Ch.* xii. 52 As capable of Governing one Kingdom, as an Utopian College of Bishops (that some dream of). 1857 W. Smith *Thorndale* v. iii. (1858) 427 An Eclectic and Utopian Philosopher. 1868 Peard *Water-farm.* xi. 114 We are not so Utopian as to assert that [etc.].

B. *sb.* **1.** A native or inhabitant of Utopia; a dweller in some Utopia. Also *Comb.*

1551 Robinson tr. *More's Utopia* II. (1895) 218 The wyttes therefore of the Vtopians..be marueluos quycke. 1597 Hooker *Eccl. Pol.* v. xxxvi. § 4 Such suttle opinions as few but Vtopians are likely to fall into. 1614 Raleigh *Hist. World* III. viii. § 1 They liued Vtopian-like, saue that they vsed no other occupation than Warre. 1684 Burnet tr. *More's Utopia* Pref. A 7 The precaution used in Marriages among the Utopians. 1771 J. Adams *Diary* 10 Nov., The good humor,..and wisdom of the Utopians, is charming. 1857 W. Smith *Thorndale* IV. v. (1858) 312, I know not precisely how his Utopians intend to deal with war. 1905 *Edin. Rev.* Oct. 426 The admiration of the Utopians..was by no means confined to the strictly classical authors.

2. One who conceives, proposes, or introduces schemes supposed or intended to bring about improved or perfect social and political conditions, etc.; an advocate of social reform.

a 1873 Lytton in *Life* (1883) I. 101 My grandfather..in youth..was a Utopian, and remained to the last much more than a 'Whig'. 1878 Seeley *Stein* II. 363 Stein..was never the utopian here described. 1887 J. C. Morison *Serv. Man* p. xxiv, He looks with coldness on Utopians who are equally ignorant of capital, labour, or hard work.

Hence **Uto·pianist,** = Utopian *sb.* 2.

1854 J. S. C. Abbott *Napoleon* (1855) II. xxix. 556 What seemed a crime to the eyes of Utopianists. 1876 *Contemp. Rev.* xxviii. 447 Neither abandoned nor disregarded by a few devoted Utopianists.

Utopianism (yutōᵘ·piăniz'm). [f. prec. + -ism.]

†**1.** A Utopian idea or condition. *Obs.*⁻¹

a 1661 Holyday *Juvenal* (1673) 194 Plato indeed would have his cittizens ambidexters:..this was but one of his vtopianismes.

2. The body of views, aims, or tenets of Utopians; impossibly ideal schemes for the amelioration or perfection of social conditions, etc.

1802–12 Bentham *Ration. Judic. Evid.* (1827) IV. 69 Such an improvement that the stamp of Utopianism..threatens to render the acceptance of it next to hopeless. 1833 Chalmers *Const. Man* (1835) I. vi. 237 The abortive enterprises of wild yet benevolent Utopianism. 1879 Kaufmann *Utopias* 258 The superiority of the most recent forms of Utopianism over previous schemes of social improvement.

Uto·pianize (yutōᵘ·piănaiz), *v.* [f. as prec. + -ize. Cf. Utopia-ize *v.*] *trans.* To render Utopian; to form a Utopia of.

1834 [implied in next]. 1913 *Public Opinion* 26 Dec. 715/1 The international aspect of Utopianising the modern world.

Hence **Uto·pianizer,** one who projects or conceives a Utopian state or polity.

1834 Southey *Doctor* ccxli, Like most Utopianisers the legislator of this Columbia had placed his Absolute King and his free People under..strict laws.

Uto·piast. [f. Utopia + -(i)st.] = Utopian *sb.* 2.

1854 tr. *Lamartine's Celebr. Char.* II. 384 The visionary Utopiasts, who advocate a purely metaphysical form of government. 1887 *Westm. Rev.* Jan. 130 It is the weakness of Utopiasts..to place themselves outside the pale of their own system.

†**Uto·pical,** *a. Obs. rare.* [f. Utop-ia + -ical.] Impracticable; chimerical.

1620 Br. Hall *Hon. Marr. Clergy* III. xiii. 805 King Edgars Vtopicall decree. *c* 1628 — *Beauty & Unity of Ch.* (1634) II. 368 Let no idle Donatist..dreame hence of an Utopicall perfection. 1628 — *Rem. Wks.* (1660) 20 There is no freedom with these unquiet dispositions, but in..their own utopical prescriptions.

Utopism (yū·tǒpiz'm). [f. as prec. + -ism.] = Utopianism 2.

1888 *Cycl. Political Sci. & U. S. Hist.* III. 258/2 It is utopism to believe that the state will have more unity, more harmony,..because [etc.]. 1901 *Field* 19 Oct. 606/2 What remains of impracticable Utopism that may cling to this new project.

Utopist (yū·tǒpist). [f. as prec. + -ist. Cf. F. *utopiste* (1857), It., Sp., Pg. *Utopista*, and Utopianist.] = Utopian *sb.* 2.

1845 Lewes *Hist. Philos.* I. 100 Like the Utopists of modern days, he [*sc.* Plato] has developed an *à priori* theory of what the State should be. 1881 Morley *Cobden* xxix. II. 263 Men..who..thought that the existing government..was better than the anarchy of utopists, anarchists, and talkers. 1898 *Salesian Bulletin* 15 Feb. 404 The indefatigable utopist of abandoned youth.

†**U·touth,** *prep.* and *adv. Sc. Obs.* Forms: 4–6 ututh, -outh, 5 -owth, 6 utoth; 4–6 vt-, wtouth (5 vttouth), 5 vtouthe, 6 vtowth; 4–5 otouth (5 otow, otowth, outhouth), 5 oututh, 6 -outh; 5 vtouthe, 6 uteucht, utewcht (6 wtew). [Sc. var. of Outwith.]

A. *prep.* **1.** Without, outside of, in respect of position.

c 1375 *Sc. Leg. Saints* xxviii. (*Margaret*) 68 Scho..gefine wes to fostir & fede wtouth the towne. 14.. *Burgh Lawes* vii. in *Sc. Acts Parlt.* I. (1844) 334/2 He sall noch mote ututh þe burgh. 1478 *Acta Auditorum* (1839) 59/2 [He] nocht being lauchfully warnit to his defensis and seruit vteuthe þe schire. 1536 [see Outwith *prep.* 1]. 1557 *Peebles Burgh Rec.* (1872) 237 Vnfremen that duellis..vtouth the burgh.

2. Out of, out or away from, throughout, in respect of motion.

1375, *c* 1375 [see Outwith *prep.* 1 b]. 1530 *Burgh Rec. Edinb.* (1871) II. 37 The said seiknes..spreddis vtouth the toun in diuers placis. 1534 Bellenden *Livy* II. vi. (S.T.S.) I. 147 Þai durst put na thing vtouth þe wallis.

B. *adv.* Without; on the outside; outwardly.

1375 Barbour *Bruce* II. 299 Till thaim wtouth send thai sone, And bad thaim herbery thaim that nycht. *c* 1375 *Sc. Leg. Saints* xxxii. (*Justin*) 170 A lytil vngument he hym tacht, & bad hyme ga..& þe wallis oututh ennoynt. 1398 *Munim. de Melros* (Bann. Cl.) 489 My demaynis.. with al þe appourtenaunce vtouth and enovth. 1455 in *Charters &c. Edinb.* (1871) 80 Baith in the watter and vtouth. 1491 *Cartular. St. Nicholai Aberdon.* (New Spald. Cl.) I. 255 Nay chapiane of the College nor vtouthe. 1512 *Acc. Ld. High Treas. Scot.* IV. 348 Ane coup..nettit with gold of florising utewcht. 1532 *Reg. Privy Seal Scot.* II. 190/2 Assemblies to be had within our realme or utouth.

transf. 1453 *Dunfermline Reg.* (Bann. Cl.) 341 Þe quhilkis ..I will all vtrali be excludit and neuer to be herd in jugement na vtouth. 1496 *Acta Dom. Conc.* II. 23 Decerning the sammyn to be of nane availe..in tyme tocum in jugment nor utouth.

Utrack, etc.: see Outrake, etc.

†**Utra·lity.** *nonce-word.* [f. L. *uter*, *utr-*, which (of two), after Neutrality.] Tendency to favour both sides; inclination towards either party.

1642 W. Price *Serm.* 2 Apostacy and neutrality, or rather utrality (if you will pardon the word).

Utraly, obs. Sc. var. Utterly.

Utraquism (yū·trăkwiz'm). *Hist.* [f. as next + -ism.]

1. The doctrine or tenets of the Utraquists.

1861 Ld. Acton *Lett.* (1906) 186 In Bohemia Utraquism was the national faith. 1892 *Athenæum* 2 Jan. 10/1 From the dawn of Utraquism to its eclipse..in the disaster of the White Mountain in 1620.

2. The use or employment of two languages on an equal footing. *rare*⁻¹.

1897 *Speaker* 10 April 392/2 The [Austrian] concession.. [*sc.* of officially recognising Czech] is spoken of as sanctioning 'the *utraquism* of German and Czech'.

Utraquist (yū·trăkwist), *sb.* and *a.* [ad. mod. L. *Utraquista*, f. L. *utraque* each, both (in the phrase *sub utrāque speciē* 'under each kind': see Species *sb.* 2, Kind *sb.* 13 b). Cf. -ist, and F. *Utraquiste*.]

A. *sb.* **1.** *Hist.* = Calixtin 1.

1836 *Pop. Encycl.* I. 814/1 *Utraquists*, a sect of Hussites in Bohemia. 1855 Milman *Lat. Chr.* VI. 248 They were called the Utraquists, as insisting on the Eucharist in both elements. 1881 Stanley *Chr. Instit.* v. 95 When the Bohemian Utraquists fought with desperate energy to recover the use of the cup.

2. 'One who composes in both Latin and the vernacular' (Webster, 1911).

B. *adj.* **1.** *Hist.* Belonging to the Utraquists; demanding, insisting on, or advocating the receiving the Communion in both kinds.

1894 F. I. Antrobus tr. *Pastor's Hist. Popes* III. 214 The Utraquist Clergy. 1900 *Pilot* 27 Oct. 539/1 The Hussites.. were pre-eminently utraquist.

2. Speaking or using both or two languages.

1867 *Chambers's Encycl.* IX. 686/1 The name Utraquist is still applied to certain districts or villages in Bohemia and Moravia..to convey that..*both languages*, Bohemian and German, are spoken.

Hence **U·traquistic** *a.*

1894 F. I. Antrobus tr. *Pastor's Hist. Popes* III. 216 This oath was thoroughly Catholic, and left no room for any Utraquistic interpretation.

Utrecht (yū·trekt, ü·trext). Also *Sc.* 5 Vtt-, Out-, Owtrecht, Outrech, -rik, 7 Utrik. The name of a town and province in Holland, used attrib. in the sense 'coined, made, etc., at Utrecht', as †*Utrecht gulden*, *noble*.

1494 *Halyburton's Ledger* (1867) 52 An Vttrecht gudlyn and a Gentis gudlyn. 1497 *Ibid.* 125 Item lent hym..7 Outrecht guldynis. 1604 *Extr. Burgh Rec. Stirling* (1887) 108 Aucht haill Utrik nobillis.

†**b.** *ellipt.* or as *sb.* A Utrecht gulden. *Obs.*

1493 *Halyburton's Ledger* (1867) 31 Item resavit fra him.. 3 Outrikis, price 4s. 1498 *Ibid.* 240 Gyffyn the Archden..at his partyn, 10 Outrech...Som of thir Owtrechtis, 2 li. 18 8.

c. **Utrecht velvet**, a strong, thick kind of plush made of worsted, mohair, or mohair and cotton, used in upholstering furniture, carriages, etc.; furniture plush.

1848 H. R. Forster *Stowe Catal.* 252 Armchairs, covered with Utrecht velvet. 1897 *Daily News* 14 June 6/6 Green Utrecht velvet upholstered oak furniture.

†**U·trechted,** *pa. pple. Obs.*⁻¹ [f. prec. + -ed.] Having its seaward defences destroyed, as stipulated in the Treaty of Utrecht (1713).

1748 H. Walpole *Lett.* (1846) II. 217 Dunkirk to remain as it is, on the land side; but to be Utrecht'd again to the sea.

Utrely, obs. Sc. f. Utterly *adv.*

†**U·tricide.** *Obs.*⁻¹ [ad. L. *ūtricīda*, f. *ūtri-s*, *ūter* leathern bottle, vessel of skin: see -cide 1.] One who stabs an inflated vessel of skin.

1566 Adlington *Apuleius* 30 That I, after the slaughter of so many enemies,..might embrace..not an homicide but an utricide. [1879 Lewis & Short, *Utricida*, one who cuts skins or bags in pieces, a skin-slayer, utricide.]

Utricle¹ (yū·trik'l). [ad. F. *utricule* (18th c.), or L. *ūtriculus* Utriculus¹.]

1. *Bot.* A small sac or bladder-shaped body; a bottle-shaped part or structure.

Primordial utricle: see Primordial *a.* 4 b.

a. 1731 Miller *Gard. Dict.* s.v. *Sap*, All Male Flowers that have Utricles at the Bottom of the Petals. 1793 Martyn *Lang. Bot.* s.v. *Vessels*, Utricles, or little Bags; usually full of a green pulp. 1826 Keith *Phys. Bot.* I. 349 The structure of the utricles of the tree is also said to be different from that of the utricles of the herb. 1875 Darwin *Insectiv. Pl.* xvii.

419 The spherical glands were still white but their utricles were broken up. **b.** 1826–34 *Encycl. Metrop.* (1845) VII. 50/1 An utricle is a membranous, elastic pericarp. 1861 Bentley *Man. Bot.* 314 The Utricle is a superior, one-celled, one or few-seeded fruit. **c.** 1849 [see Primordial *a.* 4 b]. 1857 Henfrey *Elem. Course Bot.* 495 The primordial utricle is a layer of substance of a dense mucilaginous consistence..,applied intimately to the inner surface of the cell-membrane of young cells [etc.]. 1875 Bennett & Dyer *Sach's Bot.* 62 The hydrostatic pressure which the vacuole-fluid exercises on the protoplasm [1882 primordial] utricle. **d.** 1858 Irvine *British Pl.* 240 The Carex Tribe... Fruit without hairs at the base, enclosed in a peculiar envelope (utricle). 1897 Willis *Flower. Pl.* II. 126 The axil of a second glume (the utricle) which closely enwraps it. **e.** 1874 Cooke *Fungi* 49 After the spores have become ripe, the free point of the utricle bursts. **f.** 1875 Darwin *Insectiv. Plants* xviii. 451 Found within the utricle or neck of one leaf.

2. *Anat.* and *Biol.* A small cell, sac, or bladder-like process.

1822 Good *Study Med.* IV. 603 Those utricles, or minute bladders of the cuticle containing a watery fluid. 1836–9 Todd *Cycl. Anat.* II. 413/2 Utricles floating loosely in the abdominal cavity. 1899 *Allbutt's Syst. Med.* VIII. 905 Microbacillus of the 'peladic utricle'.

b. The larger of the two sacs in the membranous labyrinth of the ear.

1837 *Penny Cycl.* IX. 239/1 The utricle, or sinus of the vestibule [in birds]. 1857 Holden *Hum. Osteol.* (ed. 2) 252 The utricle occupies the upper half of the vestibule. 1886 *Buck's Handbk. Med. Sci.* II. 563/2 The vestibular membranous labyrinth is divided into sacs: (1) the oblong utricle or..common sinus [etc.].

3. *gen.* A small bladder-like body; a globule.

1858 Graham & Watts *Elem. Chem.* (ed. 2) II. 681 Vapour of sulphur, when it comes in contact with cold bodies, condenses in the form of *utricles*, that is to say, of globules composed of a soft external pellicle filled with liquid sulphur. ..This utricular condition has also been observed in selenium.

U·tricle². *Anat.* [ad. F. *utricule*, or L. *utriculus* Utriculus².] A small cul-de-sac in the prostatic portion of the urethra in man; the prostatic vesicle.

1861 Sir H. Thompson *Dis. Prostate* (ed. 2) 28 The Utricle..is a small sac..opening on the anterior aspect of the verumontanum. 1888 *Cassell's Encycl. Dict.* s.v., There is a utricle of the male urethra.

b. In the cat: (see quot.).

1881 Mivart *Cat* 242 A small, ridge-like prominence, called the *verum montanum*, in the midst of which is a narrow, slit-like depression, named the utricle.

Utricular (yutri·kiŭlăı), *a.*¹ [f. L. *ūtricul-us* small leathern bag, Utriculus¹ + -ar¹. Cf. F. *utriculaire*.]

1. Of the nature of, resembling or like, a utricle.

1760 J. Lee *Introd. Bot.* III. xviii. (1765) 211 *Utricular*, like little Bottles. 1775 Ellis in *Phil. Trans.* LXVI. 8 The Gorgonia..has no series of utricular vessels, as the transverse vessels of wood are called by Malpighi. 1822 J. Parkinson *Outl. Oryctol.* 92 The bottle encrinite, possessing a utricular form. 1856 W. Clark *Van der Hoeven's Zool.* I. 184 Body utricular, roundish, marked with transverse rugæ. 1858 [see Utricle¹ 3]. 1881 Bentham in *Jrnl. Linn. Soc.* XVIII. 367 A single utricular glume enclosing the flower.

2. Composed of utricles or small bladders.

1835 Lindley *Introd. Bot.* (ed. 2) 5 Cellular, Utricular, or Vesicular tissue, generally, consists of little bladders..adhering together in masses. 1849 Henfrey in *Rep. & Papers Bot.* (Ray Soc.) 163 In such cases the cavities appear like utricles. This utricular structure [etc.].

Utri·cular, *a.*² [f. L. *utricul-us* little womb, etc. (Utriculus²) + -ar¹. Cf. F. *utriculaire*.] Of or pertaining to the uterus or abdomen; uterine.

1827 J. Forbes tr. *Laennec's Dis. Chest* (ed. 2) 58 The entrance and escape of the air through the wound gave rise to an extremely distinct utricular bursting. 1857 Bullock *Cazeaux' Midwif.* 180 The utricular glands also become visibly enlarged. 1871 A. Meadows *Man. Midwifery* (ed. 2) 21 The lining membrane of the uterus..appears to be made up of a countless number of small tubes, the utricular glands or follicles.

‖**Utricularia** (yutrikiŭlē·riă). Pl. **-ariæ.** [mod.L. (1737), f. L. *ūtricul-us* Utriculus¹.] A genus of scrophulariaceous plants, characterized by bearing small bladders at the margins of their leaves; bladderwort, hooded (water) milfoil; a species or plant of this.

1753 *Chambers' Cycl.* Suppl., *Utricularia*,..the name of a plant used by Linnæus for..hooded water milfoil. 1793 Martyn *Lang. Bot.* s.v. *Folliculus*, Follicles..are vessels distended with air; as at the root in *Utricularia*. 1819 *Rees' Cycl.* XXXVII. 4 F 2/2 Almost every morning's walk afforded them a new Utricularia. *Ibid.*, Twenty-four Utricularie, natives of New Holland alone. 1863 T. W. Higginson *Out-Door Papers* 278 The slender Utricularia, a dainty maiden whose light feet scarce touch the water.

Utriculate (yutri·kiŭlĕt), *a. rare.* [ad. mod. L. *ūtriculāt-us*, f. L. *ūtriculus* Utriculus¹.] (See quots.)

1860 Mayne *Expos. Lex.* 1318/1 *Utriculatus*, Bot. having the form of a small leathern bottle..: utriculate. 1864 Dana in *Webster's Dict.* 1457/1 *Utriculate*, a., swollen like a bladder; inflated; utricular.

U·tricule. *Bot. rare*⁻¹. [a. F. *utricule*: see Utricle¹.] A small bladder-like sac or body.

1830 Lindley *Nat. Syst. Bot.* 240 The reservoirs of oil in the leaves of Labiatæ..are little utricules having an open orifice.

Utri·culoid, *a. rare*⁻⁰. [f. L. *ūtricul-us* Utriculus¹ + -oid.] Resembling a bladder; utricular. 1864 Dana in *Webster's Dict.* 1457. [Hence in later Dicts.]

‖**Utriculus**¹ (yutri·kiŭlŏs). [L., dim. of *ūter* leathern bag or bottle: see -culus. Cf. Pg. *utriculo*.]

1. *Bot.* (See quots. and Utricle¹ 1.)

1753 *Chambers' Cycl.* Suppl. s.v., The leaves of trees, whose cuticle has been eat off on one side by small insects, sometimes afford views of these *Utriculi*. 1793 Martyn *Lang. Bot.*, *Utriculi*,..utricles; reservoirs to secrete and receive the sap. 1838 *Penny Cycl.* XI. 346/1 Fruit [of grasses]..occasionally an utriculus. 1857 Henfrey *Bot.* 428 (Sedges), A single erect anatropous ovule, forming in fruit an utriculus. 1866 *Treas. Bot.* 1197/2 *Utriculus*,.. the two confluent glumes of *Carex*. 1885 Goodale *Physiol. Bot.* 346 Utricularia, a genus named from the utriculi or little bladders found on the dissected leaves of some of its species.

2. *Anat.* Of the ear; = Utricle¹ 2 b.

1847 Todd & Bowman *Phys. Anat.* II. 82 As the osseous canals open into the vestibule, so the membranous ones open at both ends into the utriculus. 1878 F. J. Bell *Gegenbaur's Comp. Anat.* 535 The sacculus and utriculus contain otoliths.

‖**Utri·culus**². *Anat.* [L., dim. of *uterus* Uterus: see -culus.] = Utricle².

1848 *Brit. & For. Med.-Chirurgical Rev.* I. 271 A canal, originating by the usual opening on the utriculus. *c* 1848 *Todd's Cycl. Anat.* IV. 152/1 That the utriculus is a male uterus. 1893 D. J. Cunningham *Man. Pract. Anat.* I. 609 This [small recess] is the *sinus pocularis* or the *utriculus*.

Utriform (yū·trifǭm), *a. rare.* [ad. mod.L. *ūtriform-is* (whence F. *utriforme*), f. L. *ūtri-s*, *ūter* bag, bottle, etc.: see -form.] Having the shape of a leathern bottle.

1860 Mayne *Expos. Lex.* 1318/2 *Utriformis*,..swoln out and without apparent pedicle, as in the *Lycoperdon utriforme*: utriform. 1889 *Quart. Jrnl. Geol. Soc.* XLV. 566 The zoœcia..have the exsert parts conical, or, again, they may be leathern-bottle-shaped (utriform).

Utrique(ing, varr. Outreik(ing *Sc. Obs.*

‖**U·trum.** *Obs.* or *Hist.* [L. *utrum*, neut sing. of *uter* which, whether.] A writ authorizing the holding of an assize to decide the status of a property (see quot. 1728). Usu. in *assize of utrum*.

c 1290 Britton (1865) II. 206 La quarte assise est de *Utrum*. *Ibid.* 207 Le bref de *Utrum* pur le clerc. 1592 Rastell *Law Terms*, *Vtrum* is a writ and it lyeth when the right of any Church is aliened and holden in lay fee. 1728 Chambers *Cycl.* [following Cowell s.v. *Assise de utrum*], *Assise of Utrum*, lies for a Parson against a Layman, or a Layman against a Parson, for Land or Tenement, doubtful whether it be in Lay-fee, or Free-alms. 1865 Nichols *Britton* II. 207 *margin*, *Utrum*, the parson's writ of right. *Ibid.* 208 *margin*, No assize of *Utrum* for land belonging to cathedral or convent. 1881 Twiss *Bracton* (Rolls) IV. 622 [Assise] of Utrum may not be brought by a vicar for a small pension paid to a religious house. *Ibid.*, Assise of utrum can never be taken upon a previous assise of utrum.

Utt, Utter, obs. ff. Out, Udder.

U·tter, *sb. Mech.* [See quot. 1879.] *pl.* Indentations or marks made on a surface by the vibration or too great pressure of a tool.

1853 O. Byrne *Artisan's Handbk.* 351 Excessive pressure ..only fills the work with furrows, or produces an irregular indented surface, which by workmen is said to be full of utters. 1879 Holtzapffel *Turning* IV. 342 Fine lines or striæ, also called 'utters',..from the sound emitted by the work when in vibration against the tool.

Utter (ʊ·tǝı), *a.* Forms: α. 1 utera, uterra, utra, 4–6 vter, *Sc.* 6 vtir, utyr, 6, 9 uter. β. 2 uttera, uttra, 3, 6 uttre, 4–6 vttre, 4– utter (4–6 uttir, 5 uttere); 4–7 vtter (4 otter, 5 outter, vttere, 6–7 *Sc.* wtter), 4–6 vttur, 5 vtture, vttir, 4 vttyr. [OE. *ūtera*, *ūterra*, *ūttera*, *ūttra*, etc. (also *ȳtera*, *ȳtra*, *ȳttra*) adj. (comparative formed on *ūt* Out *adv.*), = OFris. *ūtera*, *uttera*, *uttra*, MLG. *utere*, *uter* (LG. *ūter*, *üter*), MDu. *utere* (Du. *uiter-*), OHG. *ūzero*, *ūzaro* (MHG. *ūzer*, G. *äusser*), also ON. *ytri*, MSw. *ytre*, etc. (Sw. *yttre*), Norw. *ytre*, Da. *ydre*. Cf. Outer *a.*

Shortening of the original *ū* of the stem is normal before the group *ttr*, which in OE. was regularly developed from *tr*.]

I. 1. That is farther out than another (implied or distinguished as *inner*); forming the exterior part or outlying portion; relatively far out, outward, external, exterior; also, indefinitely remote. Cf. Outer *a.* 1. Now only *poet.*

In very frequent use from *c* 1400 to *c* 1620. App. in disuse *c* 1670–*c* 1825, except in *utter bar*, *barrister* (see Bar *sb.*¹ 24, Barrister).

α. *a* 901 *Ælfred Laws* c. 44 § 1 Ȝif ðæt uterre [*v.rr.* utre, uttere] ban bið þyrel. 13.. [see 1 b]. 1507 *Acc. Ld. High Treas. Scot.* III. 292 The Kingis offerandis in the utir kyrk. 1535 Stewart *Cron. Scot.* (Rolls) III. 48 Suppois than of that toun The vter wallis win war and put doun. 1592 *Reg. Mag. Sig. Scot.* 753/1 Lie uter port de Halyrudhous. 1887 *Jamieson's Suppl.* 257/2 The uter door.

β. *c* 1125 [see α]. *c* 1374 Chaucer *Troylus* III. 664 (Camb. MS.), In his vttir [*v.rr.* vtter, outter] hous. *a* 1400–50 *Bk. Curtasye* 444 in *Babees Bk.* 313 For lordys two beddys schalle be made, Bothe vtter and inner. *c* 1435 *Chron. London* (Kingsford, 1905) 40 By the kennel of the kyngis cote, vndir his vttir garnement. 1471 *Paston Lett.* III. 20 Opyn the cofyr that standyth in the utter chambyr. 1526 Tindale *Matt.* xxv. 30 Cast that vnprophetable servaunt into vtter derckness. 1542 Boorde *Dyetary* iv. (1870) 239 If there be an vtter courte made. 1578 Lyte *Dodoens* 752 An ounce of the utter barke taken with wine. 1614 Sylvester *Little Bartas* 432 Earth's but a Point, compar'd to th' upper Globe; Yet, who hath seen but half her utter Robe? 1661 P. Gordon *Diary* (Spalding Club) 49 Whilst my servants were cleansing the inner room, he breake downe the oven in the utter roome. 1667 Milton *P. L.* VI. 716 Drive them out From all Heav'ns bounds into the utter Deep. 1827 Pollok *Course T.* IX. 1180 They heard, Afar to left, among the utter dark, Hell rolling o'er his waves of burning fire. 1848 Bailey *Festus* (ed. 3) 107 From Time's last orb which eyes The inner and the utter infinite. 1870 J. Payne *Masque of Shadows* Ded., Whoso is fain To enter in this shadow-land of mine, He must forget the utter summer's shine.

fig. 1608 B. Jonson *Masques* Wks. (1616) 934 I,..who haue neuer touch'd so much as to the barke, or vtter shell of any knowledge. 1877 L. Morris *Epic Hades* II. 147 So high a strain arose As trembled on the utter verge of being.

b. Freq. with partitive terms, as †*deal*, *end*, *part*, †*party*, and esp. *side*. Also *fig.* Now *rare.*

a 1300 *Cursor M.* 9912 Þis castell..es painted a-bute þe vtter [*Gött.* vter] side. *c* 1340 Hampole *Pr. Consc.* 4815 Þe world sal bryn on ilk syde,..Until þe utter end of alle belle. 1387 Trevisa *Higden* (Rolls) I. 59 For betynge of veynes is bettre i-knowe in þe vttre parties of bodies þan ynward. *Ibid.* VI. 251 Þe utter deel of his oost. *c* 1400 *Beryn* 3928 [He] had a mantell..; The vttir part of purpill. 1457 *Cov. Leet. Bk.* 298 The newe Crosse vppon the heth at the vtter syde of theyre fraunchice. 1508 *Bk. Keruynge* A iv, The vtter ende of the clothe on the vtter syde of the table. 1526 Tindale *Matt.* xxiii. 25 Ye make clene the vtter side off the cuppe, and off the platter. 1577 B. Googe *Heresbach's Husb.* I. 21 b, A little rayne falling, hath but wette the vtter part, and not gone deepe. 1629 Sir W. Mure *True Crucifixe* 485 Like painted Tombs who clense the vtter side, [Cf. Matt. xxiii. 27]. 1637 Rutherford *Lett.* (1671) 183 For two feathers or two straws of the devil's painted pleasures, onely lustred in the utter side. 1848 Bailey *Festus* (ed. 3) 59, I have looked down upon the utter side Of such thoughts from the leeming room of reason.

†**2.** = Outer *a.* 2. *Obs.*

c 900 tr. *Baeda's Hist.* IV. xiii. (1890) 304 Þæt heo seolfe wæron ȝe on þæm nearran [*v.r.* inneran] godum, ȝe on þæm utteran [*v.r.* uttran] mid heofonlice ȝife geweløade. *c* 1000 *Ags. Ps.* (Thorpe) xv. 7 Þeah he me þara uterrena ȝewinna ȝefreode, þeah winnað wið me þa inran unrihtlustas. *a* 1225 *Ancr. R.* 92 Hwo se ȝemeleasliche witeð hire uttre eien,.. heo ablindeð in þe inre eien. 1357 *Lay Folks' Catech.* (L.) 330 The be-houys to know þy fyue wyttys þe vttyr and þe ynnyr. *c* 1386 Chaucer *Sec. Nun's T.* 498 (Camb. MS.), Teere lakkyth no thyng to thyn vtter Iyen. 1398 Trevisa *Barth. De P. R.* III. ix. (1495) 54 The vtter wytte conteyneth the syghte,..taastynge and towchynge. *c* 1450 tr. *De Imitatione* III. xiv. 82 For þe utter enemy is sonner ouercomen, if þe ynner be destroied.

†**b.** *Utter man*, = Outward *a.* 2 c. (Cf. Outer *a.* 2 b.) *Obs.*

a 1050 *Liber Scintill.* x. (1889) 53 Þæt ys fullfremed & ȝesceadwislic fæsten þænne ure mann uttra fæst, se inra gebitt. *a* 1340 Hampole *Psalter* ix. 20 Þat..þe utter man haf noght maistry of þe inere. *c* 1380 Wyclif *Sel. Wks.* I. 53 Þis is bifore spiritual joy, as utter man is bifore spiritual. 1388 — *2 Cor.* iv. 16 Thouȝ oure vtter man be corruptid. 1565 Jewel *Reply Harding* 430 Simple folke, beinge not hable to discerne, what thinges they be in the Holy Scriptures, that are to be applied to the Inner Man, and what to the Vtter.

†**3.** = Outward *a.* 4. *Obs.*

a 1225 *Ancr. R.* 4 Ye schullen alles weis..wel witen þe inre & þe uttre [*sc.* riwle] vor hire sake. *a* 1275 *Ibid.* 420 *note* (Cotton MS.), Understondeð þet of alle þeose þinges nis nan hest ne forbot; for alle ha beoð of þe uttere riwle, þet is lute strencðe of. 1526 Tindale *John* vii. 24 Judge not after the vtter aperaunce. 1548 Hoby in Strype *Eccl. Mem.* (1721) II. App. Y. 80 He..is even now..as content to the utter shew, as he was at any time of his most prosperity. 1558 Br. White *Ibid.* III. App. lxxxi. 279 You in time of divine service, do..both in heart and utter gesture..adore the same flesh. 1563 *Homilies* II. *Place & Time of Prayer* 282 Strayghtly to obserue and kepe the vtter ceremonyes of the Saboth-day. 1593 Nashe *Christ's T.* R 4 b, Lyke the Geometritians, they square about poyntes and lynes, and the vtter shew of things.

II. 4. Going to the utmost point; extreme, absolute, complete, entire, total.

In very frequent use from *c* 1515.

c 1430 *Generides* (Roxb.) 3040 This wer to vs..an vttir shame for euermore. 14.. *Lydgate's Thebes* 4121 (MS. Laud Misc. 557, fol. 58), It were to hem a perpetuall shame, An vtter [*v.r.* outre] hyndryng vnto Grekes name. *a* 1513 Fabyan *Chron.* vi. clxxxix. 191 To the..vtter displeasure of the Kynge. 1550 Crowley *Epigr.* 1241 Ambition was punished wyth vtter exile. 1562 Winȝet *Cert. Tract.* Wks. (S.T.S.) I. 7 Ane manifest confusion and vter extermination of this realme. 1606 Dekker *Newes fr. Hell* Wks. (Grosart) II. 143 Burning Riuers In which..are [*sic*] no vtter danger. 1662 Stillingfl. *Orig. Sacræ* I. ii. § 1 We have seen already an utter impossibility of having any ancient Records among them. 1718 Prior *Poems* Dedication b j, Two Things which were his utter Aversion. 1778 Miss Burney *Evelina* xxi, I saw they were in utter amazement. 1812 J. Wilson *Isle of Palms* III. 535 A graceful calm is seen All foreign to this utter solitude. 1849 Ruskin *Sev. Lamps* vii. § 11. 184 Restraint, utter and unrelaxing, can never be comely. 1871 Tylor *Prim. Cult.* I. 277 Her utter belief that in her vision she had really seen this bright being. 1889 Clark Russell *Marooned* xii, The arrest of his movements could not have been more spasmodic and utter.

b. Freq. said of destruction, ruin, loss, etc.

1412–20 Lydg. *Chron. Troy* IV. 2443 He him [Agamemnon] had brouȝt in gret distresse, To outter meschef and confusioun. †1456– [see Undoing *vbl. sb.*¹ 3 c]. 1523 *Act* 14 & 15 *Hen. VIII*, c. 1 § 1 The utter ruyne, decaye, impoverysshyng and undoyng of a great nombre of the Kynges owne naturall Subjectes. 1560 Daus tr. *Sleidane's Comm.* 40 To the vtter destruction of the common wealthe. 1591 Shaks. *1 Hen. VI*, v. iv. 112 The vtter losse of all the Realme. 1667 Milton *P. L.* III. 308 Thou hast..quitted all to save A World from utter loss. 1674 *Jackson's Recant.* B 1 b, Turn'd out of Doors, to their utter ruin and destruction. 1772 Priestley *Inst. Relig.* (1782) I. 408 The utter ruin of their city..was foretold. 1827 Keble *Chr. Y.*, *11th Sunday after Trinity* v, Full many a soul..To utter death that hour shall sweep.

1841 Miss Mitford in L'Estrange *Life* (1870) III. viii. 125 Dark depression and utter failure of intellect. 1846 Mrs. A. Marsh *Father Darcy* II. xxi. 359 The utter destruction of all reverence for the unseen.

c. Of answers, decisions, etc.: Given without reserve or qualification; unmodified, decisive, definite. In early use chiefly *Sc.*

1456 Sir G. Haye *Law Arms* (S.T.S.) 173 As for utter ansuere to this questioun,..lawe and gude faith avidis that ..he is behaldin [etc.]. 1472 *Stonor Papers* (Camden) I. 126 But and [= if] ye..conceyve þat shee hath yoven you an utter nay. 1515 Q. Marg. in Ellis *Orig. Lett.* Ser. I. I. 117 Send me ȝour uter mynd and ansuer in all thyng. 1560 Rolland *Seven Sages* 33 This is my vtter minde and wili, That ȝe prepair [etc.]. *a* 1600 Montgomerie *Misc. Poems* xxxii. 86 Ȝour vter ansueir courteously I crave. 1647 Clarendon *Hist. Reb.* VIII. § 15 The utter refusal of the auxiliary regiments of London and Kent to march farther. 1828–32 Webster s.v., An utter refusal or denial.

d. Of darkness, etc: Complete, absolute.

1596 Shaks. *1 Hen. IV*, III. iii. 42 But thou..wert indeede, but for the Light in thy Face, the Sunne of vtter Darkenesse. 1814 Wordsw. *Excurs.* VII. 357 Then, shall the slowly-gathering twilight close In utter night. 1825 Scott *Talism.* v, They blew out their lights at once, and left the knight in utter darkness. 1830 Tennyson *Confess. Sens. Mind* 95 What if Thou..seest me drive Through utter dark a full-sailed skiff Unpiloted. 1868 — *Lucretius* 70 Then, from utter gloom stood out the breasts..of Helen.

e. Pure; unalloyed. *rare*⁻¹.

1875 Morris *Æneis* IX. 262 Two cups of utter silver wrought.

5. Of persons: That is such to an absolute degree; out-and-out, complete, 'perfect'.

In early use, usu. with 'enemy'; in 19th c., freq. with 'stranger'.

c 1420 Lydg. *Assembly of Gods* 594 He hathe be euer myn vtter enemy. 1555 J. Bradford in Strype *Eccl. Mem.* (1721) III. App. xlv. 131 That he shoulde be..the Kinges utter enemye. 1560 Daus tr. *Sleidane's Comm.* 82 b, Their moste vtter and mortall enemie. 1633 G. Herbert *Temple*, *Method* vii, Those Who heare not him, but quickly heare His utter foes? 1662 Trenchfield *Chr. Chym.* 39 Julius Cæsar having taken..the Cabinets of Pompey and Scypio his utter enemies. 1678 Bunyan *Pilgr.* I. 163 Ye be utter strangers to me; I know you not. 1828 Scott *F. M. Perth* xiii, Some of them are yet utter heathens. *a* 1845 Hood *Lamia* vi. 80 And thou wilt..say the outer woman is utter woman, And not a whit a snake! 1849 Lever *Con Cregan* xviii, To win some acknowledgment of confidence from an utter stranger. 1875 Jowett *Plato* (ed. 2) III. 70 The persons..are utter rogues.

b. *ellipt.* (in affected use).

1881 W. S. Gilbert *Patience* II, (The Officers have some difficulty in maintaining their constrained [æsthetic] attitudes.)..*Ang.* Oh, Saphir, are they not quite too all-but? *Saph.* They are indeed jolly utter. 1882 H. S. Leigh *Strains fr. Strand* 5 You and I have been together Dining up at Eaton Square. Pretty creature, tell me whether All was not 'quite utter' there. *Ibid.* 131 My wife has gone 'utterly utter'.

†**6.** Uttermost, utmost. *Obs.*

Freq. in Sc. use in 16th cent., with *power*.

1513 Douglas *Æneis* IX. ix. 16 Quham to assailȝe,..all the Italianis At vtir power onbeset atanis. 1533 Bellenden *Livy* I. iv. (S.T.S.) I. 30 Þare husbandis wald gif þare vter besines..to recovir baith [etc.]. 1576 Fleming *Panopl. Epist.* 59 My request, which yᵗ you wold accomplish to my utter expectation, we..beseech you most earnestly. 1590 *Hecuba's Mishaps* in T. Fenne *Frutes* Ff 2 b, When that I had..shewed my utter might.

†**b.** Ultimate, original. *Obs.*⁻¹

1634 Sir T. Herbert *Trav.* 141 They haue neuer altered the Dialect [of Persia] from its vtter sence, at this day being cald *Pharsee*.

†**7.** Final; last. *Obs.*⁻¹

1558 Phaer *Æneid* II. D iii b, Our vtter houre is comen alas, fell destinies death hath brought.

8. *The utter*, that which is utter or extreme; = Uttermost *a.* 7, Utmost *a.* 5, 5 b. *rare.*

1584 Raleigh *Let.* in Aubrey *Lives* (1898) II. 192 Readie to countervaile all your courtesies to the utter of my power. 1894 *Athenæum* 29 Sept. 418/1 Nothing suits him but the utter. His heroine is 'beautifully modelled' [etc.].

III. †**9.** *Combs.* (hyphened, or as one word): *utter-bark*, *-brass*, *-court*, *-deal* (Deal *sb.*¹ 1 d), *-end*, *-gate*, *-room*, *-shape* (see sense 3), *-side*; **utter-ward** (see Ward *sb.*² 14 c); also *fig.* (quot. *c* 1440); **utter-wit**, knowledge of things external to one.

1398 Trevisa *Barth. De P. R.* v. xxx. (Bodl. MS.), Þe vtterdele þereof is clene and bright. *c* 1440 *Jacob's Well* 222 As þou hast v. watyrgatys in þe vttere-warde, owtward in þe pytt of þi body. *c* 1450 *Brut* II. 545 The vtterward of the castell of Chestre. 1483 Caxton *Gold. Leg.* 309/2 The towne..in the utterende of Dalmace. 1485 *Rolls of Parlt.* VI. 353 The Uttergate of the Castell of Flynte. 1495 *Trevisa's Barth. de P. R.* III. vi. c viij/1 Felynge, bodyly wytte and Ymagynacyon arne sytuate in the soule that he is onid to the body, and yeue it lyfe, & Innerwytte & vtterwytt to perfeccion of the body. *c* 1530 Ld. Berners *Arth. Lyt. Bryt.* (1814) 139 One [bed]..yᵉ vtterbrasses therof were of grene jasper. 1530 Palsgr. 286/1 Utterbarke of a tree, *escorche*. *Ibid.*, Uttercourt, *basse court*. *a* 1550 Leland *Itin.* (1769) VII. 118 Estward to the utterward of the Chyrch. 1567 Drant *Horace*, *Sat.* iii. G 4 To folow showes, and utter-shapes,..Is folie leude. 1577 Harrison *England* II. xii. (1877) I. 236 The vtterside of their mansions. 1603 Daniel *Def. Rhime* H 6, When we heare musicke, we must be in our eare, in the vtter-roome of sense. 1675 Hobbes *Odyssey* XXI. 258 [He] shut the utter-Gate.

†**Utter,** *adv. Obs.* Forms: 1 utor, 6 *Sc.* uter; 1 uttor, 2, 7, 9, utter, 3–5 uttere (6 *Sc.* uttir), 4–7 vtter (5 vttir, vttyr), 4–5 vttere. [OE. *ūtor*, *ūttor*, *ūtter* (compar. of *ūt* Out *adv.*), = MLG. *uter*, G. *ausser*, ON. *útarr*.]

1. Farther out, away, or apart; out, outside, without.

c 888 *Ælfred Boeth.* xxxiv. § 12 Nabbað hi nan god ofer þæt to secanne, ne hi nanwuht ne maȝonne ufor ne utor findan. *c* 1000 *Ags. Gosp.* Matt. xx. 28 Þonne byþ ðe arwurðlicor þonne þe man uttor scufe. *c* 1200 *Trin. Coll. Hom.* 73 [He] ne dar his sinnes seien þe prest leste hit uttere cume þat hie twien witen. 13.. *E. E. Allit. P.* B. 42 He schulde be halden vtter, With mony blame ful bygge... Hurled to þe halle dore. 13.. *Gaw. & Gr. Knt.* 1565 Þer he..made hym, maw-gref his hed, forto mwe vtter. 1399 Langl. *Rich. Redeles* III. 232 Þe portir with his pikis þo put him vttere. *c* 1440 *Pallad. on Husb.* v. 112 In wynter to his codde an heep of stonys Is good, that in the somer vtter don is. *c* 1450 *Mirk's Festial* I. 258 Þys man..set to þe roches his schuldyr, and bade hom..sterte vttyr. *c* 1500 *World & Child* 527 Stonde vtter, felowe! Where duest thou thy curtesy preue. *a* 1529 Skelton *E. Rummyng* 535 A strawe, sayde Bele, stande vtter.

2. From among others; = Out *adv.* 1 e. Cf. Out-try *v.* 1. *rare*⁻¹

c 1440 *Pallad. on Husb.* II. 294 In Nouember kitte of the bowes drie, Superfluent & thicke ek vtter trie.

3. To an utter degree; quite, altogether.

1611 Beaum. & Fl. *King & No K.* IV. i, I know they will deny me gracious Madam, Being..So utter empty of those excellencies That tame Authority. 1652 G. Sandys *Trav.* (ed. 5) 47 It utter [*earlier edd.* utterly] excludes his former excuse of an allegory. 1816 Accum *Chem. Tests* (1818) 139 Exposed in an utter dark place, to a brisk current of air.

4. *Utter-fine*: **a.** Of metals: Superfine. *Sc.*

1562–3 *Reg. Privy Council Scot.* I. 232 Fourtie five unce of uter fyne silvir. 1641 in Cochran-Patrick *Rec. Coinage Scot.* (1876) I. Introd. 31 Vtter fynne gold. 1641 *Reg. Mag. Sig. Scot.* 366/2 Per ferramenta trium petrarum purissimi lie utter fyne argenti.

b. *ellipt.* A superfine make or quality of cloth. *Sc.* (Freq. *c* 1537–50.)

1529 *Acc. Ld. High Treas. Scot.* V. 365 Ane eln tua quarteris, and ane half of uterfyne to be tua pair of hois. 1537 *Ibid.* VI. 351 Ten elnis uter fyne to be ane goun. 1564 *Reg. Privy Council Scot.* I. 309 Sevintene cairsayis and fyve stekis of uttir fyne.

Utter (ʊ·tǝı), *v.*¹ Forms: α. 5 outer, outre (ottre, *Sc.* vtre), 6 vter, outter. β. 5 utterne, uttren, 5–7 vtter (6–7 *Sc.* wtter), vttre, 5 vttyr, 6 vttar; 5– utter, 6–7 uttre. [Partly from Out *adv.* or *v.* (with shortening of the vowel as in Utter *adv.*), partly ad. MDu. *uteren* (also *uyteren*, Du. *uiteren*, WFris. *uterje*) to drive away, announce, speak, show, make known, or MLG. *ūteren*, *ūtern* to turn out, sell, speak, demonstrate, etc. (LG. *ūtern*), = MHG. *ūzeren*, *ūzern*, *iuzern* (G. *äussern* to speak, declare, †bring forth); Da. *ytre*, *yttre*, Sw. *yttra*, Norw. *ytra*, are from LG. The AF. *uttrer* (1463), Anglo-L. *utterare* (1551) are obviously from the English word.

For the earlier *oute(n*, *owten*, in Chaucer *Wife's Prol.* 521 and *Canon Yeom. Prol. & T.* 281, two later readings are respectively *outer*, *vttren*.]

I. †**1.** To put (goods, wares, etc.) forth or upon the market; to issue, offer, or expose for sale or barter; to dispose of by way of trade; to vend, sell. *Obs.*

In very frequent use from *c* 1540 to *c* 1655.

α. ?*c* 1400 *Chaucer's Wife's Prol.* 521 (Petw. MS.), With daungere outer [*v.rr.* oute, outen, owten] we al oure chaffare. 1423 *Rolls of Parlt.* IV. 255/1 Swiche warkes..[they] kepen and senden unto the fayres.., and ther thei outre hem. 1483 in J. H. Glover *Kingsthorpiana* (1883) 43 Yf any man brewe for the avayle of the Churche, that all other brewers cesse for the tyme uppon lefulle warnynge tyll that be outred.

β. 1425 *Rolls of Parlt.* IV. 307/2 Þat your said Commens may utter and sende her Corn, Bestus and Merchaundise over the see, into the parties abovesaid. 1436 *Pol. Poems* (Rolls) II. 175 At Venice of them men wol it bye, Then utterne [*v.r.* Thei utter] there the chaffare be the payse. *c* 1450 *Harl. Contin. Higden* (Rolls) VIII. 450 These men of Flaundres commynge to londe to utter theire merchandyse. 1523 *Act* 14 & 15 *Hen. VIII*, c. 1 § 1 Yf any person..doo nat ther or elles where bargayne utter and sell the sayed Clothe. 1570 Foxe *A. & M.* (ed. 2) 1206/1 Seeing good wyne noldeth no tauerne bushe to vtter it. 1607 Middleton *Michaelmas Term* IV. ii. 13 Do they [*sc.* traders] not thrive best when they utter most? 1649 Br. Hall *Cases Consc.* III. vii. 296 When they gathered their Frankincense, none of it might be uttered till the Priest had the tithe of it. *a* 1668 Lassels *Voy. Italy* (1698) I. 68 Besides they utter a world of Taffataes, Velvets,..and other things of value. 1735 Berkeley *Querist* § 544 Whether she [*sc.* Lyons] doth not receive and utter all those commodities. 1764 Burn *Poor Laws* 243 To keep a common ale-house.., and to utter and sell therein victuals. 1825 Scott *Betrothed* xxiii, Where other men are admitted that have wares to utter. [1863 H. Cox *Instit.* I. xi. 279 Booksellers were, by statute.., prohibited from uttering Tindal's translation of the Bible.]

fig. and in fig. context. *c* 1430 Lydg. *Poems* (Percy Soc.) 150 Uttre nevir no darnel with good corn, Begyn no trouble whan men trete of pees. 1588 Shaks. *L. L. L.* II. i. 16 Beauty is bought by iudgement of the eye, Not vttred by base sale of chapmens tongues. 1613 J. Taylor (Water P.) *Waterman's Suit* Wks. (1630) 174/1 [The waterman's] worke and ware is seene and knowne, and hee vtters it with the sweat of his browes. 1624 Quarles *Job* v. 60 Earth's black babbling Daughter (she that heares, And vent alike, both Truth and Forgeries, And vtters, often, cheap as then she buyes). 1828 Scott *F. M. Perth* vi, The devil has factors enough to utter his wares.

absol. 1600 Cornwallis *Ess.* II. C 5, Let vs receiue, and vtter, be capable, and returne increase of this fruite.

b. To announce for sale; = Cry *v.* 5 b. *rare.*

1806–7 J. Beresford *Miseries Hum. Life* (1826) IV. i, The infernal dialects in which their goods are *uttered*.

†**c.** *intr.* Of goods: To find purchasers; = Sell *v.* 6. *Obs.*⁻¹

1611 Cotgr., *Marchandise d'emploiste*, ware that sells well, that vtters quickly.

2. To give currency to (money, coin, notes, etc.); to put into circulation; *esp.* to pass or circulate (base coin, forged notes, etc.) as legal tender.

c 1483 *Chron. London* (1827) 110 Every man, because of the said newe exchange, outred gold, and kept sylver. *c* 1550 *Disc. Common Weal Eng.* (1893) 78 Strangers haue conterfeted oure coine,..and heare vttered it, as well for oure gold and silver, as for oure chefe commoditie. 1554–5 *Act* 1–2 *Philip & Mary* c. 1 To the intent to utter or make paiment withe the same [*sc.* counterfeit foreign coin] within this Realme. 1602 Fulbecke *1st Pt. Parall.* 86 To utter or cause to be uttered false mony knowing it to be false. 1697 Evelyn *Numism.* i. 16 Tokens which every Tavern.. presumed to stamp and utter. 1718 S. Sewall *Diary* 21 Sept., Found Guilty of uttering Counterfeit Bills of Credit. *c* 1740 Fielding *Ess. Char. Men* Wks. 1784 IX. 417 Uttering great number of promissory notes. 1780 H. Walpole in Jesse *Selwyn & Contemp.* (1844) IV. 317 Last night I saw a proof-piece of seven-shilling pieces...I know they were not uttered, but could you get me one from the Mint? 1825 W. O. Russell & Ryan *Crown Cases* 455 The prisoner was ..convicted..of the offence of uttering and publishing, as true, a forged promissory note. 1848 Akerman *Introd. Study Anc. & Mod. Coins* i. 7 The earliest coins..bearing the symbol of the state by which they were uttered. 1861 *Act* 24–25 *Vict.* c. 99 § 9 Whosoever shall tender, utter, or put off any false or counterfeit Coin.

absol. 1863 Stephen *Blackstone's Comm.* (ed. 5) IV. 227 The punishment of forging, uttering, and the like at common law. 1905 *Daily Chron.* 22 May 5/7 Charged with being in the possession of counterfeit coins and plant for making them, and..accused also of 'uttering'.

b. *fig.* and *transf.* Also *absol.*

1588 Kyd *Househ. Philos.* Wks. (1901) 274 Memory,..imprinting in it selfe al the Images and formes of visible.. things, could not vtter them in time conuenient..vnlesse it had so ordered. 1609 B. Jonson *Sil. Wom.* IV. vi, Mavis was more deceiu'd then we; 'twas her commendation vtter'd 'hem [*ante* 'these adulterate knights'] in the colledge. 1800 Addison *Amer. Law Rep.* 44 Misner was indicted..for uttering this assignment. 1839 Bailey *Festus* 145 The great bards Of Greece, of Rome,..Men who have forged gods— uttered—made them pass.

†**c.** To issue by way of publication; to publish. *Obs.*

1561 in Haynes *Cecil Papers* (1740) 368 Sondry Bookebynders and Stationers do utter certen Papers, wherein be prynted the Face of hir Majesty. *c* 1567 Stowe in *Surv.* (1908) I. p. li, Ye same [book] was well vtteryd by ye printar. 1584 *Star Chamb. Decree Printers & Stationers* (1863) 9 Bokes printed in England are uttered no where els.

3. †**a.** To send out; *esp.* to issue or give out from or as from a store. *Obs. rare.*

1529 More *Dyaloge* III. Wks. 213/2 To by [= buy] many of the same suyte.., whiche were by them vttred to diuers yonge scolers such as thei founde properly witted. 1578 in *Househ. Ord.* (1790) 272 All those [pieces] that have beene uttered out of the store.., for the supplie of the fortes. 1617 Moryson *Itin.* II. 243 Such victuals as are..vnfit to be vttered to the souldier.

b. To put or thrust forth, shoot or urge out; to discharge, emit, eject, exhale. Also with *forth*, *out*. Now *dial.*

1536 Latimer in Strype *Eccl. Mem.* (1721) I. 260 God prosper you, to the uttering all hollow harts of England. 1565 Cooper *Thesaurus*, *Tortuosa vrina*, vrine vttered with payne. 1579 Spenser *Sheph. Cal.* March 15 Thilke same Hawthorne studde..beginnes to budde, And vtter his tender head. 1607 Breton *Murmurer* Wks. (Grosart) II. 10/1 His Tongue like the sting of a Serpent, which vttereth nothing but poison. 1673 R. Head *Canting Acad.* 168 He that utters his Stomach in his next fellows Boots. 1820 W. Irving *Sketch Bk.* (1821) I. 69 The sage Nicholas Vedder, with his..fair long pipe, uttering clouds of tobacco smoke. 1821 Lamb *Elia* I. *Old Benchers*, The little cool playful streams those exploded Cherubs uttered [*sc.* from Lincoln's Inn Square fountain]. 1905 *Eng. Dial. Dict.* s.v., The spouts couldn't utter the water.

transf. 1881 P. Brooks *Candle of Lord* 14 Every candle of the Lord must utter its peculiar light.

fig. *a* 1586 Sidney *Arcadia* II. iv, She might give passage to her thoughts, and so as it were utter out some smoke of those flames. 1588 Shaks. *Tit. A.* v. iii. 12 My tongue may vtter forth The Venemous Mallice of my swelling heart.

†**c.** To produce or yield; to send out, supply, or furnish. Also in fig. context. *Obs.*

1547 *Homilies* I. *Faith* B iiij b, They that..doe lyue in sinne.., not vttering the frutes that do belong to suche an high profession. 1603 Owen *Pembrokeshire* (1892) 54 The cheeffest and greatest comoditie that this sheere vttereth. *Ibid.* 57 It also vttereth yerelie great store of oysters. 1640 Markham *Farw. Husb.* 8 The mixt Earth, which vtters Whynnes, Bryars [etc.].

†**4.** *intr.* Of a horse: To go out of the lists or course at a tournament. *Sc. Obs. rare.*

1550 Lyndesay *Sqr. Meldrum* 306 Bot Talbartis Hors, with ane mischance, He outterit, and to ryn was laith. *a* 1578 Lindesay (Pitscottie) *Chron. Scot.* (S.T.S.) I. 234 Schir Patrickis horse wtterit witht him and wald on noways reconter his marrow.

II. 5. *trans.* To send forth as a sound; to give out in an audible voice; to give vent or expression to (joy, etc.); to burst out with (a cry, yell, etc.).

c 1400 [see Uttering *vbl. sb.*]. 1530 Palsgr. 769/2, I utter ..my voyce, *je profere*. 1560 Daus tr. *Sleidane's Comm.* 215 b, He vttereth great gladness. 1611 Shaks. *Wint. T.* IV. iv. 185 Hee singes seuerall Tunes, faster then you'l tell money: hee vtters them [etc.]. 1612 Brinsley *Lud. Lit.* iii. 13 They [*sc.* vowels] being rightly vttered. 1621 J. Taylor (Water P.) *Sir G. Nonsence* Wks. (1630) Aa 1 b, Three sighs, smilingly vttered in the Hebrew Character. 1667 Milton

V.

V (vī), the 22nd letter of the modern English and the 20th of the ancient Roman alphabet, was in the latter an adoption of the early Greek vowel-symbol V, now also represented by U (q.v.), but in Latin *u* was employed also with the value of the Greek digamma (*viz. w*), to which it corresponds etymologically. When not purely vocalic, it still denoted this sound at the time the earliest Latin loan-words were adopted in the Teutonic languages; consequently such words beginning with *v* appear in Old English ...

Uvulatome (yū-viślā'tōm). [f. UVULA + Gr. τομ-ός cutting.] An instrument for cutting or removing the uvula.

Uvulatomy (yūvūlə'tŏmi). [See prec. and -TOMY. Cf. UVULOTOMY.] The operation of cutting off the uvula.

Uvulitis (yūvūlāi'tis). *Path.* [mod.L., f. UVULA + -ITIS. Cf. F. *uvulite*.] Inflammation of the uvula.

Uvulotome (yū'vūlŏtōm). *Surg.* [See prec. and -TOME.] = UVULATOME.

Uvulo'tomy. [See prec. and -TOMY.] = UVULATOMY.

Uvula (yū'vūla), *sb.* [a. med.L. *Sous-lātvīs* (whence also F. *uvīlvrīts*), f. med.L. *ūvula* UVULA.]

1. Used in disorders of the uvula. *rare*.

2. Pertaining or belonging to the uvula.

3. Produced by vibration of the uvula.

Uvular (yū'vūla), *a.* (*sb.*). [ad. mod.L. *Sous-lātvīs* (whence also F. *uvīlvrīts*), f. med.L. *ūvula* UVULA.]

Uxorial (ŏksō'riăl). [f. L. ūxōri-us (f. ūxor wife) + -AL.]

Uxorious (ŏksō'riŏs). [f. L. ūxōri-us + -OUS.]

Uxoriousness. [f. prec. + -NESS.]

Uxoricide (ŏksō'risăid). [ad. mod.L. *ūxōri-cīda*, f. L. *ūxor* wife: see -CIDE 1, 2.]

Uzzle, dial. var. OUZEL.

Vacabuncy ...

Vacancy (vē'kănsi). Also 6 vacantie, 7 Sc. vacancie, 7-8 vacancy; ad. late med.L. *vacantia* (Sp. and Fig. *vacancia*; It. *vacanza*), f. L. *vacāre*.

Vacand, *ppl. a.* and *sb.* Sc. *Obs.* Also 5 wak-, vakand, 5-6 vakand, 6 vacan-.

Vacant (vē'kănt), *a.* and *sb.* Forms: 3-6 vacaunt (5 vacaunt), 4-vacant; [a. OF. (also mod.F.) *vacant* (= It., Pg. *vacante*), or ad. L. *vacant-, vacans*, pres. pple. of *vacāre* to be empty, etc.]

Vacantly (vē'kăntli), *adv.* [f. VACANT + -LY 2.] In a vacant manner; in freedom from business or work.

Vacat (vē'kăt). *Obs.* [L. *vacat* 3rd sing. pres. ind. of *vacāre* to be empty.]

Vacatable, a.

Vacate, v.

Vacating, vbl. sb.

Vacation (vækē·ʃən), sb.

Vacatura.

Vaccary (væ·kəri).

Vacci-, combining form of L. *vacca* cow.

Vaccigenous, a.

Vaccina.

Vaccinable, a.

Vaccinal, a.

Vaccinate, v.

Vaccination (væksinē·ʃən).

Vaccinator.

Vaccine (væ·ksin, -ain), a.

Vaccinia (væksi·niă), Path.

Vaccinine.

Vaccinifer.

Vaccine, v.

Vaccinist (væ·ksinist).

Vaccinium (væksi·niəm).

Vaccination.

Vaccino-, combining form of L. *vaccinum*.

Vaccinogenous, a.

Vaccinoid, a.

Vaccinola.

Vaccinulation.

Vaccinulous, a.

Vach, obs. St. Watch.

Vachery (væ·tʃəri).

Vacillant (væ·silant), a.

Vacillate (væ·silēt), ppl. a.

Vacillate, v.

Vacillating, ppl. a.

Vacillation (væsilē·ʃən).

Vacillator (væ·silētər).

Vacillatory (væ·silətəri), a.

Vacive (vē·iv), a.

Vacuate, v.

Vacuation. Obs. rare⁻¹.

Vacuist (væ·kiuist).

Vacuitous, a.

Vacuity (vækiū·iti).

Vacuolar (væ·kiuōlər), a.

Vacuolate (væ·kiuōlēt), a.

Vacuolated (væ·kiuōlētid), ppl. a.

Vacuolation.

Vacuole (væ·kiuōl).

Vacuoly.

Vacuous (væ·kiuəs), a.

View Nat. IV. 3 He contended, that thunder or sound would not be able to pass through walls,..unless there were some vacuous spaces in those bodies. 1813 T. Busby Lucretius II. vi. Comm. p. xxiii, He notices many natural circumstances which..demonstrate the vacuous natures of all substances. 1860 Tyndall Glac. II. xxiv. 356 The water..is not able to fill it, hence a vacuous space must be formed in the cell.

b. Empty of air or gas; in which a vacuum has been produced.

1669 Boyle Contin. New Exp. II. (1682) 158, I put Pears bruised into a vacuous Reciever. 1842 E. A. Parnell Chem. Anal. (1845) 490 The difference between its weight when containing the gas, and when vacuous. 1862 Grove Corr. Phys. Forces (ed. 4) 59 No air is given off from the bubbles, so they seem to be vacuous. 1892 Photogr. Ann. II. 233 In incandescent lamps the electric current heats up a carbon filament inclosed in a vacuous globe.

c. Bot. Not containing some part or feature usually present.

1866 Treas. Bot. 1199/2 Bracts which usually support flowers are said to be vacuous when they have no flower in their axils.

d. Empty of any visible object.

1877 Morley Crit. Misc. Ser. II. 255 As the flies of a summer day dart from point to point in the vacuous air.

3. Empty of ideas; unintelligent; expressionless. Cf. Vacant a. 5.

1848 Thackeray Bk. Snobs x, A vacuous, solemn..Snob. 1883 Standard 2 Jan. 5/2 The absence of anxiety..leaves their minds vacuous. 1889 Times 26 Oct. 9/1 That gift of oppressive familiarity which by some vacuous people is taken to indicate..sterling sense.

Comb. 1895 'H. S. Merriman' Grey Lady I. iii. (1899) 28 He was rather a vacuous-looking young man.

b. Indicative of mental vacancy.

1855 Thackeray Newcomes II. 25 With that vacuous leer which distinguishes his lordship. 1858 O. W. Holmes Aut. Breakf.-t. vi. 55 These negative faces with their vacuous eyes and stony lineaments. 1873 Black Pr. Thule xx. 320 There was a cheery, vacuous, smiling expression on his round face.

Comb. 1879 McCarthy Own Times v. I. 116 A huge white-headed, vacuous-eyed man was to be seen.

4. Devoid of content or substance.

1870 Swinburne Ess. & Stud. (1875) 56 The vacuous monotonous desire and discontent, the fitful and febrile beauty of Alfred de Musset. 1879 Howells L. Aroostook (1883) I. 45 Mrs. Erwin wrote an epistolary style exasperatingly vacuous and diffuse.

5. Unoccupied, idle, indolent; not filled up with any (profitable) employment or activity.

1872 Morley Voltaire 334 It cannot for ever be tolerable that the mass should wear away their lives in unbroken toil without hope or aim, in order that the few may live selfish and vacuous days. 1897 Review of Rev. 37 There are many rich people who..lead such mean and vacuous lives.

Hence **Va·cuously** adv.; **Va·cuousness.**

1648 W. Mountague Devout Ess. I. 352 In that vacuousness the winds and vapors of tediousness and displicence rise. 1816 J. Gilchrist Philos. Etym. 226 The mistiness and vacuousness of abstract expression. 1860 All Year Round No. 88. 283 He had..a broad fair face, rather vacuously good natured in its ordinary expression. 1880 Daily Tel. 14 Feb., So there he stood, with his hands in his pockets,.. gazing vacuously at the fighting and rough play.

‖ **Vacuum** (væ·kiu,ŏm). Pl. **vacua** and **vacuums.** [L. vacuum, neut. of vacuus empty: cf. Vacuous a. So F. vacuum, It., Sp., Pg. vacuo.]

1. Emptiness of space; space unoccupied by matter. Now rare or Obs.

1550 Cranmer Lord's Supper 21 Naturall reason abhorreth vacuum, that is to say, that there shoulde be any emptye place, wherin no substance shoulde be. 1570 Dee Math. Pref. 35 This Arte is very profitable: to proue, that Vacuum, or Emptines is not in the world. 1626 Bacon Sylva § 83 The more gross of the Tangible Parts do contract and serve themselves together..to avoid Vacuum. 1657 Trapp Ezra ix. 6 For beyond the moveable Heavens, Aristotle..saith there is neither body, nor time, nor place, nor vacuum. 1676 Poor Robin's Intell. 30 May–6 June 1/1 Having his head as ful of Vacuum as his small proportion of brains was capable of. 1795 W. Blake Bk. Los i, Round the flames roll,..mounting on high Into Vacuum, into nonentity, Where nothing was. 1843 Penny Cycl. XXVI. 76/1 The astronomical argument, therefore, in favour of absolute vacuum has fallen.

2. A space entirely empty of matter.

1607 A. Brewer Lingua IV. i. H i b, First shall the whole Machin of the world..returne to..Chaos, then the least vacuvm be found in the vniuerse. 1638 Wilkins New World I. (1684) 23 To dispute against Democritus, who thought, that the World was made by the casual concourse of Atoms in a great Vacuum. 1714 Let. from Layman (ed. 2) 7 A Government can't rightfully restrain a Man's professing the Belief of a Vacuum, or a Plenum. 1763 Johnson in Boswell 21 July, There are objections against a plenum, and objections against a vacuum; yet one of them must..be true. 1865 J. Grote Plato I. i. 80 Proceeding upon his hypothesis of atoms and vacua as the only objective existences. 1884 F. Temple Relat. Relig. & Sci. i. (1885) 8 The reasons why.. Nature abhors a vacuum were discovered.

b. A space empty of air, esp. one from which the air has been artificially withdrawn.

sing. 1652 French Yorksh. Spa ii. 7 So much air being spent, there would of necessity follow a vacuum. 1660 Boyle New Exp. Phys. Mech. Proem 2 The Interest of the Ayr, in hindring the descent of the Quick-silver, in the famous Experiment touching a Vacuum. 1713 Derham Phys.-Theol. 8 note, The Ear-wig..and some other Insects would seem unconcerned at the Vacuum a good while, and lie as dead; but revive in the Air. 1758 Reid tr. Macquer's Chym. I. 299 The air contained therein is condensed, and leaves a vacuum, which the external air..tends to occupy. 1829 Nat. Philos., Heat I. ii. 2 (L.U.K.), Count Rumford proved the passage of heat through a Torricellian vacuum, that is, the space left at the top of a barometer by the mercury falling. 1860 Maury Phys. Geog. i. § 6 At the height of 80 or 90 miles there is a vacuum far more complete than any which we can produce by any air-pump. 1872 J. P. Cooke New Chem. 17 Alcohol expands more slowly into the aqueous vapor than it would into a vacuum.

pl. 1777 Phil. Trans. LXVII. 679 That the vacua be as nearly as possible compleat. 1832 Brewster Nat. Magic x. 262 The plates, being raised or depressed by the voluntary muscles, form so many vacua.

3. An empty space; a portion of space (left) unoccupied or unfilled with the usual or natural contents.

1589 Nashe in Greene's Menaphon (Arb.) 12 The Scythians, who..swaddle themselues streighter, to the intent no vacuum beeing left in their intrayles [etc.]. a 1635 T. Randolph Poems, Parley with his Empty Purse (1640) 113 Unnatural vacuum, can your emptinesse Answer to some slight questions? 1700 T. Brown tr. Fresny's Amusem. viii, He made a Dive into my Pocket, but encountring a Disappointment, Rub'd off, Cursing the Vacuum. 1758 J. S. Le Dran's Observ. Surg. (1771) 141, I discovered a Vacuum upon the intercostal Muscles, from whence about a Spoonful of..Matter was discharged. 1791 H. Walpole in Miss Berry's Jrnl. I. 328, I shall fill my vacuum with some lines that General Conway has sent me. a 1838 C. Morris Lyra Urban. (1840) II. 97 The Dandy's head, A vacuum dead, Ne'er tries for thought to seek!

b. In various fig. uses.

1617 Middleton Fair Quar. II. D iij b, I cannot see that vacuum in your bloud. 1630 Lennard tr. Charron's Wisd. vii. 33 It were a vacuum, a defect, a deformitie too absurd in nature..that betwixt two extreames..there should be no middle. a 1670 Hacket Abp. Williams I. (1692) 10 Commonly they misspent that triennial probation, and left upon that place a vacuum of doing little or nothing. 1710 Palmer Prov. 384 'Tis infinitely pleasing to observe there has been no Vacuum in our Life. 1772 Phil. Trans. LXII. 317 It should therefore seem that the larks from the more adjacent parts croud in to supply the vacuum occasioned by the London Epicures. 1829 Marryat F. Mildmay ix, The.. vacuum occasioned by my mother's death. 1846 Grote Greece (1862) I. xvi. 294 They filled up the vacuum of the unrecorded past. 1879 R. H. Elliot Written on Foreh. I. 140 So Martin Kerr..was left with a sheer, hopeless vacuum to fill up as best he could.

4. attrib. and Comb., as vacuum-brake, cleaner, cleanser, disk, distillation, engine, -made, -pan, -pump, -vessel.

Also vacuum-apparatus, -cylinder, -filter, -gauge, -shunt, -valve (Knight, 1875–84).

1875 Knight Dict. Mech. 2636/1 *Vacuum-brake, a form of steam-operated car-brake. 1889 G. Findlay Eng. Railway 168 The train is fitted throughout with vacuum brakes. 1903 Hardwareman 23 May 395 A decision of..serious import as regards the operations of the *Vacuum Cleaner Co. 1903 Westm. Gaz. 30 May 5/3 There is a machine at work, called the '*vacuum cleanser', which gives them all, in turn, a thorough 'spring cleaning'. 1860 Tyndall Glac. I. xxiii. 163 Sometimes the *vacuum disks were parallel to the veins [of the glacier]. 1899 tr. R. von Jaksch's Clin. Diag. v. (ed. 4) 170 Still better for this purpose is the method of *vacuum distillation. 1825 J. Nicholson Operat. Mechanic 670 The application of Mr. Brown's pneumatic, or *vacuum engine. 1853 Ure Dict. Arts (ed. 4) II. 879 *Vacuum-made liqueurs. 1839 Ibid. 1208 An apparatus inserted air-tight into the cover of the *vacuum-pan. 1857 Miller Elem. Chem., Org. 66 The syrup..is boiled down again in the vacuum pan, and is obtained in the form of..crushed sugar. 1858 Simmonds Dict. Trade, *Vacuum-pump, a pump attached to a marine steam-engine. 1899 Edin. Rev. Apr. 323 Professor Dewar's coils and *vacuum-vessels.

Vad, southern ME. var. Fade a.²; obs. Sc. f. Wed sb., Woad.

† **Va·dable,** a. Obs. rare. Also **vadeable.** [ad. med.L. vadābilis (f. vadāre to wade through) or a. Sp. vadeable (Pg. vadeavel, OF. vadable).] Fordable.

1555 Watreman Fardle Facions Pref. 11 To the ende thei [sc. the rivers] might not onely be vadable, but passed also with drie foote. 1578 T. N. tr. Conq. W. India 65 After hee had iourneyed three leagues, hee came to a faire vadeable Riuer. 1611 Florio, Vadoso, vadable, or foardable.

Vadam, southern ME. var. Fathom.

Vaddah, obs. form of Veddah.

† **Vade,** sb. Obs.⁻¹ [ad. L. vadum.] A shallow place in a river.

1538 Leland Itin. (1769) V. 94 Irwel is not navigable but in sum Places for Vadys and Rokkes.

† **Vade,** v.¹ Obs. [var. of Fade v.¹, chiefly used in fig. senses (very common c 1530–1630) and app. to some extent associated with L. vādĕre to go: see next, to which some of the quotations placed under 3–3 c may really belong.

This association may be the real explanation of the form, but see the note to Fade a.²]

1. intr. Of colour: = Fade v.¹ 4.

1471 Ripley Comp. Alch. Pref. in Ashm. (1652) 127 Colour whych wyll not vade. c 1532 Du Wes Introd. Fr. in Palsgr. 956 To vade, ternir. a 1586 Sidney Astr. & Stella (1622) 578 How doth the colour vade of those vermillion dies. 1594 Plat Jewell-ho. III. 45 As soone as the beautiful hew of the leaues begin to vade. 1613 Answ. Uncasing Machiav. E iv b, Whose colours never vade. 1647 C. Harvey Schola Cordis xvii. 4 The staines of sin I see Are vaded all, or di'd in graine.

2. Of flowers, etc.: = Fade v.¹ 1.

1492 [see 3 b]. c 1532 Du Wes Introd. Fr. in Palsgr. 894 Rose that can nat vade, rose immarcessible. 1578 Lyte Dodoens I Small grayish leaves..the whiche do perish and vade in winter. 1593 Shaks. Rich. II, I. ii. 20 One flourishing branch of his most Royall roote..Is hackt downe, and his summer leafes all vaded. 1621 Lady M. Wroth Urania 22 Do not the flowers vade, and grasse die for her departure?

3. To pass away, disappear, vanish; to decay or perish; = Fade v.¹ 6.

1495 Trevisa's Barth. De P. R. XVI. xxxvi. 564 Aege that passyth & vadyth chaungyth tymes of thynges. a 1548 Hall Chron., Hen. IV (1550) 4 When he departed, the only shelde, defence and comfort of the common people was vadid and gone. 1568 T. Howell Arb. Amitie (1879) 19 Forme is most frayle,..it vadth as grasse doth growe. 1607 Middleton Fam. Love I. i, I know how soon their love vadeth. 1641 Brathwait Eng. Gentlew. 324 Where..beauty never fadeth, love never faileth, health never vadeth. a 1678 Marvell Poems, Clorinda & Damon (1681) 12 Grass withers; and the Flow'rs too fade. Seize the short Ioyes then, ere they vade.

b. Const. from, into, to.

1492 Ryman Poems lxxxiv. 2 in Archiv Stud. neu. Spr. LXXXIX. 253 As medowe floures..Vadeth to erthe..Likewise richesse and grete honoures Shall vade fro euery creature. c 1537 Thersites D ij, The cowherd of Comertowne, with his croked spade, Cause frome the the wormes soone to vade. 1596 Spenser F. Q. v. ii. 40 How euer gay their blossome or their blade Doe flourish now, they into dust shall vade. 1663 Cane Ep. to Author of Animad. Fiat Lux 96 All your talk in this your eighteenth chapter vades into nothing.

c. With away.

1530 Proper Dyaloge in Roy's Rede me, etc. (Arb.) 133 Affermynge that oure loue shuld a-way vade Without any memory of them at all. 1587 M. Grove Pelops & Hipp. (1878) 38 The time thus doth consume & wear, the night doth vade away. 1625 Purchas Pilgrims II. 1761 The bankes of sand doe fleet and vade away out of the river.

† **Vade,** v.² Obs. [ad. L. vādĕre to go; cf. prec.]

1. To go away, depart. rare.

1569 Elviden Pesistratus & Catanea (Bynneman), Then proclamation made That Pisistrate to proper soile should vade. 1638 Brathwait Barnabees Jrnl. II. (1818) 67 Beauty feedeth, beauty fadeth, Beauty lost, her lover vadeth.

2. To proceed, advance.

a 1660 Contemp. Hist. Irel. (Ir. Archæol. Soc.) II. 5 You are too yonge to vade unto these graue matters.

Vade, obs. Sc. form of Wade v.

† **Vadelect.** Obs. Also 6 -liet. [ad. Anglo-L. vadelectus, vadlectus (13th c.), ad. AF. vadlet, var. OF. vaslet, vallet, varlet: see Valet sb. and Varlet.] A servant, serving-man.

1586 Ferne Blaz. Gentrie 161 The same French king, for want of a Hereald..., was constrained to subbornate a vadeliet, or common seruing-man. 1628 Coke On Litt. 156 But if the sherife be a Vadelect of the crowne or other meniall seruant of the King, there the challenge is good. 1661 Blount Glossogr. (ed. 2), Vadelet or Vadelect..signifies a servant, and is used in the accounts of the Inner Temple, for a Benchers Clerk or Servant.

So **Vadelet, Vadlet.** arch.

1661 [see prec.]. 1813 Williams Law of Clergy 398 The King as founder of..many religious houses had a corrody for his vadelets, and a pension for a chaplain. 1861 Riley tr. Carpenter's Liber Albus 40 As soon as the Sheriffs are sworn, all the Servants of their office—clerks, serjeants and their vadlets..—shall also be sworn.

‖ **Vade-mecum** (vē·di mī·kŏm). Also **vade mecum.** [L., vāde imper. sing. of vādĕre to go + mēcum with me. So F., Sp., Pg. vademecum (Pg. also -meco).]

1. A book or manual suitable for carrying about with one for ready reference. (Sometimes used as the title of such a work.)

1629 (title), Vade Mecum: A Manuall of Essayes Morrall, Theologicall. 1649 F. Roberts Clavis Bibl. 405 Among the very Ethiopians this book was in such repute, that the Ethiopian Eunuch made it his (Vade mecum) his companion in his journey. 1679 (title), A Vade-mecum for the Lovers of Musick. 1731 Fielding Grub St. Op. Introd., It is a sort of family Opera. The husband's vade-mecum; and is very necessary for all married men to have in their houses. 1797 Monthly Mag. III. 128 The Odéon shall possess a literary journal,..to be a valuable vade-mecum for such persons as are not in the habit of deciding on the merits of theatrical performances. 1818 Byron Juan I. cci, Aristotle's rules, The Vade Mecum of the true sublime, Which makes so many poets, and some fools. 1880 Muirhead Gaius Introd. p. xv, It is the remains..of a handbook for the practitioner; a vade mecum, as modern law-writers would call it.

fig. a 1631 Donne Select. (1840) 51 His vade mecum, the abridgment of all nature, and all law, his own heart, and conscience.

2. A thing commonly carried about by a person as being of some service to him.

1632 Lithgow Trav. VIII. 355 Gold..was my continuall vade Mecum. 1654 Whitlock Zootomia 71 Whose Vade mecum is an Aqua vitæ Bottle. 1678 Yng. Man's Call. 50 You may safely take it [a maxim] as your vade mecum along with you, in reference to the things of this life. 1774 'J. Collier' Mus. Trav. App. 23 To write a pamphlet against the use of a medicine which had been his vade mecum in all his journies.

Vader, southern ME. variant of Father.

Vadiation (vædiē¹·ʃən). Law. rare. [ad. med. L. vadiātio, f. vadiāre to give security.] The action of requiring or giving surety or pledges.

1753 Chambers' Cycl. Suppl. s.v., Vadiation, Vadiatio, in the civil law. 1802–12 Bentham Ration. Judic. Evid. (1827) IV. 557 note, Remedy against..sequestration, or vadiation in this or that shape.

† **Vadimony.** Obs. Also 6 vady-, 7 vademony. [ad. L. vadimōnium, f. vad-, vas bail, surety.] A pledge or recognisance.

1502 Arnolde Chron. (1811) 2 That they haue ther vadymonies [printed -memes] and weddes; the xiiii. artycle. c 1620 A. Hume Brit. Tongue (1865) 22 The accent in the fourth syllab from the end; as in mătrimonie, pătrimonie,

vădimonie. 1654 Warren Unbelievers 48 His Obligation was arbitrary and voluntary; not arising from the guilt of ..sin, but by way of vadimony, and susception. 1699 J. Barry Reviv. Cordial (1802) 80 In this work,..which he himself, as vademony and surety for God's elect, hath undertaken to..perform.

† **Va·ding,** vbl. sb. Obs.⁻¹ [f. Vade v.¹] The action or process of disappearing, declining, etc.

1570 Foxe A. & M. (ed. 2) I. 254/2 Yᵉ lyke vadyng of the water happened also in the floode of Medewaye.

† **Va·ding,** ppl. a. Obs. Also 7 vaid-. [f. as prec.] Fading, passing away, fleeting, transitory.

1566 Adlington Apuleius Ep. Ded., The vaine and soone vadynge beautie of the worlde. 1577 Grange Golden Aphrod., etc. R j, My Lady fayre whose shape doth shine And glyster in my vading sighte. 1596 Warner Alb. Eng. II. lxv. (1612) 279 What els is Forme but vaiding aire? 1615 Brathwait Strappado (1878) 53 Thy form's Diuine, no fading, vading flower. 1661 Sir A. Haslerig's Last Will & Test. 2 What a vading breath, or light blast is this flash of Honour.

Vadlet: see Vadelet.

Vadmal, -mel, varr. (after mod. Scand. forms) of Wadmal.

[1797 Stat. Acc. Scot. XIV. 326 The old men and women.. continue to wear good strong black clothes without dying, called by the ancient Norse, Vadmell.] 1851 Thorpe Northern Myth. I. 112, I am Kraka, Coal-black in vadmel! 1881 Du Chaillu Land Midnight Sun II. 78 The tent was made of coarse heavy vadmal.

Vadome, southern ME. variant of Fathom sb.

† **Vado·sity.** Obs.⁻¹ [f. L. vadōs-us, f. vadum ford.] The fact of being fordable.

1658 Burton Comm. Itin. Antoninus 224 The word Ford, by reason of the vadosity of the River there, being added.

Va·dy, a. south-w. dial. [Of obscure origin.] Damp, moist.

1880 Mrs. Parr Adam & Eve xiii. 188 The grass was too 'vady' for him to sit down upon.

‖ **Væ.** Obs. Also 6 **ve.** [L. væ alas!] A denunciation or threatening of woe.

1559 Abp. Parker Corr. (Parker Soc.) 79 We should.. deserve the wrathful væ and vengeance of God. 1584 Lodge Alarm agst. Usurers F iiij, The Lord shal place you among the goates, and pronounce his Ve against you. 1602 W. Watson Quodl. Relig. & State 9 With how many væs and woes to you Scribes and Pharisees did he come vpon them? a 1636 Westcote View Devonsh. (1845) 61 There was a væ or woe pronounced against them in these words,—'Woe unto you Piltonians, that make cloth without wool'.

Væder, Væie, Vælde, Væle, Væren, Værne, Væx, Væȝer, southern ME. varr. Father, Fey a., Field sb., Fele a., Fere v.¹, Fern sb., Fax, Fair a.

Vafand, Vaffand, obs. Sc. ff. waving Wave v.

Vafroun, var. Wafroun Sc. Obs.

† **Va·frous,** a. Obs. Also 6 **vaffrous.** [f. L. vafer, vafr- + -ous.] Sly, cunning, crafty, shifty.

a 1548 Hall Chron., Hen. VII, 11 Thinkyng surely that they..would neuer..longe agree with the Englishmen, accordyng to their olde vaffrous [1550 crafty] varietie. 1630 R. Johnson's Kingd. & Commw. 17 Divine providence.. adjudged it best..not to bestow..upon subtle and vafrous people, Courage, and Strength of body. 1650 B. Discolliminium 17 These are subtle, and vafrous Men, who are never solidly, nor honestly Wise. 1664 H. More Myst. Iniq. 106 This vafrous and bloudy Treason against the holy Majesty of Christ. 1721 in Bailey.

Vag, sb. Devon. dial. [Cf. Fag sb.²] Dried turf or peat used as fuel; a piece of this.

1796 W. H. Marshall W. England II. 6 Towards the Mountains, Turf (provincially 'Vags') and Peat (provincially 'Turf'). 1889 Portfolio Jan. 11/2 In the winter he may turn many an honest penny by the sale of 'vags'. 1895 G. Mortimer Tales Moors 224 You can cut as much vag— or peat, as you calls it up country—as you'm a mind to.

Vag, v. U.S. slang. [f. vag. abbrev. of Vagabond.] trans. To treat or deal with (one) as a vagabond or vagrant.

1891 C. Roberts Adrift Amer. 169, I was arrested as a vagrant As the popular expression went, I got 'vagged'.

Vag, dial. var. Fag v.²; obs. Sc. f. Wage sb.

Vagabond (væ·găbǫnd), a. and sb. Forms: 5–6 vagabound(e, -bunde, 5–6, 8 -bund, 5–7 -bonde, 7– vagabond; 6 Sc. wagabund, -bond; 7, 9 dial., vagabone, 9 dial. -bon. [a. OF. vagabond (14th c.) or ad. L. vagābund-us, f. vagārī to wander. Cf. mod.F. vagabond, It. vagabondo, Sp. and Pg. vagabundo, vagamundo; also G. vagabund, -bond, Sw. vagabond, Du. vagebond. As a sb. the form finally takes the place of the earlier Vacabond.]

A. adj. 1. Of persons, etc.: Roaming or wandering from place to place without settled habitation or home; leading a wandering life; nomadic.

a. In predicative use.

1426 Lydg. De Guil. Pilgr. 16842 O thow blyssed Lady, hyde hem that flen vnto the for helpe, and they that be vagabonde, dyscoure hem nat. 1533 Bellenden Livy I. xii. (S.T.S.) I. 71 Mony of þir pepill vagabound and ouresett with pouerte tuke wagis of þe sabynis. a 1578 Lindesay (Pitscottie) Chron. Scot. (S.T.S.) I. 322 He staw away..and ȝeid wagabund dissagyssit ane lang quhill. 1838 Stephens Trav. in Russia 96/1 Dispersed and vagabond, exiled from their native soil and air, they wander over the face of the earth.

fig. c 1430 Lydg. Min. Poems (Percy Soc.) 256 My look, myn eyen, unswre and vagabounde. 1667 Milton P. L. XI. 16 To Heav'n thir prayers Flew up, nor missd the way, by envious windes Blow'n vagabond or frustrate.

b. In attrib. use (occas. hyphened).

1555 Eden Decades I. ix. (Arb.) 97 Owre men suppose them to bee a vagabunde and wanderinge nacion lyke vnto the Scythians. 1602 Mountjoy Letter in Moryson Itin. (1617) II. 233 How, as a Vagabond Woodkerne hee may preserve his life,..I know not. 1640 tr. Verdere's Rom. of Rom. III. 31, I have for my brother and Soveraign, the Prince of Greece, whom but even now I beheld to be a vagabond Girle. 1691 tr. Emiliane's Observ. Journ. Naples 226 They become soon weary of it and then turn Vagabond-Hermits. 1726 Ayliffe Parergon 181 A vagabond Debtor may be cited in whatever Place or Jurisdiction he is found. 1784 Cowper Task I. 559 A vagabond and useless tribe there eat Their miserable meal. 1819 Scott Ivanhoe xxix, Those ballads which vagabond minstrels sing to drunken churls. 1857 Hughes Tom Brown i, We are a vagabond nation now.

transf. 1606 Shaks. Ant. & Cl. I. iv. 45 This common bodie, Like to a Vagabond Flagge vpon the Streame, Goes too, and backe. 1638 Wilkins New World xii. (1707) 98 The Concourse of many little Vagabond Stars, by the union of their Beams. 1868 Lockyer Guillemin's Heavens (ed. 3) 299 Those vagabond bodies, the comets.

† c. spec. Of soldiers or sailors. Obs.

1748 Lind Lett. Rel. Navy (1757) ii. 85 If they are to be set at liberty, who are accused of perjury, how is a vagabond seaman to be found, when he comes to England? 1813 Wellington in Gurw. Desp. (1838) X. 519, I do not know what measures to take about our vagabond soldiers.

† 2. (See quot. and cf. Extravagant a. 2.) Obs.

1456 Sir G. Haye Law Arms (S.T.S.) 258 ȝit is thare othir lawis callit lawis extravaganis, that is for to say lawis vagaboundis, that ar nocht incorporit in othir bukis of lawis of Lombardy.

3. Inclined to stray or gad about without proper occupation; leading an unsettled, irregular, or disreputable life; good-for-nothing, rascally, worthless.

1630 Greene's Fr. Bacon II. i. (Q.²), Where be these vagabond [1594 vacabond] knaues, that they attend no better on their Master? 1682 Burnet Rights Princes ii. 66 Some idle vagabond Clarks that had procured themselves to be put in Orders. 1741–3 Wesley Jrnl. (1749) 9 A clergyman came into the..room, and ask'd aloud, with a tone unusually sharp, 'Where those vagabond fellows were?' 1777 W. Dalrymple Trav. Sp. & Port. civ, A most vagabond crew! 1836 W. Irving Astoria II. 123 He took a ceremonious leave of the Crow chieftain, and his vagabond warriors. c 1870 B. Harte Coyotte Poems (1886) 16 Lop-eared and large-jointed, but ever alway A thoroughly vagabond outcast in gray.

4. Of or pertaining to, characteristic or distinctive of, a homeless wanderer.

1585 T. Washington tr. Nicholay's Voy. III. xviii. 104 By suche vagabounde beggerie, they make..beleeue, that they canne foresay and deuine. 1607 Shaks. Cor. III. iii. 89 Let them pronounce the steepe Tarpeian death, Vagabond exile, ..I would not buy Their mercie. 1653 R. Sanders Physiogn. 40 Voyages by Sea and Land, and a vagabond life. 1698 Crowne Caligula IV. Dram. Wks. 1874 IV. 406 Rase from thy memery my sinful hours, And all my little vagabond amours. 1726 De Foe Hist. Devil I. vi. (1840) 73 Satan being confined to a vagabond, wandering, unsettled condition. 1824 W. Irving T. Trav. II. 27 They have the true vagabond abhorrence of all useful..employments. 1841 Borrow Zincali I. i. 7 Abandoning his vagabond propensities and becoming stationary. 1872 Blackie Lays Highl. Introd. 13 This book is well-suited for your migratory needs, and vagabond habits.

5. fig. Roving, straying; not subject to control or restraint.

1635 Quarles Embl. IV. i, My heart is a vain heart, a vagabond and unstable heart. 1643 Milton Divorce Introd., The brood of Belial,..to whom no liberty is pleasing but unbridl'd and vagabond lust without pale or partition. a 1680 Butler Rem. (1759) II. 455 The Inconstant has a vagabond Soul, without any settled Place of Abode. 1878 Morley Carlyle 195 In that house are many mansions, the boisterous sanctuary of a vagabond polytheism.

B. sb. 1. One who has no fixed abode or home, and who wanders about from place to place; spec. one who does this without regular occupation or obvious means of support; an itinerant beggar, idle loafer, or tramp; a vagrant.

α. c 1485 Digby Myst. (1882) IV. 653 Now shall all the cursinges of your lawe, Opon yow [i.e. the Jews] fall most myschevose, & be knawen of vagabundes ouer awe. 1496 Ld Bothwell in Ellis Orig. Lett. Ser. I. I. 24 Every day throw þam þir vagabunds escapis, cummyn to Perkin. 1582 Stanyhurst Æneis I. (Arb.) 25 And yeet theese wretched vagabunds hard destenye scourgeth.

β. 1495 Act 11 Hen. VII, c. 2 Every vagabounde, heremyte, or beggar able to labre, or clerk, pilgryme, or shipman. 1533 Bellenden Livy I. xii. (S.T.S.) I. 69 Gif þai suld pas as vagaboundis and vncertane pepill throw þare howsis. 1576 Fleming Panopl. Epist. 354 The dogge..defend[s] our houses from theeues, vagaboundes, lewde fellowes. 1594 R. Ashley tr. Loys le Roy 60 b, Some of them hauing bin vagabounds and beggers. 1635 Reg. Privy Counc. Scotl. Ser. II. VI. 5 Haveing corrupted all the equipage of the ship, who are bot vagabounds. 1706 Stevens Span. Dict., Vagamundear, to play the vagabound, to strole about.

γ. 1526 Tindale Acts xvii. 5 The iewes..toke vnto them evyll men wich were vagabondes and gadered a company. 1575 in Maitland Club Misc. I. 120 All wagabondis and idill personis that hes nocht quhairupoun to sustene thame selfis. 1577 Holinshed Descr. Brit. III. v. 106 b, The third [sort] consisteth of thriftlesse poore, as..the vagabond that will abide no wheres, but runneth vp and downe from place to place (as it were seeking woorke and finding none). 1605 London Prodigal v. i, For shame, betake you to some honest Trade And liue not thus so like a Vagabond. a 1629 Hinde J. Bruen xxx. (1641) 94 Such assemblies are..a very randavous of all rogues, and vagabonds. 1684 Burnet tr. More's Utopia 22 If they do this, they are put in Prison as idle Vagabonds. 1736 Gentl. Mag. VI. 718/1 A Bill..for the more effectual punishing Rogues and Vagabonds. 1796 H. Hunter tr. St.-Pierre's Stud. Nat. (1799) I. 376 His relations, dishonoured in the public estimation, abandon their home, and become vagabonds. 1833 Ht. Martineau Three Ages III. 95 Issuing forth as a vagabond to spread the infection of idleness and vice. 1849 James Woodman xviii, We have more vagabonds in the forest than I like. 1873 'Ouida' Pascarèl II. III. i. 8 He was a stroller and a vagabond, so far as social status went, an idle rogue.

transf. 1602 2nd Pt. Return Parnass. III. iv. 1352 You grandsyre Phœbus with your louely eye, The firmaments eternall vagabond.

Comb. 1579–80 North Plutarch (1657) 233 They were loose people and abjects..who vagabondlike wandred up and down the Countrey. 1816 Tuckey Narr. Exped. R. Zaire i. (1818) 16 This corps being composed of the most ragged, bare-legged, sans-culotte vagabond-looking wretches.

δ. 1567 Harman (title), A Caueat..for Commen Cursetors Vulgarely called Vagabones. 1602 Narcissus (1893) 124 Wee ar noe vagabones, wee ar noe arrant Rogues that doe runne with plaies about the country. [1842 (see 2 b).] 1901 Trotter Gail. Gossip 188 Rogues an vagabons.

b. A nomad. rare.

1756 Nugent Montesquieu XX. ii. (1758) II. 3 Hospitality ..is found in the most admirable perfection among nations of vagabonds. 1837 W. Irving Capt. Bonneville III. 108 They claimed..to be thorough mountaineers, and first-rate hunters—the common boast of these vagabonds of the wilderness.

c. Vagabond's discoloration, disease, skin (see quots.).

1876 Greenhow in Trans. Clinical Soc. IX. 46 These cases..have received the special name of 'Vogt's Vagabonden-Krankheit', which I have rendered into English as 'Vagabond's Discoloration'; because this discoloration of skin..is..brought on by long-continued exposure, dirty habits and the irritation of vermin. 1890 F. Taylor Man. Pract. Med. (1891) 803 The disease has then been called prurigo senilis, and also vagabond's disease. 1899 Allbutt's Syst. Med. VIII. 701 The vagabond's disease, or Morbus errorum of Greenhow. Ibid. 866 Excoriations, wheals and pustules are produced by scratching which, if long continued, may produce a brown, leather-like condition—the so-called vagabond's skin seen in tramps.

2. A disreputable or worthless person; an idle, good-for-nothing fellow; a rascal or rogue (sometimes without serious implication of bad qualities).

1686 tr. Chardin's Trav. Persia 178, I spoke in the mildest Terms imaginable: which nothing mov'd this Vagabond. 1848 Dickens Dombey vi, No young vagabond could be brought to bear its contemplation for a moment. 1887 Hall Caine Son of Hagar III. iii, I couldn't be such a vagabond of a husband. 1890 'R. Boldrewood' Col. Reformer (1891) 316 The dishonest, scheming vagabonds!

b. Used as a term of reproof or abuse.

1842 Lover Handy Andy x, Mind, on your peril, you old vagabone, don't let them fight that badger without me. 1844 Dickens Mart. Chuz. iv, You were eaves-dropping at that door, you vagabond! 1884 Pae Eustace 66 'What are you lying there for, you lazy vagabond?' roared Randolph.

Vagabond (væ·găbǫnd), v. Also 7 vagabound, -bund. [f. Vagabond sb. Cf. F. vagabonder (1526).] intr. To roam or wander (about) as or like a vagabond or vagrant; to vagabondize. Also with it.

a 1586 Sidney Arcadia IV. (1598) 414 In this sort vagabonding in those vntroden places, they were guided [etc.]. 1611 Cotgr. s.v. Rodé, That hath roamed, wandered, vagabonded it all the countrey ouer. c 1614 Sir W. Mure Dido & Æneas III. 27 [Dido] vagabounding in ane heavy cace Through fields vnknowne, accompanyed by none. 1748 Richardson Clarissa (1811) VI. 357 Vagabonding about from inn to inn. 1861 Reade Cloister & H. lvi, Why is he not in my counting house at Amsterdam, instead of vagabonding it out yonder? 1901 Westm. Gaz. 18 Oct. 2/1 The said son went vagabonding about the world.

Hence **Va·gabonding** vbl. sb.

a 1628 F. Grevil Cælica xii, Cupid, thou naughtie Boy, when thou wert loathed, Naked and blind, for Vagabunding noted.

Vagabondage (væ·găbǫndēdʒ). [f. Vagabond sb. + -age, or a. F. vagabondage (1798).]

1. The state, condition, or character of a vagabond; life or conduct characteristic of or resembling that of a vagabond; idle or unconventional wandering or travelling; vagabondism.

1813 [implied in Vagabondager: see below]. 1823 New Monthly Mag. VIII. 336 That love of..bird's-nesting and vagabondage, which..is inherent in all boys. 1858 Times 4 Nov. 6/2 [The Ionians] have been elevated from the lowest grade of Mediterranean vagabondage. 1871 Holme Lee Miss Barrington I. vii. 102 Spring arrived and he grew restless again and betook himself to vagabondage and the streets.

fig. 1863 Lecky in Mem. (1909) II. 34, I have been indulging in an enormous amount of literary vagabondage. 1871 Miss Braddon Lovels of Arden xxii. 171 Her random sketches—some of them mere vagabondage of the pencil, jotted down half unconsciously.

2. Vagabonds collectively; persons of a vagabond class or order.

1855 [J. D. Burn] Autobiogr. Beggar Boy (1859) 137 One of the immediate consequences of their conduct would be, to let loose the whole vagabondage of the country. 1903 Times 14 Feb. 11/5 They are already bringing a good deal of rural vagabondage to London.

Hence **Vagabo·ndager,** one who practises vagabondage.

1813 Sir R. Wilson Priv. Diary (1862) II. 52 At midnight I entered my carriage, and found myself in solitude with a cheerless imagination...Thus vagabondagers pay for their temporary pleasures.

† **Vagabo·ndial,** a. Obs.⁻¹ In 7 -bundiall. [f. as prec. + -ial.] = next.

1615 J. H. Worlds Folly C b, The recollection of the vagabundiall Iewes into the sheepe-fold of Iesus Christ.

Vagabo·ndical, a. rare. Also 6–7 vagabund-. [f. as prec. + -ical.] Roaming, wandering; vagabondish.

1576 Fleming tr. Caius' Dogs (1880) 35 Dogges..which are taught and exercised to daunce in measure,..and sundry such properties, which they learne of theyr vagabundicall masters. 1658 Cokaine Obst. Lady II. i, He..vaticinated future Occurents by the mysterious influences of the sublime Stars, and vagabundical Planets.

a 1864 G. Daniel Merrie Eng. xiv, Joe Haynes..was the hero of a variety of vagabondical adventures.

Vagabonding (væ·găbǫndiŋ), ppl. a. [f. Vagabond v.]

1. That roams or wanders as, or in the manner of, a vagabond. Also transf. and fig.

a 1586 Sidney Songs in Astr. & Stella v. xii. (Grosart) I. 86, I now then staine thy white with vagabonding shame. 1603 Florio Montaigne III. xiii. 610 Even vagabonding roagues..have their magnificences and voluptuousnesse. 1614 Drumm. of Hawth. Wks. (1913) I. 13, I..On euery part my vagabounding Sight Did cast. 1632 Lithgow Trav. III. 111 A vagabonding Guest, Transported here and there. Ibid. 118 Concerning vagabonding Greekes, and their counterfeit Testimonials. 1881 Blackw. Mag. May 571 The sword..went fairly straight along its vagabonding road.

2. Characterized by roaming or wandering; vagabondish.

Not clearly distinct from the vbl. sb. used attrib.

a 1586 Sidney Arcadia (1622) 472 These iewels certainely with their disguising sleights, they haue pilfred in their vagabounding race. 1824 New Monthly Mag. X. 283 Some would spend our prime's best age In vagabonding pilgrimage. 1904 A. B. Paterson Poems 92 And through our blood there runs The vagabonding love of change.

† **Vagabo·ndious,** a. Obs.⁻¹ [f. Vagabond sb.] Vagabond, vagrant.

1661 in MSS. Ho. Lords (Rep. Hist. MSS. Comm.) VII. 153 [The whole trade of cardmaking and wire drawing was nearly spoiled by] vagabondious persons.

Vagabondish (væ·găbǫndiʃ), a. [f. as prec.]

1. Pertaining or appropriate to, characteristic of, a vagabond or vagabonds.

1826 J. Scott Vis. Paris (ed. 5) 97 All this has a shew of business, though of a light vagabondish kind. 1868 Miss Braddon Birds of Prey II. i, There was a vagabondish kind of foppery in his costume. 1884 Harper's Mag. May 871 The vagabondish spirit engendered by their long..journey.

2. Of the nature of a vagabond; somewhat like a vagabond in conduct or life.

1854 Greenwood Haps & Mishaps 105 By far the larger number of those who apply to the traveller for charity are vagabondish in their instincts and indolent in their habits. 1881 Times 5 July 9 This vain and vagabondish mendicant.

Vagabondism (væ·găbǫndiz'm). [f. as prec.]

1. = Vagabondage 1.

1822 Blackw. Mag. II. 139 Who, after forty years of indigence and vagabondism, is admitted into the first societies. 1859 Hist. Cant in Slang Dict. p. ix, The Gypsies were not long in the country before they found native imitators. Vagabondism is peculiarly catching. 1888 Charity Organis. Rev. April 145 Vagabondism as a licit mode of life.

b. A rascally or knavish act. rare.

1840 Carlyle Heroes v. (1904) 188 All errors and perversities of his, even those stealings of ribbons, aimless confused miseries and vagabondisms.

2. = Vagabondage 2. rare⁻¹.

1872 Brewer Eng. Studies (1881) IV. 196 All the vagabondism of the kingdom had scented the fray.

Vagabondize (væ·găbǫndaiz), v. [f. as prec. + -ize.] intr. To live, wander, or go about as, or in the manner of, a vagabond; to roam or travel in a free, idle, unconstrained, or unconventional manner; to play the vagabond.

a. With indefinite it.

1611 Cotgr., Roder, to roame, wander, vagabondize it. 1776 Ann. Reg., Charact. 35/2 After thus vagabondizing it for some time, he was discovered by the consul. 1861 Reade Cloister & H. iiii, How much earlier he would have found her by staying quietly at Tergou, than by vagabondizing it all over Holland.

b. In ordinary use. Freq. with advs. and preps.

1794 Mrs. A. M. Bennett Ellen III. 39 No modest woman would go vagabondizing about the country. 1795 tr. Mercier's Fragm. Pol. & Hist. II. 223 The streets would be filled with wretches, vagabondizing round the palaces of sloth. 1832 Westm. Rev. July 38 Peoples among whom his fortunes cast him while vagabondizing in the remotest corners of the globe. 1868 Holme Lee B. Godfrey xxvi, That..scapegrace..had vagabondised all over Europe as a newspaper correspondent. 1894 D. C. Murray Making of Novelist 87, I..acquired a taste for vagabondising about among the poor.

fig. 1864 Miss Braddon Doctor's Wife iii, The surgeon's thoughts went vagabondizing away from the little coffee-room. 1868 — Birds of Prey v. iii, My thoughts went vagabondising off to Charlotte.

Hence **Va·gabondizer.**

1860 All Year Round No. 42. 362 The itinerant traveller and poetical or artistic vagabondizer.

Vagabondizing (væ·găbǫndaiziŋ), vbl. sb. [f. prec. + -ing ¹.] The action of the verb; idle or unconventional wandering; an occasion of this.

1829 Sir A. W. Calcott Lett. to Chantrey 18 Aug., A note we have had from the Phillips to join you in a vagabondizing to Hampstead. 1849 W. Irving Goldsmith xviii. 203 The Continental tour..had, with poor Goldsmith, been little better than a course of literary vagabondizing. 1853 Dickens Bleak Ho. xxi, Then, vagabondising came natural to you, from the beginning?

Va·gabondizing, ppl. a. [-ing ².]

1. That vagabondizes; vagabond.

1830 Fraser's Mag. II. 200 We have a pretty considerable ..idea of how those vagabondising ragamuffins spend the hours of the day. 1855 Household Wds. XII. 168 Her wicked, vagabondising, brandy-drinking..husband.

2. Characterized by, devoted or inclined to, wandering or vagabondage.

1841 Fraser's Mag. XXIII. 349 [They] would prefer labour to a vagabondising life. 1859 Sala Tw. round Clock (1861) 175 They..fade away with the dawn..and are not beheld any more till vagabondising time begins again. 1883 Miss C. F. Woolson Anne 377 July..already felt a strong affection in his capacious vagabondizing heart for the stranger.

Va·gabondry. Now rare or Obs. [f. Vagabond sb. + -ry.] = Vagabondage 1.

1547 Act 1 Edw. VI, c. 3 Preamble, Idlenes and Vagabundrye is the mother and roote of all theftes. 1611 Cotgr., Marandise, beggerie, roguerie, idle knauerie, base vagabondrie. 1681 W. Robertson Phraseol. Gen. (1693) 1257 A base vagabondry, mendicimonium. 1869 W. Cory Lett. & Jrnls. (1897) 257 We went through Dropmore with unusual vagabondry.

† **Vagabuncy,** later f. Vacabuncy. Obs.

-1549 Coverdale, etc. Erasm. Par. Thess. Ded., To banysh ..ryot, idlenes, ruffianynge vagabuncie [etc.].

† **Vagabundulo.** nonce-word. [f. vagabund Vagabond sb.] ? A roguish trick.

1631 Shirley School of Complement v. iii, Gorgon has had his deuices and vagabunduloes as well as the best on yee.

Vagal (vē¹·găl), a. Anat. and Path. [f. Vag-us + -al.] a. Vagal nerve, the vagus or pneumogastric nerve. b. Of, pertaining to, or affecting this.

1854 Orr's Circ. Sci., Org. Nat. I. 205 The exoccipitals.. are perforated to give exit to the vagal and hypoglossal nerves. 1885 McWilliam in Jrnl. Physiol. VI. 223 The effects of vagal stimulation were frequently investigated. 1899 Allbutt's Syst. Med. VI. 816 The upper vagal roots are more concerned in inspiration than the lower ones.

† **Va·gancy.** Obs. rare. [f. Vagant a.: see -ancy.] A wandering or strolling. Also fig.

1641 Milton Ch. Govt. I. i, That our happinesse may orbe it selfe into a thousand vagancies of glory and delight. 1641 Brome Joviall Crew v, Springlove. My humble suit is that you will be pleas'd To let me walk upon my known occasions this Sommer. Lawyer. Fie! Canst not yet leave off those Vagancies?

† **Va·gant,** a. (and pres. pple.). Obs. Forms: 4–5 vagaunt, 5–6 -aunte, 5–6, 8 vagant, 5 -ante. [a. OF. vagant, vagaunt, or L. vagant-, vagans, pres. pple. of vagārī to wander.]

1. Wandering, roaming, roving; travelling or moving from place to place; having no settled home or abiding-place. Cf. Vagrant a. 3.

1382 Wyclif Gen. iv. 12 Vagaunt and fer fugitif thow shalt be vpon the erthe alle the daies of thi lijf. 1432–50 tr. Higden (Rolls) II. 135 In the tyme of Hinguar and Hubba, Ardulphus the bischop was vagante longe with þe body of Seynte Cuthberte. 1480 Caxton Ovid's Met. XIV. x, For al we haue be disparblid & longe haue be vagant on the see. 1483 — Gold. Leg. 407 b/1 Thus Josaphat was two yere vagaunte & erryd in deserte. 1517 Watson Shyppe of Fooles A ij, I am the fyrste in the shyppe vagaunte with the other fooles. 1578 Sc. Poems 16th C. (1801) II. 170 Thocht vagant freirs faine wald lie, The trueth will furth.

2. Devious, erratic. rare.

1382 Wyclif Prov. v. 6 Bi the path of lif thei gon not: vagaunt ben the goingus of hir, and vnserchable. 1708 Brit. Apollo No. 30. 1/1 By so Vagant a Proceedure, it is a Chance but he must hear some points of Duty..repeated.

3. Of thoughts: Wandering.

c 1450 Myrr. our Ladye 42 Yt can not sturre vp yt selfe from wandryng and vagant thoughtes that yt is accustomyd in. Ibid. 165 Also the harte oughte fulle besyly to be kepte from all vagaunte thoughtes.

Vagara(u)nt, -ent, obs. forms of Vagrant.

Vagare, obs. form of Vagary.

Vaga·rian. rare⁻⁰. [f. as next + -an.] One given to vagaries or whims.

1891 in Cent. Dict.

Vagarious (văgē³·riəs), a. [f. Vagary sb.]

† 1. Variable, inconstant, changing. Obs.⁻¹

1798 R. P. Tour in Wales (MS.) 36 Thus life's vagarious tenure passes on! And thus, the scenic vision glows with change!

2. Marked or characterized by, full of, subject to, vagaries; erratic.

1827 Examiner 70/1 The Travels of Wilhelm Meister, wild, vagarious, and disconnected as it is. a 1871 De Morgan Budget Parad. (1872) 153 Mr. Wirgman's mind was somewhat attuned to psychology; but he was cracky and vagarious. 1897 Atlantic Monthly LXXIX. 134 The work..is free from the vagarious theorizing.

3. Wandering, roaming, roving.

1882 Harper's Mag. April 661 Sharp interruption from the vagarious borned enemy. 1888 Sat. Rev. 22 Sept. 363/2 The history of the vagarious canary, Kiki.

Hence **Vaga·riously** adv.

1892 Dispatch (Columbus) 17 Nov., An idly planned and vagariously disposed though always picturesque college retreat.

Vaga·rish, a. Now rare or Obs. [f. as prec.]

1. Of the eyes: Disposed to wander; wandering.

1801 Wolcot (P. Pindar) Tears & Smiles Wks. 1812 V. 40 His eyes were oft vagarish. 1823 New Monthly Mag. VII. 230 My people's eyes were all vagarish While striving your hard phrases to conjecture.

2. Somewhat vagarious or whimsical.

1819 Keats in Ld. Houghton Life (1848) II. 26 But you knowing my unsteady and vagarish disposition will [etc.].

Vaga·risome, a. [f. as prec. + -some.] Vagarious, capricious.

1883 Bazaar 5 Sept. 259 Early autumn clothing is slightly vagarisome, and steady observation is necessary in order to determine what is 'worn' from what is 'put on'.

Vaga·rist. rare. [f. as prec. + -ist.] One who is subject to vagaries; a vagarious person.

1888 The Voice (N.Y.) 24 May, The Prohibition party are now free from..suspicion of being vagarists.

Vagarity (văgē³·rĭti). rare⁻¹. [f. as prec. + -ity.] Capricious irregularity or variability.

1886 N. & Q. 7th Ser. II. 89/1 Instances of vagarity are noticeable with each Prince of Wales, many of whom seem to have ignored..the title [of Duke of Cornwall].

Vagary (văgē³·ri), sb. Also 6–7 vagare, 6 -arie. [prob. ad. L. vagārī (It. vagare) to wander. Cf. Fegary.]

† 1. A wandering or devious journey or tour; a roaming about or abroad; an excursion, ramble, stroll. Obs.

Freq. in the 17th c., chiefly in verbal phrases as to fetch, make, or take a vagary.

1577 Stanyhurst Descr. Irel. in Holinshed (1808) VI. 24 The Irish enimie spieing that the citizens were accustomed to fetch such od vagaries,..they..laid in sundrie places for their comming. 1582 — Æneis II. (Arb.) 44 Thee gates vncloased they skud with a liuely vagare. 1600 Pory tr. Leo's Africa I. 19 These haue often vagaries ouer the deserts vnto the prouince of Tedgear. c 1613 Sec. Cond. People Anglesey (1860) 40 To entice his neighbours wifes..to leave their husbands..and to follow him by turns, into other countreys, and after a long vagare, to return again. 1657 S. Purchas Pol. Flying Ins. I. v. 12 A hot Sun-shine..will quickly prompt them out of their Hives to take a short vagary. 1677 Gilpin Demonol. (1867) 320 The like did Dinah, when she made a needless vagary to see the daughters of the land. 1826 W. E. Andrews Crit. Rev. Fox's Bk. Mart. II. 413 Whether..it is likely that such a person should be permitted to make a walking vagary throughout all London.

transf. and fig. c 1630 Risdon Surv. Devon § 225 (1810) 237 Torridge, after a long vagary, making many meanders, emptieth itself in the..sea. 1655 Gurnall Chr. in Arm. XVI. (1665) 359 Our hearts are soon gone away from the duty in hand, and taken a vagary to the furthest part of the world. 1759 Sterne Tr. Shandy I. xxii, My aunt Dinah and the coachman..led us a vagary some millions of miles into the very heart of the planetary system.

† b. To play his vagary, of a horse, to leave or refuse to follow the proper or desired course. Obs.⁻¹

1580 Blundevil Art of Riding I. 11 If he will then play his vagarie, beate him forthwith with your wand.

† 2. A wandering in speech or writing; a rambling from the subject under consideration; a digression or divagation. Obs. (passing into sense 5).

1579 G. Harvey Letter-bk. (Camden) 67 Countenauncinge oute the matter either with tunge or penne withoute the same discoursinge vagaries. 1596 R. H. tr. Lavaterus' Ghostes & Sp. To Rdr. a ij, His histories seeme not idle tales, or impertinent vagaries, but very truthes. 1651 Baxter Inf. Bapt. Apol. 15 When ever he was at a loss, that the people might not perceive it, he presently would fall into a wordy vagary. 1681 — Answ. Dodwell iv. 54 You must talk at other rates than you have done in your tedious fallacious Vagaries. 1762 in Ellis Orig. Lett. Ser. II. IV. 451 Mr. Beckford..had his vagaries as usual, and gave the House a little prelude of what they were to expect.

3. A departure or straying from the ordered, regular, or usual course of conduct, decorum, or propriety; a frolic or prank, esp. one of a freakish nature. Now rare or Obs. (passing into sense 4).

1588 Babington Prof. Exp. Lord's Pr. (1596) 274 A short vagare..layde a grinding griefe vpon his conscience during life. 1593 B. Barnes Parth. & Parth. vi, I will be His bail for this offence; and if he make Another such vagary, take of me A pawn. 1609 W. M. Man in Moon (1849) 21 Hee that might doe well and would not, when hee wanteth shal be unpittied..; then shall you hear of your olde vagaries. 1667 Milton P. L. VI. 614 Strait they chang'd thir minds, Flew off, and into strange vagaries fell, As they would dance. 1693 Locke Educ. § 96 Would your Son engage in some Frolic, or take a Vagary, were it not..better he should do it with, than without your Knowledge? 1714 Gay What d'ye call it I. iv, Ye Goblins and Fairys, With Frisks and Vagarys. 1785 Grose Dict. Vulgar T., Vagaries, frolicks, wild rambles. a 1845 Barham Ingol. Leg. Ser. III. House-Warming, That should she incline to play such a vagary..She could turn a knight into a wagon of hay. 1862 C. Stretton Chequered Life II. 100, I could not sleep: I was too much amused at the vagaries of my new acquaintances [sc. rats], and kept watching them.

fig. 1794 Mrs. Radcliffe Myst. Udolpho i, Let us hear what vagaries fancy has been playing in your mind.

† b. Without article: Frolic, gambolling. Obs.

1791 Wolcot (P. Pindar) Rights of Kings Wks. 1812 II. 401 Here—there, Up, down, she dances it; now far, now near, In mad and riotous vagary.

4. A capricious, fantastic, or eccentric action or piece of conduct.

1629 Massinger Picture v. iii, An old bachelor, as I am, ..is not troubled With these fine vagaries. 1711 Steele Spect. No. 260 ¶ 1 The Vagaries of a Child are not more ridiculous than the Circumstances which are heaped up in my Memory. 1753 Richardson Grandison (1781) IV. xxi. 162 She..., not having so great a fortune to support vagaries, would have shone...in Italy. 1831 Carlyle Sart. Res. III. vi, A noble natural Courtesy shines through him, beautifying his vagaries. 1861 Tulloch Eng. Purit. iv. 409 Ignorance and vanity once unbridled knew no limit to the vagaries ..into which they ran. 1888 Bryce Amer. Commw. III. lxxxvi. 150 The sentiment of the nation at large..acts but slowly in restraining the vagaries..of one particular State.

b. A caprice or trick of fortune, fancy, the brain, a malady, etc.

1717 Dennis Remarks Pope's Homer Pref. A, A vagary of fortune who is sometimes pleased to be frolicsome. 1840 Hood Up Rhine 27 The vagaries of the perspective, originating in such an arrangement, were rather amusing. 1862 Burton Bk. Hunter (1863) 17, I must yet notice another and a peculiar vagary of his malady. 1871 Napheys Prev. & Cure Dis. I. iv. 123 To follow the vagaries of fashion.

5. An erratic play of fancy; a fantastic, eccentric, or extravagant idea or notion. (Cf. 2.)

1753 Richardson Grandison (1781) VI. xxxii. 218 These ideal vagaries, which, for the time, realize pain or pleasure to us. 1771 Gray in Corr. w. Nicholls (1843) 137 But by all means curb these vagaries and wandering imaginations. a 1806 H. K. White To Contemplation Rem. (1825) 384, I alone, A wayward youth, misled by Fancy's vagaries, Remain'd unsettled. 1856 Dove Logic Chr. Faith I. § 2. 77 Every system that would land in such a conclusion is a mere logical vagary. 1882 Farrar Early Chr. II. 270 note, But it is worse than useless to record the vagaries of Apocalyptic interpretation.

† **Vaga·ry,** v. Obs. [Cf. prec.] intr. To wander or roam. Also transf.

1598 Florio, Vagare,..to vagarie, or range, to straie abroade. 1599 Nashe Lenten Stuffe Wks. (Grosart) V. 224 The marishes and lower grounds lying vpon the three riuers that vagary vp to her. 1611 Cotgr., Vancrer, to raunge, roame, vagarie, wander, idle it vp and downe. 1656 S. H. Gold. Law 60 Though he might decline Law, yet he vagari'd not therefrom. 1681 W. Robertson Phraseol. Gen. (1693) 1257 To vagary, vagari, palari.

† **Vaga·tion.** Obs. Also 4 vagacyone, 5–6 -cion, 6 -cyon, -tione. [ad. L. vagātiōn-, vagātio, n. of action f. vagārī to wander. Cf. OF. vagation (Godef.), Pg. vagação.] The action of wandering, straying, or departing from the proper or regular course; an instance or occasion of this; a wandering, rambling, roaming; an aberration. In lit. and fig. use.

c 1340 Hampole Prose Tr. (1866) 14 Whene þe mynde es stablede sadely with-owtten changynge and vagacyone in Godd. c 1450 Myrr. our Ladye 42 For this vagacion is caused of dulnes, and of heuynes of harte. 1502 Atkynson tr. De Imitatione III. xxvii. 219 Chase fro myn hert all maner darkenes, stablysshe the great vagacions of my mynde that I suffre. 1549 Compl. Scot. xiii. 111 Ane of his familiar frendis inquyrit hym of the cause of his inconstant vagatione. 1597 Harvey Trimming T. Nashe Wks. (Grosart) III. 53 Neuerthelesse can I accuse you of lazines; for all this time of your vagation, with you I thinke the Signe hath been in Pisces. 1652 Gaule Magastrom. 291 Socrates, offended at the bold and blind vagations of men, in their disputations about the measures of the sunne. 1713 Derham Phys.-Theol. IV. ii. 100 By this so curious and exact a Libration, unseemly Contortions and Vagations of the Eye are prevented. 1714 — Astro-Theol. IV. v. (1769) 118 But I have myself observed a greater vagation in the third satellite.

† **Vage,** a. Obs. rare⁻¹. [app. ad. It. vago. Cf. Vagisness.] Fine, handsome.

1604 T. Wright Passions v. § 4. 198 The finer gold, the richer stones,..the more vage and beautifull iewell.

Vage, southern dial. var. Fage v.; obs. f. Vague sb. and v.; obs. or dial. f. Voyage; obs. Sc. f. Wage v., Wedge sb. **Vageit,** obs. Sc. f. Waged ppl. a. **Vageowr,** obs. Sc. f. Wager (soldier). **Vager,** obs. Sc. f. Vaguer (wanderer), Wager (soldier). **Vagging,** dial. var. Fagging vbl. sb.

Vagi- (vē¹·dʒi), comb. form of L. vagus Vague a., occurring in a few botanical terms, as va·giform, vaginervose adjs. (see quots.).

1859 Mayne Expos. Lex., Vagiformis,..applied by de Candolle to leaves of cellular plants when their false nervures are dispersed without order or regularity; vagiform. 1866 Treas. Bot. 1199 Vaginervose, having the veins arranged without any order.

† **Va·gient,** a. Obs. [ad. L. vāgient-em, pres. pple. of vāgire to cry, squall.] Of infants, infancy, etc.: Crying, squalling, wailing.

1628 Gaule Pract. Theo. (1629) 417 There shall be nor vagient Youngling, nor decrepit Ageling. 1642 H. More Song of Soul II. iv. III. xlii, But for the cradle of the Cretian Jove, And guardians of his vagient Infancie, What sober man but sagely will reprove? 1659 — Immort. Soul (1662) 142 The vagient cries of the Infant Jupiter amidst the..dancings of the Cretick Corybantes.

‖ **Vagina** (vădʒai·nă). Pl. **vaginæ** (-ai·nī), **vaginas.** [L. vāgina sheath, scabbard. Cf. F. vagin (1762), † vagina, Pg. vagina.]

1. Anat. and Med. The membranous canal leading from the vulva to the uterus in women and female mammals.

1682 Gibson Anat. 20 It has passages..for the neck of the Bladder, and in Women for the vagina of the Womb. 1754–64 Smellie Midwifery I. 95 The upper end of the vagina is joined to the circumference of the lips of the os uteri. 1805 Med. Jrnl. XIV. 21 Neither could we discover by the touch any communication between the rectum and vagina. 1847 Youatt Horse viii. 174 The true polypus..is usually found in the nostrils, the pharynx, the uterus, or the vagina. 1896 tr. Boas' Text-bk. Zool. 490 In the Marsupials..the two vaginæ open separately on the floor of the urinogenital sinus.

b. A canal or organ having similar form or function in other animals; a genital passage.

1826 Kirby & Sp. Entomol. IV. 146 This vessel, which consists of a double tunic, in the cabbage-butterfly terminates the vagina. 1871 T. R. Jones Anim. Kingd. (ed. 4) 358 Female generative organs of the Queen Bee:..e, vagina, or common excretory duct.

2. A part or formation serving as or suggestive of a sheath; a sheath-like covering, organ, or part; a theca.

1713 Derham Phys.-Theol. VIII. iv. (1727) 363 note, The Female hath vaginæ prettily furrow'd; the Male smooth. Ibid. 365 Many of them provided with the finest Articulations, and Foldings, for the Wings to be withdrawn, and neatly laid up in their Vaginæ, and Cases. 1771 Encycl. Brit. I. 191/1 The fibres [of the muscles] are..distinguished by membranous, cellular, or adipose septa, as by so many particular vaginæ. 1826 Kirby & Sp. Entomol. III. 361 Vagina (the Vagina), the jointed sheath of the Promuscis, representing the Labium in a perfect mouth.

b. Bot. = Sheath sb.¹ 2 b.

1720 P. Blair Bot. Ess. i. 28 Sometimes they are covered with a Vagina or Sheath at the top. 1731 P. Miller Gard. Dict. s.v. Narcissus, The Empalement, which commonly rises out of a membranous Vagina. 1832 Lindley Introd. Bot. I. ii. 95 Occasionally the petiole embraces the branch from which it springs, and in such cases is said to be sheathing; and is even called a sheath or vagina, as in grasses. 1857 Henfrey Bot. § 75 The sheathing portion..or vagina.

c. Sculpture. The lower part of a terminus, out of which the bust or figure appears to rise. (So F. gaine.) rare⁻⁰.

1728 Chambers Cycl. s.v., The Vagina is that long Part between the Base and the Capital; and is found in divers Manners, and with divers Ornaments.

Hence **Vagi·na-less** a.

1897 Allbutt's Syst. Med. II. 1061, I have recently pointed out..the process by which the embryo dracunculi quit the body of the vaginaless parent worm.

Vaginal (vădʒai·năl, væ·dʒinăl), a. and sb. [f. prec. + -al. Cf. F. vaginal (1762), Pg. vaginal.]

A. adj. 1. Anat. and Med. Of the nature of, having the form or function of, a sheath; serving as a sheath. Vaginal process, a process or apophysis of the lower portion of the temporal bone, partially enclosing the styloid process.

1726 Monro Anatomy 164 The Cavity between the Zygomatic, Auditory and vaginal Process. 1767 Phil. Trans. LVII. 295 The vaginal coat of the testicle. 1831 R. Knox Cloquet's Anat. 55 A bony lamina, called the vaginal process..., which forms the posterior limit of the glenoid cavity. 1873 Mivart Elem. Anat. 80 A sharp ridge runs inwards and forwards from the root of the styloid process. This ridge is termed the vaginal process. 1899 Syd. Soc. Lex. s.v., Vaginal coat of the eye, capsule of Tenon. Ibid., Vaginal tunic.

b. Bot. = Vaginant a.

1857 Henfrey Bot. § 75 The vaginal petiolar region is more or less distinctly evident in many Monocotyledonous leaves.

2. Of, pertaining to, or affecting the vagina.

1825 Good Study Med. (ed. 2) V. 156 marg., The vaginal polypus sometimes dispersed by stimulants and astringents. 1840 E. Wilson Anat. Vade M. (1842) 314 The Uterine and Vaginal arteries of the female are derived from the internal iliac, or Ischiatic arteries. 1855 Ramsbotham Obstet. Med. & Surg. 36 The vaginal canal becomes much contracted in advanced life. 1878 T. Bryant Pract. Surg. I. 688 Vaginal and labial hernia may be mistaken for the mucous cysts of those parts.

b. Of instruments: Used in dealing with, or operating on, the vagina.

1875 Knight Dict. Mech. 2687/2 Vaginal speculum. Ibid., Vaginal syringe. 1895 Arnold & Sons' Surg. Instr. Catal. 411 Vaginal and uterine instruments.

B. sb. A vaginal artery or muscle.

1872 F. G. Thomas Dis. Women (ed. 3) 52 Sim's instrument, on the other hand, elevates the posterior vaginal.

Vaginalitis (vædʒinălai·tis). Path. [f. prec. + -itis.] Inflammation of the vaginal coat or tunic of the testicles.

1861 Bumstead Ven. Dis. (1879) 134 Vaginalitis, although a very frequent, is not a constant symptom, and is always consecutive to the inflammation of the epididymis.

Vaginant, a. Bot. [ad. mod.L. vāginant-, vāginans, f. vāgina sheath. So F. vaginant.] = Sheathing ppl. a. b.

1760 J. Lee Introd. Bot. III. vii. (1765) 191 Vaginant, forming a Vagina or Sheath; when the Base of the Leaf forms a cylindric Tube that invests the Branch. 1851 G. F. Richardson Geol. vii. 203 Sessile leaves are sometimes vaginant, that is, sheathing, as in grasses.

Vaginate, a. rare. [ad. mod.L. vāgināt-us, f. as prec.: cf. next and Vaginated ppl. a.] Enclosed in a sheath or vagina; invaginate.

1849 Craig, Vaginate, Vaginated, in Botany, sheathed, invested by the tubular base of the leaf, as a stem. 1856 W. Clark Van der Hoeven's Zool. I. 190 Penis vaginate simple, with a small posterior accessory part. Ibid. 300 Mouth..composed of a rostellum, retractile, vaginate at the base. 1859 Mayne Expos. Lex. 1320 Vaginatus, cased, sheathed, vaginate.

† **Vaginate,** v. Obs.⁻⁰ [f. L. vāgina: cf. prec.] To sheathe (Blount Glossogr. 1656).

Phillips (1658) substitutes 'Vagination, a sheathing'.

† **Vaginated,** ppl. a. Obs. rare. [f. as prec. + -ed ¹.] = Vaginate a.

1698 Phil. Trans. XX. 402 Those above are wholly vaginated (or sheathed) and come trifoliate at every Joynt. 1776 Evelyn's Silva viii. 445 The rest of the vaginated stem touches no other part of the whole cavity. 1849 [see Vaginate a.].

Va·gine. Obs.⁻⁰ [ad. L. vāgina Vagina.] A scabbard (Cockeram, 1623).

Vagini-, comb. f. of L. vāgina sheath (see Vagino-) in a few scientific terms, as vaginiform adj.; vaginiglutæus, a muscle acting upon the sheath of the thigh; also vaginigluteal adj.; † vaginipennous a., of beetles, having the wings covered with a sheath; coleopterous.

A few other instances of scientific or technical usage are given in some recent Dicts., as vaginicoline, vaginicolous, vaginiferous, vaginipennate adjs.

1646 Sir T. Browne Pseud. Ep. III. xv. (1686) 141 All vaginipennous or sheath-winged insects, as Beetles and Dorrs. 1656 Blount Glossogr., Vaginipennous, pertaining to such flies, which have their wings cloased as it were in sheaths or cases, as the Beetle hath. Dr. Br[owne]. 1859 Mayne Expos. Lex. 1320 Vaginiformis,..vaginiform.

‖ **Vaginismus** (vædʒini·zmŏs). Path. [mod. L. (Sims), f. vāgina.] Painful spasmodic contraction of the vagina; vulvismus.

1866 J. M. Sims Uterine Surg. 326 By the term vaginismus I mean an excessive hyperæsthesia of the hymen and vulvar outlet. 1879 St. George's Hosp. Rep. IX. 443 The patient then left for two months, but was readmitted as the vaginismus still persisted.

Vaginitis (vædʒinai·tis). Path. [f. as prec. + -itis. Cf. F. vaginite.] Inflammation of the vagina.

1846 G. E. Day tr. Simon's Anim. Chem. II. 96 He found other forms of infusoria in the pus from syphilitic vaginitis. 1861 Bumstead Ven. Dis. (1879) 137 Vaginitis is more common than any other form of gonorrhœa in women. 1879 St. George's Hosp. Rep. IX. 443 Spasm of sphincter vaginæ marked, with some vaginitis and endocervicitis.

Vagino- (vădʒai·no), used as a comb. form of L. vāgina in some scientific terms, as † vaginopennous, = vaginipennous; vagi·noscope, an instrument for examining the vagina; vaginovesical, pertaining to the vagina and the bladder.

Recent Dicts. give a number of others in Med., Path., or Surg., as vagino-fixation, vaginotomy; vagino-abdominal, -labial, -vulvar adjs. (Cf. F. vaginolabial, -péritonéal, -vésical, etc.)

1755 Johnson, Ladybird, a small red insect vaginopennous. 1825 Good Study Med. (ed. 2) V. 154 Vagino-vesical prolapse. Prolapse of the vagina dragging the bladder along with it. 1866 J. M. Sims Uterine Surg. 33 Dr. Routh..has detected pregnancy..by means of his vaginoscope.

‖ **Vaginula** (vădʒai·niŭlă). Pl. **vaginulæ.** Zool. and Bot. [L. vāginula, dim. of vāgina Vagina.] A little sheath or vagina; esp. in Bot. the capsule or theca enclosing the base of the seta in certain mosses.

a. 1843 Wilkinson tr. Swedenborg's Anim. Kingd. I. i. 18 The external..membrane of the mouth forms a number of pyramidal and globular pouches or vaginulæ.

b. 1849 Balfour Man. Bot. § 1114 Urn-shaped pistillidia ..., enclosed at first within a calyptra..., which is ultimately carried up with them..., leaving often a sheath (vaginula) round the bottom of the fruit-stalk. 1863 M. J. Berkeley Brit. Mosses iii. 20 In Sphagnum the vaginula is lifted up on a cylindrical hyaline stalk. 1882 Vines tr. Sachs's Bot. 360 The basal portion of the growing archegonium becomes swollen out and penetrates down into the tissue of the stem, being nourished and firmly enclosed by it (the vaginula).

Vaginule. Bot. [Anglicizing of prec. or a. F. vaginule.] = prec.

1861 Bentley Man. Bot. 380 In Jungermannia the sporangia are elevated upon stalks arising out of the vaginule.

† **Vagisness.** Obs.⁻¹ [? f. It. vaghezza, f. vago Vage a.] Handsomeness, elegance.

1604 T. Wright Passions v. § 4. 197 All these [parts of the world]..are inameled with a most gratious vagisnesse, lustre, and beautie.

† **Va·git.** Obs.⁻¹ [ad. L. vāgīt-us, f. vāgīre to cry, squall.] A cry, lamentation, wail.

1627 Hakewill Apol. (1630) 294 His cruell altars with sad vagits sounde.

† **Va·gitate,** v. Obs.⁻¹ [ad. med.L. vagitāre, f. L. vagārī to wander.] intr. To roam or travel.

1614 Raleigh Hist. World I. viii. (1654) 103 Before the use of the compass was known it was impossible to vagitate a-thwart the Ocean.

Vago- (vē¹·go), used as comb. f. of Vagus in a few terms of Anat. or Med. in the sense 'of or pertaining to, denoting, the vagus or pneumogastric nerve (and some other nerve or part)', as vago-accessory, -glossopharyngeal, -sympathetic adjs.

1877 M. Foster Physiol. III. i. (1878) 392 In the mixed vago-sympathetic trunk. 1897 Allbutt's Syst. Med. IV. 660 Among bulbar nerves the vago-accessory is by far the most frequently attacked. 1899 Ibid. VI. 811 The hypoglossal root fibres lie in close proximity to those of the vago-glossopharyngeal nerve.

† **Va·gous,** a. Obs. [ad. L. vagus: see Vague a.] Vagrant or vague, in various senses; departing from or exceeding just or ordinary bounds; irregular, inordinate; unsettled, wandering.

1660 tr. Amyraldus' Treat. conc. Relig. I. i. 15 We have no other assurance of it then so wild and vagous a tradition. Ibid. iii. 32, I know not what natural vagous and indetermin'd notion. 1684 N. S. tr. Crit. Enq. Edit. Bible ix. 67 The first is only a Vagous way of Disputation, propounding now one thing, now another. 1710 T. Fuller Pharm. Extemp. 78 The whole throng of Physicians..crieth it up.. to..cure vagous Pains. 1726 Ayliffe Parergon 107 Such as were born and begot of a single woman, through a vagous Lust,..were called Spurii. 1737 Bracken Farriery Impr. (1757) I. 319 [They] were no doubt liable to vagous and wandering Pains.

Va·grance. rare. [f. as next: see -ance.] Vagrancy.

1751 Johnson Rambler No. 85 ¶ 9 The understanding may be restrained from that vagrance and dissipation by which it relieves itself after a long intenseness of thought. 1871 B. Taylor Faust (1875) I. xxii. 197 You'll never mount the airy steep With all your tripping vagrance.

Vagrancy (vē¹·grănsi). [f. Vagrant a.: see -ancy.]

Supplement, p. 3873; Corrigenda, p. 4092; Spurious words, p. 4093; Books quoted, p. 4094

VAGRANT.

1. *fig.* The action or fact of wandering or digressing in mind, opinion, thought, etc.; an instance of this. (Cf. 3.)

2. The state, condition, or action of roaming abroad or wandering about from place to place.

b. *spec.* Idle wandering with no settled habitation, occupation, or obvious means of support; conduct, life, or practices characteristic of vagrants or idle beggars.

3. An instance or occasion of wandering or roaming; a rambling journey; a straying.

Vagrant (vē·grǎnt), *sb.* and *a.* Forms: *a.* 5-6 vagaraunt, 6, 6-7 vagarant, 6 vagerant. *β.* 6. vagrant, 7 vag rant.

B. sb.

1. One of a class of persons who having no settled home or regular work wander from place to place, and maintain themselves by begging or in some other disreputable or dishonest way; an itinerant beggar, idle loafer, or tramp.

2. One who wanders or roams about; a person who leads a wandering life; a rover.

3. *fig.* Something that wanders; a person who has no fixed purpose or principles; a waverer.

A. adj.

1. Wandering about without proper means of livelihood; living in vagrancy or idle vagabondage; of or belonging to the class of vagrants or itinerant beggars.

b. Of a disease or pain: Not local or confined to one particular part. *Obs.*

Vagrantly, *adv.* [f. prec.] *intr.* To behave like a vagrant; to stray, wander. *Obs.*

Vagrantism. [f. VAGRANT *sb.* or *a.*] Inclination to, love of, vagrancy.

Vagrantize, *v. rare.* [f. VAGRANT *sb.* + -IZE.] †a. *trans.* To arrest as a vagrant. *Obs.* b. To reduce to the condition of a vagrant. In quot. *absol.*

Va·grant-life, *adv.* [f. VAGRANT *sb.*] In or after the manner of a vagrant.

Vagrom (vē·grŏm), *a.* [Illiterate alteration of VAGRANT *a.*: cf. INGRAM *a.* In mod. use only after Shakspere.]

VAGUE

Vague (vēg), *a.*, *adv.*, *sb.* Also 7 vage. [a. F. vague, ad. L. vagus wandering, uncertain, etc.]

1. Of statements, etc.: Couched in general or indefinite terms; not definitely or precisely expressed; deficient in details or particulars.

2. Of words, language, etc.: Not precise or exact in meaning.

3. *absol.* as *sb.*, esp. the vague, the vague aspect or consideration of things. In the vague, in a vague condition; uncertain; without entering into details or particulars.

4. The vague of uncertain future. *rare.*

5. Of ideas, knowledge, etc.: Lacking in definiteness or precision; indefinite, indistinct.

6. Of persons, the mind, etc.: Unable to think with clearness or precision; indefinite or inexact in thought or statement.

Vaguely (vē·glĭ), *adv.* [f. VAGUE *a.*] In a vague, indefinite, or indeterminate manner; with vagueness or lack of precision.

Vagueness (vē·gnĕs), *sb.* [f. prec. + -NESS.] The quality or condition of being vague; lack of distinctness or preciseness; indefiniteness.

Vaguish (vē·gĭʃ), *a.* [f. VAGUE *a.* + -ISH.] Somewhat vague or indefinite.

Vagus (vē·gŏs), *Anat.* and *Path.* Pl. vagi (vē·dʒai). [L.]

Vaidie, obs. Sc. f. VAUDIE.

VAIL

Vaifor, obs. Sc. f. WAVER *v.* **Vaig**, obs. Sc. f. VAGUE, WAGE. **Vaik** (e, later ff. VAKE *v. Sc.*; obs. Sc. ff. WAKE *v.*, WEAK *a.* and *v.*

Vail (vēl), *sb.*[1] Now *arch.* or *dial.* Forms: 5 vayll (e), 7 vaile, 6 vaile, 6-7 vaile, 6-9 vaill (e), dial. vaal; 6 veyle, 7 veile, 8 veil. *β.* 5-9 vaile. [f. VAIL *v.*[1]]

1. *fig.* Advantage, benefit, profit. *Obs.*

2. Value or worth; account, estimation. *Obs.*

II. 4. A casual or occasional profit or emolument in addition to salary, stipend, wages, or other regular payment, esp. one accruing or attached to an office or position; a fee or offering of this nature. Usu. in pl. Now *arch.* or *Obs.*

5. A gratuity given to a servant or attendant; a tip; *spec.* one of those given by a visitor on his departure to the servants of the house in which he has been a guest. Now *arch.* a. In pl.

Vail (vēl), *v.*[1] Now *arch.* Forms: *a.* 4-7 vayl (e), 6-7 vaile, 6-7 vaile (6 vayll); 6-7 vaill, vail; 6-8 vaile; *β.* north. vaile; *a* (vaile) lower *c.* to descend or sink.

1. *trans.* **1.** To lower (a weapon, banner, etc.); to cause to sink or descend or sink.

2. To lower or bring down (the eyes); to bend, bow down (the head, etc.); to bend (*the knee*).

3. *spec.* To lower in token of submission or respect.

Vail (vēl), *v.*[2] Now *arch.* Forms: *a.* 4-7 vaile (6 vaylle), vaile; 6 vaile; 6-7 vaill, vaile. [f. OF. *valer* (rare), or aphetic f. AVALE *v.*]

1. To lower (a weapon, banner, etc.); to cause to sink or descend.

2. *intr.* To sink or descend; to fall (down); to descend.

†8. To bow or bend down *to* the ground in obeisance or salutation. *Obs.*

9. To manifest submission; to acknowledge oneself overcome or surpassed; to yield.

III. *absol.* or *fig. Naut.* To lower the sail. (Cf. AVALE.)

VAIN

Vain (vēn), *a.* (*sb.* and *adv.*) Forms: 3-6 vein (e), 3-7 veine; 4 veyn (e); 4-6 veyne, vaine; 4-7 vayn (e), 4-7 vane; 5-7 vaine; 4 *Sc.* wayne; 6 *Sc.* vayne, vaine; 5-9 vaine; 6-7 vayn (e). [a. F. *vain*, *vaine*, ad. L. *vānus* empty, void, etc.]

1. Devoid of real value, worth, or significance; idle, unprofitable, useless, worthless; of no effect, force, or power; fruitless, futile, unavailing.

2. Without result or effect. *In vain*, to no effect or purpose; uselessly, ineffectually; fruitlessly.

Vaily, obs. f. VAILE *a.*

Vainglorious (vēˈnglōˌri·əs), a. Also 6–8 vainglorious. [f. VAINGLORY sb. + -OUS.]

1. Filled with, given to, indulging in, vainglory; inordinately boastful or elated on account of one's abilities, actions, or qualities; excessively and ostentatiously vain.

b. Without consent.

c. Characterized by, indicative of, or proceeding from vainglory.

d. With *name* as object.

Vaingloriously, adv. [f. prec.] In a vainglorious manner.

Vaingloriousness. [f. as prec.] The quality or character of being vainglorious.

Vainglory (vēˈnglōˌri), a. Also vain-glory, vain glory. [tr. med.L. *vāna glōria*. Cf. OF. and mod.F. *vaine gloire*, It. *vanagloria*, Pg. *vangloria*.]

1. Glory that is vain, empty, or worthless; inordinate or unwarranted pride in one's accomplishments or qualities; disposition or tendency to exalt oneself unduly; idle boasting or vaunting.

2. Foolishness, stupidity. *Obs.*

Vainly, adv. Also 4–6 vaynly, 4–5 vaineli, 5 vainli, 5–6 vaineli, 5–7 vaine-, 6–7 vainely, 7–9 vaine-ly, 6 *Sc.* vainelie, 8–9 vaynly.

1. In a vain or futile manner; without advantage, profit, or success; to no effect or purpose; in vain; uselessly, fruitlessly, ineffectually.

Vairhede, ME. var. FAIRHEAD. **Vairlooh**, variant of VARIOLA.

Vairy (vēˈri), a. Her. Forms: 4 varri, 6–7 varrye (7–8), varry, 6–7, 9 varrey, 8, 7–9 vairy. See also VERRY a. [a. OF. *vairy*, *vairié*.]

Vair (vē·r). *Obs.* Sc. In 5 wayre, wa(i)re. [ad. ONF. *vair*, OF. *veir*, *vair*:—L. *vārium*, neut. of *vārius* VARIOUS a.]

Vaivode (vāˈivōd). Now Hist. Forms: 6–7 vayuod(e, 7 vayvod, 7, 9 vayvode, 8 vay-

Vake (vēik), v. *Obs.* Forms: 4 vacke, 7 vaike, 7 vaick, 7 vaike. [ad. L. *vac-āre* to be empty.]

Valance (væˈlæns). Also 4 valaunce, 6–7 valans, 6 valanse. [Of uncertain origin.]

Valanced (-anst), *ppl. a.* Also 6–7 val-anced (6 -ened), 7, 9 valanced.

Valanche. *Obs.* rare. [ad. F. dial. (Savoie &c.) *valanche* (for F. *avalanche*) = AVALANCHE.]

Vale (vēil), sb. Forms: 4 val, 4–5 vaal, 5 vaille, 6–7 *Sc.* vail, 6 vayle, 6– vale. [a. OF. *val* (mod.F. *val*) = Pr. *val*, It. *valle*:—L. *vallem*, *acc.* of *vallis*, *valles* valley.]

Valediction (vælidiˈkʃən). [f. L. *valedict-*, ppl. stem of *valedīcere* to say farewell, f. *vale* farewell + *dīcere* to say, speak.]

Valedictory (væliˈdiktəri), a. and sb. [f. L. *valedict-* (see prec.) + -ORY.]

Valicoot, obs. form of *waycoat* WYLIECOAT.

Valid (væ'lid), *a.* (*sb.*) Also 6 *valide*, 8 valed, 7–8 F. *valide* (OF. *valide*, *Sp.*, *It.*, *Pg.*, *valido*) or L. *valid-us* strong, powerful, effective, f. *valēre* to be strong, etc.

Validate (væ'lideit), *v.* [med.L. *validāt-*, ppl. stem of *validāre* (1294 in Du Cange), or after F. *valider* (1586 in Godef. *Compl.*) = Sp. and Pg. *validar*, It. *validare*]; see VALID *a.* and -ATE[3].

Validation (vælidei'ʃən). [n.: prec.: cf. F. *validation* (16th c.), Sp. *validacion*, Pg.-*açāo*, It. *-azione*]

Validity (væli'diti). Also 6 valydyty, 6–7 validitie, 7 vallydity, Sc. validate. [ad. late L. *validitās*, f. *valid-us* VALID *a.* Cf. F. *validité* (16th c.), It. *validità*]

Validly (væ'lidli), *adv.* [as prec. + -LY[2]] In a valid manner; with legal authority, force, or strength.

Validness (væ'lidnes), *sb.* [-NESS.] Validity.

Va·lidous, *a.* Obs. [L. *valid-us* VALID *a.* + -OUS.] Valid, in various senses.

Valienton. Obs.[-1] [a. Sp. *valenton*.] A bully, braggart.

Valient, obs. form of VALIANT.

Valiente, obs. form of VALIANT.

Valincia, obs. form of VALENCE[1].

Valinch-er, **volinche**[?]. see quots. and VALENTIA.

Valise (vali·z, val·iz). Forms: 7 *valise*, 8 valise, valis, valaise, 9 Sc. wal-, walliss and *north.* 9 valis, wally, wallay, 9 valley. [ad. F. *valise*, vallie, *pl.* 6–valises. — It. valiscia, valigia, *pl.* -ge.

Vall. Obs.[-1] [ad. L. *vall-i.*] A valley.

Vallant, obs. form of VALIANT.

Vallen·cia, obs. form of VALENCE[1].

Vallenge, obs. form of VALANCE.

Vallet, obs. Sc. form of VALET.

Valley (væ'li), *sb.* Forms: 2–4·5 valeie (4 valeye), 4–6 valei (5 *Sc.* walei, waie, vale, 4 valee; 5 valeye, 4 valaye (4 valley); 4–5 valy, 5 vale (6 vale), 6 valey, 6 vally, vallie, *pl.* 6–vallies. 1, vallis, vallit: see VALE *sb.*

Va·llidnes, *rare.* [-NESS.] Validity.

Va·lidous, *a.* Obs. [L. *valid-us* VALID *a.* + -OUS.]

Valley-lily, the lily of the valley.

Valley-yne[?], *sb.*

Va·lleyed, *ppl. a.* Also valleyed.

Vallidum, *north. dial.* [f. valley VALUE *sb.*] The value or worth of a thing.

Va·llie. Obs.[-1] [f. val + VALLUM.] Rampart, wall.

Vallisneria, *sb.* Also valisneria. [mod.L. *Vallisneria*, named after Antonio *Vallisneri* (1661–1730), Italian botanist.]

Vallon, obs. form of VALLUM.

Vallonia, var. VALONIA.

Vallor, **-ow**, obs. forms of VALOUR *dial.*

Vallota (vælou·ta), *sb.* [f. VALLOT]

Vallum (væ'löm), *sb.* [L. *vallus* stake, palisade.]

Valonia (valou·nia), *sb.* Also valanea, valonea, whence also F. *vallonea*, +valonées.

Valor, obs. form of VALOUR.

Valorous (væ'lɔrəs), *a.* Also 6 valorouse, 7 valerous. [a. OF. *valeros*, *-us*, *-eux*]

Valorously (væ'lɔrəsli), *adv.* [f. prec. + -LY[2]] In a valorous manner; with valour.

Valour (væ'lə), *sb.* Forms: 4–valour (5–6 Sc. wa-), valowre, 5–6 valoure, valur, 5–6 vo-), 6 valoer (*Sc.* wa-), 5 vallour, valeour.

Valuable (væ'liuæb'l), *a.* and *sb.* Forms: 6 valuable, 6–7 valewable, etc.

Value (væ'liu), *sb.* Also 8 *volus.* [a. F. *value* (= Sp., Pg., valía, It. valuta), f. *valu-*, ppl. stem of *valoir*.]

married to a very valuable person. 1730 Southall *Treat. Buggs* 3 The late Learned and truly Valuable Dr. Woodward..approv'd the Design.

†3. That can be valued; capable of having the value estimated. *Obs. rare.*

1627 Sanderson *Serm.* (1682) I. 263 That sin..from which he hath once escaped without shame, or so much as valueable loss. 1690 Locke *Govt.* i. ix. P 10 We are..now speaking..of Possessions and Commodities of Life Valuable by Money.

†4. Capable of being compared or equated in value *with* something. *Obs.*

1646 Quarles *Judgem. & Mercy* Wks. (Grosart) I. 86/2 Is..a puffe of breath wee call life, valuable with his honour, in comparison of whom the very Angels are impure? 1651 Hobbes *Govt. & Soc.* ii. § 14. 28 His Will..hath simply before it, for its object, a certain good valuable with the thing promised.

†5. Valid, sound. *Obs.*—1

1647 N. Ward *Simple Cobler* 8 He that will rather make an irreligious quarell with other Religions then try the Truth of his own by valuable Arguments.

B. *sb.* An article of worth or value. Usually in pl., valuable goods or possessions.

1775 in Ash. 1797 S. & H. Lee *Canterb. T.* I. 188 With such valuables and papers as he deemed most likely to secure him either impunity or revenge. 1829 Lytton *Devereux* iii. v, I did not long wrestle with my pride before I obtained the victory, and sent all my valuables to the hammer. 1842 R. I. Wilberforce *Rutilius & Lucius* 22 No one but had furnished himself with some valuable. 1878 Bosw. Smith *Carthage* 123 Which the crews helped by throwing overboard their valuables.

Valuableness (væ·liu,ăb'lnès). [f. prec.] The character or condition of being valuable.

1683 Lorrain tr. *Muret's Rites Fun.* To Rdr. 4 Which having said with regard to the valuableness of the Subject, I shall only add [etc.]. 1721 T. Thomas *Pref. Urry's Chaucer* p. l, The valuableness of it will appear by the use which has been made of it in the Glossary. 1768 Tucker *Lt. Nat.* I. ii. xxiv. 134 There lies a nearer way for good qualities to arrive at their valuableness. 1865 J. Grote *Moral Ideals* vi. (1876) 71 And then it may be that the valuableness of actions varies as their usefulness.

Valuably (væ·liu,ăbli), *adv.* [f. as prec.]

†1. a. With equivalence of value. *Obs.*—1

1629 Gaule *Holy Madn.* 137 A great Patrimony may be valuably transubstantiated into the quantity of a little stone.

†b. At a high rate or value. *Obs.*

1755 Johnson, *Preciously*, valuably; to a great price.

2. With valuable or precious articles.

1780 *Gentl. Mag.* L. 617 Danford gained intelligence at an inn in the country of a box valuably filled. 1805 *Naval Chron.* XIII. 83 She is valuably laden.

3. In a valuable manner; so as to be valuable or highly useful.

1865 *Sat. Rev.* 5 Aug. 177/2 Mr. Palgrave's sombre picture must be treated as..valuably qualifying, not as superseding, such standard representations as that by Layard. 1895 *Review of Rev.* Aug. 167 If he had lived only to write that, he would have lived valuably. 1896 *Pop. Sci. Monthly* L. 285 Which perplex and exhaust the pupil without contributing valuably to his mental discipline.

Valuate (væ·liu,eit), *v.* [Back-formation from next.] *trans.* To estimate the value of (something); to appraise.

1873 *Lond. Soc.* Feb. 140 It will be important to valuate the influence of this extraordinary man. 1892 Stevenson & L. Osbourne *Wrecker* 291 The actual harm I can do I leave you to valuate for yourself.

Valuation (væliu,ē¹·ʃən). Also 6 **valewacion, valuacion, -atioun,** 7 **valueacion, valluacon, waluation.** [a. OF. *valuacion, -ation* (cf. mod.F. *évaluation* Evaluation), = Sp. *valuacion*, f. *valuer* (Sp. *valuar*) Value *v.*]

1. The action of valuing; the process of assessing or fixing the value of a thing.

1529 More *Suppl. Soulys* Wks. 294/2 For surely it might be that he was not ware of the newe valuacion: for he ranne awaye before the valuacion changed. 1551 Sir J. Williams *Accompte* (Abbotsf. Cl.) 13 Myters, ornamentes, and other thinges received without weight or valuacion. 1577–87 Holinshed *Chron.* II. 313/1 The valuation of their goodes and substance, as well in cattell as in readie monie. 1672 Petty *Pol. Anat.* (1691) 61 These Valuations were made as Parties interested could prevail upon and against one another by their Attendance, Friends, Eloquence, and Vehemence. 1737 H. Walpole in *10th Rep. Hist. MSS. Comm.* App. I. 270, I..would give more for them on a reasonable valuation than a Bookseller would doe. 1781 Gibbon *Decl. & F.* (1787) II. 71 The secret wealth of commerce, and the precarious profits of art or labour, are susceptible only of a discretionary valuation. 1839 Thirlwall *Greece* xlii. V. 205 A new valuation of all private property had been made. 1858 Ld. St. Leonards *Property Law* vii. 42 If they refuse to value the estate, or disagree in the valuation, you cannot enforce the performance of the contract.

attrib. 1855 *Statutes Gt. Brit. & Irel.* XXII. 514 Valuation (Ireland) Act Amendment; further to amend 15 & 16 Vict. c. 63 relating to the Valuation of rateable Property. 1892 *Pall Mall G.* 19 Dec. 2/1 The amendment of the valuation law.

b. Estimated value; worth or price as determined by deliberate estimation.

1631 Weever *Anc. Funeral Mon.* 816 The valuation of this religious structure..was three hundred eight pounds. 1757 Washington *Lett.* Writ. 1889 I. 437 There are many Masters of Servants yet unpaid, who are very anxious to receive their valuation. 1775 S. J. Pratt *Liberal Opin.* cxx. (1783) IV. 119 The ear-rings were no trifles in point of price.., bearing no less a valuation than 200 guineas. 1812 G. Chalmers *Dom. Econ. Gt. Brit.* 456 The fair valuation, at which our commercial concerns might be calculated. 1844 H. H. Wilson *Brit. India* i. vii. I. 445 The money valuation of the estimated produce of the land in cultivation. 1888 Annie S. Swan *Doris Cheyne* vii. 122 Mr. Hardwicke had paid the sum required for the goodwill, and had also taken the furniture at a valuation.

†2. Value or worth, esp. of a material nature.

1567 *Trial Treas.* (Percy Soc.) 6 It is not golde alwayes that doth shine, But corrupting copper, of small valuation. 1583 Melbancke *Philotimus* N j b, Diuers precious Iewells.., whereof two or three Gemmes were of more valuation in his accounte, then all the rest. 1622 R. Preston *Godly Man's Inquisition* i. 20 If any man hath lost any matter of valuation, how diligently will they set themselues to Inquisitions. 1655 tr. *Sorel's Com. Hist. Francion* ii. 44 Without receiving any considerable valuation for so precious a Jewell. 1669 Worlidge *Syst. Agric.* (1681) 145 Which casualties..makes their Price and valuation so uncertain, and proves so great a discouragement to the Countryman.

†b. *spec.* Current value (of money). *Obs.*

1551 Robinson tr. *More's Utopia* i. (1895) 88 One councelleth to rayse and enhaunce the valuacion of money, when the king must paye any. 1622 Malynes *Anc. Law-Merch.* 486 By aduancing the Valuation of gold..in England, when Crowne gold was valued from fiftie fiue shillings the ounce to three pound. 1699 Bentley *Phal.* 454 Here are four Authorities then..for the low valuation of the Sicilian Talent. 1776 Adam Smith *W. N.* i. v. (1869) I. 46 No creditor could..be cheated in consequence of the high valuation of silver in coin.

†c. = Value *sb.* 7 a. *Obs.*—1

1636 *Recorde's Gr. Artes* 43, I may reckon them simply without any respect of their valuation or place: saying, 2 and 3 make 5.

3. Appreciation or estimation of anything in respect of excellence or merit.

1548 Elyot, *Aestimatio*, a valuacion, consideracion, or weying of a matter. 1597 Shaks. *2 Hen. IV*, iv. i. 189 Our valuation shall be such, That euery slight, and false-deriued Cause, Yea, euery idle..wanton Reason,..Shall, to the King, taste of this Action. 1617 Moryson *Itin.* iv. (Roxb.) 281, I obserued in England the same superstitious neglect of Common Prayer, and excessive valuation of Preaching, to haue infected some places among vs. 1650 Earl Monm. tr. *Senault's Man bec. Guilty* 256 The very Theater whereupon things are acted, serves to put a valuation upon them. *a* 1676 Hale *Prim. Orig. Man.* (1677) 356 The admirable Solution of many of those difficulties..doth give a very great valuation and esteem to the truth..of the Scriptures. 1745–6 Fielding *True Patriot* Wks. 1775 IX. 318, I believe it is difficult to find any two persons, who place an equal valuation on any virtue, good or great quality whatever. 1884 *Manch. Exam.* 14 May 5/5 The outside public appear disposed to take Mr. Chaplin at his own valuation.

Hence **Valua·tional** *a.*

1887 *Contemp. Rev.* Feb. 285 They proposed a geometrical survey, detailed and valuational.

†**Va·luative**, *a. Obs.*—1 [f. Value *v.* + -ative.] Expressive of value.

1566 Stapleton *Ret. Untr. Jewel* iv. 62 The Sacramentary off Geneua will haue the verbe *est* is, to stand for, is in value, not is in substance, and so (*est*) must not be a verbe substantiue, but a verbe valuatiue.

Valuator (væ·liu,ē¹tə̆ɹ). [f. Value *v.* + -ator, after Valuation.] One who estimates the value of things; *esp.* one appointed or licensed to do so; an appraiser.

1731–2 Swift *Consid. two Bills* Wks. 1841 II. 225/1, I am therefore at a loss what kind of valuators the bishops will make use of. 1820 Hogg *Tales & Sk.* (1837) II. 197 The valuator of books made toward the door as fast as his loosened and yielding joints could carry him. 1848 *Chambers's Jrnl.* X. 423 A small daily stipend from government as a valuator of Books. 1886 C. Scott *Sheep-Farming* 114 The price is not always agreed upon that day; the valuators sometimes considering it advisable to wait for a time before deciding.

Value (væ·liu), *sb.* Forms: 4–5 **valu**, 4– **value** (4 **ualue**, 5 **walue, valwe**), 4 **valuwe**; 4, 7 **valeu**, 5 **-ieu, -eue**, 7 **valleu**; 5–7 **valewe** (5–6 **walew**, 5 **-ewe, -ywe**); 4–5 **valow(e**; 9 *dial.* **vally**. [a. OF. *value* (13th c.), *vallue* (F. dial. *vaillue*), fem. pa. pple. of *valoir* to be of worth:—L. *valēre*. Cf. med.L. *valua* (1235, from OF.), Sp. *valua*, It. *valuta*.]

I. 1. That amount of some commodity, medium of exchange, etc., which is considered to be an equivalent for something else; a fair or adequate equivalent or return.

1303 R. Brunne *Handl. Synne* 5966 But þou ȝyve hyt hym aȝeyn, Or þe valeu.., Þou art falle þan yn þe vyce Of coueytyse. 1338 — *Chron.* (1810) 163 Amendes I wille make, ..Þi godes þe biken, or þe valow verray. *c* 1440 *Gesta Rom.* lxv. (Harl. MS.) 288, I saide to you þat I myȝte not seille you þe ston, no lesse þan I recyvid þerfore the trewe value. 1687 A. Lovell tr. *Thevenot's Trav.* i. 254 The other two Consuls..were not released, till their Nations..promised the Basha to pay..the value of the Ships Loadings. 1716 *Lond. Gaz.* No. 5472/4 A Bill..for Value received, for 60 *l.* 1735 Johnson *Lobo's Abyss., Descr.* vii. 86 On Condition he paid a certain number of Cows, or the Value. 1806 Cumberland *Mem.* (1807) II. 151 We hardly could be said to have had value for our money. 1817 W. Selwyn *Law Nisi Prius* (ed. 4) II. 1286 For the recovery of the goods in question, or the value thereof, if the plaintiff cannot have the goods. 1868 Rogers *Pol. Econ.* (1876) 147 To pay at a given date..a specified sum of money, for which value has been received.

†b. A standard of estimation or exchange; an amount or sum reckoned in terms of this; a thing regarded as worth having. *Obs.*

1398 Trevisa *Barth. De P. R.* vi. xvii. (Bodl. MS.), Vma is a certeyne weiȝt and valewe. *c* 1460 *Play Sacram.* 290 For so lytelle a walew in conscyence to stond bownd. 1555 Waterman *Fardle Facions* ii. xi. 249 Thei game not for money, or any valewe elles. 1655 Milton *Lett. State* Wks. 1851 VIII. 333 We thought it requisite to remit beforehand two thousand Pounds of the Value of England, with all possible speed. 1754 Hanway *Trav.* vi. i. II. 146 They stripped their habitation of everything that was valuable. The Russians lost a great value [*note*, About one hundred thousand pound].

†c. *spec.* = Valour 3 d. *Obs.*

1607 [see Valour 3 d]. *a* 1631 Donne *Sat.* iii. 62 As Wards still Take such wives as their Guardians offer, or Pay valewes. 1660 *Act 12 Chas. II*, c. xxiv. § 2 Values and forfeitures of marriage and all other charges incident to tenure by Knights service. 1684 Manley, *Value of Marriage* [copying Cowel: see Valour 3 d].

2. The material or monetary worth of a thing; the amount at which it may be estimated in terms of some medium of exchange or other standard of a similar nature.

Sometimes, esp. in recent use, as the second element in combs., as *assay-, coin-, house-, land-value*.

1338 R. Brunne *Chron.* (1810) 83 Extendours he sette forto extend þe land...Alle þei did extend to witte þe verrey valowe. *c* 1380 Wyclif *Wks.* (1880) 414 God..wole not þat men chaffere but in þingis whoos valu þei knowen. *c* 1407 Lydg. *Reson & Sens.* 2812, I ha no konnyng dywe To declare the walywe So ryche of stonys and tresour. 1474 *Cov. Leet Bk.* 413 That ye..certifie vs as-wel of the names of all the seid gentilmen..as for þe very value of their said lyvelodes and goodes. 1552 in Feuillerat *Revels Edw. VI* (1914) 117 An Estimate of the contentes and valewe of soche parcelles and stuffe as was delyuered owte of the storehouses. *Ibid.* 118 Pantacles one paier of bridges satten in valewe iijii iiijd. 1560 Daus tr. *Sleidane's Comm.* 119 b, Whan a benefice or prebende is fallen..what diligent inquisition is made to knowe the yearely value. 1602 *Ld. Cromwell* ii. iii. 56 The King of late hath had his treasurie rob'd, And of the choysest iewelles that he had: The value of them was some seauen thousand pound. *a* 1680 Butler *Rem.* (1759) I. 53 As Metals mixt, the rich and base Do both at equal Values pass. 1771 *Encycl. Brit.* III. 255/2 Were pounds sterling, livres, florins, piastres, &c...invariable in their values. 1776 Adam Smith *W. N.* i. v. (1904) I. 43 In England ..the value of all goods and of all estates is generally computed in silver. 1809 Bawdwen *Domesday Bk.* 4 In the time of King Edward the value of the city to the King was fifty-three pounds. 1859 Tennyson *Elaine* 1208 To loyal hearts the value of all gifts Must vary as the giver's. 1885 Meredith *Diana* I. 116 The value of the stock I hold has doubled.

attrib. and *Comb.* 1854 in Tomes *Amer. in Japan* 410 In Japan, as in European countries, the standard of value-weight, and that of currency-weight, differ. 1878 F. A. Walker *Money* xiii. 263 The bi-metallic theory proposes to harness two metals of somewhat diverse tendencies value-wards.

†b. Valuation, appraisement. *Obs.*—1

c 1488 *Plumpton Corr.* (Camden) 68 It was sene by our tenants, & set to a valow what should be our charge to do, & that shall he have.

c. In phrases. *Under value*, below the proper value. † *To good value, at a small value*, at a low or small price.

1638 Featly *Transubst.* 9 The fifth was nominated to a poore Vicaridge under vallew. 1699 Bentley *Phal.* 387 How is his Edition so scarce, that..may be purchas'd at a small value? *a* 1700 Evelyn *Diary* 14 July 1683, He..shew'd me some very rare and curious bookes, and some MSS. which he had purchas'd to good value.

3. *Of value*, valuable. *Of..value*, possessed of (a specified) material or monetary worth.

c 1340 Hampole *Pr. Consc.* 9199 To precyouse stanes of vertew, And to sylver and gold and thing of valow. *c* 1400 Maundev. (Roxb.) xxvi. 124 Oile of olyfe of grete valu. *c* 1400 *Pilg. Sowle* (Caxton, 1483) iv. ix. 62 The prys of myn Appel is of suche valewe that it passeth the estymacion of ony creature. 1436 *Libel Eng. Policy* in *Pol. Poems* (Rolls) II. 162 Hit is of lytelle valeue,..Wyth Englysshe wolle but if it menged be. 1485 Caxton *Paris & V.* (1868) 33 Not al onely these Iewelles whyche been of lytel valewe. *a* 1548 Hall *Chron., Edw. IV* (1550) 35 When he knewe the two Erles to be a praye of suche a greate value, he determined not to deliuer theim. 1556 Olde *Antichrist* 198 b, So noble a garment, of more value than al yͤ treasures of golde. 1600 Pory tr. *Leo's Africa* iii. 133 Their shops are full of fine earthen vessels, which are of much greater value then the things contained in them. 1628–9 Digby *Voy. Medit.* (Camden) 22 Shee [a boat] had little of value in her. 1634 Sir T. Herbert *Trav.* 19 Gold and Siluer is of no value amongst them. 1709 T. Robinson *Nat. Hist. Westmld. & Cumbld.* vii. 37 Lead and Coal,..being of a disagreeable Nature, the one makes the other of little Value. 1771 *Encycl. Brit.* III. 260/2 The old [guineas] must be of less value still. 1861 M. Pattison *Ess.* (1889) I. 45 A tower, with a fireproof chamber for the muniments and jewels of especial value.

4. The equivalent (in material worth) *of* a specified sum or amount.

1362 Langl. *P. Pl.* A. xi. 34 Wolde neuer kyng ne kniht.. ȝeuen hem to heore ȝeres-ȝiue þe value of a grote! *c* 1386 Chaucer *Frankl. T.* 845 He..broghte gold vn-to this Philosophre The value of fyue hundred pound I gesse. 1412–20 Lydg. *Chron. Troy* ii. 124 We trewly may adverten ..þat for the valu of a þing of nouȝt, Mortal causes and werris first bygonne. *c* 1450 *Merlin* vii. 120 Of all the harneys that thei hade brought thider, thei hadde not with hem the valew of ijd. *a* 1533 Ld. Berners *Huon* xliii. 145 Thou shalt not lese the valew of one peny. *Ibid.* lxviii. 234 They left not in yͤ abbey the valew of a floren. 1613 Purchas *Pilgrimage* (1614) 652 A Bason, wherein each puts the value of twelue pence in Gold. 1771 *Encycl. Brit.* III. 260/2 If..the new guineas are below the value of a pound sterling in silver. 1839 *Penny Cycl.* XV. 322/2 A gold coin of the assayed value of 5*l.* 18*s.* 8*d.* 1887 *Whitaker's Alm.* 183 Bronze coinage..to the value of £57,563.

b. In contemptuous comparisons. Now *rare*.

c 1380 *Sir Ferumb.* 124 Ne douteþ he kyng ne Emperour þe value of a rysshe. *Ibid.* 5441 Þat þe Amerel ne dredeþ hym noȝt..þe value of a kerse. *c* 1386 Chaucer *Shipman's T.* 171 He is noght worth at al In no degree the value of a flye. *c* 1400 *Laud Troy Bk.* 17506, I ȝeue right not of alle his tene, Not the value of a bene. *c* 1425 Wyntoun *Cron.* vi. xviii. 2170, I cowntyt noucht þe tobir twa Wicis þe walew of a stra. 1798 Wordsw. *P. Bell* 239 But not the value of a hair Was heart or head the better.

c. The extent or amount *of* a specified standard or measure of length, quantity, etc. Now only *dial.*

1600 Surflet *Countrie Farme* iii. vi. 433 They must be sharpened like a stake for the value of the length of halfe a foote. 1731 P. Miller *Gard. Dict.* s.v. *Sap*, Flowing out very plentifully..to the Value of several Gallons in a few Days. 1764 *Museum Rust.* II. i. 10 Give each of them the value of three large table spoonfuls of the mixture for a dose. 1791 Mrs. Radcliffe *Rom. Forest* (1820) I. 67, I jogged on, near the value of a league, I warrant, and then I came to a track. 1794 — *Myst. Udolpho* lii, They stood in the same posture for the value of a minute. 1818 Wilbraham *Chesh. Gloss.* s.v., When you come to the value of five feet deep. 1854 Miss Baker *Northampt. Gloss.* 374 There was only the vally of a bushel of apples in all the orchard. *Ibid.*, Dig down to the vally of seven or eight feet.

II. †5. Worth or worthiness (of persons) in respect of rank or personal qualities. *Obs.*

c 1330 R. Brunne *Chron. Wace* (Rolls) 4911 Alle of valow, moste & leste, Suld com to London to his feste. 1338 — *Chron.* (1810) 100 Þerfor þe duke him dight, as man of grete value. *c* 1386 Chaucer *Parson's T.* P 378 Insolent is he þat dispisith in his Iugement alle oþer folk as to regard of his valieu. *c* 1400 *Brut* 248 Eueryche of ham hade ful riche ȝiftes, euery man as he was of value and of State. *c* 1425 Wyntoun *Cron.* ii. viii. 771 Þai þat duelt that ile wiþ in War sottis wylde of na walew. 1483 Caxton *Cato* A iiij, Thou oughtest to gyue place to hym that is gretter and more of valewe than thou arte. 1590 Greene *Mourn. Garm.* Wks. (Grosart) IX. 154 Some were Caualiers, and men of great value. *a* 1639 Wotton in *Reliq.* (1651) 484 A young Widow of value: Who lately dying..left order by Will that her body should be buried in her dwelling Parish.

†b. Worth or efficacy in combat or warfare; manliness, valour. *Obs.*

1590 Spenser *F. Q.* ii. vi. 29 Who..his sword forth drew, And him with equall value counteruayld. 1591 Harington *Orl. Fur.* xxxiv. xii, Alceste by his value brought My father and his friends to such distress. 1614 Lodge *Seneca* 7 The Emperour..giveth a chaine of gold to some one souldier of his that approved his valew in some difficult enterprise.

6. The relative status of a thing, or the estimate in which it is held, according to its real or supposed worth, usefulness, or importance.

c 1380 Wyclif *Sel. Wks.* I. 195 Oure bileve techiþ us þat God kepiþ þingis after her valu, for if ony þing be betere, God makiþ it to be betere. *c* 1385 Chaucer *L. G. W.* 602 *Cleopatra*, Loue hadde brought this man in swich a rage.. That al the world he sette at no value. 1470–85 Malory *Arthur* ii. ii. 78 Your bounte..may no man preyse half to the valewe. 1584 B. R. tr. *Herodotus* i. 68 These words with Cyrus came in at one eare and went out at the other, lighter in value then the wynd in waight. 1651 Hobbes *Leviath.* i. x. 42 [Let men] rate themselves at the highest Value they can; yet their true Value is no more than it is esteemed by others. 1779 *Mirror* No. 5. 33 It unfortunately happens, that we are very inadequate judges of the value of our own discourse. 1828 Duppa *Trav. Italy*, etc. 21 These landscapes have no value but as being the earliest attempts to represent scenes from nature. 1844 H. H. Wilson *Brit. India* I. 217 Attaching to its commerce and alliance more value than belonged to either. 1884 J. Gilmour *Mongols* xvii. 205 Buddhism..tells him that each prayer repeated has a certain value in cleansing away sin.

attrib. 1899 Garvie *Ritschlian Theol.* 176 The theoretical judgments cannot give an intelligible unity to the world-whole, but the value-judgments can.

b. In the phr. *of* (..) *value*. (Cf. 3.)

1375 Barbour *Bruce* i. 372 Quhar it failȝeys, na wertu May be off price, na off valu. 1396–7 in *Eng. Hist. Rev.* (1907) XXII. 299 Þe correlari is þe preyere of ualue spring-and out of parfyth charite. 1422 Yonge tr. *Secreta Secret.* 171 That appurtenyth to a feynte herte to lowe myche a thynge of lytill walue. 1555 Eden *Decades* (Arb.) 133 Yf this opinion bee of anye value. 1849 James *Woodman* iii, There may be news of value indeed. 1855 Brewster *Life of Newton* II. xviii. 166 Observations of such value, that without them they could not proceed in their researches.

c. *To set a..value on* or *upon*, to estimate at a specified rate.

1651 Hobbes *Leviath.* ii. xviii. 92 Considering what values men are naturally apt to set upon themselves. 1693 Locke *Educ.* § 62 But the Backwardness Parents shew in divulging their Faults, will make them set a greater Value on their Credit themselves. *a* 1763 W. King *Pol. & Lit. Anecd.* (1819) 101 My Lord Hardwick..who is said to be worth 800,000 *l.* sets the same value on half a crown now as he did when he was only worth one hundred. 1782 Burke *Corr.* (1844) III. 7 You set too much value on the few and slight services, that I have been able to perform. 1842 Combe *Digestion* 260 No one who sets any value on the lives of his horses or dogs, ever allows it to be disregarded. 1868 J. H. Blunt *Ref. Ch. Eng.* I. 64 Wolsey set much value upon the study of Greek. 1890 *Cornhill Mag.* Oct. 353, I must see what value the kafir sets on his services.

†d. Estimate or opinion *of*, liking *for*, a person or thing. *Obs.*

(*a*) 1652 Loveday tr. *Calprenede's Cassandra* iii. 232 Thus parted those two great men, preserving in their soules such a value of one another as you may easily imagine. 1677 in *Cleveland's Poems* Ep. Ded., Such competent Judges,..in whose just value of him Cleveland shall live..the pattern of succeeding Ages.

(*b*) 1686 tr. *Chardin's Trav. Persia* 204 He has a very great Value for her by reason of her great Estate. 1709 Steele *Tatler* No. 33 P 5 Nay, child, do not be troubled that I take Notice of it; my Value for you made me speak it. 1749 Fielding *Tom Jones* xiv. v, I must esteem one for whom I know Mr. Allworthy hath so much value. 1773

Life N. Frowde 182 In a few days she conceived a Value for me, which she expressed in the warmest Terms. 1794 Mathias *Purs. Lit.* (1798) 434 Men of learning have always had a proper value for the Greek language.

†e. *ellipt.* Esteem, regard. *Obs.*—1

1700 Dryden *Fables Anc. & Mod.* Ded., I am not vain enough to boast that I have deserv'd the value of so Illustrious a Line.

7. a. *Math.* The precise number or amount represented by a figure, quantity, etc.

1542 Recorde *Gr. Artes* (1575) 43 Euery Figure hathe two values: One..which it hath of his Forme, and yͤ other ..whiche he taketh of his Place. *a* 1680 Butler *Remains* (1759) II. 80 A huffing Courtier is a Cypher, that has no Value himself, but from the Place he stands in. 1715 tr. *Gregory's Astron.* (1726) I. 477 The Resolution whereof will give the Value of the Root. 1737 *Gentl. Mag.* VII. 134/2 That he can get a Value of *v* to substitute in the first Equation, to bring out the Value of *z* true. 1823 H. J. Brooke *Introd. Crystallogr.* 255 As the value of *p* increases, the planes *b* incline more and more on the primary planes. 1867 J. Hogg *Microsc.* i. i. 2 The values of these angles..prove that the glass of the ancients differed very little from that manufactured in our own times. 1881 *Nature* No. 618. 417 So boron in the crystalline salt..has a higher atomic value than in its fluoride.

b. *Mus.* The relative length or duration of a tone signified by a note.

1662 Playford *Skill Mus.* i. vii. (1674) 25 The Semibreve ..is called the Master-Note. All the other Notes..are measured or Proportioned to its value. 1728 Chambers *Cycl.* s.v. *Measure*, The Measure is regulated according to the different Quality or Value of the Notes in the Piece. 1840 *Penny Cycl.* XVI. 333/2 The value, or length in time, of the Semibreve may be considered as unity. 1869 Ouseley *Counterp.* xix. 157 It is not allowed, in making the answer, to change the value of the notes of the subject.

c. Of cards, chessmen, or the like: Relative rank or importance according to the conventions of the game; the amount at which each (or each set) is reckoned in counting the score.

1670 Cotton *Gamester* (1680) 76 The value of the Cards [in Cribbage] is thus: Any fifteen upon the Cards is two. *Ibid.* 87 The rest of the Cards are best according to their value in pips. 1742 Hoyle *Whist* 27 Suppose you have.. four other Cards of no Value. 1850 *Bohn's Hand-bk. Games* (1867) 152 If in cutting there be two lowest cards of a like value, the holders cut again for the deal. 1874 H. Gibbs *Ombre* (1878) 5 'French Ruff,' 'Five-cards' and other games in which the cards have the same value or nearly the same value as in Ombre.

d. *Painting.* Due or proper effect or importance; relative tone of colour in each distinct section of a picture; a patch characterized by a particular tone.

1778 Sir J. Reynolds *Disc.* viii. (1876) 453 A certain quantity of cold colours is necessary to give value and lustre to the warm colours. 1892 Mrs. H. Ward *David Grieve* II. 312 Working [at a painting] now in the forest, now at home, the lights and values had suffered. 1896 *Daily News* 10 Feb. 3/4 The new French stamp..is printed in two impressions full and mezzo-tint, white spaces furnishing a third value.

attrib. 1902 *Academy* 12 Apr. 392/1 Replace it in the picture, it is still a vase, but quite without value relation to the other parts of the picture.

Value (væ·liu), *v.* Forms: 5–6 **valew**, 6–7 **valewe**, 7 **vallew**; 7 *Sc.* **walow, wallow**; 6–7 **vallue**, 6– **value**. [f. the sb. Cf. Sp. *valuar*, It. *valutare*.]

I. 1. *trans.* To estimate or appraise as being worth a specified sum or amount. Const. *at*, †*to*, or with inf.

1482 Caxton *Trevisa's Higden* viii. i, They hadde as moche good and Jewellys, as was valewyd to fyve honderde thousand motons of Golde. 1535 Coverdale *Lev.* xxvii. 16 It shalbe valued after fiftye Sycles of syluer. 1548 Elyot s.v. *Aestimo*, He valewed it at iii. pence. 1627 *Rep. Parishes Scotl.* (Bann. Cl.) 2 We wallow it to be worth sex bollis off wictuall. *Ibid.* 3 Quilkis we walow at sex bollis. 1632 Lithgow *Trav.* viii. 355 Their Rings..were valued to a hundred Chickens of Malta. 1686 tr. *Chardin's Trav. Persia* 339, I valued it at Ten Pounds. 1734 R. Seymour *Compl. Gamester* i. 27 [In the game of Codille] a Fish is generally valued at Ten Counters. 1760–72 H. Brooke *Fool of Qual.* (1809) I. 151 The appraisers..valued the same to four pounds. 1835 *Tomlins' Law Dict.* (ed. 4) s.v. *Insurance*, After stating that the goods should be valued at so much.

†b. To equate in value *with* something. *Obs.*

1560 Bible (Geneva) *Job* xxviii. 16 Wisdome..shal not be valued with the wedge of golde of Ophir, nor with the precious onix. *Ibid.* 19.

2. To estimate the value of (goods, property, etc.); to appraise in respect of value.

1509–10 *Act 1 Hen. VIII*, c. 20 § 1 Merchaundisez..to be valued after that they coste at the firste byeng or achate. 1523 Fitzherb. *Bk. Surv.* 3 b, To value what the grasse of the gardens..be worth by the yere. 1535 Coverdale *Lev.* xxvii. 12 Yͤ prest shal value it, whether it be good or bad, & it shal stonde at the prestes valuynge. 1662 J. Davies tr. *Olearius' Voy. Ambass.* 19 The Presents had not yet been valu'd, among which was the Cabinet.., which could not be valu'd but by them. 1755 Magens *Insurances* I. 197 For Labour and Wood..which has not been valued, but put at least at 25 Rixdollars. 1780 Burke *Œcon. Reform.* Wks. III. 272, I propose to have those rights of the crown valued as manerial rights are valued on an inclosure. 1872 Morley *Voltaire* (1886) 206 Voltaire got his bill back, and the jewels were to be duly valued.

absol. 1667 Milton *P. L.* viii. 571 Weigh with her thy self; Then value.

†b. To rate for purposes of taxation. *Obs.*—1

1526 Tindale *Luke* ii. 1 All the woorlde shulde be valued.

c. With immaterial object. † Also *absol.* with *of*.

1592 Greene *Upst. Courtier* Wks. (Grosart) XI. 228 The country swaines cannot value of my worth. 1623 Heming & Condell *Ded. Shaks. Folio*, When we valew the places your H. H. sustaine, we cannot but know their dignity greater, then to descend to the reading of these trifles. 1676 Hale *Contempl.* i. 513 The Lord, who can best try, And value what is best, did pass it by.

3. To estimate or regard as having a certain value or worth: †a. With various constructions. *Obs.*

1589 Warner *Alb. Eng.* vi. xxix. 129 And all their Styles together Are lesser valewed than to liue beloued of my Tuder. 1599 Shaks. *Much Ado* iii. i. 53 And her wit Values it selfe so highly, that to her All matter else seemes weake. ? 1634 Earl Stirling *Anacrisis* P 2, I value Language as a Conduit..: I compare a Poem to a Garden. 1661 Glanvill *Van. Dogm.* xxiv. Apol. Philos. 247 The Swine may see the Pearl, which yet he values but with the ordinary muck. *a* 1667 Jer. Taylor *Serm.* (1673) 124 He must by it regulate his life, and value it above secular regards. 1726 Leoni *Alberti's Archit.* I. 26/1 In India the Cypress is valu'd almost equal with the Spice Trees.

†b. With complementary predicate. *Obs.*

1593 Shaks. *3 Hen. VI*, v. iii. 14 The Queene is valued thirtie thousand strong. 1619 in *Eng. & Germ.* (Camden) 107 His Master is here valued to be but a silly Jesuited soule. 1638 R. Baker tr. *Balzac's Lett.* (vol. II) 138 He valewes himself to be worthy of an informer, and of commissioners. 1737 Franklin *Ess.* Wks. 1840 II. 286 Caligula valued himself a notable dancer.

c. Const. *at* or †*of* (a specified amount). Also without prep. Usually in negative clauses.

1614 Raleigh *Hist. World* iv. i. § 1 To value at little the power of the Macedonians. 1667 Dryden *Sir Martin Mar-all* i. i, I will not value any man's fortune at a rush, except he have wit. 1751 Lavington *Enthus. Meth. & Papists* iii. (1754) 42 They don't value Ignatius of a Hair. 1754 Richardson *Corr.* (1804) III. 218 If I am angry, you can't help it (as much as to say you value it not a farthing). 1848 J. Grant *Aide-de-C.* xxiv, He would not value his ducats..a rush. 1892 R. N. Bain tr. *Jókai's Pretty Michal* iv. (1897) 50 He cares not a fig for muskets, and does not value his life at a boot-lace.

II. 4. To consider of worth or importance; to rate high; to esteem; to set store by.

1549 J. Cheke in *Lett. Lit. Men* (Camden) 8 Your sight is ful of gai things abrode, which I desire not, as things sufficientli known and valewd. 1592 Greene *Upst. Courtier* Wks. (Grosart) XI. 227 Though I am disdained of a few ouerweening fooles, I am valued as well as thy selfe with the wise. 1600 Shaks. *A. Y. L.* i. iii. 73, I was too yong that time to value her, But now I know her. 1656 in *Verney Mem.* (1907) II. 50, I hope..that you will pries that which is most to be valewd, which is virtue. 1703 De Foe in *15th Rep. Hist. MSS. Comm.* App. IV. 62, I value the esteem of one wise man above abundance of blessings. 1771 *Junius' Lett.* liv. (1778) 293 Perhaps the example might have taught him not to value his own understanding so highly. 1828 Scott *F. M. Perth* xii, Stir not your tongue,..as you value having an entire tooth in your head. 1844 Lingard *Anglo-Sax. Ch.* (1858) II. 195 Instead of despising, he will approve and value their exertions. 1880 L. Stephen *Pope* iv. 94 He valued money, as a man values it who has been poor.

†b. To commend or praise (*to* another); to vaunt. *Obs.*

1670 R. Montagu in *Buccleuch MSS.* (Hist. MSS. Comm.) I. 473 That your Lordship may value it to their Ministers in England, if you find them complaining. 1672 *Ibid.* 513, I have not omitted to value to them the business of the Banquiers. *a* 1700 Evelyn *Diary* 23 Apr. 1646, In this room stands the glorious inscription of Cavaliero Galeazzo Arconati, valueing his gift to the librarie of severall drawings by Da Vinci.

†5. With negatives: To take account of; to heed or regard; to be concerned about; to care. *Obs.*

Freq. *c* 1630–1730 with various constructions.

1591 Greene *Maidens Dr.* xix, But like to Scæuola, for countries good, He did not value for to spend his blood. 1634 Sir T. Herbert *Travels* 10 The foolish quality of which Bird [the booby] is to sit still, not valuing danger. 1661 in *Extr. St. Papers Friends* Ser. ii. (1911) 125 My opinion is thay will not vallew their Oath. 1722 De Foe *Plague* (1754) 84 People infected..valued not who they injur'd. 1726 Shelvocke *Voy. round World* (1757) 423 You are in a condition of not valuing whether the coasts are alarm'd or not. 1765 Earl Haddington *Forest Trees* 19 They do not value what soil they are set in.

6. *refl.* a. To pride or plume (oneself) *on* or *upon* a thing. † Also *to* a person.

1667 Pepys *Diary* 27 May, He..values himself upon having of things do well under his hand. 1699 Bentley *Phal.* 232 Mr. B. was not ashamed to write it, nay to value himself upon 't. *a* 1715 Burnet *Own Time* (1766) I. 20 Pierpont valued himself to me upon this service he did his country. 1748 *Anson's Voy.* iii. x. 413 The calm and patient turn of the Chinese, on which they so much value themselves. 1838 Lytton *Alice* ii. ii, A sensible and frequent..speaker,..valuing himself on not being a party man. 1855 Motley *Dutch Rep.* ii. v. (1866) 224 Moreover... the learned Doctor valued himself upon his logic.

b. To think highly of (oneself) *for* something.

1687 T. Brown *Saints in Uproar* Wks. 1730 I. 75 What sort of an animal was the dragon, which thou valuest thyself so much for slaying? 1725 *Portland Papers* (Hist. MSS. Comm.) VI. 118 They value themselves here for making very fine kid gloves for ladies. 1743 J. Morris *Serm.* ii. 53 Those extraordinary gifts, for which the Corinthians so highly valued themselves. 1837 J. H. Newman *Par. Serm.* I. xvii. 251 Every one is in danger of valuing himself for what he does.

†7. To give greater value to; to raise the estimation of. *Obs. rare.*

1614 Raleigh *Hist. World* v. iii. § 1. 421 Hanno..and his Partisans, being neither able to taxe the vertue of their enemies,..nor to performe the like seruices vnto the Common-weale, had nothing left, whereby to value them-

selues, excepting the generall reprehension of Warre. *a* 1635 Naunton *Fragm. Reg.* (Arb.) 16 It valued her the more,.. and it took best with the people. 1673 Temple *United Prov.* Wks. 1720 I. 54 The same Qualities and Dispositions do not value a private Man and a State.

III. †8. To equal in value; to be equivalent to. *Obs.*

1561 T. Hoby tr. *Castiglione's Courtyer* i. (1577) G j, Seeming unto them no golde nor siluer was inough to value them. 1624 Middleton *Game at Chess* iii. i, This goodness Whose worth no transitory piece can value. *a* 1642 Rowley *Birth Merlin* iv. ii, What articles or what conditions Can you expect to value half your wrong?

†b. *esp.* To have the value of (so much money).

1577 Hanmer *Anc. Eccl. Hist.* (1663) 12 In the Greek he writeth δραχμας, valuing six half pence a piece, the hundredth part of an Attick pound. 1611 Bible *Mark* xii. 15 A penny [*marg.* Valewing of our money seuen pence halfe penie. 1634 Sir T. Herbert *Trav.* 41 An English shilling values twentie two Pice. 1658 Phillips, *Julio*, a kind of Italian coin,..valuing about six pence.

†c. To be worth (nothing, more, etc.). *Obs.*

1544 tr. *Littleton's Tenures* 57 The parte of that one valueth much more than the part of the other. 1602 Marston *Antonio's Rev.* iv. i, Whose reeling censure, if I valew not, It valewes naught. 1613 Shaks. *Hen. VIII*, ii. iii. 52 What wer't worth to know The secret of your conference? *Anne*...Not your demand; it values not your asking. 1632 Lithgow *Trav.* iii. 113 Gold..values more in purest prise, Then drosse. 1799 Southey *Lett.* (1856) I. 69 The 'Maid of the Inn' you selected for censure, and in my own mind it values little.

Hence **Va·luing** *vbl. sb.*

1535 [see Value *v.* 2]. 1565 Cooper *Thesaurus, Aestimatio*, the prisyng or valuing of a thing. 1593 Q. Eliz. *Boeth.* i. pr. iv. 12 The valuing of most, regardes more fortunes event, than causes merit. 1621 *Stationers' Reg.* 16 Nov. (Arb.) IV. 23 A Booke for the true valewing of anie commoditie.

Valued (væ·liud), *ppl. a.* [f. prec.]

†1. In which value is indicated. *Obs.*—1

1605 Shaks. *Macb.* iii. i. 94 The valued file Distinguishes the swift, the slow, the subtle.

b. *Valued policy* (see quot. 1848).

1761 in Burrow *Law Rep.* II. 1171 A valued Policy is not to be considered as a Wager Policy. 1766 *Ibid.* IV. 69. 1848 Arnould *Marine Insur.* i. v. (1866) I. 218 A valued policy is one in which the agreed value of the subject insured..is expressed on the face of the policy. 1903 *Daily Chron.* 25 Sept. 6/7 Let..the private individual demand a 'valued' policy, and the monopoly of the big companies collapses.

2. Estimated, appraised; to which a definite value has been assigned.

1607 Middleton *Fam. Love* i. ii. 58 Art or nature never yet could set A valued price to her unvalued worth. 1613 Tapp *Pathw. Knowledge* 258 Now out of 252 li. the valued price of 12 peeces of Linnen cloth ready money, substract 46 li. [etc.] 1752 McDouall *Inst. Laws Scot.* II. 333 There is no mention in the brieve or service of the Valued rent. 1798 in *Hist. Moray* (1882) I. i. 172 The valued rent is £350.

3. Highly esteemed or appreciated.

1665 Glanvill *Defence Van. Dogm.* 79 Laertius sayes in his [book that] the Epicureans..were the only valued Sects of Philosophers. 1725 Pope *Odyssey* xv. 129 This silver bowl,..this valued gift be thine. 1746 Francis tr. *Horace, Epist.* i. xviii. 138 You..boldly guard the injur'd Fame Of a well-known, and valued Friend. 1803 Visct. Strangford *Poems of Camoens* (1810) 107 Within my bosom's cell I bear A recent wound—a valued woe. 1841 D'Israeli *Amen. Lit.* (1867) 160 The exposition of a political transaction is never without some valued results. 1856 Kane *Arct. Expl.* II. xxvii. 272, I have omitted that which was its most valued characteristic. It abounded in life.

Valueless (væ·liulės), *a.* [f. Value *sb.*]

1. Destitute of value; having no value.

1595 Shaks. *John* iii. i. 101 You haue beguil'd me with a counterfeit Resembling Maiesty, which being touch'd and tride, Proues valuelesse. 1684 *Foxe's A. & M.* III. 102/1 The Sentence..might not be found faulty and valueless [*earlier edd.* valureless]. 1782 Miss Burney *Cecilia* vii. vi, One single obstacle has power to render them valueless. 1819 Scott *Leg. Montrose* vi, Take them, therefore—they are to me valueless trinkets. 1848 Thackeray *Van. Fair* lxvii, It was found that all his property..was represented by valueless shares in different bubble companies. 1871 Freeman *Hist. Ess.* Ser. i. ix. 262 Like all chronicles of the kind, it is valueless alike for prophecy and for early history.

2. Priceless, invaluable. *rare*—1.

1820 Shelley *Prometh. Unb.* iv. 281 Infinite mines of adamant and gold, Valueless stones, and unimagined gems.

Hence **Va·luelessness.**

1838 *Lond. & Westm. Rev.* XXIX. 58 The valuelessness of all prior statistics of crime. 1881 Bruce *Chief End Revelation* iv. 189 The Spinozan doctrine as to the valuelessness of miracles for the purpose of revealing God.

Valuer (væ·liu,əɹ). [f. Value *v.*] **a.** One who estimates or assesses values; a valuator. **b.** One who values, or sets a value upon something; an appreciator.

1611 Cotgr., *Appreciateur*, a praiser, rater, valuer. 1638 R. Baker tr. *Balzac's Lett.* (vol. II) 66 To say nothing more hardly of you, you are too unjust a valuer of your selfe. 1660 tr. *Amyraldus' Treat. conc. Relig.* ii. viii. 266 What miserable valuers were they of its dignity. 1730 Bailey (fol.), *Appraiser*, a Valuer of Goods. 1854 *Act 17 & 18 Vict.* c. 229 § 29 To appoint a valuer to value the same. 1888 Bryce *Amer. Commw.* I. 493 The varying scales on which valuers proceed. 1893 *The Voice* (N. Y.) 31 Aug., A chairmaker..might bring a chair, and receive from the valuer..notes for as many hours' value [etc.].

†**Valure**, *sb. Obs.* Also 5 **valur, wallure**, 6 **valuer, va(l)lewer.** [app. an alteration of OF. *valur* or *valeur* Valour, after forms in -ure.]

1. a. Worthiness or merit; = Valour 1 a.

1422 Yonge tr. *Secreta Secret.* 139 What glory or what valure the may be-tyde. *c* 1440 *Ipomydon* 284 She saw also by his norture, He was a man of grete valure. *c* 1481 Caxton *Dialogues* 4 Be swyft and redy Hym or hem first to grete, Yf he be or they be men of valure. 1577 Stanyhurst *Descr. Ireland* vii. in *Holinshed*, I doubt not, but hys fame and renowme in learnyng, shall be aunswerable to his desert and valure in writyng. 1592 Wyrley *Armorie* 65 As to the gaser well it might appeere That all the Vallewer in the world was heere.

b. Physical strength or ability; power, might. *rare.*

1574 Hellowes *Guevara's Fam. Ep.* (1577) 3 Of our selues we are so weake, and our abilitie so small, our valure so litle, and haue so few things, that..of our selues we haue not what to giue. 1605 Willet *Hexapla Gen.* 440 Causing the Cananites to feare his force and valure.

c. Courage, bravery; = Valour 1 c.

Common *c* 1580–1610.

1577–82 Breton *Flourish upon Fancy* Wks. (Grosart) I. 18/2 Thy valure is but vauntes, thy weapons are but wordes. 1585 T. Washington tr. *Nicholay's Voy.* iv. xii. 125 The Arabians..beleue that in valure & hardines they doe surpasse al the other nations. 1606 Chapman *Gent. Usher* i. i, This is your old valure, nephew, that will fight sleeping as well as waking. 1640–1 *Kirkcudbr. War-Comm. Min. Bk.* (1855) 50 Barrones and gentilmen of good soirt..by quhas valure the kingdome hath ever been defendit.

2. Worth, importance, efficacy. Freq. in the phr. *of no valure*.

(*a*) *c* 1400 *Pilgr. Sowle* i. xxiv. (1859) 29 This excusacyon is of no valure. 1509 Fisher *7 Penit. Ps.* xxxviii. Wks. (1876) 81 Good hope,..without the whiche euery thynge that we do is of no valure. 1594 Carew *Huarte's Exam. Wits* v. (1596) 61 We call memory a reasonable power, because without it the vnderstanding and the imaginatiue are of no valure.

(*b*) 1456 Sir G. Haye *Law Arms* (S.T.S.) 214 For ellis war it litill of valure the privilege that the Emperour has gevin to the haly kirk. *a* 1533 Ld. Berners *Gold. Bk. M. Aurel.* (1546) B vj b, Wordes, whiche were not mete,..rude, and least of valure. 1577 Harrison *England* ii. vi. (1877) ii. 149 These [wines] are not least of all accompted of, bicause of their strength and valure. 1596 Bell *Surv. Popery* iii. ix. 397 The naturall valure only of good words. *Ibid.*, The valure and just estimation of eternal life.

3. = Value *sb.* 2.

1453 *Rolls of Parlt.* V. 269/1 Decreas of the pris and valure of the wolles. *c* 1489 Caxton *Sonnes of Aymon* xvi. 374 And whan Reynawde saw that that gyfte was so riche he was glad of it, bycause of yͤ grete valure of it. 1523 *Act 14 & 15 Hen. VIII*, c. 2 [They] shall..put to such markes to every of the same wares..upon payne of forfeyture the double valure of the same wares. 1568 Grafton *Chron.* II. 387 Swearing vnto him that he would prouyde other for him, that should amount to as good a valure. 1588 J. Mellis *Briefe Instr.* E j, Putting the valure of them, how much they be, after the common price in ready money.

b. In the phr. *of* (*great*, etc.) *valure*.

1485 Caxton *Paris & V.* (1868) 7 A shelde of crystalle of grete valure. 1491–2 *Sarum Church-w. Acc.* (Swayne) 41 Smalle peces of clene golde of litelle valure. 1523 Ld. Berners *Froiss.* I. cccxx. 495 He reputed this aduenture of more valure than v. hundred thousande frankes. 1553 Eden *Treat. New Ind.* (Arb.) 14 Hys horse is judged to be of such valure if you respect ye price, as is one of our cities. 1599 Hakluyt *Voy.* II. 234 There they put all their goods of any valure.

4. = Value *sb.* 4. Const. *of* (so much).

c 1480 *Childe of Bristowe* in Hazl. *E. P. P.* I. 124 Alle that for me thu dos pray, helpeth me not..the valure of a pese. 1485 Caxton *Chas. Gt.* 110, I doubte the not the valure of an olde dede bounde. 1518 *Star Chamber Cases* (Selden Soc.) II. 138 Robert edward wyll spende..to the valuer of twenty markys to helpe them with all. 1534 More *Comf. agst. Trib.* ii. Wks. 1184/1 He neuer vsed to passe vpon himselfe the valure of six pence at a meale.

5. = Value *sb.* 7 b.

1597 Morley *Introd. Mus.* Pref., With what toyle and wearinesse I was enforced to compare the parts for trying out the valure of some notes.

Hence †**Valure** *v. trans.*, = Value *v.* 2. *Obs.* Also †**Valureless** *a.*, valueless. *Obs.* †**Valurous** *a.*, valuable (cf. Valorous *a.* 3). *Obs.*

1487 *Act 3 Hen. VII*, c. 7 § 1 The nature, weight, content, or valure of all maner other merchandises used to be weyed or valured. 1563 Foxe *A. & M.* 1028/2 The sentence thereof might not be founde fautye and valureles by me. 1586 Marlowe *1st Pt. Tamburl.* i. ii, Thy Garments shall be.. Enchast with precious iuelles of mine owne. More rich and valurous than Zenocrates.

Valure, obs. variant of Velure.

Valuwen, southern ME. var. Fallow *v.*

Va·lval, *a. Bot.* [f. Valve *sb.* 3 b.] *Valval view*, that aspect of a diatom in which one of the valves is turned to the observer; the side-view.

1891– in *Cent. Dict.* and later Dicts.

Valvar (væ·lvăɹ), *a. rare.* [f. Valve *sb.* + -ar.] Of the nature of, pertaining to, a valve.

1831 Macgillivray tr. *Richard's Elem. Bot.* 420 Their calyx is superior with four or five valvar divisions. 1859 Mayne *Expos. Lex.*, *Valvaris*,..of or belonging to a valve: valvar.

Valvassor, variant of Vavasour.

Valvate (væ·lvēt), *a. Bot.* [ad. L. *valvāt-us* having folding-doors, f. *valva* Valve *sb.*]

1. Of sepals or petals: Applied to each other by the margins only.

1830 Lindley *Nat. Syst. Bot.* 51 Hamamelideæ, which are known by their habit,..and also by their valvate sepals and petals. 1870 Hooker *Stud. Flora* p. xi, Malvaceæ:..Sepals 5, valvate.

b. Of a calyx: Composed of sepals so united.

1858 Carpenter *Veg. Phys.* § 536 The calyx of the Rhamneæ being valvate (i. e. the sepals, before expanding, having their edges in proximity with each other). 1877 Hulme *Wild Flowers* I. p. xiii, Calyx five-partite, valvate in bud.

2. Of æstivation or vernation: Characterized by this arrangement of parts.

1829 Lindley *Synops. Brit. Bot.* 72 Calyx monophyllous, 4–5 cleft, with a valvate æstivation. 1849 Balfour *Man. Bot.* § 186 Sometimes they are..placed so as to touch each other by their edges; thus giving rise to valvate vernation. 1861 Bentley *Man. Bot.* 218 The valvate æstivation may be seen in the calyx of the Lime.

Valve (vælv), *sb.*¹ Also 5 **valwe**, 7 **value.** [ad. L. *valva* leaf of a door (usu. pl. *valvæ* a folding door). So F. *valve* (1611), Pg. *valva*.]

I. 1. One or other of the halves or leaves of a double or folding door.

1387 Trevisa *Higden* (Rolls) IV. 449 At þe laste þey brende þe valves of þe temple þet were i-heled wit gold. *c* 1440 *Promp. Parv.* 508/1 Valwe, *valva, vel valve*. 1661 Blount *Glossogr.* (ed. 2), *Valves*, folding doors or windows. 1718 Pope *Odyss.* i. 555 The bolt, obedient to the silken cord, To the strong staple's inmost depth restored, Secured the valves. 1834 Beckford *Italy* I. 326 Throwing open the valves, we entered the chapel. 1863 Baring-Gould *Iceland* 280 The outside of the valves [of the triptych] was painted with figures of S. John the Baptist and Moses 1871 B. Taylor *Faust* (1875) II. iii. 164 Ye valves of yon dark iron portals!

transf. *c* 1530 *Judic. Urines* i. iii. 8 For to delyuer and purge them oute by that membre, that is to say, by the matryce, and so out by the value, that is to say, by yͤ gate of hyr body.

b. A door controlling the flow of water in a sluice.

1790 *Act 33 Geo. III*, c. 90 § 65 If any Person..cause to be opened..any Lock Gate, or any Paddle, Valve, or Clough, belonging to any Lock..on the said Canal. 1847 Dwyer *Princ. & Pract. Hydraul. Engin.* 74 The gate or valve of a sluice is generally made to move by machinery in a vertical position.

2. a. *Conch.* One of the halves of a hinged shell; a single shell of similar form; a single part of a compound shell.

1661 Lovell *Hist. Anim. & Min.* Isagoge b 7 b, Some are covered on every side, as oisters, cocks, and tellinæ; others have but one valve, the other side sticking to rocks. 1771 *Phil. Trans.* LXI. 232, I separated the valves, and the rising part of the hinge to the edge shewed them to be shells. 1774 Goldsm. *Nat. Hist.* (1776) VII. 69 These shells take different forms, and are often composed of a different number of valves; sometimes six; sometimes but three. 1828 Stark *Elem. Nat. Hist.* II. 80 The hollow valve of this species..was formerly used as a drinking cup. *Ibid.*, The lower valve white, and longitudinally sulcated; upper valve rufous. 1871 T. R. Jones *Anim. King.* (ed. 4) 540 The elastic ligament for opening the valves..being placed externally instead of within the shell.

b. *Ent.* (See quot.)

1826 Kirby & Sp. *Entomol.* xxxiii. III. 390 *Valvæ* (the Valves), two lateral laminæ, often coriaceous, by which the ovipositor when unemployed is covered.

3. *Bot.* a. One of the halves or sections of a dehiscent pod, pericarp, or capsule.

1760 J. Lee *Introd. Bot.* i. vi. (1765) 13 *Siliqua*, a Pod, is a Pericarpium of two Valves, wherein the Seeds are fastened along both the Sutures or Joinings of the Valves. 1796 Withering *Brit. Plants* (ed. 3) I. 294 Pod long, cylindrical; ..valves 2, opening with a jerk, and the valves rolling back. 1861 Bentley *Man. Bot.* 452 The valves of the fruit opening longitudinally, and bearing transverse septa in their interior. 1870 Hooker *Stud. Flora* 235 Capsule globose;..valves septiferous.

b. In various applications (see quots.).

1785 Martyn *Lett. Bot.* xiii. (1794) 130 The inner [chaff] consisting also of two parts or valves, which you may call petals. 1796 Withering *Brit. Plants* (ed. 3) I. 176 Bloss[om]. 1 petal, funnel-shaped. Tube cylindrical, crooked... Mouth closed by 5 prominent convex, approaching valves. 1812 *New Bot. Gard.* I. 23 The stamina have six filaments, subulate, inserted into the valves of the nectary. 1832 Lindley *Introd. Bot.* 104 The pieces of which these three classes of bracteæ are composed are called valves or valvulæ by the greater part of botanists. *Ibid.* 126 In the most common state of the anther the cells..open with two valves, by a longitudinal fissure from the base to the apex. 1857 Henfrey *Bot.* § 629 The cells [of Diatomaceæ]..enclosed by a membrane..impregnated with silex and separable into valves. 1870 Hooker *Stud. Flora* 12 Anthers opening by 2 ascending lids or valves.

II. 4. *Anat.* A membranous fold in an organ or passage of the body (esp. in the heart, arteries, and veins), which automatically closes after the manner of a trap-door to prevent the reflux of blood or other fluid.

1615 Crooke *Body Man* 180 In each of these passages there are Values which hinder the refluence of the choler. 1653 More *Antid. Ath.* Scholia ii. xii. § 6 As to the Fabrick of the Valves and Veins of the Heart. 1688 Boyle *Final Causes* iv. 157 Our famous Harvey..took notice that the valves in the veins..were so placed that they gave free passage to the blood towards the heart. 1799 *Med. Jrnl.* II. 371 This foramen in the embryo..is closed by a valve which prevents the reflux of the blood. 1830 R. Knox *Béclard's Anat.* 208 The valves..close the vein, sustain the blood, and prevent its reflux towards the capillary vessels. 1870 Rolleston *Anim. Life* p. xlv, The valves, which in other Vertebrata guard the entrance of the great veins into the right auricle.

b. A similar part or structure serving to close a passage for other reasons.

1805 Bingley *Anim. Biog.* (ed. 3) I. 97 Within each [ear] there is a kind of secondary auricle..so placed as to serve for a valve or guard to the auditory passage. 1813 *Ibid.* (ed. 4) I. 110 The ears are short, and have each a very small inner valve. 1835–6 *Todd's Cycl. Anat.* I. 322/1 The pyloric orifice of the gizzard is guarded by a valve in many birds. 1863 A. M. Bell *Princ. Speech* 192 When the Stammerer has brought the *valve* of the throat—the glottis —under due control.

fig. 1871 R. H. Hutton *Ess.* (1877) I. 74 Animals..have, so to say, fewer valves in their moral constitution for the entrance of divine guidance.

†5. A supposed check (similar to above) to the reflux of sap in plants. *Obs.*

1664 *Phil. Trans.* I. 30 About the Pores of bodies, and a kind of Valves in wood. 1673–4 Grew *Anat. Pl., Anat. Trunks* (1682) 126 Which..plainly shews, That in the Sap-Vessels of a Plant, there are no Valves. *a* 1704 Locke *Elem. Nat. Phil.* ix. (1754) 35 The heat dilating, and the cold contracting those little tubes; supposing there be valves in them, it is easy to be conceived how the circulation is performed in plants. 1807 Vancouver *Agric. Devon* (1813) 435 These valves possess a contractile force,..whereby the regress of the moisture is prevented, and of course it is taken up by the tree.

6. *Mech.* A device of the nature of a flap, lid, plug, etc., applied to a pipe or aperture to control the passage of air, steam, water or the like, usually acting automatically by yielding to pressure in one direction only.

Many classes and varieties of valves are in use, and are distinguished by special epithets denoting form or purpose, as *ball-, clack-, cone-, disk-, flap-valve*; *air-, escape-, feed-, injection-valve*, etc. See also Safety-valve.

1659 Leak *Waterwks.* 13 Of the Valve or Suspiral. It will be also necessarie..to demonstrate the manner of the value of Copper which openeth itself by intervals. 1667 *Phil. Trans.* II. 447 A Square Wooden Bucket..on the ends of which are the moveable bottoms or Valves *EE.* 1702 Savery *Miner's Fr.* 68 Will not these Brass Valves.. in your Engine speedily ware out? 1800 Vince *Hydrost.* ix. (1806) 91 Each sucker has a valve opening upwards. 1839 R. S. Robinson *Naut. Steam Eng.* 11 The pressure shuts the valve in the neck of the air vessel, and opens the valve in the piston. 1889 Welch *Naval Archit.* 133 Self-acting or automatic valves are fitted where watertight bulkheads.. are pierced for ventilation purposes.

fig. 1830 Gen. P. Thompson *Exerc.* (1842) I. 295 The slightest degree of popular interference which can act as a valve to the great boiler, and prevent the whole from blowing up. 1847 De Quincey *Secr. Soc.* Wks. 1863 VI. 236 There was a valve in reserve, by which your perplexity could escape.

7. *attrib.* and *Comb.* a. In sense 6, as *valve-board, -box, casing, chest, engine, face*, etc.; *valve governor, lifter*; *valve-like, -shaped* adjs.; also in collocations used attributively, as *valve-guide stem, valve-rod end*.

The number of attributive uses is very great, esp. in recent technical works.

1869 *Eng. Mech.* 24 Dec. 352/3 There is a board screwed down on the top of A. That is the *valve-board. 1885 C. G. W. Lock *Workshop Receipts* Ser. iv. 290/2 The valve-boards are next hinged on to the feeder-boards. 1797 *Encycl. Brit.* (ed. 3) XVII. 766/2 Above..is the seat of the lower steam valve, opening into the *valve box. 1869 *Eng. Mech.* 3 Dec. 282 2 Take the high pressure valves out of the valve-box. 1839 R. S. Robinson *Naut. Steam Eng.* 44 The flange to which is bolted the *valve casing. 1887 D. A. Low *Machine Draw.* (1892) 74 An elevation of the valve casing with the cover and the valve removed. 1839 R. S. Robinson *Naut. Steam Eng.* 62 The blow-through pipe, terminating in a *valve chest. 1889 Welch *Naval Archit.* xi. 124 In the former, a suction-box or valve chest V is fitted beneath the pump. 1797 J. Curr *Coal Viewer* 44 The plug floor in all the common engines falls 17½ inches below the top of the boiler, and in the *valve engine it falls 2 feet 1 inch below. 1864 Webster, *Valve face. 1887 D. A. Low *Machine Draw.* (1892) 70 The angle which the valve face makes with its axis is generally 45°. 1842 *Penny Cycl.* XXII. 508/2 To bring the *valve-gear within.. reach of the engineer. 1835 Ure *Philos. Manuf.* 27 *Valve governors, shafts, and other geering of mills. 1875 Knight *Dict. Mech.* 2476/1 The *valve-guide stem has an end knob, by which its falling out is prevented. 1839 R. S. Robinson *Naut. Steam Eng.* 97 The eccentric rod pulled backwards and forwards by means of the *valve lifter. 1851 S. P. Woodward *Mollusca* (1856) 34 The in-coming and out-going currents..are kept apart by a *valve-like fringe. 1859 Semple *Diphtheria* 296 A valve-like sound or a peculiar hissing noise. 1836–41 Brande *Chem.* (ed. 5) 524 A slender pipe, open at both ends, inserted into the *valve-plug. 1831–3 *Encycl. Metrop.* (1845) VIII. 187/1 In this engine the working the valves is effected by eccentrics..below the *valve rods. 1861 Sir W. Fairbairn *Iron* 123 To knock off the point of the trigger from the shoulder on the valve-rod. 1887 D. A. Low *Machine Draw.* (1892) 119 Valve-rod end for a marine engine. 1841 *Civil Eng. & Arch. Jrnl.* IV. 379/2 H, the *valve-seat. 1844 *Ibid.* VII. 190/2 The next valve was composed of several triangular pieces, opening on leather joints, from the circumference of the *valve seating. 1879 *St. George's Hosp. Rep.* IX. 365 Small *valve-shaped wound over outer side of fracture. 1844 *Civil Engin. & Arch. Jrnl.* VII. 192 It was quite clear the *valve-spindle must be of adequate strength. 1827 Faraday *Chem. Manip.* xv. (1842) 373 Applying the mouth to the lower aperture of the *valve tube.

b. In sense 4, as *valve-flap, -lesion, segment*.

Many others occur in recent medical works.

1879 *St. George's Hosp. Rep.* IX. 433 The junction of two of the aortic valve-flaps. 1898 *Allbutt's Syst. Med.* V. 952 A deformed valve segment must..be a strained segment. *Ibid.* 1024 In the remainder there was no valve-lesion.

c. Special Combs.: **valve-shell**, a gasteropod of the genus *Valvata*; **valve-tailed bat** (see quot.).

1851 Woodward *Mollusca* i. 140 *Valvata*,..Valve-shell. 1871 *Cassell's Nat. Hist.* I. 316 *note*. The Valve-tailed Bat ..is remarkable..for the presence of a curious horny case, composed of two parts, which covers the extremity of the tail.

†**Valve**, *sb.*² *Obs.* [perh. an error for *volve, by confusion with prec.] A turn of a bandage.

1689 J. Moyle *Abstr. Sea Chyrurgery* i. vi. 45 Then a soft Rouler to come several turns about it, and every valve as it comes over the wound cut..in the middle. *Ibid.* 45.

Valve, *v. rare.* [f. Valve *sb.*¹]

1. *trans.* To furnish with a valve or valves; to govern or check, to hold *back*, by a valve or similar device.

1861 Smiles *Engineers* II. 160 Whilst the fresh waters should be allowed freely to escape, the sea should be valved back, and prevented flowing in upon the land. 1899 *Allbutt's Syst. Med.* VI. 512 It is probable that by these synapses the circuits of the nervous system..are..securely valved against regurgitation.

2. *intr.* To make use of a valve or valves; *spec.* in ballooning, to open a valve in order to descend.

1906 *Westm. Gaz.* 3 Oct. 8/1 All we could do was to undulate, alternately valving and ballasting.

Valved (vælvd), *a.* [f. Valve *sb.*]

1. With limiting terms: a. Of a door: Having (so many) leaves. *rare.*

1676 Hobbes *Iliad* 375 In the pale a high two-valved door For chars and waggons to go in and out.

b. *Bot.*, etc. Having (so many) valves.

See also *two-valved* s.v. Two a.

1771 *Encycl. Brit.* I. 637/2 *Siliqua*, is a double-valved pericarpium. 1796 Withering *Brit. Plants* (ed. 3) III. 867 Capsule 4-valved: seeds roundish. 1831 South *Otto's Path. Anat.* 74 There are some which..live for protection..even in the double-valved muscles. 1847 W. E. Steele *Field Bot.* 73 Fruit mostly a dry or fleshy capsule, 1 or many-celled and valved.

2. Provided with a valve or valves, in various senses.

1793 Martyn *Lang. Bot.*, *Valvatum petalum*, a valved petal. 1842 Francis *Dict. Arts*, *Valved*, anything that opens upon hinges or to which a valve of any kind is attached. 1852 Th. Ross tr. *Humboldt's Trav.* I. i. 12 We made several experiments by means of a valved thermometrical sounding lead, on the temperature of the ocean. 1873 *Routledge's Young Gentl. Mag.* Feb. 170/1 A complete set of valved instruments, consisting chiefly of cornets, clavicors, and trombones. 1899 *Allbutt's Syst. Med.* VII. 254 The blood is returned to the heart by means of muscular movements acting on the valved veins.

Valveless (væ·lvlės), *a.* [f. Valve *sb.*] Having no valve; destitute or devoid of valves.

1830 Lindley *Nat. Syst. Bot.* 219 Capsule..sometimes valveless, or dehiscing transversely. 1851 Woodward *Mollusca* (1856) 69 Animal and pen like Loligo in most respects;..funnel valveless. 1881 Mivart *Cat* 216 The hepatic veins are valveless. 1884 Knight *Dict. Mech.* Suppl. 919 The 'Wardwell' valveless engine..is horizontal.

Va·lvelet. *rare.* Also 9 **valvlet.** [f. Valve *sb.* + -let.] A small valve.

1793 Martyn *Lang. Bot.*, *Valvula*, a..Valvelet, or Valvule. [Hence in later Dicts.] 1870 tr. *Pouchet's Universe* 125 Two large openings, each furnished with two valves or valvlets intended to prevent the reflux of the blood.

Va·lviform, *a. rare.* [ad. mod.L. *valviformis* or F. *valviforme*.] Valve-shaped.

1819 Samouelle *Entomol. Compend.* 268 Valviform parts of oviduct. 1859 Mayne *Expos. Lex.* 1321.

‖**Valvula** (væ·lviŭlă). *Anat.* Pl. **valvulæ.** [med. or mod.L., dim. of *valva* Valve *sb.* Cf. L. *valvolæ* pod of legumes.] A valve or valvule.

Usually with Latin qualifying term, as *valvula coli, valvulæ conniventes*.

1615 H. Crooke *Body of Man* (1631) 853 Some men had rather call them [*sc.* valves in the veins of the joints] *Ostiolæ* than *Valvulæ*. 1653 More *Antid. Ath.* ii. xii. § 6 You may add to these the notable contrivance of the Heart, its two Ventricles and its many *Valvulae*. 1832 [see Valve *sb.*¹ 3 b]. 1859 *Todd's Cycl. Anat.* V. 346/2 Opposite the attached border of the *valvula*, this layer is somewhat thick.

Valvular (væ·lviŭlăɹ), *a.* [f. prec.]

1. Having the form or function of a valve; composed or consisting of valves. Chiefly *Anat.* and *Bot.*

(*a*) 1797 M. Baillie *Morb. Anat.* (1807) 32 The valvular apparatus between the auricles and ventricles is also occasionally thickened. *Ibid.* 104 The œsophagus necessarily acquired a valvular communication with it. 1843 J. J. Wilkinson tr. *Swedenborg's Anim. Kingd.* I. ii. 68 Among these glands..we observe a great number of transparent vessels, with valvular divisions. 1878 T. Bryant *Pract. Surg.* I. 25 It may appear as a direct or as a valvular opening, depressed, or raised.

(*b*) 1829 Lindley *Synops. Brit. Bot.* 54 Sepals 4–5, with a valvular æstivation. 1830 — *Nat. Syst. Bot.* 141 The calyx is valvular, and the petals only 2. 1870 Hooker *Stud. Flora* 298 Ovary superior. Capsule valvular.

(*c*) 1876 J. J. Wilkinson *Hum. Sci. & Div. Rev.* 67 The gates of science are valvular, and open from above downwards, but cannot be opened from below upwards.

2. Furnished with a valve or valves.

1808 Barclay *Muscular Motions* 233 Valvular veins, when divided across, require a ligature only at the orifice which points towards the heart.

3. Of or pertaining to a valve or valves.

1866 A. Flint *Princ. Med.* iii. 308 The structural lesions relate, in the first place, to the valves and orifices of the heart. These are known commonly as valvular lesions. 1876 Bristowe *Th. & Pract. Med.* 492 Valvular defects may be of two kinds; they may be obstructive,..or such as admit of regurgitation. 1881 *Med. Temp. Jrnl.* XLVIII. 209 Valvular disease of the heart.

Va·lvulate, *a. rare.* [f. as prec. + -ate ¹.] Furnished with small valves.

1838 Rolleston & Jackson *Anim. Life* 564 The length of the valve is greater than its breadth, except in the form known as valvulate pedicellariae.

Valvule (væ·lviul). [Anglicized f. Valvula or a. F. *valvule*.] A small valve, in various senses.

1755 in Johnson. 1760 J. Lee *Introd. Bot.* i. vi. (1765) 13 The Inclosure of the Capsule, which surrounds the Fruit externally, is called a Valvule. 1831 T. Hope *Ess. Orig. Man* II. 62 Their weight, pressing backwards on the parietes of the vessels, scoops these out at certain distances into bags or valvules. 1870 tr. *Pouchet's Universe* 126 In the interior of this lengthened heart larger valvules..are folded back against the wall to let the blood pass forward. 1879 *Trans. Linn. Soc.* II. i. 31 The edge..is not straight, but cut into a series of minute valvules, the crescentic or respiratory leaves.

‖**Valvuli·tis.** *Path.* [f. Valvula + -itis.] Inflammation of the valves of the heart.

1891 in *Cent. Dict.* 1897 *Allbutt's Syst. Med.* III. 43 A grave sign indicative of serious and generally persistent or recurrent valvulitis. 1898 *Ibid.* V. 866 Endocarditis affects principally the valves of the heart, hence the name valvulitis.

Valwe, southern ME. var. Fallow *sb.* and *v.*²

Valx, obs. Sc. form of Wax *sb.*

Valyaunce, obs. form of Valiance.

†**Va·lyl(e.** *Chem. Obs.* [f. Val-erian *sb.* + -yl(e).] = Butyl.

1850 Daubeny *Atom. The.* viii. (ed. 2) 249 The previous discovery made by Dr. Kolbe, of a compound of carbon and hydrogen derived by electrolysis from the valerianic acid, and hence called valyle. 1857 Miller *Elem. Chem., Org.* 195 Tetryl, Butyl, or Valyl.

Va·lylene. *Chem.* [f. as prec. + -ene.] (See quots.)

1868 Watts *Dict. Chem.* V. 982 *Valylene*...This hydrocarbon is found..among the products of the action of alcoholic potash on dibromide of valerylene. 1868 *Fownes' Chem.* (ed. 10) 564 Quintone or Valylene.

Vambrace (væ·mbrēs). Now only *Archæol.* Forms: α. 4 **vaumbras**, 4–6 **vambras** (-**brase**, 5 **uambras**, 6 *Sc.* **wambraiss**), 7 **vambrasse** (8 -**brass**). β. 4– **vambrace** (5 **wam-**, 7 **van-**). [var. of *vaunt-* Vantbrace, through elision of *t* and change of *nb* to *mb* by assimilation.] Defensive armour for the (fore-) arm.

α. *c* 1330 R. Brunne *Chron. Wace* (Rolls) 10030 Vaumbras & rerbras, wyþ coters of stel. 1385–6 *Durham Acc. Rolls* (Surtees) 133, ij palets, j brestplat, vambras. 1392 *Test. Ebor.* (Surtees) I. 171 Unum bonum par cerotecarum de plate, cum vambrase et rerebrase. 1461 *Will of Benney* (Somerset Ho.), j salett garnisshed cum argento, legharnes, vambras, & rerebras. *a* 1548 Hall *Chron., Hen. IV*, 12 One sorte had the vambrases, the pace gardes, the grandgardes..parted with golde and azure. 1581 Styward *Mart. Discipl.* ii. 165 To haue good..poldrones and vambrases for their shoulders & armes. 1627 Drayton *Agincourt* 8 [Whether] The Vambrasse, or the Pouldron, they should prize.

β. 1411 *E. E. Wills* (1882) 19 A pare of vambrace and rerebrace. *c* 1450 Metham *Wks.* (E.E.T.S.) 37 Thys knyghtys vambracys in coloure Alle depeyntyd with red were. 1513 *MS. Papers 5 Hen. VIII*, No. 4101 (P. R. O.), His vambraces, polvorines, ij Salettes (etc.). 1581 Styward *Mart. Discipl.* i. 44 A fayre Corslet, with all the peeces appertaining to the same, that is the curats, yͤ collers, the poldrens with the Vambraces. 1624 Capt. Smith *Virginia* iii. ii. 47 On his arme..an Otters skinne, or some such matter for his vambrace. 1687 A. Lovell tr. *Thevenot's Trav.* iii. 44 They have likewise the Coat of Mail, the Cuirats, the Head-piece, and a Vambrace fastened to the Sword. 1734 tr. *Rollin's Rom. Hist.* (1827) II. 379 The vambraces or greaves which covered the arms, thighs, and legs of the horsemen. 1829 Scott *Anne of G.* xxxii, Among gauntlets, boots, vambraces, and such like gear. 1850 Boutell in *Gentl. Mag.* CXX. ii. 44 The arms are cased in brassarts and vambraces of plate.

transf. 1766 *Phil. Trans.* LVI. 274, I supported the arm with a vambrace, or half-canal, made of one very thin piece of wood.

Va·mbraced, *a. Her.* [f. prec.] Of an arm: Defended or covered by a vambrace.

1610 Guillim *Heraldry* iv. xv. (1611) 232 He beareth Gules, three Dexter Armes Vambraced and Proper. 1688 Holme *Armoury* iii. xvii. 109/2 He beareth Gules a dexter Arme Vambraced, Or. *c* 1828 Berry *Encycl. Her.* I. Gloss., *Vambraced*, a term which implies that the arm is wholly covered with armour. 1868 Cussans *Her.* vi. 92 An Arm encased in armour is Vambraced.

†**Vambrash**, *v. Obs. rare.* Also -**brishe**. [Of obscure origin.] *trans.* To brandish.

1577 Grange *Golden Aphrod.* N j, For Iupiter touching the heauens with his wande, caused them to thunder & vambrishe lightnings. 1593 Nashe *Christ's T.* 27 b, With glistering naked swords, which..he made semblance as if hee shaked and vambrasht. 1623 Cockeram i, *Vambrash*, to shake a staffe or launce.

Vame, obs. Sc. f. Wem *sb.*, Womb.

Vamer, Vameure, varr. *vamure* Vaumure.

Vamose (vămōᵘ·s), **vamoose** (vămū·s), *v.* *U.S. colloq.* Also **vamos, vamous, vamoos, varmoose.** [ad. Sp. *vamos* let us go.]

1. *intr.* To depart, make off, decamp, disappear.

α. 1848 in Bartlett *Dict. Amer.*, Its occupants..forthwith vamosed with their baggage. 1855 Haliburton *Nat. & Hum. Nat.* I. 112, I makes a spring in after him, and caught him by the hair of the head, just as he was vamosing. 1893 McCarthy *Red Diamonds* I. 173 The fifth name was that of Ratt Gundy, opposite to which Seth Chickering had written the one word: 'Vamosed'.

β. 1859 *Slang Dict.* 114 *Vamous*, to go, or be off. 1862 *Illustr. Lond. News* 24 May 540/3 Guess, they'd better varmoose. 1874 M. Collins *Frances* III. 80 If I can get money down for some of my gold bonds, we'll vamoos at once. 1895 J. G. Millais *Breath fr. Veldt* (1899) 175 The hunter was voted a fraud..and was..told to 'vamoose'.

VAMP

Vanquished (væ·ŋkwiʃt), *ppl. a.* Also 5-6 *Sc.* vencust, 6 *Sc.* vinuast, vanquest, -queist; 6 vanquished, 7 vanquisht. [f. as prec.] Defeated, overcome, subdued.

Vanquisher (væ·ŋkwiʃəɹ). Also 5-6 *Sc.* venquiser, vanquesser. β. 5 vaynquyeshar, -our, 6 venquessehour, vanquisher, -an-quisher. [f. as prec.] A conqueror, subduer.

Vanquishing, *vbl. sb.* [f. as prec.] The action of overcoming or subduing.

Vanquishing, *ppl. a.* [f. as prec.] That overcomes or conquers.

Vanquishment (væ·ŋkwiʃmənt). [f. as prec.] The act of vanquishing or overcoming.

†**Vanquisant**, *a. Obs.⁻¹* [ad. obs. F. *vainquissant*, pres. pple. of *vainquir*: see VANQUISH v.] Victorious.

Vansire (væ·nsaɪɹ). *Zool.* [a. F. *vansire*, ad. Malagasy *vontsira*.] The marsh-ichneumon (*Herpestes galera*) of South Africa.

Vanston(e, southern ME. *var.* FONTSTONE.

Vant, southern *var.* FONT *sb.* [f. VAUNT *sb.* and *v.*: obs. *Sc.* f. WANT v.]

Vantage (vɑ·nteˈdʒ), *sb.* Also 4-7 vauntage, 4 vantayge; 5-6 *Sc.* wantage, 7-8 'vantage. [a. AF. *vantage* (1305), *var.* of OF. *avantage*. Cf. the later aphetic VANTAGE *sb.* and *v.*]

1. Advantage, benefit, profit, gain. Now *arch.*

2. Superiority, mastery; ascendancy; pre-eminence. *Obs.*

3. Advantage or superiority in a contest; position of superiority.

Vantage, *v.* [f. prec. sb.] *trans.* To benefit, profit.

Vantage-ground. [VANTAGE *sb.* 7.] A position which places one at an advantage for defence or attack.

Vant-guard, *v. Obs.⁻¹* [f. GUARD *v.*; prob. after VANT-GUARD *sb.*] *trans.* To defend in front.

Vantbrace. Now *arch.* or *Hist.* Forms: a. 4-5 vauntbras, 6-brace; 5-7 vantbras, 7-8 vantbrace. b. AF. *vantbras*, aphetic f. *avantbras*, i. *avant*-before + *bras* arm.] = VAMBRACE.

Vantaged, *a.* Not having any advantage or superiority.

Vantageous, *a. Obs. rare⁻¹* [f. VANTAGE *sb.* + -OUS.] Advantageous, profitable.

Vantageable, *a. Obs. rare* Also 6 vantagable. Advantageous, profitable.

Vantageless, *a.* [VANTAGE *sb.*] Not having any advantage or superiority.

Vantation. *Obs.⁻¹* [app. f. *vaunt* or VAUNT v.] Ostentation, display.

Vantward. Forms: a. 4-5 vauntbras, 6-brase; 5-7 vantbras. [f. as prec.]

Vanward, *a.* [VAN *sb.*¹ + -WARD.] Situated, having place or position, in the van or front.

Vanward, *adv.* [f. as prec.] Towards or in the front; forward. Also with *to*.

2. A vapid remark, idea, feature, etc.

Vapidly, *adv.* [f. as prec. + -LY².] In a vapid manner.

Vapidness (væ·pidnəs), *sb.* [f. as prec. + -NESS.] The quality of being vapid.

Vapography. [See quot.]

Vapon, obs. *Sc.* form of WEAPON.

Vapor, *var.* of VAPOUR *sb.* and *v.*

Vaporiality. Also *vapour*. [f. next.] Capacity of being vaporized.

Vaporable (ˈvæpəɹabl), *a.* Also *vapour*. [ad. med.L. *vapōrābilis*: see VAPOUR *sb.* and -ABLE. Cf. F. *vaporable*.] Capable of being converted into vapour.

Vaporate, *ppl. a. Obs.⁻¹* [ad. L. *vapōrāt-us*, pa. pple. of *vapōrāre*: see next.] Capable of converting substances into vapour.

Vaporate, *v. Obs.* Also *vapour*. [f. L. *vapōrāt-*, ppl. stem of *vapōrāre* to convert into, become, vapour.]

Vaporer. Also *vapour*. [f. as prec. + -ER¹.] One that vapours.

Vaporiferous, *a. rare⁻¹* [f. L. *vapōrifer* + -OUS.] That makes or stirs up vapour.

Vaporific (væˌpəɹi·fik), *a.* Also *vapori*-. [f. L. *vapōri*-VAPOUR *sb.* + -FIC.] Associated or connected with, producing or causing, vaporization.

Vaporiform (ˈvæpəɹifɔɹm), *a.* Also *vapour*-. [f. L. *vapōri*-, stem of *vapor* VAPOUR *sb.* + -FORM.] Of the nature of, or resembling, vapour; in the vaporiform state.

Vaporimeter. Also *vapour*. An instrument for measuring the amount of vapour.

Vaporish, *a.* Also *vapourish*. [f. VAPOUR *sb.*]

Vaporizable (ˈvæpəɹaizəbl), *a.* Also *vapour*-. [f. VAPORIZE v. + -ABLE.] Capable of being vaporized; vaporable.

Vaporization (væˌpəɹaiˈzeiʃən). Also *vapour*. [f. next + -ATION.] The action or process of converting, or of being converted, into vapour.

Vaporize (ˈvæpəɹaiz), *v.* Also *vapour*-. [f. L. *vapōr*-, VAPOUR *sb.* + -IZE.]
1. *trans.* To convert into vapour.
2. *intr.* To rise in or as vapour.
3. To give off vapour.

Vaporose, *a.* Also *vapour*-. [ad. L. *vapōrōs-us*: see VAPOROUS.] Full of vapour; vaporous.

Vaporosity. Also *vapour*. [f. as prec.] The quality of being vaporous.

Vaporous (ˈvæpəɹəs), *a.* Also *vapour*-. [ad. L. *vapōrōs-us*: see VAPOUR *sb.* and -OUS.]
1. Of, pertaining to, or of the nature of, vapour.
2. Full of, or abounding in, vapour.
3. Filled with, thick or dim with, vapour; foggy, misty.
4. Having the form, nature, or consistency of vapour.

Vaporously, *adv.* [f. prec. + -LY².] In a vaporous manner.

Vaporousness. [f. as prec. + -NESS.] The quality of being vaporous.

Vaporulent. *rare⁻¹* [f. VAPOUR *sb.*]

Vapour (ˈvæpəɹ), *sb.* Forms: 4-5 vapoure, vapur, 4-6 vapor, vapour. [a. AF. *vapour* (OF. *vapor*) or ad. L. *vapōr*-, *vapor* steam. Cf. F. *vapeur*, Sp. and Pg. *vapor*, It. *vapore*.]
1. Without article: Matter in the form of a steamy or imperceptible emission; *esp.* the form into which liquids are naturally converted by the action of a sufficient degree of heat.
2. *pl.* In older medical use: Exhalations supposed to be developed within the organs of the body (*esp.* the stomach), and to have an injurious effect upon the health.
3. *pl.* In older medical use: = VAPOURS.
4. An exhalation of the nature of steam, or an emanation consisting of imperceptible particles, usually due to the effect of heat upon moisture.
5. Something unsubstantial, transitory, or worthless.
6. A morbid condition supposed to be caused by the presence of such exhalations; depression of spirits, hypochondria, hysteria, or other nervous disorder.
7. *fig.* Vain imagination, fancy, or whim.
8. *fig.* of persons or minds: Inclined to be fanciful, vague, or frothy, in ideas or discourse.

Vapour, *v.* [f. prec. sb.]

VARNISHED.

Varnishing, vbl. sb.

1. The action of applying varnish or of coating anything with varnish.

2. A coating of varnish. *in quot. fig.*

3. *attrib.*, as **varnishing brush**, **varnishing day**.

Varnish-tree, Sc. var. WARNINN(ING.

Varnisoun, Sc. var. WARNISON.

Varon, *a. Obs. [ad. L. vārōnem]* Wall-eyed.

Varnish, variant of VARNICE.

Varp, *obs. Sc. f.* WARP *v.* **Varra,** *dial.* var.

Varramine, *(varə-mīn), n.* [ad. L. *Varrōniān-us*, *Varro-* (see def.).] Of or pertaining to the Roman author M. Terentius Varro.

Varsal, *(vā-sal), a.* and *adv. Also 7* varsall.

Varsovienne, *[F., fem. of Varsovien, f. Varsovie* (see def.).] A dance, app. of French origin, resembling some of the Polish national dances.

Varsovy, na. var. of WARSAW.

Vart, *obs. f.* WART.

Vartiwell, *dial. Also 8* vartuale. *Obs.*

Varus, *(vēə-rəs). Path.* [L. *vīrus* knock-kneed.] A physical deformity in which the foot is turned inwards.

Varus, *(vēə-rəs). Path.* [L. *varus* pimple.] A stone-pock.

Varvicite, variant of VARVICITE.

Varvel, *(vā-vel). Forms: a. 6* vervel, **varuel**, **vervile,** 7-9) vervel, 7 vell, vervail (a. vervil, 8. 7 **varuell**, varvell, 8. 7 **varviel**(e, etc. [a. OF. *vervelle* (1350), *vervele*, *varvele*, etc. [F. *vervelle*] in the same sense.

Varvicite, variant of VARVICITE.

VARVICITE.

Varsatile, obs. variant of VERSATILE *a.*

Varsity *(vā-siti). Also* varsity. [Colloquial abbreviation of UNIVERSITY.]

Varso *(vā-so). Obs. Also* varso.

Varsovian *n. ... warsaw.* Belonging to Warsaw.

Varus, *[var. of next, after It. or I. forms.]*

Vartiwell, *dial. Also 8* vartuale. *Obs.*

Varvel, *(vā-vel).*

Varvicite *(vā-visəit). Min. [f. med.L. Varvicia Warwickshire: see -ITE. Named by Phillips (1829).]* An impure pyrolusite or wad, resulting from the alteration of manganite (Chester).

VARY.

Vary, *sb. Obs. [f. VARY *v.*]*
A variation; a hesitation or vacillation.

Vary, *v. Forms: 4-7* varie, varye, **vari,** **varry**, 5-7 varye. [a. L. *variāre*, f. *varius* various.]

I. *intr.* 1. Of things: To undergo change or alteration; to pass from one condition, state, etc., to another, esp. with frequent or ready change or difference within certain limits.

b. *Without concr.*

II. *trans.* 8. To cause to change or alter; to introduce changes or alterations into (something).

VARYING.

Varying, *vbl. sb. [f. as prec.]*

1. That varies, in senses of the verb; tending to vary or change.

2. Varied in colour; variegated. *Obs.*

3. *Varying hare,* a species of hare, inhabiting northern or elevated regions, that of changing to white in winter; the Alpine, blue, or mountain hare.

Varyingly *adv.*

Varyer, obs. form of VERITY.

VASCULAR.

Vas, *sb.* Pl. **vasa** (vē-sa). [L. *pl. vāsa*.]

1. *a. Anat.* A hollow organ serving for the conveyance of a liquid in the body.

Vase *(vāz). Also 6* vase, 7 vaze, vaze. *Obs.*

Vascular *(væ-skiūlăr), a. ad. mod.L. vāscul-āris, f. L. vāscul-um, dim. of vās VAS. So F. vasculaire, It. vascolare, Sp. and Pg. vascular.]*

1. *Bot.* Of fibres, tissue, etc.: Having the form of tubular vessels; consisting of continuous tubes of simple membrane.

Vascularity *(-æ-riti). [f. VASCULAR a. + -ITY.]* Vascular form or condition.

Vascularization.

Vascularize *(væ-skiūlăraiz), v. [f. VASCULAR a. + -IZE.]* To increase the vascularity.

Vasculose, Vasculous.

Vasculum *(væ-skiūləm). [L., dim. of vās VAS.]*

1. *Bot.* = ARCIDIUM 2.

2. *Bot.* Having the character or properties of a conveying vessel; vascular.

Vase *(vāz). Also 6* vase, 7 vase. [a. F. *vase*, ad. L. *vās* vessel.]

1. A vessel of circular section.

2. *Archit.* The body of the Corinthian or Composite capital.

VASE.

Vasculiferous *(-lī-fərəs), a. [See quots.]*

Vasculiform, *a. [f. L. vāsculum, combining form of vāsculum, + -FORM.]*

Vascular, etc.

VASECTOMIZED.

o. A calyx or other growth resembling a vase.

Vasculated *(væ-skiūlātid), ppl. a. [f. L. vāscul-um VASCULUM.]* Provided with small vessels.

Vaseline *(væ-sĕlĭn, -in), sb. [Irreg. f. G. *wasser* water + Gr. *élaion* oil + -INE.]* A soft, greasy substance used as an ointment for lubricating etc., by evaporating petroleum and passing the residuum through animal charcoal. (Cf. PETROLATUM.)

Vase-motor, *a.* and *sb. Phys.*

Vasectomized, *ppl. a. [f. next.]* That has had the *vas deferens* removed.

Vasectomy, *Surg. [f. L. vās- VAS + -ECTOMY.]* Excision of the *vas deferens* or a portion of this.

VASSAL.

Vassal *(væ-sal), sb.* and *a. Forms: 4* vassale, 6 vassall, 6-7 vassal. [a. F. vassal, ad. med.L. vassallus.]*

I. *sb.*

1. In the feudal system, one holding lands from a superior on conditions of homage and allegiance; a feudatory; a tenant in fee.

2. A humble servant or subordinate; one devoted to the service of another.

3. *attrib.* and *as adj.* a. Having the status of, subject to, subordinate; a vassal.

4. *attrib.* or *as adj.* a. Having the status of, subject, subordinate.

VASSAL. 60	VAST.	VAST. 61	VASTLY.

Vassal. ... *Now rare.* Also 7 *vassall(e, -ayl, -ail.*

1. *trans.* To make subject or subordinate to some thing or person.

Vassaldom. *rare⁻¹.* [f. VASSAL *sb.* +-DOM.]

Vassaless. *rare.* [f. VASSAL *sb.* +-ESS.] A female vassal.

Vassalic. *rare⁻¹.* [f. VASSAL *sb.* +-IC.] Of or pertaining to vassals or vassalage.

Vassalize. (væˈsəlaiz), *v.* [f. VASSAL *sb.* +-IZE.]

Vassalry. Also 7 vasselry, 6 vassalrie, -rey. [f. VASSAL *sb.* + -RY. Cf. vassalerie.]

Vassalship. [f. VASSAL *sb.* + -SHIP.]

Vassalage. (See quots.)

Vassality. [f. VASSAL *sb.*]

Vassalry. Vassalage.

Vassaless. See -ESS.

Vast (vast), *a.* (*adv.*), *and sb.* [ad. L. *vastus* void, immense, extensive, etc., var. of *vāstus* (1611), Fr. Sp. Pg. *vasto.*]

1. Of very great or large dimensions or size; huge, immense, enormous.

2. Of great or immense extent or area; extensive, far-stretching.

Vast, *sb.* [ad. L. *vastus* WASTE.]

Va'stacy. *Obs.⁻¹* [ad. L. *vast-āre* to lay waste, *vastity.*] Vastness.

Va'state, *v.* *rare.* [f. L. *vastāt-*, ppl. stem of *vastāre.*]

Vastation. (vəsˈteɪʃən). Also 6 vastacioun. [ad. L. *vastātiōn-, vastātio,* n. of action f. *vastāre.*]

Vasty (vasˈti), *a.* [f. VAST *a.* + -Y.]

Vastly (vastˈli), *adv.*
1. In a waste or desolate manner.

Vastitude. (vasˈtitiud). [ad. L. *vastitūdō,* f. *vastus* VAST.]

Vastity. [ad. L. *vastitās,* f. *vastus* VAST.]

Vastland. *Obs.* Sc. form of WESTLAND.

VASTNESS. 62	VATICAL.	VATICAN. 63	VATINIAN.

Vastness (vastˈnes). [f. VAST *a.* + -NESS.]

Vastness. (vaˈstnes). [f. VAST *a.*]

Vasty. (See VAST.)

Vat (væt), *sb.* Forms: 3 yeat, 3-4 uat, 5 -vat, 4, 6 vatte, 6 vatt; 4-5 vaet, 6, 8 vaotte.

Vat (væt), *v.* [f. prec.] *trans.* To place or store in a vat.

Va'tful. [f. VAT *sb.* + -FUL.]

Vatch, southern dial. var. of VETCH.

Vatch., variant of FETCH *sb.*

Vates (vēˈtiːz), *sb.* [L.] A poet or bard, esp. one who is divinely inspired.

Vatful. See VA'TFUL above.

Vath., southern ME. variant of FATHOM *sb.*

Vatican (væ'tikæn). Also 6-7 Vaticane. [a. F. *Vatican* (= It. Sp., Pg. *Vaticano*; or ad. L. *Vaticān-us, -um* (sc. *mons* or *collis*); see def.]

1. (With initial capital, and now always with *the.*) The palace of the Pope built upon the Vatican Hill in Rome.

Vaticanize. *v.* [f. VATICAN + -IZE.] *trans.*

Vaticide (væˈtisaid). [ad. L. *vātēs* prophet + -CIDE.] One who kills a prophet.

Vaticinal (vaˈtisinal). [f. L. *vāticin-us* prophetic + -AL.]

Vaticinate (vaˈtisineit), *v.* [f. L. *vāticināt-,* ppl. stem of *vāticinārī.*]

Vaticination (vatisineɪˈʃən), *sb.* [ad. L. *vāticinātiōn-, vāticinātio,* n. of action.]

Vaticinator. Now *rare.* [a. obs. F. *vaticinateur* (Cotgr.) or ad. L. *vāticinātor,* agent-n. f. *vāticinārī* to VATICINATE.]

Vaticinatress. [f. VATICINATOR + -ESS¹, after L. *vāticinātrix.*] A female vaticinator; a prophetess.

Vaticinatrice. [ad. L. *vāticinātrix.*] Prophetess.

Vaticine. *Obs.* [ad. L. *vāticinium,* prophecy.]

Vatician. Variant of VATICINE. *Obs.*

Vaticinism. [f. L. *vāticini-um* prophecy + -ISM.]

Vatinian (vaˈtinian), *a.* [ad. L. *Vatīniān-us.*] Vatinian. A Roman, whom all men hated for his odious behaviour (Blount 1674).

of troops; a soldier or horseman sent out in advance of the main body. Usually in pl. *Obs.*

α. 1560 Daus tr. *Sleidane's Comm.* 433 b, He by his vauntcurrers levied as muche power as he possible mighte. 1569 Stocker tr. *Diod. Sic.* II. x. 55 The vauntcurrers of eche side gaue intelligence of the approch of one an other. 1570 R. Hichcock *Quintess. Wit* 68 b, In the spyes, in the guides, in the vantcorrours, in the principall officers. 1601 R. Johnson *Kingd. & Commw.* 184 Vpon the head of the battell ranged 200 thousande horsemen in small troupes, like our vantcurrers. 1614 Raleigh *Hist. World* III. x. II. 114 On the sodaine one of their Vaunt-currors brought newes of the King's approch. 1650 R. Stapylton *Strada's Low C. Wars* IX. 50 Some Vantcurrers advancing a little before the Army.

β. 1579–80 North *Plutarch, Publicola* (1895) I. 275 Lucretius..was appointed to make head against the vauntcurriers of the Sabynes. 1600 Dymmok *Ireland* (1843) 31 The rebel..deliveringe some few shott out of the woods and ditches upon our vaunt-curriers. *a* 1642 Kynaston *Leoline & Sydanis* 1265 How as the swift vant-curriers rode about As sentinell perdue. *a* 1670 Hacket *Abp. Williams* I. (1692) 190 Unless the leader look about him in his march and search every hedge by vant-curriers.

γ. 1609 Dekker *Gull's Hornbk.* Wks. (Grosart) II. 219 Thou dost not only send out the lively spirits, like vauntcouriers, to fortify and make good the uttermost borders of thy body.

δ. 1604 R. Cawdrey *Table Alph., Vauntcourers*, forerunners. 1614 Raleigh *Hist. World* v. iii. II. 449 The Carthaginian Horse, and light Armature, fell vpon the Roman Vant-courrers.

ε. 1677 W. Hubbard *Narrative* 73 A party of Indians..fired upon the front and mortally wounded two of the vaunt Carriers.

2. *transf.* One who goes or is sent out in advance in order to prepare the way or to announce the approach of another; a forerunner.

α. 1561 Daus tr. *Bullinger on Apoc.* (1573) 177 And this latter so impugned the supremacie of the Patriarch of Constantinople, that he sticked not to call hym the vauntcurrour of Antichrist. 1567 Drant *Horace, Ep.* iii. c v, And those that wil vauntcurrers be Not I wil draw theim backe. 1607 Dekker *Northward Hoe* II. Wks. 1873 III. 29 Ile send my vant-currer presently. 1709 Strype *Ann. Ref.* I. II. xliv. 479 All such as had been vantcurrors in private colleges to enter into this apostasy.

β, γ. 1603 Harsnet *Pop. Impost.* 12 The harbinger, the host, the Steward, the Vauntcourrier. 1606 Dekker *News from Hell* Wks. (Grosart) II. 137 To all which questions the vant curier answers briefly. 1886 R. F. Burton *Arab. Nts.* (abr. ed.) I. 4 He despatched vaunt-couriers and messengers of glad tidings.

b. Of things.

1598 Barkcley *Felic. Man* v. (1603) 472 The crying and lamenting of a childe when hee first entereth into this world, doth seeme to presage his painefull life, as a vauntcurrer of his miseries to come. 1605 Shaks. *Lear* III. ii. 5 You Sulph'rous and Thought-executing Fires, Vaunt-curriors to Oake-cleauing Thunder-bolts. 1639 Chapman & Shirley *Chabot* III. ii, I will relate to your honours his most cruel exactions upon the subject—the old vantcouriers of rebellions. 1821 Milman *Fall Jerusalem* 39 And gloom of deepest midnight the vaunt-courier Of your dread presence. 1849 Longf. *Kavanagh* xix, These were the vaunt-couriers and attendants of the hot August.

†**Vaunt-currying,** *a.* *Obs.*⁻¹ [? f. *vauntcurrier* Vaunt-courier. Cf. Curry *v.*²] (Meaning not clear.)

1606 *Sir G. Goosecappe* I. iii. in Bullen *Old Plays* (1884) III, *Will.* How will they digest it thinkest thou, when they shall finde our Ladies not there? *Ia.* I haue a vaunt-Curriing deuise shall make them digest it most healthfully.

Vaunted, *ppl. a.* Also 7 **vanted.** [f. Vaunt *v.*] Boasted or bragged of; highly extolled.

1635 A. Stafford *Fem. Glory* (1869) 123 Whose meanest Perfection so farre excels all your so long vanted masculine merits. 1667 Milton *P. L.* III. 251 My Vanquisher, spoild of his vanted spoile. 1789 Mrs. Piozzi *Journ. France* II. 42, I have seen the vaunted present of porcelain. 1825 Scott *Talism.* xiii, Our cousin Edith must first learn how this vaunted wight hath conducted himself. 1838 Prescott *Ferd. & Is.* (1846) II. I. xvii. 124 Their vaunted purity of blood. 1893 Pember *Earth's Earliest Ages* 67 How..all our vaunted wisdom in this life is said to be at best but a knowledge in part.

Vauntegarde, variant of Vantguard *Obs.*

Vaunter (vǭ·ntəɹ). Now *arch.* Forms: 5–6 **vantour,** 6 **vauntour**; 6 *Sc.* **vantar**; 6–7 **vanter,** 7– **vaunter.** [ad. OF. *vantere, vanteor* (AF. *vanteour*), *vanteur* (F. *vanteur*), f. *vanter* Vaunt *v.* Cf. Prov. *vantaire, -ador,* It. *vantatore.*] A boaster or braggart.

1456 Sir G. Haye *Law Arms* (S.T.S.) 30 Thai ar..grete vantouris of litill forededе. 1484 Caxton *Chivalry* 65 By surete ben mesprysed many cowardes, vauntours, and many vayne semblaunces. 1525 Ld. Berners *Froiss.* II. xxxiv. 104 These frenchmen ar great vantours and hyghe mynded. 1573 Tyne in *Cath. Tract.* (S.T.S.) 29 Tratours,..vantars, luffars of thame selues mair than of God. 1588 Shaks. *Tit. A.* v. iii. 113 Alas you know, I am no Vaunter I. *a* 1610 Healey *Theophrastus* (1636) 79 A vanter or forth-putter is he, that boastes upon the Exchange, that he hath store of banke mony. 1640 Gent *Knave in Gr.* II. i. E b, If it prove not correspondent to my word, thinke me an idle vanter. 1716 Pope *Iliad* v. 347 Mistaken vaunter! (Diomed replied;) Thy dart has err'd, and now my spear be tried. 1718 Hearne *Collect.* (O.H.S.) VI. 125 A very pert, conceited Person, full of himself, and a mere Vaunter. 1831 Trelawny *Adv. Younger Son* III. 222 De Ruyter's curled lip indicated his contempt of the vaunter. 1848 Lytton *Harold* VII. iii, Now thou shalt see if the Norman is the vaunter thou deemest him. 1888 Doughty *Arabia Deserta* II. 146 Such is the unmasking of vaunters, who utter their wishes, as if they were already performances.

b. A boastful assertor, extoller, commender or praiser, *of* something.

1553 T. Wilson *Rhet.* 95 b, By vocation of life a souldiour is counted a great bragger, and a vaunter of hymselfe. 1623 Cockeram II, A Vaunter of his owne vertues, *aretalogon.* 1700 Dryden *Homer, Iliad* I. 336 Tongue-valiant Hero, Vaunter of thy Might. 1789 Mrs. Piozzi *Journ. France* I. 222 They are really no puffers, no vaunters of that which they possess. 1856 Mrs. Browning *Aurora Leigh* VII. 1079 The large-mouthed frogs (Those noisy vaunters of their shallow streams). 1866 *Fortn. Rev.* V. 540 The proud vaunter of universal knowledge had been transformed into the humble student of the Bible.

Vau·ntery. Now *Obs.* or *arch.* Also 5, 7 **vaunterye,** 6 **-erie,** 7 **vanterie,** 7–8 **-ery.** [a. OF. (also mod.F.) *vanterie*, f. *vanter* to vaunt (cf. Avauntry), or in later use f. Vaunt *v.* + -ery.]

1. Vaunting, boasting; boastful or vainglorious bearing or show.

1491 Caxton *Vitas Patr.* (W. de W. 1495) II. 272 b/1 She was not so indyscrete for tenhaunce her self by ouer moche vaunterye. 1592 *Conspiracie for Pretended Reform.* 5 [He] held it vp triumphantly, and shewed it with great vaunterie and glorie. 1603 Holland *Plutarch's Mor.* 303 This vanterie and glorious boasting of a mans selfe. 1636 in *4th Rep. Hist. MSS. Commiss.* 291/1 In Wentworth's Declaration ..there was much smoke of the vanterie of his own service. 1755 T. H. Croker *Orl. Fur.* XXXIII. lxxi, They gave themselves too lofty vantery, That France no knight or Paladin could shew To stand before the weakest of them three. 1814 Southey *Roderick* XXII. 23 She had led The infatuate Moor, in dangerous vauntery, To these aspiring forms. *Ibid.* XXV. 308 The same [horse] on whom The apostate Orpas in his vauntery Wont to parade the streets of Cordoba.

†**2.** A boast, a vaunt. *Obs.*

1603 Holland *Plutarch's Mor.* 476 They stood much upon promises of future prowesse or vanteries of present valour. 1605 Daniel *Queen's Arcadia* I. iii, That Touch Of deep Dislike of both their Vaunteries. 1626 T. H[awkins] tr. *Caussin's Holy Court* 432 She shewed to take not much pleasure in these his vaunteryes.

Vau·ntful, *a.* and *adv.* Now *arch.* [f. Vaunt *sb.*¹ + -ful.] Boastful.

1590 Spenser *Muiopot.* 54 Yong Clarion with vauntfull lustie hed After his guize did cast abroad to fare. 1608 Sylvester *Du Bartas* II. iv. *Decay* 532 Rabsakeh..Thus braves the Hebrewes and upbraids their Prince (Weening, them all with vaunt-full threats to snib). 1838 *Tait's Mag.* V. 707 The English King forthwith entrusted to the vauntful captain his two sons. 1850 Blackie *Æschylus* II. 180 His lightnings and his thunders Recking no more—so speaks the vauntful tongue—Than vulgar noonday heat. 1890 *Blackw. Mag.* CXLVIII. 513 Invincible men call her [*i.e.* the Armada]:..Well won that vauntful title by the dread, That all around is by her coming spread.

b. As *adv.* Boastfully. *rare*⁻¹.

a 1814 A. Becket *Genii* I. in *New Brit. Theatre* I. 499 Albeit the agent only Of him who bears it [a name] vauntful, man's prime enemy.

Vauntgard(e, -guard, varr. Vantguard *Obs.*

Vau·ntiness. *rare.* [f. Vaunty *a.*] Boastfulness.

1820 in Jodrell (citing Bailey, app. in error: see Vauntingness). 1851 Spurgeon *Treas. David* ii. 2 Peaceful and joyful notwithstanding the proud and boastful vauntiness of his enemies.

Vau·nting, *vbl. sb.* Now *arch.* [f. Vaunt *v.*] The action of the vb.; boasting, bragging.

c 1340 Hampole *Pr. Consc.* 1145 Honours nuryshes, als men may se, Vayn glory, vauntyng and vanite. 1586 Day *Eng. Secretary* II. (1625) 51, I could alwaies find an Asse by his braying, and scorne a rascall though he were neuer so full of vaunting. 1601 Shaks. *Jul. C.* IV. iii. 52 You say, you are a better Souldier: Let it appeare so; make your vaunting true. 1611 Bible *Wisdom* xvii. 7 As for the illusions of arte Magicke, they were put downe, and their vaunting in wisedome was reproued with disgrace. 1826 Scott *Woodst.* vii, Be moderate in speech, and forbear oaths or vaunting. 1849 Macaulay *Hist. Eng.* iii. I. 349 To our generation the honest vaunting of our ancestors must appear almost ludicrous. 1864 Burton *Scot Abroad* I. iii. 112 The Earl of Flanders..having, in his vain vaunting, defeated so important a project.

attrib. *c* 1586 C'tess Pembroke *Ps.* LXIV. v, The hartes uprightly playn Shall have their vaunting scope.

b. An instance of this; a boast.

1793 Ld. Auckland *Corr.* (1862) III. 27 His vauntings increase with his disgraces. *a* 1800 Cowper *Iliad* (ed. 2) XXI. 550 Let me never in my father's courts Such vauntings hear of thine again. 1838 Dickens *Lett.* (1880) I. 8 We had many delightful vauntings of the same kind. 1877 *Smith's Dict. Chr. Biog.* I. 133/2 The hypocritical vauntings of Clytemnestra.

Vau·nting, *ppl. a.* [f. as prec. + -ing ².]

1. That vaunts or boasts; given or addicted to boasting.

1589 Nashe *Anat. Absurditie* Wks. (Grosart) I. 51 No matter though such vanting vpstarts..become the scoffe of a Scholler. 1596 Shaks. *1 Hen. IV*, v. iii. 43 Many a Nobleman lies starke and stiffe Vnder the hooues of vaunting enemies. 1601 Holland *Pliny* II. 231, I my selfe have seen these vaunting Mountebanks calling themselves Psylli. 1632 Sherwood, A vaunting woman, *ostentatrice.* 1714 Gay *Sheph. Week* i. 39 Begin thy carols, then, thou vaunting slouch. 1730 Bailey (fol.), *Braggard*, a bragging, vaunting, vain glorious fellow. 1819 Scott *Ivanhoe* xxxix, Would to God, Richard, or any of his vaunting minions of England, would appear in these lists! 1853 Lynch *Self-Improv.* ii. 45 An empty, vaunting person who has brass enough to face the world and to say there is no God in it. 1884 *Marshall's Tennis Cuts* 195 In the evenings he was vaunting, boastful, and declared he could play even Renshaw at evens.

transf. 1599 Shaks. *Hen. V*, II. iii. 4 Nim, rowse thy vaunting Veines: Boy, brissle thy Courage vp.

2. Of a boastful nature or character; indicative of, proceeding from, boasting or vainglory.

1647 Hexham I. s.v., Vaunting and bragging wordes. 1748 *Anson's Voy.* II. xi. 252 The vaunting accounts given by the Spaniards of her size, her guns, and her strength. 1770 Langhorne *Plutarch's Lives* (1879) I. 134/1 The vaunting shouts and songs of the barbarians. 1802 *Med. Jrnl.* VIII. 66 Does not Pyrrho likewise speak in a 'vaunting manner' on several occasions? 1855 Macaulay *Hist. Eng.* xxi. IV. 583 Over one gate had been placed a vaunting inscription which defied the allies to wrench the prize from the grasp of France. 1897 Sarah Tytler *Lady Jean's Son* 205 Rejoicing over him in a vaunting and insolent manner.

Vau·ntingly, *adv.* [f. prec.] In a vaunting manner; boastfully, ostentatiously, vaingloriously.

1593 Nashe *Christ's T.* (1613) 16 Let me speake truely and not vauntingly. 1593 Shaks. *Rich. II*, IV. i. 36, I heard thee say (and vauntingly thou spak'st it) That thou wer't cause of Noble Glousters death. 1611 Cotgr., *Piaffeusement*, braggingly,..stroutingly, vauntingly. 1636 Prynne *Unbish. Tim.* Ded. (1661) 1 Whether seriously or vauntingly only, let the event determine. 1689 T. Plunket *Char. Good Commander*, etc. 6 Who threatned vauntingly That he..would England Invade. 1798 Ellis in *Anti-Jacobin* 1 Jan. (1852) 28 And dare you vauntingly decide, The fortune we shall meet. 1804 Eugenia de Acton *Tale without Title* II. 100 Should the scrutiny proclaim your innocence, receive not vauntingly the clearing verdict. 1836 W. Irving *Astoria* I. 91 Upon which Mr. M'Dougal would vauntingly lay down Mr. Astor's letter,..a document not to be disputed.

†**Vau·ntingness.** *Obs.*⁻⁰ [f. Vaunting *vbl. sb.*] Boastfulness.

1727 Bailey (vol. II), *Ostentatiousness*, vauntingness, bragging, shewiness.

†**Vauntise.** *Obs.*⁻¹ [ad. OF. *vantise* vaunting, vanity, pride: see -ise ².] A vaunt or boast.

c 1477 Caxton *Jason* (1913) 22 Moche was Iason desplaysaunt whan he had vnderstande the vauntises of his mortall ennemy.

Vauntlay. Now *arch.* Also 5 (9) **vauntelay.** [f. Vaunt- + *-lay* as in Relay *sb.* The compound may have existed in AF. Cf. Vanlay *v.*] The releasing or setting on of a relay of hounds before the other pursuing hounds have passed; the relay of hounds so released.

1486 *Bk. St. Albans* E viij b, Even at his comyng yf thow lett thy howndys goo While the oder that be behynde fer arn hym froo That is a vauntelay. 1616 Bullokar *Eng. Expos., Vauntlay*, a terme of hunting, when they sette hounds in readynes, where they thinke a chace will passe, and cast them off before the rest of the kennell come in. [Hence in Blount (1656), Phillips, Holme, etc.] *a* 1700 B. E. *Dict. Cant. Crew, Vauntlay*, Hounds or Beagles set in readiness [etc.]. 1842 Sir H. Taylor *Edwin the Fair* I. vi, She holds them all together; Relay or vauntlay 'tis the same to her.

†**Vauntmure.** *Obs.* Also 6 **vauntemure, vauntmire, vantmure.** [Aphetic form of Avantmure: see Vant-, Vaunt-.] = Vaumure.

1562 J. Shute tr. *Cambini's Turk. Wars* 16 b, Throughe their long..neglygence of the Greekes for want of reparation, their vauntemures were utterlye decaied in many places. 1583 Stocker *Civ. Warres Lowe C.* III. 135 b, There fell downe a pane of the wall, and vauntmire of the Towne..sixe and twentie Poles longe. 1596 Danett tr. *Comines* (1614) 231 Wherewith the wals, towers, and vantmures of the castell and towne were throughly battered. 1605 Camden *Rem.* (1623) 206 He with another engine named the Warwolfe pierced with one stone, and cut as even as a thread, two Vauntmures.

†**Vauntparler.** *Obs.* Also **vaunt(e)perler, vauntperlor, -parler, vantperlor, -parlar.** [ad. AF. *vaunt-parlour*, obs. F. *avant-parleur* 'fore-speaker'.]

1. 'One that is too forward to speak' (Cotgr.).

a 1529 Skelton *Sp. Parrot* 427 He tryhumfythe, he trumpythe, he turnythe all vp and downe, With, skyregalyard, prowde palyard, vaunteperler, ye prate! *a* 1548 Hall *Chron., Hen. VIII*, 36 Then sodainly was ther in yᵉ counsaill, a vauntparler, a botcher which beryng this, called a great number of his affinitie and went out of the counsayll. 1577 Holinshed *Chron.* I. 408/1 This Prince..followed vpon a wilfull pretence..the councell and aduice of vauntperlors, and suche as (being aduanced from base degree vnto hygh authoritie) studyed more to keepe them-selues in fauoure than [etc.].

2. One who speaks for or on behalf of others; a spokesman.

1534 *St. Papers, Hen. VIII* (1830) I. 424 It shuld be best bestowed..upon Frire Whitford, and upon Lache, whiche bee the vauntperlers, and heddes of thair faction. 1579 Fulke *Heskins's Parl.* 66 He doeth honestly confesse, that ..Damascen [was] the first and chiefest of the lower house, he may make him Vantparlar if he will. 1586 J. Hooker *Hist. Irel.* in *Holinshed* II. 120/1 Their vantparler was sir Christopher Barnwell knight, who being somewhat learned, his credit was so much the more, and by them thought most ..worthie to haue beene the speaker for that house.

†**Vauntpe.** *Obs.*⁻⁰ [ad. older F. *vantpié*.] = Vamp *sb.*¹ 1.

1530 Palsgr. 284/1 Vauntpe of a hose, *mantpie.*

†**Vauntplate.** *Obs.*⁻¹ [f. Vaunt- + Plate *sb.*] = Vamplate.

1632 J. Hayward tr. *Biondi's Eromena* 145 He bore him a thrust under the vauntplate.

†**Vauntsquare,** *v.* *Obs.*⁻¹ [f. Vaunt- + Square *v.*] *intr.* To face or front squarely.

1562 Phaer *Æneid* IX. A a ij, Messapus voward helde, the rerward kept yong princes twayne Of Tirrhus, but himself king Turnus midst in battaile mayne, Vauntsquaring spreds his armes.

Vauntward(e, variants of Vantward *Obs.*

Vau·nty, *a.* *dial.* (chiefly *Sc.*). Also 9 *Sc.* **vanty.** [f. Vaunt *v.*] Boastful, proud, vain.

1724 Ramsay *Tea-t. Misc.* (1733) I. 21 Altho' my father was nae laird, 'Tis daffin to be vaunty, He keepit ay a good kail-yard. 1789 Burns *To Dr. Blacklock* i, Wow, but your letter made me vauntie! 1821 [see Vaudy *a.*]. 1842 Louisa S. Costello *Pilgr. Auvergne* II. 120 Certainly he had reason to be 'vaunty', for his grand new house was worthy of a more populous town than Thiers. 1875 Porson *Quaint Words S. Worcs.* 19 A vaunty dame,..proud woman.

Vaupyn, obs. Sc. form of Weapon.

†**Vau·queline.** *Obs.* [a. F. *vauqueline*, f. the name of the French chemist L. N. *Vauquelin* (1768–1829).]

1. *Chem.* Strychnine.

1819 J. G. Children *Chem. Anal.* 290 Vauqueline..was discovered by M. M. Pelletier and Caventou, in the bean of St. Ignatius, and the nux vomica.

2. *Min.* Vauquelinite.

1823 in W. Phillips *Min.* (ed. 3) 350.

Vauquelinite (vōᵘ·klinəit). *Min.* [f. as prec. + -ite. Named by Berzelius (1818).] Chromate of lead and copper, found in amorphous masses or crystalline crusts of a green colour (Chester).

1823 W. Phillips *Min.* (ed. 3) 350 Vauquelinite. Chromate of Lead and Copper. 1836–41 Brande *Chem.* (ed. 5) 914 The mineral called Vauquelinite is a double chromate of lead and copper.

‖**Vaurien** (vōryẽ̄). Also **vaut-rien, vaut rien.** [F. *vaurien*, f. *vaut* 3rd pers. sing. pres. of *valoir* to be worth + *rien* nothing.] A worthless, good-for-nothing fellow; a scamp.

α. 1825–9 Mrs. Sherwood *Lady of Manor* V. xxx. 152 Then to be called an idle fellow—a *vaut rien*—a Miss Molly —it is what I cannot bear. 1880 Ruskin *Fors Clav.* lxxxix. 142 You will have every blackguard and vaut-rien in the world claiming his share.

β. 1868 M. Collins *Sweet Anne Page* II. 118 Leaving her to be slowly murdered by the vaurien who possesses her. 1874 Lisle Carr *J. Gwynne* II. vii. 189 When that *vaurien* St. Clair's health broke down. 1885 *Diary Actress* 133 They are only vauriens who loaf about town.., not men of honour.

†**Vau·sing,** *vbl. sb.* *Obs.*⁻⁰ (See quots.)

1688 Holme *Armoury* III. 112/2 Vausing, is to make the Jaumes or sides of Stone Windows and Doors,..to over sail the other part of the Wall they are set in. *Ibid.* 473/2 The Vausing, is to make the Jaumes to over sale the Mullions, and that is wrought into severall kind of Mouldings.

Vaustity, obs. form of Vastity.

Vaut, southern dial. var. *faut* Fault *sb.*

1568 Fulwel *Like will to Like* A iij b, It is a common trade...A small vaut as the world is now brought to passe.

Vaut(e, obs. forms of Vault *sb.* and *v.*

†**Vau·terer.** *Obs. rare.* [ad. med.L. *vautrarius*, f. OF. *vautre* hunting-dog.] = Fewterer.

1679 Blount *Anc. Tenures* 35 To be the Kings Vauterer or Dog-leader in Gascoigny.

Vauxhall (vǫ·kshǭ·l). [The name of a locality in London on the south bank of the Thames, where Vauxhall Gardens (see def.) were situated.] Used *ellipt.* for Vauxhall Gardens, a popular pleasure resort from the 17th to the middle of the 19th century; a place of resort or amusement resembling or imitating this.

Evelyn records in his memoirs under the date 2 July 1661, 'I went to see the New Spring Garden at Lambeth, a pretty contriv'd plantation'. The gardens were finally closed on 25 July 1859.

1769 *Ann. Reg., Chron.* 111 Sieur Torre opened his new Vauxhall, near St. Martin's gate [in Paris], under the denomination of the Feasts of Tempe. 1815 *Ibid., Chron.* 50 Mr. Sadler appeared in Mr. Harper's gardens, or the Vauxhall of this place [*sc.* Norwich], in the evening.

attrib. 1822 *Lond. Lit. Gaz.* 61/1 But the portions [of food] are of the Vauxhall order. 1892 Dobson *18th Cent. Vignettes* 253 The popular legend that an expert Vauxhall waiter could cover the entire garden (about eleven acres) with slices from one ham.

Hence **Vauxha·llian** *a.*, **Vauxha·llify** *v. trans.*

1815 Southey *Lett.* (1856) II. 429 There is an illumination to-night in the Allée Vert, or Green Walk, which is to be Vauxhallified in honour of the Emperor. 1827 *Westm. Rev.* VIII. 353 Here follows a description of a very gay festival, much more Vauxhallian than Attic.

Vav (væv), variant of Vau. *Vav conversive*: see Conversive *a.*¹ 3 b.

1828 Gibbs *Gesenius' Hebr. Lex.* (1833) 54/1 A prefix.. usually called Vav conversive of the future. 1869 Liddell & Scott *Gr. Lex.* s.v. δίγαμμα, But the Lat. F. holds the same place in the alph[abet] with the Hebr. *vav.* 1870 J. F. Smith *Ewald's Introd. Hebr. Gram.* 229 Then the calm regular narration may come in with the Vav of sequence.

Va·vasory. Also 7 **valuassorie,** 9 **vavassory.** [ad. OF. *vavas(s)orie, va(u)vasserie*, or med.L. *vavasoria*, f. *vavasor*: see next.] An estate held by a vavasour.

1611 Cotgr., *Vavassorie*, a Valuasserie; th'estate, land, or territorie of a Vavassor, Mesne Lord. 1656 Harrington *Oceana* (1700) 65 The Middle-Thane..was also call'd a Vavasor, and his Lands a Vavasory. *Ibid.* 67 It cannot be imagin'd, that the Vavasorys or Freeholds in the People amounted to any considerable proportion. 1728 Chambers *Cycl.* s.v., There are base Vavasories, and frank, or noble Vavasories, according as it hath pleas'd the Lord to make his Vavasour. 1839 Stonehouse *Isle of Axholme* 124 He was enfeoffed with the vavasories of Camville and Wyville. *a* 1861 Sir F. Palgrave *Norm. & Eng.* III. 405 It is not practicable to ascertain the others who received their rewards by Vavassories or Sub-tenancies.

Vavasour (væ·văsŭᵊɹ). Now *arch.* and *Hist.* Forms: α. 4 **vauasour(e,** 4, 7– **vavasour** (4 **-oure),** 5 **favasour,** *Sc.* **wawasour, vauesowre,** 7 **vavesour**; 5 **vavyssoure, vauyssour,** 7 **vauessour, vauassour,** 9 **vavassour.** β. 5 **vauaser,** 7, 9 **vavasor, vavassor.** γ. 6–7 **valuasor,** 6–8 **-vasor,** 7–8 **valvasour,** 9 **valvassor.** [a. OF. *vavas(s)our, vavas(s)or, vavasseur* (so mod.F.), or med.L. *vavassor, valvassor*, also *vasvassor*, app. f. *vassi vassorum* 'vassals of vassals'. Cf. OProv. *va(l)vasor*, It. *varvassore, -oro, barbassore, -oro.*] A feudal tenant ranking immediately below a baron.

α. 13.. *K. Alis.* 3300 (Laud MS.), Noot ich no tale of his squyers, Ne of vavasours, ne of Bachilers. *c* 1330 R. Brunne *Chron. Wace* (Rolls) 10996 He gaf giftes of honurs, & landes & rentes, to vauasours. *c* 1380 *Sir Ferumb.* 430 Litel prowesse for me it were wiþ a vavasour for to melle. 1456 Sir G. Haye *Bk. Knthood.* iii. (S.T.S.) 21 All kingis suld have under thame dukkis and princis, Erllis and vicountes, and vauvassouris and barouns. *a* 1500 *Lancelot* 1729 Syne to thi tennandis & to thi wawasouris, If [= give] essy haknays, palfrais, and cursouris. 1614 Selden *Titles Honour* II. v. § 4 Now for the nature of a vavasour;..it is plaine that he was ever beneath a baron. 1647 N. Bacon *Disc. Govt. Eng.* I. xxxi. (1739) 47 Others served on horseback, and were called Rad-Knights,..and these I take to be the Vavasours, noted in the Conqueror's Laws. 1660 Sheringham *King's Supremacy Asserted* (1682) v. 32 There are other great men under the King which are called Barons, and other which are called Vavasours, men of great dignity. 1756 *Connoisseur* No. 102 ¶ 1 Upon my accession..to my elder brother's estate and title of a Baronet I received a visit from Rouge Dragon..to congratulate me upon my new rank of a Vavasour. 1766 Blackstone *Comm.* II. 65 William the conqueror ..directing..that a certain quantity..should be paid by the earls, barons, and vavasours respectively. 1831 Scott *Cast. Dang.* vii, One or two Scottish retainers or vavasours..sat at the bottom of the table. 1848 Lytton *Harold* III. ii, The ..ignominious flight of the counts and vavasours of great William the Duke. 1875 Stubbs *Const. Hist.* II. xv. 207 It was ordered that the sheriff should be a vavasour of the County.

β. *c* 1386 Chaucer *Prologue* 360 A schirreue hadde he ben and a counter, Was nowher such a worthi vauaser. 1605 Camden *Rem., Surnames* (1623) 110 Baron, Knight,.. Vavasor, Squire, Castellan. 1642 Bird *Mag. Honour* 8 There be others which are called Vavasors,..men of great dignity. 1656 Harrington *Oceana* 35 The Middle-Thane was feudall, but not honorary; he was also call'd a Vavasor. 1818 Hallam *Mid. Ages* (1872) I. 194 The vassals of this high nobility, who..were usually termed Vavassors. 1875 K. E. Digby *Real Prop.* (1876) 41 *note*, Similar provisions follow as to the relief to be paid by barons, vavassors, and villeins.

γ. 1577 Harrison *England* II. v. (1877) I. 113 As for the valvasors, it was a denomination applied unto all degrees of honor under the first three. 1610 Holland *Camden's Brit.* 696 The Kings Valvasors in times past they were. 1614 Selden *Titles Hon.* 289 For a Corollarie to this Discourse of Barons, we add..the ancient title of Vauassours or Valuasors. 1708 J. Chamberlayne *St. Gt. Brit.* I. III. iv. (1710) 185 Baronets..are constituted in the Room of the Ancient Valvasours, between the Barons of England, and the Orders of Knights. 1765 Blackstone *Comm.* I. 403 The first name of dignity, next beneath a peer, was antiently that of *vidames, vice domini*, or *valvasors.* 1840 Browning *Sordello* I. 768 Lord, liegeman, valvassor and suzerain, Ere he could choose, surrounded him. 1854 Milman *Lat. Chr.* III. 57 Heribert refused to admit the valvassors of the Church of Milan to this privilege.

Vavengeour (obs. Sc.): see Wavenger.

†**Vaver,** obs. southern variant of Favour *sb.*

1536 *Cal. Anc. Rec. Dublin* (1889) 439 That he mythe the rather bye youre grases mene obtayne the kyng his vaverys.

Vavte, obs. form of Vault *sb.*¹

Vaward. *Obs.* exc. *arch.* Forms: α. 4– **vaward** (6 **va-ward),** 5–6 **vawarde.** β. *Sc.* 5 **waward(e, waywarde,** 5–6 **wawart.** γ. 5 **vauwarde, fauward,** 6–7 **vauward**; 5–6 **vawe-,** 6 **vawwarde,** 6, 8 **vawward.** δ. 5 **wowarde,** 5–6 **vowarde,** 6–7 **voward.** [Reduced form of *vaumward* Vamward. See Vant- *prefix.*]

1. *Mil.* = Vanguard 1.

α. 1375 Barbour *Bruce* VIII. 48 Thai saw in battale cum arayit The vaward with baner displayit. *a* 1400–50 *Alexander* 3617 Þe men out of Medy he mas..To enverom alle þe vaward of all þe vile yndes. *c* 1430 *Syr Gener.* (Roxb.) 3554 Abel, his son bold and hard, Bare the baner in the vaward. *c* 1471 *Arriv. K. Edw. IV* (Camden) 29 His vawarde so sore oppressyd them, with shott of arrows, that they gave them right-a-sharpe shwre. *a* 1548 Hall *Chron., Hen. V*, 48 Beside this, be appoincted a vawarde, of the which he made capitayne Edward duke of Yorke. 1579 Digges *Stratiot.* 132 To give their attendance at the lodging of their Chiefes of the Armie, whether it be of the Battaile, or Vawarde. 1610 Holland *Camden's Brit.* II. 178 The English were the first that entered with great vigour upon the front and vaward. 1640 Habington *Edw. IV*, 81 The Vaward commanded by the Duke of Glocester, the Rere by the Lord Hastings. [1706 Phillips (ed. Kersey), *Vaward*, an obsolete Word for Van-Guard.] 1828 Tytler *Hist. Scot.* (1864) I. 116 He intrusted the command of the vaward, or centre, to the Earl of Moray. 1846 Torrens *Rem. Milit. Hist.* 148 The disposition of troops seems..to have been a vaward, or advance, a centre, and rear.

β. 1375 Barbour *Bruce* XII. 340 And thai haf tald thair reboyting, Thai of the waward. *c* 1425 Wyntoun *Cron.* VI. xix. 2261 He askyt at þe kynge Til haf þe wawarde [*v.r.* wawart] of his batale. 1500–20 [see b].

γ. *c* 1400 *Sege Jerus.* 430 Þe fauward Titus toke,..With six þousand soudiours. *c* 1440 *Bone Florence* 604 The vawewarde and the myddyll soone, And the rere-warde owte of Rome The grete oost removyd and yode. 1529 Rastell *Pastyme* (1811) 222 Havinge the rule of the Frenche kynges vawewarde. 1570 Foxe *A. & M.* (ed. 2) I. 127 Sebastian.. was Lieue tenant generall of the Vawward of Diocletian the emperour. 1603 Knolles *Hist. Turks* (1621) 39 The Vauward of his armie was conducted by Iohn and Andronicus. 1791 Cowper *Iliad* VIII. 119 Then, Diomede, unaided as he was, Rush'd ardent to the vaw-ward.

δ. 1430–40 Lydg. *Bochas* IX. xxviii, In his passage to gouerne the wowarde. 1432–50 tr. *Higden* (Rolls) VII. 241 In the vowarde of whom were foote men with bawes. 1526 *Pilgr. Perf.* (W. de W. 1531) 179 Whiche is more fered of the feendes than ony vowarde of a batayle. 1543 *St. Papers Hen. VIII* (1849) IX. 393 The other galees of thEmperour appoynted for the vowarde. 1577 Holinshed *Chron.* II. 1593/1 Forthwith the Lord Lieutenant sent to the vowarde, commaunding that they shoulde marche towarde the towne. 1631 Chapman *Cæsar & Pompey* Plays 1873 III. 162 The voward of the foe Is ranged already.

b. In fig. context.

1401 *Pol. Poems* (Rolls) II. 57 It ar ȝe that stonden bifore, in Anticristis vauwarde. 1500–20 Dunbar *Poems* xlii. 58 Than to battell thai war arreyit all, And ay the wawart kepit Thocht. 1561 T. Norton *Calvin's Inst.* I. (1634) 10 And therefore he doubteth not to set their mouthes in the vaward, as being strongly armed to subdue their madnesse. *a* 1586 Sidney *Arcadia* I. viii. (1622) 30 Her haire being laide at the full length downe her backe, bare shew as if the voward fayled, yet that would conquer.

c. *fig.* The forefront; the early part.

In later use only as an echo of Shakspere.

1597 Shaks. *2 Hen. IV*, I. ii. 200 We that are in the vaward of our youth. 1599 Nashe *Lenten Stuffe* 22 The vaward or subburbes of my narration. 1827 Scott *Jrnl.* I. 378 She is not in the vaward of youth. — *Chron. Canongate* vi, Those who write themselves in the vaward of youth. 1884 A. Birrell *Obiter Dicta* Ser. I. 208 He.. states that he and his accomplices..are in the vaward of their youth.

2. *attrib.* (Cf. Vanward *a.*)

1808 Scott *Marm.* VI. xxiv, Myself will rule this central host,..My sons command the vaward post. *Ibid.* xxxiii, Where's now their victor vaward wing? 1814 — *Lord of Isles* VI. xii, To centre of the vaward-line Fitz-Louis guided Amadine.

Vawe, ME. var. Fain *a.* and *adv.*, Few *a.*

†**Vawegard,** obs. variant of Vanguard (after Vaward).

a 1548 Hall *Chron., Hen. VI*, 176 b, The vawegard was conducted by the erle of Warwycke.

Vawght, obs. form of Vault *sb.*¹

Vawmer, -meure, -mure, varr. Vaumure *Obs.*

Vawmewarde, variant of Vamward *Obs.*

†**Vaws-cornice.** *Obs.*⁻⁰ (See quot.)

1688 Holme *Armoury* III. 102/1 *Vaws-Cornice*, is any small Cornish lying under a great swelling out peece, as under a Planchier, or swelling Friese.

Vawt(e, obs. ff. Vault *sb.*¹ and *v.*¹ **Vawthe,** obs. f. Vault *v.*¹ **Vax,** obs. Sc. f. Wax *sb.* and *v.* **Vax-cayme,** obs. Sc. f. Wax-comb.

†**Vay(e,** obs. southern variants of Fay *sb.*¹

1586 Ferne *Blaz. Gentrie* 27 By my vaye, shee looketh lyke a foule Kite that haunteth our yarde at home. 1602 *Contention betw. Liberality & Prodigality* IV. iii, Come on, surrah, chill make you vast, bum vay.

Vay, southern dial. var. Fay *v.*¹; obs. Sc. f. Way. **Vayage,** obs. Sc. var. Voyage. **Vayd,** obs. Sc. f. Wade *v.* **Vaye,** obs. Sc. f. Way *sb.* **Vayk,** obs. Sc. f. Weak *a.* **Vayle,** obs. f. Veil *sb.* **Vaylliaunce,** obs. f. Valiance. **Vayn,** southern ME. var. Fain *a.*; obs. Sc. f. Wain; Sc. var. Wane *sb. Obs.* **Vaynd,** var. Waind *v. Sc.* **Vayndis,** Sc. var. Wandish *v.* **Vayne,** obs. f. Vein *sb.* **Vayowre,** var. Veyour *Obs.* **Vayr,** southern ME. var. Fair *a.* **Vayrd,** obs. Sc. f. Ward *v.* **Vayre,** southern ME. var. Fair *a.*; obs. f. Vair. **Vaȝ,** southern ME. var. Faw *a. Obs.* **Vaȝt,** southern ME. var. *fought* Fight *v.* **Vch(e,** ME. varr. Each *a.* **Vddir, Vder,** obs. Sc. ff. Other *a.* **Ve,** obs. Sc. f. We *pron.*, Wee *a.*

†**Vea,** *int.* *Naut. Obs.* (See quots.)

1626 Capt. Smith *Accid. Yng. Seamen* 30 To row a spell, bold-water, trim the boate, *vea, vea, vea, vea, vea.* 1627 — *Seaman's Gram.* vi. 27 One and all, Vea, vea, vea, vea, vea, that is they pull all strongly together.

Veadge, Veage, obs. varr. Voyage *sb.*

Veak, obs. Sc. form of Vake *v.*

Veal (vīl), *sb.*¹ Forms: 4 **vol** (5 **vell),** 5–7 **vele;** 5 **veel** (**feel),** 6 **veele;** 5 **veylle,** 6 **veyle** (*Sc.* **veil, weill);** 6–7 **veale** (6 **ueale, feale),** 6– **veal** (*Sc.* 7 **weall,** 8 **veall).** [a. AF. *vel*, OF. *veel* (*viel, veal, vael*, etc.; mod.F. *veau*), *vedel*, = Prov. *vedel(h*, Cat. *vedel*, It. and Pg. *vitello*:—L. *vitellus*, dim. of *vitulus* calf.]

1. The flesh of a calf as an article of diet.

c 1386 Chaucer *Merch. T.* 176 'Bet is,' quod he, 'a pyk than a pikerell, And bet than olde boef is the tendre vel'. *c* 1400 Maundev. (1839) vi. 72 Thei eten but lytille or non of Flessche of Veel or of Beef. *c* 1420 *Liber Cocorum* (1862) 28 A sawce hit is For vele and venyson, iwys. *c* 1440 *Promp. Parv.* 508/2 Veel, flesche, *vitulina.* 1515 Barclay *Egloges* II. (1570) B iii/2 Fat porke or vele, & namely such as is bought For easier price when they be leane & nought. 1555 Eden *Decades* (Arb.) 177 They also coompare the fleshe of these tortoyses to be equall with veale in taste. 1620 Venner *Via Recta* iii. 51 Veale is a more odoriferous flesh then any other. 1653 H. Cogan tr. *Pinto's Trav.* xxxiv. 137 These people feed on all, as Veal, Mutton, Pork,..and finally of all other beasts whatsoever. 1706–7 Farquhar *Beaux' Strat.* I. i, *Aim.* Have you any Veal? *Bon.* Veal! Sir, we

had a delicate Loin of Veal on Wednesday last. 1780 Beckford *Biog. Mem.* 125 The most perfect fillet of veal that ever made the mouth of man to water. 1846 J. Baxter *Libr. Pract. Agric.* (ed. 4) II. 127 In the rearing of calves for veal in Holland, it is usual to confine them in..pens. 1890 *Spectator* 4 Oct., What insipid and tasteless cheer does veal afford!

2. A calf, esp. as killed for food or intended for this purpose. Now *rare.*

1422 Yonge tr. *Secreta Secret.* 244 Flesh of Velis, Vynegre, hemroll, and Potage of oot-mell. *c* 1450 *Mirour Saluacioun* (Roxb.) 71 The ydolatiers of the golden veel. 1466 *Paston Lett.* II. 269 For purveying of all the velys, lambes, ..certain piggs and polaly. 1513 Douglas *Æneid* XII. Prol. 185 Tydy ky lowys, veilys by thame rynnis. 1544 in *Star Chamber Cases* (Selden) II. 305 The prices of Flesh, as of Beefes, Muttons, Veales, & Porkes. 1582 *Nottingham Rec.* IV. 199, vj. fatte wethres, at viij s. viij d. a pece, and ij. veyles, at vjs. viij d. a pece. 1601 R. Johnson *Kingd. & Commw.* 25 The flesh..of their swine, oxen, and veales haue the best relish. 1648 Herrick *Hesper., Paneg. Sir L. Pemberton* 63 When guests make their abode To eate thy Bullocks thighs, thy Veales, thy fat Weathers. 1688 Holme *Armoury* III. 315/1 Upon these [drag hooks] are hung two Veals or Muttons at a time. 1737 *Ochtertyre House Bk.* (S.H.S.) 13 Killd a Veall. 1801 *Farmer's Mag.* Aug. 319 In selling veals to butchers, their haggling was extremely disagreeable. 1855 Thackeray *Newcomes* I. 265 My mother..would receive her prodigal and kill the fatted veal for me. 1898 Westcott *David Harum* xvii, Jim brought three or four veals into town one spring to sell.

collect. 1710 Addison *Tatler* No. 148 ¶ 1 The Flesh of Lamb, Veal, Chicken, and other Animals under Age.

3. *attrib.*, chiefly in names of dishes, etc., made from veal, as *veal broth, cutlet, gravy, pie*, etc.

a 1625 Fletcher *Hum. Lieut.* III. vii, Ye Porridg gutted Slaves, ye Veal broth-Boobies! 1630 J. Taylor (Water P.) *Gt. Eater Kent* 14 Three sixe-penny veale pyes..were presented to the scalado. 1675 E. W[ilson] *Spadacrene Dunelmensis* 39 This [water]..helpeth all internal corrosions, if taken in Veal Broath fasting. 1725 *Fam. Dict.* s.v., Put your Veal Stakes into the Pan again, and finish the dressing with Veal Sweet-Breads. *Ibid.*, Some Veal Gravy must be pour'd upon it. 1747 tr. *Astruc's Fevers* 340 Let the patient also drink plentifully of veal broth. 1769 Mrs. Raffald *Eng. Housek.* (1778) 19 About a pound of beef or veal suet. 1827 Scott *Surg. Dau.* ii, Lamb and spinage, and a veal Florentine. 1833 L. Ritchie *Wand. by Loire* 182 A large baby in one arm, and a basket of..cold veal-pie in the other. 1848 Dickens *Dombey* xviii, He treats Mrs. Perch to a veal cutlet and Scotch ale. 1858 Simmonds *Dict. Trade, Veal-tea*, a thick gelatinous soup or broth made of the fleshy part of the fillet or knuckle of veal. 1885 Jerome *On the Stage* 48 Property Man, behind, making a veal and ham pie, out of an old piece of canvas and a handful of shavings.

b. Special Combs.: **veal-bled** *a.*, bled to exhaustion, like a calf intended for veal; **veal-bones,** *fig.* youth, nonage; **veal calf,** (*a*) = sense 2; (*b*) a variety of leather; **veal-farmer,** one who rears calves for the butcher; **veal-like** *a.*, resembling (that of) veal; †**veal money** (see quot.); **veal-skin,** (*a*) the skin of a calf; (*b*) a skin-disease characterized by white shining spots.

1899 *Westm. Gaz.* 8 Sept. 3/1 The exhausted, and almost *veal-bled and forlorn bull. 1785 R. Cumberland *Observer* No. 92, Our process seldom fails in either case, when we apply it timely, and especially to young poets in their *veal bones*, as the saying is. 1888 Addy *Sheffield Gloss.* 272 There is a saying 'married in the veal bones always a calf'. ?1556 *Wills & Inv. N. C.* (Surtees, 1835) 153 To Thomas morison..for ij *veale calves. 1895 *Boston Herald* 21 March 5/6 Colored leather is firmer and selling more freely: Grain, 12 @ 14c; veal calf, 16 @ 18½c. 1844 H. Stephens *Bk. Farm* II. 469 The *veal-farmers keep from 6 to 12 cows each. 1822–7 *Veal-like [see *veal-skin* below]. 1897 W. Anderson *Surg. Treat. Lupus* 7 An unwholesome, veal-like whiteness, diversified by tiny blood-vessels. 1684 Manley *Cowell's Interpreter* s.v., *Veale money or Veale noble money. The Tenants of one of the Tythings within the Manor of Bradford in Wiltshire, pay a yearly Rent by this name..in lieu of veale paid formerly in kind. 1591 *Exch. Rolls Scotl.* XXII. 171 [10s. of certain] barkit *weillskynnis. 1822–7 Good *Study Med.* (1829) V. 694 *Epichrosis Leucasmus.* Veal-Skin...This is the vitiligo or veal-skin of Willan, so called from the veal-like appearance which these spots produce on the general colour of the surface. 1858 Simmonds *Dict. Trade, Veal-skins*, an Irish trade-name for hides of the calf, which are dearer than other leather.

Hence **Veal** *v. trans.*, to rear (calves) for use as veal; **Vea·ler,** a calf intended or fit for veal. *U.S.* 1901- in American Dicts.

Veal, *sb.*² *Sc. Mining.* (See quots.)

1883 Gresley *Gloss. Coal-M.* 269 *Veal*, a tank or waterbarrel placed upon a cage for emptying the sump. 1886 J. Barrowman *Sc. Mining Terms* 69 *Veal*, or *voun*, a water box or chest, usually on wheels, for removing water.

Veale, var. Vele *Obs.*; obs. Sc. f. Well *adv.*

Vea·ling, *vbl. sb.*¹ [f. Veal *sb.*¹] **a.** *A-vealing*, procuring veal. **b.** Conversion into veal.

1664 Cotton *Scarron.* I. 47 And up he starts, to go a stealing, Either a Mutt'ning, or a Vealing. 1847 *Jrnl. R. Agric. Soc.* VIII. II. 394 It is equally suitable, whether the calf is intended for vealing or to be reared.

†**Vea·ling,** *vbl. sb.*² *Obs.* (See quot.)

1688 Holme *Armoury* III. 86/2 Working, is to lay them on the Beam and with the Fleshing Knife and Vealing Knife, to scrape off the Lime and cleanse them from their Fleshyness.

Vea·ling, *vbl. sb.*³ *Sc. Mining.* [f. Veal *sb.*²]

1886 J. Barrowman *Sc. Mining Terms* 69 *Vealing*, or *vouning*, chesting; getting out water by means of veals.

Vealinous, obs. form of Villainous *a.*

Vealy (vī·li), *a.* [f. Veal *sb.*¹]

1. Resembling veal.

1769 Mrs. Raffald *Eng. Housekpr.* (1778) 17 Then put in a few boiled forcemeat balls, which must be made of the veally part of your turtle. 1864 Lowell *Fireside Trav.* 259 When we were fairly at anchor..they crawled out again,.. their vealy faces mezzotinted with soot.

2. *fig.* Imperfectly developed; immature; characterized by youthful immaturity.

1890 *Columbus* (Ohio) *Dispatch* 17 July, A vealy medical-school graduate, whose employment is an insult to intelligent people. 1907 *Outlook* 19 Jan. 80/1 The sylvan thief shared our vealy homage with moonlighters, smugglers [etc.].

Hence **Vea·liness,** want of maturity.

1895 in *Funk's Stand. Dict.*

Veand, obs. Sc. variant of *weighing* Weigh *v.*

Veany, variant of Veny ² *Obs.* **Vear,** obs. f. Veer *v.*; obs. Sc. f. War *sb.*; south-w. dial. f. Fear *v.* **Veare,** southern ME. variant of Fare *v.*

Vearie, obs. Sc. form of Very *adv.*

Vease. Now only *south-w. dial.* Forms: 4 (9) **vese** (9 **veze);** 6–7 (9) **vease,** 7 **veaze;** 7 **veeze** (9 **veese);** 9 **vaise, vaze,** etc. [Southern var. of Feeze *sb.*] A rush, impetus; a run before a leap. (Cf. Feeze *sb.* 1 and 1 b.)

c 1386 Chaucer *Knight's T.* 1127 And ther out cam a rage, and such a vese, That it made al the gate for to rese. 1573 Twyne *Æneid* XII. Nn 4 b, This vp in hand be caught, and tremblyng at his foe did flyng, Arysing up therwith, and forth his vease he fet withall. 1614 Gorges *Lucan* I. 41 In this flitting whirle-winde vease, I passe the Mountaines Pyrinees. *Ibid.* VIII. 346 O Marriners stay not my veaze, Headlong to plunge into the seas. *a* 1618 J. Davies (Heref.) *Wit's Pilgrimage* Wks. (Grosart) II. 31/2 From whence Loues lightest Muses take their veeze To leape into those Seas, which cares destroy. 1646 in Dircks *Life Marq. Worcester* x. (1865) 171, I only would retire myself from further present charge, as a ram doth to take a greater vease. 1678 Ray *Prov.* 78 Every pease hath its veaze, and a bean fifteen..signifies Pease are flatulent, but Beans ten times more. 1825 Jennings *Dial. W. Engl.* 80 *Vaze*,..the distance employed to increase the intensity of motion or action from a given point. 1875 Porson *Quaint Words S. Worcs.* 26 What a vese they [*sc.* the hounds] did go, surely.

Vease, dial. var. Feeze *v.*¹ **Veasy,** var. Vasy *a. Obs.* **Veawe,** southern ME. var. Few *a.*; obs. var. View *v.* **Veaze,** var. Vease. **Veb,** obs. form of Web *sb.* **Vecche, Vechche,** southern ME. varr. Fetch *v.*

‖**Vecchio.** *Obs.* [It.] An old man.

c 1570 *Bugbears* I. ii. 61 Yet it dothe not content our pinchefiste, the old vecchio. *Ibid.* 79 The three thousand Crownes that our vecchio dothe require.

Vech(e, obs. ff. Vetch. **Vecht, Vechtie,** obs. Sc. ff. Weight *sb.*, Weighty *a.*

†**Vecke.** *Obs.* Also 5 **vekke, wekke.** [app. ad. It. *vecchia*, fem. of *vecchio* old.] An old woman.

As direct adoption from Italian would be remarkable in the 14th cent., it is possible that the word existed in OF. colloquial use.

1390 Gower *Conf.* I. 98 This olde wyht him hath awaited ..: Florent his wofull heved uplefte And syh this vecke wher sche sat. *c* 1400 *Rom. Rose* 4495 A rympled vekke, ferre ronne in age, Frownyng and yelowe in hir visage. 1412–20 Lydg. *Chron. Troy* I. 2793 Sche cleped anoon vn-to hir presence An aged vekke, fer in ȝeris ronne. 1426 — *De Guil. Pilgr.* 12752 An olde wekke a-noon I mette. 1430–40 — *Bochas* I. xx. (1554) 36 b, Whan these veckes, ferre yronne in age, Within them selfe hath vaine glory and delite For to farce and poppe their visage.

†**Vecked,** *ppl. a.* *Obs.* = Invecked *ppl. a.*

1562 Legh *Armory* II. 56 b, Hee beareth Azure, a crosse formye vecked Argent.

Veeord. *rare*⁻¹. = next.

1788 tr. *Swedenborg's Wisdom of Angels* v. § 378. 364 Hence too the Terms Concord, Discord, Vecord (malicious Madness) and other similar Expressions.

Vecordy. *rare*⁻⁰. [ad. L. *vēcordia*, f. *vēcors* senseless, foolish.] (See quot.)

1656 Blount *Glossogr.* [copying Cooper], *Vecordy*, madness, trouble of minde, folly, doting.

Vecount, obs. Sc. form of Viscount.

Vecta·rious, *a.* *rare*⁻⁰. [f. L. *vectāri-us* (*equus*), f. *vectāre* to convey.] (See quot.)

1656 Blount *Glossogr.*, *Vectarious*, belonging to a coach, waggon or any carriage. [Hence in Phillips (1658); in later edd. (1671–96) *Vectorious.*]

Vectayllys, obs. variant of Victuals.

Ve·ctible, *a.* *rare*⁻⁰. [f. L. *vect-*, ppl. stem of *vehĕre* to carry.] (See quot.)

1656 Blount *Glossogr.*, *Vectible*, that is or may be carried.

Vectigal (vektəi·găl), *sb.*¹ Now only *Rom. Hist.* Also 6 **vecti-,** *Sc.* **victigall.** [a. L. *vectīgal* a payment to the State, etc.] A payment of the nature of tribute, tax, or rent, made to a superior or to the State.

1535 Stewart *Cron. Scot.* II. 243 Grit tribute and victigall alsua, Ilk ȝeir by ȝeir to king Arthure till pa. 1538 Leland *Itin.* (1769) IV. 111 Thereupon they give a Fee Farme or Vectigall of an 100 l. yearely. The Vectigall is as it was. 1656 Blount *Glossogr.*, *Vectigal*,..used substantively for toll, impost-money or tribute it self. 1774 T. West *Antiq. Furness* (1805) 104 His lands and tenants were exempted from all regal exactions of talliage, toll, passage, pontage, and vectigal. 1838 Arnold *Hist. Rome* (1846) I. xvii. 366 The tribunes demanded..that the occupiers of the remainder should pay their vectigal regularly.

†**Vectigal,** *sb.*² and *a.* *Obs. rare.* Also 6 *Sc.* **victogall.** [ad. L. *vectīgāl-is*, f. *vectīgal*: see prec.] **a.** *sb.* A collector of tribute. **b.** *adj.* (See quot. 1656.)

1535 Stewart *Cron. Scot.* I. 188 Mark Terebell..Hes constat him his victogall that tyde, For to collect his tribute and his rent. 1656 Blount *Glossogr.*, *Vectigal*, that pays or pertains to paying tribute, subsidy, pension or rent.

†**Vection.** *Obs. rare.* [ad. L. *vectiōn-*, *vectio*, n. of action f. *vehĕre* to carry.] The action of carrying; vectitation.

c 1610 Sir C. Heydon *Astrol. Disc.* (1650) 42 For whatsoever moveth another, it doth it either by impulsion, attraction, volutation, or vection. 1635 Swan *Spec. M.* (1670) 198 Albertus calls this motion a vection or a carrying. 1654 Z. Coke *Logick* 40 Local motion...Traction or drawing. Vection or carrying.

‖**Vectis** (ve·ktis). [L. *vectis* lever, crow-bar.]

†**1.** A lever. *Obs.*

1648 Wilkins *Math. Magic* I. v. 33 Rather suppose B C, to be a Vectis or Leaver, towards the middle of which is the place of the fulciment. 1674 Petty *Disc. Dupl. Proportion* 119 In the Fuze of a Watch, the greatest strength of the Spring is made to work upon the shortest Vectis.

2. *Surg.* **a.** An obstetrical instrument employed as a lever to free the head of the child.

1790 *Med. Comm.* II. 397 It is now near forty years since an account of the vectis or lever of Roonhuysen was published. 1822–7 Good *Study Med.* (1829) V. 190 If, at the same time, the head be lying clear on the perinæum, the vectis or forceps should be had recourse to. 1841 Ramsbotham *Obstet. Med. & Surg.* 314 Another instrument that has been much employed with the view of extracting the child living, is the vectis or lever. 1881 *Trans. Obstet. Soc. Lond.* XXII. 78, I passed in a vectis, and by its aid as a lever..I brought down the second larger head and left arm.

b. An instrument employed in operations on the eye.

1881 *Illustr. to Maw's Price-current* 77 [Eye instruments.] Vectis, Taylor's. 1891 *Ibid.* 42 Ophthalmoscope lamp, operation scissors,..and vectis. 1895 *Arnold & Sons' Catal. Surg. Instr.* 158 Vectis (Taylor's), for Extraction of Soft Lens.

Vectita·tion. *rare.* [f. L. *vectitāre* (rare), freq. of *vectāre* to carry, convey.] The action of carrying or conveying (frequently); the fact of being carried or conveyed.

1656 Blount *Glossogr.*, *Vectitation*, an often carriage. 1727 Pope, etc. *Martinus Scriblerus* vi, Whilst their enervated Lords are lolling in their chariots (a species of Vectitation seldom used amongst the Ancients, except by old men). 1823 *New Monthly Mag.* VIII. 253 A method of aerial vectitation.

Ve·ctitory, *a.* *rare*⁻¹. [Cf. prec.] Of the nature of carrying or conveying.

1822 *Examiner* 8/1 Heaven forbid that..the bodies of Turks should be applied to vectitory purposes.

Vector (ve·ktəɹ). [a. L. *vector*, agent-noun f. *vehĕre* to carry. So (in sense 1) Sp. and Pg. *vector*, F. *vecteur.*]

†**1.** *Astr.* (See quot. 1704.) Also *vector radius*, = *radius-vector* Radius 3 e. *Obs.*

1704 J. Harris *Lex. Techn.* I. s.v., A Line supposed to be drawn from any Planet moving round a Center, or the Focus of an Ellipsis, to that Center or Focus, is by some Writers of the New Astronomy, called the Vector; because 'tis that Line by which the Planet seems to be carried round its Center. 1796 Morse *Amer. Geog.* I. 28 If a right line, called by some the vector radius, be drawn from the sun through any planet, and supposed to revolve round the sun with the planet [etc.].

2. *Math.* A quantity having direction as well as magnitude, denoted by a line drawn from its original to its final position.

a 1865 Sir W. R. Hamilton *Elem. Quaternions* I. i. 1 A right line AB, considered as having not only length, but also direction, is said to be a Vector. 1881 J. C. Maxwell *Electr. & Magn.* II. 28 The vector, whose components are F, G, H., is called the vector-potential of magnetic induction. 1882 Minchin *Unipl. Kinemat.* 109 The resultant of a system of vectors whose type is $\omega . IP\,d\omega$, if each were directed from I to P, would be a vector $= M . IG$ directed from I to G.

attrib. 1878 W. K. Clifford *Dynamic* 95 We are led to two different kinds of product of two vectors,..a vector product..and a scalar product. 1880 *Nature* XXI. 256 Some vector property (such as rotation about an axis). 1897 Curry *Theory Electr. & Magnetism* 361 If we replace the vector-equation by its three component-equations and the vector-integrals of the latter by the above values.

Vectorial (vektō·riăl), *a.* [f. L. *vectōri-us* or directly f. prec.]

†**1.** Capable of carrying or conveying. *Obs.*

1715 Derham *Astro-Theol.* (1726) 66 From a Vectorial Power, or Emanations from the Sun. *Ibid.* 68 If..we should imagine the Moon to be wheeled about our Earth, by the Motion and Vectorial Power of the Earth.

2. *Math.* Of or pertaining to, connected with, a vector or radius vector.

1882 Minchin *Unipl. Kinemat.* 84 The vectorial area of the complex path thus traced out..is the area of the roulette. 1882 C. Smith *Conic Sect.* (1885) 10 The radius vector is considered positive if measured from O along the line bounding the vectorial angle.

Vecto·rian, *a.* *rare*⁻⁰. [Cf. prec.] (See quot.)

1656 Blount *Glossogr.*, *Vectorian*, apt to carry, serving for carriage.

†**Ve·ctorship.** *Obs.* [f. L. *vector* Vector.] Conveying agency or activity.

1649 Bulwer *Pathomyot.* I. iv. 19 This Animall Faculty.. by the vectorship of the spirit flowes from the Braines into every particle.

†**Ve·cture.** *Obs.* [ad. L. *vectūra*, f. *vect-*, *vehĕre* to carry.] Carriage, conveyance.

1625 Bacon *Ess., Sed. & Troubles* (Arb.) 405 There be but three Things, which one Nation selleth vnto another; The Commoditie..; The Manufacture; and the Vecture or Carriage. *a* 1643 [see Secture].

Ved, obs. Sc. form of Wed *v.*, Weed *sb.*

‖**Veda** (vē·dā). Also 8 **Beda; Vidam, Viedam, Vedam.** [a. Skr. *vēda* knowledge, sacred knowledge, sacred book, from the root *vid-* to know: see Wit *v.* The *a*-forms are from the Skr. nom. and acc. *vēdam*, perh. partly through Tamil. The Urdū form *bed* (Hindī *ved*) is also represented in older use by *Bead* (1698), *Beid* (1776), and *Bede* (1789).] One or other of the four ancient sacred books of the Hindus (called the *Rig-*, *Yajur-*, *Sāma-*, and *Atharva-vēda*); the body of sacred literature contained in these books.

α. 1734 Picart tr. *Roger's Relig. & Manners Bramins* in *Cerem. & Relig. Customs Var. Nations* III. 353 The Vedam is the Book of the Law among these People, and contains all they are to believe or practise. 1763 Scrafton *Indostan* (1770) 4 The Bramins say, that Brumma, their law-giver, left them a book, called the Vidam, which contains all his doctrines and institutions. 1766 J. Z. Holwell *Interesting Hist. Events* (ed. 2) I. 12 The great absurdities and impurities of the Viedam. 1778 Orme *Hist. Milit. Trans.* VI. II. 5 The Shaster..they assert to be the genuine scripture of Bramah, in preference to the Vidam. 1794 R. J. Sulivan *View Nat.* IV. 295 The Vedams, or texts of scripture, were published by Brahma, together with the Shasters, or commentaries, about six hundred years afterwards.

β. 1776 Justamond tr. *Raynal's Hist. Ind.* I. 33 The Bramin..promised to pardon him on condition that he should swear never to translate the Bedas, or sacred volumes. 1788 *Asiatic Researches* I. 340 The first four [parts of knowledge] are the immortal *Véda's* evidently revealed by God. 1808 Colebrooke *Ibid.* VIII. 387 It may be here proper to remark, that each Véda consists of two parts, denominated the Mantras and the Bráhmanas; or prayers and precepts. 1841 Elphinstone *Hist. Ind.* I. 71 The religion taught in the Institutes is derived from the Védas, to which scriptures they refer in every page. 1871 Mateer *Travancore* 35 Accordingly, as a matter of fact, the Sudras never do read the Sanscrit Vedas.

attrib. 1841 *Penny Cycl.* XX. 403/1 In like manner, the Veda-hymns..led to the consideration of the laws of metre. 1843 *Ibid.* XXVI. 171 These various schools of the Veda theology.

Hence **Veda·ic** *a.*, = Vedic *a.*; **Ve·daism,** = Vedism.

1865 Baring-Gould *Werewolves* x. 176 In ancient Indian Vedaic mythology the upsaras were heavenly damsels who dwelt in the æther, between Earth and Sun. 1887 L. Parks *Star in East* viii. 202 Their religion sprung from the same root as Vedaism.

‖**Veda·nta.** Also **Vedânta, Vedânta.** [Skr. *vēdānta*, f. *vēda* Veda + *anta* end.] One of the leading systems of Hindu philosophy. Also *attrib.*

The Hindī form *Vedant* has also been occas. used.

1823 Colebrooke *Philos. Hindus* in *Trans. Roy. Asiatic Soc.* (1827) I. 19 The latter (Uttara) commonly called Védánta, and attributed to Vyása, deduces from the text of the Indian scriptures, a refined psychology, which goes to a denial of a material world. 1849 C. S. Henry tr. *Epit. Hist. Philos.* 28 The Vedanta philosophy is an exhibition of pantheism in its greatest metaphysical strictness. *Ibid.* 29 The Vedanta system shows us..how pantheism must logically result in scepticism. 1895 *Westm. Gaz.* 23 Oct. 1/3 The philosophy of Vedânta is the abstract science which embraces all these methods.

Hence **Veda·ntic** *a.*, **Veda·ntism, Veda·ntist.**

The Skr. *Vedāntin* and Hindī *Vedānti* have also been used instead of 'Vedantist'.

1882 Max Müller *India* vii. 270 The Brahma-Samāj.. was 'Vedāntic in spirit. 1882 *Athenæum* 8 July 41/1 He commences his enumeration with that system which is furthest removed from Vedāntic speculation,..omitting, however, the Vedānta itself. 1849 C. S. Henry tr. *Epit. Hist. Philos.* 29 *Vedantism embraces in its wide comprehension, a multitude of other conceptions, which are common to it and to the other philosophies of India. 1880 Birdwood *Ind. Arts* I. 4 But Vedantism is really nothing else than Nihilism. 1849 C. S. Henry tr. *Epit. Hist. Philos.* 26 Brahma alone exists; everything else is an illusion. The *Vedantists prove this capital axiom by [etc.]. *Ibid.* 29 In order to avoid misconception of the Vedantist reasoning. 1864 Trevelyan *Compet. Wallah* (1866) 215 His sect went by the name of 'Vedantists;' in fact, the 'Evangelicals' of the East.

Ve·dda. Also 7 **Vaddah,** 9 **Veddah, Wedda.** [Sinhalese *veddā* archer, hunter.] A member of a primitive race inhabiting the forest districts of Ceylon.

1681 R. Knox *Hist. Ceylon* 61 In this Land are many of these wild men, they call them Vaddahs. 1851 Carpenter *Man. Phys.* (ed. 2) 289 The Veddahs or wild hunters of Ceylon. 1875 Jevons *Money* iv. 28 Somewhat similar pieces circulated in Abyssinia, the Soulou Archipelago.., and among the Veddahs. 1881 Tylor *Anthropology* vi. (1904) 164 In the forests of Ceylon are found..the Veddas or 'hunters', shy wild men who build bough huts, and live on game and wild honey.

Vedde, obs. Sc. f. Withy. **Vedder, -ir,** obs. Sc. f. Weather, Wether. **Vede,** obs. Sc. f. Weed *sb.* **Vede(n,** southern ME. varr. Feed *v.* **Veder,** southern ME. var. Father, Feather.

‖**Vedette** (vĭde·t). Also 9 **vedet;** 7– **vidette.** [F., ad. It. *vedetta*, prob. f. *vedere* to see. The incorrect spelling *vidette*, now rare, was common in the first half of the 19th cent.]

1. *Mil.* A mounted sentry placed in advance of the outposts of an army to observe the movements of the enemy.

α. 1690 Davies *Diary* (Camden) 129 And then lay down to sleep..without posting any scouts or videttes abroad. 1778 Gouv. Morris in Sparks *Corr. Amer. Rev.* (1853) II. 228 A few good cavalry may be requisite for the videttes. 1812 *Examiner* 7 Sept. 561/2 He fell in with the enemy's videttes. 1843 Prescott *Mexico* III. iii. (1864) 152 One of the videttes perceived..a large body of Indians moving towards the Christian lines. 1868 *Regul. & Orders Army* § 892 Instructions for the guidance of Outposts,..videttes, and sentries. 1902 R. W. Chambers *Maids of Paradise* xxii. 376 The rigid system of patrol which brought death..to our sleep-soaked videttes.

β. 1702 *Milit. Dict.*, *Vedette*, a Sentinel of the Horse.. detached from the main Body of the Army [etc.]. 1746 *Rep. Cond. Sir J. Cope* 78 To post the Out-Guard, and see the Vedettes placed properly. 1786 Gillies *Hist. Greece* III. I. 100 The order of their guards and watches was highly judicious; they employed, for their security, out-sentries and vedettes. 1809 Wellington in Gurw. *Desp.* (1836) V. 355 *note*, The vedettes of the outposts were within shot of each other. 1844 *Queen's Reg. & Ord. Army* 394 Whether they have been in the habit of placing piquets, posting vedets, conducting patrols, &c. 1879 *Blackw. Mag.* July 23 A vedette was killed to-day. Half-a-dozen Zulus rushed out on him soon after he had been posted for the day.

transf. 1807 Pike *Sources Mississ.* (1810) 248, I made a pretext to halt—established my boy as a vedet, and sat down peacably under a bush and made my notes. 1812 Col. Hawker *Diary* (1893) I. 53 An old cock, who was the vidette. 1878 L. W. M. Lockhart *Mine is Thine* xxii. II. 98 The blackcock *vedette* rolled his burnished plumage leisurely against the sun.

fig. 1801 Jefferson *Writ.* (1859) VII. 483 Philosophical vedette at the distance of one thousand miles..is precious to us here. 1880 *Spectator* 13 Nov. 1439 They cannot bear to see the landlords, whom they regard as their own vedettes, terrorized.

2. *Vedette boat*, a small vessel used for scouting purposes in naval warfare.

1884 *Pall Mall G.* 6 Oct. 6/1 Building armour-clads, fast cruisers, vedette and torpedo boats. 1892 *Times* (weekly ed.) 7 Oct. 7/2 They are vedette boats and not torpedo boats in the proper sense.

Vedic (vē·dik), *a.* and *sb.* [f. Ved-a + -ic.] **a.** *adj.* Of or pertaining to, contained or mentioned in, contemporary with, the Vedas. **b.** *sb.* The language of the Vedas, an early form of Sanskrit.

1859 Max Müller *Anc. Sanskrit Lit.* 10 The sacred literature of the Vedic age. *Ibid.* 11 The..publication of all Vedic texts and commentaries. 1864 Pusey *Lect. Daniel* ix. 558 The old Vedic worship was a libation to the god of fire. 1873 Whitney *Oriental & Ling. Stud.* 1 A general view of the whole body of Vedic literature. 1884 *American* VIII. 90 There are still orthodox Brahmans, who..maintain old Vedic sacrifices. 1890 Schrumpf *First Aryan Reader* p. xi, Specimen B ought to have preceded specimen A, as Vedic is older than Sanskrit.

Vedir, obs. Sc. f. Weather.

Ve·dism. [f. Ved-a + -ism. Cf. Vedaism.] The system of religious beliefs and practices contained in the Vedas.

1882 *Athenæum* 29 Apr. 542/3 In this paper he showed the relationship between the Vaishnava religion and three other forms of the Hindu religious system, viz., Vedism, Brāhmanism, and Saivism. 1895 J. Kidd *Morality & Relig.* v. 191 Vedism, then, generally speaking, was a religion of nature.

Ve·dist. [f. as prec. + -ist.] A student of, or authority on, the Vedas.

1896 Seeley *Introd. Pol. Sci.* (1902) 364 Not dealing with the new matter introduced by Egyptologists or Assyriologists or Vedists.

Vedlak, obs. form of Wedlock.

Vedo(u, obs. Sc. ff. Widow.

‖**Vedro.** Also 8 **wedro.** [Russ. ведрó pail.] A Russian liquid measure equal to 2.7 imperial gallons.

1753 Hanway *Trav.* VI. lxxxi. (1762) I. 371, 8 Krushquas, 1 wedro—13 english quarts. 1799 W. Tooke *View Russian Emp.* II. 523 The greater part was then already podraded (contracted) for at 146 kopecks for every vedro. 1802–3 tr. *Pallas's Trav.* (1812) I. 234 Boiled in large kettles containing from forty to forty-three Russian vedros, or eimers, of water. 1833 R. Pinkerton *Russia* 77 The..distilleries.. issue about twenty-five millions of vedros. 1907 *Edin. Rev.* Jan. 224 The peasants of that province..drank this year 62,924 vedros of vodka more than last.

Vee. *Mining.* (See quot.)

1883 Gresley *Gloss. Coal-M.* 269 *Vee*, the junction of two underground roadways meeting in the form of a V.

‖**Veedor.** *Obs.* Also 6 **veadore, viador.** [a. Sp. and Pg. *veedór*, Pg. *vedor, veador, viador*, f. *ver* to see.] An official invested with inspecting or controlling power.

α. [1555 Eden *Decades* (Arb.) 158 One Gonzalus Fernandus Ouiedus beinge one of the maiestrates appointed in that office which the Spanyardes caule *Veedor.*] 1595 T. Scarlett *Est. Engl. Fugitives* G, Sammariba, the Veedors chiefe officer. 1612 Shelton *Quix.* III. viii. 192 The office of a Bawde..should not be practised but by people well borne; and ought besides to haue a Veedor, and examinator of them.

β. 1599 Hakluyt *Voy.* II. II. 129 We spake with his Veadore, or chiefe man, that hath the dealing with the Christians. 1625 Purchas *Pilgrims* II. vii. 949 (Guinea), They haue one attending on them, whom they call Viador (which word they haue learned of the Portugals); hee is the Kings Treasurer, and keepeth his Gold and other Riches.

Veel, southern dial. var. Feel *v.*, Field *sb.*

Veer (vīəɹ), *sb.* [f. Veer *v.*²] An act or instance of veering; a change of direction.

1611 Cotgr., *Virevoulte*, a veere, whirle,..friske, or turne. 1633 T. James *Voy.* 70 Wee..expected a lower veere of the water. 1871 Tennyson *Last Tourn.* 231 Till the warm hour returns With veer of wind. 1890 *Daily News* 21 Aug. 5/7 This project of the Emperor William would explain the sudden veer round a short time ago against Prince Ferdinand.

Veer, southern ME. var. Fir; var. Vere (Spring) *Obs.*

Veer (vīəɹ), *v.*¹ *Naut.* Forms: 5–7 **vere** (6 *Sc.* **vire);** 6 **vyere,** 7 **vier-;** 6–7 **veare,** 7 **vear:** 7 **veere,** 7– **veer.** [a. MDu. *vieren* to let out, slacken, = OHG. *fieren, fiaran* to give direction to. Hence also G. *vieren, fieren*, Da. *fire*, Sw. *fira* in nautical use.]

1. *trans.* To allow (a sheet or other sail-line) to run out to some extent; to let out by releasing. Also with *out.* ? *Obs.*

So Du. and Flem. *(di) schoot vieren*, freq. used fig.

c 1460 *Pilgrim's Sea-Voy.* 25 Hale the bowelyne! now, vere the shete! 1522 *Lett. & Papers Hen. VIII*, III. II. 975 [The galley was next them, but if she] may vyere the shut, she will go from us all. 1530 *Hickscorner* 302 A-le the helme! a-le! vere! shot of! vere sayle! 1549 *Compl. Scot.* vi. 41 Vire the trossis, nou heise. *Ibid.*, Vire ȝour liftaris and ȝour top sail trossis. 1590 Spenser *F. Q.* I. xii. 1 Behold I see the hauen nigh at hand,..Vere the maine shete, and beare vp with the land. 1626 Capt. Smith *Accid. Yng. Seamen* 28 Loure the maine top saile, veare a fadome of your sheat. 1627— *Seaman's Gram.* ix. 39 Veere more sheat, or a flowne sheat, that is, when they are not haled home to the blocke. 1669 Sturmy *Mariner's Mag.* I. ii. 17 Vere out some of your Fore and Main-sheets. *Ibid.* 18 Vere out the main Sheet, and fore Sheet. 1694 [see Main-sheet 1].

absol. 1530 [see above]. *a* 1658 Cleveland *Inund. of Trent* 74 Now Bedfellows do one another greet I' th' Saylors Phrase, Vere, vere, more Sheet.

b. To let *out* (any line or rope); to allow to run *out* gradually to a desired length.

1574 W. Bourne *Regiment for Sea* xiv. (1577) 42 They haue a pece of wood, and a line to vere out ouer borde. 1628–9 Digby *Voy. Medit.* (Camden) 75, I bore vp to her, and by a barrell viered her out a long hawser. 1690 Leybourn *Curs. Math.* 608 As you veer out the Log-Line, set the Drift of the Log with your Compass. 1721 *Phil. Trans.* XXXI. 178 [He] marches on the bottom of the Sea, vearing out the Coiles of his Pipe. 1793 Smeaton *Edystone L.* § 63 They rowed it towards the rock, veering out a rope, which they had fastened to the large boat. 1839 *Civil Eng. & Arch. Jrnl.* II. 178/2 They had the appearance of a single rope capable of being coiled and veered out conveniently. 1893 W. R. Mackintosh *Around Orkney Peat Fires* (1905) II. 136 [He] veered out the boat's tether till he came alongside the vessel.

†**c.** Similarly without adv. *Obs. rare.*

1624 Capt. Smith *Virginia* VI. 219 As fast as you can hale and vere a line. 1787 Best *Angling* (ed. 2) 169 *Veer your line*, let it off the reel after striking.

2. To allow (a boat, buoy, etc.) to drift further off by letting out a line attached to it. Usually with *away* or *out.*

1539 in R. G. Marsden *Sel. Rec. Crt. Adm.* (Selden) I. 67 The marinars of the sayd Venys shippe did vere owt there grete bote. 1824 *Mechanic's Mag.* No. 41. 215 They tried the means of veering away a buoy. 1831 Trelawny *Adv. Younger Son* lxxiv, We veered an empty cask astern, with a rope attached to it. 1834 Marryat *P. Simple* (1863) 207 They veered out a buoy with a line, which we got hold of. 1846 A. Young *Naut. Dict.* 357 To veer a buoy in a ship's wake, means to slack out a rope to which the buoy has been attached, in order to let it go astern.

3. To let out or pay out (a cable).

1604 *Adm. Ct. Exam.* 21 May, The cables were not viered. 1622 R. Hawkins *Voy. S. Sea* (1847) 203 On both sides was crying out to veere cable. *Ibid.*, Those [cables were] very short, and vered to the better end. 1627 Capt. Smith *Seaman's Gram.* vii. 30 Veere more Cable, is when you ride at Anchor. 1745 P. Thomas *Jrnl. Anson's Voy.* 156 Tho' they immediately let go the Sheet-Anchor, and veer'd almost two Cables on it, yet they drove out to Sea. 1789 *Trans. Soc. Arts* VII. 211 Cables veered astern, with tackles leading from them to the ship's quarters. 1854 G. B. Richardson *Univ. Code* v. (ed. 12) 1280, I cannot veer more cable. 1870 Meade *New Zealand* 290 After veering cable we went to quarters. 1899 F. T. Bullen *Way Navy* 41 Every anchor fell and cable was veered to five shackles.

fig. 1616 B. Jonson *Devil an Ass* v. v. 46 Traines shall seeke out Ingine,..every cable Is to be veer'd.

absol. 1769 Falconer *Dict. Marine* (1780) A a a 4 b, *Ne file plus amarre!* keep fast the cable! stopper the cable! veer no more! 1775 *Phil. Trans.* LXVIII. 404 At 4 a.m. found ship drove, veered to a whole cable.

b. With *away* or *out.*

(*a*) 1697 Dampier *Voy.* I. 437 This obliged us to let go our Sheet Anchor, veering out a good scope of Cable. 1769 Falconer *Dict. Marine* (1780) A a a 4 b, *Filer le cable bout par bout*,..to veer out the cable end-for-end. 1899 F. T. Bullen *Log Sea-waif* 74 The warships, which, with topmasts housed and cables veered out to the clinch, were all steaming full speed ahead.

(*b*) 1748 *Anson's Voy.* II. iii. 138 To veer away the cable briskly. *Ibid.* III. ii. 319 After we had veered away one whole cable. 1765 Commodore Byron *Voy.* (1773) I. 79 A thick fog coming on with hard rain, we veered away the stream cable. 1846 A. Young *Naut. Dict.* 357 'Veer away the cable,' that is, slack it and let it run out.

fig. 1769 M. Cumberland *Brothers* in *Brit. Theat.* (1808) XVIII. 17 I'll veer away no more good advice after you.

c. To put *on* (cables) end to end. *rare*⁻¹.

1806 A. Duncan *Nelson* 86 The latter continued..to drop to leeward, and the Theseus was obliged to veer on two cables to keep within reach of them.

4. *To veer and haul*: (see quots.).

1769 Falconer *Dict. Marine*, *To Veer and haul*, to pull a rope tight, by drawing it in and slackening it alternately,.. so that the rope is straitened to a greater tension. 1841 R. H. Dana *Seaman's Man.* 133 *To veer and haul*, is to haul and slack alternately on a rope, as in warping, until

Veer

Veerable, a.

Veering, ppl. a.

Veering, vbl. sb.

Veery.

Vees, south. dial. variant of FEES sb.¹

Vefa ¹

Vegetability (vedʒĭtăbi·lĭti). [ad. med.L. *vegetabĭli·tāt-em*]

Vegetable (ve·dʒĭtǎb'l), sb. Also 6 vegitable. [f. the adj.]

Vegetable (ve·dʒĭtǎb'l), a. and sb. Also 5 vegytable.

Vegetablize, v. rare.

Vegetal (ve·dʒĭtǎl), a. and sb.

Vegetalize, v. rare.

Vegetarian (vedʒĭtɛə·riǎn), a. and sb.

Vegetarianism (vedʒĭtɛə·riǎniz'm).

Vegetate (ve·dʒĭteit), v.

Vegete (vĭdʒī·t), a. Obs. rare.

Vegetism.

Vegetive (ve·dʒĭtiv), a. Obs. rare.

Vegetation (vedʒĭteiˑʃǎn). Also 6 vegetacion.

Vegetated (ve·dʒĭteited), ppl. a.

Vegetating, ppl. a.

Vegetative (ve·dʒĭteitiv), a. and sb. Also 5 vegetatyf, -tyfe, 6 -tife, 6, 7 -tius. So F. végétatif.

(Oxford English Dictionary — densely set dictionary columns. Principal headwords on this page:)

Vegetity. Obs.

† Vegetous, a. Obs.

Vegit, obs. f. VEGETE a.

Vehemence (vī'hĕmĕns, vī'hĭmĕns).

Vehemency.

Vehement (vī'hĕmĕnt, vī'hĭmĕnt), a. and adv.

Vehemently adv.

Vehementness.

Vehicle (vī'ĭk'l, vī'hĭk'l), sb. Also 7 vehicolo.

Vegete (vĭdʒī't), a. Now rare. Also 7 veget, vegit.

Vegetist, nonce-word.

Vegetivorous, a.

Vegetizing, ppl. a.

Vegeto- (vĕ'dʒĕtŏ), irregular combining form of the L. stem veget-, used in the sense of 'vegetable'... or 'having a vegetable origin'.

Vehicled, ppl. a. rare⁻¹.

Vehicular (vĭhĭ'kiˇŭlar), a.

Vehicularly adv.

Vehiculary (vĭhĭ'kiˇŭlari), a.

Vehiculate, v. rare⁻¹.

Vehiculation. rare.

Vehiculatory, a.

† Vehicle, v. Obs.

† Vehiculate, v. Obs.

Vehicula, pl. of VEHICULUM.

Vehicular, (vĭhĭ'kiˇŭlar) a.

Vehiculum. Now rare or Obs. Pl. vehicula; also 7 -are.

Vehmgericht (vā'mˌ), [Ger.], Hist. Also Vehme-, Fehm-, Fem-.

Vehmic (vā'mĭk), a. Also Vehmique, Femic.

Veh'mist. A member of the Vehmgericht.

Veik, obs. Sc. form of WEAK a.

Veil (vēl), sb. Forms: 4-5 veile, 4-5 (7) veyl, veylle, 4-6 veyle, 4-7 veyll, veil (and many variant spellings).

Veigh, obs. f. WEIGH.

Veigle, v. Irreg. Obs.

Veign, obs. f. VEIN.

Veigh'tour, obs. variant.

VEIL (continued)

Veil, sb. Forms: 4–7 veil, 4 veyle, vaill, 6–7 vayle, veyll, 7 veile, vele, 6–8 vail; 7– veil.

Veil, v. Forms: 4, 7 veil, 4 vaile, 5 veyle, veyll; 7 vēlre.

Veiled, ppl. a. [f. VEIL v.]
1. Covered with or wearing a veil; shrouded in a veil.

2. Concealed, covered, hidden, as if by a veil; obscure, unrevealed.

Veiledly, adv.

Veiless (vēˈllˈes), a. [f. VEIL + -LESS.]
1. Having no veil; unprovided with or unprotected by a veil.

Veiling, vbl. sb.
1. Something serving as a veil, cover, or screen; a veil or curtain.

2. Material of which veils are made. Also pl.

Veiling, ppl. a. [f. VEIL v.]
That covers, or conceals.

Veilless, var. VEILESS.

Veilmaking.

Veilme, obs. form of VELLUM.

Veily (vēˈli), a. [f. VEIL sb. + -Y.] Veil-like.

Vein (vēˈin), sb. Forms: 4–5 veyne, 4–6 veyn, 4–7 veyne, 4–7 vayne (5 wayne), 6–7 veine, 5–7 vaine (6 vayn, wayn), 5–7 vain (6 5, 5C. vaine), 4 vene, 4–7 vayne (5 wayne), 7– vein.
1. One or other of the tubular vessels in which blood is conveyed through the animal body.

2. Material or substance of which veins are made.

3. fig. Fixed in the blood; ingrained.

4. Lodged or distributed in veins.

Vein (vēˈin), v. Forms: 6 veyne, 6–7 vayn, 7 veine; 7– vein. 6C. vaine (2C. usaine, wayne), 7 vain. [f. prec. Cf. VEINED.]
1. trans. To ornament (a garment, etc.) with narrow stripes of some suitable material.

2. To furnish or mark with veins (in various senses).

Veinage, rare⁻¹. [f. VEIN sb.] The course of a vein or veins; a collection or system of veins.

Veinal (vēˈnal), a. rare⁻¹. [f. VEIN sb.]

Veined (vēˈnd), ppl. a.
1. Furnished or marked with veins (in various senses).

Veiner. [f. VEIN v. + -ER.]

Veininess. [f. VEINY a.] The condition of being veiny.

Veining (vēˈniŋ), vbl. sb. [f. VEIN sb. or v.]
1. The action or process of ornamenting with vein-like markings.

Veinless (vēˈnles), a. [f. VEIN sb.] Having no veins; destitute of veins.

Veinlet (vēˈnlet). [f. VEIN sb. Cf. VEINULE.] A small or minor vein (in various senses).

Veinous, VEINY a.

Veinstone. Also veinstone. [f. VEIN sb.]
1. Stone or earthy matter composing a vein and containing metallic ore; gangue; matrix.

Vein-stone.

Veinule, rare. [f. VEIN sb. Cf. VENULE.] A small vein or veinlet.

Veiny (vēˈni), a. Forms: 6 veiny, 7 vainie, 7– veiny. [f. VEIN sb.]
1. Full of or having many veins; marked by veins.

Velvet-head *a.* Also **6 vellet head**, **7 velvet head**.

Velveting.

Velvetleaf.

Velvetlike *a.*

Velvety (velveti), *a.* [f. VELVET *sb.*]

Venable, *v. rare.* [? prec.]

Venal (vīˈnal), *a.*[1] Also **6 venall**. [ad. L. *vēnālis*, f. *vēnum* that which is sold or for sale.]

Venal, *a.*[2] Now rare or Obs.

Venal (vīˈnal), *sb.* [ad. L. *vēnālis* VENAL *a.*[1]] (See quot.)

Venality (vīnæˈliti). [ad. F. *vénalité*, or late L. *vēnālitās*, f. *vēnālis* VENAL *a.*[1] So It. *venalità*, Sp. *venalidad*, Pg. -*dade*.]

Venatic (vīnæˈtik), *a.* [ad. L. *venāticus-us*, f. *vēnāt-* pa. ppl. stem of *vēnārī* to hunt.]

Venatical, *a.*

Venatically, *adv.*

Venation[1]. Now rare or Obs. Also *a* **venacyon**.

Venation[2], *a.* [f. *vēnāt-*, L. *vēna* vein.]

Venator. *rare.* [a. L. *venātor*, agent-noun f. *vēnārī* to hunt.]

Venatory, *a.*

Venatorial (venătɔ̄ˈriăl), *a.* [f. L. *vēnātōri-us* (see VENATORY *a.*) + -AL.]

Vench, obs. Sc. form of WENCH *sb.*

Vencus, *v. Obs. rare.* In *a* **venkis**, *4* **venqus**.

Vend, *v.* [ad. F. *vendre* = It. *vendere*, Sp. and Pg. *vender*; or L. *vendere*.]

Vend, *sb.* [f. VEND *v.*]

Vendace (venˈdās). Also *8* **vangis**, *9* **vendis**, **vendise**; *pl. 8* **vendices**, *vendace* (mod.F.), *vandoise*.

Vendage, Obs. Also mod.*-vyndage.*

Vendean (vendēˈan), *sb.* and *a.* Also **Vendéan**.

Vendee (vendīˈ). [f. VEND *v.* + -EE.] The person to whom a thing is sold; the purchaser.

Vender (veˈndəɹ). [f. VEND *v.* + -ER[1].]

Vendibility (vendibiˈliti). [See next and -ITY.]

Vendible (veˈndibˈl), *a.* and *sb.* [ad. L. *vendibilis*, f. *vendere* to sell. So Sp. *vendible*, It. *vendibile.* Cf. VENDABLE *a.*]

Vendibleness.

Vendibly, *adv.*

Vending, *vbl. sb.* [f. VEND *v.*] The action of selling or retailing.

Vendication, Obs.[-]

Venditate, *v. Obs. rare.* [f. L. *venditāt-*, ppl. stem of *venditāre*, freq. of *vendere* to sell.]

Venditation (vendităˈiʃən), *sb.* [ad. L. *venditātiōn-em*, noun of action from *venditāre*. See prec.]

Vendition (vendiˈʃən). [ad. L. *venditiōn-em*, noun of action from *venditāre*: see VENDITATE.]

Venditor. *Obs. rare.* Also *8 Sc.* **venditer**. [a. L. *venditor*, agent-noun from *vendere* to sell, or ad. It. *venditore.*]

Vendor (veˈndəɹ, -ɔɹ). [a. late AF. *vendor*, earlier *vendour*.] A seller.

Vendue (vendiūˈ). *U.S.* and *W. Indies.* Also *7 vendu*, *9 vendoo*, **vendew.** [ad. Du. *vendu*, F. *vendue* = Sp. *venduta*; cf. med.L. *vendita* (1553).]

scene is renewed..after as many successive venesections. 1845 G. E. Day Simon's Anim. Chem. I. 248 The three following tables show the mean results of the first, second, and third venesections. 1876 tr. Wagner's Gen. Path. 2 Change in the fibrin after frequent venesections.

Venesector. rare^{-1}. [Cf. Venesect v.] One who practises venesection; a blood-letter.

1890 Cosmopolitan June 139 Our barber also acts as venesector.

Venesion, obs. form of Venetian.

Veneso(u)n, -sun, obs. forms of Venison.

†Venet, a. Obs. rare. [ad. L. venet-us.] Venet colour, a greyish-blue colour.

c 1425 MS. Digby 233 fol. 224/2 Loke þat..þe mennes clothing by coloured with venet colour þat is water coloure. a 1661 Holyday Juvenal 226 Vegetius..says that ships, which are sent out as spies, should have their sails of the venet colour, that they may not be discerned by the enemies.

Venet, obs. form of Vignette.

†Venetia. Obs.$^{-1}$ = Venetian sb. 2.

1579 G. Harvey Letter-Bk. (Camden) 72 Eloquence, if a man had it, were more worth then..a payer of tatterid venetias in his presse.

Venetian (vǐnī·ʃăn), sb. and a. Forms: α. 5 **Venycyen, Venecien, 6 Venesien.** β. 5–6 **Venecian, 6 -ycian, -esyan, -etyan, 7– Venetian; 5 Venicyan, 7, 9 Venitian.** γ. 6 **Venytyon, Venyscyon, Venecyon, Venesion, 8 Venition.** [ad. med.L. Venetiān-us, f. Venetia Venice: cf. It. and Pg. Veneziano, Sp. Veneciano. In early use also a. OF. Venicien, -esien, etc. (mod.F. Vénitien).]

A. sb. **1.** A native or inhabitant of mediæval or modern Venice; a member of the mediæval republic of Venice; more rarely, one of the ancient Veneti inhabiting the district of Venetia.

1432 Lydg. Minor Poems (Percy Soc.) 4 Other alyens:..Florentyns, and Venycyens. c 1436 Libel Eng. Policy in Pol. Poems (Rolls) II. 172 The commodites..of Venicyans and Florentynes. Ibid. 175 These seyde Veneciance. 1528 in Ellis Orig. Lett. (1824) I. 294 His Highnes also liketh wel the Frenche Kings Lettres to the Venecians for Ravenna and Servia. 1547 Boorde Introd. Knowl. xxiiii. (1870) 181, I am a Venesien both sober and sage. Ibid. 185 The Venyscions hath great prouision of warre. 1621 in Foster Eng. Factories Ind. (1906) I. 257 Two gentlemen, Venetians, who are not unknowne to you. 1695 Luttrell Brief Rel. (1857) III. 447 The Venetians, we hear, have taken several French ships. a 1715 Burnet Own Time v. (1734) II. 129 The Venetians and the Great Duke had not thought fit to own the King till then. 1756–7 tr. Keysler's Trav. (1760) IV. 57 German bravery under the auspices of the Venetians. 1841 W. Spalding Italy & It. Isl. II. 164 There were other slaves besides Mohammedans in the service of the rich Venetians. 1876 Bancroft Hist. U.S. I. v. 129 The Venetians..purchased alike infidels and Christians. 1880 Encycl. Brit. XIII. 446/1 The Gauls, the Ligurians, and the Veneti or Venetians.

†2. pl. Hose or breeches of a particular fashion originally introduced from Venice. Obs.

1582 in Feuillerat Revels Q. Eliz. (1908) 350, vi paire of venetians of Russet gold tyncell. 1586 Fermor Acc. in Archæol. Jrnl. (1851) VIII. 183 It. for an ell half of brod taffaty to make him a dublet and venytyons. 1598 Florio, Brache, all maner of breeches, slops, hosen, breekes, gascoines, venetians. 1611 Cotgr., Chausses à la gigotte, a fashion of very close Venitians; old fashioned Venitians. a 1612 Harington Epigr. (1618) I. xx, A Captaine..brought three yards of Veluet, & three quarters To make Venetians downe below the garters.

†**b.** In sing. with the. Obs.$^{-1}$

1592 Greene Def. Conny-catching Wks. (Grosart) XI. 95 The venetian and the gallogascaine is stale, and trunke slop out of vse.

†3. A sequin of Venice, as current in India and adjacent countries. Obs.

1698 Fryer Acc. E. India & P. 406 The Money which passes is a Golden Venetian, equivalent to our Angel. 1752 in J. Long Sel. Unpubl. Recs. 32 (Yule & B.), At this juncture a gold mohur is found to be worth 14 Arcot Rupees, and a Venetian 4½ Arcot Rupees. 1835 Burnes Trav. Bokhara (ed. 2) I. 90 You are then to present a handsome bow, and each of you eleven gold Venetians.

4. A closely-woven cloth having a fine twilled surface, used as a suiting or dress material.

1710 Lond. Gaz. No. 4706/4 For Sale.., Venitions,..Tabbies,..and other Stuffs. 1883 Simmonds Dict. Trade, Venetian, a fine twilled fabric of carded wool for gentlemen's suits. 1899 Daily News 30 Oct. 2/6 The newest designs in coloured tweeds, serges, coverts, meltons,..Venetians, beavers, and cashmeres.

5. ellipt. †**a.** A Venetian window. Obs.

1766 Entick London IV. 376 The body of the church is enlightened by two ranges of windows, with a Venetian in the center. 1779 Mirror No. 61, His dusky Gothic windows have been contrasted to great advantage, with their Bows and Venetians.

b. A Venetian blind.

1816 'Quiz' Grand Master vii. 167 They're soon disturb'd—a sudden rap 'Gainst the Venetians spoil'd their nap. 1881 Emma J. Worboise Sissie xvi, It was observed that no one, all through the day, proposed raising that side-venetian.

c. pl. (See quot.)

1882 Caulfeild & Saward Dict. Needlew. 514/1 Venetians, a heavy kind of tape or braid, resembling double Londons. They are employed more especially for Venetian blinds, whence the name.

6. = Domino 1.

1891 Century Mag. June 283, I then put off my sword, and put on my Venetian or domino, and entered the bal masqué.

B. adj. **1.** Of or pertaining to Venice.

1554 in Feuillerat Revels Q. Mary (1914) 166 A maske of viij patrons of galleis like venetian Senatours. 1593 G. Harvey New Lett. Wks. (Grosart) I. 264 Who honoureth not..the security of the Venetian state. 1642 Howell For. Trav. (Arb.) 53 There is in Italy the Toscan, the Roman, the Venetian, the Neapolitan [languages],..and all these have severall Dialects and Idiomes of Speech. 1648 Hexham II, De Venetiaensche Zee, the Venetian Sea, or, the Gulfe of Venice. 1756–7 tr. Keysler's Trav. (1760) III. 578 It is now some centuries since Padua has been brought under the Venetian yoke. 1841 W. Spalding Italy & It. Isl. III. 37 The republic at first embraced..the Venetian provinces of Bergamo, Brescia, and La Polesina. 1893 W. G. Collingwood Life Ruskin I. II. iv. 147 The treatment..of Venetian matters had to be indefinitely postponed.

b. Venetian School, (a) a school of painting, distinguished by its mastery of colouring, which originated in the 15th century and reached its climax in the 16th; (b) a school of Italian architecture originating in the early part of the 16th century.

(a) 1748 Melmoth Fitzosborne Lett. lxi. (1749) II. 116 On the contrary, the Venetian school is said to have neglected design a little too much. 1859 Ruskin Two Paths I. § 20 The Venetian school proposed to itself the representation of the effect of colour and shade on all things.
(b) 1842 Gwilt Archit. § 349 The Venetian School is characterised by its lightness and elegance; by the convenient distribution it displays; and by the abundant, perhaps exuberant, use of columns, pilasters, and arcades.

2. In special collocations, denoting things characteristic of Venice, esp. articles actually produced there, or others made in imitation of these. (Cf. similar uses of Venice.)

Venetian ball (see quots.). Venetian bar, in needlework, a bar formed by means of button-hole work on a thread or threads. Venetian blind, a window-blind composed of narrow horizontal slats so fixed on strong tapes as to admit of ready adjustment for the exclusion or admission of light and air. †Venetian breeches, = Venetian sb. 2. Venetian brown, a variety of brown used for colouring glass. Venetian carpet, a common make of carpet, usually striped, in which the warp alone is shown. Venetian chalk (see quots.). Venetian cloth, = Venetian sb. 4. Venetian dentil (see quot.). Venetian door (see quot. 1842). †Venetian earth, ? Venetian chalk. Venetian embroidery (see quot.). Venetian enamel, a hard enamel used for the dials of clocks and watches. Venetian filigree, a variety of coloured glass. Venetian frame, a form of window-frame (see quot. 1833). Venetian glass, Venice glass. Venetian-Gothic adj. (see quot.). †Venetian hose, = Venetian sb. 2. Venetian mast, a tall pole ornamented with spiral bands of colour, used in the decoration of streets or open spaces on special occasions. Venetian pearl, a solid artificial pearl. Venetian point, a variety of point-lace. Venetian red, satin (see quots.). Venetian shutter, a shutter constructed on the same principle as a Venetian blind; hence Venetian-shuttered adj. Venetian sole, stitch (see quots.). †Venetian sublimate (?). Venetian sumach, the southern European shrub Rhus Cotinus. Venetian swell, an organ-swell having the front constructed like a Venetian shutter. Venetian talc, a hydrous silicate of magnesia. †Venetian thyme (see quot.). Venetian turpentine, Venice turpentine. Venetian varnish (see quot.). Venetian vetch: see Vetch. Venetian white (see quot.). Venetian window (see quot. 1842). Venetian window-blind, = Venetian blind. Also Venetian bead, †dollar, lace.

1851–4 Tomlinson's Cycl. Usef. Arts (1866) I. 783/2 The *Venetian ball consists of a number of pieces of filigree glass packed into a pocket of transparent colourless glass. 1875 Knight Dict. Mech. 2702/2 Venetian ball, an ornamental form of glass for paper-weights, etc. 1882 Caulfeild & Saward Dict. Needlew. 511/2 *Venetian bar..is used in modern Point Lace. 1660 F. Brooke tr. Le Blanc's Trav. 195 Some bracelets made of *Venetian Beads of several colours. 1791 in Harper's Mag. March (1885) 535/2 Surcharge for *Venetian blinds. 1794 W. Felton Carriages I. 148 The Venetian blind..[is] frequently used as a substitute for the common shutter and spring curtain. 1840 Dickens Old C. Shop xiv, It was easy to hear through the Venetian blinds all that passed inside. 1882 Caulfeild & Saward Dict. Needlew. 514/1 Another kind of braid or tape is made for Venetian blinds. 1587 Fleming Contn. Holinshed III. 1354 Walton..rent his *venecian breeches of crimsin taffata, and distributed the same peecemeale. c 1791 Encycl. Brit. (ed. 3) VII. 774/2 *Venetian brown, with gold spangles, commonly called the philosopher's stone. 1845 G. Dodd Brit. Manuf. IV. 95 '*Venetian' carpets were never, it has been asserted, made at Venice at all. 1868 Rep. U.S. Commissioner Agric. (1869) 51 Carpets, treble ingrain, three-ply, and worsted chain Venetian. 1839 Ure Dict. Arts 1271 *Venetian chalk is Steatite. 1883 Simmonds Dict. Trade, Venetian chalk, a white compact talc or steatite, used for marking on cloth. c 1790 Encycl. Brit. (ed. 3) VI. 404/2 A new suit of French and *Venetian cloths. 1900 Daily News 6 Jan. 6/6 Venetian cloth is, next to panne, still the favourite material for dresses. 1881 Archit. Dict., *Venetian dentil, a molding consisting of a fillet with its sides cut alternately into notches, which reach the middle of the face, and produce the effect of a double row of dentils. 1626 in Foster Eng. Factories India (1909) III. 156 The *Venetian doller will yeald 5 mahmudis if full weight. 1731 Pope Ep. Burlington 36 Imitating-Fools Who..[are] Proud to catch cold at a *Venetian door. a 1744 — Hor. Sat. II. vi. 191 Palladian walls, Venetian doors, Grotesco roofs, and Stucco floors. 1842 Gwilt Archit. 1050 Venetian door, a door having side lights on each side for lighting an entrance hall. 1660 J. H[arding] Basil. Valent. Chariot Antimony 123 Mix one part of this Salt with three parts of *Venetian Earth. 1882 Caulfeild & Saward Dict. Needlew. 512/1 *Venetian embroidery..is work resembling Roman Work and Strasbourg Embroidery, but is lighter than either in effect. 1837 Hebert Engin. & Mech. Encycl. I. 468 [In] hard enamelling..the *Venetian enamels are chiefly employed. 1851–4 Tomlinson's Cycl. Usef. Arts (1866) I. 783/2 The *Venetian filigree consists of plain and coloured enamel. 1833 Loudon Encycl. Archit. § 1585 Fix a large solid *Venetian frame (a frame in three divisions, the two side divisions being narrower than the centre one). 1842 Gwilt Archit. 639 Venetian deal cased frames. 1845 Encycl. Metrop. Index 139/2 *Venetian Glass. 1875 Knight Dict. Mech. 2703/1 The Venetian-glass ball [see Venetian ball, quot. 1851–4]. 1867 Chambers's Encycl. IX. 748/1 '*Venetian-Gothic' [style of architecture] indicates the peculiar phase of that style so common in Venice and the north of Italy. 1583 Stubbes Anat. Abus. E 3, The *Venetian-hosen, they reach beneath the knee to the gartering place of the Leg. 1882 Caulfeild & Saward Dict. Needlew. 513/1 In 1654 Colbert prohibited the exportation of the *Venetian Laces into France. 1883 Harper's Mag. Jan. 311/2 The Strand being one blaze of colour with *Venetian masts, and streamers overhead. 1886 Besant Childr. Gibeon II. xxxiii, There should have been joy-bells and..Venetian masts with streamers and flags. 1864 Chambers's Encycl. VI. 5/1 *Venetian-point,..Maltese-point: in all these the pattern is flatter than in the Rose-point. 1877 W. S. Gilbert Foggerty's Fairy I, Look at the lace! It's Venetian point. 1883 Mag. of Art Dec. 66/2 Richard III wore Venetian point at his coronation. 1753 Chambers' Cycl. Suppl., Veneta bolus, a fine red earth used in painting, and called in the colour-shops *Venetian red. 1823 P. Nicholson Pract. Build. 413 Venetian-Red is a native ochre, rather inclining to scarlet. 1849–50 Weale Dict. Terms, Venetian-red:..the colours sold under this name are prepared artificially from sulphate of iron, or its residuum in the manufacturing of acids. 1867 Bloxam Chem. 322 Red oxide of iron has been already..referred to as occurring in commerce under the names of colcothar, jeweller's rouge, and Venetian red. 1786 Sixth Rep. Dep. Kpr. Public Rec. App. II. 175 A method..of manufacturing Silk and Mohair,..with materials which have never before been combined or manufactured together [as wood, reed, cane, straw, etc.], and which is called (by the Specifier) '*Venetian Sattin'. 1844 H. Stephens Bk. Farm I. 142 *Venetian shutters, which may be opened more or less at pleasure. 1892 Photogr. Ann. II. p. cxxxiii, The Plate, after exposure, goes into back chamber, a Venetian shutter being opened and closed. 1897 Mary Kingsley W. Africa 86 An infinity of flies going into the venetian shuttered window. 1803 Shaw Gen. Zool. IV. II. 304 *Venetian Sole, Pleuronectes Linguatula. 1882 Caulfeild & Saward Dict. Needlew. 514/1 *Venetian stitch, a term sometimes applied to close rows of Buttonholes as Fillings in Needlepoint Laces. 1725 Fam. Dict. s.v. Ulcer, A Solution of *Venetian Sublimate. 1755 Dict. Arts & Sci. IV. s.v. Sumach, *Venetian Sumach, cotinus, in botany. 1846 Lindley Veg. Kingd. 467 R[hus] Cotinus,..Venetian Sumach of the English, has wood called Young Fustick. 1882 Garden 19 Aug. 163/3 There are few more striking objects than a large bush of the Venetian Sumach. 1852 Seidel Organ 27 The *Venetian Swell..is the only sort used in England. 1881 C. A. Edwards Organs 121 It is to Green that we owe the Venetian swell, which took its name from the resemblance it bears to the Venetian shutter. a 1728 Woodward Fossils I. 62 This very much resembles what is sold in the Shops for *Venetian Talc. 1836 T. Thomson Min., Geol., etc. I. 186 This mineral..was formerly carried to Venice as an article of commerce, being employed in medicine. Hence the name Venetian talc. 1548 Turner Names Herbes (E.D.S.) 78 The greate kynde of thyme, wherof Dioscorides maketh mention of in Epithymo, is called nowe *Venetian thyme. 1597 A. M. tr. Guillemeau's Fr. Chirurg. 42 b/2 *Venetiane Terebentine. 1857 Miller Elem. Chem., Org. 505, 48 parts of shell-lac, 12 of Venetian turpentine. 1755 Dict. Arts & Sci. s.v. Varnish, White varnish, called also *venetian varnish, made of oil of turpentine, fine turpentine, and mastic. 1867 Ure's Dict. Arts (ed. 6) III. 984 *Venetian white, a carefully prepared carbonate of lead. 1779 Shaw Hist. Moray (1882) I. 347 It is lighted, besides several windows in the side-walls, by a *Venetian window..in the western gavel. 1837 Lockhart Scott IV. v. 148 A square small room...It had but a single Venetian window. 1842 Francis Dict. Arts, Venetian window, a window in three separate apertures, the two side ones being narrow, and separated from the centre by timber only. 1769 Public Advertiser 25 May 3/2 *Venetian Window Blinds made by Edward Bevan.

Venetianed (vǐnī·ʃănd), a. [f. Venetian sb. 5 b.] Furnished with Venetian blinds or shutters.

1839 Fraser's Mag. XIX. 366 Through the open Venetianed window I caught a passing glimpse. 1854 Stocqueler Handbk. Brit. India 125 The airy little bauleahs, with their light venetian'd rooms. 1881 Mrs. C. Praed Policy & P. III. 37 Along the white road, past the row of neat venetianed houses.

Venetic (vǐne·tik), a. [f. L. Venet-ī or Venet-ia + -ic.] Of or pertaining to the ancient Veneti or their country, or to the modern province of Venice.

1880 Encycl. Brit. XIII. 494/1 The population of the Venetian cities is 'Venetian' in language, but the country districts are in various ways Venetic. 1902 Nature 2 Jan. 212/2 Inscriptions on the outside of their rims, said to be in Venetic or old North Etruscan alphabet. 1903 Ibid. 29 Oct. 635 A large admixture of Albanian, Venetic, or Slav intruders.

Venett, obs. form of Vignette.

Venev, Venew(e, obs. forms of Venue.

Veney, variant of Veny^{2} Obs.

Veneymen, obs. form of Venom v.

Venezuelan (venĕzwī·lăn), a. and sb. [See def.] **a.** adj. Of or pertaining to the republic of Venezuela in the north of South America. **b.** sb. A native or inhabitant of Venezuela.

1836 Penny Cycl. V. 81/2 The congress of the Venezuelan Republic..at Angostura. Ibid. 82/1 The Venezuelan congress. 1881 W. H. Brett Mission Work Guiana vi. 109 From the Spaniards and Venezuelans they have suffered greatly. 1882 Caulfeild & Saward Dict. Needlew. 514/1 Venezuelan drawn work..resembles the Oriental Drawn Thread Work and the Italian and Swedish Drawn Works.

Veng(e, southern ME. variant pa. t. Fang v.

†Venge, sb. Obs. [f. Venge v. Cf. Avenge sb.] Vengeance.

1587 T. Hughes Misf. Arthur I. ii, Why shunst thou fearefull wrath? Adde coales afreshe—preserve me to this venge.

1632 Chapman & Shirley Ball II. D 2 b, You must Lay in betimes to prevent mutinie Among the small guts, which with winde of venge else Will breake your guarde of buttons.

Venge (vendʒ), v. Now arch. Forms: 4–5 **vengyn** (5 **vengy**), 4– **venge** (4 **venie, uenge**); 4–5 **wenge**, 4, 5 Sc., **weng.** [ad. OF. vengier, venger (mod.F. venger, = It. vengiare, Sp. vengar, Pg. vingar):—L. vindicāre Vindicate v. Cf. Avenge v.]

1. a. refl. = Avenge v. 1 b.

a 1300 Cursor M. 5345 For þat þai na wight drightin dred, He wenged him o þam ful sare. a 1340 Hampole Psalter ii. 5 When he venges him, his vengaunce is cald woednes. c 1386 Chaucer Melib. ¶ 45 But lete us now putte, that ye han leve to venge yow; I say ye ben nought of might ne power as now to venge you. c 1430 Lydg. Min. Poems (Percy Soc.) 31 Be nat to hasty to venge the on thi foo. c 1450 Miroure Saluacioun (Roxb.) 72 He vengid hym on his enemys horribly. 1509 Fisher 7 Penit. Ps. vi. Wks. (1876) 18 Grete laude and prayse is in wylde beestes lackynge reason, that they wyll forgyue and not venge themselfe vpon other weyker beestes. 1581 A. Hall Iliad II. 29 Til that ech one here of vs al, at wil and ease be plast With Troyan Dames..to venge vs of Paris. 1599 Shaks. Hen. V, I. ii. 292 Tel you the Dolphin, I am comming on, To venge me as I may. 1817 Scott Harold II. xv, Thou shalt know, If I can venge me on a foe. 1914 Contemp. Rev. April 578 To venge themselves they pursued a policy of obstruction in the Diet.

b. trans. = Avenge v. 1.

c 1325 Metr. Hom. 137 Ef thou prai Godd that he Apon thi fais venge the. c 1340 Hampole Pr. Consc. 5533 Haly Loverd,..How lange sal be ar þow venge our blude Of our enemys þat in erthe duellis. c 1440 Gesta Rom. x. 29 (Harl. MS.), Do vs to knowe, if þer be ony þat þretenith þe; For we ben redy to venge þe. c 1450 Lovelich Grail lvi. 435 Thus owre lord venged kyng Lawncelot certayn. 1581 A. Hall Iliad I. 16, I greatly dread, his sonne to venge, obtainde some suit she hath. 1590 Greene Orlando Furioso 1093 Now let vs seeke to venge the Lampe of France That lately was eclipsed in Angelica. 1613 Heywood Braz. Age II. ii, I sweare..to..venge the Gods that gouerne Sea and Sunne. 1814 Scott Lord of Isles III. xxix, With this he cross'd the murderer's path, And venged young Allan well! 1887 Bowen Æneid IV. 656, I have..Venged a beloved one, meted a brother measure for guilt.

c. pass. = Avenge v. 1 c.

c 1380 Wyclif Wks. (1880) 24 For to plede, for to fiȝtte and..to be vengid on men þat don aȝenst here wille, worschipe, or profit. 1390 Gower Conf. I. 202 Bot I wol make this beheste, I schal be venged er I go. c 1400 Pilgr. Sowle (Caxton) II. lvii. (1859) 55. I myght haue ben fully venged vpon the. 1480 Cov. Leet Bk. II. 441 Be-cause he seid Laurens..feyned maters to þentent to haue be venged for þe due punysshement yeven to hym be þe seid Maire. 1489 Caxton Faytes of A. I. i. 7 They that gretly be vengid on their enemyes. 1611 B. Jonson Catiline II. i, I should be right sorry To have the means so to be venged on you.

†d. intr. = Avenge v. 1 d. Obs.

13.. E. E. Allit. P. B. 201 [He] Ne venged for no vilte of vice ne synne,..Ne neuer so sodenly soȝt vnsoundely to weng. Ibid. 559 Felly he uenged Quen fourferde alle þe flesch þat he formed hade. c 1400 Destr. Troy 7333 Achilles ..Of þo kynges, þat were kild,..Wold haue vengit of þe velany, & þe vile harme. 14.. in Arnolde Chron. (1811) 208 A priest ought to be swete and softe more rather to foryeue than to vengy. a 1500 Ratis Raving 3540 Traist nocht thine honore in a fulle, Na weng nocht quhil thi blud be cule.

2. trans. = Avenge v. 2.

1303 R. Brunne Handl. Synne 3806 Þys yche chylde toke hym to rede For to venge hys fadrys ded. c 1374 Chaucer Troylus I. 62 (Harl. MS.), In dyverse wise..The ravys-hyng to vengyn of Heleyn, By Paris done, they wroughten all hir peine. a 1450 Mirk's Festial 44 The thre oþer also deyden on spytues deþes, so þat, wythyn þre ȝere aftyr, Thomas deth was thus venget. c 1489 Caxton Sonnes of Aymon ix. 244, I praye god that I maye venge your deth vpon theym or ever I deceasse. 1538 Starkey England 141 That hys ennemy may not pluke hym out at hys lyberty, nor yet in such place to venge hys iniury. 1587 Turberv. Trag. Tales (1837) 160 To venge which deede, and cursed cruell acte, He slue them all. 1620 Pyper tr. Hist. Astrea I. II. 13 Venge not my death vpon this faire Lady. 1638 Sanderson Serm. (1681) II. 111 We find our selves ready to fret at any cross occurrent, to venge every injury, to rage at every light provocation. 1802 Leyden in Life & Poems (1875) 39 Thine the mighty boast..To venge each ancient violated bust. 1851 C. L. Smith tr. Tasso XVIII. xlviii, And much he hoped with such a fiery brood To venge the felling of the precious wood.

†b. To punish (wrongdoing). Obs.

a 1340 Hampole Psalter xxix. 5 Wreth, þat is vengaunce, þat he vengid in ȝow þe first syn with ded. c 1375 Sc. Leg. Saints xxv. (Julian) 116 Syk wykyt wordis of dyspyt In þat dekine ware wengyt tyt. 1401 Pol. Poems (Rolls) II. 111 Thou seist..that charite is chacid, to vengyn oure defautis, and mende us of oure mysse.

†3. = Avenge v. 3. Obs.$^{-1}$

a 1470 Harding Chron. LXV. iii, The Scottes and Peightes be venged & ouercam.

†4. To execute (vengeance); to wreak (anger) by vengeance. Obs. rare.

1382 Wyclif Jer. li. 36 Lo! Y shal deme thi cause, and venge thi vengyng. a 1470 H. Parker Dives & Pauper (W. de W. 1496) IV. xv. 179/2 He is goddes mynystre, to venge the wrath of god in hym that dooth amys.

Vengeable, a. and adv. Obs. or dial. Forms: 4–5 **veniable**, 5–7 **vengable, vengeable** (6 **uen-**); 5 **vengeabyl, -yll(e, -abil.** [a. AF. vengable (Gower), f. venger Venge v. Cf. Vengible a.]

1. Inclined or ready to take vengeance or inflict retaliative injury. (Cf. Vengeful a. 1.)

a. Of persons (or animals).

Very common c 1400–1550; in mod. dial. use = destructive.

c 1380 Wyclif Sel. Wks. II. 189 For ȝif he were veniable here no man myȝte suffre his veniaunce. 1390 Gower Conf. II. 119 Such a Sor is incurable, And ek the goddes ben vengable. c 1400 Lydg. in Pol., Rel. & L. Poems (1903) 48 Where god list spare, a tygre is not vengeable. 1421 Hoccleve Min. Poems 153 Al-thogh þat shee were in this cas vengeable,..Shee was in þat in partie excusable. c 1450 Mirk's Festial 140 Forto schew you how vengabull God ys apon hom þat ben lef forto sched Cristys blod. 1529 S. Fish Supplic. Beggers 3 Whate tiraunt euer oppressed the people like this cruell and vengeable generacion? 1547 Boorde Introd. Knowl. xvii. (1870) 167 There is a beast called a Bouy, lyke a Bugle, whyche is a vengeable beast. 1573 G. Harvey Letter-bk. (Camden) 138 To be notoriously revenged on this vengeable feende. c 1610 Sir J. Melvil Mem. (1735) 206 The Appetites of envious, vengeable and greedy Counsellors. 1640 Bastwick Lord Bishops iii. C 3, Who should prove the most vengable Instruments of persecuting and oppressing Gods true children. 1866 Gregor Banffsh. Gloss. 232 Rottans are vengeable craiturs on young deuks.

b. Of the mind, will, etc.

1411–12 Hoccleve De Reg. Princ. 2330 He rathir chees be disobedient To his vengeable wil,..Than be forsworn of þat he swoor so depe. 1513 Bradshaw St. Werburge I. 1041 His vengeable mynde was hymselfe to magnyfy..Or destroye hymselfe. 1539 Cromwell in Merriman Life & Lett. (1902) II. 169 His Inique covetous and vengeable disposicion. 1540 Hyrde tr. Vives' Instr. Chr. Wom. (1592) H iiij, To keepe her vengeable mind unto..occasion of revengement.

c. Of weapons.

c 1400 Hoccleve Compl. Virgin 179 Wel feele I þat deeth his vengeable bowe Hath bent, & me purposith doun to throwe. 1430–40 Wycliffite Bible, Rom. xiii. 4 (Cardwell MS.), For not withoute cause he berith the vengeable swerd.

2. Characterized by, arising from, vengeance or revenge; cruel, dreadful.

c 1430 Hoccleve Min. Poems 71/128 Þat the feend..Ne sese hem nat in the vengeable day! c 1440 Capgrave Life St. Kath. IV. 1414 Ȝe shulde not suffren þis cristen foolk here Repreue oure goddis with swiche veniable manere. 1509 Barclay Shyp of Folys (1570) 201 For none..This hurt outchaseth which is so vengeable. 1582 Stanyhurst Æneis I. (Arb.) 29 Such folck as the tyrant pursude with vengeabil hatred. 1627 H. Burton Baiting Pope's Bull 18 Iezabell, for all her vengeable malice and impotent fury, yet could not wreck it vpon Elias.

3. As an intensive: Very great, severe, strong, intense, etc.

1532 More Confut. Tindale Wks. 655/2 As the church of Christe is but one, so be there of those [heretics] a vengeable maynye. 1542 Udall Erasm. Apoph. 49 b, He gave a vengeable check to those persones. 1583 Stocker Civ. Warres Lowe C. IV. 61 A mischeuous mistakyng of a matter ..bredde a vengeable suspition in the heddes of many. 1601 Deacon & Walker Spirits & Divels To Rdr. 13 [They] will courtly flutter their wings, and keepe a vengeable coyle in Conuenticles and corners.

b. As adv. = Vengeably adv. 2.

1542 Udall Erasm. Apoph. 7 Socrates asked wherfore he was so vengeable eagre. 1566 Pasquine in Traunce 48 A vengeable long leape, or a vengeable lowde lye. 1866 Gregor Banffsh. Gloss. 232 He's vengeable greedy; he can hardly be honest.

4. Punishable. rare^{-1}.

1650 S. Clarke Eccl. Hist. I. (1654) 488 [He] delivered him over to the secular power; Declaring that..it was a vengeable matter to eat or drink with him.

Vengeably, adv. Now arch. or Obs. Also 5 **vengably**, 6 **vengeablie, -eiably, veangeably.** [f. prec.]

1. In a revengeful manner; vindictively; cruelly, pitilessly.

1412–20 Lydg. Chron. Troy IV. 2775 Þis Achille of cruelte ..þe dede cors toke oute of þe taas, And vengably bond it. a 1450 Knt. de la Tour (1868) 105 Right so it plesed vnto God that he shulde deye vengeably. c 1489 Caxton Sonnes of Aymon xx. 453 He..smote a knyghte soo vengably that he cast hym doun deed to the erthe. 1549 Latimer 4th Serm. bef. Edw. VI (Arb.) 103 So that they do it charitiablye louyngelye, not of malyce, not vengeably, not couetouslye. 1586 J. Hooker Hist. Irel. in Holinshed II. 78/1 The Irish enimie..vengeablie haue brent a great towne of mine inheritance in Meth, called Ramore. 1848 Anne Brontë Agnes Grey xiv, Miss Matilda, having ..vengeably thumped the piano for an hour, in a terrible humour both with me and it.

2. Exceedingly, greatly, very.

c 1550 Bale Apol. 113 But ye are lyke to come vengeably short. 1575 Laneham Let. (1871) 12 It woold haue made mee, for my part, az hardy az I am, very veangeably afeard. 1607 R. C[arew] tr. Estienne's World of Wond. 291 Some [priests and monks]..haue bin so vengeably learned.

Vengeance (ve·ndʒăns), sb., adv., and a. Forms: α. 4 **veniance, -iaunce, -y(e)aunce**, 4–5 **venieaunce**, 5 **veniauns, -iawnce, weniaunce**; 4 **veniounse**, 5 **venions.** β. 4 **vengaunse**, 4–6 **-aunce**, 4–5 **-ance, -ans**; 4 **vengiaunce**, 5 **-ause**, 6 **-ans**; 4 **vengeans**, 4–6 **-aunce**, 4– **vengeance** (7 **veng'ance**), 6 **vengence**; 4 **wengans, -ans, -aunce, -eans, -eance**, 4, 6 Sc., **wengance**, 6 Sc. **wengence.** [a. AF. veniaunce, -ance, veng(e)aunce, -ance, = OF. and F. vengeance (It. vengianza, Sp. venganza, Pg. vinganza), f. venger Venge v.]

1. The act of avenging oneself or another; retributive infliction of injury or punishment; hurt or harm done from vindictive motives.

a 1300 Cursor M. 827 Son bigan wenganz to kiþe. Ibid. 13184 But þis ded was sald ful dere,..Wit a greithful soth vengeance. c 1315 Shoreham III. 248 He þat spilleþ mannes lyf, Veniounse hyt schel acwyte. c 1380 Wyclif Serm. Sel. Wks. I. 149 Þis is noo good praier, but more axinge of Goddis venjaunce. a 1450 Knt. de la Tour (1868) 37 She tolde..that it was the uengeaunce of God that fell on her, the whiche she had welle deserued. 1474 Caxton Chesse II. iv. (1883) 53 For hit is the most hyest and fayr vengeance that a man may doo. 1535 Coverdale Ps. xciii. 1 Thou God to whom vengeaunce belongeth, shewe thy self. 1592 Kyd Murther I. Brewen Wks. (1901) 287 The blood of the iust Abel cried..for vengeance and reuenge on the murderer. 1613 Purchas Pilgrimage (1614) 156 Diuine mercie..remoued the Christians to Pella out of the danger, that without any impediment the floud-gates of vengeance might bee set wide open for Desolations black-guard to enter. 1667 Milton P. L. I. 170 But see the angry Victor hath recall'd His Ministers of vengeance and pursuit Back to the Gates of Heav'n. 1757 Gray Bard 96 Stamp we our vengeance deep, and ratify his doom. 1769 Junius Lett. xv. (1788) 92 The injuries you have done..demand not only redress, but vengeance. 1837 W. Irving Capt. Bonneville III. 67 Alarm signals, to arouse the country and collect the scattered bands for vengeance. 1891 Farrar Darkn. & Dawn xxv, That in some way she regarded Britannicus..as the ultimate resource of her vengeance and despair.

b. In the phrase to take (also †nim) vengeance.

1297 R. Glouc. (Rolls) 6859 þe king..suor he nolde abide, Þat he nolde uerst nyme vengaunce in is side. a 1300 Cursor M. 6094 þair goddes i me on wil wrake, O þam mi wengeance sal i take. c 1386 Chaucer Melib. ¶ 49 Savinge your grace, I can nat seen that it mighte greetly harme me though I toke vengeaunce. c 1400 Rom. Rose 5780 God can wel vengeaunce therof take. c 1400 Maundev. (Roxb.) xii. 51 In taken of þe vengeaunce þat Godd tuke on þa fyue citeez. 1460 Capgrave Chron. (Rolls) 106 He receyved him with grete worchip, took veniauns on his enimes. c 1489 Caxton Sonnes of Aymon ii. 59 Vengance we sholde take therof. 1526 Tindale Rom. xiii. 4 To take vengeaunce on them that do evyll. 1611 Shaks. Cymb. v. i. 8 Gods, if you Should haue 'tane vengeance on my faults, I neuer Had liu'd to put on this. 1727 Bailey (vol. II), Avenger, one who takes Vengeance on an Offender. 1808 Scott Marmion II. xxxi, Full soon such vengeance will he take, That [etc.]. 1847 Sarah Austin Ranke's Hist. Ref. III. 17 The strong city of Pavia, on which cruel vengeance was taken for the resistance it had made.

c. Personified or otherwise regarded as an entity.

1602 Shaks. Ham. II. ii. 510 Arowsed Vengeance sets him new a-worke. 1642 D. Rogers Naaman 39 Left to conflict nakedly with hell and vengeance, till it carry them away quicke. 1721 Young Revenge II. i, Vengeance is still alive; from her dark covert..She stalks in view. 1799 Campbell Pleas. Hope I. 395 Where was thine arm, O Vengeance! a 1839 Praed Red Fisherman, Look how the fearful felon gazes On the scaffold his country's vengeance raises. 1891 Marie A. Brown tr. Runeberg's Nadeschda 67 Then saw I vengeance beckon, it lit my path In years of woe.

2. With a and pl. An act or instance of retributive or vindictive punishment. (Also as in 1 c.)

a 1300 Cursor M. 1592 For-þi in forme of iugement He thoght a neu wengaunce to sent. c 1400 Sowdone Bab. 14 For the offences to God i-doon Mary vengeaunces haue befalle. c 1440 Jacob's Well 41 Feure vengaunces comyn to man here in erthe for fals tythyng. c 1480 Henryson Fables, Wolf & Lamb xxi, It cryis ane vengeance vnto the heuinnis hie. 1659 Hammond On Ps. cix. 6–10 Sad executions, judgments, and vengeances. a 1704 T. Brown Sat. agst. Woman Wks. 1730 I. 56 He falls a willing pris'ner to her arms, There meets a vengeance of ne'er-ending harms. 1718 Pope Iliad XIII. 832 With his full strength he bent his angry bow, And wing'd the feather'd vengeance at the foe. 1728 P. Walker Life Peden (1901) I. 155 Hasty marriages are sudden vengeances. 1791 Burke App. Whigs Wks. VI. 220 Taking..a cruel vengeance on these deluded wretches. 1838 Thirlwall Greece xxxi. IV. 201 Thrasybulus..animated his men by..the prospect of a just vengeance. 1873 Miss Broughton Nancy I. 45, I am planning five distinct and lengthy vengeances against Bobby.

b. In imprecations, usually with on. Also rarely without article. Obs. or arch.

? a 1500 Chester Pl. XIII. 164 Must we afore the pharisies appeare? A vengeance on them, far and neere! 1562 J. Heywood Prov. & Epigr. (1867) 178 A vengeance on that lame iade. 1591 Shaks. Two Gent. II. iii. 21 A veng'ance on't, there 'tis. 1604 [? Chettle] Wit of Woman G 4 b, A vengeance pepper such braines, as cannot beare one draught of Ipocras. 1814 Scott Wav. xxx, D'ye think the lads..will care for..yer stool o' repentance? Vengeance on the black face o't!

c. A person of a violent temper.

1711–2 Swift Jrnl. to Stella 21 Mar., The D— he is! married to that vengeance!..Who would have her?

3. Used to strengthen interrogations. ? Obs.

1598 R. Bernard tr. Terence (1607) 167 Thr. Where are the other? San. What other in a vengeance. 1607 Shaks. Cor. III. i. 262, I would they were in Tyber. What the vengeance, could he not speake 'em faire? 1620 Frier Rush 28 His wife..said vnto him: what a vengance needest thou to take a seruant? 1663 Butler Hud. I. iii. 213 But what a-vengeance makes thee fly From me too, as thine Enemy? a 1779 D. Graham Writings (1883) II. 40 What the vengeance uncle, sudna fouks die when they're auld? 1828 Scott F. M. Perth vi, Art thou beside thyself, boy? or what a vengeance takes thee from the city, like the wing of the whirlwind?

4. With a vengeance: †**a.** With a curse or malediction. Obs.

1525 W. Smith Merry Iests Widow Edyth (1573) D j b, In she goth,..And came out agayne, saying wt a vengeaunce: They must go by water. 1581 Hanmer Jesuites Banner E 2 b, Let such then goe with a vengeaunce, and leaue those toyes for Poets to prate of and let them preach better stuffe vnto the people. 1598 R. Bernard tr. Terence, Andria II. i, Abi hinc in malam crucem. Away with a vengeance: get thee hence with a mischiefe: goe hence with sorrow enough. 1635 R. N. tr. Camden's Hist. Eliz. IV. 493 The Queene..waxing impatient gave him [Essex] a cuffe on the eare and bade him be gone with a vengeance.

1673 Vinegar & Mustard (Hindley) III. 8 You are land-sick now, and not sea-sick, with a vengeance to you for me. 1836 Carlyle in Froude Life in London I. 70 Why not quit literature—with a vengeance to it—and turn, were it even to sheep herding?

b. As an intensive: With great force or violence; in an extreme degree; to an unusual extent.

1568 V. Skinner tr. Montanus' Inquisition 24 b, He shall come downe with a vengeaunce. 1594 Greene & Lodge Looking Gl. I. ii. 236 A plaister..that mends him with a verie vengeance. 1611 Middleton & Dekker Roaring Girle M j, Are you too well, too happy? Alex. With a vengeance. 1654 H. L'Estrange Chas. I (1655) 88 The furious multitude..struck him down, and malled him with a vengeance. 1673 [R. Leigh] Transp. Reh. 63 Accordingly he lays it on with a vengeance. 1711 'J. Distaff' Char. Don Sacheverellio 6 This..is proving the..Existence of Gyants ..with a Vengeance. 1761 Foote Liar II. Wks. 1799 I. 293 His friends..gloss over his foible, by calling him an agreeable novelist: and so he is, with a vengeance. 1834 L. Ritchie Wand. by Seine 94 Some readers will think that we are drawing our traveller's bow with a vengeance. 1867 M. Arnold Celtic Lit. 29 Here, at any rate, are materials enough with a vengeance.

†c. So With the vengeance. Obs.$^{-1}$

1693 Humours Town 29 This is following the Dictates of Reason with the vengeance.

†5. As adv. **a.** Extremely, intensely. Obs.

1548 [L. Shepherd] John Bon & Mast person (1808) 5 Is not here a mischeuous thynge? The Messe is vengaunce holye for all ther sayeinge. 1566 Pasquine in Traunce 41, I remember that disputation. It is vengeaunce subtile. Ibid. 44 They were also vengeance angry against the Pope. 1607 Shaks. Cor. II. ii. 6 That's a braue fellow: but hee's vengeance prowd. a 1616 Beaum. & Fl. Little Fr. Lawyer II. i, How it grumbles! This Sword is vengeance angry. 1710–11 Swift Jrnl. to Stella 21 Jan., It has snowed terribly all night, and is vengeance cold.

†b. Not at all, never. Obs.

1556 J. Heywood Spider & Fly xxxix. 7 Vengeance the whit I am for their woordes the nere.

†6. As adj. Very great or large. Obs.$^{-1}$

1602 Fulbecke 2nd Pt. Parall. Introd. 4, I bought the booke..because it was in English: yet there is a vengeance deale of Latin in it.

7. attrib. and Comb., as vengeance-cryer, -crying, -oath, -scathed, -sword, -taking.

c 1386 Chaucer Melib. ¶ 65 For al-be-it so that alle tarying be anoyful, algates it is nat to repreve in yevinge of Iugement, ne in vengeance-taking, whan it is suffisant and resonable. c 1515 Cocke Lorell's B. 11 Cursers, chyders, and grete vengeaunce cryers. 1608 Sylvester Du Bartas II. iv. Schisme 1061 Lord, sheath again thy vengeance-sword a space. 1617 A. Newman Pleas. Vis. 15 Haples wretches, with the memory Tortur'd of woe, and vengeance-crying Sins. 1838 S. Bellamy Betrayal 43 When o'erthrown In first rebellion, vengeance-scathed he fled. 1844 Mrs. Browning Duchess May xxviii, Thou and I have parted troth,—yet I keep my vengeance-oath.

Hence **†Vengeancely** adv.; **†Vengeancer.**

c 1440 Promp. Parv. 508/2 Veniawncere,..vendicator, ultor, vindex. 1622 Fletcher Prophetess I. iii, Yet I could poyson him in a Pot of Perry, He loves that veng'ancely.

†Vengeant, a. Obs.$^{-1}$ In 4 **vengaunt.** [a. AF. vengant (F. vengeant), pres. pple. of venger Venge v.] Avenging; executing vengeance.

a 1340 Hampole Psalter xcviii. 9 Lord oure god þou herd þaim: god þou was til þaim merciabil, and vengaunt in all þaire fyndyngis.

Vengear, obs. form of Venger.

Vengeful (ve·ndʒfŭl), a. [f. Venge v., after revengeful. Cf. Avengeful a.]

1. Harbouring revenge; seeking vengeance; prone or inclined to avenge oneself; vindictive.

a 1599 Spenser F. Q. VII. vi. 48 [She] thinkes what punishment were best assign'd And thousand deathes deuiseth in her vengefull mind. 1701 F. Manning Poems 77 A worse Event..The vengeful Cupid sent. 1713 Swift On Himself Wks. 1755 IV. I. 12 The queen incens'd, his services forgot, Leaves him a victim to the vengeful Scot. a 1763 Shenstone Inscription vi. 24 Fair and flow'ry is the brake, Yet it hides the vengeful snake. 1812 Combe Syntax, Picturesque xxv. 452 Again the vengeful foes appear'd, Again their angry standards rear'd. 1856 Kane Arct. Expl. I. xxx. 414 One of them, the male, is excited—the other, the female, collected and vengeful. 1873 Symonds Grk. Poets i. 9 Ulysses is..pitiless in his hostility; subtle, vengeful, cunning.

transf. c 1600 Shaks. Sonn. xcix, But for his theft..A vengfull canker eate him vp to death. 1848 Faber Spir. Confer. (1870) 124 Wasted time is a vengeful thing. 1879 Geo. Eliot Theo. Such iv. 159 An abandoned belief may be more effectively vengeful than Dido.

b. Inflicting vengeance; serving as an instrument of vengeance. Said of a weapon, the hand or arm, etc.

(a) a 1586 Sidney Ps. xxi. xii, Thou shalt..ready make thy vengefull bow Against their guilty faces. 1593 Shaks. 2 Hen. VI, III. ii. 198 Here's a vengefull Sword, rusted with ease. a 1623 Fletcher Love's Cure v. iii, I pray His vengeful sword may fall upon thy head Successfully. 1725 Pope Odyss. I. 154 The proud oppressors fly the vengeful sword. 1807 G. Chalmers Caledonia I. II. iii. 253 The victorious career of Ida was stopt..by the vengeful sword of the valorous Owen. 1869 Goulbourn Purs. Holiness i. 1 So could he bid the vengeful fire fall from heaven.

(b) 1696 Tate & Brady Ps. cvi. 17 Her vengeful Jaws extending wide. 1729 T. Cooke Tales, etc. 140 Of all who fought beneath this Chief's Command Not one escap'd the Critic's vengeful Hand. 1748 Johnson Van. Hum. Wishes 168 Rebellion's vengeful talons. a 1800 Cowper Iliad (ed. 2) XXI. 343 Allow no respite to thy vengeful arm Till ev'ry Trojan..within Ilium's lofty walls Be fast enclosed.

2. Of actions or feelings: Characterized or prompted by revengeful motives; arising from a desire for vengeance.

1635–56 Cowley Davideis III. Poems (1905) 328 Full thrice six years they felt fierce Eglons yoke, Till Ehuds sword Gods vengeful Message spoke. 1649 Milton Eikon. viii. Wks. 1851 III. 392 That cholerie, and vengefull act of proclaiming him Traitor. 1709 Prior Carm. Sec. xvii. With wise Silence pond'ring vengeful Wars. 1774 Goldsm. Nat. Hist. VII. 193 To us who seldom feel the vengeful wound, it is merely a subject of curiosity. 1818 Scott Hrt. Midl. xxix, The fury darted her knife at him with the vengeful dexterity of a wild Indian. 1845 Ld. Campbell Chancellors liv. (1857) III. 77 In no composition that I have met with is there a greater display of vengeful malignity. 1874 Green Short Hist. viii. § 7. 534 The Massacre had left them the objects of a vengeful hate.

Hence **Vengefully** adv., **Vengefulness.**

1830–1 Ruskin Iteriad II. 300 His dark lightning-eye made him seem..like his own Thalaba, *vengefully fired. 1844 Kinglake Eothen iv, On he goes vengefully thirsting for the best blood of Troy. 1897 Advance (Chicago) 31 July 143/1 He looked at his mother vengefully. 1727 Bailey (vol. II), *Vengefulness, vindictive or revengeful Temper or Nature. 1862 Meredith Poet. Wks. (1912) 134 He fainted on his vengefulness, and strove To ape the magnanimity of love.

†Vengement. Obs. [a. OF. vengement, f. venger Venge v. Cf. Avengement.] Vengeance.

1338 R. Brunne Chron. (1810) 197, I wille of þat feloun tak vengement, þat so fordos my coroun. 1390 Gower Conf. III. 282 His oghne brother therupon..Tok of that Senne vengement. 1484 Caxton Curiall 2, I telle to the that thy vengement shal engendre to the more greuous aduersytes. 1555 Watreman Fardle Facions App. 351 That thei should take vengemente vpon them, bothe by officer, and without. 1596 Spenser F. Q. VI. iii. 18 Witnesse thereof he shew'd his head there left, And wretched life forlorne for vengement of his theft.

Vengence, -ency, varr. Vengeance, -ancy.

†Vengeously, adv. Obs. rare. [Irreg. f. Venge v. Cf. Vengeancely adv.] Violently, viciously.

1599 Breton Miseries Mavillia Wks. (Grosart) II. 43/1 If I did but even touch her, the monkie would set out the throate, and crie so vengeouslie, that to it must the mother come. 1824 in Spirit Pub. Jrnls. (1825) 312 He came up to me so vengeously in the street, and I said to him, 'Can't it be done without fighting?'

Venger (ve·ndʒəɹ). Forms: 4–5 **veniour, -iere, vengere**, 5– **venger** (5 **wen-**), 6 **vengear** (**van-**). [a. AF. or OF. *vengeour (vangeor, vencheur, F. vengeur) and vengiere, agent-n. f. venger Venge v.] An avenger. Now poet. or rhet.

a 1340 Hampole Psalter viii. 3 Þat þou distroy the enmy & þe vengere. c 1380 Wyclif Sel. Wks. III. 297 He is Goddis mynystre, vengere into wraþþe to hym þat doþ evyl. 1382 — Hosea v. 13 And Effraym wente to Assur, and sente to the kyng veniour. 1447 Bokenham Seyntys (Roxb.) 54 And this I wyl thou know for sekyrnesse That god is wenger of wyckydnesse. 1483 Cath. Angl. 400/1 A venger, vindex, vindicator. 1526 Tindale Prol. Ep. Romans A iij, Thou woldest thatt their were no..God, the auctor and vangear of the lawe. 1590 Spenser F. Q. I. iii. 20 His bleeding hart is in the vengers hand. 1601 Yarington Two Lament. Trag. IV. viii. in Bullen O. Pl. IV, I, he is well, in such a vengers handes, As will not winck at your iniquitie. 1865 Reader 16 Sept. 309/2 Other champion of our cause shall come,..venger of his sire. 1881 H. Phillips tr. Chamisso's Faust 10 The Venger's Vengeance smites the guilty head.

†Vengeress. Obs. rare. [a. OF. vengeresse: cf. prec. and -ess.] A female avenger.

In quot. c 1450 as the name of a spear.

c 1374 Chaucer Boeth. III. met. xii. (1868) 107 Þe þre goddesses, furijs, and vengerisse of felonies. c 1450 Merlin xiv. 229 This kynge alain was seke of the woundes of the spere vengeresse [F. la lance vengeresse]. 1490 Caxton Eneydos xxvii. 99 O cruelle vitryces, wycked vengeresses, Furyes infernalle & Iusticers of helle. 1647 Hexham I, A vengeresse, een wreeckster.

†Vengesour. Obs. rare. [f. OF. vengeis-on vengeance.] An avenger.

1382 Wyclif Lev. xxvi. 25 And I shal brynge vpon ȝow a swerd, vengesoure [1388 vengere] of my boond of pees. — Numb. xxxv. 25 The hoond of the vengesour.

†Vengible, a. and adv. Obs. [var. of Vengeable a.]

1. Vengeful, vindictive.

1548 Cooper Elyot's Dict., Dirus,..vengible, cruell, terrible. 1595 Locrine I. ii. 16 The desperate god Cuprit, with one of his vengible birdbolts, hath shot me vnto the heele. 1607 Topsell Four-f. Beasts 461 These also are the Epethites of the Lionesse:..bold, stony-harted, vengible. 1609 Holland Amm. Marcell. 321 A vengible wayt-layer,..by bloudie grudges and displeasures doing much mischief.

b. Grievous, severe.

1601 Holland Pliny I. 4 Impose they doe upon them hard and vengible charges to execute.

2. Remarkable, extraordinary. Also as adv.

1594 Lyly Mother Bombie III. ii, He spake nothing but sentences, but they were vengible long ones. 1602 Contention betw. Liberality & Prodigality IV. ii, Thornes, thistles, and nettles most horrible stingers, Rauens, grypes, and gryphons, oh vengible wringers. 1610 Holland Camden's Brit. I. 78 Hee was a vengible fellow in linking matters together, whereupon he came to be surnamed Catena, that is, a chain.

Hence **†Vengibly** adv. Obs.

1580 G. Harvey Three Lett. Wks. (Grosart) I. 40 Some as vengibly and frowardly bent, as for Example, Woormes, and Moules, and Cunnyes.

Venging, vbl. sb.: see Venge v. 4 (quot. 1382).

Venging, ppl. a. [f. Venge v.] Avenging; executing vengeance.

c 1470 Gol. & Gaw. 759 Thay fechtin sa fast, With vengeand wapuis of were throu wedis thai wet. 1598 Sylvester Du Bartas II. i. Imposture 495 So that th' old yeers' renewed generations Cannot asswage his venging indignations. 1605 Ibid., Sonn. Late Peace xxvi, The furie of Heav'ns venging Sword.

Vengit, obs. Sc. form of Winged a.

‖Vengolina. Obs. [mod.L., = F. vengoline (Buffon), from the native name in Angola, given as benguelinba by Edwards.] The Angola finch (Serinus angolensis).

1773 Phil. Trans. LXIII. 254, I therefore educated a young linnet under a vengolina, which imitated its African master so exactly,..that it was impossible to distinguish the one from the other.

Veniable, obs. form of Vengeable a.

†Veniable, a. Obs. rare. [ad. late L. veniābilis, f. venia: see Venial a.^{1}] Venial, excusable, pardonable.

1646 Sir T. Browne Pseud. Ep. III. xxiii. 168 It is an insufferable delusion, and with more veniable deceit it might have beene practised in Harts horne. Ibid. VII. xix. 385 In things of this nature silence condemneth history, 'tis the veniable part of things lost.

So **†Veniably** adv. Obs.$^{-1}$

1646 Sir T. Browne Pseud. Ep. V. xxi. 268 The Pictures of the Ægyptians were more tolerable, and in their sacred letters more veniably expressed the apprehension of Divinity.

Venial (vī·niăl), a.^{1} and sb. Forms: α. 4 **uenial, veniale**, 4–7 **veniall**, 4– **venial**; 4–5 **venyal** (5 **-ale**), 4–6 **venyall.** β. 4 **veniele**, 4–5 **veniel.** [a. OF. venial, veniel (mod.F. véniel, = Sp. and Pg. venial, It. veniale), or ad. L. veniālis (rare), f. venia forgiveness, indulgence, pardon.]

A. adj. **1.** Worthy or admitting of pardon, forgiveness, or remission; not grave or heinous; pardonable, light: **a.** Of sin; spec. in Theol. as opposed to deadly or mortal.

a 1300 Cursor M. 27541 Bot þar-of es oþer sines smale, Þat clerkes clepes veniale. Ibid. 27545 Man cals þam venial and light. c 1340 Hampole Pr. Consc. 2638 Þe saul þat es clensed wele Of al dedely syn and of veniele. c 1386 Chaucer Pars. T. 287 In þis wise skippith venial in to dedly synne. c 1400 26 Pol. Poems ix. 85 In venyale synne longe to byde, Makeþ dedly synnes to growe grete. 1483 Caxton Gold. Leg. 60/2 To swere lyghtly without hurte or blame is venyal synne. 1526 Pilgr. Perf. (W. de W. 1531) 180 Whome no synne sholde defoule, neyther originall nor actuall, mortall ne venyall. 1558 Bp. Watson Sev. Sacram. i. 5 If he hath lightly offended in any venyall synne, he pardoneth him. 1615 Brathwait Strappado (1878) 83 If I but tutch, to tutch 's a veniall sin, The pretty circle of thy dimpled chin. 1682 Burnet Rights Princes Pref. 33 That it is only a Venial Sin in any, to lessen the great authority of another. a 1700 in Cath. Rec. Soc. Publ. IX. 360 She had rather have suffered a thousand deaths, then wittingly commite ye least veniall sinne. 1737 Challoner Cath. Chr. Instr. (1753) 116 By what Rule shall a Person be able to make a Judgment whether his Sins be mortal or venial? 1830 Scott Demonol. ii. 56 The crime of the person who..consulted the oracle of Apollo;—a capital offence in a Jew, but surely a venial sin in an ignorant and deluded pagan. 1875 Jowett Plato (ed. 2) I. 408 Those who have only committed venial sins are first purified of them.

b. Of crimes, offences, etc.

1604 Shaks. Oth. IV. i. 9 If they do nothing, 'tis a Veniall slip. 1622 J. Taylor (Water P.) Sir Gregory Nonsence Wks. (1630) 4/1 The man that seeketh straying minds to weane all, From veniall vices, or offences penall. 1665 Boyle Occas. Refl. Pref. p. x, I hope it will be thought a venial Crime, if in some of these Meditations I have not aim'd to express Eloquence, but only to cherish Piety. 1746 Francis tr. Hor., Sat. I. iv. 174 Thus, pure from more pernicious crimes I live: Some venial frailties you may well forgive. 1796 W. H. Marshall Rur. Econ. II. 115 The practice of pruning off the side boughs of Hedgerow Elms is a venial crime. 1872 Yeats Growth Comm. 56 Our own laws not long ago punished forgery and even more venial crimes with death. 1876 Farrar Marlb. Serm. xiv. 134 Laughter may be the right cure for venial follies.

†c. Of an offender: Committing a venial sin or offence. Obs.$^{-1}$

1796 Mme. D'Arblay Camilla I. 225 The venial offender had been released with a gentle reprimand.

2. Of an error or fault: That may be excused or overlooked; of a light, unimportant, or trivial nature; excusable.

1581 Pettie Guazzo's Civ. Conv. II. (1586) 66 b, Whereby we may gather, that if the fault in wordes be veniall, the fault in sentence and matter be mortall. 1639 Fuller Holy War v. ix. 243 In the prosecuting and managing thereof, many not only veniall errours but unexcusable faults were committed. 1699 Bentley Phal. 326 He thinks it a more venial fault to make a mistake at Second hand after others. 1735 Bolingbroke On Parties xix. 235 He, who would have been ashamed to participate in Fraud, or to yield to Corruption, may begin to think the Faults venial, when he sees Men, who were far below Him, rise above Him by Fraud and by Corruption. 1784 Cowper Task VI. 418 Witness at his foot, The spaniel dying, for some venial fault. 1825 Scott Betrothed Concl., This is a venial error compared to that of our ancestors. 1876 Farrar Marlb. Serm. xxxvi. 362 If a boy has committed some..quite venial fault.

b. In general use.

1806 in Mrs. Hutchinson's Mem. of Col. H. 304 note, The account here given of Col. Hutchinson's motives..lays his conduct fairly open to the discussion..of the reader, who..will determine it for himself to be commendable, censurable, or venial. 1809–10 Coleridge Friend (1865) 138 This was indeed a gross delusion, but, assuredly for young men at least, a very venial one too. 1850 W. Irving Mahomet xvi. (1853) 96 An act of plunder and revenge—a venial act in the eyes of the Arabs. 1880 R. G. White Every-Day Eng. 79 Mere provincialism in pronunciation..is venial in comparison with slovenly speech.

†3. Allowable, permissible; blameless. rare.

1597 Hooker Eccl. Pol. v. lxxi. § 8 The Iewes..not doubting that bodily labours are made by necessitie veniall, though otherwise, especially on that day [i.e. the Sabbath], rest be more conuenient. 1667 Milton P. L. IX. 5 Where God..With Man..familiar us'd To sit indulgent,..permitting him the while Venial discourse unblam'd. 1725 Pope Odyss. I. 219 With venial freedom let me now demand Thy name, thy lineage, and paternal land.

†B. sb. A venial sin or offence; a light fault or error. Obs.

c 1380 Wyclif Sel. Wks. III. 452 Þouȝ þis be synne, ȝit it is venyal, and not dedly, and venyals ben waschen awey wiþ preieris of a Pater-noster. a 1395 Hylton Scala Perf. I. xxxiii. (W. de W. 1494), Neuertheles yet shalt thou for this defawte & all other venyals whyche may not be eschewed in this wretchyd lyf lyft up thyn hert to god. c 1425 St. Mary of Oignies I. vi. in Anglia VIII. 138/47 Þof she so eshewed fro smal [sins] and veniels. c 1540 Schole House Women (1572) D iij b, And were not two small venialles, The feminine might be glorifide. 1596 Bell Surv. Popery III. ix. 364 Howsoeuer our late papists flatter themselues in their venials. 1609 Bp. Hall Disswas. Poperie Wks. (1627) 642 It..gently blanches ouer the breaches of Gods law with the name of venialls, and fauourable titles of diminution. 1671 Woodhead St. Teresa I. iv. 15, I was careful not to commit any Mortal sin;..but of Venials I made no great account.

†Venial, a.^{2} Obs. rare. [Irreg. var. of Venal a.^{2}] Venous.

1574 J. Jones Nat. Beginn. Growing & Living Things 8 When the heart is opened, it receueth Aire by the veniall arterie. 1578 Banister Hist. Man v. 70 Galen seemeth rather willyng to call this veyne a certaine veniall passage or way.

‖Venialia, sb. pl. Obs.$^{-1}$ [L. veniālia, neut. pl. of veniālis: see Venial a.^{1}] Venial sins or offences.

1654 Gayton Pleas. Notes IV. ii. 183 The peccadillo's and venialia, which never come into the black book.

Veniality. ? Obs. [f. Venial a.^{1} + -ity; cf. Sp. venialidad, Pg. venialidade.] **a.** The property or quality of being venial. **b.** A matter of favour or grace.

1628 Bp. Hall Serm. Westm. 54 They palliate wickednesse with the faire pretence of Venialitie. 1654 H. L'Estrange Chas. I (1655) 138 The Flemish Busses..were soon reduced..to intreat the favour of fishing by his Majesties commission: a veniality the king was most ready to indulge them.

Venially (vī·niăli), adv. [f. Venial a.^{1} + -ly^{2}.] In a venial manner, esp. in the way of venial sin; pardonably, excusably.

a 1340 Hampole Psalter xvii. 26 Na man is in erthe þat synnes noght venyally. c 1386 Chaucer Pars. T. ¶ 288 Þylk worldly thynges þat he loueth, þurgh which he synneth venially. c 1440 Jacob's Well 80 Þerfore, takyth heed be my woordys, whanne ȝe synnen in pride venyally, & whanne dedly. 1534 More Comf. agst. Trib. II. Wks. 1183/1 Wher as els in dede he had offended but venyally. 1588 A. King tr. Canisius' Catech. 227 Thay ar aduersaries to the doctrine of trew religion quha sayis that ane iust man sinnes at leist veniallie in euery guid wark. 1608 Willet Hexapla Exod. 659 A iust man in his good workes doth not sinne so much as venially. 1658 Sir T. Browne Hydriot. Ded., The Antients venially delighted in flourishing Gardens. 1740 Cibber Apol. (1756) I. 128 All the faults, follies, and affectation of that agreeable tyrant were venially melted down into so many charms and attractions. 1847 Fraser's Mag. XXXVI. 53 So it fares with genius which, when only venially erroneous, is not to be forgiven. 1878 tr. Villari's Machiavelli II. I. viii. 249 If he sinned again however venially, he would certainly be hung.

Venialness. rare^{-0}. [f. as prec. + -ness.] = Veniality.

1727 Bailey (vol. II), Venialness, Pardonableness. 1755 Johnson, Pardonableness, venialness; susceptibility of pardon.

Veniance, etc., obs. ff. Vengeance.

Venice (ve·nis). Also 6 **Venysse, Venise, Ven(i)ys, Vennys, Venes**, 7 **Vennis, Venis.** Also Venus^{2}. [a. F. Venise:—L. Venetia (It. Venezia, Sp. Venecia, Pg. Veneza): see def.]

1. The name of the city (the capital of the province of the same name) in the north-east of Italy, used attrib. to designate various articles made there or having some connexion with the locality, as Venice looking-glass, paper, point (lace), tinsel, vial, work, etc. (Cf. Venetian a. 2.)

†Venice beam: see Roman a.^{1} 15. Venice blue (see quot.). Venice crown, Her. (see quot.). Venice gold, silver (cf. Gold sb. 4, Silver sb. 4). Venice lac (see Lac^{1} 2, quot. 1763). Venice soap (see quots.). †Venice sumach, Venetian sumach. Venice talc, white (see quots.).

1611 Cotgr., Traineau à plommée,..a Roman, or *Venice beame, for the weighing of things. 1598 Florio, Veneto, a light or *Venice blew, a Turkie colour. c 1828 Berry Encycl. Her. I. Gloss., *Venice Crown, the crown, or cap of state, worn by the Doge, is made of cloth of gold,..covered with precious stones, and having two long ears, or lappets, pointed at the ends, hanging down at the sides. 1506 Paston Lett. III. 404 The [horse-] harnes of *Venys gold. 1520–1 Rec. St. Mary at Hill (1905) 310 Item, paid for a vnce of venes golde iijs viijd. 1535 Wardr. Kath. Arragon 26 in Camden Misc. III, Fringid withe grene silke and Venysse golde. 1558 in Feuillerat Revels Q. Eliz. (1908) 40, viii Aperns of white gowlde sarsnet edged with veniys gowlde frenge. 1821 Scott Kenilw. ii, Her hat..being of tawny taffeta, embroidered with scorpions of Venice gold. c 1645 Howell Lett. (1655) IV. 43 A new *Venice Looking-Glasse, wherin you may behold that admired Maiden-Citty in her true complexion. 1848 Thackeray Van. Fair lxiv, The great Venice looking-glasses, framed in silver. a 1661 Fuller Worthies, Cambridge I. (1662) 149 To such who object that we can never equall the perfection of *Venice-paper. 1882 Caulfeild & Saward Dict. Needlew. 513/1 The fine Needlepoints made at Brussels..were worn..in preference to the heavier *Venice Points. 1883 Mag. of Art Dec. 66/2 Louis XIV. had a passion for Venice point. 1574 in Feuillerat Revels Q. Eliz. (1908) 234 Ritchly wroughte with *venys sylver. 1842 Penny Cycl. XXII. 171/1 White soda soap..in a less pure state..is called Alicant, *Venice, or Spanish soap. 1858 Simmonds Dict. Trade, Venice-soap, a mottled soap made with olive-oil and soda, with a little sulphate of iron in solution, or sulphate of zinc. 1597 Gerarde Herbal 1293 The first is called Coggygria and Coccygria: in English *Venice Sumach, or Silken Sumach. 1728 Bradley Dict. Bot. s.v. Rhus, The Venice Sumach, or Coggygria, sive Colinus Coriaria. 1867 Chambers's Encycl. IX. 109/1 Steatite, or Soap-stone,..is sold..under the names of Briançon Chalk, French Chalk, and *Venice Talc. 1547 in Feuillerat Revels Edw. VI (1914) 23 Tilsent [= tinsel] whyte and *venice. 1697 T. Brown Dispensary II. Wks. 1709 III. III. 77 My cordials are all put into *Venice Vials. 1839 Ure Dict. Arts & Manuf. 1298 When white lead is mixed in equal quantities with ground sulphate of barytes, it is known in France and Germany by the name of *Venice white. 1860 Chambers's Encycl. VI. 722/1 Venice White contains 1 part of Baryta, and 1 part of White Lead. 1555 Eden Decades (Arb.) 257 They esteeme nothyng more precious then drynkyng glasses of *Venice woorke.

2. a. Venice glass, (a) a very fine and delicate kind of glass, originally manufactured at Murano, near Venice; (b) an article made of this, esp. a drinking vessel or vial; (c) a Venetian mirror.

The extreme brittleness of vessels made of this glass is freq. alluded to in the 17th century.

(a) 1527 Andrew Brunswyke's Distyll. Waters A ij b, They must be made of venys glasse bycause they sholde the better withstande the hete of the fyre. a 1583 in Halliwell Rara Mathem. (1841) 41 Then they must prepare very cleare and white Glasse..as fyne and white Vennys Glasse. 1626 Bacon Sylva § 770 The Crystalline Venice Glass is reported to be a mixture, in equal portions, of Stones brought from Pavia, by the River Ticinum, and the Ashes of a Weed called by the Arabs, Kall. 1673 A. Walker Lees Lachrymans 13 Their Venice-glass..cracks with as slight a blow as pots of courser clay.

(b) 1587 Harrison England II. vi. in Holinshed I. 166/2 As for drinke it is vsuallie filled in..bols of siluer in noble mens houses, also in fine Venice glasses of all formes. 1591 Sylvester Du Bartas I. ii. 72 In a Venice Glass before our eyne, We see the Water intermix with Wine. 1620 Gataker Marriage Duties 41 The more brittle a Venice glasse is, the more gingerly we handle it. 1669 Boyle Certain Physiol. Ess. (ed. 2) Absol. Rest Bodies 22 Having enquired of a famous..Maker of Telescopes..whether he did not observe that the Venice-Glasses he employed would sometimes crack of themselves whilst they were yet in Plates. 1688 On Death in Jane Barker Poet. Recreations II. 44 Life is a Bubble;..Tis far more brittle than a Venice-Glass.

(c) 1850 Mrs. Browning Sonn. fr. Portug. ix, I will not ..breathe my poison on thy Venice-glass. 1852 Thackeray Esmond I. ix, On which poor Lady Castlewood gave a rueful smile, and a look into a little Venice glass she had.

b. Venice treacle, in old pharmacy, an electuary composed of many ingredients and supposed to possess universal alexipharmic and preservative properties. Cf. Treacle sb. 1 c. Now arch.

Also occas. called treacle of Venice.

1612 Woodall Surg. Mate Wks. (1653) 95 A little Venice Triacle or other Triacle. 1635 J. Taylor (Water P.) Life Thomas Parr C 3, And Garlick hee esteem'd above the rate Of Venice-Triacle, or best Mithridate. 1691 T. H[ale] Acc. New Invent. p. xxv, And as well may we be afraid to take the Venice Treacle, because of its being long kept in boxes of Lead. c 1720 W. Gibson Farrier's Dispens. III. (1721) 146 Venice Treacle. This is also called the Theriaca, or Treacle of Andromachus. 1753 J. Bartlet Gentl. Farriery xliii. (1754) 323 Internally, for bites from vipers, may be given cordial medicines, such as Venice treacle and salt of hartshorn. 1797 Encycl. Brit. (ed. 3) XVI. 573/2 The Muscovites at all times reject as impure..rabbit, ass's milk, mare's milk, and Venice-treacle. 1821 Scott Kenilw. xiii. footnote, Orvietan, or Venice treacle, as it was sometimes called, was understood to be a sovereign remedy against poison.

c. Venice turpentine (see quots. c 1789, 1800, and Turpentine sb. 1 b).

1577 Frampton Joyful News 45 Adde therto three ounces of Venise Turpentine. 1736 Bailey Househ. Dict. s.v. Ague, Mix the powder of white Hellebore roots with right Venice Turpentine. c 1789 Encycl. Brit. (ed. 3) IV. 567/1 The kind now called Venice turpentine, is no other than a mixture of eight parts of common yellow or black rosin with five parts of oil of turpentine. What was originally Venice turpentine is now unknown. 1800 E. Darwin Phytol. vi. 84 Thus what is called Venice turpentine is obtained from the larch by wounding the bark about two feet from the ground, and catching it as it exsudes. 1846 J. Baxter Libr. Pract. Agric. (ed. 4) II. 278 The ointment is made as follows:—Quicksilver, 1 lb.; Venice Turpentine, ½ lb. 1857 Miller Elem. Chem., Org. 503 The common varnish used for oil paintings and maps consists of 24 parts of mastic, 3 of Venice turpentine, and 1 of camphor.

Venie, var. Veny Obs. **Venieaunce**, obs. f. Vengeance. **Venifice**, var. Venefice Obs.

Venigenous, a. Geol. [f. L. type *vēnigena] Of rock-masses: Bearing or containing veins of metal or quartz.

1817 Blackw. Mag. I. 421 A series of specimens of the diamond imbedded in a venigenous mass. 1833–4 J. Phillips Geol. in Encycl. Metrop. (1845) VI. 762/2 The intricate character of the venigenous masses of Mousehole.

Venim(ous, obs. ff. Venom(ous.

†Venin, sb.^{1} Obs. In 4–5 **venyn.** [a. OF. venin:—L. venēn-um.] Venom, poison.

c 1330 R. Brunne Chron. Wace (Rolls) 9005 Venyn for salue wyþ hym he nam, Als a monk to court be cam. c 1380 Wyclif Three Treat. (1851) p. xxxvi, As Crist techiþ in his gospel, hou þat men shulden..forsake her cumpenye as venyn [v.r. venym]. c 1400 Apol. Loll. 57 Triacle is turnid in to venyn, and þis þat was foundun to remedie, is foundun to deþ.

Hence **†Venin** v. trans., to poison. Obs.$^{-0}$

a 1500 Prompt. Parv. 508/2 (MS. H.), Venynyn or venymyn, veneno.

Venin, sb.^{2} Chem. Also -ine, -ene. [f. Venom + -in^{1}.] A toxic substance forming the distinctive element in snake-venom. (In recent Dicts.)

Veniour, obs. var. Venger.

‖Venire (vĭnəi·ri). Law. [Ellipt. for next]

1. = next 1.

1665 Ever Tryals per Pais iii. 31 Therefore where the Sheriff ought not to retorn the Venire, he cannot retorn the Tales. 1676 Office Clerk Assise 82 In the mean time doth the Clerk of the Peace file the Venire, and the pannel with the Indictment. 1722 Beverley Hist. Virginia IV. vi. 223 A Writ of Venire issues in such Cases, to summon six of the nearest Neighbours to the Criminal. 1771 E. Long in Hone Every-day Bk. (1826) II. 200 You must have a venire for a jury. 1821 Archbold Digest Law Pleading & Evidence 415 Stating the names, &c. of the knights and recognitors, as in the venire. 1825 Act 6 Geo. IV, c. 50 § 16 marg., If Plaintiff sue forth a Venire, etc. in order to Trial, and proceed not, he may afterwards sue forth another Venire, etc. and try at any subsequent Assizes.

b. Venire de novo, = next 1 b.

1797 Tomlins Jacob's Law Dict. s.v. Venire Facias de novo, The following seem to be the cases in which a Venire de Novo is grantable. 1885 Law Rep. 10 App. Cas. 414 Without some such power [of ascertaining what the circumstances were] no judgment, except a venire de novo, could be given.

c. Venire man, one summoned to serve on a jury under a writ of Venire facias, a juryman. U.S.

1780 Virginia Statutes at Large X. 489 An act for regulating tobacco fees, and fixing the allowance to sheriffs, witnesses, and venire-men. 1895 Weekly Examiner (San Francisco) 5 Sept. 2/1 Sheriff Whelan's deputies had apparently summoned most all of the veniremen from the foreign sections of the city.

†2. = next 2. Obs.

1763 Ld. Hardwicke in Harris Life (1847) III. 344, I believe he came in upon the venire or capias, & put in bail. 1769 [see Venire facias 2].

†3. The place from which the jurors were to be summoned or in which the cause was to be tried; = Venue 5. Obs.

1682 Luttrell Brief Rel. (1857) I. 185 Mr. Graham haveing moved once or twice the court of kings bench that the venire might be laid in another county. 1682 Lond. Gaz. No. 1720/7 This day the great Case between the Earl of Shaftsbury and Mr. Cradock came on in the Kings-Bench about changing the Venire out of London.

‖Venire facias (vĭnəi·ri fēi·ʃiæs). Law. [L., lit. 'that you cause to come'. Cf. prec.]

1. A former judicial writ directed to a sheriff requiring him to summon a jury to try a cause or causes at issue between parties. Obs. or Hist.

1444 Rolls of Parlt. V. 112/1 Thissue joyned and entred of record, and a venire fac' of ye Jure retorned. 1531 Star Chamber Cases (Selden) II. 189 They have pursued seuerall venire facias retornable the First day of the terme of seynt Hillary next comyng. 1543 Ludlow Churchw. Acc. (Camden) 14 Payde for a venire facias, xvj d. 1607 Middleton Phœnix B 4 b, Youl get a Venire facies to warne your Iurie, a Decem tales to fill vp the number. 1665 Ever Tryals per Pais iii. 24 Of a Venire facias: To whom it shall be directed [etc.]. 1768 Blackstone Comm. III. 352 When therefore an issue is joined,..the court awards a writ of venire facias. 1790 Amer. State Papers Misc. (1834) I. 32 (Stanf.), Juries shall be summoned by writs of venire facias. 1821 Archbold Digest Law 414 The jury process is the same as in ordinary cases, namely, a venire facias and a habeas corpora juratorum. 1825 Act 6 Geo. IV, c. 50 § 16. 125 No former Writ of Venire Facias had been prosecuted in that Cause.

b. Venire facias de novo (lit. 'that you cause to come anew'), an order for a new trial of a cause, upon the same record, owing to some defect or irregularity in the first trial.

1797 Tomlins Jacob's Law Dict. s.v., New Trials are generally granted where a General Verdict is found; a Venire Facias de Novo, upon a Special Verdict.

†2. A writ issued against a person indicted of a misdemeanour, summoning him to appear before the court. Obs.

1463–4 Plumpton Corr. (Camden) 10, I shall send you another [capias] with the Copie of your new suites and a venire facias against the ministre. 1769 Blackstone Comm. IV. 313 The proper process on an indictment for any petty misdemesnor, or on a penal statute, is a writ of venire facias, which is in the nature of a summons to cause the party to appear. And if by the return to such venire [etc.].

Venis(e, obs. forms of Venice.

Venison (ve·nz'n, ve·niz'n). Forms: α. 3–5 **venesun**, 3–6 **veneson**, 4 **veneison, ueneysun**, 4–5 **venesoun**, 5 Sc. **wennesone**, 6 **vennesoun**, 7 **venneson**; 4 **venisun**, 4–5 **venisoun**, 5 **venisyn**, 6 **venicen, vennisone**, 7 **venizon**, 4– **venison**; 4–5 **venysoun**, 4–6 **venyson**, 5 **venysone, -soune, -sowne, vennysoun**, Sc. **wenysoune, -son.** β. 5 **vensoun**, 6–8 **venson**, 7–8 **ven'son**, 7 (9) **venson.** [a. AF. veneso(u)n, veneysun, venysoun, venison, OF. veneson, veneisun, venison, venoison (mod.F. venaison, = Pr. venaiso,

Supplement, p. 3873; Corrigenda, p. 4092; Spurious words, p. 4093; Books quoted, p. 4094

VENISON.

1. The flesh of an animal killed in the chase or by hunting and used as food; formerly applied to the flesh of the deer, boar, hare, rabbit, or other game animal, now almost entirely restricted to the flesh of various species of deer.

2. With *of* (an animal); or defining term.

3. Any beast of chase or other wild animal killed by hunting, esp. one of the deer kind. Now *arch.*

Venison*-sauce***,** *-soup***, etc.**

Venitary, *rare.*

Venite (vĭnaiˈti).

Venitian, obs. f. VENETIAN, VENISON.
Venk, southern ME. f. FANG v.
Venkest, *-is*, obs. var. VANQUISH *v.*
Venlin, obs. f. VENISON.

Venn, southern ME. variant of FEN *sb.*[1]

VENOM.

1. A narrow lane, passage, or thoroughfare in a town or city; an alley or wynd. Chiefly *Sc.*

2. *north.* An open drain or gutter; a sewer.

Venison*-soun, -ōn***.** f. VENISON, Venney, Vennie, *var.* VENNY[1], obs. f. VENISON.
Vennie, Vennisone, *-ȝocun*, obs. ff. VENISON.
Venny, *var.* VENT[2], *Sc.*; dial. f. FENNY *a.*[1]

VENOM (venˈəm), *sb.* [a. OF. *venim*, *venin* ...]

1. The poisonous fluid normally secreted by certain snakes and other animals and used by them in attacking other living creatures.

2. *fig.* Something comparable to or having the effect of poison; any baneful, malign, or noxious influence or quality; bitter or virulent feeling, language, etc.

3. *fig.* Something comparable to venom as a cause of poison.

Venom, v. Now *Obs.* or *arch.* Forms:

1. *trans.* To injure by means of venom; to poison (a person, etc.).

VENOMED

1. Of reptiles, insects, etc.: Endowed with venom.

2. Covered, charged, imbued, impregnated, or smeared with venom; full of venom; poisoned, poisonous.

Venomed, *ppl. a.* [f. VENOM *sb.* & v. Cf.
ENVENOMED *ppl. a.*]

VENOMER.

Venomer, *rare.* [f. VENOM *v.*] One who administers venom; a poisoner.

+Venomful, *a. Obs.* [f. VENOM *sb.* + -FUL.] Venomous, poisonous.

Venoming, *vbl. sb.* [f. VENOM *v.*] The action of the verb; poisoning.

Venomization (venomaizeiˈʃən). [f. VENOM *sb.* + -IZATION.] The action or process of treating with venom.

+Venomly, *adv. Obs. rare.* [f. VENOM + -LY.] Venomously.

Venomous (venˈəməs), *a.* Now *rare.* [f. VENOM + -OUS.]

Venomo-sa livary, *a. Zool.* [Irreg. f. VENOMO- + SALIVARY.] Of or pertaining to, secreting or conveying, venomous saliva.

Venomous (venˈəməs), *a.* — Forms: 4–7 venymus, venum, 4–6 -ous, 5 -ows, venymo(u)s (venymouse) ...

VENOMOUSLY.

6 venumous, venomous. [a. AF. *venimus*, *venimous*, — OF. (also mod.F.) *venimeux*, f. *venim* VENOM *sb.*; later L. *venēnōsus*: see VENENOUS *a.*]

1. *fig.* Morally or spiritually hurtful or injurious; pernicious.

2. Containing, consisting or full of, infected with, venom; possessing poisonous properties or qualities; destructive of, harmful or injurious to, life on this account.

3. *fig.* Having the virulence of venom; rancorous, spiteful, malignant, virulent; embittered, envenomed.

4. Of a wound, etc.: Marked or characterized by the presence of poisonous matter; full of venom; envenomed.

Venomously (venˈəməsli), *adv.* [f. prec. + -LY.]

1. In a venomous manner; [with venom or poison; envenomed, poisoned. *Obs.*

VENOMOUSNESS.

Venomousness. [f. as prec. + -NESS.] The condition or quality of being venomous; venomous matter.

Venomo-reticulated, *a. Nat.* (See quot.)

Venose (viˈnəus), *a.* [ad. L. *vēnōsus*, f. *vēna* VEIN *sb.*] Venous.

1. Filled with, full of, or having veins; veined.

2. *Anat.* and *Phys.* Of or pertaining to, of the nature of, a blood-vein or veins; having the form or function of a vein.

+Venosity, *rare.* Also f. *venosite*, -*y*. [f. VENOSE *a.* + -ITY.]

Venosity (vinoˈsiti), *rare.* Also f. *venosi*-, -*y*. [f. VENOSE *a.* + -ITY.]

Venous (viˈnəs), *a.* [ad. L. *vēnōsus* VENOSE *a.*]

VENT.

Vent (vent), *sb.*[1] [Partly a. F. *vent* (earlier L.), *venter* belly, stomach.]

1. The action of emitting or discharging

2. *Anat.* and *Phys.* Of, or pertaining to, of the nature of, a blood-vein or veins; having the form or function of a vein.

Vent (vent), *sb.*[2] Also 5 vente, 5–6 vente. [Variant of FENT *sb.*]

1. A slit or opening in a garment, a fent[1]; now *spec.* slit at the back of a coat or jacket.

Vent, *sb.*[3] [a. F. *vente*, f. *vendre*.]

Vent (vent), *v.*[1]

Hence Venously *adv.*, **Venousness.**

+Venge, etc. (See VENT *sb.*[1])

Vent, v. [Partly a. F. *venter*, partly aphetic f. *event* v.]

Ventil.

Ventile, *a. U.S.* [f. VENTIL-ATE v. +-ABLE.] Capable of being ventilated.

Ventilating-fan, *rare* −¹. [f. L. *ventilāre*-ans winnowing-fan +-AL.] Concerning or pertaining to fanning.

Ventilary, *a. Obs.* −¹ [f. L. *ventil-āre* VENTILATE v.+-ARY.] Due to or caused by the wind.

Ventilate, *pa. pple.* or *ppl. a. Obs.* [ad. L. *ventilāt-us*, pa. pple. of *ventilāre*: see next.]

Ventilate (ve'ntile̯t), *v.* Also 5 ventilate, 6 -tylate, 7 -tulate, -titate. [f. L. *ventilāt-*, ppl. stem of *ventilāre* to brandish, fan, winnow, agitate (whence It. *ventilare*, Prov., Sp., Pg. *ventilar*, F. *ventiler*); f. root *ventus* wind.]

Ventilated, *ppl. a.* [f. prec.] Purified by or exposure to air; provided with means of ventilation.

Ventilating, *vbl. sb.* [f. as prec.] The action of the verb in various senses; ventilation.

Ventilation (ventile̯'ʃən). Also 5 -cion, -cioun. [ad. L. *ventilātiōn-em*, n. of action from *ventilāre*: see VENTILATE v.]

Ventilative (ve'ntile̯tiv), *a.* [f. VENTILATE v.+-IVE.] Pertaining to, producing or promoting, ventilation.

Ventilator (ve'ntile̯tər). [agent-n. in L. form from *ventilāre*: see VENTILATE v.]

Ventose (ventōus'), *a.* [a. OF. *ventose*, L. *ventōs-us* windy, f. *ventus* wind.]

Ventosity (vento'siti). *Obs.* Forms: 5 ventose-, 5-yte, -ytie; 4-6 -ite, 6 -itee, -itye, 6-7 -tie, 6-9 -ventosity. [a. OF. *ventosité* (1314), or ad. L. *ventōsitātem.*]

Ventose, -ous. *Obs. rare.* [ad. L. *ventosus*: see VENTOSE.]

Vent-peg. [VENT *sb.²*] A small peg for inserting in the vent-hole of a cask; a spile.

Ventralward, *adv.* [f. VENTRAL *a.* +-WARD.] To or towards the belly or ventral surface of the body.

Ventral (ve'ntral), *a.* and *sb.* [ad. L. *ventrāl-is*, f. *venter, ventr-* belly.]

Ventrally (ve'ntrali), *adv.* [f. prec. +-LY².] In a ventral direction; on or toward the venter.

Ventre (ve'ntr). *Obs.* [a. F. *ventre*, L. *ventr-em.*]

Ventricle (ve'ntrik'l). *Anat.* and *Zool.* Also 6 ventricule, ventrycle, 7 ventricle. [ad. L. *ventricul-us*, dim. of *venter*: see VENTER.]

Ventricose (ve'ntrikōus), *a.* [ad. mod.L. *ventricōsus*, f. L. *venter, ventr-*: see +-OSE.]

Ventricous (ve'ntrikǝs), *a. rare.* [See -OUS.] = VENTRICOSE.

Ventricule. *Obs.* [a. F. *ventricule*, L. *ventriculus*: see VENTRICLE.]

Ventricular (ventri'kiūlər), *a.* Chiefly *Anat.* and *Path.* [f. L. *ventricul-us* (see next) +-AR, or ad. mod.L. *ventriculāris.*]

Ventriculite. *Zool.* [f. mod.L. *Ventriculītes*: see below.]

Ventriculus (ventri'kiūlǝs), *pl.* -li. [L.: see VENTRICLE.]

Ventriloqual (ventrilō'kwəl), *a.* = VENTRILOQUIAL.

Ventriloquial (ventrilō'kwiəl), *a.* [f. VENTRILOQU-Y +-IAL.]

Ventriloquism (ventri'lǝkwiz'm). [f. VENTRILOQU-Y +-ISM.]

Ventriloquist (ventri'lǝkwist), *a.* *rare.* [Cf. next and *-AL.*]

Ventriloquial (ventrilō'kwiəl), *a.* [f. VENTRILOQU-Y +-IAL.]

Ventriloquous (ventri'lǝkwǝs), *a.* [f. as prec. +-OUS.]

Ventriloquistic, a. [f. prec. + -IC.]

1. Using or practising ventriloquism.

2. Of or pertaining to ventriloquism; of or pertaining to a ventriloquist; to cast the voice.

Hence **Ventriloquistical**, a. *nonce-word.*

Ventriloquize (ventri'lŏkwəiz), v. [f.]

1. *intr.* To use or practise ventriloquism; to speak or produce sounds in the manner of a ventriloquist; to cast the voice.

2. *trans.* To utter as a ventriloquist.

Hence **Ventriloquizing** vbl. sb. Also attrib.

Ventriloquous (ventri'lŏkwəs), a. [f. L. ventriloqu-us (see prec.) + -OUS.]

1. Of persons: = VENTRILOQUIAL a.

2. Produced by or as by ventriloquism; ventriloquial.

Ventriloquy (ventri'lŏkwi). L., ventri-, venter belly + -loqui to speak, after Gr. ἐγγαστρίμυθος. Cf. VENTRILOQUY.]

1. = VENTRILOQUISM (in quots.)

Ventriloquy (ventri'lŏkwi). [ad. med. or early mod.L. ventriloquium (It. ventriloquio, Sp., Pg. ventriloquia, F. ventriloquie), f. L. ventriloquus : see prec.]

1. = VENTRILOQUISM (in quot.)

Ventrine, a. *rare⁻¹*. [f. L. ventr-, venter belly + -INE¹.] Of or pertaining to the abdomen.

Ventriose, a. *Obs. rare.* [ad. L. ventriōs-us, f. venter, ventri-, belly.] = VENTRICOSE a.

Ventripotent (ventri'pŏtent), a. [ad. L. ventripotent- (Rabelais), f. L. venter, venter belly : potens powerful, etc.]

1. Having a large abdomen; big-bellied.

2. Having great capacity of stomach; gluttonous.

Hence **Ventripoten'tial** a. *nonce-word.*

Ventro- (ventrǫ), comb. form, on Gr. models, of VENTER, occurring in various terms (chiefly *Anat.* and *Surg.*), as ventro-a'xial a., of or pertaining to the ventral and axial portions of the human trunk; ventro-do'rsal a., of sections or lines of direction : extending from venter to back; hence ventro-dorsally adv., ventro-i'nguinal a., of or pertaining to the abdominal cavity and the inguinal canal; ventro-la'teral a., of or belonging to the ventral and lateral sides of the body; hence ventro-laterally adv., ventro-me'sal, -me'sial adj., of or pertaining to, situated at or near the middle of, the venter; ventro-nu'bona'la a. [cf. NUBONAL], ventronudbrea'nchiate a., ventro-os'tal a., ventro'podal a., ventro-po'sterior a., situated on, pertaining to, the outer and hinder part of an organ, etc.; ventro'tomy, the operation of opening the abdomen by incision; abdominal section.

Ventrous, var. VENTUROUS a.

Ventry, obs. form of VENTURY.

Ventous, -ly, adv. Obs. Also ¢ ventous.

Venture (ve'ntiūɹ), sb. Also 5-6 aventure. [Aphetic f. aventure VENTURE.]

Ventured | 114 | **Venturing** | **Venturously** | 115 | **Venus.**

Venturing, ppl. a. Now *rare.* [f. as prec.]

Venturous (ve'ntiūɹəs), a. Also 4-7 ventrous. [Aphetic f. ADVENTUROUS a. after VENTURE sb. and v.]

Venturously, adv. [f. prec. + -LY²]

Venturousness. [f. prec. + -NESS.]

Venue (veniū). Forms: 4 venu, venuw, venwe, 4 venow, 6-7 venewe, 6 venu, venvew, 7 venue, venew, venne, venu. [a. OF. venue coming, in order to strike; an assault or attack, etc.]

Venued, variant of VINEWED ppl. a.

Venuline, var. of VENULE.

Venus (vī'nŭs). Pl. Venuses (7,9 Veneres).

1. The action of coming : arrival. *Obs.⁻¹*

2. *Astr.* The second planet or orb of distance from the sun, revolving in an orbit between that of Mercury and the earth.

Verbalizing.

1. intr. To use many words; to talk diffusely; to be verbose.

2. trans. To make into a verb.

3. To express in words.

Verbally (vɜ̄·băli), adv. **1.** Word for word; in respect of each word.

2. In or with (mere) words, without accompanying action or reality.

3. So far as words (only) are concerned.

4. In natural language; by means of words or speech.

Verba (vɜ̄·bă), sb. pl. Word or words.

Verbate, v. Obs.⁻¹

Verbatical, a. Obs.⁻¹

Verbatim (vɜbē·tim), adv., a., and sb.

Verbena (vɜbī·nă), sb.

Verbenaceous (vɜ̄bĭnē·ʃəs), a. Bot.

Verbene. rare.

Verberate (vɜ̄·bĕrēt), v.

Verberation (vɜ̄bĕrē·ʃən), sb.

Verberate (vɜ̄·bĕrāt), ppl. a.

Verberating, ppl. a.

Verbiage (vɜ̄·biĭdʒ), sb.

Verbicide (vɜ̄·bĭsəid), sb.

Verbid, sb.

Verbigerate (vɜbĭ·dʒĕrēt), v.

Verbile (vɜ̄·bĭl), a. and sb.

Verbless, a.

Verbose (vɜbōu·s), a.

Verbosely, adv.

Verboseness, sb.

Verbosity (vɜbɒ·sĭti), sb.

Verbous, a. Obs. rare.

Verbum sap.

Verd, sb. Obs.

Verdage.

Verdancy (vɜ̄·dănsi), sb.

Verdant (vɜ̄·dănt), a.

Verdantly, adv.

Verdantness, sb.

Verd-antique, verd antique (vɜ̄d ăntī·k).

Verdasure, sb.

Verde, southern ME. var. FEED sb.¹

Verdea (vɛə·dĭă).

Verde antico.

Verderer (vɜ̄·dĕrăr), sb.

Verdetto (vɛədē·tōu), sb.

Verdict (vɜ̄·dĭkt), sb.

Verdite, Chem. Obs.

Verditel ... A salt produced by the action of verdous acid on a base.

† Verditol. Obs. — next 1.

† Verditer (və̆ˈdītə̆r). Forms: 6 -verditter, 5 verditere, 5 verdeter, 6-7 verditor, 7-9 verditure. [...]

Verditure, obs. variant of VERDICT c.

† Verditure. [Sp., f. verde green.] A variety of wine (see quot.).

† Verdour. Obs. Forms: a. 5 verdour, 5-7 verdour (6 Sc. wor-), 6 vardour, Sc. ver-dour; 5 Sc. wardur, Sc. wardour (5-...

† Verdour¹. Obs. variant of VERDURE.

Verdous, a. Chem. [...]

† Verdugo. [Sp. (also Pg.) verdugo ...] A bangman or executioner. Obs.

Verdumal, Verdumate ... variants of next.

Verdunt, -dutt, obs. variants of VERDANT.

Verdure (və̆ˈdi̇ŭr). Also 5 verdure, 6 verdur, 7 verdeur, 8 verdeur. [a. OF. verdure ... f. verd, verde green ... + -URE. Cf. VERDOUR¹.]

† Verdour². Obs. variant. Also 6 verdour, 6-7 verdor. [a. A.F. verdour (1327), var. of verder VERDER²]

† Verdous¹. a. Chem. [...]

Verdurous (və̆ˈdi̇ŭr-rəs). Also 7-9 verd'rous. [f. VERDURE + -OUS.]
1. Of vegetation: Rich or abounding in verdure; flourishing thick and green.
2. Consisting of or composed of verdure.
3. Of or pertaining to, characteristic of, verdure.

Hence Verdurousness.

Verdy, obs. variant of VERDICT.

Verdyngald, variant of VARDINGALE Obs.

† Vere, sb. Obs. Forms: 4-5 veir, 5 verr, 4-6 vere, 5-6 veer, 4 (6 vere sb.). The season of spring; spring-time.

† Vere, sb. Obs. [Of obscure origin.] trans. To raise up; to uplift.

Vere, ME. var. FERE sb., FIRE sb.; obs. f. VEER.

Verecund (veˈrĭkʌnd), a. [ad. L. verēcund-us (whence obs. F. verecond (Cotgr.).) Pg. verecundo.], f. verēri to reverence, fear.] Modest, bashful; shy, coy.

† b. A rod or wand put in a person's hand ...

Watchmaking. The spindle or arbor of the balance in the old vertical escapement.

† Verge-board. Also vulg. varge-. [...]

Verge-line, rare. [f. VERGE sb.]

Vergency (və̆ˈdʒĕnsi). Also rare -ency. [f. next.] The fact of verging or inclining.

† Vergent, a. and sb. Obs. [a. L. vergent-, vergens, pr. pple. of vergěre to VERGE.] Constituting, ...

Verger. belonging to, a series of Appalachian strata corresponding in age to the middle Devonian strata of British geologists.

Vergeous, obs. form of VERJUICE.

† Verger¹. Also § vergere, vergier, Sc. virger. 1. Of. *verger* (11th c.; so in mod.F.), vergier (12th c.) = Pr. *vergier*, Sp. *vergel*, It. *verziere*, med.L. *viridarium*, also *viridiarium*, f. L. *viridis* green.] A garden or orchard ; a pleasure-garden.

Verger² (və̄ɹdʒəɹ). [prob. a. AF. *verger*, f. *verge* VERGE sb.] Of. *vergiere* (vergeur) *gauger, vergier* maker of rings, obs. F. *verger* verger (Cotgr.); also med.L. *virgārius*, and VIRGER.]
1. An official who carries a rod or similar symbol of office before the dignitaries of a cathedral, church, university (or before justices).

† Verger³. Obs. [? a. AF. *vergier* (Gower).] A rod carried as a symbol of office.

† Verger⁴. Obs.⁻¹ Also § vergerar—[. Hence † Vergererhip.** Obs.

Vergeress (və̄ɹdʒərɛs). [-ESS.] A female verger or caretaker of a church.

Vergerism. Action, etc., characteristic of a verger.

Vergery (və̄ɹdʒəɹi). *rare*⁻¹. [f. as prec. + -Y.] A sacristy.

† Verge-salt. Obs.⁻¹ (Meaning obscure.)

† Verge-sauce. Obs. *rare* — VERD-SAUCE.

Vergier, variant of VERGER¹ Obs.

Vergiform (və̄ɹdʒifɔɹm), a. Zool. [f. VERGE + -I- + -(U)FORM.] Of the feet of certain crustacea: Resembling a rod; rod-like.

Vergilian, var. VIRGILIAN, Vergine, obs. f. VIRGIN. **Vergious,** -in, -ius, obs. ff. VERJUICE.

Vergobret² of Gaulish origin. So obs. F. *vergobret*.] The chief magistrate among the ancient Ædui of Gaul.

† Vergoine. Obs. Of. (also mod.F.) *vergogne* = it. *vergogna*, Sp. *vergonha*]—Sc. *vericonelis, verimentus* VEREMOND §] Shame.

Vergoynous, a. Obs. [as prec. + -OUS, f. *vergoine* = It. *vergognoso*, Pg. *vergonhoso*, f. *vergoyne* q.v.] Ashamed.

Vergrese, obs. ff. VERDIGRIS, *Vergus, obs. ff. VIRGIN, Verhede, southern dial. var. forbede FERED Obs. Veri, obs. f. VERY.

Veridical (vĕrĭdĭkăl), a. [f. L. *vēridic-us* (hence F. *véridique*, It., Sp., Pg. *veridico*), f. *vērum* truth, and *dic-* stem of *dicĕre* to speak.]
1. Speaking, telling or representing the truth; truthful, veracious.

Veridicous, a. Obs. [f. L. *vēridic-us* + -OUS.] Veridical, veracious.

Veridity. [f. as prec. + -ITY.] Veracity.

Verie, southern ME. var. FERRY v.
Verier, Veriest, compar. and superl. VERY a.
Verifiable, obs. form of VERILY adv.

Verifiability (vĕrĭfaɪəbɪlɪti). [f. next + -ITY.] The fact of being verifiable.

Verificative (vĕrĭfĭkeɪtɪv), a. [f. L. *vērificāt-*, ppl. stem of *vērificāre* + -IVE. Cf. OF. *vērificatif*, Sp., Pg. f. *verificativo.*] Verificatory.

Verifiable, a. (vĕrĭfaɪəb'l), a. Also § verefiable.

Verification (vĕrĭfĭkeɪʃən). [ad. F. *vérification* (1606), or ad. med.L. *vērificātiōn-em*, n. of action f. *vērificāre*: see VERIFY and -ATION.]
1. The action of demonstrating or proving to be true or legitimate by means of evidence or testimony; formal assertion of truth.

† Verificatory, a. [f. as prec. + -ORY².] That verifies; having the property of verifying; of the nature of, serving as, a verification.

† Verified, *ppl. a.* [f. VERIFY v. + -ED¹.] Proved to be true by verification.

Verifier (vĕrĭfaɪəɹ). [f. VERIFY v. + -ER¹.]
1. One who verifies, bring witnesses.

Verify (vĕrĭfaɪ), v. Forms: 4-6 *verify*, 5 -fye, Sc. *werfy*, 6 *veryfie*; 4-7 *verifie*, 6 *verilye*, 5- *verify* ; 4 *verifie* *verefy* ; *verely* (5 Sc. *werafye*), 5-6 *verefie*. [ad. OF. *verifier* (1348) = mod.F. *vérifier*, Sp., Pg., It. *verificar*, ad. med.L. *vērificāre*, f. L. *vērus* true + *facĕre* to make.]
1. *trans.* Law. To prove by good evidence or valid testimony; to testify or affirm formally or upon oath.

Verily (vĕrĭli), *adv.* (and *a.*). Now *arch.* or *dial.* Forms: 4-5 *verraily, verrayly*, 4-6 *verayly*, 4 *veraily*, 4-5 *verrely*, -li, *verreli*, 4-5 y, 5 *verailly*, *verrelly*; 4 *verrayli*, 5 *veryly*, -ly, *veriely*, 4-7 *verelye*, 5 *verelich*, -liche, -lyche, 4-6 *verely*, 4- *verily*. [f. VERY a. + -LY².]
1. adv. In truth or verity; as a matter of truth of fact ; indeed, in fact, or reality; really, truly.

Verjuice ...

Verk, obs. Sc. forms of WORK *sb.*

Verken, obs. form of FIRKIN.

Verlay, Verlet(te, obs. ff. VIRELAY, VARLET.

Verloth(e, ME. vart. FERLY *a.* and *adv. Obs.*

Verlore, var. f. pa. t. and pa. pple. FORLESE *v. Obs.*

Verma, southern dial. var. FARM *sb.*; So. var. WORM *sb.* Vermayn(e, obs. ff. VERMIN *sb.*

Verme. *Her. Obs.*

Vermen, *a. rare⁻⁰.* [f. VERME-s + -AN.]

Vermeil, vermil (vɜːˈmɪl), *a.* and *sb. Poet.*

Vermeil, vermil (vɜːˈmɪl), *v. Chiefly poet.*

Vermellon, -meloon, obs. ff. VERMILION.

Vermelet, obs. form of VERMICEL.

Vermelon(e, -oun, etc., obs. ff. VERMILION.

Vermen, obs. form of VERMIN.

† Verment, *Obs.⁻¹* Aphetic f. AVERMENT.

Vermicelli (vɜːmɪˈtʃɛlɪ), *sb.* [pl. of vermicello.]

Vermiceti, variant of VERMICET *Obs.*

Vermicel, variant of VERMICEL *Obs.*

Vermicelly, obs. f. VERMICELLI.

Vermicili *Obs.*

Vermicelli ...

† Vermicell. *Sc. Obs.⁻¹*

Vermiculi ...

Vermicelli ...

Vermiculated ...

Vermicidal ...

Vermicide ...

Vermicular (vɜːˈmɪkjʊlə), *a.* and *sb.*

Vermiculate (vɜːˈmɪkjʊleɪt), *v.*

Vermiculate (vɜːˈmɪkjʊlət), *ppl. a.*

Vermiculated ...

Vermiculation ...

Vermicule (vɜːˈmɪkjuːl), *sb.*

Vermiculist ...

Vermiculite (vɜːˈmɪkjʊlaɪt), *sb.* [f. L. *vermiculus* + -ITE.]

Vermiculose, -ous ...

Vermiculus ...

Vermiform (vɜːˈmɪfɔːm), *a.*

Vermiformous ...

Vermifugal (vɜːˈmɪfjʊɡəl), *a. Med.*

Vermifuge (vɜːˈmɪfjuːdʒ), *a.* and *sb. Med.*

Vermil(e, obs. ff. VERMEIL.

Vermilion (vɜːˈmɪljən), *sb.*

Vermilion, *v.*

Vermilion-coloured ...

Vermilionette ...

Vermilionize ...

Vermily ...

Vermin (vɜːˈmɪn), *sb.*

hended in this versicle: *Quis, Quid, Vbi, Quibus auxiliis, Cur, Quomodo, Quando.* 1652 NEEDHAM *Selden's Mare Cl.* Ep. Ded. 8 According to that old Versicle *Frangit & attollit vires in Milite causa.* 1817 BYRON *Let. to Moore* 25 Mar., Here are some versicles. 1849 THACKERAY *Pendennis* (1850) II. 257 To these pretty little compositions Mr. Pen replied..with points of wit, nay, with pretty little verses very likely, in reply to the versicles of the Muse of 'Mes Larmes'. 1893 McCARTHY *Red Diamonds* III. 143 She was fond of writing versicles and setting them to music.

†d. Without article. *Obs.*⁻¹

1589 PUTTENHAM *Eng. Poesie* I. v. (Arb.) 26 How the wilde and sauage people vsed a naturall Poesie in versicle and rime as our vulgar is.

Hence †**Ve·rsicle** *v. intr.* (with *it*), to sing versicles. *Obs.*⁻¹

1550 BALE *Apol.* 131 b, I knowe theyr progresse was great, as ye were wont to versycle it on theyr daies.

Ve·rsicler. *rare*⁻¹. [f. VERSICLE *sb.*] A writer of versicles or short verses; a versifier.

1885 MEREDITH *Diana* xxx, I'll read your versicler to-morrow morning early.

Versicolorate, *a. Ent.* [-ATE².] = VERSICOLOURED *a.*

1826 KIRBY & SP. *Entomol.* IV. xlvi. 292 *Versicolorate*,.. when a surface changes its colour as the light varies.

Versicolo·rous, *a. rare*⁻¹. [f. late L. *versicolōrus*: cf. VERSICOLOUR *a.*] = prec.

1847 HARDY in *Proc. Berw. Nat. Club* II. 242 Abdomen shining, versicolorous.

†**Ve·rsicolour,** *sb. Obs.*⁻⁰ (See quot. and next.)

1775 ASH, *Versicolour*, a variegated or changeable colour.

Ve·rsicolour, *a. rare.* Also 7, 9 -color. [ad. L. *versicolor*, f. *vers-*, ppl. stem of *vertĕre* to turn, change, VERSE *v.*² + *color* COLOUR *sb.* So F. *versicolore.*] = next.

1628 BURTON *Anat. Mel.* (ed. 3) 264 Neate gardens full of exotick, versicoloure, diuersly varied, sweete smelling flowers. 1632 *Ibid.* (ed. 4) 478 Why doe they..decke themselues with..chaines, girdles, rings,..versicolor ribbands? [1828–32 WEBSTER, *Versicolor*, .. having various colors; changeable in color.]

Versicoloured (vǝ̄·ɹsikɒ̆ləɹd), *a.* [f. as prec. + COLOURED *ppl. a.* Cf. the earlier VERSE-COLOURED.] Changing or varying in colour; iridescent; also, of various colours, variegated.

1721 BAILEY, *Versicoloured*, changing Colour, of sundry and changeable Colours. 1822–7 GOOD *Study Med.* (1829) I. 421 Under these circumstances, the bile has at different times..been found..whitish, black, green, eruginous, and versicoloured. 1846 LANDOR *Imag. Conv.* Wks. I. 467/1 If thou hadst enveloped him in thy versicoloured and cloud-like vestiary. 1873 M. COLLINS *Squire Silchester* III. xxii. 246 A rocket..drops its versicoloured shower.

fig. 1867 VISCT. STRANGFORD *Selection* (1869) I. 135 Such views..on the subject of the versicoloured policy of France in the East.

Hence **Versicolouredness**, 'the being of changeable Colours' (Bailey, 1727, vol. II).

†**Versi·cular,** *sb. Obs.*⁻¹ [ad. med.L. *versiculārius*, f. L. *versiculus* VERSICULUS: see -AR².] One whose office it was to say or sing the versicles.

c 1450 in Aungier *Syon* (1840) 364 Of the versiculars for the wyke. The two sustres that be tabled to synge the versicles schal synge the *Venite.*

Versicular (vǝɹsi·kiŭlǎɹ), *a.* [f. L. *versicul-us* VERSICLE *sb.* + -AR¹.] Of or pertaining to, characterized by, consisting of, versicles or verses, esp. Biblical verses.

1812 J. JEBB *Corr.* (1834) II. 72 The theological uses of the hebraic versicular system. 1840 G. S. FABER *Christ's Disc. Capernaum* 20 That the sort of unconscious delusion, produced by the versicular figures, may be dissipated, I have ..omitted those figures altogether. 1882–3 *Schaff's Encycl. Relig. Knowl.* III. 2242 It was in this edition that the versicular division of the New Testament was..introduced.

Versicula·tion. *rare.* [f. L. *versicul-us* or VERSICULE.] The action or practice of making versicules; the result of this.

1893 *Edin. Rev.* Oct. 484 But here we will escape from the polyglot versiculations of Sir Edwin Arnold.

Versicule (vǝ̄·ɹsikiul). *rare.* [a. OF. (also mod.F.) *versicule* (14th c.; = It., Sp., Pg. *versiculo*), or ad. L. *versiculus*: see next and VERSICLE *sb.*] A versicle; a short verse or poem.

1491 *Cartul. St. Nicholai Aberdon.* (New Spald. Cl.) I. 256 Gif he be ane choristar and playne Sangster þat can singe Anthoms, Responseris and Versiculis. 1517 in *Archaeol.* LXI. 84 A booke with the Invitatorys and the versiculis noted. *a* 1550 *Wyntoun's Cron.* (Wemyss MS.) v. xi. 3625 Versiculis thare to he can write, And ympnis alsua maid in dite. 1861 W. H. RUSSELL in *Times* 14 May, A variety of versicules, songs, and rhetorical exercitations.

‖**Versiculus** (vǝɹsi·kiŭlŏs). Pl. -culi. [L., dim. of *versus* VERSE *sb.* Cf. prec. and VERSICLE *sb.*] A versicle. Chiefly in pl.

1755 *Gentl. Mag.* XXV. 93 The late bishop Hare..began his enquiry by attempting to discover the length of the versiculi or lines. 1820 *Blackw. Mag.* June 323 A sentence of panegyric on my own *versiculi.* 1820 BYRON *Lett. & Jrnls.* (1900) IV. 395 Pray let not these versiculi go forth with *my* name, except among the initiated.

Versie: see VERSY *a. Obs.*

Versifiable (vǝ̄·ɹsifəiǎb'l), *a. rare*⁻¹. [f. VERSIFY *v.* + -ABLE. Cf. OF. *versifiable.*] That can be versified or put into verse.

1828 SOUTHEY *Lett.* (1856) IV. 107 Names and dates, &c., will precede it [i.e. the epitaph] in the usual form, telling all that is not versifiable.

†**Versi·fical,** *a. Obs.*⁻¹ In 6 versyfycall. [f. late L. *versific-us* (cf. L. *versificāre* to versify) + -AL.] Of or pertaining to the making of verse.

1545–7 in *Archaeol.* XXXIV. 40 They have the versyfycall rulys of Sulpice gevyn in the mornyng of one of the vjth forme.

†**Ve·rsificate,** *v. Obs.*⁻⁰ [f. L. *versificāt-*, ppl. stem of *versificāre* to versify.] *intr.* 'To make verses' (Bailey, 1721).

Versification (vǝ̄ɹsifikēⁱ·ʃən). [ad. L. *versificātiōn-*, *versificātio*, noun of action f. *versificāre* to versify. So F. *versification* (1680), Sp. *versificacion*, Pg. *-ação*, It. *-azione.*]

1. The action of composing verse; the art or practice of versifying.

In Rolland *Crt. Venus* (*c* 1550) II. 176 'Versification, meter' should perhaps be read for 'Versificat in meter' of the text.

1603 HOLLAND *Plutarch's Mor.* 1198 The order of writing an historie..came downe as one would say from the stately chariot of versification, to prose, and went a foot. 1658 PHILLIPS, *Versification*, a making of Verses. 1706 POPE *Lett.* Wks. 1736 V. 53 The thoughts I have already sent you on the subject of English Versification. 1774 WARTON *Hist. Eng. Poetry* I. II. 27 Camden affirms, that Aldhelm.. taught his countrymen the art of Latin versification. 1790 COWPER *Lett.* 13 Sept., After perpetual versification during five years I find myself..reduced to read for my amusement. 1824 COLERIDGE *Table-t.* 7 June, How lamentably the art of versification is neglected by most of the poets of the present day! 1861 WRIGHT *Ess. Archæol.* II. xx. 153 The southern ecclesiastics..adopted this new style of versification for their chant music. 1875 OUSELEY *Mus. Form* ii. 3 You may teach a man the rules of versification or of melody.

2. The form or style in which the words in a poetical composition are arranged; the structure of poetry or verse; measure, metre.

1693 DRYDEN *Juvenal* Ded. p. v, Donn alone, of all our Country-men, had your Talent; but was not happy enough to arrive at your Versification. 1780 J. WELWOOD *Pref. to Rowe's Lucan* p. xliii, As to the Translation it self, ..the Language is pure, and the Versification both musical and adapted to the subject. 1729 T. COOKE *Tales*, etc. 137 His Versyfycation is mostly as faulty as his Sentiment. 1759 JOHNSON *Idler* No. 60 ⁋ 7 The versification of Rowe he thought too melodious for the stage. 1813 BYRON *Corsair* Ded., I shall..take my chance, with that versification in which I have hitherto published nothing. 1841 W. SPALDING *Italy & It. Isl.* I. 139 Virgil was the great model, and his picturesque groups and flowing versification were imitated by many men of letters. 1880 L. STEPHEN *Pope* iii. 75 To make the versification as smooth and the sense as transparent as possible.

3. A poetical or metrical version *of* something.

1821 *Q. Rev.* XXV. 36 Of this song we have been favoured with the following beautiful versification. 1858 DORAN *Crt. Fools* 154 Many of his epigrams..are said to have been versifications of his own jokes.

Versificator (vǝ̄·ɹsifikēⁱtəɹ). [a. L. *versificātor* (whence also It. *versificatore*, Sp., Pg. *versificador*, F. *versificateur*), f. *versificāre* to versify.] One who writes verse; a poet, versifier.

1611 COTGR., *Versificateur*, a versificator, versifier, maker of verses. 1682 SHADWELL *Medal* Ep. A j b, His Fort is, that he is an indifferent good Versificator. 1693 DRYDEN *Juvenal* Ded. p. xi, Statius, the best Versificator next to Virgil. 1746 W. HORSLEY *Fool* (1748) I. 15 The Sons of Imagination, whether Lovers or..Prose-Writers, or Versificators. 1760 JORTIN *Erasm.* II. 105 Erasmus was very far from being as mean a poet as this versificator. 1805 *Edin. Rev.* VI. 291 The system, upon which a certain sect of versificators have lately proceeded. 1841 D'ISRAELI *Amen. Lit.* (1867) 477 Alliterations and epithets..with mechanical versificators are a mere artifice.

†**Versificatory,** *a. Obs.*⁻⁰ [f. VERSIFICATE *v.*] 'Belonging to versifying' (Bailey, 1727, vol. II).

Versifica·trix. [a. L. type **versificātrix*, fem. of *versificātor* VERSIFICATOR.] A female versifier; a poetess.

1784 BEATTIE in Forbes *Life* (1806) II. 147 Johnson told me, with great solemnity, that she [Hannah More] was 'the most powerful versificatrix in the English language.

Versified (vǝ̄·ɹsifəid), *ppl. a.* [f. VERSIFY *v.* + -ED.] Written or composed in verse.

1841 W. SPALDING *Italy & It. Isl.* III. 205 His versified epistles are greatly prized..for their taste and feeling. 1874 L. STEPHEN *Hours in Libr.* (1892) II. vii. 210 His poems were versified sermons.

Versifier (vǝ̄·ɹsifəi,əɹ). Forms: α. 4–5 versifiour, 5 -fyowre; 5 versefiour, -fyour. β. 5 versyfyer, -fyar, 6 vercyfyer, 5 vercifier, 5– versifier, 6 -fiar, 6, 8 -fyer; 5 versefier, 5–6 -fyer. [a. AF. *versifiur* (13th c.), *versifiour*, OF. *versefiere*, *-fierre* (13th c.), *versifieur* (14th c.), f. *versifier*: see VERSIFY *v.* and -ER.]

1. One who versifies or composes verses; a verser or verse-maker; a poet.

α. *c* 1340 HAMPOLE *Pr. Consc.* 897 He suld fynd ful litel matere To mak ioy whilles he here duelles, Als a versifiour in metre þus telles. 1382 WYCLIF *Job* Pref., The whiche thing versifioures more than a symple redere vnderstonden. 1398 TREVISA *Barth. De P. R.* XVIII. xci. (Bodl. MS.), It is seide þ' versifiours likned þe lelye to mannes inwitte. *a* 1425 tr. *Arderne's Treat. Fistula*, etc. 4 Wherfore seiþ a versifiour,..'lat werke ouercome thi worde, for boste lesseneþ gode lose'. *c* 1440 *Promp. Parv.* 508/2 Versifyowre (*H.* versyowre), *versificator.*

β. 14.. *Voc.* in Wr.-Wülcker 681 *Hic versificator*, a versyfyer. *a* 1450 *Mankind* 746 in *Macro Plays* 27 As a nobyll versyfyer makyth mencyon in þis verse. 1477 EARL RIVERS (Caxton) *Dictes* 13 Omer was an auncient vercifier in Grece. *a* 1513 FABYAN *Chron.* VII. 405 Of this noble prynce a vercyfyer made these .ii. verses folowynge. 1567 DRANT *Horace, Ep.* II. ii. H iv, Euil versefyers mocked be, yet haue they to theire ioy. 1603 DANIEL *Def. Rhime* Wks. (1717) 32 This Self-Love, whereunto we Versifiers are ever noted to be especially subject. 1670 MILTON *Hist. Eng.* v. Wks. 1851 V. 227 Other pretious things, .. describ'd in Malmsbury, tak'n..out of an old versifier, some of whose verses he recites. 1741 WATTS *Improv. Mind* I. xvi. § 1 More elevated language than the fondest critics have ever found in any of the Heathen versifiers either of Greece or Rome. 1789 BELSHAM *Ess.* I. xii. 232 Pope has often been stiled the best versifier in the English language. 1828 *Harrovian* 46 He was a good classic, and an excellent versifier. 1873 SYMONDS *Grk. Poets* x. 333 Those purely rustic poems which..have.. been imitated by versifiers emulous of his gracefulness.

2. With depreciative force: A mere or poor writer of verse(s); a rimester, a poetaster.

1531 ELYOT *Gov.* I. xiii, Semblably they that make verses, expressynge therby none other lernynge but the craft of versifyeng, be..of auncient writers..onely called versifyers. 1581 SIDNEY *Apol. Poetrie* (Arb.) 28 Now swarme many versifiers that neede neuer aunswere to the name of Poets. 1589 PUTTENHAM *Eng. Poesie* I. i. (Arb.) 19 The translator, who..may well be sayd a versifier, but not a Poet. 1642 MILTON *Apol. Smect.* Wks. 1851 III. 262 Rather nice and humerous in what was tolerable, then patient to read every drawling versifier. 1652–62 HEYLYN *Cosmogr.* IV. (1682) 85 Philip whom the Versifier (I do not say the Poet) called Philippus Hispanus. 1696 PHILLIPS (ed. 5), *Versifier*, a maker of Verses, generally taken in an ill sense. 1781 SIR J. REYNOLDS *Journ. Flanders* Wks. 1797 II. 112 The modern versifiers,..carrying no weight of thought, easily fall into that false gallop of verse. 1821 BYRON *Diary* Wks. (1846) 531/2 As different from an orator as an improvisatore or a versifier from a poet. 1880 MISS BRADDON *Just as I am* xi, She thought Byron an ephemeral versifier.

Ve·rsiform, *a. rare*⁻⁰. [ad. L. *versiformis* (post-class.): see -FORM.] (See quots.)

1727 BAILEY (vol. II), *Versiform*, that changes its Shape. 1884 *Imp. Dict.*, *Versiform*, varied in form; changing form: used in botany.

Versify (vǝ̄·ɹsifəi), *v.* Also 4–7 versifye, -fie (5 uersefiȝe, versfy), 5 versyfyyn, wersyfy, 5–6 versyfy. [ad. OF. *vercifier*, *versifier* (13th c. in Godef. *Compl.*, = Prov. *versifiar*), ad. L. *versificāre* (whence It. *versificare*, Sp., Pg. *versificar*), f. *versus* VERSE *sb.* + *facĕre* to make.]

1. *intr.* To make or compose verses; to write poetry; = VERSE *v.*¹ 1. Also const. *upon* (or †*of*) a theme.

1377 LANGL. *P. Pl.* B. xv. 367 For is none of þis newe clerkes..þat can versifye faire ne formalich enditen. *c* 1440 *Promp. Parv.* 508/2 Versyfyyn, *versificor.* 1483 *Cath. Angl.* 401/1 To versifye, *versificare, versiculare.* *c* 1520 SKELTON *Magnyf.* 1162 Yes, in faythe; I can versyfy. 1579 LODGE *Def. Poetry*, etc. (Hunt. Club) 15 Tully attributeth it for prais to Archias yᵗ vpon any theame he cold versify extempory. 1612 BRINSLEY *Lud. Lit.* viii. (1627) 121 To learne to versifie, *ex tempore*, of any ordinary Theame. 1656 H. MORE *Enthus. Tri.* (1712) 8 Maracus a Poet of Syracuse, who never versified so well as when he was in his distracted fits. 1693 DRYDEN *Juvenal* I. 24 Since the World with Writing is Possest, I'll versifie in spite. 1718 *Free-thinker* No. 136. 236 The Subject..promises no small Glory to the Genius who shall versify upon it. 1798 LADY BEDINGFIELD in *Betham Lett.* (1905) 51 Cannot you versify as you walk? 1824 BYRON *Juan* XV. xix, Speculating..On what may suit ..my story, And never straining hard to versify. 1841 D'ISRAELI *Amen. Lit.* (1867) 394 A few scholars..had the intrepidity to versify in French with the ancient metres. 1897 *Pop. Sci. Monthly* L. 391 The true poet does not versify because he would, but because he must.

2. *trans.* To narrate or recount in verse; to treat as the subject of verse.

c 1386 CHAUCER *Monk's Prol.* 90 They [tragedies] ben versified communely Of vj. feet which men clepen Exametron. 1596 DANIEL *Civ. Wars* I. vi, I versify the truth, not poetize. 1766 GOLDSM. *Vic. W.* xvii, The silly poet runs home to versify the disaster. 1868 FREEMAN *Norm. Conq.* II. App. 533 The story is versified at great length in the French Life. 1871 LOWELL *Study Wind.*, *Pope* 315 His more ambitious works may be defined as careless thinking carefully versified.

3. To turn or convert (a literary piece) into verse; to change from prose into verse; to translate or rewrite in verse-form.

1735 POPE (*title*), The Satires of Dr. John Donne,..Versified. 1756 J. WARTON *Ess. Pope* I. 11 The exalted prophesy of Isaiah, which Pope has so successfully versified. 1789 BURNEY *Hist. Mus.* III. 35 *note*, The 30th. Psalm was the first which Luther versified. 1824 D'ISRAELI *Quarrels Auth.* (1867) 256 Bolingbroke really wrote the 'Essay on Man', which Pope versified. 1837 LOCKHART *Scott* I. viii. 247 These are all in prose like their originals; but he also versified..some lyrical fragments of Goethe.

Versifying (vǝ̄·ɹsifəi,iŋ), *vbl. sb.* [f. prec. + -ING¹.] The act or practice of making verses; an instance of this; the art of composing verse; versification.

c 1450 *Cov. Myst.* (Shaks. Soc.) 189 No clerke abyl to bere oure book Of versyfyeng, nor of other scyens. 1479 *Paston Lett.* III. 241, I lake no thynge but wersyfyynge, whyche I troste to have with a lytyll contynuance. *a* 1568 ASCHAM *Scholem.* II. (Arb.) 147 Yet neither of them hath fullie hite perfite and trew versifying. 1580 SPENSER *Let. to Harvey* Wks. (1912) 636, I perceiue you other whiles continue your old exercise of Versifying in English. *a* 1653 GOUGE *Comm. Hebr.* v. 14 A scholar exercised in versifying will readily distinguish between a true and false verse. 1677 J. PETER (*title*), Artificial Versifying; a New Way to make Latin Verses. 1740 J. CLARKE *Educ. Youth* (ed. 3) 61 Of what Use Versifying is,..I do not understand. 1830 SOUTHEY *Bunyan* p. xlix, In versifying he was attempting an art

which he had never learnt, and for which he had no aptitude. 1892 *Athenæum* 6 Aug. 190/1 What really genuine poetic inspiration he showed is lost in the commonplace of too idle versifyings.

b. *attrib.*, as *versifying dialogue*, etc.

1686 in *Verney Mem.* (1907) II. 424 As to y[ou]r Versifying Dialogue with Him, I like it very well. 1725 WATTS *Logic* III. ii. § 3, I confess some of these logical Subtilties have much more Use than those versifying Tables. 1737 *Gentl. Mag.* VII. 148/1, I shall exemplify by a Text, where a Singing, or mere Versifying Repetition, is literally express'd. 1787 SKINNER *Let.* in *Wks. Burns* (1800) II. 127, I know a classical education will not create a versifying taste. 1811 BYRON *Hints fr. Hor.* 839 If free, all fly his versifying fit. 1885 *Athenæum* 11 July 50/1 Godwin desired Wordsworth to undertake the versifying part of the business.

Ve·rsifying, *ppl. a.* [f. as prec. + -ING².] That versifies or writes verses.

1580 *2nd & 3rd Blast Plays & Theatres* 110 These versifieng Plaie-makers. 1750 GRAY *Long Story* 18 Shame of the versifying tribe! 1893 WALKER *Three Churchmen* 134 The reviewers he looks upon as 'gamekeepers', doing invaluable service to literature by keeping the versifying 'poachers' off Parnassus.

†**Versi·loquy.** *Obs.*⁻⁰ [Cf. late L. *versiloquus* that speaks in verse.] (See quot.)

1727 BAILEY (vol. II), *Versiloquy*, speaking in Verse.

Versin, contracted f. *versed sine* VERSED *a.*

1827 AIRY in *Encycl. Metrop.* (1845) I 685 Versin *c* = 1 – cos *c*. *Ibid.*, Versin *c* = versin *a* – *b* [etc.]. 1859 PARKINSON *Optics* (1866) 254 The quantity of light received by the disc is $2\pi^2a^2B$ versin *a*.

Versine, variant of VERZINE *Obs.*

Versing (vǝ̄·ɹsiŋ), *vbl. sb.* [f. VERSE *v.*¹ + -ING¹.] The action or practice of writing verse; an instance of this; the art or science of verse-making.

1581 SIDNEY *Apol. Poetrie* (Arb.) 49 That which gyueth greatest scope.., is ryming and versing. 1613 W. BROWNE *Brit. Past.* II. i. (1616) 9 For well it seemes in versing he hath skill. 1633 G. HERBERT *Temple*, *Flower* vi, I once more smell the dew and rain, And relish versing. 1644 BULWER *Chirol.* A iij b, Physick and Versing in his flaming Chaire Plac'd Phoebus, and bestow'd that blazing Haire. 1856 ANNE MANNING *Tasso & Leonora* 46 Charmed with his smooth versings. 1874 M. COLLINS *Transmigr.* II. ix. 162 The man who can..relish versing has nothing much the matter with his..psychical health. 1892 STOPFORD BROOKE *Early Eng. Lit.* I. vii. 146 He had before him some ancient versings of the fight.

attrib. 1645 G. DANIEL *Poems* Wks. (Grosart) II. 51 What mad men are wee of the versing trade!

†**Versing box.** *Obs.*⁻¹ (Of obscure meaning; perh. connected with VERSE *v.*³ and VERSER².)

a 1529 SKELTON *Bouge of Court* 232 As I stode musynge in my mynde, Haruy Hafter came lepynge, lyghte as lynde. Vpon his breste he bare a versynge boxe.

Version (vǝ̄·ɹʃən), *sb.* [a. F. *version* (= It. *versione*, Sp. *version*, Pg. *versão*), or ad. L. *versiōn-*, *versio*, noun of action from *vertĕre* to turn.]

1. A rendering of some text or work, or of a single word, passage, etc., from one language into another; a translation; also (rarely), the action or process of translating.

Freq. with adjs. denoting the language into which the translation is made.

1582 N. T. (Rhemish) Pref. b ij, Trusting that it may giue occasion to you..to lay away at lest such their impure versions as hitherto you haue ben forced to occupie. 1607 TOPSELL *Four-f. Beasts* 435, I vtterly seclude al their opinions, which translate this word Arabian wolues, for the Hæbrew names cannot admit such a version or exposition. *c* 1645 HOWELL *Lett.* (1650) II. 61 Things translated into another tongue lose of their primative vigor and strength, unless a paraphrasticall version be permitted. 1682 GREW *Anat. Plants* Pref., The Second Lecture..is also translated into French, by Mons. Mesmin,..whose Version is very well approved by those who are competent Judges. 1718 PRIOR *Poems Several Occas.* Pref., His excellent Version of the *Carmen Seculare.* 1794 BURKE *Pref. to Brissot's Addr.* Constit. Wks. VII. 327 The translator has only to say for himself, that he has found some difficulty in this version. *c* 1806 H. K. WHITE *Rem. Eng. Poets* Remains (1825) 156 None of our better versions have been able to preserve the original graces of these verses [of Ps. xviii]. 1841 ELPHINSTONE *Hist. India* I. III. vi. 293 Such of those literal versions as we possess in English (which are mostly from the 'Rámáyana'). 1874 GREEN *Short Hist.* viii. § 1. 448 The English version of the Bible remains the noblest example of the English tongue.

b. *Sc.* A translation from English into Latin prose done as a school or university exercise; a piece of English prose set for translation into Latin.

1711 *Burgh Rec. Aberdeen* (1872) II. 345 Ther proficiency in themms, versions, poeticall composurs, and orations. *c* 1850 HURRY in Walker *Bards Bon-Accord* (1856) 629 When we our versions wrote, nae Lexicon had we To help us.

2. The particular form of a statement, account, report, etc., given by one person or party; an account resting upon limited authority or embodying a particular point of view.

1788 in *Ld. Auckland's Corr.* (1861) II. 93 The version which we received here respecting the famous Scarborough cruise. 1855 MACAULAY *Hist. Eng.* xviii. IV. 214 The Whig version of the story was that the old robber Mac Ian had laid an ambuscade for the soldiers... The Jacobite version..appeared in the Paris Gazette of the seventh of April. 1879 FROUDE *Cæsar* xi. 140 The version generally received of what he actually did say. 1907 *Verney Mem.* II. 154 Sir Roger sends his version of the reconciliation between Monk and the City.

b. A special form or variant of something.

1835 I. TAYLOR *Spir. Despot.* viii. 345 To see Christianity freed from the bonds of every peculiar version. 1858 MASSON *Milton* (1859) I. 679 In the cause of true religion, or of the Scottish version of it. 1908 SIR H. MAXWELL *Guide Holyrood* 20 This painting is a larger version of one at Windsor Castle.

†3. A turning about; a change of direction. *Obs.*

1625 BACON *Ess., Viciss. of Things* (Arb.) 571 What Kinde of Comet, for Magnitude, Colour, Version of the Beames,..or Lasting, produceth what Kinde of Effects. 1706 CONGREVE *Disc. Pindaric Ode* A j b, The first was call'd the Strophé, from the Version or circular Motion of the Singers in that Stanza from the Right Hand to the Left.

b. *Obstet.* The operation of manually turning the child so as to facilitate delivery.

1853 J. Y. SIMPSON *Obstet. Path. & Pract.* 17, I now found an obstruction to the complete version of the infant. 1889 *Buck's Handbk. Med. Sci.* VII. 628/2 The term version is applied to all operations by which the long axis of the child is changed in its relation to the long axis of the uterus.

†4. Conversion, transformation. *Obs.*

1626 BACON *Sylva* § 27 Springs, which the Ancients thought..to be made by the Version of Aire into Water. 1626 — *New Atl.*, *Magn. Nat.* g iij, Version of bodies into other Bodies. 1666 BOYLE *Orig. Forms & Qual.* 407 As to the version of Water into Earth, by a seemingly slight Operation.

Hence **Ve·rsion** *v. trans.*, to translate. **Ve·rsional** *a.*, pertaining to a version or translation. **Ve·rsioner, Ve·rsionist**, one who produces a version; a translator. **Ve·rsionize** *v. trans.*, to render into another tongue, to translate.

1716 M. DAVIES *Athen. Brit.* III. *Arianism* 19 Biddle's brief Scripture-Catechism was caus'd to be *version'd into Latin. 1884 *Advance* (Chicago) 3 Jan., At the time the Scriptures had been versioned into the King James version. 1871 *Independent* (N.Y.) 23 Mar. (Cent.), All the suggestions for emendations [of the Bible], whether textual or *versional. 1910 *Expositor* Nov. 409 The versional variants rest on divergent Hebrew texts. *c* 1806 in *H. K. White's Rem.* (1825) 159 Our *versioner, by adding an *s* to it, has rendered them both plurals. 1782 ELPHINSTON tr. *Martial* Pref. p. iv, His [*sc.* Martial's] Editor and *Versionist. 1811 R. DIXON *Interpr. Sixty-eighth Ps.* 46 *note*, All the ancient versionists seem to have thought, that the valley in this verse received its name [etc.]. 1861 I. TAYLOR *Spir. Hebr. Poetry* 338 Serviceable as Jewish versionists..are, it was not their function to concern themselves with the soul ..of the national literature. 1874 H. COPPÉE *Eng. Lit.* (ed. 3) 52 Wace's poem..was soon again..to be *versionized into English.

†**Versipellous,** *a. Obs.*⁻¹ [f. L. *versipell-is*, f. *vers-*, *vertĕre* to turn + *pellis* skin.] Having the faculty of changing the skin. In quot *fig.*

1650 B. *Discolliminium* 28, I could demonstrate it to be Heterogeneous, Heterodoxous, Incongrous,.. Versipellous.

†**Ve·rsity.** *Obs.* [Abbrev. of UNIVERSITY.] = VARSITY.

c 1680 HICKERINGILL *Hist. Whiggism* I. Wks. 1716 I. 37 M. Tantivee is a Graduate, and no small Fool, I assure you, he has been at the—Versity. 1691 MRS. D'ANVERS *Academia* 8 When e're he's sent to th' Versity.

†**Ve·rsle,** *v. Obs. rare.* Also 3 uerslen, uersalien, 4 versail. [ad. OF. *verseiller*, *-sailler*, *-seller*, etc.:—L. type **versiculāre*, f. L. *versiculus* VERSICLE *sb.*] *intr.* To say or sing versicles or verses of the Psalms, esp. during Divine Office. Also *trans.*

a 1225 *Ancr. R.* 44 Mid him ne schule ȝe nouðer uerslen ne singen þet he hit muwe iheren. *Ibid.* 120 Þauh heo uersalie, & sigge hire vres, & hire Pater nosters. *a* 1325 *Prose Psalter* c. 1 Lord, y shal synge mercy and iugement to þe; y shal versail and vnderstonde in wai unfiled. *c* 1330 R. BRUNNE *Chron. Wace* (Rolls) 16472 Þys salme þey songe, & versled hit al wyþ o tonge.

Hence †**Ve·rsling** *vbl. sb. Obs.*

a 1225 *Ancr. R.* 44 Verslunge of hire sautere; redinge of Englichs, oðer of Frenchs; holi meditaciuns.

‖**Verso** (vǝ̄·ɹso). [L. *verso* (sc. *folio* leaf), abl. sing. neut. of *versus*, pa. pple. of *vertĕre* to turn. So F. and Pg. *verso.*]

1. The back of a leaf in a manuscript or printed book; the side presented to the eye when the leaf has been turned over. Also abbrev. *v.*, *vº*

The left-hand page of a book is the verso of that leaf, and faces the RECTO of the next.

1839 HALLIWELL *Maundevile* Introd. p. xiii, See f. 2, vo. 1850 FORSHALL & MADDEN *Wycliffite Bible* I. p. lxi, The verso commences with the eleventh chapter of the Epistle to the Romans. 1873 *Rep. Brit. Assoc.* I. 43 Sines, cosines, and secants are given on the versos of the pages in columns. 1898 *Athenaeum* 12 Nov. 676 The text begins on the verso of the title-page.

fig. 1873 J. HENRY *Aeneidea* I. Pref. 77 It was not long before I had the verso of this agreeable recto of one leaf of my library life.

2. The reverse of a coin, medal, or the like.

1891 *Cent. Dict.* 1914 P. E. NEWBERRY in *Anc. Egypt* 6 On the verso of the same palette there is a scene [etc.].

Versoke, southern ME. pa. t. FORSAKE *v.*

†**Versor**¹. *Obs.* In 5 versour(e. [a. AF. **versour* (F. *verseur*), f. *verser* to pour, VERSE *v.*²] (See quots.)

a 1483 *Liber Niger* in *Househ. Ord.* (1790) 77 One chief sobyr yeoman versoure, to resceyve all the ale or beere that shall be pourveyede. *Ibid.*, Othyr twoe groomes versours in this office to helpe to lodge theyre ale, to helpe drawe it [etc.].

Versor² (vǝ̄·ɹsǫ̆ɹ). [a. L. type **versor*, f. *vers-*, *vertĕre* to turn.]

†1. The needle of a compass. *Obs. rare.*

1640 G. WATTS tr. *Bacon's Adv. Learn.* v. ii. 229 So the versor of a Mariners needle applies it selfe to the Poles of the world.

2. *Math.* In quaternions, an operator which changes the direction of a vector without altering its length.

a 1865 SIR W. R. HAMILTON *Elem. Quaternions* II. i. (1866) 133 We shall now say that every Radial Quotient is a Versor. A Versor has thus, in general, a plane, an axis, and an angle. 1886 W. S. ALDIS *Solid Geom.* (ed. 4) xiv. 235 If the two vectors OA and OB be of equal length the change of one into the other is merely an operation of rotation. In this case the quaternion is called a versor.

Verss(e, southern ME. varr. FRESH *a.*

Verst (vǝ̄ɹst). Forms: α. 6–8 werste, 6, 8–9 werst, 7 worst, 7–8 wurste. β. 6– verst, 6–8 verste, 7 vorst; 6 verse (*pl.* versse), 7 ferse. [ad. Russ. верстá, partly through G. *werst* and F. *verste.*] A Russian measure of length equal to 3500 English feet or about two-thirds of an English mile.

α. 1555 EDEN *Decades* (Arb.) 322 From Moscouia to the citie of Vuolochda, are numbered [500] Werstes, one Werst conteynynge almoste the space of an Italyan myle. 1662 J. DAVIES tr. *Olearius' Voy. Ambass.* 27 We left Novogorod and got forwards 36. Werstes, or seven Leagues. 1715 *Lond. Gaz.* No. 5293/2 He was not gone above 12 Wurstes or Russian Miles. 1774 *Ann. Reg.* II. 151 Having approached this island within almost three wersts, or two English miles, their vessel was suddenly surrounded by ice. 1818 BYRON *Mazeppa* xvii, Many a werst, Panting as if his heart would burst, The weary brute still stagger'd on. 1841 MOTLEY *Corr.* (1889) I. iv. 73 The road from Tauroggen to Petersburg is 14 wersts.

β. 1557 JENKINSON in Hakluyt *Voy.* (1886) III. 198 Vologhda and Mosco..are accompted 500 verstes asunder. *c* 1571 J. STOW *Voy. & Trav.* (Hakl. Soc.) II. 339 The ryuer oca, which is 20 versse distant from ye moscow; a verse is iii quarters of an yngleshe myle. 1591 G. FLETCHER *Russe Commw.* (Hakl. Soc.) 7 A little isthmus or narrow slippe of lande, a fewe versts ouerthwart. 1617 MORYSON *Itin.* I. 295 In Russia among the Moscovites confining upon Poland, a mile is called a ferse. 1635 PAGITT *Christianogr.* 23 From the furthest part westward..to Siberia Eastward, is 4400. verst or thereabouts. *a* 1670 [S. COLLINS] *Pres. St. Russia* (1671) 83 Some ran away ten Versts before they could be overtaken. 1760 *Phil. Trans.* LI. 490 It runs from a great lake, which lies a verste and a half from its mouth. 1775 WRAXALL *Tour North. Europe* 218 Muscovite lords commonly go fifty and sixty versts..to make visits to each other. 1808 R. K. PORTER *Trav. Sk. Russ. & Swed.* (1813) I. iv. 27 Seventy or eighty versts above St. Petersburgh. 1864 BURTON *Scot Abr.* II. ii. 204 A country house of the Tzaar's seven versts from Moscow. 1879 BROWNING *Iván Ivánovitch* 194 No strength, old crone,— not she!—to crawl forth half a verst!

Verst(e, southern ME. varr. FIRST *a.* and *adv.*; obs. Sc. ff. WORST *a.* **Versuore,** southern ME. var. *forswore* FORSWORN.

‖**Versus** (vǝ̄·ɹsŏs), *prep.* [L.] Against; employed in *Law* to denote an action by one party against another. Also *transf.* Freq. abbrev. *v.* (also *ver.*, *vs.*).

1447–8 SHILLINGFORD *Lett.* (Camden) 53 Also the jugement by twene..John Husset *versus* John Notte. 1451 *Paston Lett.* I. 221, I send yow the *scire facias* for Osbern and Foke *versus* Heydon and Wyndam. 1621 *Debates Ho. Lords* (Camden) 26 Suyt per Fowles in the Starr-chamber *versus* Lake and others. 1744 J. COMYNS *Reports of Cases* 634 Wallis *ver.* Pain and Underhill. 1774 J. ADAMS in *Fam. Lett.* (1876) 19, I am engaged in a famous case,— the cause of King, of Scarborough, *versus* the mob that broke into his house. 1822 SCOTT *Peveril* Pref. Ep., She may sue me for damages, as in the case Dido *versus* Virgil. 1839 DE QUINCEY *Casuistry Rom. Meals* Wks. 1890 VII. 22 Generally such a person is 'rather yellow, rather yellow' (to quote Canning *versus* Lord Durham). 1873 H. SPENCER *Stud. Sociol.* ii. 38 The old battle-ground of free will *versus* necessity. 1894 *Outing* Feb. 397/2 The Rambler *vs.* the Lumberman; an indictment for the larceny of a path.

Versute (vǝɹsiū·t, vǝ̄·ɹsiūt), *a.* [ad. L. *versūtus*, f. *vers-*, *vertĕre* to turn.] Cunning, crafty, wily.

1616 J. LANE *Contn. Sqr.'s T.* IX. 15 Her artishe liers, wittie versute theeves. *Ibid.* 73 Ne bee out reachd at versute pollecie, or once out runn at hardie chivalrie. 1659 GAUDEN *Tears Ch.* I. xiv. 132 A person of very supercilious gravity, also of versute and vertiginous policy. 1790 PALEY *Horæ Paul.* i. 6 The second, which is a more versute and specious forgery.

Hence **Versutely** *adv.*; **Versuteness.**

Also *Versutiloquent*, 'a crafty talker, one using words craftily' (Blount *Glossogr.*, 1656), and *Versutiloquous*, 'talking cunningly or craftily' (Bailey, vol. II, 1727): both after L. *versūtiloquus.*

1616 J. LANE *Contn. Sqr.'s T.* x. 128 Now guiltie Horbell, Leifurcke, Gnartolite, castinge on chaunge, the lip versutlie bite. 1685 H. MORE *Cursory Refl. Baxter* 29 That he may become really sensible and ashamed of his present Crooked Versuteness and Hypocrisie. 1710 R. WARD *Life H. More* 81 Some Neatness of Stile, Versuteness of Temper, and Hypocrisie in Religion. 1857 MAURICE *Mor. & Met. Philos.* IV. vi. § 89. 286 An ingenious explanation of astuteness and versuteness.

†**Versutious,** *a. Obs.*⁻¹ [f. L. *versūt-us.*] = prec.

1660 *3rd Conf. betw. Cromwell & H. Peters* 7 What do I not ow thee for thy versutious Complements to my Lady Lambert.

†**Ve·rsy,** *a. Obs.*⁻¹ *Her.* In 6 versie. [a. F. *versé*, pa. pple. of *verser*: see VERSE *v.*² F. *versé* has been used in some mod. heraldic books] Renversé, reversed.

1572 BOSSEWELL *Armorie* II. 36 b, He beareth d'Or, a Cheuron Versie d'Azure.

Versycle, obs. form of VERSICLE *sb.*

Versyowre: see VERSER¹.

Vert (vǝ̄ɹt), *sb.*¹ (and *a.*). Also 5 veert, 5–7 verte. [a. AF. and OF. *vert* (so mod.F.; formerly also *verd* VERD *sb.*), = Prov. *vert*, Cat. *verd*, Sp., Pg., and It. *verde*:—L. *virid-em*, *viridis* green, VIRID *a.*]

1. Green vegetation growing in a wood or forest and capable of serving as cover for deer.

14.. *Forest Laws* (MS. Douce 335) fol. 73 As touching the kinges veert, that is to say, the kinges wodes; if ther be ony mann, that hath felled ony gret okes [etc.]. 1577 HARRISON *England* II. xv. in *Holinshed* I. 89 b/1 The better preseruation of such venery and vert of all sortes as were nourished in the same. 1598 MANWOOD *Lawes Forest* vi. § 1. 33 b. [Hence in later Dicts., etc.] 1702 *Phil. Trans.* XXIII. 1073 While this Country was a Chace, and while the Vert was preserv'd. 1768 BLACKSTONE *Comm.* III. 71 The punishment of all injuries done to the king's deer or *venison*, to the *vert* or greenswerd. 1818 CRUISE *Digest* (ed. 2) III. 143 Destruction of vert is destruction of venison. 1839 STONEHOUSE *Axholme* 62 A royal demesne..covered with vert, and well stocked with deer. 1871 *Daily News* 18 Sept., The Lord of the Manor..had..enclosed four hundred acres of waste land, and had destroyed the vert on parts thereof.

transf. 1635 A. STAFFORD *Fem. Glory* c vij b, The fourth is humble Ivy, intersert, But lowlie laid,..Preserved, in her antique bed of Vert, No faith's more firme,..then where't doth creep.

b. Coupled with *venison.* (The common use.) Freq. without article.

1455 *Rolls of Parlt.* V. 319/2 The oversight of verte and venyson, in all the Parkes. 1577 HOLINSHED *Chron.* II. 459/2 The k[ing]..appointed foure iustices..to be as surueyers aboue all other Foresters of vert & venison. 1598 MANWOOD *Lawes Forest* xvii. 102 b, That which tendeth to the hurt and annoyance of the Vert and the Venison. 1612 SIR J. DAVIES *Why Ireland*, etc. (1747) 164 The great plenty both of Vert and Venison within this land. 1700 TYRRELL *Hist. Eng.* II. 820 Every Forester in Fee shall..Attach Pleas of the Forest, as well concerning Vert as Venison. 1772 *Junius Lett.* lxviii. (1788) 347 If a man was taken with vert, or venison, it was declared to be equivalent to indictment. 1835 J. P. KENNEDY *Horse Shoe R.* xxxvii, He gave much of his time to the concerns of vert and venison. 1840 *Penny Cycl.* XVI. 175/1 The master-keepers' and groom-keepers' duty is to preserve the vert and venison in their respective bailiwicks and walks.

†c. *Nether, over, special vert*: (see quots.). *Obs.*

1598 MANWOOD *Lawes Forest* vi. § 2. 34 There are two sorts of Vert in euery Forrest, that is to say, Ouer vert, and Neather vert: Ouer vert is that, which the Lawiers do call Hault Boys, and Neather vert is that, which the Lawiers do call South Boys, and in the Forrest lawes, Ouer vert is all manner of Hault Boys, or great wood, aswel such as beareth fruit, as such as beareth none. *Ibid.* 35 Speciall vert, which is euery tree and bush within the Forrest, that doth beare fruite to feed the Deere withall, as Peare trees, Crabtrees, Hawthornes,..and such like. [Hence in later Law Dicts., etc.] 1727 NELSON *Laws conc. Game* 231 *Special-vert*, which may be either over or nether-vert, or both if it bears fruit, for nothing is accounted special-vert but such which beareth fruit to feed the deer.

2. *ellipt.* The right to cut green trees or shrubs in a forest. Now *arch.*

1639 in Maitland *Hist. Edinburgh* (1753) II. 151/1 All their antient Rights,..with Pit and Gallows, Sack and Soke, Thole, Theam, Vert, Wrack, Waifs [etc.]. 1707 in *State, Fraser of Fraserfield* 310 (Jam.), Cum furca, fossa,..vert, veth, venison,..pit et gallows. 1819 SCOTT *Ivanhoe* xl, The Holy Clerk shall have a grant of vert and venison in my woods of Warncliffe. 1843 JAMES *Forest Days* vii, His rights of vert and venison, extended over a wide distance around. 1864 KINGSLEY *Rom. & Teut.* 257 The nobles about gave up to him their rights of venison, and vert, and pasture, and pannage of swine.

†3. A green plant or shrub. *Obs.*⁻¹

1648 J. RAYMOND *Il Merc. Ital.* 129 Bayes, Locusts, Pomegrannets, and such like Verts, that grow wild in the Hedges.

†4. A green colour or pigment. *Obs.*

1481–90 *Howard Househ. Bks.* (Roxb.) 339 Item,..for iiij. dos. of golde paper, and silver rowche clere and verte, viij. s. 1572 in Feuillerat *Revels Q. Eliz.* (1908) 178 Vert,.. Sapp,..Crymsen,..White,..Broune. 1582 *Ibid.* 359 Paste bord, paper, and paste, white, sise, verte, Syneper.

5. *spec.* in *Her.* The tincture green. Also as *adj.*

c 1507 *Justes Moneths May & June* 28 in Hazl. *E. P. P.* II. 114 For a cognysaunce Of Mayes month they bare a souenaunce, Of a verte cocle was the resemblaunce, Tatched ryght fast. 1562 LEIGH *Armorie* 15 b, That is greene, & blased Vert. *Ibid.*, And nowe we to the fourth colour, Vert. *a* 1586 SIDNEY *Astr. & Stella* xiii, In vert field Mars bare a golden speare. 1622 PEACHAM *Compl. Gentl.* xv. (1906) 194 A plaine crosse Vert, by the name of Hussey. 1646 G. DANIEL *Poems* Wks. (Grosart) I. 44 [To] tell you how they beare Gules, or, vert, azure,—heathen words for Red, Yellow, green, blue. 1655 FULLER *Antheologia* (1867) 278 The whole field was vert or green. 1656 BLOUNT *Glossogr.* [Hence in Phillips, etc.] 1727 BAILEY (vol. II), *Vert* (in Heraldry) signifies Green, and in Graving, is expressed by Diagonal Lines, drawn from the Dexter Chief Corner, to the Sinister Base. 1815 KIRBY & SP. *Entomol.* I. (1816) I. 10 Some [insects] she [*sc.* Nature] blazons with heraldic insignia, giving them to bear in fields..vert—gules—argent and or, fesses—bars..and even animals. *c* 1828 BERRY *Encycl. Her.* I. Gloss., *Vert*, the common French term for green, and the proper heraldic term for that colour.

Vert (vǝ̄ɹt), *sb.*² Also 'vert. [Shortened f. CONVERT *sb.*, PERVERT *sb.*] A pervert or convert from one religion to another, esp. to the Roman Catholic faith.

1864 *Union Rev.* May 277 Old friends call me a pervert: new acquaintances a convert: the other day I was addressed as a 'vert...This term ''vert' I have every reason to believe has been only just coined. 1886 *Pall Mall G.* 25 May 4/2 Cardinal Manning stands alone.., and as he is an Anglican 'vert he does not count.

transf. 1886 *North Star* 5 May, Your 'vert [to Home Rule] is ever vigorous.

Vert, *v.*¹ [ad. L. *vertĕre* to turn, overturn, etc.]

†1. *trans.* To turn up, root up (the ground).

1578 *Burgh Rec. Aberdeen* (1848) II. 32 It sall be lesum to quhatsumewir personne apprehendand the said swyne.. vertand the ertht, to distroy the samen.

2. To turn in a particular direction; to turn or twist out of the normal position. Now *spec.* in *Path.* or *Anat.* Hence **Ve·rting** *ppl. a.*

c 1590 J. STEWART *Poems* (S.T.S.) II. 47 His sound..did clinck and clak, Quhair euir he verts his force And awfull face. 1659 FULLER *App. Inj. Innoc.* III. 21 When a Writer's words are madly verted, inverted, perverted, against his true intent, and their Grammaticall sense. 1883 DUNCAN *Clin. Lect. Dis. Wom.* (ed. 2) viii. 59 A lady had ulceration of the interior of the body of the uterus, which was not flexed or verted. 1903 *Med. Record* 7 Feb. 210 All of the muscles of the eyes may be relatively weak. The ducting or verting power is not as great as it should be.

3. *intr.* To change direction; to dart about.

1859 MEREDITH *R. Feveril* II. x. 198 He flew about in the very skies, verting like any blithe creature of the season.

Vert, *v.*² Also 'vert. [f. VERT *sb.*²] *intr.* To become a pervert or convert from one religion to another, esp. to Roman Catholicism.

1888 *Echo* 17 Mar. (Cassell's), As a man he is welcome to vert and re-vert as often as he pleases. 1891 *Hist. Sk. Par. St. Martin, Colchester* 7 William Murray..'verted to the Roman Church after J. H. Newman.

Vertant, *a. Her.* [a. F. *vertant*, = L. *vertent-*, *vertens*, pres. pple. of *vertĕre*: see VERT *v.*¹] Bending, curving.

1688 R. HOLME *Armoury* II. 473/1 He beareth Argent, eight Leaves, the Stalks conjoyned and contrary bowed.. But the most compendious, is to blazon them conjoyn'd dorse endorse: though good Artists will say, conjoyned and vertant to the Dextre and Sinister. *c* 1828 BERRY *Encycl. Her.* I. Gloss., *Vertant* and *Revertant*, or *Verted* and *Reverted*, the same as *flexed* and *reflexed*, or *bowed embowed*, that is formed like the letter S reverted. [Hence in later Dicts.]

Vertdegrease, Vert de grece, obs. forms of VERDIGRIS. **Verte,** southern ME. var. FART *v.*

Verteber, var. VERTEBRE.

Vertebra (vǝ̄·ɹtĭbrǎ). Pl. **vertebræ** (vǝ̄·ɹtĭbrī); also 7–8 vertebras. [a. L. *vertebra* joint, joint of the spine, f. *vertĕre* to turn. Hence It., Sp., Pg. *vertebra*, F. *vertèbre*: cf. VERTEBRE.]

1. *Anat.* and *Zool.* One or other of the joints composing the spinal column in man or other vertebrate animals; any segment of the backbone.

α. *c* 1615 CROOKE *Body of Man* (1631) 930 The vertebra in the middest receiueth that spondell which is aboue it. 1634 A. READ *Descr. Body Man* C vj/1 The transvers processe of the first vertebra. *a* 1728 WOODWARD *Fossils* (1729) I. II. 82 A large Vertebra of a Fish. 1767 GOOCH *Treat. Wounds* I. 367 The Thoracic Duct or canal runs..as far as the fifth vertebra of the back. 1788 *Encycl. Brit.* (ed. 3) I. 726 The œsophagus..terminates in the stomach about the eleventh or twelfth vertebra of the back. 1840 E. WILSON *Anat. Vade M.* (1842) 7 A Vertebra consists of a body, two laminæ, a spinous process, two transverse processes, and four articular processes. 1881 MIVART *Cat* 35 Each of these small bones is called a vertebra.

Comb. 1839 G. ROBERTS *Dict. Geol.* 180 *Vertebralis*,.. vertebra-like.

β. 1664 POWER *Exp. Philos.* I. 42 The Lamprey..hath a Cartilaginous flexible Tube or Channel, without any Vertebræ or Spondyls in it. 1666 J. DAVIES *Hist. Caribby Isles* 132 Having no vertebræ in the back-bone,..he [*sc.* the crocodile] goes straight forwards, not being able to turn. 1732 ARBUTHNOT *Rules of Diet* 362 For there be some with fewer Vertebræ in their Necks than others. 1774 GOLDSM. *Nat. Hist.* (1824) II. 140 The vertebræ of the neck [of the ourang-outang] also were shorter. 1851 S. P. WOODWARD *Mollusca* I. i. 3 A backbone, composed of numerous joints, or vertebræ. 1867 F. FRANCIS *Angling* iii. 73 The angler should..sever the vertebræ at the back of the neck.

transf. 1864 LOWELL *Fireside Trav.* 233 The shattered vertebræ of the [Roman] aqueducts.

γ. 1661 LOVELL *Hist. Anim. & Min.* Isagoge b 8 b, Their vertebra's are cartilagineous and flexile. 1667 *Phil. Trans.* II. 461 The Vertebra's descending from the Back. 1706 PHILLIPS (ed. Kersey), *Cyphoma*,..a bending backwards of the *Vertebra's*, or Turning-joynts of the Back. 1770 *Phil. Trans.* LXI. 134 It..extended..to the right ovarium, and vertebras of her back.

b. With particularizing terms.

1726 MONRO *Anat. Bones* 178 The Spine is commonly divided into true and false Vertebræ. 1771 *Encycl. Brit.* I. 169 The lumbar vertebræ, as they descend, have their oblique processes at a greater distance from each other. 1847–9 *Todd's Cycl. Anat.* IV. I. 624 The cervical vertebra..differs in this respect from the dorsal vertebra; this from the lumbar vertebra; this from the sacral vertebra; and this from the coccygeal vertebra. 1854 OWEN in *Orr's Circ. Sci.*, *Org. Nat.* I. 193 This unusually developed spine of the mesencephalic vertebra. *Ibid.* 236 In the odd-toed..ungulates, the dorso-lumbar vertebræ differ in different species. 1866 HUXLEY *Preh. Rem. Caithn.* 109 A horse's skull with its upper cervical vertebræ. 1872 — *Phys.* vii. 171 The odontoid peg of the axis vertebra.

2. *pl.* (with *the*). The vertebral column; the spine or backbone.

a 1627 MIDDLETON *Anything for Quiet Life* III. i, I will finde where his Disease of Cozenage lay, whether in the Vertebræ, or in Oscox-Index [= Os Coxendix]. *a* 1700 EVELYN *Diary* 2 May 1644, They show also the ribs and vertebræ of the same beast. 1728 CHAMBERS *Cycl.* s.v., A Weakness of the Ligaments and Muscles fasten'd to the backside of the *Vertebræ.* 1759 STERNE *Tr. Shandy* II. ix, Dr. Slop's figure, coming..waddling thro' the dirt upon the vertebræ of a little diminutive pony. 1834 McMURTRIE *Cuvier's Anim. Kingd.* 27 They are articulated at one extremity with the vertebræ. 1856 KANE *Arct. Expl.* II. xv. 160 The vertebræ of a whale similar to that at the igloë of Anoatok. 1872 HUXLEY *Phys.* i. 6 The bones thus cut through are called the bodies of the vertebræ.

fig. 1768 TUCKER *Lt. Nat.* (1834) I. 429, I should have known you for a true Search by the pliableness of your neck: the Knowals have a wonderful stiffness in the vertebræ.

b. Without article.

1849 MURCHISON *Siluria* xx. 478 Large fossil fishes with vertebræ sometimes ossified. 1861 MUSGRAVE *By-roads* 314 He had made the tour of all Europe without once leaning back in his carriage! This indicated matchless rigidity of fibre and strength of vertebræ.

3. In sing. = sense 2 *rare*⁻¹.

1791 WALKER *Pron. Dict.* s.v. 1876 J. G. WOOD *Nat. Hist.* 501 We now enter upon another vast division in which there is no true brain and no vertebra.

4. *Zool.* (See quots.)

1704 RAY *Disc.* II. iv. (1713) 182 Great Stones, and even broken Pieces of Lime-stone Rocks,..almost wholly compos'd of those *Vertebræ*, or broken Pieces of the *Radii* of Sea-Stars, which are commonly call'd Fairy-Stones. 1891 *Cent. Dict.*, *Vertebra*, in echinoderms, any one of the numerous axial ossicles of the arms of starfishes.

Vertebral (vǝ̄·ɹtĭbrǎl), *a.* and *sb.* [ad. med. or mod.L. *vertebrālis* (= F. *vertébral*, Sp., Pg. *vertebral*, It. *vertebrale*), or f. prec. + -AL.]

A. *adj.* 1. Of or pertaining to, situated on or near, the vertebræ; spinal.

1681 tr. *Willis' Rem. Med. Wks.* Vocab., *Vertebral*, belonging to the joynts of the back-bone. 1704 RAY *Creation* II. (ed. 4) 319 The carotid, vertebral and splenick Arteries are..variously contorted. 1737 BRACKEN *Farriery Impr.* (1756) I. 83 The Carotidal and the Vertebral Arteries. 1771 *Encycl. Brit* I. 218 Of the Vertebral Muscles. 1831 R. KNOX *Cloquet's Anat.* 27 Vertebral Canal..extends along the whole length of the spine, following its various curvatures. 1840 E. WILSON *Anat. Vade M.* (1842) 342 The Vertebral vein descends by the side of the vertebral artery. 1854 OWEN in *Orr's Circ. Sci.*, *Org. Nat.* I. 197 The pleurapophyses or vertebral ribs in serpents. 1887 *Encycl. Brit.* XXII. 111/2 A sort of bony canal in which runs the vertebral artery.

transf. 1824 GALT *Rothelan* I. i, The acts of..the Black Prince constitute the vertebral portion of his history.

b. *Ent.* 'Situated on or noting the median line of the upper surface' (*Cent. Dict.* 1891).

2. Composed of vertebræ; spinal. Freq. in *vertebral column.*

1822 J. FLINT *Lett. Amer.* 234 The vertebral column was completely pliant, her body..bent in every direction successively. 1847–9 *Todd's Cycl. Anat.* IV. I. 632/1 Every lesser unit of the vertebral chain. 1877 J. A. ALLEN *Amer. Bison* 449 The smaller size of the posterior part of the vertebral column in the American bison.

3. Of the nature of a vertebra.

1847–9 *Todd's Cycl. Anat.* IV. I. 648 The vertebral pieces hold their own serial order, and thus we know them. *Ibid.* 670 These two iliac bones (*c*, *c*) are homologous..to the two vertebral laminæ of A.

b. *Zool.* (See quots.)

1877 HUXLEY *Anat. Inv. Anim.* 563 [In] the Ophiuridea, ..each of these [quadrate axial] ossicles (which are sometimes termed *vertebral*) is surrounded by four plates. 1877 F. BUTLER in *Encycl. Brit.* VII. 633 The deep ambulacral grooves which occupy the middle of the lower face of each ray [in star-fishes] are formed each by a series of plates, the *vertebral ossicles.*

4. Of animals: Having a spinal column; = VERTEBRATE *a.* 1.

1816 J. SCOTT *Vis. Paris* (ed. 5) 299 Cuvier, who was the first to divide animals into vertebral and invertebral. 1822–7 GOOD *Study Med.* (1829) IV. 16 All the classes of vertebral animals possess the same number of senses as man. 1854 H. MILLER *Sch. & Schm.* xxi. (1860) 229/1 Under what peculiarities of form..vertebral life existed in the earlier ages of the world.

B. *sb.* 1. A vertebral artery or vein.

1718 J. CHAMBERLAYNE *Relig. Philos.* (1730) I. iii. § 3 We here see the Jugular Veins, and the Vertebrals. 1755 *Dict. Arts & Sci.* s.v. *Medulla*, The arteries and veins of the spinal marrow..are derived from the vertebrals of the neck, the intercostals, and the lumbar. 1880 BARWELL *Aneurism* 53 If we ligature the first part of the subclavian, ought we also to occlude the vertebral? 1899 *Allbutt's Syst. Med.* VII. 390 The arteries of the medulla oblongata..arise from the vertebrals.

2. A vertebrate animal. *rare*⁻⁰.

1828–32 WEBSTER, *Vertebral*, n., an animal of the class which have a back-bone.

3. One of the unpaired dorsal plates in the carapace of a turtle.

1883 *Encycl. Brit.* XXIII. 456 Dermal Scutes [of *Testudo pardalis*]:—*co*, costals; *v*, vertebrals; *m*, marginals.

Hence **Ve·rtebrally** *adv.*

1891 *Cent. Dict.* s.v., Segmented vertebrally; vertebrally articulated ribs.

Vertebrarte·rial, *a. Anat.* and *Zool.* [f. VERTEBR-A + ARTERIAL *a.*] Of or belonging to a vertebra and an artery; vertebro-arterial.

1884 COUES *N. Amer. Birds* 139 The series of these foramina is called the vertebrarterial canal. 1902 *Cunningham's Text-bk. Anat.* (1906) 75 The vertebrarterial foramen..is traversed by the vertebral artery and vein in the upper six vertebræ.

‖**Vertebrata** (vǝɹtĭbrēⁱ·tǎ). *Zool.* [mod.L. (Cuvier), a. L. *vertebrāta* (sc. *animālia*), neut. pl. of *vertebrātus* VERTEBRATE *a.*]

1. With *the.* A division of the animal kingdom including all animals which have a backbone or its equivalent.

1826 KIRBY & SP. *Entomol.* xxviii. III. 44 The difference here between Insects and the Vertebrata seems very wide. 1834 McMURTRIE *Cuvier's Anim. Kingd.* 232 The blood of the Mollusca..appears to contain a smaller proportionate quantity of fibrine than that of the Vertebrata. 1843 *Penny Cycl.* XXVI. 277/2 In the *Vertebrata* the brain and principal trunk or chord of the nervous system is enclosed in a bony or gristly case composed of the skull and the vertebræ. 1877 HUXLEY *Anat. Inv. Anim.* 49 Even the hiatus between the *Vertebrata* and the *Invertebrata*, is partly, if not wholly, bridged over.

2. A group or class of these; a number of vertebrate animals.

1851 D. WILSON *Preh. Ann.* IV. vii. 644 The geologist, without seeking to reanimate these extinct vertebrata, learns much regarding the past from..their colossal remains. 1855 H. SPENCER *Princ. Psychol.* (1872) I. I. i. 4 Between the water-breathing vertebrata and..air-breathing vertebrata there is an equally conspicuous unlikeness in energy. 1870 ROLLESTON *Anim. Life* 5 In every Mammalian skeleton.. the vertebrae in the trunk always differ from those of the different lower vertebrata in..the following points.

Vertebrate (vǝ̄·ɹtĭbrĕt), *a.* and *sb.* [ad. L. *vertebrāt-us* (Pliny), jointed, articulated, f. *vertebra* VERTEBRA. Cf. prec. and INVERTEBRATE.]

A. *adj.* 1. *Zool.* Of or belonging to the Vertebrata; characterized by having a backbone or spinal column. Freq. in *vertebrate animal.*

1826 KIRBY & SP. *Entomol.* xxviii. III. 42 Size forms a pretty accurate distinction between insects and the great bulk of vertebrate animals. *a* 1843 *Encycl. Metrop.* (1845) VII. 292 The passive motive Organs or Skeleton of the Vertebrate Series of Animals. 1870 GILLMORE tr. *Figuier's Rept. & Birds* Introd. 4 A bountiful Creator appears to have adopted one general plan in the organization of all the vertebrate creation. 1881 MIVART in *Nature* No. 615. 337 The highest of them, called the vertebrate sub-kingdom ..comprises ourselves, with all beasts, birds, reptiles, efts, frogs and toads, and fishes.

Comb. 1863 DANA *Man. Geol.* 276 In most of these vertebrate-tailed species the vertebral column extends into the upper lobe of the tail.

b. *Bot.* (See quot.)

1832 LINDLEY *Introd. Bot.* 390 *Vertebrate*,..when the leaf is contracted at intervals, there being an articulation at each contraction; as in Cussonia spicata.

2. Of or pertaining to, characteristic of, found in, a vertebrated animal or animals.

1848 OWEN (*title*), On the Archetype and Homologies of the Vertebrate Skeleton. 1854 H. MILLER *Sch. & Schm.* xxi. (1860) 229/1 The second age of vertebrate existence on our planet. 1857 H. SPENCER in *Westm. Rev.* Apr. 450 The earliest known vertebrate remains are those of Fishes. 1883 *Encycl. Brit.* XVI. 663/2 In the vertebrate eye, the filaments of the optic nerve penetrate the retina.

fig. 1872 MINTO *Eng. Prose Lit.* I. iii. 201 A vertebrate skeleton of the work.

3. *fig.* a. Of persons: Having connective mental powers.

1879 O. W. HOLMES *Motley* xix. 146 The archivists and annalists will pile up facts..until the vertebrate historian comes with his generalizing ideas.

b. Of writings, etc.: Connectedly put together; characterized by strength or consistency.

1882 GOSSE in Grosart *Spenser* III. p. xlvi, Ramsay's *Gentle Shepherd*..remains the most vertebrate and interesting bucolic drama produced in Great Britain. 1884 *Athenæum* 15 Nov. 635/2 The new comedy..is more than a little lachrymose and is scarcely vertebrate. 1900 *Sat. Rev.* 24 Mar. 367 We have the right..to expect something more vertebrate, if he is to take place in literature.

B. *sb.* A member of the Vertebrata; a vertebrate animal.

1826 KIRBY & SP. *Entomol.* xlv. IV. 240 The antennæ of insects are analogous to ears in Vertebrates. 1840 *Cuvier's Anim. Kingd.* 33 The general plan of their organization is not so uniform..as that of the vertebrates. 1870 F. BOWEN *Logic* vi. 155 Some wingless animals are not vertebrates.

Ve·rtebrate, *v.* [f. prec.] *trans.* To connect or join after the manner of vertebræ.

1891 in *Cent. Dict.* 1894 BLACKMORE *Perlycross* 129 As like each other as three peas vertebrated in one pod. 1910 *Q. Rev.* Jan. 69 They [*sc.* satires] were written in rough dialect and vertebrated with peasant phrases and peasant wit.

Vertebrated (vǝ̄·ɹtĭbreⁱtĕd), *ppl. a.* [f. VERTEBRATE *a.* + -ED.]

1. = VERTEBRATE *a.* 1. Freq. in *vertebrated animal(s).*

1828 STARK *Elem. Nat. Hist.* I. 371 Vertebrated animals with cold red blood, respiring by gills or branchiæ. 1835 J. DUNCAN *Beetles* (Nat. Lib.) 74 Certain relations of analogy which some of the species are thought to bear to the vertebrated tribes. 1849 SAXE *Poems* (1873) 120 One of those vertebrated vermin That lie in the grass so prettily curled. 1874 CARPENTER *Ment. Phys.* I. ii. § 57 (1879) 57 The Vertebrated series, of which Man is the highest representative.

2. Consisting of, provided with, vertebræ.

1863 DANA *Man. Geol.* 276 All these ancient fishes [Ganoids] have vertebrated tails. 1864 BOWEN *Logic* x. 323 Among inorganic bodies,..the metallic property is an instance of the former class; among animals, the possession of a vertebrated column or backbone.

3. *transf.* Constructed in a manner suggestive of vertebræ.

1840 *Civil Eng. & Arch. Jrnl.* III. 56/2 A vertebrated carriage..left the station at Euston Square with one of the trains for Birmingham. *Ibid.*, The vertebrated carriage.. adapted itself to all curves with the greatest facility.

Vertebration (vǝɹtĭbrēⁱ·ʃən). [f. VERTEBRA.]

1. Vertebral formation; division into segments like those of the spinal column. Also in fig. context.

1888 *Encycl. Brit.* XXIV. 179/2 Some writers have maintained that the vertebration of the *Vertebrata* may be understood as having reference to the segmentation of the muscles of the body-wall. 1889 *Theol. Monthly* Jan. 48 His style rather resembles a cellular tissue..which may advance by growth on many sides, rather than a..compact logical vertebration.

2. *fig.* 'Backbone'; strength or firmness.

1884 W. G. WILLS in *Pall Mall G.* 28 July 4/2 Poetry and rhetoric,..which have not the heart, life, and vertebration behind, are an impertinence and intrusion. 1892 W. S. LILLY *Gt. Enigma* 313 Doctrine is the vertebration of religion.

Vertebratist. *rare*⁻¹. [f. VERTEBRATE *sb.* + -IST.] An authority upon the spine or back-bone.

1866 *Reader* 31 Mar. 331 (Theory of the skeleton), The 'orthodox' ideas of ordinary vertebratists.

Ve·rtebre. *Anat.* and *Zool.* ? *Obs.* Also 7, 9 verteber. [a. F. *vertèbre*: see VERTEBRA. In sense 1 ad. L. *vertebrum.*]

†1. The rounded top of the thigh-bone. *Obs.*⁻¹

1541 R. COPLAND *Guydon's Quest. Chirurg.* I v, The endes of the bones of the thyghes, called vertebres.

2. = VERTEBRA 1.

α. 1578 BANISTER *Hist. Man* I. 19 b, The first Vertebre ..of the necke is more solid,..then all the bones els of the backe. 1650 BULWER *Anthropomet.* 9 That part of the neck which is next to the Atlantick Vertebre. 1692 RAY *Disc.* 109 The Vertebres of Thornbacks and other Cartilagineous Fishes. 1738 *Phil. Trans.* XL. 37 The upper extremity of the *medulla spinalis*, in the first vertebre of the neck. 1759 *Ibid.* LX. 32 A kitten..had its head cut off betwixt the first and second vertebre of the neck. 1834 CAUNTER *Orient. Ann.* viii. 107 A morah, or footstool, formed of a vertebre of some huge creature. *Ibid.* 108 The attendants brought away the jaw and half a dozen of the vertebres.

β. 1828–32 WEBSTER, *Verteber.* *a* 1843 *Encycl. Metrop.* (1845) VII. 292/2 The spine consists of a set of consecutive, cartilaginous, horny pieces,..called Vertebers.

†3. The spine; = VERTEBRA 2. *Obs.*⁻⁰

1623 COCKERAM I, *Verteber*, the chine or backe bone.

†b. *pl.* = prec. *Obs.*⁻⁰

1696 PHILLIPS (ed. 5), *Vertebers*, the whole Ridge of the Back-Bone.

Vertebriform, *a. rare.* [f. VERTEBR-A + -(I)FORM.] Having the form of a vertebra.

1847–9 *Todd's Cycl. Anat.* IV. I. 672/2 The mode in which the vertebriform scapulæ contract a connection with the costiform clavicles and coracoid bones. *Ibid.*

Vertebro- (vǝ̄·ɹtĭbro), comb. form, on Greek models, of VERTEBRA, occurring in various terms of *Anat.*, as *vertebro-arterial*, *-basilar*, *-chondral*, *-costal*, *-femoral*, *-iliac*, *-sacral*, *-sternal.*

In recent medical and other Dicts.

Ve·rted, *ppl. a. Her. rare*⁻⁰. [f. VERT *v.*¹] (See quot. *c* 1828 s.v. VERTANT *a.*)

Verte(e)go, obs. ff. VERTIGO.

†**Vertely,** *adv. Obs.*⁻¹ [After OF. *vertement*, *verdement* (15th c.) in the same sense, f. *verte* green, youthful, energetic, etc.] With activity or readiness; quickly, readily.

? *a* 1400 *Morte Arth.* 3168 Vertely the avawmwarde voydez theire horsez, In the Vertennone vale, the vines i-mangez.

†**Vertent,** *a. Obs. rare.* [ad. L. *vertent-*, *vertens*, pres. pple. of *vertĕre* to turn, etc.] *Vertent year*, a cycle of the celestial bodies, containing 15,000 solar years.

After L. *annus vertens* (Cicero *Rep.* vi. 22, 24).

1635 HEYWOOD *Hierarch.* III. 147 This great and vertent yeare is, when we see All stars and planets brought to their first station After their much and long Peregrination. 1636 — *Love's Mistress* and Prol., Who so un-read, doth not of Plato heare, His Annus Magnus, and his Vertent yeare?

Verteous, -ly, obs. forms of VIRTUOUS, -LY.

Vertew, obs. form of VIRTUE.

Vertex (vǝ̄·ɹteks). Pl. **vertices** (vǝ̄·ɹtisīz); also **vertexes.** [a. L. *vertex* whirl, whirlpool, VORTEX; crown of the head, highest point, summit, etc., f. *vertĕre* to turn. Cf. VERTICE.]

1. *Geom.* The point opposite to the base of a (plane or solid) figure; the point in a curve or surface at which the axis meets it; an angular point, as of a triangle or polygon.

1570 DEE *Math. Pref.* Cij, From the vertex, to the Circumference of the base of the Cone. 1571 DIGGES *Pantom.* IV. xxv. Hhij, A transfigured Icosaedron may be resolued into 12 Pentagonal and 20 hexagonal Pyramides, concurring with their toppes or vertices all in the centers of this transformed body. *a* 1608 DEE *Relat. Spir.* I. (1659) 355. 4 Triangles or rather Cones, of water, whose vertices rest cut off (as it were) by the middle stream of water. 1672 BOYLE *Virtues Gems* 12 So as to make six triangles, that terminated like those of a Pyramid in a Vertex. 1715 DESAGULIERS *Fires Impr.* 13 Two half Parabolas's whose Vertex's are C c. 1743 EMERSON *Fluxions* 150 In the vertices of Curves, where they cut the Abscissa at right angles. 1840 LARDNER *Geom.* ii. 17 These lines are called the sides of the angle, and the point C where the sides unite, is called its vertex. 1860 TYNDALL *Glac.* I. vii. 54 Along the two sides of a triangle, the vertex of which was near the centre of the glacier. 1882 MINCHIN *Unipl. Kinemat.* 12 The parallelogram must now be jointed at its four vertices.

b. *Optics.* (See quots.)

1704 J. HARRIS *Lex. Techn.* I, *Vertex of a Glass* (in Opticks) is the same with its Pole. 1797 *Encycl. Brit.* (ed. 3) XIII. 288 Draw the ray RC through the centre, cutting the [spherical] surface in the point V, which we shall denominate the *vertex*, while RC is called the *axis.* 1803 IMISON *Sci. & Art* I. 348 To find the vertex or centre of a lens. 1867 J. HOGG *Microsc.* I. ii. 18 The point where the axis cuts the surface is called the vertex of the lens.

c. *Astr.* (See quot.)

1876 G. F. CHAMBERS *Astron.* 922 *Vertex*.., a term used to designate that point in the limb of the Sun, the Moon, or of a planet, intersected by a circle passing through the zenith and the centre of the body.

2. The point in the heavens vertically overhead, or directly above a given place; the zenith. *Latitude* or *meridian of vertex* (see quot. *c* 1850).

1646 SIR T. BROWNE *Pseud. Ep.* II. ii. 62 The true meridian is a major circle passing through the poles of the world, and the Zenith or Vertex of any place. 1665 SIR T. HERBERT *Trav.* (1677) 5 These sorts of people freeze within the polar circles,..the Pole being their vertex, and the Æquator.. their direct Horizon. *Ibid.* 29 The heat, when the Sun comes to the Vertex, is much more intense..than it is about the Polar Circles. 1715 tr. *Gregory's Astron.* (1726) I. 346 When the Phænomenon..is in XLZ the common Azimuth ..of the two places on the Earth pitch'd upon for this purpose, whose Vertices are *X* and *Z.* 1748 *Anson's Voy.* II. v. 182 The Sun was within about three degrees of the vertex. *c* 1850 *Rudim. Navig.* (Weale) 54 Either of these points is called the *vertex* of the great circle to which it belongs; the arc intercepted between the vertex and the equator is the *latitude of vertex*; the meridian that passes through the vertex is the *meridian of vertex.* 1867 SMYTH *Sailor's Word-bk.*, *Vertex*, the zenith, the point overhead.

3. *Anat.* (and *Zool.*). The crown or top of the head; *esp.* in man, the part lying between the occiput and the sinciput.

[1615 CROOKE *Body Man* VII. ii. (1631) 434 The middle part of the scalpe..is gibbous or round;..the Latins call it *Vertex*, because in that place the haires runne round in a ring as waters doe in a whirle-poole.] 1638 A. READ *Man. Anat.* III. i. 389 *Vertex*, the crown, that which is betweene the former two, somewhat arched. 1680 S. HAWORTH *Disc. Conc. Man* 115 The middle Part between these which is Gibbose is called Vertex. 1754–64 SMELLIE *Midwif.* I. 86 [In child-birth] the crown or vertex is the first part that is pressed down, because..the bones at that part of the skull make the least resistance. 1771 *Encycl. Brit.* II. 226/2 The [Columba] turbita, with..a short bill, and a plain vertex. 1840 E. WILSON *Anat. Vade M.* (1842) 43 The skull..is divisible into four regions,—a superior region or vertex, a lateral region, an inferior, and an interior region. 1873 COUES *Birds N.W.* (1874) 281 That the young males have more or less of the vertex red or yellow, instead of an occipital crescent of scarlet. 1888 P. L. SCLATER *Argentine Ornith.* I. 137 Vertex more or less tinged with rufous.

attrib. 1899 *Allbutt's Syst. Med.* VII. 482 In these vertex cases [of tuberculous meningitis]. *Ibid.* VIII. 8 The forceps was employed fifteen times in vertex presentations.

b. *Ent.* (See quots.)

1826 KIRBY & SP. *Entomol.* III. 365 *Vertex*, the horizontal part of the *Facies*, next the front, that lies behind the eyes and between the temples. *Ibid.* 487 In *Blatta* and some other *Orthoptera* the posterior angle of the head is the vertex. 1861–2 LE CONTE *Classif. Coleoptera N. Amer.* I. Introd. p. x, The upper surface is divided into regions, the back part being called the *occiput*, the middle the *vertex*, and the anterior the *front.* 1897 W. F. KIRBY in Mary Kingsley *W. Africa* 719 *Trichomera insignata*... Face nearly smooth, shining black below the vertex.

4. The top, summit, or highest point of something, esp. a hill or structure; the crown of an arch. †Also, a high piece of land, an eminence (*obs.*).

1641 R. BROOKE *Eng. Episc.* 21, I am neere the Apex of this question, which yet (Pernassus-like) hath a double Vertex, a twofold toppe. 1691 RAY *Creation* I. (1692) 203 The great diversity of Soyls that are found there, every Vertex, or Eminency, almost affording new kinds. 1762 FALCONER *Shipwr.* III. 243 Its [an altar's] vertex thirty cubits from the ground. 1770 PENNANT *Brit. Zool.* (1777) IV. 142 *Patella vulgata*...Vertex pretty near the centre. 1811 PINKERTON *Petralogy* II. 338, I was not more than a hundred and fifty paces distant from the vertex of the cone. 1827 *Gentl. Mag.* XCVII. II. 9 A conical dome, on the vertex of which is a gilt cross. 1879 *Cassell's Techn. Educ.* I. 197/1 The highest point in the intrados is called the vertex or crown.

fig. 1865 MOZLEY *Mirac.* vi. 130 The question whether man is or is not the vertex of nature.

Vertgrees, -gres(s)e, etc., obs. ff. VERDIGRIS.

Verþe, Verþing, Verþore, Verþuorþ, southern ME. variants of FOURTH, FARTHING, FARTHER, FAR-FORTH.

†**Vertibi·lity.** *Obs.* Also 5 vertybylyte, 6 vertibilite. [ad. med.L. *vertibilitāt-*, *vertibilitās*: see next and -ITY. Cf. Sp. *vertibilidad.*] Capacity for turning or changing; changeableness, inconstancy, mutability.

1447 BOKENHAM *Seyntys* (Roxb.) 255 Whom fro servyl condycyoun fortune up hente Of hyr whele by vertybylyte And put hym in the state of hy degre. *a* 1529 SKELTON *Agst. Venemous Tongues* Wks. I. 134 Ye are so full of vertibilite, And of frenetyke folabilite. *a* 1617 P. BAYNE *On Eph.* I. 11 (1618) 268 God may..will that his creature shall sinne, being suffered to it selfe, by accident of it own liberty and vertibilitie. 1675 H. MORE in R. Ward *Life* (1710) 296 In this capacity of being United with the Matter, consists the Liberty and Vertibility of the Soul.

†**Ve·rtible,** *a. Obs.* Also 5 vertybyl. [a. OF. *vertible*, or ad. med.L. *vertibilis*, f. L. *vert-*, stem of *vertĕre* to turn: see -IBLE.] Capable of turning or being turned; changing, inconstant, mutable.

1447 BOKENHAM *Seyntys* (Roxb.) 272 By the vertybyl cours of fatal deth. 1657 J. SERGEANT *Schism Dispach't* 134 A parallel of your vertible and Wind-mill uncertainty. 1667 H. MORE *Div. Dial.* II. xx. (1713) 151 But were it not better

10–2

Supplement, p. 3873; Corrigenda, p. 4092; Spurious words, p. 4093; Books quoted, p. 4094

Supplement, p. 3873; Corrigenda, p. 4092; Spurious words, p. 4093; Books quoted, p. 4094

Vestal (ve·stăl), a. and sb. [ad. L. vestāl-is, f. Vesta.] So Sp. and Pg. vestal, It. and F. vestale.]

A. adj. 1. Vestal virgin, one of the priestesses of Vesta, bound, subsequently six in number, who had charge of the sacred fire in the temple of Vesta at Rome.

2. Of or pertaining to Vesta.

3. Resembling a priestess of Vesta in respect of chastity; chaste, pure, virgin.

4. Pertaining to, characteristic of, a vestal virgin or virgins; marked by chastity or purity.

B. sb. 1. A vestal virgin.

Vestale, obs. form of VESTRY.

Veste. [Fr.] rare. A vest.

Vestiary (ve·stiări), sb. Forms: 3-6 vesti-arie, 4 vestiare, 5 vestyarye, -iarye, 6- vesti-ary, etc.

Vestiarium, rare. [L. vestiārium, f. vesti-, vestis clothing.]

Vestiary (ve·stiări), a. [f. L. vestiāri-us.]

Vestibular (vesti·biŭlăr), a. [f. next + -AR².] Of or pertaining to, or situated in, a vestibule.

Vestibule (ve·stibiūl), sb. Also a. 7-8 vestible. [ad. L. vestibulum (hence F. vestibule, OF. vestible, It., Sp. and Pg. vestibulo), entrance-court, fore-court, vestibule.]

Vestibule, v. [f. prec.] trans. To provide or supply (a railway carriage) with vestibules; to unite by means of vestibules.

Vestibuled (ve·stibiūld), ppl. a. [f. prec. + -ED.] Of a train: Provided with vestibules. Orig. U.S.

Vestibulitis, Path. [f. VESTIBULE sb. + -ITIS.] Inflammation of the vestibule of the vulva.

Vestibulotomy, Surg. [f. as prec.: see -TOMY.] The operation of cutting or opening the vestibule of the vulva.

Vestibulum (vesti·biŭlŏm). [L.: see VESTIBULE sb.]

Vestige (ve·stidʒ), sb. [a. F. vestige, L. vestigium footstep, footprint, trace, mark, etc.]

Vestigial (vesti·dʒiăl), a. [f. L. vestigi-um (see VESTIGE) + -AL.] Of the nature of a vestige; remaining or surviving in a degenerate, atrophied, or imperfect condition or form: applied esp. in Biol.

Vestigially (vesti·dʒiăli), adv. [f. prec. + -LY².] In a vestigial fold.

Vestigian, a. and sb. rare. [f. VESTIGE + -IAN.]

Vestigiary, a. rare. [f. L. vestigi-um + -ARY¹.]

Vestigiate, v. [f. L. vestigi-um + -ATE.]

Vestigium. Pl. vestigia (-dʒiă). [L.: see VESTIGE.]

Vestigy, obs. f. VESTIGE.

Vestiment. Obs. Forms: 3-4 vestiment, 4-6 vestyment (5 -mente).

Vesting, vbl. sb. [f. VEST v. + -ING².]

Vestiment, var. VESTMENT.

Vestimentary (vestimĕ·ntări), a. [f. as prec.: see -ARY¹.] Of or pertaining to, in respect of, clothes or dress; vestiary.

Vestin, obs. form of WESTERN.

Ve·sting, vbl. sb. [f. VEST v. 3 b.] Cloth or material for making vests or waistcoats.

Vestlet. Zool. [f. VEST sb.] A sea-anemone of the genus Cerianthus, which is invested with a tube-like stem.

Vestment¹ (ve·stmĕnt), sb. Forms: α. 4 veste-ment, 4-6 vestement(e, 4-6 vestment(e, 5- vestment (7-8 vesment), etc. [a. AF. and OF. vestement (mod.F. vêtement), etc.; ad. L. vestimentum, f. vestīre to clothe.]

Vestment², rare⁻⁰. [f. VEST v. Cf. INVEST-MENT.] A right or privilege with which a person or body is invested or endowed.

Vestmented, a. [f. as prec.] Of a service: Celebrated or conducted in vestments.

Vestry¹ (ve·stri). Forms: 4-6 vestre, (6 vestere), 7 vesterie, 6-7 vestree, 6 vestrie, vestory, -urie, -urye, -ury, etc. [Prob. a. AF. *vest(i)erie, f. VEST v. + -(E)RY, substituted for OF. vestiarie, vestuarie; repr. med.L. vestiāria, vestuāria.]

Vestry², Mining. [Of uncertain origin.]

Vestryman. Also vestry-man, vestry man. [f. VESTRY sb. + 2.] A member of a parochial vestry.

Vestrymanship. The position of a vestryman.

Vestry-room. Also vestry room. [f. VESTRY sb.] The vestry of a church; the room in which a parochial vestry assembles.

Vestuous. See EASTSHIP Obs.

Vestury. Now arch. [ad. OF. vestuaire (= Fr. and Cat. vestuari, Sp. and Pg. vestuario), or med.L. vestuarium, t. vestura VESTURE sb.] A vestiary or vestry; a wardrobe. Also [many].

† **Vesturage.** Obs. [f. VESTURE sb. + AGE.] An allowance for vesture or clothing.

Vestural (ve'stiŭl), a. [f. as prec. + -AL.] Of or pertaining to vesture or clothing; vestiary.

Vesture (ve'stiŭr), sb. Also vestoure, wester (9 dial. vester), 6-7 vestur. [a. AF. and OF. vesture (mod.F. vêture), f. vestir VEST v. Cf. med.L. and It. vestura.]

I. 1. That with which a person is clothed or dressed; a. With a or pl. An article of apparel or clothing; a garment or vestment.

† **b.** Solemn investiture of a person or thing; investment.

II. 4. [See quot. under INVENTIONE.] Obs.

‡ **b.** Law. (See quot. and INVENTURE.) Obs.

Vestured, ppl. a. [f. prec.] Clothed or dressed in vesture; wearing vesture. Also transf.

Vesturer. [f. VESTURE sb. + -ER.] The keeper of the vesture of a church.

Vesturing, vbl. sb. [f. VESTURE v.]

Vesuvian (vĭsū'viăn), a. and sb. [f. Vesuvius, the name of the active volcano on the Bay of Naples in Italy. Cf. Campania Vesuvius, etc.]

A. adj. Of or pertaining to Vesuvius; esp. (a) like or resembling Vesuvius, or that of Vesuvius, in volcanic violence or power.

B. sb. **1.** = VESUVIANITE sb. 1.

2. a. Min. A silicate of aluminium, lime, and iron, or other base, occurring native; *idocrase*.

Vesuvianite. Min. [f. prec. + -ITE[1].] = VESUVIAN 2.

Vesu-viate, v., nonce-wd. [f. VESUVIUS.] To blow up.

Vesuvin (vĭsū'vĭn). Chem. [a. G. vesuvin, f. Vesuv, from its explosive properties.]

Vesyyus. Sc. Obs. [f. vesy, aphetic f. ADVISE v. + -NESS.]

Vet, sb. [Colloquial contraction for VETERIN-ARIAN or VETERINARY.] A veterinary surgeon.

Vet, v. [f. prec.] **1.** trans. To submit (an animal) to examination or treatment by a veterinary surgeon.

2. To examine or treat (a person) medically.

3. fig. To examine critically.

Vet, southern ME. var. FAT a., feet VETE v.

Vetall. obs. form of VICTUAL.

Vetayll. obs. form of VICTUAL sb.

Vetch (vetf). Forms: 4-5 feech(e, 5 fechche, fecche, 6-6 feche, 4-7 fetche, 4-8, 9 dial. fetch. [a. ONF. veche, veche, veiche, teiche, — OF. vece, vece, vesse (mod.F. vesce).—L. vicia, science also It. veccia.]

1. The bean-like fruit of various species of the leguminous plant *Vicia*.

2. pl. Plants belonging to the genus *Vicia*, the common tare.

Vetch, v., rare. [f. VETCH sb.]

Vetchling (ve'tʃlĭŋ). Bot. Also 6 vitchlings, 7 fotchling. [f. VETCH + -LING.]

Veteran (ve'tĕrăn), sb. and a. Also [F. veteran (F. vétéran), Sp. and Pg. veterano), and L. veter-, veterano, veteran-us (whence It. veterano, Sp. and Pg. veterano); a. L. veteranus old, f. veter-, vetus old.]

A. sb. **1.** One who has had long experience in military service; an old soldier.

2. Of persons in general: Grown old in service; experienced by long usage or practice.

Veterance v. U.S.A. trans. To render a veteran.

Veteranize v. U.S.A. a. trans. To make into a veteran. b. intr. To re-enlist as a soldier.

Veterascent, a. rare—1. [ad. pres. pple. of L. veterascere to grow old.] Growing old.

† **Veterate,** a. Obs. rare. [ad. L. veterat-us, f. veter-, vetus old.] 1. Of long standing; inveterate. 2. Having the authority of age or antiquity.

Veterated, a. Obs.—1.

Veteratorian, a. Obs.—1. [f. late L. veterātor.]

† **Veteratorian,** a. Obs.—1. [f. veterātor an old hand.]

Vetere, southern ME. variant of FETTER sb.

Vetere, obs. form of VETERAN.

Veterinarian (vetĕrinɛˈriăn), sb. and a. [f. L. veterīnāri-us (see next) + -AN.]

A. sb. **1.** One who is skilled in, or professionally occupied with, the medical and surgical treatment of cattle and domestic animals; a veterinary surgeon.

B. adj. = VETERINARY a.

Veterinary (vetĕˈrinǎri), a. and sb. [ad. L. veterīnāri-us, f. veterīnae beasts of burden.]

A. adj. Of or pertaining to, connected or concerned with, the medical or surgical treatment of cattle and domestic animals.

B. sb. = VETERINARIAN sb. 1.

Veterity. Obs.—1.

Vetitive (ve'titiv), a. rare—1. [f. L. vetit-, pa. ppl. stem of vetāre to forbid.] Amounting to a veto.

Vetiver (ve'tivǎr). Also -vayr, -vert, ttt- [ad. F. vétiver, ad. Tamil vettivēru (f. vēr root).] = CUSCUS[2].

Veto (vī'tō), sb. Pl. -toes. [a. L. veto I forbid (1st pers. sing. pres. ind. of vetāre), the word by which the Roman tribunes of the people opposed measures of the Senate or actions of the magistrates. Hence also F., Sp., Pg., It. veto.]

Veto (vī'tō), v. [f. prec.] trans. To put a veto on, to refuse consent to; to stop or block by this means.

Vetour, obs. form of VETTURINO.

Vetticare. rare. [ad. It. vetticare.]

Vettura (vettū'ra), sb. [It. vettura.] In Italy: One who lets out carriages or horses on hire; also, a driver of a vettura.

Vetturino (vetturī'no), sb. [It.]

Vetus, obs. var. of VETUST a.

Vetust (vĭtʌst), a. Obs. rare. [ad. L. vetust-us old, ancient.] Old, ancient.

Vetustness. Obs. rare.—1.

Vetusty. rare—1. [ad. L. vetustas, f. vetustus.] Antiquity.

Veuglaire. Obs. [a. F.]

Veve, southern dial. var. FEW a. VEWAR, obs. Sc. f. VIVER, a fishpond. VEWE, southern ME. f. VIEW. Vewlie, obs. VIEWLY. Vewter (in hunting): see FEWTERER, and cf. VENTERER Obs.

Vex, sb. [f. the vb.] **1.** A state or cause of vexation or grief. **2.** transf. and fig.

Vex, v. [a. F. vexer, ad. L. vexāre to shake, agitate, trouble, annoy.]

1. trans. To trouble, afflict, or harass (a person, etc.) by aggression, encroachment, or other interference with peace and quiet.

2. To grieve, afflict, or distress physically; to affect with pain or suffering. Now dial.

3. To distress or trouble (a person) in mind; to feel or cause to feel annoyance, vexation, or irritation; to cause (one) to fret, grieve, or feel indignant.

b. In pa. pple. freq. const. at or with.

Vexable (ve'ksăb'l), a. rare. [ad. L. vexābilis.]

Vexation (veksē'ʃən). Forms: 5-6 vexacyon, -cione, -cyoun, -cyoune; 6 vexacyon, 6 vexacioun. [a. F. vexation (14th cent.), ad. L. vexātiōn-em, f. vexāre. Cf. Sp. vejacion, It. vessazione.]

1. The action of troubling or harassing by aggressive or hostile measures; the fact of being troubled or harassed in this way.

VEXATIOUS ... *Vexatiously* ... *Vexatiousness* ... *Vexatory* ... *Vexation* ... *Vexed* ...

VEXILLATION ... *Vexedly* ... *Vexer* ... *Vexful* ... *Vexil* ... *Vexillar* ... *Vexillary* ... *Vexation* ...

VEXILLATOR ... *Vexillifer* ... *Vexillum* ... *Veyre* ... *Vezant* ... *Vezon* ... *Via* ... *Vexing* ... *Vexingly* ... *Vexor* ... *Vey* ... *Veygne* ... *Veyne* ...

VIAL ... *Via* ... *Viability* ... *Viable* ... *Viaduct* ... *Viage* ... *Viador* ... *Vial* ...

VIAL ... *Viand* ... *Viander* ... *Viandry* ... *Viatour* ...

VIATICUM ... *Viandry* ... *Viary* ... *Viatic* ... *Viatica* ... *Viatical* ... *Viaticum* ... *Viander* ...

VIATOR ... *Viator* ... *Viatore* ... *Viatory* ... *Vibex* ... *Vibrable* ... *Vibracula* ... *Vibraculoid* ... *Vibraculum* ...

VIBRATE ... *Vibrancy* ... *Vibrant* ... *Vibrate* ... *Vibrated* ...

Vicarious (vəi-, vikē·riəs), a. [f. L. vicari-us adj. and sb., f. vic-is change, turn, stead, office, etc.: see -OUS.]

1. That takes or supplies the place of another thing or person; substituted instead of the proper thing or person.

2. Of a person; Endured or suffered by one person in place of another; accomplished or attained by the substitution of some other person, etc., for the actual offender.

3. Of power, authority, etc.: Exercised by one person, or body of persons, as the representative or deputy of another.

4. Performed or achieved by means of another, or by one person, etc., on behalf of another.

5. Possessed or enjoyed in place of, or in succession to, another.

a. Of qualities, etc.: Possessed by one person but reckoned to the credit of another.

b. Of methods, principles, etc.: Based upon the substitution of one person for another.

6. Physiol. Denoting the performance by or through one organ of functions normally discharged by another; substituted.

Vicariously (vəi-, vikē·riəsli), adv. [f. prec. + -LY[2].]

1. By substitution of one thing or person for another; by means of a substitute.

2. As a substitute for another.

Vicarship (vi-kər-ʃip). rare⁻¹. [f. VICAR + -SHIP.] The office or position of a vicar.

Vicarly, a. Obs.⁻¹ [VICAR + -LY[1].] Holding the position of a vicar.

Vicarship. Also 6 -shyp, vycarship/pe. [f. VICAR + -SHIP.] The office or position of a vicar, in various senses of the word.

Vicary, sb.[1] Obs. Forms: 4-5 vicarie (4 vik-), -aryə, 4-6 vycary (4 -arye), -cary (-arie), 5 -ary, 5 vykary. 8. 4-5 vicorie, vicoorie (4 vycorye, vecory, 6 vicoorye. 7. 4 vi(o)kary, 5 vekery. [ad. L. vicāri-us VICAR.]

1. = VICAR 1 and 1 b.

2. = VICAR 2.

3. = VICAR 3.

Vice (vəis), sb.[1] Forms: 3- vice (5-6 Sc. vyis, 4-5 vyse, 4-6 vys, vise, wise, 5 vyis, vijs (vyhis, 5- Sc. wys. 5 wyse. AF. and OF. vice (mod.F. vice, = It. vici, Sp. and Pg. vicio, 1t. vizio), ad. L. vitium fault, defect, failing, etc.]

1. Depravity or corruption of morals; evil, immoral, or wicked habits or conduct; indulgence in degrading pleasure or practices.

2. A character in a morality play representing one or other vice; hence, a stage jester or buffoon.

3. Moral fault or defect (without implication of serious wrongdoing); a flaw in character or conduct.

4. Personified.

5. A fault, defect, blemish or imperfection, the action or procedure or in the constitution of a thing.

b. A physical defect or blemish; a deformity; a taint, imperfection, or weakness in some part of the system.

c. Const. of (the vice in question).

6. Viciousness, harmfulness.

7. Comb. a. With pa. pples., as vice-blotten, -corrupted, -created, -haunted, -polluted, -worn; also vice-sick.

Vice (vəis), sb.[2] Forms: (4 vis, vise), 4-6 vys (also mod.F.), vis, vijs, vice, 4-5 vyse, 5-7 vyse (6 fyces), 5- vice. [a. L. vis (also mod.F.), vis, vijs, tic.—1, vitz, vine, with reference to the spiral growth of the tendrils.]

1. A winding or spiral staircase. Obs. exc. arch.

2. The case or shaft of a spiral stair. rare.

3. A screw. Obs.

4. A tool or instrument of the nature of a screw, used for pressing, crushing, or holding anything tightly; spec. an instrument having two jaws closed by means of a screw.

5. A tool composed of two jaws, opened and closed by means of a screw, which firmly grip and hold a piece of work in position while it is being filed, sawn, or otherwise operated upon; used especially by workers in metal or carpenters.

b. A screw-stopper.

†b. A mechanical contrivance or device by which some power of apparatus, etc., is worked.

†c. A spoiled or vitiated condition. Obs.

†d. A clasp or fastening for a hood. Obs.

VICE. 178 **VICE.**

6. A tool used for drawing lead into grooved rods for lattice windows.

Vice (vəis), sb.[3] Also 4 vyis, vyse, 4-5 vyse (4 vise), 5 vyce. [a. OF. vis (mod.F. vis).] One who acts in the place of another; a substitute or deputy.

Vice, sb.[4] Obs. exc. dial. Also 4 vyse, 6 Sc. wise, vyse, 9 dial. vise. [Aphetic f. avise, arys, etc., ADVICE.] Counsel; advice.

Vice, sb.[5] T. Univ. Text. Low t. ii. [Sensel 1, to Now thou comest goodly by thyn owne vys, to comforts me with wordes.] 9 vyce (see VICE 5 of vicet Glass. (E.D.S.) 40 Vice, or Vise, advice.

† **Vice,** sb.[6] Obs. Also 5 vyse, 6 vise. [Aphetic f. DEVICE.] Design, figure, device.

Vice (vəis), v.[1] Obs. exc. dial. Also 4 vyse, 5-6 wyse, 6 vyse (vise), Sc. wyis, vice. [ad. L. vitiāre, f. vitium: see VICE sb.¹]

1. trans. To make vicious, deprave, corrupt; to vitiate.

2. Turn (in sequence or alternation). Obs.

Vice (vəis), v.[2] [f. VICE sb.²]

1. trans. To fix on with a screw. Obs.

2. To force, strain, or press hard as by the use of a vice; to fix, jam, or squeeze tightly.

3. intr. To employ or apply a vice. rare⁻¹

b. intr. To employ or apply a vice. rare⁻¹

Vice (vəis), v.[3] [f. VICE sb.³]

1. trans. [L. vice: see VICE sb.⁵] To fix on with a screw.

2. To perform the office or duty of, to act as substitute or deputy for.

Vice (vəis), v.[4] [ad. L. vitiāre, f. vitium.]

Vice (vəis), adv., prep. and sb. [L. vice, abl. of vicis (gen. sing.), change, turn, stead, place, etc.]

1. Stead or place (of another). Now rare.

2. In place of (another person).

Vice (vəis), a.[2] Chiefly Sc. [a. L. vice, abl. of vicis (gen. sing.), change, turn, stead, place, etc.]

Vice-admiral. Also 6 Sc. wice admerall, weis admirall, 6 vicea.-, vicadmirall, orall. [a. AF. vice-admiral (OF. visamiral, F. vice-amiral): see VICE- and ADMIRAL. So It. vice-ammiraglio, Sp. and Pg. vice-almirante.]

1. A naval officer ranking next to an admiral.

2. Vice-admiralty court (see quot. 1867).

Vice-admiralty. [f. prec.+ -TY. Cf. F. vice-amiral.] The office or jurisdiction of a vice-admiral (in sense 1 b); an area under the jurisdiction of a vice-admiral. Court of vice-admiralty, see vice-admiralty court.

Vice-chamberlain. [VICE-.] A subordinate or deputy chamberlain; spec. an officer of the Royal Household under the Lord Chamberlain.

Vice-chancellor. Forms: 5 viohaun-celler, 6 vychancellor, vychancelar (-ler), 6-7 vice-chancellor, vice-chauncelour, etc. [a. AF. vice-chanceler, etc.; see VICE- and CHANCELLOR. So It. vicecancelliere, Sp. vicecanciller.]

1. The deputy or representative of an ecclesiastical chancellor; spec. the cardinal at the head of the Papal Chancery.

2. The acting representative of the Chancellor of a university, usually the head of a college specially appointed to the office for a limited time, or the principal of the university.

Vice-consul. [VICE-.] An officer subordinate to a consul; spec. one who acts as consul in some small port, or who assists the consul of a larger district.

b. spec. One of the higher judges in the former Court of Chancery.

Vice-chancellorship. The office or dignity of a vice-chancellor; the period during which this is held.

Vice-consul. [VICE-CONSUL 2 and CONSUL.]

Vice-consulate. [VICE-CONSUL 2 and CONSULATE.] The district or jurisdiction of a vice-consul.

Vice-consulship.

Vice-county. [VICE-, after med.L. vice-, vicecomitatus: see VICE and COUNTY.]

† **Vice-count.** Obs. [VICE-, after med.L. vicecomes.]

† **Vice-countess.** [VICE-, after med.L.]

† **Vice-ountess-ship.** † **Vice-county-ship.**

Supplement, p. 3873; Corrigenda, p. 4092; Spurious words, p. 4093; Books quoted, p. 4094

Vicegerence. Now *rare*. [Cf. next and -ENCE. So older F. *vicegerence* (1601 in Du Cange), It. *vicegerenza*.]

1. The office, dignity, or rule of a vicegerent; the fact of ruling or administering as representative of another.

2. Vicarious nature or character. *Obs.*

Vicegerent. (*vəisˈdʒiˈrɛnt*), *sb.* and *a.* Also 6 vite-, 7 vise-gerent, etc. [ad. med.L. *vicegerent-*, *vicegerens*, l. la *vicem* (acc.) stead, place, office, etc., and *gerent-*, pple. of *gerĕre* to carry, hold. So F. *vicegérent* (also -*gérant*), It. Sp., Pg. *vicegerente*. The hyphen, formerly not uncommon, is now rarely used in this and the preceding words.]

A. *sb.* **1.** A person appointed by a king or other ruler to act in his place or exercise certain of his administrative functions.

2. Applied to magistrates and rulers as representatives of the Deity.

3. Applied to priests, and *spec.* to the Pope, as representatives of God or Christ.

Vicegerency, *rare*.

Vice-governor. One of several acting under, or in place of, a governor; a deputy-governor.

Vicegerentship.

Vice-king. One who rules as the representative of a king; a viceroy. Also *attrib.*

Vice-legate. [VICE-, after F. *vice-légat* or l. *vicelegāt-* (Sp. and Pg. *vicelegado*).] One who acts as the representative or deputy of a (Papal) legate.

Vice-legateship. Hence **Vice-le'gateship.**

Viceless (*vəisˈlɛs*), *a.* [f. VICE *sb.*¹ 1.] Free from vice.

Vice-like. Also U.S. **vise-like.** Resembling (that of) a vice; firmly tenacious or compressive.

Vice-rector. [VICE-. Cf. F. *vice-recteur*.]

Vicegodhead. Hence **Vice-godhead.**

Viceni'mal, Sc. *Law.* [f. L. *vicēni-um*: see next. Cf. L. *vicennālis*, f. *vicennium*.] Extending to twenty years.

Vice-president. [VICE-. So F. *vice-président* and Pg. *vicepresidente*.] One who acts as the representative or deputy of a president (in various senses); an official ranking immediately below a president.

Hence **Vice-presi'dential.**, **Vice-president'ship.** Also **Vice-pre'sidency.**

Vice-queen. [VICE-.] **a.** A woman ruling as the representative of a queen. **b.** the wife of a viceroy. (Cf. VICERINE.)

Viceregal, *a.* [f. VICE- + REGAL *a.*, after VICE-ROY *sb.*] Of or pertaining to, associated with, a viceroy.

Hence **Vice-re'gally** *adv.*

Vice-regent. [VICE-. Cf. F. *vice-régent*.]

Viceroy (*vəisˈroi*), *sb.* Also 6–7 -roye, -roie, viceroye; 6-7 -roy. [a. OF. *vis-roy*, *vice-roy* (mod.F. *vice-roi*, Sp., Pg. *vi-rey*, -*rei*, It. *vicere* + *roi* king. So It. *viceré*.]

1. One who acts as the governor of a country, province, etc., in the name and by the authority of the supreme ruler; a deputy king.

Hence **Vicero'ydom.**, **Vicero'yship.**

Viceroyal, *a.*

Viceroyalty.

Vicerine, *rare*.

VICESIMAL. 182 VICINE. VICINITY. 183 VICIOUS.

Vicesimal. (*vəiˈsɛsiˌməl*), *a.* *rare*. [f. L. *vicēsimus* twentieth, f. *vicēnsi-*: see VIGESIMAL.]

Vice-treasurer. [VICE-.] One who acts as the deputy or representative of a treasurer; *spec.* an official acting in this capacity in the government of Ireland.

Hence **Vice-tre'asurership.**

Viety. *rare*. [App. f. VICE *sb.*¹ + -TY, for the sake of rime.]

Vice versa (*vəiˈsi vəˈsa*), *adv. phr.* Also *vice versá* [L. (also *versā vice*), from *vice*, abl. of *vicis* turn, place, course, and *versā*, abl. sing. fem. of *versus*, pa. pple. of *vertĕre* to turn. So F. *vice versa*, Sp., Pg., It. *vice versa*, *viceversa*.] With a reversal or transposition of the main items in the statement just made; contrari-wise, conversely.

Vice-warden. [VICE-.] A deputy warden (esp. of the Stannaries or the Borders).

Hence **Vice-wa'rdenry**, -ship.

Vichy. [F.: The name of a town in the department of Allier in Central France, used *allusively* to designate a mineral water obtained from springs there.]

Vicinage (*vəiˈsinədʒ*). Also *Obs.* or *dial.* vicenage, visinage. [a. OF. *visenage* (*visnage*), *vicinage*, or *voisinage* (see VOISINAGE), which is assimilation of the stem to the original *L. vicīn-us* (: see VICINITY).]

1. A number of places lying near to each other taken collectively; an area extending to a limited distance round a particular spot; a neighbourhood.

2. Neighbouring, adjacent, near.

Vicinal. (*vəiˈsinəl*, *visəˈnal*), *a.* [ad. L. *vicīnālis*, f. *vicīn-us* neighbour. So OF. and F. *vicinal*.]

1. Belonging to neighbours or neighbourhood.

2. *Vicinal* way or road, a local common way as distinguished from a highway; a by-road or cross-road.

Vicine (*vəiˈsəin*), *a.* and *sb. rare.* [ad. L. *vicīn-us* neighbouring, near.]

Vicinity (*viˈsiniti*), *sb.* [ad. L. *vicīnitās*, *vicīn-us*: see prec. and -ITY. So It. *vicinità*, *vicindad*.]

1. The state, character, or quality of being near in space; propinquity, proximity.

2. Nearness in degree or quality; close relationship or connexion; close relation.

3. Neighbouring, adjacent, near.

Vicinous. [f. L. *vicīn-us*: see VICINE and -OUS.] Extending to immediately adjoining things.

Vicine. *a.* Now *rare*. Also 6 vyeune, 7 vicine.

Viciosity, variant of VITIOSITY.

Vicious (*vəiˈʃəs*), *a.* Forms: *a.* 4- vicious (5–6 -ouse, -os), 4 vicyous, 6 vycyous (5 -ouse), 5 vyciouse, 6 vycious (4 -owse, -ouse), 5 vysyous; 4-5 vicious (4 vyoios). *b.* 4- vicious (4 vicius), 5- vicious (*vitious*), 6 vicyous, *vitious* such.

I. 1. Of habits, practices, etc.: Of the nature of vice; contrary to moral principles; depraved, immoral, bad.

2. Of conduct, etc.: Of the nature of vice; contrary to moral rectitude.

3. Falling short of, or varying from, what is morally or practically commendable; reprehensible, blameworthy, mischievous.

4. Of animals (*esp.* horses): Inclined to be savage or dangerous, or to bad temper; not submitting to be thoroughly tamed or broken-in.

5. Of feeling or expression: Spiteful, malignantly bitter or severe.

Victual (vit'l), *sb.* Forms: a. 4–6 vitaile, vitail(e ...

Victoryless, *a.* [-LESS.] Lacking victory.

Victress (vi'tres). [f. L. *victor* + -ESS.] A female victor; a victress.

Victrice. Also 5 victrych, 6–9 *pa.* victris. [ad. OF. *victrice* or L. *victrix*; *victrice*; see next.]

Victrix (vi'triks). [L. *victrix*, fem. of *victor* VICTOR.] A female victor; a victress.

VICTORY.

a. With *the*, as in the phr. *to have (get, win) the victory*. ...

b. Without article.

c. *personif.*

d. Used interjectionally as an expression of triumph or encouragement. (cf. VICTORIA 1.)

2. An instance or occasion of overcoming an adversary in battle, etc.; a triumph gained by force of arms. ...

3. Supremacy or superiority, triumph or ultimate success, in any contest, struggle, or enterprise.

a. With *the*, or in *pl.*, etc.

VICTUAL.

† A female victor; a victress.

b. Produce of the ground capable of being used as food. *Obs.*

† b. *Clerk of the victuals*, = *clerk of the market*, a mote). *Obs.*

2. *pl.* Animals serving for food. *Obs.*

a. An article of food. *Obs.*

† b. Military stores; munitions of war. *Obs.*

Victual (vit'l), *v.* Forms: a. 4–5 vitaile β. 5 vitaill, 5-ayle, -ayle 6 vitaill 5- vittaile ...

1. *trans.* To supply or furnish (a ship, castle, garrison, body of troops, etc.) with victuals, esp. with a store to last for some time.

b. To lay in or obtain a supply of victuals.

VICTUALAGE.

Victualage, *rare.* [f. VICTUAL *sb.*] Victualling; victuals.

Victualler (vit'lǝr), *sb.* a. 4 vit-, 4,6 vittailler, 5–6 vitaile (6 vitt-), 6 vi(c)tayler (vict-) ...

VICTUALLING-OFFICE.

Victualling-office. [f. as prec.] An office concerned with the victualling of ships, esp. for the Royal Navy.

VICUNA.

‖ **Vicuña** (vikū·nˌɑ), vicuna. Forms: a. 7 becunia, 7- vicuna, 8–9 vicunia, 9va-, vecuna, vicugna, 9- vecuña. β. 7 vigonia, 9 vicune. [a. Sp. *vicuña* (Pg. *vicunha*), ad. Quichuan name of the animal, VIGOGNE, VIGONE.]

1. A South American animal (*Auchenia vicunna*), closely related to the llama and alpaca, inhabiting the higher portions of the northern Andes and yielding a fine silky wool used for textile fabrics.

2. *attrib.* and *Comb.*, as *vicuña-fur*, *-wool*; *vicuña-cloth*, cloth made of vicuña-wool (hence *ellipt. vicuña-*(*costume*)).

VIDUATE

Viduate (vi·diuǝt), *a. and sb.* [ad. L. *viduātus*, pa. pple. of *viduāre* to bereave, deprive, f. *vidua* widow.]

1. *adj.* Widowed.

2. Widowed.

Vide (vai·di), *v. imp.* [L. *vidē*, imp. sing. of *vidēre* to see.] 'See', refer to, consult'; a direction to the reader to refer to some other heading, passage, or work.

Videlicet (vide·liset, vi·-), *adv.* and *sb.* [L. *vidēlicet*, f. *vidēre licet* it is permissible to see.]

Vidimus (vai·diməs), *sb.* [L., = 'we have seen', 1st pers. *pl. perf.* of *vidēre* to see. So F. *vidimus* (from 14th c.).]

Vidonia (vidǝu·niǝ), [Of doubtful origin.]

Viduage (vi·diuǝdʒ), [f. L. *vidua* widow + -AGE.] Widowhood.

Vidual (vi·diuǝl), *a.* [ad. med. L. *viduāl-is*, f. *vidua* widow. So OF. *vidual.*]

Viduate (vi·diuǝt), *v.* [f. L. *viduāt-*, ppl. stem of *viduāre*: see VIDUATE *a.*]

Viduated, *ppl. a.* Left widowed, desolate, or destitute.

Viduation. *rare.* The state of being widowed or bereaved.

Viduity, *obs. or arch.* Widowhood; the time during which a woman is a widow; widowhood.

Viduous (vidiu,ǝs), *a. rare.* Empty, unoccupied.

Vie, *sb.* Also 4, 6 vye, vys, vie, vi.

Vie, *v.[1]* An account of the life of a saint.

Vie, *v.[2]* Way of, or put in life.

Vie, *sb.[3]* Also 6–7 vy.

Vidual, *a. Sc.* form of WIDOW.

Vidual, *ppl.* see prec.

Viduæne, *a.* Belonging to the *Viduinæ* or widow-birds.

Vie, *sb.* and *v.*

Vieing (vai,iŋ), *vbl. sb.* and *ppl. a.*

Vielle (vi,ɛl), *sb.* A musical instrument with four strings played by means of a small wheel; a hurdy-gurdy.

Vienna (vi,ɛnɑ), *sb.* The name of the capital of Austria used in various collocations.

Viennese (vi,ɛni·z), *sb.* and *a.* A native or an inhabitant of Vienna.

Vier (vai·ǝr), *rare.* [f. VIE *v.*] One who or that which vies with another.

Vierd, southern ME. variant of FAT *n.[1]*

Vierdour, variant of VERDOUR *Obs.*

Vierge, var. VERGE *sb.[1]*

Viess, var. VIES *v.*

View (viu), *sb.* Forms: 4–6 vewe, 5–7 veue, vue; 5, 7 vewes, 5–7 vewe; 5–8 vieu, 6 vieue, 8 vieu, etc.; 6 veue, 7 veue, pl. *v.*; 6–7 view.

View (viu), *v.* Forms: 6–7 vewe (6 view), vewe, vu; 6–viewe (6 views), 6 vieu; [f. the *sb.*]

Viewer. Also 5 **vywer**, 5-6 **vewer**, 6 **vewar**. [f. VIEW v. + -ER.]

Viewed, a. rare—¹. [f. VIEW sb.] Inclined or given to views or theories.

Viewably, adv. [f. next.] Visibly.

View-halloo (viū-ha·lō)

Viewly (viū·li), a. Now only dial. [f. VIEW sb. + -LY.]

View-point. Also **viewpoint.**

Viewy (viū·i), a. [f. VIEW sb.]

Viewiness (viū·inės)

Viewing, vbl. sb. [f. VIEW v.]

Viewless, a. [f. VIEW sb. or v.]

Vif, southern ME. var. FIVE; obs. Sc. f. WIFE.

Vifda, var. VIVDA, Sc. ... Vifelie, var. VIVELY adv. Obs.

Vig, southern dial. var. FIG sb. and v.

Vigesimal (vai·dże·simăl), a. [f. L. vigesim-us]

Vigenary, a. rare—¹. [f. L. vigēni-, var. of vicēni-]

Vigesm- see VICES-.

Vigentes (vai·dże·ntiz)

Vige-milon-qua-rto. = TWENTYFORMO.

Vigeur, obs. form of VIGOUR.

† Vigia (viǵa). [Sp. or Pg. vigia a lookout, etc.] A warning on a sea chart to denote some hidden danger.

† Vigi·dity. Obs.—¹. [Irreg. f. L. vig-ēre to flourish.]

Vigil (viǵil). Forms: 4-6 **vigile**, 4-6 **vygyle**, 5 **vigell**, 5-6 **vygyll**, 5 vigell, vygyll, wygell, 6 vyggyll, 6-7 vigill, 6 AF. and F. (also mod.F.) vigilia—L. vigilia watch, watchfulness, wakefulness, f. vigil awake, alert. Cf. VIGILANT.]

Vigilance. Obs. [ad. L. vigilant-.]

Vigilancy. Obs. [f. vigilant: see next and -ANCY.]

Vigilant (viǵilănt), a. [ad. L. vigilant-, vigilāns, pres. pple. of vigilāre to keep awake, f. vigil awake.]

† Vigilante. Obs. rare—¹.

Vigilant. a. U.S. Also pl. **vigilantes.**

Vigilantial, a.

Vigilantly, adv. [f. VIGILANT a. + -LY.]

Vigilantness. Obs. rare—¹.

Vigily. Obs. Also 5 vigile, rigilye. [var. VIGIL sb.]

Vigilion (viǵilion), a. rare—¹. [f. L. vigil wakeful, watchful + -OUS.] Of or pertaining to the vigil.

Vigini-. = VICENA. Also 7 vigine.

Vigintangular. rare—¹.

† Vigintivirate. Rom. Hist. Obs.

Vignette (viṅ·ne·t), n. Also 5 vigneron, 6 vigneroun, 7 vigneron. [f. F. vigneron.] One who cultivates grape vines: a wine-grower.

Vignetter (viṅe·tē). [f. VIGNETTE sb.]

Vignetting, vbl. sb.

Vignettist (viṅe·tist). [f. VIGNETTE + -IST.]

Vignette (viṅ·ne·t), n. [a. F. vignette]

Vignoble. Obs. rare. Also 5 vygnoble. [a. F. vignoble, L. vinea-.] A vineyard.

Vigogne (viṅ·gōn). [a. F. vigogne]

† Vigone. Obs. [ad. F. vigogne: see prec.]

Vigoroso (vigorō·sō), a.

Vigorous (viǵorus), a. Forms: 4-7 vigorous, 5-6 vigorouse, 5-6 vygorous, 4 vigerous, etc. [a. OF. vigoros, -us (mod.F. vigoureux)]

Vigorously, adv. [f. VIGOROUS a. + -LY.]

Vigour (viǵə̄), sb. Forms: 4- vigour, 4-5 vigoure, 4-6 vigor, 5 wygour, 5-6 vygour, etc. [a. AF. vigur, vigour, OF. vigor (mod.F. vigueur)]

Vigorousness. The quality or state of being vigorous; vigorous condition.

‖ Villanella (vilǎne·lǎ). Pl. **-elle**. [It., fem. of *villanello* rural, rustic, f. *villano* : see VILLAIN sb. and a.] (See later quot.)

Villanelle (vilǎne·l). *a.* f. *villanella* : see prec.

‖ Villanette. *rare.* [f. VILLAN + -ETTE.] A little villa.

Villar (vi·lǎr), sb. and a. *rare.* [ad. L. *villāris*, f. *villa* VILLA : see -AR.] A. sb. A peasant holding land in the feudal vill; a villein. B. adj. Pertaining or relating to, concerned with, the feudal vill or villa.

Villarsite (vilā·rsǎit), Min. [f. F. *villarsite*, name of the French botanist D. *Villars* (1745–1814) : named in 1842 by Dufrenoy.] A hydrous silicate of magnesium occurring massive or in rounded grains at Traversella, Piedmont.

Villate (vi·lǎt). Hist. [ad. med.L. *villāta*, f. *villa* VILLA.] A feudal territorial division consisting of a number of *villæ*.

Villatic (vilæ·tik), a. [ad. L. *villāticus*, f. *villa* VILLA.] Of or pertaining to a villa or, or the inhabitants, a *vill*. (after the original sense of) rural, rustic, f village.

Villein (vi·lǎn, ·lĕin). *a.* and *sb. Hist.* Forms: a. 4 *villein*, 5 *vileyn*, 6 *veleyn*, 6 *vyllayne*, 6–7 *villeyne*, 6– *villein*. β. 5 *vylayn*, 5–6 *vyllayn(e*, 5–7 *villayne*, 6– *villaine*. γ. 5 *vylayn*, 5–6 *villane*, 6– *villan*. [a. AF. *villein*, *villain*, etc., VILLAIN.]

Villeinage (vi·lǎnĕdʒ). *Now Hist.* Forms: a. 4–9 *villenage* (6 *vyllenage*, *vyllynage*, *veelenage*), 5 *villanage*, 6–9 *villanage*, 7– *villeinage*. β. 6 *villinage*. γ. 7– *villenage*, etc. [a. AF. *villenage*, *villanage*, OF. *vilenage*, *vilainage*, *villen-age*, *villain-age*, *vill(e)inage*, *vill(a)nage*, *villainage*, *vilen-age*, *vill(e)nage*, from the same source : see VILLEIN and -AGE.]

Villeiness (vi·lǎnĕs). *rare.* [f. VILLEIN + -ESS.] A female villein.

† Villeining. *Obs.—¹* = VILLENAGE.

Villenous, -enye, obs. varr. VILLAINOUS a.

Villenie, -enye, obs. varr. VILLAINY. Villi, pl. of VILLUS.

† Villicated, ppl. a. [f. L. *villicāt-*, ppl. stem of *villicāre* to act as bailiff.]

‖ Villication [ad. L. *villicātiō*.]

Villiche, obs. form of VILLELY adv.

Villiform (vi·lifǫrm), a. Zool. [ad. mod.L. *villiformis* : see VILLUS and -FORM.] So f. *villiforme.*

Villose (vi·lōᵘs), a. = VILLOUS.

Villosity (vilǫ·sĭti). [ad. L. type *villōsitās* : see prec. and -ITY.] **1.** *Bot., Zool.,* etc. The condition or fact of being villose or villous.

Villous (vi·lǎs), a. Also 5–7 *villose*, 6–7 *villous.* [ad. L. *villōsus*, f. *villus* VILLUS : see -OUS.]

Vim (vim). Orig. U.S. [Commonly regarded as a. L. *vim*, acc. sing. of *vis* strength, energy.]

Vimana (vimā·nǎ). [Skr. and Hindī *vimāna*.] An Indian musical instrument consisting of a fretted fingerboard, to which seven strings fitted with pegs are attached, with a gourd at each end ; an Indian lyre.

Vimineous (vimi·niǎs), a. Now *rare.* Also 7 *viminious* (f. *vimin-*, *vimen* : see prec.)

‖ Villus (vi·lǎs). *Bot.* and *Anat.* Pl. **villi** (vi·lǎi). [L. *villus* tuft of hair, shaggy hair, etc.]

Vimineous (vimi·niǎs), a. Now *rare.* Also 7 *viminious.*

Vinaceous (vǎinē·ǎs), a. [f. L. *vināceus*, f. *vinum* wine : see -ACEOUS.]

Vinagarette, obs. form of VINAIGRETTE.

Vinaigrette (vinĕgre·t). Also 7–8 *vinaigret*, 7 9 *vinegrette*, 9 *vinaigarette*. [F.]

Vinager, obs. form of VINEGAR.

Vinaigrous (vinē·grǎs), a. *rare.* [f. F. *vinaigre* VINEGAR.]

Vinal (vǎi·nǎl), a. [ad. L. *vīnālis*, f. *vīnum* wine.]

Vinnew, var. directly f. *vin-*, *vin-* + -AL.

Vine (vǎin), sb. Forms: 3–7 *vyne*, etc. [a. OF. *vine*, *vigne* (mod.F. *vigne*).]

Vindemiate (vinī·miĕit), v. *rare.* [f. L. *vindēmiāt-*, ppl. stem of *vindēmiāre*.]

Vindemial (vindī·miǎl), a. *rare.* [ad. L. *vindēmiālis*.]

Vindemiation (vindīmiē·ʃǎn). [ad. med.L. *vindēmiātiō*.]

‖ Vindemiatrix (vindīmiē·triks). [med. or mod.L. *vindēmiātrix.*] A bright fixed star in the constellation Virgo.

Vindemy (vi·ndĕmi), sb. *Obs.* Also 5 *vindemie* vintage, grape-gathering.

† Vindemy, v. *Obs.—¹* [f. L. *vindēmiāre.*]

Vinder, southern Sc. variant of FINDER.

Vindicability (vi·ndikǎbi·lĭti). rare.—¹ [f. next.] The quality of being vindicable, or capable of support or justification.

Vindicable (vi·ndikǎb'l), a. [ad. late L. *vindicābilis* (Du Cange), f. L. *vindicāre* to vindicate.]

Vindicate (vi·ndikĕit), v. [ad. L. *vindicāt-*, ppl. stem of *vindicāre* to claim, to set free, to punish, etc.]

Vindicated (vi·ndikĕitĕd), ppl. a.

Vindication (vindikē·ʃǎn). Also 5 *vyndy-cacion*. [ad. OF. (now F. dial.) *vindication* vengeance, or ad. L. *vindicātiō*.]

Vindicative (vi·ndikǎtiv), a. Also 6 *vendicative*, -yue, *vindicatyfe*, -tiue. [ad. OF. *vindicatif* (now dial.), or ad. med.L. *vindicātīvus.*]

Vindicator (vi·ndikĕitǎr). [ad. late L. (eccl.) *vindicātor*, agent-n. f. *vindicāre* VINDICATE v.]

Vindicatorship, the personality of a vindicator.

Vindicatorily, *adv.* [f. VINDICATORY.] In a vindicatory or justifying manner.

Vindicatory (vi'ndikǝtǝri), *a.* [f. -OR + -Y.]
1. Serving to vindicate; justificatory, defensive.
2. Avenging; punitive, retributive.

Vindicatress (vindikǝtrĕ's), *sb.* [VINDICATOR] A female vindicator.

†Vindict. *Obs. rare.* [ad. L. *vindicta*.] Vengeance, revenge; retribution.

Vindictive (vindi'ktiv), *a.* and *sb.* [f. L. *vindicta* vengeance, revenge + -IVE.]
A *adj.* 1. Of persons: Given to revenge; having a revengeful disposition. (Cf. VINDICATIVE *a.* 1.)
B. Of actions, qualities, etc.: Characterized by a desire for, or the exercise of, revenge.

Vindictively (vindi'ktivli), *adv.* [f. prec. + -LY.] In a vindictive manner; revengefully.

Vindictiveness (vindi'ktivnĕs), [f. as prec. + -NESS.] The state or character of being vindictive; revengefulness.

†Vindicative, *nonced.* [L. *vindica* vengeance, after *malevolence*.] The desire of revenging oneself or of taking vengeance.

†Vindicature. *Obs.* [irreg. f. L. *vindica*.]

Vindo, obs. Sc. form of WINDOW.

Vine (vain), *sb.* Forms: 4 α *vyngne* (*vigno*), *vinyhe*, 5 *vyny*. β 4-6 *vyne*, 5 *vyn*, *vyin*, 5 -6 *vine* (5 *vene*), 4, 6 *wine*, 5-6 *wyne*. 7, 6 *vinde*, *vynde*. [a. OF. *vigne* and *vine*: -- L. *vīnea* vineyard, vine, etc., f. *vīnum* wine.]
I. 1. The trailing or climbing plant, *Vitis vinifera*, bearing the grapes from which ordinary wine is made (= GRAPE-VINE); also generally, any plant of the genus *Vitis*.
II. +5. A vineyard. *Obs.*

VINEGAR. 214 VINE. VINEGAR. 215 VINET

Vineal (vi'nĭal), *a. rare.* [ad. L. *vineālis*, f. *vinea*.] Of pertaining to vines or wine; living on vines; consisting of vine.

Vineat, variant of VINET? *Obs.*

Vineatu, *a. rare.* -- [a. L. *vinēdĭcus*, f. *vines* VINE sb.] (See quot.)

Vine-branch. Also *vine branch*. [VINE *sb.*]
1. A branch of a vine.
2. *Ornamented* with the representation of a vine.

Vined, *a. rare.* [f. VINE *sb.*]

Vine-dresser. [VINE *sb.*] One occupied in the pruning, training, and cultivation of vines.

Vine-fretter. Now *rare* or *Obs.* [VINE *sb.*]

Vinegar (vi'nĭgǝr), *sb.* Forms: α. 4-6 *vyne-gre* (5 *vyn-*), 5-7 *vynegar*, 6-7 *vyne-ger*, 5-7 *vinegre*, 7 *vin'ger*, 5-7 *vineger*; also 7 *vineyger*.

Vinaigre (so mod.F.), [. *vin-*:--L. *vinum* wine + *egre*, *aigre* EAGER *a.*]
3. *fig.* Speech, temper, etc., of a sour or acid character.

Vinegar (vi'nĭgǝr), *v.* [f. prec.] *trans.* To treat with vinegar in some way; to add or apply vinegar to; to restore by means of vinegar.

Vinegarish (vi'nĭgǝriʃ), *a.* [f. VINEGAR sb.] Somewhat resembling vinegar.

Vinegarist, a vinegar-maker.

Vinegary (vi'nĭgǝri), *a.* [f. VINEGAR sb.] Resembling vinegar; sour vinegar. Chiefly *fig.*

Vinelet [f. VINE *sb.* + -LET.] A young vine.

Vineless (vai'nlĕs), *a.* [f. VINE *sb.*] Having no vines; destitute of vines.

Vinet (vi'nĕt), *sb.* Obs. [a. OF. *vignet*. Readopted in the 18th century as Vignette *sb.*]

| VIOLANTIN. | 220 | VIOLATION. | VIOLATIVE. | 221 | VIOLENCE. |

Violantin (*Elem. Geol. Min. etc.*), variety of Pistacite...

Violant, obs. form of VIOLET D.

Violantin *v.* Variant of VIOLA I (Allox)antin.]

Violary, variant of VIOLER.

Violate, *ppl. a.* [ad. L. *violātus*, *l. viola*.]

Violate, *v.* [f. L. *violāt-*, ppl. stem of *violāre* to treat with violence, to outrage, dishonour, injure, etc.]

1. *trans.* To treat, or injure or transgress unjustifiably; to fail duly to keep or observe: a. An oath or promise, one's faith, etc.

2. To violate, corrupt, or spoil, esp. in respect of physical qualities.

3. To ravish or constrain (a person's chastity) by force.

4. To damage or injure by violence.

Violated, *ppl. a.*

Violater (*vai'lātə_r*). Now *rare.*

Violation (*vaiolēi'ʃən*). Also 5–6 vyolacion, 6–7 -acyon, -atioun. [a. OF. *violacion* (F. *violation*), Sp. *violacion*, It. *violaciones*, or ad. L. *violātiōn-*, *violātio*, noun of action f. *violāre* to violate.] The action of violating in various senses.

Violator (*vai'lēitə_r*, -o_r). Also 6–7 -our. [a. L. *violator* (OF. *violateur*), It. *violatore*, Sp. and F. *violateur*. Cf. VIOLATER.]

Violatory, *a. rare.* [f. VIOLATE D. + -ORY.]

Viol da gamba (*viol da 'gæmbə*). Also 7 di gamba, 8 gamboy; 7– de gamba, 7 gamba. [ad. It. *viola da gamba* 'leg-viol'. Cf. VIOLA and GAMBA 2.]

Viole, *v. Obs. rare.* Also 5 vyole. [ad. OF. *violer*.] *trans.* To violate.

Violence (*vai'ŏlens*). Also 4 violaunce, 4–6 vyolence, 5 Sc. wyol-, violens, 5–6 vio-lens (7 voyolence). [a. F. *violence* (12th c.), = Pr. *violensa*, Sp. and It. *violenza*, ad. L. *violentia*, f. *violent-*, VIOLENT.]

Violator (*vai'ŏlēitə_r*).

1. The exercise of physical force so as to inflict injury on, or cause damage to, persons or property; action or conduct characterized by this; treatment or usage tending to cause bodily injury or forcibly interfering with personal freedom.

| VIOLENCE. | 222 | VIOLENT. | VIOLENT. | 223 | VIOLENTLY. |

Violent (*vai'ŏlent*), *a.* (*adv.*, *sb.*). Also 5 wyolent, 5–6 vyolent, violente, violent. [a. OF. (also mod.F.) *violent*, or ad. L. *violent-*, *violentus* (whence It., Sp., and Pg. *violento*) or *violent-*, *violens*, *violentis* violently forcible, impetuous, vehement, etc. f. *vis* strength.]

Violent, *v.* [ad. OF. (also mod.F.) *violenter*, or ad. med.L. *violentāre* to compel by force; see *prec.*]

1. *trans.* To strain or wrest the meaning of (words, a passage, etc.), *rare.*

2. To force, constrain, or oblige (one); to compel or coerce (a person).

Violently (*vai'ŏlentli*), *adv.* [f. VIOLENT a. + -LY.]

1. By means of physical strength or violence; by the exercise of improper or unlawful force; forcibly.

2. By or with great or extreme force, strength, or vigour; with impetuous or violent motion or action; so as to produce a violent effect.

3. In intensive or emphatic use: To a very great or extreme degree; very greatly, excessively.

4. Strongly, in respect of feeling; with deep feeling or emotion; ardently, passionately, vehemently.

Violentness. colloq. In a flashy or showy manner; 'loudly'.

Violentness. ? Obs. [f. VIOLENT a.] The state or quality of being violent; violence.

Violento. Obs.— [It.—L. violentus violent.] A violent person; one using or inclined to use violence.

Violer (vəiˈlər). Obs. Also 4-6 Sc. veolar, 6, 9 violar, 7 violer. [ad. OF. violeur, viëlur; see VIOL sb.[1]] A player of the viol, in early use esp. one attached to the household of the king, a noble, etc.; a fiddler.

Violescent (vəiəˈlɛsənt), a. [f. L. viola + -ESCENT. Cf. VIOLASCENT a.] Tending to a violet colour; tinged with violet.

Violet (vəiˈlɛt), sb.[1] Forms: 4- violet (5 vyolet), 4-7 violette (5-6 -ette), 5-7 vyolett; 5-6 violotte (5-6 -ote), vyolette (5 -yte); 5 vyalett, violed, 6 vilet, 7-9 v'let. [a. F. violette, Sp. and Pg. violeta), dim. of OF. viole, violet, violette fem., = violet, violet, violet (mod.F. violet masc., of similar origin.]

1. A plant or flower of the genus Viola, esp. V. odorata, the sweet-smelling violet, growing wild, and cultivated in gardens; the flowers are usually purplish blue, mauve, or white.

Violet (vəiˈlɛt), sb.[2] [ad. It. violetta, dim. of viola VIOLA[2].] (See quot., and cf. VIOLETTE.)

Violet, a. (adv.) Also 4-6 violett, 5 vyolet, violet, violet, 6 violitt. [f. OF. violet, violet, villet (mod.F. violet). Cf. It. violetto, Pg. violete.]

Violetish (vəiˈlɛtiʃ), a. [f. VIOLET sb.[1] + -ISH.] Somewhat violet in colour.

Violet-te. rare— [It. violetta.] = VIOLET sb.[2]

Violety (vəiˈlɛti), a. [f. VIOLET sb.[1] + -Y.] Of or belonging to violets; more or less violet in colour.

Violin (vəiˈlɪn, vəiˈlɪn), sb. Forms: 6 viol—, violine; also 7 violin, violln. [a. It. violino, dim. of viola VIOLA[2].]

1. A musical instrument in common use, having four strings tuned in fifths and played with a bow; a fiddle.

3. A variety of organ-stop. rare—[1].

4. attrib. and Comb., as violin-bow, -case, -class, -family, etc.; violin-maker, -making, -player; violin-like, -shaped adjs.

Violon (vəiˈlɒn), a. Also and, of ent, violon, phisalon. [a. F. violon (16th c.) violin, or (in sense 2) It. violone bass-viol.] Cf. VIOLIN.

Violoncello. [It., dim. of violone VIOLON.] Hence also Pg. violoncello. A large stringed instrument of the violin class; a bass violin. Cf. 'CELLO.

Violoncellist. [f. next + -IST.] One who plays the violoncello.

Violonist. rare— [ad. It. violonista, -lsta, f. violone VIOLON.] = VIOLINIST.

Violin, v. rare. [f. prec.]

Violinist (vəiˈlɪnɪst). [ad. F. violiniste, It. violinista.] A player of, or performer on, the violin.

Violism. rare— [f. VIOLIN sb.] Violin-playing.

Viola. n. Chem.— [INA[1].] = next.

Violin[1]. Chem. Also -in. [a. F. violine; f. viola VIOLA[1].]

Violine[2]. Chem. Also -in. [a. F. violine, f. viole Viola.] a bitter-emetic principle found in the root.

Violuric (vəiəˈljuərɪk), a. Chem. [f. viol- + URIC a.] Applied to an acid produced by the action of nitric on hydurilic acid.

Viper (vəiˈpər), sb. Also 6 vyper, vypar, veper. [a. F. vipère, Pr. vibora, vibra fem., víbre masc., Sp. and Pg. vibora, It. vipera) or ad. L. vipera viper, snake, serpent, contracted from vivi-pera, f. vivus alive, + parĕre to bring forth. See also WIVER.]

1. The small ovo-viviparous snake Pelias berus (formerly Coluber berus or Vipera communis), abundant in Europe and the only venomous snake found in Great Britain; the adder. In general any venomous, dangerous, or repulsive snake or serpent.

Viperal. Obs.— [f. L. viperālis, f. vipera.]

Viperine (vəiˈpərəin, -in), a. and sb. [ad. L. viperīnus, f. vipera viper.]

Viperish (vəiˈpəriʃ), a. [f. VIPER + -ISH.] Venomous, viperous, spiteful.

Viper-like, a. and adv. Also -lyke. Resembling or characteristic of a viper; venomous, viperous; viper-like.

Viperling. [f. VIPER + -LING.] A young viper.

Viperous (vəiˈpərəs), a. Also 6 vyperous, -ouse, vipourous; 7-8 viprous; 6 viprous, 7-8 poet. vip'rous. [f. VIPER + -OUS.]

Viperously, adv., in or after the manner of a viper; venomously; **Viperousness**, viperous nature or character; venomosity. rare.

Vipery, a. rare. [f. VIPER + -Y.] Consisting of vipers; viperous.

†Vi-politic, Obs. [Vi- pref.] (See quot.)

†Vi-president Obs. [f. VI- + PRESIDENT sb.] A vice-president.

Vipseys, obs. var. of or error for GIPSIES.

Viqueen, obs. var. of VICE-QUEEN.

Vir, variant of VIR b.

†Viragin. Obs. rare. [ad. L. virāgin-, stem of virago.]

Viragination, **Viraginity** (see prec.).

Viraginian (virædʒiˈniən), a. and sb. [f. L. virāgin- (see prec.) + -AN.]

Virago (viˈrāgo). Also 6 vyrago, 7 veryr-, rago. [a. L. virāgo a man-like or heroic woman, a female warrior, etc., f. vir man. Cf. Sp. virago.]

Viragoish a., somewhat resembling, or having the characteristics of, a virago; **Viragoship**, the character of a virago.

Virial, obs. f. VIRILE.

Viranda, etc., obs. f. VERANDA.

†Vire, sb.[1] Obs. Also 4 fyre, 4-6 vyre, 5 wyr, wyre. [a. OF. vire (= Prov., Sp., Pg. vira), f. virer to turn.]

Virecome, sb. Obs. rare. [f. L. viredo, -inis green ...]

Virescence (viˈresəns). [ad. L. virescent-, virescens.]

Virescent (viˈresənt), a. [ad. L. virescent-, virescens.]

†Vireton. Obs. In 6 yr(e)-. [a. OF. vireton.]

Virgal, a. rare. [f. L. virga rod.] Made of rods.

Virgate, a. rare. [L. virgātus: see prec.]

Virgate (vəˈgeit), sb.[1] Hist. [ad. med.L. virgāta.]

Virgate (vəˈgeit), v. [L. virga twig.]

Virgilian (vəˈdʒiliən), a. and sb. Also 5 virgilien, 6 Virgillian, 6-7 Virgilian-, -ell-, 7-9 Virgilian. [ad. L. Virgiliānus, f. Virgilius, name of the poet: see -AN.]

Virgilianism. [f. prec. + -ISM.]

Virgin (vəˈdʒin), sb. and a. Forms: 1-3 virgine, 3-7 virgine (6 wir-), 4, 6 virgyne (5 wir-), 4-5 vyrgine (4 wyr-), 5 vyrgine (4 wer-), vorgyn. 5-7 virgyn (6 vir-), 4-7 virgin. [a. AF. and OF. virgine, virgene, etc. (= Pr. virgena, It. vergine, Sp. virgen, etc.), ad. L. virgin-, virgo maiden.]

Virgin, v. rare.

18. Comb., as virgin-eyed, -minded, -vested adjs.

Hence **Virgin** v. intr. with it. To remain a virgin. **Virginal**, sb. Forms: 6 virginalles, -ynall(e)s, 6-7 virginalls, 6-7, 9 -virginalles. [App. of obscure formation as Virginal a., but the reason for thename isobscure.]

1. b. A pair of virginals, in the same sense.

Virgin (vā̆ rd'z̆ in), sb. Forms: 6 virginalles, -ynall(e)s.

1. b. Of or pertaining to a virgin or to virginity.

† Virgin-ility. Obs. rare. [f. prec.+-ITY.]

† Virginally (vɜ̄ʼdʒinăli), adv. [f. VIRGINAL a.+-LY².]

† Virg neous, a. Obs. rare. [f. L. virgineus+-ous.]

† Virginet, var. of (or error for) VIRGINAL sb.

Virginhood. [f. VIRGIN sb.+-HOOD.]

Virginia (vɜ̄dʒíniă). [f. Virginia, in honour of Queen Elizabeth[1]+-IA².]

Virginian (vɜ̄dʒíniăn), a. and sb. [f. prec.+-AN.]

Virginity (vɜ̄dʒíniti). Forms: 4-5 virgynyte, 6 -ite, 4-7 virgynite, 5 -onyte, 6 -inite; 4-6 virginite (itee, 4 wirginite, 5 Sc. wergintie); 3 -tie, 5-7 -ti, 6 virginitie, 4-7 -tie. [a. AF., and OF. virginité, virgineté, -inited, ad. L. virginitāt-, virginitas, f. virgin-, stem of virgo: see VIRGIN sb. and -ITY.]

Virgin-like, a. and adv. [f. VIRGIN sb.]

A. adj. Resembling a virgin or that of a virgin; characteristic of or befitting a virgin; maidenlike.

† Virginship. Obs. rare. [-SHIP.]

Virgin's bower. [VIRGIN sb. 11.] The British climbing shrub Clematis Vitalba, traveller's joy.

Virgo (vɜ̄ʼgo). Astr. [L.: see VIRGIN sb.]

Virgin's milk. [transl. med. L. loc virginis.] A chemical preparation having a milky appearance.

Virgin wax. = VIRGIN-WAX.

Virgin's wax. [tr. med. L. cera virginea.] = VIRGIN-WAX.

Virgo (vɜ̄ʼgo). Astr. [L.: see VIRGIN sb.]

Virgular (vɜ̄ʼgiŭlăr), a. [L. virgula.]

Virgouleuse (vɜ̄ʼgŭleuz), Obs. Also 7 vergoule. [a. F.]

Virgulate, a. [L. virgulātus.]

Virgule (vɜ̄ʼgiul). Obs. [a. L. virgula.]

Viriality, rare. [f. VIRIAL.]

† Viridant. Obs. [ad. L. viridans.]

Viridate, v. Obs. rare-¹. [L. viridātus.]

Viride scent, a. rare. [ad. L. viridescent-, viridescens.]

Viridian (virídiăn), sb. [f. L. viridis green.]

Viridic, a. Chem. [f. VIRID- + -IC.] Viridic acid.

Viridine, sb. Chem. [f. VIRID-.]

Viridite, sb. Min. [f. L. viridis green + -ITE¹.]

Viridity (viríditi). [ad. L. viriditāt-, viriditas, f. viridis green.]

Viridour. Obs. rare.

† Viridour, v. Obs.

Viri-fic, a. rare⁻¹. [L. *viri-us* VIRUS + -(¹)FIC.] Virulent, poisonous.

Virile (virəil, -il, voiə·rəil, -il), a.

Virilescence [...] The condition of becoming virile, *spec.* of assuming physical characteristics of the male.

Virilescent (virile·sĕnt), a.

Virilify (viri·lifəi), v. [f. VIRILE a. + -IFY.] *trans.* To make virile or manly.

† Viriliously, adv. Obs. rare.

Virilism (viri·liz'm).

Virility (viri·lĭti).

† Viri-potence. Obs.⁻⁰ [f. VIRIPOTENT a.]

Viri-potent, a.¹ Obs. [ad. late L. *viripotent-em*.]

Virl, obs. or dial. var. FIRK v. Virk(e, obs. Sc. ff. WORK v. Virkin, dial. var. FIRRIN, Virking, obs. Sc. f. WORKING ppl. vb.

Virl. Now only Sc.

Viron, v. Obs. Also 5 viron (6 vyron); 5 -yrryn.

† Viron, prep. and adv. Obs.⁻¹ [f. ENVIRON v.]

† Viront, Obs. rare. [ad. L. *viro-us, f. virus VIRUS.*] Poisonous; suggestive of poisonous qualities; rank and noisomeness.

Virose (vairəu·s).

† Virory. Obs.⁻¹ [f. prec. and ENVIRON v.]

† Virtrate. Obs.⁻¹ [Of obscure origin.]

Virtu (vɜːtuː·). Sc. Also vir.

Virous, a.

Virr (vɜːr). Sc. Also vir.

Virtual (vɜː·tiuæl), a. (and sb.)

Virtualism (vɜː·tiuæliz'm).

Virtuality (vɜːtiuæ·lĭti).

Virtually (vɜː·tiuæli), adv. Also 5 vertualy or -liche, 5, 7 vertually.

† Virtuate, v. Obs.

Virtue (vɜː·tiuː), sb.

Visage

Visa, v. trans.

†Vi·sable, a.

Visage (vi·sedʒ), sb. Forms: 4-6 vysage, 4-5 visage, 5-7 vysage, vyssage, vysage, 5 visache, 6 visage, 5-7 visage, 7 visage. [a. F. vis-age]

Visaged

Visaged (vi·zedʒd), a. [f. VISAGE sb.]

Visar(e, obs. form of VISOR.

Vis-à-vis (vizavi·), sb., prep., and adv.

Viscacha

Viscacha (viskæ·tʃa), sb. Also 8-9 viscacho, 8-9 vizcacha. [Sp.]

Viscera

Viscera (vi·sera), sb. pl.

†Viscate, ppl. a. Obs.

Visceral (vi·seral), a. [ad. med.L. visceralis]

Viscero-, combining form.

Vi·scerate, v. trans.

Vi·scid, v. intr.

Vi·scidly, adv.

Viscidness.

Viscid

Viscid (vi·sid), a. [ad. late L. viscid-us, f. viscum birdlime (see VISCOUS a.).]

Viscidity (visi·diti).

Viscin

Viscin (vi·sin), Chem. [a. F. viscine (Macaire), f. L. viscum birdlime (see VISCOUS a.).]

Viscoid, a. rare⁻¹.

Viscometer, variant of VISCOSIMETER.

Viscontal, a. Obs.

Viscontiel, variant of VICONTIEL.

Viscose

Visco·se, sb. [f. L. viscum birdlime + -OSE²]

Viscose, a. Obs.

Viscosimeter. Also viscometer.

Viscosity

Viscosity (viskɒ·siti). Also 5-6 viscosite, 6 -yte, 6-7 -tie.

Viscount

Viscount (vai·kaunt), sb.

Viscountcy (vai·kauntsi).

Viscountess (vai·kauntes).

Viscountship.

Viscounty (vai·kaunti).

Viscous

Viscous (vi·skəs), a. Forms: 5-7 viscouse, 6-9 viscous, 6-9 -ose. [a. AF. viscous, ad. L. viscos-us, f. viscum]

Viscus

Viscus (vi·skəs). Anat. [L. viscus, usually in pl. viscera VISCERA.]

Vise, obs. Sc. var. of WISE v. (to direct).

†Visé (vi·ze), sb.

Vise, obs. form of VICE.

Viselike, adv.

Visement, obs. form of AVISEMENT.

Visenomy, obs. var. of VISNOMY.

Viser, v. rare.

†Visern, obs. form of VISOR.

Vishnu

Vishnu (vi·ʃnu).

Vishnuism.

Vishnuite (vi·ʃnuait).

Visibility

Visibility (vizibi·liti). Also L. visibili-tas. [ad. late L. visibilitat-, -tas, f. visibilis VISIBLE.]

Supplement, p. 3873; Corrigenda, p. 4092; Spurious words, p. 4093; Books quoted, p. 4094.

3641

Supplement, p. 3873; Corrigenda, p. 4092; Spurious words, p. 4093; Books quoted, p. 4094

b. *transf.* (In modern use denoting especially those parts of a machine, ship, etc., essential to its proper working.)

1647 CLARENDON *Hist. Reb.* I. § 76 Their submiss Reverence to their Princes being a vital part of their Religion. 1698 KEILL *Exam. Th. Earth* (1734) 181 If these he has mentioned be the substantial and vital parts [of his theory]. 1866 CRUMP *Banking* v. 134 Erasure of any vital part of the bill..would justify the banker in refusing payment. 1873 J. RICHARDS *Wood-working Factories* 12 The piston, cross-head connecting rod, and main bearings, are the vital parts to be looked after. 1889 WELCH *Naval Archit.* 141 To preserve intact such vital parts as the machinery, magazines, and steering gear.

4. Of, pertaining, or relating to, accompanying, or characteristic of life; inherent in or exhibited by living things or organic bodies.

1565 COOPER *Thesaurus* s.v. *Vitaliter*, To haue liuely or vitaille motion. 1599 SHAKS. *Hen. V*, III. vi. 49 Let not Bardolphs vitall thred bee cut with edge of Penny-cord. 1604 — *Oth.* v. ii. 14 When I haue pluck'd thy Rose, I cannot giue it vitall growth againe. 1652 FRENCH *Yorksh. Spa* ii. 13 In which as in a vital abode, and natural place, the water, whilest it remains, is living. 1697 DRYDEN *Æneid* VI. 1075 There mighty Cæsar waits his vital hour, Impatient for the world. 1705 J. DUNTON *Life & Errors* 311 The last sands in his Life were run, and there was no turning the Vital-glass. 1784 COWPER *Task* III. 509 When the temper'd heat, Friendly to vital motion, may afford Soft fomentation. 1816 SHELLEY *Alastor* 238 Red morning..Shedding the mockery of its vital hues Upon his cheek of death. 1844 G. BIRD *Urin. Deposits* (1857) 47 In every case in which we endeavour to explain vital phenomena by the physical or chemical laws governing dead matter. 1873 H. SPENCER *Stud. Sociol.* xiv. 330 All actions of individuals being vital actions that conform to the laws of life at large.

b. Of faculties, functions, powers, etc.

1593 SHAKS. *2 Hen. VI*, III. ii. 41 Came he right now to sing a Rauens Note, Whose dismall tune bereft my vital powres. 1634 SIR T. HERBERT *Trav.* 169 It immediatly ouer-charged my vitall sences, and put mee..into a deadly trance. 1696 PHILLIPS (ed. 5), *Vital* Faculty, an Action whereby a Man lives..as the Motions of the Heart, Respiration, Nutrition, &c. 1805 WORDSW. *Prelude* VIII. 299 Whose truth is not a motion or a shape Instinct with vital functions. 1826 S. COOPER *First Lines Surg.* (ed. 5) 38 By a gradual decay of the vital powers from old age. 1857 HENFREY *Bot.* § 782 The vital forces appear to be of more than one kind. 1878 HUXLEY *Physiogr.* xvii. 275 The whole mass has been constructed..of the products of denudation, or of those of vital processes.

c. *Geol.* Produced or formed by vital action or force; of vital or organic origin.

1855 J. PHILLIPS *Man. Geol.* 49 Proportions of Chemical, Vital, and Mechanical Deposits. 1880 HAUGHTON *Phys. Geogr.* iii. 164 *note*, It is converted into Chemical and Vital work done by the vegetable and animal organisms that clothe the surface of the earth.

d. Of statistics: Concerned with or relating to the facts of life, e. g. birth, marriage, death, etc.

1837 [W. FARR] in McCulloch *Acc. Brit. Emp.* II. 567 Vital Statistics; or, the Statistics of Health, Sickness, Diseases, and Death. 1885 J. NICOL (*title*), Vital, Social, and Economic Statistics of the City of Glasgow, 1881–85.

e. In special collocations:

Vital affinity (see quot. and AFFINITY 9). *Vital capacity*, in *Phys.*, the breathing or respiratory capacity of the lungs (cf. quot. 1852). *Vital contractility*, in *Phys.* = IRRITABILITY 3. *Vital germ theory* = *Germ theory* GERM *sb.* 6 (1891 *Cent. Dict.*). †*Vital indication* (see quot.). *Obs.*[−1] †*Vital line*, in palmistry, the line of life: see LINE *sb.* 8 b. *Vital sister* (see quot.). *Vital union*, a union involving common life; also *fig.*

1850 DAUBENY *Atom. The.* xi. (ed. 2) 359 *Vital affinity—a force, which is supposed to come in aid of common chemical attraction, and to render the union between the particles of a body more stable. 1852 J. HUTCHINSON *Spirometer* § 4 The most complete voluntary expiration immediately following the most complete inspiration, which we denominate the '*vital capacity'. 1876 BRISTOWE *Th. & Pract. Med.* (1878) 372 The vital capacity of women is much less that of men. 1830 R. KNOX *Béchard's Anat.* 216 These vessels are extensible, and are even possessed of a high degree of retractility...Their irritability or *vital contractility is not less evident. 1704 J. HARRIS *Lex. Techn.* I, **Vital Indication*, in the Art of Medicine, is such an one as requires the restoring and reserving of the Natural Strength of the Body. 1653 R. SANDERS *Physiogn.* 100 The *Vital line forked in the end, towards the wrist. *Ibid.* 102 The Liver line at a distance, and not touching the Vital line. 1824 *Encycl. Metrop.* (1845) XVI. 602/2 The Vital line thicker than ordinary..denotes a laborious old age. *Ibid.* 604 Of the Via Martis, the way or Line of Mars, or the *Vital-sister. 1662 STILLINGFL. *Orig. Sacræ* III. iii. § 6 Those inferiour terrestrial Beings with which it [i.e. the soul] communicates through the *vital union which it hath with the body. 1690 LOCKE *Hum. Und.* II. xxvii. § 25 Several substances..which, whilst they continued in a vital union with that,..made a part of the same self. 1742 YOUNG *Nt. Th.* II. 57 Is this our duty, wisdom, glory, gain? (These heav'n benign in vital union binds). 1746 WESLEY *Princ. Methodist* 49, I believe there was a supernatural Power.. which occasion'd their Bodies to be so affected by the natural Laws of the vital Union.

5. Conferring or imparting life or vigour; invigorating, vitalizing; life-giving. Chiefly *poet.*

1590 SPENSER *F. Q.* II. i. 12 Liues he yet..that wrought this act, And doen the heauens afford him vital food? 1601 HOLLAND *Pliny* I. 56 The whole temperature of the aire is evermore so vitall, healthie, and holesome. 1608 WILLET *Hexapla Exod.* 245 Vitall and comfortable heate..from the bodie of the sunne. 1667 MILTON *P. L.* III. 22 Hail holy light, ofspring of Heav'n first-born..: thee I revisit safe, And feel thy sovran vital Lamp. 1719 YOUNG *Revenge* III. i, O Joy, thou welcome stranger! twice three years I have not felt thy vital beam. 1744 AKENSIDE *Pleas. Imag.* I. 72 Till in time complete, What he admir'd and lov'd, his vital smile Unfolded into being. 1865 NEALE *Hymns Paradise* 8 There they quaff the vital sweetness of the Well of Quickening. 1872 HUXLEY *Physiol.* vii. 156 The vital foods are derived directly, or indirectly, from the vegetable world.

6. Affecting life; fatal to or destructive of life.

1612 ROWLANDS *Knaue of Harts* (Hunter. Cl.) 46 This Picke-pocket suffer'd vitall losse, Betweene the Court-gate hang'd, and Charing-crosse. *a* 1645 MILTON *Arcades* 65 The celestial Sirens..That sit upon the nine enfolded spheares, And sing to those that hold the vital shears, And turn the Adamantine spindle round. 1776 S. J. PRATT *Pupil of Pleas.* II. 238 The surgeon, to whom I went myself, in defiance of danger, assures me the wound is vital. 1812 CALHOUN *Speech* 24 June, Wks. 1864 II. 29 Throw him into battle, and he is scarcely sensible of vital gashes.

7. *fig.* That is essential to the existence of something expressed or implied in the context; constituting or involving an essential part or feature; absolutely indispensable, necessary, or requisite. Also, in wider sense, of supreme importance.

Common in recent use, freq. const. *to* something (*b*).

(*a*) 1619 LUSHINGTON *Resurrect. Rescued* (1659) 70 The three vital circumstances of a well-ordered Action, Person, Time and Place. 1692 ATTERBURY *Serm. bef. Queen* 29 May 3 The weakness and worthlessness of external Performances, when compar'd with more vital and substantial Duties. 1708 — *Serm. bef. Queen* 31 Oct. 8 A thorough Sense, and Vital Experience of his Paternal Care over us, and Concern for us. 1809–10 COLERIDGE *Friend* (1865) 169 At a time when the views of France became daily more and more incompatible with our own vital interests. 1849 MACAULAY *Hist. Eng.* ii. I. 273 If one of them differs from the rest on a vital point. 1879 F. HARRISON *Choice Bks.* (1886) 10 The really vital books for us we also know to be a very trifling portion of the whole.

(*b*) 1742 YOUNG *Nt. Th.* VI. 506 A competence is vital to content. 1856 STANLEY *Sinai & Pal.* iv. 215 Hence it was that the raising of the siege of Gibeon..was so vital to the conquest of Canaan. 1860 MOTLEY *Netherl.* vi. (1868) I. 289 A cause which was so vital to both nations. 1893 A. CAWSTON *Street Improv. London* 1 Doubtless many will gladly take up a work so vital to the welfare of the whole community.

b. Of questions, problems, etc.

1822 HAZLITT *Table-T.* xxxiii. II. 389, I should like to live to see the downfall of the Bourbons. That is a vital question with me. 1825 COBBETT *Rur. Rides* 278 He and I never agreed upon this subject; and this subject was, with him, a vital one. 1850 CARLYLE *Latter-d. Pamph.* i. (1872) 31 The 'Organisation of Labour'..is the universal vital Problem of the world. 1865 RUSKIN *Sesame* ii. § 54 Respecting this question—quite vital to all social happiness.

c. Paramount, supreme, very great.

1810 WELLINGTON in Gurw. *Desp.* (1838) V. 529 In order to concentrate our troops on other points of greater and more vital importance. 1849 MACAULAY *Hist. Eng.* vii. II. 233 Questions respecting postures, robes, festivals and liturgies, be considered as of no vital importance. 1850 GLADSTONE *Glean.* (1879) V. viii. 180 This inquiry..is indeed of vital moment to those who [etc.].

II. 8. Endowed with, or possessed of, life; animate, living. Now *poet.* or *rhet.*

1513 BRADSHAW *St. Werburge* I. 3470 Than this vitall glebe [*sc.* the body of St. Werburge] by divine ordinaunce voluntary permytted naturall resolution. 1561 DAUS tr. *Bullinger on Apoc.* (1573) 185 b, For who soeuer shew not themselues obedient,..onto this beast..are accompted for dead and rotten members, and therfore to be cut of from this vitall body. 1621 T. WILLIAMSON tr. *Goulart's Wise Vieillard* 30 Of the dismall day, that doth threaten with death, Things vitall feele the smart, and things without breath. 1667 MILTON *P. L.* VI. 345 For Spirits that live throughout Vital in every part..Cannot but by annihilating die. 1745 WATTS in *Trans. & Paraphr. Scripture* XXXVII. vii, Out of the Deep, th' Almighty King did vital Beings frame. 1774 J. BRYANT *Mythol.* II. 206 He called the winds, and made them breathe into each, and render them vital. 1817 SHELLEY *Rev. Islam* II. xxvi. 6 Some monument Vital with mind. 1820 — *Witch Atl.* xxxv, That bright shape of vital stone which drew the heart out of Pygmalion.

transf. 1667 *Decay Chr. Piety* v. ¶ 25 That mind..that can be free when the body is fast bound..is never more strong and vital, than when that languishes and expires.

fig. 1837 J. H. NEWMAN *Par. Serm.* (ed. 2) III. xiv. 219 His creed may be orthodox, but his religion is not vital. 1842 MRS. BROWNING *Grk. Chr. Poets* (1863) 97 The live grasshopper, called..an emblem of the vital Greek tongue. 1873 SYMONDS *Grk. Poets* x. 320 Every line of Theocritus is vital with a strong passion for natural beauty.

b. Of places: Full of life or activity.

1742 YOUNG *Nt. Th.* I. 115 This is the desart, this the solitude: How populous! how vital, is the grave! 1817 SHELLEY *Rev. Islam* II. vi. 1 This vital world, this home of happy spirits.

c. Endowed with spiritual life. *rare.*

1807 SYD. SMITH *Lett. Catholics* (1808) 81 Those groaning and garrulous gentlemen, whom they denominate..Gospel preachers and Vital clergymen.

9. Employed as an epithet of *life*.

1597 J. PAYNE *Royal Exch.* 13 You must be changed you know not when, from your ritches, from this vitall lyfe and the whole worlde vnto a nother place paynefull or Joyfull. 1633 BP. HALL *Occas. Medit.* § 61 I cannot tell whether I should say those Creatures live which doth nothing; Sure I am their life is not vital. 1645 — *Rem. Discontents* 122 Neither indeed is any other life truly vital, but this; for hereby we enjoy God in all whatsoever occurrences.

†10. Having the qualities essential to life; capable of living; = VIABLE *a.*[1] *Obs.*

1608 TOPSELL *Serpents* 108 When the Butterflyes do ioyne together very late,..they doe lay or cast theyr eggs which will continue vitall, and that may liue till the next Spring. 1615 CROOKE *Body of Man* 336 The nine-moneth birth is of all other the most vitall and legitimate. 1646 SIR T. BROWNE *Pseud. Ep.* IV. xii. 218 Pythagoras, Hippocrates,..and others..affirming the birth of the seventh month to be vitall.

B. *sb.* †1. The vital spirit or principle. *Obs.*[−1]

1670 CAPT. J. SMITH *Eng. Improv. Reviv'd* v. 246 When the ulcerous Lungs cannot with dexterity enough perform their Office of cooling the Heart, the Vital is generated more hot than it should be.

2. A vital part or organ. *rare.*

Formed from the collect. pl. VITALS.

1710 OLDISWORTH tr. *Quillet's Callipædia* I. 492 A florid Bloom with Blushes decks the Face,..And every Vital breathes the sweets of Love. 1847 C. BRONTË *J. Eyre* xxxiv, Forced to keep the fire of my nature continually low, to compel it to burn inwardly..though the imprisoned flame consumed vital after vital.

3. *Palmistry.* The vital line.

1824 *Encycl. Metrop.* (1845) XVI. 602/2 This also frequently shows a most perilous Saturnine disease in that part whereien it touches the Vital.

Vitale, Vitale(e)r, obs. forms of VICTUAL *sb.* and *v.*, VICTUALLER.

Vita·lic, *a.* *rare*[−1]. [f. VITAL *a.*] Vital.

1848 POE *Eureka* Wks. 1865 II. 173 The successive geological revolutions which have attended,..these successive elevations of vitalic character.

Vitalism (vəi·tăliz'm). *Biol.* [a. F. *vitalisme*, or independently f. VITAL *a.* + -ISM.] The doctrine or theory that the origin and phenomena of life are due to or produced by a vital principle, as distinct from a purely chemical or physical force.

1822 W. TAYLOR in *Monthly Rev.* XCIX. 514 His perfect knowledge of anatomy..succeeded in erecting..the vitalism of Bichot. 1877 SHIELDS *Final Philos.* 267 Leading biologists also have maintained a duality of matter and life known as vitalism. 1889 *Nature* 26 Sept. 525 But even at the height of this movement there was a reaction towards vitalism, of which Virchow,..was the greatest exponent.

Vitalist (vəi·tălist). [Cf. prec. and F. *vitaliste.*] An advocate of or believer in vitalism. Also in recent use as *adj.*, = next.

1860 LAYCOCK *Mind & Brain* I. Contents p. xviii, Conflicting theories of Life and Mind resulting from the Dogmas of the Vitalists. 1870 MAUDSLEY *Body & Mind* 169 The obvious refuge of the vitalist is to the facts that it is impossible now to evolve life artificially out of any combination of physical and chemical forces [etc.]. 1884 *Pop. Sci. Monthly* XXIV. 763 Cuvier..was a vitalist, and thought the vital properties of the body a kind of entity.

Vitalistic (vəităli·stik), *a.* [f. prec. + -IC.]

1. Of or pertaining to, involving or denoting, vitalism or a hypothetical vital principle.

1865 *Englishw. Mag.* Feb. 158 Though Homer assures us that..Polybius and Machaon excelled in the healing art, nothing..remains to throw any light upon their vitalistic theories. 1871 TYLOR *Prim. Cult.* I. 395 The Karen doctrine of the là is indeed a perfect and well-marked vitalistic system. 1889 DUNCAN *Clin. Lect. Dis. Women* (ed. 4) xxviii. 224 The great question implied in vitalistic doctrine.

2. Pertaining to or denoting the germ-theory (see GERM *sb.* 6), esp. in its relation to fermentation.

1891 *Nature* 26 Mar. 482/1 It was no easy thing for him to justify the study of fermentation on the lines suggested by what was called the vitalistic germ-theory.

Vitality (vəitæ·lĭti). Also 6–7 **vitalitie.** [ad. L. *vītālitāt-*, *vītālitās* (Pliny) vital force, life, f. *vītālis* VITAL *a.*: see -ITY. Cf. F. *vitalité*, It. *vitalità*, Sp. *vitalidad*, Pg. *-idade.*]

1. Vital force, power, or principle as possessed or manifested by living things (cf. VITAL *a.* 1); the principle of life; animation.

1592 *Soliman & Pers.* v. iii. 65 Death..Hath depriued Erastus trunke from breathing vitalitie. 1614 RALEIGH *Hist. World* I. i. § 6. 6 Whether that motion, vitality and operation, were by incubation, or how else, the manner is onely knowne to God. 1628 FELTHAM *Resolves* II. [I.] xxxii. 102 When a man shall exhaust his very vitalitie, for the hiiling vp of fatall Gold. 1659 PEARSON *Creed* iv. 432 When by an act of his will he had submitted to that death,..it was not in the power of his soul to continue any longer vitality to the body. 1700 ROWE *Amb. Step-Moth.* III. ii, Let thy vitality impart New Spirits to his fainting Heart. 1812 *Times* 6 Mar. 2/2 They perceived that vitality had been actually extinct in two of them for some time, the bodies being perfectly cold. 1844 G. BIRD *Urin. Deposits* (1857) 338 Those which we have now to investigate are organic substances, often possessing organization, and sometimes enjoying an independent vitality. 1873 SYMONDS *Grk. Poets* i. 1 The mysteries of organized vitality remain impenetrable.

transf. 1652 FRENCH *Yorksh. Spa* ii. 13 Which sand hath in it a vitality, and in which..the water, whilest it remains, is living. 1816 BYRON *Ch. Har.* III. xxxiv, There is a very life in our despair, Vitality of poison. 1831 CARLYLE *Sart. Res.* I. v, Not Mankind only, but all that Mankind does or beholds, is in continual growth, re-genesis and self-perfecting vitality. 1837 WHEWELL *Hist. Induct. Sci.* IV. i. I. 240 All such writers ..have in them no principle of philosophical vitality.

b. Of plants or vegetative organisms. Also *spec.* of seeds: Germinating power.

(*a*) 1829 T. CASTLE *Introd. Bot.* 262 Vitality of Plants. 1842 WORDSW. *Sonn.*, '*A Poet!*' i, And so the grandeur of the Forest-tree Comes..from its own divine vitality. 1848 LINDLEY *Introd. Bot.* (ed. 4) II. 150 The experiments.. prove indeed conclusively that whatever the true seat of vegetable vitality may be, it is similar in its nature to that of the Animal Kingdom.

(*b*) 1832 LINDLEY *Introd. Bot.* 271 The power [in seeds] of preserving their vitality is also extremely variable. 1861 BENTLEY *Man. Bot.* 767 By retaining vitality we mean preserving their power of germinating.

2. *fig.* The ability or capacity on the part of something of continuing to exist or to perform its functions; power of enduring or continuing.

Merging insensibly into next.

1844 H. H. WILSON *Brit. India* III. III. ix. 563 The dependance of ministerial vitality upon parliamentary majorities. 1866 R. W. DALE *Disc. Spec. Occas.* viii. 275 There is terrible vitality both in truth and error. 1874 L. STEPHEN *Hours in Library* I. 113 The vitality of Pope's writings, or at least of certain fragments of them, is remarkable.

3. *fig.* Active force or power; mental or physical vigour; activity, animation, liveliness.

Common from *c* 1860.

1858 O. W. HOLMES *Aut. Breakf.-t.* xii. 110 Which shows that their minds are in a state of diminished vitality. 1860 MOTLEY *Netherl.* I. ii. 45 Such was the intense vitality of the Béarnese prince. 1869 TOZER *Highl. Turkey* I. 358 A country whose vitality is strong, and where the administrative power is active and vigorous. 1884 *Manch. Exam.* 9 May 5/4 To the strong vitality which distinguishes his race, he united intellectual power of the highest order.

4. With *a* and pl. Something possessed of vital force. Also *fig.*

1851 CARLYLE *Sterling* II. iii, He was full of bright speech and argument; radiant with arrowy vitalities. 1853 KANE *Grinnell Exp.* v. (1856) 36 There was no vegetation to define its course, not even the green conferva, that obscure vitality, which follows water at home. 1898 MEREDITH *Odes Fr. Hist.* 91 Shall, then, the great vitality, France, Signal the backward step once more?

Vitaliza·tion. Also **-isation.** [f. VITALIZE *v.* + -ATION.] The action or process of vitalizing, or the state of being vitalized; an instance of this.

1846 J. HUDSON in *Rep. & Papers Bot.* (Ray Soc.) 306 The phenomenon of the vitalization of cells is brought about only by an excessive endosmose or nutrition. 1891 T. HARDY *Tess* xxxvi, Her love..might result in vitalisations that would inflict upon others what she had bewailed as a misfortune to herself. *a* 1901 F. W. H. MYERS *Human Personality* (1903) I. p. xxxiv, An increased subliminal vitalization of the organism.

Vitalize (vəi·tăləiz), *v.* Also 9 **-ise.** [f. VITAL *a.* + -IZE.]

1. *trans.* To give life or animation to (the body, etc.); to endow with vital force or principle.

1678 CUDWORTH *Intell. Syst.* I. v. 784 By the Idol of the soul Plotinus seems to mean an airy or spirituous Body, quickned and vitalized by the soul, adhering to it after death. 1813 T. BUSBY *Lucretius* I. III. 797 Seeds which now the body vitalise. 1846 J. HUDSON in *Rep. & Papers Bot.* (Ray Soc.) 305 How does it happen that a cell is so vitalized as to be able to produce a phyton? 1868 PEARD *Water-farm.* xi. 113 Every year..millions of eggs are regularly vitalised and transmitted over the Continent.

transf. 1858 J. H BENNET *Nutrition* ii. 43 The intellectual man..who has vitalized..his brain by brain exercise.

b. *Path.* To excite activity in (an ulcer, etc.).

1884 M. MACKENZIE *Dis. Throat & Nose* II. 277 For the purpose..of 'vitalizing' the borders of an indolent ulcer in the nasal cavity.

2. *fig.* To make living or active; to infuse vitality or vigour into (something); to animate.

1805 FOSTER *Ess.* I. iv. 50 A malignant quality appears vitalized into a powerful demon. *a* 1853 ROBERTSON *Lect.* (1859) 124 What he wanted was to vitalize the system—to throw into it not a Jewish, but a Christian feeling. 1873 SYMONDS *Grk. Poets* v. 111 The Greek genius was endowed with the faculty of distinguishing, differentiating, vitalizing, what the Oriental nations left hazy and confused and inert.

b. To put life into (a literary or artistic conception); to present or depict in a lifelike manner.

1884 *Athenæum* 8 March 319/3 Lord Tennyson..always allows himself room not only to vitalize his characters, but to let them grow. 1907 *Ibid.* 16 March 313/1 He is not an artist. He cannot vitalize his material.

Hence **Vi·talized** *ppl. a.*

1843 R. J. GRAVES *Syst. Clin. Med.* xxvii. 350 The seminal fluid of the male is a highly vitalized product. 1868 PEARD *Water-farm.* xiii. 127 The largest quantity of this vitalised seed was sown in the rivers of France. 1874 H. R. REYNOLDS *John Bapt.* viii. 505 Those who..regard Christianity as an etherealized or vitalized morality.

Vi·talizer. [f. prec. + -ER.] One who or that which vitalizes.

1882 J. BROWN *John Leech*, etc. 375 He was not only..an organiser and vitaliser of hunting, he was a great breeder. 1883 *Advance* (Chicago) 21 June 383 Life is the revealer and vitalizer of truth.

Vi·talizing, *ppl. a.* [f. VITALIZE *v.*] That vitalizes or endues with vitality; animating, invigorating.

1813 T. BUSBY *Lucretius* I. III. *Comm.* p. xxvii, The seeds ..do not possess..any vitalizing quality. 1857 MILLER *Elem. Chem.*, *Org.* 742 The principal change is that described by Prout as the vitalizing action of the stomach. 1880 BROWNING *Dram. Idylls* II. 149 Not one flower-dust fell but straight its fall awoke Vitalizing virtue.

Vitall, -er, obs. ff. VICTUAL, -ALLER.

Vitally (vəi·tăli), *adv.* [f. VITAL *a.* + -LY [2].]

†1. In a manner which imparts life or vitality; so as to cause or produce life. *Obs.*

1661 RUST *Origen & Opin.* 78 The Body wherewith she [the Soul] is vitally united. 1664 H. MORE *Apology* 499 What Body more radiant and refulgent then the Sun in his greatest brightness can be vitally organized? 1690 LOCKE *Hum. Und.* II. xxvii. § 4 Though that Life be communicated to new Particles of Matter vitally united to the living Plant. *a* 1791 WESLEY *Serm.* lxxx. Wks. 1811 IX. 395 You are not now vitally united to any of the members of Christ.

† 2. By means of vital force or power. *Obs. rare.*

a 1676 HALE *Prim. Orig. Man.* I. ii. (1677) 50 The Mixt sort of Reason seems to be when a thing concurrs actively and from an internal principle, and (in things that have life) vitally, to the production of a reasonable effect. *Ibid.*, This reasonable work [of ploughing] is performed actively and vitally by my Brute in the virtue of my direction.

†3. In a living state; alive. *Obs.*[−1]

1692 BENTLEY *Boyle Lect.* v. 174 Nature may bring forth the young infants vitally into the world.

4. In a way or to an extent which is vital or absolutely essential; essentially, indispensably.

1770 BURKE *Pres. Discont.* Wks. II. 303 The first franchise of an Englishman, and that on which all the rest vitally depend. 1795 — *Scarcity* Wks. VII. 381 Affairs that vitally concern the agriculture of the kingdom. 1852 MISS YONGE *Cameos* II. xxxi. 325 It was vitally necessary to Henry to keep himself respected and feared. 1861 FLOR. NIGHTINGALE *Nursing* ii. (ed. 2) 11 Due attention would be bestowed on this vitally important matter. 1881 MASSON in *Macm. Mag.* Dec. 150/1 His Edinburgh life during those five years divides itself, however, very vitally, in the retrospect of it now, into two portions.

b. In an important or high degree; intensely, powerfully. *rare.*

1787 JEFFERSON *Writ.* (1859) II. 187 The effect of this operation was vitally felt by every farmer in America.

5. With life-like or vivid realization; vividly.

1865 RUSKIN *Sesame* ii. § 72 She should be taught to enter with her whole personality into the history she reads; to picture the passages of it vitally in her own bright imagination.

6. So as to affect or destroy life; fatally, mortally.

1891 *Cent. Dict.* s.v., The animal was vitally hit or hurt.

Vitals (vəi·tălz), *sb. pl.* [ad. L. *vītālia*, neut. pl. of *vītālis*, or directly f. VITAL *a.*]

1. Those parts or organs of the body, esp. the human body, essential to life, or upon which life depends; the vital parts.

Usually as a vague or general term, but sometimes applied specifically to the brain, heart, lungs, and liver.

For the phr. *stop my vitals*, see STAP *v.* and STOP *v.* 9 c.

a 1610 HEALEY *Cebes* (1636) 134 Now hee..purgeth away the causes and nutriment of the maladie, and then corroborates the vitals. 1641 TATHAM *Distracted State* IV. i. (1651) 24, I feel my vitals fail me. 1690 C. NESSE *O. & N. Test.* I. 52 Like the wound in the heel, far from the vitals, the head or heart. 1708 SWIFT *Sacram. Test* Wks. 1755 II. I. 125 If..you think a poultice made of our vitals will give it any ease, speak the word. 1760–72 H. BROOKE *Fool of Qual.* (1809) III. 117 The weapon has missed your vitals. 1792 COWPER *Odyss.* IX. 347 Me, then, my courage prompted to approach The monster..And to transfix him where the vitals wrap The liver. 1861 PALEY *Æschylus* (ed. 2) *Choeph.* 264 *note*, The notion in the mind of the speaker is that of a cold chill at the vitals. 1897 MARY KINGSLEY *W. Africa* 246 A miscellaneous collection of bits of broken iron pots and lumps of lead frisking among their vitals.

b. *fig.* or in fig. context.

1641 MILTON *Reform.* II. 64 Now heare how they [i.e. the prelates] strike at the very heart and vitals [of monarchy]. 1671 TRENCHFIELD *Cap Gray Hairs* (1688) 32 The dainty Tooths of some corroding so far into their estates, as to reach the very vitals. 1719 W. WOOD *Surv. Trade* 56 The truest Sign of our Vitals not being tainted, and that we are not wounded in any Noble Part, but go on increasing in Trade. 1790 BURKE *Fr. Rev.* 350 Such immense sums, drawn from the vitals of all France. 1802–12 in Bentham *Ration. Judic. Evid.* (1827) V. 536 The very life and vitals of the cause lies in secreting the evidence. 1853 MERIVALE *Rom. Rep.* i. (1867) 7 Tiberius..continued to brood over the plague-spot he had discovered in the vitals of his country. 1868 FARRAR *Seekers* I. iii. (1875) 37 To have fastened upon the very vitals of the national existence.

2. *transf.* Parts or features essentially necessary to something; essential points, essentials.

1657 J. WATTS *Vind. Ch. Eng.* 30 So long as the vitals and fundamentals of faith and truth abide. 1657–8 in *Burton's Diary* (1828) II. 433 If the vitals were preserved, I should not differ for the rest. 1689 *Myst. Iniq.* 9 Tho all English Protestants have ever been at an Accord in all the Essentials and Vitals of Religion. 1702 C. MATHER *Magn. Chr.* III. II. xxviii. (1852) 504 Of pernicious consequence to the very vitals of religion. 1887 *Pall Mall G.* 4 May 11/1 When the Parnellite leaders approached the vitals of the issue.

b. The vital parts of a ship. Cf. VITAL *a.* 3 b.

1884 *Pall Mall G.* 13 Nov. 5/1 *Riachuelo*...Speed 17 knots; 6,200 tons; 8½ in. armour over vitals. 1894 C. N. ROBINSON *Brit. Fleet* 288 The armour..shielding the gun, the machinery, and 'vitals' of the vessel.

†**Vitaly.** *Obs.*[−0] In 5 vytaly. [var. of ME. *vitaille* VICTUAL *sb.* Cf. obs. Flem. *victalie* (Kilian).] Victual, victuals.

c 1440 *Promp. Parv.* 511/1 Vytaly, or vytayl, *victuale.*

Vitalyge, obs. f. VICTUALAGE.

Vitascope (vəi·tăskōup). *U.S.* [f. L. *vita* life + -SCOPE.] A variety of kinematograph.

1896 *Columbus* (Ohio) *Dispatch* 4 Apr. 1/2 The vitascope throws upon a screen by means of bright lights and powerful lenses the moving life size figures of human beings and animals. 1896 *N. Amer. Rev.* Sept. 380 As yet, vitascope exhibitions are confined to episodes lasting from two to five minutes. 1897 *Pop. Sci. Monthly* Dec. 180 In some forms of apparatus, such as the vitascope,..the shutter is omitted.

†**Vita·tion.** *Obs.*[−0] [ad. L. *vītātio*, f. *vītāre* to avoid.] 'An eschewing, voiding, or shunning' (Blount).

1623 COCKERAM I. [Hence in Blount and Phillips.]

Vita·tiveness. *Phren.* [Irreg. f. L. *vīta* life.] The love of life, the desire to live, regarded as a special faculty of the mind or brain.

1843 G. COMBE *Syst. Phrenol.* (ed. 5) I. 292 Dr. Spurzheim was disposed to admit the existence of this faculty, which he calls Vitativeness. 1884 G. COHEN *Mod. Self-Instr. Phrenol.* 131 To cultivate Vitativeness people should lead a natural and healthy life.

Vitayle, -ayll(e, obs. forms of VICTUAL.

Vitayler, -lour, obs. forms of VICTUALLER.

†**Vitch**, obs. var. FITCH *sb.*[1] (Cf. VETCH.)

1598 FLORIO, *Vesza*, the pulse Veccie, or Vitches.

Viteilour, Vitel, obs. ff. VICTUAL(LER.

†**Vitele.** *Obs.*[−1] [a. obs. Pg. *vitele.*] = BETEL.

1582 N. LICHEFIELD tr. *Castanheda's Conq. E. Ind.* I. xvii. 44 In this was ye Vitele which the king doth chaw in his mouth.

Viteler, Vitell, obs. ff. VICTUAL(LER.

Vitellarian (vitelē·riăn), *a.* *Anat.* [f. next.] Of or belonging to the vitellarium.

1877 HUXLEY *Anat. Inv. Anim.* i. 67 The function of the vitellarian gland may be taken on by cells of the ovary, or oviduct. *Ibid.* iv. 199 Passing between the anterior vitellarian masses.

‖**Vitellarium** (vitelē·riŏm). *Anat.* Pl. **-aria.** [mod.L., f. *vitell-us* VITELLUS.] An accessory gland in the female productive organs of some worms, by which the vitellus for the eggs is secreted; a yolk-gland.

1865 *Nat. Hist. Rev.* July 336 There is added a highly specialised yolk-forming apparatus, or 'vitellarium'. 1877 HUXLEY *Anat. Inv. Anim.* iv. 178 The two vitellaria, which are long and simple or branched tubes, open into the oviduct.

Vitellary (vi·telări, vite·lări, vəi-), *sb.* and *a.* [f. L. *vitell-us* VITELLUS + -ARY.]

A. *sb.* †1. The place or part where the yolk of an egg is formed. *Obs.*

1650 SIR T. BROWNE *Pseud. Ep.* (ed. 2) III. xxviii. 151 A greater difficulty..is, how the sperm of the Cock..attaineth unto every egg, since the vitellary or place of the yelk is very high. 1687 *Phil. Trans.* XVI. 482 Now this Fecundation seems to be in the Vitellary, and not in the Uterus.

†2. (See quot.) *Obs.*[−0]

1736 BAILEY (fol.) Pref., *Vitellary*..the Yolk of an Egg; but some use it to signify a Cluster of Eggs.

B. *adj.* Of or belonging to the vitellus; vitelline.

1846 *Proc. Amer Philos. Soc.* IV. 307 There can be no mammiferous germ independent of vitellary matter. 1854 S. P. WOODWARD *Mollusca* II. 161 The contractions of this caudal vesicle and of the vitellary vesicle alternate. 1877 HUXLEY *Anat. Inv. Anim.* vi. 323 A caecal process, the remains, according to Rathke, of one lobe of the vitellary sac of the embryo.

Viteller, obs. form of VICTUALLER.

Vitelli-, combining form of L. *vitellus* VITELLUS, employed in a few scientific terms, as **vitelli·ferous, vitelli·genous, vitelli·gerous, vite·lligine** *adjs.*, producing the vitellus or yolk.

1819 LINDLEY tr. *Richard's Obs. Fruits & Seeds* 52 The most simple *vitelliferous embryo. *Ibid.* 59 This embryo is composed, like those which are called vitelliferous, of two distinct bodies. 1859 *Todd's Cycl. Anat.* V. 121*/1 The ova, as they continue to descend in the *vitelligenous part of the tube,..assume the form of sub-triangular flattened bodies. 1870 ROLLESTON *Anim. Life* p. cxxv, A complicated reproductive apparatus, in which..vitelligenous exist independently of germigenous glands. 1877 HUXLEY *Anat. Inv. Anim.* vii. 442, I am inclined to believe that..these epithelial cells..play the part of vitelligenous cells. 1898 *Proc. Zool. Soc. London* 555 The larvæ of many Teleosteans..in the *vitelligerous condition. 1864 COBBOLD *Entozoa* 214 The female organs..consist of two masses of *vitelligine glands occupying a limited space.

Vite·llicle. *Biol.* [f. L. *vitell-us* VITELLUS + dim. ending *-icle.*] A vitelline sac; a yolk-sac.

1852 BRANDE *Dict. Sci.*, etc. (ed. 2) Suppl. s.v., In man and mammalia the vitellicle is called the 'umbilical vesicle'.

Vitellin (vite·lin, vəi-). *Chem.* Also **-ine.** [f. VITELL-US + -IN [1].]

1. The albuminoidal substance in the yolk of egg, a mixture of albumin and casein.

1857 MILLER *Elem. Chem.*, *Org.* 647 These bodies of minor importance, such as globulin and vitellin. 1867 BLOXAM *Chem.* 614 Yolk of egg contains a modification of albumen termed vitelline. 1886 *Buck's Handbk. Med. Sci.* II. 640/1 The yolk..is a bright yellow mixture of about sixteen per cent. of vitellin, a substance resembling albumen.

2. A related substance found in the seeds of plants. Also *attrib.*

1882 BENTLEY *Man. Bot.* (ed. 4) 35 The proteids exist in these grains as globulins, which hitherto have been known only to occur in animals, that is, as myosin-globulin and vitellin-globulin. 1885 GOODALE *Physiol. Bot.* (1892) 364 Weyl..holds that legumin is a mixture of vegetable vitellin and casein.

Vitelline (vite·ləin, -in, vəi-), *a.* and *sb.* Also 5–6 vitellyn(e, 6 vytellyn, 7 vitellin. [ad. med.L. *vitellin-us*, f. L. *vitell-us* VITELLUS. Cf. OF. *vitellin* (in sense 1).]

A. *adj.* 1. Coloured like the yolk of an egg; deep-yellow with a tinge of red. In early use *spec.* of bile.

?*a* 1412 LYDG. *Two Merchants* 307 Yif of colre be take his groundement Pure or vnpure, citryn or vitellyne. *c* 1530 *Judic. Urines* II. viii. 33 Color Prassyn is gendred of a color vitellyn. *Ibid.* ix. 36 b, Coler citrin & Coler vytellyn be all one. 1596 BARROUGH *Meth. Physick* (ed. 3) 293 Matter cholericke and filthie (as one would say) vitelline, the which causeth feuers. 1666 G. HARVEY *Morbus Angl.* xxv. (1672) 56 If we should commit the first of these, namely yellow, or vitellin choler to the test. 1684 tr. *Bonet's Merc. Compit.* VI. 244 A yellow colour arises, which indicates vitelline Bile. 1887 W. PHILLIPS *Brit. Discomycetes* 144 Hymenium vitelline; stem rather long.

2. *Biol.* Of or belonging to the vitellus or yolk of an egg.

1835–6 *Todd's Cycl. Anat.* I. 545/1 Only the..oily particles

of the vitelline nidus could be expected to be seen. 1849 OWEN *Parthenogenesis* 73 An ovum..may contain a supplementary nutrient vitelline mass, properly called yelk. 1883 *Science* I. 431/2 This sac..was connected with the foetal vascular system by a vitelline artery and two veins.

b. *Vitelline membrane, sac*, the transparent membrane which surrounds the yolk of an egg; the yolk-sac; the investing membrane of the embryo.

1845 TODD & BOWMAN *Phys. Anat.* I. 48 The first, or the vitelline membrane of the ovum, is the wall of a cell. 1861 J. R. GREENE *Man. Anim. Kingd.*, *Cœlent.* 15 In addition to these parts, many ova are provided with an outer envelope, known as the yolk-sac or 'vitelline membrane'. 1880 GÜNTHER *Fishes* 166 Generally the vitelline sac of the embryoes is free.

B. *sb.* The yolk, the vitellary substance.

1891 *Cent. Dict.*

Hence †**Vitellinous** *a.* (See quot.) *Obs.*

1786 ABERCROMBIE *Arr.* 35 in *Gard. Assist.*, Vitellinous, or yellow barked [willow-tree].

Vite·llo-, combining form (cf. VITELLI-) of VITELLUS, used in a few terms (*Biol.* and *Chem.*), as **vitello-duct, -intestinal** *a.*, **-lutein, -phag, -rubin** (see quots.).

1888 ROLLESTON & JACKSON *Anim. Life* 647 Internally it opens, when single, into the *vitello-duct, or germ-duct. 1854 BUSHMAN in *Orr's Circ. Sci.* II. 84 A communication is found to have arisen between the yolk and the intestine, by a wide duct termed the *vitello-intestinal duct. 1886 *Buck's Handbk. Med. Sci.* II. 247/2 In the red eggs of *Maja squinado* R. Maly found two kinds of coloring matter, which he named *vitellolutein and vitellorubin. *Ibid.* 248/1 Vitellolutein is soluble in alcohol to a clear yellow solution. 1904 *Science* 8 April 588/2 There is no satisfactory evidence to show that the cells..are really such, and not dividing cleavage cells or possibly *vitellophags. 1886 *Buck's Handbk. Med. Sci.* II. 248/1 *Vitellorubin occurs in an amorphous form, soluble in alcohol to a brown fluid.

Vitello·genous, *a.* [f. prec. + -GEN + -OUS.] Producing the vitellus or yolk.

1872 E. R. LANKESTER *Advancem. Sci.* (1890) 265 The others disappear as..vitellogenous cells. 1878 F. J. BELL *Gegenbaur's Comp. Anat.* 301 This vitellogenous layer occupies the portion of the chamber behind the egg-cell.

‖**Vitellus** (vite·lŏs, vəi-). [L. *vitellus* yolk of an egg.]

1. *Embryol.* The yolk of an egg; the germinative contents of an ovum-cell.

1728 CHAMBERS *Cycl.* s.v. *Egg*, In the middle of the inner White, is the *Vitellus* or Yelk. 1826 GOOD *Bk. Nat.* (1834) I. 165 In this respect the albumen of the cotyledon corresponds with the vitellus of the hen's egg. 1857 BERKELEY *Cryptog. Bot.* xv. 26 Nothing can be more close than the mode of development in these..and of the vitellus in the eggs of certain *Mollusca*. 1877 HUXLEY *Anat. Inv. Anim.* 367 In certain Amphipods..the vitellus undergoes complete division.

2. *Bot.* A fleshy sac situated between the albumen and the embryo in a seed.

1807 J. E. SMITH *Phys. Bot.* 292 The *Vitellus* is esteemed by Gærtner to compose the bulk of the seed in Fuci, Mosses and Ferns. 1829 T. CASTLE *Introd. Bot.* 245 The vitellus is an organ of a fleshy but firm texture, situated, when present, between the albumen and embryo. 1861 BENTLEY *Man. Bot.* 444 Embryo minute, enclosed in a vitellus, and outside of abundant fleshy albumen.

b. (See quot.)

1900 B. D. JACKSON *Gloss. Bot. Terms*, *Vitellus*,..an oily substance adhering to the spores of Lycopodium.

Viterde, variant of VITTERED *a.* *Obs.*

†**Viteroke.** *Obs.*[−1] [app. related to VITTERED, FITTERED *a.*] A ragged upper garment.

a 1225 *Ancr. R.* 328 Heo hudet eke here ihole cloðes, & doð an alre vuemeste on viterokes al to torene.

Vith, ME. form of WITH.

Vipele, southern ME. var. FIDDLE *sb.*

Viti-, combining form of L. *vitis* vine, occurring in a few forms, as **viti·ferous** *a.* [L. *vītifer*], †**vitigi·neous** *a.* [L. *vitigineus*] (see quots.).

Also (in recent dicts.) *viticide* something which kills or destroys vines; *viticolous* adj., living on or in vines.

1656 BLOUNT *Glossogr.*, *Vitiferous*, that bears Vines. 1721 BAILEY, *Vitigineous*, that cometh of a Vine. 1753 *Chambers' Cycl.* Suppl. s.v. *Porrum*, The vitigineous wild leek of Gerrard.

†**Vitial**, *a.* *Obs.*[−1] [f. L. *viti-um* + -AL.] Vicious.

1614 T. ADAMS *Sinners Passing Bell* Wks. (1629) 253 There is nothing on it [*sc.* earth] that is of it, which is not become more vitiall, then vitall.

Vitiate (vi·ʃiĕt), *ppl. a.* Now *rare.* Also 5–6 **viciat(e, 6 vicyate, vycyat(e.** [ad. L. *vitiāt-us* (med.L. also *viciāt-us*), pa. pple. of *vitiāre*: see next.]

1. Vitiated, depraved, infected, spoiled: **a.** In predicative use.

1432–50 tr. *Higden* (Rolls) IV. 427 Peple viciate and pollute, to whom hit was not lawefulle to offre. *Ibid.* V. 213 A man viciate of body scholde not receyve ordres. 1539 ELYOT *Cast. Helthe* I. (1541) 1 b, Fyre..is the clarifyer of other elementes if they be vicyate or out of theyr naturall temperaunce. 1545 RAYNALD *Byrth Mankynde* 79 Yf the matrice be perysshed or otherwyse viciate. 1737 BRACKEN *Farriery Impr.* (1756) I. 14 The Blood is..vitiate or corrupt.

b. Const. *by* or *with*.

c 1450 tr. *De Imitatione* III. lx. 140 Nature sliden & viciat by þe first man Adam þoru3 synne. 1460 CAPGRAVE *Chron.* Ded. 1 For the elde bokes..thou3 thei were mad ful treuly, 3et be thei viciat be the writeres. 1533 MORE 2nd *Pt. Confut. Tindale* II. Wks. 636/2 The scripture adulterate and viciate with false gloses & wronge exposicions. 1572 BOSSEWELL *Armorie* III. 7 Neyther with the sonne beame is viciate the sterre, Nor yet by the bearing of a sonne, the mother.

c. Used attributively.

1551 ROBINSON tr. *More's Utopia* II. (1895) 202 In their viciate and corrupt taste. 1665 G. HARVEY *Advice agst. Plague* 15 Add thereunto the vitiate disposition of the air. 1913 A. NOYES *Tales of Mermaid Tavern*, *Raleigh*, He never stooped, Never once pandered to that vitiate hour.

†2. *Sc. Law.* Rendered null or void; interfered or tampered with. *Obs.*

1585 in *Dunfermline Regr.* (Bann. Cl.) 449 Ye auld assumptioun of ye said thrid is vitiat be ye said commendatouris proper deidis. 1593 *Sc. Acts Parlt.*, *Jas. VI* (1816) IV. 25/2 As ony pairt of the rent of dumfermling now viciat salbe recoverit. 1678 SIR G. MACKENZIE *Crim. Laws Scot.* I. xxvii. § 2. (1699) 135 It is said to be suspect, if..it appear vitiat by ocular inspection.

Vitiate (vi·ʃieʹt), *v.* Also 6–8 **viciat(e, 7 vitiat, vitiatt.** [f. L. *vitiāt-* (med.L. also *viciāt-*), ppl. stem of *vitiāre* (whence It. *viziare*, Sp. and Pg. *viciar*, F. *vicier*), f. *vitium* VICE *sb.*[1] Cf. prec.]

1. *trans.* To render incomplete, imperfect, or faulty; to impair or spoil.

1534 MORE *Treat. Passion* Wks. 1303/1 Hym must we serue, though specially wyth the mynde (whych if it be not good, viciateth all together) yet..also wyth body and goodes and al. *a* 1631 DONNE *Serm.*, *Matt.* v. 16 (1640) 82 A superstitious end, or a seditious end vitiates the best worke. 1665 MANLEY *Grotius' Low C. Wars* 453 Other Advices were prefer'd, which..do many times vitiate, if not ruine, the most noble and valiant Undertakings. 1678 BARCLAY *Apol. Quakers* vii. § 2. 197 This Doctrine of Justification hath been, and is greatly vitiated in the Church of Rome. 1711 ADDISON *Spect.* No. 25 ¶ 5 A continual Anxiety for Life vitiates all the Relishes of it, and casts a Gloom over the whole Face of Nature. 1738 WARBURTON *Div. Legat.* I. 166 Time, which naturally and fatally vitiates and depraves all things. 1794 HUTTON *Philos. Light*, etc. 124 It would only lead us into error, and thus vitiate the science or philosophy in which it were employed. 1808 J. HASLAM *Observ. Madness & Mel.* i. (1809) 31 It might be urged, that in these instances, the perception was vitiated. 1851 NICHOL *Archit. Heav.* (ed. 9) 60 Considering that a deviation from truth by the fraction of a hairbreadth, would vitiate the figure.

b. To corrupt (*a*) literary works or (*b*) language by carelessness, arbitrary changes, or the introduction of foreign elements.

(*a*) 1659 BP. WALTON *Consid. Considered* 198 The Septuagint..which we now have is the same for substance with that anciently used, though..by the injury of time, and frequent transcriptions vitiated. 1788 REID *Aristotle's Logic* i. § 1. 5 There is reason to doubt whether what [works] are his be not much vitiated and interpolated.

(*b*) 1690 TEMPLE *Ess.*, *Poetry* Wks. 1720 I. 243 Where-ever the Roman Colonies had remained, and their Language had been generally spoken, the common People used that still, but vitiated with the base Allay of their Provincial Speech. 1742 *De Foe's Tour Gt. Brit.* (ed. 3) III. 4 It is observable, that the Normans could not well pronounce Lincoln, but vitiated it to Nichol. 1756 JOHNSON *Dict.* Pref., Many barbarous terms and phrases, by which other dictionaries may vitiate the style, are rejected from this. 1790 'CASSANDRA' (J. Bruckner) *Crit. Tooke's Purley* 55 Those who consider how much the language had been vitiated at the time they lived, by the importation of foreign words.

2. To render corrupt in morals; to deprave in respect of principles or conduct; to lower the moral standard of (persons).

1534 MORE *Treat. Passion* Wks. 1311/2 We shulde note well and marke thereby, that the vice of a vicious personne, viciateth not the company or congregacion. 1658–9 in *Burton's Diary* (1828) IV. 59 This will not vitiate persons, but your nature and your posterity. 1682 BURNET *Rights Princes* Pref. 13 Mankind is not so vitiated with prejudice. 1751 JOHNSON *Rambler* No. 177 ¶ 12 The suppression of those habits with which I was vitiated. 1770 *Junius Lett.* xxxvii. (1788) 199 If any part of the representative body be not chosen by the people, that part vitiates and corrupts the whole. 1853 C. L. BRACE *Home Life Germany* 258 In 1806, the army had become thoroughly vitiated by luxury. 1880 E. KIRKE *Garfield* 55 In short, he had only one fault, but that was radical, and in the end, vitiated the whole man. He was thoroughly selfish.

b. Similarly with impersonal objects.

1584 R. SCOT *Discov. Witchcr.* v. v. (1886) 80 He being a spirit, may with Gods leave and ordinance viciat and corrupt the spirit and will of man. 1598 MARSTON *Pygmal.*, *Sat.* ii, Many spots my mind doth vitiate. 1634 HABINGTON *Castara* Pref. (Arb.) 12, I encounter'd there..Innocencie,..not vitiated by conversation with the world. 1675 TRAHERNE *Chr. Ethics* 324 So doth one vice cherished and allowed corrupt and viciate all the vertues in the whole world. 1714 R. FIDDES *Pract. Disc.* II. 93 Sufferings vitiate the best tempers. 1751 JOHNSON *Rambler* No. 172 ¶ 2 Many vitiate their principles in the acquisition of riches. 1837 HT. MARTINEAU *Soc. Amer.* III. 263 The encouragement of an amusement which does seem to be vitiated there. 1847 HAMILTON *Rewards & Punishm.* viii. (1853) 362 One sin of youth vitiates a protracted life. 1861 MILL *Utilit.* i. 4 To what extent the moral beliefs of mankind have been vitiated ..by the absence of any distinct recognition of an ultimate standard.

c. To pervert (the eye, taste, etc.), so as to lead to false judgements or preferences.

1806 A. HUNTER *Culina* (ed. 3) 120 Stomachs may be so far vitiated as to lose all relish for plain roast, or boiled meat. 1881 CRAIG *Lect. Drawing*, etc. ii. 103 This practice has such a tendency to vitiate the eye and to mislead the mind. 1845 MCCULLOCH *Taxation* I. vi. (1852) 245 It had the mischievous effect of vitiating the public taste and stimulating the consumption of ardent spirits.

†3. To deflower or violate (a woman). *Obs.*

1547–50 [see *Vitiating* vbl. sb.]. 1624 HEYWOOD *Gunaik.* I. 35 Till she returned into her owne naturall forme, in which he vitiated her, and of her begat Achilles. *c* 1645 HOWELL *Lett.* (1650) I. 49 This beutious Maid [Venice] hath bin often attempted to be vitiated. 1675 BAXTER *Cath. Theol.* I. 107 Being not..moved by him (as David to murder Urias, and to vitiate his wife). 1710 STEELE *Tatler* No. 198 ¶ 8 He confessed his Marriage, and his placing his Companion on Purpose to vitiate his Wife. 1769 BLACKSTONE *Comm.* IV. 81 It was a felony and attended with a forfeiture of the fief, if the vasal vitiated the wife or daughter of his lord. 1791 BURKE *Let. Member Nat. Assembly* Wks. VI. 36 Pedagogues, who betray the most awful family trusts, and vitiate their female pupils.

4. To corrupt or spoil in respect of substance; to make bad, impure, or defective.

1572 J. JONES *Bathes Buckstone* 15 For blood is the treasure of lyfe, not viciated. 1599 SANDYS *Europæ Spec.* (1632) 103 As a dead Flie doth vitiate a whole boxe of sweet oyntment. 1608 TOPSELL *Serpents* 125 Euen as women in their monthly courses doe vitiat their looking-glasses. 1652 L. S. *People's Liberty* iii. 6 As much water cannot so soon be viciated as a lesser quantity. 1674 R. GODFREY *Inj. & Ab. Physic* 33 The very texture of his Stomach and other vital bowels was vitiated. 1759 MILLS tr. *Duhamel's Husb.* I. xvi. 93 Farmers distinguish the wheat thus vitiated by saying that it is blacked in the point. 1789 W. BUCHAN *Dom. Med.* (1790) 465 When the saliva is vitiated,..the curing of the disorder is the cure of this symptom. 1863 GEO. ELIOT *Romola* xxxiv, The oncoming of a malady that has permanently vitiated the sight. 1882 *Med. Temp. Jrnl.* No. 52. 177 As I shall endeavour to show you, it vitiates the blood.

b. *esp.* To render (air) impure and so inadequate for, or injurious to, life.

1715 DESAGULIERS *Fires Impr.* 34 The ill Humours which go out of their Bodies..vitiate the Air more and more. 1793 BEDDOES *Consump.* 137 Only a very small portion of the air was vitiated, i.e. converted into fixed air. 1869 E. A. PARKES *Pract. Hygiene* (ed. 3) 118 The impurity of the air vitiated by respiration. 1878 HUXLEY *Physiogr.* 84 This gas would unduly accumulate, and..vitiate the entire bulk of the atmosphere.

5. To render of no effect; to invalidate either completely or in part; *spec.* to destroy or impair the legal effect or force of (a deed, etc.).

1621 SANDERSON *Serm.* I. 170 An earthly judge is subject to misprision, mis-information, partiality, corruption, and sundry infirmities that may vitiate his proceedings. 1726 AYLIFFE *Parergon* 104 A Transposition of the Order of the Sacramental Words, does, in some Mens Opinion, vitiate Baptism. 1790 BURKE *Fr. Rev.* 37 If all the absurd theories of lawyers and divines were to vitiate the objects in which they are conversant, we should have no law, and no religion left in the world. 1827 JARMAN *Powell's Devises* II. 21 If an undefined portion of a bequest is to be applied to a purpose void by the statute, it vitiates the whole. 1853 LYTTON *My Novel* XII. xxvii, I told them flatly..that, as Mr. Egerton's agent, I would allow no proceedings that might vitiate the election. 1883 *Law Rep.* 11 Q. B. Div. 568 The plaintiff is engaged in carrying out the illegal objects of the association;..and this circumstance alone vitiates the contract for repayment.

b. To render (an argument, etc.) inconclusive or unsatisfactory.

1748 HARTLEY *Observ. Man* I. iii. § 1. 308 This will not vitiate the foregoing Conjectures. 1846 MILL *Logic* I. v. § 3 The theory of that intellectual process has been vitiated by the influence of these erroneous notions. 1866 HERSCHEL *Fam. Lect. Sci.* (1867) 73 His proof is vitiated by an enormous oversight: and the thing..is a physical impossibility. 1878 STEWART & TAIT *Unseen Univ.* ii. § 84. 94 It is this eternity of atom which vitiates the hypothesis.

†6. a. To adulterate. *Obs.*[−1]

1728 SHERIDAN tr. *Persius* ii. (1739) 35 It was Luxury first made us vitiate our Oyl with Cassia.

†b. To alter feloniously. *Obs.*[−1]

1753 *Scots Mag.* Aug. 420/1 And William Taylor, for vitiating a bank-note.

Hence **Vi·tiating** *vbl. sb.* and *ppl. a.*

1547 HOOPER *Declar. Christ & Office* xii. L viij, The deathe of his chyldre, the conspyricie of Absolon, the uiciating of his wiues. *a* 1550 LELAND *Itin.* (1769) V. 21 The Collegiate Church..was translatid to Aberguili for vitiating of a Maide. 1647 CLARENDON *Contempl. Ps. Tracts* (1727) 392 The yielding to every corrupt affection and passion is as great a vitiating and weakening of the mind. 1669 BOYLE *Certain Physiol. Ess.* (ed. 2) *Absol. Rest Bodies* 27 Finding its passage obstructed..by the vitiating of the Pores of the Glass. 1858 J. MARTINEAU *Stud. Chr.* 275 A certain vitiating unsoundness of mind. 1859 GEO. ELIOT *A. Bede* xxix, No man can escape this vitiating effect of an offence against his own sentiment of right.

Vitiated (vi·ʃieʹtĕd), *ppl. a.* [f. the vb.] That has undergone vitiation; corrupted, spoiled, impaired: **a.** In respect of substance.

1620 VENNER *Via Recta* vii. 135 Those [almonds] that.. [are] reserued all the yeare, so that they waxe not too dry, or in their colour and substance vitiated [etc.]. 1644 MILTON *Areop.* (Arb.) 43 Wholesome meats to a vitiated stomack differ little or nothing from unwholesome. 1688 BOYLE *Vitiated Sight* 271 Some may think that [such] a man has rather an excellent, than a vitiated sight. 1747 tr. *Astruc's Fevers* 285 These cells becoming turgid with this vitiated matter, raise the *cuticula*. 1770 *Phil. Trans.* LX. 400 It might..seem possible, that blood-letting had only let out the vitiated part. 1813 J. THOMSON *Lect. Inflam.* 648 When the vesications pass into the state of sloughing, or vitiated ulcers. 1826 S. COOPER *First Lines Surg.* (ed. 5) 38 Certain deleterious kinds of food, such as the ergot or vitiated rye. 1867 A. BARRY *Sir C. Barry* vi. 166 The smoke and vitiated air of every room in the building. 1892 *Photogr. Ann.* II. 213 Confinement in the vitiated atmosphere of an ill-ventilated dark room.

b. In some abstract quality or principle.

1660 R. COKE *Power & Subj.* 189 No affliction, or the keeping the thing detained, ought to injure the Appellant, or the vitiated Cause ayded by remedy of the Appeal. 1719 DE FOE *Crusoe* I. 201 To have no other Guide than that of their own abominable and vitiated Passions. 1740 CIBBER *Apol.* iv. 68 It is..to the vitiated and low Taste of the Spectator, that the Corruptions of the Stage..have been owing. 1790 BURKE *Fr. Rev.* 100 It is in us the degenerate choice of a vitiated mind. 1833 I. TAYLOR *Fanat.* I. 1 Vitiated religious sentiments have too much connexion with the principles of our physical constitution to [etc.]. 1841 D'ISRAELI *Amen. Lit.* (1867) 97 This vulgar or corrupt Latin..was the vitiated mother of the sister-languages of Europe. 1871 DARWIN *Desc. Man* II. xiv. 115 Vitiated instincts may also account for some of the hybrid unions above referred to.

Vitiation (viʃiē·ʃən). [ad. L. *vitiātio* (rare), or f. VITIATE *v.*] The action of vitiating, the fact or state of being vitiated, in senses of the verb.

1635 JACKSON *Creed* VIII. xx. § 5 No addition is forbidden, but such as includeth a vitiation of the text. 1658 PHILLIPS, *Vitiation*, a corrupting or defiling; also a deflowring. 1666 G. HARVEY *Morb. Angl.* xvii. (1672) 35 The cause of the foresaid extenuation of body..is imputed to the bloods vitiation by malign putrid vapors, smoaking throughout the vessels. 1802 PALEY *Nat. Theol.* xxvi. (1819) 429 That vitiation of taste which frequently occurs in fevers, when every taste is irregular and every one bad. 1809 W. IRVING *Knickerb.* (1861) 61 The original name of the island..has already undergone considerable vitiation. 1843 MILL *Logic* I. ii. § 5 With the least vitiation of the truth of any propositions. 1863 GEO. ELIOT *Romola* xxv, No man ever struggled to retain power over a mixed multitude without suffering vitiation.

Vi·tiator. *rare*[−1]. [ad. L. *vitiātor* (rare) or f. VITIATE *v.*] One who or that which vitiates.

1846 LANDOR *Imag. Conv.* Wks. I. 68/2 The worst vitiator and violator of the Muses and the Graces.

Viti·culated, *a.* *Bot.* *rare*[−1]. [f. L. *vīticula*, dim. of *vītis* vine.] (See quot.)

1727 P. BLAIR *Pharmaco-Bot.* v. 215 Viticulated, or Vine-like Leaves.

Viti·culo·se, *a.* *Bot.* [ad. mod.L. *vīticulōs-us*, f. L. *viticul-a* (see prec.).] (See quot.)

1865 *Treas. Bot.* 1222/1 *Viticulose*, furnished with trailing stems or viticulæ.

Viti·culous, *a.* *rare*[−1]. [See prec. and -OUS.] Resembling the shoots of a vine.

1657 TOMLINSON *Renou's Disp.* 264 Out of which [*sc.* the root of scammony] slender and viticulous branches [L. *viticulosi surculi*] issue.

Viticultural (vitikʌ·ltiŭrăl, vəiti-), *a.* [f. VITICULTURE + -AL.] Of or pertaining to viticulture; connected with the growing of vines.

1865 *Pall Mall G.* 7 Nov. 9 All viticultural operations not requiring the muscular strength of a man. 1888 *Encycl. Brit.* XXIV. 610/2 Hungary, from a viticultural point of view, forms by far the most important part.

Viticulture (vi·tikʌltiŭr, vəiti-). [f. VITI- + CULTURE.] The cultivation of the vine; vine-growing.

1872 THUDICHUM & DUPRÉ (*title*), A Treatise on the Origin, Nature, and Varieties of Wine: being a complete Manual of Viticulture and Œnology. 1881 *Spectator* 12 March 345 Viticulture can only be successfully followed by those who give to it constant personal attention. 1902 A. DOBSON *S. Richardson* iii. 66 His latest idea was to establish viticulture in England.

Hence **Viticu·lturer, Viticu·lturist**, one who is engaged in the cultivation of the vine; a vine-grower.

1882 *St. James' Gaz.* 29 March 6/1 A process of elimination..turned to account by the viticulturists. 1890 *Nature* 13 Nov. 38/2 To aid in these researches, relations have already been opened with horticulturists and viticulturists. 1907 *Westm. Gaz.* 20 June 2/2 Then the viticulturers tried to carry on the trade themselves.

Vitiliginous (vitili·dʒinəs), *a.* [f. L. *vitīligin-*, stem of *vitīligo* (see next) + -OUS.] Of or connected with, of the nature of, vitiligo.

1898 P. MANSON *Trop. Diseases* xxvi. 392 They [leprosy spots] may be mere vitiliginous patches.

‖**Vitiligo** (vitiləi·gō). *Path.* [L. *vitiligo* tetter.] A skin disease characterized by the presence of smooth white shining tubercles on the face, neck, and other parts of the body; a species of leprosy.

1657 *Physical Dict.*, *Vitiligo*, a foulness of the skin with spots of divers colours. Morphew. 1693 tr. *Blancard's Phys. Dict.* (ed. 2), *Vitiligo*, a sort of Leprosie; there are Three kinds of them [etc.]. 1814 BATEMAN *Cutaneous Dis.* (ed. 3) 274 The disease, which is here intended to be designated by the term *Vitiligo*, is..somewhat rare. 1864 W. T. FOX *Skin Dis.* 21 Albinism, vitiligo, deformities of vascular and sebaceous structure. 1889 *Buck's Handbk. Med. Sci.* VIII. 604/1 The dark-skinned races are rather more subject to vitiligo than those of fair skin and light hair.

Hence ‖**Vitiligoi·dea**, a skin-disease resembling vitiligo.

1873 F. T. ROBERTS *The. & Pract. Med.* 779 A peculiar enlargement [of the liver] associated with vitiligoidea. 1899 *Allbutt's Syst. Med.* VIII. 767 Two cases are..discussed by Addison and Gull..in relation to vitiligoidea.

Vitili·tigate, *v.* *rare.* [f. ppl. stem of L. *vitilitigāre.*] (See quot.) Hence **Vitilitigating** *ppl. a.*

1670 BLOUNT *Glossogr.* (ed. 3), *Vitilitigate*,..to backbite, to detract, to wrangle, or make bate. *Hudebras.* [Cf. next.] 1819 H. BUSK *Vestriad* III. 717 In heaven yclept Alecto.. But Discord called by mortals here on earth; A vitilitigating horrid girl.

Vitilitiga·tion. *rare.* [See prec. and -ATION.] Contention, wrangling.

1647 N. WARD *Simple Cobler* 14 It is a most toylsome taske to runne the wild-goose chase after a well breath'd Opinionist: They delight in vitilitigation. 1663 BUTLER *Hud.* I. iii. 1262 I'll force you by right ratiocination To leave your Vitilitigation.

†**Vitiliti·gious**, *a.* *Obs.*[−1] [f. L. *vitilitig-āre* (see above), after *litigious*.] Contentious, quarrelsome.

1683 E. HOOKER *Pref. Pordage's Mystic Div.* 19 Most inevangelicly malevolous, vitious, vitilitigious.

Vitiosity (viʃiǫ·sĭti). Also 6–7, 9 **viciosity** (6 -itie, -itee), 7 **visiositie.** [ad. L. *vitiōsitās*, f. *vitiōsus*: see next and -ITY. So OF. *viciosité* (*vicieusité*, *-eté*), It. *viziosità*.]

†1. A defect or fault; an imperfection. *Obs.*

1538 ELYOT *Dict.* Addit., *Cacia*, viciositie, or that whiche we commonly doo calle, a faute in a thynge. 1563 ABP. PARKER *Corr.* (Parker Soc.) 199 With my natural viciosity of overmuch shamefastness I am so babished..that [etc.]. 1589 PUTTENHAM *Eng. Poesie* (Arb.) 167 It may come to passe that what the Grammarian setteth downe for a viciositee in speach may become a vertue and no vice. 1665 JER. TAYLOR *Unum Necess.* vi. § 16 Any person that hath a fault or a legal impurity, a debt, a vitiosity, defect, or imperfection.

2. The state or character of being morally vicious.

1603 HOLLAND *Plutarch's Mor.* 247 Reason by little and little doth illuminate, purge and cleanse the soule in abating and diminishing evermore the visiositie thereof. 1643 SIR T. BROWNE *Relig. Med.* I. § 42 My untamed affections and confirmed vitiosity makes mee dayly doe worse. 1678 CUDWORTH *Intell. Syst.* I. iii. Contents 104 It is not only moral vitiosity which inclines men to atheize. 1782 J. BROWN *Compend. View Nat. & Rev. Relig.* I. 13 An inconceivable vitiosity of nature absolutely inconsistent with godhead. 1836 GILBERT *Chr. Atonem.* Notes (1852) 380 The vitiosity of sin and public injury are here correlative.

†b. An instance of this; a vice. *Obs.*

1643 SIR T. BROWNE *Relig. Med.* II. § 7 There are certaine tempers of body, which..doe hatch and produce viciosities, whose..monstrosity of nature admits no name. 1657 GAULE *Sap. Just.* 9 That, after Baptism, it is no real viciosity, but only a penalty.

†3. The quality of being physically impaired or defective. *Obs.*

1647 A. ROSS *Mystag. Poet.* i. (1672) 9 In this Gum [*sc.* myrrh] Venus is much delighted, as being a help to..the vitiosity of the Matrix. 1651 N. BIGGS *New Disp.* ¶ 223 If the more waterish and yellow bloud doth denote its vitiosity.

4. *Sc. Law.* The quality of being faulty or improper in a legal aspect.

1765–8 ERSKINE *Inst. Law Scot.* III. ix. § 52 Such confirmation..purges the vitiosity of his former intromissions. 1838 W. BELL *Dict. Law Scot.* 529 It infers an intention on the part of the intromitter to account for his intromissions, which takes off the vitiosity, and renders him liable only to the extent of his intromissions.

Vitious(**ly, -ness**, varr. VICIOUS(LY, -NESS.

Vitivert, var. VETIVER. **Vitle, Vitler**, obs. ff. VICTUAL(LER. **Vitles**, obs. Sc. f. WITLESS *a.* **Vitnes**, obs. Sc. f. WITNESS. **Vitoll**, obs. f. VICTUAL. **Vitraell**, obs. f. VITRIOL.

‖**Vitrage** (vitra·ʒ). [F. *vitrage* glass-windows, f. *vitre* glass.] *Vitrage net* (also *cloth*), a lace-net or thin fabric suitable for window-curtains.

1886 *Daily News* 14 June 2/7 Window-blinds, vitrage nets, and other goods made upon curtain-machines are only in moderate request. 1894 *Times* 19 April 4/3 A steady business is being done in curtains, antimacassars, vitrage nets, &c.

Vi·trailed, *a.* *rare*[−1]. [f. F. *vitrail* (usu. in pl. *vitraux*) a glass-window.] Having glazed windows or compartments (of a specified colour).

1884 RUSKIN *Bible Amiens* iv. § 10 This Lord's House and blue-vitrailed gate of Heaven.

Vi·traillist. *rare.* [f. as prec.] A maker of glass; an artist in glass-work for windows, etc.; a designer in stained-glass.

1607 B. BARNES *Divils Charter* III. v. F 3, Th' Italian Vitraillist, Which in the fierie Phlegitonian flames, Did worke strange vitriall diddidoes for Dames. 1904 *Daily News* 28 July 4/1 In the inner gallery is a large and ambitious picture,..and some drawings by the young artist. But it is as a vitraillist that he excels.

†**Vitre**, *sb.* *Obs. rare.* Also 5 vytre. [a. F. *vitre*, ad. L. *vitrum* VITRUM.] Glass.

c 1420 LYDG. *Ballad Commend. Our Lady* 113 O glorious viole, O vitre inviolate! 1599 A. HUME *Hymnes* iii. 55 The glansing thains, and vitre bright, Resplends against the sunne.

†**Vitre**, *a.* *Obs. rare.* [ad. F. *vitré*, or L. *vitreus*, f. *vitrum* glass.] = VITREOUS *a.* 2 a.

c 1530 *Judic. Urines* II. v. 24 The .v. spice of flewme is called fleume vitrium, anglice a flewme vitre. *Ibid.* II. ix. 36 b A fleume vitre, and a whyte fleume be all one.

Vitre, variant of VITRY *Obs.*

†**Vitreal**, variant of VITRIAL *a.* *Obs.*

1658 PHILLIPS, *Vitreal*, or *Vitrine*, belonging to, or made of glasse.

†**Vi·trean**, *a.* *Obs. rare.* [f. L. *vitre-us* vitreous + -AN.] Of or resembling glass.

1656 BLOUNT *Glossogr.*, *Vitrean*, *Vitrine*,..belonging to Glass, glassie, glassie-green; clear like glass, or resembling glass. 1778 W. PRYCE *Min. Cornub.* 60 Vitrean Ore of an irregular figure.

Vitree, variant of VITRY *Obs.*

Vitrefacture. *rare*[−1]. [Cf. VITRI- and FACTURE.] (See quot.)

1842 R. PARK *Pantology* (1847) 478 Under the head of *Vitrefactures*, we include glass, pottery, and porcelain. [Hence *vitrifacture* in Worcester (1846), and later Dicts.]

†**Vitremyte.** *Obs.*[−1] (Of obscure meaning.)

c 1386 CHAUCER *Monk's T.* 382 And she that helmed was in starke shoures..Shal on hir heed now were a vitremyte [*Harl.* wyntermyte].

Vitreo-, combining form, on Greek models, of L. *vitreus* VITREOUS *a.*, employed in a few special terms having little or no currency.

1828–32 WEBSTER, *Vitreo-electric*, containing or exhibiting positive electricity, or that which is excited by rubbing glass. *c* 1840 *Encycl. Metrop.* (1845) VI. 496 Lustre [of thraulite] vitreo-resinous. 1875 KNIGHT *Dict. Mech.* 2713/2 *Vitreograph*, a photograph on glass. 1891 *Cent. Dict.* s.v., Vitreo-dentinal, -dentine.

Vitreole, obs. form of VITRIOL.

Vitreo·sity. *rare.* [f. L. *vitre-us* (see next) + -OSITY.] The state or quality of being vitreous.

1889 A. IRVING *Metamorphism of Rock* 110, I have been led to recognise vitreosity as a phenomenon occasionally exhibited by water.

Vitreous (vi·triəs), *a.* Also 8 **vitrious.** [f. L. *vitre-us* of glass, glassy, bright, etc., f. *vitrum* glass, VITRUM: see -OUS. Cf. F. *vitreux*, *-euse*.]

1. Of or belonging to, consisting or composed of, glass; of the nature of glass; glassy.

1646 SIR T. BROWNE *Pseud. Ep.* II. i. 51 Calcination or reducing it by Arte, into a subtile powder, by which way and a vitreous commixture, glasses are sometime made hereof. 1711 SHAFTESB. *Charac.* III. 15 The tumid Bladder bounds at every Kick, bursts the withstanding Casements, the Chassys, Lanterns, and all the brittle vitrious Ware. 1784 COWPER *Task* v. 161 Mirrour needed none Where all was vitreous. 1791 W. HAMILTON *Berthollet's Dyeing* II. II. IV. iv. 275 A vessel of earthenware with a vitreous coat. 1827 FARADAY *Chem. Manip.* vii. (1842) 224 Glass would then be easily acted upon, and..the product obtained would not be pure, but a combination, with part of the vitreous matter. 1852 DICKENS *Repr. P.*, *Plated Article*, Of course, you saw the glaze—composed of various vitreous materials —laid over every article. 1882 GEIKIE *Text-bk. Geol.* II. II. § 4. 105 The final stiffening of a vitreous mass into solid stone.

fig. 1836 *New Monthly Mag.* XLVI. 206 He had left the vitreous and mercurial clime of France..for the voluptuous and indolent air of Italy.

b. *Geol.* and *Min.* Resembling glass in brittleness, hardness, lustre, and mode of cleavage.

1774 in Forster *Voy.* (1777) I. 587 Some of them carried arms,..which were headed with a black vitreous lava. 1796 KIRWAN *Elem. Min.* (ed. 2) I. 409 All real lavas except those of the vitreous kind affect the magnetic needle, unless the iron they contain be much oxygenated. 1811 PINKERTON *Petral.* I. 45 There are..evidences of a vitreous lava in one of the isles of Faroe. 1849 MURCHISON *Siluria* iii. 38 It is often intersected by veins of vitreous quartz. 1855 *Orr's Circ. Sci.*, *Geol.*, etc. 498 Redruthite.—Vitreous Copper. Prismatic Copper Glance. 1868 WATTS *Dict. Chem.* V. 306 *Vitreous Silver.* Native argentic sulphide. 1882 GEIKIE *Text-Bk. Geol.* II. II. § 4. 100 Crystallites..seem to be earlier or peculiar forms of crystallization developed..in many vitreous rocks.

c. *Chem.* Resembling glass in composition.

1800 tr. *Lagrange's Chem.* I. 369 There remains in the retort a vitreous mass,..which is very pure arsenic acid. 1826 HENRY *Elem. Chem.* I. 363 Equal parts of potassium and very pure and vitreous boracic acid were put into a copper tube. 1866 ROSCOE *Elem. Chem.* xiv. 122 Like sulphur, it is capable of existing in various allotropic modifications, one of which is crystalline, the other vitreous.

d. *Anat.* and *Zool.* (See quots.)

(*a*) 1858 HUMPHRY *Hum. Skeleton* 206 The separation of the outer and inner tables of the skull by the intervening diploë...The inner, or 'vitreous' table, which is the most dense. 1866 *Chambers's Encycl.* VIII. 759 An inner dense, brittle, and somewhat glass-like layer, known as the vitreous table or layer.

(*b*) 1873 C. W. THOMSON *Depths of Sea* vii. 422 When the first specimen of *Hyalonema* was brought home, the other vitreous sponges..were unknown. 1879 CARPENTER in *Encycl. Brit.* IX. 378/2 The Vitreous *Foraminifera* may be grouped into three families. *Ibid.* 385/1 The material of their 'porcellanous' or 'vitreous' skeletons. 1896 tr. *Boas' Text Bk. Zool.* 121 Vitreous sponges (*Hexactinellidæ*) are silicious forms, characterised by the striking beauty of the skeleton, which is like spun-glass.

2. †a. *Med.* Of phlegm: Having the thick viscid consistency of molten glass. *Obs.*

1661 LOVELL *Hist. Anim. & Min.* 437 Of phlegme, if salt, from thirst...If vitreous, from fixed paine. 1684 tr. *Bonet's Merc. Compit.* III. 98 She voided much vitreous phlegm and bilious humours. 1707 FLOYER *Physic. Pulse-Watch* 75 A moderate degree of Cold produces a sweet Phlegm.. and the greatest an *Acerbe* vitrious slime towards the coldest time of Winter.

b. *Vitreous humour* (or *body*), the transparent gelatinous substance occupying the posterior and larger part of the eyeball. †*Vitreous tunicle* (see quot. 1704).

1663 BOYLE *Usef. Exp. Nat. Philos.* I. 96 We have sometimes..speedily frozen Eyes, and thereby have turn'd the Vitreous humor into very numerous and Diaphanous Films. 1676 *Phil. Trans.* XI. 747 As to the Vitreous humor, he judges it to be of that nature, that being once lost, it can never be repaired. 1704 J. HARRIS *Lex. Techn.* I, *Vitrious Tunicle*, a thin Film, or Coat, which is said to separate the Glassie Humour from the Chrystalline. 1710 J. CLARKE tr. *Rohault's Nat. Philos.* (1729) I. 237 The Vitreous Humour ..being one of the most transparent Things that we know of in the World. 1793 *Phil. Trans.* LXXXIII. 175 Its elasticity will assist the cellular texture of the vitreous humour..in restoring the indolent form. 1831 R. Knox *Cloquet's Anat.* 559 The Vitreous Body is a soft, perfectly transparent, tremulous mass, occupying the three posterior fourths of the cavity of the ball of the eye. 1877 M. Foster *Physiol.* III. ii. (1878) 398 The rays of light traverse in succession the cornea, the aqueous humour, the lens and the vitreous humour.

c. *ellipt.* as *sb.* = prec.

1869 G. Lawson *Dis. Eye* (1874) 144 He has succeeded in thus extracting the lens without the loss of any vitreous. 1879 *St. George's Hosp. Rep.* IX. 479 A quantity of the thin fluid vitreous escaped.

3. *Vitreous electricity*, positive electricity obtained from glass by friction.

1759 *Phil. Trans.* LI. 308 Experiments..respecting the vitreous and resinous electricities, as they are called. 1799 [see Electricity 1 b]. 1840 Carlyle *Heroes* i. (1904) 18 Thunder was not then mere Electricity, vitreous or resinous. 1860 Emerson *Cond. Life, Wealth* Wks. (Bohn) II. 357 The genius of reading and of gardening are antagonistic, like resinous and vitreous electricity. 1879 Proctor *Pleas. Ways Sc.* xi. 238 If glass is briskly rubbed with silk it becomes charged..with positive electricity,formerly called vitreous electricity for this reason.

4. Resembling that of glass; characteristic of glass.

1811 A. T. Thomson *Lond. Disp.* (1818) 196 The tears are..brittle, and break with a vitreous fracture. 1841 Brande *Chem.* (ed. 5) 130 This change from the vitreous to the crystalline state sometimes takes place suddenly. 1854 Ronalds & Richardson *Chem. Technol.* (ed. 2) I. 42 They form a..perfectly black mass,..generally possessing a fatty or vitreous lustre. 1863 A. C. Ramsay *Phys. Geog.* i. (1878) 20 Modern lavas have often a vitreous structure (glassy) such as obsidian.

b. Having the colour or appearance of glass.

1874 R. Buchanan *Pan* Poet. Wks. I. 90 What time the pallid sickle wax'd Blue-edged and vitreous o'er the blackning West. 1882 — *Annan Water* i, The vitreous rays of the moon began playing on the window panes. 1900 B. D. Jackson *Gloss. Bot. Terms*, *Vitreous*,..transparent, hyaline; formerly used for the light green of glass.

5. *Comb.*, as *vitreous-like*, *-shelled* adj.

1879 Carpenter in *Encycl. Brit.* IX. 378/1 The vitreous-shelled *Foraminifera* constitute the most elevated division of the group. 1902 *Westm. Gaz.* 22 Sept. 6/3 Some of the finer wares will break showing a vitreous-like substance.

Hence **Vi·treousness.**

1727 Bailey (vol. II), and later Dicts.

Vitreously (vi·triəsli), *adv.* [f. prec. + -ly [2].] In a vitreous manner: **a.** With positive electricity.

1794 G. Adams *Nat. & Exp. Philos.* IV. xlvi. 264 Those attracted by excited wax, are vitreously..electrified. 1844 Noad *Electricity* (ed. 2) 9 We are led to the inference that the cloth is vitreously electrified. 1885 Watson & Burbury *Math. The. Electr. & Magn.* I. 75 The outside of the vessel will be found to be vitreously electrified.

b. Glassily; like glass.

1904 Howells *Son of Royal Langbrith* 62 In the moonlight Hawberk's face had a greenish hue, and his eyes shone vitreously.

Vitrescence (vitre·sěns). [f. Vitrescent *a.*: see -ence.] The state of becoming vitreous or glassy; vitrified or vitreous condition.

1796 Kirwan *Elem. Min.* (ed. 2) I. 279 Mineral alkali promotes their [*sc.* zeolytes] vitrescence most, next borax, microcosmic salt least. 1888 *Encycl. Brit.* XXIV. 264/1 The vitrescence was produced by beacon fires lighted during times of invasion. 1903 *Academy* 24 Jan. 75/2 The difficulty in most cases arises from the high vitrescence of surface [of Chinese porcelain].

So **Vitre·scency.** *rare.*

1756 F. Home *Exper. Bleaching* 116 Their junction with oils, and their vitrescency. 1847 H. Miller *Rambles Geol.* (1858) 365 They are artificial structures, in which vitrescency was designedly induced.

Vitrescent (vitre·sěnt), *a.* [f. L. *vitr-um* glass + -escent. Cf. It. *vitrescente.*] Tending to become glass; susceptible of being turned into glass; glassy.

1756 P. Browne *Jamaica* 48 They seem to be formed chiefly of the vitrescent fluor, debased by a less agitated or divided clay. 1767 *Phil. Trans.* LVII. 440 The stone is of an extreme hardness, and almost a petrifaction..of many different stones, but all vitrescent. 1778 Pryce *Min. Cornub.* 262 The nitre and tartar are..rendered still more vitrescent by the borax. 1825 J. Nicholson *Oper. Mech.* 756 Iron ores..require calcareous additions, and the copper ores, rather slags or vitrescent stones, than calcareous earth. 1855 tr. *Labarte's Arts Mid. Ages* viii. 289 A vitrescent coating.

Vitrescible (vitre·sib'l), *a.* [f. L. type **vitresc-ĕre* to become glass + -ible, or directly a. F. *vitrescible* (a 1762), = It. *vitrescibile*, Pg. *-ivel.*] That can be vitrified; vitrifiable.

1754 Huxham in *Phil. Trans.* XLVIII. 841 Loosely combined with the vitrescible earth. 1786 Wedgwood *Ibid.* LXXVI. 400 This effect is constant in certain clays, and begins earliest in those which are most vitrescible. 1794 R. J. Sulivan *View Nature* I. 450 They have likewise been ranked among vitrescible stones. 1825 Hibbert in *Trans. Soc. Antiq. Scot.* (1831) IV. 166 The interstices between them being filled full of this vitrescible iron ore. 1872 Yeats *Techn. Hist. Comm.* 266 Vitrescible colours..are now laid on the glass, and burned into it.

Hence **Vitrescibi·lity.** [Cf. F. *vitrescibilité.*]

1786 Wedgwood in *Phil. Trans.* LXXVI. 401 Enabling us to ascertain the degree of vitrescibility of bodies that cannot actually be vitrified by any fires which our furnaces are capable of producing.

† **Vi·trial,** *a. Obs.* [f. L. *vitr-um* glass + -ial.] Composed of glass; glassy, vitreous.

1605 Timme *Quersit.* I. xii. 50 Their fixed heauen, or vitriall and chrystalline circles, is a salt body. 1608 Topsell *Hist. Serpents* 161 As for the flesh, it is of a vitriall or glassie colour. 1609 Armin *Maids of More-Cl.* (1880) 125 Place your plate, and pile your vitriall boales Nest vpon nest.

Vitrial(l, obs. forms of Vitriol.

† **Vi·triary,** *a. Obs.*[−1] [f. L. *vitr-um* glass. Cf. L. *vitreārius* glass-worker.] Relating to the making of glass.

1668 Sir T. Browne *Let. Merritt* 29 Dec., Wks. (Bohn) III. 508 Though I have not been a stranger unto the vitriary art, both in England and abroad.

† **Vi·triate,** *v. Obs.*[−1] [f. as prec.] *trans.* To make clear like glass.

1631 A. Wilson *Swisser* II. i. 106 An ownce of Honestie, Cleare, Pure, well vitriated.

† **Vi·triature.** *Obs.*[−1] [f. as prec.] (See quot.)

1560 R. Androse tr. *Alexis' Secr.* IV. III. 32 It helpeth maruelouslye to take a dramme of the vitriature or glasing of vessels made in pouder.

Vi·trics. *rare*[−0]. [f. L. *vitr-um* glass + -ic 2.] (See quot.)

Hence *Vitric* adj., in some later Dicts.

1875 Knight *Dict. Mech.* 2713/2 *Vitrics*, this term includes the fused compounds in which silex predominates, such as glass and some of the enamels; in contradistinction to the ceramics, in which alumina predominates.

† **Vi·trid,** *a. Obs.*[−1] [f. as prec. + -id [1].] Glass-like, vitreous.

1777 J. Williams *Acc. Anc. Ruins* 11 In some others, the stones seem to have been partly run down, and partly enveloped by the vitrid matter.

Vitrie, variant of Vitry *Obs.*

Vitrifaction (vitrifæ·kʃən). [See Vitrify *v.* and -faction.] = Vitrification.

1728 Chambers *Cycl.*, *Vitrification*, or *Vitrifaction*, the Act of converting a Body into Glass, by Fire. 1840 Vyse *Oper. Pyramids Gizeh* I. 228 In some instances the glaize was of an extremely brilliant colour, and a perfect vitrifaction. 1845 Lady Eastlake *Jrnls. & Corr.* I. 163 We now come nearer into granite Edinburgh: such petrifactions or vitrifactions, of houses. 1888 *Encycl. Brit.* XXIV. 264/2 In Scandinavia, where there are hundreds of ordinary forts, ..no trace of vitrifaction has yet been detected.

Vitrifacture: see Vitrefacture.

Vitrifiable (vitrifəi·ăb'l), *a.* [f. Vitrify *v.* + -able. Cf. F. *vitrifiable* (1734).] Capable of being vitrified; admitting of conversion into a glassy substance by means of heat.

1646 Sir T. Browne *Pseud. Ep.* II. iii. 69 Vitrification is the last or utmost fusion of a body vitrifiable, and is performed by a strong and violent fire, which keeps the melted glasse red hot. 1684 Boyle *Porousn. Anim. & Solid Bod.* vii. 98 We are wont to add to the vitrifiable matter, either some prepared metal, as calcined Copper [etc.]. 1709 *Phil. Trans.* XXVI. 382, I believe that with this Oil there is mixed a great deal of the earthy, vitrifiable part of the Metal. 1756 C. Lucas *Ess. Waters* I. 3 The primary, or vitrifiable, earth..he looks upon as the basis or matrix of all other earths. 1796 Kirwan *Elem. Min.* (ed. 2) I. 53 Mr. Achard found a mixture of two parts calcareous earths and one part magnesia vitrifiable. 1839 Ure *Dict. Arts* 574 The same mixture of vitrifiable materials will yield very different results. 1878 Miss J. J. Young *Ceramic Art* 132 The compartments are then filled with vitrifiable enamels.

Hence **Vitrifiabi·lity.** [Cf. F. *vitrifiabilité.*]

1891 *Cent. Dict.*

Vi·trificable, *a. rare*[−0]. [Cf. Vitrificate and -able. So Sp. *vitrificable*, Pg. *vitrificavel*, It. *vetrificabile.*] Vitrifiable.

1727 Bailey (vol. II), and in later Dicts.

† **Vitrifica·cious,** *a. Obs.*[−1] [Cf. next and -acious.] Resembling glass.

1794 R. J. Sulivan *View Nat.* II. 105 A black, compact, hard bitumen; brittle and vitrificacious in breaking.

† **Vitrificate,** *pa. pple. Obs.* [ad. med.L. *vitrificāt-us*, pa. pple. of **vitrificāre* to vitrify.] Vitrified. Also † **Vitrificate** *v. trans.*, to vitrify.

1471 Ripley *Comp. Alch.* v. xviii. in Ashm. (1652) 152 And make thy fyre so temperat, That by the sydys thy Water be never vytryfycate. 1626 Bacon *New Atl.* (1635) 162 We have..crystals likewise, and glasses of divers kinds, and among them some of metals vitrificated. 1721 Bailey, *Vitrificate*, to turn into Glass.

Vitrification (vitrifikē[i]·ʃən). [ad. med. or mod.L. **vitrificātio*, f. **vitrificāre* to vitrify. Cf. F. *vitrification* (16th c.), Sp. *vitrificacion*, Pg. *-ação*, It. *vit-*, *vetrificazione.*]

1. The action or process of vitrifying; conversion into a glassy substance by fusion due to heat; the fact of being so converted.

1612 Woodall *Surg. Mate* Wks. (1653) 274 Vitrification is Combustion, converting Calk and Cineres into transparant glasse. 1643 Sir T. Browne *Relig. Med.* I. § 50 The last and proper action of that element [fire] is but vitrification, or a reduction of a body into Glasse. 1661 Boyle *Scept. Chem.* v. 322 Cuppels..ought to be Destitute of Salt, lest the Violence of the Fire should bring them to Vitrification. 1709 *Phil. Trans.* XXVI. 378 We may look on it as the beginning of Vitrification, or a middle state between Metal and Glass. 1773 Franklin *Lett.*, etc., Wks. 1840 V. 454 There is no earth known so vitrifiable as not to require some auxiliary solvent to facilitate its vitrification. 1804 P. F. Tingry *Paint. & Varnish. Guide* 301 This vitrification is facilitated by the addition of a certain quantity of carbonate of potash.., or carbonate of soda. 1851 D. Wilson *Preh. Ann.* II. III. iii. 416 Sandstone, though *per se* infusible, is perfectly capable of vitrification. 1863 A. C. Ramsay *Phys. Geog.* xxxv. (1878) 613 Stones originally separate, get, so to speak, glued together in the process of vitrification.

b. With *a* and pl.: An instance of such conversion.

1626 Bacon *Sylva* § 291 Likewise in their Putrefactions, or Rusts; as Vermilion, Verdegrease, Bise, Cirrus, &c. and likewise in their Vitrifications. 1646 Sir T. Browne *Pseud. Ep.* II. i. 53 Crystall..is not onely triturable, and reduceable into powder, by contrition, but will subsist in a violent fire, and endure a vitrification. 1759 Delaval in *Phil. Trans.* LI. 86 Because all vitrifications must proceed from previous calcinations.

2. The result or product of vitrifying; a vitrified substance or body.

1651 Biggs *New Disp.* ¶ 136 We yet more detest the precipitations, vitrifications, and preparations of Mercury, Antimony, Tuty, Sulphur, &c. 1762–71 H. Walpole *Vertue's Anecd. Paint.* (1786) II. 235 Sir Theodore..communicated to them the process of the principal colours which ought to be employed in enamel, and which surpassed the famous vitrifications of Venice and Limoges. 1769 *Phil. Trans.* LX. 17 Both abound with pyrites and crystallizations, or rather vitrifications. 1845 Petrie *Eccl. Archit. Irel.* 89 This is also observable in the interior of the building, where there is a slight superficial vitrification. 1860 Smiles *Self Help* ii. 41 He had but to cover this material with a vitrification of transparent glaze.

† **Vitrificatory,** *a. Obs.*[−1] [Cf. prec. and -ory.] Causing, or resulting in, vitrification.

1678 R. R[ussell] tr. *Geber* II. i. II. vii. 54 Having no good Fusion in Heat of Fire but a vitrificatory Fusion only.

Vitrified (vi·trifəid), *ppl. a.* [f. Vitrify *v.*]

1. Converted into glass or a glassy substance by exposure to heat; rendered glassy; glazed.

1646 Sir T. Browne *Pseud. Ep.* II. i. 53 Vitrified and pellucide bodyes are of a clearer complexion in their continuities, then in their powders and Atomicall divisions. 1690 T. Burnet *Theory Earth* II. 49 The sun..would..convert it at length either into an heap of ashes, or a lump of vitrified metal. 1777 J. Williams *Acc. Anc. Ruins* 15 It was all one heap of vitrified ruins from top to bottom. a 1787 G. White *Selborne* iv, The sand..fluxes and runs by the intense heat, and so cases over the whole face of the kiln with a strong vitrified coat like glass. a 1817 T. Dwight *Trav. New Eng.*, etc. (1821) II. 80 At a little distance from the pit there was a large pile of calcined and vitrified ore. 1857 Toulmin Smith *Parish* 349 Glazed or vitrified pipes should only be used in or under buildings. 1869 J. Phillips *Vesuv.* ii. 37 That foul vitrified matter called lava!

b. *fig.* Icy, frozen.

c 1779 Crabbe *Midnight* 216 The winds that in converging Furrows plough The freezing pool..Are arm'd with pain, and vitrified their Wings.

2. *Vitrified fort*, a hill-fort of a type occurring in Scotland and some parts of the Continent, the stones of which have been converted into a vitreous material by the action of fire.

1777 J. Williams *Acc. Anc. Ruins* 25 The largest vitrified fort I ever saw, is on the south side the Grampians, in the shire of Angus. 1792 Newte *Tour Eng. & Scot.* 115 Upon the top of an insulated hill adjoining, there appears to have been what some would call a vitrified fort; though others will have it to be the vestiges of a volcano. 1825 Hibbert in *Trans. Soc. Antiq. Scot.* (1831) IV. 180 The name of *vitrified fort* may with much advantage be exchanged for the more comprehensive and untheoretical one of *vitrified site.* 1851 D. Wilson *Preh. Ann.* II. III. iii. 413 One of the most remarkable specimens of a vitrified fort in Scotland. 1879 Lubbock *Addr. Pol. & Educ.* ix. 173 The vitrified fort on the Hill of Noath.

Vitriform (vi·trifǭɹm), *a.* [f. L. *vitr-um* glass.] Having the form or appearance of glass.

1796 Kirwan *Elem. Min.* (ed. 2) II. 449, 120 [grains] of the Vitriform Phosphoric Acid. 1800 tr. *Lagrange's Chem.* I. 431 You will obtain a vitriform matter, of the colour of an animal's liver. 1834 J. Forbes *Laennec's Dis. Chest* (ed. 4) 217 The tuberculous induration is semi-transparent, vitriform, and humid. 1857 Bullock *Cazeaux' Midwif.* 176 The space between the amnios and chorion..principally filled with a liquid called by M. Velpeau the reticulated or the vitriform body.

Vitrify (vi·trifəi), *v.* [ad. F. *vitrifier* (16th c.), or med.L. **vitrificāre* (Sp. and Pg. *vitrificar*, It. *vit-*, *vetrificare*), f. *vitr-um* glass: see -fy.]

1. *trans.* To convert into glass or a glass-like substance; to render vitreous by fusion due to heat.

1594 Plat *Jewell-ho.* I. 25 Stones which..endure the strength of fire, and are not consumed therewith, but rather vitrified. c 1645 Howell *Lett.* I. I. xxix, Surely, that grand Universal-fire..at the day of judgment may by its violent ardor vitrifie and turn to one lump of Crystal, the whole Body of the Earth. 1665 Hooke *Microgr.* 45 Sometimes also is that heat so very intense, as further to melt it and vitrifie it. 1690 T. Burnet *Theory Earth* II. 46 Clayey soils, and such like, may by the strength of fire be converted into brick, or stone, or earthen metal, and so melted down and vitrified. 1728 in *6th Rep. Dep. Kpr. Rec.* App. II. 118 Vitrifying the dross of metals so as to mould the same like Bricks or Tiles. 1750 Franklin *Lett.*, etc., Wks. 1840 V. 239 The metal appeared to have been not only melted, but even vitrified. 1800 tr. *Lagrange's Chem.* I. 418 This glass pierces crucibles and vitrifies them. 1863 A. C. Ramsay *Phys. Geog.* iv. (1878) 39 Shales, sandstones, &c., are often..vitrified at the points of junction with greenstone, basaltic, and felspathic rocks. 1866 Livingstone *Last Jrnls.* (1873) I. iii. 79 The clay pipes..are met with everywhere, often vitrified.

fig. a 1618 Raleigh *Rem.* (1644) 155 Every ordinary wit can vitrifie, and make transparent pieces, and discern their corruptions. a 1678 Marvell *Appleton House* Wks. 1786 III. 221 By her flames, in heaven try'd, Nature is wholly vitrify'd. 1846 Mrs. Gore *Eng. Char.* (1852) 102 The soys, ketchups,..and other..compounds, with whose astringent juices we vitrify the coats of our stomachs.

absol. 1664 Power *Exp. Philos.* I. 54 That..so small a fire can vitrify, will be better understood by him that knows how small a heat at a Lamp-Furnace will melt Glass.

2. *intr.* To become vitreous; to turn into glass or a substance resembling this.

a 1626 Bacon *Physiol. Rem.* (1679) 101 We see Metals will vitrify. 1712 tr. *Pomet's Hist. Drugs* I. 103 These are apt to vitrifie, and make Glass and Crystal withal. 1770 *Phil. Trans.* LX. 226, I imagined that metals might not calcine or vitrify except in the same circumstances. 1813 Sir H. Davy *Agric. Chem.* (1814) 328 Such lime easily vitrifies, in consequence of the affinity of lime for silica and alumina. 1876 Page *Adv. Text-bk. Geol.* xiv. 252 Resisting heat without slagging or vitrifying.

Hence **Vi·trifying** *vbl. sb.* and *ppl. a.*

1674 Boyle *Grounds Corpusc. Philos.* 32 So strictly united..as to maintain their union in the vitrifying violence of the fire. 1756 F. Home *Exper. Bleaching* 155 The heat was just below the vitrifying point. 1839 Ure *Dict. Arts* 1019 White vitrifying pastes, fit for receiving all sorts of metallic colours. *Ibid.* 1159 The vitrifying colours are laid on by means of larger hair pencils.

Vitrine (vi·trin), *sb.* [a. F. *vitrine*, f. *vitre* glass.] A glass show-case for specimens or for objects of art. (Also *attrib.* in *vitrine table.*)

1886 *Athenæum* 27 Mar. 430/2 Four large vitrines in the Vase Room are now appropriated to the display of the Greek examples.

† **Vitrine,** *a. Obs.*[−0] [ad. med.L. *vitrīn-us*, f. L. *vitrum* glass.] Vitreous.

1656 [see Vitrean *a.*].

Vitrinopal: see Vitrite.

Vitriol (vi·triǫl), *sb.* Forms: 4–5 **vitriole,** 5 **vit-, vytreole,** 5–6 **vytryol(e,** 6–7 **vitrioll** (6 -olle), 5– **vitriol;** 5–7 **vitriall,** 6–7 **vitrial,** 7 **vitraell.** [a. OF. (also F.) *vitriol* (13th c.; = Sp. and Pg. *vitriolo*, It. *vetriolo*, *-iuolo*, *vitriolo*, *-iuolo*, *-ivuolo*) or directly ad. med.L. *vitriolum* (Albertus Magnus) f. *vitrum* glass.]

1. One or other of various native or artificial sulphates of metals (see 2 and 3) used in the arts or medicinally, esp. sulphate of iron: **a.** Used in *sing.* without article.

c 1386 Chaucer *Can. Yeom. Prol. & T.* 255 Vnslekked lym, chalk,..Poudres diuerse, asshes,..Cered pottes, sal peter, vitriole. 14.. *Voc.* in Wr.-Wülcker 579 *Draganti*, vytryole, or coporose. a 1425 tr. *Arderne's Treat. Fistula*, etc. 40 Puluerez of alume, zucarine brent, of attrament, and of vitriol. 1471 Ripley *Comp. Alch.* Adm. iv. in Ashm. (1652) 190 Also I wrought in Sulphur and in Vitriall, Whych folys doe call the Grene Lyon. 1527 Andrew *Brunswyke's Distyll. Waters* F j b, Halfe an ounce of vytryol wherof the ynke is made. 1599 A. M. tr. *Gabelhouer's Bk. Physicke* 317/1 Bloodstenchinge. Take of the best Vitriolle, beate it smalle, and boulte it through a fine cloth. 1612 Woodall *Surg. Mate* Wks. (1653) 210 Copperas or Vitriol..is a mineral salt which..doth farre excel many other kinds of salts. 1681 tr. *Belon's Myst. Physick* Introd. 38 Those Acides, and acrimonious Particles of the Salt and Vitriol which had caused its Sublimation. 1718 Quincy *Compl. Disp.* 8 The last is what is forced from Vinegar, Vitriol, and such like acid Substances. 1728 Chambers *Cycl.* s.v., The Antients give the Name *Chalcitis*, or Chalcite, to native Vitriol;.. which is a kind of mineral Stone, of a reddish Colour. 1756–7 tr. *Keysler's Trav.* (1760) III. 124 Besides sulphur, vitriol is also made here, of a sapphire colour. 1854 Ronalds & Richardson *Chem. Technol.* (ed. 2) I. 359 The chloride of calcium melting easily in the still, enables the whole of the acetic acid to be evolved at a lower temperature than when vitriol is employed. 1879 McCarthy *Own Times* xviii. II. 26 The use of vitriol was recommended among other destructive agencies.

b. In *pl.* (or with *a*).

a 1425 tr. *Arderne's Treat. Fistula*, etc. 79 Of atramentez, i. of vitriolez, bene many kyndez. 1605 Timme *Quersit.* I. ix. 37 Some of these salts are bytter as wormewood, some sharpe as vitriolls. 1656 J. Smith *Pract. Physick* 6 They that drink of them purge forth black excrements by reason of the vitrials. 1728 Chambers *Cycl.* s.v., According to Boerhaave, Vitriols consist of a metallic Part with a Sulphur adhering, a menstruous Acid, and Water. 1799 Kirwan *Geol. Ess.* 395 Vitriols have been discovered buried in the ancient sandy bed of that sea. 1868 Watts *Dict. Chem.* V. 1004 The several vitriols being distinguished by their colours, or by the metals which they contain.

2. With distinguishing epithets: **a.** With adjs. of colour. *Blue, green, red, white vitriol*, sulphate of copper, iron, cobalt, and zinc respectively.

c 1400 tr. *Lanfranc's Cirurg.* 24 Grene vitriol, & he be do to a man of a drie complexioun, engendrith fleisch. [a 1425 tr. *Arderne's Treat. Fistula*, etc. 79 Þer is a spice of vitriol þat is called vitriolum romanum, i. coporose; And it is of ȝalow colour in reward of þe grenner vitriol. And þer is one of white colour bot noȝt schynyng.] 1611 Cotgr., *Marcassin iaulne*, Red vitrioll. 1676 *Phil. Trans.* XI. 617 A salt that had some resemblance to white Vitriol. 1728 Chambers *Cycl.* s.v., In Blue Vitriol, the Metal, wherewith the Acid, etc. is join'd, is Copper. 1751 Gibson *Diseases Horses* III. iii. 193 In some cases it [*sc.* the horse's eye] may be touched with the blue Vitriol stone, or the Lunar caustic. 1758 Reid tr. *Macquer's Chym.* I. 66 Green Vitriol hath a saltish and astringent taste. 1819 Brande *Chem.* 247 Copper and Sulphuric Acid—Oxysulphate of Copper—Blue Vitriol. 1837 Dana *Min.* 180 Cobalt Vitriol ..Red Vitriol. Sulphate of Cobalt. 1858 Simmonds *Dict. Trade* s.v., White vitriol is a combination of sulphuric-acid and oxide of zinc. 1887 *Buck's Handbk. Med. Sci.* IV. 224/2 Ferrous sulphate is the salt so well known as green vitriol, and also in the impure state as copperas.

b. With other adjs., as *English, German, Hungarian, Roman vitriol.*

1573 *Art of Limming* 7 Then put in it two unces of greene Coporas, or els of Romayne Vitrial, which is beste. 1611 Cotgr., *Vitriol d'Allemagne*, German Vitrioll. *Ibid.*, *Vitriol d'Hongrie*, Hungarie Vitrioll. 1617 Moryson *Itin.* III. 134 The English bring into France..Leade, Tynne, English Vitriall, or Shoemakers blacke. 1651 French *Distill.* iii. 66 Take of Hungarian, or the best English Vitriall. 1728 Chambers *Cycl.* s.v., Roman Vitriol is made by exposing these Pyrites to the Air, till such time as they calcine. 1741 *Compl. Fam.-Piece* I. i. 46 Take Hungarian Vitriol, Allum, of each half a Pound, Phlegm of Vitriol 10 Pounds. 1837 *Penny Cycl.* VII. 505/1 Sulphuric acid and copper form sulphate of copper, blue vitriol, or Roman vitriol, or blue copperas.

3. With term indicating the base, as *vitriol of cobalt, copper, iron, lead, silver*, etc.

1695 W. W. *New Light Chirurg. Put out* 61 The Pouder consists of a Vitriol of Copper. 1699 Salmon *Bate's Dispens.* (1715) 453/1 Of this opened Sol, to make Vitriol of Gold. 1704 Harris *Lex. Techn.* I, *Vitriol of Copper* or *Venus*, is Blue Chrystals made by a Solution of Copper in Spirit of Nitre, Evaporation, and Chrystallization in a cool place. *Ibid.*, *Vitriol of Silver*, or of the *Moon.* 1753 *Chambers' Cycl.* Suppl. s.v., Of this kind are the Vitriols of gold, silver, copper, iron, lead, and tin. *Ibid.*, Vitriol of Quicksilver, the name of a chemical preparation of quicksilver, with acid spirits. *Ibid.*, Another method of making the Vitriol of mercury. 1791 *Phil. Trans.* LXXXI. 381 Fused..on a plate of platina, with the vitriols of tartar and soda, it appeared entirely to resist their action. 1796 Kirwan *Elem. Min.* (ed. 2) II. 90 If they are considered..as Vitriols of Cobalt and Nickel, they are ranged among Ores. 1800 *Med. Jrnl.* IV. 288 The patient bore large doses of the vitriols of copper and of zinc.

† b. *Vitriol of Mars, Moon, Venus*, etc. (see quots. and 1704 in prec.). *Obs.*

1678 Salmon *Pharm. Lond.* 836/2 Filings of Steel are digested in Spirit of Vitriol, to make Vitriol of Mars. 1696 Phillips (ed. 5), *Vitriol of Mars*, Iron and Spirit of Vitriol mix'd and distill'd together. 1704 J. Harris *Lex. Techn.* I, *Vitriol of Mars*, or *Salt of Steel*, is made by dissolving Steel in some proper Acid Menstruum then Evaporating and Chrystallizing to gain the Salt as above in Copper. 1758 Reid tr. *Macquer's Chym.* I. 66 These crystals are called Green Vitriol, and Vitriol of Mars.

4. **a.** *Oil of vitriol*, concentrated sulphuric acid.

1580 Frampton tr. *Monardes' Med. agst. Venome* 117 b, In our time there hath been compounded and drawen out an Oyle, which they call Oyle of Vitrioll or Coporace. 1611 Cotgr., *Huile de vic*, Oyle of Vitrioll. 1660 Boyle *New Exp. Phys. Mech.* xxii. 176 This we fill'd with Oyl of Vitriol and fair water. 1728 Chambers *Cycl.* s.v., Oil of Vitriol, which comes out after the Spirit, by heightning the Fire wherewith that had been rais'd. 1779 *Phil. Trans.* LXX. 31 Add, by a little at a time, as much vitriolic acid, commonly sold by the name of oil of vitriol, as will re-dissolve the whole. 1827 Faraday *Chem. Manip.* xv. (1842) 391 Pouring in so much concentrated oil of vitriol as shall moisten the fragments. 1878 Huxley *Physiogr.* 102 Water made slightly sour by addition of a little oil of vitriol.

b. *Spirit(s) of vitriol*, a distilled essence of vitriol.

1671 R. Bohun *Wind* 175 Such as Oyl of Tartar and Spirit of Vitriol. 1674 *Phil. Trans.* IX. 44 As for the Acid Saline Principle, I suppose no person who hath tasted the Spirit of Vitriol,..will question its abounding in that subject. 1728 Chambers *Cycl.* s.v. *Salt*, Spirit of Nitre,..Spirit of Salt,..and Spirit of Vitriol. 1771 *Encycl. Brit.* II. 72/1 If the vitriolic acid contain much water, it is then called spirit of vitriol. 1789 W. Buchan *Dom. Med.* (1790) 223 This may be sharpened with the spirits of vitriol. 1859 Mayne *Expos. Lex.* 1336 *Vitriol, Sweet Spirit of*,..a term for..sulphuric ether.

fig. 1679 Alsop *Melius Inq.* II. i. 174 The Medicine is the same; only Rome has added a few drops of the Spirits of Vitriol.

† c. *Colcothar, earth, salt, of vitriol*: see quots. Also *elixir of vitriol*: see Elixir *sb.* 4.

1684 tr. *Bonet's Merc. Compit.* I. 21 Comatous children are..cured by Vomitive Salt of Vitriol. 1699 Salmon *Bate's Dispens.* (1715) 453/1 *Terra Vitrioli dulcis*, sweet Earth of Vitriol. 1753 *Chambers' Cycl.* Suppl. s.v. *Sulphur*, Colcothar, or fixed salt of vitriol. 1755 *Dict. Arts & Sci.* s.v., A fine purple matter, called colcothar of vitriol. 1799 G. Smith *Laboratory* I. 95 Take red calcined vitriol, or colcothar of vitriol.

5. *fig.* (In allusion to the corrosive properties of vitriol.) Virulence or acrimony of feeling or utterance.

1769 *Junius Lett.* xv. (1788) 90 Flat and insipid in your retired state, but brought into action you become vitriol again. 1872 Spurgeon *Treas. David* Ps. lv. 3 They..cast the vitriol of their calumny over me. 1895 *Literary World* (Boston) 8 Nov. 359/1 This introduction, with its mixture of genius, shrewdness, and vitriol, is a piece of prose not to be missed.

6. *attrib.* and *Comb.*, as *vitriol bath, chamber, -maker, marcasite, -thrower, -throwing, water*; **vitriol ochre,** a former name of glockerite; † **vitriol stone,** a native vitriol or sulphate.

1669 Boyle *Certain Physiol. Ess.* (ed. 2) *Absol. Rest Bodies* 15 A bulky Marchasite that I procur'd from a Virtuoso that lives just by a Vitriol-work, whither these among other Vitriol-Stones are brought. 1670 [see Vitriolic *a.* 1]. 1675 E. Wilson *Spadacr. Dunelm.* 43 Two vitriol waters in the Copper Mine of Herongrundt. 1676 Wiseman *Surg. Treat.* v. ix. 378 If in the incarning the Wound the Flesh grows luxurious, touch it with a Vitriol-stone, and it will..dispose it to cicatrize. 1755 *Dict. Arts & Sci.* s.v., The old iron, picked up by the poor people about our streets, is sold to the vitriol or copperas makers. 1843 Thackeray *Irish Sk.-bk.* viii, We had a talk about the vitriol-throwers at Cork, and the sentence just passed upon them. 1849 Ht. Martineau *Hist. Peace* v. v. (1877) III. 263 They mourned over the murders, and vitriol-throwing of the operatives, who were enslaved by mercenary delegates. 1867 Bloxam *Chem.* 203 Reactions in the Vitriol Chambers. 1867 Augusta Wilson *Vashti* iv, Compassion is about as welcome to my feelings as a vitriol bath to fresh wounds.

Hence **Vi·triol** *v. trans.*, to injure (a person) by means of vitriol; to expose (a thing) to the effects of vitriol.

1897 *Westm. Gaz.* 16 Dec. 5/2, I do not want to be killed, and I have a particular objection to being vitrioled.

† **Vi·triolate,** *a. Obs.* Also 7 **vitriolet.** [ad. med. or mod.L. **vitriolāt-us*, f. *vitriolum* vitriol. Cf. It. *vitriolato*, Sp. and Pg. *vitriolado*, F. *vitriolé.*]

1. Of or belonging to, resembling that of, vitriol.

1646 Sir T. Browne *Pseud. Ep.* vi. xii. 336 A vitriolate or copperose quality conjoyning with a terrestrious and astringent humidity. 1665–6 *Phil. Trans.* I. 323 This had somewhat of a Vitriolate taste. 1672 Boyle *Ess. Gems* 159 Particles which..I observ'd to be of a Vitriolate nature.

2. Treated with vitriol. *Vitriolate tartar* (see Vitriolated 3 a).

1665 Needham *Med. Medicinae* 513 As we see in Tartar Vitriolate. 1671 Salmon *Syn. Med.* III. lxxxiv. 730 Vitriolate Tartar taken in Broath,..extract of Hellebore [etc.]..are here good. 1684 tr. *Bonet's Merc. Compit.* III. 95, I gave him Spring-water corrected with Vitriolate Syrup of Rasberries. 1704 [see Tartar [1] 3 b]. 1782 Kirwan in *Phil. Trans.* LXXIII. 40 The same double decomposition will be produced if, instead of tartar vitriolate, glauber's salt be used.

3. Affected by, impregnated with, vitriol.

1666 Boyle *Orig. Forms & Qual.* 339 This Vitriolate Nitre (if I may so call it). 1670 H. Stubbe *Plus Ultra* 131 It is also..manifest, that there are in the bodies of men.. solutions or liquors imbued with sundry salts, as aluminous, acid, and vitriolate, etc. 1684 Boyle *Porousn. Anim. & Solid Bod.* viii. 125 So that their Texture was spoiled by the saline and vitriolate Corpuscles.

b. Of water, springs, etc.

1666 *Phil. Trans.* I. 359 That Pool..seems to be of Vitriolate water. 1667 *Ibid.* II. 469 The Iron, that is said to be turned into Copper, by the Vitriolate Springs at Cremnitz.. in Hungary. 1670 *Ibid.* V. 1043 There are also two Springs of a Vitriolat water, which are affirm'd to turn iron into Copper. 1751 *Eng. Gazetteer* s.v. *Worton-Lower*, A vitriolate ferrugineous spring.

Vi·triolate, *v. rare.* [Cf. prec and -ate [3].] *trans.* To affect or treat with vitriol; to render vitriolic.

1605 Timme *Quersit.* I. vii. 27 By reason of a singular temper of sharpness vitriolated by sweet and sulphurus spirits. 1828–32 Webster, *Vitriolate*, to convert, as sulphur in any compound, into sulphuric acid, formerly called vitriolic acid.

Vi·triolated, *ppl. a.* [f. prec. or Vitriolate *a.*]

† 1. = Vitriolate *a.* 1. *Obs.*[−1]

1651 Biggs *New Dispens.* ¶ 144 The acid saline vitriolated qualities of wine, vineger, or juice of Limons.

2. Impregnated with vitriol: **a.** Of liquids.

a 1626 Meverel in *Bacon's Physiol. Rem.* (1679) 125 Iron may be dissolved by any tart, salt, or vitriolated Water. 1670 H. Stubbe *Plus Ultra* 154 The vitriolated Serum would not flame; the vitriolated blood did burn with a brisk but short flame. 1756 F. Home *Exper. Bleaching* 185 The liquor more acid than the vitriolated liquor in the foregoing experiment.

b. Of minerals, etc., affected by native sulphates.

1794 R. J. Sulivan *View Nat.* I. 250 Vitriolated clay, or alum, is rarely found. 1796 Kirwan *Elem. Min.* (ed. 2) II. 113 Mr. Bergman..deduces the origin of Vitriolated Silver, from the withering and Acidification of the Sulphurated Silver Ores. 1802–3 tr. *Pallas's Trav.* (1812) I. 87 The vitriolated layers of mire still exhibit traces of sea-weeds and marshes. 1805 W. Saunders *Min. Waters* 49 Any spring of water that flows in the neighbourhood, will hence contain both alum and vitriolated iron.

3. Treated with vitriol: **a.** *Vitriolated tartar*, sulphate of potassium. (Cf. Tartar [1] 3 b.)

1694 Salmon *Bate's Dispens.* (1713) 628/1 Antimonial Tartar vitriolated. 1728 Chambers *Cycl.* s.v. *Tartar*, Tartar Vitriolated, which some call Magistery of Tartar, is Oil of Tartar mix'd with rectify'd Spirit of Vitriol. 1758 Reid tr. *Macquer's Chym.* I. 25 Vitriolated Tartar is almost as hard to dissolve in water as the Selenites. 1789 *Trans. Soc. Arts* I. 183 An innocent neutral salt, vitriolated tartar. 1836 Brande *Chem.* (ed. 4) 36 The residuum in the retort furnishes vitriolated tartar. 1887 *Buck's Handbk. Med. Sci.* V. 795/2 Potassic sulphate..is the salt formerly called vitriolated tartar and *sal de duobus.*

b. With other sbs., as *ammonia, iron*, etc.

1788 *Phil. Trans.* LXXVIII. 395 Of vitriolated natron (Glauber's salt) four parts. 1799 *Monthly Rev.* XXX. 67 Eight grains of myrrh, a grain and a half of vitriolated iron. 1801 *Encycl. Brit.* Suppl. I. 360/1 Sulphat of ammonia..was also called vitriolated ammoniac. 1804 Abernethy *Surg. Obs.* (1827) 169, I gave her emetics of vitriolated zinc and copper. 1823 Crabb *Technol. Dict.*, *Vitriolated Alkali* (Chem.), the sulphate of potash.

Vitriola·tion. [f. Vitriolate *v.*] (See quot.)

1828–32 Webster, *Vitriolation*, the act or process of converting into sulphuric acid or vitriol.

† **Vitriole·scent,** *a. Obs.*[−1] [f. Vitriol *sb.* + -escent.] Passing into a vitriolated state. Hence **Vitriole·scence.**

1757 tr. *Henckel's Pyritol.* 60 Dissolved, crumbled, vitriolescent copper-pyrites. *Ibid.* 296 The spontaneous vitriolescence of pyrites.

Vitriolet, variant of Vitriolate *a.*

Vitriolic (vitriǫ·lik), *a.* and *sb.* Also 7–8 **vitriolick,** 7 **-ike, -iq(ue.** [ad. F. *vitriolique* (16th c., = It., Sp., Pg. *vitriolico*), or f. Vitriol *sb.* + -ic.]

A. *adj.* 1. Of or belonging to vitriol; having

the nature or qualities of vitriol; impregnated with vitriol.

1670 W. Simpson *Hydrol. Ess.* 61 The solution of the vitriol marcasite..precipitates the same vitriolick oaker. 1676 Grew *Anat. Pl.*, *Exper. Luctation* ii. § 4 Irish Slat.. seems to be nothing else but a Vitriolick Bole. 1707 Floyer *Physic. Pulse-Watch* 257 In the Quartans, the..Pain is from the vitriolic Cacochymia. 1760 *Phil. Trans.* LI. 470 It is of a subacid taste, and very nauseously vitriolic. 1774 Goldsm. *Nat. Hist.* (1862) I. xi. 215 A mucous substance, which had something of a vitriolic quality, settled under the reticular membrane. 1802 Playfair *Illustr. Hutton. The.* 33 This compound of metal and sulphur..is destroyed by the contact of moisture and resolved into a vitriolic salt. 1844 *Civil Eng. & Arch. Jrnl.* VII. 108/1 If the pit water be vitriolic..it becomes necessary to use every means to procure better water. 1899 F. T. Bullen *Log Sea-waif* 49 A fiery white spirit, fresh from the still...This vitriolic stuff seemed to meet every emergency.

b. *Vitriolic acid*, oil of vitriol.

1747 Wall in *Phil. Trans.* XLIV. Suppl. 588, I acidulated the Liquors with the vitriolic Acid. 1778 W. Pryce *Min. Cornub.* 54 It entirely resists the vitriolick acid, which dissolves or corrodes every other known metallick body, except Gold. 1802 Mar. Edgeworth *Moral T.*, *Forrester*, *Banknotes*, The large bottle of vitriolic acid was broken. 1842 Orderson *Creol.* xiii. 137 The gas was generated from steel filings and vitriolic acid.

2. *fig.* Of language, persons, etc.: Extremely sharp, caustic, or scathing; bitterly ill-natured or malignant.

1841 H. F. Chorley *Music & Mann.* III. 31 Venting a flood of vitriolic sarcasm, or a flight of high-toned poetry. 1866 E. P. Whipple *Characters & Charac. Men* 5 Robespierre..[and] Frederick of Prussia..were both bitter and vitriolic natures. 1879 McCarthy *Hist. Own Times* II. 197 He never became more than a great Parliamentary critic of the acrid and vitriolic style. 1903 Coleman *C. Reade* III. v. (1904) 324 For vitriolic vigour this epistle excels anything in the language.

B. *sb.* A vitriolic substance. *Obs.*[−1]

a 1700 Evelyn *Diary* 7 Nov. 1651, It had a taste of a strong vitrioliq, and smelt like aqua fortis.

Vitriolico-, combining form of prec., employed in a few chemical terms, as *vitriolico-antimoniated*, *-muriated*, *-neutral.*

1782 Kirwan in *Phil. Trans.* LXXIII. 49 Whenever a vitriolico-neutral salt..is evaporated to a certain degree, the vitriolic expels these acids in its turn. 1796 — *Elem. Min.* (ed. 2) II. 113 [Silver] Vitriolico muriated, or Corneous Silver Ore. *Ibid.* 122 Vitriolico Antimoniated Silver Ore.

Vitrio·lify, *v. rare*[−0]. [f. Vitriol *sb.* + -(i)fy.] *trans.* To vitriolize. Hence **Vitrio·lifying** *ppl. a.*

1674 *Phil. Trans.* IX. 71 The expansion of some of those prodigiously active Springy particles..which together with the Aerial Salt were arrested by the Vitriolifying principle.

† **Vi·trioline,** *a. Obs.* [f. Vitriol *sb.* + -ine [1].] Resembling vitriol; vitriolic.

1651 French *Yorksh. Spa* iii. 34 Astringing waters, as Alluminous, and Vitrioline almost every where. a 1661 Fuller *Worthies*, *Yorks.* (1662) III. 188 In a morish boggy ground ariseth a spring of a Vitrioline tast and odour. 1684 tr. *Bonet's Merc. Compit.* III. 52 The Bath waters, wherein the vitrioline virtue is most eminent. 1703 *Phil. Trans.* XXV. 1573 How far these Stones are the effect of a Vitrioline Juice, I will not determin.

Vitrioli·zable, *a.* [f. Vitriolize *v.* + -able.] That may be vitriolized; capable of being converted into vitriol.

1796 Kirwan *Elem. Min.* (ed. 2) II. 82 That the Iron, in Pyrites, [is] spontaneously Vitriolizable. 1828–32 Webster. [Hence in later Dicts.]

Vitrioliza·tion. [f. next + -ation.] The process of converting, or of being converted, into a vitriol.

1757 tr. *Henckel's Pyritol.* 109 The vitriolisation of pyrites. 1782 Kirwan in *Phil. Trans.* LXXIII. 74 As Mr. Monnet has observed in his excellent Treatise on Vitriolization. 1804 *Ibid.* XCIV. 318 The magnetical pyrites..seems to be liable to oxidizement, but not to vitriolization.

Vitriolize (vi·triŏləiz), *v.* [f. Vitriol *sb.*]

1. **a.** *trans.* To convert into vitriol; to vitriolate. Also *absol.*

1694 Salmon *Bate's Dispens.* (1713) 453/1 Dissolve again in fair Water and crystallize or vitriolize as before. 1799 Kirwan *Geol. Ess.* 395 By long exposure to the air and moisture they are at last vitriolized.

b. *intr.* To become vitriolated or vitriolic.

1757 tr. *Henckel's Pyritol.* 327 Such pyritæ as vitriolise sparingly and leisurely. 1796 Kirwan *Elem. Min.* (ed. 2) II. 80 There are some that spontaneously effloresce and vitriolize.

2. *trans.* To injure with vitriol; to throw vitriol at (a person) with intent to injure.

1886 *Daily News* 15 March (Cassell's), The jury did not believe that the child from the same motive vitriolized himself. 1901 *Daily Chron.* 24 July 4/6 The painful case of a handsome girl who was 'vitriolised' by a rival.

Hence **Vi·triolized** *ppl. a.* Also **Vi·triolizer,** one who throws vitriol with intent to injure.

1882 *Pall Mall G.* 13 Nov. 2 Thinking he had to deal with a vitriolizer the servant ran down to call a policeman. 1891 *Ibid.* 9 Nov. 7/1 Vitriolized spices and arsenicated coffee. 1894 *Westm. Gaz.* 17 Oct. 6/3 With vitriolised drink supplied to you at fabulous prices.

† **Vi·triolous,** *a. Obs.* [f. Vitriol *sb.* + -ous. Cf. OF. *vitrioleux.*] Of the nature of vitriol; vitriolic.

1646 Sir T. Browne *Pseud. Ep.* III. xxii. 164 Some attrition from an acide and vitriolous humidity in the stomack. *Ibid.* VI. xii. 336, I say, a vitriolous or copperous quality; for vitrioll is the active or chiefe ingredient in Inke. 1707 *Curios. in Husb. & Gard.* 56 Vitriolous, nitrous, &c. Spirits.

Vitrious, obs. form of Vitreous *a.*

Vitrisch, variant of Vitry *Obs.*

Vitrite (vi·trəit). *Min.* [f. L. *vitr-um* glass + -ite [1].] (See quots.)

1866 Lawrence tr. *Cotta's Rocks Class.* (1878) 341 Opal, as a rock, usually only forms very subordinate masses, e.g. the so-called vitrite, which occurs at Meronitz, in Bohemia. 1868 Watts *Dict. Chem.* V. 1004 *Vitrinopal*, *Vitrite*, the matrix of Bohemian pyrope, related to pitchstone.

Vi·tro-, combining form on Gr. models of L. *vitrum* glass, used in a few terms, as **vitro-de·ntine,** the hard external layer of dentine in a tooth; **vi·trophyre,** a subdivision of porphyritic rocks; hence *vitrophyric* adj.; **vi·trotype** (see quot. 1875).

1849–52 *Todd's Cycl. Anat.* IV. 882/1 The dental plate consists..of a central mass of coarse osseous substance.. and an external sheath of very hard 'vitro-dentine'. 1870 tr. *Stricker's Man. Histology* xv. (N. Syd. Soc.) 471 The central portion [of a tooth] consists of vaso-dentine, which is covered with true dentine; external to which again is a thin layer of vitro-dentine. 1875 Knight *Dict. Mech.* 2713/2 *Vitro-type* (Photography), a name given to the processes which involve the production of collodion film pictures on glass. 1882 Geikie *Text-Bk. Geol.* II. II. iii. 90 Vogelsang has proposed to classify this type [Porphyritic] in three divisions: 1st, Granophyre,..2nd, Felsophyre,..3rd, Vitrophyre, where the ground-mass is a glassy magna. 1890 *Philos. Mag.* March 288 Among the pyroxenic rocks the most noticeable varieties are the labradorite-audesites, the pyroxene-audesites—of which both 'trachytoid' and 'vitrophyric' forms occur.

† **Vitrose,** *a. Obs.*[−0] [ad. L. type **vitrōs-us*, f. *vitrum* glass.] 'Glassy, full of glass.'

1727 Bailey (vol. II).

Vi·trous, *a. rare.* [f. L. *vitr-um* glass. Cf. F. *vitreux*, and med.L. *vitrus* adj.] Vitreous.

1657 *Physical Dict.*, *Vitrous humor*, a moisture like to molten glass or chrystal, which is a part of the eye. 1779 Sir W. Hamilton in *Phil. Trans.* LXX. 51 *note*, A flexible, capillary, yellow glass,..with small vitrous globules at a little distance one from the other. 1859 Mayne *Expos. Lex.* 1336 Omalius admitted a genus of vitrous rocks comprehending the silicated, vitrified stones or rocks.

† **Vi·trum.** *Obs. rare.* [L.] Glass; a glassy substance; a glass vessel.

1657 *Physical Dict.*, *Vitrum*, glass: it's used to signifie glass distilling vessels, or any other vessels made of glass. 1665 Hooke *Microgr.* 51 A certain thin Lamina of a vitrum or vitrified part of the Metal. 1694 Salmon *Bate's Dispens.* (1713) 547/1 Le Febure makes the Salt..of the Glass..,but he mingles the Vitrum with its equal Weight of Sulphur in Pouder.

Vitruvian (vitrū·viăn), *a.* [f. the name of M. *Vitruvius* Pollio, a Roman architect and writer on architecture (c 10 B.C.).] Of, relating to, or in the style of Vitruvius.

1762 H. Walpole *Vertue's Anecd. Paint.* (1765) I. 116 Our buildings must be as Vitruvian, as writings in the days of Erasmus were obliged to be Ciceronian. 1835 R. Willis *Archit. Mid. Ages* ii. 23 *note*, The latter [Alberti] published the first treatise on the Vitruvian architecture, in 1485. 1893 Symonds *Michelangelo* xiii. II. 217 Church, cupola, and spires are built up by a succession of Vitruvian temples.

b. *Vitruvian scroll*, a convoluted scroll-pattern employed as an architectural ornament.

1837 *Antiq. Athens* 19 A sort of thatch of laurel leaves, surrounded by an ornamental edge, usually termed a Vitruvian scroll. 1886 G. Schumacher *Across the Jordan* iii. 173 A lintel-stone..which is..ornamented with the seven-branched candlestick and a sort of vitruvian scroll.

Hence **Vitru·vianism,** the style or principles of architecture favoured by Vitruvius.

1859 Jephson *Brittany* viii. 115 Going straight from the delased flamboyant or perpendicular to Vitruvianism.

† **Vi·try.** *Obs.* Forms: 5 **vettris,** *Sc.* **vitrisch;** 6 **vitre,** 7 **vitree, vitrie, vittry,** 8 **vitry;** 6–7 **vittery,** 9 **vittory.** [ad. F. *Vitré*, the name of a town in Brittany. The early forms in *-is*, *-isch* prob. represent F. *Vitrées* pl., canvas cloths made at Vitré.] *Vitry canvas*, a kind of light durable canvas. (Cf. Vandelas.) Also *ellipt.*

c 1425 *Foreign Accts.* 59 m. 23 a (P. R. O.), [A ship's bonnet containing] iiij di' uln' canab' de vettris. 1497 *Acc. Ld. High Treas. Scot.* I. 345 For xiiij elne of vetrisch cammas to ane litil palȝoune of the Kingis, xiiij s. 1534 *Exch. Acc.* 58/13 Vittery canvas. 1599 Nashe *Lenten Stuff* 27 For which is alwaies paide ready Golde, with salt, Canuas Vitre, and a great deale of good trash. 1612 *Ledger A. Halyburton* (1867) 319 Vandolose or Vitrie canves the eln, xs. 1617 Moryson *Itin.* III. 134 And they bring from thence Linnen cloathes, called white Roanes and Vitree Canvas. 1640 in Entick *London* (1766) II. 167 Linnens,.. narrow vandales, or vittry canvas. 1721 C. King *Brit. Merch.* I. 181, 17000 Hund. of Vitry and Noyals Canvas. *Ibid.* 284 Canvas Vitry,..Canvas Norman. 1757 J. H. Grose *Voy. E. Indies* 176 Holland's duck, or vitry, is whilst in use, more pliant, and less apt to split. 1867 Smyth *Sailor's Word-bk.* 714 *Vitry*, a light and durable canvas. *Ibid.*, *Vittory*, a fine canvas, of which the waist-cloths were formerly made.

Vitsonday, obs. Sc. form of Whitsunday.

‖ **Vitta** (vi·tă). Pl. **vittæ** (vi·tī). [L. *vitta* a band, fillet, chaplet, esp. one worn round the head.]

† 1. *Anat.* (See quot.) *Obs.*[−0]

1693 tr. *Blancard's Phys. Dict.* (ed. 2), *Vitta*, that part of the Coat call'd *Amnion*, which sticks to the Infants Head when 'tis just Born. [Hence in Phillips, 1706, etc.]

2. *Rom. Antiq.* (See quots.)

Neither of the applications rests upon L. usage.

1726 A. Gordon *Itin. Sept.* 77 He [*sc.* a Roman soldier] has a Sash or Vitta coming over his Breast, reaching to his Middle. 1847 *Kitto's Cycl. Bibl. Lit.* I. 227/2 The objects above denominated appendages and vittæ..were straps of leather secured to the lower rim of the barrel of a suit of armour, and to the openings for arm-holes.

3. *Zool.* A band or stripe of colour.

1819 Stephens in *Shaw's Gen. Zool.* XI. II. 346 The hypochondria [of the Guernsey Partridge] marked with a double black vitta. 1849 Johnston in *Proc. Berw. Nat. Club* II. 365 Mite..marked on the back with a dark vitta or line forming two sigmoid flexures. 1875 G. N. Lawrence *Birds S. W. Mexico* 51 *Larus californicus*..bill grayish-white, behind the yellowish-white tip a black vitta.

b. *Bot.* (See quot.)

1843 *Penny Cycl.* XXVI. 403/2 The term vittæ is also sometimes applied to the various stripes which are found upon leaves, and which either arise from irregular distribution or entire deficiency of colouring-matter.

4. *Bot.* **a.** One of a number of elongated club-shaped canals or tubes occurring in the pericarp of the fruit of most umbelliferous plants and containing their characteristic oil. Usually in pl.

1830 Lindley *Nat. Syst. Bot.* 4 The ridges are separated by channels, below which are often placed, in the substance of the pericarp, certain linear receptacles of coloured oily matter, called *vittæ.* 1847 Steele *Field Bot.* 30 Vittæ on the upper half of the fruit only..*Heracleum.* Vittæ as long as fruit..*Peucedanum.* 1870 Hooker *Stud. Flora* 156 Trinia..primary ridges subequal, thick, smooth, rugose or plaited, with a large *vitta* inside each.

b. One of a number of internal projections occurring in the valves of diatomaceous plants.

1888 *Cassell's Encycl. Dict.* 1900 Jackson *Gloss. Bot. Terms.*

Vittail(e, obs. forms of Victual *sb.* and *v.*

Vittandly, obs. Sc. variant of Wittingly *adv.*

Vittate (vi·tĕt), *a.* [ad. L. *vittāt-us* bound with a fillet or chaplet, f. *vitta* Vitta + -ate [2].]

1. *Zool.*, *Bot.*, etc. Marked or striped with vittæ. Cf. Vittated *a.*

1826 Kirby & Sp. *Entomol.* IV. xlvi. 290 Vittate (*Vittata*), painted with several such stripes. 1866 *Treas. Bot.* 1224/1 *Vittate*, striped lengthwise.

2. *Bot.* Having a vitta or vittæ (sense 4 a).

Chiefly in combination, *1-vittate.*

1870 Hooker *Stud. Flora* 153 Eryngium;..primary ridges obscure 1-vittate.

Vi·ttated, *a. Zool.*, *Ornith.*, etc. *rare.* [f. as prec. + -ed [2].] = prec. 1.

Only in the specific names of a few birds, reptiles, etc.

1790 Latham *Ind. Ornith.* II. 827 *Procellaria vittata*,.. Vittated Petrel. 1802 Shaw *Gen. Zool.* III. II. 533 Vittated Snake. *Coluber Vittatus.* 1804 *Ibid.* V. I. 22 Vittated Silure. *Silurus Vittatus.*

Vitte, obs. f. Wit *sb.* **Vittee,** dial. var. Fitty *a.*[1] **Vittel(l,** obs. ff. Victual *sb.* and *v.* **Vitteller, -lour,** etc. obs. ff. Victualler. **Vittely,** obs. Sc. f. Wittily *adv.* **Vitten,** dial. var. Fitten *sb.* and *a.*

† **Vittered,** variant of Fittered *ppl. a. Obs.*

a 1400 *Minor Poems fr. Vernon MS.* 335/265 Viterde hodes and Clokes also, Al þat vile pride schal don hem ful wo. 1578 Lyte *Dodoens* 609 The wilde Ache or Parseley hath large leaves, al jagged, cut, and vittered, much like the leaves of the wilde Carrot.

Vittering, Sc. form of Wittering.

Vitterly, Sc. form of Witterly *adv. Obs.*

Vittery, var. Vitry *Obs.*

Vittie-vayr: see Vetiver.

[1843 *Penny Cycl.* XXVI. 403 *Vittie-vayr*, the Tamool name, sometimes written *Woetiwear*, of the highly fragrant roots of a grass which is found in many parts of India.] 1861 Bentley *Man. Bot.* 699 *Andropogon muricatus*, Vittie-vayr or Cuscus, yields a fragrant oil according to Dr. Hooker.

Vitting, obs. Sc. form of Witting *vbl. sb.*

Vittle, obs. or dial. f. Victual *sb.*; obs. f. Victual *v.*

† **Vittorin,** Anglicized f. Vetturino. *Obs.*

1613 Sir A. Sherley *Trav. Persia* 24 He brought me to a Vittorin, of whom he had already hired Horses, Camels, and Moiles for me.

Vittory, Vittry, var. Vitry *Obs.* **Vitty,** dial. or slang var. of Fitty *a.*; obs. Sc. f. Witty *a.* **Vittyng,** obs. Sc. f. Witting *vbl. sb.*

† **Vi·tulate,** *v. Obs.*[−0] [f. L. *vitulāt-* ppl. stem of *vitulārī* to celebrate a festival, keep holiday, be joyful.] *intr.* 'Wantonly to rejoice' (Cockeram I, 1623).

† **Vitula·tion.** *Obs. rare.* [ad. late L. *vitulātio* (Macrobius), noun of action f. L. *vitulārī*: see prec.] A public thanksgiving or festival.

In quots. erroneously associated with L. *vitulus* a calf.

1607 Topsell *Four-f. Beasts* 90 The auncients called Victoria by the name of the Goddesse Vitula, bycause they sacrificed vnto hir calues, which was termed a Vitulation: and this was vsuall for victory and plenty. 1623 Cockeram, *Vitulation*, a reioicing like a calfe.

Vituline (vi·tiŭləin), *a. rare.* [ad. L. *vitulīnus*, f. *vitulus* calf. Cf. F. *vituline* (Balzac).] Of or belonging to a calf or calves; resembling that of a calf.

Vitular, *vitulary*, with similar sense, are recorded in the *Cent. Dict.* and other recent Dicts.

1656 Blount *Glossogr.* 1786–1805 Tooke *Purley* (1829) II. 444. 1860 Wraxall *Life in Sea* ii. 27 In spite of their [i. e. seals'] clumsy form, the vituline countenance wears an expression of calmness and peace. 1870 Lowell *Among my Bks.* Ser. I. (1873) 167 If a double allowance of vituline brains deserve such honor, there are few commentators on Shakespeare that would have gone afoot.

† **Vituper,** *sb. Obs.* Also 5 **vi-, vytupere,** 6 *Sc.* **witupér.** [a. OF. *vituper*, *-ere* (obs. or arch. F. *vitupère*, = Pr. *vetupier*), ad. late or med.L. *vituperium* Vitupery.] Vituperation.

1456 Sir G. Haye *Law Arms* (S.T.S.) 188 Thir fals Jowis ..revy[l]is thame and dois all the vituper thai may to haly kirk and to the sacrament. 1484 Caxton *Fables of Auian* xv, Suche is now in grete honour and worship that herafter shalle falle in to grete vytupere shame and dishonour. c 1500 *Melusine* xxxiii. 233 To the moost vytupere & shame of the Catholycal feyth. 1571 *Satir. Poems Reform.* xxvii. 109 Mark als þe wite, vise, witupér, and the waige Off wntried traisoun and of tyrannye.

† **Vituper,** *v. Obs. rare.* In 5 **vytuper.** [a. OF. *vituperer* (10th c.; obs. or arch. F. *vitupérer* = Pr., Sp. and Pg. *vituperar*, It. *-are*), ad. L. *vituperāre* to Vituperate. Cf. prec.] *trans.* To vituperate or revile; to dishonour or disgrace.

1484 Caxton *Fables of Æsop* III. vii, Men preysen somtyme that that sholde be blamed & vytupered And ofte men ..vytuperen that that shold be preysed. c 1489 — *Sonnes of Aymon* xiv. 337 O, gode lord..deliver me from the handes of my enmyes that I be not vytupered nor brought to shame.

Vitu·perable, *a.* ? *Obs.* Also 6 **vytuperable.** [a. OF. *vituperable* (obs. F., Sp. *vituperable*, Pg. *vituperavel*, It. *vituperabile*), ad. L. *vituperābil-is* (rare) blameworthy, censurable, f. *vituperāre* to Vituperate.] That deserves or merits vituperation; blameworthy, censurable, reprehensible; disgraceful, shameful.

c 1450 tr. *De Imitatione* I. xix. 22 Yf an accustumed exercise ..be liȝtly forsaken þorugh hevynes of soule or negligence, it is vituperable, & wol be founde noyous. 1481 Botoner *Tulle on Old Age* (Caxton) C vij, Cecilyus saide of olde age a thyng is no more vituperable and lothyng, thenne is the same that he seeith here before. c 1510 Barclay *Mirr. Gd. Manners* (1570) G v, But a famous merchaunt, great, riche, and haboundant, And rightwisely dealing, is not vituperable. 1547 Boorde *Brev. Health* § 163. 58 b, There be many other myrthes & consolacions, some beynge good & laudable & some vytuperable. 1586 Day *Eng. Secretary* I. (1625) 61 To ouercome others by vertue is a thing most honourable, but in pursuite thereof to be conuinced of any other, is a thing most vituperable. 1603 H. Crosse *Vertues Commw.* (1878) 99 Nothing doth more corrupt and wither greene and tender wits, then such vnsauoury and vituperable bookes. 1822 T. Taylor *Apuleius* 357 Of vituperable men there are four species; of which the first consists of the ambitious.

Vitu·perant, *a.* and *sb. rare.* [ad. L. *vituperant-*, *vituperans*, pr. pple. of *vituperāre* to Vituperate. Cf. OF. *vituperant* (Godef.).] **a.** *adj.* Abusive, vituperative. **b.** *sb.* A vituperator.

1864 *Realm* 17 Feb. 7 We do not think..that the most vituperant colonel would express such strong opinions. 1889 *Pall Mall G.* 16 Oct. 5/1 Whilst Lord Salisbury came here as your most exalted vituperant, you are journeying hither as his most obedient and faithful adulator!

Vitu·perate, *ppl. a. rare*[−1]. [ad. L. *vituperāt-us*, pa. pple. of *vituperāre*: see next.] Vituperated; worthy of vituperation.

1832 *Westm. Rev.* XVI. 7 Wealth was to be discreditable, unmanly, vituperate, because it was found greatly to indispose men to be active thieves.

Vituperate (vəitiū·pĕrē[i]t, vi-), *v.* [f. L. *vituperāt-*, ppl. stem of *vituperāre* to censure, blame, disparage, find fault with, etc., f. *vitu-* for *viti-*, stem of *vitium* blemish, fault, Vice *sb.*[1] + *parāre* to prepare. See also Vituper *v.*] *trans.* To blame, speak ill of, find fault with, in strong or violent language; to assail with abuse; to rate or revile.

Not in common use until the beginning of the 19th c.

1542 Boorde *Dyetary* xvi. (1870) 273 They louyth not porke nor swynes flesshe, but doth vituperat & abhorre it. 1611 Cotgr., *Vituperer*, to vituperate, dispraise, discommend. [Hence in Cockeram, Blount, Bailey, etc.] 1638 Penkethman *Artach.* C ij, Whatsoever transcends their sedulous apprehension..without any favourable expostulation..they will unworthily and unwittingly vituperate and reprehend.

1819 Scott *Ivanhoe* xxxiii, The incensed priests..continued to raise their voices, vituperating each other in bad Latin. 1826 Lamb *Elia* Ser. II *Pop. Fallacies* iv, A speech from the poorest sort of people which always indicates that the party vituperated is a gentleman. 1860 Froude *Hist. Eng.* V. 477 He vituperated from the pulpit the vices of the court. 1883 A. Forbes in *Fortn. Rev.* 1 Nov. 671 Englishmen are not in the habit of vituperating Monk as a traitor.

refl. 1812 H. & J. Smith *Rej. Addr.* x. (1873) 96 Deviation from scenic propriety has only to vituperate itself for the consequences it generates.

b. *absol.* or *intr.* To employ abusive language.

1856 R. A. Vaughan *Mystics* VIII. v. 46 Vituperated and vituperating, he became a wanderer throughout Germany. 1877 Mrs. Oliphant *Makers Flor.* vi. 168 He loses his temper and begins to vituperate.

Hence **Vitu·perated** *ppl. a.*

1841 Emerson *Conservative* Wks. (Bohn) II. 272 You are yourself the result of this manner of living, this foul compromise, this vituperated Sodom.

Vituperation (vəitiūpĕrē[i]·ʃən, vi-). Also 5 **-acyon.** [a. OF. *vituperaciun*, *-acion*, *-ation* (obs. F. *vitupération*, = Sp. *vituperacion*, Pg. *vituperação*, It. *vituperazione*), or ad. L. *vituperātiōn-*, *vituperātio* blaming, censuring, etc., noun of action f. *vituperāre*: see prec. and -ation.]

1. The action, fact, or process of vituperating; blame, censure, reproof, or (esp. in later use) the expression of this, in abusive or violent language; abuse, railing, rating. Also, vituperative or abusive language.

There are few instances of the use of the word before the beginning of the 19th c.: cf. Vituperate *v.*

1481 Botoner *Tulle on Old Age* (Caxton) C viij, The third part..which Caton answerith,..repreuith them of the seconde defaulte of uituperacyon opposed ayenst olde age. 1602 (*title*), Ane Satyre of the thrie Estaits, in commendation of Vertew and Vituperation of Vyce; maid be Sir Dauid Lindesay. 1633 J. Done *Hist. Septuagint* 155 When a man becomes vntractable, by fiercenesse and pride:..then vituperation comes vpon him, and priuation of honour followes him. 1656 Stanley *Hist. Philos.* v. (1687) 165 Of Rhetoric are six kinds..[6] Vituperation, when we declare a Man to be wicked.

1821 Scott *Kenilw.* xx, It was one of these old women who..answered his petition..with a volley of vituperation. 1845 Ford *Handbk. Spain* I. 35 Few nations can surpass the Spaniards in the language of vituperation. 1887 Ruskin *Præterita* II. 193 A rhyme written..in vituperation of the idle people at Conflans.

† 2. A cause of blame or censure. *Obs.*[−1]

1726 Ayliffe *Parergon* 305 (*bis*) Such a Writing ought to be clean and free from any Cavil or Vituperation of Rasure.

† **Vitupera·tious,** *a. Obs.*[−1] [f. prec.: see -ious.] Vituperative.

1797 Southey *Let. to J. Cottle* 13 Mar. in *Life* (1849) I. 306 Language is not vituperatious enough to describe the effect of its downward elongation.

Vituperative (vəitiū·pĕrĕtiv, vi-), *a.* [ad. L. type **vituperātīv-us*, f. *vituperāt-*, ppl. stem of *vituperāre*, or directly f. Vituperate *v.* + -ive. Cf. obs. F. *vituperativement* adv. (Godef.), It. *vituperativo.*]

1. Of words, language, etc.: Containing, conveying, or expressing strong depreciation; violently abusive or fault-finding; contumelious, opprobrious. Also, of or pertaining to vituperation.

Freq. in the 19th c.

1727 Pope, etc. *Art of Sinking* 115 The vituperative partition will as easily be replenished with a most choice collection [of arguments]. 1759 Sterne *Tr. Shandy* I. xix, Tristram!—Melancholy dissyllable of sound! which, to his ears, was unison to Nincompoop, and every name vituperative under heaven. 1816 Scott *Antiq.* xxx, In utter despair at this vituperative epithet. 1856 Kane *Arct. Expl.* II. xii. 129 His eloquence becoming more and more licentious and vituperative. 1859 Mill *Liberty* ii. (1865) 32/1 It is far more important to restrain this employment of vituperative language than the other.

b. Const. *of* (a person). *rare*[−1].

1823 Scott *Quentin D.* viii, Had I..heard by report that a question vituperative of my Prince had been asked by the King of France, I had..instantly mounted and returned.

2. Characterized or accompanied by vituperation or abuse.

1754 Chesterfield in *World* No. 101 ¶ 3 The torrents of their [*sc.* female] eloquence, especially in the vituperative way, stun all opposition. 1844 Disraeli *Coningsby* II. i, The indignant, soon to become vituperative, secession of a considerable section of the cabinet. 1871 'Holme Lee' *Miss Barrington* I. ix. 129 When they have been most in fault themselves, they are most prone to shower a general vituperative blame and condemnation on the other side.

3. Of persons: Given to vituperation; employing or uttering abusive language.

1819 *Blackw. Mag.* V. 90 A Whig is a vituperative animal. 1843 Carlyle *Past & Pr.* III. v, Quietly hearing all manner of vituperative able editors speak. 1904 H. Paul *Hist. Mod. Eng.* I. xii. 208 The violent and vituperative champion of the Protestant religion.

Hence **Vitu·peratively** *adv.*, in a vituperative manner; with vituperation or abuse.

1831 Carlyle in Froude *First 40 Years* (1882) II. 159 The critical republic will cackle vituperatively, or perhaps maintain total silence. 1852 *Fraser's Mag.* XLVI. 456 [He] continues his vituperatively shrill demands. 1884 J. Parker *Apost. Life* III. 115 They would not speak their mother tongue if they did not speak vituperatively.

Vituperator (vəitiū·pĕrē[i]tǫɹ, vi-). [a. L. *vituperātor*, agent-noun f. L. *vituperāre* to Vituperate. Cf. Sp. and Pg. *vituperador*, OF. *vitupereur.*] One who vituperates; an abuser.

1837 *Chambers' Jrnl.* 19 Aug. 239 To stigmatise the vituperators would be now of little service. 1841 Hor. Smith *Moneyed Man* II. iv. 116, I was tempted to chastise the vulgar vituperator. 1884 *Manch. Exam.* 9 May 5/1 That indignant declamation which is a favourite weapon with the vituperators of the Government.

Vitu·peratory, *a.* ? *Obs.* [f. L. type **vituperātōri-us*, f. *vituperāre*: see Vituperate *v.* and -ory [2].] Expressive of blame or censure; vituperative, violently abusive.

1586 Day *Eng. Secretary* I. (1625) 20 Laudatorie [Epistles] wherein is specially praised any thing, and Vituperatorie, in which is misliked or condemned whatsoeuer may be thought worthy either to be abhorred or dispraised. 1660 *Charac. Italy* To Rdr. A 5, For that [proverb] hath two ends..the one Vituperatory, and the other Laudatory. a 1832 Bentham *Deontol.* (1834) I. 315 The very same desire having ordinarily three designations, one laudatory, one vituperatory, and the other neutral. 1843 *Tait's Mag.* X. 343 A fluent array of vituperatory and laudatory phrases.

† **Vitupe·rious,** *a. Obs.* [a. OF. *vituperieus* (implied in the adv. *vituperieusement*; cf. Sp. *vituperioso*), or ad. late or med.L. *vituperiōsus* (Diefenbach), f. *vituperium* Vitupery: see -ious.]

1. Vituperative, strongly abusive or censorious.

1604 Drayton *Moyses* I. 2 Muse, I inuoke the vtmost of thy might,..Gainst the vile Atheists vituperious sting. 1632 Lithgow *Trav.* x. 490 To confound the calumnious and vituperious Papists. 1667 Waterhouse *Fire Lond.* 88 Vituperious Sarcasms, Secret rejoycings at their ruins.

2. Worthy of blame, vituperable; hence, shameful, discreditable, disgraceful, ignominious.

1612 tr. *Benvenuto's Passenger* I. iv. 281 O what doe I see, and what doe I heare in my dayes, what vituperious crimes? 1624 *Gag for Pope* 12 Clothed with the Sambenito, a punishment as vituperious as the carting of Bawdes in England. 1688 R. Holme *Armoury* II. 15/2 The bearing of these Hellish Vituperious, horrid and vile things, is to deter..the beholder from becoming like them.

Hence † **Vitupe·riously** *adv.*, vituperatively; shamefully. *Obs.*

1632 Lithgow *Trav.* I. (1906) 3 The name and fame of the most righteous alive,..be thus diversly taxed and vituperiously calumniated. 1650 Howell *Giraffi's Rev. Naples* I. 130 So they concluded to die sooner,..then to live so vituperiously in such a basenesse and servitude.

Vitu·perize, *v. nonce-word.* [irreg. f. L. *vituper-āre* + -ize.] *trans.* To vituperate.

1894 T. Wright *Life Defoe* 52 Whoever vituperised 'The True-born Englishman', it is not to be supposed that the ladies did.

Vitu·perous, *a.* ? *Obs.* [ad. obs. or arch. F. *vitupéreux* (= Pr. *vituperos*), or Sp. (also It. and Pg.) *vituperoso*, ad. late or med.L. *vituperōsus*, f. *vituperium* Vitupery: see -ous.]

1. = Vituperious *a.* 1.

1588 Parke tr. *Mendoza's Hist. China* 33 Then they returne againe with vituperous and vile words.

2. = Vituperious *a.* 2.

1620 *Chester's Tri.* To Rdr. A 2 b, Let him be prest without pity.., and like a vituperous offender, be stamped and stared at. 1651 Culpepper *Astrol. Judgem. Dis.* (1658) 173 White clouds in the Urine, and neer the bottome, are commendable; black clouds, and neer the top, are bad and vituperous.

Hence **Vitu·perously** *adv.*, vituperatively.

1892 E. L. Wakeman in *Columbus* (Ohio) *Dispatch* 18 Aug., Authorities differ not only widely but vituperously as to the origin of practical effort for their betterment.

† **Vitu·pery.** *Obs.* Also 5 **vituperye,** 6 **-ie.** [a. AF. *vituperie* (Gower), OF. **vituperie* (= Pr. *vituperi*, Sp., Pg., and It. *vituperio*), ad. late or med.L. *vituperium* (Diefenbach), blame, dishonour, shame, f. L. *vituperāre* to Vituperate. Cf. Vituper *sb.*] Dishonour, reproach, shame; blame, vituperation.

1489 Caxton *Faytes of A.* IV. i. P iiij, It may be yt som ..wolde gladly vse therof [*sc.* a safe-conduct], whiche ought to tourne them in to grete vituperye and blame. 1572 Bossewell *Armorie* II. 105 He ought..to defende the same (euen to the death) from all challenge or vituperie. 1590 Barrow & Greenwood in *Coll. Lett. & Confer.* 36 The rest of the vituperie wherwith you haue laden vs. 1608 H. Clapham *Errour Left Hand* 35 Emulations, heart-burnings, vituperies, bloody practises. 1680 Shelton *Quix.* II. liii. 357 At whose perswasions & vitupery, the poore Gouernour tried if he could mooue himselfe.

Vitus, in *St. Vitus's Dance*: see Dance *sb.* 6 b. Similarly *St. Vitus' fits.*

a 1845 Hood *Sniffing a Birthday* xv, Ring Tom of Lincoln till he splits, And dance into St. Vitus' fits.

Viue, southern ME. variant of Five.

Viurie *Her.*: see Vivry.

‖ **Viva** (vī·vă), *sb.*[1] and *int.* [It., lit. 'live', 3rd pers. sing. pres. subj. of *vivere* (:—L. *vīvĕre*) to live. So Sp. and Pg. *viva.* Cf. Vivat.] A cry of 'long live' as a salute or greeting; a shout of applause; a cheer or hurrah: **a.** As a sb., in the pl. *vivas.*

a 1700 Evelyn *Diary* 23 Nov. 1644, The multitude..were ..looking out of their windows and houses, with loud *viva's* and acclamations of felicity to their new Prince. 1728 [? De Foe] *Capt. Carleton's Mem.* 268 The Cavaliero.. received the repeated *Vivas* of that vast Concourse. 1818 Lady Morgan *Autobiog.* (1859) 53 He kept bowing and scraping,..answering the paid vivas of the populace with one of his *jolis mots.* 1851 Mrs. Browning *Casa Guidi Wind.* I. 490 Whereat the popular exultation drunk With indrawn 'vivas' the whole sunny air. 1882 'Ouida' *Under Two Flags* (1890) 411 Lifting her, with wild vivas that rent the sky, on to the shoulders of the four tallest men.

b. As an exclamation.

1841 Barham *Ingol. Leg.* Ser. II. *Auto-da-Fé*, How they shouted, and fired the great guns in the square, Cried 'Viva!' and rung all the bells in the steeple.

Viva (vəi·vă), *sb.*[2] *Univ. colloq.* [Abbrev. of Viva voce.] = Viva voce *sb.*

1891 *Athenæum* 19 Dec. 825/2 The description of his *vivâ* will bring vivid recollections of similar tortures to many minds. 1897 *Westm. Gaz.* 27 July 1/3 If a man has done his paperwork either very well or very badly, the 'viva' is almost entirely formal.

Hence **Vi·va** *v. trans.*, to subject to a viva voce examination; also *intr.*, to examine viva voce.

1893 in J. B. Firth *Minstrelsy of Isis* (1908) 190 We shall laugh at our Tutors and leave them to 'viva' themselves and be free. 1907 'Barbara Burke' *Barbara goes to Oxford* 132 Facing them..sat the youth who was being vivâed.

†Vivace, a. Obs.⁻¹ [ad. L. *vīvāc-*, *vivāx* VIVACIOUS a., after *vivace*.] Lively.

‖Vivace (vivā̆'tʃe), adv. and sb.) Mus. [It. *vivace* brisk, lively:—L. *vīvāc-*, *vivāx*: see next.] A direction indicating brisk or lively performance (quots. 1).

Vivaciously, adv. [f. prec.+-LY².] In a vivacious or lively manner; with vivacity or sprightly animation; †vigorously.

Vivaciousness. [f. VIVACIOUS a.+-NESS.]
1. Tenacity of life; longevity. *rare.*
2. Vivacity of manner or speech; liveliness, sprightliness.

Vivacious (vivēi'·ʃəs, vi-), a. Also 7 -eous. [f. L. *vīvāc-*, *vivāx* (whence F. *vivace*, Sp. and It. *vivace*), tenacious of life, long-lived, lively, vigorous, f. *vīvere* to live: see -ACIOUS.]
1. Full of, characterized by, or exhibiting vivacity or liveliness; animated, brisk, lively, sprightly.
2. Of persons, the mind, disposition, etc.

Vivacity (vivæ'siti, vi-). Also 5-6 vivacite, 6-7 -tie, 7 vivasity. [ad. OF. *vivacite* (F. *vivacité*, Sp. *vividad*), or ad. L. *vīvācitāt-, vīvācitās* natural vigour, vital force, liveliness, f. *vīvāx, -ācit-* VIVACIOUS a.: see -ITY.] The state or condition of being vivacious.
1. Intellectual or mental animation, acuteness, vigour; quickness or liveliness of conception or perception.

†Vive, v. Obs.⁻¹ [ad. F. *vivre*.]

‖Viva, int. [It.:—L. *vīvat.*]

‖Viva voce (vai'vǎ vō̆u'sē), adv., adv. phr., a. and sb. [L. *vivā vōce*, abl. sing. fem. of *vīvus* living, and *vōx, vōcem* voice.]

Vivarium (vaivē̆a'riŏm, vi-). Pl. -ia, also -iums. [L. *vivārium* enclosure for live game, warren, fish-pond, etc., neut. sing. of *vivārius*, f. *vivus* alive, living.]
1. A place where living animals, esp. fish, are maintained or preserved for food; a fish-pond or fish-pool.

Vivandier, vivandière (F. *vivandier* masc. (= Sp. *vivandero*), Fg. *vivandeiro*, It. *vivandiere*) A supplier of victuals or provisions, f. pop.L. **vīvanda* for *vīvenda*: see VIAND¹. Cf. VIANDER¹.]

‖Vive-roy, vive-voce. See VIVA VOCE.

Vively, adv. Now Sc. or Obs. [f. VIVE a. + -LY².]
1. Physically lively, forcible, or brisk. *rare.*

Vivify (vi'vifǎi), v. [ad. F. *vivifier* (OF. from *vivifier*), or ad. late L. *vīvificāre* to make alive, f. *vīvus* alive + *-ficāre*: see -FY.]
1. trans. To give life to, to animate, to enliven or quicken.

Vivency (vi'vensi). *rare.* [f. L. *vīvere* to live + -ENCY.] Manifestation of the principle of life; vitality.

Vive, sb. Now *dial.* or Obs. Forms: vivers, 5 vyveros, wyvers; 9 vyver, Sc. wivar). 9 vives (9 vyver, Sc. *wewar*), 5 vyvors, OF. (also mod.F.) *vivier* (= Sp. *vivero*), ad. L. *vīvārium* VIVARIUM.] A fish-pond.

Viver, sb. Now *dial.* or Obs. Forms: 7 viver, 5 vyvere, 9 vyvers, wyvers. [a. OF. *vivier*.]

†Viver², a. Obs.⁻¹ serpent:—L. *vipera* VIPER.]

Viver³ (vai'var). *dial.* [Alteration of *fiver* FIBRE.] A fibre or rootlet.

Viverra (vivē̆'ra, vai-). [mod.L. use of L. *viverra* a ferret: see next.] Zool. The civet-cat (*Viverra civetta*), or other species of the type-genus of the civet family (*Viverridae*). Also *attrib.*

Viverridous, a. Zool. [f. mod.L. *Viverrid-æ* (see VIVERRA) + -OUS.] Of or belonging to the *Viverridæ* or civet family.

Viverrine (vivē̆'rǎin, vai-), a. and sb. Zool. [ad. mod.L. *viverrīn-us*, f. *viverra* VIVERRA: see -INE¹.]
A. adj. Resembling or related to the civet, the civet family; *spec.* belonging to the sub-family *Viverrinæ*.
B. sb. An animal of the sub-family *Viverrinæ*.

Vives (vaivz). *sb. pl.* Also 6 vyves, 6-8 vives, 7 vives, Vees †, and VIVES.] Cf. FIVES, VEES †, and VIVES.] Hard swelling of the submaxillary glands of a horse; the presence of these regarded as a specific morbid condition in a horse.

Vivianite (vi'viănǎit). Min. [f. name of the discoverer, J. G. *Vivian*; named by Werner, 1817.] A phosphate of iron usually occurring in crystals of blue and green colour.

Vivid (vi'vid), a. [ad. L. *vīvid-us* living, animated, lively, f. *vīvere* to live. Cf. It. *vivido*.]
1. Full of life; vigorous, active, or energetic (in this account); lively or brisk. *a.* Of persons (or animals), their attributes, etc.

Vividity (vivi'diti). *rare.* [f. VIVID a. + -ITY.]
The quality or state of being vivid; vividness.

Vividly, adv. [f. VIVID a. + -LY².]
1. Brightly, brilliantly, in respect of colour or light.

Vividness. [f. prec. + -NESS.]
The quality or state of being vivid, in senses of the adj.
1. Of colour, light, etc.

Vivific, a. Obs. [ad. L. *vīvific-us*: see next.] Vivifying; life-giving, enlivening.

Vivificate, v. Obs. [f. L. *vīvificāt-*, ppl. stem of *vīvificāre* VIVIFY: see -ATE³.]

Vivificant, a. Obs. [ad. L. *vīvificant-*, pr. pple. of *vīvificāre*: see next.]

Vivification (vivifikēi'ʃən). [ad. late L. *vīvificātiōn-em*, n. of action f. *vīvificāre* VIVIFY.]

Vivificative, a. Obs. [f. L. *vīvificāt-* (see VIVIFICATE) + -IVE.] Vivifying, life-giving.

VIVIFYING.

3. *absol.* To impart life or animation.

Vivifying, *ppl. a.* [f. prec. + -ING².]

1. That vivifies or animates physically; life-giving, quickening.

2. That vivifies spiritually or mentally; imparting interest or energy.

Vivifyingly, *adv.*

† b. Of medicines: Restorative.

Vivi-para, *sb. pl.*

Viviparity. [f. *viviparous* + -ITY.]

Viviparous, *a.*

Viviparously, *adv.*

Vivisect, *v.* [Back-formation from VIVISECTION.]

Vivisection. [f. L. *vīvī-* ... + *sectiō* cutting.]

Vivisectional, *a.*

Vivisectionist.

Vivisective, *a.*

Vivisector.

VIXEN.

Vixen (vi·ks'n), *sb. and a.*

1. The female of the fox; a she-fox.

2. An ill-tempered quarrelsome woman; a shrew, a termagant.

3. *fig.*

4. *attrib.*

Vixenish (vi·ks'niʃ), *a.* [f. prec. + -ISH¹.]

1. Resembling a vixen in disposition; cross, ill-tempered, snappish.

2. Characteristic of, appropriate to, a vixen.

Vixenishly, *adv.*

Vixenly, *adj. and adv.*

VIZARD.

Vizard (vi·zəɹd), *sb. and a.* Now *arch.*

Forms: α. 6 **vysard**, 6 **visarde**, 7 **vizarde**...

VIZARD.

Vizard, *obs. or dial.* form of WIZARD.

Vizard, *v.* Now *rare.* Also 7 **visard.**

1. *trans.* To conceal or disguise (something) under a false outward show or appearance; to represent falsely or speciously.

2. To cover or disguise (the face, etc.) with or as with a vizard or visor; to mask.

Vizarded, *ppl. a.*

1. Disguised with a vizard; wearing a vizard; visored, masked. Used *(a)* predicatively or *(b)* attributively. Also *fig.*

Vizardless, *a. rare.* [f. VIZARD + -LESS.] Having no vizard; visorless.

Vizard-mask. Now *arch.*

1. A mask worn to conceal or disguise the face; a vizard.

2. A woman who wears such a mask; a prostitute.

VIZY.

Visier (viziəɹ). Forms: α. 7, 9 **visir**, **visire**. β. 8 **visiar**, 8–9 **visir**, 9 **visier**, ...

1. The dignity, position, or authority of a vizier; the period during which a particular vizier held office.

Visierate (viziərət). Forms: α. 7, 9 **visirate**, 8–9 **visierate**. β. 8 **visiarate**, ...

1. The office or function of a vizier; rule or government as a grand vizier. Also *transf.*

Visierial (viziəˈriːal). Also **visirial**, **visirial**.

Visiership (viziˈəɹʃip). Also **visirship**.

VIZY.

Vizy, visy, vizzy (vi·zi), *sb. Sc.* Forms: 5–6 **vesy**, **wesy**, 6 **wysy**, **vesey**...

1. An aim or act at an object which it is desired to hit.

2. To look at closely or attentively; to regard, see, view.

Vizier (vi·ziəɹ, viˈziəɹ), *sb.* Also 7 **vizir**, **vizier**.

VOCABULARY.

Vo, southern ME. var. FY n., FOE, WHO.

Vocable (vɒkəbl), *sb. and a.* [ad. F. *vocable* (16th c., = Pr. *vocable*, Sp. *vocablo*, It. *vocabolo*...), or ad. L. *vocābulum*, f. *vocāre* to call, name.]

1. A word or term.

Vocable, *a.*

Vocability. [f. next + -ITY.] A spoken or shouted amount or extent of voice.

Vocabulary (vɒˈkæbjʊləri), *sb. (and a.)* [ad. med.L. *vocābulāri-us*, *-um*, f. L. *vocābulum* VOCABLE.]

Vocabular (vɒˈkæbjʊlaɹ), *a.* [f. as prec.] Of, pertaining to, or consisting of words.

Vocabularian. [f. prec. + -IAN.]

Vocabularied, *ppl. a.*

Vocabulist (vɒˈkæbjʊlist), *sb.* [ad. F. *vocabuliste*, or med.L. *vocābulista*, f. L.]

Vocabulary (vɒˈkæbjʊləri), *sb.* Also 6 *-arie*. [ad. med.L. *vocābulāri-um*, *-us*, f. L.]

Vocabulary.

Vocable.

Vocabulist.

Vocabulous.

Vocal.

Vocalic.

Vocalism.

Vocalist.

Vocality.

Vocalize.

Vocalized.

Vocalizer.

Vocally.

Vocalness.

Vocate.

Vocation.

Vocational.

Vocative.

Vocatively.

Vociferant.

Vociferate.

Vociferation.

Vociferator.

Vociferize.

Vociferosity.

Vociferous.

Vociferously.

Vociferousness.

Vocule.

Vod.

Vodder.

Vodka.

Voder.

Voe.

Voet.

Vogal.

Vogie (vō'gi), a. Sc. Also 8 **vougy**, 9 **vogey**. [Of obscure origin.]

1. Vain, proud, conceited.

2. Merry, cheerful, delighted, gay.

Voghte, obs. variant of VAULT sb.[1]

Vogue (vōg), sb. Also 6 vogt, Sc. wogue, 7 voug, vouge, 7, 8 *F. vogue* roving, course, success, [vogart, ad. It. voga to row. So It. and Pg. voga, Sp. boga.]

1. *F. i.* The vogue, the principal or foremost place in popular repute or estimation; the most pronounced success or general acceptance; the greatest currency or prevalence.

2. Without article: Popularity; general acceptance or currency; success in popular esteem.

Vogue, v.[1] *Obs.* [f. the sb.]

1. *trans.* To row or float.

Vogue, v.[2] *Obs.* [ad. F. *voguer*: see VOGUE sb.] Naut. To float.

Voiage, obs. form of VOYAGE.

Voice (vois), sb. Forms: 4-4 voiz (4 noyz), 3-5 voys (5 voys, 5-6 woys), 4-5 voise (4 uoise), 4-7 voyce (5 woyce), 4-7 voice (4 voyce, 5-6 voice); also 5 wyce, 8-9 dial. vice.

Voice (vois), v. Also 5 voyse, 6-7 voyce, 7 vouce. [f. prec.]

Voiced (voist), ppl. a.

Voiceful (vois·fŭl), a. Chiefly *poet.* or *rhet.*

1. Endowed with, or as if with, a voice; having voice or power of utterance; vocal.

2. Much or highly spoken of; commended.

3. *Phonology.* Uttered with voice (or vibration of the vocal chords) as opposed to breath; sonant.

Voiceless, a.

Voicelessly, adv.

Voicelessness.

Voicelet. [f. VOICE *sb.* + -LET.] A little voice.

Voicing (vois·iŋ), *vbl. sb.* [f. VOICE *v.*]

Void (void), *a.* and *sb.*[1] Forms: 3-7 voyde (4-6 woyde, 6 wyde), 4-7 voide (6 voyede), 4-6 voyd, 5-6 voide, 6 voyd.

I. 1. Of a space, etc.: Having no occupant or possessor; unoccupied, vacant.

2. Of places: Destitute of occupants or inhabitants; unoccupied or frequented by living creatures; deserted, empty.

3. *spec.* Having the centre empty or hollow.

4. Of a house or room: Unoccupied; untenanted. Now chiefly *dial.*

5. Of paper, etc.: Blank, not written on; containing no writing or lettering. *Obs.*

6. Empty-handed; destitute. *Obs.*

7. Of (of) course, said of a planet: (see quot. 1679). *Obs.*

8. Of time: Free from work or occupation; unemployed, idle, leisure. Now *rare.*

9. Of persons, etc.: Empty or destitute of good qualities; worthless. *Obs.*

10. Devoid of (some quality); without.

11. Devoid of (some thing), not tainted with (some bad quality, fault, or defect).

II. 12. Destitute of, not graced or ennobled by some virtue or good quality.

Void (void), *v.* Forms: 4-5 voyden, 4-7 voyde (4 woyde, 5 voyd, voyde), 4-6 voiden, 4-6 void, -voyd (5 voyd), 4-7 voide, 4-7 voyde, -voide (OF. voider, voidier (OF. also *voutier*, *mod.F. vider*; = Pr. *voidar*, *sujar*, *sujier*, etc., (F. adj. *vuide*)...

1. *trans.* To clear (a room, house, place) of occupants; to empty or clear (a place, receptacle, etc.) of something.

2. To depart, withdraw, go away.

3. To deprive of efficacy, force, or value; to render inoperative or meaningless; to set aside or nullify.

Volate. 1. A large bird-cage; an aviary. Also *fig.* and in fig. context.

2. **collect.** The birds kept in an aviary. Also *fig.*

Volate, *v.* *Obs.* (Meaning uncertain.)

Volatic (vǫ·lătik), *a.* *rare*. Now *rare* of *volare* to fly.]

A. *sb.* A winged creature.

B. *adj.* That flies or flits about; *spec.* in *Path.*, of a variety of itch.

Volatile (vǫ·lătil, -il), *sb.* and *a.*

2. **collect.** Birds, *esp.* wild-fowl. *Obs.*

Volatile, *v.* *Obs.*

2. A winged creature; a bird, butterfly, or the like; a fowl. Usually in plural.

Volatileness.

Volatility.

a. Readily changing from one interest or mood to another; changeable, fickle; marked or characterized by levity or flightiness.

b. Of persons.

5. Evanescent, transient; readily vanishing or disappearing; difficult to seize, retain, or fix permanently.

6. Of the air: Light; not oppressive. *Obs.*

Volatileness. The character or state of being volatile; volatility. Chiefly *fig.*

b. *Volatile salt* or *salts.*

Volatility.

1. Readiness to vaporize or evaporate, tendency to be readily diffused or dissipated in the atmosphere, especially at ordinary temperatures.

2. **intr.** To become volatile; to evaporate.

Volcanically, *adv.* In a volcanic, eruptive, or fiery manner; with sudden violence.

Volcanicity.

Volcanism.

Volcanist.

Volcanity. *rare.*

Volcano.

Volcanoism.

Volcanology.

Vole, *sb.* 1. A small short-tailed mouse.

Vole, *v.*

Volet.

Volency.

Volens nolens, *advb. phr.* NOLENS VOLENS.

Volent, *a.* Exercising, or capable of exercising, will or choice in respect of one's conduct or course of action.

Volente, variant of VOLUNTY *Obs.*

Volentine. *Obs.*

Volery, *sb.* var. of VOLARY.

Volet, *sb.* 8 *dial.* violet.

Volge, *Obs. rare.*

Voligvagant.

Volible, *a.* *Obs. rare.* [ad. L. *volūbilis,* f. *volvĕre* to roll.] Capable of turning or being turned round.

Voligvagant.

Volition, *a.* *rare*. [f. VOLITE + -IVE.]

Volition.

1. An act of willing or resolving.

2. The action of consciously willing or resolving; the making of a definite choice or decision.

3. The power or faculty of willing.

B. *sb.* A desiderative verb, mood, etc.

Volitional, *a.*

Volitionally, *adv.*

Volitive, *a.*

Volitorial, *a.*

Volkameria. *Bot.* Also *Volkamer,* a German the name of Johann G. *Volkamer,* a German

botanist (1616–93).] A Linnean genus of verbenaceous shrubs, characterized by their fleshy or corky fruit; a shrub or plant of this genus.

1753 *Chambers' Cycl.* Suppl., *Volkameria*, in botany, the name of a genus of plants..The fruit is a roundish bilocular capsule. 1823 Crabb *Technol. Dict.* s.v., The species are shrubs, as—*Volkameria aculeata*,..Prickly Volkameria, &c. 1833 B'ness Bunsen in Hare *Life* (1879) I. ix. 403, I have replanted with roses, oleanders, volcamerias, and geraniums. 1866 *Treas. Bot.* 1225.

‖ **Volksraad** (vo·lksrāt). [f. Du. *volk* people, Folk *sb.* + *raad* senate, council, Rede *sb.*] The chief legislative assembly in either of the former South African republics of the Transvaal or the Orange Free State.

1852 Barter *Dorp & Veld* xiii. 194 A resolution of the *Volksraad*, that no additional natives should be allowed to take up their residence within the colony. 1865 *Chambers's Encycl.* VII. 25/2 While the volksraad, or peoples' council [of Orange River Free State], exercise legislative functions. 1881 Earl Selborne in *Personal & Pol. Mem.* (1898) II. 5 The Volksraad must yield, or the war be renewed.

† **Voll**, shortened f. of, or error for, Volley *sb.*

1574 B. Rich *Dial. betw. Mercury & Soldier* A 4, Too my farewell, certayne voll of shot discharged in hope of my good speede.

Vollary, obs. f. Volary. **Vol'le**, southern ME. var. Fill *sb.*^{1}, Full *v.*^{1} (to baptize), Full *a.* and *adv.*

† **Vollenge.** *Obs.*$^{-1}$ [Cf. Valanche and It. *valanga*.] An avalanche.

1830 W. Taylor *Hist. Surv. Germ. Poetry* II. 456 The vollenge, which overwhelms the whole village, was at first but a little snowball.

Vo·ller, vo·llier. *s. dial.* Forms: 7 **vallor, vallow**, 9 **valler**; 8 **voler**, 9 **voller, vollier.** [Southern dial. var. of Follower (5 a).] That part of a cheese-press (or cider-press) to which pressure is applied.

1675 Worlidge *Syst. Agric.* (ed. 2) 323 *Vallor*, or *Vallow*, ..a Concave-Mold wherein a Cheese is pressed. [Hence in some later Dicts.] 1730 Budgen *Hurricane fr. Bexhill to Newingden-level* 2 A Cheesebail and Voler were taken from a Shelf in a Chamber. *Note*, The Voler is a round Piece of Inch Board, fitted into the Bail, that communicates the Force of the Press upon the Cheese. 1853 Cooper *Sussex Gloss.* 84. 1891 *Hartland Gloss.* 82 *Voller*,..that part of a cider or cheese press to which the pressure is applied by screw or lever.

Vollere, southern ME. variant of Fuller *sb.*^{1}

Volley (vǫ·li), *sb.* Forms: α. 6 **volée, volee, (valee), vole**, 7 **vollee, volle.** β. 6 **vallew**, 6–7 **volue.** γ. 6–8 **vollie** (6 **vallie**, *Sc.* **wollie**), 7 **volie**, 7–9 *pl.* **vollies**; 6 **voly**, 6–7 **volly**, 7 *Ir.* **voylly.** δ. 6–7 **voley**, 7 **wolley, valley**, 6– **volley.** [ad. F. *volée* (12th c. in Godef. *Compl.*), = Pr. and Sp. *volada*, It. *volata*:—Romanic *volāta*, fem. sb. f. L. *volātus*, pa. pple. of *volāre* to fly.

The spellings *volue*, *vallew*, are prob. on the analogy of *venue*, *vinew* beside *veny*, *vinny*.]

1. A simultaneous discharge of a number of fire-arms or artillery; a salvo.

α. 1587 Holinshed *Chron.* III. 1219/2 The whole fire began to plaie in such sort, that within foure volées both sides of the house were battered through. 1591 *Garrard's Art Warre* 48 They must abide at ye least a volee of Canons.
γ. 1573 *Satir. Poems Reform.* xxxix. 93 For ordinance thay dung at day and nycht By weirlyk wollyis. *a* 1578 Lindesay (Pitscottie) *Chron. Scot.* (S.T.S.) I. 143 The king ..commandit to charge all the gunnis to gif the castell ane new wollie. 1617 Moryson *Itin.* II. 163 The enemy played all the night upon them with great vollyes, but hurt onely three men. 1688 Holme *Armoury* III. xix. (Roxb.) 214/2 In grand Battalia's or feild service the souldier fires by Vollies or as some terme it, by Salves of shot. 1700 S. L. tr. *Fryke's Voy. E. Ind.* 318 A Dutch Company that conducted us out of Town gave three Vollies and went back again. 1745 P. Thomas *Jrnl. Anson's Voy.* 282 We then kept a continual Fire upon her of both great and small Arms, not firing in set Broadsides and Vollies. 1826 J. F. Cooper *Mohicans* (1829) I. viii. 101 Rifles which sent their leaden messengers across the rock in vollies.
δ. 1591 in *Lyly's Works* (1902) I. 440 But from the Snail-mount and the Ship-Ile in the Pond..there was a long volley of Chambers discharged. 1600 E. Blount tr. *Conestaggio* 203 They forced the gallions with a fewe volleies. 1625 Markham *Souldiers Accid.* 9 Let the first Ranke onely giue their volley,..and the second to passe through it, and so giue their volley. 1662 J. Davies tr. *Olearius' Voy. Ambass.* 169 We made some stay before the City,..and saluted it with a Volley both of all our great Guns, and of small shot. 1719 De Foe *Crusoe* I. (Globe) 304 We were by this Method able to fire six Volleys, half of us at a Time. 1817 J. Scott *Paris Revisit.* (ed. 4) 293 A loud coarse laugh burst out from each,—united as a volley of musquetry, and ending as abruptly. 1844 H. H. Wilson *Brit. India* II. 219 After firing a volley, the troops charged and put the enemy to the rout. 1879 Browning *Martin Relph* 103 They level: a volley, a smoke and the clearing of smoke.

b. Const. *of* (shot, etc.).

α. 1583 Stocker *Civ. Warres Lowe C.* III. 83 b, The valee of an 130. Canon shot. 1590 Sir J. Smyth *Disc. Weapons* 12 If our..Mosquettiers would give their volees of Mosquet shot uppon these shipboates full of men. 1623 in Foster *Eng. Factories Ind.* (1908) II. 231 At his putting into the grave 3 volles of smale shotte.
β. 1579 Digges *Stratiot.* 105 These Troupes..hauing deliuered their Volue of Shot, shall marche away. *c* 1595 Capt. Wyatt *Dudley's Voy.* (Hakl. Soc.) 19 Givinge whole vallews of shott at our meetinge. *Ibid.* 43 Wyatt..receaved his Generall with a vallew of small shott.
γ. 1584 Lyly *Campaspe* v. iii. 37 There is more pleasure in tuning of voyce, then in a volly of shotte. 1599 Dallam in *Early Voy. Levant* (Hakl. Soc.) 59 Betwyxte everie greate shott a vallie of smale shott. 1650 R. Stapylton *Strada's Low C. Wars* VII. 76 A great joy expressed by three Vollyes of shot, and the cheerfull sound of Drums. *a* 1660 *Contemp. Hist. Irel.* (Ir. Archæol. Soc.) I. 261 The relife gaue a voylly of foure score shott amonge them. *a* 1700 Evelyn *Diary* 8 Oct. 1641, From whence we received many vollies of shot in compliment to my Lord Marshall.
δ. 1591 Raleigh *Last Fight Revenge* (Arb.) 20 After many enterchanged voleies of..small shot. 1604 T. Wright *Passions* v. § 4. 172 Resembling a volley of shot speedily deliuered. 1625 in Ellis *Orig. Lett.* Ser. I. III. 199 Which gave her a volley of fifteen hundred great shot. 1725 De Foe *Voy. round World* I. 143 His Men fell..as flat to the Ground, as if they had been shot to Death with a Volley of our Shot. 1748 *Anson's Voyage* II. v. 186 He fired a volley of small shot between the masts. 1803 Scott *Let.* in *Lockhart* (1837) I. xi. 390 A volley of small shot fired through the window. 1847 James *Convict* xvi, Another volley of shot rang from behind the gateway of the town.

c. *transf.*, *fig.*, and in fig. context. Also without article (quot. 1749); cf. next.

1629 H. Burton *Truth's Triumph* 232 Thus haue we.. spent a small volley vpon the Pontifician forces. 1738 Mrs. Delany *Life & Corr.* (1861) II. 15 Every one was pleased with your..compliments, and volleys have been shot off in return this afternoon, when I said I was coming to my room to write to you. 1749 Smollett *Regicide* III. viii, I will pour My vengeance in full volley; and the earth Shall dread to yield you succour or resource! 1749 Fielding *Tom Jones* IX. v, She discharged a volley of small charms at once from her whole countenance in a smile. 1817 Byron *Beppo* xlv, Large black eyes that flash on you a volley Of rays. 1836–7 Dickens *Sk. Boz, Scenes* xii, Ginger-beer corks go off in volleys.

† **d.** *In volley*, by simultaneous firing. *Obs.*$^{-1}$

1598 Barret *Theor. Warres* III. i. 42 There is yet another order of discharging of troupes of Muskets in vollie.

e. *Mining.* 'The act of exploding blasts in sections.'

1895 *Funk's Stand. Dict.*

2. A shower or simultaneous flight of many missile weapons, as arrows, stones, etc. Also in fig. context.

1598 Barret *Theor. Warres* I. i. 3 Our bowmen may shoot by vollies, as thick as hayle. 1611 Speed *Hist. Gt. Brit.* VI. xiv. § 11. 91 The Britaines..auoided the volue of the Romans, showring downe withall great store of theirs vpon them. 1667 Milton *P. L.* VI. 213 Over head the dismal hiss Of fiery Darts in flaming volies flew. 1697 Dryden *Æneid* I. 215 Stones and brands in rattling volleys fly. 1808 Scott *Marm.* VI. xxxiv, The English shafts in volleys hail'd. 1820 — *Abbot* xviii, Even thus fly all your shafts.., but a breath of foolish affection ever crosses in the mid volley, and sways the arrow from the mark.

b. Const. *of.*

1590 Sir J. Smyth *Disc. Weapons* 31 b, The Archers with their volees of arrowes did breake both horsmen and footmen. 1600 Holland *Livy* XXVIII. xxxvi. 696 The Romans ..at the first onset and volie of shot..put them to flight. 1625 Bacon *Apophth.* § 126 It was told him, that the enemie had such volleyes of arrowes, that they did hide the Sunne. 1686 tr. *Chardin's Trav. Persia* 210 The People.. ply'd the Top of the Mosque with .. Volleys of Stones. 1734 tr. *Rollin's Anc. Hist.* (1827) I. 345 Numerous volleys of arrows and stones. 1788 Gibbon *Decl. & F.* xlvi. IV. 520 Their engines discharged a perpetual volley of stones and darts. 1850 Marsden *Early Purit.* (1853) 437 The mob rushed upon them with a volley of stones.

c. *poet.* A storm or shower of hail, rain, etc.

1737 *Gentl. Mag.* VII. 630 Wintry clouds, Surcharg'd with vollies of tumultuous hail, Or stores of sounding rain. 1784 Cowper *Task* v. 141 The gloomy clouds find weapons, arrowy sleet, Skin-piercing volley, blossom-bruising hail.

† **3.** A company or troop of birds, etc., in flight; a flight. *Obs. rare.*

1601 Dolman *La Primaud. Fr. Acad.* (1618) III. 760 The ringe doues are seene to come euery yeere in great vollies ouer the sea. *Ibid.* 843 Birdes of prey doe not flie togither in vollies or troopes. 1610 G. Fletcher *Christ's Vict.* II. lxi, But to their Lord, now musing in his thought, A heavenly volie of light Angels flew.

† **b.** A crowd or large number *of* persons or things. *Obs.*

1595 Daniel *Civil Wars* V. cvii, Therefore easily great Sommerset..With all the vollie of disgraces met. 1639 Fuller *Holy War* II. xxxvii. 94 King Almerick himself wearied with whole volleys of miseries, ended his life of a bloody flux. *a* 1656 Ussher *Ann.* VI. (1658) 564 The Souldiers ..finding their return intercepted by a valley of Archers. 1693 *Humours Town* 97 The Vollies of Duns, of believing Vintners, Tailors, Sempstresses.

4. An uttering or outpouring *of* numerous words, oaths, shouts, etc., in smart or rapid succession. Also without const.

1590 Nashe *Pasquil's Apol.* I. C ij b, He giues vs a voley of Scriptures against Non Residents. 1591 Shaks. *Two Gent.* II. iv. 30 A fine volly of words, gentlemen, & quickly shot off. 1620 [G. Brydges] *Horæ Subs.* 455 Whatsoeuer by them is performed, shall be sure to finde whole vollies of praises. 1647 N. Ward *Simple Cobler* (1843) 54, I am resolved ..to storme you with volyes of Love and Loyalty. 1649 Milton *Eikon.* x. Wks. 1851 III. 412 Those thousands of blaspheming Cavaliers about him, whose mouthes let fly Oaths and Curses by the voley. 1710 Steele & Addison *Tatler* No. 254 ¶ 5 We heard a Volley of Oaths and Curses, lasting for a long while. 1779 Sheridan *St. Patrick's Day* I. i, Let him have our grievances in a volley. 1782 Miss Burney *Cecilia* v. vii, [He] poured forth..a volley of compliments. 1820 W. Irving *Sketch Bk.* I. 64 This, however, always produced a fresh volley from his wife. 1847 *Illustr. Lond. News* 2 Oct. 219/2 Between them continuous volleys of what is called 'chaff' were kept up. 1874 Lisle Carr *J. Gwynne* I. v. 163 A volley of dire anathemas against those scoundrelly insurance chaps.

b. Similarly of sighs, groans, cheers, laughter, etc. Also without const.

1589 Greene *Tullies Love* Wks. (Grosart) VII. 189 After a vole of broken sighes tempered with some teares, hee fell a sleepe. 1640 Sandys *Christs Passion* IV. 270 Cries Of weeping Women, in lowd Vollies rise. 1648 Crashaw *Music's Duel* 63 A Throng Of short thicke sobs, whose thundring volleyes float..In panting murmurs. 1727 Gay *Begg. Op.* I. xii, What vollies of sighs are sent from the windows of Holborn. 1786 tr. *Beckford's Vathek* (1868) 103 They burst out into volleys of laughter. 1877 Talmage *Serm.* 334 Let this religion of Christ go down under a volley of merriment. 1882 B. D. W. Ramsay *Recoll. Mil. Serv.* II. xv. 65 Giving a volley of British cheers.

c. A succession of words of command rapidly or smartly delivered.

1796 *Instr. & Reg. Cavalry* (1813) 27 The repetition of them by every other individual concerned, must not be strictly successive, but as much as can be in a volley.

† **5.** *At* (*the* or *a*) *volley*, *on* (or *o'*) *the volley*, at random, without consideration. Usu. with verbs, esp. *speak. Obs.*

After F. *à la volée*.

(*a*) 1578 H. Wotton *Courtlie Controv.* 252 The king.. they knew loued hir feruently,..although it were begun at the volue. 1596 Harington *Metam. Ajax Apol.* Aa vj b, The sundrie censures I shoulde incurre, by letting such a pamphlet fly abroad at such a time, when euerything is taken at the voley. *c* 1620 Z. Boyd *Zion's Flowers* (1855) 125 Like those who speake at random at a voleye. 1625 B. Jonson *Staple of N.* IV. i, 'Tis like a Ball at Tennis..When we doe speak at volley, all the ill we can one of another. 1686 F. Spence tr. *St. Evremont's Misc.* Pref., Otherwise we cannot lay hold of him, he speaks at volley and universally. [1820 Scott *Monast.* xvii, I have always known you..prompt to speak at the volley and without reflection.]
(*b*) 1629 Massinger *Picture* III. vi, What we spake on the voley begins to work. 1630 B. Jonson *New Inn* I. vi, You must not giue credit To all that Ladies publiquely professe, Or talke, o'th vollee, vnto their seruants. 1831 *Fraser's Mag.* Sept. 161/1 He never speaks 'on the *voley*' (that is to say, at random).

6. *Tennis.* The flight of a ball in play before it has touched the ground. Cf. Fly *sb.*^{2} 2 b.

1596 Nashe *Saffron Walden* To Rdr. 24 One that stands, as it were, at the line in a Tennis-court, and takes euerie ball at the volly. 1878 Marshall *Ann. Tennis* 112 He frequently takes a difficult service (at the volley) off the penthouse.

b. *Tennis*, *Lawn-tennis*, *Cricket*, etc. A return stroke or hit at a ball before it has touched the ground; the action of so returning the ball. (Cf. *half-volley* Half- II. i.)

1862 *Temple Bar* VI. 282 [Mr. Pudd] is said to have hit a volley to long-field for nine. 1884 *Marshall's Tennis Cuts* 124 The match was..loudly applauded every now and then by the spectators, when a brilliant volley was called, or a smash was declared. 1902 *Sat. Rev.* 12 July 51/1 Instruction is given in the underhand volley [in lawn-tennis].

c. = Volleyer.

1878 Marshall *Ann. Tennis* 112 He was a powerful *force*, and a capital volley.

7. *attrib.* and *Comb.*, as *volley-boast*, *loophole*, † *-shot*, *system*; **volley-ball** *U.S.*, a game in which a ball is struck from alternate sides of a high net without touching the ground (*Cent. Dict.* Suppl.); **volley-firing**, simultaneous firing at the word of command by successive parties of soldiers; also *fig.*; **volley gun**, a form of machine-gun which fires bullets successively or in a volley (Knight, 1884).

1878 Marshall *Ann. Tennis* 197 He..would generally return it by a *volley-boast against the main-wall. 1859 *Musketry Instr.* 62 Every file is to have its own target, and the hits are to be counted as in *volley firing. 1879 *Cassell's Techn. Educ.* III. 267 The superior efficacy of volley-firing and reserved fire. 1891 *Daily News* 2 Oct. 5/5 In the.. Town Hall of Newcastle the representative fighting men of the Liberal party were assembled for volley firing. 1898 Sir G. S. Robertson *Chitral* xxiii. 225 *Volley loopholes are good against an enemy that attacks with a masterful rush. 1689 *Lond. Gaz.* No. 2433/3 The Night concluded with Dancing, Bells Ringing, Bonfires, *Volly-shots. 1702 *Ibid.* No. 3793/3 The 2 Companies of Foot..gave a Volley Shot at each Proclamation. 1899 *Westm. Gaz.* 15 Sept. 2/3 There has for some time been a feeling in the air that the *volley system was going.

Volley (vǫ·li), *v.* Forms: 7 **volly** (8–9 *pa. t.* **vollied**); 6– **volley.** [f. prec.]

1. *trans.* **a.** To utter (words, etc.) rapidly or impetuously. Usually with advs., as *forth*, *off*, *out.*

1591 *Troub. Raigne K. John* I. (1611) 62 A prophet new sprung up, whose diuination volleis wonders foorth. *Ibid.* II. 73 If sobs would helpe,..My heart should volley out deepe piercing plaints. 1593 Shaks. *Ven. & Ad.* 921 Another flapmouthd mourner, blacke, and grim, Against the welkin, volies out his voyce. 1754 P. H. *Hiberniad* 37 She raves, and vollies off an horrid Cry. 1824 Scott *St. Ronan's* xx, The bursts of applause which were vollied towards the stage. 1859 Meredith *R. Feverel* xxxviii, Sir Julius turned one heel, and volleyed out silver laughter. 1885–94 R. Bridges *Eros & Psyche* Aug. xii, She saw an uncouth form..whose parted lips Volley'd their friendly warning in a storm.

b. To discharge (arrows, shot, etc.) in a volley. Cf. Volleyed *ppl. a.* 3.

1839 Bailey *Festus* 139 When the storm bends his bow, And volleys all his arrows off at once.

c. *Tennis*, etc. To return (a ball) in play before it touches the ground; to reply to (a service) in this way.

1875 'Stonehenge' *Brit. Rur. Sports* (ed. 12) III. I. v. 690/1 The service must not be volleyed. 1878 [see 2 b]. 1902 *Sat. Rev.* 12 July 51/2 It is bad policy to give the advice not to volley a lob.

d. *Cricket.* To bowl or deliver (a ball) which reaches the batsman before bouncing. ? *U.S.*

1909 *Cent. Dict.* Suppl.

2. *absol.* **a.** To fire a volley (or volleys). Also in fig. context.

Freq. in recent journalistic use, prob. after quot. 1854.

1606 Shaks. *Ant. & Cl.* II. vii. 119 Then the Boy shall sing, The holding euery man shall beate as loud, As his strong sides can volly. 1854 Tennyson *Lt. Brigade* v, Cannon behind them Volley'd and thunder'd. 1899 *Westm. Gaz.* 2 Jan. 2/1 A large line of guerillas..decided swiftly that their presence and position were discovered, and swiftly they volleyed.

b. *Tennis*, etc. To hit or return the ball before it bounces; to make a volley-stroke.

1819 in Hone *Every-day Bk.* (1825) I. 867 He never volleyed [i.e. at fives], but let the balls hop. 1878 Marshall *Ann. Tennis* 197 A young player, if he fancies he can volley well, will always be apt to volley balls which would come well off the end-walls. 1892 *Pall Mall G.* 20 July 7/2 F. Rooke..volleyed more effectively than his opponent.

3. *intr.* **a.** To emit or produce sounds simultaneously or continuously, in a manner suggestive of firearms or artillery.

In recent use freq. in 'to volley and thunder', after quot. 1854 in sense 2 a.

1810 Southey *Kehama* XXIII. xi, When its thunder broke,.. while it vollied round the vault of Hell, Earth's solid arch was shaken with the shock. 1875 L. Morris *Children Street* i, Every day come they there, Afternoon foul or fair, Shouting and volleying. 1886 Stevenson *Kidnapped* xxix, For some time Alan volleyed upon the door, and his knocking only roused the echoes of the house.

b. To rush, roll, or stream with simultaneous motion; to shoot rapidly.

1853 C. Brontë *Villette* vii, About a hundred thoughts volleyed through my mind in a moment. 1880 Blackmore *Mary Anerley* I. x. 129 The crest of the wave volleys up the incline.

c. To issue or be discharged in, or after the manner of, a volley.

1887 Bowen *Æneid* I. 150 Firebrands fly, stones volley, the weapons furnished of wrath. *Ibid.* III. 577 Molten masses of stone to the skies with a groan and a roar Volley in showers.

Volley, southern dial. var. Follow *v.*

Volleyed (vǫ·lid), *ppl. a.* Forms: 7 **volied**, 7–9 **vollied**; 8 **volly'd**, 8–9 **volley'd**, 9 **volleyed.** [f. Volley *v.* + -ed.]

1. Shouted or uttered in the manner of a volley.

a 1616 Beaum. & Fl. *Bonduca* III. v, Heark..how the air Totters and reels, and rends apieces, Drusus, With the huge vollied clamours. 1813 Scott *Rokeby* v. xxxiii, He strove, with vollied threat and ban,..To rally up the desperate fight.

2. Of thunder or lightning: Discharged with the noise or continuous effect of a volley.

Very common in poetry of the 18th cent.

1667 Milton *P. L.* IV. 928 When in Battel to thy aide The blasting volied Thunder made all speed. 1726 Pope *Odyss.* XX. 212 Some pitying God..With vollied vengeance blast their towering pride! 1744 Akenside *Pleas. Imag.* I. 188 She springs aloft Thro' fields of air; pursues the flying storm; Rides on the volley'd lightning thro' the heav'ns. 1812 H. & J. Smith *Rej. Addr.* 38 The vollied flame rides in my breath, My blast is elemental death. 1821 Clare *Vill. Minstr.* II. 60 While skies in vollied rolls are rent.

b. Of the nature of a volley.

1835 J. Harris *Gt. Teacher* (1837) 25 He discharged its tremendous contents in one volleyed and prolonged explosion.

3. Of missiles, etc.: Discharged or cast in or as in a volley. Also in fig. context.

1759 W. Mason *Caractacus* Poems 1830 II. 127 Our vollied darts, That thick as hail fell on their helms. 1791 Cowper *Iliad* VIII. 78 The vollied weapons on both sides their task Perform'd effectual. 1797 Park *Sonn.* 78 Then will we fire a vollied round, And uncharg'd goblets shall resound. 1856 Bryant *Winter Piece* 122 And bounding on the frozen earth Shall fall their [sc. clouds'] volleyed stores rounded like hail.

4. *Tennis.* Returned by volleying.

1878 Marshall *Ann. Tennis* 226/2 Volleyed service.

Volleyer (vǫ·li,əɹ). *Tennis.* [f. as prec. + -er.] One who returns the ball before it bounces.

1878 Marshall *Ann. Tennis* 196 When the ball is judged and met by the racket of the volleyer. 1879 in *Marshall's Tennis Cuts* (1884) 36 A generation of volleyers will rise up who will volley from the service-line.

Vo·lleying, *vbl. sb.* [f. as prec. + -ing^1.] The action of returning the ball (in tennis and other ball games) before it bounces. Also *attrib.*

1837 D. Walker *Games & Sports* 256 (Rackets), This last stroke is termed volleying. 1882 *Daily Tel.* 18 July 2 The volleying and low play gaining repeated rounds of applause. 1883 *Pall Mall G.* 1 Sept. 8/2 He exhibited splendid volleying ability, and won by three sets to one.

Vo·lleying, *ppl. a.* [f. as prec. + -ing^2.] That volleys, in senses of the verb.

(*a*) 1796 Coleridge *Destiny of Nations* v. 53 Some drive the mutinous clouds to clash in air, And..Yoke the red lightning to their volleying car. 1805 Scott *Last Minstrel* IV. ii, When the volleying musket play'd Against the bloody Highland blade. 1849 J. Grant *Kirkaldy of Grange* xxvi. 301 The booming cannon, the volleying harquebusses. 1852 Tennyson *Ode Wellington* 62 Let..the volleying cannon thunder his loss.
(*b*) 1816 Byron *Siege Corinth* ii, There the volleying thunders pour, Till waves grow smoother to the roar. 1822 — *Juan* VIII. vi, The volleying roar, and loud Long booming of each peal on peal, o'ercame The ear far more than thunder. 1894 *Outing* (U.S.) XXIV. 50/2 The volleying boom of giant trees, uprooted from their rocky foundations, sounded above the shriek of the wind.
(*c*) 1844 Hood *Forge* I. 170 The Forge..With volleying smoke, and many a spark, Vomiting fire. 1866 M. Arnold *Thyrsis* vi, So have I heard the cookoo's parting cry,.. Come with the volleying rain and tossing breeze.

Volliche, southern ME. var. Fully *adv.*

Vollier. *s.w. dial.* Also **volyer.** [dial. var. of Follower: cf. Voller.] (See quot. 1855.)

1855 *Househ. Wds.* 23 Sept. 130/1 [In pilchard fishing] there is a second or assisting boat, called the volyer, which carries another net, called the tuck-seine. *a* 1870 J. Couch *Hist. Polperro* vi. (1871) 106 A second boat, the *volyer*,.. has another sean-net of a hundred or more fathoms in length, and eighteen in depth.

Vollier, variant of Voller *dial.*

† **Volliere.** *Obs. rare.* Also **-yere, -ier.** [a. F. *volière*, f. *voler* to fly.] = Volary.

1638 Sir T. Herbert *Trav.* (ed. 2) 148 His Gardens are.. prettily contrivd into grotts, mazes, vollieres, and the like. *Ibid.* 156 [The] ayery Citizens..returne their thankfull notes in a more swift melodious consort, than if they were in the exactest vollyere in the Vniverse.

Vollit, obs. Sc. form of Wooled *a.*

† **Vollouth**, variant of Fullought *Obs.*

c 1330 Herebert in *Rel. Ant.* I. 87 Crist..so com to seynt Jon, And of hym was y-wasȝe..,To halewen our vollouth water, that sunne havet vor-don.

Volly, southern dial. var. Follow *v.*, Folly *sb.*^{1} and *sb.*^{2}

† **Volo-nola.** *Obs.*$^{-1}$ [f. L. *volo* I am willing + *nolo* I am unwilling.] A vacillation or wavering in decision.

1672 Marvell *Reh. Transp.* I. 14 His story of the Bookseller, and all the Volo-Nola's, and shall-I, shall-I's betwixt them, was nothing but fooling.

Volontary, obs. form of Voluntary.

Volonteer(e, obs. forms of Volunteer.

† **Volow**, var. of *folowe* Full *v.*^{1} Hence † **Volower**, one who baptizes; † **Volowing** *vbl. sb.*, baptism. *Obs. rare.*

1528 Tindale *Obed. Chr. Man* 107 b, Baptism is called volowinge in many places of Englonde. *Ibid.*, The child was well volowed (saye they); yee and our vicare is as fayre a volower as ever a prest within this twenty myles. 1530 — *Answ. More* Wks. (1573) 277/1 They brought them to confirmation straight from Baptisme: so that now oftymes they be volowed and bishoped both in one day.

Volowynge, error for *bolnynge* Bolning *ppl. a.*

c 1450 tr. *De Imitatione* III. xiv. 82 Be wrothe ayeins thi selfe, and suffre no volowynge pride [L. *tumorem*] to lyve in the.

Volplane (vǫ·lplēⁱn), *sb.* [Orig. two words, *vol plane*, properly *vol plané*, f. F. *vol* flight + *plané*, pa. pple. of *planer* Plane *v.*^{2}] A dive, descent, or downward flight at a steep angle on the part of an aeroplane under control, and with the engine stopped or shut off.

1910 in Hamel & Turner *Flying* (1914) 17 The 'vol plané', or aerial dive. 1911 Grahame-White & Harper *Aeroplane* 121 He was diving down from an altitude of about 1,000 feet. It was not a *vol plane* that he was making, as he had his engine running.

Hence **Volplane** *v. intr.*, to make a volplane.

1911 *Daily News* 21 July 1 He volplaned from about 200 feet to 20 feet of the ground, which he skimmed for about a hundred yards.

† **Volpo·ne.** *Obs.* Also **vulpone, -ony.** [The name of the chief character in B. Jonson's play *Volpone, or the Fox*, a. It. *volpone*, f. *volpe* fox; the forms in *vulp-* are after L. *vulpis*.] A cunning schemer or miser. Also *Comb.*

1672 G. Thomson *Let. to H. Stubbe* 25 To observe their Vulpone-like windings, intrigues and nimble diversions. 1685 South *Serm.* (1715) I. 408 Come to an old, rich, professing Vulpony, and tell him, that there is a Church to be built [etc.]. 1709 Sacheverell *Serm. 5 Nov.* 21 In what.. lively Colours does the Holy Psalmist paint out the crafty Insiduousness of such wilely Volpones? 1710 *Acc. Last Distemper Tom Whigg* I. 4 Certain Beasts of Prey, Vultures and Vulpones.

† **Volsce.** *Obs.* Also 4 **Vulce**, 6 *Sc.* **Wolche**, 7 **Volce** (*pl.* **-es, -ies**). [ad. L. *Volscus*, pl. *Volscī*: cf. next.] = Volscian *sb.* 1.

1387 Trevisa *Higden* (Rolls) III. 159 He ouercame þe Vulces and þe Gabies, and made pees wiþ Tuscans. 1533 Bellenden *Livy* I. xx. (S.T.S.) I. 114 To seik supporte of þe pepill namyt Wolchis [*v.r.* Wolches]. 1579–80 North *Plutarch* (1612) 234 Vpon returne of the Volsces ambassadors..Tullus caused an assembly generall to be made of the Volsces. 1607 Shaks. *Cor.* I. i. 228 The newes is, sir, the Volcies are in Armes. *Ibid.* 253 The Volces haue much Corne. *Ibid.* IV. 28 He that retires, Ile take him for a Volce.

Volscian (vǫ·lʃiăn), *sb.* and *a.* Also 6 *Sc.* **Volscan**, 7 **Volcian, Volcean.** [f. L. *Volscī* + -an. Cf. prec.]

A. *sb.* **1.** *Hist.* One of an ancient warlike people formerly inhabiting the east of Latium, subdued by the Romans in the 4th century B.C.

1513 Douglas *Æneid* XI. xi. 29 Wyth armyt men and wageouris the Volscanis So neir almost bylappit hym at anis. 1607 Shaks. *Cor.* v. iii. 178 This Fellow had a Volcean to his Mother. *Ibid.* vi. 116 Like an Eagle in a Doue-coat, I Flatter'd [*sic*] your Volcians in Corioles. 1697 Dryden *Virg. Georg.* II. 233 Volscians armed with iron-headed darts. 1770 Langhorne *Plutarch* II. 163 Corioli was the capital of the country of the Volscians. 1841 *Penny Cycl.* XX. 105/2 M. Valerius, who, with an army of 40,000 plebeians, defeated the Volscians, Aequians, and Sabines.

2. The Italic language spoken by the Volscians.

1897 R. S. Conway *Italic Dialects* I. 273 The majority of scholars incline to regard them as borrowed from Oscan. From geographical considerations I think Volscian is a more likely source. *Ibid.* 288 The Osco-Umbrian family of dialects (to which Volscian belonged).

B. *adj.* Of, pertaining or belonging to, the Volscians; that is a Volscian.

1601 Holland *Pliny* I. 58 The towne Tarracina, called in the Volscian tongue Anxur. 1607 Shaks. *Cor.* v. iii. 3 My partner in this Action, You must report to th' Volcian Lords. 1700 Dryden *Pal. & Arc.* II. 639 The Volscian Queen extended on the Plain. 1770 Langhorne *Plutarch* II. 186 This proclamation exasperated the whole Volscian nation against the Romans. 1841 W. Spalding *Italy & It. Isl.* III. 289 The Pontine Marshes..were once covered with Volscian towns. 1880 *Encycl. Brit.* XIII. 443/1 The volcanic region of Terra di Lavoro is separated by the Volscian mountains from the Roman district.

‖ **Volse·lla.** *rare.* Also 7 **vulsella.** [L. *volsella*, *vulsella* tweezers, forceps, f. *vols-*, *vuls-*, ppl. stem of *vellĕre* to pluck.] (See quot. 1693 and next.)

1693 tr. *Blancard's Phys. Dict.* (ed. 2), *Volsella*, or *Vulsella*, an Instrument to pull up Hairs with by the Root, Tweezers: Or a Chyrurgions little Tongs, which are of different shape according to the Diversity of their Use. [Hence in Harris, Phillips, etc.] 1728 Chambers *Cycl.*, *Acanthabolus*, a Surgeon's Instrument; called also *Volsella*. 1889 Duncan *Clin. Lect. Dis. Women* (ed. 4) ii. 5 A Volsella is fixed in the cervix.

‖ **Volse·llum.** *Surg.* [mod.L., perhaps from mistaking L. *volsella* (see prec.) for a neuter pl. Cf. Vulsellum.] A kind of forceps used in surgical operations. Also *attrib.*

1876 Curling *Dis. Rectum* 53 The hæmorrhoidal growths are to be seized separately with the volsellum forceps. *Ibid.* 75 A fold of membrane..is to be seized with a volsellum, or the hæmorrhoidal forceps. 1898 *Baldy's Amer. Text-Bk. Gynecol.* (ed. 2) 375 A double tenaculum or volsellum forceps.

Volt (vǫlt, vōᵘlt), *sb.* [f. the name of *Volta*: see Voltaic *a.*] The practical unit of electromotive force; the difference of potential capable of sending a current of one ampere through a conductor whose resistance is one ohm.

1873 F. Jenkin *Electr. & Magn.* x. § 2 There is already a unit of electromotive force in practical use called a *volt*. The volt is intended to represent 10^8 absolute units. 1881 Sir W. Thomson in *Rep. Brit. Assoc.* 518 Nothing above 200 volts ought..to be admitted..where safeguards against accident cannot be made absolutely..trustworthy. 1892 *Electr. Engin.* 16 Sept. 283/1 The small glow lamp requires from 0·6 to 0·8 amperes and four volts to fully light it.

b. *attrib.* (with numeral preceding).

1881 Sir W. Thomson in *Rep. Brit. Assoc.* 518 To take energy direct from the electric main with its 80,000 volts, and supply it by secondary 200-volt dynamos or 100-volt dynamos. 1890 *Anthony's Photogr. Bull.* III. 223 Five cells of this battery will light the six volt lamp.

Volt, obs. var. Vault *sb.*^{1} and *v.*^{1}; var. Volte *sb.*; var. obs. Sc. Vult (face).

Volt (vǫlt, vōᵘlt), *v.* [ad. F. *volter* (f. *volte* Volte or ad. It. *voltare*); or (in sense 4) variant of Vault *v.*^{2} under the influence of this.]

† **1.** *refl.* To turn or roll over. *Obs.*$^{-1}$

1658 Franck *North. Mem.* (1694) 67 See where he comes tumbling and tossing, and volting himself in the stiffest Streams.

† **2.** *intr.* (See quot.) *Obs.*$^{-1}$

1688 Holme *Armoury* II. 150/1 [A horse is said to] Voult, when he Raires, or stands upright.

3. *Fencing.* To make a volte. Also *fig.*

1692 Sir W. Hope *Fencing Master* 101 You must Volt, or leap with both your feet in the Air at once, quite by your Adversaries left shoulder. 1696 R. H. *Sch. Recreat.* 72 Fourthly, you may Volt, and in your so doing, give him the Thrust, which being clearly done, will mainly surprize him. 1771 Lonnergan *Fencer's Guide* 215, I parry you with a Prime, and cut at your head with a Medium as I volt. 1897 *Westm. Gaz.* 14 July 3/2 When Mr. Chamberlain volts, it is not only his face, but his whole personality he turns round.

† **4.** = Vault *v.*^{2} 2. *Obs. rare.*

1753 Young *Brothers* III. i, This pass'd, as suits his Wisdom, Macedonians! Who volts o'er elder Brothers to a Throne. 1757 — *Love Fame* v. 124 Some nymphs affect a more heroic breed, And volt [*earlier edd.* vault] from hunters to the manag'd steed.

Hence **Vo·lting** *vbl. sb.*

1692 Sir W. Hope *Fencing Master* 10 Volting is the leaping by your adversaries left side, quite out of his measure. 1823 G. Roland *Treat. Art Fencing* 151 The same may be said of volting, or any manœuvre that does not give the opponent a fair opportunity of hitting the right breast. 1861 G. Chapman *Foil Practice* 34 Volting is prohibited in teaching with the foil, and condemned in fencing.

‖ **Volta** (vǫ·ltă). [It. *volta* turn, etc., fem. pa. pple. of *volgere*, *volvere* to turn, employed as a sb.] = Lavolta.

1642 Kynaston *Leoline & Sydanis* 1005 These with ten Satyrs danc'd an antique round With Volta's, and a Saraband. 1656 Blount *Glossogr.*, *Volta*,..a turning Dance so called. 1753 *Chambers' Cycl.*, Suppl. s.v., Volta is also a sort of dance of Italian origin, in which the man turns the woman several times, and then assists her to make a leap or jump; it is a species of galliard. 1823 Crabb *Technol. Dict.*, *Volta*, an old three-timed air, peculiar to an Italian dance of the same name. 1910 *Times* 8 Aug. 10/4 At His Majesty's Theatre..the court dances will include a 'volta' with its light-hearted leaps into the air.

Volta- (vǫ·ltă), combining form of Voltaic used in a few technical terms, as *volta-electric*, *-electrometer*, *-inductric*; **voltaplast** (see quot.); **voltatype** *sb.*, an electrotype; *v. trans.*, to electrotype.

Voltagraphy, given in some Dicts. as a synonym of 'electrotypy', after *Penny Cycl.* (1843) XXVI. 434/2, was coined specially for use in that work, and appears to have had no real currency.

1834 Mrs. Somerville *Connex. Phys. Sci.* xxxiii. 338 *Volta-electric induction is instantaneous. 1862 *Catal. Internat. Exhib., Brit.* II. No. 3578, The instantaneous generation of volta-electric currents of intensity. 1834 Faraday in *Phil. Trans.* CXXIV. 85 On a new Measure of *Volta-electricity. *Ibid.* 93 The instrument offers the only actual measurer of voltaic electricity which we at present possess...I have therefore named it a *Volta-electrometer. 1839 Noad *Electricity* iii. 130 Its terminal wires are soldered to a Faraday's volta-electrometer. 1875 Knight *Dict. Mech.* 2714/1 *Voltaelectrometer*, an instrument for indicating the degree of electrical excitation. 1849 Noad *Electricity* (ed. 3) 491 The manner in which this machine acts will be clearly understood by reference to the general principles of *volta-inductric action. 1842 Francis *Dict. Arts*, **Voltaplast*. Such is the name given to that form of galvanic battery which is adapted to the electrotype. 1842 Brande *Dict. Sci.* 1309/2 Gold, silver, and other metals may..be substituted for copper, and thus a variety of *voltatypes may be obtained. *Ibid.*, It often happens that the article to be *voltatyped*, as this process is now called, is not a conductor of electricity. 1875 Knight *Dict. Mech.* 2714/2 *Volta-type*, a cast of an object obtained by the gradual deposition of a metal from a metallic solution, through the agency of electric action.

† **Vo·ltage**^{1}. *Obs.*$^{-1}$ [f. F. *volte* Volte + -age.] The action of causing a horse to move in voltes.

1606 Ford *Fame's Mem.* xxxii, He assaies, Which way to manage an vntamed horse When, how, to spur, and rayn, to stop, and raise, Close sitting, voltage of a manlike force.

Voltage^2 (vǫ·ltédʒ, vōᵘ·ltédʒ). [f. Volt *sb.* + -age.] Electromotive force reckoned or expressed in volts.

1890 *Pall Mall G.* 8 Aug. 4/3 The voltage varied between 700 and 1,300 volts. 1894 Bottone *Electr. Instr.* 111 In calculating the voltage, the desired current must also be considered, and allowance made both for the internal and external resistances. 1898 *Allbutt's Syst. Med.* V. 855 It is difficult to say what voltage is fatal to man.

fig. 1904 *Spectator* 30 Apr. 670/1 Pope..was seldom the subject of currents of high voltage like..the emotional Hazlitt.

b. *attrib.* (esp. with adj. preceding).

1890 *Daily News* 4 Jan. 6/7 There is as much danger from the low voltage as there is from the high voltage system, as far as fire is concerned. 1894 *Ibid.* 22 Jan. 2/8 The question of high voltage electricity.

Voltaic (vǫltēⁱ·ik), *a.* [From the name of the Italian physician and scientist, Alessandro *Volta* (1745–1827) + -ic.]

1. Of apparatus: Used in producing electricity by chemical action after the method discovered by Volta; esp. *voltaic battery* (Battery 10), *voltaic pile* (Pile *sb.*^{3} 5).

(*a*) 1813 Sir H. Davy *Agric. Chem.* (1814) 41 It has been shown by Experiments made by means of the Voltaic battery..that compound bodies in general are capable of being decomposed by Electrical powers. 1850 Grove *Corr. Phys. Forces* (ed. 2) 81 A voltaic battery, which consists usually of alternations of two metals, and a liquid capable of acting chemically upon one of them,..is incapable of acting. 1879 G. Prescott *Sp. Telephone* 1 When galvanism was discovered, at the beginning of the present century, and the voltaic battery invented.
(*b*) 1815 J. Smith *Panorama Sci. & Art* II. 275 The voltaic pile, as well as the battery last described, are now but little used. 1839 Noad *Electricity* iii. 97 To Volta's experiments we are indebted for the first galvanic instrument, namely, the voltaic pile; it was described by him in the Philosophical Transactions of 1800. 1896 *Allbutt's Syst. Med.* I. 332 After the discovery of the voltaic pile the use of the electrical machine gradually fell into disuse.
(*c*) 1812 Sir H. Davy *Chem. Philos.* 54 Without the voltaic apparatus, there was no possibility of examining the relations of electrical polarities to chemical attractions. 1827 Faraday *Chem. Manip.* xvii. 460 Voltaic arrangements, consisting of a few large plates rather than many small ones. 1855 Bain *Senses & Int.* I. ii. § 22 In a voltaic cell, an energy is generated and transmitted along a wire with inconceivable rapidity. 1884 Knight *Dict. Mech.* Suppl. 930/2 A voltaic pencil, by the use of which designers and draughtsmen may be enabled to dispense entirely with the aid of the engraver.

2. Of electricity: Generated by chemical action.

1816 Accum *Chem. Tests* 223 When the precipitation of the metallic lead takes place in the surface of the zinc, voltaic electricity is evolved. 1836 Mrs. Somerville *Connex. Phys. Sci.* (ed. 3) xxviii. 305 Voltaic electricity is of that peculiar kind which is elicited by the force of chemical action. 1890 *Nature* 4 Sept., The application of voltaic electricity to the welding and fusion of metals.

b. Of a current: Consisting of voltaic electricity.

1834 Mrs. Somerville *Connex. Phys. Sci.* xxxi. 324 The magnetic and electric fluids,..arising from all possible positions of the conducting wire, and every direction of the voltaic current. 1860 Piesse *Lab. Chem. Wonders* 180 The effect of a continued voltaic current.

3. Of or pertaining to, connected with, caused by, electricity due to chemical action.

1820 Faraday *Exp. Res.* (1859) 65 The little bars..evidently produced voltaic action. 1827 — *Chem. Manip.* xvii. 461 This formed a voltaic combination with the platina and the fluid. 1855 Bain *Senses & Int.* II. ii. § 23 The voltaic shock is very different, in consequence of the altered character of the discharge. 1879 *Cassell's Techn. Educ.* IV. 309/1 The invention of voltaic deposition..created a new era for the manufacture of silver-plated wares.

b. *Voltaic brass*, brass deposited by the action of electricity.

1860 *Ure's Dict. Arts* (ed. 5) II. 94 Voltaic brass does not appear to have been obtained in a solid distinct form, but has been successfully produced as a coating upon a copper surface.

Hence **Volta·ically** *adv.*, by means of, in respect of, voltaic electricity; after the manner of a voltaic battery.

1843 Grove *Corr. Phys. Forces* etc. (1874) 303 Besides employing the usual chemical tests, I analysed it voltaically. 1844 Noad *Electricity* (ed. 2) 144 When a series of some hundred couples of zinc and copper cylinders are arranged voltaically, and charged with common water, a battery is obtained. 1865 Mansfield *Salts* 12 One of these, the Chlorine, is said to be voltaically or chemically negative.

Voltairean, Voltairian (vǫltē·riăn), *sb.* and *a.* [f. the later name of the French author François Marie Arouet (1694–1778), who from 1718 styled himself *de Voltaire*.]

A. *sb.* A follower or adherent of Voltaire in respect of opinions or the manner of expressing them; one whose views on social and religious questions are characterized by a critical and mocking scepticism.

α. 1871 Morley *Condorcet* in *Crit. Misc.* Ser. I. (1878) 51 He [Condorcet] was a Voltairean in the intensity of his antipathies to the Church. 1885 *Athenæum* 2 May 567/1 His father, a country squire, and, as the fashion then was, a thorough-going Voltairean, had married one of his own serfs.
β. 1875 Gladstone *Glean.* (1879) VI. 225 We are now engaged in training a nation to consist of Voltairians and of Clericals. 1883 M. Pattison *Mem.* (1885) 212 If it is against the Church it is a fiction of the Voltairians.

B. *adj.* Of, belonging to, or resembling Voltaire; holding opinions like those of Voltaire, or expressing them in his style.

α. 1879 Morley *Burke* viii. 176 The eager, bustling, shrill-tongued crowd of the Voltairean age. 1885 'Mrs. Alexander' *At Bay* i, A shrewd, worldly, voltairean woman.
β. 1876 L. Stephen *Hours in Library* 189 Walpole must be reckoned as belonging both in his faults and his merits to the Voltairian school of literature. 1896 W. K. Leask *H. Miller* v. 125 There is still the Voltairian type of thinker.

Hence **Voltai·rianism** (also -ean-), = Voltairism.

1848 W. K. Kelly tr. *L. Blanc's Hist. Ten Y.* II. 187 In order not to offend the Voltairianism of several of his friends, he had forborne to base his constitution on religion. 1890 *Athenæum* 19 July 92/2 He interprets Voltairianism as 'a school based on destructive irony,..and incapable of raising or fortifying the human mind'.

Voltai·rianize, *v. rare.* [f. prec. + -ize.] *trans.* To render Voltairian. Hence **Voltai·rianized** *ppl. a.*

1872 Liddon *Elem. Relig.* ii. 49 It was..quite another [thing] permanently to control the heart and convictions even of the Voltairianized multitudes of Paris. 1902 *Academy* 3 Jan. 7/2 Hamlet is completely Voltairianised, in the most audacious fashion.

Voltai·rish, *a. rare*$^{-1}$. [f. *Voltaire* (see above) + -ish.] Resembling Voltaire.

1842 Mrs. Browning *Bk. Poets* Poet. Wks. (1904) 639/2 We will not..set up its grand, luxurious, melancholy devil against Goethe's subtle, biting, Voltairish devil.

Voltairism (vǫltē·riz'm). Also **-eism.** [f. as prec. + -ism.]

1. Something characteristic of Voltaire.

1776 Mickle tr. *Camoens' Lusiad* Introd. p. cxxvi, The error confessed, and still retained, is a true Voltairism.

2. The body of opinions or views expressed by Voltaire; the mocking and sceptical attitude characteristic of these.

1840 Carlyle *Heroes* i. (1904) 14 Truly, if Christianity be the highest instance of Hero-worship, then we may find here in Voltaireism one of the lowest! 1872 Morley *Voltaire* (1886) 1 We may think of Voltairism in France, somewhat as we think of Catholicism or the Renaissance or Calvinism.

Voltaism (vǫ·ltă,iz'm). [f. *Volta* (see Voltaic *a.*) + -ism.] The production of an electric current by the chemical action of a liquid on metals; galvanism as produced by Volta's methods.

1811 R. Turner *Arts & Sci.* xxix. 271 In voltaism, it is necessary that the bodies by which it is exhibited should have some chemical agency on each other. 1826 Good *Bk. Nat.* (1834) I. 219 Every one has now some knowledge of Galvanism and Voltaism. 1844 Noad *Electricity* (ed. 2) 132 That remarkable form of Electricity, known by the name of Galvanism or Voltaism.

Voltaite (vǫ·ltă,əit). *Min.* [f. as prec.; named by A. Scacchi in 1840.] A hydrous sulphate of iron occurring in green, black, or brown crystals.

1846 Worcester (citing Dana). 1852 Dana *Min.* 228 Voltaite is a double sulphate of iron, alumina, potash and water crystalising like alum in octahedrons. 1868 Watts *Dict. Chem.* V. 1005 *Voltaite*, a ferroso-ferric sulphate, containing alumina, occurring at the Solfatara, near Naples.

Voltameter (vǫltæ·mĭtəɹ). [See Volta- and -meter.] An instrument used for the quantitative measurement of electricity by means of the results of electrolysis.

1836 Brande *Chem.* (ed. 4) 385 When the quantity of products was examined by the voltameter, the oxygen..was always in the same proportion as from water. 1866 R. M. Ferguson *Electr.* (1870) 140 To measure one or other of these is the object of a galvanometer or voltameter. 1881 S. P. Thompson *Electr. & Magnetism* 179 The voltameter gives us the 'time integral' of the current.

attrib. 1844 Noad *Electricity* (ed. 2) 222 One equivalent of lead was reduced in the voltameter tube.

Volte, volt (vǫlt, vōᵘlt). [a. F. *volte*, ad. It. *volta*: see Volta.]

† **1.** A kind of dance; = Volta, Lavolta. *Obs.*

1586 Sir E. Hoby tr. *Cognet's Polit. Disc. Truth* xi. 39 The Voltes, courantes, and vyolent daunses proceede from furie. 1597 T. Morley *Introd. Mus.* 181 Like vnto this [the Bransle] (but more light) be the voltes and courantes which being both of a measure, are notwithstanding daunced after sundrie fashions. 1610 Dowland *Var. Lute-lessons* R 2, Voltes for the Lute.

2. *Fencing.* A sudden dexterous movement to avoid a thrust.

1688 Holme *Armoury* III. xix. (Roxb.) 160/1 A Volt..is when thy adversarie doth thrust at thee which thou perceiueing, dost first put by his thrust; and just turne [*sic*] thy body round about, with thy back towards thine aduersarie thrusteth him with a quarte in his right brest. 1765 Angelo *Sch. Fencing* 44 You must..with swiftness and agility perform this turn of the body called volte. 1771 Lonnergan *Fencer's Guide* 104 When I disengage a Quarte, single your body from the thrust, by quickly forming a Volt. 1861 G. Chapman *Foil Practice* 34 The volt or spring to the right or left [being] occasionally put in practice. 1889 A. Hutton *Cold Steel* 90 Make a complete volte or turn about on the toe of the right, bringing the left foot well behind it.

† **b.** *Volt-coupe*, a feint in fencing.

1692 Sir W. Hope *Fencing Master* 46 The Volt-coupe, single and double. *Ibid.* 65 Then make use of the Double Volt-Coupe..after you have made your Feint. 1696 R. H. *Sch. Recreat.* 87 Lesson 12. Of Volt Coupe.

3. In the manège, a circular movement executed by a horse. (Cf. the earlier Demi-volte.)

1727 Bailey (vol. II), *Volte* (in Horsemanship) signifies a round or a circular Tread. 1728 Chambers *Cycl.* s.v., A Renversed Volt, is a Track of two Treads, which the Horse makes with his Head to the Centre, and his Croup out. 1884 E. L. Anderson *Mod. Horsem.* II. xvii. 148 The school gallop is employed in traversing, and for voltes and pirouettes. The horse may be made to traverse and to do the voltes in the ordinary gallop.

4. Turn, change. *rare*$^{-1}$.

1901 Meredith *Hueless Love* viii, So has there come the gust at South-west flung By sudden volt on eves of freezing mist.

† **Vo·lted**, *ppl. a. Obs.* (Meaning not clear.)

1613–39 I. Jones in Leoni *Palladio's Archit.* (1742) II. 45 The Roses fretted, not volted.

‖ **Volte-face** (volt,fas). [Fr., ad. It. *volta faccia*, f. *volta* turn + *faccia* face.] The act of turning so as to face in the opposite direction; *fig.* a complete change of attitude or opinion.

1819 Scott *Leg. Montrose* xvi, Your Excellency has only to hint that the M'Aulays are going in that direction, and my friends of the Mist will instantly make volteface, and go to the right about. 1822 — *Peveril* xxxiv, At last we were obliged to make volte-face. 1883 *Athenæum* 20 Oct. 493/2 He is getting to believe in evolution and has to make some curious *voltes-face* in order to retain at the same time his belief in theism. 1889 *Spectator* 9 Nov. 627/1 The sudden *volte-face* which Mr. Gladstone and Sir William Harcourt performed in 1886.

Volter, variant of Walter *sb. Obs.*

‖ **Voltigeur** (voltiʒö·r). [F., agent-n. f. *voltiger* to flutter, hover, vault, etc.] Formerly in the French army, a member of a special skirmishing company attached to each regiment of infantry.

1807 *Hist. Europe* in *Ann. Reg.* 25/1 They were received at the mouth of the musket by the voltigeurs. [*Note.* Sharp-shooters, or marksmen, mounted on horseback, whose business it is to hover around the enemy,. and annoy him (etc.).] 1827 Southey *Hist. Penins. War* III. 430 The enemy's chasseurs and voltigeurs advanced in considerable bodies under General Lorset.

attrib. 1805 James *Milit. Dict.* (ed. 2) s.v., They submitted to a long..training, before they were admitted in the voltigeur companies. 1824 De Quincey *Pol. Econ. Dial.* vi. Misc. (1854) 259 Go on,..and skirmish with him a little more in this voltigeur style.

transf. 1809 W. Irving *Knickerb.* (1861) 221 The Van Bunschotens..would have been put to utter rout but for the arrival of a gallant corps of voltigeurs. 1817 Keatinge *Trav.* I. 155 The most active and habituated voltigeurs of the community..contrive to anticipate, and *font main basse* on whatever can be found.

Voltmeter (vǫ·ltmītəɹ). [f. Volt *sb.*^{2} + Meter.] An instrument for measuring the pressure of electricity in volts.

1882 *Eng. Mech.* 10 Mar. 4/3, I have two instruments devised by Prof. Perry and myself, an Am-meter, and a Volt-meter, the one for measuring a strong current, and the other a large electromotive force. 1884 C. G. W. Lock *Workshop Rec.* Ser. III. 132/1 This can be verified by connecting one terminal of a voltmeter to the negative brush. 1898 *Engin. Mag.* XVI. 139/2 Plan of the plant is given, showing how the dynamo, voltmeter, switchboards, and tanks should be connected.

‖ **Vo·lto.** [It. *volto* = *volta* vault (the same word as Volta).] = Vault *sb.*^{1} 1.

a 1700 Evelyn *Diary* 22 Oct. 1644, Entring the Church [St. Peter's, Rome], admirable is the bredth of the volto or roofe. *Ibid.* 18 Jan. 1645, The Consistory, a noble roome, the volto painted in grotesq. 1880 Shorthouse *J. Inglesant* xxvi. 375 The garden [at Rome] was entered by a portico or door-case adorned with ancient statues, the volto or roof of which was painted with classic subjects.

Vo·ltzine. *Min.* Also **volz-.** [-ine^5.] = next.

1836 T. Thomson *Min., Geol.*, etc. I. 540 *Voltzine.* Oxysulphuret of zinc. This mineral occurs at Rosiers. 1850 Ansted *Elem. Geol., Min.*, etc. § 470 Volzine. 1855 *Orr's Circ. Sci., Geol.*, etc. 503 *Voltzine*..Found in a vein of quartz..and in some zinc furnaces.

Voltzite (vǫ·ltzəit). *Min.* [f. the name of P. L. *Voltz*, inspector of mines; named by Fournet, 1833.] A native oxysulphide of zinc.

1835 *R. D. & T. Thomson's Rec. Gen. Sci.* I. 274 Voltzite. This mineral is found at Pont Gibaud, in Puy de Dome. It possesses a pearly lustre; colour rose-red, or yellow. 1852 Dana *Min.* 252 *Voltzite.* A compound of sulphuret and oxyd of zinc. Occurs in implanted globules of a dirty rose-red color.

Volu·bilate, *a. Bot.* [f. next + -ate.] = next.

1819 Rees *Cycl.*, *Volubile*, or *Volubilate* Stem or Stalk,.. a name given to those of many plants, as all those the stems or stalks of which are of a twining or winding climbing nature.

Volubile, *a. Bot. rare.* [ad. L. *volūbilis.* So F. *volubile.*] = Voluble *a.* 4.

1819 [see prec.]. 1838 J. Murray *Econ. Veg.* 48 Some stems are volubile; or 'twine' as the hop and honeysuckle, convolvulus, and 'scarlet runner.' 1849 Balfour *Man. Bot.* § 66 Stems have usually considerable firmness and solidity, but sometimes they..twist round other plants in a spiral manner like Woodbine, becoming volubile.

‖ **Volu·bilis.** *Bot. Obs.* [L.; see prec. So F. *volubilis.*] Convolvulus.

1664 Evelyn *Kal. Hort.* Mar. 63 Sow on the Hot-bed such Plants as are late bearing Flowers or Fruit in our Climate; as Balsamine,..Volubilis, Myrrh, Carrobs, [etc.]. 1712 tr. *Pomet's Hist. Drugs* I. 132 This Pod is the Fruit of a Kind of Volubilis.

Volubility (vǫliubi·lĭti). Also 6–7 **-itie**, 7 **-itye.** [ad. F. *volubilité* (15–16th cent.; = It. *volubilità*, Sp. *-idad*, Pg. *-idade*), or ad. L. *volūbilitās*, f. *volūbilis*: see next and -ity.]

I. † **1.** Quickness in turning from one object to another; versatility. *Obs. rare.*

1579 Fenton *Guicciard.* I. (1599) 3 The wisedome and reputation of the man, togither with the naturall volubilitie of his wit. 1605 Bacon *Adv. Learn.* II. xviii. § 5 Orators.. by the obseruing their well graced fourmes of speech..leese the volubilitie of Application.

† **b.** Ready variation of expression. *Obs.*$^{-1}$

1659 Harrington *Valerius & Publicola* 18 If you speak of Israel, Athens, Rome, Venice, or the like, they hear you with volubility of countenance.

2. The capacity of revolving, rolling, or turning round; aptness to rotate about an axis or centre.

1594 Hooker *Eccl. Pol.* I. iii. § 2 If Celestiall Spheres should forget their woonted Motions, and by irregular volubilitie turne themselues any way as it might happen. 1601 Holland *Pliny* I. 31 The world with continuall volubilitie and turning about it, driveth the..globe thereof into the forme of a round ball. 1656 Stanley *Hist. Philos.* VIII. (1687) 432/2 He who thrust the Cylinder, gave it the beginning of motion, but did not give it volubility. 1687 A. Lovell tr. *Bergerac's Com. Hist.* 86 It began to be out of my power any more to discern the Diversity of their several Motions by reason of their extream Volubility. 1705 Purshall *Mech. Macrocosm* 236 They lose their Fluidity, which depends upon the Volubility of Globular Particles at liberty. 1740 Cheyne *Regimen* 75 Blood Globules, by their Rotundity, Volubility, and Elasticity, resist Trituration, that is, Digestion. 1754 *Dict. Arts & Sci.* s.v. *Needle*, In the construction of the horizontal needle a piece of pure steel is provided, of a length not exceeding six inches, lest its weight impede its volubility. 1871 Browning *Pr. Hohenst.* 1920 Under pretence of making fast and sure The inch [of ascent] gained by late volubility.

b. Of the eye: Readiness in moving. *rare*$^{-1}$.

1603 Holland *Plutarch's Mor.* 1275 The cheerefull cast & amiable volubility of his quicke eie.

† **3.** Capacity for moving in an easy or gliding manner. *Obs.*

1605 Bacon *Adv. Learn.* II. xxi. § 9 Except men know exactly all the conditions of the serpent; ..his volubility and lubricity. 1610 Guillim *Heraldry* III. xviii. 153 Such Creatures..which..as it were slide from place to place, some more slowlie, but othersome with a certaine Volubility and flexible Agitation of the Bodie. 1653 T. Watson *Art Div. Contentm.* xi. (1668) 185 The Poets painted Time with wings, to shew the volubility and swiftness of it.

† **4.** Tendency to change or turn from one condition to another; changeableness, mutability, inconstancy. *Obs.* **a.** Of persons.

1603 Florio *Montaigne* II. i. 195 Whosoever shall heedefully survay and consider himselfe, shall finde this volubilitie and discordance to be in himselfe. 1613 Shirley *Trav. Persia* 135 The world by taking notice of your infirmitie will alwayes feare volubilitie in all your actions. *a* 1660 *Contemp. Hist. Irel.* (Ir. Archæol. Soc.) I. 204 All the lawe, phisicke, and poetrie in the world canot cure or amende the flexibilitie, volubilitie, inconstancie, and treacherie of this man.

b. Of fortune or affairs.

1609 Holland *Amm. Marcell.* 286 The volubilitie of inconstant fortune produceth these occurrences in the East parts. 1670 *Moral State Eng.* 1 All affairs do resemble the great Machines of Heaven and Earth, in their motion and volubility. 1699 T. C[ockman] tr. *Tully's Offices* (1706) 88 The great Volubility and Changeableness of Fortune.

II. 5. Ready flow *of* speech, etc.

1589 Puttenham *Eng. Poesie* II. v. (Arb.) 91 Which flowing of wordes with much volubilitie smoothly proceeding from the mouth is in some sort harmonicall. 1653 Jer. Taylor *Serm. for Year* I. ii. 15 Some men..explicate our praying in the Spirit, by a mere volubilty [*sic*] of language. 1656 Stanley *Hist. Philos.* v. (1687) 228/2 Cicero being at Athens heard him, and was much taken with the eloquence and volubility of his discourse. 1670 Clarendon *Hist. Reb.* XVI. § 122 The General was not a Man of Eloquence or Volubility of Speech. 1729 Butler *Serm.* Wks. 1874 II. 43 This unrestrained volubility and wantonness of speech is the occasion of numberless evils. 1791 Cowper *Odyss.* XVIII. 32 Gods! with what volubility of speech The table hunter prates. 1823 Lamb *Elia* II. *Old Margate Hoy*, A..young man..with..an insuppressable volubility of assertion. 1836 Thirlwall *Greece* III. 11 The sweetness of voice, and the volubility of utterance, with which both [Pisistratus and Cimon] expressed themselves.

b. Smooth, easy, or copious flow of verse or poetic utterance.

1589 Nashe in Greene *Menaphon* Pref. (Arb.) 6 The spacious volubilitie of a drumming decasillabon. 1751 Johnson *Rambler* No. 92 ¶ 11 The verse intended to represent the whisper of the vernal breeze, must be confessed not much to excel in softness or volubility. 1779 — *L. P., Pomfret* (1838) 113 In his other poems there is an easy volubility.

6. The character or state of being voluble in speech; great fluency of language; readiness of speech; garrulousness.

1596 Shaks. *Tam. Shr.* II. i. 176 Say she be mute, and will not speake a word; Then Ile commend her volubility. 1602 Marston *Ant. & Mel.* II. Wks. 1856 I. 23 You have the most gracefull presence,..amazing volubility,..delicious affabilitie. 1670 G. H. tr. *Hist. Cardinals* I. I. 13 It was my fortune to hear a Franciscan Preach.., but with more Volubility than Virtue. 1710 Steele *Tatler* No. 115 ¶ 5 His great Volubility and inimitable Manner of Speaking. 1751 Johnson *Rambler* No. 157 ¶ 8 Long familiarity with my subject enabled me to discourse with ease and volubility. 1781 R. King *Mod. Lond. Spy* 118 The following account, which she delivered with great volubility. 1826 F. Reynolds *Life & Times* II. 11 He took the lead in conversation, and his natural volubility, increased by sudden joy, carried all before it. 1855 Macaulay *Hist. Eng.* xi. III. 25 Before he had been a member three weeks, his volubility, his asperity, and his pertinacity had made him conspicuous. 1875 H. James *Mme. de Mauves* i, Her volubility was less suggestive than the latter's silence.

7. Extreme readiness *of* the tongue in respect of speech or discourse.

1612 W. Martyn *Youths Instr.* 99 The volubilitie of a smooth tongue is nothing profitable. 1650 R. Stapylton *Strada's Low C. Wars* III. 67 A Counsellour of great subtilty and volubility of tongue. 1699 Garth *Dispens.* III. 36 Both had the Volubility of Tongue, In Meaning faint, but in Opinion strong. 1711 Steele *Spect.* No. 252 ¶ 3 You have mentioned only the Volubility of their Tongue. 1755 Smollett *Quix.* (1803) II. 6 All this preamble was uttered.. with such volubility of tongue,..that they admired her good sense as much as her beauty.

b. Similarly of the throat, voice, etc.

1740 Cibber *Apol.* (1756) I. 232 In volubility of throat the former [singer] had much the superiority. 1769 Goldsm. *Hist. Rome* (1786) II. 225 Nero..used all those methods which singers practice either to mend the voice, or improve its volubility. 1884 *Encycl. Brit.* XVII. 98/2 These [harmonics on horns and trumpets] they executed with volubility akin to that displayed on fingered instruments.

† **Volu·bilous**, *a. Obs.*$^{-1}$ [f. L. *volūbil-is*: see next.] Apt to roll or turn.

1658 Rowland tr. *Moufet's Theat. Ins.* 1059 It hath a broad round volubilous body.

Voluble (vǫ·liŭb'l), *a.* Also 7 **volubil.** [a. older F. *voluble* (= Sp. *voluble*, Pg. *voluvel*, It. *volubile*) or ad. L. *volūbilis*, f. *volū-*, *volvĕre* to turn: see -ble.

In some instances the use of the word echoes Horace *Ep.* I. ii. 43 (Amnis) in omne volubilis ævum.]

I. 1. Liable to change; inconstant, variable, mutable. Now *rare.*

1575 Fenton *Gold. Epist.* (1582) 21 As of all voluble things there is nothyng more light than renown. 1578 Wotton *Courtlie Controuersie* 29 Poets, and Painters..testifye the loue of men to be voluble and vnconstant lyke a birde. 1604 T. Wright *Passions* VI. 339 Perceive how vain fancies, and voluble crosses vanish away as little cloudes before the northerne winds. 1647 J. Carter *Nail & Wheel* 71 Nothing abides at a stay; all things are unstable, and voluble. 1652 N. Culverwel *Lt. Nat.* I. xii. (1661) 104 The noblest Perfections..are but voluble, and uncertain. 1678 Alsop *Melius Inq.* II. v. 243 The Lot, wherein the..Alruling God Controuls the Contingency of the voluble Creature. 1898 Meredith *Odes Fr. Hist.* 28 He waves, and the voluble scene is a quagmire shifting block.

2. Capable of ready rotation on a centre or axis; apt to revolve or roll in this manner. Now *rare.*

1589 Puttenham *Eng. Poesie* II. xi. (Arb.) 111 He [the round or sphere] is euen and smooth, without any angle, or interruption, most voluble and apt to turne, and to continue motion. 1609 Bible (Douay) *Ezek.* x. 13 And these wheeles he called voluble, my self hearing it. 1637 Gillespie *Eng. Pop. Cerem.* A ij b, Like Diogenes turning about the mouth of his voluble hoggeshead. 1667 Milton *P. L.* IV. 594 Or this less volubil Earth By shorter flight to th' East had left him there. 1726 Leoni *Alberti's Archit.* III. 2/1 A Sphere is..a round body voluble on every side. 1784 Cowper *Task* III. 490 Thrice must the voluble and restless earth Spin round upon her axle. 1812 Cary *Dante, Purg.* XXII. 41, I had met The fierce encounter of the voluble rock. 1822 Hazlitt *Table-T.* Ser. II. xvii. 397 Go thy ways old world, swing round in blue ether, voluble to every age; you and I shall no more jostle!

fig. 1598 Dallington *Meth. Trav.* B j b, His imagination shall be carried in the voluble Sphere of diuers mens discourses. 1605 Bacon *Adv. Learn.* II. xxiii. § 33 Nothing is more politique then to make the wheels of our mind concentrique and voluble with the wheel of fortune. 1632 J. Hayward tr. *Biondi's Eromena* 106 Fortune (Sister) is unstable, and her wheele voluble.

† **b.** Of the eye: Moving readily. *Obs.*$^{-1}$

1661 Lovell *Hist. Anim. & Min.* 91 He hath..high eyebrowes, eyes not very voluble or prominent.

c. Capable of being rolled up.

1662 Evelyn *Chalcogr.* 19 Which from the German *Bucher* ..were called Books, to whatever voluble or folding matter applyed.

3. Moving rapidly and easily, esp. with a gliding or undulating movement.

1589 Puttenham *Eng. Poesie* III. iv. (Arb.) 156 A broad and voluble tong, thinne and mouable lippes, teeth euen and not shagged. 1608 Topsell *Serpents* 11 The Tongue of a Serpent..is also thinne, long, and black of colour, voluble; neither is there any beast that moueth the tongue so speedily. 1667 Milton *P. L.* IX. 436 Neerer he drew, and many a walk travers'd Of stateliest Covert, Cedar, Pine, or Palme, Then voluble and bold, now hid, now seen. 1695 Woodward *Nat. Hist. Earth* III. 131 The parts of it [*sc.* water] being very voluble and lubricous, as well as fine and small, it easily..distends the Tubes and Vessels of Vegetables. 1856 Bryant *Summer Air* 25 Why so slow, Gentle and voluble spirit of the air?

fig. 1862 Thackeray *Philip* xvii, Would you like to hear yesterday's sermon over and over again—eternally voluble?

4. *Bot.* Twining, twisting. Cf. Volubile *a.*

1753 *Chambers' Cycl.* Suppl. s.v. *Stalk*, *Voluble stalk*, that which twists round other things. 1789 E. Darwin *Bot. Gard.* II. (1791) 108 *note*, Some of the plants with voluble stems ascend other plants spirally, east—south—west. 1835 Kirby *Power, Wisd. & Goodn. God* II. 247 Some with a climbing or voluble stem, constantly turn one way, and some as constantly turn another. 1857 A. Gray *First Less. Bot.* (1866) 37 *Twining*, or *voluble*, when stems rise by coiling themselves spirally around other stems or supports. [Also in later botanical works.]

II. 5. Characterized by fluency or glibness of utterance; rapid and ready of speech; fluent:

a. Of persons.

1588 Shaks. *L. L. L.* III. i. 69 A most acute Iuuenall, voluble and free of grace. 1604 — *Oth.* II. i. 242 A knaue very voluble...A slipper, and subtle knaue, a finder of occasion. 1621 T. Williamson tr. *Goulart's Wise Vieillard* 14 There be found men aboue a hundred yeares old, that are very voluble and fluent in talke and discourse. [1704 Steele *Lying Lover* v. i, Oh this unhappy Tongue of mine! Thou lawless voluble destroying Foe.] 1726 Pope *Odyss.* XXII. 319 There end thy pompous vaunts and high disdain; Oh sharp in scandal, voluble and vain! 1807 Crabbe *Par. Reg.* II. 158 Fierce in his air, and voluble of tongue. 1840 Thirlwall *Greece* lvi. VII. 138 A school of oratory, which produced a long series of voluble sophists. 1890 M. Williams *Leaves of Life* II. xvii. 150 Of all the voluble men I have encountered in the course of my career, he is the most voluble.

absol. 1762 Foote *Orator* II. Wks. 1799 I. 219 You will have at one view, the choleric, the placid, the voluble,..and the clamorous.

b. Of the tongue.

1608 Middleton *Trick to catch Old One* I. ii, 'Tis a fine little voluble toung mine Hoste, that wins a widdow. 1650 R. Stapylton *Strada's Low C. Wars* III. 63 A man naturally eloquent, of a voluble fluent tongue. 1699 Burnet *39 Art.* xxiii. 257 Hot-headed Men of warm Fancies, and voluble Tongues..would be apt to thrust themselves on to the Teaching and Governing others. 1720 Prior *Truth & Falsehood* 45 Her tongue, so voluble and kind, It always runs before her mind. 1791 Cowper *Iliad* XX. 309 The tongue of man is voluble, hath words For every theme. 1817 Chalmers *Life Churchyard* 8 Churchyard was, plainly, a plausible man, who had many tales to tell, with a voluble tongue.

Comb. 1604 Dekker *Honest Wh.* v, A notable-voluble tongde villaine.

transf. 1820 Keats *Eve St. Agnes* xxiii, But to her heart, her heart was voluble, Paining with eloquence her balmy side.

6. Of discourse, words, etc.: Characterized by great fluency or readiness of utterance.

1588 Shaks. *L. L. L.* II. i. 76 Aged eares play treuant at his tales..So sweet and voluble is his discourse. 1590 — *Com. Err.* II. i. 92 If voluble and sharpe discourse be mar'd, Vnkindnesse blunts it more then marble. 1649 Milton *Eikon.* 32 A discours, voluble anough, and full of sentence. 1690 *Lond. Gaz.* No. 2612/4 One John Waterhouse of full middle Stature,..and of a large Voice, and voluble Speech. 1782 J. Warton *Ess. Pope* II. xiv. 473 *note*, The style of which is certainly not so melodious and voluble as that of Dryden's enchanting prose. 1791 Boswell *Johnson* an. 1750, His periods, though not diligently rounded, are voluble and easy. 1849 Robertson *Serm.* Ser. I. ii. (1855) 25 In such persons words are ever at command—voluble and impassioned words. 1870 L'Estrange *Life Miss Mitford* I. vi. 170 At length 'madame' began a very voluble oration, intended to express the extent of our delinquency.

transf. *a* 1721 Prior *Dial. betw. Locke & Montaigne* ¶ 5, I find the same strain run with a most voluble impetuosity almost thro every Chapter of your Book. 1802 Mar. Edgeworth *Moral T.*, *Forester*, *Catastrophe*, The joy of the poor dancing-master .. was rapturous and voluble. 1849 Miss Mulock *The Ogilvies* xvi, The good woman went on in her voluble grief. 1871 Macduff *Mem. Patmos* xxii. 308 Oh, the jarring discord of voluble sympathy!

† **b.** (See quot.) *Obs.*$^{-1}$

1745 P. Thomas *Jrnl. Anson's Voy.* 243 They [the Chinese] have contrived a fourth Kind of Writing, the Strokes whereof ..are made with more Ease and Expedition; on which Account they are called Voluble Letters.

Hence **Vo·lubleness**, the quality or character of being voluble.

1610 Guillim *Heraldry* III. xxii. 168 Such Reptiles as hauing no feet doe with a kind of volublenesse make their way in the waters with many intricate doublings. 1727 Bailey (vol. II), *Volubleness*, an Aptness to roll; also a round Delivery or Utterance, an easy Pronunciation. 1895 *Advance* (Chicago) 10 Oct. 517/3 In general there is..a certain volubleness among the ministers, and forgetfulness..to give the laymen a chance [to speak].

Volubly (vǫ·liŭbli), *adv.* [f. prec. + -ly^2.] In a voluble manner; fluently, glibly.

1615 Chapman *Odyss.* XVIII. 41 O Gods (saide he) how volubly doth talke This eating gulfe. 1663 Butler *Hud.* I. i. 105 This he as volubly would vent As if his stock would ne'er be spent. 1671 Clarendon *Dial.* Tracts (1727) 339 A Secretary of State who..spoke French as volubly and as exactly as he needed to do, without ever having been in France. 1765 Johnson in *Shaks. Wks.* (1778) X. 489 *note*, One that discourses fearlessly and volubly. 1796 Mme. D'Arblay *Camilla* III. i, She talked volubly of what she was about, as if it were the sole subject of her thoughts.

Supplement, p. 3873; Corrigenda, p. 4092; Spurious words, p. 4093; Books quoted, p. 4094

Voluary, rare⁻¹. [f. L. *voluer-is* bird + -ART.] A treatise on birds.

Volucrine, a. rare⁻¹. [f. as prec. + -INE.] Of pertaining to, arising from, birds.

Volue, obs. var. VOLLEY sb.; obs. Sc. f. WOLF sb.

Volume (vŏliūm), sb. Forms: a. 4–6 volym, 5 volom, 5–8 volum (5–6 vollum, 5 sc. wolum), 6 volume, 6–7 volumne, volumne (6 Sc. wolume). 7. volume, 7–9 volume. OF. *volum, volume, volumme* (F. *volume*,—It. and Pg. volume, Sp. volumen), ad. L. *volumen* roll, scroll, etc. f. *volvere* to roll. The chief senses of the English word also exist in French.]

I. 1. *Hist.* A roll of parchment, papyrus, etc., containing written matter; a literary work, or part of one, recorded or preserved in this form, which was customary in ancient times. Also *fig.*

2. A separately bound portion or division of a work; one of two or more portions into which a work of some size is divided with a view to separate binding; one of a number of books forming a related set or series.

3. Something which in character or nature is comparable to a book; *esp.* something which may be studied after the manner of a book.

4. A separately bound portion or division of a work; one of two or more portions into which a work of some size is divided with a view to separate binding; one of a number of books forming a related set or series.

II. 1. § 6. Size, bulk, or dimensions (of a book).

III. 2. *part.* A coil, fold, wreath, convolution, esp. of a serpent.

Volumed (vŏliūmd), *a.* [f. VOLUME sb. and -ED.]

Volumen (vŏliū'men). [L. *volumen* : see VOLUME sb.]

Volumenometer. = VOLUMENOMETER.

Volumeter (vŏliū'mĕtĕr). [f. VOLUME sb. + -METER.]

Volumetric (vŏliūmĕ'trik), a. [Cf. prec. and METRIC a.]

Volumetrical (vŏliūmĕ'trikăl), a. [f. as prec. + -AL.]

Voluminosity (vŏliūminŏ'sĭti). [See next and -OBITY.]

1. The state of being voluminous in respect of literary production.

Voluminous (vŏliū'minŏs), a. Also f voluminous. [ad. late L. *voluminosus* (Sidonius), f. L. *volumen-*, volumine VOLUME sb. Cf. F. *volumineux*, It., Sp., Pg. *voluminoso*.]

Voluminously, adv. [f. prec. + -LY².]

Voluminousness. [f. prec. + -NESS.]

Volumy, a. rare⁻¹. [f. VOLUME sb.] Swelling, rounded.

Volunt. Obs. rare. [a. late AF. *volunt* for earlier voluntY.] a. (See first quot.) b. One's own will.

Voluntariate. [f. VOLUNTARY + -ATE.]

Voluntarily (vŏ'lŏntărĭli), adv. Forms: 4–5 voluntarely, 5– voluntarily, 6 -lyre, -lie, 6 -ilie, -olye; 6–9 y-lye, 7-ylio. [f. VOLUNTARY a. + -LY².]

Voluntarious, a. Obs. rare⁻¹. [ad. L. *voluntárius* VOLUNTARY a.] Free, voluntary.

Voluntariness. [f. voluntarius (1866), l. voluntáre VOLUNTARY a.] Voluntary service, *spec.* of a military character. Also *attrib.*

Voluntarism (vŏ'lŏntărĭzm). [Irreg. f. VOLUNTAR-Y + -ISM. Cf. VOLUNTARYISM.]

Voluntarist (vŏ'lŏntărĭst). [f. as prec. + -IST.]

Voluntaristic, a. [prec. + -IC.] Pertaining or belonging to the philosophical theory of voluntarism.

Voluntarity. Obs. [f. VOLUNTAR a. : see VOLUNTARY.]

Voluntary (vŏ'lŏntărĭ), a., adv., and sb. Also 7 voluntarye, -arie, 5 voluntarie. [ad. F. *volontaire* (14th c.), *voluntaire* (16th c. :— mod.F. *volontaire* = It. *volontario*, Sp., Pg., voluntário; ad. L. *voluntárius.*]

Voluntaryism (vŏ'lŏntărĭĭzm). [f. VOLUNTARY a. + -ISM. Cf. VOLUNTARISM.]

Voluntaryist. [f. prec. + -IST.]

Voluntaryism.

Voluntary, *sb.*

Voluntaryism.

Voluntative, *a.*

Volunteer, *sb.* and *a.*

Volunteer, *v.*

Volunteerism.

Volunteership.

Voluntive, *a.*

Voluntary, *v.*

Volunto-motory, *a.*

Voluntly, *adv.*

Voluptuary.

Volupe.

Voluper.

Voluptuary.

Volute.

Voluptuate, *v.*

Voluptuosity.

Voluptuous, *a.*

Voluptuously, *adv.*

Voluptuousness.

Voluta.

Voluptuary.

Volu'ptuousness.

Volutation.

Volute, *sb.*

Volute, *v.*

Voluted, *a.*

Volutin.

Volution.

Volvox.

Volvulus.

Volymare.

Vomating, obs. Sc. f. VOMITING vbl. sb.

Vomative, variant of VOMITIVE Obs.

†**Vome**, sb. Obs. rare. Also vome.
[f. next.] Vomit.

†**Vome**, v. Obs. rare. Also vome.
[ad. L. vomere.] Vomit. Also fig.

Vomecue Lev. vbl. 97 Who blows spews t' thal
vome.

Vomicene, -ine, var. (Nux) VOMICA.

Vomio-se, v. Path. [L. VOMICA 2 a] Abounding in ulcerous cavities.

†**Vomish**, v. Obs. rare. [f. vomit-, length-ened stem of vomit to vomit.] trans. To vomit.

†**Vomisement**. Obs.⁻¹
[a. OF. vomissement.] The act or fact of vomiting.

Vomit (vǫ'mit), sb. Forms: 4–5 vomyt (5 vomyt, vomyght), 5–6 vomyte, 5–7 vomite, 6 vomitte (7 womit), 7–8 vomet, 5 -ete, -ette, 6 womett, 7 vomett, 5 AF. vomit, -ite, OF. vomite (1. Sp., Pg. vomito), or ad. L. vomit-us, f. vomere : see next.]

1. The act of ejecting the contents of the stomach through the mouth: a. With and pl.

b. Without article.

2. Matter ejected from the stomach by vomiting; – SPEW sb. 1.

Vomit (vǫ'mit), v. Forms: 5–6 vomyte, 6–7 vomete, womet [a. 1. vomite, vomere, ppl. stem of vomere (whence it. vomitare, F. vomir; see VOMIT sb.)]

1. intr. To bring up and discharge the contents of the stomach through the mouth.

2. trans. To bring up and discharge (swallowed food or drink) through the mouth; to cast out (a matter or substance) in this way; – SPEW v. 2.

b. Freq. with abs., as forth, out, up.

c. transf. To cause (a person) to vomit.

Vomit-, the stem of VOMIT 2b, used in a few combinations, as † vomit-grass, a grass causing vomiting in dogs; vomit-nut, VOMIT NUT (Simmonds Dict. Trade, 1858); vomit-wort U.S., Indian tobacco (Lobelia inflata).

Vomiter (vǫ'mitǝr), [f. VOMIT v. + -ER¹.]
One who, or that which, vomits.

Vomiting (vǫ'mitiŋ), vbl. sb. [f. VOMIT v. + -ING¹.]
1. The act of ejecting the contents of the stomach through the mouth; an instance of this.

Vomitingly, adv. rare⁻¹. [f. as prec. + -LY².] In a manner suggestive of vomiting.

Vomition, rare. [ad. L. vomition-, vomitio, noun of action f. vomere to vomit.]

Vomitive (vǫ'mitiv), a. and sb. Also 7 vomitif, -ive, 6–8 vomitive. [a. F. vomitif, -ive (Sp., Pg. vomitivo), ad. L. type *vomitivus, f. vomit-: see VOMIT v.]

B. sb. An emetic: = VOMITORY sb. 1.

†**Vomiture**. Obs.⁻¹ [f. VOMIT sb. + -URE.]

†**Vomiturient**, a. Obs.⁻¹ [f. L. vomiturire, desiderative of vomere.]

Vomiturition. [a. F. vomiturition or mod.L. vomiturition, vomituritio, noun of action f. *vomiturire to vomit.]

Vomito (vǫ'mito), [Sp., and (fig.) vomito, ad. 1. vomitus to vomit.] The yellow fever in its virulent form, when it is usually accompanied by black vomit. Cf. VOMIT sb. 2 b.

Vomitory (vǫ'mitǝri), sb. [ad. L. vomitorium.]

Vomitory, a. [ad. L. vomitori-us, f. vomitor to vomit: see -ORY.]

Voodoo (vū'dū), sb. Also voudoo, voudou, vudu, voudu, and VAUDOUX. (Cf. HOODOO.) [African (Dahomey) origin.]

Voodooism (vū'dūiz'm), [f. prec. + -ISM.]

Voracious (vǫrē'ʃǝs), a. [f. L. voraci-, vorax voracious + -OUS.]

Voraciously, adv. [f. prec. + -LY.]

Voraciousness. [f. as prec. + -NESS.]

Voracity (vǫræ'siti). [a. F. voracité, ad. L. voracitat-em, f. vorax: see VORACIOUS.]

Vorago (vǫrē'go). Now rare. Cf. VORAGE. [L. vorago, gulf, chasm.]

Vorant (vǫ'rant), a. [f. 1. vorant-, vorans, pres. pple. of vorare to devour.]

‡**Voration**. Obs.⁻¹ [ad. L. vorāti-o, f. vorāre.] A devouring, or eating up greedily.

†**Voralite**. Min. Obs.⁻¹ [f. Vorau in Styria + -LITE. Named in 1806.] = LAZULITE.

Vorax, a. rare⁻¹. [a. L. vorax devouring.] Voracious, ravenous.

Vorbrod-, **bede**, **bisne**, southern ME. varr.

†**Vorage** (vǫ'rėdʒ). Obs. rare. [a. OF. vorage, or ad. L. voràgo.] A whirlpool, gulf, chasm.

†**Vorageous**, a. Obs.⁻¹ [f. VORAGE + -ous.] = VORAGINOUS.

†**Voraginous**, a. [ad. L. voraginos-us, f. voragin-, vorago: see -OUS, and cf. F. voragineux, It., Sp., Pg. voraginoso.]

Vore, Voregard, Voreward, southern ME. varr. of FORE adv., FOREGARD, FOREWARD.

Vortex (vǫ'rtĕks). Pl. vortices (vǫ'rtisīz), rarely vortexes. [a. L. vortex, vertex: see VERTEX.]

Vortice, v. rare⁻¹. [Cf. prec.] trans. To bring by vortical motion.

Vorticel, variant of VORTICELLA.

Vorticella (vǫ̆ɹtise·la). Zool. [mod.L., dim. f. L. vortex, vortic-: see VORTEX.] The typical genus of Vorticellidæ (cf. next): an individual belonging to this genus; a bell-animalcule.

Vorticellid (vǫ̆ɹtise·lid). Zool. An animal belonging to the Vorticellidæ.

Vorticellidæ (vǫ̆ɹtise·lidī). Zool. [mod.L.] A family of sedentary infusorians.

Vortical a.d. = VORTICAL.

Vorticism, a. [L. vortici-, vortex: see VORTEX and -ISM.] Of or belonging to the theory of a vortex or vortices.

Vorticiform, a. rare⁻¹. [L. as prec.: see -FORM.] Having the form of a vortex.

Vorticist (vǫ̆ɹtisist). [f. as prec. + -IST.] An advocate of the theory of vortices.

Vorticity (vǫ̆ɹti·siti). [f. as prec. + -ITY.] The condition of a fluid, etc., with respect to vortical motion.

Vorticle, Obs. rare. [f. L. vortic-, vortex, after diminutives in -cle.] A little vortex.

Vorticordinous, a. Obs.⁻¹. [f. L. Vorti-, Vorticordia: see VERTICORDIOUS a.] Turning the heart.

Vorticose (vǫ̆ɹtikǫus). a. [ad. L. vorticōs-us. f. vortic-, vortex VORTEX: see -OSE.]
1. Of motion = VORTICAL a. 1.
2. Resembling a vortex.

Vorticular, Of motion: Vortical, vorticose.

Vorticulous, a. Obs. [f. L. vortic-, vortex + -ULAR.] Of motion: Vortical, vorticose.

Vortiginous, var. VERTIGINOUS a.]
1. Of motion: Vortical, vorticular.

Votable, a. rare⁻¹. [f. VOTE v. + -ABLE.] Capable, or having the right, of voting.

Votal, a. [f. VOTE + -AL.]
1. Existing in will or wish, though not carried out in fact. Obs.
2. Of the nature of a vow; consisting of or expressed by a vow.

Votaress (vǫu·tǝres). [f. VOTARY + -ESS.] A female votary; cf. a woman devoted to a religious life or to a special saint.

Votarian, Obs. rare⁻¹. [f. VOTARY.]
A female votary of a special saint.

Votarist (vǫu·tǝrist). [f. as VOTARY + -IST.] One bound by a vow; a devotee, a votary.

Votary, a. Obs. [Cf. prec.]
1. Of persons: Consecrated by a vow; devoted to a religious life.
2. Of mode of life.
3. Of the nature of a vow.

Votary (vǫu·tǝri). sb. Also [- to 7 vowtary.] [f. L. vōt-um, VOW + -ARY.]
1. One who is bound by vows to a religious life; a monk or nun.
2. One who is devoted to a particular religion, or to some form of worship or religious observance; a devotee.
3. One who is devoted or passionately addicted to some particular pursuit, occupation, study, aim, etc.
4. One who is devoted to or worshipper of God, Christ, one of the saints, etc.

Votation (vǫutēi·ʃǝn). [f. VOTE v. + -ATION.] The action of voting in an election or at a meeting.

Voteless (vǫu·tles), a. [f. VOTE sb. + -LESS.] Having no vote.

Voteen (vǫtī·n). Irish. [app. f. DEVOTEE; the equivalent Ir. móidín is however connected with Ir. móidim I devote or devote.]
A very religious person.

Voteen, attrib. or adj.

Vote (vǫut). sb. Also 7 voate; 5 G. 6 volt, voit, wott, 7 woote, wots, wott, 7 woatt. [ad. L. vōtum vow, wish, prayer; the pa. pple. neut. of vovēre to vow, desire.]
1. A vow; a solemn promise or undertaking. Obs.
2. A prayer or intercession. Obs.
3. An aspiration; an ardent wish or desire. Obs. (Common 1630–60.)

Vote (vǫut), v. [f. VOTE sb.]

Voteen var. VOTAREE, VOTEN.

Votesave, var. VOUCHSAFE. With var. WOTȜ (Obs.)

Voting (vǫu·tiŋ), vbl. sb. Also 6–7 -ing, 7 -ingg.
1. The action of giving a vote.
2. attrib. and Comb.

Voting, ppl. a. [f. VOTE v.]
1. That votes.

Votive (vǫu·tiv). a. and sb. [ad. L. vōtīv-us, f. vōt-um VOW: see -IVE.]
1. Offered, consecrated, or dedicated in consequence of a vow; given or instituted in fulfilment of, or as a token of, a vow.
2. Consisting in, expressive of, a vow, desire, or wish.

Votive, sb.

Vouch (vautʃ). v. Forms: 4 vouch- (5 Sc. wouche), 5 vouch, 6 vowche, voutch, 6 vouche, voucher (Of.: also vouch-, voukier, vougier, vonkier) to call, summon, invoke, cite, obscurely [. L. vocāre to call.
1. trans. Law. To vouch to warrant or (in refer. +or) warranty, to cite, call, or summon (a person) into court to give warranty of title. (After AF. and OF. voucher à garant.)
2. trans. To assert or maintain (a thing) to be true.

Voucher (vau·tʃǝɹ). [f. VOUCH v. + -ER.]
1. One who vouches or gives warranty.
2. A document which serves to confirm or establish the truth of something.

Vouchsafe (vautʃsēi·f). v. [orig. two words, vouch safe.]
1. trans. To grant or bestow in a gracious or condescending manner.

VOUCH. 316 VOUCHEE

VOUCHER 317 VOUCHSAFE

VOUCHSAFE 318 VOUR. VOURER. 319 VOW

VOW.

Vow (vɑu), *n.*¹ Forms: 4–6 **vowe** (4 vowȝ, 5 vowyn), 4 **vou**, 5–7 **Sc. wow**; 4 **vou**, wou, 5–7 Sc. wow; 6 **OF. vouer, vover** (F. vouer), 5 **vou Vow st.**]

1. *trans.* To promise or undertake solemnly, *spec.* by a vow to a deity or saint; to swear: **b.** With subordinate clause (or equivalent).

b. **With infinitive.**

c. To dedicate, consecrate, or devote to some person or service.

d. **With cognate object.**

Vow (vɑu), *n.*¹ Forms: 4–6 **vowe**, 4 **vowes** (4 vows, 5–7 *Sc.* wow); 4 **vou**, wou, 5–7 *Sc.* wow; 6 **OF. vouer, vover**, [f. vow *st.*]

VOWED.

Vowed, *ppl. a.* [f. Vow *v.*¹ + -ED¹.]

1. Of persons : **+b.** Of things : **c.** Solemnly sworn or threatened.

VOWEE.

Vowee. *Obs.* Also **vowe.** [Aphetic form of *avowé* Avowee.] Advocate, patron.

Vowel.

Vowel (vɑu·el), *n.* Also 4 **vowail** (6 eil), [a. OF. *vouel, voȝel* (*vouyel, voy-, voiel*) masc. : — *vōcālem* or *vōcāle*, neut. acc. sing. of *vōcālis* VOCAL *a.* The later OF. *voielle*, mod.F. *voyelle*, Prov. and Sp. *vocal*, It. *vocale* are fem., after the L. sb. *vōcālis*.]

VOWESS.

Vowess (vɑu·es), *n.* Also 5 **vowes**, 6 **vowisse.** [f. Vow *v.*¹ + -ESS.] A woman who makes a vow of devotion to a religious life ; a nun.

VOWGARD.

Vowgard, *Obs.*²

Vox.

Vox, south-western dial. var. Fox *sb.* ; obs. Sc. var. Voice *sb.* ; obs. Sc. pa. t. Wax *v.*

VOYAGE.

Voyage (voi·ědʒ), *n.* Forms: α. 3–4 **veage, wyage** (4 veyage, viage, wayage), 5 *Sc.* **veedge** ; 3 **voyage, viage, viuage, vyage** ; 4– **voyage.** [a. OF. *veiage, viage, voiage*, etc. (mod.F. *voyage*) : — L. *viāticum* VIATIC *sb.*]

VOYAGER.

Voyager (voi·ědʒəɹ), *n.* Also 6 **vyager, -our**, 6–7 **viager.** [f. OF. *veager, voi-, voyager* (F. *voyageur*) or f. prec.]

1. One who journeys ; a traveller by land.

2. One who goes upon, or takes part in, a voyage.

Voyageur (voi-idʒiŋ), vbl. sb. [f. VOYAGE v. +-ING.] The action of the verb (now usually of journeying by sea).

Voyaging (voi-idʒiŋ), vbl. sb.

Vraisemblance (vɛʁsɑ̃blɑ̃s). [F. (16th c.), f. vrai true + semblance appearance, semblance.]
1. An appearance of truth; verisimilitude.
2. a representation, picture.

Vrouw (vrou). Also ? vrow, var. **Frau**.

Vug (vʌg), southern ME. var. FALL v., var. FULL adv.

Vulcan (vɔ·lkăn), sb. [ad. L. Vulcān-us, the god of fire, son of Jupiter and Juno. Cf. F. Vulcain, † Vulcan.]
1. Rom. Myth. The god of fire and of metal-working, corresponding to the Greek Hephaestus.

Vulcanalia, sb.

Vulcanalian, a. Of or pertaining to the Vulcanalia.

Vulcanian (vɔlkē·niăn), a. and sb. Also 2 vulcanean. [f. L. Vulcāni-us, f. Vulcān-us VULCAN sb. + -AN. Cf. F. vulcanien.]
A. adj. 1. Of or pertaining to, characteristic of, associated with, Vulcan.

Vulcanic (vɔlkæ·nik), a. [f. VULCAN sb. + -IC.] = VOLCANIC.

Vulcanicity, sb.

Vulcanism (vɔ·lkăniz'm), sb.

Vulcanist (vɔ·lkănist), sb.

Vulcanite (vɔ·lkănəit), sb.

Vulcanizable, a.

Vulcanization (vɔlkănəizē'·ʃən).

Vulcanize (vɔ·lkănəiz), v.

Vulcanized (vɔ·lkănəizd), ppl. a.

Vulcanizing, vbl. sb.

Vulcano, obs. variant of VOLCANO.

Vulcanological, **Vulcanology** (Also VOLC-).

Vulgar (vɔ·lgăʁ), sb. Also 5-6 vulgare, vulgaris. [f. VULGAR a.]
1. The common or usual language of a country, etc.; the vernacular. Obs.
2. The common people.

Vulgar (vɔ·lgăʁ), a. Also 4-6 vulgare, 6 St. vlgare, wlgair. var. Vulgar, vulguar, voulger, 7 vulgar. [ad. L. vulgār-is, f. vulgus the common people. Cf. OF. and F. vulgaire, Sp. and Pg. vulgar, It. volgare.]

I. 1. Employed in common or ordinary reckoning of time, distance, etc.; common, customary, ordinary, usual; that is in general or common use or practice.

2. In common or general use; common, customary, or ordinary, as a matter of use or practice.

3. Of language or speech: Commonly or customarily used by the people of a country; ordinary, vernacular.

4. Used to designate the Vulgate version of the Bible. (Cf. VULGAR sb.)

5. Common, ordinary, commonplace.

6. Common or ordinary in character. Obs.

7. Common or mean in character. Obs.

II. 8. Of persons: Belonging to the ordinary or common class in the community; not distinguished or marked off from this in any way; plebeian.

9. With collective terms, as people, sort.

10. Of an ordinary or unartificial type; not refined or advanced beyond the common.

11. Of an ordinary unartificial type; not refined or advanced beyond the common.

12. Common in respect of use or association. Obs. rare.

13. Having ordinary or commonplace qualities.

14. Marked by, or indicative of, lack of refinement or good taste; coarse, low.

Vulgar, v. rare. [f. VULGAR a. + -ISH.] Commonly.

Vulgarian (vʌlgēə·riăn), sb. and a.

Vulgarise, v. = VULGAR a. (in later use in sense 13).

Vulgarism (vɔ·lgărizm). [f. VULGAR a. + -ISM.] Cf. Sp. and Pg. vulgarismo, It. volgarismo.
1. A common or everyday expression. Obs.
2. A vulgar phrase or expression; a colloquial or low expression.
3. The quality or character of being vulgar; vulgarity.

Vulgarist. Vulgarity. Vulgarize. Vulgarization. Vulgate. Vulgarly. Vulgarness. Vulgarism. Vulgo.

Vulnerability. Vulnerable. Vulnerate.

Vulnerated. Vulneration. Vulnerative. Vulnerose. Vulnific. Vulnific. Vulpanser. Vulning. Vulpecide. Vulpicide. Vulpicidism. Vulpine. Vulpinarines. Vulpinary. Vulpinate. Vulpinic. Vulpinism. Vulpinite. Vulture. Vulturn. Vulturine. Vulturism. Vulva. Vulviform. Vulvitis. Vulvo-. Vum.

Supplement, p. 3873; Corrigenda, p. 4092; Spurious words, p. 4093; Books quoted, p. 4094

1881 *Harper's Mag.* Jan. 249 Darius was piqued, and he said, with a vum, 'I'll pay for the wood, if you'll send it hum'.

†**Vumbard.** *Obs.*⁻¹ [app. a late form of VANWARD: for the sense cf. VANTGUARD 2.] ? A front guard.

1464 *Mann. & Househ. Exp.* (Roxb.) 195 My mastyr lent hym a payr of smale curas wyth gardys and vumbarde.

Vunde, southern ME. pa. t. FIND *v.*

Vur, Vurness, Vurther, southern dial. varr. FAR *adv.*, etc., FARNESS, FURTHER.

†**Vusse.** *Obs. rare.* [? Alteration of FAITH *sb.*] *By my vusse*, used as an asseveration.

1608 ARMIN *Nest Ninn.* F ij b, But are you my vncle indeed? By my vusse I am sayes the old man. Then vncle by my vusse welcome to Court.

Vuste, southern ME. variant of FIST *sb.*[1]

Vuzeer, variant of VIZIER.

1847 *Gentl. Mag.* March 299/2 The Vuzeer Lall Singh.. has been deposed...Unable to select a Vuzeer from among their own number [etc.].

Vuz(z, southern dial. variant of FURZE.

Vy, obs. form of VIE *sb.*[3] and *v.*

Vyall, obs. form of VIOL *sb.*

Vyalett, obs. form of VIOLET *sb.*[1]

Vyce, obs. Sc. form of WISE *a.*

Vych, Vychou, southern ME. varr. EACH (*one*).

Vychancellour, obs. f. VICE-CHANCELLOR.

Vyche, obs. form of WITCH *sb.*

Vycht, obs. Sc. form of WIGHT *sb.* and *a.*

Vychtie, obs. Sc. form of WEIGHTY *a.*

Vyckyr, obs. form of VICAR.

Vycle, southern ME. var. FICKLE *v.*[1]

Vycytar, obs. form of VISITER.

Vycyte, obs. form of VISIT *v.*

Vy'd, Vyde, obs. ff. VIED *ppl. a.*

Vyd(e, obs. Sc. forms of WIDE *a.*

Vydam(e, obs. forms of VIDAME.

Vydele, southern ME. variant of FIDDLE.

Vydour, obs. Sc. form of VOIDER.

Vye, var. VIE *sb.*[1], *sb.*[2], *sb.*[3] *Obs.*; obs. f. VIE *v.*

Vyend, southern ME. var. FIEND.

Vyer, occas. printed for *vþer* OTHER *a.*

Vyf(e, Vyff, obs. Sc. ff. WIFE *sb.*

†**Vyfnes.** *Obs.*⁻¹ [f. F. *vif* VIVE *a.* + -NESS.] Liveliness, vivacity.

1475 *Bk. Noblesse* (Roxb.) 4 Therfor..every man in hym silf let the passions of dolours be turned and empressid into vyfnes of here spiritis.

Vyftene, -teoþe, southern ME. varr. FIFTEEN(TH. **Vygne,** obs. f. VINE *sb.*

Vyhs, obs. form of VICE *sb.*[1]

Vyhte, southern ME. var. FIGHT *sb.* and *v.*

Vyijs, Vyild, obs. Sc. f. WISE *sb.*, WILD *a.*

Vying, obs. form of VIEING *vbl. sb.*

Vyir, occas. printed for *vþir* OTHER *a.*

Vyiss, variant of VISE *v. Obs.*

Vyis(e, Vyit, Vyl, Vyld(e, obs. Sc. ff. WISE *sb.* and *a.*, WITE *sb.* and *v.*, WILL *sb.*, WILD *a.*

Vylarde, variant of VIEILLARD *Obs.*

Vylence, -ens, variants of VILLAINS *a. Obs.*

Vyleny(e, etc., obs. forms of VILLAINY.

Vylette, southern ME. variant of FILLET *sb.*

Vylie, obs. form of VILELY *adv.*

Vylie, Vyling, obs. Sc. variant of WILY *a.*, WILING *vbl. sb.*

Vylney, obs. form of VILLAINY.

Vyloyns, variant of VILLAINS *a. Obs.*

Vyn, southern ME. var. FIN *sb.*; obs. Sc. f. WIN *v.*, WONE *v.*

Vynacre, -eker, obs. variants of VINEGAR.

Vynd, obs. form of WYND *sb. Sc.*

Vyndage, variant of VENDAGE *Obs.*

Vynde, southern ME. var. FIND *v.*; obs. f. VINE *sb.*; obs. Sc. f. WIND *sb.*

Vyndle, obs. Sc. form of WINDLE *v.*

Vyndok, obs. Sc. variant of WINDOW.

Vyne, obs. f. VINE; obs. Sc. f. WIN *v.*, WINE.

Vynet(t, Vyniet, variants of VINET *Obs.*

Vynetree, obs. form of VINTRY.

Vynk, obs. Sc. form of WINK *v.*

Vynne, southern ME. variant of FIN *sb.*

Vynnett, variant of VINET *Obs.*

Vynour, obs. variant of VINER[2].

Vyntre, obs. form of VINE-TREE, VINTRY.

Vynued, variant of VINEWED *a. Obs.*

Vyny, Vynye, obs. var. VINE *sb.*, VINNY *v.*

Vynyette, variant of VINET *Obs.*

Vyral, obs. form of VIRL *sb.*

Vyrchippe, obs. form of WORSHIP.

Vyre, variant of EURE *sb. Obs.*, VIRE *sb.*[1] *Obs.*

Vyrelle, -ille, obs. forms of VIRL *sb.*

Vyrk, obs. Sc. form of WORK *v.*

Vyrne, variant of VERNE *sb.* and *v. Obs.*

Vyrre, southern ME. variant of FIR.

Vysard(e, obs. forms of VIZARD.

Vyscele, obs. Sc. form of VESSEL *sb.*

Vyse, obs. var. USE *v.*, VICE *sb.*, VISE *v.*, VISS, WISE *sb.* and *v.*

Vysenamy, obs. form of VISNOMY.

Vyseuase, Vysiere: see VISEVASE, VISIERE.

Vysilie, Vysly, obs. forms of WISELY *adv.*

Vyss, Vyssyon, obs. ff. VICE *sb.*[1], VISION.

Vyss, Vyssare, Vysycyon, southern ME. varr. FISH, FISHER, PHYSICIAN.

Vyt, Vytch, Vyte, obs. Sc. ff. WIT, WITCH, WITE.

Vythulare, Vythule, southern ME. variants of FIDDLER, FIDDLE.

Vyue, southern ME. var. FIVE; obs. f. VIVE *a.*

Vyuer, Vyver(e, obs. forms of VIVER[1].

Vyveri, obs. variant of IVORY.

Vywe(r, obs. forms of VIEW *sb.*, VIEWER.

W.

W (dʌ·b'l,yū), the 23rd letter of the modern English alphabet, is an addition to the ancient Roman alphabet, having originated from a ligatured doubling of the Roman letter represented by the U and V of modern alphabets. When, in the 7th c., the Latin alphabet was first applied to the writing of English, it became necessary to provide a symbol for the sound (w), which did not exist in contemporary Latin. This sound, a gutturally-modified bilabial voiced spirant, is acoustically almost identical with the devocalized (*u*) or (u), which was the sound originally expressed by the Roman U or V as a consonant-symbol; but before the 7th c. this Latin sound had developed into (v). The single *u* or *v* therefore could not without ambiguity be used to represent (w), though this was occasionally done, and in some Northumbrian texts was the regular practice. The ordinary sign for (w) was at first *uu*, but in the 8th c. this began to be superseded by ƿ, a character borrowed from the Runic alphabet, in which its name was *wyn* (Kentish *wen*). Eventually the use of ƿ became almost universal, but in the mean time the *uu* was carried from England to the continent, being used for the sound (w) in the German dialects, and in French proper names and other words of Teut. and Celtic origin. In the 11th c. the ligatured form was introduced into England by Norman scribes, and gradually took the place of ƿ, which finally went out of use about A.D. 1300. The character W was probably very early regarded as a single letter, although it has never lost its original name of 'double U'.

In OE. the sound (w) occurred initially not only before vowels but also before (l) and (r). The combination *wl* became obsolete in the 15th c. (in Sc. poetry *wlonk*, alliterating with *w-* words, was used in the 16th c.); *wr* is still written, but the *w* is silent in standard English, though in some dialects it is sounded as (w) or as (v). OE. had also the initial combination (hw), written *hu(u*, *hƿ*, and subsequently *ƿh*, *wh*; for the later development of this phonetic combination, and the history of the associated symbols, see WH.

The chief etymological sources of the Eng. (w) are: (1) OE. (w), mainly representing Indogermanic *w*, *gʰʷ*, *kw*, or *kʷ*; (2) ON. (w) of the same origin (in cited words expressed by *v*, according to Icelandic usage); (3) OF. (w), retained in north-eastern Fr. dialects, but elsewhere becoming (gw) and ultimately (g), whence in English such doublets as *wage* and *gage*, *warranty* and *guaranty*. The sound also occurs, represented otherwise than by *w*, in words of Latin origin containing the combinations *qu* (kw) and *su* (sw), as *question*, *suavity*, *persuade* (in 16–18th c. often written with *sw*); also in a few Fr. words, as *reservoir* (-vwāɪ).

So far as it remains a consonant-symbol, the letter never denotes any other sound than (w), but in a few words it has ceased to be pronounced, though still written, as in *answer*, *sword*, *two*, and in the combination *wr* referred to above. In the unstressed second element of a compound, (w) tends to be elided in colloquial speech. This contracted pronunciation is in some words a mere vulgarism (marked as such by spellings like *back'ard*, *forrard*, *allus* for *always*); in *Norwich* and some other place-names in *-wich* it is the only one regarded as correct, and the same may be said with regard to the nautical term *gunwale*; in *midwife* the contraction (mi·dif), formerly general, is now rarely heard. The tendency to elision of *w* beginning an unstressed second syllable is shown also in the change of *housewife* into *huzzif*, *huzzy*, where the spelling has followed the pronunciation, though the uncontracted form is now restored exc. in a special disparaging sense.

In some ME. MSS. (northern and north midland), and in many Scottish texts of the 15th and 16th centuries, *w* is written for *v*, and vice versa. In the 16th and 17th c., books printed from continental type often have the letter in the divided form VV, vv.

In ME. a new (w) arose from the development of intervocalic or final (γ), inherited from OE., as in *bowe*:—earlier *boȝe*:—OE. *boga*. This sound, however, has not survived as a consonant, because every (w) after a stressed vowel became a *u*-glide, the terminal element of a diphthong. From the early ME. period *w* was often substituted for *u* in vowel-digraphs (whether denoting diphthongs or simple vowels). In modern spelling *aw*, *ew*, *ow* are phonetically equivalent to *au*, *eu*, *ou*, though *ow* never stands for (ū), as in the older *yow* = *you* (except in the surname Cowper); the choice between *u* and *w* has been determined to some extent by etymological tradition, but is mainly arbitrary; at the end of a word *w*, not *u*, is used all but invariably. The traditional statement of grammarians that 'W is a vowel as well as a consonant' refers to its use in these digraphs; but in the 14–15th c., and in Sc. also in the 16th c., *w* occasionally represents (ū), as in *trw* = true, *swne* = soon, *swth* = sooth.

In south-eastern dialects (w) is regularly substituted for (v), and many writers of the first half of the 19th c. attribute to the Cockney dialect the habit of misusing (v) for (w) and (w) for (v) on all occasions. No trace of this survives in present-day London speech; and although there is no doubt that the Kentish (w) for (v) at one time extended to London, it is probable that the reverse substitution was merely an occasional (if perhaps rather frequent) result of the endeavour to speak correctly.

1763 FOOTE *Mayor of G.* I. (1764) 21 *Sneak.* Yes, werry like Wenus. 1803 PEGGE *Anecd. Engl. Lang.* (1814) 77 The.. most offensive error in pronunciation among the Londoners ..lies in the transpositional use of the letters *W* and *V*, ever to be heard where there is any possibility of inverting them. Thus they always say, *W*eal, instead of *v*eal; and *W*inegar, instead of *v*inegar; while, on the other hand, you hear *V*icked, for wicked—*V*ig, for wig; and a few others. 1805 T. HARRAL *Scenes of Life* III. 26 'Last night thou gavest me to a willain's arms!'—'A villain?'..'Ay, a willain!' 1837 DICKENS *Pickw.* xxxiv, 'Do you spell it [Weller] with a V or a W?'..'I spells it with a V'..'Quite right too, Samivel...Put it down a we, my lord'. 1844 T. H. KEY *Alphabet* 107 London too is remarkable for the confusion of the sounds, though this confusion does not seem to arise from any inability to pronounce either a *w* or a *v*, each being substituted for the other with a most amusing perversity.

A mispronunciation of (w) for (r), in some persons due to a physical defect, has sometimes been a fashionable affectation.

1837 DICKENS *Pickw.* xxxv, 'Gwacious heavens!' said his lordship. 'I thought evewebody had seen the new mail-cart; it's the neatest, pwettiest, gwacefullest thing that ever wan.' 1844 T. H. KEY *Alphabet* 93 The letter *r* is at times confounded with *w*. Thus it is not a very rare variety of articulation that *rubbish* is pronounced *wubbish*.

1. The letter, its sound or name.

c 1465 in *Pol. Rel. & L. Poems* 2 A Doble W. for Warwike, þat god be his gide. 1552 HULOET Kk ij b, Because there is a diuersitie betwene the single V and the dowble W, therfore the alphabet of them shalbe set diuersly. [The sequence is: *Va*, *Wa*, *Vd*.] 1580 W. BULLOKAR *Bk. at large* 8 W. I account also misnamed to call it double: v: for then shoulde we sounde it: v: v: but his sounde agreeth to the olde name of: y: (which is wy). *c* 1595 R. CAREW in G. G. Smith *Elizab. Crit. Ess.* (1904) II. 286 For letters, wee haue Q. more then the Greekes; K. and Y. more then the Latynes; and W. more then them both, or the French and Italians. 1599 THYNNE *Animadv.* (1875) 65 The latyne, Italiane, frenche, and spanyshe haue no doble W. *a* 1637 B. JONSON *Engl. Gram.* iii. (1640) 40 W, Is but the V. geminated in the full sound, and though it have the seate of a Consonant with us, the power is alwayes Vowellish, even where it leades the Vowell in any Syllabe: as if you marke it, pronounce the two *uu*. like *w*, quicke in passage and these words: 8-ine. 8-ant. 8-ood. 8-ast. ʃ8-ing. ʃ8-am. Will sound wine. want. wood. wast. swing. swam. 1697 DRYDEN *Æneis* Ded. (e) 1, [In the English *Aeneis*] where a Vowel ends a word, the next begins either with a Consonant, or what is its equivalent; for our W and H aspirate..are plainly such. 1704 *Expert Orthographist* in Ellis *E. E. Pron.* I. iii. (1869) 160 All polysyllables ending in obscure *o* have *w* added for ornament's sake as *arrow*, *bellows*, &c. 1796 PEGGE *Anonym.* (1809) 454 One would wonder how the *w* could ever come to be a letter in our language, for it is plainly nothing else but the *u* vowel; for..*will* spells will, as much as *will*. 1836 CAR. B. SOUTHEY *Birth-day* I. 37 And sprawling W's, and V's, and Y's, Gaped prodigiously. 1869 ELLIS *E. E. Pron.* I. iii. 187 In Europe (w) is thought to be peculiar to England...In Arabic however (w) is quite at home. *a* 1890 W. B. SCOTT *Autob.* (1892) I. ii. 29 He went over the letters, giving them the broad old Scotch pronunciation: A was *awe*, B was *bay*, C was *say*, and so on, ending with U sounded like *oo* in good, W as *duploo*, Z as *izzid*. 1899 *Allbutt's Syst. Med.* VII. 440 *note*, The voiceless *W* and the voiceless *L* have been given

above within brackets, the former being now almost confined to Scotland and the latter being peculiar to Wales.

2. The letter considered with regard to its shape. Also *attrib.*

1798 *Hull Advertiser* 28 July 2/1 Chairs in sets..with W, tableau and X backs. 1871 *Cassell's Nat. Hist.* I. 266 The molars show sharp tubercles separated by transverse furrows, generally producing a sort of W-like pattern on each tooth. 1882 FLOYER *Unexpl. Baluchistan* 17 The walls..are.. rendered ornamental by triangular recesses fitting one into another like an endless W, each triangle being filled up with lines of smaller W's.

3. Abbreviations. W. = various personal names, as William, Walter, Winifred; † W. (*Calendar*) = Whitsunday; W. = West (W.N.W. west-north-west, W.S.W. west-south-west; W.C. the West Central postal district of London); W (*Chem.*) = tungsten (mod.L. *wolframium*); W (*Electr.*) = watt; W.C. = water-closet; W.I. = West Indies; W.S. (*Scotland*) = Writer to the Signet.

1513 SIR E. HOWARD in *Lett. & Papers War France* (1897) 94 The wynd feeryd owt off the W.N.W. into the E.N.E. *c* 1565 *Gude & Godlie Ball.* (S. T. S.) Calendar 1 2 b, Ye shal finde..at the 29. of April this letter W where begine for Whitsonday. 1708 *Lond. Gaz.* No. 4422/7 We came to an Anchor about Noon, the Wind at W. by S. 1778 *Engl. Gazetteer* (ed. 2) s. v. *Fale*, It rises about 2 miles W. of Roche Hills. 1815 *Corr. W. Fowler* (1907) 330 Apparatus for W.C. at Normanby, which had to come from London. *a* 1874 R. CHAMBERS in *Casq. Lit.* Ser. II. I. 262/1 Served a regular apprenticeship to a double-you-ess. 1891 W. CLARK RUSSELL *Marriage at Sea* v, The..compass was about W. S. W. 1892 EMINSON *Epidemic Pneumonia at Scotter* 11 No W.C. or slaughter-house drains into them.

W, obs. form of HOW *adv.*

Wa: see WAW, WAY, WHA *int.*, WOE.

Wa', Sc. form of WALL.

Waa, north. form of WAY, WHA *int.*, WOE.

Waaffery, Waale, obs. ff. WAFERY, WALE *sb.*[1]

Waam, var. WAME, north. form of WOMB.

Waam(m)le, var. WAMBLE *v.*

Waand, var. WONDE *v. Obs.*, to fear, hesitate.

Waar, -ness: see WARE, -NESS.

Waarnyng, obs. form of WARNING.

Waast, obs. form of WAIST, WASTE.

Waat, obs. pa. pple. of WET *v.*

Wab, north. form of WEB.

Wabain, Wabaio: see OUABAIO.

Wabble: see WOBBLE.

Wabble, var. WARBLE.

Wabster, north. form of WEBSTER.

Wac, obs. form of WEAK *a.*

†**Wacadash.** *Obs.* Also 7 **wacca-, waka-, wag(g)adash, wakedas(s)h.** [a. Japanese *wakizashi*.] A Japanese short sword.

1613 W. EATON in W. Foster *Lett. recd. E. Ind. Co.* (1897) II. 20 He had given her his wacadash or little catton. 1613 J. SARIS *Voy. Japan* (Hakl. Soc.) 124 Next those weapons resembling a Welch-hooke called Waggadashes. 1615 R. COCKS *Diary* (1883) I. 81, 10 pike heades, 100 arowheades, and three waccadashes. 1615 W. ADAMS *Log-bk.* (1916) 34 Kattannes wakedasshes and pikes. 1620 *Will of W. Adams* in *Athenæum* (1910) 21 May 610/1, I..bequeath vnto..Richard Cock..my best Cattane the other of my Cattans and wagadashes I..bequeath vnto my aforesaid sonne Joseph.

Wacance, -and: see VACANCE, VACAND.

Wacche, -man, obs. forms of WATCH, -MAN.

Wace, obs. f. *was*, pa. t. of BE *v.*

c 1380 *Sir Ferumb.* 389, 421.

Wace, Wach: see WAX *sb.*, WASH *v.*

Wach(e, -man, obs. forms of WATCH, -MAN.

Wachel, wachle, var. forms of WAUCHLE.

Wachet(t, obs. forms of WATCHET.

Wacht, obs. f. WAUGHT *sb.* and *v.*, *Sc.* and *north.*

Wack: see WAK, WAKE, WALK *v.*[2], WHACK.

Wacke (wæ·kə). *Geol.* Also 9 **wacca, wake, wacké.** [a. Ger. *wacke*, dial. *wake* (MHG. *wacke* large stone, OHG. *waggo* pebble), a miners' word, adopted by Werner as a geological term.] A sandstone-like rock, resulting from the decomposition of basaltic rocks *in situ*. Cf. GRAUWACKE, GREYWACKE.

1803 tr. *Pallas' Trav.* II. 115 The calcareous rock above described..sometimes also occurs under the form of Wacca, which is again composed of gritty fragments, caused by the destructive effects of past ages. 1811 PINKERTON *Petral.* I. 171 Two [German] papers..'On argillaceous schistus, hornslate, and on wake'. 1816 P. CLEAVELAND *Min.* 284 Basalt often forms one member of a series, beginning with gravel, sand, and clay; this clay gradually becomes less sandy and harder, till it passes into wacke, and the wacke is by insensible degrees lost in Basalt. 1839 MURCHISON *Silurian Syst.* I. xxxvi. 499 The chief portion of the hill consists of a dull rotten wacke.

†**Wa·cken.** *Geol. Obs.* [app. a. G. *wacken-*, combining form of *wacke*: see prec.] = WACKE.

1796 KIRWAN *Elem. Min.* (ed. 2) I. 219 [Basaltine] is most found in basalts, wacken, and lava. 1802 PLAYFAIR *Illustr. Hutton. Theory* 67 The wacken, mullen and crag of Kirwan.

b. Comb.: **wacken porphyry.**

1796 KIRWAN *Elem. Min.* (ed. 2) I. 355 Wacken Porphyry. 1807 HEADRICK *Arran* 61 The hills at the head of Glencloy are composed of wacken porphyry.

Hence **Wackeni·tic** *a.*, of the nature or composition of wacke.

1866 LAWRENCE tr. *Cotta's Rocks Classified* (1878) 88 We shall use the adjective 'wackenitic' to designate this [decomposed] state of those rocks.

Wacker, var. WHACKER.

Wackerell, var. WAKERELL, Sanctus bell.

Wad (wǫd), *sb.*[1] Also 7 **wadd(e, wade.** [Of obscure origin; the identity of the word in all the senses is not quite certain.

With sense 3 cf. mod. Sw. *vadd*, G., Du. *watte*, Fr. *ouate* (whence It. *ovatta*), wadding; the etymology and mutual relation of these words are unknown.]

1. A bundle of hay or straw (occas. of hemp, etc.); esp. a small bundle of hay, peas, beans, vetches, etc., made at the time of cutting or reaping; a portion of a sheaf of cereal plants or of reed. Now *dial.*

1573 TWYNE *Æneid* XI. 26 Hereon the lad aloft on wad of cuntrey straw they lay. 1596 SPENSER *Hymn Heav. Love* 226 Where he encradled was In simple cratch, wrapt in a wad of hay. 1601 HOLLAND *Pliny* XVII. ix. I. 503 When it [a crop of lupines] is cut downe, to make it into wads or bottles, and so to burie them at the roots of trees. 1620 MARKHAM *Farew. Husb.* ix. 65 Laying before the Plow long wades or roules of the straw of Lupyns, Pease, or else Fetches,..you shall turne the furrowes..vpon the waddes. 1622 J. TAYLOR (Water-P.) *Arrant Thief* (1625) C 2, A wispe of Rushes, or a clod of land, Or any wadde of Hay that's next to hand They'l steale. 1647 TRAPP *Comm.* 1 *Cor.* vii. 31 In the Popes in-thronization,..a piece of tow, or wad of straw is set on fire before him, and one appointed to say, *Sic transit gloria mundi.* 1693 EVELYN *De la Quint. Compl. Gard.* Dict., To wrap up Plants, or tender Trees with Wads or Wisps of Straw. 1706 ESTCOURT *Fair Example* III. i, You shall find her upon a Wad of Straw, with one Brat at her Breast. 1763 *Museum Rust.* I. 24 The reapers lay it on the land in wads as they call them, or parcels about the quantity of half a sheaf of wheat unbound. 1799 WOLCOT (P. Pindar) *Nil Admirari* III. iii. Wks. 1816 III. 447 At times she finds of hemp a little wad, Begs some young Levite spin it. 1807 SIR R. C. HOARE *Tour Irel.* 302 A wad of straw, or perhaps heath laid on a damp clay floor. 1813 VANCOUVER *Agric. Devon* 123 A cylindrical pearl barley machine, is also used to cleanse the wad of its smut. 1886 *W. Somerset Word-bk.*, *Wad*, a bundle of straw tied up by a thatcher....A bundle of reed less than a full sheaf of 28 lbs. weight is also called a wad.

fig. 1607 HEYWOOD *Fayre Mayde Exch.* I. C 2 b, Yonder bundle of sighes, yonder wad of grones.

b. A heap; also, a swath. *dial.*

1750 ELLIS *Mod. Husb.* IV. iii. 51 [To mow vetches] cock them in little wads as we do the Clover-grass. 1805 R. W. DICKSON *Pract. Agric.* II. 589 It is the usual practice to put them [cut pea crops] up into small heaps, termed wads, which are formed by setting small parcels against each other. 1856 J. C. MORTON *Cycl. Agric.* II. 726 *Wad*, a heap of beans or pease laid out to dry, previous to binding. In the county of Devon, applied to a handful of thatch. 1906 *Times* 25 June 14/4 The wet wads formed by the horse rake are avoided.

2. A small bundle of a soft, flexible material; esp. for use as a plug, pad, or rubber.

1580 HOLLYBAND *Treas. Fr. Tong*, *Torche*..a wad of strawe or cloutes that wenches vse to put on their heds when they cary any thing. 1622 MABBE tr. *Aleman's Guzman d'Alf.* II. 355 It was injoyned me..of old ends of Ragges, or of Flax and Tow, to make wads and wisps for those that goe to the Long-house. 1752 SIR H. BEAUMONT *Crito* 17 The vast Wad of Linen that they [women] carry upon their Head. 1781 HAYLEY *Tri. Temper* IV. 85 She on the types her inky wad let fall. 1861 MUSGRAVE *By-Roads* 173 The neck of the flask being closed with only a mere wad of cotton. 1887 *Poor Nellie* (1888) 398 I've to go about with wads of cotton-wool ready in my pocket for my two ears.

b. Something rolled up tightly, as a roll of bank notes. Chiefly *U.S.*

1778 *Exmoor Scolding* Gloss. (E. D. S.) 151 A garment rumbled [*sic*] up to a Wad, with many Plaits and Wrinkles. 1864 SALA in *Daily Tel.* 27 Sept., A little wallet containing one or more dollar bills, or at least a wad of fractional currency. 1888 *Bow-Bells Weekly* 22 June 396 Never roll gloves into each other in a wad, for they will never look as well after. 1890 GUNTER *Miss Nobody* ii. (1891) 24 Handing Everett a wad of greenbacks. 1899 MRS. F. H. BURNETT *De Willoughby Claim* x. 132 He..finally rolled his paper into a hard wad and threw it at the counter. 1899 CROCKETT *Kit Kennedy* lii, MacWalter pulled a thick wad of bank notes out of his pocket. 1908 S. E. WHITE *Riverman* xix, Dabbing at her eyes with a handkerchief dampened into a tiny wad.

transf. 1895 HOWELLS *Impress. & Exp.* (1896) 164 Such a small, dull wad of out-worn womanhood!—her grey old head bent upon her knees, and her withered arms wound in her thin shawl. 1913 *Sat. Rev.* 22 Mar. 365/2 He will find them well padded by wads of extracts from second-hand authorities.

†**3.** A material composed of matted fibres of silk, raw cotton, etc. = WADDING 3. *Obs.*

1540 *Act 32 Hen. VIII* c. 14 Item for every tonne Tolose wadde accompting viij hole bales..for a tonne xx s. 1695 P. MOTTEUX *St. Olon's Morocco* 139 The Traffick of Provence consists in..Velvet, Cottons, Wadds [Fr. *cottonines*], and other Commodities from the Levant. 1706 PHILLIPS (ed. Kersey), *Wad*, a sort of Flocks of Silk, course Flannel, or Cotton. 1761 *Ann. Reg.*, *Chron.* 132/1 The plant known by the name of..*Asclepias*...From the silky wad it affords we [in France] call it *Soyeuse*.

4. A plug of tow, cloth, etc., a disk of felt or cardboard, to retain the powder and shot in position in charging a gun or cartridge.

1667 *Phil. Trans.* II. 476 Another [experiment]..is a Wooden Tampion..hollow'd towards the Bullet,..and.. hollow likewise towards the Powder, and serving instead of a Wadd. 1669 STURMY *Mariner's Mag.* V. xii. 68 Put the Powder home gently, and after put in a good Wad..; then put in the Shot.., and after him another Wad. 1769 FALCONER *Dict. Marine* (1780), *Wad*, a quantity of old rope-yarns, hay, &c. rolled firmly together into the form of a ball, and used to confine the shot or shell..in the breech of a piece of artillery. 1856 'STONEHENGE' *Brit. Sports* I. I. ii. § 5. 24 After using the powder-flask..drive down..a single piece of wadding; then pour in the charge of shot, drive down another wad, [etc.]. 1862 F. A. GRIFFITHS *Artil. Man.* (ed. 9) 112 No. 5 serves No. 3 with projectiles, wads, if necessary, and traverses. 1879 *Cassell's Techn. Educ.* I. 194/1 The escape of gas was prevented by means of a felt wad attached to the back of the cartridge. 1881 GREENER *Gun* 300 Wads are punched out of sheets of various materials by cutters fixed in a press. Those most commonly used are made of felts, cardboard, or jute. 1890 D. DAVIDSON *Mem. Long Life* ii. 34 We..rowed too closely past the *Victory* as she was firing her royal salute, and one of her wads just cleared our heads.

5. A lump of a soft or plastic substance. *rare.*

1775 SHERIDAN *Duenna* III. vii, Eyes like two dead beetles in a wad of brown dough! 1838 THACKERAY *Fashnable Fax* Wks. 1900 XIII. 254 The haldermin, who was helpin the tuttle, puts on Biffeter's plate a wad of green fat.

b. A mass, heap, large quantity. *Sc.* and *north.*

1828 *Craven Gloss.*, *Wad*, a large quantity. 'We've a wad o' hay to year.' 1915 *Chamb. Jrnl.* 12 June 442/1 True, we haven't got a great wad of it on hand; but I don't like the idea of that silver being on the premises.

6. *Ceramics.*

1825 J. NICHOLSON *Oper. Mech.* 468 When a sagger is filled with clay ware, on its outer edges are placed thick pieces of coarse clay, called *wads* from their being employed to wedge or closely join the interstice between two saggers. 1891 *Century Dict.*, *Wad*, 3. In *ceram.*, a small piece of finer clay used to cover the body of an inferior material in some varieties of earthenware; especially, the piece doubled over the edge of a vessel.

7. *attrib.* and *Comb.*: (sense 4) as *wad gauge*, *punch*, *room*; **wad hook**, (*a*) a spiral tool for withdrawing wads or charges from guns; (*b*) *Mining* (see quot. 1881).

1828 SPEARMAN *Brit. Gunner* (ed. 2) 73 *Wad Gauges. 1611 FLORIO, *Cauafieno*, Gunners call it a *wad-hooke. 1766 ENTICK *London* IV. 344 Rammers, hand-spikes, wad-hooks. 1879 *Man. Artill. Exerc.* 199 The shell extractor and wadhook [are placed] outside the pit. 1881 RAYMOND *Mining Gloss.*, *Wad-hook.* A tool with two spiral steel blades for removing fragments from the bottom of deep bore-holes. 1875 KNIGHT *Dict. Mech.*, **Wad-punch*, a tubular steel punch used for cutting gun-wads, etc. 1756 *Gentl. Mag.* XXVI. 426 His gunner concealed 43 barrels of powder in the *wad room, covering them with wads and lumber.

Wad (wǫd), *sb.*[2] In 7 **wadd.** [Perh. cogn. w. ON. *vað-r* masc., measuring line, MSw. *vaþi* wk. masc., boundary-line between properties (cf. sense 2 below), or with OE. *wadan* to go, WADE *v.*]

1. *Surveying.* A straight line taken in measuring from one mark to another. ? *Obs.*

1610 W. FOLKINGHAM *Feudigr.* II. iv. 53 These dimensions are found or performed either *Cominus* or *Eminus*...The first..needes no amplification, but for precise keeping in the Wadd or right line. The Wadd is delineated either to a marke in sight or out of sight. If the First; let the Chaine-leaders Wadd vpon the marke by some intermediall eminence and at the setting down of euery pricke, let each man waue his mate into the right Wadd.

2. *dial.* 'A line, esp. one marked out between two parcels of land' (*Eng. Dial. Dict.*); also see quots.

1869 *Lonsdale Gloss.*, *Wad*, a line or rank. 1886 *S. W. Linc. Gloss.*, *Wad*, a mark set up as a guide to plough straight by. Hence Line, order, position. 1889 *N. W. Linc. Gloss.*, *Wad*, a mark in shooting, ploughing, land measuring, &c.

b. Way or course of travel, track. *lit.* and *fig.*

1854 MISS A. E. BAKER *Northampt. Gloss.*, *Wad*, 3. A way or beaten track, a line of conduct pertinaciously adhered to. 'He goes on in the old wad,' i.e. in the same manner as formerly.

3. *Comb.*: **wad-staff, -stick** (see quots.).

1856 J. C. MORTON *Cycl. Agric.* II. 726 *Wadstaff*, (Notts.), guide staff to plough by. 1889 *N. W. Linc. Gloss.*, *Wad-staff*, *wad-stick*, a tall white wand painted with rims of various colours, used as a mark for ploughmen in setting out furrows.

Wad (wǫd), *sb.*[3] Also 7 **wadt,** 8 **wadd.** [Of obscure origin.]

1. A local name for plumbago or black lead; also called *black wad.* Also *dial.* a black-lead pencil (see *Eng. Dial. Dict.*).

1614 in *Mem. Lit. & Philos. Soc. Manch.* Ser. II. (1819) III. 169 Except the wad holes and wad, commonly called black cawke, within the commons of Seatollor, or elsewhere within the commons and wastes of the said manor [of Borrowdale]. 1698 PLOT *Black-lead* in *Phil. Trans.* XX. 183 The Mineral Substance, called, Black Lead...found only at Keswick in Cumberland, and there called, *Wadt*, or *Kellow*. 1876 *Penny Cycl.* V. 225 (Borrowdale) The most remarkable product of the valley is graphite, plumbago, or black-lead (provincially wad). 1872 JENKINSON *Guide Eng. Lakes* (1879) 129 The lead, or plumbago, locally termed 'wad,'..is the best material ever discovered for making lead pencils.

2. An impure earthy ore of manganese.

1783 *Phil. Trans.* LXXIII. 284 Some Experiments upon the Ochra friabilis nigro fusca of Da Costa..; and called by the Miners of Derbyshire, Black Wadd. 1796 KIRWAN *Elem. Min.* (ed. 2) II. 465 Mr. Wedgewood dissolved a quantity of black wadd in a large quantity of nitrous acid heated. 1839 URE *Dict. Arts*, *Wadd*, is the provincial name..of an ore of manganese in Derbyshire, which consists of the peroxide of that metal, associated with nearly its own weight of oxide of iron. 1884 *Athenæum* 16 Aug. 212/3 The not very interesting manganese mineral wad.

3. *Comb.*, as (sense 1) *wad-hole*, *-lead*, *-mine*, *-pencil*.

1614 *Wad hole [see 1]. 1780 G. JARS *Voy. Metall.* II. 554 (*Philol. Soc. Trans.* 1908, p. 148) Mine de plomb pour les crayons nommés Black-lead or *Wad-Lead. 1747 *Gentl. Mag.* XVII. 583 *Wadd mines in the Cumberland Dialect, signifies the black-lead mines. 1836 *Penny Cycl.* V. 225 (Borrowdale) The wad mine. 1825 BROCKETT *N. C. Gloss.* s.v., A *wad pencil.

†**Wad,** *sb.*[4] *Obs. rare*⁻¹. Origin and sense obscure: only in proverbial phrase, app. meaning 'in that course there is danger'.

1524 WOLSEY in *St. Papers Hen. VIII*, IV. 92 Praying you eftsones, that the ereccion of the yong King be not dilayed by any diet to be kept upon the Bordre or other communicacion; for in that pad there lyeth a wad.

Wad (wǫd), *v.*[1] Also 6 **wadde.** [f. WAD *sb.*[1]]

I. To form into a wad.

1. *trans.* To lay up (the cut haulm of beans, peas, etc.) in bundles.

1677 PLOT *Oxfordsh.* ix. § 101. 256 After the sithe they wad both Beans and Peas. 1733 W. ELLIS *Chiltern & Vale Farm.* 341 They take care to Wad them [*sc.* beans] as soon as Mown, and put them into single small Parcels. 1778 [W. MARSHALL] *Minutes Agric.*, *Observ.* 93 In dry weather, Pease properly wadded with a Prong are much sooner ready to carry than those left in hard bundles by the Foot and Sithe. 1805 R. W. DICKSON *Pract. Agric.* II. 891 When..crops of this sort that have run to seed,..are left..it is the usual practice to cut and wad them in the same manner as for peas. 1813 T. BATCHELOR *View Agric. Bedfordsh.* 108 (E.D.D.) The process of wadding, and gleaning beans..is rather a tedious one.

2. To press (loose or fibrous material) into a small compass or into a close, compact mass; *U.S.* to roll up tightly. Also with *up*.

1675 EVELYN *Terra* (1776) 74 If you lay about them [*sc.* the roots] any fern-brakes or other trash capped with a little Earth..let it not be Wadded too close. 1896 *N. Y. Weekly Witness* 23 Dec. 16/4 A most peculiar cholera-remedy was in use in Persia. It consisted in wadding-up a leaf from the Koran and forcing it down the patient's throat. 1915 MRS. STRATTON-PORTER *M. O'Halloran* viii, 'Can you help me?' 'Sure I' said Mickey, wadding his cap into his back pocket.

3. *transf.* To pack (persons) closely.

1850 THACKERAY *Pendennis* lviii, An honest holiday-maker with his family wadded into a tax-cart.

II. To furnish with or as with a wad or wadding.

4. To put a wad in (a gun, a cartridge).

1579 DIGGES *Stratiot.* 113 His Gunner..to wadde and ramme, to cleanse, scoure, and coole the Peeces. 1881 GREENER *Gun* 301 When loaded with shot, the cartridges are wadded in the Erskine machine. 1894 CROCKETT *Mad Sir Uchtred* 83 He had wadded it [*sc.* a gun] with three leaves of the Bible.

5. To line, fill out, pad, as with wadding; to quilt.

1759 J. G. COOPER *Ver-Vert* IV. 212 His skin with sugar being wadded, With liquid fires his entrails burn'd. 1788 COWPER *Gratitude* 11 This wheel-footed studying chair,.. Wide-elbow'd, and wadded with hair. 1842 THACKERAY *Miss Tickletoby's Lect.* iii, Straight the King's great chair was brought him..Languidly he sunk into it, it was comfortably wadded. 1846 — *Bk. Snobs* xiv, Lord Glenlivat..playfully wadded the insides of the boots with cobbler's wax. 1848 — *Lett.* 1 Nov., You say your prayers in carved stalls wadded with velvet cushions. 1862 C. A. COLLINS *Cruise upon Wheels* xxiv. (1863) 413 My thick flannel dressing-gown, lined and wadded. 1883 MISS M. BETHAM-EDWARDS *Disarmed* xxiii, She wore a loose gown of crimson satin, wadded after the fashion of the olden time.

fig. 1871 GEO. ELIOT *Middlem.* xx, If we had a keen vision and feeling of all ordinary human life,..we should die of that roar which lies on the other side of silence. As it is, the quickest of us walk about well wadded with stupidity.

†**6.** ? To rub with a wad. *Obs.*

1688 HOLME *Armoury* III. xix. (Roxb.) 184/2 Wad or wash him [*sc.* a horse] round.

7. To plug (the ears) with wads.

1876 'OUIDA' *Winter City* iii, They have wadded their ears and..would not hear.

Wad (wǫd), *v.*[2] In 7 **wadd.** [f. WAD *sb.*[2]] *intr.* To walk with the chain in a straight line from one mark to another in land-surveying.

1610 W. FOLKINGHAM *Feudigr.* II. iv. 53 Let the Chaine-leaders Wadd vpon the marke by some intermediall eminence. 1688 HOLME *Armoury* III. 139/1 Geometrical Terms used in Surveying and Measuring of Lands...*Wadding*, keeping in a right Line. 1869 *Lonsdale Gloss.*, *Wad*, to set out a line, in land-surveying or engineering, by putting in a series of stakes or stubs.

Wad: see WED, WOAD; also WILL *v.*

Wadable, wadeable (wē^i·dăb'l), *a.* Also 7 *Sc.* **weadable.** [f. WADE *v.* + -ABLE.] That can be waded.

1611 FLORIO, *Vadasile*, foardable, wadable. 1611 COTGR., *Gayer*, a Foord, or wadeable passage ouer a riuer. *Ibid.*, *Gueable*, wadeable; fit, likely, or easie, to be waded ouer. 1622 MOLLE *Camerar. Liv. Libr.* IV. xx. 317 Vnderstanding that the Marishes were wadeable. 1693 J. FRASER in *W. Macfarlane's Geogr. Collect.* (S. H. S.) II. 218 Severid by a small streame weadable sometymes when it is low water. 1823 GALT *R. Gilhaize* xxii, As soon as the fugitives were within wadeable reach of the bank, they jumpit out of the boat. 1864 CARLYLE *Fredk. Gt.* XVII. vi. (1873) VII. 62 Where the Brook withal is of firmer bottom and more wadeable.

[**Wadage.** A spurious word, repr. AL. *vadia* 'wages' in the writ appointing a serjeant; the other words represent *feoda* 'fees', *vestura* 'vesture' and *regarda* 'rewards'.

1679 E. CHAMBERLAYNE *Pres. St. Eng.* II. (ed. 12) 262 Out of the Sergeants afore-mentioned, the King by Writ, usually calls some to be his Council at Law, allowing each one Wadage, Feodage, Vesturage, and Regardage.]

Wadd, obs. f. WAD; dial. form of WOLD.

Wadded (wǫ·dėd), *ppl. a.* Also 6 **wadid.** [f. WAD *v.*[1] + -ED[1].] Lined with wadding.

1595 *Acc. Bk. W. Wray* in *Antiquary* XXXII. 317, i pece wadded buffinge. *Ibid.* 281 Ite' i pece blacke wadid buffinge. 1710 STEELE *Tatler* No. 245 ⁋ 2 A thick wadded Callico Wrapper, [etc.]. 1835 *Ladies' Cabinet* Jan. 65 Wadded pelisses are expected to be very generally adopted. *Ibid.* Oct. 269 A white *gros de Naples* slip, which..had a deep wadded hem. 1880 'OUIDA' *Moths* I. 20, I thought Miladi was made..in Giroux's shop, and was kept in a wadded box when her mechanism was not wound up. 1890 D. DAVIDSON *Mem. Long Life* viii. 196 His costume..consisted of a hunting cap with a white wadded cover.

Wadder[1] (wǫ·dəɹ). [f. WAD *v.*[1] + -ER[1].]

†**1.** An implement for wadding a gun. *Obs.*

1579 DIGGES *Stratiot.* 115, I mighte here adioyne sundrye Tables..what Bullets, Wadders, Rammers, Ladles,..were conueniente to bee hadde in readinesse.

2. One who lays up (the cut haulm of beans, etc.) in bundles or 'wads'.

1763 *Museum Rust.* (ed. 2) I. 236 This..lays the beans in regular rows, and saves the expense of a wadder.

†**Wa·dder**[2]. *Land-surveying. Obs.* [f. WAD *v.*[2] + -ER[1].] One who is engaged in determining a 'wad' or line of direction.

1610 W. FOLKINGHAM *Feudigr.* II. iv. 53 If out of sight.. place two Assistants, the one at the marke, and the other at the eminentest Medium, and then your selfe standing at ..the station giuen, and the first Assistant erecting some visible obiect, waft the Wadders into the Wadd.

Wadder, obs. Sc. form of WETHER.

Waddie, Waddin, var. ff. WADDY, WALDIN.

Wadding (wǫ·diŋ), *vbl. sb.* [-ING[1].]

1. The action of WAD *v.*[1]

1778 [W. MARSHALL] *Minutes Agric.* 14 Sept. 1776, Whether the crop be thick or thin, Wadding puts it equally out of harm's way.

2. *concr.* Any soft, pliable material from which gun-wads are made; also, a wad.

1627 CAPT. J. SMITH *Sea Gram.* xiv. 66 Waddings is Okum, old clouts, or straw, put after the powder and the Bullet. 1664 PEPYS *Diary* 8 Nov., To the Office of the Ordnance, to discourse about wadding for guns. 1742 *Phil. Trans.* XLII. 175 The Waddings used in all these..Experiments, were of thick Leather cut round, to fit the Bore of the Piece. 1815 CROKER in *Croker Papers* (1884) I. iii. 73 The whole of the extent..was strewed with the cartridges and waddings of the cannon. 1833 *Reg. Instr. Cavalry* I. 31 The recruit is to be instructed..to ram the paper, as wadding, home. 1853 DICKENS *Bleak Ho.* liv, I found the wadding of the pistol with which the deceased Mr. Tulkinghorn was shot.

3. Any loose, fibrous material for use as a padding, stuffing, quilting, etc. Now chiefly, cotton-wool formed into a fleecy layer.

1734 *Grub St. Jrnl.* 2 May 4/1 Handsome Gowns for Ladies, with Silk Waddings. 1737 DYCHE & PARDON *Dict.*, *Wadding*, a thin, coarse, woollen Manufacture made to line Men's Morning Gowns, the Plaits of their Coats, &c. 1755 JOHNSON, *Wadding*, a kind of soft stuff loosely woven, with which the skirts of coats are stuffed out. 1784 COWPER *Task* I. 31 A generation more refin'd Improv'd the simple plan;..And o'er the seat, with plenteous wadding stuff'd, Induc'd a splendid cover. 1802 M. CUTLER in *Life, Jrnls. & Corr.* (1888) II. 113, I presented him a specimen of wadding for Ladies' cloaks. 1839 URE *Dict. Arts* s.v., Wadding [for garments] is now made with a lap or fleece of cotton prepared by the carding-engine, which is applied to tissue paper by a coat of size. 1865 *Routledge's Ev. Boy's Ann.* 493 A small ball of cotton wool or wadding enclosed in a piece of linen rag. 1902 HANNAN *Textile Fibres* 54 The raw material..when beaten out soft is used for wadding in clothing and coverlets. 1904 *Woollen Draper's Terms* in *Tailor & Cutter* 4 Aug. 480/2 Wadding: A loose fibrous material made of cotton waste; one side is finished with paper face; used for padding purposes.

fig. 1846 LANDOR *Imag. Conv.*, *Diogenes & Plato* Wks. I. 455/1 Aristoteles, and all the rest of you, must have the wadding of straw and saw-dust shaken out, and then we shall know pretty nearly your real weight and magnitude.

Waddle (wǫ·d'l), *sb.* [f. WADDLE *v.*]

1. The action of waddling; a waddling gait. Also, rate of progress by waddling.

1691 SHADWELL *Scowrers* II. i. 15 That must be my sweet Duckling—I know her by her pretty Waddle in her Gate. 1853 READE *Chr. Johnstone* ii. 38 A fisherman's natural waddle is two miles an hour. 1857 KINGSLEY *Two Yrs. Ago* xxv, The lighter woman's step was inaudible to Tom; but the heavy deliberate waddle of the banker was not. 1859 *Todd's Cycl. Anat.* V. 168/2 In the *Natatores*..the great intercotyloid distance gives to their gait its peculiar waddle.

fig. 1827 HOOD *Monkey-Martyr* 50 Striding with a step that seem'd design'd To represent the mighty March of Mind, Instead of that slow waddle Of thought, to which our ancestors inclined.

†**2.** The wane of the moon. *dial. Obs.*

[Perh. a distinct word: cf. OHG., MHG. *wadal*, MLG. *wadel* (:—*waþlo-*) phases or change of the moon.]

1678 *Ray's Prov.* (ed. 2) 343 Sow or set beans in Candlemas waddle, *i.e.* Wane of the Moon. Somerset.

Waddle (wǫ·d'l), *v.* Forms: 5 **wadill,** 6–8 **wadle,** 7– **waddle.** Also *quaddle*, QUODDLE. [freq. f. WADE *v.*: see -LE.]

†**1.** *intr.* ? To fall heavily or as an inert mass.

c 1400 *Song of Roland* 901 He rent hym vnredly euyn to the sadill: on ether sid of his horse doun did he wadill.

2. To walk with short steps, swaying alternately from one leg to the other, as is done by a stout short-legged person.

1592 SHAKS. *Rom. & Jul.* I. iii. 37 Then she could stand alone, nay bi' th' roode she could haue runne & wadled all about. 1620 J. TAYLOR (Water P.) *Jack a Lent* B 1 b, Alwayes before Lent there comes wadling a fat grosse burstengutted groome, called Shroue-Tuesday. 1681 T. D[URFEY] *Progr. Honesty* xii. 13 Next a fat Author wadled into view. 1760–2 GOLDSM. *Cit. W.* lxviii, This great man is short of stature, is fat, and waddles as he walks. 1809 MALKIN *Gil Blas* II. vii. ⁋ 20 The old procuress waddled out of sight. *c* 1860 B. HARTE *Arctic Vision* 1 Where the short-legged Esquimaux Waddle in the ice and snow. 1893 F. ESPINASSE *Lit. Recoll.* ii. 14 So fat that he waddled rather than walked.

b. said of animals; esp. of ducks or geese.

1611 COTGR., *Caneter*, to waddle, or goe, like a ducke. 1691 *Lond. Gaz.* No. 2686/4 She [a mare] wadles in her Trot. 1728–42 POPE *Dunc.* II. 63 As when a dab-chick waddles through the copse On feet and wings. 1819 CRABBE *Tales of Hall* XIII. 516 And a fat spaniel waddled at his side. 1840 DICKENS *Old C. Shop* xv, Ducks and geese..waddling awkwardly about the edges of the pond. 1845 J. COULTER *Adv. in Pacific* ix. 115, I caught sight of a huge seal waddling up out of the water. 1888 F. HUME *Mme. Midas* II. i, The parrot..waddled clumsily across the table to the inkstand.

c. *transf.* said of things.

1728 POPE *Dunc.* I. 172 Like bias to the bowl, Which, as more pond'rous, made its aim more true, Obliquely wadling to the mark in view. 1858 *Straith's Fortif. & Artillery* (ed. 7) II. 121 The nave need not be more than 12 or 14 inches in length; if too short, the wheel would waddle (or, as it is sometimes called, wabble).

†**d.** *Stock Exchange slang.* To become a 'lame duck' or defaulter (see DUCK *sb.*[1] 9). In full, *to waddle out*. *Obs.*

1771 GARRICK *Prol. to Foote's Maid of B.* 31 Change-Alley bankrupts waddle out lame ducks! 1799 in *Spirit Publ. Jrnls.* III. 72 A *bear* who pretends to sell what he is not possessed of, and is obliged frequently to *waddle out* at a great loss. 1814 *Stock Exch. Laid Open* 20 A Jobber was never known to waddle (to be a lame duck). 1823 'JON BEE' *Dict. Turf*, s.v., Jobbers, usually brokers, who cannot make good their engagements for the delivery of stock, or run short in funds to pay for what they have bought,..become lame ducks and waddle out. 1834 MARRYAT *P. Simple* lxv, He's been neither bull nor bear for these three years. He was obliged to *waddle*.

†**3.** *trans.* ? To cause to wallow *in*. *Obs.*

1569 CROWLEY *Sophistrie Dr. Watson* ii. 26 We, whom you would haue men thinke to be defiled with it, are cleare from it, and you your selfe most filthily wadled in it.

4. Of animals: To trample or tread down (grass). Now *dial.*

1627 DRAYTON *Moon-Calf* Batt. Agincourt, etc. 183 They tread and waddle all the goodly grasse, That in the field there scarse a corner was Left free by them.

†**5.** ? To delude, befool. *Obs.*

1606 N. B[AXTER] *Sydney's Ourania* I 4, Browne Paper, Lute-strings, buckles for a Saddle, Perwigs, Tiffany, Paramours to waddle.

Waddle, obs. and dial. f. WATTLE.

Waddler (wǫ·dləɹ). [f. WADDLE *v.* + -ER[1].] A person or animal that waddles.

1828 *Lights & Shades* II. 121 A basket containing half a dozen defunct waddlers [ducks]. 1830 J. WILSON in *Blackw. Mag.* XXVIII. 849 A flock of those noisy waddlers [geese]. 1859 *Sporting Mag.* July 3 Many thought Musjid [a race-horse] a 'waddler' with his hind legs. 1893 EARL DUNMORE *Pamirs* I. 143 These waddlers had waddled sufficiently.

b. A defaulter (see WADDLE *v.* 2 d).

1831 *Westm. Rev.* XV. 208 Were he of the Stock Exchange he would rail against waddlers and men of straw.

Waddling (wǫ·dliŋ), *ppl. a.* [-ING[2].] That waddles (see the verb).

1662 GURNALL *Chr. in Arm.* III. verse 17. xii. § 5. 90 Thus the little wadling child comes to go strongly, by going often. 1678 OTWAY *Friendship in F.* IV. i, You..Addle-pated, wadling brace of Puppies. 1714 GAY *Sheph. Week* iii. 62 Let the fox..join in wedlock with the waddling goose. 1729 T. COOKE *Tales*, etc. 96 A short squad Figure, with a wadling Pace. 1863 GEO. ELIOT *Romola* lvi, She saw..a little child ..pause from a waddling run and look around him.

Hence **Wa·ddlingly** *adv.*

1882 O'DONOVAN *Merv Oasis* I. i. 23 Great flocks of wild geese marched waddlingly on either side.

Waddy (wǫ·di). *Austral.* Also 9 **waddie, whaddie.** [In use among Australian aboriginals; perh. a native word, but possibly a corruption of Eng. *wood*.] An aboriginal war-club.

'The word is sometimes used for a walking-stick' (Morris).

1814 FLINDERS *Voy.* II. 189 Something resembling the *whaddie*, or wooden sword of the natives of Port Jackson. 1818 OXLEY *Jrnls. Two Exped. N. S. Wales* (1820) 226 After beating their spears and waddies together for about a quarter of an hour,..they went away. 1852 MUNDY *Our Antipodes* iv. (1855) 101 The waddy is a heavy, knobbed club, about two feet long. 1890 'R. BOLDREWOOD' *Col. Reformer* xviii, Blows from the unerring waddy. 1892 J. FRASER *Aborigines of N. S. Wales* 74 A general name for all Australian clubs is 'waddy', and, although they are really clubs, they are often used as missiles in battle.

attrib. *a* 1904 W. CRAIG *Adv. Austral. Goldf.* 283 The waddy blows inflicted..resulted in terrible injuries.

Hence **Wa·ddy** *v. trans.*, to strike, beat, or kill, with a waddy.

1855 LD. SHERBROOKE *Poems* (1885) 100 The black thieves appeared, My shepherds they waddied, my cattle they speared. 1869 HUXLEY *Let.* 25 June in L. Huxley *Life & Lett.* (1903) I. xiii. 252 The fellows who waddied the Amphitherium and speared the Phascolotherium. 1890 *Melbourne Argus* 16 Aug. 4/8 He waddied Kate pretty near to death when he got to camp that night.

†**Wade,** *sb.*[1] *Obs.* [= MLG. *wade*, MHG., mod.G. *wate* fem., seine; cf. ON. *vaðr* masc., fishing-line, Sw. *vad* masc., Norw. *vad* neut., Da. *vod* seine.] Some kind of fishing net. Also *wade-net*.

1388–9 *Acc. Obedientiars Abingdon* (Camden) 57, j rete vocatum wade et j flowe, cum alio rete vocato chanenet. 1630 in *Binnell's Descr. Thames* (1758) 75 Nor shall fish ..except with a Wade Net for Bait only.

Wade (wē^i d), *sb.*[2] *rare.* [f. WADE *v.*] An act of wading.

1665 BRATHWAIT *Comment Two Tales* 166 It is a dear wade, when your Life lies upon the last Stake. 1904 *Daily Chron.* 7 May 5/2 The Japanese..have already begun to erect piers so as to avoid the necessity of that long wade.

Wade (wē^i d), *v.* Pa. t. and pa. pple. **waded.** Forms: 1 **wadan,** 4–6 *Sc.* **waid, vaid, vayd,** 8 *Sc.* **wide,** 6 **waade,** 3– **wade.** *Pa. t.* 1 **wód,** 3 **wode,** (4 **woude),** 4–6 **wod,** 6 *Sc.* **woed, woide, woyd;** 6– **waded.** *Pa. pple.* 4 **waad, wad,** 8 *Sc.* **wid,** 7 **wade,** 6– **waded.** [A Com. Teut. (orig. strong) verb (not recorded in Gothic): OE. *wadan* (also *gewadan*), pa. t. *wód*, pl. **wódon*, pa. pple. **gewaden*, corresp. to OFris. *wada* str. vb. (WFris. *wâdsje* wk., NFris. *waar* str., to wade), MDu. *waeden* str., later wk. (Du. *waden* wk.) to wade, MLG. *waden* str. and wk. (LG. *waden*, *waen* wk.) to wade, OHG. *watan* str., to go, press forward, wade (MHG., mod.G. *waten* wk., to wade), ON. *vaða* str., to go through, wade (Norw. *vada*, *vadda*, *vaa* str., Sw. *vada*, Da. *vade* wk., to wade), f. OTeut. **wad-*: **wōd-*:— pre-Teut. **wădh-* = L. *vādĕre* to go, proceed, walk. The root, which occurs only in Teut. and L., is represented also by the sb. OE. *wæd*, ON. *vað*, L. *vadum* neut., ford, shallow water.

The mod. Eng. specific sense, 'to walk in water', though prominent in the other Teut. langs., is not recorded in OE. (unless perhaps in the compound *oferwadan* OVERWADE *v.*). In OE. the vb. is almost confined to poetical use.

The strong inflexion became obsolete in the 16th c.]

1. *intr.* To go (physically). †**a.** Of persons and animals: To go, advance, move onward; *chiefly*, to go *over* or *through* something. *Obs.*

Beowulf 2661 [He] wod þa þurh ðone wælrec. *a* 1000 *Andreas* 1271 (Gr.) Ða com hæleða þreat wadan. *c* 1375 *Sc. Leg. Saints* xxviii. (*Margaret*) 250 Þi mawmentis.. gerris in hel þare makaris wad. *Ibid.* xxix. (*Placidas*) 750 As he towart me cuth wad, a gredy wolf hynt me. *a* 1400 *Alexius* (MS. Laud 622) 548 Alexius fer and ner gan wade, For nouȝth wolde he spare. 1581 STYWARD *Mart. Discipl.* I. 85 You maie send certaine rankes of Pikes vnto the Front towards the enimie, which shall wade through to strengthen the battaile. *c* 1648–50 BRATHWAIT *Barnabees Jrnl.* IV. (1818) 153 Farewell,..Steepy wayes by which I waded, And those trugs with which I traded.

†**b.** Of inanimate things, esp. of a weapon: To go *through*, to penetrate *into* something. *Obs.*

993 *Battle of Maldon* 157 Ord in ȝewod. *c* 1290 *S. Eng. Leg.* 69/51 Þe harde scourgene in is tendre flechs deope gonne wade. *c* 1300 *Havelok* 2645 He..bi þe shu[l]dre blade þe sharpe swerd let wade þorw the brest unto þe herte. 13.. *Northern Passion* II. 138/1210 *a* Þe þornes wode in his flesse. *c* 1386 CHAUCER *Monk's T.* 504 Whan myght is ioyned vn-to crueltee Allas to depe wol the venym wade. *c* 1400 *Rowland & O.* 478 Thurgh the horse schuldirs the swerde gan wade.

†**2.** *fig.* To go (in action, thought, or discourse); to proceed. *Obs.*

Often difficult to distinguish from 3 c, in which it ultimately merged.

c 1374 CHAUCER *Troylus* II. 150 They..gonnen wade In meny an uncouthe glad and depe matere, As freendes don, whan they ben met yfere. 1412–20 LYDG. *Chron. Troy* II. 5762, I holde hym eke vnable To ben acceptid..Whan þat her tonge wadeth on þe lye. *c* 1440 CAPGRAVE *St. Kath.* 1624 What wil ȝe ferthere in this mater wade? *c* 1535 FISHER *Wks.* (E. E. T. S.) 441 To reherse his reasons, and so waade in this matter with them, it were inough for an holle daye. 1538 BALE *Thre Lawes* 1029 Lucifer I made So hyghly to wade To God he wolde be equall. 1549 LATIMER *1st Serm. bef. Edw. VI* (Arb.) 22, I might seme.. to take this parte of scripture because I woulde wade easilye awaye there wyth, and dryue my matter at my pleasure. 1568 GRAFTON *Chron.* II. 877 Which secret Serpent caused their furie to wade farther then reason could retract or restrayne. 1587 GOLDING *De Mornay* xxv. (1617) 424 Well may mans skill wade into weekes & moneths: but considering the vncertainty of worldly matters, it can neuer wade into yeeres. 1589 R. ROBINSON *Golden Mirr.* (Chetham Soc.) 60 Thy grace extend to guide my feete Least I should wade awry. 1605 VERSTEGAN *Dec. Intell.* vi. (1628) 156 Martin Luther wadeth further, and will haue England also to be a part of Germany. 1616 JAS. I *Sp. Star-Chamb.* 20 June D 2, That which concernes the mysterie of the Kings power, is not lawfull to be disputed, for that is to wade into the weakenesse of Princes. 1642–7 H. MORE *Song of Soul* II. iii. IV. xxxiv, If this Out-world continually hath wade Through a long long-spun-time. 1653 R. SANDERS *Physiogn.* 279, I have sufficiently waded in this various Doctrine. 1691 RAY *Creation* I. (1704) 64, I will not wade further into this Controversie. 1709 J. LOGAN in *Pennsylv. Hist. Soc. Mem.* X. 381 Thus far I have waded thro' some parts of his conduct in relation to the Proprietor.

†**b.** To 'go', be (in a certain condition), 'go about' (in certain attire). *Obs.*

1593 NORDEN *Spec. Brit.*, *Essex* (Camden) Introd. p. xii, Husbandmen..who wade in the weedes of gentlemen. 1576

Waft (wǒ·ft), *sb.* Also 6 **waftage.**

I. The action of wafting.

1. The action of conveying merchant-vessels.

2. Conveyance across water by ship or boat.

Wafter (wǒ·ftǝɹ), *sb.* [f. WAFT *v.* + -ER 1.] One who wafts.

Waftage (wǒ·ftǝdʒ). Also 6 **waftage.**

II. Vessels for the conveyance of merchandise or passengers by water.

Wafting, *ppl. a.* [-ING 2.] That wafts.

Wafture (wǒ·ftiǝɹ). In 7 **wafter.**

Wafty.

Waftage.

Wag (wæg), *sb.*[1] Also 6–7 **wagge.**

Wag, *sb.*[2], forms of WOEFUL *a.*

Wag, *v.* [ME. *waggen.*]

I. Intransitive uses.

II. Transitive uses.

Wagadash, Wagan: see WACADASH, WAGON.

+ Wagand, *var. wagand, pr. pple.* of VAGUE *v.*

Wage (wēdʒ), *sb.*

Wage (wēdʒ), *v.* Inflected **waging, waged.**

Supplement, p. 3873; Corrigenda, p. 4092; Spurious words, p. 4093; Books quoted, p. 4094

Wagon, waggon (wɐˈgən), v. [f. WAGON sb.]

Wagonage, waggonage (wɐˈgæˈnéd). [f. WAGON sb. + -AGE.]

Wagoner, waggoner (wɐˈgənəɹ). Obs.

Wagoner, waggoner. Also 6 waggon, 7 wagon. [f. WAGON sb. + -ER; perh. orig. a. Du. wagenaer (now waggoner) of equivalent formation.]

Wagonette, waggonette (wɐgɒnˈet). Also 9 wagonet. [f. WAGON sb. + -ETTE.]

Wagonful, waggonful (wɐˈgənful). Also -full.

Wagon-head, waggon-head. Arch. A

Wagoning, waggoning (wɐˈgəniŋ), vbl. sb. [f. WAGON v. + -ING.]

Wagon-load, waggon-load. As much as a wagon can carry.

Wagon-lit (vagɔ̃li). [Fr.: wagon railway carriage + lit bed.]

Wagonry, waggonry (wɐˈgənri), rare.

Wagon-way, waggon-way.

Waif (weif), sb. Pa. waife.

Wail (weil), sb. [f. WAIL v.]

Wail (weil), v. Forms: 3 weile, waile, 4-7 wayle, 4 waille, 6 waill, weale (wealle), 4-7 wale. [a. ON.]

Wailer (weiˈləɹ). [f. WAIL v. + -ER.]

Waileway, Wailaway var. of WELLAWAY.

Wailful (weilˈful), a. Chiefly poet. [f. WAIL sb. + -FUL.]

Wailing (weilˈiŋ), vbl. sb. [f. WAIL v. + -ING.]

Wailing, ppl. a.

Waily (weilˈi), a. [f. WAIL v. + -Y.]

Waiment (weiˈment), v. Obs. [ME. weimenten, etc.]

Waimenting, vbl. sb.

Wain (wein), sb. Forms: 1 wægn, wægen, wæn, wen, 3-5 wain(e), 4-7 wayn(e), 4-5 wayne, wan(e)... [OE. wægen, wæn.]

Wain (wein), v. Obs. [f. WAIN sb.]

Waining. Obs. Also 4 wamming, 5 mynge.

Waint. var. WAYMENT v. and sb. Obs.

used at Scoreby. 1868 ATKINSON *Cleveland Gloss.* s.v., The veritable Wain, now never seen, was a narrow, long-bodied vehicle, with two wheels only, and these at the hinder end. The front or foremost end trailed along the ground.

c. *poet.* A car or chariot. Chiefly *fig.* or in mythological use. In ME. often applied to the Four Gospels, symbolized as a four-horsed chariot (= L. *quadriga*).

c 1200 ORMIN Pref. 21 Þatt waȝȝn iss nemmnedd quaþþrigan Þatt hafeþþ fowwre wheless. a 1300 *Cursor M.* 21264 Four ar þai tald, þe wangelistes Þat draues þe wain þat es cristes. c 1380 WYCLIF *Wks.* (1880) 258 See now þe secunde wheel in þis deuelis wayn. 1412–20 LYDG. *Chron. Troy* I. 630 Wher halved is þe standyng estyval Of fresche Appollo with his golden Wayn. 1579 SPENSER *Sheph. Cal.* Jan. 74 Phœbus gan auaile, His weary waine. 1590 — *F. Q.* I. iv. 19 May seeme the wayne was very euill led When such an one had guiding of the way, That knew not, whether right he went, or else astray. 1638 R. BAKER tr. *Balzac's Lett.* (vol. III) 86 Not when the moon accomplishing her way Upon her silver wayne..presents the day. 1706 DE FOE *Jure Divino* II. 239 [They] jointly drive the Wain of Government. 1714 *Steele's Poet. Misc.* 112 He..charm'd the Wain of Night along, With his soft harmonious Song. 1885–94 BRIDGES *Eros & Psyche* April xx, They set on high upon the bridal wain Her bed for bier, and yet no corpse thereon.

Proverb. 13.. *All too Late* 7 in *Pol. Rel. & L. Poems* (1903) 250 Al to late. al to late. þen is te wayn atte yate. c 1420 WYNTOUN *Cron.* I. 640 Than to cry mercy is to lait, The wane þan standis at þe ȝate.

d. A wain-load, wagon-load.

1613 PURCHAS *Pilgrimage* IV. x. (1614) 395 Thither they bring euery yeare an hundred and fiftie waines of twigges.

† e. poet. *Winged wain*, a ship. *Obs.*

1598 SYLVESTER *Du Bartas* II. i. III. *Furies* 194 The Masters skilfull most, With gentle gales driv'n to the wished Coast, Not with lesse labour guide there winged wayns On th'azure fore-head of the liquid plains.

2. The group of seven bright stars in the constellation called the Great Bear: more fully CHARLES'S WAIN. *Lesser Wain*: the similarly shaped group of seven stars in the Little Bear.

OE. had *wǽnes þísl* or *þísla*, 'pole or poles of the wain'. With Scott's 'Arthur's slow wain' cf. 'Arthouris Plowe', Lydg. *Chron. Troy* I. 682; Arthur here represents Arcturus, regarded as the teamster or wagoner of the plough or wain.

c 888 ÆLFRED *Boeth.* xxxix. § 3 Swa swa tunglu..þe we hatað wænes ðisla. c 1374 CHAUCER *Boeth.* IV. met. v. 5 Who so þat..wot nat why þe sterre Bootes passeþ or gadereþ his weynes. 1555 EDEN *Decades* (Arb.) 280 We iudged them to bee the chariotte or wayne of the south. 1601 HOLLAND *Pliny* VI. xxii. I. 130 The starres about the North pole, called Septentriones, the Waines or Beares. 1669 STURMY *Mariner's Mag.* VI. 95 The..two Bears..Whose hinder parts and Tails contain The lesser and the greater Wain. 1703 POPE *Thebais* 521 When clouds conceal Boötes golden wain. 1805 SCOTT *Last Minstr.* I. xvii, Arthur's slow wain his course doth roll In utter darkness round the pole. 1812 CARY *Dante, Parad.* XIII. 7 The wain, that, in the bosom of our sky, Spins ever on its axle night and day. 1850 TENNYSON *In Mem.* ci, At noon or when the lesser wain Is twisting round the polar star. 1879 MISS JACKSON *Shropsh. Word-bk.* 437 *The-wain-and-horses*, sb., Ursa Major. 1887 BOWEN *Æneid* I. 744 Bright Arcturus, the showery Hyads, the Bear, and the Wain.

¶ 3. A rendering of L. *plaustrum* (lit. 'wagon') used in the Vulgate for a kind of thrashing instrument with wheels.

1382 WYCLIF *Isa.* xli. 15, I haue set thee as a newe wayn [1609 *Douay*, a newe threshing wayne] thresshende. 1778 LOWTH *Isa.* xxviii. 27–28 Nor is the wheel of the wain made to turn upon the cummin: But the dill is beaten out with the staff; And the cummin with the flail: but the bread-corn with the threshing-wain.

4. *attrib.* and *Comb.* a. Obvious combinations, as † *wain-axtree*, *-blade* (BLADE *sb.* 10 b), *-body*, † *-cart*, *-driver*, *-felloe*, † *-folk*, *-gear*, *-head* (also attrib.), *-horse*, *-load*, *-wheel*.

1559 *Richmond Wills* (Surtees) 136 One pare of newe car wheles, both *wane ashe tres [etc.]. 1557 *Ibid.* 101 A pare of *wayne blayds. 1390–91 *Durham Acc. Rolls* (Surtees) 392 In factura unius *waynbody, 6 d. a 1566 R. EDWARDS *Damon & P.* (facs.) F ij, One preached of late not farre hence, in no Pulpet, but in *Waayne carte, That spake enough of this. 1552 HULOET, *Wayne dryuer, *aurigarius*. 1360 *Priory of Finchale* (Surtees) p. liii, j gange de *wainefelies de fraxino. 1558 *Wills Northern C.* (Surtees) I. 162 Twoo gang of wayne fellowes wth heades and moldeburdes. 1641 BEST *Farm. Bks.* (Surtees) 53 It is a greate furtherance to have one to teame the waines whiles that the *wainefolkes are att breakefast. 1538 *Test. Ebor.* VI. 75 All maner of..*wayne geir. 1557 *Lanc. Wills* (Chetham Soc.) II. 128 Waynes and wayne geare. 1551 *Knaresb. Wills* (Surtees) I. 59 One *waynehedeyoke, one bolt and one shakill. 1557 *Richmond Wills* (Surtees) 101 One yron bound wayne..with wayne hed, [etc.]. 1562–3 *Durham Wills* (Surtees) III. 28 An yrone bounde wayne with a turne teame and a waine head shakle. 1727 E. LAURENCE *Duty of Steward* 71 The Steward should see that the *Wain-Horses and Oxen be muzzled, to prevent their cropping the young Springs. 1800 HURDIS *Favourite Village* 57 The stout wain-horse of encumbrance stript. 1577 B. GOOGE *Heresbach's Husb.* II. 101 b, An other [oak] in an other place, that being cutte out, made a hundred *Wayne lode. 1700 O. HEYWOOD *Diaries* (1885) IV. 238 A wainload of timber, 8 oxen and an horse. 1559 *Richmond Wills* (Surtees) 136 One pare of newe *waine wheles.

b. Special comb.: † **wain-beam**, the pole of a wagon (used to translate L. *temo*); † **wain-clout**, the iron covering for the axle-tree of a wagon (see CLOUT *sb.*[2] 2); † **wain-cope** (see quot. and COPE, COP *sb.*[4]); **wain-flakes** *dial.* [= MLG. *wagenvleke*], the movable side-boards of a wagon, used to increase its carrying capacity; † **wain-fork**, a fork used in the loading of a wagon; † **wain-gate**[1] [GATE *sb.*[1]], a gate for wains to pass through; † **wain-gate**[2] [GATE *sb.*[2]], a cart-track, wagon-road; **wain-house** (*obs.* exc. *dial.*), a wagon-house, cart-shed; † **wain-money**, ? tolls collected from wains (*E.D.D.*); † **wain-rake**, a rake used in the loading of a wagon with hay, etc.; † **wain-shackle**, ? a coupling for a wagon (see SHACKLE 6 a); **wain-stang** *dial.*, the projecting pole of a cart on either side of which oxen or horses may be yoked; † **wain-string**, ? = WAIN-ROPE; † **wain-stroke**, a curved segment forming part of the iron rim or tire of a wagon wheel (cf. STROKE *sb.*[4]); **wain-trees** *dial.*, the axle-beams supporting the wagon; † **wain-way**, a wagon-road; † **wain-weight**, ? a wagon-load.

1589 FLEMING *Virg. Georg.* III. 42 Let it creake afterwards, and let the brasen *wainbeame strong Draw both the wheels together ioind. 1650 HORN & ROB. tr. *Comenius' Gate Lang. Unl.* Foundat. T 9 One overcom with wine guid's the wain-beam [L. *temonem*] rashly. 1454 *Durham Acc. Rolls* (Surtees) 149, ij *wayneclowtez. 1523–34 FITZHERB. *Husb.* § 5 The wheles..must haue an axiltre, clout with .viii. wainclouts of yren. 1596 *Durham Wills* (Surtees) II. 259, v teames, ij horse-teames.., vij wayne cloutes [etc.]. 1688 HOLME *Armoury* III. 339/2 The *waine Cop, that part which the hinder Oxen are yoked unto to draw the Waine. 1726 *Dict. Rust.* (ed. 3) s.v. *Cart*, The Wain-Cope, is a long piece that comes out from the Wain-body, to which Oxen are fasten'd. 1570 *Richmond Wills* (1853) 101 In the yard and parke..a pare of *wayne fleaks. 1876 *Whitby Gloss.*, *Wainfleeaks*, the moveable side-boards of the waggon, adapted to heighten it. 1641 BEST *Farm. Bks.* (Surtees) 46 Allowinge to each waine two folkes, viz., a forker and a loader; and theire implements which they are to carry to field with them is a *waine-forke and a waine-rake; theire waineforke should bee in length aboute two yardes and a quarter. c 1680 in *Sussex Archæol. Collect.* (1849) II. 108 Richard Butcher..took out of 3* highway well nigh an acre of land, and made an enclosure of it, and set up a *wean gate and horse gate. 1596 in *Reg. Mag. Sig. Scot.* 1601, 414/1 Cum lie cairt and wane gait ad easdem [moras]. 1661 *Reg. Gt. Seal Scot.* 18/2 Therefra alongst ane old waingate till you come to the Seggiesyke. 1569 *Lanc. Wills* (Chetham Soc.) I. 34 With other out howses as followith..the furmost barne..the *wayn howse [etc.]. 1791 *Gentl. Mag.* LXI. I. 116/1 After supper, the company all attend the bailiff (or head of the oxen) to the Wain-house. 1828 CARR *Craven Gloss.*, *Wain-house*, wagon house or cart house. 1626 *Gateshead Church Bks.* (E. D. D.) Recaved of the hie ward ffor *wane money, 16s. 1641 BEST *Farm. Bks.* (Surtees) 46 Theire *wainerakes haue (for the most parte) theire shaftes made of saugh, theire heade of seasoned ashe, and theire teeth of iron. 1559 *Richmond Wills* (1853) 136, iij *waine shackles. 1876 *Whitby Gloss.*, *Wainstang*, the pole projecting in front of the wagon for carrying stone blocks. 1464 *Inv.* in *Feodar. Priorat. Dunelm.* (Surtees) 120, 1 cowpe-wayne cum *waynstrynges, precium iij s. 1596 *Durham Wills* (Surtees) II. 259, vij wayne cloutes, ij hay spades,..*wayne stroke [etc.]. 1876 *Whitby Gloss.*, *Waintrees, the axle-beams supporting the wagon. 1579 *Nottingham Rec.* IV. 189 The *whene waye goinge vpp they hill. 1641 BEST *Farm. Bks.* (Surtees) 38 The waine-way into this close is aboute the middle of Pinder lane, wheare yow are to pull downe a gappe. 15.. *Burgh Rec. Edin.* (1869) I. 241 Item of a *wayne weicht of leid, that is to say xiiij futemellis, iiij d.

† **Wain**, *sb.*[2] *Obs.* Forms: 3–4 wayne, 4 wayn. [a. OF. *wain* masc., *waaigne* fem., dial. varr. of *gain*, *gaaigne*: see GAIN *sb.*[2]]

1. Profit, advantage.

c 1315 SHOREHAM *Poems* I. 2207 Þe fyfte, þat hys Elyynge, Cryst onleke to oure wayne. 1340 *Ayenb.* 43 Him ne dret naȝt to done..grat harm to oþren uor a lite wayn oþer uor ureme to him.

2. Conquest, possession gained by conquest; also, booty, spoil.

c 1330 R. BRUNNE *Chron. Wace* (Rolls) 1481 Þeyr ffiote wyþ al þer wayne Turnede fro þe lond of Spaigne. *Ibid.* 1857 Albion was Brutes wayne, Þerfore he dide hit calle Brutayne. 1338 — *Chron.* (1810) 257 We rede ȝe sende to þe kyng of Almayn, & ȝour londes to defende, & reue Philip his wayn. *Ibid.* 297 Þe Scottis bare þam wele, þe Waleis had þe wayn, als maistere of þat eschele.

† **Wain**, *sb.*[3] *Obs.* In 5 wayn(e, wayyn. [Of obscure origin.] A hem, border.

c 1440 *Promp. Parv.* 513/2 Wayne, of a garlement [*v.r.* wayn, wayyn, *Pynson* of a garment], *lacinia*.

† **Wain**, *v.* *Obs.* Forms: 2–3 *Orm.* waȝȝnenn, 4 vayne, 4–6 wayne, 6 waine, 7 wein. [f. WAIN *sb.*[1]]

1. *trans.* To transport in a wain or carriage.

c 1200 ORMIN Pref. 37 Goddspell forr þatt illke þing Iss Currus Salomoniss, For þatt itt..Waȝȝneþþ soþ Crist fra land to land. *Ibid.* 5909 Þær iss þe Laferrd Crist himm sellf, & tiderr iss he waȝȝnedd Uppo þatt hallȝhe waȝȝn. 1531–2 *Durham Househ. Bk.* (Surtees) 62 Pro navigacione ultra aquam cum le waynnyng 1 but malvaseti, 6 d. 1606 BIRNIE *Kirk-Buriall* (1833) 10 Before that by the Libitinarian cure the dead was weind, the Pollinctors inbalmed the corps of the great.

2. To carry, bring, convey.

13.. *Gaw. & Gr. Knt.* 2459 Ho wayned me þis wonder, your wyttez to reue. 13.. *E. E. Allit. P.* A. 249 What wyrde has hyder my iuel vayned. 1540 PALSGR. *Acolastus* III. ii. O ij, Pamphagus wold wayne or bring no geste to Sannios howse, but he were riche. 1573–80 TUSSER *Husb.* (1878) 107 Then neighbour..if any you see, good servant for dairie house, waine her to mee.

b. ? To bring a report of.

c 1400 *Destr. Troy* 11520 He couet at the kyng,..Eneas eftsones þat erend for to wend..All þere wille for to wete & wayne at þe last.

3. *intr.* To go, rush. [Perh. a different word: cf. ON. *vegna* to proceed, go on.]

c 1400 *Destr. Troy* 7621 A thondir with a thicke Rayn thrublit in þe skewes,..As neuer water fro the welkyn hade waynit before. *Ibid.* 7655 Ector, wrathed at his wordis, waynit at the kyng, þat he gird to þe ground and the gost yald. *Ibid.* 13796 [Ho] Waynyt vp to the welkyn, as a wan clowde.

Wain: see VAIN *a.*, WANE *sb.*[1], *v.*, WEAN *v.*

† **Wai·nable**, *a.* *Law.* *Obs.* [AF. dial. var. of *gaignable* GAINABLE.] = GAINABLE.

1706 PHILLIPS (ed. Kersey), *Wainable*, (in old Deeds) that may be Manured, or Ploughed; Tillable.

Wainage (wē·nēdʒ). *Hist.* Also 6 waynage. [ad. Anglo-L. *wainnagium*: see GAINAGE.]

1. = GAINAGE 3 (q.v. with regard to erroneous interpretations).

c 1500 tr. *Gt. Charter* in *Arnolde's Chron.* (1811) 217 A villayne other than ours the same wise shalbe amercyed, sauyng his waynage yf he falle into our handis. a 1632 COKE *Inst.* II. xiv. (1642) 28 It was great reason to save his wainage, for otherwise the miserable creature, was to carry it on his back. 1700 J. TYRRELL *Hist. Eng.* II. 814 His Wainage (i.e. his Carts and Implements) to Till his Land.

2. Land under cultivation.

1875 STUBBS *Const. Hist.* I. xii. 510 That they would..declare how many carucates, or what wainage for ploughs, there were in each township. 1898 W. FARRER *Cartul. Cockersand Abbey* II. i. 362 With acquittance of multure at the grantor's mill of his house and wainage.

† **Wainbote**. *Law.* *Obs.* Also wesne-boot. [f. WAIN *sb.*[1] + *bote*, BOOT *sb.*[2] Cf. MLG. (13th c.) *wagenbote*.] The allowance of timber which a tenant had the right to cut for the repair of his wains.

1772 in *Sussex Archæol. Collect.* VI. 61 (Customs of Manor of Batell) Plough-boot and wesne-boot. 1828–32 WEBSTER.

Wainoot, obs. form of WAINSCOT.

Waine: see VAIN *a.*, WANE *sb.*[1], *v.*, WEAN *v.*

Wainer (wē·nəɹ). *rare.* In 5 wenyher, 6 weyner. [f. WAIN *sb.*[1] + -ER[1] (in 15th c. -YER).] The driver of a wain, a wagoner.

a 1500 *Tretyce* in *Walter of Henley's Husb.* (1890) 50 Se þat yor wenyheris haue no poketes betwene þer legges to stelle withe. 1566 *S'hampton Crt. Leet Rec.* (1905) I. 35 Weyners. 1840 GALT *Demon of Destiny* 77 Aghast the wainers stood.

Wainescot, obs. form of WAINSCOT.

Wai·nful. *rare.* [f. WAIN *sb.*[1] + -FUL.] As much as a wain will hold, a wain-load.

1713 LADY G. BAILLIE *Househ. Bk.* (S. H. S.) 246 For a wainfull Dails bringing from Berwick, o 6 10.

† **Wai·ning**, *vbl. sb.* *Obs.*[−0] [Of obscure origin.] (See quots.)

1585 HIGINS *Junius' Nomencl.* 385/2 *Versura*,..the waining or turning at ye lands end, where one furrow endeth and another beginneth. 1611 COTGR. s.v. *Reversure*.

Waining, obs. f. WANING; var. WONING *Obs.*

Wainman (wē·nmăn). Also 4 waynesman. [f. WAIN *sb.*[1] + MAN.]

1. = WAINER. *Obs.* exc. *Hist.*

1392 *Earl Derby's Exped.* (Camden) 180 Duobus waynemen de Dansk pro eodem viagio, iiij marcz. pr. Cuidam waynesman de Dansk pro eodem viagio, ij marcz. pr. c 1450 *St. Cuthbert* (Surtees) 5833 Þe wayne men wer noȝt ware. 1580 H. F. *Pelegrom. Syn. Sylvæ* 42 A Carter, a Waine man, *Auriga* [etc.]. 1609 *Churchw. Acc. Pittington*, etc. (Surtees) 154 Item paid to the wainmen that brought the lyme and sand for there drinkes, ix d. 1627 *Act 3 Chas. I*, c. 2 § 1 No Carrier with any Horse or Horses..nor Waynemen with anie Wayne or Waynes..shall..travell upon the said Day. 1756 P. BROWNE *Jamaica* 193 The leaves..yield a strong thready substance..which is commonly used in ropes and whips by the wainmen in that part of the world. 1880 F. G. LEE *Ch. under Q. Eliz.* I. 15 At Canterbury..a holy-oil stock was emptied of its sacred contents, in order to grease the creaking wheels of a wainman's cart.

† 2. The constellation Boötes, regarded as the teamster of 'Charles's Wain'. *Obs.*

1588 A. ASHLEY *Mariners Mirr.* A 6 b, A catalogue of the more famous fixed starres..The Wainmans right shoulder. 1594 KYD *Cornelia* III. i. 69 And now the sleepie Waineman softly droue His slow-pac'd Teeme. 1598 SYLVESTER *Du Bartas* I. iv. 290 Besides these Twelve, toward the Artick side, A flaming Dragon doth Two-Bears divide; After, the Wainman comes, the Crown, the Spear [etc.].

Wainny, obs. form of WANEY *a.*

Wain-rope. *Obs.* or *arch.* a. A rope used as a trace for drawing a wain. (Cf. *cart-rope*.) b. A rope used for binding or securing a load on a wain.

1371 *Durham Acc. Rolls* (Surtees) 129, ij waynraps novi. 1441–2 *Ibid.* 79 Item in 2 Waynrapes et 4 helteres empt., 12 d. 1523–34 FITZHERB. *Husb.* § 5 And or he shall lode his corne, he muste haue a wayne, a copyoke, a payre of sleues, a wayne rope, and a pykforke. 1581 *Inv.* in *Trans. Cumb. & Westm. Arch. Soc.* X. 40 Item Waine Ropes, xvj d. 1601 SHAKS. *Twel. N.* III. ii. 64, I thinke Oxen and waine-ropes cannot hale them together.

Wainscot (wē·nskǫt, -skǫt), *sb.* Forms: α. 4–5 waynescot, (4 -scote), 4–7 waynscot, 5–6 wayn(e)scotte, wayneskote, weynscot, (5 -scotte, 6 -skot), 5–7 waynscote, -scott, (5 wenscote, wansqwatte, waneskott, waynskote, waynscowttes (*pl.*), *Sc.* wanskoth), 6 wayn(e)skott, wenskot(te, weinscot, wainescot, (weanscott, wainscoate, wanskot(t, wenskett, *Sc.* wynscott), 6–7 wa(i)nscote, wainskot, wanescot, (6 -skot, 7 -scott), 6–8 wain-

scott, wanscot, (7 vain-, *Sc.* vandscott, weanscot, waynskot, wayn-scote, waincot), 7–9 wainscoat, (8 wanscoate), 6– wainscot. β. 4 *north.* vaynescotte, wandschoth, 5 weynshet, 6 wa(y)ne-, weyneschot. [ad. MLG. *wagenschot* (1389 in Schiller and Lübben), app. f. *wagen* carriage, WAGON + *schot* (of uncertain meaning; cf. *bōkenschot*, mod.LG. *bökenschot*, beechwood of superior quality). Cf. 16th c. Flemish *waegheschot*, *waeghenschot* (Kilian), WFlemish *wageschot* (De Bo), Du. *wagenschot*, WFris. *wagenskot*. The synonymous Flem. or Du. *wandschot* (Kilian), which may be the source of some of the Eng. forms, is either an etymologizing perversion of *wagenschot* or an independent formation on *wand* wall of a room. The Eng. examples of the word are earlier than those given in the MLG. and MDu. dicts., and the first element appears already in the earliest instances assimilated to the Eng. WAIN *sb.*[1]

The etymology as above stated does not clearly account for the meaning, and there have been attempts to explain the first element differently. Kilian (1598) identifies it with Flem. *waeghe* wave, taking it to refer to the undulation in the grain of the wood. Some modern scholars regard it as an alteration of MDu. *weeg* wall (= OFris. *wāch*, OE. *wāh*, WOUGH). These suggestions are however open to strong objection, and the probability is that the first element is really *wagen*, though the original meaning of the compound remains for the present obscure.]

1. A superior quality of foreign oak imported from Russia, Germany, and Holland, chiefly used for fine panel-work; logs or planks of this oak; oak boarding for panel-work. Now only *technical*.

1352–3 *Ely Sacr. Rolls* (1907) II. 153 Item solut. pro cc et dimid. de Waynscot empt. ad Lenne prec. de cent. xvs. xd. 1l. 19s. 7d. 1391–2 *Norwich Sacrist's Roll* (MS.), Pro tabulis de Waynscot. 1404 in *Royal & Hist. Lett. Hen. IV* (Rolls) I. 262 Nova navis cum tritico, braseo, farina..et lignis voaghenschot [? *read* waghen-] onustata. [1407 in Hakluyt *Voy.* (1599) I. 173 The said marchants [of the Hans of Almaine] doe alleage, that the customers & bailifs of the town of Southhampton do compel them to pay..for ech hundreth of bowstaues & boords called *Waghenscot*, 2. d.] a 1419 *Liber Albus* (Rolls) 238 De chescun c du bord appelle 'weynscotte' obole. 1426–7 *Rec. St. Mary at Hill* (1904) 66 Also for wayneskote, vj d. 1483 *Churchw. Acc. S. Mary Virg., Oxford* in *MS. Wood D.* 3 fol. 260 De 4s solut pro 4 asseribus vocat: weynshet. 1495 *Naval Acc. Hen. VII* (1896) 270 Chayres of waynscotte. 1496 *Acc. Ld. High Treas. Scot.* I. 290 Item, for xxiij burdis callit wanskoth, xvj s. viij d. 1522 *Bury Wills* (Camden) 117 A brode cheste of wayneskott. a 1548 HALL *Chron., Hen. VIII*, 60 The Dutchemen bryng ouer Iron, Tymber, lether and Weynskot ready wrought. 1550 *Reg. Mag. Sig. Scot.* 104/2 Exceptis..300 asseribus querneis *lie waneschot* nuncupatis. 1583 *Rates of Customs* D vij b, Playing tables Flaunders making of wainscot the dosen xvs. 1589 [? NASHE] *Almond for Parrat* 1 A brother in Christ of his..kept his wainscot from waste, and his linnen from wearing; sufficeth he tombled his wife naked into the earth at high noone. 1611 CORYAT *Crudities* 231 In the midst of the Synagogue they haue a round seat made of Wainscot. 1652 URQUHART *Jewel* 252 Seeing a wedge of Wainscot is fittest and most proper for cleaving of an oaken tree. 1670 EACHARD *Cont. Clergy* 108 An unlearned rout of contemptible people ..who perhaps shall understand very little more than a hollow pipe made of tin or wainscot. 1732 M. GREEN *Grotto* 161 As spiders Irish wainscot flee. 1842 GWILT *Encycl. Archit.* § 1686 The wood [of *Quercus robur*] is tolerably straight-grained and pretty free from knots, in many instances resembling the German species called wainscot. *Ibid.* 1689 There is a species of oak..imported from Holland, known under the name of Dutch wainscot, though grown in Germany, whence it is floated down the Rhine for exportation.

† b. A piece or a board of wainscot oak. *Obs.*

1388 in Nicolas *Hist. Royal Navy* (1847) II. 476 Parcels in the store-house..'xiiij. barrell de tarre,..cc. waynscots'. 1396 *Mem. Ripon* (Surtees) III. 123 Et in iij vayneschotes emp. pro j selour et j reredos..18 d. 1486–7 *Priory of Finchale* (Surtees) p. ccclxxvi, Pro xvj waynscowttez ad vjd., viij s. 1532 *Lett. & Papers Hen. VIII*, V. 448 To John de Garnatboo of the Company of the Easterlings, for 100 wainscots, 66s. 8d. 1603 *Reg. Mag. Sig. Scot.* 515/2 Ilk geist, corball and waynescott..ane penny. 1641 S. SMITH *Royal Fishings* 4 Waynskots, Clapboards, Deale.

† c. Furniture made of wainscot. *Obs.*

1589 *Wills & Inv. N. C.* (Surtees) 144, I will my wainscott, as well chamberes and parleres, all wainscot beddes covered with wainescott. 1597 *Lanc. Wills* (Chetham Soc.) II. 227, I give to my sonne..all the waynescott glasse painted clothes borders above the waynscott tables.

2. Panel-work of oak or other wood, used to line the walls of an apartment.

1548 in Glasscock *Rec. St. Michael's, Bp.'s Stortford* (1882) 131 Item the weyneschot of the rode loft that was taken downe. 1555 EDEN *Decades* (Arb.) 194 Chambers boarded after the maner of owre waynscotte. 1584 *Leycesters Commw.* (1641) 154 The greedy Burglarer is lesse patient of stay..when he..perceiveth only some partition of wane-skot or the like, betwixt his fingers and the cofers or money bags. 1600 SHAKS. *A. Y. L.* III. i. 88 This fellow wil but ioyne you together, as they ioyne Wainscot, then one of you wil proue a shrunke pannell. 1611 CORYAT *Crudities* 244 In the Quire the whole history of St. Bennet is very curiously made in Wainscot. a 1667 COWLEY *Ess., Greatness* (1906) 432 A convenient brick house, with decent Wainscot, and pretty Forest-work hangings. a 1701 MAUNDRELL *Journ. Jerus.* (1732) 77 It was carv'd in such a manner, as to resemble a piece of wainscot. 1711 ADDISON *Spect.* No. 235 ¶ 2 A certain Person..who when he is pleased with any Thing that is acted upon the Stage, expresses his Approbation by a loud Knock upon the Benches or the Wainscot. 1715 — *Drummer* I. i, Like a rat behind a wainscot. 1730 W. WARREN *Collectanea* in Willis & Clark *Cambridge* (1886) I. 225 The Stair-case new lin'd with Deal wainscot painted. 1768–74 TUCKER *Lt. Nat.* (1852) I. 290 When we look upon the wainscot of a room where the panels are painted of a different colour from the stiles and mouldings. 1781 COWPER *Conversat.* 116, I twirl my thumbs, fall back into my chair, Fix on the wainscot a distressful stare. 1815 SCOTT *Guy M.* xlii, The great oak-parlour, a long room, panelled with well-varnished wainscot. 1830 TENNYSON *Mariana* vi, The mouse Behind the mouldering wainscot shriek'd. 1855 MACAULAY *Hist. Eng.* xv. III. 613 The Jacobite country gentlemen..burned their commissions signed by James, and bid their arms behind wainscots or in haystacks. 1875 MISS BRADDON *Strange World* II. i. 3 The wainscot was almost black with age.

† 3. *transf.* and *fig.* (Cf. 5 b.) *Obs.*

1588 *Marprel. Epist.* (Arb.) 31 His face is made of seasoned wainscot, and wil lie as fast as a dog can trot. 1607 MIDDLETON *Fam. Love* III. iii, Cedars to make good wainscot in the House of Sincerity. 1611 BEAUM. & FL. *King & No King* v. i, This Rascal fears neither God nor man, he has been so beaten: sufferance has made him Wainscot. 1630 D. DYKE *Myst. Selfe-Deceiuing* 374 Howsoeuer sometimes this kind of men haue faces of wainscote. a 1659 OSBORN *Charac. &c.* (1673) 640 How a few years hath changed Alabaster into Wainscot, and ruffled her Neck like a walking Buskin.

4. A book-name for several moths. (See 5 c.)

1819 SAMOUELLE *Entomol. Compend.* 399. *Ibid.* 419. 1832 J. RENNIE *Butterfl. & Moths* 87.

5. *attrib.* passing into adj. a. Made of wainscot. Of a room, lined with wainscot panelling.

1575 in *Archæologia* XXX. 8 Item..ij waynscot chaires viije. *Ibid.* 14 Item a waynscott cheste, vs. 1580 *Ibid.* LXIV. 357 To mak..tow dores on for the portall and on other for the lytle wayneschot chambre. 1585 HIGINS *Junius' Nomencl.* 229/2 *Mensa vndulata vndatim crispa*,.. a wainscot table. 1593 DRAYTON *Ecl.* iv. 91 The loftie Pines were presently hew'd downe, And Men, Sea-Monsters, swam the bracky Flood, In Wainscote Tubs to seeke out Worlds vnknowne. 1594 NASHE *Terrors Nt.* Wks. (Grosart) III. 265 Through him my tender wainscot doore is deliuered from much assault and battrie. 1649 DAVENANT *Love & Hon.* III. iii. 124 Look for one of my cheek teeth That dropt under the wainscote bed. 1702 *Post Man* 6–8 Jan. 2/1 Advt., At Stanmore..is a fair House to be let, 4 Wainscot rooms on a Floor, with a Kitchin, [etc.]. 1711 in G. Lorimer *Leaves fr. Bk. West Kirke* vii. (1885) 64 Item,..a green pulpit cloath with silk fringes, six wainscot stools for the Collections. 1748 RICHARDSON *Clarissa* (1811) II. 205 They all remained in the next parlour, a wainscot partition only parting the two. 1796 J. OWEN *Trav. Europe 1791–2* I. 85 Those sculptural vagaries, in which a human figure is often made..the support of a wainscot pulpit. 1833 HT. MARTINEAU *Vanderput & S.* i. 6, I am in the wainscot parlour to-day. 1848 DICKENS *Dombey* liii, My room..was divided from the Manager's room by a wainscot partition. 1851 W. LAXTON *Builder's Price Bk.* (ed. 28) 58 Wainscot floors. 1862 *Catal. Internat. Exhib., Brit.* II. No. 5719, A wainscot sideboard. 1913 *Blackw. Mag.* July 14/2 The room..had..a wainscot table, rosewood chairs [etc.].

† b. Resembling wainscot, hardened or coloured like old wainscot. *Obs.*

1577 GRANGE *Golden Aphrod.* K ij b, Your waynscot face and brasen countenaunce. 1586 A. DAY *Eng. Secretorie* I. (1595) 91 b, Audacious and wainscot impudencie on the other side returneth the greatest impediment in anie thing to bee obtained. 1593 G. HARVEY *Pierce's Super.* Wks. (Grosart) II. 117 But it is not the wainscott forhead of a Rudhuddibras, that can arreare such an huge opinion. 1599 NASHE *Lenten Stuffe* 47 If you marke it, mustard looks of the tanned wainscot hue, of such a withered wrinklefaced beldam as she was, that was altred thereinto. 1626 MIDDLETON *Quiet Life* IV. ii, How does thy Mistriss that sits in a Wainscot Gown, like a Citizens Lure to draw the Customers? 1707 J. STEVENS tr. *Quevedo's Com. Wks.* (1709) 169 They are Wainscot Faces compair'd with white men. a 1745 SWIFT *Dick, a Maggot* 11 'Tis beyond the pow'r of meal The gypsey visage to conceal; For, as he shakes his wainscot chops, Down ev'ry mealy atom drops.

c. In book-names of certain moths: see 4.

1832 J. RENNIE *Butterfl. & Moths* 187.

6. *attrib.* and *Comb*: a. simple attrib., as *wainscot board*, *colour*, *log*, *oak*, *rafter*, *timber*, *work*; b. parasynthetic, as † *wainscot-faced* adj.; c. similative, as *wainscot joined* adj.

1420 in *For. Acc.* 3 *Hen. VI*, G/2 In diuersis peciis maeremii *Waynescotbordes. 1594 BLUNDEVIL *Exerc., Navig.* xxiv. (1597) 331 Another square box of thinne wainscot boorde. 1741 *Compl. Fam.-Piece* III. 525 Most Rooms are now Painted *Wainscot Colour. 1588 *Marprel. Epist.* (Arb.) 30 Our impudent, shamelesse, and *wainscote faced bishops. 1640 HOWELL *Dodona's Gr.* 22 But now mee thinkes I spie againe a Sunn burnt wainscot-fac'd Satyr. 1554 in Feuillerat *Revels Q. Mary* (1914) 164, viij targettes of tree shelboard of *waynscot ioyned fair worke for the said maskers. 1812 J. SMYTH *Pract. Customs* 249 *Wainscot logs, 8 inches square or upwards, are charged by the load of 50 cubic feet. 1832 *Planting* 130 in *Libr. Usef. Knowl., Husb.* III, That which is brought down the Rhine from the forests of southern Germany, and imported into this country by the name of *wainscoat oak. c 1560 *Aberd. Reg.* (MS.) XXVI. (Jam.) *Wynscott rauchter. 1875 T. LASLETT *Timber* xvi. 96 Riga *wainscot timber passes through the process of bracking prior to its being shipped. 1585 HIGINS *Junius' Nomencl.* 198/2 *Wainscot or seeling worke. 1609 *Acc. Balliol Coll., Oxford* (MS.), Item, for 2 seates, and wainscott worke, in the librarie, 5 *li*.

Wainscot (wē·nskǫt, -skǫt), *v.* Inflected wainscot(t)ed, -ing. Forms: see the sb. [f. prec. Cf. Flemish † *waeghenschotten* (Kilian).]

1. *trans.* To line (a wall, roof, etc.) with panelwork of wood.

1570 LEVINS *Manip.* 177 To Waynscotte, *contabulare*. 1599 *Rutland MSS.* (Hist. MSS. Comm. 1905) IV. 415 For waynscotting the roofes of his chamber, xxs. a 1650 BOATE *Ireland's Nat. Hist.* (1860) 121 To mend this inconvenience the English did wainscot those walls with oak or other boards. 1676 GLANVILL *Ess. Philos. & Relig.* VII. 3 He led me into an handsome square Chamber wainscotted with Cedar. 1678 MOXON *Mech. Exerc.* vi. 105 Of Wainscoting Rooms. *Ibid.* 106 In Wainscoting of Rooms there is, for the most part, but two heights of Pannels used; unless the Room to be Wainscoted be above ten foot high. 1730 W. WARREN *Collect.* in Willis & Clark *Cambridge* (1886) I. 232 The Treasury..is wainscotted with Deal. 1821 SCOTT *Kenilw.* vi, This apartment..was now beautifully wainscoted with dark foreign wood. 1839 LONGF. *Hyperion* III. iii. Pr. Wks. 1886 II. 162 It was a large room..wainscoted with pine. 1883 G. MOORE *Mod. Lover* xiv, [The room] was wainscotted in light oak.

in fig. context. a 1704 T. BROWN *Quakers Grace* Wks. 1730 I. 107 That we..may live to be saw'd out into deal-boards, to wainscoat thy New Jerusalem.

b. To grain in imitation of oak.

1835 DICKENS *Sk. Boz, Parish* iii, The house..was fresh painted and papered from top to bottom; the paint inside was all wainscoted.

2. *transf.* To line (the walls of an apartment) with marble, tiles or the like; to panel (a wall with mirrors or pictures).

1613–39 I. JONES in Leoni *Palladio's Archit.* (1742) II. 50 To wainscot their Buildings with rich Stones. 1630 DONNE *Serm.* 2 Apr. (1661) III. 138 The Scriptures are as a room wainscotted with looking-glass, we see all at once. a 1668 LASSELS *Italy* (1698) I. 93 Witness those chambers..wainscoted with great Looking-glasses and rich gilding. 1718 LADY M. W. MONTAGU *Let. to C'tess Mar* 10 Mar., The winter apartment was wainscoted with inlaid work of mother of pearl. 1745 POCOCKE *Descr. East* II. II. i. 5 The east side of it within is wainscotted with jasper and beautiful marbles. 1775 JOHNSON in *Boswell* 14 Oct., The ladies' closet wainscotted with large squares of glass over painted paper. 1806–7 J. BERESFORD *Miseries Hum. Life* XVIII. viii. (1826) 154 But enough..of Portraits; though, in truth, the walls are wainscotted with them.

Hence **Wai·nscot(t)ed** *ppl. a.*

1605 ERONDELLE *Fr. Gard.* N 2 b, God grant me alwaies the key of the fieldes, I would like it better, then to be in bondage in the fayrest wainscotted or tapistred Chamber. 1694 WESTMACOT *Script. Herb.* 40 Solomon and others..did build their Magnificent Houses,..and Wain-scotted Rooms therewith [Cedar]. 1814 SCOTT *Wav.* lv, The apartment of Colonel Talbot..was divided from his own by a wainscotted partition. 1848 DICKENS *Dombey* iv, The little wainscoted back parlour. 1866 MRS. GASKELL *Wives & Dau.* xiii, They were taken..into a wainscoted parlour.

transf. and *fig.* 1602 F. H[ERING] tr. *Oberndoerffer's Anat. True Physit.* I, This lost Companion [a quack], hauing a Foxes Head and an whorish and wainscotted Face.

† **Wainscotage**. *Obs. rare*[−1]. [f. WAINSCOT *v.* + -AGE.] Wainscot-work, wainscoting.

1677 tr. *Tavernier's Gr. Seignor's Seraglio* xv. 73 Yet is there a delicate piece of Wainscotage, of about the height of a man's waste, carried quite round the Room.

Wainscot(t)ing, (wē·nskǫtiŋ), *vbl. sb.* [f. WAINSCOT *v.* + -ING[1].] The action or process of lining a room, its walls, etc. with wainscot; also *concr.*, panelling of wainscot; also, wainscots collectively.

1580 HOLLYBAND *Treas. Fr. Tong*, *Lambris*, a seeling, wanscotting. 1611 COTGR., *Lambrissage*, a wainscotting, or seeling; also, an embowing, or frettizing in wainscot. 1631 WEEVER *Anc. Funeral Mon.* 870 He..bestowed 100. markes vpon wainscotting of the Library there. 1682 BURNET *Life Hale* 39 He laid by all his Collections.., and that they might not fall into ill hands, he hid them behind the Wainscotting of his Study. 1727 DE FOE *Eng. Tradesm.* xxii. (1841) I. 206 He must sink perhaps a third part, nay, half his stock, in painting and gilding, wainscoting and glazing. 1764 HARMER *Observ.* iii. § 8. 97 Their carved wainscottings of wood heightened with painting and gilting. 1836 DICKENS *Sk. Boz, Doctor's Commons*, An old quaint-looking apartment, with sunken windows, and black carved wainscotting. 1859 GEO. ELIOT *Adam Bede* i, The afternoon sun was warm on the five workmen there, busy upon doors and window frames and wainscoting. 1869 'LEWIS CARROLL' *Phantasmag.* 37 But after twenty years or so The wainscotings begin to go.

Waint, obs. Sc. form of VAUNT *v.*

1563 WINȜET tr. *Vincent. Lirin.* xvi. Wks. (S.T.S.) II. 37 Bot Apollinaris in a manere crakis and waintis that he consentis in deid to the vnitie of the Trinitie.

Wainwright (wē·nrait). [f. WAIN *sb.*[1] + WRIGHT. In OE. *wægn-wyrhta*. Not found in ME., but its existence is attested by the surname *Wainwright*.] A wagon-builder.

c 1000 ÆLFRIC *Gloss.* in Wr.-Wülcker 112 *Carpentarius*, wænwyrhta. 1855 HYDE CLARKE *Dict.*, *Wainwright*, wagon-wright. 1891 MEREDITH *One of our Conq.* xix, A rill, that was lured a little further down through scoops, ducts, and scaffolded channels to serve a wainwright.

Wainy, variant of WANEY *a.*

Waipone, Waippin, obs. Sc. ff. WEAPON.

† **Wair**, *sb.* *Obs. rare*[−1]. A piece of timber two yards long and one foot broad.

1664 EVELYN *Sylva* xxix. 85 A Tree [an oak]..which yielded of sawn Wair fourteen hundred, and by estimation, twenty Chords of wood. A Wair is two yards long, and one foot broad, sixscore to the hundred: so that, in the said Tree was 10080 foot of Boards. Hence 1674 BLOUNT *Glossogr.* (ed. 4), and in later Dicts.

† **Wair**, *a.* *Sc.* *Obs. rare*[−1]. ? Wild, stormy.

c 1480 HENRYSON *Preach. Swallow* xii, Bewis bene are laifit bair of blis, Be wickit windis of the winter wair.

Wair, obs. form of *were*, pa. ind. pl. of BE *v.*

Wair(e, Waird, Wairding, Wairdour, Wairdrope, Sc. or north. ff. WARE, WEIR, WARD, WARDING, WARDER, WARDROBE.

Wairn, obs. Sc. form of WARN.

Wairsche, wairsh, var. ff. WERSH *a.*

Wairstall, -staw, var. ff. WARESTALL *Sc.*

Wais: see WALL, WASE, WAVE, WAY.

Waisall, waissel, var. ff. WASSAIL.

Waische, waisshe, obs. forms of WASH *v.*

Waiscot, obs. form of WAISTCOAT.

Waist (wēⁱst). Forms: 4–6 waast, 4–7 wast, 4–8 waste, 6 *Sc.* west, 7 wayst, 5, 7– waist. [14th c. *wast*, believed to represent an OE. *wæst, *weahst, corresp. to ON. *vahstu-r (Icel. *vǫxt-r*, Sw. *växt*, Da. *vœxt*), Goth. *wahstu-s*, growth, size, f. Teut. root *wahs-: see WAX *v.*[1] With regard to the form cf. OE. *wæstm*, growth, fruit:—OTeut. type *waχstmo-z from the same root. With regard to the meaning cf. F. *taille*, where the sense 'waist' appears to be developed from the sense 'size (of body)'. The word (in the form *wacste*, which may be either native or Scandinavian) app. occurs with the sense 'greatness' in the following quot.

c 1175 *Lamb. Hom.* 77 Þe fader is ine þe sune on þre wise. On wacste [*Trin. Hom.* iv. on westme], for he is muchel and mihti ouer alle þing.

The spelling *waist* was rare until it was adopted in Johnson's Dict. 1755.]

1. The portion of the trunk of the human body that is between the ribs and the hip-bones; the middle section of the body, normally slender in comparison with the parts above and below it.

In quot. c 1480 humorously misused.

13.. *Gaw. & Gr. Knt.* 144 Bot his wombe & his wast were worthily smale. c 1386 CHAUCER *Sir Thopas* Prol. 10 He in the waast is shape as wel as I. 1390 GOWER *Conf.* II. 373 Whan I beclippe hire on the wast. c 1400 *Destr. Troy* 9902 Dyomede..Halfe-lyueles..felle, With a wicked wound thurgh the wast euyn. c 1420 *Anturs of Arth.* 578 (Douce MS.) He bronched him yne withe his bronde..þorghe þe waast of þe body. c 1440 *Promp. Parv.* 517/2 Waste, of a mannys myddyl.., *vastitas*, Cath. 1470–85 MALORY *Arthur* XI. xii. 589 There he fond a knyght that was bounden with a chayne faste aboute the wast vnto a pyller of stone. c 1480 HENRYSON *Fox, Wolf & Husbandman* 192 The tod lap on land..And left the wolf in watter to the waist. 1500–20 DUNBAR *Poems* xxxii. 29 He grippit hir abowt the west. 1509 HAWES *Past. Pleasure* xxix. (Percy Soc.) 135 His necke shorte,..His breste fatte and bolne in the wast. 1571 R. BANNATYNE *Memor.* (Bannatyne Club) 170 Culan and his men..waide to their westis befoir thei come to dry land. 1579 SPENSER *Sheph. Cal.* Apr. 134 Gird in your waste..with a tawdrie lace. 1605 SHAKS. *Lear* IV. vi. 127 Downe from the waste they are Centaures, though Women all aboue. 1650 BULWER *Anthropomet.* xx. (1653) 338 Young Virgins..who thinking a slender waste a great beauty, strive all that they possibly can by streight-lacing themselves, to attaine unto a wand-like smalnesse of waste. 1667 MILTON *P. L.* IX. 1113 Those Leaves They gatherd.. And..together sowd, To gird thir waste. 1687 A. LOVELL tr. *Thevenot's Trav.* I. 29 Over the Doliman, they gird themselves about the small of the waste with a Sash. 1774 GOLDSM. *Nat. Hist.* II. 260 He was so tall, that the Spaniards only reached his waist. 1839 LANE *Arab. Nts.* I. 105 And, lo! half of him, from his waist to the soles of his feet, was stone. 1860 TYNDALL *Glac.* I. xviii. 131 Hitherto my guides in dangerous places had tied the ropes round their waists also. 1871 *Figure Training* 17 It is not to be wondered at that ten years ago a waist of sixteen inches in circumference, for a lady of average height, should be regarded as a..much-to-be-admired achievement. 1880 'OUIDA' *Moths* I. 5 She made her waist fifteen inches round.

? *Proverbial phrase.* 1611 CHAPMAN *May-day* v. Wks. 1873 II. 401 Hauing chaster and simpler thoughts then Leonoro imagines because he measures my wast by his owne.

b. Applied to the corresponding part in an insect.

1713 J. WARDER *True Amazons* 3 The Bee is..very slender in the Waste [1741 p. 15 Waist] or middle part. 1871 STAVELEY *Brit. Insects* xiii. 155 The insects belonging to these two subsections can at once be distinguished from each other by their waists being large or small.

c. *transf.* The middle narrower part (of something compared in shape to the human body). Cf. 4.

1612 DRAYTON *Poly-olb.* vi. 194 That part of Wales,.. Which (as her very waste) in breadth from East to West In length from North to South, her midst is every way. 1817 BYRON *Manfred* I. i, Mont Blanc is the monarch of mountains,..Around his waist are forests braced. 1862 MERIVALE *Rom. Emp.* lxi. (1865) VII. 325 He had quitted the waist and had here reached the neck of Britain.

2. † a. A girdle. *Obs.*

1550 CROWLEY *Epigr.* 1315 Hyr mydle braced in as smal as a wande; And some by wastes of wyre at the paste wyfes hande. 1588 PARKE tr. *Mendoza's Hist. China* 77 They do weare wastes or girdels imbossed with gold. 1595 SHAKS. *John* II. i. 217 Those sleeping stones, That as a waste doth girdle you about By the compulsion of their Ordinance. 1599 PEELE *David & Bethsabe* G iij b, I might haue giuen thee for thy paines Tenne siluer sickles and a golden wast. 1611 CHAPMAN *Iliad* VII. 264 A faire well glossed purple waste [ζωστῆρα..φοίνικι φαεινόν].

transf. and *fig.* 1579 FENTON *Guicciard.* IX. 478 The enemies abandoned suddeinly the towne wherein the french being bestowed, planted their artillerie against the first wast [It. *contro al primo procinto*]. 1591 SHAKS. *1 Hen. VI*, IV. iii. 20 Spurre to the rescue of the Noble Talbot, Who now is girdled with a waste of Iron. 1599 MARSTON *Ant. & Mel.* I. Wks. 1856 I. 12 Weele girt them with an ample waste of love.

b. The part of a garment that covers the waist; the narrowed part of a garment corresponding to the narrowing of the body at the waist (but sometimes, in accordance with fashion, worn higher or lower than the position of this); the place in a woman's dress where the bodice and skirt meet.

1650 BULWER *Anthropomet.* App. (1653) 539 The waste (as one notes) is now come to the knee; for, the Points that were used to be about the middle, are now dangling there. 1711 STEELE *Spect.* No. 109 ¶ 4 The Modern [petticoat] is gather'd at the Waste. 1836 MARRYAT *Midsh. Easy* xix, They loaded the pistols, took a pair each and put them in their waists. 1871 *Figure Training* 25 Ladies of fashion in England might be said to have at that period [c 1806] abandoned waists altogether. 1885 *Fairholt's Costume Engl.* I. 405 In 1794 short waists became fashionable. *Ibid.* 408 Open gowns were discarded, and waists about 1798 became longer, until at the end of the century they regained their proper shape.

c. The part of a garment between the shoulders and the 'waist' or narrowed part (see 2 b).

1607 DEKKER & WEBSTER *Northw. Hoe* III. i, What fashion will make a woman haue the best bodie Taylor? *Tay.* A short dutch wast with a round cathern-wheele fardingale. 1837 DICKENS *Pickw.* ii, 'Rather short in the waist, an't it?' said the stranger, screwing himself round to catch a glimpse in the glass of the waist buttons which were half way up his back. 1853 — *Bleak Ho.* vi, Ladies haymaking, in short waists, and large hats tied under the chin.

fig. 1590 NASHE *1st Pt. Pasquil's Apol.* C iij, These places are too short in the waste to serue hys turne.

d. A bodice, blouse. Chiefly *U.S.*

1816 *Sporting Mag.* XLVIII. 189 A lady observing her neighbour in a public room, dressed very tawdrily in a satin waist, drily remarked, it was a waste of satin. 1878 H. JAMES *Europeans* II. ii. 44 She wore a white muslin waist with an embroidered border. 1893 MRS. CUSTER *Tenting on Plains* 85, I had exchanged the waist for a jacket, and left it under a tree. 1908 W. CHURCHILL *Mr. Crewe's Career* xix. 317 Mrs. Fitch..had run from the wash-tub to get into her Sunday waist.

e. *U.S.* 'An undergarment worn specially by children, to which petticoats and drawers are buttoned' (*Cent. Dict.*).

1893 HELEN CAMPBELL in *Arena* 435 Two and a half cents each is paid for the making of boys' gingham waists.

3. *Naut.* The middle part of the upper deck of a ship, between the quarter-deck and the forecastle.

1495 *Naval Acc. Hen. VII* (1896) 194 Stone gonnes of yron in the Wast of the seid Shipp. 15.. *Batayll of Egyngecourte* 90 A ij, These goodly shyppes lay there at rode.. The wastes decked with serpentynes stronge. 1530 PALSGR. 287/1 Waste of a shyppe, *cors de nauire*. a 1586 SIDNEY *Arcadia* II. xxiv. § 5 Already it [the fire] did embrace and deuoure from the sterne, to the wast of the ship. 1610 SHAKS. *Temp.* I. ii. 197. c 1618 MORYSON *Itin.* IV. viii. (1903) 136 Being built large in the Wast and Keele for Capacitye of Marchandize, they are vnfitt to fight at Sea. 1748 *Anson's Voy.* I. iii. (ed. 4) 41 The waste of the ship was filled with live cattle. 1816 'QUIZ' *Grand Master* I. 18 Neptune will presently be here, And as his godship is in haste, Muster the people in the waste. 1883 *Man. Seamanship Boys* 9 Q. Which is the waist? *A.* That portion of the upper deck contained between the fore and main hatchways. 1915 BADEN-POWELL *Ind. Mem.* i. 5 The heavy seas had..carried away the ladders leading from the upper deck into the waist.

b. In occasional uses: (*a*) pl. = *waist-rails*; (*b*) each of the two sides of the waist.

1667 *Lond. Gaz.* No. 127/4 She has been 52. dayes beating at Sea in fowl weather, in which she spent her Main-Top-Mast and her Wasts. 1679 A. LOVELL *Indic. Univ.* 199 The waste, or defences of the sides of a 'Ship'. 1820 W. SCORESBY *Acc. Arctic Reg.* II. 196 A ship having seven boats carried one at each waist.., two at each quarter.., and one across the stern.

4. Applied to the narrowest or slenderest part of an object which is smaller in breadth or girth near the middle than at the extremities; esp. of a bell, a violin or similar instrument, a boot or shoe.

1612 S. RID *Art of Jugling* E 2, A peece of lether..which being trust vp hard to the middle or waste of the said bell, will sticke fast. 1676 MOXON *Print Letters* 26 Describe the outer Arch under the Waste of g on the left hand. 1791 SMEATON *Edystone L.* (1793) § 80 It also seemed equally desirable, not to increase the size of the present building in its Waist; by which I mean that part of the building between the top of the rock, and the top of the solid. 1862 *Catal. Internat. Exhib.* II. xxvii. 51 The 'Cremerian boot', with elastic spring in waist or arch of foot. 1872 ELLACOMBE *Bells of Ch.* viii. in *Ch. Bells Devon* 407 The waist of the bell is studded with stars. 1874 J. D. HEATH *Croquet Player* 26 The amount of spring or elasticity in the handle varies according to the thickness of the waist or thinnest part of it. 1895 HASLUCK *Boot Making* viii. 132 To make a square waist, an iron similar to a double iron is used; for other waists, irons are used according to the shape required.

¶ 5. Affectedly used for: Middle (of day or night). *Obs.*

1602 SHAKS. *Ham.* I. ii. 198 In the dead wast [Qq. 1, 5, 6 vast] and middle of the night. 1604 MARSTON *Malcontent* II. v. D 3 b, Tis now about the immodest waste of night. 1622 J. TAYLOR (Water-P.) *Merrie-Wherrie-Ferrie Voy.* Wks. 1630 II. 7/1 About the waste or Nauell of the Day [*note*, Noone if you'l take it so]. 1644 — *Crop-eare Curried* 1 About the Waste or Navel of the night, Drowsie Somnus came stealing to me. 1651 *Loves of Hero & Leander* (1653) 2 This was about the wast of day: The middle, as the vulgar say.

6. *attrib.* and *Comb.* a. With sense 'intended to be placed, or worn, on or round the waist', as *waist-belt*, *-buckle*, *-clout*, † *-doublet*, *-girdle*, *-piece*, *-plate*, *-pocket*, *-scarf*; with sense 'outlining or following the contour of the waist', as *waist-line*; objective, as *waist-gripping*, *-hold*, *-pressing*, *-tightening*; with adjs., as *waist-deep*, *high*.

1672 DRYDEN *1st Pt. Conq. Granada* Prol. 10 I'll write a Play, sayes one, for I have got A broad-brim'd hat, and *wastbelt tow'rds a Plot. 1868 *Queen's Regul.* § 1128 Both straps of the havresack are to be worn outside the waist belt, so that the havresack may be easily shifted. 1805 *Ann. Reg., Chron.* 394/2 Her Majesty has recovered a diamond *waist-buckle which she had lost, and for which 10 guineas reward had been offered for the recovery. 1864 LOWELL *Fireside Trav.* 4 The merest *waist-clout of modesty. 1763 SCRAFTON *Indostan* (1770) 117 There was no way of approaching it [*sc.* the place], but through a morass *waist-deep. 1814 SCOTT *Ld. of Isles* v. xiv, The eager Knight leap'd in the sea Waist-deep. 1855 TENNYSON *Brook* 118 Waist-deep in meadow-sweet. 1553 in J. C. Jeaffreson *Middlesex County Rec.* (1886) I. 14 Unum diploidem vocatum a *wastdublett. *Ibid.*, Duos velvet *wast gyrdles. 1908 SIR H. JOHNSTON *Geo. Grenfell & Congo* II. xxiii. 589 A waist-cloth is worn all round the body from below a waist-girdle, down to the knees. 1600 FAIRFAX *Tasso* XI. xxvii, *Wast high Argantes shew'd himselfe withall. 1875 MEREDITH *Beauchamp's Career* xii. (1897) 95 A fence waist-high enclosed its plot of meadow and garden. 1904 *Daily Chron.* 12 Jan. 8/4 Two minutes passed before the men sought the mat, and then Cherpillod got a *waist hold, but failed to turn the American over. 1897 *Westm. Gaz.* 2 Sept. 3/2 The most critical place in the shirt and skirt costume is the *waist-line...One rule is universal in every well-made French gown—that the waist-line slopes downward to the front. 1870 C. C. BLACK tr. *Demmin's Weapons of War* 228 *Waist-piece, or great brayette (Vorderschurz) belonging to a Gothic suit of the fifteenth century. 1902 *New Reg. War Office* 58 *Waist-plate. Frosted Gilt Rectangular Plate with Burnished Edges. On the Plate the Royal Cypher and Crown in Silver within an Oak-leaf Wreath. On the lower part of the Wreath a Scroll inscribed 'Dieu et mon droit'. 1858–61 E. B. RAMSAY *Remin.* v. (1870) 129 His snuff he kept..in a leathern *waist-pocket. 1841 LEVER *C. O'Malley* xxxv, And the free and easy chuck under the chin, cherishing, *waist-pressing kind of a way we get with the ladies. 1853 KANE *Grinnell Exped.* xxx. (1856) 264 A long *waist-scarf, worn like the kummerbund of the Hindoos, is a fine protection while walking, to keep the cold from intruding at the pockets and waist. 1882 BESANT *All Sorts* xxi, The Professor was already come to the period of *waist-tightening.

7. Special comb.: **waist-anchor** *Naut.*, an anchor stowed in the waist of a vessel, a sheet-anchor; **waist-board** *Naut.* (see quots.); **waist-boat** *Naut.*, a boat carried in the waist of a ship, *esp.* of a whaling-vessel; hence **waistboater**, the officer in charge of such a boat; **waist-hammer**, **-iron**, shoemakers' tools (see 6); **waist-nettings** *Naut.* (see quots.); **waist-panel** *Carriage-building* (see quot.); **waist-torque** (see quot.). See also WAISTBAND, -CLOTH, -COAT, etc.

1846 A. YOUNG *Naut. Dict.*, *Waist-Anchor*, a spare bower anchor in a ship of war. 1891 H. PATTERSON *Naut. Dict.* 160 Sheet Anchor, the anchor carried in the waist on board men-o'-war. It is the same in weight as the bowers; sometimes called the waist anchor. 1627 CAPT. J. SMITH *Sea Gram.* ii. 9 The *Waist boords are set vp in the Ships waist, betwixt the Gun-waile and the waist trees, but they are most vsed in Boats, set up alongst their sides to keepe the Sea from breaking in. 1725 DE FOE *Voy. round World* (1840) 326 A kind of waste board, about two feet high, built up on the sides, without any calking or pitching, or anything to keep out the water. 1867 SMYTH *Sailor's Word-bk.*, *Waist-boards*, the berthing made to fit into a vessel's gangway on either side. 1891 *Century Dict.*, *Waist-boat*, a boat carried in the waist of a vessel; specifically, in whaling, the second mate's boat, carried in the waist on the port side. *Ibid.*, *Waistboater*, the officer of the boat carried in the waist of a whaler; the second mate. 1895 HASLUCK *Boot Making* vi. 89 The waist..should be treated with a *waist- or cramp-hammer. *Ibid.* viii. 130 The *waist-iron. 1849 TER REEHORST *Mariner's Friend* 198 *Waistnetting. 1867 SMYTH *Sailor's Word-bk.*, *Waist-nettings*, the hammock-nettings between the quarter-deck and forecastle. 1884 FORNEY *Car-Builder's Dict.* (Cent.), *Waist-panel*, the panel immediately above the lowest panel on the outside of a carriage-body. 1891 *Century Dict.*, *Waist-torque*, a girdle, properly one of twisted or spiral bars, worn by the northern nations in the early middle ages.

Waist, obs. form of WASTE.

Wai·stband. Also 6–7 wastband, wastebande. [f. WAIST + BAND *sb.*[2]]

1. Anything in the fashion of a girdle intended to go round the waist.

1584 B. R. tr. *Herodotus* I. 14 Herewith also were offered the chaynes of the Queene his wyfe, not sparing so much her girdles & wastbands, al which he caused to be dedicated at Delphos. 1884 *Pall Mall Gaz.* 6 Feb. 5/2 The..messages from Gordon..were..concealed in a quill thrust into the hair or sewn on the waistband of the natives employed.

2. *esp.* A band fitting about the waist that forms the upper part of a lower garment (skirt, pair of trousers or drawers, or the like) and serves to stiffen or maintain it; sometimes used as a receptacle for money, etc.

1686 PLOT *Staffordsh.* 294 He only took him up by the wastband of his breeches, and hung him upon one of the hooks in the shambles. 1722 DE FOE *Col. Jack* (1840) 134, I pulled it out of the waistband of my drawers. 1859 DICKENS *T. Two Cities* II. v, For the most part reclining with his hands in his waistband, looking at the fire. 1881 'OUIDA' *In Maremma* I. 43 A labourer that had got his wages in his waistband.

Waist-cloth.

† 1. *Naut.* *pl.* Coloured cloths hung about the upper works of a ship as an adornment on occasions of ceremony, or on going into action, when they also served to screen the men aboard. *Obs.*

1613 R. COCKS *Diary* (Hakl. Soc.) I. 31 The China Capt. being ready to goe for Goto, I lent hym our boate and wastclothes, and delivered hym back 120 Rs. of 8. 1627 CAPT. J. SMITH *Sea Gram.* xiii. 59 Out goes his flag and pendants, also his waste clothes and top armings, which is a long red cloth..that goeth round about the ship on the out sides of all her vpper workes fore and aft, [etc.]..as

well for the..grace of the ship, as to couer the men for being seene. 1660 PEPYS *Diary* 16 May, We..had our guns ready to fire, and our scarlet waist-cloathes out and silk pendants. 1840 HOR. SMITH *O. Cromwell* I. 284 Hundreds of lighters, pinnaces, and longboats, dressed up with waistcloths and with streamers.

2. *Naut.* A hammock-cloth stowed in the waist of a vessel.

1815 *Falconer's Dict. Marine* (ed. Burney), *Waist-cloths*, coverings of canvas or tarpauling for the hammocks, which are stowed on the gang-ways, between the quarter-deck and fore-castle. 1867 SMYTH *Sailor's Word-bk.*, *Waist-cloths*, the painted canvas coverings of the hammocks which are stowed in the waist-nettings.

3. A loin-cloth that the natives of hot climates wear round the waist, either hanging down in front or passed between the thighs.

1810 T. WILLIAMSON *E. Ind. Vade Mecum* I. 247 The dress of the *doby* is generally very plain, consisting of a turban, a *dotee*, (or waist-cloth,) and a *chudder*, (or sheet). 1835 *Court Mag.* VI. 65/2 Sometimes black glazed jackets formed part of their attire: but generally it consisted of nothing more than a blue chequered dotee, or waistcloth. 1882 DE WINDT *Equator* 81 The deceased is then brought up attired in his waistcloth and ornaments.

Waistcoat (wē·s(t)kōᵘt; *colloq.* or *vulgar* we·skǝt). For forms see WAIST and COAT *sb.* also 6 wascoat, 7 waiscot, wasecoat, -cote, wascoate, -cot, -coto, -cott.

In representations of vulgar pronunciation written *weskit*, *veskit*, etc.

A garment covering the upper part of the body down to the waist.

1. A garment forming part of ordinary male attire, worn under an outer garment (a doublet, later a coat, jacket, or the like), and intended to be partly exposed to view when in wear.

The earliest waistcoats, intended to show through the slashings and other openings of the doublet, were often extremely elaborate and costly. They were sometimes provided with sleeves, and appear to have reached to or below the hips. The waistcoat has now armholes, but not sleeves; it may be made of the same material as the coat, or of different materials, and is sometimes embroidered or otherwise ornamented. The back is now of inferior or thinner material.

1519 *Nottingham Rec.* III. 354 For makyng of a waste cotte. 1599 B. JONSON *Cynthia's Rev.* II. i, Hee has a rich wrought wast-coat to entertaine his visitants in. 1649 *K. Chas. Sp. Scaffold* 7 The King..being in his Wastcoat, put his Cloak on again. 1666 PEPYS *Diary* 20 June, I have of late taken too much cold by washing my feet and going in a thin silke waistecoate, without any other coate over it, and open-breasted. 1711 SWIFT *Jrnl. to Stella* 28 Nov., Domville saw Savage in Italy, and says he is a coxcomb, and half mad: he goes in red, and with yellow waistcoats. 1791 BOSWELL *Johnson* an. 1781, 1 Apr., Sir Philip Jennings Clerk..wore..an embroidered waistcoat, and very rich laced ruffles. 1837 DICKENS *Pickw.* x, He was habited in a coarse-striped waistcoat, with black calico sleeves, and blue glass buttons. 1869 'LEWIS CARROLL' *Phantasmagoria* 71 He would keep his right-hand buried (Like Napoleon) in his waistcoat.

† b. Applied to a plainer and less costly garment, usually of knitted wool, worn chiefly for additional warmth. *Obs.*

1585 HIGINS *Junius' Nomencl.* 163/2 *Indusium*,..a waste coate, or wollen peticoate. 1591 FLORIO *2nd Fruites* 5 *T.* Giue me my wastecote. *R.* Which will you haue, that of flannel? *T.* No, giue me that which is knit. 1617 MORYSON *Itin.* I. 68, I hauing for the cold at Dantzke, in the beginning of September, put on a wollen wasecoat, was forced now at the entring of Italy, for the great heat in the end of October, to put off the same. 1698 *Ogilby's Brit., Itin.* 4/1 Doncaster...Enjoys a good Trade for Stockings and Knit Wastcoats, &c. 1711 SWIFT *Jrnl. to Stella* 5 Oct., It grows bloody cold, and I have no waistcoat here.

c. phr. † *In one's waistcoat*; *esp.* as the typical undress of exercise implying the casting aside of an upper garment (cf. mod. *in one's shirt-sleeves*). (obs.) *Under one's waistcoat*: in one's breast.

1607 B. BARNES *Divils Charter* IV. v. I 2 b, Enter Astor and Philippo in their wast-cotes with rackets. 1859 H. KINGSLEY *G. Hamlyn* xxxix, With all our vanity and absurdity, we Irish have good warm hearts under our waistcoats.

† d. Applied to a child's first garment. *Obs.*

1538 ELYOT *Dict.*, *Crepundia*..the fyrst apparayle of chyldren, as swathels, wastcotes, and such lyke.

e. *transf.* Applied to the plumage of birds, or the coat of animals, about the breast or stomach, *esp.* where this is strikingly different in colour or marking from that of the rest of the body.

1898 J. D. REES in *19th Cent.* June 1024 A woodpecker with black wings, a white waistcoat, and a crimson crest.

† 2. A short outer coat or jacket; a 'jersey'.

a 1628 F. GREVIL *Life Sidney* (1652) 24 His wast-coat..not unlike the best sort of those woollen knit ones, which our ordinary watermen row us in. 1765 in *Sixth Rep. Dep. Kpr. Publ. Rec.* App. II. 134 Floats made of cork in the form of seamen's waistcoats..to prevent drowning.

3. A short (woollen) garment worn next the skin.

1606 HOLLAND *Sueton.* 75 In winter time clad he went against the colde with foure coates, together with a good thick gowne, and his Wastcoate or Peticoate bodie of woollen. 1789 W. BUCHAN *Dom. Med.* (1790) 347 A flannel waistcoat worn next the skin has often a very good effect in the dysentery. 1806–7 J. BERESFORD *Miseries Hum. Life* xx. § 32 Putting on a cold shirt, for the first time after throwing off the under flannel waistcoat.

4. As an article of feminine attire.

† a. A short garment, often elaborate and costly, worn by women about the upper part of the body (usually beneath an outer gown, but so as to be seen). *Obs.*

In the 16th and early 17th c. the waistcoat was one of the normal garments of women, having superseded the *placard* and *stomacher*. Later in the 17th c. (when going out of fashion), *esp.* if worn without an upper gown, it appears to have been considered a mark of a low-class woman of ill-repute (see WAISTCOATEER 1).

1547 BOORDE *Brev. Health* cxxxviii. (1557) 51, I cause a man to lye in his doublet, and a woman in her waste cote. 1603 DEKKER *Batch. Banq.* iii. C 2 b, Then comes downe mistresse Nurse, as fine as a farthing fiddle, in her petticoate and kertle, hauing on a white wastcoate, with a flaunting cambricke ruffe about her neck. 1688 HOLME *Armoury* III. 95/1 Wastcoat or Waistcoat..is an Habit or Garment generally worn by the middle and lower sort of Women. 1711 ADDISON *Spect.* No. 15 ¶ 4 A Furbelow of precious Stones, an Hat buttoned with a Diamond, a Brocade Waistcoat or Petticoat, are standing Topicks.

† b. Applied to garments of foreign women that resembled the contemporary feminine waistcoat.

1600 HAKLUYT *Voy.* III. 369 The [Indian] women weare of the sayd Turqueses at their nostrils and eares, and very good wast-coats and other garments. 1648 GAGE *West. Ind.* xii. 56 Their Wascoats made like bodies, with skirts, laced likewise with gold or silver. 1653 GREAVES *Seraglio* 130 They [the women] likewise sleep as the men do, in their linnen breeches, and quilted waste-coats. 1707 FUNNELL *Dampier's Voy.* ix. 254 [The Malayan women] wear a Linnen Waste-coat, which reaches no lower than the lower part of their Breasts.

† c. A short (sleeveless) undergarment worn about the upper part of the body; a camisole. *Obs.*

1580 HOLLYBAND *Treas. Fr. Tong*, *Vne Chemise de drap, or chemiselle*, a wastcoat. 1747 LADY M. W. MONTAGU *Town Ecl., St. James's Coffee-house* 75 Her night-cloaths tumbled with resistless grace, And her bright hair play'd careless round her face; Reaching the kettle, made her gown unpin, She wore no waistcoat, and her shift was thin. 1785 MISS FIELDING *Ophelia* I. vii, I [a woman] had never worn any thing round my waist but thin waistcoats.

d. A garment or a bodice-front designed in imitation of the masculine waistcoat.

1711 TICKELL *Spectator* No. 104 ¶ 3. 1824 SCOTT *Redgauntlet* ch. xvii, Trolloping things our mothers must have looked [in riding dress of the 18th c.], with long square-cut coats,..and with waistcoats plentifully supplied with a length of pocket, which [etc.]. 1883 *Truth* 31 May 768/2 The bodice had a sweet little waistcoat, over which the edges of the embroidered linen almost met. 1913 *Play Pictorial* No. 134 p. ii./1 Waistcoats [for ladies] are growing more and more in popularity, and the waistcoat blouse is one of the latest novelties.

5. *attrib.* and *Comb.*, as *waistcoat button*, *-piece*, *-pocket* (hence *-pocketful*), *-string*.

1787 in *Sixth Rep. Dep. Kpr. Publ. Rec.* App. II. 178 Of a new method of making..Coat and *Waistcoat Buttons. 1859 *Habits of Gd. Society* iii. 142 Elaborate studs, waistcoat-buttons, and wrist-links, are all abominable. 1832 HT. MARTINEAU *Hill & Valley* i. (ed. 4) 12 There is not a shop within twenty miles that would furnish me with such a *waistcoat-piece as I should choose to wear. 1760 JOHNSON *Idler* No. 95 ¶ 12 He now openly declares his Resolution to become a Gentleman;..carries Silver, for Readiness, in his *Waistcoat pocket. 1887 RUSKIN *Præterita* II. 153 The portress receiving a sort of dirty flattened sixpence..and returning me a waistcoat-pocketful of the loveliest clean-struck centimes. 1835 DICKENS *Sk. Boz, Mr. Watkins Tottle* ii, Watkins falling bump on his knees, and breaking two brace-buttons and a *waistcoat-string in the act.

Hence **Wai·stcoatful** *nonce-wd.*, as much (of anything) as would fill, or cover, the waistcoat. **Wai·stcoating**, a textile fabric made esp. for men's waistcoats. **Wai·stcoatless**, *a.*, wearing no waistcoat.

1824 LANDOR *Imag. Conv., Cav. Puntomichino & Mr. Talcranagh* Wks. 1853 I. 171/2 The people..would have added new decorations to his *waistcoatful of orders. 1809 MAR. EDGEWORTH *Tales Fash. Life* II. *Dun* 315 Mrs. Carver bespoke from him two pieces of *waistcoating. 1862 *Catal. Internat. Exhib., Brit.* II. No. 4071, Fancy waistcoatings and skirtings. a 1876 M. COLLINS *Pen Sk.* (1879) I. 10, I sat in his courtyard, coatless and *waistcoatless.

Waistcoated (wē·s(t)kōᵘtĕd), *a.* [f. WAISTCOAT + -ED[2].] Provided with a waistcoat.

1798 CHARLOTTE SMITH *Yng. Philos.* I. 27 He..was pantalooned and waistcoated after the very newest fashion. 1897 MARIE CORELLI *Ziska* i, His paunch..a kind of waistcoated air balloon.

b. with defining word prefixed.

1838 DICKENS *O. Twist* ii, As I purpose to show in the sequel whether the white-waistcoated gentleman was right or not. 1896 R. B. MANSFIELD *Chips* 224 Magpies..the black-coated and white-waistcoated gentry.

Wai·stcoatee·r. Also 7 wastecoateer, -coater, wastcoateer, -coatier, westecoateer, 8 wastecateer, 9 waistcoatteer. [f. WAISTCOAT + -EER.]

† 1. A low-class prostitute. *Obs.* exc. *Hist.*

a 1616 BEAUM. & FL. *Wit without Money* IV. iv, *Luce.* Doe you thinke you are here sir amongst your wastcoateers, your base Wenches that scratch at such occasions? 1675 *Char. Town-Gallant* 3 Every thing with him is an Incentive to Lust, and every Woman Devil enough to tempt him, Covent-Garden, Silk-gowns, and Wapping Wastcoatiers, are equally his Game. 1822 SCOTT *Nigel* xvii, 'I know the face of yonder waistcoateer', continued the guide.

2. *nonce-use.* A person wearing a waistcoat of a specified fashion.

1825 T. L. BEDDOES *Let.* 11 Jan. (1894) 49 Here followed a long Brutus & Cassius discourse between a shilling-buttoned waist-coatteer of a porter and myself.

Waisted (wē·stĕd), *a.* [f. WAIST + -ED[2].] Having a waist (usu. of specified size or form). (For parasynthetic formations, as *deep-*, *fair-*, *long-*, *short-waisted*, see the first element.)

1582 STANYHURST *Æneis* etc. (Arb.) 141 Shee limps in the going,..And as a cow wasted plods on, with an head like a lutecase. 1824 *New Monthly Mag.* XI. 124 Beautiful as youth; Waisted like Hebe; and with Dian's step. 1913 E. T. LEEDS *Archæol. Anglo-Sax. Settlements* vii. 132 A peculiar waisted beaker with rounded base often terminating in an excrescent knob.

Waister (wē·stəɹ). *Naut.* [f. WAIST + -ER[1].] (See quots.)

1815 *Falconer's Dict. Marine* (ed. Burney), *Waisters*, a name given, to the men stationed in the waist in working the ship. 1846 A. YOUNG *Naut. Dict.*, *Waisters*, 'green hands, or broken-down seamen', placed in the waist of a ship of war, to do duty not requiring a knowledge of seamanship. 1850 H. MELVILLE *White Jacket* I. iii. 12 Then, there are the Waisters, always stationed on the gun-deck. These haul aft the fore and main-sheets, besides being subject to ignoble duties; attending to the drainage [etc.]. 1854 J. HANNAY *Sand & Shells* 13 Mr. Crabb relieved his feelings by pegging into an idle 'waister' with his 'colt'.

Waistless (wē·stlĕs), *a.* [f. WAIST + -LESS.] Having no waist; having the appearance of being without a waist.

1500–20 DUNBAR *Poems* xxvi. 97 Full mony a waistless wallydrag With wamiss vnweildable, did furth wag, In creische that did incress. 1796 *Sporting Mag.* VIII. 185 To conform to fashion's sway, Betsey is become waistless. 1870 MISS BROUGHTON *Red as Rose* I. 122 Their little, bustless, waistless, hipless figures. 1910 SUFFLING *Eng. Ch. Brasses* 128 It is a life size figure habited in a long flowing gown, waistless and without ornament of any kind.

Waist-rail.

1. *Naut.* (See quot. 1867.)

1804 DUNCAN *Mariner's Chron.* Pref. p. xix, Drift-rails, fife-rails, sheer-rails, waist-rails, &c. 1867 SMYTH *Sailor's Word-bk.*, *Waist-rail*, the channel-rail or moulding of the ship's side.

2. *Carriage-building.* (See quot.)

1884 FORNEY *Car-builder's Dict.* (Cent.), *Waist-rail*, a horizontal piece in the framing of the side of a passenger-carriage.

Waist-tree. *Naut.* (See quot. 1846.)

1485 *Nav. Acc. Hen. VII* (1896) 50 Wast trees..ij. 1627 CAPT. J. SMITH *Sea Gram.* ii. 9 The Waist boords are set vp in the Ships waist, betwixt the Gun-waile and the waist trees. 1704 J. HARRIS *Lex. Techn.* I, *Wast-Trees*, are those Timbers of a Ship which lie in the Waste. 1846 A. YOUNG *Naut. Dict.*, *Waist-Tree* or *Rough-Tree*, a spare spar placed along the side of a ship's waist where there happens to be no bulwark, in order to protect persons from falling overboard.

Wait (wēⁱt), *sb.* Forms: 3–7 wayte, waite, (5 wayet, whayte), 4–7 wayt, 4, 7 weyte, (6 weytte, wette), 5–6 wate, (5 watte), 6 waytte (waitte, wayght, weyght, wyethe, whet), 7 waight, (weight), 4– wait. [Partly a. ONF. *wait, *wet* masc. (= OF. *guait*, *gait*, *guet*, mod.F. *guet*, Pr. *gach*, *gait*), vbl. noun f. *waitier* (see WAIT *v.*) and ONF. *waite* fem. (OF. *guaite*, *gaite*, mod.F. *guette*, *guète*, Pr. *gacha*, *gaita*); it is uncertain whether the fem. sb. is f. the vb., or a direct adoption from Teut. (cf. OHG. *wahta*, Goth. *wahtwō*): see WAIT *v.* The word adopted from Fr. has coalesced with an Eng. formation on WAIT *v.* Cf. AWAIT *sb.*

Many apparent examples of this word in texts of 14–16th c. really belong to the synonymous AWAIT *sb.*, which, like other words beginning with a prefix, was often written as two words. It is possible that the *a* was in the 16th c. sometimes apprehended by writers and readers as the indefinite article, but distinct evidence of this is wanting.]

I. The action of WAIT *v.*[1]

1. In various phrases with the general sense: To take up a concealed position in order to make an unforeseen attack, or to be in readiness to intercept one's enemy or intended prey in passing; to lurk in ambush.

† a. *To sit in wait('s*. *Obs. rare.* (cf. AWAIT *sb.*)

a 1300 *E. E. Psalter* ix. 29 He sites in waites [Vulg. *in insidiis*] with riche of land In derne, to sla þe vnderand. 1667 MILTON *P. L.* IV. 825 Why satst thou like an enemie in waite Here watching at the head of these that sleep?

b. *To lie* (or † *lay*) *in wait*. † Also, *to lie at (the) wait*, *to lie on wait*.

c 1440 *Pallad. on Husb.* IV. 157 For moldywarpes cattes is to kepe To ligge in wayte to touche hem with her cle. c 1449 PECOCK *Repr.* I. xix. 113 As if perauenture in oon of thilk weies a man liggith in wait for to sle my seid seruaunt. 1450–1530 *Myrr. our Ladye* 311 The faythful saynge of the crede chaseth away fendes whiche lye on wayte to hynder men. 1503–4 *Act 19 Hen. VII*, c. 36 Preamb., Stanhop..lay in wayte uppon the seid sir William and hym grevously wouneded. 1530 PALSGR. 605/2, I ley in wayte of one to do him a displeasure. a 1578 LINDESAY (Pitscottie) *Chron. Scot.* (S.T.S.) I. 31 Or evir he cuild persawe the chancellaris folkis lyand in the wait for him he was invironit and circuatt round about with thame. 1611 BIBLE *Ps.* x. 9 He lieth in waite secretly as a lyon in his denne, he lieth in wait to catch the poore. 1668 H. ROLLE *Abridgm.*, *Action sur Case* 50 Si home dit dun auter, que il lay in wait at shooters hill to rob him, action sur le case gist. a 1672 WOOD *Life* Sept. (O.H.S.) I. 123 Some of their partie were upon London road neare Thame to lay in wait for provision or wine that came from London towards Aylesbury. 1709 STEELE *Tatler* No. 34 ¶ 5 The five Fields where the Robbers lie in wait. 1794 MRS. RADCLIFFE *Myst. Udolpho* xxviii, His friend advised that

Supplement, p. 3873; Corrigenda, p. 4092; Spurious words, p. 4093; Books quoted, p. 4094

theyshould lie in wait for the enemy. 1879 Cassell's Techn. Educ. IV. 95/2 Full of rage, he lay in wait for Rosen, and as the latter left the Senate, he rushed upon him sword in hand. 1904 Lady M. Verney Verney Mem. II. 341 Lying in wait for dowagers' coaches in tortuous lanes.

fig. 1500–20 Dunbar Poems xxi. 34 May no man lang in welth indure, For wo that evir lyis at the wait. 1553 Gresham in Burgon Life (1839) I. 118 To the intent to prevent the marchaunts, bothe strangers and Englishe, who allwayes lay in wayte to prevent my devisses. a1613 Overbury Characters, Meere Fellow Wks. (1856) 129 His religion lies in wait for the inclination of his patron. 1704 Swift T. Tub ii, A ring of disciples, who lie in wait to catch up their droppings. 1784 Cowper Task iii. 553 Ten thousand dangers lie in wait to thwart The process. 1785 T. Balguy Disc. 47 He is constantly lying at wait to correct them. 1791 Charlotte Smith Celestina III. 212 He..had indeed no other design than to lay in wait for traces of that involved mystery. 1865 Dickens Mut. Fr. ii. i, The habit..had given him a suspicious manner, or a manner that would be better described as one of lying in wait.

†c. *To lie wait.* Obs. rare.

1445 in Anglia XXVIII. 269 Ambicion..which evir lyeth waite at chambir dorys. a1578 Lindesay (Pitscottie) Chron. Scot. (S.T.S.) I. 55 Thair followit na thing bot slaughter.., ilk ane lyand wait for wther as they had ben settand tinchellis for the murther of wyld beistes.

d. *To lay wait*, †*lay one's wait.*

1577 Hanmer Anc. Eccl. Hist., Euseb. x. viii. 206 But God being the friend..of Constantinus brought to light the wayte layde for him in secret. 1586 Thynne Contn. Ann. Scot. 457/1 in Holinshed, But, hauing wait laid for him by an ambush of his enimies, he was in his iorneie towards his castell intercepted. 1597 Beard Theatre God's Judgem. (1612) 333 Wherefore they layed wait for him as hee came one day from hunting, and murdered him. 1653 J. Mayer Expos. Ps. xxxi. 4 When wait was layd for him to kill him in his house. 1665 Manley Grotius' Low-C. Warrs 169 Although they could escape all the wait laid for them by Pirates. 1841 James Brigand ii, They were known to lay wait in all the principal passes, both of Piedmont and Savoy.

transf. and fig. 1535 Coverdale Acts xx. 19, I haue.. serued ye Lorde..with many teares and tentacions, which happened vnto me by ye layenges of wayte of the Iewes. 1599 T. Storer Life & D. Wolsey G 2 b, Those vnbaptised sacrilegious hands, That onely for Gods vestrie laide their waite. 1611 Bible Jer. ix. 8 One speaketh peaceably to his neighbour with his mouth, but in heart he layeth his waite. 1755 Monitor I. 27 Can a free constitution be out of danger, where one part of it lays wait to destroy the energy of another? 1799 E. Du Bois Piece Family Biog. II. 42 By laying wait for a favourable moment, she might ultimately obtain the enjoyment of her criminal passion. 1891 Sat. Rev. 14 Nov. 563/2 Their..followers laid perpetual wait to steal.

†e. *To take under wait*: to capture or surprise by an ambush. Obs.

1533 Bellenden Livy (S.T.S.) I. 180 Þai war na less astonist þan þai had bene tane vnder wait [haud secus quam si in insidias incidissent].

†f. The sb. used without the phrasal context: Ambush. Obs. rare.

1533 Bellenden Livy (S.T.S.) I. 149 Als sone as hermyneus herde the noyis of Valerius company, he Ischit with his buschement haistely fra þe wate [concurrit ex insidiis]. 1788 Burns Written in Friars-Carse Hermitage 20 Check thy climbing step, elate, Evils lurk in felon wait. 1796 Mme. D'Arblay Camilla IV. 375 He was..always in wait to converse with her when she was seated.

2. The action of watching.

†a. In phrases. *At (the) wait*, on the watch. *To do, make wait*, to keep watch. *To have in wait*, to have under observation. Also, *to lie in great wait, lay good wait* (cf. 1), to be carefully on the watch. Obs.

c1440 Partenope 6715 (B. M. MS.) His ffrendes had nym so in watte..That his purpose myght not be Atte Bleys parfouremed. c1460 in Archæologia XXIX. 339 Þe Fisshe drewe nere vnto þe bayte; Nede haþe no lawe,..þe Egle þerto euer layde goode wayte. c1470 Henry Wallace x. 379 A suttell knycht tharat had gret despyt, Folowyt at wait. 1500–20 Dunbar Poems xlii. 21 And in thir termis can thai say, Do wait, and lat him nocht away. 1509 Fisher Funeral Serm. C'tess Richmond Wks. (1876) 293 Her sobre temperaunce..wherin she lay in as grete wayte of herself as ony persone myght. 1513 Douglas Æneis xi. xiv. 83 Quhen as ane Aruns, by hys mortal fait Onto myschewos deid predestinate, Circulis at the wayt. c1520 Everyman (facs.) B j, I haue a great enemy that hath me in wayte Whiche intendeth me for to hyndre. 1523 Berners Froiss. I. cclxi. 144/2 The moost parte of the state of the prince..was well knowen with the kynges there about..for they layed great wayte to knowe it. 1535 Hen. VIII in Strype Eccl. Mem. 1733 I. App. liv. 141 That they..do make & cause to be made diligent search, wait & espyal, whether the said Bps. & Clergy do..execute..their said charge.

†b. Watchfulness. Obs.

1575 Laneham Let. (1871) 18 It waz a sport very pleazaunt ..to see..the nimblness and wayt of the dog too take hiz auauntage.

3. a. (*Day's*) *wait*: the duty of keeping guard by day performed by the warders of the Tower.

1694 E. Chamberlayne Pres. St. Eng. iii. 608 The Yeoman Warders of the Tower are 40 in number....Ten of them are usually upon the Days-wait. 1733–47 in Pegge Curialia iii. (1791) 103 When the Man waiting for another hath performed such Wait, he shall not be permitted to wait again, so as to continue his Wait for divers Men one after another.

b. The period of attendance at court of a lord- or lady-in-waiting.

1884 World 20 Aug. 10/1 The Queen always likes the yearly rota of waits to be arranged so that her favourite ladies shall be with her at Balmoral. 1893 Westm. Gaz. 7 July 1/2 He will have no duties..as his appointed 'wait' is from October 3 to 17, when the Queen will be at Balmoral, where the attendance of a Lord-in-Waiting is always dispensed with.

4. The state or condition of waiting or remaining expectant. *At wait*: in an expectant attitude. *In wait*: waiting, remaining in a place in expectation of some one coming. rare.

1873 Longf. Wayside Inn iii. Mother's Ghost xviii, When she came to the castle gate, There stood her eldest daughter in wait. 1875 Swinburne Ess. & Stud. 344 Next to this we find a sudden sunny bank in the dim depth of a wood, with a wolf at watch and a rabbit at wait.

5. A period of waiting; spec. *Theatr.*, the time of an audience's waiting between the acts, or of an actor's waiting between his appearances in the piece.

1855–6 Dickens in Forster Life (1874) III. v. 107 The waits between the acts being very much longer than the acts themselves. 1863 Le Fanu House by Churchyard III. ix. 93 This was said after a wait of nearly ten minutes. 1876 Daily News 27 Oct. 5/6 What a long, tedious wait it was up there on the edge of the wood while we listened..for some sign of Graf Keller's approach. 1884 Manch. Exam. 16 Oct. 5/4 The audience..passed a long wait pleasantly in singing a number of political songs. 1886 C. E. Pascoe London To-day iii. (ed. 3) 50 The Criterion has a chorus of glee singers to wile away waits through the courses.

II. A person who watches or waits.

†6. A watchman; a scout, spy. Obs.

a. A military watchman, sentinel, or look-out; also a scout, spy; esp. a watchman in a camp, castle, or fortified place who was furnished with a horn or trumpet to sound an alarm or to make a signal.

a1300 Cursor M. 11541 He [Herod] sett his waites bi þe stret, If þai moght wit þaa kinges mett, He commandid son þai suld be slan. 13.. K. Alis. 4312 Theo knyghtis beore body dubbeth: The waytes bleow, the belle rynges. c1325 Coer de L. 2281 The wayts of that host that did espie, And ful loud began to crie: We are betrayd and y-nome! 1340 Ayenb. 121 Þet is þe wayte of þe castele þet neure ne slepþ. c1380 Wyclif Wks. (1880) 395 Þe holy prophete Ezechiel saiþ: 'If þe wayte or þe wacche-man se ennemys cum [etc.].' 1387 Trevisa Higden (Rolls) II. 191 A knyghte þat highte Strabo stode in a weytes place. 1398 — Barth. De P. R. v. v. (1495) 108 And for the eye is in stede of a wayte, kynde settyth hym in the hyghest place of the body. c1400 Laud Troy Bk. 7222 Euery man to his In owe, The wayte be-gan nyght to blowe. c1435 Torr. Portugal 1065 Waytes on the walle gan blowe, Knyghtis assemled on a rowe. c1440 Promp. Parv. 513/2 Wayte, speculator (v.r. explorator). 1450–80 tr. Secreta Secret. lxi. 37 Loke thou haue good waytes and aspies in thyn oste. 1470–85 Malory Arthur vii. xxxi. 263 At the last by fortune he came to a Castel and there he herd the waytes vpon the wallys. 1513 Douglas Æneis iii. iv. 60 Mysenus, the wait, on the hie garret seyis, And, with his trumpet, thame a takin maid.

transf. 1398 Trevisa Barth. De P. R. xvii. clxxx. (1495) 721 A vynyerde is ofte vysyted and ouerseen of the erthe tylthers and kepers of vynes and a wayte is there set in an hyghe place.

b. A watchman attached to the royal household who sounded the watch, etc., by the blowing of a pipe, trumpet, or other wind-instrument.

13.. K. Alis. 7769 When theo table was y drawe, Theo wayte gan a pipe blawe. c1430 Pilgr. Lyf Manhode iv. xlvii. (1869) 198 The ladi that thou hast herd pleye with instrumentes and bereth an horn that is the waite that awaketh the king alle times that he slepeth bi hire blowinge. a1440 Sir Eglam. 1097 Grete lordys were at the assent; Waytys blewe, to mete they wente. a1483 Liber Niger in Househ. Ord. (1790) 48 A Wayte, that nyghtly, from Mighelmasse till Shere-Thursday, pipeth the watche within this courte fower tymes,..and he to make bon gayte, and [? read at] everey chambre door and office, as well for fyre as for other pikers or perelles...And under this yoman, a groome wayte. 1802 Mrs. Radcliffe Gaston de Blondeville (1826) I. 185 And thus it kept, until the wayte piped his second watch in all the courts.

c. A municipal watchman.

1418 Maldon (Essex) Court-Rolls Bundle 11, no. 3, [Ordered, by consent] ballivorum et magnatum ville, in defectu ministrorum alias dictorum waytes, quod quedam campana ecclesie Omnium Sanctorum et alia campana ecclesie Sancti Petri congruis horis noctis pulsentur, viz., in mane Daybeli, et in vespere Curfewe. 1419 Liber Albus (Rolls) 646 Quod qualibet Porta custodiatur per diem per duos homines bene armatos, et de nocte claudetur per Servientem eam inhabitantem; et quod quilibet Serviens habeat unum Wayte, sumptibus suis propriis.

†7. collect. A body of guards. Obs.

1704 in Pegge Curialia iii. (1791) 81 Which Twelve Men [of the Guard] are to be chosen by the Six Waits then out of Waiting. 1747 Ibid. 104 Upon Forfeiture of his or their share of such Bounty-Money among the rest of the Wait then and there in waiting.

8. †a. pl. A small body of wind instrumentalists maintained by a city or town at the public charge. Also sing., a member of this body. Obs.

They played for the daily diversion of the councillors, on ceremonial and festive occasions, and as a town or city band they entertained the citizens, perambulating the streets, often by night or in the early morning.

1298 [see Waitmeat]. 1438 in Cov. Leet Bk. 189 Hyt is ordeyned that they [sic] Trumpet schall haue the rule off the whaytes, and off hem be Cheffe. 1467 Ibid. 335 Also þat þe Waytis of þis Cite..shall not passe þis Cite, but to abbottis & priours within x miles of þis Cite. 1499 in W. Kelly Notices illustr. Drama (1865) 189 Thomas Wylkyns Wayte. 1541 Ibid. 192 Item paed to Thomas Goldsmyth ffor mendyng of the Towne Waytes Collars iijs. iiijd. 1548 Ibid. 193 Item pd to Mr. Gyllott for the Waughts gownes xxxvjs vjd. 1553 Machyn Diary (Camden) 47 [The new Lord Mayor went] toward Westmynter [attended by the] craftes of London.. with trumpets blohyng and the whets playing. 1571 in Picton L'pool Munic. Rec. (1883) I. 118 Lewis Lockwood, Bagpiper was admitted Wayte of this town. 1587 Fleming Contn. Holinshed III. 289/2 The waits of the citie were placed with lowd musicke, who cheerefullie & melodiouslie welcomed hir maiestie into the citie, this song being soong by the best voices in the same. 1589 [? Nashe] Almond for Parrat 2 Who hearing the waites play vnder his window very early, insulted..that [etc.]. a1596 Sir T. More (Malone Soc.) 944 Where are the waytes? goe, bid them play, to spend the time awhile. 1609 B. Jonson Silent Wom. i. i, Tru. A Trumpet should fright him terribly, or the Hau'-boyes? Cle. Out of his senses. The Waights of the citie haue a pension of him, not to come neere that ward. 1617 Moryson Itin. iv. iv. i. (1903) 301 In like sorte many Cittyes mantayne at publike charge Musitians, vsing Sagbutts, Hoboyes, and such loude Instruments, which wee call the waytes of Cyttyes, and these play at the publicke house of the Citty each day at Noone, when the Senatours goe to dinner, and at all publike Feasts. a1625 Fletcher Captain ii. ii, Jac. Hark, are the Waits abroad? Fab. Be softer prethee, 'Tis private musick. ..Jac. Well I will hear, or sleep, I care not whether. 1667 Lond. Gaz. No. 189/1 The Mayor, Aldermen and Common Council of this Town, after a Sermon Preached to them, went to the Market-Cross in their Formalities, the Waytes playing before them. 1670 Moral State Eng. 132 The Weights of the Town who played upon Cornets and Haut-bois. 1687 Wood Life 3 Sept. (O.H.S.) III. 230 When he came to Quartervois he was entertaind with the wind musick or waits belonging to the city and Universitie. 1731 Fielding Letter Writers ii. ii, You are a couple of wretched Scrapers, and play ten Degrees worse than the University Waits. 1736 F. Drake Eboracum i. vi. 197 [The sheriffs] are preceded by the city's waites, or musicians, in their scarlet liveries and silver badges playing all the way through the streets. 1762 Goldsm. Nash (Globe) 524/1 Upon a stranger's arrival at Bath he is welcomed by..the voice and music of the city waits. 1764 in Picton L'pool Munic. Rec. (1886) II. 202 Ordered that John Bolton and John Langhorn be appointed two publick Waites of this town.

b. pl. A band of musicians and singers who perambulate the streets by night at the approach of Christmas and the New Year playing and singing carols and other seasonable music for gratuities.

1773 Archæologia II. 66 What we at present call the Waits, or the music on the nights of the Christmas holydays. 1801 Busby Dict. Mus. s.v. Wayghtes, Those persons who annually, at the approach of Christmas, salute us with their nocturnal concerts, were, and are to this day, called Wayghtes. 1820 Irving Sketch Bk. II. 37 The sound of the Waits,..breaks upon the mid-watches of a winter night. 1889 Grove's Dict. Mus. IV. 375 Waits, The. A name given, from time immemorial, to the little bands of rustic Musicians who sing and play Carols, by night, in country places, at Christmas-time.

†c. gen. A player on the flute, hautboy, trumpet, etc. Obs.

1510 Stanbridge Vocabula (W. de W.) Div, Tibicen, a wayte. 1585 Higins Junius' Nomencl. 501/1 Spondiales vel spondiauli,..such as plaied vpon long pipes at diuine seruice, they may be called the waytes. 1600 Holland Livy xvii. Brev. 390 That..as he returned home to his owne house, the waits should sound the hautboies all the way [tibicine canente]. 1648 Gage West Ind. 12 Whom travelling, Indian Waites and Trumpets should accompany.

†9. One who waits in service, an attendant. Obs.

1652 Benlowes Theoph. xi. xxx, Still to have toting Waits unseel thine Eyes, In Bed, at Board, when sit, when rise: Such, Card'nal-like, their Paris prize 'bove Paradise.

†III. 10. [Originally a transferred use of 8 c.] pl. Wind instruments, either hautboys, shawms, or flutes. Also sing. (rare). Obs.

[Cf. Sp., Pg. gaita, a kind of flute; the word seems to have been adopted from OF., though no examples of the sense have been found in French of any period.]

1530 Palsgr. 286/1 Wayte an instrument, hauboys. 1556 Withals Dict. (1562) 68, 2 The trumpet or waytes, tuba. 1592 Doctor Faustus in Thoms E. Eng. Prose Rom. (1858) III. 178 Lutes, viols, citterns waits..and all manner of other instruments. 1620 Shelton 2nd Pt. Quixote xxvi. 173 For amongst Moores you haue..a kinde of Shaulmes that bee like our Waytes. [1703 Motteux, like our Waits or Hautboys.] 1636 C. Butler Princ. Mus. ii. i. 93 [Wind-instruments, as] Waits or Hobois. 1683 Tryon Way to Health 654 Waits are under the dominion of Jupiter, in the Sign Libra; the Sounds and harmonious Consorts of this Instrument are great, noble and pleasing to Nature.

IV. 11. attrib. and Comb., as *wait-pipe, player, -song*; †**wait captain**, the chief of the municipal waits; †**wait fee** (see quot. 1706); †**wait-layer**, one who lies in wait; †**waitmeat**, food supplied to the municipal waits.

1565 in Picton L'pool Munic. Rec. (1888) II. 35 Mr. Mayor called James Atherby then being *Waite Captain. 1563 in Spelman Gloss. s.v., Per redditum 14s. pro *Wayte fee, and Castle garde. 1706 Phillips (ed. Kersey), Wayt-fee, (old Law-word) Ward-penny, or a Fee anciently paid for keeping Watch and Ward. 1600 Holland Livy xl. xii. 1067 He..will..have the world beleeve that I play the part not onely of a secret and cunning *wait-laier, but of an open theefe. 1632 — Cyrupædia 30 Who ever shall effect this, had need be a waitlayer, a deepe dissembler. 1298 Yorks. Inquisit. (Yorks. Rec. Soc. 1902) III. 84, 2s. for *Waytemete and Schirrefstuthe. 14.. Nom. in Wr.-Wülcker 694/40 Hec colomaula,..*waytepype. 1610 in T. Sharp Cov. Myst. (1825) 210 Every Maior shall pay to the *waite players iiij d. 1872 Whittier Penn. Pilgrim 501 On frosty Christmas eves..he..closed his eyes, and listened to the sweet Old *wait-songs sounding down his native street.

Wait (wēt), v.[1] Pa. t. and pa. pple. **waited.** Forms: 2–7 **waite**, 3–8 **wayte**, 4–7 **wayt**, (4 *erron.* **whaite, whayte**), 3–4, 6 *Sc.* **waitte**, 4–6 *Sc.* **vaitte**, 5 **waytte**, 6–7 **waight**, 4–6 *Sc.* **watte**, 8 *dial.* **watt**, 3–4 **weite**, 4–6 **weyte**, 7 **weight**, 3–6, 8 *dial.* **wate**, 4 **vate**, 4– **wait.** [Early ME. waite-n, a. ONF. waitier (Central OF. guaitier, gaiter, mod.F. guetter) = Prov.

gaitar, It. guatare, to watch, lie in wait for; a. OHG. wahtēn (mod.G. wachten) to watch, guard, f. wahta fem. (mod.G. wacht) watch, f. OTeut. *wak-: see Wake v.]

I. The simple verb.

†1. trans. To watch with hostile intent; to spy upon; to lie in wait for. Obs.

c1200 Vices & Virtues 103 Ðat bið ðo werewede gostes ðe waitið ðo soules hier buuen on ðe wolkne. c1200 Trin. Coll. Hom. 43 For ure gult god man bicom and ure eldre waiteden him to deaðe. Ibid. 87 Þanne ferde þe fule gost, and seuene oðre gostes mid him forcuðere þen him self were, and bitrumede þat child, and waiteden hit on eche wise. a1300 Cursor M. 23731 Euer he wates vs þat fede, es nathing certainur þan dede. c1300 Havelok 512 He may [me] waiten for to slo. 1340 Hampole Pr. C. 1186 His despisers he waytes ay, Als shadow to tak to his pray. c1375 Sc. Leg. Saints ii. (Peter) 22 In Jerusalem he wes bofte, spyit, waitit, and bundyn ofte. c1420 Wyntoun Cron. v. xi. 3062 (MS. Cott.) Ane erl of his compauny Waytit Traen sa besely Þat wiþe a buschement he has [slayn] Traen. a1450 Le Morte Arth. 74 Sir agravayne at home is he, nyght & day he waytes vs two. 1530 Palsgr. 770/2, I wayte, I lye awayte for one to hurte hym, or to spye what he dothe. Je guette. I wyll wayte him here tyll to morowe but I wyll have him. 1596 Dalrymple tr. Leslie's Hist. Scot. (S. T. S.) II. 22 He thairfor appoynted certan cutthrots to wayt thame as fra the Banquet thay return. 1597 J. Melvill Autob. & Diary (Wodrow Soc.) 421 They steir upe and incitats four deboshit young limmers, and wattes.. James Smithe, as he was coming ham at night from the cost syde.

†b. intr. To keep hostile watch; to lie in wait.

a1225 Ancr. R. 196 Iðe wildernesse heo aspieden [MS. C. in þe wildene weiteden] us to slean. a1300 E. E. Psalter ix. 30 He waites (Vulg. insidiatur) in hidel als lioun in den. a1300 Cursor M. 899 Þou sal waite womman for to sting, And sco sal yiet þi hede bring. 1362 Langl. P. Pl. A. vii. 149 To kepen him..From wastors þat wayten winners to schende. ?1404–8 Wyt & Wille 30 in 26 Pol. Poems 23 Echon wayte oþer for to kille. 1535 Coverdale Obad. i. 14 Nether shalt thou stonde waytinge enymore at ye corners of the stretes, to murthur soch as are fled. 1573–80 Tusser Husb. (1878) 125 Lay pease vpon stacke,..And couer it straight, from doues that waight.

†2. trans. To be on the watch to inflict (injury): = Await v. 2. Obs.

The sense is app. due to the confusion of this vb. with Wait v.[2]

c1400 Destr. Troy 13012 Noght warre of the weghes, þat waited his harme, [He] past furth thurgh the pase with his proude knightes.

†3. To watch, keep one's eye upon, observe constantly; to look out for, watch for. Obs.

a1300 Cursor M. 13285 At see sant Iohn and Iam he fand, Quils þai þair lines war waitand. c1300 Havelok 1754 And bad him..Haue'ok wel yemen..And wel do wayten al þe nith. 13.. E. E. Allit. P. B. 99 Fechez mo gester, Waytez gorstez & greuez, if ani gomez lyggez,..fechez hem hider. c1386 Chaucer Sqr.'s T. 121 He wayted many a constellacion Er he had doon this operacion. c1400 Destr. Troy 2883 Wemen waited hym well, hade wondur of hym one, That of shap for to shew was shene to beholde. c1400 Rule St. Benet 863 And when so we ȝern ony thing þat may fall vnto flesch likyng, Thinke we god waites vs weterly. c1450 St. Cuthbert (Surtees) 1698 Whethir þou wayted our nyght wayes? Ibid. 3761 A monk to wayte þis taken stode.

†b. To watch mentally, observe, consider attentively. Obs.

1382 Wyclif Phil. iii. 17 Britheren,..wayte ȝe (Vulg. observate) hem that walken so as ȝe han oure foorme. 1399 Langl. Rich. Redeles Prol. 45 Ther nys no gouernour on þe grounde ne sholde gye him þe better..ȝif he waite well be wordis, and so werche þerafter. c1430 God's Complaint 57 in Pol. Rel. & L. Poems (1866) 165 Waite what y dide to marie maudeleyne, And what y seide to thomas of ynde.

†c. To watch over, take charge of, care for (a person's interests). Obs.

13.. Cursor M. 5416 (Gött.) Þus coude ihoseph, i said ȝou, waite his lauerd þe kinges prou. 1362 Langl. P. Pl. A. vi. 37, I haue ben his felawe þis fiftene wynter..With-Innen and withouten I-wayted his profyt. ?a1400 Morte Arth. 164 If thou my wyrchipe wayte..Thou salle haue gersoms fulle grett. c1400 Rule St. Benet 2471 Þeir awn winyng þai sal noȝt wayt, Þat oþer win þai sal couayt.

†d. To search for. Obs.

1340–70 Alisaunder 808 Hee wendes too a wildernes & waites him erbes. c1400 Beryn 424 Þe Pardonere, þat drewe apart, & weytid hym a trest ffor to hyde hym selff.

†4. intr. To keep watch; to look intently. Also with adv. or phrase, *to wait about, about one, on every side*, etc. Obs.

1338 R. Brunne Chron. (1725) 120 Hir frendes fulle fast waited aboute & woke, & Mald at þe last kyng Steuen scho toke. 13.. Gaw. & Gr. Knt. 2163 Þenne he wayted hym aboute. 13.. E. E. Allit. P. B. 1423 He waytez onwyde, his wenches he byholdes. 1362 Langl. P. Pl. A. viii. 128 And þorw heore wordes I awok and waitide [MS. V. lokede] aboute, And sauh [etc.]. 1377 Ibid. B. xiii. 343, I wayted wisloker, and thanne was it soiled With lykyng of lecherye, as by lokyng of his eye. c1400 Destr. Troy 376 He waites vmbe hym wightly, & was ware sone Of þe orible oxin. c1400 Ywaine & Gaw. 1815 Sho..waited obout fer and ner. a1400–50 Wars Alex. 1585 And as he waytis in a wra, þan was he ware sone Of þe maister of þat meneyhe. 1470–85 Malory Arthur vi. xvi. 209 Ther with he wayted aboue hym and vnder hym, and ouer his hede he sawe a rownsepyk. c1480 Henryson Fox & Wolf 150 On euerilk syde full warlie couth he wait. a1500 Flower & Leaf 106 Wherfore about I waited busily On every syde, if I her mighte see.

†b. To act as a watchman. Obs.

1436 Siege of Calais in Polit. Poems (Rolls) II. 153 The porters kept the gattes full manly,..To wate they wer not irk. c1470 Harding Chron. cxxxviii. xii, To castell Pilgrym ..there was no waye but one full straite, On a cawsey.. Strongly walled, with towres on to wayte. 1591 Shaks. 1 Hen. VI, i. iii. 3, I am come to suruey the Tower this day; ..Where be these Warders, that they wait not here? 1605 Verstegan Dec. Intell. x. (1628) 327 Wee call him that waiteth at the Towre one of the ward, or a warder.

†c. To observe carefully. Obs.

1399 Langl. Rich. Redeles iii. 128 Ȝit swiche ffresshe floodis beth..ffor her dignesse endauntid of dullisshe nollis, And, if þou well waite, of no wight ellis.

†d. With indirect question: To watch, observe carefully *what, when, how*, etc. Obs.

c1275 Lay. 23077 Þis ileueþ Bruttus þat he wole come þus and lokeþ and waiteþ wane he come to londe. c1290 S. Eng. Leg. 268 Euere he waytede, ȝif ore louerd ani grace him wolde sende. c1330 R. Brunne Chron. Wace (Rolls) 1495 He sente knyghtes & squiers To waite who made on hym pres. c1350 Will. Palerne 1821, I wol..waite ȝif any weiȝh comes wending alone. c1391 Chaucer Astrol. ii. § 25 Now yif so be þat the semith to long a tarienge.., thanne whaite whan the sonne is in any other degree of the zodiak. c1470 Henry Wallace v. 902 A suerd he drew, rych manlik him to wer, Ay wayttand fast gyff he can get a sper. 1598 R. Bernard tr. Terence (1607) Andria i. i, Observes illum quid agat: quid captet consilii. Watch him what hee doth, wait what he intendeth.

†e. To take precautions, be watchful or cautious. In imperative: Take care, see to it that.

13.. E. E. Allit. P. B. 292, I schal wayte to be war her wrenchez to kepe. c1386 Chaucer Prol. 571 Algate he wayted so in his achat That he was ay biforn and in good stat. c1460 J. Russell Bk. Nurture 436 in Babees Bk., Euer of a sharpe knyff wayte þat ye be sure. 1470–85 Malory Arthur i. ii. 37 But wayte ye make not many questions with her nor her men, but saye ye are diseased, and soo hye yow to bedde. 1522 World & Child (facs.) A iv, Wayte well that thou suffre no shame.

5. trans. To look forward (esp. with desire or apprehension) to (some future event or contingency); to continue in expectation of. Now somewhat rare: usually superseded by Await v.

a1400 Minor Poems fr. Vernon MS. 527/80 Ȝif þou waxe pore he wol skorne þe—Wayte of him neuere oþer bounte. c1400 Destr. Troy 3322, I wot, sir, witterly, will I or noght, Your wille I moste wirke, waite I non other. c1586 C'tess Pembroke Ps. lxix. i, Waiting aid, with ernest eying. 1634 Massinger Very Wom. iv. i, Ped. I thank ye, And soon I'll wait your promise. 1671–2 Sir C. Lyttelton in Hatton Corr. (Camden) 75 Wee waite much wht ye Spaniards will returne to ye King of France message. 1746 Francis tr. Hor., Epist. i. xviii. 21 Admitted as an humble Guest, Where Men of Money break their Jest, He waits the Nod, with Awe profound, And catches, ere it reach the Ground, The falling Joke. 1802 H. Martin Helen of Glenross II. 57 If Harry really loves me.., bid him wait futurity with composure. 1830 Tennyson Adeline iv, What aileth thee? whom waitest thou? 1837 Carlyle Fr. Rev. I. i. i, Or they that in the Bicêtre Hospital, 'eight to a bed', lie waiting their manumission. 1848 Thackeray Van. Fair xl, She took up her residence with Mr. Bowls..and waited the result of the advertisement. 1885 J. H. Dell Dawning Grey, Higher Creed 6 We wait the harps of sounder string, Than [etc.].

b. intr. (Chiefly *to wait for* = sense 5).

1577 Hanmer Anc. Eccl. Hist., Socr. i. xix. 245 When the woman perceaued her selfe to be daungerously sicke, and wayted for no other then present death. 1581 Satir. Poems Reform. xliv. 266, I knaw thou vaittis Lieutenentis place to haue. a1591 H. Smith Serm., Noah's Drunk. (1602) G 4 b, The ground..wayted for nothing now, but a paynefull labourer to till and dresse it. 1621 T. Granger Expos. Eccles. xi. 5. 297 And hee that waiteth for olde mens shoes, may happily goe bare foote in the meane time. 1641 Milton Reform. ii. 87 These importunate Wolves, that wait and thinke long till they devoure thy tender Flock. 1805 Med. Jrnl. XIV. 374 We wait with anxiety but not with impatience for the succeeding numbers. 1833 Tennyson Dream Fair Wom. xxviii, Dimly I could descry The stern blackbearded Kings.., Waiting to see me die.

c. To remain for a time without something expected or promised.

1550 Crowley Last Trumpet 935 If thou be a mans atturney, ..Let him not waite and spende money, If his dispatch do lie in the. 1897 Hall Caine Christian x, That was the only condition on which he would agree to wait for his money.

6. trans. To continue stationary or quiescent, in expectation of (a person or thing, an event); to defer departure or action until the arrival or occurrence of. Now rare: superseded by *wait for* (see 7) and Await v.

1375 Barbour Bruce v. 36 Tharfor thair cummyng vaitit he, And met thame at thair ariving. 14.. Pol. Rel. & L. Poems (1903) 273 Mary hys moder went þe weye To caluery þer he xuld deye, And waytyd þer here chylde. 1578 in Feuillerat Revels Q. Eliz. (1908) 297 To waight my Lord Chamberlaines comyng thither. a1604 Hanmer Chron. Irel. (1633) 59 From thence he went to a place called Lothra, where he builded another Monasterie, and lyeth there wayting the generall resurrection. 1662 Stillingfl. Orig. Sacræ ii. vi. § 2 That where there were any other evidences, that the Prophet spake by Divine Revelation, there was no reason to wait the fulfilling of every particular Prophecy before he was believed as a Prophet. 1667 Dryden & Dk. Newcastle Sir M. Mar-all i. i, This Tide will bring them from Gravesend. You had best let your man go, as from me, And wait them at the Stairs in Durham-yard. 1771 Mrs. Griffith Hist. Lady Barton II. 253 We had before agreed to wait the return of the chancellor's messenger at St. Omers. 1797 Ht. Lee Canterb. T., Frenchm. T. (1799) I. 293 Without waiting her answer..he would have led her down stairs. 1802 Noble Wanderers II. 128 One of the slaves, whom he had commanded to wait his return. 1808 Pike Sources Mississ. ii. App. 22 We were requested to halt and wait the arrival of the chief, who was half a mile from us. 1816 Scott Old Mort. xxxviii, Lady Emily's servant was waiting orders in the kitchen. 1819 — Leg. Montrose xxiii, She now waits you at the altar. 1883 Whitelaw Sophocles, Philoct. 123 Now then remain, and wait his coming here, Whilst I go hence. 1899 Quiller-Couch Ship of Stars xxvi, The Vicar clambered out to wait it [the coffin].

b. transf. Of things: To remain in readiness for, to await; to be in store for, to be reserved for. Cf. Await v. 8 a.

1745 Sc. Transl. & Paraphr. li. i, But better mansions wait the just, prepar'd above the sky. 1761 Churchill Rosciad 512 Public Contempt shall wait the Public Fool. 1850 Robertson Serm. Ser. iii. xviii. (1853) 233 The same ..calculations wait us when we bend our eyes on that which is to come. 1854 Surtees Handley Cr. xl. (1901) II. 36 'Tea and coffee wait your pleasure in the drawing-room', observed the stiff-necked footman.

7. intr. or absol. Often *to wait for* = sense 6.

a. To remain in a place, defer one's departure until something happens.

c1386 Chaucer Knt.'s T. 71 And certes lord, to abyden youre presence Heere in the temple of the goddesse clemence We han ben waitynge al this fourtenyght. 1535 Coverdale Judith x. 6 Now whan she came to the porte of the cite, she founde Osias and the elders of the cite waitinge there. 1568 Grafton Chron. II. 642 But he was espyed by diuerse watermen..which wayted for his foortbcomyng on the Thamys. 1599 Shaks. Much Ado i. iii. 17, I must bee sad when I haue cause, and smile at no mans iests, eat when I haue stomacke, and wait for no mans leisure. 1628 Ford Lover's Mel. iii. i, At the back dore Tatter-demallians waite, who know not how To get admittance. 1711 Steele Spect. No. 132 ¶ 1, I..dressed immediately, that I might make no one wait. 1779 Mirror No. 57 Allowing ladies to go unattended to a public place, to wait there four hours in expectation of the gentlemen with whom they were to dance. 1835 Dickens Sk. Boz, Parish iii, The old adage, 'time and tide wait for no man'. 1856 Ruskin King Golden River i. (ed. 3) 12 What did you keep us waiting in the rain for? 1860 Tyndall Glac. i. xxii. 152 At the summit of these rocks I again waited for him. 1896 Conan Doyle Rodney Stone xxii, Sir James Ovington's carriage was waiting without. 1905 R. Bagot Passport xi. 104, I must drive back to Genzano. I told the vetturino to wait.

b. colloq. *To wait about*: to linger expectantly, 'hang about' where something is likely to happen. Also (chiefly *U.S.*) *to wait around*.

1879 Miss Braddon Cloven Foot xxix. II. 268 'What has become of your brother?' Laura asked, as she and Celia waited about, side by side, watching the assembly of the field. 1886 Besant Childr. Gibeon ii. xxx, The street was, however, well enough lighted for Claude to see a figure waiting about on the pavement. 1895 M. Halstead Hundred Bear Stor. 57 It grew sort of monotonous waiting around. 1899 J. L. Williams Stolen Story etc. 175, I suppose they're waiting around till it stops raining.

c. To defer action until some event has taken place; also with inf., to delay to do something.

a1633 G. Herbert Outlandish Prov. (1640) 25 Hee puls with a long rope, that waights for anothers death. 1800 Med. Jrnl. III. 460 To wait 'no longer than ten or fifteen minutes for the efforts of nature', is a position which cannot be too strongly reprobated. 1836 J. H. Newman Par. Serm. III. xxi. 342 If we wait till all the world are worshippers, we must wait till the world is new made. 1843 Carlyle Past & Pr. iii. xv, A whole Eternity I waited to be born. 1852 Thackeray Esmond i. viii, Beatrix..waited even to burst out a-crying until she got to the door. 1874 Green Short Hist. viii. § 6. 519 He had shown he knew how to wait, and when waiting was over he knew how to act. 1875 Jowett Plato (ed. 2) I. 434 A man should wait, and not take his own life until God summons him. 1883 Whitelaw Sophocles, Philoct. 837 Thou seest, now is the time. Why should we wait to do this deed?

d. *To wait on*: (a) *Sc.* to linger about a place; (b) *Sc.* also. to linger in expectation of death; (c) *Hawking* (see quot. 1891).

(a) 1818 Scott Hrt. Midl. xii, It's a sair thing to hae to do wi' courts of law, unless it be to improve one's knowledge ..by waiting on as a hearer.

(b) 1836 J. M. Wilson's Tales Borders II. 377, I did hear tell that his faither was waitin on, but I hope he's no that far gane yet.

(c) 1773 J. Campbell Mod. Faulconry 158 If your hawk wait well on at her being first entered. 1828 Sir J. S. Sebright Hawking (1828) 17 He [the hawk] may thus be made to follow the falconer wherever he pleases; this is called waiting on. 1891 Harting Bibl. Accipitr. 231 A hawk is said to 'wait on' when she soars in circles over the head of the falconer, waiting for the game to be flushed.

e. Racing. *To wait off*: to allow oneself to be distanced by other competitors in order to 'romp in' when their energies are exhausted. Cf. Waiting vbl. sb.[1] 2 c.

1856 'Druid' Post & Paddock vi. 91 He patiently waited off, while Sancho forced the running.

f. *To wait up*: to defer going to bed in expectation of the arrival of some one.

1855 Trollope Warden xviii, Dr. Grantly..and Mrs. Grantly..are waiting up for you. 1892 Temple Bar Oct. 169 Don't wait up for me.

g. *To wait and see* (with indirect question or ellipsis of this): to await the course of events.

Recently often used with allusion to Mr. H. H. Asquith's repeated reply of 'Wait and see' to a succession of questions in parliament.

1719 De Foe Crusoe i. (Globe) 267 However, we had no Remedy, but to wait and see what the Issue of Things might present. 1836 Dickens Sk. Boz, Scotland-Yard, The tailor..bid them wait and see what happened. 1848 — Dombey xxxv, Mr. Towlinson..says wait and see. 1883 Miss M. Betham-Edwards Disarmed viii, When we have had dinner, we will do something better than have stories. Wait and see.

attrib. 1915 F. S. Oliver Ordeal by Battle i. vii. 82 History..shows us at every other crisis of this sort always the

same triangle of forces—a War party, a Peace party, and a Wait-and-See party.

h. transf. Of a thing: To remain in readiness for some purpose. Also, to remain for a while neglected.

1838 Lytton Alice i. iii, 'So you are come for your daily lesson?' 'Yes; but Tasso can wait if [etc.].' 1876 J. Parker Paracl. i. ii. 14 John's gospel is waiting until the Church becomes mature enough to understand it. 1894 Hall Caine Manxman vi. xvii, There was a letter waiting for Philip at home. Mod. This letter must be answered at once; the others can wait.

i. quasi-trans. To postpone (a meal) in expectation of the arrival of some one. colloq.

1838 Dickens O. Twist li, 'It's a trying thing waiting supper for lovers,' said Mr. Grimwig, waking up. 1862 Trollope Orley F. xxi, Who asked you to wait tea till near eleven o'clock?

8. Phrases. *To wait one's* (or *the*) *time, hour, opportunity*, etc. †a. (sense 3) To watch, look out for an opportunity (obs.). b. (sense 6) To defer action until a fitting season or opportunity shall present itself.

a. a1300 Cursor M. 19715 Þair redes þar-for can þai run, ..Night and dai to wait þe time Quen þai moght cum to murther him. 1303 R. Brunne Handl. Synne 825 Weyte þy tyme, and be not þe last To come whan holy watyr ys cast. 1338 — Chron. (1725) 94 To triste was he sette, forto waite þe chance. 1375 Barbour Bruce v. 523 He hame till his houss is gane, And vaitit oportunite For to fulfill his mawite. c1386 Chaucer Frankl. T. 535 Nyght and day he spedde hym þat he kan To wayten a tyme of his conclusion. c1420 Wyntoun Cron. vi. xiii. 1220 (MS. Cott.) Twa men he bade in prewate To wayt ane oportunyte, And stel þat barn. 1526 Pilgr. Perf. (W. de W. 1531) 83 Waytynge theyr vauntage whan they may smyte the & slee the.

b. c1375 Sc. Leg. Saints iii. (Andrew) 909 Þe bischope had gret will his fellone lust to fulfill, waitand bot lasare quhen he mycht purchess oportunite. 1626 B. Jonson Staple of N. ii. ii, Well, Sir, I'll wait a better season. 1701 W. Wotton Hist. Rome, Marcus iv. 59 Cassius was obliged to wait his opportunity. 1799 Dundas in Owen Wellesley Desp. (1877) 644 We cannot at present materially meliorate his government, but must wait favourable opportunities. 1813 Scott Rokeby i. xxix, She comes not—He will wait the hour, When her lamp lightens in the tower.

9. To be in readiness to receive orders; hence, to be in attendance as a servant; to attend as a servant does to the requirements of a superior. Chiefly const. *on*: see *wait on*, 14 j.

1526 Tindale 1 Cor. ix. 13 They which wayte att the aulter are partakers with the aultre. 1617 Moryson Itin. ii. 49 Yea, his Lordships very Grayhound, likewise vsing to waite at his stirrop, was shot through the body. c1655 Milton Sonn., 'When I consider' 14 They also serve who only stand and waite. 1818 Scott Br. Lamm. xviii, He..dropped a little behind the lady, at whose bridle-rein he had hitherto waited with such devotion.

b. To serve as an attendant at table; to hand food and drink to persons at a meal. Phr. *to wait at table* (cf. 14 j), †*to wait at a trencher.*

1568 T. Howell Arb. Amitie 36 b, (Iacke showes his qualities) Yee and ich can, if neede be than, waight at the table well. Ibid., Where ich did waite, at euerye baite. 1592 in Sir J. Harington's Nugæ Antiq. (1804) I. 106 Item, That no man waite at the table, without a trencher in his hand. 1605 Breton I pray you (Grosart) 8/2 To spend my time.. onely for..waighting at a trencher, looking on a faire house. c1618 Moryson Itin. iv. ii. (1903) 90 These gentlemen servants waite with their hatts on, and sett at their masters table, both at home and abroad where their masters are invited. 1742 Fielding J. Andrews i. ii, Joey was now preferred from the stable to attend on his lady, to..wait at her tea-table [etc.]. 1796–7 Jane Austen Pride & Prej. xlvii, She had not prudence enough to hold her tongue before the servants, while they waited at table. 1853 Dickens Bleak Ho. iv, The young woman with the flannel bandage waited, and dropped everything on the table wherever it happened to go. 1905 E. T. Thurston Traffic v. iv, 'Is she a musician then [at the restaurant]?' asked Mr. Puckle. 'No—she waited.'

†c. *To wait up*: to be in attendance at the head of the table. Obs.

a1634 Chapman Alphonsus iii. i, As for the Chambermaid and my self, we will take our places at the neither end, the Jester is to wait up, and live by the crums that fall from the Emperours trencher.

d. quasi-trans. *To wait (the) table* = to wait at table. Sc.

1879 Stevenson Trav. Cevennes 152 She waited the table with a heavy placable nonchalance. a1894 — St. Ives xi. (1898) 82 We had a good many pleasant passages as she waited table or warmed my bed for me.

†e. quasi-trans. *To wait attendance*: to remain in attendance. Obs.

1590 [see Attendance 3]. 1607 Shaks. Timon i. i. 161.

†10. trans. To attend or escort, to accompany for the purpose of rendering service or showing respect. Obs.

c1384 Chaucer L. G. W. 1269 This Troyan, that..can so well doon alle his obeisaunces, And waytyn hire at festis & at dauncis. 1598 Greene Jas. IV, v. i, I must to Edenbourg, vnto the King, There to take charge and waight him in his warres. 1633 Massinger Guard. ii. i, Jol. Waite me. Calyph. As your shadow. Exeunt Jol. Calyp. 1687 Dryden Hind & P. i. 557 She made a mannerly excuse to stay, Proffering the Hind to wait her half the way. 1697 — Æneis viii. 734 Steeds are prepar'd to mount the Trojan Band; Who wait their Leader to the Tyrrhene Land. Ibid. xi. 92 He..chose a thousand Horse..to wait the Funeral. 1725 Pope Odyss. iv. 61 Refresh'd, they wait them to the bow'r of state. 1728 — Dunc. i. 265 She bids him wait her to her sacred Dome: Well pleas'd he enter'd. 1816 L. Hunt Rimini i. 242 His shield Borne by the squire that waits him to the field.

†b. absol. Obs.

1599 B. Jonson Cynthia's Rev. ii. iii, One, that hath newly entertain'd the begger to follow him, but cannot get him to wait neere enough.

†11. To attend as a concomitant or consequence.

1675 Traherne Chr. Ethics 330 Prudence consists most in attempting the business, for it will go on, and is ever waited with success when undertaken. a1718 Prior First Hymn Callimachus 64 Swift Growth and wond'rous Grace, O heav'nly Jove, Waited Thy blooming Years.

II. Special constructions with preps.

†12. **Wait after**—. a. To expect, look forward to; to be ambitious or desirous of, seek for. Obs.

1393 Gower Conf. III. 323 This Leonin..waiteth after gret beyete; But al for noght. 1393 Langl. P. Pl. C. ii. 124 Hewes in þe halyday after hete wayten. c1440 Generydes 2440 He is descendid of an high lenage, And..waytith after right grete heritage. c1449 Pecock Repr. ii. i. 135 That we waite not aftir to be hoosilid with the sacrament of the auter. Ibid. v. ii. 489 Certis he may not waite aftir that the conclusioun of this argument be proued or be trewe. c1489 Caxton Sonnes of Aymon xix. 423 It is not for vs to wayte after pyte of hym, for he is over cruell a kyng vpon us. 1533 tr. Erasm. Comm. Crede 52 b, They do wayte after a kynge plentuously appoynted with ryches, with armies or hostes of men, and with other worldly aydes.

†b. To look out for; to watch, keep in observation. Obs.

c1400 Beryn 1589 Beryne clepid a Marynere, & bad hym 'sty on lofft, And weyte aftir our four Shippis, [þat] aftir vs doith dryve.' 1450–1530 Myrr. our Ladye i. xx. 54 He sawe a fende that..wayted bysely after all letters, and syllables, and wordes, and faylynges, that eny made. c1489 Caxton Sonnes of Aymon xxvi. 553 Thenne they set theymselfe doun vpon the fayr grasse, waytynge after theyr adverse party.

Wait for—: see 5 b, 7.

13. **Wait of**—.

†a. To execute the commands of. Obs.

a1586 Sidney Arcadia i. xi. (1912) 69 He would extol the deeds of Philoxenus, who indeede had but waited of him therin. Ibid. v. (1598) 465 A Counseller, who hath..the reasonable excuse of a seruant, that did but wait of his mistresse.

†b. To escort, accompany on the way, as a mark of honour: = *wait on*, 14 k. Obs.

1563 Foxe A. & M. 860/1 This deponent..receyued the kynges maiesties Visitors at Chichester,..and conducted and wayted of them into the dioces of Wynton. 1606 Chapman Gent. Usher iii. ii. 77 Waite of Master Usher to the doore. 1709 N. Blundell Diary (1895) 78, I Wated of ye Duke and Dutches of Norfolk &c. out of Wigan part of their way towards Preston. 1724 Briton No. 25. 110 Footmen..return when the Play is done to wait of them home. 1734 Adm. Gordon in 10th Rep. Hist. MSS. Comm. App. i. 193 At 9 acloake I sent my pinnace to wayte of General Lacy.

†c. To pay a respectful visit to: = *wait on*, 14 m. Obs.

1555 in Lodge Illustr. Brit. Hist. (1791) I. 211 Trustyng shortely to wayte of yor Lordshyppe. c1673 W. Mountagu in Buccleuch MSS. (Hist. MSS. Comm.) I. 320 My Lord and his sons have been to see me at my chamber, but I had the misfortune to be abroad; and upon that score..I will wait of them again. 1677 Ibid. 324, I..shall acquaint his Lordship myself with it on Saturday, before which I cannot wait of him. 1707 N. Blundell Diary (1895) 55, I went to Bold to wate of Mr. Molin[eux] but he was gon a hunting.

d. = *wait for*: see 7 a. Now dial.

1712 Tyldesley Diary (1873) 23 Stayed alday at Dick Jackson's watting of Mr. Blackborne, who came not till affter nine att night. 1828 Trial Wm. Dyon at York Assizes 8, I was up waiting of my master until two o'clock.

14. **Wait on** or **upon**—.

†a. To observe, watch; to fix one's eyes upon, gaze at. Obs.

c1384 Chaucer H. Fame 342 For though your loue laste a seson, Wayte vpon the conclusyon. c1394 P. Pl. Crede 361 Þei wilneþ worshipes—but waite on her dedes! c1400 Rowland & O. 444 To þe castelle he wendes a pase And appone þe kirnells gase, to wayte appon þat were. c1400 Destr. Troy 13055 So Eger were all men Elan to se, For to waite on þat worthy went þai belyue. c1430 Syr Gener. (Roxb.) 6344 Anoon Jewel to his ship sent To warn his men to be redie, On his comyng to waite and spie. 1538 Elyot Dict., Inspecto, to behold attentiuely, to wayte on.

†b. To lie in wait for. Obs.

1390 Gower Conf. I. 349 Of his men a gret partie He made in buisshement abide, To waite on him in such a tide That he ne mihte here hond ascape. 1595 Locrine iv. i. 183 Millions of diuels wayt vpon thy soule! 1628 Hobbes Thucyd. ii. (1629) 128 As they sayled along the shore, Phormio waited on them till they were out of the streight, intending to set vpon them in the open Sea.

†c. To secure, protect (oneself). Obs.

c1400 Destr. Troy 12722 Þan he counseld Clunestra,..To be war of þat wegh, & wait on hir-seluyn.

†d. To attend to (a business, a duty). Obs.

1526 Tindale Rom. xii. 7 Let hym that hath an office, wayte on his office. [Similarly in later versions.]

†e. With clause as obj.: To take care *that*. Obs.

1596 Dalrymple tr. Leslie's Hist. Scot. (S.T.S.) I. 255 He wayted weill onn, be all meines possible, that nathyng dekayet of Justice in his Realme.

†f. To await, expect with desire or anxiety. Obs.

c1400 Destr. Troy 7944. I wot the in witte to waite on myn end. 1608 Yorks. Trag. viii. 23 Was this the answear I long waited on? 1642 Milton Apol. Smect. 37, I perceave how hopelesse it will be to reach the heigth of their prayses at the accomplishment of that expectation that weights upon their noble deeds.

†g. To await the action of; to look to (a person) *for* something. Obs.

1682 Bunyan Holy War (1905) 253 That the Prince that lay in the Leaguer without the Wall, waited upon them [the townsfolk] for an answer.

h. In Bible phrase, to place one's hope in (God).

Very common in the Bible of 1611; rendering several Heb. verbs of identical meaning.

1535 Coverdale Ps. lxi[i]. 1 My soule wayteth only vpon God, for of him commeth my helpe. 1611 Bible Ps. xxv. 3 Let none that wait on the be ashamed.

†i. To remain in one place in expectation of = *wait for* (7 a). Obs.

1694 tr. Marten's Voy. Spitzbergen in Acc. Sev. Late Voy. ii. 7 We were forced to wait on him above half an hour, before he came from underneath the Ice.

j. To attend as or in the manner of a servant to the personal requirements of; to minister to the comfort of. † Also in phrases, *to wait on the cup, the trencher, the table* (cf. 9 b).

To wait on (a person) *hand and foot*: see Hand sb. 56.

1509–10 Act 1 Hen. VIII, c. 14 § 1 No servyng manne waytyng uppon his maister..were eny garded Hose. c1550 Cheke Matt. iv. 11 Then let ye devel him go, and lo angels cam vnto him and waited on him. 1552 Huloet, Wayte on the cup, ad cyathos stare. 1575 Gascoigne Glasse of Govt. Wks. 1910 II. 66 Wee should have beene fayne to wayte on the table, and to bee contented with their leavings after supper. 1602 Kyd's Sp. Trag. ii. v. (Addit.), His Maiestie the other day did grace him With waiting on his cup. 1615 G. Sandys Trav. 80 When they grow old, they most grow contemptible, being put to do the drudgeries of the house, and many times to waite on their children. 1749 Fielding Tom Jones vii. xv, It is not my business, answered the Drawer, to wait upon the Chambers. If you come to that, answered the Maid, it is not my business to wait upon Gentlemen. 1847 Marryat Childr. New Forest iv, You can have no servants to wait upon you. 1866 Mrs. H. Wood Mildred Arkell xi, When I was only six years old I had to wait on Mamma and Charlotte. 1901 Alldridge Sherbro xii. 114 He is waited upon hand and foot.

k. To accompany on one's way (as a mark of respect or to render service or assistance); to escort. Now rare (? exc. U.S.).

1450 W. Lomner in Paston Lett. I. 124 With other shippis waytyng on hym. 1481 Cov. Leet Bk. (1908) 486 There shuld be xl sowdyers mo waged for a quarter of þe town wages to make vp a C men to wayte vppon the kyng in þis viage etc. c1530 Tindale Jonas Prol. A vj b, Ande one yt cast out deuels in Christes name they forbade because he wayted not on them. 1585 Higins Junius' Nomencl. 517/1 Pronuba,..a bridemaid, or she that trimmeth and maketh ready the bride, and waiteth vpon her homeward to her husbands house. 1595 Shaks. John v. vii. 98 Let it be so, and you my noble Prince,..Shall waite vpon your Fathers Funerall. 1601 Ld. Mountjoy Let. 13 Nov. in Moryson's Itin. ii. (1617) 155 We entertained them so well, that we waited on them to the walls of the Towne, and made them leave some of their dead bodies behind them. 1628 T. Ball Life Preston (1885) 175 His friends at Cambridge, who did highly honour him, and desired nothing more then to have wayted on his dust to his long home. 1654 Evelyn Diary 4 July, On a letter from my wife's uncle, Mr. Pretyman, I waited back on her to London. 1713 Tyldesley Diary (1873) 107 Then went to wate on Judge Dormr out off the toun. Ibid. 125 He watted on her home. 1807–8 W. Irving Salmag. iii. (1860) 51 On landing we were waited upon to our lodgings ..by a vast and respectable escort. 1880 P. Ludlow Nick Hardy at College vi. (1882) 29 Nick complied, and was waited on into the drawing-room.

transf. 1691 Tate Petty's Pol. Anat. Ded. to Dk. Ormond, Be pleas'd to permit this useful Treatise to wait on you to the Camp.

l. Hence (?) in Hunting, *to wait close upon*: to keep close to (the horse immediately in front).

1861 Whyte-Melville Market Harb. xxv, Crasher..and Sawyer take their leaps abreast, the latter riding very quietly and carefully...Luxury is waiting close upon them.

m. To pay a respectful visit to; to call upon with the intention of showing respect, asking a favour, or the like.

1501 Plumpton Corr. (Camden) 161 Also I shall wate one you at Nottingham one sunday next, except ye comand me contrary. 1594 O. B. Quest. Profit. Concern. 5 God willing he shall one day waight vpon you to better his knowledges. 1638 in Verney Mem. (1892) I. 279, I have A greate ambition yt you would please to honour me so farre as..to admitt me to waite upon you. 1664 Sir A. Bateman in Extr. St. P. rel. Friends iii. (1912) 215 It is my Lord Chanselors comaund to mee, that I waite vpon your Honor to deliuer this inclosed letter to you. 1713 Addison Guardian No. 107 ¶ 3 She will wait upon any Lady at her own Lodging, and talk by the Clock after the Rate of three Guineas an Hour. 1765 R. Gem in Jesse Selwyn & Contemp. (1843) I. 367 The Baron D'Olbach and I intend ourselves the pleasure of waiting on you to dinner to-morrow. 1766 Goldsm. Vicar W. xxx, A person of distinction..sent his respects to the gentleman that was with us, and begged to know when he should think proper to be waited upon. 1848 Dickens Dombey xxvi, I took the liberty of waiting on her..to inquire if she could charge me with any little commission. 1849 Macaulay Hist. Eng. ix. II. 474 The Primate and the few Spiritual Peers who happened to be then in London had orders to wait upon the King. 1885 Manch. Exam. 6 July 4/7 A deputation had waited upon Lords Salisbury, Redesdale, and Roxburghe.

†transf. 1762 Wilkes Let. 21 Sept. (1769) I. 15 Sunday's post brought me your lordship's [letter] of the 17th, and by the return of it this waits on your lordship.

n. Of things: To accompany; to be associated with; to attend as a concomitant or consequence.

1579–80 North Plutarch, Lycurgus (1595) 52 For no man is so..simple witted, as to bring into so povre and meane houses, bedsteads with siluer feete, imbrodered couerlets.. nor such other like costly furniture and finenesse, as those things require to waite vpon them. 1605 Shaks. Macb. i. vii. 44 Letting I dare not, wait vpon I would, Like the poore Cat i' th' Addage. 1611 — Wint. T. v. i. 142 Infirmitie (Which waits vpon worne times). 1622 J. Taylor (Water P.) Farew. Tower Bottles A 7, For 'tis a Maxim held in euery Nation, Great men are wayted on by Adulation. 1646 Crashaw Steps to Temple 33 To them shee gave the first and fairest Beame That waited on her Birth. 1657 Heylin Eccles. Vind. ii. iii. § 6. 146 Prayer..being an action meerly moral, was notwithstanding to be waited on with such rites and gestures. 1692 Prior Ode Imit. Hor. xi, Justice and Freedom on his Conquests wait. 1746 Hervey Medit. (1818) 60 Her form was symmetry itself; every elegance breathed in her air; and all the graces waited on her motions. 1842 Lover Handy Andy i, Disappointment waited on all affairs in which he bore a part. 1859 Mill Liberty i. (1864) 2/2 Elective and responsible government became subject to the observations and criticisms which wait upon a great existing fact. 1875 Jowett Plato (ed. 2) V. 299 Retribution is the suffering which waits upon injustice.

†o. To support the opinion of. Obs.

1639 Fuller Holy War iv. v. (1640) 175 The Master of the Sentences (waited on herein with other learned men) is of opinion, That [etc.].

†15. **Wait over**—. To watch over. Obs.

Cf. Overwait v. (= supervise, Pecock).

1659 Hammond Paraphr. Ps. lxxviii. 52 His..providence ..continually waited over them, and provided supplies for all their wants.

†16. **Wait to**—. To keep watch upon, attend carefully to. Obs.

c1440 York Myst. xxxiii. 253 Sirs, waites to þer wightis þat no wiles be wrought. c1449 Pecock Repr. iii. xviii. 405 And skile whi al this is trewe may be perceyued weel ynowȝ of a diligent considerer, waiting weel to ech word which is now bifore here seid. 1508–13 Bk. Keruynge in Babees Bk. (1868) 270 And wayte well to ye sewer how many dysshes be couered.

III. 17. Comb.: †**wait-gleed** [= OF. *gaitetison*], one who sits lazily watching the fire.

c1310 in Wright Lyric P. xv. 47 Me calleth me fulle flet, ant waynoun wayte-glede.

†**Wait**, v.[2] Obs. Also 4 **weyte, waite, wayte.** [app. a. ON. *veita* to show or do (kindness, etc.), less frequently to do (an ill turn), = OHG. *weizen*:—OTeut. type *waitjan, f. *wait- abl.-var. of *wit-: see Wit v. Confused with Wait v.[1]: see Await v. 2.]

1. trans. a. With thing as direct obj. and dative of person: To show (unkindness) to, to put (disgrace, suffering, etc.) on. b. In similar sense, but with changed construction: To treat (a person) *with* (unkindness, cruelty, etc.), to affect *with* (disgrace, suffering, etc.).

a. 1303 R. Brunne Handl. Synne 5987 Þeft he wyl vpon hym wyte, Or ouþer skaþe he wyl hym weyte. c1330 Arth. & Merl. (Kölbing) 352 Ac ferst þai sworen him an oþ, Þai schuld him neuer waite loþ. c1350 Will. Palerne 148 He.. þouȝt..he wold..wayte hire sum wicked torn. Ibid. 4051 Þat no burn nere so bold..to wayte þe werwolf no maner schaþe. c1400 Rom. Rose 3938 Therfore close I shall the weie Fro hem that..come to wayte me vilonye. c1450 Erle Tolous 296 Certys hyt were a traytory, For to wayte hym velany. 1450 Rolls of Parlt. V. 183/2 Ye shall not shewe nor wayte..noo malice..to any persone. 1548 Udall, etc. Erasm. Par. Matt. iv. 23–5 Sum came for malice with a myndo to wayte displeasure. 1601 Holland Pliny x. lxxiv. I. 308 The bird Ægithus, (the least in manner of all others) waiteth the Asse a shrewd turne.

b. a1300 Cursor M. 4330 Sco waited him wit a werr turn. 1303 R. Brunne Handl. Synne 4186 Whan þys Iudas.. weytede Ihesu with tresun. c1320 Sir Tristr. 2175 Meriadok wiþ ille Waited hem ful neiȝe Of her dede. c1330 R. Brunne Chron. Wace (Rolls) 7122 For þou art no knyght of armes, Þe more þey wayte þis lond wyþ harmes. 1352 Minot Poems i. 64 Ay er þai boune To wait Ingland with sorow and schame. a1400 Sir Perc. 92 Was noȝte the rede knyghte so rathe For to wayte hym with skathe. c1430 Syr Tryam. 101 Yf ye be so hardy To wayte me wyth velanye. c1470 Henry Wallace viii. 900 We sall be bundyn yow to,..nocht efftyr to wait yow with na ill. c1475 Rauf Coilȝear 913 'Sa thrine I', said the Sarazine, '..Quha waitis the Cristin with cair, my cusingis ar thay'. 15.. Murning Maiden 81 in Maitl. Fol. MS. (S.T.S.) I, And heir to ȝow my treuth I plycht That I sall nowder day nor nycht No wyld beist wait with wrang. 1581 Satir. Poems Reform. xliii. 83 Did sho not wait him with sic foule inuy.

2. Comb. **wait-scathe** (as a nickname or quasi-proper name), a perpetrator of mischief.

1481 Caxton Reynard xxviii. (Arb.) 70 Ther is prentout, wayte scathe, and other of my frendis and alyes. a1500 Henryson Fox & Wolf 54 Freir Wolf Waitskaith.

Wait, obs. and dial. f. Wet, Wite, Wot.

Wait-a-bit. Also **wait-a-while.** [tr. Cape Du. *wacht-een-beetje.*] Usually *attrib.* with *thorn, thorn-tree*, etc.

a. A name given to various S. African plants and shrubs with humorous reference to their hooked and clinging thorns; e.g. various species of *mimosa.*

1785 G. Forster tr. Sparrman's Voy. Cape G. H. I. 236 A new species of callophyllum, which from its catching..fast hold of the traveller with its hooked prickles..is commonly called here wakt een betje, or wait a bit. 1850 R. G. Cumming Hunter's Life S. Afr. (ed. 2) I. 152 This variety of mimosa is waggishly termed by the Boers 'vyacht um bige', or wait-a-bit thorns; as they continually solicit the passing traveller not to be in a hurry. 1857 Livingstone Trav. iii. 61 The 'wait-a-bit thorn', or Acacia detinens. 1863 W. C. Baldwin Afr. Hunting vii. 239 The Kaffirs throw in the most virulent 'wait-a-while' thorn branches into the pits, to prevent the oxen from trampling. 1899 Bertrand Kingd. Barotsi 48 Various species of thorn, of which the most formidable is the 'wacht-een-beetje', appropriately interpreted as the 'wait-a-bit', a crooked, steely, regular fishhook of a thorn, that stops and tears everything that comes in its way. 1913 Pettman Africanderisms, s.v. Wacht-en-beetje, The familiar Zizyphus mucronata, W., is popularly known all through Kaffraria and the Eastern Districts as the 'wait-a-bit thorn tree'.

b. Applied by travellers to different plants of similar character in other parts of the world.

1865 Tristram Land of Israel 202 The principal tree was the zizyphus spina-Christi..with long pointed and rather reflex thorns, very strong,—a true wait-a-bit tree. 1894 Dennys Dict. Malaya 415 Wait-a-bit. A name conventionally applied to a species of rattan armed with powerful curved thorns.

Waitchfull, obs. Sc. form of Watchful.

Waite, obs. form of Wite.

Waiter (wēi·təɹ). Forms: 4 **weyter**, 4–5 **waytar**, 4–7 **wayter**, 5 **waytere**, 5–7 **waitor**, **waytor**, 6 **weighter**, **waitour**, **water**, **weighter** (*Sc.* **vyttar**), 6– **waiter.** [Orig. a. AF. *waitour, OF. *weitteor, gaiteor*, agent-n. f. *weitier, gaitier* Wait v.[1] In later use f. Wait v.[1] + -er[1].]

I. †1. One who watches, or observes closely; one who is on the look-out. Obs.

1382 Wyclif 2 Sam. xiii. 34 And the child weyter [Vulg. puer speculator] heuede vp his eyen and bihelde. c1420 Wyclif Bible, Pref. Epist. St. Jerome 70 Sophonyas the wayter [L. speculator] and the knower of the priuetees of the Lord, herith a cry. 1549 Coverdale etc. Erasm. Par. 1 John i. 1–4 Euen the thing which we yt were continual waitours heard with our eares, saw with our eies. 1554 Aberdeen Reg. (1844) I. 281 That the saidis baillies suld..apprehend the said John Chalmer, and put him in custodie..with vyttaris and vaychearis to awyt and keip him fra doing of skayth. 1672 Swinnock Life T. Wilson 21 Accordingly, he thus clad came forth, not knowing but that the Waiter was still at the door. 1687 A. Lovell tr. Thevenot's Trav. i. 285 The Health-boat came, and put Waiters on board of us, to keep the People of the Town from mingling with us.

2. †a. A watchman at the city gates. Sc. Obs.

1684 in G. Sinclair Satan's Invis. World (1685) Postscr. ¶ 1 b, He had..some charge over the Waiters at the Ports of the City [Edinburgh]. 1737 in Crim. Trials illustr. 'Heart of Mid-Lothian' (1818) 294 William Lindsay, waiter at the Netherbow port of Edinburgh..deponed, That [etc.]. 1818 Scott Hrt. Midl. vi, During this parley the insurgents had made themselves masters of the West Port, rushing upon the Waiters (so the people were called who had the charge of the gates), and possessing themselves of the keys.

b. A warder of the Tower of London. More fully *yeoman waiter.*

1551 T. Wilson Logic N viij b, Yeomen of the gard, and all other waiters. 1592 in 3rd Rep. Hist. MSS. Comm. 6/2 [Ralph Smythe] one of your highness ordinary yeomen waiters. c1600 in Peck Desid. Curiosa (1732) I. ii. 16 The Towre..Yeoman Waighters or Warders.

†c. An officer in the employ of the Customs. Obs. exc. Hist. See Coast-waiter, Tide-waiter.

1473 Stonor Papers (Camden) I. 134 For þer be so many wayters and controllers. 1556 Acts Privy Counc. (1892) V. 295 They have, neverthe'es of late byn troubled and disquieted by diverse Wayters at the portes in London. 1561 Clough in Burgon Life Gresham (1839) I. 407 So many Quays crowne-serchers, wayters, and other powlyng offycers. 1612 Proclam. Transport. Corn 19 Jan., All our Customers, Comptrollers, Searchers, Waitors, and other the Ministers of our Ports. 1685 Sc. Proclam. 28 Apr. in Lond. Gaz. No. 2032/3 We hereby Require and Command all Our Collectors, Customers, or Waiters, to make strict and diligent Search and Inquiry in all Ships. 1818 Scott Hrt. Midl. xvi, Some tuilzies about run goods wi' the gaugers and the waiters.

†3. An observer in secret. a. A spy, scout. Obs.

1471 Caxton Recuyell (Sommer) 133 Diuerse espies and waytars that were sent out..to see and to descouuere the state..of their enemyes.

†b. In *Hunting*, one set to watch the movements of the intended game. Obs. rare.

c1400 Master of Game (MS. Digby 182) xxxiii, Þei shulde goo forthe þider as þe deere is herbowred and sette redy wayters aboute þe quarter, or þe wode þat þe deer is Inne to se what commeth oute.

†c. One who lies in wait. Obs. rare.

c1430 Pilgr. Lyf Manhode ii. xii. (1869) 79 An espyour of weyes, and a waytere [aguetteur] of pilgrimes.

II. 4. One who waits expectant of some event, opportunity, appointed time, etc.

1655 R. Capel Tentations iv. iii. (ed. 5) 124 The expectation of the waiter shall not fail for ever, that is, never. 1870 R. Buchanan Bk. Orm ii. ii. 50 O Shadow sad, Monitor, haunter, waiter till the end. 1900 F. G. Kenyon in Egypt Explor. Fund, Archaeol. Rep. 45 Students of papyri will indeed be expectant waiters for gifts from their rich table for a long time to come.

b. *Waiter upon God* (see Wait v.[1] 14 h). † *Waiter upon time* (obs.), *waiter upon Providence*, one who awaits the turn of events when required by duty or honour to come to a personal decision; a temporizer.

1592 Bacon Observ. Libel Resusc. (1657) 132 The Spaniards are great Waiters upon Time, and ground their Plots deep. 1836 Marq. Londonderry in Dk. Buckhm. Mem. Crts. Will. IV & Vict. (1861) II. 228 Such as are rats, and waiters upon Providence, who have now deserted us. 1907 P. T. Forsyth Positive Preaching vii. 231 It is the waiters on God that renew their strength.

III. †5. One who waits in the presence of another (of superior rank); one who visits, or pays court to a superior.

1530 Palsgr. 286/1 Wayter, qui baille attendance. 1542 Udall Erasm. Apoph. 41 b, Diogenes called Aristippus the kynges hownde, because he was a dayly waiter, and gaue contynuall attendaunce in the Courte of Dionysius. 1591 Savile Tacitus, Agricola (1622) 200 Being admitted to the princes presence, and receiued with a short salutation and no speech, he sorted himselfe with the rest of the wayters [turba servientium inmixtus est]. 1611 Bible Judith xiii. 1 Bagoas shut his tent without, and dismissed the waiters from the presence of his lord.

†b. *Waiter at the table*: a parasite. Obs. rare.

1552 Huloet, Wayter at the table as vncommaunded to ye entent to get hys dynner, parasitaster.

†6. A man (more rarely, a woman) whose office or privilege it is to attend upon a superior. a. A regular member (often a person of high rank) of the retinue or household of a royal or noble personage. Obs.

14.. 15th Cent. Courtesy Bk. (1914) 14 Then shall be þer redy yemen of the chambre yef it be þer, yemen waytors yef it be in þe hall, to take away stolis and bordes and trestelies. a1548 Hall Chron., Hen. VIII, 12 The kyng & his thre felowes entred into the felde their bardes and bases of Crimosyn and blew Veluet..and all the wayters in sylke of the same colour. a1562 G. Cavendish Wolsey (1893) 45 Whan he came to the gallerye's end, he satt hyme down uppon a forme that stode there for the wayters some tyme to take ther ease. 1594 R. Carew Huarte's Exam. Wits (1616) 228 The sixt thing which honoureth a man, is the seemely ornament of his person, and his going well apparelled, and attended with manie waiters. 1630 R. Johnson's Kingd. & Commw. 142 They which were wont to be called Pantlers, Tasters and Carvers, are now called Gentlemen Wayters of the Court. 1678–9 Dryden & Lee Œdipus ii. i, Each trembling Ghost shall rise, And leave their grizly King without a waiter.

†b. An attendant upon the bride at weddings; a bridesmaid. Obs.

1537 in Lett. & Papers Hen. VIII, XII. i. 11, 3 goodly ladies in cloth of gold gorgeously decked following as waiters of the bride. c1680 Roxb. Ballads (1891) VII. 458 Then come let us be, blithe, merry and free, Upon my life all the waiters are gone!..The Bride-Maids that waited are gone.

†c. = Acolyte. nonce-use.

1563 Man Musculus' Commonpl. 275 Thei do reckon up, dore keepers, readers, conjurers, wayters [L. acolytos], sub deacons, deacons, and priestes, whiche all thei do call clerkes.

†d. One who out of courtesy waits at table on special occasions. (Cf. sense 7 c.) Obs.

1605 Camden Rem., Wise Sp. 196 The Archebishop of Yorke saide vnto the yoong king..'there is never a Prince in the world that hath this day such a waiter at his Table [viz. K. Henry II] as you have'. a1641 Bp. Mountagu Acts & Mon. (1642) 434 The waiters are all free men, who willingly proffer attendance at such feasts;..their waiters are clad in long loose garments to distinguish them from servants. a1714 Parnell in Steele Poet. Misc. 65 Each sweet engaging Grace Put on some Cloaths to come abroad, And took a Waiters Place.

†e. *Waiter at the altar*: (a) *gen.* (after 1 Cor. ix. 13), a priest or other minister of the altar; (b) one in minor orders (cf. 6 c).

1648 Fanshawe Il Pastor Fido iv. iii. 137 The waiters at the altar [It. i ministri minori]. 1711 G. Hickes Two Treat. Chr. Priesth. (1847) II. 70 Ministers about holy things, and waiters at God's altar.

7. A man (rarely a woman) of lower rank employed as a household servant.

†a. A servitor, groom, footman, etc. Obs.

a1483 Liber Niger in Househ. Ord. (1790) 41 Dayly iiii other of these groomes, called wayters, to make fyres, to sett up tressyls and bourdes. c1586 C'tess Pembroke Ps. cxxiii. i, Right as a waiters eye on a graceful master is holden. 1611 Beaum. & Fl. Philaster ii. (1620) 24 What sawcy groome knocks at this dead of night, where be our waiters? 1655 E. Terry Voy. East India xiii. 244 Death made many breaches into my Lord Ambassadors family, for of four and twenty wayters, besides his Secretary and my self, there was not above the fourth man returned home. 1788 Massachusetts Spy 29 May 3/4 A considerable number of the respectable inhabitants of Princeton, consisting of 37 gunners and their waiters, spent the day past in hunting.

†b. A waiting-woman. Obs. rare.

1639 Massinger Unnat. Combat i. i, Bid your wayters [two waiting-women] Stand farther of.

c. esp. A servant (in a private house) whose particular duty it is to wait upon those seated at table. Obs. (? exc. U.S.); cf. sense 8.

1528 Roy Rede me (Arb.) 98 Then proll the servynge officers, With their yemen that be wayters, So that their levettis are but thynne. 1609 Holland Amm. Marcell. d 4 b, Butlers, carvers, yeomen of the cellar, wayters at the table. a1674 Milton Hist. Moscovia v. Wks. 1851 VIII. 507 In dinner time he twice chang'd his Crown, his Waiters thrice thir Apparel. 1856 Mrs. Stowe Dred xi, She was in the middle of the saloon again, just as the waiter announced dinner.

8. A man employed, at inns, hotels, eating-houses, or similar places, to wait upon the guests (esp. during meals). Also a man hired for a similar purpose on special occasions to supplement the staff of a private household.

This sense probably arose in England about the middle of the 17th c., and superseded the older term *drawer*. From the 18th c. onwards it appears to have been the most usual sense of the word.

a1663 Killigrew Parson's Wedd. iii. v. (1664) 120 Drawer. ..The sum is six pounds, and be pleased to remember the Waiters. 1712 Steele Spect. No. 508 ¶ 3 We change our Taverns according as he suspects any Treasonable Practices in the settling the Bill by the Master, or sees any bold Rebellion in point of Attendance by the Waiters. 1779 Mirror No. 26 But there is another set of persons still more exposed to be treated roughly than even domestic servants, and these are, the waiters at inns and taverns. 1818 Hazlitt Table-t., Knowl. Charact. (1822) II. 351 After a familiar conversation with a waiter at a tavern. 1837 Dickens Pickw. xxxv, The White Hart hotel..where the waiters, from their costume, might be mistaken for Westminster boys. 1874 Ruskin Fors Clav. xlviii. IV. 271 Presently afterwards, an evidently German-importation of waiter brings me up my breakfast.

IV. A contrivance to supply the place of a waiter or facilitate waiting.

†9. = DUMB-WAITER 2.

10. A silver, small tray (cf. *waiting-board*).

†11. (See quot.)

Waiteráge (wēˈtǎrėdʒ). [f. WAITER + -AGE.]
†1. The office of warder, or watchman. *Obs. rare.*
2. A position as a waiter in an inn, etc.

Wai'terdom. The performance of a waiter's duties. Waiters considered as a class. **Wai'terism**, waiters collectively. **Wai'terhood**, the state or condition of a waiter. **Wai'tering**, the occupation of a waiter.

Waitersh'ip (wēˈtǎʃip). [f. WAITER + -SHIP.]
†1. The office of warder, or watchman. *Obs. rare.*
2. A position as a waiter in an inn, etc.

†Waith, *sb.¹ Sc. and north. Obs.* Forms: [f. wathe, β waith, γ waithe, 4 waithe, 5 wathe.

Waith (wēiþ), *sb.² Sc. Obs.*

†Waith, *sb.³ Sc.*

Waith, *sb.⁴ Sc. Also 8 weeth.*

†Wai'thman. *Sc. Obs.*

Waiting (wēiˈtiŋ), *vbl. sb.* [f. -ING¹.]
1. The action of WAIT in various senses.
†b. Watching, observation. *Obs.*

Waiting-, comb.

Waiting-maid. [WAITING *ppl. a.*]

†Waiting-ma·n. *Sc. Obs.* [WAITING *ppl. a.*]

Waiting-room. [WAITING *vbl. sb.*]

Wai'ting-woman. Now *arch.* [WAITING *ppl. a.*]

Waitress (wēiˈtrės). *Also 6* **waiteresse.** [f. WAITER + -ESS.]

†Wai'ting, *sb.* [f. WAIT *v.*]

Waivable (wēiˈvăb'l), *a.* [f. WAIVE *v.* + -ABLE.]

†Waive, *sb. Law. Obs.*

Waive (wēiv), *v.¹* Forms: 3-4 **weyve, 5 weyfe, 6 pa. pple. waived, weth**, etc.

Waiver (wēiˈvǎ(r)). *Law.*

Waivery. *Law. Obs.* [a. AF.]

Waiving (wēiˈviŋ), *vbl. sb.* [f. WAIVE *v.* + -ING¹.]

Waivling, var. WAVELING *a. Sc.*

†Wak, *a. ON.*

Waivode, waiwode : see WAYWODE.

Wak, Wakande : see WEAK *a.*, VACAND.

Wake (wēik), *sb.¹* Forms: 4 wak, woke, 6 wakke, 6 wacke, 7 *dial.* wake; 2 waxen, waakes, etc. ; β wake.

1. The state of wakefulness *esp.* during normal hours of sleep.

2. Abstinence from sleep, watching, practised as a religious observance.

3. The watching (*esp.* by night) of relatives and friends beside the body of a dead person from death to burial.

4. *transf.* Applied to similar periodic festivals or occasions of revelry.

5. Used by Hogg for : A nocturnal song.

Wake, sb.²

Wake (wēk), sb.² Also 6 7 walk, 7 wack.

Wake (wēk), v.¹ Forms: Inf. and Present stem.

Wake, a. Obs. exc. dial.

Wake, sb.³ Obs. rare⁻¹.

Wake, a. Obs. exc. dial.

Wakeful (wēk·fŭl), a. [f. WAKE sb.¹ + -FUL.]

Wake-goose. Obs. rare⁻¹.

Wakeless, a.

Wakeman (wēk·măn). Obs. exc. arch.

Waken (wēk·ĕn), v.

Waker, a. Obs.

Wakeness. Obs.

Wakener (wēk·ĕnăɹ).

Waker (wēk·ăɹ). Also 4 Sc. walk(y)nar.

Wakerell. Obs. Forms: 5 **wakerell**, 5 **wag(e)rell**, **wak(e)rell**, (5 **wakerong**). 7 **wakerell**. [App. f. WAKER sb. + -EL.] The name given in Kent to a church bell (f. the sancta bell). Also **wakerell bell**, **rope**.

Wakerife, a. Sc. and north. dial. Forms: 6 **wauryff**, **wakrife** (wakryfe, waloryf), 5-7 **walkryf** 6, 6-7 **wakryf**, 8 **wakryfe**, 9 **-rife**, 8, 9 **wakerife**. [f. WAKE v. + -RIFE a. cf. LATEGIFE.] Indisposed to sleep, wakeful, vigilant.

+ Wakerly, a. Obs. [f. WAKER a. + -LY¹.] Wakeful, watchful.

+ Wakerly, adv. Obs. In 4 **wokyrly**. Nimbly.

Wake-robin. [App. f. WAKE v. + ROBIN.] The plant Arum maculatum, also commonly called cuckoo-pint, lords-and-ladies, etc.

Waking, vbl. sb.¹ [-ING¹.] The action of the verb WAKE.

Waking, vbl. sb.² [-ING¹.] The action of remaining awake or sitting up at night.

Waking, ppl. a. [-ING².] That remains awake; that keeps watch; fig.

Wale, sb.¹ Also **weal**, **wheal**.

Walach, **Wallach** (wǫ'lăk). Also 8 **Woloch**, 9 **Wallack**. [See VLACH.] A member of a Romanic-speaking race widely disseminated in south-eastern Europe, principally in Rumania: = VLACH.

Walachian, **Wallachian** (wǫlā'kiăn), sb.

Walchowite (wæ'lkǫǐt). Min. [Named by Haidinger 1845 from Walachow in Moravia where it was found: see -ITE.] A honey-yellow resin similar to amber.

Walcry (obs. form of WAKERIFE).

Wald (wōld). Obs. [OE. wald.] A wood, forest.

Waldenses (wǭldenzīz), sb. pl. [med.L. Waldenses (Valdenses).] A body of Protestant reformers originating in the south of France about 1170 through the preaching of Peter Waldo.

Waldhorn (va'ldhôrn). [G. waldhorn, forest or hunting horn, French horn.]

+ Waldin, a. Obs. Forms: 5 waldin, 9 waldyng, waddin. [Pa. pple. of weald.]

Walding, Sc. form of WELDING, WIELDING.

Wale, sb.¹ 1 walu, 5-6 Sc. wail, 6-7 wale, wayle (whale, waol, woale), 5 Sc., 8-9 wall, 4- wale. [OE. walu wk. fem. (also 6-8 wall) 4- wale. [OE. walu wk. fem.]

Wale, sb.¹ (continued)

Waler. [f. (New South) Wales + -ER¹.] A horse imported from New South Wales.

Walesman. [Wales + man.]

Walk, v. [OE. wealcan, to roll, to full.]

Walk, sb.

d. A public promenade in or near a town.

1840 Dickens Old C. Shop xliv, In the public walks and lounges of a town, people go to see and to be seen. 1842 Louisa S. Costello Pilgr. Auvergne II. iii. 43 This public walk is prettily arranged on the site of a Roman amphitheatre.

e. The circular pavement on which the mill-horse walks in driving the mill.

1734 Phil. Trans. XXXVIII. 403 Their Muscles and Tendons..are unequally strain'd, as the Duty is hardest on one Side, even tho' their Walk is large. 1744 Desaguliers Course Exper. Philos. II. 536 Those plain and simple Instruments used at the Coal-pits, call'd Barrel-Gins, where an Horse going round in a sufficiently large Walk draws round an Axis in Peritrochio. 1834–6 Barlow in Encycl. Metrop. (1845) VIII. 91/1 The diameter of a walk for a horse mill ought to be at least 25 to 30 feet.

f. = Rope-walk.

1794 Rigging & Seamanship I. 54 A Capstern..is fixed in the ground at the lower-end of the walk. Ibid. 56 Rope-house-ground, or Walk, should be four-hundred yards long. 1839 Ure Dict. Arts 1070 (Rope-making.) As soon as he has reached the termination of the walk, a second spinner takes the yarn off the whirl, and gives it to another person to put upon a reel.

10. A tract of forest land comprised in the circuit regularly perambulated by a superintending officer (cf. 3); a division of a forest placed in the charge of a forester, ranger, or keeper.

1541 N. Country Wills (Surtees 1908) 190 To poor housholders and other honest people within my walkes within the forest of Wyndesore. 1593 Shaks. 3 Hen. VI, v. ii. 24 My Parkes, my Walkes, my Mannors that I had, Euen now forsake me. 1642 Docq. Lett. Pat. at Oxf. (1837) 330 The Office of Keeper of the lower walke of the great Parke of Windsor. Ibid. 338 The Offices of the foure Bayliwickes or eight walkes, and of Ranger and Launderer of the Forrest of Whichwood. 1679–88 Moneys Secr. Serv. Chas. II & Jas. II (Camden) 125 To Sr Eliab Harvey, Lieut. of Waltham forest,..for the repayres of Low-Layton Lodge, wherein he lives, being under-keeper of that walk. a 1700 Evelyn Diary 23 Oct. 1686, Went with the Countesse of Sunderland to Cranbourn, a lodge and walke of my Lord Godolphin's in Windsor Parke. 1778 Engl. Gazetteer (ed. 2) s.v. New Forest, There are 9 walks in it; and to every one a keeper, under a lord-warden, besides 2 rangers, and a bow-bearer. 1810 J. Evans & Britton Beauties Eng. & Wales XI. Northampt. 31 The Forest of Whittlewood...The whole is divided into five walks, viz. Hazleborough, Sholbrook, Wakefield, Hanger, and Shrobb. 1819 Scott Ivanhoe xxxii, If the Normans drive ye from these walks, Rowena has forests of her own, where her gallant deliverers may range at full freedom.

†b. Agric. A tract of land used for corn-growing.

1797 in A. Young Agric. Suffolk 39 A walk that is laid down with plenty of seeds for two years, never grows so much corn as when first broke up again.

c. West Indian. A plantation.

1793 Ann. Reg., Nat. Hist. 310 The usual method of forming a new piemento plantation (in Jamaica it is called a walk) is nothing more than to appropriate a piece of woodland, [etc.]. 1901 Westm. Gaz. 13 June 2/3 Many sugar estates in the West Indies have of late years been converted into banana walks.

11. a. An enclosure in which poultry or other birds are allowed to run freely; a fowl-run. Also (cf. sense 13), a place to which fowls are sent in order that they may have more space to run about than can be allowed them where they are bred: in phrase at walk.

1538 Elyot Dict., Viuarium, a place, where wylde beastes, byrdes, or fyshes be kepte. It may be callyd as welle a ponde, as a parke, a counnyngar, a walke for byrdes. 1600 Surflet Country Farme I. xvi. 107 Likewise you must not let them [geese] lay out of their walke or fold. 1880 Jessopp Arcady i. (1887) 10 He eats the eggs for breakfast and the chickens for dinner, goes in for fancy breeds [of fowl], and runs up an ornamental 'walk' for them.

¶b. A walk of snipes (†snites). In the early lists of 'proper terms' the meaning is uncertain; later writers interpret it as a 'company term' (cf. 'congregation of plovers' in the same lists).

c 1450 MS. Egerton 1995 fol. 19 A Walke of Snytys. 1801 Strutt Sports & Past. I. ii. 33. 1859 Folkard Wild Fowler i. 6 A walk of snipes.

c. The place in which a game-cock is kept. Cock of the walk (fig.): a person whose supremacy in his own circle is undisputed (see Cock sb.[1] 7).

1615 T. Savile in J. J. Cartwright Chapters Hist. Yorks. (1872) 350, I have..borowed my father's cocks...I go..to get walkes for them. 1688 Holme Armoury II. 251/2 The Cocks Walk is the place where he is bred, which usually is a place that no other Cock comes to. c 1770 T. Fairfax Compl. Sportsm. 4 Let the cock chickens go with their hens, till they begin to fight one with another; but then separate them into several walks, and that walk is the best, that is freest from the resort of others. 1823 Grose's Dict. Vulgar T. (ed. Egan), Cock, or Chief Cock of the Walk. The leading man in any Society or body; the best boxer in a village or district. 1823 'Jon Bee' Dict. Turf, Walk (in cocking)—the ground for keeping them. 1857 Trollope Barchester T. xvii. heading, Who shall be cock of the walk? 1875 Whyte Melville Katerfelto i, Mr. Gale, to use his own phraseology, was accustomed to consider himself Cock of the Walk in every society he frequented.

12. Land, or a tract of land, used for the pasture of animals, esp. sheep. Obs. exc. in Sheepwalk.

1549 Latimer 1st Serm. bef. Edw. VI (Arb.) 40 He had walke for a hundred shepe, and my mother mylked .xxx. kyne. 1573–80 Tusser Husb. (1878) 62 The housing of cattel while winter doth hold..spareth the pasture for walke of thy sheepe. a 1647 Habington Surv. Worcs. (Worcs. Hist. Soc.) I. 254 A large walke for sauage beastes, but nowe more commodiously chaunged to the civill habitations of many gentellmen. 1808 Jamieson, Gang,..a pasture or walk for cattle.

13. A farm or cottage to which a young hound is sent in order to get accustomed to a variety of surroundings. Phrases, at walk, to put to walk.

1735 Somerville Chase iv. Argt., Of the litter of whelps..of setting them out to their several walks. 1781 P. Beckford Thoughts Hunting v. 60 The distemper makes dreadful havoc with whelps at their walks. 1840 Blaine Encycl. Rur. Sports iv. v. § 3. 474 Hounds are usually named at the time they are sent out to their walks. 1845 Youatt Dog ii. 36 There is a difference of opinion whether the [greyhound] whelp should be kept in the kennel and subjected to its regular discipline, or placed at walk in some farm-house. 1854 Surtees Handley Cr. (1901) I. i. 4 The hounds were still kept at walks during the summer. 1856 'Stonehenge' Brit. Sports II. iv. § 340 The Walks for the Young Hounds should be chosen in such situations as that they shall be accustomed to all sorts of company from children to horses. 1881 E. D. Brickwood Hound in Encycl. Brit. XII. 315/2 When about ten or twelve weeks old [foxhound] puppies are sent out to walk.

14. The 'beat', round, or circuit of an itinerating official, workman, tradesman, beggar, etc.; the district within which a person is accustomed to practise his occupation without interference from a rival. ? Obs.

1703 Lond. Gaz. No. 3910/4 Making use of the Company's Pavior of that Walk to Dig the same. 1705 tr. Bosman's Guinea 98 The last and most contemptible Office is that of Under-Fiscal, commonly called by us, Auditor, though in his Walks, Informer, as he really is no better. 1824 Scott Redgauntlet let. xii, The old man [the blind fiddler] struck the earth with his staff...'The whoreson fisher rabble! They have brought another violer upon my walk!' 1825 Hone Every-day Bk. I. 571 Milk people of less profitable walks. 1848 Sinks of Lond. 97 Beat, a watchman's walk. 1851 Mayhew Lond. Labour I. 435/2 'My father had a milk-walk', he said. Ibid. (1861) II. 8/2 He had thoughts at one time of trying to establish himself in a cats'-meat walk.

15. A distance or length of way to be walked; esp. such a distance as defined by a specified length of time spent in walking. (Often in phrases used advb.)

1562 J. Heywood Prov. & Epigr. (1867) 79 Dwellyng a good walke from hir at the townes eende. a 1700 Evelyn Diary 15 Sept. 1685, Her house being a walke in the forest, within a little of a quarter mile from Bagshot towne. 1808 Scott in Lockhart I. i. 59, I agreed to go every morning to his house, which, being at the extremity of Prince's Street, New Town, was a walk of two miles. 1834 Dickens Sk. Boz, Boarding-ho. i, 'A cheerful musical home in a select private family, residing within ten minutes' walk of'—everywhere. 1859 Mrs. Carlyle Lett. III. 4 Within a quarter of an hour's walk of it. 1875 Ruskin Morn. Florence i. 5 A few hundred yards west of you, within ten minutes' walk, is the Baptistery of Florence. 1883 C. Howard Roads Eng. & Wales (ed. 3) 123 Beginning with a ¼ m. walk out of the town, it is an almost continual ascent for 7 m. Ibid., There is a mile run down to the railway, followed by a mile walk up into Stow.

b. U.S. (See quot.)

'1901 P. Fountain Deserts N. Amer. vii. 118 The Indians had a singular custom in parting with their land. They sold it by the 'walk'. Ibid. 119 The duration of a walk was always a day in time, no matter what the distance.

16. A course or circuit, in the country or in a town, which may be chosen for walking.

1617 Moryson Itin. I. 32 In the valley under this Mountaine of Goates, towards the City, is a pleasant walk, of the sweetnes called the Phylosophicall way. 1687 A. Lovell tr. Thevenot's Trav. I. 28 Though the Countrey about Constantinople be not so delightful, nor so well peopled, as in France; yet it is not without pleasant Walks. 1693 Dryden Ovid's Metam. xiii. Acis etc. 51 A Promontory..over-looks the Seas: On either side, below, the water flows: This airy walk the Giant Lover chose. 1757 Mrs. P. L. Powys Passages fr. Diaries (1899) 32, I..thought myself most happy when I got into the grove, one of the sweetest walks in Matlock. 1786 Cowper Let. to J. Hill 9 Dec., Weston is one of the prettiest villages in England, and the walks about it at all seasons of the year delightful. 1850 J. Martineau in J. Drummond Life (1902) I. 337 We can find walks that will vie with the Thiergarten even in this desolate country. 1860 Tyndall Glac. I. xv. 100 This walk was full of instruction and delight.

III. Department of action.

17. A department of action; a particular branch or variety of some specified activity, e.g. trade, literature, science, etc.; a special line of work.

1759 Franklin Ess. Wks. 1840 III. 145 Two thirds were to be a quorum in the upper walk of business, and one third in the lower. 1762 H. Walpole Vertue's Anecd. Paint. (1786) I. Pref. p. vii, It would be difficult..to assign a physical reason, why a nation that produced Shakespear, should owe its glory in another walk of genius to Holbein and Vandyck. 1776 Mickle tr. Camoens' Lusiad Dissert. 167/1 However superior Voltaire may be in the other walks of poetry, certain it is, no originality, no strength of colouring, shines in the Henriade. 1806 Beresford Miseries Hum. Life vi. Introd., As you appear to have a peculiar kindness for Inns, I will treat you with a choice sample of satisfactions in that walk of enjoyment. 1809 Malkin Gil Blas vii. xiii. ¶ 9 He had..taken upon himself to eclipse the best writers each in their own favourite walk. 1815 W. H. Ireland Scribbleomania 147 Three sisters..displayed much talent in pursuing this walk of literature. 1823 De Quincey Lett. Educ. i. (1860) 12 He seeks to renew that elevated walk of study at all opportunities. 1833 Chalmers Const. Man (1835) I. ii. 137 Each affection has its peculiar walk of enjoyment. 1838 Prescott Ferd. & Is. I. xix. II. 293 A similar impulse was felt in the other walks of science. 1856 Masson Ess. iv. 112 Butler had shewn the more original vein of talent in one particular walk. 1857 Dickens Dorrit II. vi, 'Does Mr. Henry Gowan paint—ha—Portraits?' inquired Mr. Dorrit. Mr. Sparkler opined that he painted anything, if he could get the job. 'He has no particular walk?'..'No speciality?' said Mr. Dorrit. 1866 Crump Banking ii. 48 It is one of the most singular peculiarities in connection with men who have had much experience in other walks of trade, as merchants, &c. 1888 Bryce Amer. Commw. xcviii. III. 370 When he [a lawyer] has attained real eminence he may confine himself entirely to the higher walks.

18. Walk of life (more rarely walk in life): a. A social grade, station of life, rank. Also walk of society. b. A trade, profession, or occupation.

a. 1752 Fielding Covent-Garden Jrnl. No. 56 ¶ 9 Both of these [sc. characters of humour] will be almost infinitely diversified according to the different..natural dispositions of each individual; and according to their different walks in life. 1766 Fordyce Serm. Young Women (1767) II. xiii. 247 Those who are placed in the higher walks of life. 1768 Goldsm. Goodn. Man Pref., The term 'genteel comedy' was then unknown amongst us, and little more was desired by an audience than nature and humour, in whatever walks of life they were most conspicuous. 1800 Asiatic Ann. Reg. II. 97/2 The walk of life from which writers are to come should be duly weighed as they are in future, perhaps, to become directors, and probably legislators of India. 1832 P. Egan's Bk. Sports No. 5. 66/2 Nature, enriched by art, had rendered the late Mr. Emery a man not often to be met with in the walks of society. 1899 Ch. Times 13 Oct. 415/2 But according to the fashion of dress of to-day, it is not easy to tell from what walk in life women may come.

b. 1848 Sinks of Lond. 3 In what is termed the 'walks of life'. 1849 Macaulay Hist. Eng. viii. II. 307 They found every walk of life towards which men of their habits could look for a subsistence closed against them with malignant care. 1861 Bright Sp. India 19 Mar. Sp. (1868) I. 119 Of course there are men of genius in very objectionable walks of life. 1888 Bryce Amer. Commw. xcviii. III. 378 The lawyers outnumber the persons belonging to other walks of life. 1912 Sat. Rev. 18 May 615/1 Emolument far greater than what was possible for them in any other walk of life.

19. (= walk of life, 18 a and b). a. Social grade or station; b. trade or profession. rare.

a. 1847 Miller First Impr. Eng. xiii. 251, I met a funeral, the first I had seen in England. It was apparently that of a person in the middle walks. 1854 — Sch. & Schm. (1858) 246 To those who move in the upper walks, the superiority in status of the village shop-keeper over the journeyman mason may not be very perceptible.

b. 1836 Dickens Sk. Boz, First of May, Certain dark insinuations..to the effect that children in the lower ranks of life were beginning to choose chimney-sweeping as their particular walk.

IV. 20. attrib. and Comb. (sense 1) as walk-companion; (sense 9 c), as walk-making, -side; (sense 14) as walk-rotation; (sense 12) as walk-land; also walk-clerk, a banker's clerk whose duty it is to collect payment of cheques in a particular district; walksman, an officer charged with the care of a certain length of the banks of a river or canal; walkway U.S. = sense 9 c.

1890 H. Price Lond. Bankers 35 note, The following misfortune that befell a *walk-clerk. 1833 Lamb Let. to Wordsw. May, I am about to lose my old and only *walk-companion, whose mirthful spirits were the 'youth of our house'. 1797 A. Young Agric. Suffolk 108 Ten loads..an acre upon good land, a middling crop; but upon *walk-land (poor sheep-walks ploughed up) less. 1849 J. Forbes Physic. Holiday i. (1850) 1 They..indulge in farming, gardening, tree-felling, *walk-making, or [etc.]. 1893 Stevenson Catriona iii, A pleasant gabled house set by the *walkside among some brave young woods. 1901 Daily Chron. 8 June 7/7 The alleged attempts of the [Post Office] department to reduce the value of Christmas boxes by the introduction of a system of '*walk-rotation'. 1794 Ann. Reg., Nat. Hist. 311 For the care of the banks [of the New River], a *walksman is appointed to every two miles. 1903 Daily Chron. 17 Mar. 9/5 A 'walksman' in the service of the New River Company. 1911 H. S. Harrison Queed xvi, He went down the broad steps of the Capitol, and out the winding white *walkway through the park.

†**Walk**, sb.[2] Sc. Obs. [repr. OE. wolc, var. of wolcen, wolcne: see Welkin.] A cloud or clouds.

1513 Douglas Æneis III. viii. 155 The mone wes vndir walk, and gaif na lycht. c 1560 Rolland Seven Sages 73 Sa as thir twa togidder was at talk, The Mone wox dark, and hid was vnder walk.

Walk (wǫk), v.[1] Pa. t. and pa. pple. walked (wǫkt). Forms: Inf. and pres. stem: 1 wealcan, wealcian, 2, 3 walki-en, 4 walc, 2–7 walke, 6 walck(e, Sc. valk, 8–9 Sc. wauk, 4– walk. Pa. t. a. strong 1 wéolc, 3–5 welk(e, 5 walke, wilke; β. weak 1 wealcede, 4 welkide, walkit, 5 walkude, walkyd, 6 walckt(e, (6 Sc. valkit), 4– walked. Pa. pple. a. strong 3 i-walken, walke; β. weak 5 walkude, 3– walked. [OE. had two forms: (1) wealcan redupl. str. vb. (pa. t. wéolc, pa. pple. gewealcen), to roll, toss (trans. and intr.); (2) wealcian weak vb., occurring only twice, in the senses 'to muffle up' (gl. obvolvere), to curl (hair: gl. calamistrare). One or both of these vbs. may have had also the sense 'to full (cloth)': see Walk v.[2] The corresponding forms in the other Teut. langs. are: OHG. walchan str. vb., recorded only in pa. pple. giwalchen, firwalchen, felted, matted (said of hair: gl. concretus); MHG. walken (pa. t. wielc, pa. pple. walken; later conjugated weak), to knead, to roll (paste) into balls in the palms of the hands; rarely, to move about (trans. and intr.), to turn into something; usually, to full (cloth), whence to cudgel, drub; mod.G. walken wk. vb., to full, to cudgel;

(M)LG., (M)Du. walken wk. vb., to full, to work (felt), to cudgel; ON. valka (Icel. válka, mod. volka) wk. vb., to drag about, to torment, refl. to wallow; MSw. valka wk. vb., to roll (a morsel) about in the mouth, Norw. valka wk. vb. to crumple in the hand, MDa. valke wk. vb. to torment; the mod.Sw. valka, Da. valke (wk.), to full, prob. take their sense from LG.

The strong pa. t. survived into the 15th c.; the weak conjugation, recorded from the 13th c. onwards, may perh. not be a survival of the rare OE. wealcian but an instance of the frequent change of inflexion from strong to weak. The corresponding weak vb. in continental Teut. is prob. to be explained in this way.

It is remarkable that to the end of the OE. period the sense of the str. vb. was 'to roll', and that from the beginning of the ME. period it was 'to move about, travel'. The explanation of this apparently sudden change may be that the ME. sense had arisen in OE. as a colloquial (perhaps jocular) use, and that when the literary tradition was interrupted after the Conquest, and people wrote as they spoke, the original meaning of the verb was no longer current.

The OTeut. root *walk- has no certain affinities in any other branch of the Indogermanic family; phonologically the Skr. valg- to leap, dance, and the L. valgus bow-legged, might be related, but there is no clear similarity of meaning.]

†**I. 1.** intr. a. In OE. (str. vb.). Of the waves: To roll, toss. b. In early ME. of persons: To toss about restlessly. Obs.

In OE. also trans. (str. vb.) to turn over, roll; also fig. to turn over in one's mind, consider; (wk. verb) to curl (hair); to press together (cf. Walk v.[2]). For examples see Bosworth-Toller.

a 1100 Aldh. Glosses in Napier OE. Gl. i. 2474 Feruentis oceani, wealcendre sæ. a 1200 Moral Ode 240 Ho [sc. souls in hell] secheð reste þer nis nan..walkeð weri up and dun, se water deþ mid winde. ? a 1200 Body & Soul (Phillips) 5 He walkeþ & wendeþ & woneþ..þes, he sæiþ on his bedde, wome þæt ic libbe, þæt æffre [etc.]. 1398 W. Paris Cristine (Horstm.) 394 Fyve daies..Sche welkide þerin [an oven] to & froo. c 1400 Pety Job 329 in 26 Pol. Poems 131 Allas, I walke in a lake Of dedly synne that doth me tene.

II. intr. To journey, move about, esp. on foot.

†**2.** To go from place to place; to journey, wander. Also with cogn. obj., to go (one's way).

In quot. a 1000 the sense appears to be 'to pass over'; if so, the gloss is the only example within the OE. period of any anticipation of the ME. development of the meaning of the word; but it may be significant that the reference is to motion on the sea.

a 1000 Prudentius Glosses in Germania XI. 400 Emensus, gewealcon ['Emensus et multum freti' Prud. Peristeph. v. 471]. c 1200 Trin. Coll. Hom. 51 Þat israelisshe folc was walkende toward ierusalem on swinche and on drede and on wanrede. c 1205 Lay. 112 Heuede Eneas be duc mid his dribt folcke widen iwalken. c 1250 Meid. Maregrete xlix, Muchel ic habbe iwalken bi water ant bi londe. a 1300 Cursor M. 6359 Queder-sum he welk her or þare, Þis wandes ever he wit him bare. Ibid. 21685 Quen þe nedders..Þe folk staunged of israel, Quen þai welk in þe wildernes. 13.. Ibid. 22063 (Gött.) Þe angel..in þe pitt [þe deuil] sperd fast..for to be laised at þe last quen þat thousand ȝere war past, to walk his wai [Edinb. MS. to walc his waiis forthe] fra þat quile. 1340–70 Alex. & Dind. 498 Vs is likful and lef in landus to walke, þere won walleþ of water in þe welle-springus. 1377 Langl. P. Pl. B. viii. 14 Þei ben men on þis molde þat moste wyde walken. c 1400 Rule St. Benet 1893 Þai þat sal walk bi way, or wirk, And may not cum to haly kirk,..Þeir seruyse sal þai not for-gete. 1513 Douglas Æneis v. x. 29 And for ilk menȝe A capitane walkis rewland all his rowt.

3. Of things.

†a. Of time: To pass, elapse. Obs.

c 1250 Gen. & Ex. 568 An hundred winter..welken or it was ended wel.

†b. Of reports, fame, also of letters, money: To circulate, pass from one to another; also with about. Also said of the person whose fame is spread abroad. Obs.

13.. Gaw. & Gr. Knt. 1521 Your worde & your worchip walkez ay quere. a 1352 Minot Poems viii. 29 Þe word of him walkes ful wide. 1387 T. Usk Test. Love I. vii. (Sk.) 95 Loke now what people hast thou served; whiche of them al in tyme of thyne exile ever the refresshed, by the value of the leste coyned plate that walketh in mony? c 1470 Henry Wallace III. 252 The worde of him walkit baith fer and ner. 1533 More Let. to Cromwell Wks. 1422/1 An vnknowen heretike which hath sent ouer a worke that walketh in ouer many mens handes named the Souper of the lord. 1549 Latimer 4th Serm. bef. Edw. VI (Arb.) 111 Ther was brybes walking, money makynge, makynge of haudes. a 1566 R. Edwards Damon & P. (facs.) Biv, And I vp and downe, Go seekyng to learne what Newes here are walkyng. 1583 Stubbes Anat. Abus. II. 13 If any man that hath freends and mony..chance to haue committed neuer so..flagicious a deed,..then letters walke, freends bestir them, and mony carrieth all away. 1601 B. Jonson Poetaster III. v. 77 For he shall weepe, and walke with euery tongue Throughout the citie, infamously song. a 1626 Bacon War with Spain (1629) 42 A wonderfull erroneous obseruation that walketh about. 1640 tr. Verdere's Rom. of Rom. II. 120 This Prince..never left praying and importuning; every day she had a Page, letters were continually walking [Fr. les lettres marchoient à toutes heures]. 1671 Milton Samson 1089, I..now am come to see of whom such noise Hath walk'd about. 1687 R. L'Estrange Answ. Dissenter 22 There may be Mony Walking on the One Side as well as on the Other.

†c. Of crime, vice, or virtue: To be rife, spread abroad. Obs.

1377 Langl. P. Pl. B. vii. 79 In hym þat taketh is þe treccherye, if any tresoun wawe [read walke (with 5 MSS.)]. 1387 Trevisa Higden (Rolls) II. 169 Þese men..beeþ i-woned to haue the victorie..in euerich fiȝt wher no treson is walkynge [L. ubi fraus abfuerit]. c 1450 in Kingsford Chron. Lond. (1905) 140 Ther whas so moch treson walkyng that men wist not what to do. 1567 Gude & Godlie B. (S.T.S.) 101 Thair violence and wrang walkis full wyde. 1573 L. Lloyd Pilgr. Princes 53 Then luste knew no way to the pallace of Cæsars, then abstinence walked in the market place, then all Rome was chast. 1626 Breton Pasquils Mad-cap (Grosart) 8/2 Wealth is a witch that hath a wicked charme, That in the mindes of wicked men doth walke.

†d. Of drink, etc.: To be handed round, pass, circulate. Obs.

1555 R. Smith in Foxe A. & M. (1563) 1254/1 My Lorde mayre being set with the bishop and one of the shriues, wine was walking on euery syde, I standing before them as an outcast. 1567 Harman Caveat (Shaks. Soc.) 32 How the pottes walke about! their talking tounges talke at large. 1594 Greene & Lodge Looking Gl. 1858 G.'s Wks. 1905 I. 201 Frolicke, my Lord[s]; let all the standerds walke; Ply it till euery man hath tane his load. 1596 Raleigh Guiana 85 Wee found them all as drunke as beggers, and the pottes walking from one to another without rest. 1622 R. Hawkins Voy. S. Sea (1847) 216 The pott continually walking, infused desperate and foolish hardinesse in many. 1691 Wood Ath. Oxon. II. 157 This Hicks..was also Author..of other little trivial matters meerly to get bread, and make the pot walk.

†e. Of various material things, e.g. a pen, a weapon, an instrument, a heavenly body: To move, be in motion. Of leaves: To come out. Obs.

a 1400 Stockh. Med. MS. ii. 753 in Anglia XVIII. 325 At euery knot ij lewys owt walke. a 1530 J. Heywood Wether (1903) 686 Whan the wynde doth blow the uttermost Our wyndmylles walk a mayne in every cost. 1549 Latimer Ploughers (Arb.) 25 And then bothe ploughes not walkyng, nothyng shoulde be in the common weale but honger. 1550 — Serm. Stamford (1562) 103, I hearde a penne walkynge in the chimney behynde the cloth. They hadde appoynted one there to wryte al myne aunsweres. 1565 J. Hall Crt. Vertue 150 The great Beare..Whych wyth the small Beare euermore Doth walke the pole about. 1575 Gascoigne Making of Verse § 1, I would..finde some supernaturall cause whereby my penne might walke in the superlatiue degree. 1580 Blundevil Curing Horses Dis. xi. 6 Of the Feuer which commeth of rawe digestion...The Horse will blowe at the nose..you shall see his flankes walke and his backe to beate. 1590 Spenser F. Q. I. vii. 45 From euery coast that heauen walks about, Haue thither come the noble Martiall crew. 1622 Drayton Poly-olb. xxii. 663 Now English Bowes, and Bills, and Battle-axes walke, Death vp and downe the field in gastly sort doth stalke. 1686 tr. Chardin's Trav. Persia 115 They did not like working, so that the Cudgel was forc'd to walk now and then to quick'n their Laziness. 1815 Scott Guy M. xxiv, [They] got me down, and knevelled me sair aneuch, or I could gar my whip walk about their lugs.

†f. Of a vehicle: To make regular journeys.

c 1450 Godstow Reg. 671, ij. cartis the which they had every day walking to busshyng in his wode of Shottore.

†g. Of the tongue, the jaws: To move briskly.

1550 Crowley Epigr. 908 No man shal fynde a tyme to speake, so faste theyr tonges shal walke. 1590 Spenser F. Q. II. iv. 5 And, ever as she went, her toung did walke In foule reproch and termes of vile despight. 1609 Dekker Guls Horne-bk. v. 24 It will adde much to your fame to let your tongue walke faster then your teeth. 1609 — Lanth. & Candle-light x. Wks. (Grosart) III. 277 If then..his chappes begin to walke as if he were chewing downe a Horse-loafe. 1673 Kirkman Unlucky Citizen 231 He could make but little defence with his hands: but his tongue walked, he stormed, raged and threatened.

h. Naut. Of a ship: To make progress.

1884 'H. Collingwood' Under Meteor Flag 159 Seeing us walking ahead, he hailed us to keep back in line with him. 1891 W. C. Russell Marriage at Sea iii, If..it lies in my power to keep this here Spitfire [the ship's name] awalking.

†i. fig. (a) ? To be successful. (b) To be a substitute, 'pass', 'go' for. Obs.

(a) a 1553 Udall Royster D. III. iii. (Arb.) 48, I doubt not but this geare shall on my side walke.

(b) 1557 Phaer Æneid v. (1558) O iv, One only man shall be, whome lost in depe seas he shall seke, One poll shall walke for all [L. unum pro multis dabitur caput]. 1617 W. Sclater Exp. 2 Thess. (1629) 299 That now, writtes walk for words.

†**4.** To go about in public, live, move (in a place or region). Also of animals: To range, be found (in a place). Obs.

a 1300 Cursor M. 17800 In mi cite of aramathi Þar ar þai [sc. the risen dead] walkand witerli. 13.. Propr. Sanct. (Vernon MS.) in Archiv Stud. neu. Spr. LXXXI. 302/310 Þer is a ffisch..Þat in þe see is walkynge: Euere he slumbreþ and eke slepeþ. c 1330 R. Brunne Chron. Wace (Rolls) 4734 Þys feste day..Were offred..þre þousand hyndes, Wylde walkande by wode lyndes. a 1350 S. Lucy 121 in Horstm. Altengl. Leg. (1881) 18 Whils he welk in þis werld here, He said to his appostels in-fere. — S. Thomas 2 (ibid. 19) Saint Thomas, þe apostill trew, Þat welk in werld here with Jhesu. 1456 Sir G. Haye Law Arms (S.T.S.) 244 Men suld nocht lichtly traist in na sauf conditis, and namely in the warld that walkis now. c 1470 Henry Wallace IV. 329 He sawe full feill bestis abide, Off wylde and tayme walkand habound-andlye. 1513 More Rich. III, Wks. 40/1 Robbers and riuers walking at libertie vncorrected. 1559 Bp. Scor in Strype Ann. Ref. (1709) I. App. x. 22 Upon the which Place St. Augustine wryteth thus, Christe tooke Fleshe of the blessed Virgin his Mother, and in the same he did walke. [1856 Aytoun Bothwell I. v, And yet—he bandies texts with Knox, And walks a pious man!]

†b. To be, live in a certain condition. Obs.

a 1300 Cursor M. 755 Adam ȝode walkand in þat welth þat halden was in micul elth. 1493 Will E. Bonde (Somerset Ho.), I Edward Bonde in hole mynde walking & some what syke.

†c. To busy oneself, be active about something. Obs. (Cf. Wake v. 4 b.)

a 1300 Cursor M. 7530 Dauid..toke bot a staf and a sling Þat be was wont to bere in hand Abute his flocke o scep walcand. c 1450 Mirk's Festial 84 And þi[l]ke folke þat han ben bysy erly and late to walke aboute worldely good, now schuld be bysy, alsoo, to vyset pore and seke.

d. With complementary adj. or phrase: = Go v. 6. Now rare or obs.

1604 Jas. I Counterbl. Tobacco (Arb.) 100 Why doe we not as well imitate them [the Indians] in walking naked as they doe? a 1625 Fletcher Custom Country II. (1647) 8/1 How long might I have walkt without a cloake, Before I should have met with such a fortune?

5. To travel or move about on foot. Also with advs. about, on, etc.

To walk with (a stick): to use it as a partial support in walking. To walk on crutches: to support oneself by crutches in walking.

a 1300 K. Horn 953 Ich habbe walke [other texts walked] wide Bi þe se side; Nis he nowar ifunde. a 1300 Cursor M. 17288+127 Þese thre maries come þiderward, for drede þai stynted oft For ferd of þe Jews, and sithen welk ful soft. c 1403 Lydg. Temple of Glas 550, I saugh a man, þat welke al solitarie. a 1535 Frere & Boy (Ritson) 63 An olde man came hym tyll, Walkynge by the waye. 1557 North Guevara's Diall Pr. III. xlii. (1568) 71 Thow walkest by the thornes: and wylt not that thy gown bee torne. 1697 Collier Ess. II. (1703) 99 To walk always upon crutches, is the way to lose the use of our limbs. 1835 Dickens Sk. Boz, Miss Evans & Eagle, They all walked on together, talking, and laughing. 1836 Ibid., Vauxhall-Gardens, We walked about, and met with a disappointment at every turn. 1908 'Violet Jacob' Sheep-Stealers viii, He carried a stick, but he did not use it to walk with. 1907 'C. E. Craddock' Windfall iv. 75 Why, I'll feel so old whenst I'm twenty that I reckon I'll hev ter walk with a stick by then.

†b. with refl. pron.

c 1450 Godstow Reg. 16, I wil now me walke from sege to sege, And pray to help me now euery saynt. 1509 Hawes Past. Pleas. xxvii. (1845) 119 As I went walkyng my selfe to and fro, Full sodaynly Venus wrought me such wo.

¶c. conjugated with to be. Also pa. pple. in intr. sense.

1770 C. Jenner Placid Man vi. v. II. 202 Mrs. Stapleton inquired after Lady Clayton; Miss Clayton said she was walked out. 1818 Scott Br. Lamm. xxxii, I shall never forget how frightened I was when I took him for the picture of old Sir Malise walked out of the canvass.

d. with cognate obj.; also, with advb. accusative of distance. Phrase, to walk a turn, to walk once up and once down.

c 1460 Towneley Myst. xxviii. 261 With lucas and with cleophas he welke a day Iurnee. 1548 [see f]. 1610 Shaks. Temp. IV. i. 162 A turne or two Ile walke To still my beating minde. 1653 Holcroft Procopius, Pers. Wars I. 6 They prayed the King to walk some turns with Arsaces in their presence, to be witnesses of what passed. 1753 Jane Collier Art Torment. II. iv. 177 Strange disorders in her head, for which she is advised to walk long walks. 1819 Scott Ivanhoe xxxiv, They walked a turn through the hall. 1833 Dickens Sk. Boz, Mr. Minns, I've walked all the way from Stamford-hill this morning. 1836 Ibid., Criminal Courts, They walked a few paces, and paused. 1895 J. Winsor Mississ. Basin 239 A scandalous act of Thomas Penn some years back (1737) had asserted inordinate claims by virtue of what was known as the 'Walking Purchase'. The extent of the concession was dependent on the distance a man could walk in a day and a half by an honest tramp.

Proverb. 1605 Erondelle Fr. Gard. M 6 b, After Dinner sit a while: After Supper walke a mile.

e. In express or implied contrast with ride. Also colloq. to walk it.

1668 Pepys Diary 16 Sept., Walking it to the Temple; and in my way observe that the Stockes are now pulled quite down. 1712 Steele Spectator No. 454 ¶ 6 When I resolved to walk it out of Cheapness. 1766 Goldsm. Vicar W. x, I therefore walked back by the horse-way. 1805 T. Holcroft Bryan Perdue III. 185, I was obliged to walk the journey. 1853 Dickens Bleak Ho. vi, We alighted and walked up all the hills. 1883 C. Howard Roads Eng. & Wales (ed. 3) 84 A dangerous descent, best walked down into Banwell. Ibid. 139 A long stiff ascent..which most tourists will walk up. 1915 Blackw. Mag. Apr. 466 He had ridden and I had walked before him.

f. More explicitly, To walk on foot, also (now rarely) afoot. †Also transf. of a stream: To flow slowly (obs.).

1362 Langl. P. Pl. A. vi. 1 (MS. H.) Now riden þis folk & walken on fote to seche þat seint in selcouþe londis. c 1375 Cursor M. 18548 (Fairf.) Þa iewes sagh þis ilk man..a-pon þe se wiþ-outen wete dry to walke a-pon his fete [Cott. and Gött. Gangand als apon a strete]. 1548 Udall, etc. Erasm. Par. John xii. 12–16 Where as before he was wunte to walke his iourneyes on foote. 1565 Stapleton tr. Bede's Hist. Ch. Eng. 114 The said..bishop Chadde was wonte alwaies to..doo the worke of the ghospell more walking a fote wher he went, than on horsebacke. 1621 H. King Serm. 37 But Kings haue walkt a'foote whilest the Pope hath rode. 1747 W. Horsley Fool (1748) II. 252 When it [the blood] walks a Foot, in an even, regular Pace, every Faculty coincides. 1749 Fielding Tom Jones IX. vi, How comes it..that such a great Gentleman walks about the Country afoot? a 1774 Goldsm. Hist. Greece II. 221 The King walked on foot among the infantry. 1810 S. Green Reformist II. 37 When he quitted Ellingford, he resolved always to walk on foot. 1849 Macaulay Hist. Eng. v. I. 561 The prisoner..walked on foot, bareheaded, up the whole length of that stately street which ..leads from Holyrood House to the Castle.

g. With advs. in, up, †forth, and const. into, the use of this vb. instead of the indefinite come or go sometimes implies an additional notion of absence of pausing or hesitation. So, 'in the ceremonious language of invitation' (J.), Walk in = 'come in' (now chiefly in rustic use). Similarly in the showman's 'Walk up! walk up!' when the show is on a raised platform.

In general, the tendency to substitute 'come' or 'go' for

this verb has become much more prevalent since the 16–17th c.

a 1300 Cursor M. 19737 Paulus þan welk forth her and þar, And spelled fast wit-vten spar. 1450 Paston Lett. I. 111 Than we welk forthe, and desyryd an answer of hem. 1598 Shaks. Merry W. I. i. 291, I pray you Sir walke in. 1614 J. Cooke Greene's Tu Quoque B 2, Prethee, walke in, what you bargaine for, Ile discharge. 1696 Vanbrugh Relapse IV. v, If your Lordship please to walk in, we'll help you to some Brown Sugar-Candy. 1797 Jane Austen Sense & Sensib. xxx, Mrs. Jennings..opened the door and walked in with a look of real concern. 1804 J. Tobin Honey Moon I. i. (1805) 12 Of as tried a courage As ever walk'd up to the roaring throats Of a deep-rang'd artillery. 1834 Mary Howitt Spider & Fly 1 'Will you walk into my parlour?' said the Spider to the Fly. 1836 Dickens Sk. Boz, Tuggs's at Ramsgate, 'Won't you walk in, sir?' said the servant. 1838 — Nickleby iii, The voice replied that the gentleman was to walk up. 1840 — Old C. Shop xlviii, Close here, sir, if you please to walk this way. 1847 Helps Friends in C. I. viii. 149 Men walk up composedly to the most perilous enterprises. 1867 H. Latham Black & White Pref. p. vi, Every American's house cannot be walked into, like the President's; but [etc.]. 1907 J. H. Patterson Man-Eaters of Tsavo ix. 101 Rather foolishly, I at once scrambled down from the tree and walked up towards him [the lion]. 1909 in I. G. Sieveking Francis W. Newman vi. 126 The door opened and the Professor walked in.

h. To move about or go from place to place on foot for the sake of exercise, pleasure, or pastime; to take a walk or walks. †Also with abroad.

a 1300 Cursor M. 4778 Jacob yode walcand be þe nile. 1362 Langl. P. Pl. A. ix. 54 And as I wente bi a wode walkyng myn one, Blisse of þe Briddes made me to Abyde. c 1381 Chaucer Parl. Foules 297 Forth welk I tho mi seluyn to solace. c 1400 Parce Mihi 1 in 26 Pol. Poems 143 By a forest syde, walkyng as I went, Disporte to take. 1569 Spenser Vis. Petrarch 73 On hearbs and flowres she walked pensiuely. 1573–80 Tusser Husb. (1878) 42 Saue sawe dust, and brick dust, and ashes as fine, for alley to walke in, with neighbour of thine. 1617 S. H. Engl. Mans Doctor II. (1624) 41 When you arise in the morning..remember to powre foorth your prayers vnto God..Then walke ye gently. a 1626 Bacon Med. Rem. Baconiana (1679) 161 Stir up the Pouder when you drink, and walk upon it. 1640 tr. Verdere's Rom. of Rom. II. 120 Carinda said he, being gone out to walk in the garden. 1653 W. Ramesey Astrol. Restored 192 And as touching walking abroad, some of the Ancients have been large. 1685 Caldwell Papers (Maitl. Club) I. 153 [At Spa] There is a pleasant garden of the Capuciners, where drinkers of the waters generallie walk. 1718 Lady M. W. Montagu Let. to C'tess Mar 10 Mar., She asked me to walk in her garden. 1745 Eliza Haywood Female Spect. XII. (1748) II. 309 That monarch being walking in the Mall one day, was infinitely charmed with the beauty of a young lady who happened to be there. 1830 Portugal; or Y'ng. Travellers 239 As he spoke, Mr. Grey rose from table and invited them to walk. 1867 Augusta Wilson Vashti xxi, 'Stay, Salome! Where are you going?' 'To walk.'

†i. transf. To take air and exercise (on horseback). Obs.

1541 Wyatt Def. in H. Walpole Misc. Antiq. II. (1772) 49 There be maynie men in the towne and most of them gentlemen, wch walke upon there horses, and here and there tawlke with those ladies.

j. To walk (out) with, to walk together: in rustic use said of a young man and young woman 'keeping company' with a view to marriage.

1876 Miss Yonge Womankind xxiii. 195 There is a semi-engaged state of 'walking' with a man on trial. 1886 Hardy Mayor Casterbr. xx, She..no longer said of young men and women that they 'walked together' but that they were 'engaged'. 1896 Housman Shropsh. Lad xxv, Rose Harland on her Sundays out Walked with the better man. Ibid., When Rose and I walk out together. 1908 W. W. Jacobs Lady of Barge (1908) 5 A certain young woman I'm walking out with. 1905 Jerome Idle Ideas xx, 'You are not engaged, I 'ope?' 'Walking out, ma'am, do you mean?' says Emma. 1906 Times 26 Nov. 3/6 Her sister knew him in the way of business, but had never walked out with him.

†k. Followed by a (= on) and vbl. sb.: = Go v. 32 e. Obs.

1533 More Answ. Poysoned Bk. Wks. 1076/2 Like as if a ryght great man woulde wantonly walke a mumming, and disguise hymself.

l. In various phrases. †To walk at rovers: to have no settled abode (cf. Rover[1] 2). To walk Spanish: see Spanish C. To walk upon air: to be in an exultant state of mind. †To walk will of one's way (Sc.): to go astray, lose oneself.

c 1475 Rauf Coilȝear 73 Or ony vther gude fallow that I heir fand Walkand will of his way. Ibid. 106 In wickit wedderis and weit walkand full will. 1528 More Dial. Heresyes III. Wks. 228/1 The order is rebuked by priestes begging and lewde liuing, which either is fayne to walke at rouers and liue upon trentalles or worse or els [etc.]. 1887 Stevenson Mem. & Portr. iv. 72, I went home that morning walking upon air.

m. Racing. Of a jockey: To weigh (so much) when going on foot.

1856 'Druid' Post & Paddock v. 83 He was about 5 ft. 5 in. in height, walked about 9 st. 5 lbs. in the winter months, and could ride, if required for a great race, 7 st. 12 lbs. to the last.

n. quasi-trans. with complementary adj., adv., or phrase. To walk off, to get rid of (the effects of liquor, an ailment) by walking exercise. Also in nonce-uses: To walk down, to counteract (poison) by walking; to exhaust (a companion) by walking; to walk out a sermon, to continue walking till it has ended.

1669 Pepys Diary 2 May, Thence with them to White Hall, and there walked out the sermon with one or other. 1823 Scott Quentin D. iii, I have walked my clothes dry, or nearly so. 1860 Sala Baddington Peerage I. vii. 131 Perhaps he wished to walk off the fumes of the punch and tobacco. 1872 Black Adv. Phaeton xix, He would have liked..to have..walked himself dead with fatigue. 1884 Harper's Mag. Jan. 302/2 A walker who gives promise of great things if he doesn't walk his short legs off within the next two or three years. 1884 Tennyson Cup II. 260, I pray you lift me And make me walk awhile. I have heard these poisons May be walk'd down. 1894 Frances P. Cobbe Life I. 341, I do believe I could walk down anybody and perhaps talk down anybody too!

o. Naut. To turn (the capstan) by walking round it; to haul by walking round the capstan or by walking away with a rope.

1836 Marryat Pirate viii, The men..walked the anchor up to the bows. 1882 Nares Seamanship (ed. 6) 118 Walk the yard up to the derrick head with the hawser. Ibid. 203 Walk the anchor up the bow. Ibid. 172 Walk back the capstan.

6. fig. a. Chiefly in religious use, after Bible examples: To conduct oneself, behave (ill or well, wisely or unwisely). Sometimes with reference to a metaphorical 'path' or 'way'. To walk with God (Gen. v. 22), interpreted to mean 'to lead a godly life' (so rendered by Coverdale, after Luther; later versions retain the Heb. phrase), or to have intimate communion with God.

Cf. Heb. hālak, Gr. περιπατεῖν, Vulg. ambulare.

1526 Pilgr. Perf. (W. de W. 1531) 213 O man (sayth scripture) walke in ye wayes of thy herte as moche as thou wylte, but [etc.]. 1526 Tindale 2 Thess. iii. 6 We requyre you..that ye withdrawe youre selves from every brother that walketh inordinatly [Vulg. ambulante inordinate]. 1550 Crowley Last Trump. 516 And then, lyke a good Christian, Thou doste walke forth in thy callynge. 1581 J. Hamilton Cath. Traict. Epist. 8 b, To..trauell to reduce yame to ye treu vay quhairin all yair forbearis valkit yir mony hundreth zeris bygane. a 1593 Marlowe Ovid's Elegies III. xiii. [xiv.] 13 Be more aduisde, walke as a puritan, And I shall thinke you chaste, do what you can. a 1629 Hinde J. Bruen xliv. (1641) 140 It was the desire and delight of his soule to walke with God. 1669 Sturmy Mariner's Mag., Penalties & Forfeit. C 2 If all..had but the knowledge of what they should know, they might prevent this loss and damage, and walk safely. 1681 Flavel Meth. Grace xxx. 323 When a man walks suitably to his place and calling in the world, we say he acts like himself. 1853 Maurice Proph. & Kings vi. 93 If he walked in God's ways he would establish a sure house. 1872 Morley Voltaire (1886) 11 Those do best who walk most warily.

b. To direct one's conduct by, after a rule, etc.

1581 Lambarde Eiren. II. ii. (1588) 113 Many other wayes there bee, after which the Iustice of Peace may walke in taking of this kind of Recognusance. 1706 E. Ward Wooden World Diss. (1708) 39 He is the great Exempler they walk by. 1711 Addison Spect. No. 25 ¶ 4 Give me more certain Rules to walk by than those I have already observed. 1821 Scott Kenilw. xxv, I give thee way, good imp, and will walk by thy counsel. 1884 W. C. Smith Kildrostan 46 We judge a stranger by our home-bred ways, Who, may be, walks by other rule of right.

†c. To be associated, act harmoniously with. Also to walk together. Obs.

1620 J. Taylor (Water P.) Jack a Lent Ep. A 3 b, And though it be written in a mery stile, yet I dare presume that mirth and truth walke together in it. 1650 H. Ellis Pseudochristus 7 After this, he walked sometime in fellowship with that Congregation. 1657 Docum. S. Paul's (Camden) 155 The congregation yt wallke wth Mr John Symson. a 1709 J. Lister Autobiog. (1842) 50 My wife and myself, were admitted into the church at Kipping, with which we walked satisfyingly many years. Ibid. 51 Some of his hearers left him [the pastor], and others walked with him till new matters of dissatisfaction broke out. Ibid., After he was gone, the church at Kipping was again united, and walked sweetly together, but could not get a pastor.

†d. To walk wide in words: to argue at cross purposes. Obs.

1529 More Dyaloge I. xviii. 23 Wythout whych we were lyke to walke wyde in wordys.

†e. To proceed, 'go' upon (grounds). Obs.

1828 Life Planter Jamaica 252 What grounds of probability have we to walk upon that the present negroes..would act otherwise.

7. To go on foot at a walk: see Walk sb.[1] 5.

a. Of human beings or other bipeds: To progress by alternate movements of the legs, so that one of the feet is always on the ground: contrasted with run, hop, etc. To walk through (a dance) = 7 e; similarly of an actor, to walk through his part (cf. quot. 1824).

1762 Foote Orator I. Wks. 1799 I. 193 Soft and fair; we must walk before we can run. 1815 Stephens in Shaw's Gen. Zool. IX. I. 65 The progressive motion of this bird is not by walking but hopping. 1824 Scott Redgauntlet ch. xix, That caprice which so often tempts painters and musicians and great actors, in the phrase of the latter, to walk through their part, instead of exerting themselves with the energy which acquired their fame. 1859 Habits of Gd. Society v. 206 'Steps,' as the chasser of the quadrille is called, belong to a past age, and even ladies are now content to walk through a quadrille. 1862 Whyte Melville Mkt. Harb. v, It must have been a fine run; but slow...It's labour and sorrow, walking after hounds, to my mind. 1868 J. Burroughs Wake-robin viii. (1884) 295 Among the land-birds, the grouse, pigeon, quails, larks, and various blackbirds, walk. 1894 Daily News 10 Aug. 5/3 A bluejacket never walks, when an order is given, but does everything at the double.

b. Of a horse, dog, or other quadruped: To advance by a gait in which there are always two feet on the ground, and during a part of the step three or (in slow walking) four feet: opposed to amble, trot, gallop, etc. Also said of a rider.

1681 Lond. Gaz. No. 1639/4 Lost..., a bright Bay Gelding, 14 hands high,..Walks, Trots, and Gallops, something dull in going, but will leap very well. 1818 Scott Br. Lamm. xxiii, Ravenswood walked on with equal deliberation until he reached the head of the avenue...When he had passed the upper gate, he turned his horse. 1863 W. C. Baldwin Afr. Hunting vii. 252 It was only the dogs walking among the dead leaves.

c. To walk over (the course): of a horse, literally, to go over the course at a walking pace, so as to be accounted the winner of a race in which there is no opposition; transf. and fig. to win a race or other contest with little or no effort. To walk away from, to outdistance easily in a race (in quot. fig.). Also (U.S. colloq.) to walk round (an opponent): to beat easily.

1779 Warner in Jesse Selwyn & Contemp. (1844) IV. 245 A little on this side the park is Sir John Thorold's, who, you see by the papers, is walking over the course for the county. 1823 'Jon Bee' Dict. Turf s.v., 'To walk over' another, is ..to set him at naught, as a racer which is so vastly superior to other cattle that none dare start, and he walks over the course. 1832 P. Egan's Bk. Sports 117/2 At Knutsford..he won the Gold Cup..; and walked over for the Pengwern Stakes at Holywell. 1862 Cornh. Mag. V. 26, I was promptly assured that..I should be elected without opposition..; in short I should walk over the course. 1883 Miss Broughton Belinda IV. iii, 'Beaten by a banjo!' says she tragically; 'if it had not been for the banjo I should have walked away from her.' 1890 Rules of Racing § 142 in Encycl. Sport (1898) II. 227 When one horse pays forfeit for a match the other need not walk over. 1901 Westm. Gaz. 29 June 9/3 To use a colloquial expression, they 'walked round' Gamble and Davies.

¶d. transf. Of a vehicle, a ship, a stream: To go very slowly. nonce-uses.

1827 Pollok Course T. I. 346 Round his sacred hill, a streamlet walked, Warbling the holy melodies of heaven. 1852 Mundy Antipodes (1857) 200 Our steamer ran, or rather walked—for she could make no running—plump upon a rock off Bradley's Head. 1865 Emerson Let. in Harper's Mag. (1884) Feb. 464/1 The train walked all the way.

e. trans. To go through (a dance, esp. a minuet) at a walk.

1810 [see Minuet 1]. 1827 Lytton Pelham xl, They just walk a quadrille or spin a waltz,..hang dancing, 'tis so vulgar. 1859 Habits of Gd. Society v. 207, I do not attempt to deny that the quadrille, as now walked, is ridiculous. 1863 Cowden Clarke Shaks. Char. xiv. 362 He walked his minuet in life, and he danced out of it with a caper.

8. To go away. a. simply or †with away, forth. Formerly often in imperative = 'begone', with a vocative of some term of opprobrium (sometimes retained in indirect narration). Now only colloq., to go away perforce, be turned out; also slang, to die.

c 1460 Towneley Myst. ii. 106 Leif brother, let vs be walkand. 1526 Pilgr. Perf. (W. de W. 1531) 140 b, Yf than the porter wold come forth sodeynly & all to beet vs, & bydde vs walke forth vnthryftes with sorowe. a 1529 Skelton Agst. Garnesche iv. 60 Sche praiid yow walke, on Goddes halfe! 1529 More Dyaloge I. xiv. 18 b, He bad hym walk faytoure. And made hym be sett openly in ye stokkys. 1530 Palsgr. 770/2 Walke, pyke you hence: tire avant. 1530 Tindale Pract. Prelates G v b, The Cardinall bad him walcke a vilayne. 1546 J. Heywood Prov. II. ii. (1867) 52 Walke drab walke. Nay (quoth she) walke knaue walke. 1605 Chapman All Fooles I. B 4 b, I like his learning well, make him your heire, And let your other walke. 1607 Middleton Mich. Term II. iii. 169 It stands upon the loss of my credit to-night, if I walk without money. 1712 Swift Jrnl. to Stella 26 Dec., Lord Bolingbroke told me I must walk away to-day after dinner, because lord treasurer and he and another were to enter upon business. 1858 Trollope Dr. Thorne iv, If the governor were to walk, I think Porlock would content himself with the thirty thousand a-year. 1902 S. E. White Blazed Trail xxviii, If I want to discharge a man, he walks without any question.

†b. transf. Of animals: To be stolen. Of a thing: To be got rid of; to be carried off. To let (something) walk: to dismiss from attention. Obs.

c 1440 Capgrave Life St. Kath. 672 Lete argumentys walk, þei ar not to our be-houe. 1573–80 Tusser Husb. (1878) 141 There horse being tide on a balke, is readie with theefe for to walke. 1596 Spenser State Irel. Wks. (Globe) 619/2 When he comes foorth, he will make theyr cowes and garrans to walke, yf he doe noe other mischeif to theyr persons. 1611 Chapman May-Day I. ii, Nay, they [sc. houses] shall walke, thats certaine, Ile turne 'em into money.

c. With off: To depart suddenly or abruptly. To walk off with: to carry away as a prize or plunder.

1604 Marston Malcontent III. v. E 4 b, I am heauie, walke of, I shall talke in my sleepe, walke of. Exeunt Pages. 1705 Vanbrugh Mistake IV. i, Jacin. Have a care he don't rally, and beat you yet tho'; pray walk off. 1836 Hawker Diary (1893) II. 107 A green sub...had walked off with my portmanteau. 1840 Thackeray Barber Cox Apr., I gave Master Baron that day a precious good beating, and walked off with no less than fifteen shillings of his money. 1848 Dickens Dombey ii, Mr. Chick..said no more, and walked off. c 1850 Arab. Nts. (Rtldg.) 147 Why dost thou not depart with the Fire? Walk off. 1888 'J. S. Winter' Bootle's Childr. ix, And then she gave another sniff and walked off to the drawing-room again. 1889 Conan Doyle Sign of Four ix, Wait a bit, my friend,.. You have important information, and you must not walk off. We shall keep you, whether you like or not, until our friend returns.

9. Of a ghost, spectre, fiend: To be seen walking, to appear. Of a dead person: To 'come back' as a ghost. Also †to walk out.

For the ghost walks (Theat. Slang), see Ghost sb. 8 b.

a 1300 Cursor M. 22611 Quen sal scine [= chine] þe heuenes open, þaa warlaus all sal walk þan vte. c 1440 Gesta Rom. 408 (Add. MS.) All the chambres were take vp, safe oon, in the which was a sperite walkyng. a 1513 Fabyan's Chron. clxxix. (1533) 105 He also for that the munkes of wynchester sayd that his father Alurede walkyd, caused hym to be remoued vnto the new abbay. 1542 Udall Erasm. Apoph. 111 b, Sore subiecte to the terrours of buggues, and spyrytes, or goblyns, that walken by night and in places solitarie. 1573 L. Lloyd Pilgr. Princes 101 We reade in Lucan how that the soules of Silla and Marius..were alwayes walking and appearing vnto men before they were purged by sacrifice. 1602 Shaks. Ham. I. v. 10, I am thy Father's Spirit Doom'd for a certaine terme to walke the night. 1611 Tourneur Ath. Trag. IV. iii, There's a talke, thou know'st, that the Ghoast of olde Montferers walks. a 1625 Fletcher Hum. Lieut. III. v, I make your Grace my Executor, and I beseech ye See my poor Will fulfill'd: sure I shall walk else. 1727 De Foe Hist. Appar. x. 201 Such a courage..would..lay all the devils that ever walked. 1801 Scott Glenfinlas xlvi, Alone, I dare not venture there, Where walks, they say, the shrieking ghost. 1882 A. Jessopp in 19th Cent. Nov. 737 Everybody knows that it's an awful thing for a dead man to walk. 1888 Stevenson Black Arrow Prol. 12 Would ye rob the man before his body? Nay, he would walk!

10. 'To act in sleep' (J.); to walk about or perform other actions as a somnambulist. rare exc. in the full phrase to walk in one's sleep.

1605 Shaks. Macb. v. i. 3 When was it shee [Lady Macbeth] last walk'd? Ibid. 66 Yet I haue knowne those which haue walkt in their sleep, who haue dyed holily in their beds. 1607 Dekker & Webster Northw. Hoe III. E 1 b, My mistris makes her husband beleeue that shee walkes in her sleepe. 1728 Chambers' Cycl., Somnambuli, an Appellation given to People, who walk in their Sleep. 1848 Dickens Dombey xxxix, Some uneasy ideas that he must be walking in his sleep, or that he had been troubled with phantoms,..beset the Captain at first.

11. To go on foot in procession; also, to go in a regular circuit or to and fro over a prescribed track in the course of official duty. Also with cognate accus., as in to walk one's round(s, the round, a round, said esp. of a sentinel.

1594–1600 Min. Archdeaconry Colchester (MS.) 99 b, 19 Apr. 1596. Our perambulacion was not walked through the defalte of our vicar. 1596 Spenser State Irel. Wks. (Globe) 673/1 The sheriff of the shire, whose peculiar office it is to walke continuallye up and downe his baly-wick,..to snatch up all those runnagates [etc.]. Ibid., The sherriff may doe therin what he can, and yet the marshall may walke his course besides. 1639 Du Verger tr. Camus' Admir. Events 102 Octavian coms accompanyed with his friend Leobell to walke his accustomed round. a 1700 Evelyn Diary 12 Sept. 1641, I was permitted to walk the round and view the workes. 1831 Scott Ct. Robt. xviii, If the lovers have agreed, Agelastes, it is probable, walks his round, to prevent intrusion. 1863 Geo. Eliot Romola xxii, He..was to walk in procession as Latin secretary.

transf. and fig. 1629 Massinger Picture II. i, Dreames and phantasticke visions walke the round About my widdowed bed. 1834 H. Miller Scenes & Leg. xxiv. (1857) 351 He continued to walk the round of his duties.

†b. Oxford University. (a) Of a proctor or pro-proctor: To perambulate the streets at night, in the exercise of his function. (b) Of the proctors: To march to and fro in the Convocation House, as part of the ceremony of conferring degrees.

1530 in W. H. Turner Select. Rec. Oxford (1880) 77 It was proved that the ij Proctors servaunts walkyd wt other persons as plesyd them, and theyr maisters walkyd not nor noe other for them. 1677 Wood Life (O.H.S.) II. 384, I [a Proproctor] walk by the authoritie of the vice-chancellour. Ibid. 391 Dr. Nicholas..verie active in walking and hauling taverns. 1906 J. Wells Oxf. Degree Cerem. 8 Within living memory it was necessary for each 'grace' to be taken separately, and the Proctors 'walked' for each candidate. Ibid. 9 It is currently believed that the Proctors walk in order to give any Oxford tradesman the opportunity of 'plucking' their gown and protesting against the degree of a defaulting candidate.

12. Walk into—. (Colloquial or slang.) a. In phrase to walk into (a person's) affections, to win the love of (a person) at once and without effort. Sometimes used jocularly for b or c.

1858 in K. Young Delhi 1857, App. 328 Major Erskine was fearful that the jolly 52th would have walked into the affections of the Madrassees, and then all would have gone a regular smash.

b. To make a vigorous attack upon.

1794 Ld. Hood 14 July in Nicolas Disp. & Lett. Nelson (1845) I. 438 note, From your rapid firing last night I flattered myself it was intended to walk into the Mozelle as this night. 1852 C. B. Mansfield Paraguay etc. (1856) 20 Some small spermaceti whales, which came in for a lark (luckily for them, after the American and French vessels had left, who would assuredly have walked into them). 1853 'C. Bede' Verdant Green I. xi, His claret had been repeatedly tapped, his bread-basket walked into, his day-lights darkened.

transf. 1840 Cockton Val. Vox xiii, The carver walked into the pie and bounteously helped each man, woman, and child, to a share. 1846 De Quincey Syst. Heavens (1862) III. 185 A call was heard for Lord Rosse! and immediately his telescope walked into Orion; destroyed the supposed matter of stars; but, in return, created immeasurable worlds.

c. To assail with invective or reproof.

1859 Lang Wand. India 399 His Excellency 'walked into' the President, and recommended him to study some catechism of the Law of Courts Martial. 1861 Hughes Tom Brown at Oxf. ix, He walks into us all as if it were our faults.

d. To eat or drink heartily of, to 'make a hole in'.

1837 Dickens Pickw. xxii, I wish you could ha' seen the shepherd walkin' into the ham and muffins. 1849 Alb. Smith Pottleton Legacy xxvi. 280 Look at that little fellow—how he is walking into the raised pie, and how ill he will

be to-morrow! 1850 Smedley F. Fairlegh xiv, I must walk into old Coleman's champagne before I make a fresh start. 1871 M. Collins Marq. & Merch. III. iii. 78 He..with most voracious swallow Walks into my mutton chops.

e. To make large inroads on (one's stock of money).

1859 H. Kingsley G. Hamlyn xv, 'And you've got her money?' 'Yes,' he said; 'but I've been walking into it.'

III. trans. To perambulate, traverse: = walk over, upon, etc.

†**13.** To travel over (a country, etc.). Cf. 2. Obs.

a 1400–50 Wars Alex. 519 Sire, þer sall borne be a barne of þi blithe lady, þat dristyn efter þi day has destaned to regne, þe quilke sall walke all þe werd & wyn it him selfe.

14. Of fame, etc.: To pervade (a country). Cf. 3 b. Obs. exc. as transferred use of 17.

c 1350 St. John 43 in Horstm. Altengl. Leg. (1881) 35 Þe word of him welk al þe land. 1806 Wordsw. Char. Happy Warrior 77 Whether praise of him must walk the earth For ever, and to noble deeds give birth, Or he must fall, to sleep without his fame.

15. To go over or traverse on foot.

a 1300 Cursor M. 3155 He welk þat fell ner dais thre To sek þe sted quar he wald be. 1576 Gascoigne Kenelworth Castle Wks. 1910 II. 108 Beware (I say) least whiles we walke these woods,..Some harmfull hart entrap your harmlesse moodes. 1748 Johnson Van. Hum. Wishes 38 The needy traveller..Walks the wild heath. 1763 P. Collinson in Darlington Memorials (1849) 257 They [Indians] were notoriously..cheated out of their land in your province [Penn.], by a man's walking a tract of ground in one day, that was to be purchased of them. 1871 Simpson Recit. 9 Hundreds of diggers daily then were walking Melbourne town with their pockets filled with gold. 1868 Browning Ring & Bk. x. 360 When man walks the garden of this world For his own solace.

b. in contrast with ride.

1864 Good Words 516/2 Devonshire, to be properly seen, should be walked.

c. Of a stallion: To travel over (a tract of country) serving mares.

1898 Daily News 9 Mar. 4/4 The judging yesterday began with stallions that are to walk the Eastern and Midland counties.

16. To walk on or along (a road). To walk the street(s: see Street sb. 2 f.

1530 Palsgr. 770/2 In dede you walke the stretes. 1577 Grange Golden Aphrod. etc. P j, They onely walke the streates, to see and to be seene. 1590 Spenser F. Q. I. x. 10 All..take delight With many rather for to go astray.. Than with a few to walke the narrow way.

b. in contrast with ride.

1883 C. Howard Roads Eng. & Wales (ed. 3) 3 The very steep ascent of Chatham Hill, which most riders will walk. Ibid. 134 A very bad hill leading down into Rickmansworth, which is best walked.

17. To walk about upon (a surface, the ground, the sea, etc.). So Naut., of an officer, to walk the deck, the quarter-deck.

To walk the plank: see Plank sb. 6.

1634 Milton Lycidas 173 Through the dear might of him, that walk'd the waves. 1667 — P. L. v. 200 Yee that in Waters glide, and yee that walk The Earth, and stately tread, or lowly creep. Ibid. vii. 503 Aire, Water, Earth, By Fowl, Fish, Beast, was flown, was swum, was walkt. 1706 E. Ward Wooden World Diss. (1708) 7 It must be a great Change of Weather indeed, when he deigns to walk the Quarter-Deck. 1814 Scott Lord of Isles IV. xvi, Edward, who walk'd the deck apart. 1840 Marryat Poor Jack vi, He was..walking the deck. 1849 Aytoun Poems, Heart of Bruce v, The good Lord Douglas walk'd the deck. 1872 M. Collins Two Plunges for Pearl III. 71 He walked the moorland as if it were his native earth. 1885 R. L. & F. Stevenson Dynamiter xiii. 197 He continued to walk the pavements.

transf. 1813 Byron Corsair I. iii, She [the ship] walks the waters like a thing of life. a 1861 T. Winthrop Life in Open Air (1863) 3 At five P.M. we found ourselves..on board the Isaac Newton, a great, ugly, three-tiered box that walks the North River.

18. To walk along (a line); to perambulate (a boundary). Cf. 11.

To walk the chalk (slang): to walk along a chalked line (as a proof of being sober). To walk one's chalks (slang): see Chalk sb. 6 b.

1602–5 Min. Archdeaconry Colchester (MS.) 104, 1604. They did not walke the bounds of ther parishe. 1823 'Jon Bee' Dict. Turf s.v., 'To walk the chalk'—a military manœuvre to discover which is drunkest. 1842 Punch II. 20 Ere death her charms should fix, Gladly I'd walk my chalks or cut my sticks. 1876 Farrar Marlb. Serm. xxiii. 226 You cannot walk the dim borderland between vice and virtue without knowing it.

†**19.** To attend, frequent (the exchange, a market). Obs.

1634 Peacham Compl. Gentl. i. (1906) 15 In Venice likewise, every Mechanique is a Magnifico, though his magnificence walketh the Market but with a Chequin. 1649 W. Bullock Virginia 43 Let him then enquire of the principallest straights and Spanish Merchants, walking the Exchange. 1750 Johnson Rambler No. 182 ¶ 6 To walk the exchange with a face of importance.

b. To walk the hospitals or a hospital: to receive regular clinical instruction and assist in surgical work.

1781 G. White Let. to S. Barker 26 Nov., I have not yet heard—whether he will walk the hospitals in town. 1807 Picture of Lond. (ed. 8) 235 The combined method of walking the hospitals and attending lectures. 1823 Ibid. (ed. 22) 211 A number of young men, who walk the hospital, as it is termed. 1887 Ruskin Præterita II. 333 He became..a ..medical student, came up to London to walk the hospitals.

20. Shooting. To start (game-birds) by beating up the ground with pointers or setters. Usually to walk up.

1873 G. S. Baden-Powell New Homes 255 A good dog for putting them [sc. quail] up would be very valuable, but [etc.]...Walking up quail, even with the help of a chain, is equally unsatisfactory. 1900 G. C. Brodrick Mem. & Impressions 8 Year in and year out they lived at home,..walking up their own game with the aid of pointers. 1913 Times 12 Sept. 12/6 Now voices are raised in favour of a return.. to the use of pointers and setters, in conjunction with the system of walking-up the birds. Ibid., Walked or driven, moreover, the partridge gives more enjoyment to many keen shots than all the pheasants in a beat.

IV. Causative uses.

21. To lead, drive, or ride (a horse) at a walk; to exercise (a horse, a dog) by causing it to walk. Also with out.

1470–85 Malory Arthur v. ix. 176 A man armed walkynge his hors easyly by a wodes syde. 1562 Child-Marriages (1897) 82 This deponent scarslie rested walkinge the horses at the doore, half or quarter of an howre, when one callid hym in to his Mistris. 1601 W. Percy Cuckqueanes & Cuckolds Errants IV. ii. (Roxb.) 48 Sirrha Rooke, take my Nagge, and see you walk him faire and soft to Colchester. 1615 G. Markham Country Contentm. I. vii. 103 Touching ayring or walking of grey-hounds,..it must dewlie be done euerie morning before sunne-rise, [etc.]. 1681 T. Flatman Heraclitus Ridens No. 32 (1713) I. 206 Let's walk them a little; for they have run Heats, and must be rubb'd down well. 1833 T. Hook Parson's Dau. I. vii, As he walked his cob [be was riding] back from the fields. 1835 H. Harewood Dict. Sports s.v. Training, Taking care that he [the horse] is walked for some time afterward, that he may become rather cool before he returns to the stable. 1866 Kingsley Herew. xvii, You may walk your bloodhound over his grave to-morrow without finding him. 1872 Black Adv. Phaeton vi, We had walked the horses nearly to the end of the pleasant stretch of beechwood. 1902 A. E. T. Watson Hunting in Encycl. Brit. XXIX. 365/2 The kennel huntsman is generally called the 'feeder'. It is his business to look after the pack which is not hunting, to walk them out, to prepare the food for the hunting pack.

transf. 1583 Melbancke Philotimus S j, If you be chafed you shal be walked, if you be hot you may be cooled.

22. To cause or induce (a person) to walk; to conduct on a walk. Also with advs., off, out, etc. †Walk your body (Sc.) = take yourself off, begone (obs.).

1630 J. Taylor (Water P.) Gt. Eater of Kent Wks. I. 144 Now Gentlemen, as I haue walked you amongst the Trees, and thorow the Wood, I pray set downe, and take a taste or two more of this Banquet. 1667 Pepys Diary 14 July, Then I carried them to see my cozen Pepys's house..; and then I walked them to the wood hard by. 1717 Berkeley in Fraser Life (1871) 547 He walked us round the town. c 1730 Ramsay To Æolus 11 Pray wauk your body, if you please, Gae gowl and tooly on the seas. 1818 T. Jefferson Writ. (1830) IV. 448 He walked me backwards and forwards before the President's door for half an hour. 1848 Thackeray Van. Fair lvii, She slaved, toiled..for old Sedley, walked him out sedulously into Kensington Gardens. 1883 Miss Yonge Armourer's Prent. ii, Stephen and Ambrose found themselves walked out of the cloister of St. Grimbald, and the gates shut behind them. 1912 J. S. Fletcher in Throne 7 Aug. 224/2 He soon drew me out of the office to walk me off in the direction of Gray's Inn Road.

b. To force to walk (by holding the arms or pushing before one). Also, to help to walk.

To walk (a person) Spanish: see Spanish C.

1809 R. K. Porter Russ. & Swed. (1813) II. 21 The poor wretch, attended by the police, had been walked through the streets; in order to shew him to the populace. 1848 Dickens Dombey xii, Mr. Feeder himself held a glass of water to his [the boy's] lips, and the butler walked him up and down several times between his own chair and the sideboard. 1853 — Bleak Ho. xxii, Thirdly, Mr. Bucket has to take Jo by the arm a little above the elbow, and walk him on before him. 1918 F. Hackett Ireland viii. 230 Good bewildered people who never knew they were deemed blameworthy until they were walked out to the guillotine.

23. a. To take charge of (a puppy) 'at walk' (see Walk sb. 13). b. To keep (a game-cock) in a 'walk'.

a. 1845 Youatt Dog iii. 75 Whelps walked, or taken care of, at butchers' houses..are apt to be heavy-shouldered and throaty. 1887 Field 19 Feb. 229/1 The practice of walking puppies is not quite so prevalent as it used to be. 1907 Times 3 Oct. 4/4 Defendant said he had walked puppies for the Southwold Hunt for 25 years.

b. 1854 Poultry Chron. I. 474 Formerly when cock-fighting was more practised, every farm-yard walked a game cock or two. 1889 Archæol. Æliana N.S. XIII. 314 'Walking a cock' was the feeding and tending of a game cock.

24. With a thing as obj.

†a. To send round (drink). Cf. 3 d. Obs.

1581 A. Hall Iliad I. 14 A seemely sight it was to see the seamen plye their teeth, Wherewith the Cups apace they walke.

b. Cribbage. (See quots.)

1803 Sporting Mag. XXI. 326 Walking the pegs—at cribbage, means either your adversary putting his own pegs forward, or those of your's back. 1865 Hotten's Slang Dict., 'Walking the pegs,' a method of cheating at the game of cribbage by a species of legerdemain, the sharper either moving his own pegs forward, or those of his antagonist backward, according to the state of the game.

c. Bell-ringing. (See quot.)

1671 [Stedman] Tintinalogia 53 All changes are to be Rang either by walking them (as the term is) or else Whole-pulls, or Half-pulls. By walking them, is meant, that the bells go round, four, six, eight times or more, in one change, which is commonly used by young Practisers.

V. 25. The verb-stem in combination: walk-around (a) Colonial, a kind of rotary mill turned by

Walk (wǫk), v.² Pa. t. and pa. pple. **walked**. Now only *dial.* and *Hist.* Also 6 woke, 7 wak, waok, 8 wawk, 9 waolk (*dial.* wauk, waok, wake- *or* wawk (*dial. Dict.*). Orig. identical with WALK v.¹ ...

Walk, obsc. Sc. form of WAKE.

Walkable (wǫ·kǎb'l), a. [f. WALK v.¹ + -ABLE.]
a. Of a road, country, etc.: Suitable or fit for walking on. b. Of a distance: That may be walked.

Walker (wǫ·kǎɹ), sb.¹
1. With the construction of the verb in various senses. ...

Walker (wǫ·kǎɹ), sb.²
2. a. 4–5 walkar, 5–6 walkare, 6 Sc. wakar; -er, wa(u)lker. [OE. wealcere (once, gl. fullo) = (M)LG., (M)Du. walker, OHG. walchari (MHG., mod.G. walker), agent-n. f. OTeut. *walkan WALK v.² ...

Walker (wǫ·kǎɹ), int. More fully Hookey Walker, Walker! ...

Walker (wǫ·kǎɹ)¹, the proper name Walker (see below) + -ITE.] A member of an extreme Calvinistic sect founded in Ireland by John Walker (1768–1833). Also *attrib.*

Walkerite² (wǫ·kǎɹǒit). Min. [Named by Heddle 1880, after Prof. John Walker (1731–1803) who discovered it + -ITE².] = TICROLITE.

Walking (wǫ·kiŋ), vbl. sb.¹ [-ING¹.]
1. The action or an act of the vb. WALK v.¹

Walking (wǫ·kiŋ), ppl. a. [f. WALK v.¹ + -ING¹.]
1. Moving about from place to place, travelling, itinerant. Now only with implication of sense 2. ...

Walking-fish (wǫ·kiŋ·fiʃ). [WALKING ppl. a.]
1. A name given to various fishes (see quots.).
2. = SILVER-FISH 2 (Cent. Dict. 1891).

Walking-leaf (WALKING vbl. sb.)
1. † a. Some unidentified plant. b. An American evergreen fern, Camptosorus rhizophyllus. ...

Walking-staff (WALKING vbl. sb.)
1. A staff or long stick which one carries in the hand for support or aid in walking, etc.

Walking-stick. A stick or short staff carried in the hand when walking.

Walking-wheel (WALKING vbl. sb.² and ppl. a.) = PEDOMETER.

Walk-mill sb. Cf. G. walkmühle. A fulling-mill.

Walk-mill, v. [WALK v.² or sb.] A mechanical contrivance or machine, the driving power of which is furnished by the walking of a horse, etc.

Walk-over, sb. [WALK v.¹ and sb.; cf. WALK over, WELKIN.]

Walkrife, a. Obs. rare⁻¹. [f. WALK v.² + -RIFE.]

† Walkster, Sc. Obs. rare⁻¹. [f. WALK v.² + -STER.] A walker or fuller.

Walkyne, obs. form of WELKIN.

Walkyrie (wǫlki·ri), repr. OE. wælcyrie. A member of a class of goddesses or female demons supposed to hover in or ride through the air over battle-fields and decide who should be slain: corresponding to the Scandinavian VALKYRIE.

Wall (wǫl), sb.¹ Forms: 1 weall, weal, wall, 2–7 wal, walle, 3–7 Sc. wall, 6 Sc. wa'3, 5 whalle, 6 wrawle, wrawle, 8–9 wa, wa'. [OE. weall (WS. weall), corresp. to OFris. wall, MLG., (M)Du. wal, MHG., mod.HLG. (mod.G.) wall, f. L. vallum; also as Anglo-Frisian adoption of L. vallum. ...

Wall (wǫl), sb.²

Wall (wǫl), v.¹

here,..but since you will needs Haue the wall, Ile take the paynes to thrust You into the kennell. 1855 Kingsley Westw. Ho! xxv, The Spaniards..had..no room, in that narrow path, to use their pikes. The English had the wall of them; and to have the wall there, was to have the foe's life at their mercy.

1587 Greene Penelopes Web Wks. (Grosart) V. 201 The wife of a poore Smith meeting the Empresse Faustina, tooke the wall of her in the streetes. 1617 Moryson Itin. III. 28 Nothing was more common with them then to fight about taking the right or left hand, or the wall. 1757 Foote Author I. Wks. 1799 I. 135 He wou'd take the wall of a Prince of the Blood. 1821 Scott Kenilw. iv, To..quarrel in her cause with any flat-capp'd thread-maker that would take the wall of her. 1840 Dickens Old C. Shop xxxiii, The parlour window..is so close upon the foot-way that the passenger who takes the wall brushes the dim glass with his coat sleeve.

b. *fig.* (In early use sometimes without article, *to give, take wall.*)

1591 Nashe Wonderf. Prognost. Wks. (Grosart) II. 157 The Bakers Basket shall giue wall vnto the Brewers Barrell. 1608 Bp. Hall Serm. Pharasaism Wks. (1625) 413 Some Traditions must haue place in euery Church; but, Their place: they may not take wall of Scripture. 1652 — Invis. World III. § 1 If a supposed and self respective good be suffered to take the wall of the best and absolute good. 1679 R. W. Cromwell's Ghost 2 Though old in Artful Wickedness I be, Yet Rome, I now Resign the Wall to thee. 1758 L. Temple Sketches (ed. 2) 59 According to nice Herald-like Ceremony, the Son, as the better Gentleman, ought to take the Wall of the Father.

†17. *To lie by the wall* (or *walls*), to lie on one side, remain idle or unused; of a ship, to lie up (in dock or harbour); also *to lay by the walls. Obs.*

1579 Tomson Calvin's Serm. Tim. 46/2 And the law in the meane time must lye by the walles (Fr. demeure là). 1656 Burton's Diary (1828) I. 82, I am glad the mariners are so sensible of the laying of our English ships by the walls. 1658–9 Ibid. III. 462 Our ships lie by the walls, and theirs ride. 1672 Wallis in Rigaud Corr. Sci. Men (1841) II. 529 To put forth what France is not willing to venture upon, provided that it do not hinder the printing those of our own nation,..which lie by the wall for want of publishing. 1725 De Foe Voy. round World (1840) 66 He walked towards that part of the Creek, where..three of their largest ships lay by the walls. 1787 Grose Provinc. Gloss. s.v. Wall, He lies by the wall. Spoken of a person dead but not buried. Norf. and Suf.

18. (To be able) *to see*, etc. *through* or *into a* (*brick, mud, stone*) *wall*: to be endowed with great keenness of perception or understanding.

1598 Marston Pygmal., Sat. ii, Thou know'st I am sure, for thou canst cast thine eie Through nine mud walls, or els old Poets lie. 1885 Illustr. Lond. News 7 Feb. 136/4 Lord Sherbrooke..can see as far as most people into a stone wall.

19. *To turn one's face to the wall*: said of a person on his deathbed conscious of the approach of the end (? after 2 Kings xx. 2, Isa. xxxviii. 2).

1579 in Narratives Reform. (Camden) 35 He turned his face to the walle in the sayd belfry; and so after his prayers sleapte swheetly in the Lorde. 16.. Barbara Allen's Cruelty ix. in Child Ballads II. 277 He turnd his face unto the wall, And death came creeping to him. 1856 Knight Pop. Hist. Eng. I. xxi. 304 He [Henry II] turned his face to the wall, and exclaimed, 'Let every thing go as it will'. [Cf. Girald. Cambrens. (Rolls) VIII. 295 iterum se lecto reclinans faciemque suam ad parietem vertens.] 1876 'Mark Twain' Tom Sawyer iii, He would turn his face to the wall, and die with that word unsaid.

IV. 20. Short for a. *wall-tree*, b. Wallflower, c. *wall butterfly*.

a. 1707 Mortimer Husb. 522 Your Trees being grafted.. the next thing to be consider'd, is which are to be for Dwarfs, Walls and Standards.

b. 1825 R. P. Ward Tremaine I. xvi. 100 There was a regular return of the same flowers..such as walls, and provence roses, convolvolus, and sweet-william.

c. 1832 J. Rennie Butterfl. & Moths 12 The Wall (Hipparchia Megæra, Leach). The Brown Wall (H. Phædra, Stephens).

V. *attrib.* and *Comb.*

21. a. simple attrib., as *wall arch, -coping, -mosaic, -nook, -side, -tiling, -top*; with the meaning 'set or fixed against a wall', as *wall candlestick, -case, -clock, -map, -plug, -press, -sconce*; with the meaning 'growing upon or against a wall', as *wall-berry, -plant, -plum*.

1886 C. E. Pascoe Lond. To-day xxx. (ed. 3) 268 On the wall of Westminster Hall..there are plainly visible the traces of *wall arches erected by Richard II. 1908 [Miss E. Fowler] Betw. Trent & Ancholme 313 Perhaps it had earlier been busy upon the *wall-berries. 1688 Holme Armoury III. 381/2 *Wall or Hanging Candlesticks. 1886 Willis & Clark Cambridge III. 181 *Wall-cases were provided, and the collections were removed from the Old Museum. 1891 Century Dict., *Wall clock. 1887 J. G. Andrew Mem. W. Graham vii. 153 Above the *wall-coping..appeared an endless row of peering sorrow-stricken faces. 1907 T. C. Middleton Geogr. Knowl. Discov. Amer. 20 The *wall-map of the world, painted in his banquet-hall at the Lateran. 1913 Eden Ancient Glass 26 Glass *wall-mosaics for interior decoration. 1847 C. Brontë Jane Eyre iii, The ground-ivy mantling old *wall-nooks. 1880 Archæol. Cant. XIII. 26 The singular thickness of the *wall-piers causes the central body of the crypt to be narrower. 1873 Mary Somerville Recoll. xviii. 372 The Trachelium cœruleum, a pretty *wall-plant. 1914 Batstone Electr.-Light Fitting 122 *Wall Plugs. 1675 Shadwell Virtuoso IV. 72, I have observ'd upon a *Wall-plum..at first beginning to turn blue [etc.]. 1844 H. Stephens Bk. Farm II. 285 A *wall-press..is necessary in a corn-barn. c 1400 Destr. Troy 861 Sho went vp wightly by a *walle syde To the toppe of a toure. 1887 P. M'Neill Blawearie 176 Many alterations on the roof and wall-sides would have to be made. 1884 Health Exhib. Catal. 83/2 Decorative *wall-tiling. 1849 Proc. Berw. Nat. Club II. 371 It is found under..lichens on *wall-tops.

b. objective, and objective genitive, as *wall-builder, -building, -peeler; wall-like, -loving* adjs.; instrumental, as *wall-bound, -fed, -girt* adjs.

1878 Bosw. Smith Carthage 375 Hannibal..taking his place..among the *wall-builders and wonder-workers of Eastern history and legend. 1823 Cobbett Rur. Rides (1885) I. 221 Paving and *wall-building. 1862 W. Barnes Dorset Dial. II. 78 There, in the geärden's *wall-bound square. 1898 Athenæum 23 July 137/3 The clinging *wall-fed ivy. 1883 Harper's Mag. Nov. 876 Gray *wall-girt stillness. 1878 Huxley Physiogr. 168 *Wall-like masses are partially detached from the cliffs. 1865 Gosse Land & Sea (1874) 120 Walls..of loose, dry stones, affording in the crevices root-space for many *wall-loving plants. 1712 Steele Spect. No. 431 ¶ 3 These craving Damsels, whether ..Coal-Scranchers, *Wall-peelers, or Gravel-diggers.

22. Special comb.: **wall-arcade** *Arch.*, an arcade (see Arcade *sb.* 3) used as a decoration of a wall; hence **wall-arcading**, the stonework composing a wall-arcade; **wall-bearing** (see quot.); **wall-border**, a garden-border at the foot of a wall; **wall-box** (*a*) an aperture made in or through a wall to accommodate a wall-bearing; (*b*) a postal collecting box affixed to a wall as distinguished from a pillar-box; †**wall-break** *a.*, that breaks down walls; **wall-casing**, the lining or superficial exterior covering of a wall; †**wall-chalker** (see quot. 1823); **wall-clamp, -coal** (see quots.); **wall-crook** *dial.*, ? a wooden hook for driving into cob walls; **wall-cutting, dock** (see quots.); **wall-dormer** *Arch.*, a dormer whose front is part of the main wall of the building carried up to the required height; **wall-earth** (see quot.); **wall-engine**, a small vertical steam engine bolted to a wall; **wall-face** (*a*) the working face in a coal-mine; (*b*) the surface of a wall; †**wall-fast** *a.*, secure within walls; **wall-fight**, a siege; **wall-fruit**, the fruit of trees grown against a wall; also a fruit tree so grown; also *attrib.*, as *wall-fruit tree*; **wall-game**, the Eton game of football played 'at the wall' (see 4 f); **wall-grenade**, a bombshell thrown from the walls by hand or by means of a small mortar called a hand-mortar (*Cent. Dict.* 1891); **wall-gun**, a large hand-gun supported on a tripod or crutch, for firing over a rampart; **wall-hangings**, tapestry hangings for walls; **wall-head** *Sc.*, the top of a wall, esp. of a house-wall; also the space on the top of a wall between the roof-beams, used as a receptacle or shelf; also *attrib.*; **wall-hold**, the end (of a beam, etc.) which is inserted in a wall as a bearing; **wall-hook**, †(*a*) a grappling-hook (*obs.*); (*b*) a hook-shaped holdfast for fastening wire, piping, etc. to a wall; †**wall lecture** *Oxford Univ.*, a lecture delivered, according to statute, by a regent-master (to empty benches); **wall-lining**, a covering for the interior surface of a wall; **wall-nail**, a kind of nail made for driving into walls; **wall-net**, a vertical fishing-net forming the wall of an inclosed space (*Cent. Dict.*); †**wall-observer**, one who is addicted to reading placards; **wall-post** *Arch.* = Pendant *sb.* 6 a; †**wall-rase** *Sc.* [cf. Rasen, Raising-piece, *-plate*] = Wall plate; †**wall-reared** *a.* = *wall-sided*; †**wall-reeve**, an official charged with keeping embankments in repair; **wall-rib** *Arch.* (see quots. 1835–50); also *attrib.*; **wall-rock** *Mining*, the rock forming the walls of a vein; **wall-saltpetre** (see quot.); **wall-shaft** *Arch.*, in *engaged wall-shaft*, a shaft or column partly let into the wall (cf. Engaged *column*); **wall-sided** *a.*, having perpendicular sides like a wall; **wall-strap** (see quot.); **wall-string**, the string-board of a staircase which is next the wall; **wall-tent**, a tent with perpendicular sides; **wall-tie**, each of the pieces of iron, slate, or other material used to bind together the two parts of a hollow wall; **wall-tile** (*a*) a tile used for lining a wall; †(*b*) *north.*, a brick as distinguished from a roofing tile; †**wall-tooth**, a cheek-tooth, grinder; **wall-tower**, a tower forming part of a fortified wall (*Cent. Dict.*); †**wall-town** *Sc.*, a walled or fortified town; **wall-tree**, a fruit-tree planted against and trained upon a wall; also *attrib.*; **wall-wash**, liquid distemper applied to the surface of a wall; **wall-wise** *adv.*, after the manner of a wall; **wall-work**, †(*a*) work done in building a wall (*obs.*); (*b*) a defensive work consisting of walls. Also Wall-paper, Wall-piece, Wall-plat, Wall-plate, Wall-stone.

1860 G. E. Street in Archæol. Cant. III. 133 The *wall-arcades in the two churches. 1863 Sir G. Scott Glean. Westm. Abb. (ed. 2) 33 The spandrels over the *wall-arcading are exquisitely beautiful. a 1878 — Lect. Archit. I. 97. 1875 Knight Dict. Mech., *Wall-bearing, a bearing for receiving a shaft when entering or passing through a wall. 1707 Mortimer Husb. 461 They are..transplanted into some *Wall-border towards the South and East. 1851 in Beck's Florist 128 A shrubbery or wall-border some four or five feet broad. 1875 Knight Dict. Mech., *Wall-box. 1887 D. A. Low Machine Draw. (1892) 34 A neat appearance is given to the opening..by building into the wall a wall box. 1598 Sylvester Du Bartas II. iv. III. Schism 727 Fell, *wall-break (all break) Famine..Howls hideously. 1858 Hawthorne Fr. & It. Note-bks. (1871) I. 28 *Wall-casings of rich, polished marble. 1823 'Jon Bee' Dict. Turf, *Wall-chalkers—fellows who..scrawl balderdash upon garden walls..Others chalk up their trades—as 'try Warren's blacking' [etc.]. 1829 T. Hook Bank to Barnes 95 The Bill-Sticker's Assistant and Wall-Chalker's Vade-Mecum. 1875 Knight Dict. Mech., *Wall-clamp, a brace or tie to hold walls together, or the two parts of a double-wall, to prevent spreading. 1886 J. Barrowman Sc. Mining Terms 70 *Wall-coal, breast coal; the middle division of three in a seam, the other two being termed top coal and ground coal. 1869 Blackmore Lorna D. xxxviii, I worked..in the copse of young ash,..making spars to keep for thatching, *wall-crooks to drive into the cob, [etc.]. 1886 J. Barrowman Sc. Mining Terms 70 *Wall cutting, side cutting or shearing the solid coal in opening out working places; trimming the sides of a sinking pit. 1833 Loudon Encycl. Archit. § 925 The *wall docks (plugs of wood) are not to be more than 16 inches apart. 1886 Willis & Clark Cambridge III. 551 The roof dormers very soon became *wall-dormers, rising in a line with the main walls of the buildings. 1723 Phil. Trans. XXXII. 420 The lower half of the Layers of Fullers-Earth, they call the *Wall-Earth. 1839 Ure Dict. Arts, etc. 982 The instant each corve arrives, from the *wall-face,..it is lifted from the tram by a crane. a 1878 Sir G. Scott Lect. Archit. (1879) II. 141 In some of the Byzantine remains.. they have architecturalised by mouldings and enrichments only just so much of the arch-stones as was needful for beauty, and left the rest to go as mere wall-face. 1593 Rites & Mon. Durham (Surtees) 53 She..laid those two without the doore that before was maid *wall-fast within her house. 1850 Grote Greece II. lxiii. (1862) V. 457 Alkibiadês warned the assembled seamen that they must prepare for a sea-fight, a land-fight, and a *wall-fight, all at once. 1669 Worlidge Syst. Agric. (1681) 266 Nail and trim *Wall-fruits. 1690 Lond. Gaz. No. 2550/4 Good Gardens and Orchards planted with all sorts of choice Wall-fruit. a 1700 Evelyn Diary 24 Mar. 1688, The wall fruit trees are most exquisitely nail'd and train'd. 1842 Loudon Suburban Hort. 582 The wall-fruits of Britain include all those which in the central districts of England require the aid of a wall to bring them to perfection. 1883 Sat. Rev. 1 Dec. 695/2 The *Wall Game [at Eton]. 1812 Col. Hawker Diary (1893) I. 63 We then fired with slugs (Colonel Douglas with a Spanish barrel, and I with a huge *wall gun). 1819 Scott Leg. Montrose x, They found themselves..exposed to a fire both of musketry and wall-guns. 1865 Carlyle Fredk. Gt. xix. iv. V. 473 Wall-guns brought from Cüstrin. 1896 Lina Eckenstein Woman under Monasticism 233 The great work of her life was the manufacture of *wall-hangings. a 1578 Lindesay (Pitscottie) Chron. Scot. (S.T.S.) II. 83 [They] laid him on the *wall heid, that all might sie him deid. 1636 in Scottish Jrnl. Topogr. (1848) II. 11/1 Item, for ten hondreth of diffeit [= divot] riggine and wae-heid towrs [= turfs]. 1898 Ld. E. Hamilton Mawkin of Flow xvii. 226 Here, Rob, rax me that bit rope that's lying in the wall-head yonder. 1833 Loudon Encycl. Archit. § 919 The inside lintels..are..to have at least 12 inches of bond (or *wall-hold) on each end. 1844 H. Stephens Bk. Farm I. 170 The steps should be droved 3 feet 6 inches clear of the wall, with 6 inches of wall hold. 1681 W. Robertson Phraseol. Gen. (1693) 739 A *wall-hook or drag; Lupus, harpago. 1823 P. Nicholson Pract. Build. 408 Fastening the pipes to the wall by means of wall-hooks of iron. 1882 Christy Joints 194 A strip of 5 lb. lead,..secured along one edge to the wall with wall hooks. 1662 Wood Life 22 Dec. (O.H.S.) I. 464 Wheras they were left of after the king was restored and *wall lectures onlie read in their places, declamations were now setled and wall lectures too. 1691 — Ath. Oxon. (1721) II. 796 He did also sometimes repair to the Ordinaries (commonly called Wall Lectures from the paucity of Auditors). 1767 J. Penn By Way of Prevention To Clergy p. i, Dry Morals and musty Doctrines have turned Sermons into Wall Lectures. 1860 G. E. Street in Archæol. Cant. III. 132 A great deal of chalk is used for *wall lining. 1892 Dict. Archit. (Archit. Publ. Soc.), Wall-lining, a thin internal wall of brick for keeping dry the interior surface of a house in exposed places. 1344–5 Exch. Acc. K. R. 492. 24 (MS.), In Ml de *Walnail empt. vjd. ob. 1864 Atkinson Stanton Grange 224 Next stood a box of shreds and wall-nails. 1673 [R. Leigh] Transp. Reh. 76 The avenue-readers, the *wall-observers, and those that are acquainted with stall-learning. 1871 T. Morris Brit. Carpentry 85 The situation of the *wall posts would seem to indicate a purpose of concentrating the weight. 1513 Acc. Ld. High Treas. Scot. V. 220 Item, for ij *wall rasis put undre the cuppill feit,..Item, for v corbalis of stane..for bering to the tua wall rasis. 1627 Capt. J. Smith Sea Gram. xi. 53 We say a Ship is..*wall reared when she is right built vp, after shee comes to her bearing. 1316 Placiterum Abbrev. (1811) 352 Et dicunt qd idem dñs & curia sua de Stebenhethe..ordinavit..duos homines qui vocantur *Walreves ad supervidendum wallias fossata seweras & gutteras praedicta. 1835 R. Willis Archit. Mid. Ages vii. 82 If the compartment be bounded by a wall as in the case of the clerestory, the rib which is placed at the intersection of the vault with the wall may be called the *Wall Rib. 1850 Inkersley Inquir. Archit. France 309 The union of the wall-rib-shaft..with the spring of the window-archway. 1877 Raymond Statist. Mines & Mining 349 On it a shaft has been sunk..showing a continuous vein with well-defined *wall-rock. 1911 Encycl. Brit. XXIV. 94/2 *Wall-saltpetre or lime saltpetre, calcium nitrate, Ca $(NO_3)_2$, is found as an efflorescence on the walls of stables; it is now manufactured in large quantities. 1865 G. E. Street Gothic Archit. Spain ix. 191 There are three-quarter engaged *wall-shafts between the windows. 1711 W. Sutherland Shipbuild. Assist. 165 *Wall-sided. 1769 Falconer Dict. Marine (1780). 1830 Lyell Princ. Geol. I. 180 A deep wall-sided valley. 1840 R. H. Dana Bef. Mast xxix, She was a good, substantial ship,..wall-sided and kettle-bottomed. 1866 Huxley Prehist. Rem. Caithn. 88 The transverse contour of the skull inclines to be pentagonal and wall-sided. 1833 Loudon Encycl. Archit. § 925 The *wall-straps (battens, or pieces of quartering on which to nail the laths) are to be 1 inch and a quarter thick. 1849 *Wall string [see String *sb.* 26]. 1862 T. W. Higginson Army Life (1870) 19 Two *wall-tents being placed end to end, for office and bedroom. 1894 Outing XXIV. 86/1 We had a single wall-tent, ten by twelve. 1884 Health Exhib. Catal. 81/2 Section of Hollow Brick Wall, showing our patent cast and wrought *wall-ties. 1358 York Mercers etc. (Surtees) 15 Pro xx mille de *Walteghill, vj li. 1465 in Paston Lett. II. 224 A thousand waltyle that his fadir had fro ye seide Williams wyfes place. 1790 Grose Provinc. Gloss. Suppl., Wall-tiles, bricks; opposed to tiles, called Thack-tiles. North. 1882 Christy Joints 68 Wall tiles are sometimes bedded in fine plaster. c 1475 Pict. Voc. in Wr.-Wülcker 748/7 Hoc maxillare, a *walthothe. (? Hence) 1847 Halliwell, Wall-tooth, a large double-tooth. c 1470 Henry Wallace VIII. 699 This war the best off all, To kepe our strynth off castell and off *wall toun. c 1480 Henryson Death & Man 7 Wal-townis, castellis, towiris, neuir so wicht, may nocht resist quhill it be at his hert. 1657 Austen Fruit Trees I. 66 As concerning the distance of *Wal-trees. 1786 Abercrombie Gard. Assist. 42 For wall-tree cherries, plums, pears, etc. allot a portion of the earliest..varieties for south walls. 1844 Zoologist II. 493 Another [nest] was completed in an adjoining wall-tree. 1898 Allbutt's Syst. Med. V. 511 We discovered arsenic in large quantity in the green unsized *wall-wash of her own sitting-room. 1596 S. Finche Let. 26 Feb., in Ducarel Hist. Croydon (1783) App. 155 We have made up that angle.. *wall-wyse with stone and morter. c 1000 Ælfric Hom. (Thorpe) II. 166 Þa ȝebroðra eodon to ðam *weall-weorce. 1581 J. Bell Haddon's Answ. Osor. A vj b, Our dutie hadd bene to direct the buildyng of our Religion by this lyne and leuell, and to ramme fast the wallworkes hereof with this cemente and morter. 1837 Penny Cycl. IX. 468/1 Other internal walls..communicate with wall-works running east and west.

b. In the names of animals frequenting or living in walls, as **wall-bee** (see quot.); **wall-bird**, a dial. name of the Spotted Flycatcher, *Muscicapa grisola*; **wall-brown**, a common British butterfly, *Satyrus megæra* = *brown wall* (see 19 c); **wall-butterfly** (see quot.); **wall-carpet**, a variety of the carpet-moth (see Carpet *sb.* 5); **wall-creeper** (see quot. 1888); **wall-fly** (see quot.); **wall-gecko** (see quot.); **wall-lizard**, a lizard of the species *Lacerta muralis*; **wall-louse**, †(*a*) the bed-bug, *Cimex lectularius*; (*b*) *dial.* the woodlouse; †**wall-newt**, ? = *wall-lizard*; **wall-usher**, a variety of moth (see quot.); **wall-wasp** (see quot.).

1774 Goldsm. Nat. Hist. (1776) VIII. 94 The *Wall Bees are so called, because they make their nests in walls. 1848 Zoologist VI. 2186 The spotted flycatcher is the '*wall-bird'. 1846 Proc. Berw. Nat. Club II. 171 Not a single specimen has been observed of the..*Wall Brown, or the Dark Green Aglaia. 1860 W. S. Coleman Brit. Butterfl. 98 The *Wall Butterfly (Lasiommata Megæra). Ibid. 99 It is called the Wall Butterfly from its frequent habit of choosing a roadside wall for a perch. 1832 J. Rennie Butterfl. & Moths 111 The *Wall Carpet (Alcis muraria Curtis). 1667 C. Merrett Pinax 177 Picus murarius, the Creeper, or *Wall-Creeper. 1678 [see Spider-catcher 2]. 1764 G. Edwards Glean. Nat. Hist. III. 284 The Wall-creeper of Surinam. 1888 Newton in Encycl. Brit. XXIII. 534/2 Allied to the Tree-Creeper [Certhia]..is the genus Tichodroma, the single member of which is the Wall-Creeper (T. muraria) of the Alps and some other mountainous parts of Europe and Asia. 1653 Walton Angler ii. 54 Nay, sometimes a worm, or any kind of fly; as the Ant-fly, the Flesh-fly, or *Wall-fly [cf. ed. 3 (1661) 63, the black Bee that breeds in clay walls]. 1886 Cassell's Dict. s.v. Platydactylus, P. fascicularis or muralis is the *Wall Gecko. c 1880 Cassell's Nat. Hist. IV. 274 The lively little *Wall Lizard, Lacerta muralis. 1540 Septem Ling. Dict. D vj, Cimices..*wallyse. 1598–1657 Wall louse [see Punaise]. 1673 [see Chinch *sb.*[1]]. 1693 S. Dale Pharmacol. 531 Cimex..The Wall-Louse or Bugg. 1899 Cumbld. Gloss., s.v. Kirk louse, Wall louse, Slater, woodlouse, millipede. Oniscidæ. 1605 Shaks. Lear III. iv. 135 Poore Tom, that eates..the Tod-pole, the *wall-Neut, and the water. 1708 Brit. Apollo No. 88. 2/1 Like the Body of a Red *Wall-Spider. 1832 J. Rennie Butterfl. & Moths 102 The *Wall Usher (Anisopteryx Æscularia, Stephens) appears on palings and trunks of trees the middle of March. 1881 Cassell's Nat. Hist. V. 372 The *Wall Wasp (Odynerus parietum)..may be almost constantly seen haunting sunny walls during the months of June and July.

c. In the names of plants growing on or by walls and in dry or stony places, as **wall barley**, the wild barley, *Hordeum murinum*; also rye-grass, *Lolium perenne*; **wall bugloss**, a plant of the genus *Lycopsis*; **wall cabbage** (see quot.); **wall-cress**, the genus *Arabis*; also (see quot. 1796); **wall fern**, the common evergreen fern, *Polypodium vulgore*; **wall gillyflower**, the Wallflower; **wall grass**, the stonecrop, *Sedum acre*; **wall hawkweed**, *Hieracium murorum*; **wall moss**, (*a*) the yellow lichen, *Parmelia parietaria* (Cent. Dict.); (*b*) *Sedum acre*; (*c*) see quot. 1855; **wall mustard** = *wall-rocket*; **wall pellitory** = Pellitory 2; †**wall penny grass**, **wall pennywort** = Pennywort 1; **wall pepper**, *Sedum acre*; **wall pie** = *wall rue*; **wall-rocket**, *Diplotaxis tenuifolia*; **wall rue**, a small fern, *Asplenium Ruta-muraria*; **wall sage**, †(*a*) a species of *Sideritis*; cf. Glidewort, Ironwort; (*b*) = Pellitory 2 (*Eng. Dial. Dict.*); **wall speedwell**, *Veronica arvensis*; **wall spleenwort** = *wall rue*; **wall weed**, ? mother-of-thousands, *Linaria Cymbalaria*. Also Wallflower, Wallwort.

1548 Turner Names Herbes (E.D.S.) 43 Phenicea or Hordeum murinum of Plinie, is the *wal Barley, whiche groweth on mud walles. 1597 Gerarde Herbal I. li. 71 Red Darnell is called..in Latin Lolium rubrum: and Lolium Murinum: in English Wall Barley. 1763 Mills Pract. Husb. III. 333 The Wall barley, or way bennet, as some people improperly term it. 1866 Treas. Bot. I. 597/1 We all remember how in our youth we put inverted spikes of the Wall Barley up our sleeves and found them travel to our shoulders. 1650 [W. Howe] Phytol. Brit. 36 Echium alterum, Dod. Lycopsis Anglica, Lob. in agris siccioribus & muris. *Wall Buglosse. 1860 Mayne Expos. Lex., Wall-Bugloss. Common name for the Lycopsis. 1796 Withering Brit. Plants (ed. 3) III. 593 [Brassica muralis] Sisymbrium murale. Linn...*Wall Cabbage. Old walls and rubbish. Ibid. 589 Turritis hirsuta..*Wall Cress. 1866 Treas. Bot. 83/2 Wall-cress, the English name [of Arabis] has similar reference to the usual place of growth. 1525 Grete Herbal cccxlix. (1529) Tv, De polytryco. *Walfarne. 1639 O. Wood Alph. Bk. Secrets 214 Walferne. 1548 Turner Names Herbes (E.D.S.) 80 Viola alba...There are diuerse sortes... One is called in english Cheiry, Hertes ease or *wal Geleflour, it groweth vpon the walles, and..hath yealowe floures. 1796 H. Hunter tr. St.-Pierre's Stud. Nat. (1799) II. 94 The butter-flower of the meadow, and the wall gilly-flower. 1882 H. Friend Devonsh. Plant-n., *Wall Grass. Sedum acre, L. 1829 Loudon Encycl. Plants (1836) 674 *Wall hawkweed. 1855 Anne Pratt Flowering Pl. II. 324 *Wall-moss (Dicranum murale). 1886 Britten & Holland Plant-n., Wall Moss. Sedum acre L.—N. and E. Yks. 1904 *Wall-mustard [see *wall-rocket*]. 1562 Turner Herbal II. 169, I knowe no English name for it [Vmbilicus veneris]: but lest it should be wythout a name I call it 'wall penny grasse. 1578 Lyte Dodoens I. xxv. 37 Cotyledon vera. *Wall Pennywurte. 1579, 1756 [see Pennywort 1]. 1855 Anne Pratt Flowering Pl. II. 320 Cotyledon Umbilicus (Wall Pennywort). 1578 Lyte Dodoens I. lxxvii. 115 Of Houselyke and Sengreene...The fourth is called..in English Stone Crop,..& of some it is called *Wall Pepper. 1861 S. Thomson Wild Flowers III. (ed. 4) 238 We find the Sedum acre, or yellow stone-crop, often called wall-pepper. 1855 Anne Pratt Flowering Pl. I. 152 Sinapis tenuifolia (*Wall-rocket). 1904 Westm. Gaz. 13 Oct. 10/1 This is the wall-rocket or narrow-leaved wall-mustard (Diplotaxis tenuifolia), a glaucous plant, one to one and a half feet high, with pale lemon-yellow flowers. 1548 Turner Names Herbes (E.D.S.) 86 Saluia vita or Ruta muralis..maye be called in english Stone Rue, or *wal Rue. 1741 Compl. Fam.-Piece I. iv. 243 Leaves of Wall-Rue 4 Ounces. 1906 J. Vaughan Wild-Fl. Selborne 92 The little wall-rue fern. 1548 Turner Names Herbes (E.D.S.) 73 Sideritis prima..may be called in englishe *walsage or stonisage. 1651 J. F[reake] Agrippa's Occ. Philos. I. xvii. 40 Geese, Ducks, and such like watery fowle, cure themselves with the Hearb called wall-sage [L. herba sideritide]. 1796 Withering Brit. Plants (ed. 3) II. 13 Veronica arvensis..*Wall Speedwell. 1866 Swinburne St. Dorothy Poems & Ballads 288 Green blossom cleaves To the green chinks, and lesser *wall-weed sweet, Kissing the crannies that are split with heat.

†**Wall**, *sb.*[2] *Sc. Obs.* Also 6 vall, wal. [var. spelling (with silent *ll*) of Waw *sb.*] A wave (of the sea).

c 1480 Wyntoun's Cron. I. vii. 399 (MS. E.) Of wellis wawerit wallis wid. c 1480 Henryson Paddock & Mouse 180 The watter is the warld, ay welterand With mony wall of trubulatioun. c 1500 Lancelot 1316 This schip, that goth apone the stormy vall. 1513 Douglas Æneis III. viii. 60 Within the havin goith loune, but wind or wall. 1549 Compl. Scot. 39 The suelland vallis of the brym seye. 1599 Alex. Hume Hymns vii. 89 The waltering wals, and raging windie blast.

†**Wall**, *sb.*[3] *Obs.* Also 7 whall. [Back-formation from Wall-eye.] *Eyes of wall* (nonce-phrase) = 'wall eyes': see Wall eye. Also *attrib.* or *adj.*, as in *wall speck*; *wall-coloured* adj.

1611 Cotgr. s.v. Oeil, Oeil de chevre, a whall, or ouerwhite eye. 1653 R. Sanders Physiogn. 27 The apple [of the eye] is half blew, and all about wall-coloured. 1663 Butler Hud. I. i. 424 The Beast was sturdy large and tall, With Mouth of Meal and Eyes of Wall. 1706 Lond. Gaz. No. 4285/8 Stolen.., a white Horse, with..a wall Speck in one of his Eyes.

Wall (wǫl), *sb.*[4] *Naut.* Short for Wall-knot.

1834 Marryat P. Simple vi, 'How is this to be finished off sir?' inquired a sailor of the boatswain. 'Why,..it must be with a double wall.' c 1860 H. Stuart Seaman's Catech. 30 Make a single wall. Ibid. 56 A 'double wall' or deck stopper-knot is made..close up to the wall. 1884 Knight Dict. Mech. Suppl., Wall and Crown. This knot should be finished with a crown.

Wall (wǫl), *sb.*[5] = Lablab.

1884 De Candolle's Orig. Cultiv. Plants 346 Lablab, or Wall..Dolichos Lablab, Linnæus. This species is much cultivated in India and tropical Africa. 1887 Moloney Forestry W. Afr. 322 'Wall' of India (Dolichos Lablab, L.) A climbing perennial largely cultivated in the Tropics for its unpalatable seeds.

Wall, *v.*[1] *Obs.* exc. *dial.* Forms: 1 weallan, 2–5 walle-n, 7– wall. *Pa. t.* 1 wéol(l, 3 weol, wul, 4 wel; *weak* 4 wallede, 7– walled. [OE. *weallan* redupl. str. vb. (pa. t. *wéoll*, pa. pple. *geweallen*) corresp. to OFris. *walla* to well up (WFris. *walle* to boil), MFlem. *wallen* (Kilian) to well up (mod.Flem. to boil), OS. *wallan* str. vb., to boil up, gush forth (MLG. *wallen*), OHG. *wallan* str. vb., to boil, gush forth (MHG. *wallen* str., mod.G. wk., to boil, be agitated, swarm, etc.).

The transitive uses do not occur in OE., and as they are found only with the weak conjugation, it is possible that they descend not from OE. *weallan*, but from *wællan* var. of *wiellan, wellan* Well *v.*; cf. mod. Sc. *wall* (Well *sb.*) repr. OE. *wælla* var. of *wiella*. The transitive senses below are closely paralleled by those of Well *v.* and its equivalents in other Teut. langs.

The Teut. *wallan (:—*waln-) redupl. vb. with the sense 'to boil, bubble up' is confined to WGer.; but a cogn. and synonymous *wellan str. vb. exists in ON. vella (vall, ollenn), MSw. välla str. vb. (Sw. välla, Da. vælde wk. vbs.), and a causative type *walljan wk. vb. in ON. vella (Sw. välla) to boil (trans.), to weld = MHG. wellen, OE. wiellan: see Well, Weld vbs. For other Teut. derivatives of the root in the same specific sense see Walm, Well sb.; cf. also Goth. wulan to be fervent. It is probable that the sense 'to boil, bubble, well up' is developed from the sense 'to roll', which belongs to the root *wel- in Teut. and Indogermanic (see Wallow v.); for the form *well- cf. OHG. wella roller, axle (MHG., mod.G. welle), wellan str. vb. trans. to roll.]

†1. *intr.* Of a liquid: To boil. Also of a person: To be in boiling liquid. *Obs.*

c 1000 Sax. Leechd. II. 358 Do ofer fyr, awyl; þonne hit wealle, sing iii. pater noster. c 1200 Moral Ode 249 (Trin. MS.) Þar is pich þat afre walleð [MS. Egerton wealð]. c 1200 Ormin 10507 To bærnnenn & to wallenn Wiþþ deofless dun in hellegrund. c 1250 Song Passion 45 in O.E. Misc. 198 Wallen in helle dep nere neuere so swet wit alle.

†b. *fig.* To 'boil' with passion. (Cf. Walling *ppl. a.*) *Obs.*

Beowulf 2113 Hreðer inne weoll, þonne he wintrum frod worn ȝemunde. a 1225 Leg. Kath. 1926 Þe king weol al inwið of wreððe. a 1225 Ancr. R. 118 Þeo hwule þet te heorte walleð wiðinnen of wreððe, nis þer no riht dom.

†2. Of liquids: To bubble up; to well up, flow abundantly. Of the sea, waves: To boil up, rage.

c 893 Ælfred Oros. IV. iii, Mon ȝeseah weallan blod of eorþan. c 1200 Trin. Coll. Hom. 167 At eche wunde wul ut atter. 1297 R. Glouc. (Rolls) 662 As þe water deþ vp walle. c 1315 Shoreham Poems III. 28 Syker þou myȝt be of þat lond Þar melke and hony walleþ. c 1330 King of Tars 1087 Þe blod out of his wounde wel. 1362 Langl. P. Pl. A. v. 71 Venim or vernisch or vinegre, I trouwe, Walleþ in my wombe or waxeþ, ich wene. c 1450 Mirk's Festial 9 Out of þe whech tombe manna and oyle walleþ out yfere. *fig.* 1449 Pecock Repr. IV. iii. 432 Thes..causis, out of whiche wallen the seid yuelis.

†b. To swarm (with vermin). *Obs.*

c 1000 Ælfric Saints' Lives IV. 212 On blindum cwearterne ..þær manna lic lagon, þe wæran ær acwealde..þa weollon eall maðon. c 1050 Voc. in Wr.-Wülcker 531/22 Scatens, weallende [gl. Aldh. Laud. Virg. (poet.) lxxxix, scatens vermibus]. 1387 Trevisa Higden (Rolls) V. 235 He wallede ful of wormes [L. vermibus scatens].

3. *trans.* To boil. Cf. Well *v.*

See *pot-walling*, quot. 1456 s.v. Pot-walloping.

c 1310 S. Margaret 287 in Horstm. Altengl. Leg. (1881) 232 Takeþ and walleþ oyle and lete opon hir renne.

b. *absol.* To boil brine in salt-making.

1600 [Implied in Waller[2]]. 1669 Phil. Trans. IV. 1063 They seldom Wall, that is, make Salt, in above 6 Houses at a time.

4. *intr.* To weld, become welded; *fig.* to blend. Cf. Well, Weld *vbs.*

1629 Sir W. Mure True Crucifixe 2692 Pleasure in Him and fleshlie pleasure fall So foull at strife, they can, nor mixe, nor wall.

Wall (wǫl), *v.*[2] Pa. t. and pa. pple. **walled** (wǫld). [OE. *weallian (only in pa. pple. *geweallod*), f. *weall* Wall *sb.*[1] Cf. LG. *wallen.*]

1. *trans.* To furnish with a wall.

a. To enclose, surround, or divide with a wall or walls; to provide (a town, etc.) with fortified walls.

[c 1000 Ælfric Num. xiii. 29 Micele burȝa þær sind and mærlice ȝeweallode.] c 1250 Gen. & Ex. 435 He ches a stede toward eden, And..Wallede a burȝ, e-no bi name. ? a 1366 Chaucer Rom. Rose 138, I saugh a Gardin.., Enclos it was, and walled wel, With hye walles enbatailled. 1387 Trevisa Higden (Rolls) VI. 339 Þe citee of Ȝork, þat was not ful i-walled. 1471 Caxton Recuyell (Sommer) 271 Laomedon the kynge of Troye was besy to walle and mure his cyte with mures and towres. 1589 Bigges Summarie Drake's W. Ind. Voy. 39 The same [Priorie] being walled with a wall of stone. 1611 Shaks. Cymb. V. iii. 14 Close by the battell, ditch'd, & wall'd with turph. 1643 R. Baker Chron. 13 King Athelstan..new walled and beautifyed the City of Exceter. 1794 Trans. Soc. Arts XII. 201 The expence of walling the forty-two acres was seventy-eight pounds. 1842 Dickens Amer. Notes iii, The House of Correction..is not walled, like other prisons, but is palisaded round about with..stakes. 1849 Lyell 2nd Visit U.S. II. 295 Some lands near the river..have risen immensely in value, being now trenched and walled. 1881 Proc. R. Geog. Soc. (N.S.) III. 31 The town of Shonga..is walled and ditched.

b. with *about, round about, round*. *To wall in*, to enclose with a wall. *To wall off, out*, to shut off or out with a wall.

1297 R. Glouc. (Rolls) 1169 Þe vif tounes of þe vif pors he let walli aboute. 1375 Barbour Bruce II. 220 Till Perth then went thai..That then wes wallyt all about. c 1420 Wyntoun Cron. V. 1303 (Cott.) He gert wal in al þat stede Qwhar Criste his passion tholit of dede. 1481 Caxton Reynard v. (Arb.) 10 They..wente in a yerde whiche was walled round a boute. c 1530 Tindale Jonas Prol. B vij, Enuironed it and walled it aboute on euery syde with yᵉ feare of god. 1600 Surflet Country Farm VII. xix. 834 Their parkes therefore must bee walled about. 1633 Stow's Surv. 761 He round walled the Church-yard. 1691 J. Gibson in Archæologia XII. 189 The garden not being walled about they have less summer fruit. 1719 De Foe Crusoe II. (Globe) 564 It was a low marshy Ground, wall'd round with a Stone-wall. 1760–72 H. Brooke Fool of Qual. (1809) IV. 48 A gravel-walk that was walled in on the left hand. 1799 Wellington Let. Lieut. Col. Close 21 Dec., in Gurwood Disp. (1844) I. 47 What I should propose would be to wall off that part occupied by him. 1848 Dickens Dombey vii, Traffic was walled out. 1860 Tyndall Glac. I. ii. 19 A space for cooking walled off from the sleeping-room. 1865 W. G. Palgrave Journ. Central & E. Arabia II. 301 The town is walled in, but not strongly, on the land side.

c. To furnish (a building) with side and partition walls; to build the wall or walls of. Also with *up*.

1377 Langl. P. Pl. B. XIX. 323 And þere-with grace bigan to make a good foundement, And watteled it and walled it with his peynes & his passioun. c 1394 P. Pl. Crede 164 And all was walled þat wone. 1523 Berners Froiss. I. ccix. 102 b/2 Therein was a square toure thick walled. 1691 Dryden K. Arthur II. 19 That Castle, were it wall'd with Adamant, Can hide thy Head, but till to Morrow's Dawn. 1726 Leoni Alberti's Archit. I. 78 The Towers..ought not to be open on the inside, but walled up quite round. 1799 A. Young View Agric. Lincoln. 34 The old buildings are of timber, walled with clay. 1911 G. Macdonald Roman Wall Scot. xii. 401 Perhaps it was now that Castlecary was walled with stone.

d. To line (a well, cistern) with a wall. Also with *round*.

1707 Mortimer Husb. 229 A Cistern of Clay walled within with Bricks. 1833 Jas. Davidson Brit. & Rom. Rem. Axminster 84 A hole in the natural soil..walled round in a circular form with flint stones.

2. *transf.* and *fig.* To enclose, defend, bound, or divide as with a wall, or as a wall does.

c 1386 Chaucer Manciple's T. 219 My sone, god..Walled a tonge with teeth and lippes eke ffor man sholde hym auyse what he speeke. 1558 A. Jenkinson in Hakluyt Voy. (1599) I. 331 We feared nothing being walled with the said riuer. 1591 Shaks. 1 Hen. VI, IV. ii. 24 On either hand thee, there are squadrons pitcht, To wall thee from the liberty of Flight. 1595 Polimanteia in Brydges Brit. Bibl. I. 278 Yet both of you [Oxford and Cambridge] so deare to me,..so walled with priuiledges, so crowned with all kinde of honor. 1603–4 Shaks. Ham. IV. v. 122 (QQ 1, 2) There's such diuinitie doth wall [Fol. hedge] a king, That treason dares not looke on. c 1620 Fletcher False One V. iv. 26 My free mind, Like to the palm-tree walling fruitful Nile, Shall grow up straighter. 1638 Sir T. Herbert Trav. (ed. 2) 165 Either side is wall'd with an amazing hill. 1639 Fuller Holy War IV. vii. 179 They..onely spoiled poore villages, which counted themselves walled with the truce as yet in force. 1667 Milton P. L. III. 721 Each [star] had his place appointed, each his course, The rest in circuit walles this Universe. 1818 L. Hunt Hero & Leander II. 7 The struggling flare Seem'd out; but then he knew his Hero's care, And that she only wall'd it with her cloak. 1834 Ld. Houghton Mem. Tour Greece 23 The tall white rock, Walled the far waste of silent sea. 1879 Daily News 18 Sept. 6/1 The enclosures were walled with Union Jacks. 1883 Bridges Prometheus 14 Where the path Is walled with corn I am found. 1913 Engl. Rev. Dec. 59 On the right hand, walling the street, [is] the great monastery to the Passion of Christ.

b. with *about, across, along, in, round*.

c 1430 Pilgr. Lyf Manhode I. xx. (1869) 15 This closure that closeth yow and walleth yow in, disseueringe yow from the world. 1588 Shaks. L. L. L. V. ii. 3 A Lady wal'd about with Diamonds. 1593 — Rich. II, III. ii. 167 As if this Flesh, which walls about our Life, Were Brasse impregnable. a 1626 Bacon War with Spain (1629) 45 The Spaniards.. casting themselues continually into Roundels, (their strongest Ships walling in the rest). 1642 Denham Sophy I. i 'Tis his single vertue And terror of his name, that walls us in From danger. 1690 C. Nesse O. & N. Test. I. 38 A weekly sabbath walls in our wild natures. 1795 Southey Joan of Arc I. 475 At length I heard of Orleans, by the foe Wall'd in from human succour. 1837 W. Irving Capt. Bonneville II. 207 The high precipices which had hitherto walled in the channel of Snake river. 1845 J. Coulter Adv. in Pacific xi. 132 The..upper part of the clearing, which was walled along for several hundred yards by solid rock. 1878 Browning Poets Croisic Prol. 3 World— how it walled about Life with disgrace. 1883 Stevenson Silverado Sq. (1886) 39 A canyon..was here walled across by a dump of rolling stones. 1890 'R. Boldrewood' Col. Reformer xiv, The..landlocked bay, with..a grand sandstone bluff guarding and walling-in the farther point like a grim jealous giant.

c. To form the sides of (a room) like walls; to line the walls of (an apartment).

1832 Lytton Eugene Aram I. iii. 20 The rest of the room was walled from the floor to the roof with books. 1846 G. B. Cheever Lect. Pilgr. Progr. x. 126 It does not take long in such employment to make the room seem walled with retributive flames. 1910 G. W. E. Russell 15 Chapters Autob. (1914) vii. 149 The great gallery, walled with the canvases of Rubens.

3. To shut up (a person or thing) within walls, to build up or entomb in a wall, to immure. Chiefly with *up*.

1530 Palsgr. 770/2, I wall, I shyt up, or close up, within walles. Je mure...It is a harde relygyon to be an anchre, for they be shytte up within walles and can go no farther. 1600 E. Blount tr. Conestaggio 243 They were walled vp within their monasterie. a 1628 Fletcher Mad Lover I. i, In three [battles] he beat the Thunder-bolt his Brother, Forc'd him to wall himself up. 1621 Lady M. Wroth Urania 133 After the sight of one dead, the other wall'd to certaine death,..what could they say? 1647 in Verney Mem. (1892) II. xii. 285 The feather bedds that were waled up are much eaten with Ratts. 1719 D'Urfey Pills (1872) VI. 87 But if ne'er so close you wall him,..Blind Love..Will find out the way. 1737 W. Cowper in F. Peck Mem. O. Cromwell etc. II. (1740) 88, I am apt to think the person found in the vault was betrayed and walled up alive by them he trusted. 1845 Poe Black Cat (end), I had walled the monster up within the tomb! *transf.* 1867 G. Macdonald Poems 87, I will be a knight Walled up in armour black.

¶ b. An alleged synonym of Gate *v.*[1]

1860 C. Benson Mr. Bedlow, Remin. Amer. Coll. Life in Macm. Mag. II. 222/1 To 'gate' or 'wall' a refractory student would be simply impossible, for want of the material masonry. 1871 Hoppe s.v. Gate gives the prec. quot.; hence the sense appears (as 'Oxford university slang') in Barrère & Leland Slang, in Farmer, and in recent Dicts.

4. To close (a gate or other aperture) with or as with a wall. Chiefly with *up*.

1503 Engl. Misc. (Surtees 1890) 30 John Mitteley & his heires frome now forthe shall wall up..the utter west syde of his swynstye. 1535 Coverdale 1 Macc. v. 47 They that were in the cite, wolde not let them go thorow, but walled vp the portes with stones. 1605 Shuttleworths' Acc. (Chetham Soc.) 168 A waller, one day wallinge uppe the dower..iiijd. 1667 Observ. Burning Lond. 23 [They] were talking of walling the Gates to prevent the coming in of the Tartarians. 1707–21 Mortimer Husb. (ed. 5) II. 192 Wall up the sides with Brick. 1848 H. Greville Leaves fr. Diary 1 July (1883) 280 The door has been walled to prevent surprise. 1861 Dickens Gt. Expect. viii, Some of the windows had been walled up. 1886 Willis & Clark Cambridge II. 125 Bishop Alcock..walled up the arches and inserted in each of them a window.

5. To build (stone) into a wall. Also of stone, to make (a specified length) of walling.

1621 Shuttleworths' Acc. (Chetham Soc.) 251 P'd for soe many stones as walled nyne y'des, ijs iiijd. 1791 Smeaton Edystone L. (1793) § 209 When it [Bath Free Stone] is walled with this kind of mortar,..the joints are more permanent. 1848–9 L'pool. Archit. Soc. (1852) II. 190 It [the rubble] may be walled with or without mortar.

6. *absol.* or *intr.* To construct a wall or walls; to build walling.

1588 Shuttleworth's Acc. (Chetham Soc.) 44 Towe mene for wallinge towe days, ijs ijd. 1598 Ibid. 112 Towe workemen, for waullynge and daubynge in the bru howse..xvjd. 1726 Leoni Alberti's Archit. I. 47 We may be said rather to wall than only to fill up.

7. *trans.* To chalk up (a score) on the wall. *slang.*

1848 Sinks of Lond. 129 Wall it, chalking a reckoning up at a public house.

†**Wall**, *v.*[3] *Obs.* [OE. *weallian* = OHG., (M)LG., MDu. *wallen*, OHG. *wallōn* (MHG., mod.G. *wallen*):—WGer. **wallōjan.*

By some scholars referred to the root of Wall v.[1]; others regard it as a contraction of *waþlōjan (cf. OHG. wadalōn to roam about).]

intr. To go on pilgrimage.

a 1000 Canons Edgar, Of Penitents § 10 in Thorpe Ags. Laws II. 280 Deoplic dæd-bot bið þæt læwede man his wæpna alecge & weallige bær-fot wide. c 1485 Digby Myst. III. 1848 With me xall ȝe wall to have more eloquens & goo vesyte þe stacyons by and by.

Wall (wǫl), *v.*[4] Now only *U.S.* Also 5–9 *Sc.* waul(e, wawl(e, 5–6 *Sc.* (? *erron.*) waill. [MSc. *wawle*:—**waȝle*, related to *waȝl-* in Wall-eyed *a.*] *trans.* To roll (the eyes). Also *absol.*, and *intr.* of the eyes. Hence **Wa·lling** *ppl. a.* (Sc. *waulen'*).

c 1480 Henryson Cock & Fox 469 The Cok..Vnwarlie winkand, wawland vp and doun. c 1500 in Makculloch MS. (S. T. S.) iv. 27 Cuttis for þi cot þai kest..out throw þi harnis þe pykis of thorne apliit, wawland [MS. Arundel wailland] þi ene. 1513 Douglas Æneis VIII. vii. 154 In the breist of the goddes graif thai Gorgones heid,..Wyth ene wauland [L. vertentem lumina]. 1818 Edin. Mag. Oct. 328/2 The sicht forhow't her waulen' een, Sho lay in the deadthraws. 1821 Scott Pirate xxx, But presently recovering himself, he wawls on me with his gray een, like a wild-cat. 1817 Hogg Gude Greye Katt xxvii. in Poetic Mirror (1817) 196 Quhill ilken bosome byrnit with lufe, And waulit ilken ee. 1876 'Mark Twain' Tom Sawyer v, The ladies would lift up their hands,..and 'wall' their eyes, and shake their heads. 1883 Trans. Amer. Philol. Soc. 55 Wall the eyes, that is, 'to roll the eyes so as to show the white.' I can remember this as a very common way among the little negroes in South Carolina of showing displeasure.

Wall (wǫl), *v.*[5] *Naut.* [f. Wall *sb.*[4]] *trans.* To make a wall-knot on (a rope).

1883 Man. Seamanship for Boys 112 The end [of the rose-lashing] is finished off by crowning and walling the end close to the crossing turns.

Wall: see Wale *sb.*[1] and *sb.*[2], Waw, Well.

Walla, variant form of Wallah.

Wallaba (wǫ·lăbă). [? a. native name.] A large South American timber-tree (*Eperua falcata*). Also *attrib.*, as *wallaba oil, tree*.

1825 Waterton Wand. S. Amer. I. (1903) 17 Here the.. wallaba, purple-heart,..and mora, are met with in vast abundance. 1845 Lindley Veg. Kingd. (1846) 550 Eperua falcata is the Wallaba-tree of Guiana. 1862 List Contrib. fr. B. Guiana to Lond. Exhib. in Veness El Dorado (1866) App. 122 Wallaba Oil. Ibid. 137 Wallaba...Used for house-frames, shingles, staves, palings, and posts. Yields an oil and gum resin having medicinal properties. 1871 Kingsley At Last vii, I passed the great Australian Blue-Gum which overhangs the road, and the Wallaba-tree.

Wallaby (wǫ·labi). Also -bi(e, -bee, walloby, whallabee. Pl. **wallabies**, †-bys. [Native Australian: spelt *wal-li-bah* by D. Collins *Acc. Eng. Colony N.S. Wales* 614, 1798. Morris suggests derivation from *walla* to leap.]

1. A kangaroo belonging to any of the small species of the genus *Macropus*, formerly grouped as the sub-genus *Halmaturus*, or of the genera *Onychogale* ('Nail-tailed Wallaby'), *Petrogale* ('Rock Wallaby'), *Lagorchestes* ('Hare Wallaby') and *Lagostrophus* ('Banded Wallaby'). All the species are confined to Australia and the neighbouring islands.

The sing. form is used in sporting language as collective plural.

1828 P. Cunningham N.S. Wales (ed. 3) I. 289 The wallabee and paddymalla grow to about sixty pounds each. 1830 R. Dawson Pres. State Australia iii. (1831) 111 A species of small kangaroo..which the natives call the 'Walloby'. 1832 Bischoff Van Diemen's Land II. 25 We.. wallabee is not very common. 1843 J. E. Gray List Specim. Mammalia Brit. Mus. 89 The Whallabee. Halmaturus Ualabatus [etc.]. 1845 J. O. Balfour Sk. N. S. Wales 25 The wallaby, or rock kangaroo, is of a dark-grey colour [etc.]. Ibid., The wallabys are to be seen only on the hottest days. 1846 J. L. Stokes Discov. in Australia I. ix. 267 The Wallaby are numerous on this part of the island [Tasmania]. 1860 G. Bennett Gather. Naturalist xiv. 286 A species of Wallaby Kangaroo was found about the rocky ranges at the Nepean. 1867 W. Richardson Tasmanian Poems 18 Go to the country a week to shoot wallaby. 1884 'R. Boldrewood' Melbourne Mem. iii. 24 Violet was so fast that she could catch the brush kangaroo (the wallaby) within sight. 1893 Mrs. C. Praed Outlaw & Lawmaker II. 35 The scared rock wallabies darted out of their holes.

2. *On the wallaby track*, hence shortened *on the wallaby*: on tramp; wandering about on foot, whether in search of work or aimlessly as a vagrant.

1869 Marcus Clarke Peripatetic Philosopher 41 (Morris) An old bush ditty, which I have heard sung when I was on the 'Wallaby'. 1890 'R. Boldrewood' Col. Reformer ix, What is the meaning of 'out on the wallaby'?..It's bush slang, sir, for men just as you or I might be now, looking for work or something to eat. Ibid. xxvii, He wanted a summer on the wallaby track to open his mind. 1896 Kipling Seven Seas, Lost Legion ii, And some of us hunt on the Oil Coast, And some on—the Wallaby track.

3. *attrib.*, as in *wallaby skin, tail*; **wallaby (-proof) fence**, a fence intended to keep out wallabies; **wallaby-grass**, an Australian grass, *Danthonia penicillata*.

1852 Mundy Antipodes ii. 43, I found myself..swallowing with relish, a plate of wallabi-tail soup. 1881 Gentl. Mag. Jan. 56 A portion of this station was fenced with wallaby-proof fence—a high, close paling, reminding one of an English park. 1890 Melbourne Argus 13 June 6/2 A wallaby-skin rug. 1897 Outing XXX. 138/2 Down the wallaby fence..the emus turned at a hurricane gait.

Wallace, variant of Wallis.

Wallach, Wallachian: see Walach, -ian.

Walladay, obs. form of Welladay.

Wallah (wǫ·lă). *Anglo-Indian.* Also wal(l)a, wollah. [a. Hindī *-wālā*, a suffix, forming adjs. with the sense 'pertaining to or connected with' what is denoted by the sb.; hence forming sbs., as in *nāo-wālā* boatman, *Dillī-wālā* inhabitant of Delhi. The suffix in this function may be compared to -er[1]; Europeans have commonly apprehended it as a sb. equivalent to 'man', 'fellow'.]

a. In certain Hindī or Hindustānī words adopted in Anglo-Indian use or cited in popular Anglo-Indian spelling, as *Agra wallah*, native of Agra, *banghy-wallah*, a porter who carries loads with a *banghy* or shoulder-yoke, *howdah-wallah*, an elephant accustomed to carry a howdah, *jungle-wallah*, man of the jungle. See also Lootie-wallah, Punkah-*wallah*, Topi-wallah.

Mrs. Sherwood's purdah-walla (see Purdah 3), applied to a woman, is a misuse.

1776 Trial Nundocomar 25/1 They were both Agra Walla's ..by Agra, I mean the place he came from. 1810 T. Williamson E. India Vade-M. I. 325 The bangy-wollah, that is, the bearer who carries the bangy. 1826 Galt Last of Lairds xvi. 146 The murderous old decoit and his Junglewallah of a servant. 1863 Trevelyan Compet. Wallah v. (1864) 113 My suite comprised sixteen bearers,..and four banghy-wallahs. Ibid. vi. 176 Strange stories these old howdah-wallahs could tell us, if they had the gift of speech!

b. Used as sb. with Eng. word prefixed attrib., in imitation of native derivatives with the suffix, as in *box-wallah* (Box *sb.*[2] 24), *competition wallah* (Competition 3).

1785 in Seton-Karr Sel. Calcutta Gaz. (1864) I. 93 A band of good Patriot-wallahs. 1834 [A. Prinsep] Baboo II. iii. 55 (Stanf.) These chits of 90, 50, and 200 rupees to box-walas from Mrs. Title. 1853 W. D. Arnold Oakfield I. 66 'Were you ever in the Lakes?' 'No, I'm a Suffolk walla.' 1894 Mrs. Dyan Man's Keeping (1899) 195 'The Inseparables' ..came in to superintend his toilet, accompanied by a ready-made clothes wallah and a barber. 1917 Blackw. Mag. Sept. 299/1 Now, those fellows..those big-ship wallahs —they're only just beginning to take Us seriously.

c. Short for *competition-wallah*.

1863 Trevelyan Compet. Wallah i. (1864) 9 Stories against the Competition Wallahs,..are told...For instance: Story showing the Pride of Wallahs.—A Wallah being invited to dinner by a Member of Council, went out before the whole company. 1872 'Aliph Cheem' (Yeldham) Lays of Ind (1876) 142 Each unemployed wallah so surely applies To be kindly allowed in that Station to stay, Doing his nothing, and drawing his pay. 1911 Sir W. F. Butler Autob. iii. 45 M. sleeps. Enter the wallahs and servants.

†**Wa·lland**, *a. dial. Obs.* [Of obscure origin. The E.Anglian glossary is prob. correct in reading *walland* as one word, not *wall and* as printed in Bloomfield's poem. Cf. the Yorkshire *wallband whip*, 'a whip of plaited leather thongs' (*Eng. Dial. Dict.*).]

(See quot. 1895.)

1802 Bloomfield Rur. Tales, Richard & Kate 29 She straight slipp'd off the Wall and Band. 1895 E. Angl. Gloss. (citing Rev. E. S. Taylor), Walland band, the leather used in spinning.

Wallaroo (wǫ·lărū). Also 9 wallooroo, wolloroo (see Morris *Austral Engl.*), walluru. [Native Australian *wolarū*: cf. Wallaby.] A large species of kangaroo, *Macropus robustus*; in Queensland and New South Wales applied chiefly to the black variety. Also *wallaroo kangaroo.*

1827 P. Cunningham Two Years N.S.W. I. xvii. 309 The wallaroo, of a blackish colour, with coarse shaggy fur, inhabiting the hills. 1845 J. O. Balfour Sk. N.S. Wales 25 The wallaroo kangaroo is of a darkish red colour, and weighs about 60 lbs. 1847 Leichhardt Jrnl. xiii. 458 He had been guided by a beaten track of Wallurus. 1890 'R. Boldrewood' Miner's Right v, The southern forest where ..the forester kangaroo and the wallaroo alone run.

Wallat, obs. variant of Wallet.

Wallaway, obs. form of Wellaway.

[**Wall-can**: perh. a misprint for **walk-can*: cf. *walk-pin*, Walk *v.*[2] 3.

1688 Holme Armoury III. 386/1 An Hatters Wall-Can,.. a Can by which the Felt-maker bears his Liquor from the Furnace to the Bench.]

Walle: see Wale *sb.*[1], *a.*, *v.*[1], Well.

Walle, obs. Sc. variant of Valley.

c 1420 Wyntoun Cron. I. 73 In þe feild of Damask faire.. Or in a walle of Ebron.

†**Walled**, *a. Obs.* [f. Wall *sb.*[3] + -ed[2]. Cf. Wall *v.*[4]] Of a horse's eye: Affected with 'wall-eye'.

1577–8 in W. H. Turner Select. Rec. Oxford (1880) 396 One grey trotting curtoll mare, crapped on the further yeare, and the neare ie walled. 1672 Lond. Gaz. No. 713/4 A dapple gray Gelding, near 15 hands high, both eies walled. 1705 Ibid. No. 4182/4 A brown bay Mare,..one walled Eye, the other about half walled.

Walled (wǫld), *ppl. a.* [f. Wall *v.*[2] + -ed[1].]

1. Furnished with or as with a wall, enclosed with a wall. Of a town, etc.: Surrounded or protected with fortifications. Of a well, cistern, pond, the sides of a cavity, etc.: Lined or faced with masonry.

c 1000 Ags. Ps. (Spelm.) xxx. 27 [22] On ceastre ȝeweal-ledre [Vulg. in civitate munita]. 13.. K. Alis. 6068 They haden wallid cite townes, In dalis, and eke in downes. 1450–1530 Myrr. our Ladye II. 72 Cytyes and Castelles and walled townes. 1591 Shaks. 1 Hen. VI, III. iv. 7 Twelue Cities, and seuen walled Townes of strength. 1605 — Lear V. iii. 18 And wee'l weare out In a wall'd prison, packs and sects of great ones. 1671 Milton P. R. II. 22 Each Town or City wall'd On this side the broad lake Genezaret. 1756–7 tr. Keysler's Trav. (1760) I. 191 On one side of this cathedral is a walled terrass. 1789 Ir. Act 29 Geo. III, c. 33 § 25 Walled deer-parks, and planted avenues excepted. 1819 W. S. Rose Lett. N. Italy II. 85 note, Oblong pieces of walled ground, planted with fruit-trees. 1839 Ure Dict. Arts, etc. 820 [These] have led to the contrivance of surrounding the area on which the roasting takes place with three little walls or with four...This is what is called a walled area. 1869 Tozer Highl. Turkey I. 376 A walled Bulgarian village. 1880 C. R. Markham Peruv. Bark 130 A succession of..terraced gardens...Their walled sides are thickly clothed with Calceolarias, Celsias [etc.]. 1895 Outing XXVII. 237/2 Neptune's Grotto is an enchanting, walled fish-pond. *fig.* 1907 Raleigh Shakespeare 201 Bereavement or crime breaking in upon the walled serenity of daily life.

b. with qualifying word prefixed.

c 1400 Maundev. (Roxb.) vii. 24 Þe whilk es a strang citee and a wele walled. 1871 W. Morris in Mackail Life (1899) I. 267 A great double-walled dyke. 1901 C. Holland Mousmé 18 Our little fragile-walled house on the hillside at Nagasaki.

2. With advs. a. *Walled-up*, closed or blocked up with masonry.

1826 Cobbett Rur. Rides (1885) II. 118 A..large walled-in garden. 1886 Willis & Clark Cambridge I. 219 The third chamber has another old walled-up window. 1903 F. W. H. Myers Human Personality 103 Like wine found in a walled up cellar. 1906 C. Bigg Wayside Sk. Eccl. Hist. i. 12 In front of the church was a walled-in court.

b. *Walled-in, -up*, entombed in a wall.

1837 Carlyle Fr. Rev. I. v. ix, Crowds..gaze on the skeletons found walled-up. 1903 Daily Chron. 11 Feb. 3/6 The remains of a walled-in nun were discovered.

3. *Anat.* and *Zool.* Furnished with a 'wall' or investing structure: chiefly in parasynthetic formations. Also *walled-off*, separated by a 'wall'.

1875 Huxley & Martin Elem. Biol. (1877) 201 The atrium: thin-walled, rounded, lies on the dorsal aspect of the truncus and ventricle. 1890 Retrospect Med. CII. 362 It was a smooth walled cavity,..about the size of a small marble. 1906 Brit. Med. Jrnl. 13 Jan. 70 A small walled-off pocket of pus.

4. Of the nature of a wall, made of stone-work.

1805 R. W. Dickson Pract. Agric. I. 115 Where stones can be easily procured,..walled fences may be preferable.

Waller[1] (wǫ·lə̆ɹ). [f. Wall *v.*[2] + -er[1].] One who builds walls (see quot. 1908).

c 1440 Promp. Parv. 514/1 Wallare, murator, machio. Wallare, þat werkythe wythe stone and morter, cementarius. 1513 Douglas Æneis I. i. 12 Fra quhame..Come..the valleris of greit Rome. c 1565 in 14th Rep. Hist. MSS. Comm. App. III. 30 Four masones and viij wallaris: viij quariouris. 1612 N. Riding Rec. (1884) I. 253 Oswald Collyson waller or rough mason. 1683 Churchw. Acc. Pittington, etc. (Surtees) 341 To the wallers for work and plastering, 1 l. 2 s. 1890 Lincoln Gaz. 30 Aug. 4/1 Choppers, Wallers, and Masons for Ancaster Stone Wanted. 1908 Remin. Stonemason 89 He himself was what is called a 'waller'—that is, he did not dress stones, but set them on the walls when dressed, or else built walls of rough, unhewn stone.

Waller[2] (wǫ·lə̆ɹ). [f. Wall *v.*[1] + -er[1].] In the Cheshire salt-works, a brine-boiler, a worker who attends to the salt-pans. Also *lead-waller* (cf. *lead-walling*, Lead *sb.*[1] 12).

1600 Camden Brit. (ed. 5) 543 Et muliercule (Wallers vocant) rastellis ligneis é fundo salem educunt. 1886 Cheshire Gloss., Lead-wallers, commonly abbreviated to Wallers. Waller, a salt-maker or boiler. At present the men call boilers those who make stoved and butter-salt, and the others wallers. 1892 Labour Commission Gloss., Waller, a local term, applied to salt boilers, i.e., those who look after the boiling of the salt. It is applied to the men who look after the making of any white salt, whether the pan is required to boil or not.

Waller[3] (wǫ·lə̆ɹ). [f. Wall *sb.*[1] + -er[1].]

1. A wall-tree.

1688 Holme Armoury II. 87/1 Wall-Trees, called Wallers, are such as are planted at Wall sides, and are pinned up to the Wall.

†2. A 'keeper of the walls'. Hence **Wallership**. *Obs.*

1578 in Househ. Ord. (1790) 264 Keeper of the Walles, alias wallership; fee 2 s. 4 d.

3. (See quots.)

1904 Daily Chron. 15 Apr. 8/2 'Wallers'..are men who find casual employment as law-writers, and have been facetiously christened 'wallers', because they are generally to be found lounging against a wall in Cursitor-street waiting on an engagement. 1908 Ibid. 3 July 6/7 'Waller', as applied to a man who does law writing...They were called 'wallers', as a term of contempt, by the regular writers.

Wallerian (wǫlī°·riăn), *a. Phys.* [f. the name of A. V. *Waller* (1816–70) + -ian.] Of or pertaining to Waller, or to the kind of degeneration of tissue discovered by him.

1877 M. Foster Physiol. III. i. (1878) 392 This method of diagnosis is often spoken of as the Wallerian method, after A. Waller. 1897 Allbutt's Syst. Med. II. 863 The part of the nerve-fibre between the rupture and the muscle now undergoes Wallerian degeneration. 1899 Ibid. VI. 492 The more active or Wallerian degeneration ensues. Ibid. 495 The operation of the Wallerian law.

Wallet (wǫ·lĕt). Also 4–6 walet, 5 wallett(e, 6 walett, wallyt, 6, 7, 9 *dial.* wallat. [Of obscure origin; the stress *wale·t* (beside *wa·let*) in Chaucer is unfavourable to the current theory that the word is a metathesis of *watel* Wattle *sb.*

Possibly a. OF. or AF. *walet, which might be derived from Teut. *wall- to go on pilgrimage (Wall v.[3]) or *wall- to roll up (see under Wall v.[4])]

1. A bag for holding provisions, clothing, books, etc., esp. on a journey either on foot or on horseback; a pilgrim's scrip, a knapsack, a pedlar's pack, or the like.

c 1386 Chaucer Prol. 681 But hood, for Iolitee, wered he noon, For it was trussed vp in his walet [rhyme let]. Ibid. 686 His walet [lay] biforn hym in his lappe, Bret ful of pardon comen from Rome al hoot. 1387–8 T. Usk Test. Love I. i. (Skeat) 106 Yet have I ensample to gadere the smale crommes, and fullen my walet of tho that fallen from the borde among the smale houndes. c 1440 Promp. Parv. 514/1 Walette, seek, or poke, sistarcia. 1506–7 Acc. Ld. High Treas. Scot. III. 372 Item, for ane wallat to John of Bute xij d. 1514 A. Barclay Eglogue iv. 9 Within his wallet were meates good and fine. 1523–34 Fitzherb. Husb. § 141 Take hede..what maner of people resorte and comme to thy house ..and specially if they brynge with them..bottelles, bagges, wallettes, or busshell-pokes. a 1529 Skelton E. Rummyng 461 Another brought two goslynges..She brought them in a wallet. 1535 Coverdale Judith xiii. 10 She..delyuered the head of Holofernes vnto hir mayden, and bad hir put it in hir walett [Gr. εἰς τὴν πήραν τῶν βρωμάτων αὐτῆς, Vulg. in peram suam]. 1577 B. Googe Heresbach's Husb. I. 11 b, Husbandry necessaries..the smaller sort be these..Sacks, Wallets, Bottels, [etc.]. 1609 Dekker Guls Horne-bk. I. 7 Neither..the Switzers blistred Cod-peece, nor the Danish sleeue, sagging downe like a Welsh wallet. 1617 Churchw. Acc. Pittington etc. (Surtees) 292 For makinge of a wallet to put the challenc and a bottle in, 1 d. 1622 R. Hawkins Voy. S. Seas xxvii. 62 Their Childe they carry in a Wallet about their necke, ordinarily vnder one arme, because it may sucke when it will. c 1670 in 10th Rep. Hist. MSS. Comm. App. I. 39 A wallet to cari books. 1712 Spectator No. 289 ¶ 9 Having looked about him for some time, he [a Dervise] enter'd into a long Gallery, where he laid down his Wallet, and spread his Carpet, in order to repose himself upon it. a 1721 Prior Cupid turned Plowman 2 A rustic wallet o'er his shoulders ty'd. 1760–2 Goldsm. Cit. W. lxii, With her scanty wardrobe packed up in a wallet, she set out on her journey on foot. 1791 A. Wilson Pack Poet. Wks. 1876 II. 30 My pond'rous Pack apo' the ground I carelessly had flung; A wallet green, wi straps fast bound. 1840 Dickens Old C. Shop xii, The old man had forgotten a kind of wallet which contained the light burden he had to carry. 1859 Thackeray Virgin. lxii, I have heard he came up to London himself as a young man with only his tragedy in his wallet. 1904 Bridges Demeter 592 Approach him with a gift: this little wallet. (Giving a little bag of seeds.) 1914 Miss. Rec. U. F. Ch. Jan. 3/2 The Highlands, where there is no more welcome visitor than the colporteur with his wallet of healthy and inspiring literature.

Proverb, *To brew in a bottle and bake in a wallet*: ? to attempt enterprises beyond one's means.

c 1540 Boorde Bk. for to Lerne B iv, These men the whiche doo brewe in a botell and bake in a walet.

b. *spec.* A bag having the opening in the middle and a receptacle at each end.

Some of the instances above may belong to this specific sense. The wallet 'with two pouches in it' was prob. originally slung across the horse, or over the shoulder of the pedestrian.

1528, 1638 [see 1 c]. 1674 Jackson's Recant. A 4 b, Being thus early up, I timely met with a long Purse lying neglected in the Street, whose entrance was on the middle like a Wallat. 1706 Phillips (ed. Kersey), Wallet, a kind of Bag with two Pouches to it. 1880 Jefferies Gt. Estate 141 The wallet is almost unknown even in farmsteads now: it is a kind of long bag closed at each end, but with a slit in the centre for the insertion of things. 1886 Cheshire Gloss., Wallet or Wally,..As a batting term it is a workbag with the entrance in the centre and made up at each end.

c. *fig.*

The fable here alluded to (Phædrus IV. x) says that Jupiter gave to every man two bags, one of which, containing his own faults, hangs at his back, and the other, containing those of his fellows, hangs at his breast.

1528 More Dyaloge III. Wks. 233/1 If we wold once tourne oure wallette..and the bagge with other folkes faultes cast at oure backe, and caste the bagge that bereth our own faultes ..before vs at our brest. 1570 B. Googe Popish Kingd. IV. 60 But sure the wallet them beguiles, that hanges behinde their backe, And better others faultes they see, than what themselues doe lacke. 1589 Cooper Admonit. (Arb.) 18 They looke not into their owne doings: they cast that end of the wallet behinde them, wherein their owne faultes are wrapped. 1638 Sanderson Serm. (1681) II. 118 Neither of both..were willing enough to look into the other end of the wallet, and to examine throughly their own spirits.

d. A beggar's bag. †Phrases, *to bear the wallet*, to be a beggar. [= Fr. *porter la besace.*]

1546 Supplic. Poore Commons (E.E.T.S.) 19 Bringing them vp other to bear wallettes, other els, if thei be sturdy, to stuffe prisons. 1561 B. Googe tr. Palingenius' Zodiac V. N vj, And se thy goodes they not decrease but may augmented be, Least in thy age the wallet come. 1608 Dekker Belman Lond. Wks. (Grosart) III. 85 Thou art likewise to Giue way to any of vs that haue borne all the Offices of the Wallet before thee. 1612 T. Taylor Comm. Titus ii. 6 (1619) 405 Needs must be beare a wallet, and die a beggar. 1622 Bacon To King Wks. 1874 XIX. 386 Pity me so far, as I that have borne a bag be not now in my age forced in effect to bear a wallet. 1654 Gataker Disc. Apol. 30 Without House or Land, or so much as a Wallet to go a begging with. 1665 Surv. Affaires of Netherlands 33 They coyned Meddals with the Kings Picture, on the one hand a Wallet, and a Dish on the other, with this Inscription, Faithful to God and the King, even to bear the Wallet. 1790 Cowper Odyss. XVII. 237 So saying, his tatter'd wallet o'er his back He cast. 1832 Ht. Martineau Hill & Valley ix. 135 Without a crust in my wallet, as beggars usually have. 1836 [Hooton] Bilberry Thurland I. vi. 124 Their appetites were now recovered, and the contributions of their collected wallets were found insufficient for the whole. 1879 Maclear Celts viii. 125 Itinerant beggars, who went about with wallets, were not regarded with favour. *fig.* 1606 Shaks. Tr. & Cr. III. iii. 145 Time hath (my lorde) a wallet at his backe Wherein he puts almes for obliuion.

e. A lawyer's bag. ? *Obs.*

1645 Milton Colast. 17 A meer and arrant petti-fogger, who lately was so bardy, as to lay aside his buckram wallet, and make himself a fool in Print.

f. *Her.* (See quot.)

c 1828 Berry Encycl. Herald. I. Gloss., Wallet, a scrip, or pilgrim's pouch.

†2. *transf.* Something (in an animal's body) protuberant and swagging. Cf. Wattle *sb.*[2] *Obs.*

1610 Shaks. Temp. III. iii. 46 Who would believe that there were Mountayneeres, Dew-lapt, like Buls, whose throats had hanging at 'em Wallets of flesh? 1698 Phil. Trans. XX. 137 Since the great Bulk or Wallet of these Intestines must incline and swag towards the Diaphragm.

3. A flat bag, usually of leather, closed by a flap fastened with a button or clasp, or secured by a band. Orig. *U.S.*

a. A pocket-book for holding paper money without folding, or documents.

1845 N. P. Willis Dashes at Life II. 245 Our several borrowings were thrust into a wallet which was sometimes in his pocket, and sometimes in mine, as each took the turn to be paymaster. 1854 Webster, Wallet,..also, a pocket-book or place for keeping money about one's person. 1884 Advt., Thin Pocket Diary, for Wallet. 1888 Cassell [as 'American']. 1913 Daily News 1 Nov. 7 The plaintiff, a diamond merchant, was carrying a wallet containing £370 in bank-notes, brilliants value £320, two necklaces.., a diamond pendant cluster, [etc.]. 1914 Ibid. 29 Jan. 2 He put his hand in his pocket and pulled out a leather dollar wallet and examined its contents.

b. A cyclist's tool-bag.

1887 Visct. Bury & Hillier Cycling 432 The wallet, or tool-bag, is generally supplied with the machine.

c. 'A small kit carried by anglers,' containing 'thread and needles, awl, waxed ends, .. a pair of small pliers, a file, etc.' (*Cent. Dict.*). ? *U.S.*

4. *attrib.* and *Comb.* as *wallet-bearer, book*; †*wallet-ways* adv.; **wallet envelope**, an envelope with a broad flap like that of a wallet.

1611 Cotgr., Besacier, the bag-bearer, or wallet-bearer of a begging, or beggarly companie. 1654 Gayton Pleas. Notes III. i. 69 You may perchance thinke it improper to behold me upon thy asse hanging Wallet-wayes. 1823 Gillies Aristotle's Rhet. III. ii. 372 In this way Iphicrates insulted Callias, by calling him the wallet-bearer of the goddess, instead of her torch-bearer. 1863 J. C. Bruce (title), The Wallet-book of the Roman Wall.

Walleteer (wǫlĕtī°·ɹ). *rare*[−1]. [f. Wallet + -eer.] One who carries a wallet.

1778 Tollet in Shaks. Wks. V. 428 At his girdle hangs a wallet for the reception of provision, the only revenue of the mendicant orders of religious; who were named Walleteers or budget-bearers.

Wallett, obs. Sc. form of Valet.

Wall eye, wall-eye (wǫ·lˌəi·, wǫ·lˌəi). Also 6 walowe yee, whal eie, 7 whall, waled eye. [Back-formation from Wall-eyed *a.* In sense 1 pronounced with level stress, the first element being apprehended as an adj.]

1. An eye the iris of which is whitish, streaked, particoloured, or different in hue from the other eye, or which has a divergent squint. (See Wall-eyed *a.* 1.) a. in human beings.

1526 Hundred Merry Tales (1866) 91, I haue a wall eye in

Wall-eyed

Wall-eyed (wǭ̧l‚aid), a. Forms c. 4 wawil-wangle-, 6 whawl-y, 7 whake-, 6-7 wall-y, 8 wawgh-eyd, 7- **Wall-eyed**.

† Wall-fair. Obs. In 1 walfair. [f. WALL sb.[1] + FAIR a.] — WALLFLOWER.

Wallflower (wǭ̧l‚flouǝr). [f. WALL sb.[1] + FLOWER.]

† German wallflower. Obs.

† Wa·lling, ppl. a.[2] Obs. [f. WALL v.[2] + -ING[2].]

4. attrib. in designations of colour, as *wallflower-brown, -red*; also separately as a colour-name.

† Wall-hot, a. Obs. [f. WALL a. + HOT a.]

Wa·lling, vbl. sb.[2] [f. WALL v.[2] + -ING[2].]

Wa·lling, ppl. a.[1] [f. WALL v.[1] + -ING[2].]

Wallis, var. Now dial. also wallace.

Wallis, Sc. form of VALISE.

Wallish-bill, variant of WELSH-BILL. Obs.

Wall-knot, variant of WALE-KNOT (wǭ̧l‚knŏt).

Wall·less (wǭ̧l‚les), a. [f. WALL sb.[1] + -LESS.] Having no wall.

Walloon (wǎlū·n), sb. and a. Also 6 Vallon, 8 Wallon, 6- Wallon. [a. F. *Wallon* (fem. *Wallonne*), sb. and a. — med.L. *Wallōn-em*, f. Teut. **walh*, foreigner (OE. *wealh*): cf. WELSH a.

B. adj. Pertaining to the Walloons.

Wallop (wǎ·lǫp), sb.[1] Also 5 valop, 6 walop, 6 wallope, 9 wallup, w(h)ollop, etc. [f. WALLOP v.[1]]

† Wallop, sb.[2] Obs. [f. WALLOP v.[2]]

† 1. A horse's gallop. Only adv. phr. (tr. or imitations of French) *(to ride, go, etc.) + a wallop*; *† a* (at the) *great wallop*, in full gallop. Obs.

† 2. The series of noisy bubbling motions made by water, etc. rapidly boiling, or approaching boiling point. Usually in phr. *to boil (seethe) a wallop, a full wallop*: to boil with a rapid noisy bubbling, to galopy. Obs. Cf. WALE sb.[3]

Wall·op, v.[1]

Walloper (wǎ·lǫpǝr), sb. [f. WALLOP v.[1] + -ER[1].]

Walloping (wǎ·lǫpiŋ), vbl. sb. [f. WALLOP v.[1] + -ING[1].]

Walloping, ppl. a. [f. WALLOP v.[1] + -ING[2].]

Wallow (wǒ·lou), sb. In 6 *walow*. [f. WALLOW v.[1]]

Wallow (wǒ·lou), v.[1] Forms: 1 *wealwian, weal(o)wian*, 3 *woelewe*, 3-5 *walewe, walwe*, 6 *walowe*, 4- *wallow*. [OE. *wealwian*]

Wallow (wǒ·lou), v.[2] Forms: 1 *wealwian, weal(o)wian*, 3-4 *walwen*, 4-6 *walowe(n*, 6- *wallow*.

Wallowish (wǒ·louiʃ), a. Now dial.

Wa·llow-ware. Obs.

Wa·llowing, vbl. sb.

Wa·llowing, ppl. a.

Wallower (wǒ·louǝr), sb. [f. WALLOW v.[1] + -ER[1].]

Wa·ll-plat, dial. Also -plot, -plit. [f. WALL-PLATE.]

Wa·ll-plate, sb.

Wa·ll-piece. Obs.

Wa·ll-spring, sb.

Wa·ll-paper, sb.

Wa·llsend, sb.

Wallman, obs. form of WEALSMAN.

Wa·ll-stone. A stone for building.

Wa·ll-tiding, a. Obs. [f. WALL v.[1] + TIDE sb.]

Wallure, variant of WALLOP.

†Wallure. Obs. rare. [f. WALL sb. + -URE.] Walls collectively.

Wallurt, variant of WALLABOO.

Wallwort (wǭˈdwǫrt). Forms: 1 walh-, weal-, wal-, welewyrt, vealwyrt, 3, 6 walwurt, 4-7 walworte, 4-5 -wourte), 6 walwrote, -woort, (wolworte, walwoort), 4 welleuuort, walle- wort. [OE. weal-, wealh-wyrt, f. WALH, WEALH (a Celtic or Roman) foreigner, a 'Welshman' (see WELSH a.) + wyrt herb, plant, WORT sb.]

Walsh.

Walsh-nut.

† Walt, sb. Obs. 1 Beaten glory.

† Walt, v. Obs. Forms: walten, weltan.

Walter, obs. form of WALTER.

Walterer. Obs.

Walth, obs. form of WEALTH.

† Waltham. Obs. exc. Hist.

Walterot, Walth : see WALTER, WEALTH.

Waltonian.

Waltrot.

Waltz (wǭls, wǫlts), sb.

Waltz, v.

Waltzer (wǭlˈtsǫr).

Walty, obs. form of WAX sb.

Walwe, obs. form of VALUE.

Waly.

Wamara (wămără). [Native name.]

Wambais.

Wamble (wǫmˈbl), sb. Now dial.

Wamble (wǫmˈbl), v. Now dial.

Walrus (wǭˈlrŭs). Also 8 walruss, wallrass, 9-russes.

Walnut (wǭˈlnŭt). Forms: 1 walhhnutu, 4-6 walnote, 5 wallnott, 5, 6 walnutte, (6-8 wall-nutt), 7 walenote, 7-8 walnut, (6-8 knutte str. fen.—WFris. walnôt, OE. walh-hnutu from Da.).

Walnut-tree.

Walm, sb.

Walm, v.

Walming, vbl. sb.

Walnut [2], Naut.

Walsh, a. and sb.

Walt, sb. Obs.

Walt, v. Obs.

WAMBLING.

b. Of things: To totter, waver; to move unsteadily, stagger, reel.

Wambly, a. dial. Also wambley, wombly. 1. Affected with nausea.

2. Causing nausea.

3. Shaky, tottering, unsteady.

Hence **Wambliness**.

Wambrace, -brass, -bras *var.* VAMBRACE.

Wambutose, -tow *(q. v.)*.

Wambus, *variant of* WAMBAIS.

Wameloweke, *variant of* WOMBLOUCT *Obs.*

Wame *(wǫm)*, *Sc. and north.* Forms: 5–6 wayms, 6 weyme, 6–7 weame, 6 waymb, wamb; 7 weamb, 7–8 wem, wemb, 8 weame, weeme, wame, 9 wame, wean. For mod. dial. forms see *Eng. Dial. Dict.* [Northern form of WOMB *sb.*]

1. The belly, abdomen: = WOMB *in obsolete senses.*

Wamble *(wǫm'b'l)*, *v. dial.* Also wamble, wommle. [f. WAMBLE *sb.* or *v.* + -L.¹]

Wameful *(wē'mful)*, *Sc.* [f. WAME + -FUL.] Cf. wombful (Trevisa).] = BELLY-FUL.

Wamel, *variant of* WAMBLE, WAYMENT.

Wame-tow *north.* Forms: 4 wambtoue, 5–tow, 4 wamb(e towe, waimto, wamtow, 4 wamtowe, -5 wamtowes. [f. WAME (Tow *sb.³*)] A girth or belly-band for a horse.

Wamfle, *v. Sc.* [? Phonetically symbolic : cf. WAMPISH and WAMBLE *v.*, *v.* b.] *intr.* To go about with flapping garments (? of garments), to flap, flutter (in the wind).

60

Hic *ahowe*, a wame. 1500–20 DUNBAR *Poems* xxvi. 90 The fowll munsit Glutteny, Off wame vnsatiable and gredy.

Wamfler *(wǫ'mflǝr)*, *Sc.* ? *Obs.* Also 6 wamfier, -ar. [? f. WAMFLE *v.* + -ER.] ? A beau, gallant.

Wamfler, -ie ...

Wam-lock. *dial.* Also 5 wamloke, 6 wemloke, 8 wanloke, wemlock. [f. WAME + LOCK *sb.³*] A twisted or tangled lock of wool from under the belly of a sheep.

Wammel, -mle, obs. form of WAMBLE.

Wammill, -mle, obs. forms of WAMBLE.

Wammus, -mus *var.* WAMUS.

Wampam, Wampe, obs. forms of WAMPUM, VAMP.

Wampee *(wǫmpī')*. Also wahampee. *Sc.* Chinese *hwang-p'i (hwang yellow, p'i skin).*

1. The fruit of an Asiatic tree *Clausena Wampi*, also the tree itself.

b. *U.S.* = PICKEREL-WEED 2. [? A different word.]

Wampish, *v. Sc.* *intr.* To wave to and fro. *b. trans.* To wave or toss (one's arms) about. *c. intr.* To make waving movements (with the arms).

2. *transf.* The cavity, or the protuberant part of a thing : — BELLY *sb.* 11, 1 *c.*

Wampum *(wǫ'mpŏm)*. Also 7 wampam, 7–8 wampon, wampom, 8 wompom. [See WAMPUMPEAG. Cf. F. *wampum* (little Suppl.).]

1. Cylindrical beads made from the ends of shells rubbed down, polished, and threaded on strings, which were often combined to form bracelets, belts, collars, etc. *See* PEAG, ROANOKE, SEAWAN.

b. Serving as currency for the N. Amer. Indians both among themselves and in dealings with Europeans: also, in early colonial times, between Europeans for the payment of small amounts. See quot. 1843, and former quots. under WAMPUMPEAG.

Wamplate. Obs. 1 WHAME-PLATE *sb.* [a] A symmetrical plate on harness to be put below the belly of a horse.

4. The belly-piece of a fur-skin. *Obs. rare.*

5. *Comb.* wame-ill *(a)* an empty stomach affecting the stomach; *(b)* = STOMACH-ACHE.

Waned *(wēnd)*, *a.* [f. WANE + -ED 2: cf. WOXEN.] Having a belly (of a specified kind); in *comb. great-wamed*, *yellow-wamed*.

Wameful *(wē'mful)*.

Wamel, *variant of* WAMBLE, WAYMENT.

2. *Wom* an ornamental garments or jewellery.

WAMPUM.

1808 JAMIESON, To *wamfle*, to move like a tattermedallion; conveying the idea of one moving about, as to make his rags flap.

Wamfler *(wǫ'mflǝr)*, *Sc.* ? *Obs.*

Wampum.

WAMPUMPEAG.

shells found on the coasts of New England and Virginia, which are sawed out into beads of an oblong form...

c. Serving (as a material for writing) a mnemonic or symbolic purpose according to the arrangement of the beads, and so used in tribal messages, treaty-records, etc. among the N. Amer. Indians.

2. *transf.* Money; in *comb.* wampum-beads, belt, collar, etc. *See* WAMPUMPEAG.

3. *transf.* *(jocular).* Money.

Wampumpeag *(wǫ'mpʌmpīg)*. Now *rare.* Forms: a. 7 wampumpeage, -peage, -peag, -peak, wampum peage, wampumpeage, -peak, wampampeage, 7 wamponeage, wampompeague, 9 wampumpeag. β. 7 wompompeag, 9 wampumpeg...

[Adopted (in 16–17th c.) from the Northerly dialects of the Algonkin language.]

WAN.

a Shell Fish; whose Shell has the tincture of Pearl colour, and the Indians make it into Wampam Pcag; which Shell is a staple Commodity. 1651 J. BACON'S Rebellion (1676) 2.

Wamtow, Wamtye, obs. ff. WAME-TOW.

Wanus *(wǫ'nǝs)*. *U.S.* also waunus, wammus. [a. Du. *wammes*, contracted f. *wambuis*, a. OF. *wambois*, -eis: see WAMBAIS, GAMBESON. Cf. G. *wams, waumus*, woollen jacket (MHG. *wambeis*), jacket worn under the armour.] In southern and western U.S., a stout jacket resembling a cardigan.

2. *transf.* or *fig.* Sad, dismal; also awful, fearful, deadly, cruel, wicked, etc. (Cf. uses of *dark, gloomy.*) *Obs.*

Wan *(wǫn)*, *sb.³ Sc. 6 pl.* wanis, wannys [Perh. a subst. use of WAN *a.¹* But cf. WAN.] A dark or livid mark produced by a blow; a bruise.

Wan, *obs. pa. t.* of WIN, contr. of WANT.

Wandale, *north. Obs.* Also 4 wandayle 7 -dill. [? Of obscure formation; perh. a derivative of DALE *sb.³*, the first element possibly WAND *sb.*] A portion of land.

WAN.

etc.: Faint, sickly, partially obscured. Also, of white objects, etc.: Dull, lustreless.

Wan *(wǫn)*, *a.* Inflected wanned, wanning.

+1. *intr.* To become dark, discoloured, or livid.

2. To beat (with a wand or switch.

Wandale. *Obs. rare⁻¹.*

Wander *(wǫ'ndǝr)*, *v.* Forms: 1 wandrian, 2–3 wandrien, wondrie(n, (wuandre), 3 wandri, 4 wandry, 4 wandir, 4–5, 7 wandyr, 4–6 wandur, 3–7 wandre, 4 wandir, wandur(e, 4–6 wandre, 5 wandyr, -yr, 4– wander. [OE. *wandrian*, frequent. related to *wendan* to WEND *v.*] = MDu. *wanderen* (Du. *wanderen*), MLG., LG. *wanderen*, G. *wandern* (whence Da. *vandre*, Sw. *vandra*).]

1. *intr.* To move hither and thither without fixed course or certain aim; to be (in motion) without control or direction; to roam, ramble, go idly or restlessly about.

Wanderer (wɒ'ndərə). Also 4 wanderrere, 5-6 wanderer, 6-7 wandrer, wand'rer.

Wandering (wɒ'ndəriŋ), vbl. sb. [-ING¹.]

Wandering (wɒ'ndəriŋ), ppl. a. [-ING².]

b. The Wandering Jew.

Wanderable, a. *nonce-word.* [f. WANDER v. + -ABLE.]

Wandered (wɒ'ndəd), ppl. a. [f. WANDER v. + -ED¹.]

Wanderingly, adv.

Wanderment. Obs. rare. [f. WANDER v. + -MENT.]

Wanderoo (wɒndərūˊ). Also 7-9 wanderow, 9 wandaru.

Wander-year. [f. WANDER v., after G. wanderjahr, the year, or one of the years, spent in travel for the purpose of perfecting one's skill and knowledge.]

Wandle (wɒ'nd'l), a. Sc. and north.

Wandle (wɒ'nd'l), v. dial. Also wannel.

Wandlessness, var. WANLASSOUR Obs.

Wandness, obs. form of WANNESS.

Wandoand, var. WANDOUND, a. Sc. pres. pple. of WIDROW v.

Wandsman. [f. WAND sb. + MAN sb.]

Wands, sb. pl. ? Obs.

Wandy, a.

Wandreth. Obs.

Wandsome, a.

Wandy (wɒ'ndi), a. [f. WAND sb. + -Y.]

Wane (wēn), sb.¹ Forms: 1 wana (wona, also won), 2 wane, 3-5 won, 4 wayn, 3-5 wan, 5 wone, 5-7 wayne, waine. [OE. wana (wona) wk. masc.]

Wane (wēn), v. Obs. Forms: 1 wana, 2-3 won, 3 wane, 4 won, woon. [part. wane; also wone. OE. wanian, wonian wk. vb., f. WANA sb.]

Wane (wēn), a. Obs. Forms: 1 wana, 3 wone, won.

Wane (wɐ̄n), v. Infected waned, waning.

Wane-cloud, a. Obs.

Wanewless, a. Obs.

Waneless, a. Obs.

Wanese, var. WANEL v. Obs.

Wanese, **Waned**, obs. Sc. ff. VANISHED, VAUNT.

Waneword, var. WAYWORTH.

Waney (wɐ̄ni), a. Also 7, 9 wanny, weyny, 9 wainy. [f. WANE sb.[1] + -Y[1].]

Wangle (wæ·ŋg'l), v.[1] [Perh. an altered form of WAGGLE v.]

Wang, var. WONG dial., field.

Wangala, variant of WANGUN.

Wangan, variant of WANGUN.

†Wangel, aphetic f. of EVANGEL. Sc. and north.

Wanglist: see WANGUN.

Wanger. Forms: 1 wongere, wangere, 4 wonger(e, wanger, 5-6 wonger, -ur = OHG. wanger, Goth. waggari, Goth. waggareis.

†Wanghee: see WHANGEE.

Wanhap. Sc. Obs. Also 6 van-. [f. WAN- + HAP sb.[1]] Misfortune.

†Wanhope. Now Hist. or arch. Also 3-4 wane-, 4 won-, 5 van-, 4-5 whan-, 5 wany-, 6-7 wanne-, 4 hop, 5 hoppe. [f. WAN- + HOPE sb.[1]]

Wanhye. Obs. rare. [f. WAN- + HUE sb.[1]]

Wanian, obs. form of WANION.

†Waniand. Obs.

Waning, vbl. sb.

Wanion (wæ·niˌən). Now arch. or dial. Forms: 6 waniam, wenyon, 6-7 wanion, wenian, -on, 6- wanion, wannion. An altered form of WANIAND.

Wanite, obs. Sc. f. VANITY.

Wankapin, **-kopin** (-ŏpin). U.S. Also wongopin (-ŏ́pin).

Wankle (wæ·ŋk'l), a. Obs. exc. dial. Forms: 1 wancol, 3 wankel, 4 -kyl, 4-5 -kill, 5, 7 wankle, wankle.

Wanmol, var. WAN + MOAL.

Wa·ning, ppl. a. [f. WANE v. + -ING[2].]

Wanless, var. WANDLE.

Wanly (wæ·nli), adv. Also 7 wanlye. [f. WAN a. + -LY[2].]

Wannel, var. WANDLE.

Wanness (wɒ·nes). Also 7 wan-, 5-6 wanness, 7 -NESS.

Wannish (wɒ·niʃ). Also 7 wanish. [f. WAN a. + -ISH[1].]

Wansome, a. Obs. [f. WAN- + SOME.]

Wanspeedy, a. Sc. Obs. [f. WAN- + SPEEDY a.]

Wanston, var. FONT-STONE Obs.

Wansum, var. WANSOME a. Obs.

Want (wɒnt), sb.[1] Dial. Forms: 1 wand, wond; 4-6 wonte, 7 wounte, 9 wont, wante.

Wannook, anglicized form of GUANACO.

†Wannow, int. Obs. rare.

†Wanny, a. Obs. [f. WAN a. + -Y[1].]

†Wanpa, Sc. var. VAMPEY. Obs.

Wanrede: see WANDRETH Obs. [f.]

†Wanrest. Sc. Obs. [f. WAN- + REST sb.[1]]

†Wanruly, a. Obs. [f. WAN- + RULY a.]

Wanshapen, a. Obs. Also wanshape.

Wansonsy, a. Sc. [f. WAN- + SONSY a. UNSONSY.]

†Wanspeed. Obs. [f. WAN- + SPEED sb.]

Wanton, obs. form of WAINSCOT.

Wanweird, Sc. form of WAINSCOT.

Want (wɒnt), sb.[2] Forms: 1 wand, wond; 2-6 wonte, 4-6 wonde, 5 wonte.

†Wanthrive, a. Obs. [f. WAN- + THRIVE.]

†Wanthriven, ppl. a. Obs. [f. WAN- + THRIVEN.]

†Wanton, a. Obs.

Wanze, var. WANSE v. Obs.

Warble, v.⁴ Obs. rare⁻¹. [Of obscure origin.] intr. ? To quarrel, wrangle. Hence **Warbling** vbl. sb. and ppl. a.

Warbled, a.² Obs. [f. WARBLE sb.²] Of hides: Injured by warbles.

1. Melodiously sung or sounded. Also, celebrated

Warbler. 1. One who, or something that, warbles or sings; a singer, songster.

b. In America: One of the small, usually brightcoloured, birds, with little power of song, of the family *Mniotiltidæ*.

c. In Australia and New Zealand: A bird of the genera *Cisticola*, *Malurus*, and others.

Warbling, vbl. sb.¹

Warblingly, adv.

Warbot, Obs. [f. Alteration of WARBLE sb.²]

Warbrece = WARBREST.

Wardcooling, Obs.

Warcraft.

Warling, ppl. a.² Obs. [f. WARBLE sb.³ + -ING.]

Warlot, Obs.

War-cry. [Cf. F. cri de guerre.] A cry

Warbling, vbl. sb.² Obs. [f. WARBLE sb.²]

Warbling, vbl. sb.³ Obs.

Warbling, ppl. a.³ [f. WARBLE v.³ + -ING.] In continual motion, quavering.

Ward, sb.¹ Forms: 1 weard, 4-5 warde, 4 Sc. ward, warth, 4 warde, 5-7 (now) word, 6-7 Sc. wairde, 4- ward. [OE. *weard*, fem. = MLG. *warde*, OHG. *warta* (MHG. *warte*, G. *warte*), ON. *varða* (Sw. *varda*), etc., f. OTeut. *wardo-*.]

I. Action of watching or guarding.

1. The action or function of a watchman, sentinel, or the like; observation for the purpose of discovering the approach of danger; look-out, watch.

b. Of discourse: ? Ineffectual. (Cf. WARBLE v.¹)

2. In name of birds, as the Warbling Flycatcher or Vireo, *Vireo gilvus*.

Wat-sling, ppl. a.³ [f. WARBLE v.³ + -ING.]

Warbot, Obs.

Ward, sb.² Also 7 Sc. wairde. Aphetic form of AWARD.

Ward, sb.³ [f. WARD v.¹ or WARE a.³ Cf. WARDED a.³]

Ward, v.¹ Forms: 1 weardian, -igan, 3 werdien, 3 wardie, 3-4 wardi, wardy (6, 7 Sc. warde), warth, 5-7 ward. [OE. *weardian* = OFris. *wardia*, OS. *wardon* (MDu. *waerden*, MLG. *warden*), OHG. *wartôn* — OTeut. *wardôjan*.]

1. trans. To guard, stand guard over; to keep in safety, take care of; to defend.

2. To defend, protect from. Now arch.

WARDEN. 90 WARDENRY. WARDENSHIP. 91 WARDING.

Warding (wǭ·diŋ), *ppl. a.* [f. WARD v.¹ + -ING³.] That wards or guards; protecting.

Wardless (wǭ·dles), *a.* [f. WARD sb. + -LESS.] That cannot be parried.

Wardlie, Wardly, obs. Sc. ff. WORDLY.

Wardman, Sc. [I. WARD + MAN sb.] Cf. WARDSMAN.]

Wardmote (wǭ·dmōt). Also 4-7 wardemote, (7 vordimote, wardmoot); (6 in combinations corruptly warmoll, warmail, warmoll). [f. WARD sb.¹ + MOTE sb.¹] A meeting of the citizens of a ward; esp. in the City of London.

Wardrape (wǭ·drēp). *see* WARDROBE.

Wardrober (wǭ·drō·bər). Obs. exc. Hist. Forms: 5 ward(e)ropere, Sc. wardropar, 5-7 wardrobere, (5 wardrope), 5-7 wardroper, -raipar, 5 wardrobar. [a. AF. wardrobier, dial. var. of garderobier, -rober, f. OF. garderobe: see prec.]

Wardship (wǭ·dship). [f. WARD sb.² + -SHIP.]
1. The office or position of guardian.
b. The guardianship of a minor; cf. in Feudal law, the guardianship and custody of the person and lands of a minor with all profits accruing during his minority.

Wardsman (wǭ·dzmän). *Obs.* [f. WARD sb.¹ (+ AWARD) + MAN sb.] An arbitrator.

Wardsman¹. *Obs.* [f. ward's genit. of WARD sb.¹ + MAN sb.] Cf. WARDMAN.]
1. In certain boroughs: A member of the governing body, consisting of representatives elected by the several wards.
2. An inmate appointed to supervise his ward in a prison or workhouse.
3. A watchman who is responsible for prisoners.

Ware (wɛə·), sb.¹ Sc. and dial. Forms: 1 waru, waur.

Ware (wɛə·), sb.² [OE. waru sb. = OFris. were, ware, OHG. wara (MHG. ware, war:)—OTeut. *warō.]

Ware (wɛə·), sb.⁴ [OE. wær.] Forms: 1-2 wær (wer), 4 waro, wayr (6 wuar), 6 waur, 4-8 ware.

Ware (wɛə·), a. Forms: 1-2 war (inflected ware), 1 war, 2-3 wær, 3 wær, 5 ware, 3-6 (7 war), 5 wore, 4-5 war, wor, 3-7 ware, 4-7 warre, (3-5 waar), 4-9 ware.

Ware, v. Obs. exc. dial.

Ware (headword continued), sb. and a.; var. **Wart** v.

Wareant, Sc. var. **Variant** a. (sense 3 b.)

Wareant-place. var. Sc. Stirling (1887) Any gowne of waraunt champit weaves; prive four li. xs.

Wareband. Obs. [f. **Ware** sb.1 + **Band** sb.1] A mill-stone, tacera.

Warsoorn: see **Ware** sb.1 b.

Wared, var. **Waried** a.

Waredly: see **Warily** adv.

Waredrop, obs. form of **Wardrobe**.

Wareful, a. [f. **Ware** sb.1 or v.1 + -ful.] Watchful, cautious.

Warefulness. Obs.

Warehouse (wɛ′ɹhous), sb. [f. **Ware** sb.1 + **House** sb. Cf. Du. warenhuis, G. warenhaus.]

1. A building or part of a building used for the storage of merchandise.

b. transf. and fig.

2. Ungeared, unconscious (of danger).

Warehousage: U.S. [f. **Warehouse** sb. or v. + -age.] The cost of warehousing.

Warehouseman (wɛ′ɹhousmən), wɛ′ɹtous-.

1. A man employed in or having the charge of a warehouse.

2. A wholesale merchant (esp. a trader in textile materials) who has a warehouse for the storing of goods.

Warehousing (wɛ′ɹhouziŋ), vbl. sb. [f. **Warehouse** v. + -ing1.] The depositing goods, etc. in a warehouse whether under bond or otherwise.

Wareless, a. Obs. Forms: 1 wærlēas, -lēs, 3 warelēs, 4 weorles, 6 -lesse. Cautionless; negligent.

Warely, adv. Obs. Forms: 1 wærlice, -lyce, 3-4 wareliche, -like, warli, (warly)the; also 3-4 warli, 6 -warliche. [OE. wǣrlice, f. wǣr **Ware** a.: see -ly2.]

Waren, obs. f. **Warren**, **Wherefore**.

Warene. Obs. [a. OF. wareinne (11th c. in Hatz.-Darm.) also 13th c. in F. garenne = Pr. warenda = Rom. WARREN.]

Wareng (wɛ′ɹɛŋg). Obs. exc. Hist.

Wareyed, ppl. a. Obs.

Warewolf, etc.: see **Werewolf**.

Warewyn, obs. form of **Warren**.

Warfare (wɔ′ɹfɛəɹ), sb. Forms: 4-6 warfare, 6-7 Sc. -fair; also 6 warefare. [f. **War** sb.3 + **Fare** sb.] A going to war (cf. b.); the action of carrying on, or engaging in, war; the act or state of conflict; military life or service.

Warfare (wɔ′ɹfɛəɹ), v. [f. prec. sb.] intr. To wage war; to take part in war; to serve in the field. Also fig.

Warfarer, a warrior. **Warfaring**, ppl. a.

Wari, var. **Wary** a. Obs., to curse.

Wariable, ave. Obs. [f. **Ware** v. + -able.] Deserving of cursing; execrable.

Wariable, -ance, -and: see **Variable**, **Variance**, **Varying**.

Warier. Obs. Also 4 -ere, 5 -iar, waryare, 6 wariour. [f. **Wary** v. + -er1.] One who curses.

Wariangle. Obs. Forms: 1? wearginael, 4-5 variangel, wero-, weryangle, wayryngle, 6-7 wariangle, -gill, 7 wireangle, werywangle, wierangle, wirangle; also 7 wearingle, wringle. [OE. wearignæl shrike.]

Warifie, v. Obs. (nonce-wd.) [f. **Wary** a. + -fy.] trans. To render wary or cautious.

Warily (wɛ′ɹili), adv. [f. **Wary** a. + -ly2.] In a wary manner, cautiously, warily.

Wariment. Obs. rarc-1. [f. **Wary** a. + -ment.] Precaution.

Warine. Obs. [a rendering of Buffon's *ouarine*, a misreading for *ouarine*, ad. Sp. *guariba* (h′ra).]

Wariness (wɛ′ɹines). [f. **Wary** a. + -ness.]

Waring, vbl. sb. Obs. exc. dial. Also 4 varinge, 5 waryinge, 6 varin, 6 wayring. [f. **Ware** v.2 + -ing1.]

Waring, obs. Sc. form of **Warland**.

Waristed. Obs. Forms: 1 wearig-, wearhbrædo, 6 warybredo, 8 wearh- = **Ware** sb.1 + **Bread** sb.

Warish, v. Obs. exc. Hist. Forms: 4-6 warisse, 6 warishe, -ysshe, var. **Warrish** sb. [a. OF. wariss-, variss-.]

Warisoun: see **Warrison**.

Wark (wɔɹk). Obs. exc. dial. Forms: 1 weorc, wærc, 3 werk, etc. Also 8 werk. [Of obscure origin.] Pain.

Wark (wɔɹk), sb. Obs. exc. Sc. and north. dial. Forms: 3 warch, 7 wark, 9 wark. [OE. weorc.] Work.

Warkfooted: see **Workmanly**.

Warland. Obs. exc. Hist. Forms: 3 warlond, 4 warelond, 6 warlonde, 5 Hist. (see **Ware** sb. + **Land** sb.)

Warless (wɔ′ɹles), a. In 1 werreles. [f. **War** sb.3 + -less.]

Warlike (wɔ′ɹlaik), a. and adv. Forms: 5 warlyke, etc. [f. **War** sb.3 + **Like** a.] 1. Of a person, nation, etc.: Naturally disposed or eager for fighting; skilled in war, martial; courageous in valiant; fond of war, bellicose.

vi. Wks. 1851 V. 584 The warlike tribes in North America. 1837 W. Irving *Capt. Bonneville* III. 200 Some trifling assistance from government, to protect them from the predatory and warlike tribes. 1837 Dickens *Pickw.* ii, Mr. Winkle retraced his steps..with the gloomy and dreadful resolve of accepting the challenge of the warlike Doctor Slammer.

b. Of actions, attributes, etc.: Martial, valiant.

1594 Kyd *Cornelia* iv. 188 And so let his warlike browes Still be deckt with Lawrel boughes. 1836 Thirlwall *Greece* xiii. II. 190 These exercises do not create and are not sufficient to keep alive the warlike spirit of a nation.

c. Of things: Martial in character.

c1470 Henry *Wallace* viii. 1021 Зeit thai within on lowd defyit Wallace, And trumpattis blew with mony werlik soun. 1595 Shaks. *John* ii. 242 For this downe-troden equity, we tread In warlike march, these greenes before your Towne. 1602 — *Ham.* v. ii. 360 What warlike noyse is this? 1667 Milton *P. L.* i. 531 At the warlike sound Of Trumpets loud and Clarions. 1811 Scott *Roderick* lvi, Then peals the warlike thunder of the drum.

d. Favouring or threatening war.

1915 *Nation* (N.Y.) 17 June 671/1 After his own outgivings he [Mr. Bryan] had the effrontery to blame the press for making people think the note would be warlike.

†**e.** *fig.* Of writings: = Polemic *a.* *nonce-use.*

a1603 T. Cartwright in *Presbyt. Rev.* (1888) Jan. 121 Ambrose and especially Austin in their warlike writinges as they are termed.

†**2.** Equipped for fighting or for war. *Obs.*

c1420 Wyntoun *Cron.* ix. xvi. 1704 Schir Henry, qwhat makis зow to be Sa wirlyk as now heyr we зow se? 1563 in Rymer *Foedera* (1719) XV. 631 With one Shippe..Marchantlike and not Warlike. 1591 Spenser *Virg. Gnat* 124 He, that..No deadly fight of warlick fleete doth feare. 1602 Shaks. *Ham.* iv. vi. 15 Ere we were two dayes old at Sea, a Pyrate of very Warlicke appointment gaue vs Chace. 1630 *R. Johnson's Kingd. & Commw.* 537 Monasteries, ancient and warlike, so built for feare of theeves and pyrats. 1697 Dryden *Virg. Georg.* iii. 285 If to the Warlike Steed thy Studies bend. 1711 in *10th Rep. Hist. MSS. Comm.* App. v. 124 They are..destitute of warlick ships and other vessells.

3. Of or pertaining to war.

1560 Daus tr. *Sleidane's Comm.* 78 b, The assemblie of the Empire..was in this warlyke preparation. 1573 *Satir. Poems Reform.* xxxix. 93 For ordinance thay dung at day and nycht By weirlyk volyis. 1585 T. Washington tr. *Nicholay's Voy.* i. xxi. 26 b, [They] surrendred the same [castle]..without any warlike reason. 1590 Spenser *F. Q.* ii. ii. 16 They were two knights of perelesse puissance, And famous far abroad for warlike gest. 1591 Shaks. *1 Hen. VI*, ii. i. 44 Since first I follow'd Armes, Nere heard I of a warlike enterprize More venturous..then this. 1610 Holland *Camden's Brit.* i. 282 Who being brought up in warlike feats..most manfully defended this Castle against King Stephen. 1675 Traherne *Chr. Ethics* 363 A warlike-field is the seed-plot of great and heroical actions. 1687 A. Lovell tr. *Thevenot's Trav.* iii. xxi. 39 He was upon his return from a Warlike expedition. 1784 Cowper *Task* v. 234 Him they serv'd in war, And him in peace, for sake of warlike deeds Rev'renc'd no less. 1817 Byron *Manfred* iii. i. 141 Mortals..who..die ere middle age, Without the violence of warlike death. 1846 Greener *Sci. Gunnery* 81 All our arrangements in warlike preparations, at present, involve [etc.]. 1847 Mrs. A. Kerr tr. *Ranke's Hist. Servia* 342 Their former glorious warlike exploits..led them to entertain very different expectations.

b. of formation, order, etc.

1599 Alex. Hume *Hymns* vii. 191 Poems (S.T.S.) 57 Euen sik..Sall armed be that day with spear and sheild, Baith horsse and fute in weirlike maner drest. 1667 Milton *P. L.* iv. 780 The Cherubim..stood armd To thir night watches in warlike Parade. 1808 Scott *Marmion* i. xx, Were I in warlike wise to ride, A better guard I would not lack. 1870 Bryant *Iliad* ix. 102 With each A hundred youths in warlike order marched.

c. Of arms, munitions, etc.: For use in war.

1561 Daus tr. *Bullinger on Apoc.* xliii. 283 We shall learne also howe to fight agaynst Antichrist, and howe he muste be ouercomen not with warlicke, but spiritual weapons. 1585 Higins *Junius' Nomencl.* 183/1 *Armamentarium*,..an armourie, or place wherein warlike furniture is kept. 1606 Shaks. *Tr. & Cr.* Prol. 13 To Tenedos they come, And the deepe-drawing Barke[s] do there disgorge Their warlike fraut-age. 1652 Wadsworth tr. *Sandoval's Civ. Wars Spain* v. xxx. 312 They were in all six thousand compleat Foot and hors, besides thirtie Carts loaden with Munition, carriages, and other warlike utensils. 1895 J. G. Millais *Breath fr. Veldt* 24 Ample provisions, ammunition, and warlike stores were deposited in the hunting-carts.

d. Of exercises, training, etc.: Of a military character, martial. ? Now *rare.*

1585 T. Washington tr. *Nicholay's Voy.* ii. xviii. 51 b, [They are] exercised..to shoote, and doe all other warlyke exercises. 1626 Gouge *Serm. Dignity Chivalry* § 7 Were Artillery Gardens, and Military Fields for Martiall discipline and warlike trainings fostered..thorow-out this land.

4. Of or belonging to a warrior or soldier.

1551 in Feuillerat *Revels Edw. VI* (1914) 59 Item for our Master of ye Ordnaunce a ffayre apparell warlyke. 1591 Shaks. *1 Hen. VI*, iv. iii. 31, I breake my warlike word. 1621 G. Sandys *Ovid's Met.* viii. (1626) 150 For when he wore his fairely plumed cask; She thought him louely in that warlick mask. 1671 Milton *Samson* 137 He..In scorn of thir proud arms and warlike tools, Spurn'd them to death by Troops. 1813 Scott *Trierm.* i. xvii, Behind him were in triumph borne The warlike arms he late had worn. 1818 Shelley *Homer's Hymn to Minerva* 5 From his awful head Whom Jove brought forth, in warlike armour dressed.

†**B.** *adv.* As is usual in war. *Obs. rare.*

1583 A. Melvill in *J. Melvill's Autob. & Diary* (Wodrow Soc.) 161 The quhilk merciless men..ar gorgiuslie arrayit, and accompanied warlyke with a sort of limmers and godles suddartes. 1632 Lithgow *Trav.* viii. 343 Some warlike maim'd, some lame.

Hence †**Wa·rlikely** *adv.*, in a warlike condition or manner. †**Wa·rlikeness**, warlike disposition.

1548 Hall *Chron.*, *Edw. IV* (1550) 2 When his army by the sea, was thus warlykely set forward. *Ibid.* 37 b, So he hym selfe with his nobilitie warlikely accompaignied, passed ouer betwene Douer and Caleys. 1605 Warlikenesse [see Warliness]. 1606 Warner *Alb. Eng.* xiv. lxxxiii. 345 We shall the warlikenesse compend of those fame-wronged Men. 1615 G. Sandys *Trav.* i. 51 Many tall ships..warlikely appointed. 1626 *Sir W. Rawleigh's Ghost* 3 The Cound.. began to repeate many relations..touching the generall warlikenesse of the British Nation.

Warlike, obs. variant of Warlock.

†**Wa·rliness.** *Obs. rare*−1. [f. Warly *a.*2 + -ness.] Warlike disposition, valiantness.

1599 Sandys *Europæ Spec.* (1629) 209 And all to keepe the Father from jealousie of his owne sonne, whose brauenesse of mind and warlinesse [*the pirated ed. of* 1605 *reads* warlikenesse] is still suspected.

†**Wa·rling.** *Obs.* Forms: 6 **werlyng**, 7 **worling, worldling**, 7– **warling**. [app. formed arbitrarily to rhyme with *darling*. The resemblance to the Sc. Wirling seems to be accidental.] One who is despised or disliked. Only in the proverb (see quots.) and allusively.

In the proverb *snarling* is sometimes substituted for *warling*; the form *worldling* is an obvious perversion.

1546 J. Heywood *Prov.* ii. vii. (1867) 65 It is better to be An olde mans derlyng, than a yong mans werlyng. 1604 [?Chettle] *Wit of Woman* F 4, A young mans worldling. 1611 L. Barry *Ram Alley* ii. i, A young mans warling. 1671 T. Hunt *Abeced. Scholast.* 91 A young mans Worling. 1857 Sir F. Palgrave *Norm. & Eng.* (1864) III. iii. 162 Fully does King Henry appear self-vindicated from the stigma of inertness, the failing assigned by his vixen Mother as justifying her schemes for aggrandizing her darling at the expence of her warling.

Warlock (wǭ·ɹlǫk), *sb.*1 Forms: 1 **wǽrloga, wérloga**, 3 **werlau, werlaw**, 3–4 **warlou**, 3–5 **warlagh(e, warlau, warlaw(e**, 4–5 **warlag, warlaȝ(e, warloghe, werlaughe**, 4–5 (6–7 *Sc.*) **warlow(e**, 4–6 (?9) *Sc.* **warlo**, 5 **warlach, warloo, warlowȝ, werlawe**, 6 *Sc.* **warloche, warlok, vairloche, varlo**, 7 ? **warelocke, warlike, warluck**, 8 (*Sc.*), 9 **warlock**. [OE. *wǽr-loga* wk. masc. traitor, enemy, devil, etc. = OS. *wâr-logo* wk. masc. ?deceiver (once, *Hêliand* 3817, in pl. *wârlogon* applied to the Pharisees). The first element is probably OE. *wǽr* str. fem. covenant = OHG. *wâra* truth, ON. *várar* str. fem. pl. solemn promise, vow (cf. *Væringi* confederate, Varangian); cf. OSlav. *věra* faith. This is a derivative from the adj. represented by OE. *wǽr* true (once, *Genesis* 681; ?a. OS.) = OS., OHG. *wâr* true:—OTeut. **wǣro-*:—Pre-Teut. **wēro-* = L. *vērus*. The second element (an agent-n. related to OE. *léogan* to Lie, belie, deny) occurs also in the similar comps. *âþ-loga, tréow-loga* (OS. *treulogo*), *wed-loga* (ME. *wedlowe*), an oath-breaker, etc.

This seems to have been the original sense of the present word, but the special application to the Devil (either as a rebel, or a deceiver) was already in OE. the leading sense. The applications to sorcerers, with especial reference to the power of assuming inhuman shapes, and to monsters (esp. serpents), appear to be developments, partly due to Scriptural language, of the sense 'devil'.

The modern forms with final *-(c)k* are of obscure origin, for they appear first in Sc. of 16th c., and owe their spread to Sc. writers, and so cannot represent, as has been assumed, a Southern sound-substitution of (k) for the *-ch* (χ) of some of the rarer North. and Sc. forms. From the first they have been used exclusively in the sense 'wizard'. Some other word, lost or not discovered, has perh. influenced both form and sense. ON. *varðlokkur* wk. fem. pl. (cf. also *urðar lo(k)kur*) ?incantation, suggested already in Johnson, is too rare (? occurring once), with regard to the late appearance of the *-k* forms, to be considered.)

†**1.** An oath-breaker, traitor. *Obs.*

Widsið 9 (Gr.) Hreðcyninges ham..Eormanrices, wraþes wærloȝan. a1023 Wulfstan *Hom.* (1883) 266 He sceal wedloȝan and wærloȝan hatian and hynan. ?a1400 *Morte Arth.* 3771 Sir Gawayne i-wysse, he waytes hym wele To wreke hyme on this werlaughe [Modred], that this werre mouede.

†**b.** A wicked person; a scoundrel, reprobate; a general term of reproach or abuse. *Obs.*

a1000 *Judith* 71 (Gr.) Weras winsade..ðone wærloȝan [Holofernus], laðne leodhatan læddon to bedde. c1275 *Serving Christ* 37 in *O. E. Misc.* 91 Bi-leueþ oure weorre warlawes wode. Al þes world is bi-heled myd heþene-hode. c1394 *P. Pl. Crede* 783 Wenest þou þer wold so fele swiche warlawes worþen, Ne were worldlyche wele and her welfare. a1400-50 *Wars Alex.* 4425 Þus fra þe rote of riȝtwisnes rauyst ere зe clene, And to þe way of wickidnes be warlaȝes gidid. c1440 *York Myst.* xxx. 141 Sir, what warlowe yow wakens With wordis full wilde, þat boy for his brawlyng were better be vn-borne. *Ibid.* xliv. 176 Undo youre dores, and haues no doute, For to зone warlowes [the Jews] will we wende. c1450 *St. Cuthbert* 4544 Þan all þe hoste with Elfride To Assendoun þai turne þat tyde, Whare þa warlowes ware. 1500-20 Dunbar *Poems* xxvi. 60 Catyvis, wrechis and okkeraris, Hud-pykis, hurdaris and gadderaris, All with that warlo [Covetousness] went.

†**c.** A damned soul in hell. *Obs. rare.*

a900 Cynewulf *Crist* 1562 Ðonne manscеaða fore meotude forht deore on þam dome standeð..bið se wærloga fyres afylled feores unwyrðe exsan ȝebread and-weard gode won & wliteleas. a1300 *Cursor M.* 23250 Þe aghtand pine it es ful grise, to se þaa warlaus in þat wise.

†**2.** The Devil; Satan. *Obs.*

Freq. in *Cursor Mundi*, where *warlau* occurs as a genitive (:—OE. *wærloȝan*).

a1000 *Cædmon's Gen.* 36 (Gr.) [God] sceop ðam werloȝan

wræclicne ham weorce to leane. a1300 *Cursor M.* 22275 [Antichrist] þe warlau aun child. *Ibid.* 23747 Vr flexs, þis werld, and þe warlau, We ar bunden vnder þair au. *Ibid.* 27060 For qua witstandes warlau will, he has na might to do him ill. c1375 *Sc. Leg. Saints* xviii. (*Egipciane*) 636 [Christ] þat ws fra þe warlo wane. c1460 *Towneley Myst.* xiii. 640 That warloo to sheynd this nyght is he borne. a1568 in *Bannatyne MS.* (Hunter. Club) 78 Betuix ws, varlo, and thy weris All Chrystis passioun we put compleit.

†**b.** A devil, demon, spirit of hell. *Obs. rare.*

a900 Cynewulf *Guthlac* 269 Wid is þes westen, wræcsetla fela, eardas onhæle earmra gæsta; sindon wærloȝan, þe þa wic buȝað. a1300 *Cursor M.* 22611 Þan sal þai þat in helle es cropen Quen sal scine þe heuennes open, þaa warlaus all sal walk þan vte. c1440 *De mirac. B. Marie* 105 in Horstm. *Altengl. Leg.* (1881) 504 Þe foulle warlawes of helle Vndir þe wallys skrykked schille.

†**3.** A savage or monstrous creature (hostile to men). The word is applied to giants, cannibals, mythic beasts, etc. *Obs.*

a1000 *Cædmon's Gen.* 1266 (Gr.) Frea wolde on wærloȝan wite settan & on deað slean dædum scyldiȝe ȝiȝantmæcgas, gode unleofe. a1300 *Cursor M.* 7478 Allas! quar sal we find a man þat dar þe fight, for mi sake, Again yon warlau [Goliath] vndertake. 13.. *E. E. Allit. P.* C. 258 Þe hyȝe heuen kyng, þurȝ his honde myȝt, Warded þis wrech man [Jonah] in warlowes guttez. c1400 *Destr. Troy* 303 So dang he þat dog [*sc.* Cerberus] with dynt of his wappon, þat þe warlag was wete of his wan atter. *Ibid.* 7765 The warlagh [the Centaur] with a wicked arowe woundit hym behynd. a1400-50 *Wars Alex.* 3795 Þai went be waldis & be wastis..And armed bud þam all bee for angwischis o bestis, As colwers & for coltris & crabbid snakis, And oþire warlaȝes wild þat in þe wod duelled. a1585 Polwart *Flyting w. Montgomerie* 634 Ane vairloche [*v.rr.* warloch(e)], ane woirwolf, ane wowbat of hair.

4. One in league with the Devil and so possessing occult and evil powers; a sorcerer, wizard (sometimes partly imagined as inhuman or demonic, and so approaching sense 2 or 3); the male equivalent of *witch*. *Sc.* and *north. dial.*

Frequently used by Scott, whence it has obtained some general literary currency. On the form *warlock*, specialized for this sense, see the etymology.

13.. *E. E. Allit. P.* B. 1560 Segges..þat wer wyse of wych-crafte & warlaȝes oþer. c1460 *Towneley Myst.* viii. 232 *Pharao*...Say, whence is yond warlow [Moyses] with his wand that thus wold wyle oure folk away? a1585 Montgomerie *Misc. Poems* iii. 25 That witch, that warlok [*sc.* Fortune]..Turnis ay the best men tittest on thair bakis. 1685 G. Sinclair *Satan's Invis. World* 45 An eminent Warlock whose name was Robert Grieve. 1689 tr. *Buchanan's De Jure Regni apud Scotos* 65 No Thief or Warlike will willingly compear before a Judge to be judged. c1730 Burt *Lett. N. Scot.* (1818) I. 234 He was himself a warlock, or wizard, which they knew by his taking the witch's part. 1795 Burns *Song, 'Last May a braw wooer'* v, I gaed to the tryste o' Dalgarnock, And wha but my fine fickle lover was there! I glowr'd as I'd seen a warlock, a warlock. 1816 Scott *Bl. Dwarf* v, 'But you forget that they say he is a warlock,' said Nancy Ilderton. 'And, if his magic diabolical should fail him,' rejoined her sister, 'I would have him trust to his magic natural'. 1822 S. Hibbert *Shetl. Isl.* iv. 576 The warlocks and witches of Thule used, by the same means, to raise tempests. 1840 Barham *Ingol. Leg., St. Aloys*, The gipsy..always sneaks out at night with the bats and the owls,—So do Witches and Warlocks, Ghosts, Goblins, and Ghouls. 1860 Longf. *Wayside Inn* i. *King Olaf* v. x, In their real forms appeared The warlocks weird, Awful as the Witch of Endor. 1865 Baring-Gould *Werewolves* 29 In like manner the Danish king Harold sent a warlock to Iceland in the form of a whale. 1882 Miss Braddon *Mt. Royal* I. ii. 51, I am prepared to believe in witches—warlocks.

b. *Sc.* In weaker sense, a magician, conjurer.

1721 Ramsay *Prospect of Plenty* 75 But gin ye be nae warlock, how d'ye ken? 1828 Scott *Aunt Marg. Mirr.* ii, 'That rascally quack would make my fortune were he to stay in Edinburgh,' said the graduate...'I suppose I must not ask your ladyship anything about this Italian warlock's proceedings?' 1877 A. J. Ross *Mem. Alex. Ewing* xiv. 197 'The Bishop..never came to my private room.. without leaving me the impression that he was—' an auditor, interrupting, said, 'A godly warlock.' 'Yes,' rejoined the speaker, 'that was just it, he was a wizard..'. 1886 Stevenson *Kidnapped* iii, I'm nae warlock, to find a fortune for you in the bottom of a parritch bowl.

†**5.** By Dryden taken to mean: A warrior magically immune from wounds inflicted by certain metals. *Obs.*

Dryden's spelling perh. indicates that he imagined the word to be f. War *sb.* + Luck.

1697 Dryden *Æneis* Ded. (b) 4 b, It seems he [Æneas] was no War-luck, as the Scots commonly call such Men, who, they say, are Iron-free, or Lead-free.

6. *attrib.* and *Comb.* **a.** Appositive or adj. †Malignant, wicked (*obs.*); in later use, That is a warlock or wizard.

c1375 *Cursor M.* 7489 (Fairf.) Agayne зone warlagh hethen þing [*Cotton MS.* wreche haiþen þing] for-soþ I drede me noȝt sir king. c1400 *Destr. Troy* 6425 Nay, warloghe wolfe, in þi wode hongur,..The tydis not to taste of þis triet meite! 1560 Rolland *Seven Sages* 131 This reid Reifar & this rank warlo witche. 1683 G. Sinclair *Nat. Philos.* 243 The Devil answered,..I and my Father will come and fetch you to hell, with Warlock-theeves. 1685 — *Satan's Invis. World* 123 Saying, You Warlok Cairle, what have you to do here? 1724 Ramsay *Ever Green* (1761) I. 51 A Bytand Ballat on warlo Wives, That gar thair Men live pinging Lives. 1786 Burns *Brigs of Ayr* 71 Our warlock Rhymer instantly descry'd the Sprites that owre the Brigs of Ayr preside. (That Bards are second-sighted is nae joke, And ken the lingo of the sp'ritual folk.) 1896 Kipling *Seven Seas, Rhyme Three Sealers*, A Stralsund man shot blind and large, and a warlock Finn was he.

b. Pertaining to a warlock or warlocks, as in

warlock claw, fight, knoll, etc.; **warlock brief**, a charter conveying magical powers; **warlock fecket** *Sc.* (see quot. 1810).

1786 Burns *To J. Smith* 3 Ye surely hae some warlock-breef Owre human hearts; For ne'er a bosom yet was prief Against your arts. 1793 — *Song, 'Now rosy May'* Chorus, Meet me on the warlock-knowe, Daintie Davie, daintie Davie. 1803 H. K. White *Lines..spoken by a Lover* Rem. 1807 II. 47 No wicked elves upon the Warlock-knoll Dare now assemble at their mystic revels. 1807 Tannahill *Soldier's Ret.* ii. i, A great red dragon, wi a warlock claw, Has come, and wi your dochter flown awa! 1810 Cromek *Remains Nithsdale Song* 281 Jackets, woven of water snake skins, at a certain time of a March moon, were much in vogue among the crusading servants of Satan; and are yet remembered by the name of warlock feckets. 1819 J. R. Drake *Culprit Fay* viii, Yet..If thy heart be pure and thy spirit right, Thou shalt win the warlock fight! 1905 *Academy* 21 Oct. 1103/1 A warlock voice from the slumber of ages stirred.

†**Warlock**, *sb.*2 *Obs. rare.* In quots. **warloc, warlok.** [Perh. repr. an OE. **wærloc*, f. OE. *waru* Ware *sb.*1 guard, safe-keeping + *loc* Lock *sb.*2 It is, however, possibly an alteration of Warrok *sb.* caused by some such etymological association as that indicated. Cf. the senses in mod. dial. of Warlock *v.*1 and Warrok *v.*]

1. ? A shackle, fetter.

13.. *E. E. Allit. P.* C. 80 Pynez me in a prysoun, put me in stokkes, Wryþe me in a warlok, wrast out myn yȝen.

2. A fetterlock.

c1440 *Promp. Parv.* 517/1 Warlok, a fetyr lok..*sera pedicalis, vel compedicalis.*

Wa·rlock, *sb.*3 *Obs.* (? exc. *dial.*) *rare.* Also 5 **warich**, (? **warkecok**), **warlok.** [Of obscure origin. The early forms *warich, warkecok* are perh. nearer to the original than *warlo(c)k*, which may be due to association with Charlock.] Apparently applied like Charlock (q.v.) to various field-weeds of the N.O. *Cruciferæ*, esp. to species of the genus *Sinapis*, Mustard.

c1425 *Voc.* in Wr.-Wülcker 644/29 *Hoc sinapium*, warkecok. c1440 *Promp. Parv.* 349/1 Mustard, or warlok, or se(n)vyne, herbe..*sinapis*. *Ibid.* 517/1 Warlok, herbe, *eruca*. c1450 *Alphita* (Anecd. Oxon.) 37/1 *Cenapium*, gall. ceneue, angl. warich, uel mostard. 1784-1815 A. Young *Annals Agric.* V. 231 (E. D. S.) Warlock, *Raphanus Raphanistrum*(?) Suff(olk). a1850 W. A. Brousfield *Flora Vectensis* (1856) 37 *Sinapis nigra*, L. Common or Black Mustard. *Vect.* Warlock.

†**Wa·rlock**, *sb.*4 *Obs.* [app. a real or supposed Norw. word: cf. Norw. *varde* (dial. *vale*) cairn.] A cairn, pile of stones (in Scandinavian regions).

1584 R. Norman tr. *Safegard of Sailers* 51 Item, if it were so that you would saile into Calfe sound, then you shall hale in by a high land which is called Winge, and there stands fiue Warlocks or Bomes vpon it. *Ibid.*, The fiue Warlocks or Beacons. *Ibid.* 52 b. 1612 Gatonbe in *Churchill's Voy.* (1732) VI. 250 We rowed about the cape and came to an island whereon was a warlock. 1614 R. Fotherby in Purchas *Pilgrims* (1625) III. 725 Here vpon the mountaine wee set vp a Warelocke, and then came downe againe.

Wa·rlock, *v.*1 *Obs.* (exc. *dial.*) *rare.* Also **warloke.** [f. Warlock *sb.*2] *trans.* †**a.** ? To secure (a horse) as with a fetterlock. *Obs. rare*−1. **b.** *dial.* (See quot.) Cf. Warrok *v.*

a1400-50 *Wars Alex.* 769* (Dubl. MS.) So carez he in þe castell-ȝarde & commez on a day By a wyndow als þis wild horse [was] warloked in bandez. 1885 *Cheshire Gloss.* s.v. 1905 *Eng. Dial. Dict.*, *Warlock*, to tighten the rope or chain which binds the load upon a waggon.

War-lock, *v.*2 *nonce-wd.* [f. War *sb.*1 + Lock *v.* (? suggested by Warlock *sb.*1)] *trans.* ? To bar against hostile invasion.

1800 Hurdis *Fav. Village* 40 The western fort, That.. war-locks imminent the mouth of Ouse.

Wa·rlockry. ? *Obs.* [f. Warlock *sb.*1 + -ry.] The practice of magic (by men, or male beings); wizardry.

1818 *Blackw. Mag.* II. 527 Hence proceed..the warlockry and fortune-telling abilities of the shrewd sagacious gypsies. 1822 Hogg *Siege of Roxburgh* i, Sin' the Rhymer's days, the spirit o' true warlockry is gane. 1831 J. Wilson in *Blackw. Mag.* XXIX. 21 The shadows o' a' the eatables and drinkables that his wild warlockry cou'd hae conjured up. 1834 Hogg in *Fraser's Mag.* X. 404 Yes, witchcraft! Wicked warlockrye!

Warlogh(e, warloo, obs. ff. Warlock *sb.*1

Warlonde, obs. form of Warland *Hist.*

War-lord. A military commander or commander-in-chief. Often used to render *Kriegsherr* as a title of the German Emperor; also *attrib.*

1856 Emerson *Eng. Traits, Aristocr.* Wks. (Bohn) II. 77 Piracy and war gave place to trade, politics, and letters; the war-lord to the law-lord. 1875 Morris *Æneids* ix. 39 Æneas, war-lord wise. 1888 *Boston* (Mass.) *Transcript* 7 July 4/4 The very bristling and 'war-lord' talk of the young Emperor William. 1897 *Edin. Rev.* Oct. 534 The officers of the [German] army, with all their traditional loyalty to their 'war-lord'.

Hence **Wa·rlordship**, the status of a war-lord.

1913 C. Tower *Germany To-day* ii. 36 The Kaisership is the old Presidency of the bund plus the warlordship.

†**Wa·rlott.** *local. Obs.* [f. *war-* as in Warland + Lot *sb.*] Some kind of waste or common lands.

c1290 *Register Malton Priory* (MS. Cott. Claudius D.xi) 206 Cum prato que dicitur Warlotes. 1614 *Terrier of Mor-*

ley of Winterton, Warlotes, the long; the short. 1794 *Act Inclos. South Kelsey* 3 Commissioners for dividing..and inclosing the said Open and Common Fields,..Warlotts, or Whoselotts, Furze Leas, and Waste Grounds, within the Manor or Lordship of South Kelsey.

Warlou, -low(e, -luck: see Warlock.

†**Wa·rly**, *a.* and *adv.* *Obs.* Forms: 5 **werly**, *Sc.* **werely**, 5–7 **war(re)ly**, 6 **warely, warlye**, *Sc.* **werelie, weirlie, -ly, weyrly**, 6–7 **warlie.** [f. War *sb.*1 + -ly1 and -ly2.]

A. *adj.*

1. Skilled in war, martial; fond of war, bellicose; valiant. = Warlike *a.* 1.

1423 Jas. I. *Kingis Q.* clv, The werely porpapyne. c1475 *Partenay* 1362 The petyuins tham bare As warly men fre;..Assautes tha[y] gafe dyuers And sondry. a1513 Fabyan *Chron.* vii. (1533) 77 b/1 Ye arche bisshop of yorke ..with great nombre of men and fewe warly or discrete cheuetaynes, yode agayne ye Scottes. 1513 More *Rich. III* Wks. (1557) 37/1 Richard the thirde sonne..was..hard fauoured of visage, and suche as is in states called warlye [L. *quale bellicosum in purpuratis, ac Martium appellari*], in other menne otherwise. 1594 T. B. *La Primaud. Fr. Acad.* i. 585 If a yoong prince..be warlie, he will hazard his subjects, his estate, and his person, to make triall of his valure. 1596 Dalrymple tr. *Leslie's Hist. Scot.* (S. T. S.) I. 86 Thay war a people baith ciuile and weirlie. 1605 Verstegan *Dec. Intell.* v. (1628) 122 The lacke of Warrely courage in the Britaines.

b. Of actions, things: Martial. = Warlike *a.* 1 b, c.

1536 Bellenden *Cron. Scot.*, Proheme Cosmogr. 262 Of feirs Achill, the weirlie dedis sprang In Troy and Grece, quhill he in vertew rang. 1599 Alex. Hume *Hymns* vii. 57 Poems (S. T. S.) 54 Mak shouting shalms and persing phiphers shill,..Cause mightily the weirly notis breik.

2. Equipped or munitioned for war. Of a horse: Equipped and trained for war. = Warlike *a.* 2.

c1470 *Golagros & Gaw.* 493 Yone is the warliest wane, said the wise king, That euer I vist in my walk. a1513 Fabyan *Chron.* vii. (1533) 123/2 The sayde sowdiours came vnto a castell..& wan it by strength, & after vytayled & manned it in moste warly wyse. 1591 Harington *Orl. Fur.* xxxiii. lxxxv, This said, he mounted on the steed so warly. 1593 G. Harvey *Pierces Super.* Wks. (Grosart) II. 104 Could the Warlie Horse speake, as he can runne and fight, he would tell them, they are hoat Knightes.

3. Of or pertaining to war. = War-like *a.* 3.

1457 in R. R. Sharpe *Lond. & Kingd.* (1895) III. 382 Ships ..in their most defensible and warrely araye. ?c1507 C. Brandon [etc.] *Justes May & June, Justes June* 233 in Hazl. *E. P. P.* II. 129 This weerly vsage and martes entrepryse These monthes twayne yonge folke dyd exercyse. 1533 Bellenden *Livy* i. i. (S. T. S.) I. 13 King latyne of laurence assemblit þe auld Inhabitantis of his realme..in þare maist werelie ordinance. *Ibid.* i. iv. I. 32. 1544 Betham *Precepts War* i. cix. F v, They being practysed in warly knowledge can discerne what is profytable. 1548 Hall *Chron.*, *Hen. V*, 45 b, Kyng Henry..determined..to set forward in performyng his intended purpose and warrely enterprise. 1570 Foxe *A. & M.* (ed. 2) II. 1000/2 The Bernates..renounced the league made before with the French king, refusing..his warly stipend, whereby they were bound at his call to fede hys warres. a1676 Hale *Prim. Orig. Man.* ii. iv. (1677) 161 The Manufacture, during those Warly times, held its course in France, the Netherlands, and the Hans Towns.

4. Belonging to a warrior. = Warlike *a.* 4.

1535 Stewart *Cron. Scot.* (Rolls) I. 277 The king of Pechtis, in his weirlie weid, With his power come and met corbreid. 1567 *Gude & Godlie B.* (S. T. S.) 107 His wingis ar thy weirlie weid [*v.r.* weerely weed], His pennis ar thy strang defence. 1609 Bible (Douay) 1 *Macc.* iii. 3 And he ..girded about him his warlie armour in battels.

B. *adv.* In a warlike manner.

c1400 *Rowland & O.* 813 Kyng askuardyn in his gere Rydis owte a course of were, Full werly and with ill will. c1475 *Partenay* 1741 Then thes brethren, ech by thaimself, tho, So ful werrely wrought, can noght be said, lo! 1592 Wyrley *Armorie, Capitall de Buz* xxiv, And goodly armd beside Him stands the Duke of Orleance warly dight.

Warly, -lyche: see Warely *a.* and *adv.* *Obs.*

Warm (wǭɹm), *sb.*1 [f. Warm *v.*] An act of warming or state of becoming warm. Phr. *to give, get, have, take a warm.* Somewhat *colloq.*

In the first quot. *warmes* is a mistake for *walmes*: see Walm *sb.*1 3 c.

[1655 Walton *Angler* (ed. 2) x. 239 Boil it [*sc.* the malt] in the kettle (one or two warmes is enough).] 1768 Ross *Helenore* 70 This morning's raw, gin ye've a' night been out, That ye wad thole a warm, I mak na doubt. 1800 in *Spirit Publ. Jrnls.* IV. 6 The dark and dreary night, the dreadful storm Drove me unwillingly to get a warm. 1838 Dickens *O. Twist* i, The surgeon had been sitting with his face turned towards the fire, giving the palms of his hands a warm and a rub alternately. 1843 — *Chr. Carol* iii, Sit ye down before the fire, my dear, and have a warm. 1861 — *Gt. Expect.* ii, When I..was taking a final warm in the chimney-corner before being sent up to bed. 1861 Flor. Nightingale *Nursing* 55 If, after washing a patient, you must put the same night-dress on him again, always give it a warm first, at the fire. 1891 C. Roberts *Adrift Amer.* 120, I made a fire, and..had a good warm.

Warm (wǭɹm), *a.* (and *sb.*2) Forms: 1 **wearm**, 2 **wærm**, 3 *Orm.* **warrm**, 3–7 **warme**, 3– **warm.** [Com. Teut.: OE. *wearm* = OFris. *warm* (mod. WFris. *waerm*, NFris. *wârəm*), MDu., Du. *warm*, OS. *warm* (MLG. *war(e)m*, LG. *warm*), OHG. *war(a)m* (MHG., G. *warm*), ON. *varmr* (Norw., Sw., Da. *varm*), Goth. *warm-* in *warmjan* to warm, cherish:—OTeut. **warmo-*, also **werm-* (in ON. *verme* wk. masc. warmth, OHG. *wirma*, MHG. *wirm(e)* fem. warmth).

The further relationship of this word is somewhat doubtful. In spite of certain difficulties it is probably to be identified with Indogermanic **gʷhormo-*, or **gʷhermo-* found in Skr. *gharmá* heat, Zend *garᵊma-* hot, Gk. θερμός hot, L. *formus* warm, OPrussian *gorme* heat, Albanian *zjarm* heat, Armenian *jerm* warm, derivatives of **gʷher-* with a radical sense of heat. For another possible example of initial *w* in Teut. from **gʷh* or **ghw* see Wild *a.* Compare also the similar phonetic phenomena in Latin whereby older *gʷ* gave *g* before *ŭ* and consonants, *v* before other vowels (e.g. *gurges, vorāre*).

Some scholars have referred the word to a root **wer-* found in Lith. *virti* to cook (trans.), OSl. *vrěti* to boil, cook (intr.), *variti* to cook (trans.), *varŭ* hot. The primary sense of this root, however, seems to be rather 'to well up, bubble' than 'to be hot'; cf. Lith. *versmė* a spring. The root is confined to the Balto-Slav. langs., and in them has no derivative corresponding in sense and suffix to the Teut. adj., which on the other view represents a widespread Indogermanic formation.]

A. *adj.*

1. Having a fairly high temperature; affording or giving out a considerable degree of heat (less than that indicated by *hot*).

a. of natural agencies and things, as the weather, air, climate, soil.

Out of God's (*Christ's*) *blessing into the warm sun*: see God *sb.* 5 c.

c888 Ælfred *Boeth.* xxxiii. § 5 Sie lyft..is ægþer ge ceald ge wæt ge wearm. a1000 *Boeth. Metr.* xi. 61 Sumor æfter cymeð, wearm ȝewideru. a1250 *Owl & Night.* 622 Þar inne ic habbe god ihold A wintre warm a sumere cold. 1377 Langl. *P. Pl.* B. xviii. 410 Is no weder warmer þan after watery cloudes. c1440 *Pallad. on Husb.* i. 219 In spryngyne of the mone is best to sowe, In dayis warm. 1540 Palsgr. *Acolastus* ii. i. H iij, To leappe out of the halle, into the kytchyn, or out of Chrystis blessynge in to a warme sonne. 1549 *Compl. Scot.* vi. 58 [Rain falls] sum tyme in soft & varme schouris. 1577 B. Googe tr. *Heresbach's Husb.* i. 34 Pease ..must be sowen in warme groundes. 1727 E. Laurence *Duty of Steward* 75 On a warm soil well shelter'd with Trees and Hills. 1750 Gray *Elegy* 87 The warm precincts of the chearful day. 1774 Goldsm. *Nat. Hist.* VI. 347 The prisoners of congelation..waiting the approach of a warmer sun, to restore them at once to life and liberty. 1833 Arnott *Physics* (1853) 35 England is much warmer in winter than central Germany, which lies south of England. 1854 *Poultry Chron.* I. 249 We..stand much in need of warm weather, and especially, warm nights for the young poultry. 1915 *Blackw. Mag.* Apr. 467 A warm south wind was melting the fall [of snow].

b. of other things, typically with reference to artificial heating.

c1385 Chaucer *L. G. W.* 914 His swerd sche tok a-swythe That warm was of hire louys blod & hot. 1577 B. Googe tr. *Heresbach's Husb.* iii. 119 b, In winter, your stable should rather be warme, then hot. 1606 Shaks. *Ant. & Cl.* iii. i. 6 Whil'st yet with Parthian blood thy Sword is warme. 1697 Dryden *Æneis* xi. 323 They rake the yet warm Ashes, from below. a1700 Evelyn *Diary* 11 Mar. 1651, They..carried him before a warme fire to bring him to himselfe. 1741 M. Grindal (*title*) Warm Beer, a Treatise proving..that Beer so qualify'd, is far more wholesome than that which is drank Cold...With a full Confutation of all the Objections..against Drink being used Warm. 1764 Whytt *Observ. Nervous Disorders* (1767) 434 The warm bath affects the nerves with an agreeable sensation, removes spasms in the small vessels, [etc.]. 1848 Dickens *Dombey* v, Promise me to take a little something warm before you go to bed. 1849 James *Woodman* vii, Our houses are more warm and air-tight than those of that day. 1871 A. Meadows *Midwifery* (ed. 2) 339 Warm poultices should also be kept over the abdomen.

c. *fig.* *To keep a seat* or *place warm*: to occupy it temporarily for another who is not yet qualified to hold it. (Cf. Warming-pan 3 c.)

1845 Jerrold *St. Giles* vi. (1851) 55 Of course, the borough will be kept warm for the young gentleman...He may count upon my vote. 1853 Mrs. Gaskell *Ruth* xxi, Before the Cranworths had determined who should keep the seat warm till the eldest son came of age.

2. Of the body, the blood, etc.: Having the degree of heat natural to the living organism.

a1000 *Riddles* v. 7 Wearm lim ȝebundenne beaȝ bersteð hwilum. c1200 Ormin 10146 Forrþi þatt itt [the tunic] iss neh þe lich & haldeþþ warrm þe mare. 1338 R. Brunne *Chron.* (1810) 36 Þe blode was boþe warme & fresh, þat of þe schankes lete. c1386 Chaucer *Sompn. T.* 119 Though I him wrye a-nyght and make hym warm. 1562 J. Heywood *Prov. & Epigr.* (1867) 148 Thou art wyse inough, if thou keepe thee warme. 1603 Shaks. *Meas. for M.* iii. ii. 9 A fur'd gowne to keepe him warme. 1693 Dryden *Persius* vi. 13 For me, my warmer Constitution wants More cold, than our Ligurian Winter grants. 1697 — *Æneis* ii. 867 Go you, whose Blood runs warm in ev'ry Vein. 1754 Gray *Progr. Poesy* 40 O'er her warm cheek, and rising bosom. 1855 *Poultry Chron.* III. 398 New milk, warm from the cow. 1878 Browning *La Saisiaz* 21 At the least warm touch of hand. 1919 *Blackw. Mag.* Nov. 644/2, I found the carcase of a hartebeeste still warm.

fig. 1737 Pope *Hor. Ep.* ii. i. 247 Then Marble, soften'd into life, grew warm.

b. Of persons: Glowing with exertion or exercise, with eating and drinking, etc.; often with mixture of one of the senses 10–12. Of exercise: Strenuous enough to raise one's temperature.

1606 Shaks. *Tr. & Cr.* iv. v. 118, I am not warme yet, let vs fight againe. 1665 Dryden *Ind. Emp.* iii. i, And Fighting gains us but to dye more warm. 1746 Francis tr. *Horace, Art of Poetry* 322 A lawless Croud, with Wine and Feasting warm. 1753 Jane Collier *Art Torment.* i. ii. 61 For although it is noble sport to have a girl of sense to work upon, yet 'tis warm exercise. 1769 *Ann. Reg.* 25 There is nothing that an army will not attempt or endure for a general who keeps the soldiers warm in continual action. 1850 Tennyson *In Mem.* xc. 9 'Twas well, indeed, when warm with wine, To pledge them with a kindly tear. 1900 *Pall*

Mall Mag. May 43, I was warm from my company, and was propelled by an abundant flow of vitality.

c. Applied to tears.

1377 Langl. *P. Pl.* B. xv. 187 And with warme water at his eyghen wasshen hem after. 1483 Caxton *Golden Leg.* 196/1 Thenne she..prayed god wyth warme teerys to helpe hyr. 1588 Shaks. *Tit. A.* iii. i. 20 In Winter with warme teares Ile melt the snow. 1648 Bp. Hall *Sel. Th.* lxxvi. 221 But if..we shall suffer our selves to be drawn away into some heinous wickedness, it must cost warm water to recover us.

d. Of a kiss, embrace (combining the literal idea of bodily warmth with that of affection).

1588 Shaks. *Tit. A.* v. iii. 153 Oh take this warme kisse on thy pale cold lips. a1764 R. Lloyd *Whim* 45 Give me the man..Who..Can meet him with a warm embrace. 1822 M. A. Kelty *Osmond* I. 29 Imprinting on it another fond warm kiss. 1866 Trollope *Claverings* iv, With the kiss of the dear, modest, affectionate girl still warm upon his lips.

e. = Warm-blooded. *rare.*

1793 T. Beddoes *Calculus* etc. 242 The ordinary temperature of the blood of warm animals.

3. Of clothing, or the natural integument of animals: Made of material which retains heat in the body.

a1225 *Ancr. R.* 418 Þet heo [i.e. your clothes] beon unorne & warme & wel i-wrouhte. a1300 *Cursor M.* 23090 (Edinb.) Of nakidhed quen I drow harme, Ye gaf me cleþing þat was warme. a1450 *Mirk's Festial* 33/36 Hit wer almes forto зeue зondyr pore man warmer cloþes þen he haþe. 1535 Coverdale *Job* xxxvii. 17 And how thy clothes are warme, when the londe is still thorow the south wynde? 1653 in *Verney Mem.* (1904) I. 547 Here is now some cold snowie weather approaching, which incites mee to putt on warmer cloths. 1774 Goldsm. *Nat. Hist.* (1776) V. 39 These are generally cloathed with a warmer coat of feathers. 1849 James *Woodman* xi, Would that I had brought warmer garments. 1917 H. Gibson *Diplom. Diary* 259 Mrs. Whitlock..is busy getting warm clothing for the poor.

4. Of a drug or edible: Producing a sensation of heat in the body.

1737 J. Stevenson in *Med. Ess.* IV. 387 Common Practice bids us..give warm, generous Medicines, Alexipharmicks, and all of that Tribe that heats, stimulates and forces Sweat. 1822-7 Good *Study Med.* (1829) I. 251 A pretty free dose of turpentine, or some of the warmer balsams. 1842 Loudon *Suburban Hort.* 689 Its seed-pods..make a warm aromatic pickle.

5. Of a scent or trail: Fresh, strong.

1713 Gay *Rural Sports* ii. 68 The scent grows warm; he stops; he springs the prey. 1832 *P. Egan's Bk. Sports* 211/2 As the scent grew warmer, the certainty of finding was confirmed.

6. Of the person chosen to seek or guess, in children's games: Being near the object sought; being on the verge of finding or guessing. Also *fig.*

1860 *All Year Round* 4 Feb. 339/2 Here I get 'warm', as children say. 1865 Dickens *Mut. Fr.* iii. vi, He's warm... He's precious warm. He's close. 1893 *Nation* (N.Y.) 24 Aug. 139/3 Showing how the author was 'warm', and passed without seeing it very near to the object of his search.

†**7.** Comfortable, comfortably settled (*in* a seat, throne, office); securely established *in* (possession of). Also, with converse construction, *to feel the crown warm upon one's head*. *Obs.*

c1374 Chaucer *Troylus* iii. 1630 Be not to rakel þough þou sitte warme. c1430 *How Wise Man taught Son* 114 in *Babees Bk.* 51 If þou be wel at eese, And warme amonge þi neiȝboris sitte. 1601 *Imp. Consid. Sec. Priests* (1675) 55 Her Highness had scarcely felt the Crown warm upon her head, but it was challenged from her. 1610 B. Jonson *Alchemist* ii. vi. A Gentleman, newly warme in his land. 1614 Ralegh *Hist. World* ii. xvii. § 4. 481 The Philistims hearing that Dauid was now anointed king..thought to try him in the beginning, before hee was fully warme in his seat. 1647 N. Bacon *Disc. Govt. Eng.* i. xlvii. (1739) 78 The conquering King was scarce warm in his Throne, whenas the Pope demanded Fealty of him for the Crown of England. a1670 Wood *Life* (O.H.S.) I. 129 A. W. seemed very sorry at this news, because he was well and warme where he was. 1715 M. Davies *Athen. Brit.* I. 47 Before he was quite warm in Winchester, he fell into the King's displeasure. 1809 W. Irving *Knickerb.* vii. iii. (1900) 258 Scarcely had the worthy Mynheer Beekman got warm in the seat of authority on the South River than enemies began to spring up all around him.

8. Comfortably off, well to do; rich, affluent. Now chiefly *colloq.*

1571 Campion *Hist. Irel.* ii. ix. (1633) 114 But you are well and warme and so hold you. 1573-80 Tusser *Husb.* (1878) 8 But I must plaie the farmer, and yet no whit the warmer. a1624 Bp. M. Smith *Serm.* (1632) 118 All things seeme to fall out alike, to the one and to the other: nay, the wicked seeme to be the warmer, and to haue a greater portion in this life. 1626 Middleton *Anything Quiet Life* i. i, You are warm, and blest with a fair wife. 1699 Farquhar *Love & Bottle* i. 2 Your warm fellows are so far above the sense of our Misery, that they can't pitty us. 1712 Steele *Spect.* No. 450 ¶ 2 For who does not know or imagine the Comforts of being warm or living at Ease? 1742 Fielding *J. Andrews* ii. xiv, 'Though I am but a curate,' says Trulliber, 'I believe I am as warm as the vicar himself.' 1766 Goldsm. *Vicar W.* xvi, They who had warm fortunes were always sure of getting good husbands. 1767 A. Young *Farmer's Lett.* 74 These farmers, and their warm, comfortable families, are of great consequence to the well being of agriculture itself. 1834 Macaulay in *Life & Lett.* (1880) I. 381 A warm man; a fellow who will cut up well. 1888 Rider Haggard *Col. Quaritch* xxviii, He is about the warmest man in our part of the country. 1908 J. S. Fletcher *Mothers in Israel* 304 With the serene consciousness of his value as a warm man. 1920 *Guardian* 5 Nov. 1034/4 In 1836 he was presented..to the very snug vicarage of Cheddar, and a year later he took to himself the still warmer benefice of Wiveliscombe.

9. Of fighting, conflict, an onset: Vigorously conducted; pressing hard on or harassing the foe; also *fig.* Of a combatant: Dangerous to tackle. Of a locality: Dangerous to live in, inhabited by turbulent spirits. Phr. *warm work*, hot fighting. *To make it* (or *things*) *warm for* (a person): to attack or 'go for' him, to involve in hostilities or broils.

1627 J. Taylor (Water P.) *Armado* C 2, The Sweat, a vessell of warme imployment or hot seruice. 1667 *Hatton Corr.* (Camden) 53 You may easily imagine this does give us a warme alarum. 1682 Bunyan *Holy War* (1905) 235 They had from the Camp of Shaddai such frequent, warm, and terrifying alarms. 1726 Shelvocke *Voy. round World* 163, I saw the Mercury standing out of the way, by which I judged the ship was too warm for her. 1759 R. Rogers *Jrnls.* (1769) 119 The Canadians and Indians..were soon stopped by a warm fire from the Rangers and Mohocks. 1760 *Cautions & Advices to Officers of Army* 182 If we had [been discovered], they might have made warm Work of it. 1793 Washington *Let.* Writ. 1891 XII. 380 If he should be detected in any knavish pranks I will make the country too warm for him to remain in. 1813 Southey *Nelson* II. ix. 255 Nelson then smiled, and said, 'This is too warm work, Hardy, to last long.' 1817 Jas. Mill *Brit. India* II. v. v. 527 The action..was close, warm, and general. 1840 Dickens *Old C. Shop* vi, This being warmer work than they had calculated upon, speedily cooled the courage of the belligerents. 1847 Yeowell *Anc. Brit. Church* iii. 28 In his Second Epistle to Timothy..there are many traces of a warm persecution. 1874 'Max Adeler' *Out of Hurly-burly* xv. (Rtldg.) 208 The bishop saw clearly enough that if he gave presents to the other children, and not to the late Simpson's, the bride would make things warm for him. 1884 *Good Words* June 399/1 The 'habituals'..are, as a body, congregated together in one particularly warm little street...Outsiders do not care to venture into this warm spot.

b. *A warm reception*: a vigorous onslaught or resistance; a demonstration of hostile feeling.

The phrase prob. belonged originally to sense 12 c, in which it is still current.

1708 [see Reception 5 a]. 1737 [S. Berington] *Mem. G. di Lucca* (1738) 37 We thought, by that warm Reception, they would have given us over. 1841 James *Brigand* xxvi, We must give him [the rival] a warm reception.

10. Of persons, party-feeling, controversy, etc.: Ardent, zealous, keen; eager, excited, heated. Const. *for, upon.*

Very common in the 17th and 18th c.; now somewhat *rare.*

1390 Gower *Conf.* III. 230 Yong conseil, which is to warm, Er men be war doth ofte harm. 1668 Temple *Let. to Ld. Keeper* Wks. 1731 II. 99 Which I could not have known, if the Marquis were not a very warm Talker, and sometimes farther than he intended. 1682 Bunyan *Holy War* (1905) 314 Then said the warm man, and true hearted Mr. Zeal-for-God, Cut them off. 1687 Atterbury *Answ. Consid. Spirit Luther* 20 Yet the Pamphlet is very warm with Luther for impiously accusing the Religious of uncleanness. 1705 Hearne *Collect.* 24 Aug. (O.H.S.) I. 34 He is now very warm for them. 1720 De Foe *Capt. Singleton* xiii. (1840) 233 So warm were the men upon it, that they grew..clamorous. 1737 Waterland *Eucharist* 113 *Smalcius*, a warm Man, and who seldom knew any Bounds. 1742 E. Montagu in *Mrs. Montagu's Corr.* (1906) I. 130 The Debates were very warm, and the Chancellor of the Exchequer was terribly roasted. 1776 *Trial of Nundocomar* 59/2 The Counsel for the Prisoner speaking in a warm and improper manner to the Jury. 1791 Burke *Th. Fr. Affairs* Wks. 1842 I. 575 Of all men, the most dangerous is a warm, hot-headed, zealous atheist. 1847 Dickens in Forster *Life* (1872) I. ii. 49, I never can forget, that my mother was warm for my being sent back. 1850 Grote *Greece* ii. lviii. (1862) V. 161 A warm and even angry debate arose upon his present speech. 1874 Geo. Eliot *Coll. Breakf.-P.* 348 Doting reasoners Who hugged some reasons with a preference As warm Laertes did. 1883 L. C. Murray *Hearts* xix. (1885) 163 They..found the young man there in a state of warm indignation at the libellous paragraph.

b. Of the passions or disposition in general: Prone to excitement, ardent, impulsive; apt to disregard the voice of cool reason.

1749 Fielding *Tom Jones* xii. xiii, As Jones had the vices of a warm disposition, he was entirely free from those of a cold one. a1768 Secker *Serm.* (1770) III. 50 They are just entering into the World..with lively Spirits and warm Passions to mislead them.

11. Hot-tempered, angry.

1547 Q. Catherine Parr in S. Haynes *St. Papers* (1740) 61 My Lord your Brother hathe thys Afternone a lyttell made me warme. Yt was fortunate we war so muche dystant, for I suppose els I schulde have bytten hym. 1581 A. Hall *Iliad* ix. 168 This warme and bitter wrath it grew of strife. 1712 Addison *Spect.* No. 440 ¶ 4 This insensibly grew into some warm Words. *Ibid.* No. 481 ¶ 3 They say he's a warm Man, and does not care to be made Mouths at. 1719 De Foe *Crusoe* ii. (Globe) 505, I..begun to be a little warm with him. 1822 Galt *Provost* xxxvii, A fine bold rattling lad, warm in the temper. 1849 Macaulay *Hist. Eng.* vi. II. 123 He was mortified and irritated by the tidings. He held warm and menacing language. 1855 D. Costello *Stories fr. Screen* 131 'It's an expression of mine when I'm angry.' 'You're warm,' says he.

12. Of the heart, feelings, etc.: Full of love, gratitude, approbation, etc.; very cordial or tender.

c1480 Henryson *Cock & Fox* 60 Quhen I behald зour fedderis fair and gent,..My hart is warme. 1526 *Pilgr. Perf.* (W. de W. 1531) 150 The soule melteth whan it waxeth warme in deuocyon. 1740 *New Hist. Jamaica* iv. 86 He had a warm Side to the Royal Party, and encouraged the loyal Sufferers. 1749 Fielding *Tom Jones* v. iii, He was not yet free from doubt of misconstruing compassion, or at best esteem, into a warmer regard. 1822 M. A. Kelty *Osmond* I. 73 Her heart was warm in the cause of her young friend. 1828 Macaulay *Ess. Hallam* ¶ 43 The conduct of Hampden in the affair of the ship-money met with the warm approbation of every respectable Royalist in England. 1834 Dickens *Sk. Boz, Boarding-ho.* ii, A very warm friendship soon sprung up between them. 1864 D. G. Mitchell *Seven*

Stories 57, I was beginning to feel a warm interest in the people over the way. 1904 *Verney Mem.* II. 239 Her warm heart..made her welcome in every household.

b. with agent-noun or equivalent sb., as *a warm friend, supporter*. Also of persons: Full of tenderness or affection.

1765 *Museum Rust.* IV. 314 A certain noble lord, a warm friend to every improvement in husbandry. 1827 Lytton *Pelham* ii, Yet to those he loved, no one could be more open and warm. 1838 — *Alice* iii. vii, We should have thought that Lord Vargrave was her warmest admirer. 1842 Dickens *Amer. Notes* ix, I have frequently heard this admitted, even by those who are its warmest advocates. 1854 Patmore *Angel in Ho.* i. ii. vii. (1879) 205 Others as chaste and warm there are. 1891 E. Peacock *N. Brendon* II. 379 They were now warm friends.

c. of utterances or manifestations.

1742 in *10th Rep. Hist. MSS. Comm.* App. i. 277, I beg you would present my warmest thanks to my Lord Carteret. 1766 Goldsm. *Vicar W.* xxxi, As you once had my warmest vows of constancy, you shall now have them repeated. 1782 Cowper *Let. to J. Hill* Nov., I received a note from old Mr. Small, which was more than civil—it was warm and friendly. 1814 Byron *Lara* i. vii, Warm was his welcome to the haunts of men. 1855 Macaulay *Hist. Eng.* xii. III. 206 He concluded by acknowledging in warm terms his obligations to the King of France. 1885 'Mrs. Alexander' *At Bay* ix, She dispatched a warm invitation.

13. Characterized by, of the nature of, prone to, sexual desire; amorous.

1592 Shaks. *Ven. & Ad.* 605 The warme effects which she in him finds missing, She seekes to kindle with continuall kissing. c1630 Milton *On May Morning* 6 Hail bounteous May that dost inspire Mirth and youth and warm desire. 1897 Flor. Marryat *Blood Vampire* iv, She's rather a warm customer, and if she takes a fancy to a man, 'e won't well know 'ow to get out of it.

14. With reference to fancy and imagination, ideas, expectations, and the like: Ardent, lively, glowing.

1668 Evelyn tr. *Freart's Idea Perf. Paint.* 49 Our Painters Idea was not, it seems, so warm. 1699 T. Allison *Voy. Archangel* 52 Notwithstanding it froze extream hard at this time, yet we had warm hopes of getting to Sea. 1702 *Post Man* 23–26 May 2/1 Yesterday there was a warm report that Her Majesty's Ship the Lenox..had attacked a Fleet of French Merchant Ships. 1746 Hervey *Medit.* (1818) 33 May we learn to renounce our own will, and be ready to make a sacrifice of our warmest wishes. 1838 Prescott *Ferd. & Is.* ii. viii. (1846) II. 424 Their imaginations were warm with the beauty and novelty of the scenes which met their eyes in the New World. 1849 Ruskin *Sev. Lamps* v. § 24. 160 There is not one tender touch, not one warm stroke, on the whole façade. 1872 E. W. Robertson *Hist. Ess.* 192 Bridferth has drawn a very warm picture of the scene from which the indignant abbot snatched the king.

b. Of imaginative composition: Indelicate in its appeal to sexual emotion.

1814 Jane Austen *Mansfield Park* xv, I do not know the play; but, as Maria says, if there is anything a little too warm..it can be easily left out. 1826 Disraeli *Viv. Grey* iii. vii, And then be stumbled on rather a warm scene in an old Château in the South of France. 1831 Scott *Ct. Robt.* x, He..avoided those warm descriptions which had given such offence to the Countess Brenhilda. 1846 *Hints on Husband-catching* 18 The most immoral doctrines, the warmest scenes.

15. Of colour: Suggestive of warmth; said esp. of rich red or yellow, and tints mingled with these.

1764 Goldsm. *Trav.* 137 The canvas glow'd, beyond e'en Nature warm. 1815 J. Smith *Panorama Sci. & Art* II. 752 Where a richer and warmer effect..is required, strong body colours must be employed. 1820 Keats *Eve of St. Agnes* xxv, Full on this casement shone the wintry moon, And threw warm gules on Madeline's fair breast. 1858 Kingsley *Misc.* (1860) I. iv. 198 The delicate yellow-green..fly, with its warm grey wings. 1860 Ruskin *Mod. Paint.* V. ix. xi. 320 If the tones of the picture are kept low.., and the reflected lights warm. 1892 *Photogr. Ann.* II. p. lv, Prints can be made either of warm or cold tones. 1897 Sarah Grand *Beth Bk.* xxxvii, The walls were painted a pale warm pink.

b. qualifying an adjective of colour.

1864 Tennyson *Aylmer's F.* 155 The warm-blue breathings of a hidden hearth.

16. Of a bill: Exorbitant in its charges. *colloq.*

1892 *Daily News* 20 July 5/4 He had expressed the opinion that a certain bill for stoves was 'a warm one.' 'Excuse my ignorance,' interrupted the Lord Chief Justice, 'but what does "warm" mean?'

17. Comb. and spec. collocations: **a.** parasynthetic, as *warm-backed, -coloured, -complexioned, -constitutioned, -tempered* adjs.; **b. warm bath**, a bath of warm water (often as a medical treatment); also **warm bathing**; †**warm head**, a warm-headed person; **warm-headed** *a.*, having a heated fancy or excitable temperament; **warm-house**, a kind of hot-house; **warm with** *colloq.*, (spirits) mixed with hot water and sugar (cf. *cold without*).

1847 R. S. Surtees *Hawbuck Gr.* iii, An atmosphere warranting the *warm-backed waistcoat. 1731 R. Porter in *Med. Ess.* (1737) III. 371, I resolved therefore to try what might be the Advantage of a *warm Bath, by relaxing the Intestine, and opening the Passage. 1858 J. H. Walsh *Dom. Med.* 370 Action on the skin by means of the warm-bath or the vapour-bath. 1744 J. Stevenson in *Med. Ess.* V. ii. 867 *Warm Bathing, by relaxing and enlarging the Capacities of the Vessels, makes a Derivation of the Fluids into the Parts bathed. 1813 J. Thomson *Inflammation* 173 Hot fomentations and warm-bathing. 1818 Scott *Br. Lamm.* xxvi, It was comfortably hung with a sort of *warm-coloured worsted. 1761 A. Murphy *All in Wrong* ii. 28 A smooth-faced, fiery eyed, *warm-complexioned, taper young fellow. 1775 Adair *Amer. Ind.* 190 The *warm-constitutioned young widows. 1684 *Def. Resol. Case of Consc. conc. Symbolizing with Ch.*

Rome 32 By what figure do you call one Start-up *Warm Head a new Generation? 1690 Locke *Hum. Und.* iv. iv. § 1 The advantage will be on the *warm-headed Man's side, as having the more Ideas, and the more lively. 1749 Lavington *Enthus. Meth. & Papists* (1820) 95 Our rambling, warm-headed, itinerant preachers. 1843 *Florist's Jrnl.* (1846) IV. 175 They may then be placed in the *warm-house. 1903 *Westm. Gaz.* 8 Oct. 10/2 The tubers..were first planted in a warm-house. 1591 Sylvester *Du Bartas* i. ii. 437 *Warm-temp'red show'rs it sendeth in the Spring. 1796 Mme. D'Arblay *Camilla* III. 244 The Ensign [was] more warm tempered and wrong-headed. 1818 Scott *Br. Lamm.* xxii, I know Lady Ashton is a warm-tempered and prejudiced woman. 1838 *Bentley's Misc.* IV. 575 A second tumbler of brandy and water, '*warm with,' stood exhaling its fragrance at my elbow. 1840 T. A. Trollope *Summer in Brittany* I. 213 They have some other object and enjoyment in life besides the consumption of 'warm with' or 'cold without'.

B. *absol.* and *sb.*2

1. That which is warm; a state, or sensation, of being warm; warmth. *rare.*

a1250 *Owl & Night.* 538 Hi beoþ houhful & wel arme And secheþ yorne to þen warme. c1350 *St. Christina* 251 in Horstm. *Altengl. Leg.* (1881) 95 Of al þe fire scho felid no warm. Þan come scho furth with-outen harm. 1379 *Glouc. Cath. MS.* 19, No. 1, fol. 9 b, The more nere the sonne ys to vs the more hete or warme. 1513 Douglas *Æneis* vi. xii. 16 A hait fyry power, warme, and dew. a1547 Surrey *'The sonne hath twise'* 7 The winters hurt recouers with the warm. 1839 A. Pike in *Blackw. Mag.* XLV. 819 A pleasant warm is felt upon the sea.

b. *In the warm*: (of a solution, etc.) in a warm state.

1903 *Brit. Med. Jrnl.* 21 Mar. 654 The union of toxin and antitoxin occurs in fixed ratios, more rapidly in concentrated solution and in the warm.

2. *British* (*Service*) *warm*, a warm short overcoat worn especially by officers of the army.

1902 *Imp. Yeom., Rep. D.A.G.* 15 May (1902) 123 The coat or jacket known as 'British Service Warm,' which is practically an overcoat made to wear over uniform, thick and warm. 1918 *Blackw. Mag.* June 803/2 In a 'British Warm' and patched breeches.

Warm (wǭɹm), *adv.* Now only quasi-adv., in predicate-extensions. [OE. *wearme*, f. the adj.] Warmly; so as to be warm.

c1000 *Sax. Leechd.* II. 116 Bewreoh ðe wearme. ?a1366 Chaucer *Rom. Rose* 409 Wel had she clad hir silf and warme. c1410 *Lantern of Light* 46 Whanne þe sunne schynneþ warme. 1596 *Edw. III*, iii. v. 90 With thy sword, yet reaking warme With blood of those that fought to be thy bane. 1707 Mortimer *Husb.* (1721) II. 356 When the South or West Winds blow, or the Sun shines warm. 1774 Goldsm. *Nat. Hist.* (1776) V. 336 They should be put nest and all into a little basket, which should be covered up warm. 1820 Keats *Lamia* i. 8 Hermes empty left His golden throne, bent warm on amorous theft. 1840 Dickens *Old C. Shop* xlvi, The women straightway carried her off to bed; and, having covered her up warm, [etc.].

b. *Comb.*, qualifying an adj. or pple., as †*warm-hot*; *warm-breathed, -contested, -sheltered*; *-kept, -lying, -reeking, -working.*

c1430 *Two Cookery-bks.* 8 Set it on þe fyre tyl it be warme hot. 1599 Shaks. *Hen. V*, v. ii. 335 For Maides well Summer'd, and warme kept, are like Flyes at Bartholomew-tyde. 1634 W. Wood *New Eng. Prosp.* i. ii. 4 The North-east and South winde..bringing in the warme-working waters of the Sea, loosneth the frozen Bayes. 1740 Somervile *Hobbinol* iii. 245 The panting Rivals..in Conceit Already grasp the warm-contested Prize. 1757 Dyer *Fleece* ii. 161 The high heath, by trees Warm-shelter'd, may despise the rage of storms. 1775 Sheridan *Rivals* ii. i, Their quivering, warm-breathed sighs impregnate the very air. 1786 Burns *To a Haggis* iii, O what a glorious sight, Warm-reekin, rich! 1786 Abercrombie *Gard. Assist.* 294 Plunge plants in pots—in some dry warm-lying ground.

Warm (wǭɹm), *v.* Pa. t. and pa. pple. **warmed** (wǭɹmd). Forms: 1 **werman, wærman, wirman, wyrman; wearmian**; 2–3 *Orm.* **warrmenn**, 3 **werme, wormie**, 3–7 **warme**, 5– **warm.** [Two formations: (i) OE. (**wierman*), *werman, wirman* trans. = OS. *warmian* (MLG., (M)Du. *warmen*), OHG. *warmen, wermen* (MHG. *wermen*, mod.G. *wärmen*), ON. *verma* (Sw. *värma*, Da. *varme*), Goth. *warmjan*:—OTeut. **warmjan*; (ii) OE. *wearmian* intr. = OHG. *war(a)mên* (MHG., early mod.G. *warmen*):—OTeut. type **warmǣjan*; both f. OTeut. **warmo-* Warm *a.*]

I. *trans.* To make warm.

1. To make (one's body, limbs, etc.) warm by approach to a fire, exposure to the sun's rays, exercise, clothing, etc.; to impart warmth to (a person or animal suffering from cold).

c900 *Bæda's Hist.* iii. xiv. (1890) 196 Se cyning þonne, forðon he of huntað cwom ȝestod æt þam fyre & hine wyrmde. c1000 *Ags. Gosp.* John xviii. 14 Þa þeȝnas stodon æt þam gledon, & wyrmdon hiȝ. c1200 Ormin 2711 To wasshenn hemm, to warrmenn hemm, To beddenn hemm & frofrenn. c1205 Lay. 12609 Nu þu scalt þe warmen [c1275 wormie] þer. c1275 *Passion of our Lord* 230 in *O. E. Misc.* 43 Peter stod..and wermede hym at the glede. a1300 *Cursor M.* 23090 O naked-hed quen i drogh arme, Yee gaf me clething me to warme. 1340-70 *Alex. & Dind.* 332 For no cold þat vs comeþ in oure kinde age, We ne faren to no fir our fingrus to warme. c1440 *Alphabet of Tales* 431 Þan he oppynd þe dure & said vnto hym: And þou be a man, þou hase myster to hafe þe dure opynd, and to hafe meatt and warm þe. 1471 Caxton *Recuyell* (Sommer) 169 Prayng hym that he wold brynge her in to some hous where she myghte warme and chauffe her wyth her chyld for he was nyhe ded for cold. a1548 Hall *Chron.*, *Hen. VIII* 238 b, All the Ladyes entered the tentes and there warmed them a space.

1604 E. G. tr. *Acosta's Hist. Indies* ii. ix. 101, I felt so great cold, as I was forced to go into the sunne to warme me. 1642 Fuller *Holy & Prof. St.* ii. xix. 121 His hands must be their own fire, and warm themselves with working. 1798 Sophia Lee *Canterb. T., Young Lady's T.* II. 74 A group of fishermen sat warming themselves in the sun. 1831 Scott *Ct. Robt.* xxvi, Think not I will once more warm in my bosom the household snake which had so nearly stung me to death. 1852 Thackeray *Esmond* i. xiv, You little serpent, warmed by my fire. 1860 Tyndall *Glaciers* i. xi. 72 We rose ..renewed the fire and warmed ourselves. 1902 R. Bagot *Donna Diana* i. 4 Shall we go to Aragno's on our way home and have some coffee to warm us?

absol. 1611 Bible *Isa.* xlvii. 14 There shall not be a coale to warm at, nor fire to sit before it.

b. Said of a fire, the sun, etc. Also *absol.*

a1548 Hall *Chron.*, *Edw. IV*, 216 b, Whiche sight as much pleased the citizens, as a fier paynted on the wall, warmed the olde woman. 1583 Babington *Commandm.* 413 When they are colde, they goe to the fire, and not to the water to warme them; and can they not tell which dooth warme and which dooth coole? 1732 Pope *Ess. Man* i. 271 All are but parts of one stupendous whole..That..Warms in the sun, refreshes in the breeze.

c. To increase the animal heat of. In quot. *absol.*

1610 Markham *Masterp.* ii. clxxiii. 483 It looseth and scattereth humors, warmeth and moisteneth.

d. Said of the blood.

1759 Sterne *Tr. Shandy* II. xvii, He was as honest a soul, added Trim, (pulling out his handkerchief) as ever blood warmed. 1810 Scott *Lady of Lake* v. xiv, For I have sworn this braid to stain In the best blood that warms thy vein. 1896 Housman *Shropshire Lad* xxxi, The blood that warms an English yeoman.

2. In various figurative uses.

a. To inspire with affection or kindly feelings; to cause to 'glow' with pleasure.

1526 *Pilgr. Perf.* (W. de W. 1531) 266 It calefyeth & warmeth the hert of man or woman with the flame of loue. 1665 Boyle *Occas. Refl.* Introd. Pref. (1848) p. xxx, Whilst pious Reflections are making, they are proper to Instruct the Mind, and Warm the Affections. 1773 Mrs. Chapone *Improv. Mind* (1774) I. 78 The effusions of a heart warm'd with the tenderest affection. 1836 J. Grant *Random Recoll. Ho. Lords* xvi. 391 That eloquence which approves itself to the judgment, though it never warms the heart by appeals to the passions. 1837 Dickens *Pickw.* lvii, It will warm my heart to witness the happiness of those friends who are dearest to me. 1847 C. Brontë *Jane Eyre* xi, The charm of adventure sweetens that sensation, the glow of pride warms it. 1864 Tennyson *Aylmer's F.* 554 Once indeed, Warm'd with his wines, or taking pride in her, She look'd so sweet, he kiss'd her tenderly. 1905 C. G. Lang *Th. Parables Jesus* 16 When the example of a true man or woman warms the heart and fires the will.

absol. 1883 R. W. Dixon *Mano* i. viii. 21 Those lightsome words that warm like summer days.

b. To render eager or zealous; to rouse from indifference. Also *absol.* Now *rare.*

c1580 Hooker *Sir P. Carew* (1857) 42 Sir Peter Carew was then present, and one unto whom, as they thought, the speeches were specially directed..and indeed, he being somewhat warmed theirin, deviseth how to compass the matter. 1638 Davenant *Madagascar* 10 When honours warmes him, and his blood is young. 1706 *Epistle after Battle Ramillies* 106 Prior's Wks. 1907 II. 372 The rescu'd chief, by the past danger warm'd, Our weaken'd houshold with new fury storm'd. 1712 Steele *Spect.* No. 521 ¶ 2, I had arrived at a particular Skill in warming a Man so far in his Narration, as to make him throw in a little of the Marvelous. 1737 Whiston *Josephus, Hist.* i. i. § 4 When he was warmed by this great success, he made an assault upon the garrison that was in the city. 1764 Goldsm. *Trav.* 380 Calm is my soul, nor apt to rise in arms, Except when fast approaching danger warms. 1764 Churchill *Gotham* iii. 323 The Soul, with great and manly feelings warm'd, Panting for Knowledge, rests not till inform'd. 1765 Burke *Corr.* (1844) I. 59, I am not used to defend my conduct;..I have been warmed to it by the imputation you threw on me. 1857 Mrs. Carlyle *Lett.* II. 308 Anne, who is so difficult to warm up to bare satisfaction point.

†**c.** To exhort to valour. (Often in Dryden and Pope.) *Obs.*

1697 Dryden *Æneis* vii. 657 The Gods invok'd, the Rutuli prepare Their Arms, and warm each other to the War. *Ibid.* viii. 927 The Queen her self,..With Cymbals toss'd, her fainting Souldiers warms. 1718 Pope *Iliad* xvi. 653 First to the Fight his native Troops he warms.

d. Of drink: To excite, stimulate.

1617 Moryson *Itin.* i. 3 When the common people are once warmed with drinke, they are apt to doe them injury. 1743 Francis tr. *Hor., Epodes* xi. 12 When the gay Liquor warm'd my opening Soul.

†**e.** To provoke, excite (temper). *Obs.*

1752 Chesterf. *Let. to Son* 26 Sept., Keep your own temper, and artfully warm other people's.

3. To make (a material object or substance) warm; to heat moderately; to 'take the chill off'.

a1000 *Riddles* xii[i]. 10 Wonfeax Wale..wæteð in wætre, wyrmeð hwilum fæȝre to fyre. c1000 in Assmann *Ags. Hom.* xi. 84 For ðy he cwæð be ðam colan wætere, ðæt nan man ne ðorfte hine beladian, ðæt he fæt næfde, on hwy he hit wyrman mihte. c1374 Chaucer *Troylus* v. 1109 The laurer crowned Phebus with his hete Gan..To warmen of þe Est See þe wawes wete. a1425 tr. *Arderne's Treat. Fistula* etc. 40 Þe Iuyse of celidone y-medled wiþ vinegre and warmed at þe fire..quenchiþ wele þe wickid hete. 1530 Palsgr. 771/2 You must warme your medecyne or you drinke it. a1589 R. Willes in Hakluyt *Voy.* 611 Before the Sunne hath warmed the ayre and dissolued the ise,..there can be no sailing. 1617 S. H. *Preserv. Health* (1624) 45 In the Winter time, warme well your garments at the fire, and warm the linings of the same. 17.. Watts *Hymns & Spir. Songs* ii. cxlvii. (1751) 259 E'er there was Rain to bless the Earth, Or Sun to warm the Ground. 1747–96 Mrs. Glasse *Cookery* xv.

269 Skim it, warm it blood warm, and drink it. 1774 Goldsm. *Nat. Hist.* VI. 168 In summer, they [*sc.* fish] are seen in great numbers in the shallows near the shore, where the sun has power to warm the water to the bottom. 1859 H. Kingsley *G. Hamlyn* xix, The tea's cold; put it on the embers and warm it a bit. 1862 Mrs. H. Wood *Mrs. Hallib. Troub.* i. i, You can get my slippers warmed, Jane. 1900 *Jrnl. Soc. Dyers* XVI. 12 Powerful jets with water warmed by steam. 1907 J. A. Hodges *Elem. Photogr.* (ed. 6) 159 The negative should be slightly warmed.

†**b.** Said jocularly for: To occupy (one's bed).

1599 Marston *Antonio's Rev.* iii. ii, I thinke we shall not warme our beds to day.

c. *To warm up* (U.S. *to warm over*): to make warm again (cooked food that has become cold). Also (*rarely*) without adv.

1848 Dickens *Dombey* lix, She requests to have that little bit of sweetbread that was left, warmed up for her supper. 1853 Soyer *Pantroph.* 380 Another custom..was that of warming the remains of a preceding banquet for other guests. 1863 W. C. Baldwin *Afr. Hunting* iii. 68 We lived for three days on a most recommendable stew,..which appeared, warmed up fresh, at every meal. 1885 'Mrs. Alexander' *Valerie's Fate* iv, Valerie went..to the kitchen to warm up an appetizing little dish prepared by the femme de ménage.

fig. 1876 Ld. Hartington in Ld. E. Fitzmaurice *Earl Granville* (1905) II. 167 All the old anti-Turk abuse was warmed up again. 1879 O. W. Holmes *Motley* xxi. 162 [The reply] took up the old exceptions, warmed them over into grievances.

d. To impart warmth of colour to.

1853 Kane *Grinnell Exp.* xxxv. (1856) 321 A peculiar purple, slightly warmed or bronzed at its margins. 1862 Miss Braddon *Lady Audley* iii, Not one glimmer of gold or auburn warmed the dull flaxen of her hair.

4. To heat (a building, a room) to a moderate temperature.

1858 Lardner *Hand-bk. Nat. Phil.* 278 Warming buildings by hot water. 1874 Micklethwaite *Modern Par. Churches* 200 A perfect method of warming churches has yet to be invented. 1915 *Blackw. Mag.* Mar. 345/1 The room was warmed by a brazier.

†**5.** To inaugurate (a new house) by a feast or entertainment. *Obs.* Cf. House-warming 2.

1617 in *Crt. & Times Jas. I* (1848) II. 50 On Monday, to warm it [the renovated house], he made a great feast. 1661 Heylin *Eccl. Restaur.* (1674) 237 Sir Thomas Tresham.. took possession of his place, which having scarce warmed, he was taken from it by the stroke of death. 1800 *Gentl. Mag.* LXX. ii. 786/2 The Prince, it is said, will be present at the first dinner that *warms* this room.

†**6.** *To be well warmed*: to be settled *in* (a residence, position of dignity or profit). *Obs.* Cf. Warm *a.* 7.

1565 Allen *Defence Purg.* (1886) 16 Ere they be well warmed in their benefices. 1711 *Country-Man's Let. Curat* 79 Even before she was well warm'd on the Throne.

†**7.** *Mil.* To throw (an enemy) into commotion by a cannonade. *To warm the field*: to carry on a furious cannonade. *Obs.*

Cf. F. *chauffer un poste*, 'le canonner vivement' (Littré).

1705 *Addr. Blessington* in *Lond. Gaz.* No. 4089/2 The English warm'd the Field to that degree, that Thirty Squadrons..were forc'd to fly. 1720 De Foe *Capt. Singleton* xi. (1840) 187 Resolving to give him a broadside that should warm him.

b. Sporting. *To warm up*: to give (one's competitor) reason to fear defeat.

1868 *Field* 4 July 14/3 First Trinity rowed over for the trial heat, and in the final heat on the second day 'warmed up' University to some tune.

8. *dial.* To beat, flog.

1824 Carr *Craven Gloss.*, *Warm*, to beat. 'I'll warm thy jerkin for the.' 1825 Brockett *N. C. Words*, *Warm*, to beat. 'Aw'l warm yor hide.' 1828 Scott *F. M. Perth* xxix, Old Dorothy, whose hand has warmed my haffits before now. 1853 'C. Bede' *Verdant Green* i. i, You take out your strap and warm him! 1862 Mrs. H. Wood *Mrs. Hallib. Troub.* i. xxi, Won't Charlotte warm his back for him! 1892 M. C. F. Morris *Yorks. Folk Talk* 95 Every Yorkshireman knows what warming a child means; perhaps not a few..by bitter experience. 1915 'Q' (Quiller-Couch) in *Blackw. Mag.* Jan. 102/2 To 'warm' a child in Polpier signifies to beat him with a strap.

II. *intr.* To become warm.

9. Of a living body, a material thing or substance: To be raised in temperature.

a1000 *Phœnix* 213 Wyrta wearmiaþ. c1000 Ælfric *Gram.* xxvi. (Z.) 154 *Caleo*, ic wearmiȝe. c1400 *Destr. Troy* 4035 Wyndis wastid away, warmyt the ayre. c1648-50 Brathwait *Barnabees Jrnl.* iii. (1818) 95 Thence to Cambridge where the Muses Haunt the Vine-bush..Like sparks up a chimney warming. 1827 Faraday *Chem. Manip.* iv. (1842) 141 A large thermometer..may from the lapse of time necessary to allow of its proper change, occasion an alteration of temperature, by allowing the body tried to cool or warm. 1868 Louisa M. Alcott *Little Women* i, Beth put a pair of slippers down to warm. 1872 O. W. Holmes *Poet* i. (1885) 19 A cold day warming up to 32°. 1889 'R. Boldrewood' *Robbery under Arms* xi, Here's some damper and mutton..while tea warms. 1904 S. E. White *Forest* xiv, The weather had warmed, the sun shone.

b. Of colour: To become 'warmer' or more ruddy.

1831 James *Phil. Augustus* xv. On a bright morning of July, when the grey of the sky was just beginning to warm with the rising day. 1906 *Westm. Gaz.* 8 June 8/1 His head and underparts are of a pearly grey that warms to a pinkish hue on the breast.

10. Of a person, his heart, feelings, etc.: To become affectionate, kindly, or genial (*to, towards* a person).

Supplement, p. 3873; Corrigenda, p. 4092; Spurious words, p. 4093; Books quoted, p. 4094

Warmable, a. *nonce-wd.* [f. WARM v. + -ABLE.] Capable of being warmed.

Warm-man. A fighting-man, warrior, soldier.

Warm-blooded, a. Having warm blood; *spec.* of mammals and birds, which have a uniform high temperature.

Warmed (wǫmd), *ppl. a.* [f. WARM v. + -ED 1.]

Warmer (wǫ'məɪ), [f. WARM v. + -ER 1.] 1. A person who warms.

Warm-hearted, a. Having a warm heart; of a generous and affectionate disposition.

Warming-pan. A long-handled covered pan of metal (usually of brass) to contain live coals, etc., formerly in common use for warming beds.

Warmful, a. *Obs. rare.* [f. WARM a. + -FUL.] Full of warmth.

Warm-hearted, *ppl. a.* Warm-heartedly.

Warmish, a. Somewhat warm.

Warmly (wǫ'mlɪ), *adv.* [f. WARM a. + -LY 2.] In a warm manner.

Warmness. Now *rare.* [f. WARM a. + -NESS.] The condition of being warm, warmth. 1. Moderate heat. 2. The state of being well to do. *Obs.* 3. Lukewarmness. *Obs. rare.* 4. Warmth of affection or devotion.

Warmonger. One who traffics in war.

Warmoth, obs. form of WARDMOTE.

Warmth (wǫmþ). [OE. *wiermþu, *wiermþo, MHG. *wermde, warmth (early mod.G. *wärmde) — OTeut. type *warmiþô.] 1. The state or quality of being warm. 2. The natural heat of a living body. 3. Pungency (of seasoning). 4. An excited or warm state of the feelings. 5. A glowing hue (of colouring in a picture, in nature); *spec.* in *Painting*.

Warmful, a. *Obs.* Full of warmth.

Warn (wǫn), *sb.* [f. WARN v.] 1. An intimation or notice of something as about to happen. 2. *poet.* Warning. 3. *Comb.* (perh. the stem of WARN v.).

Warn (wǫn), v. 1 Pa. t. and pa. pple. **warned.** Forms: 1 *warnian, wearnian,* 2 *warnian, -en, (wernin),* 2–6 *werne,* 2–3 *warni, warni,* 3 *werne, (werche),* 3–4 *warny, 6 wam;* also 5 *warn, 3–7 warne,* 6 *dial.* [OE. *warnian, wearnian, wear-nian* = MLG. *warnen* to warn, inform, Flem. *warnen* to warn, put on one's guard.]

Warn, v. 1 (*continued*) 1. To give (a person) cautionary notice or advice with regard to actions or conduct; to caution against neglect of duty or against wrong or mistaken action or belief. 2. To give previous notice to. More definitely *to warn before*. *Obs.* b. *absol.*

Warned *ppl. a.*

Warn, v. 3 Forms: a. 1 *wiernan, wyrnan, wyrnian, wernen,* 3–5 *werne,* 1–5 *werne, 3–5 warne, wern,* a. 3 *Sc.* varn, 4 *werne.* [OE. *wiernan, wyrnan,* ON. *varna* to refuse, deny.] 1. To prohibit (a person) from doing something; to hinder or restrain. 2. To refuse to allow (some action or course of action) to a person; to forbid (a person) to do something. 3. To refuse, forbid, deny (entry, the gate, door, etc.). 4. To refuse to take or accept. 5. To refuse to allow (some action or course of action) to a person.

Warnable, a. *Obs. rare.* [f. prec.] 1. That may be warned.

Warnage. *Obs.* *Sc. var.* VERNAGE.

Warne, *conj.* *Obs.* Also *warn.* [app. a northern var. of unless.]

Supplement, p. 3873; Corrigenda, p. 4092; Spurious words, p. 4093; Books quoted, p. 4094

WARP. (continued)

18. trans. To turn aside or divert (a moving body) from its path or orbit. Also, to deflect, change the direction of (one's journey). *rare.*

b. intr. To turn or incline in a (specified) direction. *rare.*

19. fig. To receive a 'twist' or bias, which influences one's judgement or sentiments; to turn from the straight path; to deviate, swerve, go astray. Const. *from, &c.*

b. To submit to do something. Obs.

III. To weave, twine.

20. trans. To weave (a web). Obs. **b.** To arrange (threads, yarn) so as to form a warp; to wind on a warp-beam. Also dial.

c. To warp one's warp.

21. a. Rope-making. To stretch (yarn) into lengths to be tarred.

b. fig. To weave, contrive, devise. Also with *up, and about.*

Warp, obs. f. WHARF, WARP v.

Warpage (wǭpǐdʒ). [f. WARP + -AGE.] App. a charge for 'warping' or hauling ships entering certain harbours.

Warped (wǭpt), ppl. a. [f. WARP v. + -ED[1].]

1. The action of throwing. Obs.

Warp-paint. Among North American Indians: Paint applied to the face and body before going into battle.

Warp-fat. Obs. [f. WARP sb. + FAT sb.[2]] = warping-fat, -trough (WARPING vbl. sb. 4 c).

Warping (wǭpǐŋ), vbl. sb. [f. WARP v. + -ING[1].]

1. The action of throwing. Obs.

Warper (wǭpǝɪ). [f. WARP v. + -ER[1].]

1. One who throws, a thrower. Obs.

2. One who winds yarn in preparation for weaving.

Warping (wǭpǐŋ), ppl. a. [-ING[2].] That swerves, deviates; distorting, perverting.

Warpis, v. sc. Obs.

Warple (wǭˑp'l), sb. dial. Forms: 6 pl. warples, warplas, 7 whaple, 7- whapple, 9 warple, wafel, warpul, worple, wopple. [Of obscure origin; cf. warp sb. 8c.]

War-proof, a. [WAR sb. + PROOF.] Able to resist a hostile attack.

Warr, obs. form of WAR sb.[1] v., WARE a., p.t.

Warra-, variant of WARRA-.

Warragal, variant of WARRIGAL.

Warral, var. WARRAY v. Obs.

Warrandice (wǭˑrǝndǝis). Chiefly Sc. Also 5 warandis, -andys.

Warrant (wǭˑrǎnt), sb. Forms: 1-2 wǭrant, 5 warantie, waranti, 4-6 warand, 5 waraunt, 5 warante, 5-7 warrant, warraunt.

1. A protector, defender. Obs.

2. One who or something which protects or authorizes.

Warrant (wǭˑrǎnt), v. Forms: 3 warante, death-warrant, press-warrant.

Cf. WARRANT OFFICER.

WARRANT.

6 warrande, (7 *pa. pple.* warand), 8 warran, 5 - warrand (*occas.* written wand). [early ME. *warant*, *waranti*, *warand*, a. OF. *warantir*, *warandir*, dial. variants of *g(u)arantir*, *g(u)arandir* (mod.F. *garantir*) = Pr. *garantir*, *guirensir*, Sp. Pg. *garantir*, It. *guarentire*, *guarentere*; a Com. Rom. formation on the vb.: see WARRANT *sb.*]

† 1. *trans.* To keep safe from danger, to protect.

9. To give (a person) warrant or authority, authorize (*to do something*); to authorize, sanction (a course of action).

WARRANTABLE.

40 'Tis therefore very Warrantable to pass a Severe Judgment upon a Man, when 'tis plain and fair of question that he deserves it.

WARRANTISE.

Warrantise (wǫ'rǎntəiz). [f. WARRANT *v.* + -ISE.]

1. *Law.* The person to whom a warranty is given.

WARRANTISE.

WARRANTY.

Warranty (wǫ'rǎnti). Forms: 4-5 warantie, 5-6 war-, 5 7 warrantie, 4-7 guarantie, &c. [AF. *warantie*, var. of *guarantie*: f. GUARANTEE *sb.*]

1. *Law.* An act of warranting; in certain specific applications.

WARRAY.

Warray, *obs.* form of VERY.

Warrayable, *a. Obs.* Of: warrantable, dial. var. of VERY.

WARREN.

Warre. *Obs.* Also 5 warre, 6 war. [repr. OE. *wearr* str. masc., recorded only in the Epinal glosses; also cf. LG. *warte*.]

Warren (wǫ'rěn), *sb.* Forms: 2 warenne, 4-5 wareyne, 5 warande, warayne, 5-6 warant(e), 5 warayne, 6-7 warreyne, 6-7 warrayne, 6 warrein(e). [ME. *wareine*, a. ONF. *warenne* (= OF. *garenne*).]

1. A piece of land enclosed and preserved for breeding game.

WASH. 128 WASH.

WASH. 129 WASH.

WASHABILITY. 130

WASHED. 131 WASHERWOMAN.

WASHERY.

Washery (wǫ'ʃəri). [f. WASH v. + -ERY.] A place at which the washing of coal, ore, wool, etc. is carried on.

†Washer. Obs. A female washer (of linen), a washerwoman.

Washery (wǫ'ʃəri). Obs. [f. WASH sb.]

Wash ground. Obs. [f. WASH sb. or v.] A drying-ground.

Wash-hand, a. In 8 wash-hands. [f. WASH v. Cf. F. lavemain(t) sb., wash-hand stand, wash-hand basin.]

Wash-house (wǫ'ʃhaus). Also 6–7 washouse, wash'us. [f. WASH sb. + HOUSE sb. Cf. Du. waschhuis, G. waschhaus.]

Washical. Obs. rare—.

Washiness (wǫ'ʃines). [f. WASHY a. + -NESS.]

Washing (wǫ'ʃiŋ), vbl. sb. [-ING.]

WASH-LEATHER. 134 **WASHY.** **WASKITE.** 135 **WASPISH.**

Wash-leather. [Cf. WASH v. Cf. G. waschleder (perh. from Eng.).]

†Washer. Obs. [f. WASH v.; cf. WASHMAID.]

Washman (wǫ'ʃmən). [f. WASH sb.]

†Washmaid. Obs. [f. WASH v.; cf. WASHER.]

Washmead. Obs. [f. WASH sb. (?and a.)]

Wash-mill. [f. WASH v.]

Wash-mouth. I. w. dial. Also washa-mouth.

Wash-off, sb. [f. Calico-printing.]

Wash-out. [f. WASH v. I.]

Wash-pool. [f. WASH sb. or v. + POOL sb.]

Wash-pot. [f. WASH v.]

Washlock. [f. WASH sb. or v. + LOCK sb.]

Washmaid. [f. WASH v.]

Wash road.

Washstand.

Washwoman. Now = WASHERWOMAN.

Wash-trough. [f. WASH v.]

Wash-tub. [f. WASH sb. Cf. Du. waschtobbe.]

Wash-up. [f. WASH v.]

Wash-water. [f. WASH v.]

Washy (wǫ'ʃi). [f. WASH v. + -Y.]

Washy-water.

Wash-work. [f. WASH sb. + WORK sb.]

Waskite, variant of VASQUINE Obs.

Waslage, contraction of VASSALAGE.

Wasp (wǫsp), sb. Forms: 1–2 wæps, wæsp, 4–6 waspe, dial. wape.

Wasp (wǫsp), v. nonce-wd.

Waspish (wǫ'ʃpiʃ), a. [f. WASP sb. + -ISH.]

Wasp-spade.

Washphood (wǫ'ʃphud).

Waspishly. [f. WASPISH + -LY.]

Wasp-kite, rare⁻⁰. [A translation of the G. name *wespenbussard*, the bird *pernis apivorus*.]

Waspling. A young wasp.

Wasp's nest, wasp-nest. The nest of a wasp. Also *fig.*

Wasp, *sb.* Obs. exc. dial. Now dial. wapy. [f. WASP *sb.* + -Y¹.]

Waspy (wɒˈspi), *a.* Resembling a wasp in form, wasp-like.

Wasp-waisted, *a.* Having the waist very slender, esp. as the result of tight-lacing.

Wassail (wɒˈseil, wɒˈsl, ˈwɒsl), *sb.* Now only *arch.* and *Hist.* Forms: 1 wæs hæil, woshail, washael, waxail, +wasseyl, 3–4, 7 wassayl, 3, 6–7, 9 *arch.* wassaile, 5 wessayle, wosasyle, (whatsaille, -aill), 6 -ayle, 6–7 was-saill, (7 vassaill, *Hist.* wa-saile, washsail), was-haal, 5–9 wassail, 7 vassaile, [ME. *wæs hæil* etc., 1. ON. *ves* (*later* ver) *heill*, corresp. to OE. *wes hál* lit. 'be in good health' or 'be fortunate': see BE *v.* and HALE *a.*]

Wassail-bowl, a large bowl or cup in which wassail (*sense* 3) was made, and from which healths were drunk; a loving-cup; also the liquor contained therein.

Wassailer (wɒˈseilər). [f. WASSAIL *sb.* or *v.* + -ER¹.] One who takes part in riotous festivities or a reveller.

Wassailing, *vbl. sb.* [f. WASSAIL *v.* + -ING¹.] The action of the verb WASSAIL; carousing, riotous festivity.

Wassail, *v.* [f. WASSAIL *sb.*]

Wassailry. [f. WASSAIL *sb.* + -RY.] Carousing, revelry.

Wassie, *local.* Also *wassel.* [Of obscure origin.] The stems of seaweed used as a manure.

Wassy, var. WAZZY.

Wast, 2nd sing. pa. t. of BE *v.*

Wast, obs. form of WAIST, WASTE, WEST.

Wastable (wéiˈstəbl), *a.* [f. WASTE *v.* + -ABLE.] 1. Liable to be wasted; subject to wastage. Also, in *Law*, said of things in respect of which a tenant may be chargeable with waste.

Wastage (wéiˈstidʒ). [f. WASTE *v.* + -AGE.] 1. Loss or diminution by wear, decay, leakage, or the like.

Waste (wéist), *a.* Forms: 3–7 wast, 4–5 wa(a)st, 6, 9 wast, 5 wayst, 4–6 *Sc.* vast(e), 3–wast(e), 6 OF. *wast(e)*, dial. variant of *guast(e)*, *gast(e)*, partly *repr.* L. *vāstum*, neut. of *vāstus* WASTE *a.* (q.v. for the phonology), partly a verbal noun 1. *waster* (*guaster*, *gaster*) WASTE *v.* Cf. *Fr.* gāt *vastum*, waste. Sp., Pg. *gasto* expense, It. *guasto* ravage, damage, injury.

Waste (wéist), *sb.* Forms: 3–7 wast, 4–5 waast, 6, 9 wast, wayste, 4–6 *Sc.* vast(e), 3–wast(e), 6 OF. *wast(e)*, dial. variant of *guast(e)*.

I. 1. Uninhabited (or sparsely inhabited) and uncultivated country; a wild and desolate region, a desert, wilderness. Somewhat *arch.*

II. The product of wear or decay, waste.

III. Refuse matter; unserviceable material remaining over from any process of manufacture; the useless by-products of any industrial process; material or manufactured articles so damaged as to be useless or unsaleable.

IV. Comparisons.

12. 1. An overflow of surplus water. *Obs.*

13. Obvious combinations, as Waste *n.* (sense 1) *waste-preventing* adj.; *-preventer* (*sense* 14) *waste-collector, -dealer, -heap, -pit, -tip* (TIP *sb.²* 4 b).

14. Special combinations: waste-basket (now chiefly *U.S.*) = WASTE-PAPER *basket*; waste-basket-n., to put in the waste-paper basket; waste-bin, a dustbin; waste-box *Mining* (see quot.); waste-cock, a stop-cock for regulating the discharge of water; waste-drain, a drain for carrying off waste water; waste-gate, -hatch, a gate or hatch for regulating the outflow of waste water; waste-pipe, a pipe to carry off waste water or steam; waste-sluice, a sluice for regulating the outflow of waste water; waste-spout, a spout for the issue of waste-water; waste-way *U.S.*, a channel for the passage of waste water; waste-weir (see quots.); waste-yard, a yard for the reception of odds and ends of little value.

Wasterful, Wasterfulness, Wasterfully

Wasterful, *a.* Obs. [f. WASTER sb. + -FUL.] Wasteful.

Wasterie, **Wasterne**, *-ine*. [Altered form (after WASTE sb.) of ONorthumb. *wœstern*, var. of *wēsten* : see WESTEN.] A wilderness.

Wasting, *ppl. a.* [f. WASTE v. + -ING.]

1. That lays waste, devastates, or destroys.
2. That is being gradually consumed or destroyed; decaying, wasting away.
3. A good-for-nothing, idle, worthless, disreputable person.

Wasting, *vbl. sb.* [f. WASTE v. + -ING.]

1. The action of laying waste; devastation.
2. The action of using or spending lavishly or to no profit.

Wastry, etc.

Wastry, *a.* Sc. [f. WASTE v., WASTER sb. + -Y. Cf. WASTRIFE *a.*] Wasteful, extravagant.

Wastrie, **Wastry**, **Wastrife**, etc.

WATCH

Wat, *sb.* [f. WATTE.] Forms: 5-6 wat, 5 watt, 6 watte, etc.

Watch, *sb.* Forms: 1 wœcce, weœe, 3-4 wacche, 3-5 wecche, wacche, etc.

as a watch dog; watch-mate, a fellow-member of a ship's watch; †watch-meal (see *watch-mail); †watch-money, a sum of money paid for watching; watch-night (see *quot.); watch-night, originally a religious service extending over midnight held monthly by Wesleyan Methodists; in later use a service held by Methodists and others) on New Year's eve, lasting until midnight; also, the night upon which the service is held; watch-officer, an officer who takes his turn in the officer in charge of the watch; watch-oil, a high refined lubricating oil used for watches and clocks; watch-paper, a disc of paper, silk, or other material, inserted or painted with an ornamental design, a picture, rhyme, or other device, inserted as a lining or pad in the outer case of an old-fashioned watch'; watch-part = *watch train; watch-peel, a warm-ing peal (of a bell); watch-pocket (see *PEEL sb.1 4); watch-pocket, a small pocket in a garment for carrying a watch; also, a pocket or pouch at the head of a bed, to hold a person's watch at night'; watch-point, a watching station or watch-box, a watchman's pole or staff; watch-post Mil., a position at which a body of soldiers, a sentinel or watchman, is stationed at watch; also, a body of guards; watch rate, a rate levied by a municipal borough to defray the expenses of watching'; watch-riband, a watch-guard in the form of a riband; watch round = ROUND sb.1 14; watch-seal = SEAL sb.2 3 f; watch-setting Mil., the posting of the watch; watch-spring, the main-spring of a watch (also without article); as a material); also astrid., a watch-stand, † (a) a look-out position for a sentinel or watchman; (2) a small case or stand in or upon which a watch may be placed so that its face may be seen; †watch-star = GUARD sb.1 12; watch-string, a watch-guard of cord; watch-tackle Naut., a TACKLE (sb. 3) by means of which the watch can perform various operations without the help of additional men; watch train, the set of wheels and pinions which drive the hands of a clock, as distinguished from the striking train; watch-wheel, the balance wheel of the 'watch-work' of a clock; also Comb.; watch-woman, (a) a woman who 'watches' in a sick room or attends a sick person; †(b) a woman who performs the duties of a night watchman; (c) a woman who keeps watch (nonce-use); †watch-wright, a watchmaker. Also WATCH-BELL, WATCH-BILL, WATCH-BOX, WATCH-CASE, WATCH-CLOCK, WATCH-DOG, WATCH-GLASS, etc.

Mayor... shall be called the *Watch Committee for such Borough. 1882 Encycl. Brit. XVII. 68/1 The mayor... is ex officio a magistrate for the borough and a member of the watch committee.

1851 SCOTT Glenfinlas xxxix, And by the *watch-fire's glimmering light... was an huntress-maid. 1864 TENNYSON Enoch Arden 570, Now the man had...

In which before the passing this Act any Rate might be levied in any Borough...for the Purpose of watching...it shall be lawful for the Council of such Borough to levy a *Watch Rate. 1880 SAILOR Self-help 314 Flaxman... was on one occasion selected by the ratepayers to collect the watch-rate. 1611 BIBLE Transl. Pref. ¶ 1 Such were the notes that from the Pirate's side Around the kindling watch-fire rang the while. 1897 DAILY NEWS 4 Jan...

Watch-house. (Watch sb.)

Watching (wǫ'tʃiŋ), vbl. sb. [-ING]

Watchless. [f. Watchless a. + -NESS.]

Watchlight. [WATCH sb.]

Watchman.

Watchmaking, vbl. sb. The making of watches.

Watchman (wǫ'tʃmæn). Pl. watchmen. [f. WATCH sb. + MAN sb.]

Watchmanly (wǫ'tʃmænli), a.

Watch-out.

Watchhole, obs. form of WATCHET.

Watoht, variant of WATCHED ppl. a.

Watch-tower. [WATCH sb.]

Watchword (wǫ'tʃwəd). [WATCH sb.]

Watchwork (wǫ'tʃwəɹk). [WATCH sb.]

Wate, obs. form of WAIT.

Wate, var. WHAT, WHATE sb. Obs., fortune.

Wate, obs. form of WET sb.

Wate, obs. pa. t. WRITE v.

Watel, obs. form of WATTLE sb. and v.

Water (wǫ'təɹ). Forms: 1–3 water, 2–5 water; etc.

WATER. 154 WATER. WATER. 155 WATER.

Water (wǫ'təɹ).

I. The liquid of which seas, lakes, and rivers are composed, and which falls as rain and issues from springs.

[Dictionary page — three-column Oxford English Dictionary text. The upper half continues the entry for the verb **Water** *with numbered senses, followed by entries for* **Water-bailage**, **Water-bailie**, **Water-bailiff**, **Waterage**, **Water-bar**, **Water-ball**, **Water-balance**, **Water- balliff**, **Water-bank**, **Water-bath**, *etc.]*

[The lower half contains the entries **Water-bear**, **Water-bearer**, **Water-bearing**, **Water-bed**, **Water-board**, **Water-boot**, **Water-boots**, **Water-borne**, **Water-bottle**, **Water-bough**, **Water-bound**, **Water-break**, **Water-buck**, **Water-budge**, **Water-bouge**, **Water-bouget**, **Water-budget**, **Water-butt**, **Water-carriage**, **Water-carrier**, **Water-cart**, **Water-caster**, **Water-cat**, **Water-chain**, **Water-clock**, **Water-closet**, **Water-colour**, *etc.]*

Water-coloured.

Water-colourist.

Water-course.

Water-cracker.

Water-craft.

Water-crane.

Water-cress.

Water-dog.

Water-doctor.

Water-drinker.

Water-drinking.

Water-drop.

Watered.

Water-engine.

Watery.

Waterfall.

Water-fast.

Water-finder.

Water-flood.

Water-flag.

Water-flower.

Water-dy.

Waterfowl.

Water-front.

Water-furrow.

Water-gall.

Water-gang.

Water-gate.

Water-gate.

Water-gauge.

Water-glass.

Water-grave.

Water-gruel.

Water-hammer.

Water-head.

Water-hen.

Water-hole.

Water-horse.
+ 1. The hippopotamus. Obs.

2. A fabled water-spirit appearing in the form of a horse.

3. (See quot.)

Water-house.
+ 1. A building in which water is raised from a river or well into a 'conduit-head' or reservoir to be conveyed by means of conduits or pipes for domestic use. Obs.

Water-ice.
1. A confection of water and sugar, flavoured and frozen.

2. Massive ice formed by the direct freezing of water, and not by the compacting of snow.

+ Wateried, ppl. a. Obs. nonce-wd. [f. WATERY.]

Waterily (wǭ'tərili), adv. [f. WATERY a. + -LY.]
In a watery manner.

Wateriness (wǭ'tərinĕs). [f. WATERY a. + -NESS.]
+ 1. concr. Watery constituent or element; aqueous matter contained in or diffused through a liquid or solid. Obs.

2. Watery secretion.

3. Watery quality.

8. Superfluity of water as a constituent, connoting poorness, thinness, insipidity. a. of the blood.

b. of an article of food.

c. fig. of literary style, composition, etc.

4. The state of being saturated with water.

5. Lachrymal moistness.

Watering (wǭ'tǝriŋ), vbl. sb. [f. WATER v. + -ING.]
+ 1. The action of carrying water. Obs.

2. The action (or an act) of pouring or sprinkling water on plants, crops, or the soil.

3. Running (of the eyes): filling with tears.

4. Salivation of the teeth, mouth, or 'chops', induced by the thought or anticipation of appetizing food.

II. Concrete senses.
+ 15. A place where horses and cattle are taken to drink. Chiefly as in b. Obs.

16. A well, spring, or other place where water is obtained for domestic use. Obs.

+ 17. A place where vessels obtain a supply of fresh water. Obs.

+ 18. Water for irrigation. Obs.

19. A ditch for draining a marsh; the tract drained by such a ditch.

20. The wavy, variegated appearance given to silk, metal, etc.

III. attrib. and Comb.

22. Special comb.: watering-bridle, a bridle with a snaffle-bit, used chiefly when taking a horse to be watered; also attrib.; watering-cap, a cavalryman's fatigue cap; watering-house, an inn or public house where stage coachmen and hackney coachmen may obtain water for their horses and refreshment for themselves; watering-man = WATERMAN; watering-order Mil.; watering-pan = WATERING-POT; watering-saddle, a saddle used by cavalry when riding their horses to water; watering-snaffle, a snaffle used for watering, etc.; watering-trough or fountain = watering-place.

Wa'tering-place. [WATERING vbl. sb.]
1. A place in a river or lake where animals are brought to obtain water; also a pool or trough prepared for the use of the cattle and horses.

b. As a designation of colour. Light grey, pale blue.

2. A place where a ship's company goes to fill the ship's casks with fresh water.

3. A resort of fashionable or holiday visitors, either for drinking or bathing in the waters of a mineral spring, or for sea-bathing.

Wa'tering-pot. [WATERING vbl. sb.]
1. A portable vessel for watering plants; now usually of tin or iron, and furnished with a long tubular spout, often ending with a rose for scattering the water.

2. fig.

Watering (wǭ'tǝriŋ), ppl. a. [f. WATER v. + -ING.] That waters.

Waterish, a. [f. WATER sb. + -ISH.] (Sweet gives an OE. wæteriric, of which no example seems to be known.)

1. Composed of water, or of the nature of water, aqueous. Obs.

2. Resembling water in appearance or sensible quality.

fig.

+ 4. Relating to or concerned with water. Obs.

+ 5. Containing an excess of water. Obs.

6. Containing excess of water. Dilute, thin, poor. Of solids: Loose in texture, not compact.

7. Next to or inhabiting the water, aquatic. Obs.

8. Of a taste: Characteristic of that which contains excess of water. Obs.

+ 9. Having a predominance of water in composition. Also, of disease, characterized by accumulation of water in some part of the body. Obs.

Wa'terishly, adv. **Wa'terishness.**

9. Of light or of luminous bodies: Dimmed by watery vapour.

Water-lapper. Obs. One who 'lappeth with his tongue' (Judges vii. 5).

Water-leaf. (-līf.)
1. A mill-leaf.

2. = Water-leaf (lēf.) A mill-leaf.

+ Water-leader. Obs.
1. One who carts water for sale.

Water-leaf.
1. Any plant of the genus Hydrophyllum.
2. Arch. An ornament used in sculptured capitals, supposed to be a conventional representation of the leaf of some aquatic plant.

Water-knot. (KNOT sb.)
A kind of knot used in joining together the several portions of a fishing line (see quot. 1847).

Waterlade. Obs. [WATER sb. + LADE sb.]
A channel for water; an aqueduct.

Waterlag. [Short for next.] An epithet of abuse.

Water-lagger. [f. LAG + 2-ER]
= WATER-CARRIER.

Waterlander. [Du. waterlander.] The name given to the anabaptists of Friesland and Germany. Also called Waterlandians.

Waterlandish.
Characteristic of the theologian Daniel Waterland (1683–1740).

coming up a waterlane, between two lines of shipping, just behind us.

+ Water-lifter. Obs. = WATER-LEADER 1.
Water-lily. The common name for many aquatic plants in flower, belonging to the N. Nymphaeaceae.

Waterless, a. [OE. wæterléas.] Destitute of water; containing no water.

Water-line.
+ 1. A rope of some kind. Obs.
2. Naut. The line of floatation of a ship; the line supposed to be described on the hull by the surface of the water when a ship is afloat. (See — LOAD-WATER-LINE) the proper line of floatation when the ship is fully laden. Light water-line: the line of floatation of a ship without cargo.
3. fig.

Water-log, v. [app. f. WATER v. + LOG sb.]
1. Of a ship, boat: Flooded with water by leakage or overflow so as to become impaired in buoyancy, heavy, and unmanageable.
2. fig.

Waterlined, ppl. a. Of paper, marked with water-lines.

Waterlog, v. [app. f. WATER v. + LOG sb.]

Waterlogged (wǭ'tǝlǫgd), ppl. a. [f. prec. + -ED.]
1. Of a ship, boat: Flooded with water by leakage or overflow so as to become impaired in buoyancy, heavy, and unmanageable.
2. Of floating bodies: Saturated with water so as to be deprived of buoyancy.
3. Suffering from deteriorated or rendered unserviceable by excessive saturation with water.
b. of butter: Containing an excess of water.

Waterlog (wǭ'tǝlǫg), v. [app. f. WATER v. + LOG sb.]

Waterloo (wǭ'tǝlū). The name given to the battle fought outside the village of Waterloo near Brussels, on June 18, 1815, in which Napoleon was decisively and finally defeated. Hence (with a hi): Something which is a 'settler'; a decisive and final defeat.
attrib.

Hence waterlooing vbl. sb.; also **Waterlooer.**

Waterlily, attrib. **Waterloo helmet,** with crest and plume as worn by the old Life Guards.

Waterlogging.

Water-mail. Sc. Obs. [MAIL sb.] A rent charged upon a piece of water.

Waterman (wǭ'tǝmăn). [f. WATER sb. + MAN sb.]
1. A man who plies for hire, or works, a wherry, boat, or other craft upon a river, etc.; a boatman, ferryman.
2. A seaman, mariner.

Watermanship.

Supplement, p. 3873; Corrigenda, p. 4092; Spurious words, p. 4093; Books quoted, p. 4094

Water-mark, *sb.*

Water-mark, *v.*

Water-marking, *vbl. sb.*

Wa·ter-mea·sure.

Wa·ter-mea·surer.

Wa·ter-me·lon.

Wa·ter-mill.

Wa·ter-mint.

Wa·ter-mole [MOLE *sb.*2]

Wa·ter-mouse.

Wa·ter-mouth.

Wa·ter-nymph.

Wa·ter-oak.

Wa·ter-of-Ayr. / **Water of Ayr.**

Water of life.

Wa·ter-par·sley.

Wa·ter-par·snip.

Wa·ter-part·ing.

Wa·ter-pep·per.

Wa·ter-pit.

Wa·ter-pitcher.

Wa·ter-plane.

Wa·ter-plant.

Wa·ter-plantain.

Wa·ter-pot.

Waterproof, *a.* and *sb.*

Waterproof, *v.*

Waterproofed, *ppl. a.*

Waterproofer.

Waterproofing, *vbl. sb.*

Wa·ter-pump.

Wa·ter-quake.

Wa·ter-rail [RAIL *sb.*3]

Wa·ter-rat.

Wa·ter-ret, *v.*

Wa·ter-rocket.

Wa·ter-rug.

Wa·ter-scape1.

Wa·ter-scape2.

Wa·ter-snake. Also = SEA-SERPENT.

Wa·ter-pepper, *sb.*

Wa·ter-shed.

Wa·ter-shoot, *sb.*

Wa·ter-shot, *sb.* [WATER *sb.* + SHOT *sb.*]

Water shot, *adv.*

Wa·ter-shut.

Wa·ter-side.

Wa·ter-snake, *sb.*

Wa·ter-soak, *v.*

Wa·ter-soaken, *ppl. a.* = WATER-SOAKED.

Wa·ter-soaked, *ppl. a.*

Water-sop.

Wa·ter-souchy.

Wa·ter-spaniel.

Wa·ter-spider.

Waterspike.

Supplement, p. 3873; Corrigenda, p. 4092; Spurious words, p. 4093; Books quoted, p. 4094.

3707

Water-spout, waterspout, 1. A spout, pipe, or nozzle, through which water is discharged; also, a water-pipe, or conduit.

Water-spring. A permanent flow of water issuing from the earth: = SPRING sb. Also fig.

Water-stone. [Cf. G. *wasserstein* in various senses.]

Water-stream. Now rare. [Cf. G. *wasserstrom*, MLG. *waterstrōm*.] A stream or current of water; a river or brook.

Water-swallow 1. A name for the water-wagtail.

Water-swallow 2. = SWALLOW sb. 2.

Water-table. 1. Arch. a. The sloping top of a plinth.

Watertight (wǫ'tǝitt), a. [See TIGHT a. 2.] 1. So closely constructed or fitted that water cannot leak through.

Water-tree. 1. A tree which grows by the water in watery ground.

Water-vine. A name for several plants which yield an abundant watery juice.

Water-wagtail. 1. The common pied wagtail, *Motacilla lugubris*.

Water-wall. [Cf. G. *wasserwall*.] A wall which rises by the side of water; a containing wall beside or around a piece of water.

Waterward, -wards (wǫ'tǝiwǝid, -wǝidz), adv. [See -WARD, -WARDS.] Toward the water; in earlier use to (the) *waterward*.

Water-tree. +1. A tree which grows by the water in watery ground.

Water-washed, pa. *pple.* and *ppl.* a. Drenched with water; swept, flushed, or inundated by running water.

Water-washen. = prec.

Water-way. 1. A way of or channel for water.

Water-weed. Any aquatic plant with inconspicuous flowers; esp. = WATER-THYME.

Water-wheel. A wheel designed to drive machinery, that of a mill or pump, with water as the motive power.

Water-willow. +1. The purple loosestrife, *Lythrum Salicaria*, or the willow-herb, *Epilobium angustifolium*.

Water-witch. 1. A witch haunting the water.

Water-withe. A West Indian plant, *Vitis caribæa* (see quot. 1756).

Waterwork (wǫ'tǝiwǝik). [f. WATER sb. + WORK sb. Cf. Du. *waterwerk*, G. *wasserwerk*.] +1. A structure built in the water or serving as a receptacle for water or a defence against the force of water, as a tank, pier, sea-wall, lock, etc.

Waterwort. A name for several chiefly aquatic plants.

Watery (wǫ'tǝri), a. Forms: 1 *wæteriᵹ, wæterīᵹ,* 5 *watery,* 5-6 *watry, watery, watri, watiry,* 5-6 *watrye,* 6-7 *waterie,* 5-9 *watery,* 7-9 *watry; +* 4 *watery.* [OE. *wæteriᵹ,* etc. f. WATER sb.] 1. Of land or soil: Full of water; moist, plashy; well-watered.

Wath. 1. = AQUEOUS 1 b. Obs.

Wath (wāᵹ, wath), sb. Obs. exc. dial. Forms: 1 *wæþ,* 4 *waþ,* 6 *wath, wathe,* 6-7 *waith; +* 4 *waed.* [OE. *wæþ* neut. = ON. *vaᵹ* neut. (MSw. *vaþ,* Sw., Da. *vad*) str. neut.:—OTeut. *waþom* = L. *vadum*; cogn. w. WADE v.] A ford; a fordable stream.

Wath(e: see WATER sb.[1], WHAT, WOTHE.

Wather, obs. form of WEATHER, WHETHER.

Wathstead, dial. Also † wrastead.

Watkin, Obs. [f. WAT[2] + -KIN.] A hare.

Watling-street (wɒˈtlɪŋstriːt). Forms: 1 Wœclinga-, Wæclinga-, 1–5 Watlinga-, Wætlinga-stret, 4 Wat(e)lynge-, 5 Watlyn-, 5 Wadlyng-, 6 Watling-. [OE. Wœclinga strœt; the word, app. the genit. pl. of the name of a (real or imaginary) family or clan, occurs also in Wœclinga ceaster ('the Wœclings' city'), the OE. name of the Romano-British Verulamium (near St. Albans), through which the 'Watling-street' passed.]

Watling-street — ... The English name given in pre-Conquest times to the Roman road running from near London through St. Albans to Wroxeter...

Watmol, Watmal, obs. form of WADMAL.

Watna (wɒˈtnə), sb. [f. wat Sc. form of WOTE + NA adv.[3]] (I) know not. Hence **Watna-what** ...

Watre, obs. form of WATER sb. and v.

Watsail, obs. form of WASSAIL.

Watschod, watashod, obs. form of WETSHOD.

Watstone, obs. form of WHETSTONE.

Watt (wɒt). Physics. [The name of James Watt (1736–1819), the inventor of the modern steam-engine, and a pioneer in the science of energy.] A unit of activity or power (used chiefly with reference to electricity)...

Wattau (wɒˈtaʊ), f. sing. [French.] The name of Antoine Watteau (1684–1721), a French painter, used attrib. in Watteau costume.

Watte, obs. form of WAT, WET, WOT v.

Wattchelt, var. WATCHET.

Watt(e)ring, obs. form of WATERING.

Wattle (wɒˈt'l). Forms: 1 watul, pl. watla (-Worf.), watelas ; watt(e)l, pl. 6 wattill, Anglo-Irish wattil, 7 pl. (-wattel, 7 wadle, 6–9 wattle ; 7 dial. waddle, 6 weattle. [OE. watul (not found in other Texts; langs.) of uncertain origin...]

Wattle and daub (dæb): interwoven twigs plastered with clay or mud, as a building material...

Wattled (wɒˈt'ld), ppl. a. [f. WATTLE v. + -ED.]

Wattless (wɒˈtlɪs), a. Electr. [f. WATT + -LESS.] Of an electromotive force, etc.; Consuming no power.

Wattling (wɒˈtlɪŋ), vbl. sb. Also 4–7 wattlyng-a, -ing, 4–6 wadlyng-a, 6 wadling-, [f. WATTLE v. + -ING.]

Wattle-head, Obs. rare. [f. WATTLE sb.1] a. designating a weak building-material.]

Waught (wɔːt), int. Also 8 wa, 9 wagh. [An instinctive exclamation.]

Waugh (wɔː), sb. Sc. var. of WALL.[1]

Waukrife, variant of WAKERIFE Sc.[1]

Waul, Wawl (wɔːl), sb. [1 next.] A loud cry or howl.

Waul, wawl (wɔːl), v. Also 6 Sc. wawill, 6–7 wawle, 6–8 waule, 9 dial. Wawil, wawl. To utter the loud harsh cry characteristic of cats or of new-born babes.

Waur, Sc. var. WAR v.[1]

Waught (wɔːt), sb. and v. : see WAUGH a., WAUGH v.[1]

Waul, waule, Sc. form of WIELD sb. and v., WOLD.

Wauld, Sc. [I would : see WILL v.

Waulk, obs. f. WALK v. ; variant of WALK sb.[1]

Waulm, Sc. variant of WALM sb.[1]

Waur, var. WAR v.[1]

Waursh, a., variant of WERSH.

Wave (weɪv), sb.[1] Forms: 4 (also 6 whave, 5 weave.)

In sense 1, which appears early in the 16th c., it seems to have been substituted by popular etymology for the older WAW sb., which it rapidly superseded in use.

I. 1. A movement in the sea or other collection of water, by which a portion of the water rises above the normal level and then subsides, at the same time travelling a greater or smaller distance over the surface...

b. Meteorol. A change of atmospheric pressure or temperature causing a gradual rise and fall or hot and cold, travelling over an extensive surface; a region in which...

II. A swelling, upward movement and subsidence (of feeling, thought, opinion, a custom, condition, etc.)...

III. The flower of the wattle.

Wave, variant of WOW. (Also 6 whave, 6 weave.)

this minimum represent..the trough of a barometric wave which at 3 A.M. was vertically over Brussels, and at 11 A.M. over London, the wave must have been travelling westwards. 1846 W. R. Birt in Rep. Brit. Assoc. I. 147 Now a wave generated in any way and approaching the continent of Europe from the north-west would most probably impinge on it with a high..crest...Again a negative wave, with a deep trough..would present large fluctuations as it impinged on the land. 1901 Scotsman 4 Oct. 5/1 When a cold wave strikes Northern Minnesota, there is no knowing where the thermometer may go.

c. *Seismol.* A seismic disturbance of a portion of the crust or surface of the earth, travelling continuously for a certain distance.

1862 R. Mallet First Princ. Observ. Seismol. I. iv. 33 If an isolated wall..be subjected to the transit of an earth wave ..the resulting fractures will vary with the direction of the wave-path. 1877 F. W. Rudler Earthquake in Encycl. Brit. VII. 609/2 From the seismic centre waves are propagated in all directions through the solid materials of the earth's crust. 1886 J. Milne Earthquakes iii. 55 Hitherto we have chiefly considered earthquake vibrations; now we will say a few words about earthquake waves.

d. Phys. *Wave of contraction*, the onward contraction of a muscle from the point where the stimulus is applied. *Wave of stimulation*, the (hypothetical) impulse of molecular vibration travelling along a nerve from the point at which it is stimulated.

1851 Carpenter Man. Phys. (ed. 2) 214 Successive contractions and relaxations may be produced..by a single prick with a scalpel; a sort of wave of contraction being transmitted in the direction of its length. 1885 Romanes Jelly Fish etc. i. 25 A stimulus applied to a nerveless muscle,.giving rise to a visible wave of contraction, which spreads in all directions. Ibid., I shall always speak of muscle-fibres as conveying a visible wave of contraction, and of nerve-fibres as conveying an invisible, or molecular, wave of stimulation.

6. A book-name of certain geometrid moths.

1819 Samouelle Entomol. Compend. 423 Geometra inornata. The plain Wave. 1832 J. Rennie Consp. Butterfl. & Moths 139 The Small White Wave (Emmelesia candidata, Stephens). Ibid. 140 The Small Fan-footed Wave (Ptychopoda dilutaria, Stephens). Ibid. 141 The Dwarf Cream Wave (Acidalia osseata, Stephens). Ibid. 143 The Subangled Wave (Timandra variegata, Stephens). 1882 Cassell's Nat. Hist. VI. 67 The Acidalidæ or 'Waves,' comprise a large number of small species.

II. An act of waving.

7. A motion to and fro of the hand or of something held in the hand, used as a signal or as an expressive sign.

1688 Holme Armoury III. xix. (Roxb.) 155/2 Termes used about the displaying or florishing of an ensigne...A Wave, or plaine wave, is A Turne or florish. 1840 Dickens Old C. Shop xv, And so, with many waves of the hand, and cheering nods,..they parted company. 1854 Surtees Handley Cr. i. (1901) I. 8 With a wave of his hat [he] brought the pack forward. 1883 D. C. Murray Hearts iii. (1885) 20 With a charming smile and a reassuring wave of the right hand. 1898 Kipling Fleet in Being i. 4 The man-of-war..must also be ready to drop three or four knots at the wave of a flag.

8. A swaying to and fro.

1648 Herrick Hesper., Delight in Disorder 9 A winning wave (deserving Note) In the tempestuous petticote. 1825 Scott Talism. x, The point at which he had seen the last slight wave of the Templar's mantle. 1849 M. Arnold Obermann xlii, Where with clear-rustling wave The scented pines of Switzerland Stand dark round thy green grave.

III. *attrib.* and *Comb.*

9. simple attrib., as *wave-crest, -head, -ridge, -top, -water*; (sense 2 d) *wave-region*; (sense 5 a) *wave-problem, -transmission, -velocity*.

1823 Scott Peveril xxvii. Motto, The restless foam Of the wild *wave-crest. 1849 Cupples Green Hand ii. (1856) 16 The *wave-heads..were crested here and there with light. 1910 S. P. Thompson Ld. Kelvin II. xxi. 862 Sir William read four papers bearing on *wave-problems. 1856 Olmsted Slave States 397 For an hour or two we got above the sandy zone, and into the..'*wave' region of the State. The surface here was extremely undulating. 1849 C. Bronte Shirley xiii, She rises high, and glides all revealed, on the dark *wave-ridge. 1893 Conan Doyle Refugees III. xxv. 30 For hours a glimpse could be caught of the boat, dwindling away on the *wave tops. 1907 V. Cornish in Geogr. Jrnl. Jan. 23 The effect of this *wave-transmission is to diminish the initial inequality of slope. 1910 S. P. Thompson Ld. Kelvin II. xxi. 861 The proposition that the *wave-velocity is double [that] of the group-velocity. 1889 Welch Text Bk. Naval Archit. iii. 59 The amount of the buoyancy in *wave-water is also constantly varying.

b. objective, as *wave-breaker, wave-drawing*; also *wave-subjected* adj.

1764 Goldsm. Trav. 297 The wave-subjected soil [of Holland] Impels the native to repeated toil. 1881 Broadhouse Mus. Acoustics 59 Constant practice in wave-drawing ..will soon familiarize the student [etc.]. 1885 L. F. Vernon-Harcourt Harbours & Docks I. 93 The open jetty does not act as a wave-breaker.

c. similative, as *wave-green*; also with the sense 'having a waved form or markings', as *wave blade, -bladed, -breasted, -edged, -haired, -leaved*, etc.

1877 Lane-Fox Catal. Anthrop. Coll. Bethnal Green Branch S. Kens. 183 Malay Krisses, with *wave blades. 1866 W. J. Fitzpatrick Sham Squire 115 He..with a *wave-bladed dagger..made some stabs at the intruder. 1811 Shaw Gen. Zool. VIII. 405 *Wave-breasted Parrakeet. Psittacus versicolor. 1884 R. F. Burton Bk. Sword vii. 137 The *wave-edged form [of blade] is well shown in an iron dagger. 1621 G. Sandys Ovid's Met. ix. (1626) 175 I..let my *waue-greene Mantle sink. 1866 Christina Rossetti Prince's Progr. x, A *wave-haired milkmaid. 1816–20 T. Green Univ. Herbal II. 828 Xysmalobium Undulatum; *Wave-leaved Xysmalobium.

d. locative, as *wave-bowered, -reflected*.

1812 Byron Ch. Har. II. xxiv, Thus bending o'er the vessel's laving side, To gaze on Dian's wave-reflected sphere. 1820 Shelley Prometh. Unb. III. ii. 32 Tracking their path..by the light Of wave-reflected flowers. 1881 Rossetti Ballads & Sonn., House of Life lvi, The wave-bowered pearl.

e. instrumental, as *wave-beaten, -buffeted, -dashed, -encircled, -hollowed, -lashed, -moist, -swept, -tossed, -washed, -wet, -worn*, etc.

a 1593 Marlowe Ovid's Eleg. I. xiv. 34 Such were they [her locks] as Diana painted stands All naked holding in her waue-moist hands. 1610 Shaks. Temp. II. i. 120 He..oared Himselfe ..To th' shore; that ore his waue-worne basis bowed As stooping to releeue him. 1741 Boyse Patience 200 On the sea-weed spray,..the wave-toss'd body lay. 1777 Potter Æschylus 51 The tort'ring sting Thence drove thee wand'ring o'er the wave-wash'd strand. 1810 Scott Lady of L. I. xiii, The shaggy mounds..wave-encircled, seem'd to float. 1819 Byron Juan II. cxcviii, Amidst the barren sand and rocks so rude She and her wave-worn love had made their bower. 1848 Lytton K. Arthur II. cvii, Wave-hollow'd caves. 1856 Lever Martins of Cro' M. xxiii, The dark cliffs and rugged crags, the wave-beaten rocks. 1857 Dickens Dorrit II. xx, Every wave-dashed, storm-beaten object. 1857 Dufferin Lett. High Lat. (ed. 3) 225 A..channel, between two wave-lashed ridges of drift ice. 1876 Morris Sigurd II. 92 So Sigurd turned to the river and stood by the wave-wet strand. 1894 Outing XXIV. 92/1 The long, wave-swept margin was left to the solitude of primeval nature.

10. Special comb.: **wave-action** (*a*) *Geol.*, the action of water flowing in waves; (*b*) *Gunnery*, 'abnormally high pressure in a gun from very large charges' (*Cent. Dict.* 1891); **wave-detector**, an instrument designed to detect very feeble electric waves in wireless telegraphy; **wave-disk**, a metal disk with a waved edge, used in the *wave-siren*; **wave-form** (see quot. 1864); **wave-front** *Physics*, the continuous line or surface including all the waves or radiatory emissions which are in the same phase; **wave-horse** = Sea-horse 5; **wave-length**, the length of a wave as measured from crest to crest or from hollow to hollow; **wave-making**, the production of waves by the movement of a floating body on the surface of the water; also *attrib.*; **wave-mark** (*a*) *Geol.* (see quot. 1863); (*b*) a wavy marking, stain, or blemish; so also **wave-marked** *a.*, **wave-marking** *Geol.*; **wave-meter** *Electr.* 'an instrument for determining the wave-form of alternating currents' (W. 1911); **wave-motion**, motion in curves alternately concave and convex; **wave-motor**, a machine or apparatus designed to utilize the energy in the waves of water as a motive power; also *attrib.*; **wave-path** *Seismol.* (see quot. 1886); **wave-rainbow**, a rainbow formed on the spray of sea-waves; **wave-rate** *Acoustics*, the rate of vibration of a sounding body in a given time; **wave resistance**, the retarding force of the action of waves of water; **wave screen** (see quot.); **wave-shell** *Physics*, each of the imaginary concentric spherical layers in any medium traversed by a wave, such that the vibration of the particles of the layer is always in the same phase; **wave-siren**, a form of the Siren (*sb.* 7) in which a current of air is driven through a narrow slit against an undulatory curve on the periphery of a cylinder or disk; **wave-slope**, the angle of inclination of the surface of a wave to the horizontal; **wave-surface** *Physics*, a geometrical surface which is the locus of all points reached at one instant by an undulatory agitation propagated from any centre; **wave-system** *Ship-building*, see quot. and Wave-line 1; **wave theory** = *undulatory theory* (see Undulatory 1 c); **wave-train** *Physics* (see quot.); **wave-trap**, **winding** (see quots.); † **wave work**, watered work (see quot.). Also Wave-like *a.* and *adv.*, Wave-line.

1880 Dana Man. Geol. (ed. 3) 910 Index, *Wave-action on coral reefs. 1886 A. Winchell Walks Geol. Field 63 Here the torrential action was less turbulent: it was perhaps wave-action along a beach. 1905 Athenæum 18 Mar. 339/2 The centre of interest in wireless telegraphy seems to be shifting from the *wave-detector or coherer to the means of producing the energy required to act upon it. 1890 S. P. Thompson in Nature (1891) 8 Jan. 226/2 Two such *wave-disks, looking rather like circular saws with irregular teeth. 1846 W. R. Birt in Rep. Brit. Assoc. I. 138 Should the rarefying process cease,..not only will the *wave-form be continued, but also the wave-motion. 1889 Welch Text Bk. Naval Archit. iii. 58 It is only the wave form which advances, and not the water composing that wave. 1867 Tait Quaternions xi. 289 The planes of polarization of the two rays whose *wave-fronts are parallel, bisect the angles [etc.]. 1888 Rutley Rock-Forming Min. 57 The plane wave-surfaces or wave-fronts of the two rays will respectively be represented by the tangent planes. 1888 Rider Haggard Mr. Meeson's Will xi. (1897) 140 They..looked out across the troubled ocean. There was nothing in sight..but the white *wave-horses. 1871 Schellen Spectrum Anal. § 18. 59 The rays of shortest *wave-length, namely the violet. 1881 Broadhouse Mus. Acoustics 66 The fork..condenses..a bulk of air equal in length to the wave-length of its own pitch. 1907 V. Cornish in Geogr. Jrnl. Jan. 25 The water may commonly be seen to..grow in the space of a few yards to a uniform wave-length of about 2 feet. 1877 W. H. White Naval Archit. xi. 447 Mr. Scott Russell first drew attention to the importance of *wave-making resistance. 1878 D. Kemp Man. Yacht Sailing vi. 41 There are only two principal sources of resistance, and they are consequent upon surface friction and wave-making. 1863 Dana Man. Geol. (ed. 3) 94 *Wave-marks.—Faint outlinings, of curved form, on a sandstone layer, like the outline left by a wave along the limit where it dies out upon a beach. 1902 Westm. Gaz. 14 Apr. 4/2 When the novice finds a few pinholes in his negatives, or wave marks on parts of the image. Ibid., The wave-marks were the result of careless development. 1903 Amer. Geol. June 356 The top of the Lorraine is formed by a *wavemarked layer of limestone. Ibid., Numerous other instances of *wavemarking at this horizon might be given. 1905 Athenæum 27 May 662/2 Prof. Fleming's direct-reading cymometer or *wave-meter, for measuring the length of the waves used in wireless telegraphy. 1846 W. R. Birt in Rep. Brit. Assoc. I. 135 In contemplating the transference of the barometric maxima and minima, we regard only the *wave-motion—but very different must be the air-motion. 1882 P. G. Tait Light in Encycl. Brit. XIV. 603 The essential characteristic of wave-motion is that a disturbance of some kind is handed on from one portion of a solid or fluid mass to another. 1898 Daily News 9 June 7/2 The Linden *wave-motor boat. 1899 Ibid. 15 Apr. 8/6 A wave motor, which may be seen working off Dover. 1862 R. Mallet First Princ. Observ. Seismol. I. iv. 35 The line of transit, or *wave-path. 1886 J. Milne Earthquakes i. 9 The radial lines along which an earthquake may be propagated from the centrum are called 'wave-paths'. 1848 Tennyson in Ld. Tennyson Mem. (1897) I. 275 Sat watching *wave-rainbows [at the Lizard]. 1903 G. M. Stratton Exper. Psychol. v. 83 Musical notes whose *wave-rates do not differ at least a fifth of a vibration a second. 1889 Welch Text Bk. Naval Archit. iii. 56 *Wave resistance is by far the most powerful agent in extinguishing the oscillations. 1883 Fisheries Exhib. Catal. 48 *Wave Screen, or Breakwater, for breaking the force of the sea, at entrance of bar..or elsewhere. 1877 F. W. Rudler Earthquake in Encycl. Brit. VII. 610/1 The points at which a *wave-shell reaches the surface form a curve which is conveniently called a coseismal line. 1881 Nature 18 Aug. 359/2 Helmholtz..has constructed a new instrument, the *wave-siren. 1890 S. P. Thompson in Nature (1891) 15 Jan. 250/2 Dr. Kœnig had recourse to the wave-siren, an earlier invention of his own. 1877 W. H. White Naval Archit. vi. 212 In considering the sufficiency of the range of the curve of stability for any vessel, it is desirable to regard it as abridged by this 8 or 10 degrees, in order to allow for the *wave slope. 1833 MacCullagh Collected Wks. (1880) 34 In this theory, the surface of waves, or the *wave surface, is a geometrical surface used to determine the directions and velocities of refracted or reflected rays, being the surface of a sphere in a singly refracting medium; a double surface, [etc.]. 1860 Cayley Math. Papers (1891) IV. 420 Some very beautiful results in relation to the Wave Surface have been recently obtained by Herr Zech. 1910 S. P. Thompson Ld. Kelvin II. xx. 820 Stokes has found by minute experiment that the Huygens wave-surface is most accurately obeyed by light. 1886 Encycl. Brit. XXI. 66/2 His [J. Scott Russell's] observations led him to propose and experiment on a new system of shaping vessels, which is known as the *wave system. 1833 MacCullagh Collected Wks. (1880) 34 On the *Wave Theory of Light. 1873 Cooke Chem. 22, I cannot agree with those who regard the wave-theory of light as an established principle of science. 1897 E. L. Nichols & Franklin Elem. Physics III. 12 A periodic disturbance sends out what is called a *train of waves*, each one of which is exactly like its forerunner...Graphic representation of *wave trains. 1875 Knight Dict. Mech., *Wave-trap (Hydraulic Engineering), a widening inwards of the sides of piers, to afford space for storm-waves which roll in at the entrance to spread and extend themselves. 1893 Sloane Electr. Dict., *Wave Winding, a method of winding disc and drum armatures. 1601 Holland Pliny VIII. xlviii. I. 228 The very roiall robe ..made..after the manner of water-chamlot in *wave worke [L. *togam undulatam*].

† **Wavé**, *a. Her. Obs.* [Hybrid f. Wave *sb.* + AF. suffix *-é*, after *undé*.] = Wavy. Cf. Undee, Undé.

1513, 1688 [see Undee]. 1572 Bossewell Armorie 26 Crosse taue, checkey, waue. 1646 Sir T. Browne Pseud. Ep. v. x. 249 Three Barres wave. 1680 Sir G. Mackenzie Sci. Her. vii. 26 The Drummonds bear three faces *undé* or *wavé*. 1684 Lond. Gaz. No. 1980/4 Two pair of Gold Buckles..dented and wave.

Wave (wēⁱv), *v.* Inflected **waved, waving**. Also ?4 *Sc.* **vaf**, **wayve**. [OE. *wafian* (twice, in sense 6), corresp. formally to MHG. (and rare mod.G.) *waben* (see Grimm s.v. *wabben*) to wave, undulate; the Teut. root **wab-* is found in ON. *vafe* wk. masc. doubt, uncertainty, and in Waver vb. and the cognates there mentioned; the ablaut-variants **web-*, **wǣb-* occur in G. *weben* to wave, move about (cf. Weave *v.*², Weve *v.*), which, however, is believed to be partly a dial. form of MHG. *wēwen* (mod.G. *wehen*) to wave, flutter, etc.; and in ON. *vífa* to swing, vibrate.

It is not always possible to distinguish between this vb. and the obsolete Waive *v.*²; the two approximate or coincide in some of their senses, and in some dialects and periods were identical in sound.]

I. To move to and fro or up and down.

*Of involuntary movement.

1. *intr.* Of a thing having a free end: To move to and fro, shake or sway in the air by the action of the wind or breeze.

1375 Barbour Bruce IX. 245 The discurrouris saw thame cumande With baneris to the vynd vafand [*v.rr.* wawand, waiuand]. 1508 Dunbar Poems iv. 14 As with the wynd wavis the wickir, [So] wavis [*v.rr.* wannis, waveris] this warldis vanite. 1523 Berners Froiss. I. ciii. 50 b/2 Whanne those fotemen..sawe the baners and standerdes waue with the wynde. 1577 Kendall Flowers Epigr. 73 His crisped locks wavde all behinde. 1593 Shaks. 3 Hen. VI, II. ii. 173 Sound Trumpets, let our bloody Colours waue, And either Victorie, or else a Graue. 1671 Milton Samson 718 Like a

stately Ship..With all her bravery on, and tackle trim, Sails fill'd, and streamers waving. 1713 Pope Windsor For. 350 High in the midst..(His sea-green mantle waving with the wind), The god appear'd. 1810 Scott Lady of L. III. xxv, No banner waved on Cardross gate. 1837 Dickens Pickw. xxxv, Dresses rustled, feathers waved,..and jewels sparkled. 1846 Ruskin Mod. Paint. II. III. I. xii. § 5 The bending trunk, waving to and fro in the wind above the waterfall. 1846 McCulloch Acc. Brit. Empire (1854) II. 7 It was then that the flag of England began to wave over every sea. 1884 Bible (R.V.) Judges ix. 9 But the olive tree said unto them, Should I leave my fatness..and go to wave to and fro over the trees?

fig. 1648 Herrick Hesper., Mrs. Eliz. Wheeler Poet. Wks. (1915) 107 In bloome of Peach, and Roses bud, There waves the Streamer of her blood.

† b. *To wave in the wind*: to be hanged. (Cf. Wag *v.* 3 d.) *Obs.*

a 1533 Berners Huon xvi. 43 Or it be nyght, I shall cause thee to waue in the wynde.

c. Of long hair: To hang down loose. *poet.*

1671 Milton Samson 1493 And view him sitting in the house, ..And on his shoulders waving down those locks. 1767 M. Bruce Last Day Poems (1796) 129 His golden hair Wav'd on his shoulders.

d. *trans.* Of the wind, etc.: To cause (a thing) to sway or move to and fro.

1602 Kyd Span. Trag. III. xii A, Behold a man hanging, and tottering, and tottering, as you know the winde will waue a man. 1817 Shelley Rev. Islam VIII. xxx, Beneath a bright acacia's shadowy hair, Waved by the wind amid the sunny noon. 1828 Lytton Pelham x, The wind waved my long curls. 1829 Scott Anne of G. xi, No sound was heard save that of the night wind, when it..waved the tattered banners which were the tapestry of the feudal hall.

† 2. *intr.* To move to and fro restlessly or uncertainly; to waver. *Obs.*

1406 Hoccleve La Male Regle 399 And whil my breeth may in my body waue, To recorde it vnnethe I may souffyse. 1500–20 Dunbar Poems xxi. 59 [This world] Quhair fortoun evir, as so, dissavis With freyndly smylingis of ane hure, Quhais fals behechtis as wind hyne wavis. 1508 [see 1 above]. 1628 [see Waving *ppl. a.* 2]. 1665 [see Waving *vbl. sb.* 1].

† b. To move to and fro unsteadily on its base or (of a person) on the feet; to totter. *Obs.*

1538 Elyot Dict., *Vacillo*, to moue inconstantly, to wagge or waue, to be vnstable, or vnsure. 1605 Sylvester Du Bartas II. iii. IV. 645 As an Infant which the Nurse lets go To goe alone, waves weakly to and fro. 1608 A. Willet Hexapla in Exod. xx. 18. 445 [Vatablus renders the verb by] *vacillabant*, they waued. 1609 Ld. Brooke Mustapha IV. iv. Chorus iv, Thus reeles our present State, And her foundation waues.

† c. Of a floating body: To move restlessly by the impulse of the air or water. Also, To hover about in the air. *Obs.*

1606 G. W[oodcocke] Hist. Ivstine xxvi. 94 b, The Ghoasts of them whose liues they had rauished from their bodies, wauing before their eyes. 1632 Milton Penseroso 148 And let som strange mysterious dream, Wave at his Wings in Airy stream. c 1639 Roxb. Ball. (1887) VI. 429 They waving up and down the Seas, upon the Ocean Main. c 1645 Howell Lett. (1650) II. xix. 32 Those, that have their heads lightly ballasted..are like buys [buoys] in a barrd Port, waving perpetually up and down. 1728 Pope Dunc. IV. 538 Int'rest that waves on Party-colour'd wings.

† d. *To wave oneself*: ?to give oneself up to the motion of the water. In quot. *fig. Obs.*

1628 Feltham Resolves I. i. 1 When a Rich Crowne ha's newly kiss'd the Temples of a gladded King, where he finds all things in a golden swimme,..hee carelesly waues himselfe in the swelling plenty.

† 3. Of a person: To be restless in mind; to alternate between different opinions or courses of action; to vacillate, waver. Said also of the mind, will, etc. *Obs.*

1387–8 T. Usk Test. Love I. ii. (Skeat) 167 'Ye wete wel, lady, eke', quod I, 'that I have not..with the wethercocke waved.' 1566 Drant Horace, Sat. I. i. A v, Thy mynde it waues and wagges, And wisheth after greater things. 1582 T. Watson Pass. Cent. Love v. Poems (Arb.) 41, I waue in doubt what helpe I shall require, In Sommer freeze, in winter burne like fire. 1597 Hooker Eccl. Pol. v. xliii. § 5 The truth is they waue in and out, no way sufficiently grounded, no way resolued what to thinke, speake or write. 1607 Shaks. Cor. II. ii. 19 If he did not care whether he had their loue, or no, hee waued indifferently, 'twixt doing them neyther good, nor harme. 1611 [see Waving *ppl. a.* 2]. 1628 Feltham Resolves II. xvi. 46 Variety, in any thing, distracteth the minde; and leaues it waving in a dubious trouble. 1642 H. More Song of Soul II. iii. I. ii, Thus waves the mind in things of greatest weight. 1796 Morse Amer. Geog. II. 62 The court waved between these two factions.

4. Of water, the sea: To move in waves, undulate.

1530 Palsgr. 772/2, I wave, as the see dothe. *Je vague.* After a storme the see waveth. 1552 Huloet, Waue as water doth in tempest, *fluctuo*. 1571 [see Waving *vbl. sb.* 2]. c 1797–1804 W. Blake Poet. Wks. (1913) 366 Wave freshly, clear waters, flowing around the tender grass. 1820 [see Waving *vbl. sb.* 2]. 1865 Tylor Early Hist. Man. iv. 63 Water is that which waves, undulates.

b. *transf.* Of a crowd: To move to and fro restlessly in a body.

1579–80 North Plutarch, Pompeius (1595) 708 Pompey.. perceiuing..that his owne battell on the other side waued vp and downe disorderly, as men vnskilfull in warres. 1591 Savile Tacitus, Hist. I. xl. 23 Galba was driuen to and fro with the crowde of the companie, as it waued up and downe [L. *vario turbæ fluctuantis impulsu*]. 1646 Sir J. Temple Ir. Rebellion 25 The people..continued waving up and down the streets. 1860 Froude Hist. Eng. V. 387 He was still speaking, when the crowd began suddenly to wave and shift.

c. Of a field of corn, etc.; To undulate like the waves of the sea.

1667 Milton P. L. IV. 981 As when a field Of Ceres ripe for harvest waving bends Her bearded Grove of ears. 1720 Pope Iliad XX. 78 The forests wave, the mountains nod around. 1725 — Odyss. IX. 124 With wheat and barley wave the golden fields. 1775 Johnson Tax. no Tyr. 20 Regions smiling with pleasure and waving with fertility. 1784 Cowper Task IV. 313 The lands, where lately wav'd The golden harvest. a 1830 H. Cockburn Memor. (1856) 171 The whole place waved with wood, and was diversified by undulations of surface. 1834 Ruskin Months iii, Rejoice! ye fields, rejoice! and wave with gold. 1851 J. H. Gurney Hymn, Fair waved the golden corn In Canaan's pleasant land.

† 5. *intr.* To turn aside. Also *trans.* To move (a person) aside. *To wave one's way*: ? to take a divergent route. [But this may belong to Waive *v.*¹]

a 1548 Hall Chron., Hen. VIII 206 b, The kynges train waued on the lefte hande, to geue the Frenche kyng and his train the right hande. 1642 Wotton Buckingham in Reliq. W. (1651) 109 Notwithstanding all which importunity, he resolved not [ed. 1642 *omits* not] to wave his way upon this reason;..that if..he should but once by such a diversion make his Enemy believe he were afraid of danger, he should never live without. 1646 Sir T. Browne Pseud. Ep. VII. xviii. 381 Æschilus..was brained by a Tortoise which an Eagle let fall upon it...Some men..would perhaps from hence confute the opinion of Copernicus, never conceiving how the motion of the earth below should not wave him from a knock perpendicularly directed from a body in the ayre above.

† b. Of the sun: To decline. *Obs. rare.*

1615 Kyd Span. Trag. I. ii. 83 Till, Phoebus wauing to the western deepe, Our Trumpeters were chargde to sound retreat.

** Of voluntary movements.

† 6. *intr.* To make a movement to and fro (with the hands). Only *OE.*

c 1000 Ælfric Saints' Lives xxvii. 151 Þeah þe man wafige wundorlice mid handa ne bið hit þeah bletsung buta he wyrce tacn þære halgan rode. c 1000 Sax. Leechd. II. 318 Ymbfo hine [a dung beetle] mid twam handum..wafa mid þinum handum swiþe & cweð þriwa Remedium facio [etc.].

† 7. To make motions (with the uplifted hands or with something held in the hands) by way of signal. Chiefly *Naut.* (Cf. Weave *v.*²) *Obs.*

Cf. the OE. sense 6, which may possibly have survived unrecorded to the 16 c.

1513 Echyngham in Lett. & Papers War France (1897) 146 He sayth he see my lord Admirall wayvyng with his handes and cryeng to the galeye: 'Comme aborde agayne!' c 1595 Capt. Wyatt Dudley's Voy. (Hakl. Soc.) 30 Wee might discrie..two or three with a flagg of truce, wavinge unto us that it might be lawfull to com and speake with us. 1611 Shaks. Cymb. I. iii. 12 He did keepe The Decke, with Gloue, or Hat, or Handkerchife, Still wauing. 1611 B. Jonson Catiline I. i. C 1 b, A Bloody arme it is, that holds a pine Lighted, aboue the Capitoll: And, now, It waues vnto vs. 1644 Manwayring Sea-mans Dict. 114 *Waving* is making a signe for a ship, or boate, to come towards them, or else to goe from them, as the signe is made, either towards or fromwards the ship.

† b. *trans.* To signal to (a person). Chiefly *Naut.* (Cf. Weave *v.*²) *Obs.*

1555 W. Towrson in Hakluyt (1599) II. II. 33 We mistrusted some knauery, and being waued by them to come a shoare, yet we would not. Ibid., Certaine Negroes..waued vs with a white flagge, but we..would not stay. Ibid. 34 A great sort came downe to the water side, and waued vs on shoare with a white flagge. c 1595 Capt. Wyatt Dudley's Voy. (Hakl. Soc.) 4 Our Generall commaunded to wave them, and balinge them..made them know their dwtie unto our English collers by vailinge theire topsailes. 1602 Shaks. Ham. I. iv. 61 Looke with what courteous action It wafts [Qos. 1605–4 waues] you to a more remoued ground. Ibid. 68 It waues me forth againe; Ile follow it. 1616 Capt. J. Smith Descr. New Eng. (Arb.) 225 We were haled by two West Indy men: but when they saw vs waue them for the King of France, they gaue vs their broad sides. 1627 — Sea Gram. xiii. 60 He waues vs to lee-ward with his drawne sword.

† 8. To move to and fro or up and down regularly or rhythmically.

a. *intr.* To move the wings up and down in or as in flight. Said also of the wings. Also *trans.*, to actuate or flap (the wings) in or as in flight. *Obs.*

1526 Pilgr. Perf. (W. de W. 1531) 202 b, Than with her wynges she fanneth & waveth vnto she haue kyndled in them fyre. 1584–7 Greene Carde of Fancie Wks. (Grosart) IV. 165 The Bird[s]..beeing young, seeing the olde ones through age growen so weake, as they are not able to waue their wings, carrie them..on their backs. 1657 [see Waving *vbl. sb.* 5]. 1667 Milton P. L. VII. 476 Those wav'd thir limber fans For wings. 1712–14 Pope Rape Lock II. 68 Colours that change whene'er they wave their wings. 1728 — Dunc. IV. 422 Of all th' enamell'd race, whose silv'ry wing Waves to the tepid Zephyrs of the spring. 1808 W. Blake Poet. Wks. (1913) 145 Before her throne my wings I wave.

† b. *intr.* To move the body from side to side. Also *refl.* (Cf. Weave *v.*²) *Obs.*

1608 Topsell Serpents 138 As fast as the bayte was to the rope and hooke, so fast is he also ensnared and tyed vnto it, which while hee waueth and strayneth to vnloose and breake, he wearieth himselfe in vaine. 1697 Dryden Virg. Georg. III. 640 A Snake..With curling Crest, and with advancing Head: Waving he rolls, and makes a winding Track. a 1700 Evelyn Diary 15 Jan. 1645 All the company fell a singing an Hebrew hymn..waving themselves to and fro.

† c. *transf.* To move (the head *up and down*) with a significant gesture; to incline (the head). *Obs.*

1602 Shaks. Ham. II. i. 93 At last, a little shaking of mine Arme: And thrice his head thus wauing vp and downe, He rais'd a sigh. 1607 — Cor. III. ii. 77 Goe to them, with this Bonnet in thy Hand,..Thy Knee bussing the stones:.. wauing thy head. 1768 Sterne Sent. Journ., Passport (Versailles), I see the injured spirit wave her head, and turn off silent from the author of her miseries.

9. *trans.* To move through the air with a sweeping gesture (the uplifted or extended arm or hand, or something held in the hand by one extremity, e.g. a wand, a hat, or something that flutters in the breeze, as a flag, a handkerchief), often as a sign of greeting or farewell, or as an expression of exultation; usually implying repeated movements to and fro or up and down.

1607 Shaks. Cor. II. iii. 175 And with his Hat, thus wauing it in scorne, I would be Consull, sayes he. 1611 — Cymb. I. iii. 6 Pisa. It [i.e. his last speech] was his Queene, his Queene. Imo. Then wau'd his Handkerchiefe. 1634, 1667, 1794 [see Wand *sb.* 10]. 1697 Dryden Virg. Georg. IV. 513 At once she wav'd her Hand on either side, At once the Ranks of swelling Streams divide. 1712–14 Pope Rape Lock V. 7 Then grave Clarissa graceful wav'd her fan; Silence ensu'd. 1784 Cowper Task VI. 699 Maidens wave Their 'kerchiefs, and old women weep for joy. 1794 Mrs. Radcliffe Myst. Udolpho xix, [He] waved his hand for him to leave the room. 1814 Scott Wav. xx, Many sprung up and waved their arms in ecstasy. 1847 Tennyson Princess IV. 501 She, ending, waved her hands: Thereat the crowd Muttering, dissolved. 1849 Macaulay Hist. Eng. viii. II. 385 Halifax sprang up and waved his hat. At that signal, benches and galleries raised a shout. 1859 H. Kingsley G. Hamlyn xli, Sam only waved his hand in good-bye, and sped on across the plain. 1896 Conan Doyle Rodney Stone vi, He waved his white hands as if to brush aside all opposition.

b. of impersonal things personified; chiefly *poet.*

1667 Milton P. L. V. 193 And wave your tops, ye Pines, With every Plant, in sign of Worship wave. 1749 Smollett Regicide I. vi, Ye spreading boughs, that wave Your blossoms o'er the stream! 1783 Crabbe Village I. 74 Above the slender sheaf, The slimy mallow waves her silky leaf. 1804 W. L. Bowles Spir. Discov. II. 271 Dark Lebanon Waved all his pines for thee. 1820 Shelley Orpheus 106 And cypresses that seldom wave their boughs. 1886 J. G. Wood Man & Handiwork iii. 31 Where the corn waves its yellow ears.

c. To brandish (a weapon).

1601 Shaks. Jul. C. III. i. 109 And wauing our red Weapons o're our heads, Let's all cry Peace, Freedome, and Liberty. 1606 — Tr. & Cr. V. v. 9 Bastard Margareion Hath Doreus prisoner, And stands Colossus-wise wauing his beame. 1718 Pope Iliad XIII. 728 King Helenus wav'd high the Thracian blade. 1799 Campbell Pleas. Hope I. 363 By that dread name we wave the sword on high, And swear for her to live! 1825 Scott Talism. xxviii, The sabre of Saladin left its sheath as lightning leaves the cloud. It was waved in the air,—and the head of the Grand Master rolled to the extremity of the tent. 1869 W. S. Gilbert 'Bab' Ballads, Ben Allah Achmet 56 'My rival!' shrieked the invalid, And drew a mighty sword and waved it. 1911 G. M. Trevelyan Garibaldi viii. 184 Men and women waved swords which they would never wield in earnest.

absol. 1607 Shaks. Cor. I. vi. 74 Let him alone: Or so many so minded, Waue thus to expresse his disposition, And follow Martius. *They all shout and waue their swords.*

d. *intr.* (for *pass.*) To be moved to and fro. Of a weapon: To be brandished. † Also *trans.*, to pass over (something) with a brandishing movement.

1605 First Pt. Jeronimo III. ii. 105 See, a reuengfull sword Waues ore my head. 1667 Milton P. L. VI. 304 Now wav'd thir fierie Swords, and in the Aire Made horrid Circles. Ibid. XII. 643 They looking back, all th' Eastern side beheld Of Paradise,..Wav'd over by that flaming Brand. 1671 T. Hunt Abeced. Scholast. 90 Give a child as long as he will crave, and a dog as long as his tail will wave. 1828 Lytton Pelham xvii, The lady's handkerchief waved in token of encouragement and triumph. 1896 Conan Doyle Rodney Stone vi, I see, too, the figures at the garden gate: my mother, with her face turned away, and her handkerchief waving.

† e. *trans.* In the Levitical law: To elevate and move from side to side (an oblation or *wave-offering*) before the altar. *Obs.*

First in Tindale, following Luther, who renders the verb by *weben*, and also has the compounds *webebrot, webebrust, webeopfer* = wave-loaf, -breast, -offering (see 13).

1530 Tindale Exod. xxix. 24 And put all apon the handes of Aaron and on the handes of his sonnes: and waue them in and out a waueoffrynge vnto the Lorde. — Lev. xiv. 21 Let him bringe one lambe for a trespaceoffrynge to waue it. [So 1535 Coverdale; and all later versions.]

f. Occasional uses. Of a dog: To wag (his tail). Of a fish: To flap (a fin).

1677 Gilpin Demonol. III. v. 31 The Devil..stands like a Fawning Dog scratching and waving his Tail. 1883 E. W. Gosse in Longm. Mag. I. 559 Beneath the granite gray The sulky ferox lay And waved a fin.

10. To signify (something) by a wave of the hand or arm. Also with dative of person.

1810 Scott Lady of L. II. v, Perchance the maiden smiled to see Yon parting lingerer wave adieu. 1847 Tennyson Princess II. 84 She spoke, and bowing waved Dismissal. 1874 Sankey's Sacred Songs (1878) 3 'Hold the Fort, for I am coming', Jesus signals still; Wave the answer back to heaven, 'By thy grace we will.' 1878 Browning La Saisiaz 16 From no far mound Waved salute a tall white figure. 1888 Besant Inner House iii, The women wept and laughed at the same time, and waved their welcome.

b. To motion (a person, etc.) *aside, away, back, in, off* by a movement of the hand, etc.; also with preps. *from, over, to*, etc. Also *fig.*

1840 Dickens Old C. Shop lxxi, Waving them off with his hand, and calling softly to her as he went, he stole into the room. 1841 C. Whitehead R. Savage I. xi. 322 He waved me from him. 1854 Surtees Handley Cr. (1901) I. i. 6 Michael took off his broad-brimmed, low-crowned hat, and waving in the pack, cheered them to the echo. Ibid. 7 He presently had the old hounds at his heels, and hat in hand he waved them over the wall. 1864 Mrs. H. Wood Ld. Oakburn's Dau.

xxxvii, An attendant opened the door to see if anything might be wanted, but was waved away again. 1883 D. C. Murray Hearts ix, 'There is a fire in the sitting-room', he said, closing the outer door and waving her along the hall. 1894 Mrs. H. Ward Marcella II. 200 Marcella waved him aside and ran on. 1914 H. James in Q. Rev. Apr. 338 If we put ourselves questions we yet wave away doubts. 1916 W. Sanday In View of End 87 Hitherto the pacifist writings have been waved aside simply on the ground that they were pacifist.

c. *intr.* To make a sign by a wave of the hand.

1803 Edwin I. xiii. 205, I waved to the door, and in silence proceeded to the tyrant. 1847 C. Bronte Jane Eyre xii, I retained my station when he waved to me to go, and announced:—'I cannot think of leaving you, sir.' 1855 Tennyson Maud I. ix. 8 Rapidly riding far away, She waved to me with her hand. 1905 Mabel Barnes-Grundy Vacill. Hazel xvi. 219 He looks very miserable and cold and pinched. Poor old Sammy! I must wave to him.

d. *trans.* To mark (musical measures) by waving something.

1851 Mrs. Browning Casa Guidi Wind. I. 804 All, to please The donna waving measures with her fan.

II. (From Wave *sb.*)

11. To ornament with an undulating design; to make (something) wavy in outline.

1547 in Feuillerat Revels Edw. VI (1914) 9, v] Couering of Bardes of clothe of golde wherof three ar waved with clothe of golde. c 1611 Chapman Iliad XXIII. 482 Arms..forged of brass, and waved about with tin. 1652 Culpeper Eng. Physit. (1656) 137 Leavs..a little unevenly waved sometimes about the edges. 1667 Milton P. L. IV. 306 Shee..Her unadorned golden tresses wore Dishevel'd, but in wanton ringlets wav'd As the Vine curles her tendrils. 1678 Moxon Mech. Exerc. vi. 104 When one end of the Riglet you wave, is with the Vice Screwed to the plain side of the Rack. Ibid. 105 The Riglet will on its upper side receive the form of the several waves on the under side of the Rack, and also the form or Molding that is on the edge of the bottom of the Iron and so at once the Riglet will be both Molded and waved. 1686 tr. Chardin's Trav. Persia 394 The lower part of which Chappel is cover'd with large Tiles of Porphiry wav'd, and painted with Flowers. 1706 Phillips (ed. Kersey), To *Wave*, to fashion, or make like the waves of the Sea; as watered Silks or Stuffs are. 1733 School of Miniature 39 Finish..by fine thin Strokes,..waving and curling them according to the turn of the Hair. 1815 J. Smith Panorama Sci. & Art II. 763 Strokes following the same direction, but gently waved. 1875 Swinburne Ess. & Studies 319 A head-dress of eastern fashion,..raised and waved and rounded in the likeness of a sea-shell. 1888 Sweet Hist. Eng. Sounds § 221 Earlier in the [11th] century they began to wave and lengthen the top tags of *i, n, h*, etc. 1909 Daily Chron. 1 Oct. 7/4 Hair that has been waved by hot irons till it is broken and irregular.

12. *intr.* To undulate in form or outline.

1789 J. Williams Min. Kingd. I. 108 The horizontal coals ..are found to wave considerably in several places. 1795 Anderson Narr. Embassy China 73 Its [*sc.* the river's] course waves in the finest meanders. 1796 W. H. Marshall W. Eng. II. 84 A slip or coomb, of water formed land, waving with the stream. 1859 Ruskin Two Paths iv. § 121 From this, and in subordination to this, waved the arch and sprang the pinnacle. 1883 Miss Broughton Belinda II. ix, Now and then the type waves up and down before her like the furrows of a ploughed field; but she reads on.

III. 13. The verb-stem in combination, in the names of the several offerings which, according to the Levitical law, were 'waved' (see 9 e) by the priest when presented in sacrifice, as **wavebreast, -loaf, -offering, -sheaf**; also **wave-bread**, a mod. synonym of *wave-loaf*.

1530 Tindale Lev. vii. 30 Euen the fatt apon the brest he shall bringe with the brest to waue it a waueoffrynge before the Lorde. Ibid. 34 For the wauebrest and the heueshulder I haue taken of the children of Israel. Ibid. xxiii. 17 And ye shall brynge out of youre habitacions two waueloaues. 1535 Coverdale Lev. xxiii. 15 From the nexte daye after the Sabbath, whan ye brought yᵉ Waueshefe [1530 Tindale, the sheffe of the waueoffrynge]. 1625 T. Godwin Moses & Aaron VI. ii. 268 These two words, Thenuphoth, and Therumoth; both signifie shake-offrings, heaue-offrings, or waue-offrings. 1879 Farrar St. Paul II. 297 Which with the wave-bread and the heave-shoulders the priest afterwards took as his own perquisites.

Wave, obs. form of Waif *sb.*¹, Waive *v.*¹, *v.*²

Wave, obs. pa. t. of Weave *v.*¹

Waved (wēⁱvd) *ppl. a.* [f. Wave *v.* + -ed ¹.]

1. Having the form of waves, presenting a wavy outline or appearance, undulating, undulated.

a. *gen.*

1599 Hakluyt Voy. II. II. 86 In the hole is laied good store of wood, whereon is raised gallantly a waued roofe. 1605 Sylvester Du Bartas II. iii. IV. Captaines 114 A large Cave, ..Whose waved Seeling,..The Nymphs..rarely had imbost With Pearls and Rubies. 1768 Boswell Corsica i. (ed. 2) 25 A rich waved country..reaches along the east and south coasts to Bonifaccio. 1808 Eleanor Sleath Bristol Heiress I. 61 This surface..is gently waved, rising with a varied swell from a small hollow, or valley. 1863 Illustr. Lond. News 1 Aug. 116/4 Advt., Crinoline.—The Patent Ondina, or Waved Jupon, does away with the unsightly results of the ordinary hoops. 1875 Knight Dict. Mech., Waved Wheel. The edge of the wheel is waved or convoluted so that as it revolves it imparts a lateral oscillation to an arm, pitman, or what not. 1890 Hessels Corpus Gloss. Introd. p. xi, [The letter] l, with a waved stroke through it, indicates uel.

b. of hair, etc.

1863 'Holme Lee' A. Warleigh III. 58 Her hat in her lap, and her waved brown hair uncovered. 1884 McLaren Spinning (ed. 2) 6 Take some hairs and some fibres of South Down wool and hold them together. The hair will hang straight and smooth, the wool will be curly, something like a corkscrew, and will have a waved appearance. 1913 Play Pictorial No. 138, p. vi/2 The waved hair is drawn smoothly back from the forehead.

c. *Her.* = Undee, Wavé, Wavy.

1610 Guillim Heraldry II. iii. 44 Of these [Lines] some are ..Waued. 1680 Sir G. Mackenzie Sci. Her. 26 Waved is so call'd, from the waves of the Sea, which it represents, and is therefore called *undé*, and is used for signifying that the Bearer got his Arms for service done at sea. Ibid. 44 A cross waved. Crux undosa. 1704 J. Harris Lex. Techn. I, Waved or Wavy.

d. Of a sword, dagger, etc.: Having the edge undulated. Also in *Her.*

1688 Holme Armoury III. xviii. (Roxb.) 126/1 He beareth Azure, a waved sword, or a sword waved, or wavey. 1780 Edmondson Heraldry II. Gloss., Waved Sword, by some erroneously called a flaming sword. 1855 tr. Labarte's Arts Mid. Ages p. xxxv, Malay knife..., blade waved.

2. Having undulated markings. Of silk, etc. = Watered. Also in comb. † *waved-wise* adv.

1547 in Feuillerat Revels Edw. VI (1914) 14 Gardyd abowtes with clothe of golde wavyd wyse. 1601 Holland Pliny VIII. xlviii. I. 228 The waved water chamelot was from the beginning esteemed the richest and bravest wearing. 1667 Milton P. L. VII. 406 Fish..through Groves Of Coral stray, or sporting with quick glance Show to the Sun thir wav'd coats dropt with Gold. 1711 Fr. Bk. Rates 378 Camblets, watered and not watered, waved, and not waved.

3. *Bot., Zool.*, and *Min.* Undulate; having a wavy form or texture; having wavy markings.

1664 Power Exp. Philos. I. 6 The Gray, or Horse-Fly. Her eye is..of a semisphæroidal figure; black and waved. 1776 J. Lee Introd. Bot. Expl. Terms 379 Flexuosus, waved, bent backwards and forwards from Bud to Bud. 1796 Withering Brit. Plants (ed. 3) III. 673 Leaves..waved at the edge. 1822 J. Parkinson Outl. Oryctol. 187 The hinge..without tooth, waved and rather sinuous and unequal. 1841 Florist's Jrnl. (1846) II. 277 The sepals and petals are very linear and waved. 1843 Humble Dict. Geol. etc. (ed. 2), Waved, ..In botany, applied to the margins of leaves, when bordered alternately with numerous minute segments of circles and angles. In entomology, applied to insects when the margin of the body is marked with a succession of arched incisions. 1845 A. Gray Bot. Text-bk. (ed. 2) 112 A slightly waved or sinuous margin is said to be *repand*. 1870 Hooker Stud. Flora 276 Lobes of lower lip subequal, waved and toothed.

b. In specific names of animals, plants, etc.

1668 Charleton Onomast. 130 Raia Vndulata..the waved Scate. 1681 Grew Musæum I. § vi. ii. 147 The Great Waved-Muscle..is commonly found in the Red-Sea. 1822 Hortus Anglicus II. 397 Aster Undulatus. Waved Star Wort. 1824 R. K. Greville Flora Edin. 20 Aira flexuosa..Waved Hair-grass. 1832 Rennie Consp. Butterfl. & Moths 139 The Waved Carpet (Emmelesia sylvata, Stephens).

Comb. 1796 Marshall Planting II. 66 The Curled Cistus, or Waved-leaved Rock Rose.

4. Moved in waves.

1820 Shelley Prometh. Unb. IV. 187 'Tis the deep music of the rolling world Kindling within the strings of the waved air Æolian modulations.

5. Held aloft and moved to and fro.

1883 Miss Broughton Belinda I. iii, A burly middle-aged figure gesticulating with raised arms and waved umbrella in mid-road. 1891 F. Tennyson Daphne 3 Beeches swung their heads Before the waved banners of the winds. 1916 Bayfield tr. Ovid's Met. xi. in 19th Cent. May 1013 She.. was the first to see Her lord..Who with waved hand made signal, and her own She waved in answer.

Wavel (wēⁱv'l), *v. Sc.* Also 7 **waivle, weavle**, 9 **wavle**. [Freq. of Wave *v.*: see -el.]

† 1. *intr.* 'To move backwards and forwards, to wave' (Jam. 1808). *Obs.*

a 1689 W. Cleland Poems (1697) 107 He making Hands, and Gown, and sleives wavel, Half Singing vents this Reavel Ravel.

† b. *trans.* To twist (the mouth). *Obs.*

1654 Sir A. Johnston (Ld. Wariston) Diary (S.H.S.) II. 277 Folks observing in the kirk..my wagging my head and weavling my mouth in the singing.

2. To stagger.

[1638: cf. *ppl. a.* below.] 1896 J. J. H. Burgess Lowra Biglan 56 (E.D.D.) So up he waavles to da door.

3. ? To embroider with a wavy pattern.

a 1844 W. Miller in A. Whitelaw Scot. Song 536 His coat's o' glowin' ruddy brown, and wavilet wi' gold.

Hence **Wa·velled** *ppl. a.* ? twisted; **Wa·velling** *ppl. a.*

1638 Sir A. Johnston (Ld. Wariston) Diary (S.H.S.) I. 383 Using al and only his auin means, without waivling steps to byrods and bypayths, they may find that sprit within telling them realy and sensibly This is not the way, walk not in it. 1886 J. J. H. Burgess Shetland Sk. 30 He's sic a wavlit ill-vyndid lookin' objec', nae manly wy wi him ava.

Waveless (wēⁱ·vlės), *a.* [f. Wave *sb.* + -less.] Having no waves or undulation; not agitated or disturbed by waves. Also *fig.*

? a 1597 Peele David & Bethsabe (1599) B j b, Thy body smoother then this wauelesse spring. 1799 Campbell Pleas. Hope II. 127 In the waveless mirror of his mind. 1804 Grahame Sabbath 212 A waveless lake, In which the wintry stars all bright appear. 1818 Shelley Eugan. Hills 91 Beneath is spread like a green sea The waveless plain of Lombardy. 1842 Barham Ingol. Leg., Fragm. Westm. Abbey 12 Above each knightly stall Unmoved, the banner'd blazonry hung waveless as a pall. 1872 M. Collins Two Plunges for Pearl III. 166 Lotos-islands in a waveless bay. 1887 G. W. Cable Grande Pointe v. in Century Mag. Mar. 668/1 Their delicately penciled brows, their dark, waveless hair. 1890 'R. Boldrewood' Col. Reformer xii, Waveless uniformity, not to say monotony, of existence.

Hence **Wa·velessly** *adv.*

1819 Blackw. Mag. VI. 136 Wavelessly the river spread Its silver mirror. 1845 Jane Robinson Whitehall iii, So placidly and wavelessly the winds of passion or guilt glide past the waters of time.

Wavelet (wēⁱ·vlėt). [f. Wave *sb.* + -let.] A little wave, a ripple.

1813 Shelley Q. Mab viii. 24 Like the vague sighings of a wind at even, That wakes the wavelets of the slumbering sea. 1856 Geo. Eliot Scenes Cler. Life, Amos Barton ii, The head, with its thin wavelets of brown hair, indents the little pillow. 1873 Black Pr. Thule v. 77 The white wavelets that were breaking on the beach.

b. *transf.* and *fig.*

c 1810 Coleridge in Lit. Rem. (1838) III. 360 You only hide it by foam and bubbles, by wavelets and steam-clouds, of ebullient rhetoric. 1874 H. R. Reynolds John Baptist i. 3 The transcendent Intelligence which presides over the law and measure of every wavelet of the universal energy. 1879 Macdonald P. Faber I. vi. 61 Slowly she rose through a sky freckled with wavelets of cloud.

Wa·ve-like, *a.* and *adv.* [f. Wave *sb.* + -like.]

A. *adj.* Resembling a wave, or what pertains to a wave.

1685 Boyle Effects of Motion iii. (1690) 18, I see no necessity of having recourse to any thing but the wave-like motion of the Air for the production of our Phænomenon. 1830 Lyell Princ. Geol. I. 468 The wave like motion of the ground during earthquakes. 1887 T. Stevens Around World on Bicycle I. 3 The wave-like macadam abruptly terminates, and I find myself on a common dirt road. 1889 Hardwicke's Sci.-Gossip XXV. 124 Every now and then a wave-like movement is seen to traverse through them.

B. *adv.* After the manner of a wave or waves.

1872 Routledge's Every Boy's Ann. 215 The dark solid wall of the enemy's infantry rolled, wave-like against this position. 1884 J. Payn Lit. Recoll. 33 When I think of that inimitable scene, the humour of it sweeps wavelike over all.

Wa·ve-line.

1. *Ship-building.* An outline recommended by some naval architects for the hull of a vessel as facilitating movement through the waves.

1846 Mechanic's Mag. 24 Oct. 391 What is the wave line? According to its ingenious author, Mr. J. Scott Russell, it differs from an ordinary ship's bow..in this, that it is 'gently hollower than such a bow towards the cutwater, and a little rounder towards the greatest breadth'. 1883 Harper's Mag. Aug. 441/2 The wave-line theories..had been adopted.

2. *Physics.* The path of a wave of light, sound, etc.; also, the graphic representation of the path.

1888 Rutley Rock-forming Min. 30 They are thrown into a wave line through the successive vibration of the other particles from the line of rest. Ibid. 31 The wave-line..is just half a wave-length.

3. Each of the lines or furrows produced by the action of the waves on a sandy beach.

1891 Century Dict.

Wavellite (wēⁱ·vělɔit). *Min.* [Named 1805 after Dr. W. *Wavel* its discoverer: see -ite.] Hydrous phosphate of aluminium, found in globular aggregates with a radiated structure.

1805 Phil. Trans. XCV. 162. 1822 G. Young Geol. Surv. Coast Yorks. (1828) 129 Silky crystals, resembling wavellite. 1885 Encycl. Brit. XVIII. 818/1.

† **Wa·venger.** *Sc.* and *north. Obs.* Forms: 5–6 vau-, 6 **wauengeour**, 9 **waff-, whiffinger, waifinger**. [App. f. Waif *sb.* after *messenger, passenger, scavenger*, etc.]

1. *Sc.* A vagabond. Also *attrib.*

1493 Sc. Acts Jas. IV (1814) II. 235/1 To causs idill men vauengeouris to laubour for þair leuing. 1513 Douglas Æneis IV. xi. 17 [Shall it be] lefull till a wauengeour strangeir Me and my realm betrump on this maneir. Ibid. XII. v. 99 Follow me Quham now 3on vauengeour, 3on ilk stranger, Affrays so.

2. *dial.* A stray animal, estray.

1825 Brockett N. C. Gloss., Waifinger, an estray. a 1864 R. B. Peacock Lonsdale Gloss., Waifinger, stray cattle.

Waver (wēⁱ·vəɹ), *sb.*¹ Also 6 **wayver, weaver**, 6–8 **waiver**. [Of obscure origin: the early forms do not favour derivation from Wave *v.* Possibly f. Waive *v.*¹, in the sense 'to leave untouched'.] A young tree left standing when the surrounding wood is felled.

1555 Anc. Deed C 7700 (P.R.O.), The said Luke shall leave ..standynge..all suche wayuers of oke and asshe that be vnder the compace of twelue ynches in thycknesse. 1590 W. West Symbol. § 267 (§ 406) Except the land and soile of the same woodes and vnderwoodes, and also wayuers called standers of &c. 1595 Holmesfield Court Rolls in Sheffield Gloss. s.v., That no persone or persons within this manor shall cutt vpp or carry away any of the lorde's woodes..vpon payne of every burden of greene wood vjd. and every weaver xij d. and every burden of dry wood being hedgwood iiij d. 1597 Ibid., Every weaver or poole. 1664 Evelyn Sylva xxvii. 71 It is a very ordinary Copse which will not afford three or four Firsts, that is, Bests; fourteen Seconds; twelve Thirds; eight Wavers, &c. according to which proportions the sizes of young Trees in Copsing are to succeed one another. 1768 Waiver [see Tiller *sb.*³ 2]. 1800 J. Tuke Agric. N. Riding Yorks. 186 Leaving at certain distances, when the timber and under-wood are cut down, the thriving young trees, which so left, are very properly called *wavers*, from their being agitated by every breeze. 1888 Sheffield Gloss.

Waver (wēⁱ·vəɹ), *sb.*² [f. Wave *v.* + -er ¹.]

† 1. One who vacillates. *Obs.*

1667 Waterhous Fire Lond. 189 No waver in Judgment, have I, through Gods mercy, ever been.

2. One who waves, or causes to undulate, swing, or flutter.

1835 T. Mitchell Aristoph. Acharn. 1059 note, Groupes of tumblers, jugglers, ball-players, and wavers of the torch. 1860 W. G. Clark in Galton Vac. Tour. (1861) 46 The wavers of flags, and the brandishers of daggers. 1869 'Mark Twain' Innoc. Abr. xiii. (1872) 91 The..house-tops..burst into a snow storm of waving handkerchiefs, and the wavers of the same mingled their cheers with those of the masses below.

† 3. A name for the star Fomalhaut in the constellation Piscis Australis. *Obs.*

1556 Recorde Cast. Knowl. IV. 267 [*marg.*] The Wauer.

4. *Printing.* See quots. Also *waver roller*.

1882 Southward Pract. Print. 471 Next set in their places the wavers and the inkers. 1888 Encycl. Brit. XXIII. 706/1 As the carriage returns, this strip of ink is distributed on the inking table by rollers placed diagonally across the machine. The diagonal position gives them a waving motion; hence they are called *wavers*. 1888 Jacobi Printers' Vocab., *Waver rollers*, rollers which distribute ink on the ink table in a diagonal direction. *Wavers*, short term for 'waver rollers'.

5. An implement for making the hair wavy.

1895 Army & Navy Stores List 15 Sept. 180/2 Hair Wavers ..Price per box, containing 5 wavers, 0/8½. 1909 Daily Chron. 1 Oct. 7/4 These wavers may be left in the slightly dampened hair for an hour or two, and the result will be a soft, natural-looking wave.

Waver (wēⁱ·vəɹ), *sb.*³ [f. Waver *v.*] The act or condition of wavering.

a. In physical sense, a flutter or trembling.

1826 J. Wilson in Blackw. Mag. XX. 90 No a bit butterflee on its silent waver, meeting the murmur of the straightforward bee. 1886 Guillemard Cruise of Marchesa I. 137 Here and there a little gap revealed a Hobbema-like scene of sunny distance, whose clearness was unbroken by the waver of a single leaf. 1891 'R. Boldrewood' Sydney-side Sax. xii, Sitting square, without the slightest waver or tremble in her saddle. 1918 Merrick When Love flies iv. 44 She sat watching the waver of the candles in the draught.

b. A condition of vacillation or faltering. † *In a waver* (obs.), *on* or *upon the waver*, in uncertainty or unsteadiness; inclining now this way, now that.

1519 Horman Vulgaria 57 b, I stande in doubte or in a wauer. *Anceps sum concilii.* 1806 Henry Siddons Maid, Wife, & Widow III. 64 His reason was on the waver. a 1809 J. Palmer Like Master (1811) I. xii. 167 His regret to leave the coppers he touch'd in his present service, and his inclination to embrace the brazier's offer, kept him upon the waver, like an ass between two bundles of hay. 1864 Sherman Let. 31 Dec. (1894) 241 Not a waver, doubt, or hesitation when I order, and men march to certain death without a murmur if I call on them. 1865 Mrs. H. Wood Mildred Arkell xlviii, 'Does she mean to accept him?' asked Travice. 'Well, she's on the waver. She does not dislike him, and she does not particularly like him.'

Waver (wēⁱ·vəɹ), *v.* Also 4 **wever**, 4–5 *Sc.* **wayver, wafer**, 4–6 *Sc.* **vaver**, 4–7 *Sc.* **wawer**, 5 **wavere, wavur, wafyr**, 6 **wavor**, *Sc.* **vaifer**, 7 **wavour**. [ME. *waver, wever* = MHG. *waberēn*, mod.G. (now dial.) *wabern, webern* to move about, ON. *vafra* to move unsteadily, flicker (cf. *vafrloge* flickering flame), Norw. *vavra* to go to and fro, stagger; a frequentative f. Teut. root **wab-*: see Wave *v.*

Shoreham's *weverinde* (c 1315, sense 5) shows that the word in the south at least is native English (cf. OE. *wæfre* unsteady, also nimble); it is possible that in the north the word may partly represent an adoption of ON. *vafra*, but the supposition is not necessary.]

I. Intransitive.

† 1. To go about or travel at random or without fixed destination; to wander, rove. Also with adv., as *about*. *Obs.*

1375 Barbour Bruce VII. 41 The sleuth-hund maid stynting thar, And vaueryt [*v.r.* waweryt] lang tyme to and fra. c 1375 Sc. Leg. Saints xxv. (Julian) 287 Waferand fra place to place. c 1440 Alphabet of Tales 490 Þai waxed so pure at þai wavurd aboute here & þer. c 1470 Henry Wallace IV. 283 He saw mony rout Off wyld bestis wauerand in wode and playne. 1483 Cath. Angl. 411/1 To Wavere Aboute (*v.r.* Wafyr Abowt), *vagari*. 1513 Douglas Æneis VI. v. 70 Quha ar vnbereit a hundreth ȝeir man byde, Wauerand and wandrand by this bankis syde. 1599 Nashe Lenten Stuffe C 1, There were two Channels..where through the fishermen did wander and wauer vp to Norwich and diuers parts of Suffolke and Norfolke.

† b. To stray *from*. *Obs.*

1456 Sir G. Haye Bk. Knighthood Wks. (S.T.S.) II. 6 He slepit aȝ on his palfray, and waverit fra his folk out of the hye way. 1599 Extracts Aberd. Reg. (1848) II. 204 The said Thomas hes bene accusit of..wavering oftentymes fra his wyff, bairnis, and famelie. 1609 Skene Reg. Maj., Quon. Attach. x. 78 Gif..he..sall sweare that, that beast did waver away from him.

2. To sway to and fro, as if in danger of falling; to reel, stagger, totter. Now *rare* (cf. 5 d, 7).

c 1400 Destr. Troy 8266 All in wer for to walt, wayuerонde he sote. c 1440 Promp. Parv. 447/2 Schoggyn, schakyn, or waveryn, *vacillo*. 1500–20 Dunbar Poems liii. 10 Bot ay his ane futt did wawer, He stackerit lyk ane strummall awer. 1531 Elyot Gov. I. xi. (1883) I. 95 Oza, for puttyng his hande to the holy shryne that was called *Archa federis*,..though it were wauerynge and in daunger to fall, yet was he stryken of god. 1691 Ray Creation I. (1692) 142 When they [*sc.* the Fins] are cut off, it [*sc.* the Body of the Fish] wavers to and fro. 1852 Mrs. Stowe Uncle Tom's C. xxxiii. 298 She was evidently in a condition of great suffering, and Tom often heard her praying, as she wavered and trembled, and seemed about to fall down.

3. To swing or wave in the air; to float or flutter.

c 1440 Promp. Parv. 518/2 Wawyn, or wauеryn, yn a myry totyr, *oscillo*. c 1514 Barclay Eclogue iii, Sometime must thou stoupe unto a rude vilayne Calling him master,.. Although thou would see him waver in a bande. 1548 Udall Erasm. Par. Matt. viii. 18–22 The byrdes fleyng and wauoring in the ayer. 1574 T. Hill Art Garden., Weather viii. 72 The kytes playing and wauering about in the aire. 1610 Guillim Heraldry III. xv. 136 Two Lions came running with their shaggy lockes wauering about their shoulders. 1726–30 Thomson Winter 230 Thro' the hush'd air the whitening shower descends, At first thin-wavering. 1818 Scott Hrt.

Midl. vii, He could discern a figure wavering and struggling as it hung suspended above the heads of the multitude. 1847 Tennyson Princess VI. 64 On their curls From the high tree the blossom wavering fell. 1864 Skeat Uhland's Poems 252 Lo! down waver clustering ringlets Round a soft and gentle face! 1883 Chamb. Jrnl. 689 Huge butterflies wavered about the cactus plants.

b. Phr. *To waver with* or *in the wind.* ? *Obs.*

c 1500 Nut-brown Maid 74 in Arnolde Chron. (1811) 200 Wythout pytee, hanged to bee, and wauer wᵗ the wynde. 1523 Berners Froiss. I. cccxxxiii. 522 With baners and penons waueryng with the wynde. 1526 Tindale Matt. xi. 7 A rede waueringe with the wynde. 1582 N. Lichefield tr. Castanheda's Conq. E. Ind. I. lxxviii. 158 After this, hee went up and downe, wauering in the winde, tarryeng for the rest of the shippes. 1725 Pope Odyss. XXII. 503 Soon fled the soul impure, and left behind The empty corse to waver with the wind. 1818 Scott Hrt. Midl. xl, Here many an outlaw..had wavered in the wind during the wars. 1828 Miss Mitford Village, Country Barber III. 165 A lank, long, stooping figure, which seemed wavering in the wind like a powder-puff.

c. *transf.*

1860 Hawthorne Transform. xxix, Now tumbling down, down, down, with a long shriek wavering after him, all the way. 1876 Morris Sigurd II. 141 The wind in his raiment wavered.

† 4. Of water, waves: To surge. *Obs. rare.*

c 1425 Wyntoun Cron. IV. 1963 As rewaris reythe for rayn wil rysse And wauer mare wiþe wawis woide þan wil a kyndly standande flude.

5. Of persons, their sentiments, etc.: To exhibit doubt or indecision; to change or vary; to fluctuate or vacillate (*between*); to falter in resolution or allegiance; to show signs of giving way.

c 1315 Shoreham Poems I. 424 And þi bi-leaue of ihesu crist His nou al weuerinde. 1375 Barbour Bruce XII. 185 Mony ane hert sal vaverand [*v.r.* waverand] be That semyt ere of gret bounte. c 1407 Lydg. Reson & Sens. 2901 And thus I stood al in a rage With look cast fix in hir visage, Wavering as in a were. c 1425 Wyntoun Cron. V. 4318 He was curyousse in his stille,..Mad in metyr meit his dyte, Litil or noucht neuir þe lesse Wauerande fra þe suythtfastnes. c 1440 Promp. Parv. 18/2 Waueron yn hert for vnstabylnesse, *muto*. c 1440 Gesta Rom. xxv. 97 Þat he sette fully his hope in god, and not be dul in the feithe, ne wauere in the comavndementes of god. 1526 Tindale Jas. i. 6 But let hym axe in faythe and waver not [1611 nothing wauering]. 1526 Pilgr. Perf. (W. de W. 1531) 223 b, That we his yongest chylden..sholde not..wauer in our fayth. 1548 Udall Erasm. Par. Matt. i. 20, 21 Why art thou vexed? why doest thou wauer in & out? 1579 Shaks. Lover's Compl. 97 And nice affections wavering stood in doubt If best were as it was, or best without. 1610 Holland Camden's Brit. (1637) 43 They that wavered betweene warre and peace. 1641 Milton Ch. Govt. I. vii. 28 Vertue that wavers is not vertue. 1714 Addison Spect. No. 585 ¶ 8 Her Mind continued wavering about twenty Years longer between Shalum and Mishpach. 1849 Macaulay Hist. Eng. v. I. 603 While he was thus wavering between projects equally hopeless. 1856 Froude Hist. Eng. (1858) I. iv. 355 The allegiance even of the bishops and the secular clergy to Rome had begun to waver. 1874 Green Short Hist. iv. § 2. 172 Only on one occasion..did the burgesses waver from their general support of the Crown. 1883 Froude Short Stud. IV. I. xi. 131 Many people had begun to waver in their allegiance. 1884 M. Creighton Hist. Ess. viii. (1902) 239 For a time opinions wavered which boundary to choose.

† b. Phr. *To waver as, like, with the wind.* Cf. 3 b. *Obs.*

c 1480 Henryson Fox, Wolf & Cadger 218 (Harl.) With that þe cadger, wauering as the wind, Come rydand on the laid. a 1548 Hall Chron., Edw. V 13 Not common people onely, which wauer with the wynde, but wyse menne also. 1565 B. Googe tr. Palingenius' Zodiac VII. A vj b, And so corrupt the mindes Of rude vnskilfull common sort, that wauer lyke the wyndes. a 1825 Child Noryce i. in Child Ballads II. 266 Child Noryce is a clever young man, He wavers wi the wind.

† c. To hesitate *to* (do something). *Ob. rare.*

1644 Milton Divorce II. xv. 61, I shall not much waver to affirm, that [etc.].

d. Of a combatant, body of troops, line of battle: To become unsteady, flinch, give way.

1831 James Phil. Augustus xlii, He wavered not a step; but, still striding over the body of the king,..maintained his ground. 1860 Froude Hist. Eng. V. xxvi. 213 The sustained fire of the Lanzknechts threw their dense and unorganized masses into rapid confusion. As they wavered, Warwick's horse were in the midst of them. 1915 J. Buchan Hist. War IV. xxvi. 75 The line wavered and broke.

6. Of things (or a person as an unconscious agent): To change, vary, fluctuate.

1490 Caxton Eneydos 2 We englysshe men ben borne vnder the domynacyon of the mone, whiche is neuer stedfaste, but euer wauerynge. a 1548 Hall Chron., Hen. VI 116 Thus the Englishe affaires..within the realme began to wauer, and waxe variable. 1560 Daus tr. Sleidane's Comm. 91 b, To suffer this gere to hange waueringe [L. *ut rem ita fluctuare sinat*]. 1565 Cooper Thesaurus s. v. Nuto, Victorie wauereth or flitteth betweene both vncertaynly. 1837 Dickens Pickw. xxxviii, During the whole space of time just mentioned, Mr. Benjamin Allen had been wavering between intoxication partial and intoxication complete. 1859 Dickens etc. Haunted Ho. iii. 14/1 He had..a waistcoat that wavered in hue between a sunny buff and a stony drab. 1922 19th Cent. Apr. 681 Among all Arabs succession is hereditary, but it wavers between the eldest son and the eldest male member of the family.

7. Of the voice, the eye, etc. (or a person with reference to these): To become unsteady; to shake, tremble, falter (through emotion or bodily weakness). † Of the wits: To become confused, reel.

1621 Fletcher Pilgr. III. iii, Keep my wits Heaven, I feel 'em wavering, O God my head. 1840 Dickens Old C. Shop xlv, 'No,' replied the old man, wavering in his voice, no less than in his manner. 1850 Susan Warner Wide World xv, Miss Fortune's conscience must have troubled her a little, for her eye wavered uneasily. 1876 Miss Broughton Joan I. ix, Her voice wavers and breaks. The tears well up into her eyes. 1883 A. K. Green X. Y. Z. iv. 63 His eye did not waver from its steady solemn look toward the door. 1886 Kipling Departm. Ditties etc. (1888) 45 The white hands wavered—the bright head drooped.

8. Of light, shade, objects seen unsteadily or through a haze: To flicker, quiver.

1664 Boyle Exper. Colours III. xiv. 227, I took..two Triangular Glasses, and one of them being kept fixt in the same Posture, that the Iris it projected on the Floor might not Waver. 1842 Tennyson Gardener's Dau. 129 The shadow of the flowers..wavering Lovingly lower, trembled on her waist..and still went wavering down. 1842 — Will Waterproof 38 The gas-light wavers dimmer. 1849 Cupples Green Hand xvii. (1856) 173 Tall palms and cocoas—their stems wavering in the thin haze. 1914 Blackw. Mag. Oct. 491/2 A little gleam wavered ahead on my right.

fig. 1837 Whewell Hist. Induct. Sci. IV. i. I. 247 It may serve to illustrate..the extent to which, under the Roman empire, men's notions of mechanical relations became faint, wavered, and disappeared, if we observe the change which took place in architecture.

II. Transitive.

† 9. *causal.* To cause to waver; to wave to and fro; to set in waving or fluttering motion; to render unsteady or unsteadfast. *Obs.*

c 1425 Wyntoun Cron. III. 798 Þus in seige a sote to se, Or do a dowde in dignyte, Sal ger standande statis stauer, And wil bathe wit and worschep wauer. c 1440 Promp. Parv. 518/2 Waueron, or mevyn or steryn, *agito*. 1456 Sir G. Haye Law of Arms (S.T.S.) 227 Nocht gaynstandand that he be wauerit [*prin'ed* wanerit] in his wit. 1561 in Tytler Hist. Scot. (1864) III. 148 Seeing he..showed himself so constant in religion, that neither the fear of his souereign's indignation could wauer him, nor great promises win him. 1583 in Hakluyt Voy. (1589) 683 Item, if the Admirall shall happen to hull in the night: then to make a wauering light ouer his other light, wauering the light vpon a pole. 1594 Nashe Unfort. Trav. E 2 b, A third wauerd and wagled his head, like a proud horse playing with his bridle. 1812 Courier in Examiner 24 Aug. 540/1 Shot, shells, grape,..could not ..waver the line of the..infantry.

† 10. To vacillate under, falter in resistance to. *Obs. rare*⁻¹.

1596 Drayton Mortimer. B 4 b, Th'vnconstant Barrons, wauering euery houre, The fierce encounter of this raging tyde.

Waver, var. Waiver.

Waverer (wēⁱ·vərəɹ). [f. Waver *v.* + -er ¹.] One who wavers; one who is undecided or vacillates in opinion or choice; one who falters in allegiance or hesitates to embrace a particular party or cause.

1592 Shaks. Rom. & Jul. II. iii. 89 But come young wauerer, come goe with me. 1640 tr. Verdere's Rom. of Rom. I. xxviii. 134, I went to Cloria, unto whom I discovered the desires of my waverer [orig. (1626) 744 *les desseins de cet inconstant*]. 1850 Grote Greece II. lx. (1862) V. 259 The waverers thought it time to declare themselves. 1855 Macaulay Hist. Eng. xiii. III. 271 More than one waverer was kept steady by being assured in confident terms that a speedy restoration was inevitable. 1885 Manch. Guard. 20 July 5/5 A section of waverers who have inclined lately to the Tory side.

b. *Hist.* The name given to a section of Peers who were willing to make terms with the Reform government of 1832 rather than wreck the Upper House.

1832 Greville Mem. 27 Mar. (1874) II. 273, I have no doubt that all the ultras will be deeply mortified at the moderation of Lord Grey and of the Duke of Wellington, and at the success *so far* of 'the Waverers'. 1886 Kebbel Hist. Toryism iv. 210 The second reading of the Bill had been carried in the Lords..with the help of the well-known 'Waverers', led by Lords Harrowby and Wharncliffe.

Wavering (wēⁱ·vəriŋ), *vbl. sb.* [-ing ¹.] The action of the verb Waver, in various senses.

1375 Barbour Bruce VI. 584 The hund alwais followit the kyng, And changit nocht for na parting, Bot ay followit the kyngis tras, But vaueryng, as he passit was. ? a 1400 Morte Arth. 2224, I watte be thi wauerynge, thow willnez aftyre sorowe. 1548 Udall Erasm. Par. Luke vi. 12–16 Whan the people wer in a wauеryng and mammeryng what he was. 1593 Nashe Christ's T. E 3 b, Had you rested them on the true Rocke, they had beene ruine-proofe; but now the raine wil rough-enter through the crannies of theyr wauering. 1605 Bacon Adv. Learn. II. § 8. 13 Massiue bodies..haue certaine trepidations and wauerings before they fixe and settle. a 1768 Secker Serm. (1770) IV. 2 Why this perpetual Wavering and Fluctuation, about the first thing, that you ought to fix. 1826 Jane Austen Emma xxii, Had there been no pain to her friend, or reproach to herself, in the waverings of Harriet's mind, Emma would have been amused by its variations. 1828–43 Tytler Hist. Scot. (1864) I. 120 The wavering of the English lines was now discernible by the Scottish soldiers. 1831 Alford in Life (1873) 68 Quick waverings about of bands of light such as take place in the Polar Auroras. 1868 E. Edwards Ralegh I. xx. 443 The King's wavering between a course of clemency and one of rigour.

Wa·vering, *ppl. a.* [f. Waver *v.* + -ing ².]

† 1. Wandering, vagrant. *Obs.*

1375 Barbour Bruce VII. 112 Thai saw on syde thre men cumand, Lik to licht men and vauerand. 1607 N. Riding Rec., Q. Sess. Rec. (1884) I. 91 Tho. Best of Wath, a wavering person, [presented] for three assaults on the Constable of Melmerby.

2. Tottering, shaking, faltering, reeling.

c 1400 Destr. Troy 13546 And wayuerand, weike, [I] wan to the lond. 1569 Roest tr. J. van der Noot's Theat. Worldlings 76 Theyr proude titles haue no sure foundation, but are buylded only vppon the wauеryng sandes of doubtefulnesse and falshode. 1816 Byron Siege of Corinth xxix,

Supplement, p. 3873; Corrigenda, p. 4092; Spurious words, p. 4093; Books quoted, p. 4094

WAX. 194 WAX. WAX. WAX. 195 WAX.

Supplement, p. 3873; Corrigenda, p. 4092; Spurious words, p. 4093; Books quoted, p. 4094

WAY.

VI. Combinations.

39. Obvious combinations. **a.** simple attrib., as *way-boat*, *-end*, *-pane* (PANE *sb.* 9), *-signal*; **b.** objective, as *way-taking*, *-traveller*, *-wanderer*; **c.** instrumental, as *way-beaten*, *-benighted*, *-sorry*, *-spent*, *-wearied* adjs.

40. Special comb.: *way-baggage* U.S., the baggage or luggage of a way-passenger; *way-beam*, a beam used in the construction of a form of longitudinal railway sleeper; *way-beaten* *a.*, exhausted by travel; *way-beater*, one who frequents the highway for felonious purposes; *way-chain*, a brake for the wheel of a vehicle; in quot. *fig.*; *way-master* U.S., a fare charged for travelling between intermediate stations on a railway; cf. *way-passenger*, *-station*; *way-fare* [FINE *sb.*], a companion in travel; *way-flax* (meaning obscure); *way-food*, provision for a journey; *way-gang*, go so WAYGATE; *way-gatherer*, a traveller by road, a wayfarer; *way-tithe* ...

way (wē*), *sb.*, exc. *north.*, and U.S. [Aphetic f. AWAY. Cf. G. *weg* similarly used.]
1. = AWAY *adv.* in various senses. † *Do way; see* 5.

way-bill, U.S. trans., to enter (goods) on a way-bill.

Waybread (wē*brēd*). Forms: 1 *wegbræde*, *-brǣde*, *-brōde*, ... Now dial. and U.S.

Wayfarer (wē*fēərər*). [f. WAY *sb.* + FARE *sb.*, after WAYFARING *vbl. sb.*] A traveller by road, esp. one who journeys on foot.

Wayfaring.

Wayfaring-tree. 1. The tall shrub *Viburnum Lantana*, with broad leaves downy underneath, white flowers in dense cymes, and green berries turning first red then black.

Waylay (wēlē*), *v.* [f. WAY *sb.* + LAY *v.*]
1. *trans.* To lie in wait for (a person or thing) with evil or hostile intent; to seize or attack in the way.

Wayleave, **way-leave.** 1. = wayfele, *-leve*. [f. WAY *sb.* + LEAVE *sb.*] Permission to make and use a way for conveying coal from the pit-head across a person's land.

Wayment, *sb.* Also 4 *weyment*. [Aphetic f. AWAYMENT.] Lamentation, grief.

Waymark, **way-mark.** An object, whether natural feature or artificial structure, that serves as a guide to the traveller. Also *fig.*

Way-side. The side of a road or path; the land bordering either side of the way.

Ways and means.

1. The methods and resources which are at a person's disposal for effecting some object.

2. *spec.* In *Legislation:* Methods of procuring funds or supplies for the current expenditure of the state.

Wayt, Waystor : see WAITE, WASTER.

Wayte (obs. ff. WAIT *sb.*1 and *v.*1, *v.*2), WEIGHT.

Wayte, variant of WAITE *sb.*1, WOTHE *Obs.*

Way-thee, *dial.* [f. WAY *sb.*1 or WEIGH *v.*]

† Wayward, *a. Obs. rare*⁻¹. [f. prec. adj.]
To be perversely prejudiced.

Wayward, *sb.* form of WAIVE *v.*2 and *v.*2 *Obs.*

Wayward (wē'wǎrd), *a.* Not now in colloquial use. Also 4 wariward, weiward, 4-5 wayward (4- werd), 6-warde), 4, 6 wayewarde, 6 -waiward (6 -warde), 7 waward). [Aphetic f. AWAYWARD. Cf. froward.]

1. Disposed to go counter to the wishes or advice of others, or to what is reasonable ; wrongheaded, intractable, self-willed ; froward, perverse. Of children: Disobedient, refractory.

2. Capriciously wilful ; conforming to no fixed rule or principle of conduct ; erratic.

Wayward, -wards. In the 17-18th c. the suffix -ward(s was often appended to phrases like this way, that way, over way, coming this way-ward.

Wayward'e, variant form of VAWARD.

Waywarden (wē'wọrd'n). [WAY *sb.*1 + WARDEN *sb.*1] A person (later, one of a board) elected to supervise the highways of a parish or district.

Waywardly (wē'wǎrdli), *adv.* [f. WAYWARD *a.* + -LY 2.] In a wayward manner.

Waywardness (wē'wǎrdnes). [f. WAYWARD *a.* + -NESS.] The quality of being wayward (see prec.)

Way-way, obs. form of WAWA.

Way-wiser (wē'wǒizǎ). Now *Hist.* Also 8-9 -weiser, 8-9 wise-guiser (= De megruiser, Sw. vägvisare, Du. wegwiser), *f. weg* WAY *sb.*1 + -wiser, agent-n. f. weisen to show.

Waywode (wē'wǒud). Now *Hist.* Forms: 7-9 waywode, -wood, weywode, 7 weiwode, 8 weywode, -wod), 8-9 waiwod, 4- waywode, woewood). [Var. of VAIVODE, rep. the Magyar form of a common Slavonic title of office.

Way-worn, *a.* Worn or wearied by travel.

Waywort (wē'wǒ̈rt), [WAY *sb.*1 + WORT.] Early mid-G. *wegwort*, synonym of Ga. *weg(e)-wart(-endive.)*

We (wī). *pers. pron.*, 1st *pl.* Forms: 1 we, wē, 3 we, 3-4 we), 4-6 whe, 5 whee, 4-7 wee, 5-6 wo, 5-6 oi, 5 uue), 6 w 9 us.

Weak (wīk), *a.* and *sb.* Forms: *a.* 3-6, 4-9 Sc. 9 dial. weik, (6 Sc. week), 4-6 wake, wayk(e, (6, 9 wayke, vaike), 5-6 weik(e, weyk(e, (6 Sc. vaek, voik), 8, 4-6 wek, 4 weck, 6 woke, 5-6 weke, 4-7 woke, (6 wake, 8-9 wick), 6- weak ; corresponding to OE. *wāc*; see WOKE *a.*

†Weal, sb.[1] Var. WEALE sb.[1] Obs.

Weal (wīl), sb.[2] [var. of WALE sb.[1]]

Wealaway, obs. form of WELLAWAY.

Wealad (wīld). Forms: 1 weald, 3–4, 6 welde, 7 weld, 5–6, 8 wald; 6–9 wild(e, wyld(e, 7 wilde; 6 weylde, 6–7 weild, 6 weald, [OE. *weald* = WOLD], normally developing into mod. spelling...

Wealden (wīldan), sb. and a. [f. WEALD + -EN.[4]]

†Weal-public. Obs. Also pl. 6–7 weale publiques, [WEAL sb.[1] + public a. 2, after F. *le tien publique* and L. *bonum publicum*.]

Wealful, var. WEALE.

†Wealman. Obs. rare.—[f. weal's genitive of WEAL sb.[1] + MAN sb.[1]]

†Wea·lsome. Obs. rare.—[f. WEAL + -SOME.]

†Wea·lsman, weolson, 5 weylsian, weoalsman. [f. WEAL sb.[1] + -SOME.]

Wealth (welþ). Forms: 3 welðe, welðhe, 3 welþe, 4 welðthe, (-þe), 4–7 welth, 5 welt, 4–5, 6 Sc. velth, 6 Sc. veilth, 4–6 welthe, (6 weilthe, 7 weaulthe, 7 wealth), 5–7 wealth...

†Wealthy, a. Obs. rare.—[f. WEALTH + -Y.[1]]

Wealthful (welþfl), a. Now rare. [f. WEALTH + -FUL.] Abounding in wealth; happy (obs.); rich, prosperous; conducive to wealth.

Wealthily (welþili), adv. Now rare. Also **Wealthly**. [-LY[2]] In a wealthy manner.

Wealthiness (welþi·nes). [f. WEALTHY + -NESS.] Wealthy quality or condition; wealth.

Wealthless (welþles), a. rare. [f. WEALTH + -LESS.] Without wealth, having no money.

†Wealthing. Obs. rare.—[f. WEALTH + -ING[1].] A wealthy wight.

Wealthy (welþi), a. [f. WEALTH + -Y[1].] 1. Possessing well-being, happy, prosperous. Obs.

Wealy, a.[1] Obs. Forms: 1 weliз, -eз, welð, 2–4 weli, 3 weoli, -03, 4–5 wely, 6 Sc. veilie, [OE. *welig*, *weliз* and MDu. *welich*, *welig*] Wealthy.

Wealy, a.[2] [f. WEAL sb.[2] + -Y.] Marked with weals.

Weam (b : see WAME.

Weame, obs. form of WAME, WEM.

†Wea·mish, a. Obs. [Variant of QUEMISH] Squeamish.

Wean (wīn, win), sb. Sc. and dial. Also 9 ween, wain, wane. [A contraction of *wee ane* (see WEE a. and ONE), the full form still appearing in the first group of quotations.

Wean (wīn), v. [OE. *wenian*...] 1. trans. To accustom (a child or young animal) to the loss of its mother's milk; to cause to cease to be suckled.

Weanable (wī·nāb'l), a. [f. WEAN v. + -ABLE] Capable of being weaned.

Wean-calf, [f. WEAN sb.[1] + CALF.] A calf newly weaned.

Weaned, variant of WAYNE sb.[3]

Weaned (wīnd), ppl. a. [f. WEAN v. + -ED[1].]

Weaner (wī·nər). [f. WEAN v.[1] + -ER.[1]]

Weanling (wī·nliŋ), sb. and a. [f. WEAN v. + -LING[1].] A. sb. A young child or animal newly weaned.

Weanyer, variant of WEANER, WEENT.

Weanyer, -scott, obs. forms of WAINSBOOT.

Weap, obs. f. WEEP.

Weapon (wē'pən, wĕ'p'n), sb.

Weaponed (wē'pənd), ppl. a.

Weaponless (wē'pənlĕs), a.

Weaponry (wē'pənri), rare.

Weapon-salve. Obs.

Wear (wɛəɹ), sb.[1]

Wear (wɛəɹ), v.[1]

Weary (wī'rį), v. Forms: see WEARY sb. and a.

Wearying (wī'rį·iŋ), ppl. a. [-ING².]

Wearyish, a. Obs. rare. [f. WEARY a. + -ISH¹.]

Weary-rish, v. Obs. rare.

Weasand (wī'zănd). Now chiefly dial. Forms: α. 1 wǽsend, 4 wosen, 7 wesen, 8. 4–8 wosand.

Weasel (wī'z'l). Forms: 1 useosule, useosule, 4 wesel, 4 weselle, 4–6 we-sell, -il, 5 wesy'l(le, wesse, weasylle, wey-syl, weesel, weselle, Sc. quhaaill, 6 weoyll, weselL, 6–7 weasell, -ill, weasel, weasele, we(e)sill, weeele, wheesle, Sc. waesel, 7–8 weesel, Sc. whasell, 8–9 weasle, 9 dial. weasl', -weesel, Sc. weesle, weezle, wheezle.

Weasel-alley, corrupt form of WEESE-ALLAN.

Weaselled, a. Obs. [f. WEASEL + -ED²]

Weaselly (wī'z'lį), a. Also -y.

Weaselship (wī'z'lʃip). [f. WEASEL + -SHIP.]

Weasen, obs. form of WEASAND.

Weaseny, variant of WEASANT.

Weasill, variant of WEEZLE Obs.

Weason, variant of WEASAND.

Wea-swa, obs. form of WHOSO.

Weasiness (Joye's suggest'n).

Weat, obs. forms of WAIT², WET.

Weather (we'ðăǝ), sb. Forms: 1 weder, 2 weder, 3–5 weder, 4 wedder, 4–6 wedyr, 4–5 wedir, -yr, weddre, wedur, wedyr, whedir, wheder, weder, wedre, wodder, 5–6 weddyr, 4–9 Sc. wather, 5 wedre, 6–7 weather.

Weather (we'ðǝr), v. Forms: 1 wederyan, 4 wedren, 6 weather.

Weavel, obs. f. WEEVIL.

Weaver (wī·vəz). [f. WEAVE v.¹ + -ER¹.]
1. One who weaves textile fabrics; a workman or workwoman whose occupation is weaving.
2. One who weaves, in metaphorical senses of the vb.; one who contrives, constructs, etc. (something specified).

Weaver, obs. f. WAVER.

Weaveress (wī·vəres). A female weaver.

Weaving, vbl. sb. Obs. rare. [f. WEAVE v.²]
Weaver's worry.

†Wea·versly, adv. rare.

Weavel(l, obs. f. WEEVIL.

Weaving (wī·viŋ), vbl. sb.¹ [f. WEAVE v.¹ + -ING¹.]
1. The action of the vb. WEAVE; the operation of forming cloth or other stuff by the interlacing of yarn or other filaments in a loom.
2. attrib. and Comb. as weaver-body, -key, -craft, -girl, -leg, -trindle; also in names of certain bands, as weaver-bird (see sense 4), -bunting, -finch, -oriole.

Weaving (wī·viŋ), ppl. a. [f. WEAVE v.¹ + -ING².] (See WEAVE v.²)

†Weavy, adv. Also WAVEY v. obs.
Suitable for weaving.

Weasand, **Weasand**: see WEASAND, WEEZLE.

Weazen, obs. f. WIZEN a.

Weasened (wī·zənd), ppl. a. = WIZENED ppl. a.

Weazeny (wī·zəni), a. [f. WEAZEN a. + -Y¹.]
Somewhat weazened.

Weason, weasond, obs. f. WEASAND.

Weazen, Weazy: see WEASE, WEAZE.

Web (web), sb. Forms: 1 web, 1–2 webb, 3 webbe, 6 webbe, 4–5 webbe, 4–7 webbe, 7–9 webb, 6 web, 5 webbe, 7 woob, 5–9 web, vob, webb(e, 6–9 web, 7 woob, 8–9 wab. [OE. web(b neut., corresp. to OFris. web, web WEB, webb, MFris. web, wobbe, MLG. and LG. webbe, MHG. weppe, webbe) neut., ON. wef-masc. (genit. vefjar; Da. væv, Sw. väf)]

Webbed (webd), ppl. a. [f. WEB sb. + -ED².]
Furnished with a web or connecting membrane.

Webby (we·bi), a. [f. WEB sb. + -Y.]

Web-beam. [f. WEB sb. + BEAM.]
The roller in a loom on which the web is wound as it is woven.

Web-footed, a. Having web-feet.

We-foot. [See WEB sb. 8.]

Webless (we·bles), a. rare. [f. WEB sb. + -LESS.]

Webster (we·bstəz). Obs. exc. Hist. [OE. webbestre.]

WEDGE (continued)

b. The V-shaped formation adopted by a number of geese or other wildfowl when flying.

2. Something in the form of a wedge; a wedge-shaped part or piece of anything.

b. A strip of land narrowing to a point.

d. A thin strip of wood used as a wedge.

e. In an opium (see quot.).

f. *Meteorol.* A narrow wedge-shaped area of high pressure between two adjacent cyclonic systems.

g. The wedge-shaped stroke in cuneiform characters. Also *attrib.*

h. Short for *wedge-shell* (see 7).

6. *Geom.* **a.** A triangular prism. **b.** A simple solid formed by cutting a triangular prism by any two planes.

7. *Her.* A charge consisting of an isosceles triangle with a very acute angle at its vertex.

8. *Cambridge University.* The *(wooden)* wedge: the student last in the classical tripos list.

9. Combinations, chiefly similative, as *wedge-block*, *-bolt*, *-friction*, *-head*, *-shape*, *-stone*, *-wad*; *wedge-billed*, *-shaped*.

Wedge, *v.*

1. *trans.* To split, fasten tight by driving in a wedge or wedges. Also *with on*, *in*, etc.

b. *trans.* To force open, split asunder, or open, by driving in a wedge. Also *fig.*

2. *trans.* To drive apart or asunder (an object) into something where it is held fast.

3. *trans.* To drive, push, or squeeze (an object) by driving in, or by pressing tight.

4. To pack or crowd (a number of persons or animals) in close formation, or in a limited space. Also *with together*.

5. *intr.* To become fixed or jammed tight by (or as by) the operation of a wedge.

6. *Geol.* The jutting out or flaking off (of rock, etc.), as if by the operation of a wedge.

Wedged, *ppl. a.*

Wedge-like, *a.*

Wedge-shaped, *a.*

Wedgewise, *adv.*

Wedging, *vbl. sb.*

1. The action of driving in a wedge or wedges, or of fixing or cleaving by this means.

2. *concr.* A wedge-shaped piece or pieces of some hard material (iron, wood, etc.) for tightening or securing.

WEDGWOOD

Wedgwood. *(attrib.)* Also incorrectly **Wedgewood**.

1. Used *attrib.* to designate the pottery made by Josiah Wedgwood (1730–95) and his successors at Etruria, Staffs.

b. Used to designate the blue colour which is characteristic of Wedgwood ware.

c. *Wedgwood pottery or ware.*

Wedgy, *a.*

Resembling a wedge; shaped like a wedge.

Wedhood.

Wedir, *Wedyr.*

Wedlock, *sb.*

1. The marriage vow or obligation. Chiefly in phrases, *to hold*, *keep wedlock*, to be faithful in marriage.

2. The married state.

3. A wife.

Wedmal, *Wednal.*

Wednesday.

The name of the fourth day of the week.

Wedow, obs. form of WIDOW.

Wedset.

Wee, *a.* and *sb.*

A. *adj.* A little or young thing; a child.

B. *adj.* Extremely small, tiny.

Wee, *v.*

Weebit.

Weeble, obs. variant of WEEVIL.

Weech, obs. variant of WYCH.

Weed, *sb.¹*

1. A herbaceous plant not valued for use or beauty, growing wild and rank, and regarded as cumbering the ground or hindering the growth of superior vegetation.

2. *spec.* Tobacco.

Weed, *sb.²*

1. An article of apparel; a garment.

Supplement, p. 3873; Corrigenda, p. 4092; Spurious words, p. 4093; Books quoted, p. 4094

Week-end, sb. (with a and pl.) The holiday period at the end of a week's work, usually extending from Saturday noon or Friday night to Monday; esp. this holiday when spent away from home.

B. The period from Saturday to Monday during which business is suspended and shops are closed.

Week-ender.

Weekly (wīˈklĭ), a. and sb. [f. WEEK sb. + -LY 2.] **A.** adj.

1. Of or pertaining to the week (either as a seven-days period or as opposed to Sunday).

2. That occurs, is done, made, given, etc. once a week.

Weekly Bill; see BILL sb. 9. Weekly tenancy; one determinable at the end of any week.

B. sb.

Weekman (wīˈkmăn), [f. week², genitive of WEEK. Cf. month's-man, MONTH sb. 6.] A functionary whose term of office is a week; spec. (see quot.).

Weekwam, obs. form of WIGWAM.

Week-work, Hist. Obs. form of WIGWAM.

Weel [1] (wīl), Sc. and north. Forms: 1 wel, wēl, 4–7 wele, 6 wyle, 6–7 weel, weele, 6–7 weil, 7 weile.

Weel [2], var. WEALY a.² Obs.

Weem (wīm), (a early Gael. uaim) caverns.] The name applied in Scotland to a cave or underground dwelling-place used by early inhabitants of the country.

Ween (wīn), sb. Forms: 1, 3–4 wen, 3–6 wene, (3 wenne), 4–5 weene; Sc. and north. 4–7 weyne, 6 wyne, (5 wene). [OE. wēn fem. (rarely masc. or neut.), corresp. to OFris. wēn opinion, OS. wān meaning, hope, OHG., MHG., G. wahn fem.]

1. Opinion, belief.

2. Expectation, hope.

3. Probability; appearance; doubt.

4. Phrases. **a.** Wen is, is ween: the probability is (that . . .), it is probable (that . . .).

b. Const. obj. and infin. (to . . .).

Ween, a. Obs. rare. [a. ON. vǣnn.—OTeut.] Beautiful.

Ween (wīn), v. In one in which fish are kept.

B. trans. To imagine or suspect to exist. Obs.

C. intr. To think.

Weener. [f. WEEN v. + -ER 1.] One who weens; easy weener, a credulous person.

Ween-ness. rare. [f. WEEN a.] Smallness.

Weening, vbl. sb.

1. The action of thinking, supposing, expecting, etc. In ME. often = mere opinion, surmise or suspicion (as opposed to certain knowledge).

2. Phrases.

Weening, ppl. a. Obs. [-ING².]

Weenong (wīˈpŏng). The Javanese name for the tree Tetrameles nudiflora.

Weent, var. WEEN sb. Obs.

Weeny, a. colloq. Also 8 weeny.

Weep (wīp), sb. [f. WEEP v.]

1. Weeping, lamentation.

2. Const. for, over, of a person or thing regretted or commiserated.

3. said of animals.

Weep (wīp), v. Pa. t. and pt. pple. wept (wept). Forms: 1 Pa. t. and pp. wept (wēpt), 2–4 wep.

1. intr.

1. To manifest the combination of bodily symptoms (instinctive cries or moans, sobs, and shedding of tears) which is the natural, audible, and visible expression of painful (and sometimes of intensely pleasurable) emotion; also, and in mod. use chiefly, to shed tears (more or less silently).

2. Proverbial expressions.

b. said of animals.

c. fig. of the heart. (Cf. 6 b.)

4. transf. Of things: To shed water or moisture in drops; to exude drops of water. Also, to waste away in drops.

II. trans.

6. To weep for; to lament with tears.

Weeper (wīˈpə), sb. [f. WEEP v. + -ER 1.]

1. One who weeps or sheds tears, esp. one who is constantly weeping; one given to weeping.

2. A hired mourner at a death-bed or funeral.

3. A kind of weeping monkey (Cebus capucinus), the weeper or capuchin monkey.

Weepered ... *weepers* for his son who fell at Culloden. ...

Weeping (wī′piŋ), *ppl. a.* [f. WEEP *v.* + -ING[1].]

Weeping, *vbl. sb.* [f. WEEP *v.* + -ING[1].] The action of the verb in the various senses; an instance of this.

Weeping ash, the Californian white oak, *Quercus lobata.*

Weeping birch ...

Weeping willow [See WEEPING *ppl. a.* 6.]

Weepingly, *adv.* [f. WEEPING *ppl. a.* + -LY[2].] In a weeping manner.

Weep-ily, *adv. Obs. rare.* [f. WEEP *sb.* + -LY[2].] Lamentable, tearful.

Weepy (wī′pi), *a. rare.* [f. WEEP *sb.* + -Y[1].] 1. Weeping, mournful. 2. Inclined to weep or shed tears, tearful.

Weeping Cross.

Weequashing.

Weer, obs. form of WEIR, and var. WERE Obs.

Weer, obs. pa. t. of WEAR *v.*, BE *v.*

Weese, var. WEASE.

Weese allan (also weese alley), an alleged local name of the skua.

Weesel, obs. form of WEASEL.

Weesel-coot, var. WEASEL-COOT.

Weest, var. WEST, WHIST.

Weet, obs. form of WET.

Weet, *a. and v.* Also 6 weete, 6-7 wiete. [repr. ME. *wēte(n.*, var. of *wē̆te* pl. ind. and subj., and *wite* imperative and sing. pres. WOT *v.*, WIT *v.*] From the middle of the 16th c., if not earlier, the form *weet* seems to be obsolete.

Weetingly, obs. form of WITTINGLY. adv. (Cf. WEET *v.* and next.)

Weetless (wī′tles), *a. arch.* [f. WEET *v.* + -LESS.] App. coined by Spenser; distinct from witless.] Unknowing, unconscious. Also (quot. 1879), unmeaning.

Weevil (wī′v'l, wī′vil), *sb.* Forms: 1 wifil, wibil, 4 wyvyl, -ill, 6 wyuell[e, 6-7 wivel(l); 3 weovel, 6-7 weevell (wew-), -7 7ll, 6-7 weevill 6-8 weevil (-7 ill), 6-7 weavill 7 weevill (-7 ill), 6-7, 7-.

Weevil, *v. rare*[−1]. [f. WEEVIL *sb.*] *refl.* To wriggle (oneself) out.

Weevilly (wī′v'li), *a.* Also 8 weavely, 9 weevily. [f. WEEVIL + -Y[1].] Infested with weevils.

Weeze, var. WEASE.

Weevil-eaten, pa. pple. Also (6 weevill), erron. var. of WEEVIL.

Weft, *sb.*[1] Forms: 1 weft, 4 waft, 6-7 weft. [OE. *weft, *weft*, *wefta*.]

Weft, *sb.*[2] Obs. Forms: 3-4 wef, 4-5 weef, 4-6 wefte. [Of obscure etymology; represented by OE. *weft.*]

Weft, *sb.*[3] *rare.* Also 6 waif, 7-8 waft. To form a weft or weft; to interlace the weft with the warp.

Weft, *v.* Obs. rare[−1]. [f. WEFT *sb.*[1]] *trans.* To weave weft or woof.

Weftage (we′ftid3). [f. WEFT *sb.*[1] + -AGE.]

Wefted (we′fted), *ppl. a.* [f. WEFT *sb.*[1] + -ED[1].] Composed of interwoven weft.

Weigela, Weigelia (waidʒī′liˌä, -li·liä). *Bot.* [mod. L., f. name of C. E. Weigel, a German physician (1748−1831).] A genus of caprifoliaceous shrubs from China and Japan cultivated for its flowers.

Weigh (wēi), *v.*[1] Forms: 1 wegan, pa. t. wǣg, weg, wǣgon, pa. pple. wegen.

Weir (wīr), sb.[1] Forms: ... A fence or enclosure of stakes set in a stream, harbour, etc., for taking or preserving fish.

Weir, v. trans. To provide with a weir.

Weiral, var. WARBAT sb. Obs.

Weird (wīrd), sb. Forms: 1 wyrd, 3–5 wird, (4 wird), 5 wyrd, 4–5 weird, (6 Sc.) wierd; Sc. 6 waird, 6–7 weard, 8 weerd. [OE. wyrd fem.,

Weird (wī·rd), a. Also 5 wyrde, 5–6 Sc. werd, 6 veird, 7 weyard (wayward) ... Of or pertaining to fate or destiny; having power to control the fate or destiny of men, etc.

Weird-like (wī·rdlaik), a. [f. WEIRD sb. + -LIKE.] Suggestive of the supernatural, ominous, eery, uncanny.

Weirdful (wī·rdful), a. [f. WEIRD sb. + -FUL.] Favoured by fate, happy, prosperous.

Weirdless (wī·rdles), a. [f. WEIRD sb. + -LESS.]

Weirdly (wī·rdli), adv. [f. WEIRD a. + -LY.] In a weird or fantastic manner.

Weirdness (wī·rdnes). [f. WEIRD a. + -NESS.] The fact or quality of being weird.

Weirdsome (wī·rdsəm), a. [f. WEIRD sb. + -SOME.] Uncanny, mysterious.

Weirdward, a. [f. WEIRD sb. + -WARD.] Bordering on or tending to the supernatural.

Weirdy, a. Sc. [f. WEIRD sb. + -Y.] Fateful.

Weird, Sc. var. WAN sb. Obs. **Weirstyle**, Obs.

Weiring (wī·riŋ), vbl. sb. [f. WEIR v.] The constructing of a weir or weirs; also, concr. materials used for making a weir or of which a weir is composed.

Weirly, -ive, etc.

Weiring, var. WARY a.

Weis, obs. form of WISE.

Weisel, var. WEASEL.

Weism (wī·z'm). [f. WE pron. + -ISM.] After egoism.] The too frequent use of "we" before "I" by a speaker or writer.

Weismannian, a. and sb. [f. as next + -IAN.] a. adj. Of or pertaining to Weismann or his biological theory. b. sb. One who accepts the theory of Weismannism.

Weismannism (vī·smänizm). The theory of evolution and heredity propounded by the German biologist, August Weismann, esp. in regard to the continuity of the germ-plasm and the non-transmission of acquired characters.

Weissite (vaī·sait). Min. [Named (G. weissit) after C. S. Weiss, German crystallographer: see -ITE.] An altered form of olivine.

Weist, obs. f. WEST, al. dial.

Weit, obs. Sc. f. WET; obs. f. WHITE, WIT v.; var. WEITH, obs. f. WOITH. **Weive**, obs. f. WEAVE; var. WAIVE v.[1]

Weize, var. WAY; Sc. var. WISE.

Wejack, earlier form of WOODCHUCK.

Wok, obs. form of WEEK.

Weka (wē·ka, wē·kā). Also waika. [Maori], so named from its cry.] The native name for the flightless rails Ocydromus australis and O. brachypterus of New Zealand. Also called weka rail.

Weke, obs. f. WEEK; WICK.

Wekit, Sc. var. WICKED.

Weks, obs. f. WEAX, WEEK sb., WICK sb.[1]; var. WEAK a.

Wel, obs. f. WAL, WEEL, WELL.

Wol, obs. contraction of we will.

Welaciate, **welaciate**, var. WELLADAY.

Welany, etc., var. VILLAINY, VILLAIN.

Welbe, **-bode**, obs. forms of WELL-BEING, WELL-BORN.

Welch, var. WELSH.

Welcome (we·lkəm), sb.[1], int., and a. Forms: a. 1 wilcuma (wilcyme), 2–3 wilcume, wilcumme, (3 wlcume), 4 wylcume, wolcume, 1 wylcyme, etc.

Welcome (we·lkəm), a.[1] [OE. wilcuma.] 1. Forms: as prec. Received with gladness; greeted with a glad welcome.

Welcome (we·lkəm), v. [OE. wilcumian.] trans. To greet the arrival of (a person) with kindly salutations.

Welcomed (we·lkəmd), ppl. a. [f. WELCOME v.] Made welcome; gladly received.

Welcomeless (we·lkəmles), a.[2] [f. WELCOME sb.[1] + -LESS.] Without a welcome; also, unwelcome.

Welcomely (we·lkəmli), adv. [f. WELCOME a.[1] + -LY.] In a welcome manner; with an expression or feeling of welcome; gladly, hospitably.

Welcomeness (we·lkəmnes). [-NESS.] The state of being welcome or of being welcomed.

Welcomer (we·lkəmər). One who, or something which, welcomes; one who greets (a person or thing).

Welcoming (we·lkəmiŋ), vbl. sb. [f. WELCOME v. + -ING[1].] The action of greeting with welcome or of making welcome.

Welcoming (we·lkəmiŋ), ppl. a. [-ING[2].] That welcomes or gives a welcome.

Welcomingly (we·lkəmiŋli), adv. [-LY[2].] In a welcoming manner.

Weld (weld), sb.[1] Forms: a. 4–6 welde, 6 uuylde, 7 welld, 4–9 wolde, (6 wolld), 9 (5 welld), 6–8 weelde, (7 wield), 8 wald. [OE. wealde, Anglian wold = MLG. walde (walds) ... 1. The plant Reseda Luteola, which yields a yellow dye. Also, the dye obtained from this plant.

2. attrib. and Comb., as weld plant, weld-dyeing, dyer-weed, dyeweed; weldwort, Lindley's name for the N.O. Resedaceae.

Weld, sb.²

Weld, v.¹

Weldable, a.

Welder, sb.

Welding, vbl. sb.

Weldless (weld-lĕs), a.

Weldom.

Wele, v. Obs.

Welfare (welf-ɛər), sb.

Welfaredness.

Welful, a. Obs.

Welk, v. Obs.

Welked, ppl. a.

Welken, v. Obs.

Welkin (welk-in).

Welky, var. WEELY a.¹

Well, sb.¹

Well, sb.²

Well, v.¹

Well-aged, a. Obs. Advanced in years, of a good age.

Well-aimed, a.

Well-⁄aired, a.

Well-anear. Obs.
1. Thoroughly ventilated; favoured with good air.
2. Damp-freed by exposure to air or heat.

Well-ali-ed, ppl. a.

Well-⁄apaid, ppl. a. Obs. exc. arch.
Heartily pleased or satisfied.

Hence **Well-apai·dness.**

Well-⁄appa·relled, ppl. a.

Well-⁄appli·ed, ppl. a.

with this well-applied inscription.

Well-appoi·nted, a. Properly equipped or fitted out.
Hence **Well-appoi·ntedness.**

Well-appro·ved, ppl. a.

Well-⁄arayed, ppl. a.

Well-a·rmed, ppl. a.
1. Adequately armed for war or combat. Also transf. and fig.
2. Furnished with a powerful armature.

Well-a·rranged, ppl. a.

Well-⁄array·ed, ppl. a.

Well away, compound adv. Obs.
1. Qualifying a comparative: Far and away, much. Cf. WELL B.
2. Used elliptically with care and a verb implied: well away until = put up with, tolerate, endure. Cf. AWAY 16.

† **Well-away,** int. and sb. Now dial.

Well-⁄becoming, a. Highly befitting or suiting.

Well-beg0·ne, ppl. a. Obs. Also 4 wel bigoo. [See BEGO v. 8.]
1. Well-contented, cheerful, joyous.
2. Fortunate, well off.

Well-a-wins, int. Sc. In quots. well-, weel-wull-. Altered form of WELLAWAY.

Wellaway (we·lăwē·), int. and adv. Obs.

Wellaway, int. and sb.

† **Well away,** = WELLAWAY B.

† **Well-beaten,** ppl. a. [BEAT v. 13, BEATEN 2.]

Well-⁄begi·rt, ppl. a.

Well-⁄begoʻtten, ppl. a. Obs. Also 4 wel begotten.

Well-being, vbl. sb. [Cf. F. bien-être, mod.L. bene esse.]

Wellaway: see WELL-ADVISED.

Well-avised: see WELL-ADVISED.

Well-⁄balanced, a.
1. Exactly poised or equilibrated.
2. Having an orderly or harmonious disposition of parts.
3. Having or belonging to a good balance of the mental faculties; sane and sensible; not flighty or eccentric.

Well-belo·ved, ppl. a. and sb.

Well-belo·ved, a.

A. ppl. adj.
1. Dearly loved, greatly beloved.
2. Much beloved, held and honoured in high esteem.

Well-⁄be·nched, ppl. a.

Well-⁄bo·ddied, ppl. a.

Well-bo·ned, ppl. a. [WELL adv. 32.] Used to render Homer's ἠΰξοος, epithet of a ship.

Well-bo·rnched, a. Obs.

Well-⁄bese·en, a. Obs. Also 4 be-, biseye. [See BESEE v. 2.] Good-looking, of good appearance; well appointed or apparelled; well furnished (with); versed or accomplished in.

Well-be·sten, ppl. a. Obs.

† **Well-bese·en,** a. Obs. Also 4 be-, biseye.

Well-⁄besto·wed, ppl. a.

Well-⁄blo·oded, a. Obs. Also 7 -blouded. [See WELL adv. 32 and BLOODED a.] Having plenty of blood.

Well-boat. [See WELL sb 6 b.]
1. A fishing-boat provided with a well or tank for the storage and transport of live fish.

Well-bo·died, a.

Well-⁄bo·iling, ppl. a.

Well-bo·nes, sb.

Well-bo·red, ppl. a.

† **Well-bo·red,** ppl. a.

Well-bo·rn, ppl. a. [See BORN 3 a. Cf. Da. velbaaren, Du. welgeboren, G. wohlgeboren (MHG. wolgeboren).]
1. Of good birth or lineage, of gentle blood.
2. Of good breed or strain.
b. absol.

Well-⁄bo·sed, a. Obs.

Well-⁄bou·ght, ppl. a. Bought at a fair price; worth the price paid. (See WELL adv. 6 d.)
b. Valiantly won. (Cf. DEAR-BOUGHT.)

Well-bred, ppl. a.
1. Of good family and bringing up. Usually: Displaying good breeding; having refined manners; courteous in speech and behaviour.
2. Of good breed or strain.
3. Of good breeding or race. Said of animals.

Well-⁄bre·wed, ppl. a.

† **Well-bri·dled,** ppl. a.

Well-⁄bu·cket. [WELL sb 1.] A bucket used to draw water from a well by means of a rope or windlass.

Well-builded, ppl. a. Also 4 -bild. = next.

Well-bu·ilt, ppl. a.

Well-built, ppl. a. Also in phr. well-built, etc.

Well-bred, ppl. a.

Well-carriaged, a. See CARRIAGED.

Well-ca·rved, ppl. a.

Well-cha·racterized, ppl. a.

Well-⁄che·wed, ppl. a.

Well-chosen, ppl. a.

† **Well-cho·sing,** ppl. a.

† **Well-(ʼ)cho·sen,** ppl. a. Carefully or happily selected.

Well-⁄clad, ppl. a.

Well-⁄clo·thed, ppl. a.

Well-co·loured, a.

Well-come·ly, a.

Well-⁄compa·nioned, ppl. a.

Well-compa·cted, ppl. a.

† **Well-comple·xioned,** a. Obs. Having good complexion (constitution, colour, etc.).

Well-conce·ited, ppl. a. Obs.

Well-(ʼ)concei·ted, ppl. a.

Well-⁄condi·tioned, ppl. a.
1. Properly directed, managed, or carried out.

Well-(ʼ)conne·cted, ppl. a.
1. Linked together in good order or sequence; exhibiting proper sequence or coherence of thought.
2. Of persons: Having a favourable opinion of a person or thing.

Well-⁄consi·dered, ppl. a.

Well-co·nstituted, a.

Well-conte·nt, a. Highly pleased, gratified, or satisfied.

Well-conte·sted, a.

Well-contrived, ppl. a.

Well-controlled, ppl. a.

Well-cooked, ppl. a.

Well-couched, ppl. a.

Well-coupled: see COUPLED 3.

Well-covered, ppl. a.

Well-crest, Now dial.

Well-cross.

Well-crested, ppl. a.

Well-cropped, ppl. a.

Well-cultivated, ppl. a.

Well-cultured, ppl. a.

Wellerism.

Well-eyed.

Welleral, var. WELLARD.

Welldraw, obs. var. WEAL, WEL-, etc.

Well-decked, ppl. a. [DECKED ppl.]

Well-deck [WELL sb.] An open space on the main deck of a ship.

Well-deed, ob. a. [WELL sb. 3]

Well-defined, ppl. a.

Well-deserve, ppl. a.

Well-deserving, ppl. a.

Well-descended, ppl. a.

Well-deserved, ppl. a.

Well(-)directed, ppl. a. Aimed, addressed, guided, conducted, with skill and care.

Well-disciplined, ppl. a.

Well-disposed, ppl. a.

Well-doer, ppl. a.

Well-doing, vbl. sb. a.

Well-drawn, ppl. a.

Well-drilled, ppl. a.

Well-dressed, ppl. a.

Well-disguised, ppl. a.

Well-dissembled, ppl. a.

Well-disposed, ppl. a.

Well-dying, vbl. sb.

Well(-)earned, ppl. a.

Well-established, ppl. a.

Welled, ppl. a.

Welled, a.

Well-educated, ppl. a.

Welleboe, obs. var. of WILLOW.

Welloword, var. WOOLWARD.

Well-enjoined, ppl. a.

Well-endowed, ppl. a.

Weller, obs. Also a welk ware.

Well-experienced, ppl. a.

Well-faced, ppl. a.

Welfare, obs. f. WELFARE.

Well-faring, vbl. sb. Obs. exc. arch.

Well-favoured, ppl. a.

Well-favouredly, adv.

Well-favouredness.

Well-fashioned, ppl. a.

Well-feathered, ppl. a.

Well-favoured, ppl. a. Handsome or attractive in appearance, good-looking.

Well-feasted, ppl. a.

Well-filled, ppl. a.

Well-favoured, ppl. a.

Well-fixed, ppl. a.

Well-flavoured, ppl. a.

Well-fleshed, ppl. a.

Well-foined, ppl. a.

Well-formed, ppl. a.

Well-fortified, ppl. a.

Well-fought, ppl. a.

Well-found, ppl. a.

Well-founded, ppl. a.

Well-flowered, ppl. a.

Well-framed, ppl. a.

Well-fraught, ppl. a.

Wellful, var. WEALFUL, Obs.

Well(-)furnished, ppl. a.

Well-furnishedness.

Hence Well-nurnishedness.

Well-gared, ppl. a.

Well-geared, ppl. a.

Well-gifted, a.

Well-girt, ppl. a. Firmly encircled or secured by a girdle or girth; esp., after Gr. εὔζωνος (εὐζώνως), girt up for exercise, in good trim for walking; hence fig. (of time) strenuously bestowed.

Well-glebed, a.

Well-go-ing, ppl. a. (Said of an animal, a machine, etc.)

Well-go-otten, ppl. a. Obtained by good means, honourably gained. (Cf. Ill-gotten.)

Well-go-verned, a.
1. Following a good rule of life and behaviour; controlled by reason.
2. Of a state or society of men: Ruled by a good government.

Well-governing, vbl. sb.

Well-governing, ppl. a.

Well-govern, -ment.

Hence Well-instrument.

Well-graced, ppl. a. Full of grace or graces.

Well-graced, ppl. a. Used to translate Homer's ἐύκνημες (pl.).

Well-grained, ppl. a. Of unmaterial things: Based on good grounds, firmly founded, having a good basis or foundation.

Well-grounded, ppl. a. Of unmaterial things: Based on good grounds, firmly founded, having a good basis or foundation.

Well-grown, ppl. a. Showing a satisfactory growth or development.

Well-groomed, ppl. a.

Hence Well-groomedness.

Well-hall. [Well sb.]
1. The place at which a spring breaks out of the ground; the head-spring or source of a stream or river.

Well-head. [Well sb.]
1. The place at which a spring breaks out of the ground; the head-spring or source of a stream or river.
2. The empty space round which the stairs of a winding staircase turn.

Well-heated, ppl. a.

Well-hearted, ppl. a.
1. Stout-hearted, courageous. Obs.
2. Well-disposed, kind-hearted, generous.

Well-hole. [Well sb.]
1. a. An opening through a floor or series of floors, for a staircase, chimney-stack, or for the admission of light, air.
 b. The empty space round which the stairs of a winding staircase turn.
 c. A vertical passage-way (for machinery, a lift, etc.); a shaft.
2. The compartment at the lower end of a ship's pump.

Well-horsed, ppl. a. Furnished with, mounted on, riding by a good horse or horses.

Well-hung, ppl. a.
1. Furnished with large pendent organs.
 b. Suspended or attached so as to hang well.
2. Of the tongue: Working readily and freely; glib, fluent.

Wellibe (we-lib), adv. dial. [L. Well adv. + -ish.] Pretty well. Wellish of, fairly well to do. Not wellish adj., rather unwell.

Welling (we-liŋ), vbl. sb.1 [f. Well v.1]
1. Boiling; a well of a liquid, of molten metal, etc.; also of a pot. Welling out, boiling foot.

Welling, vbl. sb.2 [f. Well v.2]
The action of making a well or shaft; in quot. conc., shaft-work.

Welling, ppl. a. [f. Well v.1 + -ing2.]
1. Boiling; that wells up, as water.
 b. fig. in phr. welling woe (of hell). Cf. Well v.1.

Well-inclined, ppl. a. Of good natural inclination or disposition; well-disposed.

Well-informed, ppl. a. Well equipped with information; fully furnished with knowledge, whether of a special subject or of things in general; having a well-stored mind.
2. Furnished with something which is good.

Well-informed, ppl. a.

Welling (we-liŋ), vbl. sb.3

Wellington (we-liŋtən). [Named after Arthur, first duke of Wellington.]
1. attrib. a. Wellington boot — sense 2.
 b. Used to designate other articles of clothing introduced by the Duke, or named after him, as Wellington cloak, coat, frock, trousers.
2. a. The melting or founding of metals. Obs.
2. a. A high boot covering the knee in front and cut away behind. Also a somewhat shorter boot worn under the trousers.
3. A variety of cooking apple, large, roundish, and with yellowish white flesh.

Wellingtonia (we-liŋtou·niă). [Named by Lindley after Arthur, first duke of Wellington (1769–1852): see -ia.] The popular name in England of Sequoia (Wellingtonia) gigantea, a large coniferous tree, native of California; the 'big tree' or Washington cedar.

Wellingtonian (weliŋtou·niăn), a. and sb. Belonging to or characteristic of the duke of Wellington.

Well-inhabited, ppl. a. Populous.

Well-instituted, ppl. a.

Well-instructed, ppl. a.
1. Well trained or instructed by teaching.
2. Well-conditioned, modest.

Wellink (we-liŋk), dial. Also wallink. [app. worn down from Well (well) sb.2] -ink: see Lewek and Brooklime.] A provincial name of the Brooklime, Veronica Beccabunga.

Well-intended, ppl. a. Characterized by a right and sincere intention; well-meant.

Hence Well-intendedness.

Well-intentioned, ppl. a.
1. Of a person: Having good intentions.
2. Of a measure: Arising from good intentions.

Hence Well-intentionedness.

Well-invented, ppl. a. Cleverly fabricated or made up. Cf. Ill-invented.

Welling-left.

Well-known, ppl. a.
1. Known to many, widely or generally known.

Welles-lettered, ppl. a. Having a good knowledge of letters; imbued with learning.

Well-liked, ppl. a. [Cf. OE. wel-licmlic.]
 b. Generally liked.

Well-liking, ppl. a. [Cf. OE. wel-licmlic.] Favourable regard, fondness; approbation or love (of).

Well-looked, a. Of good appearance, good-looking.

Well-liking, ppl. a.
1. In good condition and of lusty appearance; thriving, healthy, plump. arch.
2. Intimately or thoroughly known.

Welles-loving, ppl. a. That leads a good life.

Well-made, ppl. a.

Well-jointed, ppl. a.

Well-judged, ppl. a. Marked by sound judgement, judicious; wisely estimated, correctly calculated.

Well-judging, ppl. a. Having or exercising sound judgement.

Well-known, ppl. a.

Well-left.

Well-labo-ured, ppl. a. Skilfully wrought or elaborated.

Well-legged, ppl. a. Having a good knowledge or letters; imbued with learning.

Well-limbed, ppl. a. Having good or fine limbs.

Well-legged, ppl. a.

Well-lined, ppl. a. [See Line v.1 2, 3, 3b.] Furnished with a good lining.

Well-lettered, ppl. a.

Well-liked, ppl. a.

Well-looking, ppl. a.

Well-loved, ppl. a. = Well-beloved.

Well-learned, ppl. a. Now rare. Having good knowledge or instruction; deeply read or versed (in a subject).

Well-learned, ppl. a. Obs. — next.
 b. Expressed in good language, well-worded.
2. Pleasant, agreeable. Obs.

Well-limned, ppl. a. Also = 7 -limb'd, lim'd.

Well-managed, ppl. a.
1. Carefully and skilfully controlled, handled, carried on, or dealt with.
2. Displaying good management. Of a horse: Well-trained.

Well-mannered, ppl. a.
 b. Of good morals, displaying virtuous conduct and behaviour.
2. Displaying good manners.

Well-married, ppl. a. Fortunate in one's marriage. Also, † nobly married.

Well-matched, ppl. a.

† Well-meaned, ppl. a.

Well-meant, ppl. a.

Well-mea·ner. One who means well or is well-intentioned.

Well-mea·ning, vbl. sb. Disposition to do what is right : good intentions.

Well-mea·ning, ppl. a. Having or actuated by good intentions ; animated by a kindly purpose or friendly disposition.

Hence **Well-mea·ningly** adv. ; **Well-mea·ning·ness**.

† Well-mo·neyed, ppl. a. Well supplied with, having plenty of, money.

Well-most, adv. Also 6–7 welmost(e. Almost, well-nigh.

Well-mou·nted, ppl. a. 1. Seated on a good horse.

2. Having a good bodily carriage, well-developed, 'well set up'.

Well-mou·thed, a. Having a good mouth (in various senses).

Well-na·med, ppl. a. 1. Called by an appropriate or suitable name.

2. Having a good name or reputation.

Well-na·tured, a. Obs. exc. Sc. and dial. 1. Having or showing a good or benevolent disposition ; kindly, good-natured.

2. Wishful or determined (to do something).

Well-near, adv. Obs. exc. dial. Nearly well, almost well, well-nigh.

Wellness (we'lnès), [f. WELL a. + -NESS] The state of being well (in good health).

Well- o·rdered, ppl. a. Having good order ; rightly regulated ; carefully arranged ; orderly.

Well-nigh (we'lnəi), adv. Almost ; very nearly.

Well-o·ffering, vbl. sb. ...

Well-oiled, ppl. a.

Well-po·lished, ppl. a. (lit. and fig.)

Well-que·me, a. (Also 6–7 welquem, -queame.) Well-pleasing, agreeable.

Well-practised, ppl. a. Skilled through long or good practice.

Well-prepa·red, ppl. a.

Well-preserved, ppl. a.

Well-pri·ncipled, a. Holding, actuated by, or founded upon, good principles.

Well-proportioned, ppl. a. Having good or correct proportions.

Well-proved, ppl. a.

Well-regulated, ppl. a.

Well-rou·nded, ppl. a.

Well-re·membered, ppl. a. 1. Remembered or appositely brought to mind.

2. Clearly or distinctly remembered.

Well-repu·nished, ppl. a.

Well-repu·ted, ppl. a.

Well-sa·nded, ppl. a. 1. Said of meat or drink (see SEASON v. 1).

2. Well matured or cured ; versed, proficient in (some science or affair).

Well-sa· ted, ppl. a.

Well-sa·ved, ppl. a.

Well-sea·soned, ppl. a.

Well-seen, ppl. a.

Well-set, ppl. a. 1. Skilfully, fittingly, or happily placed, fixed, settled, arranged, or adjusted.

Well-spo·ken, ppl. a. Also 5 -spoke.

Well-spread, ppl. a.

1. Widely extended; † spec. of a horse, broad in the rear (obs.).

2. Of a surface: Plentifully or elegantly covered with articles spread over it. Of a table: Laid out for a good meal.

Well-spring. [OE. *welspryng, wylspring*; see WELL sb. and SPRING.]

1. The source or head-spring of a stream; a fountain-head.

2. *fig.* A source of perennial emanation or supply.

Well-staid, ppl. a.

1. Produced or formed by careful study.

† 2. Of a person: Well read, learned. Also, *Well-stayed*.

Well-stricken, -strooken, -strucken (in years) a.

Well-stuff-tied, ppl. a.

** 2. Of climate or season: Temperate. Obs.

** 3. a. Of steel: Brought to the right degree of hardness and elasticity.

Well-timbered, ppl. a.

1. Strongly built or constructed of wood.

2. Having a good structure or constitution; well-framed, well-built. Chiefly of persons and animals.

Well-timed, ppl. a.

1. Occurring, done, or made at a good or fitting time; timely, opportune.

Well-toned, ppl. a. Having a good tone, in various senses: see TONED.

Well-trod, -trodden, ppl. a.

Well-trimmed, ppl. a.

Well-tended, ppl. a. [See TASTED B.]

1. Having a good taste or flavour.

Well-ta·sted, a. Now *rare*. [See TASTED B.]

Well-taught, ppl. a.

1. † a. Having a good bodily 'temperament' or constitution. Obs.

b. Having a well-balanced mental temperament (*obs.*). In later use, good-tempered.

Well-thewed, ppl. a. Obs. [See THEWED.]

Well-thought, ppl. a. In comb. with a prep. or adv., as *of, on, upon*, out.

Well-to-do, adj. phr. [See WELL a. 3.]

1. Possessed of a competency, in easy circumstances; thriving, prosperous: as predicate (with or without hyphens).

b. *transf.* Indicative of easy circumstances, prosperous-looking.

Well-pass, adj. phr. [See WELL a. 3.] In predicate: Well off, well to do. Also *well to pass in the world*.

Well-to-passer nonce-vo., a person of good estate.

Well-trussed, ppl. a.

Well-trusted. 306 **WELL-WILLER.** **WELL-WILLING.** 307 **WELL-WOVEN.**

Well-trusted, ppl. a.

Well-tuned, a. Melodious, in good tune.

Well-turned, ppl. a.

1. Skilfully turned or rounded.

2. Of speech: Neatly finished, felicitously expressed.

† 4. Of the mind: Having a good bent, well disposed. Obs.

Well-(-)used, ppl. a.

1. Rightly or effectively used.

2. Much or often used.

Well-used, ppl. a.

Wellvet, obs. Sc. form of VELVET.

Well-wa·nged, ppl. a.

Well-wa·red, ppl. a. (Having good walis. (Cf. Gr. εὐτυχέως.)

Well-warmed, ppl. a.

Well-warranted, ppl. a.

Well-wa·rrant, v. [WELL adv. + WARRANT v.] Water issuing, or drawn, from a well.

Well-wa·tered, ppl. a.

Well-wea·poned, ppl. a.

Well-wea·ring, ppl. a.

Well-wi·ller. Now rare.

Well-wi·lling, vbl. sb.

1. The act of wishing well (to another); good will, favour, kindly regard.

2. (One's) good pleasure; what seems good to a person to do, intend, or allow.

Well-willed, a. Kindly or favourably disposed.

Well-wi·lling, a. (Cf. MHG. *wolwellende*.)

Well-wi·ller. One who bears good will to another, a cause, etc. Const. *to, of*, or with possessive.

Well-wisher. One who wishes well to another, a cause, etc.

Well-wishing, vbl. sb. The action of wishing well to another; the expression of good wishes.

Well-wishing, ppl. a. That wishes well to others, beneficent, etc.

Well-willy, a. Obs. exc.dial. Cf. Sw. *välvillig*, G. *wohlwollen*.

Well-won, ppl. a. Gained by hard or honourable effort.

Well-wooded, a.

Well-woven, ppl. a. lit. and fig.

Westering, vbl. sb. [f. Wester v.] Westward movement, declension westwards.

Westering (we'stəriŋ), ppl. a. [f. Wester v.]

1. That declines from the meridian towards the west. (Said chiefly of the sun when it is nearing the western horizon.)

2. That moves in a westward direction. Of the wind : That shifts to the west.

Wester·lines [-ness.] Westerly situation.

Westerling (we'stərliŋ), sb. [f. Wester a. + -ling.] An inhabitant of a western country or district.

Westerly (we'stərli), a. and sb. [f. West a. Cf. easterly, and next.]

A. adj.

1. Coming from the west.

2. Situated in or towards the west.

3. Situated near the western horizon.

B. adv.

Western (we'stən), a. and sb. [f. West sb.]

A. adj.

1. Of or belonging to the west; found or produced in the west.

B. Of or belonging to the west : as, the place of the sun's setting ; also of the sun, or the evening star (cf. next.).

C. Of or pertaining to the Western or European countries or races as distinguished from the Eastern or Oriental.

B. sb.

1. A member of a Western race ; a native or inhabitant of the West, as distinguished from an Oriental or Asiatic.

Westerly (we'stəmli), a. Now rare. [f. Western a. + -ly¹. Cf. Westerly a.]

Westerner (we'stənəɹ).

1. An inhabitant or native of the Western States of America.

Westernism (we'stəniz'm).

Westernize (we'stənəiz), v. [f. Western a. + -ize.] trans. To make western in character; esp. to make (a person of another country or race) more Western in regard to its institutions, ideas, etc.

Hence **Westernized** ppl. a.; **Westernizing** vbl. sb. and ppl. a.; also **Westerniza·tion** sb.

West India. Now only attrib. Also 7 pl. Indies. [West a. Cf. East India.]

West Indian, sb. and a. Also 9 vulgar Injun. [West a. Cf. East Indian.]

West Indies.

Westland, sb.

Westlin, a. Sc. [var. of westland.] Western; westerly.

Westlins, adv. Sc. rare⁻¹. [f. prec. + -lins.] Westerly.

Westlooker. Obs. rare⁻¹. A name for the sun.

Westly, adv. Obs. rare⁻¹. [West adv. Cf. MLG.] Westwards.

Westm, var. Wastum Obs.

Westminster. The name of the abbey on the north bank of the Thames at London.

West-north-west, adv., etc.

Weston, obs. form of Whetstone.

Westphalia (westfēˈliă). Also 7 Westfalia.

West-some, ME. form of OE. West-sáwan.

West side.

Westphalian (westfēˈliăn), a. and sb. [f. prec. + -an.]

West-some, var. Westsome.

Westralia (westrēˈliăn), a. and sb. [f. West + Australia, a telegraphic abbrev. of West Australia.]

Hence **Westra·lianism**.

Westro, obs. form of Westward.

Westring, var. of Westering.

West-south-westerly, adv.

Westvale. Obs. Also 4-5 -vall (-uall), 7 westvals. [f. MLG. westvale, var. Westfale.] A variety of cloth of Westphalian manufacture.

Westward, adv., sb., and a. Also West-ward. [f. West a. + -ward. Cf. MLG.]

Westwardly, adv. [as prec.] In or to the westward; in a westerly direction.

Supplement, p. 3873; Corrigenda, p. 4092; Spurious words, p. 4093; Books quoted, p. 4094

VI. *a-al* Adapting my phraseology to the author's, I would say such parts of the book are very "wet-blankety".

Wetche, obs. form of WATCH.

Wet-dock. (a contrast to DRY DOCK.)
+ 1. = DOCK *sb.*² 1 (where see quot. 1627). *Obs.*
2. (See DOCK *sb.*² 4.)

We'the, obs. form of WITH.

Wet-shod (†-shoed), *a. Obs. exc. dial.*
Forms: *a.* 4-5 wete-schood, -shoed, -shode; 1 wet-schoede, wētschode, *a* wētschood (wheteshood); 6 -shode, † -shoed; 5 wate-shod(e; 7-9 wete-shod, -shodde; 6-7 wet-shode, -shodde; 8-9 wet-shod. In many dialect forms: see *Eng. Dial. Dict.* [f. WET *a.* + SHOED, SHOD, *ppl. adjs.*] Having the feet wet.

Wethen, witherwine, var. ff. WITHERWIN *Obs.*, WEATHERWINE *Obs.* v. WEATHER, WITHER.

Wetness. Also † wētnis, 5-6 wetenes, 6 -ness(e; 7 weatnes; 4-6 wetness(e. [f. WET *a.* + -NESS.]

Wetschede, obs. form of WATCHET.

Wet-safe, obs. form of VOUCHSAFE.

Wetter.
1. One who wets; *spec.* one who damps paper to be used in printing.

Wet-nurse, wet-nurse, *sb.*
A woman who is hired to suckle and nurse another woman's child.

Wetting, *vbl. sb.* [f. WET *v.*]

Wettish, a. [f. WET *a.* + -ISH.] Somewhat wet.

Wh.

WH, a consonantal digraph, normally representing initial *hw* in words of OE. origin, as in *hwæt what, hwisperian* to whisper. In words of other origin, its occurrence may be due to analogy or to the silent *h* being restored, etc.

Wevestirte. *Obs.* In quot. wevestrote.

Wewt. *south-west. dial.* [f. WEFT *sb.*¹] A cobweb. * Also *collect.*

Wey, *sb.*¹ Forms: 1 wēᵹ, wǣᵹ, 4-8 wey, 5 wygh, 5-7 wēgh. [Identical in origin with WAY *sb.*¹ Cf. WAY *sb.*¹]
1. A standard of dry-goods weight, varying greatly with different commodities. (See quots.)

Wh. (see main column)

Weymouth (wēᵐmᵊþ). [The title of the first Lord Weymouth, by whom the tree was extensively planted after its introduction into England in 1705.] *Weymouth Pine*, the American white pine, *Pinus Strobus*.

Weyn, obs. f. WAIN, VEIN *sb.*; north. f. WHEN *sb.*, *v.*
Weynd(e, obs. ff. WIND *sb.*, WIND *v.*
Veyn, Wayr (obs. WE; north. f. WATER *sb.*, v.
Weyng, obs. ff. WING. **Weynote**, -soote, skot, obs. ff. WAINSCOT.

Whack (hwæk), *v. colloq.* Also 8-9 wh-whauk.
1. *trans.* To beat or strike vigorously, as with a stick; *tr.* to thrash.

Whacker (hwæk'ᵊɹ). *colloq.* [f. WHACK *v.* + -ER¹.]

Whacking (hwæk'iŋ), *vbl. sb.* [f. WHACK *v.*] 1. Beating.

priest in our neighbourhood. 1889 — *Jrnl.* 16 Apr. (1890) II. 268 This whacking reason. 1853 G. J. Cayley *Las Alforjas* II. 193 We saw a whacking great building. 1873 C. M. Davies *Unorth. Lond., Walworth Jumpers* 91 A good whacking kiss that echoed all over the archway.

Whad, Whaddie: see What, Waddy.

Whaey, Whafer, Whaff, Whaffle: see Whey, Wafer *sb.*, Waff *v.*1, Waffle *v.*

Whahoo, variant of Wahoo.

Whaies: see Why.

Whaiet, obs. dial. f. Quiet.

1581 N. Woodes *Confl. Consc.* III. iv, Ay wawd he wer brunt that ay mawght be whaiet.

Whaile, obs. var. Quail *v.*2, to curdle.

c1440 *Anc. Cookery* in *Househ. Ord.* (1790) 453 At the first boyling take hom off the fyre that they whaile noght.

Whaint, Whair(e, Whaish, Whais(h)le, whaizle, Whaite, Whake: see Quaint, Where, Wheyish, Wheeze, Wheezle, Wait *v.*1, Quake.

Whaker, north. dial. form of Quaker.

1700 in Sir C. Sharp *Chron. Mirab.* (1841) 51 Att ye Whakers metting house. 1802 R. Anderson *Ball. Cumbld.* (1805) 22 The neist was a Whaker, caw'd Jacob, He turn'd up the wheyte o' his een.

Whale (hwēl), *sb.* Forms: 1 hwæl, 3–4 **whal, wal, 4–5 wall, 4–7 whall, 5 wale, 5–6 whalle, 7 whaill, wheal, 4– whale**; chiefly *Sc.* and *north.* **3 qual, 4 quale, 5 qwal, qwall(e, qwaylle, 5–6 quhail(l, 6 quhale, quhell.** [OE. *hwæl*, corresp. to OHG., MHG. *wal* (G. *walfisch* Whale-fish, q.v.), ON. *hvalr* (Sw., Da. *hval*), related to OHG. *wâlira, welira*, MHG. *wâlre*, and MHG., G. *wels* (:— **χwalis*) sheath-fish; cf. Pruss. *kalis* sheath-fish.

The present form *whale* represents oblique forms (OE. *hwalas*, etc.); the OE. nom. *hwæl* gave 14th–17th cent. *whall* (cf. *small, awl*, † *all*, from *smæl, æl*).]

1. Any of the larger fish-like marine mammals of the order *Cetacea*, which have fore-limbs like fins and a tail with horizontal flukes, and are hunted for their oil and whalebone; in wider (scientific) use, any cetacean of the groups *Mystacoceti* or whalebone-whales, and *Odontoceti* or toothed whales (which are distinguished by the names dolphin, grampus, porpoise, etc.).

c893 Ælfred *Oros.* I. i. § 16 Se hwæl bið micle læssa þonne oðre hwalas. c1000 Ælfric *Gen.* i. 21 God gesceop þa micelan hwalas and eall libbende fisc-cinn. c1055 *Byrhtferth's Handboc* in *Anglia* VIII. 310 Þa myclan hwælas, & þa lytlan sprottas. c1220 *Bestiary* 735 He is blac so bro of qual. c1300 *Havelok* 753 He tok þe sturgiun, and þe qual. c1325 *Metr. Hom.* 136 Riht als the quale fars wit the elringe, And riht als sturioun etes merling. c1330 *Arth. & Merl.* 2495 He hadde a bodi as a whal. c1386 Chaucer *Sompn. T.* 222 Me thynketh they been lyk Iovinyan Fat as a whale and walkynge as a swan. 14.. *Metr. Voc.* in Wr.-Wülcker 625/11 Wale, *cete*. 14.. *Nom.* ibid. 704/15 *Hic cetus*, a whalle. c1440 *Promp. Parv.* 523 Whale, or qwal, grete fysche. 1513 Douglas *Æneis* vii. Prol. 23 Fludis monstreis, sic as meirswyne or quhailis. 1606 Shaks. *Tr. & Cr.* v. v. 23 And there they flye or dye, like scaled sculs, Before the belching Whale. 1707 *Curios. Husb. & Gard.* 140 Steep your Corn, or any other Seed, in Oil of Whale. 1769 Pennant *Brit. Zool.* III. 35 Whales are still seen one hundred and sixty feet long. 1843 *Penny Cycl.* XXVII. 272/2 The Toothed Whales are subdivided into those which have teeth in both jaws and those which have teeth in the lower jaw. 1860 Gosse *Rom. Nat. Hist.* x. 259 The pursuit of the whale, whether that species which our hardy mariners seek amidst the ice-floes of the Polar Seas, or the still huger kind which wallows in the boundless Pacific. *collective sing.* 1637 I. Jones & Davenant *Brit. Tri.* 15 And then on Rock he [*sc.* the giant] stood to bob for Whale. 1845 Coulter *Adv. Pacific* vii. 78 While cruising for whale, the look-outs are on the cross trees.

b. With defining words for various species: e.g. Bottle-nose(d *w.*, Ca'ing-whale, Fin-, Finback(ed, Finner, Greenland, Grey (*a.* 8 b), Humpback, Ice-, Pike-, Piked, Pike-headed, Pilot, Rostrated, *round-lipped* (Round *a.* 16 b), Scrag (*sb.*1 5), Spermaceti *w.*, Sperm whale, Whalebone-*w.* Also **Beaked, Black, Bowhead, Sowerby's, White Whale**: see quots.

1755 tr. *Pontoppidan's Nat. Hist. Norway* II. 123, I shall call it Balæna rostrata, or Nebbe-hval, the *Beaked Whale. 1920 *Brit. Mus. Return* 89 Cuvier's Beaked Whale (*Ziphius cavirostris*). 1834 Dewhurst *Cetacea* 16 *note*, *La Baleine Franche*,..Common *Black Whale. 1840 Marryat *Poor Jack* vi, The sparmacitty don't take the harpoon quite so quietly as the black whale does. 1843 *Penny Cycl.* XXVII. 296/1 The Whalebone Whale or Black Whale of the South Seas. 1883 *Fisheries Exhib. Catal.* (ed. 4) 201 Slabs of whalebone of *Bowhead Whale. 1920 *Brit. Mus. Return* 101 Tooth of a *Sowerby's Whale (*Mesoplodon bidens*). 1834 Dewhurst *Cetacea* 190 *Delphinapterus Beluga*, or the *White Whale.

(*b*) **Right Whale**, a whalebone-whale, esp. of the genus *Balæna*. Hence *right-whaling, right-whaler*, etc.

1725 P. Dudley in *Phil. Trans.* XXXIII. 256 The Right or Whalebone Whale is a large Fish, measuring sixty or seventy Feet in Length. 1824 J. F. Cooper *Pilot* xvii, 'Tis a right whale,..I saw his spout. 1874 Darwin *Desc. Man* II. xvii. (ed. 2) 516 The males of the right-whales do not fight together. 1888 *Encycl. Brit.* XXIV. 527/2 A right whale fishery of great importance. 1895 *Pall Mall Gaz.* 16 Dec. 2/1 Just before I took to 'right' whaling.

2. Applied to the 'great fish' which swallowed Jonah (*Jonah* i. 17).

c950 *Lindisf. Gosp.* Matt. xii. 40 Sua forðon wæs ionas in innað vel in wom huales ðrim dagum & ðrim næhtum [1382 Wyclif As Jonas was in the womb of a whall three days and three niȝtis]. 13.. *E. E. Allit. P.* C. 247 Now is Ionas þe Iwe iugged to drowne;..A wylde walterande whal..bi þat bot flotte. c1450 *St. Cuthbert* (Surtees) 572 Grete god..þat saued þe prophete with in þe whall. 1548 Udall, etc. *Erasm. Par. Acts* ii. 22–28 Euen as did ye whale reuomit the prophet Ionas. a1586 Montgomerie *Misc. Poems* xxxi. 35 Ionas, in þe quhellis bellie, þow safit thre dayis. 1687 A. Lovell tr. *Thevenot's Trav.* I. 41 Jona's Whale is also to go to Paradise.

†**3.** *Whale of the river, river-whale*: = Sheath-fish 1, a large freshwater fish, *Silurus glanis*. *Obs.*

1585 Higins *Junius' Nomencl.* 69/2 *Silurus*,..a fish much like a Sturgeon: a sheathfishe; a whale of the riuer. 1611 Cotgr., *Silure*, the rauening sheat fish, or Whall of the riuer.

4. *transf.* (from 1). An object resembling a whale; *Astron.* (with cap.) the constellation *Cetus*.

1551 Recorde *Cast. Knowl.* (1556) 267 The greate Whale, contayning 22 starres. 1664 *Phil. Trans.* I. 5 In the evening of that day it [*sc.* a comet] was to come into the jaw of the Whale. 1760 *Ann. Reg., Chron.* 66/1 The comet..passed..toward the whale's jaw. 1866 Lockyer *Guillemin's Heavens* (ed. 2) 356. 1905 F. M. Crawford *Glean. Venet. Hist.* I. 5 When the first fugitives, blind with terror, stumbled ashore upon the back of one of the sand whales in the lagoon.

5. Allusive, proverbial, transf., and fig. uses of sense 1. **a.** Prov. phr. (*To throw out*) *a tub to the whale*: see Tub *sb.* 9 b. *Very like a whale* (after Shaks. *Ham.* III. ii. 398): see quot. 1859.

[1591 *1st Pt. Troub. Raigne K. John* (1611) C 3 b, The mariner, Spying the hugie Whale, whose monstrous bulke Doth beare the waues like mountaines fore the wind, That throwes out emptie vessels, so to stay His fury.] 1859 *Slang Dict.* 115 *Very like a whale*, said of anything that is very improbable.

b. *allusively.*

1601 Shaks. *All's Well* IV. iii. 249 A..lasciuious boy, who is a whale to Virginity, and deuours vp all the fry it finds. 1606 Dekker *Seuen Deadly Sinnes* Wks. (Grosart) II. 27 Be wise therefore,..play with these Whales of the Sea, till you escape them that are deuourers of your Merchants. 1914 Marriott in *Edin. Rev.* July 1 Amid a shoal of minnows they promptly pose as authoritative whales.

c. fig. phr. *A whale on . . .*, having a great capacity or appetite for . . ., very good at or keen on . . . *A whale of* (U.S.): 'no end of'. *colloq.*

1893 McCarthy *Red Diamonds* xxiii, He was not, as he put it himself graphically, a whale on geography. 1899 A. Marshall *Peter Binney* xvi. 326, I should be a whale on parental authority myself if I were in your place. 1913 *19th Cent.* Sept. 621 [They] had what the Americans call 'a whale of a good time'.

6. *attrib.* and *Comb.*, as *whale-blubber* [Blubber *sb.*1 4], *-butt, -calf* [Calf 1 3], *-catching, -cub, -cutter, -drive* [Drive *sb.* 1 c], *-duty, -guts, -hunter* (cf. OE. *hwælhunta*), *-hunting* (cf. OE. *hwælhuntaþ*), *-killer, -killing, -kind, -meat, -spoilt, -steak, -striker, -striking, -trade, -vessel*; also in names of weapons, etc. used in hunting whales, as *whale-gun, -lance, -line, -net, -rope, -spade*; also *whale-like, -mouthed, -tailed* adjs. **b.** Spec. Combs.: **whale-acorn-shell** (see quot.); **whale-barnacle** = Coronule 2; **whale-brit** [Brit *sb.*1] = *whale-food*; **whale-deep** = *whale-hole*; **whale-feed** = *whale-food*; **whale('s) food** [tr. G. *walfischaas*, 1747], a general name for the small animals upon which whales feed; *spec.* a mollusc, *Clio borealis*; **whale-foots** [Foot *sb.* 22], the refuse in refining whale-oil, used by soap-makers and tanners; **whale-gull**, the ivory gull (Gull *sb.*1); **whale-head**, the shoebill or whale-headed stork, *Balæniceps rex*; also called **whale-headed** *stork*; †**whale-horn**, whalebone; **whale-laid** *a.* of a rope (see quot.); **whale-louse**, a small crustacean of the genus *Cyamus*, parasitic on whales; **whale-mouse** = *whale's guide*; **whale-pool** *humorous*, the Atlantic ocean (cf. *herring-pond*); **whale's belly, -tail**, etc., stars in the constellation *Cetus* (see 4); †**whale's guide**, the animal called by Pliny *musculus piscis* (cf. note s.v. Mysticete 1); **whale-shark**, (*a*) a very large shark, *Rhinodon typicus*; (*b*) the basking-shark (Basking *ppl. a.* 2); **whale-ship** = Whale-boat; †**whale-shot** [Shot *sb.*1 19], spermaceti. Also Whaleback, -bird, -boat, -bone, -fin, etc.

1815 Burrow *Elem. Conchol.* 194 *Balanoides*, Small, striated Acorn S[hell]. *Diadema*, *Whale Do. 1854 A. Adams, etc. *Man. Nat. Hist.* 305 *Whale-Barnacles (*Coronulidæ*). 1844 H. Stephens *Bk. Farm* II. 646 *Whale-blubber..forms a good compost for turnips. 1845 Darwin *Voy. Nat.* x. 214 A piece of putrid whales-blubber. 1835 Batman in K. Cornwallis *New World* (1859) I. 369 The 'Belinda', of Sydney, with a cargo of *whale-butts. 1867 Smyth *Sailor's Word-bk.*, **Whale-calf*, the young whale. 1685 R. Turner in W. Penn *Furth. Acc. Pennsylv.* 13 Three Companies for *Whale catching. 1885 J. G. Wood in *Longm. Mag.* Mar. 552 The *whale-cub, when first formed, has no baleen. 1631 Pellham *Gods Power* A 4 b, Thomas Ayers, *Whale-cutter. 1668 Prynne *Aurum Reg.* 127 This *Whale Duty hath been totally suspended..from the death of King Henry the 8, till the first year of King James, for want of a Queen Consort. 1853 *Househ. Words* VI. 402/2 The little red creatures ('*whale feed', sailors call them) are retained by the fringe [of the baleen]. 1767 tr. *Crantz'* *Hist. Greenland* I. 109 This *whale's-food is found in the greatest quantity between Spitzberg..and Greenland. 1865 Gosse *Land & Sea* 166 The immense aggregations of close-packed swimming invertebrata so well known to mariners in Arctic regions under the appellation of 'whale-food'. 1852 Macgillivray *Brit. Birds* V. 508 *Cetosparactes eburneus*. The Ivory *Whale-gull. 1858 *Merc. Marine Mag.* V. 149 The crew..murdered the Captain and third officer by shooting them with a *whale-gun. 1780 Coxe *Russ. Discov.* 256 Cloaks..made of thin *whale guts. 1884 Coues *Key N. Amer. Birds* (ed. 2) 654 *Balæniceps rex*, the Shoe-bill or *Whale-head, of Africa. 1875 *Encycl. Brit.* III. 759/1 The gigantic *Whale-headed Stork, *Balæniceps rex*. 1562 in *Inv. Mary Q. Scots* (Bannatyne Club) Pref. p. xxviii. *note*, xij bowtis of *quhaill horne. 1598 Hakluyt *Voy.* I. 4 He was come as far towards the North, as commonly the *whale hunters vse to trauell. 1851 H. Melville *Whale* xvi, Some of these same Quakers are the most sanguinary of all sailors and whale-hunters. 1615 *Trade's Incr.* 52 The Greenland company, out of the pretence of their first *Whale-hunting. 1868 Gorrie *Summ. & Wint. in Orkneys* viii. 323 The whale-hunting fleet. 1613 *Voy. Spitzbergen* in *Archæol. Amer.* (1860) IV. 305 When he enters into the sounds, our *whal-killers doe presentlie sallie forth to meet him. 1625 Purchas *Pilgrims* III. III. 461 The first setled, ordinary, and orderly Voyages for the *Whale-killing. 1703 Dampier *Voy.* III. ii. 57 About Christmas these are mostly imployed in Whale-killing. 1706 Phillips (ed. Kersey), *Manati*, a Fish of the *Whale-kind that breeds about the Island of Hispaniola. 1812 Manby *Ess. Preserv. Shipwr. Persons* 17 It may likewise be coiled in the manner used in the whale fishery. *Whale laid. 1823 Scoresby *Voy. N. Whale-fishery* 112 Armed only with a *whale-lance, he..set out on his adventurous exploit. 1608 Sylvester *Du Bartas* II. iv. *Schisme* 1016 This mighty Fish, of *Whale-like hugenesse. 1855 Leifchild *Cornwall* 166 The large whale-like back of a prostrate pillar. 1785 *Act 25 Geo. III* c. 56 § 2 Short Chucking, Half Clean, *Whale-line, or other Toppings. 1897 F. T. Bullen *Cruise of 'Cachalot'* 12 The whale-line, manilla rope like yellow silk, 1½ inch round, was brought on deck. 1774 Goldsm. *Nat. Hist.* (1824) III. 21 A small animal, of the shell-fish kind, called the *Whale-louse, that sticks to its body. 1875 Knight *Dict. Mech.* s.v. *Whalebone*, Time has passed since the people of England reveled in *whale meat. 1607 Topsell *Four-f. Beasts* 504 A little fishe called..in Greeke Mystocetos, the *Whale-mouse. 1656 Osborn *Adv. Son* (ed. 4) To Rdr., As I did then, in imitation of Sea-men by designe, so I may perhaps now cast out some empty stuffe, to find play for the *Whale-mouth'd gapers after Levity. 1853 Kane *Grinnell Exp.* xlvi. (1856) 426 Stalwart fellows, practiced in the kayack, and the sledge, and the *whale-net. a1876 M. Collins *Pen Sketches* (1879) II. 145 This is one of the good turns for which I am grateful to our friends across the *whale-pool. 1857 in Trevelyan *Compet. Wallah* (1866) 342 A coil of *whale rope. 1573 W. Bourne *Regim. Sea* (1580) 59 b, The names of the Starres..*Whales backe. Whales belly... Whales tayle. 1668 Charleton *Onomast.* 125 *Cetorum Dux*..the *Whales Guide. 1706 Phillips (ed. 6), *Mysticetus*, a Fish, call'd the Whale's Guide. 1884–5 *Riverside Nat. Hist.* (1888) III. 78 The Rhinodontidæ embraces only two species of large sharks, one of which well deserves the name *whale-shark, which is applied to it. 1820 Scoresby *Acc. Arctic Reg.* II. 199 The crew of a *whale-ship usually consists of 40 to 50 men. 1612 *Sc. Bk. Rates* in *Halyburton's Ledger* (1867) 332 *Whale shote the barrell, xx li. 1852 Mundy *Antipodes* (1857) 104 The harpoon, the axe, the lance, and the *whale-spade. 1836 *Uncle Philip's Convers. Whale Fishery* 349 They heard *whale-spouts near them. 1613 *Voy. Spitzbergen* in *Archæol. Amer.* (1860) IV. 289 Then the Basks, our *whale-strikers, went presentlie back againe to the Foreland wth their shallops. 1821 Scott *Pirate* xx, No *whale-striking, bird-nesting favourite for me. 1781 Pennant *Hist. Quadrup.* II. 537 *Whale-tailed Manati. 1840 R. H. Dana *Bef. Mast* v, He had been forty years in the *whale-trade. 1821 Scott *Pirate* xxxviii, A garland of faded ribbons, such as are used to decorate *whale-vessels.

Whale (hwēl), *v.*1 [f. prec.] *intr.* To engage in whale-fishing; see also Whaling *vbl. sb.*1

c1700 in *Cheever's Whalem. Adv.* i. (1850) 5 [To] whale out in the deep for sperm whales. 1812 *Sydney Gaz.* in *O'Hara's Hist. N. S. Wales* (1817) 386 The brig Active..was at Frederick Henry Bay whaling.

Whale, *v.*2 Now *U.S. colloq.* [Of obscure origin. Commonly regarded as a spelling of Wale *v.*1, but there are difficulties of form, chronology, and meaning. Perhaps orig. = to thrash with a whalebone whip (see Whalebone 3 b).]

1. *trans.* To beat, flog, thrash.

1790 Grose *Prov. Gloss.* (ed. 2), *Whale*, to beat with a horsewhip or pliant stick. 1801 Col. G. Hanger *Life* II. 162 Whaleing a gentleman is but a vulgar revenge. 1884 'Mark Twain' *Huck. Finn* iii, He used to always whale me when he was sober and could get his hands on me.

2. *transf. intr.* To do something implied by the context continuously or vehemently.

1897 Barrère & Leland *Dict. Slang*, *To whale away*, (Amer.), to preach, talk, or lecture away continuously or vehemently. 1908 H. Day *King Spruce* xxiv, You don't think I've whaled up here..to..talk about women, do you? 1915 *Morning Post* 1 June 4/4 They..snatched these rifles up, and whaled away at our chaps.

Whale, var. Wale.

Whaleback (hwēi·lbæk). [f. Whale *sb.* + Back *sb.*]

1. An arched structure over the deck of a steamer; = Turtle-back 1.

1886 *Times* 20 Apr. 10/2 He was standing under the whale-back.

2. A kind of steam vessel having a spoon bow and the main decks covered in and rounded over, suggesting the back of a whale.

1891 *Pall Mall Gaz.* 10 June 2/2 The Americans claim that, in Captain Macdougall's steel 'whalebacks', they possess the universal ship of the future.

3. *Geol.* A large mound of the shape of the back of a whale.

1893 Howorth *Glacial Nightmare* II. 774 Glaciers cannot explain the mounds called eskers, kames, or whalebacks.

4. *attrib.* or as *adj.* Furnished with a whale-back (sense 1); of the shape of the back of a whale.

1891 *Daily Graphic* 24 July 14/1 The first 'whaleback' boat which has crossed the Atlantic arrived at Liverpool on Monday. 1894 *Engineer* 13 July 33/3 A new craft is expected to take part in the yacht races at Galveston. She was built in Fort Worth, and may be classed as a whale-back yacht. 1908 *Daily Chron.* 29 July 4/4 Beneath a hot sun Belgrade lies bleaching on her whaleback promontory.

Hence **Wha·lebacked** *a.*, shaped like a whale's back; **Wha·lebacker**, a whaleback steamer.

1879 *Daily News* 8 Nov. 5/7 Whale-backed station of the London and South Eastern Railway Company. 1891 *Daily Graphic* 24 July 14/1 These 'Whalebackers' as they are termed offer very little resistance to the sea. 1903 Kipling *Five Nations, Sussex* 19 Our blunt, bow-headed, whale-backed Downs.

Wha·le-bird. Name of various birds which inhabit the places where whales are found, or which feed on their oil or offal: (*a*) a petrel of the genus *Prion* or *Procellaria*; (*b*) the turnstone, *Strepsilas interpres*; (*c*) the red or grey phalarope; (*d*) the ivory gull.

1768 *Phil. Trans.* LX. 117 Another bird, not much unlike a quail, which they call here the whale-bird, from its feeding on the offal of those fish. 1867 Smyth *Sailor's Word-bk.*, *Whale-bird*, a beautiful little bird seen hovering in flocks over the Southern Ocean. 1875 Melliss *St. Helena* 200 The Whale Bird (*Procellaria glacialoides*). 1879 *Bulletin U.S. Nat. Mus.* No. 15. 85 *Phalaropus fulicarius*,..'Shatgak', Cumberland Eskimo. 'Whale-bird', or 'Bow-head Bird', of whalemen.

Wha·le-boat. A long carvel-built boat, sharp at both ends, and steered with a rudder or an oar, used in whale-fishing. **b.** A boat of this kind carried as a life-boat by large passenger-steamers and warships.

1756 R. Rogers *Jrnls.* (1769) 13 Our rendezvous was appointed at Albany, from thence to proceed in four whale-boats to lake George. 1824 W. Irving *T. Trav.* IV. iv. (1849) 415 A picked crew of daring fellows set off for her in a whale-boat. 1871 *Good Words* 713 Having come to her moorings, she is immediately surrounded by a multitude of whale-boats.

Whalebone (hwēi·lbōun), *sb.* Forms: see Whale *sb.* and Bone *sb.*; also **4 huelbon, 7 whel-, whal-, whealbone, quhallbon**; (in sense 1) **whales bone**, etc.

†**1.** Ivory from the walrus or some similar animal confused with the whale: chiefly in phr. *white as whale's bone*. *Obs.*

c1205 Lay. 2363 Þe walles of stone, þe duren of whales bone [c1275 wales bone]. a1310 in Wright *Lyric P.* xi. 38 A wayle whyt as whalies bon. 13.. *E. E. Allit. P.* A. 212 Her ble more blaȝt þen whallez bon. a1400 *Sqr. lowe Degre* 537 Lady, as whyte as whales bone. ?1467 *Paston Lett.* II. 298 But yef ye purposid to falle hastely in my Lady Anne P. lappe, as white as whales bon, &c. c1520 Skelton *Garl. Laurel* 472 An hundred steppis mountyng to the halle, One of iasper, another of whalis bone. 1567 Turberv. *Epit.*, etc. 138 Hir Mouth so small, hir Teeth so white as any Whale his bone. 1588 Shaks. *L. L. L.* v. ii. 332 This is the flower that smiles on euerie one, To shew his teeth as white as Whales bone. 1590 Greene *Never too Late* Wks. (Grosart) VIII. 213 Legges as white as whales bone. 1610 Toffe *Hon. Acad.* IV. 162 Her hands were white, as Whale his bone. 1848 Kingsley *Saint's Trag.* III. i, Purer than white whales' bone.

β. 13.. *Coer de L.* 62 All it was whyt of huel-bon. c1400 *Destr. Troy* 3055 Alse qwyte & qwem as any qwalle bon. 1500–20 Dunbar *Poems* xxi. 46 Toungis now are maid of quhyte quhaill bone, And hairtis ar maid of hard flynt stone.

2. The elastic horny substance which grows in a series of thin parallel plates in the upper jaw of certain whales in place of teeth; baleen: used esp. for stiffening parts of the dress, etc.

Formerly supposed to be obtained from the whale's fins.

1604 *Lismore Papers* Ser. II. (1887) I. 107 For whelbone to ye bodes ixd. 1613 *Voy. Spitzbergen* in *Archæol. Amer.* (1860) IV. 311 They cut of his head, containing his toung and his finnes, commonlie called whalbone. 1711 Addison *Spect.* No. 127 ⁋ 4 A Female who is thus invested in Whalebone is sufficiently secured against the Approaches of an ill-bred Fellow. 1712 Budgell *ibid.* 277 ⁋ 8 The Petticoat has no Whale-bone. 1820 Scoresby *Acc. Arctic Reg.* I. 457 Fifteen feet is the greatest length of the whalebone. 1878 J. W. Hayes *Draper & Haberd.* (ed. 4) 87 Stay Whalebone is prepared and cut into suitable lengths for corsets. *Ibid.*, Dress Whalebone is sold in lengths varying between 27 in. and 54 in. 1887 Ruskin *Præterita* II. xi. 390 At a Christmas party, [she] acted any part—that depended on whalebone [*i.e.* stays]—admirably.

3. A strip of whalebone, esp. used as stiffening in women's stays, dresses, etc.

1601 [? Marston] *Jack Drums Entert.* IV. F 4, Oh I could crack my Whalebones, breake my Buske, to think what laughter may arise from this. a1635 Corbet *Iter Bor.* 391 She was barr'd up in Whale-bones that did leese None of the Whales length, for they reach'd her knees. 1674 tr. *Scheffer's Lapland* 107 If they fish with a Cane or Whale-bone. 1712–14 Pope *Rape Lock* v. 40 Fans clap, silks rustle, and tough whalebones crack. 1871 *Figure Training* 106 In order to insure a good fit, and to keep it perfectly in place, the busk in front, and the whalebones behind, are made somewhat longer than the present fashion.

b. A riding-whip of whalebone.

1842 Lover *Handy Andy* iii, Smarting under a sense of injury and whalebone. 1867 A. L. Gordon *Poems* (1912) 96 Ah! there goes Fred's whalebone a flanker.

4. The jaw-bone of a whale. (Cf. G. *walfischbein*.)

1846 R. E. E. Warburton *Hunting Songs* viii. 25 Where 'twixt the whalebones the widow [*sc.* Maria Hollingsworth, a German by birth] sat down.

5. *attrib.* and *Comb.*, as *whalebone-cutter, -kind, -man*; **whalebone-hair**, the hairy fringe of whalebone; **whalebone-tree**, an Australian urticaceous tree, *Pseudomorus brunoniana*; **whalebone-whale**, a whale of the family *Balænidæ*, having plates of whalebone developed from the palate instead of teeth; a right whale.

1761 *Brit. Mag.* II. 672 Philip Benton, of Cainsborough,..*whalebone-cutter and merchant. 1820 Scoresby *Acc. Arctic Reg.* II. 451 Large shreds of old thin canvas, *whale-bone-hair, and a quantity of ashes. 1708 J. Chamberlayne *St. Gt. Brit.* II. I. iii. (1743) 331 Great whales of the Baleen, or *whale bone kind. a1637 B. Jonson *Underwoods* lx. Wks. (1641) 208 The *whale-bone man That quilts those bodies, I have leave to span. 1889 Maiden *Useful Pl. Australia* 591 *Pseudomorus Brunoniana*,..called *Whalebone Tree in Southern New South Wales. 1725 *Whalebone whale [see Whale *sb.* 1 b (*b*)]. 1843 *Penny Cycl.* XXVII. 272/2 The Toothless or Whalebone Whales.

b. as *adj.* Stiffened with strips of whalebone; made of or containing whalebone; also *fig.*, 'stiff', affected.

1601 B. Jonson *Poetaster* II. i. (1905) 28 Your whale-bone-bodies. 1603 in *10th Rep. Hist. MSS. Comm.* App. I. 31 Ane par of quhallbon bodis. 1650 Bulwer *Anthropomet.* 193 And to that end..shut up their Wastes in a Whale-bone prison. 1711 Swift *Jrnl. to Stella* 10 Nov., Have you got the whalebone petticoats among you yet?..a woman here may hide a moderate gallant under them. 17.. in *Lyra Elegant.* (1867) l. 3 Last Sunday at St. James's prayers I, drest in all my whale-bone airs. 1802 Maria Edgeworth *Moral T., Good Fr. Gov.*, A few words in defence of sacks, long waists, and whalebone stays. 1807 W. Irving *Salmag.* No. 6 (1811) I. 119 A plentiful stock of whims, and oddities, and whalebone habits. 1866 Le Fanu *All in Dark* lxviii, To make his bow before the world in the picturesque long robe and whalebone wig which everyone of taste admires. 1908 [Eliz. Fowler] *Betw. Trent & Ancholme* 382 A light umbrella was one not made with whalebone ribs.

Hence **Whaleboned** (hwēi·lbōund) *pa. pple.* and *ppl. a.*, stiffened with whalebone.

1641 J. Day *Parl. Bees* (1881) 29 Such whale-bon'd-bodied rascals. 1835 *Court Mag.* VI. p. vii/2 A mantelet..whale-boned in such a manner as to prevent it from crushing the dress. 1908 Edith Wharton *Hermit*, etc. IV. 150 A laced, whaleboned, frizzle-headed, high-heeled daughter of iniquity.

Whale-eyde, obs. f. Wall-eyed.

Wha·le-fin. ? *Obs.* Also 7 **whales-finne**. Whalebone, formerly supposed to be the fin of the whale.

1612 *Sc. Bk. Rates* in *Halyburton's Ledger* (1867) 332 Whale fin the fin, xls. 1614 Purchas *Pilgrimage* IV. xvii. (ed. 2) 433 The Inhabitantes holde trade with other Samoeds ..for..Beauers, Downe, Whales-Finnes. 1741 *Daily Post* 11 Apr. 1/3 On Tuesday was imported..from Holland 9 C. Whale-fins. 1809 Kendall *Trav.* II. iii. 207 By whale-fin has always been meant the barb, from which the whale-bone is really obtained. 1820 Scoresby *Acc. Arctic Reg.* II. 415 Whale-bone, or whale-fins, as the substance is sometimes, though incorrectly named.

†**Whalefish.** *Obs.* Also 6 **wall-, whal(le)-, 6–7 wale-**. [repr. unrecorded OE. **hwælfisc*, or a. MLG., MDu., Du. *walvisch* = OHG. *walvisc* (MHG. *-visch*, G. *walfisch*), ON. *hvalfiskr*: see Whale *sb.* and Fish *sb.*1] A whale.

c1511 *1st Eng. Bk. Amer.* (Arb.) Introd. 28/1 There by be many walefysshes & flyinge fysshes. 1535 Coverdale *Ps.* cxlviii. 7 Prayse the Lorde vpon earth, ye whalfishes and all depes. 1546 *Gasser's Prognost.* A v b, The Son in the same euening shall go doune or set with the tayle of the Whalle fish. 1582 N. Lichefield tr. *Castanheda's Conq. E. Ind.* I. ii. 6 b, These people doe mainteine themselues with rootes of hearbes, with Sea Woulfes, and Whale fish. 1615 R. Cocks *Diary* (Hakl. Soc.) I. 91, 2 pec. wale fyshe. 1635 R. Johnson *Hist. Tom a Lincolne* (1828) 105 The whale fishes lay wallowing in the waves. 1712 *Phil. Trans.* XXVII. 440 About two Years ago there came a Stranger to me, who had two Penis's of the Whale Fish.

Wha·le-fisher. [f. Whale-fishing: see -er 1.] = Whaler 1. So **Wha·lefisherman**, = Whaler 1 and 2; **Wha·le-fishery**, (*a*) the occupation or industry of whale-fishing; (*b*) a locality where whale-fishing is carried on or where whales abound.

1773 Berridge *Chr. World Unmasked* (1805) 43 In Greenland among the *whale-fishers. 1820 Scoresby *Acc. Arctic Reg.* I. 271 The salt in the sea..destroys the tenacity of the bay-ice,..and, in the language of the whale-fisher, completely rots it. 1874 A. H. Markham *Whaling Cruise* i. 1 Hither [*sc.* to the Arctic Regions] our brave whale-fishers have annually ventured for many years. 1724 *Phil. Trans.* XXXIII. 193 Our *Whale Fishermen of Nantucket. 1820 Scoresby *Acc. Arctic Reg.* II. 74 Foreign Protestants also, who had served three years on board of any British whale-fishermen. 1704 *Phil. Trans.* XXIV. 1723 When our Ships return'd from the *Whale-Fishery. 1752 J. Hill *Hist. Anim.* 555 About Greenland, and in other places where there are whale-fisheries. 1820 Scoresby *Acc. Arctic Reg.* II. 76 The British whale-fishery of 1758 was very unsuccessful. 1874 A. H. Markham *Whaling Cruise* i. 8 The ships engaged in the whale fishery are all most substantially built.

Wha·le-fishing. [f. Whale *sb.* + Fishing *vbl. sb.*] The occupation of taking whales, whaling.

1580 in Hakluyt *Voy.* (1589) 460 To the end we may turne our new found land fishing or Island fishing or our whale-fishing that way. 1699 T. Allison *Voy. Archangel* 109 A Flemish Fly-boat bound to Greenland, for Whale-fishing. 1722 Elking *View Greenland Trade* (1859) 95 We can..carry on the whale-fishing trade..much cheaper than the Hollanders. 1820 Scoresby *Acc. Arctic Reg.* I. 257 Ice becomes exceedingly fragile towards the close of the whale-fishing season. 1889 C. Edwardes *Sardinia* xviii. 345 The industry [of tunny-fishing] is as speculative as whale-fishing or silver-mining.

Whal eie, obs. f. Wall eye.

Whaleman (hwēi·lmæn). [Man *sb.*1 4 p, 14.]

1. = Whaler 1.

1716 B. Church *Hist. Philip's War* (1867) II. 133 And Whale-men then will be very serviceable in this Expedition, which having a promise made to them, that they shall be released in good season to go home a Whaling in the Fall. 1850 H. Melville *White Jacket* I. iv. 21 He launched out..into tremendous laudations of whalemen; declaring that whalemen alone deserved the name of sailors. 1898 F. T. Bullen *Cruise of 'Cachalot'* xvi. 198 A smarter whaleman than Mistah Jones did not live.

2. = Whaler 2.

1767 M. Cutler in *Life*, etc. (1888) I. 19 Whalemen fitted out for the Straits of Belle Isle, and Davis Straits. 1840 R. H. Dana *Bef. Mast* vii, The ship was the Cortes, whaleman, of New Bedford. 1860 *Merc. Marine Mag.* VII. 254 There were two or three whalemen in port.

Wha·le-oil. Oil obtained from whale-blubber.

1435–6 in Heath *Grocers' Comp.* (1869) 418, ii shippes of waloill, conteynyng xlviij.° iii. v. oyil. c1580 in *Engl. Hist. Rev.* (1914) July 520 Whale oyles that come frome newfound Land. 1672 *Act 25 Chas. II* c. 7 § 4 Noe English built Shipp..importing Whale oyle or Blubber or other Fish, Oyle. 1712 tr. *Pomet's Hist. Drugs* I. 157 We have Oil of Camomile and Linseed..when Train or Whale-Oil is dear. 1896 Brannt *Anim. & Veg. Fats* (ed. 2) II. 57 The pure whale oils, pale, brownish-yellow or brown.

attrib. 1853 *Zoologist* XI. 4044 Syringing the young tree well with whale-oil-soap. 1885 *Harper's Mag.* Feb. 368/2 Flavilla lit the..whale-oil lamp.

Whaler (hwēi·ləɹ). [f. Whale *sb.* or *v.*1 + -er 1.]

1. A person engaged in whaling; a whale-catcher.

1684 *Roxb. Ball.* (1885) V. 457 Without you do now imploy the Wheelers to do 't, Ye ne'r will be able to bring all about. 1775 Romans *Florida* App. 79 The North, or Grand Bahama bank, is little frequented but by whalers and turtlers. 1843 *Penny Cycl.* XXVII. 752/1 The whalers kill the calves in order to capture the mother. 1895 Gore-Booth *Sea Fishing* (Badm. Libr.) xvi. 476 Two bollard heads (pronounced 'bullet heads' by the Scotch whalers).

2. a. A vessel used in whale-fishing. **b.** = Whale-boat b.

1806 *Sydney Gaz.* in *O'Hara's Hist. N. S. Wales* (1817) 270 Arrived..same day, the Aurora south whaler. 1817 Byron *Beppo* lxi, Stopp'd by the elements, like a whaler. 1893 *Times* 3 July 6/2 Some loose oars..with which I supported myself until picked up by the Dreadnought's whaler. 1898 Kipling *Fleet in Being* v. 62 The First Lieutenant..had the whaler's crew sleeping all handy by. 1909 *Athenæum* 13 Mar. 320/1 The original plan was to descend the Mackenzie to the Beaufort Sea, leaving the stores to come round by whaler.

3. Anything unusually large of its kind; a 'whacker', 'whopper'. *U.S. slang.*

a1860 *Georgia Scenes* 184 (Bartlett) 'He's a whaler!' said Rory; 'but his face is mighty little for his body and legs.' 1873 Leland *Egypt. Sketch-Bk.* 25, I shared..a cabin with a captain who had been a whaler for forty years; and he *was* a whaler! and great at 'whalers'.

Whalery (hwēi·ləri). [f. Whale *sb.* + -ery.]

1. The industry of whale-fishing, or the establishment for carrying it on.

1683 W. Penn *Let. to Free Soc. Traders* 9 The Whalery [is conveniently posted] for a sound and fruitful Bank. 1685 — *Furth. Acc. Pennsylv.* 8 We justly hope a considerable profit by a Whalery. 1878 Susan Phillips *On Seaboard* 15 Since I sailed away to the whalery, When I was a bit of a lad. 1899 *Daily News* 2 Dec. 6/4 South Sea whaleries.

2. A tank to keep a whale in.

a1880 F. T. Buckland *Notes & Jottings* (1882) 345 When the whale had been in his whalery about three hours, he had quite recovered himself both in mind and body.

Whales bone: see Whalebone.

Whaling (hwēi·liŋ), *vbl. sb.*1 [f. Whale *sb.* or *v.*1 + -ing 1.] The action, practice, or business of catching whales.

1716 B. Church *Hist. Philip's War* (1867) II. 133 Whale-men..having a promise made to them, that they shall be released in good season to go home a Whaling in the Fall. 1851 H. Melville *Whale* xvi, 'But what takes thee a-whaling?'..'Well, sir I want to see what whaling is.' 1895 Gore-Booth *Sea Fishing* (Badm. Libr.) xvi. 497 The Arctics seem to have an extraordinary and incomprehensible attraction for some people; and when it is coupled with whaling, to the author it becomes almost irresistible.

b. *attrib.* or as *ppl. a.*

1821 Scott *Pirate* v, Ill-faur'd tools they had in their hands, whaaling knives they ca'ed them. 1823 Scoresby *Voy. N. Whale-fishery* 34 The practice of such kinds of harmless frolic, as the circumstances of a whaling voyage will admit. 1836 *Uncle Philip's Convers. Whale Fishery* 6 There was a whaling ship fitting out for her voyage. 1843 *Penny Cycl.* XXVII. 752/1 The number of whales has greatly decreased on the whaling-ground. 1860 Wraxall *Life in Sea* ii. 33 He listened to the brilliant promises of a whaling captain. 1863 Mrs. Gaskell *Sylvia's Lovers* xvi, Stores had to be purchased by the whaling-masters. 1890 'R. Boldrewood' *Col. Reformer* xvi, The barque was empty and the whaling gear in trim.

Wha·ling, *vbl. sb.*2 *dial.* and *U.S.* [f. Whale *v.*2 + -ing 1.] Beating, thrashing.

1852 Mrs. Stowe *Uncle Tom's C.* xxxvi, How did yer whaling agree with yer, Tom? 1885 'C. E. Craddock' *Proph. Gt. Smoky Mts.* ii. 44 From fear of a whaling by his active parent.

Whalish (hwēi·liʃ), *a. rare.* [f. Whale *sb.* + -ish 1.] Of the nature of or resembling a whale.

a1892 G. H. Kingsley *Sport & Trav.* (1900) 424 A big, wide-flippered whalish-looking creature.

Whalke, Whall(e: see Walk *sb.*1, Wall.

Whallabee, var. Wallaby. **Whallup**, obs. f. Wallop *v.*

Whally (hwǭ·li), *a. rare.* Also 9 **-ey**. [? f. *whall*, Wall *sb.*3, 'whally eyes' being equivalent to 'eyes of wall', i.e. wall-eyes.] Of the eyes: Showing much white, glaring.

1590 Spenser *F. Q.* I. iv. 24 A bearded Goat, whose..whally eyes (the signe of gelosy). 1828 J. Wilson in *Blackw. Mag.* XXIV. 669 His low vile forehead, whalley eyes, pendulous cheeks.

Whalm, Whalp: see Walm, Whelm, Whelp.

Whaly (hwēi·li), *a. rare.* [f. Whale *sb.* + -y 1.] Of whales.

1600 Tourneur *Transf. Metam.* xxxix, The ocean's monarch..The great controller of the whaly ranckes.

†**Wham.** *Obs. nonce-wd.* [A factitious word made by altering the vowel of Whim.] A whimsical or fantastic person.

1691 Wood *Ath. Oxon.* II. 253 The Author of it was a whim and a wham, a Fellow that invented ridiculous Principles.

Wham, Sc. and north. dial. form of Whom.

Whamble, var. Whemmel *Sc.*, overturn.

Whame. *Obs.* or *dial.* A gadfly.

1658 Rowland tr. *Moufet's Theat. Ins.* 937 This Fly [*Curvicauda*] the English in their proper tongue call a Whame and a Burrell-fly. 1775 Romans *Florida* App. 51 *note*, *Tabona* [*sic*] is Spanish for a whame or horsefly. 1829 *Glover's Hist. Derby* I. 177 *Oestrus Bovis*, Whame or Burrel Fly. 1881 Blackmore *Christowell* ii, He mistook a large stone-fly..for a genuine oestrus, a bot-fly, whame, or tabanus.

Whamera, var. Woomera. **Whamire**, dial. var. Quamire *Obs.* **Whammel**, var. Whemmel *Sc.*, overturn. **Whampee**, var. Wampee. **Whan**, obs. f. When, Whom; obs. pa. t. of Win. **Whand**, Sc. var. Wand *sb.* **Whane, Whanene**: see When, Whenne.

Whang (hwæŋ), *sb.*1 *Sc.* and *dial.* Also 6 *Sc.* **quhayng, quhaing, 7 whange, 9** *Sc.* **quhang; 7 whanck, 7– whank.** [Variant of *thwang*, Thong.]

1. = Thong *sb.*

1536 Bellenden *Cron. Scot.* (1821) II. 32 Quhen Hengist had gottin the grant of sa mekill land as he micht circle about with ane bull hide, he schure it in maist crafty and subtell quhaingis. a1578 Lindesay (Pitscottie) *Chron. Scot.* (S.T.S.) I. 117 Ane gret scheiff of arrowis knet together in ane quhange of leathir. a1598 D. Fergusson *Scot. Prov.* (1785) 647 Mony ane tines the haff-merk whinger for the halfpenny whang. 1670 Ray *Prov.* 289 Of other mens lether, men takes large whanges. 1691 — *Coll. Words* (ed. 2) 151 Shoe-whang. 1717 De Foe *Mem. Ch. Scot.* III. 268, I had not the worth of a Spur Whang of any Man's, but was mounted of Horse and Arms of my own. 1737–8 *MS. Par. Bk., Pannal, Yks.*, Church gate mending a beast face and Whangs, 1s. od. 1818 Scott *Rob Roy* xxxiii, Never weigh a MacGregor's bluid against a broken whang o' leather. 1837 Sir F. Palgrave *Merch. & Friar* i. 16 Their sacks..tightly bound by many a whang and thong.

2. A large or thick slice, esp. of cheese, bread, etc.

1684 Meriton *Yorksh. Dial.* 57 What a whanck's there. a1700 *Gaberlunzie Man* viii. in Ramsay *Tea-t. Misc.* (1733) I. 86 The twa, with kindly sport and glee, Cut frae a new cheese a whang. 1818 Hogg *Tales & Sk., Adv. Allan Gordon* (1836) I. 264 A good whang of solid fish. 1866 W. Henderson *Folk Lore N. Counties* 3 The whang must be taken from the edge of the cheese, and divided into portions. 1879 Stevenson *Trav. Cevennes* 33 With a glass, a whang of bread, and an iron fork, the table is completely laid.

Whang, *sb.*2. Chiefly *dial.* [Echoic. Cf. Whang *v.*2] A resounding blow or stroke, or the sound of such a blow; a bang.

1824 Mactaggart *Gallovid. Encycl.*, *Whang*..a blow, or rather a lash with a whip. 1868 Kinglake *Crimea* IV. v. 79 The 'whang' of the round-shot. 1889 'Q' *Splendid Spur* ix. 130 Soon the whang-whang-I of the hammer below rous'd me. 1891 *Century Mag.* Dec. 246 Our gear came down with a whang as the ship forged ahead.

Whang, *v.*1 *Sc.* and *dial.* [Variant of Thong *v.*; cf. Whang *sb.*1]

1. *trans.* To beat as with a thong; to lash (also *fig.*); *gen.* to beat, strike, hit or knock violently.

1684 Meriton *Yorksh. Dial.* 54 If she hear she'l whang the varra sayer. 1786 Burns *Ordination* iii, Heresy is in her pow'r, And gloriously she'll whang her. 1889 Baden-Powell *Pigsticking* 21 A savage would consider it the height of sport to go and whang a pig on the head.

b. To throw, drive, pull, etc. with force or with violent impact.

1880 Clare *Rural Life* (ed. 2) 60 I'd just streak'd down, and with a swish Whang'd off my hat soak'd like a fish. 1899 Crockett *Black Douglas* xix, Whang the steel bolt through his ribs. *Ibid.* xxxiv, Bring back every true lad that can whang bow, or gar sword-iron whistle.

2. To cut in 'whangs' or large slices. Also *absol.* or *intr.*

a1743 *Argyll is my name* in Whitelaw *Bk. Scot. Song* (1866) 224 I'll aff to the Highlands as hard's I can reel. And whang at the bannocks o' barley meal. 1802 W. Beattie *Tales* (1813) 8 At last, came cheese..My uncle set it to his breast, And whang'd it down.

Whang, *v.*2 [Cf. Whang *sb.*2] *intr.* To make a loud resounding noise, as of a heavy blow or explosion, of shot flying through the air, etc.

1875 Kinglake *Crimea* V. vi. 426 Another of the mighty 18-pounder shot flew whanging over the heads of our soldiery. 1912 Masefield *Widow in Bye Street* II. liv, The organ whangs, the giddy horses reel.

b. The vb.-stem used adverbially: cf. Bang *v.* 8.

1844 Kinglake *Eothen* xxi. 335, I..went falling, and falling through air till my crown came whang against the ground. 1855 Browning *Up at a Villa* ix, Bang, whang, whang goes the drum.

Whang, dial. f. Wang 1.

Whangee (hwæŋgī·) Also **w(h)anghee.** [Chinese *huang* bamboo sprouts too old for eating, a hard white-skinned bamboo (Giles).] A cane made of the stem of one or other species of *Phyllostachys*, Chinese and Japanese plants allied to and resembling bamboos. Also *whangee-cane*.

1813 W. Milburn *Oriental Comm.* II. 545 Wanghees, sometimes called Japan canes, should be chosen pliable, tough, round and taper. 1836 *Act 3 & 4 Will. IV*, c. 56 Duties of Customs Inwards... Canes, *viz.*.. Whangees, Jumboo..and other Walking Canes or Sticks, the 1,000.. o. 5. o. 1891 A. Dobson *Hogarth* ii. 31 A short-trowsered tar of the Tom Bowling era is deliberately executing a nautical *pas seul*..with the aid of a whangee. 1906 Oxenham *Profit & Loss* vi, A tough flexible whangee cane.

Whanger (hwæ·ŋəɹ). [f. Whang *v.*1 + -er 1.] (See quot.)

1867 Smyth *Sailor's Word-bk.*, *Whangers*, or Cod-whangers. Fish-curers of Newfoundland. An old term for a large sword.

Whanhope, obs. form of Wanhope.

Whanne, obs. f. When; var. *wan*, obs. pa. t. of Win *v.* **Whannen**, var. Whenne *Obs.*, whence. **Whannes**, obs. f. Whence.

†**Whannow**, *int. Obs.* Also **wannowe.** [? f. What + Now. Cf. Whau, which is similarly used.] What! I say! Come, come!

c1450 *Northern Passion* (MS. Addit.) 147/59* 'Wannowe', sayde kayme, 'her es Envy; My smoke gose down and thyne gose hye.' c1460 *Towneley Myst.* xxviii. 184 *Thomas.* Whannow, peter! art thou mad?

Whanse, var. Wanze *v. Obs.* **Whante**, **Whantite**, obs. ff. Quant, Want, Quantity. **Whap**, var. Wap *v.*3 *Obs.*, to bark, Whaup *Sc.*, curlew, Whop.

†**Whaped**, *pa. pple. Obs.* Also 4 **whaaped**, 5 **waped.** [Cf. Awhape.] Bewildered, dismayed.

c1374 Chaucer *Anel. & Arc.* 215 Turnid is in quakynge all my daunce My suretee in a whaaped [*v.rr.* waped, wayped, whaped] countenaunce. c1403 Lydg. *Temple of Glas* 401 That þei wiþ derknes were waped & amate. 1426 — *De Guil. Pilgr.* 1297, I was so whapyd & amaat.

Whapper, etc.: see Whopper, etc.

Whappet (hwǫ·pėt). *dial.* Also 9 **wappet.** [f. **whap*, Wap *sb.*2 + -et.] A small dog addicted to 'wapping' or yelping.

1577 Harrison *England* III. vii. (1878) 48 The whappet or prick-eard curre. 1622 S. Ward *Life of Faith* (1627) 62 As the sturdie Steede dashes out the little Whappets braines, so easily doth Death with the least kicke..the stoutest Constitution. a1825 Forby *Voc. E. Anglia*, *Wappet*, a yelping cur.

Whapple, var. Warple. **Whapto**, var. Wapato(o. **Whar**, obs. f. *were*, pl. pa. t. indic. of Be *v.*; obs. f. Ware *a.*; Sc. and n. dial. f. Where; obs. contr. f. Whether.

†**Whar**, *v. Obs.* Imitative of a rumbling sound.

13.. *Gaw. & Gr. Knt.* 2203 What! hit wharred, & whette, as water at a mulne.

‖**Whare** (hwā·re, hwǫ·ri, wǫ·ri). Also **ware, warree, warré, wharre, wharry.** [Maori *whare*, *ware* house.] A Maori hut or native dwelling.

1833 H. Williams in H. Carleton *H. W.* (1874) 151 The Europeans, who were near us in a raupo whare (rush house). 1852 Mundy *Antipodes* (1857) 179 A capital breakfast..was served in a handsome glass-windowed and carpeted warree. 1865 *Pall Mall Gaz.* 28 Sept. 9/2 Lounging among the wharres of a pah. 1875 Wood & Lapham *Waiting for Mail* 31 He pulled up..beside a wharry. 1892 E. Reeves *Homeward Bound* 63 A smart man he, and transacted his business in a very handsome whare.

Whare, obs. shortened form of Wharrow.

1688 Holme *Armoury* III. 272/1 A Ropers Whare or Wharve, or Wheele Spindle.

Whare, obs. form of Where.

Wharel, obs. f. Quarrel *sb.*2, quarry.

c1356 *Durham Acc. Rolls* (Surtees) 557 Wharel-wegges.

Wharf (hwǫɹf), *sb.*1 Pl. **wharfs** (hwǫɹfs), **wharves** (hwǫɹvz). Forms: 1 **hwearf, wearf, hwerf, 1, 4 warf, 4 wherf(e, warffe, wharghffe, quarf, 5 qwerf, 5–7 warff, wharff(e, 5–8 wharfe, 6 quarfe, (wharthe), 7 hwarf, 7– wharf.** [Late OE. *hwearf* (cf. earlier poetical comp. *merehwearf* sea-shore), corresp. to MLG. *warf, werf* mole, dam, wharf, raised site protected from flooding (LG. *warf*), whence EFris. *warf, werf*, Du. *werf* shipyard, G. *werf* wharf, pier, *werft* dockyard. Ultimately related to Wharf *sb.*2, Wharve *sb.* and *v.*

¹ Mr. Pickering notices this form of the plural of *wharf*, as peculiar to Americans. The English say *wharfs*. In the Colony and Province Laws of Massachusetts, Mr. Pickering says he has observed the plural *wharfs* (or *wharfes*) as late as the year 1735; but after that period the form *wharves* is used' (Bartlett *Dict. Amer.*, 1848).]

1. A substantial structure of timber, stone, etc., built along the water's edge, so that ships may lie alongside for loading and unloading.

Often with prefixed sb., as *fish-wharf, gun-wharf*.

10.. *Charter of Eadweard* in Kemble *Cod. Dipl.* IV. 221 Ic wille ðat sainte Petre and ða gebroðera in Westminstre habben ðat land and ðone wearf..ðe Ulf and his wif..gafon. 1067 in *Charter Roll 9 Edw. III*, m. 18 De uno hwearfo quod est ad applicationem navium ad caput pontis illius civitatis [*sc.* London]. 1080–5 in H. W. C. Davis *Regesta Regum Anglo-Norm.* (1913) 126 Unum warf quod est ad caput pontis Londonie. c1320 *Domesday of St. Paul's* (Camden) 158* An qwarvæ sive kayæ, muri sive wallæ..debite reparentur. 1320 *Rolls of Parlt.* I. 370/2 In shopis suis super Warfam predictam. 1397 *Ibid.* III. 371/1 De la novell Keye autrement appelle le Wherf [1432 *Act 10 Hen. VI*, c. 5 § 2 Qwerl] a le cost du dit Port de Caleys. 1442 *Ibid.* V. 54/2 Diverse Wharves and Keyes beyng by the water sides. 1485 *Cal. Pat. Rolls* 6 [Keeping the] hawes and wharfes of Walton and Waybrigge. 1503–4 *Act 19 Hen. VII*, c. 37 § 5 Too Cotages or Meses wyth Howses & Wharfes..in Stepeney. 1669 Sturmy *Mariner's Mag.*, *Pen. & Forf.* 8 If any Custom-house Officer..keep any Wharfe, or hold any Hostelry, or Tavern. a1700 Evelyn *Diary* 17 Aug. 1654, A wharfe of hewn stone, which makes the river appeare very neate. 1815 J. Smith *Panorama Sci. & Art* I. 241 Its [*sc.* Blackfriars bridge] length, from wharf to wharf, is about nine hundred and ninety-five feet. 1834 Dickens *Sk. Boz, Steam Excurs.*, The bell at London-bridge Wharf rang; and a Margate boat was just starting. 1878 Nares *Polar Sea* I. i. 1 H.M. ships 'Alert' and Discovery' cast off from the dockyard wharf, Portsmouth. 1882 J. Rhys *Celtic Brit.* ii. 46 The wharfs for the tin-barges were erected.

†**2. a.** An embankment, mole, or dam. *Obs.*

1038 *Charter of Harold* in Thorpe *Charters* 341 Þa gyrnde he þæt he moste macian foran gen Mildryþe æker ænne hwerf wið þon wodan to werianne. 1567 Golding *Ovid's Met.* xv. 196 b, Untill that hee the bowwing wharf besyde the hauen tooke [orig. *Tendit ad incurvo munitos aggere portus*]. 1600 Holland *Livy* xl. lv. 1091 Lepidus..raised the great causey or wharfe at Tarracina. 1601 — *Pliny* vi. xxviii. I. 140 The Apamians..set open the sluces, and breake up the wharfes and bankes that keepe these two rivers asunder.

†**b.** A terrace or raised platform. *Obs.*

1533 in W. H. St. John Hope *Windsor Castle* (1913) I. 249 The makyng off a new wharff upon the north syde of the said Castell. 1535 *Ibid.* 262 The buttresses made on the bakesyde of the new Wharffe.

c. † The bank of a river (*obs.*); also, a gravel or sandbank.

1602 Shaks. *Ham.* I. v. 33 The fat weede That rots it selfe in ease, on Lethe Wharfe. 1606 — *Ant. & Cl.* II. ii. 218 From the Barge A strange inuisible perfume, hits the sense Of the adiacent Wharfes. 1867 Smyth *Sailor's Word-bk.*, *Wharf*, in hydrography, is a scar, a rocky or gravelly concretion, or frequently a sandbank,..where the tides throw up dangerous ripples and overfalls.

†**d.** A large raft. *Obs. rare.*

1662 J. Bargrave *Pope Alex. VII* (1867) 119 They were brought upon warffs or raffts of many pines and firs.

e. A place raised or otherwise marked out on which stuff is deposited for subsequent removal to another place.

1785 in *Dig. Proc. Crt.-leet Savoy* (1789) 22 For making a dung wharfe or lay stall at the lower end of Fountain Court.

3. *attrib.* and *Comb.*, as *wharf-end, -frontage, -head, -holder, -house, -land, -man, -master, -measure, -property, -side, -stead, -wall*; **wharf-boat**, (*a*) *U.S.* a boat supporting a platform and moored at a bank, used as a wharf; (*b*) a boat employed about a wharf; †**wharf-gelt**, ? an impost levied on shipping for the use of a wharf; **wharf-rat**, (*a*) the common brown rat, *Mus decumanus*, which infests wharfs; (*b*) a man or boy who loafs about wharfs, often with the intention of stealing (*slang*).

1849 Lyell *2nd Visit U. S.* II. 227 In the *wharf-boat..I expected to find a bed for the first night. 1860 Bartlett *Dict. Amer.* s.v., On the Western rivers the height of the water is so variable that a fixed wharf would be useless. In its place is used a rectangular float...It is generally aground on the shore side, and is entered by a plank or movable platform. This is a *wharf-boat*. 1878 *N. Amer. Rev.* CXXVII. 225 She was used as a 'wharf-boat' or store-ship. 1897 Kipling *Capt. Cour.* iv. 95 Her rigging flew knotted and tangled like weed at a *wharf-end. *Ibid.* x. 216 Statistics of boats, gear, *wharf-frontage, capital invested,..and profits. 1505 *Cal. Pat. Rolls Hen. VII*, 404 [Without paying any] sandegelt, *wharfgelt. 1800 *Asiat. Ann. Reg., Chron.* 35/1 All goods whatsoever, that are not disembarked at the *Wharf Head. 1883 *Law Rep.* 11 Q. B. Div. 486 Whether the persons for whom the weighing was done were *wharfholders or not. 1698 in *Hertford Sess. Rolls* (1905) I. 428 [Encroaching upon the river Lea] by building a *wharfe house..thereon. 1895 *Daily Tel.* 5 Aug. 5/3 Converting a piece of *wharfland on the Isle of Dogs into a public pleasure-ground. 1848 Mill *Pol. Econ.* I. ii. § 6 Bargemen, sailors, *wharfmen. a1628 Raleigh in *Rem.* (1661) 179 From any Port Town..the Bridge-master or the *Wharfmaster..will deliver a true Note of the number of Lasts of Herrings brought to their Wharfes. 1821 *Acc. Peculat. Coal Trade* 13 All coals sent out, *wharf measure. 1877 Burroughs *Taxation* 140 The whole *wharf property ..was liable to be taxed. 1860 Bartlett *Dict. Amer.*, **Wharf-Rats*. 1. Rats that inhabit wharves. 2. Thieves that infest the wharves of seaport towns. 1863 Hawthorne *Our Old Home, Boston* I. 269 Lolling on long-boats,..as sailors and old wharf-rats are accustomed to do. 1842 Dickens *Amer. Notes* xi, A crowd of high-pressure steam-boats, clustered together by a *wharf-side. 1891 Meredith *One of our Conq.* xxv, A hanged heavy look, suggestive of a wharfside crane. 1828 *Craven Gloss.*, **Wharf-stead*, a ford in a river. In Ray, it is *warstead*, q.d. waterstead. 1831–3 in *Encycl. Metrop.* (1845) VIII. 604/1 A *wharf wall ..at the East end of His Majesty's dock-yard, Woolwich.

†**Wharf**, *sb.*2 *Obs.* [OE. *hwearf* (poet., alliterating on w), corresp. to OS. *hwarf* crowd, MLG. *warf, werf* circle, assembly sitting in a circle, court of justice, OHG. *warb* (MHG. *warp, warf*): cf. prec.] A crowd, assembly.

In the first quot. from Laȝamon's *Brut* perh. = change (OE. *hwearf*: cf. OFris. *hwarf, werf*, OHG. *warba*, MHG. *warbe* (with numerals) time(s, (M)LG. *werf, warf*, (-*ve*) turn, time; cf. Wharve *v.*).

a1000 *Guthlac* 234 Beorg ymbstodan hwearfum wræcmæcgas. c1205 Lay. 2070 Þus is þis eitlond igon from honde to hond, þet alle þa burhȝes þe Brutus iwrohte..beoð swiðe afelled þurh warf of þon folke. *Ibid.* 17485 Þider com Aurilie..& al his folc mid him. Whiten-sunendæie he þer warf makede [Wace *Altre gent assés assambla Feste tint*].

Wharf (hwǫɹf), *v.* Also 7 **warfe.** [f. Wharf *sb.*1]

†**1.** *trans.* To strengthen or make firm (e.g. the bank of a river) with a wall of timber or stone. *Obs.*

1569 *Surrey & Kent Sewers Comm.* (1909) 6 To..cope and wharfe xxiiijte roddes of the walle. 1615 *Crt.-roll of Gt. Waltham Manor, Essex* (MS.), Preceptum est.. sufficienter cumulare (Anglicè, to wharfe) fossatum suum. 1618 in F. Devon *Issues Exch.* (1836) 335 For three bridges to go over the sewers, and for wharfing the sides with strong timber. 1674 Josselyn *Two Voy. New-Eng.* 162 The houses are for the most part raised on the Sea-banks and wharfed out with great industry and cost. a1706 Evelyn *Diary* 6 Mar. 1667, I proposed to my Lo. Chancellor Monsieur Kiviet's undertaking to warfe the whole river of Thames, or Key, from the Temple to the Tower ..with brick. 1724 [see Wharfing 2]. 1793 R. Mylne *Rep. Thames* 37 The Road ought to be raised and wharfed. *transf.* 1623 Wither *Brit. Rememb.* I. 192 Is this the Iland, which our love..Did wharfe about (within her watry Dike) With mighty Rocks, and Cliffes?

2. To bring to shore or discharge at a wharf.

1629 Wadsworth *Pilgr.* viii. 87 A Master of an English Barke..who had wharft ouer a hundred French. 1694 *Lond. Gaz.* No. 3024/4 Goods will be Wharfed here at easier Rates than heretofore. 1798 in *Spirit Publ. Jrnls.* (1799) II. 351 Every species of property (whether landed, funded, wharfed, warehoused, or shipped). 1803 W. Tatham *Rep. Imped. Thames* 73 Nor would it be a very difficult matter to dock or wharf the whole of their commerce.

3. To accommodate (vessels) at a wharf.

1902 *Times* 1 Nov. 5/6 A large stone basin, capable of wharfing a dozen battleships of the first class.

4. *intr.* To come to wharf.

1891 *Voice* (N.Y.) 1 Jan., When the Mayflower wharfed at Plymouth Rock. 1901 *Daily Chron.* 4 June 3/4 The Royal Squadron wharfed..at half-past seven.

Wharfage (hwǭ·ɹfėdʒ). Also [3 **wheruagium**, 4 **querfage, werphagium**], 5, 8 **wharffage**, 6 **warfeage**, 8 **warf(f)age.** [f. Wharf *sb.*1 + -age.]

1. The provision of or accommodation at a wharf; the stowage of goods on, or loading or unloading at, a wharf.

[1295 *Memoranda K. R.* 23 & 24 Edw. I (P.R.O.), In cariagio dicte lane..vsque London..cum wharuagio et portagio eiusdem. 1376 *Rolls of Parlt.* II. 351/1 Ore sont il constreintz de paier pur Messuage de chescune Sarp' ob. Et un autre ob. pur Querfage. 1395 *Compotus Will. Chert custodis collegii Cantuar. Oxon.* (1881) 28 Item pro werphagio eiusdem meremii capelle) iiijs. iiijd.] 1469–71 *Stonor Papers* (Camden) I. 106 Paid..for C and vj li. of Iren, iiij. s. v. d, for the wharfage, j d., for bringyng of the seid stuffe to Derteford, vj. d. a1552 Leland *Itin.* (1768) II. 29 There is great Warfeage of Timbre and fier Wood on the West Ende of the Bridge. c1640 J. Smyth *Lives Berkeleys* (1883) I. 341 Renting out the Toll or profit of the wharfage. 1687–8 in Willis & Clark *Cambridge* (1886) II. 545 Expences for sawing, carriage, and wharfage of Cedar. 1795 J. Phillips *Hist. Inland Nav.* Addenda 109 For wharfage exceeding six months, to make a reasonable recompence. 1848 Mill *Pol. Econ.* III. v. § 3 The rents of wharfage, dock and harbour room. 1885 *Law Times* LXXIX. 189/2 Duties for defraying the expenses of pilotage, wharfage, lighthouses, and lights and buoys.

2. The charge or dues exacted for the use of a wharf.

1535 *Act 27 Hen. VIII*, c. 26 § 23 Lordes Marches..shall have within..their said Lordeshipps.. wreke de mere, wharfage and customes of Strangers. 1598 Hakluyt *Voy.* I. 135 All marchants..may come into our kingdome..without paying wharfage, pontage, or pannage. c1683 *Citizens Loss* in Somers *Tracts* (1748) I. 180 Wharfage, with Power to distrain for the same. 1715 *Lond. Gaz.* No. 5387/3 The Wharfage, Duties, and Profits arising..by and out of Billingsgate-Dock. 1795 J. Phillips *Hist. Inland Nav.* Addenda 105 Wharfage for more than twenty-four hours, to be a reasonable allowance. 1894 *Times* 25 Aug. 5/4 The company is gradually issuing through rates, inclusive of Ship Canal toll and wharfage.

3. Wharfs collectively; wharf accommodation.

1807 *Ann. Reg., Chron.* 406 The company assembled on the insular wharfage. 1836 Jesse *Angler's Rambles* 295 The little secluded harbour, with its small planked wharfage. 1848 Mill *Pol. Econ.* I. i. § 4 The wharfage or harbour-room. 1899 *Westm. Gaz.* 26 Sept. 9/1 At the terminus of the railway the Dominion Government is erecting complete wharfages to make the harbour suitable for oil vessels.

4. *attrib.*

1714 Lady G. Baillie *Househ. Bk.* (S.H.S.) 30 For warfage porters carts to the Lodging etc., 1. 9. 1..For warfage bale and cariing to the Lodgine, o. 2. 6. 1862 G. T. Lloyd *33 Yrs. Tasmania* xvi. 415 Wharfage accommodation. 1867 Smyth *Sailor's Word-bk.*, *Wharfage dues*, the dues for landing or shipping goods at a wharf; customs charges in particular... Wharfage charges are demanded even from a ship of war!

Wharfe (hwǭɹf). Short for **Wharfedale** (*machine*): see quots.

1888 Jacobi *Printers' Vocab.*, *Wharfedale machine*, a cylindrical machine manufactured in Yorkshire and called after the place of that name. *Wharfe*, short term for the Wharfedale printing machine. 1890 W. J. Gordon *Foundry* 210 The Wharfedales, Bremners, and other machines on which is printed most illustrated work. 1901 *Daily Chron.* 3 Dec. 9/7 Printer's Minder, 31, seeks Situation; Wharfes, platens, gas engine.

Wharfing (hwǭ·ɹfiŋ). [f. Wharf *sb.*1 + -ing 1]

†**1.** = Wharfage 1, 2. *Obs. rare.*

1466–7 *Mann. & Househ. Exp.* (Roxb.) 392 Item, fore warffenge at the keye, ob.

2. A structure in the form of a wharf; materials of which a wharf is constructed; the facing of sea-walls, etc. by planks secured by ties.

1691 T. H[ale] *Acc. New Invent.* p. lxxviii, To go into the Thames..will cost a Man 300 l. with the slighter sort of Wharfing. a1700 Evelyn *Sylva* I. ii. (1776) 49 A..strong stone-wall, which was a kind of wharfing against a river running by it. 1724 De Foe *Tour Gt. Brit.* I. III. 87 The Mill Tayl, or Floor for the Water below the Wheels is Wharft up on either Side with Stone,..at the End of this Wharfing is a Grating of Wood. 1791 R. Mylne *2nd Rep. Thames* 7 An old Wharfing, bent over into the Stream, which formerly supported a Parish Road along the Shore. 1809 *Naval Chron.* XXIII. 81 The destruction of the wharfing of the basin. 1897 *Jrnl. R. Agric. Soc.* Dec. 612 Wharfing along the sides with short posts and rough boards.

Wharfinger (hwǭ·ɹfindʒəɹ). Also 8 **wharfenger.** [app. for earlier **wharfager* (f. Wharfage + -er 1), like *harbinger, passenger, messenger* for earlier *harbeger, passager, messager*.] An owner or keeper of a wharf.

1552–3 *Act 7 Edw. VI*, c. 7 § 3 No person..shall buy any suche Wood Coles or Fuell but onelye suche as will..consume the same,..without fraude or covine, or Wharfingers or Bargemen. 1642 *Two Orders of Lds. & Comm.* 3 Dec. 2 No Carrier, Waggoner, Watchman, Wharfinger. 1704 *Lond. Gaz.* No. 4024/4 Francis Haslewood, of London, Cornfactor, and Wharfenger. 1761 *Ann. Reg., Chron.* 119 Whether the wharfingers are accountable for the thefts committed on board their lighters. 1858 Redfield *Law Railways* xvi. § 7. 250 *note*, A delivery to the wharfinger without notice, if warranted by the usage of the place, was sufficient. 1911 Sir H. Craik *Life Clarendon* I. ii. 42 Their goods were thus delayed at the caprice of the wharfinger.

Wharfless (hwǭ·ɹflės), *a.* [f. Wharf *sb.*1 + -less.] Having no wharf.

1822 W. Taylor in *Monthly Rev.* XCVII. 35 Wharfless shores. 1906 *Daily Chron.* 10 Mar. 1/7 Exercises in embarkation and disembarkation on a wharfless beach.

Wharl (hwāɹl), *v.* Also 5 **warl-.** [Imitative.] *intr.* To pronounce the letter *r* with a burr or guttural sound; = Burr *v.*3 1. Hence **Wharl** *sb.* = Burr *sb.*6, **Wha·rler, Wha·rling** *vbl. sb.*

c1440 *Promp. Parv.* 37/2 Blaffoorde or warlare, *traulus*. (P. *Traulus peccat in R, peccat in S sidunus.*) *Ibid.* 523/2 Wha[r]lare, in speche. 1610 Holland *Camden's Brit.* I. 517 As for Carleton, as one would say, the husbandmens towne,..wherein..all in maner that are borne,..have an ilfavoured, untunable, and harsh maner of speech, fetching their words with very much adoe deepe from out of the throat, with a certaine kind of wharling. 1634 W. Wood *New Eng. Prosp.* II. xviii. 92 The Tarrenteens, whose Tongues runne so much upon *R*, that they wharle much in pronunciation. 1656 Duch. Newc. *Natures Pict.* etc. 376 Not stuttering, nor wharling in the throat, or speaking through the Nose. 1661 Childrey *Brit. Baconica* 109, I have heard from some that were this Country [Leicestershire] men, that it is Breson that is the Town of the Wharlers, and not Carleton. 1769 *De Foe's Tour Gt. Brit.* (ed. 7) III. 251 The Northumberland R, or Wharle. 1825 Jamieson.

Wharl(e: see Quarrel *sb.* 1, 2, Whorl.

Wharp, erron. form of Warp *sb.* (sense 6).

Wharre, wharry, Wharrel, var. Whare, Quarrel *sb.*2, quarry.

Wharrow (hwæ·rou). Also 6 **whar(r)owe, wherrow(e, 9 worra.** [By-form of Wharve *sb.*] = Wharve *sb. Obs.* exc. *dial.* (= grooved pulley in spinning-wheel). Also attrib. *wharrow-spindle* (a heraldic bearing).

[c1475 *Pict. Voc.* in Wr.-Wülcker 794/18 *Hoc vertebrum*, a aworowylle.] 1519 Horman *Vulg.* 149 b, I wotte nat where is my spyndel with the wharowe. a1529 Skelton *E. Rummyng* 298 Theyr wharrowe, Theyr rybskyn and theyr spyndell. 1578 Lyte *Dodoens* VI. xxix. 693 The fruite whiche is large, and almost fashioned lyke to a wherrowe or buckler. 1610 Guillim *Heraldry* IV. vii. 204 The round Ball at the lower end serueth to the fast twisting of the threed, and is called a Wharrow: and thereof this is called a Wharrow Spindle. 1716 S. Kent *Gram. Her.* s.v. *Trefuses of Cornwall*, A Chevron between three Wharrow Spindles Sable. 1825 Jennings *Obs. Dial. W. Eng.* 84 The spill and worra are attached to the common spinning-wheel. c1828 Berry *Encycl. Her.* I. Gloss., *Wharrow-Spindle* is represented in heraldry with a hook at the end, to spin with a distaff.

Wharry, dial. f. Quarry *sb.*2

Whart(e, Wharter, Whartfull: see Quart, Thwart, Wart, Quarter, Quartful *a.*

Wharth, obs. var. Warth.

c1450 *St. Cuthbert* (Surtees) 5717 How anes at eland at full se, On þe wharth sodanly, A way wex dry. *Ibid.* 5797–9.

Whartonian (hwǭɹtōu·niăn), *a. Anat.* Applied to certain structures discovered or described by Thomas Wharton, English anatomist (1610–73), as *Whartonian* (also *Wharton's*) *duct, gelatine* (*jelly*): see quots.

1840 W. J. E. Wilson *Anat. Vade M.* 474 The excretory duct (Wharton's) of the submaxillary gland commences upon the papilla, by the side of the frænum linguæ. 1857 Bullock tr. *Cazeaux' Midwifery* 209 These vessels are surrounded by a gelatinous substance called Wharton's gelatine. 1860 Mayne *Expos. Lex.*, Whartonian Duct. 1874 C. H. Jones & Siev. *Path. Anat.* (ed. 2) 137 The Whartonian jelly of the umbilical cord.

Wharve (hwǭɹv), *sb.* Forms: 1 **hweorfa, 5–7 wherve, (5, 7, 9 warve, 9 warf), 9 wharve.** [OE. *hweorfa* = OHG. *werbo, werfo* wk. masc., *werbâ* wk. fem. rotating object, whirl, vortex :— **χwerbon*, f. *χwerb-*, as in OE. *hweorfan*, Goth. *hwairban* (see next).] The whorl of a spindle.

c1000 *Sax. Leechd.* II. 310 Wið ceoc adle, nim þone hweorfan þe wif mid spinnað. 14.. *Lat.-Eng. Voc.* in Wr.-Wülcker 618/46 *Verticrum*, a wherve, or a reele. 14.. *Metr. Voc.* ibid. 627 Colus cum fuso uertebrum [*glossed* warve, *misprinted* warbe] filum, alabrumque. 1538 Elyot, *Spondilus*, a wherue, whyche is a rounde thynge of stone, or wodde, or leadde, put on a spyndell to make it runne rounde. 1582 Stanyhurst *Æneis*, etc. 95 Three wheru's [*orig.* *radios*] fyerd glystring, with Soutwynds rufflered huffling. 1590 Barrough *Meth. Phisick* v. xxiv. (1596) 339 He did lay and bind vnto Ganglium, a thick round peece of lead like vnto a wherue. 1601 Holland *Pliny* xi. xxiv. I. 323 So fine..a thread she [*sc.* the spider] spinnes, hanging thereunto her selfe, and using the weight of her owne bodie in stead of a wherve. 1688 Holme *Armoury* III. xxi. (Roxb.) 266/2 The Warve or small Pullas. a1693 Urquhart's *Rabelais* III. xxviii. 237 Wouldst thou..blunt the Spindles, joynt the Wherves, slander the Spinning Quills,..of the weer'd Sister Parques? 1805 in *Abridgm. Specif. Patents Spinning* (1866) 125 The making the haft or warf at times to shift or remove from off the spindle. 1831 *Ibid.* 236 The warve is driven by a band passing round it and round the spindle drum. 1884 W.S.B. McLaren *Spinning* (ed. 2) 171 The wharve, *B*, together with sliding tube, *c*, runs loosely on the spindle and carries the bobbin.

†**Wharve**, *v. Obs.* Forms: 1 **hwearfian, hweorfan, hwierfan, hwerfan, hwyrfan, 2 hwærfan, 3 whærfen, whæruen, weruen, hwarefen, warfen, (**Orm.**) wharrfenn.** [Three (for the most part) synonymous vbs. existed in OE.: (1) *hweorfan* = OFris. *hwerva* to turn, OS. *hwerban* to turn, change (MLG. *werven* to be active or busy, gain, obtain), OHG. *hwerban, hwerfan* (MHG. *werben, werfen*) to be active, turn, return, set or be in motion, ON. *hverfa* to turn, return, disappear, Goth. *hwairban* to go; (2) *hwearfian* = OS. *hwarbôn*, OHG. *warbôn, warpôn* to wander, proceed, ON. *hvarfa* to turn round, wander, Goth. *hwarbôn*; (3) *hwierfan, hwirfan*, etc. = OS. *gihwerbian* to turn, change, OHG. *hwarban, hwerban* (MHG. *werben*) to turn, roll, return, *giwerben* to turn, divert, ON. *hverfa* to cause to turn: all f. *χwerb-* : *χwarb-* to turn (cf. prec. and Wharf *sbs.*1 and 2).]

1. *trans.* To change, turn. Cf. Blindwharved.

c897 Ælfred *Gregory's Past. C.* xxxvi. 256 He hwierfde his stemne nalles his mod. c1200 Ormin 13289 & forrþi wass he wurrþ þatt Crist Hiss name hinm shollde wharrfenn. *Ibid.* 14137 Forr þatt he wollde..þurrh þe ȝife off Haliȝ Gast Uss wharrfenn all fra sinne. c1200 *Trin. Coll. Hom.* 173 Gief hie wunienge hwarefeð, hie turneð fram iuele to werse. c1205 Lay. 6319 Alfred..wharfde hire nome on his dæȝe and cleopede heo Mærcene laȝe. *Ibid.* 30738 Wið him warfte Brien al his iweden. [13.. *Gaw. & Gr. Knt.* 2220 He ruschedon þat rurde,..& wyth quettyng a-wharf, er he wolde lyȝt.]

2. *intr.* To turn, revolve.

c888 Ælfred *Boeth.* xxxix. § 3 Þære eaxe þe eall þes rodor on hwerfð. c1200 Ormin 3641 All þiss middellærdess þing Aȝȝ turrneþþ her & wharrfeþþ..swa summ þe wheol.

3. To roam, wander.

c890 Wærferth tr. *Gregory's Dial.* IV. lix. (1900) 347 Swa oft swa he wæs hwearfiende mid þam ilcan scipe. c1200 *Trin. Coll. Hom.* 87 He wandrede wide weruende longe sechende him. c1205 Lay. 31680 Eiðer freten oðer, swa hund deð his broðer, and leten heore whelpes whæruen heom bi-sides elc oðer quelle.

4. To proceed, turn out, happen.

c888 Ælfred *Boeth.* iv, Ȝif seo wyrd swa hweorfan mot on yfelra manna gewill. c1200 Ormin 8420 Swa shall itt tanne wharrfenn Bitwenenn Cristess hallȝhe þeod & deofless laþe genge.

Hence †**Wharfed** (*wherrfedd, warrfedd*) *ppl. a.*, perverse; whence †**Wha·rfedlaik**, perversity, error.

c1200 Ormin 9721 Forr i þatt wherrfedd follc hemm hallt Forr gode & forr rihhtwise. *Ibid.* 9825 & tatt wass mikell wherrfeddleȝȝc þatt dide hemm swa to wenenn.

Wharve(s: see Wharf *sb.*1

Whas, obs. f. *was*, pa. t. of Be, Wash *v.*

Whasche, etc.: see Wash *v.*

Whas(e: see Whose, Whoso.

Whasp(e, obs. ff. Wasp *sb.*

What (hwǫt), *pron.*, *a.*1, *adv.*, *conj.*, *int.* (*sb.*) Forms: 1 **hwæt, huæt, huæd, 1–4 hwet, 2–4 hwat, wet, 2–5 wat, 3 (Orm.) watt, whæt, wæt, (waht, wæht, whæht, weht, ȝwat), 3–4 whet, (4 huet, wad), 3 (Orm.), 5 whatt, 3–6 whate, (5 whad, wath), 5–6 whatte, (9 dial. or vulgar wot), 3– what; 3–5 north. quat, (3 quuat, 4–5 quatt, qwat, 5 qhat), 4–8 Sc. quhat.** [OE. *hwæt* = OFris. *hwet, wet, haet, hat*, etc. (Fris. *wæt, wat, wut, haet*, etc.), OS. *huat*, (M)LG., (M)Du. *wat*, OHG. *hwaz, waz* (MHG. *waz*, G.

Whereinne. *Obs.* [f. WHERE + INNE.]

Whereinsoever, *adv.* Now *formal* or *arch.* [f. WHEREIN + SOEVER.] In whatever matter, respect, etc.

Whereintill, *adv.* *Sc. Obs.* In 6-7 quha(i)r-. [f. WHERE + INTILL.]

Whereinto. [f. WHERE + INTO.]

Whereness (hwēɹ·nĕs). [f. WHERE + -NESS.]

Whereof (hwĕɹov). Now *formal* or *arch.* [f. WHERE 15 + OF *prep.* Cf. (M)Sw. *hwaruf*, Du. *waarvan*.]

Whereon (hwĕɹon). *adv.* [f. WHERE 15 + ON *prep.* Cf. Du. *waaraan*, G. *woran*.]

Whereout (hwĕɹaut), *adv.* *arch.* [f. WHERE 15 + OUT *adv.* Cf. Du. *waaruit*, G. *woraus*.]

Whereover, *adv.* *rare.* [f. WHERE + OVER.]

Whereround: see WHERE 15.

Whereso (hwĕɹsō·), *adv.* *arch.* [ME. *hwar-swa*, *hwar-se*, repr. OE. *hwǣr swā*; see WHERE and So 41. Cf. WHERESOEVER.]

Wheresoever, *conj. Obs. exc. dial.* [f. WHERE + SOEVER.]

Wheresome, *adv. dial.* and *Obs.* [f. WHERE + SOME.]

Wherethorough. *Obs.* [f. WHERE 15 + THOROUGH *prep.*]

Wherethrough (hwĕɹθru·). Now *formal* or *arch.* [f. WHERE 15 + THROUGH *prep.*]

Wheretill (hwĕɹti·l), *adv.* [f. WHERE 15 + TILL *prep.* Cf. (M)Sw. *hvartill*.]

Whereto (hwĕɹtū·). Now *formal* or *arch.* [f. WHERE 15 + To *prep.* Cf. Du. *waartoe*.]

Wheretoever.

Whereunder (hwĕɹ·ndaɹ), *adv.* *arch.* Cf. Du. *waaronder*.

Whereunto (hwĕɹʌntū·, -ʌ·ntu), *adv.* Now *formal* or *arch.* [f. WHERE 15 + UNTO.]

Whereuntill (hwĕɹʌnti·l), *adv.* *dial.* [f. WHERE + UNTILL.]

Whereupon (hwĕɹʌpon·), *adv.* (*conj.*) *rare.* [f. WHERE 15 + UPON.]

Wherever (hwĕɹe·vaɹ), *adv.*, *conj.*

Wherewith (hwĕɹwi·θ), *adv.* [f. WHERE 15 + WITH *prep.*]

Wherewithal (hwĕɹwiðǭ·l), *adv.*, *sb.*

Wherret (hwĕ·rĕt), *sb.* Now *dial.*

Wherret (hwĕ·rĕt), *v.* Now *rare.*

Wherrit (hwe·rit).

Wherrow: var. WHARROW.

Wherry (hwe·ri), *sb.*

Whey. The whey is derived by the veters into the bladder...

Wheyey (hwē·i), a. Forms: 6 wheye, 6-7 wheyey, -yneye, 8 wheyie, wheyy, 7- wheyey. [f. WHEY sb. + -Y¹.] Of the nature of whey; consisting of, containing, or resembling whey.

A. Illustration of Forms.
1. I twela, huele, hwele, huele, huoele, 3 hwelk, 4-5 whulke, 5 whilke, 4-6 whech, quoche, (qheche); 3 qwel, 4 quelk.

Wheyish, a. Also 6 whaish, 6-7 whayish(e. [f. WHEY sb. + -ISH¹.] Having the nature or quality of whey; like or resembling whey in consistence, colour, or other quality; watery, thin; palish.

Wheyl, obs. forms of WHEEL.

Whi, var. WHEY, WHY, WHI.

Whib(b)le, etc., obs. variants of QUIBBLE, etc.

Whin. Of doubtful origin and meaning...

Whicche, see WHICH, WITCH.

Which (hwitf), a. and pron. Forms: see C.

B. Signification.

I. Interrogative and allied uses.

†Whey, north. f. QUEY, heifer, WAY int.

Which (ch)e, var. WHICH Obs., chest.

Whichever, (hwitferaɪ), a. and pron. [Orig. two words, WHICH and EVER adv. B 5.]

Whider, Whie, Whieale, whiel, Whiet, Whieu, obs. forms of WHITHER, QUEY.

Whiff (hwif), sb.¹ Also 6-7 whiffe, 8-9 whif.

Whimsically, *adv.* [f. WHIMSICAL + -LY.] In a whimsical manner; capriciously; oddly, fantastically.

Whimsicalness. [f. prec. adj. + -NESS.] The quality of being whimsical; whimsicality.

Whimsy, whimsey, *sb.* (a.) Forms: 7 whim-, whimsie, whimsey, 8-whimsy, whimzy. [Of obscure origin. See WHIM-WHAM.]

†Whimsy-whamsy. [f. WHIM after next.] — next 2.

Whim-wham, *sb.* (Whimsie.) Also 6-7 whym wham, 7 whimwhom, 8-9 whimwam, 9 wimwam, whim-, whim-wham. [A reduplication with vowel-variation, like *fim-fam*, *jim-jam*, *trim-tram*, all of which are similarly applied to trivial or frivolous things.]

Whin, *sb.* [Of obscure origin.]

Whin-bush. Forms: see WHIN and BUSH. Also 6 wyn- 7 wine. A furze-bush.

Whinberry. see WHINBERRY.

Whinchat (hwin'tʃæt). [f. WHIN + CHAT.] A small European bird, *Pratincola rubetra*, closely allied to the stonechat.

Whindle (hwin'd'l), v. Obs. exc. dial. + -LE.] to Whine, whimper. Hence **Whin'dling** *vbl. sb.*

Whine (hwain), *sb.* [f. WHINE v.] An act of whining; a low, somewhat shrill protracted cry, usually expressive of pain or distress.

Whiner. One who or that which whines.

Whing (hwiŋ), *int.* and *sb.* [Imitative.] A word expressing a high-pitched ringing sound.

Whinge (hwindʒ), v. Sc. and *north. dial.* Forms: [Onomatopœic; cf. WHINGE.]

Whine, *obs. form of* WINE.

Whinge (hwindʒ), v. Sc. and *north. dial.*

Whing'ing *vbl. sb.* and *ppl. a.*

Whining, *ppl. a.* [f. as prec. + -ING 2.]

Whinny-whanny. Obs. [Cf. WHIM-WHAM, WHIMSY-WHAMSY.] A trivial thing, trifle.

Whinner, v. *Obs. exc. dial.* [Frequentative of WHINE v. : see -ER 5.] *intr.* To whine (feebly). Hence **Whin'nering** *vbl. sb.* and *ppl. a.*; **Whin'nery**, a feeble whine.

Whinnock (hwin'nɒk), v. *dial.* to whine, snivel, whinnock.

Whinnock, *sb.* dial. Also 9 whinook, win-, cuinnoog, W.; cuinnog. A pail.

Whin'nock, dial. Also 9 whinook, win-.

Whinny (hwin'i), v. [f. WHIN 1 + -Y 1.] An act of whinnying; a (low or gentle) neigh, or similar sound.

Whinny, *ppl. a.* 1 [f. WHIN 1 + -Y 1.] Covered or abounding with whins or furze-bushes.

Whinny (hwin'i), v. [f. WHIN 1 + -Y 1.] Of the nature of or containing whin or whinstone.

Whinstone, obs. form of WINE. A name for various very hard dark-coloured rocks or stones, as greenstone, basalt, chert, or quartzose sandstone.

Whip (hwip), *sb.* Forms: 3-4 whippe, quippe, 4-7 whippe, 5-6 wyppe, whyppe, whyp, 7- whippe, etc. [Of obscure origin.] An instrument for flogging or beating.

Whip, *sb.2* Forms: see prec. Pa. t. and pple. whipped (hwipt).

Whippy (hwi'pi), a.

Whip-saw (hwi'pɑ̈), sb.

Whippy, -adder(y); see WHIPPET-DERRY.

Whipsnip (hwi'pjp), nonce-wd.

Whip-snake.

Whip-stitch. Needlework.

Whip-stitch (hwi'pstit∫), sb. (adv.)

Whip-stitch. Needlework.

Whipstock (hwi'pstƆk), sb. [STOCK sb. 1]

Whipstaff (hwi'pstɑf). [STAFF sb.]

†Whipstalk, dial. = WHIPSTOCK 1.

†Whipstart. Obs. rare⁻¹. [ʔf WHIP v. D. UPSTART.]

Whipster (hwi'pstər).

Whipstress (hwi'pstrĕs). rare⁻¹.

Whippy-derry. Also whipsider(y), whip-sey-derry.

Whiptail (hwi'ptĕl). [WHIP sb. 1 + TAIL]

Whip-tom-kelly.

Whir, sb. and v.: see WHIRR.

Whirohe, obs. var. WORE v.

Whirken, obs. f. QUIRKEN v., to suffocate.

Whirl (hwə:l), sb.¹ Forms: 5 qwherel, qwerle, wherwille, Sc. quhirl(l, 6 whirell(l, wherle, whyrle, whirroll, 6-7 whurle, 6-8 whirle, 7 werrell, whurl, 6- whirl. [Partly a. MLG., MDu. wervel or ON. hvirfill: see WHIRL v.], partly f. the verb itself.]

I. Denoting a material object.

Whirl (hwə:l), v. Forms: 3 zwirle, 4 werel, 4-6 whyrle, 4-7 whirle, 5 quirle, 6 whyrl, Sc. quherle, quhirl(l)e, whirlo, 6-7 wherwhirl, whirl. [prob. a. ON. hvirfla to turn about, whirl: see WHIRL sb. 1]

Whirl-about. Also whirl-a-bout.

Whirl-bone (hwə:l-bōn). Obs. or dial. Forms: 4-8 whirlebone, 5 wherylbone, 6 whyrlbone, 6-7 wheel-, whirl-, whorle-, whorlebone, 6-8 whirl-bone, 6 whorlebone.

Whirled (hwə:ld). a. = WHORLED.

Whirler (hwə:lər).

Whirly¹ (hwə:li), a. [WHIRL v. + -Y¹.]

†Whirlbat, whirlbatt. β. 7-8 whirl(e)bat. [Alteration of HURLBAT by substitution of WHIRL for the first element.]

Whirly², a.

Whirl-blast.

Whirley. Whirlicote. Obs. exc. Hist. Forms: 5 whirlecole, whirlecote, whorlecole, 8-9 whirlicote.

Whirley. Whirlicote.

Whirligig (hwə:ligig). Forms: 5 whyrlegyge, 6 whirligig, 6-7 whyrligig, 7 whirligig, 6-7 whirle-gig, 6 whirlegig(ge, 7 whirligige, 6 whirlie-gig(e, whirlie-gig, (6 whirligig, 9 whirligig.

Whirling, ppl. a. [f. WHIRL v. + -ING²]

Whirling, vbl. sb. [f. as prec. + -ING¹.] The action of the verb WHIRL.

Whirlpool (hwə:lpūl). Also 6 whrpole, whoorlpool, etc. [WHIRL + POOL sb.]

Whirl-puff. Obs. exc. dial. (also whirli-puff).

†Whirlwater. *Obs.* [f. WHIRL- + WATER *sb.*] A waterspout.

Whirling (hwə̄·lɪŋ), *vbl. sb.* [-ING¹.] 4.

Whirling, *ppl. a.* [-ING².]

Whirl-worm (hwə̄·lwə̄m). Also 7 *whyrl-.*

Whirly, *sb.*, or dial. *var.* in comb.

Whirry, *sb.* Forms: 5 *whirie.*

Whirra, -oo, Whirret: see WIRRA, WHERRET.

Whirrick, variant of WHERRET.

Whirring (hwə̄·rɪŋ), *vbl. sb.* [f. WHIRR v. + -ING¹.]

Whirring, *ppl. a.*

Whirry, *sb.* Forms: 5 *whirry.*

Whirr, whir (hwə̄r), *sb.* Forms: 5, 6 *qwirre.*

Whirl-wind-cloud.

Whirr, whir (hwə̄r), *v.*, (*adv., int.*) Forms: 5 6 *whirre.*

Whirring, *ppl. a.*

Whirry, *v. Obs.* In 7 *whyrry, whurrie.* [f. *whirr* v.]

Whirl, Whirrul, obs. ff. WHERRET, WHERLE, WHIRL.

Quiris [*v. var.* whirrs] furth all in quite. 1523 DOUGLAS

Whirry, obs. form of WHERRY.

Whirtle, variant of WORTLE.

Whirtud, obs. Sc. form of WHIRL *sb.*¹

Whish (hwɪʃ), *int.* [Imitative.] A soft sibilant sound, as that of something moving rapidly through the air or over the surface of water.

Whish, a² *Obs. exc. dial.* [Cf. WHIST *sb.*² and WHIST², Hushed, silent:— WHIST *a.*², WHIST¹, WHIST *int.*¹]

Whish, a² (*dial.*): see WISHT.

Whish, v¹. Now *dial.* Also 6 *whyash.* [f. WHISH *int.*¹ & WHIST², WHISH *v.*²]

Whish, v².

Whisher (hwɪ·ʃəɹ), *sb.* [f. WHISH *v.*² + -ER¹.]

Whish, v³.

Whishin, Whilllin, obs. form of CUSHION.

Whisht, Whist, a.

Whisht (hwɪʃt), *int.* Also 9 *sc.* *wheesht, wheisht.*

Whisht, v.

Whishtly *adv.*, silently, quietly.

Whisk (hwɪsk), *sb.¹* Forms: 4-6 *wysk,* 5-6 *Sc. quhisk, 5-9 wisk, 6 whiske, 7 wiske, 6- whisk.*

Whisk, *sb.²* [Cf. Sw. *visk.* wisp, cluster, pull, tug.—OHG. *wisc* wisp, etc.]

Whisk, *v.* [f. WHISK *sb.*¹]

Whisk, *sb.³* *Obs. or dial.* [Perh. f. WHISK *v.*] The earlier name of the card-game now called *whist.*

Whisk, *v.* [f. WHISK *sb.*¹]

Whisker (hwɪ·skəɹ), *sb.¹* Forms: 5-7 *wisker,* 6 *whysker,* (7 *whisquer*). [f. WHISK v.]

Whiskered (hwɪ·skəɹd), *a.* [f. WHISKER *sb.*¹ + -ED².]

Whiskerando (hwɪskəræ·ndɒ), *sb.* *humorous.* [f. *Whiskerandos,* with ending in imitation of Spanish words.]

Whiskerandos, Whiskerandoed.

Whiskerlike, *a.*

Whisket. var. WHISKET.

Whiskey. see WHISKY.

Whiskified, Whiskeyfied.

Whisking, *vbl. sb.* [-ING¹.] The action of the verb WHISK, in various senses.

Whisking, *ppl. a.* [as *prec.* + -ING².]

† Whiskish, *a.* *Obs. rare⁻¹.* [f. WHISK *sb.*³ or *v.* + -ISH¹.] Lively, frisky.

Whisky, *a.* *rare.* [f. WHISK *v.* + -Y¹.] Light and lively, flighty.

Whisky-bae, whisquy-beath, *var.* USQUEBAUGH.

Whisky, whiskey (hwɪ·skɪ), *sb.* [app. f. WHISKY-BAE, USQUEBAUGH.]

Whisky john.

Whistle, var. WHISTLE.

Whisket.

Whisp, -ler, -ling, obs. ff. WHISTLE, etc.

Whisper (hwɪ·spəɹ), *v.* Forms: 1 *hwisprian,* 3 *wispren,* 3-6 *whispre, 6-7 whis-, 6- whisper.* [OE. *hwisprian* (= Northumb.) — Early Flem. *wisperen* (Kilian), *wispern* (— MLG., MDu.), Sw. *hwiskra,* Da. *hviske,* f. *hwis-.*]

Whisper (hwɪ·spəɹ), *sb.* Forms: 1 *hwisprung,* etc.; 3-6 *whispre; 6- whisper.* [OE. *hwisprung,* etc.]

White fisher. ... Hence **White fisher**, one who catches white fish (sense 1); **White fishery, fishing**, the occupation of catching white fish.

Whitefoot (hwəi·tfut). [Cf. OE. hwít-fót.]

White friar.

Whitehead.

White-headed.

White-heart.

White-hearted.

White-gum.

White-haired.

White horse.

White line, white-line.

White iron.

White lead.

White-lead.

White-lime, white-lime.

White heat.

White-livered.

White-liver.

White-livered.

White monk.

Whitener.

Whiteness.

Whitening (hwəi·tniŋ), vbl. sb. [f. WHITEN v. + -ING[1].]

Whitening, ppl. a.

White-pot, whitepot.

Whitesmith.

Whitester.

White-skin.

White staff.

Whitethroat.

Whitewashed.

White wine.

Whitewash.

White stick.

White-tail.

White-tailed.

White-tawer.

Whitethorn.

Whitethroat (hwəi·tþrout), sb. (a.) (Also with hyphen, and formerly as two words.)

Whitewasher.

White-winged.

White witch.

White water.

Whiteweed.

Whitewood (hwəi·twud). (Also with hyphen, and formerly sometimes as two words.)

Supplement, p. 3873; Corrigenda, p. 4092; Spurious words, p. 4093; Books quoted, p. 4094

Whitewort. rare. Obs.

Whitey: see WHITY.
Whitfieldian, etc.: see WHITEFIELDIAN.
Whitflaw, -flow, obs. var. WHITFLOW.
Whith, obs. form of WHITE, WITH.
Whither, sb.¹ Sc. and dial. Forms: see the vb. [f. WHITHER v.]

Whi ther, sb.² Sc. and dial. Forms: see WHITHER sb.¹

Whither, v. Sc. and dial.

Whither, adv. (sb.) Forms: see the vb.

Whitherso, adv. arch. [ME. hwiderse, repr. OE. swā hwider swā: see So adv. 17 d.]

Whithersoever, adv.

Whitherto, adv.

Whitherward, adv.

Whiting, vbl. sb. Forms: 1 hwit-ing, 5 whytyng, wytyng, whyting, whytyng, 6-7 whiting, 7 whyting, wyting, whytting, 8 whiten, 6- whiting. [f. WHITE v.]

Whiting, sb.¹ Forms: 4 whyt-ynge, whytyng, 4-5 whiting, 5-6 whytyng, -yng, 6 whyting, -inge, 7 whytting, Sc. quhiting, quhittine, 8 whiting; also 4 wittyngis, MLG. wítínc 'aculeja', 'amia 'asellus'; app. f. WHITE a. + -ING³.

Whitish, a. [f. WHITE a. + -ISH¹.]

Whitishness.

Whitleather. Forms: 4 whit-leqtr, 5 whittlether, 5-7 whit(e)lether, 4 whit-leather, — whitleather. [WHITE a. 2 (with normal shortening in Obs.) and LEATHER sb.]

Whitling. (hwit'lŋ). Sc. and north. Also 6 whiddelynge, 9 whitlin. [f. WHITE a. + -LING.]

Whitret, Whitrit, -rat, -rack: see WEASEL, WHITTRET.

Whitster (hwit'stər). Whitester (hwit'təstər).

Whitsour (hwit'sauər). [? f. WHITE a. + SOUR a.] A variety of apple.

Whitster Whittster.

Whitster [f. WHITE a. + -STER.] A woman that whitens the walls (Sewel).

Whitsun (hwit'sən). Forms: 3 witsonne, witsun, 4 wytsun, 4-5 Wysp-, Wyt-, Wyte-, Whypst-, (St.-Vt.), 5-7 Wit-, 5-8 Whitsun, 6 Whitson, Wyt-sone, -sen, Witteson, (Sc. Vitson), 7-8 Whit-sun, 9 dial. Whuson. [See following words.]

Whit Sunday, Whitsunday (hwit' sənd-).

Whitsuntide (hwit'səntəid).

Whittaw (hwit'tǫ). Now only Hist. or dial. Forms: 4 whitawere, white-tawer, whit(e)wyer, 5 whyttawer, 5-7 whitawer, 6-7 whitaw(e)r, 5-, whittawer, 6-8 whit-tawer, 7-8 white-tawer, 9 whittawer, dial. [f. WHITE a. (Cf. the synonymous ME. wíght-wergere, Q. weissgerber.)]

Whitten (hwit'n). Also Sc. weyton, 7 whitting, whitten, 9 witten.

Whitter, v.¹ [Later form of QUITTER v.²]

Whitter, v.² Sc.

Whitter, sb. [Cf. WHITTLE v.¹]

Whitteret, -tck, var. WHITRET.

Whitterish adv.

Whittie-whattie

Whittie-whattie (ʍitiʍɔti), sb. and north. dial. Also 7 whytie whatie, 8 whity-whaty, 9 whittie-whattie, 9 whitty-whatty. [Reduplicated f. WHAT int. pron.] 1 Vague or undecided talk or statement; indecision, shilly-shallying; a frivolous excuse. So Whittie-whattie v. intr., to be undecided, to shilly-shally; also, to speak low or secretly, to mutter, whisper.

Whittle, sb.[1] Obs. Also 6 whittel, whytell(e, whittyll, 6–7 whittle. [Unsually taken to be a fig. use of next (cf. WHET v. 6), but evidence is wanting.] trans. To ply with drink, to make drunk, intoxicate; in pa. pple. excited by drink, drunk, intoxicated. Hence Whittled ppl. a., Whittling vbl. sb.

Whittle, sb.[2] (slang), var. WHIDDLE, to 'peach'.

Whittle, sb.[3] Obs. exc. dial. Also 6 whytel, etc. Now dial. Forms: 1–3 hwitel, 4 whitel, wytel, 5 wytele, 6 whittel. [OE. hwítel, covering.] 1. A white bed-cover (Norw. kvítel blanket), f. hwít WHITE a. + -EL1.] A cloak, mantle, flannel petticoat. †b. A shawl or wrap. c. A baby's woollen napkin or blanket. d. A shawl or wrap.

Whittle, sb.[4] Now dial. Forms: 4 qwytyll, 5 whytel, 6 whittall, 6 quhittil, 7 whittle, 6– whittle. (Variant of THWITTLE (cf. whack, whang).] A knife, esp. one of a large size, as a carving-knife, a butcher's knife, or one carried as a weapon; also, a clasp-knife.

†b. transf. To wear away or reduce by a process analogous to paring : see quota.

2. transf. To cut into slices or shavings from the surface (of a stick, etc.); to dress or pare with a knife; to reduce or sharpen by doing this.

Whitworth (ʍitwəθ), [f. name of the inventor : see below.] In full, Whitworth gun or rifle : a form of rifle (either cannon or small arm) invented by Sir Joseph Whitworth of Manchester (1854), having a hexagonal bore with a rapid twist, and firing an elongated shot. Also attrib.

Whity (ʍai·ti), sb. in quot. as a quasi-proper name : cf. BLACKY sb.[1]

Whity, whity (ʍai·ti), a. (adv.) Also 6 whitty. [f. WHITE a. + -Y[1]] = WHITISH.

Whity-brown, a. (sb.) [WHITE a.] 1. Of a brown colour inclining to white; whitish brown; pale brown : most commonly of paper. As sb. (properly two words) a whitish brown; ellipt. – whity-brown paper.

2. fig. Neither one thing nor another, neutral, undecided, half-and-half.

Whizz, whiz (ʍiz), sb.[1] [f. next.] 1. An act, or the action, of whizzing; a sibilant sound somewhat less shrill than a hiss, and having a trace of musical tone like a buzz; a swift movement producing such a sound.

2. fig. slant. An agreement, 'bargain'.

Whittle (ʍiti), v.[1] Obs. Also 9 whity. Usually whitty-tree — WHITEN-tree.

Whittle (ʍi·tl), v.[2] (slang). Also 9 WHIDDLE, to 'peach.'

Whizz, whiz, v. Also 6 whisse, 7 whisse, 6, 9 dial. whiz. [Echoic. Cf. FIZZ.] 1. intr. To make a sound as of a body rushing through the air (see WHEEZ sb.); (of trees) to rustle; (of a burning or hot object) to hiss, sizzle. Now dial.

b. Of a sound : To be of the nature of a whizz.

2. To move swiftly with or as with such a sound.

Whizz, whiz, int. and adv. An exclamation imitating the sound described under WHIZZ sb. and v.; as adv. – with a whizz.

Whizzer (ʍi·zə), [f. WHIZZ v. + -ER1.] Something that whizzes; spec. a. a toy that makes a whizzing noise when whirled round; b. a machine for drying various articles by the centrifugal force of rapid revolution; a hydro-extractor.

Whizzing (ʍi·ziŋ), vbl. sb. [f. WHIZZ v. + -ING1.] The action or sound denoted by WHIZZ.

Whizzing (ʍi·ziŋ), ppl. a. [f. WHIZZ v. + -ING[2]] That whizzes : see the verb.

Whiz-kile, v. Also 6 whisle, whysle. [f. WHIZ + -LE.] 1 intr. To whiz or whistle.

Whizzy (ʍi·zi), a. rare. [f. WHIZZ sb. or v.] 1 Characterized by whizzing. fig. (slant. dizzy, giddy. Hence Whizzaness, quality or state of whizzing.

WHO

Who (hū), pron. Forms : 1–3 hwa, (1 hua), 2–3 hwo, hwoa, 2–4 wa, (3 wha, wo, wes, wah, hwoo, 3wo), 3–5 hoa, 3 who, whoa, 4–9 (Sc. etc.) quha, whoa, 4–5 (6 dial. wha, wo, (Sc. who, 5 Sc. qua), hoa, 6 hou, (5 Sc. vbs), 6–7 whoe, (7 Sc. whae), 3 quho, (4–5 quo, quod, 4 qwo, 5 quha, quo, quhay), 4–5 quho, (6 Sc. qwha, quhe), wha. [OE. hwá – OFris. hwā, OS. hwe, hwie (MDu., Du. wie), OHG. (h)wer (Ger. wer)]

Whole, a. [OE. hál. From the same stem are also Ofris. oil, QSl. cēlū, whole, OPrus. kailū stas acc. health (f. haïlūstas); Gr. κοîλoς only κoῖλoς (Hesychius)], OS. hēl omen, OHG. (MHG., G.) heil health, (good or bad) fortune, ON. heill omen, fem. good luck, happiness, Goth. hails health (also gahails). The gradation-variant *gailo- is represented by OIr. cēl

WHOLE

Supplement, p. 3873; Corrigenda, p. 4092; Spurious words, p. 4093; Books quoted, p. 4094

Whole cloth. A piece of cloth of the full size as manufactured, as distinguished from a piece that may be cut off or out of it for a garment, etc.

Whole-footed (-fūted), a.

Wholer (hōʻlɛɹ). local. (See quot.)

Wholesale (hōʻlsēl), sb., a., adv.

Wholesome (hōʻlsŭm), a., (sb.)

Wholeness (hōʻlnɛs). [f. WHOLE a. + -NESS.] The quality or condition of being whole.

Wholesomely (hōʻlsŭmli), adv. [f. prec. + -LY.] In a wholesome manner.

Wholesomeness. [f. as prec. + -NESS.] The quality or condition of being wholesome.

Wholewise, (hōl·wīz), *adv. nonce-wd.* [f. WHOLE *sb.* or *a.* + WISE.] As a whole, completely, all at once.

Wholey, wholie, obs. forms of WHOLLY.

Wholl, wholly, var. WALLOP *sb.* and *v.*

Wholly (hōl·li, hōu·li), *adv.* Forms: *a.* HALELY, 3-5 holliche, 4-6 hoolly, holy, holly, 5-6 hooly, 6-8 wholy (4 hoolliche, hollche, holyliche, holyliche, holych, holli, hollicke, holie, whol(1)y, whol(l)ie, 7 wholy, wholi-, wholly-, 7-9 wholely, 6- wholly. [ME. *hol(liche*, *hollīche*, repr. OE. *hāllīce*: see WHOLE *a.* and -LY². For the northern form see HALELY.]

Whom (hūm), *pron.* Forms: *sg.* 1 *masc.* 1–3 hwam, 3–5 wam, 3–5, 8–9 *Sc.* wham, 4–5 whame, whome, 4 (whom 3 quhom, quhome, 4–6 quhome, 4–7 quhom, (3–4 quam, 4 quham, quohm, quhowm, 5 qwhom(e, qwom(e, whom). [Inflexion of WHO.]

Whom, obs. form of WHEN, var. WONE.

Whom, whome, obs. ff. HOME.

Whomsoever (hūmsoēvĕr), *pron.*; also *pcl.* † *literary.* The objective case of WHOSOEVER. (More freq. than WHOMEVER.)

Whon, obs. form of WHEN, var. WONE.

Whon, whone, obs. ff. OON, var. WONE.

Whonde, wa- : see WONDE *v.* Obs.

Whone, whon(d)one, var. WHENNE Obs.

Whoo (hwū), *v.* [Cf. next.]

Whoop (hŭp), *v.* Forms: 4–7 whope, 5 whowpe, 5–6 whoupe, 6 whoup, whup, 6–7 whoope, (6 whoppe, whowpe, 6– whoop. [Parallel with WHOOP *int.*; cf. HOOP *v.*²]

Whoop (hŭp), *int.* and *sb.*² Forms: 4–7 whope, 5 whowpe, 6–7 whoope, 6 whoup, 6– whoop, etc. [Cf. HOOP *int.*¹]

Whooper (hū·pĕr). Also 7 whopper. [f. WHOOP *v.* + -ER¹.]

Whooping (hū·piŋ), *vbl. sb.* [f. WHOOP *v.* + -ING¹.]

Whooping-cough (hū·piŋ,kǫf), now the prevalent spelling of HOOPING-COUGH.

Whoosh (hwụʃ, hweʃ), *v.* [Imitative; the vowel expressing a duller sound than that of WHISH *v.*]

Whore (hōᵊ), *sb.* Forms: 1–6 hore, 3 hoore, 4–6 hoore, houre, 5–6 hour, 6 howr(e, 5– whore. [OE. *hōre*;]

Whore (hōᵊ), *v.* [f. prec. *sb.*]

Whore-, comb. form of WHORE *sb.*

Whoredom (hōᵊdəm), *sb.* Forms: 1–6 hordom, 4–6 hoordom, hordome. [ON. *hórdómr* (Sw. *hordom*) = WHORE *sb.* + -DOM.]

Supplement, p. 3873; Corrigenda, p. 4092; Spurious words, p. 4093; Books quoted, p. 4094

Wickedness ... *sb.* 1. The quality or being wicked; wicked character or disposition; depravity, iniquity, immorality. ...

2. Wicked action or conduct; iniquity as committed or perpetrated; *occas.* wicked speech or statement. ...

b. *with sing.* and *pl.* A piece of wickedness; a wicked act or proceeding. ...

†c. In physical sense: Malignancy, corruption: cf. **Wicked** 3 c. *Obs.* 1440 ...

†4. In the concrete. *Obs.* ...

Wicken, variant of **Quicken** *sb.*[1], *sb.*[2]

Wicker (wi·kəɹ), *sb.* Forms: 4–5 wyker, 4–6 wekir, 6–7 wycker, 5 wikre, wikir, wykyr, qwykyr, wekker, 6 wycre, wykir, -ur, wicker, wikkyer, wickar, -ir, 7 wykkier), 6– wicker. [East Scandinavian (MSw. and Sw. dial. *viker*, early Da. *viger*, Da. dial. *vigger* willow, osier, branch of willow; f. root of Sw. *vika* to bend (cf. OE. *wícan* to give way, collapse, and **Weak** *a.*, **Week**).]

1. A pliant twig or small rod, usually of willow, esp. as used for making baskets and various other objects; an osier; a withe. Chiefly in *pl.* (= 2). ...

b. *attrib.* Of or belonging to wickers; made of wickers or wickerwork. ...

Wicker, *v.* [f. prec. sb.] *trans.* To furnish, fit, cover, or inclose with wicker. ...

Wickered (wi·kəɹd), *a.* [f. **Wicker** *sb.* or *v.* + -ED[2].] 1. Encased in wicker; inclosed or surrounded by wickerwork. ...

Wickerwork (wi·kəɹwəɹk). [f. **Wicker** *sb.* + **Work** *sb.*] Work consisting of wickers; a structure of flexible twigs, osiers, or the like plaited together; basket-work. ...

Wicket (wi·ket). Forms: [3 wicat], 3–5 wykote(e, 5–6 wyket, wiket, 4–5 whett, wekett, 4–6 wyketz, wycott, wikett, 5 wikette, wokyt, (wigate), 5–6 wekee, 6 woket, 6– wicket. [ME. AF. – ONF. *wiket* (Norman *viguet*, Walloon *wichet*) – OF. *guichet*; usually referred to the Teut. root appearing in ON. *víkja* to move, turn (Sw. *vika*, Da. *vige*: but the forms of F. *guichet*, *wiket*, Pr. *guisquet* indicate the possibility of another source.]

1. A small door or gate made in, or placed beside, a large one, for ingress and egress when the large one is closed; also, any small gate for foot-passengers, as at the entrance of a field or other inclosure. ...

Wickyberry, Wickey-up: see **Wicky**, **Wickup**.

Wishtalk. *Obs.* [app. f. **Wick** *a.* + **Halse** *sb.*[1], neck.] app. a gallows-bird, rogue. ...

Wicking (wi·kiŋ), *vbl. sb.*[1]. = **Wick** *v.*[3], 2. ...

Wickit, obs. form of **Wicked**.

Wicker, *obs. Sc. dial.* var. Forms: 1 = 1 wickner. 1 wickness, 4–5 wig-r·ber, 6– wickner. ...

Widdendream, wi·ddrim (-drem). *Sc.* *Obs.* Also **wuddendream, widdrum, -dreme, windrem, woo-, wudrum**. [OE. *wēdendréam* and *wuddi-daemonium* (also *plu.*, on *weddandréam* in delirium, lit. *mad men's joy*: see **Wood** *a.*, **Dream** *sb.*[2]). For the survival in Sc. **Wether·ham**: see **Wither·ham**.] ...

Widdy (wi·di). Chiefly *Sc.* Forms: 5 widde, wedde, *pl.* wedeis, -ys, wyddie, 6 wedy, widdy, -ie, woddie, *pl.* widdeis, weddeis, 6–9 widdy, 7 wyddie, 6–9 woddie, woody, 9 widdey, waddy-ie, 9– widdy. [Sc. and north. dial. variant of **Withy**.]

1. A band or rope, properly one made of interwined osiers or the like. ...

Widdy (wi·di), *v.* [abbrev. of **Widows**.] *Obs.*

Wide (waid), *sb.* [absol. use of **Wide** *a.* (OE. *wíd* sb.)] ...

Wide (waid), *a.* Forms: 1–4 wid, 3–5 wyd, 4–6 wyde (4, 5 wydde, wyyd, 7 weede), 3– wide. Comp. widder (wᵻ·dəɹ), also, with shortened vowel, 1 widdra, 4 wyddre (wᵻ·dəɹ). [Com. Teut. (wanting in Gothic): OE. *wíd* = OFris., OS. *wid* (MLG. *wide*, MDu., Du. *wijd*), OHG. *wit* (MHG. *wit*, G. *weit*), ON. *víðr* (Sw. *vid*, Da. *vid*). Not known outside Teut.] ...

Wide, *adv.* Forms: 1 wide, wid, 3 wide, 3–4 wyde, 4–6 wyd, 6– wide. (OE. *wíde*; cf. the adj.) In various senses. ...

Supplement, p. 3873; Corrigenda, p. 4092; Spurious words, p. 4093; Books quoted, p. 4094

Widower [1] (wi·dǫǝ). Forms: 4 wid(e)wer, wydewer, 4–5 wedower, 5 wyduare, 5–6 wydower, (wydward), 6 wedower, wydoer, 7 widdower, 9 dial. widiwer, 7–widower. [A new formation with -ER[1] on WIDOW sb.[1]; appearing in late ME as an unequivocal form for WIDOW sb.[1] 4 b. Cf. MHG. wîtewœre, MDu. wedewître.]

1. A man whose wife is dead (and who has not married again); a husband bereaved of his wife.

Widowhood (wi·dǫhud). Forms: see WIDOW sb.[1] and -HOOD; also 5 wydewood; 1 gen. of WIDOW sb.[1] or 2 + -HOOD.

Widowie see widowy, after WIDOW sb.[1]
Widow-wail [See quot. 1597]. 2. A name for the shrub Daphne Mezereum) or other species of Daphne.

Width (widþ). [A literary formation of the 17th century, taking the place of widness WIDENESS (which in the usual word in modern dialects), the short vowel of breadth (6–7 bredth) providing an analogy. Johnson 1755 calls it 'a low word'.]

1. Extent across, or from side to side; transverse dimension = BREADTH 1; across, extent of opening, distance apart (of the two parts of something, as a pair of compasses).

2. Large extent across. Also fig. (cf. BREADTH 2, WIDENESS 1, 2.

Wield (wîld). Forms: see below. [Two OE. verbs here represented: (1) a Com. Teut. reduplicating strong vb. OE. (WS.) wealdan, (Anglian) wældan, pa. t. wéold, (pa. pple. ge·wealden) (see WALD[1]) = OFris. walda, OS. gi-waldan, pa. t. giwéld, OHG. waltan, (pa. t. wialt (MHG. welt), pres. wildu, pa. t. weltu)...]

A. Illustration of Forms.

I. Infin. and Present Stem.

2. Power, might, force, strength.

3. Meaning, significance (cf. 4 c).

Wife (waif). pl. wives (waivz). Forms: Sing. α. 1–5 (6 Sc.) wíf, 3–4 wyf, 4–6 wyffe, wyffe, (chiefly Sc.) vif, vyffe, 5–6 (6 Sc. vyff, (4 wiif, 4 wife, wiefe, wyefe, wyfe, wyffe, 4 wif, 5–6 wive, wive, wyve, 5 wyef, wyfe, 6 wyef...

1. A woman: formerly in general sense; in later restricted to a woman of humble rank or of low employment (J.), esp. one engaged in the sale of some commodity.

Wieldy, a. Obs. rare. [f. WIELD v. + -Y[1].] 1. weldable, manageable. b. capable of being wielded; = WIELDABLE.

Wield, a. Obs. Forms: 1 wielde, wylde, 2–3 wilde, 3 wilde. [OE. wielde, ge-wielde, f. root of WIELD v.] 1. Strong, powerful, mighty.

Wieldsome, a. Obs. rare. [f. WIELD v. + -SOME.] = WIELDY 2.

Wieldy (wîldi), a. Forms 1–4 weldi (-y), 5 weoldy, 6 wyldy, 7 wieldie, weldy, 7–wieldy. [f. WIELD v. + -Y[1].]

Wifedom (wai·fdǫm). [f. WIFE + -DOM.] The position or condition of a wife, married womanhood.

†Wifehood, sb.

Wifeless, a.

†Wifelet. **Wifeling**

Wifelike. A. adj. B. adv.

†Wifely, a.

Wifeship.

†Wifen

†Wife, sb.

†Wifkin.

†Wifely, a.

Wift.

†Wifthing, sb.

†Wifing.

Wig, sb.[1]

Wig, sb.[2]

Wig, sb.[3]

Wig, sb.[4]

Wig, sb.[5]

Wig, v.[1]

Wig, v.[2]

Wigan (wī'găn).

Wigen, wigeon: see WIDGEON.

Wigg, wigeon: f. WIG, WIG.

Wigged, a.

Wiggery (wī'gări).

Wiggle (wī'g'l), v.

Wigging (wī'giŋ).

Wiggish, Wiggism

Wiggle (wī'g'l).

Wiggle-waggle

Wiggly

Wi'ggling

Wiggy (wī'gi).

Wight (wəit), a.

Wightly (wəitli), adv.

Wightness.

Wighty (wəiti), a.

Wiglet.

†Wiglomeration.

†Wiglouse.

Wigster.

Wig-wag (wī'gwæg), v.

Wig-wagger.

Wigwam (wī'gwæm, wī'gwām).

Wikonare, Wiker: see WICKER.

Wikke, Wikked, Wikken: see WICK, WICKED.

Wild (wəild), a.

WILD. 122 WILD. WILD. 123 WILD CAT.

WILD-CATTER. 124 WILDERNESS. WILD-FIRE. 125 WILD GOOSE.

Wild goose chase

Wildish (waiˈdiʃ), a.

Wilding (waiˈldiŋ).

Wildgrave. Obs.

Wildhede. Obs.

Wilding (waiˈldiŋ), n. and a.

Wildly (waiˈldli), adv.

Wild man.

Wildness.

Wildwood (waiˈldwud).

Wile (waiˈl), n.

Wile, v.

Wileful, a.

Wilely (waiˈllli), adv. Obs.

Wilful (wiˈlful), a.

Wilfulhead.

Wilfulness (wiˈlfulnes).

Wiliness (waiˈlinɛs).

Wilga (wiˈlgə).

Wilger (wiˈlgər).

Wilghe, obs. form of WILLOW.

Wilghode. Obs. rare.

Wilily (waiˈlili), adv.

Wiling (waiˈliŋ).

Wilk, obs. form of WHELK, WHICH.

Wilkats, obs. form of WILD CAT.

Wilkin.

Wilkume, obs. form of WELCOME.

Will (wil), n.[1]

Will, v.[1]

Supplement, p. 3873; Corrigenda, p. 4092; Spurious words, p. 4093; Books quoted, p. 4094

Wimpler. A female wimpler.

Wimplie, v. ... [f. WIMPLE v. + -ER¹.]

Wimpling, vbl. sb. In 3 wimlunge. [f. WIMPLE v. + -ING¹.]

Wimpling, ppl. a. [f. WIMPLE v. + -ING².]

Win, sb.¹ Forms: 1-3 winn, (2 walmen), 4-5 winne, wynne, wyn(e. 3- win. [OE. *win(n)* labour, strife, conflict (cf. MG. *win*), more frequently *gewinn*: see I-WIN sb. The modern senses are from WIN v.¹]

+Win, sb.² Forms: 1 wynn, 1 wunn, wenn), 3 winne, (also 7 wun), 3-4 winne (also 7) wunne, 3-5, 7 win, 4-5 wyn, wynne, 4-6 wynne, 4 wyn. [OE. *wyn*(n), *wynn*, fem. *i*-stem (also 7 to OS. *wunnia*, OHG. *wunni*, *wunnia* in OE. *gewun*, *wunian* (see WONT) ...and related to *wen*-(see WEN sb. and v.) and WINE v.² friend. Cf. WINSOME.]

+Win, sb.³

Win, sb.⁴ Also 6-7 wyn, 9 whinn, winn, wing.

+Win, sb.⁵ Obs.

Win, v.¹ Pa.t. and pple. won (wʌn).

+Win, v.² Obs. Forms: 1 wunnian, (wann, wunnen), variably give to the smaller boy...

+Win, v.³

Wince, sb.¹

Wince, v.¹

Wince, sb.²

Wince, v.²

Wincer¹

Wincer²

Wincey (wɪnsi). Also winsey. [Variant of WINCEY sb.²]

Winch, sb.¹ Forms: 3 wynci, 4-5 wynche, (5 wynce, winche), 6-7 wynche, 6-9 win, 8-9 winch. [OE. *wince*, ... rel. to WINK v.]

Winch, sb.²

Winch, v.¹

Winch, v.²

Wind, v.

Windas. Obs.

Wind-bag, windbag (windbæg).

Wind-ball.

Wind-band.

Windbound, wind-bound.

Wind-break, v.

Wind-cutter.

Wind-drift.

Wind-egg.

Winded.

Winder, Winderous: see WINDOW, WONDER, WONDROUS.

Windermost. Obs.

Winder, v.

Windfall.

Windfallen, wind-fallen.

Wind-flower.

Wind-gall.

Wind-gauge, -gage.

Wind-gun.

Windhover.

Windi-

†Windfucker. Obs.

Windic, var. WINDIE.

Windill, obs. form of WINDLE v.

Windily, adv.

Windiness.

Winding, vbl. sb.

Windle.

Windli, obs. form of WINDLE.

Winding (wai'ndiŋ), *ppl. a.* [f. WIND *v.*[1] + -ING[1].] That winds, in various senses.

Winding (wai'ndiŋ), *vbl. sb.*[1] [f. WIND *v.*[1] + -ING[1].]

†Winding-cloth. Obs. [f. WINDING *vbl. sb.*[1] + CLOTH *sb.*] = WINDING-SHEET 1.

†Winding-cloth[2] = WINDOW, WINDOWCLOTH.

Winding-sheet (wai'ndiŋʃiːt). [f. WINDING *vbl. sb.*[1] + SHEET *sb.*[1].] A sheet in which a corpse is wrapped for burial; a shroud.

Wind-instrument. (Often as two words.) 1. A musical instrument played by means of 'wind' (WIND *sb.*[1] 12), supplied either by the breath of the player or by bellows: most commonly applied to portable instruments of this kind.

Hence **Wind-instru'mental a.; Wind-instru'mentalist.**

Windish, var. WINNOWISH Obs.

Windlass (wi'ndlas), *sb.*[1] Forms: 5 wyn-las(e), wyndlase, 5–6 wyndlas, 6 -lasse, wyn-las, 6–7 windlase, -lasse, 6 (also 9) windlace, 6–8 windlas, windlesse, 7 wyndeles, 7–8 windlass, windlace, 8 windlas, 7–windlass, etc.

Windlass, *sb.*[2] [f. WINDLASS *sb.*[1]]

Windlass, *v.*[1] [f. WINDLASS *sb.*[1].]

Windlass, *v.*[2] [f. WINDLASS *sb.*[2].] To hoist or haul with a windlass. Hence **Wi'ndlassing** *vbl. sb.*[2]

Windle (wi'nd'l), *sb.*[1] Now *dial.* or *local.* Forms: 1 wyndel, (1 -il), 3–6 wyndel, 4 -dille, -doll, 3–9 *dial.* winnel, 6 -wyndle, -dille, 6–9 windle; also *Sc.* windel, windal, etc. [OE. *windel sb.*, 'cartelius', 'fiscella', 'canistrum'.]

†Windle, *v.*[1] Obs. *rare.* [as WINDLE *sb.*[2] + -LE[3].] *trans.* To winnow.

Windle (wi'nd'l), *v.*[2] *trans.* 1. Now dial. or local. Forms: 1–2 windlian, 3–9 -windel, *dial.* wyndle.

†Windling, *vbl. sb.* Forms: 1 windling, 8 windlin, wonlyne, 9 winlin, windlin, windling. [?f. WIND *v.*[1] + -LING[1] 2.]

Windle-straw (wi'nd'lstrɔː). *Sc.* and *dial.* Forms: 8–9 *Sc.* winnel, wi(n)le, 7—windle-straw, 8–9 *Sc.* -windlestrae, stray, etc., -windlestraw, 9 *Sc.* strae; also *dial.* windle (winnelstraw, straw, etc.), windle-stra, winnelstrae, -stray, etc.

Windle-straw 1 A dry withered blade of grass, such as is left standing after the flower or seed is shed.

†Windless, *sb.*[3] Obs. Forms: 6 wynd(e)-, winlesse, wyndla(s)se, (-laies?), wyndlas(s)e, -lace, 6–7 windlace, -lasse, 7 -lace, windlasse (8 windlasch). [Alteration of WANLACE, by association with WIND *v.*[1] and *perb*. with *prec. sb.*]

Hence **Wind-law.** to intercept the game in hunting (= WANLACE 1); *gen.* a circuit, circuitous movement.

Windless (wi'ndlɛs), *a.* [f. WIND *sb.*[1] + -LESS.] 1. Breathless, out of breath.

2. Free from wind; not exposed to or stirred by the wind, in or upon which no wind blows.

Windless, *ppl. a.*: see WINDLE *v.*[1] and *v.*[2]

Windmill (wi'ndmil, winmil), *sb.* (Formerly also as two words.) [f. WIND *sb.*[1] + MILL *sb.*[1]; cf. MHG. *wintmül*, G. *windmühle*, LG., Du. *windmolen*, and F. *moulin à vent* (from 13th c.).] 1. A mill the machinery of which is driven by the wind acting upon sails, used (chiefly in flat districts) for grinding corn, pumping water, etc.

Windo(e, -dok, obs. ff. WINDOW, WINNOCK.

Windola. Obs. [= WINDOW *sb.* + -LE?] = WINDOW. Also *fig.*

†Windolf. Obs. [f. E. *Anglia*.] In 5 wyn-dolf(e. [Obscure. The second syllable is prob. related to DELF[2], DELVE *v.*] = E. Anglian *delf*, a drain, ditch.] A refuse pit.

Windore. Obs. or *dial.* Also 6 wyndoor(e, 7 windoor, 8 windore, vindore. [Altered form of WINDOW 2, by assimilation to DOOR *sb.*[1] + cf. WIND-DOOR.] A window.

Windore (wi'ndɔːr), var. WINNOWSTER Obs.

Windows (wi'ndoz), *sb.* Forms 3 windowe, -dowe, -owe(?), wyndowe, 3–4 windoz, 4 vyndow, 4–6 wyndowes, 6–7 windoe, wyndowe, 9 windowe, 6–7 windo, windo(e, wyndo(e, (wyndough, windowgh, 5–7 windowe, windo, windowe), 7–windowe. [ME. *windoge,* a. ON. *vindauga* (Sw. and Da. *vindöge*, Norw. dial. *vindauga*, MDa. *vind-öje* = 'wind-eye', f. *vindr,* WIND *sb.*[1] + *auga,* EYE *sb.*[1]), finally superseded OE. *éagþyrel* EYETHURL, *éagduru,* but the French-derived FENESTER was in continued use to the beginning of the modern period.]

1. An opening in a wall or side of a building, ship, or carriage, to admit light or air, or both, and to afford a view of what is outside or inside.

Windowful (windō·ful), sb. FULL. As much as fills or will fill a window or the space which a window gives a view of.

†Windowing. Obs. [f. WINDOW sb. + -ING¹.] The fittings or furniture of a window.

Windowless (windō·lĕs), a. [-LESS.] Not having or furnished with windows.

Window-sill = SILL sb.¹

Window-sole. dial. [SOLE sb.¹ + -¹.] Full of windows or openings.

†Windowy, a. Obs. rare. [f. WINDOW sb. + -Y¹.] Full of windows or openings.

Windpipe (wi·ndpəip, -pai̯p). [f. WIND sb.¹ + PIPE sb.¹ Cf. Du. + windpijp (Kilian).]
1. The tube which leads from the throat and (dividing into the two bronchi) conveys air to and from the lungs in breathing: = TRACHEA 1 a.

Wind-row (wi·ndrō·). See WINDROW.

Windsail (wi·ndsē·l). [f. WIND sb.¹ + SAIL sb.]
1. Naut. A long wide tube or funnel of sail-cloth used for ventilating a ship.

Wind-shake, sb.

Windrow (wi·ndrō·), sb. Forms and etym.

Window (wi·ndō), sb. Also 4-5 wyndown, 9 dial. windon. Obscure var. WINDOW sb.

†Window, v. Obs. rare. [f. prec.]
1. trans. To furnish with windows (see WINDOWED 1) or window-like openings.

Windowed (wi·ndōd), ppl. a. [f. WINDOW sb. + -ED.] partly after OF. fenestré.]
1. Furnished with or having windows. Also with prefixed word in comb.

Windy (wi·ndi), a. Forms: 1 windig, 4 windi, 4-7 windie, 4-6 wyndy, 6 -die, -dye, windye, Sc. vyndie, wondie, 6-7 windie, 9-windy. [OE. windig, f. WIND sb.¹ + -Y¹.]
1. Consisting of wind; of or pertaining to (the) wind; having the command of the winds, as a heathen deity; indicating or suggesting wind.

Wine (wəin), sb.¹ Forms: 1-4 win, (2-3 uin), 3-6 wyn, 4-6 Sc. wyne, 4 wyin, wyn, 4-6 wine, (OE. wín, OFris., OS., MLG., MDu. wīn (Du. wijn), OHG., MHG. wīn (G. wein), ON. vín (Sw., Da.), Goth. wein) < OL. vīnum, the source also of the Balto-Slavic (OSl. vino, Lith. vynas) and Celtic words (Ir. fín, W. gwin).]
1. The fermented juice of the grape used as a beverage.

Supplement, p. 3873; Corrigenda, p. 4092; Spurious words, p. 4093; Books quoted, p. 4094

Wine-bibber. [f. WINE sb.1 + BIBBER sb.]

Wine-dibber.

Wine-fat: see WINE-VAT.

Wi'ne-glass. [f. WINE sb.1 + GLASS sb.]

Wine-grape. [f. WINE sb.1 + GRAPE sb.]

Wine-house. [OE. wínhús = MLG., MDu., MHG. wínhús (Du. wijnhuis, G. weinhaus), ON. vínhús.]

Wine-lees. [f. WINE sb.1 + LEES.]

Winery: [f. WINE sb.1 + -ERY.]

Wine-press. [WINE sb.1 + PRESS sb.]

Wine-vat, wine-fat. [f. WINE sb.1 + VAT, FAT sb.]

Winey: see WINY.

†Winful, a. Obs. rare.

†Winful, a.2 rare.

Wine, sb.1 [OE. wín = OFris. wín, winne, OS., OHG. wín (MHG. wín), ON. vín; a friend. Also attrib. wine and OE. winemæg; a kinsman.]

Wine-cellar. [f. WINE sb.1 + CELLAR sb.]

Wined (wəind), ppl. a. [f. WINE sb.1 or v. + -ED.]

Wine (wəin), v. [f. WINE sb.1]

Wineless (wəi·nlĕs), a. [f. WINE sb.1 + -LESS.]

Wineberry (wəi·nberi). Forms: 1 winber(i)ge, 6 winberi, 3-rom. wind, 6 wyneberry. [OE. wínberige.]

Winebibber (wəi·nbibər). [OE. wínbibere.]

Wine-drunk(en, a. Obs. [OE. wíndruncen.]

†Winedrunkenness.

Wine-drunk: see WINE-DRUNK.

Wine-pot. [f. WINE sb.1 + POT sb.]

Wing (wiŋ), sb. Forms: 4 wenge, winge, wynge, 4-6 wyng(e, -es, 5 yr. whynge, 5-6 whynges, 5-7 wynge, 5 weng(e, 6-7 wig. Sing. 4-5 wenge, wing, wynge, 5-6 weyng, weyngis, 5-6 wing, weing; 4-6 wynge, wyrghe, 5 wheng, wykng, 4-7 wyng, 6 winge. [ME., first in 12th cent., early north. acc. wæng, pl. of vængr; da. vinge) wing of bird, aisle, etc.; replacing OE. féþra wings, pl. of feþer, and feþere (see FEATHER sb.).]

†2. To make wing (cf. 3 a and MAKE v. 59):

18. To wing (see WING v. 4 b): see 7 b.

To take (sit, etc.) wing (see TAKE v. 24 c).

21. Special Combs.: **wing-band** = next, (f.) **wing-bar**, (a) a lateral bar to a wading-plough; (b) a bar used for attaching to the feathers of a bird's wing; (c) one formed by distinctive coloration of the greater or median coverts of the wing; **wing-case**, each of the small feathers overlying the flight-feathers of a bird's wing; **wing-covert** (COVERT sb.), any of the small feathers overlying the flight-feathers of a bird's wing...

†wing-fashion adv., in the form of wings;

Wing-fish. (a) = PLECTHYS; (b) a flying-fish, esp. of the genus *Prionotus*; wing-snail, a herring winged feet, swiftly-moving; wing-game, game-bird.

Wing, v. Forms: see prec.; also *pa. pple.* 5 wynged, wyngged. [f. prec. sb.]

1. Senses derived from senses 1–4 of the sb.

2. *intr.* To carve (a quail or partridge). *Obs.*

II. Senses derived from senses 6–9 of the sb.

Winged (wiŋd), *ppl. a.* [f. WING *sb.* + -ED[1].]

1. Shot or wounded in the wing.

Winger (wiŋˈər). [f. WING *sb.* + -ER[1].]

1. *Naut.* A small cask or tank stowed in the wing of a ship's hold.

2. *Football.* A player in the (right or left) wing in the Rugby game, a forward whose place is on the wing.

Wingless (wiŋˈlɛs), *a.* [f. WING *sb.* + -LESS.] Having no wings; destitute of wings.

Hence **Wi·nglessness.**

Winglet (wiŋˈlɛt). [f. WING *sb.* + -LET.]
1. A little wing; a small wing, something resembling a little wing, as in bird.

Wing·manship (wiŋˈmanʃip). [f. WING *sb.* after such words as *oarsmanship, penmanship.*] Skill in the use of the wings; flying regarded as an art or accomplishment.

Winy. variant of WINEY.

Wining (waɪˈniŋ), *vbl. sb.* [f. WINE *v.* or *sb.*] The drinking of wine in excess.

Winish (waɪˈniʃ), *a.* Now *rare.* [f. WINE *sb.* + -ISH[1].] Having the taste or quality of wine; somewhat vinous.

Wink (wiŋk), *sb.*[1] [f. WINK *v.*[1]]
1. A closing of the eyes for sleep; a (short) spell of sleep.

Wink (wiŋk), *v.*[1] Forms: 1 wincian, 3 winken, 4–5 wynk(e, 4–7 winke, winck, 6–7 winck(e, 4– wynke, wynck, wonk, 6 wynck(e, 9 *dial.* winc, *Sc.* wunk; 4– wink.

Wink (wiŋk), *sb.*[2] Short for WINKLE *sb.*

Wink-a-peep (wiŋkəpiːp). Also *f.* wink-apin, winkopipe. [f. WINK *sb.*[2] + PEEP *sb.*]

Winkel (wiŋkəl). [WINK *sb.* + -EL.]

Winker (wiŋˈkər). [f. WINK *v.*[1] + -ER[1].]

Winking (wiŋˈkiŋ), *vbl. sb.*[1] [f. WINK *v.*[1]]

Winking (wiŋˈkiŋ), *ppl. a.*[1] [f. WINK *v.*[1] + -ING[2].]
1. That winks.

Winter, v. [ME. *winter*: after L. *hiemare* (in senses 1, 2), *hibernare* (in sense 1; cf. MHG., MLG., Du. *winteren* (G. *wintern*), ON. *vetra*.]

Winter cherry.

1. Name for several plants of the nightshade tribe (N. O. *Solanaceæ*) with cherry-like fruit which is ripe in winter; also, the fruit itself.

Winter corn. [Cf. Du. *winterkoren*, G. *winterkorn*.] Corn sown in winter, or in autumn and remaining in the ground through the winter.

Winter-cress. [After Du. *winterkers*.] Any of the cruciferous herbs of the genus *Barbarea*, the leaves of which were formerly used as a winter salad; esp. *B. vulgaris* (Winter Rocket, Yellow R.).

Winterage (wi'ntərédʒ), *local*. Also -*age*. [f. WINTER v. + -AGE.] The action of wintering cattle; food or pasture for cattle in winter.

Winterberry (wi'ntəberi). Any of several N. American species of holly (*Ilex*, formerly *Prinos*) with berries, usually scarlet, which persist through the winter.

Winterbourne (wi'ntəbuɒn). [OE. *winterburna*, f. WINTER sb.[1] + *burna*, BOURN sb.[1], BURN sb.[1]]

Winter, sb.[2] [Origin uncertain.]

Winter-day. [OE. *winterdæg* = MLG., MDu. *winterdach*, -*dagh* (Du. *winterdag*, G. *wintertag*), ON. *vetrardagr*.] A day in winter.

Wintered (wi'ntəd), *ppl. a.*

Winterden, corrupt form of WITHERDEN.

Winterer (wi'ntərəɹ). [f. WINTER v. (or sb.[1]) + -ER.] One who winters, in various senses.

Winter-fallow, *sb.* (and *v.*)

Winter-feed, *v. trans.* To feed or maintain (animals, etc.) during winter.

Wintergreen (wi'ntəgriɪn). [After Du. *wintergroen*, G. *wintergrün*.]

Wintering (wi'ntəriŋ), *vbl. sb.* [f. WINTER v. + -ING[1].]

Wintering, *ppl. a.* [f. WINTER v. + -ING[2].] That winters, in various senses.

Winterish (wi'ntəriʃ), *a.* [f. WINTER sb.[1] + -ISH[1].] Belonging to winter.

Winterless (wi'ntələs), *a.* [f. as prec. + -LESS.] Having no winter; free from or not experiencing winter.

Winterling, [f. as prec. + -LING.] An ox, sheep, or other animal of a year old; a yearling.

Wintery (wi'ntəri), *a.* [OE. *winterlic*, -*lig*.]

Winter quarters. (Also with hyphen.) [See QUARTER sb.]

Winter's bark. [= mod. L. *cortex Winteranus* (see WINTERA), named from its discoverer Captain William Winter.]

Winter solstice. The time at which the sun reaches the winter tropic, i.e. in the northern hemisphere the tropic of Capricorn.

Winter-tide. Now somewhat arch. [OE. *wintertíd* (G. *winterzeit*).]

Winter-time. [f. WINTER sb.[1] + TIME sb.] The season of winter.

Winterward, *adv.* [f. WINTER sb.[1] + -WARD.] Towards winter.

Wintery: see WINTRY.

Wintle (wi'nt'l), *v.* Sc. Also 9 wuntle. [early Flem. *windtelen*, frequent. of WIND sb.[1]]

Wintery: see WINTRY.

Wintry (wi'ntri), *a.* Also 4, 6-7 wyntry, 6 wynle, 6-7 wintre. [OE. *wintrig*.]

Winx, *v.* [Cf. dial. *winsk* to bark, yelp, whinny?] *intr.* To bray as an ass.

Winy, winey (wai'ni), *a.* Also 4, 6-7 wyny, 6 wynie, 6-7 winie. [f. WINE sb. + -Y[1].] Of, belonging to, or characteristic of wine; having the nature or properties (taste, colour, etc.) of wine.

Winx, *v.* [Cf. dial. *winsk* to bark, yelp.]

Wipe (wəip), *v.* Pa. t. and *pple.* wiped (wəipt). Forms: 1 *wipian*, 3-6 wype, 4 wype, wyp, 6 wype, 4-5 wipe, 5 wippe, etc.; 6-7 wipe, 7- wipe.

Wird: see WEIRD, WERD, WORD, WORTH.

Wire (wəiəɹ), *sb.* Forms: 1–4 wir, 4–5, 7 *Sc.* wyr, 4–7 wyro, 5–7 wyer, (5 were, whir, 6 wyere, wheaire, wiar; *Sc.* 6 wyir, 7 wyre), 5–7 wyer, wyar, *sc.* wire; (6–8 wyre). … [OE. wir, corresp. to MLG. wire (LG. wîr), ON. *wîr* in wiravirki filigree work, related further to OHG. wiara (MHG. wiere) fine gold, ornament; prob.: referred to the base *wî-* of L. *viēre* to plait, weave, etc. (cf. WITHE sb.)]

I. Denoting the substance.

1. Metal wrought into the form of a slender rod or thread, formerly by hammering, now by the operation of wire-drawing. **a.** of precious metal, esp. gold, used chiefly in ornamentation.

Wiping (wəiˈpiŋ), *vbl. sb.* [f. WIPE v. + -ING[1].] The action of the verb WIPE, in various senses.

Wiper (wəiˈpəɹ). Also 6 in sense 3) wyper. [f. WIPE v. + -ER[1].]

Wipe, obs. f. WEEP v.; var. WYPE, lapwing.

Wiping, *ppl. a.* [f. as prec. + -ING[2].] That wipes, in various senses: see the verb.

Wippe, obs. (sc. f. WEEP O.; ffe. f. WHIP.
Wipped, **wipt** (e, obs. pa. t. and pple. of WIPE v.
Wips, obs. form of WISP.
Wirble (wəiɹbl), *v.* (individual.) Also *wirbel*. [ad. G. *wirbeln*.]

Wirchep, **-ip**, obs. ff. WORSHIP.

Wire (wəiəɹ), *v.* [f. WIRE sb.]

Wired (wəiəɹd), *ppl. a.* [f. WIRE v. + -ED[1].]

Wire, var. VIRE sb. Obs., dart.
Wire, var. WEIR sb.

Wird, obs. form of WEIRD sb.

Wire-drawer (wəiəɹˌdrɔːəɹ). [f. WIRE sb. + DRAWER.]

Wire-drawing, *vbl. sb.*
1. The action or operation of making wire by drawing a piece of ductile metal through a series of holes, successively decreasing in diameter, in a steel plate called a draw-plate.

Wireless (wəiə·les, *a.* (*sb.*) [f. WIRE *sb.* + -LESS.] 1. Without a wire or wires; spec. Electr. dispensing with the use of a conducting wire.

Wireman (wəiə·mæn), *sb.* [f. WIRE *sb.* + MAN *sb.*]
1. One who makes or works in wire.

Wire-pull, *v.*

Wire-puller (wəiə·pu·lər).

Wirework (wəiə·wəːk).

Wire-worker.

Wireworm (wəiə·wəːm).

Wiring (wəiə·riŋ), *vbl. sb.* [f. WIRE *v.* + -ING¹.]

Wirk(e, obs. form of WORK *v.*

Wirling, dial. [? OBSCURE.]

Wirra (wiɹ·a), *int.* *Irish.*

Wirry, var. of WORRY.

Wiry, **Wirykow**: see WORRY, WORRICOW.

Wis (wis), *v.¹*

Wisard, obs. f. WIZARD.

Wisdom (wizdəm). Forms: 1- wisdom. [OE.]
1. Capacity of judging rightly in matters relating to life and conduct; soundness of judgement in the choice of means and ends.

Wisdom-tooth.

Wise (wəiz), *a.* [OE. wís.]
1. Having or exercising sound judgement or discernment.

Wise (wəiz), *sb.¹* [OE. wíse.]
1. Manner, mode, fashion, style.

ys. 1526 Tindale *Luke* xvi. 8 The chyldren of this worlde, are in their kynde [1611 generation] wyser then the chyldren off light. 1539 Taverner *Erasm. Prov.* 18 He is in vayne wyse yt is not wyse for hym selfe. [See *Prov.* ix. 12.] 1562 J. Heywood *Prov. & Epigr.* (1867) 132 Who wedth ere he be wise, shall die ere he thriue. 1596 Shaks. *Merch. V.* II. ii. 83 It is a wise Father that knowes his owne childe. 1617 B. Rich *Irish Hubbub* 16 We were wont to say, it was a wise childe that did know the owne Father. 1717 Wodrow *Corr.* (1843) II. 319 The proverb of being wise behind the time. 1745 B. Franklin *Poor Richard* (1890) 157 Fools make feasts and wise men eat them. 1879 Dixon *Windsor* II. xix. 204 Men who are wise are wise in time. 1881 Saintsbury *Dryden* i. 10 Sir Gilbert Pickering..was wiser in his generation.

b. Of action, speech, personal attributes, etc.: Proceeding from, indicating, or suggesting sound judgement or good sense; 'becoming a wise man' (J.); sage.

a 900 Cynewulf *Crist* 922 Þam þe hafað wisne ȝeboht. a 1225 *Ancr. R.* 198 So þet non wisure read ne mei bringen hire ut of hire riote. *Ibid.* 338 Of þe axunge mei uallen vuel bute ȝif þe axunge beo þe wisre. 1362 Langl. *P. Pl.* A. x. 71 Vche wiȝt in þis world þat haþ wys vnderstondinge. 1422 Yonge tr. *Secr. Secr.* 134 Anothyr yewyth a vyse consail. c 1480 Henryson *Fables* Prol. 17 (Makculloch MS.), A doctryne wiss anewch, and ful of fruyt. 1597 Shaks. *2 Hen. IV*, v. i. 84 It is certaine, that either wise bearing, or ignorant Carriage is caught, as men take diseases, one of another. 1600 — *A. Y. L.* II. vii. 156 Full of wise sawes, and moderne instances. 1667 Milton *P. L.* xi. 666 One..eminent In wise deport, spake much of Right and Wrong. a 1672 Wilkins *Nat. Relig.* I. vi. (1675) 84 It must be a Wise Being that is the Cause of those Wise Effects. 1753–4 Richardson *Grandison* II. xxiii. 166 My father also thought fit (perhaps for wise reasons) to acquaint us, that he designed for us but small fortunes. 1821 Scott *Kenilw.* xvi, Teach your affection to see with a wiser eye. 1849 Macaulay *Hist. Eng.* vi. II. 89 By a wise dispensation of Providence. 1860 Tyndall *Glac.* I. xi. 71 He thought it wise not to attempt the ascent farther.

ironically. 1535 Joye *Apol. Tindale* (Arb.) 28 S. Paule (by this wyse reason) playd bo peep wythe hys pistle to the hebrews. 1822 Shelley *Scenes fr. Faust* ii. 227 'Twere a wise feat indeed to wander out Into the Brocken upon May-day night.

†2. Having practical understanding and ability; skilful, clever; skilled, expert (const. *of*). *Obs.*

a 900 Cynewulf *Elene* 592 Wordcræftes wis. c 1300 *Havelok* 282 Of alle þewes was she wis, Þat gode weren. c 1320 *Sir Tristr.* 1270 In warld was non so wiis Of craft þat men knewe. ? a 1400 *Morte Arth.* 2745, I rede ȝe wyrke aftyre witte, as wyesse men of armes. c 1400 *Destr. Troy* 1530 Wise wrightis to waie, werkys to caste. 1508 Dunbar *Tua mariit wemen* 462 Ȝit am I wise in sic werk. a 1548 Hall *Chron., Hen. VII* 32 b, He secretly sent wise espialles..to searche & prye oute of what progeny thys..Rycharde was dissended.

b. *spec.* Skilled in magic or hidden arts. Now only *dial.*, as in *wise wife*, Wise man 3, Wise woman 1.

a 1639 Spottiswood *Hist. Ch. Scot.* vi. (1655) 383 Agnes Samson (commonly called the wise wife of Keith) was..a woman not of the base and ignorant sort of Witches. 1653 H. More *Antid. Ath.* III. vi. § 6 (1712) 102 While he wish'd to himself that some wise body would help him to his..money again there appeared unto him a Spirit.

3. Having knowledge, well-informed; instructed, learned (*in*, earlier *of*, *upon*). *Obs.* exc. as in b. (See also Wise man 2 a, Wise woman 1.)

c 1000 *Sax. Leechd.* II. 146 Læcas lærdon, þa þe wisoste wæron, þæt nan man on þam monþe ne drenc ne drunce. c 1250 *Gen. & Ex.* 331 Sone ȝe it ðor of hauen eten,..ȝe..sulen..ben so wise alle euene So ðo ðe wunen a-buuen in heuone. 13.. *Gaw. & Gr. Knt.* 1605 Wys vpon wodcraftez. c 1375 *Sc. Leg. Saints* xxxi. (*Eugenia*) 61 In al science at dewyce, þar mycht na woman wysare be. c 1400 *Rule St. Benet* (prose) lxiv. 42 Sho aȝht at be wise in goddis law. c 1505 (*title*) Here begynneth thystorye of yᵉ .vii. Wyse Maysters of rome. 1591 Shaks. *1 Hen. VI*, II. iv. 18 But in these nice sharpe Quillets of the Law, Good faith I am no wiser then a Daw. 1651 Hobbes *Leviathan* II. xxx. 179 Wiser and better learned in cases of Law,..than themselves. 1742 Gray *Eton* 100 Where ignorance is bliss, 'Tis folly to be wise.

b. Informed or aware *of* something specified or implied. Now only in such phrases as *none the wiser*, *as wise as before* = knowing no more than before (i.e., usually, nothing) about the matter.

c 1200 Ormin 2279 Forrþi wollde ȝho ben wis off þatt þurrh Godess enngell. c 1220 *Bestiary* 799 In water ȝe is wis of beuekes come. c 1375 *Sc. Leg. Saints* ii. (*Paulus*) 424 Þat god wyss þame wald make Peteris banis quhilk war of þai, And quhilk war paulis banis alsa. 1377 Langl. *P. Pl.* B. x. 372 Þis is a longe lessoun,..and litel am I þe wyser. c 1470 Henry *Wallace* viii. 580 Thai maid him wys off all that suttell cace. 1599 Shaks. *Hen. V* IV. i. 206. 1616 *Withals' Dict.* 574 *Obscurum per obscurius*, I am as wise as I was before. 1635 D. Dickson *Hebr.* viii. 8. 156 The Church was made wyse of the imperfection of the Olde Covenant. 1712–13 Swift *Jrnl. to Stella* 2 Mar., I went into the city to see Pat Rolt, who lodges with a city cousin, a daughter of cousin Cleve (you are much the wiser). 1714 — *Let. to Miss Vanomrigh* 8 June, The pretender, or duke of Cambridge, may both be landed, and I never the wiser. 1838 Dickens *O. Twist* xxxi, Messrs. Blathers and Duff came back again as wise as they went. 1889 *Century Mag.* July 343/1 Not one whit the wiser of the world than when he left home.

(*b*) U.S. colloq. *To be* (or *get*) *wise to*, to be (or become) aware of; *to put* (one) *wise* (*to*), to inform one (of), enlighten one (concerning).

1901 H. McHugh *John Henry* 69 When I hear a pool-room comedian speaking lines about getting seasick on the B. & O., I'm wise to the fact that he dips in the Farmers' Almanac for his comedy stuff. 1918 Bindloss *Agatha's Fortune* xvii. 158, I suppose it was because the drummer put you wise that you went to Miss Strange? 1923 F. H. Kitchin *Divers. Dawson* 103 There would be the very devil to pay if Crutchley..got wise to their existence.

4. In one's right mind, sane. Now *Sc.* and *dial.* So Du. *wijs*. Cf. Wisdom 4.

Cf. *Beowulf* 3094 wis and ȝewittiȝ (= fully conscious).

c 1290 *S. Eng. Leg.* I. 412 Here men miȝhten iseo Hou he pleiȝez with þis ȝongue brid; he ne miȝhte nouȝt wys beo. a 1400, 1481 [implied in Unwise 3]. a 1598 D. Fergusson *Scot. Prov.* (S.T.S.) 8 Anes wood, never wise. 1604 Shaks. *Oth.* IV. i. 245 *Oth.* Fire, and brimestone. *Des.* My Lord. *Oth.* Are you wise? *Des.* My Lord? *Oth.* I am glad to see you mad. 1881 'Sarah Tytler' *Three Frights* (1882) 9 They were each, according to a significant old Scotch phrase, 'wise (pronounced *wice*, and meaning rather rational than sagacious) and warld-like'.

5. †a. *To make it wise* (see Make *v.*[1] 68 b): to deliberate, hesitate. *Obs.*

c 1386 Chaucer *Prol.* 785 Vs thoughte it was noght worth to make it wys And graunted hym wit outen moore auys.

b. *To make wise* (see Make *v.*[1] 69): to behave as if one were 'wise' about a matter; to pretend, 'make as if...' *Obs.* exc. *dial.*

1447 Shillingford *Lett.* (Camden) 14 Hengston seide but litell therto, but made wise as thogh hit were yes. 1561 Hoby tr. *Castiglione's Courtyer* II. (1577) M vj, The two..wente to bed darkelong, laughing and making wise to beleeue that hee wente about to mocke them. 1589 Puttenham *Engl. Poesie* III. xxii. (Arb.) 265 He makes wise, as if he had not bene a man learned in some of the mathematickes. 1604 Hieron *Preachers Plea* Wks. 1614 I. 511 Hee..made wise, as if he could haue tolde great tydings. 1834 Mrs. Bray *Warleigh* x, Whether she really felt desirous to take this opportunity of gaining repose, or whether, to use a Devonshire phrase, she only 'made wise' to do so.

6. *absol.* or as *sb.* **†a.** *sing.* usually with def. article or demonstrative: A or the wise man; *spec.* a sage. *Obs.*

c 897 Ælfred *Gregory's Past. C.* xxxiii. 220 Se dysega..all his inȝeðonc he ȝeypt, ac se wisa hit ieldcað. a 1250 *Owl & Night.* 176 Wel fyht þat wel flyhþ, seyþ þe wise. c 1374 Chaucer *Troylus* I. 79 Þis forknowyng wyse. 1390 Gower *Conf.* I. 268 Upon the sol, upon the wise Siknesse and hele entrecomune. 1401 *26 Pol. Poems* iii. 12 Do euene lawe to fooll and wyse. c 1440 *Alphabet of Tales* 484 Þe wise sayd vnto hym: 'þis way is bothe fayr & gude'.

b. *pl.* Wise men or persons: now always with *the*; †formerly also with demonstrative, possessive, etc.

c 1000 *Ags. Gosp.* Matt. xi. 25 Þu þe behyddyst þas þing fram wisun & gleawun. c 1205 Lay. 16817 He bi-heold..wulc of wiisen ærest spæken wolden. a 1300 *Cursor M.* 20794 Disput, he sais, es na mister, Bituix te wis in swilk a wer. 1340–70 *Alex. & Dind.* 973 Dindimus þe dere king, the docktour of wise. 1390 Gower *Conf.* I. 1 Som matiere, Essampled of these olde wyse. *Ibid.* 26 The wisest of Caldee Ne cowthen wite what it mente. c 1400 *26 Pol. Poems* i. 167 Fle fro fooles, and folwe wise. 1535 Coverdale *Isa.* xxix. 14, I wil destroye the wisdome of their wise. 1670 Dryden *1st Pt. Conq. Granada* II. (1672) 21 The bold are but the Instruments o' th' wise. 1784 Cowper *Task* III. 562 The learn'd and wise Sarcastic would exclaim. 1833 Tennyson *Pal. Art* 105 O silent faces of the Great and Wise.

c. *A word to the wise* (*is enough*): = Verbum sap. Also †*Few words to the wise suffice*, etc.

1500–20 Dunbar *Poems* xv. 24 Few wordis may serve the wyis. 1562 Mountgomery in *Archaeologia* XLVII. 241 Feawe woordes to the wise doeth suffice. 1639 J. Clarke *Parœm.* 51 Few words to the wise suffice. *Verbum sapienti sat est.* A word to the wise. 1754 Richardson *Grandison* I. xix. 127 Nay, if she can withstand him—But a word to the wise, Mr. Reeves! Hem!

d. The comp. *wiser* as sb. (with pl. *wisers*): One who is wiser; usually with possessive, (one's) superior in wisdom. Now *rare*.

(Cf. Better A. 7, Elder *sb.*[2] 2, Greater C b.)

a 1300 *Cursor M.* 26180 Ga til a wijser to scou þi wond. c 1385 Chaucer *L. G. W.* 2634 *Hypermnestra*, And werke aftyr thyn wisere euere mo. 1447 Bokenham *Seyntys* v. 292 And of þi wysers lern bettyr gouernaunce. c 1480 Henryson *Want of Wise Men* 22 For warldly wyn sik walkis, quhen wysar wynkis. 1818 Scott *Hrt. Midl.* i, Since it is well known these Delilahs seduce my wisers and my betters. 1838 Hare *Guesses* Ser. I. (1847) 161 All writers who feel an itching..to be carping at their wisers and betters. 1843 Carlyle *Past & Pr.* III. xiii, If thou really art my Senior, Seigneur, my Elder,..if thou art in very deed my Wiser.

7. Used as *adv.* = Wisely. In later use only in comparative. *rare*.

1375 Barbour *Bruce* xvii. 52 Thou vroucht has vis, That thou discouerit first till me. 1600 Shaks. *A. Y. L.* II. iv. 58 Thou speak'st wiser then thou art ware of. 1797 Mrs. M. Robinson *Walsingham* IV. 153, I cannot act wiser than to take the little Welsh girl off the hands of her dragon.

8. *Comb.* **a.** advb. with adj. or pple., as *wise-bold*, *-hardy* (opp. to Foolhardy), *-valiant*; *wise-framed*, *-judging*, *-reflecting*, *-said*. **b.** attrib. with sb., as *wisebones* sb. (humorous appellation for a wiseacre), *wise-heart* adj. (= wise-hearted). **c.** parasynthetic, as *wise-hearted*, *-lipped*, *-worded* (ME. *wis iworded*).

1600 Tourneur *Transf. Metam.* liv, With a *wise-bold heed. 1894 Alma-Tadema *Wings of Icarus* v. 26 There you go, old *wisebones! Here's a storm in a tea-cup! 1642 H. More *Song of Soul* III. II. xli, *Wise framed questions. 1575 Laneham *Let.* (1871) 44 Valiant, & *wizehardy. 1587 Holinshed *Chron.* III. 583/2 Of courage invincible,..wisehardie alwaies. 1887 Morris *Odyssey* viii. 327 The cunning of *wise-heart Hephæstus' snare. 1535 Coverdale *Exod.* xxxv. 26 Soch wemen as were *wyse herted. 1867 Morris *Jason* II. 862 Men there are Wise-hearted. 1644 Milton *Divorce* II. xvii. (ed. 2) 66 Why men so disesteem this *wise judging Law of God. 1821 Scott *Kenilw.* vii, Many wise-judging men. 1818 Milman *Samor* I. 384 *Wise-lipp'd chief. 1848 Buckley *Iliad* vi. 110 By no means could she persuade just-minded, *wise-reflecting Bellerophon. 1597 *Pilgr. Parnass.* I. 113 Youre *wise-said says Keepe mee from devious..wayes! a 1586 Sidney *Astr. & Stella* lxxv, He could young wise, *wise valliant frame His Syres revenge. a 1225 *Ancr. R.* 64 Sum is so wel ilered, oðer se *wis iworded [etc.].

Wise (waiz), *v.*[1] *Obs.* exc. *Sc.* and *north. dial.* Forms: 1 wisian, 3 wisie, 4–6 (8–9 *Sc.* and *dial.*) wyse, (5 vyse, 6 *pa. pple.* wizde), 7 (9 *dial.*) wize, 3–7 (9 *dial.*) wise, 9 *Sc.* weise, weize. [OE. *wisian* to show the way = OFris. *wisa*, OS. *wîsian*, MLG., MDu. *wisen* (Du. *wijzen*), OHG. *wîsan* (MHG. *wîsen*, G. *weisen*, now conjugated as a str. vb.), ON. *visa* (Sw. *visa*, Da. *vise*), Goth. *fulla-weisjan* πείθειν: f. OTeut. *wîsaz Wise *a.* (Cf. Wis *v.*[1])]

1. *trans.* To show the way to (a person); to guide, direct; †hence, to direct or manage the affairs of, govern, rule (*obs.*); also in mod. dial., to induce, entice *away*, *from*...; to instruct, inform.

Beowulf 320 Stræt wæs stanfah, stiȝ wisode gumum ætgædere. c 1000 Ælfric *Gen.* xxxv. 5 Iacob ferde þa mid ealre his hiwrædene, swa him god wisode. c 1205 Lay. 1200 Wise mi & witere..whuder ich mæi liðan. a 1250 *Owl & Night.* 973 Þu..seist þu uisest [*v. r.* wisest] mankunne þat hi biwepen hore sunne. c 1250 *Prayer to Our Lady* 2 in *O. E. Misc.* 192 Þu wisie me nuþe for ich eom eirede. 1297 R. Glouc. (Rolls) 10755 Sire steuene of segraue was imad þo hei iustise In sire hubertes stude de boru þut lond wel to wise. 13.. *Cursor M.* 17931 (Gött.) Quen i þe gan wis To þe ȝatis of paradis. c 1320 *Cast. Love* 297 Wiþ-oute whom he ne mai His kindom wiþ pees wysen. a 1400–50 *Wars Alex.* 2988 Alexander..trottis him to þe trod-gate, as him þe torche wyssis [*Dubl.* vysys]. c 1400 *Song Roland* 303 'Now wise vs crist!' quod Rouland. c 1460 *Towneley Myst.* ix. 122 Mahowne he wyse the on thi way. 1575 Turberv. *Faulconrie* 130 Alwayes wysing and making your bawke to leane in vpon you. 1594 Carew *Tasso* II. xli, To be wizde what cause her thither drew. 1604 H. Broughton *Advt. Corrupt. Relig.* E 3 b, Tremelius might haue wised M. Lively. 1606 N. B[axter] *Sydney's Ourania* D 2, She [*sc.* the Moon] wizeth Surgeons when to ope a veine. 1610 H. Broughton *Job* xxxv. 11 Who doth teach us more than the beasts of the earth: and wiseth us above the foules of the heaven. 1657 Trapp *Comm. Ezra* viii. 16 Being themselves wise, and willing to wise others. a 1810 Tannahill *Song, Dear Highland Laddie* ii, The Laird's wys'd awa' my braw Highland laddie, O. 1821 Galt *Ann. Parish* xxxviii. 310 She..took me by the hand, and wised me to go back. 1825 Brockett *N. C. Gloss.*, *Wise*, to shew or direct. 'Wise him in.' 'Wise him out.'

2. To direct the course or movement of; to move in some direction or into some position; to convey, conduct; to turn (in various connexions: see quots.); also *fig.*

a 1300 *Cursor M.* 21272 A..wain men wit four quelis wises. c 1330 R. Brunne *Chron. Wace* (Rolls) 13698 His hors on hym [*sc.* Bokkus] his bridel wysed. c 1440 *Pallad. on Husb.* II. 78 The forgh is best, ille humour out to wise. 1606 N. Baxter *Sidney's Ourania* C 3, Planets..Knowne to each Figure-flinger..That wize from thence many an vncouth-tale. 1816 Scott *Antiq.* vii, Now, weize yoursell a wee easel-ward—a wee mair yet to that ither stane. 1825 Brockett *N. C. Gloss.* s.v., Wise off that rope there. a 1827 in Scott *Jrnl.* 2 Aug., Stuff with moss, and clog with clay, And that will weize the water away. 1830 Galt *Lawrie T.* IV. x. (1849) 179 Mr. Bell quietly wised the conversation upon juvenile indiscretions. 1862 Smiles *Engineers* III. 113 Wise on the Hydrogen, Nichol! 1862 Hislop *Prov. Scot.* 58 Every miller wad weise the water to his ain mill. 1867 J. K. Hunter *Retrospect Artist's Life* xiv. (1912) 135 The little fish rushed to the shore before him, as he quietly wysed them shoreward.

b. To direct, aim, 'send', shoot (a missile) (*Sc.*); †*fig.* to utter.

a 1300 *Cursor M.* 24103 Quen i wend word to wise. 1721 Ramsay *Ode to Fh—* ii, Fowk wysing a Jee The Byass Bouls on Tamson's Green. 1814 Scott *Wav.* lviii, Mony o' them wadna mind a bawbee the weising a ball through the Prince himsell.

c. *intr.* for *refl.* To direct one's course, make one's way, betake oneself, go.

c 1330 R. Brunne *Chron. Wace* (Rolls) 10956 Vnto þer contres he bad þem wyse. 1721 Ramsay *Richy & Sandy* 69 But see the Sheep are wysing to the Cleugh.

3. *trans.* To show, point out (the way). †Also, to cause to be seen, show, reveal (*obs.*).

13.. *E. E. Allit. P.* A. 1135 A wounde ful wyde..con wyse An-ende hys hert þurȝ hyde to-rente. c 1400 *Rule St. Benet* (verse) 138 Wysand vs þe way to heuen. c 1450 *Pol. Poems* (Rolls) II. 226 The printe of a palsy wisith the thy way. 1818 Scott *Rob Roy* xxiii, I'll hae somebody waiting to weise ye the gate to the place.

Wise (waiz), *v.*[2] [f. Wise *a.* 3 b (*b*).] *To wise up* (U.S. slang): to 'get wise'; to 'put wise'.

1919 J. Buchan *Mr. Standfast* iii. 70 You've got to wise up about Gresson with the whole forces of the British State arrayed officially against you. 1922 P. G. Wodehouse *Girl on Boat* i. 25 You won't wise him up that I threw a spanner into the machinery?

Wise: see Vaisya.

1665 Sir T. Herbert *Trav.* (1677) 53 The last Sect or Cast of Gentiles are the Wises.

Wise, obs. f. Vice *sb.*[1] and [2], Vise *v.*

-wise: see Wise *sb.*[1] II.

Wiseacre (wai·zěikəɹ). Forms: 6–7 wise-aker, 7 wiseaker, wisacre, 7–8 wise acre,

7– wise-acre, wiseacre. [ad. (with unexplained assimilation to *acre*) MDu. *wijsseggher* (wai·sɛgər) soothsayer, app. ad. OHG. *wîzago*, MHG. *wîzage* (= OE. *witega* Witie *sb.*), with assimilation to *wijs* Wise *a.* and *segher* Sayer.]

1. One who thinks himself, or wishes to be thought, wise; a pretender to wisdom; a foolish person with an air or affectation of wisdom.

1595 *Eng. Tripe-wife* (1881) 146 Shall he run vp and downe the town,..accompanied with some such wise-akers as himselfe. 1609 Dekker *Gulls Horn-bk.* Proemium 5 Thou Lady of Clownes and Carters, Schoolemistres of fooles and wisacres. 1654 Whitlock *Zootomia* 47 Syrupe of Poppy, (that edged Tool in the hands of such Doctor Wiseakers). 1711 Steele *Spect.* No. 138 ¶ 6 This Wiseacre was reckoned by the Parish, who did not understand him, a most excellent Preacher. 1810 Scott *Fam. Lett.* 31 Dec. (1894) I. vi. 202 This wise-acre thinks he should have a finger in every man's pie. 1852 Thackeray *Esmond* I. xiii, I have heard politicians and coffee-house wise-acres talking over the newspaper. 1874 Micklethwaite *Mod. Par. Churches* 115 The architect..is lectured on his own art by wiseacres, whose whole stock of knowledge is got up from 'Parker's Glossary'.

†b. Used in pl. form of a single person; sometimes as a *quasi*-proper name. *Obs.*

? 1613 J. Taylor (Water P.) *Laugh & be fat* Wks. (1630) II. 71/1 A learned wiseakers. 1615 Tofte *Varchi's Blazon Jealousie* 24 *note*, Wiseakers her Husband, neuer so much as once doubting or dreaming of any such matter. 1673 *S'too him Bayes* 9 When he has done (like a wise-acres) he makes nothing of it.

¶c. With allusion to *acres* as = 'lands'; in first quot. app. applied to a landed estate.

1608 *Yorksh. Trag.* I. iii, Is the rubbish sold, those wiseakers your lands? a 1734 North *Exam.* II. v. § 128 (1740) 394 If wise by their Acres, or, in a word Wiseacres, it was expected the Guineys should come out, for the Uses of Mobbing.

2. A wise or learned person, a sage. (Usually contemptuous.)

1753 in *Gentl. Mag.* XXIII. 417 (spuriously archaic) Pythagoras lerned muche—becomming a myghtye wyseacre. 1814 *Sporting Mag.* XLIV. 271 The concourse of wiseacres..was truly astonishing. 1842 Thackeray *Fitz-Boodle's Conf.* Pref., It requires no great wiseacre to know that. 1902 *Sat. Rev.* 29 Nov. 677/2 The stoic paradox that the cobbler who has got wisdom is the universal wiseacre.

Hence (*nonce-wds.*) **Wi·sea:cred** (-əɹd) *a.*, having the character of a wiseacre (in quot. with allusion to *acre*: cf. 1 c above), whence *wi·seacredness*; **Wi·sea:credom**, the realm of wiseacres, wiseacres collectively; **Wi·sea:creish** (-əriʃ) *a.*, like or characteristic of a wiseacre (whence *wiseacreishness*); **Wi·sea:creism** (-əriz'm), **Wi·sea:crery** (-əri), something characteristic of a wiseacre; pretension to or affectation of wisdom, or a remark exhibiting this.

1603 Dekker *Wonderful Year* B 3, Each *wise-acred Landlord. 1848 Earl Northbrook in Mallet *Mem.* (1908) 39 The conceited phraseology and would-be *wiseacredness of its professors. 1885 A. Dobson *Don Quix.* in *Sign of Lyre* 93 To make *Wiseacredom, both high and low, Rub purblind eyes. 1834 J. Wilson in *Blackw. Mag.* XXXVI. 415 He..then perpends, in a *wiseacreish pause, to consider if they are all to be found. 1895 Saintsbury *Corrected Impr.* ii. 12 *Ex post facto* *wiseacre-ishness. 1861 T. L. Peacock *Gryll Grange* xiii, Whist is more consentaneous to modern solemnity: there is more *wiseacre-ism about it. 1917 Saintsbury *Hist. Fr. Novel* I. 371 Interrupting his vizier and the other tale-tellers with *wiseacreries.

Wisedam, -dom(e, obs. ff. Wisdom.

Wisehead (wai·zhed). [f. Wise *a.* + Head *sb.*] One who has a wise head; always in ironical sense, One who fancies himself wise, a wiseacre.

[1378 *Poll Tax Yorks* 158 in Bardsley *Surnames*, Johannes Wysehede.] 1796 *Monitor* No. 64. II. 123 The wise-heads..have been a good deal troubled to invent proper subjects for this purpose. 1862 Miss Braddon *Lady Audley* xxxvi, The wiseheads of the servants' hall. 1875 H. James *Rod. Hudson* iii. 94 There were naturally a great many wiseheads who smiled at his precipitancy.

†Wi·sehede. *Obs. rare.* In 4–5 wys-. [f. Wise *a.* + -hede, -head. Cf. OFris. *wîshêd*, Du. *wijsheid*, G. *weisheit*.] Wisdom.

1340 *Ayenb.* 68 Zuyche uolke þet wylleþ him benyme his lhordssip and his wyshede. 1481 Caxton *Reynard* xxviii. (Arb.) 68 The ouerest wysehede.

Wise-like (wai·z,laik, *dial.* wai·s-, wei·slaik), *a.* (*adv.*) *Sc.* and *dial.* [f. Wise *a.* + -like 2.]

1. Reasonable, rational.

1816 Scott *Old Mort.* xiv, It wad hae been lang or my Leddy Margaret..wad hae fund out sic a wise-like doctrine in the Bible! 1818 Susan Ferrier *Marriage* I. xii, It wad set her better to be carrying a wise-like wean in her arms, than trailing aboot wi' thae confounded dougs an' paurits. 1893–4 *Northumbld. Gloss.* s.v., That's a wise-like dog o' yors.

2. Becoming, seemly, respectable, proper: esp. in appearance.

1820 *Blackw. Mag.* Nov. 148 Talking..o thrashing ripe rigs wi' the west wind..may look very wiselike in rhyme. 1842 J. Aiton *Dom. Econ.* (1857) 123 Make it something 'wiselike' and substantial, that it may remain as a monument of your own liberality and good sense. 1881 *Academy* 15 Oct. 289/3 Jane..wice-like rather than pretty. 1894 *Blackw. Mag.* June 754/1 He was considered by..many ladies of the parish to be a very personable man, comely.., and altogether a wyss-like man.

B. as *adv.* Fittingly, becomingly, respectably.

1822 *Blackw. Mag.* Sept. 313 They ought to hire a chaise, and gang in till Edinburgh wiselike. 1841 *Fraser's Mag.* Jan. 109/2 Dinna gang ramstam in, saying, 'Janet, here's meal; and Janet, here's butter';..slip cannily and wiselike in.

Wiseling (wai·zliŋ). Now *rare*. [f. Wise *a.* + -ling [1] 2.] A pretender to wisdom; a wiseacre.

1633 J. Done *Hist. Septuagint* 214 These wiselings, that shew themselues fooles in so speaking, and discoursing without Discourse. 1649 J. Ellistone tr. *Behmen's Epist.* (1886) 3 Those Luciferian wiselings that thought none could teach them anything. 1765 Law *Behmen's Myst. Magnum* xxxix. 222 Let Master Sophister or Wiseling of Babel look us right in the Face. 1914 Nellen & Craig tr. *Ozanam's Franciscan Poets Italy* v. 245 He praises the wisdom which shrinks from the wiselings.

Wisell, var. Wizle, stalk, etc.

†Wi·sely, *a.* *Obs. rare.* Forms: 1 wislic, 3 wislich, 4 *comp.* wislier, 5 wysely, 6 wysley, 7 wisely. [OE. *wîslic*: see Wise *a.* and -ly [1].] = Wise *a.* 1.

c 900 tr. *Bæda's Hist.* II. xiii. (1890) 134 Me þynceð wislic, ȝif þu ȝeseo þa þing beteran,..þæt we þam onfon. a 1023 Wulfstan *Hom.* i. (1883) 4 Ðonne is eac wislic ræd, þæt manna ȝehwylc ȝeornlice smeage. a 1300 *Cursor M.* 28116 Wit wislier þat i was amang Haue i striued oft-sithes wrang. 1436 *Libel Engl. Policy* in *Pol. Poems* (Rolls) II. 183 Yf men were wysely, the Frenshmen and Flemmynge Shulde bere no state in see by werrynge. 1556 *J. de Flores' Aurelio & Isab.* E 8, Vnto howre wysley wordes.

Wisely (wai·zli), *adv.* Forms: see Wise *a.* and -ly [2]; also 5 wisily, vi-, vysilie, 5–6 wys(e)-, wyislie, 6 wyslye, wislie. [OE. *wîslîce* = OS. *wîslîco*, MLG., MDu. *wislik* (Du. *wijzelijk*), OHG. *wîslîcho* (MHG. *wîslîche*), ON. *vísliga* (in the sense of *víssuliga* certainly): f. Wise *a.* + -ly [2].] In a wise manner.

1. With wisdom, sound judgement, or sagacity. Also more widely, with good sense or discretion.

c 888 Ælfred *Boeth.* xviii. § 1 Se þe wile wislice & ȝeornlice æfter þam hlisan spyrian. c 897 — *Gregory's Past. C.* xviii. 131 Ðæt he meahte ðæt folc ðy wislicor & ðy rædlicor læran. c 1175 *Lamb. Hom.* 105 Þet mon wisliche spene þa þing þe him god lene on þisse liue to brukene. c 1200 Ormin 2199 Ȝho toc wisliȝ to fraȝȝnenn himm whatt itt bitacnenn mihhte. c 1250 *Gen. & Ex.* 1091 Loth hem warnede, wislike and wel, Oc he ne troweden him neuere a del. a 1300 *Cursor M.* 18852 Clerli spak he þat he wald, And al his skil wiseli he tald. c 1374 Chaucer *Troylus* I. 956 He hasteþ wel þat wysly kan a-byde. c 1400 *Lanfranc's Cirurg.* 70 Alle þese þingis I haue told, þat he þat rediþ hem mai þe visiloker [*v. r.* wyslocor] in semblable causis worchen. a 1450 *Le Morte Arth.* 1158 Thou ne woste not Ryght wiseliche What harme hathe falle. c 1489 Caxton *Sonnes of Aymon* xxv. 539 See that ye revenge yourself wysly. 1551 Robinson tr. *More's Utopia* I. (1895) 113 Thys I suppose is the chiefe cause whie theyr common wealthes be wyselyere gouerned. a 1586 Sidney *Arcadia* III. (1922) 78 Young men, who thinke, then they speake wiseliest, when they cannot understand themselves. 1604 Shaks. *Oth.* v. ii. 344 One that lou'd not wisely, but too well. 1610 — *Temp.* II. i. 21 *Gon.*..You haue spoken truer then you purpos'd. *Seb.* You haue taken it wiselier then I meant you should. 1667 Milton *P. L.* x. 1023 Doubt not but God Hath wiselier arm'd his vengeful ire then so To be forestall'd. 1765 A. Dickson *Treat. Agric.* (ed. 2) 63 This method of conveying the vegetable food from the earth to the air, and from the air to the earth, is wisely established, for making a just distribution of it upon all parts of the earth. 1829 Southey *Sir T. More* I. 280 Men judge wiseliest, when they judge most charitably. 1847 Helps *Friends in C.* I. v. 85 From a genial, wisely-developed man, good things radiate. 1925 E. Phillpotts *Voice from Dark* xvi. 199 He would have done wiselier to be home before it came.

b. With an air or assumption of wisdom; sagely, knowingly.

1585 T. Washington tr. *Nicholay's Voy.* IV. xiii. 126 b, [I asked him..what religion he kept, wherupon wisely he gaue me to vnderstand that [etc.]. 1600 Shaks. *A. Y. L.* II. vii. 22 He..looking on it, with lacke-lustre eye, Sayes, very wisely, it is ten a clocke. 1888 'J. S. Winter' *Bootle's Childr.* iv, 'Ah! but there's very few Captain Ferrers about,' said Lassie wisely.

†2. Attentively, carefully, heedfully. *Obs.*

c 1000 *Inst. Polity* x. in Thorpe *Laws* II. 318 Beþencan heora dæda wislice & wærlice. a 1225 *Ancr. R.* 104 Þe heorte is wel iloked ȝif muð & eien & earen wisliche beoð ilokene. a 1225 *Leg. Kath.* 82 Ha heold hire aldrene hird wisliche & warliche. 1377 Langl. *P. Pl.* B. xiii. 343, I wayted wisloker. ? a 1400 *Morte Arth.* 1613 That they be weisely wachede and in warde holdene. c 1400 Maundev. (Roxb.) xxvi. 123 Qwhen þai ga to were, þai hafe þam riȝt warly and wysely. c 1475 *Rauf Coilȝear* 587, I raid on full richt, To watche wyselie the wayis. 1558 Warde tr. *Alexis' Secr.* 111 Powre the said water fynely and wisely into some other vessel that is cleane. 1594 Plat *Jewell-ho.* III. 28 If you holde the same [glass] wisely..you shall see the wine ascende in the forme of a clowd.

†3. Skilfully, cleverly, ingeniously; cunningly.

a 1000 *Cædmon's Gen.* 456 Oð ðæt he Adam on eorðrice, godes handȝesceaft ȝearone funde, wislice ȝeworht, & his wif somed. a 1000 *Boeth. Metr.* xx. 15 Þu þe unstilla aȝna ȝesceafta to ðinum willan wislice astyrest. c 1250 *Gen. & Ex.* 3630 God it taȝte al ear moysen Wislike hu it wroȝt sulde ben. 1390 Gower *Conf.* I. 255 With his wordes slyhe and queinte, The whiche he cowthe wysly peinte. c 1430 *Pilgr. Lyf Manhode* I. lxxiv. (1869) 44 She wolde it were so wysliche moolded and so subtylliche that bi seemynge it were litel. a 1586 Sidney *Arcadia* Ecl. ii. (1922) 231 The hives of wisely painfull Bees. 1601 Shaks. *Twel. N.* I. v. 33 Here comes my Lady: make your excuse wisely, you were best.

Wise man. (Formerly often as one word, or with hyphen; cf. the surname *Wiseman*.)

1. *gen.* A man who is wise; a man of good judgement or discernment; a discreet or prudent man. (Often opposed to *fool*.)

Worldly wiseman: see Worldly.

c 888 Ælfred *Boeth.* xl. § 3 Fordy ne scyle nan wis mon forhigan ne to swiðe ymb þæt gnornian, to hwæm his wise weorðe. c 1000 Ælfric *Saints' Lives* xiii. 116 Ne sceal se wise mann beon butan godum weorcum. a 1225 *Ancr. R.* 214 Wel understond euerich wis mon þis. c 1300 *Havelok* 180 Wis man of red, wis man of dede. 1390 Gower *Conf.* I. 46 It myhte make a wisman madd. c 1400 *Rule St. Benet* (prose) 15 Þe wyse man musters hym wid fa wordis & welle sitande. 1481 Caxton *Godfrey* xxv. 57 There ben more fooles than wysemen. a 1548 Hall *Chron., Edw. IV* 207 This mariage semed very straunge to wise men. 1549 *Compl. Scot.* Prol. 16, I hope that vyise men vil reput my ignorance for ane mortifeit prudens. a 1619 Fotherby *Atheom.* I. xiv. § 3. (1622) 150 Wisemen indeed haue euer reputed them, for no better then mad-men. 1702 H. Dodwell *Apol.* § 13 in S. Parker *Cicero's De Finibus*, He took Cato for a perfect Stoick, and for a Wiseman, in the Sense of the Philosophers. 1770 Bridges *Burlesque Transl. Homer* II. 26 Old Nestor,..Who always counted was a Wise-man. 1853 Lynch *Self-Improvem.* i. 2 He is a wise man who has an instructed mind and a regulated choice. 1859 Geo. Eliot *Adam Bede* xix, A fool 'ull hit on't sometimes when a wise man misses.

b. Ironically applied to a fool or simpleton, as in *the wise men of Gotham* (see Gotham 1).

[1471 *Paston Lett.* III. 32 Yonge Wyseman othyrwy[s]e callyd Foole.] 1525, c 1560 [see Gotham 1]. 1596 Raleigh *Discov. Guiana* 5 Who like Wise men in the absence of their Captaine followed the Indians. 1711 *Countrey-Mans Lett. to Curate* 32 It were..too Churlish to grudge these talkers the Character of the only Wisemen of G——.

2. *spec.* **a.** A man deeply versed in some subject of study, or in studies generally; a learned man, scholar, philosopher, sage. Now *rare* or *arch.*

The seven wise men = the seven sages: see Sage *sb.*[2] 1.

a 1000 *Cædmon's Exod.* 377 Wise men wordum secgað, þæt from Noe nigoða wære fæder Abrahames on folctale. 1338 R. Brunne *Chron.* (1810) 114 Wis man in þe lawe. 1379 *Glouc. Cath. MS.* 19 I. I. iv. If. 1 Iff þu will wysman be in demyng of vryn. 1387 Trevisa *Higden* (Rolls) III. 63 Tales Millesus..þe firste of þe seuene wise men. 1450–80 tr. *Secr. Secr.* iii. 6 His philesofris and grete wisemen of clergie. 1588 Kyd *Househ. Philos.* Index, Thales one of the seauen wise men of Greece. 1655 Stanley *Hist. Philos.* Pref. (1687) 2 Hermippus in his Treatise of the seven wise Men saith, they were in all seventeen, of which seven were variously named. 1656 Blount *Glossogr.*, *Solon*, one of the seven wisemen of Greece. 1842 W. C. Taylor *Anc. Hist.* ix. § 5 (ed. 3) 240 Periander, who is sometimes ranked among the Seven Wise Men of Greece. 1850 Ld. Kelvin in S. P. Thompson *Life* (1910) I. v. 223 The steamer appeared about 4 P.M.—contrary to the expectation of the nautical wise men about the harbour.

b. A man who utters wise sayings or maxims; *esp.* as a title for any of the writers of the Jewish 'Wisdom Literature'.

a 1225 *Ancr. R.* 64 Þe wise mon [*sc.* Solomon] askeð in his boc hweðer [etc.]. 1375 Barbour *Bruce* I. 121 And wys men sayis he is happy, That be othir will him chasty. c 1400 *Rule St. Benet* (verse) 1080 Þus þe wisman sais þerbi. 1542 Boorde *Dyetary* ix. (1870) 251 The wyse man sayth, that surfetes do kyll many men. 1587 T. Newton *Herbal for Bible* l. 274 So doth the Wiseman [*marg.* Eccle. i. 24] vse it, whereby he promiseth felicitie..to him that..embraceth Wisedom. 1611 *Bible* Transl. Pref. ¶ 3 There is no new thing vnder the Sunne, saith the wiseman. 1649 Wilkins *Beauty Provid.* 92 Like snow in Harvest (as the Wiseman speaks). 1659 *Gentl. Calling* v. § 13 The wise-man hath assured us this, Prov. 11. 4. Riches profit not in the day of wrath. c 1705 Pope *Jan. & May* 153 Yet you pursue sage Solomon's advice,..But, with the wiseman's leave, I must protest. c 1750 *New Whole Duty of Man* viii, The threatening of the Wise-man, who..declares, that the eye that mocketh his father,..the ravens of the valley shall pick it out.

†c. One of a body of men chosen for their sagacity as advisers in matters of state; a councillor. *Obs.* as a specific sense.

By 16th–18th century historians used in pl. to render Witan.

c 1250 *Gen. & Ex.* 2649 Ðe king wið-stod & an wisman, He seide, 'ðe child doð als he can'. 1488 *Cely Papers* (Camden) 169 That eueryche of thes contreys doo send..serten wysemen wᵗ full auctoryte..for to coomen..wᵗ the Gauntnersse. 1502 Arnolde *Chron.* (1811) p. xx, This yere wer chosen be wise men of the cite, xxxv men,..sworne to mayntene the Assisis. 1591 Lambarde *Archeion* (1635) 256 All the Acts are said to passe from the King, and his Wise-men both of the Clergie and Laitie. 1648 Prynne *Plea for Lords* 3 Lordes and Peeres; anciently stiled Aldermen, Heretockes, Senators, Wisemen,..by our Historians. 1714 Fortescue-Aland *Pref. Fortescue's Abs. & Lim. Mon.* 18 King Alfred..with the Thought, i.e. Advice of his Wisemen, or Parliament.

3. A man versed or skilled in hidden arts, as magic, witchcraft, and the like; a magician, wizard; *spec.* applied in biblical versions and allusions to the three Oriental astrologers or Magi (see Magus 2) who came to worship the infant Jesus. In general sense now *dial.* or *vulgar* (cf. Wise woman 1).

1382 Wyclif *Matt.* ii. 1 When Jhesus was born in Bethlem ..loo! kyngis, or wijs men [1388 astronomyenes; Vulg. *Magi*], camen fro the eest. 1552 Latimer *Serm. Lincs.* v. (1562) 100 b, Whan we be in trouble, or sicknes, or lose any thing: we runne hither and thither to wyssardes, or sorcerers, whome we call wyse men. 1561 S. Wythers tr. *Calvin's Treat. Relics* G iv b, Yᵉ wysmen which came to worshipe our lord Iesus after his natiuitie. 1573 Twyne *Æneid.*, *Life Virgil* A 3, That he was at the first couenaunt seruant wᵗ a traueilinge wyseman. 1595 Peele *Old Wives T.* (facs.) C i b, I pray you tell where the wise man the Coniurer dwells? 1612 Cotta *Discov. Dang. Pract. Phys.* I. ix. 71 A sort of practitioners, whom our custome..doth call wisemen and wisewomen, reputed a kind of good..harmles witches or

wisards, who by good words..promise to allay..diuels, practises of other witches, and the forces of many diseases. 1731 *Flying Post* 29 Apr. 2/1 George Raunsforth, ..a reputed Conjurer, or (as the Country People call him) a Wise Man. 1802 R. Anderson *Cumbld. Ball.* 39 The wise man lives nit far frae this,..He telt Nan Dobson whee she'd wed. 1839 [see Magus 2].

Wisen, obs. form of Wizen *v.*

Wiseness (wai·znės). *rare.* [f. Wise *a.* + -ness. Cf. OE. *unwîsnes*.] The quality of being wise; wisdom; occas. *ironical*.

c 1320 *Cast. Love* 292 To vchone sunderlyng He ȝaf a dole of..his wysnesse. 1387–8 T. Usk *Test. Love* II. vi. (Skeat) l. 119 For his goodnesse and wysnesse wolt thou nat do him worship? 1579 E. K. *Ded. to Spenser's Sheph. Cal.* § 1 His morall wisenesse. 1602 Shaks. *Ham.* v. i. 286 Yet haue I something in me dangerous, Which let thy wisenesse feare. 1634 Massinger *Very Woman* III. ii, Your wives wonderful wiseness. 1796 Mme. D'Arblay *Camilla* vii. viii, Which is a wiseness that does honour to her education. 1820 Coleridge in *Blackw. Mag.* Sept. 629 This chilly, doubting, qualifying *wiseness*. 1907 *Sat. Rev.* 8 June 702/2 This report..is full of touches that illustrate his wiseness.

¶ *Right wiseness*, erron. division of *rightwiseness*, Righteousness.

1447 *Shillingford Lett.* (Camden) 134 Of your grete right wisnesse and speciall grace. 1493 *Festivall* (W. de W. 1515) 49 Come to this byleve by doynge of werkes of ryght wysenes. 15.. *New Notbroune Mayd* 172 in Hazl. *E. P. P.* III. 8 By ryght wysenes. 1638 *Dial. on Laws of Eng.* I. xv. 26 b, Truth in his word, & right wisenes in his deed.

Wisent (wī·zĕnt). *Antiq.* [a. G. *wisent* (OHG. *wisunt*): see Bison.] The aurochs.

1866 J. E. Lee tr. *F. Keller's Lake Dwellings* 356 The urus..as well as the bison (or wisent)..are found to have been the most abundant animals in the forests of the stone age. 1889 I. Taylor *Orig. Aryans* iii. 152. 1893 Lydekker *Horns & Hoofs* 31 The true, or European, bison..also known as the wisent or zubr.

Wise woman. (For the general sense 'a woman who is wise' see Wise *a.* 1.)

1. A woman skilled in magic or hidden arts; a female magician, soothsayer, etc.; a witch, sorceress; *esp.* a harmless or beneficent one, who deals in charms against disease, misfortune, or malignant witchcraft. Now *dial.* or *arch.*

1382 Wyclif *2 Sam.* xiv. 2 Joab..sente to Thekuam, and took thens a wise womman. 1552 Huloet, Wise woman that telleth fortune. 1598 Shaks. *Merry W.* IV. v. 27 Was't not the Wise-woman of Brainford? 1601 W. Percy *Cuckqueanes & Cuckolds Errants* v. vi. (Roxb.) 74, I haue haunted a wise woman of our Parish in Maldon, hath taught mee the spell of eury each of them. 1612 [see Wise man 3]. 1653 H. More *Antid. Ath.* III. vii. § 8 (1712) 107 The help and skill of the Witch or Wise-woman. 1828 Hone *Table Bk.* II. 777 An old woman..who was..accounted a wise woman, and a practiser of the 'art that none may name'. 1875 in Miss Jackson *Shropsh. Folk-lore* (1883) 146, I asked him if Mrs. P—— was a witch? He answered, she was a wise woman, and only used her knowledge to stop others doing wrong. 1885 A. H. Bullen in *Dict. Nat. Biog.* I. 112/2 In his extremity he sought the assistance of a wisewoman, Alison Pearson, who treated him so successfully that he completely recovered. His enemies ascribed his cure to witchcraft.

2. A midwife (= F. *sage-femme*): cf. Sage *a.* 2 b.

1821 Scott *Kenilw.* xxiv, O, what, you have got the wise woman, then?' said Varney.

Wish (wiʃ), *sb.*[1] [f. Wish *v.*, q.v. for forms.]

1. An instance of wishing; a feeling in the mind directed towards something which one believes would give satisfaction if attained, possessed, or realized. (With const. as in Wish *v.* 1 (*b*), (*c*), (*d*).)

Most commonly denoting a desire for something not attainable by one's own effort, felt in the mind but not impelling to action; a passive or inactive desire.

The ordinary word for this affection of the mind; less emphatic than *craving*, *longing*, or *yearning*, but including these as particular cases.

1390 Gower *Conf.* III. 254 Bot if mi wisshes myhte availe, I wolde it were a groundles pet. c 1440 *Promp. Parv.* 535/1 Wusche, or wuschynge, *exoptacio*. c 1480 Henryson *Prais of Aige* 6 My wys Of al þis warld to mak me lord & kyng. 1530 Palsgr. 289/2 Wysshe desyre, *souhait*. 1591 Shaks. *Two Gent.* I. iii. 62 As one relying on your Lordships will, And not depending on his friendly wish. 1597 — *2 Hen. IV*, IV. v. 93 Thy wish was Father (Harry) to that thought. 1600 Dekker *Old Fortunatus* D 2 b, This Hat..clapt vpon my head, I (onely with a wish) am through the ayre, Transported in a moment ouer Seas. 1648 Fanshawe *Il Pastor Fido* II. iv. 64 Fortune beyond my wish hath favoured me. 1694 Atterbury *Serm., Prov.* xiv. 6 (1726) I. 191 He comes with strong Wishes that he may find it all a Mistake. 1750 Gray *Elegy* 74 Their sober wishes never learn'd to stray. 1751 Johnson *Rambler* No. 178 ¶ 12 The whole world is put in motion by the wish for riches, and the dread of poverty. 1825 Scott *Betrothed* v, Form but a wish for her advantage, and it shall be fulfilled. 1850 Tennyson *In Mem.* lv. 1 The wish, that of the living whole No life may fail beyond the grave. *Ibid.* xc. 24, I find not yet one lonely thought That cries against my wish for thee. 1850 G. C. Lewis *Lett.* (1870) 223 He..has no wish to be a Church dignitary. 1876 Mozley *Univ. Serm.* xi. 213 The power of prayer..is..the power of strong wishes.

Proverbs. 1665 Wither *Lord's Prayer* 50 If (as the Proverb is) wishes were Thrushes, we might all eat Birds. 1670 Ray *Prov.* 157 If wishes would bide, beggers would ride. 1721 Kelly *Sc. Prov.* 178 If Wishes were Horses, Beggars would ride. 1880 Meredith *Tragic Com.* (1881) 89 He had a saying: Two wishes make a will.

†b. in generalized use: Desire. *Obs. rare.*

c 1430 *Hymns Virgin* (1867) 62 Pride..ȝeueþ but woo & wyssche to wage. a 1716 South *Serm., Matt.* xxvi. 41 (1717) VI. 416 Prayer..was never designed to supply the room of Watchfulness, or to make Wish instead of Endeavour.

c. In phrases with prepositions. †*With* or *upon one's wish* or *wishes*, †*at wish*, according to one's wish, just as one wishes; in readiness for one as one wishes, at one's disposal (= *at will*, Will *sb.*[1] 15 b, c). †*At high wish*, at the height of the fulfilment of one's wishes. *To* (*one's*) *wish* (rarely *wishes*), as one wishes; *esp.* to the full extent of one's desire, as much as one wishes. (Now *rare* or *Obs.*) *To a wish* (Sc.), †*till a wish*, just as one would wish, perfectly, exactly.

13.. *Cursor M.* 23412 All þat wit-standand þe es Thoru sal þou thril it wit þi wiss [*Gött.* Thoru sal þou thril wid þi suiftnes]. 1390 Gower *Conf.* I. 330, I have ben ofte moeved so, That with my wisshes if I myhte,..I hadde storven in a day. *Ibid.* II. 39 He ne wol no travail take To ryde for his ladi sake, Bot liveth al upon his wisshes. c 1450 Holland *Howlat* 847 All thus thir hathillis in hall heirly remanit, With all welthis at wiss. c 1489 Caxton *Blanchardyn* ix. 37 Well syttyng on horsbacke, and tyl a wysshe wel shapen of alle membres. a 1542 Wyatt *Poems*, '*Unstable Dream*' 13 Where it was at wysshe it could not remain. a 1568 Ascham *Scholem.* (Arb.) 40 Though a child haue all the giftes of nature at wishe. 1586 Whitney *Choice Emblems* 144 [He] to his wishe, of pilottes made his choise. 1601 Shaks. *Jul. C.* III. ii. 271 He comes vpon a wish. 1607 — *Timon* IV. iii. 245 The one is filling still, neuer compleat; The other, at high wish. 1667 Milton *P. L.* IX. 423 When to his wish, Beyond his hope, Eve separate he spies. a 1674 Clarendon *Hist. Reb.* VIII. § 153 Though the relief of Banbury succeeded to wish, yet the King paid dear for it soon after. 1779 Forrest *Voy. N. Guinea* 56 The people, who assisted us so opportunely, were rewarded to their wish. 1787 [J. Beattie] *Scoticisms* 106 Every thing succeeds to a wish. 1823 Byron *Juan* xv. lxviii, A dish Of which perhaps the cookery rather varies, So every one may dress it to his wish.

2. A desire expressed in words, or the expression of such; sometimes nearly = 'request': = Desire *sb.* 4. (Cf. Wish *v.* 3–5.)

1513 Douglas *Æneis* VIII. ix. 31 The wyssis and avowis..By women and the matronys doublit were. a 1533 Ld. Berners *Huon* lxxxiv. 264 He sayd 'I wysshe them here on this table'. He had no sooner made his wysshe but they were set on the table. 1598 J. Melvill *Autob. & Diary* (Wodrow Soc.) 443 My opiniouu and wis was, ther sould be na generall meitings. 1714 Pope *Let. to Jervas* 27 Aug., I admire your whig principles of resistance exceedingly, in the spirit of the Barcelonians; I join in your wish for them. 1819 Shelley *Cenci* I. iii. 27 One supplication, one desire, one hope, That he would grant a wish for his two sons. 1908 R. Bagot *A. Cuthbert* xxvi. 339 At Anthony's wish she wore the Cuthbert diamonds.

b. *spec.* An expression of desire for another's welfare: often as a farewell greeting. Usually, now always, in *pl.*

1593 Shaks. *Rich. II*, I. iii. 94 Take from my mouth, the wish of happy yeares. 1601 — *All's Well* I. i. 68 Maddam I desire your holie wishes. 1627 J. Taylor (Water P.) *Armado* Ep. Ded., With my best wishes for the perpetuity of your..felicity. 1735 Pope *Let.* Sept., Wks. 1741 II. 148 Pray tell him my best wishes for his health and long life. 1860 Tyndall *Glac.* I. xxv. 177 We quitted Chamouni, bearing with us the good wishes of a portion of its inhabitants. 1883 D. C. Murray *Hearts* v, I know nothing about it, Tom,..but you have my best wishes.

c. An imprecation, a malediction. *Obs.* or *dial.*

1592 Shaks. *Rom. & Jul.* III. ii. 91 Blister'd be thy tongue For such a wish, he was not borne to shame. 1594 — *Rich. III*, IV. i. 72 This was my Wish: Be thou (quoth I) accurst. 1820 *Marmaiden of Clyde* x. in *Edin. Mag.* VI. 423, I flang the renyie on his neck With a wiss that sould nae been. 1854 Miss Baker *Northampt. Gloss.* s.v., 'He took a many wishes', was an expression used by a witness in the Sessions Court at Northampton.

3. *transf.* An object of desire; what one wishes or wishes for: = Desire *sb.* 5.

a 1300 *Cursor M.* 10406 Þai þat stad er in þair blis, Wit-vten want has alle þair wis. c 1400 Maundev. xvii. [xiii.] (1919) 97 Þat faire lady schal ȝeuen him..the first wyssche þat he wil wyssche of erthely thinges. 1591 Shaks. *Two Gent.* IV. ii. 93 *Sil.* What's your will? *Pro.* That I may compasse yours. *Sil.* You haue your wish. 1611 — *Cymb.* III. v. 20 Your valiant Britaines haue their wishes in it. 1667 Milton *P. L.* VIII. 451 Thy fit help, thy other self, Thy wish, exactly to thy hearts desire. 1713 Addison *Cato* IV. iii. 80 My joy! my best belov'd! my only wish! [1761 Foote *Lyar* I. ii. (1786) 15 Surely, the wish of every decent woman is to be unnotic'd in public. 1849 Macaulay *Hist. Eng.* v. I. 566 The wish of the government was that he should be executed in England.]

4. *Comb.*: wish-bone = Merrythought (q. v. for reason of the name); wish-wife [after ON. *óskmær* (see Wishmay)], a light woman.

1860 Bartlett *Dict. Amer.* (ed. 3), *Wish-Bone. 1884 Roe *Nat. Ser. Story* vi, If I bring you a canvas-back [duck], Amy, will you pat the wish-bone over the door? 1886 Corbett *Fall of Asgard* I. 227 Her wouldst thou profane as though she were some *wish-wife.

Wish (wiʃ), *sb.*[2] *local* (now *Sussex*). [OE. *wisc*, corresp. to OLG. *wisc* (in place-names), (M)LG. *wisch*(*e*, *wisk*(*e*, repr. OTeut. *wisko-, f. *wais-: *wîs-, whence OE. *wâs* Ooze, G. *wiese* meadow.] A piece of meadow, now of marshy meadow; a piece of flat ground lying in the bend of a river and thus liable to be flooded.

898 in Birch *Cart. Sax.* II. 219 Concedo..terram..in loco qui dicitur Fearnleaȝ & an miclan wisce vi æceres mæde. c 1150 in Kemble *Cod. Dipl.* III. 175 To stucan wisc æt ðæne mearcbeorh. 1516–17 *Ledger Bk. Battle Abbey* in *Trans. Philol. Soc.* 1895–8 542 Menewyssh..Borderswyssh..Hodisdaliswyssh. a 1600 in *Sussex Archæol. Collect.* (1851) IV. 306 A true & certeine note how yᵉ Drinker dooth faule to everymans lande or yard wishe in the parishe of Kingston, nigh Lewis, at yᵉ time of trading of yᵉ wishe. 1651 *Ibid.* (1872) XXIV. 282 Lands settled vpon her by the name of Marshland, called Castle Wish als Colbrands lying within the parish of Westham. 1696–7 *Ibid.* (1849) II. 121 Yᵉ two acres croppe in yᵉ Northwish. 1850 *Ibid.* IV. 305 In both these parishes [*sc.* Lewes and Southease] were particular brooks [*i.e.* marshes] called Wishes, and in each also there was a small piece of brookland called the Drinker. 1857 *Ibid.* IX. 156 'The Wish' in East Bourn, close to the sea.

Wish, *a.* (*dial.*): see Wisht.

Wish (wiʃ), *v.* Pa. t. and pa. pple. **wished** (wiʃt). Forms: *α.* 1 wȳscan, wiscan, 3–5 wusshe, 4–5 wysche, (7 *Sc.*) wische, 4–6 wisshe, 5–6 wys(s)he, (3 wusse, wisse, 4 wussche, whusshe, wiche, wesche, wesse, 5 wusche, wiesshe, wosshe, weesshe, 6 wys(c)h, wishe, whysshe, wysshe), 6– wish. *β.* *Sc.* (and *north.*) 4–6 wisse, wis, 4–9 wiss, 6 wys(s, whise, 6–7 viss, 7 wosse, 9 wuss. *Pa. t.* 1 wyscte, wiscte, 5 wyst, weste, 6 (9) wisht; 3 wissede, etc., 4–6 wisshed, 5–6 *Sc.* wissit, etc., 6– wished. *Pa. pple.* 3 iwist, 6 wysht, 6–8 wisht; 4–6 wisshed, etc., 6– wished. [OE. *wȳscan* = OHG. *wunskan* (MHG., G. *wünschen*), ON. *œskja* (MSw. *yskia*, Sw. *önska*, Da. *önske*):—OTeut. *wunskjan, f. *wunska-, -skô- (represented by OE. *wúsc*, OHG. *wunsc*, MHG., G. *wunsch*, ON. *ósk*); cf. Skr. *vāñchā*:—*wānskā-: f. base *wen-* to hold dear, love, desire, whence also Wine *sb.*[2], Win *sb.*[2], Ween *sb.* and *v.*, Wone.

Another form of the stem appears in (M)Du. *wensch*: see Winze [1].]

1. *trans.* To have or feel a wish for; to desire.

The ordinary word for this; now always less emphatic than the synonyms *covet*, *crave*, *long* (*for*), *yearn* (*for*); in earlier use occas. in the sense of these. Sometimes softened by *could* or *should* (*would*): cf. Can *v.*[1] 7, Shall *v.* 19 c, Will *v.*[1] 40 b; or strengthened before a dependent clause (*b*, *c*) by such phrases as *to God*, *to goodness*, *to heaven*.

(*a*) with simple obj. (in OE. usually in the genitive). Now *dial.*; superseded in standard English by *wish for* (see 2), or colloq. in certain contexts by *want* (Want *v.* 5).

c 897 Ælfred *Gregory's Past. C.* i. 29 Ne cuæð he ðæt forðyðe he ænegum men ðæs wyscte oððe wilnode. 971 *Blickl. Hom.* 103 [Hie] his tocymes wyscton. c 1000 Ælfric *Hom.* I. 594 Ic sceal his rode sigor swiðor wiscan ðonne ondrædan. c 1200 *Trin. Coll. Hom.* 165 Ðe sune wusshed þe fader deað, ar his dai cume. 13.. *E. E. Allit. P.* A. 14 Ofte haf I wayted wyschande þat wele. c 1470 Henry *Wallace* ix. 1413 Sum wald haiff had Boyd at the suerdis lenth; Sum wyst [*ed.* 1570 wissit] Lundy. c 1489 Caxton *Sonnes of Aymon* xxiii. 496 Now haue I that I desired and wysshed soo longe. a 1510 Douglas *K. Hart* II. 3 [He] wantis nocht in warld, that he wald wis. 1567 *Gude & Godlie B.* (S.T.S.) 9 Thy nychtbouris wyfe..Thow couet not to the, nor wis His hors, his oxe, [etc.] 1597 Morley *Introd. Mus.* 116 Causing you thinke the night long and wish the daylight. 1610 Shaks. *Temp.* III. i. 54, I would not wish Any Companion in the world but you. 1651 Hobbes *Leviath.* II. xxvii. 159 Not as wishing liberty of private revenges. 1748 Richardson *Clarissa* VI. lxxxiii. 305, I charge you,..as you wish my peace, not to say any-thing of a letter you have from me. 1816 Scott *Bl. Dwarf* i, 'Wussing your health, sirs,' said the shepherd. 1819 Shelley *Cenci* I. ii. 40 You know My zeal for all you wish, sweet Beatrice. 1854 Dickens *Hard T.* II. i, Would you wish a little more hot water, ma'am? 1901 W. R. H. Trowbridge *Lett. her Mother to Eliz.* xxix. 144 [The maid] flew into a rage, and wanted to know if I wished a month's notice.

(*b*) with obj. clause with *may* or (formerly) pres. subj., occas. indic.: expressing a desire that the event may happen or that the fact may prove to be so, and often implying some want of confidence or fear of the opposite (now commonly expressed by *hope*: see Hope *v.* 3 b). Also expressing a request (see 5).

a 1000 *Deor* 25 Secg moniȝ..wyscte ȝeneahhe þæt þæs cynerices ofercumen wære. c 1000 Ælfric *Gen.* xvii. 18 Ic wisce þæt Ismahel lybbe ætforan ðe. a 1586 Sidney *Arcadia* II. x. (1912) 208, I wish that it may not prove ominous foretoken of misfortune. 1591 Shaks. *Two Gent.* IV. iii. 41, I wish all good befortune you. 1649 in *Spalding Club Misc.* (1852) V. 381, I heartellie wosse that anie that lowes religione..keepe themselwes free of anie accessione..to swche wnhape men. 1661 P. Henry *Diaries & Lett.* (1882) 86, I wish I suffer no prejudice by it. 1691 Shadwell *Scowrers* IV, I wish the house is not robb'd. 1715 Addison *Drummer* II. i, He say's he's a Conjurer, but he looks very suspicious; I wish he ben't a Jesuit. 1756 *Monitor* No. 35. I. 325 He is certainly bewitched: I wish the old hag upon the green has done him no mischief. 1808 Jane Austen *Lett.* (1884) II. 6 She hears that Miss Bigg is to be married in a fortnight. I wish it may be so. 1823 Scott *Quentin D.* xxi, I wish we have not got King Stork, instead of King Log. 1860 Emily Eden *Semi-attached Couple* xii, Mrs. Tomkinson wished to goodness there might soon be..'a little staying company' in the house. 1872 Geo. Eliot in J. W. Cross *Life* (1885) III. 157, I wish that you may happen to know her.

(*c*) with obj. clause with past subj. (or indic., e.g. *was* for *were*): expressing an unrealized or unrealizable desire (see also Will *v.*[1] 46), or in mod. use sometimes a mild request (cf. 5).

971 *Blickl. Hom.* 93 Hie..wyscaþ þæt hie næfre næron acennede fram fæder ne from meder. c 1000 Ælfric *Deut.* xxxii. 29 Ic wisce ðæt hi wisdom & underȝeaton..hyra ende [Vulg. *utinam saperent*]. 1340 *Ayenb.* 56 Hi wesseþ þet hi hedden nykken of crane and wombe of cou. 1362 Langl. *P. Pl.* A. v. 92 Þenne I wussche hit weore myn. c 1385 Chaucer *L. G. W.* 755 *Thisbe*, Thys wall they woldyn threte And wysshe to god hyt were doun ybete. 1476 *Stonor Papers* (Camden) II. 11 Wherfore I wyst fulle hertly dyuerse tymez þat ȝe hadde ben here. a 1568 G. Cavendish *Poems* (1825) II. 40 Therfor my fraylte I may both curse and ban, Whissyng to God I had never known man. 1579 Lyly *Euphues* 31, I wish my wish were as effectually ended as it is heartely looked for. 1605 Shaks. *Macb.* I. v. 26 That which rather thou do'st feare to doe, Then wishest should be vndone. 1624 Ussher *Lett.* (1686) 315, I could wish that Mr. Lisle would take some pains in translating the Saxon Annals into our English Tongue. 1681 in *10th Rep. Hist. MSS. Comm.* App. I. 133, I haiue gotten a tasch upon me that I wisch from my hart it was well of my handes to your satisfaction. 1711 I could wish [see Can *v.*[1] 7]. 1817 Byron *Let. to Moore* 25 Mar., Heigh ho! I wish I was drunk—but I have nothing but this damned barley-water before me. 1833 Tennyson *May Queen, New Year's Eve* iv, I wish the snow would melt...I long to see a flower so. 1885 'F. Anstey' *Tinted Venus* ii. 24, 'I wish to heaven I did,' cried the manager. 1890 [see Goodness 5].

(*d*) with inf. as obj. (usually, now always, with *to*).

Occas. with admixture of the idea of intention or request for permission (cf. 5), as 'I wish to say a few words'.

c 1250 *Gen. & Ex.* 1060 He wisten him bergen fro ðe dead. 1390 Gower *Conf.* I. 149 Sche wissheth forto ben unbore. c 1450 *Merlin* vii. 113 So that the moste hardy of hem..sholde wiesshe to be at home in his owne contree. 1500–20 Dunbar *Poems* liii. 33, I wissitt to be The gyrtast erle, or duik, in France. 1513 Douglas *Æneis* XII. xiv. 17 Wys now to fle vp to the starnis on hycht. 1560 *Bible* (Geneva) *Jonah* iv. 8 Ionah fainted, and wished in his heart to dye. 1611 Shaks. *Wint. T.* II. i. 123, I neuer wish'd to see you sorry, now I trust I shall. 1630 Milton *On Shakespear* 16 Kings for such a Tomb would wish to die. 1776 *Trial of Nundocomar* 23/2 Any body that wishes to see him may. 1850 Miss Mulock *Olive* xxv, I wish to talk to you. 1876 Mozley *Univ. Serm.* xi. 213 If men really wish to be good, they will become good. 1893 *Law Times* XCV. 305/2 If she wished to be sure of her income she should of all things avoid dabbling in the shares of new companies.

(*e*) with acc. and inf., or in pass. with inf. (usually, now always, with *to*).

Sometimes expressing a request: see 5 b.

1538 Starkey *England* II. i. (1878) 176 Aftur a maner..the wych I wold wysch to be put in vse wyth vs. c 1560 A. Scott *Poems* (S.T.S.) xv. 39 Away I went,..Wissing all luvaris leill to haif sic chance. ? 1567 [M. Parker] *Whole Psalter* cx. vii, Pursued to death, and wysht to sinke. a 1585 Sidney *Astr. & Stella* x, I rather wish thee clim̃e the Muses hill. 1603 Shaks. *Meas. for M.* IV. iii. 138 If you can pace your wisdome, In that good path that I would wish it go. 1657 J. Sergeant *Schism Dispach't* 406, I love the Presbyterians so well as not to wish them renounce their reason. 1753–4 Richardson *Grandison* I. xix. 130 [He said that] every man who saw me must wish me to be his. 1891 Farrar *Darkn. & Dawn* xv, Nero..wished Junia Silana and Calvia Crispinilla to be of the party.

(*f*) with obj. and compl. (sb., adj., pple., advb. phrase): now chiefly in imprecations or the like.

14.. *How Plowman learned Paternoster* 152 in Hazl. *E. P. P.* I. 215 He wysshed them at the devyll therfore. 1477 *Stonor Papers* (Camden) II. 22, I thank you hertely þat hyt plesyd you to wyshe me with you. c 1520 Skelton *Magnyf.* 2306, I se well there is no better rede, But sygh, and sorowe, and wysshe my selfe dede. 1532 Tindale *Exp. Matt.* v–vii vii. (? 1550) 88 b, Who is so wel beloued..but that ther be ynow..that woulde, for hys good, wishe him to hel? a 1533 [see Wish *sb.*[1] 2]. 1579 Lyly *Euphues* (Arb.) 70, I wyshed my selfe heere. 1591 Shaks. *Two Gent.* I. i. 14 Wish me partaker in thy happinesse, When thou do'st meet good hap. 1605 — *Macb.* v. viii. 49 Had I as many Sonnes, as I haue haires, I would not wish them to a fairer death. 1621 [see Further *adv.* 4 b]. 1711 Steele *Spect.* No. 27 ¶ 2 We every day wish ourselves disengaged from its allurements. 1724 Ramsay *Vision* ix, Mailpayers wiss it to the devil. 1797 Jane Austen *Sense & Sensib.* xxxvii, We all wish her extremely happy. 1819 Crabbe *T. of Hall* xvii. 364 Perch that were wish'd to salmon for her sake. 1823 Lamb *Let. to Southey* 21 Nov., I wished both magazine and review at the bottom of the sea. 1848 Dickens *Dombey* xxii, Let us remember James by name, and wish him happy. 1902 'Violet Jacob' *Sheep-Stealers* xi, She could only move uneasily on her seat, and wish him miles away.

(*g*) after *as* or *than*: often *ellipt.* (so also with rel.) for various constructions, esp. (*c*), (*d*), (*e*).

1523 Ld. Berners *Froiss.* I. clxiv. 83/1 The adventures of amours and of war, are more fortunate and marueilous, than any man canne thynke or wysshe. 1530 Palsgr. 783/1, I am as well nowe, I thanke God, as I coulde wysshe. 1560 *Bible* (Geneva) *Ps.* lxxiii. 7 They haue more then heart can wish. 1698 Collier *Immor. Stage* 227 He..goes off as like a Town Spark as you would wish. 1750 Gray *Elegy* Ep. 8 He gain'd from Heav'n ('twas all he wish'd) a friend. 1866 Geo. Eliot *Felix Holt* i, Nothing had come just as she had wished. 1868 Louisa M. Alcott *Little Women* xiii, You should do just what your grandfather wishes.

(*h*) in passive: esp. in predicative phr. *to be wished* = desirable.

1531 Elyot *Gov.* II. ix, It is to be wisshed, that they, whiche..haue any autoritie, maye be like to the lawes, whiche in correctynge be ladde only by equitie. 1597 Morley *Introd. Mus.* Ded., More to be wished and much more durable. 1602 Shaks. *Ham.* III. i. 64 'Tis a consummation Deuoutly to be wish'd. 1697 De Foe *Ess. Projects* 232 'Twere to be wish'd our Gentry were so much Lovers of Learning, that Birth might always be join'd with Capacity. 1786 Clara Reeve *Exiles* II. 124 At length the day so long wished and expected came. 1876 *Jrnl. Soc. Arts* 2 June 708/1 The returns from the Cheltenham district were not so complete as might be wished. 1918 *Pall Mall Gaz.* 29 June 8/1 The first venture..was not, perhaps, as successful as could have been wished.

†b. *fig.* of a thing: To 'require': = Desire *v.* 3.

1600 Abbot *Jonah* 599, I do not find that expositors speake so fully to the matter of this wind, as me seemeth this text doth wish.

2. *intr.* To have or feel a wish; in early use

often, to long, yearn. **a.** with *after* (obs.), *for*: = 1 (*a*); also *indir. pass.* = 1 (*h*).

c 1200 *Trin. Coll. Hom.* 3 Men..wisten ȝerne after ure lauerd ihesu cristes tocume. *Ibid.* 135 Þu hauest longe iwist after strene, and god haueð herd þine bede. 13.. *Cursor M.* 23548 (Edinb.) Ilk man sal haf til his, Al þat he wil eftir wis. 1481 Caxton *Myrr.* 107 The deth wold they haue and weesshe after it incessantly. 1526 Tindale *Acts* xxvii. 29 They cast iiij. ancres out of the sterne: and wysshed for the daye. 1579 Lyly *Euphues* (Arb.) 69 By so much the more you are welcome, by how much the more you were wished for. 1740 Richardson *Pamela* II. 263, I can only wish for more worthiness. 1757 Eliz. Griffith *Lett. Henry & Frances* (1767) I. 84, I wished for you..in vain all night, the life-long night. 1834 Dickens *Sk. Boz*, *Boarding-ho.* ii, Having nothing to do and nothing to wish for, she naturally imagined she must be very ill. 1867 Spedding *Publ. & Authors* 75 Buy the volumes as they come out, if you wish for them.

b. *absol.*

1546 J. Heywood *Prov.* (1867) 50 Better to haue then wishe. 1570 *Satir. Poems Reform.* xii. 185 Than war I fane, bot all in vane, To wis and will nocht be. 1596 Dalrymple tr. *Leslie's Hist. Scot.* (S.T.S.) I. 228 Quha can wiss aboue thir thrie? 1601 Shaks. *All's Well* I. iii. 218 If your selfe..Did euer, in so true a flame of liking, Wish chastly, and loue dearely. 1850 Miss Mulock *Olive* xxi, It had been one of her childish superstitions always 'to wish at the new moon'. 1904 W. W. Jacobs *Dialstone Lane* iii. 37, 'I could see it at any time I wished', she said sharply. 'Well, wish now', entreated Mr. Tredgold.

c. *trans.* with cognate obj.

c 1400 [see Wish *sb.*[1] 3]. 1588 Shaks. *L. L. L.* II. i. 179 Thy own wish wish I thee, in euery place. 1849 Mrs. Gaskell *Lizzie Leigh*, etc. (1913) 426 Wishing all manner of idle wishes. 1914 'Ian Hay' *Knt. on Wheels* xi, If you wish a wish and then feel in my pocket, old lady, you may find something.

3. *trans.* To express a wish for; to say that one wishes...(with various const. as in 1); *spec.* to imprecate, invoke (an evil or curse).

c 1000 Ælfric *Hom.* II. 308 Alexander ða wiscte: 'Eala ȝif ðu wære hund!' 1476 *Paston Lett.* Suppl. (1901) 149, I wysshed to hym that he and I hadde been at Norwyche. 1526 *Pilgr. Perf.* (W. de W. 1531) 7 Than he cryeth out and wyssheth that he neuer had had eyes to se. 1560 *Bible* (Geneva) *Job* xxxi. 30 Nether haue I suffred my mouth to sinne, by wishing a cursse vnto his soule. 1594 Shaks. *Rich. III*, I. iii. 218 If Heauen haue any grieuous plague in store, Exceeding those that I can wish vpon thee. 1673 Cave *Prim. Chr.* III. i. 221 He was consumed by such a disease as he had wished upon himself. 1715 Atterbury *Serm., Matt.* xxvii. 25 (1734) I. 134 The profane Folly..of wishing that Damnation to ourselves, which we otherways but too well deserve. 1724 Ramsay *Vision* xxvii, He..wischt I happyness micht bruke. 1781 in *Jrnl. Friends Hist. Soc.* (1918) 72 She was senceable to the last..often wished she might be like her..D[ea]r Grandmother.

4. *spec.* (with *to* or simple object) To desire (something, usually good) for or on behalf of a person, etc.: esp. in formulæ of greeting or expressions of goodwill; hence as in 3, to express such a wish for, esp. as a formal greeting:

e.g. *to wish* (*one*) *good morning*, *good-bye* (= Bid *v.*[1] 9), *a merry Christmas*, *a happy New Year*, *many happy returns of the day* (see Return *sb.* 2 b), etc.; also intr. in *to wish* (*one*) *well* (see Well *adv.* 2 d), and intr. or trans. (usually with neg.) in *to wish* (*one*) *ill* (where *ill* may be taken as adv. or sb.). *To wish* (*one*) *joy of*: see Joy *sb.* 9 d.

c 900 *Laws Alfred* Introd. xlix. § 3 Ða apostolas & þa eldran broðor hælo eow wyscað. c 1374 Chaucer *Troylus* II. 406, I bidde wisshe yow no more sorwe. 1393 Langl. *P. Pl.* C. xx. 328 Þer ne is syk ne sory..Þat he ne may..boþe wusshen and wylnen Alle manere of men mercy and for-ȝeuenesse. 1516 *State Papers Hen. VIII*, VI. 50 Not to thintent he schulde have hys parte off thys intolerable troble.., for I wolde not wysche itt to a dogge. 1535 Coverdale *Ps.* cxxix. 8 We wish you good lucke in the name of the Lorde. — *Job* xxxi. 30, I neuer suffred my mouth to do soch a sinne, as to wysh him euell. 1552 Huloet, Wyshe ille to any thinge, *fascino*. 1579 Lyly *Euphues* (Arb.) 97, I would neither wish thee a greater plague, nor him a deadlyer poyson. a 1586 Sidney *Apol. Poetrie* (Arb.) 72, I will not wish vnto you..to be rimed to death. 1596 Dalrymple tr. *Leslie's Hist. Scot.* x. (S.T.S.) II. 359 To salute thame baith, wisse thame gude morne. 1610 Shaks. *Temp.* v. i. 215 Let griefe and sorrow still embrace his heart, That doth not wish you ioy. 1623 Heminge & Condell *Shaks. Wks.* To Rdrs., And such Readers we wish him. c 1720 De Foe *Mem. Cavalier* I. 29 They wished the Swedes Success. 1816 Jane Austen *Emma* x, I wish Jane Fairfax very well; but she tires me to death. 1821 Scott *Kenilw.* vii, I have been prayed for, and wished well to, in your congregations. 1885 *Law Times* LXXIX. 345/2 [He] wished the officials good night, and left the room.

b. To desire, or express a desire for, the welfare or misfortune of (a person); only in *evil wished*, Ill-wish *v.*, Well-wished.

1577 Hellowes *Gueuara's Chron.* 325 All three were so euil wished in the Common wealth, that the least euill which they would them..was but death. 1604 Bodley in *Buccleuch MSS.* (Hist. MSS. Comm.) I. 48, I leave you both as well wished, as if you were to enjoy the best wishes bestowed this new year's day in England.

5. In expressions of desire for something to be done by another, thus conveying a request; hence, to request, entreat; formerly sometimes, to bid, command: **a.** a thing or action (with various const. as in 1): cf. Desire *v.* 5.

a 1533 Ld. Berners *Huon* lxxxiii. 259 He came to Huon & wysshyd yᵉ fetters fro all there fete [orig. *soubhaita leurs fers hors de leurs iambes*]. 1553 T. Wilson *Rhet.* 38 To wishe of God to purge oure hartes from all filthines and vngodlie dealinge. 1596 Dalrymple tr. *Leslie's Hist. Scot.* ix. (S.T.S.) II. 236, I wisse rather..that in hope of barnes he take Margaret rather than Magdalen for his bedfallow. 1596 Bacon *Max. Com. Law* ix. (1636) 36 The Statute of 27. H. 8. of uses, that wisheth that the *cestui que use* shall have the possession in quality and degree as hee had the use. 1671 Milton *Samson* 1414 Brethren farewel, your company along I will not wish. a 1674 Clarendon *Hist. Reb.* VIII. § 272 To confer with lord Digby, who..should find the best way to make the earl of Antrim to communicate the affair to him, and to wish his assistance. 1842 Dickens *Amer. Notes* xiv, Whatever we wished done was done with great civility and readiness. 1875 Jowett *Plato* (ed. 2) I. 429, I wish that you would tell me about his death.

b. a person *to do* something: cf. Desire *v.* 6.

1537 Stocker *Civ. Warres Lowe C.* IV. 55 [The] Captaine ..wished them quietly departe, without they liked to be saluted with Cannon shotte. 1603 Shaks. *Meas. for M.* v. i. 79 *Duk.* You were not bid to speake. *Luc.* No,..Nor wish'd to hold my peace. 1604 Dekker & Middleton *Honest Wh.* I. C 2 b, Hie to the Constable, And in all calme order wish him to attach them. 1716 Swift *Poems*, *Phyllis* 35 The Groom was wish'd to saddle Crop. 1854 Dickens *Hard T.* II. i, Would you wish the gentleman to be shewn in, ma'am? 1859 Ruskin *Two Paths* i. § 35 There is another thing I wish you to notice specially in these statues.

†c. To invite, 'bid' (a person to a place). *Obs. rare.*

a 1533 Ld. Berners *Huon* lxxxiii. 259 He..causyd them to syt downe at his owne table that he had wysshyd thether [orig. *ent fait venir*].

6. To recommend (a person) *to* another, or *to* a place, etc. *Obs.* or *dial.*

orig. prob. belonging to Wis *v.*[1] 2, to direct.

1596 Shaks. *Tam. Shr.* I. i. 113 If I can by any meanes light on a fit man to teach her that wherein she delights, I will wish him to her father. 1610 B. Jonson *Alch.* I. iii, I was wish'd to your worship, by a gentleman,..That say's you know mens planets. 1633 Rowley *Match at Mid-n.* IV. i, He sayes he was wisht to [a] very wealthy Widdow, but of you he has heard much Histories, that he will marry you. 1751 Eliza Heywood *Betsy Thoughtless* I. xvi. 196 Now I have been wished to several fine women, but my fancy gives the preference to you. 1818 Scott *Hrt. Midl.* xxiii, She passed that interval of time in the lodging of a woman, an acquaintance of that person who had wished her to that place. 1846 Brockett *N. C. Gloss.* (ed. 3) s.v., Can you wish me to a customer?

7. To influence in a magical or occult way by wishing; to bewitch by a desire or imprecation. *dial.*

1848 Mrs. Gaskell *Mary Barton* vii, We mun get him away from his mother. He cannot die while she's wishing him. 1865 Tylor *Early Hist. Man.* vi. 134 When he hears that he has been 'wished,' he..takes to his bed at once.

¶ *I wish*, corrupt form of *iwis*: see Wis *v.*[2]

Wish, var. Wis *v.*[1] *Obs.*

Wishable (wi·ʃăb'l), *a.* *rare.* [f. Wish *v.* + -able.] That may be wished for; desirable.

1548 Udall *Erasm. Par. Luke* iv. 20–24 The glad & wishable tidynges of saluacion. 1611 Cotgr., *Souhaitable*, ..wishable, desirable. 1905 W. A. Ellis *R. Wagner to M. Wesendonck* 165 Wisdom is so excellent and wishable.

Wishe, obs. pa. t. of Wash *v.*; obs. f. Wish.

Wished (wiʃt, *poet. also* wi·ʃĕd), *ppl. a.* [f. Wish *v.* + -ed [1].]

1. That is the object of a wish; desired, longed-for. Now *rare* exc. as in b.

15.. *Fickle Estate of Our Vncertayn Lyfe* (MS. Rawl. poet. 112, lf. 10 b), What if a day or A moneth or a yeare Crowne thy delightes with a thousand wisht contentinges? 1577 Grange *Golden Aphrod.* etc. P iv b, So friendly Venus is, so friendly Cupid was, That fancie brought hir soone, vnto my wished passe. 1583 Melbancke *Philotimus* C c iij, My wished frend, and welcomde guest. 1602 Marston *Antonio's Rev.* III. ii, We touch the shore Of wisht revenge. 1667 Milton *P. L.* I. 208 While Night Invests the Sea, and wished Morn delayes. 1748 Richardson *Clarissa* VII. lxii. 221 At length..every thing is in the wished train. 1811 W. R. Spencer *Poems* 17 Oh! why so late thy wish'd return? 1812 Cary *Dante*, *Par.* xxiii. 4 The bird..With her sweet brood; impatient to descry Their wished looks. 1906 Charl. Mansfield *Girl & Gods* xxvii, Psyche..held out her hand in token of a wished farewell.

b. with *for*: cf. Wish *v.* 2 a.

1586 T. B. *La Primaud. Fr. Acad.* I. 1 The wished-for newes of peace. 1725 Ramsay *Gentle Sheph.* III. iv, When wished-for pleasures rise like morning light. 1812 Byron *Ch. Har.* I. xlv, Yet is she free—the spoiler's wish'd-for prey! 1888 Burgon *Lives 12 Gd. Men* I. i. 32 [They] declared their inability to render America the wished for assistance.

2. Entertained as a wish: cf. Wish *v.* 2 c. *rare.*

1580 Lyly *Euphues* (Arb.) 467 Hauing thus made ech other priuie to our wished desires.

Wishedly (wi·ʃĕdli), *adv.* Now *rare* or *Obs.* [f. Wished *ppl. a.* + -ly [2].] As is or was wished; according to desire.

1573 Twyne *Æneid.* x. E e 3, Like as wisshedly when winds in sommer season blowe. 1603 Knolles *Hist. Turks* (1621) 620 What could have happened unto him more wishedly? 1624 Capt. J. Smith *Virginia* v. 174 Sir George Somers..most wishedly and happily descried land. 1633 Heywood *Eng. Trav.* IV. G 4 b, Of all my friends to me Most wishedly, you are welcome.

Wisher (wi·ʃəɹ). Now *rare*. [f. Wish *v.* + -er [1].] One who wishes.

† *Wishers and woulders*: see Woulder.

15.. *Parl. Byrdes* 91 in Hazl. *E. P. P.* III. 171 Wysshers want wyll. a 1586 Sidney *Arcadia* III. (1922) 15 Many times he wished himself the back of an Asse,..(an unfortunate wisher, for if he had as well wished the head, it had bene graunted him). 1606 Shaks. *Ant. & Cl.* IV. xv. 37 Wishers were euer Fooles. 1670 Eachard *Cont. Clergy* To Rdr., I am..only an honest and hearty wisher, that the best of our clergy might forever continue as they are. 1760 Sterne *Tr. Shandy* III. i, The safest way..to take off the

Supplement, p. 3873; Corrigenda, p. 4092; Spurious words, p. 4093; Books quoted, p. 4094

WITCH.

1. A female magician, sorceress; in later use *esp.* a woman supposed to have dealings with the devil or evil spirits and to be able by their co-operation to perform supernatural acts. See also WHITE WITCH.

2. With masculine prefix.

Witch, wych (witʃ), *sb.²* Forms: 1 wiɔe, wiɔ, wyɔ, 5-7 wyche, 6-8 wich, 6(9)the, wiech, weech, weoche, wytche, vyche, wyche, weyche, 6 witch, wetch.

Witch (witʃ), *v.*

Witched (witʃt), *ppl. a.*

Witchen. Now *dial.* Also 7 witchen.

WITCHERY.

WITCHET.

Witchet.

Witchety (witʃi). *Austral.* [Native name.]

Witch-finder.

Witch knot, wych hazel.

Witchmonger (witʃmʌŋgər).

Witchy (witʃi), *a., rare.*

†Wite, *sb.¹* Obs.

†Wite, *sb.²* Obs.

Witching (witʃiŋ), *vbl. sb.*

Witching, *ppl. a.*

Wite, wyte (wəit), *sb.³* Obs. exc. *Hist.* and *dial.*

WITE.

†Wite, *v.¹* Obs.

†Wite, *v.²* Obs.

+Wite, *v.³* Obs.

†Wite, *sb.* Obs. Forms: 1 witan, 2-4 wite.

Wite, *obs.* f. WHITE, WIGHT, *v.*

†Witeless, *a.* Obs. Blameless.

Witenagemot (witənəgəˌmoːt), *popularly* **Witan.** *Hist.*

Witer, Witing *vbl. sb.²*

Witeredem.

Witereden.

Witful (witˌfuːl), *a.*

Witsafe, obs. f. VOUCHSAFE.

Witson, etc., obs. forms of WHITSUN.

Wit-tee. *dial.*

Witter (witər), *v.*

Wittereden.

whyt(h, whith, witȝ, weþ, Sc. wygh(e, wyghte, wycht, 6 wight, witht, Sc. vitht, quhit, wutht, 7–9 n. dial. wud, 8–9 Sc. and n. dial. wi', 9 dial. wiv, way), 2– with; abbreviated 4–7 w^t, 5–7 wth (6 wth). [OE. wið = OFris. with, OS. wið, ON. við (Sw. vid, Da. ved): app. a shortening (peculiar to the Anglo-Frisian and Scandinavian areas) of the Com. Teut. *wider- (see s.v. WITHER a. and adv. and WITHER-[1]), perh. taking place orig. in compounds (cf. WITH- and the parallelism of OE. wiþcéosan and wiþercéosan to reject, wiþstandan and wiþerstandan to withstand, etc.).

As an adv., with occurs as the second element in composition with other advs. denoting direction, motion, or extension: FORWITH (FOROUTH, FORROW), FORTHWITH, INWITH, OUTWITH (UTOUTH), DOWNWITH, UPWITH.]

The prevailing senses of this prep. in the earliest periods are those of opposition ('against') and of motion or rest in proximity ('towards', 'alongside'), which are now current only in certain traditional collocations or specific applications. These notions readily pass into fig. uses denoting various kinds of relations, among which those implying reciprocity are at first prominent. The most remarkable development in the signification of with consists in its having taken over in the ME. period the chief senses belonging properly to OE. mid MID prep.[1] (cognate with Gr. μετά with). These senses are mainly those denoting association, combination or union, instrumentality or means, and attendant circumstance. These are all important senses of ON. við, to which fact their currency and ultimate predominance in the English word are partly due. The last important stage was the extension of with from the instrument to the agent, in which use it was current for different periods along with of and through, and later with by, which finally superseded the other three. The range of meanings in general has no doubt been enlarged by association with L. cum. The interaction of senses and sense-groups has been such that the position of a particular sense in the order of development is often difficult to determine.

In common with other preps. with can be postponed to the end of an interrogative or relative clause introduced by its regimen; but in ME. it was freq. placed immediately after the verb in relative clauses, e.g. þes rentis þat þe fend haþ dowed wiþ clerkis = these revenues with which the Devil has endowed clerics. In postposition it was for a long period extensively replaced by WITHAL (q.v. B).

I. Denoting opposition and derived notions (separation; motion towards).

†1. In a position opposite to; over against: = AGAINST 1. Chiefly in advb. phrases with repeated sb., as face with face, where to is now used.

c 893 ÆLFRED Oros. I. i. § 31 Be norðan is se sæ, be æȝþer his ȝe nearo ȝe breoh, wið Italia þam lande. c 950 Lindisf. Gosp. Mark xii. 41 Sætt se hælend wið..ðæs dores. c 1175 Lamb. Hom. 61 Cristes wille bo us bitwon neb wið neb for him to son. c 1200 Trin. Coll. Hom. 105 His wise wordes þe he wiþ hem spec muð wið muðe. c 1205 LAY. 8253 Breoste wið breoste banes þer craekeden. a 1300 [see FACE sb. 2 d].

b. In exchange, return, or payment for: = AGAINST 14, FOR 6. Obs. exc. dial.

The related senses 'in compensation for', 'in comparison with' are only OE.

c 893 ÆLFRED Oros. IV. xiii. § 1 Hit Scipia nolde him aliefan wið uanum oþrum þinge butan hie him ealle hiera wæpeno aȝeafen. 993 Battle of Maldon 35 We willað wið þam golde grið fæstnian. c 1000 ÆLFRIC Exod. xxi. 24 Eȝe wið eaȝan, toþ wiþ teð. 1442 in Reg. Mag. Sig. Scot. 1424 64/1 The landis of..Pettendrech, the quhilkis war changeit with the landis of Dunottir. a 1568 ASCHAM Scholem. I. (Arb.) 27 If the childe misse, either in forgetting a worde, or in chaunging a good with a worse. 1570 in Shropsh. Par. Doc. (1903) 63 Rec. at the chaunge of the cupp with the chaliers vii^s. ii^d. 1637 RUTHERFORD Lett., to M. Mowat 7 Sept. (1671) 165 We might barter or niffer our lazie ease with a profitable cross.

2. Of conflict, antagonism, dispute, injury, reproof, competition, rivalry, and the like: In opposition to, adversely to: = AGAINST 12, 12 b, 12 d.

Still the normal prep. with such words as battle, chide, compete, conflict, contend, dispute, fight, quarrel, strive, struggle, vie, war, and phrases like go to law, at odds, but now associated with or merged in 8, 13 b, or 20.

Beowulf 152 Grendel wan hwile wið Hroþgar. a 900 CYNEWULF Elene 836 Hie wið Godes bearne nið ahofun. 900–30 O. E. Chron. an. 853 (Parker MS.), Ealhere mid Cantwarum, & Huda mid Suþriȝium ȝefuhton on Tenet wiþ hæþnum herige. a 1000 Gnomic Verses II. 187 Weriȝ sceal wiþ winde roweþ. c 1175 Lamb. Hom. 19 Þet he ne misdude wið oderne. Ibid. 129 Of þan icompe þe ure drihten hefde wið þene feond. c 1200 ORMIN 16981 Ȝiff þa mihhtenn witenn itt þatt haffdenn niþ wiþþ Criste. 1338 R. BRUNNE Chron. (1810) 57 He praied him for his nauy to help him with summ. c 1440 Alphabet of Tales 124 Þis knight askid hym if he kend oght with hym selfe. 1590 [see CONFLICT sb. 1]. 1596 Edw. III, II. ii, Poore shipskin, how it braules with him that beateth it! 1611 SHAKS. Wint. T. I. ii. 355 One, Who in Rebellion with himselfe, will haue All that are his, so too. 1668 WALTON Angler iv. (ed. 4) 66 He [sc. the trout] may justly contend with all fresh-water-Fish, as the Mullet may with all Sea-Fish. 1719 DE FOE Crusoe II. (Globe) 357 Let us go and have t'other Brush with them. 1736 Gentl. Mag. VI. 334/1 Let the Boys be set a running, as it were, with one another, in getting without Book. 1851 NEWMAN Pres. Pos. Cath. vi. § 7 Invention cannot run with prejudice. Prejudice wins. 1909 Dublin Rev. Jan. 128 Amazons at handgrips with a long-suffering police.

†3. Of resistance, defence, protection, warning, caution: = AGAINST 13, 13 b. Obs.

Beowulf 540 Wit unc wið hronfixas werian þohton. 971 Blickl. Hom. 171 Þa woldan hie on ecnesse hæle & trume wið deofla niþum & helle witum. c 1000 Sax. Leechd. II. 130 Wiþ bryne ȝenim finules niþewearde. c 1040 Bidding Prayer in Lay Folks Mass Bk. 62 Þæt hy us ȝehealdan & ȝescyldan wið ealra feonda costnunga. c 1175 Lamb. Hom. 53 Þe feder and þe sune and þe halie gast iscilde us..wið alle sunnen. a 1225 Ancr. R. 224 Hu ȝe schulen witen ou wið þes deofles wieles. c 1320 Cast. Love 826 Þe seue berbicans abouten,..witeþ þis Castel so wel Wiþ arwe and wiþ qwarel. c 1375 Sc. Leg. Saints xi. (Symon & Iudas) 203 For þat þu suld mar vnwar be Vith þi fais.

†4. Of separation or deliverance: = FROM 6, 6 b. Obs. (See also 19 c.)

Beowulf 2423 Sundur ȝedælan lif wið lice. a 1000 Cædmon's Gen. 127 Þa ȝesundrode sigora waldend..leoht wið þeostrum, sceade wið sciman. a 1250 Owl & Night. 610 Me is lof to cristes huse To clansi hit wiþ fule muse.

5. †a. Towards, in the direction of: = AGAINST 5. (Only OE.) Obs.

Beowulf 213 Streamas wundon sund wið sande. Ibid. 1880 Ac him on hreþre hygebendum fæst æfter deorum men dyrne langað beorn wið blode. 900–30 O. E. Chron. an. 894 (Parker MS.), Þa wende he hine west wið Exanceastres. a 1000 Riddles iv. 42 Þonne scearp cymeð sceo wiþ oþrum, ecg wið ecge. c 1000 ÆLFRIC Saints' Lives xxvi. 204 Sum weȝfarende man ferde wið þone feld.

b. Near or close to, against, alongside. Now only Naut. with words denoting proximity and consequently belonging more properly to 18.

Beowulf 326 Setton..rondas regnhearde wið þæs recedes weal. Ibid. 2566 Stiðmod ȝestod wið steapne rond winia bealdor. 900–30 O. E. Chron. an. 878 (Parker MS.), Æt Alre, & þæt is wiþ Æþelingga eiȝe. c 1000 Ags. Gosp. Luke viii. 5 Þa he þæt seow sum feoll wið þæne weȝ. c 1050 Voc. in Wr.-Wülcker 447/25 Murotenus, wið ðone weall. 13.. Gaw. & Gr. Knt. 113 Bischop Bawdewyn abof bi-ginez þe table, & Ywan, Vryn son, ette wit hymseluen. 14.. Sailing Directions (Hakl. Soc.) 12 Than go your cours with the horse shoo south southwest. Ibid. 13 Fro Seint Margret steyers and ye will go with Dengenes, your best way is south south west. 1579–80 NORTH Plutarch, Theseus (1595) 10 By force of weather driven with the coast of Sicile. 1591 RALEIGH Last Fight Rev. (Arb.) 24 A fourth ranne her selfe with the shore to saue her men. 1625 PURCHAS Pilgrims II. 1133 An houre after Sunne rising, we were with a very long and faire point. 1708– [see IN adv. 9 b]. 1748 Anson's Voy. II. vii. 212 One of our prizes was ordered to stand close in with it [sc. the land]. 1788 J. WHITE Jrnl. Voy. N. S. Wales (1790) 108 As we run in with the land,..we were surprised to see..some small patches of snow. 1849 O'BYRNE Naval Biogr. Dict. 661/2 At the cutting out, close in with the enemy's batteries of La Guêpe privateer. 1860 DICKENS Uncomm. Trav. ii, A man..saw..some dark troubled object close in with the land.

c. Into the presence or immediate proximity of (and in derived fig. uses): following such verbs as encounter, fall in, meet, etc., q.v. (Now associated with 19.)

†6. Governing a demonstrative pronoun, forming conjunctive phrases: with than (the, that), with that, with thi (that), wiþi, wyþy, rarely with this (that) [see THAN dem. pron., THAT conj. 1 c, THY adv.]: a. On condition that, provided that, if.

c 1000 ÆLFRIC Saints' Lives xii. 118 Nolde he syllan ealle his æhta þeah þe he weliȝ wære, wið þan þe he libban moste. a 1200 Moral Ode 132 in O. E. Hom. I. 169 Eure he walde her inne wawe and ine wene wunien Wið þet he mihte belle pine bi-flien. c 1205 LAY. 8253 Al þine wille he wule don, wið þon þe þu him ȝeue grið. a 1300 Siriz 192 Ich wile ȝeve the riche mede With that hit be so. a 1300 St. Thomas 184 in Horstm. Altengl. Leg. (1881) 22 Grete bewtes to him he bed..Withi he wold dwell with him still. c 1300 Havelok 532, I shal maken þe fre,..With-þan þu wilt þis childe take. 1375 BARBOUR Bruce I. 493 With-thi ȝe giff me all the land, That ȝe haiff now in-till ȝour hand. c 1400 Beryn 3972 Tomorow I woll be redy his best to fulfill, With this I have save condit. 1473 Paston Lett. III. 100, I wolde he had it for vij. yeer, with thys that my moodre be agreable to the same. 1497 in Somerset Med. Wills (1901) 353, I will that Isabell my doughter, shal haue all suche stuffe [etc.] whit that she marie by thaduyce of my executours. c 1500 Lancelot 960, I grant yow leif, withthy Your name to me that ȝe wil specify. c 1500 Crow & Pie v. in Child Ballads II. 478 Haue ye thys, my dere swetyng, With that ye wylbe lemman myn.

†b. With the intention that, in order that, to the end that. Obs.

c 888 ÆLFRED Boeth. xxxiii. § 2 He..forlæt mænigne weoruldlust wið þæm þe he þone welan beȝete & ȝehealde. Ibid. xl. § 5 Me wære leofre þæt ic onette wið þæs þæt ic þe moste ȝelæstan þæt ic þe ær ȝehet. a 1225 Juliana 3 Þe liflade of a meiden þat is of latin iturnd to englische leode, wið þon þat teos hali leafdi in heouene luuie us þe mare.

II. Denoting personal relation, agreement, association, connexion, union, addition.

* Senses denoting primarily activity towards or influence upon a person or thing.

7. After words denoting speech or other verbal communication between persons (with the person as obj.); properly of mutual communication, but formerly sometimes merely = to, as in quot. 1480.

Beowulf 365 Hy benan synt þæt hie..wið þe moton wordum wrixlan. a 1000 Riddles xl. 12 Ne hafað hio fot ne folm,..ne muð hafaþ ne wiþ monnum spræc. c 1205 LAY. 14069 He wolde wið þan kinge holden runinge. c 1300 Harrow. Hell 123 Y shal speke þe wyht Ant do þe to holde gryht. c 1386 CHAUCER Melib. ¶ 755, I prey yow lat me speke with youre Aduersaries in priuee place. c 1420 Prose Life Alex. 14 He went..for to consaile wit a godd þat þay called Amon. 1470–1760 [see QUESTION v. 2]. c 1480 HENRYSON Bludy Serk 106 Scho said nay, With men þat wald hir wed. 1500–20 DUNBAR Poems xiii. 15 Sum with his fallow rownis. 1555– [see CONFERENCE 4]. 1588 SHAKS. L. L. L. v. ii. 230 White handed Mistris, one sweet word with thee. 1670 in 12th Rep. Hist. MSS. Comm. App. v. 16 Give me leave to be ingennuous with your Honour, that mannifacture grows worse daylie. a 1700 EVELYN Diary 9 Feb. 1665, I had much discourse with his Lordship. 1753–4 RICHARDSON Grandison III. viii. 109 But, unseasonably, as the event shewed, Father Marescotti, being talked with, was earnest to be allowed to visit her. 1884 CONWAY Bound Together I. 181 For many years Mrs. Blatchford had held little communication with her family.

b. Followed by refl. pron., in reference to soliloquy, consideration, determination, etc. arch.

1530 PALSGR. 514/2 Whan I determyne with my selfe to do a thyng. 1553 [see WEIGH v.[1] 12 c]. 1564 HARDING Answ. Jewel 180 Saye this with thy selfe. 1580 LYLY Euphues (Arb.) 443 Bicause you are braue, disdaine not those that are base, thinke with your selues that russet coates haue their Christendome. a 1592 GREENE Alphonsus IV. iii, Remember with your selues. 1707 Curios. Husb. & Gard. 201, I imagin'd with my self..that..we might multiply..the very same curious Plants. 1741 WATTS Improv. Mind I. i. § 1 (1786) 5 Think seriously with yourselves how many follies and sorrows you had escaped.

†c. After communicate, impart (information), orig. = 'share' (cf. 20). Obs. (now replaced by to).

1559, 1704 [see COMMUNICATE v. 2]. 1571 [see IMPART v. 2]. 1612 BRINSLEY Lud. Lit. 4 More readie..to impart your experiments with me. 1623 BINGHAM Xenophon 65 He..communicated his dream with him.

8. a. After words expressing transaction or dealing between persons (with the person as obj.).

Beowulf 155 Grendel..sibbe ne wolde wið manna hwone mæȝenes Deniȝa. c 893 ÆLFRED Oros. III. v, Æfter þæm þe Perse frið ȝenaman wið Romanum. a 1300 Cursor M. 5848 (Gött.) Wid þe eldest folk of israel, Wid pharao þai went to dele. ? c 1360 Alexius 123 (MS. Ashmol. 42) in Horstm. Altengl. Leg. (1881) 177 He..chaungid..his riche wede Wiþ a beggar. a 1400–50– [see COVENANT sb. 1 γ]. c 1450– [see TREATY sb. 2, 3]. 1481 Cely Papers (Camden) 72 Ye schall receyve..a lytyll fardell of felles that ys alowyd for iij felles with the costomer. 1591 SHAKS. Two Gent. III. i. 3 What's your will with me? 1637 RUTHERFORD Lett., to A. Colvill 19 Feb. (1671) 194, I will neither borrow nor lend with it [sc. this world]. 1659 in Engl. Hist. Rev. (1920) Apr. 254, I will keepe my dayes with you as long as I am able. 1661 in Extr. St. Papers rel. Friends Ser. II. (1911) 139 Such of his Maiesties freindes as euer had occasion with me. 1780 Mirror No. 110 ¶ 1 To do justice to those with whom they have had dealings. 1838 THIRLWALL Hist. Greece xl. V. 115 To give audience to all who had business to transact with him. 1861 M. PATTISON Ess. (1889) I. 41 During Edward's wars our commerce with France was wholly broken off.

b. After words expressing conduct or feeling towards (a person, etc.).

In some cases now replaced by other prepositions, e.g. envious of. In expressions of hostile action or feeling, this coincides with 2.

c 888 ÆLFRED Boeth. vii. § 3 Hwi murcnast ðu wið min? c 1000 ÆLFRIC Gen. xii. 18 Hwi dydest ðu swa wið me? c 1175 Lamb. Hom. 27 Ȝif þu ert swiðe for-gult wið þine eorðliche lauerd. a 1200 Moral Ode 216 in O. E. Hom. I. 173 Ac helle king is are-les with þa þe he mei binden. a 1250 Owl & Night. 62 Ich wot þat þu art unmilde Wiþ hom þat ne muȝe from þe schilde. c 1300 Havelok 2705 Godrich, wat is þe Þat þou fare þus with me? c 1400 Brut I. 18 Corneil his eldest douȝter..was so annoyed wiþ him and wiþ his peple. 1470–85 MALORY Arthur X. xxvii. 457 Thenne was kyng Arthur wroth with kynge Marke. 1526 TINDALE Matt. xviii. 29 Have pacience with me, and I will paye the all. 1577– in love with [see LOVE sb. 7 d]. 1599 B. JONSON Ev. Man out of Hum. II. vi, I am come to haue you play the Alchymist with me. 1601 SHAKS. Twel. N. II. v. 162 Be opposite with a kinsman, surly with seruants. 1601 — Jul. C. III. i. 255 O pardon me..That I am meeke and gentle with these Butchers. 1636 Bk. Com. Prayer, Catechism, To ..be in charity with all men. 1677 EARL ESSEX in Essex Papers (Camden) II. 108 Ye soldier being very rough with ye Corporall, and refusing to pay. 1709 ADDISON Tatler No. 108 ¶ 3 Out of Humour with [see HUMOUR sb. 8 a]. 1736– vexed with [see VEX v. 4 b]. 1889 J. K. JEROME Three Men in Boat 172, I..lost my temper with him.

9. Expressing a general relation to a person or thing, usually as affected in some way by the action, etc. spoken of: In the matter of, in regard to, towards, to, at, upon, about, concerning; in regard to the condition or fortune of.

Sometimes approaching the instrumental use, 37; or (with personal obj.) 8 b.

c 897 ÆLFRED Gregory's Past. C. xxix. 200 Ðæm ðeowan is to cyðonne ðæt he wiete ðæt he nis freoh wið his hlaford. c 1205 LAY. 19057 Þe king hire wende to..& hæfde him to done wið leofuest wimmonne. c 1300 Havelok 901 Þan men haueden holpen him doun With þe birþene of his croun. c 1394 P. Pl. Crede 712 Y miȝt tymen þo troiflardes to toilen wiþ þe erþe. c 1400 26 Pol. Poems iv. 8 How it is wiþ hym, y kan not say. 14.. Tundale's Vis. 2366 (MS. A.) How þei schuld be with don as Godus wyll wold. 1502 Plumpton Corr. (Camden) 164 There was a servant of yours..was myschevously made away with. 1595 SHAKS. John v. vii. 111 Let vs pay the time but needfull woe, Since it hath beene before hand with our greefes. 1595– [see BEFOREHAND 1 c]. 1596– [see BEHIND adv. 5 b]. 1603 SHAKS. Meas. for M. I. i. 33 Heauen doth with vs, as we, with Torches doe. 1610 B. JONSON Alch. I. iii, You shall deale much with mineralls. 1624 CAPT. J. SMITH Virginia I. 16 We tooke more Cod then we knew what to doe with. 1660 SOUTH Serm., Matt. xiii. 52 (1727) IV. 27 When the Rooters and Through-Reformers made clean Work with the Church. a 1715 BURNET Own Time (1724) I. 557 He told me, it was not decent to be merry with such a matter. 1715– [see MATTER sb.[1] 25 b]. 1753–4 RICHARDSON Grandison II. xv. 116 Things,..that we have no business with. 1755 Connoisseur No. 100 ¶ 5 All these indignities I very patiently put up with. 1799 G. S. CAREY Balnea (ed. 2) 159 The walks.. have been taken a great deal of pains with. 1802 MARIA EDGEWORTH Moral T., Prussian Vase (1816) I. 211 What do you want with me? 1814 WORDSW. Excurs. VII. 194 The ..Master's hand Was busier with his task. 1816 LADY GRANVILLE Lett. (1894) I. 101 His manner is brusque and short, and I got on but little with him. 1818 SCOTT Hrt. Midl. xxxviii, He knows how to manage with her. 1823 SCORESBY Jrnl. 391 This anxiety with myself. 1841 BROWNING Pippa Passes I. 228 God's in his heaven—All's right with the world! 1865 KINGSLEY Herew. viii, He surpassed Ptolemy with the astrolabe. 1873 H. E. ROSCOE in Owens Coll. Ess. & Addr. (1874) 56 Experiments on the properties of vanadium..made with much larger quantities than it fell to the lot of the Swedish chemist to work with. 1887 LEWIS CARROLL Game of Logic iv. 95 She is perhaps a little overdoing it, in the way of lessons, with her children. 1923 Times Lit. Suppl. 18 Jan. 34/3 Getting through with work as quickly as possible.

(b) 1809 MALKIN Gil Blas I. vi. ¶ 4 Get along with you, and go to bed. 1897 go along with you [see GO v. 72 a].

b. After an adv. or phr. with ellipsis of or equivalent to a verb, usually imperative: e.g. away with it = 'take it away', down with it = 'put or throw it down', etc.

c 1377 in Minor Poems Vernon MS. 718/99, I ou Rede.. Þat vch a Mon vp wiþ þe hede, And Mayntene him boþe heiȝe and lowe. c 1388 in Wyclif's Sel. Wks. III. 472 His proude clerkis schal downe wiþ þer pride. 1477 SIR J. PASTON in P. Lett. III. 199 My charges be gretter than I maye a weye with. 1528 Impeachm. Wolsey in Furniv. Ballads from MSS. I. 360 Down with thy tayle, and of with thy goldyn shone. 1535– [see DOWN adv. 25 b]. 1598 SHAKS. Merry W. IV. ii. 239 Come, to the Forge with it. 1603 — Meas. for M. v. i. 121 To prison with her. Ibid. 313 To th' racke with him. 1708 [see IN adv. 1 c]. 1843 Blackw. Mag. LIV. 75 To the foul fiend with Rosley Castle!

†c. In case of, in the event of. Obs. rare.

1625 PURCHAS Pilgrims II. 1140 A good Hauen with all weathers. 1751 R. PALTOCK P. Wilkins (1884) II. 209, I don't know what we should do with fires; we see the dread of them sufficiently.

d. In phr. with reference, regard, respect to: see REFERENCE sb. 3 b, REGARD sb. 13, RESPECT sb. 7. So † with (now in) comparison to.

1669 Hist. Pope's Nephews (1673) I. 38 When once he had put on the habit of a Priest, he could hardly..know himself with comparison to what he was before.

10. In the opinion, view, or estimation of; 'in the sight of'.

a 1000 Cædmon's Gen. 507 Nu þu..hæfst þe wið drihten dyrne ȝeworhtne. c 1000 ÆLFRIC Saints' Lives xxvii. 171 Scyldiȝ wið god. a 1300 Cursor M. 9521 He had an anlepe son, Þat wit his fader was sa wele þat [he] wist his wisdom ilk dele. c 1430 Life St. Kath. (1884) 92 He was so gret wyth þe Emperour. 1474 Stonor Papers (Camden) I. 149 Remembryng how grettely in consette ye stonde..with a gentylwoman. 1572 Treat. of Treasons agst. Q. Eliz. 61 b, To discredite those Noble persons with the people. 1598 HAKLUYT Voy. I. 56 To slay men, to inuade the dominions of other people, and to rifle their goods..are with them no offences at all. 1608– go down with [see GO v. 78 g]. 1611 Bible 1 Pet. ii. 20 This is acceptable with God. 1634 SIR T. HERBERT Trav. Table Gg 3/2 Cycala-Bassa..is out of credit with the Grand Signior. c 1646 MILTON New Forcers Consc. 10 Men whose Life, Learning, Faith and pure intent Would have been held in high esteem with Paul. 1681 DRYDEN Abs. & Achit. I. 558 Every man with him was God or Devil. 1709 POPE Ess. Crit. 338 Most by Numbers judge a Poet's song; And smooth or rough, with them is right or wrong. 1823 BYRON Juan XIII. xxiv, Juan stood well both with Ins and Outs. 1841 BROWNING Pippa Passes ad fin., All service is the same with God.

11. In the practice or experience of, in the life or conduct of, in (one's) case; sometimes spec. in the language or statement of, according to. (With pl. obj. = AMONG A. 6.)

a 1310 in Wright Lyric P. v. 25 He is coral y-cud with cayser ant knyht. a 1352 MINOT Poems (ed. Hall) iii. 69 Þan with þam was none oþer gle. ? 1478 Stonor Papers (Camden) II. 35 Schepe was neuer so der with vs. 1526 TINDALE Matt. xix. 26 With men this is vnpossyble, but with God all thinges are possyble. 1605 SHAKS. Macb. v. i. 32 It is an accustom'd action with her, to seeme thus washing her hands. 1615 T. MAXFIELD in Cath. Rec. Soc. Publ. (1906) III. 51 Julie the 16, wth y^u 26. 1676 DRYDEN Aurengz. III. i, 'Tis not with me as with a private Man. 1678 CUDWORTH Intell. Syst. I. iv. § 32. 516 This notion was so familiar with these Pagans. 1796–7 JANE AUSTEN Pride & Prej. xliii, 'And this is always the way with him', she added. 1841 FITZGERALD Lett. (1889) I. 77 These fits of exaltation are not very common with me. 1864 MRS. H. WOOD Trevlyn Hold xli, 'Were the ricks insured?' 'No. There's the smart with Chattaway.' 1881 RUSSELL Haigs xiv. 426 With the rough-riding men on both sides of the frontier to meet was to fight. 1909 BYWATER Aristotle on Art Poetry 172 Πολιτικῶς is with him the practical wisdom of the statesman. 1910 BOLLAND Eyre of Kent (Selden Soc.) I. Introd. 95 These omissions would be impossible with a copyist who read over what he had copied.

b. After words expressing influence or the like: sometimes replaceable by over or upon.

1573–80 BARET Alv. P 696 With whom when she could nothing preuaile. 1631 WEEVER Anc. Funeral Mon. 512 His all-potencie with the King. 1712 P. METCALFE Life S. Winefride (1917) 16 He had great Power and Authority with them. 1814 JANE AUSTEN Mansf. Park xiii, She has no influence with..my sisters that could be of any use. 1865 RUSKIN Sesame i. § 4 Most honest men..would..acknowledge its leading power with them as a motive.

** Senses relating to agreement (or disagreement) in some respect.

Senses 16 and 18 are closely allied to those under ***, involving the idea of proximity or accompaniment in space or time.

12. Following words expressing comparison, likeness, equality, or identity.

In some cases varying with or now replaced by to, e.g. after compare, comparison, equal, resemblance; after same, as is more usual; but with is still regular after some derived sbs., as equality, sameness, and also after even adj., identical, identity, level adj., one adj., rank vb., etc. See the various words.

c 888 ÆLFRED Boeth. xvi. § 2 Hu micle mare is ðonne þæs monnes lichoma to metenne wið þæt mod þonne seo mus wið ðone mon. c 1200 ORMIN 3090 Þatt wass inoh all an wiþþ þatt þatt Godess enngell seȝȝde. Ibid. 7931 Þeȝȝre sang iss lic wiþþ wop. 1387 TREVISA Higden (Rolls) II. 259 Of þe same age wiþ þe kyngdom of Assiries. c 1450 Merlin xx. 317 Thei ben so fewe that thei may not compare with hem. 1513 MORE Rich. III, Wks. 47/1 Waye [= weigh] the good that they dooe, with the hurte that commeth of them. 1526 TINDALE Phil. ii. 6 Which beynge in the shape off god, and thought it not robbery to be equall with god. 1677– [see IDENTICAL 2]. 1710 HEARNE Collect. 24 Feb. (O.H.S.) II. 348 A sniveling Gentleman of not half the sense with the late poor spirited Dick Cromwell. 1836 MACAULAY Life & Lett. (1883) I. 456 His style affects me in something the same way with that of Gibbon. 1879 WHITNEY Sanskrit Gram. 337 Some of the apparent roots..with sibilant final are akin with the desideratives. 1885 Act 48 & 49 Vict. c. 58 § 1 This Act shall be read as one with the Telegraph Acts, 1863 to 1878.

13. Following words expressing agreement, conformity, sympathy, and the like.

c 893 ÆLFRED Oros. IV. viii, For þon hie on symbel wið Romanum sibbe heoldon. a 1000 Guthlac 382 Þæt frið wið hy ȝefreoþad wære. 1123 O. E. Chron. (Laud MS.) an. 1120 Se arceb[iscop] Turstein..wearð þurh þone papan wið þone cyng acordad. c 1200 Trin. Coll. Hom. 105 Hie ben þenne sahtnede wið þe heuenliche fader. 1390 GOWER Conf. I. 6 At his commandement, With whom myn herte is of accord. 1398 TREVISA Barth. De P. R. XVI. xliv. (1495) L ij/2 Yren hath agrement with the stone Adamas. c 1430 Hymns Virgin (1867) 13 God wiþ man is maade at oone. 1535 JOYE Apol. Tindale (Arb.) 11 Henrichus Bullyngerus.. consenteth with me in the significacion of this worde. 1605 B. JONSON Volpone III. iv, There was but one sole man.. With whom I ere could sympathise. 1611 SHAKS. Cymb. III. iii. 31 Hap'ly this life is best..Well corresponding With your stiffe Age. 1642– fall in with [see FALL v. 90 b–e]. 1662– [see SYMPATHY 3 b]. 1761 MRS. F. SHERIDAN Sidney Bidulph II. 310 How ill does the vanity of pomp suit with a house of mourning! 1796 Ann. Reg., Hist. 115 Spain was..on friendly terms with France. 1821 SHELLEY Hellas 537 The tiger leagues not with the stag at bay Against the hunter. 1849 MACAULAY Hist. Eng. I. I. 107 He declared his determination to govern in harmony with the Commons. 1913 W. M. RAMSAY Teaching of Paul 158 His heart became ..more..sympathetic with their trials.

b. By extension, after words expressing disagreement.

1646 SIR T. BROWNE Pseud. Ep. I. viii. 30 It containeth impossibilities and things inconsistent with truth. 1735–8 BOLINGBROKE On Parties 81 They [sc. the Tories] had only differ'd with the Whigs about the Degree of Oppression. 1791–1823 D'ISRAELI Cur. Lit. (1866) 208 Every edition varies with the preceding ones. 1868 GLADSTONE Juv. Mundi i. (1870) 16 Testimony..in no case discordant with that of the Iliad.

14. On the side or party of; in favour of; on behalf of; 'for': opp. to AGAINST 12. (See also 22 c.)

c 1200 ORMIN 4675 Swa forrwerrpesst tu þin Godd, & haldesst wiþþ þatt anhte. c 1300 Havelok 2308 He swore, Þat he sholde with him halde Boþe ageynes stille and bolde. 1382 WYCLIF Matt. xii. 30 He that is nat with me, is aȝeinus me. c 1420 LYDG. Assembly of Gods 1058 Vertu was full heuy, when he sy Frewyll Take part with Vyce. 1478 Acta Audit. (1839) 66/2 Ilk baroun and freehaldare þat..geve voce with þe said dome. c 1489 CAXTON Sonnes of Aymon ix. 238 Nevertheles he came, and helde syde wyth his broder. 1509 FISHER Serm. Wks. (1876) 277 What sentence he shal gyue wheder with me or ayenst me. 1534 Star Chamber Cases (Selden Soc.) II. 317 They were at issue and by a substancyall Jury..Founde with the seid inulsho. 1582 N. T. (Rhem.) Acts xiv. 4 Certaine of them..were with the Jewes, but certaine with the Apostles. 1600 HOLLAND Livy XXIX. vi. 713 The citie of Locri..had sided also with the Carthaginians. 1633 EARL MANCH. Al Mondo (1636) 171 When a man comes to be judged; his life..shal give the evidence with, or against him. 1653 CROMWELL Sp. 4 July in Carlyle, He hath appeared with them. 1697 DRYDEN Æneis XII. 827 Jove is with us. 1709 STRYPE Ann. Ref. I. xlix. 492 There being with the bill 60, against it 75. 1842 DICKENS Amer. Notes xv, The soldiers rather laughed at this blade than with him. 1845 BROWNING Lost Leader 14 Shakespeare was of us, Milton was for us, Burns, Shelley, were with us. 1886 Manch. Exam. 9 Jan. 5/3 M. Granet, Minister of Posts and Telegraphs, has usually voted with M. Clemenceau.

b. In reference to wind, tide, etc.: Favourable to, in a favourable direction for.

1647 SANDERSON Serm. (1674) II. 218 As a Boat that (having wind and tide with it) runneth glib and merrily down the stream. 1719 DE FOE Crusoe II. (Globe) 378 They had.. the Flood-Tide with them.

15. In the same way as; as — does or did, is or was, etc.; like. (Cf. 17.)

c 1340 Medit. in Hampole's Wks. (1895) I. 94 So þat þoru þi merci and grace we moun repente of oure..mys-dedis with seint Petir. 1362 LANGL. P. Pl. A. VIII. 71 He is Fals with þe Fend. c 1400 Rule St. Benet (prose) 11 Of mekenes spekis sain benet..& sais with hali scripture: 'Omnis qui se exaltat &c.' 1433 LYDG. S. Edmund & Fremund 1034–6 in Horstm. Altengl. Leg. (1881) 395 He..Hadde with Nestor manly auysynesse;..With Tideus he badde eek hardynesse. 1589 NASHE Returne Pasquill Wks. (Grosart) I. 121 A crooked generation, that loues to swym side-long with the Crabbe. 1600 — Summer's Last Will Prol. 73 Euery man cannot, with Archimedes, make a heauen of brasse. 1634 RAINBOW Labour (1635) 35 With stomackefull children we bawle for Rattles. 1711 ADDISON Spect. No. 227 ¶ 5, I must cry out with Dido..'Ah! cruel Heaven, that made no Cure for Love!' 1809 BYRON Bards & Rev. 102 Better to err with Pope, than shine with Pye. 1861 PALEY Æschylus (ed. 2) 7 agst. Thebes 759 note, Hermann gives ἀλκὰν with one of the most recent MSS. 1905 CHESTERTON Heretics 37 Whether we should love everybody with Tolstoy, or spare nobody with Nietzsche.

b. Followed by the and a superlative used absol.: As well or thoroughly as; (as) one of, 'among', 'of': forming adverbial (or † predicative) phrases denoting 'to the full or fullest extent', '(nearly) as — as any or as possible', 'very —', 'highly —': e.g. with the best = among the best, as well as any, very well; with the first, as one of the first, very early, chiefly, especially (see FIRST 6 c); with the least = at the lowest estimate; † with the most inclined = highly inclined. Obs. or arch.

a 1300 K. Horn 1119 (Harl.) Þou shen[c]h vs wiþ þe vurste. 13.. Seuyn Sag. (W.) 1656 The king..kep the leuedi with the best. 1445 in Anglia XXVIII. 281 Why is not he redde with the worthiest? 1470–85 MALORY Arthur x. lxviii. 531 Soo that nyghte they were lodged with the best. 1477 Paston Lett. III. 183, I wold have hym [sc. a horse] sumwhat large, not with the largest. a 1533 LD. BERNERS Huon clxii. 634 Thyne armure is good and thy sworde is with the best. 1553 GRIMALDE Cicero's Offices I. (1556) 41 b, If ther be anie somewhat with the moste enclined to pleasures. 1573–80 TUSSER Husb. (1878) 51 Who pescods delighteth to haue with the furst, If now he do sowe them, I thinke it not wurst. 1577 GOOGE tr. Heresbach's Husb. 45 Not to mowe your Grasse with the latest, but before the seede be ripe. a 1592 GREENE Jas. IV, I. ii, A young stripling..that can sleep with the soundest, eate with the hungriest. 1629 GAULE Pract. Theories 376 Of all the difficulties of Truth and Faith, the Article of Christs Resurrection is with the formost. 1671 H. M. tr. Erasm. Colloq. 494 There was no year, wherein he did not gain a thousand Duckats, to speak with the least. 1826 Priestley's Rudim. 55 The preposition with is..sometimes used in conversation, to express a degree ..something less than the greatest; as 'They are with the widest.' 1859 TENNYSON Grandm. 20 At your age, Annie, I could have wept with the best.

16. Expressing simultaneous occurrence and association (cf. 25), often also implying causal connexion (cf. 39). a. At the same time as; at the time or instant of; on the occurrence of (often with implication 'and because of'); at, on, upon.

(a) Followed by a sb. (often qualified).

Before occasion, opportunity, now replaced by on or (less usually) at.

13.. Cursor M. 19462 (Gött.) Vtayne wid þis word gan tene. 1456 SIR G. HAYE Law Arms (S.T.S.) 145 The payment cessis with the impossibilitee of the service. 1592 SHAKS. Ven. & Ad. 900. 1655 Theophania 89 With a resolution to hire a ship,..and with the first occasion to follow her into Sicily. 1697 DRYDEN Virg. Georg. IV. 273 Nor ends their Work, but with declining Day. 1719 PHILIPPS tr. Thirty-four Conferences 338 He hath promised to send you a Copy with the first Opportunity. 1748 THOMSON Cast. Indol. II. x, Sometimes with early morn, he mounted gay The hunter-steed. 1822 T. L. PEACOCK Maid Marian x, John..was determining to take possession with the first light of morning. 1870 LOWELL Study Wind. (1871) 157 Browning.. draws nearer to the all-for-point fashion of the concettisti, with every poem he writes. 1926 Times 15 Mar., With his death, his younger brother..becomes heir to the barony.

(b) Followed by a demonstrative pron.: with that († than), when (and, often, because) that occurred, thereupon; † at that instant, just then (obs.); saying or having just said that; with this, hereupon. Cf. HEREWITH 2, THEREWITH 2 c, WHEREWITH 4 b.

c 1250 Gen. & Ex. 1409 Laban and his moder wið-ðan Faȝneden wel ðis sondere man. a 1300 Cursor M. 1203 Wit þis [Trin. Here aftir] was born an hali child, Seth þat meke was and mild. Ibid. 3308 And þof sco scamful was, i-wiss, Sco tint na contenance wit þis. 1375 BARBOUR Bruce XV. 168 Syne..[The] myddis of the toune he tais, With that neir command war his fais. c 1425 WYNTOUN Cron. I. v. 203 A child..said, he saw a dere. Wiþ þat þe takill wp he drew. 1470–85 MALORY Arthur XVI. xvi. 687 With that Bors lyfte vp his hand & wold haue smyten his broder. 1592 SHAKS. Ven. & Ad. 25. 1603 in Cath. Rec. Soc. Publ. (1906) II. 218 And with this I byd you most hartely farewell. 1681 DRYDEN Abs. & Achit. I. 717 'Take then my tears' (with that he wiped his Eyes). 1779 Mirror No. 35 ¶ 11 'Who shall decide when doctors disagree?' And, with that, he made one of the finest bows in the world. 1847 TENNYSON Princess II. 290 'Our mother, is she well?' With that she kiss'd His forehead.

b. Followed by a sb. or pron., forming a phrase equivalent to a clause with when, in which the sb. or pron. is the subj. (or obj.), and the vb. is identical with that in the principal clause; e.g. our hopes died with him, i.e. when (and because) he died; to rise with the lark, i.e. when the lark rises (= early in the morning): see LARK sb.[1] 1 b.

†Formerly also with vbs. of durative meaning: = contemporaneously with.

1432–50 tr. Higden (Rolls) VIII. 497 But mony abusions

comme from Boemia into Englonde with this qwene. 1592 SHAKS. Ven. & Ad. 1019 He being dead, with him is beautie slaine. 1614 RALEIGH Hist. World III. v. § 8. 57 Where the Persians, so many of them as lost not their wits with their courage [etc.]. 1697 DRYDEN Virg. Georg. IV. 673 His Griefs with Day begun. 1742 MIDDLETON Cicero (ed. 3) II. vi. 31 Lentulus and Metellus, whose consulship expired with the year. 1791 BOSWELL Johnson 10 Apr. an. 1775, What was said by Johnson, or other eminent persons who lived with him. 1812 CRABBE Tales xi. 376 With virtue, prudence fled. 1891 FARRAR Darkn. & Dawn xliii, I hear rumours that another large vessel..foundered at sea. I expect that some of the accusers of Paulus perished with her.

c. In the course or duration of, in process of, 'in' (time, etc.); often with admixture of the instrumental sense: By, or in consequence of, the passage or lapse of (cf. 37, 39).

c 1440 Alphabet of Tales 329 With a few yeris þai war passand riche men. 1560 WHITEHORNE tr. Macchiavelli's Arte of Warre 87 All other thyng..maie with tyme be ouercome, this onely with tyme ouercometh thee. 1610 SHAKS. Temp. IV. i. 164 Come with a thought. 1611 FENTON Usurie II. xiii. 95 Mans labours and skill wil faile with yeeres. 1627 W. D. tr. Andiguier's Lisander 15 To render you more signal offices, which, with time, I hope to performe. 1784 in B. Ward Dawn Cath. Revival (1909) I. iv. 81 [Prejudices] will die away with time. 1855 TENNYSON Will ii, Bettering not with time. 1875 M. ARNOLD God & Bible p. xxviii, Christianity's admixture of popular legend and illusion was sure to be cleared away with time. 1884 W. C. SMITH Kildrostan 74 Unripe fruit..mellows with the months.

d. After words denoting change or variation: At the same rate as; at a rate, or in a manner, corresponding to that of; in proportion to, according to.

1697 DRYDEN Virg. Georg. III. 322 His stout Stomach with his Food will grow. 1701 SWIFT Contests Nobles & Comm. iii, Their Insolence and Power encreased with their Number. 1712 ARBUTHNOT John Bull I. v, His Spirits rose and fell with the Weather-glass. 1838 DE MORGAN Ess. Probab. 140 The probability of an error diminishes with its magnitude. 1839–47 Todd's Cycl. Anat. III. 516/2 The diameter of the capillaries of muscle varies..with the size of the blood-particles of the animal. 1857 BUCKLE Civiliz. I. ii. 58 The rate of wages fluctuates with the population. 1910 H. A. DALLAS Mors Janua Vitæ? 17 Her conviction as to the importance of the script naturally increased with the evidence for its veridical character.

17. Expressing agreement or accordance, esp. in opinion or statement. To be with, to be of the same opinion as, to agree with. (See also 15.)

1456 SIR G. HAYE Gov. Princis (S.T.S.) 99 Thai speke quhilum with the and othir quhilis aganis the. 1565 ALLEN Def. Purg. xi. 104, I am not afraide to vse the word Satisfaction, with Cyprian, Origen, Ambrose, Augustin. 1611 TOURNEUR Ath. Trag. IV. iv. I 4 b, Enter the Watch. Belfo. The Watch? Met with my wish. 1625– run with [see RUN v. 71 b]. 1648 HEXHAM, Ick ben Met u, I am With you, or, I am of your opinion. 1796 in B. Edwards Maroon Negroes 20, I am perfectly with you, that the pin ought not to receive another screw. 1883 STEVENSON Treas. Isl. xxix. Ah, it's a fine dance—I'm with you there. 1886 W. S. BLUNT Diary 22 Apr. in Land War Irel. (1912) ii. 79 Morris is with me about Ireland. 1916 J. R. MOZLEY Div. Aspect Hist. I. ix. 235 It was heart beating with heart.

18. In the same direction as; along the course of: opp. to AGAINST 9: esp. in such phrases as with the grain, with the hair, with the stream, with the tide, with the wind.

c 1489– [see STREAM sb. 2 f]. 1577– [see WIND sb.[1] 29]. 1597 BACON Coulers Good & Euill Ess. (Arb.) 154 If it be with the streame or with the hill. 1651 H. MORE Enthus. Tri. (1712) 37 With thankfulnesse and reverence he doth receive whatever Divine Providence brings upon him, be it sweet or sour, with the hair, or against it. 1678 MOXON Mech. Exerc. iv. 66 As well upon the Traverse ..as with the Grain of the wood. 1688 [see METAL sb. 7]. c 1710 CELIA FIENNES Diary (1888) 75 The Gardens runns down a great way, you descend with them by severall stepps. 1712 with the tide [see SWIM v. 1 c]. a 1774 GOLDSM. Surv. Exp. Philos. (1776) II. 386 A field of corn, viewed with the wind, is of a different shade from the same field viewed against the wind. 1786, 1816 [see STROKE v.[1] 1 d]. 1810 CRABBE Borough xviii. 183 The black footway winding with the wall. 1840 with the tide [see DROP v. 8]. 1867 SMYTH Sailor's Word-bk., With the sun, ropes coiled from the left hand towards the right; but where the sun passes the meridian north of the observer, it is of course the reverse. 1891 with the tide [see GO v. 85 f].

*** Senses expressing accompaniment or addition.

19. Following words expressing such meanings as are indicated above, as accompany (see note s.v.), ally, alternate, associate, blend, combine, confront, connect, couple, entangle, incorporate, join, link, marry, mix, partake, share, unite, wed (etc.) vbs. (and derived sbs., as association, connexion, etc.); communion, company, contact, intercourse (etc.) sbs.; together adv.: see the various words. See also ALONG adv. 3.

Beowulf 1088 Þæt hie healfre geweald wið Eotena bearn agan moston. c 888 ÆLFRED Boeth. xxxvi. § 8 Se yfla willa næfð nænne ȝeferscipe wið þa ȝesælða. a 900 CYNEWULF Elene 307 Swa ȝe modblinde mengan onȝunnon liȝe wið soþe. a 1240 Ureisun in O. E. Hom. I. 201 Hwoa so euer wule habben lot wið þe of þine blisse, he mot delen wið þe of þine pine on eorðe. 13.. Cursor M. 18019 (Gött.) Aisel haue i blend wid gall. c 1400 Lanfranc's Cirurg. 201 Þei ben maad fast wiþ þe botme of þe stomac. 1557 Dunfermline Reg. (Bann. Club) 400 To pay..Twelf caponis to giddir wutht hariage careage and due serwice. 1665 WALTON Hooker Introd., About forty years past..I began a happy affinity with William Cranmer. 1671 MILTON P. R. IV. 412 Fierce rain with lightning mixt, water with fire In ruine reconcil'd. 1759 GOLDSM. Bee No. 4 ¶ 6, I was once determined to throw off all connexions with taste. 1785 REID Intell. Powers II. xiv. 214 A kind of feeling, or immediate perception of things present, and in contact with the percipient. 1836 THIRLWALL Greece xvi. (1838) II. 345 The Lacedæmonians, whose force, together with the Tegeans and forty thousand light troops, amounted to upwards of fifty thousand men. 1889 SWINBURNE Study B. Jonson 87 The collocation of such names..as those of Æglamour and Earine with such others as March and Maudlin.

b. Following words expressing acquaintance or familiarity. (After accustome(d, known, now replaced by to.)

c 1220 Bestiary 113 His muð is ȝet wel unkuð wið pater noster and crede. a 1225 Juliana 14 Ne ich neuer þat ich wite nes wið him icnawen. 1338 R. BRUNNE Chron. (1810) 225 Þan went þis Ottobone þorghout þe cuntre, & quaynted him with ilkone. c 1369 CHAUCER Dethe of Blaunche 532, I..gan me aqueynt With hym. c 1386 — Prol. 216 Famulier was he With frankeleyns ouer al in his contree. 1535 COVERDALE Ecclus. xxiii. 9 Let not thy mouth be accustomed with swearinge. 1611 Bible Isa. liii. 3 He is..a man of sorrows, and acquainted with griefe. 1719 in 10th Rep. Hist. MSS. Comm. App. I. 197 They could not..undergoe the fatigue that the natives were accustomed with. 1880 L. STEPHEN Pope iii. 61 Pope was not disinclined to pride himself upon his familiarity with the great.

c. By extension, following words expressing separation: e.g. to break with = to break off connexion with (BREAK v. 34); to part with = to cease to be with or to have with one (PART v. 6 c). (After take leave now replaced by of.)

a 1300 Cursor M. 17022 Kynd na saul suffers ar to part wit man o-liue. c 1485 Digby Myst. (1883) III. 102 O ye good fathyr of grete degre, thus to departe with your ryches. 1486 Bk. St. Albans E iij b, In iij. degrees he hem berith or he with hem twyn. 1607 SHAKS. Cor. IV. vi. 48 It cannot be The Volces dare breake with vs. a 1629 HINDE J. Bruen lxvii. (1641) 224 My wife..and my selfe, came to take leave with him. 1808 SOUTHEY Lett. (1856) II. 110 For more than a year, Scott has cut with the Edinburgh Review. 1885 Manch. Exam. 28 Mar. 5/5 The imminence of a rupture with Russia.

20. Expressing association or participation in some act, proceeding, or experience; spec. = acting on the same side as (another lawyer) in an action at law.

c 1290– [see SIN v. 1 c]. a 1300– [see PLAY v. 10]. c 1440 Jacob's Well 201 Ȝif þou be partenere in dede of thefte,..or of ony oþer wronges, þat is for to seyne, in folowynge wyth suche doers. 1526 TINDALE Rom. xii. 15 Be mery with them that are mery. wepe with them that wepe. 1533 [see ADULTERY 1]. 1596 SHAKS. Merch. V. I. iii. 36, I will buy with you, sell with you, talke with you, walke with you, and so following: but I will not eate with you, drinke with you, nor pray with you. 1711 STEELE Spect. No. 53 ¶ 7, I will..for the future be merry with the Vulgar. 1816 SCOTT Old Mort. xxxviii, My lot is cast with Evandale, and with him I am resolved to bear it. 1837 DICKENS Pickw. xxxiv, 'I am for the plaintiff, my Lord,' said Mr. Serjeant Buzfuz. 'Who is with you, brother Buzfuz?' said the judge. 1848 — Dombey xxxviii, Rob..ran sniggering off to get change, and tossed it away with a pieman. 1883 Manchester Exam. 7 Nov. 5/2 A new weekly mail service with Australia.

21. a. (with such vbs. as bring, take, come, go) Followed by a sb. or (most commonly) pron. denoting the person (vessel, etc.) that leads, conveys, or carries a person or thing, thus having it in charge (cf. 23, of which this use is the converse).

Also fig. after take: see TAKE v. 59 b, c.

c 1290 St. Matthew 9 in S. Eng. Leg. 77 He bi-lefde þo is weork, and wiz ore louerd eode. c 1290 Beket 1213 ibid. 141 With him a-morewe he nam his oste. a 1300 Cursor M. 5297 To mi lauerd yee com wit me, I sal yow do a-quentid be. 1432–50 tr. Higden (Rolls) I. 133 [Nilus] makethe the londe plentuous thro slycche that hit drawethe with hit. c 1475 Rauf Coilȝear 6 Thay past vnto Paris..With mony Prelatis and Princis. 1591 SHAKS. Two Gent. IV. i. 74 Come, goe with vs, we'll bring thee to our Crewes. a 1596 Sir T. More I. ii. 28 Ten poundes..To carie in your pursse about with ye. 1697 DRYDEN Virg. Georg. III. 534 The Shepherd last appears, And with him all his Patrimony bears. 1776 Trial of Nundocomar 68/1 My uncle used frequently to go to Maha Rajah's: when I was little I used to go with him. 1812 JEFFERSON Writ. (1830) IV. 178 The truth is that we brought with us the rights of men. 1869 FREEMAN Norm. Conq. III. xi. 61 They took with them no force capable of controlling..the country.

b. In the possession, keeping, care, or charge of (a person); in the hands of. (lit. and fig.)

a 1300 Cursor M. 4403 His mantel es bi-left wit me. 1340–70 Alex. & Dind. 32 Whan no wordliche wele is wiþ us founde. 1528 in Pocock Rec. Ref. (1870) I. 81 Leaving with the master of the Rolls such things as might..instruct him. 1649 BP. HALL Cases Consc. III. ix. 341 That..commissionary authority, which is by Christ entrusted with them. c 1720 W. HAMILTON Descr. Lanark & Renfrew (Maitl. Club 1831) 64 Douglass parish..continued with the Earles of Douglass untill their fatall forfeiture. 1776 Trial of Nundocomar 68/1 You have for a long time had my money; it shall remain no longer with you. 1825 JEFFERSON Autobiog. Wks. 1859 I. 6 The committee..left it in charge with their chairman to forward them by express. 1828 WHATELY Rhet. (1850) I. iii. § 2 The 'burden of proof' lies with the accusers. 1896 CONAN DOYLE Expl. Gerard iii. 121 The deal lay with him. 1911 Act 1 & 2 Geo. V c. 46 § 17 The ownership of an author's manuscript after his death..shall be primâ facie proof of the copyright being with the owner of the manuscript.

c. In the nature or character of; as a quality or attribute of. Now chiefly after way: see WAY sb.[1] 22 d. (The converse of 31.)

14.. Tundale's Vis. 31 With hym was no charyte. 1553 Douglas' Æneis IX. Prol. marg., Vertue..has euer this rewill with hyr: do as thou wald be done to. 1650 TRAPP Comm. Gen. xxv. 30 This hunter hath no ho with him. 1678 DRYDEN Kind Keeper I. i, She has a notable Smack with her! 1711 R. MARTIN in E. H. Burton Life Bp. Challoner (1909) I. iii. 33 He had such an honest way with him. 1848 NEWMAN Loss & Gain II. xx. (1904) 254 What a way those fellows have with them!

22. In the company, society, or presence of.

Face to face with: see FACE sb. 2 d. With God, in heaven: see GOD 5 c. With oneself (dial.): by oneself.

a 1300 K. Horn 363 (Camb.) He schal wiþ me bileue Til hit beo nir eue. a 1300 Cursor M. 5706 Þat fot moyses ful skete, And wit þe preist raguel he ete. 13.. Gosp. Nicod. (S.) 1579 Withe me þis ilk day be þou sall, With me in heuenryke. 1377 LANGL. P. Pl. B. v. 234 Ones I was herberwed..with an hep of chapmen. a 1400–50 Wars Alex. 1613 Þan Wer þair common whit hym kyngez. c 1450 Mirk's Festial 61 Then sate scho done all othyr wyth. 1526 TINDALE John xii. 8 The poore all wayes shall ye have with you, butt me shall ye nott all wayes have. 1553 Dioc. Reg. Glasgow (1875) I. 209 The said contrak..subscrivit wyth Schir Jhone Alaine, notair publik. 1709 STEELE Tatler No. 26 ¶ 11 This Gentleman who has arrived with you is a fool of his own making. 1791 BOSWELL Johnson June 1763 (1904) I. 267, I begged I might be allowed to pass an evening with him there soon. a 1814 Sailors' Ret. I. i. in New Brit. Theatre II. 313 This whipper-snapper of mine.. sets off with himself, and no one knows where. 1820 KEATS St. Agnes xvi, Alone with her good angels, far apart From wicked men like thee. 1857 M. ARNOLD Rugby Chapel 25, I..think Of bygone autumns with thee. 1891 FARRAR Darkn. & Dawn lviii, He found Nero sitting with Poppæa and Tigellinus. 1914 'IAN HAY' Knt. on Wheels xvii, I don't go very often...Perhaps it is because I have no one to go with.

b. spec. At the house of, or in the same house or meeting-place as; in the household, retinue, or service of, attending upon; on a visit to, being the guest of (hence be with sometimes = 'visit', 'call upon').

c 1250 Gen. & Ex. 466 Sella wuneð oc lamech wið. c 1275 LAY. 6 He wonede at Ernleie wid þan gode cniþte. c 1386 CHAUCER Prol. 65 This ilke worthy knyght hadde been also Somtyme with the lord of Palatye Agayn another hethen in Turkye. a 1400 in Halliwell Early Hist. Freemasonry (1840) 20 He most love..his mayster also, that he ys wyth. c 1440 Alphabet of Tales 171 When sho had ligen þus many day sho dyed, & no body with hur. c 1440 Jacob's Well 286 Þei..weryn barberwyd wyth a ryȝt good man. c 1465 Stonor Papers (Camden) I. 71 Squier for þe body with Kynge H. 1482 Cely Papers (Camden) 121, I thank yow of the grette cher that ye dydde me at my laste beyng wytthe yow. 1551 ROBINSON tr. More's Utopia II. viii. (1895) 253 For them, whomewyth they be in wayges, they fyghte hardelye. 1583 in Cath. Rec. Soc. Publ. V. 38 Somtyme Apprentice with oon Mr Bannester of Preston. 1651 CROMWELL Let. 12 Apr. in Carlyle, If Dick Cromwell and his Wife be with you, my dear love to them. 1711–12 SWIFT Jrnl. to Stella 22 Jan., He was glad to find I was not with James Broad. 1715 C'TESS COWPER Diary (1864) 44 This Day Madame Selnave was with me to thank me for her Affair being ended. a 1752 in Jrnl. Friends' Hist. Soc. (1918) 21 Went..to Yealand Scool..to learn Wrighting and Arithmatick with Michael Jenkinson. 1803 T. JEFFERSON Let. Writ. 1854 IV. 470 He will be with you in Philadelphia in two or three weeks. 1878 HARDY Ret. Native v. vi, Have you heard that Eustacia is not with me now?

c. fig. in reference to an abstract thing: to be with, to accompany, 'attend'. Also in reference to God, combining the ideas of presence or companionship and favour, assistance, or the like (cf. 14).

Cf. God be with you, GOOD-BYE.

13.. Gosp. Nicod. (G.) 1020 Goddes bliscing be all his puple with. 1382 WYCLIF Judges vi. 12 The Lord with thee, moost stroong of men. c 1400 MAUNDEV. (Roxb.) iii. 10 Godd be with þe, for Godd es with vs. 1526 TINDALE Eph. vi. 24 Grace be with all them which love oure lorde Jesus Christ. 1634 SIR T. HERBERT Trav. 7 This calme and immoderate heate continued with vs seuen dayes. 1788 BURNS 'Of a' the Airts' i, Day and night my fancy's flight Is ever wi' my Jean. 1825 BROCKETT N. C. Gloss. s.v. Wud, 'God be wud her'—God rest her soul. 1896 HOUSMAN Shropsh. Lad xxxvii, Luck, my lads, be with you still. 1897 KIPLING Recess. i, Lord God of Hosts, be with us yet.

d. The phrase to be with, used in menace, etc. = to be avenged on, chastise, be even with (cf. 12), perh. belongs here (cf. VISIT v. 3), but has affinities with other senses.

1590 SHAKS. Mids. N. III. ii. 403, I will be with thee straight. 1592 — Rom. & Jul. II. iv. 78 Was I with you there for the Goose? 1596 — Tam. Shr. IV. i. 170 What, do you grumble? Ile be with you straight. 1825 JAMIESON s.v. With, 'I'll be wi' him for that yet', Roxb.

23. Having in one's hold, keeping, or charge; having within its compass, limits, area, etc.; leading, bringing, conveying, carrying, wearing, containing, etc.

With bag and baggage: see BAG sb. 19. (Found or taken) with the mainour (manner): see MAINOUR 1.

c 1300 Havelok 52 Þanne micthe chapmen fare Þuruth englond wit here ware. a 1400 Pist. Susan 5 His Innes and his orchardus were with a dep dich. c 1400 Ywaine & Gaw. 759 A pot with riche wine. c 1400 Destr. Troy 5564 Palomydon..presit into hauyn,..With xxx^{ti} shippes full shene, shot full of pepull. c 1430 Chev. Assigne 23 A pore womman.. Withe two chylderen her by-fore. 1488 Acc. Ld. High Treas. Scot. I. 80 A poik of canwes with demyis contenand aucht hundreth ane les. 1523 LD. BERNERS Froiss. I. ccxxvi. 123 b/1 The erle..toke hym a flagon with wyne, wherof he had dronke. 1539 Bible (Great) 2 Sam. xviii. 27 He is a good man, and commeth with good tydinges. 1596 SHAKS. Merch. V. II. ii. (stage-direction) Enter old Gobbo with a Basket. 1722 Lond. Gaz. No. 6054/2 A tall..Man,..with Ruffles and a light bag Wig. 1849 MACAULAY Hist. Eng. v. I. 609 He ordered Grey to lead the way with the cavalry. 1888 BARRIE Auld Licht Idylls iv. 105 The crowd..was back in a moment with a handful of small change.

b. In phr. with child, with young, etc., said of a pregnant woman or animal (also in fig. phr. from these).

See CHILD sb. 17, EGG sb. 4, FOAL sb. 1 b, WHELP sb. 1 b, YOUNG B. 2 c; also BIG a. 4, 5, GREAT a. 3, PREGNANT a.[1] 1, 2 b, 4, 5 (where the sense approaches 39); BEGET v. 2 c, CONCEIVE v. 3, GET v. 27 c, GO v. 7.

c 1200 ORMIN 2455 Þu best wiþþ childe off Haliȝ Gast. a 1300 Cursor M. 10572 Anna wit child was of a mai. c 1450 St. Cuthbert (Surtees) 391 Þe childe mett a cowe with' calfe. 1491 Acta Audit. (1839) 148/1, xxxij ȝowis with lamb. 1504 Lincoln Wills (1914) I. 21 If my wyfe be wyth a sonne. ? 1556 Wills & Inv. N. C. (Surtees 1835) I. 152, IX whies calved and w^t calve. 1575 TURBERV. Faulconrie 269 When hawkes fall to laying egges, and to be with egge in the mewe. 1585 Knaresb. Wills (Surtees) I. 149 The childe my wief is now conceyvid with. 1633 G. HERBERT Temple, Ch. Porch vi, He that is drunken, may his mother kill Bigge with his sister. a 1756 ELIZA HAYWOOD New Present (1771) 23 If they are with egg, their vents will be open. c 1850 Arab. Nts. (Rtldg.) 388, I have also to inform you, that I am with child, and if Heaven so much favours me as to give me a son [etc.].

†c. In ownership of, as owner of, having in possession. Sc. Obs.

1406 in Reg. Mag. Sig. Scot. 1427 17/2 Quhyl we remane wyth the said landis. 1483 Acta Audit. in Acta Dom. Conc. II. Introd. 114 The said Thomas sall remain with the said land and tenement.

d. In phr. with costs, with damages (in a lawsuit): in early use said in ref. to the winning party = 'in possession of', 'having as awarded'; later, in ref. to the verdict = 'accompanied by an order to the losing party to pay' (cf. 32).

1466 Stonor Papers (Camden) I. 76 Richard..prayeth þat he may be dismissed out of this Courte with his costes and damages. 1775 G. WILSON Cases Comm. Pleas III. 319 A verdict was given for the plaintiff, with one pound eleven shillings and sixpence damages. 1830 BARNEWALL & CRESSWELL Rep. K. B. IX. 528 They..recovered 25l. penalty, together with taxed costs. 1866 Scott. Law Reporter III. 81 The defender [was] assoilzied with expenses.

24. Accompanied by; having as an addition; having in one's company. Often connecting the two sbs. or prons.: = 'and in addition', 'and besides', or simply 'and'. Occas. in compound place-names: = CUM. † With the mare (Sc. obs.): = and more, and something over: see MORE B. 4 d.

c 1200 ORMIN 14792 Faraon wiþþ all hiss ferd comm affterrwarrd. a 1300 E. E. Psalter ciii. 27 [civ. 25] Bestes smaller with þe mare. 1370–80 Visions St. Paul 247 in O. E. Misc. 230 Þer as was wepyng wiþ muche vnseeþe. c 1380 WYCLIF Sel. Wks. I. 205 Þe Sixte, wiþ Clementyns, done myche harm to Goddis lawe, and enfeblen bileve. 1432–50 tr. Higden (Rolls) I. 367 The water was so habundante that hit pereschede þe woman with here childe. 1494 Acta Audit. (1839) 205/2 Alexander..tuk fra him out of his maling v^{xx} of ȝowis with the may. 1502 Reg. Privy Seal Scot. I. 112/2 Half a ȝere, with the mare, befor the date hereof. 1563 T. WILSON Logic 54 Beauuis with Alexander are comprehended vnder manne, as their kinde and speciall. a 1706 EVELYN Hist. Relig. (1850) I. 410 The permitting female slaves to be corrupted by their masters, with the like. 1719 DE FOE Crusoe I. (Globe) 296 We readily agreed to follow him, as did also twelve other Gentlemen, with their Servants. 1859 'GEO. ELIOT' Adam Bede xviii, These grey pews, with the buff-washed walls, gave a very pleasing tone to this shabby interior. 1911 Act 1 & 2 Geo. V c. 6 § 1 Imprisonment with or without hard labour.

in attrib. phr. 1898 Westm. Gaz. 17 May 8/1 To inaugurate some with-profit scheme.

b. Comprising in the whole number or total; including.

c 1250 Gen. & Ex. 86 Til ihesus crist fro helle nam His quemed wid eue and adam. 1836 DICKENS Sk. Boz, Tuggs's at Ramsgate, 'What's the terms?'..'Five guineas a week, ma'am, with attendance.' Mod. 'How many were there in the party?' 'I should say about twenty, with the children.'

c. Accompanied by (favourable wind, weather, etc.); having the advantage of.

1536 in Sel. Pleas Crt. Admiralty (1894) I. 58 Goyng from the porte of London at a full see with a full wynde. 1600 FAIRFAX Tasso XV. xlv, This evening (if you make good speed) To that hils foote with day-light might you passe. 1686 tr. Chardin's Trav. Persia 75 We put again to Sea with fair Weather.

25. Expressing association, conjunction, or connexion in thought, action, or condition.

One (day, etc.) with another: see ONE 17 b.

1387 TREVISA Higden (Rolls) II. 91 And so is Cornewayle acounted wiþ þe oþere schires. 1472 Stonor Papers (Camden) I. 124 For the certente what my cosen shall have with her, yf God provide for them that they shall go throwe in mariage. 1678 PRIDEAUX Lett. (Camden) 64 Livy may be read with him [sc. Dionysius of Halicarnassus]. 1784 Unfortunate Sensibility II. 7 One week with another she earned about half-a-crown. ? 1807–8 WORDSW. Somnambulist 162 And thou, in lovers' hearts forgiven, Shalt take thy place with Yarrow! 1820 SHELLEY To a Skylark xvi, With thy clear keen joyance Languor cannot be. 1834 DICKENS Sk. Boz, Boarding-ho. i, He was to his wife what the o is in 90—he was of some importance with her—he was nothing without her. 1918 Act 8 Geo. V c. 4 § 6 This Act..may be cited with the Trustee Savings Banks Acts 1863 to 1904.

26. Expressing collocation in space.

1480 Cely Papers (Camden) 54 Aull iij sortes lyes togyddyr whon w^t anothyr. 1480 Acta Dom. Conc. (1839) 47/1 Þe castin of petis in a mosse merchand with þe landis of Dalruskane. 1662 J. DAVIES tr. Olearius' Voy. Ambass. 21 We thought it enough to put it [sc. a paper] in with that of the Suedish Ambassadors. 1664 J. WEBB Stone-Heng (1725) 105 The most conspicuous [entrance]..into the Work it self lyeth North-East, whereby it fronteth rightly with the publick or high Road. 1815 WELLINGTON in Gurw. Desp. (1838) XII. 484, I send with this dispatch three eagles, taken by the troops in this action. 1831 SCOTT Cast. Dang. i, The bonnet usually worn with this showy dress. 1849 RUSKIN Samuel Prout (1870) 8 The angle formed by St. Mark's Church with the Doge's palace. 1914 F. GRIBBLE Francis Joseph xxxi. 331 The aristocracy dare not ask the professors to dinner for fear lest..they should wear green ties with their dress clothes.

b. Expressing mixture or combination of material substances.

c 1400 Lanfranc's Cirurg. 199 Ȝeue him tiriaca maior wiþ a litil musco. c 1430 Two Cookery-bks. 13 Take gode Mylke of Almaundys, an drawe it wyth Wyne. c 1440 Pallad. on Husb. III. 829 Take peres right mature, And with hool salt hem trede. 1697 DRYDEN Virg. Georg. IV. 194 Potherbs.. Which..bruis'd with Vervain, were his frugal Fare. 1753 Chambers' Cycl. Suppl. s.v. Lime ¶ 3 They work up the chalk rubbish into a sort of stiff paste with water. 1841 Penny Cycl. XX. 354/2 When hydrate of salicyle is heated with potash, an acid is formed.

(b) ellipt. in slang use, in ref. to liquor = mixed with sugar, having sugar added; usually in phr. hot (warm) or cold with.

1835 DICKENS Sk. Boz, Miss Evans & Eagle, Two glasses of rum-and-water 'warm with—'. 1854 SURTEES Handley Cr. xiv, Fatch me up a glass of cold sherry with. Ibid. xxiv, 'Take a glass of brandy,' said she...'Ot with? or cold without?'

†27. In addition to, besides; with neg., except.

c 1305 St. Edward 8 in E. E. P. (1862) 106 He nadd neȝ him noþing For to ȝyue þis pore man wiþ a goldene ring. c 1425 WYNTOUN Cron. V. x. 2252 Thre ȝhere and monethis twa, And ful ellewyn dayis withe þai. 1426 LYDG. De Guil. Pilgr. 8703 A myghty kyng,..And wyth al thys, a famous knyht. c 1470 HENRY Wallace IX. 43 With that thai war a gudly cumpany Off waillit men. 1530 TINDALE Exod. xx. 23 Ye shal not make therfore with me goddes of syluer nor goddes of golde. 1579–80 NORTH Plutarch, Agis & Cleom. (1595) 484 Very wise,..and with his wisdome..very valiant. 1599 THYNNE Animadv. 11 All whiche make xxx persons with Chaucer.

28. After a sb., in a qualifying phrase indicating a characteristic or distinctive part or adjunct: Having, possessing; having in or upon it, containing, bearing (cf. 23).

In this and sense 31 the phr. is sometimes equivalent to a descriptive adj.: e.g. with corners = 'angular'; with four wheels = 'four-wheeled'.

c 1300 Havelok 701 Shep wit wolle, neth wit horn,..and gate wit berd. 1377 LANGL. P. Pl. B. II. 16 Hire robe.. With ribanes of red golde. 1398 TREVISA Barth. De P. R. XVII. cxlv. (1495) T v/1 Harde stalkes wyth corners. a 1400 Minor Poems fr. Vernon MS. 626 His Innes & his orchardus were with a dep dich. c 1400 MAUNDEV. xxvi. [xxii.] (1919) I. 159 A charett with .iiij. wheles. 1432–50 tr. Higden (Rolls) VIII. App. 497 Schoone with longe pykes. 1500–20 DUNBAR Poems liv. 5 My ladye with the mekle lippis. 1599 SHAKS. Much Ado II. i. 15 With a good legge,..and money enough.., such a man would winne any woman in the world. 1663 GERBIER Counsel 28 Stone with Sandy veines. 1711 ADDISON Spect. No. 86 ¶ 2 A Man with a sour rivell'd Face. 1842 Penny Cycl. XXII. 429/2 The consonants are conveniently classed into those with and those without voice. 1848 THACKERAY Lett. 28 July (1887) 9 A paper-knife with a mother of pearl blade. 1892 Speaker 3 Sept. 289/2 The high road, with its shrieking steam-tram.

29. Indicating a quality or attribute of the action spoken of: forming phrases equivalent to adverbs, e.g. with one accord or consent = unanimously, with care = carefully, with ease = easily, with impunity = L. impune, with severity = severely, etc. (Sometimes closely approaching the instrumental use 37, esp. in such phrases as with a curious eye, with all one's heart, etc.) Similarly after an adj., in phr. expressing a particular kind or degree of the quality denoted by the adj.

c 1200 ORMIN 1395 Enngless haffdenn heoffness ærd forrlorenn all wiþþ rihhte. c 1250 Gen. & Ex. 1598 Fro bersabe he ferde wið sped. Ibid. 1668 Aske it wið skil and ðu salt hauen. a 1300 Cursor M. 4430 Now es ioseph in prisun strang Don..wijt wrang. 13.. Northern Passion (1913) I. 5/16 Þe Iewys..sayd he ferid all wyth foly. 13.. K. Horn 1353 (Harl.) He louede horn wiþ mihte & he him wiþ ryhte. c 1350 Will. Palerne 163 Alle wiȝth on hol hert. c 1400 Rule St. Benet (prose) 45 Whit mekenes sal sho muster to þabbes hir sekenes. 1528 Star Chamber Cases (Selden Soc.) II. 174 To get hys money with crafte and suttully. 1535 COVERDALE Deut. vi. 5 Thou shalt loue the Lorde thy God with all thy hart, with all thy soule, & with all thy mighte. 1599 SHAKS. Much Ado I. i. 300, I look'd vpon her with a souldiers eie. 1660 R. COKE Power & Subj. 45 This unlimited power of doing anything with impunity. 1671 MILTON P. R. I. 319 Who first with curious eye Perus'd him. 1710 STEELE Tatler No. 208 ¶ 8 He replied with a very angry Tone. 1760–72 H. BROOKE Fool of Qual. (1809) III. 116 A little stage was erected..that the spectators might see with the better advantage. 1771 GOLDSM. Hist. Eng. III. 351 He always travelled with hurry. 1780 COWPER Progr. Err. 562 They sidle to the goal with awkward pace. 1848 DICKENS Dombey xxxviii, Polly, who, with a woman's tact, understood this at once. 1856 MRS. CARLYLE Lett. II. 269 To-day I walked with effort one little mile. 1875 JEVONS Money (1878) 25 We use a great many words with a total disregard of logical precision.

30. Indicating a feeling, purpose, or other mental state accompanying the action spoken of: e.g. with approval, awe, horror, indifference, pleasure, regret, (due) respect, etc.; with (a, the, etc.) determination, hope, intent(ion, view, etc.: see also the sbs.

The phrase thus formed is often equivalent to an adv., as in 29, from which this use is not always distinguishable.

c 1250 Gen. & Ex. 128 God..bliscede it wid milde mood. c 1330 Spec. Gy. de Warw. 93 To don penaunce Wid sorwe at þin herte rote. c 1350 Libeaus Desc. (Kaluza) 1029 Sir Giffroun..Was bore hom on his scheld Wiþ care and rufull roun. 1382 WYCLIF Phil. ii. 12 Worche ȝe with drede and tremblinge ȝoure heelthe. 1526 TINDALE Heb. xii. 28 Grace, wherby we maye serve god..with reverence and godly feare. 1581 RICH Farew. D ij b, With this resolution he began to relate [etc.]. 1601 HOLLAND Pliny II. cv. I. 47 Shee approched neere to the altars, with purpose to sacrifice. 1714 in Jrnl. Friends' Hist. Soc. (1918) 28 We left New England with peace of mind. 1748 Anson's Voy. II. xiv. 285 They still remember, with the utmost horror, the sacking of their cities. 1786 tr. Beckford's Vathek (1868) 51 Vathek applied his ear with the hope of catching the sound of some latent runnel. 1798 SOUTHEY Pious Painter I. i, Still on his Madonnas the curious may gaze With applause and with pleasure. 1820 KEATS Lamia II. 100 If, as now it seems, your vision rests With any pleasure on me. 1849 MACAULAY Hist. Eng. vii. II. 183 A land of exile, visited with reluctance and quitted with delight. 1885 Law Rep. 29 Chanc. Div. 482 It is wholly immaterial with what object the lie is told.

b. In expressions of devotion, affection, or gratitude accompanying what is said or written, esp. by way of greeting, as in a message or the conclusion of a letter.

1454 Paston Lett. I. 273 Right wurshipfull and myn especiall good maister, I recomaund me to you with all service and prayer to my power. 1521 in Acts Parlt. Scot. (1875) XII. 40/1 Ȝoure humile oratouris and servandis with all lauchfull service. 1679 in Jrnl. Friends' Hist. Soc. (1912) IX. 191 G. F[ox] ordered me to signifie thus to thee with his deare Love. 1685 PETT in Engl. Hist. Rev. (1920) Jan. 114 Two Dorsetshire regiments..were dismissed..with thanks for their good service. 1744 in 10th Rep. Hist. MSS. Comm. App. I. 283 Laying the aff^r before my Ld Harrington with my best complim^{ts} desiring the fav^r of him just to sound the Count upon it. 1789 [see REMEMBRANCE sb. 4 d]. 1793 [see LOVE sb. 1 e]. 1835 [see REGARD sb. 10 c]. 1898 G. B. SHAW Mrs. Warren's Prof. II, Here: take George his hat and stick with my compliments.

31. Indicating an attribute, quality, or condition of the person or thing spoken of: Having, possessing, characterized by. (Often scarcely distinguishable from 28 or 29.)

c 1450 HOLLAND Howlat 18 The land lowne was and le, with lyking and luf. 1587 HOLINSHED Hist. Scot. 246/2 The Englishmen (with the number of 1500, vnder the conduct..of Talbot). 1593 SHAKS. 2 Hen. VI, I. i. 105 What meanes this passionate discourse? This peroration with such circumstance. 1610 — Temp. II. ii. 52 She had a tongue with a tang. 1671 MILTON Samson 271 Bondage with ease. 1702 DE FOE Shortest Way w. Dissenters 28 Why shou'd the Papist with his Seven Sacraments be worse than the Quaker with no Sacraments at all? 1712 STEELE Spect. No. 438 ¶ 4 A very learned Man with an erect Solemn Air. 1776 Trial of Nundocomar 32/2 He was then in a cool sweat, with a low pulse. 1812 CRABBE Tales xi. 385 Retiring late, at early hour to rise, With shrunken features, and with bloodshot eyes. 1864 TENNYSON Aylmer's Field 387. 1883 Law Times 22 Sept. 356/1 A colony with a constitution like that of the Cape Colony. 1893 Atalanta Jan. 269 Many another man with less heart and less imagination.

b. With special implications: (a) Still having; without loss of or detriment to; so as to keep or retain; consistently with.

c 1440 Alphabet of Tales 25 He vnnethis gatt away with his life. 1568 GRAFTON Chron. II. 224 He could not long continue in the seruice of princes with the sauetie of his lyfe. 1600 in J. Morris Troubles Cath. Foref. (1872) Ser. I. iv. 195 Another gentleman..was beaten down from his horse and hardly escaped with life. 1615 in Buccleuch MSS. (Hist. MSS. Comm.) I. 163 The King's letter was, that he ..could not with his greatness answer the proposition. 1654 in J. Morris Troubles Cath. Foref. (1872) Ser. I. vi. 307 He said she could not pass the next winter with life, if she took not this remedy. 1865 RUSKIN Sesame i. § 31 A nation.. cannot with impunity,..cannot with existence,..go on..concentrating its soul on Pence.

(b) Though having; notwithstanding, in spite of. (Usually followed by all qualifying the sb.; cf. FOR prep. 23 a, b.)

13.. Sir Beues (A.) 1105 Ȝet wiþ þan Ichauede þe leuer to me lemman,..Þan al þe gold þat Crist haþ maked. 1557 NORTH Gueuara's Diall Pr. (1582) 409 All these things notwithstanding they are dishonest are sometimes tollerable ..,so y^t with these faults they would be diligent to dispatch men. 1561 HOBY tr. Castiglione's Courtyer II. (1577) K j b, He hath suche straunge conceites.., that with all ye painting he hath he can not paint them. 1693 DRYDEN Juvenal Sat. Ded. (1697) p. lxxxv, Ancient Words..which, with all their Rusticity, had somewhat of Venerable in them. 1779 Mirror No. 34 ¶ 9 Umphraville, with all his dignity, his abilities, and his knowledge, felt himself uneasy and ridiculous. 1784 COWPER Task II. 206 England, with all thy faults, I love thee still. 1881 STEVENSON Virg. Puerisque Ded., But, with the best will, no man can be twenty-five for ever. 1908 R. BAGOT A. Cuthbert vi. 50 With all her apparent roughness of disposition..she was by no means a heartless woman.

32. Indicating an accompanying or attendant circumstance, or a result following from the action expressed by the verb.

c 1350 Will. Palerne 1851 Þe werwolf..went to him euene, Wiþ a rude roring. 1500–20 DUNBAR Poems viii. 2 Thou may complain with sighis lamentable The death of Bernard Stewart. 1563 FOXE A. & M. 621/2 To passe it ouer with sylence. 1621 LADY M. WROTH Urania 459, I looked vpon him, and with teares told him, his censure was harder, then the Prince his. 1677 MOXON Mech. Exerc. i. 10 Afterwards smooth it with a Blood red Heat. 1703 ROWE Fair Penit. I. i, She, with Looks averse, and Eyes that froze me, Sadly reply'd. 1793 SMEATON Edystone L. § 265 Our men went out with a declaration that they would not return till they

had found the moorings. 1806–7 J. Beresford *Miseries Hum. Life* (1826) vii. 13 The frosty silence..with which it is received by the different auditors. 1809 Malkin *Gil Blas* I. xvii. ¶ 11, I do not in the least doubt it, interrupted Fabricio with a horse-laugh. 1872 Morley *Voltaire* (1886) 1 With as far-spreading and invincible an effect. 1912 *Engl. Hist. Rev.* Oct. 672 The value of a papal dispensation is considered, with the conclusion that it is valid in some cases but not in all.

b. (after *find, take*, etc.) In the actual commission of (a crime or misdemeanour). *Obs.* or *arch.*

c 1430 *Syr Tryam.* 185 Y trowed in hur no false-hedd, Tylle y fonde them with the dede. 1510 *Reg. Privy Seal Scot.* I. 314/2 Taken in redehand with any crime. 1530–1611 [see Mainour 2]. 1572 R. H. tr. *Lavaterus' Ghostes* (1596) 40 Albeit they were..almost taken tardy with the deede doing. 1586 T. B. *La Primaud. Fr. Acad.* I. 227 His sonne being taken with the fact,..Zaleucus would never suffer the punishment to be..lessened.

33. Indicating something granted, received, or assumed: often with conditional implication, as in *with your leave* (or *permission*) = 'if you will allow me'.

13.. *Gaw. & Gr. Knt.* 971 Wyth leue la3t of þe lorde he went hem a3aynes. c 1400 *Apol. Loll.* 70 Weþ þe lefe or conferming of þe kirk, swilk mariage is rate. 1436 in *Rep. Hist. MSS. Comm., Var. Coll.* IV. 199 To caste this land oute of alle reputacion..yf so falle, as with oure Lord mercy it never shal falle. 1539 *Bible* (Great) 2 Chron. xviii. 12 The wordes of the prophetes speake good to the kyng with one assent. — *Ps.* xviii. 29 Wt the helpe of my God I shall leape ouer the wall. 1610 B. Jonson *Alch.* IV. i, Madame, with your pardon, I kisse your vesture. 1648–9 in *Engl. Hist. Rev.* (1917) Oct. 570 Hee..had alsoe the Keyes of the Castle (but not with Thompson's good will). 1660 *Act 12 Chas. II* c. 19 Bee it Enacted by the Kings most Excellent Majesty by and with the advice and consent of the Lords and Commons..That [etc.]. 1779 *Mirror* No. 33 ¶ 4 We were accordingly married with the universal approbation of my friends. 1794 J. H. Moore *Pract. Navig.* (ed. 10) 87 With the course and distance find the difference of latitude and departure. 1838 Dickens *Nich. Nick.* xv, Another gentleman comes and collars that glass of punch, without a 'with your leave', or 'by your leave'. 1856 Froude *Hist. Eng.* I. i. 77 So the law of England remained..with the deliberate approval of both the great parties. 1879 E. Waterton *Pietas Mariana Brit.* 226 With these general data, I now proceed to examine some of the details.

34. Followed by a sb. denoting some alteration or modification, or something imposed in the way of a demand or requirement: e.g. *change, condition, exception, loss, proviso, qualification*, etc. (Before *condition* now replaced by *on*.)

c 1450 *Merlin* xiv. 203 We be come to serue yow, with this condicion, that ye desire not to knowe oure names. 1489 in *Trevelyan Papers* (Camden) 93 With the same condicions and provisoes. 1626 W. Sclater *Exp. 2 Thess.* (1629) 210 With exception of the crosse. 1629 Hobbes *Thucyd.* I. 59 The Athenians..made peace, with condition to haue their Prisoners released. 1779 *Mirror* No. 7 ¶ 2 With these qualifications, Sir, I am held in considerable estimation by the wits of both sexes. 1849 Macaulay *Hist. Eng.* ii. I. 165 Such a body..is composed, with scarcely an exception, of sincere persons. 1861 M. Pattison *Ess.* (1889) I. 44 With the exception of a dwelling-house.., the remainder of the area was covered with warehouses.

35. a. Followed by a sb. denoting misfortune or evil, in imprecations and intensive phrases: also *with a* Wanion, *with a witness* (see Witness *sb.* 14). Now chiefly in *with a vengeance* (in intensive sense: see Vengeance *sb.* 4).

a 1300 *K. Horn* 326 (Camb.) Went [= go] vt of my bur Wiþ muchel mesauentur. c 1386 Chaucer *Manciple's Prol.* 11 Is that a Cook of London, with meschance? a 1529 Skelton *E. Rummyng* 346 As thou, wyth shamfull deth! 1538– [see Mischief *sb.* 9 a]. 16.. Middleton, etc. *Old Law* III. ii, *Ly.* I will send it through you with a powder. *Sim.* Let come, with a Pox! 1663 Dryden *Wild Gallant* I. ii, I'll put you out of your Pater Nosters, with a sorrow to you.

b. Introducing a refrain (often meaningless) in a poem or ballad.

[13.. *Coer de L.* 2522 They rowede hard, and sungge ther too, With heuelow and rumbeloo.] c 1400 *Pety Job* 96 in *26 Pol. Poems* 124 Nowe yeue me mercy, and say nat nay, Wyth *Parce michi, domine.* 15..– [see Hey-ho]. 1519 [see Hey *int.* 2]. a 1529 Skelton *E. Rummyng* 289 Wyth Hey and wyth howe. 1633, 1672 [see Fading *sb.*]. 1665, a 1800 [see Fa-la a]. 1780 *British Grenadiers*, With a tow, row, row, row, row.

36. In various preceding senses, followed by object and complement (phr. with prep., pple., adj., adv., or inf. with *to*).

c 1290 *Beket* 1169 in *S. Eng. Leg.* 140 With one haltre ope þe mere forth rod þis holi man. 1375 Barbour *Bruce* VIII. 48 Thai saw in battale cum arayit The vaward with baner displayit. c 1386 Chaucer *Doctor's T.* 211 With fadres pitee stikynge thurgh his herte. 1443–50 in W. P. Baildon *Sel. Cases Chanc.* (1896) 134 His purse with xxv. s. of money therin. c 1482 *Paston Lett.* III. 295 Fayne she wold be redde of it with hyr onowt savyd. 1527 *Test. Ebor.* (Surtees) VI. 13 The lesse leede with the hole in the bothom. 1534 More *Comf. agst. Trib.* III. xix. (1553) R vij, The..prieste..that had..vsed to say *Dominus* with the seconde sillable long. 1611 Shaks. *Cymb.* II. i. 26 You crow Cock, with your combe on. 1630 Pagitt *Christianogr.* I. iii. (1636) 133 Standing..with their armes foulded. 1745 Pococke *Descr. East* II. II. 231 There are six youths in each room, with a master over them. 1760–2 Goldsm. *Cit. W.* lxxi, He sat with rapture in his eye. 1831 Scott *Cast. Dang.* xiv, The shield represented an owl with its wings spread. 1842 Tennyson *Lady Clare* xv, She went by dale, and she went by down, With a single rose in her hair. 1842 Browning *Through the Metidja to Abd-el-Kadr* i, As I ride, as I ride, With a full heart for my guide. 1848 Dickens *Dombey* v, An iron-grey autumnal day, with a shrewd east wind blowing. 1859 Geo. Eliot *Adam Bede* xviii, They..stood with their hats off. 1866 Ruskin *Let.* 10 May, Joan has written another long letter to you with something about me in it. 1870 Morris *Earthly Par.* III. 455 Life seemed not so cursed With this to think of.

III. Denoting instrumentality, causation, or agency.

37. Indicating the means or instrument (material or immaterial) of any kind of action: By means of, by the use of.

c 1200 Ormin 5524 Þe bodi3 forr to pinenn wiþþ swinnc. c 1220 *Bestiary* 9 He..Drageð dust wið his stert. *Ibid.* 627 He ne hauen no lið Ðat he mu3en risen wið. a 1250 *Prov. Alfred* 90 in *O. E. Misc.* 108 For to werie þat lond wiþ hunger and wiþ herivnge. c 1250 *Gen. & Ex.* 44 Al was ðat firme ðrosing in ni3t, Til he wit hise word made li3t. a 1300 *K. Horn* 439 (Camb.) Wiþ seluer & wiþ golde Hit wurþ him wel i3olde. *Ibid.* 514 Þin armes he haþ & scheld To fi3te wiþ vpon þe feld. a 1300 *Cursor M.* 14427 Þat he suld flexs take o þair kin, For to ranscun wit adam sin. 13.. *E. E. Allit. P.* B. 1438 He with keyes vncloses kystes ful mony. 1382 Wyclif *Mark* xiv. 58, I schal vndo this temple maad with hondis. c 1386 Chaucer *Prol.* 1 Whan that Aprille with hise shoures soote The droghte of March hath perced to the roote. c 1400 Maundev. (1919) xxvii. 165 A lytille whippe in hire hondes for to chacen with hire hors. 1413 *E. E. Wills* (1882) 22 The residue of my gode, y bequethe tho Amys my wyf, an my son, to kepe hem boþ wyt. 1479 *Cely Papers* (Camden) 18, v c or vj c baras canvase for to packe woll wyt. 1491 Caxton *Vitas Patr.* (W. de W. 1495) II. 247/2 Oonly as moche as suffysed to bye with his brede cotydyan. 1523 Ld. Berners *Froiss.* I. ccxxvi. 123/1 He lost euer after ye syght with that eye. 1526 Tindale *Matt.* xx. 22 Are ye able..to be baptised with the baptism that y shalbe baptised with? — *Mark* ix. 49 Every sacryfyse shalbe seasoned with saltt. 1591 Spenser *Virg. Gnat* 432 All slaine with darts. 1634 Sir T. Herbert *Trav.* 145 They build with vnburnt clay. 1671 Milton *Samson* 1621 The people with a shout Rifted the Air. 1748 *Anson's Voy.* I. i. 9 The ships were disappointed of provisions for want of a cargo to truck with. 1766 Goldsm. *Vicar W.* iii, We lightened the fatigues of the road with philosophical disputes. 1855 Macaulay *Hist. Eng.* xi. III. 44 Some acts which in the citizen are punished with fine or imprisonment must in the soldier be punished with death. 1877 Ruskin *St. Mark's Rest* i. § 18 There is nothing like a little work with the fingers for teaching the eyes. 1890 *Law Times' Rep.* LXIII. 691/2 A publican runs a greater risk of being cheated with false money than other tradesmen.

†(*b*) Through the medium of (a person). *rare.*

c 1000 Ælfric *Gen.* xxxviii. 20 Iudas sende an ticcen wið hys Odolamitiscean hyrde. a 1300 *Cursor M.* 1274 He wald send me word wit þe. c 1375 *Sc. Leg. Saints* xxviii. (*Margaret*) 135 Tyne nocht my sawle with fellone mene. 1590 Shaks. *Com. Err.* V. i. 230 He did arrest me with an Officer.

b. Formerly used in many cases where *by* (By *prep.* 30, 32) is now the usual or only construction; e.g. with obj. a person, or an action (esp. when expressed by a gerund or vbl. sb. in *-ing*).

a 1300 *Cursor M.* 882 Scó fild wit hir sin. 13.. *Guy Warw.* (A.) 129 He wald do nimen him anon, & wiþ strengþe him nim wolde. 1375 Barbour *Bruce* I. 521 Wes nocht all Troy with tresoune tane..? c 1386 Chaucer *Doctor's T.* 217 To dyen with a swerd or with a knyf. c 1450 tr. *De Imitatione* II. xii. 57 It shal not lye in þy power to be esid ner delyuered wiþ no remedy ner no solace. c 1450 Capgrave *Life St. Aug.* 112 Þou wer led in-to þis place wit3 þe handis of many men. 1513 Bradshaw *St. Werburge* I. 2461 And it to confyrme..With charters and dedes. 1523 Ld. Berners *Froiss.* I. ccciii. 183 b/1 The towne was taken with assaute, and robbed. 1539 *Bible* (Great) 1 Kings vi. 8 Men went vp with windyng steares into the myddle chambre. 1571 Digges *Pantom.* IV. vi. X j, If by the second rule ye diuide 100 with 24, the quotient is 4⅙. 1667 Dryden tr. *Life S. Francis Xavier* vi. 667 Many sick persons..were cur'd with only seeing it. a 1715 Burnet *Own Time* (1724) I. 409 With all this the King was convinced. 1750 Johnson *Rambler* No. 43 ¶ 10 Distant countries are united with canals. 1837 Dickens *Pickw.* iii, Will you oblige us with proceeding with what you were going to relate? 1859 Geo. Eliot *Adam Bede* xvi, I don't believe there's anything you can't prevail on people to do with kindness.

c. Used where other prepositions are now usual, as *at* (a charge or cost), *in* (a receptacle or something figured as such), *of* (a material or constituent, after *make*), *on* or *upon* (food, etc.).

a 1300 *Cursor M.* 11109 Ion..liued wit rotes and wit gress, Wit honi o þe wildernes. c 1450 *Godstow Reg.* 530 The forsaid Adam shold susteyn the said mese..with his owne costis. 1564 Harding *Answ. Jewel* 40 S. Augustine vttereth the same thinge almost with the same wordes. a 1586 Sidney *Astr. & Stella* Sonn. xcix, When farre spent night perswades each mortal eie..To laye his then marke wanting shaftes of sight, Clos'd with their quivers in Sleeps armorie. 1588 Shaks. *L. L. L.* I. i. 303 You shall fast a Weeke with Branne and water. 1598 Greneway *Tacitus, Ann.* I. xv. (1622) 29 Germanicus..furnished the rest with his owne charges. 1617 Moryson *Itin.* III. 83 They dine with dried pork. 1633 J. Clarke *Two-fold Praxis*, I lived..with sevenpence a day. 1709 Strype *Ann. Ref.* I. xl. 410 That she would wrap up all such matters with oblivion. a 1774 Goldsm. *Surv. Exp. Philos.* (1776) II. 239 Burning instruments of this kind are usually made with glass. 1785 Cumberland *Nat. Son* I. i, When he shall see what frippery a woman is made up with. 1802 Strutt *Sports & Past.* III. vi. 221 Diminutive imitations of muskets made with wood. 1840 Pereira *Elem. Mat. Med.* II. 1269 A sinapism made with flour.

†**d.** In reference to procreation, with obj. either the male or the female parent: = By *prep.* 32 c.

c 1450 *Merlin* 20 Thow wast with childe with hym. 1593 in *Maitl. Club Misc.* I. 56 The barne gottin be him with the said Margaret Steyne. 1603 Shaks. *Meas. for M.* II. ii. 143 Shee speakes, and 'tis such sence That my Sence breeds with it. a 1709 J. Lister *Autobiog.* (1842) 51, I had but two children with my wife.

e. After *begin* or *end* and words of like sense, in various shades of meaning: indicating (*a*) that which constitutes the beginning or end, i.e. the initial or final part, element, stage, proceeding, etc. (after a personal subj. and before a gerund now *by*, as in b above); (*b*) a person or thing acted upon or treated first or last (coinciding with 9); (*c*) (after *begin, originate*, etc.) the agent or source from which something takes its rise (allied to 11).

Phr. (with ellipsis of obj.) *to begin with*: to take what is mentioned or indicated as one's starting-point.

1412–20 Lydg. *Chron. Troy* I. 2414 For my behest with deth I schal conclude. c 1550 Bale *K. Johan* (Camden) 47 Fyrst to begyne with, we shall interdyte the lond. 1570 Foxe *A. & M.* (ed. 2) I. 494/2 First begynnyng with that godly man..the autor of the boke. a 1619 in S. Atkinson *Gold Mynes Scot.* (Bann. Club) 2 It is true that 'say well and doe well ends both with one letter'. 1677 in *Essex Papers* (Camden) II. 110 The Commoners..take distaste that anything which relates to mony, should..begin with the Lords. 1683 Tryon *Way to Health* 642 Drawing towards a Conclusion of this Treatise, I shall put a period thereto with some unvulgar Considerations of the Nature of Sounds and Melody. 1713 Berkeley *Guardian* No. 69 ¶ 2 He has ended his Discourse with a Prayer. 1768 Sterne *Sent. Journ.* II. 51 (*Le Patisser*) He finish'd the scene with winning my esteem. 1833 Ht. Martineau *Brooke Farm* i. 6, I must begin my lecture with you. 1843 *Fraser's Mag.* XXVIII. 657 The evening generally closed with music. 1861 T. L. Peacock *Gryll Grange* xxix, I will be bound every one of this company could..find a quotation in point. —Miss Gryll, to begin with. 1879 Ruskin *St. Mark's Rest* iv. § 56 We may close her national history with the seventeenth century. 1887 'L. Carroll' *Game of Logic* i. § 2. 22 'Middle' begins with 'm'. 1918 in *Engl. Hist. Rev.* (1919) July 442 Newcastle's response..did not stop with sending Warren for the defence of the Northern Colonies.

38. After words of furnishing, filling, covering, adorning, and the like. (Allied to II. ***, involving the notion of addition.)

After *full* now replaced by *of*.

c 1200 Ormin 994 Bulltedd bræd..smeredd wel wiþþ elesæw. c 1290 *S. Eng. Leg.* I. 384/256 For-to..crouni him with golde. a 1300 *Cursor M.* 852 God..fild þis werld al wit his grace. *Ibid.* 1046 Wit gress and leues he clad. a 1310 in Wright *Lyric P.* xxxiv. 96 To presente hyre sone With myrre, gold, ant encenz. ?a 1366 Chaucer *Rom. Rose* 1076 It [*sc.* a robe] ful well With Orfrays leyd was euerydeell. c 1394 *P. Pl. Crede* 116 Cloþ to coveren wiþ our bones. c 1425 *Engl. Conq. Irel.* 130 Encombret whyth syn. 1445 in *Anglia* XXVIII. 277 Histirlonde he plantith with vyne. 1506 in *Mem. Hen. VII* (Rolls) 285 The third chamber..was hanged with a very rich arras. c 1511 *1st Engl. Bk. Amer.* (Arb.) Introd. 28/1 Ledder to kyuer they members with. 1526– [see Endow *v.* 3 b]. 1590 Shaks. *Mids. N.* II. i. 131 Her wombe then rich with my yong squire. 1590 Spenser *F. Q.* III. iii. 4 That doest ennoble with immortall name The warlike Worthies. 1610 Shaks. *Temp.* I. ii. 154 Infused with a fortitude from heauen. *Ibid.* 283 Then was this Island..not honour'd with A humane shape. 1621 Lady M. Wroth *Urania* 229 As full of spite and ill nature as a Spider with poyson. 1633 J. Clarke *Two-fold Praxis* 63 It is very expedient for us scholars to be instructed with good manners. c 1646 Milton *New Forcers Consc.* 7 To force our Consciences..And ride us with a classic Hierarchy. 1713– [see Litter *v.* 5, 6 a]. 1734 Sale *Koran* Prelim. Disc. § 1. 3 A stony and barren valley, surrounded on all sides with mountains. 1849 Robertson *Serm.* Ser. I. vi. (1866) 99 Christianity..permeates all evil with good. 1878 Hardy *Ret. Native* VI. i, Wreathing it [*sc.* a pole] with wildflowers. 1884 W. C. Smith *Kildrostan* 86 A..breeze..Tipping the waves with foam.

39. Indicating the cause or reason: In consequence of, as a result of, by the action of; because of, by reason of, on account of; from, through, by.

In some cases now replaced by *of* (e.g. after Come *v.* 11 c); in others *of* and *with* are used with distinction of meaning (see e.g. Die *v.*[1] 1 b, 7 c, Weary *a.* 1 c, 2).

13.. *Cursor M.* 1058 (Gött.) For-þi was he witt þat for lorn. 13.. *K. Alis.* 1058 Mony a baner..rotled with the wynde. ?a 1400 *Arthur* 466 And deyde wyþ strokis þat þey hente. 1476 *Paston Lett.* III. 161, I am somewhatt crased, what with the see and what wythe thys dyet beer. 1591 Shaks. *Two Gent.* I. i. 69 Hart sick with thought. 1593 — *2 Hen. VI*, IV. vii. 111, I feele remorse in my selfe with his words. 1596 — *Tam. Shr.* III. ii. 243 Went they not quickly, I should die with laughing. 1600 G. Abbot *Exp. Jonah* 54 These did perish in their owne sinne, although they perished with his fault. 1601 Shaks. *Twel. N.* III. iv. 366 This comes with seeking you. a 1604 Hanmer *Chron. Irel.* (1633) 202 The Lord Iames Audley..dyed with the fall of a horse. 1671 in *12th Rep. Hist. MSS. Comm.* App. v. 23 She was so ill with wearing a paire of perfumed bodyes that she was forced to go to bed. 1682 Wood *Life* (O.H.S.) III. 12 July, Sir Jonas Moore..died with a fall from his horse. 1784 Cowper *Tiroc.* 833 Flush'd with drunk'ness. 1826 Byron *Pris. Chillon* i My hair is grey, but not with years. 1837 Hawthorne *Twice-told T., Gt. Carbuncle*, The..branches..mossy with age. 1889 J. K. Jerome *Three Men in Boat* 4 Zymosis I had evidently been suffering with from boyhood. *Mod. colloq.* Harry Wood is in the Cottage Hospital with his knee.

b. After a trans. vb. (usually in pass.), or a pa. pple. or ppl. adj., indicating the immediate cause or ground of the action or state spoken of: often approaching or coinciding with 37 or 40 b.

After certain pples., as *pleased, surprised*, etc., varying with or now replaced by *at*. After *trouble* vb. sometimes approaching 9.

c 1250 *Gen. & Ex.* 3690 Ðor wurð ȝhe ðanne wið lepre smiten. a 1300 *Cursor M.* 4076 Þai soght him ai to greue wit wrang. 1387 Trevisa *Higden* (Rolls) VIII. 149 Þe pepil was i-plesed wiþ his faire speche. c 1400 *Rom. Rose* 5628 Contente with his pouerte. c 1440 *Generydes* 2221 With tho wordes the kyng liked full ill. 14.. in *Guillim's*

Heraldry IV. vii. (1632) 296 Worne wud Age. 1535 Coverdale *Prov.* vi. 25 Lest thou be taken with hir fayre lokes. 1553 T. Wilson *Rhet.* 115 b, Because I haue halfe weried the reader.., I will harten him agayne wyth a merye tale. 1603– [see Spent 3 b]. 1652 Wadsworth tr. *Sandoval's Civ. Wars Spain* 342 Hugging himself with that small victorie. 1655–1768 [see Surprise *v.* 5]. a 1745 Swift *Ess. Faculties Mind* Ded., Wks. 1841 II. 284/2 To suppose you would be very much obliged with anything that was new. 1792 Jefferson *Writ.* (1859) III. 494, I am rejoiced with the account he gives me. 1807 Earl Malmesbury *Diaries & Corr.* III. 363, I am..not surprised with the opiniativeness of Lord Grenville. 1839 Thirlwall *Greece* li. VI. 243 His men and horses were now nearly spent with toil. 1891 Conan Doyle *White Company* xx, A face which was distorted with rage.

c. After an intr. (rarely a trans.) vb. or an adj., combining the sense 'by reason of' with 28 ('having in or upon it') or 38 ('filled, covered, etc. with'). Also more vaguely, indicating a substance (esp. a liquid) which is the logical subject of the vb.: e.g. *it is pouring with rain* = rain is pouring; (*flowers*) *dripping with dew* = having dew dripping from them.

1388 Wyclif *Exod.* iii. 8 A lond that flowith with milk and hony. 1390 Gower *Conf.* I. 98 Hire chekes ben with teres wet. c 1400 *Ywaine & Gaw.* 1397 The castel and cete rang With mynstralsi and nobil sang. c 1450 Holland *Howlat* 5 With alkyn herbes..The feldis flurist. 1508 Dunbar *Gold. Targe* 28 Doun throu the ryce a ryuir ran wyth stremys. 1513 Douglas *Æneis* VII. viii. 93 Hir figoure sa grisly gret aboundis, Wyth glowand ene birnand of flawmis blak. 1565 Cooper *Thesaurus*, *Manantia vlcera*, sores runnyng with matter. 1606 Shaks. *Ant. & Cl.* I. iii. 45 Our Italy, Shines o're with ciuill Swords. 1622– [see Heavy *a.* 4]. 1667 Milton *P. L.* IV. 605 Now glow'd the Firmament With living Saphirs. 1697 Dryden *Virg. Georg.* III. 235 Th' Alburnian Groves, with Holly green. *Ibid.* 559 The Garment, stiff with Ice, at Hearths is thaw'd. 1746 Smollett *Reproof* 28 Hallowed be the mouth That teems with moral zeal and dauntless truth! 1798 Coleridge *Kubla Khan* 8 Gardens bright with sinuous rills. 1799 Wordsw. *Fountain* viii, My eyes are dim with childish tears. 1849 [see Pour *v.* 6 b]. 1899 T. S. Moore *Vinedresser* 6 Banks more soft with moss than any bed.

d. Following words of blame or the like (after *charge* orig. fig. from 38); also after *credit* vb.: indicating the ground of the charge, etc.

After *accuse, suspect*, now replaced by *of*.

c 1440 *Alph. Tales* 318 Þis preste..tolde hur cowncell, & vpbrayed hur þerwith. 1559 *Mirr. Mag., Dk. Clarence* l. 7 To charge me with offence. 1579–80 North *Plutarch, Demetrius* (1595) 946 Hee..was most detected with this vice of lechery. 1591 *Troub. Raigne K. John* i. 147 A Man, Whom be accuseth with adulterie. 1665 Dryden *Ind. Emperor* III. ii, None shall tax me with base Perjury. 1670 Stubbe *Reply H. More* (1671) 75 The World will condemn you with Blasphemy for that comparison. 1715 De Foe *Fam. Instruct.* (1841) II. I. i. 10 The blot with which I reproach myself. 1814 Mrs. J. West *Alicia de Lacy* IV. 298 There seems no just cause for accusing the King with the premature fate of this nobleman. 1877 Froude *Short Stud.* (1883) IV. I. iii. 27 To credit him with a desire to reform the Church.

40. After a passive verb or participle, indicating the principal agent: = By *prep.* 33. **a.** (a person or animal). *Obs.* exc. *dial.*

c 1300 *Havelok* 2489 He was wit þe prestes shriue. 13.. *Cursor M.* 15908 (Gött.) Sare he dred þat syden fell Wid þaim he suld be slaine. 13.. *Gaw. & Gr. Knt.* 1229 Your honour..is hendely prayсed With lordez, wyth ladyes, with alle þat lyf bere. 1375 Barbour *Bruce* XVIII. 128 And be the armys led wes he With twa men. c 1400 Maundev. (Roxb.) vi. 19 Þis same sowdan..was slayne with his awen seruands. 1456 Sir G. Haye *Law Arms* (S.T.S.) 38 The first quhete that ever was sawin with man. c 1489 Caxton *Sonnes of Aymon* i. 52 They all were eten wyth bores and of lions. 1535 Stewart *Cron. Scot.* (Rolls) II. 56 So awful rumour..Wes neuir hard with no man in this erd. 1579 Lyly *Euphues* (Arb.) 110 There was a Towne in Spayne vndermined with Connyes, in Thessalia with Mowles, with Frogges in Fraunce. 1611 Shaks. *Wint. T.* V. ii. 68 He was torne to pieces with a Beare. 1632 Lithgow *Trav.* III. 86 It was miserably sacked, and burned with Turkes. 1670 Dryden *Conq. Granada* III. i, As I were stung with some tarantula. 1707 Mortimer *Husb.* 165 If the Ass, you design to breed on, be suckled with a Mare. a 1715 Burnet *Own Time* (1724) I. 250 He rode thro' London, accompanied with the most popular men of his Court. 1727 *Philip Quarll* (1816) 19 This island is inhabited..with monkies and myself. 1735 J. Hughes tr. *Fontenelle's Dial.* I. viii. (ed. 3) 32, I went attended with a numerous train. *Mod. dial.* You never hear of horses being bit with snakes.

†**b.** (a thing, material or immaterial). *Obs.*

c 1375 *Sc. Leg. Saints* xii. (*Mathias*) 65 With wawis castine to be land. 1387 Trevisa *Higden* (Rolls) III. 295 Awaked wiþ crienge of gandres. c 1450 *St. Cuthbert* (Surtees) 5866 In to eland war þai kest with' a flowyng flode. 1571 Digges *Pantom.* I. xxxi. K j, Intercepted with the perpendicular lyne. 1634 Sir T. Herbert *Trav.* 94 Hyrcania..is limited on the North with the Caspian Sea. 1729 Law *Serious C.* xix. 354 Her other entrails were much hurt by being crush'd together with her stays. 1760 R. Brown *Compl. Farmer* II. 2 Overflowed with rivers or land-floods.

B. *adv.*

†**1.** With it (me, them, etc.); in collocation, company, or association; together; occas., at the same time, simultaneously. *Obs.*

c 888 Ælfred *Boeth.* xvi. § 3 Hit nis nauht ȝecynde..þæt æniȝ wiðerweard þing bion ȝemenged wið oðrum wiðerweardum, oððe æniȝe ȝeferrædenne wið habban. c 1000 *Sax. Leechd.* II. 54 Meng þonne hwitcwudu wiþ. c 1440 *Pallad. on Husb.* I. 711 Ley nettelys vndir with. *Ibid.* VI. 10 Al doubil seed, as benes,..And other puls, a xl dayes floure, And greteth with [orig. *simulque grandescunt*]. c 1450 tr. *De Imitatione* III. lxiv. 150 Defende and kepe þe soule of þy..seruaunt..and, þy grace goyng wiþ [orig. *comitante gratia*], dyrecte hym by þe wey of pes.

†**b.** *With also*: nonce-substitute for Withal (= 'also'). *Obs. rare.*

1586 G. Whetstone *Engl. Mirr.* I. xv. 95 Frauncis the second..beeing both very young, and with also married to the Queene of Scots.

†**2.** *With and with*: **a.** Immediately, forthwith (= By and by 3); **b.** From time to time, again and again, every now and then. *Obs.*

c 1200 Ormin 5628 Icc wile wiþþ & wiþþ þa seoffne seollþess shæwenn. c 1205 Lay. 20747 We sendeð wið and wið and ȝeornen Arðures grið. *Ibid.* 30177 Adwine..seide auere wið and wið: ich wulle makien un-frið. c 1440 *Pallad. on Husb.* XI. 175 Delue hit ofte, and..Ay with and with lycour on hit to trete.

†**3.** With that, or with which; therewith, wherewith: = Withal *adv.* 2. *Obs.*

a 1300 *Cursor M.* 936 God mad þam kyrtels þan of hide, And cled þar flexs wit for to hide. a 1425 *Ibid.* 8597 (Trin.) Her modris..had no cradles ne wiþ to by. 1566 in Picton *L'pool Munic. Rec.* (1883) I. 48 The said earl..had a couple of partridges, and to drink with of his lordships cost.

†**C.** *conj.* **a.** To the time that, until. (Only OE.) **b.** During or at the time that; while; when. (Cf. sense 16 of the prep.) *Obs. rare.*

c 950 *Lindisf. Gosp.* Matt. x. 11 Ðer wunas wið ȝe ðona ȝeonga. 1375 Barbour *Bruce* XVII. 455 It wes nocht eyth till ta The toune, with [*v. rr.* quhill; *ed.* 1570 while] sic defens wes maid. c 1450 *St. Cuthbert* (Surtees) 1685 With þir thinges were done.

D. *Comb.*, as **with-worker** (*nonce-wd.* after G. *mitwerker*), a fellow-worker, co-worker.

1884 R. F. Burton *Camoens, Lyricks* I. 4, I have been aided by a host of 'with-workers'.

With: see Withe.

With, obs. form of White, Wight.

With-, representing OE. *wiþ-* (see With *prep.*) used as a prefix to verbs (and derived sbs.) with the meanings: (1) away, back, as in OE. *wiþblāwan* to blow away, *wiþfaran* to escape, *wiþgān* to disappear, *wiþtēon* to withdraw; so Withdraw, Withhold; a few modern words come under this heading, which are formed by substituting *with-* for *re-*, as *withcall*; (2) away from one, as in several OE. verbs meaning 'reject', 'refuse', *wiþcēosan*, *wiþcweþan*, *wiþhogian*, *wiþlecgan*, *wiþsacan* Withsake *v.*, *wiþweorpan*; (3) against, in opposition, as in OE. *wiþfeohtend* adversary, *wiþhabban* to resist, *wiþlicgan* to oppose, *wiþsprecan* to contradict, *wiþstandan* Withstand *v.*; (4) together, in *withjoin*.

The following is a list of the less important verbal formations (transitive verbs except where otherwise marked); mostly obs. (see quots.).

†**Withbere** [Bear *v.*[1]], to carry away; see also b; †**withbo3t** *pa. pple.* [Buy *v.*] redeemed; †**withbrast** *pa. t.* [Burst *v.*] *intr.* burst asunder; †**withbreide** [OE. *wiþbregdan*, Braid *v.*[1]], to withdraw; †**withbuwe** [Bow *v.*[1]], to avoid; **withcall**, to recall; †**withclepe**, to recall, revoke, repeal; †**withdrive**, to drive away, repel; †**withhuhe** [OE. *wiþhogian*], to despise; †**withjoin**, to join together, conjoin (*intr.* and *trans.*); †**withleft** *pa. pple.* left behind; †**withlosen** *pa. pple.* [Leese], lost; †**withnay** [Nay *v.*; cf. Renay], to deny, refuse; †**withnim** [= L. *reprehendere*; see Nim *v.*], to reprove, rebuke; †**withpass**, to escape the lips of; †**withquethe**, to deny, contradict, refuse; †**withscape**, to escape; †**withschadowid** *pa. pple.*, darkened; †**withschild** [Shield *v.*], in *God w.*, God forbid; †**withscore**, to cut away, detach; †**withshonte** [Shunt *v.*], *intr.* to shrink back; †**withslip**, to escape; †**withso3t** *pa. t.* [Seek *v.*], pursued, persecuted; †**withsperre** *v.* [Spar *v.*[1]], to bar (the way); †**withstad**, **-sted** *pa. pple.* [Stead *v.*], beset; †**withstarte** [Start *v.* 6], *intr.* to escape; **withstay** [Stay *v.*[1] III], to hold back, oppose, withstand; †**withstew** [Stew *v.*[1]], to check; **withstrain**, †(*a*) to constrict; (*b*) to restrain; †**withtee** [Tee *v.*[1]], to withdraw; *refl.* and *intr.* to abstain; †**withtelle**, to gainsay; †**withturn**, to avert.

c 1500 *Melusine* 196 Other thing ye shal not haue ne *withbere fro me. 1340 *Ayenb.* 186 Alle we byeþ *wiþbo3t of one zelue pris. 1448–9 Metham *Amoryus & Cl.* 1520 The dragon ..*with brast in þe myddys. c 890 Wærferth tr. *Gregory's Dial.* (1900) 203 Þara oðre se cniht *wiðbræd..& þa oðre brohte to ðam Godes men. c 1000 Ælfric *Hom.* I. 88 Ðæt hi heora handa fram ðam blodes gyte ne wiðbrudon. c 1230 *Hali Meid.* (1922) 11 In wunne stude þu hauest her ofte helle; & bute þu wið-breide þe, bredes te þat oðer. a 1225 *Ancr. R.* 116 Uorte *wiðbuwen sunne. c 1230 *Hali Meid.* (1922) 52 Hwase þencheð on al þis,..& nule wiðbuhe þet þing þet hit al of awakeneð. 1901 J. Prior *Forest Folk* x. 105 Do yo *withcall them saving tears shed years and years agoo, Sister Morris? 1904 'H. S. Merriman' *Flotsam* xiv. 159 The troops were withcalled. 13.. *K. Alis.* 1301 Y *withclepe and withstonde Theo truage of Grece londe. 1340 *Ayenb.* 189 Uor alle time y-confermed ne neure in none time wyþcleped. *Ibid.* 215 Þer me ssel wyþ-clepie his herte to him. 1387 Trevisa *Higden* (Rolls) VI. 267 He..wiþcleped al þat was i-doo by his predecessour. c 1440 *Promp. Parv.* 530/2 Wythe clepyn', or reuokyn. 1617 Holyoke *Rider's Dict.*, To Withclepe, *revoco*. c 1000 *Ags. Ps.* (Th.) xciii[i]. 13 [14] Næfre *wiðdrifeð Drihten ure his aȝen folc. 1527 Andrew *Brunswyke's Distyll. Waters* II. ii. A ij/2 The same [Sorell] water withdryueth impetigines. a 1000 *Cædmon's Gen.* 2864 Nalles nergendes hæse *wiðhogode. c 1230 *Hali Meid.* (1922) 53 Nule wiðhuhe þat þing þat hit al of awakeneð. c 1450 *Merlin* 282 Holde we vs to-geder cloos and make semblaunte as we wolde *with Ioyne. 1630 J. Hayward *Edw. VI*, 10 It had bin agreed..they should withjoyne forces. c 1375 *Cursor M.* 4403 (Fairf.) Hys mantel ys *wiþleft [*Cott.* bileft] wiþ me. a 1300 *Ibid.* 10855 (Cott.) Ne sal þe nawight be *wit-losen þe maidenhed þat þou hast chosen. *Ibid.* 14109 Þe better lott has mari chosen, Þat hir mai nagat be witlosin. 13.. *E. E. Allit. P.* A. 915 As þou art gloryous with-outen galle, *With-nay þou neuer my ruful bone. c 1440 *Pallad. on Husb.* III. 1151 If thai withnay Her fruit. c 1450 *Brut* II. 480 Then she withneyed and withseyd all the poyntez þat were put. c 1315 Shoreham *Poems* vii. 308 By ry3tte he my3tte be *wyþ-nome Ry3t ase a qued. 13.. *S. E. Leg.* (MS. Bodl. 779) in Herrig's *Archiv* LXXXII. 374/297 Ic am a-knowe þat ic whyl-er þe wit-nom amys. 1340 *Ayenb.* 17 Þe more þet me him wyþ[þ]nimþ and blameþ..þe more he him wreþeþ. *Ibid.* 66 Efter þan comeþ þe wyþnymynges,..huanne me atwyt ane man oþer his zennes. c 1340 *Nominale* (Skeat) 290 Woman thretith and withnemyth. a 1340 Hampole *Psalter* xxxviii. 2 Þat nane reprouabil word *withpassid me. c 888 Ælfred *Boeth.* x. § 1 Ne mæȝ ic na *wiðcweðan ne andsacigan þæt þe þu me ær sædest. c 1200 *Trin. Coll. Hom.* 137 He wið-quað and seide *Non sum ego christus*. a 1300 *Cursor M.* 20726 *Witschap scho vs, we sal ha blam. a 1400 *Sir Degrev.* (Linc. MS.) 1180 (Luick) Withscapid nane hym fra. 1398 Trevisa *Barth. De P. R.* VIII. xl. (Tollem. MS.), [Light] putteþ nou3t it selfe deep into a body þat is *withschadowid [orig. *umbrosi*]. a 1300 *Cursor M.* 2893 Godd *wit schild 3e do þat sin. 13.. *Ibid.* 5011 (Gött.) 1340 *Ayenb.* 254 *Wyþscore [*MS. Bodl.* 283 fol. 178 kit a weye] and wyþdra3 þine willes and zete ane brydel to þine couaytises. a 1400 *Pistill of Susan* 231 (Cott. MS.) Sche *withe-shoute for no shame. a 1300 *Cursor M.* 12900 Moght it nangat þe *witslip þat he-self said o þi wirscip. c 1375 *Ibid.* 16196 (Fairf.) Herode..asked him..Quy þai him squa *wiþso3t [*Cott.* bisoght]. c 1330 R. Brunne *Chron. Wace* (Rolls) 15660 Toward þe southe he wolde haue fled, But Edwyn his weye *wyþ-sperd. *Ibid.* 13503 Þat weye þey haue vs *wyþ-sted þat y scholde 3ow haue inne y-led. 14.. *Tundale's Vis.* 1628 (MS. A.) In grett povertte was he *wiþstadde. c 1460 *Pol. Rel. & L. Poems* (1903) 204, I knowe wele I may nat *with-starte. I have so doone, I ought to dreede. 1854 S. Dobell *Balder* iii, Death, careful of my learning, hath *withstayed His final presence. 1885–94 R. Bridges *Eros & Psyche* May v, It fill'd the passage of the rising glade, And there withstay'd the sun in dazzling sheen. *Ibid.* July xix, There was no repentance coud atone For her dishonour, nor her fate withstay. c 1175 *Lamb. Hom.* 15 Heoreuuel þe heo doð þu a3est to hetiene and *wið-stewen. c 1400 *Lanfranc's Cirurg.* 65 Þat poudre *wiþstreyneþ [orig. *constringit*] þe blood. 1904 Ryle *Holy Script. & Crit.* 122 With difficulty is the multitude withstrained from doing sacrifice. c 897 Ælfred *Gregory's Past. C.* xxxvi. 254 Balaham..wolde feran ðær hiene mon bæd, ac his estfulnesse *wiðteah se esol þe he onuppan sæt. c 1175 *Lamb. Hom.* 143 Þa þe heom wið-teoð of flesliche lustes. c 1200 *Trin. Coll. Hom.* 63 Þe lichames festing is wiðtiȝing of estmetes. *Ibid.* 79 Þat he us wissie to wið-tien of alle flesliche lustes. c 1275 Lay. 13242 Nas þar neuere man so bold þat þis wolde *wiþ-telle. 1563 *Mirr. Mag., Ld. Hastings* lxxxvii, God of Justyce had *withturnd that fate.

b. In the earlier version of the Wycliffite Bible it is used in nonce-formations modelled upon L. compounds of *con-, co-*: see quots.

Withheezing [Hie *v.*, to hasten] is an erron. rendering of L. *cum festinatione* with haste. *Withhilden* covered over [Hill *v.*[1]] represents a L. compound of *ob-*.

1382 Wyclif *Isa.* lxii. 9 Thei..that *with bern [*comportant*] it, shul drinken in myn hoeli porches. *Ecclus.* xii. 19 Many thingus grucchendeli whistrende shal *with chaunge [*commutabit*] his chere. *Ibid.* i. 24 Kunnyng and vnderstonding of prudence wisdam shal *with departen [*compartietur*]. *Ps.* xxxi[i]. 4, I am turned in my myseise, whil *with ficchid [*configitur*] is the thorn. *Gen.* xxiv. 59 The *withfolweris [*comites*] of hyr. *Ps.* lxxvii[i]. 33 The 3eeris of hem [faileden] in *withheezing. Pref. Ep. vii. 70 Micheas of Moraschym, the *witheire [*coheres*] of Crist. *Gen.* vii. 24 The watris of the flood..*with bilden [*obtinuerunt*] the erthe. *Gen.* xxi. 6 Who so euer shal here shal *with lawe to me [*corridebit mihi*]. *Ecclus.* li. 15, I shal preisen thi name bysyly, and I shal *withpreisen [*collaudabo*] it in confessioun. *Gen.* xxii. 3 Abraham on the ny3t *with rysynge [*consurgens*], di3te his asse.

Withal (wiðǭ·l), *adv.* and *prep. arch.* [Properly two words, orig. *with al(le* (see With *prep.* and All A. 9 c); in the earliest instances predominantly northern; ultimately superseding the older *mid alle* (see Mid *prep.*[1] 7 a). The spelling *withall* continued till nearly 1800.]

A. *adv.* **1.** Along with the rest; in addition; besides; moreover; likewise; as well. Often in the collocations *and withal* (so-and-so), *and* (so-and-so) *withal*. See also Forthwithal.

c 1200 Ormin 2572 Ne nan ne beoþ..þatt mu3he..tredenn dun þe deofless mahht, swa summ 3ho tradd wiþþ alle. *Ibid.* 2997 Þatt Godess Gast iss soþfast Godd & Allmahhti3 wiþþ alle. *Ibid.* 4203 He beoþ all unnbeshorenn þa swa þwerrt ut wel wiþþ alle. 1297 R. Glouc. (Rolls) 7012 Seint edward heid at windelsore a uair feste wiþ alle. a 1300 *Cursor M.* 3491 He þat was rugh was rede wit-al. 13.. *K. Horn* 424 (Harl.) Ich am ybore þral, Þy fader fundlyng wiþ al. 13.. *Guy Warw.* (A.) 2984 Romiraunt com forþ snelle A Sarrazin a strong wiþ elle. 1393 Langl. *P. Pl.* C. XI. 143 The constable of þat castel..Is a wys knyght with-alle. c 1470 Henry *Wallace* IV. 549 A bow he bair..And arrous als, bath lang and scharpe with aw. 1528 More *Dyaloge* III. Wks. 224/1 Thereupon they burne up the booke and sometime the good manne withall. 1542 Udall *Erasm. Apoph.* 35 Meryly spoken & nippyngly withall. 1611 *Bible Acts*

xxv. 27 It seemeth to me vnreasonable, to send a prisoner, and not withall to signifie the crimes laid against him. 1643 Sir T. Browne *Relig. Med.* II. § 2. 139 He that shall consider how many thousand severall words have beene..composed out of 24. Letters; withall how many hundred lines there are to be drawn in the fabrick of one man; shall [etc.]. 1671 Milton *P. R.* IV. 128, I shall, thou say'st, expel A brutish monster: what if I withal Expel a Devil who first made him such? 1771 Franklin *Autobiog.* Wks. 1840 I. 11 When he played and sung withal, it was extremely agreeable to hear. 1808 Scott *Marm.* I. xxviii, Nor lord nor knight was there more tall Or had a statelier step withal. 1837 Southey *Let. to Wynn* 24 May, Withal I have not often read a book that interested me so much. 1883 D. C. Murray *Hearts* viii, She..was so sweet and kind, and withal seemed ..so dependent on him. 1897 Mary Kingsley *W. Africa* 266 Of such peculiar suppleness that you could wind it round anything,..and as strong withal as a hawser.

b. Contextually: 'At the same time'; in spite of all; notwithstanding, nevertheless.

1596 Danett tr. *Comines* VIII. v. 326 Yet is it verie troublesome for horsemen, because it is full of ditches like to Flaunders,..but withall it is much pleasanter. 1654 Bp. Bramhall *Just Vind.* vi. (1661) 124 St. Gregory..disliked the Law, but withall according to his duty published it. 1794 Southey *Let. to G. C. Bedford* 11 May, They have shown me that happiness is attainable; but, withal, taught me by repeated disappointments never to build on so sandy a foundation. 1802 Wordsw. *To the Small Celandine* 17 Modest, yet withal an Elf Bold, and lavish of thyself. 1859 Lang *Wand. India* 161 He confessed that his master was rather severe, but withal a very good man. 1880 *Academy* 23 Oct. 299/2 This impressive, though withal faulty, work.

2. = Therewith 2, 3.

a 1300 *Cursor M.* 12318 Iesus..bar it ham als in a ball, And present þan his moder wit-all. 1389 in *Engl. Gilds* (1870) 101 Ye Den schal gedren ye forseyde halpenys, and bywyht-al breed. 1390 Gower *Conf.* I. 83 Lok thou dele noght withal. c 1400 *Rule St. Benet* (prose) 29/33 Yef any es tan wid-al. 1535 Coverdale *1 Macc.* iv. 44 He toke aduysement, what he might do withall. 1586 T. B. *La Primaud. Fr. Acad.* I. 301 A Philosopher..taking a lanterne and a candle lighted at midday..was demanded what he ment to do withall. 1605 A. Wotton *Answ. to late Popish Articles* 78 We are not ashamed of our small nomber: though the Papists twight vs with all, in comparison of their huge multitudes. 1657 Sanderson *Serm.* Pref. § 4 The Papists,..escaping in the mean while Scot-free, seldome or never meddled withall in any of their Sermons. 1833 Mrs. Browning *Prometh. Bound* 92 Having spoiled the gods Of honours, crown withal thy mortal men Who live a whole day out.

To begin withal: see With *prep.* 37 e.

1531 Tindale *Expos. 1 John* v. (1538) 83 And to begynne wythall, they sayde *Confiteor*. 1553 Bradford *Serm. Repentance* (1574) B vij b, I wyll (to begyn withal) shew you what repentance is. 1590 Marlowe *2nd Pt. Tamburl.* V. i, Then have at him, to begin withal.

†**b.** *I cannot do withal*: I cannot help it.

1470–1611 [see Do *v.* 54].

B. *prep.* Substituted for With *prep.* in postposition, esp. at the end of a relative clause or its equivalent or of a direct or indirect question, governing a relative (expressed or implied) or an interrogative; †occas. = Wherewithal 2 b.

The relative may be either expressed (e.g. *that..withal* = with whom or which; *as* after *such*, etc.) or not expressed (freq. in the inf. construction, e.g. *a rod to be beaten withal* = a rod with which to be beaten).

The advs. *herewithal, therewithal, wherewithal*, were modelled upon the earlier *herewith, therewith, wherewith*.

a 1300 *Cursor M.* 6174 Bot tel yew of his suinc i sall, He drou þat fraward folk wit-all. c 1400 Maundev. (Roxb.) xxvi. 122 Þai giffe a grete soume of monee for to bye oute þaire penaunce withall. 1477 Earl Rivers (Caxton) *Dictes* 7 Leste ye resemble hym that seketh a rod to be betyn with all. 1517 in Glasscock *Rec. St. Michael's, Bp.'s Stortford* (1882) 35 A skeyn to kefer wt alle the same booke. 1523 Ld. Berners *Froiss.* I. cxlvi. 71 b/2 And we be so sore strayned that we haue nat to lyue withall. 1526 Tindale *Matt.* xvi. 26 What shall a man geve to redeme hys soule agayne with all? 1531 *Test. Ebor.* (Surtees) VI. 25 Suche tithes as I was behind withall. 1555 R. Pownall *Musculus' Temporiser* i. B vj b, Yonder commeth be that I haue dyuers tymes desyred to talke withall. 1600 Shaks. *A. Y. L.* III. ii. 328 *Ros.* Ile tel you who Time ambles withall, who Time trots withal,..and who he stands stil withall. *Orl.* I prethee, who doth he trot withal? a 1628 Preston *Breastpl. Faith* (1630) 30 Whatsoever you part withall, you shall have a hundred fold in this life. 1665 in *Extr. St. Papers rel. Friends* Ser. III. (1912) 236 P. J...tooke one Rebecah who he liues withall as his wife. 1703 Moxon *Mech. Exerc.* 238 Which sort of Bricks, is commonly used..to pave Yards or Stables withal. a 1774 Goldsm. *Surv. Exp. Philos.* (1776) I. 365 Though we took the best telescope to observe him withal. 1821 Scott *Kenilw.* iv, But for hurting a man I have drunk my morning's draught withal, 'tis clean against my conscience. 1884 Lowell *Democr.* (1887) 6 Such eyes and ears as Nature had been pleased to endow me withal.

†**b.** In other cases, esp. with indirect passive.

1556 in Lodge *Illustr. Brit. Hist.* (1791) I. 215 Notwithstanding ther layt brags and doings, wherin they have ben somwhat met withall. a 1568 Ascham *Scholem.* I. (Arb.) 45 Will in children, wiselie wrought withall, maie easelie be won. 1642 Tasman *Jrnl.* in *Acc. Sev. Late Voy.* I. (1694) 141 From that time they were better to be spoken withal. 1680 Allen *Peace & Unity* Pref. p. xv, If such were indulgently dealt withal and tolerated. c 1685 *Roxb. Ball.* (1891) VII. 477 Full six legs she travels withal. 1700 T. Brown tr. *Fresny's Amusem.* 28 The Devil's Broker may be spoken withal every Sunday.

Witham (wi·təm). Also 6 **wyttam, wittam, wittome,** 7 **wittham**. The name of certain villages in Lincolnshire and Essex. *Little* (or *small*) *Witham* was used proverbially (with pun on Wit *sb.*) for a place of which the inhabitants were remarkable for stupidity. Hence (app.), without qualification, used for: A witless person, a fool.

1538 Bale *Thre Lawes* B ij, Small wyttam be your spede. 1562 J. Heywood *Prov. & Epigr.* (1867) 182 Whens come great breeches? from little wittam. 1589 Nashe *Anat. Absurditie* C 3 b, Who so snatcheth vp follies too greedilie ..may happes proue a wittome whiles he fisheth for finer witte. 1589 *Martins Months Minde* G 2 b, I appoynt..to each of them an Aduouson: To the former of small Wittam: and to the other of little Brainford. 1589 *Almond for Parrat* D 4, G. W. of Wig. house, in the land of little Wittam, chosen to the place and function of a pastor. a 1661 Fuller *Worthies, Lincs.* (1662) 153 Lincolneshire..Proverbs. He was born at Little Wittham..It is applyed to such people as are not overstock'd with acutenesse.

Withamite (wi·ðəmait). *Min.* [f. the name of its discoverer, H. *Witham*: see -ite[1].] A red or reddish-yellow variety of epidote, found at Glencoe in Scotland.

1825 D. Brewster in *Edin. Jrnl. Sci.* II. 218.

†**Withbind.** *Obs. rare.* Forms: 1 **weoþobend,** 4 **weþebond, withbinde.** [OE. **wiþobend*, *weoþobend* (cf. OLG. *widebinde* 'ligustrum'), f. *wiþ-* in Withe + *bend* Bend *sb.*[1] (Cf. Bindwith, Bendwith.)] A name for certain plants having pliant stems.

c 1000 *Sax. Leechd.* II. 312 Nim þas wyrte, sæfenan & mersc mealwan..& weoþobend. 1362 Langl. *P. Pl.* A. VI. 9 He bar a bordun I-bounde wiþ a brod lyste, In A weþebondes [*v. r.* wodebyndes] wyse I-wriþen aboute. [1551: see Weedbind.] 1648–58 Hexham, *Mondt-hout*,..Privet, Prime-print, or White-withbinde.

†**With-child,** *v. Obs. nonce-wd.* [With *prep.* 23 b.] *trans.* To 'get with child', make pregnant.

1591 Sylvester *Du Bartas* I. ii. 390 The lusty Heav'n with Earth doth company: And with a fruitfull seed..Withchildes..his own lawfull wife. 1598 *Ibid.* II. ii. IV. 355.

Withdraught. *Obs.* exc. *arch.* Forms: see With *prep.* and Draught *sb.*; also 5 **wedraught,** 6 **wyddra(u)ght, -drought, weydraught, widdrawte,** 6–7 (8–9 *arch.*) **wydraught,** 7 **widraught.** [f. With- + Draught *sb.*, after *withdraw*.]

1. Withdrawal.

1340 *Ayenb.* 240 Þe castel of þe wombe..ne may him hyealde aye þane gost þanne he is asterued be uestinges and be wyþdra3þes. 1437 *Rolls of Parlt.* IV. 508/2 The..hurtes..doone..to you..in withdraught of your due Custumes. 1442 *Ibid.* V. 64/2 Withoute fraude, embeselyng or withdraught therof in eny wise. c 1475 *Partenay* 5927 Thys knight saw hir come, with-draught wold not gette. 1623 T. Adams *Peace-offering* (1624) 42 May not a withdraught of all Gods fauours..be..foreseen?

b. *spec.* Withdrawal from an action in court (= Retraxit); a fine or fee imposed for this.

Cf. Withdraw *sb.*, quot. 1444.

[?1402, 1455: see *Essex Rev.* (1907) XVI. 128, 133.] 1600 *Maldon (Essex) Docts.* Bundle 162 lf. 3 (MS.) Withdraughts. Item, they are charged with xxxiiii s. by them receyved for lycenses of concord in accions personalls. 1635 *Maldon (Essex) Borough Deeds* Bundle 80 No. 2 (MS.) Allowance to the said seriants for collecting of withdrafts behind.

†**2.** A place of retirement or retreat; a retreat; a private chamber, retiring-room; a closet or recess.

1480 Caxton *Myrr.* III. xxi. 175 He that hath none other wythdraughte ne other dwellyng place. 1481 Botoner *Tulle on Old Age* (Caxton) b vj, [He] fled by the withdraught into the toure of the same castelle. 1509 *Will Earl of Oxford* (Prerog. Crt. Cant.), ij peces of Rede Worstede vsed to be in the Wydraught of my Chamber. 1530 Palsgr. 288/2 Wydraught, *basse chambre*; *retraict*; *retraict*.

3. A privy; a sewer: = Draught *sb.* 45, 46.

Survives locally in leases.

1493–4 *Leicester Borough Rec.* (1901) II. 344 For borde & tymbre for the wedraught. a 1513 Fabyan *Chron.* VI. cciv. (1811) 215 Whan the Kynge was at the withdraught to purge nature. c 1516 in Willis & Clark *Cambridge* (1886) II. 245 A Hows for the comyn wyddrowght of the said College. 1559 *Boke Presidentes* 26 The sayde mesuage.. with thappurtenances with the pauementes, and wydraughtes of the same. 1671 in Birch *Hist. Charters* (1884) 247 That no man shall make or continue any widraughts, seat or seats, for houses of easement. 1702 J. K. *New Eng. Dict.*, A *Wy-draught*, a Water-course, or Water-passage. 1846 (25 Aug.) *Lease* (Surrey), Privies, sinks, sewers, wydraughts, drains and houses of office. 1896 *Lease*, Fences, pavements, gutters, pipes, drains, wydraughts.

Withdraw, *sb. rare.* [f. Withdraw *v.*] Withdrawal, removal; *spec.* = Withdraught 1 b.

1444 *Maldon (Essex) Docts.* liber 'A' lf. 32 b (MS.) For a defaute, or a withdrawe of courte, a freman shall be amerced at iii d. 1693 C. Mather *Wonders Invis. World* 64 One of these Witnesses was over-perswaded by some Persons, to be out of the way upon G. B.'s Tryal; but he came afterwards with Sorrow for his withdraw. 1720 S. Sewall *Diary* 11 Nov. (1882) III. 276 Went not to Mrs. Winthrop's. This is the 2d Withdraw. 1727 C. Mather (*title*) Christian Loyalty, Or, some Suitable Sentiments On the Withdraw of King George the First,..and the Access of King George the Second.

Withdraw (wiðdrǭ·, wiþ-), *v.* Pa. t. **withdrew** (wiðdrū·); pa. pple. **withdrawn** (wiðdrǭ·n). Forms: see With *prep.* and Draw *v.*; also 4 **widdraw**; *pa. t.* 4 **wid-drogh, widrouh**; *pa. pple.* 5 **othedraw,** 6 **withdrawed.** [f. With- (1) + Draw *v.* (Cf. L. *retrahĕre* to Retract, Retray, F. *retirer* to Retire.)]

I. *trans.* **1.** To take back or away (something that has been given, granted, allowed, possessed, enjoyed, or experienced).

a 1225 *Ancr. R.* 230 Ure Louerd..wiðdraweð his grace, & his cumfort. c 1315 Shoreham *Poems* VII. 450 Ich mey 3yuen, and eke wyþ-dra3e, Al þat myn hys. 13.. *Guy Warw.* (A.) 332 Þat he no may his loue haue, Grete strengþe him doþ wiþ-drawe. 1390 Gower *Conf.* II. 91 Lich unto the greene tree, If that men toke his rote aweie, Riht so myn herte scholde deie, If that mi love be withdrawe. a 1400 *Prymer* (1891) 41 The sonne with drow3 his li3t. c 1400 *Pilgr. Sowle* (Caxton 1483) IV. xx. 65 Now the from me withdraweth bytter deth. 1535 Coverdale *1 Chron.* xvii[i]. 13, I wyl not withdrawe my mercy from him. 1597 Hooker *Eccl. Pol.* V. lv. § 3 Impossible it is that God should withdrawe his presence from any thing. 1602 Marston *Ant. & Mel.* II. Wks. 1856 I. 23 My mistresse..withdrewe her gratious aspect even now. 1611 *Bible* Transl. Pref. ¶ 1 Those noursing fathers and mothers..that withdraw from them who hang vpon their breasts..liuelyhood and support. 1815 Shelley *Alastor* 16 Withdraw No portion of your wonted favour. 1833 Tennyson *Two Voices* 145 When Life her light withdraws. 1854 R. S. Surtees *Handley Cr.* xxxvi. (1901) I. 288 They..said they'd withdraw their subscriptions from the hounds. 1874 Green *Short Hist.* ii. § 8. 105 The office of sheriff was withdrawn from the great nobles of the shire. 1898 'H. S. Merriman' *Roden's Corner* xiv, Then you are not disposed to withdraw your name from the concern?

†**b.** To subtract (arithmetically). *Obs.*

c 1391 Chaucer *Astrol.* II. § 45 Vnder that nombere [1400] I wrote a 1397; þan withdrowe I the laste nombere owte of þat, and þan fond I þe residue was 3 3ere. c 1400 *Pilgr. Sowle* (Caxton) V. xiv. (1859) 81 Where that it nedeth oughte to adden, or withdrawen. c 1430 *Art of Nombryng* (E.E.T.S.) 6 The figures that thow hast withdraw, adde them ayene to the omyst figures.

†**c.** To cause to decline, decrease, or disappear.

c 1450 Capgrave *St. Augustine* xxxv. 45 Þat 3e schuld..not be lettyd with no cold whech schuld withdrawe 3our deuocion. 1546 *Gassar's Prognost.* b viij, The heat of Summer shalbegynne to be wythdrawne by rayne. 1563 Shute *Archit.* B ij b, It hath ben withdrawen and hidden (as almost al other knowlages..hath bene) through ignoraunce.

2. To draw back, take away, remove (a thing) *from* its place or position.

c 1250 *Gen. & Ex.* 3803 Aaron..ðis fier blessede and wiðdro3. c 1386 Chaucer *Can. Yeom. Prol. & T.* 870 Withdraweth the fir, lest it to faste brenne. 1387–8 T. Usk *Test. Love* II. v. (Skeat) l. 129 Whan the see ebbeth and withdraweth the gravel. c 1400 tr. *Secr. Secr., Gov. Lordsh.* 70 Reubard ..withdrawys þe fleume fro þe mouth of þe stomake. c 1400 Maundev. (Roxb.) vi. 21 Syrus..withdrew þe water and destruyd þe citee. 1422 Yonge tr. *Secr. Secr.* 241 Whan a man sittyth atte mette he sholde wythdrawe his honde afor that he be y-fillit. c 1489 Caxton *Sonnes of Aymon* xiv. 352/12 Whan charlemagne sawe that reynawde had wythdrawe his baner, he was glad of it. 1648 Gage *West Ind.* 176, I withdrew my foot a little. 1671 Milton *Samson* 192 In prosperous days They swarm, but in adverse withdraw their head. 1834 Hook *Gilbert Gurney* iii, This speech..induced me suddenly to withdraw my head. 1842 Loudon *Suburban Hort.* 463 So as to admit of withdrawing, and reintroducing the vines without injuring them. 1848 Dickens *Dombey* lviii, Harriet was withdrawing her hand to open the book, when Alice detained it for a moment. 1854 Ronalds & Richardson *Chem. Technol.* (ed. 2) I. 168 The most appropriate spot for withdrawing the gases from this furnace. 1898 'H. S. Merriman' *Roden's Corner* xxv, As he spoke he had withdrawn from his pocket a folded paper.

b. To take (one's eyes, etc.) off something.

1477 Earl Rivers (Caxton) *Dictes* 5 He is happy that withdraweth his ere & his eye from alle vyle thinges. 1542 Elyot, *Oculorum remissio*, a withdrawyng of the loke. 1836 Dickens *Sk. Boz, Tuggs's at Ramsgate*, As her eye caught that of Mr. Cymon Tuggs, she withdrew it from his features in bashful confusion. 1838 — *O. Twist* xxxviii, Till even she, who was not easily cowed, was fain to withdraw her eyes, and turn them towards the ground.

c. To remove (money) *from* capital, or *from* a bank or other place of deposit.

1776 Adam Smith *W. N.* II. iii. I. 403 That part is, from that moment, withdrawn from his capital. 1828 *Act 9 Geo. IV* c. 92 § 38 After having withdrawn any Sum or Sums of Money from or out of any Savings Banks. 1861 *Act 24 Vict.* c. 14 § 4 The Officers of the Postmaster General ..shall not disclose the Name of any Depositor nor the Amount deposited or withdrawn.

d. To draw (a veil, curtain, etc.) back or aside; to draw back (a bolt). Now *rare.*

1797 Mrs. Radcliffe *Italian* xi, The veil was at length withdrawn. 1833 L. Ritchie *Wand. Loire* 170 The sound of opening doors, withdrawing bolts, and hoarse voices hallooing from tower to tower. 1841 Dickens *Barn. Rudge* ix, Withdrawing the little window curtain, she gazed out. 1878 Browning *La Saisiaz* 106 Here's the veil withdrawn from landscape.

3. *fig.* †**a.** To retract, revoke, rescind. *Obs.*

c 1290 *Beket* 1829 in *S. Eng. Leg.* 159 3if þov wenest wel for-to do, with-drau3 þine dede sone. c 1300 *St. Nicholas* 265 ibid. 248 With-drau3 þi red, ich þe rede. c 1400 *Ywaine & Gaw.* 3459 The king withdrogh his jugement. c 1480 Henryson *Test. Cress.* 327 Withdraw thy sentence, and be gracious.

b. To remove *from* the scope of an inquiry, *from* a particular category, or the like.

1725 Broome *Notes Pope's Odyss.* VI. 331 Nausicaa..is withdrawn, and a whole nation introduced for a more general praise of Ulysses. 1839 Hallam *Lit. Eur.* II. v. § 97 One [poem] by Hercules Rollock..is..equal, a few names withdrawn, to any of the contemporaneous poetry of France. 1848 H. R. Forster *Stowe Catal.* 236 The next two lots were withdrawn. 1869 Tozer *Highl. Turkey* II. 259 The marvellous element..withdraws the narrative.. from the course of ordinary occurrences. 1895 *Law Times Rep.* LXXIII. 637/2 It was not a case which should have been withdrawn from the jury.

c. To take back, retract (one's words, an expression). Often *absol.* in imper., in parliamentary

procedure, to demand the withdrawal by a member of an expression or a statement.

1793 in *Ld. Auckland's Corr.* (1862) III. 37 Burke got up twice, but the House was so satisfied, that it would hear nothing, and nothing was heard but *Withdraw, withdraw.* 1837 Dickens *Pickw.* i, The Chairman was quite sure the hon. Pickwickian would withdraw the expression he had just made use of. 1880 *Hansard's Parl. Deb.* 20 Aug. 1756, I call upon the hon. Member to withdraw the word 'offensive'..(Cries of 'Withdraw!')

d. To refrain from proceeding with or prosecuting (a course of action, a proposal, etc.); to cease to support or present (a candidate, etc.).

1781 Blackstone *Rep.* II. 1028 The Court allowed the Plaintiff to withdraw his Demurrer. 1834 Dickens *Sk. Boz, Steam Excurs.*, Mr. Alexander Briggs moved as an amendment, that [etc.]..; but after some debate consented to withdraw his opposition. 1844 H. H. Wilson *Brit. India* I. 555 The latter proposition was withdrawn. 1880 *Hansard's Parl. Deb.* 20 Aug. 1739 Amendment, by leave, withdrawn. 1891 Farrar *Darkn. & Dawn* xxiii, Nero..neither repeated nor withdrew his command. 1913 *Act 3 & 4 Geo. V*, c. 6 § 1 If the candidate is withdrawn or deemed to be withdrawn.

4. †**a.** To keep back or hold (one's hand); also, to withhold (a blow). *Obs.*

a 1300 *K. Horn* 859 (Camb.) His dent he gan wiþ-dra3e, For hi were boþe asla3e. 1390 Gower *Conf.* I. 369 Achilles tho withdrow3 his hond. c 1400 tr. *Secr. Secr., Gov. Lordsh.* 52 Whanne kynges..withdrawes her hondys frome þe..posсessiouns of her subgitz.

†**b.** To keep back, withhold (something due, customary, or necessary); hence *gen.* to withhold.

a 1300 *Cursor M.* 21906 Þai serue him all apon þair wise, And man wit-draus his seruise. c 1386 Chaucer *Wife's Prol.* 617, I koude noght withdrawe My chambre of Venus from a good felawe. c 1450 *Godstow Reg.* 231 They haue preuyd þat þey with-drowe no dewete þat was wonyd & vsyd. 1510 in Leadam *Sel. Cases Star Chamber* (Selden Soc.) II. 70 The seid priour..withdraweth suche duties as they of Right owght to take. 1526 *Pilgr. Perf.* (W. de W. 1531) 6 b, Whan god withdraweth his rayne,..than shall there be neyther oxe ne cowe. 1580 [see Withdrawer].

†**c.** To keep back, restrain (a person, his desires, etc.). *Obs.*

1340 *Ayenb.* 254 Þe guode man and þe wyse wyþdraȝeþ hare wyl and hare lostes..be temperance. 1390 Gower *Conf.* II. 393 Withdrawh thi lust and hold the stille. c 1450 *Mirk's Festial* 96 Forto wythdraw all men of such opes and wordys Seynt Poule..forbedyth yche cristen man not to speke al maner ydull speche. 1450–1530 *Myrr. our Ladye* I. xix. 51 Yf yt happe..that any..be dystracte from saynge ..eny..verse..and may not say yt, but yf he withdrawe his voyce from syngynge. 1530 Palsgr. 781/2 Let him go whan he wyll, he shall nat be withdrawen for me.

5. To draw away, deflect, divert (a person, his mind, etc.) *from* an object, pursuit, line of conduct, etc.; †also, to draw, attract; to distract. Now *rare.*

†Occas. const. inf.: To divert from doing something.

1340 *Ayenb.* 58 Þet hi my3ten his..uram þe guode þet hi habeþ y-conceyued wyþdra3e. *Ibid.*, Yef þou be þine tonge wyþdra3st ane man oþer a child wel to done. c 1380 Wyclif *Sel. Wks.* II. 215 Þat man leve no worldly goodis þat wiþdrawiþ his wille fro God. ?1477 *Stonor Papers* (Camden) II. 34 Parauenture more chargeful besynes hathe othedraw yower mynde. 1489 Caxton *Faytes of A.* I. xxix. F iv, Withdrawe towardys the, the hertes of straungers by yeftes. 1542 Elyot, *Avocamentum*,..recreation, that withdraweth the mynde from heuynes or melancholy. 1563 Golding *Cæsar* III. (1565) 76 Those sorte of rascals whom hope of spoile..had wythdrawen from husbandrye and daylye labor. a 1592 Greene *Jas. IV*, II. ii, With how contrarious thoughts am I withdrawne! Why linger I twixt hope and doubtfull feare? 1606 Shaks. *Tr. & Cr.* V. iv. 23 Aduantagious care Withdrew me from the oddes of multitude. 1606 *Reg. Privy Council Scot.* (1885) VII. 181 To alienat and withdraw thaim from thair due obedience to his Majestie. 1651 Hobbes *Leviath.* I. viii. 33 Whatsoever is new, or great,.. withdrawes a man..from the intended way of his discourse. 1667 Milton *P. L.* VII. 612 They thought Thee to diminish, and from thee withdraw The number of thy worshippers. 1841 Elphinstone *Hist. India* I. 593 It would have been happy if he had never been withdrawn from those pursuits. 1859 W. Collins *Q. of Hearts* i. The circumstances which have withdrawn us from the world for the rest of our days.

6. To remove (a person) *from* a position; to cause to retire or recede; †occas. to take aside; *spec.* to cause (a force, troops) to retire *from* a position; to draw off *from* an engagement.

a 1450 *Knt. de la Tour* (1868) 107 Mani that haue be withdrawe oute of abbeyes, for thaire londes. 1471 Caxton *Recuyell* (Sommer) 149 Saturne wythdrowe his peple on that oon syde. a 1548 Hall *Chron., Edw. IV* 206 His onely sauegarde and comforte, were to withdrawe hym and his compaignie into Fraunce. a 1592 Greene *Jas. IV*, III. iii, A shining blade Withdrawes a coward theefe that would inuade. 1615 in *Buccleuch MSS.* (Hist. MSS. Comm.) I. 160, I presently did withdraw him..until I had discovered that which I desired. 1621 Elsing *Debates Ho. Lords* (Camden) 87 The prisoner withdrawen. 1805 C. James *Milit. Dict.* (ed. 2), To *withdraw*, to call back; to make to retire. 1821 Shelley *Adonais* xlii, Where'er that Power may move Which has withdrawn his being to its own. 1823 Scott *Quentin D.* ix, A sounder..had..withdrawn in pursuit of him all the dogs..and the greater part of the huntsmen. 1836 Thirlwall *Greece* xxi. III. 175 She would be compelled to withdraw her forces from Lesbos. 1848 Thackeray *Van. Fair* lx, Walter Scape was withdrawn from Eton, and put into a merchant's house. 1891 Farrar *Darkn. & Dawn* xx, She has withdrawn her spies.

b. *Law.* To remove (a juror) from the panel in order to put an end to the proceedings.

a 1676 Hale *De Jure Maris* I. vi. (1787) 36 The court and the king's attorney-generall..were so well satisfied with the defendant's title, that they moved the defendant to consent to withdraw a juror. 1789 *New Lond. Mag.* Sept. 458/2 And Mrs. Phillips agreed on her part that a Juror should be withdrawn. 1866 Foster & Finlason *Nisi Prius Cases* IV. 942 The plaintiff's counsel proposed to withdraw a juror, which was assented to. 1881 Odgers *Libel & Slander* 550 Actions of defamation are often compromised before the judge comes to sum up the evidence. A juror is often withdrawn, sometimes at the suggestion of the judge.

†**7.** = *withdraw from* in various senses. *Obs. rare.*

1340–70 *Alex. & Dind.* 895 Sin 3e maugray 3our miht mote hit wiþ-drawe. c 1400 *Beryn* 1257 Yff þow wolt drawe the to wit, & rebawdry withdrawe. c 1450 *Godstow Reg.* 304 He with-drow the kyngis court, by the mean of a frendly accorde.

II. *refl.* **8.** To remove oneself *from* a place or position; = 12. Now *rare* or *arch.*

a 1300 *Cursor M.* 19175 Þai badd þat þai þam suld witdrau Quils þai samen spak a thrau. 13.. *Ibid.* 21654 (Edinb.) Adam quen he wro3t hauid wo3 Vndir þis tre he him wiþ-dro3. 1390 Gower *Conf.* I. 73 He him withdrowh So privly that sche ne wiste Wher he becom. c 1410 *Master of Game* xxvi. (1904) 83 Þei ought to wiþdrawe hym in þe softest maner..and þan go preuyli to þei be vndir þe wynde. c 1450 Capgrave *Life St. Aug.* 39/19 He wepte, and with-drow him. 1485 *Rolls of Parlt.* VI. 314/1 The said William had withdrawn him out of thys Lande. 1530 Palsgr. 783/1 He hath withdrawen him selfe in some corner. 1593 Shaks. *Rich. II*, V. iii. 28 Withdraw your selues, and leaue vs here alone. 1610 Holland *Camden's Brit.* I. 627 Vortigern had withdrawen himselfe into these parts. 1718 Atterbury *Serm., Acts* i. 3 (1734) I. 177 It was requisite that he should not withdraw himself from their Sight, at once. 1839 Lane *Arab. Nts.* I. 103 The King disguised himself, and..withdrew himself from the midst of his troops.

†**b.** Of combatants, troops, etc.: = 12 b. *Obs.*

1297 R. Glouc. (Rolls) 3253 Þe brutons hom wiþdrowe, & þe saxons hom reste. c 1300 *K. Horn* 886 (Laud MS.) Hys feren gonnen hem wyt drawe. 1387 Trevisa *Higden* (Rolls) III. 169 Cirus..feyned hym to flee and wiþdrow3 hym.

†**c.** Of water: = 12 c. *Obs.*

c 1400 Maundev. (Roxb.) xxiv. 111 Þe see, þat before bette apon þe mount, withdrewe it. 1422 Yonge tr. *Secr. Secr.* 196 The See meveth and hym wyth-drawyth aftyr the mewynge..of the mone.

9. To remove oneself *from* a condition, sphere, society, etc.; = 13. Now *rare* or *arch.*

a 1300 *Cursor M.* 28136 Oft als haue i me wit-draun Til vncuth pryst, and fra myn aun. 1553 Eden *Treat. Newe Ind.* G j b, Voyces of deuyls..withdrawing them from the right waye. 1560 Daus tr. *Sleidane's Comm.* 102 b, It is also to be feared lest suche as would haue ioyned them selues vnto this league, wyll be affrayde nowe of this, and withdrawe them selues. 1612 Sir J. Digby *Let.* 10 Oct. in *10th Rep. Hist. MSS. Comm.* App. I. 609 Some of the beste of them have withdrawen themselves from their trade. 1638 Junius *Paint. Ancients* 24 Let our Imagination therefore among multitudes of people..withdraw it selfe to some secrecie. 1663 *Sc. Acts Chas. II* (1820) VII. 455/2 All..persons who shall..wilfully withdraw and absent themselffs from the ordinary meitings of divine worship. 1770 *Junius Lett.* xxxix, He cannot withdraw himself from the Complaints.. of his Subjects. 1798 Malthus *Popul.* (1878) 448 Every man may..have the redress of withdrawing himself from the club. 1812 Belsham *Mem. Lindsey* 348 Withdrawing himself from an office the duties of which he was so fully competent to discharge. 1865 Dickens *Lett.* (1880) II. 233, I am withdrawing myself from engagements of all kinds.

†**10.** To cease, refrain; = 14. *Obs.*

c 1290 *St. James* 159 in *S. Eng. Leg.* 38 Of is luþere þou3t þat he þou3te for drede he him with drou3. 1297 R. Glouc. (Rolls) 10221 Þe king of alimayne sende..To king Ion, þat he wiþdrewe him of is wou. 1303 R. Brunne *Handl. Synne* 10872 Of þat man hyt ys grete drede, Þat wyþdraghþ hym fro gode dede. 1340 *Ayenb.* 52 Huanne hi wyþ-dra3eþ to do wel. 1422 Yonge tr. *Secr. Secr.* 243 He that is custumet to ette two tymes in the day, yf he wythdrawe hym sodaynly, anone he may grevaunce take.

†**11.** To contract. *Obs. rare.*

1471 Caxton *Recuyell* (Sommer) 497 His synewis shronke and withdrewe them.

III. *intr.* **12.** To go away, depart, or retire *from* a place or position, *from* some one's presence, to another room or a private place, etc.; †to draw back or turn aside.

c 1250 *Gen. & Ex.* 3983 If ðin asse ne were wið-dra3en, Her suldes ðu nu wurðen sla3en. [*Vulg.* nisi asina declinasset de via..te occidissem, Num. xxii. 33.] 1398 Trevisa *Barth. De P. R.* VIII. xxii. [xi.] (Tollem. MS.), Nou3t withdrawinge towarde þe lyfte side, oþer towarde þe ry3t side. 1471 Caxton *Recuyell* (Sommer) 170 He made his marouners to saylle and rowe with alle diligence for to withdrawe fro the porte. *Ibid.* 239 Whan she was a lytill withdrawen fro the temple. 1577 Holinshed *Chron.* II. 302/2 The people with their goodes and Cattell being fled and withdrawen into the Wooddes and Mountaynes. 1599 Shaks. *Much Ado* III. iv. 100 Madam, withdraw, the Prince..and all the gallants of the towne are come to fetch you to Church. 1600 *1st Pt. Sir J. Oldcastle* V. x. 43, I will withdraw into some other roome. 1691 Wood *Ath. Oxon.* II. 711 Who was there, but withdrawn under a hedge with the Prince and Duke. 1697 Dryden *Virg. Past.* viii. 19 Scarce from our upper World the Shades withdrew. 1711 Addison *Spect.* No. 108 ¶ 6 Upon withdrawing into my Room after Dinner. 1712 *Ibid.* 536 ¶ 1 She delivered the remaining part of her Message, and withdrew. 1749 Fielding *Tom Jones* XVIII. xiii, Sophia now took the first Opportunity of withdrawing with the Ladies. 1781 Cowper *Retirem.* 447 A man..Who comes when call'd, and at a word withdraws. 1810 Scott *Lady of L.* II. xxxvii, The Minstrel..from the shore withdrew. 1828 Lytton *Pelham* III. iii, I bowed slightly, and she withdrew to the countess. 1860 Tyndall *Glac.* I. xxvii. 209 The men..withdrew from me, and approached the eastern boundary of the glacier. 1874 Green *Short Hist.* iii. § 3. 127 By the treaty of Lambeth, Lewis promised to withdraw from England.

b. Of combatants, troops, etc.: To retire *from* the field of battle or any contest, or *from* an advanced position.

1297 R. Glouc. (Rolls) 3681 Prest a3en him he was & slou of hom to grounde, so þat hii gonne wiþ drawe. c 1330 R. Brunne *Chron. Wace* (Rolls) 12746 Lenger to iuste my3ht þey nought stande, But þem defended al wyþdrawande. a 1400–50 *Wars Alex.* 2015, I..will at þou knaw þat for na drede I with-draw. 1471 Caxton *Recuyell* (Sommer) 401 Whan the two oostes were withdrawen. a 1533 Ld. Berners *Huon* lix. 203 Cause your men to withdraw fro the batayle. 1594 Shaks. *Rich. III*, V. iv. 8 Withdraw my Lord, Ile helpe you to a Horse. 1697 Dryden *Æneis* XI. 559, I beg your Greatness..beaten, to withdraw. 1709 Steele *Tatler* No. 83 ¶ 10 The Confederates are preparing to withdraw into Winter Quarters. 1880 Hensman *Afghan War* (1881) 449 The Amir's troops..only withdrew at daylight.

†**c.** Of water: To subside, ebb. *Obs.*

c 1250 *Gen. & Ex.* 596 In armenie ðat arche stod, Ðo was wið-dra3en ðat ilc flod. *Ibid.* 599 Dunes wexen, ðe flod wið-dro3. a 1300 *K. Horn* 1399 (Camb.) Whanne þe se wiþ dro3e. c 1400 *Destr. Troy* 2608 The wodenes of waghes wightly with droghe. 1471 Caxton *Recuyell* (Sommer) 280 Whan the see was withdrawen & ferre ebbed. 1525 Ld. Berners *Froiss.* II. liii. [lii.] 76/2 They founde ye ryuers withdrawen. 1618 Bolton *Florus* III. x. (1636) 199 The Tide withdrawing upon course.

13. To draw away *from* a person; to remove oneself or retire *from* a society or community, *from* publicity, etc.; to retire from participation in or pursuit of something; †to resign.

c 1385 Chaucer *L. G. W.* 257 [331] Thow..makyst wise folk fro me withdrawe. 1540 *Bible* (Cranmer) Prov. xix. 7 Hys awne frendes withdrawe from him. 1667 Marvell *Corr.* Wks. (Grosart) II. 227 A large petition from the Earle of Clarindon, intimating that he was withdrawn. 1677 *Reg. Privy Council Scot.* Ser. III. (1912) V. 120 Withdrawing from the publik ordinances in their owne paroch kirkes. 1697 Dryden *Æneis* XII. 757 [He] wisely from th' infectious World withdrew. 1715 Pope *Iliad* II. 448 Now great Achilles from our aid withdraws. 1746 Hervey *Medit.* (1818) 108 Wisely they withdrew from that immense multiplicity of learning. 1798 Ferriar *Illustr. Sterne* iii. 63 An ideal world, into which we can withdraw at pleasure. 1849 A. Scratchley *Build. Societies* 100 Desirous of withdrawing from the society. 1853 Newman *Hist. Sk.* (1873) II. I. iv. 174 Classes and ranks withdraw from each other more and more. 1870 J. E. T. Rogers *Hist. Glean.* Ser. II. 23 Wiklif withdrew from his political and social projects. 1892 Gladstone in *Daily News* 4 Nov. 5/4, I have..withdrawn from all attendance at public banquets. 1911 Marett *Anthropology* ix. 237 No one has a chance of withdrawing into his own soul.

†**b.** Of an immaterial thing, a condition, etc.: To depart, disappear.

1297 R. Glouc. (Rolls) 6583 [He] biheld toward þe water, & is grete herte wiþdrou. *Ibid.* 9189 Þe verste tuo 3er god cas & hap inou..com to king steuene, ac suþþe it wiþ drou. 13.. *Cursor M.* 4698 (Gött.) Bot alkines welth bigan widdrau. 1426 Audelay *Poems* 25 Dredles deuocioun hit is with draw. 1450–1530 *Myrr. our Ladye* II. 151 Then grace withdrawyth and the fende enteryth.

†**14.** Const. *of* or inf. To cease or refrain from, or from doing, something. *Obs.*

1297 R. Glouc. (Rolls) 10893 Seint edmond..ofte him bisou3te þat he wiþdrowe of is dede. 1340 *Ayenb.* 53 Ich wille þet þou loki and wyþdra3e. c 1375 *Cato Major* 523 in *Minor Poems fr. Vernon MS.* 598 Þou most with-drawe of diuers metes, And vse no glotenie. 1450–80 tr. *Secr. Secr.* v. 8 Whan he withdrawith forto take the goodis and possessiones of his sugetis.

Withdrawable (wiðdrǭ·ăb'l), *a.* [f. prec. + -able.] Capable of being withdrawn.

1850 Herschel *Ess.* (1857) 392 Its deposits being withdrawable only at a market value. 1876 Gladstone in *Contemp. Rev.* June 6 All other rights..are called rights only by way of accommodation, for they are withdrawable at will. 1903 in *Q. Rev.* (1905) Jan. 67 Half..had to be invested in stock and the other half was withdrawable.

Withdrawal (wiðdrǭ·ăl). [f. as prec. + -al. (Superseding Withdrawment, which took the place of the earlier Withdraught and Withdraw *sb.*)]

1. The act of taking back or away what has been held, occupied, or enjoyed.

1839 Lane *Arab. Nts.* I. 80 Thou deservest..the withdrawal of protection from thee. 1860 Tyndall *Glac.* I. xxv. 189 The cold, resulting from the withdrawal of the sunbeams.

b. The removal of money or securities from a bank or other place of deposit.

1861 *Regulations P. O. Savings Banks* § 15 If any person shall fraudulently represent himself to be a Depositor, and by forwarding the proper notice of withdrawal,..shall obtain any sum of money. 1884 *Manch. Exam.* 28 May 5/3 The bank was in difficulties through large withdrawals.

2. The act of withdrawing a person or thing *from* a place or position, *esp.* the removal of troops by way of retreat.

1838 Meeson & Welby *Cases Exch.* II. 36 It was no part of the agreement between the parties that the withdrawal of a juror should put an end to the suit at all events. 1844 H. H. Wilson *Brit. India* II. 480 He urged the withdrawal of the British officers, as their presence was no longer necessary. 1877 Huxley *Physiogr.* 37 The artificial withdrawal of water to feed the canal. 1892 Hardy *Well-beloved* I. v, Their application for admission led to the withdrawal of a bolt.

3. The retractation of a statement, proposal, etc.

1835 T. Hook *G. Gurney* xiv, I thought perhaps the news ..might have induced you to retract; and that you might have considered it a perfect justification of your withdrawal. 1885 *Law Times* LXXVIII. 384/2 In consequence of his resignation, and notwithstanding his withdrawal of it.

4. The act of retiring or retreating *from* a place or position.

1824 Miss Mitford *Village* Ser. I. 190 Perhaps, indeed, Joel's rapid improvement might be one cause of William's withdrawal. 1836 *Act 6 & 7 Will. IV*, c. 32 § 1 The With-

WITHHOLDABLE.

Withholden, pa. pple.

Withholder.

Withholding, ppl. a.

Withholdment, rare.

WITHIN.

Withi, var. *with thi*: see WITH *prep.* 6.

Within (wiðin), *adv., prep., (adj.)*

WITHIN-DOOR.

Withinside, *adv., prep.,* (*sb.*).

Within-door(s), *adv.* (*adj.*), *sb.*, *arch.*

Within-forth, *adv.* Obs.

Withinside *adv. arch. or dial.*

Within-wards, *adv. nonce-wds.*

Withinth, *obs. form of* WITHIN *prep.*

Withnay, *var.* WITH-.

Withness (wi'ðnes), *nonce-wd.*

Without (wiðau't), *adv., prep., conj.*

WITHOUT.

8903 Þi louerd ssal abbe an name..vair wiþoute blame. a 1300 Cursor M. 102 Mild and mek, witouten gall. c 1380 Sir Ferumb. 4112 Neuere ne was he with-oute strif, Bot ay wykkeliche lyuede ys lyf. 1390 Gower Conf. I. 45 To grounde I was withoute breth. 14.. Tundale's Vis. 32 He was a man withoute pyte. 1509 Fisher Funeral Serm. C'tess Richmond Wks. (1876) 309 Be not sad..as men withouten hope. 1626 Bacon Sylva § 499 It is obserued by some, that there is a vertuous Bezoar, and another without vertue. 1690 Locke Hum. Und. I iv. § 1 There was a time, when the Mind was without those Principles. 1719 De Foe Crusoe II. (Globe) 422 All sorts of Tools and Iron-work, they had without Tale. 1758 Hume Ess., Eloquence 66 'Tis vehement reasoning, without any appearance of art. 1859 Hawthorne Fr. & It. Jrnls. (1871) II. 284 It resembled an unspeakably bad dough nut, without any sweetening. 1869 Ruskin Q. of Air § 77 They are white, without purity; ..massive, without strength; and slender, without grace.

c. With no possibility of; so, or such, as not to admit of; so, or such, that there can be no . . .

a 1300 Cursor M. 25821 For þair wanhopping Þai fall witvten vp-couering. c 1470 Henry Wallace I. 113 Our men was slayne with outyn redemptioune. Ibid. 226 With out reskew he stekyt him to dede. 1530 Palsgr. 329/2 Without remedy, irremediable. 1670 [see Clergy 6]. 1751 Johnson Rambler No. 174 ¶ 14 These wounds..are without cure. 1762 Hume Hist. Eng., Jul. C. to Hen. VII, I. App. I. 151 The great lords and abbots among the Anglo-Saxons..could punish without appeal any thieves..they caught. 1766 [see Remedy sb. 3].

d. In such phrases as *without comparison, controversy, doubt, †nay*, etc. the meaning app. varies between 'beyond' (sense 2 or 3) and 'involving the absence of', 'not admitting of', 'so that there is or can be no . . .'.

a 1300– [see Doubt sb.[1] 4 d]. 1340–1578 [see Comparison sb. 2 b]. 1547–1777 [see Controversy sb. 1 c]. 1557 N. T. (Geneva) Heb. vii. 7 Without all nay, he which is lesse, receaueth blessyng of hym which is greater. 1605 Bacon Adv. Learn. II. xix. § 3 These things are without Contradiction, and could not otherwise be. 1621–1709 [see Compare sb.[1] 2].

†e. *Without day* = Sine die. *Obs.*

1607 Cowel Interpr. s.v. Day, To be dismissed with out day, is to be finally discharged the court. 1713 Mod. Cases VI. 262 He doubted of the Effect of a Nolle Pros'..if it discharged the Indictment, or only put the Defendant without Day.

11. Followed by a gerund or vbl. sb. in *-ing*: equivalent to 'so as not to' or 'and not' with the corresponding vb., or 'not' with the pres. pple.; e.g. *to pass by without seeing* = 'to pass by so as not to see', 'to pass by and not see', 'to pass by, not seeing'.

c 1320 Sir Tristr. 2620 Tristrem is went oway Wiþ outen coming oȝain. 1377 Langl. P. Pl. B. xi. 144 He..wilned me were graunted Grace, wyth-outen any bede-byddynge. c 1400 Destr. Troy 2992 Tite, withoutyn tariyng, atirit were all. 1515 Reg. Privy Seal Scot. I. 407/1 To pas and repas als oft as thai ples..without ony..aresting. a 1548 Hall Chron., 14 Edw. IV, 235 The Frenche kyng..callyng for water, washed and rose without any answere makyng. 1639 S. Du Verger tr. Camus' Admir. Events To Rdr. a vij, Drones which do but humme about flowers, without gathering any honey from them. 1734 Berkeley Let. Wks. 1871 IV. 217, I can hardly stir abroad without catching cold. 1779 Mirror No. 2 ¶ 1 No child ever heard from its nurse the story of Jack the Giant Killer's cap of darkness, without envying the pleasures of invisibility. 1836 Dickens Sk. Boz, Shops & Tenants, We never passed at night without seeing the eldest girl at work. 1849 Macaulay Hist. Eng. ii. I. 169 He was a slave without being a dupe. 1877 Ruskin St. Mark's Rest iv. § 51 A solemn piece of old Venetian wall..which you might pass under twenty times without seeing. 1885 Law Times LXXIX. 119/2 No person was..to blast coal without the charge having been inspected by the underlooker.

†b. Governing an infinitive with *to*. [After Fr., etc.]

c 1489 Caxton Sonnes of Aymon xxii. 470 That we maye retourne agen hole and sounde..wythoute to be dyshonoured. 1556 J. de Flores' Aurelio & Isab. F 6, Without to see it whiche is written.

c. By ellipsis of the gerund: Not counting, leaving out of account. *colloq.*

1871 Geo. Eliot Middlem. xxxv. II. 212 My father has enough to do to keep the rest, without me.

†12. *Without mo* or *more*: in various senses (see Mo B. 3 c, More a. B. 4 c). Often used as a tag.

c 1290, etc. [see Mo, More, as above]. c 1350 Will. Palerne 2573 Þe werwolf..went wiȝtly a-wei wit-oute any more. c 1350 Leg. Rood iii. 148 By þat ilk way went we twa, Þi moder and I with-outen ma. 14.. Guy Warw. (Camb. MS.) 719 Wythowtyn more forthe they rode. c 1470 Henry Wallace I. 61 Till Noram kirk he come with outyn mar. 1500–20 Dunbar Poems xxxiv. 89 The Deuill said then, withouttin mair, 'Renunce ȝour God, and cum to me.'

13. In senses 7–11 often with conditional implication (mostly with negative, expressed or implied): If one have (or had) not, if there be (or were) not, unless one have or there be, in the absence of, in default of, 'supposing the negation or omission of' (J.).

a 1300 Cursor M. 126 Na werc may stand Wit-outen grundwall to be lastand. 1387 Trevisa Higden III. 161 Noþer man ne womman schulde be punsched wiþ oute gilt. c 1450 Capgrave Life St. Aug. 99 Þat swech þingis myte not be do wit3-outen vertuous lyuyng. 1526 Tindale Heb. xi. 6 With out faith it is vnpossible to please him. 1661 Godolphin View Adm. Jurisd. Introd. a 6, The Mariner..may not sail without one Cat or more in his Vessel. 1748 Thomson Cast. Indol. I. i, Withouten that would come an heavyer bale. 1766 Goldsm. Vicar W. xv, What is genius or courage without an heart? 1834 Marryat Peter Simple xxxvii, Without a sense of your fault, how can repentance and amendment be expected? 1857 Buckle Civiliz. I. x. 617 The people believed that without the nobles there was no safety; the nobles believed that without the crown there was no honour.

14. With ellipsis of the obj. (cf. 4). Now *colloq.* (except in contrast with *with*).

In negative contexts, as in quots. 1733, 1898, virtually = otherwise; this use is further extended in unstudied speech, e.g.: 'You can go, if you can find somebody to go with,—not without'.

c 1400 Rule St. Benet (prose) 16 Þe nihend-ferþe salme wid þe antefen ouþir wid-vten. 1597 Shaks. Lover's Compl. 98 Smal shew of man was yet vpon his chinne..Yet..nice affections wauering stood in doubt If best were as it was, or best without. 1654 Dorothy Osborne Lett. (1888) 233 Here is a ring:..'tis indifferent whether there be any word in't or not; only 'tis as well without. 1672 Wiseman Wounds I. viii. 70 We threw out our Tent, and by Sarcoticks cured this wound without. 1681 T. Flatman Heraclitus Ridens No. 27 (1713) I. 178 Come, it is a great while since we had a Pindarick; have you never a one in your Budget? Earn. I am seldom without. 1720 Lady B. Germaine in C'tess Suffolk's Lett. (1824) I. 73 Though you should take the four [thousand pounds], still I shall have enough without. 1733 Tull Horse-Hoeing Husb. vii. 26 All the former Roots being broken off at the Ends in taking up (for 'tis impossible to do it without). 1741 Richardson Pamela III. 27 Pray don't! You'll have enough on your hands without. 1800 Mrs. Hervey Mourtray Fam. IV. 57 Well, promise nothing, Mr. Chowles; but do it without. 1834 Newman Lett. (1891) II. 48 [He] was afraid to tell me, and left Oxford without. 1878 E. A. Freeman Let. in W. R. W. Stephens Life & Lett. (1895) II. 161, I don't get any worship here; but I am better without. 1898 W. W. Jacobs Sea Urchins, Grey Parrot (1906) 208 You must have given him some encouragement... A man wouldn't offer to lend a lady his opera-glasses without.

b. *slang.* in reference to liquor: Not mixed with sugar: cf. With *prep.* 26 b (*b*).

1835 Dickens Sk. Boz, River, Glasses of brandy-and-water cold without. 1837 Barham Ingol. Leg., Execution 71 There is 'punch,' 'cold without,' 'hot with,' 'heavy wet.' 1854 [see With prep. 26 b (b)].

15. Qualified by a negative: *not without* = not lacking, with or having some (implying or suggesting a somewhat slight or not very great amount).

Cf. *not* with negative adj. or adv. (Not adv. 10 c).

1596 Dalrymple tr. Leslie's Hist. Scot. (S.T.S.) I. 42 Sa sure a havin..that nocht w[t]out cause the historiographours named it, the Porte of saifgaird and saiftie. 1605 Shaks. Macb. I. v. 20 Thou would'st be great; Art not without Ambition. 1766 Goldsm. Vicar W. iv, Nor were we without guests. 1807 Southey Espriella's Lett. xxxvii. (1808) II. 71, I looked back upon Birmingham not without satisfaction at thinking I should never enter it again. 1855 Macaulay Hist. Eng. xi. III. 113 Many..were not without hopes that mild and liberal counsels might prevail. 1879 McCarthy Donna Q. I. 61 She remembered not without a pang that [etc.].

C. *conj.* (or in *conj. phr.*)

1. The prep. governing a clause introduced by *that*, so that *without that* becomes a conjunctional phr.: †a. (*a*) Except that. (*b*) In addition to the fact that. *Obs. rare.*

c 1200 Ormin 1022 Þatt wasȝerifft wass henngedd tær, forr þatt itt hidenn sholde All þatt tatt tær wiþþinnenn wass ..Wiþþutenn þatt te bisscopp sellf..Þær sholde cumenn o þe ȝer ann siþe, & all himm ane. 1489 Acc. Ld. High Treas. Scot. I. 145 Laide downe in redy siluer for rybbanis to the King,..withowte at the Master of the Wardrop hes boycht v dussane of rybbanis..summa iij[li].

b. (in sense B. 10) Without its being the case that: now expressed by the construction with gerund (B. 11), with or without poss., e.g. *without that you shall need* = 'without your needing'; *without that he led me* = 'without leading me'. Now *rare* or *Obs.*

c 1450 in W. T. Barbour Hist. Contract (1914) 201 Withoute þat ever eny accord..were made or had bitwene þe seid John Mercer and John Halsnoth. 1471 Fortescue Wks. (1869) 525 Sainte Edwarde reyned..peseably..with oute eny clayme made vppon him, by hyr, or by her husbande, and without that eny of ther heirs have claymed this londe. c 1489 Caxton Sonnes of Aymon xxvi. 560 The speres flew in peces wythout that ony of theym felle to the grounde. 1594 R. Carew Huarte's Exam. Wits xiii. (1596) 203 Himselfe will deliuer them into your hands, without that you shall neede to conquer them. 1596 Danett tr. Comines (1614) 86, The captaine at the castell gate..offred me a cup of wine, without that he led mee into the castell as he was accustomed. a 1648 Ld. Herbert Hen. VIII (1683) 162 This seemed to be done, without that the King was fully informed thereof. Ibid. 230 Your Actions (without that I or any else speak of them) make you a lyar. 1853 C. Bronte Villette xii, It was next to impossible that a casket could be thrown into her garden..without..that she should have caught intimation [etc.].

†c. (with conditional implication as in B. 13) If it be or were not the case that, unless: = 2. *Obs.*

c 1440 Generydes 475 Withoute that she myght have his loue ageyn, She were on don for euere in certayne. c 1450 Capgrave Life St. Aug. ii. 4 This myth not be do withouten þat þei had substauns of possession. 1523 Q. Marg. in M. A. E. Green Lett. Royal Ladies (1846) I. 266 (MS.) The lordes wilbe..ferd to leve the governours wayes, without that they may fynd some suyrtie to take ther partt.

†d. *Without that* (or *this*) *that*: legal phr. introducing an exception, *spec.* in pleading [tr. law-L. *absque hoc quod*, law-Fr. *sans ceo que*], a form, obsolete since 1852, whereby a defendant asserted special matter of exception or justification against the plaintiff's claim while reserving his denial of the whole cause of action.

1518 Star Chamber Cases (Selden Soc.) II. 150 That all the said mesuages and londes shuld be in the rule..of the Chamberleyne..Without that that the said mesuages and londes extend to the yerely value of cxl li. 1592 B. N. C. (Oxf.) Docts. B 2 37 (MS.) Without that, that H. P. was never properly enfeoffed. 1601 Fulbecke 1st Pt. Parall. 72 b, The plaintife replyed, that..the defendant..assaulted him and beate him..and the defendant reioined that..by their common accorde they played together, without that that he beate him in other maner. 1651 tr. Kitchin's Jurisd. (1653) 422 Conspiracy, he is alive, with out that, that he is dead. Ibid. 423 Where one pleads out of his Fee, the other saith within, without that, that it was out in manner and forme. 1824 H. J. Stephen Treat. Princ. Pleading ii. 211 The defendants delivered their petition to the common council, complaining of an undue election; *without this that* the jurisdiction..belonged to the court of the mayor and aldermen.

2. Hence, by omission of *that*, simply as a conjunction: If..not, except, unless.

Formerly common in literary use, most frequently with verb in subjunctive; later *colloq.* ('not in use, except in conversation' J. 1755) or *arch.*, and now chiefly *illiterate*. Often replaceable by the const. with gerund (B. 11), e.g. *without he be compelled* = 'without being compelled'; esp. with clause referring to an attendant circumstance or result rather than a condition, as in quot. 1467.

1393 Langl. P. Pl. C. v. 176 Quath conscience to þe kynge with-oute þe comune help, Hit is ful hard..þer-to hit to brynge. 1467 Marg. Paston in P. Lett. II. 308 If I wer ther withought I had the mor..wurchepfull persones abought me..it shuld be to me but a vylney. 1477 Stonor Papers (Camden) II. 28 She is displeside and I know nat whereffore, with owte hir olde sekenes be fallen on hir agayn. 1523 Ld. Berners Froiss. (1812) I. xii. 12 All the moost parte of the realme were right joyouse, withoute it were a fewe parsones..fauourable to syr Hewe Spencer. 1534 More Comf. agst. Trib. I. xii. (1553) Ciij b, Good workes to godwarde worketh no man without god woorke with him. 1565 Reg. Privy Council Scot. I. 410 [He] will nocht deliver..the said hors without he be compellit. 1591 Shaks. Com. Err. III. ii. 92 Such a one, as a man may not speake of, without he say sir reuerence. a 1643 J. Shute Judgem. & Mercy (1645) 129 He may barke, but he cannot bite without a man come within his reach. 1695 Congreve Love for L. IV. i, If he can't be cur'd without I suck the Poyson from his Wounds. 1754 Shebbeare Matrimony (1766) I. 143 Do not think of marrying this young Lady, without you are convinced you can love her. 1787 Beattie Scoticisms 101, I will not go without I am paid for it. Scottish and obsolete and vulgar English. 1802 Mrs. E. Parsons Myst. Visit III. 57, I shall never intrude without you invite me. a 1814 Fam. Politics II. i. in New Brit. Theatre II. 207 I'm but a working woman, and cannot live without I gets my due. 1834 T. Arnold Let. 14 Apr. in Stanley Life (1898) I. vii. 328 Not allowing God's seal, without it be countersigned by one of their own forging. 1859 Tennyson Elaine 1411 Not without She wills it. 1860 O. W. Holmes Elsie V. xv. (1891) 211, I know these people..so as all the science in the world can't know them, without it takes time about it. 1868 J. H. Blunt Ref. Ch. Eng. I. 437 No canons were to become law without they were assented to..by the crown. 1887 Daily News 21 Nov. 2/7 Without a great change takes place the meeting is sure to commence to-morrow.

D. *sb.* That which is external; the outside. *nonce-use.*

1899 C. F. D'Arcy Ideal. & Theol. Introd. 22 Necessity is determination from without, determination by the not-self. It belongs therefore to whatever has a 'without.'

Without, obs. pa. t. of Withhold *v.*

†**Withou·t door**, *adv. phr.* (*adj.*) *Obs.* = next.

c 1205 Lay. 2382 Þat neuer ne ferde heo wið uten dore. 1570 Levins Manip. 229/8 Wythout dore, extrà, foris. 1621 in Foster Engl. Factories Ind. (1906) 280 A storme of..rayne ..that wett these bales which weare without doare in the street. 1649 C. Wase Sophocles, Electra 30 Enter in, and let her without door Her own distresses, and her friends deplore. 1739 Johnson Boerhaave in Gentl. Mag. IX. 174/1 His..Friend..found him sitting without Door.

b. *attrib.* or as *adj.* (with hyphen). = Out-door *a.*; in quot. *transf.* or *fig.* relating to the outer world, outward, external.

1611 Shaks. Wint. T. II. i. 69 Prayse her but for this her without-dore-Forme.

Withou·t doors, *adv. phr.* (*adj.*) *Obs.* or *rare arch.* (Also with hyphen.) [See Without *prep.* I. and Door 5.]

1. Out of doors, outside the house, in the open air.

1617 Moryson Itin. I. 63 Our meat we bought our selues, ..and we fetched our beere without doores. 1663 Gerbier Counsel 27 At the latter end of the year..no brick-work without doores ought to be laid. 1695 A. Telfair New Confut. Sadd. (1696) 4 The Family being all without-doors. 1711 Addison Spect. No. 83 ¶ 1 When the Weather hinders me from taking my Diversions without Doors. 1796 Morse Amer. Geog. II. 621 Without doors they use a kind of wooden patten. 1840 Dickens Old Cur. Shop xxviii, The preparations without doors had not been neglected.

2. *transf.* and *fig.* Outside the community (family, nation, etc.); †*spec.* outside Parliament (= Out-of-door, -doors A. 2 a).

1697 C. Davenant Ess. E. India Trade Wks. 1771 I. 96 Some persons (without doors)..profess themselves open enemies to the traffic in general. 1709 Swift Adv. Relig. Misc. (1711) 224 Senates are like to have little Regard for any Proposals that come from without Doors. 1723 Dk. Wharton True Briton No. 5. I. 43 Those who are Without-Doors should do their Duty by supporting such Patriots. 1769 Junius Lett. xvii. (1812) I. 281 It will not be necessary.. to take the trouble of answering..the quotation from a speech without doors. 1792 Burke Sp. 11 May (1816) IV. 51 The House was untainted..by those false principles which had been so amply circulated without doors. 1823 Scott Quentin D. xiv, He who beat all enemies without doors, found a fair foe who could belabour him within.

3. *attrib.* or as *adj.* = prec. b.

1654 Fuller Comm. Ruth 139 The Daughters of Sarah, whom the meeknesse of their Sex hath priviledged from following without doors affairs.

†**Withou·tforth**, *adv. Obs.* (or *rare arch.*) Also with hyphen, or as two words, or as three. [f. Without *adv.* + Forth *adv.*] Properly, Everywhere without or outside (see Forth *adv.* 2 b); but in use a mere synonym of *without*. (Opp. to Withinforth.) a. = Without *adv.* 1.

c 1380 Wyclif Sel. Wks. II. 384 Woo worþe ȝou,..ypocritis, þat clensen wiþout-forþ of þe cuppe and of þe dishe. c 1380 — Wks. (1880) 46 Þei weren apeied wiþ o cote or kirtil with-ynne forþe & with-oute forþ. c 1450 Mirk's Festial 72 When þay wern alle in, God closud þe dore aftyr hom wythout-forth. 1474 in Litt. Cantuar. (Rolls) III. 272 Yowre powche and key-band with the keverynge; on the which are..set ij. porses with owteforth. 1511 Guylforde's Pylgr. (Camden) 23 Withoute forthe byfore the entre into this Temple. 1601 Holland Pliny xxxv. vi. II. 528 The peeces of this earth, if a man doe breake, shew the own naturall colour which is not mixt: without-forth they be spotted. 1894 F. S. Ellis Reynard the Fox 247 Withoutforth of the ring ..A stone..of colours three.

b. = Without *adv.* 2, 2 b.

1382 Wyclif Matt. xii. 46 His modir and his bretheren stoden with outeforth [1388 withouteforth]. 1388 — Acts v. 34 Gamaliel..comaundide the men to be put without forth. 1467 in Engl. Gilds (1870) 373 That euery citezein..w[t]outforth paye alle maner chargs as citezens do that dwelle w[t]ynforth. 1470–85 Malory Arthur xx. xxii. 836 They ..kepte the syege wyth lytel warre withoutforth. 1530 Tindale Deut. xxxii. 25 Without forth, the swerde shall robbe them off theire childern. 1600 Holland Livy VII. xxi, All was quiet withoutforth. 1609 — Amm. Marcell. 132 The space..between the wall and the heape of earth cast up withoutforth.

c. = Without *adv.* 3.

1357 Lay Folks Catech. (L.) 758 Thou schalt not do leccherye noþer in consent in hert ne spekynge ne in countenaunce withowte-forþ. c 1374 Chaucer Boeth. v. pr. iv. (1868) 164 Þe wit comprehendiþ fro wiþ outen furþe þe figure of þe body of þe man. c 1400 Love Bonavent. Mirr. (1907) 123 The schame that sche hadde of hir synne was so grete withynneforth that sche forȝat al schame and reproue withouteforth. 1491 Caxton Vitas Patr. (W. de W. 1495) I. i. 4 b/2 Faynynge wythoute fourthe by theyr couuert maners and symple habyllemens to be Innocentes. 1530 Palsgr. Introd. 34 The verbes actyves betokyng some acte to passe from the doer without forth.

d. quasi-*sb.* (preceded by *of*): That which is without; external region or action.

1474 Caxton Chesse III. iv. (1883) 114 Hyt befelle that a marchant of withoute forth herd the..fame of this man. 1491 — Vitas Patr. (W. de W. 1495) II. 277 b/2 That the werkes of withoutforth be fyrst withinforth ruled after the Iugement of right & reason.

e. *attrib.* or as *adj.* Outside, external.

c 1500 in Arnolde Chron. (1811) 9 The wythoutforth landys and tenementis.

Withou·tside, *adv.* and *prep.* Now *rare* or *Obs.* (Also with hyphen, or as two words.) [f. Without + Side *sb.*, after *outside*.] Opp. to Withinside or Within. A. *adv.*

1. On the outer side or surface: = Outside *adv.* 1 (in part), Without *adv.* 1.

1578 Lyte Dodoens I. v. 11 The roote is..blacke withoutside. 1668 H. More Div. Dial. II. v. (1713) 97 Nor do we our selves grow by being liquored without side, but within. 1695 Congreve Love for L. IV. i, Why does that Lawyer wear black?—Does he carry his Conscience without side? 1727–38 Chambers Cycl. s.v. Mould, The Moulds..are of wax, supported within-side by what they call a core, and covered without-side with a cap or case. 1794 C. Smith Wand. Warwick 19 Barricading the cabin door withoutside. 1849 Chr. G. Rossetti Testimony 20 Poet. Wks. (1904) 119 We build our houses on the sand Comely withoutside and within. c 1850 [see Withinside A. 1].

2. In (or to) the place or space without: = Outside *adv.* 1 (in part), 2, Without *adv.* 2.

a 1700 Evelyn Diary 21 Sept. 1644, The Cathedrall,..full of sepulchres without-side. 1706 E. Ward Hud. Rediv. (1707) II. vi. 4 Without side warm, within side merry. 1710 Mrs. Centlivre Marplot II. Wks. 1760 II. 147 When I came without-side, I saw nobody there. 1800 Ann. Reg., Chron. 414 Within this temple is an altar, and without-side, near the entrance, another. 1831 Trelawny Adv. Younger Son I. xx. 148 A wild shout from without-side.

3. *Withoutside of*, *prep. phr.* = *outside of*, Outside *adv.* 3 a.

1638 in Collect. Mass. Hist. Soc. Ser. III. VI. 23 Placing the Indians..without side of our soldiers in a ring battalia. 1711 in 10th Rep. Hist. MSS. Comm. App. v. 169 A very narrow bridge,..without-side of the gate. 1751 R. Paltock P. Wilkins (1884) II. xi. 108 Without-side of these mountains, it was scarce darker than at my arkoe. 1769 J. Bush Hibernia Curiosa 163 Wearing their shirts withoutside of their cloaths. 1865 W. G. Palgrave Arabia I. 345 All the world withoutside of Nejed.

B. *prep.* = A. 3, Outside *prep.* 1, 2, Without *prep.* 1, 1 b.

1686 [see Withinside B. 2]. 1760 Impostors Detected I. iv. I. 31 The monk's sandals which he had left without side the door. a 1774 Goldsm. Surv. Exp. Philos. (1776) II. 176 Succeeding each other, one without side the other, like circles in disturbed water. 1809 A. Henry Trav. 133 A fire was made without side the cabin, in the open air. 1831 T. Hope Ess. Origin Man I. 8 Modifications existing withoutside my person.

†**Withou·t-take**, *prep. Obs. rare.* [f. Without *adv.* after Out-take *pple.*, *prep.*] Except.

1422 Yonge tr. Secr. Secr. 185 With al the Princes and men of value of the lande, wythout-take the Pepill of Vilystere.

Withou·twards, *adv. nonce-wd.* [f. Without + -wards.] Towards the exterior.

1865 [see Withinwards].

Withpraise, etc.: see With- b.

Withsafe, -saif, obs. ff. Vouchsafe.

†**Withsake**, *v. Obs.* Forms: 1 wiþsacan, 3 -saken; *pa. t.* 3 -soc(k, *pa. pple.* 4 -saken. [OE. *wiþsacan*, f. With- + *sacan* to contend, dispute, deny; cf. MHG. *widersachen.*] = Withsay *v.* 1, 2, 3.

971 Blickl. Hom. 53 Wiþsacaþ nu þam leasum welum. c 1000 Ags. Gosp. Matt. x. 33 Se þe me wiðsacð beforan mannun, & ic wiþsace hyne beforan minum fæder. c 1205 Lay. 10898 Þa wiðsaken wolde cristindom he dude his marken him on. Ibid. 13000 Imong þan eorlen he stod & fastliche hit wið-soc. a 1225 Ancr. R. 88 Ich hit ne mei nout wiðsaken. a 1375 Joseph Arim. 178 His grete folk þat him wiþ-saken hedde.

†**Withsave**, obs. f. Vouchsafe, used by Wyatt in the sense: To preserve.

a 1542 Wyatt 'Syns love ys suche' 20 Hencefonhe my fredome to withsave [rime have]. — 'Now must I lerne' 22 Now must I seke som other ways My self for to withsave.

†**Withsaw**. *Obs.* [f. With- + Saw *sb.*[2], after Withsay *v.*] = Withsaying.

a 1225 Ancr. R. 288 Hwon þe delit iðe luste is igon so ouerurð þet ter nis non wiðsigginge [v.r. wiðsahe]. a 1300 Cursor M. 5877 Now wald þai mak þam a witsau Fra þair warkes for to drau. a 1325 MS. Rawl. B. 520, lf. 28 Manie lordes of wastes..habbez i ben desturbed þoru with sawe of hoere neȝeburs [orig. per contradiccionem vicinorum].

†**Withsay·**, *sb. Obs.* [f. next.] = prec.

c 1315 Shoreham VII. 369 Þer nere stryf ne contekynge, Ne no wyþ-sey.

†**Withsay·**, *v. Obs.* [OE. (rare Northumb.) *wiðsæcga*: see With- and Say *v.*[1] Cf. OFris. *withsedza.*]

1. *trans.* To renounce. *rare.*

c 960 Rituale Dunelm. (Surtees) 34 Terrena desideria respuentes, eardlico lusto wiðsæcgende. c 1386 Chaucer Sec. Nun's T. 447 Euery cristen wight shal han penaunce But if that he his cristendom withseye. Ibid. 457 We that knowen thilke name [of Christian] so For vertuous, we may it nat withseye.

2. a. To affirm the contrary of, contradict, deny (a fact or statement); also, to deny the existence of.

a 1225 Ancr. R. 86 Ȝif a mon..deð so much mis þat hit beo so open sunne þat he hit ne mei nonesweis allelunge wiðsiggen. 1297 R. Glouc. (Rolls) 2309 To londone he gan him bringe, & sede he was purost eyr to be icrouned to kinge. Nomon ne miȝte it wel wiþ segge. 1303 R. Brunne Handl. Synne 9800 Syker ys, þat yn volle ys leyde, For þan may hyt neuer be wyþseyde. 1387 Trevisa Higden (Rolls) I. 19 Sawes þat wiþseiþ nouȝt oure byleue. 1443–50 in W. P. Baildon Sel. Cases Chanc. (1896) 136 He withseieth not the matier conteigned in the seid bille of complainte. 1493 Cov. Leet Bk. 57 To which the Recordour..seid that he withseith not þe ffraunchis of Couentre, nor the allowance þerof had at Bristoll. 1530 Palsgr. 783/2 Sythe I have sayd it, I wyll never withsay it. 1567 Turberv. Ovid's Ep. 136 That Dian witnesde thou canst not withsaye.

b. To contradict, deny the statement of (a person).

1297 R. Glouc. (Rolls) 10349 Wan þou seist, quaþ þe king, þat þat was mi þouȝt, So gret louerd as þou art, Ine wiþsegge þe nouȝt. 1387–8 T. Usk Test. Love I. ii. (Skeat) I. 184 To withsaye thilke men that of thee speken otherwyse than the sothe. 1426 Lydg. De Guil. Pilgr. 5594, I ne may Suffre.. But that I muste yow with-seyn. 1530 Rastell Bk. Purgat. I. vii, As beyng and not beynge be two contraryauntys [etc.] the one alway doth denye and with saye the other.

c. *intr.* To make denial or contradiction; to speak in opposition *to*; also *trans.* to utter by way of contradiction.

a 1300 Cursor M. 17288 + 11 In witnes þai ros with him,..For þe Iews suld not with-say þat gart to ded him bring. 1382 Wyclif Job xvi. 9 The false seiere is rered vp aȝen my face, withseiende to me. — Judith i. 11 To alle these Nabugodonosor..sente messageres; the whiche alle with o wil withseiden. 1390 Gower Conf. I. 341 Whan Nestor hath his tale seid, Ayein him was no word withseid. a 1400 Engl. Gilds (1870) 355 Þat euerych bakere habbe hys seal y-knowe vpon hys loff, þat he mowe wiþ-segge ȝif he is of take oþer þan weel. c 1430 Pilgr. Lyf Manhode I. lxxiii. (1869) 48, I may not to that of no thing wel withseye. 1463 Cases bef. King's Council (Selden) 113 b, Forasmoch as they withsey not by dedez and actez of their factours.

3. *trans.* To speak or act against, oppose, resist; = Gainsay *v.* 3; occas. to say (a thing) in opposition. Also, to disallow, forbid. Also *absol.*

c 1200 Ormin 17826 Fele þede modiliȝ wiþþstodenn, & wiþþseȝȝdenn..heffness lihht. c 1200 Trin. Coll. Hom. 139 Bi þo daȝes luuede heroudes..his broðer wif, and binam hire him, and Seint Iohan hit wið seide. a 1225 Ancr. R. 204 Hwonne þe schil & te heorte ne wiðsiggeð nout. c 1275 Passion our Lord 422 in O. E. Misc. 49 Euereych mon þat makeþ hym king..He wyþ-seyþ cesare. c 1380 Wyclif Wks. (1880) 160 Þat no man dar wiþ-seie hem in here wrong. c 1386 Chaucer Prol. 805 Who so wole my Iuggement withseye. 1390 Gower Conf. I. 312 Ther mai noman his happ withsein. 1471 Caxton Recuyell (Sommer) 88 That ther be not oon man that is so hardy to withsaye ony thynge contrarye to my will. 1483 — G. de la Tour xxix. c vj, He was..patron of the parysshe and the parson durst not withsaye hym. Ibid. cxxxiii. mij b. I defende and withsaye to them the kyssyng. 1523 Ld. Berners Froiss. I. cclxxxiv. 174/1, I may nat nor dare nat withsay yor noble pleasure. a 1529 Skelton Sp. Parrot 395 Moloc, that mawmett, there darre no man withsay.

4. a. To refuse to do or perform. Also *absol.*

a 1225 Ancr. R. 238 Þeo..wiðsegged þe graunt þerof mid unwille heorte. a 1225 Juliana 26 Ȝet tu maht ȝef þu wult burþen þe seoluen, ant ȝef þu mare wiðseist [etc.]. 1297 R. Glouc. (Rolls) 7689 To hom þat wolde is wille do debonere he was & milde & to hom þat wiþsede strong tirant & wilde. c 1385 Chaucer L. G. W. Prol. 367 Or hym was bodyn make thilke tweye Of sum persone & durste it not with-seye. 1485 Caxton Chas. Gt. 49 Gladly he wold haue doo the batayle yf he had not wythsayed it..whan he was requyred.

b. To decline to give, grant, or allow; to refuse. Also with dat. of person (sometimes without dir. obj.).

1297 R. Glouc. (Rolls) 4920 + 6 Þe bysscop yt nolde grante ac outlych yt wyþ seyde. 13.. K. Alis. 2905 (Laud MS.) Homage nolde hym non wiþsaye. 1402 Hoccleve Let. Cupid 108 She..So lyberal ys, she wol no wyght with-sey. c 1430 Lydg. Min. Poems (Percy Soc.) 32 She..Halsethe and kissethe and wol hym not with-seyne. c 1450 Merlin xiv. 204, I will in no wise with-sey that ye requere. c 1475 Partenay 86 No man shall ther-of you werne ne withsay. 1531 Dial. on Laws Eng. I. vi. 10 b, I wyll nat withsay thy desyre. 1545 Ascham Toxoph. (Arb.) 165 Thanke your selfe, whiche woulde haue me rather faulte..than..withsay your request. 16.. Eger & Grine 590 in Furniv. & Hales Percy Folio I. 372 Soe he desired that sword soe bright That shee was loth to with-say that Knight. 1661–85 in Househ. Ord. (1790) 372 This is in noe wise to bee withsaid, for it is the King's honour.

Hence †**Withsay·er**, a gainsayer, opponent.

c 1420 Wycliffite Bible Pref. Ep. iii. 63 The withseieris to withstonde [orig. contradicentes revincere]. c 1450 Godstow Reg. 267 All withseyers and attemptours to breke this writyng.

†**Withsay·ing**, *vbl. sb. Obs.* [f. Withsay *v.* + -ing [1].] Contradiction, gainsaying, opposition.

a 1225 [see Withsaw]. 1340 Ayenb. 233 Þou sselt louye god..mid ale þine wylle wyþ-oute wyþziggnge. 1387 Trevisa Higden (Rolls) I. 71 Fame of Paradys haþ i-dured wiþoute wiþseienge sexe þowsand ȝere and more. c 1450 Godstow Reg. 194 To distreyne aftir their owne wil, without ony withseiyng of them or ther successours. c 1475 Partenay 482, I shal do With all my hole hert, without withsaing, Al that which ye wyll be me commaunding.

†**Withse·t**, *v. Obs.* [OE. *wiþsettan*: see With- and Set *v.*]

1. *trans.* To resist, oppose, withstand. Also occas. const. inf.: To prevent from doing something.

c 1000 Lambeth Ps. xvi[i]. 9 Ȝescyld me fram ansyne arleasra þa þe me ȝeswenctun vel wiðsettun. c 1000 in Assmann Ags. Hom. vii. 186 Ðonne sende he heom fultum ðurh sumne deman, ðe wiðsette heoræ feondum. c 1175 Lamb. Hom. 113 Deus superbis resistit..Drihten widset þan prudan. a 1330 Roland & V. 834 No hadde ben þe bacinet, þat þe strok wiþ sett. c 1330 R. Brunne Chron. Wace (Rolls) 2921 Hauen to aryue þey hym wyþsette. 1393 Langl. P. Pl. C. I. 174 Myȝte we with eny wyt hus wil with-sette, We myȝte be lordes aloft. a 1430 Pol. Rel. & L. Poems (1903) 215/394 Holi writt, Þat cleerli schewiþ þee goostli liȝt, How þou schuldist deedli synne with-sett. c 1430 Syr Gener. (Roxb.) 4518 Generides and his feres to lete, And here entre to withsett. c 1440 Promp. Parv. 530/2 Wythe settyn', obstc, obsisto. c 1450 Cov. Myst. (Shaks. Soc.) 212 If thou with-sett the deuyl in his deede.

2. To beset (a way, etc.) so as to prevent a person from passing. (In early use with dat. of person.)

a 1300 Cursor M. 23727 Ded has vs wit-sett vr strete, Nil we, wil we, we sal mete. 1338 R. Brunne Chron. (1810) 337 Als þei fro kirke cam, Þer way he þam witbsette. 1375 Barbour Bruce XIV. 107 Twa of thame..With-set ane place in-till his way..With twa thousand of men. c 1400 Ywaine & Gaw. 1921 Sir Ywayne sone with-set the yate, That the eril myght noght in tharate. 1426 Lydg. De Guil. Pilgr. 10527 Thys..iii. confederat, Causen..a perillous mortal stryff To pylgrymes..Ther weyes, when they ha wyth-set.

3. To seize in compensation for a debt, etc.

1445 Paston Lett. I. 58 He hathe suffrid the corne to ben with sette for viijs. of rentte..wich yowre fadre paide nevere. 1477 Ibid. III. 211 Mastras Clere hath sen down hyr men, and with set alle the stuff and wrekke.

Hence †**Withse·tting** *vbl. sb.*

1340 Ayenb. 39 Þe ualse yulemde þet..zecheþ wyþsetti[n]gges and respit uor to bynime oþren hare oȝen. c 1440 Promp. Parv. 530/2 Wythe settynge, obsistencia.

†**Withsi·t**, *v. Obs.* [f. With- + Sit *v.*]

1. *trans.* To oppose, resist, withstand. Also, to prevent; to ward off.

c 1300 Havelok 1683 Hauelok ne durste..Nouth withsitten þat ubbe bad. c 1330 R. Brunne Chron. Wace (Rolls) 8138 Ȝyf ȝe ne conne nought do hym wyte What þe fallyng may wyþ-syt. c 1330 Arth. & Merl. 9055 King Rion wiþsat þat dent. 1387–8 T. Usk Test. Love III. viii. (Skeat) I. 87 This rightfulnesse..helpeth the spirit to withsitte the leude lustes of flesshly lykinge. 1393 Langl. P. Pl. C. xix. 251 Ich with-sat nat hus heste. 1412–20 Lydg. Chron. Troy I. 3003 To with-sitte þe force of sorcerye. c 1425 Seven Sag. (P.) 518 None durste wyth-sytte hys heste, Nouthir the lest no the moste. c 1430 Pilgr. Lyf Manhode II. liii. (1869) 96 He shulde not mown with sitte thee ne ayens stonde thee.

2. *intr.* To fail. *rare.*

c 1330 Arth. & Merl. 8457 Hir eiȝen turned, hir voice wiþsat.

Hence †**Withsi·tting** *vbl. sb.*, opposition.

1387–8 T. Usk Test. Love II. vii. (Skeat) I. 142 The fleshly body of a man, over whiche have oftentyme flyes,..mokel might in grevaunce..withouten any withsittinge.

Withstand (wiðstæ·nd), *v.* Pa. t. and pa. pple. withstood. (Also 5 *pa. t.* wiþstonded.) [OE. *wiþstandan*, = OFris. *withstonda*, ON. *viðstanda*: see With- and Stand *v.* Cf. OS. *wiðarstandan* (MLG. *wedderstān*), OHG. *widarstān*. For the separable form *stand with* see Stand *v.* 79 a.]

1. *trans.* To stand or maintain one's or its position against; to offer resistance to, resist, oppose: often with implication that the resistance is successful or effectual.

(*a*) a person, his will, desire, power, etc.

c 888 Ælfred Boeth. vi. § 1 Swa doð nu ða þeostro þinre

ȝedrefednesse wiðstandan minum leohtum larum. 971 Blickl. Hom. 161 Hi cyningum & yfelum ricum ealdormannum wiþstandan mihtan. c 1000 Ælfric Hom. II. 434 Nis nan ðing þe his mihte wiðstande. a 1122 O.E. Chron. (Laud MS.) Introd. 3 Ȝif hwa eow wiðstent, we eow fultumiað. c 1200 Ormin 16143 & tatt all forr to cwemenn Godd & defell to wiþþstanndenn. a 1225 Ancr. R. 264 Þet we muhten wiðstonden þes deofles ferde, þet is so strong uppon vs. 1377 Langl. P. Pl. B. Prol. 156 Myȝte we wiþ any witte his wille withstonde. c 1386 Chaucer Monk's Prol. 32, I dar hire [sc. my wife] nat withstonde For she is bigg in Armes. 1434 in Ellis Orig. Lett. Ser. II. I. 111 To withstand your enemyes in tyme of nede. c 1450 Brut 432 She withstode the Duke of Burgoyne and alle his malice. 1530 Palsgr. 783/2 All the worlde can nat withstande the wyll of God. 1581 J. Bell Haddon's Answ. Osor. 212 Seeing that not their willes, but Gods predestination withstandeth them so, that they cannot be able to come. 1592 Shaks. 2 Hen. VI, IV. v. 4 They haue wonne the Bridge, Killing all those that withstand them. 1642 J. Taylor (Water P.) Mad Fashions 3 Thou Lord of Hosts,..Thy foes (Thine Anti-christian foes) withstand. 1708 Prior Turtle & Sparrow 106 Grim Pluto will not be withstood By Force or Craft. 1857 Buckle Civiliz. I. vi. 296 His might nothing was able to withstand. 1882 Miss Braddon Mt. Royal v, You have not the will to withstand your aunt.

(*b*) a blow, force, attack, impulse; a destructive, oppressive, or hostile agency or influence.

a 1000 Wanderer 15 Ne mæȝ weriȝ mod wyrde wiðstondan. c 1000 Sax. Leechd. II. 236 Þisse adle eac wiþstandeþ tosnidenre breaþemuse blod. a 1300 Cursor M. 19105 Yur sin witstand, þat yee mai rise Wit þat parti þat es rightwise. 13.. Ibid. 10523 (Gött.) Ioseph..þat styward was,..wele widstode þe hunger þat egipt ouer-ȝode. 1390 Gower Conf. I. 68 He was noght of such myht The strengthe of love to withstonde. 1430–40 Lydg. Bochas VIII. vii. (1558) 4 b, The stroke of fortune withstant no creatures. 1558 Phaer Æneid. V. Nij b, And sturdy strokes he did withstand. 1593 Shaks. Rich. II, I. i. 173 Rage must be withstood. 1610 Holland Camden's Brit. 509 It valiantly withstood the siege. 1667 Milton P. L. VI. 253 Such destruction to withstand He hasted. 1741 Butler Serm. Wks. 1874 II. 264 The love of liberty..carries us to withstand tyranny. 1842 Dickens Amer. Notes viii, Having withstood such strong attacks upon my fortitude. 1852 Malpas Builder's Pocket-bk. 56 The pressure is..withstood by the abutments. 1860 Tyndall Glac. I. xi. 76 Ground to mud by an agency which the hardest rocks cannot withstand. 1912 Sphere 28 Dec. 326/2 Armour to withstand the terrific hitting power of the latest naval gun.

(*c*) a material thing.

a 1400 Octouian 1120 He ne fond neuer boon ne lyre Hys ax withstent. 1581 A. Hall Iliad II. 22 Yet they our Machins haue withstoode. 1638 Junius Paint. Ancients 209 An oxe doth withstand the yoke, and a horse doth withstand the bridle. 1697 Dryden Æneis VIII. 396 Nor thy resistless Arm the Bull withstood. 1721 Prior Predestination 332 A Casual Fabric built upon the sand Which can nor winds nor falling rains withstand. 1870 Bryant Iliad I. IV. 130 Their limbs Are not of stone or iron to withstand The trenchant steel ye wield.

†b. To oppose in statement; to controvert, contradict, deny. *Obs.*

1513 Thomas Ld. Howard in Ellis Orig. Lett. Ser. III. I. 160 Trustyng that ye woll..withstonde all ill reports undeserved made of me. 1526 Pilgr. Perf. (W. de W. 1531) 66 b, To withstande and stoppe the tonges of them that..sclaundreth them. 1581 J. Bell Haddon's Answ. Osor. 170 b, This withstandeth our disputation of Necessitie nothyng at all.

c. To resist the attraction, influence, or cogency of; occas. to abstain from (doing something).

1725 De Foe Voy. round World (1840) 292 A curiosity that I could scarce withstand. 1781 Cowper Charity 31 The wretch that slighted or withstood The tender argument of kindred blood. 1798 Ferriar Illustr. Sterne ii. 25 Religious disputes were subjects of ridicule too tempting to be withstood. 1852 Disraeli Bentinck 18 He could scarcely have withstood contemplating what might perhaps have been his own position. 1877 Freeman Norm. Conq. (ed. 3) I. App. 753 It seems impossible to withstand this evidence.

†2. a. To refuse to allow (a person) the possession of (something). *Obs.*

a 1300 Cursor M. 24772 (Edin.) [William] sloh þe king þat Harald hiht Þat born was of þe danis blod For qui þe land he him wit stod.

†b. Const. inf. or clause: To prevent. *Obs.*

a 1300 Cursor M. 6973 Þai fand strang folk..Þat..wit-stode þam þe land to win. c 1400 Rom. Rose 3807 He myght not his tunge withstonde Worse to reporte than he fonde. 1542 Udall Erasm. Apoph. 278 marg., What..Caesar saied vnto Metellus withstandyng that he should not take any money out of the treasourie [Metello obsistenti ne pecunias ab ærario tolleret]. 1581 J. Bell Haddon's Answ. Osor. 177 b, Nothyng withstandeth truely, but that both may bee true.

†c. To keep off or away, withhold, withdraw.

1398 Trevisa Barth. De P. R. v. xxiv. (Bodl. MS.), He haþ bondes and obstacles to withstonde & lette þe poudre. c 1485 Digby Myst. III. 284 Lord, with-stond þis duresse! 1508 Fisher 7 Penit. Ps. xxxviii. Wks. (1876) 82 He may no more withdrawe from them the bemes of his grace.. than the sonne may withstande his bemes out of wyndowes whan they be open.

d. To stand in the way of; to oppose or hinder the performance, operation, or progress of. *Obs.* or merged in 1.

c 1385 Chaucer L. G. W. 1183 Dido, Hyre systir Anne as she that coude hire good Seyde as hire thoughte & sumdel it with stod. a 1425 tr. Arderne's Treat. Fistula, etc. 51 When þer growed..any superflue flesch.., I withstode it or mette it with poudre of creoferoboron. a 1548 Hall Chron., Edw. V, 1 b, He spared no mannes deathe, whose life withstode his purpose. 1584 Cogan Haven Health cix. (1636) 110 Raysons..concoct raw humors, and withstand putrifaction. 1621 G. Sandys Ovid's Met. v. (1626) 90 His sword withstood Their re-ascent. c 1680 Roxb. Ball. (1891) VII. 358 Then prethee Love make no delay, let's not our precious time withstand. 1697 Dryden Æneis II. 155 The Wintry Seas, and Southern Winds, Withstood their passage home. 1737 Glover Leonidas I. 228 Leonidas awake! Shall these withstand The public safety? Lo! thy country calls. 1742 Fielding J. Andrews II. iv, I hope you will not withstand your own preferment. 1814 Scott Ld. of Isles III. iv, His frantic mood Was scarcely by the news withstood, That Moray shared his sister's flight. 1825 — Talism. xvii, The entrance of Queen Berengaria..was withstood..by the chamberlains.

3. *intr.* To offer resistance or opposition.

c 950 Lindisf. Gosp. Luke xi. 53 Ongunnun ða ældu.. heȝlice wiðstonda. a 1122 O. E. Chron. (Laud MS.) an. 2070 Þa utlaȝa..woldon into þam mynstre, & þa munecas wiðstoden þæt hi na mihton in cumen. c 1175 Lamb. Hom. 131 Ne mihte þer [in hell] nan wiðstonden, ne prophete ne patriarche. c 1200 Vices & Virtues 39 Strengþe to wiðstanden aȝeanes dieules fondinges. c 1250 Gen. & Ex. 2649 Ðe king wið-stod. 13.. K. Alis. 2062 (Laud MS.), Þise shulden wiþstonde hard And sauen al þe forme ward. 1340 Ayenb. 22 Huanne þe man wyþstant to alle ham þet guod him wolde. 1375 Barbour Bruce I. 456 Quhar God helpys, quhat may withstand? ?a 1400 Morte Arth. 1747 Ȝife we in the stour withstondene the better. 1530 Palsgr. 781/2 Agaynst the wyll of God no man may withstande. 1618 Bolton Florus (1636) 183 The City was encouraged to withstand upon the news of Lucullus his approach. 1667 Milton P. L. II. 610 They..wish..to reach The..stream,..But fate withstands. 1676 S. Sewall Diary (1876) I. 31 He was here with Mr. Broughton earnestly urging [etc.]..Mr. Broughton withstood. 1874 Green Short Hist. iii. § 2. 122 Langton prepared to withstand and rescue his country from the tyranny of John.

†4. To come to a stand, halt, stop. *Obs.*

c 1250 Gen. & Ex. 3646 Ðre daies and niȝtes faren it gan And wið-stod in ðe deserd pharan. c 1330 R. Brunne Chron. Wace (Rolls) 12780 Þey come & passed to þe wodes side, & þere wyþstode for to abyde. c 1430 Pistill of Susan 285 (Cott. MS.) Alle were a-stonyed and with-stood.

Withsta·nder. [f. Withstand *v.* + -er [1].] One who withstands; a resister, opponent.

a 1325 MS. Rawl. B. 520 lf. 25 b, Þe schirreue..sal..chastise þe withstonderes þoru þe prison. 1382 Wyclif Num. xxii. 33 Ȝyuynge stede to the withstonder. 1550 Bale Engl. Votaries II. 49 To terryfye their withstanders. 1567 Reg. Privy Council Scot. I. 569 A withstandar of his Hienes authoritie. 1588 Marprel. Epist. (Arb.) 6 Proud prelates, intolerable withstanders of reformation. a 1618 Raleigh Judic. & Sel. Ess. II. (1650) 1 War..may be defined the exercise of violence under Soveraigne Command, against withstanders force. 1745 Dodsley Rex et Pontifex Misc. I. 155 Silence every bold withstander That shall dare to disobey. 1880 Examiner No. 645. 530/1 It has seen him withstand the withstanders of those despotisms. 1877 Morley Crit. Misc. Ser. II. 199 Obstinate withstanders of all novelty.

Withsta·nding, *vbl. sb.* [f. Withstand *v.* + -ing [1].] The action of the verb Withstand; opposition, resistance.

13.. K. Alis. 2168 (Laud MS.), Stif wiþstondyng & wiȝth fleiȝeyng. 1303 R. Brunne Handl. Synne 12049 Þy wyþstondyng haþ hym rafte Of hys temptyng alle þe crafte. 1340 Ayenb. 29 Wy[þ]stondinge, þet is hardnesse of herte. 1493 [H. Parker] Dives & Pauper III. xiii. (1496) 148/2 They shall haue sotylte of bodye without ony withstandynge, for ther shal no thynge withstande them. 1525 Ld. Berners Froiss. II. vi. 6 b/1 The first went with ladders in to the dykes. They founde no withstandyng. 1650 Trapp Comm. Deut. xii. 3 Notwithstanding the withstandings of the rude rabble. 1696 Aubrey Misc. ii. 28 To make several withstandings against the Shock of Fortune. 1842 Newman Corr. (1917) 174 No one can tell how much there is in sympathy, over and above the influence one may have in withstanding.

So **Withsta·nding** *ppl. a.*, that withstands.

1711 Shaftesb. Charac. III. Misc. I. ii. 15 The tumid Bladder..bursts the withstanding Casements.

†**Withsta·nding**, *prep.* (*conj.*) *Obs.* (Only in Caxton.) [pr. pple. of Withstand used as a prep. (conj.) in imitation of OF. *obstant* (*que*). Cf. Notwithstanding (= F. *non obstant*).] Having regard to, on account of; seeing *that*.

c 1489 Caxton Sonnes of Aymon xxvi. 566 Why dyde ye calle my fader of treyson, wythstandyng that men know well that he is one of the trueste knyghtes of the worlde? 1490 — Eneydos xvi. 65 Thynkyng in hymselfe to be in daunger of his persone..wythstandyng the innuectyue moneycyons doon to hym. 1491 — Vitas Patr. (W. de W. 1495) II. 186 b/2 The marchaunt..wolde not by it withstandynge this that be knewe not how moche it myght well be worth.

Withstart to **Withstrain**: see With-.

†**Withta·ke**, *v. Obs.* [f. With- + Take *v.* Cf. ON. *viðtaka* resistance.]

1. *trans.* To 'take up', reprove, rebuke.

a 1340 Hampole Psalter xlix. 9 Noght in þi sacrifice i sall wiþtake þe [Vulg. arguam te]. c 1340 — Prose Treat. 8 Þay ere in trauayle..with takand ydill mene. c 1400 Titus & Vesp. (Roxb.) 1403 For he withtoke hem in her lawe þei wratthede hem sore with his sawe.

2. ? To rescue.

c 1400 Destr. Troy 11036 Phylmen þe freke, þat fuersly withtakon,..Lut to þe lady.

3. To keep back, retain, or withhold unlawfully.

14.. Siege Jerus. (E.E.T.S.) 48 His tribute..þat þey withtake wolde. a 1450 Myrc Par. Pr. (1902) 1185 Hast þow werkemen oght wyth-tan Of any þynge þat þey schulde han?

Hence †**Withta·ker**, a rebuker, reprover.

a 1340 Hampole Psalter ix. 24 Þat thynge has man delite to doe in þe whilk þai hafe sum louere & nan with takere.

†**Withward**, *prep. Obs.* [f. With *adv.* + -ward, after *toward*.] ? Along with.

a 1225 Leg. Kath. 1983 Þis pinfule gin wes o swuch wise iginet, Þæt te twa turnden eiðer wiðward oðer.

Wi·thweed. *Obs.* or *dial.* [A blending of Withwind and Bindweed.] = next.

1567 Maplet Gr. Forest 34 Bindweede, of some Withweede. 1766 Compl. Farmer s.v. Bindweed P 2/1, I had a very good crop of wheat; but a with-weed came up to every plant. [Reproducing Lisle Husb. (1757) 393, which, however, has withwind.]

Withwind (wi·þwəind). Now *dial.* Forms: 1 wiþo-, wiþewinde, 2 wiþwinde, 4 weþewinde, withe-, wythe-, weythwynde, 6 with-, wythwynde, 6–7 withwinde, 6– withwind. [OE. *wiþowinde*, *wiþe-*, later *wiþwinde*, f. *wiþo-*, *wiþe-* (related to Withe) + *winde* Wind *sb.*[2]; corresp. to OS. *withewind* 'caprifolium', MLG., MDu. *wedewinde* 'caprifolium', 'periclymena', 'hedera', 'ligustrum'; for the first element cf. OE. *weoþobend* Withbind, for the second, OE. *widuwinde* ivy, convolvulus; see also Withywind.] Bindweed, *Convolvulus arvensis* or *C. sepium*; also *C. Soldanella* (Sea Withwind: see Sea *sb.* 23 f). Applied also, like Bindweed, to other climbing plants, e.g. dodder, smilax, traveller's joy.

c 1000 Sax. Leechd. II. 34 Wiþ eaȝece ȝenim wiþowindan twiȝu. Ibid. 122 Wiþewindan twiȝ foreweard. c 1050 Voc. in Wr.-Wülcker 428/36 Inuoluco, wiþewinde. c 1100 Gloss. ibid. 138/28 Uiticella, wiþwinde. 1377 Langl. P. Pl. B. v. 525 In a withewyndes wise ywounden aboute. 1398 Trevisa Barth. De P. R. XVIII. xxix. (Bodl. MS.), A tree þat is biclipped w[t] yuye oþer wiþ weþewinde. 1533 Elyot Cast. Helthe (1541) 11 b, Thynges good for the Lyuer: Wormewode: Wyth wynde. 1548 Turner Names Herbes (E.D.S.) 30 Conuoluulus..called of the herbaries Volubilis, in english wythwynde or byndeweede. 1552 Huloet, Withwinde herbe, cassutha, cascuta, cissampelos, conuolulus. 1580 T. Newton Approved Medicines 20 b, Smilax hortensis, Gardein withwinde. a 1722 Lisle Husb. (1757) 382 Giving their lands a second tillage, perhaps to destroy the withwind. 1899 R. Bridges Idle Flowers xiv, Thro' the hedgerow peer Withwind and Snapdragon.

attrib. 1891 Hardy Noble Dames ii. 90 One of those sweet-pea or with-wind natures which require a twig of stouter fibre than its own to hang upon and bloom.

Withy (wi·ði), *sb.* Forms: 1 wiðiȝ, 3 wiþi, 4 wiþie, wiþge, (w(h)itheye, wytie, weþie), 4, 6–7 (9 *Sc.*) withie, 5–6 wythy, 5–7 withye, wythie, 6 wythye, 6–7 withee (5 withi, wethei, -ie, *pl.* wetheis, wethiss, 5–6 wethy, whythy, 6 wethye, *pl.* wythiese), 7, 9 withey, 6– withy. [OE. *wiþig* (= L. *vitex*, *vitic-* Agnus Castus), for the connexions of which see Withe. Cf. Widdy.]

1. A willow of any species: sometimes *spec.* the osier willow, *Salix viminalis*.

961 in Birch Cartul. Sax. III. 289 On þone haran wiðiȝ. a 1225 Ancr. R. 86 He is ase þe wiði þet sprutted ut þe betere þet me hine ofte croppeð. 1325 in Kennett Parochial Antiq. (1695) 395 Tres acræ apud le Whitheyes. Ibid. 400 A quo quidem prato dimidia roda jacet atte Witheyes juxta pratum Prioris. c 1325 Gloss. W. de Bibbesw. in Wright Voc. 163 Sauz [glossed wytie (wilwe)]. 1382 Wyclif Lev. xxiii. 40 Ȝe shulen take to ȝow..withies of the rennynge water. 1398 Trevisa Barth. De P. R. XIII. xi. (Bodl. MS.), In som partie of his brymme he haþ plente of wiþges and of segge as it is seide. 1523 Fitzherb. Husb. § 24 The rakes..be moste comynly made of hasel and withe [ed. 1534 withee]. 1578 Lyte Dodoens III. lxii. 403 [Polypody] growing vppon olde wythiese. c 1640 J. Smyth Lives Berkeleys (1883) I. 123 To be a bendinge withy, not a stubborne Oke. 1661 Boyle Style Script. 180 Withees, whilst they are sound grow Unregarded Trees; but when they once are Rotten, Shine in the Night. 1791 W. Gilpin Forest Scenery I. 64 The withy, or salix fragilis, is the most inconsiderable of it's tribe. 1866 Blackmore Cradock Nowell I, The witheys were gloved with silver and gold. 1889 Conan Doyle Micah Clarke xxix, The moaning of the breeze among the withies.

b. With qualification, applied to various species of willow; also to other plants, as the laserwort, *Laserpitium Siler*: see quots.

Hoop withy: see Hoop *sb.*[1] 13 b. †Rose withy = Willow-herb 2.

14.. Metr. Voc. in Wr.-Wülcker 629/9 Wythy, siler. 1523–34 Fitzherb. Husb. § 130 Whyte wethy..wyll not grow in marsshe ground. 1585 Higins Junius' Nomencl. 152/1 Siler,..spert withie, ozier withie, or small withie. 1612 R. Ch. Olde Thrift newly revived 49 The Withie, of which are said to be 4 kinds, that is, the white withy, blacke Withie, and red Withie, osier Withie. 1650 [W. Howe] Phytol. Brit. 27 Chamænerion sive Epilobium..Rosebay willow-herb, Rose withy, or Willow-flower. 1733 W. Ellis Chiltern & Vale Farm. 191 This Withy often arrives to a large Stature, especially the red Sort. 1860 Warter Sea-board II. 35 The yellow withy which lived on the moisture in the hollow. 1866 Treas. Bot. 1235/2 Withy, Laserpitium Siler:..—, Hoop, Rivina octandra.

2. A flexible branch of a willow, esp. as used for tying or binding, as a halter (cf. Widdy 2), etc.; any similar flexible branch or twig; a leash, hoop, or the like made of a withy.

a 1400 Sir Perc. 444 Therto his mere he bande With the withy. c 1425 Wyntoun Cron. VII. ix. 2874 Withe rapis and wetheis about þar hals. c 1460 Sir R. Ros La Belle Dame 186 With grene wythies ybounden. 1564 Bullein Dial. agst. Pest. (1573) 6, I had better be hangad in a withie or in a cowtaile, then be a rowfooted Scot. 1587 Fleming Contn. Holinshed III. 1348/2 Which tempest.. rent up manie great trees,..or woond them like withies. 1658 N. Riding Rec. VI. 34 He is a rogue and deserves a withy. 1727 A. Hamilton New Acc. E. Indies II. xlv. 149 A Rattan Withy to lift them by. 1787 W. Hutton Courts of Requests 324 The ties of honour..are as easily broken through, as Sampson's withies. 1790 Grose Prov. Gloss. (ed. 2), Withy, a round hoop of osier. 1805 Southey Madoc I. v, Canes and withies formed the walls and roof. 1818 Scott Br. Lamm. vii, In order to save himself from the withie. 1865 W. G. Palgrave Arabia II. 219 Palm-huts unroofed, despite of their strong lacings and withies. 1893 Conan Doyle Refugees xxxiv, They were lashed to low posts with willow withies.

b. *coll. sing.* Withies as a material.

1833 Ht. Martineau Brooke Farm viii. 95 The harness was made of withy. 1915 Q. Rev. July 4 Pots of withy or of stout netting..are used for crabs.

†3. = Widdy 3. *Obs.*

1438 Exch. Rolls Scot. V. 58 Pro fabrica septem wethyis erri. 1456 Ibid. VI. 278. 1484 Ibid. IX. 239.

4. *attrib.* and *Comb.*, as *withy band, basket, bed, blossom, bough, cutting, holt, labyrinth, leaf, pollard, pot, prison, rope, shoot, tree, twig, wood*, etc.; *withy-bound* adj.; †*withy-cole*, ?charcoal made of willow wood; †*withy-cragged* [Cragged *a.*[2]], see quots.; *withy-fly*, an artificial fly used in angling; †*withy-herb*, purple loosestrife: = Willow-herb 1.

a 1685 Stradling Serm. (1692) 176 Those Shackles..which could no more hold him, than the *withy bands could Sampson. 1820 Shelley Hymn Merc. lxix, He..bound Stiff withy bands the infant's wrists around. 1891 Hardy Tess xlix, She ..packed up as many of her belongings as would go into a *withy basket. 956 in Birch Cartul. Sax. III. 96 On ðæt *wiðiȝ bed. 1420 Chertsey Cartulary 41 b (P.R.O.), Duas acras terre et dimidiam super le Whythybed. 1583 in Wadley Notes Wills Bristol (1886) 237 The withie Bedd or twigg bedd. 1844 J. T. Hewlett Parsons & W. xxxix, And now, sir, do you push on to that corner of this withy-bed. 1898 J. A. Gibbs Cotswold Village 106 When November frosts begin to attract snipes to the withybeds. 1707 Mortimer Husb. 203 As soon as the Willow or *Withy Blossoms appear. c 1440 Pallad. on Husb. III. 412 An arm gret *withi bough. 1862 W. Barnes Hwomely Rhymes II. 85 Grey-leav'd withy-boughs. 1898 A. Austin Lamia's Winter Quarters 8 The *withy-bound flask of ruby wine. 1657 Reeve God's Plea 254 Fumigations of Storax,..Nemphar, Dragagant, *Withy-cole. 1607 Markham Cavel. III. ii. 14 His necke straight..and..of one peece with his bodie, and not (as my countrey-men say) *withie cragged, which is loose and plyant. 1766 Complete Farmer s.v. Stable 7 B 1/1 The continual lifting up of the head to feed out of the rack..makes him, as they express it, withy-cragged. 1813 Vancouver Agric. Devon 137 Two rows of *withy or sallow cuttings. 1799 G. Smith Laboratory II. 298 Alder-fly, *withy-fly, or bastard-caddis. 1578 Lyte Dodoens I. li. 75 Red Lysimachus, or *wythie herbe. 1856 Mrs. Tennyson in Mem. Ld. Tennyson (1897) I. 412 Went to our *withy holt. 1633 P. Fletcher Purple Isl. I. lv, When a fisher-swain..hath spi'd A big-grown Pike..He sets a *withy Labyrinth beside. c 1460 J. Russell Bk. Nurture 995 *Wethy leves, grene otes boyled in fere fulle soft. 1578 Lyte Dodoens I. li. 71 The leaues be..like willow, or wythie leaues. 1863 Kingsley Water-Bab. iii, The great *withy pollard which hangs over the backwater. a 1700 Evelyn Diary 9 Feb. 1665, *Withy-potts or nests for the wild fowle to lay their eggs in. 1633 P. Fletcher Purple Isl. III. ii, Thirsil from *withy prison..Lets out his flock. 1815 Simond Tour Gt. Brit. II. 240 The *withy rope lasts good two years. a 1722 Lisle Husb. (1757) 375, I gathered *withy-shoots over which the cart-wheel had run. 1398 Trevisa Barth. De P. R. XVII. cxliv. (Bodl. MS.), Þerfor it [is] nouȝt seker to slepe vnder þe *webie tree. 1664 Evelyn Sylva xxix. 82, A..Withy-tree ..which is increased to a most stupendious bulk. 1820 Shelley Hymn Merc. xiii, He..bound them in a lump with *withy twigs. 1523 Fitzherb. Husb. § 24 Than maye he.. tothe the rakes with drye *wethy wode.

Wi·thy, *a. rare.* Also -ey. [f. Withe *sb.* + -y [1].] Resembling a withe or withy in flexibility.

1598 Florio, Vencido, tractable, yeeldinge,..plyable, withie. 1756 P. Browne Jamaica 244 A strong withey shrub. 1822 W. Irving Braceb. Hall xxxvii. (1845) 229 The long withy ends of the branches.

Withywind (wi·ðiwəind). Now *dial.* [Alteration of Withwind, after Withy *sb.*] = Withwind.

1578 Lyte Dodoens III. lii. 391 Of smothe Bindweede, or Withiwinde. The great white Bindeweede or soft withiwinde. Ibid. liii. 393 Of blacke Withiwinde, or Bindeweede. 1591 Percivall Sp. Dict., Campanilla yerva, withie winde, Smilax. 1621 Burton Anat. Mel. II. ii. III. 610 Whiter Galat then the white withy-wind. 1658 tr. Porta's Nat. Magic III. xix. 105 The seed of withy-winde being planted neer to Basil, [etc.]. 1825 Jennings Obs. Dial. W. Eng., Withy-wine, the plant bindweed. 1829 J. L. Knapp Jrnl. Nat. 114 The clematis, the 'withy-wind' of our peasantry. 1878 Hardy Ret. Native I. x, You could twist him to your will like withywind, if you only had the mind.

†**Wi·tie**, *sb. Obs.* Forms: 1 wit(e)ȝa, -iȝa, (1 witȝe, -eȝa), 2–3 witiȝe, -eȝe, witie, (3 witeie, witti(e, -y). [OE. *wit(e)ga*, *-iga* = OHG. *wiz(z)ago*, altered (by association with *wis* Wise *a.* and *sagen* Say *v.*[1]) to *wissago* (MHG. *wissage*, *-ag*), ON. *vitke*: f. *wit-*: see Wit *v.*[1]] A prophet. Also *adj.*, prophetic.

c 897 Ælfred Gregory's Past. C. xxxii. 213 Ne eow..ne ondrædað for nanes monnes wordum, ne for nanes witȝan gæste. c 950 Lindisf. Gosp. Mark i. 2 Suæ awritten is in esaia ðone witȝo. c 1175 Lamb. Hom. 43 Of þas pinan spekeð dauid þe halie witeȝe. c 1200 Trin. Coll. Hom. 83 Salemon and alle wise witeȝe. Ibid. 127 Þis childes witiȝe gost. c 1205 Lay. 15877 To þan kinge was ibroht Joram þe witie [c 1275 witti]. a 1225 Juliana 39 Þen muchele witti witeȝe ysaie.

†**Wi·tie**, *v.*[1] *Obs.* In 1 wit(e)ȝian, 2–3 witeȝen. [OE. *wit(e)ȝian* = OFris. *witgia* (MLG. *wittigen*), OHG. *wizagōn* (MHG. *wissagen*, G. *weissagen*); f. *witeȝa* Witie *sb.*] To prophesy.

c 950 Lindisf. Gosp. Matt. xxvi. 68 Witȝa us, crist, hua is se ðe ðec of-slog. c 1000 Ælfric Num. xi. 27 Ða hi witeȝodon on wicstowe. c 1175 Lamb. Hom. 7 Þis he witeȝede bi drihtene þurh þene halie gast. c 1200 Trin. Coll. Hom. 127 Hie witeȝede..of ure louerd ihesu cristes to cume.

†**Wi·tie**, *v.*[2] *Obs.* Forms: 3 witeȝen, -iȝe, -ien, -ye, wete (?), 3–4 witi(e, wytie, 4 -ye, wetye; *pa. t.* 4 wited. [OE. **witian*, as in be-

witian Biwitie.] *trans.* To keep, guard, protect: = Wite *v.*[2]

c 1205 Lay. 2753 Heo biȝeten men þe heom cuðen witen [c 1275 witie]. Ibid. 23738 Þat he..mid his riht honde witeȝe me wið sconde. Ibid. 32155 Þe pape hatte Sergius, he weteð Peteres hus. a 1290 St. Eustace 92 in Horstm. Altengl. Leg. (1881) 213 Wendeþ..godes way, Wytieþ oure soule niȝt and day. c 1290 St. Brendan 299 in S. Eng. Leg. 227 Þat euerech frere of þat him leuez witiez to is soper. 1297 R. Glouc. (Rolls) 9875 Saladin..let witie þe sepulcre þat no cristine ne com þer. 1340 Ayenb. 122 Þe baylifs þet gouerneþ and wytyeþ þe kingriche. c 1350 Will. Palerne 176 Þis litel barn..couþe..kepe alle here bestes,..& wited hem so wisly. a 1400 Engl. Gilds (1870) 357 And þat seluer..be y-take to sexe godemen..for þe Commune assent, and treweleche wetye, and trewleche spende.

Hence †**Wi·tier**, protector, guardian; †**Wi·tiing** *vbl. sb.*, guarding.

1340–70 Alex. & Dind. 678 [Bacus] wis witiere of win þat alle won bryngus. 13.. Pol. Rel. & L. Poems (1903) 268 Of vr vife wittes a wel witiynge.

Witie, obs. form of Witty.

†**Wi·tieng.** *Obs.* Forms: 1 witeȝung, witȝiung, witȝeong, 2 witeȝung, 3 witieng, *Orm.* witeȝhunnge. [OE. *witegung* (= OHG. *wizagunga*, MHG. *wissagunge*), f. *witegian* Witie *v.*[1] + *-ung*, -ing [1].] Prophecy. Also *attrib.*

c 950 Lindisf. Gosp. Matt. xiii 14 Witȝiung essaies. c 1000 Ælfric Saints' Lives xxiv. 115 Hit is awriten be me on witeȝung bocum [etc.]. c 1200 Trin. Coll. Hom. 127 Þis childes witiȝe gost lihte þe moder gost of witienge. c 1200 Ormin 15174 All þatt witeȝhunnge wass þurrh himm onn erþe cwiddedd. Ibid. 15188 All þatt witeȝhunngeboc þatt witess haffdenn cwiddedd.

Witin, obs. pa. pple. of Wit *v.*[1]

Witing, -liche, obs. ff. Witting, -ly.

Witless (wi·tlės), *a.* Now only *literary* and somewhat *arch.* [OE. *witlēas*, also *gewitlēas*: see Wit *sb.*, Iwit, and -less.]

1. Lacking wisdom or sense; not guided by reason; unreasonable, foolish, heedless.

[a 1000 Boeth. Metr. xix. 46 Wenað þonne swa ȝewitlease ðæt hi þa soðan gesælða hæbben.] c 1200 Ormin 6197 Ȝiff þin macche iss wis & god, & tu wittiæs & wicke. c 1290 S. Eng. Leg. 248/263 Þov witiese wrechche. c 1400 26 Pol. Poems iii. 90 Witteles wordes in ydel spoken. c 1400 Brut ccxiii. 249 Longe berde hertles, peyntede Hode witles, Gay cote graceles, makeþ Englissheman þriftles. 1559 Mirr. Mag., Dk. Clarence xiii, I was witlesse, wanton, fond, and yong. 1581 Burne in Cath. Tractates (S.T.S.) 170 Ane..confused rabil of vitles Bisbopis. 1587 Turberv. Trag. Tales 73 b, O wilfull witlesse acte, Which no man well aduisde would do. a 1676 Hale Prim. Orig. Man. (1677) 356 To keep in and regulate the extravagant and witless Spirit of Man. 1724 Ramsay Tea-t. Misc. (1733) II. 149 Why did I, young witless maid Believe the flatt'ring tale? 1794 Godwin Cal. Williams 42 Intended (witless and miserable precaution!) for the safeguards of the poor. 1803 Jane Porter Thaddeus xxxvi, This witless coxcomb. 1860 Motley Nether. v. (1868) I. 153 It was witless to believe that Parma contemplated any such measure. 1879 Butcher & Lang Odyssey 25 Telemachus, even hereafter thou shalt not be craven or witless. 1910 Times 13 July 12/3 Mr. Rolls..had..to drop suddenly to the ground..owing to some witless spectators running into his way.

2. Mentally deficient or deranged; out of one's wits, crazy, lunatic. † Also, stupefied, dazed.

c 1000 Sax. Leechd. III. 146 On þam fiftan monþe he [sc. the fœtus] biþ cwica and weaxeð and seo modur lið witleas. c 1290 Beket 1906 in S. Eng. Leg. 161 He eode op and doun ase witles. 1297 R. Glouc. (Rolls) 4414 He werde as a witles mon, hit was deol to be him ney. c 1375 Sc. Leg. Saints xxix. (Placidas) 440 Sa lang witias stil he stud, Til þat nere he dronyt in þat flud. 1377 Langl. P. Pl. B. XIII. 1, I awaked þere-with, witles nerehande. c 1470 Gol. & Gaw. 573 Wraithly wroht, as thei war witlese and wode. 1571 Golding Calvin on Ps. xxxiv. 1 The woord (witlesse) ..will well agree, bycause Dauid feyned himself too bee out of his wittes. 16.. Young Musgrave xix. in Child Ballads II. 249/2 She'll gae witless wud. 1900 H. Sutcliffe Shameless Wayne iii. (1905) 26 It would never do to leave this witless body to the night-rain and the cold.

†3. Devoid of understanding; having no intellectual faculty; irrational. *Obs.*

1382 Wyclif Wisd. xv. 18 Thei most wrecchid herien bestes; witles forsothe, comparisouned to these. c 1395 Plowman's T. II. 523 They..liven wors than witles beestes. 1577 T. Kendall Flowers Epigr. 50 This Image..Tongles and witles. 1587 Golding De Mornay xiv. 236 Sillie Soules which go on still like witlesse Beastes.

4. Deficient in understanding; having undeveloped or imperfect intellectual power; unintelligent, undiscerning; stupid, dull-witted.

1562 A. Brooke Romeus & Jul. 2470 Euen from the hory head vnto the witles childe She wan the hartes of all. 1612 Woodall Surg. Mate (1639) 6, I hold none so witlesse which cannot make use thereof, when they once see but the instrument. 1625 Purchas Pilgrims II. vi. i. 777 The Inhabitants ..are most base and witlesse people. 1822 Praed Lillian I. 140 The witless Child grew up alone. 1855 M. Arnold Balder Dead I. 98 Of ignorant witless mind Thou barest me, and unforeseeing soul.

b. Not understanding (something specified or implied); inapprehensive.

1614 R. Wilkinson Paire Serm. 2 Witlesse to discerne what he is himselfe. 1637 Rutherford Lett., To Jas. Lindsay 7 Sept. (1671) 138 A witless and lazie observer of the Lord's way and working. 1855 Browning An Epistle 143 The man is witless of..The value in proportion of all things. 1856 R. A. Vaughan Mystics III. iv. (1860) I. 85 The blue aether..at which to look up with smiles of witless wonder.

5. Not knowing; unaware, unconscious *of*.

In quot. 1827, incapable *of*.

1584 Reg. Privy Council Scot. III. 691 Ignorant and wytles of thair rysche and insolent behaviour. 1597 Beard Theatre God's Judgem. I. ii. (1612) 232 Guiltlesse and witlesse of the crime. 1827 Hood Mids. Fairies lxxxi, His pretty pouting mouth, witless of speech. 1850 P. Crook War of Hats 34 Witless of the storm his words excite. 1872 Blackie Lays Highl. 82 He lay all witless of his doom.

6. Devoid of wit (Wit *sb.* 8). *rare.*

1753 Richardson Grandison II. xxvi. 200 Repartee and smartness; the current wit of that witless place. 1859 Habits of Gd. Society 93 He can no longer claim exemption from solemn dinners,..and witless tea-parties.

Hence **Wi·tlessly** *adv.*, foolishly, stupidly; **Wi·tlessness**, senselessness, folly, stupidity.

a 1100 in Napier OE. Glosses (1902) 213 Socordia, torpor, dementia, witleasnes. 1598 Florio To Rdr. 7 Had not H.S... so witlesly prouoked me. 1599 Sandys Europæ Spec. (1632) 178 Divine blessing, which accompanieth good causes, where wickednesse or wilfull witlessenesse doth not barre against it. 1608 T. Morton Preamb. Encounter 72 Rather..accounted lyingly witty, than witlesly rash. 1766 Fordyce Serm. Yng. Women (1767) I. vii. 302 The admiration raised by 'a set of features..', is often by the witlessness of the possessor thrown down in an instant. 1855 Anne Manning Old Chelsea Bun-ho. xix. 317 Everybody conceived themselves safe, as witlessly as they had previously held themselves to be in Danger. 1860 Pusey Min. Proph. 239 Wisdom was turned into witlessness. 1879 Butcher & Lang Odyssey 282 He kicked Odysseus on the hip in his witlessness. 1910 Times Lit. Suppl. 10 Mar. 82/3 An artist..choosing to portray..the havoc and witlessness of mankind.

Witling (wi·tliŋ). [f. Wit *sb.* + -ling [1] 2.] A petty wit (see Wit *sb.* 9, 10); one who fancies himself a wit; a pretender to wit (see Wit *sb.* 5, 7); one who utters light or feeble witticisms.

1693 Dryden Persius Sat. I. Prol. 17 Let Gain, that gilded Bait, be hung on high, The hungry Witlings have it in their Eye. 1702 Engl. Theophrastus 6 There are many impertinent Witlings at Will's. 1712–14 Pope Rape of Lock v. 59 A Beau and Witling perish'd in the throng, One died in metaphor, and one in song. 1807 W. Irving Salmag. No. 2 ¶ 5 Does any witling want to distress the company with a miserable pun? 1876 Meredith Beauchamp's Career xx, 'What's in hand?'..Luckily some witling said, 'Fours-in-hand!' and so drily that it passed for humour.

attrib. 1817 J. Scott Paris Revisit. (ed. 4) 228 The miserable witling captiousness of an opposition. 1845 Miall in Nonconf. V. 45 A witling poet.

‖**Witloof** (wi·tlōf). [Du., lit. 'white leaf'.] = Chicory 1, Succory 1. Also *attrib.*

1885 Bazaar 2 Jan. 7/2 Chicory, or witloof, as some choose to call it, is a useful winter salad plant. 1925 W. Watson Gard. Assist. I. 79 Witloof Chicory...Large Brussels (Witloof)..has large leaves with wide midribs and stalks.

†**Wi·tly**, *adv. Obs.* Also 5 wittle. (Of doubtful authenticity; in some instances perh. a spelling of *wittely* Wittily, in others of *wihtly* Wightly.)

c 1350 Will. Palerne 259 Þe child witly þanne wende wiþoute ani more. c 1380 Wyclif Sel. Wks. II. 275 Siþ þis martirdoom of Crist was so swete bifore God, Poul clepiþ it witly siche an offryng bifore God into smelling of swetnesse. 1426 Audelay Poems (Percy Soc.) 30 Wysele and wytle and wittie the leud thai wyl here.

†**Wi·tne**, *v. Obs.* Also 4 witt(e)ne, (wythene). [a. ON. *vitna*, related to *vitni* witness, f. *wit-* Wit *v.*[1] (Cf. etym. note s.v. Witness *v.*)]

1. *trans.* To bear witness to; to attest, testify. Also *absol.* or *intr.* to bear witness.

a 1225 Ancr. R. 30 Þet ich þurh hore bonen mote habben þe tweolf bowes þet bloweð of cherite, ase seinte Powel witneð. Ibid. 384 Seint Powel witneð þet alle uttre herdschipes..al is ase nout aȝean luue. 1340 Hampole Pr. Consc. 5355 Als þe buke wythenes. a 1400–50 Wars Alex. 2900 With slike a reryd þan it rynnes, þe romance it witnes, Þat, qua so tuke it in þat tyme, tint ware for euire. c 1400 Rule St. Benet (verse) 753 For þe wisman witnes & sais [etc.].

2. To invoke, entreat.

c 1200 Trin. Coll. Hom. 171 Iob witnede ure drihten, þat of þis deað him redde, on þe carefuldai.

3. To impute, ascribe.

c 1350 Will. Palerne 3462 Holli williams werkes þei wittened it alle, nade his douȝhi dedes þe þei hade be dede alle.

Witne, obs. pa. pple. of Wit *v.*[1]

Witness (wi·tnės), *sb.* Forms: 1–7 witnes, 3–5 wittnesse, 3 *Orm.*, 6 wittness, 3–6 wittenes, wytnesse, 3–7 witnesse, 4–5 witenes, 4–6 wittnes, wytnes(s, (2 witnys, 3 -nesce, 4 wijtnes, wittenesse, 4–5 whitnes, 4, 6 wytnes, wetness(e, witnese, (7 *Sc.*) vitnes, 5 wytt(e)nesse, -(e)nes, witnesh, wetenesse, whetnesse, vitness(e)), 5– witness. [OE. *witnes*, more freq. *gewitnes*, f. (*ge*)*wit* Wit *sb.*, Iwit + *-nes* -ness. Cf. OHG. *giwiznessi*, MDu. *wetenisse*. The passage in sense from abstract to concrete is paralleled in F. *témoin* (:– L. *testimonium*). The uninflected pl. was frequent in early use; for separate illustration see sense 4.]

I. †1. Knowledge, understanding, wisdom. *Obs.*

c 950 Rituale Eccl. Dunelm. (Surtees) 194 Fore wisdom vel witnes ðæs biscop..propter scientiam episcopi. c 1250 Gen. & Ex. 507 He sal..wenden iewes..To ðe wittenesse of iesus crist. c 1380 Wyclif Sel. Wks. II. 225 Whanne a symple man seiþ a treuþe, we trowen it not for he seiþ it,.. but Crist is man of greet witnesse. 1382 — Prov. viii. 5 Vnderstondeth, ȝee litle childer, witnesse [1388 wisdom; Vulg. astutiam]. 1433 Rolls of Parlt. V. 435/1 The connyng and witnes that resten in his persone. 1482 Monk of Evesham (Arb.) 27 His owne seyng that he had tolde before to a few persons of wytnesse [orig. perpaucis arbitris].

2. Attestation of a fact, event, or statement; testimony, evidence; †evidence given in a court of justice. *See* also †1.

†**b.** The action or condition of being an observer of an event.

α. *spec.* in reference to the inward testimony of the conscience.

†**d.** In some versions of the Bible: = TESTIMONY *sb.* 4. *Obs.*

3. Testimony by signature, oath, etc. Chiefly in phr. *in* (*rarely* †*onely witness of*) *hand*, *hereof*, etc.

4. One who gives evidence in relation to matters of fact under inquiry; *spec.* one who gives or is legally qualified to give evidence upon oath or affirmation in a court of justice or judicial inquiry.

†**b.** A bishop or godparent at baptism. *Obs.*

5. One who is or was present or able to testify from personal observation; one present as a spectator or auditor. (Cf. EAR-WITNESS, EYE-WITNESS.) Usually *with of*, *occas. to.*

†*fig.* Something that furnishes evidence or proof of the thing or fact mentioned; an evidential mark or sign, a token.

6. One who is or was present or able to testify from personal observation; *one* present as a spectator or auditor. (Cf. EAR-WITNESS, EYE-WITNESS.)

II. Introd. 104 The Lordis .. ordaina him to haue lettera to summond his witnes, and the party to here them.

b. in asseverative formulæ, in which a deity or a human being is invoked as one who is cognizant of a fact; as *God is my witness*, *Be my witness that* ... Most often in phr. *to call* or *take to* (†*one's*) *witness*: to call upon or appeal to as one's surety; to aver by.

7. Technical uses (see quots.; cf. F. *témoin*).

8. *Referring* to, usually introducing, the designation of an authority for a statement. (Cf. 7 *b*.)

II. Phrases. (See also above.)

9. *a.* *witness* as a testimony or piece of evidence. Now *rare* or *Obs.* exc. as in 3.

10. *To bear witness*: (said properly of a person, a book, etc.) to give oral or written testimony or evidence of; to testify, vouch, witness of (occas. *of*). *To bear* (one) *witness*: to corroborate one's statement or affirmation.

IV. xvii. 8 Gifts yet more costly were now the witness of his personal presence.

5. Introducing a name, designation, phrase, or clause denoting a person or thing that furnishes evidence of the fact or exemplifies the statement. Also *as witness*, and, in early use, †*witness on*. (Alter L. *teste* , -*e*.)

6. To bring witness (TEEN *v.* 1) to witness': to bring under examination. *Obs.*

† **12.** *To bring*, *make* (TEEN *v.* 1) *to witness*: to bring under examination.

(8) *with obj. clause.*

† **13.** *To take witness of*: to call or take to witness (see 6 *b*); to appeal to as an authority for a statement or source of information. *Obs.*

10. *With a witness*: with clear evidence, without a doubt, †*with a vengeance,*' 'and no mistake'. *Obs.* or *rare arch.*

III. 13. *attrib.* and *Comb.*, as *witness-bearer*, *-bearing* *sb.* and *adj.* (*see* 10), *-chair*, *-room* (see quots.).

† **11.** *To take witness* (*by* or *of*): to take example by. *Obs.*

12. *To bring* ...

†**d.** To give evidence by one's behaviour; to make evident; to evince. *Obs.*

b. To furnish evidence or proof of.

c. To give evidence of or about; to attest.

2. *intr.* To bear oral or written witness; to testify. Now usually *with to* or *against.*

Witnessable (wi'tnesăb'l), *a.* [f. WIT-NESS *v.* + -ABLE.] That may be witnessed.

Witnessed (wi'tnest), *ppl. a.* [f. WITNESS *sb.* + -ED².]

1. Furnished with evidence or proof.

b. Attested by a witness or witnesses.

Witnesser (wi'tnesăɹ). [f. WITNESS *v.* + -ER¹.] One who witnesses a witness.

Witnessing (wi'tnesiŋ), *vbl. sb.* [f. WITNESS *v.* + -ING¹.]

1. The action of bearing witness or giving testimony. *In witnessing* (as a witness to); †*to witness.*

b. *attrib.*

Witryff, Witryffe, obs. forms of WITTERING.

Witryff (wi'tni). Also 3–8 -aye.

A heavy loose woollen material with a nap, manufactured and made up into blankets at Witney, a town in Oxfordshire; also, formerly, a kind of cloth of coating made there. Also *attrib.* esp. in *Witney blanket* (for which the single *Witney* is occas. used.)

2. *Curling.* The tee (TEE *sb.*²³) towards which the stone is to be urged.

3. *attrib.* *witter hole*, a hole serving as a mark for the curler.

1598 Spalding Club *Misc.* (1841) I. 122 The crawis ar witryff beastis, and the Devil will cun in thair likenes.

Witsach, -safe, -saufe, -save, -schaif, obs. ff. VOUCHSAFE, WITSAU, var. WITHSAW OS.

† **Wi'tship¹.** [OE. (*ge'witscipe* = OFris. *wit-skipe*, OS. *giwitscepi* (MLG. *getwitschap*), OHG. *giwizscaf*: see WIT and -SHIP.] Witness, testimony; knowledge.

Wi'tship², [f. WIT *sb.*¹ + -SHIP.] With possessive pron. used as a fanciful title for a witty person.

Witt, obs. form of WIT.

Wittebeem (vi'tabēm). *S. Afr.* [Cape Du.] *pl.* The barks of any tree, the like. (*rare in sing.*)

Witted (wi'ted), *ppl. a.* [f. WIT *sb.*¹ + -ED².]

1. Having wit or wits of a specified quality or amount; with qualifying adv., as WELL-WITTED, etc. (*obs.*), or in parasynthetic comb. with an adj. as *dull-*, *fine-*, *half-*, *light-*, *quick-*, *sharp-*, *slow-witted*, etc.; also in combinations after *half-witted*, as *two-third-witted*, *whole-witted.*

Witter (wi'tăɹ), *sb.*² *Sc.* and *north.* Also 8 weiter, 9 wither, wi'tter. (Also 5 *D. D.*) [Of obscure origin; cf. however, MG. *wither-kabel* (WITHER-¹ 2) and dial. *witter-hukul* (Lonsdale Gloss. 1869)] *pl.* The barbs of an arrow, fishing-spear, fish-hook, or the like. (*rare in sing.*)

Wi'ttered *a.*, barbed.

1773 H. Foord in *Trans. Soc. Arts* (1789) 92 To the other [whale] was lost... by the Wetters, or Feathers of the Harpoon, which were laid in proper order on the Iron.

Witterly, f. WIT *sb.* + -LY.] With possessive pron. used as a fanciful title for a witty person.

Wi'ttiness. [f. WITTY + -NESS.] The quality of being witty.

Wittily (wi'tili), *adv.* Forms: see WITTY *a.*; also 4–6 *witly* (*Sc. vittely*), 5 *witteli*. [f. WITTY + -LY².]

† **1.** Intelligently, cleverly, ingeniously. *Obs.*

2. Wisely, discreetly, sensibly. *Obs.*

3. In a manner characterized by wit (WIT *sb.* 7, 8); in a cleverly amusing way; with smart sarcasm.

WITTINESS. 234 WITTY. WITTY. 235 WIVE.

WIVEN. 236 WIZEN. WIZENED. 237 WLONK.

WLONKFUL. 238 WOADED. WOADER. 239 WOE.

WOE. 240 WOE. WOE. 241 WOEFUL.

Supplement, p. 3873; Corrigenda, p. 4092; Spurious words, p. 4093; Books quoted, p. 4094

Wolf's-fist. *Obs.* In 3 wolvesfest, 6 woolfes fistes, 7 wolues fyste; also 6 wolfy-, woolf-fist. [f. gen. of WOLF *sb.* + FIST *sb.*², of which LYCOPERDON (Tournefort) is a translation.] The puff-ball, *Lycoperdon Bovista*. Also used as a term of abuse.

Wolf's-head, wolf-head. Forms: *see* WOLF *sb.* and HEAD *sb.*

1. The head of a wolf; a figure of this, e.g. as a heraldic bearing.

2. Old English Law. A cry for the pursuit of an outlaw as one to be hunted down like a wolf; *transf.* (*orig.* in phr. *to cry wolf's head*) an outlaw.

Wolfkin. The skin or pelt of a wolf; garment, etc. made of this. Also *attrib.*

Wolf's-milk. [Cf. LG. *wulfsmilk*, MHG. *wolfmilch*, (G. *wolfs-*), Da. *ulvemelk*, etc.]

1. a. A spurge, esp. the sun-spurge, *Euphorbia Helioscopia*; so called from the acrid milky juice.

2. The milk of a wolf.

Wolfwort (wu'lfwɔɪt). *Obs.* [WOLF *sb.* + WORT.] a. A plant of the genus *Periploca*, the juice of which was used for poisoning wolves.

Wolfyt: *see* WOLF'S-FIST.

Wolhe, nolhe: *see* WILL *sb.* ¹ *sb.* Wolken (e-, -in, obs. f. WELKIN. Woll: *see* WHILE, WILL, WOOL, WHOLE.

Wollastonite (wu-lʌstɒnəit). *Min.* Named by Lehman (1818) after the chemist and physicist W. H. Wollaston (1766–1828); *see* -ITE¹.] Native metasilicate of calcium; tabular spar.

Wolle: *see* WALL *sb.*¹, WILL *v.*¹, WOOL.
Wolle bode, obs. var.¹ WOOLLBODE.

† **Wolleyn,** apparently by-form of WOOLLEN, 3.9. q.] as an alternative for MULLEIN.

Wollop, var. WALLOP *v.*

Wollow, obs. form of WALLOW *v.*²

Wollyn, obs. form of WOOLLEN.
Wolp, obs. form of WOP *v.* Sc.
Wolroch, var. WILROONE *sb.*

Wolsome, var. WHOLESOME *a.*
Wolsted, obs. form of WORSTED.

Wolt, (obs. var. of WIELD, WOLD), obs. var. VAULT *sb.*; *see* WILL *v.*¹ A WOLTE.

Wolve (wulv), *n.* [f. inflexional stem of WOLF *sb.*]

Wolveling. *Obs. rare*⁻¹ [*wolv-*, inflectional stem of WOLF *sb.* + -LING.] = WOLFLING.

Wolver (wu'lvəɪ), *rare.* Also 6–7 woolver. [f. WOLVER, or inflexional stem of WOLF *sb.* + -ER.]
1. One who behaves like a wolf; a ravenous or savage creature.
2. One who searches or hunts for wolves.

Wolverine, -ine (wɒlvəɪiːn). Forms: 6–9 wolvering, 8–wolvereen, 7–9 (6 wool-, ulver-ing(e, 7 woolverin(e, Sc. voluering). [app. f. *wolv-*, inflexional stem of WOLF *sb.*, but the formation is obscure.]
1. The glutton (*Gulo luscus*), now esp. the North American variety; *see* GLUTTON A. 4.
2. The fur of the wolverine.

Wolvish, var. WOLFISH *a.*

Wolwarde: *see* WOOLWARD *adv.*

Woman (wu'man), *sb.* Pl. women (wi'men). Forms (case-inflexions in OE. and early ME. as in MAN *sb.*²): *Sing.* α. 1–5 wifman, 2–3 -mon, 2–4 wiman, (3 wim'on, 4 -mun), 3–4 wymon, 3–5 wumman. 7. 3–5 womman, wom-mon, 4–6 woman, 5 womman, woman(n)e, 9 (*dial.*) wooman, womanne, woumman. 7 Anglo-Welsh o'man, 7–9 uman, 9 'ooman, umman. *Pl.* a. 1–4 wifmen, 1–4, 8 wimmen, 3–4 wymmen (4 wymen, wimen, wymmen), 4–5 wymyn, wemen, 4–7 weomen, 5 wemyn, whemen, weymen, 6–7 weomen, 6 wemen, 6–7 weemen, 7 weamen. [OE. *wifmann*, *-mon* mascu., later *wimman*, WIFE *sb.* + MANN, mann(e, human being, MAN *sb.*² A formation peculiar to English, and not extant in the earliest period of OE., the ancient word being WIFE.

Woman-hater. Also (in pl.) women-. One who hates women; a misogynist.

Womanhead. *Obs. or rare arch.* Forms 4–5 wommanhede, -hed, 5 wommanhode. = WOMANHOOD.

Womanhood (wu'manhud). Forms and varieties. *see* WOMAN *sb.* and -HOOD.
1. The state or condition of being a woman.

Womanish (wu'manij), *a.* [f. WOMAN *sb.* + -ISH¹.] Advocacy of, or enthusiasm for the rights, achievements, etc. of woman.

Womanize (wu'mənəiz), *v.* [f. WOMAN *sb.* + -IZE.]
1. *trans.* To make into (a) woman; *gen.* to render effeminate, to emasculate.

Womanized (wu'mənəizd), *ppl. a.* [f. prec. + -ED¹.]

Womanly (wu'manli), *a.* [f. WOMAN *sb.* + -LY¹.]

Woman-child. *Obs. Pl.* wo-men-child-ren. Forms: 4–5 wo-man-child. A female child.

Womanishness. The realm of woman.

Womanish *a.*

Womanist (wu'mənist), *sb.* [f. WOMAN *sb.* + -IST.]

Womanly (wu'mənli), *adv.*

Womanizer.

also, rendered womanly; Womanising vbl. sb. and ppl. a.; Womanising vbl. sb. one who goes after or consorts illicitly with women.

Womankind (wu·mǎnkǎind). [f. WOMAN sb. + KIND sb. Cf. WOMENKIND.]
1. The female part of the human race; the female sex; women in general.

Womanless (wu·mǎnles), a. [f. WOMAN sb. + -LESS.] Without a woman or women; having or containing no women.

Womanlike (wu·mǎnlǎik), a. and adv. [f. WOMAN sb. + -LIKE.] **A** adj. Like, resembling, or characteristic of a woman or womankind.

Womanly (wu·mǎnli), a. and adv. [f. WOMAN sb. + -LY.] 1. Possessing the attributes proper to a woman.

Womanness (wu·mǎnnes). rare. [f. WOMAN sb. + -NESS.] The quality of being womanly.

Womaniness (wu·mǎnines). [f. WOMANLY + -NESS.] The quality of being womanly; womanly character.

Woman-servant. Pl. women-servants. A female servant.

Woman's rights. The rights claimed for women of equal privileges and opportunities with men.

Womar, var. WOOMERA.

Womb (wūm), sb. Forms 1–4, wamb, 4–5 wambe; see also WAME.

Wombat (wǫ·mbæt). Also womat, wombach, or wombadey. (Native Australian name.) Any of the burrowing marsupials of the genus *Phascolomys*, native to South Australia and Tasmania.

Womby (wū·mi), a. rare. [f. WOMB sb. + -Y.] Having a womb (empty); hollow.

Women, pl. of WOMAN.

Womenkind (wi·menkǎind). Also dial. -folks. [f. woman pl. of WOMAN sb. + FOLK.] The women of a household, a party, or the like: dial.

Won (wǫn), sb. [OE. wunn.] 1 wounde, 2 wnede, 3 wunde, wunn.

Wonable, a. Sc. var. of WINNABLE (see WIN 2).

Wonde, obs. form of WIND, WOUND, WONT, WOUND.

Wonder (wǫ·ndǝɹ), sb. Forms 1 wundor, 2–3 wunder, 3 wonder, Orm. wunnderr.

Wondrous (wǫ·ndrǝs), a. and adv.

Supplement, p. 3873; Corrigenda, p. 4092; Spurious words, p. 4093; Books quoted, p. 4094

WOOD

1875 Bennett & Dyer *Sachs' Bot.* 100 Whether *wood-fibres occur in Cryptogams is at least doubtful. 1493 *Festivall* (W. de W.) 131 b, A *wode fyre, for peple to syt & wake therby. 1794 Mrs. Radcliffe *Myst. Udolpho* xlii[i], The dying embers of a wood fire still glimmered on the hearth. 1823 J. Badcock *Dom. Amusem.* 185 Bugs never infest houses..in which wood-fires only are used. 1867 Morris *Jason* I. 262 All about The *wood-folk gathered. 1398 Trevisa *Barth. De P. R.* xii. i. (Bodl. MS.), *Wood foules..dwelleþ in woodes and in þikke coppes of treen. 1787 Burns *'Admiring Nature in her wildest grace'* 13 The lawns *wood-fring'd in Nature's native taste. 1828 G. W. Bridges *Ann. Jamaica* II. xv. 227 Surprised to find their *wood-girt town surrounded by an armed force. 1590 Spenser *F. Q.* i. vi. 9 The wyld *woodgods. 1610 Fletcher *Faithf. Sheph.* i. i, No Goblin, Wood-god, Fairy, Elfe, or Fiend. 1820 Keats *Lamia* i. 34 Full of painful jealousies Of the Wood-Gods, and even the very trees. c1843 Carlyle *Hist. Sketches* (1898) 270 The *wood-goddess with her nymphs. 1581 *Cov. Leet Bk.* 824 & so followe the broke into another *woodground. 1611 Cotgr., *Laie*, Wood-ground, by measure, or quantitie of *Arpens*. 1835 Ure *Philos. Manuf.* 258 [He] has to pay..more for his timber, to protect the *wood-grower. 1851 Mayne Reid *Scalp-Hunters* vi. 48 The water-drawing, *wood-hewing pueblos. 1891 Hardy *Tess* xxvii, The *wood-hooped pails..hung..ready..for the evening milking. 1537 *Wood hoy [see Wend *v.* 6 c]. 1483 *Cath. Angl.* 423/1 A *Wodde keper, *lucarius*. 1519 *Pres. Juries* in *Surtees Misc.* (1890) 32 That noo wode kyeper take no swyn into the woddys for akecornes. 1868 'Holme Lee' *B. Godfrey* xvii. 95 He is woodkeeper to Squire Gisborne. 1874 Thearle *Naval Archit.* 27 The pieces of which it is composed are connected by *wood-keyed hook scarphs. 1845 Browning *Flight of Duchess* xvii. 78 Like Orson the *wood-knight. 1548 Thomas *Ital. Dict.* (1550), *Seluaggio*, wilde, or *wooddelike. 1713 *Phil. Trans.* XXVIII. 224 A sort of sullen greenish Wood-like rust. 1785 Cowper *Let. to Newton* 19 Mar., We..have..more than two waggon loads of them in our *wood-loft. 1796 T. Townshend *Poems* 104 For many a long and languid day Upon the *wood-moss laid. a1586 Sidney *Arcadia* iii. (1922) II. 74 The Nightingale *woodmusiques King. 1757 *Refl. Importation Bar-Iron* 17 The *Wood-Owner..divides his Wood into a Number of Cuts. 1832 *Gentl. Mag.* CII. i. 578/2 The *wood panneled ceiling. 1827–35 N. P. Willis *Idleness* 60 *Woodpath or stream, or slope by hill or vale. 1856 Vaughan *Mystics* (1860) I. 139 These *wood-pathways ..led up a steep hill. 1842 *Civil Eng. & Arch. Jrnl.* V. 281/1 To *wood-pave all the turnpike roads. 1887 *Pall Mall Gaz.* 14 Nov. 2/1 The *wood-paved part of the Space. *Beowulf* 3144 *Wudu-rec astah. [1895 W. Morris *Beowulf* 109 The wood-reek went up.] 1898 *Pall Mall Mag.* May 87 That the blue wood-reek might chase away the flies. 1869 Blackmore *Lorna D.* x, The bark from the *wood-ricks [being] washed down the gutters. 1827 Clare *Sheph. Cal.* 9 Beside the *woodride's lonely gate. 969 *Lease* in Birch *Cartul. Sax.* III. 528 Of swepelan streame west be *wudu riman. c1205 Lay. 739, I þon wode rime. 1837 *Civil Eng. & Arch. Jrnl.* I. 24/1 The *wood-roofed house. c1205 Lay. 467 Leouere heom his to libben bi þan *wode-roten. 1825 Hazlitt *Spirit of Age* i. Wks. 1902 IV. 198 Wreaths of snow under which the wild *wood-rovers bury themselves ..in winter. 1817 Lady Morgan *France* (1818) II. 309 Our celebrated landscape-painter, Robert,..assisted me in laying out the grounds, and disposing of my *wood scenery. 1479 in *Engl. Gilds* (1870) 425 Prouydid..that the *woddesillers leve not the bak..bare of wodde. 1554 in Wadley *Notes Wills Bristol* (1886) 189 Wodseller and Citesin of the Citie of Bristowe. 1755 Johnson, *Woodmonger*, a woodseller. 1828 Mrs. Hemans *Peasant Girl Rhone* 16 Sad and slow, Through the *wood-shadows, moved the knightly train. 1691 T. H[ale] *Acc. New Invent.* 9 *Wood-sheathed Ships. 1844 Louisa S. Costello *Bearn & Pyrenees* I. 282 We were glad to take shelter in a *wood-shed. c1440 *Promp. Parv.* 531/2 *Wodeschyde.., *teda*. 1577 in J. R. Boyle *Hedon* (1875) 65 For nailes and wodshiddes and two skottells vjd. 1842 J. Aiton *Dom. Econ.* (1857) 299 Take the *wood-shoots close by their roots, so that the bark may grow over the wound. 1822 Home *Fatal Discov.* iii, On the *wood-skirted lawn. 1858 O. W. Holmes *Aut. Breakf.-t.* ix. (1891) 211 The creaking of the *wood-sleds, bringing their loads of oak and walnut. 1847 Mrs. Gore *Castles in Air* vii. (1857) 48 Smelling of fresh straw in summer, and *wood-smoke in winter. 1601 *Death of Robt. Earl of Huntington* D 2, Fall to your *wod-songs therefore, yeomen bold. 1834 Mrs. Hemans *Poems, Happy Hour* 7 The sweet wood-song's penetrating flow. 1538 Elyot *Dict.*, *Lignile*, fuell, or a *wodde stacke. 1707 Mortimer *Husb.* 379 The size of Faggots and Wood Stacks..differs in most Countries. 1913 'Q' *Hetty Wesley* ii. v, The wood stack hid her from the Parsonage windows. c1820 Mrs. Hemans *Tale 14th C.* 322 The *wood-stream's plaintive harmony. a1585 Montgomerie *Flyting* 737 *Woodtyk, hoodpyk, ay like to liue in lacke! 1794 Mrs. Radcliffe *Myst. Udolpho* xxxi[i], The passing gleam fell on the *wood-tops below. 1839 in *Inquiry, Yorksh. Deaf & Dumb* (1870) 22 William..Sedgwick, *wood-turner. 1901 *Scotsman* 5 Apr. 7/2 *Wood-turning tools. 1791 Charlotte Smith *Celestina* (ed. 2) I. 228 Birds, who found food and shelter amid the shrubberies and *wood-walks. 1595 Markham *Trag. Sir R. Grinuile* (Arb.) 46 The *wood-walled Cittizens at sea. c1325 in Kennett *Par. Antiq.* (1818) I. 566 Duæ acræ..juxta le *wode wey. 1906 S. W. Mitchell *Pearl* 19 The beauty of those wood-ways green. 1850 *Household Words* I. 29/1 *Wood-weeds, river-weeds, and other weeds. a1887 Jefferies *Field & Hedgerow* (1889) 331 The humble-bee the wide *wood-world may roam. 1579 Fulke *Conf. Sanders* 587 To proue them *woode worshippers and idolaters.

f. In ME. poetry, in combs. *wood bough, lay* (Lea *sb.*[1]) = ? glade or grove, *lind* (= tree), *rise* (Rice [1], small branch), esp. in phr. *under wood bough*, etc. = in the woods, in the leafy shade: sometimes with allusion to secret love-making.

Cf. J. Hall's ed. of *King Horn* 1227 note.

a1225 *Ancr. R.* 96 Buer is þe eie to þe wude leie [*v.r.* wodeleȝe], þerinne is þet ich luuie. a1290 *S. Eustace* 20 in Horstm. *Altengl. Leg.* (1881) 212 Þe bert wes muchel..þer he wes ounder wode linde. *Ibid.* 32 Þere he wes ounder wode leye. *Ibid.* 76 [He] wes ounder wode-bowe. 13.. *K. Horn* 1160 (Harl.) Ȝef þou horn euer seȝe vnder wode leȝe. c1320 *Sir Tristr.* 2485 Vnder wode bouȝ Þai knewen day and niȝt. c1330 R. Brunne *Chron. Wace* (Rolls) 4734 Wylde walkande by wode lyndes. 1387–8 T. Usk *Test. Love* iii. vii. (Skeat) l. 53 Beware of thy lyfe, that thou no wodelay use, as in asking of thinges that strecchen in-to shame! c1400 *Gamelyn* 633 Adam loked tho vndir wode bough. *Ibid.* 676 As men that ben..hard be-stad vnder wode lynde. c1470 *Gol. & Gaw.* 1344 Rachis can ryn vndir the wod rise.

g. attrib. uses and comb. of pl. (sense 2). *U. S.*

1849 F. Douglas *Life* 59, I stopped my oxen to open the woods gate. 1868 *Rep. U. S. Comm. Agric.* (1869) 391 Any land..may be improved by the addition of vegetable matter, such as woods litter. 1880 S. Lanier *Hymns of Marshes, Sunrise* 47 The woods-smell. 1902 S. E. White *Blazed Trail* v, Bands of woods-creatures. 1904 — *Forest* xiv, He was.. comparatively inexperienced in woods-walking. *Ibid.*, A good woods-walker progresses without apparent hurry. 1908 — *Riverman* vii, Still lingering at the woods camps,..five hundred woods-weary men.

10. Special Combs.: **wood-acid** = *wood-vinegar*; **wood-agate**, agatized wood (*Cent. Dict.*); **wood-alcohol** = Wood-spirit 2; **wood-axe**, an axe for hewing wood or felling trees; **wood-block**, a block of wood, *esp.* one on which a design is cut for printing from (cf. *wood-engraving*, Woodcut); **wood-block** *v.*, to pave with wood-blocks; †**wood-bone** [Boon *sb.*[1] 6], ? a boon-day for wood-cutting; **wood-borer**, something that bores wood; *esp.* any one of certain insects and other invertebrates which make perforations in wood; so **wood-boring** *a.*; **wood-bound** *a.*, (*a*) bound or fastened with wood; (*b*) of land, encumbered with woody hedges or trees; (*c*) enclosed by woodland; (*d*) see quot. 1892; **wood-branch**, a branch of a fruit tree kept primarily for growth of wood (6 d); **wood brick**, a block of wood cut to the size and shape of a brick, inserted in the interior walls of a building as a hold for joinery (Gwilt); **wood-bud**, a bud forming the rudiment of a wood-branch; †**wood-bush** [1] [Buss *sb.*[1]], a vessel for conveying wood, a wood-barge; **wood-bush** [2] [Bush *sb.*[1] 9], name of a wooded region in S. Africa; **wood-butcher** *U.S. slang*, an inexperienced carpenter; **wood-carpet**, (*a*) a floor-carpet made of thin pieces of wood arranged in patterns (Knight *Dict. Mech.* 1875); (*b*) the geometer moth *Melanippe rivata* (E. Newman, 1869); †**wood-carriage**, a tenurial obligation to carry wood; **wood-carving**, the ornamental carving of wooden utensils, furniture, etc.; *concr.* a piece of such carving; hence **wood-carved** *a.*, **-carver**; †**wood-cast** [Cast *sb.* 13], a pile or stack of wood; **wood-colour**, the colour of wood; a pigment of such a colour; **wood-copper**, a wood-brown fibrous variety of olivenite; **wood-corn**, 'some quantity of Oats or other Grain, paid by Customary Tenants to the Lord, for liberty to pick up dead or broken Wood' (*Cowel's Interpr.* 1701); **wood-draughtsman**, one who draws for wood-engraving; so **wood-drawing**; **wood-dried** *a.*, dried by the heat of burning wood; **wood-drink**, a decoction of some medicinal wood (cf. 6 g); **wood-engraver**, (*a*) one who engraves on wood, an artist who does wood-engraving; (*b*) a name for various species of N. American wood-boring beetles, esp. *Xyleborus cælatus*; **wood-engraving**, the process or art of engraving on wood or of making wood-cuts; *concr.* a design so cut upon a wood-block or obtained by impression from it, a woodcut; **woodfall**, a felling of trees for their wood, a cutting of timber; **wood-farm**, (*a*) a farm on which trees are grown for timber; †(*b*) an office in the Port of London, which dealt with the delivery of wood and other goods discharged; **wood-farmer** (see quot.); **wood-flour**, (*a*) a substance obtained by grinding wood containing starchy matter, proposed as a substitute for flour; (*b*) a very fine sawdust obtained from pine-wood, used as an absorbent surgical dressing; †**wood-fold**, a wood-yard; **wood-forester** *Sc.*, one who has charge of woods; †**wood-free** *a.* [cf. Free *a.* 27 b], entitled to take wood gratis; **wood-fretter** (cf. *wood-borer*); **wood-fungus**, a fungus that infests wood; †**wood-garth** = Wood-yard; **wood-gas**, gas for illumination obtained from wood; †**wood-geld** [Geld *sb.*], money paid for the privilege of cutting or gathering wood in a forest; also (according to 17th c. legal writers), the privilege of immunity from such payment; **wood-gum** = Xylan; †**wood-hag** [Hag *sb.*[3]], the right to cut wood; †**wood-hagger**, a wood-cutter, wood-hewer; **wood-hanging**, 'thin veneer on a paper backing, to be used as wall-paper' (Knight *Dict. Mech.* 1875); **wood-hewer**, (*a*) one who hews wood, a wood-cutter; (*b*) a bird of the family *Dendrocolaptidæ*, a South American tree-creeper; †**wood-hire**, payment or outrent for wood; **wood-hole**, a hole or recess in which wood is stored for fuel (cf. *coal-hole*); †**wood-honey** [OE. *wuduhunig* = L. *mel silvestre*, Gr. μέλι ἄγριον], wild honey; **wood-hook**, a hook for cutting off pieces of wood from trees; **wood-horse** *U.S.*, (*a*) a sawing-horse; (*b*) the walking-stick insect (*Cent. Dict.*); **wood-hung** *a.*, bordered with hanging woods; †**wood-iron**, ? iron smelted by means of wood; †**wood-leave** (Sc. *-leif, -lief, -leive*), leave or permission to cut or procure wood; *transf.* a duty charged for this; **wood-lock** *Naut.*, a piece of hard wood sheathed with copper, fitted closely beneath the pintle of a rudder to prevent the latter from rising; hence **wood-locked** *a.*, secured by a wood-lock; †**wood-lode**, the carriage or conveyance of wood; the right or privilege of carrying wood; **wood-lot** *U.S.* [Lot *sb.* 6 a], a plot of land containing or consisting of woodland; **wood-maid, -maiden**, a mythical female being dwelling in or haunting woods; †**wood-maker** = Woodman 2; **wood-master**, now *Hist.* the master or overseer of a wood; **wood-meal**, (*a*) a kind of flour, resembling sawdust in appearance, prepared from the root of the manioc or cassava-plant; (*b*) the powdered wood produced by the wood-worm; **wood-money** (see quot.); **wood-mote**, now *Hist.*, a court for determining cases in forest law, later called *court of attachments* (Attachment 3); **wood-mould**, mould consisting of decayed wood; **wood naphtha** = Wood-spirit 2; **wood-note**, a natural untrained musical note or song like that of a wild bird in a wood (in later quots. echoing Milton); **wood offering**, an offering of wood to be burnt in sacrifice; **wood-opal** [G. *holzopal*], opal formed by petrifaction of wood, opalized or silicified wood; **wood-paper**, paper made from wood-pulp; **wood-peat**, peat formed from decayed wood (*Cent. Dict.*); †**wood-penny**, (*a*) ? = *wood-silver*; cf. *woodland penny*; (*b*) Paul's betony, *Veronica officinalis*; **wood-piercer, -piercing** *a.* = *wood-borer, -boring*; **wood-pile**, a pile or stack of wood, esp. for fuel; **wood-plant**, (*a*) a plant with woody stem and branches; (*b*) a plant that grows in woods, a woodland plant; †**wood-plea court**, ? = *wood-mote*; †**wood-pleck** [Pleck], ? an enclosure in which wood is stored; **wood post**, a station where wood is procured; **wood powder**, (*a*) powder made by disintegration of wood, as sawdust; (*b*) a kind of gunpowder made from light porous wood; **wood-print**, a print from an engraved wood-block, a woodcut; **wood-pulp**, a pulp made by mechanical or chemical disintegration of wood-fibre, and used for making paper; also *attrib.*; **wood-ranger** *U.S.*, one who ranges woods; a scout or sharpshooter in American armies (cf. Ranger [1] 3); †**wood-rent**, ? = *wood-silver*; **wood-rock**, a compact variety of asbestos resembling dry wood, also called *mountain wood* (Cent. Dict.); **wood-saw**, a saw for cutting wood, as a buck-saw (Knight 1875); **wood-sawyer**, (*a*) a man employed in sawing wood; (*b*) the larva of a wood-boring beetle or other insect, which cuts off twigs, etc. (*Cent. Dict.*); †**wood-scathe** [Scathe *sb.* 1], a fiend or monster of the wood; **wood-screw**, a metallic screw specially adapted for fastening together parts of woodwork or wood and metal; **wood-service**, service as a wood-ranger; †**wood-silver**, ? a payment made in lieu of a supply of wood; cf. *woodland silver*; **wood-skin**, a light canoe made of bark, used by native tribes in Guiana; **wood-soot**, the soot of burnt wood, formerly recognized in the British Pharmacopœia as *fuligo ligni*, and used in dyeing; †**wood-speech** [Speech *sb.*[1] 10 b], a kind of wood-mote; **wood-still**, a still for distilling tar or turpentine from pine-wood (Knight *Dict. Mech.* 1875); **wood-stone**, petrified wood, *esp.* a form of quartz consisting of silicified wood; **wood-stove**, a stove adapted for burning wood (Knight 1875); **wood-sugar** = Xylose (*Cent. Dict. Suppl.*); †**wood-tale**, a quantity of wood supplied as a due; **wood-tar**, a bituminous liquid obtained in the destructive distillation of pines and other trees; **wood-tin** [G. *holzzinn*], a variety of cassiterite or tin-stone of brownish colour and fibrous structure, resembling dry wood; **wood-vessel**, (*a*) a vessel carrying a cargo of wood; (*b*) *Bot.* a sap-conducting vessel in the woody tissue of a plant; **wood-vinegar**, vinegar or crude acetic acid obtained by distillation of wood, also called *pyroligneous acid*; †**wood-waste** (meaning unknown); **wood-wharf**, a wharf at which cargoes of wood are landed or shipped; so *wood-wharfing*;

†**wood-whistle**, ? the bishop's weed, *Ammi majus*; **wood-wind**, the wooden wind-instruments in an orchestra collectively (cf. 7 e above, and Wind *sb.*[1] 12 b); **wood-wool**, †(*a*) cotton; (*b*) fine shavings of wood, usually pine-wood, used as a surgical dressing and for various other purposes; **wood-wright**, a worker in wood, as a carpenter.

1858 Simmonds *Dict. Trade*, **Wood-acid*, an inferior pyroligneous acid, distilled from oak, beech, ash, &c. 1861 *Wood alcohol [see Pyroligneous]. c1356 *Durham Acc. Rolls* 557 In factura unius *Wodeax. 1535 Stewart *Cron. Scot.* II. 454 With ane wod-ax thair tha straik of his heid. 1625 *Reg. Mag. Sig. Scot.* 300/2 Lie schaft of the wode aix. 1900 R. W. Chambers *Cardigan* xxix, I..unslung my wood-axe. He drew his hatchet. 1837 Hebert *Engin. & Mech. Encycl.* II. 825 Two specimens of *wood-blocks, cut by Mr. Wightman. 1877 H. Law & D. K. Clark *Constr. Roads* 17 Following the experience of stone-set paving, the wood blocks of narrower dimensions answered better. 1883 *Builder* 24 Nov. 704/2 The prejudice against the use of good elm for purposes such as wood-block floors. 1908 *Westm. Gaz.* 13 Aug. 4/2 The road leading from Shepherd's Bush to Uxbridge,..the major part of which was *wood-blocked by the United Tramways Company. 1524 *Compotus of monastic property in Cottingham, Northants* (MS.), Vnu' *Wodbone in autumpno, vnam Gallinam ad Natale D'ni, et decem oua ad Pascha. 1850 A. White *List Crustacea B. Mus.* 56 *Chelura terebrans*. Sea *Wood-Borer. 1815 Kirby & Sp. *Entomol.* viii. (1818) I. 240 The little *wood-boring beetles..(*Anobium pertinax* and *striatum*) also attack books. 1875 Knight *Dict. Mech.* 2275/1 *Spiral Bit*, a wood boring tool..made of a twisted bar of metal. 1570 *Richmond Wills* (Surtees) 229 Two paire of *wood boune wheills. 1710 Hilman *Tusser Rediv.* Mar. (1744) 35 Where it fronts the Sea, pois'nous Marshes, Wood-bound, over-shelter'd by Woods, and the like. 1796 Marshall *Planting* I. 56 High Hedges, and low Pollards, are the bane of corn fields..in Norfolk, lands thus encumbered are..said to be wood-bound. 1876 Hardy *Hand of Ethelberta* xv, Ethelberta and Christopher stood within the wood-bound circle alone. 1892 *Labour Commission* Gloss., *Wood-bound Trade*, in the coopering industry making packing casks in which to put bottles for export from breweries. 1706 London & Wise *Retir'd Gard'ner* I. ii. iii. 111 The *Wood-Branches are those that form the Shape of the Tree. 1842 *Wood Bricks [see Nog *sb.*[1]]. 1763 Mills *Syst. Pract. Husb.* IV. 249 Care should..be taken to cut them a little sloping behind a *wood bud, which may be easily distinguished from the blossom buds. 1840 *Penny Cycl.* XVII. 346/1 The flower-buds are plump and roundish; the wood-buds are more oblong and pointed. 1587 *K. R. Mem. Roll* 392 Mich. v. 3 Navis Angl' voc' *woodbushe. 1896 *Westm. Gaz.* 14 Sept. 2/3 Majajie, the mystical Queen of the *Wood-bush tribes. 1903 J. Buchan *Afr. Colony* 114 A delight in the Wood Bush is apt to spoil a man for other scenery. 1890 in Barrère & Leland *Dict. Slang* s.v., Counting carpenters and *wood-butchers together, it is estimated that about 20,000 men make their living in London as carpenters and joiners. 1557 *Acts Privy Counc. Irel.* (Hist. MSS. Comm.) 39 The freholders..hathe been accustomed..to pay..certain *woodd cariages and other duties. 1885 Halliwell *Life Shaks.* (ed. 5) 521 The elegant *wood-carved roof. 1859 W. S. Coleman *Woodlands* (1862) 62 The wood [of the alder]..is a favourite material for many purposes of the turner and the *wood-carver. 1847 Ld. Lindsay *Chr. Art* I. p. ccix, Artists in *wood-carving. 1862 *Catal. Internat. Exhib., Brit.* II. No. 5723, Book-case, wood-carvings, stone-sculpture. 1483 *Cath. Angl.* 423/1 A *Wodde caste, *strues*. 1612 *N. Riding Rec.* (1884) I. 259 Chr. Wright..[presented] for building his wood-cast and laying his tymber in the Kinges street whereby the people..cannot conveniently passe. 1622 Peacham *Compl. Gent.* xii. 116 Your *Wood colours are compounded either of Vmber and White, Char-coale and White [etc.]. 1884 Bower & Scott *De Bary's Phaner.* 507 The sap-wood..has a light whitish or yellowish wood-colour. 1823 W. Phillips *Introd. Min.* (ed. 3) 320 Hæmatitic Arseniate. *Wood Copper. 1235–52 *Rentalia Glaston.* (Somerset Rec. Soc.) 76 Facit easdem consuetudines sicut Robertus de Stodlegh' preter *Wdecorn unum ferdellum. 1894 Herkomer in *Daily News* 28 Apr. 6/7 Nearly all the *wood-draughtsmen of my time have become painters of eminence. *Ibid.*, He watches over the welfare of the artists now as much as he did in my *wood-drawings days. 1577 Harrison *England* iii. i. 96/1 The *woode dryed mault..doth..annoye the heade of him that is not vsed thereto because of the smoke. 1591 R. Hitchcock in Arb. *Garner* II. 216 Wood-dried malt will make unsavoury drink. 1611 Florio, *Pigliare il legno*, to take the *wood or dyet drinke for the pox. 1696 Floyer *Humours* 190 Drinking Wine, and two parts of Water, or Wood-Drinks. 1816 Ottley *Hist. Engraving* I. 97 It appears that the old German *wood engravers manufactured prodigious quantities of these religious cuts. *Ibid.* 31 The professors of *wood engraving. *Ibid.* 32 Another large wood engraving, representing the Madonna. 1588 Walsingham in *Collect.* (O.H.S.) I. 230 Yearely *woodfals in Middlesex. 1619 T. Clay *Chorol. Disc.* 25 To see that the Woodfalls be made at seasonable times. 1767 A. Young *Farmer's Lett. to People* (1771) I. iii. 153 *note*, *Wood-farms..not being very common. 1812 J. Smyth *Pract. Customs* (1821) 388 The business of the Woodfarm or River Office in the Port of London. 1831 Loudon *Encycl. Agric.* (ed. 2) 1123 *Wood-farmers, such as rent woodlands, to be periodically cut for fuel [etc.]. 1845 Dodd *Brit. Manuf.* Ser. v. 18 The wood is next dried.., and is afterwards ground repeatedly, till it assumes the form of a rough flour. The *wood-flour is then formed into small flat cakes by the addition of water. 1885 *Buck's Handbk. Med. Sci.* I. 265/2 Wood-wool and wood-flour, the latter the finest, are made from pine wood. 1570 Levins *Manip.* 219/20 A *Wodfould, *lignarium*. 1865 Q. Victoria *More Leaves* (1884) 32 The Duke's head *wood-forester. 1899 Crockett *Kit Kennedy* 175 Kit's uncle Rob, the wood forester. 1554 *Charters rel. Glasgow* (1906) II. 513 Archinbalde salbe *wod fre and querell fre to the bigging..of the saidis mylne and hir dame. 1611 Cotgr., *Tavelliere*, the little worme called a *Wood-fretter. 1876 Preece *Telegraphy* 161 Dry-rot..is due to a species of *wood-fungus—the *Merulius lachrymans*—which destroys the tensile and cohesive power of the wood, and gradually reduces it to..a fine powder. 1343 *Durham Acc. Rolls* (Surtees) 39 Lapides pro paviamento del *Wodegarthe. 1570 Levins *Manip.* 34/5 Yᵉ Wodgarth, *lig[n]arium*. c1865 Letheby in *Circ. Sci.* I. 125/2 The..city of Heilbronn has recently been lighted up with *wood-gas. 1220 in Spelman *Gloss. Archæol.* (1664) 260 Et sint quieti..de omnibus geldis, & danegeldis, & *vodegeldis. 1334 in *N. Riding Record Soc.* N.S. III. 108 Quod ipse et homines sui sint quieti de omnibus geldis..Et de wodegeldis. 1594 Crompton *Jurisd.* 197 Woodgeld, is properly to be discharged of gathering within the forest, for the behoofe of the foresters, and other ministers there. 1628 Coke *On Litt.* 233 Pudzeld [*i.e.* pudȝeld] or Woodgeld is to be free from payment of money for taking of Wood in any Forest. 1894 Muir & Morley *Watts' Dict. Chem.* IV. 868/1 Tree gum. *Wood gum. 1569 in *Reg. Mag. Sig. Scot.* 1580, 810 Cum..lapicidiis, silvis, nemoribus cum lie *wode hage. 1569 *Charters Crosraguel Abbey* (1886) I. 195 Cum earundem silvis et nemoribus cum lie Wodhag. 1295 *Acc. Exch. K. R.* 5/8 m. 2 (P.R.O.) In stipendiis Walteri Le *Wodhagger pro meremio prosternendo in bosco de Stagholme. 1624 Capt. J. Smith *Virginia* iii. vii. 69 Let no man thinke that..these gentlemen spent their times as common wood-haggers at felling of trees. 1868 *Rep. U. S. Comm. Agric.* (1869) 15 The American *wood-hanging..has been applied for the finish of the suite of rooms. c1000 Ælfric *Deut.* xxix. 11 Butan *wuduheawerum & ðam ðe wæter berað. 1300 *Rolls of Parlt.* I. 255/1 Roberto le Wodehyewere. 1483 *Cath. Angl.* 423/1 A Wodde hewer, *lignarius*. 1867 Sclater & Salvin *Exotic Ornith.* (1869) 71 *Xiphocolaptes major.* (Rusty Wood-hewer). 1361 in Blount *Fragm. Antiq.* (1815) 368 Pro *wodehyre ob'. 1438–9 *Durham Acc. Rolls* (Surtees) 74 Pro Wodhire apud Aldyngrige, Brome, et Rylley, hoc anno, iiij *d.* 1511–12 *Ibid.* (MS.), Pro Wodbire in Aldyngryge et Rylley, iij d. ob. 1668 Etheredge *She Wou'd if she Cou'd* i. i, Creep into the *Wood-hole here. 1703 J. Philips *Splendid Shilling* 44 Confounded, to the dark recess I fly Of wood-hole. c950 *Lindisf. Gosp.* Mark i. 6 *Mel siluestrae*, *wudu hunig. 1398 Trevisa *Barth. De P. R.* xvii. lxiii. (1495) P vj/2 Been haunte the floures [of beech] and gadre wode hony in holowe trees. c1450 *Mirk's Festial* 184/30 Saynt Ion ete leues, brod and rownd and whyt,..and when þay byn frotude..thay byn swete as hony..and byn callyd wod-hony. c1440 *Promp. Parv.* 531/2 *Wodehoke, or wedehoke, *sarculus*. 1598 Barret *Theor. Warres* v. iii. 134, 1500 wood hookes, and tooles to make faggots. 1849 F. Douglas *Life* 116 Mr. Johnson kindly let me have his *wood horse and saw. 1745 Warton *Pleas. Melanch.* 315 *Wood-hung Menai, stream of druids old. 1536–7 *Durham Acc. Rolls* (Surtees) 694 Et in 4ᶜᶜ petr. ferri de stauro dni Prioris pro le *Wodyron ad 4*d.*, 26*s.* 8*d.* 1503 *Acc. Ld. High Treas. Scot.* II. 283 Payit be the said Robert for *wod leif in France, xviij frankis. 1610 in *Rec. Convent. Burghs Scot.* (1870) II. 300 Dewteis for grundlieve and woodlieve. 1805 *Shipwright's Vade-m.* 142 *Wood-lock*, a piece of elm or oak..in the throating or score of the pintle, near the load-water line. 1867 Smyth *Sailor's Word-bk.* 529 The pintles are hooks which enter the braces, and the rudder is then *wood-locked. 1263 *Cal. Inquis. p. M. Hen. III* (1904) 563, 15*s.* 4*d.* *wodelode. 1377 in *Somerset & Dorset N. & Q.* (1911) Dec. 342 Johannes Purdy tenet unam virgatam..reddet per annum vijs. vj d. pro Wodelode iiij d. 1742 in W. M. Sargent *Maine Wills* (1887) 473 A third part of a *Wood Lott for Cutting of yᵉ wood or for feeding. 1866 Lowell *Among my Bks., Lessing* (1870) 304 He would soon be driven to the cutting of green stuff from his own wood-lot, more rich in smoke than fire. 1616 *MS. Acc. St. John's Hosp., Canterb.*, For bread and drink to the teners and *wood makers. 15.. in Blount *Anc. Tenures* (1679) 168 The *Woodmaster and Kepers of Needwoode shale every yere mete at..Birkeley Lodgge ..one Seynt Laurence dey; at which dey and place a Woodmote shal be kept. 1826 Hor. Smith *Tor Hill* I. 292 A Woodmote having been held on the same day,..the wood-master and his men came to swell the procession. 1760–72 J. Adams tr. *Juan & Ulloa's Voy.* (ed. 3) II. 324 The common food of the inhabitants..throughout Brazil, is the farina de Pau or *wood-meal, which is universally eaten instead of bread. 1852 J. J. Seidel *Organ* 121 Pipes..so completely eaten by the wood-worm, that the wind blows out the dust or wood-meal through all the holes. 1892 *Labour Comm.* Gloss. s.v. *Money*, Some yards in the barge-building industry allow the men to take home..small pieces of wood: others allow 2*d.* per day in lieu of wood; this is termed *wood money. 15.., 1826 *Wood-mote [see *wood-master*]. a1610 Manwood *Lawes Forest* xxii. § 1 (1615) 207 The said Court of attachments then called the Wood-mote Court. 1768 Blackstone *Comm.* III. vi. 71 The court of attachments, wood-mote, or forty days court, is to be held before the verderors of the forest once in every forty days. 1868 *Rep. U. S. Comm. Agric.* (1869) 424 A small portion of the field was manured with a compost of night-soil and *wood-mold. 1842 *wood-naphtha [see Wood-spirit 2]. 1632 Milton *L'Allegro* 134 If..sweetest Shakespear fancies childe, Warble his native *Wood-notes wilde. 1789 Burns *Let. to M'Auley* 4 June, Mrs. Burns..has a glorious 'wood-note wild' at either old song or psalmody. 1887 S. Colvin *Keats* v. 105 Wild wood-notes of Celtic imagination. 1611 *Bible* Neh. x. 34 We cast the lots among the priests, the Leuites, and the people, for the *wood offering..to burne vpon the altar. 1816 R. Jameson *Syst. Min.* I. 246 *Wood-Opal. 1800 Koops *Hist. Acc. Inv. Paper* 88 The substance of the *Wood Paper on which these lines are printed. 1261 *Cal. Inquis. p. M. Hen. III* (1904) 502, 2 d, *Wudepanies. 1570 Levins *Manip.* 102/29 Wodpenie, *betonica Pauli*. 1713 Petiver *Aquat. Anim. Amboinæ* Tab. 19/8 *Pholas Lignorum*..*Wood Peircer. 1802 Bingley *Anim. Biog.* (1813) III. 279 The *Wood-Piercing Bee. 1552 Huloet, *Woode pyle, *strues*. 1696 Aubrey *Misc.* vi. 68 The Cook Maid, going to the Wood-pile to fetch Wood to dress Supper. 1699 Dampier *Voy.* II. i. 107 They built a Town and fenced it round about with a kind of Wood-pile, or Wall of great Timber Trees. 1883 'Mark Twain' *Life on Mississippi* xxi. 222 The seldomest spectacle on the Mississippi to-day is a wood-pile. 1773 *Holme on Spaldingmoor Incl. Act* 18 Banks, *Wood-Plants, Quicksets, or Fences. 1908 [Eliz. Fowler] *Betw. Trent & Ancholme* 19 Wood-plants flourish about this border. 1672 *Cowel's Interpr.*, **Woodplea-Court*, is a Court held twice in the year in the Forest of Clun in Con. Salop,..and perhaps was anciently the same with Woodmote-Court. 1521 *Cov. Leet Bk.* 668 That no inhabitant..make eny gardeyn or *wodpleck with-in xlᵗⁱ fote [of the town wall]. 1904 *Brit. Med. Jrnl.* 17 Sept. 662 Leisha *wood post is on the bank of the river surrounded by forests. 1870 in *Boorde's Introd. Knowl.* 99 *Wood-powder, Boorde's remedy for Excoriation. 1881 Greener *Gun* 322 In combustion wood powder is far more rapid than black. 1816 W. Y. Ottley *Hist. Engraving* I. 91 The very early *wood-prints of Germany. 1908 *Dublin Rev.* July 216 The book is adorned with charming wood-prints. 1866 *Patents, Abridgm. Specif. Manuf. Paper* ii. (1876) 427 Improvements in preparing..*wood pulp for the manufacture of paper. 1757 [Burke] *Europ. Settlem. Amer.* vii. xxvii. II. 270 A company of *wood rangers..to scour the country near our settlements. 1896 *Harper's Mag.* XCII. 712/1 The white wood-rangers were as ruthless as their red foes. 1774 T. West *Antiq. Furness* 109 These [iron forges] were destroyed..at the request of the customary tenants, who charged themselves with paying the rent of 20 *l.* by a rate which is now called *Woodrent or Bloomsmithy rent. 1844 Emerson *New Eng. Reform.* Wks. (Bohn) I. 260 The labour of the porter and *wood-sawyer. c1275 Lay. 25859 Wola þat þe *wode-scaþe haueþ þe þus for-fare. 1733 Tull *Horse-hoeing Husb.* xxiv. 402 What is meant by *Wood Screws, are taper Screws made with Iron, having very deep Threads, whereby they hold fast when screw'd into Wood. 1868 *Rep. to Govt. U. S. Munitions War* 222 These plates ..are attached to the ship's side by a plentiful supply of wood-screws, screwed into the timber backing. 1757 R. Rogers *Jrnls.* (1769) 52 Volunteers in the regular troops, to be trained to the ranging, or *wood-service. c1245 in Lysons *Environs Lond.* (1796) IV. 131 [In this survey two payments are mentioned called] *wodeselver [and] averselver [a composition for labour]. 1355–6 *Abingdon Obedientiars Acc.* (Camden) 5 De redditu de wodeseluer x li. iij s. 1510–11 in Eyton *Antiq. Shropsh.* (1856) III. 325. 1825 Waterton *Wand. S. Amer.* i. (1903) 32 There is neither curial nor canoe, nor purple-heart tree in the neighbourhood to make a *wood-skin to carry you over. 166. Sir W. Petty in Sprat *Hist. Roy. Soc.* (1667) 296 In Cloth Dying *wood-soot is of good use. 1728 Chambers *Cycl.* s.v. *Dy(e)ing*, Wood-soot, containing not only a colour, but a salt, needs nothing to..make it strike on the stuff. 1770 *Cook's Voy. round World* iii. viii. (1773) 632 Of the colour of wood soot, or what is commonly called a chocolate colour. 1222–3 in Dugdale *Monast. Angl.* (1825) V. 268/1 In curiis nostris.. shiris, halemotis, et *wodespeches. 1796 Kirwan *Elem. Min.* (ed. 2) I. 315 *Woodstone..is commonly..the substance of petrified wood. 1839 Ure *Dict. Arts* 647 Hornstone occurs under three modifications; splintery hornstone, conchoidal hornstone, and woodstone. 1235–52 *Rentalia Glaston.* (Som. Rec. Soc.) 83 Et debet habere *wdetale contra Natale, scil. unum truncum [etc.]. 1857 Miller *Elem. Chem., Org.* iv. § 6. 198 *Eupione*, which Reichenbach obtained during the rectification of the products from *wood-tar. 1787 Groschke tr. *Klaproth's Observ. Fossils Cornw.* 13 The most remarkable species of stream-tin is a tin-ore like haematites, or what is called *Wood-tin. 1855 Leifchild *Cornwall* 201 The famous wood-tin, so called from the woody appearance of some of the pebbles, was formerly found in the Loth stream works in abundance. 1796 Nelson 26 July in Nicolas *Disp.* (1845) II. 220 Not a *Wood-Vessel bound to Piombino would go out of the Port. 1883 McNab *Bot., Morphol. & Physiol.* ii. 42 The xylem..consists..of three sets of cells, viz. the wood vessels, the wood prosenchyma, and the wood parenchyma. 1837 Hebert *Engin. & Mech. Encycl.* II. 849 There are four principal kinds: namely, wine vinegar, malt vinegar, sugar vinegar, and *wood vinegar. 1235–52 *Rentalia Glaston.* (Som. Rec. Soc.) 135 Et debet cariare bladum cum careta sua per j diem et debet auxiliari ad *wddewaste. 1279 *Liber Cust.* (Rolls) 150 Q'i serra lie au pilier qi estet en Tamise a *Wodehwarfe. 1554 Norden *Spec. Brit., Essex* (Camden) 10 Places wher they take in wood,..wᶜʰ places are called vpon the Thames, westward, haws or woodwharfes. a1700 Evelyn *Diary* 5 Sept. 1666, The coale and wood wharfes. 1902 Cornish *Naturalist Thames* 212 A tug was taking a couple of deal-loaded barges to a woodwharf. 1840 *Evid. Hull Docks Comm.* 136, I propose what in the neighbourhood of Hull is called *wood-wharfing. a1400 *Alphita* (Anecd. Oxon.) 8 *Ameos agreste*, similis fraxinarie, anglice, *wodewhisgle [*v.r.* wodewhistle]. 1876 *Wood wind [see Wind *sb.*[1] 12 b]. 1901 W. J. Henderson *Orchestra* 19 Next in importance to the strings is the wood-wind, which is divided into three families—flutes, oboes, and clarinets. 1559 Morwyng *Evonymus* 323 With a little *wode woul dipte therein rub the teethe. 1885 [see *wood-flour*]. 1887 *Advance* (Chicago) 7 July 431 In workshops, the wood-wool is even replacing cotton waste for cleaning machinery. 1867 Morris *Jason* iii. 75 All who chanced to know The *woodwright's craft. 1883 J. Parker *Tyne Chylde* 6 At a wood-wright's door, where I stood on a large block of old oak.

b. In names of animals, chiefly birds and insects: (i) that live in woods, as *wood bee, fly, gnat, hornet, moth*; esp. in designations of particular species or groups, as *wood Argus* (Argus 3), *dormouse, fly, lady* (Lady *sb.* 9), *mite, rattlesnake, red-bird, sandpiper, swift* (Swift *sb.*[2] 4), *tattler, tiger* (Tiger *sb.* 11), *wagtail* (see quots.); *wood* Mouse, Pewee, Pie (*sb.*[1] 3 b), Swallow (*sb.*[1] 2 b); (ii) that live, bore, or burrow in wood; e.g. in local names of species of woodpecker, as *wood-jobber, -knacker, -tapper*, and in *wood-borer, -fretter, -piercer, -sawyer* in 10; **wood-ant**, (*a*) a large ant, *Formica rufa*, living in woods; (*b*) a termite or white ant, which burrows in wood; **wood baboon** = Drill *sb.*[3]; **wood-beetle**, a wood-boring beetle; **wood bison, wood buffalo**, a variety of American bison (*Bison bison athabascæ*) found in the wooded parts of the west of Canada; **wood-bug**, an insect of the genus *Pentatoma*; **wood-cat**, †(*a*) a fanciful name for the hare; (*b*) a wild cat living in woods, *spec.* the S. American species *Felis geoffroyi*; **wood-cracker** *dial.*, the nuthatch, *Sitta cæsia*; **wood-cricket**, a species of cricket found in woods, as *Nemobius sylvestris*; **wood-culver** = Wood-pigeon; **wood-deer** = *wood-goat*; **wood-digger**, a West Indian

insect (see quot.); **wood-drake**, the male of the *wood-duck*; **wood-duck**, a species of duck inhabiting woods, *esp.* the N. American summer duck, *Æx sponsa*, and the Australian *Bernicla jubata*; **wood-frog**, a species of frog found in woods, as the N. American *Rana sylvatica*; **wood-goat**, a S. African species of antelope, *Antilope sylvatica*; **wood-grouse**, (*a*) the capercailye *Tetrao urogallus* (see Grouse *sb.* 1); (*b*) the spotted Canada grouse, *Canace (Dendragapus) canadensis*, or allied species; **wood-ibis**, a stork of the subfamily *Tantalinæ*, esp. *Tantalus loculator*, which inhabits wooded swamps in southern U.S.; a wood-stork; **wood-kingfisher**, a name for birds allied to the kingfisher, living in woods: = *king-hunter* (King *sb.* 13 b); **wood-leopard** (*moth*), a species of spotted moth (*Zeuzera pyrina*), the larva of which bores into the wood of trees; **wood-owl**, any species of owl living in woods, as the tawny or brown owl, *Syrnium aluco*; **wood-partridge** = *wood-grouse*; **wood-pelican** = *wood-ibis*; **wood-pheasant**, (*a*) = *wood-grouse* (a); (*b*) in Zanzibar (see quot. 1892); **wood-quail**, any bird of the genus *Rollulus*, of the Malay archipelago; **wood-rabbit**, the common rabbit of U.S., *Lepus sylvaticus*, also called *cotton-tail*; also, any rabbit living in a wood; **wood-rat**, any rat of the American genus *Neotoma*; **wood-robin**, a local name of the American *wood-thrush*; **wood-shrike**, (*a*) = Woodchat; (*b*) an African shrike of the genus *Prionops*; **wood-shrimp**, a crustacean of the family *Cheluridæ*, as *Chelura terebrans*, which bores in submerged wood; **wood-slave**, a West Indian lizard of the species *Mabouya*; **wood-snail**, any species of snail inhabiting woods, esp. *Helix nemoralis*; **wood-snake**, a snake that lives in woods, as those of the family *Dryophidæ*; **wood-snipe, -snite**, names for the woodcock (British or American); **wood-star**, a name for several species of humming-birds, as those of the genus *Calothorax* and the Bahama sheartail, *Doricha evelynæ*; **wood-stork** = *wood-ibis*; **wood-swine**, a swine living in woods; *spec.* the bosch-vark, a ferocious wild swine of S. and E. Africa; **wood-tantalus** = *wood-ibis*; **wood-thrush**, (*a*) a species of thrush of the eastern U.S., *Turdus* (*Hylocichla*) *mustelinus*, noted for its beautiful coloration and sweet song; (*b*) a local name of the missel-thrush, *T. viscivorus*; **wood-tick** [Tick *sb.*[1]], a tick of the family *Ixodidæ*, found upon plants; **wood-warbler**, (*a*) the wood-wren, *Phylloscopus sibilatrix*; (*b*) a general name for the American warblers (Warbler 2 b), esp. those of the genus *Dendrœca*; **wood-wasp**, (*a*) a wasp that lives in woods, as *Vespa sylvestris*; (*b*) a wasp that burrows in rotten wood, as some species of *Crabronidæ*, or a wasp-like insect whose larvæ bore in wood, as the horn-tails; **wood-worm**, an insect larva or other invertebrate, as the ship-worm (see Teredo), which bores in wood (also *fig.*); **wood-wren**, a species of warbler, *Phylloscopus sibilatrix*, or its congener the willow-wren, *P. trochilus*. See also Woodcock, etc.

1709 T. Robinson *Vind. Mosaick Syst.* 92 The *Wood-Ant feeds upon Leaves. 1781 *Phil. Trans.* LXXI. 140 In the West Indies, [they are called] Wood Lice, Wood Ants, or White Ants. 1889 *Science-Gossip* XXV. 33 Length of the wood-ant (*F. rufa*) three-eighths of an inch. 1781 Pennant *Hist. Quadrup.* I. 176 *Wood Baboon...Inhabits Guinea. 1398 Trevisa *Barth. De P. R.* xviii. xii. (Bodl. MS.), Some beþ feelde been and some beþ *wood been. 1609 C. Butler *Fem. Mon.* H 5 b, The wood-pecker..doth more harme to wood-bees then garden-bees. 1795 Winterbotham *View U.S.* IV. 413 *Wood-beetle, Leptura. 1825 R. T. Gore *Blumenbach's Nat. Hist.* 190 Leptura..1. Aquatica...The Wood-beetle...On aquatic plants of all kinds. 1843 Johnston in *Proc. Berw. Nat. Club* II. No. xi. 78 As thoroughly drilled as ..a piece of wood that has been eaten with the maggot of the wood-beetles. 1895 C. W. Whitney in *Harper's Mag.* Dec. 10/2 To hunt *wood-bison,..now become the rarest game in the world. 1892 W. Pike *Barren Ground N. Canada* 143 These animals go by the name of *wood buffalo. 1836 Redding *Hist. Mod. Wines* iii. (ed. 2) 47 A nauseous odour ..from a vast number of *wood bugs which had been.. crushed in the [wine] press. c1280 *Names of Hare* in *Rel. Ant.* I. 133 The frendlese, the *wodecat. 1892 W. H. Hudson *Nat. La Plata* 15 It is called wood-cat, and..is an intruder from wooded districts north of the pampas. 1898 Stanley J. Weyman *Shrewsbury* xxvi, Speak, you viper, and don't stand there glowering like a wood-cat! 1677 Plot *Oxfordsh.* 175 A little Bird, somtimes seen, but oftner heard in the Park at Woodstock, from the noise that it makes, commonly called the *Wood-cracker. 1774 Goldsmith *Nat. Hist.* VII. 350 The *wood-cricket is the most timorous animal in nature. a1100 *Gloss.* in Wr.-Wülcker 131/32 *Palumbus*, *wudeculfre. 1533 Elyot *Cast. Helthe* (1541) 15 Meates and drynkes makynge good juyce...Wodde culvers. 1662 J. Chandler *Van Helmont's Oriat.* 201 Mice, Dormice, and Swine do sooner perish with hunger, than they do eat of a Ring-Dove or Wood-Culver. 1812 Plumtre *Lichtenstein's S. Africa* I. 194 Large animals, such as buffalos, *wood-deer (*antilope sylvatica*). 1838 W. P. Hunter tr. *Azara's Nat. Hist. Paraguay* I. 145 Laborde says that his first species is called red deer and wood deer (*Cierba roxa y cierba de Bosques*) in Cayenne, being always met with in woods. 1756 P. Browne *Jamaica* 433 The *Wood-Digger. This insect..digs frequently into soft places of timber, where it keeps a throbbing noise, not unlike our death-watches in Europe. 1801 Shaw *Gen. Zool.* II. 166 *Wood Dormouse. *Myoxus Dryas*...It is said to be a native of Russia, Georgia, &c. inhabiting woods, &c. 1814 A. Wilson *Amer. Ornith.* VIII. 97 Summer Duck, or *Wood Duck. *Anas sponsa*. 1847 Leichhardt *Jrnl.* v. 147 The wood-duck (Bernicla jubata) abounded on the larger water-holes. 1827 Clare *Sheph. Cal.* 54 Green *wood-fly, and blossom-haunting bee. 1854 A. Adams, etc. *Man. Nat. Hist.* 258 Wood-Flies (Platypezidæ). 1698 M. Lister *Journ. Paris* 73 Very large *Wood-Frog, with the extremity of the Toes webbed. 1895 Swettenham *Malay Sketches* 288 The fitful and plaintive croak of a wood-frog. 1882 *Cassell's Nat. Hist.* VI. 77 The *Wood Gnat (*Culex nemorosus*) frequents woods and does not come into houses. 1785 G. Forster tr. *Sparrman's Voy. Cape Gd. Hope* vii. I. 276 This *wood-goat, or, as it is called, *bosch-bok*. 1776 Pennant *Brit. Zool.* (ed. 4) I. 223 *Wood Grous...It inhabits wooded and mountanous countries. 1658 Rowland tr. *Moufet's Theat. Ins.* 928 The *wood or wilde Hornet (saith Pliny) live in hollow trees all the winter. 1785 Latham *Gen. Syn. Birds* V. 104 *Wood Ibis...found in Carolina, and in various parts of South America. 1875–84 *Layard's Birds S. Afr.* 735 *Pseudotantalus ibis*. African Wood-Ibis. 1856 *Knight's Eng. Cycl., Nat. Hist.* IV. 1276 *Zeuzera Æsculi*, the *Wood-Leopard, is a rare species, of a white colour, with numerous steel-blue spots. 1854 A. Adams, etc. *Man. Nat. Hist.* 277 *Wood-Mites (Orbitidæ). a1678 Marvell *Appleton Ho.* 542 The hewel..Doth from the bark the *wood-moths glean. 1601 Holland *Pliny* xxx. viii. II. 384 If the seat be galled, it is thought that the ashes of the *wood-Mouse tempered with honey, cureth the same. 1834 Mary Howitt in *Tait's Mag.* I. 445/2, I saw a little Wood-mouse..Sit under a mushroom tall. 1809 Shaw *Gen. Zool.* VII. 253 *Wood Owl...As the bird seems to be the only British species..more particularly found in woody than in other situations, the title of Wood Owl seems best adapted to its nature. 1772 *Phil. Trans.* LXII. 389 *Woodpartridge. 1830 Galt *Lawrie T.* viii. v. (1849) 370, I heard the wood-partridge drumming on a neighbouring tree. 1754 Catesby *Carolina* I. pl. 81 *Pelicanus Sylvaticus*. The *Wood Pelican. 1810 A. Wilson *Amer. Ornith.* II. 81 *Wood Pewee Fly-catcher. *Muscicapa rapax*. 1705 tr. *Sir J. Ware's Antiq. Irel.* vii. 20 The Cock of the Wood, which Giraldus Cambrensis calls the *Wood Pheasant. 1892 *Pall Mall Gaz.* 12 Nov. 3/1 What is called the 'wood-pheasant' is a big long-tailed bush cuckoo. 1891 *Cent. Dict.* s.v. *Rollulus*, The red-crested *wood-quail is *R. cristatus* or *roulroul*. *Ibid.*, *Wood-rabbit. 1902 Cornish *Naturalist Thames* 73 These wood-rabbits differ in their way of life from those in the open warren outside. 1766 J. Bartram *Jrnl.* 10 Jan. 30 We found a great nest of a *wood-rat, built of long pieces of dry sticks. 1879 W. L. Lindsay *Mind in Lower Animals* II. xi. 151 The Californian wood-rat. 1802 Shaw *Gen. Zool.* III. 335 *Wood Rattle-Snake. *Crotalus Dryinas*. 1805 Mitchell & Miller *Med. Repos.* 122 Fire-bird or *wood red-bird with blue wings. 1808 A. Wilson *Amer. Ornith.* I. 29 Wood Thrush. *Turdus melodus*...It is called by some the *Wood Robin. 1882 *Garden* 11 Nov. 425/1 The chief bird friend and companion of the wanderer in the New Zealand bush is the wood robin. 1784 Pennant *Arctic Zool.* II. 482 *Wood.. Sandpiper...*Tringa Glareola*...Inhabits the moist woods of Sweden. 1824 [see Sandpiper 1]. 1875–84 *Layard's Birds S. Afr.* 401 *Bradyornis mariquensis*. Mariqua *Wood-Shrike. 1725 Sloane *Jamaica* II. 18?, I saw one of these Spiders eat a small lizard call'd a *Wood-slave. 1864 *N. Brit. Rev.* Dec. 404 The baleful race of woodslave and slippery-back, those hideous brown and yellow lizards of the West Indies. 1831 Audubon *Ornith. Biog.* I. 19 They now and then descend..to pick up a *wood-snail or a beetle. 1865 Gosse *Land & Sea* (1874) 118 The pretty banded wood-snail (*Helix nemoralis*). 1585 Higins *Junius' Nomencl.* 75/2 *Coluber*,..a landsnake or *woodsnake. 1887 *St. James's Gaz.* 14 Mar. 6/1 It would seem that in times past the '*woodsnipe' was considered a stupid bird. c1050 *Voc.* in Wr.-Wülcker 363/27 *Cardiolus*, *wudusnite. 1655 Moufet & Bennet *Health's Improv.* xi. 96 There is a kind of Wood-Snite in Devonshire, greater than the common Snite. 1859–62 Sir J. Richardson, etc. *Mus. Nat. Hist.* (1868) I. 311 The Short-tailed *Woodstar (*Calothorax macrurus*)..is one of the most diminutive even in the family of dwarfs, measuring rather less than two inches and a half in length. 1884 Coues *N. Amer. Birds* (ed. 2) 653 American *Wood Stork. 1854 A. Adams, etc. *Man. Nat. Hist.* 37 *Wood-Swallows (*Artamidæ*). 1869 E. Newman *Brit. Moths* 19 The *Wood Swift (*Hepialus sylvinus*). c1480 Henryson *Trial of Fox* 894 The Uild *wod Swyne. 1785 G. Forster tr. *Sparrman's Voy. Cape Gd. Hope* x. II. 23, I saw..a herd of *bosch-varkens*, or, as they are likewise called, *wilde-varkens*, (wood-swine, or wild-swine). 1834 [see *bosch-vark* s.v. Bosch [1]]. 1824 Stephens in Shaw's *Gen. Zool.* XII. 3 *Wood Tantalus. (*Tantalus loculator.*) 1852 Macgillivray *Brit. Birds* IV. 346 *Totanus Glareola*. *Wood Tatler. 1791 W. Bartram *Trav. N. & S. Carolina* (1792) 179 The shrill tuneful songs of the *wood-thrush! 1817 Stephens in Shaw's *Gen. Zool.* X. 179 Wood Thrush. (*Turdus melodes.*) 1841 W. C. Bryant *Earth's Children* 11 Wks. 44 Dark maples where the wood-thrush sings. 1668 Charleton *Onomast.* 49 *Ricinus*..the *Wood Teek, or, Dogs Teek. 1819 D. B. Warden *Acc. United States* II. 180 The wood tick.. resembles a bug, and lives upon trees and rushes. 1869 E. Newman *Brit. Moths* 32 The *Wood Tiger..(*Chelonia Plantaginis*). 1868 J. Burroughs *Wake-robin* v. (1884) 207 The well-known golden-crowned thrush (*Sciurus aurocapillus*) or *wood-wagtail. *Ibid.* viii. 296 [see Wagtail 2 a]. 1817 Stephens in Shaw's *Gen. Zool.* X. 748 *Wood Warbler. (*Sylvia Sylvicola.*) 1868 *Rep. U. S. Comm. Agric.* (1869) 310 The *wood-wasps..are often seen resting on leaves in the sunshine. 1871 Staveley *Brit. Insects* 203 The second division of the predaceous stinging Hymenoptera, known as *Fossores* or diggers, consists of the Sand-wasps and Wood-wasps. 1895 Rider Haggard *Heart of World* x. (1899) 135 Tiny grey flies, wood-wasps, and ants..tormented us with their bites and stings. 1540 *Septem Ling. Dict.* D vj, Teredo ..a *woodworme. 1607 B. Barnes *Divils Charter* (ed. McKerrow) 1376 Now skelder yee scounderels,..you wood-wormes. 1725 Swift *Wood an Insect* 17 An Insect we call a Wood-Worm, That lies in old Wood like a Hare in her Form. 1855 Browning *Mesmerism* 7 At night, when..the wood-worm picks, And the death-watch ticks. 1792 T. Lamb in *Trans. Linnean Soc.* (1794) II. 245 A New Species of Warbler, called the *Wood Wren...It..comes with the rest of the summer warblers. 1839 Macgillivray *Brit. Birds* II. 371 *Phyllopneuste Trochilus*. The Willow Woodwren.

c. In names of plants or their products (usually designating particular species) growing in woods, as *wood calamint, fern, germander, horsetail, hyacinth, liverwort, pea, pimpernel, rasp, reed, rose, sedge, violet*, etc. (see quots. and Calamint, etc.); **wood-almond**, a West Indian shrub, *Hippocratea comosa*, producing edible seeds like almonds; **wood-anemone**, the common wild anemone, *A. nemorosa*, abundant in woods, and blossoming in early spring; also applied to other species; **wood-apple**, (*a*) a wild apple, crab-apple; (*b*) the fruit of *Feronia elephantum*, an East Indian gum-yielding tree allied to the orange, or the tree itself; also called *elephant-apple*; **wood betony**, the common betony, *Stachys Betonica*; **wood crab** = *wood-apple* (a); **wood cranesbill**, *Geranium sylvaticum*, a wild species with light purple flowers; **wood-grass**, any species of grass growing in woods; **wood-lily**, †(*a*) ? the meadow-saffron, *Colchicum autumnale*; (*b*) the lily-of-the-valley, *Convallaria majalis*; (*c*) the common winter-green, *Pyrola minor*; (*d*) any plant of the N. American genus *Trillium*, grown here as a spring-flowering perennial; †**wood-march** [OE. *wudumerce*: see March *sb.*[1]], the common or wood sanicle, *Sanicula europæa*; †**wood-mint**, pennyroyal, *Mentha Pulegium*; †**wood-nep** [Nep *sb.*[1] or [2]], see quots.; **wood nut** (**tree**), the hazel, *Corylus avellana*; **wood-spurge**, a species of spurge, *Euphorbia amygdaloides*, with greenish-yellow flowers; **wood strawberry**, the common wild strawberry, *Fragaria vesca*; **wood-vetch**, any species of vetch growing in woods, esp. *Vicia sylvatica*, with pink or white flowers streaked with purple; **wood-vine**, (*a*) the bryony, *Bryonia dioica*; (*b*) *yellow wood-vine*, a species of mulberry, *Morus Calcar-galli*. See also main words.

1657 W. Coles *Adam in Eden* ccxci, The *Wood Anemone or Wind-flower. 1816–20 T. Green *Univ. Herbal* I. 100 *Anemone Ranunculoides*; Yellow Wood Anemone. c1000 *Sax. Leechd.* II. 100 Ȝesodene *wudu æpla. 1430 in *Engl. Hist. Rev.* (1899) July 514 Ooke, esshe, holyn, wodapiltre and crabtre. 1858 Simmonds *Dict. Trade*, *Vellanga, Yelanga*, vernacular Indian names for the wood-apple, *Feronia Elephantum*. 1859 Miss Pratt *Brit. Grasses* 121 *Hordeum sylvaticum* (Lyme-grass, or *Wood Barley). 1657 S. Purchas *Pol. Flying-Ins.* i. xv. 92 Bees gather not of flowers which have deep sockets, as..*Wood-bettony. 1747 Wesley *Prim. Physick* (1762) 117 Apply Wood Betony bruised. 1712 J. James tr. *Le Blond's Gardening* 152 The Box proper for planting Palisades, is the *Wood-Box. 14.. *Nom.* in Wr.-Wülcker 715/38 *Hec arbitus*, *wodcrabtre. 1483 *Cath. Angl.* 423/1 A Wodde crab, *acroma*. 1525 *Grete Herbal* cclxxxiii. (1529) Q ij, Wood crabbes, or wyldynges. 1796 Withering *Brit. Plants* (ed. 3) III. 602 *Geranium batrachoides alterum*...*Wood Cranesbill. 1863 Baring-Gould *Iceland* 214 A hill purpled with wood cranesbill. 1884 Miller *Plant-n.*, *Aspidium nevadense*, Nevada *Wood-fern. *Ibid.*, *Polypodium vulgare*, Adder's Fern, Common Polypody,..Wood Fern. 1844 Whittier *Pumpkin* 26 When *wood-grapes were purpling. 1597 Gerarde *Herbal* i. vi. 7 *Wood grasse hath many thicke and threadie rootes. *Ibid.* 8 *Gramen sylvaticum*..is called in our toong Wood grasse or Shadow grasse. 1882 *Proc. Berw. Nat. Club* IX. No. iii. 475 *Listera ovata* was plentiful, as well as *Calamintha Clinopodium*, and several wood-grasses. 1597 Gerarde *Herbal* ii. ccccxlii. 957 *Wood Horse taile. 1871 Ruskin *Fors Clav.* vi. 7 The *wood-hyacinth is the best English representative of the tribe of flowers which the Greeks called 'Asphodel'. a1400 *Stockholm Med. MS.* ii. 517 in *Anglia* XVIII. 320 *Wode-liiie with..Blo purpre flowres, no lefe on stele. 1579 Langham *Gard. Health* 679 Wood-lillie, or Lillie conuaile. 1882 *Garden* 20 May 352/1 The Virginian Cowslip..attains true development in semi-shady spots..and so does the large white Wood Lily. 1884 Miller *Plant-n.*, *Pyrola minor*, Common Winter-green, Wood Lily. *Ibid.*, *Trillium*, American Wood-lily. c1000 *Sax. Leechd.* II. 22 Ȝenim..*wudumerce. c1265 *Voc. Plants* in Wr.-Wülcker 554/8 *Saniculum, i. sanicle, i.* wudemerch. a1387 *Sinon. Barthol.* (Anecd. Oxon.) 38 *Sanicula*, i. wodemerche. 1597 Gerarde *Herbal* Suppl., Wood March is Sanickle. c1265 *Voc. Plants* in Wr.-Wülcker 557/20 *Origanum, i. puliol real, i.* *wde-minte. 1525 *Grete Herbal* xlviii. (1529) C v b, Ameos, *woodnep, or penywort. 1599 Gerarde *Catal. in horto* 19 *Sison*. Wood Nep. 1597 — *Herbal* ii. lviii. 279 The later Herbarists haue named this plant *Dulcamara, Amaradulcis*, and *Amaradulcis*..we call it Bitter sweete, and *Woodnightshade. 1578 *Wood Nut tree [see Hazel [1] 1]. 1634 T. Johnson *Merc. Bot.* 24 *Astragalus sylvaticus*. *Wood-pease, or Heath-pease. 1820 Hogg *Tales, Bridal of Polmood* (1836) II. 82 Gathering *wood-rasps for a delicate preserve. 1816–20 T. Green *Univ. Herbal* I. 129 *Arundo Calamagrostis*. *Wood Reed-grass. c1000 *Sax. Leechd.* II. 90 Ȝenim *wudu rosan. 1614 Markham *Cheap Husb.* Table Hard Words, Woodrose or wilde-Eglantine. 1705 tr. *Cowley's Plants* Wks. 1711 III. 363 Nought by Experience than the Wood-Rose found, Better to cure a mad Dog's poisonous Wound. 1597 Gerarde *Herbal* i. xvi. 20 *Wood Rushie grasse. 1816–20 T. Green *Univ. Herbal* I. 256 *Carex Sylvatica*; *Wood Sedge. 1597 Gerarde *Herbal* ii. cxxxii. 403 Sweete *wood Spurge...Vnsauorie wood Spurge. 1707 *Curios. Husb. & Gard.* 154 Spurges of Different Kinds..the Wood-Spurge, the Cipress-Spurge, and the Mirtle-Spurge. a1860 Rossetti *Songs, Woodspurge* 12 Among those few..The woodspurge flowered, three cups in one. 1731 Miller *Gard. Dict.*, *Fragaria vulgaris*. Common or *Wood-Strawberry. 1766 *Complete Farmer* s.v. *Pulse* 6 G 1/2 Dr. Lister..recommends for the improvement of sandy, light ground,..all plants of the..pea kind, and particularly..the *wood vetch. 1813 Scott *Rokeby* iv. ii, Where profuse the wood-vetch clings Round ash and elm,..Its pale and azure-pencill'd flower Should canopy Titania's bower. 1861 Miss Pratt *Flower. Pl.* II. 312 This Bryony is commonly called also Wild Vine, or *Wood-vine. 1866 *Treas. Bot.* s.v., Woodvine, Yellow, *Morus calcar galli*.

Wood, *a.* (*sb.*[2], *adv.*) *Obs.* exc. *dial.* or *rare arch.* Forms: 1–6 (9 *Sc.*) wod, 3–7 (9 *arch.*) wode, (4 *Sc.* vode), 4–5 wood, 4–6 woode, woud(e, wodde, (5 ode, oothe, *Sc.* woide, void, 5–7 *Sc.* woid), 6 wodd, (oode, wyd, *Sc.* vod, wuid), 6–7 woodde, (6, 9 *Sc.* wid, 7 would, 8– *Sc.* and *dial.* wud), 4– wood. [OE. *wód* = OHG. *wuot* (in *ferwuot* raging, frantic), ON. *óðr*, Goth. *wôþ-*, *wôþs* possessed (cf. OHG., MHG. *wuot*, G. *wut* rage); f. Teut. *wôð-* (to which belong also OE. *wóþ* song, sound, ON. *óðr* poetry, and Woden):—Indo-Eur. *wāt-*, represented by L. *vātēs* seer, poet, OIr. *fáith* poet, W. *gwawd* song of praise, the fundamental meaning being 'to be excited or inspired'. From the mutated stem are OE. *wéde* mad, *wédan* Wede *v.*, *wéden* in Wedenonfa', Widdendream. The form *oothe* is from Scand. Compounds are Brain-wood, Red-wood *a.*]

1. Out of one's mind, insane, lunatic: = Mad *a.* 1.

c725 *Corpus Gloss.* (Hessels) E 249 *Epilenticus*, woda. c1000 *Ags. Gosp.* John x. 21 Ne synt na þis wodes mannes word. c1200 Ormin 15506 He draf ut off wode menn Defless. 1303 R. Brunne *Handl. Synne* 11026 A wode man touched on hys bere,..And a-none he hadde botenyng. c1350 *Will. Palerne* 554 Ȝif i told him treuli my tene..He wold wene i were wod. c1430 *Hymns Virgin* (1867) 46 Woode men, he ȝeueþ hem þer mynde, And makiþ mesels hool. c1440 *York Myst.* xi. 334 His folke sall no ferre Yf he go welland woode. c1440 *Promp. Parv.* 372/2 Oothe, or woode, *amens*. 1540 Hyrde tr. *Vives' Instr. Chr. Wom.* (1592) G, They bee bitten of the wood dog the devil, & be fallen wood themselves. 1572 *Satir. Poems Reform.* xxxviii. 101 Anis wod and ay the war. 1590 Spenser *F. Q.* i. iv. 34 Through vnaduized rashnesse woxen wood. 1609 Skene *Reg. Maj.* 82 b, Gif any man is Lunatick, woodde, or furious, with space of manifest wit and judgement betwix ilk time. 1627 J. Taylor (Water P.) *Armado* D 1 b, In the North parts of England,..when they thinke that a man is distracted or frenzy, they will say the man is Wood. 1724 Ramsay *Tea-t. Misc.* (1733) I. 86 The wife was wood, and out o' her wit. c1730 — *Betty & Kate* iv, That's like to put us wood. 1816 Scott *Old Mort.* xxxvii, Some folk say, that pride and anger hae driven him clean wud. 1828 *Craven Gloss.*, *Wood*, mad, rhyming with *food*. This word is rarely used. 1843 Lytton *Last Bar.* i. ix, Am I dement? Stark wode?

b. Of a dog or other beast: Rabid: = Mad *a.* 6.

c1000 *Sax. Leechd.* I. 4 Wið woden hundes slite. 1398 Trevisa *Barth. De P. R.* xii. iv. (Tollem. MS.), [Honey] heleþ þe bitynge of a wood hounde. 1481 Caxton *Reynard* xviii. (Arb.) 44 Ye sawe neuer wood dogges do more harme. 1549 *Compl. Scot.* vi. 57 Quhen it [*sc.* the dog-star] ringis in our hemispere, than dogis ar in dangeir to ryn vod. 1551 Turner *Herbal* i. B v, Garlyke..is good agaynst the bitinges of madd or wood beastes. 1608 *Melrose Regality Rec.* (S.H.S. 1914) 60 Scho [*sc.* a mare] ran woid and drouneit hirself in Tueid. 1610 Fletcher *Faithf. Sheph.* ii, Bitten by a wood-Dogs venom'd tooth. 1733 *Culross Town Rec.* (MS.), There has been some wood dogs going through the town. 1856 G. Henderson *Pop. Rhymes* 58 The bull ran wud. a1869 Spence *Braes of Carse* (1898) 181 The dog ran wud that barkit at her.

c. In phr. of comparison, often expressing fury or violence (cf. 3): e.g. *as (if) he* (etc.) *were wood*; *as* or *like wood* (cf. Mad *a.* 1 c).

c1220 *Bestiary* 338 We brennen in mod, And wurðen so we weren wod. c1300 *Havelok* 508 Starinde als he were wod. 1340 *Ayenb.* 140 Hi yerneþ hi lheapeþ ase wode. c1420 *Chron. Vilod.* 3859 He cryedde & rorede as þaw he were wode. a1450 *Knt. de la Tour* xxviii, They..beganne to crye lyke wode folke. c1460 *Play Sacram.* 403 in *Non-Cycle Myst. Plays* (1909) 70 Yt bledyth as yt were woode, I wys. a1510 Douglas *K. Hart* i. 224 Thai preik, thai prance, as princis that war woude. 1568 T. Howell *Newe Sonets* (1879) 121 From me he fled as woode. 1591 Shaks. *Two Gent.* ii. iii. 30 Like a would-woman. 1647 H. More *Song of Soul* i. ii. xciii, Thou..rav'st as thou wert wood. 1721 Ramsay *To Earl Dalhousie* 13 Some like to..gar the Courser rin like wood.

d. With qualification, as *half, near* (*nigh*), *worse than*, etc., the combined phrase becoming virtually equivalent to one of the derived senses below.

1297 R. Glouc. (Rolls) 3840 He was ney uor wraþþe wod. c1350 *Will. Palerne* 36 He gan to berke on þat barn..Þat it wax neiȝ of his witt wod for fere. 14.. *Childh. Jesus* 133 in Horstm. *Altengl. Leg.* (1878) 113 Frawdys was wroþe & nydel ode [*v.r.* nerehande wode]. c1440 *Gesta Rom.* xxvi. 99 Þe knight was halfe woode for wo. c1470 Henry *Wallace* vi. 418 In propyr ire he wox ner wode for teyne.

2. Going beyond all reasonable bounds; utterly senseless; extremely rash or reckless, wild; vehemently excited: = Mad *a.* 2, 4, 7.

c900 Ælfred *Solil. August.* (1922) 25 Hwa is swa wod þæt he dyrre cweðan þæt God ne se æce? c1205 Lay. 1714 Swa wod he was to fehte. a1225 *Ancr. R.* 120 Þet tu schalt demen þi suluen wod, þo þu þer touward þouhtest. 1340 Hampole *Pr. Consc.* 99 Þat man may be halden wode, þat cheses þe ille and leves þe gude. ? a1366 Chaucer *Rom. Rose* 203 Coueitise is euere wode, To gripen other folkis gode. 1390 Gower *Conf.* I. 164 Aweie he fledde..As he that was for love wod. c1460 *Pride of Life* 409 in *Non-Cycle Myst. Plays* 104 Be he so hardy or so wode In his londe to aryue, He wol se his herte blode. c1430 Lydg. *Min. Poems* (Percy Soc.) 76 A woode wisdom, and a wise woodenesse. 1435 Misyn *Fire of Love* ii. viii. 89 Wode luste, made lufe. 1509 Barclay *Shyp of Folys* (1874) I. 116 Whiche of theyr myndes ar so blynde and wode And so reted in theyr errour and foly. 1579 Spenser *Sheph. Cal.* Mar. 55 Thelf was so wanton and so wood. 1584 *Mirr. Mag.* 26 b, Incontinent desire maketh him wood of their societie. 1617 Collins *Def. Bp. Ely* ii. x. 413 Vnles you wil be so wood now, as to adde brutish Ubiquitisme, to your barbarous Cyclopisme. a1708 T. Ward *Eng. Ref.* 14 What sees he in her, he's so wood for? 1818 Scott *Rob Roy* xiv, The folk in Lunnun are a' clean wud about this bit job. 1895 Crockett *Men of Moss-Hags* liv. 382 The lassie's gane wud! There's nae reason in her.

¶**b.** Used inaccurately to render L. *furialis*.

1387 Trevisa *Higden* (Rolls) I. 197 In þat lond is a lake wonderful and wood [L. *furialis*], for who þat drynkeþ þerof he schal brenne in woodnesse of leccherie.

3. a. Extremely fierce or violent, ferocious; irascible, passionate.

a1225 *Ancr. R.* 66 Monie cumeð..ischrud mid lombes fleose, & beoð wode wulues. 1340 Hampole *Pr. Consc.* 2224 Als wode lyons þai sal þan fare. 1435 Misyn *Fire of Love* ii. viii. 89 A scheep cled in foxis skyn, & a dowe wodar þen any wode best. c1480 Henryson *Cock & Fox* 195 A nyce proud man, void and vaneglorious. 1538 Starkey *England* (1878) 12 Ther ys no best..so wyld, oode, or cruel, but to man by wysdom he ys subduyd. 1556 Lauder *Tractate of Kyngis* 286 Ȝe sulde nocht chuse vnto that cure Ane Vinolent nor wod Pasture. 1590 Barrough *Meth. Phisick* i. xxvii. (1596) 44 They that haue this disease [*sc.* mania] be wood & vnruly like wilde beasts. 1747 Upton *New Canto Spenser's F. Q.* xxvi, Guileful Dissimulation, and pale Fear, And Discord wood.

b. Violently angry or irritated; enraged, furious.

c1205 Lay. 2189 Humber wes swa swiðe wod for al þat lond on him stod. 1297 R. Glouc. (Rolls) 5979 Suan..þo he hurde of þis cas Made him wroþ & wod ynou. c1380 Wyclif *Wks.* (1880) 25 Þei..ben wode ȝif men speken treuly aȝenst their cursed synnes. 1422 Yonge tr. *Secr. Secr.* 229 Tho that haue a brandynge colure like the lye of fyre, lightly wexen woode. 1481 Caxton *Godfrey* lxvii. 112 The gretestedes..becam alle araged and wood for thurst. a1540 Barnes *Wks.* (1573) 282 Yᵉ more it is preached the more they grudge, and the woodder bee they. a1578 Lindesay (Pitscottie) *Chron. Scot.* (S.T.S.) I. 146 To quhome scho turnit about witht ane wode and furious contienance. 1590 Shaks. *Mids. N.* ii. i. 192 Heere am I, and wood within this wood, Because I cannot meet my Hermia. 1654 Gayton *Pleas. Notes* iv. xix. 267 Be not thou wood too, nor a jot inraged. 1682 Shadwell *Lanc. Witches* i, Pray now do not say ought to my Lady, by th' Mass who'l be e'en stark wood an who hears on't. 1786 Burns *Sc. Drink* xiii, When neebors anger at a plea, An' just as wud as wud can be. 1816 Scott *Old Mort.* xlii, Now he's anes wud and aye waur, and roars for revenge. 1858 Kingsley *Red King* 23 King William sterte up wroth and wood.

c. *transf.* of rage, pain, etc. (Cf. Mad *a.* 5.)

1297 R. Glouc. (Rolls) 4415 In is wod rage he wende Vor to awreke is vncle deþ. c1374 Chaucer *Boeth.* iii. met. ii. (1868) 68 Þe woode wraþþes of hem. 1390 Gower *Conf.* I. 287 In this wilde wode peine. a1400–50 *Wars Alex.* 1168 Þar is na wa in þe werd to þe wode hunger. c1500 *Lancelot* 2695 Thar was the batell furyous and woud. 1607 J. Carpenter *Plaine Mans Plough* 193 To execute..against them (in his wood furie) whatsoever he listeth.

d. *fig.* of inanimate things, as the sea, wind, fire: Violently agitated; 'furious', 'raging'. (Cf. Mad *a.* 7 b.)

c1100 *O. E. Chron.* an. 1075 (MS. D) Seo wode sæ & se stranga wind hi on þæt land awearp. c1320 *Sir Tristr.* 371 Þe wawes were so wode Wiþ winde. c1386 Chaucer *Miller's T.* 331 A reyn..so wilde and wood That half so greet was neuere Noees flood. c1400 *St. Alexius* (Laud 622) 593 Wynde aroos wiþ wood rage. 1477 Norton *Ord. Alch.* vi. in Ashm. (1652) 98 Flames brenning fierce and woode. 1490 Caxton *Eneydos* x. 39 Temppestes horrible of the woode see. a1510 Douglas *K. Hart* i. 75 About the wall thair ran ane water void, Blak, stinkand, sowr, and salt as is the sey. 1593 Q. Eliz. *Boeth.* i. met. iv. 7 Wood Vesevus..that burstz out his smoky fires.

†**B.** quasi-*sb.* (*a*) madness; (*b*) in phr. *for wood* (see For- *pref.*[1] 10), 'like mad', madly, furiously.

c1275 *xi Pains of Hell* 48 in *O. E. Misc.* 148 Snaken and neddren stingeþ for wod. 1297 R. Glouc. (Rolls) 6201 Þeruore hii flowe vor wod. ? a1366 Chaucer *Rom. Rose* 276 She..hath such wo, whan folk doth good, That nygh she meltith for pure wood. c1384 — *H. Fame* iii. 657 Lat vs.. seme..That wommen louen vs for wode. 1390 Gower *Conf.* I. 286 Betwen the wawe of wod and wroth Into his dowhtres chambre he goth. c1430 *Syr Gener.* (Roxb.) 5777 Out of witt he was for wode.

†**C.** *adv.* Madly, frantically, furiously (chiefly in *wod wroth*). *Obs.*

1297 R. Glouc. (Rolls) 6109 Þe king knout wiþ hom was þo so wod wroþ. c1380 Wyclif *Wks.* (1880) 5 Ȝif þei.. haten and ben woode wroþ with men þat trewly dispisen synne. c1425 *Engl. Conq. Irel.* xxxvii. 94 The knyght.. bytwene twe perylle: on on halue, þe wode-yernynge watyr so grysly; on other halue, hys fomen. c1430 *Syr Gener.* (Roxb.) 4913 The king of kinges quoke woode That any shuld be hold..bettre than him self were. a1513 Fabyan *Chron.* vii. (1811) 515 The more the Kynge spake for the Englysshe men, the more woder were they dysposyd agayne them. 1513 Douglas *Æneis* xii. vii. 9 Wod wroth he worthis, for dysdene and dyspyte That he ne mycht his feris succur. 1535 Coverdale *Hosea* vii. 5 They begynne to be woode droncken thorow wyne. 1569 Blague *Sch. Conceytes* 94 The pacient hearing this..was wood angrie, and commaunded all yᵉ Phisitians to be put out of doores. 1602 Dent *Pathw. Heaven* (1831) 142 They are so extraordinarily enamoured..and are so wood-mad of it, that they will have it.

D. *Comb.*: †**wood-like** *a.* = Woodly *a.*; †**woodsek** [Sick *a.*], mad. See also Woodman [2].

1578 T. Proctor *Gorg. Gallery* O iv b, Wherwith distinct

with *woodlike rage, the[se] words he out abrade. c890 Wærferth tr. *Gregory's Dial.* (1900) 135 Þa wæs ȝelæded se *wodseoca [*v.r.* wedendseoca] man to..Benedicte. 14.. in Wr.-Wülcker 595/25 *Meger*, wode sek.

†**Wood**, *v.*[1] *Obs.* Also 4–5 wode. [f. prec.] *intr.* To go mad; to rave, rage (also *fig.*).

c1374 Chaucer *Boeth.* iv. met. iii. (1868) 123 Þouȝ þei ne anoye nat þe body, ȝitte vices wooden to distroien men by wounde of þouȝt. c1386 — *Sec. Nun's T.* 467 He stareth and he woodeth in his Aduertence. 1390 Gower *Conf.* I. 282 Whan I ne may my ladi se, The more I am redy to wraththe,..I wode as doth the wylde Se. c1430 *Pilgr. Lyf Manhode* i. cxvi. (1869) 61 Deth is a beste so wylde that who so seeth it he woodeth. c1440 *Ipomydon* 1144 The kynge..began to wode, That his knyghtes bore downe were.

Wood (wud), *v.*[2] [f. Wood *sb.*[1] (Cf. OE. *wudian* to fell wood.)]

I. †**1.** *trans.* To surround with or inclose in a wood or trees; *refl.* and *intr.* to hide or take refuge in a wood. *Obs.*

1538 in *Lett. Suppr. Monast.* (Camden) 195 The howse.. ys metely wodeyd in hege rowys. a1589 R. Lane in *Hakluyt's Voy.* 741 The Sauages..betooke themselues to flight: we..followed for a smal time after them, who had wooded themselues we know not where. 1645 *City Alarum* 13 We should not tread those Mazes of fortune, wherein we have often wooded.

2. *trans.* To cover (land) with wood, as trees; to plant with trees, convert into woodland.

In this sense a back-formation from Wooded *ppl. a.*, q.v. for earlier quots.; cf. also Wooding 2.

1807 Southey *Espriella's Lett.* xxxiv. (1808) II. 36, I was delighted with the fine pear-trees which wooded the country. 1828 Steuart *Planter's Guide* (ed. 2) 10 Transplanting could do this;..an entire Park could be thus wooded at once. 1896 Howells *Impressions & Exp.* 6 The primeval forests densely wooding the vast levels.

II. 3. a. *trans.* To supply with wood for fuel; to load (a vessel) with wood.

1628 in Foster *Engl. Factories India* (1909) III. 260 Wee woodded and ballasted our shipps. 1712 E. Cooke *Voy. S. Sea* 117 This Island where we careen'd, wooded, water'd, and fitted our Ships. 1748 *Anson's Voy.* i. v. 42 Our next employment was wooding and watering our squadron. 1804 Nelson 22 Mar. in Nicolas *Disp.* (1845) V. 471 Seahorse being in want of wood, to be ordered..to the Island of Asinara, to cut wood, for which purpose she may remain forty-eight hours. In much less time the Victory could be wooded. 1902 Lennox *James Chalmers* x. 72 The people helped in wooding the vessel.

b. *intr.* To procure or take in a supply of wood for fuel. Also (in mod. use) with *up*.

1630 Capt. J. Smith *Trav. & Adv.* ii. 57 In this little Ile of Mevis,..I have remained..to wod and water and refresh my men. 1726 Shelvocke *Voy. round World* 76 In this river I imagined we might wood and water. 1856 Olmsted *Slave States* 369 Soon after leaving, we passed the Zephyr, wooding-up: an hour later, our own boat was run to the bank,..and we also commenced wooding. 1891 C. Roberts *Adrift Amer.* 220 We went on down the river,..stopping.. occasionally to 'wood up', as taking in fuel was termed. 1921 W. P. Livingstone *Laws of Livingstonia* 56 The vessel was wooding..with rosemary and ebony logs.

4. Bowls. *To be wooded*: see quot.

1897 *Encycl. Sport* I. 130/2 The jack is said to be 'wooded' when surrounded by bowls.

5. *trans.* To furnish with a wooden support; to prop with wood.

1918 *Glasgow Her.* 14 June 6 Simpson wooded the place [in a coal-mine] temporarily, in order..to prevent a further fall.

Wood, obs. form of Woad.

†**Woodage.** *Obs. rare.* [f. Wood *sb.*[1] + -age.]

1611 Cotgr., *Lignade*, woodage; prouision of wood.

Woo·d-ash, *pl.* **-ashes.** [Wood *sb.*[1], Ash *sb.*[2]] The ash or ashes of burnt wood.

1748 *Anson's Voy.* ii. ii. 135 This oil served..,when mixed with wood-ashes, to supply the use of tallow. 1836 C. Wordsworth *Athens* v. (1855) 26 Kneading some cakes to be placed among the wood-ashes of the fire, and baked. 1884 *Littell's Living Age* 659 Natives who had rubbed themselves with wood-ash until their complexions were 'the color of slate-pencil'.

¶ See Woad-ashes.

Wood-bill (wu·dbil). [OE. *wudubil*(*l*: see Wood *sb.*[1] and Bill *sb.*[1]] An implement used for cutting wood, pruning, etc.: = Bill *sb.*[1] 4.

c725 *Corpus Gloss.* (Hessels) F 48 *Falcastrum*, wudubil. c890 Wærferth tr. *Gregory's Dial.* (1900) 113 Sume dæge sealde he him irengeloman, þæt is baten wudubill. 1356 in Riley *Mem. Lond.* (1868) 284, 3 twybilles, 3 wodbilles. 1485 in *Ripon Ch. Acts* (Surtees) 373, j wodbill. 1660 Blount *Boscobel* i. (1680) 44 His Name was agreed to be Wil-Jones, and His arms a wood-Bill. 1788 Cowper *Let.* 28 July, The axe and the woodbill..have..been constantly employed.

Woodbine (wu·dbəin), **woodbind** (-bəind). Forms: see Wood *sb.*[1]: α. 1 -bind, -bend, 1–6 -binde, 4–7 -bynde, 5 -bende, 5–6 -bynd, 6– woodbind; β. 6 -byne, -bin, (9 *dial.* wid(d)bin), 6– woodbine. (Also with hyphen, formerly occas. as two words.) [OE. *wudubind*, *-binde*, also *-bend*, f. *wudu* Wood *sb.*[1] + root of Bind *v.* (*bend-*, *band-*); cf. Da. *vedbende* ivy, and, for the second element, Withbind. For the loss of final *d* cf. *line* for *lind*, *rine* for *rind*.

Similar formations are OE. *widuwinde* 'volvola', 'edera', 'viburna', 'convolvulus', *widubindle* 'involuco', ON. *viðvindill* ivy, Norw. *vi(d)vendel, vivendel, vibendel* 'caprifolium'.]

1. A name for various plants of a climbing habit; in early use (later only dial.), convolvulus and ivy;

Supplement, p. 3873; Corrigenda, p. 4092; Spurious words, p. 4093; Books quoted, p. 4094

now chiefly (U.S.) the Virginia Creeper *Ampelopsis quinquefolia*, and the West Indian *Ipomœa tuberosa* (Spanish Woodbine).

Woodchat (wu'dtʃæt). [First found in a posthumous work of Ray's (see first quot.), where it is *wood-cat*, a literal rendering of G. *waldkatze* (Naumann) or *waldhatze* (Brehm): thus not connected with CHAT *sb.*¹] A species of shrike. Latin *rutilus* (*rufus*, or *auriculatus*), a rare summer visitor to England; also called *woodchat-shrike*.

Woodchuck (wu'dtʃʌk). [Alteration, by association with *wood sb.*¹, of American Indian name: cf. *Cree ouchek* (Watkins), *otchock* (J. Richardson), WEJACK.] A common N. American species of marmot, *Arctomys monax*, of a large stout form, which burrows in the ground, and hibernates in winter.

Wood-coal.
1. Charcoal obtained from wood; *with pl.*, a kind of charcoal.
2. = LIGNITE.

Hence **Woo'd-coaler**, **-collier**, a maker of or dealer in 'wood-coal' (sense 1): = COLLIER 1, 2.

Woodcock (wu'dkɒk). Forms: see WOOD and COCK *sb.*¹; also 2–3 **wide cok**, 4 **wodcock**, 6 **wodkoke**, 6 **wodkoos**, Sc. **widcok**. (Late OE. *wudu-*, *cwudecoc*, (1 WOOD *sb.*¹ and COCK *sb.*¹) Appears in OF. as *buitcocs*, *witcocs*, *videcoc*, etc., and in Norman dial. as *videcoq*.)

Wood-cutter (wu'dkʌtəʒ).
1. One who cuts wood; one who cuts down or fells trees, or cuts off their branches, for fuel; a wood-hewer.
2. A maker of woodcuts, a wood-engraver.

Wood-cutting (wu'dkʌtɪŋ).
1. Wood-engraving. Also *attrib.*

Wooden (wu'd'n). *a.* Also 6–7 **wodden**, **woodden**, 6–8 **wouden**. [f. WOOD *sb.*¹ + -EN⁴.]
I. 1. Made of or consisting of wood.

Woo'der (wu'dəʒ). *Obs.* [OE. *wuders*, f. *wudian* to cut wool; later directly f. WOOD *sb.*¹ or *v.* + -ER¹.] A wool-gatherer.

Woo'd-evil. [f. WOOD *a.* + EVIL *sb.*] Name for dysentery or a similar disease in sheep and cattle; also called *moor-evil* or *black-leg*.

Woodhouse, var. WOODWOSE.

Woodie, var. WIDDY; *obs.* f. WOODY.

Wood-kern, **kerne**. *Hist.* Also 6- **karne**, 7 **carne**, **cerne**. [tr. *ceithearnach coille* (*ceithearn* kern *sb.*¹, *coill* wood).] An Irish outlaw or robber haunting woods or thickets; such outlaws collectively.

Woodland (wu'dlænd). *sb.* 1. See WOOD *sb.*¹ and LAND *sb.* Land covered with wood, with trees; a wooded region or piece of ground.

Woodlark (wu'dlɑːk). Forms and etym.: see WOOD *sb.*¹ and LARK *sb.*² A small brown bird allied to the skylark but distinguished from the skylark by having a shorter tail, more variegated plumage, and a shorter.

Woodman (wu'dmæn). Also 4–5 **wode-**, 5 **woed-**, 6–7 **wood(e)-**. 1. Speke I like Herne the Hunter; *Mery Wives* Exp. A man who cuts or fells trees, who hews timber; a forester, a woodcutter.

Woodmonger (wu'dmʌŋgəʒ). Now *rare exc. Hist.* Forms and etym.: see WOOD *sb.*¹ A seller of wood; a timber-merchant.

Wood·ness. Obs. exc. dial. or arch. Forms: see WOOD (also WOOD-a. and -NESS.)

1. Mental derangement, insanity, mania, frenzy, lunacy, craziness: = MADNESS 1.

2. Extravagant folly or recklessness; vehemence of passion or desire; wildness, infatuation. Cf. MADNESS 2.

3. Violent anger, wrath, fury, rage; extreme fierceness, ferocity, savageness, cruelty. Cf. MADNESS 3.

b. fig. Excessive violence or severity, 'fury' (of pain, or of inanimate things, as wind, fire, etc.)

Wood-nymph. A nymph of the woods: superhuman being imagined as a naiad maiden inhabiting woods; a dryad or hamadryad.

b. transf. Cf. DRYAD 2, NYMPH 3.

2. a. Name for certain species of humming-bird, esp. of the genus Thalurania (Gould). b. Collectors' name for moths of the genus Eudryas.

Wood-oil. A name for several oils or oily substances obtained from various trees (a) from the East Indian Dipterocarpus alatus and other species (= GURJUN balsam or oil); (b) from the East Indian Sastiwood, Chloroxylon Swietenia; (c) from the seeds of the Chinese Oil-tree or Varnish-tree, Aleurites cordata (also called tung-oil, from Chinese yu·t'ung or t'ung-tsã-shu, native names of the tree), and chiefly for varnishing woodwork. Also attrib.

Woodpeck. Also 6 -pyke. Obs. alteration of WOODPECK after next. = next.

Woodpecker (wu·dpekǝɹ). Also 7 -picker.
[f. WOOD sb.1 + PECK v. + -ER.] (Cf. the synonymous words woodhack, woodhacker, woodjobber, woodspeck, etc.)

1. A bird of the family Picidæ, esp. of the subfamily Picinæ, comprising very numerous genera and species found in most parts of the world; usually having variegated plumage of bright contrasted colours with various markings; characterized by their habit of pecking holes in the trunks and branches of trees.

b. With defining words, denoting various species.

2. Extended to other species of Asperula.

Wood·rush. [RUSH sb.1] Any plant of the genus Luzula, comprising grass-like herbs allied to the rushes, with clusters of chaffy brown flowers.

Wood·sage. [SAGE sb.1] A common name for Wood Germander (Teucrium Scorodonia), a labiate herb with dull greenish-yellow flowers, and leaves having a heavy aromatic smell like sage and a bitter flavour like hops.

Wood·shaw. Obs. Forms and etym.: see WOOD and SHAW sb.1 also with gen. 4 wodeschawe. A thicket: see -SHAW.

Wood·sour. Obs. Forms: see WOOD sb.1, 4-6 -sour, -sower, -soure, -sowre, -sour. [WOOD sb.1 + SOUR a.] Wood-sorrel.

Wood·ship. Obs. [OE. wódscipe: see WOOD a. and -SHIP.] Madness; = WOODNESS 1.

Woodshock. dial. = WOODWOSE.

Wood·spite. Now dial. [f. WOOD sb.1 + SPITE sb.] A woodpecker; esp. the Green Woodpecker, Gecinus viridis.

Woodsman (wu·dzmǝn). Pl. woodsmen. (Chiefly U.S.) [f. wood's, gen. sing. of wood(p.) + MAN.]
1. A man who inhabits, frequents, or ranges the woods, as a huntsman, sportsman, wood-cutter, etc.
b. Crude method of obtaining wood by destructive distillation.

Wood·sorrel. [Englishing of sorrel de boys, superseding WOODSOUR: see WOOD sb.1, SORREL sb.1 (3 a.): so called from the sour taste of the leaves, resembling that of sorrel.]

Wood·ward (wu·dwǝɹd). Now arch. Forms: 3 wode-, 3-5 wodeward(e, 5 -wal, woodward, 6- woodward. See also dial. WOODERD, WOODWARDE.

Wood·wax (wu·dwæks). 7 Also 6 wood-weasen, -croass, 3 dial woodwish, etc. Co-extensive form with WOAD.
1. The plant's broom or greenweed, Genista tinctoria.

Wood·work, wood·work (wu·dwɜːk).
1. Work or things made of wood; an article made of wood, or articles collectively. Obs.

Wood-pigeon. Any of the species of pigeon that live in woods; esp. the ring-dove, Columba œnas, and (now esp.) the ring-dove, C. palumbus.

Wood·sale. [SALE sb.1] A periodical sale of wood or timber from an estate.

Wood·dwose, woo·dhouse, sb. Obs. (exc. dial.). Forms: 1 wuduwasa, 4 wodwos(e, 4-5 wodwose, 4-6 wodewose, 5 wodwos(e -wous(e, -woys, -wosh(e, -wysah(e, wode-wyse), 5-6 woodwose, wyas, 6 -wose, 4-6 woodys, -wodys, 6 -woodwos, 8 woodehous, -howse, wood(e)house.
1. A wild man of the woods; a satyr, a savage; a faun; a person dressed to represent such a being in a pageant.

Wood-yard. Forms and etym.: see WOOD sb.1 and YARD sb.1 A yard or inclosure in which wood is stored; a wood-yard.

I. 1. Covered or overgrown with wood; having a growth of trees or shrubs; full of or abounding in woods or forests; wooded.

Woodyer (wu·djǝɹ). Obs. Forms and etym.: see WOOD sb.1 and YARD sb.1

Woody (wu·di). a. Forms: 4 wodi, 4-5 woddi, 4-7 woddy, 6-7 woodye, 6-8 woody, 7 wodye.
1. Abounding in wood; wooded, covered with trees; sylvan.

Wool (wul). sb. Forms: 1-5 wol, wull, 3-6 woll, 4-5 wolle, wulle, 3-6 wole(wal, 5 Sc. voll, wyl, 4-5 wowl(l, wo(u)l(l, 4-6 wouell), 5-7 woole, 7 wooll; 5-6 wul(l, 5-6 wull(e, 6 woll(e; 3 Sc. woo; also 1 wull, wal; 4-5 wll, woll; OFris. wolle, ulle, MDu. wolle, wulle (Du. wol), OHG. wolla (MHG. wolle, G. wolle), ON. ull (Sw. ull, Da. uld), Goth. wulla.
1. The fine curly hair forming the fleecy coat of the domesticated sheep (and similar animals), characterized by its property of felting (due to the imbricated nature of the filaments); in a prepared state for making cloth (yarn), the material in a prepared state as a commodity.

Wool-bearing a.

Wool-blade. Obs. [ad. MDu. *wolblat*, f. *wolle* Wool + *blad* Blade sb.] Mullein.

Wool-card. [Cf. LG. *wullkaarten*, MDu. *wullkaert*, etc.] An instrument (see Card sb.1) used in carding wool. Also in comb.

Wool-comb. The toothed instrument used in carding wool by hand; later also, a machine to perform the same operation.

Wool-comber, one who cards wool; **Wool-combing** vbl. sb. and ppl. a.

Woold (wūld), v. Forms: 7 wolde, 9 woold. [Related to next.] a. *Naut.* = Woolding. b. *attrib.* in *woold cord*, *rope* (cf. Wflem. *oeltorde*): binding cord or rope.

Woolded (wūlded), ppl. a. [f. prec.] = Woolled, woollit (6 wollit, 6– woolled, 8– Sc. and U.S.) wooled, [f. Wool sb.]

Wooler, obs. form of Weld sb.2

Woolder (wūldar). Also 6 wolder, 8 woolder, woulder. [f. Woold v.+-er1.] 1. *Naut.* A woold rope. 2. A stick used as a lever in woolding; also, a woman operating this.

Woolding (wūlding), vbl. sb. Forms: 4, 5 wolding, 5-6 woolynge, 6 woolding (etc. β. 5 woldynge, 7 pl. wouldens, 7-8 wouldings, late ME. *wef-fling*, prob. ad. MLG. *woolling*, Du. *wueling*; whence G. *wuhling*, *wuling*, Du. *wuling*; cf. Sw. *vuiming*), f. MLG. *wolen*, cf. Woold v.

Woolf(e, obs. forms of Wolf sb.

Wool-fell *hist.* [Fell sb.1] = Wool-skin.

Woolf's-fist, var. Wolf's-fist.

Wool-gathering, vbl. sb. and gerund.

Woollen (wū-lĕn), a. and sb. Forms: 1, 5 wullen, 4-6 wolen, 4-7 wollen, 5 -ene, wolyn, wullan, 4-8 wollin, 5 vollen, 6 wolon, woolen, 7, 9 wollan, -on, 6- woollen, (now U.S.) woolen, [Late OE. *wullen*, f. *wull* Wool + -en4, replacing the mutated form *wyllen* (= OHG., MHG. *wullin*, G. *wollen*), (M)Du. *wollen*, Fris., G. *wollen*] A. *adj.*

Woollen-draper. Now *Hist.* [prec. sb. + Draper sb.] A dealer in woollen goods.

Woollen-drapery. *Now rare.*

Woollet, var. Woollit.

Woollette. [Woollet a. +-ette.] A thin woollen.

Woolly (wū-li), a. Forms: α. 5 woly, 6 wolie, 7 wooly, 8-9 wolly, 7 woolly. β. 6 wollie, (7 wullig, Du., G. *wollig*).

(remaining dense dictionary text illegible at this resolution)

Woollyer, obs. form of WOOLLIER.

Woollyhead. A person with woolly hair.

Wool-man. Now chiefly *Hist.* A dealer in wool, a wool-merchant.

Woollyish, somewhat woolly.

Wool-pack. 1. A large bag into which a quantity of wool or fleeces is packed for carriage or sale.

Wool-packer. One who makes up packages of wool for transport or sale.

Woollyin.

Wool-staple. A market appointed for the sale of wool.

Woolsack. 1. A large package or bale of wool.

Woolskin.

Woolward. *adv.* 1. *trans.* to turn WOOL-to-WARD.

Woolwich.

Woon. *(Burmese* woon*.)* A Burmese administrative officer.

Woorali, wourali.

Wootz.

Word. *sb.*

Word. *sb.*

I. Speech, utterance, verbal expression.

1. *collect pl.* Things said, or something said; speech, talk, discourse, utterance.

II. A combination of vocal sounds, or one such sound, used in a language to express an idea.

III. Phrases.

Word (wəəd), *v.* [f. WORD *sb.*; cf. OHG. *wortōn*, MHG. *worten*, to convert, discourse, ON. *orða* to talk, Goth. *-waurdjan* to speak).]

1. *intr.* To utter words: to speak, talk. *Obs.* or *arch.*

2. *trans.* To utter in words, to express, phrase; *also,* to speak (occas. or arch.).

3. *trans.* To bring by the use of words (into or out of a specified condition or course of action). *Obs.*

4. To express in or put into words; to compose, draw up. *Obs.* exc. in 5.

5. *intr.* To pit or urge with words. *Obs. rare.*

Word-book. [f. WORD *sb.* + BOOK *sb.*; cf. Du. *woordboek*, *woordenboek*, Swed. *ordbok*, Da. *ordbog*.]

Worded (wəədəd), *ppl. a.* [f. WORD *sb.* + -ED.]

Worder (wəədəə), *rare.* [f. WORD *v.* + -ER.]

Wordish, *a. Obs.* [f. WORD *sb.* + -ISH.]

Wordily (wəədili), *adv.* [f. WORDY *a.* + -LY.]

Wording (wəədiŋ), *vbl. sb.* [f. WORD *v.* (or vbl. sb.)]

Wordless (wəədles), *a.* [f. WORD *sb.* + -LESS.]

Wordless (wəədles), *a.* [f. WORD *sb.* + -LESS.]

Wordlessly, *adv.* **Wordlessness.**

Wordl(e-, l-ioh(e, Wordling, obs. ff. WORLD, WORLDLY, WORLDLING.

Wordlore (wəədlōəə), *rare.* [f. WORD *sb.* + LORE *sb.*]

Wordly, obs. forms of WORLDLY.

Wordman (wəədmæn), *rare.* [f. WORD *sb.* + MAN *sb.*]

Wordmonger (wəədmʌŋgəə). [f. WORD *sb.* + MONGER.]

Wore, *v.* *Obs.* Also *worl.* [perh. to WORE *v.*]

Wori, obs. form of WORRY.

Wori, *v.* *Obs.* [f. stem of WORE *v.* + -I. 'Troubled,' disturbed, wrath.]

Wordsworthian (wəədzwəəðiən), *a.* (sb.) [f. the name of the English poet William Wordsworth (1770–1850) + -IAN.]

Wordy (wəədi), *a.* [Late OE. *wordig*, f. WORD *sb.* + -Y[1].]

Work (wəək), *sb.* Forms: 1–3 weorc, 2–4 worc, werk, werc, 3–6 werke, wark, Orm. werrc, 3–6 werc,

38. Work out. *a. trans.* To bring, fetch, or get out by some process or course of action; to get rid of, or effect a riddance of; to expel, deliver, efface, etc.

39. Work up. †*a. trans.* To build up, construct, 'raise' (a wall, etc.): usually with special reference to the actual process.

Workable (wɜ̄·kăb'l), *a.* [f. WORK *v.* + -ABLE.]
I. Of substances or materials : That can be worked, fashioned, or manipulated for use; said also of the state in which they are capable of being worked.

Workaday, work-a-day (wɜ̄·kădeĭ), *sb.* and *a.* Forms: *a.* 3 (Orm.) werkedæȝȝ, workedi, 4 werkeday'n. β. 6 wurke-, worky-, 7–9 work(e)a-day, work-a-day.

Worked (wɜ̄kt), *ppl. a.* [f. WORK *v.* + -ED¹.]
1. Used for turn-ware.

Worker (wɜ̄·kăɹ). Forms: *see* WORK *sb.* [f. WORK *v.* + -ER¹. Cf. OE. *wyrcere*, MHG. *wercher* (G. *werker*).]
1. One who makes, creates, produces, or contrives.

Workability (wɜ̄kăbi·lĭti). [f. next + -ITY.] The condition of being workable; capability of being worked.

Work-brittle, *a. dial.* Also -brattle, -brackle, etc. (see *Eng. Dial. Dict. s.v. Work-bracco*). [f.

Workhouse (wɜ̄·khous). [OE. *weorchús*: f. WORK *sb.* + HOUSE *sb.*¹ Cf. MDu. *werchuus*, Du. *werkhuis*, MHG. *werchūs* (G. *werkhaus*), ON. *verkhús* (in comb.).]
1. A house, shop, or room in which work is regularly performed; a workshop or factory.

Workfolk (wɜ̄·kfōuk). Also (*now rare*) -folks. [f. WORK *sb.* + FOLK *sb.* Cf. Du. *werkvolk*.]
WORKPEOPLE, *esp.* farm labourers.

Workful (wɜ̄·kfŭl), *a.* [f. WORK *sb.* + -FUL.]
Cf. OE. *weorcful* 'operosus.']
1. Active, operative.

14. A place in which mineral is or has been worked; a mining or excavation.

III. 15. With adverbs, as *work-out*, *working-up* (see WORK *v.* 39); also *attrib.*

16. *Involuntary* movement of the face or mouth, due to emotion.

Hence **Workhoused** *a.*, lodged in, or habituated to, a workhouse.

Working, *vbl. sb.* ...

Working.

b. Of a thing (concr. or abstr.): Operative, effective. *Obs.*

2. That works or labours: *esp.* that works for an employer in a manual or industrial occupation (see also WORKING-CLASS, -MAN).

b. In contrast with: (*a*) 'master'; 'managing', etc., in designations of trade or occupation; (*b*) 'sleeping', in reference to partners in a firm. Also in designations of persons or animals that work or are active in a special way.

Working-class. Chiefly *attrib.* working old uses.

† **2. Of faith:** Without works. *Obs.*

Working-day. (Also **6 warkyday**, 6-7 **workynday.**) [f. WORKING *vbl. sb.* + DAY *sb.*]

1. A work-day

2. The portion of a day devoted to work or allotted to labour by custom, etc.

8. Of a majority: Sufficient to secure the passing of measures.

† **Working-house.** *Obs.* [WORKING *vbl. sb.*]

Working-man. A man of the working classes; a man employed to work for a wage, *esp.* in a manual or industrial occupation: a term inclusive of 'artisan', 'mechanic', and 'labourer'.

Working-woman.

Workless (*wǝˈ·ǝkles*), *a.* [f. WORK *sb.* + -LESS.]

1. Doing no work: inactive, idle. *Obs.* or *arch.*

2. Unprovided with work; having no work to do; out of work, unemployed. Often *absol.*, with the.

Hence **Worklessness**, the condition of being workless; unemployment.

Work-loom. *Sc.* and *north.* (now in form **wark-loom.**) [f. WORK *sb.* + LOOM *sb.*]

Workman (*wǝˈǝkmǎn*), *sb.* Forms: see WORK *sb.* and MAN *sb.*; 4 **werkman**, *Sc.* **warman.** [OE. *weorcman* = Du. *werkman*, OHG. *werchman* (MHG. *werc-*, *wercman*), ON. *verk-maðr.*]

1. A man engaged to do work or (usually) manual labour, *esp.* one employed upon some particular piece of work: an operative; often (contextually) a skilled worker: † *occas.* a worker (in a medium).

Workmanlike (*wǝˈǝkmǎnlɑik*), *a.* and *adv.* [See -LIKE.]

Workmanly (*wǝˈ·ǝkmǎnli*), *a.* and *adv.* [f. WORKMAN *sb.* + -LY.]

1. Of or pertaining to a workman; characteristic of or suitable to a workman.

2. Characteristic of or resembling (that of) a good workman; *esp.* said of the execution of a work; later applied also to persons or animals having an efficient, 'business-like', or 'smart' appearance or action.

Hence **Workmanliness.**

Workmanship (*wǝˈ·ǝkmǎnʃip*), *sb.* [f. WORKMAN *sb.* + -SHIP.]

1. The performance or execution of a work; work, labour: in early use often, the labour or amount of labour performed on a particular task or piece of work. *Obs.*

† **b.** Creation, making, manufacture, production.

Workpeople (*wǝˈ·ǝkpiːpˀl*). [f. WORK *sb.*] People employed in manual or industrial labour for a wage; workmen and (or) workwomen.

Workshop (*wǝˈ·ǝkʃɒp*). [f. WORK *sb.* + SHOP *sb.*] A room, apartment, or building in which manual or industrial work is carried on.

Work-silver. *Obs.* [WORK *sb.*] A customary money payment made in lieu of service.

Worksome, *a.* *nonce-wd.* [f. WORK *sb.* + -SOME.] Explained in Dicts. as = Industrious, diligent; but perh. intended to mean Laborious.

Workwoman (*wǝˈ·ǝkwumǎn*). [f. WORK *sb.* + WOMAN *sb.*, after *workman.*] A woman who works; a female worker or operative; a woman who does needle-work.

Workyday, obs. var. WORKADAY.

Work-master. *Now rare.* [Cf. MLG. *werkmester*, ON. *verkmeistari* (MSw. *werkmästare*).] A master workman; an overseer or employer of workmen.

Work-mistress. [f. WORK *sb.* + MISTRESS, after *-mest.*] A woman who controls or superintends work: only *fig.*, chiefly of Nature (personified).

Work-out. *Pugilism.* [See WORK *v.* 38 f.] A boxing bout for practice.

World (*wǝld*), *sb.* Forms: *a.* 1 **weorold**, **wuruld**, **worold**, **woruld**, **woruld**, 1-3 **woruld**, **woruld**, -**old**, -**uld**, 2 **worold**, 3 **wo(o)rld**, **werold**, **weoreld**, **werld**, **weorld**, **wereld**; *b.* 1 **weorld**, 4-6 **worlde** (3 **werld**, 3 **wurld**, **worldl(e)**); 2-3 **werld**, 3 **wereld**, 3-5 **world**, 3 **wordle**, 3-5 **warld**, 5-6 **wardle**, (5-6 **wordle**, **wardil**, (5 **weorld**); *north.* and *Sc.* 5-7 **warld**, 6 **wardill**, **warld**; *north.* 5-7 **warld**; 3-9 **world**.

[OE. *weorold*, *woruld*, *world* = OFris. *wrald*, *warld* (EFris. *warld*, OS. *werold* (MDu. *werelt*, Du. *wereld*), OHG. *weralt* (MHG. *werelt*, *welt*, G. *welt*), ON. *verǫld* (Sw. *verld*, Da. *verden*); f. formation (peculiar to Germanic, *wer-* man WERE *sb.*1 + *ald* (cf. OLD *a.*, ELD *sb.*2), the etymological meaning being, therefore, 'age' or 'life of man'.]

I. **1. a.** (Chiefly *the world, the world's*) The earthly state of human existence; this present life.

2. The pursuits and interests of this present life; *esp.* in religious use, the least worthy of these; temporal or mundane affairs.

3. The affairs and conditions of life; chiefly in *phr.*, with the verb *go* (*q.v.*): *how the world goes*, how events shape themselves; *how goes the world with* (a person), how are his affairs; as (*or* this) *world goes*, as things are, considering the state of affairs; also *to live* (*or be*) *at deadly world*, to live in enmity (*Sc.*).

4. *World without* (ME. *abuten* or *buten*) *end;* later used hyperbolically: Endlessly, eternally.

Supplement, p. 3873; Corrigenda, p. 4092; Spurious words, p. 4093; Books quoted, p. 4094

Worldly-wise a. [stress variable], a. Wise in a worldly manner or in respect of conduct. Also *absol.*

World-man (OE. *woruldman*), f. *woruld* WORLD sb. + MAN sb. 1. A man of this world, a human being.

World-power. 1. The power of 'this world' (as distinguished from the higher world); secular power. 2. Any of the powers (Nations, empires) that dominate the world.

+World-riche. *Obs.* Also 4 *worldæriche*. [OE. *woruldrīce* sb. The kingdom of the world.]

+Worldling. *Obs.* Obs. A worldly creature.

Worldward (wɜːldwəd), adv. [f. WORLD + -WARD.] 1. (orig. *To the worldward*) In regard to the world; in worldly respects.

Towards or in the direction of the world.

World-wide a. [f. WORLD sb. + WIDE a.] As wide as the world; extending over or covering the whole world.

Worldy, var. *Obs.* rare. [f. WORLD sb. + -Y.] Worldly.

Worley, worlia, var. forms of WURLEY.

Worm (wɜːm), sb. Forms: 1 wyrm, 3, 5–6 werm, wurm (3, 4 wurme), 3 wrm, 4 worme, wyrme, &c.
1. An animal of the invertebrate type; any of the creeping or crawling animals; a reptile, an insect.
2. The larva of an insect; a maggot, grub, or caterpillar.
3. A member of the genus *Lumbricus*; a slender, creeping, naked, limbless animal, usually brown or reddish, with a soft body divided into a series of segments; an earthworm.

Worm (wɜːm), v. Forms: 3 wyrme, 6–7 worme, 7 worme.

Supplement, p. 3873; Corrigenda, p. 4092; Spurious words, p. 4093; Books quoted, p. 4094

Worriless, a. [f. WORRY v. + -LESS.] Free from worry.

Worriment (wǒ'riment). Chiefly U.S. [f. WORRY v. + -MENT.] The act of worrying or causing anxiety; the state of being worried or troubled in mind. Also, something that harasses or worries.

Worrisome (wǒ'risǒm), a. [f. WORRY vb. or n. + -SOME.] Apt to cause worry or distress; given to worrying.

Worrit (wǒ'rit), sb. colloq. Also 9 -et. [f. the vb.] A state of worry or mental distress; a fretting care or anxiety. Also, a person that worries others or himself.

Worrit (wǒ'rit), v. colloq. Also 9 -et. [Cf. WHERRIT, WHERRIT.]
1. trans. To worry, distress, vex, pester.
2. intr. To give way to worry; to experience or display mental disquietude, impatience, etc.

Worry (wǒ'ri), sb. [f. WORRY v.]
1. A troubled state of mind arising from the frets and cares of life; harassing anxiety or solicitude.
2. The act of biting and shaking an animal so as to injure or kill it. (Properly of hounds when they seize their quarry.)
3. trans. To seize by the throat with the teeth and tear or lacerate; to kill or injure by biting and shaking.

Worry (wǒ'ri), v. Pa. t. and ppl. a. worried. Forms: a. 1 wyrᵹan, 4 wyrye, 4-5 wirwe, wirie, wyrie, wyrye, 6 wyrwyn, wyrhy, 4-7 wirrie, wyrye, 5-6 worry, 6-9.9 wirry. β. 4 worow, 5c. ver(r)y, 4-6 wor(r)e, (5 were, weruy), 5-7, 9 dial. weary, 6 6-9 wearie, weary. γ. 4 wood, 6 3 sing. worosh, 5 worwryn, 6-7 worrow, 7 wurrow, 6-7 worry, 6 worie, 6-7 woorry, 6-7 worry(e, 6-7 wory), worie, 6 wurry, 7-9 worrye, 6 wurry, 6 worry, 7 wory (in nerv), 6-7 OFris. worgia to kill, MLG. worgen, MDu. worghen (Du. worgen, wurgen), to strang-e, throttle, OHG. wurgen, ꝩurchjan (MHG. würgen, worgen), to strangle, worry, kill by violence.—OTeut. *wurᵹjan, related to *wearᵹ-, a strong vb. stem found in MHG. erwergen to throttle—Indo-Eur. *wergh-.
1. trans. To kill (a person or animal) by compressing the throat; to strangle.
2. To choke (a person or animal) with a mouthful of food. Const. on (the food); hence to be worried, or worry oneself, (on) to devour greedily.
3. trans. To bite at or upon (an object); to kiss or bug vehemently; to utter (one's words) with the teeth nearly closed, as if biting or champing them.
4. trans. To swallow greedily, devour.

Worse (wōrs), a. and sb. Forms: a. 1 wiersa, 3 wirse, wrse, worse, 1 wyrsa, -e, wirsa, 2-3 wurse, -a, wrse, (3 -4 werse), 3-4 worse, 3-7 wors, 6 worse, worse, 7 wors, 9 ulᵹar wuss. β. 1 weorsa, 2-6 wers, wers, 2-6 werse, 3-7 wurse, wursa, 2-6 north. warse. [OE. wyrsa, wiersa = OFris. wirra, 'worsa' by assimilation), OS. wirsa (Du. wirser), OHG. wirsir, MHG. wirser, Goth. wairsiza — OTent. *werisizon-, f. *weris- to entangle, confound (see WAR sb.) + -izon- compar. suffix.]
I. More reprehensible morally; more wicked, depraved or vicious; more cruel, unkind, or ill-conditioned.

Worrying, vbl. sb. [f. WORRY v. + -ING¹.]
1. The action of strangling or of biting and tearing by the throat.
2. The action of harassing, pestering, or distressing.

Worrying, ppl. a. [f. WORRY v. + -ING².]
1. Given to harrying or raiding.
2. Harassing; distressing to the mind or spirits.

Woman, var. of WOSSUM Obs., pus.

OHG. wirsōn (MHG. wirsen, wuirsen) to make worse.

Worse, v. Obs. Forms: a. 1 wiers, wyrsᵹ, 2 wurs, 2-6 wurs, 3 wyrsᵹe; 3-6 wors, 6-9 worsse; 2 worsᵹ; 7 warse, 6 warsen. [OE. wyrs, wiers = OS. wirs, OHG. wirs (MHG. wirs), Goth. wairs.]

1. intr. To become or grow worse, deteriorate.
2. trans. To make worse, impair; injure, blemish.

Worse

Worsen (wəˈz'n), v. [f. WORSE a. + -EN 1.]

Worsement. [f. WORSE + -MENT.]

Worsenment. [WORSEN v. + -MENT.] Occas. used in preference to WORSEMENT as a more analogical form.

Worser (wəˈzər), a. [f. WORSE + -ER.]

Worserer (wəˈzərər), a. A further extension (jocular or vulgar) of WORSER a.

Worset, worsett, north. ff. WORSTED.

Worship.

Worship (wəˈʃip), sb. Forms: 4. worp, worshippe; 4-5 worshepe, -shupe, 5-6 -shoppe(6 -sch-prpe(n); 4-5 worschip(e, -ashipe, -shepe(n), 4-5 shupe; 4-5 worshippe, 5-shippe, 5-6 -whyppe; 4 worschip, 5 -chep, -chypp, -chyppyn), 5-6 worshypp(e, -chep, -obepyn), 8. 4 worscippe (5 -schipe, -chip, -ahyn, -shippe, -shep, 4 wyrschip-, etc. [Early ME. worþ, worþscipien, f. worþ-, worþship; ...]

Worshipable (wəˈʃipˌab'l), a. [f. WORSHIP sb. + -ABLE.]

Worshipability (Lit. Rem. (1836) I. 378.) Capability of being worshipped.

Worshipful (wəˈʃipˌfʊl), a. (sb., adv.) Forms: 4. worshipful; 4 worschip-, 5 worschyp- ... 7. 4 wir-, wyrschip-ful; 6 wire-; [f. WORSHIP sb. + -FUL 1.]

Worshipfully, adv. Now rare. Forms: 4. 4-worschipfully, 5 worschupeliche, worschep-, wor-chipp-, 5-7 worshipfully, 4 wurchip-, 5 worchefully; [f. prec. + -LY 2.]

Worshipped (wǒ·ʃipt), ppl. a. [f. WORSHIP v.] Regarded with worship; adored, venerated.

Worshipper (wǒ·ʃipǝr). Also 4 worschiper, 4 wor-, 7, 9 wor-shipper.

1. One who worships. Freq. const. of (the deity or thing worshipped).

Worshipping, ppl. a. [f. as prec. + -ING 2.] That worships; engaged in worship.

Worship·ping, vbl. sb. [f. WORSHIP v. + -ING 1.]

Worst (wŏrst), a. and adv. Forms: a. 1 wyrrsta, wyrsta, wierresta, (wyrrest); 1 North-umb. wyrresta, 2–4 wurst, 3–4 wrst; 3–6 worste, 2–4 worst, 6 worst, 5 vilgar-west. β. 1 werresta, 1–2 werste, 6 worset. γ. etc.

1. Most bad or evil, in regard to moral character or behaviour; most vicious, wicked, cruel, etc.

2. Most wanting in the good qualities required or expected; least good, valuable, desirable, or successful; most inferior; meanest or poorest in quality; least considerable or important.

3. What is most grievous, unlucky, painful, and to bear; a state of things that is most undesirable or most to be dreaded.

Worst (wŏrst), sb. Forms: see prec.

1. Most evil or ill; that which is worst.

2. That which is most objectionable or deplorable in regard to morals, taste, etc.

Worst (wŏrst), v. [f. WORST a.]

1. trans. To make worse, impair, damage, inflict loss upon.

2. To get the better of, to defeat, overcome, get the better of (an adversary) in a fight or battle.

Worsted (wŭ·stéd), sb. Forms: 3–4 worth-, 4 wurthstede, worthestede, 6 worstede, 5 wor-, 6 wursted, etc.

1. A woollen fabric or stuff made from well-twisted yarn spun of long-staple wool combed to lay the fibres parallel.

2. A woollen thread or yarn spun of long-staple wool in which the fibres are arranged to lie parallel to each other.

Worsted (wŭ·stéd), ppl. a. [f. WORST v.]

Worsted-man, worsted-weaver.

Worsten, worsten, sb.

Wort (wŏrt), sb.[1] [OE. wyrt = OS. wurt, MDu. worte, MLG., OHG., MHG. wurz, Goth. waurts.]

1. A plant, herb, or vegetable, used for food or medicine: often = pot-herb.

2. A general name for any plant of the cabbage kind, genus Brassica; colewort. Obs.

Wort (wŏrt), sb.[2] [OE. wyrt.]

1. The infusion of malt or other grain which after fermentation becomes beer (or may be used for the distillation of spirits), unfermented beer.

Worthing. *Obs.* [app. f. ME. *wurþ* WORTH *sb.* + Cf. *Goozong old sb.*] Dung; manure. Also *fig.*, moral corruption or filth.

Worthless, *a.* [f. WORTH *sb.* + -LESS.]

1. Of things, etc.: Destitute of (material) worth; having no intrinsic value.

2. Of persons: Lacking worth or merit; destitute of moral character; contemptible; despicable.

Worthlessness.

Worthy, *sb.*

1. Of things: Having great value or importance; noble, fine, excellent, worthy.

2. Of persons: Estimable, honourable, worthy.

Worthy, *Obs.* Forms: 3 wurðe-liche, -like, wurðliche (wrðliche, *Orm.* wurrþlike), -lich, -lic; 3-6 worþliche, 3-6 worþlich, 5 worthely, -ly, 6 worthlye, [f. WORTH *a.* + -LY¹.]

2. Of persons: Distinguished by good qualities; entitled to honour or respect on this account; estimable.

b. Sufficiently heavy or severe; deserved, merited by default or wrong-doing, condign. *Obs.*

Worth (*wɔːθ*), *a.* [OE. *weorþ*, *wurþ*, *wyrþ*.]

Worthy, *v.*

1. *trans.* To honour, or hold, worthy of (some-thing); to raise to honour or distinction.

Worths (*wɔːθs*). Forms: 4 *swirtil*, *writel*, 9 *whirle*, *worle*. [f. 2 *wurdle*, 9 *wordle*. Of obscure origin.] An implement used in the manufacture of lead-pipe (see quot. 1875).

Worthle, *as worthle-maker*, *plait*.

Wortle, *var.* WARTWALE *Obs.*

Wortworm. *Obs.* [f. WORT *sb.*¹ + WORM *sb.*] A caterpillar that feeds on worts or cabbages.

Worwrv, *obs.* forms of WORRY *v.*

Wos, obs. form of WORT *sb.*

Wose, obs. form of OOZE, WOO.

Wosith. *Obs.* Also 3 *wasið*, [*wel-sið*]. Trouble, affliction.

Wot (*wɔt*), v.¹ pres. indic. Sc. *a.* 4-5 wat, 4-6 wate, (4 whate, quat, vat), 6 wait, (vait), 8. 4 wyte.

Wote, var. of *woghe* WOUGH *sb.²*

Wother, obs. form of OTHER.

Wother-weight (Sc.): see WHETHER.

Wo-tless, *a.* [Irreg. f. WOT *v.¹*] Unknowing, ignorant.

Wotsave, obs. form of VOUCHSAFE *v.*

Wott, obs. Sc. form of WIT *v.¹*

Wotte, obs. inf. pres. of WIT *v.¹*

† Wo-tingly, *adv. Obs.* [f. *woting*, pres. ppl. of WOT *v.*¹] Wittingly, knowingly.

Wough (*woχ, wou*), *sb.¹* *Obs.* exc. *dial.* Forms: 1-4 *wah* (3. Sc. *wacht*).

Wough, *sb.²* *Obs.* Forms: α. 1-4 *woh*, 3 *woch*, 3 (5 *Sc.*) *wocht*, 4 *woȝ*, (3 *woȝe*), 4-5 *wogh*, 4 (9 *dial.*) *wow*, (4 *woȝ*, 5 *wowe*), 5 *woh*, 5 *wough*. [OE. *wōh*.]

1. Wrong, evil; harm.

2. Mining. The side of a vein.

Column 1 (p. 334)

†**Wough**, a. Obs. (or dial.) Forms: 1–4 woh (3 woʒ), 4 wouʒ, 9 dial. wow, 5–9 wough, wohe, wowe. [OE. wōh (inflected wōh, wōʒ-), of obscure origin. Hence WOUGH sb.²]

1. Crooked, bent.

2. Wrong, evil, bad.

†**Wough**, int. Obs.¹ = WAUGH, Wow.

†**Woulleche**. Obs.⁻¹ [f. wouh-, repr. OE. wōh, or *wōʒ-an to WOO + -LECHE¹.] Wooing, courtship. So also †Woullechung.

Wouke, obs. form of WEEK sb.

†**Woul**, v. Obs. rare. [Imitative. Cf. WAWL v.] intr. To howl, cry.

Would (wud), sb. The subj. of WILL v.¹ used substantively.]

Would-be (wudbe), a. and sb. The phrase would be (see WILL v.¹ 40) used attributively and absolutely.

Would-have-been, a. [The verbal phrase would have been to be, that aimed at being.]

†**Woung**, sb. Obs. [irreg. f. would pa.t. of WILL v.¹] The action or fact of desiring. Usually coupled with wishing.

†**Wouldingness**. Obs. nonce-wd. [f. as prec. + -NESS.] Desire, inclination.

†**Woulfe**. Also Woulf. [The surname of Peter Woulfe (1727?–1803), a chemist.] Woulfe's apparatus, a series of glass receivers (Woulfe's bottles) formerly used in distillation.

Woulk, obs. Sc. form of WEEK sb.¹

Woult, obs. Sc. var. of VAULT sb.¹

Woman, obs. form of WOMAN.

Wound (wŏnd), sb.¹ Forms: 1 wund, 3 wunde (wende), 4–6 wond (6 Sc. vond), 5 wownde, 6–7 wownd, 7– wound; (common Teutonic: OE. wund = OFris. wunde, wund (WFris. wounte, EFris. wūn), MDu. wonde (wunne), (MHG. wunte, wunde, G. wunde), ON. (Icel., MSw.) und (LG.), of uncertain relationship.

Column 2 (p. 335)

Wound, sb.¹ *continued.* An injury to the body caused by the laceration or separation of the tissues of the body by a hard or sharp instrument, a bullet, etc.; an external injury.

Surgery. An incision or opening made by a surgical operation.

Column 3 (p. 336)

Wound (wound), ppl. a. [Pa. pple. of WIND v.³]

Woundable, a. rare. [f. WOUND v. + -ABLE.] Capable of being wounded; vulnerable.

Wounded (wŏndid), ppl. a. [f. as prec. + -ED.]

Wounder (wŏndaᵊ). One who or that which wounds.

Wounder, obs. form of WONDER sb. and v.

Woundikins, int. [WOUND int.] sec -KIN.]

Woundily (wŏndili), adv. Obs. exc. arch. [f. WOUNDY a. + -LY².] Excessively, extremely, dreadfully.

Wounding (wŏndiŋ), vbl. sb. [f. WOUND v.]

Wounding, ppl. a. [f. as prec. + -ING².] That wounds or injures; capable of causing hurt or pain.

Column 4 (p. 336–337)

Woundless (wŏndles), a. [f. WOUND sb.¹ + -LESS.]

Woundly (wŏndli), adv. Obs. exc. arch. [= WOUNDILY.]

Woundrous, obs. form of WONDROUS.

Wounds (wŏndz), int. Obs. exc. arch. Also **Zwounds**. [Aphetic f. GOD'S WOUNDS.]

†**Woup**, Sc. Obs. Forms: 6 wowp, wop, 6–8 woup, 7 woupe, 8 woop. [Of obscure origin.]

Wour, var. WORE; southern ME. of FOUR.

Wous, var. of VOUS int. Obs.

Wousel, **woust**, obs. forms of WEASEL, WOOST.

Woundwort (wŏndwºⁱt), sb. [WOUND sb.¹ + WORT sb.¹]

Column 5 (p. 337)

Wove, pa. t. and pple. of WEAVE v.¹

Woven (wºᵘv'n), ppl. a. Also 6 wouen, wovyn. [Pa. pple. of WEAVE v.¹]

1. That has undergone the process of weaving; formed or fabricated by weaving.

Woundy (wŏndi), adv. and a.² Obs. exc. arch. Also 6 wowndy, 6 wolvin, 7 woldin. [See WOUNDY a.]

Wow, sb.¹ [Imitative: cf. BOW-WOW.] A bark or similar sound.

Wow-wow¹ (wᵘᵘ'wᵘ'). Also wou-wou, wau-wau. [Native name.] = WOU-WOU.

Wow-wow², [Imitative.] A bird of British Guiana.

Column 6 (p. 337)

Wove, obs. pa. pple. of WEAVE v.¹

Wovel, var. WOOVE.

†**Wowell**. Obs. [Of obscure origin.]

Wowen, obs. pa. pple. of WEAVE v.¹

Wowf (wouf), a. Sc. [Of obscure origin.]

Wowp, obs. var. of WUP sb.

Wowt, obs. form of WOULD v.

Wowy, obs. form of WOOING sb.

Woxen, **Woxin**, etc., obs. pa. pple.

Woy, int. var. woyh. [Exclamatory.] A call used in driving pigs.

Woy, obs. form of WAY.

Wr.

Wr- (r), a consonantal combination occurring initially in a number of words (frequently implying twisting or distortion), the earlier of which usually have cognates with the same initial sounds in the older Germanic languages. The combination is regularly preserved in Gothic, OS., OFris., and OE., but in OHG. is reduced to *r*. In ON. the *w* was lost before *rō*, *rū*, at an early date over the whole Scandinavian area; at a later period in all other words in ONorw. and OIcel. In the modern Germanic tongues *wr-* remains in Du., Flem., LG., and Fris., and is represented by *vr-* in Da., Sw., and some Norw. dialects.

Some 130 words in *wr-* are recorded from the OE. period, and a number of these survive in the later language, while others have been added from Du. and LG. Early difficulty in pronouncing the combination may be indicated by the Old Northumbrian spellings with *wur-*, and by the 14–15th cent. *weritt* 'writ', *werangus* 'wrongous'. The *r* is sometimes separated from the *w* by metathesis, as in ME. *wærð* for *wræð* 'wroth', *werch* for *wrech* 'wretch', *wirten* for *written*; but conversely *wr-* may arise from the same cause, as in OE. *wryhta* 'wright', for *wyrhta*. Signs of the dropping of the *w* begin to appear about the middle of the 15th cent. in such spellings as *ringe* for *wring* v., *rong* for *wrong* adj.; these become common in the 16th cent. (for examples see Wrangle, Wrap, Wreak, Wreck, Wrench, Wrest, etc.). Reduction of the sound is also indicated by the converse practice of writing *wr-* for *r-*, which similarly appears in the 15th cent. (in *wrath* for *rathe*), and becomes common in the 16th; for examples see the subordinate entries under Wrack, Wracked, Wragged, Wrap, Wrape, Wretchless, etc. In standard English the *w* was finally dropped in the 17th century; it has remained (though now obsolescent) in Scottish, and in some south-western English dialects is represented by *v*, which is also regular in north-eastern Scottish.

The phonetists Bullokar (*Amendment of Ortographie*, 1580) and Gill (*Logonomia*, 1621) have *wr-* throughout, and no doubt pronounced the *w*. Later authorities, e.g. R. Hodges (*English Primrose*, 1644), mark the *w* in this combination as silent.

Wr, obs. var. Our *pron.* **Wra**, ME. var. Wro. **Wraak**, var. Wrake *sb.*[1] *Obs.* **Wraaste**, obs. var. Wrest *sb.*[1] **Wrabbe**, var. Wrob *v.* *Obs.*

† **Wrabbed**, *a.* *Obs. rare.* [Of obscure origin. Cf. Wrawed *a.*] Perverse; difficult to manage.

1540 J. Heywood *Four P. P.* 986 By theyr condicions so croked and crabbed, Frowardly fashonde, so waywarde and wrabbed. 1568 *Jacob & Esau* ii. ii, Haue any mo maisters suche a man as I haue?..so eluishe, so frowarde? So crabbed, so wrabbed, so stiffe, so vntowarde?

† **Wra·bble**, *v.* *Obs. rare.* In 6 **wrabel-**, *Sc.* **wrabill.** [Of obscure origin. Cf. Warble *v.*[3], Worble *v.*] *intr.* To wriggle.

1513 Douglas *Æneid* viii. x. 84 About hir palpis..The tua twynnis..Sportand full tyte gan to wrabill and hing. 1534 More *Answ. Poysoned Bk.* i. iii. 7 The hote fyre of hell shalbe so fast tayed in all theyr tayles wrabelynge there together, yt neuer shall they gete ye fyre fro theyr taylys.

Wrable, obs. Sc. variant of Warble *sb.*[1]

1513 Douglas *Æneid* xii. Prol. 245 In wrablis [*ed.* 1553 werblis] dulce of hevynly armonyis The larkis..Lovys thar lege with tonys curyus. [Cf. Wrible.]

Wrache, obs. Sc. var. Wretch *sb.*

Wrachit(ness, obs. Sc. ff. Wretched(ness.

Wrack (ræk), *sb.*[1] Forms: 1 **wræc**, 3–5, *Sc.* 6 **wrak**, 4 **wrac**, 4– **wrack**, 6–7 **wracke.** [OE. *wræc* neut., f. pret. stem of *wrecan* to drive, etc., Wreak *v.* Cf. Wrack *sb.*[2], by which the later senses (esp. sense 5) may partly have been influenced; in writers of the 16–17th cent. it is sometimes uncertain which word is intended.

The evidence of rhymes shows that early northern ME. instances of the spelling *wrak* usually have a long vowel, and belong to Wrake *sb.*[1]]

I. 1. Retributive punishment; vengeance, revenge; in later use also, hostile action, active enmity, persecution. *Obs.* exc. *arch.* or *poet.*

Freq. coupled with words of similar meaning, as *war*, *wrath*, *wreak*, and tending to pass into sense 2.

c 900 tr. *Baeda's Hist.* iv. xxv. (1890) 356 Hi..mid þy wiite ðæs forespreceenan wræces slægene wæron. 971 *Blickl. Hom.* 25 Þæt unasecgenlice wræc & þæt ungeendode wite, þæt þon unlædon þær ʒeteohhod biþ. 13.. *Cursor M.* 890 (Gött.), Til þat worm vr lauerd þan spack wordis bath of wreth and wrack. 1535 Stewart *Cron. Scot.* (Rolls) I. 24 Sic diuisioun may nocht lest rycht lang, But weir and wrak and mekle opin wrang. 1575 Turberv. *Venerie* 177 And yet can man..Use wracke for rewth! can murder like him best? c 1586 C'tess Pembroke *Psalms* lxxviii. xix, Now pine and paine conspire With angry angells wreak and wrack to frame. 1596 Spenser *F. Q.* vi. ii. 21 There gan he ..with bitter wracke To wreake on me the guilt of his owne wrong. 1863 Longf. *Wayside Inn*, *K. Olaf* ii. v, Strange memories crowded back Of Queen Gunhild's wrath and wrack. 1870 Morris *Earthly Par.* II. iii. 516 Will it bring him back To let loose on the country war and wrack?

fig. 1590 Shaks. *Com. Err.* v. i. 49 Hath he not lost much wealth by wrack of sea?

† **b.** In the phr. *to do* or *take wrack* (*on* one).

12.. *Mem. Ripon* (Surtees) I. 91 Tol Tem Sok et Sak with yryn' and with water deme and do wrak. 1426 Lydg. *De Guil. Pilgr.* 1585 Myn hornys [are made] for to take wrak On shrewes, & to putte abak.

2. Damage, disaster, or injury to a person, state, etc., by reason of force, outrage, or violence; devastation, destruction.

In very frequent use from c 1580 to c 1640.

c 1407 Lydg. *Reson & Sens.* 5426 The tother [bow], hydouse and ryght blak, Wrought al oonly for the wrak, Ful of knottys. 1412–20 — *Chron. Troy* i. 2184 For lak of manhod drawiþ hym euer a-bak; He is so dredful and ferful of þe wrak. 1557 *Tottel's Misc.* (Arb.) 188 The golden apple that the Troyan boy Gaue to Venus.., Which was the cause of all the wrack of Troy. 1561 Norton & Sackv. *Gorboduc* v. ii, Loe, here..the wofull wracke And vtter ruine of this noble realme! 1581 A. Hall *Iliad* vi. 120 On this odde knight alacke We neuer shall set eyes againe, this day wil be his wracke. 1596 Spenser *F. Q.* iv. ix. 25 Eftsoones the others..on their foes did worke full cruell wracke. 1634 *Malory's Arthur* i. cxxxix. Ff 2, If he be angry he wil.. worke you much wrack in this countrey. 1640 T. Carew *Perswasions to love* 69 Time and age will worke that wrack Which time or age shall ne'er call back. 1659 *Bibliotheca Regia* (title-p.), Such of the Papers..as have escaped the wrack and ruines of these times. 1817 Scott *Harold* i. i, When he hoisted his standard black, Before him was battle, behind him wrack. 1853 M. Arnold *Sohrab & Rustum* 414 The wind in winter-time Has made in Himalayan forests wrack. 1873 Dixon *Two Queens* I. 122 While the country was a prey to fire and sword, the Church stood high above the wrack and waste.

b. In the phr. *to bring, go, put, run to wrack* (*and ruin*). Also *fig.* Cf. Rack *sb.*[5] 1.

In freq. use, esp. with *go* (*went*), c 1560–c 1680.

1412 Lydg. *Chron. Troy* Prol. 161 For nere writers, al wer out of mynde, Nat story only, but of nature and kynde The trewe knowyng schulde haue gon to wrak. 1420–2 — *Thebes* ii. 2215 Vpon his foon he rolled it [*sc.* a huge stone] at onys, That ten of hem wenten vnto wrak. 1528 Roy *Rede Me* (Arb.) 41 What did monkes and fryeres thanne, When masse went thus to wracke? 1540 Palsgr. *Acolastus* iii. iii. P iij b, He whose shyppe is gone to wracke. 1581 Marbeck *Bk. of Notes* 70 This Arke..by diuine prouidence..was gouerned from running to wracke. 1591 Spenser *Tears of Muses* 400 Thy scepter rent, and power put to wrack. 1601 R. Johnson *Kingd. & Commw.* (1603) 111 Arezzo beeing by long dissention amongest themselues almost brought to wracke. 1606 G. Woodcock *Hist. Iustine* xvi. 67 The greater part of his army..were all put to wrack. 1667 Milton *P. L.* vi. 670 And now all Heav'n Had gone to wrack, with ruin overspred. 1692 R. L'Estrange *Josephus, Antiq.* v. ii. (1733) 115 All their Affairs went to wrack upon it. 1757 Hume *Ess. & Treat.* (1777) II. 421 All nature was going to wrack...Gods and men were perishing in one common ruin. 1864 Kingsley *Roman & T.* ii. (1875) 31 All things were going to wrack. 1876 Browning *Pacchiarotto*, etc. 129 The man but for whom had gone to wrack All that France saved from the fight.

(*b*) 1577 Hanmer *Anc. Eccl. Hist.* i. ix. 12 Herod..supposing..his rule to goe to wracke, and ruine. 1577 H. Bull tr. *Luther's Comm. Ps.* (1615) 287 Whiles all things seeme to fall to wracke and ruine. 1585 Abp. Sandys *Serm.* 196 Gods familie and the common wealth goe to wracke and ruine.

c. In other phrases, as † *at, in wrack.* *rare.*

1592 A. Day *Eng. Secretorie* i. (1595) 51 When Rome was now at wracke, her Nobilitie spoyled, and her glorie trode vnder foote. 1901 J. Barlow *Ghost-bereft* 113 Round his gang crashed roof and wall in wrack.

d. *dial.* The brunt or consequences *of* some action. (Cf. Racket *sb.*[3] 4.)

1844 W. Barnes *Dorset Gloss.* s.v., 'Mind you'll stan' the wrack o't'. 1871– in south. dial. use (Oxf., Berks., Devon): *Eng. Dial. Dict.* s.v.

3. A disastrous change in a state or condition of affairs; wreck, ruin, subversion. ? *Obs.*

c 1400 *Found. St. Bartholomew's* 49 Where oure dede and purpos ys of the wracke of chastite. 1557 *Tottel's Misc.* (Arb.) 256 A frend no wracke of wealth, no cruell cause of wo, Can force his frendly faith vnfrendly to forgo. 1588 Greene *Metam.* Wks. (Grosart) IX. 87 Wit oft hath wracke by selfe-conceit of pride. 1591 *2nd Pt. Troubl. Raigne K. John* (1611) 108 What haue I lou'd but wracke of others weale? 1595 Markham *Sir R. Grinvile* (Arb.) 42 The wet worlds sacke Swells in my song, the Dirge for glories wracke. 1601 Shaks. *All's Well* iii. v. 24 The miserie is example, that so terrible shewes in the wracke of maidenhood. 1692 Locke *3rd Let. Toleration* x. 281 Toleration then does not..make that woful wrack on True Religion which you talk of. 1823 Scott *Peveril* xxvii, He that serves Peveril munna be slack, Neither for weather, nor yet for wrack. 1862 Lytton *Strange Story* II. 159 Have all those sound resolutions..melted away in the wrack of haggard dissolving fancies!

† **b.** The ruin, downfall, or overthrow of a person or persons; adversity, misfortune. *Obs.*

1426 Lydg. *De Guil. Pilgr.* 7727 Lat no man..with hys wordys falsly smyte, Malycyously to make wrak Off hys neyhebour. a 1578 Lindesay (Pitscottie) *Chron. Scot.* (S.T.S.) I. 21 Tyrantis settand thair haill purpois and intent vpone mischeiff and wrack of vtheris. a 1586 Sidney *Astr. & Stella* Sonn. xix, On Cupids bowe, how are my hart strings bent, That see my wracke, and yet imbrace the same? 1595 Markham *Sir R. Grinvile* lvii, To flye from them..Were to ..crush my selfe with shame and seruile wrack. 1625 A. Gil *Sacred Philos.* i. 119 By sinne there was a generall wrack of mankinde. 1667 Denham *Direct. Painter* 55 Presuming of his certain wrack, To help him late, they send for Rupert back. a 1699 J. Beaumont *Psyche* ii. cxxxvii, That smooth-tongu'd Gale whose whispers woke That Wrack which stole on me.

II. † **4.** An instance of suffering or causing wreck, ruin, destruction, etc. *Obs.*

1594 Kyd *Cornelia* v. i, Amongst so many wracks As I haue suffred both by Land and Sea. 1613 Purchas *Pilgrimage* 609 The new Conquerours..by wrackes testified to the earth, that they had wrecked themselues on her and their enemies. 1630 Lord *Banians* 33 Thunder and lightning..such as seemed to threaten a finall wracke to the earth. 1632 Heywood *1st Pt. Iron Age* i. i, Troy was twice rac't, and Troy deseru'd that wracke.

† **b.** A means or cause of subversion, overthrow, or downfall. *Obs.*

1579 Gosson *Sch. Abuse* (Arb.) 20 The Syrens song is the Saylers wrack. 1593 Shaks. *2 Hen. VI*, i. ii. 105 And thus I feare at last, Humes Knauerie will be the Duchesse Wracke. c 1611 Chapman *Iliad* ii. 781 The fool Amphimachus, to field, brought gold to be his wrack. 1613 Day *Festivals* (1615) ix. 248 How at length might it haue prooved a wrack to his owne Person. 1650 W. Brough *Sacr. Princ.* (1659) 183 When shall I be delivered from thee, gaol of my soul, and wrack of my salvation. 1682 Cochran in Howie *Cloud of Witnesses* (1778) 199 Jugling with the Lord..hath been our ruin and wrack.

5. A thing or person in an impaired, wrecked, or shattered condition. (Cf. Wrack *sb.*[2])

a 1586 Sidney *Psalms* xxxvii. xv, The mann whom God directs,..Though he doth fall, no wrack he proveth. 1611 Shaks. *Cymb.* iv. ii. 366 Young one,..who is this Thou mak'st thy bloody Pillow?..What's thy interest in this sad wracke? a 1803 in Child *Ballads* IV. 187/2 O spare me, Clyde's water,..Mak me your wrack as I come back, But spare me as I gae. 1866 Gregor *Banffshire Gloss.* 204 *Vrack*, ..a broken down person. 1888 *Scot. Sermons* in *Brit. Workman* May, Doon gaed the biggin', an unco wrack.

b. That which remains after the operation of any destructive action or agency; a vestige or trace left by some subversive cause. Also *fig.*

In later use, esp. with *leave*, freq. by misapprehension of Shaks. *Temp.* iv. i. 156, where the reading (altered by Malone to *wrack*) is *racke*: see Rack *sb.*[1] 3 b.

1602 Marston *Antonio's Rev.* iv. iv, I am a poore, poore orphant—a weake, weake childe, The wrack of splitted fortune. 1656 Cowley *Pindar. Odes*, *Muse* iii. note, Poetry.. makes what Choice it pleases out of the Wrack of Time of things that it will save from Oblivion. 1793 Wordsw. *Evening Walk* 360 No wrack of all the pageant scene remains. 1813 Byron *Giaour* 1237 The wither'd frame, the ruin'd mind, The wrack by passion left behind. 1878 Bosw. Smith *Carthage* 406 An ancient seat of civilisation..was swept away at a single stroke, leaving hardly a wrack behind.

† **c.** A damaged or injured part; damage, impairment. Also *fig.* *Obs.*

1601 Donne *Progr. Soul* i. vii, This soule which oft did teare And mend the wracks of th' Empire. 1610 Guillim *Heraldry* iii. xvii. 151 With the threeds..[the spider] repaireth all rents and wracks of the same [web]. *Ibid.*, A man carefull of his priuate estate, and of good foresight, in repairing of small decaies and preuenting of wracks. a 1631 Donne *Paradoxes* (1652) 9 We mend the wrack and stains of our apparel.

Wrack (ræk), *sb.*[2] Forms: 4–5, *Sc.* 6–7 **wrak**, 5 *Sc.* **wrac**, 6–7 **wracke**, 6– **wrack** (9 *Sc.* **vrack**). [a. MDu. (also mod. Du.) *wrak* neut. (older Flem. *wracke*, Kilian), or MLG. *wrak*, *wrack* (whence G. *wrack*), = MDa. *vrak* (Da. *vrag*) neut., MSw. *vrak* (*wrack*, *wragh*; Sw. *vrak*) neut., Norw. dial. *rak* neut., wreck, wrecked vessel, a parallel formation to OE. *wræc* Wrack *sb.*[1]

Except for its frequent use by southern writers between 1508 and 1690 (cf. the note to Wrack *sb.*[1]), the form is predominantly northern and Scottish.]

1. A wrecked ship or other vessel; a vessel ruined or crippled by wreck. Now *dial.*

c 1386 Chaucer *Man of Law's T.* 513 The Constable of the Castel down is fare To seen this wrak and al the shipe he soghte. 1626 Capt. Smith *Accid. Yng. Seamen* 29 She will..split or billage on a Rocke, a wracke. 1636 G. Sandys *Paraphr. Ps.* xlviii. 76 Blacke Eurus roars, And spreads his wracks on Tharsian shores. 1687 A. Lovell tr. *Thevenot's Trav.* i. 126 Close by shoar we saw the wrack of that Saique, which stranded the same day. 1692 in *Rec. Convent. Burghs Scot.* (1880) IV. 594 His ship become a wrak. 1756 in *Hist. Coll. Essex Inst.* (U.S.A.) V. 158/1 Drowned from the wrack of the sch[ooner]. *Ibid.*, The sea came and washed them over from the said wrack. 1772 Anne Lindsay *Auld Robin Gray* v, But hard blew the winds, and his ship was a wrack. 1862 Longf. *Birds of Passage* ii. *The Cumberland* vi, Down went the Cumberland all a wrack. 1905 *Cornh. Mag.* Feb. 209 'Wracks, man,' he shouted,..pointing to the double lighthouse,..' there is no chance of wracks for a puir fisherbody noo'.

transf. (of persons). 1589 Greene *Menaphon* (Arb.) 27 Menaphon..espied certain fragments of a broken ship floating vpon the waues, and sundrie persons driuen vpon the shore...These three (as distressed wrackes) preserued by some further forepoynting fate [etc.]. 1594 Shaks. *Rich III*, i. iv. 24 Me thoughts, I saw a thousand fearfull wrackes: A thousand men that Fishes gnaw'd vpon. 1601 — *Twel. N.* v. i. 82 That most ingratefull boy..From the rude seas.. Did I redeeme: a wracke past hope he was.

b. Remnants of, or goods from, a wrecked vessel, esp. as driven or cast ashore; shipwrecked effects or property, wreckage; also in earlier use, the right to have such. Now *arch.*

1428 *Excheq. Rolls Scotl.* IV. 439 Le wrak cujusdam navis combuste infra portum de Leth. 1452 *Reg. Mag. Sig. Scot.* 125/1 Invenerunt dictum forestarium custodem de *Wrac* et *Waif* infra dictum dominium de Coldingham. 1501 *Extr. Aberd. Reg.* (1844) I. 428 Ane brokin schip,..quhilk, throw storme of sey, happin to brek, and the wrak of hir come in on the cost of Croudane. 1584 Greene *Morando* Wks. (Grosart) III. 84 Tis an ill flaw that bringeth vp no wracke. 1599 Shaks. *Hen. V*, i. ii. 165 As rich..As is the Owse and bottome of the Sea With sunken Wrack. 1639 in Maitland *Hist. Edinburgh* (1753) II. 151/1 All their antient Rights,..with Pit and Gallows, Sack and Soke, Thole, Theam, Vert, Wrack, Waifs [etc.]. a 1662 Heylin *Cosmogr.* i. (1669) 71 Charybdis is a Gulf..which violently attracting all Vessels that come too nigh it, devoureth them, and casteth up their wracks [*ed.* 1652 wrecks]. 1670 Dryden *Conq. Granada* iv. i, My own lost Wealth thou giv'st not only back, But driv'st upon my Coast my Pyrat's Wrack. 1759 Philipott *Villare Cant.* 11 Witsom were goods driven to the shore, when there had not been for some space any wrack visible. 1883 Whitelaw *Sophocles, Antigone* 591 Casting up mire and blackness and storm-vext wrack of the sea. 1897 *Longm. Mag.* Feb. 333 Through the heaped mysteries of waith and wrack, When the long wave from the long beach draws back.

† **c.** *pl.* Fragments of wreckage. Also *fig.* *Obs.*

a 1586 Sidney *Arcadia* ii. (1912) 350 Who then myselfe should flie So close unto my selfe my wrackes doo lie.

2. The total or partial disablement or destruction of a vessel by any disaster or accident of navigation; = Shipwreck *sb.* 2. Now *rare.*

1579 Gosson *Sch. Abuse* (Arb.) 41, I haue in my voyage suffred wrack with Vlisses. 1590 Spenser *F. Q.* i. vi. 1 As when a ship..An hidden rocke escaped hath vnwares, That lay in waite her wrack for to bewaile. 1615 G. Sandys *Trav.* 2 Glad that with wracke of ship, and losse of goods they may prolong a despised life. 1648 G. Daniel *Eclog.* v. 331 In a wracke, wee trust A Sayle-yard, or a Planke of broken Chest, To carrie vs. 1673 Dryden *2 Pt. Conq. Granada* (ed. 2) iii. 105 As Seamen, parting in a gen'ral wrack, When first the loosening Planks begin to crack Each catches one. 1706 Phillips (ed. Kersey) s.v. *Flotson*, Jetson, or Goods cast out of the Ship, being in danger of Wrack. a 1879 H. Dewar in *Poems of Places, Brit. Amer.* 35 In the wrack tall masts would crack.

b. *fig.* and in fig. context.

1580 H. Gifford *Posie of Gilloflowers* (1870) 52 Fell Sathan is chiefe rular of these seas: Hee seekes our wracke, he doth these tempestes rayse. a 1586 Sidney *Arcadia* v. Wks. 1922 II. 130 Yet being imbarqued in the same ship, the finall wrack must needs be common to them all. 1600 Dekker *Fortunatus* Wks. 1873 I. 114 Ryot sets up sayles, And.. Drives your unsteddie fortunes on the point of wracke inevitable. 1611 Speed *Hist. Gt. Brit.* vi. iii. § 7 When Seas did foame..His force effecting with his cares preuented still my wracke. 1628 Feltham *Resolves* ii. ii. 5 Hee that steeres by that gale, is euer in danger of wracke. 1649 G. Daniel *Trinarch., Rich. II*, vii, The greater winds of Faction broke in here, To make a wracke. a 1699 J. Beaumont *Psyche* i. ccxxxiv, That venturing any longer stay to make, Was but to run upon a certain wrack.

3. Marine vegetation, seaweed or the like, cast ashore by the waves or growing on the tidal seashore. (Cf. Wreck *sb.*[1] 2, Varec 1.)

Also *cart-*, *grass-*, *kelp-*, *lady-*, *sea-wrack*.

In first quot. the precise sense is not quite clear.

1513 Douglas *Æneid* iii. ix. 34 Rent me in pecis, and in the fludis swak, Or droun law vndir the large seis wrak. 1551– [see Sea-wrack 2]. 1650 [Howe] *Phytol. Brit.* 101 Divers sorts of Sea-Oake, or Wrack. 1668 Wilkins *Real Char.* 71 Herbs..growing commonly upon Stones and Rocks in the Sea: 14. Wrack. †1700 Wallace *Descr. Orkney* (1883) 42 *note*, When the sea-weed is driven in greater plenty, all the people..divide the wrack according to the proportion of land they have. 1716 *Petiveriana* i. 159 Full of small seedy Warts as in our common Wrach or *Quercus maritima*. 1785 Martyn *Lett. Bot.* xxxii. 500 Fucus, Wrack, or Sea-weed properly so called, has two kinds of bladders. 1849 H. Miller *Footpr. Creat.* i. 10 The shores..of the lake were strewed..by a line of *wrack*, consisting..of marine plants [etc.]. 1855 Kingsley *Glaucus* 57 The purple and olive wreaths of wrack, and bladder-weed, and tangle. 1880 *Antrim & Down Gloss.* 78 The farmers grow sea-weed for manure, cutting the wrack periodically...Stones are placed for the wrack to grow on.

b. Weeds, rubbish, waste, etc., floating on, or washed down or ashore by, a river, pond, or the like; = Wreck *sb.*[1] 2 b.

1598– water-wrack [see Water *sb.* 29]. 1851 H. Stephens *Bk. Farm* (ed. 2) I. 396/2 To prevent the *wrack* floating on the surface of the water finding its way into the sluice. 1865 Livingstone *Zambesi* i. 14 When we came within five or six miles of the land, the yellowish-green tinge of the sea.. was suddenly succeeded by muddy water with wrack, as of a river in flood. *Ibid.*, The wrack, consisting of reeds, sticks and leaves. 1877 V. L. Cameron *Across Africa* I. 63, I observed wrack of grass and twigs in the branches of small trees..,showing how high the floods..must be at times.

c. Field-weeds, roots of couch-grass or the like, esp. as loosened from the soil to be collected for burning; vegetable rubbish or refuse found on agricultural lands; = Wreck *sb.*[1] 2 c.

1715 Pennecuik *Tweeddale* 6 [They] will not suffer the *Wrack* to be taken of their Land, because (say they) it keeps the Corn warm. 1825 Jamieson, *Wrack*, Dog's grass,.. *Triticum repens*, Linn.; Roxb. Perhaps denominated *Wrack*, because..it is harrowed out in the fall, and burnt. 1883 *Longm. Mag.* April 658 Seed has to be sown, turnips have to be thinned and hoed..and 'wrack' gathered. 1894 Heslop *Northumb. Gloss.* 799 *Wrack*, weeds; especially 'whickens' and sea-weed.

4. *attrib.* and *Comb.*, as † *wrack-ship* (= sense 1); † *wrack-rich*; *wrack-threatened*, *-threatening*; also † **wrackfree**, = Wreckfree *a.*; † **wrack-goods** [cf. Du. *wrakgoederen*, G. *wrackgut*] *Scots Law*, = sense 1 b; **wrack-spangle** *local* (see quot. 1856).

1570 in W. Boys *Hist. Sandwich* (1792) 775 Savyng that we shalbe wrakfree of our owne goodes whatsoever. 1594 Shaks. *Lucr.* 590 All which together like a troubled Ocean, Beat at thy rockie, and wracke-threatning heart. 1598 J. Dickenson *Greene in Conc.* (1878) 138 More deafe.. then are the wrack-rich Libique rocks. 1603 J. Davies (Heref.) *Microcosmos* Wks. (Grosart) I. 38/2 A Sternelesse Shippe..On mightiest Seas, wrack-threatn'd on each syde. 1671 *Shetland Docum.* in *Proc. Soc. Ant. Scot.* (1892) XXVI. 194 To..secure all wrack and waith goods. 1681 Stair *Instit.* vii. 76 Our Custome agrees with..other Nations, except in the Matter of waith and wrack Goods. 1693 *Ibid.* (ed. 2) iii. iii. 420 Where the Wrack ship is, the Owner may be known by Writs in the Ship. 1706 Phillips (ed. Kersey), *Wrecfry*,..wrack-free, exempt or freed from the forfeiture of Shipwracked Goods and Vessels to the King. 1856 *Househ. Words* 8 Nov. 391/1 Wrack-spangle, the popular name of these things, implies that they deck the sea-weeds as spangles adorn robes. The savans call them Serpulæ.

Wrack (ræk), *sb.*[3] Also 5, 6 *Sc.* **wrak**, 6 **wracke**, 9 *Sc.* **vrack.** [a. (M)LG. or Du. *wrak* (whence MHG. and G. dial. *wrack* refuse, rubbish, Da. *vrag*, Sw. *vrak*, refuse); see also Wrake *sb.*[3], Wreck *sb.*[2], and cf. Wrack *a.*]

1. That which is of an inferior, poor, or worthless quality; waste material; rubbish. Now *rare.*

1472–5 *Rolls of Parlt.* VI. 156/1 Such [bowstaves] as were called the wrak, not goode ne able to make of but Childern' Bowes. 1492–3 *Durham Acc. Rolls* (Surtees) 249 Reparaciones [on a mill]:..pro cariagio le ramell et wrak a scacaric usque Viram. 1542–3 *Act 34 & 35 Hen. VIII*, c. 9 § 4 That no persone or persones doo caste or unlade out of any maner of Ship..any maner of Balaste rubbishe gravell or any other wracke or filthe, but oonelie upon the Lande. 1866 Gregor *Banffshire Gloss.* 204 *Vrack*, anything worthless. *Ibid.*, 'His nout's jist mere vrack.' 1885 *Pall Mall G.* 27 March 4 They send anything—the very wrack of towns—instead of the valuable agricultural labourer which we want.

† **b.** *Sc.* *World's wrack*, earthly 'pelf' or 'dross'; worldly possessions, goods, or gear. *Obs.*

c 1480 Henryson *Swallow & Birds* 307 (Bann.), Our wickit ennemye..evir is reddye, Quhen wretchis in þis warldis wrak do scraip, To draw his nett. 1500–20 Dunbar *Poems* xxiii. 10 For warldis wrak but weilfair nocht awailis. a 1568 in *Bannatyne MS.* (Hunter. Cl.) 223 Quhill..stuffit weill with warldis wrak, Amang my freindis I wes weill kend. a 1586 in *Maitland Fol. MS.* (S.T.S.) 241 Now he hes gold and warldis wrak ȝand him besyd. 1792 Burns *My Wife's a winsome wee thing* iv, The warld's wrack we share o't, The warstle and the care o't.

2. An inferior grade of flax. Also *attrib.*

1879 J. Paton in *Encycl. Brit.* IX. 298/1 Of the lower qualities of Riga flax the following may be named:—Wrack flax, White picked wrack,..Picked wrack flax. *Ibid.*, The lowest quality of Riga flax is..Dreiband Wrack.

Wrack, freq. erron. f. Rack *sb.*[1] 3, 3 b.

1794 Mrs. Piozzi *Synon.* II. 397 Observing how the wrack rides before the wind. 1848 Lytton *Harold* v. i, The smoke rises..to join the wrack of clouds. 1878 H. S. Wilson *Alpine Ascents* ii. 57 A filmy wrack wreathes round and upward.

Wrack, erron. f. Rack *sb.*[3] 1, 1 b, 1 c.

1591 Shaks. *1 Hen. VI*, ii. v. 3 Euen like a man new haled from the Wrack, So fare my Limbes with long Imprisonment. 1666 *Boyle's Orig. Formes & Qual.* a 2 Mystical Notions, which put the Understanding upon the Wrack. 1866 Swinburne *Poems & Ballads* 306 For the pure sharpness of her miseries She had no heart's pain, but mere body's wrack.

Wrack, erron. f. Rack *sb.*[6]

1829 H. Murray *N. America* II. iii. iv. 442 They abhor a trot, and instruct the animal only in a pace and a wrack.

† **Wrack**, *a.* *Obs. rare.* Also 4 **wrac**, 6 *Sc.* **wrak.** [a. MLG. *wrak*, *wrack*, LG. *wrak* (whence G. dial. *wrack* worthless, Sw. *vrak-*, Da. *vrag-*), or MDu. *wrac*, *wrak* (Kilian *wrack*, *wraeck*, Du. *wrak*), OFris. *wrak*, *wrac* base (WFris. *wrak* shaky): cf. Wrack *sb.*[3]]

1. Of persons: Worthless, base, evil.

c 1375 *Kindheit Iesu* 315 in Horstm. *Altengl. Leg.* (1875) 12 Bote a giw of heorte wrac Alle hise lawes þare he to brac.

2. Damaged, impaired, injured; unsound.

1487 *Cely Papers* (Camden) 164, iiij last heryng, iij wrack & on rooue; the wrack cost viijli & the roue ixli. 1496–7 *Rec. St. Mary at Hill* (1905) 32 Item, a diaper clothe, wrack, content in lengthe iij yardes di. 1584 *Burgh Rec. Edinb.* (1882) IV. 343 To devyde the guid and sufficient fische fra the wrak and evill.

† **Wrack**, *v.*[1] *Obs.* Forms: 3 **wracken**, 4–5 **wrak**, 6 **wracke.** [Irreg. var. of Wreak *v.* Cf. *brack*, *brak*, for Break *v.*]

1. *trans.* To avenge or revenge (a person, deed, etc.); to punish. Also const. *on.*

c 1205 Lay. 20256 Baldulf..þencheð in þissere nihte to slæn þe..to wracken his broðer. a 1300 *Body & Soul* in *Map's Poems* (Camden) 338 Merci criende lutel availede, ȝwan Crist it wolde so harde wrac. [1871 Waddell *Psalm* xviii. 47 The God wha wracks a' right for me.]

2. To give vent to or wreak (spite, malice, etc.).

1635 J. Hayward tr. *Biondi's Banish'd Virg.* 199 The King went to wrack his spite on their corpes. 1644 J. Fary *Gods Severity* (1645) 21 You..must needs wrack your malice by revenge. 1720 Prior *Cupid Mistaken* iii, Couldst thou find none other, To wrack [*ed.* 1709 wreck] thy spleen on?

Wrack (ræk), *v.*[2] Now *arch.* or *dial.* Also 5–7 **wracke**, 6–7 *Sc.* **wrak**, 9 **rack.** [f. Wrack *sb.*[2] Cf. Wreck *v.*[1]]

† **1.** *intr.* To suffer or undergo shipwreck. *Obs.*

1470–85 Malory *Arthur* viii. xxxviii. 331 One told hym there was a knyghte of kyng Arthur [tha]t had wrackyd on the rockes. 1596 [A. Munday] tr. *Sylvain's Orator* 333 The ship happened to wracke, so that the poore man and his daughter saued themselues in a little Island. a 1620 J. Dyke *Sel. Serm.* (1640) 146 When a Shippe wrackes at Sea, the goods are utterly lost. 1632 Sanderson *Serm.* 56 We may..cast our wares into the Sea, to lighten the ship that it wracke not.

fig. and in fig. context. a 1592 Greene *Alcida* (1617) C 1 b, Thus selfe-loue..Makes beautie wracke against an ebbing tide. 1596 Bp. Andrewes *Serm.* (1629) 327 Their Love hath wracked, and from kind love, beene turned to deadly hate. 1616 B. Jonson *Forrest* iii. 95 God wisheth none should wracke on a strange shelfe. 1622 Bacon *Hen. VII*, 223 Sir, you haue beene saued vpon my coast, I hope you will not suffer mee to wrack vpon yours.

2. *trans.* To wreck (a vessel, mariners, etc.); to ruin or cast ashore by shipwreck. Chiefly *pass.*

1562 A. Brooke *Romeus & Jul.* 1368 Driuen hard vpon the bare and wrackfull shore, In greater daunger to be wract, then he had been before. 1593 Marlowe *Edw. II*, ii. ii, I feare me he is wrackt vpon the sea. 1596 Bacon *Max. & Use Com. Law* i. (1636) 44 Goods wrackt..shall be preserved to the use of the owner. 1614 Raleigh *Hist. World* iii. (1634) 86 They pursuing the victorie, had left part of the fleet..to save those that were wrackt. 1683 *Brit. Spec.* 86 Most of the Fleet, wrackt that Night by a sudden Tempest, lay split on the Shore. 1699 T. Allison *Voy. Archangel* 22 Putting provision therein for subsistance, in case we should be forced ashore and wracked. 1755 Johnson. 1838 J. F. Cooper *Homeward Bound* xxiv, I esteem it a great privilege..to have the honour of being *wracked*.. in such company. *Ibid.*, If she [the ship] had been honorably and fairly wracked. 1871 Palgrave *Lyr. Poems* 19 The seas..With outstretch'd angry arms..Wracking whole fleets in pride like riven toys.

fig. and in fig. context. 1583 Greene *Mamillia* Wks (Grosart) II. 193 A professed Curtizan, whose honestie and credit is so wracked in the waues of wantonnesse. *Ibid.* 242 No..tempests of aduersitie shal..wracke my fancie against the slipperie rockes of inconstancie. 1594 *Selimus* G 3 b, My feeble barke,..while thy foamie floud doth it immure, Shall soon be wrackt vpon the sandie shallowes. 1598–9 B. Jonson *Case Altered* ii. vii, O! in what tempests do my fortunes saile, Still wrackt with winds more foule and contrary, Then any other northern guest. 1670 Dryden *1st Pt. Conq. Granada* iii. (1672) 23 Though wrack'd and lost, My Ruines stand to warn you from the Coast. a 1699 J. Beaumont *Psyche* i. ccxvii, Till miserably wrack'd, most woful she Quite sinks in this self-torments monstrous Sea. [1897 W. Beatty *Secretar* x. 77 The wind that drave them ..was the same that had wracked..Darnley, and Bodwell.]

3. To cause the ruin, downfall, or subversion of (a person, etc.); to ruin, overthrow. Also *refl.*

1564 Queen Mary in *Reg. Privy Council Scot.* XIV. 201 Seing the puir men, awnaris of the saidis ship and guidis, ar ..uterlie heriit and wrakkit. 1567 *Gude & Godlie B.* (S.T.S.) 186 Suppose we suld wrack [1621 wrake] our self, and tyne The feild, and all our kin be hangit syne. a 1586 Sidney *Ps.* xli. iv, Now he is wrackt, say they, loe their he lies. 1604 A. Craig *Poet. Ess.* A 4, When Troy was wrackt,..He came...Yet sayd he nought. 1628 Prynne *Love-lockes* 59 Externall Beautie..betrays and wrackes the Soules of many. 1792 Burns '*What can a young lassie*' iv, I'll cross him, and wrack him, until I heart-break him. 1810 in R. H. Cromek *Remains* 27 He'll dance wi' ye, 'O'er Bogie', Maiden, and wrack ye.

refl. 1595 Daniel *Civ. Wars* iii. xvi. 47 b, That weake, and enuied if they should conspire They wracke themselues, and he hath his desire.

b. To render useless by breaking, shattering, etc.; to injure or spoil severely; to destroy.

1587 Fleming *Contn. Holinshed* III. 1310/2 In the towne of Bedford the water came vp to the market place..; their fewell, corne and haie was wrackt & borne awaie. a 1593 Marlowe *Dido* i. i, Of them all scarce seuen [ships] doe anchor safe, And they so wrackt and weltred by the waues [etc.]. a 1678 Marvell *Bermudas* 9 Where he the huge Sea-Monsters wracks, That lift the Deep upon their Backs. 1817 Shelley *Rev. Islam* vii. xxxviii, As if the world's wide continent Had fallen in universal ruin wracked. 1845 Mrs. S. C. Hall *Whiteboy* vi. 56 The [castle]..is wracked by the Saxon's breath. 1899 S. Macmanus *Chimney Corners* 252 His queeny bee..was wrackin' an' ruinin' all afore her.

transf. a 1586 Sidney *Astr. & Stella* Sonn. lxvii, Doth Stella now beginne with pitteous eye The raigne of this her conquest to espie? Will she take time before all wracked be? 1594 Shaks. *Rich. III*, iv. i. 97 Eightie odde yeeres of sorrow haue I seene, And each howres ioy wrackt with a weeke of teene. 1648 J. Beaumont *Psyche* iii. cxxxii, The Precedent may dangerous prove, and wrack Thy Throne and Kingdome.

4. *intr.* To undergo ruin or subversion.

a 1586 Sidney *Ps.* xxxvii. xviii, [Those] who be swarved To ill, both they and theirs shall wrack. 1599 Sandys *Europæ Spec.* (1632) 191 Ayde..without which the whole Empire were in daunger of wracking. a 1600 Montgomerie *Misc. Poems* xlvi. 56, I smore if I conceill, I wrak if I reveill, My hurt. 1607 J. Carpenter *Plaine Mans Plough* 89 What gaine these..when they..themselves remaine castawayes, wracking in the depth of hell.

Hence **Wra·cking** *vbl. sb.* and *ppl. a.*

1611 Cotgr., *Ruinement*, a ruining, *wracking, spoyling. 1642 Vicars *God in Mount* 13 The utter wracking and worrying of the..holy lambes of Christ. 1611 Cotgr., *Naufrageux*, *wracking, shipwrack-bringing.

† **Wrack**, *v.*[3] *Sc.* *Obs.* [ad. MLG. *wracken* (whence G. *wracken* to sort), to reject, refuse, var. of *wraken*, Wrake *v.*[3]] *trans.* = Wrake *v.*[3]

1609 in *Rec. Convent. Burghs Scot.* (1870) II. 284 Ilk last vesetit urackit, jadget and brunt be thame [*sc.* inspectors]. 1611 *Ibid.* 326 Anent the mater of the hering and barrells thairof, sufficiencie of pakking and wrakking of the same.

† **Wrack**, *v.*[4] *Obs.*[−1] (? ad. Du. *wraken* to make leeway. Cf. G. *wrak*, *wraking*, leeway.)

1635 L. Foxe in *North-West Fox* 180 In that distance holding the same course, I had 2 deg. 14 min. to wracke upon, and within one point at most of my paralell.

Wrack, freq. erron. f. Rack *v.*[3]

1553–5 Latimer in Strype *Eccl. Mem.* (1721) III. App. xxxv. 98 The Martyrs in the old Time were wracked. 1622 Fletcher *Sea Voy.* i. i, The Money I ha wrackt by usury. a 1637 B. Jonson *Discov.* Wks. (1641) 118 Doubtfull writing hath wrackt mee beyond my patience. 1674 N. Fairfax *Bulk & Selv.* To Rdr., As the one had wrackt and limm'd my thoughts, with endless tenters. 1683 Cave *Ecclesiastici, Eusebius* 33 The Church rather expounds the Opinion..into a favourable sence, than nicely weighs and wracks their words. 1720 Welton *Suffer. Son of God* II. xiv. 370 What great Concern wracks the Spirit of a faithful Servant of God. 1721 Strype *Eccl. Mem.* II. ii. xiv. 353 Landlords had now so wracked their rents. 1756 *Monitor* No. 72 II. 197 If they wrack their brains..to find out [etc.]. 1785 Burns *Scotch Drink* i, Let..Crabbit names an' stories wrack us, An' grate our lug. 1895 Parkhurst in *Advance* (Chicago) 7 Mar. 808/2 Sin..wracks the machinery of the mind. 1898 *Daily News* 31 Aug. 5/3 They themselves are wracking their busy brains.

absol. 1607 Shaks. *Cor.* v. i. 16 A paire of Tribunes, that haue wrack'd for Rome, To make Coales cheape.

Wracked (rækt), *ppl. a.* [f. Wrack *v.*[2] + -ed[1].] That has undergone or suffered wreck, esp. shipwreck; ruined, destroyed.

1581 A. Hall *Iliad* i. 15 Yeelding the Greekes a thorough feare, the Troyans courage hie, So that the wracked Campe restore his credite worthilie. 1608 Sylvester *Du Bartas* ii. iv. *Schisme* 371 A hundred Prophets..from sad drowning keep The wracked planks on th' Idol-Ocean deep. 1648 J. Beaumont *Psyche* iv. lxxxv, When loe an angry Sea..on its proud waves bears In dreadfull triumph a wrack'd Man. 1652 Needham tr. *Selden's Mare Cl.* 157 Those wrack't goods that had been seized by the Receivers of his Customs. 1747 *New Canto Spenser's F. Q.* xxiii, The wrack'd Merchant, now secure, from Shore Looks back with Dread on all his Perils past. 1864 Mrs. Lloyd *Ladies Polc.* 17 Every body's troubles is her troubles, from a wracked boat to a broken putcher! 1875 Morris *Æneid* ix. 263 Two cups..which my father took from wracked Arisbe's hold.

Wracked, erron. f. Racked *ppl. a.*[3]

1606 Sylvester *Du Bartas* ii. iv. *Tropheis* 823 Hee makes th' whole Kingdom's wracked ribs to meet. 1656 Cowley *Davideis* iii. 683 Merab rejoyc'd in her wrackt Lovers pain. a 1699 J. Beaumont *Psyche* x. ccxxxiv, New fear Stormed their wracked Souls.

Wracker[1] (ræ·kəɹ). *rare.* [f. Wrack *v.*[2] + -er[1].] One who wrecks, ruins, or subverts.

1611 Cotgr., *Ruineur*, a ruiner, wracker, spoyler.

† **Wracker**[2]. *Obs. rare.* [f. Wrack *v.*[3] + -er[1], or ad. MLG. *wraker* (whence Da. *vrager* sorter).] = Wraker.

1584 [see Wraker]. 1719 in *Rec. Convent. Royal Burghs Scot.* (1885) V. 217 By means of wrackers of herrings to be imported there. *Ibid.*, To appoint..ane overseer of these wrackers.

Wracker[3] (ræ·kəɹ). *rare.* [f. Wrack *sb.*[2] 3 + -er[1] 1. Cf. Vraicker.] One who collects wrack, vraic, or seaweed.

1833 *Fraser's Mag.* VII. 293 The Norman wrackers, as they gathered sea-weed on the beach.

Wracker, obs. var. Racker[1].

1736 Ainsworth i, *Contortor*,..a wracker, or wrester.

† **Wra·ckful**, *a.*[1] *Obs.* Also 3 **wracful**, 4 **wrakful**, 5 **-fulle.** [f. Wrack *sb.*[1] + -ful.] Characterized by resentment or anger; vengeful, angry.

c 1230 (implied in next). 13.. *E. E. Allit. P.* B. 302 Now God in nwy to Noe con speke Wylde wrakful wordez. *Ibid.* 541 Suche a wrakful wo for wlatsum dedez Parformed þe hyȝe fader. ? a 1400 *Morte Arth.* 3818 He wente at the gayneste, Wondis of thas wedirwyns with wrakfulle dynttys.

Hence † **Wra·ckfully** *adv.*, vengefully. *Obs.*

c 1230 *Hali Meid.* 41 Hwen godd se wracfulliche fordemde his heh engel.

† **Wra·ckful**, *a.*[2] *Obs. rare.* In 4 **wrecful.** [OE. *wræcful*, f. *wræc* Wrack *sb.*[1] + -ful.] Full of misery; wretched.

c 1311 in Wright *Pol. Songs* (Camden) 256 For wille is red, the lond is wrecful; For wit is qued, the lond is wrongful.

Wra·ckful, *a.*[3] Now *arch.* and *rare.* [f. Wrack *sb.*[2] + -ful.]

1. Causing shipwreck; wreckful.

1558 Phaer *Æneid* ii. 64 To Syllas wrackfull shore with shypps approche we nye. 1583 Melbancke *Philotimus* T iv b, That..shears the fruitles sande with wrackfull waues. 1591 Sylvester *Du Bartas* i. ii. 353 To stand still firm against the roaring noise Of wrackfull Neptune. 1612 Drayton *Poly-olb.* i. 326 Where king Latinus lent safe harbor for his Ships, with wrackfull tempests rent. 1623 Drumm. of Hawth. *Flowres of Sion* xii. 6 These Lockes, of blushing deedes the gilt attire, Waues curling, wrackfull shelfes to shadow deepe. 1633 T. Bancroft *Gluttons Feauer* F 2 b, A Vessell, neare some wrackfull strand.

2. Causing destruction or devastation; effecting damage or harm; destructive.

1578 *Mirr. Mag.* 23 b, Then my delight was in the diery dent Of wrackfull warre. 1594 Carew *Tasso* (1881) 24 Eu'n so the king of streames..Beyond his banckes abroad all wrackfull goes. c 1600 Shaks. *Sonn.* lxv. 6 O how shall summers hunny breath hold out Against the wrackfull siedge of battring dayes? 1633 T. Bancroft *Gluttons Feauer* B 6 Cracke all mine arteries with tortures tride, Yet must more stormes, more wrackfull woes abide? 1921 *Chambers's Jrnl.* Jan. 50/1 A people that..has not had its mind and feelings warped by that wrackful war.

3. Subject to, attended by, injury, harm, etc.

1581 T. Howell *Deuises* B iv, To shunne the sheete of shame, Which had bewrapt her wrackfull blemisht name. 1612 J. Davies (Heref.) *Muses Sacr.* Wks. (Grosart) II. 82/1 This Life, a Way! (a wrackfull way) that Wisedome lothes to proue. 1811 Scott *Don Roderick* iii. vi, What wanton horrors marked their wrackful path!

Wracking, erron. f. Racking *vbl. sb.*[3] (also *attrib.*).

1676 *Lond. Gaz.* No. 1083/1 Certain Instruments..made use of for the wracking of Criminals. 1688 Holme *Armory* iii. 311/1 A Wracking Plank, with a Rowling Wheel of so many Spokes. 1803 W. Blake '*I saw a Monk*' ii, Voltaire [arose] with a wracking wheel.

Wracking, erron. f. Racking *ppl. a.*[1] 2.

1749 *Milton's P. L.* (ed. Newton) ii. 182 We perhaps.. shall be hurl'd Each on his rock transfix'd, the sport and prey Of wracking whirlwinds. 1837 Carlyle *Misc. Ess.*, *Mirabeau*, The sport of wracking winds.

Wrack-rider. Also **rack-**. *north. dial.* (See quots.)

1794 Hutchinson *Hist. Cumbld.* I. 460 [The] Brandling.. is the Rackrider of the county of Durham, and the Samlet. 1825 Brockett *N. C. Words*, *Wrack*, or *Wrackrider*,..the same species of trout as the brandling.

† **Wra·cksome**, *a.* *Obs. rare*[−1]. [f. Wrack *v.*[2] + -some[1].] Destructive.

1584 Hudson *Du Bartas' Judith* ii. 361 Then mine not you their towers and tourets tall, Nor bring the wracksom engine to their wall.

Wrackstaff, obs. erron. form of Rack-staff.

1706 E. Ward *Hud. Rediv.* i. xii. 6 If he eat Nothing but Wrack-staves for his Meat.

Wrae, Sc. var. Wro *sb.* **Wræche**, obs. var. Wretch. **Wræstlen**, obs. f. Wrestle *v.* **Wræð**, obs. pa. t. of Writhe; obs. var. Wroth *a.*

Wrag, obs. erron. f. Rag *sb.*[2] 2.

1844 *Civil Eng. & Arch. Jrnl.* VII. 63/1 Two stone offices ..formed of Kentish wrag ashlar.

† **Wrag**, *v.* *Obs. rare*[−1]. [Of imitative origin. Cf. Wraggle *v.*[1]] *intr.* To struggle or strive; to resist. Hence **Wragging** *vbl. sb.*

a 1225 *Ancr. R.* (MS. Cleopatra C. vi) fol. 173 b, For þeo ȝet [*sic*] fondunges..wragged oðer hwiles, & [heo] mote wresten aȝein wið strong wraggunge.

Wrag, erron. f. Rag *v.*[2]

1841 J. Blackwood in Mrs. Oliphant *Blackwood & Sons* (1898) II. 261, I do not forget to wrag the Doctor on this subject.

† **Wragged**, obs. erron. f. Ragged (rough).

c 1600 Shaks. *Sonn.* vi, Then let not winters wragged hand deface, In thee thy summer ere thou be distil'd.

† **Wra·gger.** *Obs.* Also **wrager.** [Cf. Wrag *v.*] One who wrangles.

c 1460 *Towneley Myst.* xii. 58 Both bosters and bragers god kepe vs fro;..Sich wryers and wragers gose to and fro For to crak. *Ibid.* xxx. 143 A bag full..Of Wraggers and wrears, a bag full of brefes, Of carpars and cryars [etc.].

† **Wra·ggle**, *v.*[1] *Obs. rare.* In 3 **wragel-**, 6 *Sc.* **wraggil**, **wraigle**, 7 **wragle.** [See Wrag *v.* and -le, and cf. WFris. *wraggelje* to waddle, LG. dial. *wraggeln* to wiggle, to wriggle.]

1. *intr.* To struggle or strive; to resist. Hence **Wra·ggling** *vbl. sb.*

a 1225 *Ancr. R.* 374 Þe oðer bitternesse is bitternesse in wrastlunge, & in wragelunge aȝean uondunges. *Ibid.*, For þe ȝet [*sic*] fondunges, þet beoð þe deofles swenges, wraggeð oðer hwules, & [heo] moten wresten aȝean mid strongre wragelunge.

2. To wriggle. Hence **Wra·ggling** *ppl. a.*

1508 Dunbar *Flyting* 195 Wan wraiglane [*Maitl.* wraggilland] wasp! 1602 Middleton *Blurt, Master Constable* C 2, I strugled and stragled, and wrigled and wragled.

Wra·ggle, *v.*[2] (See quot. and cf. Raggle *v.*)

1875 Gillies in *Trans. N. Z. Inst.* (1876) VIII. 246, I could make out two or three holes..where the silk lining.. was raised and wraggled.

Wragh, obs. var. Wrath *sb.*; var. Wraw *a.*

Freq. in the Egerton and Harleian copies of the *E. E. Psalter*, e.g. ii. 13, xvii. 9, lix. 1, lxxiii. 1.

† **Wragland.** *Obs. rare.* [Of obscure origin. Perh. merely a var. of the erroneous form *wranglan(d)* cited s.v. Wranlons; but cf. Wraggle *v.*[1]]

1. (See quot. and cf. Wranlons.)

1611 Cotgr., *Raboudris*, wraglands; crooked, or misgrowne trees which will neuer proue timber.

2. (See quot. and cf. Wreckling.)

1611 Cotgr., *Rabougrir*,..to wax mishapen, or imperfect of shape; to become a wragland, or grub.

Wrah, variant of Wraw *a.* *Obs.* **Wraht**, var. *wrought*: see Work *v.* **Wrai(e, Wraier**, varr. Wray(er *Obs.*

† **Wrain-bolt**, variant of Ring-bolt. Also † **Wrain-stave**, a staff for inserting in an eye of this.

1750 Blanckley *Naval Expos.* 17 *Wrain Bolts.* [Each] has a ring at one End for a Staff to go through, [etc.]. *Ibid.* 190 *Wrain Staves* are a Sort of thick Billets, tapered so at each End that they may go into the Ring of the Wrain Bolt. [Hence in Rees' *Cycl.* (1819), Young *Naut. Dict.* (1846), Smyth *Sailor's Word-bk.* (1867), etc.]

Hence † **Wrai·ning-bolt, -staff.** *Obs.*[−1]

1769 Falconer *Dict. Marine* (1776), *Antoit*, a crooked instrument of iron, used to bind the side-planks round the timbers in ship-building. The English artificers perform this operation by wraining-bolts and staffs.

Wraist(e, obs. variants of Wrest *sb.*[1], *a.*, and *v.*

Wrait, obs. or Sc. pa. t. of Write *v.*

Wraith (rēɪþ), *sb.* Orig. (and chiefly) *Sc.* Also 6 **wrath**, **wrayth**, **wraithe**, 7 **wreath.** [Of obscure origin.]

1. An apparition or spectre of a dead person; a phantom or ghost.

1513 Douglas *Æneid* x. x. 112 Norȝit na vane wrathis nor gaistis quent Thi char constrenyt for to went. *Ibid.* xi. 93 In diuers placis The wraithis walkis of goistis that ar deyd. a 1585 Polwart *Flyting w. Montgomerie* 658 Thy speach ..is espyed, That wrytes of witches, warlocks, wraiths, and wratches. 1786 Burns '*When Guilford good*' viii, Chatham's wraith, in heavenly graith,..cry'd, 'Willie, rise!' 1808 Scott *Marm.* vi. Introd. 146 In realms of death Ulysses meets Alcides' wraith. 1861 E. S. Kennedy in *Peaks, Passes & Glaciers* Ser. ii. I. 170 She..died broken-hearted. ..Afterwards, in the still of the evening,..the damsel's wraith would enter the dairy department. 1866 Alger *Solit. Nat. & Man* vi. 288 While Winander, Fairfield and Rydal remain, to all visionary minds his [*sc.* Wordsworth's] wraith will haunt them. 1893 T. E. Brown *Old John*, etc. 44 While I..Drift vaporous to the ancient sea, A wraith, a film, a memory. 1900 A. Upward *E. Lobb* 226 Tall, pale and hollow-eyed, with gaunt cheek-bones,..like a wraith from an extinct world.

fig. 1880 G. Macdonald *Diary Old Soul* Feb. ix, Duty's firm shape thins to a misty wraith.

b. An immaterial or spectral appearance of a living being, freq. regarded as portending that person's death; a fetch.

1513 Douglas *Æneid* x. xi. 127 Thydder went this wrath or schaddo of Ene. 1597 Jas. VI *Dæmonol.* iii. i. 60 These kindes of spirites..when they appeare in the shaddow of a person..to die, to his friendes,..are called Wraithes in our language. 1691 R. Kirk *Secr. Commonwealth* i. § 7. 18 What the Low-countrey Scotts calls a Wreath, and the Irish *Taibhshe* or Death's Messenger. 1772–3 R. Fergusson *To Mem. Dr. W. Wilkie* 35, I dream't yestreen his deadly wraith I saw Gang by my ein as white's the driven snaw... I kent that it forespak approachin' wae. 1802 Scott *Minstr. Scott. Bord.* I. p. cxxxvi, The wraith..of a person shortly to die, is a firm article in the creed of Scotish superstition. 1824 Mrs. Grant in *Mem. & Corr.* (1844) III. 66 A wraith ..is the shadowy likeness of an absent living person. 1838 Lytton *Alice* xi. ii, As the shape of the warning wraith haunts the mountaineer. 1870 Myers *Poems* 92 She and her love,—how dimly has she seen him Dark in a dream and windy in a wraith! 1871 Tylor *Prim. Cult.* I. 404 This is well shown by the reception not only of a theory of ghosts, but of a special doctrine of 'wraiths' or 'fetches'.

transf. 1849 C. Brontë *Shirley* xvii, An opposition procession was there entering, headed also by men in black... 'Is it our double?' asked Shirley: 'our manifold wraith?'

fig. 1850 Tennyson *In Mem.* lxxii. 13 O hollow wraith of dying fame, Fade wholly, while the soul exults.

c. Without article.

1884 E. Gurney in *19th Cent.* 796 The coincidences of death and wraith are due to chance. 1898 H. Newbolt *Island Race* p. x, O Strength divine of Roman days, O Spirit of the Age of Faith, Go with our sons on all their ways When we long since are dust and wraith.

2. A water-spirit.

1742, etc. [see Water *sb.* 24 q]. 1801 M. G. Lewis *Bothwell's Bonny Jane* ii, I hear, with mournful yell, The wraiths of angry Clyde complain. 1832 J. Baxe *St. Herbert's Isle* 132 Wraiths and warlocks by the rush-grown mere. 1854 H. Miller *Sch. & Schm.* x. (1858) 203 Highlanders.. cutting down their corn, when the boding voice of the wraith was heard.

3. An appearance or configuration suggestive of a wraith or spectre.

1882 Whittier *Storm on Lake Asquam* iii, A fire-veined darkness swept Over the..range; A wraith of tempest,.. From peak to peak the cloudy giant stepped. 1912 L. Tracy *Mirabel's Isl.* i, Through the wraiths of scud he thought he had seen something.

4. *attrib.* and *Comb.*, as *wraith-land*, *-seeing*, *-spell*; *wraith-like* adj.

1756 *Yorkshire diary* in *N. & Q.* (1922) 390/2 For the warding off of all things whatsoever from the dead—be they imps, wraithspells, wick things and the like ket. 1865 J. Young *Homely Pictures* 126 Their leggies gat wraith-like, their cheekies gat death-like. 1871 Tylor *Prim. Cult.* I. 405 In Silesia and the Tyrol the gift of wraith-seeing still flourishes. 1893 *Columbus* (Ohio) *Dispatch* 27 Apr., What challenges are prompted to the great..to come from their wraithlands!

Wraith, obs. Sc. var. Wrath *sb.*, *v.*, Wroth *a.*

Wraith(e, erron. varr. Rathe *sb.*[2]

1824 Carr *Craven Gloss.*, *Wraiths*, shafts of a cart. 1851 L. D. B. Gordon *Art Jrnl. Illustr. Cat.* p. vii**, The 'wraithe' is for the purpose of keeping the threads separate. 1897 *Westm. Gaz.* 2 Feb. 7/2 He got a rope, fastened it.. to the cart wraiths, and..strangled himself.

Wraithly, etc., obs. Sc. varr. Wrothly, etc.

Wrak: see Wrack *sbs.*, Wrake *sb.*[1], *sb.*[3]

† **Wrake**, *sb.*[1] *Obs.* Forms: 1 **wracu**, 3–5 **wrak**, 4 *north.* **wrac**, 5 **wraak**, *Sc.* **vrak**; 2– **wrake**, 5–6 *Sc.* **wraik.** [OE. *wracu* (oblique cases *wrace*, *wræce*), f., revenge, vengeance, etc., = Goth. *wraka* persecution, f. the same stem as OE. *wræc* neut., Wrack *sb.*[1] For the related OS. *wrâka*, OHG. *râhha*, see Wreche *sb.*]

1. Suffering that comes or is inflicted as a retribution or penalty; retributive punishment, vengeance, revenge. Also (*b*) coupled with cognate terms.

Beowulf 2336 Him ðæs guðkyning, wedera þioden, wræce leornode. c 825 *Vesp. Psalter* lvii. 11 Bið geblissad se rehtwisa ðonne he ȝesið wrece ðeara arleasra. c 1050 tr. *Bæda's Hist.* i. xv. § 2 (MS. Corpus Camb.), Ne wæs unȝelic wracu þam ðe iu Caldeas bærndon Hierusaleme weallas. c 1200 *Trin. Coll. Hom.* 61 Bute we turnen to gode anradliche, he wile his swerd draȝen, þat is his wrake. a 1225 *Juliana* 50 Ah we schulen sechen efter wrake on alle þat we biwiteð. a 1300 *Cursor M.* 13055, I dred bot þou ne bete þi sake, þou sal noght dei wit-vten wrake. 13.. *E. E. Allit. P.* B. 386 [On] þe moste mountayner..flokked þe folke, for ferde of þe wrake. c 1375 *Sc. Leg. Saints* xii. (*Matthias*) 179 At þe laste Iudas for wrake Rubene in þe nek..strake. c 1430 *Chev. Assigne* 72 Wolt þou werne wrake to hem þat hit deseruethe? a 1500 *Hist. K. Boccus & Sydracke* (? 1510) U j b, That scourge is a swerd of wrake That one shal agayne a nother take. 1513 Douglas *Æneid* ii. ii. 120 The cruell wraik of that dissaitfull slycht.

(*b*) c 1175 *Lamb. Hom.* 13 ȝif ȝe..to-breċað mine lare.., þenne scal eou sone ȝewaxen muchele wrake and sake, here and hunger. a 1250 *Owl & Night.* 1194 Ic wot hwar sal beo niþ & wrake. c 1250 *Gen. & Ex.* 552 So cam on werlde wreche and wrake. a 1300 *Cursor M.* 890 Til þat worm þan drightin spak wordes bath o wrath and wrak [*Trin.* wrake]. 1303 R. Brunne *Handl. Synne* 3389 Þer shewed God weyl by þat kas Þat þe kote a-cursed was, And tokened wel sorowe and wrake. 1382 *Pol. Poems* (Rolls) I. 252 The grete vengaunce and wrake That schulde falle for synnes sake. c 1400 *Sowdone Bab.* 2446 Vengeaunce shalle than on you come, With sorowe, woo and wrake! a 1450 *Le Morte Arth.* 1451 The knyghtis answerd with wo and wrake. 1513 Douglas *Æneid* vii. x. 117 Hevy wraik and sorofull vengence ȝit sall the ourtak.

b. In the phr. *to do*, *have*, *nim* (= take), *ta*, or *take wrake* (*of*, *on*, or *upon* a person or thing, or with indirect object).

In freq. use c 1375–c 1480, esp. with *take*.

†a 900 *Laws of Ine* ix, Ȝif hwa wrace do, ærðon he him ryhtes bidde. c 1000 *Ags. Gosp.* Luke xviii. 7 Ne deð god his gecorenra wrace..? c 1175 *Lamb. Hom.* 9 Þa ilke wrake þe ic dude þe, þu scoldest don me. a 1200 *Moral Ode* 205 God nom..muchele wrake for are misdede. a 1275 *Prov. Alfred* 647 in *O. E. Misc.* 136 For he þe wile wrake don. a 1300 *Cursor M.* 11554 On þe saklés he suld ta wrake. 1357 *Lay Folks' Catech.* (T.) 485 For to take wrake Or wickedly to venge him opon his euen-cristen. c 1450 *Ludus Cov.* 375 Mercy nay nay they xul haue wrake. c 1489 Caxton *Blanch.* xxvi. 95 To be pressented..to the kynge of salamandrye,.. for to haue wrake vpon hym. a 1500 *Hist. K. Boccus & Sydracke* (? 1510) E j, On thy goddes we shall do wrake. 1513 Douglas *Æneid* xi. vi. 80 The montane Caphareus,..That vengeans tuke and wraik apon our floit. 1533 Bellenden *Livy* iii. xxiii. (S.T.S.) II. 40 We desire nowther þe goddis nor men to tak ony wraik or punyssement on ȝow. 1613 Chapman *Hymn to Hymen* Plays 1873 III. 122 Let Peace grow cruell, and take wrake of all.

c. *In wrake of*, in revenge or punishment for. *Sc.*

c 1375 *Sc. Leg. Saints* xxx. (*Theodera*) 799 In wrak of hyr fals plicht [the accuser] deit sodanely in þare sicht. 1513 Douglas *Æneid* iii. iv. 91 For strang hunger sall ȝe stand in sic state, In wraik of our iniuris and bestis slane.

2. Adverse action; active enmity; hostility; mischief.

a 1023 Wulfstan *Hom.* (1883) 106 His sunu hatte Mars, se macode æfre ȝewinn, and wrohte, and saca and wraca he styrede ȝelome. c 1205 Lay. 4040 Wrake wes on londe; wa wes þone vnstronge. a 1327 *Metr. Treat. Dreams* in *Rel. Ant.* I. 262 Armes y-sen ant eke bataille, Hit is strif ant wrake withoute faille. c 1330 *Amis & Amil.* 397 All thus the wrake gan biginne, And with wrethe thai went atvinne, Tho bold bernes to. 1393 Langl. *P. Pl.* C. xviii. 85 What þorw werre and wrake and wycked hyfdes, May no preiour pees make in no place. c 1430 Lydg. *Min. Poems* (Percy Soc.) 125 Hertis devided have caused mochel wrake. a 1450 *Le Morte Arth.* 1675 Syr gawayne And mordreite that mykelle couthe of wrake. 1470–85 Malory *Arthur* xx. i. 797 For and there ryse warre and wrake betwyx syr launcelot and vs, wete you wel [etc.].

3. Distress of body or mind; pain, suffering, misery.

a 1000 *Phœnix* 51 (Gr.), Nis þær on þam londe..ne wop ne wracu, weatacen nan. c 1320 *Bonaventura's Medit.* 366 My breþren also, kepe hem fro wrake. 13.. *Sir Beues* (A.) 328 A was ibrouȝt in tene & wrake Ofte for þat childes sake. 13.. *Leg. St. Gregory* 338 He tok þat child wiþouten hete and bar it hom wiþouten wrake. c 1440 Capgrave *St. Kath.* 866 Þis wille turne vs all to wrake & to dole. c 1450 *Ludus Coventriæ* 189 He xall suffer for mannys sake..moch gret sorow and wrake.

4. Destructive harm or injury; wrecked, ruined, or impaired state or condition; ruin, destruction, wreck.

a 1275 *Prov. Alfred* 142 in *O. E. Misc.* 111 For God may giuen wanne he wele goed after yuil, wele after wrake. c 1380 *Sir Ferumb.* 1815 He wol þe chacy as ys fo & werche þe sorwe & wrake. a 1400 *R. Gloucester's Chron.* (Rolls) II. 786 Her was muche manqualm, wrake was in londe. c 1400 *Anturs of Arth.* xvii, These wrechut wurmus..wurchen me this wrake. Thus to wrake am I wroȝte, Waynor, i-wis. c 1450 *Guy Warw.* (C.) 1158 For thy sake To vs ys comen moche wrake, And all for the loue of the. 1470–85 Malory *Arth.* vii. xx. 244 He wil doo moche harme.., and worche you wrake in this countray. a 1586 Montgomerie *Banks Helicon* 47 Fals Helene..causd King Priamus wraik [*v. r.* wrake] In Troy. 1596 Dalrymple tr. *Leslie's Hist. Scot.* (S.T.S.) II. 178 That sik hatred war nocht the occasioun of the wrake of the hail Realme. 1602 Chettle *Hoffman* i. (1631) B 4 b, Newes..more welcome then the sad discourse Of Leninberg our nephewes timeles wrake.

b. In the phr. *to bring unto*, *to fall into*, *to go*, *put*, or *work to wrake.*

a 1425 *Cursor M.* 9204 (Trin.), Ierusalem was stroyed & take; þat kyngdome fel in to wrake. c 1425 *Non-Cycle Myst. Pl.* 35 Alas, all þen had gone to wrake; Wold ye haue slayne my son Isaac! c 1435 *Chron. London* (Kingsford, 1905) 15 Jurrours went also to Wrake, wher that they myht be ffounde. 1513 Douglas *Æneid* ii. vii. 110 By multitude and nomer on ws set All ȝeid to wraik. c 1550 R. Bieston *Bayte Fortune* A ij b, Displeasure and thought doth bring him vnto wrake. 1565 *Satir. Poems Reform.* i. 107 W[hi]ch made muche myserye, and wrought this realme to wrake. 1596 Dalrymple tr. *Leslie's Hist. Scot.* (S.T.S.) I. 158 Quhen his armie was al put to wrake.

5. An instance or occasion of suffering or inflicting vengeance, harm, injury, or the like.

c 1300 *Cursor M.* 4950 Now es vs comen our ald sakes In to wandret new, and wrakes. 13.. *E. E. Allit. P.* B. 235 Þat oþer wrake þat wex on wyȝez. 13.. *Coer de L.* 1562 Kyng Rychard hys hostel gan take, Thar he gan hys fyrste wrak. c 1425 Wyntoun *Chron.* i. 1361, V. wrakys syndry has our tane..þis Brettane. *Ibid.* ii. 533 The wrakys ten in Egipte rasse. c 1440 *Bone Florence* 1977 God had sende on hym a wrake, That in the palsye can he schake. a 1450 *Le Morte Arth.* 948 The quene..swore to venge hyr of that wrake. a 1578 Lindesay (Pitscottie) *Chron. Scot.* (S.T.S.) I. 125 Seand nathing bot wraikis to come to hir pretendit husband.

Hence † **Wra·kedom**, revenge. *Obs. rare*[−1].

c 1205 Lay. 76 For þe wrake-dome of Menelaus quene,.. for hire weoren on ane daȝe hund þousunt deade.

† **Wrake**, *sb.*[2] Chiefly *Sc.* *Obs.* Also 6–7 *Sc.* **wraik** (6 **vraik**), 7 **wraick.** [var. of Wrack *sb.*[2]; the form may be due to the influence of the preceding word.]

1. Shipwreck; = Wrack *sb.*[2] 2.

1513 Douglas *Æneid* i. iii. *heading*, How that Enee wes withit the tempest schaik, And how Neptune his navy saifit fra wraik. 1530 Palsgr. 290/2 Wrake of a shippe, *naufraige.*

2. Wreck, wreckage; = Wrack *sb.*[2] 1 b.

1544 *Aberdeen Reg.* (1844) I. 205 Ane schip of fyr, quhilk wes storit as vraik in hir cumin in the havyn. 1581 *Sc. Acts Parlt.*, *Jas. VI* (1814) III. 255/2 The haill wraik and wayth that sal happin to be fund..within the boundis of the saidis landis or sie cost thairoff. 1610 *Reg. Mag. Sig. Scot.* 146/1 Cum lie wraik et wair, piscaria de lie yair de Avach, silvis lie scroggis et bussis. 1615 [see Waith *sb.*[2]]. 1632 *Extracts Burgh Rec. Lanark* (1893) 327 With furk, fork, ..vert, vair, wraik, vennysone.

3. Sea-wrack; = Wrack *sb.*[2] 3.

1547 Salesbury *Welsh Dict.*, *Brock mor*, Wrake of the sea. 1597, 1657 [see Sea-oak]. c 1690 Kennett in *Promp. Parv.* (1865) 533 Reits, sea-weed, of some..called reits, of others wrack or wraick.

4. *Sc.* A wrecked edifice, etc. *rare*[−1].

c 1625 A. Craig in H. Bisset *Rolment* (S.T.S.) I. 23 One man..consecratis religius workis to Gods: ane Other leavs sad wraiks, and Ruynis now.

† **Wrake**, *sb.*[3] *Obs. rare.* Also 6 *Sc.* **wraik.** [var. of Wrack *sb.*[3]; for the long vowel cf. Wrake *v.*[3]] Refuse, rubbish; something worthless.

a 1350 *Northern Passion* (G.) 1372 Þe met of þat oþir [tree] ne wol it notht del. Hit was schortir þan þe make. Awei þei slongen hit alle for wrake. a 1586 *Maitland Quarto MS.* (S.T.S.) 111 Sum houpe is ȝit that my seruice sall speid, Without ye quhill I wait I am bot wraik. 1604 A. Craig *Poet. Ess.* C 3, Then should we not bin poynted at for wrake, scorne, and disgrace.

† **Wrake**, *v.*[1] *Obs.* Also 4 *north.*, 5 *Sc.* **wrak**, 8 **rake**; 6 *pa. pple.* **ywrake.** [Irreg. var. of *wreke* Wreak *v.*, prob. influenced by Wrake *sb.*[1] Cf. MDu. *wraken*, var. of *wreken*; MLG. *wraken* to torture.

OE. *wraciende* occurs as var. of *wrecende* (=carrying on) in *Oros.* i. xi.]

1. *trans.* = Wrack *v.*[1] 1. Occas. *refl.* Also *fig.*

c 1205 Lay. 6015 Wrake we us on Bruttes & in to þan londen we sullen faren. a 1300 *Cursor M.* 6256 Bot þan i sal me on him wrake. *Ibid.* 6597 Drightin sal me on yow wrak [*v.r.* wrake], To sauue þaa men þat has na sak. c 1400 *Pride of Life* 88 in *Non-Cycle Myst. Plays* 90 Deth & Life ..striuith a sterne strife King of Life to wrake.

2. *intr.* To execute vengeance (*on* a person).

a 1300 *Cursor M.* 25458 O mans-slaghter had I na mak, Ne nan sa wild in wa to wrak [*Fairf.* wrake], To riue þe grene and gra. *Ibid.* 27459 Quare euer he mai þat man ouer-tak, He sal wit suerd apon him wrak [*Fairf.* wrake].

3. a. To be wroth or angry. *rare*[−1].

a 1300 *E. E. Psalter* vii. 12 (E.), God demer riht, þoland, and strang, Nou wrakes [*v.r.* wrathes] he daies alle lang?

b. To wax violent or furious; to rage.

c 1330 *King of Tars* 148 Gret werre tho bigon to wrake, For the mariage ne moste he take Of that mayden beende.

4. *trans.* To vent (one's wrath); = Wreak *v.* 3.

1596 Spenser *F. Q.* iv. viii. 14 Ah wofull man, what..wrath of cruell wight on thee ywrake..doth thee thus wretched make?

b. To take (vengeance) *on* some one.

1755 *Mem. Capt. Peter Drake* I. xiii. 102 In the End, I sufficiently raked my Vengeance on Mrs. Dickering.

† **Wrake**, *v.*[2] *Sc.* *Obs.* Also **wraik(e.** [var. of Wrack *v.*[2] Cf. Wrake *sb.*[2]]

1. *trans.* To bring (a person) to ruin; = Wrack *v.*[2] 3. Also *refl.*

1571 *Satir. Poems Reform.* xxviii. 141 And schoo wer wrakit, all the warld may wene, Than sould the Duke but dout ressaif ye croun. a 1578 Lindesay (Pitscottie) *Chron. Scot.* (S.T.S.) I. 71 They thocht no thing better nor to wraike them and that witht extreme weiris. 1599 Alex. Hume *Poems* (S.T.S.) 41 The Lord the wicked wraikes. 1603 *Philotus* liii, Quhome haue ȝe wraikit bot ȝour awin. 1621 [see Wrack *v.*[2] 3, quot. 1567].

b. To subvert or overthrow.

1570 *Satir. Poems Reform.* xii. 74 Apperandly thir plaigis ar powrit out To wraik this warld, and wait ȝe quhair about? 1574 *Ibid.* xliii. 447 Quhen the Kirk sa ȝe haue wraikit, ȝit all the Kirkis sall not be stakit. a 1614 J. Melvill *Diary* (Wodrow Soc.) 246 The presuming..of the cheiff corrupt members..had vitiat and wrakit the esteat of the Kirk.

2. To hurt, harm, or injure severely; to damage, wreck, or ruin materially.

1570 *Satir. Poems Reform.* xxiv. 8 Quhair furious Fleming schot his Ordinance, Willing to wraik him wantit na gude will. 1578 *Sc. Acts, Jas. VI* (1814) III. 113/2 Sum of thair housis wyiffis and bairnis being thairin wer allutterlie wraikit and brount. 1596 in *Spalding Club Misc.* (1841) I. 88 His haill geir surmounting to mair nor thrie thowsand lib...ar altogidder wrakit and away. 1607 *Extr. Aberd. Reg.* (1848) II. 295 Dumbartane..is liklie to be wraikit be the inundatioun of the watter of Clyde. 1692 in *Rec. Convent. Burghs Scot.* (1880) IV. 595 Ane bush..named the Generall, was wraked in this harbour.

3. *intr.* = Wrack *v.*[2] 4. *rare*[−1].

1570 *Satir. Poems Reform.* xii. 67, I dout not, in our dayis, Hepburnis will wraik for wyrrying of the King.

Hence † **Wra·king** *vbl. sb.* *Obs.*

1569 *Diurn. Occurr.* (Bann. Cl.) 147 The wraiking of James erle of Mortoun and his assistaris.

† **Wrake**, *v.*[3] *Sc.* *Obs.* Also 7 **wraik.** [a. (M)LG. *wrāken* (whence Sw. *vraka*, Da. *vrage*), older Du. *wraaken*, Du. *wraken*, older Flem. *wraecken* (Kilian), to reject, etc. Cf. Wrack *v.*[3]] *trans.* To examine (goods, etc.) with a view to rejecting or destroying the unsound, faulty, or damaged. Hence **Wraking** *vbl. sb.*

1584 *Burgh Rec. Edinb.* (1882) IV. 343 All the beiring and quhyte fische that sall cum within the said port..to be strukin vp, visitet and wraket. 1599 in *Rec. Convent. Burghs Scot.* (1870) II. 60 Anent the office of jedgerie wraking and burneing of all boghedis and barrellis of herings. 1609 *Ibid.* 284 Nane to be transportit furth of the realm quhill thai [*sc.* herring-barrels] be packit, wraikit and merkett as followis.

† **Wra·keful**, *a.* *Obs.* [f. Wrake *sb.*[1] + -ful. Cf. Wrackful *a.*[1], Wreakful *a.*]

1. Vengeful; = Wrackful *a.*[1]

a 1225 [implied in Wrakefully]. c 1480 Henryson *Test. Cres.* 329 Ane wraikfull sentence geuin on fair Cresseid.

2. Of persons: Revengeful, vindictive.

a 1300 *E. E. Psalter* xvii. 51 (E.), Leser min be niht and dai Fra mi faes wrakeful [*v.r.* wrathful] are.

3. ? Wicked; sinful.

c 1310 in Wright *Lyric P.* iv. 23 This wrakeful werkes under wede in soule soteleth sone.

4. *Sc.* Destructive.

c 1625 *Bisset's Rolment* (S.T.S.) I. 22 Evin in this act, thow rearest a Monument That all the spyte of wraikfull tyme out faces.

Hence † **Wra·kefully** *adv.*, vengefully. *Obs.*

a 1225 *Ancr. R.* 364 Wule God so wrakefuliche awreken him upon sunne? a 1225 *Leg. Kath.* 2047 (Royal MS.), Hu wrakefulliche [*Cott. MS.* wrakeliche] wenestu wule he ant wreððe uppon þe, wrecche!

† **Wra·ker.** *Sc.* *Obs.* [f. Wrake *v.*[3] + -er[1] or a. (M)LG. *wraker*. Cf. Wracker[2].] One who inspects goods and rejects or destroys the faulty.

1584 *Sc. Acts, Jas. VI*, III. (1814) 302 [To] appoint ane discrete man to be visitour, wraker [*v.r.* wracker], gager, and birnar of the saidis treis. 1584 *Burgh Rec. Edinb.* (1882) IV. 343 Jadgeares, wrakeris, visitouris and markeris of the haill hering and quhyte fishe that sall cum within the port. 1598 in *Rec. Convent. Burghs Scot.* (1870) I. 31 Iadger burnear, or wraker of all barrellis and hogheidis of salmond and hering.

† **Wrakling.** *Sc.* *Obs.* Also **-lin, -lyne, -lene.** [ad. MLG. *wrakelinge*, MDu. *wrakeline* (whence also Fris. *wrakling* plank-nail, Da. dial. *vrækling*).] A large make of nail, esp. used in shipbuilding. Also *collect.*

1494 *Acc. Ld. High Treas. Scot.* I. 250 The expensis..for the macken of the erne grathe of the barge [include]..for wraklynys bocht, xvjd. *Ibid.* 253, vij stane and xij pundis of boltis and wrakling. 1496 *Ibid.* 310 Ane thousand of singil bowssleit, and iiijm wraklene.

attrib. 1497 *Acc. Ld. High Treas. Scot.* I. 334, iijc gret wraklin nalis.

† **Wrall**, *sb.* *Obs. rare.* Also **wrawl.** [f. next.]

1. A winding or twisting; a twist or coil.

1398 Trevisa *Barth. De P. R.* xviii. ix. (Camb. MS.), Þe eddir amphibena..wigleþ wiþ wralles [*ed.* 1495 wrynkles] corckles & drauȝtis of þe bodi.

2. A wreathed decoration or ornamentation.

1540 in V. Green *Hist. Worcs.* (1796) II. App. p. iii, Item, vj spones with wrawles. *Ibid.* p. iv, vj spones with wralls.

† **Wrall**, *v.* *Obs.* [Of obscure origin; cf. Unwrall *v.*] *trans.* To wreathe, wind, or twist; to convolve.

1398 Trevisa *Barth. De P. R.* v. xii. (Tollem. MS.), These holes ben set in þe stony bon [of the ear]..and ben wrallid and wounde as a spyndel of a presse. *Ibid.* xvii. lxxx,

Wrall, obs. var. Wrawl, etc.

Wramp (ræmp), sb. Also 9 wramp. [Of obscure origin. Cf. MLG. *wrampachtich*, Du. *wrampet* warped, twisted.] A twist or sprain.

Wramp (ræmp), v. *trans.* To twist or sprain the ankle, etc.; to rick or wrench.

Wran, Sc. or dial. var. Wren.

+ Wranchooved. Obs.

Wrancke, obs. erron. f. Rank a. Wranckle, obs. erron. f. Rankle v. Wrang, obs. or dial. pa. t. of Wring v.

+ Wrangel, Obs.

Wrangle (ræŋg'l), sb. [f. next.] 1. An angry dispute or noisy quarrel; an altercation or bitter disputation.

+2. a. A disputation answer or argument. b. A controversy. Obs.

Wrangle (ræŋg'l), v. Also 7–8 rangle. 1. intr. To dispute angrily; to argue noisily or vehemently; to altercate, contend; to bicker.

2. Without article. The action of wrangling; angry altercation or argument; noisy dispute or controversy.

Wrangle (ræŋg'l), v. Also 7–8 rangle. [f. prec.]

Wrangler (ræŋg'lər), sb. [f. as prec. + -er.] 1. One who wrangles or quarrels; an angry or noisy disputer or arguer.

b. One who engages in argument, debate, or controversy; a debater, disputant, or controversialist.

2. The name for each of the candidates who have been placed in the first class in the mathematical tripos at Cambridge University. See Tripos 2, and cf. Optime.

Wrangler (ræŋg'lər), v.

Wranglership (ræŋg'lər-ʃip). [f. prec. + -ship.] The position or rank of a wrangler at Cambridge University.

Wranglesome (ræŋg'lsəm), a. *collog.* or *dial.* Given to wrangling; quarrelsome; contentious, peevish.

Wrangling, *vbl. sb.* [f. Wrangle v. + -ing.] 1. The action of the verb; noisy quarrelling.

Wrangling, *ppl. a.* [as prec. + -ing2.] 1. That wrangles, quarrels, or disputes; engaged or embroiled in, given or addicted to, noisy altercation or dispute; contentious.

Wrang-nail, -rope: see Wrong sb.3
Wrangous(lie, -uis(lie, -us(lie, etc., obs. var. Wrongous.
Wrangus(e, -ly, -ness, obs. ff. Wrongous, -ly, -ness.
Wrankle, obs. erron. f. Rankle v.
+ Wranions. Obs. rare—1 [Of obscure origin. Cf. Waggland 2.] *pl.* Unthriving trees that will never become timber.

Wrap (ræp), sb.1 Also 5 wrappe. [f. the vb. Not usual before the 19th cent.] 1. A wrapper or covering.

2. A loose garment or article of feminine dress used or designed to envelop or fold about the person; a shawl, scarf, or the like.

Wrap (ræp), v. Also 4–7 wrappe (6 *arch.* 9 *dial.* wrap, 7 *pa. pple.* wrapt).

2. To cover or envelop (an object) by winding or folding something round or about it; to surround with or enwrap in a covering, wrapper, or the like, esp. so as to protect from injury, damage, loss, etc. Also *transf.*

3. To envelop or enclose in a surrounding medium, as flames, water, etc. Freq. in *passive*.

Wrap, *sb.* and *v.*, var. Warp.
Wrap-rascal

Wrapped (ræpt), *ppl. a.* and *pa. pple.* 1. Concealed, covered, hidden.

Wrapper (ræ'pər). Also 6 rapper, 8 wraper, 9 *dial.* wropper. [f. Wrap v. + -er1.] 1. That which anything is wrapped, enveloped, or enclosed; a piece of fabric or other material forming a wrapping; esp. in later use, a protective covering for a parcel or the like.

2. An article of apparel for wrapping, rolling, or coiling about the head, face, or person.

Supplement, p. 3873; Corrigenda, p. 4092; Spurious words, p. 4093; Books quoted, p. 4094

Wrapper.

3. An outer garment, esp. for indoor wear or in household work, designed for loosely enveloping the whole (or nearly the whole) figure; a loose robe or gown. In later use *chiefly U.S.*

4. An article of dress, esp. for masculine wear, intended to wrap about or envelop the person; a wrap. Now *dial.*

5. *Bot.* = INVOLUCRE.

6. *Anat. & Surg.* (See quot.) *Obs.*

7. *Lumbering.* A chain for binding logs on a skid.

II. 8. One who wraps or packs up anything; *spec.* one whose occupation consists in wrapping parcels. Also *with agent.*

III. 8. *attrib.* and *Comb.*, as *wrapper-apron-*, *brat*; *wrapper-addresser*, *-writer*.

Wrapping, *vbl. sb.* [f. WRAP *v.* + -ING.] App. rare between the 16th and 19th cent.

1. The action of covering with or enveloping in a wrap or wrapper.

2. A loose outer garment; a wrap or wrapper.

3. *concr.* That which wraps or envelops; a wrapping, covering, or wrapper.

II. 4. The action of interlacing or intertwining; the fact of being interwoven. Also *fig.*

Wrapping-gown. *Obs.* [f. WRAPPING *vbl. sb.* + GOWN *sb.*] A nightgown.

Wrap-rascal (ræˈpraskal). Now *arch.* or *dial.* [WRAP *v.* + RASCAL *sb.*] A loose overcoat or great-coat, esp. worn in the 18th century.

Wrasse (ræs). Also 6-9 wrass. [ad. Cornish, *wrach*, mutated form of *gwrach* = Welsh *gwrach* wrasse, also old woman (cf. OLD WIFE *b*). Mod. Cornish *dial.* has also the form *wrath*, and *wrase* may be an E. plural in *-s*.]

Wrast, *south. dial.* var. WREST *sb.*

Wrast, *v.* *Obs.⁻¹* [Meaning obscure.]

Wrastle, var. WRESTLE *v.*

Wrat, *v.* Now *dial.* or *Obs.* Also 6 wratte, 9 wraght. [a. (M)LG. *wratte* (LG. *wrat*), Du. *wrat*, or metathetic var. WART *sb.*]

Wrath, *sb.* [OE. *wrǽþþo*, *wrǽþþu*, f. *wráþ* WROTH *a.*]

Wrath (rǫþ), *a.* [var. of WROTH *a.*, prob. by association with WRATH *sb.*] Wroth, angry, irate; deeply resentful.

Wrathe, *v.* Also: Forms: α. 3-6 wreþþen, wreppe, wreiþe, 4-5 wreothe. β. 3 Orm. -oun), 4-5 wraiþe, 5 wraþþe; 3 wrað, -en, 4-5 wrathen, wratheð etc. γ. 3 wraþen, wrathen, wraþþen, wrathe(n. δ. 5-6 wraith. [Early ME. *wreþþen*, *wraþþen*, f. the *sb.* (see WRATH *sb.*), *wreþþen*, etc. of the earlier verbum WRETHE *v.* Cf. AWRATH, WRETHE *v.*]

1. *intr.* To be or become angry, wrathful, or wroth; to feel, manifest, or express rage.

2. *trans.* To make angry or indignant; to incense; to treat with anger; to grow resentment.

3. *trans.* To afflict, harm, or injure; to bring to grief or disaster.

4. *refl.* To be or become angry with any one.

Wrathful, *a.* [f. WRATH *sb.* + -FUL.] Full of wrath.

1. Of persons, etc.: Harbouring wrath; full of anger; enraged, incensed.

2. *transf.* To make angry, irate; angry, or wroth; to move to wrath, ire, or deep resentment; to anger, enrage; to annoy, vex.

Wrathfully, *adv.* [f. prec. + -LY.] Cf. WRETHFULLY *adv.*] In a wrathful manner; angrily, resentfully.

Wrathfulness. [f. prec. + -NESS.] Cf. WRETHFULNESS *sb.*] The state, condition, or quality of being wrathful; wrath, ire.

Wrathhede. *Obs.⁻¹* wrath: deep anger.

Wrath-thede, wrath: deep anger. *Obs.⁻¹*

Wrathless, *a.* and *b.* = wrappelee. [f. WRATH *sb.* + -LESS.] Free from, devoid of, wrath.

Wrathly, *a.* and *adv.* [f. WRATH *sb.* + -LY.] **A.** *adj.* Full of or characterized by wrath; wrathful. **B.** *adv.* In a wrathful manner; angrily.

Wrath money. *local.* [var. of *warth-money*: cf. WARD-PENNY.] = WARDPENNY.

Wrathyhe. *Obs.⁻¹* [Of obscure origin; perh. f. Cornish *wrath* WRASSE + *bihan* small.] (See quot.)

Wratten, *dial.* var. WRETHEN *ppl. a.*

WRAW. 348 349 WRAYER

Wraw, *a.* Now *dial.* Forms: 4 wrau, 4-5 wra, 4 wrawe, 5 wrawe. [Of obscure origin.]

Wrawful, *a.* *Obs.* [f. prec. + -FUL.] Angry, wrathful.

Wrawl, *v.* *dial.* Also 5-6 wrawl. 6 wraule, 7 wraule(d), 7 wrawle, 8 wrawl. [Imitative. Cf. WRAW *a.*]

1. *intr.* To utter an inarticulate noise or sound; to bawl, squall.

2. *intr.* To scream.

Wrawlingly, *adv.*

Wrawly, *adv.* [f. WRAW *a.* + -LY.] Perversely.

Wrawness, perverseness. [f. WRAW *a.* + -NESS.]

Wraw, *v.* *Obs. rare.* Also 3 wrawon. [ad. MDu. *wrauwen*, of imitative origin.] *intr.* To miaul, as a cat; to mew.

Wraxle, *dial.* var. WRESTLE *v.*

Wray, *v.* *Obs.* var. WROY *v.*

Wrayer. *Obs.* [f. WRAY *v.* + -ER.]

†Wrayful, a. Obs. rare. In 3 wreiful. [f. WRAY sb.[1] + -FUL.] Containing or involving an accusation; accusatory.

Wraytic, obs. f. WRECK sb.

†Wrayward, a. Obs. rare. [Perh. an alteration of WAYWARD a.] Perverse, froward.

Wrd, obs. form of WORD.

Wre, obs. Sc. variant of ORE[2].

Wreachednesse, obs. var. WRETCHEDNESS.

Wreade, obs. var. WREATHE v.

Wreak (rɪk), sb. Now arch. or Obs. Forms: 1 wrǣc, wrēc, 2–5 wreche, 3–4 wreke, 3–5 wrake, 4–6 wreke ... [OE. wrǣc ...] 1. Pain or punishment inflicted in return for injury wrong, offence, etc.; hurt or harm done from vindictive motives; vengeance, revenge.

Wreak (rɪk), v. Forms: 1–2 wrecan, 2 wrecen, 2–4 wreken (3 wreken, werken, wreoken ...) [OE. wrecan ...] 1. trans. To drive, press, force to move. Obs.

Wreake, obs. f. REEK sb.[1] — RECKLESS a.

†Wreaks, erron. f. REAKS (pranks) Obs.

Wreal, var. WREATHE (Obs.)

Wreap, var. WREATHE (Obs.); Wreast, obs. f. WREST sb. and v. ... obs. f. WRIST sb.

Wreath (riθ). Pl. wreaths (riδz). Forms: 1 wrǽð, wriþa, 4–5 wreþe, 4–6 wreth, 5–6 wrethe, wreyth, 6–7 wreathe, 6 wreath ... [OE. wriða, wriþa ...]

Wreath (riθ), v. [f. WREATH sb.]

Wreathe (riδ), v. Forms: 1 wreóðan ... [OE. wríþan ...]

Wreathed (riδd), ppl. a. [f. WREATHE v. + -ED.]

oratory in England. 1828 TENNYSON *Lover's Tale* II. 43 They vanish'd..Beneath the bower of wreathed eglantines. *transf.* 1782 WARTON *On Sir J. Reynolds's Painted Window* 24 Where Superstition with capricious hand In many a maze the wreathed window plann'd. *fig.* 1820 KEATS *Ode to Psyche* 60 A rosy sanctuary will I dress With the wreath'd trellis of a working brain.

5. Covered, decked, or encompassed by a wreath or wreaths; garlanded.

1819 KEATS *Lamia* I. 38 When from this wreathed tomb shall I awake? 1847 LONGF. in *Life* (1891) II. 76 Byron's wild and wicked travesty..hits the Laureate [*sc.* Southey] hard on his wreathed head. 1897 *Daily News* 30 June 6/2 The wreathed coffin was conveyed..to the burial ground.

b. *Her.* Encircled with a twisted band or wreath.

1688 HOLME *Armoury* II. 473/2 A Flower de Lis Wreathed, or in the middle Wreathed. *Ibid.* 393/2 A Sarazens Head.. wreathed about the temples. 1838 *Penny Cycl.* XII. 143/2 Heads are also blazoned wreathed or banded, as the case may be.

c. In the specific names of birds (see quots.). Frequently used by Latham.

1781 LATHAM *Gen. Synop. Birds* I. 358 Wreathed Hornbill; ..on the top of the upper mandible is an appendage..rounded at top. 1785 *Ibid.* V. 216 Wreathed Plover;..round the crown runs a list of white, encircling the head like a wreath. 1819 STEPHENS in Shaw's *Gen. Zool.* XI. 488 Wreathed Pluvian. *Pluvianus coronatus*,..[= Latham's] Wreathed Plover. 1823 LATHAM *Gen. Hist. Birds* VII. 140 Wreathed Warbler...From the eye round to the nape a white line, passing backwards, and surrounding it as a wreath at the back part.

Hence **Wrea·thedness.** *rare*⁻⁰.

1730 BAILEY (fol.), *Contorteousness*, wreathedness.

Wreathen (rī·ðʼn), *ppl. a.* Also 4–6 **wrethen**, 5 **-yne, -in**, (?) **wrethe.** [ME. *wrēðen*, normal variant of *wrīðen*, pa. pple. of *wrīðen* WRITHE *v.* Cf. WRITHEN *ppl. a.*]

1. = WREATHED *ppl. a.* 1.

a. *a* 1400–50 *Wars Alex.* 5526 All þe watir of þe werd [to him seemed] bot as a wrethen neddire. 1401–2 *Durham Acc. Rolls* (Surtees) 393, vj libr. de wrethyn candell, xs. *a* 1450 *Songs & Carols 15th C.* (Warton Club) 85 My baselard haȝt a wrethin hafte. 1465 *Will of Pachett* (Somerset Ho.), A wrethyne rynge of golde. *c* 1530 in Gutch *Coll. Cur.* II. 310 Great gilte Candilsteks costid withe wrethin shanks. *a* 1548 HALL *Chron., Hen. VIII*, 207 b, Veluet..fret with flowers of Siluer, and small twigges of wrethen worke. *a* 1600 MONTGOMERIE *Misc. Poems* iv. 5 Mercure with his wrethin wand. 1887 *Suppl. Jamieson* 280 Wrethin' strae-rapes.

β. 1568 BIBLE (Bishops') *Exod.* xxviii. 22 Chaynes of pure golde and wreathen worke. 1598 DELONEY *Jacke Newb.* i. Wks. (1912) 7 The Bel-weather..by the force of his wreathen hornes..slew him. 1608 TOPSELL *Serpents* 245 Many..are the Epithets which are giuen to Snakes, as..Gorgonean, wreathen, slyding. 1611 BIBLE *Exod.* xxviii. 14 Thou shalt make..two chaines of pure gold..; of wreathen worke shalt thou make them. 1792 *Mass. Mag.* Nov., Imagination very easily giving them [*sc.* stalactites] pedestals and chapiters, and even wreathen-work. 1871 J. HAY *Pike County Ball.* (1880) 154 Wreathen amulet Forged against sword-stroke. 1872 RUSKIN *Aratra Pentelici* 51 The wreathen work of its doors, ..the foliage of its capitals. 1875 — *Fors Clav.* lviii. 288 The pierced fractional coins will only bear a chased wreathen fillet. 1877 BLACKMORE *Erema* li, The glorious woods of wreathen gold..all were mine.

Comb. 1796 WITHERING *Brit. Plants* (ed. 3) III. 566 Wreathen-podded Whitlowgrass. [Grows in] Fissures of limestone rocks.

2. Formed or arranged by or as by twining or interweaving; entwined, intertwined.

1611 SPEED *Hist. Gt. Brit.* VI. ix. § 21. 81 Their Oratory, built onely of wrethen wands. 1631 WEEVER *Anc. Funeral Mon.* 58 To build a Church or Oratorie of wreathen wands. 1713 C'TESS WINCHELSEA *Misc. Poems* 39 The Flowers..In wreathen Garlands dropt agen On Lucullus. *a* 1850 in Mrs. Jameson *Leg. Monast. Orders* (1852) 45 A church of wreathen wands.

Wreather (rī·ðəɹ). [f. WREATHE *v.* + -ER[1].] One who or that which wreathes, twists, or twines. Also *transf.*

1566 STAPLETON *Ret. Untr. Jewel* IV. 62 To proue you wresters and wrethers of Gods holy worde. 1579–80 NORTH *Plutarch* (1595) 5 Pityocamtes, that is to say, a wreather or bower of pine apple trees. 1648 HEXHAM II, *Een Wrijter*, an Extorter, a Wreather, or a Wrester. 1817 KEATS *Sleep & Poetry* 14 Sleep,..Soft closer of our eyes!..Wreather of poppy buds, and weeping willows!

Wreathing (rī·ðiŋ), *vbl. sb.* [f. as prec. + -ING[1].]

1. The action of twisting or contorting; the fact of writhing; an instance of this.

1580 HOLLYBAND *Treas. Fr. Tong*, *Torsement*, a wreathing. 1587 GOLDING *De Mornay* xiii. 223 Leauing their mouings free; which yet..shall come to the end which God hath listed to appoint vnto them, whatsoeuer windings and wreathings they seeme to themselues to make. 1615 G. SANDYS *Trav.* 34 By the wreathing of their bodies..they seek to avoid the pursuer. 1668 CULPEPPER & COLE *Barthol. Anat.* I. v. 8 Touching the Contorsion or Wreathing of the recurrent Nerve. 1721 BRADLEY *Philos. Acc. Wks. Nat.* 130 The Earth-Worm..by a sort of wreathing..takes hold of the Ground with its small Feet. 1794 R. J. SULIVAN *View Nat.* II. 456 The sun,..whose oblique course is not unaptly represented by the wreathings of a snake. 1800 *Med. Jrnl.* III. 451 The attendants told me, from the wreathing of her body.., that she would soon have another fit. 1823 JOANNA BAILLIE *Poems* 260 [Steam] With tressy wreathings playing in the air. 1885 R. BRIDGES *Eros & Psyche* Oct. 23 Mid the wreathings of the vapour dim The goddess grew in glory visible.

fig. 1612 SHELTON *Quix.* I. IV. vi. (1620) 343 His Friend did notable injurie to their amitie in searching out wreathings and ambages in the discovery of his most hidden thoughts to him. 1641 FANNANT *True Relat. Parl. Rich. II*, 37 Those infinit wreathings of contention.

b. *concr.* That which is wreathed or twisted.

1600 SURFLET *Countrie Farme* III. xiii. 449 And for these grafts it is ynough, if euerie one of them, haue one good eielet or two aboue the wreathing. 1634 PEACHAM *Compl. Gentl.* (ed. 2) xii. 110 To Painters, for the picturing of some exquisit arme, leg. torse or wreathing of the body.

†**2.** A wresting of the sense or meaning of something. *Obs.*

1628 PRYNNE *Cens. Cozens* 67 Which is a grosse abuse, a wreathing, a peruerting of the Scriptures.

3. The action or fact of entwining or intertwining; an instance of this.

1553 [see WRAPPING *vbl. sb.* 1 b]. 1590 SPENSER *F. Q.* II. xii. 53 Boughes and braunches..did..dilate Their clasping armes, in wanton wreathings intricate. 1661 BOYLE *Spring of Air* II. ii. (1682) 32 In strings there is required either wreathing or some..texture of component parts. 1844 MRS. BROWNING *Cry of Children* viii. Let them touch each other's hands, in a fresh wreathing Of their tender human youth! *a* 1901 W. BRIGHT *Age of Fathers* (1903) II. 23 The wreathing of a garland for the Penates.

4. The action of investing with a wreath.

1852 GROTE *Greece* II. lxx. IX. 137 The operations of wreathing and unwreathing must here have been performed by the soldiers symbolically.

Wrea·thing, *ppl. a.* [f. as prec. + -ING[2].]

1. That wreathes, twists, or twines; enwreathing.

1677 DRYDEN *State Innoc.* III. 16 When your kind Eyes look'd languishing on mine, And wreathing Arms did soft embraces joyn. 1697 — *Virg. Past.* IV. 22 Unbidden Earth shall wreathing Ivy bring. 1718 ROWE tr. *Lucan* 180 To cast from off her Brow the wreathing Green. 1816 BYRON *Siege Cor.* vi, In red and wreathing columns flash'd The flame. 1842 DICKENS *Amer. Notes* xiv, [To] see the wreathing water in the rapids hurrying on to take its fearful plunge. 1887 HISSEY *Holiday on Road* 327 The wreathing mists and wandering clouds of such a day.

†**2.** *Wreathing-team*, part of the gear of a plough. Perhaps an error for *wrethen* WREATHEN *ppl. a.*

1523 FITZHERB. *Husb.* § 5 He muste haue his ploughe and his..horses, and the geare that belongeth to them;..bowes, yokes, landes, stylkynges, wrethynge-temes.

Hence **Wrea·thingly** *adv.*

1845 J. C. MANGAN *German Anthol.* II. 59 That lone Gate which the tall wild weeds encircle wreathingly. 1891 *Temple Bar Mag.* Aug. 542 [The smoke] falls wreathingly upon the face of the sleeping child.

Wreathless (rī·þlės), *a.* [f. WREATH *sb.* + -LESS.] Having no wreath; destitute or devoid of a wreath or wreaths.

1825 COLERIDGE *Work without Hope* 11 With lips unbrightened, wreathless brow, I stroll. 1878 SWINBURNE *Poems & Ball.* 139 While youth with burning lips and wreathless hair Sang toward the sun. 1903 *Daily Chron.* 30 March 5/7 The almost clandestine removal of the coffin.. wreathless and flowerless to the numbered luggage-van.

Wreathlet (rī·þlėt). [f. as prec. + -LET.] A small wreath.

1833 *Blackw. Mag.* XXXIV. 258 From that Wreath he has woven wreathlets. 1857 *Fraser's Mag.* LVI. 491 These tiny wreathlets wandered hither and thither. 1887 [C. MACKAY] *Twin Soul* I. xxii. 235 The blue smoke curled in beautiful wreathlets to the sky.

Wreathy (rī·þi), *a.* [f. as prec. + -Y[1].]

1. Of the form of a wreath, coil, or twisted band; marked or characterized by convolution, twisting, or twining; wreathing, curling.

1644 DIGBY *Nat. Bodies* xxiii. § 1. 203 A vast multitude of seuerall little ioyntes, and wreathy labyrinthes of nature. 1658 SIR T. BROWNE *Pseud. Ep.* (ed. 3) III. xxiii. 135 That famous one [*sc.* horn] which is preserved at St. Dennis near Paris, hath wreathy spires, and cochleary turnings about it. 1798 JOANNA BAILLIE *Fugitive Verses* (1840) 3 Slowly mounts the smoke in wreathy clouds. *Ibid.* 110 Wreathy folds. 1817 MOORE *Lalla R., Nourmahal* 411 Those wreathy, Red Sea shells, Where Love himself, of old, lay sleeping. *a* 1851 MOIR *Evening Tranquillity* vi, Above yon cottage..The wreathy smoke ascends. 1853 KANE *Grinnell Exp.* xxxvi. (1856) 332 The long, wreathy brown clouds.

transf. 1784–5 *Ann. Reg., Poetry* 137 Wreathy smiles, and roseate pleasures, Are thy richest, sweetest treasures. 1853 *Fraser's Mag.* XLVII. 513 The very foam of the sea, flung in all its wreathy airiness from the crest of a wave.

2. Decked with a wreath or wreathing.

1697 DRYDEN *Æneis* IV. 438 The Bacchanalian Dames.. houl about the Hills, and shake the wreathy Spear.

b. *Her.* (See quot.) *rare*⁻⁰.

1894 *Parker's Gloss. Her.*, *Tortilly*,..a term applied to Ordinaries which are wreathed; the term *wreathy* is also found.

3. Of the nature of, forming or constituting, a wreath or garland. Also *transf.*

1718 ROWE tr. *Lucan* 181 Her bristling Locks the wreathy Fillet scorn. 1725 POPE *Odyssey* VI. 152 Around his loins the verdant cincture spreads A wreathy foliage. *c* 1750 R. CUMBERLAND in *Mem.* (1806) 62 The victim beast,..With all its wreathy honours on its head. 1818 *Blackw. Mag.* III. 90 On Carmel's brow the wreathy vine Had all its honours shed. 1828 MISS MITFORD *Village* Ser. III. 146 A wilderness of blossom, interwoven, intertwined, wreathy, garlandy. 1830 [see GARLANDY *a.*]. 1845 BROWNING *Flight of Duchess* xvii. 59 His forehead chapleted green with wreathy hop.

Wreat(t, obs. Sc. forms of WRITE *sb.*[1]

†**Wrecche,** *v. Obs.* [OE. *wreccan* (*wreahte, wrehte*; *wreaht, wreht*) to arouse, undertake, raise. Cf. MDu. *wrecken*, NFris. *wräki* to waken, *wräken* (adj.) awake.] *trans.* To rouse, arouse; to bring to life.

c 897 ÆLFRED *Gregory's Past. C.* xxviii. 193 Ne sceal he no ðæt an don ðæt he ana waciʒe, ac he sceal eac his friend wreccean [*v.r.* wreccan]. *c* 1000 ÆLFRIC *Saints' Lives* xi. 241 We feollan on slæpe... ac he læʒ burh-wacol.., and wræhte us siððan. *a* 1250 *Owl & Night.* 106 Þo hit bycom þat he hayhte [= hatched] & of his eyre briddes wrauhte [*Cott.* wraȝte].

Wrecche, Wreche, etc.: see WRETCH, etc.

Wrecful, variant of WRACKFUL *a.*[2] *Obs.*

†**Wreche,** *sb. Obs.* Forms: *α.* 3 **wræche**, 3–6 **wreche**, 4–6 **wrech**, 4 **wrieche**, 4–5 **wreeche**, 5 **wreach**. *β.* 3–4 **wrache**, 5 **wrach**. *γ.* 4–5 **wrecche** (4 **vrecche**), 5–6 **wretche**. [The normal representative of an OE. *wrǣc* (with palatal *c*) fem., of which however the existing texts present no example which can be definitely distinguished from *wrǣc* neut., WRACK *sb.*[1] (A possible instance occurs in *Riddles* ii. 4, if the reading *wræce* is correct.) The vowel of *wrǣc* (:—earlier **wrāk-jō*) corresponds to that of OFris. *wrēke*, *wrētse* (NFris. *wrēk*, *wrāk*), OS. *wrāka*, *wrēka* (MLG. *wrāke*; MDu. *wrāke*, Du. *wraak*), OHG. *rāhha* (MHG. *rāche*, G. *rache*), Goth. *wrēkei*.

The *β*-forms partly represent a south-eastern variant of *wræche*, and are partly due to confusion with *wrake* WRAKE *sb.*; the *γ*-forms show assimilation (in some instances merely graphic) to *wrecche* WRETCH *sb.* The normal spelling, if the word had survived into modern English, would have been *wreach* or *wreech*.]

1. Retributive punishment; vengeance; = WREAK *sb.* 1.

In very frequent use from *c* 1290 to *c* 1450.

α. *c* 1200 ORMIN Introd. 19 Forr þatt wass mikell wræche wiss þatt all follc for till helle. *c* 1205 LAY. 29581 Vre drihte ..his wreche sende an wræstliche þan folke. *c* 1250 *Gen. & Ex.* 552 So cam on werlde wreche and wrake. *a* 1333 W. HEREBERT in *Relig. Lyrics 14th C.* (1924) 20 Nou, dame, ich þe byseche At þylke day of wreche..spek uor me. 13.. *E. E. Allit. P.* B. 230 Ȝet wrathed not þe wyȝ, ne þe wrech saȝtled. *c* 1386 CHAUCER *Monk's T.* 625 The wreche of god hym smoot so cruelly, That thurgh his body wikked wormes crepte. *c* 1400 *Pilgr. Sowle* (Caxton, 1483) III. viii. 55 Euer haue they in theyr hertes holden wreeche and rancour. 1477 NORTON *Ord. Alch.* i. in Ashm. (1652) 15 For doubt of such pride and wreach, He must be ware that will this Science teach. *c* 1485 *Digby Myst.* (1882) III. 469 To kepe þis place from wreche.

Personif. 1413 26 *Pol. Poems* 53 Euere by troube stondes wreche, For wreche is goddis champioun. *c* 1460 *Wisdom* 698 in *Macro Plays* 58 Let se: cum in, Indignacion & Sturdynes,..Wreche, & Dyscorde expres.

β. *c* 1200 [see 1 b *β*]. *c* 1320 *Cast. Love* (H.) 1560 The eyȝhte day betokynth gret wrache. 13.. *E. E. Allit. P.* B. 204 He forȝet alle his fre þewes, & wex wod to þe wrache, for wrath at his hert. *c* 1450 *Mirk's Festial* I. 36 And for wrach schuld falle on hymselfe yn party, þerfor [etc.]. 1535 *Trevisa's Barth. De P. R.* XVIII. xii. 315 b/1 Some [bees] for grete wrath and desyre of wrache stingethe soo depe, that [etc.].

γ. 1297 R. GLOUC. (Rolls) 1585 Þus him vel vrecche of god, vor he þe apostles slou. *c* 1330 *King of Tars* 658 Leef on hym that strengor is, For doute of more wrecche [*rimes* teche, leche]. 1387 TREVISA *Higden* I. 253 Anon þe pride of Romayns,..oþer som oþer wrecche of God all myȝti falleþ vppon hem. *a* 1470 H. PARKER *Dives & Pauper* (W. de W. 1496) I. xxix. 67/2 Harde wretche was comyng but yf they wolde amende them of her falshode. *a* 1513 FABYAN *Chron.* VI. (1811) 147 Hir eyen dystylled dropes of blode,..the which, in token of Goddes wretche, in yᵉ boke remayne at this day.

b. In the phr. *to do, have, make, nim, seek*, and esp. *take wreche.* (Cf. WREAK *sb.* 1 b.)

α. *c* 1200 *Trin. Coll. Hom.* 29 Ȝef þu wreche ne secst hwanne þu time siest. *a* 1240 *Ureisun* 107 in *O. E. Hom.* I. 197 Ȝif þu heuedest wreche inumen of mine luðernesse. *c* 1275 *Duty of Christians* 56 in *O. E. Misc.* 143 Elles vre louerd god on vs wulle don wreche. 1297 R. GLOUC. (Rolls) 1334 Icnabbe of him wreche inou, wanne he bisecþ min ore. *a* 1300 in *E. E. P.* (1862) 4 Tak wrech of sinful man. 13.. *K. Horn* 1292 (Harl. MS.), Þat lond ichulle þorhreche & do mi fader wreche. 1340 *Ayenb.* 45 He heþ ynome to lite wreche. *c* 1350 *Will. Palerne* 3404 [They] bouȝt manli to make wreche here lorde to queme. *c* 1425 *Eng. Conq. Ireland* 120 Yn hope þat god shold take wrech of ham. *c* 1430 *Syr Gener.* (Roxb.) 6396 Generides, youre lord, now besech On this mater to doo som wrech. *c* 1450 LOVELICH *Grail* xii. 244 Be war lest god wele taken wreche. *a* 1513 FABYAN *Chron.* II. (1811) 24 This Appolyn toke wreche of theim that spoyled the goddes & theyr Temples. 1529 RASTELL *Pastyme* (1811) 138 To take wrech for the cruell murder of his nevew.

β. *c* 1200 *Trin. Coll. Hom.* 51 He nam stronge wrache þer-of. *c* 1325 *Chron. Eng.* 724 in Ritson *Metr. Rom.* II. 300 Hou schulde he speren eni mon Wen be of bestes wrache nom?

2. An act or instance of vengeance; = WREAK *sb.* 2.

c 1250 *Gen. & Ex.* 641 On wreche ðat sal ȝet wurðen sent, wan al ðis werld wurðe brent. *Ibid.* 2985 De ðridde wreche dede aaron Bi-foren ðe king pharaon. 13.. *E. E. Allit. P.* B. 229 Fro heuen to helle þat hatel schor laste...Þis hit was a brem brest & a byge wrache. 1387 TREVISA *Higden* II. 329 Egipte was i-smyte wiþ ten grete wreches. 1398 — *Barth. De P. R.* XXI. (Tollem. MS.), God sente mo wreches upon þe Egypcians þan ten. *a* 1425 *Cursor M.* 5943 (Trin.), Fast on god þo gon þei cal To delyuer þe folke of þat wreche. *a* 1513 FABYAN *Chron.* VII. (1811) 241 By reason of a wreche done..vpon one of Kynge Wyllyams knyghtes.

3. Affliction or calamity; deep distress, misery.

c 1250 *Gen. & Ex.* 3306 Ȝet sal ðe kinde of amalech Ben al fled dun in deades wrech. 1387–8 T. USK *Test. Love* I. i. (Skeat) l. 60 Thinke on your wreche and your daunger. *a* 1400 *Leg. Rood* (1871) 138 Lord of loue..For þe was set sely sacrynge, To winne þe world þat was in wreche. *c* 1450 *LudusCoventriæ* 327 Cryst..hath us wonnyn owt of wreche. 1460–70 *Bk. Quintessence* 19 Siþ þat deuelis be dampned, & ful of wreche of helle.

b. *To go to wreche*, to go to wrack. *rare*⁻¹.

13.. *Body & Soul* 242 in *Map's Poems* (Camden) 343 Thyn other thing, nou thou art ded, Al schal geynliche gon to wreche.

†**Wreche,** *v. Obs. rare.* [f. prec.]

1. *trans.* To rescue or deliver; = WREAK *v.* 5 d.

c 1330 R. BRUNNE *Chron. Wace* (Rolls) 16076 Þat bischop cam, his folk to preche, Þer Cristendam fro Paen wreche [*v.r.* to reche].

2. *refl.* To avenge (oneself).

1398 TREVISA *Glanvil De P. R.* XVIII. vii. (Bodl. MS.), Þe bore..takeþ herte and strengþe to wreche hym of his adversarye wiþ his tuskes.

3. To give effect to (wrath, etc.); = WREAK *v.* 3.

c 1420 LYDG. *Ballad Commend. Our Lady* 41 Or þe wycked fend his wrath up on us wreche [*rime* leche].

Hence †**Wre·cher,** an avenger (*of* some wrong).

a 1325 *Prose Psalter* viii. 3 Þat þou destruye þe enemy and þe wrecher [L. *ultorem*] of Adam sinne.

†**Wre·cheful,** *a. Obs.* Also 3–4 **wrech-**; 4 **wrac(o)h-**, 5 **wreechful.** [f. WRECHE *sb.* + -FUL. Cf. WREAKFUL *a.*] Vengeful; revengeful.

c 1290 *St. Edmund* 333 in *S. Eng. Leg.* I. 309 God..nis nouȝt so wrechful ase men weneth. 1387 TREVISA *Higden* I. 377 Seyntes and halowes of þis lond beeþ more wrecheful þan seyntes of oþer londes. 1398 — *Barth. De P. R.* XVIII. xii. (B.M. Add. MS.), No creature is more wrecheful..þan is þe bee whanne he is ywraþþed. *a* 1400 *New Test.* (Paues) 1 Thess. iv. 6 God is wrachful of alle suche men. *c* 1410 *Lantern of Light* 99 He smytiþ not to venge is owene wreechful herte but to do þe wille of God & saue his neibours soule.

Wrecht, obs. Sc. form of WRIGHT *sb.*[1]

Wreck (rek), *sb.*[1] Forms: [1–3 **wrec** (1 **wereo, waerece, wareo**), 2 **wrech**, 3–4 **wrek**, 3 **wreck-**, 4 **wreck**,] 3, 5–6 **wrek**, 5–7 **wrekke, wrecke**, 6– **wreck.** [a. AF. *wrec*, *wrech*, *wrek* (also *werec*, *waerec*, *warec*, whence F. *varech*, *varec* VAREC), a. ON. **wrec*, **wrek* (Norw. and Icel. *rek* n.), f. the stem of *wrekan* to drive: see WREAK *v.*, and cf. WRACK *sb.*[2] The AF. word is also the source of med.L. *wreccum*, *warectum*. The ON. variant **wreke* (Icel. *reki*) is represented in English by the obsolete WREKE. Another French form appears in VRAIC.]

I. 1. *Law.* That which is cast ashore by the sea in tidal waters; esp. goods or cargo as thrown on land by the sea from a wrecked, stranded, or foundered vessel. Occas. *wreck of the sea* (med.L. *wreccum maris*, AF. *wrec* or *wreck de mer*), †*wreck of the king* (med.L. *wrech regis*). Cf. SHIPWRECK *sb.* 1, SHIPBRECHE.

[1077 WM. I in *Chron. Abb. Ramsey* (Rolls) 201 Bramcestre ..cum omni maris ejectu quod nos *wrec* (*v.r.* *waerec*) nominamus. 1175–6 *Pipe Roll Hen. II* (1904) 83 Quia accepit wrech regis. 1200 K. JOHN *Charter to Dunwich* in *Rotuli Chart.* (1837) 51/2 De ewagio de wrec et lagan et de omnibus aliis consuetudinibus. *a* 1268 BRACTON *De Leg.* I. xii. (Rolls) I. 60 Item ubi non apparet dominus rei, sicut est de wrecco maris. 1292 BRITTON I. 216 Par fraunchises de aver wrek de mer trové en soen soil. 1343 in *Rymer's Fœdera* (Rolls) II. II. 1225 Wreccum maris..tam de piscibus regalibus, quam de aliis rebus quibuscumque, ad terram ibidem projectis. 1600: see JETSAM 1.]

1228 in *Mem. Ripon* (Surtees) I. 52 Wrek, weyf, stray, merchet, lechewyt, blodewyt. *Ibid.* 57 Wrek et weyf, stray. 1455 *Rolls of Parlt.* V. 311/2 Wrecke of the Sea, Weyves, Estrayes. 1477 *Paston Lett.* III. 211 Mastras Clere hath sen down hyr men, and with set alle the stuff and wrekke. 1482 *Rolls of Parlt.* VI. 205/1 The same Duc shall have.. Wrekke of the See, Tresour founde. 1570 LAMBARDE *Peramb. Kent* (1576) 229 If a ship were cast on shoare..and were not repaired by suche as escaped on liue within a certaine time, ..this was taken for Wreck. *Ibid.*, If from thencefoorth any one thing (being within the vessell) arriued on liue, then the ship and goods should not be seised for wrecke. 1630 *Aldeburgh Rec.* in *N. & Q.* May (1921) 427/2 Burying a man that came ashore when the Kings wreck came ashore. 1651 tr. *Kitchin's Courts Leet* (1657) 24 The Kings Prerogative, chap. 11. the King shall have Wreck of the Sea throughout the whole Realm. 1666 *N. Riding Rec.* VI. 101 A warrant against 11 Britton men for riotously taking a whale and other wrecke. 1728 CHAMBERS *Cycl.* (1738) s.v., Wreck, antiently, not only comprehended goods..from a perishing ship, but whatever else the sea cast upon land; whether it were precious stones, fishes,..or the like. 1765 BLACKSTONE *Comm.* I. 283 If any persons..take any goods so cast on shore, which are not legal wreck. 1768 *Ibid.* III. 106 The court of the admiral [had]..no manner of cognizance..of any wreck of the sea: for that must be cast on land before it becomes a wreck. 1800 ADDISON *Amer. Law Rep.* 63 *Wreck*, in its legal signification, is confined to such goods as, after shipwreck at sea, are by the sea cast upon the land. 1821 *Act* 1–2 *Geo. IV*, c. 75 § 26 That no..person who may be entitled..to Wreck of the Sea..shall be entitled to appropriate such Wreck or Goods..until he [etc.]. 1866 *Daily Tel.* 3 Nov., The more scrupulous deliver up their spoil to the receiver of wreck. 1888 J. WILLIAMS in *Encycl. Brit.* XXIV. 687/1 As wreck in the last resort became crown property, it was never subject to forfeiture. *Ibid.*, Wreck was frequently granted to subjects as a franchise.

2. = WRACK *sb.*[2] 3, SEA-WRACK 2 a, VAREC 1. Latterly *Sc.* and *north. dial.*

Cf. *tangle-wreck* TANGLE *sb.*[1] 3, *sea-wreck* s.v. SEA-WRACK. 1499 *Promp. Parv.* (Pynson) s v b, Wrek of the see, *alga, norga.* 1500 *Ortus Vocab.* B iii, *Alga*,..*herba marina*, i.e. *illud quod mare projicit*, wrekke or frothe of the see. 1634–5 BRERETON *Trav.* (Chetham Soc.) 97 The grass, weeds and wreck, brought by the sea..and left upon the sands. 1728 CHAMBERS *Cycl.* (1738) s.v., Wreck..in some places..is used to manure the ground. 1752 in *Scots Mag.* (1753) July 335/2 He was then employed in gathering wreck. 1791 *Statist. Acc. Scotl.* I. 113 The shores [of Ayrshire] abound with..rich sea-weed or wreck for manure. 1806 FORSYTH *Beauties Scotl.* III. 351 Sea-ware..driven upon the shore by the tides..is commonly called *blown wreck.* 1876 in *Cleveland Gloss.* Suppl. 1894 K. HEWAT *Little Scottish World* vii. 112 The 'Wreck Brethren'..annually..raised funds for their purposes and regulated the carting of the wreck.

b. = WRACK *sb.*[2] 3 b. Now *dial.*

c 1440 *Promp. Parv.* 533/2 Wrek, of a dyke, or a fenne, or stondynge watyr, *ulva.* 1742 *N. Riding Rec.* VIII. 242 The Treasurer to pay £1 for clearing away the wreck from How and Kirby Misperton Bridges. 1851 MAYNE REID *Scalp Hunt.* II. 298 Our faces were concealed by the 'wreck' that covered the stones. 1877–86 in Lincoln and Chesh. glossaries. 1884 G. S. STREATFIELD *Lincoln. & Danes* 376 Wreck, weeds and other rubbish floating down streams or on ditch water.

c. *Sc.* and *dial.* = WRACK *sb.*[2] 3 c.

1743 R. MAXWELL *Sel. Trans. Soc. Improv. Agric. Scot.* 11 Cause pull up and gather carefully the Wreck, or Roots of Weeds and Grass, into Heaps. 1787 W. H. MARSHALL *Norfolk* II. 392 *Wreck*, dead undigested roots and stems of grasses and weeds in plowland. 1801 *Farmer's Mag.* Jan. 59 A field..where dung was applied amid mountains of wreck, or couch grass.

3. A vessel broken, ruined, or totally disabled by being driven on rocks, cast ashore, or stranded; a wrecked or helpless ship; the ruins or hulk of such. Occas. also *wreck of a ship.*

[*c* 1290 *Fleta* I. xliv. (1647) 61 Item dicitur wreckum navis vel batellus fractus, de quibus nihil vivum evaserit.] ? *a* 1500 *Chaucer's Man of Law's T.* 415 Wks. (1532) 24 b, The constable of the castel downe is fare To seen this wrecke, & al the shyp he sought. 1611 COTGR., *Vuaresque*, a wrecke, or ship cast away. 1652 HEYLIN *Cosmogr.* I. 67 Charybdis is a Gulf..which violently attracting all Vessells that come too nigh it, devoureth them, and casteth up their wrecks. 1698 FRYER *Acc. E. India & P.* 80 He shall restore whatever Wrecks may happen on his Coasts. 1719 DE FOE *Crusoe* I. (Globe) 189, I could plainly see..the Wreck of a Ship cast away in the Night. 1743 BULKELEY & CUMMINS *Voy. S. Seas* 14 The Ship is a perfect Wreck. 1762 FALCONER *Shipwr.* III. 669 Three..from the wreck on oars and rafts descend. 1805 J. TURNBULL *Voy. World* (1813) 391 The ship..struck upon a reef of rocks.., and shortly became a total wreck. 1812 J. WILSON *Isle of Palms* I. 32 Fast the miserable Ship Becomes a lifeless wreck. 1865 H. KINGSLEY *Hillyars & Burtons* lxxix, The wreck of a little coasting craft still lay about two hundred yards to sea.

fig. and in fig. context. 1781 COWPER *Retirem.* 386 To the fair haven of my native home, The wreck of what I was, fatigu'd, I come. 1796 BURKE *Corr.* (1844) IV. 350 Such is the person you come to see, or rather the wreck of what was never a first-rate vessel. 1883 S. C. HALL *Retrospect* I. 322 All of manhood in him..had given way and left him a stranded wreck. 1885 TENNYSON *The Wreck* 5 My life itself is a wreck,..I am flung from the rushing tide of the world as a waif of shame.

b. An unserviceable or crazy old vessel.

1896 *Westm. Gaz.* 5 Dec. 5/1 There are too many of these old wrecks [= barges] on the river.

4. a. *Law.* A piece or article of wreckage; a fragment of a wrecked vessel or its cargo. Freq. *pl.*

1570 in Boys *Sandwich* (1792) 775 Wrecks and fyndalls floating, and the half of all wrecks and fyndalls jottsome. 1577 HOLINSHED *Chron.* II. 489/2 [Richard I] pardoned al wreckes by sea..., releasing for euer al his right to the same. 1579 [RASTELL] *Termes Lawes* 187 b, The Lorde shall haue that as a wreck of yᵉ sea. 1652 NEEDHAM *Selden's Mare Cl.* I. xxv. (1663) 167 The Question is, whether the Goods bee.. called Spoils or Wrecks. 1729 JACOB *Law Dict.* s.v. *Lagan*, [If] these Goods..are cast away upon the Land, they are then a Wreck. *Ibid.* s.v., It was usual to seise and forfeit Wrecks to the King, only when no Owner could be found. 1768 [see 1].

b. Without article. = WRECKAGE 2.

1744 *Gentl. Mag.* 616/2 Several chests, broken masts, and other pieces of wreck floating in the sea. 1796 CHARLOTTE SMITH *Narr. Loss Transports* 34 The Chissel-bank..was strewn..with pieces of wreck, and piles of plundered goods. 1815 *Ann. Reg., Chron.* 42 Six men reached the shore..upon planks, being much bruised by the surf and wreck. 1833 REDDING *Shipwrecks* I. 194 All the crew believed the ship was crushed to pieces, but no wreck floated up. 1865 SWINBURNE *Felise* 80 [Such things] As the sea feeds on, wreck and stray and castaway.

5. A drifted or tossed-up mass; a large heap; a great quantity; an abundance. Now *north. dial.*

1612 DRAYTON *Poly-olb.* II. 34 Where Chesill lifts Her ridged snake-like sands, in wrecks and smouldring drifts. 1683 G. M[ERITON] *Yorks. Dial.* 15 There's sike a wreck, it [*sc.* corn] liggs all down o'th Land. 1846 BROCKETT *N. C. Words* (ed. 3), *Wreck*, a great quantity..as a confused heap. 1876 *Whitby Gloss.* 224/1, I saw wrecks on 't.

6. That which remains *of* something that has suffered ruin, demolishment, waste, etc.; the dilapidated, disorganized, or disordered residue or remainder *of* anything. Also (*a*) with *a* and pl.

(*a*) 1713 ADDISON *Cato* v. i, But thou shalt flourish..Unhurt amidst..The Wrecks of Matter, and the Crush of Worlds. 1756 MRS. CALDERWOOD in *Coltness Collect.* (Maitl. Cl.) 250 His freinds..got him, out of the wrecks of his estate, betwixt L.30 or L.40 *per annum.* 1780 *Westm. Mag.* 371 He continued obstinate and mad, going..over the wrecks of the house. 1821 SHELLEY *Epipsych.* 493 An envy of the isles, a pleasure-house.., It scarce seems now a wreck of human art. 1888 BRYCE *Amer. Commw.* II. lv. 335 The Republican party was formed..out of the wrecks of the Whig party.

(*b*) 1743 R. BLAIR *Grave* 30 Names once famed, now dubious or forgot, And buried 'midst the wreck of things which were. 1751 SMOLLETT *Per. Pic.* ix, From the wreck of the hammock [she] made an occasional bed for herself on the floor. 1794 MRS. RADCLIFFE *Myst. Udolpho* xxviii, Assisted with suggestions which they had since executed with the wreck of their fortunes. 1804 W. L. BOWLES *Spir. Discov.* III. 46 My destined voyage, by the shores Of Asia, and the wreck of cities old. 1840 ARNOLD *Hist. Rome* II. xxxi. 255 There he was joined by the wreck of the consul's army. 1854 R. S. SURTEES *Handley Cr.* lxxvi, As Mamma surveyed the wreck of luncheon.

transf. and *fig.* 1791 BURNS *Song of Death* iii, Thou strik'st the dull peasant—he sinks in the dark, Nor saves e'en the wreck of a name. 1813 SHELLEY *Q. Mab* v. 109 He sheds A passing tear perchance upon the wreck Of earthly peace.

b. The broken-down, debilitated, or emaciated form *of* a person. (Cf. 7 b.)

1820 W. IRVING *Sketch Bk.* I. 225 It was, indeed, the wreck of her once noble lad. 1836 LYTTON *Duchess de La Vallière* V. iii, These wrecks of man Worn to decay. 1893 SELOUS *Trav. S. E. Africa* 62 All the Portuguese here were mere wrecks of men—frail, yellow, and fever-stricken.

7. That which is in a state of ruin; anything that is broken down or has undergone wrecking, shattering, or dilapidation.

1814 SOUTHEY *Roderick* XVI. 62 Amid heaps Of mountain wreck, on either side thrown high,..The tortuous channel wound. 1816 SCOTT *Antiq.* iii, This wreck of ancient books and utensils. 1842 MACAULAY *Horatius* lv, Like a dam, the mighty wreck [*sc.* of a bridge] Lay right athwart the stream. 1855 KINGSLEY *Westw. Ho!* xx, Alas! a crack, a flap, a rattle, ..and all forward was a mass of dangling wreck. 1889 MRS. E. KENNARD *Landing a Prize* i. (1891) 4 What was left of the wreck had to be given up to creditors.

fig. 1849 ROBERTSON *Serm.* Ser. I. viii. (1866) 145 The life-hopes have become a wreck.

b. A person of undermined, shattered, or ruined constitution; one who is debilitated by ill-health, hardship, etc. (Cf. 6 b.)

1795–6 WORDSW. *Borderers* I. 336 *Osw.* But how fare you? *Her.* Well as the wreck I am permits. 1828 LYTTON *Pelham* I. xxxi, 'Yes,' continued the venerable wreck, after a short pause. 1857 MRS. CARLYLE *Lett.* (1883) II. 335 It is easy to see you have suffered! an entire wreck, like myself. 1899 E. W. HORNUNG *Dead Men* xii, I was slowly dying of insomnia. I was a nervous wreck. 1901 W. R. H. TROWBRIDGE *Lett. of her Mother to Eliz.* xxxi. 154, I think I am in for influenza. I feel a perfect wreck.

8. [By misapprehension.] = WRACK *sb.*[1] 5 b.

1787–9 WORDSW. *Evening Walk* 306 No wreck of all the pageantry remains. 1813 SHELLEY *Q. Mab* IX. 130 These ruins soon left not a wreck behind. 1835 I. TAYLOR *Spir. Despot.* v. 185 Other systems have..been swept away, leaving hardly a wreck behind.

II. 9. The disabling or destruction of a vessel by any disaster or accident of navigation; loss of a ship by striking on a rock, stranding, or foundering; an instance of this; = SHIPWRECK *sb.* 2. *To make wreck*: cf. MAKE *v.*[1] 64.

1463–4 *Rolls of Parlt.* V. 507/1 Yf eny of the forseid Wares or Chaffares..come into this Reame or Wales by wey of wrek. 1477 *Paston Lett.* III. 211 There is a grete chyppe go to wrekke be for Wynterton. 1568 GRAFTON *Chron.* I. 4 This Arke..by diuine prouidence..was gouerned from running to wreck. 1577 HOLINSHED *Chron.* II. 490/1 That euery person makyng wrecke by sea, and comming aliue to lande, shoulde haue all his goodes free. 1590 SPENSER *F. Q.* II. x. 6 Learning his ship from those white rocks to saue,.. Threatning vnheedie wrecke and rash decay. 1607 COWELL *Interpr.* s.v. *Flotsen*, Jetson is a thing cast out of the shippe being in danger of wrecke. 1672 DRYDEN *2nd Pt. Conq. Granada* III. 107 As Seamen, parting in a gen'ral wreck, When first the loosening planks begin to crack, Each catches one. 1749 *Gentl. Mag.* 396/1 The ill behaviour of his crew, and the bad condition of the ship occasioned its wreck. 1795 BURNS *O Mally's meek* iii, Her two eyes..Would keep a sinking ship frae wreck. 1809 R. WARNER *Tour Cornwall* 158 A range of rocks, the terrible scene of many a disastrous wreck. 1845 C. WILKES *Narr. U.S. Explor. Exped.* II. 91 In leaving the harbour we had a narrow escape from wreck. 1888 F. HUME *Mme. Midas* I. Prol., We are..shipwrecked sailors; and I will tell the story of the wreck.

fig. and in fig. context. 1564 BULLEIN *Dial. agst. Pest* (1888) 93 The ship of fooles..wanteth a good Pilot, the storme, the rocke, and the wrecke at hand. 1770 COWPER *Let.* 25 Sept., The storm of sixty-three made a wreck of the friendships I had contracted.

b. *Stock Exchange.* (See first quot.)

1876 'E. PINTO' *Ye outside Fools!* 360 A *Corner*, *Pool*, *Clique*, *Ring* are all terms equivalent to a *Rig* or *Wreck.* *Ibid.* 408 The seductive interest of Rigs and Wrecks.

10. The action of subverting or overthrowing an established order of things, etc.; the fact of being brought to disaster; downfall, overthrow, ruin.

1577 HANMER *Anc. Eccl. Hist.* 494 He came into Mesopotamia, not without plaine daunger and wrecke to the state. 1594 SPENSER *Amoretti* xxv, Then all the woes and wrecks which I abide, as meanes of blisse I gladly wil embrace. 1608 *Great Frost* ad fin., Being..thus round beset with the horrors of so present a wreck, he fell down on his knees. 1763 J. BROWN *Poetry & Music* v. 78 The most celebrated bards of ancient Greece, whose songs have perished in the wreck of time. 1775 SHERIDAN *Rivals* III. iii, Proud of calamity, we will enjoy the wreck of wealth. 1838 PRESCOTT *Ferd. & Is.* Introd. (1846) I. 23 The wreck of their ancient liberties. 1839 TALFOURD *Glencoe* I. i, You come To share the wreck of the Macdonalds. 1885 J. PAYN *Talk of Town* I. 182 It was not that she feared to risk the wreck of her own happiness.

fig. 1793 BURNS '*Where are the joys*' iv, A' that has caused this wreck in my bosom, Is Jenny.

b. The action of wrecking or breaking apart; the fact of being materially wrecked or ruined; destruction or demolition.

1711 ADDISON *Spect.* No. 166 ¶ 2 Books, which..may last as long as the Sun and Moon, and perish only in the general Wreck of Nature. 1774 GOLDSM. *Nat. Hist.* (1776) I. 25 The manner in which he relieves the earth from this universal wreck. 1839 MURCHISON *Silur. Syst.* I. xxix. 376 In accounting for these extraordinary accumulations of broken coal we may undoubtedly refer their origin to the wreck of the regular seams. 1864 LOWELL *Fireside Trav.* 31 Dealing thunderous wreck to the two hostile vessels. 1886 J. BARROWMAN *Sc. Mining Terms* 73 *Wreck*, a break-down, as in a shaft or on an incline.

c. In the phr. *to go to wreck* (*and ruin*).

a 1547 SURREY *Æneid* II. 542 Our fained shields and wepons then they found, And..our discording voice they knew. We went to wreck, with nomber ouerlayd. 1548 UDALL, etc. *Erasm. Par. Mark* v. 11–17 The flocke goeth to wrecke and vtterly perisheth. 1600 HOLLAND *Livy* 676 All things els about him went to wreck. 1721 DE FOE *Mem. Cavalier* (1840) 65, I saw our men go to wreck. 1789 BURNS *Elegy on Year 1788* 4 A Towmont, sirs, is gane to wreck! ? 1834 DE QUINCEY *Autob. Sk.* Wks. 1858 I. 126 To wreck goes every notion or feeling that divides..the brave man from the brave. 1877 BLACK *Green Past.* i, The whole estate is going to wreck and ruin. 1883 STEVENSON *Treas. Isl.* xxviii, Here you are in a bad way: ship lost,..your whole business gone to wreck.

ellipt. 1782 BURNS '*No Churchman am I*' v, A letter inform'd me that all was to wreck.

III. 11. *attrib.* and *Comb.*, as *wreck buoy*, *case*, *chart*, *flag*; objective and instrumental, as *wreck-finder*, *raiser*, *-seeker*; †*wreck-fishing*, *-raising*, *-threatening*; also *wreck-devoted*, *-strewn.*

1874 BEDFORD *Sailor's Pocket-bk.* v. 109 *Wreck buoys are painted green. 1892 MARSDEN *Sel. Pleas* p. xliv, In 1377 a *wreck case was tried before justices. 1862 *Catal. Internat. Exhib., Brit.* No. 2747, Large *wreck chart of the British Isles for 1861. 1819 SHELLEY *Cenci* v. iv. 42 A *wreck-devoted seaman thus might pray To the deaf sea. 1902 *Daily Chron.* 29 Oct. 7/1 (citing *N. Y. Tribune*), The wreck of a coal barge was first located...Two boats, termed '*wreck-finders', then..by means of derricks or suction pumps raise the coal to the surface. 1674 TEMPLE *Let.* Wks. 1720 II. 310 This Invention of *Wreck-fishing [by Sir Edmund Curtis], for the Recovery of His Majesty's Tin, cast away before Ostend. 1897 *Daily News* 15 Sept. 8/4 The Thames Conservancy have hoisted their green '*wreck flag', warning all craft to steer clear of the debris. 1881 *Instr. Census Clerks* (1885) 36 Wharfinger, Wharf Agent,.. *Wreck Raiser. 1898 *Westm. Gaz.* 14 July 5/2 The *wreck-raising vessels that are to make an attempt to save some of Admiral Cervera's unfortunate squadron. 1843 CAPT. MARRYAT *M. Violet* xxviii, The unconscientious *wreck-seeker of a captain. 1821 SHELLEY *The Fugitives* 21 The Earth is like Ocean, *Wreck-strewn and in motion. 1757 DYER *Fleece* IV. 620 Inaccessible *Wreck-threatening Staten Land's o'erhanging shore.

b. Attrib. in names of persons having, or appointed to take, charge of wreck or wreckage, as **wreck commissioner, -master.**

1846 WORCESTER (citing *Lee*), *Wreck-Master*, a master of a wreck. *a* 1868 in Grant *Rep. Wrecking Bahamas* 77 The first-licensed wreck-master boarding a vessel wrecked, stranded, or in distress..shall..become the master of all wreckers employed on such vessel, and shall be styled the 'wreck-master'. 1876 *Act* 39–40 *Vict.* c. 80 § 29 It shall be the duty of a wreck commissioner..to hold any formal investigation into a loss. 1891 *Cent. Dict.* s.v., *Receivers of wrecks* (in Great Britain), *wreck-masters* (in New York and Texas), officers whose duty [etc.]. 1898 *Engineering Mag.* XVI. 70 Instructions for the handling of explosives..should be placed in the hands of the railroad staff, including wreckmasters.

c. Special Combs., as **wreck-fish**, the stone-bass; †**wreck-goods** *Sc.*, goods cast ashore from a wreck; †**wreck-make**, *poet.* that which causes wrecks; **wreck-ware** *Sc.*, **-weed**, = sense 2; **wreck-wood**, wood washed up or ashore from a wreck; also *attrib.*; **wreck-works**, salvage-works for raising a wreck or wrecks.

1880 DAY *Fishes Gt. Brit.* I. 18 This fish..is called in Devonshire, *Wreck fish, because it follows floating timbers. 1883 *Fisheries Exhib. Catal.* 270 Special Line, furnished with all accessories, used in fishing for Stone Bass or Wreck-fish. 1693 STAIR *Instit.* (ed. 2) Alph. Index K 2, '*Wreck-goods.. become Escheat as Publick. 1765–8 ERSKINE *Inst. Law Scot.* II. i. § 13 Wreck-goods..were not claimed as escheat, but secured for the owners. 1582 STANYHURST *Æneis* III. (Arb.) 88 And Caulons castels we doe spy, with Scylla the *wreckmake. 1865 WAY *Promp. Parv.* 533 *note*, On the coasts of Scotland sea-weed is called '*wreck-ware'. 1821 SCOTT *Pirate* x, One whom the sea flung forth as *wreck-weed. *Ibid.* v, The *wreck-wood that the cailants brought in yesterday. 1843 *Times* 25 July 3/2 The mast is still standing, and very little wreck-wood has driven from her. 1895 QUILLER COUCH *Wandering Heath* 5 The rain drove.. aslant like threads of gold silk in the shine of the wreckwood fire. 1903 E. CHILDERS *Riddle of Sands* xx, The *wreck-works were evidently what they purported to be.

†**Wreck,** *sb.*[2] *Sc. Obs.* [var. of WRACK *sb.*[3], after prec.] 'Pelf'; 'dross'; = WRACK *sb.*[3] 1 b.

1562 WINȜET *Cert. Tractatis* Wks. (S.T.S.) I. 8 Hauand regarde to the wrek of this warld or lustis of thair bodyis. *a* 1568 BLYTH in *Bannatyne MS.* (Hunt. Club) 321/11 Ane wreche sall haif no mair, Bot ane schort scheit at heid and feit, For all his wrek and wair.

†**Wreck,** *sb.*[3] *Obs. rare.* [Alteration of WREAK *sb.*: cf. WRECK *v.*[2]] Vengeance; revenge.

1591 *Legh's Armory* 96 b, His irefull heart straight braided out wrothfull wordes of wrecke [1562 wreke] and reuenge. 1596 SPENSER *F. Q.* IV. vi. 16 Ah cruell hand, and..hart That workst such wrecke on her.

Wreck, obs. erron. var. RACK *sb.*[1] 3.

1707 E. SMITH *Phædra & Hipp.* III. 30 Why did you raise me to the heighth of Joy, Above the wreck of Clouds and Storms below?

Wreck, var. RECK *sb.*[2] (= RACK *sb.*[2] 5 d).

1674 RAY *Coll. Words, Smelting Tin* 122 The head tin passes to the *wreck*, where they work it with a wooden rake in Vessels. 1800 MISS EDGEWORTH *Lame Jervas* ii, I had new models made of the sieves for lueing, the box and trough, the buddle, wreck, and tool.

Wreck (rek), *v.*[1] Also 5–6 **wrek-.** [f. WRECK *sb.*[1] Cf. med.L. *wrecare* (12th cent.).]

In various senses common only in passive use.

†**1.** *trans.* To cast on shore. *Obs.*

c 1420 *Sir Amadas* (W.) 475 Folke fordryvon in the schores, ..Brone stedes,..All maner of ryches,..Wrekkyd with the water lay. [= xliv. (Camden), He fond wrekun a-mung the stones Kny3tes in meneuere.] *a* 1440 *Sir Eglam.* 894 He say that lady whyte as flowre, Was wrekyd on the sonde. *a* 1509 in *Rep. Hist. MSS. Comm.* Var. Coll. (1907) IV. 87 [Seizing them] as goodes wrekked, which neither can ne may soo bee taken as long as the veray owners thereof be certainly knowen. 1596 SPENSER *F. Q.* V. iv. 5 A Coffer strong,.. seeming to haue suffred mickle wrong by being wreckt vppon the sands. 1729 JACOB *Law Dict.* s.v., If Goods wreck'd are seised by Persons having no Authority. 1821 *Act* 1–2 *Geo. IV*, c. 75 § 26 That Part of the Coast where the same [goods] shall have been stranded, wrecked or found.

2. To cause the wreck of (a vessel); to wreck (a ship); = SHIPWRECK *v.* 1 b. Chiefly *passive.* Also *fig.* and in fig. context.

1570 LAMBARDE *Peramb. Kent* (1576) 228 A shippe laden with the Kings owne goods was wrecked within the precinct of this libertie. 1590 SPENSER *F. Q.* II. xii. 7 The ribs of vessels broke, And shiuered ships, which had bene wrecked late. 1732 *Gentl. Mag.* 976 A great Number of Ships were wrecked..by stormy Weather. 1774 GOLDSM. *Nat. Hist.* (1776) VI. 395 Brought into the European seas, in some India ship that might be wrecked upon her return. 1845 J. C. MANGAN *German Anthol.* II. 100 The shallop of my peace is wrecked on Beauty's shore. 1846 MRS. A. MARSH *Father Darcy* II. ii. 60 So bravely as we have struggled against the overwhelming waters! The vessel is finally wrecked! 1865 H. KINGSLEY *Hillyars & Burtons* lxxvii, If the *Wainoora* has sailed,..she is wrecked somewhere on the coast.

refl. 1864 TENNYSON *Aylmer's F.* 716 This frail bark of ours, when sorely tried, May wreck itself without the pilot's guilt.

b. To make or cause (a person) to suffer or undergo shipwreck; to involve in wreck; also, to cause the loss of (goods or cargo) by shipwreck; = SHIPWRECK *v.* 1. Chiefly *passive.*

1617 MORYSON *Itin.* II. 8 The..Spaniards, last yeere wrecked on the Coasts of Connaght..had left..great store of treasure. 1796 CHARLOTTE SMITH *Narr. Loss Transports* 14 A young Gentleman,..wrecked himself, and wandering along the unhospitable shore. 1836 MARRYAT *Midsh. Easy* xx, We were wrecked in our boat last night. 1877 TENNYSON *Harold* II. i, Thy villains with their lying lights have wreck'd us! 1903 S. E. WHITE *Forest* vii, A big roller rips along your gunwale [of a canoe]. You are wrecked.

fig. 1821 SHELLEY *Epipsych.* 148 The rocks on which high hearts are wrecked. 1845 BAILEY *Festus* (ed. 2) 323 Bound to earth, Wrecked in the deeps of Heaven, in Death's expiring birth! 1880 W. H. D. ADAMS *Wrecked Lives* Ser. I. p. vi, If he would not wreck his life amid the rocks and quicksands of worldly lusts.

absol. 1881 H. D. RAWNSLEY *Sonn. Eng. Lakes* 115 So may it be when storms my life shall strand On treacherous shoal,..May..waves that wrecked reach out a pitying hand To gulf my sorrow.

c. *transf.* (See quot.)

1617 MORYSON *Itin.* III. 144 There be some quicksands, wherein footemen are in danger to be wrecked.

3. To cause or bring about the ruin or destruction of (a structure, etc.) as by violence or misuse; to reduce to a ruinous condition in this way; to shatter, ruin, destroy.

1510 in Leadam *Star Chamber Cases* (Selden) II. 70 [He] maketh Fysch garthes & weeres..by reason wherof the seid porte is so wrekked & shallowed, that [etc.]. 1594 SPENSER *Amoretti* lvi, That tree..am I, whom ye do wreck, do ruine, and destroy. 1821 SHELLEY *Epipsych.* 370 Thou too, O Comet..., Who drew the heart of this frail Universe Towards thine own; till, wrecked in that convulsion,..Thine went astray. 1865 *Pall Mall G.* 14 July 9/2 The mob..commenced 'wrecking' Conservative houses, stoning one sick old gentleman as he lay in his bed. 1878 BROWNING *La Saisiaz* 34 The everyway external stream..leaves it [*sc.* a rush]..wrecked at last. 1899 *Allbutt's Syst. Med.* VII. 123 The joint is found to be completely wrecked.

transf. 1878 BROWNING *Poets Croisic* xli, How now? My Duke's crown wrecked?

b. To cause or bring about the subversion or overthrow of (some condition or order of things); to shatter, ruin.

1749 SMOLLETT *Regicide* I. vi, O recal Those flatt'ring arts thy own deceit employ'd To wreck my peace! 1791 BURNS *Fair Eliza* ii, Can'st thou wreck his peace for ever? 1826 in *Sheridaniana* 334 Their want of tact and judgment has wrecked the party. 1858 CARLYLE *Fredk. Gt.* VII. iv, Do not wreck, upon trifles, a noble interest we have in common. 1883 SIR C. S. C. BOWEN in *Law Times Rep.* XLIX. 251/2 We hear of abuse of different kinds of process..which amounts to wrecking credit. 1884 *St. James's Gaz.* 11 Jan. 6/1 His Administration was very nearly wrecked at the outset.

c. To frustrate or thwart; to prevent the passing of (a measure, etc.).

1855 MOTLEY *Dutch Rep.* V. v, Every fresh attempt at an amicable compromise was wrecked upon the obstinate bigotry of the leading civic authorities. 1901 *Scotsman* 28 Feb. 7/2 The measure will, it is pretty certain, be wrecked before it gets out of committee.

4. To bring (a person) to ruin or disaster; to subvert, ruin. Also *refl.*

1590 SPENSER *F. Q.* III. ix. 4 All his mind is set on mucky pelfe, To hoord vp heapes of evill gotten masse, For which he others wrongs, and wreckes himselfe. 1594 [see 3]. 1644 *Raleigh's Remains* 48 If he resolve..to wreck him, and to have his life. 1732 POPE *Ess. Man* I. 254 Let ruling Angels from their spheres be hurl'd, Being on Being wreck'd, and world on world. 1782 WOLCOT (P. Pindar) *Ode R.A.'s* iii. Wks. 1812 I. 20 Despising Pride, whose wish it is to wreck 'em.

b. To shatter (a person's health, constitution, or nerves) by sickness, hardship, or the like; to destroy the quality or tone of. Usu. in *passive.*

1850 ROBERTSON *Serm.* Ser. III. (1857) 125 The drunkard ..discovers that he is unexpectedly degraded, his health wrecked. 1897 KIPLING *Capt. Cour.* 213, I wonder your nervous system isn't completely wrecked.

5. *intr.* **a.** To suffer or undergo shipwreck; = SHIPWRECK *v.* 2. Also *fig.* and in fig. context.

1671 MILTON *P. R.* II. 228 Honour, glory, and popular praise; Rocks whereon greatest men have oftest wreck'd. 1671 — *Samson* 1044 What Pilot so expert but needs must wreck Embarqu'd with such a Stears-mate at the Helm? 1729 BERKELEY *Lett.* Wks. 1871 IV. 161 My letters were in one of the vessels that wreck'd. 1860 MRS. C. CLIVE *Why Paul Ferroll* iv, With all her early impressions wrecking around her, she did not know to what to cling. 1864 LOWELL *Fireside Trav.* 172 The *montagna bruna* on which Ulysses wrecked. 1884 TENNYSON *Becket* II. ii, Holy Church May rock, but will not wreck, nor our Archbishop Stagger on the slope decks for any rough sea.

b. To break down in health.

1876 R. BRIDGES *Growth of Love* xiv, What is this wreck of all he hath in fief, When he that hath is wrecking?

6. a. To cause damage by washing *up.*

1634 *Rotherham* (Yorks.) *Feoffees Accounts* (MS.), P[ai]d to Tho. Sandall..for paveing at the bridge where the water had wreckt up.

b. To silt *up*, as with tide-driven sand, etc.

1786 in *Trans. Soc. Arts* (1789) VII. 56 By a gradual, continual loss of out-fall amongst the sands, and by the sluice on the marsh and other parts wrecking up.

7. To seize or collect wreck or wreckage; to search *for* wreck. Also *transf.*

1843 *Times* 28 Mar. 7/1 The news of the wreck spread rapidly.., and in the evening a large mob assembled with a view of 'wrecking'. 1897 *Westm. Gaz.* 2 Oct. 3/1 [Your job,] perhaps, is to go 'wrecking' for firewood. Down upon the rocks the friendly tide casts many a spar and log.

†**Wreck** (rek), *v.*[2] *Obs.* Also 6–7 **wrecke**, 6–7, 9 **reck**, 7 **recke.** [Late variant of WREAK *v.*; the exact reason for the shortening of the vowel is not clear, but cf. dial. *breck* for BREAK *v.*]

1. *trans.* = WREAK *v.* 5, 5 b. Chiefly *refl.*

1570 LEVINS *Manip.* 54 To Wreck, *vindicare.* 1583 BABINGTON *Commandm.* (1590) 331 Any larger commission granted to vs to wreck our selues vpon our brethren. 1612 T. TAYLOR *Comm. Titus* i. 10 The minde and intention of the Apostle here..was not..to wrecke himselfe vpon them. 1622 P. HANNAY *Philomela* lxxxiv, The world shall know I was not slow To wreck a wronged maid. 1670 MILTON *Hist. Eng.* VI. Wks. 1851 V. 242 They wreck'd themselves on the Countries round about, wasting..all Essex, Kent, and Sussex.

2. = WREAK *v.* 3.

1658 *Whole Duty Man* xv. § 31 It is a kind desire of his amendment (and not a willingness to wreck his own rage) which [etc.]. 1672 MARVELL *Reh. Transp.* I. 11 Being ready at once to asswage his Concupiscence, and wreck his Malice. 1681 *Character Ill-Court-Favourite* 5 These insufferable Grandees, who reck their Private Spleens.

b. With preps., as *on*, *upon*, *against* (a person, etc.); = WREAK *v.* 3 b. Also with *out.*

1577 GRANGE *Golden Aphrod.*, etc. Q ij b, She sought on me to wrecke hir spight. 1583 GREENE *Mamillia* II. Wks. (Grosart) II. 151 With what greater plague..can..the vniust gods..wreck their wrath and extreme rigour vppon any man. 1613 PURCHAS *Pilgrimage* (1614) 25 That malice.. which he could not there so easily wrecke on their Creator. 1649 MILTON *Eikon.* xxvi, To wreck his spleen, or ease his mind upon the Parlament. 1702 ROWE *Tamerl.* IV. i, Give him Pow'r to wreck his Hatred Upon his greatest Foe? 1712 ADDISON *Spect.* No. 439 ¶ 3 [They] often wreck their particular Spite or Malice against the person whom they are set to watch. 1777 WATSON *Philip II*, I. 191 The king.. was determined to wreck his resentment on all concerned. 1793 R. GRAY *Poems* 25 Some in the fray wreckt out his spleen On some sly pate or sawney.

3. = WREAK *v.* 6, 7.

1593 MARLOWE *Edw. II*, IV. iv, For the open wronges and iniuries Edward hath done to vs,..We come in armes to wrecke it with the swords. 1596 SPENSER *F. Q.* V. iv. 24 He Talus sent To wrecke on them their follies hardyment. 1667 MILTON *P. L.* IV. 11 Satan..came down..To wreck on innocent frail man his loss Of that first Battel.

4. = WREAK *v.* 8.

1764 GOLDSM. *Hist. Eng. in Lett.* (1772) II. 231 There was no object on whom to wreck their vengeance. *a* 1790 HENRY *Britain* (1793) VI. 419 They not only wrecked their vengeance on the living, but on the ashes of dead heretics.

Wreck, obs. erron. var. RACK *v.*[3] 2 c.

1776 G. SEMPLE *Building in Water* 101 Splicing the long Sides of the Belts, so as they may not wreck in dropping them down. [Cf. WRECKING.]

Wreck, obs. erron. form of RECK *v.*

Wreckage (re·kėdʒ). [f. WRECK *v.*[1] + -AGE 3.]

1. The action or process of wrecking; the fact of being wrecked. Also *fig.*

1837 CARLYLE *Fr. Rev.* II. v. ii, Wreckage and dissolution are the appointed issue for both [*sc.* wisdom and folly]. 1890 GASQUET & BISHOP *Edw. VI & Bk. Com. Prayer* 272 A lively picture of the wreckage of ecclesiastical structures at that time [1548–9]. 1899 MACKAIL *Life Morris* II. 291 There had been much wreckage of unverified beliefs and extravagant hopes.

2. Fragments or remains of a shattered or wrecked vessel; wreck.

1846 WORCESTER (citing *Times*). 1867 *Morn. Star* 4 Feb., A large quantity of timber, ship's spars, &c...The wreckage appeared to be that of a large ship. 1885 T. P. BATTERSBY *Elf Island* 36 The deck was..covered with wreckage. 1899 DOYLE *Duet* (1909) 119/2 Some of the wreckage from those vanished vessels.

attrib. 1898 MEREDITH *Odes Fr. Hist.* 23 His wreckage-spars, His harried ships.

b. *pl.* Pieces or fragments of wreck. *rare.*

1864 CARLYLE *Fredk. Gt.* XVII. vii, A bolt shot into the storm-tost Sea and its wreckages.

3. Material of or from a wrecked or shattered structure; a ruined fabric, building, etc.

1874 J. GEIKIE *Gt. Ice Age* xvi. 208 The ice-current.. would leave upon their frozen shores the wreckage of the distant mountains. 1891 BARING-GOULD *In Troubadour-Land* viii. 112 They form the wreckage of a palace for princes. 1894 DOYLE *Mem. Sherlock Holmes* 103 The venerable wreckage of a feudal keep.

b. *fig.* Persons whose lives have been wrecked, who have failed to maintain a position in society.

1883 F. PEEK (*title*) Social Wreckage; a Review of the Laws of England as they affect the Poor. 1888 *Pall Mall G.* 26 Nov. 6/1 Twenty beds..are nightly filled by wreckage, more or less battered, from the stress of life. 1898 *Daily News* 18 Apr. 5/1 What a line of flotsam and jetsam it is!..that mass of human wreckage.

Wrecked (rekt), *ppl. a.* [f. WRECK *v.*[1] + -ED[1].]

1. That has undergone or suffered shipwreck; destroyed, lost, or cast ashore by shipwreck; = SHIPWRECKED *ppl. a.*

1729 WOODWARD *Fossils* I. 116 The Coral found affix'd and growing upon wreck'd Ships. 1795 W. LEE *Hist. Lewes* 547 It has..been the practice of many lords to keep the wrecked goods. 1818 SHELLEY *Rosal. & Helen* 394 Wrecked mariners, Who cling to the rock of a wintry sea. 1821 SCOTT *Pirate* vii, One wave..made the wrecked vessel completely manifest in her whole bulk. 1850 W. IRVING *Mahomet* II. 483 Whether the old man..was one of the wrecked cruisers, or a wrecker,..is not specified. 1869 *Daily News* 11 Aug., Throwing upon the holders of wrecked goods the burden of accounting for their possession.

2. Damaged or destroyed by wreck, violence, or disaster; shattered, ruined.

1818 SHELLEY *Julian* 224 Like weeds on a wrecked palace growing. 1818 — *Marenghi* vii, Thou shadowest forth that mighty shape in story, As ocean its wrecked fanes, severe yet tender. 1867 SMILES *Huguenots Eng.* ix. (1880) 150 Amidst the ruins of a wrecked church. 1875 KNIGHT *Dict. Mech.* 2821/1 Removing obstructions from the track, such as wrecked cars or locomotives.

b. *fig.* That has suffered wreck; brought to ruin or disaster.

1819 KEATS *Lines to Fanny* 33 That most hateful land, [where]..my friends..live a wrecked life. 1855 G. BRIMLEY *Ess.* (1858) 84 The incipient stage of madness, springing from the wrecked affections. 1879 FROUDE *Cæsar* xviii. 301 He flung into bribery what was left of his wrecked credit. 1901 *Munsey's Mag.* XXIV. 470/2 He was thinking of the old king with the wrecked mind.

Wrecker[1] (re·kəɹ). [f. WRECK *v.*[1] + -ER[1].]

1. One who causes shipwreck, esp. for purposes of plunder by showing luring lights or false signals; a person who makes a business of watching for and plundering wrecked vessels; also, one who wrongfully seizes or appropriates wreck washed ashore.

1820 W. IRVING *Sketch Bk.* (1821) I. 27 The good people.. thronged like wreckers to get some part of the noble vessel.. driven on shore. 1843 *Times* 20 Jan. 3/6 Although the officers of the coast-guard keep a sharp look-out, considerable depredation was carried on by the wreckers. 1882 FARRAR *Early Chr.* xxii, Cornish wreckers went straight from church to light their beacon-fires.

fig. 1865 THOREAU *Cape Cod* vi. 105 Are we not all wreckers contriving that some treasure may be washed up on our beach?

b. One who wrecks or ruins a structure, institution, concern, etc.

1882 C. G. WALPOLE *Short Hist. Irel.* 441 The Defenders especially had begun to turn the tables upon the 'wreckers', and were the terror of the country side. 1889 GASQUET *Hen. VIII & Eng. Monast.* II. 426 Like a swarm of locusts the royal wreckers went forth over the land.

fig. 1883 *American* VI. 37 Lawyers and agents, who might be described with fairness as 'wreckers' and who generally manage to absorb the assets. 1903 *Westm. Gaz.* 28 Feb. 10/1 As a wrecker of Cabinets Ireland holds a proud position.

c. *fig.* One who wrecks, or successfully obstructs the passing of a measure, etc.

1892 *Pall Mall G.* 12 July 1/2 If..they are not able to reckon more than 8 Parnellite 'wreckers'. 1901 *Scotsman* 20 Nov. 8/4 The wreckers in the Senate claimed for America the right of fortifying the Canal.

2. *Stock Exchange.* (See first quot.)

1876 'E. PINTO' *Ye Outside Fools!* 359 *Wreckers*,..those who make a similarly-organized attack as bears upon some stock, rotten or good,..and force down the price by large and successive sudden sales. 1884 *American* VIII. 84 The clamor of contending inflaters and wreckers at the stock exchange.

Wrecker[2] (re·kəɹ). Orig. (and chiefly) *Amer.* [f. WRECK *sb.*[1] + -ER[1].]

1. A person engaged in salving wrecked or endangered vessels or cargo; a salvager, salvor.

1804 M'KINNON *Tour West Indies* ix. 137 Those persons called wreckers, who are licensed by the Governor of the Bahamas, and cruise amongst these islands for the benefit of salvage. 1819 *Edwards' Hist. W. Indies* (ed. 5) IV. 225 The business of wreckers..consists in giving assistance to those who are wrecked, or in danger of being so, upon the almost endless rocks and shoals [of the Bahamas]. 1851 *Rovings in Pacific* I. 173 Our own vessel..had heeled on to a sunken patch in the offing...It gave us wreckers a tremendous fright. 1875 TALMAGE *Old Wells* 273 The wreckers shoot a rope out to the suffering men.

2. A ship or vessel employed in salvaging sunk, wrecked, or stranded vessels.

1864 WEBSTER. 1868 [see WRECKING *vbl. sb.*[2] 2]. 1898 *Westm. Gaz.* 14 July 5/2 The Wreckers and Admiral Cervera's Vessels.

†**Wreck-free,** *a. Obs.* [Early ME. *wrec-fri*, f. WRECK *sb.*[1] 1 + FREE *a.*] Exempted or free from the forfeiture of wrecked vessels and goods.

1205 *Rot. Chart.* (1837) 153/2 Cum socca & sacca & thol & theam & infangenthef & wrecfri & witefri & lestagefri & locofri. 1278 *Charter to Cinque Ports* in *Rymer's Fœdera* (1816) I. II. 558/1 Et quod habeant infangenethef; & quod sint wrecfry, & wytefry & lestagefry. 1598 HAKLUYT *Voy.* I. 117 (tr. quot. 1278), That they shall be wreckefree, lastagefree, and louecopfree. [1706 PHILLIPS (*Wrec-fry*); and in later Dicts.]

Wreckful (re·kfŭl), *a.*[1] [f. WRECK *sb.*[1] + -FUL.] Causing shipwreck, ruin, or disaster; dangerous, destructive.

1596 SPENSER *F. Q.* VI. viii. 36 Straungers..which on their border Were brought..by wreckfull wynde. 1810 SCOTT *Lady of L.* V. i, The wreckful storms that cloud the brow of War. 1848 MANGAN *Poems* (1903) 106 This dull world still slumbers...In a midnight dream, Drifts it down Time's wreckful stream. 1876 TENNYSON *Harold* III. i. 51 A summer mere with sudden wreckful gusts From a side-gorge.

†**Wre·ckful,** *a.*[2] *Obs.* [f. WRECK *sb.*[3] + -FUL. Cf. WRACKFUL *a.*[1], WRAKEFUL *a.*, WREAKFUL *a.*] Full of, manifesting or taking, revenge; marked or characterized by vengeance.

1557 NORTH *Gueuara's Diall Pr.* IV. xvii. (1568) 158 Per force my self dooth straine the wreckfull gods, vouch saue it doo not so. 1601 W. T. *Ld. Remy's Civ. Consid.* 36 If a man haue to deale with some manner of men which are wreckfull, of a strange nature, hard to please. 1610 HOLLAND *Camden's Brit.* I. 709 The Earle in wreckfull displeasure..laid his Castle even with the ground.

Wre·cking, *vbl. sb.*[1] [f. WRECK *v.*[1] + -ING[1].]

1. The action of destroying by shipwreck or causing wreck; the fact of having suffered wreck.

1775 ASH, *Wrecking*,..the act of destroying by dashing against rocks or sands at sea; the act of destroying by violent means. 1851 W. COLLINS *Rambles beyond Railw.* v. (1852) 108 'Wrecking' is a crime unknown in the Cornwall of our day. 1868 M. PATTISON *Academ. Org.* 3 Wrecking was no longer permitted by public morality. 1891 C. DAWSON *Avonmore* 46 Till drunk with wrecking's awful toil, Havoc will laugh and Ruin smile!

attrib. 1885 *N. & Q.* 6th Ser. XI. 428/1 The Wrecking system once practised on the English coasts.

2. *concr.* That which is wrecked; *pl.* wrecked remains.

1855 SINGLETON *Virgil* I. 200 The more vigorously all will toil To mend the wreckings of a fallen race.

Wre·cking, *vbl. sb.*[2] *Amer.* [f. WRECK *sb.*[1] 3.]

1. The action or business of salvaging a wreck or wrecks.

1804 (see 2). 1868 H. D. GRANT *Rep. Wrecking in Bahamas* 35 Wrecking has become a regular vocation for a considerable portion of the population.

2. *attrib.*, esp. in sense 'used for, or in connexion with, relating to, salvaging wreck', as *wrecking car*, *crane*, *outfit*, *pump*, *train*; also *wrecking law*, *operation.*

1804 M'KINNON *Tour West Indies* ix. 144 Effecting an immediate escape in a wrecking-vessel from this wild and inhospitable spot. 1868 H. D. GRANT *Rep. Wrecking in Bahamas* 36 Copies of abstract of the wrecking laws. *Ibid.* 62 The harbour-master.., who formerly commanded a wrecker and now owns licensed wrecking vessels. 1875 KNIGHT *Dict. Mech.* 644/1 Fairbairn's traveling-crane..is adapted for a wrecking-crane for railroad use. *Ibid.* 2821/1 *Wrecking-car*, one carrying devices for removing obstructions from the track, such as wrecked cars or locomotives. *Ibid.* 2821/2 *Wrecking-pump*, a steam-pump specially designed for pumping the water out of bilged or sunken vessels, in order to raise them. 1891 *Harper's Weekly* 19 Sept. 914/2 A wrecking train soon removed the débris. 1898 *Engineering Mag.* XVI. 68 The wrecking outfit should be immediately available. *Ibid.*, Wrecking operations.

b. In sense 'engaged in salvaging wreck or wrecks', as *wrecking company*, *crew*, *expedition.*

1851 *Rovings in Pacific* I. 149 Bound on a wrecking Expedition. 1878 B. HARTE *Man on Beach* 33 A wrecking crew of curlew hastily manned the uprooted tree that tossed wearily beyond the bar. 1891 in *Leeds Mercury* 19 Sept. 12 Captain Merritt, of the Merritt Wrecking Company.

Wrecking, obs. errron. var. RACKING *vbl. sb.*[3] 1.

1776 G. SEMPLE *Building in Water* 128 That the Timber ..be both firmly spliced and bolted together..to prevent their wrecking, swagging or dislocating.

Wre·cking, *ppl. a.* [f. WRECK *v.*[1] + -ING[2].]

1. That wrecks; causing wreck, ruin, or destruction; destructive.

a 1677 BARROW *Serm.* Wks. 1686 III. 228 [Industry] is in itself..satisfactory; as freeing our mind from distraction, and wrecking irresolution. 1809 MALKIN *Gil Blas* XII. ix. ¶ 4 The wrecking fury of the storm. 1880 R. BRIDGES *Shorter Poems* Wks. (1912) 275 The moon, That poured her midnight noon Upon his wrecking sea. 1893 *Westm. Gaz.* 9 Feb. 7/2 Playing a wrecking game towards the present Government.

2. Going to wreck; becoming wrecked.

1903 S. E. WHITE *Forest* viii, A man..scaled the face of the moving jam, and reached the top just as the two sections ground together with the brutish noise of wrecking timbers.

Wreckle, variant of WRIGGLE *sb.* 3.

1816 BINGLEY *Usef. Knowl.* III. 225 Sand-launce, Sand Eel, or Wreckle (*Ammodytes tobianus*) is a small fish distinguished by its eel-shape.

Wre·ckless (re·klės), *a. rare.* [f. WRECK *v.*[1] + -LESS.] That cannot be wrecked.

1821 BYRON *Heaven & Earth* iii. 753 Hence to where our all-hallow'd ark uprears Its safe and wreckless sides!

Wreckless, obs. erron. f. RECKLESS *a.*

Wre·ckling. Now *dial.* [var. of RECKLING. Cf. WREGLING.] A weak, puny, or dwarfish animal (or plant); *spec.* the smallest and weakest of a litter.

1601 HOLLAND *Pliny* I. 530 It causeth it [*sc.* the vine] to seeme scortched and full of knots, yea and to grow like a dwarfe or wreckling. 1607 MARKHAM *Cavel.* I. 48 When shee shoulde come to foale, shee would bring foorth nought but a wreckling. 1614 — *Cheap Husb., Swine* xi. 94 Take the wreckling, or worst Pigge, and annoint it all over. 1781 [see RECKLING]. 1825– in dialect glossaries, etc. (N. Cy.; Nhb. to Warw.).

attrib. 1602 tr. *Pastor Fido* IV. viii. M 2 b, Too much I honour thee, poore weake and wreckling child.

Wree, Sc. variant of WRY *v.*[2]

†**Wreekes,** erron. f. REAKS (pranks) *Obs.*

1628 BURTON *Anat. Mel.* (ed. 3) III. ii. VI. iii. 515 Fawnes and Satyrs will certainely play wreekes.

Wreest(e, obs. or dial. var. WREST *sb.*

†**Wre·gling.** *Sc. Obs.* = WRECKLING.

1679 in Wodrow *Ch. Hist.* (1828) IV. 501 What through grace he will make such a weak wregling able to endure.

Wrehche, obs. f. WRETCH *sb.* **Wrei,** etc.: see WRAY *v.*, etc. **Wreicht, Wreight,** obs. ff. WRIGHT *sb.*[1] **Wreist,** obs. Sc. var. WREST. **Wreithe,** obs. f. WREATHE *v.* **Wreitt, Wreitten,** obs. Sc. pa. t. and pa. pple. of WRITE *v.*

Wrek, alteration of WRACK *v.*[4]

a 1635 L. FOXE *North-West Fox* in *Voy.* (Hakl. Soc. 1894) II. 280 In that distance holding the same course, I was 1 d. 17 m. wrekt from my true course.

†**Wreke.** *Obs.* Also 6 **reke.** [a. early ON. **wreke* m. (Icel. *reki*, Norw. *reke*), from the same stem as **wrek* neut.: see WRECK *sb.*[1]]

1. = WRECK *sb.*[1] 1.

1420 *Stonor Papers* (Camden) I. 32 Every man here knoweth wel þat þe wreke is parcel of þe enheritance of Ermyngton. 1477 *Paston Lett.* III. 213 Remembir your ryth of your wreke at Wynterton. *Ibid.*, Gret plante of wreke of the schyppe..worth meche mony. 1495 *Act* 11 *Hen. VII*, c. 34 *Preamble*, With wreke of the Sea and all other forfaitures. [1535 *Act* 27 *Hen. VIII*, c. 26 § 23 Lordes marchers..shall have, hold, and kepe within..the precincte of their said Lordeshipps..wreke de mere, wharfage.]

2. = WRECK *sb.*[1] 2.

c 1440 *Promp. Parv.* 533/2 Wreke, of þe see, *alga*, *norga.* 1500 *Ortus Vocab.* BB viij b/1 *Norga*, *fex maris*,..wreke. 1545 ELYOT, *Vlua*, reke or wiedes of the see.

Wreke, etc., obs. ff. WREAK *sb.* and *v.*

†**Wrele,** *v. Sc. Obs.* [? Of imitative origin.] *intr.* To struggle or move about writhingly.

1513 DOUGLAS *Æneid* I. Prol. 298 Quha is attachit on till a staik..Ma go no ferrar, but wrele about that tre. *Ibid.* V. iv. 114 First Sergest behind sone left l.es he, Wreland [L. *luctantem*] on skelleis and wndepis of the see.

Wren (ren). Forms: *α.* 1 **wrenna** (**werna**), 3–7 **wrenne**, 5 **wrenn**, 5–6 **wrene** (6 *pl.* **wreneys**), 5– **wren.** *β.* 1 **wrænna** (**wærna**), 3, *Sc.* 6–7 **wranne**, 5 *Sc.*, 9 *Sc.* and *dial.* **wran** (7 **wrane**, 9 **ran**), *Sc.* 6, 9 **vran** (9 **vraun**). [OE. *wrenna* (also with metathesis *werna*), *wrænna* (*wærna*), obscurely related to OHG. *wrendo*, *wrendilo*, Icel. *rindill.*]

1. *Ornith.* One or other species of small dentirostral passerine birds belonging to the genus *Troglodites*, esp. the common wren (jenny- or kitty-wren), *T. parvulus*, native to Europe.

In quot. *c* 1450 used in some allusive sense.

α. *c* 725 *Corpus Gloss.* (Hessels) B 136 *Birbicariolus*, werna. *a* 1100 *Gloss.* in Wr.-Wülcker 132 *Parrax*, wrenna, *uel* hicemase. *a* 1250 *Owl & Night.* 564 (Jesus Coll. MS.), Hwat dostu godes among monne? Na mo þene doþ a wrecche wrenne [*Cotton MS.* wranne]. *Ibid.* 1717 Þe wrenne [*Cotton MS.* wranne] for heo cuþe singe Þar com..To helpe þare nyhtegale. 13.. in *Rel. Ant.* II. 107 Levere is the wrenne, Abouten the schowe renne, Than the fithel draut, Other the floute craf. 1390 GOWER *Conf.* III. 349 So that the litel wrenne in his mesure Hath yit of kinde a love under his cure. *c* 1401 LYDG. *Flour of Curtesye* 57 The sely wrenne, the titmose also,..have free eleccioun To flyen..Wher-as hem liste. *c* 1450 *Merlin* xxviii. 573 Thus shull the knyghtes of the rounde table go to a-venge the deth of the wrenne. *a* 1529 SKELTON *P. Sparowe* 600 The prety wren, That is our Ladyes hen. 1593 MARLOWE *Edw. II*, V. iii, The Wrenne may striue against the Lions strength, But all in vaine. 1613 W. BROWNE *Brit. Past.* I. iv. 13 As little wrens, but newly fledge, First by their nests hop up and downe the hedge. 1652 BENLOWES *Theoph.* I. xcviii, Shrubs cannot cedars, nor wrens eagles praise. 1710 ADDISON *Tatler* No. 224 ¶ 2 Thus the fable tells us, that the wren mounted as high as the eagle, by getting upon his back. 1750 C. SMITH *State Co. Cork* II 334 The Wren makes but short flights..; to hunt and kill him is an antient custom of the Irish on St. Stephen's day. 1768 PENNANT *Brit. Zool.* II. 268 The wren may be placed among the finest of our singing birds. 1825 WORDSW. *The Contrast* 30 This moss-lined shed, green, soft, and dry, Harbours a self-contented Wren. 1864 BRYANT *Little People of Snow* 21 A pleasant spot in spring, where first the wren Was heard to chatter. 1888 NEWTON in *Encycl. Brit.* XXIV. 688/2 The range of the Wren in Europe is very extensive.

β. *c* 1050 *Voc.* in Wr.-Wülcker 260 *Litorius*, wærna. *a* 1100 *Voc.* Ibid. 286 *Bitorius*, wrænna, *uel pintorus.* *a* 1250 [see *α*]. *c* 1450 HOLLAND *Houlate* 649 The litill we Wran, That wretchit dorche was. 1549 *Compl. Scot.* vi. 39 Robeen and the litil vran var hamely in vyntir. 1823 JENNINGS *Observ. Dial. W. Eng.* 128 Wrans an robin-riddicks. *a* 1842 in Halliwell *Nursery Rhymes* 184 We'll hunt the wran, says Robin to Bobbin. *a* 1859 in *N. & Q.* 2nd Ser. VIII. 209/1 The wran, the king of all birds. 1880–91 in Antrim, Cornwall, and Devon glossaries. 1899 SOMERVILLE & ROSS *Some Exper. Irish R. M.* i, The carpenter..wished the divil might run the plumber through a wran's quill.

Phrases. *a* 1550 *Image Hypocr.* III. 105 in *Skelton's Wks.* (1843) II. 434 As wise as any wrenne And holy as an henne. *a* 1598 FERGUSSON *Prov.* (S. T. S.) 10 As sair fights wranes as cranes.

transf. 1601 SHAKS. *Twel. N.* III. ii. 70 [Stage direction] Enter Maria. *Toby.* Looke where the youngest Wren of mine comes.

b. With distinguishing epithets.

1638 W. LISLE *Heliodorus* VI. 87 A bird no bigger then.. the Iynny Wren. 1648– [see JENNY WREN]. 1808–14 A. WILSON *Amer. Ornith.* (1831) II. 188 *Sylvia troglodytes*,

Supplement, p. 3873; Corrigenda, p. 4092; Spurious words, p. 4093; Books quoted, p. 4094

Wre·stable, a. rare. [f. WREST v. + -ABLE.] Capable of being wrested.

Wrest-balk, obs. erron. f. REST-BALK D.

Wrest-boar, obs.

Wrest-boor.

Wre·sted, ppl. a. [f. WREST v. + -ED.] 1. That has undergone wresting or wringing; twisted. Also *transf.*

2. *fig.* Deflected or turned from the true meaning or natural application; strained, perverted.

Wre·ster. [f. as prec. + -ER.] 1. One who wrests or wrenches; a twister; ✝one who tunes with a wrest.

2. An implement for picking locks. *Obs.*

Wre·sting, *ppl. a. rare.* [f. as prec. + -ING.] That wrests or twists; in quot. *fig.*

Hence **Wre·stingly** adv.

Wre·stle (re·s'l), *sb.* [f. next. Cf. WARSLE *sb.*]

Wre·stle (re·s'l), v. Forms 1–2 ... (many forms listed)

We·stling (re·sliŋ), *vbl. sb.*

1. The action or exercise of two persons grappling or gripping in a contest of strength and adroitness, either in sport or in earnest, each striving to throw the other by tripping or overbalancing him; the sport or pastime of throwing in this manner. Also in *fig.* context.

Wre·stling, *ppl. a.* in various senses.

Wret, obs. or dial. var. WART *sb.*

Wretar, obs. Sc. f. WRITE.

Wretch (retʃ), *sb.* and *a.* Forms 1–4 wrecca, 2–5 wrecche, 2–3 wrecche, 3–4 wrochche, 3–5 wrecche, 4–5 wrecche, wrocheth, 5 wreche, 6 wreche, 6 wretch (6 wreatch), 4–6 wretche, 5– wretch. [OE. *wrecca*, *wrecca*, *wrecche*, = (applied to the Magi) OHG. *reccho*, *recho*, etc., exile, adventurer, knight errant (MHG. and G. *recke* warrior, hero)—OTeut. **wrakjo-*, f. the stem **wrak-*, **wrēk-* in WREAK v.]

A. *sb.* 1. One driven out of or away from his native country; a banished person; an exile.

2. One who is sunk in deep distress, sorrow, misfortune or poverty; a miserable, unhappy, or unfortunate being.

3. A vile, sorry, or despicable person; a mean or contemptible creature. Also without article.

✝Wretch, *v. Obs.* Also 5 wreche, Sc. 7 wreche, 8–9 wratch [f. the sb.]

Wretched (re·tʃed), *a.* Forms 4– 3–5 wrecched, 4–5 -id, -yd; 3–5 wreched (3–4 -id, -yd), 4–5 wrichede, 5 -ed, 5 -id, 4– wretched. [Irreg. f. WRETCH *sb.* + -ED. Cf. WICKED *a.*]

1. Of persons, etc.: Living in a state of misery, poverty, or degradation; sunk in distress or dejection; very miserable or unhappy.

2. Of conditions, etc.: Marked or distinguished by misery or unhappiness; attended by distress, discomfort, etc.

✝Wretchdom. *Obs.* In 3–4 wrecchedom, 5 wrecche-, 4 -dom, -dum. [f. WRETCH *sb.* + -DOM.] Misery; distress; baseness.

Wretche, var. WRECHE *sb.*, *Obs.*

✝Wretched, *ppl. a. Obs.*

✝Wretchedful, *a. Obs.* [var. of WRETCHFUL *a.*] Full of misery; miserable; wretched.

† **Wretchedhede**, *Obs.*

Wretchedly (reʧedli), *adv.* [f. as prec. + -LY¹.]

Wretchedness (reʧednes), *sb.* [f. as prec. + -NESS.]

† **Wretchful**, *a. Obs.*

Wretchhede, *Obs.*

Wretchly, *Obs.*

† **Wretchness**, *Obs. rare.*

Wretchock, *Obs. rare.*

Wrethe, *sb.*

Wrethe, *v.*

Wrethe, *v.²*

Wrethful, *a. Obs.*

Wrethly, *var. of* WROTHLY *a. and adv. Obs.*

Wrethness, *Obs. rare.*

Wrewe, *var. of* WROW *Obs.*

† **Wrevoke**, *Obs.*

Wriannes, *var.*

Wribbe, *Obs.*

† **Wrible**, *v. Obs.*

Wrick (rik), *sb. dial.*

Wrick (rik), *v.*

Wride, *Obs.*

† **Wrimpled**, *a. Obs.*

Wriggle (rig'l), *sb.*

Wriggle (rig'l), *v.*

Wriggled, *ppl. a.*

Wriggler (rig'lə). [f. WRIGGLE *v.* + -ER¹.]

Wriggle-wag, *a. Obs. rare⁻¹.*

Wriggling, *vbl. sb.*

Wriggling, *ppl. a.*

Wrigglingly, *adv.*

Wriggly (rig'li), *a.*

Wright, *sb.*

Wright, *sb.² Obs.*

Wright (rəit), *v.*

Wrighting, *vbl. sb.*

Wrigwrag. *Obs. rare.*

Wrimple, *sb. Obs.*

Wrimple, *v. Obs. rare.*

Wrinch, *var. of* WRENCH *sb.*

Wrinch, *var. of* (or error for) *winch* WINCE *v.*

Wring (riŋ), *sb.¹*

Wring (riŋ), *sb.²*

Wring (riŋ), *v.*

WRIT. 376 WRITE. WRITE. 377 WRITE.

Writhe (raiðð), v. Forms: 1 wriðan, 3 wriðen, 4 wryþen, 4–5 wrythe, 4 wrythen; pa. t. 1 wraþ, 3 wroþ, 4–5 wrothe, wrathe; pa. pple. 1 writhen, 4 wrythen, writhen.

Write (rəit), v. rare. [f. prec. + -ER.] One to or for whom something is written; a reader.

Writer (rəi´tər). Forms: 1–5 writere, 3–writer, 6–7 wrightere, Sc. writter (6–wrate, -air, -ar), 4–7 wryter, 5–ere, -are, 6 Sc. 6–ar, Sc. 6 wreitar, vryter, wrytter, 6 wrester, -ar, wrettar. [OE. writere, f. writan + -ER.]

Writer-up.

Writership (rəi´tərʃip). [f. prec. + -SHIP.]

Writhable. [f. WRITHE v. + -ABLE.] Capable of being writhed.

Write. [OE. writan.]

Writhe ... *fig.* To divert or deflect from or to a person, course, etc.; to cause to turn away, bend, or incline towards another. Cf. WRENCH *v.* 4.

5. To subject (the body, limbs, etc.) to a contorting or twisting movement; to twist, contort; to writhe or wreathe. Also with *advs.*, as *around*, *round*, *together*, *up*, and *about*.

b. To distort (the face, etc.); to draw awry; — WRITH *v.* 2 b.

6. To twist or wrench (something) out of place, position, or relation; — WREST *v.* Const. with *advs.*, as *asunder*, *failure*, *off*, *out*, or *preps.*, as *from*, *off*, *out of*. Also *refl.* Occas. *fig.*

7. To wrest, strain, or pervert the meaning of (a writing, passage, word, etc.); to deflect, misapply. — WRENCH *v.* 7, WREST *v.* 5, 6, WRING *v.* 9 b. *Obs.*

Writhen (rī'ð'n), *ppl. a.* [pa. pple. of WRITHE *v.*] Cf. WREATHEN *ppl. a.* 2.

1. Subjected to writhing, twisting, or turning; twisted out of regular shape or form; contorted; † also, closed, clenched (quot. 1377). *b.* Of things...

2. Fashioned by or as by twisting or convolution; twisted, wreathed, or wound one in another as a cord or rope is; linked to linck, ... **b.** *Her.* ...

3. Of pillars, etc. † — WREATHEN *ppl. a.* 3.

4. Of the features, etc.: Subjected to contortion or writhing; contorted, wry.

5. Characterized by sinuous or tortuous movement.

Writhing, *vbl. sb.* [f. as prec. + -ING [1].]

Writher (raī'ðər). Also *5-6 wryther.* [f. WRITHE *v.* + -ER [1].] One who writhes or twists; † one who perverts.

Writhing (raī'ðiŋ), *vbl. sb.* [as prec. + -ING [1]]

1. The action of the verb in various senses; an instance of this. Also with *away*. Occas. *fig.*

2. Fashioning by or as by twisting or convolution; ...

3. *Her.* ...

Writhing-, *ppl. a.* [f. as prec. + -ING [2].]

Writhle, *v. Obs.* [Of obscure origin.] ... Wild lettuce.

Writhled (rī'ð'ld, -LE-); but *perh.* an alteration of KIVELLED *a.*]

1. Of persons, the skin, etc.: Wrinkled; shrivelled, withered. Now *Obs. exc. arch.*

2. Combined or made by, subjected to, twining or plaiting; intertwined, entwined, or plaited. Cf.

Writhy (raī'ði), *a.* [f. WRITHE *v.* [1] + -Y [1]. Cf. Da. *vridig* flexible.] Moving sinuously; writhing.

Writing (raī'tiŋ), *vbl. sb.* [f. WRITE *v.* + -ING [1].]

1. The action of one who writes, in various senses; the penning or forming of letters or words; the using of written characters for purposes of record, transmission of ideas, etc.

b. *At this (present) writing*, at the time of writing this.

2. The action of composing; the expression of thoughts or ideas in written words; literary composition or production; literary work or composition.

3. Style or manner of composition or writing.

4. Manner of setting down in written form; spelling, orthography.

5. The composition of music.

6. That which is in a written (now also typewritten) state or form; something penned or recorded; written composition, composition, or production; literary work or compilation.

Writing, *ppl. a.* [f. as prec. + -ING [2].]

Writing-board. [WRITING *vbl. sb.* 12 e + BOARD *sb.*] A board on which to rest the paper while writing.

Writing-book. [WRITING *vbl. sb.* 12 d +...] A blank book in which to write for purposes of record, etc.; a book containing or consisting of writing-copy.

Writing-box. [WRITING *vbl. sb.* 13 + BOX *sb.* [2]] A small box for containing paper and other writing requisites.

Writing-desk. [WRITING *vbl. sb.* 12 c + DESK.] A desk used or designed for writing on; such a desk fitted with conveniences for holding writing materials, papers, etc. Also *transf.*

Writing-ink. Also *writing-ink.* [WRITING *vbl. sb.* 12 b + INK *sb.* [1].] A make of ink or writing-fluid prepared or suitable for writing with the pen.

Writing-master. [WRITING *vbl. sb.* 13 +...] A teacher or instructor in writing, penmanship, or calligraphy. Also *transf.*

Writing-paper. [WRITING *vbl. sb.* 12 d +...] A special make of paper, usu. with a smooth surface and sized, for writing upon; now *esp.*, note-paper.

Writing-pen. [WRITING *vbl. sb.* 12 b + PEN *sb.* [2].] A pen suitable or adapted for writing.

Writing-school. [WRITING *vbl. sb.* 13 +...] A school in which writing or calligraphy is taught. *Obs.*

Writing-schoolmaster. *Obs.*

Writing-table. [WRITING *vbl. sb.* 12 c + TABLE [2].] A small thin tablet, sheet, or plate of wood, ivory, or other material for writing (esp. notes or memoranda) upon; a writing-tablet; — TABLE [2]...

Writ, *obs. f.* WRIT.

Writer (rī'tər). [f. WRITE *v.* + -ER [1].] One who writes.

Writto, *obs. f.* WRITTEN *ppl. a.*

Wrizzle, *v. Obs.* Also *wrixel, wryxle.* [OE. *wrixlian*, -*an* to vary, change, exchange, etc.; also *gewrixlan*, altered from gewrixl ...]

1. To alter, change, contrast.

2. To exchange.

Wrizzled (rī'z'ld), *ppl. a. Now dial.* Also *wrizled.* [Var. of WRINKLED *a.*] Marked with creases, wrinkles, or corrugations; wrinkled, shrivelled.

Wro. Now *north. dial.* Forms: *a. north.* and *wro*, *vro*, *wrote*, *wroth*, *vro*. [a. ON. *vrá*, *rá* nook, cabin (whence MSw. *vraa*, Sw. *vrå*, Norw. *raa*, ro).]

1. A nook or corner; a retired or sheltered spot. *Obs.*

Wrong (rǫŋ), *a.* [Late OE. *wrang* (in comb.), a. ON. *rangr* wrong, wry, unjust, a. pa. pple. of *wring-an* to WRING *v.*]

1. Having the character or shape of something bent or twisted out of a straight line; crooked, bent, curved, wry. *Obs.*

2. Deviating from rectitude or uprightness; contrary to what is morally right; unrighteous. *Obs.*

3. Not in consonance with moral rectitude, law, or fairness. Also *absol.*

4. Of letters, etc.: Traced or formed with the fingers, etc.

5. That has been written in. Also with *in*.

Wrong, *sb.* [f. prec. *a.*, or a. ON. *rangr* *sb.*] ...

Wrong, *adv.* ...

Wrong, *v.* Also *wrang.* [f. WRONG *a.*]

Wrong-doer. Also wrongdoer.

Wrong-doing, ppl. a. and vbl. sb.

Wrouged, ppl. a.

Wrongen, obs. var. WRUNG ppl.

Wronger (ʳŋɑɹ). Also 4 wronger.

Wrong-doing (ppl. a. and vbl. sb.)

Wronged, ppl. a.

Wrongful (ʳŋfŭl), a. Also 3 wrongful.

Wrongfully (ʳŋfŭli), adv.

Wrongfulness (ʳŋfŭlnes).

Wronging, vbl. sb.

Wrong-head. Also wronghead.

Wrong-headed, a. Also wrongheaded.

Wrong-headedness. Also wrongheadedness.

Wrongness (ʳŋnes).

Wrongous (ʳŋɑs), a.

Wrongously (ʳŋɑsli), adv.

Wrongousness (ʳŋɑsnes).

Wrong-wise, adv.

Wrongwende, a.

Wrongwiseness, Obs. rare.

Wroot, obs. form of ROOT.

Wroot-, obs. form of ROOT.

Wroothe, obs. form of WROTH a.

Wrooting, vbl. sb. Obs.

Wroot, sb. Obs. Forms.

Wroper, dial. 1 Wrapper.

Wroth, sb.[1] Also 5 wroth.

Wroth (roʳ), a. Cornish dial.

Wroth, obs. var. tvrought, pa. pple. of WORK v.

Wrothe, obs. Obs. Forms: 1 wrathe.

Wroter, obs. form of Flem. wroeter.

Wroth-heal, sb. and adj. Obs.

Wrothful, a. Obs. or arch. [f. WRATH-FUL a. after WRATHFUL.]

Wrothly, adv. Obs. In 4 wrathli.

Wro-thliche, adv. Obs. Forms: 1 wraðlice, 2 wr.

X.

III. Abbreviations.

6. In writing the name CHRIST, esp. in abbreviated form, X or x represents the first letter (kəi) of Gr. ΧΡΙϹΤΟϹ *khristos*, and XP or xp the first two letters (kəi rōu). Hence in early times Xp̄, in modern times Xt, Xᵗ, and X, are used as abbreviations of the syllable *Christ*, alone or in derivatives; thus †Xp̄en, Xp̄n = CHRISTEN, †Xp̄enned = CHRISTENED; †Xpian, Xtian(ity) = CHRISTIAN(ITY); XMAS (*Xstmas*, *Xtmas*) = CHRISTMAS.

†Xp̄c stands for X̅P̅C̅ contracted form of ΧΡΙϹΤΟϹ; cf. IHS.

a 1100 *O.E. Chron.* an. 1021 On Xp̄es mæsse uhtan. *c* 1380 WYCLIF *Serm.* Sel. Wks. I. 337 In þis word Vix ben but þree lettris, V, and I, and X. And V bitokeneþ fyve; I bitokeneþ Jesus; and X bitokeneþ Crist. 1426 LYDG. *De Guil. Pilgr.* 19951 Xp̄c þi sone, þat in þis world alighte, Vp-on þe cros to suffre his passioun. 1485 *Rolls of Parlt.* VI. 280/1 The most famous, blessed and Xp̄en Prince. *Ibid.* 336/1 Any Kyng or Prynce in England Xp̄enned. 1573 BARET *Alv.* s.v. *Y*, The long mistaking of this woorde Xp̄s, standing for Chrs by abbreuation which for lacke of knowledge in the greeke they tooke for x, p, and s, and so likewise Xp̄ofer. 1598 ROWLANDS *Betraying of Christ* (Hunter. Cl.) 25 Xpian the outward, inward, not at all. 1634 *Documents agst. Prynne* (Camden) 33 Such right..as your Xtianity, place, and function joyntly require. 1685–6 MS. in *Bk. Com. Pr. 1662* (Bodl.), My first child..Xstened on thursday the 28 of the same month. *a* 1697 AUBREY *Lives, Milton* (MS. Aubrey 8, lf. 63), He was so faire, that they called him the lady of Xᵗˢ coll. 1711 HEARNE *Collect.* (O.H.S.) III. 155 This Note I took out of a Book of Mʳ. Urry of Xᵗ. Church. 1842 FRANCIS *Dict. Arts*, etc. s.v., Xmas. for Christmas, Xpher. for Christopher, &c.

7. Put for the initial syllable *ex-* of a word, or as an abbreviation for a word beginning with *ex-*. *X's* (slang): expenses. Also, in Stock Exchange quotations, *xd* = ex dividend, etc.

1838 MANNING *Let.* in Purcell *Life* (1896) I. xi. 230 All the 'Xs', I fear,..would go out. [*Note.* 'X's and Peculiars' were the nicknames given by the Tractarians to the Evangelicals ..who called themselves Christians *par excellence.*] *Ibid.*, He writes as tenderly as if he thought you a serious 'X'. *a* 1849 POE *Tales, X-ing a Paragrab*, One gentleman thought the whole an X-ellent joke. 1885 *Daily News* 13 Mar. 2/1 New York Central Railway 92⅜ 92⅝ xd. 1894 LOUISE J. MILN *Strolling Players East* xv. 132, I think we might clear our X.'s...Perhaps I should explain that 'X.'s' means expenses. 1910 *Encycl. Brit.* V. 197/2 Canonists have continued to refer to the decretals of Gregory IX by the abbreviation X (*Extra*, i.e. *extra Decretum*).

8. *Chem.* = XENON.

Hence **X** *v. trans.*, to supply with x's in place of types that are wanting.

a 1849 POE *Tales, X-ing a Paragrab*, I shell have to *x* this ere paragrab', said he to himself, as he read it over... So *x* it he did, unflinchingly, and to press it went *x-ed.*

Xa, Xabandar, obs. ff. SHAH, SHABUNDER.

Xal, xall(e, obs. ff. SHALL.

Xanthæmatin to **Xanthelene**: see XANTHO-.

Xanthate (zæ·nþeɪt). *Chem.* [f. XANTHIC + -ATE⁴.] **a.** A salt of xanthic (sulphocarbethylic) acid. **b.** A compound of xanthic oxide (xanthine) with an alkali.

1831 [see XANTHIC 1 b]. 1868 WATTS *Dict. Chem.* V. 498 Xanthate of sodium forms yellow needles. *Ibid.* 499 Xanthate of Antimony..forms large, lemon-yellow, triclinic crystals...Xanthate of Bismuth..crystallises in shining golden-yellow laminæ. 1887 A. M. BROWN *Anim. Alkaloids* 79 [Xanthine] combines with the alkalies,..forming xanthates.

Xanthein (zæ·nþiˌin). *Chem.* Also **-ine.** [ad. F. *xanthéine* (Frémy & Cloez, 1854), arbitrarily f. Gr. ξανθός yellow, to distinguish it from *xanthine* XANTHIN (1 b).] That part of the yellow colouring-matter of flowers which is soluble in water: cf. XANTHIN 1 b.

1857 MILLER *Elem. Chem., Org.* 546 The yellow substance which is soluble in water is termed xantheine: it..may be obtained from the yellow dahlia. 1864 WATTS tr. *Gmelin's Hand-bk. Chem.* XVI. 513 Yellow of Flowers...The insoluble substance, called Xanthin by Frémy & Cloez, appears to correspond with Marquart's anthoxanthin; their Xanthein, soluble in water, with Marquart's colourless extractive matter.

‖**Xanthelasma** (zænþɪlæ·zmă). *Path.* [mod.L., f. Gr. ξανθός yellow + ἔλασμα metal plate.] = XANTHOMA. Also *attrib.* Hence **Xanthela·smic** *a.* = XANTHOMATOUS; ‖**Xanthelasmoidea** [see -OID], a disease resembling xanthelasma, which leaves yellowish or brownish patches on the skin; also called *vitiligoidea.*

1867 W. J. E. WILSON *Diseases of Skin* (ed. 6) xxiv. 773 Epithelial hypertrophy..to which from its colour and laminated appearance we have given the name of xanthelasma. 1900 J. HUTCHINSON in *Archives Surg.* XI. No. 41. 10 There is none of the characteristic xanthelasma leather. *Ibid.* 18 She..had xanthelasma spots on the eyelids. *Ibid.* 2 The xanthelasmic [form of jaundice]. 1899 *Syd. Soc. Lex.*, Xanthelasmoidea. 1903 *Lancet* 30 May 1521/2 If further investigation should prove that in xanthelasmoidea the coagulability is high it will thus be more decisively separated from the urticarias.

Xanthian (zæ·nþiăn), *a.* and *sb.* Also 7 **Zanthian.** [f. *Xanthus* (see def.) + -IAN.] Of or pertaining to (or an inhabitant of) Xanthus, an ancient town in Asia Minor; *spec.* of a collection of marbles discovered near it.

1685 COTTON *Montaigne* I. xl. (1711) I. 363 The Zanthians, who being besieg'd..precipitated themselves..into such a furious Appetite of dying,..that Brutus had much ado to save but a very small number. 1697 DRYDEN *Æneid* I. 662 Ere yet the Food Of Troy they taste, or drink the Xanthian Flood. 1770 LANGHORNE *Plutarch* IV. 244 (*Alexander*) A spring in Lycia near the city of the Xanthians. 1842 SIR C. FELLOWS (*title*) The Xanthian Marbles, their acquisition and transmission to England.

Xanthic (zæ·nþik), *a.* [ad. F. *xanthique*, f. Gr. ξανθός yellow: see -IC.]

1. *Chem.* Epithet of certain compounds which produce substances of a yellow colour, or of bodies connected with these. **a.** *Xanthic oxide*, the original name of XANTHINE; so *xanthic calculus*, a urinary calculus containing xanthine.

1817 MARCET *Ess. Chem. Hist. Calculous Disorders* iv. 99 If the potash be added to the pure xanthic substance,..no change of colour takes place. The residue of the solution of xanthic oxyd in water produces the yellow substance, when treated with nitric acid. *Ibid.* 101 Xanthic oxyd. *Ibid.* 102 In burning, it emitted an animal smell, which did not at all resemble that of the lithic, cystic, or xanthic calculus. 1857 MILLER *Elem. Chem., Org.* 642 Xanthic or Uric Oxide ($C_{10}H_4N_4O_4$) was discovered by Dr. Marcet as the principal constituent of a very rare variety of urinary calculus. 1872 T. BRYANT *Pract. Surg.* (1879) II. 84 Calculi of uric acid and the urates, with their modifications the oxalates, xanthic and cystic oxide.

b. *Xanthic acid*, a complex acid containing sulphur and carbon, also called sulphocarbethylic or ethyldisulphocarbonic acid ($C_3H_6OS_2$), many of whose salts (*xanthates*) are yellow. So *xanthic ether*, etc.

1831 T. THOMSON *Syst. Chem.* (ed. 7) II. 176 Xanthic acid is characterized by precipitating the salts of copper yellow. *Ibid.*, During the distillation of xanthate of potash, a substance comes over which Zeise has distinguished by the name of xanthic oil. 1857 MILLER *Elem. Chem., Org.* 146 Xanthic or Sulphocarbethylic Acid. 1868 WATTS *Dict. Chem.* V. 498 Ethyldisulphocarbonic or Xanthic Acid..is a colourless oil, heavier than water,..its taste is acid, astringent, and bitter. *Ibid.* 500 Ethylic Disulphocarbonate or Xanthate, Xanthic Ether, $C^5H^{10}OS^2$..has a pale-yellow colour, a sweetish taste.

2. *Bot.* De Candolle's name for a series or class of colours in flowers, of which the type is yellow: opp. to *cyanic.*

1843 *Florist's Jrnl.* (1846) IV. 34 A most uncommon combination of colours—cyanic and xanthic tints in one and the same flower. 1885 GOODALE *Physiol. Bot.* (1892) 454.

Xanthide (zæ·nþəid). *Chem.* [f. Gr. ξανθός yellow + -IDE.] **a.** A compound of xanthogen (XANTHOGEN 1). **b.** A salt of xanthydric (persulphocyanic) acid.

1823 HENRY *Elem. Chem.* (ed. 9) II. 667 The oxides of common metals (copper, lead, mercury, &c.) decompose it [*sc.* hydroxanthic acid] by giving up their oxygen to the hydrogen of the acid, and the xanthogene unites with the metal, forming xanthides. 1868 WATTS *Dict. Chem.* V. 1050 *Xanthides*, syn. with *Persulphocyanates.*

Xanthin (zæ·nþin). *Chem.* Also **xanthine,** (**zanthin**). [ad. F. *xanthine* or G. *xanthin*, f. Gr. ξανθός yellow: see -IN¹.]

1. a. A yellow colouring-matter obtained from madder.

1838 T. THOMSON *Chem. Org. Bodies* 387 Madder, according to Kuhlmann, contains two colouring matters, one, which is yellow, is soluble in cold water. Kuhlmann, who first obtained it, has given it the name of *xanthin.* 1839 URE *Dict. Arts*, etc. 1329 *Xanthine*, is the name given by Kuhlmann to the yellow dyeing-matter contained in madder. *c* 1865 J. WYLDE in *Circ. Sc.* I. 421/1 Other principles may be extracted from madder, such as purpurine, alizarine, xanthine.

b. That part of the yellow colouring-matter of flowers which is insoluble in water: cf. XANTHEIN.

1857 MILLER *Elem. Chem., Org.* 546. 1868 WATTS *Dict. Chem.* V. 1050.

2. (See quot.)

1868 WATTS *Dict. Chem.* V. 1050 *Xanthin*,..applied..3. By Couerbe to a gaseous product of the decomposition of xanthates, to which he assigned the formula $C^2H^2S^2O^2$.

3. *attrib.* **Xanthin-spar,** yellow lead-spar or WULFENITE.

1868 WATTS *Dict. Chem.* V. 1052.

Xanthine (zæ·nþəin). Also **-in.** *Chem.* [ad. F. *xanthine*, f. Gr. ξανθός yellow: see -INE⁵.] A substance ($C_5H_4N_4O_2$) allied to uric acid, found in various organs and secretions of the animal body; originally called *xanthic oxide* (see XANTHIC 1 a), from its forming a lemon-yellow compound with nitric acid.

1857 G. BIRD *Urin. Deposits* (ed. 5) 46 This interesting body..bears so close a resemblance to xanthine or uric oxide, that Scherer has named it hypoxanthine. 1862 H. BENCE JONES in *Jrnl. Chem. Soc.* XV. 78 (*heading*) On a Deposit of Crystallized Xanthin in Human Urine. 1880 J. W. LEGG *Bile* 582 The liver contained..leucin, tyrosin, and xanthin. 1887 A. M. BROWN *Anim. Alkaloids* 78 Xanthine may be extracted from muscular tissue in the same way as the sarkine.

attrib. and *Comb.* 1868 WATTS *Dict. Chem.* V. 1050 *Xanthine*..was discovered by Marcet in a urinary calculus weighing only 8 grains. Liebig and Wöhler afterwards found it in a larger calculus weighing between 18 and 20 grammes; these are the only known examples of xanthine calculi. 1873 RALFE *Phys. Chem.* 93 Dr. Bence Jones has recorded an interesting case of xanthin gravel occurring in a lad aged nine and a half years. 1883 *Science* 23 Feb. 75/1 By heating xanthine-silver [= the silver-compound of xanthine] with methyl iodide, a methyl group was introduced. 1897 *Trans. Amer. Pediatric Soc.* IX. 123 Convulsive seizures,..produced by the action of the poisonous xanthin bodies on the nerve centres. 1907 *Sat. Rev.* 16 Mar. 338/1 So called food reformers..bandy about their catchwords—flesh-forming,..xanthin-forming and the like.

Hence **Xa·nthinine,** ‖**Xanthinu·ria** (see quots.).

1868 WATTS *Dict. Chem.* V. 1051 *Xanthinine.* $C^4H^5N^3O^2$. ..A base produced..by heating thionurate of ammonium to 200°...On boiling the resulting mass with water, the xanthinine remains as a yellow powder. 1890 BILLINGS *Nat. Med. Dict.*, *Xanthinuria*, passage of xanthin in the urine.

Xanthippe: see XANTIPPE.

Xanthitane (zæ·nþiteɪn). *Min.* [f. next + -ANE.] A mineral produced by alteration or decomposition of sphene or titanite: see quot.

1856 C. U. SHEPARD in *Amer. Jrnl. Sci.* Ser. II. XXII. 96 *Xanthitane.* In hollow crystals with the form of sphene, and pulverulent. Color pale yellowish white...It is found in a decomposing feldspar,..and probably proceeds from the decomposition of sphene.

Xanthite (zæ·nþəit). *Min.* [f. Gr. ξανθός yellow + -ITE¹.] A variety of vesuvianite or idocrase, occurring in yellowish crystals.

1828 THOMSON *Ann. Lyc. N. Hist. N. Y.* III. 44 (Dana). 1843 *Penny Cycl.* XXVII. 615/1 *Xanthite* consists of a congeries of small rounded grains,..not larger than small grains of sand. 1851 MANTELL *Petrifactions* iv. § 1. 364.

Xantho- (zænþo), before a vowel **xanth-,** repr. Gr. ξανθο-, combining form of ξανθός yellow; occurring as the first element in various compounds and derivatives, chiefly terms of chemistry, mineralogy, and pathology; the more important of these are given in their alphabetical places.

(Sometimes also erroneously *Zantho-*: see X.)

1. *Chem.* In names of, or adjectives relating to, various compounds: (*a*) of a yellow colour, as *xanthæ·matin, xa·nthaline, xa·nthoco·balt, -coba·ltic, xanthocre·atine* (*-crea·tinine*), *xantho·phane* [Gr. φαν-, stem of φαίνειν to cause to appear], *xanthopi·crin* (*-pi·crite*) [Gr. πικρός bitter], *xanthopro·tein, xantho·psin* [Gr. ὄψις sight], *xanthopu·ccine* [PUCCOON], *xanthopu·rpurin, xanthorha·mnin; xanthophe·nic, xanthoprote·ic, xanthota·nnic, xanthy·dric* [Gr. ὕδωρ water] adjs.; (*b*) derived from or related to xanthic acid (XANTHIC 1 b), as *xa·nthamide, xa·ntharin, xa·nthelene; xanthe·ic, xa·nthomethy·lic* adjs.; (*c*) derived from or related to xanthydric acid, as *xa·nthane* (*-an*): see quots.

1860 MAYNE *Expos. Lex.*, *Xanthæmatin..Term by Brett and Bird for a yellow, bitter substance found by dissolving hematin in weak nitric acid. 1893 *Pharmaceut. Jrnl.* 25 Mar. 793/2 *Xanthaline—A New Opium Alkaloid ($C_{37}H_{36}N_2O_9$). 1855 WATTS tr. *Gmelin's Chem.* IX. 276 *Xanthamide. $C^6NH^7S^2O^2$. *Ibid.* 277 Xanthamide exposed in a distillatory apparatus to a gradually increasing temperature is resolved into mercaptan and cyanuric acid. 1868 — *Dict. Chem.* V. 1049 **Xanthan*, Berzelius's name for the group Cy^2S^3, regarded as the radicle of persulphocyanic or xanthydric acid. *Ibid.*, **Xantharin*, or *Xanthil*, an oily fetid compound, $C^4H^{10}O^2$, supposed by Couerbe..to be produced by the dry distillation of xanthic ether. 1843 *Penny Cycl.* XXVII. 614/2 When xanthate of potash is subjected to distillation a limpid yellow coloured fluid comes over, which Zeise has called **xantheic oil.* 1868 WATTS *Dict. Chem.* V. 1049 **Xanthelene.* Zeise gave this name to an oil..produced..by precipitating potassic ethylsulphocarbonate with a cupric salt. 1856 GIBBS & GENTH *Res. Ammonia-cobalt Bases* in *Smithsonian Contrib. Knowl.* (1857) IX. v. 48 The salts of *Xanthocobalt. 1863 WATTS *Dict. Chem.* I. 1054 *Xantho-cobaltic Salts. 1891 *Cent. Dict.*, **Xanthocreatine.* 1913 DORLAND *Med. Dict.* (ed. 7), *Xanthocreatin*, xanthocreatinin. 1887 A. M. BROWN *Anim. Alkaloids* 85 *Xanthocreatinine $C^5H^{10}N^4O$.. closely resembles kreatinine...It shows in pellets of sulphur yellow, of slightly cadaveric odour. 1868 WATTS *Dict. Chem.* V. 1052 **Xanthoglobulin.* This name was given by Scherer..to a substance which he obtained in yellow globules. 1880 J. W. LEGG *Bile* 515 Hypoxanthin and xanthoglobulin were also found. 1868 WATTS *Dict. Chem.* V. 501 Methyl-disulphocarbonic Acid $(CH^3)HCOS^2$. *Xanthomethylic Acid...Methylic Disulphocarbonate, $C^3H^6OS^2$. ..Xanthomethylic Ether. 1890 BILLINGS *Nat. Med. Dict.*, **Xanthophane*, an orange-yellow pigment obtained from the retina. 1868 WATTS *Dict. Chem.* V. 1052 **Xanthophenic acid.* A yellow colouring-matter,..produced..by heating phenol or cresol with arsenic acid...The xanthophenates dye silk and wool red, of various shades. 1852 W. GREGORY *Handbk. Org. Chem.* 301 **Xanthopicrine* is a bitter crystalline substance from the bark of *Zanthoxylum Clava Herculis.* 1868 WATTS *Dict. Chem.* V. 1053 *Xanthopicrin, Xanthopicrite.* These names were given..to a yellow colouring-matter from the bark of *Xanthoxylon caribæum*, since shown..to be identical with berberine. 1838 T. THOMSON *Chem. Org. Bodies* 710 *Xanthopicrite..was detected by Chevalier and Pelletan [1826], in the bark of the *Xanthoxylon carybæum*...It has..a very bitter and astringent taste. 1847–9 *Todd's Cycl. Anat.* IV. 164/1 The alkaline *xanthoproteates. 1843 T. THOMSON *Chem. Anim. Bodies* 178 *Xantho-proteic Acid.* This name [*Xantho-proteinsäure*] has been given by Mulder [1838] to a yellow coloured acid, obtained first by Fourcroy, by treating fibrin or albumen with nitric acid. 1873 RALFE *Phys. Chem.* 130 Heated with strong nitric acid pepsin does not give the xantho-proteic reaction; hence it would appear that pepsin is not an albuminoid substance. 1904 *Brit. Med. Jrnl.* 10 Sept. 601 The normal gland extract gave a positive result with the xanthoproteic test. 1883 OGILVIE (Annandale), **Xanthoprotein*, a yellow acid substance formed by the action of nitric acid upon fibrine. 1890 BILLINGS *Nat. Med. Dict.*, **Xanthopsin*, yellow pigment of the retina. 1901 DORLAND *Med. Dict.* (ed. 2), *Xanthopsin*, visual purple partially discolored or bleached by light; visual yellow. 1890 BILLINGS *Nat. Med. Dict.*, **Xanthopuccine*, name proposed by Lercben (1878) for an alkaloid found in hydrastis. 1877 WATTS *Fownes' Chem.* II. 588 *Purpuroxanthin* (or **Xanthopurpurin*)..is formed from purpurin by reduction with stannous chloride in alkaline solution. 1843 KANE in *Lond., Edinb., & Dubl. Philos. Mag.* July 3 The dark-coloured [Persian] berries.. give out to boiling water an olive-yellow material, to which ..I give the name of **xanthorhamnine.* 1862 WATTS tr. *Gmelin's Hand-bk. Chem.* XV. 533 *Xanthotannic Acid. Obtained from elm-leaves reddened in the autumn. 1868 WATTS *Dict. Chem.* V. 1054 **Xanthydric acid.* Syn. with *Persulphocyanic Acid* [obtained as 'a pale yellow crystalline powder', *ibid.* IV. 378].

2. In various compounds. **Xantha·rsenite** *Min.*, a mineral allied to chondrarsenite, occurring in sulphur-yellow masses. **Xanthoca·rpous** *a. Bot.* [Gr. καρπός fruit], having yellow fruit. **Xanthocomic** (-kǫ·mik) *a.* (*nonce-wd.*) [Gr. κόμη hair], yellow-haired. **Xa·nthocone** (-con), **Xantho·conite** *Min.* [G. *xanthokon* (Breithaupt, 1840), f. Gr. κόνις dust], an arseniosulphide of silver, of a dull red or brown colour, yellow when pulverized. **Xanthocy·anopsy, Xanthocya·nopy** (-kyan-) *Path.* [Gr. κύανος blue + ὄψις, ὠπή sight], a form of colour-blindness in which yellow and blue are the only colours discerned. ‖**Xanthode·rma, -de·rmia** *Path.* [mod.L., f. Gr. δέρμα skin], yellowness of the skin. **Xa·nthodont, Xanthodo·ntous** *adjs. Zool.* [Gr. ὀδούς, ὀδοντ- tooth], having yellow teeth, as certain rodents. **Xantho·meter** [-METER], an instrument for determining the colour of sea or lake water by comparison with a scale of different-coloured solutions. ‖**Xanthopa·thia, Xantho·pathy** *Path.* [Gr. -πάθεια -PATHY] = *xanthoderma.* ‖**Xantho·psia, Xa·nthopsy** *Path.* [Gr. ὄψις appearance, sight], an affection of the eyes in which objects appear yellow; yellow vision. **Xantho·rthite** *Min.*, a yellow variety of orthite. **Xanthosi·derite** *Min.* [Gr. σίδηρος iron], a native hydrated oxide of iron, occurring in needle-shaped or fibrous crystals, or as an ochre, of a yellow, brown, or reddish colour. **Xanthospe·rmous** *a. Bot.* [Gr. σπέρμα seed], having yellow seeds.

1892 DANA *Syst. Min.* 796 *Xantharsenite...Occurs with hausmannite,..in crystalline limestone. 1861 MAYNE *Med. Vocab.* (ed. 2) 436/1 *Xanthocarpous. 1861 WYNTER *Soc. Bees* 497 Europe is the chief seat of the *xantho-comic or light-haired races. 1846 WORCESTER, *Xanthocon (citing DANA). 1868 WATTS *Dict. Chem.* V. 1052 *Xanthocone*...A silver-ore from the Himmelfürst mine, near Freiberg in Saxony. 1868 DANA *Min.* (ed. 5) 108 **Xanthoconite*...Color dull-red to clove-brown; crystals orange-yellow on the edges by transmitted light. 1891 *Cent. Dict.*, *Xanthocyanopsy. 1890 BILLINGS *Nat. Med. Dict.*, *Xanthokyanopy. 1867 W. J. E. WILSON *Diseases of Skin* (ed. 6) 695 *Xanthoderma represents the yellow complexion of certain of the races of mankind. 1900 *Lancet* 11 Aug. 414/1 The mucous membranes were not coloured and the urine..never showed a trace of bile pigment. This was in favour of the diagnosis of *xanthodermia. 1891 *Cent. Dict.*, *Xanthodont. 1861 MAYNE *Med. Vocab.* (ed. 2) 436 *Xanthodontous. 1902 *Westm. Gaz.* 8 April 8/3 When the Queen visited the Antarctic exploration ship *Discovery* she was particularly interested in Forel's *xanthometer. 1867 W. J. E. WILSON *Diseases of Skin* (ed. 6) 695 *Xanthopathia, or yellow discoloration of the skin, consists in the deposit in the cells of the rete mucosum of a yellow colouring principle. 1848 DUNGLISON *Med. Lex.* (ed. 7), **Xanthopsia*, yellow vision,—as sometimes occurs in jaundice. 1875 H. C. WOOD *Therap.* (1879) 603 A very curious symptom caused by santonin..is xanthopsia. 1868 DANA *Min.* (ed. 5) 287 *Xanthorthite, of Hermann,..is apparently an altered variety [of orthite]. 1868 WATTS *Dict. Chem.* V. 1054 **Xanthosiderite.* A hydrated ferric oxide. 1861 MAYNE *Med. Vocab.* (ed. 2) 436/2 *Xanthospermous.

‖**Xanthochroi** (zænþǫ·kroˌəi, -ōu·kroi), *sb. pl. Anthropology.* [mod.L. (Huxley), app. meant as a transliteration of an assumed Gr. *ξάνθωχροι, f. ξανθός yellow + ὠχρός pale (the regular L. form of which would be **xanthōchri*); by later writers and in Dicts. taken as *xanthŏchroi* (sing. *-chrous*), ad. Gr. ξανθόχροος, f. ξανθός yellow + χρόα skin: cf. MELANOCHROI.] In Huxley's classification of the varieties of mankind: A subdivision of the *Leiotrichi* or smooth-haired class, having yellow or light-coloured hair and pale complexion.

1866 [see XANTHOMELANOI]. 1875 TYLOR in *Encycl. Brit.* II. 113/2 The Xanthochroi, or fair whites..are the prevalent inhabitants of Northern Europe.

Hence **Xanthochroic** (-krōu·ik), **Xanthochroid** (-ōu·kroid), **Xanthochrooid** (-ǫ·kroˌoid), **Xanthochroous** (-ǫ·kroˌəs), **Xanthochrous** (-ōu·krəs) *adjs.*, of, pertaining to, or having the characters of the *Xanthochroi.* So ‖**Xanthochroia** (-kroi·ă) [mod.L. f. Gr. χροιά = χρόα skin], yellow discoloration of the skin from change in the pigment; **Xanthochroism** (-ǫ·kroˌiz'm), *Ornith.*, abnormal replacement of another colour by yellow in the plumage of certain birds.

1867 W. J. E. WILSON *Diseases of Skin* (ed. 6) 695 Xanthopathia. Syn. Xanthoderma; *xanthochroia. 1870 HUXLEY in *Contemp. Rev.* July 515 The *Xanthochroic area. 1878 BARTLEY tr. *Topinard's Anthrop.* II. i. 202 The xanthochroic group: pale skin, blue eyes, and abundant fair hair. 1865 LUBBOCK *Preh. Times* xii. (1869) 378 [The] *Xanthochroid [group]. 1893 NEWTON *Dict. Birds* 421 There seems to be a certain correlation of colours in most cases of Heterochrosis:..green feathers exhibit *xanthochroism. 1909 *Cent. Dict. Supp.*, **Xanthochroöid*, same as *Xanthochroic.* 1891 *Cent. Dict.*, *Xanthochroous. 1865 *Xanthochrous [see MELANOCHROUS]. 1901 *Q. Rev.* July 230 Great stature and a xanthochrous complexion were..the characteristics of the Celt or German.

Xanthogen (zæ·nþǫdʒen). *Chem.* [f. XANTHO- + -GEN, after G. *xanthogensäure* (Zeise, 1822).]

1. The hypothetical radical of xanthic acid. Also *attrib.*

1823 HENRY *Elem. Chem.* (ed. 9) II. 665 This new acid contains sulphur, carbon, and hydrogen, the two first of which probably form a compound base, analogous to cyanogen...To the base, Mr. Zeise..has given the name of *xanthogene*..on account of the yellow colour of its compounds. 1868 WATTS *Dict. Chem.* V. 1052 *Xanthogen-oil.* Zeise's name for an oily product formed by the dry distillation of potassic xanthate.

2. A substance supposed to be contained in flowers: see quot.

1864 WATTS *Dict. Chem.* II. 668 According to Filhol, nearly all flowers contain a substance which forms colourless solutions with acids, and acquires a fine yellow colour when treated with alkalis: this substance was designated by Marquart as resin of flowers, and by Hope..as xanthogen, which name is also retained by Filhol. He describes it as solid, of a light yellow colour,..soluble in water, alcohol, and ether.

Xantholiniform (zænþoli·nifǭrm), *a. Entom.* [f. mod.L. *Xantholinus* (f. Gr. ξανθός yellow, with ending of *Staphylinus*, an allied genus) + -(I)FORM.] Resembling in form the beetles of the genus *Xantholinus.*

1847 HARDY in *Proc. Berw. Nat. Club* II. No. 5. 250 *Ph[ilonthus] procerulus*..Narrow, elongate, sub-parallel, xantholiniform.

‖**Xanthoma** (zænþōu·mă). *Path.* [f. Gr. ξανθός yellow + -ωμα (cf. *sarcoma*).] An affection of the skin, characterized by the growth of yellowish patches or tubercles. Also *attrib.* Hence **Xanthomatous** (-ōu·mătəs) *a.*, pertaining to or of the nature of xanthoma.

1876 DUHRING *Dis. Skin* 410 Xanthoma is a connective-tissue new growth, characterized by the formation of yellowish, circumscribed, irregularly shaped,..non-indurated patches or tubercles. 1899 *Allbutt's Syst. Med.* VIII. 484 The chamois-leather-like patches may simulate xanthoma. *Ibid.* 896 The so-called 'xanthoma cell' is..a fragmented muscle fibre in a state of granulo-fatty degeneration. 1914 *Lancet* 13 June 1697/1 Xanthomatous nodules in the liver.

‖**Xanthomelanoi** (zænþome·lănoi), *sb. pl. Anthropology.* [mod.L. (Huxley), transliteration (instead of the regular L. form **xanthomelanī*) of an assumed Gr. *ξανθομέλανοι, f. ξανθός yellow + μέλας, μελαν- black: cf. MELANOI and XANTHOCHROI. (On the analogy of the other terms, the word should have been *Melanoxanthoi*, the first element referring to the hair, the second to the skin.)] In Huxley's classification of the varieties of mankind: A subdivision of the *Leiotrichi* or smooth-haired class, having black hair and yellow, brown, or olive complexion. Hence **Xanthome·lanous** (-əs) *a.*, belonging to or having the characters of the *Xanthomelanoi.*

1865 HUXLEY *Crit. & Addr.* (1873) 153 The 'xanthomelanous,' with black hair and yellow, brown, or olive skins. 1866 — *Laing's Preh. Rem. Caithn.* 132 The *Leiotrichi* may be best subdivided, according to their complexion, into *Xanthochroi, Melanochroi, Xanthomelanoi*, and *Melanoi.*

Xanthone (zæ·nþoun). *Chem.* [f. Gr. ξανθός yellow + -ONE.] A compound which forms the basis of various natural colouring matters.

1894 MUIR & MORLEY *Watts' Dict. Chem.* IV. 867 *Xanthone* is Diphenylene ketone oxide.

Xanthophyll (zæ·nþǫfil). *Chem.* [ad. F. *xanthophylle* (Berzelius), f. Gr. ξανθός yellow + φύλλον leaf.] The yellow colouring-matter of leaves in autumn, a constituent or derivative of chlorophyll; also called *phylloxanthin.*

1838 R. D. THOMSON in *Brit. Ann.* 334. 1868 WATTS *Dict. Chem.* V. 1052 *Xanthophyll*...Nothing certain is known respecting its composition, or of the manner in which it is formed from chlorophyll. 1891 *Science-Gossip* XXVII. 46/2 When the life of the leaf is destroyed by frost or drought, the chlorophyll is rapidly changed to xanthophyll.

Xanthophyllite (zænþofi·ləit). *Min.* [ad. G. *xanthophyllit* (G. Rose, 1840), f. Gr. ξανθός yellow + φύλλον leaf + -ITE¹ 2 b.] A micaceous mineral, a species of seybertite, occurring in yellowish crusts or implanted globules in talcose schist.

1844 DANA *Min.* (1862) 149.

‖**Xanthorrhœa** (zænþorī·ă). [mod.L., f. Gr. ξανθός yellow + ῥοία flowing, flow.]

1. *Bot.* A genus of Australian liliaceous plants, some species of which (called Grass-trees or Grass Gum-trees) yield a yellow resin.

1868 WATTS *Dict. Chem.* V. 1054 Xanthorrhœa resin.

2. *Path.* A morbid affection resembling leucorrhœa (see quot.).

1891 *Lancet* 7 Nov. 1037/1 There is..more or less leucorrhœa, or xanthorrhœa, as it should rather be called, because the discharge is yellow, not white.

‖**Xanthosis** (zænþōu·sis). *Path.* [mod.L., f. Gr. ξανθός yellow: see -OSIS.] (See quots.)

1857 DUNGLISON *Med. Lex.*, *Xanthosis*, a term applied to the yellow discolouration often observed in cancerous tumours. 1890 BILLINGS *Nat. Med. Dict.*, *Xanthosis*, formation of a yellow skin or pigment.

Xanthous (zæ·nþəs), *a. Ethnology.* [f. Gr. ξανθός yellow + -OUS.] Applied to those races, or that type, of mankind characterized by yellow or yellowish hair and light complexion; fair, blond. Also said of the hair, complexion, etc. Opp. to MELANIC 1, MELANOUS.

1829 T. PRICE *Ess. Physiogn. & Physiol. Inhab. Brit.* 3 It is true that the Greek and Roman writers do describe the various barbarous tribes of Europe,..representing some to be of the fair, or, as it has been styled, Xanthous complexion; others of the dark, or Melanic. 1834 *Nat. Philos., Phys. Geog.* 64/1 (U.K.S.) Men of the xanthous variety of colour are known to spring up among the negroes in Africa. 1876 W. F. SKENE *Celtic Scot.* I. I. ii. 126 The Caledonii.. were larger in body,..and less xanthous. 1896 *Allbutt's Syst. Med.* I. 35 The xanthous type with chestnut, red, or fair hair.

‖**Xanthoxylon** (zænþǫ·ksilǫn). *Bot.* Also 8 **zanthoxylon, -um.** [mod.L. *Xanthoxylon*, *-um* (by Linnæus spelt *Zanthoxylum*), f. Gr. ξανθός yellow + ξύλον wood.] A large and widely distributed genus of trees and shrubs of the N. O. *Rutaceæ* (type of the suborder *Xanthoxyleæ*, sometimes reckoned as an order *Xanthoxylaceæ*), yielding various products, esp. pungent and aromatic drugs and condiments; it includes the N. American Prickly Ash or Toothache-tree (*X. americanum* and *fraxineum*), the Chinese or Japanese Pepper (*X. piperitum*), the Prickly or W. Indian Yellow-wood (*X. Clava-Herculis*), etc. Hence **Xantho·xyl,** a plant of this genus, or of the order or suborder of which it is the type; **Xanthoxyla·ceous** (-ē¹·ʃəs), **Xanthoxyleous** (-i·lǐəs) *adjs.*, belonging to the *Xanthoxylaceæ* or *Xanthoxyleæ* (see above); **Xantho·xylene** (-īn) *Chem.*, an aromatic volatile oil obtained from the fruit of *Xanthoxylon piperitum*; **Xantho·xylin** (-in) *Chem.*, (*a*) a crystalline resin or camphor obtained from an oil distilled from the seeds of *X. piperitum*; (*b*) a crystallizable bitter principle contained in the bark of *X. Clava-Herculis* and other species; **Xanthoxy·loïn,** a neutral principle obtained from the bark of *X. americanum.*

1846 LINDLEY *Veg. Kingd.* 473 Several *Xanthoxyls have in their habit, and especially in their foliage, a marked resemblance to the Ash. 1876 HARLEY *Mat. Med.* (ed. 6) 679 The Xanthoxyl Family of the Rutal alliance. 1852 TH. ROSS tr. *Humboldt's Trav.* I. vi. 213 *note*, Among *zanthoxylaceous plants, the Cuspare of Angostura, known in America under the name of Orinoco bark. 1857 STENHOUSE in *Pharmaceut. Jrnl.* July 20 The pure hydrocarbon, to which I propose to give the name of *Xanthoxylene, is colourless, [etc.]. *Note*, The pleasant aromatic odour of Japanese pepper is due to Xanthoxylene. 1830 LINDLEY *Nat. Syst. Bot.* 131 Several *Xanthoxyleous plants have.. a marked resemblance to the Ash. 1854 STENHOUSE in *Lond., Edin., & Dubl. Philos. Mag.* Jan. 28 The crystals of *xanthoxyline belong to the oblique system. 1765 J. BARTRAM *Jrnl.* 21 Dec. in Stork *Acc. E. Florida* (1766) 3 Some curious shrubs..we had never seen before,..large *zanthoxylum, and purple-berried bay. 1799 *Med. Jrnl.* II. 32 A Negro woman, who had been affected for many years with several large phagædenic ulcers..was put under my care. I commenced the use of the Zanthoxylon, by bathing the sores with the decoction. 1868 WATTS *Dict. Chem.* V. 1054 *Xanthoxylon.* The bark of *X. caribæum*..or *X. Clava Herculis* ..used in the Antilles as a febrifuge.

‖**Xantippe** (zænti·pĭ). Also 7 **Zentippe, Zantippe.** [Properly *Xanthippe*, Gr. Ξανθίππη.] The name of the wife of Socrates; hence *allusively*, an ill-tempered woman or wife, a shrew, a scold (with pl. *Xantippes*).

1596 SHAKS. *Tam. Shr.* I. ii. 71 As curst and shrow'd As Socrates Zentippe [*1st Fol., Qo.*; *2nd–4th Fol.* Zantippe, *mod. edd.* Xanthippe]. 1691 WOOD *Ath. Oxon.* I. 262 Richard Hooker..married a clownish silly Woman and withal a meer Xantippe. 1749 FIELDING *Tom Jones* VIII. xi, An errant Vixen of a Wife...By this *Xantippe* he had two Sons. 1859 *Habits of Gd. Society* xiii. 339 For the time being the worst of Xantippes must turn into an angel of amiability if she gives a ball.

Xaraf, -affe, -off, obs. ff. SARAF.

1628 in Foster *Eng. Factories India* (1909) III. 296 We lye at the mercy of the xaroffs or exchangers of monie. 1662 J. DAVIES tr. *Mandelslo's Trav.* 93 In the presence of the Xaraf, or Money-changers.

Xebec (zī·bek; *also* zĭbe·k). Also 8–9 **-eck, -eque, -ecque;** β. 8–9 **zebec(k,** 9 **zebecque.** See also CHEBEC. [Altered form of CHEBEC (F. *chebec*) after Sp. *xabeque*, now *jabeque.*] A small three-masted (originally two-masted) vessel, commonly lateen-rigged but with some square sails, used in the Mediterranean, formerly as a ship of war, now as a merchant-ship.

1756 *Gentl. Mag.* Aug. 409/2 Capt. Fortunatus Wright, of Liverpool, in the *King George* privateer off Leghorn, engaged a xebeck which had 280 men on board. 1760 *Ann. Reg., Chron.* 148/2 An Algerine xebeque of 20 guns..was driven on shore near Penzance. 1762 MORE in *Phil. Trans.* LII. 450 There came a Spanish xebeck from the West,..and ..was becalmed. 1769 FALCONER *Dict. Marine* (1780) s.v., The sails of the xebec are in general similar to those of the polacre, but the hull is extremely different...The extremity of the stern..projects further behind the counter and buttock than that of any European ship. 1794 *Rigging & Seamanship* I. 237 *Xebec.* A small vessel with three masts, navigated in the mediterranean. The fore and main-masts are called block-masts, being short...The mizen-mast is fitted with a topmast, &c.,..and..has been lately added, to keep them better to the wind...The fore-mast rakes much forward. 1816 *Ann. Reg., Gen. Hist.* 133/2 A large Tunisian xebeck..putting out two boats, gave a general chase. *a* 1829 I. TAYLOR *Ship* v. (1846) 118 The xebec very much resembles the galley in shape.., in its triangular sails and low masts. It is the corsair of the Algerines,..and mounts from sixteen to twenty-four guns. 1851 KIPPING *Sailmaking* (ed. 2) 158 The Spanish xebec has in general a lateen fore, with a square main-sail and mizen. 1884 MISS C. F. WOOLSON in *Harper's Mag.* Feb. 368/2 The coasting xebecs.

β. 1769 *Ann. Reg., Chron.* 164/1 A large Algerine zebeck, of 30 guns and 300 men. 1839 MARRYAT *Phant. Ship* xix, A three-masted zebecque. 1844 HOOD *The Key* iv, The last Zebeck that came And moor'd within the Mole.

attrib. and *Comb.* 1780 CAPT. KNOWLES in *Naval Chron.* II. 518 Two Spanish Xebec Ships, polacre rigged. 1801 LD. COCHRANE *ibid.* VI. 151 A Spanish xebeck frigate, of 32 guns. 1812 *Examiner* 4 May 280/2 A French xebeck-rigged privateer, of two guns.

Xel, obs. form of SHALL *v.*

1429 in *Calr. Pat. Rolls 8 Hen. VI.* 30 A comon assemble which xel ben ordeyned be the mair.

Xeme (zīm). *Ornith.* [ad. mod.L. *Xema* (Leach, 1819), an arbitrarily formed word.] A bird of the genus *Xema*; a fork-tailed gull.

1836 EYTON *Rarer Brit. Birds* 64 Sabine's Xeme...was first observed by Captain Sabine in Greenland.

Xenacanthine, Xenarthral: see XENO-.

†**Xenagogue** (ze·năgǫg). *Obs.* In 7 **zen-.** [ad. Gr. ξεναγωγός, f. ξένος stranger + -αγωγός leading.] One who conducts strangers; a guide. So †**Xenagogy,** conduction of strangers: used as the title of a guide-book.

1570–6 LAMBARDE *Peramb. Kent* 386 The places, whereof I ment to make note in this my Xenagogie and perambulation of Kent. 1583 in Thynne *Animadv.* (1875) p. lxii, The Xenogogie of Bedfordshire. 1674 JOSSELYN *Voy. New Eng.* 136 They are generally excellent Zenagogues or guides through their Countrie.

Xenelasy (zenī·lăsi). *Gr. Hist.* [ad. Gr. ξενηλασία, f. ξενηλατεῖν, f. ξένος foreigner + ἐλα- (ἐλαύνειν) to drive away.] A measure at Sparta for expulsion of foreigners.

1846 GROTE *Greece* II. vi. II. 515 Nor were strangers permitted to stay at Sparta; they came thither it seems, by a sort of sufferance, but the uncourteous process called xenêlasy was always available to remove them.

‖**Xenia** (zī·niă). *Bot.* [mod.L., ad. Gr. ξενία state or relation of a guest, f. ξένος guest: see -IA¹.] A supposed direct action or influence of foreign pollen upon the seed or fruit which is pollinated.

1899 *Nat. Sci.* May 393 *Xenia*..,the direct action of the male element on the mother-plant, is an extremely hypothetical theory. 1901 *Nature* 12 Dec. 126/2 Xenia is the name given to the results of the crossing of the plant by a foreign pollen, exhibited in some peculiarity which appears in the seed itself.

Xenia, pl. of XENIUM.

Xenial (zī·niăl), *a. Gr. Antiq.* [f. Gr. ξενία XENIA + -AL.] Of the nature of, or pertaining to, the relation between host and guest: applied to a friendly relation between two persons of different countries, or between a person and a foreign country. So **Xe·nian** *a.* (in quot. 1834 rendering Gr. ξένιος, a title of Zeus as protector of the rights of hospitality).

1834 *Fraser's Mag.* X. 533 The holy customs of the Xenian Jove. 1858 GLADSTONE *Homer* I. 220 The Taphians,..from the xenial relation of their Lord Mentes to Ulysses, must in all likelihood have lived in the neighbourhood of Ithaca. 1869 — *Juv. Mundi* iii. 87 Demetor Tasides..is represented..as being in xenial relations with Egypt.

‖**Xenium** (zī·niŏm); usually in pl. **xenia.** [L., ad. Gr. ξένιον, prop. neut. of ξένιος adj. pertaining to a guest, f. ξένος guest, stranger.] **a.** In *Gr.* and *Rom. Antiq.*, a present (esp. of table delicacies) given to a guest or stranger; *transf.*, in mediæval usage, an offering made (sometimes compulsorily) by subjects to their prince on the occasion of his passing through their estates; also extended to other kinds of offerings (see quots.).

1706 PHILLIPS (ed. Kersey), *Xenia*, Presents bestowed by the Greeks to their Friends, Guests, or Strangers...In our old Records, it is taken for such Presents or Gifts as us'd to be made to Princes, or to the Governours of Provinces. 1772 [S. DENNE] *Hist. Rochester* 106 That there be reserved to me..out of the estates which I have assigned for the maintenance of the monks, such a xenium [orig. *exenium*] as is here specified. 1865 STUBBS *Chron. & Mem. Rich. I* (Rolls) II. Introd. p. xxx, The xenia, or Easter and Christmas offerings from [the monks'] manors, which were settled on the cellarer for the use of the sick and strangers.

b. (See quots.)

1791 NEWTON tr. *Vitruvius' Archit.* VI. x. 145 The pictures representing the sending of gifts to strangers are by the painters called *xenia.* 1854 FAIRHOLT *Dict. Terms Art, Xenia.* ..Pictures of still-life, fruit, fish, &c., many of which have been found as decorations on the walls of houses in Pompeii.

Xenization (zenəizē¹·ʃən). *rare*⁻¹. [f. Gr. ξενίζειν, trans. to entertain strangers, intr. to be a stranger, f. ξένος stranger: see -IZE and -ATION.] The fact of sojourning as a stranger.

1818 G. S. FABER *Horæ Mosaicæ* I. 231 The xenization of Abraham's seed in a foreign land.

Xeno- (zeno), before a vowel **xen-,** repr. Gr. ξενο-, ξεν-, combining form of ξένος a guest, stranger, foreigner, adj. foreign, strange; used in various scientific and other terms; for those not found here, see their alphabetical places. **Xenacanthine** (-ăkæ·nþəin) *Zool.* [ad. mod.L. *Xenacanthini* pl., f. Gr. ἄκανθα spine], *a.* belonging to the extinct order *Xenacanthini* of selachian fishes, with long slender spines; *sb.* a fish of this order. **Xena·rthral** *a. Zool.* [Gr. ἄρθρον joint], having peculiar accessory articulations in the vertebræ, as the American edentates. **Xenobiosis** (-bəiˌōu·sis) *Zool.* [Gr. βίωσις manner of life], a form of symbiosis among ants in which two colonies of different species live together on friendly terms without rearing their broods in common. **Xe·noderm** *Zool.* [mod.L. *Xenoderma*, f. Gr. δέρμα skin], a snake of the genus *Xenoderma* or sub-family *Xenodermatinæ* (mod. Dicts.). **Xeno·gamy** *Bot.* [Gr. γάμος marriage], fertilization by pollen from another plant of the same species; cross-fertilization. **Xenogenesis** (-dʒe·nĭsis) *Biol.* [GENESIS], (supposed) production of offspring permanently unlike the parent (cf. HETEROGENESIS 3); so **Xenogene·tic, Xenoge·nic** *adjs.*, pertaining to or of the nature of xenogenesis; **Xenogeny** (zenǫ·dʒĭni), xenogenesis. **Xeno·genous** *a. Path.* (see quot.). **Xenolite** *Min.* [-LITE], a silicate of aluminium, allied to fibrolite. **Xenomania** (-mē¹·niă), a mania or insane fancy for foreigners, or for something foreign; hence **Xenoma·niac,** a person affected with 'xenomania'. **Xenomorphic** (-mǭ·ɹfik) *a. Geol.* [Gr. μορφή form], applied to mineral constituents of a rock having a form different from the normal in consequence of the pressure of other constituents. **Xenopa·rasite, Xenopa·rasitism** *Biol.* (see quot.). **Xenophilism** (-ǫ·filiz'm) *nonce-wd.* [Gr. φίλος loving, friendly], love of foreigners or of something foreign. **Xenophoby** (zenǫ·fŏbi) *nonce-wd.* [Gr. φόβος fear], fear of foreign persons or things; so **Xenophobic** (zenofǫ·bik) *a.* characterized by this. **Xenophoran** (-ǫ·fŏrăn) *a. Zool.* [f. mod.L. *Xenophora*, f. Gr. -φορος carrying], belonging or allied to the genus *Xenophora* (carrier-shells) of gastropod molluscs, distinguished by the habit of cementing stones and other foreign bodies to their shells. **Xenopterygian** (-ptĕri·dʒiăn), *Zool.* [Gr. πτέρυξ wing, fin], *a.* belonging to the suborder *Xenopterygii* of fishes, with spineless fins, scaleless skin, and a complex sucking-disk between the ventral fins; *sb.* a fish of this suborder. **Xenurine** (ze·niurəin) *Zool.* [f. mod.L. *Xenurus*, f. Gr. οὐρά tail], *a.* belonging to the genus *Xenurus* of armadillos, having the tail nearly naked; *sb.* an armadillo of this genus, a kabassou.

1885 *Stand. Nat. Hist.* (1888) V. 66 The geographical distribution of the Edentates...To America belong the *xenarthral or many-jointed forms. 1901 W. M. WHEELER in *Amer. Naturalist* July 535 *Xenobiosis...The best-known guest ant is the European *Formicoxenus nitidulus.* 1877 DARWIN *Lett.* (1903) II. 413 Some such terms as autogamy, *xenogamy, etc. 1870 HUXLEY *Pres. Addr. Brit. Assoc., Rep.* p. lxxvii, The term Heterogenesis..has..been used in a different sense, and M. Milne-Edwards has therefore substituted for it **Xenogenesis. Ibid.* p. lxxxv, The analogy of pathological modification..is in favour of the *xenogenetic origin of microzymes. 1901 DORLAND *Med. Dict.* (ed. 2), **Xenogenous*, caused by a foreign body, or originating outside the organism. 1913 *Ibid.* (ed. 7) *adds* 2. Formed or developed in the host: a term applied to toxins formed by the action of stimuli on the cells of the host. 1844 DANA *Min.* (1868) 374 *Xenolite..resembles fibrolite..excepting in the high specific gravity. 1879 K. HILLEBRAND in *19th Cent.* Oct. 626 Germany received the first caresses of this strange *xenomania from the hands of youthful Carlyle and old Coleridge. 1887 SAINTSBURY *Hist. Elizab. Lit.* iv. 136 No writer of the period has such a command of pure English, unadulterated by xenomania and unweakened by purism, as Daniel. 1879 *Daily News* 30 Sept. 5/1 Are we all *Xenomaniacs? 1891 *Illustr. Lond. News* 7 Feb. 168/2 Sir Arthur Sullivan was never the least bit of a *xenomaniac.* 1888 HATCH in Teall *Brit. Petrography* Gloss. 423 *Allotriomorphic*, a term applied by Rosenbusch..in contradistinction to idiomorphic. It is synonymous with *xenomorphic. 1905 E. S. SALMON in *Ann. Bot.* Jan. 127 To describe cases where a form of a Fungus which is specialized to certain host-plants..proves able to infect injured parts of a strange host, I propose the terms '*xenoparasite and *xenoparasitism.' 1912 W. SICKERT in *English Review* Apr. 147 Lest the writer be accused of *Xenophilism. 1912 *Nation* 11 May 214/1 The popular attitude with regard to external politics is one of crude and *xenophobic Imperialism. 1909 *Athenæum* 13 Mar. 325/3 Those whose sense of justice..is not impaired by prejudice or '*xenophoby'. 1898 *Q. Jrnl. Microsc. Sci.* June 308 No Stromboid, Naticoid, or *Xenophoran molluscs have been found hitherto in any fresh water that is known. 1885 *Stand. Nat. Hist.* (1888) V. 50 The Kabassous, or *Xenurines, have the third as well as the fourth and fifth metacarpals abbreviated and broad.

†**Xenodo·chial,** *a. Obs. rare*⁻¹. [f. Gr. ξενοδοχία (XENODOCHY²) + -AL.] Given to receiving strangers; hospitable.

1716 M. DAVIES *Athen. Brit.* II. 402 The Insuperable Aversion, that those three Xenodochial Prelates seem'd always to exert against the French Nation. *Ibid.* 404.

‖**Xenodochium** (zenǫdǫ·kiŏm). Also **-ion, -eum.** Pl. **-a.** [Late L. *xenodochīum, -ēum*, ad. late Gr. ξενοδοχεῖον, f. ξένος stranger + δέχεσθαι to receive.] A house of reception for strangers and pilgrims; a hostel, guest-house, esp. in a monastery.

1612 CORYAT in Purchas *Pilgrims* (1625) II. 1829 In Constantinople, Pera, and Galata, there are..Karabassaries or *Xenodochia* foure hundred and eighteen. 1736 DRAKE *Eboracum* I. vii. 246 [A] spital..was an house of entertainment for poor travellers or pilgrims..this [*sc.* spital of St. Catherine] was a *Xenodochium* of that kind. 1832 GELL *Pompeiana* II. xiii. 18 Many have supposed that the xenodochium, or hospitium, for the reception of strangers was placed in this division of the mansion. 1844 LINGARD *Anglo-Saxon Ch.* (1858) I. vi. 246 Within the precincts of the monastery stood an edifice, distinguished by the Greek name of *Xenodochium*, in which a certain number of paupers received their daily support, and which was gratuitously opened to every traveller who solicited relief. 1865 LECKY *Ration.* II. vi. 263 Long before the era of persecution had closed, the hospital and the Xenodochion, or refuge for strangers, was known among the Christians.

†**Xenodochy**¹. *Obs. rare*⁻¹. [Anglicized form of prec.] = prec.

c 1540 tr. *Pol. Verg. Eng. Hist.* (Camden No. 29) 121 Ther was at York an auncyent and welthy xenodochye that ys to say, an hospytall..wher powre and nedye people wer enterteynyd.

†**Xenodochy**². *Obs. rare*⁻¹. In 7 **xenodechie, zenodochie.** [ad. Gr. ξενοδοχία: cf. XENODOCHIUM.] Entertainment of strangers; hospitality.

1623 COCKERAM, *Xenodechie*, hospitality. 1674 JOSSELYN *Voy. New Eng.* 181 Sincere and religious people..descryed by their charity and humility..by their Zenodochie or hospitality.

Xenon (ze·nǫn). *Chem.* [ad. Gr. ξένον, neut. of ξένος strange.] A heavy inert gaseous element present in minute quantity in the atmosphere, discovered by Sir William Ramsay in 1898. Symbol Xe or X.

1898 RAMSAY & TRAVERS in *Rep. Brit. Assoc. Bristol* 830 The last fractions of liquefied argon show the presence of three new gases. These are krypton..metargon..and a still heavier gas,..which we propose to name 'xenon'.

Xenophontean, -ian (zenǫfǫ·ntiăn), *a.* [f. Gr. Ξενοφῶν, -ῶντος Xenophon, name of an ancient Greek historian and biographer (*c* 444–354 B.C.) + -EAN, -IAN.] Pertaining to, characteristic of, described by, or resembling (that of) Xenophon.

1593 G. HARVEY *Pierce's Super.* Wks. (Grosart) II. 99 M. Thomas Blundeuil,..whose painefull, and skillfull bookes of Horsemanship, deserue also to be registred in the Catalogue of Xenophontian woorkes. 1834 GEN. P. THOMPSON *Exerc.* (1842) III. 127 In all European services there is a class of officers who might not unaptly be termed Xenophontean; men..zealous to know the most that is possible, for the sake of acting under its guidance. 1875 JOWETT *Plato* (ed. 2) I. 338 The Apology appears to combine the common characteristics both of the Xenophontean and Platonic Socrates.

So **Xenopho·ntic** *a.*

1822 T. MITCHELL *Aristoph.* II. 27 What..authority the poet had for engaging his Socrates in these ridiculous speculations, it is now impossible to ascertain; but..the Platonic, and even the Xenophontic, Socrates is sometimes almost as absurd. 1864 SALA in *Daily Tel.* 15 Aug., Colonel Fremantle, in one of the most Xenophontic little books that has seen the light within these latter days, tells us [etc.]. 1882 A. S. WALPOLE *Xenophon's Anab.* I. (1900) p. x, A Greek of Xenophontic age. 1904 *Times* 27 Aug. 10/1 A mere Xenophontic record of the length of stages in a journey.

Xenotime (ze·nǫtəim). *Min.* [Named (in Fr.) by Beudant, 1832, as if f. Gr. ξένος strange + τιμή honour, but app. in error for **kenotime*, f. Gr. κενός empty, vain: see quot. below.] A native phosphate of yttrium.

1844 DANA *Min.* (1868) 528 Xenotime...Lustre resinous Color yellowish-brown, reddish-brown, hair-brown, flesh-red, grayish-white [etc.]..Beudant named the species *xenotime* (apparently from ξενός, stranger to, and τιμή, honor), but in the next line gives the derivation 'κενός, vain, et τιμή, honneur', as if the word were *kenotime*, and adds.. that this name is intended to recall the fact that the mineral was erroneously supposed by Berzelius..to contain a new metal. 1907 *Athenæum* 20 Apr. 479/1 M. Jean Becquerel ..has been engaged in magneto-optical researches...Most of his experiments have been made with crystals of xenotime (a magnetic phosphate of yttrium).

Xeque, var. (Pg. spelling) of SHEIKH.

Xerafeen, -in, var. SERAPHIN *Obs.*

‖**Xeranthemum** (ziəræ·nþĭmŏm). *Bot.* [mod.L. (Tournefort, 1700), f. Gr. ξηρός dry + ἄνθεμον blossom.] A plant of a genus of composites of the Mediterranean region, having flower-heads with dry chaffy bracts of a purplish or whitish colour; the genus itself; one kind of the plants commonly called *everlasting* or *immortelle.*

1741 *Compl. Fam.-Piece* II. iii. 385 Seeds of Jacea's,.. Xeranthemums,..and sweet Sultan. 1751 HILL *Hist. Plants* 574 The longleaved xeranthemum with paleaceous receptacles. It is a native of Germany and France; the flowers retain their beauty many years. 1786 ABERCROMBIE *Gard. Assist.* 116 Virginia and English tobacco, Indian corn, xeranthemum, ten-week's stocks.

Xerapheen, -phin, var. SERAPHIN *Obs.*

‖**Xerasia** (ziərē¹·siă). *Path.* [mod.L., a. Gr. ξηρασία dryness, also in sense below (Galen).] A disease of the hair characterized by excessive dryness.

1706 PHILLIPS (ed. Kersey), *Xerasia*, a fault in the Hairs when they appear like Down, as it were sprinkled with Dust. 1896 tr. *Balzac's César Birotteau* 152 To prevent xerasia and baldness.

Xeres (ze·rĕs, zīə·rĕz). Also 7 **Zeres.** Name of a town in Andalusia, famous for its wine; in full, *Xeres sack, wine* = SHERRIS (*sack*), SHERRY *sb.*¹ 1.

a 1661 FULLER *Worthies, Bristol* (1662) III. 34 *Bristol Milk*...This Metaphorical Milk, whereby Xeres or Sherry-Sack is intended. 1662 MERRET in Charleton *Myst. Vintners* (1675) 233 Most of the Canary is made with Malago and Zerez Sack. 1841 *Fraser's Mag.* XXIV. 26 The xeres and port Are of the right sort. 1869 BLACKMORE *Lorna D.* I, Do you like the wine of Oporto, or the wine of Xeres? 1872 RUSKIN *Fors Clav.* II. xvi. 13 So many skins of Xeres wine.

Xeriff (ze·rif, zīə·rif), var. of *sheriff*: see SHERIFI.

1690 DRYDEN *Don Sebastian* I. i, I ask Six Hundred Xeriffs for him [*sc.* a horse]. 1858 SIMMONDS *Dict. Trade*, *Xeriff*, a former gold coin, current in Egypt and Turkey, for about 9s. 6d. Another name for the ducat in Morocco.

Xeriff, obs. form of SHEREEF.

Xero- (zīə·ro), before a vowel **xer-,** repr. Gr. ξηρο-, ξηρ-, combining form of ξηρός dry, occurring in several scientific and technical terms. ‖**Xerode·rma, -de·rmia,** *Path.* [mod.L., f. Gr. δέρμα skin], one of several diseases characterized by excessive dryness of the skin; hence **Xerodermatic, -de·rmatous, -de·rmic** *adjs.*, pertaining to or characteristic of xeroderma. **Xe·roform** *Med.* [after *chloroform*]: see quot. **Xerophilous** (-ǫ·filəs) *a. Bot.* [Gr. -φιλος loving], adapted to a dry climate or habitat, or to conditions of scanty available moisture; so **Xerophil(e** (zīə·rofil), *sb.* a xerophilous plant; **Xero·phily,** the condition or character of being xerophilous. **Xe·rophyte** (-fəit), *Bot.* [Gr. φυτόν plant], a xerophilous plant (see above); so **Xerophytic** (-fi·tik) *a.*, pertaining to or having the character of a xerophyte, xerophilous; **Xero·phytism,** xerophytic character, xerophily. ‖**Xerostomia** (-stōu·miă), *Path.* [mod.L., f. Gr. στόμα mouth], dryness of the mouth from insufficient secretion of saliva. **Xerothe·rmic** *a.* [Gr. θερμός hot], dry and hot.

1848 DUNGLISON *Med. Lex.* (ed. 7), **Xeroderma*, diminution of secretion of the sebaceous glands. 1864 W. T. FOX *Skin Dis.* viii. 222 True xeroderma is in reality the early stage of ichthyosis, a true epithelial disease. 1899 *Allbutt's Syst. Med.* VIII. 786 [*Lichen pilaris*] is only a part of a general xeroderma. 1913 DORLAND *Med. Dict.* (ed. 7), *Xerodermatic. 1899 *Allbutt's Syst. Med.* VIII. 851 The skin is dry and thin but not *xerodermatous. 1891 *Cent. Dict.*, **Xerodermia*, same as Xeroderma. 1899 [see XEROSIS]. 1890 *Retrospect Med.* CII. 92 Minute white, gray, or red scaly *xerodermic prominences, having a hair in the centre. 1901 DORLAND *Med. Dict.* (ed. 2), **Xeroform*, a yellow neutral powder derived from tribromphenol and bismuth, ($C_6H_2Br_3O_2BiOH + Bi_2O_3$): useful in the treatment of wounds, abscesses, etc., and as an intestinal antiseptic. 1884 *Trans. Victoria Inst.* 38 *Xerophiles—plants such as pertain to very dry climates. 1863 J. G. BAKER *N. Yorksh.* xxii. 316 The *Xerophilous and Maritime species [of mosses] are very few in number. 1893 *Athenæum* 2 Dec. 774/3 A paper..by the Rev. G. Henslow 'On the Origin of Plant Structures by Self-adaptation to the Environment, exemplified by Desert and Xerophilous Plants.' 1904 *Science* 3 June 866/2 The causes of *xerophily in bog plants. 1897 WILLIS *Flower. Pl. & Ferns* I. 178 In countries with long dry seasons [etc.] .., the plants..agree in having a lower rate of transpiration than plants living where there is plenty of available water. Plants of this kind are termed **xerophytes.* 1906 G. HENSLOW in *19th Cent.* Nov. 801 *E[uphorbia] Paralias* is a xerophyte with coriaceous leaves, because it has adapted itself to a maritime situation in England. 1897 WILLIS *Flower. Pl. & Ferns* I. 185 No plants..can be regular epiphytes unless they possess well-marked *xerophytic characters, including as a rule the capacity for water-storage. 1900 *Nature* 13 Dec. 150/1 Every one is aware how extremely intolerant of moisture are the cacti and some other xerophytic plants. *Ibid.* 15 Nov. 53/2 The stomatal grooves on the lower surface of the leaf [of *Lepidodendron*] suggest a xerophytic adaptation. Indications of *xerophytism are afforded by other anatomical characters in certain Palæozoic types. 1890 BILLINGS *Nat. Med. Dict.*, **Xerostomia*, dryness of the mouth. 1897 *Allbutt's Syst. Med.* III. 310 The salivary and buccal secretions may be totally arrested as in cases of xerostomia. 1904 *Bot. Gaz.* Apr. 312 (Cent. D. Suppl.) Jerosch holds that an interglacial *xerothermic or steppe period has been proved by the facts of plant geography, paleontology, and geology.

‖**Xeroma** (ziərōu·mă). *Path.* [mod.L., f. Gr. ξηρός dry, after *sarcoma*, etc.] Abnormal dryness of some part from lack of fluid secretion; *spec.* = XEROPHTHALMIA. Hence **Xero·matous** *a.*, of the nature of or affected with xeroma.

1848 DUNGLISON *Med. Lex.* (ed. 7), *Xeroma*, xerophthalmia...*Xeroma, lachrymal*, suppression of the lachrymal secretion. 1860 MAYNE *Expos. Lex.*, Xeromatous. 1875 H. WALTON *Dis. Eye* (ed. 3) 876 The cornea passes into complete pannus or xeroma.

Xerophagy (ziərǫ·fădʒi). Also 7 **-fag-.** [ad. Gr. ξηροφαγία: see XERO- and -PHAGY.] The eating of dry food, esp. as a form of fasting practised in the early church.

1656 BLOUNT *Glossogr.*, *Xerophagy*..the eating dry meats. 1671 F. S. tr. *Daillé's Serm. Colossians* ii. 2 The stations, the xerofagies, and other disciplines of the Montanists. 1725 tr. *Dupin's Eccl. Hist. 17th C.* I. v. 157 In the Week which precedes the Feast of Easter, the Fast was more rigorous, and in some Places they eat nothing but dry'd things; which they call'd Xerophagy. 1884 *Catholic Dict.* (1897) 558/2 (*Lent*) Some kept the fast of extraordinary strictness known as xerophagy for one day. 1889 FARRAR *Lives Fathers* I. v. 190 *note*, As for xerophagies, says Tertullian, they charge them with being a novel title for a pretended duty.

‖**Xerophthalmia** (ziərǫfþæ·lmiă). *Path.* Also formerly anglicized as **xerophthalmy, -ie.** [L., ad. Gr. ξηροφθαλμία, f. ξηρός dry + ὀφθαλμία OPHTHALMIA.] An ophthalmia without discharge; inflammation of the conjunctiva of the eye with abnormal dryness and corrugation.

1656 BLOUNT *Glossogr.*, *Xerophthalmy*..soarness or bleeredness of the Eyes, when they neither swell, nor run. 1658 PHILLIPS, Xerophthalmie. [1684 tr. *Blancard's Phys. Dict.* (1693), *Xerophthalmia*, a dry Bleardness or Blood-shot of the Eyes.] 1875 H. WALTON *Dis. Eye* (ed. 3) 885 (*heading*) Cuticular conjunctivitis or xerophthalmia.

‖**Xerosis** (ziərōu·sis). *Path.* [mod.L., a. Gr. ξήρωσις, f. ξηρός dry: see -OSIS.] = XEROMA; spec. = *xeroderma* (see XERO-). Also *attrib.*

1890 BILLINGS *Nat. Med. Dict.*, *Xerosis*, a drying, dryness. 1899 *Allbutt's Syst. Med.* VIII. 661 To the milder forms [of ichthyosis] the names *xerodermia* and *xerosis* are frequently..applied. 1900 *Brit. Med. Jrnl.* 17 Mar. 622/2 Xerosis bacilli were present.

So **Xerotic** (ziərǫ·tik) *a.* [see -OTIC], affected with xerosis: **Xerotine** (zīə·rŏtəin) *a.*, in *xerotine siccative*, trade-name of a substance used for drying ships' bottoms.

1882 *Standard* 14 Jan. 5/8 We have had a terrible explosion of xerotine siccative on board here. 1890 BILLINGS *Nat. Med. Dict.*, *Xerotic*, dry. 1893 *Westm. Gaz.* 5 Oct. 3/1 The sad loss of H.M.S. *Dotterel*..., presumably from the effects of an explosion..of Xerotine Siccative, supplied as patent driers. 1901 DORLAND *Med. Dict.* (ed. 2), *Xerotic*, characterized by xerosis, or dryness.

†**Xesturgy.** *Obs. rare*⁻¹. [ad. Gr. ξεστουργία, f. ξεστός, vbl. adj. f. ξεῖν to polish: see -URGY.] The process of polishing.

1592 R. D. *Hypnerotomachia* 48 Diuers coulered stones.. so glistering and seuerly set of a diligent Xesturgie [orig. *xesturgia*].

Xil-: see XYL-.

†**Xilinous,** *a. Obs. rare*⁻⁰. [f. L. *xilinus*, *xylinus* (Pliny), a. Gr. ξύλινος, f. ξύλον cotton-tree: see -OUS.] Of cotton.

1656 BLOUNT *Glossogr.*, Xilinous.

Xinto, etc., obs. ff. SHINTO, etc.

1776 JUSTAMOND tr. *Raynal's Hist. Indies* I. 108 The sect of Xinto...The Xinto sect...The deity of the Xintoists [orig. *Sintos, Sintoistes*].

†**Xiph.** *Obs. rare.* In 6 **zyphe.** [ad. L. *xiphias*: see next.] The swordfish, *Xiphias gladius.*

1572 BOSSEWELL *Armorie* II. 66 The fielde is of the Jacinthe, a pyle in pointe d'Ermyne, betwene two Zyphes hariante, Lunæ. This is a fishe whiche is named a sworde fishe.

Xiphias (zi·fiæs). Also 9 *erron.* **xy-.** [L., a. Gr. ξιφίας, f. ξίφος sword.]

1. A swordfish, esp. *X. gladius*; in mod. *Zool.*, the genus of fishes of which this is the common species, characterized by having the upper jaw prolonged into a sword-like weapon.

1667 *Phil. Trans.* II 492 Having..dissected the head of a *Xiphias* or Sword-fish. 1763 C. SMART *Song to David* lxxv, Strong through the turbulent profound Shoots xiphias to his aim. 1860 WRAXALL *Life in Sea* v. 108 The heel of an East Indiaman was once bored by a twenty-foot Xyphias so violently, that the sword went in up to the root, and the fish was killed by the force of the blow.

2. *Astron.* A southern constellation, also called Dorado or the Sword-fish.

1728 CHAMBERS *Cycl.* s.v. *Constellation.* 1771 [see SWORD-FISH 2].

Hence **Xiphiad** (zi·fiæd), a fish of the family *Xiphiidæ.*

1859–62 SIR J. RICHARDSON, etc. *Mus. Nat. Hist.* (1868) II. 137 Xiphiads or Sword-fishes.

Xiphioid (zi·fiˌoid), *a.* and *sb. Zool.* [f. prec. + -OID.] **a.** *adj.* Resembling or allied to the genus *Xiphias*; belonging to or having the characters of the family *Xiphiidæ.* **b.** *sb.* A xiphioid fish.

1851 MANTELL *Petrifactions* v. § 1. 416 Cycloid Order... Xiphioids. 1891 *Cent. Dict.*, Xiphioid, *a.* and *n.*

‖**Xiphiplastron** (zifiplæ·strǫn). *Anat.* and *Zool.* Pl. **-a.** Also (more correctly) **xipho-.** [mod. L., properly *xiphoplastron*, f. Gr. ξίφος sword + PLASTRON.] Each of the fourth or hindmost pair of lateral plates in the plastron of a turtle. Hence **Xiphipla·stral** *a.*, pertaining to or constituting a xiphiplastron; *sb.* a xiphiplastral plate, a xiphiplastron.

1871 HUXLEY *Anat. Vert.* v. 202 In the Turtle the plastron consists of nine pieces..the fourth [lateral], xiphiplastron. 1889 NICHOLSON & LYDEKKER *Palæont.* liii. II. 1084 [The pubis and the ischium] may be anchylosed to the xiphiplastral. 1889 LYDEKKER in *Q. Jrnl. Geol. Soc.* 1 Aug. 511 The imperfect left xiphiplastral [of a Chelonian].

Xiphisternal (zifistǭ·ɹnăl), *a.* and *sb. Anat.* and *Zool.* Also (more correctly) **xipho-.** [f. *xiphi-* for *xipho-*, Gr. ξίφος sword + STERNUM + -AL.] **a.** *adj.* Belonging to or constituting the xiphisternum (see below). **b.** *sb.* A xiphisternal part or appendage. So ‖**Xiphiste·rnum** (**xipho-**), the posterior division of the sternum, in some animals osseous and in others cartilaginous, in man constituting the xiphoid or ensiform cartilage; also sometimes applied to the XIPHIPLASTRON of a turtle.

1835–6 *Todd's Cycl. Anat.* I. 284/1 The posterior cartilaginous appendages [of the sternum in birds] he [*sc.* Geoffrey St. Hilaire] terms xiphi-sternals. 1839–47 *Ibid.* III. 838/1 The posterior [of the two pairs of elements of the 'sternum', i.e. plastron, of *Chelonia*] are fitly denominated the xiphosternal pieces. 1870 ROLLESTON *Anim. Life* 15 The posterior or xiphisternal end of the sternum. 1872 H. A. NICHOLSON *Palæont.* 399 The xiphisternum is the 'xiphoid cartilage' of human anatomy. 1888 ROLLESTON & JACKSON *Anim. Life* 362 The sternum [in *Mammalia*]..is divisible into three regions—a praesternum or manubrium sterni..; a mesosternum..; and a xiphisternum, sometimes cartilaginous, sometimes ossified. *Ibid.* 384 [The] bilateral origin [of the sternum in some *Lacertilia*] is evidenced..by the prolongation backwards..of two xiphisternal horns.

Xiphocostal (zifokǫ·stăl), *a. Anat.* [f. Gr. ξίφος sword + COSTAL.] Pertaining to or connected with the xiphoid cartilage and the ribs.

1899 in *Syd. Soc. Lex.*

Xiphodyme (zi·fodəim). [ad. mod.L. *xiphodymus*, contr. f. *xiphodidymus*, f. Gr. ξίφος sword + δίδυμος twin.] = XIPHOPAGUS.

1861 *N. Syd. Soc. Year-bk. Med.* 404 A Monstrosity of the Genus Xiphodyme.

Xiphoid (zi·foid), *a.* (*sb.*) *Anat.* Also *erron.* 8–9 **xyphoid,** 9 **ziphoide.** [ad. mod.L. *xiphoidēs*, a. Gr. ξιφοειδής, f. ξίφος sword + εἶδος form: see -OID.] Sword-shaped, ensiform: a descriptive epithet of the cartilaginous or bony process at the lower or posterior end of the sternum in man and other animals (also called XIPHISTERNUM), and of a projecting bone at the back of the head in the cormorants and related birds (also called *occipital style*).

1746 GLASS *Dropsy* in *Phil. Trans.* XLIV. 338 We found the Circumference of her Abdomen to be just six Feet four Inches, and from the Xyphoid Cartilage to the Os Pubis it measur'd four Feet and half an Inch. 1782 A. MONRO *Anat.* 172 The outer surface of the xiphoid bone. 1802 HOME in *Phil. Trans.* XCII. 351 In the Hystrix, there is a xiphoid cartilage. 1847–9 *Todd's Cycl. Anat.* IV. 202/1 [The sternum] is connected..with a xyphoid appendix. 1848 DUNGLISON *Med. Lex.* (ed. 7), *Xiphoid ligament*..is a small, very thin, ligamentous fasciculus, which passes from the cartilage..of the 7th rib to the anterior surface of the xiphoid cartilage. 1873 MIVART *Elem. Anat.* 35 The narrow lower end [of the sternum], which projects freely and remains cartilaginous till late in life, is called the xiphoid process. *Ibid.* 65 In Frogs and Toads we have a middle and xiphoid sternum.

So **Xiphoi·dal, Xiphoi·dan, Xiphoi·dian** *adjs.*

1653 R. SANDERS *Physiogn.* 276 The brest..extended from the throat to the Diaphragma or Cartilagian Xiphoidan muscle or Midriff, which is round, lying overthwart the lower part of the brest, separating the heart and lights from the stomach. 1860 MAYNE *Expos. Lex.* 1345/2 Xiphoidian. 1904 *Amer. Nat.* Jan. 20 (Osteology of Pygopodes) A pair of flaring external xiphoidal processes, which curve outwards, then inwards.

Xiphonite (zi·fŏnəit). *Min.* [Named from *Xiphonia*, an ancient city in Sicily, where found: see -ITE¹.] A variety of amphibole, occurring in minute light yellow crystals in cavities of a volcanic rock.

1899 DANA *Syst. Min.* App. I. 3 Xiphonite is a name given by G. Platania..to a variety occurring in minute crystals with hematite in cavities of a slag-like rock.

‖**Xiphopagus** (zifǫ·păgŏs). Pl. **-gi** (-dʒəi). [mod.L., f. Gr. ξίφος sword (here referring to the xiphoid cartilage) + πάγος something firmly fixed or set (: πηγνύναι to fix).] A twin monster united by a band extending downwards from the xiphoid cartilage, as in the case of the Siamese twins. Hence **Xiphopagic** (zifopæ·dʒik), **Xiphopagous** (zifǫ·păgəs) *adjs.*, constituting a xiphopagus.

1848 DUNGLISON *Med. Lex.* (ed. 7), *Xiphopages* [sic]. 1890 BILLINGS *Nat. Med. Dict.*, Xiphopagus. 1894 BATESON *Variation* 560 *note*, The relative position of xiphopagous twins may result simply from the way in which they happen to be laid by the mother or the midwife. 1901 *Brit. Med. Jrnl.* 6 Apr. 874/2 A new case of xiphopagous twins in two Chinese boys..who are united by a bridge running from the xiphoid cartilage to the umbilicus. 1901 *Lancet* 13 July 108/1 A Case of Xiphopagus or Double Monster. 190. *Buck's Handbk. Med. Sci.* VII. 685 (Cent. D., Suppl.) Xiphopagic.

Xiphosuran (zifosiūə·răn), *a.* and *sb. Zool.* [f. mod.L. *Xiphosūra* pl. (irreg. f. Gr. ξίφος sword + οὐρά tail, instead of the correct form *Xiphūra*) + -AN.] **a.** *adj.* Belonging to the order *Xiphosura* of *Arachnida*, including the king-crab (*Limulus*)

with a long sharp telson, and the extinct genus *Belinurus*. b. An arachnid of this order. So **Xiphosure** (= b); an **Xiphosurous**, **Xiphosurous** adj. (= a).

Xmas, common abbreviation for the word *Christmas*: see X. Also **Xmassing**.

X rays (eks rēs), *sb. pl.* (Also with hyphen.) [tr. Ger. *x-strahlen*, the name given by Röntgen to the rays in question, expressing the fact that their essential nature is unknown; cf. X.] A form of radiation discovered by Prof. W. C. Röntgen of Würzburg in 1895, capable of passing through many substances impervious to light, and affecting a sensitized plate.

Xylate (zɔiˈleⁱt). *Chem.* [f. XYL-IC + -ATE⁴.] A salt of xylic acid.

Xylene (zɔiˈlīn). *Chem.* [f. Gr. ξύλον wood + -ENE.] A mixture of three isomeric hydrocarbons having the formula $C_6H_4(CH_3)_2$.

Xylic (zɔiˈlik), *a. Chem.* [f. XYL-ENE + -IC.] attrib. or comb. f. of ξύλον wood.

Xylidic (zɔiˈlidik), *a. Chem.* [f. XYL-IO + -ID + -IC.]

Xylidine (zɔiˈlidīn). *Chem.* [f. XYL-IO + -ID + -INE⁵.]

Xylite (zɔiˈlɔit). *Chem.* A volatile liquid obtained from wood-spirit.

Xylo-, comb. form of Gr. ξύλον wood; repr. Gr. ξύλο-, ξυλο-, comb. form of ξύλον wood.

Xylobalsamum (zɔiloˈbalsəm). Also XYLO-BALSAM, BALM.

the more important of which see in their alphabetical places. **Xylochlore** (-klōⁱr). **Xylochlor** (von Walterahausen, 1853). **Xylochlorite** (-klōⁱrɔit). **Xylochrome** (-krōⁱm) *Chem.* **Xyloxan** (-zan), *Bot.* **Xyloiamin** (-iˈamin). **Xylobacter.** **Xylobalsamum.**

Xylograph (zɔiˈlograf), *sb.* A wood-engraving. So **Xylographer** (-grafəⁱr), **Xylographist** (-grafist), **Xylography** (-grafi). **Xyloma** (-loˈmə) *Bot.* **Xylophilous** (-ˈfiləs) *a.* **Xyloidin** (zɔiˈloidin), *formerly* xɔiˈlōⁱdin).

Xylose (zɔiˈlōs). *Chem.* [f. Gr. ξύλον wood + -OSE.]

by the Name of *Balm of Gilead*...The *Xylo-balsamum* is reputed good to strengthen the Brain, and Stomach.

Xyloi'm (zɔiˈlōⁱlin). Also **Xyloin** (zɔiˈlōⁱin). [f. xylo- + -IN.] *Chem.*

Xylonite (zɔiˈlonɔit). *Chem.* [Early form *xylonite*, irreg. f. XYLOIDIN + -ITE.]

Xylophagous (zɔiˈlofəgəs), *a. Zool.* [f. Gr. ξύλον wood + -φαγος eating: see -OUS.]

Xylyl (zɔiˈlil). *Chem.* [f. XYL-ENE + -YL.] The hypothetical radical (C_8H_9) of xylene and its derivatives. Hence **Xylylamine**, **Xylylene**.

Xylite (zɔiˈlɔit). *Chem.* **Xylol** (zɔiˈlol) *Chem.* Also-ol. [f. XYL- + -OL.] = XYLENE.

Xylidin (zɔiˈlidin). *Chem.* [f. XYL- + -ID + -IN.]

Xylonite (zɔiˈlonɔit). *Chem.*

Xyloid (zɔiˈloid), *a.* Also **xyloid-**. [f. Gr. ξύλον wood + -OID.] = XYLENE.

Xyster (zɔiˈstəⁱr). *Surg.* [mod.L., a. Gr. ξυστήρ, f. ξύειν to scrape.] An instrument for scraping bones.

Xystus (zɔiˈstəs). *Gr. Antiq.* [L. *xystus*, a. Gr. ξυστός scraped, polished, f. ξύειν to scrape, polish.]

Supplement, p. 3873; Corrigenda, p. 4092; Spurious words, p. 4093; Books quoted, p. 4094

Y.

Y (wai), *n.* Pl. **Y's, Ys** (waiz), the twenty-fifth letter of the modern and twenty-third of the ancient Roman alphabet, representing ultimately Υ, Τ (Greek *upsilon*), a pison) of the Greek alphabet, a differentiated form of the primitive V which has given also U and V. It was adopted first in the Latin alphabet in the form V to express (u) and (w), and was later (after B.C. 100) readopted in the form Y to represent the Τ of borrowed Greek words.

number, such as *gehieran* YHERE, *gesēon* YSEE, continued in use in present and past tenses till 1400 or later; very few lasted till 1500 or beyond. But from the middle of the 16th century onwards archaizing poets created (orig. after pa. ppl. forms) new formations in which the prefix was meaningless. Such are *yclepe* (after *yclept*), *yglaunst*, and *yshrilled* (Spenser), *ycharm'd*, *ysprout* (Robinson's *Mary Magdalene*), *ysteer* (Gosson), *ydrop* (Henry More); there are also pres. pples. like Sackville's *ycausing* and Milton's *star-ypointing*.

4. The use of perfective or completive *ge-* had its most extensive development in the formation of pa. pples., a function common to the Low German and High German groups but not found in Gothic and Scandinavian. The prefix could be employed with any uncompounded verb, but the verbs corresp. to OE. *bringan* to bring, *cuman* to come, *findan* to find, *weorþan* to become, did not normally take it. In OE. and in ME. (where the prefix continued in full use) it is often impossible to determine whether a particular pa. pple. with *ge-* (*i-*, *y-*) belongs to a simple verb or to its compound with *ge-*.

In OE. the prefix was employed in forms derived from Latin, as *geplantod* = *plantatus*. Similarly in ME. it was freely employed with verbs of French origin, as *ybaptised*, *yblamed*, *ycircumcysed*, *iclosed*, *igranted*, *ikupled*, *ymartred*, *yoccupied*, *ipaied*, *ipassed*, *irobbet*, *isturbed*, *isued*, *isustened*, *iwarised*. Early loanwords from Scandinavian also took it, as *itaken* (12th cent.).

It came down into ME. as a peculiar characteristic of the language of the south and west-midland regions, and examples are consequently abundant in such texts as (in the 13th cent.) Layamon's Brut, the texts of 'the Katherine group', Owl and Nightingale, Robert of Gloucester, (in the 14th cent.) Ayenbite, Shoreham's poems, Piers Plowman, Trevisa's works, Sir Ferumbras, (in the 15th cent.) Yonge's translation (Anglo-Irish) of Secreta Secretorum and the anonymous Two Cookery Books (E. E. T. S.); its frequency in Lydgate is presumably due to metrical exigencies and to imitation of Chaucer, in whom it is fairly common, whereas it is almost entirely absent from the works of Gower. In the 16th century it was adopted as an archaistic feature from Chaucer and Lydgate by many poetical writers, among whom are Phaer, Sylvester, Arthur Hall, and, above all, Spenser. In the 17th cent. Henry More is a prominent user of these pa. pples., and in the 18th cent. Thomson and other Spenserians have many examples. Some of the most commonly occurring words are *ybent*, *ybound*, *ybrought*, *yclad*, *yclept*, *ydight*, *ydrad*, *ypent*, *ypight*, *ywrought*.

In modern dialects its use in the form *a* (ə) extends over a triangular area of which the angles lie in Worcestershire, Surrey, and Cornwall; it is found also in Pembrokeshire and Wexford. Modern examples of dialectal usage are:—

1568 HOWELL *Arbor of Amitie* 36 b, In husbandry, icham truely, ycounted to excell. 1605 *London Prodigal* IV. i. E 3 b, Such a lerripoope as thick ych was nere a sarued. 1640 JOHN SMYTH *Descr. Hundr. Berkeley* (1885) 23 A native hundreder, beinge asked where hee was borne, answereth, where shu'd y bee y bore, but at Berkeley hurns, And there, begis, each was y bore. Or thus, Each was 'geboren at Berkeley hurns. 1746 *Exmoor Courtship* (E.D.S.) 26 Tha hast a creem'd ma Yearms, and a most a bost ma Neck. 1863 BARNES *Dorset Dial.* 27, I shall've a-meäde. *Ibid.* Gloss., *A-zet*, set, or planted. 1886 *W. Som. Word-bk.*, *Adood*, done.

5. In OE. *ge-* was used in the formation of adjs. from substantival stems to express the possession of, or being provided with, something, as *gefeax* having hair (of a certain colour), *geheort* courageous, *gestence* odorous, *gewurms* purulent (f. *wurms* corruption; cf. Goth. *gaskōhs* shod), but esp. with the ppl. ending *-od*, *-ed*, as *gefeaxod* (beside *gefeaxen*) having hair, *gehelmod*, *gehilmed* helmeted, *gehyrnd* horned, *gesperod* armed with a spear. The number of the latter was added to in ME., e.g. *ybonchyd* humped, (*wel*) *ycheryd* well-favoured, *ifeðered* (cf. OE. *gefeðerian*), *ileaded*, *ileðered*, *ypavylyound*, *iteiled*, (*old*) *i-yeerid*; in some instances the forms with the prefix are the more original forms of such adjs.: see e.g. FEATHERED, LEADED, LEATHERED, TAILED, YEARED. A few compounds of this class were coined by archaists of the 16th century; e.g. *ycrested* (A. Hall, 1581).

-y *suffix* 1 (Forms: 1 **-iȝ**, 2–5 **-i**, 4–6 **-ye**, 4–7 **-ie**, 4– **-y**, 6– now only in certain cases **-ey**), descending from the OE. adj. suffix *-ig*, which represents under a common form two OTeut. suffixes **-īga-*, *-aga-*, still distinguishable in OE. by the presence or absence respectively of mutation of the stem vowel of the sb. to which it is added, e.g. *mōdig* MOODY :- **mōdaga-*, f. **mōda-* MOOD *sb.*1, *mihtig* MIGHTY :- **mahtīga-*, f. **mahtis* MIGHT, *stānig* STONY beside *stǣnig*, *þurstig* beside *þyrstig* THIRSTY.

OTeut. **-īga-*, *-aga-* are differentiated forms of Indo-eur. *-qo-* (Skr. *-ka-*, Gr. *-κο-*, L. *-cu-*) arising from application of the suffix to *i-* and *a-* stems respectively. In other Teut. languages the following forms are found: OFris. *-ig*, OS. *ig*, (MDu. *-ig*, *-ich*, Du. *-ig*), OHG. *-ig* (MHG. *-ic*, *-ec*, G. *-ig*), ON. *-igr*, Goth. *-eigs*, *-igs*; OS. *-ag*, OHG. *-ag*, *-ah*, ON. *-agr*, Goth. *-ags*, *-ahs*; also OHG. *-uh*, ON. *-ugr*, Goth. *-ugs*.

When the suffix is appended to a sb. ending in *y*, the convention of modern spelling requires it to be spelt *-ey*, as in *clayey*, *skyey*, *wheyey*. When the sb. ends in *-e* preceded by a vowel, the *e* is retained, as *bluey*, *gluey*; in other cases there may be variation, as *homey*, *homy*, *liney*, *liny*, *nosey*, *nosy*.

1. The general sense of this suffix is 'having the qualities of' or 'full of' that which is denoted by the sb. to which it is added, as *icy* = (1) of the nature of, having the appearance, hardness, coldness, slipperiness, transparency, etc. of ice; (2) full of or covered with ice. In OE. there was a very large number of such adjs., many of which have a continuous history from the earliest times to the present day; in the case of some, however, e.g. *clayey*, *icy*, *rainy*, *wintry*, there is a significant gap in the evidence, which suggests that they may have dropped out of use and have been formed afresh later. There are some noteworthy instances of new formations in late OE., e.g. *dohtig* DOUGHTY replacing *dyhtig*, *dūstig* DUSTY, *snāwig* SNOWY replacing *snāwlic*. To several OE. adjs. in *-ig* there were parallel formations in *-iht*, as *īsig*, *īsiht* icy, *sandig*, *sandiht* sandy, *þornig*, *þorniht* and *þyrniht* thorny; the disappearance of this latter suffix left freer scope of development for the forms in *-ig*.

In ME. the number of these derivatives does not seem to have been at first greatly increased; the following fresh coinages are exemplified first from texts before 1300, *dready*, *fiery*, *frighty*, *hairy* (cf. OE. *hǣriht*), *happy*, *needy*, *sleepy* (but cf. OE. *unslǣpig*), *tidy* (*c* 1250 = in good condition); there are occasional parasynthetic compounds, as *sortleui* short-lived. The addition of the suffix to non-native sbs. is at least as early as the 13th cent., e.g. *savoury* in the Ancren Riwle. The fourteenth cent., esp. the later half, was prolific in new formations; to this period belong *angry*, *bushy*, *earthy*, *fatty*, *flowery*, *heady*, *hearty*, *milky*, *miry*, *mouldy*, *mucky*, *naughty*, *smoky*, *sweaty*, and many more. The sixteenth cent. was also a prolific period; to it belong, e.g., *cottony*, *frothy*, *dirty*, *healthy*, *leafy* (but *leavy* is 15th cent.), *mealy*, *saucy*, *sugary*, *viny*, *woolly*, *yeasty*. Others, such as *bulky*, *measly*, *noisy* (Dryden), *peppery*, *racy*, *skyey* are recorded first from the 17th cent.

Later new derivatives tend in a large measure to be colloquial, undignified, or trivial, as *bumpy*, *dumpy*, *flighty*, *hammy*, *liney*, *loopy*, *lumpy*, *lungy*, *messy*, *oniony*, *treey*, *verminy*, *vipery*; some are from verbs, as *dangly*. Contextually, the application of the adj. may be narrowed in any direction, as *mousy* = (1) resembling a mouse, (2) quiet as a mouse, or (3) infested with mice. A sense 'addicted to' (cf. 3), as in *booky*, *doggy*, *horsy*, is of modern growth.

1850 THACKERAY *Contrib. to Punch* Wks. 1900 VI. 163 Grizzel had brought me an oniony knife to cut the bread. 1869 MRS. WHITNEY *We Girls* ii, Bedsteads and washstands and bureaus—the very things that made up-stairs look so very bedroomy. 1891 M. MURIEL DOWIE *Girl in Karp.* xi. 144 Fretwork brackets and crystal dangly things.

2. In the 15th cent., if not earlier, certain monosyllabic adjs. were extended by means of this suffix, app. with the design of giving them a more adjectival appearance, e.g. *hugy* f. *huge*, *leany* f. *lean*. The majority of such words arose in the 16th and 17th cent.; examples are: *bleaky*, *chilly*, *cooly*, *dusky*, *fainty*, *haughty*, *hoary*, *lanky*, *paly* adj.1, *plumpy*, *slighty*, *slippery*, *stouty*, *swarty*, *thicky*, *vasty*. In this application the suffix has not infrequently come to express much the same notion as *-ish*; this is particularly so with colour-epithets, as *blacky*, *yellowy*, and esp. when these are used quasi-advb., as *greeny-blue*, *bluey-green*, *reddy-brown*.

3. As early as the 13th c. this suffix began to be used with verb-stems to express the meaning 'inclined or apt to' do something, or 'giving occasion to' a certain action; in the Ancren Riwle alone we have *slibbri*, *sliddri*, *sluggi*, *slummi*. Chaucer has *sleepy* = soporific. In the 16th cent. arose *choky*, *drowsy*, *slippy*, *sticky*; later we find *blowy*, *clingy*, *floaty*, *quavery*, *rollicky*. The immediate etymon of such adjs. cannot always be ascertained.

4. From the early years of the 19th cent. the suffix has been used still more freely in nonce-words designed to connote such characteristics of a person or thing as call for condemnation, ridicule, or contempt; hence such adjs. as *beery*, *catty*, *churchy*, *jumpy*, *newspapery*, *piggy*, *tinny*.

-y *suffix* 2 (1–3 **-ian**, **-iȝan**, **-ia**, 2–4 **-ien**, **-ie**, 3 **-iȝen**, **-eȝen**, **-ye**(**n**, **-in**, 3–4 **-i**, 4–5 **-ey**, 8 **-ee**, 3– **-y**) represents OE. infin. ending *-ian* of the 2nd class of weak verbs (having pa. t. in *-ode* and pa. pple. in *-od*), corresp. to OFris. *-ia*, OS. *-ōian*, *-ōn*, (MLG., MDu. *-en*), OHG. *-ōn* (MHG., G. *-en*), Goth. *-ōn* :— OTeut. **-ōjan*. This class of verbs is denominative; e.g. OE. *sealfian* to anoint :— **salbōjan*, f. **salbō* ointment, salve, *hearpian* to harp, f. *hearp* harp, and contains many intrans. verbs derived from adjs., e.g. *cōlian* to be cool (= OS. *cōlōn*) :— **kōlōjan*, f. **kōluz* cool, *nearwian* to be narrow, f. *nearu* narrow; it was swelled in prehistoric OE. by the passing over to it of many verbs that orig. belonged to the *-ǣjan* class, as *hatian* :— **hātōjan*, *-ǣjan* to hate (cf. OHG. *hazzōn* beside *hazzēn*). Adoptions of foreign verbs were regularly taken into this class, e.g. OE. *fersian* to versify, (*ge*)*temprian* to moderate, *offrian* to sacrifice.

By the 13th century this suffix had become restricted to the southern and western districts of England, and in the course of the century became generalized in those parts as the infin. ending of all verbs of whatever origin. The following are some examples of the extension of its use: in verbs orig. belonging to other conjugations, *brukien* (OE. *brūcan*) to enjoy, *nemni* (OE. *nemnan*) to name (Layamon); in new derivatives on native stems, *chapfari* to chaffer (Ayenbite), *grundien* to sink (Layamon), *kniȝti* to knight (King Horn); in verbs from Scandinavian, *lastin* (ON. *lasta*) to blame, *trosti* (Ayenbite); in verbs from French, not only those in *-ier*, *-ir*, *-ire* (the similarity of which to the ME. suffix would naturally suggest adoption into the *-ien* conjugation), *boili* (OF. *boillir*) to boil, *consenti* (OF. *consentir*), *herberȝi* (OF. *herbergier*) to harbour, *saisi* (OF. *saisir*) to seize, *trety* (OF. *traitier*) to treat—including those of the *-iss-* conjugation, *norisi*, *norischei* (OF. *noriss-*) to nourish, *perissy* (OF. *periss-*) to perish—but many also of other classes, *anuri* (OF. *anourer*) to worship, *fausie* (OF. *fauser*) to fail, *granti* (AF. *graunter*) to grant, *ioyni* (OF. *ioign-*) to join, *tempti* (OF. *tempter*) to tempt (these forms occur in various texts from Layamon to Ayenbite).

This suffix has been in continuous use in the south-west until the present day, when it is the regular infin. ending of verbs when used intrans. in the counties of Somerset, Devon, and Dorset. Examples and illustrations since 1400 are:—

c 1430 *Two Cookery-bks.* 7 Gadere alle þe kreme in þe clothe, an let hongy on an pyn. *Ibid.* 31 Take Porke or Beef, wheþer þe lykey. 1484 *Yatton Churchw. Acc.* (Som. Rec. Soc.) 115 To costs to rydy for the Chals that waste ystole xijd. 1746 *Exmoor Scolding* (E.D.S.) 143 Thee wut ruckee, and squattee, and doattee in the Chimley Coander lick an Axwaddle. 1825 JENNINGS *Observ. Dial. W. Eng.* 7 Another peculiarity is that of attaching to many of the common verbs in the infinitive mode, as well as to some other parts of different conjugations, the letter *y*. Thus it is very common to say *I can't sewy*, *I can't nurzy*, *he can't reapy*, *he can't sawy*; as well as *to sewy*, *to nursy*, *to reapy*, *to sawy*, &c. but never, I think, without an auxiliary verb, or the sign of the infinitive *to*. 1863 BARNES *Dorset Dial.* 28 The truth is, that in the Dorset the verb takes *y* only when it is absolute, and never with an accusative case. We may say, 'Can ye zewy?' but never 'Wull ye zewy up theäse zēam?' 'Wull ye zew up theäse zēam?' would be good Dorset. Belonging to this use of the free infinitive *y*-ended verbs, is another kindred one, the showing of a repetition or habit of the action, as 'How the dog do jumpy,' i.e. keep jumping. 'The child do like to whippy,' amuse himself with whipping. 'Idle chap, He'll do nothen but vishy, (spend his time in fishing,) if you do leäve en alwone.' 'He do markety,' He attends market.

-y *suffix* 3 (also 3–7 **-ie**, 4–6 **-ye**) represents ultimately, through F. *-ie*, Com. Romanic *-ia* = L. *-ĭa*, which comprised under one graphic form the Greek suffixes *-ία* and *-εια*, as in L. *mania* = Gr. *μανία*, whence F. *manie*, ME. MANIE, L. *sympathīa* = Gr. *συμπάθεια*, whence F. *sympathie*, Eng. SYMPATHY. Romanic *-ia* displaced L. *-ĭa* and became a living formative for abstract nouns of quality or condition; e.g. in OF. from *corteis* (COURTEOUS) was formed *corteisie* COURTESY, from *fol* (FOOL), *folie* FOLLY, from *gelos* (JEALOUS), *gelosie* JEALOUSY, and the like. When learned adoptions were made of L. nouns in *-ĭa*, this suffix was also represented by *-ie*, and so assimilated to *-ia*; e.g. F. *furie* FURY, ad. L. *furia* (whence also organic OF. *fuire*). In AF. preference was given to such forms as these over popular or semi-popular forms, e.g. AF. *accidie*, *glorie*, *estorie*, *victorie* = central F. *accide*, *gloire*, *estoire*, *victoire*, L. or med.L. *accīdia*, *glōria*, *historia* (Gr. *ἱστορία*), *victōria*; it is the AF. forms of such words that were adopted into English (see ACCIDIE, GLORY, STORY, VICTORY).

There were various new formations in late or med.L., in Romanic, or in individual Romance languages; examples are Romanic **libraria* LIBRARY, **poesia* (for *poesis*) POESY, OF. *navie* NAVY.

This suffix has never been in English a prolific formative, but from time to time new coinages have been made, e.g. in the 14th cent. *beggerie* BEGGARY and in the 16th COOPERY (= cooper's work or ware), f. *beggar* and *cooper*, both doubtless furthered by the prevalence of the suffix -ERY. Nonce-words like *orphany* and *tenanty* are of doubtful status, but the correspondence of adjs. in *-ic* and *-ous* to sbs. in *-y* has made possible in modern times the formation after Gr. types of such words as *brachycephaly*, *gymnospermy*, *synchrony*, *syntony* from *brachycephalic*, *gymnospermous*, *synchronous*, *syntonic*. The domain of the suffix is much enlarged by its constituting the final element of many compound suffixes, which receive separate treatment in this Dictionary in their alphabetical places; e.g. -ACY, -CY, -ERY, -GRAPHY, -LATRY, -LOGY, -MACHY, -PATHY, -PHAGY, -PHILY, -RY, -TOMY, -TONY.

Many important sbs. having this suffix appear as English adoptions of French words in the 13th century, as *barony*, *blasphemy*, *company*, *courtesy*, *felony*, *folly*, *jealousy*, *litany*, *story*, *villainy*; others, such as *comedy* and *tragedy*, *fury*, *glory*, *harmony*, *honesty*, *library*, *melancholy*, *memory*, *misery*, *navy*, *victory* date from the 14th century; in the 15th and 16th centuries another series of borrowings from French or from Latin appears, such as *family*, *industry*, *irony*, *liturgy*, *modesty*.

The majority denote a state, condition, or quality; others denote an activity or a result of it, as *blasphemy*, *felony*, *fury*, *harmony*, *history*, *liturgy*, *memory*, *phantasy*, *poesy*, *victory*. From either signification a definitely concrete meaning may be readily developed, which is found in *barony* (= baronial domain, body of barons), *company*, *family*, *library*, *navy*, *sacristy*, etc. The concrete application is abundantly illustrated also by names of countries, as † *Armony* (Armenia), *Italy*, † *Syrie* (Syria), *Brittany*; cf. -IA *suffix* 1.

-y *suffix* 4, representing, first through AF. forms in *-ie*, later by direct adaptation, L. *-ium*, which was added to verbal roots (primarily *i-* and *e-* stems) to denote an act, as in *beneficium* well-doing, good action, f. *beneficĕre* to do good, *colloquium* conference, conversation, f. *colloquī* to speak with, *gaudium* joy, f. *gaudēre* to rejoice, *suspīrium* sigh, f. *suspīrāre* to sigh. The earliest derivatives of this formation that were introduced into English are *remedy* (Ancren Riwle), through AF. *remedie*, from L. *remedium*, and † *sacrilegy* (early 14th c.), from AF. **sacrilegie* or L. *sacrilegium*. To both of these there are parallel forms, † *remede* and *sacrilege*, derived from continental Fr. forms *remede* and *sacrilege*; there are several similar pairs, of which the shorter form represents a continental Fr. form, the longer the corresponding AF. form or the orig. Latin, viz. † *augure* 1 and *augury*, *benefice* and † *beneficie* (rare), † *colloque* and *colloquy*, *empire* (F. *empire*) and † *empery* (AF. *emperie*, L. *imperium*), *homicide* sb.2 and † *homicidie* (rare), † *perjure* sb.2 (rare) and *perjury*, † *subside* (*c* 1450–1553) and *subsidy*; † *ingeny* 'mind', 'intellect' has its etymological doublet in *engine* 'native talent, genius, ingenuity, mechanical contrivance'. Most of these words, together with *obloquy*, came into the language before 1500. † *Relevy* sb.1 (med. L. *relevium*) and *suspiry* (L. *suspīrium*) are rarities; *gaudy*, though partly from L. *gaudium*, is prob. of mixed origin; the derivation of *larceny* is somewhat obscure. *Horology* 1 (beside *horologe*) and *mystery* 1 are derived, through the medium of L. *-ium*, from Greek forms having the cognate termination *-ιον*.

This cannot be said to have been at any time a living suffix in Eng., but there appears to have been reminiscence of its function, combined with the false analogy of words in -RY, in the coining of a few nouns from verbs ending in an *r*-sound, viz. *enquery* (*c* 1440), *inquery*, *inquiry* (16th c.), f. *enquere*, *inquire*, *expiry* (from 1752) f. *expire*, and a rare *transpiry* f. *transpire*. *Entreaty* (16th c.) is f. *entreat* vb. on the analogy of *treat*, *treaty*.

-y *suffix* 5, representing AF., OF. *-é*, *-ée*, mod.F. *-é*, *-ée* :— L. *-ātu-*, *-āta-* (see -ATE 1, -ATE 2).

a. In sbs. = -ATE 1, as in (i) COUNTY 1, OF. *counte*, F. *comté*, L. *comitātus*, f. *comit-*, *comes* count, DUCHY, F. *duché*, L. *ducātus*, f. *duc-*, *dux* duke, TREATY, F. *traité*, L. *tractātus*, f. *tractāre* to treat, (ii) ARMY, F. *armée*, Romanic **armāta* armed force, f. *armāre* to arm, DELIVERY, AF. *delivree*, ppl. sb. f. *delivrer* to deliver, ENTRY, F. *entrée*, Romanic **intrāta*, f. *intrāre* to enter.

This suffix is represented under other forms in certain words, e.g. *assignee*, *committee*, *refugee* (F. *assigné*, *comité*, *refugié*), *attorney* (OF. *atorné*), *alley*, *journey*, *valley* (F. *allée*, *journée*, *vallée*).

b. In adjs. = -ATE 2, as in *easy*, OF. *aisié* (F. *aisé*), f. *aisier* to ease. There are few general adjs. of this kind, but there is a considerable number of heraldic descriptive terms having this termination, the earliest example of which is *jerownde* (14th cent.), *gerundi* (1486), GYRONNY, a. OF. *geroné*, *gironné*, f. *giron* GYRON. Early adoptions of this class have the ending *-e*, later *-ee*, and (as early as the Book of St. Albans, 1486) often *-i*, later *-y*. With some, *-y* has become the regular form, as *barry*, *bendy*, *fretty*, *fusilly*, *gyronny*, *lozengy*, *nowy*, *paly* adj.2, *sarcelly*; others are found commonly with either *-é*, *-ée*, *-ee*, or *-y*, as *botoné*(*e*, *-y*, *checky*, *chequee*, *nébulé*, *-y*, *tenné*, *-y*, *undé*(*e*, *undy*; others, of more modern introduction, usually retain the French spelling, as *coupé*, *dancetté*(*e* (cf. † *dancy*), *écartelé*, *renversé*, *semée*; some have been anglicized with the native ppl. suffix, either temporarily or permanently, as † *besantid* (= *bezanty*), *escarteled*, *paled* ppl. adj.1, *resarcelled*, *sarcelled*. In *wavy* (after *undy*) we have a rare instance of an analogical use of the suffix with a sb. of native origin.

-y *suffix* 6, **-ie** (also 7–8 **-ee**, 7– **-ey**), used to form pet names and familiar diminutives. The forms *-y* and *-ie* are now almost equally common in proper names as such, but in a few instances one or other spelling is preferred, as *Annie*, *Betty*, *Sally* (rather than *Anny*, *Bettie*, *Sallie*); in the transferred applications of these, as *jemmy*, *tommy*, *dicky*, and the like, *-y* prevails; in general hypocoristic forms *-ie* is the favourite spelling after Scottish usage, as *dearie*, *mousie*. The use of *-ey* is subject to the same rules as for -Y *suffix* 1.

The use of this suffix in pet forms of proper names is found in Sc. as early as 1400; and in the 15th and 16th centuries instances become frequent; examples are *Cryste*, *Cristi* (f. *Cristin*, *Cristian*), *Pery* (f. *Pere* Peter), *Sandy* (f. *Sandre* for *Alisandre* Alexander), *Jamy* (f. *James*), *Michy* (f. *Michel*), *Richy* (f. *Richard*), *Roby* (f. *Robert*), *Edi* (f. *Ede*, *Ade* Adam), *Anny* (f. *Anne*), *Bessy* (f. *Elizabeth*). Such names were prob. modelled orig. upon forms like *Davy*, *Mathy* (= OF. *Davi*, *Mathé*), which have the appearance of being pet forms of *David*, *Mathou*. (Many have survived in Sc. surnames, as *Christie*, *Eadie*, *Pirrie*, *Ritchie*, *Christison*, *Mathieson*, *Robison*; *Davy* occurs as a surname in English use in the early 14th cent.)

The formation was greatly extended in Scottish and English use; whence *Annie*, BILLY, *Carrie* (f. *Caroline*), CHARLIE or CHARLEY, *Fanny* (f. *Frances*), JACKY, JENNY, JIMMY, JOHNNY, NANNY, *Nellie* (f. *Ellen*), PATTY, *Reggie* (f. *Reginald*), TOMMY, *Willie*. Many female names have corresponding forms in Du. names with the suffix *-je*, as in *huisje* little house, f. *huis* HOUSE *sb.*1; e.g. *Betty*, *Elsie*, *Hetty*, *Katy*, *Lottie*, *Matty*, *Sally* correspond to Du. *Betje*, *Elsje*, *Jetje*, *Kaatje*, *Lotje*, *Matje*, *Sellie*; but there is no evidence of historical contact.

The earliest recorded instances of the use of such proper names as appellatives are Scottish and belong to the beginning of the 16th century: viz. *Lowrie* (f. *Lowrens* Laurence) used for 'fox'; *Katy* and *Kitty* (f. *Katherine*), with the meaning 'lass, wench', tending to a specifically depreciatory sense, 'wanton, loose woman', which senses belong also to the 18th century *Molly* and *Nanny* (as in *Nanny-house* brothel); a few female names, viz. *Molly* and (dialectally) *Peggy*, have been used to designate an effeminate type of man.

The application of the female names to birds dates, according to our evidence, from the close of the 16th century; the wren is designated by *Kitty* and (more commonly) *Jenny*; in 1616 Ben Jonson calls a parrot *Polly*; in modern dialects *Peggy* is applied to various warblers and the pied wagtail, and *Betty* to the hedge-sparrow. Then, in the course of the 17th century, these names came to be applied to various mechanical contrivances, among which machines for spinning processes and the burglar's jemmy are prominent. This transference of application is illustrated by *Betty* (a burglar's jemmy, 1700), *Jenny* (in SPINNING-JENNY, 1783), *Jinny* (a stationary engine at a mine), *Peggy* (a washing-tub dolly, in various dialects).

Among male names the following are typical: *Johnny* is used for fellow, chap, *Jemmy* for the burglar's weapon, *Billy* for a roving machine; *Bobby*, *Charley*, *Dicky*, *Geordie*, *Jacky*, *Jockey*, *Tommy* exhibit a great variety of modes of application.

The first known instance of the application of the suffix to a common noun is LADDIE which appears in 1546 in the form *laddy*, used by John Bale; but there is no evidence until the 18th century of the generalization of *-y* for pet diminutives. Early instances are *dummie* (1595), *grannie* (1663), *dearie* (1681), *mousie* (1693, Sc.); *laddie*, *lassie*, and *sweetie* were used by Allan Ramsay, and these, with Burns's *birdie* and *mousie*, helped to popularize such formations in English generally; hence the appearance in the late 18th and early 19th century of *cooky*, *doggie*, *froggy*, *mannie*, *slavey*. In *blacky* and *darky* = 'nigger' there remains something of the status of a proper name; cf. *Fatty* as a nickname. *Bookie* for *bookmaker* is a formation of a rare type; cf. *nighty* for *nightdress*.

1885 *Eng. Illustr. Mag.* Apr. 509/2 No rowdy ring, but a few quiet and well-known 'bookies', who were ready enough to lay the odds to a modest fiver.

There are two words that are generally held to contain this suffix, viz. *baby* (late 14th c.) and *puppy* (late 15th c.). With *baby* may perhaps be coupled *daddy* and *mammy*, although the evidence for these is not earlier than the 16th century; the pairs *babe* and *baby*, *dad* and *daddy*, *mam* and *mammy*, may have resulted from different phonetic reductions of original reduplicated forms **baba* (cf. BABAN), **dada*, **mama*. The source of *puppy* (spelt *popi* in the Bk. St. Albans) is doubtful; *pup* is a back-formation from it.

Ya: see ONE, YAH, YE, YEA, YOU.

Yabber (yæ·bəɹ), *sb. Australia.* ['It is pronounced by the aborigines *yabba*, without a final *r*. *Ya* is an aboriginal stem, meaning to speak' (Morris *Austral Eng.*).] Speech, language, talk: applied to the speech of the Australian aborigines. So **Yabber** *v.* (*intr.* and *trans.*), to talk, esp. in an aboriginal Australian language.

1874 BEVERIDGE *Lost Life* III. 37, I marked Much yabber that I did not know. 1885 MRS. C. PRAED *Austral. Life* 19 They yabbered unsuspiciously to each other. *Ibid.* 28 Longing to fire a volley of Black's yabber across a London dinner-table. 1887 FARRELL *How He Died* 126 He's yabbering some sort of stuff in his sleep. 1888 'R. BOLDREWOOD' *Robbery under Arms* xxvii, They could speak a little Spanish and French, and got on with them. But Jim and I could only stare and stand open-mouthed..while they'd yabber away quite comfortable.

Yabble, Sc. var. GABBLE *sb.* and *v.*; hence **Yabbler** = GABBLER. (Cf. *yab*, *yabber* = GAB, GABBER.)

1808 JAMIESON, To *yabble*, *v. n.*, to gabble, Fife. 1819 W. TENNANT *Papistry Storm'd* (1827) 204 And than sic skellochin' and shout,..Was never sic a yabble! 1871 W. ALEXANDER *Johnny Gibb* xi, There was a general..clustering about him..as Samie 'yabbled' out the particulars. 1901 LAWSON *Remin. Dollar Acad.* 48 An outpost of these cacklers and yabblers sounded the alarm.

‖**Yaboo** (yabū·). Also 8 **yabou**, 9 **yabu**. [Hindustani = Persian یابو *yābū*.] One of a breed of large ponies or small stout horses in Afghanistan, Persia, and adjacent countries.

1753 HANWAY *Trav.* (1762) II. XIV. vii. 367 *note*, There are in the highland country of Kandahar and Cabul a small kind of horses called yabous, which are very serviceable. 1831 *Lit. Souvenir* 153 What in England would have been termed a capital punch pony,—in Persia, a good stout yaboo. 1880 in Ld. Roberts *41 Years in India* lxi. (1897) II. 353 Yabus 1,592, mules and ponies 5,926.

‖**Yacca** (yæ·kă). [Native name.] A West Indian evergreen tree, of either of two species of *Podocarpus* (*P. coriacea* and *P. Purdieana*, N. O. *Taxaceæ*), or its wood, used in cabinet-work, etc. Also *attrib.*

1843 HOLTZAPFFEL *Turning* I. 109 Yacca Wood, or Yacher, from Jamaica, is sent in short crooked pieces like roots. 1864 GRISEBACH *Flora W. Ind. Isl.* 789 Yacca tree, *Podocarpus coriacea*. 1890 H. THOMAS *Untrodden Jamaica* 10 A gate composed of closely set pales of Yacca.

Yacht (yɒt), *sb.* Forms: 6 **yeagh**, 7 **yoath**, **yolke**?, **yaugh**, **yuaght**, **yought**, **y(e)aught**, (*Sc.* **ȝ(e)aught**, with *ȝ* for *ȝ*), **yaucht**, **jacht**, **yach**, (**yacth**), **yat**, **yott**, 7–9 **yatcht**, **yatch** (*pl.* 7–8 **yatchs**, 8 **yatches**), 7– **yacht**. [ad. early mod. Du. *jaght*(*e* (now *jacht*) = *jaghtschip* (lit. ship for chasing), light sailing vessel, fast piratical ship, f. *jag*(*h*)*t* hunting, chase (= G. *jagd*), f. *jagen* to

hunt, chase (see -T *suffix* 3 a). Owing to the presence in the Du. word of the unfamiliar guttural spirant denoted by *g*(*h*), the English spellings have been various and erratic; how far they represent varieties of pronunciation it is difficult to say. That a pronunciation (yɒtʃ) or (yatʃ), denoted by *yatch*, once existed seems to be indicated by the plural *yatches*; it may have been suggested by *catch*, *ketch*.

The word has been adopted in many European languages: F. *yacht* (yak), G. *jacht-*, *yacht*(*schiff*), Da. *jagt*, MSw. *jackt* (15th c.), Icel., Sw. *jakt*, Sp. *yacte*, *yate*, *yac*, Pg. *hiate*, Russ. якта.]

A light fast-sailing ship, in early use esp. for the conveyance of royal or other important persons; later, a vessel, usually light and comparatively small, propelled by motive power other than oars, and used for pleasure excursions, cruising, etc., and now esp. one built and rigged for racing.

1557 *Voy. Stephan Burrough* in Hakluyt *Voy.* (1598) I. 294 A barke which was of Dronton, and three or foure Norway yeaghes, belonging to Northberne. 1613 PHINEAS PETT *Autobiogr.* (Navy Rec. Soc. 1918) 109 [We anchored] thwart of Sluis, where came on board us with his] yoathes [the Prince of Orange]. 1616 R. COCKS *Diary* (Hakl. Soc.) I. 118, I esteemed he came to spie..whether our shipp and the Duch yaught staid for to take the Amacon shipp. 1622 in Foster *Eng. Factories Ind.* (1906) 303 This smalle shippe or yolke is mostly ladne with pepper. 1630 R. *Johnson's Kingd. & Commw.* 40 The Emperour (who yet had never greater vessell than a Punt or Yaugh upon the Danuby). 1645 in *Sussex Archæol. Coll.* XLVIII. 129 Paid for tow and nails used aboute my Lords Yought at Pemsie. *Ibid.*, To unrig my Lord's Yaught. 1660 SIR W. LOWER *Voy. Chas. II*, 12 Jachts or pinnaces. 1664 in *Maitl. Club Misc.* (1840) II. 518 To the sailors whair his Lordship breakfast in the Zeaught 001 10 00. To the sailleris of the Zaught at Owlage 003 12 00. 1666 in *10th Rep. Hist. MSS. Comm.* App. v. 10 Gunner of his Majestie's vessell the Mary yaucht. 1673 H. STUBBE *Further Justif. War Neth.* 5 They who had struck their Flags..unto a Ketch of two Guns in the time of Cromwel, refuse to do it unto a Yacht of his Majesties. 1678 R. FERRIER *Jrnl.* 25 in *Camden Misc.* (1895) IX, A fair small River which ye King has there cut to take his pleasure on, there being severall yotts. 1680 ALSOP *Mischief Impos.* vi. 36 A..Man of War as big as 2 or 3 Yatchs. 1688 in Boys *Sandwich* (1792) 759 About 20 small smacks and yats in the Downs. *a* 1700 EVELYN *Diary* 1 Oct. 1661, I sailed this morning with his Majesty in one of his Yatchts (or pleasure boats), vessels not known among us till the Dutch East India Company presented that curious piece to the King. 1710 J. HARRIS *Lex. Techn.* II, *Yatches*, are Vessels with one Deck carrying from 4 to 12 Guns, with from 20 to 40 Men; and are of Burden from 30 to 160 Tun. 1766 *Ann. Reg., Chron.* 137/1 Admiral Keppel set out for Harwich, to take the command of the yatchs intended to carry over her R. Highness the Princess Carolina Matilda to Holland. 1769 FALCONER *Dict. Marine* (1780) s. v., The royal yachts are commonly rigged as ketches, except the principal one reserved for the sovereign, which is equipped with three masts like a ship. 1790 H. WALPOLE *Let. to Miss Mary Berry* 10 July, The river was covered with little yatches and boats. 1811 *Self Instructor* 587 The Dutch yatchts are chiefly used on their rivers and canals. 1839 DARWIN *Voy. Nat.* xxiii. 602 A yacht now with every luxury of life can circumnavigate the globe.

b. *attrib.* and *Comb.*, as *yacht-berth*, *-builder*, *-building*, *-club*, *-race*, *-racing*, *-sailing*, *-sailor*, *-squadron*.

1846 MRS. GORE *Engl. Char.* (1852) 46 Insensible to the perils of any uneasy *yacht-berth. 1868 *Trollope's Brit. Sports* 195 The Swedes are skilful *yacht-builders. *Ibid.* 217 The progressive improvement in *yacht-building during the last twenty years. 1837 in *Yachting* (Badm. Libr.) II. 12 That the Commodore be requested to seek an..audience with Her Majesty, with a view to the continuance of the Royal Cup to be presented to the *Yacht Club at Cowes. 1867 DICKENS *Lett.* (1880) II. 271 The American *yacht race is the last sensation. 1868 *Trollope's Brit. Sports* 196 We do not mean to say that *yacht-racing has wholly escaped those sharp practices. 1833 W. H. MAXWELL *Field Bk.* Introd., *Yacht-sailing has been slightly noticed. 1856 MARETT *Yachts and Yacht Bldg.* Introd. p. ix, The designer [of a yacht] should..be..an experienced *yacht sailor. *Ibid.* 74 For many years after the establishment of the Royal *Yacht Squadron.

Hence (*nonce-wds.*) **Ya·chtdom**, **Ya·chtery**, yachts collectively; **Ya·chtian**, **Ya·chtist**, a yachtsman; **Ya·chtling**, a little yacht; **Ya·chty**, *a.*, pertaining to or characteristic of a yacht.

1901 *Pall Mall Gaz.* 12 Jan. 1/3 A yacht for her Majesty that would eclipse all examples in modern *yachtdom for luxurious comfort and sea-going qualities. 1861 J. G. FRANCIS *Beach Rambles* 60 The flower of the *yachtery of England. 1842 *Blackw. Mag.* LI. 419 The assembled Thames *yachtians. 1895 *Nat. Observer* 21 Sept. 542 They went the way all *yachtists go. 1872 *Daily News* 21 Aug., The tiny *yachtlings (the largest of them measures but 10 tons, the smallest but four or five). 1892 *Field* 27 Feb. 279/2 The latest craft on the stocks—though of size that might be called '*yachty'—is..thoroughly of the canoe family.

Yacht (yɒt), *v.* [f. prec. sb., or back-formation from YACHTING *sb.*] *intr.* To make a trip in a yacht. (Chiefly in gerund or pres. pple.)

1836 MARRYAT *Midsh. Easy* xix, We must swear that it is a party of pleasure, and that we are gentlemen yachting. 1858 S. WILBERFORCE *Sp. Missions* (1874) 243 Sir James Brooke..not content with yachting it about amidst orange flowering groves,..conceived a great work amongst the Malay race. 1863 SPEKE *Jrnl.* 260 Sometimes the king spends a fortnight yachting. 1867 *Nation* (N.Y.) 3 Jan. 1/2 The only one of the owners who *yachted* as well as raced, by being on board his own craft.

Yachter (yɒ·təɹ). [f. YACHT *sb.* or *v.* + -ER 1.] One who makes a trip in a yacht; a yachtsman.

1828 *Sporting Mag.* XXI. 341 Several East India ships.. with such saucy rigging that would have made the Yachters raving in envy. 1892 *Daily News* 22 Mar. 5/4 When in Bombay he was an enthusiastic yachter.

Yachting (yɒ·tiŋ), *vbl. sb.* [f. YACHT *sb.* or *v.* + -ING 1.] The action, practice, or amusement of cruising in a yacht; the art of navigating a yacht.

1836 MARRYAT *Three Cutters* i, Of all amusements, give me yachting. 1874 BURNAND *My Time* xxix. 279 He..never missed a season's yachting with them.

attrib. 1850 OGILVIE s. v., A yachting voyage. 1868 A. K. H. BOYD *Less. Mid. Age* 327 We had a pleasant yachting excursion. 1884 *Harper's Mag.* Aug. 465/2 Invited to a yachting party. 1887 *Times* 27 Aug. 9 A sad yachting disaster occurred at Ilfracombe.

So **Ya·chting** *ppl. a.*, that sails in a yacht; addicted to yachting.

1848 THACKERAY *Van. Fair* xxxix, Yachting men from Southampton. 1862 *Lond. Rev.* 16 Aug. 138 The yachting world is very variously composed.

Yachtman (yɒ·tmæn). Now *rare*. Pl. **-men**. [f. YACHT *sb.* + MAN *sb.*1] = YACHTSMAN.

1820 *Examiner* No. 662. 807/1 The Royal Yachtman. 1856 'STONEHENGE' *Brit. Rur. Sports* 460/2 A variety of sails called flying-jibs, &c., which vary with every yachtman's fancy. 1868 *Trollope's Brit. Sports* 205 First-class yachtmen from Harwich.

Yachtsman (yɒ·tsmæn). Pl. **-men**. [f. gen. of YACHT *sb.* + MAN *sb.*1] A man who owns, manages, or sails in a yacht; a man addicted to yachting.

1862 *Lond. Rev.* 16 Aug. 138 It..requires a combination of those attributes which distinguish the modern Briton to make a great racing-man or a genuine yachtsman. 1868 *Trollope's Brit. Sports* 219 Nine out of ten yachtsmen build or buy their vessels in the dark.

Hence **Ya·chtsmanship**, the practice or skill of a yachtsman.

1862 VANDERDECKEN (*title*) The Yacht Sailor; a treatise on Practical Yachtsmanship. 1886 *St. James's Gaz.* 8 Sept. 4/2 The partisans of English yachtsmanship.

So **Yachtswoman** (yɒ·tswumăn).

1888 *Athenæum* 1 Sept. 294/1 The Sea-Eagle..is much exposed to the attacks of marauding yachtsmen and yachtswomen. 1906 *Daily Tel.* 29 Jan. 9/6 A well-known American yachtswoman.

Yack (yæk). A syllable imitative of a snapping sound; hence as vb.

1861 MEREDITH *Evan Harrington* xli, Tom..with a sound translated by 'yack', sent his leg out a long way. 1873 W. CORY *Lett. & Jrnls.* (1897) 318 He opens his beak, and yacks like the young jackdaw.

Yack, var. YERK, to beat; dial. f. OAK.

Yad, obs. pa. t. of GO.

1424 in Picton *L'pool Munic. Rec.* (1883) I. 23 The Sheriffs..yadden up to the West Derby fen. *c* 1435 *Torr. Portugal* 1193 His squiers habite he had, Whan he to the deyse yad.

Yad, var. YAUD *Sc.* and *north. dial.*, mare.

Yadder, var. EDDER: see YEDDER *sb.* and *v.*

Yae, Sc. dial. var. AE *a.*, one, only. Hence **Yaefauldness**, 'onefoldness', simplicity.

a 1771 *Bonny Hind* viii. in Child *Ballads* (1884) I. 446/2 I'm Lord Randal's yae daughter, He has nae mair nor me. 1864 J. BROWN *Jeems* 8 His absolute downrightness and yaefauldness.

Yaf, **yafe**, obs. pa. t. of GIVE *v.*

Yaff (yæf), *v.* *Sc.* and *north. dial.* [Echoic: cf. YAFFLE *v.* and WAFF.] *intr.* To bark, yelp; also, to prate, nag. Hence **Ya·ffing** *vbl. sb.* and *ppl. a.*; also **Yaff** *sb.*, a bark or yelp.

1609 *Ravenscroft's Deuteromelia* 21 With all the hounds at her tail! With 'yeaffe a yaffe! yeaffe a yaffe!' 1808 JAMIESON, To *Yaff*, ..1. To bark,..to yelp,..2. To prate, to talk pertly. 1815 SCOTT *Guy M.* i, Will ye no let me hear what the man wants, wi' your yaffing? 1844 G. J. PENNINGTON *Pronunc. Gk.* 22 A yaffing cur. 1910 G. J. LAURIE in *Poets of Ayrshire* 205 He'll row for fun amang the snaw And syne yaff at the moon.

Yaffe, obs. pa. t. of GIVE.

Yaffingale (yæ·fingeᵗl). *s.* and *s.w. dial.* Also 7 **yippingale**, 9 **yelpingal**, **yappingal**(**e**. [f. various echoic syllables with termination modelled on *nightingale*.] The green woodpecker; = YAFFLE *sb.*1

1609 C. BUTLER *Fem. Mon.* vii. § 5. H 5 b, The woodpecker or yippingale. 1802 [see YAFFLE *sb.*1]. 1865 *Cornh. Mag.* July 35 Mr. Matthew Arnold has very justly praised Maurice de Guérin for speaking of the woodpecker's laugh. But the West-country peasant ages ago called it the 'yaffingale', that is, the laugh-singer. 1866 BLACKMORE *Cradock Nowell* i, The tap of the yaffingale. 1871 TENNYSON *Last Tourn.* 696 The garnet-headed yaffingale. 1888 *Berksh. Gloss.*, *Yelpingal*, the woodpecker. 1906 G. A. B. DEWAR *Faery Year* 198 The statement of the gamekeeper that he had seen a 'black yappingal'.

Yaffle (yæ·f'l), *sb.*1 *dial.* Also **-el**, **-il**. [Echoic of the laughing cry of the bird: cf. YAFFLE *v.* (See also HICKWALL.)] The green woodpecker.

1792 CHARLOTTE SMITH *Desmond* I. 173, I remember the cry of the wood-peckers, or yaffils, as we call them in that country [*sc.* Kent]. 1802 MONTAGU *Ornith. Dict.* (1831) 385 Green Woodpecker...Yappingale. Yaffle or Yaffler. 1856 KINGSLEY *South Wind* ii. Poems (1889) 292 O blessed yaffil, laughing loud! 1893 D. JORDAN & JEAN A. OWEN *Forest Tithes* 126 On their grey trunks the yaffle shins about, yells, laughs, and yikes to his heart's content.

Yaffle, *sb.*2 *dial.* [f. YAFFLE *v.*] A bark, a yelp.

1836 *Fraser's Mag.* XIII. 662 My faithful dog..sent up a loud 'yaffle'. 1856 AIRD *Winter Day* Poet. Wks. 192 The petulant yaffle of the cottage cur.

Yaffle, *v. dial.* [Echoic.] *intr.* **a.** To bark sharply, as a dog; to yelp. (Cf. YAFF *v.*) **b.** To talk indistinctly, to mumble. **c.** Of a woodpecker: To utter its characteristic cry. (Cf. YAFFLE *sb.*1, YAFFLER.) Hence **Ya·ffling** *ppl. a.*

1847 HALLIWELL, *Yaffle*,..to bark. Same as *Yaff*. 1848 A. B. EVANS *Leicestersh. Words*, *Yaffle*, to yelp, or bark like a little dog...A yaffling little cur. 1875 *Anderida* xvi. II. 26 Then came three or four sounding taps from a woodpecker's beak, and a yaffling laugh as he flew away. 1887 *L'pool Daily Post* 12 Aug. 4/5 Yaffling little pet dogs.

Yaffler (yæ·flər). *dial.* [f. YAFFLE *v.* + -ER 1.] The green woodpecker: = YAFFLE *sb.*1

1802 [see YAFFLE *sb.*1]. 1840 MACGILLIVRAY *Brit. Birds* III. 91 *Picus viridis*. The Green Woodpecker...Yaffler. Yappingale. 1863 J. C. ATKINSON *Stanton Grange* 70 Ta'n't a yaffler's [nest]; it's a black and white woodpecker's. 1906 *Sat. Rev.* 10 Feb. 169/1, I thought that would touch you, woodpecker! Ha, ha, ha—who's the yaffler now?

†**Y-aforsayde** [Y- 4], aforesaid. 1422 YONGE tr. *Secr. Secr.* 147 And as y-aforsayde thes bene the foure cardynall vertues.

Yager (yēⁱgəɹ). Anglicized spelling of G. *jäger*, *jaeger*: see JÄGER 1, 2.

1804 *Ann. Reg., Chron.* 424/2 The light companies and yagers were sent out and skirmished. 1809 BYRON *Bards & Rev.* xv, All hail, M. P....At whose command 'grim women' throng in crowds..With 'small gray men', 'wild yagers', and what not. 1809 CAMPBELL *Gert. Wyom.* III. xxi, And first the wild Moravian yagers pass. 1812 *Examiner* 7 Sept. 562/1 The 8th Uhlans, and the 10th regiments of foot Yagers; both Poles, are nearly cut up. 1876 BANCROFT *Hist. U.S.* V. lvii. 176 He [*sc.* the landgrave] bargained to supply four hundred Hessian yagers, armed with rifled guns.

b. A rifle. *U. S.*

1840 C. F. HOFFMAN *Greyslaer* I. i, He instantly brought his yager to his shoulder. 1848 H. W. HERBERT *Field Sports U. S.* II. 254 Throughout the South and South-West, ..the *yager*, as it is called, or short-barrelled, large-bored piece, is universally preferred.

Yager, **yagger**, var. JAGGER 3.

Yagger, var. JAGGER 2 *dial.*, pedlar.

1821 SCOTT *Pirate* v, I would take the lad for a yagger, but he has rather ower good havings, and has no pack.

Yaguarondi, **-undi**, var. JAGUARONDI.

Yah (yā), *int.*1 (and *sb.*). Also **ya**, **yar**. [Echoic.] An exclamation of disgust, aversion, or malicious defiance. Also a vague or meaningless exclamation used by or attributed to negroes.

1812 H. & J. SMITH *Rej. Addr.*, *Rebuilding* v, While shout and scoff, Ya! ya! off! off! Like thunderbolt on Surya's ear-drum fell. 1840 DICKENS *Old C. Shop* lxii, 'A very excellent lodger, sir. I hope we may not lose him.' 'Yah!' cried the dwarf. 'Never thinking of anybody but yourself.' 1863 KINGSLEY *Water-Bab.* iv, He turned to bay..and bit the professor's finger till it bled. 'Oh! ah! yah!' cried he. *Ibid.* v, 'Yar!'..'you little meddlesome wretch.' 1863 READE *Hard Cash* xi, 'What him mean? what him mean? Yah! yah!' 1868 HOLME LEE *B. Godfrey* xxxvi, Gerrard, with a 'yah!' of repulsion, dropped the thing. 1890 HENTY *With Lee in Virg.* 299 'Yah!' the old man shouted. 'Do you suppose we are going to give in to five men?'

Hence **Yah** *v. intr.*, to shout 'yah!' *nonce-wd.*

1904 *Sat. Rev.* 23 Jan. 101 Yahing at Russia and cheering the 'brave little Japs'.

Yah, *int.*2 Repeated, *yah! yah!*, denoting a perverted or affected pronunciation of 'hear! hear!'

1886 H. W. LUCY *Diary Gladstone Parlt.* 349 There are cheers of various kinds. There is Mr. Alderman Fowler's deep-chested 'Yah, yah, yah!' 1887 *Punch* 21 Mar. 132/1, I used to call out Yah! yah! as I do in House of Commons.

Yah (yā, ya), *adv.* Dialectal for 'yea' or 'yes'; or in representations of Ger. or Du. speech. Cf. the earlier YAW *adv.*

1889 RIDER HAGGARD *Allan's Wife* iv, 'Yah! yah! hold a light', put in one of the Boers. 1899 *Daily News* 5 Apr. 5/1 'Yah,' which the rustics of the Peak frequently use for 'Yes,' and which they employed exclusively thirty years ago. 1905 *Ibid.* 23 May 4/7 America ..has two substitutes for 'yes.' One of them is 'yep' and the other is 'yah.'

Yahoo (yahū·), *sb.* A name invented by Swift in *Gulliver's Travels* for an imaginary race of brutes having the form of men; hence *transf.* and *allusively*, a human being of a degraded or bestial type. (Cf. HOUYHNHNM.)

1726 SWIFT *Gulliver* IV. ii, The Fore-feet of the Yahoo differed from my Hands in nothing else, but the Length of the Nails, the Coarseness and Brownness of the Palms, and the Hairiness on the Backs. 1764 REID *Inquiry* i. § 5. 28 At the expence of disgracing reason and human nature, and making mankind yahoos. 1772 GRAVES *Spir. Quix.* IV. x, To see a noble creature start...at the passionate exclamation of a mere Yahoo of a stable-boy. 1829 MACAULAY *Mill on Govt.* Misc. Writ. (1868) 143/1 Because civilised men, pursuing their own happiness in a social state, are not Yahoos fighting for carrion. 1861 H. KINGSLEY *Ravenshoe* lv, 'And what sort of fellow is he?..a Yahoo, I suppose?' 'Not at all; he is..a perfect gentleman.' 1904 ASHBEE *Last Rec. Cotswold Community* p. xxiii, To have..the pleasant valleys of Saintbury and Weston tramped by armed bands of Birmingham yahoos.

attrib. 1726 SWIFT *Gulliver* IV. iv, I told him, we had great Numbers [of Houyhnhnms]..[that] Yahoo-Servants were employed to rub their Skins smooth [etc.]. 1735 *Ibid.*, *Let. to Sympson*, I must..confess, that..some Corruptions of my Yahoo Nature have revived in me. 1751 WARTON *Newmarket* 192 That hated animal, a Yahoo-Squire. 1888 F. HARRISON in *Fortn. Rev.* Nov. 681 Pessimist pictures of human destiny and Ya-hoo theories of human life.

Hence (*nonce-wds.*) **Yahoo·** *v. intr.*, to behave like a yahoo; **Yahoo·dom**, the realm of yahoos, yahoos collectively; **Yahoo·ish** *a.*, resembling or characteristic of a yahoo; **Yahoo·ism**, style or quality characteristic or suggestive of a yahoo.

1868 YATES *Rock Ahead* III. v, A dam low-bred lot, *yahooin' all over the place. 1906 *Sun* (N. Y.) 17 Aug. 4/1 One dictum in a Judge's mouth can..unleash all *Yahoodom. 1885 MASSON *Carlyle* i. 37 The infrahuman, the *Yahooish, the diabolic. 1862 ROSSETTI in *Fraser's Mag.* July 70 Those '*yahooisms' are degrading in art. 1901 *Speaker* 5 Jan. 374/1 In the '*Scotsman*' we have Yahooism militant.

Yahveh, **-vism**, etc., **-weh**, etc.: see JEHOVAH, JAHVISM. **Yai**, graphic variant of *þai*, obs. f. THEY: see TH and Y. **Yaid**, **ȝaid**, var. YAUD. **Yaik**, **ȝaik**, obs. Sc. ff. ACHE *v.* **Yailing**, variant of YILING.

†**Yain**, *v. Obs.* Forms: 1 **ȝiȝeȝnian**, 3 **aȝeine**, **ȝene**, 4 **ȝeyne**, **ȝayne**. [OE. (Northumb.) *gigegnian*, **ongegnian*, corresp. to OHG. *gaganan*, *gegenan*, ON. *gegna* (whence GAIN *v.*1), f. *gegn-*, *ongegn* against (see AGAIN *adv.*).]

1. *trans.* To meet, encounter, oppose.

a 1000 *Rit. Dunelm.* (Surtees) 45/23 [*Justitia*] *obviabit illi quasi mater honorificata*, [soðfæstnis] ȝiȝegnað him svoelce moder arwyrðe. *c* 1205 LAY. 17854 He..aȝeineden þere uerde þe icumen wes to ærde. *a* 1250 *Owl & Night.* 845 Abid abid me shal þe ȝene [*v. r.* yene]. 13.. *Gaw. & Gr. Knt.* 1724 Loude he was ȝayned, with ȝarande speche.

2. *intr.* To avail: = GAIN *v.*1 1.

c 1325 *Minor Poems fr. Vernon MS.* 661 For heer but ȝif we make vs euene, Þer may no miht ne ȝiftes ȝeyne.

Yair, **yare** (yē³ɹ). *Sc.* and *north. dial.* Forms: 2–3 **ihar**, **yhar**, 3 **yhare**, (**yere**), 3–9 **yare**, 4 **yar**, 4–6 **yaire**, 5 **ȝar**, 6–9 **yair**, 9 **yaar**. [OE. *gear*, *ger*, recorded in comb. *mylengear*, *-ger* 'mill-yair'.] An inclosure extending into a tide-way in a river or on the sea-shore, for catching fish; a fishgarth.

1178–1219 *Chartulary of Abbey of Lindores* (S.H.S.) 11 Omnes piscarias in they .. preter vnam piscariam meam, scilicet, vnam iharam ad colcrike. *c* 1200 *Newminster Cartul.* (Surtees) 15 Piscarias meas de Benton in Tyna, &c. Hames yhare et Burnemuth yare. 1369 *Reg. Mag. Sig. Scot.* (1814) 66/1 Cum piscariis infra aquas de Northesk, et Suthesk, in crois, yaris, et Rethibus. 1408 *Durham Acc. Rolls* (Surtees) 53 In cccc sperlynges de nostro ȝar, ij s. 1511 *Exch. Rolls Scot.* XIII. 443 *note*, With all woddis, forestis, wateris, lowis, yairis and fischingis thaireof bath in fresch watir and in salt. 1580 *Burgh Rec. Edin.* (1882) IV. 553 The demolescheing and doun casting of the cruvis and yairis on the watter of Forth. *c* 1680 *Macfarlane's Geogr. Collect.* (S.H.S.) III. 211 Some of them [*sc.* herrings]..are taken in the Yairs. 1791 *Statist. Acc. Scot.* I. 282 There are a good number of salmon caught on the sea coast [Kiltearn]..by means of yaires, or small inclosures, built in a curve or semicircular form near the shore. At high water the salmon comes within these yaires, and at low water is easily taken. 1793 *Ibid.* VIII. 597 They erect what are called *yares*, a sort of scaffold projecting into the water; upon which they build little huts..; from these scaffolds they let down..their nets. 1883 *Standard* 10 May 3/6 He ..destroyed a yare in which they often caught a number of herrings.

b. *attrib.* and *Comb.*: **yair-fishing**, fishing by means of yairs; **yair-net**, a long net fixed by poles and extending into a river so as to form a yair.

1796 *Statist. Acc. Scot.* XVII. 217 The Zair or Yair Fishings, so productive in this parish [*sc.* Cardross]. 1805 *State v. Leslie of Powis* 109 (Jam.) The yare-net is about thirty-six fathoms in length, and about two and one-half fathoms in depth. *Ibid.* 356 The..yare nets extend at least three fourths across the channel of the river.

Yair, graphic variant of *þair*, obs. f. THEIR, THERE: so **yairfor**, **yairof**, etc., obs. Sc. ff. THEREFORE, THEREOF, etc. **Yait**(**t**: see GATE *sb.*1

Yak (yæk, yāk). [Tibetan གཡག *gyag* (Jäschke).] A bovine animal (*Poephagus grunniens*), found wild and domesticated in Tibet and other high regions of central Asia, having the body and tail covered with long silky hair, which is made into various fabrics; the tails are used for decoration, and in India as fly-flappers (see CHOWRY).

1799 S. TURNER *Embassy Tibet* (1800) 186 The black chowry-tailed cattle..the Yak of Tartary. 1862 TORRENS *Trav. Tartary* etc. 125 The oxen mostly used in Ladak are hybrids between the yâk and the common cow. 1893 DUNMORE *Pamirs* I. 246, I remounted my yak. 1903 *Athenæum* 1 Aug. 163/1 Only in the valleys does scanty scrub give sustenance to the yaks, on whose services the travellers depended.

b. *attrib.* and *Comb.*, as *yak corps*, *-hair*, *-tail*; **yak lace**, a heavy kind of lace made from the hair of the yak.

1904 *Times* 18 Jan. 5/6 The transport difficulties are still enormous, though the *Yak Corps is working well. 1905 E. CANDLER *Unveiling of Lhasa* xiv. 268 A heavy curtain of *yak-hair hangs above the entrance-gate. 1882 CAULFEILD & SAWARD *Dict. Needlework* 525 **Yak Lace*..is a coarse Pillow Lace, made in Buckinghamshire and Northampton. ..The material used is from the fine wool of the Yak. 1902 *Q. Rev.* July 42 Strange gifts from the East..*yak-tails and peacock feathers.

Yak, obs. Sc. f. ACHE *v.*; dial. f. OAK.

‖**Yakamik** (yæ·kămik). Native name of a South American bird allied to the cranes, *Psophia crepitans*, also called Trumpeter, domesticated by the Indians. In recent Dicts.

Yakmak, erron. form of YASHMAK.

Yald, obs. f. OLD *a.*, YAUD; var. YAULD *a.*; Sc. pa. t. of YIELD *v.*

Yaldran, **-drin**, var. YOLDRING.

Yale (yēⁱl). Also 5 **gaill**, **gale**, 6 **jall**, 7 **yeale**. [ad. L. *eale* (Pliny *Nat. Hist.*).] A fabulous beast with horns and tusks, perhaps the two-horned rhinoceros; used *Her.* (see quot. 1910).

c 1425 WYNTOUN *Cron.* I. ix. 754 In to þat lande [*sc.* India] þai say sulde be Ane oþer best, callyt Eale [*v. r.* Ane oþir beist is callit Gaill Into þat land foroutin faill], Þat is lik al til a hors..And has a gret tusk as a bare..And in his hewide ar hornys twa. 1536 in *Archæologia* (1910) LXII. 311 Paid to Ric. Rydge..for lyke cuttyng carvyng..and makyng of..and jall and Iunecorne a dragon, a lyan a greyhonde [etc.] [1601 HOLLAND *Pliny* VIII. xxi. I. 206.] *a* 1660 *Contemp. Hist. Irel.* (Ir. Archæol. Soc.) I. 264 The Ethiopian yeale hath two hornes of a cubit longe. 1910 *Archæologia* 313 The jall or yale..is a rare and strange animal partaking of the nature of the heraldic antelope, that is to say, wearing horns and a large pair of projecting tusks:..and he is silver bezanty, that is, white with yellow spots. He is one of the supporters of the Dukes of Somerset. *Ibid.* 314 *note*, The yale occurs as one of the supporters of the arms of the Lady Margaret Beaufort, mother of King Henry VII.

Yale, **yall**, obs. forms of ALE, YAWL.

Yalloch, **Yal(l)ow**, **Yalp**: see YELLOCH, YELLOW, YAWP. **Yalt**, obs. pa. t. of YIELD *v.*

Yam 1 (yæm). Forms: [6 **nname**, **inany**, **ignane**, **iniamo**, 6–7 **inamia**, 6–8 **igname**, 7 **ignaman**, **ighname**, **iniamu**, 7–8 **inhame**], 7 **yeam**(**e**, **yawm**, **yaum**, **jamoo**, 7–8 **yame**, 8 **jamme**, **jamb**, **guam** (?), **yamm**, 7– **yam**. [a. Pg. *inhame* (Clusius 1567) or Sp. *igname* (Scaliger 1557), *iñame*, †*name*, whence F. *igname* (Thevet 1575); the ultimate origin is uncertain.

The foll. quots. contain unanglicized forms:—

1588 HICKOCK tr. *Frederick's Voy. E. Indies* 18 A fruite called Inany [It. *Ignami*]:..lyke to our Turnops, but is verye sweete and good to eate. 1588 PARKE tr. *Mendoza's Hist. China* Comm. xi. 342 These people [*sc.* of the Philippine Islands] do more esteeme yron than siluer or golde, and gaue for it fruites nnames [Sp. *ñames*] patatas, fish. 1588 in Hakluyt *Voy.* (1599) II. II. 129 Their bread is a kind of roots, they call it *Inamia*, and when it is well sodden I would leaue our bread to eat of it. 1598 W. PHILLIP tr. *Linschoten's Voy.* I. lv. 99/2 Iniamos were this yeare brought hether out of Guinea, as bigge as a mans legge. 1600 J. PORY tr. *Leo's Africa* Descr. Places 52 They haue good sustenance also by meanes of a root, called there Igname, but in the west Indies Batata. 1640 PARKINSON *Theat. Bot.* XV. xxix. 1383 This manner of planting this Inhame savoureth something of that of the Manihot or Iucca, wherof the Cassavi is made. 1665 *Golden Coast* 65 The Battatas are..in form almost like Iniamus. 1703 PETIVER in *Phil. Trans.* XXIII. 1460 A sort of Inhame *vulgo* Yam or Potatoe. 1759 tr. *Adanson's Voy. Senegal* 165 The roots of manioc, igname [Fr.], and batatee multiply greatly in open places.]

1. The starchy tuberous root of various species of *Dioscorea*, largely cultivated for food in tropical and subtropical countries, where it takes the place of the potato; also, any plant of the genus *Dioscorea* (or, by extension, of the N. O. *Dioscoreaceæ*), comprising twining herbs or shrubs with spikes of small inconspicuous flowers.

With defining words, applied to various species of *Dioscorea*, and to plants of other genera in some way resembling these. **Chinese** or **Japanese Yam**, *D. Batatas*. **Coco** or **Koko Yam** = Cocco, Koko. **Common Yam**, *D. sativa*. **Granada** or **Guinea Yam**, *D. bulbifera*. **Indian Yam**, *D. trifida*. **Long Yam**, of Australia, *D. transversa*. **Native Yam**, a name for Australian species of *Ipomæa* (N.O. *Convolvulaceæ*) with edible tubers. **Red**, **White**, **Negro Country**, or **Winged Yam**, *Dioscorea alata*. **Round Yam**, (*a*) a species of yam with a round tuber; (*b*) the Burdekin Vine of Australia, *Vitis* (*Cissus*) *opaca*, with an edible tuberous root. **Wild Yam**, *Dioscorea villosa* of N. America, the root of which is used medicinally, also called *colic-root*; also applied to two W. Indian climbing shrubs, *Rajania pleioneura* (N.O. *Dioscoreaceæ*) and *Cissus sicyoides* (N.O. *Vitaceæ*); also to an Australian parasitic orchid (*Gastrodia sesamoides*) with edible roots, called *native potato* in Tasmania.

1657 R. LIGON *Barbadoes* (1673) 94 Planting provisions of Corn, Yeams, Bonavista, Cassavie. 1659 in *Engl. Hist. Rev.* (1919) July 285 To procure..planton rootes, cassada-sticks, large jamooes, potatoes and bonavist [in Cape Verde Is.]. 1661 HICKERINGILL *Jamaica* 16 Plentifull produce of Sugar-Canes, Tobacco, Cotten, Maiz.., Potato's, Yames [*printed* Yarnes]. 1697 DAMPIER *Voy.* (1699) 12 Yams, Potatoes and Plantains served us for Bread. 1699 WAFER *Voy.* 101 Yams, of which they have two sorts, a White and a Purple. 1705 tr. *Bosman's Guinea* i. 7 Jammes [orig. F. *jammes*]. *Ibid.* ii. 16 Jambs, Potatoes, and other Fruits. 1720 DE FOE *Capt. Singleton* xiv. (1840) 236 Guams, potatoes. 1729 *Dampier's Voy.* III. 460 *Round Yam*. From the Root which is white raw, but when boyl'd red...*White Yam*. Its Root being of that Colour, the Leaves single and cordated. 1756 P. BROWNE *Jamaica* (1789) 360 The Wild Yam. This plant grows wild in the inland woods of Jamaica. *Ibid.* 359 The Negro Yam. 1830 LINDLEY *Nat. Syst. Bot.* 278 The yams, so important a food in all tropical countries, because of their large, fleshy, mucilaginous, sweetish tubers. 1858 HOGG *Veg. Kingd.* 718 The Chinese Yam (*D. Batatas*), recently introduced to this country as a substitute for the potatoe. 1864 GRISEBACH *Flora W. Ind. Isl.* 789 Yams, Indian, *Dioscorea trifida*... Yams, white, *Dioscorea alata*. Yams, wild, *Cissus sicyoides* and *Rajania pleioneura*. 1866 *Treas. Bot.* 411 Yams vary greatly in size and colour..; many attain a length of two or three feet, and weigh from 30 to 40 lbs.; some are white, others purplish throughout, while some have a purple skin with whitish flesh, and others are pink, or even black. 1887 MOLONEY *Forestry W. Afr.* 433 White Bockra or Winged Yam (*Dioscorea alata*, L.).—Square-stemmed climbing plant. The roots of this species afford a much more delicate..food than those of *D. sativa*. 1889 MAIDEN *Useful Native Pl. Austral.* 67 *Vitis opaca*,..Round Yam.

2. Applied to † (*a*) the mangrove, of which some species have an edible fruit; (*b*) varieties of the common potato (*Solanum tuberosum*), cultivated in Scotland; (*c*) a variety of the sweet potato (*Batatas edulis*), largely eaten by negroes in America.

1753 *Chambers' Cycl. Suppl.* App., *Yams*,..a name sometimes used for the *rhizophora* of Linnæus. *c* 1775 T. L. *Yankee Doodle* (song) ii. in *N. & Q.* 1st Ser. V. 87 Farewell all de yams, and farewell de salt fish. 1805 FORSYTH *Beauties Scot.* II. 84 To give them [*sc.* horses]..a considerable quantity daily of potatoes, especially of the coarse sort, called yams. 1815 *Pennecuik's Wks.* 78 *note*, There is a demand for the large coarse varieties of potatoe, improperly called yams. 1844 H. STEPHENS *Bk. Farm* II. 30 The varieties raised exclusively for cattle are the common yam, red yam, and ox-noble. 1862 WHITTIER *At Port Royal*, *Song of the Negro Boatmen*, De yam will grow, de cotton blow, We'll hab de rice an' corn. 1892 *Kilmarnock Standard* 30 July 5/2 The Negro likes his yam.

3. *attrib.* and *Comb.*, as *yam-hill*, *-root*; **yam-bean**, either of two species of leguminous plants, *Pachyrrhizus* (*Dolichos*) *tuberosus* and *angulatus*, cultivated in the tropics for their pods and tubers, both of which are edible; **yam potato** = sense 2 (*b*); **yam-stick**, a long stick sharpened at the end, used by Australian natives for digging and as a weapon; **yam-stock**, a nickname for an inhabitant of St. Helena; **yam-vine**, (*a*) a species of yam (*Dioscorea bulbifera*); (*b*) the 'vine' or climbing stem of the yam-plant.

1864 GRISEBACH *Flora W. Ind. Isl.* 789 *Yam-bean, *Dolichos tuberosus*. 1887 MOLONEY *Forestry W. Afr.* 321 Yam Bean (*Pachyrhizus angulatus*), its tubers are like turnips. 1867 EMERSON *Lett. & Soc. Aims*, *Progr. Cult.* Wks. (Bohn) III. 228 Even the races that we still call savage..vindicate their faculty by the skill with which they make their *yam-cloths. 1864–5 WOOD *Homes without H.* iii. 85 A *Yam-hill—i.e. a bank of mould prepared for the purpose of growing yams. 1801 *Farmer's Mag.* Aug. 324 The *yam potatoe. 1829 LOUDON *Encycl. Plants* (1836) § 2085 The juice of *yam-roots fresh is acrid. 1861 BP. MACKENZIE in H. Goodwin *Mem.* (1864) 349 Huge yam-roots, some weighing fifty pounds. 1863 M. K. BEVERIDGE *Gatherings* 27 One leg's thin as Lierah's *yam-stick. 1833 T. HOOK *Parson's Dau.* I. ii, The blonds of the Baltic, the brunettes of the Mediterranean,..and the fair *yam-stocks of St. Helena. 1792 MAR. RIDDELL *Voy. Madeira* 89 The *dioscorea bulbifera*, or *yam vine. 1894 B. THOMSON *S. Sea Yarns* 186, I should soon..see the green yam-vines.

† **Yam** 2. *Obs. rare.* [a. Russ. ямъ *yam* posting stage or house, Pers. یام *yām* post-horse.] A posting house.

1569 TURBERV. *Trag. Tales*, etc. (1587) 147 b, If riding poast vpon a trotting Nagge. If homely yammes, in stead of Innes at night [etc.].

1800 *Asiat. Ann. Reg.*, *Misc. Tracts* 236/2 Each night they reached a yam, and each week a city.

Yam(**e**, graphic var. *þam*(*e*, THEM: see Y (3).

Yamboo, var. of (or error for) *jamboo*, JAMBO.

1777 G. FORSTER *Voy. round World* II. 302 The yamboos, (*eugenia*,) a cooling watery fruit, of the size of pears.

Yamen, **Yamf**: see YAMUN, YAMPH.

Yammer (yæ·məɹ), *sb. Sc.* and *dial.* Forms: 6 **ȝawmer**, **ȝamer**, 8 **yaumour**, **yaummer**, 8– **yammer**. [f. next. Cf. MDu., MLG. *jammer*.] An act, or the action, of 'yammering'; a cry of lamentation, a wail; a loud outcry, shout, yell; lamentation, complaint, querulous utterance.

1500–20 DUNBAR *Poems* xxxiii. 122 The air was dirkit with the fowlis, That come with ȝawmeris and with ȝowlis. 1552 LYNDESAY *Monarche* 6002 Than sall those Creaturis forlorne Warie the hour that thay wer borne, With mony ȝamer, ȝewt, and ȝell. 1792 A. WILSON *Watty & Meg* xxxix, While the weans, wi' mornfu' yaummer, Round their sabbin mother flew. 1894 CROCKETT *Lilac Sunbonnet* ix, Gin ye dinna tak' tent to yersel'..wi' yer eternal yammer o' 'Peats, Jock Gordon', an' 'Water, Jock Gordon', ye'll maybes find yersel' whaur Jock Gordon 'll no be there to serve ye.

Yammer (yæ·məɹ), *v. Obs.* exc. *Sc.* and *dial.* Forms: 5, 8 **yamer**, 6 **ȝammer**, **-ar**, **ȝalmer**, 7 **yalmer**, **-ur**, 8 **yommer**, 8–9 **yaumer**, 9 **yaummer**, **yawmer**, **yammar**, 6, 9 **yammer**. [Alteration of ME. *ȝomer*, YOMER, after MDu., MLG. *jammeren*.]

1. *intr.* To lament, mourn; to utter cries of lamentation or distress, to wail; to whine, whimper.

[*c* 1400 *Anturs Arth.* ix, Hit ȝaulut, hit ȝamurt, lyke a woman.] 1481 CAXTON *Reynard* xix. (Arb.) 47 He..fayned as he had wepte, right as he hadde yamerde in his herte. 1603 *Proph. of Waldhaue* (Bannatyne) 20 Thou shalt yalmur and yell: that al York shal it heare. 1818 MISS FERRIER *Marriage* xviii, It [*sc.* the child] does yammer constantly. 1820 SCOTT *Monast.* iv, The White Maiden of Avenel..is aye seen to yammer and wail before ony o' that family dies. 1861 WAUGH *Birtle Carter's Tale* 27 To see poor wortchin folk's little bits o' childher yammerin' for a bite o' meight—when there's noan for 'em.

YAMMERING. 14 YANKEE.

b. To murmur, complain, grumble; also *trans.* to say in a complaining or querulous tone.

Yamp (yæmp), *v.* dial. and *U.S.* [Origin unknown.]

1. *intr.* To pull with a sudden vigorous movement; to jerk or twitch vigorously.

2. To make a loud unpleasant noise or outcry; to howl; yell; to roar, shout.

3. To long; yearn, crave.

Hence **Yamping** *vbl. sb.* and *ppl. a.*

Yampee. = YAM sb.

Yamph [+əmf], *v.* Sc. and north. dial. Also **yaraf**. [Echoic.] *intr.* To bark, as a dog, esp. a small dog; to yelp.

Hence **Yamphing** *ppl. a.*

Yamstchik, yemstchik, var. YAMSHCHIK.

Yamun, yamen (yɑˈmun). Also -oun, -ên. [Chinese *ya-mun* or *ya-mên* the office of a Chinese mandarin.]

Yan. Yanoe, north. dial. ff. ONE, ONCE.

Yando. obs. form of YOND.

Yang, north. dial. f. ONE: dial. f. YAWN.

Yanglour, obs. form of JANGLER.

Yanizari: see JANIZARY.

Yank (yæŋk), *v.* dial. and *U.S.* [f. YANK v.] *a.* Sc. A sudden sharp blow or stroke. *b.*

Yank, *sb.²* f. [Colloq. abbreviation of YANKEE.]

Comb. **Yankland** *nonce-wd.*, the land of the Yankees, America.

Yank (yæŋk), *v.* dial. and *U.S.* [Origin unknown.]

1. *trans.* To pull with a sudden vigorous movement; to jerk or twitch vigorously.

2. *intr.*

Yankee (yæˈŋkɪ), *sb.* (a.) active; 'pushing' (Sc.); (*b.*) jerking; twitching.

1. *a.* A nickname for a native or inhabitant of New England; or, more widely, of the northern States generally; during the War of Secession applied by the Confederates to the soldiers of the Federal army.

b. trans.

Yankee (yæˈŋkɪ), *adj.* n. dial. Also b. **Yanky, Yanky.** [Source unascertained.]

1. *a.* A nickname for a native or inhabitant of New England, or more widely, of the northern States generally; during the War of Secession applied by the Confederates to the soldiers of the Federal army.

b. Special combinations and collocations.

2. *adj.* That is a Yankee; pertaining to or characteristic of Yankees (often with connotation of cleverness, cunning, or cold calculation); *loosely*, belonging to the United States, American.

Hence **Yankee** *v. (rare⁻⁰)*, *trans.* to deal cunningly with like a Yankee; to cheat; **Yaˈnkeedom**, the realm or country of Yankees, the United States of America; Yankees as a body; **Yaˈnkeyness**, a depreciatory term for an American woman; **Yaˈnkeefied** (-faɪd) *ppl. a.*, made or become like a Yankee; characteristic of a Yankee; **Yaˈnkeeish** *a.*, resembling a Yankee (whence **Yaˈnkeeishly** *adv.*, like a Yankee); **Yaˈnkeeism**, Yankee characteristic or idiom; **Yaˈnkeeize**, *v. trans.* to make Yankeeish, give a Yankee character to.

YANKEE DOODLE. 15 YARD.

Yankee Doodle (yæˈŋkɪ duːˈdəl). [Origin uncertain.]

The tune is said to have been composed in 1755 by Dr. Shuckburgh, a surgeon in Lord Amherst's army, in scorn of the provincial troops (*Hist. & Misc. Coll. New Hampsh.*)

1. The title of a popular air of the United States, considered to be characteristically national.

2. A name for various special tools of American origin, or of ingenious design. (Cf. *Yankee notions.*)

3. *adj.* That is a Yankee; pertaining to or characteristic of Yankees (often with connotation of cleverness, cunning, or cold calculation); *loosely*, belonging to the United States, American.

Yankee gang, name in Canada for a special arrangement of gang-saws (see quot.); **Yankeeland**, the land of Yankees, New England; *loosely*, the United States; **Yankee notions** [NOTION 9 b.], small wares or useful articles, such as those made or dealt in by New Englanders; **Yankee State**, a nickname for Ohio.

Yanolite (yæˈnəlaɪt). *Min.* [a. F. *yanolithe*, f. Gr. *lawbos* violet; see -LITE.] = AXINITE.

Yaoor, var. YAOURT.

Yaourt (yaˈurt). Also yao(o)rt, you(a)rt. [Turkish *yoġhurt* (with quiescent *ġh*) YOGURT.] A fermented liquor made by the Turks from milk.

Yap (yæp), *sb.* [Echoic. Cf. YAWP.]

1. A dog that yaps; a yelping cur. Now *dial.*

2. A sound expressible by the syllable 'yap'; a short sharp bark or cry.

Yap, yaup (yæp, yɔːp), *v.* Chiefly Sc. and *U.S.* [Echoic; cf. YAWP.]

1. *intr.* To bark sharply, as a small dog; to yelp.

2. *trans.* To speak snappishly.

Hence **Yapping** *vbl. sb.* and *ppl. a.*; also **Yap-per**.

Yappy (yæˈpɪ). Chiefly Sc. and north. Forms: 4-5 yap(e), 5 ȝappe, 8-9 yappy. [prob. f. YAP *a.*]

Yapock, yapok (yæˈpɒk). [f. *Oyapok*, name of a river between French Guiana and Brazil, spelt earlier *Wiapoco* (Harcourt *Voy.*)]

Yapon, yaupon (yɔːˈpɒn). Also 8 yaupon, yopon, yaupon. [North Carolina.] An evergreen shrub or small tree (*Ilex Cassine* or *vomitoria*), allied to the holly, growing in Texas and Southern U.S.; a decoction of the leaves (*yapon* tea) is used medicinally.

Yapp (yæp). [Name of a London bookseller.]

1. A comparatively small uncultivated area attached to a house or other building or enclosed.

2. A piece of enclosed ground or enclosure, usually of comparatively small extent, attached to a building or house.

YARD. 16 YARD.

Yard (jɑːɹd), *sb.¹* Forms: 1 ȝeard, 4-5 ȝerd(e), yard, -e, 4-5 ȝard(e), 4-7 yarde, (5 ȝeordde, ȝeord, ȝeorde, yherde, 4 ȝierd(e, ȝeird, yerde, 5 ȝeorde, 5 yordde), 5-6 yard. [OE. *ġeard*, *ġerd*, *gird*, Angl. *gerd* = OFris. *ġerde* (Fris. *jerd*), WFris. *gaerde*, OS. *gard* (MLG. *gard*, LG. *jaard*), MDu. *gaert*, Du. *gaard*, gard, OHG. *gartja*, *gardea*, *garta*, MHG. *garte*, G. *garten*), Goth. *gards* enclosure, house; OHG. *garto* (MHG. *garte*, *garten*), OS. *gardo*, Goth. *gards* garden.]

YARD. 17 YARD.

Yard (jɑːɹd), *sb.²* Forms: 1 ȝyrd, ȝerd (ierd), 1-ȝird, 3-ȝierd(e, ȝeord, 4-5ȝerde, 4-7 ȝarde, (3ȝeorde, ȝeord, ȝeorde, yherde, 4ȝierd(e, ȝeird, yord, ȝeerde, yorde, 5 ȝeorde, ȝeerde, 5 yarde. [OE. *ġierd, ġyrd, gird*, Angl. *gerd* = OFris. *ġerde* (Fris. *jerd*), etc.]

Yare (jɛə(r)), *a.* and *adv.* Forms: 1 ȝearu, ȝearo, 3 ȝare, (ȝar, ȝer, ȝeru, ȝerewe), 4-6 yare. [OE. *ġearu*, *ġearo* = OFris. *gere*, OS. *garo* (MLG., MDu. *gare*), OHG. *garo* (MHG. *gar(e*, G. *gar*), ON. *gǫrr*, *gerr*; not in Goth.]

Yark (jɑːɹk), *v.* dial. Also 6-7 yerk. [var. of YERK.]

Yarr, dial. form of HERB.

Yarborough (jɑːˈbərə). Cards. [Said to be so called because a certain Earl of Yarborough used to bet 1,000 to 1 against the occurrence of such a hand.]

Yardage¹ (yäˈdḗdʒ). [f. YARD *sb.*¹ + -AGE.]

Yardage² [f. YARD *sb.*³ + -AGE.]
1. The cutting of coal at a fixed rate per yard.
2. The aggregate number of yards; amount estimated in yards.

Yard-arm, *sb.*, *Naut.* Also 6 *yarde-*, 7 *yarde-*, -8 *yard'e-*. [f. YARD *sb.*² + ARM *sb.*¹ b.] Either of the two ends of a yard; *esp.* that part of either end which is outside the sheave-hole. Often used for the yard as a whole.

Yardman (yäˈdmän). [f. gen. of YARD *sb.*¹ + MAN *sb.*¹]

Yardland.

Yard-measure.

Yard-rope, *Naut.*

Yards-man (yäˈdzmän). [f. gen. of YARD *sb.*¹ + -MAN.]

Yards-man, *Naut.*

Yarding, *vbl. sb.*

Yardel. *Obs. rare.* A yard-measure.

Yard-wand, *sb.*

Yare, *adv. Obs.* or *arch.* and *dial.* Forms: 1 ȝearo, ȝearu, ȝearw-, -ow-, -ow-, 2-3 ȝaru, 3 ȝareou, -ow, -ua, -yw, ȝearewe, ȝar, ȝer, etc.
1. Ready, prepared.
2. Incorrectly used for YARD *sb.*¹

Yare (yē·ə), *a.*, *arch.* and *dial.* Forms: 1 ȝearo, ȝearu, ȝearw-, -ow-, -ow-, 3 ȝareou, 4 ȝare, ȝere, 4-7 ȝare, 7 yare, youre, etc.

Yare, *var.* YARE.

Yarely, *adv. Obs.* or *arch.* Forms: ... [OE. ȝearolíce]

Yare, *v. Obs.*

Yarkeh.

Yarke, áke (yäˈrkê). [Native name.] A South American monkey of the genus *Pithecia*.

Yarken, *v. Obs.* [f. YARE *v.* + -EN²] *trans.*

Yarn (yärn), *sb.* Forms: 1 ȝearn, 4 ȝarn, iern, ȝaarn, 4-6 yern, 5 ȝieren, yoern, 6-7 yearne, 7 ȝarn, *dial.* yern.
1. Originally, spun fibre, as of cotton, silk, wool, flax; now, usually, fibre spun and prepared for use in weaving, knitting, the manufacture of sewing-thread, etc.
2. *To spin a yarn* (*fig.*, orig. *Naut. slang*), to tell.

Yarn, *v.*, *colloq.* [f. prec. *sb.*]
intr. To 'spin a yarn', tell a story.

Yarn-beam, *Weaving.* [Cf. *G. garnbaum.*]

Yarned (yärnd), *a.* [f. YARN *sb.* + -ED².]

Yarnen, ene. [OE. *ȝearnen.*]

Yarnels, its. *Sc.* [Of obscure formation.]

Yarn-spinner.

Yarned.

Yarnwindle (yäˈrnwindl). *Sc.* Also 9 yarewind.

Yarn-winder.

Yarrow (yæˈroʊ), *sb.*¹ Forms: 1 ȝearwe, 5 ȝarow, 5-6 yarow, 6 yarowe, yarrowe, *yarrow*; *dial.* 7 ȝarrow, 9 yarrow, yarra, etc.

Yarrow, *a. dial.* [dial. var. ARGH *a.*]

Yarrum. *Thieves' Cant.* Also 6 yaram, 6-7 yarum. *Milk.*

Yart, *var.* YARD *sb.*¹

Yarta, *Obs.*

Yarth, *obs.* form of EARTH.

Yarthe, *obs.* form of EARTH.

Yarto, yaspin, *var.* YEPSEN.

Yasured.

Ya·shmak (yæˈʃmæk). Also *-mack, -mac, yasmak, yashmak* (yæˈsmæk). [Arab., *Turk.* ...] The veil worn by Mohammedan women in public.

Yatagán, Yataghan (yæˈtəgæn). Also *yatagan,* ATAGHAN. [Turkish ...] A sword of Mohammedan countries, having a handle without a guard and then a double-curved blade.

Yate, *v. Obs.* Forms: 1 ȝeátan, ȝetan, ȝeoten, (Orm.) ȝatenn, north. ȝate, 4-5 ȝete, north. ȝlate, 4-5 north. ȝate, ȝete, 6 ȝate, ȝeote. [OE. *ȝeátan*]

Yate, var. GATE *sb.*¹, YET.

Yatte, obs. form of GATE *sb.*¹

Yaucht, obs. form of YACHT.

Yauld (yǭld), *a. Sc.* and *north. dial.* Also 8 *yaul.* [Origin unknown.] Active, sprightly, nimble; strong, vigorous.

Yaule, Yaulew, Yaulpe, Yaumer, -our: see YOWL, YELLOW, YAWP, YAMMER.

Yaup, see YAP *a.*, YAWP.

Yaund, pa. ppl. *Sc.* [Related to Yaw?] An act of yawing; a movement of deviation from the direct course, as from bad steering.

Yaug, *Sc.* [f. Du. *jagt, jacht* YACHT.]

Yaught, yaughl, *obs.* ff. YACHT.

Yauld: see YAULD.

Yaup, see YAP, YAWP.

Yaut, *v. Obs.*

Ya·tagan: see YATAGHAN.

Yat, see GATE *sb.*¹, THAT, YACHT.

Yaw (yǭ), *sb.*¹ [Of obscure origin.] *Naut.*
1. A movement of a vessel by which she temporarily departs from the straight course, as through faulty or inexpert steering.

Yaw, *v.* *intr.* *Naut.* To deviate temporarily from the straight course, as through faulty or inexpert steering; to turn out of the line to one side or the other.

Yaw, *adv.* [Used in representations of Ger. and Du. speech: cf. YAH *adv.*] Yes.

Yawd, *var.* YAUD, JADE.

Yaw-haw, Yaw-haw: see YAW-HAWING.

Yawl (yǭl), *sb.*¹ Forms: 7 yaule, yale, 7-8 yall, yaul, 8 yawle, 9 yoll, yoll; *dial.* 7-8 yaul, yowl, yoll, jolle. [a. MLG. *jolle* (LG. *jölle*, whence Da. *jolle*), also of obscure origin.]
1. A ship's boat resembling a pinnace, but some-

Yawl (yǭl), *sb.*² A small sailing vessel.

Yawl, *v.* *intr. dial.* To howl.

Yawler ... **Yawling** ... **Yawmer** ... **Yawn** ... **Yawl** ...

Yawn (yǭn), *sb.* [f. YAWN *v.*]

Yawn (yǭn), *v.* [OE. *gánian*, etc.]

Yawner (yǭnər). [f. YAWN *v.* + -ER.]

Yawning (yǭniŋ), *vbl. sb.* [f. YAWN *v.* + -ING.]

Yawning, *ppl. a.*

Yawp ... **Yaws** ... **Yawy** ...

Yblessed, **yblest**, *pa. pple.* Obs.

Ybleured ... **Ybore** ... **Ybrent** ... **Ybound** ... **Yborn** ...

Ycleped, **ycleapt**, etc.

Yclept (iklē'pt), *ppl. a.*

Ye (yī, unstressed yi), *pers. pron. 2nd pers. nom. (obj.), pl.*

Yearful ... sb. nonce-wd.

Yearing, sb. and a. Obs. Forms: see YEAR; also 6 yeoryng.

Yearling, sb. and a. Forms: 6 yerling; also 6 erlynge.

Yearly, sb. and a.

Yearlong, a.

Yearn, v.[1] ... Forms: 1 ziorna, zeornan, ziernan, zirnan, zyrnan, 3-4 zierne, ierne, 2-5 ʒeorne, ...

Yearn, v.[2]

Yearn, sb.

Yearnful, a. Obs. rare.

Yearning, vbl. sb.[1]

Yearning, ppl. a.[1]

Yearn's day: see YEAR-DAY.

Yearmain, yr-mind.

Yearth, etc., obs. or dial. ff. EARTH.

Yeast, sb.

Yeasty, a.

Yeast, v.

Yeaster, ... see YEAST.

Yeasty, a.

Yeat, Anglo-Irish f. GET v.

Yeate: see GATE sb.[1], YET.

Yeather, var. YEDDER sb. and v.

Yeaven, obs. form of GIVEN.

Yeaven, obs. pa. pple. of GIVE v.

Yeavling, ...

Yeender, sb.

Yedder, sb. north. dial.

Yee, obs. f. EYE, YE, YEA.

Yeek, obs. f. ITCH.

Yeel, obs. form of EEL.

Yeelman, variant of HIELAMAN.

Yeeld, etc., obs. ff. of GUILD, YIELD, etc.

Yee-o, ...

Yeet, obs. f. YET.

Yeyn, obs. forms of IRON.

Yeik, dial. var. of OAK.

Yeke, sb. Obs. Forms: 5 ʒaeo, ʒaeo, ʒeo ...

Yelde, variant of YOLDEN.

Yeldrin, -rine, etc., var. YELDRING.

Yeke, v.

Yekesterne

Yeld, v.

Yeld, a.

Yelden, var. YILDING.

Yelk (yelk), var. of YOLK.

Yelke, obs. f. ILK, YELK.

Yell, sb.

Yell, v.

Yell, obs. form of YELK.

Yelloch (ye·lŏx), *sb.* *Sc.* Forms: 6 ȝelloch, ȝalloch, 7 yellough, 9 yill-, yelloch, [app. f. YELL with symbolic ending.] A yell.

Yelloch (ye·lŏx), *v.* *Sc.* Also 6 ȝellowch, 9 yello-. To yell; *trans.* to utter with a yell. *Yellooching* vbl. sb.

Yellow (ye·lo), *a.* and *sb.* Forms: 1 ȝeolu, ȝeolo, ȝeolo, ȝeolu, ȝeolow, -uw-, -ew-, 2 ȝeoluw, ȝeoluu, 3 ȝelu, 4 ȝeluȝh, ȝeloȝh, ȝelowȝ, 4-5 ȝolȝ, yolu, (ȝelhȝ, ȝelewȝ), 4-6 ȝelowe, -uwe, yelowe, (ȝealwe), 5 ȝelow, ȝelwe, 6 yelow, yellow, yelowe.

I. Of the colour of gold, butter, the yolk of an egg, various flowers, and other objects; constituting one (the most luminous) of the primary colours, occurring in the spectrum between green and orange.

Yell, obs. form of AIEL.

Yell, *sb.* *Sc. and north.* Trade Suppl., *Yells*, in weaving, guides for the warp-threads.

Yell, obs. var. ELE, form of l ALE, EVIL, HALE *a.*, YELL.

Yelld, var. YELD, obs. form of YELD.

Yelling (ye·liŋ), *vbl. sb.* [f. YELL *v.* + -ING¹.] The action of the verb YELL; the utterance of a sharp loud cry of rage, agony, etc.

II. Having a naturally yellow skin or complexion, as those of the Mongolian races; hence = MONGOLIAN 2, MONGOLOID 1. (Also applied in U.S. to mulattos or dark quadroons.)

III. With allusion to the use of yellow starch (coloured with saffron). *Obs.*

IV. = jealous. *Obs.*

V. Denoting various epithets of yellow colour, as the yolk of an egg, the stigmas of the saffron crocus (quot. 1587), a yellow carriage (quot. 1833).

B. *sb.*

1. Special collocations and Combinations.
 a. In names of species varieties of animals distinguished by their yellow colour or colouring.
 b. With qualifying words, denoting different shades of the colour, as brass-, bronze-, canary-, gold-, Isabella-, lemon-, primrose-, rust-, straw-, sulphur- (etc.); yellow, or various pigments and dyes, as amber-y, Chinese-, cobalt-y, imperial-; yellow earth, a yellow-y.

Yellowing, *vbl. sb.* [f. YELLOW *v.* + -ING¹.] The action of imparting a yellow colour.

2. Combinations. a. Qualifying other adjs. (or sbs.) of colour = yellowish, inclining to or tinged with yellow; as yellow-black, -brown, -dun, -green, -grey, -olive, -red, -white; also advb., as yellow-pale.

b. Parasynthetic and instrumental combs. (many of which are used in the names of species or varieties of animals or plants); as yellow-backed, -banded, -barred, -bellied, -billed, -blossomed, -bodied, -bearded, -browed, -cheeked, -chinned, -coloured, -covered, -crested, -crowned, -faced, -fingered, -fleshed, -flowered, -footed, -fringed, -haired, -hammered, -headed, -killed, -horned, -jerkined, -leaved, -legged, -painted, -ringed, -ringleted, -ruled, -seamed, -sealed, -shafted, -shouldered, -skinned, -spotted, -sprinkled, -striped, -throated, -tinged, -tinted, -winged, etc., adjs.

c. Forming sbs. (or adjs.), the names of (a) descriptive epithets of animals and other objects; in which yellow qualifies the name of some part or distinctive feature: yellow-back, (a) some kind of fish (see quot. 1796); (b) a cheap yellow-backed crop, French novel; yellow-beak of a young bird; yellow-bill, name for various birds with a yellow bill or yellow coloration on the bill, as the American scoter (*Oedemia americana*), yellow-bunting; yellow-coot, yellow-foot; -legs (Sc. -fit), yellow-fishes yellow-foot, an African plant of the genus *Helichrysum* having brilliant yellow flowers; (b) a species of moth (see quot. 1832); (c) the American yellow-headed blackbird, *Xanthocephalus icterocephalus*; yellow-jacket, (a) U.S. colloq., name for a wasp or hornet; (b) any of various species of *Eucalyptus* with yellowish bark (Morris Austral Eng.); yellow-juice, either of two N. American sorts of jundices, *Iris fcetidus* and *T. melanoleucus*; yellow-nine, collectors' name for species of moths of the genus *Ordinia* (see quots.); yellow-ochre = yellow-oat, plants yellow-pate (warbler), the summer yellow-bird; yellow-rump (warbler), *Dendroica coronata*, also called yellow-crowned warbler or myrtle-bird; yellow-seal (nonce-use), wine in bottles bearing a yellow seal; yellow-shank, -shanks = yellow-leg; yellow-shell, collectors' name for a species of moth (see quot. A. 1 d); yellow-spot, collectors' name for a species of skipper (butterfly), *Pelites pechisa*, having a yellow-up and orange wing; also (yellow-gill unicorn hawk) for a species of hawk-moth, *Sphinx quinque-maculata*; yellow-throat, any species of warbler of the N. American genus *Geothlypis*, esp. G. trichas, the Maryland yellow-throat; yellow-tail, a N. American species of reed-grass, *Calamagrostis hyperborea* Americana, valued for hay; (b) a variety of turnip, having the top of the root of a yellow colour. See also YELLOW-BELLY, YELLOW-BILL, YELLOW-WOOD.

Yellow-belly.
1. A name for a toad.
2. A native of the fens of Lincolnshire.

Yellow-fish. Name for several kinds of fish.

Yellow-hammer, -ammer. Forms: 6 yelambre, 7 yelamber, yellow-hamer, 7-8 amber, -9 ammer, dial. -oam-ber, -oim-ber, 6-9 yellow-hammer. [app. f. YELLOW *a.* + AM(M)ER.] A species of bunting, *Emberiza citrinella*, common in Britain and Europe generally, having the head, throat, and under parts of a bright yellow.

Yellow-bottle. [f. BLUEBOTTLE I, BOTTLE *sb.*] The marigold (*obs.*); the corn-marigold (*dial.*).

Yellow-boy. *slang.* *Obs.* (Also as two words.) A gold coin; a guinea.

Yellow fever. A highly fatal infectious febrile disease of hot climates, characterized by vomiting, congestion, fatty degeneration of the liver, jaundice, etc.

Yellowed (ye·lod), *ppl. a.* [f. YELLOW *v.* + -ED.] Made yellow.

Yellow-haired (-hēəd), *a.* Having yellow (flaxen, auburn, or golden) hair.

Yellow-ham, var. YELLOW-HAM (under an-).

Yellow-bird (ye·lobɜːd), Name for several birds having yellow plumage, *esp.* the North American goldfinch or thistle-bird, *Chrysomitris tristis*.

Yellowing, *vbl. sb.³* [f. YELLOW *v.* + -ING¹.] The action of imparting a yellow colour.

Yellowing, ppl. a.

Yellowish, a. [f. YELLOW + -ISH.] Somewhat yellow; of colour inclining or approaching to yellow; having a tinge of yellow.

Yellowishness, yellowish colour or tinge.

Yellowly (yeˈloˌli), adv. [f. as prec. + -LY.] With a yellow colour or light.

Yellowness (yeˈlones). Forms: see YELLOW + -NESS.
1. The quality or state of being yellow; yellow colour.
2. fig. Jealousy.

Yellowplush. Plush of a yellow colour, as worn by footmen; hence transf. as a humorous appellation for a footman.

Yellow-rattle : see RATTLE sb.

Yellow-root. (Also as two words.) Name for two N. American ranunculaceous plants, the one a herb, *Hydrastis canadensis*, of Canada and Northern U.S. (*Canadian yellow-root, goldenseal, or yellow puccoon*); the other a shrub, *Xanthorrhiza apiifolia*, of Southern U.S. (*shrub yellow-root*), or the root roots, which yield yellow dyes, and are used in medicine as tonics.

Yellows (yeˈloˌz). [Plural of YELLOW sb., used in specific senses.]
1. Jaundice, chiefly in horses and cattle.
2. A disease in plants, in which many sterile shoots are produced and the leaves turn yellow (= *peach-yellow*: see PEACH sb.).

Yellowy (yeˈloˌi), a. [f. YELLOW a. + -Y.] Having a yellow tinge; yellowish.

Yellow-root (yeˈlo, ruut), sb. and a.

Yelm (yelm), sb. Now dial. [OE. *gielm, gelm*, *gilm*.] A handful, bundle, sheaf, as of reaped corn; in mod. dial. use, a bundle of straw laid straight for thatching (see YELM v.).
Yelm (yelm), v. dial. [f. prec.] Also **yelm**, **yalm**, **yolm**. 1. trans. and intr. To separate and draw straw and lay it in order for thatching.

Yelp (yelp), sb. Forms: 1 *ʒielp, ʒelp, ʒylp*, 2-6 *yelp*, *3elp, 4-7 yelpe, yelp*. [OE. *gielp*, *gelp*, *gilp*, *ʒelp*.] 1. Boasting, vainglory, pride = OS. *gelp* (defiant or arrogant speech, OHG. *MHG. gelph, gelf* loud crying, outcry, cheerfulness, exultation, insolence). Obs.

Yelp (yelp), v. Forms: 1 *ʒielpan, ʒelpan, ʒylpan*, 3 *ʒelpen*, 4 *yelpe*, *3elpe, yolpe*, 4-6 *yelpe, yelp*. [OE. *ʒielpan, ʒelpan, ʒylpan*.]
1. intr. To boast, speak vaingloriously. Const. *of* (= OE. *gen.*). Obs.
2. To utter a yelp or yelps; said of dogs and related animals, and certain birds.

Yelper (yeˈlpɚ). [f. YELP v. + -ER.]
1. A boaster.
2. An animal that yalps or gives a sharp shrill cry; also, a person who 'yelps', etc.

Yelping, vbl. sb. [f. YELP v. + -ING.]
1. Boasting, proud or pompous talk. Obs.
2. The uttering of a sharp shrill cry.

Yeme (yeem), sb. and v. Obs. [OE.]

Yend, obs. or dial. var. YOND.

Yengee (ye'ngi), also -cee, -ci, whence N. American Indian corruption of *English*.

Yenite, obs. form of EVEN sb.

Yenough, obs. form of ENOUGH.

Yeo, obs. form of EVE sb.

Yeoman (yoˈmn). Forms: 1 *ʒemann*, (3omann), 3-7 *yoman, yeman*, 4-7 *yeoman*, 5-6 *yoman*, etc.
1. A servant or attendant in a royal or noble household, usually of a superior grade, ranking between a sergeant (SERGEANT sb.) and a page (PAGE sb.); or between a squire and a page.

YEOMANESS. 42 YEPE. YEPHEDE. 43 YERK.

Yeomaness.

Yeomanly, a. and adv. [f. YEOMAN + -LY¹.]

Yeomanry.

Yeoman's service.

Yeorling, var. YORLING dial., yellow-hammer.

Yeorned, ME. pa. pple. of EARN v.

Yeoven, obs. pa. pple. of GIVE.

Yeowe, obs. f. EWE.

Yeoxe, var. YEX Obs.

Yep, int. (? yeap.) A call to urge on a horse.

Yepe, a. (sb.) Obs.

Yepsen, var. YESPEN.

Yer, obs. f. ERE, IRE, YEAR; obs. graphic var. THEIR, THERE; dial. or vulgar f. YOU, YOUR.

Yerabull, var. EARABLE Obs.

Yerb, dial. or U.S. f. HERB.

Yerba, in full yerba-maté.

Yerbal.

Yercum, (yẽrkŭm). [Tamil.] An East Indian shrub, Calotropis gigantea.

Yerd, v. Obs.

Yerd-hunger.

Yere.

Yeply, adv. Obs.

Yer, sb.

Yepsen.

Yerk (yẽrk), yark (yärk), v. Now Sc. and dial.

Yerk, sb.

YERKER. 44 YERT. YES. 45 YESTER.

Yerker.

Yerl, -ly, obs. f. EARL, EARLY, YEARLY.

Yern, variant of YARN.

Yerne, v. Obs.

Yern-bliter, var. EARN-BLEATER, snipe.

Yerne, adv. Obs. Forms: 1 georne, 2–4 3eorne, 3–4 3erne, 3–5 (6 Orm.) 4–6 3erne, yerne, yarne, 5 yerne, yarne, 6 yerne.

Yerr, sb. Obs. Forms: 1 3eorr, 3 3orn.

Yerne, adv. Obs. Forms: 1 georne, yorne.

Yersal, Sc. form of YOURSELF.

Yert, obs. form of EARTH.

Yerva: see HERBA, YERBA.

Yes, adv. and sb.

Yesk, var. YEX.

Yeso.

Yesso, Obs. [Sp. yeso GYPSUM.] = GESSO.

Yest, obs. var. of YEAST.

Yeste, obs. graphic var. of JEST, GEST sb.¹

Yester (yẽ·stər), a. and adv. sb. [The first element is yester-, yesterve, etc., used as a separate word. Cf. next.]

Yester-, *adj.* Of or belonging to yesterday. *poet.*

Yester-, in comb. or as prefix = immediately preceding the present, last, in YESTEREVE, etc., after YESTERDAY, YESTERNIGHT: e.g. *yester-afternoon*, *-dawn*, *-morn*, *-noon*, *-year*, etc.

Yestereve (yestər'iv), *adv.* Chiefly *poet.* [f. YESTER- + EVE sb. 1] = YESTER-EVENING.

Yester-even (yestər'iv'n), *adv.* and *sb.* *arch.* and *dial.* Forms: 3 yistir-, yistir-. β. YESTER- + EVEN *sb.* [f. YESTEREN.]

Yestereven (yestər'iv'n), *adv.* = YESTER-EVENING *adv.*

Yester-evening, *adv.* and *sb.* *arch.* [f. YESTER- + EVENING *sb.*]

Yesterdaw (yestər'dɔ), *sb.* Obs. [f. YESTER- + DAW.]

Yesterday (yestər'dei), *adv.*, *sb.*, and *a.* Forms: a. 1 ȝeostran-, ȝystran-, ȝioster-, ȝeoster-, 3-6 ȝister-, 3 yhistre-, 4 ȝistir(e-, ȝystre-, ȝistre-, ȝister-, ȝustir-, ȝuster-, 3 ȝister-, 4 ȝirsday, 5-7 ȝisterdaie... B. 1 ȝystran-, ȝiestrandæges, 3 ȝerstan-, ȝuster-, ȝersten-, ȝeresten-, 4 ȝirsday, 5...

Yesterdayness.

Yestereve (see above)

Yestereven (see above)

Yesterfang (yestər'faŋ), *sb.* Obs.

Yestermorn (yestər'mɔrn), *adv.* Chiefly *poet.* [f. YESTER- + MORN *sb.*] Yesterday morning.

Yester-morning, *adv.* and *sb.* *arch.* and *dial.*

Yestern (yestə'rn), *a.* and *adv.* Obs. or *arch.*

Yesternight (yestər'nait), *adv.*, *sb.*, and *a.*

Yesterreve, *adv.* Obs. Chiefly *poet.*

Yestreen (yestri'n), *adv.* and *sb.* Chiefly *Sc.* and *poet.* Forms: 4 ȝhistrewyn, ȝystrewine, 5 ȝistrewyn, β. ȝesterevin, ȝestreuen, ȝestreuine, 8-yestreen... Yesterday evening; last night.

Yester-year. [Coined by D. G. Rossetti to render F. *antan* (= L. *ante annum*) in François Villon's *Grand Testament*, 1461.]

Yestreward, *adv.* Obs.

Yestreen (see above)

Yet (yet), *adv.* (*adj.*) and *conj.* Forms: a. 1 ȝiet, ȝit, ȝieta, 2-3 ȝiete, 3-5 (6-7 *Sc.*) ȝit, 3-4 ȝiet, ȝite, ȝeot, 3-5 ȝyt, 3-6 ȝett, 4 ȝeet, 4-5 ȝhit, (ȝhit), 4-7 ȝit, (5 ȝit), 6-7 ȝitt, 4-6 ȝet, 4-7, 8 *dial.* yit... A. *adv.* 1. In addition, in continuation; besides, also; further, furthermore, moreover; with a numeral or the like = 'more', as *yet a* foot, *another*', 'one more'; (*as yet a* foot) = 'one more'...

Yew (yu), *sb.* Forms: 1 *iw*, *eow*, *eoh*, 4-7 *ewe*, 4-6 *ew*, 5 *yewe*, 5-9 *yew*, (6 *ewe*, 8 *dial.* *yow*, *yowe*, *eugh*), 6-7 *yough*, 6-8 *yew*, (7 *ew*, 8 *dial.* *you*), 7-9 *yew*...

Yip (yip), *v. Obs.* or *dial.* In 5 ȝyppe, ȝippe, yepe. [Echoic.] *intr.* To cheep, as a young bird.
c 1440 *Promp. Parv.* 401/2 Pypyn, or ȝyppe, as henn byrdys (*K., H.* ȝippyn, as bryddys, *P.* yepyn). a 1825 FORBY *Voc. E. Anglia, Yip, v.* to chirp like a newly hatched chicken, or other very young bird.

Yir, graphic var. *þir* THIR, these.
1572 *Satir. Poems Reform.* xxxi. 199 Thairfor, yir plaigs wald yai eschew.

Yirb, Sc. and n. dial. f. HERB.

Yird (also 4 ȝerd(e, 4, 8–9 yerd, 5 yherde, 6 ȝird). Sc. and north. f. EARTH *sb.*, and *v.* (to bury).
c 1375 *Sc. Leg. Saints* i. (*Petrus*) 681 Ihesu,..þat in þis ȝerd com fra hewine. 1433 *Deeds rel. Orkney* vi, Aisiamentis.. as weill vnder yherde as boufe yherde. 1550 *Rental Bk. Cupar-Angus* (1880) II. 74 All..pertenens quhatsumeuir.. als weill vnder the ȝird as abouf. 1562 *Acc. Ld. High Treas. Scot.* XI. 214 To David Ellis for ȝerding of Johnne Gordoune..xx s. a 1670 SPALDING *Troub. Chas. I* (Bannatyne Club) II. 221 They fand yirdit in the yaird of Drum ane trunk full of silver plait. 1785 BURNS *Jolly Beggars* Recit. i, When lyart leaves bestrew the yird. 1824 MACTAGGART *Gallovid. Encycl.* s.v. *Yird-fasts,* The cauld yird, the grave. 1825 JAMIESON s.v., '*Fairly yirdit*', dead and buried. 1851 *Cumbld. Gloss., Yerd,* a fox-earth. 1882 *Proc. Berw. Nat. Club* IX. No. 3. 511 The 'Yirding of a live Cock' to cure epilepsy. 1894 CROCKETT *Raiders* xxiv, To afford yirds and secret caves for our Solway smugglers.
b. *Comb.*: esp. in *yirdfast* = EARTHFAST (cf. ON. *jarðfastr*). See also YERD-HUNGER.
1545 *Aberd. Reg.* XIX. (Jam.) Tuelf pennis Scottis of yerd-siluer. 1785 *Poems in Buchan Dial.* 6 Whare now thy groans in dowy dens The yerd-fast stanes do thirle. 1808 JAMIESON, *Yirdin,* thunder [see EARTH-DIN]. 1820 *Blackw. Mag.* VI. 568 A penetrating and even suffocating yird-drift. 1824 MACTAGGART *Gallovid. Encycl., Yird-fasts,* large stones sticking in the yird, or earth, that the plough cannot move. 1825 JAMIESON, *Yird-drift,* snow, not in the act of falling, but lifted up from the ground, and driven by the wind, after it has lain for some time.

Yire, Yirk, Yirm, Yirn: see IRE, YERK, YARM, IRON.

Yirr (yer), *v. Sc.* [Possibly repr. OE. *gyrran,* **girran* (see YERR), but probably an independent echoic formation.] *intr.* To snarl, growl. So **Yirr** *sb.*, a snarl, growl.
1786 BURNS *Ep. to Maj. Logan* ii, When idly goavan whyles we saunter; Yirr! fancy barks. 1815 G. BEATTIE *John o' Arnha'* (1826) 63 The watch-dogs yirr'd and yowf'd wi' fright. 1825 JAMIESON, *Yirr,* the growl of a dog. 1890 SERVICE *Notandums* xix. 125 If ony whillywha o' an Englisher should yirr and mak a kilfudyoch aboot the words he doesna ken.

Yirth, Sc. form of EARTH.

Yis, obs. pl. of EYE *sb.*[1]
c 1425 *Found. St. Bartholomew's* (E.E.T.S.) 11 Beholdyng ..thynges to cumme..with the yis of his soule.

Yis: see THIS, YES.

Yisce, variant of YISSE.

Yise, obs. f. ICE, YES.

†**Yisel.** *Obs.* Forms: 1 ȝisel, 2 ȝysel, 3 ȝisel, ȝæsel. [OE. *gísel* = OHG. *gîsal* (MHG. *gîsel,* G. *geisel*), ON. *gísl* (Sw. *gislan,* Da. *gidsel, gissel*) GISEL; cf. OIr. *giall.*] A hostage.
c 893 ÆLFRED *Oros.* III. vii. § 2 Philippus þa he cniht wæs, wæs Thebanum to ȝisle geseald. c 1205 LAY. 21103 Bringeð her þa ȝæsles Biforen ure cnihtes. *Ibid.* 22790 He wes iȝefen Arður To halden to ȝisle.

Yisk, Sc. f. *yesk*, YEX.

†**Yisse**, *v. Obs.* Forms: 1 ȝitsian, ȝietsian, ȝidsian, 2–3 ȝitsen, 2–4 ȝissen, (2 ȝitcen, 3 ȝiscen, ȝyscen, ȝescen, ȝietcen, ȝetsen, 4 yisse; in vbl. sb. 3 ȝittsunng, ȝssyng, 4 icinge). [OE. *gītsian, gīdsian* = OHG. **gîtisôn* (MHG. *gîzen, gîtsen,* G. *geizen*), f. Teut. *gîd-*, whence also OHG. *kît* (MHG. *gît,* G. *geiz*) covetousness, OHG. *kîtac* (MHG. *gîtec,* G. *geizig*) covetous; ultimately related to Lith. *geidžu* to covet, Lettish *gaida* desire, OSl. *židati* to expect.] *trans.* (in OE. const. gen. or dat.) and *intr.* To covet. Hence **Yisser**, a covetous person; **Yissing** *vbl. sb.*, coveting, covetousness.
Beowulf 1749 [He] ȝytsað gromhydiȝ. c 700 *Epinal Gloss.* 82 *Appetitus,* ȝitsung [*Corpus Gloss.* ȝidsung]. c 888 ÆLFRED *Boeth.* xiii. § 1 Sio ȝitsung ȝedeð heore ȝitseras laðe. *Ibid.* xxvi. § 2 Ælc bit þæs reaflaces þe him on ȝenumen bið, oððe eft oðres ȝitsað. c 897 — *Gregory's Past. C.* xli. 298 (Cotton MS.) Hu ȝewitende ða ðing sint þe hie ȝidsiað [*v. r.* ȝietsiað]. a 1175 *Cott. Hom.* 233 He wat wel þat maniȝe men bieð sa ful of ȝescung. c 1200 *Moral Ode* 271 (Trin. Coll. MS.) Þo þe waren ȝietceres of þis wereldes aihte. c 1200 ORMIN 4560 Ȝæn ȝittsunng & grediȝleȝc. c 1205 LAY. 5332 Þe kinges beoð ȝunge Of æhte ȝissinge. a 1225 *Ancr. R.* 202 Al so ȝisceð a ȝissare [*v. r.* ȝiscere] þet moni þusunt muhten biflutten. c 1250 *Gen. & Ex.* 3515 Ne ȝisce ðu noȝt ðin nestes ðing, Hus, ne aȝte, ne wif, in ðin ȝiscing. c 1275 *Passion our Lord* 35 in *O.E. Misc.* 38 Mid yuernesse and prude and yssyng wes þat on. c 1315 SHOREHAM IV. 357 Þorȝ ȝeskynge after gode. 1340 *Ayenb.* 16 Icinge, in cle[r]gie auarice oþer couaytise. a 1400 in *Pol. Rel. & L. Poems* (1903) 251 Ȝissinge and glosinge and felsship beon riue. *Ibid.* 269 Worldes yissyng Me haueth schent.

Yisse, ȝ-, obs. ff. YES. **Yist**, dial. f. YEAST *sb.*

Yistai, -ay (ȝistai, -ay), contr. f. YESTERDAY.

Yister-, ȝister-, etc., obs. or dial. ff. YESTER-.

†**Yit**, *2nd pers. pron. dual nom. Obs.* Forms: 1 ȝit, ȝyt, 2–3 ȝit, 3 ȝet, (*Orm.*) ȝitt. [OE. *git* = OFris. **jit* (NFris. *jat, jæt,* Sylt *at*), OS. *git,* ON. (MSw.) *it*; f. unstressed form of YE with an obscure dental element.] Ye two, both of you.
Beowulf 508 Ðær ȝit for wlence wada cunnedon. 971 *Blickl. Hom.* 187 Ȝyt ȝit þurhwuniað on incre anwilnesse. c 1000 *Ags. Gosp.* Matt. xx. 22 Ȝyt nyton hwæt ȝyt biddaþ. c 1175 *Lamb. Hom.* 93 Hwi iwearð hinc swa þet ȝit dursten fondian godes? c 1200 ORMIN 4498 Butt iff ȝitt muȝhenn betenn itt Onn aniȝ kinne wise. c 1205 LAY. 5020 Ne beon ȝit [c 1275 ȝe] bute tweien, mine sunen ȝit [c 1275 ȝeo] beoð beien.

Yit(e, ȝit(e, obs. ff. YET.

Yite (yəit). *dial.* Also **yeite, yoit.** [Obscure.] The yellow-hammer, *Emberiza citrinella.*
1812 P. FORBES *Poems* 104 (E.D.D.) Herryin' linties, yites an' kays. 1830 J. WILSON *Noctes Ambr.* Wks. 1856 III. 4 Lark, lintie, yellow-yite,..shilfa, and goldfinch. 1888 BARRIE *Auld Licht Idylls* ii. 54, I have known a black-fishing expedition stopped because a 'yellow yite', or yellowhammer, hovered round the gang when they were setting out.

†**Yiug(g)ed** [Y- 4], judged. 1297 R. GLOUC. (Rolls) 7082 Þo was it iIugged þat he ssolde be..Hardi kniȝt. c 1315 SHOREHAM V. 101 Y-iuged by þe lawe To by stend wyþ stone. 1387 TREVISA *Higden* (Rolls) V. 45 Geta was i-iuged [*MS.* γ y-juget] for a comoun enemy.

Yive, ȝive, obs. ff. GIVE, IF.

Yk, obs. form of I *pers. pron.*

Ykeld, Ykend, Ykened, ME. pa. pples. of KILL, KEN *v.*[2], KENE.

†**Ykep(t** [Y- 4, KEEP, I-KEPE *vbs.*], kept. 13.. *Seuyn Sag.* 460 To the ich have i-kept mi maidenhod. c 1380 *Sir Ferumb.* 2125 Þis ys þat tresour..Which þat my fader.. haueþ y-kept hit in-to þis day. 1399 *Pol. Poems* (Rolls) I. 365 Roton corne, So long ykep, hit is forlorne. 1422 YONGE tr. *Secr. Secr.* lxix. 246 Als longe as the natural hette duryth ..the helth of man shal be y-keppit. 1593 [see KEEP *v.* 14].

Ykest: see CAST *v.*, YCAST.

†**Ykeuered** [Y- 4, COVER *v.*[1]], covered. 1393 LANGL. *P. Pl.* C. x. 138 Vnder godes secre seel here synnes ben ykeuered. 1420 *E. E. Wills* (1882) 45, I ȝewe to Iohn Forster my godsonne a becure of seluer y-keueryd.

†**Ykid**, *pa. pple.* and *ppl. a. Obs.* Forms: 1 ȝecyd, 2 ȝekyd, 3 ikud(d, 3–4 icud(de, 3–5 ykud, 4–5 ykid(de, ykyd, 5 ykyde, (4 ykudde, ycud, ikid, yked, ikedde). [OE. *ȝecýd,* contracted pa. pple. of *cýþan, ȝecýþan*: see KID *ppl. a.* and KITHE *v.*] Made known; hence, well known, renowned: sometimes (like YCORE) a vague epithet of commendation.
a 1100 in *Leg. Rood* (1871) 3 Þa wearð hit sona þam mæran constantine þam kasere ȝecyd. a 1122 *O. E. Chron.* (Laud MS.) an. 1093 Se cyng..wæs ofer eall dead ȝekyd. c 1205 LAY. 24671 Þat nan lauerd taken nolde..Næuer nænne cniht,..Bute he icostned weoren Þrie inne compe, & his oht-scipen icudde. a 1225 *Leg. Kath.* 1295 Italde bi tale, fif siðe tene, icudde & icorene. *Ibid.* 1933 O icudd keiser! c 1315 SHOREHAM I. 633 Bote wanne þer hys o þyng yked, An oþer to onderstonde Þerinne. 13.. *K. Alis.* 3359 (Linc. Inn MS.) Y say Darie..Þat he was god knyȝt y kud. 1340–70 *Alex. & Dind.* 64 Þe king cortais i-kid cofliche saide. 1362 LANGL. *P. Pl.* A. IV. 140 Bote he beo A Cokewold I-kore [*MS. H.* ykyd] cut of boþe myn Eres! c 1380 *Sir Ferumb.* 4344 Y schal..haue wyþ me of ȝour knyȝtes .V. hundred gode y-kudde. 1393 LANGL. *P. Pl.* C. XIII. 196 A confessour ykud [*MSS. M., T.* i-kid] that counteþ nat a ruysshe Fere, ne famyne, ne false menne tonges. 14.. *K. Sol. Bk. Wisd.* 78 Wisdom yheled, litel is worþ oiþer treuþ ihyd; Bot boþe þai wexen swiþe ȝif þai ben y-kyd.

†**Ykitt, ykut, ykutted, ykyt** [Y- 4], cut. c 1300, c 1330 [see CUT *v.* I, 7]. 1387 TREVISA *Higden* (Rolls) V. 391 He made alle þe hedes and lymes of mawmettes i-kut [*MS.* γ ykitt] of. a 1425 tr. *Arderne's Treat. Fistula,* etc. 69 Smal y-kutted. c 1430 *Two Cookery-bks.* 55 Taylid Datys y-kyt a-long. **Yknet(t, yknit, yknyt**, knit. 13.. *Leg. Greg.* 481 Þe ropes wer fast yknett. c 1374 CHAUCER *Boeth.* IV. pr. vi. (1868) 134 While þat I weue..to þe resouns yknyt by ordre. 1426 LYDG. *De Guil. Pilgr.* 4924 Whan thys lettrys [*sc.* P, A, X] ben yknet,..Parfyt pes they sygnyfye. c 1440 *Promp. Parv.* 154/1 Felowys, y-knytte to-gedyr in wykydnesse, *complices.*

†**Yknow**, *v. Obs.* Forms: 1 ȝecnawan, 2 ȝecnowen, ikna(u)wen, 2–3 icnawe(n, 3 i-cnowe(n, 3–4 iknowe(n, 3–5 yknowe(n, 4 y-knawe(n, yknaue(n, 5 iknow. *Pa. t.* 1 ȝecneow, 2–3 icnew, 2 ȝecnew, ȝicneow(e, 3–4 iknewe, ikneu. *Pa. pple.* 1 ȝecnawen, 2–3 icnawe(n, 2 ȝecnowe, 3 icnowe(n, iknowe, 4 yknawe, yknowe(n, ycnowen, 5 yknow. [OE. *gecnáwan*: see Y- 3 c and KNOW *v.*] To know (in various senses); to acknowledge.
971 *Blickl. Hom.* 71 He wæs..of cilda muþe ȝecnawen & weorþad. a 1000, etc. [see KNOW *v.* I, II, etc.]. c 1175 *Lamb. Hom.* 49 Betre hit is þet mon ne iknawe noht þe wei to godalmihtin þe he hine icnawe and seodðe hine for-hoȝie. c 1200 *Trin. Coll. Hom.* 143 Ða biðohte heo on hire liflode and ȝe-cnew þat hie was lað gode. c 1205 LAY. 24805 Ȝif þu wult icnawen þat he is king ouer þe. a 1240 *Lofsong* in *O. E. Hom.* I. 205 Ich icnowe me gulti and creie þe leafdi merci. 1297 R. GLOUC. (Rolls) App. H. 122 Ich ne dar þat þe folc yhure þat ich yknowe þe. c 1320 *Cast. Love* 36 For him þat con not i-knowen Nouþer French ne Latyn. c 1330 *Arth. & Merl.* 9049 Herui Riuel þis iknewe. 1340 *Ayenb.* 104 He is þe eldeste and þet he meste yknawe and þe meste beloued. *Ibid.* 201 Zuo þet he ne may y-knawe his sseppere. 1377 LANGL. *P. Pl.* B. XI. 225 In her lyknesse owre lorde ofte hath ben y-knowe. 1387 TREVISA *Higden* (Rolls) VII. 205 A lewed goost, þat kouþe not y-knowe þe cause..of verray martirdom. c 1394 *P. Pl. Crede* 252 We ben clerkes y-cnowen cunnynge in scole. 1422 YONGE tr. *Secr. Secr.* 123 Whath awaylyth Sotilte of vndyrstondynge and connynge, and how thay byth y-know. c 1430 *Syr Gener.* (Roxb.) 6737 If ye can me tech Hou I may I-know him.
b. To make known; = KNOW *v.* 13.
a 1400 *New Test.* (Paues) Col. i. 27 To whom God wolde y-knowe þe richesse of þe blisse of þis sacrement.

†**Ykorve(n**: see YCORVE(N. **Ykoweryn**, ME. pa. pple. of COVER *v.*[1] ?1466 *Stonor Papers* (Camden) I. 77 To send hym worde wher to [= whether the] Mylle of Ermyngton schall be y-koweryn with stone or strawe. **Ykoyned** [Y- 4, COIN *v.*[1]], coined. 1423 *Rolls of Parlt.* IV. 256/2 Silver is ..no better..thenne xxxii *s.* the seid pound of troie ykoyned. **Ykremyd** [CRIM *v.*], crumbled. c 1430 *Two Cookery-bks.* 40 A fewe ȝolkys of hard Eyroun y-kremyd þer-on. **Ykuenct**: see YQUENCT. **Ykynde** [Y- 5, KIN *sb.*[1]], of (high) kin or lineage. 1420 *Proc. Privy Council* (1834) II. 273 The whiche partyes bothe beth weel ykynde and of gret allyaunce. **Ykyt**: see YKITT.

Yl, obs. form of ILL, ISLE.

-yl (il), formerly occas. **-ule**, a terminal element of chemical terms, ad. F. *-yle* (also *-ule*), f. Gr. ὕλη wood, matter, substance (see HYLE), used for 'chemical principle, radical'. It was introduced by Wöhler and Liebig (*Ann. de Chimie,* 1832, LI. 286), and first used by them in the term *benzoyle*; other early names were *éthyle* (*éthule*), *élayle* (Berzelius), *dadyle, peucyle, citronyle, citryle* (Blanchet and Sell). Some fifteen in anglicized form, including *acetyl, amyl, cinnamyl, glyceryl, salicyl,* appear in the *Elements of Chemistry* by T. Graham, 1842, who also invented the general term *basyle* for a body which unites with oxygen to form a base. *Methyl* is peculiar in being a back-formation from *methylene.*
-yl is used in forming the names of radicals compounded of two or three elements in various atomic proportions, which behave in combination like simple elements and are the constant bases of series of compounds (though they may not be themselves obtainable in a free state). Thus *carbonyl* CO, *hydroxyl* HO, *sulphuryl* SO_2, are compounds of carbon, hydrogen, and sulphur respectively. The greater number are compounds of carbon and hydrogen, either alone, as *amyl, ethyl, deutyl, trityl,* or with oxygen, as *acetyl, lactyl.*

Ylacay, obs. Sc. var. LACKEY.
1512 *Acc. Ld. High Treas. Scot.* IV. 342 Item, to ane Franche ylacay,..xiiij s.

†**Ylacet** [Y- 4, LACE *v.*], laced. c 1425 *Engl. Conq. Irel.* 52 Þay..turneden toward weysford by Odroon, wyth baners y-lacet. **Ylad(d** [LEAD *v.*[1]], led, conveyed, carried. 1297 R. GLOUC. (Rolls) 2424 Mercurius us aþ ylad in to þin londe. 1387 TREVISA *Higden* (Rolls) V. 99 Numerianus was y-lad in a liter. c 1400 MAUNDEV. (1839) ii. 13 Oure Lord Jesu, in that Nyghte that he was taken, he was y lad in to a Gardyn. 14.. *K. Sol. Bk. Wisd.* 211 Þo Ely in þis fair cart to heuen was ylad, Elisee his felawe was sory. 1426 LYDG. *De Guil. Pilgr.* 9772 The maryner..Ledeth the shyp,..And ys hym sylff ylad also. **Ylaft(e**: see YLEFT. **Ylaht** [LATCH *v.*[1], I-LECCHE], seized, caught. c 1306 *Pol. Songs* (Camden) 214 The Bisshop of Glascou ychot he was y-laht. **Ylaid, ylayd, yleid, yleyd**, ME. pa. pple. of LAY *v.*[1] 12.. *Moral Ode* vi. in *E. E. P.* (1862) 22 Al to muchel ic habbe i-spend, to litel y-leid an horde. c 1330 *Assump. Virg.* (B.M. MS.) 842 It was in þe tumbe ylaide. c 1380 *Sir Ferumb.* 2427 Þe cloþes þat wern on hure bed ilaid. 1426 LYDG. *De Guil. Pilgr.* 5415 Ther was no chaff ysene, And the strawh yleyd a-syde. **Ylakked** [LACK *v.*[1]], blamed. 1377 LANGL. *P. Pl.* B. II. 21 That is Mede þe Mayde..hath noyed me ful oft, And ylakked my lemman.

Yland(e, obs. forms of ISLAND.

Ylang-ylang (ī·læŋ ī·læŋ). Also **yhlang-, i(h)lang-.** [Tagalog *álang-ilang.*] An anonaceous tree (*Canangium odoratum*) of Malaysia, the Philippines, etc., with fragrant greenish-yellow flowers from which a perfume is distilled; hence, the perfume itself.
1876 *Jrnl. Chem. Soc.* I. 243 Oxidation of Essential Oils. ..*Citronella* and *ylang ylang* developed no hydrogen peroxide. 1881 *Ibid.* XL. 916 Cananga Oil...This oil, also known as Hang-lang or Alanguilan oil. 1882 *Englishman* (Calcutta) 2 Dec. 4/5 Atkinson's Perfumery. Ess. Ylang Ylang, Frangipanne. 1884 MILLER *Plant-n., Cananga odorata,* Ilang-Ilang-tree.
Hence **Yla·ngol** *Chem.* (See quot.)
1895 *Jrnl. Chem. Soc.* LXVIII. I. 243 Ylangol, $C_{10}H_{18}O$, the isomeride of geraniol.

†**Yla·st**, *v. Obs.* Forms: 1–5 ȝelæstan, etc. as in LAST *v.*[1]; also 3–4 ylaste, yleste. *Pa. t.* 1 ȝelæste, 2 ȝelest, 3–4 ilast(e, ilest(e, 3–5 ylast(e. *Pa. pple.* 1 ȝelæst, ȝelæsted, 2 ȝelest, 3 ilæst, ilast, 4 ylast(ed. [OE. *gelǽstan*: see Y- 3 c and LAST *v.*[1]]
1. *trans.* To carry out, perform: = LAST *v.*[1] I b.
Beowulf 524 Beot eal wið þe sunu Beanstanes soðe ȝelæste. c 888 ÆLFRED *Boeth.* xxxvi. § 4 Ic eac nauht ne tweoȝe ðæt ðu hit mæȝe ȝelæstan. a 1000 *Cædmon's Gen.* 2762 He..hæfde wordbeot leofum ȝelæsted. a 1122 *O. E. Chron.* (Laud MS.) an. 1012 Ða þet gafol ȝelest wæs. a 1200 *Moral Ode* 242 Þa þe gode biheten heste and nolden hit ileste. c 1205 LAY. 31109 Ȝif þu miht under criste þis forward me ileste.
2. *intr.* To last, continue, endure: = LAST *v.*[1] 2.
a 1000 *Boeth. Metr.* 19 Ne mæȝ hælеþa gehwæm hus on munte lange ȝelæstan. c 1175 *Lamb. Hom.* 157 Wa is mine saule þet mi lif þus longe ilest. c 1200 *Trin. Coll. Hom.* 151 Letitia sempiterna, þat is ilestende liht. a 1250 *Prov. Ælfred* 387 in *O. E. Misc.* 126 Alle world-ayhte schulle bi-cumen to nouhte...And vre owe lif lutel hwile ileste. 1297 R. GLOUC. (Rolls) 208 Þe bataile of troye þat ilast vale ȝer. 1377 LANGL. *P. Pl.* B. III. 191 [Þow] wendest þat wyntre wolde han y-lasted euere. c 1400 *St. Jer.* 15 Tokens 32 Leuere had his owen moder in helle pyne to be, Al þe while þe dom ylast, þan her sones face to see.
b. To stretch, extend; = LAST *v.*[1] 4.
a 1175 *Cott. Hom.* 231 His land ȝelest wide and side.

†**Ylat**: see YLET. **Ylauenyt**, ME. pa. pple. of LEAVEN *v.* 1422 [see LEAVEN *v.* 1]. **Ylauȝte, ylauȝthe**, ME. pa. pples. of LATCH *v.*[1], I-LECCHE. **Ylay(e, yleie, yleighe, yleiȝe, yleine, yleye(n, yly**, ME. pa. pple. of LIE *v.*[1] 1297 R. GLOUC. (Rolls) 5729 He sein swithin..Þat longe adde vnder erþe ybe [*v.r.* yleye] verst broȝte in to ssryne. 13.. *K. Alis.* 508 (Linc. Inn MS.) A god..þat haþ ylaye by þe quene. 1377 LANGL. *P. Pl.* B. V. 82 As a leke hadde yleye longe in þe sonne. c 1400 MAUNDEV. xiii. [ix.], Ȝif here fader had not ben dronken he hadde not yleye with hem.

Ylde, obs. by-form of ISLE.

Yle: see AIL *sb.*[2], AISLE, HYLE, ILL, ISLE.

†**Yleave.** *Obs.* [OE. *gelēaf*: see Y- 3 a, LEAVE *sb.*] Permission; leave.
a 1050 *Liber Scintill.* l. (1889) 165 *Iniquorum potestas super te ex dei datur licentia,* unrihtwisra miht ofer þe of godes ys ȝeseald ȝeleaf. a 1122 *O. E. Chron.* (Laud MS.) an. 1043 Be þes cynges ȝelæfan. c 1315 SHOREHAM I. 1269 Ȝef eny oþer hyt doþ, Nys hyt ordre, ac ileaue. 1340 *Ayenb.* 50 God yaf yleaue þe dyeulen to guo in to þe zuyn. *Ibid.* 112 At his yleaue nymynge.

Ylechyd, ME. pa. pple. of LEACH *v.*[1]

†**Yle·ft, yla·ft**, *pa. pple. Obs.* Forms: 1 ȝelæfed, 3 ileaued, ileued, 4 yleued, -yd, 4–5 yleft(e, ylafte, 7 ylaft. [OE. *gelǽfed,* pa. pple. of (*ge*)*lǽfan*: see Y- 4 and LEAVE *v.*[1]] Left.
c 950 *Lindisf. Gosp.* Matt. xv. 37 *Et quod superfuit de fragmentis,* & þ ȝelæfed wæs of screadungum. a 1225 *Ancr. R.* 168 Oure large relef þet we habbeð ileaued. c 1275 LAY. 28583 Þo nas þar na more ileued in þan fihte.. bote Arthur þe king. 1297 R. GLOUC. (Rolls) 6722 He was al one of þe tem bileued [*v.r.* yleft] there. c 1380 *Sir Ferumb.* 3349 Þe Assege þanne þay y-lafte. *Ibid.* 5121 Tho was þe assaut y-leuyd clene. 1405 in *Royal & Hist. Lett. Hen. IV* (Rolls) 158, I have nought ylefte with me over two men. 1422 YONGE tr. *Secr. Secr.* lxiv. 240 Yf anythynge be y-lefte in the stomake. c 1634 W. CARTWRIGHT *Ordinary* II. ii. (1651) 25 None pleasaunce is me ylaft.

†**Yleid, Yleie, yleighe, yleine**, etc.: see YLAID, YLAY(E.

Ylend, ylent, pa. pples. of LEND *v.*[1] and *v.*[2] a 1310 [see LEND *v.*[1] 2]. 13.. *Leg. Greg.* 259 Þat day was hem no grace ylent. 1340 *Ayenb.* 19 Þe greate guodes þet god ham heþ ylend. 1647 H. MORE *Song of Soul* II. II. II. iv, The hearing never knew the verdant peint Of springs gay mantle, nor heavens light ylent That must discover all that goodly pride. *Ibid.* IV. xxii, Their life ylent And subtill being quite away are flone. **Ylengd**, pa. pple. of LENG *v.*

†**Yleo·f**, *a.* (*sb.*) *Obs.* Forms: 1 ȝeleof, 3 *pl.* yleoue, ilоue. [OE. *geléof* = MHG. *geliep* (also as sb. pl.): see *ge-* Y- 1 b, 2 and *léof* LIEF.] Mutually loving or beloved; *sb. pl.* a pair of lovers.
a 1000 *Confess. Ecgberti* xxviii. in Thorpe *Laws* (1840) II. 152 On þære fiftan cneorysse ȝeleofe men hiȝ moton ȝesamniȝan. c 1000 *Ags. Gloss.* in Haupt's *Zeitschr.* (1853) IX. 461 *Contubernali sodalitate,*..mid ȝeleofre ferrædene. a 1250 *Owl & Night.* 1047 Þar two yleoue [*Cott.* ilove] in one bedde Liggeþ iclupt & wel bihedde.

†**Ylepe, ylope** [Y- 4, LEAP *v.*[1]], leapt. c 1380 *Sir Ferumb.* 4626 Many wer ouer y-lepe. *Ibid.* 5059 Þe tour þay hauede y-take þo Nadde duk Naymes y-lope hem to.

†**Yle·re**, *v. Obs.* [OE. *gelǽran*: see Y- 3 c and LERE *v.*] To teach; to learn.
Beowulf 3079 Ne meahton we ȝelæran leofne þeoden.. ræd æniȝne. c 1290 *Beket* 216 in *S. Eng. Leg.* 112 Seli child is sone i-lered. c 1300 *Havelok* 12 Þat ye mowen nou y-here, And þe tale ye mowen y-lere. 1393 LANGL. *P. Pl.* C. XII. 128 Thus þorw my lore beþ men ylered.

†**Ylered**, *ppl. a. Obs.* [OE. *gelǽred,* pa. pple. of (*ge*)*lǽran*: see prec.] = LERED, learned.
c 897 ÆLFRED *Gregory's Past. C.* 8 Uncuð hu longe þær swæ ȝelærede biscopas sien. 11.. *Fragm. Ælfric's Gram.* (1838) 6 Ilærede men. c 1205 LAY. 21858 Þreo biscopes wise, a boke wel ilæred. a 1225 *Ancr. R.* 64 Sum is so wel ilered, oðer se wis iworded. 1377 LANGL. *P. Pl.* B. XIII. 213 My denore to shewen, And conformen fauntekynes and other folke ylered. c 1440 *Partonope* 1994 And eke in armes full wele ylered.

†**Ylerned** [Y- 4], learnt. 1340 *Ayenb.* 70 Non wel libbe ne ssel conne þet to sterue ylyerned ne heþ. 1362 LANGL. *P. Pl.* A. IX. 10 Ich heilede hem hendeli as Ich hedde I-leorned [*C-text* hadde ylerned]. 1387 TREVISA *Higden* (Rolls) VII. 219 Þat þey hadde i-lerned [*MS.* γ ylurned] of here sovereynes to meyntene fredom.

Yleslipe, ylespile, var. *ilespil*: see under IL, ILE. **Ylessed**, ME. pa. pple. of LESS *v.*

Ylet, obs. form of EYELET.
14.. *Voc.* in Wr.-Wülcker 598/39 *Ocellulus,* an ylet.

†**Ylet**[1], **ylat**, earlier *gelæten, ileten, ilate(n* [Y- 4, LET *v.*[1]], let, allowed, left, etc. 13.. *K. Alis.* 2414 (Linc. Inn MS.) Þer was..mony a veyne ylat blode. 1340 *Ayenb.* 115 Þe guodes þet ich habbe uoryete and ylete to done. 1387 TREVISA *Higden* (Rolls) V. 109 He was i-closed wiþ ynne þe citee, and y-let out by a roop over þe wal. **Ylet**[2], **ylettyd**, earlier *gelett(e, ilet* [LET *v.*[2]], hindered. 13.. *K. Alis.* 1776 (Linc. Inn MS.) Ac he was y-lat by þe way. *Ibid.* 3221 Þer þey weoren fouly ylet, Þe gates weoren ageyns him scheet. 1422 YONGE tr. *Secr. Secr.* xxxi. 174 He was moche y-lettyd by an hugy ryuer. **Ylettert, ylettred**, early var. of LETTERED. 1303 y-lettrede [see LETTERED *ppl. a.*]. 1387 TREVISA *Higden* (Rolls) VI. 141 Well i-lettred [*MS.* γ ylettert].

†**Yleve**, *sb. Obs.* Forms: 1 ȝeleafa, 2 ȝe-l(e)afe, ileafe, ileave, 2–3 ileve, 3 ȝielefe, ilæfe. [OE. *geléafa*: see LEVE *sb.*] Belief, faith.
c 888 ÆLFRED *Boeth.* v. § 3 Nu þu ðone ȝeleafan hæfst. c 1175 *Lamb. Hom.* 5 Þet we sulen..habben godne ileafe to ure drihten. *Ibid.* 73 Þet an is rihte ileue, þet oðer fulluht. c 1200 *Trin. Coll. Hom.* 143 Þurh rihte ȝielefe, and clene liflade. c 1205 LAY. 2974 Swa helpe me Apollin, for min ilæfe is al on him.

†**Yleve**, *v. Obs.* Forms: 1 ȝeliefan, ȝelyfan, ȝelefan, 2 ȝelifen, ȝelyfen, ileafen, 2–5 ileve(n, 3 ilæiven, ilæfen, iluven, 3–4 ilefe(n, ylefe(n, ileove(n, 4 ileave, ileeve, ilyve, yleve, ylif. [OE. *gelíefan* = OS. *gilôbjan* (MDu. *ghelooven,* Du. *gelooven*), OHG. *gilouben* (MHG. *gelouben, glouben, glöuben,* early mod.G. *gleuben,* G. *glauben*), Goth. *galaubjan*: f. Teut. *ga-* Y- + *laub-* dear (related to *leub-* LIEF and *lub-* LOVE).] To believe.
c 888 ÆLFRED *Boeth.* v. § 3 Ȝelefst ðu þet sio wyrd wealde þisse woruldе? a 1000 *Boeth. Metr.* xxvi. 99 Ða dyseȝan men þe ðysum drycræftum long ȝelyfdon. c 1175 *Lamb. Hom.* 65 Wenne ic ileue and wel iso þet no gult me forȝeuen bo. c 1205 LAY. 29022 Karic ileouede to soðe Sexisce monne lare. a 1250 *Prov. Ælfred* 352 in *O. E. Misc.* 124 Ne ilef þu neuer þane mon þat is of feole speche. c 1380 *Sir Ferumb.* 4097 Þou ne dost noȝt ase þe wys If þow y-lyuest sir Alorys. 1387 TREVISA *Higden* (Rolls) VIII. 177 Men of þe contray aboute longe tyme þerafter myȝte unneþe i-leve þat þat citee was i-take. c 1400 *Lanfranc's Cirurg.* 267 I-leue þe wordis þat I seie.

Yleve: see YLIVE, to live.

Yleved, Yleyd, Yleye, Yliac: see YLEFT, YLAID, YLAY, ILIAC.

†**Ylight(ed** [Y- 4, LIGHT *v.*[2]], lighted. 1422 YONGE tr. *Secr. Secr.* lxi. 237 The mecche of a candill whych is y-lyghtid. c 1450 *Brut* II. 313 With candels ylight.

†**Ylike**, *a.* and *sb. Obs.* Forms: α. 1 ȝelic, 2 ȝelic(h), 2–5 ilich(e, ylych(e, 3–5 ylich(e, 4 ileche, 4–5 yleche, ilyche. β. 2–5 ilik(e, 3–5 ilyke, 4 ylik, ilek, 4–5 ylyk(e, illike, ylike. [OE. *gelíc*: see Y- 1 b and LIKE *a.* Represented now by ALIKE, q. v.; see also INLIKE.]
A. *adj.* 1. Like, similar (const. dat. or *to*).
a 900 CYNEWULF *Juliana* 549 Ic ær ne sið æniȝ ne mette in woruldrice wiþ þe ȝelic. c 900 tr. *Bæda's Hist.* IV. xix. (1890) 322 [Se lichoma] wæs slæpendum men ȝelicra þonne deadum. c 1175 *Lamb. Hom.* 109 Þe alde mon þe bið butan treowscipe bið iliche þan treo þe bereð lef and blosman and nane westmas ne bereð. c 1200 *Vices & Virtues* 9 Ic scal bien ȝelich ðan heisten [orig. *ero similis altissimo*]. a 1225 *Ancr. R.* 200 Hwose haueð eni undeau of þeo þet ich er nemde, oðer ham iliche. 1340–70 *Alex. & Dind.* 792 Ȝe ben to þe helle-hond holliche i-like. c 1380 *Sir Ferumb.* 2336 A semede þe diuel ileche. 1422 YONGE tr. *Secr. Secr.* xxii. 149 None afore the hath be y-lyke the, ne aftyre the shall come. c 1474 CAXTON *Recuyell* (1894) 321 A geant named Cerberus ynowh ylyke vnto pluto of condicions.
2. Of a number of things: Like one another; alike; equal. *Ever ylike*: always the same.
Beowulf 2164 Feower mearas..ȝelice. c 980–c 1060 *Laws of Æthelred* VI. iii. (Liebermann) 258 Se maȝa & se unmaȝa ne beoð na ȝelice, ne ne maȝon na ȝelice byrþene ahebban. a 1240 *Ureisun* in *O. E. Hom.* I. 203 Þet naueþ nouðer ende ne biginnunge þet is euer iliche wiðute sturiunge. 1387 TREVISA *Higden* (Rolls) IV. 355 Þinges þat beeth i-liche [*MS.* γ buþ ylyche] acordeþ to gidres. c 1391 CHAUCER *Astrol.* I. § 17 Than ben the daies & the nyhtes illike of lenghthe in al the world. c 1420 *Chron. Vilod.* 399 Thre waxe-candels he let make þen, Euery candelle y-leyche of weyȝt. 1422 YONGE tr. *Secr. Secr.* xxiii. 151 Yestyrday he hadd frendys Speciall, but to-day he haue ham all y-lyke. 1430–40 LYDG. *Bochas* IV. xi. (1558) 103 Fortunes gyftes be nat aye ylyche.
3. Fitting, suitable. (Cf. LIKE *a.* 6 a.)
c 1205 LAY. 15117 Nusten heo an world-riche ræd þat heom weore ilike.
B. *sb.* 1. (One's) like, equal, counterpart.
a 1000 *Boeth. Metr.* xx. 37 Nan þing nis þin ȝelica. c 1175 *Lamb. Hom.* 151 Iob wes..swa godmon þet ure drihten.. seide þet under houene ne nan his ilike. c 1205 LAY. 25378 Nes þer na king his ilike. c 1305 *Judas* 66 in *E. E. P.* (1862) 109 Ech þing loueþ his iliche.
2. Outward appearance, likeness, semblance; *concr.* an image, 'likeness'.
a 1225 *Leg. Kath.* 1843 Crist..þurh his ahne engel i culurene iliche, fedde hire. a 1225 *Ancr. R.* 136 Loke þet tu habbe his iliche, þet is þet crucifix. a 1300 *K. Horn* 305 In hornes ilike þu schalt hure biswike. c 1315 SHOREHAM VII. 883 Ase mannes ylyche ymad of tre May nauȝt be al ase man may be..Ne godes ylyche, man, y-wys Ne may nauȝt be al ase god ys.

†**Yli·ke**, *adv. Obs.* Forms: 1 ȝelíce, 2 ȝe-lic(h)e, 3–5 iliche, yliche, 4–5 ilike, 4–7 ylike, etc. (cf. prec.); also 4 eliche, elike, elyke, 5 yeliche. [OE. *gelíce* = OS. *gilîco* (MDu. *gelike,* Du. *gelijk*), OHG. *galîhho, g(i)lîcho* (MHG. *g(e)lîche, g(e)lîch,* G. *gleich*), Goth. *galeikô*; f. prec.]
1. Similarly; likewise; alike; equally. *Everylike*: unceasingly, continuously.
971 *Blickl. Hom.* 119 Ne wæron þas ealle ȝelice lange. c 1000 *Ags. Gosp.* Matt. xx. 5 Eft he ut-eode embe þa sixtan & niȝoþan tide & dyde þam swa ȝelice. c 1200 *Moral Ode* 66 (Trin. Coll. MS.) Africh man mid þat he haueð mai bugge heueriche þe þe more haueð and þe þe lasse boðe iliche. 1297 R. GLOUC. (Rolls) 152 Þat water of baþe is þat on þat euere is iliche hot. 1377 LANGL. *P. Pl.* B. XIX. 436 Al tymes ylyke. c 1386 CHAUCER *Knt.'s T.* 1668 Til that the Thebane knyghtes bothe yliche Honured, were in to the paleys fet. c 1391 — *Astrol.* II. § 39 The longitude of a clymat ys a lyne ymagined fro Est to west, illike distant by-twene them alle. a 1395 HYLTON *Scala Perf.* (W. de W. 1494) I. xxxiv, Who soo is euer ylyke wyse in knowyng of god & ghostly thynges. c 1400 LYDG. *Chorle & Bird* 48 (MS. Harl. 116) Of lengthe and brede yeliche square and longe. c 1403 CLANVOWE *Cuckow & Night.* 64 The floures and the gras y-lyke hye. 1423 JAS. I *Kingis Q.* lxx, Tantalus..That euer ylike hailith at the well Water to draw with buket botemles. c 1460 *Towneley Myst.* viii. 106 A bush I se burnand full bryght, and euer elyke the leyfes are greyn. 1486 *Bk. St. Albans* c vj b, Take Fenell Maryall and Kersis ilich moch.
2. Const. dative: In the same manner (as), like, as. Also with *as* (OE. *swá*), as conj. or conj. adv.
c 893 ÆLFRED *Oros.* V. vii. § 2 Þe elpendes hyd wile drincan wætan, ȝelice & spynge deð. 971 *Blickl. Hom.* 17 He him gehet his æriste,..ȝelice swa he ær þa þrowunge dyde. 1393 LANGL. *P. Pl.* C. XX. 330 Wusshen and wylnen Alle manere of men mercy and forȝeuenesse, And louye hem yliche hym-sylf. 1579 SPENSER *Sheph. Cal.* May 4 How falles it then, we no merrier bene, Ylike as others, girt in gawdy greene? c 1634 W. CARTWRIGHT *Ordinary* II. ii. (1651) 25 If I kissen, These thick stark bristles of mine beard will pricken Ylike the skin of Hownd-fish.

†**Yli·ke**, *v. Obs.* [OE. *gelícian* (cf. MDu. *gheliken,* MHG. *gelichen,* Goth. *galeikan*): see Y- 3 c and LIKE *v.*[1]] *trans.* To please.
c 893 ÆLFRED *Oros.* V. i, Ascian þonne Italie hiera aȝne londleode, hu him þa tida ȝelicoden. 1340 *Ayenb.* 109 Leue uader ylyky þe þet þe holy gost ous wille alyȝte þe hert.

†**Ylik(e)ned** [Y- 4], likened. 1340 *Ayenb.* 234 No þing ne is worþi to be ylykned to þe chaste herte. 1393 LANGL. *P. Pl.* C. XVII. 265 Ypocrisie is..ylikned in latyn to a lothliche dounghep. 1422 YONGE tr. *Secr. Secr.* lviii. 228 They bene folis y-lykenyd to assis. **Yli·kewise**, *adv.* = ALIKEWISE: cf. YLIKE *a.* 1460 *Cal. Anc. Rec. Dublin* (1889) 305 And of fysherys ylykewis for the fysch. **Ylin(c)ked** [Y- 4], linked. a 1565 SIR T. CHALLONER in Q. Eliz. *Boeth.* etc. 156/56 What ere thow be that thinges ylynked hast In league so olde. 1590 [see LINKED *ppl. a.*]. **Yliþe** *v.* [Y- 3 c, LITHE *v.*[2]], to hearken, listen. a 1300 *K. Horn* (Harl. MS.) 2 Alle heo ben bliþe þat to my song ylyþe.

†**Ylive**, *v. Obs.* Forms: 1 ȝelifian, 4 yleue; *pa. pple.* 1 ȝelifd, 3–4 ilyued, yliued, ylyued, 4 yleued. [OE. *gelibban, gelifian* (cf. OHG. *gileben*): see Y- 3 c and LIVE *v.*[1]] To live.
c 950 *Lindisf. Gosp.* Luke x. 28 *Hoc fac et uiues,* ðis do þætte ðu ȝelifiȝe. c 1000 in *Narrat. Angl.* (1861) 30 Fulne ende þines lifes þu hæfst gelifd. 1297, etc. Ylived, etc. [see LIVE *v.*[1]]. 1340 *Ayenb.* 93 Þet is guod lyf and yblyssed þet cristene ssolle yleue. *Ibid.* 130 Huanne þe man þengþ.. ine huet trauail he heþ yleued. 1393 LANGL. *P. Pl.* C. XII. 255 A goode fryday..a felon was ysaued That vnlawefulliche hadde ylyued.

Ylk(e, Ylkan, Yll, obs. ff. ILK, ILKA, ILL.

Ylle, obs. form of AISLE, ILL, ISLE.

Yllischman, yllisman, obs. ff. ISLESMAN.
a 1578 LINDESAY (Pitscottie) *Chron. Scot.* (S. T. S.) I. 29 Of grett oppressioun maid be the yllismen [*cf. infra* men of the yllis]. 1610 *Reg. Privy Council Scot.* VIII. 615 What cours salbe takin with these Yllischmen.

Yllond, obs. form of ISLAND.

Ylls, obs. form of ELSE.
1461 in *Jarrow & Wearmouth* (Surtees) 245 Yt he..apper be for ye said holy fader ye pope, or ylls ye wirschipfull doctour Bernardus Romia.

†**Ylog(g)ed** [Y- 4], lodged. 13.. *K. Alis.* 3132 (Laud MS.) Forto he com to þat plas, Þer Alisaunder yloged was. c 1380 *Sir Ferumb.* 4001 Wel y-loged ther on pauylliouns. **Yloȝe, ylow(e**, ME. pa. pple. of LIE *v.*[2] **Yloȝed, ylowed** [LOW *v.*[1]], subjected, humbled. 1340 *Ayenb.* 144 Hi ham byeþ zuo moche yloȝed. 1422 YONGE tr. *Secr. Secr.* xxx. 172 He ne holdyth hym not y-lowet ne vndyrfote of the dyssayses whyche he hathe escapid. **Yloke, ylokked**, ME. pa. pples. of LOCK *v.*[1] 13.. *K. Alis.* 2769 (Laud MS.) Ar þe ȝates weren yloke. 1399 LANGL. *Rich. Redeles* I. 44 With lewte and loue yloke to þi peeris. c 1400 *Trevisa's Higden* (Rolls) VII. App. 525 That the dores be fast y-loke and barred. c 1400 y lokked [see LOCK *v.*[1] 3]. **Yloked** [LOOK *v.*], looked, observed, etc. 1340 *Ayenb.* 7 Þe sabat, þet wes straytliche y-loked ine þe yalde laȝe.

†**Ylome**, *adv. Obs.* Forms: 1 ȝelome, 2–5 ilome, 3 ȝelome, 3–5 ylome. [OE. *gelóme,* f. *ge-* Y-, with an element of obscure origin: see LOOM *sb.*[1]] Frequently, often; phr. *oft and ylome.*
a 1000 *Cædmon's Gen.* 1539 Ȝe on wolcnum þæs oft ȝelome andȝiettacen maȝon sceawiȝan. c 1175 *Lamb. Hom.* 13 Westmes þorð uuele wederas oft and ilome scal for-wurðan. c 1200 *Trin. Coll. Hom.* 31 Heald þin cunde, and þine licames lust kel ilome. a 1250 *Owl & Night.* 595 Þar me mai þe ilomest finde, Þar men worpeþ hore bihinde. 1340–70 *Alisaunder* 521 A Lioun in a launde may lightlych driue Of hertes an bolle herde, as happes ilome. c 1400 *St. Alexius* (Laud 622) 69 Men speken of hym ylome In alle þinges wiþouten strijf.

Ylond, obs. form of ISLAND.

†**Ylong**, obs. var. ALONG *a.*[1] (in sense 'depending *on*'). 1297 R. GLOUC. (Rolls) 2711 Þe king esste at enchantors war on it were ylong. a 1310 in Wright *Lyric P.* xxi. 61 My joie ant eke my blisse on him is al y-long. c 1400 *Pilgr. Sowle* (Caxton 1483) IV. xxx. 78 Yf it soo be that in his hede be founde ony defaute, hit wylle seme.. that hit is y long vppon his counceyl. **Ylope**: see YLEPE. **Ylore(n, ylorn(e**, ME. pa. pple. of LEESE *v.*[1] to lose. 1297 R. GLOUC. (Rolls) 5133 Hii ssolleþ ȝut keuery moche lond þat hii abbeþ y lore. a 1310 in Wright *Lyric P.* xxxix. 110 Al is dayes werk ther were y-loren. 1393 LANGL. *P. Pl.* C. XIII. 182 Oþer sedes..That ben leide on louh erthe ylore as hit were. c 1430 *Hymns Virg.* (1867) 79 At euery hour a poynt is y-loore. **Ylosed, ylost(e**, ME. pa. pple. of LOSE *v.*[1] 13.. *K. Alis.* 4284 (Linc. Inn MS.) Darie haþ ylost his pray. 1387 TREVISA *Higden* (Rolls) IV. 461 Allas! my freendes, þis day I have y-lost. 1407 SCOGAN *Mor. Balade* 36 Tyme y-lost in youthe folily Greveth a wight goostly and bodily. **Ylоused**[1], loosed, loosened. 1387 TREVISA *Higden* (Rolls) VII. 151 Þe skyn y-loused [orig. *soluta cute*]. **Ylоused**[2], freed from lice. 1387 TREVISA *Higden* (Rolls) III. 353 Þey hadde i-lowsed [*MS.* γ ylоused] her cloþes. **Yloved, ylowid**, ME. pa. pple. of LOVE *v.*[1] 13.. *Coer de L.* 1744 Friends, with the best That might be in any lond Y-loved. 1422 YONGE tr. *Secr. Secr.* vii. 137 Wyrchippyd, ylowid, and ydreddyd. **Ylow(e, Ylowed**: see YLOȜE, YLOȜED. **Yluggyd**, lugged, pulled. 1399 LANGL. *Rich. Redeles* III. 336 He was lyghtliche y-lauȝte and y-luggyd of many. **Ylurned, ylyerned**: see YLERNED.

Yly: see YLAY(E. **Ylych(e, ylyk(e**, var. YLIKE. **Ylyft(e**, lifted. 1387 TREVISA *Higden* (Rolls) VI. 9 Þanne he was i-left [*MS.* γ ylyft] an hiȝe. **Ymaad, ymad(e**, obs. pa. pple. of MAKE *v.*[1] **Ymaced**, ME. pa. pple. of MASS *v.*[2]

Ymadge, ymag(e, etc., obs. ff. IMAGE, etc.

†**Ymake, ymaked**, ME. pa. pples. of MAKE *v.*[1] **Y-manered, ymanerit(e** [Y-5, MANNER *sb.*[1]], mannered. 1393 LANGL. *P. Pl.* C. XI. 260 A mayde wel ymanered of good men ysponge. 1422 YONGE tr. *Secr. Secr.* lviii. 226 Tho that haue the flesshe of the brestis lytill and dry bene ille-ymanerite. **Ymanned, -yd** [Y-4], manned. c 1450 *Brut* II. 434 The toune of Orliaunce was..well ymannyd and vitailid. **Ymaried**, married. 1377 LANGL. *P. Pl.* B. II. 39 Now worth þis Mede ymaried al to a mansed schrewe. **Ymariss(ch)ed**, pa. pple. of MARISSE *v.* **Ymarked, -yd**, ME. pa. pple. of MARK *v.* 13.. *Sir Orfeo* 546 (Zielke) A way!..þat him was so hard Grace yȝarked, And so vile deþ ymarked! 1422 YONGE tr. *Secr. Secr.* xl. 199 Euery manes lyfe is y-markyd by kynde, how longe he shal mow doure. **Ymart(i)red, ymartyred**, ME. pa. pple. of MARTYR *v.* 1297 R. GLOUC. (Rolls) 1819 Ymartred [*v. rr.* y martired, y martred] uor vre louerdes loue. 1387 TREVISA *Higden* (Rolls) V. 19 Þat ȝere Eustas..was y-martired. **Ymasked, Ymaymed**, ME. pa. pples. of MASK, MAIM.

Ymbar, obs. form of EMBER[2].
1550 *Acts Privy Council* (1891) III. 68 Holiedaies or fastinge daies as Lent, Ymbar daies, or any such lyke.

Ymbarge, obs. form of EMBARGE *v.*
1585 *MS. Tanner* 78, 52 They shall ymbarge or arrest the Duke of Florrences Gallion.

Ymbassator, -bassutt, obs. var. AMBASSADOR, AMBASSADE.
1484 *Cely Papers* (Camden) 149 To goo as ymbassutt for the stappell to Dewke Phyllypp. 1543 in Lodge *Illustr. Brit. Hist.* (1791) I. 45 The Frenche Ymbassator has not proponyt that matt⁹ as yet.

Ymber, ymbre, obs. forms of EMBER[1].
c 1450 *Mirk's Festial* 254 Our old faders wolden ete þes dayes kakes bakyn yn þe ymbres. 1588 KYD *Househ. Phil.* Wks. (1901) 273 She gins the ymbers vp to rake.

Ymbir-, ymbre(n, etc., obs. ff. EMBER[2].

Ymbolden, obs. f. EMBOLDEN, IMBOLDEN.
1611 W. ADAMS *Let.* in Rundall *Mem. Japon* (Hakl. Soc.) 31, I haue ymboldened my selfe to write these few lines.

Ymbrasour, obs. form of EMBRACER[2].

Ymbroder, obs. form of EMBROIDER.
1562–3 *N. Country Wills* (Surtees 1912) 37 A suyte of blewe velvet ymbrodered. 1638 *Abridgm. Specif. Patents, Furniture* (1869) 1 Ymbrodering or hufling of guilded leather.

†**Ymed(e)led** [Y-4, MEDDLE *v.*], mixed. c 1374 CHAUCER *Troylus* III. 815 So worldly selynesse..y-medled is with many a bitternesse. c 1394 *P. Pl. Crede* 177 Wyde wyndowes..Schynen wiþ schapen scheldes..Wiþ merkes of marchauntes y-medled bytwene.

Ymedicable, Ymedyat, obs. ff. IMMEDICABLE, IMMEDIATE.

†**Ymeint**, pa. pple. (ME. and 7 *arch.*) of MENG *v.*, to mix. **Ymelked** [Y-4], milked. 13.. *St. Kenelm* 234 in *E.E.P.* (1862) 54 As ful heo wolde a morwe beo, þeȝ heo were ymelked an eue.

Ymel(le: see IMELLE.

†**Ymelled, -yd** [MELL *v.*[1]], mixed. 1387 TREVISA *Higden* (Rolls) III. 469 Þe elementes i-medled [*MS.* γ ymelled] to gidres. c 1430 *Two Cookery-bks.* 28 Pouder Gyngere y-mellyd with Sugre. **Ymelt(ed**, ME. pa. pple. of MELT *v.*[1] 1387 TREVISA *Higden* (Rolls) III. 13 A streem of gold of nayles i-melt [*MS.* γ ymelt]. 1432–50 tr. *Higden* (Rolls) IV. 187 Golde y-meltede. **Ymende** [Y- 3 c, *mende* MIND *v.*[1]], to remember. 1340 [see MIND *v.* 2 c]. **Ymene**: see I-MENE. **Ymeneȝed**, pa. pple. of MING *v.* **Ymeng, ymeng(e)d, -id, -yd**, ME. pa. pples. of MENG *v.*, to mingle. 1297 R. GLOUC. (Rolls) 2541 Þo were among cristinemen þis paiens þus imengd [*v. r.* y menged]. *Ibid.* 3437 Þus were in worre & in wo ymeng þe saxons..myd þe brutons. 1340 *Ayenb.* 196 Loke þet ydele blisse..ne by naȝt y-mengd. c 1430 *Two Cookery-bks.* 38 Ȝolkys of Eyroun y-mengyd with þe Ius of haselle leuys. **Yment**, ME. pa. pple. of MEAN *v.*[1] **Ymered**, pa. pple. of MERE *v.*[1], to purify. **Ymesurid**, ME. f. MEASURED; *well y-mesurid*, well-proportioned. 1422 YONGE tr. *Secr. Secr.* lxix. 236 The hede well y-mesurid. **Ymet**[1], ME. pa. pple. of METE *v.*[2], to dream. c 1380 *Sir Ferumb.* 335 Þou hast y met of venysoun; þou mostest drynke a torn. c 1430 [see METE *v.*[2] 2]. **Ymet**[2], pa. pple. (ME. and 6–7 *arch.*) of MEET *v.* 1522 *World & Child* (facs.) C v b, Well ymet syr, well ymet. 1642 H. MORE *Song of Soul* I. III. ii, Last time we were together here ymet.

†**Ymete**, *v. Obs.* [OE. *gemétan*: see Y- 3 c and MEET *v.*] To meet, meet with, encounter.
c 893 ÆLFRED *Oros.* VI. xxxi. 286 Mid þæm þæt hiene ȝemette an mon, þa he for from Actesiphonte þære byriȝ. c 1175 *Lamb. Hom.* 109 Iselie beoð efre þa mildheortan for þi heo imetað þa mildheortnesse. c 1275 *Wom. Samaria* 67 in *O. E. Misc.* 86 To alle þat heo myhte iseon oþer y-mete. 1297 R. GLOUC. (Rolls) 1437 Him þouȝte imete mid is ost ar he at hom were. c 1300 *Names of Hare* 1 in *Rel. Ant.* I. 133 The mon that the hare i-met, Ne shal him nevere be the bet. c 1305 *St. Christopher* 37 in *E.E.P.* (1862) 60 Þe maistre þat was firs ynouȝ com & ymette him anon.

†**Ymete(n**, ME. pa. pple. of METE *v.*[1], to measure. c 1380 *Sir Ferumb.* 2092 Fuliche ne is he noȝt now fram þe vj fet ymete in brede. **Ymeved, ymeoved, ymoved**, ME. pa. pple. of MOVE *v.* 1387 TREVISA *Higden* (Rolls) III. 301 Þe Frensche men..were i-meved [MS. γ ymeoued] by likynge of þat wyn. 1422 YONGE tr. *Secr. Secr.* xxxiv. 189 Yf he thyn answere in dispite haue, neuer for that be thow ymeuet. 1432–50 tr. *Higden* (Rolls) V. 143 To decide the maters y-movede. **Ymeynd, ymeynt** = YMEINT.

Ymgrame, error (in T. Wilson's *Rhet.* p. 37, edd. 1580, etc.) for *yngrame*, INGRAM.

Ymidde, ymydde, var. IMID *Obs.*
c 1400 26 *Pol. Poems* xi. 66 God may say, fern ȝere, folk were fayn To resceyue me ymydde here brest. c 1450 *St. Cuthbert* (Surtees) 7794 He..went forth his enmys y midde.

†**Yminne** *v.* [Y- 3 c, MIN *v.*[2]], to mention. a 1325 *Maundelain* 579 in Horstm. *Altengl. Leg.* (1878) 169 Herdestow euer in spelle yminne Of a woman þat was in sinne? **Yminted**, pseudo-arch. pa. pple. of MINT *v.*[2] 1835 CLARE *Rural Muse* 10 Like gold yminted new. **Ymixt**, mixed. a 1600 MONTGOMERIE *Misc. Poems* xxxv. 38 Hir comelie cheeks of vive colour, Of rid and vhyt ymixt.

Ymnake, error for *ynmake*, INMAKE, inmate.
1536 *Act 28 Hen. VIII.* c. 24 in Bolton *Stat. Irel.* (1621) 175 Euery person and persons..which in the haruest season, receiue..in his or their houses..any person or persons called ymnakes.

Ymne, etc., obs. forms of HYMN, etc.

†**Ymolt(en** = YMELT(ED. 1387 TREVISA *Higden* (Rolls) VIII. 129 Golde i-schave of seyntes schrynes and i-ȝote [*MS.* β y-molt]. a 1425 tr. *Arderne's Treat. Fistula,* etc. 31 Whiche y-molten and þe forseid þingis beyng hote. 1590 [see MELT *v.*[1] 8]. 1748 [see MELT *v.*[1] 11].

†**Ymo·ne**, *sb. Obs.* [OE. *gemána*: see MONE *sb.*[1], MENE, MEAN *a.*[1]]
1. Companionship, fellowship.
c 888 ÆLFRED *Boeth.* v. § 1 Þonne wære he mid his aȝnum cynne..þonne he wæs on ðara ryhtwisena ȝemanan. a 1175 *Cott. Hom.* 245 For ðan þe se helende underfeng þa sinfullan, and ham mid imone hafede. c 1205 LAY. 21308 Þeh þe wulf beon ane buten ælc imane [c 1275 one..imone]. c 1260 *K. Horn* (Camb. MS.) 834 Sire, ischal al one Wiþute more ymone..Bringe hem þre to deþe.
2. Sexual intercourse.
c 950 *Lindisf. Gosp.* Mark xii. 25 *rubric,* Ne ceorl hæfis wifes ȝemana. c 1275 *Wom. Samaria* 32 in *O.E. Misc.* 85 Nabbe ich of wepmonne nones kunnes y-mone. c 1275 *Annunc. Virg.* 10 ibid. 100 Hw myhte hit iwurþe þat ich were myd childe, Monnes imone on me ne may nomon fynde. c 1275 LAY. 25916 Ne mihte þat maide his imone [c 1205 mone] þolie. c 1315 SHOREHAM V. 28 Hy wyþ-oute mannes ymone In body,..To manne hyne broute.
3. A companion. (? A scribal error.)
a 1300 *K. Horn* (Harl. MS.) 530 He nolde gon is one, Athulf wes hys ymone [*Camb. MS.* mone].

†**Ymone**, *a.* and *adv. Obs.* [Alteration of I-MENE *a.* and *adv.* after YMONE *sb.*]
A. *adj.* Common, shared by two or more.
1205 LAY. 978 Ȝif we sceoteð to heora mæðe, þat bið ure imone deað. 1297 R. GLOUC. (Rolls) 6359 He..sede, hail þou be King one. So nis it noȝt, quaþ þe King, uor mi Kinedom is ymone.
B. *adv.* Together.
c 1300 *St. Brandan* 380 Anon so hi seȝe the monekes come, hi gonne to singe ymone. c 1380 *Sir Ferumb.* 99 If þat on of hem ne dar him self wiþ me fiȝte al one Send hem boþe on þyn helf to fiȝte wiþ me ymone.

†**Ymong**, *sb. Obs.* [OE. *gemang,* f. *ge-* Y- 3 a + root *mang-* to mix, found in MENG *v.* Cf. next.] Mixture (OE. only); company, assembly.
a 1000 *Judith* 193 Berað..Scire helmas in sceaðena ȝemong. c 1205 LAY. 10868, & sloh þene king..Imong þissen imonge [c 1275 motinge].

†**Ymo·ng**, *prep.* and *conj. Obs.* Forms: 1 ȝemang, ȝemong, 2–3 imong, 3–7 ymong, 4 imang(e, 4–5 ymang(e, 4–6 ymonge; also 5 *Sc.* ymangis (after *amonges,* AMONGST). [OE. *gemang, gemong,* used beside *ongemang* AMONG *prep.,* which is f. *on* ON *prep.* + *gemang* company, YMONG *sb.*] A. *prep.* Among, in the midst of.
c 893 ÆLFRED *Oros.* IV. iv, & þeah ȝemong þære heringe þyllica bismra on hie selfe asædon. c 1000 *Ags. Gosp.* Matt. x. 16 Nu ic eow sende swa sceap ȝemang [*Lindisf.* inmong, *Hatton* onmang] wulfas. *Ibid.* John xxi. 23 Ðeos spræc com ut ȝemang broþrum þæt se leorning-cniht ne swylt. c 1175 *Lamb. Hom.* 27 Hu derst þu mon þer on-ȝein underfon drihtenes fleis and his blod in þine licome imong þan unwreste sunne and ec imong þan deofle þe wuneð in him? c 1205 LAY. 13116 Þe þer sæt..imong alle þan cnihten. c 1250 *Gen. & Ex.* 3419 If ymong .x. wurð oȝt mis-don. c 1325 *Metr. Hom.* 48 Imang yow wonand he isse. c 1330 R. BRUNNE *Chron. Wace* (Rolls) 369 Y-monge þe pres. a 1400 *Isumbras* 368 In his mantille of skarlet rede Y-mange his golde he did his brede. c 1450 *St. Cuthbert* (Surtees) 5646 Be takyns he aspyed þe these ymang ilkane. 1474 *Acc. Ld. High Treas. Scot.* I. 53 Item to the batis that carijt our the King, the Quene, and the Courte, ymangis thaim,..xl. s. c 1500 *Lancelot* 820 He goith ymong them in his hie curage. 1536 in J. Nicolson & R. Burn *Westmld. & Cumbld.* (1777) 613 *note,* Every on of the other iiii prysts to have vi d, and to have to drynke ymonge theym viii d. 1642 H. MORE *Song of Soul, Paraphr. Interpr. Answ. Apollo* 15, I Phœbus with my lovely locks ymong The midst of you shall sit.
b. *Her* (*þer*)..*ymong*: among or with them; herewith, therewith.
c 1205 LAY. 22702 Her wes fiðelinge and song, her wes harpinge imong. *Ibid.* 24194 Þer wes harepinge and song, þer weoren blissen imong. a 1225 *Leg. Kath.* 1580 Heo wes hire seolf þer imong, as hire þuhte.
B. *conj. Ymong þat*: while.
Cf. OE. *gemang þám,* meanwhile.
c 893 ÆLFRED *Oros.* IV. i. § 9 Ȝemong þæm þe Pirrus wið Romane winnende wæs. c 1205 LAY. 18174 Imong þat he king wæs..Merlin him æt-wende.

†**Ymorþred**, ME. pa. pple. of MURDER *v.* 1297 [see MURDER *v.* 1 a]. 1393 LANGL. *P. Pl.* C. XIII. 243 And so is meny man ymorþred for hus money and goodes. **Ymortified**, of MORTIFY. a 1425 tr. *Arderne's Treat. Fistula* etc. 45 A gret quantite y-mortified. **Ymoselyd**, of MUZZLE *v.*[1]

Y-moth: see Y 3 b.

Ymounted, pseudo-arch. pa. pple. of MOUNT *v.*
1590 MARLOWE *2nd Pt. Tamburl.* IV. iii, Like to an almond tree ymounted high.

Ymovede: see YMEVED.

Ympes(c)he, obs. forms of IMPEACH.

Ymplịȝeply, obs. form of IMPLIEDLY.

Ympn(e, obs. forms of HYMN.

Ympreif, var. IMPREVE *v. Obs.*

Ymree, obs. form of EMERY.

Ymston, var. ME. *ȝymston*: see GEMSTONE.
a 1272 *Luue Ron* 175 in *O. E. Misc.* 98 Among alle oþre ymstone þes beoþ deorre in vyche place. *Ibid.* 178 Mayde al so ich þe tolde þe ymston of þi bur.

Ymulis, obs. Sc. form of EMULOUS.

†**Ymummyd**, ME. pa. pple. of MUM *v.* **Ymund, -munt**: see YMINT. **Ymunde**: see MIND *sb.*[1], *a.* **Y-mundified**, ME. pa. pple. of MUNDIFY *v.* a 1425 tr. *Arderne's Treat. Fistula* etc. 27 Þe wounde ymundified if it be wele tretable.

†**Ymur.** *Obs.* [?a. dial. var. of OF. *umor* HUMOUR *sb.* (cf. Picard *himeur,* Walloon *imeure*).] ? Atmospheric moisture.
c 1400 *Destr. Troy* 897 All cold it became & the course helde, Bothe of ymur & aire after I-wise. *Ibid.* 1575 The Stretis were streght & of a stronge brede, For ymur & aire opon in þe myddis.

†**Ymurdred**, arch. pa. pple. of MURDER *v.* 1581 A. HALL *Iliad* v. 95 Here dy thou shalt ymurdred by my hand. **Ymuwed**, ME. pa. pple. of MEW *v.*[1]

Ymyd(de, Ymyddes, -is, -ys, Ymydward, obs. var. AMID (cf. YMIDDE), AMIDST, AMIDWARD.
c 1400 *Destr. Troy* 8769 The body..Was..set in a seate vnder, Ymydward the mayne towmbe.

†**Ymylded**, ME. pa. pple. of MILD *v.* **Ymynced, y-mynsyd**, ME. pa. pple. of MINCE *v.* c 1430 *Two Cookery-bks.* 6 Oynons y-mynced. *Ibid.* 13 Oynonys y-mynsyd. **Ymyned**, ME. pa. pple. of MINE *v.* **Ymynt(e**: see YMINT. 1297 R. GLOUC. (Rolls) 4920+31 Þe nyȝt þet he adde imund [*MS.* δ ymynte] vort abbe ywend a-morwe. c 1380 *Sir Ferumb.* 576 Hadd y þat stronge strok y-take þou haddest to me ymynt. **Ymynused**, pa. pple. of MINISH *v.* a 1400 *New Test.* (Paues) Col. i. 21 Whan ȝe weren sumtyme y-alyened & y-mynused in wyt in efel werkes.

Yn, obs. f. IN *prep.* and *adv.*, INN *sb.*

Ynail(l)ed, Ynamyd, ME. pa. pples. of NAIL *v.*, NAME *v.*[1] **Ynca**, obs. f. INCA. **Ynce**, obs. Sc. form of HENCE *adv.* **Ynch(e**, obs. ff. INCH. **Yncke, Ync(k)le, Ynclynge, Yncorne**, obs. ff. INK, INKLE, INKLING, INK-HORN. **Ynd(e**: see END *sb.*, HIND *sb.*[1], IND, INDE. **Yndeen, -ien, Yndewes**, obs. ff. INDIAN, INDIES. **Yndling**, var. INDLING, EYNDLING *Sc. Obs.*, jealous. **Yndoys**, var. *Yndes* (see IND 2). **Yndrest**, var. INNEREST *Obs.*, innermost. **Yne**, obs. pl. of EYE *sb.*[1], obs. f. IN *prep.*

†**Ynem(p)ned**, pa. pple. of NEMN *v.*, to name. 1297 R. GLOUC. (Rolls) App. H. 10 After þe quene y nempned heo was. 1340 *Ayenb.* 66 Alle þise zennes þet we habbeþ hyer ynemned. 1417 *E. E. Wills* (1882) 27 All my pourest tenauntes..excepte ham þat I haue ynemned in þis bok.

†**Ynence, -ens, -entes**, *prep. Obs.* [var. ff. *enence, anentes* ANENT.] Towards; in relation to.
a 1340 HAMPOLE *Psalter* ix. 2 Ynence my selfe i. sall be glad in þe. *Ibid.* x. 8 Euennes is sen in his knawynge, ynentes bath þe partis of goed and ill. c 1340 — *Prose Treat.* 8 Many are þat neuer haue halde þe ordyre of lufe ynesche [*read* ynence] þaire frendys sybbe or ffremede. a 1400 *Relig. Pieces fr. Thornton MS.* (1914) 26 Thurghe þis commandement es man ordaynede ynence God þe Fadire. c 1400 MAUNDEV. (Roxb.) x. 40 Ynentes þe kirk of þe Sepulchre es þe citee maste wayke. c 1400 tr. *Secr. Secr., Gov. Lordsh.* 106 Conferme my louynge in þe, ynens þis Iew.

Yneuch(t, ynew(cht: see ENOUGH, ENOW.

Ynewe, obs. var. ANEW *adv.*
c 1380 *Sir Ferumb.* 626, & þo by-gan ynewe fiȝt be-twene þis knyȝtes tweye.

†**Ynewed** [Y- 4, NEW *v.*], renewed. 1340 *Ayenb.* 107 Ynewed and eft ycristned ine þe bloode of Iesu crist.

Yngde, obs. f. IND. **Ynge**, obs. f. HINGE, ING, YOUNG. **Ynȝoin, ynion**, obs. ff. ONION.

Yngles, -is(se, etc., obs. ff. ENGLISH, INGLIS.

Yngynore, obs. form of ENGINEER.

Ynke, Ynkell, obs. forms of INK, INKLE.

Ynkirly, -urly, var. ENKERLY *adv. Obs.*

Ynkleth: see INKLETH.

Ynmast, -most, obs. forms of INMOST.

Ynn(e, Ynner: see IN, INN, INNE, INNER.

Ynnion, obs. form of ONION.
c 1580 in *Engl. Hist. Rev.* (1914) July 529 Greate ynnions that be xij or xiiij ynches abowte.

Ynogh(e, ynoh(e, etc.: see ENOUGH, ENOW.

†**Ynombred**, ME. pa. pple. of NUMBER *v.* 1470–85 MALORY *Arthur* x. 178 His armye..with the garneson of godard and sarasyns of Southland ynombred lx M of good men of armes. **Ynome(n, ynume**, ME. pa. pple. of NIM *v.*, to take. c 1275 in *O. E. Misc.* 43/206 So me doþ to þeoue þat schal beon ynume. 1297 R. GLOUC. (Rolls) 2421 Vor to be maistres of þis folc we beþ ychose & ynome. 13.. *K. Alis.* 4668 (Laud MS.), Þe boweles weren ynomen oute. c 1380 *Sir Ferumb.* 1105 Erld Olyuer & his felawes þat Sarazyns habbeþ ynome. c 1470 HENRY *Wallace* IX. 53 Leyt salys fall, and has thar cours ynom.

Ynon, obs. form of ONION.

†**Ynorisched, -issed, Ynorsched**, ME. pa. pples. of NOURISH, NORSH. 1297 R. GLOUC. (Rolls) 1450 He spac engliss vor he was at rome inorssed [*MS. B.* ynorisched] biuore. 1340 *Ayenb.* 205 Þe children þet weren y-norissed mid greate metes. 1387 TREVISA *Higden* (Rolls) VIII. 35 While he was a child y-norsched in þe kynges court of Fraunce. c 1450 *Mirk's Festial* 9, I..haue ben cheresly ynorysched.

Ynot = *y not*, I do not know: see NOT *v.*[2]
1297 R. GLOUC. (Rolls) 5628 Þere he liþ ȝut to þis day ac ynot to wuche dome þe toun suþþe of pokel chirche fram glastingbury came. 13.. in Ritson *Anc. Songs* (1877) 57 Ynot non so freoh flour, Ase ledies that beth bryght in bour.

Ynou(gh, ynow(gh, etc.: see ENOUGH, ENOW.

Ynoumbred, ME. pa. pple. of NUMBER *v.*

Ynpossybull, Ynpugne, obs. ff. IMPOSSIBLE, IMPUGN. **Yn sted, stude, styd**, obs. ff. INSTEAD.

Ynsyte, obs. form of INCITE.

†**Ynued** [Y- 4, NOY *v.*], harmed. 1422 YONGE tr. *Secr. Secr.* xxx. 170 By this vertu Is the herte of a man I-Stabelid, in so myche that for no chaunce hit is not y-nued.

Ynug(h, Ynume(n: see ENOUGH, YNOME(N.

Ynuste = *y nuste*, I knew not: see NIST.

Yo (yōᵘ), *int.* (*sb.*) Forms: 5 ȝo, io, ȝaw, 9 yo, yeo(h. An exclamation of incitement, warning, etc. (also repeated). In nautical use = YOHO. Occas. as sb. and in vbl. sb. *yo-yoing.*
c 1420 *Avow. Arth.* vii. [*To hounds*], Ȝaw thar suche him no mare. c 1450 *Mankind* 450 in *Macro Plays* 17 Myscheff. How, New-gyse, Now-a-days! herke or I goo! When owur hedis wer to-gethere, I spake of 'si dedero'. *New-gyse.* Ȝo! go þi wey! we xall gaþer mony on-to. c 1460 *Towneley Myst.* II. 25 Io furth, greyn-horne! and war oute, gryme! 1772 *Monthly Rev.* XLII. 191/1 The scene was quite chang'd, 'twas no more yo, yo-ho. 1806 PINCKARD *Tour W. Indies* III. 343 A string of negroes singing out in the sailors' cry—yeoh-yeoh, yeoh-yeoh, and hauling at a long rope. 1837 DICKENS *Pickw.* ix, He was roused by a loud shouting of the post-boy on the leader. 'Yo—yo—yo—yo—yoe,' went the first boy. 'Yo—yo—yo—yoe!' went the second...And amidst the yo-yoing..the chaise stopped. 1839 HOOD *Storm at Hastings* xiii, Sundry boatmen, that with quick yeo's, Lest it should *blow,*—were pulling up the *Rose.* 1859 DICKENS *T. Two Cities* I. ii, Yo there! Stand! I shall fire!

Yo, obs. f. YOU. **Yoak(e**: see OAK, YOKE, YOLK.

Yoaks, yoax (yōᵘks), *int. Obs.* exc. *dial.* (**yooks**). A hunting cry; also as vb. (Cf. YOICKS.)
1778 GARRICK in *Monthly Rev.* (1779) LX. 59 'Squire Western, reeling, with October mellow, Tall, yo!—Boys!—Yoax—Critics! hunt the fellow! 1828 *Sporting Mag.* (N. S.) XXII. 129 He yoaksed in a whisper, he cheered in a whisper. 1905 *Eng. Dial. Dict., Yocks,* a call of encouragement to a dog hunting rabbits, &c. n. Yks.

Yoalk, obs. form of YOLK.

Yoberte, obs. form of JEOPARDY.
1539 *St. Pap. Hen. VIII* III. 161 Yn gret yoberte of lyff.

Yobliged, ME. pa. pple. of OBLIGE *v.*

Yochomdale, yockynggale, var. YOKINDALE.

Yock, yocke, obs. forms of YOKE.

Yod (yǫd, yōᵘd). [See JOD.] Name of the tenth (the smallest) letter of the Hebrew alphabet.
1735 LYONS *Scholars Instr.* (1757) 25 Those Verbs which have Vau Consonant, or Yod Consonant for the second Radical. 1769 PARKHURST *Grk. Eng. Lexicon N. T.* (1794) 385/2 An Iota, Jod, or Yod. 1879 FARRAR *St. Paul* I. II. viii. 143 They remembered..what He had said about the permanence of every yod and horn of a letter in the Law.

†**Yode, yede**, *v. Obs.* Past tense of GO *v.* (= went, went away, proceeded, took his course). [12th cent. ME. (north-east midland) *ȝeode, ȝede* (*iede*), prob. altered form of OE., ME. *eode* (*ede, ode*), pa. t. of GO *v.*, by prothesis of *ȝ*-glide induced by the hiatus in such collocations as *he eode, we eoden.* Later, when the form *ȝode,* arising from the development of *eo* as a rising diphthong, became established, it would help to extend the currency of the form *ȝede* by analogical influence upon *ede,* the normal representative of *éode* with a falling diphthong. A parallel development is furnished by ME. *York, Yerk*:—OE. *Eoforwīc* (see YORK). Moreover, the OE. compound form *geéode,* pa. t. of *gegán* IGO *v.*, examples of which are here given with the meaning of the simple *éode,* may have survived in localities where the prefix *ȝe-* = Y- persisted in ME., and so have furthered the spread of *ȝede* and *ȝode.*
Beowulf 1967 Hi sið druȝon, elne ȝeeodon. *Ibid.* 2676 Ac se maȝa ȝeonga under his mæȝes scyld elne ȝeeode. c 725 *Corpus Gloss.* (Hessels) A 217 *Adgrediuntur,* ȝeeodun [*Epinal* 76 ȝihiodun]. c 950 *Lindisf. Gosp.* Matt. xx. 5 *Exiit,* ȝe-eode. *Ibid.* John x. 23 *Ambulabat,* ȝe-eade.]
Illustration of Forms.
α. 2–4 ȝeode (4 ȝiode).
a 1122 *O. E. Chron.* (Laud MS.) an. 1070 Hi..ȝeodon into þe mynstre. c 1260 *K. Horn* (Camb. MS.) 401 He ȝeode in wel riȝte To Rymenhild þe briȝte. c 1275 LAY. 25331–2 Ofte hii ȝeode [c 1205 eoden] to reade, ofte hii ȝeode to roune. c 1305 *Judas* 31 in *E. E. P.* (1862) 108 Þe quene ȝeode adai and pleide bi þe stronde. 13.. *Cursor M.* 19920 (Edin.) Quen þai of Petir undirstode, His coming, sone gain him þai ȝiode. 1387 TREVISA *Higden* (Rolls) IV. 397 A lampe..in þat hevene..þat ȝede [*MS.* γ ȝeode] adoun westward as it were þe sonne. a 1400 *Pistill of Susan* 228 To the ȝate ȝaply þei ȝeoden [*v.rr.* ȝedyn, ȝede] wel ȝare. c 1400 *R. Gloucester's Chron.* (Rolls) 8409 (MS. α) Þoru wham þe heþene men ȝeoden al to schonde.
β. 2 ȝæde, iede, iæde, 2–5 ȝede, 3–4 ȝiede, 4 ȝide, ȝed, yhed, *Sc.* ȝheid, 4–5 ȝeide, ȝhede, ȝeede, 4–6 yeede, (also 9 *Sc.*) yede, 5 ȝeyde, ȝhed, *Sc.* ȝheide, 5–6 *Sc.* ȝeid, yeid, 5–6 (8 *Sc.*) yeed, 6 yheid, yead(e, 8 yee'd.
a 1122 *O. E. Chron.* (Laud MS.) an. 1070 Syððon ȝeden heom to scipe, ferden heom to Eliȝ. 1154 *Ibid.* an. 1137 Sume ieden on ælmes þe waren sum wile rice men. *Ibid.*, Me dide cnotted strenges abuton here hæued & uurythen to ðet it ȝæde to þe hærnes. *Ibid.* 1140 Scæ fleh & iæde on fote to Walingford. c 1200 *Vices & Virtues* 69 Ðies ȝunge mann ȝiede awei sari. 1297 R. GLOUC. (Rolls) 1766 Ac basian & al is folc ȝede anon to gronde. a 1300 *Cursor M.* 1086 Quen caym had don þat dreri dide, Til his fader hamward he ȝeide. *Ibid.* 21093 He prechid þare wiþ fote he ȝide. c 1330 R. BRUNNE *Chron. Wace* (Rolls) 14308 Þyse were þe lordes of renoun Þat on Moddredes side ȝed doun. 1340 HAMPOLE *Pr. Consc.* 4851 Þat day, þat Loth yhed out of Sodome. 1340–70 *Alisaunder* 304 Hur ȝates ȝeede þei too & youlden hem soone. 1375 BARBOUR *Bruce* I. 90 Bot othir wayis all ȝheid the gle. *Ibid.* 333 And till swylk thowlesnes he ȝeid, As the courss askis off ȝowtheid. 1423 *Acts Privy Council* III. 97 He yeed in ambassiate to..ye Kyng of Polayn. c 1470 *Gol. & Gaw.* 228 The day yeid doun. 1487 *Cely Papers* (Camden) 158, I had xx[li] more wheyr of ȝeyde xij[li] and mor for carryayge of wholl. 1508 DUNBAR *Kynd Kittok* 33 Becaus the wif ȝeid wrang. 1566 DRANT *Horace, Sat.* v. C vij, When you..yeade to Louaine there to heare the Latine Romishe worde. 1575 *Gammer Gurton* IV. ii, My Gammer then she yeede, see now hir neele againe to bring. 1583 *Leg. Bp. St. Androis* 327 With this the word yead through the toun. a 1600 MONTGOMERIE *Devot. Poems* iii. 29 That leddir..Quhairby the angels come and ȝeid From hevin to earth. 1768 ROSS *Helenore* I. 7 They Yeed hand in hand together. 1808 JAMIESON, *Yede* is still used in Ang[us] although almost obsolete.
β². 3–4 ȝet.
c 1275 LAY. 2647 Þis wes þe ereste king þet ȝet vt to reuing. c 1375 *Sc. Leg. Saints* xxix. (*Placidas*) 297 Þane wes þe feynd wondir wa, Þat placydas lewit hym sa & ȝet on crist.
γ. 3–5 ȝod, 4–5 yhode, (also 6 *Sc.*) ȝode, (also 7–8 *dial.*) yod, (4 ȝood, ȝodd, yoede, 5 ȝ-, yoode, 6 yood, *Sc.* ȝoid, 7 youd), 4–6 (6–9 *arch.*) yode.
c 1250 *Gen. & Ex.* 2030 Sone ȝhe mai hire louerd sen, Ȝhe ȝod him bitterlike a-ȝen. a 1300 *Cursor M.* 1806 He wist noght wyder-ward he ȝodd. *Ibid.* 6264 Þe see on aiþer side þam stod Als walles tua, quils þai for yod. 13.. *Ibid.* 24360 (Gött.) Þe nailes þat him fest on rode Thoru in hend and fete þai ȝode. 13.. *Gaw. & Gr. Knt.* 1146 A hundreth of hunteres..To trystors vewters ȝod. c 1400 *Melayne* 449 The fire ȝode owtt þat come þer nee. c 1400 [see GO *v.* B. 21 b]. c 1440 *York Myst.* ix. 151 My frendis þat I fra yoode Are ouere flowen with floode. c 1450 *St. Cuthbert* (Surtees) 643 Him thoght oute of þe shipp he yhode. 1513 DOUGLAS *Æneis* II. xii. 21 Throw howsis and the citie quhar I ȝoid. 1524 in Ellis *Orig. Lett.* Ser. I. I. 244 Saing if he yode awaye she must neds do for her self. a 1533 LD. BERNERS *Huon* clxiii. 636 He issued out of the gate and yode towardes the tentes of his enemyes. 1590 SPENSER *F. Q.* I. x. 53 Such one, as that same mighty man of God, That bloudred billowes..disparted with his rod, Till that his army dryfoot through them yod. 1596 *Ibid.* IV. viii. 34 So forth they yode, and forward softly paced. 1600 FAIRFAX *Tasso* XX. xcii, An armed stead fast by the Soldan yood. 1615 BRATHWAIT *Strappado* (1878) 130 A lang youd I. a 1650 *Glasgerion* 46 in Furniv. & Hales *Percy Folio* I. 250 He did not kisse that Lady gay when he came nor when he youd. 1748 THOMSON *Cast. Indol.* II. xxxv, And much they moraliz'd as thus yfere they yode. 1808 SCOTT *Marm.* III. xxxi, In other pace than forth he yode, Returned Lord Marmion.
γ². 4 ȝot, yot.
13.. *E. E. Allit. P.* A. 10, I leste hyr in on erbere, Þurȝ gresse to grounde hit fro me yot. c 1380 *Sir Ferumb.* 3690 A rideþ to Richard wyþ a spere,..& on þe scheld hym smot; þorȝ-out ys scheld..& iakke & ioupoun, þorȝ-out al it ȝot.
δ. 4 ȝud, 4–5 yude, (yhude, ȝhude, 5 ȝhuyde), 4–6 ȝude, 7 *dial.* yud, 7–8 *dial.* yewd.
1375 BARBOUR *Bruce* XII. 560 Quhill throu the byrneis brist the blud, That till the erd doune stremand ȝud [*MS. Edin.* ȝhude]. 1387 TREVISA *Higden* (Rolls) V. 423 Þe kyng meked hym, and ȝeede [*MS.* γ ȝude] barfoot. c 1425 WYNTOUN *Cron.* II. v. 330 His breþir..Slew a kyde and in þe blude Wet þe gowne þat he in ȝhuyde. ? a 1550 *Freiris of Berwik* 563 in *Dunbar's Poems* 303 And throw the myre full smertly than he ȝude. 1674 RAY *N. C. Words* 55 *Yewd* or *Yod*: Went, *Yewing*: Going.
ε. 5 yad.
1424 in Picton *L'pool Munic. Rec.* (1883) I. 23 The Sheriffs ..yadden up to the West Derby fen. c 1435 *Torr. Portugal* 1192 His squiers habite he had, Whan he to the deyse yad.

†**Yode**, *v. Obs. rare.* [Pseudo-archaic use of prec. as infin. or pres.; cf. YEDE *v.*] *intr.* To go.
1587 M. GROVE *Pelops & Hippod.* (1878) 42 Then foorth one yodeth fast And sayes [etc.].

Yode, var. YAUD, mare.

Yodel (yōᵘ·dĕl), *sb.* Also **jodel, yodle,** *erron.* **jödel.** [f. next.] A melody or musical phrase inarticulately sung with interchange of the ordinary and falsetto voice, as by Swiss and Tyrolese mountaineers. Also *transf.* any cry resembling this.
1849 THACKERAY *Pendennis* lxv, Fanny's little sisters were taught a particular cry or *jödel,* which they innocently whooped in the court. 1864 *Cornh. Mag.* Aug. 230, I heard singing and wild jodels about this dissipated city of Innsbrück. 1883 *Harper's Mag.* July 907/2 As he joined his own vibrant baritone to the Tyrolese song-music, his yodel drowned all other sounds. 1894 DU MAURIER *Trilby* I. 22 The British milkman's yodel, 'Milk below!'
Comb. 1874 MISS R. H. BUSK *Vall. Tirol* Pref. p. vi, Just as the shriek of the whistle overpowers the Jödel-call.

Yodel (yōᵘ·dĕl), *v.* Also **youdle, yoddle, yodle, jodel,** *erron.* **jödel.** [ad. G. *jodeln* (Bavarian dial. *jodln, jolen*), properly, to utter the syllable *jo.*] *intr.* To sing or warble with interchange of the ordinary and falsetto voice, in the manner of Swiss and Tyrolese mountaineers. Also *transf.*
1838 LADY GRANVILLE *Lett.* (1894) II. 266 Listening to three little peasant girls, all youdling to perfection in parts. 1841 in J. F. Campbell *Frost & Fire* (1865) I. 156 We went yoddling and shouting to rouse the echoes. 1850 *The Initials* v, A loud gay voice was heard in the distance jodling. 1876 BESANT & RICE *Gold. Butterfly* xxv, The shepherds jodel in the valleys. 1878 H. S. WILSON *Alpine Ascents* i. 21 Our guides shout and jödel. 1890 LOWELL *Let. to Miss E. G. Norton* 7 Sept., The screech-owl..every night yodels mournfully about the house like a banshee.
b. *trans.* with the melody as object.
1839 LONGF. *Hyperion* III. iii, A single voice..was heard yodling forth a ballad. 1879 BARING-GOULD *Germany* xi. II. 52 From far away comes the refrain jödeled back to her.

Hence **Yodel(l)ing** (yoddling, jodel(l)ing) *vbl. sb.*; also **Yodel(l)er** (yodler, jodler), **Yodelist**, one who yodels.
1830 SCOTT *Jrnl.* 4 June, Anne wants me to go to hear the Tyrolese Minstrels, but..I cannot but think their yodelling..is a variation..upon the tones of a jackass. 1841 in J. F. Campbell *Frost & Fire* (1865) I. 155 We stepped out for our stone house, from which came yoddling and screaming and all sorts of noises. 1885 MRS. C. PRAED *Head Stat.* xxviii, Clephane and Wyatt executed..an effective jodelling chorus. 1885 *Detroit Free Press* 7 Nov. (Cassell), The yodelist began to play once more. 1910 *Blackw. Mag.* Oct. 469/2 A Swiss yodeler.

Yoe, obs. form of JOY. **Yoede**: see YODE.

Yoelle, obs. form of JEWEL.
1536 in Archbold *Somerset. Relig. Houses* (1892) 62 The crosses, chalysshes and other yoelles of the churches.

Yoeman, obs. form of YEOMAN.

Yoen, yoene, obs. forms of YON.

Yof, graphic var. *þof*, obs. f. THOUGH: see Y (3).

Yof, variant of YOUF.

Yoff, intended to imitate the grunt of a pig.
c 1630 *Song* ii. in De Foe *Mem. Cavalier* (1840) Notes 323 Yoffing, crying, youlling, yelling, Lyk ane citie swyne summonds out with an horne.

†**Y-offred** (earlier *ioffred,* OE. *ȝeoffrod*), offered, sacrificed. 1340–70 *Alex. & Dind.* 738 Of swiche bestus þat ben of burnus yofreed. 1387 TREVISA *Higden* (Rolls) IV. 427 Þe bisshop acountede þis nombre by þe nombre of oystes þat were y-offred. 1432–50 tr. *Higden* (Rolls) V. 169 The bowelles of a beste y-offrede.

‖**Yoga** (yōᵘ·gă). [Hind., Skr. *yoga* lit. union: see YOKE *sb.*] In Hindu religious philosophy, Union with the Supreme Spirit; a system of ascetic practice, abstract meditation, and mental concentration, used as a method of attaining this. Also *attrib.*
1820 W. WARD *View Hindoos* (ed. 3) IV. 125 Clear knowledge of spirit arises from yogŭ, or abstraction of mind. 1832 H. H. WILSON in *Asiatic Researches* XVII. 184 The Yoga, or Pátanjala school of philosophy. 1843 *Penny Cycl.* XXVII. 657/2 *Yoga*..chiefly consists in a continual meditation on the sacred monosyllable *Om*.., profound contemplation of the divine excellence, and various acts of self-denial. ..The *Yoga* is often practised for the purpose of obtaining the eight magical properties of power...In the Purân'as and other works, Yoga very often means magic. 1881 *Contemp. Rev.* Oct. 583 The *yoga* faculty, or the power of spiritual communion and absorption, is specially claimed for the Hindu race. 1886 'F. ANSTEY' *Fallen Idol* viii, A yogi performing his *japa* in the yoga posture.

Yogee: see YOGI.

Yogh (yoγ). Also **ȝok, ȝoch**, etc. (see quots.). [See *Mod. Lang. Review* VI. (1911) 441 seqq., VII. (1912) 520–1.] The name of the ME. letter ȝ: see G, Y.
The use of L. *jugum* 'yoke' to designate this letter (see quot. a 1440) points to the prevalence of the English form *ȝok.*
c 1300 *MS. McClean* 123, lf. 114 b in *Mod. Lang. Rev.* (1911) VI. 442 ·Yoȝ·ȝ·[*examples*] ȝef·ȝus·ȝer·ȝender·draȝ·sclaȝ·arȝ·marȝ. a 1400 *Maundeville's Travels* (Fr. text, MS. Brit. Mus. Harl. 4383, lf. 31) ibid. 444 Nous auons en nostre parleure en Engleterre deux lettres pluis qils nount en lour a b c, cest assauoir þ et ȝ, qi sont appelez thorn et yogh [*v.rr.* ȝogh, iogh, ȝok]. 1410–20 *Ibid.* (Eng. text, MS. Cott. Tit. C. xvi, lf. 60 b) ibid. 445 Þ & ȝ, the whiche ben clept þorn and ȝogh [*v. rr.* ȝoch, ȝoche, ȝoghe, ȝoub, yowh, yough, þouȝ, ȝowȝe, ȝow, ȝoux, youx]. 14.. *MS. Reg.* 17, *B.* 1, lf. 14 b, ibid. 442 Þe carect yogh, þat is to seie ȝ is figurid lijk a ȝed. [a 1440 THOMAS ELMHAM *Liber Metr. de Hen. V* ii. in *Mem. Henry V* (Rolls) 195 Praeposita litera Anglica, scilicet ȝ quae jugum sonat. c 1465: see Y 1].

Yogh, obs. form of YAW *sb.*[1]

Yoghourt, yoghurd, var. YOGURT.

‖**Yogi** (yōᵘ·gi). Forms: 7 ioggue, iogue, 7, 9 jogue, 8 jougie, joguey, 9 yoguee, yogue, yogee, yogi; yogin. [Hind. *yogī* (Skr. *yogi-n*), f. *yoga*: see YOGA.] An Indian devotee or ascetic who practises the system of YOGA, q.v.
1619 PURCHAS *Microcosmus* lvii. 543 The Indian Gymnosophists..offering violence to Nature in nakednesse, and strict absurd Niceties, wherein they are followed to this day by the Bramenes, Ioggues, and others. 1625 — *Pilgrims* I. II. 31 An Indian Iogue, a begging Frier of that Bramene Religion. 1727 A. HAMILTON *New Acc. E. Ind.* I. 152 There is another Sort called *Jougies,* who..go naked, except a Bit of Cloth about their Loyns. 1734 *Cerem. & Relig. Customs Nat.* III. 480 The *Joguis,* who affect to devote themselves to the most dreadful Torments, from a Principle of Pride and Fanaticism. 1810 SOUTHEY *Kehama* XIII. xvi, A band Of Yoguees, as they roam'd the land Seeking a spouse for Jaga-Naut their God. 1813 J. FORBES *Oriental Mem.* III. 14 A Yogee, who lives under the tree on the skin of a tiger or leopard, which they are very fond of. 1824 HEBER *Narr. Journ.* (1828) I. 133 A 'Yogi' (a religious mendicant). 1841 *Penny Cycl.* XX. 402/1 Hence has arisen the saying, that the 'yogin' is exalted above the Vedas. 1854 MILMAN *Lat. Christ.* VIII. iv. III. 335 He attained a height of abstraction from earthly things which might have been envied by an Indian Yogue. 1871 TYLOR *Prim. Cult.* II. xviii. 375 No wonder that..the Hindu yogi should bring on by fasting a state in which he can with bodily eyes behold the gods.
So **Yo·gism, Yo·geeism**, the system of yoga or of the yogis; **Yo·gist**, a yogi.
1881 SINNETT *Occ. World* 27 The ethereal yogeeism which is called *Ragi yog.* 1881 *N. & Q.* 6th Ser. III. 291 The Indian yogist (or fakeer) Haridas. 1893 A. LANG in *Daily News* 20 Apr. 5/1 He reckons about 90,000 believers in Yogism.

‖**Yogurt** (yōᵘ·gŭət). Forms: 7 yoghurd, yogourt, 9 yahourt, yaghourt, yogurd, yo-

Yo-hah, *yohay*, *int.* (*sb.*) An exclamation of pleasure among N. American Indians.

Yo-heave-ho (yōʹhēv-hōʹ), *int.* (*sb.*) Also **-oh, -o**; **yo-heave-o, -yeo.** [See Yo *int.* and Heave *sb.*] An exclamation of sailors when hauling at a rope or a capstan, heaving an anchor up, etc. Hence **Yo-heave-hoing** *vbl. sb.*

Yohimbenine, Yohimbine, *Chem.* Also **-in.** [See *sb.* and -ine[2].] Names of two colourless alkaloids obtained from the bark and leaves of the *yohimbé*, a West African rubiaceous tree. Also **Yohimbic acid.**

Yoho (yōʹhōʹ), *int.* Also as two words, or with hyphen; also **Yo hoho, -ho-ho, -hoy, yo(o)y-ho.** An exclamation used to call attention: orig. in nautical use, hence generally; also sometimes used like Yo-Heave-Ho, q.v.

Yoi, *int.* ? Obs. Also *yool.* A huntsman's cry to encourage the hounds. Cf. Voicks.

Yoicks (yoiks), *int.* Also **8-9 yoias, 9 yotx.** [? Cf. Voicks, Yo, and Hoicks.]

Yojan (yōʹjan), **yojana** (yōʹjāna). Also **-an, -una.** *E. Indian.* [Hindi *yōjan*, Skr. *yōjana*.] A measure of distance (lit. that travelled at one time without unyoking), t. *yoke* t. see Yoked *sb.*

Yoke (yōk), *sb.* **1.** Forms: 1 xeo, 2OE, ioo, iuo, 2-3 ioo, 3 iok, (*Orm.*) ʒooc, 3-5 (6 Sc.) ʒok, 4 ʒook, 4-5 (6 Sc.) ʒoke, (6-7 *dial.*) ʒook, 5 yok, 5 yoke, youk; k, 6-7 yooke, 6 youck, youwg, yolke, (*pl.* yoixe?), Sc. 3olk (3oilt), 6-7 yoake, (7 yolke, oak), 6-8 yoak, (8 yolk), *pl.* 9 yokes.

Yoke, *sb.*

I. 1. A contrivance, used from ancient times, by which two animals, esp. oxen, are coupled together for drawing a plough or vehicle...

II. 4. wooden frame or collar fitted on the neck of a hog or other animal, to prevent it from breaking...

III. 5. *Sc.* **a.** A pair, couple. **b.** The shafts of a cart...

YOKE. YOKE.

Yoke (yōk), *v.* Forms: see *sb.*; also 1 *pa. pple.* ʒetūkod, 3 *pa. t.* ʒeokede, ʒeocede, 4 iok, *pa. pple.* ʒoked, 7 yoakt, (*pa. pple.* ʒeokyd, 7 yokte). [OE. *ʒeocian, pa. pple.* ʒeūkod.]

1. *trans.* To put a yoke on (a pair of draught-animals, etc.); to couple with a yoke.

2. To attach to draught-animal(s) to a plough or vehicle (orig. with a yoke)...

Yokeable *a. (for ref.)* To join, associate oneself, or become connected or linked. Now *rare.*

Yoke-fellow (yōʹkʹfelo), [f. Yoke *sb.* + Fellow *sb.*], *transl. of* Gr. σύζυγος.

Yoker (yōʹkər). *rare.* [f. Yoke *v.* + -er[1].] One who yokes.

Yokewise (yōʹkʹwaiz), *adv.* *rare*-[1]. [f. Yoke *sb.* + -wise.] In the manner of a yoke.

†**Yokinable**, *Obs.* Also **yoorhomable, youk-yndall, yoykyngagle; yoghendalle;** *Sc.* **yopondali, ʒʒogo; jowp, yopindaili, -dale, -dall, yopindaal.** [ad. early L.L. *jachimdaler-*, ʒodndalar, var. of *joachimsdaler* Joachimsdaler, -dale, and 16th c. F. *joachimsdale* or *-thaler,* f. Joachimsthal a mining town in Bohemia, the mod. name of which is Jachymov.]

Yoking (yōʹking), *vbl. sb.* [f. as prec. + -ing[1].] That yokes, in various senses : see the verb.

Yoking *ppl. a.* [f. as prec. + -ing[2].]

Yoke-mating, marriage.

Yoking, *Sc. and north. dial.* Also **youking, yowdring, yoldrin, yaldrin, -an,** yeld(e)rin, yieldrin. [Variant of Yowling-ring.]

Yolde, yold, *ppl. a. Obs. exc. Sc.* Forms: see Yield *v.*, q.v. **1.** [pa. pple. of Yield *v.*]

Yolk, yelk, *sb.* Forms: a 1 ʒeoleca, ʒeolca, ʒioleca, 3 ʒeolke, 4 yholk(e; a 4-5 yelke, 5 yolk, 7 yoalk, 6 yelk.

Yolk (yōk), *sb.*[2] Also 6 yolky, 9 yolky. [OE. *eow, eowk.*] Resembling or consisting of egg yolk.

Yolk-stone, a local name for a kind of conglomerate.

Yolky (yōʹki), *a.* Also 6 **yelky, 9 yolky.** [f. Yolk *sb.*[1] + -y[1].] Resembling or consisting of (egg) yolk; of or pertaining to yolk; full of or abounding in yolk.

Yoll (yōl), *v. Obs. exc. dial.* Also **6 yoll, 9 yaul, 4 yolling.** [Imitative. Cf. N.Fris. *jolli,* and similar forms.] *intr.* To yell; to howl. Hence **Yolling** *vbl. sb.*

(Top row, columns)

Youthhead ... Chiefly Sc. Forms: 3 ȝuþhede, 4 ȝouþehede, -hede, ȝhouthede, juthed, 4-5 ȝowthede, 5-6 ȝouthhede, youthhede, (ȝouthed, -e), 4 ȝowthede, youthhed, jeutheid, ȝowth-heid, -houthede, 9-hed, 9 youth-head, youthhead (Sc. -heid). [f. YOUTH + -HEAD.]

1. The state of youth, youngness = YOUTH 1.

2. The time of youth, adolescence = YOUTH 2.

3. Youths collectively = YOUTH 3.

Youthhood [or-hod]. Now rare or obs. Forms: 1 ȝeoȝoþhad, ȝeoȝuþhad, 3 ȝeowehode; 7-9 youthhood, youth-hood, youthhode. [OE. ȝeoȝuþhad, f. ȝeoȝuþ YOUTH + -had -HOOD; cf. OS. juguðhēd, MHG. jugentheit. In mod.E. a new formation.]

1. = YOUTH 1, 2, 3.

2. = YOUTH 3.

Youthily, adv. ... see after YOUTHY.

Youthiness, sb. Sc. [f. YOUTH + -Y + -NESS.] ... A youthful person.

Youthy, a. Sc. [f. YOUTH + -Y.] ... Having or affecting the character of youth; usually connoting a youthful appearance or behaviour inconsistent with the person's years.

Youward, **Youwards**, etc. ... see after YOU.

Yow, ... see YOU, EWE.

Yow, int. [Imitative.]

Yowden-drift, variant of EWDEN-DRIFT, snow driven by the wind.

Yowl, v. Forms: 3 ȝoȝele, ȝule, jule, 4-5 (6 Sc.) ȝoule, ȝowle, 5-6 yowle, 5-7 youle, 5, 7, 9 yooll, 7 9 yowl, 9 yowll, 8- yowl. [ME.]

Yowl, sb. Also 5-6 jowle, 7 youle, 9 yowll. ... [f. prec.]

Yowl, obs. form of YULE.

Yowley, north. dial. [f. YOWLBING + -ey, -y.] A yellow-hammer.

Yowling, vbl. sb. [f. YOWL v. + -ING[1].] The action of the verb YOWL.

Yowt, v. Forms: 3 ȝoȝele, juhele ... [ME.] intr. To cry out loudly from pain, grief, or distress.

Yowth, variant of YOUTH.

Yowx, yox(e (ȝoxe), obs. or dial. ff. YEX.

Yoxe, ȝoyx: see JOY, YEA.

Yoyle, Yoyln, Yoyn, Yoyntor, Yoyste, obs. ff. OIL sb.[1], YULE, JOIN, JOINTURE, JOIST sb.[1]

Ypaid, ypayrid (V-4, PAY v.[1]), paid, pleased.

Ypsiloid [ip'siloid], a. [f. YPSILON + -Y-shaped.] Shaped like the Greek letter upsilon, Y-shaped. Cf. HYPSILOID.

Ypsilon (ip'silɒn). rare. [So mod. L., OF-., etc.] = UPSILON.

Ypurified ... **Ypurveyd** ... obs. pa. pples. of PURIFY, PURVEY.

Yrad (V-4), counselled.

Yrayn, e ... variant of RAIN.

Ysame ...

Yrain, e ...

Yuke, Yuck, Yucca, Yttria, Yttric, Yttrium ... (bottom row headwords)

Yschue, obs. form of ISSUE sb.

Yse, Yso, obs. ff. ICE, etc.

Ytent, Ytented ...

Yuke, Yuck, sb. and north. dial. Forms: ... Itching, itch.

Z.

ZAPPE

ZAPPE 86 ZEAL · ZEAL 87 ZEBRA · ZEBRAED 88 ZEMBLAN. · ZEMBLETE. 89 ZENITH.

Supplement, p. 3873; Corrigenda, p. 4092; Spurious words, p. 4093; Books quoted, p. 4094.

ZIMME

ZINC.

Zinc (ziŋk), sb. Forms: 7-9 zink, 7-8 zinck, 8- zinc. [ad. G. zink (of obscure origin), whence also late 17th c. F. zinc (+zinck, zinch), Sw., Da. zink, etc., mod.L. zincum.] 1. A hard bluish-white metal (commercially known as SPELTER), brittle at ordinary temperatures, but malleable and ductile between 100° and 150° F.; obtained from various ores, esp. the sulphide (BLENDE), the carbonate and silicate (CALAMINE, SMITHSONITE), and the red oxide (ZINCITE), and used for roofing, for coating or 'galvanizing' sheet-iron, and for numerous other purposes; it forms several alloys, of which the best known is that with copper called Brass.

Zinco ...

Zincograph ...

Zincography ...

Zinco- ...

Zincoid ...

Zincous ...

Zincite ...

Zincke ...

Zincky ...

Zing ...

Zingaresca ...

Zingaro ...

Zingiber ...

+Zingho ...

Zingiberaceous ...

Zinke ...

Zinkenite ...

Zinking ...

Zinky ...

Zinnia ...

Zinnwaldite ...

Zinsang ...

Zion ...

Zionism ...

Zionist ...

Zip ...

Ziphioid ...

Ziphius ...

Zippeite ...

Ziracote ...

Zircon ...

Zirconate ...

Zirconia ...

Zirconic ...

Zirconium ...

Zither (ziðər, -tər). [ad. G. zither.] A musical instrument (introduced into England c1850 from Austria) having from thirty to forty strings fitted into the lower rim of a shallow resonance-box, and played by striking with the fingers and thumb.

Zitherist ...

Zithern ...

Ziz ...

Zizania ...

Zizany ...

Zizel ...

Zizyph- ...

Ziz ...

Zloty ...

Zoantharian ...

Zoanthropy ...

Zoarium ...

Zobo ...

Zocco, zoccolo ...

Zocle ...

Zodiac ...

Zodiacal ...

Zodiographer ...

Zodiography ...

Zoea ...

Zoetrope ...

Zoic ...

Zoid ...

Zoisite ...

Zoism ...

Zoist ...

Zokor ...

Zoismus ...

Zol ...

Zoll ...

Zollverein ...

Zolotnik ...

Zolow, Zona, Zomboruk, Zomer ...

Zomotherapy ...

Zona ...

Zonal.

Zonal (zō·nǎl), a. [ad. mod.L. zonālis, f. L. zōna ZONE.] 1. Characterized by or arranged in zones, circles, or rings: of the nature of a zone.

ZONALITY ... ZONE ... ZONED ... ZOO- ... ZOOPHILY

Zonary. 1. Having the form of a zone or girdle: applied to the placenta in certain mammals, as the *Carnivora*, forming a broad girdle round the chorion. 2. Occurring in a zone or zones, i.e. within definite limits of depth (see ZONE *sb.* 6).

Zonate, *a.* Marked with zones, rings, or bands of colour; zoned. Also Zo·nated *a.*

Zonation. a. Distribution in zones or regions of definite character (see ZONE *sb.* 7). b. Formation of zones or concentric layers, as in a growing water-shell.

Zone, *sb.* 1. Each of the 'belts' or encircling regions, distinguished by differences of climate, into which the surface of the earth (and, in ancient cosmogony, the celestial sphere) is divided by the tropics (Cancer and Capricorn) and the polar (arctic and antarctic) circles.

Zone, *v.* 1. *trans.* To furnish with, or surround like, a zone or girdle; to gird, encircle.

Zoneless, *a.* Not confined by a zone; not wearing a zone or girdle; ungirt.

Zonelet, *sb.* A little zone.

Zonic, *a.* Belonging to a particular zone or region.

Zonite, *sb.* 1. A snail of the genus Zonites.

Zooid, *sb.* Something that resembles an animal.

Zoogamous, *a.* Of or pertaining to zoogamy.

Zoogamy, *sb.* Sexual reproduction of animals.

Zoography, *sb.* 1. Description of animals; descriptive zoology.

Zoolatry, *sb.* The worship of animals.

Zoological, *a.* Of or pertaining to zoology.

Zoology, *sb.* 1. The science which treats of animals.

Zoophily, *sb.* Love of animals.

ZOOPHYTE

Zoophorus, etc.: see ZOPHORUS.

Zoophyte (zōᵘ·ŏfəit). Forms: α. 7–8 **zoophyton** (7 **zoophiton**), 7–9 *pl.* **zoophyta** (zoǫ·fită). β. 7 **zoophyt**, **-phit**, 7–9 **-phite**, 7– **zoophyte**. [ad. mod.L. *zōophyton*, a. Gr. ζωόφυτον (Aristotle), f. ζῷον animal + φυτόν plant, f. φύεσθαι to grow. Cf. F. *zoöphyte* (Rabelais).]

†**1.** Applied to certain plants having or supposed to have some qualities of animals, as the 'sensitive plant' and the 'vegetable lamb' or BAROMETZ. *Obs.*

1621 LODGE *Summary Du Bartas* I. 132 There is mention of the Boranets, Zoophites, or Plant-animals of Moscouy, in the first Booke of the second Weeke. 1653 W. HARVEY *Anat. Exerc.* xvii. 95 The sensative Plant, and other Zoophyta. 1680 MORDEN *Geog. Rect., Muscovy* (1685) 67 In this Country grows the Plant Zoophyte that resembles a Lamb.

2. A general name for various animals of low organization, formerly classed as intermediate between animals and plants, being usually fixed, and often having a branched or radiating structure, thus resembling plants or flowers: as crinoids, hornwracks, sea-anemones, corals, hydroids, sponges, etc.; any member of the group *Zoophyta*.

Formerly sometimes applied to the branched connecting structure in hornwracks, corals, etc. as distinct from the 'polyps' inhabiting it; but often also a synonym of 'polyp'. In early modern Zoology the term *Zoophyta* was applied systematically but with varying extent, sometimes including all the Echinoderms, Polyzoa, Cœlenterates, Sponges, and Protozoa, in other cases more restricted, esp. to the Cœlenterates; it is now almost or entirely disused.

α. 1635 PERSON *Varieties* I. § 9 Mid creatures which wee call Zoophyta, and Plantanimalia. 1651 J. F[REAKE] *Agrippa's Occ. Philos.* 74 The Zoophyton [*mispr.* Zeo-] (*i. e.*) half Animall, and half Plant. 1682 H. MORE *Annot. Glanvill's Lux O.* 53 To blame her [*sc.* Providence] for making Zoophiton's, or rather Amphibion's. 1743 *Phil. Trans.* XLII. 590 A Zoophyton, somewhat resembling the Flower of the Marigold. 1855 J. PHILLIPS *Man. Geol.* 46 The innumerable tribes of zoophyta, mollusca, and other [in]vertebrata.

β. 1621 BURTON *Anat. Mel.* II. ii. III. 319 Many strange creatures, mineralls, vegetalls, Zoophites. 1640 HOWELL *Dodona's Grove* 23 Those Zoophits or Plant-Animals the Philosophers write of. 1644 DIGBY *Nat. Bodies* xxiii. (1658) 259 Under the title of plants I include not zoophytes or plant animals. 1752 WATSON in *Phil. Trans.* XLVII. 457 If..some will still consider these marine productions as plants, they are truly zoophytes, formed by the labour of the animals, which inhabit them. 1762 NASMYTH ibid. LII. 556 Whether animal, zoophite, or submarine plant, I leave to your determination. 1828 STARK *Elem. Nat. Hist.* II. 395 Polypi or Zoophytes; comprehending all those small, gelatinous, and compound or aggregated animals which have a mouth surrounded by tentacula, and conducting into a simple stomach. 1847 WHEWELL *Hist. Induct. Sci.* (1857) III. 463 Suppose the coralline zoophytes to go on building. 1877 THOMSON *Voy. Challenger* I. iv. 255 Very elegant alcyonarian zoophytes.

fig. 1865 O. W. HOLMES *Aut. Breakf.-t.* viii. 75 When the whole human zoöphyte flowers out like a full-blown rose.

3. *attrib.* and *Comb.*

1753 *Chambers' Cycl.* Suppl. s.v. *Marygold*, Zoophyte Marygold..the name of a species of sea animal, of a very beautiful kind, and of the nature of those commonly called Zoophytes,..by the old naturalists. 1856 CARPENTER *Micros.* § 69 For the examination of living aquatic objects, too large to be conveniently received into the Aquatic Box, the Zoophyte-trough contrived by Mr. Lister may be employed with great advantage. 1889 *Science-Gossip* XXV. 38 The zoophyte-clothed rocks.

Hence **Zo·ophytal**, **Zo,ophytic** (-fi·tik), **-ical** *adjs.*, of or pertaining to a zoophyte or zoophytes; of the nature of a zoophyte; produced by zoophytes; **Zo·ophytish** *a.*, having the character of a zoophyte; **Zo·ophytist**, a naturalist who studies zoophytes, a zoophytologist; **Zo:ophyto·graphy**, description of zoophytes; **Zo,ophy·toid** *a.*, resembling a zoophyte, or related to the zoophytes; **Zo:ophytolo·gical** *a.*, pertaining to zoophytology; **Zo:ophyto·logist**, one versed in zoophytology; **Zo:ophyto·logy**, that department of zoology which treats of zoophytes.

1838 MANTELL *Wonders Geol.* II. 468 In the flustra..we have the elements of *zoophytal organization. 1818 *Q. Jrnl. Sci.* V. 375 Molluscous and *zoophytic animals. 1830 LYELL *Princ. Geol.* I. 128 The zoophytic, and shelly limestones..sometimes alternate with the rocks of mechanical origin. 1851 RICHARDSON *Geol.* (1855) 216 The ocean's bed, on which the foundations of the zoophytic structure are laid. 1838 G. JOHNSTON *Brit. Zooph.* 8 Bernard de Jussieu and Guettard proceeded..to different parts of the coasts of France with the view of examining their *zoophytical productions. 1850 W. SCORESBY *Cheever's Whalem. Adv.* iv. (1858) 53 Many of the zoophytical and molluscous orders. 1854 *Chamb. Jrnl.* 28 Oct. 280/1 The home of some human reptile or *zoophytish monster. 1862 ANSTED *Channel Isl.* II. ix. 242 Caverns..worthy the careful examination of the *zoophytist. 1736 BAILEY (folio) Pref., **Zoophytography*..a Treatise or Discourse of animal Plants, as Cockles, Muscles, Oysters. 1861 R. E. GRANT *Tabular View Rec. Zool.* 66 Physograda ..*Zoophytoid. 1828–32 WEBSTER, *Zoophytological. 1849–52 *Todd's Cycl. Anat.* IV. 1307/1 The modern *Zoophytologist. 1828 *Athenæum* 6 Aug. 651/1 *Zoophytology. Respiration of Animalcules. 1883 *Knowledge* 13 July 22/1 Ellis..has been called the father of English Zoophytology.

Zoopraxiscope (zōᵘǫpræ·ksiskoᵘp). Also **-praxeoscope**, and erron. **-praxinoscope** (cf. PRAXINOSCOPE). [f. ZOO- + Gr. πρᾶξις (acc. πρᾶξιν, gen. πράξεως) action + -SCOPE.] A modified form of the ZOOGYROSCOPE.

1881 *Leeds Merc.* 31 May 5 The Zoöpraxeoscope is..the zoögyroscope in an improved form. 1882 *Athenæum* 16 Mar. 352/3 Mr. Muybridge, of Philadelphia, lectured on 'The Science of Animal Locomotion in its Relation to Design in Art.'..The lecturer by the zoopraxiscope and its limelight displayed a great number of illustrations.

‖**Zoosporangium** (zōᵘ:ǫsporæ·ndʒiə̆m). *Bot.* Pl. **-ia.** Also in anglicized form **zoosporange** (zōᵘ·ǫsporændʒ). [mod.L., f. next after SPORANGIUM.] A receptacle containing zoospores. Hence **Zo:osporangiophore** (-fōᵊɹ) [see -PHORE], a structure bearing zoosporangia.

1874 COOKE *Fungi* 170 Thick filaments or tubes, similar to those which form the Zoosporangia. 1882 HUXLEY in *Nature* 9 Mar. 438 The zoospores are set free through an opening formed at the apex of the zoosporangium. 1889 A. W. BENNETT & MURRAY *Crypt. Bot.* 326 The..zoospores are borne in zoosporanges at the end of cylindrical or club-shaped zoosporangiophores.

Zoospore (zōᵘ·ǫspōᵊɹ). *Biol.* [f. ZOO- + SPORE.] A spore having the power of spontaneous movement, occurring in certain Algæ, Fungi, and Protozoa; a motile spore, swarm-spore.

1846 LINDLEY *Veg. Kingd.* 8 Cellular flowerless plants,..propagated by zoospores, coloured spores, or tetraspores. 1858 — *Veg. Phys.* § 767 For the propagation of their kind, ..the Confervae have two different modes; the one being the liberation of moving particles, termed zoospores, from the interior of the cells. 1888 ROLLESTON & JACKSON *Anim. Life* 821 The spores [in Protozoa]..may when they become motile be amoeboid or flagellate, and to these two states respectively the terms *amoebula*, or *zoospore* s. *flagellula* may be applied.

Hence **Zoosporous** (zo,ǫ·spŏrəs) *a.*, producing, of the nature of, or effected by zoospores.

1846 LINDLEY *Veg. Kingd.* 1 The spores of those Confervæ which are sometimes called Zoosporous. 1859 *Todd's Cycl. Anat.* V. 212/2 Zoosporous reproduction.

Zooster, var. ZOSTER.

Zo,o·tic, *a.* [ad. mod.L. *zōoticus* (Mayne *Expos. Lex.*), f. Gr. ζῷον animal: see -OTIC.] (See quots.)

1868 WATTS *Dict. Chem.* V. 1085 Zootic Acid, syn. with Hydrocyanic Acid. 1879 WEBSTER, *Zootic*..containing the remains of organized bodies;—used of rock or soil.

Zootomy (zo,ǫ·tŏmi). [ad. mod. L. *zōotomia* (M. A. Severinus, 1645): see ZOO- and -TOMY.] The anatomy of animals; the dissection, or the science of the structure, of animal bodies; in mod. use *esp.* comparative anatomy.

1663 BOYLE *Usef. Exp. Nat. Philos.* II. i. 21 The naturalist by his Zootomy, may be very serviceable to the Physitian in his anatomical inquiries. 1697 *Phil. Trans.* XIX. 558 Zootomy is either for compleating natural History,..or for the better Attainment of the Cure of Diseases. 1797 S. JAMES *Narr. Voy.* 156 The cook..lives in East Smithfield, where he exercises the trade of zootomy. 1870 ROLLESTON *Anim. Life* Pref. p. v, To combine the concrete facts of Zootomy with the outlines of systematic Classification. 1872 MIVART *Anat.* 74 This lower jaw—or, as it is called in zootomy, mandible. 1875 W. TURNER in *Encycl. Brit.* I. 799/1 [Anatomy] resolves itself into..Animal Anatomy or Zootomy,..and Vegetable Anatomy or Phytotomy.

So **Zootomic** (zōᵘǫtǫ·mik), **Zo,oto·mical** *adjs.*, belonging or relating to zootomy; **Zo,oto·mically** *adv.*, in relation to or in the way of zootomy; **Zo,o·tomist**, one versed in zootomy; one who dissects, or who studies the structure of, animal bodies; in mod. use *esp.* a comparative anatomist.

1887 *Nature* 17 Nov. 70/1 The *zootomic and embryological works of the last ten years. 1833 R. E. GRANT in *Lancet* 12 Oct. 93/2 The *zootomical investigations of Moreschi of Milan. 1870 ROLLESTON *Anim. Life* Pref. p. v, A Zootomical account of its various Sub-kingdoms. 1849–52 *Todd's Cycl. Anat.* IV. 873/1 The investigation of the whole of this vast subject, *zootomically. 1688 BOYLE *Final Causes* iv. 223 The remarks of *Zootomists. 1797 S. JAMES *Narr. Voy.* 156 The cook..by profession a zootomist. 1879 LEWES *Probl. Life & Mind* Ser. III. I. 132 If the biologist recognises the many points of community in animal structures, the zootomist has to insist on the points of diversity.

Zootrope (zōᵘ·ǫtroᵘp), corrected form of ZOETROPE, with substitution of the more normal combining form *zoo-* [Gr. ζωο-] for *zoe-*.

1872 HUXLEY *Physiol.* x. 245 The curious toy called the thaumatrope or 'Zootrope' or 'wheel of life'.

Zope (zōᵘp). [a. G. dial. *zope* (F. *sope*), prob. Slav. (cf. Russ. *sapá*).] A bream, *Abramis ballerus*.

1880 GÜNTHER *Fishes* 603 In Europe there occur the 'Common bream', *A. brama*; the 'Zope', *A[bramis] ballerus*.

‖**Zophorus** (zōᵘ·fŏrə̆s), **zoophorus** (zo,ǫ·fŏrə̆s). *Anc. Arch.* Pl. **-i.** Also 8 anglicized **zoophore**. [L. *zōphorus*, *zōophorus* (Vitruvius), ad. Gr. ζωφόρος, ζῳοφόρος adj. bearing figures of animals, f. ζῷον animal + -φόρος -bearing. Cf. F. *zoophore* (Rabelais).] A continuous frieze bearing figures of men and animals carved in relief.

1563 SHUTE *Archit.* Bij, Vpon their heddes, he laide Epistilia, and Coronas, setting betwixt them Zophorus. 1694 MOTTEUX *Rabelais* v. xliii. 199 The Architraves, Zoophores and Cornishes. 1706 PHILLIPS (ed. Kersey), Zophorus or Zoophorus. 1823 P. NICHOLSON *Pract. Builder* 586. 1905 *Times* 25 Apr. 5/2 The sculptures on the zophorus of the west front..should be taken down and stored in a museum.

So **Zo(o)phoric** (-fǫ·rik) *a.*, bearing the figure of an animal.

1728 CHAMBERS *Cycl.*, *Zoophoric Column*, is a Statuary Column; or a Column that bears or supports the Figure of an Animal. 1752 *Ibid.*, *Zophoric*.

‖**Zopilote** (zōᵘ·pilōᵘt). Also **-ot.** [Sp., a. Mexican *azopilotl*.] A vulture of the family *Cathartidæ*, esp. the American carrion vulture or turkey-buzzard, *Cathartes aura*.

1787 CULLEN tr. *Clavigero's Mexico* I. 47 The *Zopilots*, known in South America by the name of *Gallinazzi*;.. There are two very different species..; the one, the Zopilote properly so called, the other called the *Cozcaquauhtli*. 1850 MAYNE REID *Rifle Rangers* II. xxx. 278 The Eagle's cliff was black with zopilotes. 1862 J. G. WOOD *Illustr. Nat. Hist.* II. 17 When in search of food, the Zopilote ascends to a vast height in the air.

‖**Zopissa** (zopi·să). [L., a. Gr. ζώπισσα, f. πίσσα pitch.] † **a.** An old medicinal application made from wax and pitch scraped from the sides of ships. *Obs.* **b.** A patent composition used as a hardening or protecting coat for metal, etc.

1601 HOLLAND *Pliny* XXIV. vii. II. 184 Zopissa, is that Pitch, which..is scraped from ships, and is confected of wax well soked in the salt water of the sea. 1712 tr. *Pomet's Hist. Drugs* I. 212 This Zopissa is a Composition of black Pitch, Rosin, Suet and Tar melted together. 1861 *Illustr. Lond. News* 2 Feb. 108/1 To experimentalise on a portion of that stone with a substance called 'zopissa'—phraseologically borrowed from Dioscorides..pitch-plaster. 1862 *Catal. Internat. Exhib., Brit.* II. No. 2653 The zopissa composition, for preserving iron and wooden ships against rust and decay, invented by N. C. Szerelmy. *Ibid.* 5089 Arabian zopissa waterproof and paper boards processes.

Zopy, obs. var. SOPIE.

1687 LOCKE in Fox Bourne *J. L.* (1876) II. 71 A hogshead of cyder, even now and then a bottle of wine or a zopy.

Zore, obs. or dial. f. SORE *a.*[1]

c 1572 GASCOIGNE *Posies* Wks. 1907 I. 73 Our landlordes a zore man: He racketh up our rentes.

Zorȝe, obs. form of SORROW.

Zorgite (zǭ·rgəit). *Min.* [f. *Zorge*, a village in the Hartz Mountains: see -ITE [1].] A lead-grey selenide of lead and copper.

1852 BROOKE & MILLER *Phillips' Introd. Min.* 153.

Zorgo, obs. variant of SORGHO.

1549 THOMAS *Hist. Italie* 5 b, He is not hable..to finde breade of Zorgo (a verie vile graine).

Zoril, **zorille** (zǫ·ril). Also **zorilla**, **-o.** [ad. F. *zorille*, ad. Sp. *zorrilla*, *-illo*, dim. of *zorra*, ZORRO.] An animal of the African genus *Zorilla*, allied to the skunks; also applied to some Central or South American skunks, as the conepatl.

1774 GOLDSM. *Nat. Hist.* (1824) II. 47 The zorille resembles the skink, but is rather smaller. 1845 DARWIN *Voy. Nat.* iv. 80 We saw also a couple of Zorillos, or skunks. 1878 *Cassell's Nat. Hist.* II. 196 The Cape Zorilla. 1883 SIMMONDS *Dict. Trade* Suppl., *Zoril*, a variety of the American skunk.

Zoroastrian (zǫro,æ·striăn), *a.* and *sb.* Also 8 **Zoroastran.** [f. L. *Zōroastrēs*, a. Gr. Ζωροάστρης, ad. Zend *Zarathustra* (Pers. *Zardusht*): see -IAN.]

A. *adj.* Of or pertaining to Zoroaster or his religious system, which is mainly dualistic.

1743 WARBURTON *Pope's Ess. Man* II. 81 *note*, This dangerous school-opinion gives great support to the Manichean or Zoroastran error. 1795 T. MAURICE *Hindostan* (1820) II. IV. iii. 249 The..heresy of Manes, which was compounded out of the ancient Zoroastrian or Magian superstition, and certain perverted doctrines of Christianity. 1892 WESTCOTT *Gospel of Life* 172 There appears to be a distinct polemical element in the earliest Zoroastrian Hymns. 1903 *Times* 5 Mar. 3/5 On no previous occasion has any one been received from Christianity into the Zoroastrian faith.

B. *sb.* A follower of Zoroaster; a Parsee.

1811 BYRON *Let. to F. Hodgson* 3 Sept., I would sooner be a Paulician, Manichæan, Spinozist, Gentile, Pyrrhonian, Zoroastrian, than any one of the seventy-two villainous sects who are tearing each other to pieces for the love of the Lord. 1864 PUSEY *Daniel* 492 The doctrine of the Resurrection..was not known to the Zoroastrians until after the Christian era. 1886 PHIL ROBINSON *Vall. Teetotum Trees* 3 The semi-sacred character of the holly..among the Zoroastrians and Fire-worshippers.

Hence **Zoroa·strianize** *v.*, *trans.* and *intr.*, to make or become Zoroastrian in character.

1891 CHEYNE *Orig. Psalter* viii. 449 Zoroastrianizing phraseology. *Ibid.* 452 The Judaism carried to Egypt.. had..already been in some degree Zoroastrianized.

Zoroa·strianism. Also **-ter-.** [f. prec. + -ISM.] The religious system taught by Zoroaster and his followers, and incorporated in the Zend-Avesta: commonly known as *fire-worship*.

1854 MILMAN *Lat. Christ.* IV. i. II. 4 Zoroasterianism had failed to propagate itself with any great success. 1874 SAYCE *Compar. Philol.* viii. 307 The deities of the Veda became the evil spirits of Zoroastrianism.

Zoroa·stric, *a. rare.* [f. L. *Zōroastrēs* Zoroaster.] = ZOROASTRIAN. So **Zoroa·st(e)rism** = ZOROASTRIANISM.

1854 T. KEIGHTLEY *Mythol.* (ed. 3) 468 The Ferwer of Zoroastric theology. 1862 tr. *Renan's Age & Antiq. Bk. Nab. Agric.* ii. 45 The old Zoroastrism of the Zend writings. 1864 PUSEY *Daniel* ix. 528 Zoroastrism betrays its original, the Aryan creature-worship, to which has been added its characteristic Dualism.

‖**Zorro** (þǫ·rro, zǫ·ro). [Sp., = fox.] The South American fox-wolf. Also **Zorri·no** [dim.], a kind of skunk (cf. ZORIL), or its fur.

1838 HUNTER tr. *Azara's Nat. Hist. Paraguay* I. 290 As to habits they vary considerably in my zorros. 1885 *Encycl. Brit.* XVIII. 353/1 The zorro or *Canis Azaræ* (a kind of fox), the zorrino or *Mephitis patagonica* (a kind of skunk), and the tuco-tuco or *Ctenomys magellanicus*. 1899 *Westm. Gaz.* 17 June 7/1 Furs in great variety (chinchilla, vicuna, guanaco, zorrino, lynx, leopard, alpaca, &c.).

‖**Zoster** (zǫ·stəɹ). Also 9 **zooster.** [L., a. Gr. ζωστήρ girdle, f. ζωννύναι to gird.]

†**1.** A kind of seaweed. *Obs. rare.*

1601 HOLLAND *Pliny* XIII. xxv. I. 401 As for the former [seaweed] called Zoster, it is found among the shelves and shallow waters not farre from the shore.

2. The disease shingles, *Herpes zoster*. Also *attrib.*

1706 PHILLIPS (ed. Kersey). 1867 O. W. HOLMES *Guardian Angel* xxv, Armed against every malady from Ague to Zoster. 1876 DUHRING *Dis. Skin* 78 Pustules are met with ..in non-parasitic sycosis, zoster, etc.

3. *Gr. Antiq.* A belt or girdle, esp. as worn by men.

1824 *Gentl. Mag.* Dec. 483 A *zooster* or girdle of the same metal, which reaches half round the body. 1906 *Academy* 1 Dec. 543/2 The Mitrē is a band of metal worn round the waist under the Chiton, the Zoster a similar belt worn over the tunic.

Zoster, obs. form of SISTER.

‖**Zostera** (zǫstīᵊ·ră). *Bot.* [mod.L. (Linnæus), f. Gr. ζωστήρ: see ZOSTER and -A[1]. So called from its long leaves.] A marine plant of the genus so named, esp. grasswrack, *Z. marina*.

1819 LINDLEY tr. *Richard's Obs. Fruits & Seeds* 54 The kernel of *Zostera* is an oblong oval. 1855 KINGSLEY *Glaucus* 57 The delicate green ribbons of the Zostera (the only English flowering plant which grows beneath the sea). 1858 *Phytologist* Nov. 601 The thin line of dry *Zostera* to be met with at high-water mark. 1865 MRS. L. L. CLARKE *Common Seaweeds* ii. 30, I have found it often in *Zostera* beds at low tide.

‖**Zosterops** (zǫ·stĕrǫps). *Ornith.* [mod. L. (Vigors and Horsfield, 1827), f. Gr. ζωστήρ girdle + ὤψ eye.] Any of the small birds of the genus so named, widely distributed chiefly in tropical and subtropical regions, and characterized by a ring of white feathers round the eye; a silver-eye or white-eye.

1867 A. L. ADAMS *Wand. Nat. India* 71 That beautiful warbler the yellow zosterops, known by the white downy ring round the eye. 1909 *Blackw. Mag.* Aug. 204/2 It is interesting to watch a Zosterops operating on a pear.

Zoþ(e, obs. forms of SOOTH *a.*

Zotie, **zoty**, variants of SOTIE [2] *Obs.*

1578 T. N. tr. *Conq. W. Ind.* (1596) 272 They burned.. three Zoties neere vnto their owne lodging. 1667 DRYDEN *Ind. Emp.* v. ii, At last Cydaria looks over the zoty.

Zouave (zwāᵊv). Also **zouava.** [F., f. native name *Zouaoua* (see below).]

1. One of a body of light infantry in the French army, originally recruited from the Algerian Kabyle tribe of Zouaoua, but afterwards composed of French soldiers distinguished for their physique and dash, and formerly retaining the original Oriental uniform.

[1830 tr. *E. Blaquiere's Sig. Pananti* (ed. 2) 56 The whole of the native warriors called the *Zouavi*.] 1848 KELLY tr. *L. Blanc's Hist. Ten Y.* II. 520 The Zouaves were standing on the breach. 1858 HAWTHORNE *Fr. & It. Note-bks.* 8 Jan., Zouaves with turbans, long mantles, and bronzed, half Moorish faces. 1897 *Harper's Mag.* Apr. 752/1 In January, 1863, the French general Forey laid siege to Puebla...In one of the many assaults on the corner held by Diaz the zouaves broke into the first court-yard of his stronghold.

fig. 1858 BEECHER *Life Th.* 135 Those sciences which might be called the light infantry of progress, the Zouaves of thought. 1903 *Speaker* 30 May 210/2 The 'Physical Force' agitators were the Zouaves of Carlton House.

attrib. 1863 E. DICEY *Six Months* II. 7 The orderly disorder of a Zouave march.

b. (Also *Papal* or *Pontifical Z.*) One of a corps of French soldiers organized at Rome in 1860 for the defence of the pope, and disbanded in 1871.

1864 MANNING in A. Reinaud *Abbé-Zouave* Pref. p. ix, Some hundreds of the Pontifical Zouaves, chiefly French and Belgian,..were seen at St. Peter's. 1868 tr. *Cardella's J. W. Russell* 38 When he returned to Rome to join the Zouaves.

c. A soldier of any of several volunteer regiments, assuming the name and in part the uniform of the French Zouaves, which served on the side of the North in the American Civil War (1861–5).

1865 SALA *My Diary* I. 292 In the beginning, when the Yankee Zouaves were young and hopeful.

2. (In full, *z. jacket*, *bodice*.) A woman's short embroidered jacket or bodice, with or without sleeves, resembling the jacket of the Zouave uniform.

1859 *Ladies' Treas.* Sept. 285/1 One of the most decided novelties of the present season is the *Zouave* jacket. 1859 *Ladies' Cabinet* Dec. 335/1 Nothing can be prettier for the interior than the little oriental jackets which we call to-day *Zouaves*. 1893 *Lady* 17 Aug. 178/1 Zouave Bodices are a feature of autumn gowns.

Zouchee: see WATER SOUCHY.

Zounds (zaundz), *int.* Now *rare* or *Obs.* In later use a literary archaism. Forms: 6 **zownes**, 7 **zoones**, **'zons**, **zons**, **zonnes**(?), **dzowns**, **sownds**, **zwounds**, **zauns**, 7–8 **'zoons**, 7–9 **zoons**, 8 **'dswounds**, 7– **zounds.** (Cf. ZINES.) A euphemistic abbreviation of *by God's wounds* (1535, 1573, s.v. GOD *sb.* 14 a) used in oaths and asseverations.

1600 ROWLANDS *Lett. Humours Blood* Sat. v. 72 If any fall together by the eares, To field cries he; why? zownes (to field) he sweares. 1605 ARMIN *Foole vpon F.* E 3 b, One comes sweating, zoones (Cobler) the boots. 1607 DEKKER *Hist. Sir T. Wyatt* Wks. 1873 III. 119 Zwounds I was talking with a crue of vagabondes. 1614 J. COOKE *Greene's Tu Quoque* C 2, *Spend.* M. Rash! zownds how does he know I am here? 1616 *Marlowe's Faustus* 1158 Zounds hee'l raise vp a Kennell of Diuels. *Ibid.* 1300 'Zons, hornes againe. 1623 *Shaks. John* II. ii. 466 Zounds, I was neuer so bethumpt with words. 1682 *Tories' Conf.* in *Roxb. Ball.* (1882) IV. 269 Dzowns, we'l have none but honest Souls. 1699 FARQUHAR *Love & Bottle* II. ii, Zoons is only us'd by the disbanded Officers and Bullies: but Zauns is the Beaux pronuncation [*sic*]. 1712 ARBUTHNOT *John Bull* II. ix, 'Dswounds! why dost thou not lay out thy money to purchase a place at court? 1739 *Joe Miller's Jests* 3 Zoons, Sir, said an old Campaigner..who's that? 1812 COMBE *Picturesque* x, Syntax look'd wild—the man said 'Zounds! You know you betted twenty pounds.' 1821 *Sporting Mag.* (N.S.) VII. 180 Zoons! said we, deranging the economy of our grey hairs. 1847 LYTTON *Lucretia* I. i, Zounds, Charles, I love you, and that's the truth. 1883 *Fortn. Rev.* July 111 Forgiven me! Zounds! I must correct him in that.

Hence † **Zounds** *v.* (*obs. nonce-wd.*) *intr.* to exclaim 'zounds'.

1680 DRYDEN *Kind Keeper* IV. i. 39 When he loses upon the Square, he comes home Zoundzing and Blooding.

Zoutchee: see WATER SOUCHY.

Zow, **Zowl**, dial. ff. SOW, SOWL *v.*[3], SULL.

Zown, obs. form of SWOON *v.*

Zoyl(e, etc.: see ZOILUS, etc.

Zubeline, obs. form of ZIBELINE.

‖**Zubr** (zūbr). [Russ. See *Columna lui Traian* (1875) 97 ff.] The European bison or aurochs, *Bos bonasus*.

1847 W. C. L. MARTIN *Ox* 8/1 He who kills a zubr without permission of the Russian government, has to pay as a fine 2000 rubles. 1882 C. ELTON *Orig. Eng. Hist.* 59 A confused account of two distinct animals, the Aurochs or Zubr of Lithuania, and the extinct Urus which Charlemagne is said to have hunted.

Zubu, var. *Zobo*: see ZHO.

† **Zucarine**, *a.* *Obs.* [ad. med.L. *zucarīnus* adj., f. *zucara* SUGAR.] *Alum zucarine*, saccharine alum (see ALUM 1).

a 1425 tr. *Arderne's Treat. Fistula* etc. 40 Tapsimel, In whiche be puluerez of alume zucarine brent, of attrament, and of vitriol. *Ibid.* 81 Alum zucaryne is called comonly alumglasse. [1616 B. JONSON *Devil is an Ass* IV. iv, Your *Allum Scagliola*, or *Pol dipedra*; And *Zuccarino*.]

Zuccary, **zucco(u)r**, obs. ff. SUGAR.

‖**Zucchetto** (tsuke·to). Also **zuchetta**, **-etto.** [Incorrect but usual form for It. *zucchetta* (tsukke·tta) small gourd, cap, f. *zucca* gourd, the head.] The skull-cap of an ecclesiastic, differing in colour according to rank.

1853 DALE tr. *Baldeschi's Ceremonial* 3 They should take off their zucchettos in the act of genuflecting. 1897 *Westm. Gaz.* 18 June 3/2 Instead of the usual college cap the Chapter will appear in *zuchettos*. 1901 M. J. F. MCCARTHY *Five Yrs. in Irel.* xx. 257 Leo XIII...took off the Zuchetta he had been wearing and gave it to Father O'Brien.

Zucer, obs. form of SUGAR.

† **Zuche.** *Obs.* [app. AN. form of OF. *çoche* (tsotʃə), mod. F. *souche*, Norman-Picard *chouque* (whence dim. *chouquet*): of unknown origin. Not known in real English use as an ordinary sb.; survives in the town-name of *Ashby-de-la-Zouch* (Leicestershire).] A tree stump.

[1220 *Close Rolls 4 Hen. III* memb. 10 (1833) I. 418/1 De auxilio faciendo burgensibus Salop. de veteribus zuchis & de mortuo bosco. 1223 *Plac. Forest. in Com. Nott.* (Cowell 1672) Omnes Zuches aridos qui Anglice vocantur stovenes infra Haiam nostram de Beskewood [now Bestwood]. 1358 *Patent Rolls 32 Edw. III.* memb. 5 (1911) I. 59 [Grant to Richard de la Vache, steward of the forest of Shirewod, of all logs (*ligna*) called] zouches in Beskwode. 1672 COWELL *Interpr.*, Zuche, *zucheus*, *stips siccus & aridus*, A withered or dry stock of wood. 1676 COLES *Dict.*, *Zuche*, *Stovene*, a withered or dry stock of wood.

Zucre, **-ur**, **Zucrish**, **-ys**, obs. ff. SUGAR, -ISH.

Zuen(c)kfeldian, obs. ff. SWENKFELDIAN.

1565 T. STAPLETON *Fortr. Faith* 9 b, Memnonites and Zuenckfeldians.

Zuft: see SUFF *Obs.*

Zugere, **-ure**, **zuker**, **-re**, **-ur**, obs. ff. SUGAR.

Zuitzer, obs. form of SWITZER.

Zule, **zulis.** *Her.* A chess rook as a bearing.

1780 EDMONDSON *Compl. Body Her.* II, *Zulis*, a German bearing, nearly resembling a chess-rook. 1874 PAPWORTH *Ord. Brit. Arm.* 1125 Gu. three zules (chess rooks?) arg. in chief a label of three points of the last.

Zull(ow, var. SULL(OW, a plough.

Zulu (zū·lu), *sb.* and *a.* Also **Zoola**, **Zooloo.** [Native name.]

1. (Also *Z.-Kaffir.*) **a.** *sb.* A member of a warlike South African race of blacks belonging to the Bantu family, of a type resembling the Kaffir, and inhabiting Natal. **b.** *adj.* Belonging to this race.

1824 in Christopher *Natal* (1850) 21 Chaka, king of the Zulus, to whom belongs the whole of the country from Natal to Dela Goa Bay. 1828 *Ibid.* 23 The country of the Zoolas, eastward of Natal. *Ibid.* 25 The interior productions of the Zoola country. 1863 W. C. BALDWIN *Afr. Hunting* ii. 40 A buffalo, which some Zulu Kaffirs had killed. *Ibid.* iii. 75 They much resemble the Zulu huts, but have larger doorways. 1895 A. H. KEANE *Africa* II. vi. 241 Tribal groups belonging either to the Bechuana, or to the Zulu-Kafir division of the Southern Bantus.

2. (*sb.* or *adj.*) Applied to the language spoken by the Zulus.

1850 CHRISTOPHER *Natal* 137 The Zulu alphabet. 1857 DÖHNE *Zulu-Kafir Dict.* Introd. p. xxxviii, The Zulu, as the high language, has ever exercised a controlling influence upon the low languages. 1861 COLENSO *Zulu-Engl. Dict.* p. v, The Zulu for dog is commonly spelt *inja*. 1869 BLEEK in *Cape & its People* (ed. R. Noble) 272 The Zulu noun a-*ba*-ntu 'men, people'. 1900 *Speaker* 24 Feb. 551/2 What we want is competent officials, with knowledge of Zulu.

3. Name of an artificial fly used in angling.

1898 *Speaker* 29 Oct. 515 General utility flies... Such are the red tag, the Zulu, the blue dun, the snipewing. 1901 *Field* 9 Nov. 739, I put up a fine cast with three biggish flies tied on fine gut (a March brown, a Zulu, and a black palmer).

Hence **Zu·lu** *v.*, *intr.* (with *it*) to act like a Zulu; **Zu·ludom**, the domain of the Zulus; **Zu·luize** *v.*, *trans.* to make into a Zulu.

1876 *Jrnl. Soc. Arts* 28 Jan. 166/2 Into the heart of savage Zuludom. 1882 PHIL ROBINSON *Noah's Ark* i, The lion, again, they say, is King in Africa, yet the gorilla Zulus it over the forests within the lion's territory. 1895 *Pall Mall Gaz.* 6 Aug. 7/1 Death of John Dunn. A Zuluized Englishman.

Zum, dial. f. SOME. **Zumate**: see ZYMATE.

† **Zumbador.** *Obs.* [Sp., f. *zumbar* to hum.] A humming-bird of S. America.

1760–72 J. ADAMS tr. *Juan & Ulloa's Voy.* VI. viii. (ed. 3) I. 436 Partridges, condors, and zumbadores or hummers. 1764 GRAINGER *Sugar Cane* I. 641 The swift-wing'd zumbadore The mountain desert startled with his hum.

Zumbooruk (zʊ·mburʊk). Also **zumbooruck**, **-boorak**, **-barak**, **zomboru(c)k**, **zamboorak**, **-borouk**, **-búrak.** [ad. Hindustani زنبورک *zambūrak*, f. Pers. زنبور *zambūr* hornet. Cf. Pers. زنبرک *zemberek* crossbow.] A small swivel-gun, esp. one mounted on the back of a camel. Hence **Zumboorukchee**, a gunner.

1825 J. B. FRASER *Journ. Khorasan* 198 One or two shots from Zumboorucks dropping among them. 1840 — *Trav. Koordistan* II. xiii. 249 Four guns, and a large body of *zumboorukchees*. 1863 R. F. BURTON *Abeokuta* I. 75 East Indian jezails and zumbaraks. 1904 *Blackw. Mag.* July 87/1 Rakish swivel-guns, bell-mouthed *zumbooraks*.

Zumeendar, **-ary**, var. ZEMINDAR, -ARY.

Zumic, **Zumologic**, etc.: see ZYMIC, etc.

Zunana, **Zundavastaw**: see ZENANA, ZEND-AVESTA.

‖**Zuñi** (zū·nyi). A Pueblo Indian inhabiting the valley of the Zuñi, New Mexico. Hence **Zuñian**, **Zunyan** *a.*

1883 *Century Mag.* XXV. 201 Zūni food prepared in Zūni fashion. *Ibid.* 202/1 The domestic life of the Zūnis. 1885 *Science* 25 Sept. 267/2 This clay model of the Zuñian owl. 1898 A. LANG *Making Relig.* xiv. 275 In the Zuñi hymn we have the myth of the marriage of Heaven and Earth.

Zunyite (zū·nyəit). *Min.* [f. *Zuñi*, name of a mine in Colorado + -ITE [1].] A fluosilicate of aluminium, occurring in transparent tetrahedral crystals. 1885 *Amer. Jrnl. Sci.* Apr. 340.

Zur, southern dial. form of SIR.

1825 J. JENNINGS *Observ. Dial. W. Eng.* etc. 118, I bag ye, zur, to take en vooäth. 1838 JAS. GRANT *Sk. Lond.* ix. 292 'Woy, yes, Zur,' said a waggon-driver, with a short smock-frock...'That's how it is, Zur.'

Zureveld, **Zurf**: see ZUUR-VELDT, ZARF.

Zurlite (zʊ·ɹləit). *Min.* [f. the name of Signor *Zurlo*, an amateur naturalist of Naples + -ITE [1].] A white or green variety of melilite.

1826 *Amer. Jrnl. Sci.* XI. 255 The zurlite was discovered by Ramondini.

Zurumbeth, var. ZERUMBET.

‖**Zuur-veldt** (zū·ᵊrvelt). *S. Africa.* Also **-feldt**, **zureveld.** [Cape Du., = sour country or pasture land: see SOUR, VELD.] A district covered with sour pasturage. Also *attrib.*

1834 PRINGLE *Afr. Sk.* vi. 203 Long, coarse, wiry grass, of the sort called sour (whence the names Zureberg and Zureveld). 1850 R. G. CUMMING *Hunter's Life S. Afr.* (ed. 2) I. 13 Black, zuur-feldt oxen.

‖**Zuz** (zūz). Pl. **zuzim**; also **zuzees.** [Rabbinical Heb. זוז *zūz*.] A silver coin anciently in use among the Jews, the fourth part of a silver shekel.

1688 HOLME *Armoury* III. 25/2 A Zuz or Zuzim shekil. 1858 SIMMONDS *Dict. Trade*, *Zuzah*, an ancient Hebrew silver coin, worth about 6d. 1877 C. GEIKIE *Christ* xxxvi, A blow on the ear was variously set at the fine of a shilling or a pound: a blow on the one cheek at two hundred zuzees.

‖**Zwanziger** (tsva·ntsigəɹ). [G., f. *zwanzig* twenty + *-er* masc. adj. ending.] An Austrian silver coin, equivalent to twenty kreutzers.

1828 R. CRAIG in *Mem.* viii. (1862) 151 A passenger pays a zwanzig[er] or 17½ sous of France per hour. 1841 BROWNING *Pippa Passes* II, I possess a burning pocketfull of *zwanzigers*. 1866 HOWELLS *Venet. Life* xix, Lest the fervid imagination of the gondolier rise to zwanzigers and florins.

Zwenckfeldian, var. SWENKFELDIAN.

1565 HARDING *Confut. Apol.* II. xi. 88 The Zwenckfeldians that spring out of the same stocke.

Zwieselite (tsvī·zĕləit). *Min.* Also **zwis-.** [ad. G. *zwiselit* (Breithaupt, 1841), f. *Zwiesel*, Bavaria.] A clove-brown variety of triplite.

1861 BRISTOW *Gloss. Min.*

Zwingfelter, aberrant f. SCHWENKFELDER.

1794 MORSE *Amer. Geog.* (1796) I. 545 Zwingfelters, who are a species of Quakers.

Zwinglian (zwi·ŋgliăn, tsvi·ŋgliăn), *sb.* and *a.* Also 6 **Zu-**, **Zwynglian**, **-lyan**, 6–7 **Swi-**, 6–9 **Zui-**, 7 **Sui-.** [f. *Zwingli* (see below) + -AN.]

A. *sb.* A follower of Ulrich Zwingli (1484–1531), the Swiss religious reformer.

1532 MORE *Confut. Tindale* Wks. 570/2 The Lutheranes & Zwinglianes haue begunne to ryse & ruffle in rebellion in soondry partes of Almayne. 1533 — *Answ. poysoned Bk.* Wks. 1051/2 These Lutherane heretikes, and these Huskins, Swinglians: and Tyndalins. 1567 ALLEN *Def. Priesth.* 146 The whole packe of Protestauntes and Zuinglians deny that sacrament also to remitte sinnes. 1615 BRATHWAIT *Strappado* (1878) 4 Yes, for want of a bush thou'd hang thy selfe, And caper like a zuinglian. 1687 T. R. *Veritas Evang.* 23 Some being Lutherans, others Swinglians, others Anabaptists. 1768 MACLAINE tr. *Mosheim's Eccl. Hist.* (ed. 2) IV. 70 This union, between the Lutherans and Zuinglians, was so ardently desired by Melancthon. 1888 SCHAFF *Hist. Church, Mod. Chr.* I. 61 He regretted the toleration of the Zwinglians in Switzerland.

B. *adj.* Of or pertaining to Ulrich Zwingli or his doctrine, esp. concerning the eucharist (see SACRAMENTARIAN B. 1).

1565 HARDING *Confut. Apol.* I. x. 36 b, Ye shall be driuen to forsake your Zuinglian doctrine which putteth signes and figures only in the sacrament of the aulter for the true and reall body of Christ there present. 1661 HEYLIN *Hist. Ref.* II. (1670) 59 Their..Leaders..being for the most part of the Zwinglian-Gospellers. 1752 CARTE *Hist. Eng.* III. 395 The Zuinglian doctrines preached by Farel and other ministers. 1898 *Expositor* Oct. 271 Mere protest is conducting us through Zwinglian attenuation to Socinian negation.

Hence **Zwi·nglianism**, the doctrines of Zwingli, or the holding of such doctrines; † **Zwi·nglianist**, a Zwinglian.

1581 ALLEN *Apol.* 35 b, In most things agreeing with Zuinglianisme, in some with Lutheranisme. 1641 'SMECTYMNUUS' *Answ.* (1653) 71 So doe the Papists upbraid the Protestants with their Lutheranisme, Calvinisme, and Zuinglianisme. 1674 HICKMAN *Quinquart. Hist.* (ed. 2) Ep. a, The Lutherans use no breaking of the Bread: So do the Zuinglianists. 1745 BUTLER *Lives of Saints* (1845) XI. 117 Where he..converted many Zuinglianists. 1857 PUSEY *Real Pres.* I. 109 Zwinglianism was consistent in itself.

Zwitzar, **-er**, obs. ff. SWITZER. **Zwookers**, **Zwop**, **Zwounds**: see ZOOKERS, SWAP, ZOUNDS.

Zy: see SEE *v.*, THE. **Zyalde**: see SELL *v.*

Zyga, plural of ZYGON.

Zygadite (zi·gădəit). *Min.* [ad. G. *zygadit* (Breithaupt), f. Gr. ζυγάδην in pairs, f. ζυγόν yoke.] A variety of albite, occurring in tabular twin crystals, of a yellowish-white or reddish colour.

1861 BRISTOW *Gloss. Min.* 1886 *Jrnl. Chem. Soc.* L. 518 *Zygadite*..occurs in druses in the slate of St. Andreasberg in association with quartz and sphalerite.

‖**Zygæna** (zəidʒī·nă). *Zool.* [mod.L., ad. Gr. ζύγαινα a kind of fish, perh. the hammer-headed shark.] **a.** *Ichth.* A fish of the genus formerly so named (now *Sphyrna*), comprising the hammer-headed sharks. **b.** *Entom.* A genus of moths (also called *Anthrocera*), comprising the burnet-moths. Hence **Zygæ·nid**, **-idan** *sbs.*, a member of the family *Zygænidæ*, typified by the genus *Zygæna*; *adjs.* belonging to the *Zygænidæ*.

1683–4 [see *balance-fish*, BALANCE *sb.* 22]. 1774 GOLDSM. *Nat. Hist.* (1824) III. 34 The Dog Fish,..the Zygæna, the Tope, the Cat Fish. 1837 SIR J. RICHARDSON *Fauna Bor.-Amer.* IV. 301 Family Zygænidæ. Zygænidans. 1913 *Oxf. Univ. Gaz.* 954/1 The Zygaenid moth *Procris geryon*.

Zygal (zəi·găl), *a.* *Anat.* [f. ZYGON + -AL.] Pertaining to or having a zygon.

1886 B. G. WILDER in *Jrnl. Nerv. & Mental Dis.* June 304 The complete or typical condition of a zygal fissure is like two y's joined by their stems,..or, viewed from the side, like an expanded H.

‖**Zygantrum** (zəigæ·ntrə̆m, zig-). *Anat.* and *Zool.* Pl. **-antra.** [mod.L., f. Gr. ζυγόν yoke + ἄντρον cave.] A double cavity on the posterior side of the neural arch of each ordinary vertebra in serpents and some lizards, into which the *zygosphene* of the next vertebra fits.

1854 OWEN in *Orr's Circ. Sci., Org. Nat.* I. 197 This wedge [*sc.* the zygosphene] is received into a cavity (the 'zygantrum') excavated in the posterior expansion of the neural arch. 1888 ROLLESTON & JACKSON *Anim. Life* 73.

‖**Zygapophysis** (zəigăpǫ·fisis, zig-). *Anat.* and *Zool.* Pl. **-physes** (-fisīz). [mod.L., f. Gr. ζυγόν yoke + ἀπόφυσις APOPHYSIS.] A lateral process on the neural arch of a vertebra, articulating with the corresponding process of the next vertebra; an articular process. There are normally four to each vertebra, viz. right and left anterior (*prezygapophyses*) and right and left posterior (*postzygapophyses*). Hence **Zygapophysial** (-ăpofi·ziăl) *a.*, pertaining to a zygapophysis.

1854 OWEN in *Orr's Circ. Sci., Org. Nat.* I. 169 The exogenous parts are the diapophysis.., the parapophysis.., the zygapophysis.., the anapophysis.., the metapophysis.., the hypapophysis.., and the epapophysis. 1870 ROLLESTON *Anim. Life* 11 Two oblique zygapophysial surfaces.

Zygge, **Zyȝt**, **Zyȝþ**, **Zyȝþe**: see SAY *v.*[1], SEE *v.*, SIGHT *sb.*[1]

Zygite (zəi·dʒəit). *Gr. Antiq.* [ad. Gr. ζυγίτης, f. ζυγόν: see ZYGON 2 and -ITE [1].] In the ancient bireme or trireme, a rower of the upper or the middle tier: cf. THALAMITE, THRANITE.

1888 WOODGATE *Boating* (Badm. Libr.) i. 17 In the bireme the zygite, as he sat on his bench, had behind him and below him his thalamite.

Zygnemaceous (zignīmēᵊ·ʃəs), *a.* *Bot.* [f. mod.L. *Zygnēmăceæ* pl., f. *Zygnēma* (Kützing, 1843), irreg. for **zygonēma*, f. Gr. ζυγόν yoke + νῆμα thread: see -ACEOUS.] Belonging to the N. O. *Zygnemaceæ* of filamentous fresh-water algæ, typified by the genus *Zygnema*, which propagate by conjugation. So **Zygnemid** (zignī·mid), a member of this order.

1887 *Athenæum* 12 Mar. 357/1 The Conjugatæ, including zygnemids and desmids.

Zygo- (zəigo, zigo), before a vowel properly **zyg-**, repr. Gr. ζυγο-, combining form of ζυγόν yoke; occurring in various scientific terms, of which the more important will be found in their alphabetical places. (In terms of Biology the prefix often refers to *conjugation* or *zygosis* as a method of reproduction: see CONJUGATION 5.)

Zygoca·rdiac *a.* [CARDIAC A. 4], denoting an ossicle in the stomach of the crayfish and other crustaceans (see quot., and cf. PTEROCARDIAC, UROCARDIAC). **Zy·godont** *a.* [Gr. ὀδούς, ὀδοντ- tooth], having molar teeth with an even number of cusps arranged in pairs; having cusps thus arranged, as a molar tooth. **Zygoneurous** (-niū·rəs) *a.* [Gr. νεῦρον nerve], applied to an arrangement of the nervous system in certain gastropod molluscs, in which the pallial nerve of each pleural ganglion unites directly with the ganglion of the visceral commissure of its own side (opp. to *dialyneurous*); so **Zygoneu·ry**, zygoneurous condition. **Zygophiuran** (-ǫfiyū·răn) *a.* and *sb.*, belonging to, or a member of, the division *Zygophiuræ* of ophiuroids, having special structures which limit the movement of the ossicles of the arms (cf. *zygospondyline* below). **Zy·gophyte** (-fəit) [Gr. φυτόν plant], a plant which reproduces by conjugation. **Zygo·pterid** *sb.* and *a.* [Gr. πτερόν wing], a member of, or belonging to, the division *Zygopterides* or *Zygoptera* of dragon-flies, having all the wings nearly or quite equal in size. **Zy·gosperm** [Gr. σπέρμα seed] = ZYGOSPORE. **Zy·gosphere** (-sfīᵊɹ) [after OOSPHERE], either of the two conjugating cells or gametes which form a zygospore. **Zygospo·ndyline** *a.* [Gr. σπόνδυλος vertebra, joint], applied to those ophiuroids in which the arms are incapable of being coiled round straight objects, the movements of their ossicles being limited by internal pits and processes. **Zy·gostyle** (-stəil) [STYLE 10] (see quot.). **Zygozo·ospore**, a zoospore formed by conjugation; a motile zygospore.

1877 HUXLEY *Anat. Inv. Anim.* vi. 319 A large, elongated postero-lateral or *zygocardiac ossicle. 1888 *Amer. Naturalist* XXII. 832 The *zygodont (quadritubercular) type. 1901 *Proc. Zool. Soc.* 466 A *Vivipara* possessing a single *zygoneurous connection on the left and the normal dialoneurous relationship of the nerves upon the right. 1892 *Ibid.* 182 For the *Zygophiurans assistance in classification will be gained from Ljungman's well-known work. 1885 GOODALE *Physiol. Bot.* 439 *note*, The sexual process in *Zygophytes is characterized by the confluence of the protoplasmic masses of two very similar cells by which a new mass is formed as the starting-point of the new individual. 1900 W. J. LUCAS *Brit. Dragonflies* 53 A *Zygopterid [wing]. *Ibid.* 34 Nymph of a Zygopterid Dragonfly. 1880 A. W. BENNETT & MURRAY in *Q. Jrnl. Microsc. Sci.* XX. 417 The conjugated *zygospheres..constitute a *zygosperm. 1892 *Proc. Zool. Soc.* 1 Mar. 178 To regard the streptospondyline type [of ophiuroids] as earlier than the *zygospondyline. 1881 MIVART *Cat* 463 The caudal vertebræ are few and end in a bone, shaped somewhat like a ploughshare, called the *zygostyle. 1881 *Nature* 28 July 292 Family *Protococcaceæ*. Genus *Chlorochytrium*...Each cell becomes resolved into spherical zoospores, which upon leaving the mother-cell conjugate within the gelatinous envelope. The *zygozoospores before becoming surrounded with a membrane make their way..into the intercellular spaces of living plants.

Zygobranchiate (zəigobræ·ŋki,ĕt, zig-), *a.* (*sb.*) *Zool.* [f. mod.L. *Zygobranchiāta* pl., f. Gr. ζυγόν yoke + βράγχια gills: see -ATE [2].] Belonging to the division *Zygobranchiata* or *Zygobranchia* of gastropod molluscs, having paired (right and left) gills or ctenidia; as *sb.* a mollusc of this division.

1883 RAY LANKESTER in *Encycl. Brit.* XVI. 655/2 The Zygobranchiate Streptoneura.

Zygodactyl (zəigodæ·ktil, zig-), *a.* and *sb.* *Ornith.* Also **-yle.** [See ZYGO- and DACTYL.] **a.** *adj.* Having the toes 'yoked' or arranged in pairs, i. e. two before and two behind, as the feet of a scansorial bird, or the bird itself; yoke-toed. **b.** *sb.* A yoke-toed bird. Also **Zygodacty·lic**, **Zygoda·ctylous** *adjs.*

[1842 BRANDE *Dict. Sci.* etc., *Zygodactyles*, the name given by M. Temminck to an order of Climbing Birds.]

1828–32 WEBSTER, *Zygodactylous*. 1831 *Gard. & Menag. Zool. Soc.*, *Birds* 73 By the structure of their toes, which are partially zygodactyle (the intermediate ones being turned forwards, and the two lateral ones most commonly taking the opposite direction). 1835 PARTINGTON *Brit. Cycl. Nat. Hist.* I. 445/1 Feet which accomplish these purposes are all zygodactylic, or yoke-toed. 1890 COUES *Handbk. Ornithol.* 187 The arrangement of toes in pairs, two before and two behind,..is called zygodactyl or zygodactylous. *Ibid.* 188 The true hind toe is wanting, the outer anterior one being reversed as usual in zygodactyls.

‖**Zygoma** (zəigōᵘ·mă, zig-). *Anat.* Pl. **zygomata**, **zygomas.** Also 8 *erron.* **zigoma.** [mod. L., a. Gr. ζύγωμα, f. ζυγόν yoke. Cf. F. *zygome*, †*zigome*.] The bony arch on each side of the skull in vertebrates, consisting of the malar or jugal bone (cheek-bone) and its connexions, and forming a junction between the cranial and facial bones; the zygomatic arch; also, in restricted sense, some part of this, as the malar bone itself, the zygomatic process of the temporal bone, or the process of the malar which articulates with this.

1684 tr. *Blancard's Phys. Dict.* (1693), *Zygoma*, the jugal Bone about the Temples. 1758 J. S. tr. *Le Dran's Observ. Surg.* (1771) 13 There appeared near the *Zigoma*.., by the Wing of the Nostril, a slender Fluctuation. 1804 ABERNETHY *Surg. Obs.* 175 The fracture ran horizontally, about a quarter of an inch above the zygoma. 1806 SIR C. BELL *Anat. Expr.* (1872) 109 The zygoma, a process of the cheek-bone, which joins the temporal bone. 1825 A. MONRO *Anat. Hum. Body* I. 379 The Temporal muscle is seen in the temples, and its tendon passing under the zygoma. 1855 HOLDEN *Hum. Osteol.* (1878) 69 At the lower part of the squamous portion there is an outgrowth of bone, termed the zygoma. 1893 H. MORRIS *Treat. Human Anat.* 37 A ridge of bone, the supra-mastoid crest, runs immediately above the external auditory meatus, and is continued onwards to the zygoma.

Zygomatic (zəigomæ·tik, zig-), *a.* (*sb.*) *Anat.* [ad. mod.L. *zygomaticus*, f. Gr. ζύγωμα, -ατ-: see prec. and -IC.] Pertaining to or forming part of the zygoma; jugal.

Zygomatic apophysis = *z. process*. *Zygomatic arch* = ZYGOMA. *Zygomatic bone*, the malar bone. *Zygomatic fossa*, an irregularly-shaped cavity on the side of the skull below and within the zygomatic arch. *Zygomatic muscle*, any one of several small muscles connected with the zygoma; *esp.* each of two pairs of muscles (*zygomaticus major* and *minor*) arising from the malar bone and inserted at the corners of the mouth, serving to draw the upper lip outward and upward. *Zygomatic process*, a process of the squamosal portion of the temporal bone, which articulates with the malar bone. *Zygomatic suture*, the suture connecting the squamosal with the malar bone.

1709 BLAIR in *Phil. Trans.* XXVII. 143 Two Zygomatic Bones. 1741 A. MONRO *Anat.* (ed. 3) 95 Immediately before the Root of the zygomatic Process. 1811 C. BELL *Anat. Hum. Body* (ed. 3) I. 180 The zygomatic muscles pull the angles of the mouth upwards as in laughter. 1825 *Zool. Jrnl.* II. 162 The zygomatic arch. 1855 HOLDEN *Hum. Osteol.* 102 The 'zygomatic fossa' is bounded externally by the zygomatic arch. 1895 *Q. Rev.* July 178 That 'sweet contraction' of the zygomatic muscles.

B. *sb.* Short for *z. muscle* or *z. bone*.

1811 C. BELL *Anat. Hum. Body* (ed. 3) I. 181 The zygomatics and levators pull the angles of the mouth upwards. 1919 *Man* XIX. 156 Prominence of the zygomatics.

Zygoma·tico-, combining form of mod.L. *zygomaticus* ZYGOMATIC, forming adjs. in sense 'belonging to the zygoma or zygomatic arch and (some other part)', as *zygomatico-auricular* (see quot.).

1890 BILLINGS *Med. Dict.*, *Zygomatico-auricular index*, ratio between the bizygomatic and the biauricular diameters of the cranium.

Zygo·mato-, combining form of ZYGOMA, used as prec., as in *zygomato-temporal*.

1831 R. KNOX tr. *Cloquet's Anat.* (ed. 2) 41 The cerebral and zygomato-temporal aspects of the sphenoid bone.

Zygomorphic (zəigomǭ·ɹfik, zig-), *a.* *Bot.* [f. Gr. ζυγόν yoke + μορφή form + -IC.] Applied to a flower that is symmetrical about a single plane, i.e. divisible into similar lateral halves in only one way; = MONOSYMMETRICAL. Also **Zygomo·rphous**; opp. to ACTINOMORPHOUS. So **Zygomo·rphism**, the character of being zygomorphic.

1875 BENNETT & DYER tr. *Sachs' Bot.* 526 In Orchids both whorls are developed in a petaloid, and like the whole flower in a zygomorphic or monosymmetrical manner. *Ibid.* 534 The zygomorphism of the flower. 1879 A. GRAY *Struct. Bot.* 175 *note*, Both these forms [*sc.* monosymmetrical and polysymmetrical] have a more expressive and older terminology, adopted by Eichler, viz.:—*Zygomorphous*, for flowers, or other structures, which can be bisected in one plane,.. (*median zygomorphous*, when this is a median or antero-posterior plane,..*transverse zygomorphous*, when the plane of section is transverse or at right angles to the median).

‖**Zygon** (zəi·gǫn). Pl. **zyga** (zəi·gă). [mod.L., ad. Gr. ζυγόν yoke.]

1. *Anat.* The bar or stem connecting the two branches of an H-shaped fissure (*zygal fissure*) of the brain.

1886 B. G. WILDER in *Jrnl. Nerv. & Mental Dis.* June 310 If..the zygon is the principal, central, and primary constituent of a fissural integer, the paroccipital.

2. *Gr. Antiq.* A cross-bench or thwart for rowers.

1888 WOODGATE *Boating* (Badm. Libr.) i. 17 When.. vessels were expressly built as triremes, we may imagine ..the benches or zyga would be a little raised.

Zygophyllaceous (zəigofilēᵊ·ʃəs, zig-), *a.* *Bot.* [f. mod.L. *Zygophyllaceæ* pl., f. *Zygophyllum*, f. Gr. ζυγόν yoke + φύλλον leaf: see -ACEOUS.] Belonging to the N. O. *Zygophyllaceæ*, typified by the genus *Zygophyllum* (bean-capers).

1887 J. BALL *Nat. S. Amer.* 198 The singular Zygophyllaceous shrub *Porliera hygrometrica*.

‖**Zygopleura** (zəigoplūᵊ·ră, zig-), *sb. pl.* *Morphol.* [mod. L., f. Gr. ζυγόν yoke + πλευρά side.] Organic forms having bilateral symmetry, with

either two or four antimeres or corresponding opposite parts (DIPLEURA, TETRAPLEURA). Hence **Zygopleu·ral** *a.*, having bilateral symmetry.

1883 [see DIPLEURA]. 1896 [see DIPLEURAL def.].

‖**Zygosis** (zəigōᵘ·sis, zig-). *Biol.* [mod.L., ad. Gr. ζύγωσις, f. ζυγοῦν to yoke, f. ζυγόν yoke.] = CONJUGATION 5.

1880 PASCOE *Zool. Chem.* (ed. 2) 297. 1882 SAVILLE-KENT *Man. Infusoria* 874.

Zygosphene (zəi·gosfīn, zi·g-). *Anat.* and *Zool.* [f. Gr. ζυγόν yoke + σφήν wedge.] A double wedge-shaped projection on the anterior side of the neural arch of each ordinary vertebra in serpents and some lizards, which fits into the *zygantrum* of the next vertebra. Hence **Zygosphe·nal** *a.*, belonging to or constituting a zygosphene.

1854 OWEN in *Orr's Circ. Sci., Org. Nat.* I. 196 A wedge-shaped process (the 'zygosphene')..is developed from the fore part of the base of the spine. *Ibid.* 197 Surfaces to which the zygosphenal surfaces are adapted. 1892 *Proc. Zool. Soc.* 1 Mar. 176 The zygosphenes and zygantra of the Ophidian vertebræ.

Zygospore (zəi·gospōᵊɹ, zi·g-). *Bot.* [ad. G. *zygospor*: see ZYGO- and SPORE.] A spore formed by conjugation; a germ-cell arising from the fusion of two similar cells (gametes), as in certain Algæ and Fungi.

1864 *Q. Jrnl. Microscop. Sci.* (N. S.) IV. 178, I have..made use of..the more apt term 'Zygospore', as suggested by Professor De Bary in his work 'Untersuchungen..' in preference to the..inaccurate term 'Sporangium' of most other authors. 1874 COOKE *Fungi* 164 The threads which conjugate to form the zygospores.

† **Zygostat.** *Obs. rare*[—0]. [ad. late L. *zygostatēs*, a. Gr. ζυγοστάτης, f. ζυγόν yoke, beam of a balance, etc. + ἱστάναι to set, place.] Hence † **Zygostatical** *a.* (*obs. rare*[—0]). (See quots.)

1623 COCKERAM, *Zygost[at]e*, one that is appointed to see the weights, a Clarke of the market. [1654 CHARLETON *Physiol. Epic.-Gass.-Charlton.* 403 Such a Zygostata or Ballance, wherewith Jewellers are to weigh Pearles and Diamonds.] 1656 BLOUNT *Glossogr.*, *Zygostatical*..belonging to the pound weight of Sixteen ounces, or to a Clark of a Market that looks to weights.

Zygote (zəi·goᵘt). *Biol.* [ad. Gr. ζυγωτός yoked, f. ζυγοῦν to yoke.] A body of living protoplasm, as a cell or cell-nucleus, formed by the conjugation or fusion of two such bodies in reproduction; a zygospore, or any germ-cell resulting from the union of two reproductive cells or gametes. Also *attrib.* or as *adj.* That is a zygote, formed by conjugation; of or pertaining to a zygote.

1891 HARTOG in *Nature* 17 Sept. 484 Paragamy or Endokaryogamy: vegetative or gametal nuclei lying in a continuous mass of cytoplasm fuse to form a zygote nucleus. 1895 OLIVER tr. *Kerner's Nat. Hist. Plants* II. 628 The cell produced by the fusion of the bodies of two gametes is called the zygote.

Hence **Zygotic** (-ǫ·tik) *a.*, pertaining to or of the nature of a zygote, produced or characterized by zygosis; **Zygo·toblast** [-BLAST], one of a number of germ-cells or sporozoites produced by budding from a *zygotomere* (see below); **Zygo·toid** [-OID], a multinucleate form of zygote in certain fungi (see quot.); **Zygo·tomere** [Gr. μέρος part], one of a number of cells formed by segmentation of a zygote in the malaria parasite or other *Sporozoa*.

1891 HARTOG in *Nature* 17 Sept. 484 In apocytial fungi multinucleated masses of protoplasm (*gametoids*) may conjugate to form a *zygotoid*. 1899 *Allbutt's Syst. Med.* VIII. 945 Nucleus and protoplasm divide into a number of zygotomeres, which become blastophores, each bearing on its surface..a large number of filamentous zygotoblasts.

Zyke, **Zykere**, obs. ff. SICK, SICKER.

Zylo-, erroneous spelling of words in XYLO-.

Zymad (zəi·mæd). [f. Gr. ζύμη leaven + -AD, after *monad*.] A micro-organism which produces zymotic disease.

1885 *Leisure Hour* Jan. 25/2 The cook..exercises zymads and parasites. 1913 DORLAND *Med. Dict.*

Zymase (zəi·mēᵊs). *Chem.* [ad. F. *zymase* (Bechamp), f. Gr. ζύμη leaven, after *diastase*.] Name given to a ferment obtained from the yeast-fungus; also extended to unorganized ferments or enzymes in general.

1875 *Jrnl. Chem. Soc.* XXVIII. 374. 1899 J. R. GREEN *Soluble Ferm.* viii. 108 Bechamp thought that the enzyme from fungi was not quite the same as that existing in the flowers...He gave to the first the name *zymase*...The name *zymase* was soon abandoned, as it began to be applied to enzymes in general.

† **Zymate** (zəi·mēᵊt), in actual use **zumate** (ziū·mēᵊt). *Chem.* *Obs.* [f. ZYM-IC (*zum-ic*) + -ATE [4].] A salt of 'zymic acid'.

1817 T. THOMSON *Syst. Chem.* (ed. 5) II. 189 Zumate of ammonia. 1819 J. G. CHILDREN *Chem. Anal.* 281 Zumate of peroxide of iron.

Zyme (zəim). [ad. Gr. ζύμη leaven.] A name for the substance or principle causing a zymotic disease: cf. ZYMOSIS.

1882 *Quain's Dict. Med.* 1806 Corresponding with the adjective *zymotic* is the substantive *zyme*.., by which we refer to the poisonous cause of zymotic diseases.

† **Zymic** (zəi·mik, zi·mik), in actual use **zumic** (ziū·mik), *a.* *Chem.* *Obs.* [f. Gr. ζύμη leaven + -IC.] Pertaining to or connected with fermentation; formerly applied to a supposed acid (afterwards shown to be impure lactic acid) obtained by fermentation of starchy substances.

1817 T. THOMSON *Syst. Chem.* (ed. 5) II. 189 Of Zumic Acid. I give this name to an acid recently discovered by M. Braconnot. 1826 HENRY *Elem. Chem.* II. 241.

Zymin (zəi·min). Also **-ine.** [f. Gr. ζύμη leaven + -IN [1].] **a.** = ZYME. **b.** A pancreatic extract used in medicine. Hence **Zy·minized** *a.*, predigested by means of zymin.

1842 W. FARR in *4th Ann. Rep. Reg.-Gen.* 201 The morbific principle (zymine). *Ibid.* 202 Some..kinds of matter (zymin) are reproduced in the organization after they have been destroyed by transformation (zymosis) in attacks of disease. 1888 M. MACKENZIE *Fredk. the Noble* vii. 99 Zyminised nutriments. 1901 DORLAND *Med. Dict.*, *Zymin*, ..a pancreatic extract prepared for therapeutic use.

Zymo- (zəimo), before a vowel **zym-**, combining form repr. Gr. ζύμη leaven, used in the general sense 'ferment', in various scientific terms. (Some of these were formerly written *zumo-*, the Gr. υ being represented, contrary to analogy, by *u*: see Y.) **Zy·mocyte** (-səit) [-CYTE], a unicellular organism which produces fermentation. **Zy:mogluco·nic** *a.*, epithet of an acid obtained by fermentation from glucose; hence **Zymoglu·conate**, a salt of this acid. ‖ **Zy:mohydro·lysis**, hydrolysis effected by the action of a ferment. **Zymo·logy** († zumo-) [-LOGY], the science of fermentation; that department of chemistry which deals with ferments and their action; hence **Zymolo·gical** († zumo-) *a.*, relating to zymology; **Zymo·logist** († zumo-), one versed in zymology. **Zymo·lysis** [Gr. λύσις loosening], decomposition by means of a (esp. an unorganized) ferment; so **Zymoly·tic** *a.*, pertaining to or involving zymolysis. **Zymo·meter** († zumo-) [-METER] = ZYMOSIMETER. **Zy·mophore** (-fōᵊɹ), **Zymophoric** (-fǫ·rik), **Zymophorous** (-ǫ·fŏrəs) *adjs.* [see -PHORE, etc.], in Ehrlich's theory of immunization, applied to a particular group of atoms in a ferment, or in the receptors of a living cell, to which the fermentative action is due (analogous to the toxophore group in a toxin). **Zy·mophyte** (-fəit) [-PHYTE], a vegetable organism which causes fermentation. **Zymopla·stic** *a.* [see PLASTIC *a.*], forming a ferment. **Zy·moscope** [-SCOPE]: see quot. **Zymotechnic** (-te·knik), **-ical** *adjs.* [Gr. τεχνή art], relating to the art of fermentation; so **Zymote·chnics**, **Zy·motechny**, the art of fermentation (cf. ZYMURGY); **Zy:motechno·logy** [-LOGY], the scientific study of the principles of zymotechny; **Zy:motechno·logist**, one versed in zymotechnology. **Zymoto·xic** *a.*, having a fermentative and toxic action.

a 1909 *Disinfectants* 14 (Cent. D. Suppl.) Salicylic acid only holding its reputation as an enemy to the *zymocytes of the cider barrel. 1887 *Jrnl. Chem. Soc.* LII. 468 The crystallised ammonium gluconate recently described by Volpert..had previously been obtained by the author [*sc.* L. Boutroux], and described by him as ammonium *zymogluconate. 1886 *Ibid.* L. 682 The *zymogluconic acid obtained by the action of *M[icrococcus] oblongus* on glucose. 1903 C. SNYDER *New Concept. Sci.* 236 Croft Hill's bold announcement, three or four years ago, of the discovery of 'reversible *zymohydrolysis'. 1828–32 WEBSTER, *Zumological, *Zumologist. 1846 WORCESTER, Zymological, Zymologist (citing OSWALD). 1753 *Chambers's Cycl. Supp.*, *Zymology [referring to W. Simpson's *Zymologia Physica*, 1675]. 1828–32 WEBSTER, *Zumology*. 1890 A. S. LEA in *Jrnl. Physiol.* XI. 254 *note*, I would suggest that the word '*zymolysis' might be..used to denote generally the changes produced by the enzymes or unorganised ferments. *Ibid.* 264 The *zymolytic activity of the digestive fluid. 1842 BRANDE *Dict. Sci.*, etc., **Zumometer*, or *Zumosimeter*... an instrument intended to show the degree to which fermentation has proceeded in different fermenting liquors. 1900 *U. S. Dept. Agric., Bur. Anim. Ind.* Rep. 257 (Cent. D. Suppl.) The hypothesis of Morgenroth in regard to the existence of a haptophore group and the [*sic*; ?a] *zymophore group in the labile ferment has been recently verified by Myers and Bashford, who have discovered zymoids analogous to the toxoids. 1902 *Brit. Med. Jrnl.* 12 Apr. 920 There is no amboceptor as such, but the body consists of a *zymophoric group. 1890 BILLINGS *Med. Dict.*, **Zymophytes*, bacteroid ferments that liberate fatty acids from neutral fats. 1868 WATTS *Dict. Chem.* V. 1086 **Zymoscope*, an instrument..for testing the fermenting power of yeast, by bringing it in contact with sugar-water, and observing the quantity of carbonic anhydride evolved. 1896 A. K. MILLER tr. *E. C. Hansen's Ferment.* 71 Ancker and Bergh's *zymotechnic laboratory, Stockholm. 1900 tr. *A. Jörgensen's Micro-org. & Ferment.* 47 *Zymotechnical examinations of water according to the principles laid down by Hansen. 1896 A. K. MILLER tr. *E. C. Hansen's Ferment.* 113 Several *zymotechnologists have made similar experiments. 1860 MAYNE *Expos. Lex.*, *Zymotechny. 1902 *Jrnl. Exper. Med.* 17 Mar. 282 The complement possesses in addition to such a..haptophore group, another group which exhibits fermentative properties (*zymotoxic or toxophore group).

Zymogen (zəi·modʒen). *Biol. Chem.* [ad. G. *zymogen* (Heidenhain, 1875): see ZYMO- and -GEN.] A substance formed in an organism, from which a ferment is produced. Also *attrib.*

1877 M. FOSTER *Physiol.* II. i. (1878) 219 A pancreas taken fresh from the body..contains but little ready-made ferment, though there is present in it a body which, by some kind of decomposition, gives birth to the ferment...To this body..Heidenhain has given the name of Zymogen. 1896 E. B. WILSON *Cell in Devel.* 288 Zymogen granules. 1897 *Allbutt's Syst. Med.* III. 306 A zymogen is the antecedent of the ferment of the secretion—pepsinogen, trypsinogen, for example.

So **Zymogene·tic**, **Zymoge·nic**, **Zymo·genous** *adjs.*, producing a ferment, or causing fermentation.

1896 *Allbutt's Syst. Med.* I. 528 Organisms..acting partly as ferments, partly as *zymogenetic cells. 1884 KLEIN *Micro-org.* xxi. 187 Putrefactive and many *zymogenic organisms thrive well at ordinary temperatures. 1900 *Nature* 13 Sept. 465 Zymogenic..bacteria.

Zymoid (zəi·moid), *a.* and *sb.* [f. Gr. ζύμη: see ZYMO- and -OID.] **a.** *adj.* Resembling a ferment. **b.** *sb.* A substance having a relation to a ferment analogous to that of a toxoid to the corresponding toxin.

1891 *Cent. Dict.* 1900 [see *zymophore* under ZYMO-].

† **Zy·mome.** *Chem.* *Obs.* Also **zimome.** [ad. mod.L. *zymōma*, It. *zimoma* (Taddei), ad. Gr. ζύμωμα fermented mixture, f. ζυμοῦν: see ZYMOSIS.] A name for that constituent of gluten which is insoluble in alcohol. Also called † **Zymomin.**

[1820 *Q. Jrnl. Sci.* VIII. 377 D. Taddei..having undertaken researches in fermentation,..in various cases has ascertained that the gluten of wheat is composed of two substances, perfectly distinct from each other, one of which he has named *gloiodina*, and the other *zimoma*.] 1820 T. THOMSON in *Ann. Phil.* May 390 M. Taddey..has lately ascertained that the gluten of wheat may be decomposed into two principles, which he has distinguished by the names, *gliadine*..and *zimome*. 1826 HENRY *Elem. Chem.* II. 268 Zimome is obtained pure by boiling gluten in alcohol. 1830 DONOVAN *Dom. Econ.* I. 345 Zimomin is of a dirty white colour, hard, and without any of the elasticity which gluten possesses. 1831 JONES *New Convers. Chem.* xxix. 292 Zymome.

Zymosi·meter. Also **zumo-.** [f. Gr. ζύμωσις (see next) + μέτρον measure: see -METER.] An instrument for measuring the degree of fermentation of a fermenting liquor.

1704 J. HARRIS *Lex. Techn.* I, Zymosimetre. 1842 Zumosimeter [see *zymometer* under ZYMO-].

‖**Zymosis** (zəimōᵘ·sis). Pl. **zymoses** (-sīz). [mod.L., ad. Gr. ζύμωσις fermentation, f. ζυμοῦν to leaven, in pass. to ferment, f. ζύμη leaven: see -OSIS.] Fermentation; *spec.* the morbid process which constitutes a zymotic disease, regarded as analogous to or involving fermentation.

1842 W. FARR in *4th Ann. Rep. Reg.-Gen.* 201 *note*, Zymosis fermentation, and zyma ferment, may also be employed in English, not in the sense which they have in Greek, but as general designations of the morbid processes and their exciters. *Ibid.* 202 [see ZYMIN]. 1876 BARTHOLOW *Mat. Med.* (1879) 523 As all fermentations are correlative of the growth and multiplication of these minute bodies, carbolic acid, by destroying their activity, arrests zymosis.

fig. 1876 EMERSON *Lett. & Soc. Aims, Eloquence* Wks. (Bohn) III. 195 In the Elizabethan Age there was a dramatic *zymosis*, when all the genius ran in that direction.

Zymotic (zəimǫ·tik), *a.* (*sb.*) [ad. Gr. ζυμωτικός causing fermentation, f. ζυμοῦν: see ZYMOSIS.] A general epithet for infectious diseases, originally because regarded as being caused by a process analogous to fermentation (cf. ZYMOSIS); pertaining to this theory of disease; causing such disease.

1842 W. FARR in *4th Ann. Rep. Reg.-Gen.* 201 The property of communicating their action, and effecting analogous transformations in other bodies, is..characteristic in these diseases, which it is proposed therefore to call..zymotic. 1851 MAYHEW *Lond. Labour* (1861) II. 395/2 The zymotic doctrine of the Board of Health as to the cause of cholera. 1896 *Allbutt's Syst. Med.* I. 528 Since many morbid processes are analogous, if not akin, to fermentative processes, ..the term *zymotic* has been applied to them,—a term, however, to be avoided rather than recommended.

b. In etymological sense: Causing or consisting in fermentation, fermentative.

1874 GARROD & BAXTER *Mat. Med.* 145 The zymotic action of yeast.

c. *transf.* Containing putrefactive germs.

1881 TYNDALL *Ess. Floating Matter Air* 208 An éprouvette containing one cubic centimeter of cold water, previously ascertained to be zymotic, was evaporated to dryness.

B. *sb.* A zymotic disease.

1842 W. FARR in *4th Ann. Rep. Reg.-Gen.* 201 A single word, such as Zymotics, is required to replace..the long periphrasis 'epidemic, endemic, and contagious diseases'. 1859 *Househ. Words* 8 Jan. 122/2 People who have died of Zymotics. 1916 *Lancet* 8 Jan. 112/1 Health of Belfast... In 1914 there were 51 notifications of typhus..; not a case of this zymotic has been reported in 1915.

Hence **Zymo·tically** *adv.*

1851 MAYHEW *Lond. Labour* (1861) II. 385/2 Whether this mass of filth be, zymotically, the cause of cholera.

Zymurgy (zəi·mɒɹdʒi). [f. Gr. ζύμη leaven + -ουργία working, as in METALLURGY.] The practice or art of fermentation, as in wine-making, brewing, distilling, etc. 1868 WATTS *Dict. Chem.* V. 1086.

Zynder, **Zyne**, **Zyphe**: see CINDER, SINE [1], XIPH. **Zyþ**, obs. (Kentish) 3rd sing. ind. pres. of SEE *v.* **Zyþe**, obs. f. SITHE *sb.*[1] **Zyxst**, obs. f. SIXTH. **Zyxt**, obs. (Kentish) 2nd sing. ind. pres. of SEE *v.*

Supplement, p. 3873; Corrigenda, p. 4092; Spurious words, p. 4093; Books quoted, p. 4094

A NEW
ENGLISH DICTIONARY
SUPPLEMENT

Column 1

A. Add: *From A to Z:* see Z 3.

Aasvogel (ä-sfōgel). [S. African Du., f. *aas* carrion (cf. KES) + *vogel* bird, Fowl.] A South African vulture, esp. *Gyps Kolbii.*

Aba, abba (ä'bä). [Arab. عباء *ʿabā.*] A sleeveless outer garment, resembling a sack with openings for the head and arms, worn by Arabs.

Aba'ctinally, *adv.* [f. ABACTINAL + -LY².] Towards the abactinal side.

Abalone (abalō'ni). [Sp., of unknown origin.] A gastropod mollusc of the genus *Haliotis,* used for food; an ear-shell or sea ear. Also *attrib.*, as *abalone meat, fishery, shell.*

Abaya (äbä'yä). An Arab shirt, abbat, abaya. [Arab. عباية *ʿabāya.*] = ABA.

Abbozzo (äbbe'tsu). An *(obs. rare.)* [It.] A rough drawing or sketch (for a portrait, etc.); an outline or draught (of a speech, essay, etc.).

Abduction. Add:

Abdominally, *adv.* = ABDOMINAL + -LY².] In or with reference to the abdomen.

Abdomino-, used as comb. form of ABDOMEN, as in *abdomino-anterior, posterior* adjs.

Aberdeen (äbə(r)dī·n). The name of a city and county in Scotland.

Aberdonian (äbə(r)dō·niăn), *a.* and *sb.* [f. med.L. *Aberdonia* : see -IAN.] Of or pertaining to, a native of, Aberdeen.

Aberglaube (ä'bərglaubə). [G., f. *aber-* additional + *Glaube* belief.] Belief beyond what is certain and verifiable.

Abernethy (äbə(r)ne'þi). Of disputed origin.

Abessive (äbe'siv), *a.* Finnish Gram. [f. L. *abesse* to be distant + -IVE.] Applied to the case which denotes absence.

Column 2

Abiturient (äbitiū·riĕnt). [G., ad. mod.L *abituriens,* pr. pple. of *abiturire,* desiderative of *abire* to go away.] In Germany, a pupil who is leaving a 'gymnasium' or high-school to enter a university.

A.B.C. (ĕbʉ·). Initial letters of *Aerated Bread Company.*

Abdominally, (abdu'minăli), *adv.* [f. ABDOMINAL + -LY².] In or with reference to the abdomen.

Adjoint (äbdʒoi·nt), *n. Biol.* [f. AB- + JOINT sb.] To separate by formation of a joint or partition, as the cells and spores in certain fungi.

Ablate, *v.* Delete † *Obs. rare,* and add after def.: *Obs.* in general sense; in recent scientific use as back-formation from ABLATION 3, 4.

Ablatival (äblätəi'văl), *a. Gram.* [f. ABLATIVE + -AL.] Pertaining to the ablative case.

Ablaut (ä'blaut), *sb. Philol.* [a. Ger. *Ablaut.*] Applied to an electric current which passes from a nerve fibre to and through a muscular fibre.

Abneural (äbniū·răl), *a. Anat.* [AB- + Gr. νεῦρον nerve + -AL.] Of or pertaining to the region opposite to the central nervous system.

Abox, *adv.* and *prep.* Add: **A.** L. *c. All aboard,* the call to warn passengers to get aboard a vessel about to start. Also *transf.*

Abracadabra. Add:

About. Add:

Abolition. Add:

Column 3

Acadian (äkē·diăn), *a.* and *sb.* Also **Akkadian.** [f. *Accad,* one of the five cities in 'the land of Shinar' or Babylonia (Gen. x. 10) + -IAN.] *A. adj.* Of or belonging to the primitive (non-Semitic) language of Babylonia; pertaining to the Accadians. *B. sb.* The Accadian language; a member of one of the primitive races of Babylonia.

Accelerans (äkse'lerănz). *Anat.* [prev. pple. of L. *accelerare* to ACCELERATE.] Applied (*attrib.* or as *sb.*) to certain fibres and nerves which accelerate the action of the heart.

Accelerate, *v.* 1. b. To increase the speed of (a railway train, motor-car, motor-engine, etc.); also *absol.* (cf. sense 3).

Acceleration. Add:

Accelerator. Add: **b.** An apparatus to regulate the speed of the engine in a motor-vehicle, for increasing speed; also *attrib.*, as *accelerator pedal,* the pedal that controls the 'throttle'; *accelerator valve* (see quot. 1901).

Accelerometer (äkselərə·mītə(r)). [f. *accelero-*, irreg. comb. f. repr. ACCELERATE, etc. + -METER.] An instrument for ascertaining the acceleration of a moving body.

Accent, *sb.* Add:

Accentor (äkse·ntə(r)). *Ornith.* [Late L. *accentor* one who sings with another (Isidore), f. *ad* + *cantor* singer, f. *cantare* to sing.] A genus of passerine singing birds (Bechstein), including the hedge sparrow or hedge accentor, *A. modularis;* a bird of this genus.

Column 4

Acclimator. *U.S.* [f. ACCLIMATE v.] One who becomes acclimatized.

Accommodate, *v.* Add: **11. b.** *spec.* Of a bank, etc.: To furnish (a person) with a loan of money. (Cf. ACCOMMODATION 8.)

Accommodation. Add: **6. b.** *spec.* To accommodate with a loan.

Accordion. Add: **b.** *attrib.* and *Comb.*, in reference to things having a series of folds like those of the bellows of an accordion; esp. *accordion pleat, pleating, skirt.*

Accretionary (äkrī·ʃənări), *a.* [f. ACCRETION + -ARY.] Characterized or formed by accretion.

Accretive. Add quots.

Accrete, *v.* Add: **3. b.** To draw or attract to oneself or itself.

Accultuation (äkʌltiū·ʃən). *U.S.* [f. AC- *pref.* + CULTURE *sb.* + -ATION.] The adoption and assimilation of an alien culture.

Accumulator. 3. Add quots.

Acquired, *ppl. a.* Add: *phr. acquired taste,* a taste for a food or drink that is gained by constant use; also *transf.* applied to any thing or person for which or for whom one has acquired a liking.

Acrobatic, *a.* Add:

b. *sb.* **Acrobatics,** Acrobatic performances or feats; also *transf.* and *fig.*

Acrochordite (ækrǫkǭ·ɹdəit). *Min.* [ad. Sw. *akrochordit* (1922), f. Gr. ἀκροχορδών wart: see -ITE¹.] Hydrated basic arsenate of manganese and magnesium found in small spherical aggregates.
1923 *Amer. Min.* VIII. 167.

Acromegaly (ækrome·gāli). *Path.* [ad. Fr. *acromégalie* (P. Marie), f. Gr. ἄκρον extremity + μέγας, μεγαλ- great.] A disease characterized by hypertrophy and enlargement of the extremities. Hence **Acromegalic** (-mĭgæ·lik), *a.* pertaining to or of the nature of acromegaly; *sb.* one affected with acromegaly.
1889 *Brain* July 59 Acromegaly. By Pierre Marie, M.D. 1896 *Godey's Mag.* Feb. 125/1 A..very rare disease,..acromegaly, or the enormous enlargement of the feet, hands, face, and chest. 1909 *Cent. Dict.* Suppl., *Acromegalic.*

Acroscopic (ækrosko·pik), *a. Bot.* [f. Gr. ἄκρον apex + -σκοπος viewing + -IC.] Looking, or on the side, towards the apex.
1882 VINES tr. *Sachs' Bot.* 450 In *Azolla*, the leaves of the one row all arise from one cell of the acroscopic part of the segment.

Across. Add: **A.** *adv.* **2.** c. *Across to* = '*up to*' (UP *adv.*² 17 d). *U.S.*
1911 R. W. CHAMBERS *Common Law* x. 303 It's across to her, now.
4. Delete † and read *Obs.* exc. *dial.*
1887 BARING-GOULD *Red Spider* vii, When folks who look straight before them fall across. *Ibid.*, The two who have got across. 1892 *Cornh. Mag.* July 28 Matters were soon across again between the pair. 1897 *Daily News* 4 Mar. 6/1 He is getting across with the farmers now, for he roundly rates them on account of their apathy.
B. *prep.* **2.** *Across lots* (U.S.): see LOT *sb.* 6 a.
b. U.S. phr. orig. *Across the footlights*: from the performers to the audience; hence advb. (by ellipsis) in *to get* or *come across* (*to*), to reach the audience or the public, to make oneself or itself understood or appreciated; similarly *to get it across*. (For *to put it across* see *PUT *v.* Cf. *OVER.)
1913 KIPLING *Diversity of Creatures* (1917) 190 Tell a fellow now, did I get it across? 1921 *Sat. Westm. Gaz.* 27 Aug. 14/2 Some vitality that may be as far away as you like from lifelikeness or psychological truth, but nevertheless gets across to the reader from the writer. 1923 *Westm. Gaz.* 27 Feb., It is very doubtful whether the play would get across the footlights in an ordinary run. *Ibid.* 26 Mar., 'Magda', dressed as a comedy of manners of a hundred years ago, would probably come across more satisfactorily than it does played as..contemporary tragedy. 1927 *Observer* 16 Oct. 15/3 The lower comedy is at present in the making, but Miss B. C., Mr. E. M. and Mr. L. H. are experts at getting it across. 1927 *Daily Tel.* 19 July 12/4 The Earl of Birkenhead..said..he had never succeeded in projecting his personality across the footlights.

Acrostical (ăkrǫ·stikăl), *a.* [f. ACROSTIC + -AL; cf. -ICAL.] Of the nature of, consisting of, or in the form of an acrostic.
1843 J. HOLLAND *Psalmists Brit.* I. 104 The whole Bible is abridged in a sort of scheme of acrostical mnemonics. 1887 LUPTON in *W. Smith's Dict. Chr. Biog.* IV. 648/1 The Eighth Book, in acrostichal verse. 1894 *Athenæum* 28 July 128/3 Chaucer's 'A B C', a curious acrostical prayer 'like Psalm cxviii'.

Act, *v.* Add:
8. b. Of a play: To be susceptible of being performed (well or otherwise).
1821 BYRON in Trelawny *Recoll. Shelley & Byron* (1858) 29 My plays won't act..my poesy won't sell. 1926 SHEILA KAY-SMITH *John Galsworthy* 17 Galsworthy's plays have the advantage of acting well—unlike much literary drama.
9. f. *To act up*, to become unruly, to make a disturbance. *U.S.*
1903 A. ADAMS *Log Cowboy* xviii. 275 The horse of some peeler..acted up one morning.

Actability (æktăbi·liti). Also irreg. **-ibility**. [f. ACTABLE: see *-BILITY.] Capability of being acted.
1836 *Fraser's Mag.* Apr. 451 Opinions..as to the actibility of certain unacted plays. 1925 *Glasgow Herald* 9 Apr. 4 When Hugh M'Diarmid's Braid Scots play, 'The Purple Patch', appeared,..doubts were expressed as to its actability.

Actinally (see ACTINAL), *adv.* [f. ACTINAL + -LY².] Towards the actinal or oral side.
1888 [see *ABACTINALLY *adv.*].

Actine. Add:
2. A 'ray' or radiating part of a sponge-spicule.
1887 SOLLAS in *Encycl. Brit.* XXII. 416/2 Two actines soldered together by intervening silica.

Acting, *vbl. sb.* **5.** Add:
Applied to versions of plays specially prepared for actors' use (provided with full stage-directions, etc.), as *acting copy, drama, edition, version*.
1834 (*title*) The Acting Drama; containing all the popular plays, standard and modern. 1850 (*title*) Lacy's acting edition of plays. 1910 W. W. GREG *Shaks. Merry W.* Introd. 31 These four scenes cannot have been altogether omitted in the acting version.

Acting, *ppl. a.* **3.** Add: Applied esp. to a person (usually in a subordinate position) taking duty as a temporary substitute, as *acting editor, head, secretary*. Hence *acting allowance*.
[1781 *Proc. Trial Lord George Gordon* 39 Q. Pray, did he, or any one else, act as President of any meeting then held? *A.* I understood him to be acting as President.] 1783 *Pol. Mag.* IV. 195 Mr. Harpley, the acting carpenter, died with fatigue. 1826 *New Monthly Mag.* II. 486 Sentence remitted by the acting governor. 1833 *Rep. Sel. Comm. King's Printers' Patents* 5 When I succeeded in 1800 Mr. Bruce, the Co-patentee, had already been appointed acting manager. 1836 MARRYAT *Midsh. Easy* xxv, He..served his time, was acting lieutenant for two years and then somehow or other he bore up for the Church. 1872 E. F. MOORE *Privy Council Rep.* (N.S.) IX. 402 Judgment was given by Sir Charles Farquhar Shand, Chief Judge, and the acting second Puisne Judge, Gorrie. 1886 KIPLING *Departm. Ditties*, etc. *Public Waste*, A Deputy-Acting-Vice-Resident-Engineer. 1888 — *Plain Tales fr. Hills* 16 Nothing matters except Home-furlough and acting allowances. 1902 BANKS *Newspaper Girl* 70 I'm acting editor, and if it's anything important I'll lay it before him and give you an answer.

Actinian (ækti·niăn). *Zool.* [f. ACTINIA + -AN.] A sea-anemone belonging to the genus *Actinia*.
1888 *Athenæum* 30 June 830 A tube-forming actinian (*Cerianthus membranaceus*). 1902 *Fortn. Rev.* June 1012 The actinian..merely responds mechanically to a chemical stimulus.

Actinium. Add:
2. *Chem.* A radio-active metallic element found, associated with thorium, in pitchblende. Symbol Ac.
1904 J. J. THOMSON *Electr. & Matter* 141 M. and Mme. Curie, with..MM. Bemont and Debierne, succeeded in establishing the existence of three new radio-active substances in pitch-blende: radium,..polonium,..and actinium.

Actinize (æ·ktinəiz), *v. Photogr.* [f. ACTINISM + -IZE.] *trans.* To affect (a photographic plate) with actinism.
1889 *Anthony's Photogr. Bull.* II. 320 It requires at noon two and one-half times longer exposure on December 21st than on June 21st to equally actinize a plate.

Actinograph. Add:
b. esp. *Photogr.* An instrument (of which there are various kinds) used for recording the actinic power of the light, to determine the correct time of exposure for a photographic plate.
1890 *Anthony's Photogr. Bull.* III. 432 The actinograph [before us] is..an ingenious application of the slide rule for the purpose of determining photographic exposures. 1902 *Encycl. Brit.* XXX. 702/1 In Hurter & Driffield's 'Actinograph', the light coefficient is given by a printed card showing the curves for every day in the year.

Actinology (ækting·lŏdʒi). [f. ACTINO- + -LOGY.] The science of the chemical action of light. Hence **Actino·logous** *a.*, exhibiting actinology. **Acti·nologue**, an actinologous part.
1883 OGILVIE Suppl., *Actinology*. 1894 GOULD *Dict. Med.*, Actinologous, Actinologue.

Actinomyces (æktinŏmǝi·sīz). [mod.L., f. Gr. ἀκτίς, -ῖν- ray (see ACTINO-) + μύκης fungus.] The ray-fungus, the presence of which, in cattle, constitutes the disease **Actinomyco·sis**, forms of which are known as *lumpy jaw* (LUMPY *a.* 1 c) and *wooden tongue* (WOODEN *a.* 9). Also *attrib.* Hence **Actinomyco·tic** *a.*, resembling, related to, or caused by actinomyces.
1882 *Times* 8 Nov. 5/6 From the peculiar manner in which the fungus grows..it has received the name of Actinomyces, and it is consequently proposed to designate the disease Actinomykosis. 1884 KLEIN *Micro-org.* xvi. 148 In the centre of the nodules lie dense groups of peculiar club-shaped corpuscles—*actinomyces*...Each of these actinomyces-corpuscles appears homogeneous. 1900–1 *Jrnl. Exper. Med.* V. 179 The actinomycotic form of the tubercle bacillus.

Action, *sb.* **6. b.** Add U.S. quots.:
a 1861 WINTHROP *John Brent* iii. (1862) 28 He trotted after, a hundred feet behind the hindmost, with large and liberal action. 1867–9 *Trans. Ill. Agric. Soc.* VII. 80 Best pair of mares, to be shown in harness—style and action to be the test.
16. Add: **action-photography**, photography representing the subject in action; hence *action-photograph*; **action-time** *Psychol.*, the period between reaction and the application of a stimulus; reaction-time.
1905 BELDAM & FRY *Great Batsmen* (title-p.), Illustrated by 600 action-photographs. *Ibid.*, Key-notes p. xi, The book is founded upon Action-Photography and Actual Experience. 1906 *Academy* 21 July 60/1 Investigations..into the action-time of stimulus upon visual sensation.

Actionability (ækʃənăbi·liti). [f. ACTIONABLE: see *-BILITY.] Liability to action at law.
1883 MOYLE *Instit. Justinian* I. 46 Actionability is only one of such usual incidents.

Actioning (æ·kʃəniŋ), *vbl. sb.* [f. ACTION *sb.* (6 c) + -ING¹.] The furnishing (of a gun) with an action.
1882 WALSH *Mod. Sportsman's Gun* I. 96 In the various forms of actioning, this breech action is slotted in different ways.

Activate, *v.* Delete † *Obs.*, and add:
1858 BENNET *Nutrition* ii. 47 Increased muscular vigour ..activates respiration. 1905 *Sat. Westm. Gaz.* 15 July 13 The young English dramatist has very few opportunities of making the hair of the Philistine stand on end or activating his digestion. 1926 J. A. THOMSON *Man in light of Evol.* 20 The rarely activated muscles of our ear-trumpet.
b. spec. in *Physics*. To make radioactive.
1902 *Jrnl. Soc. Chem. Industry* 30 Aug. 1102/2 Schönbein ..found that sulphurous acid had a remarkable 'activating' (*activirende*) effect on various oxidising substances, *i.e.*, they were considerably more active in the presence of small quantities of sulphurous acid. 1903 *Electr. World & Engineer* 10 Jan. 86 (C. D. Suppl.) Underground air is not like activated air. 1907 *Med. Record* 3 Aug. 171 The former [ferment, viz. enterokinase] activates the pancreatic juice. 1921 *Glasgow Herald* 13 Aug. 5 The new process of producing activated sludge by which complete purification of the sewage is achieved.
Hence **Activation** (æktivē·ʃən), the action of activating; the state of being activated; spec. in *Physics*, the method or process of producing radio-activity.
1906 *Practitioner* Dec. 747 Mixed sera from several animals might be used, in the hope of finding one suitable for activation with human serum.

Active, *a.* **4.** Add:
active list, a list of officers in the army and navy who are performing, or are available for, military service, and are receiving full pay; *active service*, war service in the field or at sea.
1838 *Navy List* 20 Sept. 118 Alphabetical List of Masters. Those in Italics are unfit for active Service. 1852 *Ibid.* 20 Dec. 327 The number of Captains on the Active List will be reduced to a number not permanently exceeding 350. 1859 *Queen's Regul. Army* 326 When a regiment is embarked for active field service, the embarkation of soldiers' wives is altogether forbidden. 1865 W. H. D. ADAMS *Famous Regim.* 284 During the remainder of the campaign he showed himself fully worthy of the responsibilities cast upon him, though it was his first essay in active service. 1880 *Army List* Nov. 109ª Mobilization of the Forces In Great Britain and Ireland. Active Army. 1899 KIPLING *Absent-Minded Beggar* i, He is out on active service, wiping something off a slate.

Activism (æ·ktiviz'm). [f. ACTIVE *a.* + -ISM.]
1. A philosophical theory which assumes the objective reality and active existence of everything.
1908 BOYCE GIBSON tr. *Eucken's Meaning & Value of Life* Pref. p. vii, Eucken's philosophy has been variously described as 'The New Idealism', a 'Religious' or 'Spiritual' Idealism, and as an 'Activism'. 1920 H. L. ENO *Activism* x. 176 Activism is..essentially realistic. It assumes the 'objective' validity and 'real' being of entities and relations, as well as the fundamental relational complexes of space, time, number, and change.
2. A policy of advocating energetic action.
1920 *Glasgow Herald* 12 Aug. 7 It is a question of repelling the fateful activism of the Entente just as it was necessary in 1916 to stand against German activism.
Hence **Activist** (æ·ktivist), an advocate of activism in either sense; also *attrib.* = **Activi·stic** *a.*
1909 *Athenæum* 17 Apr. 469/3 Pragmatism..is tainted with the characteristic activist fallacy of making process as active account for the structural form of process which it implies. 1913 E. UNDERHILL *Mystic Way* 31 The positive and activistic mysticism of the West. 1915 *Times* 7 Aug. 7/6 For some, neutrality simply means a passive aloofness. For others, neutrality should be active, and these are divided, in the current jargon, with active and passive 'activists'. 1920 *Glasgow Herald* 30 Sept. 6 The activist and dominant section of Sinn Fein. 1923 J. W. HARPER *Essentials Relig.* vi. 96 The activistic factor is indeed supreme. 1927 *Public Opinion* Feb. 206/1 We are no longer all Socialists, to recall Harcourt's classic gibe, but we are certainly all 'activists'.

Actualist (æ·ktiŭălist). [f. ACTUAL *a.* 3.] One who aims at actuality or realism.
1887 *Harper's Mag.* Jan. 324/1 In his first essay in the field of fiction he turns out an actualist, whose first wish seems to be truth to his facts and the meaning of them.

Actuarially (æktiŭē·riăli), *adv.* [f. ACTUARIAL *a.* + -LY².] In relation to actuarial principles, on an actuarial basis.
1884 *Athenæum* 12 July 39/3 That..every society hereafter formed has its actuarially certified table. 1886 *N. Amer. Rev.* Sept. 233 The trade-unions of England are, actuarially speaking, bankrupt. 1905 *Daily News* 12 Apr. 9/3 These schemes..were found..to be actuarially sound.

Actuate, *v.* **6.** Delete † *Obs.* and add:
1920 *Chamb. Jrnl.* 25 Dec. 55/1 The [human] mass..came round with an almost dismaying swiftness. 'How could such a bulk actuate with such rapidity?' Clement thought. 1924 O. LODGE *Making of Man* v. 113 He is beginning to learn.. that the portion of consciousness now actuating and made manifest in his brain is but a small part of the whole.
Hence **A·ctuator**, one who or a thing which actuates.
1890 C. MERCIER *Sanity & Insanity* xii. 299 The higher nerve regions are the actuators of conduct.

Acyclic, *a.* Add:
b. *Dynamics*, etc. That does not move in circles.
1873 MAXWELL *Electr. & Magn.* I. 137 As the negative region continues to expand till it fills all space, it loses every degree of cyclosis it has acquired, and becomes at last acyclic. 1902 *Encycl. Brit.* XXVII. 57c/2 The system now behaves, as regards the co-ordinates $q_1, q_2, \ldots q_m$, exactly like the acyclic type there contemplated.
c. *Chem.* That contains no cycle or ring of atoms. (Said of an organic compound.)
1913 BLOXAM & LEWIS *Chem.* 544 There are two great divisions of organic compounds (*a*) The acyclic, open-chain, fatty or aliphatic..series..; (*b*) the cyclic or closed-chain series.

Ad, colloq. abbrev. of ADVERTISEMENT.
1868 *Putnam's Mag.* Aug. 215/2 In the newspaper offices and the advertising business they say 'ad'. 1884 *Milnor (Dakota) Teller* 4 July, Mr. P. Wicklund, merchant, has recovered the stray advertised two weeks ago. The ad in The Teller found her. 1902 HOWELLS *Lit. & Life* 268 Ad is a loathly little word, but we must come to it. It's as legitimate as lunch.

-ad, *suffix* invented by J. Barclay in *A new anatomical nomenclature*, 1803, in the sense of 'towards' (the part denoted by the main element of the word), as *caudad* towards the tail (L. *cauda*), *cephalad* towards the head (Gr. κεφαλή), DEXTRAD DORSAD, LATERAD, NEURAD.

Adalin (æ·dălin). *Chem.* [a. G. *adalin*.] (See quots.)
1911 *Jrnl. Chem. Soc.* C. II. 1120 Adaline is a sedative producing light, but lasting, sleep. 1912 *Ibid.* CII. I. 244 Adaline (α-bromo-α-ethylbutyrylcarbamide).

Adam¹. Add: Phr. *Not to know* (a person) *from Adam*: not to recognize him. (*As*) *old as Adam*: primevally old. Also, *since Adam was a boy*, etc.
1840 DICKENS *Old C. Shop* xxxviii, He called to see my Governor this morning,..and beyond that I don't know him from Adam. 1854 SEBA SMITH *Way down East* 60 We didn't know one of 'em from Adam. 1862 'E. KIRKE' *Among Pines* xvii. 289 Ever sense Adam was a young un'. 1867 'COLONIST' *Life's Work Austral.* 82 Though old as Adam, love is still the theme that interests all hearts in all countries. 1900 BUCHAN *Half-Hearted* xx, I found people I didn't know from Adam drinking the old toasts. 1928 MULFORD *Man fr. Bar-20* ii. 25 You hunt up that pen you've had since Adam was a boy.

Adam², proper name used *attrib.* (at first in pl.) to designate buildings, furniture, etc., designed by the brothers *Adam*, Robert (died 1792) and James (died 1794).
1898 *Lady's Realm* July 389/1 Adams rooms. 1900 *Jrnl. Soc. Arts* XLVIII. 374/2 The 'Adams' is the most delicate and refined of all styles founded on the classic. *Ibid.* 380/1 'Adams' decoration. 1903 *Connoisseur* Mar. 21 Adam, and other Furniture. 1914 H. A. VACHELL *Quinney's* iv. § 1 The sweetest table, genuine Adam. 1918 J. ALFRED GOTCH *The English Home* ix. 280 Robert was the most gifted, and it is his work which gave rise to the well-known 'Adam' style. 1920 GALSWORTHY *In Chancery* I. xii. 99 The fine reading-room was decorated in the Adam style. 1926 — *Silver Spoon* I. ii, A blend between Adam and Louis Quinze. 1926 *Times* 31 Mar. 28 Beautiful Adam Residence.

Adaptation. Add:
5. *Biol.* Organic modification by which an animal or plant becomes adapted to its environment.
1892 *Westm. Rev.* Sept. 315 Where life exists in these depths it is due to special adaptations. 1897 H. F. OSBORN in *Science* 15 Oct., The hypothesis is briefly as follows: That ontogenetic adaptation is of a very profound character. It enables animals and plants to survive very critical changes in their environment. 1904 H. E. CRAMPTON in *Biometrika* III. 114 A rigid..organization, incapable..of structural alterations as the result of 'functional adaptation'.
6. *attrib.* *Adaptation-product*, in *Biol. Chem.*, a substance produced in the body as the result of an effort to adapt itself to the presence of a foreign body (e.g. a toxin), and acting in antagonism to such foreign body, thus guarding against infection. (Cf. *ANTIBODY.) 1909 in *Cent. Dict.* Suppl.

Add, *v.* Add:
5. *intr.* in colloq. phr. *to add up*, to make the desired, expected, or correct total.
1850 DICKENS *Dav. Copp.* xli, The figures made her cry. They wouldn't add up, she said. 1864 *Good Words* 316/2 On one occasion, it struck me that a series of figures just given by the traffic-manager of a railway company, would not add up. 1885 *Sat. Rev.* 21 Feb. 243 Of the sixteen articles of diet enumerated, the percentages of five only will 'add up'. 1893 *Chamb. Jrnl.* 26 Aug. 532/1 Account books that would not add up right.

Addephagia (ædĭfē·dʒiă). Also ade-. [mod. L., f. Gr. ἅδ(δ)ην 'satis' + -φαγία -PHAGY.] = BULIMY I.
1820 GOOD *Physiol. Syst. Nosol.* 19. 1848 DUNGLISON *Med. Lex.* (ed. 7).

Adder¹. Add: **2.** An adding-machine.
1890 *N. Y. Herald* Jan. Advt., The Adder is so called because really too simple to be styled a 'machine'.

Addict (æ·dikt), *sb.* [f. ADDICT *v.*] One who is addicted to the habitual and excessive use of a drug; chiefly with qualifying sb., as *drug, morphia addict*. Also *transf.*
1909 OSCAR JENNINGS *Morphia Habit* vi. 78 As shown by *post-mortem* examinations in morphia addicts. 1920 *Glasgow Herald* 18 Oct. 9 The Chicago Bridewell Institute for drug addicts. 1920 *Outward Bound* Oct. 38/2 The morphia addict is a doomed man. 1924 *Westm. Gaz.* 19 Dec., People who..get into the habit of going to the chemist for drugs to induce sleep, and often end up by becoming opium, morphine, or heroin addicts. 1925 *Ibid.* 27 Jan., Even many working men are night club addicts.

Addiment (æ·dimĕnt). *Biol. Chem.* [ad. L. *addimentum*, f. *addere* to ADD; see -MENT.] = *COMPLEMENT *sb.* 5 i.
1901 *Lancet* 19 Oct. 1030/1 If an animal be..given two M. L. D. [minimum lethal dose] and two serum equivalents it..dies from the infection. This has been explained as due to a deficiency of addiment in the animal concerned. 1903 *Jrnl. Hygiene* Jan. 52 The supposed ferment (complement, addiment) upon which this power depends.

Adding, *vbl. sb.* Add:
b. *attrib.*: **adding-machine**, an instrument for the mechanical adding up of numbers.
1874 KNIGHT *Dict. Mech.* 1911 H. S. HARRISON *Queed* viii. 102 He was as definite as an adding machine, as practical as a cash register. 1929 *Times* (weekly ed.) 7 Feb. 147/4 Clerks recording quickly on adding machines.

Addition, *sb.* Add:
7. *attrib.* Chem. *Addition compound* or *product*, one formed by the direct addition of one element or compound to another; opposed to *substitution compound, product* (see SUBSTITUTION 7). So **A·dditive** *a.* (*additive compound*, etc.), whence **Additivity** (æditi·viti).
1875 BLOXAM *Chem.* (ed. 3) 84 The carbonates may be expressed either by additive formulæ, showing the bases which combine with carbonic acid to produce them, or by substitutive formulæ. 1876 *Jrnl. Chem. Soc.* I. 338 The Laws which regulate Direct Additive Reactions. 1888 ROSCOE & SCHORLEMMER *Treat. Chem.* III. IV. 469 Addition Products of Phthalic Acid. 1899 PATTISON MUIR *Wand. Atoms* 101 Compounds..that are produced by the addition of an atom, or atoms, to the molecules of a compound..are named additive compounds. 1906 *Jrnl. Chem. Soc.* XC. I. 729 The oxidation of amines is initially an additive process. 1908 *Ibid.* XCIV. II. 937 Connexion between Residual Affinity and Additivity.

Additory, *a.* Delete † *Obs.* and add:
1805 *Miniature* No. 26 P 3 Others..have divided them [lies] into the Additory, Detractory, and Translatory. 1897 *Amer. Jrnl. Philol.* XVIII. 27 The three distinct values of *etiam*..the temporal ('still', with negative 'yet'), the additory ('also') and the intensive ('even').

Address, *sb.* Add:
7. b. *To the address of*: addressed to, esp. in the way of criticism. *U.S.*
1928 *Times* 13 Aug. 12/1 (Washington corresp.) Much of the speech was to the address of the farmers of the Western States.
c. = *place of address*.
1886 GUNTER *Mr. Potter of Texas.* xix, He doesn't know where his son is to be found.., otherwise he would drive to his address at once.

Addressing, *vbl. sb.* Add:
b. *attrib.*: **addressing-machine**, a machine for cutting out and pasting on, stencilling, or printing addresses on newspaper-wrappers, etc.
1874 KNIGHT *Dict. Mech.*

Addressograph (ădre·sograf). [f. ADDRESS *sb.* + -O + -GRAPH.] An addressing-machine for printing addresses by means of embossed type.
1908 *Modern Business* Sept., Index to Advertisers p. iii/2. 1924 *Public Opinion* 11 July 37/1 The addresses have that dull, uninteresting look that an addressograph gives them.

Adelo- (ădī·lo, æ·dĭlo), comb. form of Gr. ἄδηλος not manifest or evident, unseen, in **Adelocodo·nic** *a.* (see quot.); **Adelomo·rphic, -mo·rphous** *adjs.*, applied to the central cells of the peptic glands.
1871 G. J. ALLMAN *Gymnobl. Hydroids* 30 The gonophore is always borne as a bud...It may be referred to one or other of two principal types, based respectively on the greater or less approach to the completely formed medusa. The peculiar condition by which one of these types is characterised may be termed phanerocodonic, while that which distinguishes the other may be designated as *adelocodonic*. 1891 W. D. HALLIBURTON *Chem. Physiol.* xxx. 633 These cells [of the cardiac glands] were called principal cells by Heidenhain, *adelomorphic cells by Rollett, and central cells on account of their position. 1875 A. GAMGEE tr. *L. Hermann's Elem. Hum. Physiol.* ii. 99 'Hauptzellen' (Haidenhain), or '*adelomorphous cells' (Rollett).

Adelphi (ăde·lfi). The name of a group of buildings in London between the Strand and Covent Garden, laid out by the four brothers, James, John, Robert, and William Adam (see *ADAM ²) and hence called *Adelphi* (Gr. ἀδελφοί brothers); the name of the theatre in the vicinity of these buildings, at which a certain type of melodrama was prevalent *c* 1882–1900, and so allusively.
1894 *Queen* 17 Mar. 432/1 Those who expected that the advent of a new Adelphi dramatist would be marked by a new development in Adelphi drama. 1902 *Encycl. Brit.* XXVII. 517/1 The 'Adelphi' as opposed to the 'Drury Lane' type of drama has recently died out in the West End. 1928 CHESTERTON *Generally Speaking* 231 His trouble cannot have been as deep as hell and as shallow as an Adelphi play.

Adenine (æ·dĕnin). *Chem.* Also **-in**. [f. Gr. ἀδήν gland + -INE⁵.] A crystallizable base, $C_5H_5N_5$, found in various glands.
1887 A. M. BROWN *Anim. Alkaloids* 75 Adenine, $C^5H^5N^5 + 3H^2O$, is in large transparent crystals, contains three molecules of water of crystallization.

Adenitis (ædĕnəi·tis). *Path.* [f. Gr. ἀδήν gland + -ITIS.] Inflammation of a gland.
1848 DUNGLISON *Med. Lex.* (ed. 7). 1853 ERICHSEN *Sci. & Art Surg.* xxxiii. 448 Inflammation of the lymphatic glands, or adenitis. 1879 *St. George's Hosp. Rep.* IX. 654 Erysipelas and adenitis in 6, 1 of whom died.

Adenodynia (ædĕnodi·niă). *Path.* [mod.L., f. Gr. ἀδήν gland + ὀδύνη pain.] Pain in a gland.
1848 DUNGLISON *Med. Lex.* (ed. 7).

Adenoid, *a.* Add earlier quots.:
1848 DUNGLISON *Med. Lex.* (ed. 7). 1863 W. TURNER *J. Paget's Surg. Pathol.* 548 *note*, The name adenoid sarcomata is sometimes applied to these tumours of the mammary gland.
B. *sb. pl.* Adenoid growths or vegetations.
1891 *Medical Annual* 347 Admitting that usually adenoids make their appearance during childhood. 1901 CHEYNE & BURGHARD *Man. Surg. Treatment* v. 365 The removal of the adenoids is more easily accomplished during the earlier and deeper stage of the anæsthesia. 1912 OSLER & MCCRAE *Princ. Med.* (ed. 8) 468 'Adenoids' have become recognized as one of the most common and important affections of childhood.

Adenoma (ædĕnō·mă). [mod.L., f. Gr. ἀδήν gland: see -OMA.] A benign tumour with the structure or appearance of a gland. Hence **Adenomatous** (-ō·mătəs) *a.*, of the nature of an adenoma, glandular.
1870 W. TURNER *Paget's Surg. Path.* xxviii. (ed. 3) 558 Glandular tumour, Adenoid tumour, or Adenoma. 1870 *T. Holmes's Syst. Surg.* (ed. 2) IV. 578 Adenomatous or Glandular Growths. 1899 *Allbutt's Syst. Med.* VIII. 737 Adenoma of the coil-gland.

Adequate, *a.* Add: **2. b.** Without const.: Equal to the occasion, competent to deal with the situation. So **Adequacy**.
1924 ANNE D. SEDGWICK *Little French Girl* II. viii, The deliberate adequacy with which madame Vervier advanced to meet the occasion. *Ibid.* ix, Alix, in Maman's place, poured out their coffee, heavy-eyed, but still adequate.

Adespota (ăde·spǫtă). *Bibliography.* [neut. pl. of Gr. ἀδέσποτος without owner, f. ἀ- priv. + δεσπότης master, DESPOT.] Literary works not attributed to (or claimed by) an author.
Orig. used as a title of collections of anonymous Greek poetry.
1897 *Times* 27 Oct. 10 A bibliographical paper on Burns's *adespota*; verses fugitive, unsanctioned, or apocryphal. 1905 A. W. POLLARD *Mem. R. Proctor* p. xxvii, The cards were then sorted out according to countries, towns and presses, with a large section of 'adespota'. 1913 R. B. MCKERROW *Printers' & Publ. Devices* Introd. p. l, To lump together a large number of blocks of every date and style in a class of *Adespota*.

Adessive (æde·siv), *a. Gram.* [f. L. *adesse* to be present + -IVE.] Denoting the case used (in Finnish, etc.) to express position in or presence at a place.
1890 ELIOT *Finnish Gramm.* 131 The first member (inessive, adessive, essive) denotes originally rest in a position. 1890 GATSCHET *Klamath Indians* II. I. 486 Adessive case in -kshi.

Ad hoc (æd hǫk). [L., lit. 'to this'.] For this purpose, to this end; for the particular purpose in hand or in view.
1659 R. BAXTER *Key for Catholics* II. iv. 351 *Ad hoc* the Magistrate is the only Judge what is sound doctrine. 1809 *Edin. Rev.* Jan. 433 The conscripts are..examined.. by a special commission, created *ad hoc* by the prefect. 1882 W. R. GREG *Misc. Ess.* vi. 147 A sum not far off two millions per annum will have to be provided *ad hoc* by the Chancellor of the Exchequer.
b. *attrib.* or as *adj.* Devoted, appointed, etc., to or for some particular purpose.
[1853 GREVILLE *Mem.* III. (1887) I. ii. 51 There are already symptoms of a possible combination *ad hoc*.] 1900 *Daily News* 18 Apr. 7/1 The discussion of the constitution of the educational authorities was sensational, inasmuch as it led to the Conference declaring for the ad hoc principle. 1904 *Fabian News* Aug. 29/1 A report..on the total abolition of *ad hoc* bodies was read. 1928 ABP. CANT. in *Daily News* 8 Feb. 10/1 A growing sense of the usefulness of Reservation of the ad hoc kind.

Adiate (æ·diēit), *v. Roman-Dutch Law.* [app. irreg. f. L. *adire* to approach + -ATE³.] *trans.* To accept (an inheritance) as heir under a will; in South Africa, to accept as beneficiary under a will. Hence **Adiation** (ædiē·ʃən).
1829 in J. W. KNAPP *Rep. Cases Privy Council* (1831) I. 111 Adiation (*aditio in hereditatem*) is a question more of intention than action. 1845 HERBERT *Grotius' Dutch Jurispr.* II. xx. 143 An instituted heir, who adiates freely the inheritance, may deduct therefrom a fourth part. *Ibid.* xxi. 147 Repudiation must take place after the inheritance falls in by death and before adiation. 1896 JUTA *Selection of Leading Cases* II. 111 If the survivor has adiated and accepted benefits under the will. 1925 R. W. LEE *Roman-Dutch Law* 313 If he [*sc.* the 'extraneus heres'] accepted or acted as heir, he was said to 'adiate' the inheritance (*adire hereditatem*), and from that moment was in the position of a universal successor.

Adiposis (ædipō·sis). *Path.* [mod.L., f. L. *adip-*, *adeps* fat: see -OSIS.] Obesity or fatness of the body; fatty degeneration (of an organ).
1848 DUNGLISON *Med. Lex.* (ed. 7).

Aditus (æ·ditŏs). *Zool.* [L., lit. 'approach', f. *adire*, f. *ad* to + *ire* to go.] An incurrent canal in a sponge. Hence **Adital** (æ·dităl) *a.*
1887 SOLLAS in *Encycl. Brit.* XXII. 415/1 The prosopyles.. may..be prolonged into..a *prorodus* or *aditus*...By the extension of the prosodal or adital canals..a still higher differentiation is reached.

Adjectivally (ædʒĕktəi·văli), *adv.* [f. ADJECTIVAL *a.* + -LY².] In an adjectival manner, as an adjective; = ADJECTIVELY *adv.*
1867 F. W. FARRAR *Greek Syntax* Introd. § 38 The fact that substantives are frequently used adjectivally. 1928 E. G. R. WATERS *St. Brendan* p. cxcvi, The tonic forms of the possessive pronouns are frequently used adjectivally.

Adjective, *sb.* Add: **1. b.** Euphemistically substituted for an expletive adjective. (Cf. next.)
1894 *Idler* Feb. 102 To know where the adjective blazes they are going. 1900 E. WELLS *Chestnuts* i. (ed. 3) 29 Now we must have some (adjective) fun.

Adjective, *v.* Add:
2. To furnish with an adjective. Also *intr.* (*colloq.*) to use adjectives. So **A·djectived** *a.* or *ppl. a.*, qualified by an adjective or adjectives.
1804 *Med. Jrnl.* XII. 335 *Vaccine*, French, is from Latin: ..Milk is by Pliny adjectived with the word, *lac vaccinum*. 1871 EARLE *Philol. Engl. Tongue* 341 Clough took the liberty of thus adjectiving Lord Macaulay..'I have only detected one error myself, but it is a very Macaulayesque one'. 1892 'H. S. MERRIMAN' *From one Generation to Another* xi, He paid for his pleasure in..the adjectived items [i.e. 'ripping', 'topping'] of hospitality. 1920 *Sunday at Home* Apr. 423/2 In her place I think I should have 'adjectived' a good deal more.

Adjectively, *adv.* Add: **b.** (Cf. *ADJECTIVE *sb.*)
1928 *Boston Pilot* 9 Feb. 4/7 The effect of zero weather.. on the public..is adjectively bad.

Adjectivism (æ·dʒĕktiviz'm). [f. ADJECTIVE + -ISM.] The (excessive) use of adjectives.
1890 *Sat. Rev.* 5 Apr. 423/1 All our isms—Romanticism, Naturalism, Socialism, Æstheticism, Undogmaticism, Adjectivism. 1904 G. S. HALL *Adolescence* II. xvi. 467 Adjectivism, adverbism, and nounism, or marked disposition to multiply one or more of the above classes of words.

Adjectivity (ædʒĕkti·viti). [f. ADJECTIVE + -ITY.] Addiction to the free use of adjectives.
1889 *Sat. Rev.* 5 Jan. 21/1 The adjectivity of his description. 1894 *Athenæum* 14 Apr. 469/1 Mrs. Ward..has checked the reckless fluency of her 'adjectivity'.

Adjectivized (æ·dʒĕktivəizd), *ppl. a.* [f. ADJECTIVE *sb.* + -IZE + -ED¹.] Turned into an adjective.
1901 *Publ. Mod. Lang. Assoc. Amer.* XVI. 142 The completely adjectivized participle.

Adjourner (ădʒǭ·ɹnəɹ). [f. ADJOURN *v.* + -ER¹.] One who adjourns or is in favour of an adjournment.
1893 *Westm. Gaz.* 25 Nov. 7/2 There were only 44 adjourners, while 142 members preferred to proceed with the.. business. 1893 *Columbus* (Ohio) *Disp.* 24 Aug., The weakening among Senators..upon which..the confidence of the early adjourners is based.

Adjunct. **B. 2.** (U.S. use.)
1851 C. CIST *Cincinnati* 69 The Classes..are divided among the Adjunct Professors of Mathematics and Languages and the Professor of Modern Languages. 1855 DUYCKINCK *Cycl. Amer. Lit.* I. 386/2 Professor Henry Drisler, adjunct professor of Greek and Latin. 1876 D. C. GILMAN *University Probl.* (1898) 29 Promoting them because of their merit to successive posts, as scholars, fellows, assistants, adjuncts, professors, and university professors.

Adjustive (ădʒv·stiv), *a.* [f. ADJUST *v.* + -IVE.] Tending to adjust, concerned with adjustment.
1888 ROMANES *Mental Evol. in Anim.* i. 17 Adjustive movements due to reflex action, and adjustive movements accompanied by mental perception. *Ibid.* 18 Adjustive action.

Adjustment. Add:
5. *attrib.* in *adjustment award, committee, levy* (see quots.).
1904 KIPLING *Traffics & Discov., Army of a dream* I. 251 The Adjustment Committee—the umpires of the Military Areas. 1920 *Act 10 Geo. V*, c. 4 § 2 If the profits..exceed the sum apportioned to that undertaking,..the excess shall be payable to the Controller by the owner of the undertaking and shall be recoverable as a debt due to the Crown, and the amount so payable is in this Act referred to as adjustment levy. *Ibid.*, Any sum so payable [by the Controller] is in this Act referred to as adjustment award.

Adjustor (ădʒv·stǫɹ). *Anat.* and *Zool.* [f. ADJUST *v.*, after L. agent-nouns in *-or*, as *retractor*.] Name for certain muscles in Brachiopoda; see quot. Also *attrib.* in *adjustor muscle*.
1895 SHIPLEY in *Camb. Nat. Hist.* III. 477 There are three pairs of adjustor muscles..called respectively the central.., external..,and posterior..adjustors, whose action adjusts the shells when all contract together, and brings about a certain sliding movement of the shells on one another when they act independently. 1923 *Glasgow Herald* 11 Aug. 4 The more adjustors a creature has, the higher its capacity for effective behaviour.

Adjuvancy (æ·dʒuvănsi). [f. ADJUVANT: see -ANCY.] Assistance, help.
1884 W. STANILAND *Songs after Sunset* 54 Whose designing flattery Bought my adjuvancy with foul intent. 1896 *Durham Univ. Jrnl.* XII. 14 The students..endeavoured to secure his adjuvancy in their theological studies.

Admedian (ædmī·diăn), *a.* [f. L. *ad* near + MEDIAN *a.*] Situated near the median plane.
1888 ROLLESTON & JACKSON *Anim. Life* 116 In *Pulmonata* a median tooth may be distinguished from an indefinite number of admedian teeth.

Admire, *v.* **1. d.** Add: *U.S.* To like, be desirous (*to* do something).
c 1770 *Lett. to B. Franklin* (1859) 194, I should admire to come and see her and hear all about every thing. 1816 PICKERING *Vocab.* s.v., *To admire*, to like very much, to be very fond of. This verb is much used in New England in expressions like the following: I should admire to go to such a place; I should admire to have such a thing, &c. 1836 W. T. PORTER *Quarter Race Kentucky* (1846) 15, I said: 'I should admire to bet some gentleman $10. on the bay'. 1839 MARRYAT *Diary Amer.* II. 223 'Have you ever been at Paris?' 'No; but I should admire to go.' 1872 'MARK TWAIN' *Roughing it* xiv. (1882) 78 They said they would 'admire' to see a 'Gentile' force a Mormon to fulfil a losing contract in Utah! 1876 B. HARTE *Gabriel Conroy* IV. i, 'Why didn't you come into the parlour?' she said,..'I didn't admire to to-night,' returned Gabriel. 1886 *Harper's Mag.* Sept. 578/2, I should admire to know what your coffee is made of. 1905 A. ADAMS *Outlet* 202 I'll be all ready to start..in fifteen minutes, and I'd admire to have you all go along.

Admission. **1.** Add: *attrib.*, as *admission fee*.
1888 GUNTER *Mr. Potter of Texas* xx, No one demands an admission fee.

Ad nauseam (æd nǭ·ʃiæm). [L., = 'to sickness'. (The earlier examples in English context have *usque ad nauseam, et ad nauseam*.)] To a sickening extent, so as to excite disgust.
1814 *Edin. Rev.* Apr. 73 He had already spoken *ad nauseam* on this very subject. 1907 W. DE MORGAN *Alice-for-Short* xxv, His frequent use of this expression compels repetition *ad nauseam*.

Adobe. Add: Also, a house made of unburnt brick.
1881 *Amer. Naturalist* XV. 25 The adobe at one moment seemed near, and the next very far off. 1898 F. REMINGTON *Crooked Trails* 25 A little broken adobe.

Adonis. **1.** Substitute for def.: A beautiful or handsome young man.
1622 MABBE tr. *Aleman's Guzman d'Alf.* II. ii. 21 My Master..made me another *Adonis*, in the neatnesse and galliantry of my cloathes, and delicacie of Perfumes. 1624 MASSINGER *Parl. Love* II. ii, A leper,..in respect of thee, Appears a young Adonis. 1768 TUCKER *Lt. Nat.* II. I. xxiii. 225 How it would divert our ladies below to hear two such Adonises talking so sweetly of our reciprocal passion! *a* 1800 COWPER *On Female Inconstancy*, She who call'd thee once her pretty one, And her Adonis, now inquires thy name. 1888 GUNTER *Mr. Potter of Texas* viii, George! in a month this chap 'll be an Adonis.

Adoptee (ădǫptī·). [f. ADOPT *v.* + -EE.] An adopted person.
1892 *Sat. Rev.* 6 Aug. 179/1 That odd provision of French law which permits adoption—in case the adoptee has saved the life of the adopter.

Adorant (ădō·rănt), *a. poet.* [f. ADORE *v.* + -ANT.] = ADORING *ppl. a.*
a 1821 KEATS *Hyperion* I. 283 'Shade of Memory!'—Cried I, with act adorant at her feet. 1893 *19th Cent.* Nov. 842, I..make petition on adorant knee.

Adradial, *a.* Substitute for def.: Situated near or beside a ray. Add:
B. *sb.* An adradial organ.
1888 ROLLESTON & JACKSON *Anim. Life* 717 The adradials open one into each of the eight meridional or ctenophoral vessels. 1892 J. A. THOMSON *Outl. Zool.* 134 Tentacles—first four corresponding to the angles of the mouth (perradials), and then other four (interradials) between these, and ..eight intervening adradials.

Adrectal (ædre·ktăl), *a. Zool.* [f. AD- + RECTUM + -AL.] Situated at or near the rectum; *spec.* of or pertaining to the purpuriparous glands of certain molluscs.
1883 *Encycl. Brit.* XVI. 648/2 The presence of glandular plication of the surface of the mantle-flap..and an adrectal gland (purple-gland).

Ad referendum (æd refĕre·ndŏm) [mod.L., = 'for reference'.] In diplomatic use, a phr. qualifying the acceptance of proposals by representatives subject to reference to their principals.
1781 J. ADAMS *Corr.* Wks. 1852 VII. 438 They will take the proposition *ad referendum* immediately. 1787 *Gent. Mag.* 1015/2 Congress have taken this generous offer of his *ad referendum*. 1815 WELLINGTON *Dispatches* (1838) XII. 287 The agreement was read to the whole, and taken *ad referendum* by the Russian and Prussian Ministers. 1906 HARDY *Dynasts* II. v. i. 238 Prince Eugène will..make the formal offer in his name...Which I can but receive *ad referendum*.

Ad rem (æd rem). [L., = 'to the matter'.] (Pertaining or pertinent) to the matter or subject in hand; to the purpose.
1608 MIDDLETON *Fam. Love* v. H 4, *Ad rem, ad rem*, master Poppin: leaue your allegories,..and to the point. 1621 BURTON *Anat. Mel.* To Rdr. 40 To speake *ad rem*, who is free from passion? 1680 J. HOWE *Let. to Person of Qual.* 23 What I can find in his Sermon hath any aspect or design that way is either *ad rem*, or *ad hominem*. 1865 RUSKIN in *Daily Tel.* 7 Sept. (Cent. Dict.) Your statements of practical difficulty are..more *ad rem* than my mere assertions of principle. 1905 *Spectator* 4 Feb. 180/2 It is more *ad rem* to consider whether a satisfactory answer to Newman's question is to be found in the second book on our list.

Adrenal (ædrī·năl), *a.* and *sb.* [f. AD- 1 + L. *rēnes* kidneys: cf. RENAL.] **A.** *adj.* = SUPRARENAL *a.* **B.** *sb. pl.* Suprarenals.
1875 HUXLEY & MARTIN *Elem. Biol.* xiii. 173 The Adrenal glands are yellow bodies imbedded in the ventral face of the kidney. 1882 *Trans. Path. Soc.* XXXIII. 341 Adrenals. 1883 *Encycl. Brit.* XV. 365/1 The 'suprarenal bodies' or 'adrenals.'

Adrenalin (ædrī·nălin). Also **-ine**. [f. prec. + -INE⁵.] A crystalline substance extracted from the adrenal glands, used medicinally as a vaso-motor and hæmostatic.
See quot. 1901 for the discovery of the substance and the invention of the name, which have, however, been claimed also for Dr. Norton L. Wilson.
1901 *Amer. Jrnl. Physiol.* V. 457 The most important contribution to our knowledge of the active principle of the suprarenal gland..is from Dr. Jokichi Takamine who has isolated the blood-pressure-raising principle of the gland in a stable and pure crystalline form...To this body..he has given the name 'Adrenalin'. 1902 *Jrnl. Chem. Soc.* LXXXII. I. 68 It is claimed that suprarenin is identical with Takamine's adrenalin. 1907 OSLER & MCCRAE *Syst. Med.* I. 758 Experimentally..adrenalin..has a powerful influence on carbohydrate metabolism. 1920 *Discovery* Mar. 88/2 Adrenaline prescribed for Addison's disease. 1922 J. C. SQUIRE in *Public Opinion* 3 Mar. 203/1 The toad secretes too much adrenalin.

Adsorb (ædsǭ·ɹb), *v.* [Back-formation from next.] *trans.* To collect by adsorption. Hence **Adso·rbent**, an adsorbing substance.
1882 *Nature* XXVI. 139 Continuing his researches on 'adsorption', or condensation of gases on surfaces of solids, Herr Kayser..has studied the influence of the adsorbing material. 1906 *Bio-Chem. Jrnl.* I. 485 As to other factors which influence the adsorption v. Bemmelen points out the following:—(1) the adsorbing substance, (2) the solvent, (3) the substance to be adsorbed. 1923 *Discovery* Sept. 231/2 Impurities deposited on or adsorbed by the crystals. 1928 W. A. CASPARI *Structure & Properties of Matter* ii. 37 Some charcoals will adsorb hundreds of times their bulk of gas. *Ibid.*, Specially prepared charcoals rank high as adsorbents. *Ibid.* 38 Animal and vegetable fibres..are tolerably good adsorbents, owing to the large surfaces presented by their internal structure.

Adsorption. Add quots. Hence **Adso·rptional** *a.*, pertaining to adsorption.
1904 tr. *W. Nernst's Theor. Chem.* 129 Adsorption.—Charcoal shaken with an iodine solution or placed in an atmosphere of iodine vapour condenses appreciable amounts of iodine on its surface; this is known as 'adsorption'. 1913 E. HATSCHEK *Introd. Physics & Chem. Colloids* i. 5 One other property of colloids..is their capacity for taking dissolved substances out of solution and retaining them...This phenomenon..is now generally called 'Adsorption'.. Specially striking is the power of 'selective absorption'..possessed by many substances. 1928 W. A. CASPARI *Struct. & Prop. Matter* ii. 37 Adsorption from liquids is of the highest technical importance. In the sugar industry, for instance, there are certain..impurities in the liquors which can only be removed by this means, so that filtration through charcoal is resorted to. *Ibid.* 35 Adsorptional effects are by no means limited to the liquid state.

Adurol (ædiū·rǫl, æ·diurǫl). [G. *adurol*.] A haloid substitution product of hydroquinone, used as a photographic developer.
1899 *Brit. Jrnl. Photogr.* 3 Mar. 139/1 Adurol is a new photographic developer, said to be obtained from hydroquinone by a patented process. 1913 G. MARTIN *Industr. Chem., Org.* 659 'Adurol' developer consists of the stock solutions: (A) 10 g. adurol + 80 g. cryst. sod. sulphite + 500 c.c. H_2O; (B) 60 g. K_2CO_3 + 500 c.c. H_2O.

Advance, *sb.* **5.** *Comb.* Add:
advance agent, announcement; **advance copy**, a copy of a book sent out in advance of publication; **advance note** (see quot. 1886).
1885 *Art Annual* Advt. 1 Advance Announcements from the Prospectus for 1885/86. 1886 *Encycl. Brit.* XXI. 606/1 Advance notes—that is, documents promising the future payment of money on account of a seaman's wages conditionally on his going to sea. 1897 *Congress Rec.* Mar. 177/1 That grand advance agent of prosperity, William McKinley. 1899 *Academy* 25 Nov. 591 Mr. Donnelly conceived the request to be for an advance copy. 1903 *Eikon Basilike* [Pref.] p. iv, The present edition has been set up from an 'advance copy' of the first edition.

Advanced, *a.* **2.** Add: sometimes *spec.* of women.
1871 *N. Y. Tribune* 2 Feb. (De Vere) The shortsightedness of the Advanced Female to the interest of her own cause.

Adventist (æ·dvĕntist). [f. ADVENT + -IST.] A member of any of the various religious sects holding millenarian views. Hence **A·dventism**, the principles or tenets of adventists.
Second Adventist, orig. the fuller designation of the followers of William Miller (died 1849), who promoted the doctrine that the second coming of Christ and the end of the world were near at hand, a Millerite.
1876 [see SEVENTH-DAY b]. 1877 BARTLETT *Dict. Amer.* (ed. 4). 1878 ELIZ. PRENTISS in *Life & Lett.* (1882) 504 Neither Mr. Prentiss or myself have ever had any sympathy with Second Adventists. 1883 *Encycl. Brit.* XVI. 320/2 At present the number of Millerites or Adventists is estimated at from 15,000 to 20,000. 1898 J. R. HARRIS *Union with God* xi. 188 The existence of an adventist movement in Jerusalem. 1927 FLINT & TAIT tr. *Fülöp-Miller's Mind & Face of Bolshevism* 78 The sects with a more rationalist tinge, the 'Adventists' and the 'New Adventists'.

Adventitial, *a.* Delete † *Obs.* and add:
1901–5 *Jrnl. Exper. Med.* VI. 69 The adventitial lymphatic sheath is in most cases distended.

Adventure, *v.* Add:
5. b. *trans.* To venture to say or utter.
1898 *Daily News* 19 Oct. 3/1 He adventured the opinion that 'some members opposite' were 'unaccustomed to the amenities of debate.' 1900 L. B. WALFORD *One of Ourselves* xiv, 'Did he tell you about us?' she adventured, cautiously.

Adventureship (ădve·ntiŭɹʃip). [f. ADVENTURE *sb.* + -SHIP.] Adventurous practice.
1879 MORLEY *Burke* ii. 33 An unpleasant taint of speculation and financial adventureship hung at one time about the whole connexion.

Advertising, *vbl. sb.* Add: **2. b.** *attrib.*
1884 H. S. CUMMINGS *Sk. Class 1862 Dartmouth Coll.* 45 On November, 1871, he was made the advertising agent of the Pennsylvania Railroad Company.

Advisory, *a.* (Earlier U.S. examples.)
1778 *Essex Result* (U.S.) 45 We think therefore that the members of that court ought never to be advisory to any officer in the state. 1789 MORSE *Amer. Geog.* (1792) 170 The churches claim no jurisdiction over each other, and the power of ecclesiastical councils is only advisory.

Adynamical (ædinæ·mikăl), *a.* [f. as ADYNAMIC *a.* + -AL.] Not dynamical.
1900 *Jrnl. Inst. Electr. Engineers* Apr. 396 The properties of electric and magnetic force are explicable upon dynamical principles; so far there is no known necessity for seeking for adynamical properties in the ether.

Ægithognathous (īdʒiþǫ·gnăþəs), *a. Zool.* [f. Gr. αἴγιθος, name of an unknown bird + γνάθος jaw.] Having the formation of palate characteristic of the family *Ægithognathæ* (perching birds, woodpeckers, swifts): see quot. 1894. Hence **Ægitho·gnathism**, the condition of being ægithognathous.
1875 W. K. PARKER in *Encycl. Brit.* III. 699/1 All the *Coracomorphæ* have the ægithognathous palate. 1884 COUES *N. Amer. Birds* (ed. 2) 172 Ægithognathism..is exhibited almost unexceptionally by the great group of Passerine birds. 1894 R. B. SHARPE *Handbk. Birds Gt. Brit.* I. 1 The palate is said to be 'ægithognathous,' or 'Passerine,' when the *vomer* is broadened and blunt, or truncated, at the anterior end, and is not connected with the *maxillo-palatines*, which, consequently, are widely separated from each other.

Æluroid (īliū·roid), *a.* (*sb.*) *Zool.* [f. mod.L. *Æluroidea* neut. pl., f. Gr. αἴλουρος cat: see -OID.] Belonging to, or having the characters of, the division *Æluroidea* of Carnivora, comprising the feline and allied families; as *sb.* an animal of this division.
1869 *Proc. Zool. Soc.* 22 Cryptoprocta is a member of the Æluroid group. *Ibid.* 27 In the presence of a short cæcum.. Hyæna conforms with the Æluroids.

Aeneolithic (ēˌīnioli·þik), *a.* [f. L. *aēneus* of brass + Gr. λίθος stone + -IC.] Of or pertaining to the period of the neolithic age in which copper was used together with flint implements.
1901 SERGI *Mediterr. Race* xii. 240 In Italy this period is termed *æneolithic*, that is to say, the period of copper and polished stone together.

Æolianly (īō·liănli), *adv.* [f. ÆOLIAN + -LY².] With an æolian sound; with a sound as of an æolian harp.
1849 SYMINGTON *Harebell Chimes* 129 Plaint melody Sung by the mermaids of the wave, Æolianly. 1886 M. F. TUPPER *My Life as an Author* 393 Moaning Æolianly as it went.

Æolienne, occas. var. of EOLIENNE.

Æonic (īǫ·nik), *a.* [f. ÆON + -IC.] Age-long.
1883 *Harper's Mag.* Sept. 622/1 Such a period of æonic sleep may have been requisite for the evolution.

Aerator. Add:
a. A contrivance for fumigating grain. **b.** An apparatus for forcing air or carbonic acid gas into liquids.
1874 KNIGHT *Dict. Mech.* 1891 *Sci. Amer.* 4 Apr. 218/1 Aerator..a portable device having a receiver near the top of a standard, the receiver having numerous small perforations, while lower on the standards are pans..for the aeration of warm and fresh milk. 1892 *Jrnl. Soc. Chem. Industry* 30 Nov. 896/1 Improvements in Æreators for Treating Liquids.

Aerial, *a.* Add, with pronunciation (ē·riăl):
5. *esp.* with reference to locomotion in the air by means of aircraft; relating to aircraft or aviation, as *aerial line*, the course followed by a service of aeroplanes.
1783 in *W. H. Robinson's* (*Newcastle-on-Tyne*) *Catal.* (1926) No. 14. 49 (*Aeronautical Cartoon*), The Montgolfier. A first Rate of the French Aerial Navy. 1784 *Universal Mag.* LXXIV. 18 A full account of the late wonderful Aërial Excursions. *Ibid.* 20 They soon lost sight of our aërial navigators. 1804 in *Times* (1927) 10 Mar. 16/1 Cayley's original draft of an unfinished essay on the 'Mechanical Principles of Aerial Navigation' bearing the early date 'October 6 1804'. 1865 *Mech. Mag.* XIV. 64/1 Mr. Low, another American aëronaut, has constructed what he terms an aërial ship. 1866 WENHAM in *Ann. Rep. Aëronautical Soc. Gt. Brit.* 10 On Aërial Locomotion and the Laws by which Heavy Bodies impelled through Air are Sustained. 1867 *Ibid.* 31 The French Aërial Screw..was now exhibited. 1879 *Encycl. Brit.* IX. 319/1 Professor Pettigrew..recommends an elastic aerial screw consisting of two blades. 1920 *Discovery* Mar. 80/1 It is probable that kite balloons will be used as landmarks for the main aerial lines over the world.
6. b. *Aerial railway* or *tramway*, a track consisting of overhead wires, cables, or rails supporting carriages, usually driven by electric force. *Aerial wire*, a wire supported in the air for radiating or receiving the waves of wireless telegraphy; an antenna. Hence applied to things connected with this, as *aerial circuit, switch*, etc. Also *sb.*, short for *aerial wire*.
1874 KNIGHT *Dict. Mech.*, *Aerial railway*, an attempt to govern the balloon or aërostat by guiding rails or wires stretched between posts. 1889 *Cent. Dict.* s.v. *Aerial*, *Aerial railway*...A name sometimes applied to systems of transportation by cars suspended from a rail or rope above them. 1899 MARCONI in *Proc. Inst. Electr. Engin.* XXVIII. 274 A vertical conductor *W*, which I will call the aërial conductor. *Ibid.* 289 The aërial wire comes through the frame-work of a skylight. 1902 [see *ANTENNA 5]. 1906 A. F. COLLINS *Man. Wireless Telegr.* 203 Aerial. A word much used instead of the longer term *aerial wire*. *Ibid.*, Aerial switch. A switch used to throw the aerial wire into connection with the spark-gap and out of connection with the detector, and vice versa. 1908 *Westm. Gaz.* 8 Dec. 9/4 The four aerials connected with the mast cover about an acre and a half. 1913 *Yr. Bk. Wireless Telegr.* 415 *Aerial Circuit*.—Starts at the free or insulated end of the aerial and ends with the connection to earth. 1921 *Chamb. Jrnl.* 24 Sept. 681/2 There was an aerial between the masts and another between the derricks.

Ae·riform, *v.* [f. AERIFORM *a.*] *trans.* To make aeriform.
1890 COUES *Ornithol.* 284 Matter diffused in air—aeriformed.

Aero- (ē·rō, ē·ərō). Add:
In various names of aeroplanes or flying-machines, or their parts, as *aero-biplane, -bus, -car, -engine, -surface*; also **Aerobatics** (-bæ·tiks) [after *acrobatics*], evolutions performed with an aeroplane, esp. for display; so **Aeroba·tic** *a.*; **A·ero-club**, a club for the pursuit and promotion of aviation; so *aero-meet, -race*; † **A·ero-curve**, an occasional substitute for *AEROPLANE 1 (the wing of a flying-machine) when of a curved form; **A·erofoil**, a proposed name for the wing of a flying-machine, whether plane or curved; **A·erogram** (*a*) a message sent 'through the air', i.e. by wireless telegraphy; (*b*) a telegram conveyed partly by aeroplane; **A·erograph** = *AIR-brush.
1917 'CONTACT' *Airman's Outings* 128 Watching the *aerobatics and shamfights of the pool pupils. 1923 *Westm. Gaz.* 2 July 3/2 Ability to perform aerobatics..gives a pilot confidence... The 'aerobatic' display that followed was, therefore, not the merely ornamental thing that some supposed. 1874 *9th Ann. Rep. Aëronaut. Soc. Gt. Brit.* The *Aero-bi-plane, or First Steps to Flight. 1906 *Daily Chron.* 11 Dec. 6/6 '*Aerobus' might be preferred [to 'airvan']. 1913 *Daily Mail* 4 Oct. 6 The Grahame-White aerobus established a new passenger-carrying record by taking up nine passengers. 1926 *Chamb. Jrnl.* 14 Aug. 581/2 *Aero-cars may take off from here. 1920 *Glasgow Herald* 28 Aug. 5/1 The Racing Committee of the Royal *Aero Club. 1897 in *Epit. Aeronautical Ann.* (1910) 64 The lower *aerocurve was..taken off,..reducing the sustaining surface to 135 square feet. 1902 F. WALKER *Aërial Navig.* 115 Aeroplanes and Aerocurves. When these are made of fabric, yacht duck may be employed. 1928 C. F. S. GAMBLE *North Sea Air Station* viii. 115 The Navy was..compelled to adapt the Army *aero-engine to its seaplanes. 1910 R. FERRIS *How it Flies* 453 *Aerofoil, another name for the aeroplane, suggested as more accurate, considering that the surfaces are not true planes. 1899 *Daily News* 20 Nov. 7/1 'Wanted, a new name for wireless telegraphy,' Miss Collett, Hyde-park-mansions, suggests..'*Aerogram.' 1901 *Westm. Gaz.* 20 Dec. 6/2 Halfpenny-a-word aerograms. 1898 *Brit. Jrnl. Photogr.* 29 Apr. 274/1 Enlargements finished with the *aerograph in water colours. 1910 *Boston Globe* 4 Sept. 12/1 *Aero meet. 1912 *World Alman.* (N.Y.) 432 Cross-country *Aero Races European Circuit Race. 1902 *Aeronaut. World* (U.S.A.) 1 Oct. 65/2 Hofman's Flying Machine ..is furnished with three large square flat *aero-surfaces.

Aerobe (ē·ərōub). *Biol.* [f. mod.L. *Aerobia* neut. pl. (F. *aërobies*, Pasteur), f. Gr. ἀήρ air + βίος life.] One of a group (*Aerobia*) of microbes or bacteria which live on free oxygen derived from the air. So **Aero·bian, Aerobic** (-ō·bik), **Aero·bious** *adjs.*, living on the oxygen of the air; of the nature of or pertaining to aerobes; **Aero·bically** *adv.*; **Aerobio·sis**, life sustained by the oxygen of the air; **Aerobio·tic** (-ǫ·tik) *a.*, pertaining to or characterized by aerobiosis, aerobic.
1879 tr. *Pasteur's Ferment.* 210 The first aërobian ferment. *Ibid.*, An aërobious ferment. 1885 VINES in *Encycl. Brit.* XIX. 51/2 In aerobiotic plants the normal processes of destructive metabolism..may be replaced for a..time by those abnormal processes of which fermentation is the outward expression. 1885 KLEIN *Micro-Org.* 34 Some bacteria require free access of oxygen, and are called *aërobic* (Pasteur); others grow without free oxygen, and are *anaërobic* (Pasteur). 1886 *Buck's Handbk. Med. Sci.* III. 64/1 Those [micro-organisms] which thrive only with free oxygen; these he calls *aerobes*. 1887 A. M. BROWN *Anim. Alkaloids* 117 Four-fifths of our tissues live aerobically; and..the remaining fifth part,..lives anaerobically, that is, after the fashion of putrid ferment. 1896 *Allbutt's Syst. Med.* I. 513 Obligatory aerobes, which must be supplied with oxygen. 1900 *Jrnl. Soc. Arts* XLVIII. 387/2 A larger number of bacteria were.. facultatively aerobic.

Aerodrome (ē·ərō-, ē·ərōdrōum). [In sense 1, ad. Gr. ἀεροδρόμος adj. running through or traversing the air; in sense 2, f. AERO- + Gr. δρόμος course, race-course (cf. *hippodrome*).]
† **1.** S. P. Langley's name for an aeroplane: = *AEROPLANE 2. Also *attrib.* *Obs.*
1891 S. P. LANGLEY *Exper. Aerodynamics* 49 An actual working aerodrome model with its motor. 1896 A. J. BELL in *Smithsonian Rep.* 6 Witnessing the successful flight of some of these aerodromes.
2. A course for practice or contests with flying-machines; a tract of level ground from which flying-machines (aeroplanes or air-ships) can start.
1902 *Westm. Gaz.* 29 Jan. 6/2 He..soared above the Prince's castle to the aerodrome. 1911 in Grahame-White & Harper *Aeroplane* 124 A circle had been whitewashed on the aerodrome..to act as a mark in which the aviators were to descend.
Hence **Aerodromic** (-drǫ·mik) *a.*, pertaining to flying-machines; **Aerodro·mics**, the art of constructing and using flying-machines.
1891 S. P. LANGLEY *Exper. Aerodynamics* 5 The yet inchoate art of constructing suitable mechanisms for guiding heavy bodies through the air..which art..I will provisionally call aerodromics. 1896 A. G. BELL in *Smithsonian Rep.* 6 Investigations connected with aerodromic problems.

Aerodynamic. Add:
2. Pertaining to **Aerodynamics** [cf. DYNAMICS 1], the art of moving through the air by some mechanism, the use of flying-machines, aviation. So **Aerodyna·mical** *a.*, **-ally** *adv.*
1891 S. P. LANGLEY (*title*) Experiments in Aerodynamics. 1921 *Glasgow Herald* 8 Sept. 10/2 Department for aerodynamical research. 1922 *Edin. Rev.* Oct. 214 The improvements in range and aerodynamic and engine efficiency of aircraft. 1926 *Glasgow Herald* 23 Apr. 5 The problem of aerodynamic safety. 1928 C. F. S. GAMBLE *North Sea Air Station* x. 147 The Wight seaplane..was of similar type to the Short, but its aerodynamical qualities were inferior to its prototype. *Ibid.* xiii. 210 Aerodynamically, it was of interest in being fitted with an air-brake in the form of adjustable flaps.

Aeroplane (ē·ərō-, ē·ərōplēin), *sb.* [Properly two words: in sense 1 f. AERO- + PLANE *sb.*²; in sense 2 ad. F. *aéroplane*, f. Gr. ἀερο-, ἀήρ AIR *sb.* + -πλανος wandering (cf. PLANET).]
† **1.** A plane (or slightly curved) light framework or 'surface' forming part of a flying-machine, and serving to sustain it in the air. *Obs.* (now called simply *plane*, also *wing*).
1866 WENHAM in *Ann. Rep. Aëronautical Soc. Gt. Brit.* 33 In the flying mechanism of beetles..when the..wing-cases are opened, they are checked by a stop, which sets them at a fixed angle. It is probable that these serve as 'aeroplanes,' for carrying the weight of the insect. *Ibid.* 37 A thin steel tie-band,..served as the foundation of the superposed aeroplanes. 1902 F. WALKER *Aërial Navig.* 117 Air-ships as combinations of aërostat, aëroplane, and propelling apparatus. 1905 G. BACON *Balloons, etc.* 111 What are called 'aeroplanes'—large flat surfaces, light but rigid, inclined at a suitable angle to the horizon.
2. A heavier-than-air flying-machine having one, two, or three such planes (*monoplane, biplane*, or *triplane*), and driven by a motor.
1884 *Pall Mall Gaz.* 28 Aug. 4/1 As soon as the Aero-Plane has been seen floating to and fro over the city of San Francisco, steered at pleasure this way and that, and carrying a number of passengers. 1892 H. S. MAXIM in *Century Mag.* Apr. 957/2 Ascertaining how much power was..required to perform flight with a screw-driven aëroplane. 1910 R. FERRIS *How it Flies* 453 *Aeroplane*—The type of flying machine which is supported in the air by a spread of surfaces or planes formerly flat and therefore truly 'plane' but of late more or less curved.
3. *attrib.*
1884 *Pall Mall Gaz.* 28 Aug. 4/1 The company is called 'Marriott's Aero-Plane Company, for Navigating the Air.' 1896 MAXIM in *Aeronautical Annual, Nat. & Artif. Flight*, The next machine..was on the kite or aeroplane system. 1902 *Aeronaut. World* (U.S.A.) 1 Oct. 58/1 This bird-like aeroplane machine. 1911 GRAHAME-WHITE *Aeroplane* 3 Wilbur and Orville Wright started their first aeroplane experiments..[in] North Carolina.
Hence **Aeroplane** *v. intr.*, to travel in an aeroplane.
1910 SHAW *Misalliance* (1925) 46 *Lina*. I never drink tea. *Tarleton*. Bad thing to aeroplane on, I should imagine.

Æsopic (īsǫ·pik), *a.* Also (now *U.S.*) **Esopic**. [ad. late L. *Æsōpicus*, f. *Æsōpus* = Gr. Αἴσωπος.] Of, pertaining to, or characteristic of Æsop, an ancient Greek fabulist. So **Æsopian** (īsō·piăn), *a.* [f. late L. *Æsōpius*: see -IAN]. Hence **Æsopism** (ī·sopiz'm), an Æsopic characteristic.
1728 CHAMBERS *Cycl.* s.v. *Fable*, Esopic Fables. 1831 CARLYLE *Misc. Ess., Early German Lit.* (1888) III. 204 The old prevalence of the Didactic, especially of the Æsopic, is everywhere manifest. 1869 TOZER *Highl. Turkey* II. 266 The Æsopic and similar fables of later date. 1905 J. M. ROBERTSON *Shaksp. Titus Andron.* 146 The Æsopism about the crow figuring at court.

Aetomorphic (ēˌētomǭ·ɹfik), *a. Ornith.* [f. mod.L. *Aëtomorphæ* fem. pl. (f. Gr. ἀετός eagle + μορφή form) + -IC.] Belonging to, or having the characters of, the division *Aetomorphæ* of *Carinatæ* in Huxley's classification, comprising the birds of prey or *Raptores*.
1893 NEWTON *Dict. Birds* 3 Prof. Huxley makes four divisions of the Aetomorphic birds.

Afeard, *a.* (Illustrations of later U.S. use.)
1807–8 W. IRVING *Salmagundi* (1824) 361 Being affeared that I might possibly appear to less advantage as a pedestrian. 1834 [C. A. DAVIS] *Lett. J. Downing* 21 And when we crossed the brook, says I, don't be afeard of the string-pieces here. 1845 S. JUDD *Margaret* I. xiv. 127, I am afeared some of us are resting upon a sandy foundation. 1876 'MARK TWAIN' *Tom Sawyer* ix. 83 Oh, don't be afeard. I don't believe they'll bother us. 1881 A. A. HAYES *New Colorado* vii. 97 That's what she's afeered of—them clouds a-droppin'. 1896 J. C. HARRIS *Sister Jane* 74 That's no reason why you should act as if you was afeared she'd eat you up. 1911 R. D. SAUNDERS *Col. Todhunter* iv. 54, I wouldn't be afeared for him in a difficulty with Stam Tucker.

Afebrile (ăfe·brəil), *a.* [f. A- 14 + FEBRILE *a.*] Unaccompanied by fever.
1875 tr. *von Ziemssen's Cycl. Med.* I. 124 The cases of febrile and afebrile abdominal catarrh. 1901 *Practitioner* Mar. 303 The afebrile cases of lobar pneumonia.

Affect, *sb.* Delete † *Obs.*, insert them in every sense already given and add:
1. e. *Psychol.* (see quots.). So **Affective** *a.* (see quot. 1926).
1891 J. M. BALDWIN *Handbk. Psychol.* II. 314 Affects..are the feeling antecedents of involuntary movements; as motives, including affects, are the inner antecedents of acts of will. 1919 HADFIELD in Streeter *The Spirit* 101 Like fear, it [*sc.* the sexual instinct] has a far greater 'affect' or emotional tone than we need for this purpose. 1921 *Sat. Westm. Gaz.* 1 Oct. 16/2 The influence of Affect on Apperception—or, in non-psychological language, the way in which feeling colours our perception of facts. 1923 *Ibid.* 24 Mar. 181 Their psychic lives are overfull of complexes, levels and affects. 1926 W. MCDOUGALL *Outl. Abnormal Psychol.* 26 The terms 'affect' and 'affective' denote the emotional-conative aspect of all mental activity.

Affectation. Add:
[After Fr.] The declared occupation or employment of a ship. 1914 in *Concise Oxf. Dict.* Addenda.

Affe·ctionize, *v.* [AFFECTION *sb.* 6.] *trans.* To regard or treat with affection.
a 1864 HAWTHORNE *Dr. Grimshawe* xvii. 233 Much as the Warden had seemed to affectionise Redclyffe hitherto.

Affiche (æfī·ʃ, ‖afīʃ). [F., f. *afficher*:—L. type *affigicare (see AFFICHE).] A paper containing a notice to be affixed to a wall, etc.; a placard, poster.
[1774 POSTLETHWAYT *Dict. Trade* (ed. 4), *Affiche*, so the French call those bills or advertisements which are pasted up in public places.] 1818 MOORE *Fudge Fam. Paris* viii. 87 Then we stare into shops—read the evening's *affiches*. 1819 H. BUSK *Vestriad* v. 241 Soon those who spell the grand affiche peruse. 1833 T. HAMILTON *Men & Mann. Amer.* (1843) I. 11 When the sphere of my intelligence became enlarged with regard to this *affiche* (*sc.* placard on a wall). 1884 J. SHARMAN *Cursory Hist. Swearing* i. 6 The usual notice-board..covered with a trellis-work of crimson tape for the purpose of retaining the various *affiches*.

Affiliate, *v.* **2. c.** (Earlier U.S. example.)
1852 *Congress. Globe* 18 Mar., App. 322/1 Can we affiliate with the Whigs? Never!

Affiliation. Add:
2. b. Association, connexion, esp. in politics. *U.S.*
1852 *Congress. Globe* 15 Mar., App. 323/3 Certain merchants with whom be has affiliations in New Mexico. 1862 *Ibid.* Jan. 589/2, I am here almost without any affiliation in political sentiment. 1893 *Congress. Rec.* Feb. 2301/1 The black man..is being educated, and can see where his political affiliation can best be allied. 1904 Roosevelt in *N. Y. Times* 23 Mar. 7, I have not the slightest idea what your political affiliations are.
c. An affiliated part of an organization.
1818 *Ann. Reg. 1817* 22 Busily..at work, establishing branches and affiliations. 1922 *Daily Mail* 14 Nov. 4 *Advt.*, The London Joint City and Midland Bank or its affiliations, the Belfast Banking Company, Ireland, and the Clydesdale Bank, Scotland.

Affirmance. 1. and **2.** (Add U.S. examples.)
1885 *Century Mag.* XXIX. 730 The affirmance of the judgment of the court below by the General Term. 1888 Bryce *Amer. Commw.* I. 505 A majority of the Supreme court seems to have placed upon this ground .. its affirmance of that competence of Congress to declare paper money a legal tender for debts.

Affli·ctedly, *adv.* In an afflicted manner, distressfully.
1888 Doughty *Trav. Arabia Deserta* II. 169 The stranger answered him afflictedly, 'Eigh me.'

Afforestable (æfǫ·restăb'l), *a.* [f. Afforest + -able.] Capable of being afforested.
1928 *Britain's Industr. Future* (*Liberal Ind. Inquiry*) Index 489 Estimate of afforestable land.

Affricate (æ·frikět), *sb. Phonetics.* [ad. L. *affricātus*, pa. pple. of *affricāre*, f. *ad* to + *fricāre* to rub.] A close combination of an explosive consonant or 'stop' with an immediately following fricative or spirant of corresponding position, as in Ger. *pf*, *z* (= ts). Also called **Affri·cative.** So **A·ffricated** *a.*, converted into an affricate.
1880 Sayce *Introd. Sci. Lang.* I. 270 Where a spirant or fricative is immediately preceded by an explosive, a double sound or affricative is the result (*e.g.* German *pf*, Armenian *t's*). 1889 *New Engl. Dict.* s.v. Ch (consonantal digraph), The combination CH..was introduced [into Roman spelling] to represent the Greek aspirate or affricate X. *Ibid.*, *Ch* ..was introduced initially, in Upper German, for the affricated sound of *c* (k) as *chamara* (kχa·māra). 1895 P. Giles *Man. Compar. Philol.* 70 Another series of sounds which must be..distinguished from spirants and aspirates is the affricates. 1905 L. A. Magnus *Respublica* 74 Here we might safely say final *c* is preserved as a sibilant or affricate.

Afghan (æ·fgæn). Also **Afghaun.** [Name of the natives of Afghanistan, a country lying north-west of British India, and their language.] A blanket or wrap of knitted or crocheted wool.
1833 Carlyle *Sartor Res.* i. v, Afghaun shawls. 1858 Eliz. Prentiss *Let.* 13 Dec. in *Life & Lett.* (1882) 260 Mr. P. has come up-stairs rolled up in your afghan. 1867 Stockton *Hundredth Man* xxxii, Miss Burns was crocheting an afghan.

Afield, *adv.* Add: **3. b.** Astray.
1887 *Nation* (N.Y.) 12 May 412/1 He is utterly afield as to Greek art.

African (æ·frikăn), *a.* and *sb.* Also 6–7 Af(f)ricane, (6 Aph-). [ad. L. *Africanus*, f. *Africa* (see below) + *-anus* -an.] **A.** *adj.* **a.** Of or pertaining to Africa (the continent, or the ancient Roman province of that name); occurring in some specific names of plants (see quots.). **b.** Belonging to or characteristic of the negro races of Africa. **B.** *sb.* A native of Africa; an African negro.
1564 Harding *Answ. Jewel* 61 b, He being an Aphricane borne, and writing to Aphricanes. *Ibid.* 89 b, This reconciliation..of the Affricane churches to the catholike church. 1624 [Scott] *2nd Pt. Vox Populi* 23 That (insolent and african pride) of restrayning him from that liberall..converse..with the Lady Maria Infanta. 1646 Carre *Occas. Disc.* 147 The Epist. of the Africane Bishops to Pope Celestine. 1706 Phillips (ed. Kersey), *Ulpicum*.. African Garlick. 1756–9 A. Butler *Lives Saints* (1780) IX. 172 The concurring suffrages of sixteen ancient and worthy bishops (two of whom were Africans). 1782 Latham *Gen. Syn. Birds* I. ii. 532 African C[uckow]. 1849 Carlyle *Latter-d. Pamph.*, *Nigger-Q.* (1858) 5 Our West-Indian policy..of keeping down the labour-market in those islands by importing new Africans. 1861 Bentley *Man. Bot.* 645 *Oldfieldia africana*, yields..African Oak or African Teak. *Ibid.* 677 *Sanseviera zeylanica*..[produces] African Hemp or Bowstring Hemp. 1869 Allies *Form. Christendom* ii. 277 Tertullian adds the witness of the African church to that of the Asiatic and Gallic churches in Irenæus.

Africander (æfrikæ·ndəɹ). [ad. Cape Du. *Afrikaander*, f. *Afrikaansch* African, with termination modelled on *Hollander* Dutchman.] A white native of South Africa, esp. one of Dutch descent. Also *attrib.* esp. in *Afrikander Bond*, a political league inaugurated in 1882, having as its object the unification of the states and colonies of South Africa with a view to independence.
Also applied to coloured South Africans of mixed descent.
[1822 Burchell *Trav.* I. 21 All those who are born in the colony speak that language [*sc.* Dutch], and call themselves Africaanders, whether of Dutch, German, or French origin.] 1834 *C. Gd. Hope Lit. Gaz.* IV. 103 (Pettman) The number of matches that have taken place between the fair Africanders. 1882 *De Patriot* (Cape Colony) in *Encycl. Brit.* (1902) XXVI. 568/2 The Afrikander Bond has for its object the establishment of a South African Nationality by spreading a true love for what is really our fatherland. 1884 *Q. Rev.* July 150 The Africanders would hoist their own flag. *Ibid.*, An Africander republic. 1904 *Ibid.* (1921) Jan. 40 A nation may be born worthy to take its place among the nations of the world, where the name of 'Africander' shall be heard with honour and applause.
Hence **Africa·nderdom,** the Africander section of the inhabitants of South Africa; **Africa·nderism,** the policy, ideals, or aspirations of Africanders; (with *a* and *pl.*) an Afrikaans word or idiom used in South African English.
1884 *Pall Mall Gaz.* 9 Oct. 2/2 Shall we throw in our lot with Afrikanderism, abjuring our nationality for evermore? 1892 *Review Rev.* 15 Jan. 53/1 The further cry of Afrikanderism, 'South Africa for the South Africans.' 1893 *Standard* 21 Apr. 6/2 The sympathy of Africanderdom. 1909 *State* Dec. 701 If an English boy learns Dutch he is apt to acquire what are popularly called Dutchisms or Africanderisms.

Africanism (æ·frikăniz'm). [f. African + -ism.] An African mode of speech or idiom. Also, African qualities or characteristics in the aggregate.
1641 Milton *Reform.* i. 38 He that cannot understand the sober..stile of the Scriptures, will be ten times more puzzl'd with the knotty Africanisms..of the Fathers. 1836 *New Monthly Mag.* XLVII. 152, I have spent some days in a town where every thing is pure Africanism. 1851 Trench *Exp. Serm. on Mt.* (ed. 2) 27 The harsh Africanisms of Tertullian and Arnobius. 1882 B. F. Westcott in Smith & Wace *Dict. Chr. Biogr.* (1887) IV. 139/2 The principles which he [*sc.* Origen] affirmed..are fitted to correct the Africanism which, since the time of Augustine, has dominated Western theology. 1885 G. W. Cable *Creoles of Louisiana* xxxiii. 260 He [*sc.* the rich Creole] dropped..the Africanisms of his black nurse.

Africanize (æ·frikănəiz), *v.* [f. African + -ize.] *trans.* To give an African character to; to subject to the influence of African negroes. Hence **A·fricaniza·tion.**
1853 Lord Clarendon in J. F. Rhodes *Hist. U.S.* (1893) II. 20 A violent..article in the Washington *Union* charging them with an intrigue with Spain to 'Africanize' Cuba. 1859 Bartlett *Dict. Amer.*, Africanization. 1864 *Handbk. Democracy* 6, 27 Africanization. 1884 *N. Amer. Rev.* Nov. 429 When the Africanizing and ruin of the South becomes a clearly seen danger. 1890 *Congress. Rec.* Jan. 806/2, I said I was not in favor of the africanization of this continent. 1905 *Tablet* 21 Oct. 649/2 They have become thoroughly Africanised, speak only the Ethiopian language.

Africanoid (æ·frikănoid), *a.* [f. African + -oid.] Resembling the African types of mankind.
1899 Ripley *Races Eur.* 397 A long-headed member of the Africanoid races. 1921 *19th Cent.* May 884 The character-making quality did not come from Asianoid or Africanoid races, it was supplied by the Teuton.

Afrikaans (æfrikā·ns). Also -caans. [= Du. *Afrikaansch*: see African and -ish.] South African or Cape Dutch; = Taal.
1908 *East London Dispatch* 20 Oct. 4 (Pettman), I have always regarded (high) Dutch as my mother tongue and Africaans (low Dutch) as a hodge-pot sort of a language. 1927 *Observer* 27 Mar. 16/6 Too many British South Africans fail to learn Afrikaans.

Afro- (æ·fro), used as comb. form of L. *Afer*, *Afr-* African, as in *Afro-American* (also *Aframerican*) adj. and sb., (a person) of African descent born in America (spec. the United States); *Afro-European* adj., African and European.
1890 *Ann Arbor R.* 23 Jan., Afro-Americans at Chicago ..The Afro-American League. 1898 *Westm. Gaz.* 31 May 3/1 She is a New Orleans Creole, her mother being an Afro-American, and her father a Louisiana Frenchman. 1910 Sir H. H. Johnston *Negro in New World* 390 In music the Aframerican..may achieve triumphs.

After. Add: **B. 6.** In expressions of the type *day after day, man after man.*
c 1175, 1866 [see Dict. s.v.]. 1611, 1830 [see Year 7]. 1631 [see Time *sb.* 31]. 1798 Coleridge *Anc. Mar.* 115 Day after day, day after day, We stuck, nor breath nor motion. 1868 Dilke *Greater Britain* I. i. iii. 34 Time after time I heard the complaint, 'The Yankees treat us shamefully, I reckon'. 1887 [see Hour 1]. 1893 Beatrice Harraden *Ships that pass* i. vii, 'It seems so little to ask', she cried to herself time after time.
8. b. Past (a certain hour). Now *dial.* and *U.S.*
1774 P. V. Fithian *Jrnl.* 271. I..rode thence to Westmoreland Court House ten Miles by half after six. 1775 *Essex Inst. Hist. Coll.* XLVIII. 52 We was preaded (i.e. paraded) about half after two in the morning. 1812 Mar. Edgeworth *Madame de Fleury* i, It was now half after four. 1899 Quinn *Pennsylv. Stories* 134 Mrs. De Lancy's dinner party..had reached the lower right-hand box by a quarter after eight. 1905 *N. Y. Even. Post* 27 Jan. 3 About half after twelve the roof of the building fell in with a crash.

A·fter-care. [f. After- 9 + Care *sb.*] Care or attention bestowed after the conclusion of a certain period of treatment, etc.; freq. *attrib.*
1894 *Daily News* 12 Jan. 5/5 The After-Care Association facilitates the readmission of poor female convalescents from lunatic asylums into social life. 1921 *Act 11 Geo. V*, c. 12 § 2 Arrangements..for the after-care of persons who have suffered from tuberculosis. 1927 *Daily Tel.* 8 Feb. 13/7 Changes which are contemplated in connection with St. Dunstan's Institute..will not affect the work of after-care. *Ibid.* 3 May 14/1 Some after-care committee should protect young people from jobs which led nowhere.

A·fter-day·s, *sb. pl.* [After- 9.] Later or subsequent days. Rarely *sing.* a subsequent day or period.
1700 Wesley *Ep. to Friend conc. Poetry* 451 Like old Ennius he design'd What After-days have polish'd and refin'd. 1795 Southey *Joan of Arc* i. 173 Happy those Who in the after-days shall live. 1828 Scott *F. M. Perth* xxi, That celebrated Lindsay, Earl of Crawford, who, in his afterdays, was known by the epithet of the Tiger-Earl. 1832 Tennyson '*Love thou thy Land*' vii, Nor toil for title,.. neither count on praise It grows to guerdon after-days. 1873 Caswall *Tale of Tintern* iv. (1907) 49 And He thine offering will repay Most fully in an after day! 1903 Hardy *Dynasts* i. i. iii, To retrospective eyes of afterdays.

A·fter-dea·th. [After- 1.] An existence that follows death; a future life.
1899 W. S. Blunt *Satan Absolved* Poet. Wks. 1914 II. 282 In the long after-death Ye shall be burned with fire. 1907 *Folk-Lore* June 164 That belief in an after-death or life of souls.

A·fter-li·fe. [After- 9.]
1. A future life.
1615 Hoby *Curry-combe* 149 Saduces..denied the Resurrection, and by consequence any after-life. 1925 F. W. Norwood in Welldon, etc. *Life after Death* 70 Concerning Jesus and the After Life. 1925 D. Thomas *Ibid.* 104 Young children whose minds were unversed in speculations about the After Life.
2. The later period of one's life.
1817 Scott *Harold* vi. xix. Eivir! since thou for many a day Hast follow'd Harold's wayward way, It is but meet that in the line Of after-life I follow thine. 1837 Lockhart *Scott* I. 323 Archibald Constable, in after life one of the most eminent of British publishers. 1862 *Chamb. Encycl.* III. 772/1 The subject-matter of the teaching would be an acquisition of great value in after-life to every one. 1878 Jevons *Pol. Econ.* Pref. (1892) 6 To instil..notions on subjects with which all must in after-life be practically conversant.

Afternoo·ner. Used in comb., as in *Saturday-afternooner*, one who has a holiday on Saturday afternoons.
1906 *Daily Chron.* 28 July 7/6 Thus giving early-closers and Saturday-afternooners a chance. 1927 *Daily Tel.* 7 June 3/1 If the amendment which I suggest is wrong for the Saturday afternooners, it is wrong for cricket.

Afterwards. Add: *sb.* The future; the future life, the after-life.
1901 'Linesman' *Words Eyewitness* (1902) 343 The little spark must keep the great cold world warm until the Afterwards. 1902 Elinor Glyn *Refl. Ambrosine* 285 An English girl would have a blank prospect in front of her for the afterwards.

A·fterword. [f. After- 9 after *foreword*.] Something written at the conclusion of a book, etc. as an epilogue or the like.
1889 *Caxton's Eneydos* (E.E.T.S.) p. xx, Afterwords by F. J. Furnivall. 1900 Mead *Fragm. Faith* 605 *heading*, Afterword. 1911 J. Gwynn (*title*) The Present Position of Protestantism in Ireland and an Afterword.

A·fter-yea·rs, *sb. pl.* [After- 9.] The years that come, came, or will come after; the later years (of a man's life, etc.). Rarely *sing.* a later year.
1837 Lockhart *Scott* I. 341 Had the subject been taken up in after years, we might have had another Marmion. 1838 *Penny Cycl.* XII. 308/2 If the growth is checked by starvation, beauty and energy will rarely be displayed in after-years. 1858 Matson *Sonn.* Poems 459 Love..sagely musing o'er Fate's riddle-book, The secret coins of many an after-year. 1869 Tennyson *Coming of Arthur* 157 In one great annal-book, where after-years Will learn the secret of our Arthur's birth. 1902 Gairdner *Engl. Ch. 16th C.* iv. 45 In spite of all the frightful demoralization of his after years he retained both characters to the very end.

Agalite (æ·gălait). *Min.* Also -lith. [Said to be f. Gr. ἀγη wonder + -lite.] A fine fibrous variety of talc used in the manufacture of paper.
1887 *Athenæum* 14 May 644 The variety of talc known commercially as agalite is now largely used in paper-making in place of kaolin.

Agamoid, *a.* Add:
B. *sb.* An agamoid lizard.
1882 *Encycl. Brit.* XIV. 736/2 *Calotes* is another genus of agamoids peculiar to the East Indies. 1886 *Ibid.* XX. 469/2 The bulk of the Lacertilian fauna is composed of Skinks, Geckos, Agamoids, and *Varanidæ*.

Agapanthus (ægăpæ·nþǫs). [mod.L., f. Gr. ἀγάπη love + ἄνθος flower.] A plant of the genus *Agapanthus* (N.O. *Liliaceæ*), having large umbels of bright blue flowers, cultivated for ornament.
1879 W. Cory *Lett. & Jrnls.* (1897) 448 He made flowering plants huddle round the trunks of trees, agapanthus under plane. 1886 Rider Haggard *Jess* i, The agapanthus which is so familiar to us in English greenhouses.

Agapemone (ægăpī·mŏni). [irreg. f. Gr. ἀγάπη love + μονή dwelling, abode (μένειν to stay, remain).] Proper name of an association of men and women established at Spaxton in Somerset by the Rev. Henry James Prince; a similar establishment conducted by his successor, the Rev. John Hugh Smyth-Pigott, at Clapton, London. Also *gen.* an establishment of this kind, an abode-of-love; esp. with unfavourable implication. Hence **Agapemonian** (-mōᵘ·niăn) *a.*, **Agape·monite** *a.*, *sb.*
1850 *Daily News* 22 Mar., The Agapemonites.—It is said that there is a general split amongst this deluded sect at their abode near Bridgewater. 1854 *Edin. Rev.* Apr. 377 The Agapemone of Bridgwater is full of crazy fanatics. 1859 *Sat. Rev.* 30 Apr. 527/2 A carriage-full of Brothers and Sisters in Love singing the Agapemonite Psalter. *Ibid.*, Any of the subsequent Agapemonian extravagances. 1888 Sir J. D. Hooker in *Life & Lett.* (1918) II. 317 The moment you allow of 'promiscuous intercourse' it is all up and the thing degenerates into an agapemone. 1908 *Daily Chron.* 24 Sept. 1/1 The Agapemonites are extremely reticent about their peculiar religion. 1908 *Times* 10 Nov. 12/4 The date.. on which a party of Cambridge undergraduates were going to raid the 'Agapemone' at Spaxton, and tar and feather the Rev. Smyth Pigott.

Agar (ā·gaɹ). Short for next.
1889 *Jrnl. Chem. Soc.* LVI. 817 Diffusion in Agar Jelly. 1892 *Pall Mall Gaz.* 3 Aug. 7/2 Cultures were made in broth, gelatine, and agar. 1929 *Practitioner* Nov. 596 An ordinary 2 per cent. agar medium.

Agar-agar (ā·gar,ā·gaɹ). Also occas. agal-agal. [Malay.] Any of certain East-Indian seaweeds, esp. the Ceylon moss *Gracilaria lichenoides*, from which a gelatinous substance is extracted and used in China for soups and the manufacture of transparent silk and paper, and in bacteriology as a solidifying agent in culture media.
1820 J. Crawfurd *Ind. Archipelago* III. ix. ii. 181 The articles of the return cargo [to China]..embrace..*agar-agar*, or sea-weed, *tripang*, or sea-slug. 1825 T. Thornton *W. Milburn's Oriental Comm.* 330 Agal Agal, a species of seaweed, dissoluble into a glutinous substance like congee. 1863 Watts *Dict. Chem.* I. 61 Agar-agar or Bengal Isinglass. 1886 Cruikshank *Bacteriology* 65 Agar-agar has the advantage of remaining solid up to a temperature of about 45°. 1896 *Lancet* 28 Mar. 835/2 Löffler's serum agar-agar.

Agate, *sb.* **6.** Add:
agate-ware, a kind of pottery coloured to resemble agate; also, enamelled iron or steel ware for household utensils. Also *attrib.*
1857 J. Marryat *Pottery & Porcelain* viii. (ed. 2) 154 *note*, Agate and jasper ware. 1865 Jewitt *Wedgwoods* Index, Agate-ware vases. 1879 *Cassell's Techn. Educ.* I. 367 During the reigns of Anne and George I, an improved ware was made of sand and pipe-clay, coloured with oxide of copper and manganese, forming the well-known 'agate-ware' and 'tortoiseshell-ware.'

Age, *sb.* Add:
6. b. *Cards.* The 'eldest hand' in the game of poker.
1882 *Poker: how to play it* 47 Before the dealer begins to deal the cards, the player next to his left, who is called the *ante-man*, or *age*, must deposit in the pool an *ante* not exceeding one-half the limit previously agreed upon. 1889 Guerndale *Poker Bk.* v. 33 It would be C's place to bet first, he being to the left of the Age.

Age, *v.* Add:
3. To calculate the age of (a horse).
1908 *Animal Managem.* 37 Dates from which horses are aged.
4. *trans.* To mature by keeping in storage, by exposing to the air, etc.
1852 J. Swindles & W. Nicholson in *Patents, Abridgm. Specif.* (1859) 379 For oxydating metallic solutions, and for ageing and raising various coloring matters. 1854 W. E. Staite *Ibid.* 480 Madder which, technically speaking, has not been 'aged'.
5. *Calico-printing.* To fix the mordants and printed colours in (cloth, etc.) by the process of ageing. Also *intr.*, to undergo this process. So **Aged** *ppl. a.*
1849 [see *Ageing 2]. 1862 C. O'Neill *Dict. Calico Printing* 8/1 The difference of appearance will be..in favour of the aged or exposed part. 1890 W. J. Gordon *Foundry* 177 The calico..has to be dried and aged. 1910 E. Knecht, etc. *Man. Dyeing* (ed. 2) II. 649 The dyeing of aged blacks. 1912 E. Knecht & J. B. Fothergill *Textile Printing* 138 If they [*sc.* the goods] are simply printed in aluminium mordants, one day may be quite sufficient to fully 'age' them. *Ibid.* 141 It is preferable to let them 'age' for a day or two in pile before dyeing.
6. *intr.* Of iron, the iron core of an electrical transformer: To suffer a continuously increased loss in hysteretic quality.
1896 [see *Ageing 4]. 1899 S. R. Roget in *Proc. R. Soc.* 23 Jan. 154 Brands of transformer steel, which are practically 'non-ageing'. 1902 *Encycl. Brit.* XXVIII. 121/1 Brands of steel are now obtainable which do not age in this manner.

Ageing, *vbl. sb.* Add (cf. *Age *v.*):
2. *Calico-printing.* The action or process of fixing the colours and mordants by exposing the printed goods to the action of a warm, moist atmosphere or by running them through hot steam. Also *attrib.*
1849 J. Thom in *Patents, Abridgm. Specific.* (1859) 304 The ageing of goods by..passing them through a chamber containing aqueous vapour. 1850 S. Pincoff *ibid.* 319 Improvements in the ageing process..consist..in the mode of introducing into the ageing room..a heated and moistened atmosphere. 1859 *Ibid.*, The ageing stove. 1862 C. O'Neill *Dict. Calico Printing* 8/2 Ageing liquor. 1881 *Instr. Census Clerks* (1885) 69 Ageing Machine Minder. 1882 *Jrnl. Soc. Chem. Industry* I. 188 To prevent condensation,..the walls of the aging [*sic*] house are double.
3. The action or process of maturing pottery clay, wine, logwood, etc. Also *attrib.*
1860 Tomlinson *Arts & Manuf.* 2nd Ser. *Pottery* 31 The mixture of clay and flint..ought to be kept..in order that the materials may become more intimately united...During this ageing, as it is called, a fermentation takes place. 1874 Knight *Dict. Mech.*, *Ageing* (Wine and Liquors). *Ibid.*, Wine-ageing Apparatus. 1910 E. Knecht, etc. *Man. Dyeing* (ed. 2) I. 331 Ageing or Maturing of Logwood.
4. The continually increasing hysteresis of iron under alternating magnetization, or when subjected to great heat.
1896 D. C. & J. P. Jackson *Alternating Currents* 539 Ageing of Transformer Cores. *Ibid.*, The ageing seems to have the greatest effect upon poor qualities of iron.
b. The deterioration in candle-power (of an incandescent lamp).
1902 *Encycl. Brit.* XXVIII. 90/1 Ageing of lamps.

Agelessness (ē·dʒlĕsnĕs). [f. Ageless *a.* + -ness.] The quality of being ageless.
1905 W. Watson *Prince's Quest* i. Poems II. 137 And so the people of this land possess, Age after age, unaltering agelessness. [Not so in earlier editions.] 1906 A. C. Benson *From a College Window* xviii, The mighty unresting Heart, to whose vastness and agelessness the whole mass of these flying and glowing suns are but as a handful of dust. 1927 J. C. Squire in *Observer* 1 May 6 He had a rare gift with boys and young men, whom he could draw out by sheer agelessness.

Agency. Add: **6.** The office of an Indian agent, or the establishment forming the headquarters of one. *U.S.*
1824 *Publ. Stat. U. S. A.* (1856) IV. 25 It shall be the duty of each Indian agent to reside and keep his agency within, or near the territory claimed by the tribe or tribes of Indians for which he may be agent. 1878 J. H. Beadle *Western Wilds* xiii. 198 We concluded we had better see the Creeks at home, and started afoot for the Agency. 1888 *Harper's Mag.* Mar. 566/2 They are fed and clothed by the government, and they camp about the agencies in idleness. 1895 C. King *Fort Frayne* xvi. 228 Eleven o'clock came and..no further authority from the agency.
attrib. 1873 J. H. Beadle *Undevel. West* xxv. 527 The last grain in the Agency storehouse was issued to them on the 14th. 1878 — *Western Wilds* xvi. 249 The band..unite in the quadrangle inclosed by the Agency buildings. *Ibid.* 252 Mr. Thomas V. Keams, Agency Clerk. 1891 *Fur, Fin & Feather* Mar. 169 A bear likes wild plums and black haws better than a Crow papoose likes agency lump sugar. 1901 S. E. White *Westerners* viii. 57 Rain-in-the-Face was at once an agency Indian and a reckless man.

Agenda. See Agend 3, and add:
b. *attrib.*, as **agenda-paper,** the paper containing the agenda of a meeting.
1887 *Westmor. Gaz.* 10 Dec. 2/5 (Stanf.) The next business stated on the agenda paper was to sign a petition [etc.]. 1905 *Westm. Gaz.* 24 July 2/2 The Czar on the *Polar Star* and the Kaiser on the *Hohenzollern* are meeting to-day in the Gulf of Finland.—We are not given the agenda-paper of their conversation at the interviews to be held on the two yachts.

Agendum (ădʒe·ndǫm). [See Agend.] = Agend 3.
1898 *Westm. Gaz.* 23 Mar. 1/2 A prearranged agendum and precise rules of debate. 1920 *Daily Tel.* 25 May 12/4 To cause the closing of the session before its agendum had been fully dealt with.

Agent, *sb.* Add:
1. b. *Telepathy.* The person who originates the impression received by the percipient.
1882 *Proc. Soc. Psychical Research* I. 119 In Thought-transference..both parties (whom, for convenience' sake, we will call the Agent and the Percipient) are supposed to be in a normal state. 1886 [see Percipient *sb.* b].
4. b. (In full *Indian agent.*) An official appointed to represent the government in dealing with an Indian tribe. *U.S.*
1816 *Register of Officers & Agents U. S.* 62 Indian agents have been allowed from 2 to 8 rations per day in addition to their annual compensation. 1818 *Publ. Stat. U.S.A.* (1856) III. 428 An Act directing the manner of appointing Indian Agents. *Ibid.* 461 The agent to the Creek nation. 1833 T. Flint *Indian Wars* 76 He there met an Indian agent from Detroit, who..exerted his influence with the savages for his release. 1878 B. P. Poore *Political Reg.* 235 The commissioner of Indian affairs..receives reports from inspectors, superintendents, agents, and traders. 1886 Capt. Bell *Report* in *Nation* (1888) 15 Mar. 211/1 There can be but one head to an Indian agency, and the agent should be that head, if discipline is to be maintained. 1901 S. E. White *Westerners* xxxv. 317 He could not recall all the story he had told the Indian agent.
c. Ellipt. for *road-agent* (see Road *sb.* 12). *U.S.*
1881 A. A. Hayes *New Colorado* xi. 154 We reached it before long, and concluded the 'agents' or robbers, had an excellent eye for position. *a* 1904 S. E. White *Blazed Trail Stories* 152 Nex' time I drives stage some of these yere agents massacrees me from behind a bush.

Agenting (ē·dʒĕntiŋ), *vbl. sb.* [f. Agent *sb.* or *v.* + -ing[1].] The work or duties of an agent.
1681 [see Agent *v.*]. 1751 [see Extractor 2 b]. 1924 Galsworthy *White Monkey* ii. i, A man called Smith.. who's done most of the agenting for the German business.

Agentive (ē·dʒe·ntiv), *a. Gram.* [f. Agent *sb.* + -ive.] Applied to the case which denotes the subject of a transitive verb in languages in which its form differs from that denoting the subject of an intransitive verb.
1903 *Amer. Anthropologist* Jan.–Mar. 26 Syntactical Cases and Appositions [in native languages of California]. Agentive, Subjective, Objective, Possessive.

Agent provocateur (aʒaṅ provokatǫ̈r). [F. = provocative agent.] An agent employed to induce or incite a person to commit a treasonable or actionable offence.
1896 Le Queux *Secret Service* viii, It was hinted to an *agent provocateur* that your death would be gratifying. 1923 *Daily Mail* 1 Mar. 8 Constantinople had long been the Mecca of the professional spy and *agent provocateur*.

Ager (ē·dʒəɹ). [f. Age *v.* + -er[1].] **a.** An ageing apparatus or chamber. Also *attrib.* as *ager man, minder.* **b.** = ager man. **c.** An inspector of electric lamps (cf. *Ageing 4 b).
1912 E. Knecht & J. B. Fothergill *Textile Printing* 143 Mather & Platt's Rapid Steam 'Ager'..was brought out in 1879. 1921 *Dict. Occup. Terms* (1927) § 308 *Ager, flash ager*; examines electric incandescent lamps, before and after cap is fitted on. *Ibid.* 298 *Ager, ager man, ager minder, age minder, ageing machine minder*..minds ageing machine.

Agglutinate, *v.* Add:
2. b. *Bacteriology.* To cause agglutination or coalescence of (bacteria or red blood-corpuscles). Also *absol.* or *intr.*, to undergo agglutination. Hence **Agglu·tinating** *ppl. a.*, **Agglu·tinable, Agglu·tinative** *adjs.*; **Agglutina·tion; Agglu·tinator; Agglu·tinin,** an agent that causes agglutination; **Agglu·tinogen,** the substance present in bacteria, which stimulates the formation of agglutinins; hence **Agglutino·genous** *a.*; **Agglu·tinoid,** an agglutinin that has lost its agglutinophoric group, but retains the haptophoric group for the cell; **Agglu·tinophore,** a molecular complex of the agglutinins to which their agglutinating property is due; hence **Agglutinopho·ric** *a.*
1896 *Lancet* 19 Sept. 806/2 The 'agglutinines' found in the serum of immunised animals. *Ibid.*, The use of the agglutinative action of human serum for the diagnosis of enteric fever. 1900 *Jrnl. Chem. Soc.* LXXVIII. ii. 560 A discussion with experimental tests of the numerous theories put forward to explain agglutination. No satisfactory theory ..has yet been offered, although Bordet's, that an agglutinating agent (agglutinine) acting upon an agglutinable substance..is regarded as most rational. 1902 *Encycl. Brit.* XXVI. 68/2 Widal..showed that serum of patients suffering from typhoid fever..agglutinated the typhoid bacillus. 1902 *Jrnl. Exper. Med.* 17 Mar. 289 Ricin, a strong agglutinator. 1903 *Jrnl. R. Microsc. Soc.* Feb. 78 The agglutinative and agglutinogenous functions are subject to the greatest variations. 1903 *Lancet* 4 Apr. 946/1 The existence of the agglutinins was one of the earliest results of modern investigations into immunity. *Ibid.* 946/2 The bacilli may lose their agglutinability,..viz., their agglutinable substance loses its functional atom-group. *Ibid.*, A higher dilution would sometimes agglutinate when a lower one would not. *Ibid.*, Agglutinins may become converted into agglutinoids. 1915 *Ibid.* 13 Nov. 1086/2 The agglutination test..gave a positive result in practically every case of enteric fever.

Aggrade (ăgrē·d), *v. Geol.* [f. L. Ag- + Grade, after *degrade*.] *trans.* To fill up (a bay, valley, etc.) with detritus. (The opposite of Degrade *v.* 6.) Hence **Aggra·ded, Aggra·ding** *ppl. adjs.*; also **Aggrada·tion,** whence **Aggrada·tional** *a.*
1905 Chamberlin & Salisbury *Geol.* I. 2 The deposition of material, whether on the land or in the sea, is aggradation. *Ibid.* 178 Streams carrying glacial drainage are usually aggrading streams. *Ibid.* 184 The stream in flood aggrades its plain, and degrades its channel. *Ibid.* 318 The degradational and aggradational work of the sea are greatest near its shores. 1906 *Ibid.* III. 296 The most distinguishing formational feature of the Pliocene is its aggradation deposits. 1915 *Nation* (N.Y.) 10 June 662/3 The distribution and origin of loess, in which insufficient emphasis is given to aggrading rivers, as supplying fine silt in their broad deposits.

Aggregable, *a.* Delete ? *Obs.* and add:
That may be aggregated *with* (other property).
1910 Ld. Halsbury *Laws Eng.* XIII. § 253. 204 Property accruing to a deceased person's estate after his death..is aggregated with the other aggregable property passing on the death of such person. 1924 *Westm. Gaz.* 12 Feb., The Parliamentary estates were aggregable with the marriage settlement funds. 1927 *Daily Tel.* 12 Apr. 9/1 Property which is [so] settled..is not aggregable when passing on the death of the life tenant with the other property passing on that death.

Aggrievedly (ăgrī·vĕdli), *adv.* [f. Aggrieved *ppl. a.* + -ly[2].] In an aggrieved manner.
1883 Miss Broughton *Belinda* viii, 'I offered to teach it to Sarah', he says aggrievedly. 1886 R. A. King *Shadowed Life* vi, He growled as aggrievedly as though it was his wife.

Agila (æ·gilă). Also 6 aguila, 7 aguala, 8 agala, 9 agilla. [ad. Sp., Pg. *aguila* in *palo de aguila*, *pao d'aguila* (= wood of a.): see Eagle-wood and Agalloch.] A resin or resinous wood: = Agalloch, Calambac. Also *agila-wood.*
1589 R. Parke tr. *Mendoza's Hist. China* 41 They do offer vnto their Idolles, frankensence, beniamin, wood of aguila and cayolaque. 1699 Dampier *Voy.* II. i. 8 Pepper, Lignum Aloes, and Aguala Wood. 1727 A. Hamilton *E. Indies* II. 153 It [*sc.* the Siam Coast] produces much Agala and Sapanwoods. 1846 Lindley *Veg. Kingd.* 579 Aloes-wood, Agila-wood, or Eagle-wood. 187: Agilla [see Calambac]. 1881 *Spons' Encycl. Industrial Arts* 1523 Agar, Agila, Akyaw, Calambak, Eagle-wood, Kayugaru, or Lignum-aloes.

Agin (ăgi·n), *prep.* Dialectal var. Again *prep.* (= against), often used jocularly and esp. in phr. *agin the government*, taken as typical of the Irishman's attitude in politics.
1878 W. S. Gilbert *H.M.S. Pinafore* ii, I'm unpleasant to look at, and my name's agin me. 1888 *Nation* (N. Y.) 2 Aug. 81/3 It was as natural for them to support the party in power..as it was for the 'Pat' of the anecdote to reply, when asked on landing which party he belonged to: 'I'm ag'in the gover'mint.' 1904 *Athenæum* 5 Nov. 615 He was by nature 'agin' the Government'. 1920 Galsworthy *In Chancery* ii. xii, Possession, vested rights; and anyone 'agin' 'em—outcast. 'Thank Heaven!' he thought, 'I always felt "agin" 'em, anyway!' 1920 *Punch* 21 July 53/1 To compel the poor thing [*sc.* the motor car] to crawl is 'agin natur''.

Agitatingly (æ·dʒitē·tiŋli), *adv.* [f. Agitating *ppl. a.* + -ly[2].] In such a manner as to cause agitation.
1819 *Blackw. Mag.* VI. 160 That such a mind should have known miserable thoughts so well as to be enabled thus agitatingly to paint them. 1887 *Pictorial World* 28 Apr. 410 He had been deeply, not to say agitatingly, impressed.

Agitatorship (æ·dʒitē·təɹʃip). [f. Agitator + -ship.] The state, condition, or *rôle* of agitator.
1836 *Fraser's Mag.* XIV. 49 That his agitatorship [i. e. O'Connell] and the rest of the tail, be respectfully reminded of their oaths. 1921 Leslie *Manning* 369 Manning..encouraged Ben Tillett upon the path of true agitatorship.

Aglist (ăgli·st), *adv.* [f. A *prep.*[1] + Glist *v.*] Glistening. Also **Agli·sten** *adv.*
1858 Mrs. Oliphant *Laird of Norlaw* lxvi, All aglist with early morning dews and sunshine. 1891 *Murray's Mag.* Aug. 291 The garden all aglisten 'twixt two showers.

Agnostical (ægnǫ·stikăl), *a.* [f. Agnostic *a.* + -al.] = Agnostic *a.*
1884 *Punch* 20 Sept. 135 The Agnostical or Nothingarian creed. 1886 *Sat. Rev.* 25 Dec. 849 Our Agnostical friend passed to the paradise of Mahomet. 1907 *Daily Chron.* 23 Mar. 6/4 Anthropomorphism is the most agnostical and atheistical habit of thought.

Agogic (ăgǫ·dʒik), *a.* [f. Gr. ἀγωγός leading, guiding (f. ἄγειν to lead) + -ic.]
†**1.** Of or pertaining to modelling in wax.
1662 Evelyn *Sculptura* i. i. 7 Neither the Paradigmatic, Agogic, or any of the Plastic [Arts], can Genuinely..be call'd Sculpture.
2. *Mus.* Applied to a kind of accent consisting in a lengthening of the time-value of the note. Also **Ago·gical** *a.* So **Ago·gics,** the use of agogic accents.
1909 C. F. A. Williams *Rhythm Mod. Mus.* 308 The slight delay by which the late Hans von Bülow gave prominence to accented notes..is called by Dr. Hugo Riemann the 'Agogic Accent'. 1919–20 *Mus. Assoc. Proc.* 23 Treatises.. on Aesthetics, Expression, Agogics, Phrasing. 1922 S. Crew *Art of Player-Piano* 62 'Agogic restraint' is the term found by German pedagogues to describe this detail of *rubato*. *Ibid.* 63 Clashings of discordant notes may be.. intensified by an 'agogical' pressure.

Agometer (ăgǫ·mĭtəɹ). *Electr.* [irreg. f. Gr. ἄγειν to lead: see -meter.] A rheostat or resistance-coil.
1855 *Chamb. Jrnl.* IV. 127 A newly invented instrument called an agometer. 1879 *Encycl. Brit.* VIII. 45 The quick-silver agometer of Müller.

Agraffe. Add:
2. Various technical uses: see quots.
1883 *Lond. & Prov. Music Trades Rev.* Mar. 13/2 Erard [in 1808]..substituting for a long, pinned wooden bridge as many little brass bridges as there were notes. The strings passing through holes bored through the little bridges, called agraffes, or studs, turned upwards towards the wrest-pin. 1901 Dorland *Med. Dict.* (ed. 2), *Agraffe*, an instrument for keeping together the edges of the wound in operation for harelip. 1919 E. S. Farrow *Dict. Mil. Terms*, *Agraffe*,.. the coupling pin in artillery.

Agraphy (æ·grăfi). Anglicization of Agraphia.
1903 Myers *Hum. Pers.* I. 65 Elements of agraphy, of word-blindness, of word-deafness appear.

Agree, *v.* **4.** Add:
1920 *Act 10 & 11 Geo. V* c. 11 § 1 So long as the tenant continues to pay rent at the agreed rate. *Ibid.* c. 76 § 21 (3) The remuneration of an arbitrator when agreed or fixed under this section. 1928 *Times* 15 Aug. 7/5 The actual figures of profits were agreed between the accountants. 1928 *Britain's Industr. Future* (*Liberal Ind. Inquiry*) 140 These councils should have power to agree factory rules.

Agreeable, *a.* Add: **6. c.** *To do the agreeable*, to make oneself pleasant, show courteous attentions.
1851 J. J. Hooper *Widow Rugby's Husb.* 168 The Colonel does the agreeable to strangers.

Agricultural, *a.* Add U.S. quot.:
1868 *Amer. Naturalist* II. 157 Such structures are remarkable..reminding us of the intelligence shown by the Agricultural Ant of Texas.

Agriculturalist. (Earlier U.S. example.)
1808 *Deb. Congress* 28 Nov. (1853) 157 What have the agriculturalists to do with your neutral commerce.

Agriculturally (ægrikǫ·ltiŭrăli), *adv.* [f. Agricultural *a.* + -ly[2].] With regard or reference to agriculture.
1821 *Examiner* 50/1 Why say a word about it—why not pass it agriculturally, in prudent silence? 1883 Holme Lee *Loving & Serving* I. xi. 211 His land is poor agriculturally. 1885 *Standard* 2 Sept. 2/4 The Board have not lost sight of the dealing with the sewage agriculturally.

Agrimotor (æ·grimōᵘtǫɹ). [f. L. *agri-*, *ager* land + Motor *sb.*] A motor tractor for agricultural work.
1917 *Town Topics* 10 Feb., The immediate future of agrimotors in this country. 1920 *Country Life* 10 Jan. p. lxi, The Crawley Agrimotor Equal to 8 men and 16 horses.

Agriology (ægriǫ·lŏdʒi). [f. Gr. ἄγριος wild, savage: see -ology.] The comparative study of the history and customs of savage or uncivilized races. Hence **Agriolo·gical** *a.*
1878 *Fraser's Mag.* XVII. 730 Trying the law..of euphony and prosody in face of the agriology of the day. *Ibid.* 733 Mr. Sayce..threatens to make agriological scalps the only wear in glottology. 1886 *Jrnl. Educ.* 1 Apr. 152/1 The new lights thrown on the early stages of society by..what may be called Agriology.

Aguacate (agwakā·te). [Sp.: see Avocado.] The alligator pear or avocado. Also *attrib.*
1897 *Blackw. Mag.* Nov. 686/1 Tall mangoes and aguacates. 1926 *Chamb. Jrnl.* 23 Jan. 126/2 Banana peelings, aguacate skins.

Aguardiente (agwardie·nte). [Sp., = brandy, f. *agua* water + *ardiente* Ardent.] A coarse kind of brandy made and consumed in Spain and Portugal. Also applied to any distilled spirituous liquor; in south-western U.S., native whisky.
1826 Capt. F. B. Head *Notes Journ. Pampas* 241 He..was drinking aquadiente [*sic*] with the Gauchos. 1848–54 [see Mescal]. 1900 St. Barbe *Mod. Spain* 67 Much of the fun of the fair consists in sipping *aguardiente*, a strong liqueur. 1922 *Chamb. Jrnl.* 7 Jan. 95/2 Alvarez left the meeting with his grievance fanned to fury by the fiery *aguardiente*.

Ahead, *adv.* Add: **1. b.** *fig.* To the good. *U.S.*
1883 J. H. Beadle *Western Wilds* xxxviii. 615 My sheep had done well, and that was all I was ahead. 1904 W. H. Smith *Promoters* i. 21 We can go on and finish our plant, and be ahead every dollar that they've blown in!

Ahem (ăhe·m), *v.* [f. Ahem *int.*] *intr.* To exclaim 'ahem!'; also *trans.*, to pass off with the exclamation 'ahem!'.
1839 *Fraser's Mag.* XIX. 125 He immediately 'a-hems' away his jocularity. 1875 Meredith *Beauch. Career* xlv, Tuckham brushed his hand over his mouth and ahemed. 1891 — *One of our Conq.* I. xiii. 240 He..pulled the waistcoat, and swelled it, aheming.

A-hold (ăhōᵘ·ld). [f. A *prep.*[1] + Hold *sb.*[1]] *A-hold of*: holding (something). Also in *to catch, lay a-hold of, on, upon*: see Hold *sb.*[1] 2.
1879 *Scribner's Monthly* May 17/1 With one bee a-hold of your collar..and another a-hold of each arm. 1879 Lanier *Marshes of Glynn* Poems (1892) 17, I will heartily lay me a-hold on the greatness of God. 1887 Morris *Odyss.* x. 264 He caught ahold upon me.

Ahorse (ăhǭ·ɹs), *adv.* [f. A *prep.*[1] + Horse *sb.*] = A-horseback.
1860 W. H. Russell *Diary India* II. 120 Young ladies and gentlemen..a-horse and a-foot. 1925 *Chamb. Jrnl.* Xmas. No. 854/2 When he and I encountered, ahorse on a road, we pulled up our horses and conversed.

Aich('s) metal. [Named after the patentee Johann *Aich* (3 Feb. 1860).] An alloy of copper, zinc, and iron, used in gun-making.
1867 Bloxam *Chem.* 342 Aich (or Gedge's) metal. 1875 Hunt *Ure's Dict. Arts* (ed. 7), *Aich metal.*

Aid, *sb.* Add: **2. b.** *To call or crave in aid*, properly a legal phrase, also in a loose transf. use.
1927 *Observer* 8 May 16/2 Imagination craves the wireless in aid. 1928 *Ibid.* 1 July 13/4 Many [bishops]..would call in aid, as justifying their action, the use of the *Jus Liturgicum* inherent in their office.
7. b. *U.S.* = Aide.
1840–32 J. P. Kennedy *Swallow B.* I. xix. 190 Ned and myself formed part of his retinue, like a pair of aids somewhat behind the commander-in-chief.
8. aid post, a post at which wounded soldiers received first medical attention.
1916 Boyd Cable *Action Front* 49 To walk..to the nearest aid-post and hospital. 1918 E. A. Mackintosh *War, the Liberator* 149 The Aid Post was like a shambles with blood and wounded men.

Aid-de-camp, occas. (chiefly *U.S.*) var. of Aide-de-camp.
1732 [see Aide-de-camp]. 1776 *Jrnl. Cont. Congress* V. 418 Resolved, That the aids de camp of the commander in chief rank as lieutenant colonels. 1808 Ann Grant *Mem. Amer. Lady* I. 190 There the general, his aid-de-camps, ..and the principal officers..were received. 1878 J. H. Beadle *Western Wilds* xxxiii. 531 He..was made full captain and aid-de-camp of General McClellan.

Aide-mémoire (ē·dmemwār, ‖ ɛdmemwār). [F., f. *aider* to help + *mémoire* Memory.] An aid to the memory.
1856 Laxton (*title*) Examples of Building Construction intended as an Aide-Memoire for the Professional Man. 1913 *Westm. Gaz.* 3 July, No written document on the subject of the British questionnaires, even in the way of an aide memoire, will be handed to the Foreign Secretary.

Aileron (ē·lĕrǫn). [a. F. *aileron*, dim. of *aile* wing.] A small hinged plane or flap on the wings and tail of an aeroplane, for maintaining or restoring its balance when flying. Also *attrib.*
1909 *Aero* 25 May 1 The ailerons or small planes between the main surfaces are used instead of wing-flexing for balancing. 1916 *Air* Dec. 11 Elevator surface and aileron surfaces of which are constructed of steel frames covered with linen.

Aim, *v.* **5. b.** Add: *dial.* and *U.S.* (with infinitive: cf. quot. 1649 in Dict.).
1665 *Rhode Isl. Col. Rec.* II. 120 And this the Court hath done, aimeing alsoe therein to save the towne. 1785 Hutton *Bran New Wark* 24 (E.D.S.) Aiming to hev a good conscience. 1878– in *Eng. Dial. Dict.* 1891 Hardy *Tess* xxv. (1892) 204 Aiming to arrive about the breakfast hour. 1903 *McClure's Mag.* July 318 Each factory aimed to add barrel works as soon as able. 1909 J. Bigelow *Retrosp.* 57 A[n].. article in which I aimed to compare and contrast the duties of Roman lawyers with those of our own time and country.

Ain't. *dial.* Variant of *hain't*, have not.
1845 Simms *Wigwam & Cabin* Ser. i. 7 But you ain't said, ..who was your Carolina gineral. 1875 in *Eng. Dial. Dict.* s.v. *Have* v. I. ii. 1880 Tourgee *Invis. Empire* x. 473 I ain't done nothing. 1880 Mary E. Wilkins *Humble Romance* 3 You've been crying, ain't you? 1910 W. M. Raine *B. O'Connor* 37 'We ain't got one chance in a hundred'. John Dillon growled. 1917 Mathewson *Sec. Base Sloan* xiv. 195 More than that I ain't got the right to say.

Air, *sb.* Add:
1. c. colloq. phr. *On the air*: broadcast by wireless telegraphy.
1927 *Observer* 11 Dec. 16 The only New York church which is 'on the air'. 1928 *Daily Express* 13 Apr. 11/1 They will speak into the microphone as usual, but before being put 'on the air' their voice modulations will be turned upside down.
15. c. *To put on airs*, to give oneself airs.
1832 *Deb. Congress* 30 Jan. 203, I am aware that, at times, States have attempted to put on airs, and set up their own against federal opinions. 1860 O. W. Holmes *Prof. Breakf.-t.* v. 93 None of them like too well to be told of it, but it must be sounded in their ears whenever they put on airs.
B. II. air-bath, the protracted exposure of the body to the free action of the air as a form of medical treatment (cf. *sun-bath*); **air-bell, -bubble,** a small bubble formed in a photographic developer, etc., and appearing as a spot on a plate, film, or paper; **air-brush,** a device for spraying colour over a surface by means of compressed air; **air cane,** a walking-stick in which an air-gun is concealed; **air channel,** a channel for the passage of air, in various structures; **air-compressor,** a machine for compressing air; **air-cooled** *a.*, cooled by means of a current of air; so **air-cooling** *sb.* and *a.*; **air-cooler,** an apparatus or appliance for reducing the temperature; **air-crossing,** a passage or arched way to carry one air-passage over another in a mine; **air-cure** [tr. G. *luftkur*], treating diseases by the use of air; **air-driven** *a.*, actuated by means of compressed air; **air-dry** *a.*, dry to such a degree that on exposure to the air no further moisture is given off; **air-filter,** an apparatus for extracting extraneous particles, germs, etc. from air; **air-flue** = *air channel*; **air-gap,** a gap or hole through which air passes; *Electr.* the air-filled space in a magnetic or electric circuit, as between the poles of a magnet, or the terminals of an electrostatic machine; **air-gas,** a mixture of air and petroleum or other vapour, used as an illuminant; **air-gauge,** an instrument for measuring and indicating the pressure of air or gases; **air-jacket,** a jacket (Jacket *sb.* 2) in which air or gas is circulated to diminish loss of heat from the enclosed vessel; **air-lock,** an air-tight chamber in a pneumatic caisson, communicating between the outer air and the compressed-air chamber; **air-machine,** in a mine, a contrivance by which pure air is forced into ill-ventilated parts; **air-pad,** a pad inflated with air; **air-passage,** (*a*) a passage through which air travels, e.g. the nasal passages, bronchial tubes, etc.; (*b*) *Bot.* the large intercellular space in the stems and leaves of some plants; **air-pit,** a ventilating shaft in a mine; **air-tube,** a tube which conveys air; the inner tube of a pneumatic tyre; **air-volcano,** an eruptive orifice from which volumes of gas are discharged with mud and stones; **air-wave,** an atmospheric wave as of compression, rarefaction, or progression; **air-wood,** wood dried by exposure to the air.
Also in various names of instruments or apparatus actuated by the elastic force of compressed or heated air (often = 'pneumatic'), as *air-brake, -cylinder, -drill, -lift, -locomotive.*
1791 Boswell *Johnson* (1887) III. 168 He..walked in his room naked, with the window open, which he called taking an *air bath. 1885 *Buck's Handbk. Med. Sci.* I. 467 It is often desirable not to employ too much water, but to expose the body freely, giving an air bath. 1889 *Anthony's Photogr. Bull.* II. 143 Carbon Printing in Winter...The difficulty I experienced in avoiding *air bells. 1873 J. H. Beadle *Undevel. West* xiv. 235 The *air-brake, which was a novelty to me, and a perfect success. 1928 C. F. S. Gamble *North Sea Air Station* xiii. 210 Fitted with an air-brake in the form of adjustable flaps in the trailing edge of the lower plane adjacent to the fuselage. 1889 *Cent. Dict.*, *Air-brush. 1901 *Brit. Jrnl. Photog.* 1 Nov. 696 The aerograph [*read* aero-] is probably better known to the majority of photographers as the air-brush. 1891 Bothamley *Ilford Man. Photogr.* (revised ed.) 67 The formation of *air-bubbles in the emulsion during coating. 1854 *Poultry Chron.* I. 389 Hidden in a secluded corner was an *air-cane, the air-receptacle being still partially charged. 1833 *Ridgemont Farm Rep.* 140 in *Libr. Usef. Knowl., Husb.* III, A tunnel is formed by placing a wooden pipe..exactly over the centre of the *air-channel. 1874 *Air-compressor [see Compressor g]. 1892 P. Benjamin's *Mod. Mechanism* 17 The Norfolk Compound Air-Compressor. 1908 *Westm. Gaz.* 21 July 4/2 An.. ingenious air-compressor, specially designed for use on motor-vehicles. 1899 *Motor-Car World* I. 59/1 An *air-cooled Aster motor of 2¼ h.p. 1909 *Westm. Gaz.* 1 Apr. 4/1 The seven cylinders of the Gnome..when they are revolving at a high speed..will be very efficiently air-cooled. 1874 Knight *Dict. Mech.* I. 34/2 Shaler's *air-cooler.. 1909 *Westm. Gaz.* 25 Mar. 2/2 The designer has adopted the expedient of revolving the cylinders en bloc around fixed cranks, whereby he is enabled to successfully adopt *air-cooling. 1874 Knight *Dict. Mech.* I. 34/1 *Air-cooling Apparatus. 1909 *Westm. Gaz.* 9 Sept. 4/3 The sparking plugs, which are provided with air-cooling ribs. 1884 Knight *Dict. Mech.* Suppl. 15/1 **Air-crossing* (Mining), an arch built over a horse-way or other road, with a passage or airway above it. 1911 *Act 1 & 2 Geo. V*, c. 50 § 42 (3) All air-crossings shall..be so constructed as not to be liable to be destroyed in the event of an explosion. 1900 *Daily News* 16 Aug. 6/7 The lower *air-cures known as the Schwarz-see, the Hörnli, and the Shoulder. 1897 *Ibid.* 1 Nov. 7/1 The *air-driven hydraulic pump. 1856 *Jrnl. R. Agric. Soc.* XVII. i. 194, I..then allowed it to become *air-dry, by

keeping it for some days in a safe place, in a heated room. 1874 Knight *Dict. Mech.*, *Air-filter. 1884 *Ibid.* Suppl. 15/2 *Air Filter*, a protective ventilator consisting of a cloth interwoven with thin brass wire to act as a filter for the air. 1927 *Daily Tel.* 10 Feb., Motor manufacturers are urged to provide air-filters on all motor vehicles. 1840 *Cottager's Man.* 23 in *Libr. Usef. Knowl., Husb.* III, Cover to the false or *air-flue, which is only kept open during summer to prevent excessive heat of that season. 1848 Mrs. Gaskell *Mary Barton* xvi, *Air-gaps were to be seen in their garments. 1899 R. Routledge *Discov. & Inv. 19th C.* (ed. 13) 541 A stout wire interrupted by an air gap in its centre provided with small brass balls. 1902 *How to make Things* 3/2 A miniature flash of lightning breaks through the insulating air-gap between the balls or oscillators. 1884 Knight *Dict. Mech.* Suppl. 16/1 **Air-gas Apparatus*, another name for the Carburetor, in which coal-gas or air is passed through a volatile hydrocarbon to increase or confer the illuminating power. 1841 *Civil Engin. & Arch. Jrnl.* IV. 13/1 The..instruments employed..to determine the pressure of the steam,..namely, the barometer-gauge, the *air-gauge, etc. 1909 *Westm. Gaz.* 4 May 4/2 An engine having specially designed *air-jackets. 1893 *Patent Specif.* No. 22372 My process..I term the '*air lift' process. 1874 Knight *Dict. Mech.*, *Air-lock. 1877 *Encycl. Brit.* VI. 63/1 A cylinder of wrought iron, within which a tubular chamber, provided with doors above and below, known as an air-lock. 1879 *Scribner's Monthly* XIX. 281 The moment you reach the men the air will escape, and the water will rise and drown them. 'Air-locks are provided,' says Birewood. 1855 Leifchild *Cornwall Mines* 282 The underground boys work the *air-machines. 1876 *Trans. Clinical Soc.* IX. 23 An *air-pad was applied to the tumour. 1835–6 *Todd's Cycl. Anat.* I. 345/1 The *air-passages in birds commence by a simple *superior larynx*. 1878 Rankine *Steam Engine* (ed. 9) 450 Air Passages—Blowing Apparatus —Chimney. 1709 T. Robinson *Nat. Hist. Westmld.* v. 30 If the Miners should not open their *Air-Pits and keep their Thurling-Ways clear. 1839 Ure *Dict. Arts* 969 These air-pits do not in general exceed 7 feet in diameter. 1877 *Engineering* 16 Nov. 381/3 The *air-tube of a diver's dress. 1894 *Work* 315/2 Repairing Air-tube of 1892 Dunlop. 1879 Geikie in *Encycl. Brit.* X. 250 Certain remarkable orifices of eruption..to which the names of mud-volcanoes, salses, *air-volcanoes, and macalubas have been applied. 1895 H. Lamb *Hydrodynamics* Index, *Air-waves, effect of viscosity on. 1676 Mace *Musick's Mon.* 49 Next, what Wood is Best for the Ribbs. The *Air-wood is absolutely the Best.
b. In numerous combinations relating to motion through the air, esp. to flying-machines or aviation, as *air armament, -boat, -car, -fleet, -liner, -mail, mechanic, -pilot, -sailer, -or* (person or machine), *service, -station, -yacht*, etc.; also **air base,** a base of operations for aircraft; **air force,** a military or naval force organized for conducting operations in the air; that part of the offensive and defensive forces of a country (in Great Britain, the Royal Air Force) which consists of officers and men with flying machines or other necessary equipment; so *air arm, air council, air-marshal, air officer* (see quots.); **air-mast,** a mast to which airships are moored; **air-pocket,** an alteration in atmospheric conditions, causing an aeroplane to drop suddenly (like a billiard ball into a pocket); **air-port** [after *sea-port*], a place containing an aerodrome with its buildings and apparatus, at which aeroplanes and other flying-machines start on, or land from, their voyages; **air raid,** a raiding attack by aircraft upon an enemy; **air-screw,** the driving screw of an aeroplane or other flying-machine; **air-sick** *a.* [after *sea-sick*], sick from the motion of aircraft (cf. *air-sickness* in Dict.); **air-speed,** the velocity of a flying-machine (or of anything flying, e.g. a bird) in relation to the air through which it is moving.
1921 *Daily Tel.* 15 Oct. 11/7 The experts in sea, land, and *air armaments. 1919 *Athenæum* 23 May 360/2 '*Air-base,' 'aircraft,' 'airman,' 'air-mechanic,' 'air-pocket,' 'air-raid,' 'air-scout,' 'airship,' and 'anti-aircraft' are now everyday terms. 1922 *19th Cent.* Sept. 356 Air bases will be liable to air attack. 1888 *Wonderful Balloon Ascents* 224 The question is, to find out a new machine capable of flying in the air, and at the same time heavier than the air...The *air-boat of M. Pline seems to us one of the best ideas. 1913 *Britannica Year-bk.* 343 The second class, variously termed 'flying-boat' and 'air-boat', consists..of a long boat-shaped hull, wherein the passengers' seats are contained, and on which the planes are built up. 1926 *Glasgow Herald* 18 Aug. 9 New British all-metal air-boats. 1829 *Mech. Mag.* XI. 164 The machine which is to carry him, may be designated an *Air-car. 1898 *Westm. Gaz.* 8 July 8/1 Five hundred ten-pound notes will enable Mr. George L. O. Davidson to commence the construction of his air-car, which will be capable of lifting itself into the air and travelling over the ground. 1911 in Grahame-White & Harper *Aeroplane* 41 Further developments, in passenger-carrying, are expected during 1911, when 'air-cars', carrying four and six occupants as their regular equipment, will be introduced. 1908 H. G. Wells *War in Air* iv. § 3 The German *air-fleet. 1917 *Act 7 & 8 Geo. V*, c. 51 An Act to make provision for the establishment, administration, and discipline of an *Air Force, the establishment of an Air Council, and for purposes connected therewith. 1920 *Act 10 & 11 Geo. V*, c. 76 § 11 (2) Where possession is reasonably required for naval, military, or air force purposes. 1922 *Glasgow Herald* 12 Oct. 9 The Napier-Instone *Air Liners..flying..from Cologne to London. *Ibid.* 4 Apr. 9 The despatch of *air-mail letters..between London and Paris. 1919 *Times* 19 Aug. 10/3 The King has been pleased to approve the promotion of Air Vice-Marshal Sir H. Trenchard, K.C.B., to *Air-Marshal. 1927 *Daily Tel.* 1 Nov. 10/6 The selection of a site on the south side of the St. Lawrence for the erection of an Imperial *airmast. 1919 *Air-mechanic [see *air-base* above]. 1928 C. F. S. Gamble *North Sea Air Station* i. 39 The term 'air mechanic' is in use, though no such naval rating really exists. By air mechanic is meant a man who has been through a course of training either at the Central Flying School or at Eastchurch. 1920 *Act 10 Geo. V*, c. 7 § 11 (3) The expression '*air officer' means any officer above the rank of group captain. 1923 J. W. Simpson *Ess. & Mem.* 169 The confident courage that inspires *air-pilots. 1914 *Aeroplane* 9 Apr. 435/1 Mr. Hucks said that the term '*air-pocket' is a misnomer. The so-called 'pocket' is nothing but a down-current of air, and not a partial vacuum of any kind. 1918 'Avion' *Aeroplanes*, etc. 79 *Air Pocket*—Otherwise called a 'remou': a patch of rarefied air, or a downward eddy, either of which causes an aeroplane to lose altitude. 1926 *Glasgow Herald* 13 Nov. 4 At Croydon ..The scene is characteristic of the *airports of all the big cities. 1929 *Times* 10 Jan. 7/1 Hull is destined ultimately to have an airport. 1915 Lanchester *Aircraft in Warfare* (1916) 190 *Air-raids on Great Britain by Zeppelin do not pay. 1917 W. Pett Ridge *Amazing Years* xii, The glass windows,..which had been broken in an air raid. 1897 *Aeronautical Ann.*, *Scientific value of flying models*, The *air-sailer who..adds the thrust of a screw to the forces he is accustomed to deal with. *Ibid.*, The development of the motorless air-sailer. 1908 H. G. Wells *War in Air* vii. § 5 Then Bert..had his first experience of the work of an air-sailor. 1923 *Daily Mail* 17 Apr. 8 The engineless air-sailor. 1895 *Aeronautical Ann.*, *At Rhinow*, The..care needed in making changes in an *air-sailing machine. 1904 *Aeronaut. Soc. Gt. Brit., Techn. Terms*, *Airscrew, used as a generic term to include both a propeller and a tractor screw. 1926 *Chamb. Jrnl.* Sept. 580/2 An aeroplane..propelled by a rapid series of explosions, no airscrew..being used. 1922 *Daily Mail* 8 Dec. 12 An 1,800 miles *air service from Copenhagen to Brindisi is being planned. 1908 H. G. Wells *War in Air* vii. § 1 One or two were *air-sick. 1918 'Avion' *Aeroplanes*, etc. 28 An action like that of the pendulum of a clock would result, and the passengers would soon be airsick. 1784 *Air-sickness [see Air *sb.* B. II. in Dict.]. 1908 H. G. Wells *War in Air* vii. § 2 For a time he was not a human being, he was a case of air-sickness. 1910 R. Ferris *How it Flies* 453 *Air-speed—The speed of aircraft as related to the air in which they are moving; as distinguished from land-speed. 1923 *Daily Mail* 17 July 10 Ocean *Air-stations. 1927 *Observer* 7 Aug. 11/3 It was an ordinary *air-taxi flight from Brooklands to Ascot. 1927 *Cornell Alumni News* Aug. 459 McGovern was attorney for both parties, designed the truck body for the plane, and invented the description '*air-truck'. 1821–2 Byron in Medwin *Conversat. Ld. B.* (1824) I. 199, I suppose we shall soon travel by *air-vessels; make air instead of sea-voyages. 1902 F. Walker *Aërial Navig.* 116 Greater efficiency to be attained by air-ships..relatively to..the one or two passenger *air-yachts.

Aircraft (ē·ɹ,kraft). [f. Air *sb.* + Craft *sb.* 9.] Flying-machines collectively; *rarely* a flying-machine. Hence **Ai·rcraftsman,** a man who manages aircraft, an aeronaut.
1907 *Navigating the Air* Introd. p. xxxix, The Wellman arctic balloon, a comparatively slow, but..skilfully constructed air-craft. 1909 *Daily Chron.* 26 Feb. 1/2 The vast commercial possibilities that the manufacture and world-wide use of air craft offer. 1910 Rotch in *Aeronautical Ann.*, [Suppose] an aircraft to possess the very moderate speed of 9 metres per second. 1920 *Glasgow Her.* 2 Aug. 6 The demand for experienced pilots and aircraftsmen.

Airedale (ē·ɹdēl). Name of a district in the West Riding of Yorkshire; hence short for *Airedale terrier*, one of a breed of large rough-haired dogs.
1880 Dalziel *Brit. Dogs* 377 The Airedale or Bingley Terrier. 1889 *Ibid.* (ed. 2) II. 385 The name Terrier, applied to the Airedale, is admittedly a stretching of the term beyond its original meaning. 1916 F. M. Jowett *Airedale Terrier* 26 A dog brimful of true Airedale character and type.

Airish, *a.* **2.** (Modern U.S. examples.)
1883 J. H. Beadle *Western Wilds* xxxvii. 613 Going westward on any line one will find the winters growing dryer, also more 'airish'. 1885 'C. E. Craddock' *Prophet Gt. Smoky Mts.* 267 It air toler'ble airish in the fog.

Airlessness (ē·ɹlĕsnĕs). [f. Airless + -ness.] The condition of being airless.
1831 J. Wilson *Unimore* ii. 186 Idle all at once her sails Hang in the airlessness. 1857 Dickens *Dorrit* ii. xxiii, The airlessness and closeness of the house. 1885 'Lucas Malet' *Col. Enderby's Wife* ii. iv, The shut and darkened windows produced an effect of airlessness.

Air-line. [See Air *sb.* B. II.]
1. A line taken direct through the air; a bee-line. Chiefly *U.S.*
1813 J. Quincy in *Deb. Congress* 1 Jan. 544 They will not rigidly observe any air-lines or water-lines in enforcing their necessary levies. 1829 J. F. Cooper *Wishton-wish* ii. 27 This clearing, which by an air line might have been half a mile from the place where his horse had stopped. 1864 *Congress. Globe* Mar. 1264/2, I invite any gentleman who supposes that by voting for this bill he is voting for an air-line, to look..and see the kind of air-line it is proposed to establish. 1890 *Harper's Mag.* Apr. 730/1 Although only fifteen miles in an air line, the renegade insisted that it would be necessary to make a detour. 1904 *Chicago Tribune* 1 Aug. 4 The judge held that distance was to be measured by air line or 'as the crow flies', not as the main traveled road leads.
attrib. 1863 *Congress. Globe* Feb. 813/1 This is a proposition to construct an air-line railroad between Washington and New York. 1895 *Outing* Dec. 214/2 Pursuing an even air-line route across the roughest country.
2. A line of airships or aeroplanes for passenger or postal service. Also *attrib.*
1888 Kipling *Soldiers Three*, etc. (1895) 293 The Religion never seemed to get much beyond its first manifestations; though it added an air-line postal service. 1908 Sir F. Maclean in *Daily Express* 9 Nov. 9/4 It is difficult to see how public air lines can compete with railways.

Airman (ē·ɹmăn). [f. Air *sb.* + Man *sb.*[1], after *seaman.*] A man who navigates a flying-machine; the pilot of an aeroplane or airship.
1910 *Daily Mail* 4 June 4/2 A flight of over forty miles above the sea, during which the airman is in continual danger. 1920 *Act 10 & 11 Geo. V*, c. 30 § 41 (5) The expression 'airman' means a man of the regular air force.
So **Ai·rwoman.**
1912 *Daily News* 11 Mar., Aviation has claimed another victim, the youngest airwoman in France.

Airmanship. Add in def. after 'balloon': 'or flying-machine'.
1908 *Daily Chron.* 15 Aug. 4/6 'Airmanship' is the newest addition to the language. 1910 *Daily Mail* 4 June 4/2 When airmanship was in the elementary stage.

Airol (ē·ɹǫl). *Med.* A greyish-green powder consisting of bismuth oxyiodogallate, used as an antiseptic.
1901 Dorland *Med. Dict.* (ed. 2). 1906 *Harmsworth Encycl.* II. 507/1 The use of anti-streptococci serum, and the application of airol and thiol.

Airplane (ē·ɹplēn). [Alteration of Aeroplane, after Air *sb.*] = *Aeroplane 2.
1907 *Westm. Gaz.* 19 July 4/2 It is this ease of going against the current, with no motive force in evidence, that is..the despair of the aeronauts with their air-planes. 1916 Buchan *Hist. War* XIV. 48 Airplane reconnaissance. 1918 *King's Regs. R.A.F.* § 1024 A The supply of patent fire-extinguishers is to be limited to the following services:— Motor boats. Motor vehicles. Airplanes. Seaplanes.

Airship (ē·ɹʃip). Formerly air-ship. [f. Air *sb.* + Ship *sb.*, after G. *luftschiff*.] A dirigible motor-driven balloon, usually of an elongated cigar-shaped form. Also *attrib.*
1888 *Wonderful Balloon Ascents* 15 The same thing would happen with the air-ship as with the water-ship. 1890 *Sci. Amer.* 19 Apr. 253/1 [In Index of Inventions for which Letters Patent of the United States were Granted April 1, 1890.] 1892 P. Benjamin's *Mod. Mechanism* 2 The accompanying table gives the principal data as to the four air-ships. 1900 [see Zeppelin]. 1902 *Westm. Gaz.* 16 July 6/1 The first prize at the St. Louis Exposition airship contest will be £20,000.
¶ This word was used for the nonce by Carlyle in the following passage:—1833 Carlyle *Sart. Res.* i. xi, What vacant, high-sailing air-ships are these, and whither will they sail with us?

Air-tight, *a.* Add: **b.** *sb.* An article of food put up in an air-tight vessel. *U.S.*
1907 S. E. White *Arizona Nights* i. xvi. 219 On top of a few incidental pounds of *chile con*, baked beans, soda biscuits, 'air tights', and other delicacies.

Airway (ē·ɹwē). [f. Air *sb.* + Way *sb.*]
1. A passage for air, esp. one for ventilation in a mine.
1859 R. Hunt *Guide Mus. Pract. Geol.* (ed. 2) 224 A rapid circulation of pure air through all the airways of the colliery. 1877 *Design & Work* III. 603/1 The wind wheel..would work in a midship air-way. 1887 in Kipling *From Sea to Sea* (1904) I. 158 A sort of loose box with a two-foot air-way all round the top. 1907 *Daily Chron.* 20 July 9/3 A longer connection is more easily attached, and the air-way in it less liable to be obstructed by flexion. 1908 *Ibid.* 7 Mar. 5/5 Free the return air-way from noxious gases.
2. The route of a service of aeroplanes or airships.
1908 *Westm. Gaz.* 3 Oct. 3/2 An impression of 1920...Extract from Passenger Handbook of the Great Eastern Airway Company for June. 1911 in Grahame-White & Harper *Aeroplane* 218 The Atlantic will,..beyond doubt, have its regular 'airway'.

Airworthy (ē·ɹwǫ̈ɹði), *a.* [f. Air *sb.* after *seaworthy*.] Of a flying-machine: In a fit condition for travelling through the air. Hence **Ai·rworthiness.**
1829 *Mech. Mag.* XI. 181 The airiner has time, in all cases (assuming that the air-car is air-worthy) to concert proper measures for his safe descent.
1909 *Westm. Gaz.* 11 May 5/2 That their vessel would be airworthy when completed. 1909 H. G. Wells *Tono-Bungay* iv. i, I had satisfied myself..of the real air-worthiness of Lord Roberts β [a dirigible balloon]. 1927 *Observer* 21 Aug. 6/2 A strength of approximately double that specified by the British Air Ministry upon the advice of the Airworthiness of Airships Panel.

Airy-fairy (ē·ri,fē·ri), *a. colloq.* [After Tennyson's 'airy, fairy Lilian' (*Lilian*, 1830).] Delicate or light as a fairy. Also as *sb.*
1869 W. S. Gilbert *Bab Ballads, Only a Dancing Girl* iii, No airy fairy she, As she hangs in arsenic green, From a highly impossible tree, In a highly impossible scene. 1898 *Westm. Gaz.* 1 Oct. 8/1 The low-necked airy-fairy ladies' ball gown. 1907 *Ibid.* 30 Mar. 16/1 To find partners for the airy-fairy creatures.

Aisle. Add: **4. b.** *Broad aisle* (U.S.): see *Broad aisle.
5. A passage-way in a building or a train. *north. dial.* and *U.S.*
1851 J. J. Hooper *Widow Rugby's Husb.* 103, I have seen him..charge..into one door of the court-house, dash furiously along the aisle [etc.]. 1873 *Sat. Rev.* 22 Nov. 662/2 The Deputy-Sheriff placed his prisoners in the smoking-car of the train...The aisle was packed. 1880 L. Wallace *Ben-Hur* v. xiii, As the four stout servants carried the merchant in his chair up the aisle [in the circus] curiosity was much excited. 1889 *Harper's Mag.* Oct. 736/2 He..collected the price of three hours reading..and went on down the aisle [of the train]. 1902 S. E. White *Blazed Trail* iii, One big fellow..swaggered back and forth down the aisle [of the train]. 1903 I. Bacheller *Darrel of Blessed Isles* xiv. 148 Small boys would be chasing each other up and down aisles [of the school]. 1904 *N. Y. Times* 9 May 4 The main aisle [of the store] is full of laces. 1909 *Daily Chron.* 16 Feb. 4/7 [In America] all gangways and narrow paths whether in theatres, shops, or omnibuses, are 'aisles'.

6. A double row of wheat-sheaves set up to dry. *local.*

1794 T. DAVIS *Agric. Wilts* 76 The general custom of Wiltshire, is, to set up the sheafs in double rows...and the sheaves so set up are called an aile. 1893 M. GRAY *Last Sentence* III. i, Paler gold of piled sheaves 'in aisle' on upland slopes. 1904 *Daily Mail* 10 Sept. 3/7 In the Isle of Wight, what is locally described as an 'aisle' of corn standing in a field..was struck by lightning.

Aisleman. [*AISLE 5.] *U.S.* A shop-assistant in charge of an aisle.

1906 *N. Y. Even. Post* 8 Oct. 12 Simplify shopping by asking questions...Ask the Aislemen and Elevator men.

Aitch (ētʃ). Name of the letter H, q.v.; cf. ACHE *sb.*[3] Also *Comb.*, as *aitch-dropping, -free* adjs. Hence **Ai·tchless** *a.*, that does not aspirate his *h*'s.

1900 G. SWIFT *Somerley* 75 The aitch-less 'Arry. *Ibid.* 115 A bounder of the aitch-dropping type. 1907 *Daily Chron.* 9 July 3/3 Humanity, with a capital aitch. 1925 *Contemp. Rev.* June 746 The aitch-free accent.

Ajoupa (ădʒū·pă). [Fr., repr. the native name.] In the West Indies, a hut or wigwam built on piles and covered with leaves or branches.

1870 KINGSLEY *At Last* viii, A tribe of Chaymas built their palm-leaf ajoupas upon the very spot where the lake now lies.

Akee, variant of *ACKEE.

A la carte, à la carte (alakā·rt). [See A LA and CARTE[1] 5.] 'By the card' (or bill of fare): said of meals which are ordered at a hotel or restaurant in separate items, each having its specified price. (Distinguished from a TABLE D'HÔTE meal, which is served at a fixed inclusive price.)

1826 SHERER *Ramble in Germany* 252 He will find comfortable apartments, civil attendance, excellent fare, *à la carte*, at any hour.

Alalonga (ælălɒ·ŋgă). Also -**lunga.** [mod.L., a. local It. *alalonga*, f. *ala* fin + *longa* (It. *lunga*) long.] A long-finned tunny, *Thunnus* (*Germo*) *alalonga.*

1854 BADHAM *Halieut.* xi. 201 The trembling thunnies, pelamyds, and alalongas, which covered the bottom of the net. *Ibid.* 203 Alalongas, whose long pectorals had been draggled in the mire.

Alamandine (ælămæ·ndin). [ad. med.L. *alamandina*, altered f. L. *alabandina* (*gemma*), f. *Alabanda* a city of Caria.] A kind of garnet. Cf. ALMANDINE.

1895 J. W. ANDERSON *Prospector's Handbk.* (ed. 6) 96 Garnet (including carbuncle, alamandine, pyrope, &c.). 1921 W. W. WATTS in *Trans. Scott. Ecclesiol. Soc.* 152 A ring with an alamandine (a garnet-coloured stone). [tr. Matt. Paris *Chron. Maj.* (Rolls) VI. 383.]

Alarm, *sb.* Add:

4. and **11.** *Alarums* (or *alarms*) *and excursions*, a stage-direction occurring in slightly varying forms in Shaks. *Hen. VI* and *Rich. III* (e.g. 3 *Hen. VI*, v. ii. *init.*); hence used playfully by recent writers for: Skirmishing, confused fighting or onsets, sudden divagations, etc.

1895 K. GRAHAME *Golden Age* 29 Alarums and Excursions. [1910 G. K. CHESTERTON (*title*) Alarms and Discursions.] 1922 BARRIE *Courage* 9, I want you to hold..That to gain courage is what you come to St. Andrews for. With some alarums and excursions into college life.

12. b. In modified sense: Apprehension, uneasiness as to consequences.

1833 *Deb. Congress* 26 Feb. 1781 This General Assembly views with alarm..the proposition..for abandoning..the principle of protection. 1834 *Ibid.* 18 Feb. 604 They regard with alarm the late measures of the President.

13. alarm-cord, the cord of an alarm-bell, *esp.* the communication-cord on a railway train. *U.S.*

1872 E. EGGLESTON *End of World* v. 40 In behind the donjon chimney he pulled an alarm cord.

Alastrim (ălæ·strim). [? Of Brazilian origin.] A contagious eruptive fever resembling smallpox.

[1926 *Encycl. Brit.* Suppl. III. 559/2 An outbreak [of mild smallpox] in South Africa was described by de Korté in 1904, under the name of Amaas or Kaffir-pox, another by Ribas in Brazil in 1910, under the name of Alastrim.] 1913 DORLAND *Med. Dict.* (ed. 7), *Alastrim*, same as *amaas.* 1922 *Times* 19 May 10/4 Last week no fewer than 38 cases of smallpox were notified in England and Wales...One of these cases was notified as 'alastrim'.

Albanian (ælbē·niăn), *a.*[1] and *sb.*[1] *Hist.* [f. med.L. *Albania* Scotland (Ir. *Albu*, genit. *Alban*) + -AN.] **A.** *adj.* Of or pertaining to Scotland. **B.** *sb.* A Scot. So **Albanic** (ælbæ·nik) *a.* [cf. Ir. *Albanac*, Gael. *Albannech*], Scottish.

1561 NORTON & SACKV. *Gorboduc* v. ii. 137 The proude attemptes of this Albanian prince. 1756–9 A. BUTLER *Lives of Saints* (1847) I. 451 St. Gildas the Albanian, or the Scot. 1865 T. M'LAUCHLAN *Early Scott. Ch.* xvi. 208 The great convention at Drumceat in Ulster, where the question of Albanic independence was fully discussed.

Albanian (ælbē·niăn), *a.*[2] and *sb.*[2] [f. *Albania* (see below) + -AN.

Albania is the med.L. and general mod. name of the country, which is called *Shkyipëria* by the natives, who call themselves *Shkyipetar*; in med.Gr. Ἀλβανία, with variants Ἀλβανητία, Ἀρβανητία, the inhabitants being called Ἀλβάνοι, Ἀλ-, Ἀρβανῆτες (in Turkish *ARNAOUT).]

A. *adj.* Of or pertaining to Albania, a country in the western part of the Balkan peninsula, its inhabitants or their language.

1813 *Q. Rev.* Oct. 283 The Hungarian and the Albanian languages have some traits of resemblance to each other. 1869 TOZER *Highl. Turkey* I. 186 The Mahometans are mostly Albanian. 1905 M. E. DURHAM *Burden of Balkans* x. 227 A young Albanian officer. 1920 — in *Contemp. Rev.* Aug. 210 The long-forbidden Albanian language was printed.

B. *sb.* **1.** A native or inhabitant of modern Albania in the Balkan peninsula.

1813 *Q. Rev.* Oct. 284 The Albanians speak a language of which a considerable portion is Greek, Latin, German, Sclavonian or Turkish. 1905 M. E. DURHAM *Burden of Balkans* xii. 299 The Albanians are fond of animals. 1920 — in *Contemp. Rev.* Aug. 210 Freed from Turkish prohibition,..the cult of the national language became almost a religion to the Albanians.

2. The language of modern Albania (the only surviving representative of the 'Thraco-Illyrian' group).

1813 *Q. Rev.* Oct. 283 The Finnish is said to have some coincidence with the Greek, the Hungarian with the Finnish, and the Albanian with all its neighbours. 1905 M. E. DURHAM *Burden of Balkans* xii. 298 Books printed in Albanian by the Church press at Skodra. 1920 — in *Contemp. Rev.* Aug. 210 Up till 1908 the foreign schools, where alone Albanian could be taught as a written language, had for political purposes frequently changed the spelling of their school books. *Ibid.* 212 He [Essad Pasha] could only understand Turkish and Albanian.

Albergo (ælbɔ̄·ɪgo). Occas. anglicized **alberg.** [It.: see AUBERGE.] An inn (in Italy).

1617 MORYSON *Itin.* I. 154 Three houses like Colledges, called *Albergi*, for those that make long stay in the Citie. 1673 RAY *Journ. Low C.* 303 The *Alberghi* or Halls of the eight several Nations..of the Order. 1808 HELEN ST. VICTOR *Ruins of Rigonda* I. 137 By your naming payment, I should suppose that you had mistaken my poor Cottage for an Albergo, some distance from this. 1889 F. PIGOT *Strangest Journ.* 149, I was thus able..to rest at the country albergs. 1926 *Spectator* 20 Feb. 318/2 Ostia..consisted of a few forlorn houses, a modest *albergo*, and a wilderness of sand.

Albigenses (ælbidʒe·nsīz), *sb. pl.* [med.L. (12th c.), f. *Albiga*, L. name of Albi, a city in s.w. France.] The name of a sect of Catharist heretics of the south of France in the 12th and 13th centuries.

1692 P. ALLIX (*title*) Remarks upon The Ecclesiastical History of the Antient Churches of the Albigenses. 1756–9 A. BUTLER *Lives of Saints, S. Dominic*, The abominations of the heresy of the Albigenses. 1832 [in title below]. 1910 *Encycl. Brit.* I. 505/2.

Hence **Albige·nsian** *a.* and *sb.*, **Albige·nsic** *a.*

1828 G. S. FABER *Sacr. Cal. Prophecy* III. 28 The Albigensic church of the south of France. 1832 S. R. MAITLAND *Albigenses & Waldenses* 14 Fugitive Waldensians (not Albigensians) driven out of Lyons. *Ibid.* 17 Either the Albigensian, or Waldensian, sect. 1922 H. J. WARNER (*title*) The Albigensian Heresy.

Albinistic (ælbini·stik), *a.* [f. ALBINISM: see -ISTIC.] Of, pertaining to, or affected with albinism.

1880 in WEBSTER *Suppl.* 1912 *Brit. Museum Return* 115 Skull of an albinistic Pekinese Spaniel, presented by G. Nettleship.

Albinotic (ælbinɒ·tik), *a.* [f. ALBINO + -OTIC.] Of, pertaining to, or affected with albinism: = prec.

1872 COUES *N. Amer. Birds* 237 Albinotic or melanotic, and other abnormally colored specimens.

Albo-carbon (ælbokā·ɪbɒn). [f. *albo-*, taken as comb. form of L. *albus* white + CARBON.] A name for naphthalene as used for carburetting gas in order to increase its illuminating power. Chiefly *attrib.*, in *albo-carbon lamp, light.*

1882 G. LUNGE *Distill. Coal-tar* 242 A gas-carburetting apparatus, called the albo-carbon light. *Ibid.* 244 The albo-carbon lamp. 1888 *Daily News* 2 June 7/1, I knew that the barrel contained albo-carbon, which we used in connection with the gas.

Albumose (ælbiūmōᵘs). *Chem.* [f. ALBUMIN + -OSE[2].] An intermediate digestion-product of albuminous matter, passing into peptone; a species of proteose.

1884 *Jrnl. Chem. Soc.* XLVI. 1389 A new method of preparation..whereby four different forms of albumose are separated. 1889 M^cGOWAN *Bernthsen's Org. Chem.* 516 Albuminous matters undergo change when acted upon by the juices of the stomach at a temperature of 30–40°, pepsin converting them in the first instance into Anti- and Hemi-albumoses, both of which then go into peptone; trypsin likewise gives rise to the two above albumoses. 1891 [see PTOMAÏNE].

Alcmanian (ælkmē·niăn), *a.* and *sb.* [f. L. *Alcmānius*, f. *Alcmān*, Gr. Ἀλκμάν, the name of a Greek lyric poet of the 7th c. B.C.] Used to designate a verse of four dactyls, or a distich consisting of a dactylic hexameter followed by this verse. Also *sb.*, an Alcmanian verse or distich.

1879 J. W. WHITE *Schmidt's Rhythmic & Metric* 95 The Alcmanian group, consisting of a dactylic hexameter followed by a dactylic tetrameter.

Alcogel (æ·lkŏdʒel). *Chem.* [f. ALCO(HOL + GEL(ATIN: see *GEL.] A gelatinous precipitate from a colloidal solution in alcohol.

1864 [see *ALCOSOL]. 1914 E. F. BURTON *Colloid. Solutions* (1921) 9, 147.

Alcoholic. B. *sb.* Add:

1. (Example.)

1870 *Food Jrnl.* 1 Apr. 141 Any restriction on the sale of alcoholics.

2. One who is addicted to excessive consumption of alcoholic drinks; a drink addict.

1891 G. T. KEMP in *Q. Jrnl. Inebriety* Jan. (Funk), Chronic alcoholics. 1907 *Daily Chron.* 4 Sept. 3/1 There is..a time coming when the alcoholic will be a rarity. 1909 *Westm. Gaz.* 25 Feb. 8/1 Warning him that deceased was a 'chronic alcoholic,' and must have a bottle of port a day.

Alcoholist (æ·lkŏhɒlist). [See -IST.] One who is addicted to, or advocates, drinking alcoholic liquors.

1888 *Forum* (N.Y.) Sept. 103 Of 250 chronic alcoholists nearly 90 % had fatty degeneration of the liver. 1894 *Pop. Sci. Monthly* Nov. 99 A moderate alcoholist. 1920 W. J. LOCKE *House of Baltazar* iii, Old Jack Bonnithorne, the champion alcoholist of the moorland.

Alcoholizer (æ·lkŏhɒlaizəɪ). = prec.

1890 'R. BOLDREWOOD' *Miner's Right* xxiv, I pity those alcoholisers...And they are often such Bayards in their sane periods.

Alcosol (æ·lkŏsɒl). *Chem.* [f. ALCO(HOL + SOL(UTION: see *SOL.] A colloidal solution in alcohol.

1864 T. GRAHAM in *Proc. Royal Soc.* XIII. 337 If I may be allowed to distinguish the liquid and gelatinous hydrates of silicic acid by the irregularly formed terms of hydrosol and hydrogel of silicic acid, the two corresponding alcoholic bodies now introduced may be named the alcosol and alcogel of silicic acid. 1922 A. W. STEWART *Physico-Chem. Themes* ix. 160.

Alderney (ɔ̄·ldəɪni). [The name of one of the Channel Islands.] Properly, the designation of the cattle bred in Alderney; but popularly used as a general name for the cattle (mostly light or dark fawn-coloured) of the Channel Islands, including those of Jersey and Guernsey; also, an individual of this breed.

1830 MISS MITFORD *Our Village* Ser. IV. 106 The wealthy yeoman gave her..a very fine young Alderney. 1834 YOUATT *Cattle* 267 The Alderney, considering its voracious appetite ..yields very little milk. 1854 DICKENS *Hard Times* II. x, She didn't give any milk, ma'am; she gave bruises. She was a regular Alderney at that. 1875 in J. Coleman *Cattle Gt. Brit.* 139 The Channel Island breed of cattle, popularly known in this country as 'Alderneys', consists of two classes. ..The Guernsey is the larger of the two, usually of a light fawn colour...The Jersey class is smaller. 1887 J. M. HALL in J. Coleman *Cattle, Sheep, & Pigs Gt. Brit.* 219 To this day Jerseys and Guernseys are still popularly included in the name 'Alderneys'. 1910 *Encycl. Brit.* V. 539/2 (*Cattle*) The term Alderney is obsolete, the cattle of Alderney being mainly a type of the Guernsey breed.

Alderwoman. Add earlier quot.:

1557 in W. H. Turner *Select. Rec. Oxford* (1880) 264 Mres Brydgman shall go nexte unto the Alderwomen.

2. A woman holding the position of an alderman.

1768 MORANT *Hist. Essex* II. 400/2 A Gild of women of our Lady's Lights, to which belonged an Alderwoman, and two wardens. 1895 *N. Amer. Rev.* Sept. 267 When women shall have become, not only votresses, but legislatresses, mayoresses, and alderwomen. 1900 *Daily News* 24 May 3/1 The London Government Act of last year..prohibited women serving as alderwomen or councillors on borough Councils.

Aldine (æ·ldəin, ɔ̄·ldəin), *a.* (and *sb.*). [ad. mod.L. *Aldinus, -a* (scil. *editio*), f. *Aldus*, latinized f. *Aldo* (see below).] The designation of the editions of Greek and Latin classics (including many *principes*) printed or published at Venice by Aldo Manuzio (the more familiar name of Teobaldo Manucci, 1450–1515), and his family (*c* 1490–1597). As *sb.*, an Aldine book or edition.

The device characteristic of Aldine books is a figure of a dolphin.

1802 DIBDIN *Classics* Introd. 27 A most beautiful copy of this Aldine edition. 1827 — *Gr. & Lat. Classics* (ed. 4) II. 342 The Aldine Demosthenes of 1504. *Ibid.* 343 This edition..departs from the Aldine in some places. 1862 BURTON *Bk. Hunter* 101 Old editions of the classics in vellum bindings—Stephenses or Aldines. 1880 A. LANG *Ballades in Blue China, Book-hunter*, In rich men's shelves they take their ease—Aldines, Bodonis, Elzevirs! 1883 *Pall Mall Gaz.* 18 Sept. 3/2 An Aldine dolphin.

Aldo- (ældo), before a vowel **ald-**, used as combining form of ALDEHYDE in the names of chemical compounds as *aldo-hexose, -pentose, -keten*; **aldoxim(e**, the oxime of an aldehyde.

1883 *Jrnl. Chem. Soc.* XLIV. 1104 Lactones are not converted into aldoximes by the action of hydroxylamine. 1906 SUDBOROUGH *Bernthsen's Org. Chem.* 308 The relationship of the aldohexoses to the aldopentoses. 1907 J. B. COHEN *Org. Chem.* 295 An aldehyde sugar containing six atoms of carbon would be termed an aldo-hexose. *Ibid.* 310 Aldo-Pentose. 1912 F. G. POPE *Mod. Research Org. Chem.* 276 Two classes of ketens have been recognized, namely, the keto-ketens.. and the aldo-ketens.

Aldose (æ·ldōᵘs). *Chem.* [f. ALD(EHYDE + -OSE[2].] An aldehyde sugar.

1900 *W. H. Howell's Physiol.* (ed. 2) I. 561 Bodies.. possessing either the constitution of an aldehyde-alcohol,—CH(OH)CHO, called aldoses, or of a ketone-alcohol. 1902 J. J. R. MACLEOD *Pract. Physiol.* 161 Chemically, monosaccharides are either aldehydes or ketones, the former are called aldoses, the latter ketoses.

Alecithal (ăle·sipăl), *a.* *Embryol.* [f. Gr. ἀ- priv. + λέκιθος yolk + -AL.] Of an ovum: Devoid of food-yolk.

1880 BALFOUR *Comp. Embryol.* I. iii. 90 It is convenient to distinguish the ova which segment uniformly by some term; and I should propose for this the term alecithal, as implying that they are without food-yolk, or that what little food-yolk there is, is distributed uniformly. [*Note*] For this term as well as for the terms telolecithal and centrolecithal I am indebted to Mr. Lankester.

Aleck (in *smart Aleck*): see *SMART *a.*

Alemanic (ælĕmæ·nik), *a.* and *sb.* Also **All-, -annic.** [ad. late L. *Alemannicus*, f. *Alemanni*, Gr. Ἀλαμανοί, ad. OTeut. **Alamannōs*, which is prob. f. ALL + MAN *sb.*[1] and denotes a wide alliance of peoples.] The name of a confederation of Germanic tribes occupying the territory between the Rhine, the Main, and the Danube; also, of the dialects of Old High German spoken by them or the modern representatives of these. Also **Alema·nnian** *a.* and *sb.* **Alema·nnish** [after G. *Alemannisch*].

1788 *Encycl. Brit.* (1797) I. 469/2 Allemannic language. 1813 *Q. Rev.* 258 German, Himina. Alemannish, Himil. Classical German, Himmel. 1814 J. JAMIESON (*title*) Hermes Scythicus: or, the radical affinities of the Greek and Latin languages to the Gothic: illustrated from the Moeso-Gothic, Anglo-Saxon, Francic, Alemannic. 1842 *Penny Cycl.* XXIV. 268/1 Suabian branch [of modern High German]...*Allemannic*, commonly so called in the south-west corner of the Black Forest. 1879 *Encycl. Brit.* X. 517/2 For Bavarian we may quote some old glossaries, for Alemannian the interlinear versions of the Benedictine Rule. *Ibid.* 519/2 Alemannian is best characterized by its rigidly keeping its original vowel qualities. 1888 WRIGHT *O.H.G. Primer* 1 Upper German, spoken in the highlands of South Germany, and consisting of the Alemanic and Bavarian dialects. 1912 BRYCE *S. America* 424 The Swiss, Alemannian Germans to begin with, grew slowly into a nation.

[Delete ALEMBICATE *v.* and substitute:]

Alembicated (ăle·mbikēɪtĕd), *ppl. a.* [f. L. type *alembicātus* + -ED. Cf. F. *alambiqué.*] Of ideas, expression, etc.: Over-refined, over-subtilized (as if by passing through an alembic).

1786 MRS. PIOZZI *Anecd. Johnson* 197 His mind was like a warm climate, which brings every thing to perfection suddenly and vigorously, not like the alembicated productions of artificial fire, which always betray the difficulty of bringing them forth when their size is disproportionate to their flavour. 1818 LADY MORGAN *Fl. Macarthy* I. i. 8 Theories of alembicated refinement. 1823 *New Monthly Mag.* VII. 194 Alembicated systems for explaining conduct, and reconciling contradictions of character, are rarely satisfactory. 1913 W. RALEIGH *Some Authors, Boccaccio* (1923) 24 The prose style of Boccaccio..is not a simple style—rather it is curious and alembicated.

So **Alembica·tion**, over-subtlety or over-refinement of expression.

1893 STEVENSON *Vailima Lett.* 2 June (1895) 271 This sort of trouble..produces nothing when done but alembication and the far-fetched.

Ale-wife[2]. The form *aloofe* in quot. 1678 in Dict. is app. a mere misprint, as all other 17th cent. instances have *ale-wife, -wives*, e.g.:

1633 *Plymouth Col. Rec.* I. 17 Whereas God, by his providence, hath cast the fish called alewiues or herrings in the middest of the place. 1634 *Mass. Col. Rec.* (1853) I. 114 [He] is to sell the Alewyves hee takes there at 5 s. the thousand. 1652 J. ELIOT *Progr. Gospel* 5 Where the Fish we call Alewives come, there we built a Bridge. 1670 S. CLARKE *Acc. Plantations* 37 Big-bellied Alewives, Mackrils richly clad With Rainbow colours.

Alexandrian (ælĕgzɑ·ndriăn), *a.*[2] (and *sb.*[2]). [ad. L. *Alexandriānus*, Gr. Ἀλεξανδρειανός, f. *Alexandrīa*, Ἀλεξάνδρεια, the capital of ancient Egypt: see -AN.]

1. Belonging or akin to the school of Greek literature, esp. poetry, which flourished at Alexandria under the Ptolemies, and is regarded as a 'silver age', derivative, imitative, artificial, addicted to recondite learning. As *sb.*, a member or imitator of this school, or a writer who shows himself to be a kindred spirit.

1840 *Q. Rev.* June 110 The great mass of Alexandrian literature has perished by its own acknowledged worthlessness. 1858 DONALDSON *Lit. Anc. Greece* II. 449 Of all the writers of the Alexandrian school, the bucolic poets have enjoyed the most universal and permanent popularity. 1877 SELLAR *Virgil* 42 Virgil..has used the Alexandrians more freely than any other Greek writers, with the exception of Homer. 1887 MAHAFFY *Gr. Life & Thought* xi. (1896) 252 Antimachus of Colophon..certainly was great enough to set a model which had fatal effects on the Alexandrians. 1904 T. R. GLOVER *Stud. Virgil* 68 Ovid adds to his Alexandrian learning an air of humour which gives it quite a new complexion.

2. Belonging or akin to the schools of philosophy in Alexandria, esp. those which produced Philo Judaeus, the Neo-Platonists Ammonius, Plotinus, Iamblichus, and the Christian fathers Clement of Alexandria and Origen. As *sb.*, a member or follower of one or other of these schools.

1788 *Encycl. Brit.* (ed. 3) I. 394/2 Alexandrian philosophers. 1809 [E. JERNINGHAM] (*title*) The Alexandrian School; or, A Narrative of the First Christian Professors in Alexandria. *Ibid.* 18 The Alexandrians at length silenced the adverse party. 1840 *Q. Rev.* June 67 What in Plato was a religious philosophy, became, in the hands of the Alexandrians, a philosophical religion. *Ibid.*, John Smith, Cudworth, Norris, and More, were Alexandrian, not Athenian Platonists. 1858 DONALDSON *Lit. Anc. Greece* III. 172 Gnosticism originated in the Orientalized Platonism of the Alexandrians. 1883 FARRAR *Ep. Hebrews* Introd. 35 The most marked feature of the Epistle to the Hebrews is its Alexandrian character. *Ibid.* 36 It is Alexandrian in its method of dealing with Scripture.

Hence **Alexa·ndrianism**, the style and characteristics of the literary school, or the method and doctrine of the philosophical and Christian schools, mentioned above.

1860 WESTCOTT *Introd. Study Gosp.* i. 75 The society of the Therapeutæ was indeed the practical corollary of Alexandrianism. 1878 J. C. COLLINS *Tourneur's Plays* II. 223 Lycophosed...This is a good instance of Tourneur's Alexandrianism. 1883 FARRAR *Ep. Hebrews* Introd. 38 The Alexandrianism of the Epistle appears most clearly in the constant parallels which it furnishes to the writings of Philo.

Alexandrine, *a.*[2] and *sb.*[2] Add: *esp.* = *ALEXANDRIAN *a.*[2] and *sb.*[2]

1877 SELLAR *Virgil* 42 Yet even in him [Horace] the influence of the Alexandrine tone is apparent, especially in his treatment of the subjects taken from the Greek mythology. 1893 C. T. CRUTTWELL *Lit. Hist. Early Christ.* II. 442 The Alexandrine Fathers. 1904 T. R. GLOVER *Stud. Virgil* 165 From Euripides and the Alexandrines the love motive found its way into Latin poetry.

Hence **Alexa·ndrinism** = *ALEXANDRIANISM.

1880 CHEYNE *Proph. Isaiah* I. 238 Hence the Greek writer of Wisdom need not be credited with Alexandrinism. 1901 J. C. COLLINS *Ephem. Crit.* 336 He [Catullus] has not, indeed, escaped the taint of Alexandrinism.

Alexia (ăle·ksiă). *Med.* [mod.L., badly f. (after AGRAPHIA) Gr. ἀ- privative + λέξις speech, f. λέγειν to speak, confused with L. *legere* to read.] Inability to see words or to read; word-blindness.

1878 tr. *von Ziemssen's Cycl. Med.* XIV. 774 It is..by no means easy to say how much of the alexia and paralexia is to be ascribed to the hemiopia. 1904 TITCHENER tr. *Wundt's Physiol. Psychol.* I. 305.

Alexin (ăle·ksin). *Biol. Chem.* [a. Ger. *alexin* (Buchner, 1888), f. Gr. ἀλέξειν to ward off + -IN[1].] Name for a class of substances found in blood-serum, having the capacity of destroying bacteria, etc. and thus guarding against infection; *spec.* = *ADDIMENT, *COMPLEMENT *sb.* 5 i.

1896 *Allbutt's Syst. Med.* I. 568 Buchner..suggested that the destructive power of serum is due to certain proteid substances, to which, unfortunately, he gave the name of alexins. 1901 *Jrnl. Chem. Soc.* LXXX. II. 256 Alexin is found in larger quantity in the polynuclear leucocytes than in normal blood serum of dogs and rabbits. 1904 [see THERMOLABILE].

Alfilaria (ælfilē·riă). Also **-eria.** [Mexican Sp., f. Sp. *alfiler* pin, from the shape of the carpels.] (See quots.)

1889 FARMER *Americanisms*, Alfilaria (*Erodium cicutarium*). Also known as Storksbill, Pin-grass, Filaree, &c. A valuable forage plant of the dry regions from Colorado and New Mexico to Southern California. 1897 BEATRICE HARRADEN *Hilda Strafford* 115 Carpets of the little pink blossom of the alfilaria, the first spring flower.

Also **Alfileri·lla.**

1897 *Outing* XXIX. 551/2 The sleek Herefords lifted their white faces from the ferny circles of alfilerilla.

Algerine (ældʒĕrī·n), *sb.* and *a.* [f. *Alger-ia* + -INE.]

1. *sb.* An inhabitant or native of Algiers; esp. a pirate from Algiers.

1669 PEPYS *Diary* 26 Jan., The Algerines have broke the peace with us. 1728 J. MORGAN *Hist. Algiers* II. 433 Hassan Basha, with his Algerines, determined to attack that small Peninsula. 1785 JEFFERSON *Writ.* (1894) IV. 25 The Algerines ..have taken two of our vessels. 1819 SALAMÉ *Narr. Exped. Algiers* 39 At a few minutes before three, the Algerines, from the Eastern battery, fired the first shot at the Impregnable. 1870 W. THORNBURY *Old Stories* 249 The Algerines stood astonished at the English audacity. 1890 S. LANE-POOLE *Barbary Corsairs* 302 The French..beating back the Algerines as they advanced.

2. *transf.* One who acts like a pirate. *U.S.* Hence **Algeri·neism.**

1841 FOOTE *Texas & Texans* 83 A transaction which will..call down retributive vengeance upon these American Algerines. 1844 *Congress. Globe* 11 Mar. 360/1 The gentleman from Rhode Island had talked of 'ruffianism' in that State, and of 'Algerines'; but if the proposition he made to this House was not a specimen of 'Algerineism', he apprehended it was not to be found in Rhode Island. *a* 1861 WINTHROP *John Brent* vii. (1862) 71 He's one er them Algerines what don't know a dark hint, till it begins to make motions.

3. *adj.* Of or belonging to Algiers; characteristic of Algiers pirates.

1682 in L. Hertslet *Treaties* (1820) I. 63 In like manner no Algerine passenger being on board any ship or vessel in enmity with the said King of Great Britain shall be in any way molested. 1728 J. MORGAN *Hist. Algiers* I. 348 The Algerine Turks. 1818 FEARON *Sketches* 150 He [the captain] is an American, tall, determined, and with an eye that flashes with Algerine cruelty. 1819 SALAMÉ *Narr. Exped. Algiers* 175 It is well known that the Algerine government are very rich, by their plundering at sea. 1870 W. THORNBURY *Old Stories* 250 An Algerine frigate. 1873 *Murray's Handbk. Algeria* 22 The audacity of the Algerine pirates at this time was unparalleled.

Algid, *a.* Add: *spec.* in *algid cholera*, Asiatic cholera, which is marked by copious watery alvine discharges, etc.

1873 ROBERTS *Theor. Pract. Med.* 685 Epidemic, Asiatic, Algide, or Malignant Cholera. *Ibid.* 690 Stage of Collapse. Algide Stage. 1889 *Buck's Handbk. Med. Sci.* VIII. 610 Algid dysentery. 1901 DORLAND *Dict. Med.* s.v. *Cholera.*

Algin (æ·ldʒin). *Chem.* Also **algine.** [f. ALGA seaweed + -IN[1].] A nitrogenous substance, resembling gelatin, obtainable from certain algæ.

1888 *Chambers's Encycl.* I. 160 The cell-walls of our common brown seaweeds..all contain algin. 1897 C. T. DAVIS *Manuf. Leather* xxxvii. 505 Algine dissolved in water in the proportion of 12 to 100.

Algometer (ælgɒ·mĭtəɪ). [f. Gr. ἄλγος pain + μέτρον measure: see -METER.] An instrument for measuring degrees of sensitiveness to pain. So **Algometric** (ælgome·trik) *a.*, pertaining to such measurement; **Algometry** (-ɒ·mĕtri), the use of the algometer.

1890 in BILLINGS *Med. Dict.* 1892 *Fortn. Rev.* Mar. 355 By experiments made with the electric algometer it is clearly shown that woman is inferior to man [in general sensibility, including sensitiveness to pain]. 1897 E. W. SCRIPTURE *New Psychol.* 303 The pressure algometer consists..of a strong spring by means of which a rubber disc or point is pressed against the surface to be tested. 1904 G. S. HALL *Adolescence* II. 4 Other algometric tests..have led to somewhat different results.

Algo·nkian, *a.* and *sb.*

1. Variant spelling of *ALGONQUIAN *a.* and *sb.*

2. *Geol.* An epithet proposed to designate a period between the Archæan and the Palæozoic; proterozoic. As *sb.* = this period or system of rocks (in the U.S.A.).

These rocks are a feature of the region of Lake Superior, a territory of the Algonquian Indians.

1890 J. W. POWELL in *10th Ann. Rep. U.S. Geol. Survey* I. 20 At a recent conference of geologists..it was decided to make but one period of the Agnotozoic, and the name 'Algonkian' was chosen to designate that period. 1893 — *14th Ann. Rep. U.S. Geol. Survey* I. 100 The chronologic series from the Algonkian up to the Cretaceous. 1893 GEIKIE *Text-bk. Geol.* VI. I. § ii. 715 Another enormous succession of rocks comprised under the general name of 'Algonkian', but consisting of several distinct formations, separated from each other by unconformabilities.

Algonquian, -kian (ælgɒ·nkiăn), *a.* and *sb.* [f. *ALGONQUIN, by alteration of ending: see -IAN.] **A.** *adj.* Of or belonging to a large family of N. American Indians which includes the Algonquin tribe proper. **B.** *sb.* **1.** A member of this family. **2.** Any one of the languages or dialects spoken by different branches of this family.

1891 J. C. PILLING (*title*) Bibliography of the Algonquian Languages. — Pref. p. iii, The Algonquian speaking peoples. 1900 DENIKER *Races of Man* 526 The original home of the Algonquians was the region around Hudson's Bay. 1907 F. W. HODGE *Handbk. N. Amer. Ind.* I. 40/1 The central Algonquians are tall. *Ibid.* 43/1 The present number of the Algonquian family is about 90,000.

Algonquin, -kin (ælgɒ·nkin), *sb.* and *a.* [a. F. *Algonquin*, perh. contracted f. *Algoumequin* (17th c.). In Micmac *algoomeaking* or *-making* is said to mean 'at the place of spearing fish and eels'.] **A.** *sb.* **1.** An Indian of a tribe encountered in the districts of Ottawa and Quebec; also used as collect. sing. = this tribe. **2.** More widely = ALGONQUIAN. **3.** The language of the tribe or family. **B.** *adj.* Pertaining to any of the above.

[1625 PURCHAS *Pilgrims* IV. 1607 The Estechemins, Algoumequins, and Mountainers. 1698 L. HENNEPIN *Contin. New Discov.* xxiv. 95 The Algoncains; *orig.* les Algonkains.] 1765 *Exped. Henry Bouquet* (1868) 153 Nipissins, Algonquins, living towards the heads of the Ottawa river. 1778 T. HUTCHINS *Topogr. Descr. Virginia* etc. 67 Algonkins. 1845 H. R. SCHOOLCRAFT *Oneóta* 171 The Algonquin tribes. 1851 — *Ind. Tribes U.S.* I. 306 Their language is pure Algonquin. 1865 PARKMAN *Pioneers of France* (1876) 347 This neighborhood was the seat of the principal Indian population of the river [Ottawa], ancestors of the modern Ottawas. [*Note.*] Usually called Algoumequins, or Algonquins, by Champlain and other early writers,—a name now always used in a generic sense to designate a large family of cognate tribes. 1867 — *Jesuits N. Amer.* (1899) Introd. 4 Tribes speaking various Algonquin languages and dialects. 1884 C. G. LELAND (*title*) The Algonquin Legends of New England, or Myths and Folk Lore of the Micmac, Passamaquoddy, and Penobscot Tribes.

Algraphy (æ·lgrăfi). [f. AL(UMINIUM + -GRAPHY, after *lithography.*] The art or process of printing from aluminium plates. Hence **Algra·phic** *a.*

1897 *Studio* Sept. 244/2 An alternative device which would give equal facilities to the artist, and would preserve the technical character of lithography, while it would remove the necessity for depending upon the use of lithographic stone itself,..a process..discovered by Mr. Scholz of Mayence, who has patented his invention under the name of 'Algraphy'. 1898 *Daily Chron.* 14 Oct. 3/1 The algraphic plate is a substitute for the ordinary lithographic stone. 1914 E. H. RICHTER *Prints* 10 Plates of metal are often substituted for stone (zincography, algraphy).

Ali- (æ·li), combining form of L. *ala* wing, denoting 'pertaining to the "wings" or lateral expansions' of certain parts, as **alie·thmoid** *a.*, pertaining to the lateral expansions of the ethmoid bone; **alina·sal** *a.*, pertaining to the lateral parts of the nostrils; **alise·ptal** *a.*, pertaining to a cartilaginous partition in the nasal passage of the embryo of a bird; also as sbs.

1875 W. K. PARKER in *Encycl. Brit.* III. 704/2 Behind the alinasal comes the aliseptal region. *Ibid.*, The hinder region or 'aliethmoid' is the true olfactory region. *Ibid.* 705/1 (Figure) Aliseptal.

Alibi. B. *sb.* Add: **b.** A plea of innocence; an excuse. *U.S.*

1921 R. D. PAINE *Comrades Roll. Ocean* viii. 130 I'm not trying to build up an alibi, but I wasn't losing much sleep over the right and wrong of it.

Hence **A·libi** *v. trans.*, to clear by an excuse. *U.S.*

1926 J. BLACK *You Can't Win* i. 3, I am not lugging in the fact..to alibi myself away from anything.

Alicyclic (ælisi·klik), *a.* *Chem.* [f. *ALI(PHATIC + CYCLIC.] Combining the properties of aliphatic and cyclic compounds (see *CYCLIC).

1891 *Jrnl. Chem. Soc.* LX. II. 1097 Alicyclic Homology. 1900 E. F. SMITH *Richter's Org. Chem.* II. 18 Aliphatic-cyclic or alicyclic saturated and unsaturated compounds. 1907 J. B. COHEN *Org. Chem.* 553.

Alienize (ē·liənaiz), *v.* [See -IZE.] *trans.* To make alien, reduce to the status of an alien (in quot. rendering W. *alltudaw*). Hence **A·lienized** *ppl. a.*, foreignized.

1841 *Anc. Laws & Inst. Wales* II. 333 Her brothers alienized her children when they gave her to an alltud. 1861 MEREDITH *Evan Harrington* iv, This extremely alienised idea of the nature of a member of the Parliament of Great Britain.

Alif (ā·lif). The first letter of the Arabic and Persian alphabets (corresponding to our *a*).

1868 E. FITZGERALD *Omar* (ed. 2) li, Yes; and a single Alif were the clue, Could you but find it, to the Treasure-house.

Alikeness. Delete †*Obs.* and add:

1920 E. V. LUCAS in *Times* 25 Sept. 11/6 This alikeness is not confined to the features and clothing of Americans, but it is noticeable in their thought and conversation. The whole tendency is towards levelling. 1924 *Public Opin.* 6 Dec. 572/1 The fundamental alikeness of God and man.

Alimonious, *a.* Delete †*Obs.* and add:

2. Laying claim to alimony.

1883 J. H. BEADLE *Western Wilds* xxxvii. 604 There they clung till his death, save for a few side disturbances most noted of which was the alimonious Ann Eliza.

Aliphatic (ælifæ·tik), *a.* *Chem.* [f. Gr. ἀλειφατ-, ἄλειφαρ unguent, fat + -IC.] Of or pertaining to fat; epithet of organic compounds having an 'open-chain' structure.

1895 F. P. MÖLLER *Cod-liver Oil & Chem.* 7 The aliphatic series. *Ibid.* 83 The aliphatic hydrocarbons. 1906 SUDBOROUGH *Bernthsen's Org. Chem.* 24 The Methane Derivatives or Fatty Compounds, or Aliphatic Compounds.

Aliturgic (ælitə·ɪdʒik), *a.* *Eccl.* [f. Gr. ἀ- privative + LITURGY. Cf. F. *aliturgique* and Gr. ἀλειτούργητος.] Of a day: On which the Liturgy is not celebrated. So **Alitu·rgical** *a.*

1872 O. SHIPLEY *Gloss. Eccl. Terms, Aliturgical Days*, those days when the holy sacrifice is not offered. 1898 *Ch. Times* 7 Apr., Those who desired to communicate on that [sc. Good Friday] and other aliturgic days. 1912 A. FORTESCUE *Mass* 186 In the Milanese rite all Fridays in Lent are still strictly aliturgical days.

Alive, *a.* Add: **5. b.** *transf.* Of things, in specific uses. (See quots.)

1845 S. JUDD *Margaret* II. i. 186 Her Mother 'stirs it off' and a due quantity of the 'quick' and 'alive' crystal sweet is the result. 1892 GUNTER *Miss Dividends* xvi. 234 The locomotives..are moving about slowly, with a view to keeping themselves what is technically called 'alive'—that is their steam up, sufficient to give them power of motion.

6. (Earlier U.S. example.)

1789 MORSE *Amer. Geog.* 205 The markets are alive with them [sc. fish].

Aliveness (ălai·vnĕs). [f. ALIVE *a.* + -NESS.] The quality of being alive or full of vigour. Also, sensitiveness *to* (one's surroundings, etc.).

1866 MRS. CARLYLE in T. W. Reid *Life Ld. Houghton* (1891) II. xv. 146 A woman..going about in society alive and well. To be sure, both the aliveness and the wellness 'may be strongly doubted', as they say in Edinburgh. 1892 *Independent* 7 Oct. 35/1 Aliveness, if we may use such a phrase, to the spirit of the age. 1901 J. WOOD in L. S. Hunter *John Hunter* ii. 18 He had all Dawson's aliveness to the world in which he lived.

Alkali, *sb.* Add: **3. b.** Native alkali (i.e. various salts) existing in excess in the soil of certain areas in the Western States; hence, a region abounding in alkali. *U.S.*

1869 S. BOWLES *Our New West* xiv. 278 In looking out.. on the starry heavens,..one almost forgets alkali. *a* 1875 'MARK TWAIN' *Sketches* Wks. XIX. 317 That awful five days journey through alkali, sagebrush, peril of body. 1878 J. H. BEADLE *Western Wilds* ix. 139 The high plains are dotted by tracts of alkali. *a* 1904 S. E. WHITE *Blazed Trail Stories* x. 181 They had ridden solitary over the limitless alkali of the Arizona plains. *Ibid.* 182 Tom, and Alfred,.. had done the alkali for three days.

attrib. 1869 S. BOWLES *Our New West* xiv. 275 The alkali dust, dry with a season's sun,..was thick and constant. *Ibid.* 276 Bare alkali plains stretch out..for miles. 1878 J. H. BEADLE *Western Wilds* xxiv. 388, I am convinced there is little to see but..alkali flats and sand-hills. 1886 *Boston* (Mass.) *Herald* 16 July, It is only an 'alkali sink'—a natural well, filled with a paste as yielding as water. 1907 S. E. WHITE *Arizona Nights* III. xiv. 348 The sparse vegetation was grey with the alkali dust.

c. *transf.* One who lives in or frequents an alkali region. *U.S.*

1907 S. E. WHITE *Arizona Nights* I. ii. 31 A white-faced woman who looked mighty good to us alkalis opened the flaps.

A·lkali, *v.* *U.S.* [f. *ALKALI *sb.* 3 b.] *trans.* To affect by life in an alkali region.

1907 S. E. WHITE *Arizona Nights* I. vii. 126 The trouble with you fellows..is that you're so plumb alkalied you don't know the real thing when you see it.

Alkaline, *a.* Add: **3.** Of soils or areas: Charged or permeated with alkali. *U.S.*

1869 S. BOWLES *Our New West* xiv. 277 It would seem as if these alkaline valleys of the Great Interior Basin were too cold. 1870 *Amer. Naturalist* IV. 29 A desert section proper and one more particularly pertaining to the alkaline flats.

Alkapton (ælkæ·ptɒn). *Med.* [Coined by Bödeker 1858; f. AL(KALI + Gr. κάπτον, neut. pres. pple. of κάπτειν to swallow greedily.] A reducing substance which causes urine, left standing, to turn dark through oxidation. Also *attrib.* Hence **Alkaptonu·ria** [Gr. οὖρον urine], the disease in which this substance is present. **Alkaptonu·ric** *a.* and *sb.*

1888 *Jrnl. Chem. Soc.* LIV. 1121 Alcaptonuria...A certain kind of human urine darkens on the addition of alkalis. Bödeker..isolated from such urine a substance to which he gave the name 'alcapton'. 1899 GARROD in *Jrnl. Physiol.* XXIII. 512 The urine of an alkaptonuric individual. *Ibid.*, Alkapton urines. *Ibid.*, Some cases of alkaptonuria. 1905 GARROD & HELE *ibid.* XXXIII. 198 An adult male alkaptonuric.

Alkyl (æ·lkil). *Chem.* [f. ALC(OHOL + -YL.] A general term for alcohol radicals of the methane series, as methyl, ethyl, etc.

1883 *Jrnl. Chem. Soc.* XLIV. 919 Action of the Alkyl-derivatives of the Halogen-substituted Fatty Acids on Aniline. *Ibid.* 276 The alkyl salts of the $C_nH_{2m}O_2$ series. 1889 M^cGOWAN *Bernthsen's Org. Chem.* 37 The halogen alkyls, $C_nH_{2n+1}X$. 1906 SUDBOROUGH *Bernthsen's Org. Chem.* 22 The monovalent residues, C_nH_{2n+1}(methyl, ethyl, etc.), which form the radicals of the monovalent alcohols, $C_nH_{2n+1}OH$, are frequently termed *alkyls*, or *alphyls*, while the divalent residues, C_nH_{2n}, are known as *alkylenes.*

Hence **A·lkylated** *a.*, containing one or more alkyl radicals. So **A·lkylating** *ppl. a.*, **Alkyla·tion.** **A·lkylene**, an ethylene or olefine.

1889 M^cGOWAN *Bernthsen's Org. Chem.* 46 Olefines or Hydrocarbons of the Ethylene Series (Alkylenes): C_nH_{2n}. *Ibid.* 272 Alkylated ureas. 1900 *Jrnl. Chem. Soc.* LXXVIII. I. 610 Dimethyl Sulphate as an Alkylating Agent. *Ibid.* LXXVII. I. 729 Alkylation by means of Dry Silver Oxide and Alkyl Halides.

All. Add:

A. 6. *All of*, as much as, altogether, quite. *For all of*, as far as concerned.

1856 *Trans. Mich. Agric. Soc.* VII. 317 He puts down the average price per bbl. at $11, which is all of $2 per bbl. too high. 1883 'MARK TWAIN' *Life Mississippi* xviii. 220 It must have been all of fifteen minutes..of dull, homesick silence. 1898 A. NICHOLAS *Idyl of Wabash* 20 There was Mr. Litledale, all of thirty-one. 1911 H. S. HARRISON *Queed* xvii. 209 Thus they parted, almost precipitately, and, for all of him, might never have met again in this world.

7. b. In scoring at games, denoting that both sides have made the stated score; e.g. *love all* = neither side has scored.

1837 T. BACON *First Impr. fr. Nat. in Hindustan* I. 252 In the fourth 20, they were even; 67 all. 1878 *Lawn Tennis Laws* 12 If both players win five games, the score is called games-all. 1883 *Nat. Hist. Jrnl. & School Reporter* VII. 155 Up to within ten minutes when time was called the score was one goal all. 1898 Love all [see LOVE *sb.* 10 b].

All- (see ALL E.). Add:

all-ages, horses of all ages entered for a race; **all-but** [see ALL A. 8 b] used *adj.*, almost complete or entire; **all-or-nothing** (**piece**), a piece of mechanism in a repeating watch; **all-through** *a.*, (of a journey) performed without a change of conveyance.

1876 *Coursing Calendar* 323 The *all-ages were not a good lot, but they contained one or two who had already distinguished themselves this season. 1816 TUCKEY *Narr. Exped. R. Zaire* i. (1818) 18 Negro washerwomen, whose state of **all but* nudity. 1881 GILBERT *Patience* II, *Col.* (apologetically). I'm afraid we're not quite right. *Ang.* Not supremely, perhaps, but, oh, so all-but! Oh, Saphir, are they not quite too all-but? 1920 W. S. PALMER *Christianity & Christ* 43 Until the great all-but-men brought forth true men. 1843 *Penny Cycl.* XXVII. 108/1 (*Watch, Repeating*) The whole..carried by the *all-or-nothing piece *TR.* *Ibid.* 108/2 When the quarter-rack is brought back to its original position..the part *m* will have passed between the end *R* of the all-or-nothing, which in its passage *m* will have pressed outwards. 1912 MRS. HUGH FRASER *Further Remin.* i. 10 After an *all-through journey from Rome, our train crawled into the Gare de Lyons.

b. In modern (esp. twentieth-century) use, *all* with a sb. forms an attrib. phr. denoting that all the persons or things, or the whole of the thing, expressed by the sb. is concerned or included.

1878 (*title*) Laws of Lawn-Tennis as adopted by The Marylebone Cricket Club and The *All England Croquet and Lawn-Tennis Club. 1909 *Westm. Gaz.* 8 Nov. 7/1 The National *All-Grades Movement of the Amalgamated Society of Railway Servants. 1928 *Manch. Guardian Weekly* 28 Sept. 242/3 The *all-India leaders. 1861 RAMSAY *Remin.* Ser. II. 133 The body-lifters, or '*all-night-men', as they were wont to be called. 1888 GUNTER *Mr. Potter of Texas* xx, The..Press Club..just beginning to assume its usual all-night gayety and brilliancy. *Ibid.*, He knows Cotton-tree is an all-night man. 1892 HOWELLS *Mercy* 214 The long, all-night ride. 1899 *Westm. Gaz.* 24 Aug. 2/3 The all-night tram system. 1904 *Daily Chron.* 25 May 8/6 Soldiers' all-night passes. 1906 O. HENRY *Four Million* 215 An all-night lunch Counter. 1928 *Manch. Guardian Weekly* 23 Nov. 401/3 The *all-parties Constitution. 1928 *Times* 3 July 16/6 The new *all-purpose Fairey Napier aeroplane. 1928 *Manch. Guardian Weekly* 26 Oct. 328/2 Six-cylinder Thornycroft *all-weather body cars. 1906 *Dublin Rev.* Oct. 332 We are forced onwards to the necessity of an *all-world State if we would escape an all-world anarchy.

Allactite (ælæ·ktəit). *Min.* [Named (*allaktit*) 1884 by A. Sjögren, f. Gr. stem ἀλλακτ-, ἀλλάσσειν to change: see -ITE[1].] A native arsenate of manganese.

1920 *Brit. Museum Return* 145 Allactite from Sweden.

Allamanda (ælămæ·ndă). Also erron. **ala-.** [mod.L., f. the name of the Swiss scientist J. N. S. *Allamand.*] A genus of apocynaceous trees of tropical America, cultivated in hothouses for their large funnel-shaped yellow flowers. Also (with small initial), a plant of this genus.

1796 CURTIS in *Bot. Mag.* X. pl. 338 Willow-leaved Allamanda. 1879 W. CORY *Lett. & Jrnls.* 7 Oct. (1897) 449 An alamanda with big petals of a very lovely yellow.

Comb. 1918 'W. H. HUDSON *Far Away* xxii. 294 The large alamanda-like flower of a purest divine yellow.

All around, all-around, *adv.* and *a.* *U.S.* = ALL-ROUND *adv.* and *a.*

1878 J. H. BEADLE *Western Wilds* xxxiii. 538 The trail shows that twelve American horses, shod all around, have passed at a walk. 1883 [see AROUND *adv.* 4]. 1886 *Harper's Mag.* June 18/2 This arrangement gives a clear sweep.. enabling the forward gun to cover an all-around fire. 1904 *Brooklyn Daily Standard Union* 7 July 6 Our army in the Philippines seems to be composed of 'all-around' men. 1904 *Forum* Oct. 257 The most comprehensive and in many ways the best all-around American city school exhibit.

Hence **All-arou·ndness.** *U.S.*

1888 *Voice* (N.Y.) 6 Sept., The all-aroundness of our chieftain's character.

Allegator. Now avoided on account of its inevitable suggestion of *alligator*: see quot.

1884 'EDNA LYALL' *We Two* iv, 'His accusation is utterly false. I deny the allegation, and I scorn the allegator—!' He was interrupted by a shout of laughter.

Allegiant. Add:

sb. One who owes or renders allegiance; a subject.

1886 *N. Amer. Rev.* CXLII. 225 Strangers shall have the same personal rights as the allegiants. 1888 TOURGEE *Lett. to King* v. 67 In the one sense it [the word 'citizen'] is used to distinguish the American people from the allegiants of a foreign power.

[Delete ALLEGORISM (in the quot., which should be attributed to Harding, not Jewel, 'allegorisme' is an error for 'algorisme') and substitute:]

Allegorism (æ·lĭgŏriz'm). [f. ALLEGORIZE; cf. *allegorist.*] The use of allegory; the allegorical method of interpreting Scripture.

1901 *Jewish Encycl.* I. *Allegorical interpretation* [of Scripture]. Expositors of this system may be called allegorists; the system itself, allegorism. 1919 P. H. OSMOND *Myst. Poets Engl. Ch.* 350 No doubt there is a rather slippery descent from this type of mysticism, through symbolism, to mere allegorism.

Allelomorph (ălī·lomɒ̄ɪf). *Biol.* [f. Gr. ἀλληλ- one another + μορφή form.] Each of a pair of mutually exclusive characters, one or the other of which is exhibited without intermixture in descendants of a cross between parental forms respectively possessing them. Hence **Alle·lomo·rphic** *a.*, pertaining to or of the nature of allelomorphs.

1902 BATESON & SAUNDERS *Rep. Evol. Com. Roy. Soc.* I. 159 [If] two similar gametes meet, their offspring will be no more likely to show the other allelomorph than if no cross had ever taken place. *Ibid.* 127 The strictly allelomorphic or Mendelian distribution of characters among the gametes. 1906 R. H. LOCK *Variation, Hered. & Evol.* vii. 184 The dominant and recessive allelomorph seem to represent respectively the presence and absence of something. *Ibid.* x. 265 Allelomorphic characters.

Allemande, *v.* [f. ALLEMANDE.] *intr.* To dance an allemande.

1835 *Nautical Mag.* July 416 A girl in the same set, who was tying her shoe-string when she ought to have been allemanding. 1890 BARING-GOULD *Arminell* xlviii, The love-making below stairs is..full of restraints and shynesses, of setting to partners, and allemanding about them.

Allergy (æ·ləɪdʒi). [ad. mod.L. *allergia*, f. Gr. ἄλλος other, after *energia* ENERGY.] See quot. 1913. Hence **Alle·rgic** *a.* Also **Allergen** (æ·ləɪdʒen) [after words in -GEN].

1913 DORLAND *Med. Dict.* (ed. 7), *Allergen*, a hypothetic substance in infectious matter capable of rendering anaphylactic an animal into which the matter is injected. Called also *anaphylactogen* and *sensibilisinogen.* *Allergia, allergie, allergy*, a condition of acquired immunity associated with anaphylaxis in which reinoculation brings about the same infection as before, but in an altered form. 1925 W. W. DUKE (*title*) Allergy Asthma, Hay Fever, Urticaria and Allied Manifestations of Reaction. *Ibid.* Introd. 20 Wells and others contend that 'allergy' is a broad useful term, for under its heading can be described a group of peculiar phenomena of altered reactivity the underlying cause of which is as yet unproved. *Ibid.* 246 A large proportion of patients with asthma, 'allergic coryza', erythema,..and even allergic shock, are actually sensitive specifically and solely to the action of a physical agent, such as light, heat, cold, or mechanical irritation. 1926 SOLLMAN *Pharmacol.* (ed. 3) 86 Allergic hypersusceptibility is a special type of idiosyncrasy in which the patient reacts to special substances.

Alleviate, *v.* **2.** Add: also *absol.*

1888 MRS. H. WARD *R. Elsmere* xli, The constant effort to serve and to alleviate.

Alley. Add: **3. b.** A back-lane running parallel with a main street. *U.S.*

1729 *Baltimore Town Rec.* 10 The commissioners..shall cause the same Sixty Acres to be..divided into convenient Streets, Lanes, and Allies, as near as may be into Sixty equal lots. 1747 *Ibid.* 22 To Survey the Same and lay it out into Lotts with convenient Streets and Alleys. 1817 S. R. BROWN *Western Gaz.* 90 There are three streets,..besides lanes and alleys. *Ibid.* 101 Each block of lots has the advantage of two 16 feet alleys. 1835 J. MARTIN *Gazetteer Virginia* 139 Fire plugs are connected with the distributing pipes at every intersection of the alleys with 2nd and 3rd streets. 1891 J. A. RIIS *How other half lives* 21 A notorious Fourth Ward alley.

Alley-way (æ·liwēɪ). orig. *U.S.* Also *colloq.* **alloway** (æ·lōwēɪ). [f. ALLEY + WAY *sb.*[1]] A narrow passage or avenue, e.g. between houses or between rows of cabins in a ship.

1869 HALE *Sybaris*, etc. 115 The same child whom I had seen faded and dead in the alley-ways of the town! 1871 in Amy Fay *Music Study Germany* xi. (1904) 134 A long alley-way or vista of trees. 1882 *Harper's Mag.* June 81 Divided..by substantial walls of adobe, with narrow alley-ways running between. 1888 *Murray's Mag.* III. 238 The covered way, or 'alloway', on the port side, which led from the quarter-deck to the fore part of the ship. 1891 C. ROBERTS *Adrift Amer.* 231 Alley-way between the after-deck house and the bulwarks. 1894 *Outing* (U.S.) XXIV. 286/2 The main street of this town was as dirty as the filthiest alley-way found in any large city of America. 1920 *Blackw. Mag.* Jan. 108/2 A local marshman as a guide, or you will soon find yourself lost in the maze of alleyways through the giant reeds.

Alligator[2]. Add: **1. b.** An inhabitant or native of the Mississippi region (freq. described as 'half horse, half alligator'). *U.S.*

1837 R. M. BIRD *Nick of Woods* II. 246 He..launched his broad-horn on the narrow bosom of the Salt, and was soon afterwards transformed into a Mississippi alligator.

c. A lean hog. *U.S.*

1852 *Trans. Mich. Agric. Soc.* III. 332 Variously known as narragansetts, alligators, land sharks and flea breeders.

2. c. *U.S.* (See quot.)

1909 *Century Dict.* Suppl., *Alligator*, a boat used in handling floating logs. It can be moved overland from one body of water to another by its own power, usually applied through drum and cable. *U.S.*

3. alligator gar *U.S.*, a large species of gar-pike, found in waters of the Mississippi region; **alligator pepper**, Melegueta pepper or grain of paradise (see GRAIN *sb.*[1] 4); **alligator snapper, terrapin, turtle** *U.S.*, various species of fresh-water turtles.

1834 *Southern Lit. Messenger* I. 121 An anomalous species called the *alligator-garr. 1836 D. B. EDWARD *Hist. Texas* 60 Then there is the Alligator Gar, a singular animal, in form half fish half alligator. 1885 *Encycl. Brit.* XVIII. 517/1 '*Alligator pepper' is the seed of..a plant of the Ginger family. 1884 GOODE *Nat. Hist. Aquat. Anim.* 153 An *Alligator Snapper of perhaps forty pounds weight. 1835 W. G. SIMMS *Partisan* 317 Three enormous terrapins of that doubtful brood which the vulgar in the southern country describe as the *alligator terrapin. 1885 *Stand. Nat. Hist.* (1888) III. 452 The elongated tail of the animal..has..given rise to the popular name, '*alligator-turtle'.

A·lligatoring, *vbl. sb.* *U.S.* The cracking and retraction of paint, varnish, etc., caused by contraction.

1911 *Engin. News* (N.Y.) 27 July 121 Many of the paints which lack any evidence of cracking, checking, or alligatoring.

All-in.

1. As predicative adj.: Exhausted.

1902 A. D. McFAUL *Ike Glidden* xxii. 201 The horse was holding steady up to his clip, but it could be easily seen that he was 'all in'. 1916 B. M. BOWER *Phantom Herd* xiv. 244 You better find him right there in the blizzard—hurt maybe—anyway just about all in.

2. As attrib. phr.: Inclusive of all.

1890 *Daily News* 17 Feb. 3/6 The all-in tournament at the Westminster Aquarium. 1908 *Westm. Gaz.* 6 June 9/3 The 'all-in' system—that is to say, railway and hotel accommodation combined. 1924 F. W. THOMAS *Rain & Shine* 125 Our Double-Decked Combination Endowment and All-in Policy. 1927 *Daily Tel.* 7 Mar. 2 The exceptionally high all-in cost of 1*s.* 11½*d.* per lb. 1927 *Manch. Guardian Weekly* Oct. 329/2 A notable appeal for disarmament and all-in arbitration. 1929 *Times* 8 Jan. 14/1 The two-part tariffs comprise a domestic 'all-in' rate and a business 'all-in' rate. The charge per unit for electricity for..lighting, heating, cooking, and domestic and business appliances is 1*d.* per unit.

Allo- (æ·lo), *Chem.*, combining form of Gr. ἄλλος other, used to distinguish one of two organic isomers, as *allo-cinnamic, -maleic, -mucic* (acids).

1893 *Jrnl. Chem. Soc.* LXIV. I. 513 Allocinnamic acid. 1894 *Ibid.* I. 173 Allofurfuracrylic Acid and the Formation of Allo-Acids. *Ibid.*, The allo-form of cynnamylacrylic acid.

Allomorph (æ·lomɒ̄ɪf). *Min.* [f. Gr. ἄλλος other + μορφή form.] A distinct crystalline form without change of chemical composition. Hence **Allomo·rphic** *a.*, **Allomo·rphism.**

1866 *Q. Jrnl. Geol. Soc.* XXII. I. 187 *note*, All these varieties are considered to belong to one axial system—the monoclinate; but being obviously of other forms than one, and as they are all chemically alike, we propose to call them *allomorphs.* Like aragonite, calcite is also subject to allomorphism. *Ibid.* 193 *note*, It is our present impression that flocculite is merely an allomorph of serpentine.

All-out, *adj. phr.*

1. Completely, fully. (Cf. OUT *adv.* 23.)

1885 MRS. HUNGERFORD *Maiden all Forlorn*, etc. III. 3 'I haven't any time for a chat', he says, glancing at his watch. 'It is seven all out.'

2. Using or involving all one's (or its) strength or resources; 'fully extended'; at top speed.

1895 *Windsor Mag.* I. 120/1 There is no fun in going all-out. 1907 *Westm. Gaz.* 10 Dec. 4/2 The proposed 300-mile all-out-through race. 1908 *Ibid.* 29 Sept. 4/2 To put a vehicle to an all-out test. 1925 E. F. NORTON *Fight for Everest 1924* 143 Irvine..was willing..to 'go all out', as he put it, in an utmost effort to reach the top. 1928 GALSWORTHY *Swan Song* II. vi. 140 He..made up his mind to go 'all out' for his Uncle Hilary's slum-conversion scheme.

All over, *adv. phr.* Add: **1. b.** Everywhere. *U.S.*

1904 *Rochester* (U.S.) *Post Express* 12 Sept. 3 News Flashes from All Over. 1906 *Harper's Mag.* Oct. 764 They'd been hunting all over for her. 1911 *N.Y. Even. Post* 12 Jan. 16 They came from all over, and showed it. They were.. from every section of the country.

4. Applied to ornamental patterns or designs: see quot. 1916.

1898 J. BILSON in C. V. Collier *Acc. Boynton Family* (1914) 79 A..plaster ceiling with an all-over honey-suckle design. 1906 *Daily Chron.* 15 Oct. 8/5 Any kind of 'all-over' lace or embroidered net. 1916 HAMLIN *Hist. Ornament* i. 4 According to the way in which ornament covers space it may be divided into linear all-over, and radiating ornament. *Ibid.* 5 In 'all-over' patterns the units are arranged along two or more intersecting systems of lines so as to cover a broad surface. *Ibid.*, Continuous 'all-overs' forming a mesh of two sets of intersecting lines are called quarries.

All-overish, *a.* (Examples.)

1834 *Sk. & Eccentr. D. Crockett* 52, I wish I may be shot if I know how I felt; but I tell you what, it made me feel quite all-overish. 1855 *Putnam's Mag.* Dec. 575/1, I felt the satire to its full extent. I grew—all-over-ish, no other phrase expresses it.

Allow, *v.* Add:

7. (Earlier U.S. examples.)

Also used in aphetic form *'low.*

1843 CARLTON *New Purchase* II. 158 She allowed her Bill could lick are a man in the 'varsal world. *a* 1861 WINTHROP *John Brent* iii. (1862) 32, I allowed from seeing you handle that thar hoss, that you had got your hand in on women. 1871 G. A. TOWNSEND *Mormon Trials* 13 Well, in the first place, he allowed he was doing his religious duties, and he allowed that he had got to live with some one else.

8. c. Also with ellipse of inf.: To permit to go or come *in, out*, etc.

1864 TROLLOPE *Small House at Allington* II. 260 He could not have been allowed again into my drawing-room. 1882 BESANT *All Sorts* xiv, Then he allows the Conservatives.. back again, and gives them another show. 1911 *Rep. Labour & Social Conditions Germany* III. Nos. vi and vii. 76 The miners who were in the company were allowed to some parts. 1915 RUPERT BROOKE *Collected Poems* (1918) Mem. p. cxlii, We were allowed ashore from 5 to midnight. 1924 D. GARNETT *Man in Zoo* 19 He was allowed out every evening after closing-time.

12. b. *refl.*

1888 MRS. H. WARD *R. Elsmere* xvii, Robert, meanwhile ..had been allowing himself a little deliberate study of Mr. Wendover. *Ibid.* xlii, Madame de Netteville allowed herself plenty of jests with her intimates. 1896 'H. S. MERRIMAN' *Sowers* vii, He would not allow himself the luxury of being the first arrival.

Allowance, *sb.* **7. a.** Add: In military use, *pl.* the sums of money (distinct from the *pay*) paid to an officer for various kinds of services.

1837 T. BACON *First Impr. fr. Nat. in Hindustan* I. 252 Upon pay and allowances not exceeding £20 a month. 1853 STOCQUELER *Milit. Encycl.* s.v. 1888 KIPLING *Plain Tales fr. Hills, False Dawn* 40 Pay and allowances of nearly fourteen hundred rupees a month.

Alloway: see *ALLEY-WAY.

All-red, *a.* Used to indicate a telegraph-line, a trading route, etc., lying throughout in territory of the British Empire. (From the practice of colouring British and Imperial territory red in our maps.)

1895 G. HUTCHISON in *N. Z. Hansard* XCI. 854 Arguments..in favour of the 'All Red' line. 1898 J. G. WARD *Ibid.* CI. 344 What further steps have been taken to have an 'all red' cable laid across the Pacific? 1902 *Westm. Gaz.* 11 Sept. 5/2 An 'all-red line' from Great Britain through Canada to Australia. 1923 *Daily Mail* 12 Mar. 9 A huge 'All-Red' aeroplane, spanning the Empire in such a series of great, long-distance night-and-day flights as shall obviate any necessity for alighting on foreign soil.

All right, sb. use of phr. *all right* (see RIGHT *a.* 15), esp. in *bit of all right*: see *BIT *sb.*[2] 4 f.

All-round. Add: **D.** *sb.* = ALL-ROUNDER.

1860 O. W. HOLMES *Prof. Breakf.-t.* vi. 134 If any of my young friends should be tempted to waste their substance on white kids and 'all-rounds',..by anything I have said.

Allure, *sb.*[1] Recently reintroduced in the sense of 'charm', 'attractiveness'.

1901 *Westm. Gaz.* 2 Jan. 1/3 Biskra..Doré like are its allures. 1925 J. FARNOL *Loring Mystery* xix. 126 He seemed to find a strange allure in this forbidding prospect.

Alluvial. Add:

B. *sb.* 'The common term in Australia and New Zealand for gold-bearing alluvial soil' (Morris).

1888 'R. BOLDREWOOD' *Robbery under Arms* lii. (1889) 403 The whole of the alluvial will be taken up, and the Terrible Hollow..will re-echo with the sound of pick and shovel. 1890 *Pall Mall Gaz.* 16 Dec. 2/1 There is..every indication of mineral wealth, but it has not been sufficiently proved yet for one to say whether there is good alluvial or not.

Allways (ɔ̄·lwēɪz), *adv.* [Properly two words: see WAY *sb.*[1] 9.] In all directions.

1838 *Fraser's Mag.* XVII. 689 They were borne about the room backwards, forwards, sideways, and allways.

Almacantar. Add:

2. A telescope fitted with horizontal wires and mounted on a float resting on mercury, used for observing the rising and setting of stars.

Transfer quot. 1880 to this sense, and add:

1900 *Proc. Durham Phil. Soc.* II. 6 In the Almacantar we claim that the telescope turns with faultless truth about its theoretical axis of rotation.

Alocasia (ælokē·ziă, -kē·ʒiă). [Said to be an alteration of COLOCASIA.] A genus of plants of tropical Asia cultivated for their foliage, closely allied to COLOCASIA; (with small initial) a plant of this genus.

1882 *Garden* 4 Feb. 86/3 Alocasias..should be potted before growth begins. 1884 *De Candolle's Orig. Cultivated Pl.* 75 Apé, or Large-rooted Alocasia—*Alocasia macrorrhiza.*

Alogical (ēɪlɒ·dʒikăl), *a.* [f. A- 14 + LOGICAL. Cf. F. *alogique.*] Non-logical; not based upon reason or formed by an act of judgement. Hence **Alo·gically** *adv.*; **A·logica·lity.**

1694 MOTTEUX *Rabelais* v. xviii, Foreign Civilians..have uncivily drawn alogical and unreasonable Consequences from it [*tiré à consequence alogicque, c'est à dire desraisonnable*]. 1907 E. B. BAX *Roots of Reality* 19 Undoubtedly the alogical is..a primary element in all experience. *Ibid.*, In ordinary consciousness..the ultimate elements of a reality or thing are an alogical feeling or sensation, and a logical form or category. *Ibid.* 161 In every process of consciousness a contradiction lies embedded, based on the antithetic character of its two ultimate elements, the mark of which we have found to consist respectively in alogicality and logicality. *Ibid.* 173 The aim of art..is to express the unity and harmony of experience..in the world of immediate feeling—in a word, *alogically.* 1908 J. M. BALDWIN *Thought & Things* II. 386 The Logical and the A-logical. *Ibid.* 387 Does any meaning persist in being a-logical?—not to be exhaustively rendered by acts of judgment? 1925 J. E. TURNER *Theory Direct Realism* 25 It is not surprising.. that this attitude..should be regarded as instinctive non-rational, and alogical. 1928 *Musical Times* Nov. 986 It is typical of the 'alogical' thinking of most musicians that these conflicts were never regarded by them as serious.

Along, *adv.* Add: **1. b.** Some way on (in the progress of time). *U.S.*

1883 'MARK TWAIN' *Life Mississippi* xxviii, Far along in the day, we saw one steamboat. 1886 *Harper's Mag.* Oct. 808/1 He come to the house 'long in the first part of the evenin'. 1897 'MARK TWAIN' *Following Equator* xxi. 200 He was along toward fifty. 1902 *N.Y. Tribune* 26 Apr. 82 The afternoon was well along by this time.

2. b. *To be along*, to come to a place, to call.

1831 MRS. HOLLEY *Texas Lett.* (1833) 21 The captain..sent word that he would be along for us about sun-set.

Aloofly (ălū·fli), *a.* and *adv.* [f. ALOOF + -LY[1, 2].] **A.** *adj.* Characterized by aloofness; 'distant', unsympathetic. **B.** *adv.* So as to keep, or as if keeping, aloof.

1901 F. CAMPBELL *Love* 118 His cold justice and aloofly Christianity. 1921 *Chamb. Jrnl.* Mar. 203/1 A tall moon rode aloofly across the sky. 1924 *Blackw. Mag.* Oct. 514/1 This aloofly displeased person now came and spoke to us.

Alopecoid (ælopī·koid), *a.* (*sb.*) *Zool.* [f. Gr. ἀλώπηξ fox: see -OID.] Belonging to the division of the genus *Canis* of which the fox is the type; vulpine. **b.** *sb.* An animal of this division.

1880 HUXLEY in *Proc. Zool. Soc.* 6 Apr. 278 Thooids and Alopecoids, similar to those which exist at present, inhabited Europe during the Quaternary epoch. *Ibid.* 286 [see THOOID].

Alpargata (alpargā·ta). [Sp.] A sandal made of hemp.

A form in earlier use was *alparca*: see Stanford Dict. Anglicised words.

1897 GADOW *In Northern Spain* iv. 63 My companions wore *alpargatas*, namely, canvas shoes with thick soles of plaited hemp or grass. 1909 BELLOC *Pyrenees* v. 169 Remember that, in Alpargatas, you will always end the day with wet feet. 1920 *Glasgow Herald* 6 Mar. 3 Spinning, and twisting heavy jute yarns for alpargatas. 1924 *Blackw. Mag.* June 797/2 A middle-aged weather-beaten man with one foot in a black boot, and the other in an alpargata came into the saloon.

Alpeen (æ·lpīn). *Anglo-Ir.* Also **-ine.** [Ir. *ailpín.*] A cudgel, stout-headed stick.

1828 BANIM *Anglo-Irish* II. 188 The..alpeens of the primitive Irish. 1844 THACKERAY *Box of Novels* Wks. 1900 XIII. 411 Here comes Rory O'More thundering down with his big alpeen. 1847 TROLLOPE *Macdermots* xiii, Thady had an alpine in his hand, and was preparing to strike a blow at the Captain.

Alpenglow (æ·lpĕnglōᵘ). [Partial transl. of G. *alpenglühen*, less freq. *alpenglut*, f. *Alpen*, gen. pl. of *Alp* + *glühen, glut* fire, flame, glow (see GLEED *sb.*).] The rosy light of the setting or rising sun seen on high mountains.

1871 TYNDALL *Fragm. Sci.* 282 On August 23, 1869, the evening Alpenglow was very fine. 1880 *Scribner's Monthly* XX. 346/2 The whole picture stood revealed in the full flush of the alpenglow.

Alpenhorn (æ·lpĕnhɒ̄ɪn). Also **alphorn.** [Both G.] (See quot. 1879.) Also *attrib.*

1864 [see ALP[1] 4]. 1879 *Grove's Dict. Mus.* I. 56 *Alpenhorn*, or *Alphorn*, an instrument with a cupped mouthpiece, of wood and bark, used by the mountaineers in Switzerland. 1895 *Westm. Gaz.* 13 Aug. 2/3 The time-honoured Alp-horn melodies.

Alpha. Add:

3. d. *Alpha rays* or *α-rays*, the first of three types of rays emitted by radium and other radio-active substances, and consisting of positively-charged particles. Also *alpha* (or *α*) *particles*, the flight of projected particles which constitute the ray.

1904 E. RUTHERFORD *Radio-activity* 91 There are three different types of radiation emitted from radio-active bodies, which..have been termed [*ed.* 2 (1905) 109 *adds* by the writer] the *α*, *β*, and *γ* rays. *Ibid.* 105 An envelope thick enough to absorb all the *α* particles. 1913 — *Radioactive Substances* 114 [Ch.-heading] The Alpha Rays. 1925 F.

Supplement, p. 3873; Corrigenda, p. 4092; Spurious words, p. 4093; Books quoted, p. 4094

Soddy in *Evolution* x. 371 The radiant α- and β-particles expelled by the radioelements.

4. An examiner's first-class mark.

1902 S. T. in *Oxford Mag.* 22 Jan., And what I deemed an a rules (Like markets) flat as β +. 1907 A. D. Godley *Ibid.* 23 Jan., One who to all Experience gave An Alpha or Epsilon. 1923 *Times Lit. Suppl.* 25 Oct., The critic (who can hardly help feeling on this occasion like an examiner with prize competition papers before him) must give the *alpha* here to Mr. Sichel. 1929 *Ibid.* 2 May, Nor can we give an alpha mark to [etc.].

Alphabetiform (ælfǣbɪ·tifǭɹm), *a.* [See -form.] Resembling the letters of an alphabet.

1901 G. Sergi *Mediterranean Race* xiv. 296 The alphabetiform signs in megalithic inscriptions. 1908 A. J. Evans in *Anthropol. & Classics* 12 Linear signs which..present a truly alphabetiform character.

Alphabetization (æ:lfăbĕtəizē·ʃən). [f. Alphabetize *v.* + -ation.] The process of arranging words in alphabetic order; the result of this, an alphabetic series or list.

1889 H. B. Wheatley *How to catalogue* 203 In the alphabetization of a catalogue. 1902 *Academy* 19 July 76/2 The index to the completed work, covering under one alphabetization the ninth edition and the new volumes.

Alphyl (æ·lfil). *Chem.* [f. Al(kyl + Ph(en)yl.] An aliphatic alkyl radical.

1906 Sudborough *Bernthsen's Org. Chem.* 22 [see *Alkyl]. *Ibid.* 365 The alphyl radicals..The purely aliphatic alkyl radicals are termed alphyl groups, and the aromatic, aryl.

Alpine, *a.* Add: **B.** *sb.* An alpine plant, or one that grows on high ground.

1830 B. Maund *Bot. Gard.* III. No. 234 *Onosma taurica.* A plant of it may also be kept in a pot amongst the alpines. 1841 Mrs. Loudon *Ladies' Comp. Fl. Gard.* (1846) 257 Of such plants as Saxifrages or other Alpines. 1896 *Daily News* 21 May 8/4 A choice collection of alpines. 1907 R. Farrer *My Rock-garden* 26 *Arenaria gothica* justly heads the list of our alpines.

Alpinism (æ·lpainiz'm). [ad. F. *alpinisme*: see Alpine and -ism.] Climbing of the Alps or of high mountains.

1884 *Standard* 5 July, Alpenism is, in this country at least, a relaxation, not a pursuit more serious than the nature of it demands. 1888 *Ibid.* 9 July 5/4 For these members of the upper crust of Alpinism, Switzerland is ceasing to have its old attractions. 1892 *Ibid.* 24 May 5/2 The Geographical Society has..admitted 'Alpinism' to be geography.

Alright, a frequent spelling of *all right.*

1893 *Durham Univ. Jrnl.* Nov. 186, I think I shall pass alright. 1897 *Westm. Gaz.* 16 Dec. 9/3 Witness said, 'Alright, come along.' 1925 Marquess Curzon in Ronaldshay *Life* (1928) III. 378, I am sure I shall get through alright.

Alsatian. B. Add:

2. In full *Alsatian wolf-dog* (occas. *wolf-hound*), the official name adopted by the Kennel Club for the German sheepdog or shepherd dog (*deutscher schäferhund*).

The name *Alsatian* was adopted in order to avoid the associations of *German.* The dog does not belong to Alsace, nor is there a wolf strain in its composition.

1917 A. Croxton Smith in *Ladies' Field* 12 May 416/3 The French or Alsatian sheepdogs, which are now becoming familiarised to us. 1922 R. Leighton *Compl. Bk. Dog* 119 The dogs lately introduced into Great Britain as the Alsatian Wolfdog and into the United States as the German sheepdog. *Ibid.* 120 The Alsatian was known in England before the war. 1923 [see Wolf-hound]. 1926 D. Brockwell (*title*) *The Alsatian* 25 The so-called Police Dog, or German Shepherd Dog,..variously known as the Alsatian Wolf Dog, Belgian Police Dog, and French Police Dog.

Also, *adv.* Add: In phr. *also ran*, applied to horses in a race which do not get a 'place'; also *fig.* of any inferior person or thing.

1908 Mulford *Orphan* xvii. 226, I won't be among the also rans...I don't weigh very much, but I'm geared high. 1908 G. H. Lorimer *Jack Spurlock* xi. 269 Sporty old three-bottle ancestors, with a genius for throwing deuces and picking also-rans. 1921 Flora Klickmann *Trail of Ragged Robin* 73 Bella's name [in a list of scholarship winners] was not even among those who 'also ran'. 1926 *Karachi Daily Gaz.* 11 Oct. 5 Karachi Autumn Meeting. Also ran: Teddy. ..Also ran: Sir Visto. 1926 B. Pain *Ess. To-day & Yesterday* 40 He is so hard that he puts the nether millstone among the also-ran.

Alstrœmeria (ælstrōmi°·riă). [mod L., f. the name of Claude *Alstrœmer*, Swedish naturalist (1736–96).] A plant of the genus of tropical American amaryllidaceous plants so named, grown in hothouses for their flowers.

1833 *Penny Cycl.* I. 447/2 Gaily-marked flowers called Alstromerias. 1882 *Garden* 30 Sept. 292/1 Alstrœmerias are real gems, and should be in every garden.

Altar. Add:

6. Each of the steps or ledges up the sloping sides of a graving-dock. [Suggested by *altar-step*: see B. II.]

1840 *Civil Eng. & Arch. Jrnl.* III. 27/2 The object of these altars is for the convenience of placing the shores against the hull of a vessel at any height, and for resting the ends of spars for staging. 1885 Vernon-Harcourt *Harbours & Docks* I. 457 The sides of a graving dock..are constructed with steps, or altars, for receiving the timber props which support the vessel in an upright position.

B. II. altar-card, any of a set of three cards placed on the altar (one in the middle, and one at either end), containing certain portions of the Eucharistic prayers to assist the priest's memory.

1865 F. C. Lee *Direct. Angl.* Index 297 *Altar-card*, no mediaeval authority for, 12. 1884 Addis & Arnold *Cath. Dict.* s.v. *Altar*, Under the crucifix there ought to be an altar-card, with certain prayers which the priest cannot read from the Missal without inconvenience. 1905 *Ch. Times* 30 June 842/2 A 'wooden altar card' of the 18th century. It is a thick wooden panel, about 2 ft. by 18 in., painted to imitate a book, bearing the words, 'The Lord Jesus after He was betrayed,' etc., from the prayer of Consecration in the English liturgy; it stood on the altar of Redbourn Church, Herts, until about 1850.

Alter *v.* Add:

1. b. *transf.* To castrate, geld (an animal). *U.S.* and *Austral.*

1889 in *Cent. Dict.* 1895 *Austr. Pastoralist Rev.* 15 Aug. 295 For this reason bulls were rarely altered (castrated) till they were four or five years old.

Alteration. Add:

5. *attrib.*: **alteration hand,** one who alters or remakes ready-made clothes to suit customers' requirements, or repairs or renovates old or second-hand garments.

1902 *Daily Chron.* 9 Sept. 9/4 Mantles.—Wanted a good alteration hand.

Alter ego (æ·ltər e·go). [L. (Cicero); *alter* another, *ego* I. Cf. Gr. ἄλλος ἐγώ, ἕτερος ἐγώ.] A second self; an intimate and trusted friend; a confidential agent or representative.

1537 in *Lett. Suppress. Monast.* (Camden) 156 Ye muste have suche as ye may trust evyn as well as your owne self, wiche muste be unto yowe as *alter ego.* 1622 Mabbe tr. *Aleman's Guzman d'Alf.* I. ii. 24 She would tell him, that I was his *alter ego*, that he and I were one. 1650 Trapp *Comm. Gen.* ii. 18 One..that may be to him as an *Alter-ego*, a second-self. 1652 N. Culverwel *Lt. Nature* etc., *Schisme* (1654) 10 We use to call a friend *Alter ego.* 1872 Geo. Eliot *Middlem.* li (end), These people might not take that high view of you which I have always taken, as an *alter ego*, a right hand. 1886 *Law Times Rep.* LIV. 856/1 He who makes the contract agrees to the condition that it shall not be binding on the person whose *alter ego* or representative he is if he has made any misrepresentation, or has been guilty of any concealment.

fig. 1856 S. Dobell *Eng. in time of War, A Shower* 39 Methinks the fruit But alter ego of the root.

Alternate. Add: **A.** *adj.* **5. b.** *Electr.* = next, d.

1858 [see next, note]. 1878 *Design & Work* 23 Feb. 234/2 In each revolution..there will have been induced 16 alternate currents.

B. *sb.* **2.** A person who alternates with another in the occupation, or performance of the duties, of an office.

Cf. F. *alternat* (used also in Eng. context), the arrangement according to which rotation of office is maintained among persons of equal rank, etc.

1898 *Westm. Gaz.* 21 Apr. 4/3 When sitting at our Board as an alternate in London for Mr. Rhodes. 1908 *Ibid.* 21 July 5/2 In 1903 he was appointed alternate to the Chief of the Admiralty Staff.

3. One who is appointed to act in place of a delegate who is unable to be present; a substitute. *U.S.*

1888 Bryce *Amer. Commw.* II. iii. lxix. 542 To every delegate there is added a person called his 'alternate,'..to replace him in case he cannot be present..; if from any cause the delegate is absent, the alternate steps into his shoes. 1895 *Denver Times* 5 Mar. 2/7 Each precinct is entitled to delegates and alternates as follows.

Alternating, *ppl. a.* Add:

d. *Alternating current*: an electric current which reverses its direction at regular intervals. So *alternating machine.*

In Wheatstone's patent specification No. 1241, of the year 1858, the terms used are *alternate current*, *alternately inverted current.*

1872 E. Atkinson *Ganot's Elem. Treat. Physics* (new ed.) 726 The pieces *o o'* are constantly poles of alternating currents which are developed in the bobbins. 1879 Tyndall *Fragm. Sci.* (1889) II. 428 M. Serrin modified his excellent lamp with the express view of enabling it to cope with alternating currents. 1879 G. Prescott *Sp. Telephone* xiv. 491 Alternating magneto machine. 1882 J. Maier tr. *Hospitalier's Mod. Applic. Electr.* 83 Machines with alternating currents. 1884 Higgs *Magn. & Dyn. Electr. Mach.* 249 The Ferranti alternating current generator. 1888 E. Atkinson tr. *Mascart & Joubert's Electr. & Magn.* II. 289 Use of the Electrodynamometer with Alternating Currents.

Alternatively. **1.** Add: Now freq. = as or by way of an alternative.

1884 *Law Reports* 13 Q. Bench Div. 674 The defendants claimed 30,000 *l.* in respect of their counter-claim, and alternatively 30,000 *l.* damages. 1912 *Times* (weekly ed.) 4 Oct. 794 Mr. Paul Taylor imposed the full penalty of £5, or, alternatively, sentenced the prisoner to one month's imprisonment. 1921 *Act* 11 & 12 *Geo. V*, c. 13 § 1 Liable..to a fine not exceeding [25 *l.*], or alternatively or in addition thereto to be imprisoned..for a term not exceeding three months. 1927 *Sunday Express* 8 May 4 What you do..is to secure a photograph of the hall...Alternatively, you may make an exact drawing of the hall.

Alternator (ǭ·ltəɹneɪtəɹ). *Electr.* [f. Alternate *v.* + -or.] A dynamo giving an alternating current.

1893 *Leisure Hour* Aug. 718/1 Six high-pressure alternators working in parallel. 1893 G. Kapp *Dynamos*, etc. 10 The alternator, in which mechanical energy of rotation is converted into the energy of an alternating current. 1919 R. Stanley *Wireless Telegr.* (ed. 2) I. 86 An alternator is a machine in which the difference of potential, or voltage, induced has not a constant value, as in an ordinary direct current generator, but rises and falls and reverses in direction many times per second.

Altimeter. Add:

2. A form of aneroid barometer used on a flying-machine for indicating the altitude above ground. Also *attrib.*

1918 B. Cable *Air Men o' War* 179 His altimeter showed him to be a bare couple of hundred feet up. 1923 *Blackw. Mag.* July 10/1 His altimeter needle crawled down from nine to eight thousand feet.

Altitudinous (æltitiū·dinəs), *a.* [f. L. *altitūdin-*, *altitūdo* Altitude.] Used affectedly for: High, lofty.

1868 H. T. Tuckerman *Collector* 55 The confined and altitudinous cells into which so many of the complacent victims of these potentates are stowed. 1890 *Cornhill Mag.* Feb. 146 The keen air of this altitudinous city exhilarated him. 1921 *Public Opinion* 15 June 57/3 Enveloped in the mists of his altitudinous thoughts.

Alto-cumulus (æ:lto,kiū·miŭlŏs). *Meteorology.* [irreg. f. L. *altus* high + Cumulus.] A fleecy cloud-formation consisting of large greyish-white rounded clouds with shaded portions. Similarly **Alto-stra·tus,** a thick veil of grey or bluish clouds sometimes showing fibrous structure, called also *alto-cirrus*; also *alto-cloud.*

1898 *Jrnl. Sch. Geog.* (U.S.) Oct. 297 The development of alto-cumulus and heavy cumulus clouds over the land, while out to sea only small cumuli were visible. 1905 Clayden *Cloud Studies* 59 From cirro-cumulus and cirro-stratus we pass through almost insensible gradations to the denser forms classed together in the alto group. *Ibid.* 62 The simplest alto cloud is alto-stratus.

Altogether. B. *adv.* Add:

4. In all, in total amount.

1797 H. Cox *Jrnl. Resid. Burmhan Emp.* (1821) 93 We were in the palace tent altogether about an hour and a half. 1797–1811 Jane Austen *Sense & Sens.* ii, Altogether, they will have five hundred a-year amongst them. 1866 S. T. Hall *Biogr. Sk. Remark. People* (1873) 158 Debt amounting altogether to not much more, perhaps, than twenty pounds. 1929 H. W. Freeman *Joseph & His Brethren* 259 Altogether they did not spend as much on the whole meal as some of his other customers on drink alone.

5. On the whole, taking everything into account.

1815–16 Jane Austen *Persuasion* xi, Though we could have wished it different, yet altogether we did not think it fair to stand out any longer. 1886 W. R. Inge *Society in Rome* (1888) 44 Altogether, Roman slavery at this time contrasts favourably in many ways with the negro slavery of Christian nations. 1927 W. E. Collinson *Contemp. Engl.* 43 Altogether I cannot think of any modern writer who has exercised so far-reaching an influence on our every-day speech.

C. *sb.* Add:

b. *The altogether* (colloq.): the nude.

1894 Du Maurier *Trilby* I. 185, I have sat for the 'altogether' to several other people. 1908 *Daily Chron.* 16 Apr. 5/7 Mme. Sarah Bernhardt frankly says she sees nothing wrong in the 'altogether.'

attrib. 1896 *Punch* 25 Jan. 45/2 O, Röntgen..Your worse than 'altogether' state Of portraiture we bar *in toto*!

c. *pl.* A set of tights for the whole body.

1927 *Observer* 24 July 13/2 Sokolova impersonated Death in scarlet altogethers.

¶ There is a common tendency to write *altogether* where *all together* is logically preferable.

1765 Mrs. Glasse *Art of Cookery* To Rdr. (ed. 9) p. iv, Put all the ingredients together again,..strain it off well,..and give it a boil altogether. 1837 T. Bacon *First Impr. fr. Nat. in Hindustan* I. 243 Of infinitely greater importance to the creation than the sun, moon and stars altogether. 1862 Trollope *Orley F.* xxix, In that field the dogs were now running, altogether, so that a sheet might have covered them. 1880 in Grove *Dict. Mus.* II. 574/2 The pipes of the early organs are said to have sounded at first altogether.

Altricial (æltri·ʃăl), *a.* *Ornith.* [f. L. *altric-*, *altrix*, fem. of *altor* nourisher (f. *alĕre* to nourish) + -al.] Of or belonging to the division *Altrices* of birds, comprising those whose young are hatched immature and fed by the parents in the nest: opp. to Præcocial, q.v.

1872 Coues *N. Amer. Birds* 224 Pigeons are altricial, and monogamous. 1885 *Athenæum* 1 Aug. 146/2 The altricial herons. 1890 Coues *Handbk. Ornithol.* 131 Altricial birds, such as are reared by the parents in the nest. 1902 [see Præcocial].

Alula (æ·liŭlă). [mod.L. dim. of *āla* wing.]

1. *Ornith.* The winglet or bastard wing of a bird: see Bastard *a.* 5 c, Winglet.

1772 [see Bastard *a.* 5 c]. 1899 A. H. Evans *Birds* i. 9 The *Casuarii* and *Apteryges* possess an index only, which in the *Sphenisci* fuses with the pollex. The basal joint of this is the normal place of attachment of the 'bastard wing', (*alula spuria*).

2. *Ent.* A small scale-like appendage at the base of each wing of many *Diptera*, above the halteres. Also, a similar appendage beneath the elytron in some water-beetles.

1817 Kirby & Sp. *Entomol.* II. 359 (*Diptera*) Their winglets (*Alulæ*). 1877 *Encycl. Brit.* VI. 127 In certain water beetles (Dytiscidæ) a pair of *alulæ*, or winglets, are developed at the inner angle of the elytra. 1899 D. Sharp *Insects* ii. 447 (*Diptera*) On the hind margin of the wing, near the base, there is often a more or less free lobe..called the 'alula.'

Alum, *v.*, **Alumed,** *ppl. a.* Add quots.:

1877 W. Grey in Mackail *W. Morris* (1899) I. 356 Silks were alumed for to-morrow's dyeing. 1889 *Anthony's Photogr. Bull.* II. 108 The plate should be alumed before and after the operation. 1893 *Pall Mall Gaz.* 30 Jan. 7/3 These harmful alumed baking powders. 1896 *Kodak News* Aug. 29/1 During development, fixing and aluming, it showed no signs of blistering...Using an alumed fixing bath ..improved matters.

Alumino·graphy. Fuller form of Algraphy.

1911 in Webster.

Alumna (ălɒ·mnă). Pl. alumnæ. [L., fem. of *alumnus.*] A female pupil or student of a school, college, or university. (Freq. in U.S.)

1892 *Wellesley Coll. Pres. Rep.* 17 The Alumnæ have special qualifications for this form of work. 1896 *Century Mag.* LI. 798/1 The average salary of the alumna teacher would be below rather than above $1000 a year. 1910 *Catal. Vassar Coll.* 3 The editors..have tried to obtain the information necessary for a complete record of the alumnæ.

Alumnus. (Examples of U.S. use, esp. of the pl. *alumni.*)

1815 in *Proc. Mass. Hist. Soc.* (1890) Ser. II. V. 180 The oldest alumnus at Com. of whom I heard was Mr. Henry Hill (1756). 1823 J. & R. C. Morse *Pocket Gaz. U.S.* 320 The number of alumni, that is, the number who have been educated at each college since its establishment. 1843 Hopkins in B. H. Hall *College Words* (1851) 7 So far as I know, the Society of the Alumni of Williams College was the first association of the kind in this country...It was formed September 5th, 1821. 1874 *Rep. U.S. Commissioner Educ.* 1873, 181 Williams College...The trustees and alumni have built and furnished a new boarding-hall. 1890 *Harper's Mag.* Apr. 799/1 The associated alumni of a college organized into a club preserve..the old feeling of comradeship.

attrib. 1843 Hopkins in B. H. Hall *College Words* (1851) 8 Last year, for the first time, the voice of an Alumnus orator was heard at Harvard. 1892 (*title*) Alumni Weekly (New Haven, Conn.). 1895 *Century Mag.* Sept. 794/2 How often at an alumni banquet is intellectual supremacy in college life praised? 1896 *Cosmopolitan* XX. 440/2 At the alumni dinners of colleges..he found himself an honoured guest. 1906 *Springfield Weekly Republ.* 28 June 10 Tuesday was alumni day at Yale, when hundreds of old graduates ..gathered in alumni hall.

Alure. Delete † *Obs.* and add quots.:

1876 McVittie *Chr. Ch. Cath.* 63 Round north and south transepts and on to the alure of choir. 1919 *Proc. Soc. Antiq. Scot.* LIII. 38 Its base in the ditch must have been visible from the allure on the curtain.

Alveolar, *a.* Add: Pertaining to an air-cell of the lungs. Cf. *Alveolus d.

1890 Billings *Med. Dict.*, *Alveolar ducts*, tubes passing from terminal bronchioles to air-vesicles of lungs. 1927 Haldane & Huxley *Anim. Biol.* vii. 153 This, which is called the alveolar air, can be obtained at the end of a deep breath out.

Alveolus. Add:

d. An air-cell of the lungs.

1890 Billings *Med. Dict.* 1909 *Practitioner* Dec. 859 The alveoli themselves are distended with a mixture of gases.

Always, *adv.* **3.** Delete †*Obs.* or *dial.*, substitute the following def. and add quots.: In any or every circumstance, whatever the circumstances; whatever happens, whatever one may do or say; in any event, anyhow.

[*c* 1460, 1488] 1600 [see Provided 5, 5b]. 1778 Miss Burney *Evelina* xxxvii, You will always make my respects to the hospitable family to which we are so much obliged. 1848 Dickens *Dombey* viii, Never so distressed as by the company of children — Florence alone excepted, always. 1872 Geo. Eliot *Middlem.* xxiii, Fred had always (at that time) his father's pocket as a last resource. 1888 Mrs. H. Ward *R. Elsmere* xxx, Always supposing there were no risk in the matter. 1910 *Punch* 9 Feb. 104/3 It don't look as if I'm goin' to 'ave a job this arternoon. 'Owever, no matter. There's always the work'us.

Alypin (ălai·pin). *Med.* Also -ine. [f. Gr. ἄλυπος painless + -in [1].] A glyceria derivative, $C_{16}H_{26}O_2N_2HCl$, used as a local anæsthetic.

1905 *Lancet* 29 July 321/2 A new anæsthetic compound termed 'alypin.' 1908 *Practitioner* Jan. 143 A 5 per cent. solution of cocaine and alypine.

Amadis (æ·mădis). *Hist.* [Name of the hero of a romance of chivalry, and title of one of Quinault's operas (1684).] A close-fitting sleeve buttoned at the wrist, which became fashionable from the costume of Amadis as worn in the opera of the name. Also, an embroidered edging on a bodice.

1835 *Court Mag.* VI. p. xxi/1 An attempt has been made to bring up again the Amadis sleeve. 1898 Lady Mary Loyd tr. *Octave Uzanne's Fashion in Paris* ii. 38 Their bodices..were known as 'canezous', a scalloped embroidery called 'amadis' was carried round the edges and wrists.

Amalgamist (ămæ·lgămist). [f. Amalgam *sb.* + -ist.] One who amalgamates ores, or makes amalgams.

1884 *L. Le C. Hamilton's Mex. Handbk.* 65 A most famous mining expert, chemist, and amalgamist.

Amatol (æ·mătǫl). [irreg. f. Am(monium + -*tol* in *trinitrotoluene.*] A high explosive consisting of a mixture of trinitrotoluene (T.N.T.) and ammonium nitrate.

1918 Colver *High Explosives* 252 In England these mixtures [trinitrotoluene and ammonium nitrate] are designated amatol. 1922 H. F. Moulton *Life of Ld. Moulton* vii. 191 Finally in February 1915 Lord Kitchener..gave his casting vote on the side of big production, and A. 6 were told that they might proceed with the production of amatol.

Amatorio (æmătō°·rio). *Ceramics.* [It., ad. L. *amātōrius* Amatory.] A decorated piece intended as a love gift; *spec.* a piece of majolica bearing the portrait of a lady with a complimentary inscription. 1889 in *Cent. Dict.*

Amatorious, *a.* Delete † *Obs.* and add to def.: Inclined to love, amorous. Hence **Amato·riousness.**

1746 Francis tr. *Horace, Ep.* i. iii. 31 Sure to gain, for amatorious Lays, The Wreaths of Ivy, with unenvied Praise. 1887 *Longman's Mag.* Nov. 108 A fine balance between domestic and 'amatorious' interest on one hand, and romance on the other. 1893 *National Observer* 1 Apr. 489/1 Girls and boys..jostle and jest at one another with a certain violence of amatoriousness. *Ibid.* 23 Sept. 482/1 The divagations of amatorious poets with fragile women. 1901 Henley in *Poetry R. Burns* IV. 249 It was natural and honourable in a young man of this lusty and amatorious habit to look round for a wife.

Amazonism (æ·măzǫniz'm). [f. Amazon + -ism.] Amazonian character or condition; a condition in which women have the supremacy. Also **Amazo·nianism.**

1874 M. Collins *Transmigr.* II. xv. 247 A world in which women were analytical..would result in absolute Amazonism. 1903 L. F. Ward *Pure Sociol.* xiv. 338 It might be supposed that woman would prove the dominant sex in primitive hordes...The..most striking form of evidence pointing this way consists in a class of facts that may be roughly grouped under the general head of *amazonism.* 1909 W. J. Locke *Septimus* ii, She had done with men... In that she prided herself on her Amazonianism.

Amban (æ·mbæn). [Manchu, lit. minister.] A Chinese resident official in Tibet, representing the suzerainty of China.

1882 *Encycl. Brit.* XIV. 8/1 In the time of the Chinese, before Yakub Beg's sway, Yangi Shahr..was the residence of the *amban* or governor. 1923 *Glasgow Herald* 24 Apr. 4 The travellers were entertained..by an Amban who spoke excellent Chinese.

Ambary (æmbæ·ri). Also -i. [Urdu *ambārā*, *ambārī.*] The fibre of an Indian plant, *Hibiscus cannabinus*, used for making ropes and coarse cloth; Brown Indian Hemp (also *ambary hemp*); the plant itself.

1887 Moloney *Forestry W. Afr.* 282 The plant is largely grown in Western India, both as a pot-herb and for its fibre, known as 'Ambari', which much resembles jute.

Ambatch (æ·mbætʃ). Also **ambach, ambash.** [app. native name.] A leguminous tree or shrub, *Herminiera* (or *Æschynomene*) *Elaphroxylon*, of tropical Africa, with very light spongy wood; also called *pith-tree.*

1884 J. Colborne *With Hicks Pasha in Soudan* 100 Here, too, we came across the famous ambatch.., one of the most extraordinary growths of African vegetation. 1887 Ambash [see *pith-tree*, Pith *sb.* 8]. 1889 H. M. Stanley in *Daily News* 4 Dec. 3/1 A..sand bank overgrown with sedge and ambatch.

A·mber-fish. [Amber *sb.*[1]] A fish of the genus *Seriola*, found in warm parts of the Atlantic; several species are esteemed as food, e.g. *S. dumerili* and *S. lalandi*, also called **A·mberjack.**

1674 Josselyn *Two Voy. New Eng.* 107 The Sea-bream, Dorado, or Amber-fish, they follow ships..and are good meat. 1706 Phillips (ed. Kersey), *Dorado*..a Fish otherwise call'd the Sea-bream; or Amber-fish, the Head of which in the Water is Green, and the Body as Yellow as Gold. 1799 A. Ellicott in *Life & Lett.* (1908) 186 A great abundance and variety of fish..such as..Amber-fish. 1888 Goode *Amer. Fishes* 232 The Amber-fish, *Seriola carolinensis*, is quite common off the West Florida coast. 1897 *Outing* (U.S.) XXIX. 330/2 Not inferior to the kingfish for sport is the amber fish, or 'amberjack'.

Amberiferous (æmbəri·fĕrəs), *a.* [f. Amber *sb.*[1] + -(i)ferous.] Producing amber.

1885 *Buck's Handbk. Med. Sci.* I. 127/1 The west coast of Denmark..is included in this amberiferous region.

Amberite (æ·mbərait). [f. Amber *sb.*[1] + -ite[1] 4.] An explosive composed chiefly of nitro-glycerine and soluble gun-cotton.

1893 *Daily Chron.* 6 Sept. 2/7 That a smokeless powder such as amberite had been used in the cartridge. 1915 A. Marshall *Explosives* 251 The older powders, Schultze and Amberite, are 42-grain powders, that is to say the charge required for an ordinary 12-bore cartridge is 42 grains.

Amberous (æ·mbərəs), *a.* [f. Amber *sb.*[1] + -ous.] Resembling amber; amber-coloured.

1890 *Century Mag.* Aug. 500 So soft, so warm, the water lay, Its chambers paved with amberous lights.

Ambi- (æmbi), repr. L. *ambi-* both, on both sides (*ambo* both) in various (chiefly scientific) terms (see words in Ambi- in Dict.). **Ambiciliate** (-si·liĕt), *a.* *Ichth.*, having the scales on both sides of the body minutely toothed along the edges; **Ambicolorate** (-kɒ·lŏrĕt,-kʊ·l-), *a.* *Ichth.*, applied to flat-fishes abnormally coloured on both sides instead of having the under side white; so **Ambicolora·tion**; **Ambivalent** (æmbi·vălĕnt), *a.* [after *equivalent*] having either, or both, of two contrary values or qualities.

1894 *Proc. Zool. Soc.* 439 *Ambicolorate fish appear to be always what one may call *ambiciliate' also. *Ibid.* 435 Why Cyclopean examples should be ambicolorate. *Ibid.* 432 On an Adult Specimen of the Common Sole..with Symmetrical Eyes, with a Discussion of its bearing on *Ambicoloration. 1916 tr. *C. G. Jung's Papers on Analytical Psychol.* vi. 200 [Bleuler] presents us with a new psychological conception.. viz. the concept of *ambivalency and of *ambitendency, thus formulating the psychological axiom that every tendency is balanced by its opposite tendency. 1921 Blanchard *Adolescent Girl* v. 125 A second case where the falsehoods were.. the result of *ambivalent desire for and fear of the erotic life.

Ambience (æ·mbiĕns). [f. Ambient: see -ence.] Environment, surrounding. In the Fr. form **ambiance** (ańbiańs) used in *Art* for the arrangement of accessories to support the main effect of a piece.

1902 W. Watson *Ode on Coronation of King Edward VII* 5 Slowly in the ambience of this crown Have many crowns been gathered. 1927 *Observer* 2 Oct. 22/3 It had lost..much of the ambience, sparkle, and caricature which makes the 'Pickwick Papers' what they are.

Ambiens (æ·mbienz). *Ornith.* [pr. pple. of L. *ambire* to go round, surround, f. *ambi-* around + *ire* to go.] A muscle in the thigh of certain birds, so called from the way in which it winds in passing from the hip to the foot.

1873 A. H. Garrod in *Proc. Zool. Soc.* 630 The ambiens and the accessory femoro-caudal are absent. 1884 Coues *N. Amer. Birds* 193 The ambiens arises from the pelvis about the acetabulum, and passes along the inner side of the thigh.

Ambitty (æmbi·ti). *Glass-making.* Also **ambitti, ambetty.** [app. ad. F. *ambité*, of obscure origin.] Applied to glass which becomes devitrified while it is being worked.

1883 H. J. Powell, etc. *Glass-Making* 104 Glass made with sulphate of soda is less liable to devitrify or as it is termed, become 'ambitty' in the pot during the time of working. 1885 Miller *Glass-painting* 51 A beautiful make of glass is anbetti [*sic*]. 1885 Spon *Mechanic's Own Book* 630 'Ambilti' [*sic*] (single and double) is a sheet glass, originally of Italian manufacture. 1902 Suffling *Art of Glass Painting* 63 Ambetty sheet.

Amboceptor (æmbǫse·ptǫɹ). *Biol. Chem.* [f. L. *ambo* both + (Re)ceptor.] In Ehrlich's theory of immunization, a receptor, esp. one set free as a *haptine* or *adaptation-product*, having two combining or *haptophoric* groups of atoms, by which it unites both with the immunizing body and with the *complement* (see these terms in Suppl.). Opp. to *Uniceptor.

1902 *Brit. Med. Jrnl.* 12 Apr. 920 There is no amboceptor as such, but the body consists of a zymophoric group. 1904 [see Thermolabile].

Ambroid (æ·mbroid). [f. Amber *sb.*[1] + -oid.] Trade name for a substance made by moulding pieces of amber with heat and pressure.

1899 *Sci. Amer.* 16 Sept. 188/2 The inferior pieces of amber are made into what is called ambroid. 1913 *Daily Mail* 4 Feb. 5/6 Charged..with keeping the trimmings and selling them to be made into pressed amber, known in the trade as 'ambroid'.

Ambrosia. Add:

9. A fungous substance which forms the food of certain N. American wood-boring beetles of various species (hence called **ambrosia beetles**).

1896 *Year-bk. U.S. Dept. Agr.* 421 Their food consists not of wood, but of a substance to which the name ambrosia has been given, and which is a coating formed by certain minute fungi and propagated on the walls of their galleries by the beetles.

Ambroty·pic, *a.* [f. Ambrotype *sb.*] Suggestive after the manner of an ambrotype.

1861 *Trans. Ill. Agric. Soc.* IV. 264, I give a voice to a few thoughts ambrotypic of what the working man is, and what he ought to be.

Ambulance. Add:

2. *attrib.* in **ambulance chaser** (U.S. slang), a lawyer who makes a business of raising actions for personal injuries.

1904 *Philad. Public Ledger* 10 June 8 The body of the unfortunate child had hardly been brought to the house before the 'ambulance chasers', as lawyers of this class are called, began to arrive.

3. A touring caravan or similar vehicle. *U.S.*

1868 *Life among Mormons* 67 The husband of one of them rushed into the room where I was, to inquire about his wife, for their ambulance had not arrived. 1875 *Fur, Fin & Feather* 105 If he wishes, he can procure..an ambulance fitted up with the necessary toilet arrangements. 1879 Tourgee *Fool's Err.* ix. 40 So he got an ambulance and we started. 1899 T. Hall *Tales* 95 Once in a while she caught sight of a muffled figure in an ambulance that stopped for water for its thirsty mules.

Ambulant, *a.* Add:

3. *Path.* and *Med.* **a.** Of a disease: Shifting from one part of the body to another: = Wandering *ppl. a.* 2 g. **b.** Of a disease: Allowing the patient to walk about, not confining him to bed; also of medical treatment in which the patient is allowed or ordered to walk about.

1882 tr. *von Ziemssen's Cycl. Med.* Suppl. 682 Ambulant œdema. 1913 Dorland *Med. Dict.*, *Ambulant, Ambulatory*...Walking or able to walk; not confining the patient to bed. 1927 *Daily Tel.* 31 May 15/5 Additional provision for what was called ambulant treatment of those suffering from lupus.

Ambulatory, *a.* Add:

5. *Path.* = prec.

1857 Dunglison *Med. Lex.* s.v., A morbid affection is said to be 'ambulatory'..when it skips from one part to another. 1883 Quain *Dict. Med.* 38 *Ambulatory*, a term given to typhoid fever, showing that the patient is able to walk about during the attack. 1903 *Westm. Gaz.* 21 Feb. 6/1 That the cause of death was ambulatory typhoid.

Ambusher (æ·mbuʃəɹ). [f. Ambush *v.* + -er[1].] One who makes an ambush.

1895 *Funk's Stand. Dict.* 1920 *Glasgow Herald* 20 Nov. 7 The ambushers, he said, were all dressed in khaki.

Amen, *int.* Add: **2. b.** *attrib.* **amen corner, amen seat,** that part of a meeting-house occupied by persons who assist the preacher with occasional and irregular responses. *U.S.*

1868 *All Yr. Round* 31 Oct. 490/1 Sunday found them, judge and lawyers, seated in the 'amen corner'. 1877 Harberton *Jericho Road* xiv. 128 In an 'amen' seat sat an old half-breed. 1904 Harben *Georgians* vii. 67 [They] were in their places in the 'amen corner', at the right of the crude pulpit.

transf. 1884 *Congress. Rec.* 24 Apr. 3207/1 When commiserated upon the fact that he was compelled to go to what is commonly known here as the amen corner, [he] frankly said that any seat in the Senate was better than none. 1894 *Ibid.* Jan. 1502 2 One of those saintly Republican monopolists who sit in the 'Amen corner' of protected privilege.

Amenability. **1.** (Earlier U.S. example.)

1789 J. Madison *Writ.* (1904) V. 373 A unity in each has been resolved on, and an amenability to the President alone, as well as to the Senate by way of impeachment.

Amendatory, *a.* (Earlier examples.)

1803 *Deb. Congress* 26 Feb. (1851) 603 Mr. Bayard..reported an amendatory bill, which was read twice. 1830 L. Lincoln *Mass. Legisl.* 29 May 382.

Amenity. **1. a.** Add: In freq. mod. use in pl., with reference to the pleasurable, as distinguished from the utilitarian, features of an estate. Also *attrib.* as in *amenity woodland.*

[1926 N. P. Lewis *Planning Mod. City* 327 The object aimed at is the securing of proper sanitation, amenity and convenience.] 1928 *Britain's Industr. Future* (*Liberal Ind. Inquiry*) iv. xxiv. § 9. 336 Amenity woodland definitely uneconomic. 1929 *Oxford Times* 8 Feb. 13/4 The payment of £88 for the purchase of the land; the payment of £250 as compensation for the loss of amenities and disturbance of existing garden and grounds.

Ament[2] (ǟme·nt). [ad. L. *āment-*, *āmens*, after *Amentia.] A person congenitally deficient in mind or intellect; a born idiot or imbecile.

1897 *Lippincott's Med. Dict.*, *Ament*, a person affected with amentia; an idiot. 1912 *Ch. Q. Rev.* LXXIII. 326 We will classify them all (idiots, imbeciles, or feeble-minded) under the name 'Ament', meaning people without mind in contrast to the class of Dement, which we will assume to mean all those who have been sane, but have lost their mind.

Amentia (ǟme·nʃiă). [L., f. *āmens*, f. *ā* = *ab* + *mens* Mind *sb.*] Total lack of intelligence, imbecility.

1801 *Monthly Mag.* Aug. 256/2 That state of intellectual derangement which Nosologists have distinguished by the term Amentia. 1887 *Buck's Handbk. Med. Sci.* IV. 88/2 The word [*sc.* idiocy] was used until Esquirol first clearly applied it..in connection with both amentia and the terminal stage of chronic insanity.

American, *a.* Add:

A. 2. c. *U.S. spec.* (See quot. *a* 1861.)

1846 E. Bryant *What I saw in Cal.* iv. (1849) 37 Such [Indians] as rode ponies were desirous of swapping them for the American horses of the emigrants. *a* 1861 Winthrop *John Brent* ii. (1862) 14 He was an American horse,—so they distinguish in California one brought from the old States. 1878 J. H. Beadle *Western Wilds* xvi. 253, I rode a good-sized American horse.

3. **American Beauty (rose),** a variety of cultivated rose; **American cloth,** (*a*) = *Americani, (*b*) an enamelled oilcloth used chiefly for covering articles, such as tables, chairs; **American ivy,** the Virginia creeper; **American leather,** also **American leather cloth,** an early name for a kind of American cloth imitating leather; **American plan,** at hotels, payment for board by time instead of by separate items (contrasted with *European plan*); **American sheeting,** = *Americani.

1904 *N. Y. Even. Post* 29 Sept. 1 Carrying an armful of *American Beauties. 1904 *N. Y. Times* 24 Nov. 14 A box of thirty-nine American Beauty roses. 1860 J. A. Grant in *Blackw. Mag.* (1865) XCVII. 107 The body sewed up in an *American cloth. 1889 Sir J. C. Willoughby *East Africa & its Big Game* App. ii. *Eng.-Swaheli Vocab.*, American cloth, *Amerikano.* 1896 C. James *Yoke of Freedom* 85 Not a single ring of stickiness was to be found upon the American-cloth table cover. 1896 H. G. Wells *Wheels of Chance* iv, A neat packet of American cloth behind the saddle contained his change of raiment. 1859 Bartlett *Dict. Amer.* (ed. 2) 497 *Virginia Creeper*,..By some it is called Woodbine, and by others *American Ivy. 1874 Knight *Dict. Mech.*, *American leather, an enameled cloth imitating leather. 1893 [see Leather *sb.* 1]. 1865 *House of Lords Cases* XI. 523 Leather Cloth Co. v. *American Leather Cloth Co. 1863 in Petherick *Trav. Central Africa* (1869) II. 179, I have already taken from your stores..96 yards of *American sheeting.

B. 4. *pl.* Short for *American stocks* or *shares.*

1886 *Times Reg. Events in* 1885 p. cliii, People..who..had come to believe that 'Americans' would never advance any more. 1897 *Daily News* 7 Sept. 7/1 A further rise in Americans. 1905 *Daily Report* 22 Mar. 1/2 Yankees. As predicted yesterday, Americans have quickly recovered their reaction.

5. American English; the form of English spoken in the United States.

1837 *Southern Lit. Messenger* III. 11 Insomuch that I speak *American* with the *brogue* of one or the other of them in spite of my teeth. 1844 'Jon. Slick' *High Life N.Y.* I. 103 She didn't speak rale American. 1869 Gillmore *Accessible Field Sports N. Amer.* 19 But it was evident I was not boss. [*Note*] American for 'master'. 1871 Schele de Vere *Americanisms* 4 Hence we still speak English, but we talk American. 1903 *Daily Chron.* 26 Mar. 3/2 The crisp American it is written in. 1908 *Ibid.* 10 June 6/7 English spoken; American understood. 1920 *Contemp. Rev.* Sept. 342, I was an unknown foreigner speaking broken American with a distinctly alien accent.

Hence (in sense A. 2 or B. 2) **Americana** (-ā·nă, -ǟ·nă) *sb. pl.* [see Ana B. 2]; **Americanese** (-ī·z) = American B. 5 (see above); **Ame·ricaness,** an American woman; **Americanitis** (-ai·tis) [see -itis], some affection characteristically American (esp. *fig.* overweening or blatant national conceit in Americans) or (*loosely*) related in some way to what is American (*e.g.* morbid fear of American competition or rivalry); **Ame·ricanly** *adv.*, in an American manner.

1890 Tregaskis *Catalogue* Sept. 3/1 America and *Americana. 1926 *Chamb. Jrnl.* Aug. 513/1 The trade in Americana is no common huckstering of second-hand volumes. 1882 Sala *Amer. Revis.* (1885) 405 A 'bull-fiddle'..*Americanese for a violoncello. 1907 *Daily Chron.* 23 Feb. 4/7 Poor Willis is almost forgotten now...He was one of the founders of 'Americanese'. 1838 Cooper *Home as Found* I. vi. 93 Every true American and *Americaness was expected to be at his or her post. 1903 Ld. R. Gower *Rec. & Remin.* 239 Mr. Washburn and his 'lady', a pert little Americaness. 1891 Annie P. Call *Power through Repose* ii. 13 Extreme nervous tension seems to be so peculiarly American, that a German physician coming to this country to practise became puzzled by the variety of nervous disorders he was called upon to help, and finally announced his discovery of a new disease which he chose to call '*Americanitis'. 1901 *Daily Chron.* 18 Oct. 4/6 We are not among those who are attacked by the disease of Americanitis in its extreme form. 1904 G. S. Hall *Adolescence* II. 411 Less perfervid Americanitis at games and in celebrating victories. 1886 Howells in *Harper's Mag.* Jan. 325/1 For our novelists to try to write *Americanly, from any motive, would be a dismal error. 1892 *Illustr. Lond. News* Summer No. 3 Horribly, incredibly, Americanly rich. 1906 *Daily Chron.* 13 Apr. 4/7 Rather than 'expect' in this sense, let us Americanly 'calculate', or even 'guess'.

Americani (ămerikā·nī). Also **Mer(c)kani.** [Swahili; also *Amerikano* (Madan, Steere), *Marekani* (Sacleux).] A kind of cotton cloth.

1864 Speke *Jrnl. Discov. Source Nile* App. B. 617 Merikani or American sheeting. 1872 Burton *Zanzibar* II. App. i. 419 The Γakah or piece..of 'Merkani American domestics is generally of 30 yards. 1894 Bell tr. *L. von Höhnel's Discov. Lakes Rudolf & Stefanie* I. 12, 600 pieces (*djora*) of white cotton goods (Merekani).

1893 *Geogr. Jrnl.* Mar. 221 Their dress is a white cloth.. of broad Americani. 1900 Grogan & Sharp *From the Cape to Cairo* 182 'Amerikani'. [*Note*] White trade cloth. 1910 Ethel Younghusband *Glimpses E. Africa & Zanzibar* 34 Boys wear a cotton singlet, a loin cloth of 'Amerikani'. 1921 *Blackw. Mag.* Jan. 118/1 A venerable savage, with a yard of tattered and dirty americani round his loins. 1925 *Chamb. Jrnl.* Apr. 352/1 The rough *Americani* curtain.

Americanism. **1.** (Earlier U.S. example.)

1797 Jefferson *Let.* 24 June, Wks. 1854 IV. 190 The dictates of reason and pure Americanism.

3. (Orig. reference for first quot.)

1781 Witherspoon in *Pennsylvania Jrnl.* No. 1391. 1/2 [Add to quot.] The word Americanism, which I have coined for the purpose, is exactly similar in its formation and signification to the word Scotticism.

Americanize, *v.* **2.** Add earlier quots.:

1797 (Oct. 27) J. Jay *Corr. & Public Papers* (1893) IV. 232, I wish to see our people more *Americanized*, if I may use that expression; until we feel and act as an independent nation. 1803 W. O. Pughe *Cambrian Biog.* 140 Him they found perfectly Americanized: before any answer was sent he must first know who would pay him for his trouble. 1824 *Blackw. Mag.* XVI. 595 His wish is to see Greece 'not Anglicized, but Americanized'.

Amerind (æ·mĕrind), **Amerindian** (æmĕri·ndiăn), *sbs.* and *adjs.*, contraction for *American Indian* (see American B. 1, Indian A. 2, B. 2).

1897–8 *Ann. Rep. Bur. Amer. Ethnol.* p. xlviii, The tribal fraternities of the Amerinds. *Ibid.* 835 The four worlds of widespread Amerindian mythology. 1900 Dellenbaugh *N.-Americans Yest.* 247 The communal principle of living had much to do almost everywhere with the size and character of the Amerind houses. 1902 *Man* II. 101 A group of Amerind tribes are known as Algonquians. 1921 *Edin. Rev.* Apr. 268 Crosses between Amerindians..and Europeans.

Ameristic (æmĕri·stik), *a.* *Biol.* [f. Gr. ἀ-priv. + μεριστός divided, divisible (f. μερίζειν to divide, f. μέρος part) + -ic.] Unsegmented.

1881 E. R. Lankester in *Encycl. Brit.* XII. 555/1 In leeches as compared with the ameristic flukes.

Amharic (æmhæ·rik), *a.* and *sb.* [f. *Amhara*, name of a province of Abyssinia.] The name of the official and court language of Abyssinia.

1813 *Q. Rev.* Oct. 258. 1907 *Camb. Univ. Press Bull.* Jan. 27 Every Amharic word is phonetically expressed in Roman letters as well as given in the Amharic character. 1923 *Blackw. Mag.* Aug. 245/2 Ancient Ge'z, the language of the Abyssinian Church and parent of the modern Amharic.

Amidol (æ·midǫl). [f. Amide + -ol.] Trade-name for a salt of diamidophenol, used as a developer in photography.

1894 *Brit. Jrnl. Photogr. Alm.* 830 Diamidophenol or amidol, both as the chlorhydrate and the sulphate, was originally prepared by T. Gauche in 1869.

Amil, variant and more modern form of Aumil.

1898 *Daily News* 15 Aug. 6/2 They kept the amils (native revenue officials) at bay. 1921 *Times Lit. Suppl.* 10 Feb. 84/4 The *amil* was exacting..66 per cent. more than the authorized revenue.

Amino- (æ·mino), *Chem.*; combining form of Amine, used *spec.* in names of compounds containing the group NH_2 combined with a non-acid radical (thus distinguished from Amido-, which in strict use denotes those with an acid radical).

1887 A. M. Brown *Anim. Alkaloids* 85 The modes of syntheses of glycocolle or aminacetic acid and cyanide. 1922 *Times Lit. Suppl.* 27 Apr. 279/1 A protein diet containing the amino-acid—lysine.

Aminol (æ·minǫl). [f. Amine + -ol.] A colourless antiseptic liquid derived from the methylamine of herring-brine.

1893 *Westm. Gaz.* May 3/2 Aminol is the new disinfectant.

Amitosis (æmitō°·sis). *Biol.* [mod.L., f. Gr. ἀ- privative + Mitosis.] Direct division of a nucleus or cell, without mitosis. So **Amitotic** (-ɒ·tik) *a.*, not exhibiting mitosis; whence **Amito·tically** *adv.*

1888 Rolleston & Jackson *Anim. Life* Introd. p. xxii, The..division of the nucleus..may be direct or amitotic... Or it may be indirect or mitotic. 1894 *Nat. Science* June 418 Amitosis is of frequent occurrence in the cells of pathological growths of all kinds. *Ibid.*, The sperm-mother-cells divide amitotically.

Ammonal (æ·mǒnæl). [f. Ammon(ium + Al(uminium.] A high explosive composed of 3 parts of ammonium nitrate with 1 part of aluminium.

1903 *Westm. Gaz.* 30 Oct. 11/1 Ammonal is being manufactured at the works of Messrs. G. and J. Roth at Felixdorf, Austria.

Ammonoid (æ·mǒnoid). [f. mod.L. *Ammonoidea*, f. *Ammonites* Ammonite: see -oid.] A fossil cephalopod of the order *Ammonoidea*, comprising the ammonites and their allies.

1889 Nicholson & Lydekker *Palæont.* (ed. 3) I. 849 The septal 'necks' of the Ammonoids are variable in their development. 1912 *Brit. Museum Return* 169 The collection of Austrian Triassic Ammonoids.

Amœbic (ămī·bik), *a.* [f. Amœba + -ic.] Pertaining to, of the nature of, or caused by an amœba.

1892 Osler *Pract. Med.* 132 Amœbic Dysentery. 1902 *Encycl. Brit.* XXXI. 536 A form [of dysentery] has been described which is said to be due to an animal parasite—amœbic dysentery or amœbic enteritis.

Amole (amō°·le). [Mexican Sp.] The root or bulb of any one of several plants found in Mexico and California, used as a detersive; also any of such plants, esp. *Chlorogalum pomeridianum*, also called *soap-plant* (see Soap *sb.* 6 b).

1884 *Encycl. Brit.* XVII. 401/2 *Yucca filamentosa*, commonly called amole or soap-weed. 1927 *Chamb. Jrnl.* 227/1 Soap grows for him..in the bulbs of the curious Amole.

Amontillado (amɒntil^yā·do). [Sp.; f. *Montilla*, a town in Spain + -*ado* -ate[2].] Formerly, a wine of the sherry type produced in Montilla; now, a matured sherry in which the 'flor' has developed.

1825 Henderson in *Q. Jrnl. Sci.* XVIII. 130 The driest species of Sherry is the Amontillado. 1833 C. Redding *Mod. Wines* 190. *a* 1845 Poe *Cask Amont.* Wks. 1864 I. 347, I was silly enough to pay the full Amontillado price without consulting you in the matter. 1886 Ruskin *Præterita* II. ix. 325 A certain quantity of the drier Amontillado, from the hill districts of Montilla.

b. *attrib.* in fig. sense.

1862 Thackeray *Philip* xvii, 'By the housekeeper, do you mean Mrs. Baynes?' I ask, in my *amontillado* manner. 1921 *Spectator* 22 Jan. 109/1 We will take as our next example of what we might call Mr. Max Beerbohm's Amontillado style 'Hosts and Guests'.

Amoral, *a.* Delete *nonce-wd.* and add quots. below. So **Amo·ralism, Amo·ralist, Amora·lity.**

1892 S. Weir Mitchell in *Century Mag.* July 343/2 You are amoral, not immoral. 1910 *Westm. Gaz.* 19 Mar. 3/2 He argued..that Nature was a-moral, ethically neutral. 1913 Kipling *A Diversity of Creatures* (1917) 176 He's the Absolutely Amoral Soul. I've never met one yet. 1920 *Glasgow Herald* 27 Nov. 6 Dada..leads to amoralism. 1923 *Observer* 10 June 8/3 Stupidity, brutality, and general amorality. 1926 *British Weekly* 16 Sept. 487/4 That great sceptic and amoralist [Anatole France]. 1927 Rachel A. Taylor *Leonardo the Florentine* II. ii. 103 The bright amoral virtue of courage.

Amorce (ǟmǭ·ɹs). ? *Obs.* [ad. F. *amorce* (OF. *amorse*) bait, lure, priming, f. OF. *amordre*, f. *à* + *mordre* to bite.] A charge of fine-grained powder for priming a small fire-arm; a cap for a toy pistol.

1802 C. James *Milit. Dict.*, *Amorce*, an old military word for fine-grained powder, such as is sometimes used for the priming of great guns, mortars or howitzers; as also for small-arms, on account of its rapid inflammation. A port fire, or quick match. 1883 *B'ham Weekly Post* 15 Dec. 7/5 Summoned for having in his possession a small quantity of manufactured amorces, he not having a license for the sale of explosives..These toy pistol caps..were made of a very dangerous explosive. 1889 *Standard* 2 Dec. 4/8 To restrain Mr. Cadwell from making amorces for toy pistols.

Amorism (æ·mŏriz'm). [f. as Amorist + -ism.] The disposition or practice of amorists; amorous sentiment or intrigue.

1897 *Star* 30 Mar. 1/7 We were in the land of romantic amorism. 1903 *Athenæum* 17 Jan. 77/1 Half old-world Spanish, half topsy-turvy Oriental in its fatalism and passionate amorism.

Amorist. Add:

2. One who treats of love; a writer of amatory literature. Also *attrib.*

1824 *Blackw. Mag.* XVI. 191 Our most eminent amorist.. Tom Moore. 1882 Palgrave in Grosart *Spenser's Wks.* IV. p. lx, Amourist literature. 1905 *Athenæum* 1 Apr. 390/3 The poet..is imagined as a mild and amiable amorist. 1909 Jusserand *Lit. Hist. Eng.* III. 468 The..amourist writers of Elizabethan times.

Amp., abbreviation of Ampère.

1907 *Install. News* July 8/2 Suction gas plant and 200 amp. dynamo...A private plant supplying 100 amps.

Ampelopsis (æmpĕlɒ·psis). *Bot.* [mod.L., f. Gr. ἄμπελος vine + ὄψις appearance.] A genus of climbing plants allied to the vine; a plant of this genus, as the various species of Virginian Creeper.

1842 *Florist's Jrnl.* (1846) III. 148 The honeysuckle, the jasmine, the ampelopsis,..may be made to contribute largely to the general appearance of a garden. 1900 *Echo* 25 Sept. 1/3 The crimsoning leafage of ampelopsis.

Amperage (æmpē°·rĕdʒ, æ·mpĕrĕdʒ). *Electr.* [f. Ampere + -age, after *voltage.*] The strength of an electric current expressed in amperes; also *fig.*

1894 *Work* 17 Mar. 139/2 The longer the length of wire you use on any armature, the higher will be the voltage, but the lower the ampèrage. 1924 Megroz *Walter de la Mare* 105 The living poet's 'Sunk Lyonnesse' in which each word has a far higher amperage of power.

Amperian (æmpē°·riăn), *a.* Pertaining to the French physicist André Marie *Ampère* or his theory of molecular currents.

1872 E. Atkinson *Ganot's Elem. Treat. Physics* (new ed.) 724 The Ampèrian currents seem to turn like the hands of a watch. 1879 G. Prescott *Sp. Telephone* xiv. 496 The Amperian currents in the inducing magnet.

Amphi- (æ·mfi). Add:

Amphidiarthrosis (æ:mfidai,aɹþrōu·sis) *Anat.*, a form of articulation (see quots.); **Amphikaryotic** (-kæriɒ·tik), *a.* *Biol.* [Gr. κάρυον nut, kernel], having both a male and a female nucleus; **Amphimixis** (æmfimi·ksis) *Biol.* [mod.L. (Weismann, 1891), f. Gr. μίξις mingling: cf. ἀμφιμιγνύναι to mix up thoroughly] (see quot. 1893); **A·mphiodont** (-ǫdɒnt), *a.* *Entom.* [Gr. ὀδούς, ὀδοντ- tooth], applied to a form of the mandibles in stag-beetles intermediate between the priodont and teleodont; **Amphipneustic** (-pniū·stik), *a.* *Zool.* [f. as Amphipneust + -ic], having breathing-pores at both ends of the body, as certain dipterous larvæ; **A:mphiprosty·lar,** *a.* = Amphiprostyle *a.*; **Amphirhine** (æ·mfirain), *a.* *Zool.* [ad. mod.L. *Amphirhinus*, neut. pl. *Amphirhina*, f. Gr. ῥίν nose], belonging to the *Amphirhina*, a division (comprising the large majority) of skulled vertebrates, having the nasal orifice double; two-nostriled; opp. to Monorhine; **Amphithect** (-þekt), *a.* *Morphol.* [ad. Gr. ἀμφιθηκτός sharpened on both sides, two-edged], applied to an irregular or unequal-sided polygon, or to a pyramid having such a polygon for base; **Amphitrochal** (æmfi·trǒkăl), *a.* *Zool.* [Gr. τροχός wheel], having two rows of cilia, ventral and dorsal, as the larvæ of certain annelids.

1848 Dunglison *Med. Lex.* (ed. 7), *Amphidiarthrosis*, a name given by Winslow to the temporo-maxillary articulation, because, according to that anatomist, it partakes both of ginglymus and arthrodia. 1890 Billings *Med. Dict.*, *Amphidiarthrosis*, joint having characteristics of two classes, both hinge and gliding, as articulation of lower jaw. 1909 J. W. Jenkinson *Experim. Embryol.* 267 One blastomere has a male and a female nucleus, and therefore 2*n* chromosomes (*amphikaryotic), while the other has only a female (thelykaryotic). 1893 tr. *Weismann's Germ-Plasm* Introd. 20 *Amphimixis..consists in the mingling of two individuals or of their germs, and owing to its constant connection with reproduction in multicellular organisms it is usually spoken of as 'sexual reproduction'...Amongst unicellular organisms..amphimixis is widely spread..in the form of conjugation. 1909 Sorley *Interpr. Evolution* 23 It throws off certain cells which have the power of reproducing organisms like itself—this result being dependent in all the higher organisms upon amphimixis. 1883 *Amphiodont [see Priodont]. 1891 tr. *Lang's Comp. Anat.* I. 482 This *amphipneustic tracheal system is found in many parasitic or half-parasitic *Diptera* larvæ. 1899 *Camb. Nat. Hist.* VI. 450 Other larvæ have a pair of stigmata placed at the termination of the body, and another pair near the anterior extremity..; these larvæ are said to be 'amphipneustic'. 1875 *Encycl. Brit.* II. 459 A temple with a portico at each end is said to be *amphiprostylar. 1871 Huxley *Anat. Vert.* 147 The other *amphirhine fishes. 1883 *Encycl. Brit.* XVI. 844/1 In the highest..group [of pyramids], the Heterostaura, the basal polygon is no longer regular but *amphithect...Ctenophores furnish examples of eight-sided amphithect pyramids. 1880 F. M. Balfour *Comp. Embryol.* I. 275 The larvæ of Nerine and Spio..are both *amphitrochal forms.

Amphiaster (æmfi,æ·stəɹ). [f. Gr. ἀμφί, Amphi- + ἀστήρ star, Aster.] **a.** *Zool.* A sponge-spicule with rays at each end. **b.** *Embryol.* A spindle-shaped formation in a developing ovum, with radiations at each end, thus resembling two star-shaped figures conjoined.

1887 *Buck's Handbk. Med. Sci.* V. 439/1. 1888 Sollas in *Challenger Rep.* XXV. p. lxiv. 1901 G. N. Calkins *Protozoa* 82 A central or 'astral' granule..which in some cases has been seen to divide..and to form an amphiaster.

Amphibian. A. and B. Add: Often *fig.* esp. of persons who have a double character or live a two-fold life; also *transf.* of seaplanes.

1902 *Daily Chron.* 5 May 4/3 These quiet, undistinguished amphibians of Sunwich. 1903 *Ibid.* 7 Jan. 4/4 Such is the natural logic of the amphibian. 1920 *Glasgow Herald* 26 June 7 A service employing flying boats or 'Amphibian' machines or a mixed service of sea and land aircraft. 1920 *Ibid.* 2 Aug. 6 The land tests for seaplanes (amphibians).

Amphibrachic (-bræ·kik), *a.* [f. Amphibrach + -ic.] Consisting of amphibrachs.

1822 *Blackw. Mag.* XI. 441 The amphibrachic verses of French poetry. 1901 *Chamb. Encycl.* VII. 162/2 In the opening of Byron's *Bride of Abydos*..each of the three lines is in a different metre, the first dactylic, the second amphibrachic, the third anapæstic.

Ample, *a.* **1. a.** Add to def.:

Of persons: Of large proportions; esp. in euphemistic use, of stout or well-covered women.

1860 Whyte-Melville *Mkt. Harb.* 60 Mrs. Dove, an ample lady, with the remains of considerable beauty. 1901 Sarah Grand *Babs* iii, She was already more ample than a woman of thirty-eight need be in active life.

Amplifier. Add:

4. An apparatus for increasing the loudness of a speaker's voice or the force of the signals in wireless operations.

1918 in J. A. Fleming *Thermionic Valve* (1919) 274 Where the de Forest valve acts as an amplifier it is outside any claim on the Fleming patent of 1904.

Amuletic, *a.* Delete †*Obs.* and add:

1742 W. Stukeley *Mem.* (Surtees) I. 326 An amuletick, averruncative or prophylactick symbol. 1855 Smedley *Occult Sciences* 359 The amuletic medicine which cured disease. 1914 *Brit. Mus. Return* 100 A large fan, with amuletic inscriptions in Arabic.

Amusedly (ămiū·zĕdli), *adv.* [f. Amused + -ly [2].] As being amused, with amusement.

1844 *Fraser's Mag.* XXX. 63/1 He looked amusedly at the baggage. 1864 Meredith *Sandra Belloni* xv, Leaning back and contemplating him amusedly. 1905 Locke *Usurper* iii, He wandered amusedly around the baccarat tables.

Amusement. Add: Frequent in recent times in *Comb.* in senses 5 and 6, as *amusement-lover* (-*loving*), -*seeker* (-*seeking*); *amusement park* (U.S.).

1898 *Daily News* 8 Sept. 5/1 It may surprise old amusement lovers to learn that one of the original troupe of Christy Minstrels..is still alive. 1904 *Westm. Gaz.* 31 Dec. 16/3 The average amusement-seeker has a limited amount to spend. 1906 *Bungalow* Dec. 4/2 The Tivoli..caters for the amusement-loving people. 1907 *Westm. Gaz.* 10 May 12/1 London in particular..is 'amusement mad.' 1909 *New York Even. Post* 13 June 4 This is, or was to have been, the year of the amusement park.

Amyloid. **A. 2.** (Read):

Path. Applied to a form of degeneration of various organs, or to the albuminoid substance (formerly supposed to be akin to starch) produced in this: = Lardaceous; (and transfer the quots. in B. 3 to this sense).

B. (For senses 1 and 2 substitute)

1. A substance akin to starch; any member of the group of carbohydrates including starch and related substances, as cellulose (with quots. 1872, 1873).

(For sense 3 substitute)

2. *Path.* The substance formed in amyloid degeneration, also called Lardacein.

Amylolysis (æmilɒ·lisis). [See Amylolytic.] The conversion of starch into soluble products by the action of enzymes.

1890 Billings *Med. Dict.* 1909 *Practitioner* Dec. 818 The contents [of the stomach] showed deficient amylolysis.

Amyloplast (æ·miloplæst). *Bot.* [f. Gr. ἄμυλον starch + πλαστός formed: see -plast.] A colourless granule in a plant-cell, around which a starch-grain is formed.

1889 in *Cent. Dict.*

Amylopsin (æmilɒ·psin). *Physiol. Chem.* [f. Gr. ἄμυλον starch, after *pepsin*: cf. Steapsin.] The amylolytic ferment of the pancreatic juice.

1886 *Buck's Handbk. Med. Sci.* II. 452/1 A third ferment, *amylopsin*, acts on starch as ptyalin does. 1894 *Jrnl. Chem. Soc.* LXVI. II. 103 The production of ferments by the pancreatic cell is successive; it is an operation of two acts, of which the first is the formation of amylopsin, the second of trypsin.

Amyrin (æ·mirin). [f. Amyris + -in[1].] A resin obtained from a Mexican species of *Amyris* (*A. elemifera*).

1889 *Chamb. Encycl.* IV. 288/1 When treated with cold alcohol, it [Elemi] partly dissolves, leaving about 20 per cent. of a white resinous substance called Amyrine.

Anabiosis (æ:năbai,ō°·sis). [mod.L., ad. Gr. ἀναβίωσις, f. ἀναβιοῦν: see Anabiotic.] A coming to life again; revival, resuscitation.

1890 Billings *Med. Dict.*, *Anabiosis*, the power which certain organisms possess of regaining vital activity after being dried and heated. 1913 J. G. Frazer *Belief in Immortality* I. iii. 85 John Hunter, supported by his experiments on *anabiosis*, hoped to prolong the life of man indefinitely by alternate freezing and thawing. 1926 *Chamb. Jrnl.* 1 May 349/2 From latent life there can be a protoplasmic resurrection, learnedly called 'Anabiosis.'

Anabolic (ænăbɒ·lik), *a.* *Biol.* [f. Gr. ἀναβολή (*lit.* a throwing up), ascent, etc. + -ic.] Pertaining to, involving, or exhibiting anabolism; constructively metabolic: opp. to Katabolic.

1885 M. Foster *Physiology* in *Encycl. Brit.* XIX. 13 An upward series of changes (*anabolic* changes). 1889 Geddes & Thomson *Evol. Sex* ii. 26 The males live at a loss, are more katabolic...The females..live at a profit, are more anabolic—constructive processes predominating in their life, whence indeed the capacity of bearing offspring. 1903 F. W. H. Myers *Hum. Pers.* II. 514 The katabolic as well as the anabolic forces, the output as well as the intake of the bodily frame, are amenable..to subliminal control.

Anabolism (ănæ·bŏliz'm). *Biol.* [f. as prec. + -ism.] The 'ascending' process in metabolism, in which simpler substances, as nutritive matter, are transformed into more complex ones, and thus built up into the living structure of the organism; constructive metabolism: opp. to Katabolism.

1886 W. H. Gaskell in *Jrnl. Physiol.* VII. 46 In other words, metabolism includes the two opposite processes of destruction and construction, or as they may be called of katabolism and anabolism. 1889 Geddes & Thomson *Evol. Sex* x. 122 These upbuilding, constructive, synthetic processes are summed up in the phrase anabolism. 1897 Willis *Flower. Pl.* I. 206 Metabolism..may be divided into anabolism, the building up, and katabolism, the breaking down, of complex materials.

Anabranch (æ·năbranʃ). *Australia.* [f. Ana- + Branch *sb.*; suggested by Anastomosis.] A branch stream which turns out of a river and re-enters it lower down, forming a *branch-island.*

1834 *Jrnl. R. Geog. Soc.* IV. 79 Thus, such branches of a river as after separation re-unite, I would term anastomosing branches; or, if a word might be coined, ana-branches. 1847 Leichhardt *Jrnl.* ii. 35 The river..divided into anabranches which..made the whole valley a maze of channels. 1849 Sturt *Central Austr.* I. 93 To ascertain how high the back-waters of the Murray had gone up the Ana-branch of the Darling.

Anachronism. **2.** Add: Also *transf.* of persons.

1899 Beatrice Harraden *Fowler* I. vii, 'Sentiment,' she repeated. 'It is absurd to try and hustle sentiment off the scenes.'..'You are always an anachronism,' he said, quietly.

Anæmic. **1.** Add to def.: Often *transf.* or *fig.*: Lacking in vigour, strength, or spirit. *colloq.*

1898 *Daily News* 16 Sept. 4/5 The Americans..are not anæmic. They are overflowing with vigour and enterprise. 1899 *Ibid.* 21 Oct. 7/7 Some of the tweeds are made in rather anæmic, sickly tones. 1906 *Westm. Gaz.* 1 Dec. 20/3 [He] must indeed have made an anæmic diamond declaration.

Anaerobe (ǣnē°·ərō°b). *Biol.* [f. mod.L. *Anaerobia* neut. pl. (F. *anaérobies*, Pasteur), f. Gr. ἀν- privative: see *Aerobe.] A microbe or bacterium of the group *Anaerobia*, which live without free oxygen. So **Anaero·bian, Anaerobic** (-ɒ·bik), **Anaero·bious** *adjs.*, of the nature of or pertaining to anaerobes; capable of living without free oxygen; **Anaero·bically** *adv.*; **Ana:erobio·sis,** life in a medium devoid of free oxygen; **Ana:erobiotic** (-ɒ·tik) *a.*, pertaining to or characterized by anaerobiosis, anaerobic.

1884 Klein *Micro-Org.* vi. 34 Some bacteria require free access of oxygen, and are called aërobic (Pasteur); others grow without free oxygen, and are anaërobic (Pasteur). 1885 Stirling tr. *Landois' Physiol.* iv. § 184. 374 This fungus [Bacillus butyricus]..is a true anaërobe, and grows only in the absence of O(xygen). 1885 Vines in *Encycl. Brit.* XIX. 51/2 It is just the anaerobiotic plants which are most highly endowed with the property of exciting fermentation. 1887 Anaerobically [see *Aerobically]. 1891 Linsley tr. *Fraenkel's Bacteriol.* 115 That the anaërobia in particular distinguish themselves by generating gases is already known. 1894 *Pop. Sci. Monthly* June 278 With special reference to anaerobiosis and gas production among bacteria.

Anallantoidian (æ:nælǣntoi·diăn), *a.* and *sb.* *Zool.* [f. An- 10 + Allantoidian.] **A.** *adj.* Having no allantois in the embryo, as the lower vertebrates. **B.** *sb.* An animal thus characterized. (Opp. to Allantoidian.)

1861 Hulme tr. *Moquin-Tandon* II. II. 62 Anallantoidians—Batrachia, Pisces, Myelairia.

Analphabet. Add:

B. *sb.* [after It. *analfabeta*, G. *analphabet*, F. *analphabète*, etc.] One who is totally illiterate or unable to read.

1881 *Encycl. Brit.* XIII. 460 As late as..1861..[in Italy] in a population of 21,777,331 there were..16,999,701 'analphabetes,' or persons..absolutely unable to read. 1914 Hauptmann in *New York Times Current History* 12 Dec. 79 There are no analphabets to be found among them.

Analyse, *v.* Add:

3. b. Short for *Psycho-analyse.

1919 M. K. Bradby *Psycho-analysis* (1920) 126, I have had no nightmare..since I was analysed. 1921 Rose Macaulay *Dangerous Ages* v. § 4, I think you'd be awfully wise to get analysed.

Analytical, *a.* Add:

1. c. *Math.* Applied to geometry treated by means of algebra, as in the Cartesian representation of curves and surfaces by equations.

1827 *Encycl. Metrop.* (1845) I. 709 This branch of the subject is usually distinguished by the name of Algebraic, or Analytical, Geometry. 1881 J. M. Dyer (*title*) Exercises in Analytical Geometry.

Analytically, *adv.* **1.** Add to def.: By the analytical method, by the method of analytical geometry.

1879 *Encycl. Brit.* X. 408/1 It would be possible, analytically, or by the method of coordinates, to develop the truths of geometry in a systematic course.

Anamesite (ănæ·mĕsait). *Min.* [f. Gr. ἀνάμεσος intermediate + -ite[1].] A fine-grained variety of basalt. Hence **Anamesitic** (ănæmĕsi·tik) *a.*, of the nature of or resembling anamesite.

1879 Rutley *Study Rocks* xiii. 253 Those [basalts] in which the constituents are too small to be recognised without a magnifying power, but in which a crystalline texture is yet clearly discernible, are styled anamesites. 1899 *Smithsonian Rep.* 233 The anamesitic basalt of the neighborhood showed a structure fully corresponding with the bauxite.

Anamnesis. Add:

b. *Liturgiology.* That part of the Eucharistic canon

in which the sacrifice of Christ is recalled and pleaded.

1894 H. Lucas in *Dublin Rev.* CXIV. 123 The Anamnesis, a prayer commencing with the words Μεμνημένοι οὖν, and answering more closely to the Roman *Unde et memores* than to any Gallican *Post Secreta* or Mozarabic *Post Pridie*. 1912 A. Fortescue *Mass* ii. 103 The next prayer (*Post pridie* or *Post mysterium*) contains the Anamnesis and Epiklesis of the Holy Ghost.

Ananas. Add: **3.** *attrib.*: **ananas oil**, trade-name for ethyl butyrate mixed with alcohol, used to imitate the flavour or odour of pine-apple.

1890 Bloxam *Chem.* (ed. 7) 570 *Ethyl butyrate*..is sold as *ananas oil*, or *essence of pineapple*, which it resembles in odour.

Anangian (ănæ·ndʒiăn), *a.* *Zool.* [f. An- 10 + Gr. ἀγγεῖον vessel + -an.] Destitute of a vascular system, as certain worms.

1896 Benham in *Cambr. Nat. Hist.* II. 253 The fluid in these 'anangian' worms..behaves like the 'blood' of Vertebrates.

Anangious (ănæ·ndʒiəs), *a.* *Zool.* [f. as prec. + -ous.] Destitute of blood-vessels (in the retina).

1901 *Phil. Trans.* Ser. B. CXCIV. 68 The eyes of these nocturnal creatures [*sc.* bats] are very small, anangious, and devoid of any traces of higher development.

Ananias (ænănəi·ăs). Name of a man who, 'with Sapphira his wife, sold a possession and kept back part of the price' (Acts v. 1, 2); used allusively for a liar.

1890 *Harper's Mag.* Apr. 795/1 Since Locke's time newspaper Ananiases have not been infrequent.

Anaphase (æ·năfēiz). *Biol.* [a. G. *anaphase*, f. Ana- + Phase.] The stage in mitosis at which the daughter chromosomes move apart just before the division of the cell. Cf. *metaphase* (Meta- 4), Prophase, *telophase* (Telo-[1]).

1887 tr. *E. Strasburger's Bot.* xxxii. 363 The further phases of the separation of the sister-segments, which appertain to the receding phases of division, the anaphases. 1901 Calkins *Protozoa* 263 Late anaphase.

Anaphora. Add:

2. *Liturgiology.* That part of the Eucharistic service which includes the consecration, oblation, and communion; in the Western Church, the canon of the mass. Hence **Ana·phoral** *a.*

1744 *Anc. Liturgy Ch. Jerus.* Pref. p. iii, All that Part, both of this and the other ancient Liturgies, which precedes the Anaphora, is a latter Addition to the Service of the Church. *Ibid.* p. v, The proper Anaphora, or Eucharistical Service, viz. from the Sursum Corda..to the Ite in Pace. 1832 W. Palmer *Orig. Liturg.* I. 27 Omitting..any comparison of the introductions of these two liturgies, I will compare their *Anaphoræ*, or solemn offices. 1859 Neale *Liturgies of SS. Mark*, etc. p. xi, The Anaphoral portion has these four divisions: The great Eucharistic Prayer: The Consecration: The Intercession for quick and dead: and The Communion.

Anapterygotous (ænæ̆pterigō·təs), *a.* *Entom.* [f. mod.L. *Anapterygota*, app. f. Gr. ἀνά back, again + πτερυγωτός winged, or f. ἀν(ά + *Apterygotous: see -ous.] Belonging to the division *Anapterygota* of insects, which are wingless but held to be descended from a winged ancestry (cf. *Apterygotous). So **Anapterygo·tism**, the condition of being anapterygotous.

1902 *Encycl. Brit.* XXIX. 503/1 [It is] probable that insects may..become wingless, though their ancestors were winged. Such insects have been styled anapterygotous. *Ibid.*, The change from exopterygotism to endopterygotism ..by an intermediate period of anapterygotism.

Anaptyxis (ænăpti·ksis). *Phonetics.* [mod.L., a. Gr. ἀνάπτυξις unfolding.] (See quot. 1895 [1].) So **Anapty·otic, -ical** *adjs.*, pertaining to anaptyxis.

1885 *Athenæum* 18 July 76/1 The irregular appearance of the anaptyctic vowel. 1895 P. Giles *Man. Compar. Philol.* 169 Anaptyxis..the development of a vowel between two consonants. 1895 *Athenæum* 14 Sept. 347/2 ['Cycular' is] formed from 'cycle' on the analogy of 'circular' from 'circle' (more correctly from *circulus*). The irregular anaptyxis cannot be defended on historical grounds.

Anarch. A. Add:

2. An advocate of anarchy, an anarchist.

1884 W. Cory *Lett. & Jrnls.* (1897) 508 We occupied the Delta in 1882 to prevent anarchs from hindering trade on the Canal. 1885 R. L. & F. Stevenson *Dynamiters* 194, I recognise in you the marks of an accomplished Anarch.

Anarchic, *a.* Add: **b.** Pertaining to *Anarchy 1 b. So **Anarchist.**

1889 W. Donisthorpe *Individualism* 256 Under a truly anarchic system. 1889 S. Webb in Shaw *Fabian Ess. Socialism* 44 The complete freedom preached by..the scientific Anarchists of to-day.

Anarchistic (ænaɹki·stik), *a.* [f. Anarchist + -ic: see -istic.] Belonging to, characteristic of, or adhering to anarchists or anarchism.

1884 *Standard* 5 Dec. 5/5 The seizure of Revolutionary and Anarchistic prints. 1900 H. G. Wells *Love & Mr. Lewisham* xxiii, That Honesty is essentially an anarchistic and disintegrating force in society.

Anarchy. Add:

1. b. A theoretical social state in which there is no governing person or body of persons, but each individual has absolute liberty (without implication of disorder).

1884 Rae *Contemp. Socialism* vii. 281 This idea of a 'genial anarchy'..has always been the favourite social remedy of the Russian revolutionary party. 1889 W. Donisthorpe *Individualism* 282 Scientific anarchy is..the end towards which society is moving. 1892 *Daily News* 27 Apr. 5/8 Anarchy means the placing in common of all this world's riches to allow each to consume according to his needs. Anarchy is a great family where each will be protected by all and will take whatever he requires.

Anastate (æ·năstēit). *Biol.* [f. Gr. ἀνά up + στατός placed.] A substance formed in the process of *Anabolism in a living organism: opp. to Katastate.

1885 M. Foster in *Encycl. Brit.* XIX. 19 The substances or mesostates appearing in the former [*sc.* the anabolic series of processes] we may speak of as anastates, those of the latter we may call katastates. *Ibid.*, In the animal-cell the initial anastates seem..generally more complex than the final katastates. 1889 Geddes & Thomson *Evol. Sex* vii. 88.

Anastigmat (ănăsti·gmæt). *Photogr.* [a. G. *anastigmat* (Miethe), back-formation from *anastigmatisch*: see next.] An anastigmatic lens or system of lenses.

1894 *Amer. Ann. Photogr.* 100 The Anastigmat..is the most rapid lens I have tried. 1902 *Westm. Gaz.* 23 June 8/2 All scientists have declared it impossible to construct a true Anastigmat lens without the aid of the Jena glass. 1908 *Ibid.* 6 June 14/2 The best lens for copying purposes is.. one of the flat field anastigmats.

Anastigmatic (ænăstigmæ·tik), *a.* [f. Gr. ἀν- privative + Astigmatic; cf. Stigmatic 9.] Not astigmatic; free from astigmatism: applied to a compound lens so constructed as to correct the astigmatic aberration.

1897 *Outing* (U.S.) XXX. 340/2 The lens must be one of the almost faultless anastigmatic type. 1901 *Brit. Jrnl. Photogr.* 22 Nov. 744/1 The anastigmatic flatness of field. 1902 *Encycl. Brit.* XXXI. 696/1 A..new type of anastigmatic objective.

Anathematical. Transfer † *Obs.* to B. and add quots.:

1882 *Liquor Christmas Ann.* 1. 27/1 To profane my lips with an anathematical expression. 1927 *Scots Observer* 22 Jan. 15/1 The tenets of militarism were fathered upon Carlyle and his name made anathematical.

Anatine (æ·nătəin), *a.* and *sb.* [ad. L. *anatinus*, f. *anat-*, *anas* duck: see -ine [1].] **A.** *adj.* Of or pertaining to, resembling or characteristic of, a duck. **B.** *sb.* A bird of the duck family.

1862 H. G. Adams *Wild Fl., Birds, & Insects* 274 Those [birds] of the Anatine group. 1875 *Encycl. Brit.* III. 712/2 The Anserines and Anatines. 1893 Newton *Dict. Birds* 543 Their [*sc.* the Mergansers'] structure does not much depart from the Anatine or rather Fuliguline type.

Anatriæne (ænătrəi,ĭn). [f. Gr. ἀνά up, back + Triæne.] In sponges, a triæne with recurved prongs. 1887 [see Protriæne].

Anatropy (ănæ·trŏpi). *Bot.* [f. Gr. type *ἀνατροπία, f. *ἀνάτροπος: see Anatropous.] The condition of being anatropous.

1848 [see Orthotropy].

Anautotomic (æn,ǭtotǫ·mik), *a.* *Geom.* [f. Gr. ἀν- privative + Autotomic.] Not intersecting itself; having no multiple point: opp. to Autotomic.

1901 A. B. Basset *Elem. Cubic & Quartic Curves* Pref. p. vii, I have..introduced the words *autotomic* and *anautotomic* to designate curves which respectively do and do not possess multiple points.

Anauxite (ǽnǭ·ksəit). *Min.* [ad. G. *anauxit*, f. Gr. ἀναυξής not increasing, so named 'because the mineral does not swell up before the blowpipe' (Chester): see -ite [1].] A pearly-white translucent variety of Cimolite.

1868 Dana *Min.* 458. 1883 *Encycl. Brit.* XVI. 424/2 Anauxite..Granular..Translucent, pearly.

Ancestor, *sb.* **1. b.** Add quots.:

1854 *Wesleyan Methodist Mag.* X. 623 Ancestor-worship ..has linked and attached itself most powerfully to the heart of every Chinese. 1869 Henry Callaway (*title*) Amatongo; or Ancestor Worship, as existing among the Amazulu. 1871 E. B. Tylor *Prim. Cult.* II. 108 In China..ancestor-worship is the dominant religion of the land. 1883 Maine *Early Law & Custom* iii. 55 Ancestor-worship, the worship of father, grandfather, and great-grandfather, has among the Hindus a most elaborate liturgy and ritual.

c. *Law.* A person who precedes another in the course of inheritance, and from whom an inheritance is derived, whether in the direct line of descent or not: correlative to *heir*. *Collateral ancestor*: see Collateral A. 4.

1628 Coke *On Litt.* 380 b, If lands had beene giuen to the husband and wife and their heires, and the husband had made a Feoffement to another, to whom a Collaterall Ancester of the wife had released and died. 1651, 1767 [see Heir *sb.* 1]. 1768, 1809 [see Ancestral 1 b].

Hence **A·ncestor** *v. trans.*, to be the ancestor of; **A·ncestored** (-əɹd) *ppl. a.*, having an ancestor or ancestors (of a specified kind); **A·ncestorship**, the position of an ancestor.

1776 H. Walpole *Let. to Cole* Wks. 1840 V. 456 Few men are so well ancestored in so short a compass of time. 1853 *Tait's Mag.* XX. 604 The thorough-bred, orientally ancestred horse. 1883 Max Müller *India, What Can It Teach Us?* vii. 239 Ancestorship as a natural ingredient of religion among all savage nations. 1921 *Times Lit. Supp.* 10 Feb. 92/2 Their younger brother ancestored the well-known family of Howard-Vyse, of Stoke Place, Slough.

Ancestrally (ænse·străli), *adv.* [f. Ancestral + -ly [2].] By or in respect of ancestry.

1883 G. Allen *Colin Clout's Calendar* xvii. 97 Ancestrally, yellow-rattle is a near relation of the pretty little blue veronicas. 1886 *Athenæum* 6 Mar. 328/3 Whether the vertebrate eye..will turn out..to be ancestrally derived from a number of modified ancestral gills.

Anchorage. Add: **3. b.** *spec.* in *Dentistry*.

1912 *Cat. Dental Manuf. Co. Ltd.* G. 71 Sufficient anchorage must be made to withstand the force of mastication, and to provide for firm retention of the inlay within the cavity. 1917 *Recalled to Life* Sept. p. xx, They have platinum anchorages baked in the teeth and large, strong pins soldered to the anchorages after baking of the porcelain is complete.

Anchor-hold [2]. *Hist.* [f. Anchor *sb.*[2] + Hold *sb.*[1]] An anchorite's 'hold', abode, or retreat; = Anchorage [2].

1631 Weever *Anc. Funeral Mon.* 150 Their solitarie little cells..carrie still the name of..Anchor-holds. *a* 1695 Wood *City of Oxford* (O.H.S.) I. 356 *note*, The Anchorhold of S. Giles Church. 1802 Fosbroke *Brit. Mon.* (1843) 372 The *Destina* (for so these anchor-holds or stalls, affixed to larger buildings were called), occupied by Dunstan soon after he became a Monk. 1922 *Times* 22 Apr. 9/4 Both the church and its 'anchorhold', or anchorite's cell, are more than once mentioned in documents of the college [*sc.* Merton].

Ancona [1] (æŋkōu·nă). [It., = med.L. (Stat. Guild of Painters at Venice, 1271 A.D.): etym. uncertain; perh. an alteration of Gr. εἰκόνα, acc. of εἰκών image, Icon.] An altar-piece, esp. one consisting of a group of pictures or painted panels connected by architectural structure.

1874 Miss R. H. Busk *Tirol* 146 A priceless work of Alb. Durer, an '*Ancona*', showing forth in its various compartments the history of the Passion. 1885 *Athenæum* 19 Sept. 377/2 The Van Eycks' 'Adoration of the Lamb' ..[is] a true representative of the Italian *ancona* or group of pictures included in a single altarpiece. 1887 *Ibid.* 20 Aug. 248/3 The work is neither more nor less than an ancona, which is different in kind as well as in scale from a triptych. 'Altarpiece' would be a correct term here, if the author fears to use 'ancona'. 1900 *Speaker* 28 Apr. 116/2. 1903 *Burlington Mag.* I. 309/2 This altar-piece now hangs on the north wall of the choir of the Collegiata. It is a Gothic *ancona* in which four scenes are represented. 1906 Molmenti *Venice, Mid. Ages* II. 123 It is in these *ancone*, sacred images painted on wood, that we find the origin of Venetian painting.

attrib. 1900 *Speaker* 28 Apr. 116/1 The ancona form of composition..was characteristic of the old Venetian school.

Ancona [2] (æŋkōu·nă). [Name of a town in Italy.] A breed of domestic fowl characterized by black and white mottled plumage and leaden-grey shanks.

1853 Wingfield & Johnson *Poultry Bk.* 110 The *Ancona* is a first cousin to the Minorca, its sole point of difference being a mottled or splashed plumage, black and white, in about equal proportions. 1874 L. Wright *Bk. Poultry* 357 We entertain scarcely any doubt that the origin of Anconas is to be found in accidental 'sports' of this colour from crossing Black and White Minorcas. 1902 *Ibid.* 412 The earliest [Ancona] we remember (about 1864) were cuckoo-coloured, and dusky or leaden in the shanks...We..put these birds down to probable crossing of black and white Minorcas, ..but there can be little doubt now that they were really Cuckoo Leghorns or Anconas.

Andalusian (ændălū·ʃiăn), *a.* and *sb.* [f. *Andalusia* (see below) + -an.] Native or belonging to Andalusia, a province of Spain; applied *spec.* to a breed of domestic fowl, a make of wool, etc.

1854 *Poultry Chron.* I. 101 Several so-called Andalusians, bred by a Minorca cock out of a Maltese hen...The Andalusian fowls were introduced to the notice of amateurs by Mr. Taylor, of Shepherd's Bush. 1882 Caulfeild & Saward *Dict. Needlework* 6/2 Andalusian Wool..is also called Victoria Wool, and is a fine soft warm make of woollen thread or yarn...It is the same wool as the Shetland, but is thicker. 1920 *Discovery* July 200/2 This form of fowl is bluish-black with black lacing, and is called the Blue Andalusian. 1927 *Blackw. Mag.* Sept. 313/1 A sky of Andalusian azure.

Anderoon, -un (ændĕrū·n). [Pers. اندرون *enderūn* prop. internal, interior, f. اندر *ender* within.] The apartments of a (Persian) harem.

1840 Savile in *New Monthly Mag.* LVIII. 189 In the anderoon..sat Khodadad, in sweet converse with his beloved Semira. 1842 Thackeray *Sultan Stork* Wks. 1900 V. 742 The ladies they keep so secretly in the anderoon. 1900 *Westm. Gaz.* 20 July 2/1 The household gathering outside the *anderoon* till the Shah emerges.

Andine (æ·ndəin), *a.* [f. *Andes* + -ine [1].] = Andean.

1900 *Daily Chron.* 23 Aug. 3/4 The explorations carried out..for the Argentine Government in the Andine region. 1924 *Chamb. Jrnl.* Mar. 188/2 A vast ancient crater of the Andine range.

Andrewsite (æ·ndruzəit). *Min.* [f. the name of Thomas *Andrews* + -ite [1].] A bluish-green hydrous phosphate of iron and copper.

1871 *Chem. News* XXIV. 99 A mineral recently found in Cornwall..has been analysed in the Museum Laboratory, and Professor Maskelyne named it Andrewsite, in honour of the distinguished President of the Chemical Section of the British Association, Dr. Andrews, of Belfast.

Andro- (before a vowel **Andr-**), repr. Gr. ἀνδρο-, combining form of ἀνήρ man, male (see words in Andro- in Dict.). **Androcentric** (ændrose·ntrik) *a.*, having man, or the male, as its centre; **Androcracy** (ændrǫ·krăsi) [-cracy], the rule of man or the male, male supremacy; **Androcratic** (-kræ·tik) *a.*, pertaining to or involving androcracy; **Andromonœcism** (-mǫnī·siz'm) *Bot.*, the condition of being andromonœcious; **Andromonœcious** (-mǫnī·ʃəs), *a.* *Bot.* [Monœcious], having male and hermaphrodite flowers on the same plant.

1903 L. F. Ward *Pure Sociol.* xiv. 292 The *androcentric theory is the view that the male sex is primary and the female secondary.., that all things center, as it were, about the male. *Ibid.* 376 The stage of gynæcocracy was succeeded by the stage of *androcracy, and the subjection of woman was rendered complete. 1893 *Athenæum* 7 Oct. 494/1 Marital relations among tribes in the enjoyment of an *androcratic government being generally far more satisfactory. 1903 L. F. Ward *Pure Sociol.* xiv. 399 The androcratic régime, during which woman had no voice in the selecting process. 1888 Henslow *Orig. Flor. Struct.* 227 *Andromonœcism signifies that the same plant bears both male and hermaphrodite flowers.

Andromedid (ændrǫ·mĭdid). *Astr.* [f. *Andromeda* + -id [3]: cf. Leonid, Perseid.] = Andromede.

1898 *Pall Mall Gaz.* 21 Nov. 2 (Cass. Suppl.), The Leonids are remarkably swift; the Andromedids strikingly slow. 1904 *Westm. Gaz.* 17 Nov. 12/1 The Andromedids form part of the débris of Biela's Comet.

Andromedotoxin (ændrǫ:mĭdotǫ·ksin), **andrometoxin** (ændrǫmĭtǫ·ksin). [f. Andromeda 2 + Toxin.] A poisonous crystalline substance found in various ericaceous plants, esp. the genus *Andromeda*.

1890 Billings *Med. Dict.* 1902 *Westm. Gaz.* 16 July 2/2 A chicken fed for four days on increasing doses of the andromedotoxin from this plant [*Kalmia latifolia*].

An-end, *adv. phr.* Add: **5.** In the direction of the length; directly ahead. Chiefly *Naut.*

1601 Deacon & Walker *Spirits & Divels* 68 You must not be haled hedlong an end with an inueterate opinion. 1769 Falconer *Dict. Marine* (1789), *Avoir vent de bout*, to have the wind right an-end, or a-head. 1802 *Ann. Reg., Chron.* 81 They were riding with two cables an end. 1867 Smyth *Sailor's Word-bk.* s.v., To strike a spar or plank *an-end* is to drive it in the direction of its length. *Ibid.*, *Every rope an end*, the order to coil down the running rigging, or braces or bowlines, after tacking, or other evolution. Also, the order, when about to perform an evolution, to see that every rope is clear for running.

Angareb, -eeb, -ep (æŋgărē·b). Also **-er-**; **-ib, -ieb.** [Native name.] A stretcher or light bedstead used by the Arabs, and in Egypt and the Soudan.

1867 Sir S. W. Baker *Nile Trib. Abyssinia* viii. 182 The angareps, or native bedsteads,..are simple frameworks upon legs, covered with a network of raw hide. 1885 *Daily News* 3 July 5/4 Camels..heavily laden with angerebs traversely placed and resting on the flank upon a huge box. 1900 Conan Doyle *Green Flag, Bimbashi Joyce* 329 He lay upon his angareeb still debating it. 1925 *Blackw. Mag.* Sept. 424/2 The harassed native Bimbashi sought his angerib.

Angary (æ·ŋgări). [ad. F. *angarie*, ad. L. *angaria*: see Angariate *v.*] In full *right of angary* (F. *droit d'angarie*): the right of a belligerent to use and destroy, if necessary, the property of neutrals.

1880 Hall *Internat. Law* 655 The most recent cases of the exercise of the right of angary occurred during the Franco-German War of 1870–71. 1902 *Encycl. Brit.* XXXI. 129.

Angeio-, variant spelling of Angio-.

1848 Dunglison *Med. Lex.* (ed. 7). 1859 Semple *Diphtheria* 316 Angeioleucitis. 1888 *Chamb. Encycl.* I. 254/1 Angeiology describes the vessels or ducts, with their complex network and ramifications.

Angekok (æ·ŋgĕkǫk). [Eskimo.] An Eskimo sorcerer or medicine-man.

1767 tr. *Crantz's Hist. Greenland* I. 206 When a dearth befalls them [*sc.* Greenlanders] at sea, an Angekok must undertake a journey thither. 1819 *Edin. Rev.* XXXI. 345 Their conjurors or angekoks are merely a superior order of jugglers. 1842 Moffat *Mission. Labours S. Africa* 305 The angekoks of the Greenlanders..and the greegrees of Western Africa.

Angel. Add:

7. *Angling.* A spinning bait.

1890 *Daily News* 10 Apr. 5/1 In Loch Leven, when the trout do not rise to fly, they are trolled for with angels, or even with the natural minnow.

8. A dead turtle.

1908 *Daily Chron.* 6 Nov. 7/3 A blazing sun will kill them, and so will a frost, and when they experience both on the voyage most of them arrive in the shape of 'angels'.

9. *Angels on horseback*, a dish consisting of oysters and bacon served on toast.

1888 Mrs. Beeton *Bk. Househ. Managem.* (new ed.) § 2078 Angels on Horseback. (Fr.—Anges à Cheval). 1901 Sarah Grand *Babs* xv, Angels on Horseback, now—those delicious little morsels of oysters rolled in bacon, and served on crisp toast.

B. 2. **angel-cake** (orig. *U.S.*), a variety of sponge-cake.

1897 *Amer. Dainties* 44 Angel Cake. 1904 *N. Y. Times* 13 June 8 To have angel cake would be sacrilegious. 1905 *N. Y. Even. Post* 4 Aug. 7 Angel cake, sponge cake, and ice-cream cake have conspired to relegate the seed cake to practical oblivion.

Angevin (æ·ndʒĕvin), *a.* and *sb.* [ad. F. *Angevin*:—med. L. *Andegavinu-s*, f. *Andegavum* Angers, capital of Anjou (*Andegavia*).] **A.** *adj.* Of or pertaining to Anjou, a former province of France, or any sovereign, government, etc. derived thence; *spec.* in *Engl. Hist.*, belonging to or characteristic of the Plantagenet kings (beginning with Henry II) descended from Geoffrey, count of Anjou, and Matilda, daughter of Henry I; pertaining or relating to their descendants, the period of history which they cover, etc. **B.** *sb.* A native of Anjou; an Angevin ruler.

1737 tr. *M. Baudier's Hist. Marg. Anjou* 4 Henry..complained of the Angevin's Escape. 1769 G. Lyttelton *Hist. Hen. II* I. 162 The Angevin family had been long very powerful and illustrious. 1834 *Penny Cycl.* II. 35/1 The Angevin prince invaded Italy with an army of 30,000 men. 1874 Green *Short Hist.* ii. § 7. 94 To understand the history of England under its Angevin rulers, we must first know something of the Angevins themselves. 1887 Kate Norgate *Eng. under Angevin Kings* I. 3 Those wonderful Angevin counts who..grew into a sovereign house. 1887 *Encycl. Brit.* XXII. 27/2 The Angevin conquest of Sicily. 1924 J. S. C. Bridge *Hist. France* II. 173 Charles had vindicated his Angevin claims.

Angico (andʒī·ko). A Brazilian name applied to the gum, etc. of the tropical S. America tree *Piptadenia rigida*, which yields a hard durable timber, and an astringent bark and a gum both used medicinally.

1863–7 Simmonds *Dict. Trade* Suppl., *Angico Gum*. 1897 Willis *Flowering Pl.* II. 298 P[iptadenia] rigida..yields Angico gum used like gum-arabic.

Anginal (æ·ndʒinăl), *a.* [f. Angina + -al.] Pertaining to angina, i.e. quinsy, or *angina pectoris*; = Anginous. Also **Anginic** (ændʒi·nik) *a.* So **Angi·niform, A·nginoid** *adjs.*, resembling *angina pectoris*.

1811 Lettsom in Pettigrew *Life* (1817) III. 4 The anginal stridula may make its onset without that exudation in the throat. 1882 Sir J. D. Hooker in *Life* (1918) II. 260, I have had a ten days' bout of my Anginic pains. 1891 *Lancet* 14 Feb. 371/2 A series of anginoid attacks. *Ibid.* 371/1 Such cases might be termed 'anginous' or 'anginal'.

Angiocarpous, *a.* Add to def.:

Also, having the apothecium inclosed within the thallus, as certain lichens.

1851 W. A. Leighton (*title*) The British Species of Angiocarpous Lichens. [So also quot. 1875 in Dict.]

Angioma (ændʒi,ōu·mă). *Path.* Pl. **-ata.** [mod.L., f. Gr. ἀγγεῖον vessel + *-oma.] A tumour produced by dilatation or new formation of blood-vessels. Hence **Angio·matous** *a.*

1873 T. H. Green *Introd. Pathol.* (ed. 2) 178 The angiomata, or vascular tumours, are tumours consisting of blood-vessels held together by..connective tissue. 1897 *Trans. Amer. Pediatric Soc.* IX. 154 Angiomatous tumours.

Angle, *v.*[2] Add:

2. Also *intr.* = *refl.*

1883 *Century Mag.* Oct. 923/2 He..once more alters his direction, and so twists off, 'angling' across the meadow.

3. *intr.* To turn or move at an angle, diagonally, or obliquely; to lie in an oblique direction.

1835 *Fraser's Mag.* XI. 39 The circuitous route you are obliged to take—angling off at an infinite variety of points. 1868 *Rep. U. S. Comm. Agric.* (1869) 258 About half the saplings may be laid along outside one stake, then inside of the next, and thence angling across to the other row. 1881 Mayne Reid *Free Lances* II. xxxii. 116 [The road] angles abruptly to the right. 1897 *Times* 5 Feb. 14/5 The Majestic ..broke her starboard quarter rope, which caused her to angle across the entrance and to become jammed.

b. *trans.* To strike or drive at an angle.

1920 *Westm. Gaz.* 16 Oct. 2/2 She attracted the returns to her by cleverly angling the ball.

4. *intr.* To obtain an angle by which to discover the location of a bee-hive. *U.S.*

1848 J. F. Cooper *Oak Open.* I. i. 21 'I must "angle" for them chaps'...'Many a man who can "line" a bee, can do nothing at an "angle"'.

Angler [1]. **2.** Add to def.:

Also applied to other pediculate fishes having a free dorsal spine, as in the family *Antennariidæ*.

1653 [see Sea-angler]. 1845 [see Toad-fish]. 1884 Goode *Nat. Hist. Aquatic Anim.* 173 Marbled Angler, *Pterophryne histrio*.

A·nglicanize, *v.* [f. Anglican *a.*] *trans.* To Anglicize.

1904 L. O. Brastow *Repres. Mod. Preachers* 50 Although in remote lineage he may have been Scotch, he had become thoroughly Anglicanized.

Anglicist (æ·ŋglisist). [f. Anglicism: see -ist.] An advocate or favourer of Anglicism, in any sense; in quots., one who advocated the use of English in Indian schools.

1878 G. Smith *Life John Wilson* xvi. 529 Dr. Duff, Macaulay, and the Anglicists under Lord William Bentinck. 1892 *Athenæum* 24 Sept. 411/3 The controversy between the 'Orientalists' and the 'Anglicists', which evoked Macaulay's famous minute.

Angling, *vbl. sb.*[2] Add: **2.** The process of obtaining an angle in tracking bees. (See *Angle *v.*[2] 4.) *U.S.*

1848 J. F. Cooper *Oak Open.* II. iii. 36 Indians are not expert..on account of the 'angle-ing' part of the process, which much exceeds their skill in mathematics.

Anglist (æ·ŋglist). [ad. G. *anglist*, f. L. *Anglus* English (see Angle *sb.*[3]): see -ist.] A student of English, or scholar versed in English.

1888 *Jrnl. Educ.* Jan. 32 The 'Anglist' is warned that he has yet stricter duties to fulfil than the 'Germanist'. Most Anglists, it appears, in Germany conceive that they have done their duty if they have studied thoroughly Gothic, German, and English.

A:nglo-Ame·rica. [f. Anglo- 1 + America.] The United States and Canada.

1846 D. J. Browne *Trees Amer.* 19 Britain and Anglo-America. *Ibid.* 106 French Illinois...Other parts of Anglo-America.

A:nglo-Ame·rican, *sb.* and *a.* [f. Anglo- 1 + American.]

1. *sb.* An American of English origin; an English settler or colonist in North America; sometimes *spec.* a Canadian.

1781–2 Jefferson *Writ.* (1894) III. 100 In case of war with our neighbors, the Anglo-Americans or the Indians. 1787 S. S. Smith *Ess. Complexion* (1788) 194 The Anglo-Americans on the frontiers of the states, who acquire their sustenance principally by hunting. 1789 J. Morse *Amer. Geog.* (1792) 63 The greater part, however, are descended from the English; and for the sake of distinction, are called Anglo-Americans. 1834 H. Brackenridge *Recoll.* ii. 27 When sent for..to act as interpreter to some stray Anglo-American, the little English boy..could not comprehend a single word. 1849 Parkman *Oregon Trail* 22 Henry had not the restless energy of an Anglo-American. 1858 *Texas Almanac* 114 The Anglo-Americans of Texas were threatened with subjection to military despotism.

2. *adj.* Of or pertaining to Americans of English origin. (Cf. F. *anglo-américain*, used by Mirabeau in 1784.)

1824 P. Horry *Life Marion* (1833) 23 The Anglo-American army then prepared themselves for a serious and bloody conflict. 1841 Foote *Texas & Texans* II. 36 The Federal model supplied by Anglo-American wisdom was imitated in Mexico. 1851 C. Cist *Cincinnati* 34 Destined to render the Anglo-American race paramount throughout this great continent. 1873 J. H. Beadle *Undeveloped West* 817 The Supreme Government..introduced troops..whose real object was to overawe the Anglo-American Colonists.

Hence **A:nglo-Ame·ricanism.**

1841 Foote *Texas & Texans* I. 110 In the land [England] whence what we now call Anglo-Americanism has derived its origin.

Anglo-Indian (æŋglo,i·ndiăn), *a.* and *sb.* [f. Anglo- 1 b + Indian.] **A.** *adj.* Of, pertaining to, or characteristic of India under British rule, or the English in India. Also, Indian-Eurasian. **B.** *sb.* **a.** A person of British birth now or formerly resident in India. **b.** A Eurasian of India.

[1838 (*title*) Anglo-India, social, moral, and political.] 1857 Gen. P. Thompson *Audi Alt.* xlvii. I. 183 It may be quite true that sensible men consider Nana Sahib as an Anglo-Indian myth. 1861 Swinhoe *N. China Camp.* 153 The Chinese *Tsaou*, called Bier by the Anglo-Indians, is a somewhat cylindrically shaped fruit. 1876 (*title*) Anglo-Indian Prize Poems, by Native and English Writers. 1882 (*title*) The Opium Question solved. By Anglo-Indian. 1887–8 Whitley Stokes (*title*) The Anglo-Indian Codes. 1907 *Westm. Gaz.* 11 Dec. 2/1 Calcutta..merits the epithet of Anglo-Indian better than anything else in India. 1919 *Cowley Evangelist* June 134 A congregation of Indian, Anglo-Indian and European people, all happily joining together. 1929 *Church Times* 14 June 726/4 The Archdeacon of Madras said that the Anglo-Indian, and particularly the lower class of Anglo-Indian, was the crux of the whole question.

A:nglo-I·sraelite. One who holds that the English-speaking peoples represent the 'lost' tribes of Israel. Also *attrib.*, as *Anglo-Israelite theory*, *theorist*; so **A:nglo-I·sraelitism.**

1886 *Brit. & For. Evang. Rev.* Jan. 65 The Anglo-Israelite Theory. *Ibid.* 72 The Anglo-Israelite theorists hold that they [*sc.* the Ten Tribes] were 'lost' first, and then their punishment and humiliation was changed to a brilliant future. 1897 *Westm. Gaz.* 22 Nov. 3/3 Anglo-Israelitism, which, judged on an historical theory, is simply a foolish craze, has yet no little importance as a sentiment.

A:nglomani·acal, *a.* [f. Anglomaniac.] Of the nature of Anglomania.

1893 *Outing* XXII. 115/1 Bunker's utmost anglomaniacal yearnings had never caused him to be taken for a Briton.

Anglophil, -phile (æ·nglofil), *a.* and *sb.* [ad. F. *anglophile*: see Anglo- and -phil, -phile.] **A.** *adj.* Friendly to England or to what is English. **B.** *sb.* One who is friendly to England. Hence **Anglophi·lia, Anglo·philism**, friendliness to England.

1867 *Contemp. Rev.* IV. 88 The *Revue des deux Mondes*, a thorough 'Anglo-phile' periodical. 1883 *Chamb. Jrnl.* 13 Jan. 18/1 This telephone..was an Anglophile, and would only respond to the honoured name of Faraday. 1892 *Athenæum* 26 Mar. 400/3 When prudence dictated assistance to the Dutch, the Huguenots, or the 'Anglophile' party in Scotland. 1896 *Westm. Gaz.* 2 Oct. 2/1 To show how Anglophilia and Anglophobia counteract each other. *Ibid.* 5 Dec. 6/3 The New York *Evening Sun*..has frequently attacked Mr. Bayard for what it regards as his extreme Anglophilism. 1920 Robb *Thre Prestis of Peblis* (S. T. S.) Introd. p. xxxv, The unpopularity he thus incurred as an anglophile.

Anglophobe. Add: *attrib.* or *adj.*

1901 *Daily Chron.* 6 Aug. 3/1 The revival of Anglophobe reaction was further strengthened by the Parliamentary activity of Clericalism.

Anglophobia. (Earlier U.S. example.)

1793 Jefferson *Writ.* (1895) VI. 250 We are going on here in the same spirit still. The Anglophobia has seized violently on three members of our Council.

Anglophobiac (æŋglofōu·biæk), *a.* and *sb.* [f. Anglophobia after *mania, maniac*.] = Anglophobe. Also **Anglopho·bian** *a.*

1893 *N. Amer. Rev.* Aug. 170 The work of an Anglophobiac who labors to widen..the schism. 1894 *Pop. Sci. Monthly* XLV. 476 The Anglophobiac American who proposed cutting a canal through Yucatan. 1896 Miss Betham Edwards in *Daily News* 11 Jan. 7/5 If..scurrilous little newspapers of Paris indulge in Anglophobian diatribes. 1908 *Daily Chron.* 26 May 5/1 The New York 'Sun,' a violently Anglophobiac paper.

A:nglo-Ro·man, *a.* **a.** English Roman Catholic. Hence **A:nglo-Ro·manism**, English Romanism. **b.** Pertaining to England and Rome.

1866 F. Oakeley (*title*) Anglo-Romanism unveiled: or, Canon Oakeley and Dr. Newman at issue with the Catholic and Roman Church, and with one another. 1892 Gladstone in *Westm. Gaz.* (1898) 20 May 8/1, I share the dissatisfaction which many feel at the attitude in England of the *Anglo*-Roman body. 1895 *Ibid.* 12 Jan. 8/2 An essential part of that history [of the sixteenth and seventeenth century] is what I may term Anglo-Roman. 1913 C. G. Bayne (*title*) Anglo-Roman Relations, 1558–1565.

A:nglo-Sa·xonize, *v.* [f. Anglo-Saxon + -ize.] *trans.* To make Anglo-Saxon.

1883 Marquis of Lorne in *Contemp. Rev.* Nov. 641 That great Anglo-Saxonizing amalgamation mill, the United States, would soon efface their [*sc.* French Canadians'] language. 1898 *Westm. Gaz.* 14 July 2/1 These silly efforts to Anglo-Saxonise the United States.

A:nglo-verna·cular, *a.* Consisting of English and an Indian vernacular.

1877 Caldwell *Evangel. Work Tinnevelly* 2 Our S.P.G. Anglo-Vernacular School. 1888 Kipling *Plain Tales fr. Hills, Madness of Priv. Ortheris* 269 He wound up with a six-shot Anglo-Vernacular oath. 1915 (*title*) A List of Educational Books..for Schools in India, Burma and Ceylon.. (Vernacular, Anglo-Vernacular and English).

Angola (*sc.* cat: see Angora 1).

1851 Borrow *Lavengro* i, The cheerful hum of the kettle and the purring of the favourite angola.

Angon (æ·ŋgǫn). [med.L., ad. Gr. ἄγγων.] (See quot. 1893.)

1875 *Encycl. Brit.* II. 555/1 Iron head of Angon from a grave at Darmstadt. 1893 *Athenæum* 9 Sept. 361/3 Among the most curious of the weapons our ancestors used was the angon, a sort of long spear with a double barb—one tongue of which was longer than the other and flame-shaped. 1908 *Victoria Hist. Kent* I. 377 One of the rare iron weapons usually called angons.

Angora. Add: Also applied to a variety of rabbit having fine white fur and pink eyes.

1849 tr. *Wyss's Swiss Family Robinson* Ser. II. xvii. 152 Fritz has two magnificent Angora rabbits in his pouch. 1908 J. A. Thomson *Heredity* x. § 4. 365 Hurst paired white Angora rabbits..with 'Belgian hare' rabbits. 1927 E. V. Knox *Awful Occasions* 56 The vexed topic of dandelions as a diet for half bred Angoras.

Ångström (unit). [The name of A. J. *Ångström*, a Swedish physicist.] A hundred-millionth of a centimetre, used in expressing short wave-lengths (abbrev. A. U.).

1921 *Discovery* Sept. 226 An X-ray of wave length equal to two-tenths of an Angström Unit (100-millionth of a centimetre). 1925 *Chamb. Jrnl.* July 421/1 The angström is so small that ten thousand million of them are needed to make one metre.

Anguipede, -ped (æ·ŋgwipīd, -ped), *a.* [ad. L. *anguipēs* (-*ped*-), f. *anguis* serpent + *pēs* foot.] Having feet or legs in the form of serpents, serpent-footed: an epithet of certain giants of ancient mythology.

1883 A. S. Murray *Gr. Sculpt.* II. 305 *note*, A winged anguipede giant. 1888 A. H. Smith *Catal. Engr. Gems Brit. Mus.* 100 Athene..treading down anguipede Giant.

Anhima (æ·nhimă). Also aniuma. [Brazilian.] The Kamichi or Horned Screamer (*Palamedea cornuta*).

1773 [see Screamer 3 a]. 1774 Goldsm. *Nat. Hist.* (1862) II. vi. iv. 180 A bird..of the crane kind..called the *anhima*, a native of Brazil. 1869–73 Aniuma [see Screamer 3 a].

Anhinga (ænhi·ŋgă). [Tupi.] Any bird of the genus *Anhinga*, esp. the American snake-bird, *A. anhinga*.

1818 Tuckey *Narr. Exped. River Zaire* 82 Mr. Cranch shot some birds amongst which..an anhinga. 1872 Coues *N. Amer. Birds* 332 Few other birds, such as cormorants and anhingas, resemble the *Pygopodes* in this respect.

Ani (ā·ni). [Brazilian.] A bird of the genus *Crotophaga* (family *Cuculidæ*), of which several species are found in the warmer parts of America and in the West Indies.

1840 *Cuvier's Anim. Kingd.* 216 The Ani (*Crotophaga*, Lin.). 1893 Newton *Dict. Birds* 191 There are other eggs, as those of the Anis, *Crotophaga*, the Grebes, *Podicipedidæ*, [etc.] which are more or less covered with a cretaceous film.

Aniconic (ænəikǫ·nik), *a.* *Gr. Antiq.* Also **anik-**. [f. Gr. ἀν- privative + Iconic.] Applied to rude material symbols of a deity, as a simple pillar or block, not shaped into an image of human form; also to the worship connected with these. Hence **Aniconism** (ǽnəi·kǫniz'm), the use of, or worship connected with, such symbols.

1892 C. Waldstein *Excav. Heraion Argos* I. 19 Clement of Alexandria..tells us that the aniconic *σανίς* was superseded by the iconic image, which he calls βρέτας. 1893 *Athenæum* 1 July 38/2 The various stages of development of her [Hera's] *agalmata*: the rudest of all, the anikonic..A..pillar which may have been the actual anikonic image of the goddess. 1907 *Academy* 24 Aug. 818/1 Aniconism does not necessarily imply..anthropomorphism. 1912 L. R. Farnell *Higher Aspects Gr. Relig.* i. 4 Certain aniconic sacred things that we may call fetishes—the hewn stock or pillar, the meteorite, the axe.

Animal. Add:

A. 1. b. The living body or soft fleshy part of a mollusc, crustacean, etc., as distinguished from its shell or other hard part.

1834 McMurtrie *Cuvier's Anim. Kingd.* 248 These Mollusca are arranged in several families according to the form of their shell, which appears to bear a constant relation to that of the animal. 1868 Dana *Min.* 677 Carbonaceous matters..derived from the animals of the shells, corals, etc. out of which the limestones were..made.

3. b. With *the*: The animal nature in man: cf. Beast *sb.* 1 c.

1809 C. Simeon in W. Carus *Life* (1847) 272 Less mixture of the *animal* I never expect to see in this world. 1907 H. A. Vachell *Her Son* i, The animal in this girl was about to spring upon her. 1919 M. K. Bradby *Psycho-analysis* 231 His fleshly desires were strong, and he was unmerciful to the animal in himself.

B. 5. b. Characteristic of or resembling (that of) a lower animal. Also *Comb.*, as *animal-bodied* adj.

1924 Hichens *After the Verdict* III. xv, Fine-souled and animal-bodied men. 1924 D. H. Lawrence *England, my England* 216 The wild, bare, animal shoulders.

Animalist. Add:

4. An artist who makes figures of animals; an animal-painter or -sculptor; also, a writer who deals with stories of animals.

1886 *Century Mag.* Feb. 584/1 [Barye] brought envy and malice on his head through the erection..in the Tuileries gardens of his colossal bronze lion and serpent. It was then the sneer of 'animalist' began. 1890 *Universal Rev.* 15 July 412 The animalists greatly repeat themselves. 1909 *Daily Chron.* 19 Jan. 4/4 The whole crowd of animalists, from Æsop to Mr. Jack London.

Animalization. Add:

1. b. The process of animalizing vegetable fibre.

1862 O'Neill *Calico Printing & Dyeing* 14 The present view of animalisation is, that it is not possible to animalise a fabric in any other way than by actually depositing upon it the animal matter in question.

4. The action of making into or representing as an animal. (Cf. Animalize 1.)

1886 Huxley in *19th Cent.* Apr. 493 In the theology of both the Babylonians and the Egyptians there is abundant evidence..of..the deification of animals, and the converse animalisation of Gods.

Animalize, *v.* **1.** Delete † *Obs.* and add:

1835 [see Animalized 2]. 1886 [implied in *Animalization 4]. 1889 *Cent. Dict.* s.v., The Egyptians animalized their deities.

2. b. To convert (vegetable fibre) into a substance resembling animal fibre.

1862 [see prec. 1 b]. 1874 Knight *Dict. Mech.*, *Animalizing Fiber*, the process of conferring upon vegetable fiber the physical characteristics of animal fiber.

Animated, *ppl. a.* Add:

1. d. In *†animated picture*, etc., early names for cinematographic picture (cf. next).

[1895 *Cassell's Fam. Mag.* Mar. 320/1 The handle is turned ..so as to move the series of photographs rapidly past the eyes, and give the impression of a single animated portrait.] 1898 *Daily News* 31 Mar. 6/3 The animated photographs of the eclipse taken by the Marquis of Graham at Viziadurg. 1900 *Westm. Gaz.* 12 Nov. 10/2 Besides the animated views of the play, there are introduced at intervals a number of still pictures. 1903 *Ibid.* 28 Aug. 8/2 The America Cup race will be shown by animated pictures.

†Animatograph (ænimæ·tograf). *Obs.* [Hybrid f. L. *animātus* Animate *a.* + -graph.] An early name for the *Cinematograph; also, a camera for taking a series of instantaneous photographs for a cinematograph. Also *fig.* in reference to literary description. Hence **†Animatographic** (-græ·fik) *a.*

1896 *Daily News* 26 Mar. 3/6 At a neighbouring house we have the 'cinematographe,' and by way of varying the title Mr. Paul calls his pictures the 'Animatographe'. 1897 *Westm. Gaz.* 25 Sept. 2/3 The animatographic fight between Fitzsimmons and Corbett. 1897 *Ibid.* 5 Feb. 7/1 Animatographic Records for British Museum...Photographs taken for the purpose of the animatograph, or theatregraph, as it is variously called. 1898 *Field* 12 Feb. 213/2, I noticed..a man with an animatograph, and, as there was a good fence to start with, and I know one spill, the photos should not lack animation. 1902 *Westm. Gaz.* 3 Oct. 6/2 Animatograph scenes of life in the Royal Navy.

Aniuma: see *Anhima.

Ankh (æŋk). [Egyptian, = life, soul.] A figure resembling a cross, with a loop or ring forming a handle instead of the upper arm: used in ancient Egyptian art as a symbol of life. Also called *crux ansata*.

1888 A. H. Smith *Catal. Engr. Gems Brit. Mus.* 49 In front, Uraeus; beneath, ☥ Ānχ and Uraei. 1895 Elworthy *Evil Eye* 279. 1896 T. Wilson *Swastika* 766 The *Crux Ansata*..according to Egyptian mythology, was Ankh, the emblem of Ka, the spiritual double of man. 1910 A. Churchward *Signs & Symb. Primord. Man* xix. 409 The cross on the church of Amba Derho is a form of the Ank-cross.

Ankle. 3. Add: **ankle-tie** = *ankle-band*.

1923 Kate D. Wiggin *Gard. Memory* 5 Children with brief legs, white stockings, and ankle-ties.

Ankylostomiasis (æŋkilostomai·ăsis). *Path.* [mod.L., f. *Ankylostoma*: see below and -asis.] An anæmic disease caused by a nematode worm (*Ankylostoma duodenale*, or some similar species) parasitic in the intestines; also called *tunnel-disease* (see Tunnel *sb.* 5).

1890 Billings *Med. Dict.* 1897 *Allbutt's Syst. Med.* II. 1043 The essential symptoms of ankylostomiasis are those of a progressive anæmia associated with symptoms of intestinal catarrh.

Anlage (a·nlāgə). Pl. **anlagen.** Also with anglicized pron. (æ·nlēdʒ). [G., = foundation, basis, f. *anlegen* to establish, f. *an-* on + *legen* Lay *v.*[1]] The rudimentary basis of an organ or organism; in *Embryology*, the first accumulation of cells recognizable as the beginning of a part or organ.

1892 Minot *Human Embryol.* (1897) 432 Comparative anatomy renders it probable that every vertebra had ribs primitively, and most of them have still in the human embryo the anlages of ribs. 1907 Driesch *Sci. and Philos. Organism* (1908) I. 81 You will get a complete larva only from that part [of the gastrula] which bears the 'Anlage' of the endoderm. *Ibid.* 112 *note*, A leaf may be formed out of the Anlage of a scale, if all the leaves are cut off.

Anlaut (a·nlaut). *Philol.* [G., f. *an* on + *laut* sound.] The initial sound of a word. Hence **A·nlauting** *ppl. a.*, serving as anlaut, initial.

1884 Einenkel *St. Kath.* p. xvii, [MS.] Z frequently softens the anlauting *f* to *u*, that is, *v*. Whenever this *u* is no more than a peculiarity of Z's,..I gave it up for the *f*, which C always has as 'anlaut'. 1892 G. Dunn in *Classical Rev.* Feb. 2/2 This representation of y by ζ only occurs with certainty as an anlaut.

Annalistically (ænăli·stikăli), *adv.* [f. Annalistic: see -ically.] In annalistic order; by way of annals.

1881 Freeman in Stephens *Life & Lett.* (1895) II. 222 The years 1088–1093 are easy to tell, almost annalistically. 1894 *Academy* 24 Feb. 164/2 Chronologically and annalistically arranged.

Annatto, annotta, annotto, var. ff. Anatta.

Annexational (æneksē^i·ʃənăl), *a.* [f. Annexation + -al.] Of, pertaining or relating to annexation. So **Annexa·tionism**, advocacy of, or a policy aiming at, annexation; **Annexative** (ăne·ksătiv) *a.*, disposed to annex territory, given to annexation.

1850 Carlyle *Latter-day Pamph.* iv. (1872) 127 A regular statistic of Annexationism. 1869 *Nation* 8 Apr. 267 They..are availing themselves of the strong annexational fever which now rages. 1918 *The Crime* II. i. 24 *note*, That a belligerent state..should..make known annexational intentions. 1921 *Contemp. Rev.* Dec. 723 A nation..insatiably aggressive and annexative.

Annexive (ăne·ksiv), *a.* *Gram.* [f. L. *annex-* (see Annex *v.*) + -ive.] Expressing annexion: = Conjunctive *a.* 3 l.

1853 Edwards & Tayler tr. *Kühner's Gr. Gram.* § 321 A copulative coördinate sentence is either annexive or enhansive. 1913 J. M. Jones *Welsh Gram.* 440 Conjunctions are ..i. annexive..ii. disjunctive.

Annexure (ăne·ksiŭɹ, -ʃŭɹ). [f. L. *annex-* (see Annex *v.*) + -ure.] Something annexed: = Annex *sb.*, Annexment 1.

1878 *Fraser's Mag.* XVIII. 85 A large and profitable annexure to our vast possessions on the Indian continent. 1902 *Westm. Gaz.* 7 July 5/4 The annexures to the petition. 1904 *Blue-bk. Papers Rel. to Thibet* 15, 17.

Annite (æ·nəit). *Min.* [Named by Dana from its locality: see def. and -ite [1].] A variety of Lepidomelane found at Cape Ann, Massachusetts.

1868 Dana *Min.* 308.

Anniversa·rian. *U.S.* [f. Anniversary *sb.*] One who delivers an anniversary address.

1898 *Official Congress Directory* 31 William Henry Fleming..was chosen private anniversarian of the Phi Beta Kappa Society in 1873.

Anno Domini. Add:

b. *jocular colloq.* as *sb.* Advanced or advancing age.

1885 F. Gale *Hon. R. Grimston* xvi. 284 Whenever he felt less able to do things than formerly, he used to say he was afraid 'Anno Domini' was the cause. 1892 Sir F. Pollock *Leading Cases, Death of College Cat*, Yet nothing mortal may deny The march of *Anno Domini* Not e'en the Senior Fellow. 1900 *Daily News* 3 Feb. 2/5, I suffer from an incurable complaint—the complaint of Anno Domini. 1906 E. V. Lucas *Fireside & Sunshine* 186 When the time came for A. to take the bat he was unable to do so. *Anno Domini* asserted itself. 1921 *Times* 31 Mar., My resignation is due to what we call the *anno Domini* clause, which has come into operation.

Annotine. Delete † *Obs. rare*[−1] and add:

2. *Ornith.* A year old. Also *sb.* A bird a year old, or that has moulted once.

1889 in *Cent. Dict.*

Announce, *v.* Add:

1. c. To make (a person) known *as* so-and-so: often *refl.*

1837 E. Howard *Old Commodore* xix. II. 184 Announcing himself as a magistrate made a considerable impression on the seamen. 1856 De Quincey *Confess.* Wks. 1856 V. 150, I announced myself as a passenger 'booked' for that night's mail. 1888 Mrs. H. Ward *R. Elsmere* ii, He announced himself as safely installed at Oxford. 1891 Hardy *Group of Noble Dames* 125 She could not live without announcing herself to him as his mother. *Ibid.* 158 She..requested him to allow her to..announce him as having died of malignant ague.

Announcer. Add:

b. In broadcasting by wireless telegraphy, the person who announces the subjects of a programme and the items of current news.

1922 *Radio Broadcast* Dec. 138 You have heard the announcer say: 'This is XYZ, the Blankety Blank station at So-and-So.' 1923 *Radio Times* 28 Sept. 19 (Announcer) 'The Stock Exchange was very lively to-day'. 1928 *Broadcast English* 19 They are recommendations made primarily for the benefit of announcers.

Annual. **B. 3. b.** Add to def.: Less frequently applied to an animal. Also *hardy annual* (lit. and fig.): see Hardy *a.* 4 b.

1767 Abercrombie *Ev. Man his own Gardener* 49 To prepare for sowing some of the more curious forms of annuals. 1834 *Paxton's Mag. Bot.* I. 18 Treatment of Hardy Annuals. 1854 *F. & A. Dickson's* (of Chester) *Catal.*, Hardy Annuals can be supplied in small packets. 1879 *Punch* LXXVII. 256 In fact, to judge by these hardy annuals, Christmas may be said to have begun about a month ago. 1883 Day *Indian Fish* (Fish. Exhib. Publ.) 31 The various modes in which the reproduction of these fishes is carried on...Whether the parents are monogamous, polygamous, or are annuals dying after the reproductive process has been accomplished. 1905 *Westm. Gaz.* 20 June 3/2 Presumably a time will come when even such a wonderfully hardy annual [as Sarah Bernhardt] will fail to reappear.

Annuity. Add: **1. c.** *U.S. spec.* A yearly supply of goods and provisions given by the Government to an Indian tribe. Also *attrib.*

1873 J. H. Beadle *Undevel. West* xxv. 530 The annuity goods and provisions of that year were soon exhausted. *Ibid.* xxvii. 586 They now receive regular annuities of Government goods.

Annulism (æ·niŭliz'm). [f. Annulus + -ism.] Annulate structure.

1841 [see Radiism].

Annunciation. Add:

4. *attrib.*: **Annunciation lily**, a Madonna lily such as is depicted in pictures of the Annunciation.

1877 Lady Wood *Sheen's Foreman* I. 234 Clusters of annunciation lilies. 1899 *Daily News* 4 Feb. 6/3 The dress is white velvet, embroidered straight up the front with long sprays of Annunciation lilies. 1907 *Daily Chron.* 2 May 4/5 The large drawing room,..decorated with tall Annunciation lilies.. and exquisite roses.

Anoa (ănōu·ă). [Native name.] An animal of the genus of the same name; a small wild ox of the Celebes.

1888 *Athenæum* 1 Dec. 740/1 Prof. J. B. Steere [read a paper] on the 'tamaron', a bovine animal found in the island of Mindoro, Philippines, which he believed to be allied to the *anoa* of Celebes.

Anodal (æ·nodăl), *a.* [f. Anode + -al.] Pertaining to the anode.

1882 *Athenæum* 8 July 50/3 The character (anodal or kathodal) of the electric charge. 1886 *Buck's Handbk. Med. Sci.* II. 651/1 The second, anodal closure contraction, occurs when the anode is applied to the nerve or muscle.

Anodic (ænǫ·dik), *a.* [f. Gr. ἄνοδος way up (f. ἀνά up + ὁδός way) or directly f. Anode + -ic.]

1. *Phys.* Of nerve force: Proceeding towards a nerve-centre; afferent. (Cf. Cathodic 1.)

1852 M. Hall *Diastaltic Nerv. Syst.* 32 The influence which has induced this effect must have been anodic and cathodic in one and the same lumbar nerve.

2. *Electr.* = *Anodal.

1849 Noad *Electricity* (ed. 3) 200 The anodic division.. will finally become colourless, owing to the separation of chlorine. 1890 Billings *Med. Dict.* s.v., *A[nodic]-closure-contraction*,..contraction of a muscle when circuit is closed by placing the anode over the motive-point. *A.-opening-contraction*,..contraction when circuit is opened by removal of anode from over motive-point.

3. *Bot.* (See quot. 1882 s.v. Cathodic 2.)

Hence **Ano·dically** *adv.*, in relation to the anode.

1905 tr. *Haeckel's Wond. Life* 101 Most of the flagellate infusoria..are anodically sensitive or positively galvanotactic.

Anodynous, *a.* (Modern U.S. example.)

1904 'O. Henry' *Cabbages & Kings* v. 89 The prestige of drifting music on moonlit waters gave it an anodynous charm.

Anoetic, *a.* Add:

2. *Psychol.* Relating to or characterized by **Anoesis** (ano,ī·sis), a hypothetical state of consciousness in which there is sensation but no thought.

1902 G. F. Stout *Anal. Psychol.* I. 51 Objective reference supervening on purely anoetic experience would be a completely new psychical fact. 1902 *Encycl. Brit.* XXXII. 63 Such a consciousness has been happily named anoetic. Whether or no it actually exists is another matter..But relative anoesis suffices here.

Anointment. Delete †, for *Obs.* read *arch.*, and add:

1868 Milman *St. Paul's* 40 The dying yearned in vain for anointment with the blessed oil. 1887 Hardy *Woodlanders* I. iv. 59 As if your knee-jints were greased with very saint's anointment.

Anolian (ănōu·liăn), *a.* and *sb.* *Zool.* [f. Anoli(s + -an.] **A.** *adj.* Belonging or related to the genus *Anolis*. **B.** *sb.* A lizard of or related to this genus.

1841 *Penny Cycl.* XX. 459/2 The Lacertian, Iguanian, Anolian, and Scincoid families.

Anomalure (ănǫ·măliuəɹ). *Zool.* [ad. mod.L. *Anomalūrus*, f. Gr. ἀνώμαλος Anomalous + οὐρά tail.] An animal of the African genus *Anomalurus* of rodents resembling the flying squirrels, and having projecting scales on the tail which serve for assistance in climbing; a scale-tailed squirrel. So **Anomalu·rid**, a member of the family *Anomaluridæ*, of which this is the only genus.

1883 *Cassell's Nat. Hist.* III. 96 Whilst in the Flying Squirrels this spur springs from the wrist.., in the Anomalures it projects from the elbow. 1920 *Brit. Museum Return* 102 An Anomalure..from Sierra Leone.

Anomœan (ænomī·ăn), *a.* and *sb.* *Theol.* [f. mod.L. *Anomœus*, ad. Gr. ἀνόμοιος unlike, dissimilar (f. ἀν- privative + ὅμοιος like, similar) + -an.] Belonging to, or a member of, an extreme sect of Arians who held that the Father and the Son are unlike in essence: = Heteroousian: opp. to Homoiousian.

[1526 R. Whytford *Martiloge* 6 Apr., Yᵉ heretykes called..anomeyes.] 1683 Cave *Ecclesiastici, Athanasius* 153 The Anomæan Heresie. *Ibid.*, *Basil* 224 The Head of the Homoiousian, against the Anomæans or Heterousian Sect. 1756–9 A. Butler *Lives Saints* (1780) V. 31 *note*, The Anomæans or rank Arians. 1840 Milman *Hist. Chr.* III. v. III. 47 The party of the Anomeans triumphed, while Aetius, its author, was sent into banishment. 1874 J. C. Robertson *Hist. Chr. Ch.* II. vi. 63 The perpetual virginity of the Saviour's mother was denied by the anomœan Eunomius. 1882–3 [see Heteroousiast].

Anopheles (ănǫ·fĭlīz). *Entom.* [mod.L. (Meigen in *Syst. Beschr. Eur. Zweifl. Ins.* (1818) I. 10), f. *Anōphelēs*, a. Gr. ἀνωφελής unprofitable, useless.] A mosquito of the genus *Anopheles*, which conveys the parasite of malaria. Hence **Ano·pheline** *a.* and *sb.*

1899 *Daily News* 28 Sept. 3/4 We could kill most of the anopheles grubs here in a few hours with kerosene oil. 1902 *Encycl. Brit.* XXIX. 498/2 The parasite has now been found to live in the body of the Anopheles. 1920 J. Ritchie *Animal Life Scot.* 511 Mosquitoes,..I mean Anopheline, or ..'spot-winged' Gnats.

Anopisthograph (ænopi·spǫgraf), *a.* [f. Gr. ἀν- privative + ὀπισθόγραφος Opisthograph.] Having no writing (or printing) on the back; inscribed only on one side. Also **A:nopisthographic** (-græ·fik), **-ical** *adjs.*; hence **A:nopisthogra·phically** *adv.*

1871 H. Bradshaw *Collected Papers* xiv. 263 If a fragment is found printed only on one side it has hitherto been described as 'a remarkably interesting specimen of anopisthographic typography'. 1887 Bigmore tr. *Bouchot's Printed Bk.* i. 15 Gutenberg..desired..that the leaves of his books should not be anopis[th]ograph, or printed only on one side. 1887 *Book-Lore* VI. 159 Two leaves were..pasted together, back to back, forming what is termed an anopist[h]ographical book. 1893 E. G. Duff *Early Printed Bks.* 13 There must have been some reason for printing these books on one side only..or, as it is called, anopisthographically.

Anorthosite (ænǫ·ɹþǫsəit). *Min.* [f. F. *anorthose* + -ite [1].] A granular igneous rock composed mainly of a soda-lime felspar.

1863 T. S. Hunt in *Amer. Jrnl. Sci.* Ser. II. XXXVI. 222 A series of strata characterized by a great development of anorthosites. *Ibid.* 224 These anorthosite rocks are often compact, but more frequently granitoid in structure. 1925 J. Joly *Surface-Hist. Earth* iii. 47 These rocks..present to our view many varieties of structure and mineral composition; e.g. in the granites, gneisses, anorthosites, diorites.

Another. **1. b.** Add to def.:

You're another! (slang or colloq.), a phrase properly used in retorting a charge upon the person who makes it (cf. Tu quoque); hence humorously as a meaningless or vaguely contemptuous retort.

a 1553 Udall *Royster D.* III. v, *R. Royster.* If it were an other but thou, it were a knaue. *M. Mery.* Ye are an other your selfe sir, the lorde vs both saue. 1569 Preston *Cambyses* (Brandl) 786 And thou calst me knave, thou art another! 1749 Fielding *Tom Jones* IX. vi, 'I did not mean to abuse the Cloth; I only said your Conclusion was a *Non Sequitur*.' 'You are another,' cries the Sergeant, 'an' you come to that. No more a *Sequitur* than yourself.' 1837 Dickens *Pickw.* xv, 'Sir,' said Mr. Tupman, 'you're a fellow.' 'Sir,' said Mr. Pickwick, 'you're another.' 1882 *Boston Lit. World* 3 June 184/3 The argument of it is simply, 'You're another,'—a retort in dignified manner to..British critics. 1887 Lowell *Democr.* etc. 10, I find little..to edify me in these international bandyings of 'You're another.'

3. Add to def.:

Another place: a euphemistic phrase used by members of parliament to designate the other House, i.e. the House of Lords or the House of Commons.

1883 [see Dict.]. 1908 *Westm. Gaz.* 27 July 1/3 Lord Lamington, was a busy member of the House of Commons.. before he went to 'another place' on his father's death in 1890. 1927 *Observer* 10 July 15/7 Usually M.P.'s speak dispassionately of 'another place', but Mr. Baldwin the other day made it 'the other end of the passage', and Mr. Snowden 'the other end of the corridor'.

Ansate (æ·nsēt), *a.* [ad. L. *ansātus*, f. *ansa* handle.] = Ansated. Also in L. (fem.) form in *ansata cross* for *crux ansata* (= *Ankh).

1891 Kinns *Graven in Rock* viii. 292 Iris and Horus are each holding the ansata cross or emblem of life. 1891 Haverfield in *Athenæum* 31 Oct. 591/1 Centurial stone, ansate, 17 in. by 8 in.

Ansated, *ppl. a.* Delete † *Obs.*[−0] and add:

1785 *European Mag.* VIII. 131 The Tau, or ansated Cross of the Egyptians. 1798 *Proc. Soc. Antiquaries* IV. 2 An ansated patera. 1891 Haverfield in *Athenæum* 16 May 644/1 [The stone has] well-cut letters..in an ansated panel.

Ansation (ænsē^i·ʃən). [f. L. *ansa* handle + -ation, after Ansate.] The provision of handles.

1859 *Jrnl. Brit. Archæol. Assoc.* XV. 69 There is rarely any attempt at ansation; the nearest approach to handles being heavy perforated knobs placed a little beneath the mouth.

Answer, *sb.* Add: **4. b.** *U.S. spec.* (See quot.)

1816 Pickering *Vocab.*, *Answer*. This term is always used by us to signify the Reply of the Senate or House of Representatives to the speech of the President (or of the Governor of a state) at the opening of a session of the Legislature.

c. *Answer-back*: a rejoinder or repartee; also *fig.*

1925 J. A. Thomson *Sci. & Relig.* vi. § 9. 194 The struggle for existence is a formula covering all the answers-back that organisms make to environing difficulties.

Answer, *v.* **12. e.** Add:

spec. in Horse-racing. *To answer* (*the question*): (of a horse) to respond to a call made by the jockey. (Cf. *ask the question*, *Ask *v.* 2 b.)

1894 H. Custance *Riding Recoll.* vii. 88, I..asked 'King Lud' the question. He answered in the most generous manner possible,..and won. 1894 *Idler* June 545 The certain winner of the Derby—if he is able to answer the question I am going to put to him.

Ant. 4. Add:

ant-bird, any bird of the family *Formicariidæ*, comprising the ant-eaters of S. America; **ant-cow**, a popular name for the aphides kept and tended by ants for the sake of the sweet fluid that they extract from them; **ant-eggs, ants' eggs**, properly, the eggs of ants; popularly applied to their larvæ or pupæ; **ant-orchis**, a terrestrial Australasian orchid of the species *Chiloglottis gunnii* (Morris *Austral English*, 1898); **ants' wood**, = *saffron plum* (Saffron B. b); **ant-thrush**, any of the South American ant-eating birds otherwise called ant-birds; also, formerly by some writers, a bird of the genus *Pitta*; **ant-wren**, W. Swainson's name for a South American ant-eating bird of the genus *Formicivora*, included by P. L. Sclater in the subfamily *Formicariinæ* in his division of the family *Formicariidæ*, the ant-thrushes.

1858 Sclater in *Proc. Zool. Soc.* 13 Apr. 202 Synopsis of the American *Ant-birds (Formicariidæ). 1875 *Encycl. Brit.* II. 98/1 The Coccidæ in America take the place of the European aphides as *ant-cows. 1666 *Phil. Trans.* No. 23. 426 Upon opening of these Banks, I observe first a white substance, which..looks like the scatterings of fine white Sugar or Salt...This same substance..I finde in the Ants themselves, which I take to be the true *Ants Eggs. *Ibid.* 427 In the Morning they bring up those of their Young (that are vulgarly call'd Ants Eggs) towards the top of the Bank. 1834 *Penny Cycl.* II. 61/1 To collect the cocoons (popularly and erroneously called ants'-eggs) in quantity as food for nightingales and larks. 1884 *Ants' Wood [see Saffron B. b]. 1783 Latham *Gen. Syn. Birds* II. 87 *Ant Thr[ush]. This is of the size of a Lark: length six inches. 1836 W. Swainson in *Zool. Jrnl.* II. 146 The *Formicivoræ*, or *Ant-Wrens, are all of them very small.

Antarian (æntē^ə·riăn), *a.* *Astr.* [f. *Antares* (æntē^ə·rīz), latinized form of Gr. Ἀντάρης (Ptolemy), f. ἀντί (Anti-[1]) + Ἄρης Mars: so named from its red colour, like that of the planet Mars: see -ian.] Pertaining to or resembling Antares, a star of the first magnitude in the constellation of the Scorpion; applied to a class of stars having a spectrum like that of Antares.

1909 *Cent. Dict.* Suppl. s.v., Antarian stars..are far less abundant than Sirian and Arcturian stars.

Ante (æ·nti), *sb.*[2] (Also erron. anti.) [a. L. *ante* before.] In *Poker*, a stake put up by a player (usually, the eldest hand) before drawing new cards. Hence, a price. Also *attrib.* in **anteman** = *Age *sb.* 6 b.

1853 J. G. Baldwin *Flush Times Alab.* 8 A negro *ante* and twenty on the call, was moderate playing. 1859 Bartlett *Dict. Amer.* (ed. 2) s.v. *Anti*, The amount placed in the pool by each player being called the *anti*. 1873 [G. A. Lawrence] *Silverland* 112 His crafty opponents read his hand like a book, and the very 'ante's' will break him at last. 1882 *Poker* 7 To begin the pool, the player next to the dealer, on his left, must put up money, which is called an 'Ante'. *Ibid.* 8 It is best generally for the ante-man to make good and go in. 1890 *Harper's Mag.* Feb. 428/2, I raised the ante, and sold three hundred papers at ten cents each.

Ante (æ·nti), *v.* [f. prec.] *trans.* To put up (an ante); also *transf.* (*U.S.*) to bet, stake; to pay *off*, *up*. Also *absol.*

1845 J. J. Hooper *Simon Suggs' Adv.* x. 129 Ante up! ante up, boys—friends I mean—don't back out! *Ibid.* xii. 144 Exsept..500 dollers I anteed off amongst the boys of a night, I couldn't git off a sent. 1854 in Thornton *Amer. Gloss.* 971 Playin' at billiards an' monte Till they've nary red cent to ante. 1857 *Knick. Mag.* Jan. 43, I did hear that you anted off 1000 shares in trade for Texas lands. 1859 Bartlett *Dict. Amer.* (ed. 2), To *Anti*, to risk; to venture a bet; as, 'I'll anti all I'm worth on that'. This term is derived from the game of poker. 1861 *N. Y. Tribune* 10 Aug. (Bartlett), I have had to ante up at the rate of $200. 1861 *Congress. Globe* Dec. 126/1 [Senator Polk] is not familiar with scenes where hundreds of dollars are 'anted up'. 1889 R. Guerndale *Poker Bk.* ii. 13 The player after the dealer must Ante first, before the draw. *Ibid.* vii. 42 B Antes one, and the cards are dealt by A. 1889 Farmer *Americanisms*, To *Ante up* is to pay, as well as to wager. 1896 Vachell *Rom. Judge Ketchum* III. viii. 267 Death.. and I hev bin pardners many a time, an' when he passes the word, I'll ante up with a smile if I kin. 1900 H. Lawson *On Track* 157 The man that doesn't ante gets the best of this world. 1910 W. M. Raine *B. O'Connor* 237 You got a right to ante up with some information.

Ante-bellum (æ·nti,be·lŏm). [Lat. phrase = 'before the war', used *attrib.* or as *adj.*] Previous to the war, i.e. *spec.* the American civil war (1861–5), the S. African war (1899–1902), or the European war (1914–18).

1879 Tourgee *Fool's Errand* xv. 80 Evidently thinking that his connection with this ante bellum barbarity had somehow increased his importance. 1882 *Rep. Ho. Repr. Prec. Met. U.S.* 306 One of the productive mines of ante-bellum days. 1905 *Westm. Gaz.* 4 Jan. 2/3 The ante-bellum negotiations. 1924 *Contemp. Rev.* Apr. 438 Deaths of infants from overlaying..were also only one-third of the ante-bellum number.

Supplement, p. 3873; Corrigenda, p. 4092; Spurious words, p. 4093; Books quoted, p. 4094

Antebrachial, *a.*, more correct f. ANTIBRACHIAL. So **Antebrachium** (anti-) *Biol.* [med.L.], in mammalia, the part of the arm or fore-limb from the wrist to the elbow; the forearm.
1877 [see BRACHIUM]. 1880 [see ANTIBRACHIAL].

Antecede, *v.* Delete *arch.* and add to 1:
1911 C. A. MERCIER *Astrol. in Med.* (1914) 1 Its origin is so remote as to antecede all written records. 1902 H. SPENCER *Facts and Comments* 204 Recognizing the properties of Space..as anteceding all creation..and all evolution.

A·ntechamber, *v.* *intr.* and *trans.* To wait or wait for in or as in an antechamber: cf. ANTECHAMBERING *vbl. sb.*
1891 *Pall Mall Gaz.* 2 Oct. 1/3 All intriguing Paris was antechambering him. 1900 W. A. ELLIS *Wagner* 291 My poor dog..was antechambering in the street in wait for his more fortunate master, allowed to antechamber among men.

Antecian, variant of ANTŒCIAN.

A:nte-Commu·nion. In full *Ante-Communion Service* [ANTE- B. 2], a popular term for that part of the Communion Service in the Book of Common Prayer which extends from the beginning of the office to 'the end of the general Prayer "For the whole state of Christ's Church militant here in earth"' and is appointed to be said 'upon the Sundays and other Holy-days (if there be no Communion)'.
According to the American rite, the Ante-Communion ends with the Gospel.
1827 *Gentl. Mag.* XCVII. II. 487 There was no offertory, and no prayer for the church militant. I am not aware by what authority this part of the Ante-Communion Service is now so commonly omitted on Sundays. 1871 F. G. LEE *Dict. Ritual Terms, Ante-Communion.* (1) An Anglican term used to designate that portion of the Liturgy or Communion service which, commencing with the Introit, or the Lord's Prayer, closes with the end of the Nicene Creed. (2) This term is also used for the introductory part of the Eucharistic office, when it only, and nothing further, is intended to be used. 1899 *Westm. Gaz.* 2 Jan. 4/2 Those of you who feel that it is not necessary to hear the ante-Communion service twice on Sunday.

Antedation (æntidēⁱ·ʃən). [irreg. f. ANTEDATE *v.*: see -ATION.] The act of antedating or fact of being antedated.
1925 *Lond. Gaz.* 29 Dec. 8652/1 The King has approved the antedation of the promotion of Lieut. L. S...to the rank of Captain to 1st Jan. 1921.

Ante meridiem (æ·nti mėri·diem), *phr.* [L. *ante meridiem* before midday.] Before midday; applied to the hours between noon and the preceding midnight; abbreviated A.M. or a.m. (q.v.).
1563 DEE *Diary* (Camden Soc.) 2, Sept. 28th, Mr. John Ask ante meridiem, by York six myle on this syde. 1647 LILLY *Chr. Astrol.* iv. 41 If your hour of the day be in the morning, or as we say *Ante Meridiem*, or before noon.

Antenna. Add:
4. A dorsal sense-organ in rotifers.
1886 A. G. BOURNE in *Encycl. Brit.* XXI. 5/2 A structure found in many Rotifers, and variously known as the 'calcar', 'siphon', 'tentaculum', or 'antenna'.
5. *Wireless Telegr.* An aerial wire, an aerial: see *AERIAL 6 b.
1902 J. A. FLEMING in *Encycl. Brit.* XXXIII. 230/2 The great improvement introduced by Marconi was the employment of this vertical air-wire, aerial, antenna, or elevated conductor. 1904 *Phys. Rev.* Sept. 197 In 1898 he [*sc.* Marconi] saw the importance of the direct grounding of the receiving antenna. 1915 tr. *Zenneck's Wireless Telegr.* 150 Every radio station has an open oscillator, the 'antenna', that part of the antenna which is suspended in the air being called the 'aerial'. 1916 J. A. FLEMING *Radiotelegr.* (ed. 3) 155 A single mast..having two sprits attached to it by means of which an antenna wire is upheld in the form of a vertical rectangle.

Ante-post (æ·nti,pōᵘst). [f. ANTE- + POST *sb.*[1] 2.] Of betting (see quot. 1902).
1902 *Encycl. Brit.* XXVI. 236/1 Betting is of two kinds: 'post', when wagering does not begin until the numbers of the runners are hoisted on the board; and 'ante-post', when wagering opens weeks or months before the event. 1914 *Daily Express* 19 Sept. 5/2 If there had been any important ante-post betting..many would have burnt their fingers badly.

Antergic (æntə̄·ɹdʒik), *a.* *Physiol.* [f. ANT- = ANTI- + Gr. ἔργον work + -IC, after *synergic.*] Acting in opposition to the action of another part, as a muscle: = ANTAGONISTIC 2: opp. to SYNERGIC.
1892 W. R. GOWERS *Man. Dis. Nerv. Syst.* I. 7 This antergic contraction is essential for the exertion of force.

Anteriad (ænti³·riæd), *adv.* *Anat.* [f. ANTERIOR + *-AD.] Towards the anterior part or surface of the body.
1903 *Trans. Amer. Microsc. Soc.* Nov. 66 (C.D. Suppl.), The rudiment of the gall-bladder which in the previous stage..opens dorsad..in the present stage..opens anteriad.

Anterior, *a.* Add:
1. b. *Anat.*, *Bot.*, and *Zool.* Situated in the front or near the head, fore-part, axis, etc.: opp. to POSTERIOR A. 3.
1733 G. DOUGLAS tr. *Winslow's Anat.* I. 75 The Clavicle is divided into a Body or middle Part, and two Extremities, one anterior, inferior, and internal..; the other posterior, superior, and external. 1826 KIRBY & SP. *Entomol.* IV. 335 *Anterior*, the fore or upper wings. *Ibid.* 339 *Anterior* or *Exterior*, the outer margin of the wing, or that from the body. 1829 LOUDON *Encycl. Plants* 1094 *Anterior*, growing in front of some other thing. 1853 DARLINGTON *Flora Cestrica* (ed. 3) Gloss., *Anterior*, in front, or below,—as that part of a flower next to the bract, or farthest from the axis of inflorescence. 1877 W. TURNER *Hum. Anat.* 213 The anterior cerebral vesicle bends downwards from the middle vesicle. 1879 A. GRAY *Bot. Text-bk.* (ed. 6) I. 160 The portion of the flower which faces the subtending bract is the anterior. 1886 *Buck's Handbk. Med. Sci.* II. 507/2 The anterior oblique dislocation of Bigelow. 1893 *H. Morris' Hum. Anat.* 1127 In front of the sterno-mastoid is the anterior triangle. 1897 D. H. SCOTT *Struct. Bot.* (ed. 4) I. 23 The two outer sepals are so placed that one lies next the axis (*posterior*), and the other remote from it (*anterior*).

Antevert, *v.* **1.** Delete †*Obs.* and add:
1914 *N. Amer. Rev.* Sept. 387 The Cossacks..rode down the sidewalks..in an effort to antevert a meeting of the students.

Anthelmi·nthic (-þik), more correct form of ANTHELMINTIC.
1684 [see ANTHELMINTIC A.]. 1702 FULLER *Pharmacopœia* (1710) 76 The Decoction called Sacrum..is a most noble..Anthelminthic. *Ibid.* 189 Give Anthelminthics..to make the Worms weak and languishing. 1871 KINGSLEY *At Last* xiii, Their bitter anthelminthic oil.

Anthilly (æ·nt,hili), *a.* [f. ANT-HILL + -Y[1].] Full of or abounding in ant-hills.
1796 W. H. MARSHALL *Rural Econ. W. Eng.* II. 212 Rough anthilly land. 1892 *Field* 19 Nov. 766/2 Anthilly fields of grass.

Anthocodia (ænþokōᵘ·diă). *Zool.* Pl. **-æ.** [mod.L., f. Gr. ἄνθος flower + κώδεια head of poppy, etc.] The free part of an alcyonarian polyp, which bears the tentacles. Cf. *ANTHOSTELE.
1900 G. C. BOURNE in *Trans. Linn. Soc., Zool.* VII. 528 Branches..each ending in a terminal anthocodia larger than the lateral anthocodiæ.

Anthodium (ænþōᵘ·diəm). *Bot.* Pl. **-ia.** [mod.L., f. Gr. ἀνθώδης (see ANTHOID) + *-ium.*] A name for the flower-head or *capitulum* in *Compositæ*.
1861 BENTLEY *Man. Bot.* 203 *The Capitulum, Anthodium, or Head.*—This kind of inflorescence constitutes the Compound Flower of Linnæus.

Anthologize (ænþǫ·lŏdʒəiz), *v.* [f. ANTHOLOGY + -IZE.] **a.** *trans.* To make an anthology of or from; to use in an anthology. **b.** *intr.* To make an anthology. Chiefly in *pa. pple.*, *vbl. sb.*, or *gerund*.
1892 *Sat. Rev.* 9 Apr. 426/2 The anthologized poet. 1892 *Daily News* 12 July 4/8 Where poets dead and gone are concerned,..the practice of selecting and anthologising is comparatively innocuous. 1923 *Times Lit. Suppl.* 4 Jan. 9/3 Many writers of verse are familiar to the public through an anthologized example. 1924 *Ibid.* 13 Nov. 724/2 The thirty-four lines..deserve to be rescued from Professor Macaulay's grim black covers and anthologized. 1928 *Manch. Guardian Weekly* 17 Aug. 133/2 The anthologising offences of Palgrave, Sir Arthur Quiller-Couch and Mr. J. C. Squire.

Anthophilous (ænþǫ·filəs), *a.* *Entom.* [f. Gr. ἄνθος flower + -φιλος loving + -OUS.] Loving or frequenting flowers, as an insect (correlative to ENTOMOPHILOUS); *spec.* belonging to the division *Anthophila* of hymenopterous insects, comprising the bees.
1883 THOMPSON tr. *Müller's Fert. Flowers* 33 The larvæ of beetles which are anthophilous.

Anthostele (æ·nþostīl). *Zool.* [f. Gr. ἄνθος flower + στήλη pillar.] The part of the body of an alcyonarian polyp by which it is fused with neighbouring polyps of the colony. Cf. *ANTHOCODIA.
1900 G. C. BOURNE in *Trans. Linn. Soc., Zool.* VII. 532 The anthostele sends up a solenium.

Anthotaxis (ænþotæ·ksis). *Bot.* [mod.L., f. Gr. ἄνθος flower + τάξις arrangement: cf. PHYLLOTAXIS.] The arrangement of flowers on the flowering stem; inflorescence.
1861 BENTLEY *Man. Bot.* 187 Inflorescence or Anthotaxis.

Anthotype (æ·nþotəip). *Photogr.* [f. Gr. ἄνθος flower + -TYPE.] A photographic process in which fugitive prints are obtained on paper treated with the expressed juice of flowers; a print so obtained.
1843 *Civil Eng. & Arch. Jrnl.* VI. 286/1 The subject in all its branches, including..Ferrotype, Anthotype. 1909 *Cent. Dict.* Suppl. s.v., The anthotype process was discovered by Sir John Herschel.

Anthracitization (ænþrăsəitəizēⁱ·ʃən). [f. ANTHRACITE + -IZE + -ATION.] The process of becoming changed from bituminous coal into anthracite.
1903 *Progr. Geol. Surv. U.K.* 1902, 49 An investigation of the anthracitisation of the coals. *Ibid.* 190 The anthracitisation is more rapid in a north and south direction.

Anthracosis (ænþrăkōᵘ·sis). [mod.L., f. Gr. ἀνθρακ-, ἄνθραξ ANTHRAX + -OSIS.] Lung disease produced by the inhalation of coal-dust. Hence **Anthracotic** (-ǫ·tik) *a.*, pertaining to or affected with anthracosis.
1848 DUNGLISON *Med. Lex.* (ed. 7), Anthracosis. 1875 *C. H. Jones & Sieveking's Path. Anat.* (ed. 2) 492 'Colliers' Phthisis', or as it has been called, anthrakosis. 1900–1 *Jrnl. Exper. Med.* V. 156 The cut section of the lungs, which were markedly anthracotic, was smooth. 1912 ADAMI & McCRAE *Pathol.* 325 Section of an anthracotic lung.

Anthropic, *a.* Add to def.: Concerned with or relating to human beings; in *Geol.* applied to the period of the deposits in which human remains are found.
1884 HARRISON in *19th Cent.* Mar. 505 The conclusion that the future of religion is to be, not only..anthropomorphic—but frankly anthropic. 1884 BLACKMORE *Tommy Upmore* xiii, My dear little anthropic nautilus, I can do nothing. 1893 J. W. DAWSON *Salient Points* 465 The age of which we have been writing the history, is that which has been fitly named the Anthropic.

Anthropogeography (ænþrǭᵘpo,dʒi,ǫ·grăfi). [f. ANTHROPO- + GEOGRAPHY, after G. *anthropogeographie* (F. Ratzel 1882).] That department of geography which treats of the relations of the earth to mankind as its inhabitants. So **Anthropogeographer** (-ǫ·grăfəɹ), one versed in anthropogeography; **Anthropogeographic** (-ogræ·fik), **-ical** *adjs.*, pertaining to anthropogeography.
1652 *Hermeticall Banquet* 120 The new Anthropogeographicall Map. *a* 1899 BRINTON *Basis Soc. Relat.* iv. (1902) 131 Even the most determined of the 'anthropo-geographers' will not deny that the power over the mind which they attribute to geographical features diminishes in proportion as culture increases. 1899 *Geogr. Jrnl.* Feb. 171 Anthropogeography is a convenient term under which to include all those aspects of geography that deal with the relations of humanity..to the earth...'Applied Geography' might be taken as an alternative term.

Anthropogony (ænþrǫpǫ·gŏni). [ad. Gr. ἀνθρωπογονία (Josephus).] **a.** The origin of man. **b.** The investigation or an account of this.
1868 MANSEL *Gnostic Heresies* (1875) 36 A scheme of cosmogony and anthropogony, running parallel to each other, man being regarded as the microcosm, or image in miniature of the world. 1874 tr. *Van Oosterzee's Chr. Dogmatics* I. 361 A comparison with other Eastern Anthropogonies gives a result most favourable to the Mosaic.

Anthropometer (-ǫ·mĭtəɹ). [See -METER.] **a.** One who studies or practises anthropometry. **b.** An anthropometrical instrument.
1881 *Ann. Rep. Smithsonian Inst.* (1883) 499 Man is an animal..exhibiting in his adult form those characteristics which engage the attention of the anatomist, the physiologist, and the anthropometer. 1898 A. C. HADDON *Study of Man* xvi. 446 The rod of the Anthropometer should be held vertically in front of the face of the subject.
So **Anthropo·metrist** = a. above.
1883 *Pall Mall Gaz.* 3 Oct. 2 Surely the anthropometrists will do harm if they encourage the craze for tallness. 1904 G. S. HALL *Adolescence* I. 19 Anthropometrists think growth in height..antagonistic to growth in girth.

Anthropomorph (ænþrōᵘ·po-, æ·nþroupomǭɹf). [ad. Gr. ἀνθρωπόμορφος: see ANTHROPOMORPHOUS.] A representation of the human form in art.
In quot. 1894 used with sarcastic application.
1894 *Daily News* 26 Nov. 6/5 Your fashionable and self-adoring man or 'anthropomorph'. 1895 A. C. HADDON *Evol. Art* 185 New Zealand is one of the places where anthropomorphs abound. 1913 J. RENDEL HARRIS *Boanerges* ii. 14 There was an ornithomorph, and..several theriomorphs, before the anthropomorph.

Anthropomorphic, *a.* Add:
2. Having a human form: = ANTHROPOMORPHOUS.
1886 [see ZOOMORPHIC 2 b]. 1905 A. S. GRIFFITH tr. *Capart's Prim. Art Egypt* iii. 59 The designs..borrowed from animals (zoomorphic designs), from the human figure (anthropomorphic), and occasionally from manufactured objects (skeuomorphic).

Anthropopsychism (ǣnþrōᵘposəi·kiz'm), *a.* [f. Gr. ἄνθρωπος man + ψυχή soul + -ISM.] The ascription of mental faculties or characteristics like those of man to the Divine Being or the agencies at work in nature. So **Anthro:popsy·chic** *a.*, **anthro:popsy·chically** *adv.*
1884 DK. ARGYLL *Unity of Nature* v. 168 It is not the Form of Man that is in question. It is the Mind and Spirit of Man—his Reason, his Intelligence, and his Will...The question is of a..fundamental analogy..between the Mind which is in us and the Mind which is in Nature. The true etymological expression for this idea..would be, not Anthropomorphism, but Anthropopsychism. *Ibid.* 191 If the human or anthropopsychic interpretation of the..actions of all living Beings is the only interpretation which explains them. *Ibid.* viii. 289 Professor Tyndall himself cannot describe this System without using the most intensely anthropopsychic language: 'The continued effort of animated nature is to improve its conditions and raise itself to a loftier level.' 1884 *Edin. Rev.* Apr. 514 The Duke admits that much of the language which is anthropopsychically used, is of a metaphorical character. 1898 *Literary Guide* 1 Jan. 10, I desire to abstain from any thoughts about the Ultimate Reality which suggest anthropomorphism or anthropopsychism.

Anti (æ·nti), *a.* and *sb.*[1] [ANTI-[1] used as a word.] (One who or that which is) against or antagonistic to some person or thing.
1852 MUNDY *Antipodes* (1857) 209 The 'Anti' journals joined with them in coarse personalities. 1889 *Pall Mall Gaz.* 27 June 1 The 'antis' have no option but to take it up. 1899 GUINNESS ROGERS in *Daily News* 28 June 9/2 Preachers of the 'Anti'.

Anti, *sb.*[2] Abbrev. of ANTI-FEDERALIST. *U.S.*
1789 (Apr. 4) FISHER AMES *Wks.* (1854) I. 33 The antis will laugh at their own fears. 1792 J. JAY *Corr.* (1891) III. 448 Furnish the Anties with materials. 1801 *Spirit of Farmers' Museum* 56 There Feds shall cease to charge the Antis With making Frenchmen rule brave yankees. 1807–8 W. IRVING *Salmag.* (1824) 183 One old tenant, who always, just before the election, became a violent anti.

Anti, erron. var. *ANTE *sb.*[2], *v.*

Anti-aircraft (æntiē³·ɹkraft). [ANTI-[1] 4.] Used for defence against hostile aircraft; esp. *a. gun*, one for firing shrapnel at a very high elevation.
1914 *Scotsman* 25 Sept. 5/4 An anti-aircraft gun of the Third Army Corps. 1919 *Athenæum* 23 May 360/2 The anti-aircraft force.

Antibiotic, *a.* Add:
2. Injurious to or destructive of living matter.

1892 *Phil. Trans.* (1894) B. CLXXXV. 312 Production of a bactericidal, or at least antibiotic, substance.

Antibody (æ·ntibǫdi). *Biol. Chem.* [tr. G. *antikörper*: see ANTI-[1] 2 a.] A body or substance formed in the blood or juices of an animal, which antagonizes the action of another substance, esp. of a toxin or the like. Also *fig.*
1901 *Hektoen & Riesman's Pathol.* 231 Substances which appear during spontaneous or artificial infection or intoxication are known as antibodies (*Antikörper*) and antitoxins. 1921 R. A. FREEMAN *Social Decay* 287 The Social Anti-body is not Mechanism itself but the domination by it of human life and human activities. 1921 R. A. FREEMAN in *Edin. Rev.* July 33 Those antibodies by which the existence of aggregates of the lower organisms is brought to an end.

A:nti-Bri·tish (stress variable), *a.* [f. ANTI-[1] 3 a + BRITISH.] Hostile to the interests of Britain, opposed to the British. Hence **Anti-Britisher,** one who is antagonistic to the British or British interests; **Anti-Britishism,** a spirit of hostility towards the British.
1845 SYD. SMITH *Irish Ch.* Wks. 1859 II. 334/1 Such a piece of anti-British villany. 1898 *Daily News* 4 Oct. 4/5 Germany has withdrawn her anti-British support from the Transvaal. 1902 *Daily Chron.* 10 Mar. 7/3 The result is that Dutch Reformed ministers are, as a rule, anti-British. *Ibid.* 15 Sept. 5/3 Commandant Wolmarans,..an extremely bitter anti-Britisher. 1909 H. G. WELLS *Tono-Bungay* III. iv, The captain helped him to express his own malignant Anti-Britishism. 1928 *Observer* 18 Mar. 17/4 There is no anti-Britishism here, but I am puzzled by the objection to our being pro-American.

A·ntical, *a.*[2] [f. ANTIC *sb.* 2.] Indulging in antics.
1890 *Harper's Mag.* Apr. 797/1 Edward S. van Zile and John Kendrick Bangs (antical Manhattaners) are writing steadily, humorously.

Anticathode (ænti,kæ·þōᵘd). *Electr.* [ANTI-[1] 2.] The metal plate opposite the cathode in a Röntgen vacuum tube, upon which the cathode rays impinge and produce Röntgen rays.
1907 A. F. HERTZ in *Practitioner* Apr. 524 A pencil, which points directly towards the anticathode, is fastened behind the fluorescent screen. 1913 *Physical Rev.* Ser. II. II. 416 The anticathode..consists of a single piece of wrought tungsten, having at the end facing the cathode a diameter of 1·9 cm. 1923 *Glazebrook's Dict. Applied Physics* 595 The electrons (cathode rays)..are directed on a heavy metal anticathode or target.

Anticipate, *v.* Add:
10. *S. African Law.* To advance (the date of a judicial hearing). Cf. *ANTICIPATION 9.
1888 *Cape Law Jrnl.* 115 The defendant..is therefore allowed to 'anticipate' or to shorten the day of hearing before the usually appointed time..by giving notice. 1907 NATHAN *Com. Law S. Afr.* § 2412 IV. 2359 In special cases, however, the law allows a respondent to anticipate the expiration of the period allowed for prosecuting an appeal.

Anti·cipatingly, *adv.* [f. ANTICIPATING *ppl. a.* + -LY[2].] With anticipation.
1888 WALT WHITMAN in *Century Mag.* (1911) Dec. 250/1 His whole face would light up anticipatingly as he spoke. 1904 *Daily Chron.* 19 Mar. 7/5 The listeners..tittered anticipatingly.

Anticipation. Add:
9. *S. African Law.* The bringing up of a matter or case for judicial hearing or action before the normal or appointed time. Cf. *ANTICIPATE *v.* 10.
1888 *Cape Law Jrnl.* 115 'Anticipation' in its legal sense is used in all cases where there is *periculum in mora*; that is where the case demands immediate attention. 1907 NATHAN *Com. Law S. Afr.* § 2412. IV. 2357 The respondent in the appeal may apply to the Court for an order of anticipation (*mandament van anticipatie*).

Anticlimactic (æ:ntikləimæ·ktik), *a.* [f. ANTICLIMAX, after CLIMACTIC.] Of the nature of an anticlimax. So **A:nticlima·ctically** *adv.*
1898 *Westm. Gaz.* 28 May 2/3 That sounds a little anticlimactic. 1914 LOCKE *Jaffery* xix, I urged, somewhat anticlimactically after my impassioned harangue [etc.]. 1927 MCKENNA *Sonia* I. 37 He began valiantly enough, and then anticlimactically as he caught sight of me, 'What d'you want?'

Anticlinal, *a.* Add:
3. *Bot.* Applied to those cell-walls at a growing-point which have a direction at right angles to the surface: opp. to PERICLINAL 2. Also as *sb.* = anticlinal wall or plane.
1882 VINES tr. *Sachs' Bot.* 951 The planes of the walls in a growing-point are classified thus: *a. Periclinal*...*b. Anticlinal*, those which intersect the surface and the periclinal walls at right angles...If the outline..of the growing-point is a parabola..the anticlinals being the orthogonal trajectories of the periclinals, constitute a system of confocal parabolas.

Anticlinorium (æ:ntiklinōᵊ·riəm). *Geol.* [mod.L., f. as ANTICLINAL + Gr. ὄρος mountain + termination *-ium.*] A mountain range or region in which the folds of the strata are chiefly anticlinal.
1893 *13th Ann. Rep. U.S. Geol. Surv.* II. 220 It often happens that the result of the combination of many anticlines and synclines is to form a complex structure, which, regarded as a whole, is either synclinal or anticlinal. The former is called a synclinorium, the latter an anticlinorium.

Anti-clockwise (æ:nti,klǫ·kwəiz), *a.* and *adv.* [f. ANTI-[1] 3 c + CLOCK *sb.* + -WISE.] = COUNTER-CLOCKWISE.
1898 G. WHERRY in *Lancet* 1 Jan. 24/1 Mathematicians often use the expression 'clockwise' or 'anticlock-wise' to indicate the way of a spiral coil. 1914 DOMVILLE-FIFE *Submarines*, etc. 163 A tiny three or four-cylinder engine which operates twin screws, moving 'clockwise' and 'anti-clockwise'. 1917 'CONTACT' *Airman's Outings* 153 A little left rudder again puts the needle into an anticlockwise motion. 1927 *Daily Express* 23 Sept. 3/3 A clockwork motor that is wound up anti-clockwise.

Anti-coherer (ænti,kohiᵊ·rəɹ). *Wireless Telegraphy.* [ANTI-[1].] A device used in connexion with the receiving apparatus as a detector of electric waves, which greatly increase its resistance.
1902 *Westm. Gaz.* 16 June 7/3 In the place of a coherer at the receiving station..[there is] an anti-coherer.

Anticryptic (æntikri·ptik), *a.* *Zool.* [f. ANTI-[1] (here used advb.) + CRYPTIC.] Applied to markings or coloration serving for concealment to the disadvantage of some other animal: distinguished from PROCRYPTIC, q.v.
1890 E. B. POULTON *Colours Anim.* xvii. 336 Protective and Aggressive Resemblances are classed as Cryptic Colours (Procryptic and Anticryptic). *Ibid.* 337 Pseudepisematic colours..are special instances of Anticryptic colours.

Antidoron (æntidǭ·rǫn). *Greek Ch.* [Gr. ἀντίδωρον return-gift, f. ἀντί ANTI-[1] + δῶρον gift.] = EULOGIA c.
1850 NEALE *Holy East. Ch.* I. 525 Before the people are dismissed, the Priest gives them the *antidoron*; i.e. a part of the bread blessed for the prothesis. 1892 MACLEAN & BROWNE *Cath. East* 209 The Syrian deacon..may also make the holy loaves for consecration and for the *Antidoron*.

Anti-enzyme (ænti,e·nzim) [f. *ANTI(BODY) + *ENZYME.] The antibody to an enzyme.
1903 *Lancet* 4 Apr. 946/1 The human stomach wall contains an anti-enzyme to its own ferment. 1906 L. HILL, etc. *Recent Adv. Physiol.* 107 The first anti-enzyme was shown to exist by Morgenroth in the case of anti-rennin.

Anti-fat (æ·nti,fæt), *a.* and *sb.* [ANTI-[1] 3 c (2).] **A.** *adj.* That counteracts the formation of, or reduces the amount of fat. **B.** *sb.* A substance used as a remedy for the prevention or reduction of obesity.
1887 BENTLEY *Man. Bot.* (ed. 5) 768 This Alga is the essential constituent in the nostrum termed Anti-Fat. 1909 *Brit. Med. Assoc., Secret Remedies* ix. 92 Anti-Fat..acts solely upon the food in the stomach.

Antifebrin (ænti,fī·brin). Also **-ine.** [ANTI-[1].] Acetanilid, used as an antipyretic.
1891 *Medical Annual* 2 We are reduced to a choice of antipyretics; this now lies between phenacetin and antifebrin. 1893 W. A. HAMMOND in *N. Amer. Rev.* CLVI. 21 Coal tar, that wonderful body to which we owe..Antifebrine.

Anti-fe·d, -fe·deral, -fe·deralist. *U.S.* [ANTI-[1] 5.] An opponent of federalism in the early years of American independence. Also **Anti-fe·deral** *a.*, **-fe·deralism.**
1788 *Maryland Jrnl.* 3 June (Th.) The famous Dr. Spring asked a lady on which side she was, fed, or 'antifed. 1798 FESSENDEN in *Spirit of Farmers' Museum* (1801) 43 These fine fellows should be led By Lyon, sturdy Antifed, Who ought to howl with broken head. 1806 — *Democr. Unveiled* I. 112 Supported by the factious heads Of ever restless anti-feds. 1789 JEFFERSON *Writ.* (1859) II. 576 They are furiously 'antifederal. 1796–1821 FESSENDEN *Orig. Poems* (1806) 55 And swears no anti-federal noddy Has half a soul to bless his body. 1806 — *Democr. Unveiled* I. 13 As Torries many of you vex'd us As Antifederals then perplex'd us. 1789 *Boston Centinel* Jan., The genius of 'Anti-Federalism..it was born in August, 1787. 1788 *Maryland Jrnl.* 18 Feb. (Th.) This town is now divided into two distinct parties, Federalists and 'Antifederalists. 1800 *Aurora* (Philad.) 28 Nov. (Th.) By anti-federalist, the same is meant as by jacobin,..and the like.

Anti-fogma·tic. *U.S.* [f. ANTI-[1] 7 + a jocular formation on FOG *sb.*] An alcoholic liquor taken to counteract the effects of damp or wet.
1789 *Massachusetts Spy* 12 Nov. 4/2 Rum. Its great utility in preserving the planters from the effects of the damp and unwholsome air of the morning, has given it the medical name of an Antifogmatick. 1813 PAULDING *J. Bull & Br. Jon.* xviii. (ed. 2) 92 They were also wonderful boys for what they called antifogmatics. 1824 P. HORRY *Life Marion* ix. (1833) 77 Now suppose you take a glass of peach ..they say it is good of a rainy morning..a mighty antifogmatic. 1840 W. G. SIMMS *Border Beagles* 99, I had just risen to take my antifogmatic. 1852 *As good as a Comedy* (Philad.) 134 (Th.) Tom Nettles [was] mixing a couple of rosy antifogmatics.

Antigen (æ·ntidʒen). *Biol. Chem.* [f. *ANTI(BODY) + -GEN.] A foreign substance which, when introduced into the cells of a living organism, causes the production of an *ANTIBODY and thus effects immunization.
1909 *Cent. Dict.* Suppl. s.v. *Immunity*, The introduction into the body of almost any foreign substance of an albuminous character (*antigen*) is followed by the production of a corresponding antagonistic or antibody. 1911 *Jrnl. Chem. Soc.* C. II. 812 When an optimum dose of antigen (goat's or rat's blood) is injected intravenously into a dog.

Antijudaic (ænti,dʒudē·ik), *a.* and *sb.* [f. ANTI-[1] 5 a + JUDAIC *a.*] That is contrary to the Jews or Jewish opinion, policy, etc. Hence **Antijuda·ically** *adv.*
1885 LIGHTFOOT *Apostolic Fathers* I. 371 Marcion was markedly Anti-judaic. 1916 J. RENDEL HARRIS *Testimonies* I. 49 ['Jeremiah prophesied by the Holy Ghost.'] It is a very favourite quotation with the earlier anti-Judaics. 1920 *Ibid.* II. 16 The passage quoted by St. Paul is used anti-Judaically.

Antilegomena (æntilĕgǫ·mĕnă), *sb. pl.* [Gr. ἀντιλεγόμενα, neut. pl. of pres. pple. pass. of ἀντιλέγειν to gainsay, pass. to be disputed.] The deuterocanonical books of the New Testament.
[1847 CRUSE tr. *Eusebius' Eccl. Hist.* (ed. 4) 247 He has given us abridged accounts of all the canonical Scriptures, not even omitting those that are disputed (The Antilegomenoi).] 1875 *Encycl. Brit.* II. 128/2 The following is a catalogue of the *Antilegomena*:—the Epistle to the Hebrews, the Epistle of St. James, the Second Epistle of St. Peter, the Second and Third Epistles of St. John, the Epistle of St. Jude, the Apocalypse.

Anti-lipoid (æntili·poid). [ANTI-[1].] An antibody having the power of reacting with any of the lipoids (Dorland *Med. Dict.* 1913).

Antilog, abbreviation of ANTILOGARITHM.
1927 CRACKNELL (*title*) Elementary Practical Mathematics. With Tables of Logs and Antilogs.

Antimacassared (æ:ntimăkæ·səɹd), *a.* Covered or adorned with an ANTIMACASSAR.
1907 ARNOLD BENNETT *Grim Smile of Five Towns*, '*Silent Brothers*' § 2. 56 Seated in the antimacassared arm-chair. 1928 *Daily Express* 31 July 8/3 The antimacassared chairs, the horse-hair sofa, and the picture of Queen Victoria's jubilee.

Anti-mason. *U.S.* [ANTI-[1] 5 b.] One who is opposed to Freemasonry.
1828 in T. W. BARNES *Life Th. Weed* (1884) I. 307 If under these multiplied difficulties the Anti-Masons incline to bestow their votes upon Mr. Southwick. 1838 *Congress. Globe* Apr., App. 273/1 Counterfeit Democrats, National Republicans, Antimasons, and Abolitionists. 1878 J. H. BEADLE *Western Wilds* xii. 186 They parted and held their own, and they daresn't an anti-mason show hisself.
So **Anti-maso·nic** *a.*; **Anti-ma·sonry.**
1826 TH. WEED (*title*) The *Anti-Masonic Enquirer. 1828–30 H. D. WARD (*title*) The Anti-Masonic Review and Magazine. 1899 QUINN *Pennsylv. Stories* 39 His grandfather..had been one of the local leaders of the Anti-Masonic party. 1827 in T. W. Barnes *Life Th. Weed* (1884) II. 31 The subject of my communication was *anti-Masonry. 1831 MRS. HOLLEY *Texas Lett.* (1833) 128 There is neither masonry, anti-masonry, nullification, nor court intrigues. 1879 H. O'REILLY (*title*) American Political Antimasonry.

Antina·tionalism. Antinational principle or policy. So **A:ntinationali·stic** *a.*
1906 MILNER in *Daily Chron.* 29 Sept. 5/7 The danger..was the growth of a spirit of what he could only call anti-nationalism. 1920 *19th Cent.* Aug. 204 Antinationalistic class war.

Anti-natural (ænti,næ·tiŭrăl, -tʃərăl), *a.* [f. ANTI-[1] 3 c + NATURAL *a.*] Contrary or antagonistic to nature.
a 1603 T. CARTWRIGHT *Confut. Rhem. N. T.* (1618) 298 Your Diuinity in the Supper is Anti-naturall..that is..contrary to nature. 1727 POPE, etc. *Art of Sinking* v, This happy and antinatural way of thinking. 1897 *Daily News* 24 Nov. 9/5 Such wealth is represented as not only 'anti-social', but 'anti-natural'. 1924 *Public Opinion* 23 May 504/3 This human conception is simply antinatural.

Anting-anting (a·ntiŋ, a·ntiŋ). [Tagalog.] A supposed supernatural influence having the power of protecting its possessor from harm; also, an amulet or charm having the same qualities.
1890 FOREMAN *Philippine Isl.* 129 The most ignorant classes..believe that certain persons are possessed of a diabolical influence called *anting-anting*, which preserves them from all harm. 1898 *Daily News* 28 July 2/2 Supernatural qualities of anting-anting. 1900 F. H. SAWYER *Inhab. Philippines* 215 The famous Tulisanes or bandits, thoroughly believe in the power of the *Antin-Antin* or amulet to render them invulnerable to bullets.

Antiniad (ænti·niæd), *adv.* *Anat.* [f. next + *-AD. Cf. INIAD.] In a direction towards the antinion; towards the anterior portion of the cranium. So **Antinial** (ænti·niăl), *a.* *Anat.*, of or belonging to the antinion.
1803 J. BARCLAY *New Anat. Nomencl.* 165 Antiniad will signify towards the antinial [aspect]. 1808 — *Muscular Motions* 277 The fulcrum..is situated between the power and the resistance, which are respectively iniad and antiniad of the centre of motion. 1852 SIR J. RICHARDSON *Zool. Voy. H.M.S. Herald* 98 From the antinial tip of the premaxillary to the occipital spine.

Antinion (ænti·niǫn). *Anat.* [f. Gr. ἀντί ANTI-[1] 2 + ἰνίον INION[1].] The medial frontal part of the head, farthest from the inion.
1803 J. BARCLAY *New Anat. Nomencl.* 146 This distant part of the face..may be called the Antinion.

Antiochene (æntəi·ŏkīn), *a.* and *sb.* [ad. L. *Antiochēnus*, f. *Antiochia* Antioch.] **A.** *adj.* Of or pertaining to Antioch in Syria, esp. to the school of theology represented chiefly by the church at Antioch in the 4th and 5th centuries. **B.** *sb.* An adherent of this school.
1884 *Encycl. Brit.* XVII. 355/2 The antagonism between the Alexandrian and Antiochene schools of theology. *Ibid.* 356/2 The Antiochenes continued to maintain for a considerable time an attitude of antagonism towards Cyril and his creed. 1894 RIVINGTON *Prim. Ch.* 192 To understand..the Antiochene troubles of that century aright, it is necessary to bear in mind that St. Meletius entered upon his episcopate at Antioch under false pretences.
Also **Antiochian** (æntiǫ·kiăn), *a.* in same sense.
1840 E. COX tr. *Döllinger's Hist. Ch.* I. ii. § 7. 176 The Antiochian fathers.

Antiopelmous (æntiope·lməs), *a.* *Ornith.* [f. Gr. ἀντίος set against + πέλμα sole of the foot + -OUS.] Applied to a disposition of the muscles of the foot of picarian birds.
1884 *Riverside Nat. Hist.* IV. 369 [It being] opposed to the above, and only found in these non-cuculine, pair-toed birds, we propose to call this arrangement antiopelmous.

Anti-papal (ænti,pē·păl), *a.* [ANTI-[1] 3.] Opposed to popery and the pope.
1649 MILTON *Eikon.* xxvii. 214 He..charges strictly his Son after him to persevere in that Anti-Papal Scisme. 1894 J. C. HEDLEY *Retreat* xxi. (ed. 4) 257 The anti-Catholic, anti-Papal,..and anti-spiritual literature. 1902 GAIRDNER *Hist. Engl. Ch. 16th Cent.* viii. (1903) 141 Some anti-papal measures.

Antipatharian (æ:ntipăpē³·riăn), *a.* (*sb.*) *Zool.* [f. mod.L. *Antipatharia* (f. *Antipathes*, name of the typical genus) + -AN.] Belonging to the order *Antipatharia* of corals (the black corals); as *sb.* a coral of this order. So **Antipathid** (ænti·păþid), a coral belonging to the *Antipathidæ*, a family of this order.
1890 *Athenæum* 17 May 644/1 Prof. F. Jeffrey Bell [read a paper on] the antipatharian corals..containing..an account of a very remarkable antipathid from the neighbourhood of..Mauritius. 1899 *Nat. Science* Jan. 90 Large numbers of hydroids, antipathids, and the crinoid *Antedon phalangium* were dredged. 1924 *Glasgow Herald* 1 Nov. 4 The black corals or antipatharians.

Antiphlogistin (æntiflodʒi·stin). [f. ANTIPHLOGISTIC + -IN[1].] A proprietary preparation used as an anodyne, antiseptic, and antiphlogistic.
1901 DORLAND *Med. Dict.* (ed. 2). 1910 SIR W. BENNETT in *Practitioner* June 750 The induction of hyperaemia is certainly sometimes beneficial and is most easily effected by the use of some such material as Antiphlogistine.

Antiplanet (æ·ntiplăne·t). *Photogr.* Also **-at.** [ad. G. *antiplanat* (A. Steinheil, 1881), f. Gr. ἀντί, ANTI-[1] + πλανᾶν to wander. The form with *-et* seems to be due to association with Gr. πλανητός wandering.] A doublet composed of unsymmetrical lenses, the opposite aberrations of which correct each other.
1892 J. T. TAYLOR *Optics of Photography* xii. 72 Steinheil makes the antiplanat in two forms, one having a larger angular aperture than the other. 1900 S. P. THOMPSON *Lummer's Photogr. Optics* x. 61 The Antiplanat of A. Steinheil. 1902 *Encycl. Brit.* XXXI. 693/2 The 'Portrait Antiplanet'..is also a distinct type, differing from the ordinary Steinheil antiplanets.

Antipodal, *a.* Add:
3. *spec.* in *Bot.* Applied to cells at the base of the embryo sac, formed by division of the nucleus.
1876 *Encycl. Brit.* IV. 146/1 In some cases at the base of the embryo-sac a few cells are formed, which have been termed antipodal cells. 1898 *Nat. Science* June 375 The variety in the place of origin of the embryos from egg-cells, synergids, antipodal cells, or nucellus.

Antipyrin (æntipəiᵊ·rin). [f. ANTIPYR(ETIC) + -IN[1].] The commercial name of a benzene derivative, $C_{11}H_{12}N_2O$, used as an antipyretic: discovered in 1884 by L. Knorr, professor at Jena.
1884 *Jrnl. Chem. Soc.* XLVI. 1378 By distillation with zinc-dust, antipyrine yields benzene. 1893 [see TOLYPYRIN]. 1902 *Encycl. Brit.* XXXIII. 271/1 Antipyrin belongs rather to the furfurol group.

Antique, *a.* Add: Applied to old furniture, pictures, china, and other articles of vertu, esp. as sought for and collected by amateurs; *absol.* with *the*, antique articles collectively. Also *sb.* such an article; freq. *attrib.* as in *antique dealer* (a dealer in antiques, who also often repairs and renovates them), *furnisher*, *shop*.
1840 *P.O. Guide* 351/1 Antique Furniture Dealers. 1851 (*title*) Antiquarian Gleanings in the North of England, being examples of antique furniture, plate, etc. drawn and etched by William B. Scott. 1868 H. T. TUCKERMAN *Collector* 99 When an ancient dame..drew one [*sc.* a miniature] of her husband from an antique cabinet. 1877 *G. Shrimpton's Oxford Direct.* 33 Walford & Son, jewellers, and dealers in antique china. 1884 *Engl. Illustr. Mag.* Dec. 210/1 Brass and copper vessels..many of them shapely as antiques. 1888 (*title*) Antique and Modern Point Lace. 1904 *Daily Chron.* 29 Jan. 8/1 A story told in the 'antique' shops shows the cunning of those concerned in the business. 1908 R. & E. SHACKLETON (*title*) The quest of the antique, being some personal experiences in the finding of old furniture. 1913 *Engl. Rev.* May 301 Genuine antiques are admitted in America duty free. 1920 *19th Cent.* July 166 Morrison was staying with a little antique-dealer in the West of England.

Antiquity. Add:
4. c. The early ages of the Christian era; the early centuries of the Church; more explicitly *Christian antiquity*.
1564 HARDING *Answ. Jewel* 173 To see antiquitie for proufe hereof..Let him reade [etc.]. 1574 BRISTOW *Motives* (1599) 54 All Antiquity is full of such practise. 1753 CHALLONER *Cath. Chr. Instr.* 77 This Custom..is as ancient as Christianity, as appears from the most certain Monuments of Antiquity. 1850 NEWMAN *Difficulties of Anglicans* I. ii. (1891) I. 40 He would...have given up the Establishment, rather than have rejected Antiquity. 1860 A. P. DE LISLE in E. Purcell *Life* (1900) I. x. 185 Christian Antiquity.

Anti-rabic (ænti,ræ·bik), *a.* [irreg. f. ANTI-[1] 3 b + RABIES + -IC.] Having the property of counteracting the virus of rabies; curing, or relating to the cure of, rabies. Also **Anti-rabietic** (ræbi,e·tik) *a.*, **Anti-rabific** (ræbi·fik), *a.*
1887 *Science* IX. 186 The Russian antirabic inoculation institution [in Odessa]. 1888 *Nature* XXXIX. 73 The anti-rabietic treatment of M. Pasteur. 1894 *Nature* 8 Mar. 437/2 The establishment in the chief town of each province of an antirabific laboratory. 1919 *Times* (weekly ed.) 25 Apr. 404 The treatment of patients with specific anti-rabic material.

Anti-Saloon. *U.S.* [ANTI-[1] 4.] Opposed to the existence of drinking-saloons; *esp.* in *Anti-Saloon League*, an organization formed in the United States in 1893.
1888 *N. Amer. Rev.* Aug. 148 In the latter convention good men..wanted an anti-saloon plank put in the platform. 1892 *Cycl. Temperance & Prohib.* 29 The Anti-Saloon Republicans prepared to test their strength in the national councils of the party. 1894 *Arena* (Boston) May 858 They organize leagues of various sorts, 'Anti-Saloon Republican Leagues,'..and the like. 1900 J. ROWNTREE & A. SHERWELL *Temperance Reform* (ed. 7) 282 This list was furnished by the State Superintendent of the Minnesota Anti-Saloon League. 1909 *Nation* (N.Y.) 29 Apr. 427/2 Brewers and distillers, who..have joined with the reform clubs and Anti-Saloon League in securing the passage of a drastic excise law.

Antise·pticism (-siz'm). [f. ANTISEPTIC + -ISM.] Antiseptic surgical treatment. So **Antise·ptize** *v.* *trans.* to treat antiseptically; to disinfect by means of an antiseptic.
1880 BARWELL *Aneurism* 14 A careful and thorough application of antisepticism renders pyæmia..very rare. 1888 M. MACKENZIE *Illness Fredk. the Noble* 109 The Professor of Surgery, in the matter of antisepticism, attended to the letter rather than to the spirit. 1901 *Contemp. Rev.* Mar. 402 The bottle and its contents must be antiseptized at a heat of 123 degs. centigrade.

Anti-serum (ænti,siᵊ·rəm). *Bacteriology.* Pl. **-serums, -sera.** [ANTI-[1] 7 b.] A serum containing a specific antibody, which, when injected, neutralizes the toxin of the micro-organism from which it is prepared.
1901 NUTTALL in *Daily Chron.* 28 Dec. 3/7 No other bloods excepting those of monkeys give a reaction to the anti-serum for human blood. 1913 *Pembrey & Ritchie's Gen. Pathol.* 138.

Antisocial, *a.* Add:
2. b. *Sociology.* Pertaining to a class of persons devoid of or antagonistic to normal social instincts.
1896 GIDDINGS *Princ. Sociol.* iv. 72 The anti-social or criminal [class], in which the consciousness of kind is approaching extinction.

Antisocialist. Delete *rare*[−1] and add:
2. One who is antagonistic to socialism. So **Antiso·cialism.**
a 1881 J. S. MILL (Annandale) The vitality of these associations must indeed be great to have enabled about twenty of them to survive the antisocialist reaction. 1905 *Daily Chron.* 26 June 5/3 Mr. Deakin declined on behalf of the Liberal Protectionists to accept Anti-Socialism as the issue at the next General Election.

Antisociality (æ:ntisōᵘʃiæ·liti). [f. ANTISOCIAL + -ITY.] The quality or condition of being antisocial: **a.** Aversion to social intercourse; **b.** Antagonism to the laws of ordered society.
1818 T. L. PEACOCK *Nightmare Abbey* vii. 100 That amiable discontent and antisociality, which you reprobate in our present parlour-window literature. 1902 *Amer. Jrnl. Psychol.* Oct. 526 The anti-sociality of so many defectives is due to the arrest which so often takes place at the end of childhood.

Anti-spadix (ænti,spē·diks). *Zool.* [ANTI-[1] 2.] A group of four tentacles situated opposite to the spadix in the male nautilus.
1883 E. R. LANKESTER in *Encycl. Brit.* XVI. 674/2 These four tentacles may be called the 'anti-spadix'. 1888 ROLLESTON & JACKSON *Anim. Life* 457.

Antistrophe. Add:
4. *Cryst.* (See quot., and cf. METASTROPHE 2.)
1895 N. STORY-MASKELYNE *Crystallogr.* v. § 80. 99 A solid figure..is [symmetrical] to a plane of symmetry when corresponding points equidistant from the plane would lie on any line drawn perpendicularly to the plane. Where the solid figure presents symmetry to only a single plane (and not to a centre also) the corresponding portions of its surface..are to each other as either would be to its own image if seen reflected by the plane of symmetry as by a mirror. *Def.*—Such a correspondence of form will be termed antistrophe, and such figures will be said to be antistrophic to each other. 1899 W. J. LEWIS *Crystallogr.* 21.

Anti-submarine (ænti,sʌ·bmărīn), *a.* [ANTI-[1] 4.] Employed or used for defence against enemy submarines.
1914 DOMVILLE-FIFE *Submarines* ix. *heading*, Anti-Submarine Tactics. *Ibid.* 80 Fast vessels required for anti-submarine operations. 1915 *Times* (weekly ed.) 22 Oct. 897 These anti-submarine craft.

Anti-sun (æ·ntisʌn). [ANTI-[1].] The point in the sky diametrically opposite the sun; *esp.* a point opposite the sun in azimuth, of the same altitude as the sun.
1902 *Encycl. Brit.* XXX. 705 Babinet located a neutral point or zone about as far from the anti-sun as was Arago's from the sun itself.

Anti-tank (æ·ntitæ·nk), *a.* [ANTI-[1] 4 + *TANK.] Used against tanks.
1919 FARROW *Dict. Milit. Terms* 26 *Anti-tank Gun*, a gun especially designed and prepared to meet the onrush of the tank or mobile fort. 1920 J. F. C. FULLER *Tanks in Gt. War* 260 During the winter of 1916 and 1917 instructions were issued on anti-tank defence.

Antitoxic (æntitǫ·ksik), *a.* (*sb.*) [ANTI-[1] 3 b.] Having the quality of counteracting the effect of a toxin; of the nature of an antitoxin. Also as *sb.*
1890 BILLINGS *Med. Dict.*, *Antitoxics*, antidotes. 1894 *Daily News* 1 Dec. 3/4 The anti-toxic serum treatment of diphtheria. 1894 *Liberal* 24 Nov. 41/2 Bacterial products being gifted with an antitoxic power. 1905 G. A. REID *Princ. Heredity* x. 124 'Passive' immunity which results from the injection of antitoxic sera.

Antitoxin (æntitǫ·ksin). Also *erron.* **-ine.** [ANTI-[1] 7 b.] A substance, esp. a protein, which has the property of counteracting the effect of a toxin: either existing normally, or produced as the *ANTIBODY to a toxin. Also *attrib.*
1892 *Pop. Sci. Monthly* Sept. 629 Acquired immunity depends upon the formation of an antitoxine in the body of the immune animal. 1893 *Fortn. Rev.* Jan. 113 Antitoxin was used, and resulted in perfect recovery. 1895 *Pop. Sci. Monthly* Sept. 715 The principles..employed in the antitoxine treatment of diphtheria. 1904 [see TOXIN].

Anti-vaccinist (ænti,væ·ksinist). [f. ANTI-[1] 6 + VACCINIST.] One who is opposed to the practice of vaccination.
1822 *Blackw. Mag.* XII. 786 [He] treated with utter scorn ..every hint of the anti-vaccinist. 1896 *Daily News* 2 Dec. 8/5 He would disfranchise the anti-vaccinist for 'bad citizenship'. 1898 *Ibid.* 20 Apr. 4/7 The anti-vaccinist agitation.

Antivenene (æntivĭnī·n). Also *erron.* **-in(e.** [f. ANTI-[1] 7 b + L. *venēnum* poison, VENOM.] An antitoxin; *spec.* that used as an antidote to the venom of serpents. Also as *adj.* = *ANTITOXIC, q.v.
1895 *Pharmaceut. Jrnl.* 20 July 59 Observations of antivenene and the production of immunity against serpents' venom. 1902 *Encycl. Brit.* XXXIII. 271/2 The serum is found to act as an anti-venin. 1904 *Brit. Med. Jrnl.* 10 Sept. 571 Polyvalent antivenenes. 1909 *Westm. Gaz.* 17 Aug. 6/3 The anti-venine treatment. 1912 ADAMI & MCCRAE *Pathol.* 168 By the repeated injection of minute quantities of venom into lower animals, antitoxins—or antivenins..can be obtained for all the animal poisons.

Antler-moth. A noctuid moth (*Charæas* or *Cerapteryx graminis*), the larva of which is destructive in meadow lands.
1832 T. BROWN *Bk. Butterfl. & M.* (1834) I. 78 The Antler Moth..devours a considerable variety of grasses. 1897 *Daily News* 13 Sept. 6/2 The grub of the antler moth..has been known to commit such havoc that..the meadows looked as if a fire had passed over them.

Antode (æ·ntōᵘd). [ad. Gr. ἀντῳδή responsive singing, f. ἀντί against + ᾠδή ODE.] An ode sung in response to another (in a Greek play).
1883 *Times* 28 Nov. 6 The piece was very well received.. the ode and antode of the parabasis meeting with special applause.

A·ntony over. *U.S.* (See quot. 1871.)
1871 SCHELE DE VERE *Americanisms* (1872) 579 *Antony Over*, a game of ball played by two parties of boys, on opposite sides of a schoolhouse, over which the ball is thrown. Used in Pennsylvania. 1899 G. ADE *Doc. Horne* xi. 118 Why he and the alligator moved the dresser out from the wall and began to play 'ant'ny over' with my eye.

Antwerp (æ·ntwə̄ɹp). The Belgian city of that name, used attrib. in *Antwerp pigeon*, a variety of homing or carrier pigeon.
1839 *New Sporting Mag.* June 378 The Antwerps are a later introduction into our country...I believe little was known of them before the famous Antwerp match in July 1830. 1876 FULTON *Bk. Pigeons* 258 A few years ago, when Antwerp fanciers were few and far between. *Ibid.* 268 The bird now known as the Antwerp Carrier, Voyageur, or Homing Pigeon. 1904–5 *Encycl. Amer.* XIV. 341 Two main types of the Belgian homer have been distinguished as the Antwerp and the Liege varieties, the former being larger but less graceful in form than the latter.

Anxious, *a.* **2.** *Anxious bench* or *seat* (additional examples; see quot. 1839). *U.S.*
1832 MRS. TROLLOPE *Dom. Mann. Americans* I. 111 The poor creatures..seated themselves on the 'anxious benches'. 1839 MARRYAT *Diary Amer.* II. xi. 184 In front of the pulpit there was a space railed off, and strewed with straw, which I was told was the *Anxious seat*, and on which sat those who were touched by their consciences or the discourse of the preacher. 1888 J. KIRKLAND *McVeys* 19 'Seekers' were sought for and urged forward to the 'anxious seat' or 'mourners bench' by zealous friends.
b. *On the anxious bench* or *seat* (fig.), in a state of anxiety. *U.S.*
1861 MRS. STOWE *Pearl Orr's Isl.* II. i. 1 What a life you did lead me in them days! I think you kep' me on the anxious seat a pretty middlin' spell. 1883 NYE *Baled Hay* 17 By telling..lies about both I managed to..keep the two elements on the anxious seat. 1894 *Congress. Rec.* Feb. 2382/1, I am glad to see so many gentlemen 'on the anxious seat'. 1906 *N. Y. Even. Post* 23 Nov. 1 The entire diplomatic corps at Havana is..on the 'anxious bench'. 1910 W. M. RAINE *B. O'Connor* 45 That extra hour and a half cinches our escape, and we weren't on the anxious seat any without it.

Any, *a.* Add: **1. e.** *Any old*: any... whatever. *slang* (orig. *U.S.*).
1911 R. W. CHAMBERS *Common Law* ii. 63 'Would you like to have a chance to study?'..'Study? What?' 'Sculpture—any old thing!' 1918 W. J. LOCKE *Rough Road* v, Mate, Bill, Joe—any old name. 1920 *Independent* (U.S.) 4 Dec. 333 Any old European war.
7. b. At all. (Without comparative adj. or adv.) *dial.* and *U.S.*
1817 *Analectic Mag.* (Philad.) IX. 437 (Th.) If our readers are any like ourselves, we think they cannot help laughing. 1823 *Nantucket Inquirer* 2 Dec. (Th.) I much need [a nap], not having slept any for several nights. 1827 *Massachusetts Spy* 8 Aug. (Th.) It can't be that he has been examined and cross-questioned, and differed any. 1834 S. SMITH *Major Downing* 6 It is not likely Mr. Ruggles will be speaker any this winter. 1857 HOLLAND *Bay Path* (1864) 32 Your words come down jest like rain spatterin' on a rock. They don't soak in any. 1869 'MARK TWAIN' *Innoc. Abroad* iv. 45 It is a good tune—you can't improve it any. 1880 P. H. BURNETT *Recoll. Old Pioneer* 12, I had never danced any, and I determined that I would break the ice. 1887 J. C. HARRIS *Free Joe* (1888) 181 It certainly had not improved any since the war. 1888 *Detroit Free Press* Aug. (Farmer), Was he hurt any? A little. 1888 *Amer. Canoeist* (Farmer), I had just enough money to pay my passage to Natchez, but the fact did not worry me any. 1896 *Harper's Mag.* XCII. 178/2, I don't think he could have suffered any, he looked so peaceful. 1904 *Booklover's Mag.* Mar. 300 One interesting speech followed which did not help matters any. 1911 H. P. FAIRCHILD *Greek Immigr. to U.S.* 101 Costa was not used to springs, and he did not mind this any.

Anywhere, *adv.* Add: **b.** Used with *from ..to*, to indicate limits of variation. *U.S.*
1897 *Outing* XXIX. 471/1 The tarpon will be anywhere from fifty to three hundred feet away when the boat is ready to follow him. 1909 'O. HENRY' *Options* (1916) 13 I'll guarantee an increase of anywhere from ten thousand to a hundred thousand a year.

Anzac (æ·nzæk). A word made up from the initials of *Australian and New Zealand Army Corps*, and used colloq. for a member of that corps. Also *attrib.*, as *Anzac Day*, the day (25 April, 1915) on which these troops effected a landing in the Gallipoli Peninsula during the war of 1914–18, or any anniversary of that day.
1916 *Daily Mail* 1 Nov. 4/4 'Anzac'..is a word that bids fair to be reckoned among the immortals. 1920 *Glasgow Herald* 26 Apr. 9 Anzac Day.

Aoristically, *adv.* Add quots.:
1860 G. P. MARSH *Lect. Engl. Lang.* xiv. 300 In most languages,..even the forms grammatically expressive of time are, in general propositions, employed aoristically, or without any reference to time. 1880 *Expositor* 381 There is no need to suppose these aorists used aoristically (as they would be in classic Greek).

Aoudad (ā·udæd). Also **audad, udad.** [Fr. form of native name.] A species of wild sheep, *Ovis* or *Ammotragus tragelaphus* (often domesticated), found in N. Africa.
1864 J. ORMSBY *Autumn Rambles* 70 The maned moufflon of the Atlas,..the Aoudad of modern naturalists. 1886 *Encycl. Brit.* XXI. 785/1 The..goat-like aoudad, *O. tragelaphus*. 1902 *Ibid.* XXXIII. 483/2 The magnificent udad or Barbary sheep.

Aoul (ā·ul). Also **aoull, aul.** [Eastern Turkish *aul.*] A Caucasian or Tartar village or encampment.
1828 J. B. FRASER *Kuzzilbash* I. iv. 48 Men, women, and children, poured tumultuously from the nearer aouls. 1877 D. M. WALLACE *Russia* xxi. II. 39 The aoul consisted of about twenty tents..scattered about in sporadic fashion. 1884 *Leisure Hour* 461/1 One or two of the mounted young men are sent from the aul..to select a suitable spot for a new encampment.

Apache (ăpæ·ʃ, ‖apa·ʃ). [Fr., a. *Apache* (apa·tʃe), one of a warlike tribe of American Indians in New Mexico and Arizona.] A member of a band of robbers and assassins in and around Paris and other European cities; also *gen.* a man of ruffianly character. Also *attrib.* (e.g. *Apache hat, scarf*).
1902 *Westm. Gaz.* 22 Oct. 8/1 The leader of the band of roughs in Paris known as the 'Apaches'. 1909 *Times* 9 Feb. 4/4 Those *apaches* with which Brussels is haunted. 1909 'O. HENRY' *Roads of Destiny* xii, Probably..you'd need him to..help stand off a band of Apaches. 1918 F. HACKETT *Ireland* iii. 80 This faith in the Apache character of Ulster Catholics. 1920 *Times Lit. Suppl.* 10 June 363/2 Something a little more Bacchic than the calculated extravagances of the drawing-room *apache* would occasionally relieve the atmosphere. 1928 *Punch* 30 May 602 Friend (referring to 'Apache' hat). 'I like that one, dear. You see, it's noticeable without being really fierce.'

Aparejo (æpărē·ho). Also **app-.** *U.S.* [Sp. *aparejo* preparation, harness, tackle.] A pack-saddle.
1845 T. J. GREEN *Texian Exped.* xiv. 228 An aparejo, a kind of pack-saddle upon which is packed all kinds of produce. 1847 RUXTON *Adv. Mexico* x. 65 Mules so lacerated by the chafings of the aparejos, that the rib-bones are plainly discernible. 1887 *Scribner's Mag.* Oct. 511/1 The traveller.. will have further to master the art..of securing his *aparejo*. 1895 C. KING *Fort Frayne* ii. 22 Ten days rations were set aside in readiness to be packed on the apparejos the moment word should come. 1907 S. E. WHITE *Arizona Nights* I. ii. 27 We skirmished around and found a condemned army pack saddle with aparejos.

Apartment. Add: **1. b.** A set of rooms forming one dwelling-house in a building containing a number of these. (Corresponding to *flat* in British use.) *U.S.*
1890 *Harper's Mag.* Jan. 327/1 Mr. and Mrs. Delancy Robinson reside in a cosy flat, or 'apartment', as they prefer to call it, in New York city. 1891 J. A. RIIS *How other half lives* 291 Of the one hundred and six 'apartments' only four were vacant in August. 1903 *N. Y. Even. Post* 12 Sept., The chief distinction between a flat and an apartment, according to the accepted definition, is that the apartment has an elevator.
c. *attrib.*: **apartment-house,** a house divided into residential suites of rooms, esp. as distinguished from one divided into flats by the absence of facilities for cooking. So *apartment hotel.*
1883 *Encycl. Amer.* I. 297/2 The rapid multiplication of apartment-houses in the larger cities brings large masses of building under the hand of the architect. 1890 *Harper's Mag.* Apr. 740/1 No. 15 in the third section of the Haworth apartment-house was vacant. 1895 *Outing* XXVI. 395/2 Will you be glad to get..back to your paved streets and apartment house? 1898 ELLEN GLASGOW *Phases of Inferior Planet* i. 8 Facing her stood the immense and unpicturesque apartment-house known as 'The Gotham'. 1902 EATON & UNDERHILL *Runaway Place* 238 The vast apartment hotels along the Park front.

Apatelite (ăpæ·tĕləit). *Min.* [Named (in French) by A. Meillet, 1841; f. Gr. ἀπατηλός illusive, deceptive + -ITE[1].] A hydrous ferric sulphate, found in yellow nodules in clay.
1862 DANA *Min.* 247 Apatelite is..peculiar in containing but 4 per cent. of water. 1883 *Encycl. Brit.* XVI. 401/2 Apatelite, reniform-earthy, yellow, from Auteuil near Paris.

Apatetic (æpăte·tik), *a.* *Zool.* [ad. Gr. ἀπατητικός fallacious, f. ἀπατᾶν to deceive: see -IC.] Applied to markings or coloration deceptively resembling those of another species or of the environment.
1890 POULTON *Colours Anim.* xvii. 338 Apatetic Colours. 1926 *Contemp. Rev.* Sept. 369 Data affecting Epigamic colours have not been collected and examined to anything like the extent of those which concern Apatetic and Sematic colours.

Ape-man. *Anthropol.* One of a hypothetical genus of mammals supposed by Haeckel to have been intermediate in character and existence between the apes and man. Cf. *missing link* (b) s.v. MISSING *ppl. a.* 4.
1879 tr. *Haeckel's Evol. Man* II. 182 The ape-men, or *Alali*, were therefore probably already in existence toward the close of the Tertiary Epoch, during the Pliocene Period. 1895 *Westm. Gaz.* 17 Dec. 8/2 Professor Virchow..held that Dubois's discoveries did not at all prove the existence of an antediluvian ape-man.

Aperigraphic (ăperigræ·fik), *a.* *Geom.* [f. Gr. ἀ- privative + περιγραφή outline, circumference (or περιγράφειν to draw a line round) + -IC.] Not having a circumference: applied to a curve with infinite branches.
1901 A. B. BASSET *Elem. Cubic & Quartic Curves* 14 A continuous closed curve will be called a perigraphic curve; whilst a curve which possesses branches extending to infinity will be called an aperigraphic curve.

Aperiodic (ē³pi³ri,ǫ·dik), *a.* [f. Gr. ἀ- privative + PERIODIC.] Not periodic; without regular recurrence; *spec.* of a galvanometer, without periodic vibrations, 'dead-beat'.
1879 *Encycl. Brit.* X. 50/2 An intermediate stage called the aperiodic state. 1884 HIGGS *Magn. & Dyn. Electr. Mach.* 228 The commutator am-meter is an aperiodic galvanometer. 1894 W. L. DALLAS in *Indian Meteorol. Mem.* VI. 2 The annual periodic changes and the aperiodic changes [are] both very slight.

Aperitif (aperitīf). [F. *apéritif*:—L. *aperitivus*, f. *aperire* to open.] An alcoholic drink taken, before a meal, to stimulate the appetite.
1894 *Idler* Mar. 187 They..sipped their *apéritifs* tranquilly. 1905 *Daily Tel.* 22 Feb. 9/2 A teacup-full of whisky which was handed to him by the cook as an aperitif. 1929 *Graphic* 12 Jan. 54 A memento of Prince George's visit to Bermuda...He is having an after-the-bathe apéritif.

Apex, *sb.* **9.** Add: **apex-right** *U.S.*, a mining-right based on the point at which a vein has its apex. (Cf. *APEX *v.* 2.)
1898 *Engineering Mag.* XVI. 121/1 Besides, of such productive work No 'apex-right' or legal quirk Could thwart the rich requittal.

A·pex, *v.* [f. APEX *sb.*] **1.** *trans.* To form with an apex or pointed top; to raise to a point or tip.
1905 HOLMAN-HUNT *Pre-Raph.* I. 87 Should the several parts of the composition be always apexed in pyramids? 1924 *Scribner's Mag.* Jan. 56/1 Phil apexed his fine even eyebrows in the direction of Mary.
2. *intr.* (*Mining.*) Of a vein of mineral: To form an apex; to run up to an edge. *U.S. local.*
1914 G. ATHERTON *Perch of Devil* I. xii. 79 'It dips towards the ranch'..'It's pretty close. That would be a kettle of fish—if it apexed on your land!'

Aphasiac. Delete *rare*[−1] and add:
b. *adj.* Affected with aphasia; also *transf.* (*jocular*), incapable of 'speaking' or sounding.
1892 STEVENSON & L. OSBOURNE *Wrecker* xxi. 326 The old familiar room,..with..the aphasiac piano. 1906 DORLAND *Med. Dict.*, *Aphasic*, *Aphasiac*..1. Pertaining to or affected with aphasia.

Aphasic, *a.* Add to A.: Of or characteristic of aphasia.
1878 tr. *von Ziemssen's Cycl. Pract. Med.* XIV. 730 As well in temporary as in permanent aphasic disturbances. 1901 *Lancet* 26 Jan. 276 Slight aphasic symptoms. 1906 *Westm. Gaz.* 2 June 9/1 A curious form of aphasic amnesia.

Aphid (æ·fid), anglicized form of APHIS (from the pl. *aphides*).
1885 BROWNING *Ferishtah's Fancies, A Bean-stripe* 176 The aphis feeds, nor finds his leaf Untenable, because..Lightning strikes sere a moss-patch close beside, Where certain other aphids live. 1925 R. W. G. KINGSTON in E. F. Norton *Fight for Everest* 285 Aphids were numerous at 15,000 feet.

Aphidid (æ·fidid). [f. mod.L. *Aphididæ*, f. APHIS: see -ID[3].] An insect of the family *Aphididæ*; an aphid or aphis.
1886 *Science* VII. 394/2 The Fenesica larva actually feeds upon the aphidids.

Apicultural (ē³pi,kʌ·ltiŭrăl, -tʃər-), *a.* [f. APICULTURE + -AL.] Of or pertaining to apiculture.
1914 KIPLING *Diversity of Creatures* (1917) 392 Apicultural exhibitions.

Apiculturist (ē³pi,kʌ·ltiŭrist, -tʃəɹ-). [f. APICULTURE + -IST.] One who practises apiculture, a bee-keeper.
1883 (*title*) The American Apiculturist. 1885 W. H. HARRIS *Honey-Bee* 271 Apiculturists, like agriculturists, are subject to many and great alternations of hope and fear.

Apioid (ē³·pi,oid, æ·p-). *Geom.* [f. Gr. ἄπιον pear: see -OID.] **a.** A species of plane curve, being that one of a pair of Cartesian ovals which is within the other. **b.** A species of solid of revolution, being the form assumed by a rotating liquid when the velocity of rotation exceeds a certain amount. Hence **Apioi·dal** *a.*, pertaining to, or having the form of an apioid.
1898 G. W. MYERS in *Astrophys. Jrnl.* VIII. 163 The distance of centers does not materially differ from the sum of the radii of the components [of the star U Pegasi], suggesting the probable existence of the 'apioidal' form of Poincaré. 1905 AGNES M. CLERKE *Mod. Cosmog.* vi. 104 An 'apioid', or pear-shaped body, replaces the antecedent ellipsoid.

Aplanat (æ·plănæt). *Photogr.* [a. G. *aplanat* (A. Steinheil, 1866), f. Gr. ἀ- privative + πλανᾶν to wander, stray, err.] A symmetrical doublet composed of achromatized lenses.
1890 *Anthony's Photogr. Bull.* III. 129 After Steinheil invented his applanat [*sic*], Dallmeyer copied the same and called it Rapid Rectilinear. 1895 J. A. HODGES *Photographic Lenses* viii. 44 Prior to 1866, when Steinheil introduced his rapid aplanat working at f/7, all doublet lenses required comparatively small apertures in order to obtain sufficient definition and flatness of field. 1901 *Brit. Jrnl. Photog.* 1 Nov. 695/1 These aplanats consist of strong refracting flint glasses, whose quotient and colour diversion do not much differ. 1902 J. WATERHOUSE in *Encycl. Brit.* XXXI. 695/1 Dr. Miethe calculated the data for two lenses brought out by Hartnack (1889), one of them a symmetrical aplanat.

Aplanogamete (æplănǫgămī·t). *Biol.* [f. Gr. ἀ- (A- *pref.* 14) + πλάνος wandering (PLANO-[2]) + GAMETE.] A non-ciliated stationary gamete or conjugating cell, as distinguished from a PLANOGAMETE.
1886 [see GAMETE].

A-plenty, *adv.* *U.S.* [See PLENTY B. 2 c.] In plenty; in abundance.
1841 *Scot. Let.* in Catlin *N. Amer. Ind.* (1844) I. iv. 25 There are cattle a-plenty on that spot. 1876 'MARK TWAIN' *Tom Sawyer* vi. 59 Sho, there's ticks a-plenty. 1891 *Harper's Mag.* July 218/1 There are Briticisms a-plenty in the talk of the Londoner. 1892 *Ibid.* Apr. 694/2 At present there are trout a-plenty in the streams. 1910 MULFORD *Hopalong Cassidy* xi. 72 There's water a-plenty there.

Aplustre (ăplʌ·strĭ). [L. (pl. *aplustria*), a. Gr. ἄφλαστον.] The curved and ornamented stern of an ancient Greek or Roman ship.
1705 ADDISON *Italy* 344 The one holds a Sword in her Hand to represent the Iliad,..as the other has an *Aplustre* to represent the Odyssy, or Voyage of Ulysses. 1842 W. SMITH *Dict. Gk. & Rom. Antiq.* 58/2 A bird..which perches on the aplustre of the ship Argo. 1880 WALLACE *Ben-Hur* 141 The aplustre of the galley. 1929 *Times* 1 Feb. 7/5 Their [Phoenicians'] earliest coins..show a long rakish vessel with ..a handsome aplustre astern.

Apocentre (æ·posentəɹ). [f. APO- + CENTRE *sb.*]
1. The point in the eccentric orbit of a body at which it is most distant from the body or point around which it moves.
1902 NEWCOMB *Study of Universe* 160 In some cases there may be two pericentres and two apocentres to the apparent orbit. 1902 *Science* 7 Feb. 221 The apparently needless introduction of new terms in place of the familiar old ones, such as the logically inappropriate apocenter, pericenter, for apastron, periastron, in connection with double star orbits.
2. *Biol.* An organic structure regarded as a modification of or divergence from the primitive or central type in the conception of evolution; distinguished from an *ARCHECENTRE.
1909 in *Cent. Dict.* Suppl.

Apocentric (æpose·ntrik), *a.* [f. *APOCENTRE + -IC.] Of or pertaining to, of the nature or condition of an apocentre; *spec.* in *Biol.*, divergent from the primitive or central type. Hence **Apoce·ntrically** *adv.*, in an apocentric manner.
1901 P. CHALMERS MITCHELL in *Trans. Linnean Soc., Zool.* VIII. 204 The former start from a metacentric position common to the Colymbomorphæ and the Ciconiiformes, but have diverged apocentrically from that position. 1902 — in *Encycl. Brit.* XXVIII. 343/2 Such modified conditions have been termed apocentric.

Apocentricity (æ:posentri·siti). *Biol.* [f. *APOCENTRIC *a.* + -ITY.] The condition or property of being apocentric.
1902 P. CHALMERS MITCHELL in *Encycl. Brit.* XXVIII. 343/2 The mere apocentricity of a character can be no guide to the affinities of its possessor.

Apochromatic (æpokromæ·tik), *a.* (*sb.*) [f. Gr. ἀπό from, after ACHROMATIC.] Epithet of an improved form of achromatic lens invented by Prof. Abbe of Jena. Also as *sb.* = *apochromatic lens*; in *Photogr.* further shortened to **A·pochromat.** So **Apochro·matism,** apochromatic condition or quality.
1887 *Jrnl. Roy. Microsc. Soc.* Feb. 23 In the new objectives..the elimination of these errors realizes an achromatism of higher order than has hitherto been attained. The objectives of this system may be therefore distinguished from achromatic lenses in the old sense of the word by the term apochromatism, and may be called apochromatic objectives. 1890 *Anthony's Photogr. Bull.* III. 318 The

apochromatic objectives give absolutely the same photographic image as that seen upon the screen. *Ibid.* 319 In 1884, before the apochromatics were brought out. 1901 *Photogr. Jrnl.* 31 July 324 Remarkably perfect microscope objectives—the Abbe apochromats. 1902 *Encycl. Brit.* XXXI. 695/1 Fritsch, of Vienna, in 1888, constructed a wide-angle 'Apochromat' of the symmetrical aplanatic type.

Apodal (æ·pǫdăl), *sb.* [f. mod.L. *Apoda* (f. Gr. ἀποδ-, ἄπους footless) + -AL.] A batrachian belonging to the order *Apoda*, a group of the Cæcilians.
1856 *Encycl. Brit.* (ed. 8) XII. 229/1 Sub-Order III.—Ribbon Apodals. 1902 G. A. BOULENGER in *Encycl. Brit.* XXV. 383 To say nothing of the scales, present in many genera of Apodals and absent in all Caudates.

Apogamy (ăpǫ·gămi). *Bot.* [ad. F. *apogamie*, f. Gr. ἀπό APO- + γάμος marriage (cf. GAMO-).] Absence of sexual reproduction; asexual reproduction, agamogenesis; *spec.* in ferns and other cryptogams, Production of the perfect plant directly from a bud on the prothallus instead of by the usual sexual process. So **Apogamic** (æpogæ·mik), **Apogamous** (ăpǫ·gămǝs) *adjs.*, characterized by or of the nature of apogamy; agamogenetic (*spec.* in the way described above); hence **Apo·gamously** *adv.* (Cf. *APOSPORY, etc.)
1878 VINES in *Jrnl. Bot.* (N.S.) VII. 360 A transition from an oophore to a sporophore without the intervention of sexual reproductive organs. Apogamy (De Bary). 1881 *Ann. Rep. Smithsonian Inst.* 403 Forms where oogonia are found without male pollinodia..considered as representing a distinct apogamous species. 1886 *Jrnl. Roy. Microsc. Soc.* Ser. II. VI. I. 298 The author could not detect any act of impregnation [in a parasite on the olive], and believes that reproduction is apogamic. 1886 VINES in *Encycl. Brit.* XX. 431/2 By the suppression either of the sexually produced spore or of the asexually produced spore; the former is an instance of apogamy, the latter of apospory. *Ibid.* 431/1 [Spores] formed..without a sexual process—in a word, apogamously.

Apohyal (æpohǝi·ăl). [f. APO- + HY(OID + -AL.] (*a*) *Ornith.*, the ceratobranchial bone. (*b*) *Ichth.*, the basihyal bone.
1890 COUES *Ornith.* 305 Ceratobranchials proper, commonly called apohyals.

Apolau·sticism (-siz'm). [f. APOLAUSTIC + -ISM.] Devotion to enjoyment.
1883 *Sat. Rev.* 15 Dec. 763 He combined the lessons of economy with apolausticism. 1894 X.L. *Aut Diabolus aut Nihil* 6 He was indeed only fervent in his apolausticism.

Apollina·rianism. The doctrine of the Apollinarians.
1884 *Encycl. Brit.* XVII. 356/2 Nestorius..was equally explicitly opposed to Arianism and Apollinarianism. 1921 *Contemp. Rev.* Nov. 623 The Dean of Carlisle warns theologians against the peril of Apollinarianism or Monotheism.

Apollinaris (ăpǫline·ris). Short for *Apollinaris water*, an effervescent mineral water produced at Apollinarisburg near Bonn in Germany, and used as a beverage.
1878 *Fun* 26 Jan. (Hoppe) Sweet champagne and Apollinaris—Sham and Polly, as it is slangily called. 1897 FLANDRAU *Harvard Episodes* 335 Mrs. Lauriston brought some apollinaris from her table. 1905 *Smart Set* Sept. 119/2 'Been here long?' I queried, after a short pause, in which I finished the remainder of the apollinaris.

Apolline (ăpǫ·lǝin, -lin), *a.* [ad. L. *Apollineus*, f. *Apollin-*, Apollo.] Pertaining to Apollo: = APOLLONIAN I. So **Apollinic, -inian** (æpǫli·nik, -i·niăn) *adjs.* in same sense.
1884 *Encycl. Brit.* XVII. 808/2 Apolline oracles, such as the Delphic. 1886 *Ibid.* XX. 360 Apollinic (Delphic) religion. 1924 tr. *Baudouin's Psychoanalysis & Aesthetics* vi. 255 Dionysian art is being converted into apollinian art.

Apologia (æpǫlǭu·dʒiă). [L. *apologia*, a. Gr. ἀπολογία speech in defence.] A written defence of the opinions or conduct of the writer.
The currency of the word is due to J. H. Newman's *Apologia pro Vita Sua*, 1864.
1883 *Sat. Rev.* 10 Nov. 613/1 The Duke [of Argyll] has put his own version of the story on record. This apologia is a pamphlet, entitled *Crofts and Farms in the Hebrides*. 1903 *Westm. Gaz.* 20 Jan. 8/2 They may be taken as his 'Apologia'—though not in any sense an apology—for the achievements of his official career.

Aponogeton (æ·ponodʒī·tǫn, gī·tǫn). [Of doubtful origin; perhaps a modified form of POTAMOGETON.] A genus of aquatic plants belonging to the order *Naiadaceæ*; also, a plant of this genus.
1829 LOUDON *Encycl. Plants* (1836) 292. 1845 SIR J. D. HOOKER in *Life* (1918) I. 441 Aponogeton, a Cape plant,..bears a freezing every winter in our ponds. 1898 HOLE in *19th Cent.* Apr. 641 The fair and fragrant aponogeton.

Apophony (ăpǫ·fŏni). *Philol.* [ad. F. *apophonie*, f. Gr. ἀπό APO- + φωνή sound.] = ABLAUT.
1883 I. SYDOW *German Convers.-Gram.* 253 The Germans call this..Ablaut, that may be rendered by apophony. 1894 V. HENRY *Compar. Gram. Eng. & Ger.* 358 Mod. German, though keeping the apophony, obscures it by borrowing the metaphony from the subjunctive.

Apophysis. Add:
3. *Geol.* A branch from the main mass of an intrusive igneous rock.
1889 in *Cent. Dict.* 1893 GEIKIE *Geol.* (ed. 3) 580 All over the world it is common for eruptive bosses of this rock to have a fringe of intrusive veins (*Apophyses*). 1925 B. N. ODELL in E. F. Norton *Fight for Everest* 293 Thoroughly metamorphosed and crystalline limestone resting on the schorl granite, which sent off apophyses into it.

Apopyle (æ·pǫpǝil). *Zool.* [f. Gr. ἀπό APO- + πύλη gate.] An aperture by which an endodermal chamber in a sponge communicates with the central cavity or *paragaster*.
1887 W. J. SOLLAS *Sponges* in *Encycl. Brit.* XXII. 414/1 A comparatively large aperture, which we may term for distinction an apopyle. 1888 [see PARAGASTER].

Aporia. Add:
2. A perplexing difficulty.
[1888 *Athenæum* 18 Aug. 219/3 No quibble was too sophistical, no ἀπορία too transparent, for him to think it worth examination.] 1893 W. CLARKE ROBINSON tr. *Ten Brink's Hist. Engl. Lit.* II. 80 The solution of many an *aporia*, as attempted by the idealistic thinker. 1902 *Daily Chron.* 12 Dec. 3/4 Mr. Kidd does not seem to us to surmount this *aporia* very successfully.

Aposaturnium (æposătū·rniǝm). *Astr.* [mod. L., f. Gr. ἀπό from + L. *Saturn-us* Saturn: cf. APOJOVE and PERISATURNIUM.] The point in the orbit of a satellite of Saturn at which it is most distant from the planet. Also in anglicized form **Aposa·turn.**
18.. AIRY (Cent. Dict.).

Aposematic (æposĭmæ·tik), *a.* *Biol.* [f. Gr. ἀπό away from + σῆμα sign (cf. SEMATIC).] Applied to colours, markings, or other attributes serving to warn or alarm, and thus to repel the attacks of enemies. So **Aposeme** (æ·posīm), an aposematic marking, etc.
1890 POULTON *Colours of Animals* xvii. 337 Pseudaposematic colours..deceptively resemble Aposematic colours. 1902 *Encycl. Brit.* XXVII. 147 We often see the combination of Cryptic and Sematic methods, the animal being concealed until disturbed, when it instantly assumes an Aposematic attitude. 1919 DIXEY *Addr. Zool. Sect. Brit. Assoc.* 4 Adopting Professor Poulton's terminology, we may say that..one form may possess..the Aposemes belonging to two distinct models. *Ibid.* 6 The..most conspicuous of these common Aposemes or danger signals belong to the under surface.

Apospory (ăpǫ·spŏri). *Bot.* [f. APO- + Gr. σπόρος seed + -Y³.] Absence or suppression of spores where they are normally produced, as in certain ferns, mosses, and other cryptogams in which the sexual organism (prothallus in ferns, etc. or perfect plant in mosses) is developed directly from the sporangium or from the leaf instead of from a spore. So **Apo·sporous** *a.*, characterized by or of the nature of apospory; hence **Apo·sporously** *adv.* (Cf. *APOGAMY.)
1878 VINES in *Jrnl. Bot.* (N.S.) VII. 361 To indicate..that no spores are..produced..by the sporophore of *Chara*, we may speak of this plant as being 'aposporous'. 1884 F. O. BOWER in *Jrnl. Linn. Soc., Bot.* XXI. 360 (*title*) On Apospory in Ferns. 1886 [see *APOGAMY]. 1886 *Encycl. Brit.* XX. 431/2 In the aposporous Ferns and Mosses and in the Characeæ the oophore is developed as a bud from the sporophore. 1892 *Athenæum* 12 Nov. 667/3 Prothalli developed aposporously.

Apostolate. Add:
b. A society or sodality of persons having as their object the propagation of a method or rule of faith, life, or conduct.
1897 *Westm. Gaz.* 1 Oct. 4/2 The little settlement is an apostolate of mercy. 1905 *Tablet* 14 Oct. 607/2 The mere mention of that oxymoron the 'lay-apostolate' causes among Catholics of the elder generation a wise shaking of heads. 1911 *Catholic Encycl.* XII. 107 Ven. Vincent Mary Pallotti..gave to his society the name of 'Catholic Apostolate', afterwards changed by Pius IX to the 'Pious Society of Missions'.

Apothecial (æpǫþī·siăl), *a.* [f. APOTHECIUM + -AL.] Of or pertaining to an apothecium.
1882 J. M. CROMBIE in *Encycl. Brit.* XIV. 559 Apothecial reactions for the most part take place either externally on the epithecium or internally on the hymenial gelatin.

Apotropaic (æ·potropē·ik), *a.* [f. Gr. ἀποτρόπαιος averting evil (f. ἀποτρέπειν to turn away, avert) + -IC.] Having or reputed to have the power of averting evil influence or ill luck.
1883 *Encycl. Brit.* XV. 570/1 The sacrifice of the 'October horse' in the Campus Martius..had also a naturalistic and apotropaic character. 1904 W. M. RAMSAY in Hastings *Dict. Bible* V. 115/1 The..employment of a bull's head on..sarcophagi..evidently..had at first an apotropaic purpose. 1918 L. STRACHEY *Eminent Victorians* 230 (*Gordon*) The same doctrine led him..to append, in brackets, the apotropaic initials D.V. after every statement in his letters implying futurity.

A-pout (ăpau·t), *adv. poet.* [f. A- *pref.* 2 + POUT.] Pouting.
1886 J. ASHBY-STERRY *Lazy Minstrel* (1892) 150 Ah! sweet are those eloquent lips a-pout. 1893 F. THOMPSON *Poems* 74 (*The Poppy*) With mouth wide a-pout for a sultry kiss.

Apparatus. **3. c.** Add: In full *critical apparatus*: = next.
1868 *Jrnl. Philol.* I. No. 2. 66 His collation of the poem, with a description of the MS., a careful apparatus, and an interesting explanatory commentary. 1876 *Hermathena* II. 389 Professor W. Ramsay compiled his text very carefully, with apparently all the requisite data and critical apparatus.

Apparatus criticus (æpărā·tǝs kri·tikǝs). [mod.L.: see APPARATUS and CRITICAL.] A collection of palæographical and critical matter accompanying an edition of a text.
1865 CONINGTON *Vergili Opera* I. p. x, The publication of Ribbeck's *apparatus criticus* has made a new recension necessary. 1867 *Athenæum* 8 June 758/1 In the notes are found all the various readings of MSS., as given by preceding editors, followed by the testimonies of ancient writers in support of them; the whole forming as complete a *criticus apparatus* as could be desired. 1887 *Classical Rev.* Mar. 17/1 The *apparatus criticus* is still simple and the new editor's personality is rarely obtruded on the reader. 1928 *Observer* 4 Mar. 7/3 The second half of the volume comprises the Geographical Text..with a complete *apparatus criticus*.

Apparitional. Add:
2. Belonging to the sphere of mere appearances or phenomena.
1899 SIR A. C. LYALL *Asiatic Studies* Ser. II. 89 The Hindu in his conviction of the illusory nature of all phenomena..will not contest the authenticity, in an..apparitional sense, of historic religions.

Appeal, *sb.* Add:
6. b. *fig.* esp. in phr. *to make an appeal to*, to attract the sympathetic attention of, exert influence upon; hence, attractive influence or power (e.g. *the sex appeal*). (Cf. APPEAL *v.* 9.)
1920 ROSE MACAULAY *Potterism* I. i. § 4 Mrs. Potter was rather sadly aware that she made no appeal to the twins. *Ibid.* I. iv. § 1 His was the sort of beauty which..makes so strong an appeal to the senses of the sex other than that of the possessor. 1926 W. DEEPING *Sorrell & Son* xxiii. § 3 The enticements that might be expected to make an appeal to a very young man. *Ibid.* xxvii. § 1 She was standing close to him,..and Kit was conscious of the sudden shock of her appeal. 1926 *Grand* Aug. 587/2 The sport of man-hunting had lost its appeal.
8. *attrib.*: **appeal tribunal**, a court of inquiry for the hearing of appeals for exemption from military service.
1916 *Act 5 & 6 Geo. V* 2nd Schedule, There shall be Appeal Tribunals, acting within such areas as His Majesty may appoint.

Appeal, *v.* **9.** Add: Also without const.: To 'make an appeal'.
1907 *Smart Set* Mar. 23/1 The speciousness of Betty's words appealed.

Appearing, *ppl. a.* Add: **2. c.** With defining word preceding, as *best-, fine-appearing*. *U.S.*
1879 HOWELLS *Lady of Aroostook* ii. (1884) 59 She is very fine-appearing' said Lydia. Stamford smiled at the countrified phrase. 1897 *Outing* XXX. 352/1 First prize for best appearing club at Long Branch.

Appeaseless, *a.* (Earlier U.S. example.)
1837 *Southern Lit. Messenger* III. 105 My morbid imagination, though glutted or half-starved, with it, was still appeaseless.

Appendical, *a.* Add: **b.** Of or pertaining to the appendix vermiformis.
1909 *Practitioner* Nov. 646 A typical history of appendical perforation.

Appendicectomy (ăpendise·ktŏmi). *Surg.* [f. L. *appendic-*, stem of APPENDIX + Gr. ἐκτομή cutting out.] Excision of the vermiform appendix of the cæcum.
1903 *Medical Record* 28 Mar. 484 (Cent. D. Suppl.). 1905 *Nursing Times* 23 Dec. 666/2 Appendicectomy: After Results..The late after-results of removal of the appendix.

Appendicitis (ăpendisǝi·tis). *Path.* [mod.L. (R. H. Fitz, 1886), f. as prec. + -ITIS.] Inflammation of the vermiform appendix of the cæcum.
1886 R. H. FITZ in *Amer. Jrnl. Med. Sci.* Oct. 323 As a circumscribed peritonitis is simply one event..in the history of inflammation of the appendix, it seems preferable to use the term appendicitis to express the primary condition. 1887 *Buck's Handbk. Med. Sci.* IV. 185/2 The symptoms of appendicitis, pure and simple, are probably very slight, and not easily recognizable. 1905 H. A. KELLY & HURDON *Verm. App.* 382 Some cases of appendicitis occasioned by influenza.

Appendix, *sb.* **3.** Add after def.: *spec.*, short for *vermiform appendix* (of the cæcum): see VERMIFORM 3 a.
1902 *Scotsman* 2 July 7/3 This operation, removal of the appendix. 1905 H. A. KELLY & HURDON *Verm. App.* 2 The first recorded case of disease of the appendix is the classical one of Mestivier, reported in 1759. 1905 H. G. WELLS *Modern Utopia* App. 377, I had seen the ancestral cæcum shrink to that disease nest, the appendix of to-day.

Apperceive, *v.* Insert **1.** before def., transfer † *Obs.* to that sense, and add:
2. *Psychol.* To be or become conscious of perceiving; to comprehend (something perceived) by a mental act which unites and assimilates the perception to a mass of ideas already possessed; to have apperception of: see below.
1876 J. SULLY in *Mind* Jan. 41 Where two impressions are simultaneously apperceived, it is because they are such as can be brought under one complex impression as parts of the whole. 1892 — *Human Mind* I. 163 The new presentative element is said..to be apperceived or assimilated by a pre-existing cluster of ideas or an ideal mass. 1894 *Academy* 7 July 6/2 A thousand people, observes Lange, may read Virgil; but every one will apperceive him differently.
Hence **Apperceiving** *ppl. a.*; whence **Apperceivingly** *adv.*
1889 C. DE GARMO tr. *Lange's Apperception* (1896) 101 When ideal norms are apperceivingly active in the field of knowledge..true culture is attained. 1902 JAMES *Varieties Relig. Exper.* 257 Some..knowing that numerous..relapses take place, make of these their apperceiving mass for interpreting the whole subject. 1914 R. M. JONES *Spir. Reformers of 16th & 17th C.* xiii. 263 The representative of the old system ..condemning a dawning movement which with his apperceiving material he could not understand.

Apperception. Add:
3. *Psychol.* The action or fact of becoming conscious by subsequent reflection of a perception already experienced; any act or process by which the mind unites and assimilates a particular idea (esp. one newly presented) to a larger set or mass of ideas (already possessed), so as to comprehend it as part of the whole: see quots.
1876 J. SULLY in *Mind* Jan. 36 The entrance of a presentation into the internal field of view is termed a Perception; its entrance into the point of view an Apperception. 1887 J. DEWEY *Psychol.* 89 Apperception is the relating activity which combines the various sensuous elements presented to the mind at one time into a whole, and which unites these wholes, recurring at successive times, into a continuous mental life, thereby making psychical life intelligent. 1889 C. DE GARMO tr. *Lange's Apperception* 28 Apperception is the subsumption of a notion, usually newly given and more or less individual, under a predicate which is more complete ..and..usually older and more familiar. Apperception does not always follow perception immediately, for years sometimes intervene between the learning of a fact and its comprehension. 1892 J. SULLY *Human Mind* I. 163 The reinforcement which a sensation secures through the revival of kindred ideal elements is spoken of by Herbart and his school as apperception. 1900 *Hand and Eye* 15 Nov. 35 Apperception may be defined as the interaction of two analogous presentations, by which the one is more or less re-formed by the other.
Hence **Apperce·ptionism** *Psychol.*, the explanation and systematization of the process of apperception; **Apperce·ptionist**, one who holds or affects the doctrine of apperceptionism; **Apperceptioni·stic** *a.*, of, pertaining to, or characterized by apperceptionism.
1903 H. MÜNSTERBERG *Harvard Psychol. Stud.* I. 644 Without returning to apperceptionism we can overcome the one-sidedness of associationism if full use is made of the means which the world of phenomena offers to theory. *Ibid.* 653 Apperceptionistic psychology. 1904 *Jrnl. Philos., Psychol. & Sci. Methods* 18 Aug. 466 (Cent. D. Suppl.) The idealist's view is that of the 'apperceptionists'.

Apperceptive (æpǝɹse·ptiv), *a.* [f. prec. after PERCEPTIVE.] Pertaining to or involving apperception; also = next.
1884 E. MONTGOMERY in *Mind* July 381 It is after all nothing but our own apperceptive faculties, potentially idealised, that are made to serve for the consciousness of a universal subject. 1886 RADESTOCK *Habit & Education* 45 Blending or apperceptive synthesis, that is, a union of impressions following one another, in which the latter exist in the new conception produced by their union. 1890 JAMES *Princ. Psychol.* II. 107 All recognition, classing, and naming; and..all further thought about our percepts are apperceptive processes.

Appercipient (æpǝɹsi·piĕnt), *a.* [f. as prec. after PERCIPIENT.] Having or exercising the faculty of apperception.
1906 H. H. JOACHIM *Nature of Truth* iii. 93 Every judgement..is informed, conditioned, and to some extent constituted by the appercipient character of the mind which makes it. 1922 SYD. GREW *Art of Player-Piano* 161 Only the musician may be entirely appercipient as regards the subtle beauty of poetry.

Appetiteless (æ·pǝtǝit,lès), *a.* [f. APPETITE *sb.* + -LESS.] Having no appetite; marked by want of appetite.
1853 SURTEES *Sponge's Sp. Tour* lx, Having finished a poor appetiteless breakfast. 1890 *Temple Bar* July 303 He sits appetiteless over his solitary breakfast.

Applanate (æ·plănèt), *a.* *Bot.* [ad. mod.L. *applānātus*, pa. pple. of *applānāre*, f. *ap-* = *ad* to + late L. *plānāre* to level, f. *plānus* PLANE.] Of a flattened or horizontally expanded form.
1887 W. PHILLIPS *Brit. Discomycetes* 2 Pileus sessile and applanate. *Ibid.* 101 *Peziza depressa*..from its applanate growth.

Apple, *sb.* Add:
6. b. A pale green colour like that of an unripe apple, apple-green.
1923 *Daily Mail* 5 Mar. 13 Colours: Peach, Apple, Apricot, Mauve.
B. II. apple-borer *U.S.*, an insect attacking apple-trees; **apple-box, -gum**, names for species of *Eucalyptus*; **apple-brandy** *U.S.* (earlier example); **apple-bug**, a water-beetle of the family *Gyrinidæ*, which exudes a milky liquid having an odour of apples; **apple-essence, -oil**, a chemical substance used to imitate the odour of apples in confectionery; **apple-jack** *U.S.* (earlier example); **apple-peru** *U.S.*, the thorn-apple; **apple-slump** *U.S.* (see quot. 1871).
1857-8 *Trans. Ill. Agric. Soc.* (1859) III. 344 The most destructive of these..is that known as the 'apple borer. 1890 *Melbourne Argus* 9 Aug. 4/6 An ironstone hill..with *apple-box and ironbark dotted about. c 1780 *Maryland Hist. Mag.* II. 256 [I] accepted 13 gals. of peach brandy in satisfaction of the damage...He cheated me with *apple brandy. 1832 J. P. KENNEDY *Swallow B.* I. xii. 129 The *apple-bugs (as school-boys call that glossy black insect which frequents the summer pools, and is distinguished for the perfume of the apple) danced in busy myriads over the surface of the still water. 1868 *Rep. U.S. Commissioner Agric.* (1869) 80 The fifth family, gyrinidae, comprises those oval water-beetles usually known by the name of 'whirligigs' or apple-bugs. 1847 LEICHHARDT *Jrnl.* viii. 264 Another Eucalyptus [*E. Stuartiana*]..with smooth upper trunk and cordate ovate leaves..; we called it the *Apple-gum. 1840 C. F. HOFFMAN *Greyslaer* III. i. 108 Wash the dust from his mouth with a cup of *apple-jack, Adam. 1883 BLOXAM *Chemistry* (ed. 5) 556 The amyle valerianate, which has the flavour of apples, and is known as *apple oil, is obtained by distilling fousel oil with sulphuric acid and potassium dichromate. 1850 HAWTHORNE *Scarlet L.* i. (1928) 64 A grass-plot, much overgrown with burdock, pig-weed, *apple-peru, and such unsightly vegetation. 1848 BARTLETT *Dict. Amer.* s.v. *Slump*, A favorite dish in New England, called an *apple slump. 1871 SCHELE DE VERE *Americanisms* (1872) 415 *Apple-Slump* is..a favorite New England dish, consisting of apples and molasses baked within a bread-pie in an iron pot. 1884 E. E. HALE *Christmas in Narragansett* i. 11 Guessed that they had done justice to..Polly's apple-slump.

Apple-butter. *U.S.* [APPLE *sb.* II.] (See quot. 1832.) Also *Comb.*
1832 *Mirror of Lit.* etc. 26 May 323/2 Apple butter..is made by stewing apples in new cider, after it has been boiled down to one-third of its bulk. 1851 C. CIST *Cincinnati* 49 Apple-butter makers. 1870 *Congress. Globe* Apr. 2685/1 Apple-butter is a substitute for butter; it is spread upon bread and eaten in like manner. 1880 *Congress. Rec.* Mar. 1534/2 If I draw my finger across the page, the ink comes off as though it were printed with apple-butter.

Apple-cart. Phr. *to upset the* (or some one's) *apple-cart*, humorously used for 'to cause an upset' (*lit.* or *fig.*); *esp.* to upset a person's plans, to ruin the undertaking. Also in similar expressions.
1796 GROSE *Dict. Vulgar Tongue* (ed. 3) s.v., Down with his apple-cart; knock or throw him down. 1796-1801 FESSENDEN *Orig. Poems* (1806) 100 He talketh big words to congress and threateneth to overturn their apple-cart. 1834 CARRUTHERS *Kentuckian in N.Y.* I. 23 You don't chaw tobacco, and you don't drink nothin; smatch my apple cart if I can see into it. *Ibid.* 101 Smash my apple-cart, if there wasn't more crying..than I've seen at many an honest man's funeral. 1847 HALLIWELL s.v. *Apple-cart*, Down with his apple-cart, knock or throw him down. *North*. 1848 in Hodder *Life Shaftesbury* (1887) xvii. 396 If the Prince goes on like this, why he 'll upset our apple-cart. 1871 G. P. R. PULMAN *Rustic Sketches* (ed. 3) Gloss. 77 s.v. *Apple-cart*, 'Don't upsit th' apple-cart.' That is—be careful you do not let fall anything carried. 1883 *Pall Mall Gaz.* 26 Oct., If the Control had done more it might have upset the apple-cart altogether. 1889 *Northumbld. Gloss.* s.v. *Apple-cairt*, 'That's upset his apple-cairt for him, as think'—that has completely stopped his project. 1896 C. RHODES in *Daily News* 24 July 5/5 Old Jameson has upset my applecart. 1897 *Review of Rev.* Aug. 114 Somebody will lose patience, and then over will go the apple-cart. 1906 G. W. CHRYSTAL tr. *Mem. Prince Chlodwig of Hohenlohe-Schillingsfürst* II. 71 It appears that the compromising papers found in possession of the Jesuits..have upset the apple-cart.

Apple-tree. Add:
2. In Australia applied to various indigenous trees, esp. to a species of Eucalyptus (= *apple-gum*: see *APPLE B. II.), and to another myrtaceous tree, *Angophora subvelutina*.
1820 J. OXLEY *Jrnl. Exped. N.S. Wales* 187 That species of eucalyptus which is vulgarly called the apple tree. 1885 MRS. C. PRAED *Head Station* (new ed.) 22 A giant eucalyptus, of the kind called 'apple-tree'. 1885 *Spons' Mechanics' Own Bk.* 127 Apple (Australian) (*Angophora subvelutina*). The so-called apple-tree of Queensland yields planks 20-30 in. in diameter.

Appliable, *a.* Transfer † *Obs.* to senses 1 and 3, and add quots. below for sense 2.
1855 *Jrnl. R. Agric. Soc.* XVI. II. 563 A practical and appliable knowledge. 1874 *Contemp. Rev.* XXIV. 731 Abundance..of wealth..appliable to other purposes.

Application. Add:
11. *Comb.*: **application money**, the sum of money paid when applying for the allotment of shares.
1900 *Westm. Gaz.* 12 Mar. 9/1 The lists may be closed earlier than Thursday..to avoid the unnecessary locking up of application money. 1907 *Ibid.* 9 Mar. 15/1 A special form of application is provided, under which the application money will have to be paid as in the case of new subscriptions.

Applied, *ppl. a.* Add:
4. *Dressmaking.* Laid on as appliqué.
1882 CAULFEILD & SAWARD *Dict. Needlework* 9/1 s.v. *Appliqué*, The various applied pieces are laid in position one at a time, and secured by being sewn round their edges. 1901 *Westm. Gaz.* 25 July 3/2 A lace applied collar. 1910 *Ibid.* 29 Jan. 15/2 Applied velvet.

Apply, *v.* Add:
1. c. *Dressmaking.* To lay on as appliqué; to trim or ornament with appliqué.
1882 CAULFEILD & SAWARD *Dict. Needlework* 12/1 The foundation was generally muslin, and the net applied or let in. 1901 *Westm. Gaz.* 14 Mar. 4/2 Everything is applied with insertions or cut-out flowers and figures of lace.

Appointing, *ppl. a.* (Later U.S. example.)
1826 T. H. BENTON in *U.S. Senate Rep.* 12 The appointing power.

Appointive, *a.* For *rare* read *U.S.* For def. read:
1. Dependent on appointment; that is filled by appointment; holding one's place by appointment.
1881 [see Dict.]. 1886 *N. Amer. Rev.* Aug. 203 Whether the entire judiciary should be appointive or elective. 1889 *Nation* (N.Y.) 4 July 1/1 Mr. Geer being an appointive officer of the Custom-house. 1914 T. C. SMITH *Wars betw. Eng. & Amer.* iii. 54 The Quebec Act altered the government of the province by the creation of an appointive council.
2. 'Of or pertaining to appointment; appointing, as, the appointive power of the President' (*Cent. Dict.*).

Apport, *sb.* Transfer † *Obs.* to senses 1 and 2, and add:
3. *pl.* Material things introduced, professedly by occult means, at a spiritualistic séance.
1902 O. LODGE in *Proc. Soc. Psych. Research* XVII. 48 Some of the physical phenomena which I have adduced as among those proclaimed to have occurred, such as *apports*, scent, movement of objects..bear a perilous resemblance to conjuring tricks.

Apportioner. Delete † *Obs.*—⁰ and add:
1885 BROWNING *Ferishtah, Cherries* 70 The apportioner of every lot of ground. 1893 *St. James's Budget* 23 June 6/3 The apportioners of the Chantrey Bequest. 1905 C. KERNAHAN *Visions* 259 The..dishonest Apportioner of life's good and evil.

Appreciation. Add:
2. b. An expression (in speech or writing) of one's estimate of something: often implying a favourable estimate (cf. 4).
1858 M. PATTISON *Essays* xix. (1889) II. 344 In the last page he has written, in his small and fine hand, a short appreciation of the book and its author. 1889 PATER (*title*) Appreciations, with an essay on style. 1907 J. A. HAMMERTON (*title*) Stevensoniana: an anecdotal life and appreciation of R. L. Stevenson.

Apprehension. Add:
7. b. *Psychol.* (See quot.)
1896 G. F. STOUT *Anal. Psychol.* I. I. iv. 95 This circumstance suggests a name for that apprehension of a whole which takes place without discernment of its parts. We may call it implicit apprehension.

Appressorium (æpresǭ·riǝm). *Bot.* [mod. L., f. L. *appress-*, ppl. stem of *apprimĕre*, f. *ad* AD- + *premĕre* to press: see -ORIUM.] The organ by which certain fungi attach themselves to their hosts.
1902 *Encycl. Brit.* XXVIII. 555/1 Appressoria are also formed by some parasitic Fungi, as a minute flattening of the top of a very short branch..or the swollen end of any hypha which comes in contact with..the host.

Appro. (æ·pro). Commercial abbrev. of *APPROBATION or *APPROVAL, in the phrase *on* (or *upon*) *appro*. Also *attrib.*, as *appro transaction*.
1901 *Punch* 26 June 467/1 You ordered it 'upon appro'. 1906 *Daily Chron.* 20 June 6/6 We have..purchases on 'appro.'. 1908 *Westm. Gaz.* 10 Jan. 2/1 The goods on appro. we left to Lavinia's maid. 1910 *Ibid.* 10 Feb. 8/1 The bead salesman..said it was not an 'appro' transaction.

Approach, *sb.* Add:
3. b. Advances made to a person for the purpose of improperly influencing his actions. *U.S.*
1893 *Congress. Rec.* Sept. 1874/1 The idea that..[Mr. Hooper] was subject to approach is ridiculous.
11. *Golf.* The play by which the player hits his ball on to the putting-green; chiefly *attrib.*, as *approach shot, stroke*.
1879 *Encycl. Brit.* X. 765/2 Having got within some moderate distance of it [*sc.* a hole], he proceeds to make his 'approach shot'. *Ibid.*, The 'approach' and the 'putting' are by far the most difficult..parts of the game. 1887 W. G. SIMPSON *Golf* viii. 155 There are four clubs used for ordinary approach work—the putter, the cleek, the iron, and the mashy.

Approach, *v.* Add:
4. b. In recent use also, To make an overture or proposal to; to seek in or for an interview; to make advances to (a person) with a view to influencing his actions; to attempt to influence or bribe.
1893 *Congress. Rec.* Sept. 1874/1 Nearly every bit of everything that is said about public men being corrupted or approached is false. 1909 *Daily News* 10 Apr. 7/3 When the 'Daily News' approached the Admiralty on the subject an official said [etc.]. *Mod.* He was approached with a view to obtaining his consent.
12. *Golf. intr.* To play the approach stroke. Hence **Approaching** *vbl. sb.* Also **Approacher**.
1887 W. G. SIMPSON *Golf* viii. 140 When the player's ball is within less than a driver shot of the hole, approaching commences. *Ibid.* 146 Approachers of equal skill indulge in all the variations [of grip]. 1903 *Westm. Gaz.* 9 Jan. 2/1 Mr. Laidlay used to approach better than any other man I have ever seen play.

Approbation. Add:
3. b. *On approbation*: phr. in commercial use denoting that goods (esp. wearing apparel) sent to a customer are submitted for his examination only without obligation to purchase (if they are returned undamaged).
1920 *Conquest* Jan. p. viii, Please send these books on Approbation.

Approfound (æprofau·nd), *v.* (A Gallicism.) [ad. F. *approfondir*, f. *ap-* AD- + *profond* PROFOUND.] *trans.* To go deeply into, to search the depths of (a subject of study).
1885 R. G. WHITE *Stud. Shakespeare* 35 Subtle theories as to Shakespeare's purpose in this play have been set forth by critics who engage in the task of approfounding him. 1897 *Sat. Rev.* 8 May 520 These seven pages of M. Mallarmé would take longer to approfound than all the back numbers of 'Cosmopolis' put together.

Approval. Add:
b. *On approval*: on approbation (see *APPROBATION). Also without prep. and attrib.
1877 *Design & Work* 15 Dec. 667/2 Watch...English lever ..approval. *Ibid.* 22 Dec. 690/3 Sheets of stamps sent on approval. 1880 *Exchange & Mart* Suppl. 2 Jan. 1/1 Breechloaders. Great Bargains...Approval. Deposit. *Ibid.* 5/2 Mulready envelope and 380 foreign stamps. Sent on approval. 1902 *Connoisseur* Jan. (Advt.), Stamps...We are sending out Approval Sheets and Books. 1906 *Drapers' Record* 27 Oct. 190 These goods cannot be sent on approval.

Aprick (ăpri·k), *adv.* or *pred. a. poet.* [f. A- *pref.* 2 + stem of PRICK *v.*] In such a position or condition as to prick; pricking.
1856 MRS. BROWNING *Aurora Leigh* VI. 237 Watching gnats a-prick upon a pond. 1898 SIR O. SEAMAN *In Cap & Bells* 15 (*At the sign of the cock*) Amazon spurs aprick at heel. 1903 *Academy* 21 Feb. 186/2 The earth was quick with green a-prick.

Apricot. Add:
1. b. *transf.* The colour of an apricot. Also Comb., as *apricot-coloured, -tinted* adjs.
1907 GALSWORTHY *Country House* II. ii. 119 The moon, tinted apricot and figured like a coin, hung above the cedar-trees. 1923 *Daily Mail* 28 Feb. 1 The newest Paris shades of Coral, Lilac,..Apricot.

Aprilian (ǟpri·liăn), *a.* [f. APRIL + -IAN.] Of or characteristic of April.
1902 *Daily Chron.* 24 Mar. 8/1 Rain of a spitefully Aprilian character. 1905 BLISS CARMAN *Songs Northern Garden* 10 Fear not the mighty instinct, The great Aprilian Creed; The House of Spring is open And furnished for thy need.

A·prilish, *a.* [f. APRIL + -ISH¹.] = APRILESQUE.
1759 *Essex Inst. Hist. Coll.* XLIX. 2 Fair aprilish Day.

Apriorism. Add to def.:
Also, the philosophical doctrine of *a priori* or innate ideas (see A PRIORI 3). So **Apriorist**, one who holds this doctrine; also *loosely*, one given to *a priori* reasoning (in quot. 1889 *attrib.* = A PRIORI 2); hence **Apriori·stic** *a.*, pertaining to apriorism or apriorists.
1874 LEWES *Prob. Life & Mind* I. 412 This will be disputed by the *a priorists*. 1874 tr. *Van Oosterzee's Christian Dogmatics* I. 141 No authority..must..be conceded to such an aprioristic criticism. *Ibid.* II. 596 However little..inclined to an abstract a-priorism. 1877 E. C. THOMAS tr. *Lange's Hist. Materialism* I. 180 *note*, The theory..was of aprioristic origin. 1889 G. B. SHAW *Fabian Ess. Socialism* 177 The apriorist notion that among free competitors wealth must go to the industrious. 1891 *Monist* I. 635 Empiricism is wrong because it can at best show the temporal succession of two phenomena, and apriorism is wrong because *a priori* knowledge lies in the subject alone and not in the object. 1914 TEIXEIRA DE MATTOS tr. *Maeterlinck's Unknown Guest* III. 42 The 'apriorists', who hold that the idea of time is innate.

Apron, *sb.* Add: **4.** (Additional quots.)
1769 FALCONER *Dict. Marine* (1789), *Apron*,..a platform, or flooring of plank, raised at the entrance of a dock, a little higher than the bottom, against which the dock gates are shut. 1791 R. MYLNE in *Rep. Engineers Thames-Isis Navig.* 31 A new Pound lock..would..amend the Shallowness over the apron of a new Arch at Radcot Bridge. 1847 CLARKE in *Jrnl. Roy. Agric. Soc. Eng.* VIII. I. 115 The waters on the cill of the South Holland Sluice have been known to rise, during the summer season, with the sand-bed 5 feet on the apron. 1882 L. F. VERNON-HARCOURT *Rivers & Canals* I. vii. 82 (*Locks*) Beyond the gate-floor, at each end of the lock, is the apron, which is generally protected from scour by pitching or masonry. 1908 *Westm. Gaz.* 17 Nov. 5/2 The dashboard is of the metal apron type.
g. *Theatr.* (See quot.) Also *apron stage*.
1903 A. B. WALKLEY *Dramatic Criticism* 108 The 'apron' is the technical name for the stage-area in front of the curtain. In the Elizabethan theatre it jutted right out among the public, who surrounded it on three sides. This 'apron' slowly shrank..till at last in our day it has altogether disappeared.
5. b. (See quot.)
1876 *Field & Forest* II. 73 This mass is very conspicuous even in the rapidly swimming crab, and causes the abdominal flap (called apron by fishermen) to be opened almost to its fullest extent.
6. apron-cloth (see sense 3).
1857 D. H. STROTHER *Virginia Illustr.* ii. 139 The apron-cloth was drawn up over their legs and with a..crack of the whip they started into the storm.

Apt, *a.* Add: **4. c.** Inclined, disposed (in a single instance).
1677 CARY *Chronology* II. II. I. iv. 195, I am apt to think, that..Vashti is meant. 1706 HEARNE *Collect.* (O.H.S.) I. 297, I am apt to think he has not consulted Books enough upon this occasion. 1899 E. E. HALE *Lowell* 126, I am apt to think that this modest man was the first person..to recognize [etc.].
d. Likely. *U.S.*
1904 'O. HENRY' *Cabbages & Kings* iii. 52 'You will be apt to find Dr. Gregg at the hotel', said the consul. 1904 *Chicago Tribune* 22 June 6 Are the republicans apt to dodge that issue.., or will they meet it? 1906 *N.Y. Even. Post* 9 Jan. 2 The incident is not apt to be followed by international complications.

Apterium (æpti·riǝm). *Ornith.* Pl. **-ia.** [mod.L. (Nitzsch 1833), f. Gr. ἀ- priv. + πτερόν feather.] Each of the featherless spaces on the skin of a bird intervening between the feathered tracts or *pterylæ*.
1867 P. L. SCLATER tr. *Nitzsch's Pterylography* (Ray Soc.) 16 To these feathered bands I give the name of Feather-tracts or Contour-feather-tracts (*pterylæ*, Federn-fluren), and to the naked bands, or those which are not beset with contour-feathers, that of featherless spaces (*apteria*, Federn-raine). 1894 [see PTERYLA].

Apterygial (æptěri·dʒiăl), *a.* *Ichth.* [f. Gr. ἀ- priv. + πτέρυξ, πτερυγ- wing, fin, or πτερύγιον fin + -(I)AL.] Destitute of fins, finless.
1902 *Nature* 25 Sept. 526 We may distinguish the Cyclostomes as apterygial and epicraniate.

Apterygotous (æpterigǭ·tǝs), *a.* *Entom.* [f. mod.L. *Apterygota* (f. Gr. ἀ- priv. + πτερυγωτός winged) + -OUS.] Belonging to the division *Apterygota* of insects, which are wingless and held to be descended from an originally wingless ancestry, as distinguished from other wingless or *apterous* insects descended from winged ancestors (see *ANAPTERYGOTOUS). So **Apterygo·tism**, the condition of being apterygotous.
1902 *Encycl. Brit.* XXIX. 502/2 Were an apterygotous insect gradually to develop wings, it would be on the exopterygotous system.

Aptian (æ·ptiăn), *a.* (*sb.*) *Geol.* [f. place-name *Apt* (Vaucluse, France) + -IAN.] Epithet of a division of the Lower Cretaceous formation in France and Belgium; belonging to or found in this, as a fossil.
1885 GEIKIE *Geol.* (ed. 2) 831 In northern France the Aptian stage is chiefly clay. 1921 *British Museum Return* 151 Aptian fossils from Whale's Head.

Aptic (æ·ptik), *a.* [app. irreg. f. L. *aptus* APT (or *aptāre* to fit, adapt) + -IC.] (See quot.)
1897 R. H. VINCENT *Elem. Hypnotism* (ed. 2) iv. 179 If the response [to a stimulus] be one which is 'physical,' *i.e.*, giving no evidence of modification due to the external environment, we include it in the elementary class of nervous action—the inaptic. If the response be of such a nature as to show that there has been a modification due to the environment of the moment, but without consciousness, then we have an easily appreciable distinction as our basis for a second classification—the aptic.

Aquake (ăkwē·k), *adv.* or *pred. a. poet.* [f. A- *pref.* 2 + stem of QUAKE *v.*] In a quaking condition, quaking.
1876 MORRIS *Æneids* III. 616 My mates aquake with dread. 1883 MEREDITH *Poems, Day of Daughter of Hades* ix, The valley aquake with the tread Of an iron-resounding hoof.

Aquarid (ăkwē·rid). Also **-iid.** *Astron.* [f. AQUARIUS + -ID².] *pl.* A group of meteors that radiate from the constellation Aquarius. Also *attrib.*
1902 *Encycl. Brit.* XXX. 691/2 The orbit of a shower of Aquarids, occurring early in May, offers a suggestive resemblance to the path of Halley's comet. 1908 *Westm. Gaz.* 7 May 10/1 The Aquarid meteors.

Aquavivarium (æ·kwăˌvǝivē·riǝm). Now disused. [irreg. f. L. *aqua* water + VIVARIUM.] = AQUARIUM.
1856 *C. Knight's Eng. Cycl., Nat. Hist.* IV. 48 Several species have lived for months in the aquavivarium at the gardens of the Zoological Society, Regent's Park. 1904 *Westm. Gaz.* 29 Apr. 12/1 The Aquavivarium, later called the Fish-houses.

Aqueous. Add:
4. as *sb.* short for *aqueous humour*: see 1 b.
1879 *St. George's Hospital Rep.* IX. 481 During one week she had the aqueous tapped daily.

Aquilegia (ækwilī·dʒiă). *Bot.* [mod.L., of uncertain origin.] A genus of ranunculaceous plants, consisting of several species the flowers of which are pentamerous with spurred petals; = COLUMBINE I.
1920 *Chamb. Jrnl.* May 326/2 Old-world flowers..as delphinium and antirrhinum and aquilegia.

Araban (æ·răbæn). *Chem.* [a. G., f. ARABIC + -AN.] = ARABIN.
1892 *Jrnl. Soc. Chem. Industry* XI. 931/1 The Pentosans (Wood-Gum, Xylan, and Araban) of Lignified Fibre.

Arabesque, *sb.* Add:
4. *Mus.* (See quot. 1880.) Also *transf.*
1880 *Grove's Dict. Mus.* I. 80/2 *Arabesque*..(1) The title has been given..by Schumann to one of his pianoforte pieces..which is written in a form bearing some analogy to that of the rondo, and it has been since occasionally used by other writers for the piano. (2) The word 'Arabesque' is sometimes used by writers on music to express the ornamentation of a theme. 1924 ANNE D. SEDGWICK *Little French Girl* III. vii, Listening to a blackbird that fluted golden arabesques.

Arabe·sque, *v.* [f. ARABESQUE *sb.*] *trans.* To ornament in arabesque. Hence **Arabesquing** *ppl. a.*
(Delete ARABESQUED *ppl. a.*, which is the pa. pple. of the vb., and incorporate the quots.)
1858 [see Dict.]. 1861 SALA in *Temple Bar* I. 306 The same embroideress who arabesqued the hems of her under-skirts pinked the shrouds. 1867 H. LATHAM *Black & White* 21 A cell in which a weaver had arabesqued the walls. 1908 SAINTSBURY in *Cambr. Hist. Eng. Lit.* II. 191 A sort of vignetting or arabesquing fringe and atmosphere of exaggeration and fantasy.

Arabe·squeness, [f. ARABESQUE *a.* + -NESS.] Arabesque quality or character: see ARABESQUE *a.* 3.
1858 MOTLEY *Let. to Wife* 30 May, Corr. 1889 I. 237 There was not a touch of Holmes's ever bubbling wit, imagination, enthusiasm, and arabesqueness.

Ara·bianize, *v.* [f. ARABIAN *a.* + -IZE.] *trans.* To make Arabian, give an Arabian character to; to assimilate to the Arabian language.
1893 F. ADAMS *New Egypt* 9 The fiercely protracted effort of Islam to Arabianise Egypt.

Arability (æræbi·lĭti). [f. ARABLE: see *-BILITY.] Capability of being used as arable land.
1879 *Athenæum* 28 June 817/2 The term [*sc.* hide] being ..variable according to the arability..of the land.

Arabis. Add: A plant of the genus.
1876 RHODA BROUGHTON *Joan* v, Milk-white arabis haunted by the drowsy booming bees. 1905 *Westm. Gaz.* 10 June 16/1 The white blossoms of the double arabis.

Arabism. Delete ? *Obs.* and add quot.:
1899 SAYCE *Early Israel* iii. 109 Hebrew had retained a few 'Arabisms', a few traces of its ancient contact with Arabic-speaking tribes.
2. Influence by or assimilation to the customs or civilization of the Arabs.
1874 DRAPER *Hist. Conflict Relig. & Sci.* iii. (1880) 99 Arabism, which had done so much for the intellectual advancement of the world, came to an end when the Turks and the Berbers attained to power.

Arabize (æ·răbǝiz), *v.* [f. ARAB + -IZE.] *trans.* To make Arab; to give an Arabian or Arabic character to. Hence **A·rabized** (-ǝizd), **A·rabizing** *ppl. adjs.*
1883 CUST *Mod. Lang. Africa* I. viii. 83 The Arabizing process [in Africa] has taken place in various ways. 1884 *Science* 12 Dec. 531/1 These Arabs of the Sudan are not true Arabs, but to a great extent merely Arabized negroes. 1899 SAYCE *Early Israel* iii. 114 The dialect of Edom agreed with Hebrew in those Arabising peculiarities. 1920 *19th Cent.* Aug. 229 The civil administration of the country should be Arabised to a greater extent.

Arachnitis (æræknǝi·tis). *Path.* [f. ARACHN(OID + -ITIS.] Inflammation of the arachnoid membrane. Also (in medical Dicts.) in more correct form **Arachnoiditis.**
1834 J. FORBES *Laennec's Dis. Chest* (ed. 4) 69, I have witnessed the supervention of peritonitis, severe dysentery, and arachnitis, to fluxes suppressed by the use of hot wine and spices. 1857 DUNGLISON *Med. Lex.*, *Arachnitis*, more properly *Arachnoiditis*.

Arahat: see *ARHAT.

Aralia (ărē·liă). [mod.L., of uncertain origin.] A genus of trees, shrubs, and herbs, the type of the N.O. *Araliaceæ*.
1829 LOUDON *Encycl. Plants* 230 *Aralia*. Aralia. *Araliaceæ*. 1908 *Westm. Gaz.* 25 Nov. 5/1 A tall aralia growing in a corner of the well-lighted entrance-hall of the hotel.

Araliaceous (ărēli,ē·ʃǝs), *a.* *Bot.* [f. mod.L. *Araliaceæ*, f. *Aralia*, the typical genus; see -ACEOUS.] Belonging to the N.O. *Araliaceæ*, comprising various herbs, shrubs, and trees, including the ivy.
1866 BRANDE & COX *Dict. Sci. & Art* II. 780/1 *Panax*, a name applied to some plants of the Araliaceous order. 1884 *Spectator* 24 May 685 Virtues..attributed to the araliaceous plant Jinseng.

Aramaicism (ærămē·isiz'm). [f. ARAMAIC + -ISM.] An Aramaic idiom: = ARAMAISM.
1898 BLASS *Philology of the Gospels* 194 In the [first twelve chapters of the Acts] Aramaicisms abound.

Aramaize (ærămē·ǝiz), *v.* [f. as prec. + -IZE.] *trans.* To render Aramaic, imbue with Aramaisms.
1868 LIGHTFOOT *Ep. to Philippians* (1885) 149 In Aramaised Greek.

Araneidal (ærănī·idăl), *a.* *Zool.* = ARANEIDAN *a.* So **Arane·idiform** *a.* = ARANEIFORM.
1826 KIRBY & SP. *Entomol.* III. xxx. 171 The *Corydalina* ..is Chilopodiform, but with a tendency to the Araneidiform Type. 1895 *Naturalist* 29 The Araneidal Fauna of the northern counties of England.

Araneology (ărēniǫ·lŏdʒi). [f. L. *arānea* spider + -(O)LOGY.] The department of zoology relating to spiders. Hence **Araneolo·gical** *a.*, belonging to araneology; **Araneo·logist**, one versed in araneology.
1798 *Monthly Mag.* Jan. 53/2 Araneology...The Araneological Calendar. 1875 *Encycl. Brit.* II. 296/1 An eminent araneologist. 1884 *Science* 4 July 24/1 Facts..new to the field of American araneology.

Arapaima (ærăpai·mă). [South American native name.] A genus of fishes of the family *Osteoglossidæ*, remarkable for their size; a fish of this genus.
1840 R. H. SCHOMBURGK *Brit. Guiana* 39 The Arapaima or Pirarucu (*Sudis Gigas*), and..the Lau-lau, are from ten to twelve feet long. 1896 LYDEKKER *Roy. Nat. Hist.* V. 478 The true arapaima (*Arapaima gigas*) of the larger rivers of Brazil and the Guianas..occupies the proud position of being the largest fresh-water bony fish. 1908 C. F. HOLDER *Big Game at Sea* xix. 288 The *arapaima*..the game fish of South American waters—a monster that attained a length of twelve feet and a weight of twelve hundred pounds.

Araroba (ærărǭ·bă). [Tupi.] A substance found in cavities of the trunk of a Brazilian tree *Andira Araroba*; also called chrysarobin and Goa powder.
1879 *Encycl. Brit.* X. 707/1 The Goa powder or araroba is contained in the trunk, filling crevices in the heartwood.

Arbitrable, *a.* (Modern U.S. examples.)
1896 *Columbus* (O.) *Dispatch* 18 July 1/4 Secretary Olney points out in support of his amendments that they make all disputes prima facie, arbitrable. 1915 ROOSEVELT in *Spectator* 6 Feb. 195/1 They would not be made arbitrable, any more than an individual's right to life which is made arbitrable.

Arbitrageur (aɹbitrăʒǭɹ). *Stock Exchange.* [Fr.] (See quot. 1875.)
1875 *Encycl. Brit.* II. 311/1 Arbitrage properly known as such, is the business of an arbitrageur, who is almost always a member of a Stock Exchange or 'Bourse', and his arbitrations..are..in Government and other stocks and shares. 1903 *Westm. Gaz.* 13 Aug. 9/1 The knowledge that these accounts had been taken over for cash by a big arbitrageur helped the Yankee Market materially.

Arbitra·ging, *vbl. sb.* [ARBITRAGE 3.] (See quot.)
1900 S. A. NELSON *A.B.C. of Wall Street* 126 *Arbitraging*, trading in two markets in order to profit by the difference in prices.

Arbitral, *a.* **1.** (Later U.S. example.)
1911 *Amer. Year Book, 1910* 103 The most significant event of the past year in the development of international

arbitration has been the virtual establishment..of the New Court of Arbitral Justice.

Arbitrary. **B.** *sb.* Add:
Printing. Short for *arbitrary character*: A character used to supplement the letters and accents which constitute an ordinary fount of type.
1890 (*title*) Clarendon Press Inventory of Accents, Arbitrary Characters, &c. compiled April 1890. 1900 H. HART *Notes Century Typogr.* 139, I thought it unnecessary to 'set' the matrices for all the arbitrary characters. 1928 *The Periodical* 15 Feb. 17 The variety of type used, the many languages involved, and the multiplication of 'arbitraries' have demanded technical knowledge and minute accuracy to an extent probably unequalled in any other work.

Arbitra·tional, *a.* [See -AL.] Pertaining to, involving, or effected by arbitration.
a 1889 A. HAYWARD *Ethics of Peace* (Cent. D.), Arbitrational settlement of the Alabama claims.

Arbitrationist (āɹbitrē·ʃǝnist). [f. ARBITRATION + -IST.] One who is in favour of arbitration.
1884 *Pall Mall Gaz.* 24 June 3/1 Fine doctrine this for the arbitrationists! 1902 *Q. Rev.* Oct. 667 As an arbitrationist, he has been a hero with the emotional Radicals.

Arbitrative (āɹbitrētiv), *a.* [f. ARBITRATE *v.* + -IVE.] Having power to arbitrate; done by arbitration.
1831 WADDINGTON *Hist. Church* xiii. 221 The arbitrative authority of the Primitive Bishops was tolerated..by the Pagan Emperors. 1861 WARDLAW *Lect. Proverbs*, The arbitrative settlement of appealed differences. 1875 R. J. HINTON *Eng. Radical Leaders* 117 He urged arbitrative tribunals as one of the better modes of treatment.

Arbor Day (āɹbǝɹ dē). orig. *U.S.* [L. *arbor* tree. Cf. ARBOR².] A day set apart by law, orig. in the state of Nebraska, afterwards observed throughout the U.S. and adopted in S. Australia to be yearly observed for the planting of trees.
1872 in *Encycl. Brit.* (1902) XXXI. 112/2 Resolved that Wednesday, the 10th day of April 1872, be..set apart..for tree-planting in the state of Nebraska, and the State Board of Agriculture hereby name it Arbor Day. 1888 *Daily Inter-Ocean* 14 Mar. (Farmer), Governor Oglesby has designated April 13 as Arbor Day in Illinois. 1889 *Harper's Mag.* July 311/2 If the name of Arbor Day may seem to be a little misleading,..yet it may well serve until a better name is suggested. 1892 *Congress. Rec.* June 5404/2 In every quarter of the country 'arbor days' are days named by law, and also by custom, for planting forest trees to make lumber for the generations yet to come. 1897 *Westm. Gaz.* 2 March 4/2 The members of the Folklore Society were..doing a good and national work in assisting in the revival of such customs as that of tree-planting on a particular day, and he hoped this arbor day would be continued in their own locality. 1902 *Encycl. Brit.* XXXII. 731/2 In order to encourage tree-planting [in S. Australia], a yearly school holiday devoted to this purpose, and known as Arbor Day, was established in 1886. 1906 *N.Y. Even. Post* 4 May 4 Arbor Day is being celebrated in the schools of Greater New York to-day.

Arboricidal (āɹbǒrisǝi·dăl), *a.* [f. L. *arbor* tree + *-cīda* -CIDE I + -AL.] Given to cutting down trees, tree-felling.
1866 BLACKMORE *Cradock Nowell* xii, Condemnation of this arboricidal age. 1877 *Celebrities at Home, Gladstone*, The arboricidal tastes of the Master of Hawarden.

Arborize, *v.* Add: *intr.* To make tree-like formations.
1907 *Practitioner* June 860 Some of the fibres from the posterior nerve-root pass directly into the posterior grey cornu, and arborise around cells at its base.

Arbutus. Add:
2. *U.S.* With the pronunciation *arbū·tus*, applied to a North American ericaceous plant, *Epigæa repens*, called also *trailing arbutus, ground laurel*, and MAYFLOWER, and prized as a harbinger of spring.
1806 SHECUT *Flora Carol.*, Trailing Arbutus. 1856 WHITTIER *The Mayflowers*, The trailing arbutus, or mayflower, grows abundantly in the vicinity of Plymouth, and was the first flower that greeted the Pilgrims after their fearful winter.

Arc, *v.* Inflected **arcked, arcking,** or **arced, arcing** (with *c* = k). [f. ARC *sb.* 5.] *intr.* To form an electric arc.
1893 *Westm. Gaz.* 20 June 6/3 In 'arcing' or jumping from one conductor to another the current damaged the [gas] pipes. 1905 *Daily Chron.* 19 Apr. 6/5 The contact or arcing between the trolley cables and the conductor rail. 1908 *Installation News* II. 19/2 The fuse is provided with a phosphor bronze arcing tongue. 1910 *Ibid.* IV. 63/1 Fires ..due to the melting of soft compo gas-pipe, by arcing.

Arcades ambo (āɹkădīz æ·mbo). [L. phr. (Vergil *Ecl.* VII. 4), lit. both Arcadians, i.e. both pastoral poets or musicians.] Two persons of the same tastes, profession, or character (often derogatory).
1820 BYRON *Juan* IV. xciii, Each pull'd different ways with many an oath, 'Arcades ambo,' *id est*—blackguards both. 1882 T. MOZLEY *Remin.* lxxxiii. II. 92 [Denison and Neate] were *Arcades ambo*. They could talk and chaff about anything...They were both good scholars, rather above the Oxford run. 1888 RIDER HAGGARD *Colonel Quaritch* xvii, 'Well, I'm a lawyer too, and a pretty sharp one—*arcades ambo*,' said Johnnie with a coarse laugh.

Arcature (āɹkătiŭɹ). *Arch.* [ad. F. *arcature*, f. late L. *arcata* ARCADE: see -URE.] **a.** A small arcade. **b.** A blind arcade.
[1845-50 PARKER *Gloss. Archit.*] 1889 *Cent. Dict.*

Arch, *sb.* Add:
7. Chiefly *pl.* Collectors' name for certain species of moths: see quots.
1832 J. RENNIE *Butterfl. & Moths* 169 The Rufous Arch (*S[emasia] rufana*, Stephens). 1869 E. NEWMAN *Brit. Moths* 407 The Gray Arches (*Aplecta nebulosa*)...The costal margin of the fore wings is very slightly arched, the margin very slightly scalloped. *Ibid.* 408 The Silvery Arches (*Aplecta tincta*)...The fore wings are slightly arched beyond the middle of the costal margin. 1921 *Conquest* Sept. 496/2 The Dark Arches (*Xylophasia monoglypha*).

A·rcha·bbey. [ARCH- 1, 4.] The head abbey of a Benedictine congregation. So **A·rchabbot**, also called *abbot-general*.
1881 B. WELDON *Engl. Congreg. St. Benedict* p. ix, The Arch-Abbey of Monte Cassino. 1889 *Cent. Dict.*, Archabbot. 1897 BEDE CAMM *Benedictine Martyr* iv. 82 In the Order of St. Benedict..a confederacy of Abbeys and Priories, ..united together under one President (somtimes called Abbot-General or Arch-Abbot). 1912 *Cath. Encycl.* XV. 648/2 The location where St. Vincent Archabbey, College, and Seminary stand to-day. 1923 ABP. SETON *Memories of many years* 264 We had dinner at different tables, in the gallery. Arch-Abbot Krug..presided at the principal one.

Archaistically (āɹkeˌi·stikăli), *adv.* [f. ARCHAISTIC: see -ICALLY.] In an archaistic way; as an archaism.
1891 DRIVER *Introd. Lit. O.T.* (1892) 327 *note*, 'Ephraim' must in this case be used emblematically or archaistically.

Archaize, *v.* Add examples of the finite verb, and **A·rchaizer**, one who uses archaisms, an archaist.
1882 *Encycl. Brit.* XIV. 332 It may be remembered that Varro was himself something of an archaizer. 1906 *Academy* 1 Dec. 543/1 Poets in uncritical times do not archaise. 1921 GLOVER *Jesus in Exper. Men* viii. 134 The rather fabulous 'Age of Faith' is not for us, however much we archaize.

Archangel¹. Add:
2. c. A book-name for *Archangelica officinalis* and allied plants, as *Angelica sylvestris* (Wild Archangel): = ANGELICA I.
1855 MISS PRATT *Flower. Pl.* III. 54 *Angelica sylvestris* (Wild Archangel). 1884 MILLER *Plant-n.*, Archangel, *Archangelica officinalis*.

Archangel² (āɹkeˈndʒěl). Name of a government of European Russia and its chief town, used *attrib.* in *Archangel mat*, a bast mat used by horticulturists as a protective covering for plants, garden frames, etc.
1854 *F. & A. Dickson's* (of Chester) *Catal.*, Mats, large Archangel. 1909 *Daily Chron.* 9 Mar. 7/5 The plants being covered..with what are known as Archangel mats.

A·rchconfrate·rnity. *R.C.Ch.* [ARCH- 1.] 'A confraternity empowered to aggregate or affiliate other confraternities of the same nature, and to impart to them its indulgences and privileges' (*Cath. Encycl.*).
1661 BLOUNT *Glossogr.* (ed. 2) s.v. *Rosary*, Such Romanists who are of the Archconfraternity of the Rosary, instituted by St. Dominick. 1844 *Dublin Rev.* Mar. 11 The wonderful blessings, which have followed in the train of this religious association, have induced his present Holiness to..raise it to the title of an arch-confraternity. 1914 GASQUET *Order of Visitation* 32 The Archconfraternity of the Guard of Honour of the Sacred Heart.

Archebiosis (āɹkĭbǝiˌǭu·sis). *Biol.* [f. Gr. ἀρχή beginning + βίος life + -OSIS (cf. βίωσις way of life).] H. C. Bastian's term for: 'Spontaneous generation'; = ABIOGENESIS.
1872 BASTIAN *Beginnings of Life* I. v. 232. 1872 DARWIN *Let.* 28 Aug. in *Life & Lett.* III. 169, I should like to live to see Archebiosis proved true. 1874 FISKE *Cosmic Philos.* II. viii. I. 430 Archebiosis, or the origination of living matter in accordance with natural laws, must have occurred at some epoch of the past.

Archecentre (āɹkĭsentǝɹ). *Biol.* [f. as prec. + Gr. κέντρον CENTRE.] An organic structure regarded as the primitive or central type from which homologous structures have been derived as modifications in the course of evolution. So **Arche·ce·ntric** *a.*
1901 P. CHALMERS MITCHELL in *Trans. Linnean Soc., Zool.* VIII. 204 It is plain that the other Anseriformes must be removed from the Palamedeæ. The latter are archecentric. *Ibid.* 258 The metacentre of the Limicoline-Gruiform assemblages..is a derivative of the archecentre in which Meckel's tract is no longer symmetrical about the middle mesenteric vein and the diverticulum.

Archenteron (aɹke·ntěrǫn). *Biol.* [mod.L., f. Gr. ἀρχή beginning + ἔντερον intestine.] The primitive intestinal or alimentary cavity in an embryo. (Cf. METENTERON, PERIENTERON.) Hence **Archenteric** (-ente·rik) *a.*, pertaining to the archenteron.
1877 [see METENTERON]. 1881 E. R. LANKESTER in *Encycl. Brit.* XII. 548/2 The archenteron or primitive digestive space. *Ibid.*, The closure or shutting off of the axial from the periaxial portion of the archenteric space.

Archespore, archispore (āɹkĭ-, āɹkispǭɹ). *Bot.* and *Zool.* [ad. mod.L. *archesporium*, f. Gr. ἀρχε-, ἀρχι- ARCHI- + σπορά, σπόρος SPORE.] A protoplasmic body from which spores or similar reproductive bodies are developed. Hence **Archespo·rial** *a.*, pertaining to or of the nature of an archespore.
1882 VINES tr. *Sachs's Bot.* 403 By repeated divisions the archesporial cell produces the spore-mother-cells. 1901 G. N. CALKINS *Protozoa* v. 151 The entire organism takes part in the formation of archispores (or sporoblasts), each archispore gives rise to spores, and each spore to sporozoites. 1902 OLIVER tr. *Kerner's Nat. Hist. Plants* II. 95 Within [the anther], large cells..form what is known as the *archesporium*. *Ibid.* 96 The archesporial cells divide, giving rise to the pollen-mother-cells.

Archibenthal (āɹkibe·nþăl), *a.* [f. mod.L. *archibenthos* (f. Gr. ἀρχι- ARCHI- + βένθος depth) + -AL.] Belonging to or inhabiting the **Archibe·nthos**, or depths of the primitive (palæozoic) ocean.
1904 *Science* 7 Oct. 463 The archibenthal species..have a greater range than those restricted to..the shallow waters of the coast. 1912 J. MURRAY & HJORT *Depths of the Ocean* 459, etc.

Archiblast (āɹkiblæst). *Embryol.* [f. Gr. ἀρχι- ARCHI- + βλαστός sprout, germ, -BLAST.] The formative yolk in an ovum, which constitutes the germ; also applied by His to the epiblast. (In both uses distinguished from PARABLAST 2, q.v.) Hence **Archibla·stic** *a.*
1876 [see ARCHI- 2]. 1876 [see PARABLAST 2]. 1885 STIRLING tr. *Landois' Human Physiol.* II. 1128.

Archicerebrum (āɹkise·rĭbrǝm). *Zool.* [mod. L., f. Gr. ἀρχι- ARCHI- 2 + L. *cerebrum* brain.] The primitive brain of an insect or other arthropod.
1881 [see *syncerebrum* s.v. SYN-].

Archie (āɹtʃi), *sb.* [abbrev. of proper name *Archibald*: see quot. 1922.] In the war of 1914–18, an anti-aircraft gun firing shrapnel, orig. applied to those used by the Germans. Hence **Archie** *v. trans.*, to fire at with an anti-aircraft gun.
1915 ROSHER *In R.N.A.S.* (1916) 116 There are some beastly Archies..which come unpleasantly near first shot. [1916 H. G. WELLS *Mr. Britling* II. iv. 334 Suddenly whack, whack, whack, came a line of little puffs of smoke behind it, and then one in front of it, which meant that our anti-aircraft guns were having a go at it. Then, as suddenly, Archibald stopped.] 1917 'CONTACT' (A. J. Bott) *An Airman's Outings* vi. 159 Only somebody who has been Archied from Pluspres can realise what it means to fly right over the stronghold at four thousand feet. 1920 *Blackw. Mag.* Dec. 757/1 So soon as they crossed the lines, they were heavily 'archied'. 1922 RALEIGH *War in Air* I. 343 The anti-aircraft guns got their name of 'Archies' from a light-hearted British pilot, who when he was fired at in the air quoted a popular music-hall refrain—'Archibald, certainly not!'

Archiepi·scopally, *adv.* [f. ARCHIEPISCOPAL + -LY².] In an archiepiscopal way; in the manner of an archbishop.
1839 *Fraser's Mag.* XX. 122 So fond is Mr. Philip of episcopacy, that at page 248 he archiepiscopally consecrates John Bunyan, 'Bishop Bunyan'. 1884 TENNYSON *Becket* III. iii, *Herbert.* And how did Roger of York comport himself? *Walter Map.* As magnificently and archiepiscopally as our Thomas would have done. 1886 F. C. PHILIPS *Jack & Three Jills* II. x. 174 His demeanour was archiepiscopally grave.

Archipelagoed (āɹkipe·lăgǭud), *pa. pple.*, interspersed (*with*...) like an archipelago.
1880 'MARK TWAIN' *Tramp Abroad* xlix, Gravy, archipelagoed with mushrooms. 1906 HOWELLS *Certain Delightful Eng. Towns* 91 The tender blue sky, thickly archipelagoed with whity-brown clouds.

Archispore; see *ARCHESPORE.

Architected (āɹkitektĕd), *pa. pple.* [f. ARCHITECT *sb.*] Designed by an architect.
1890 *Harper's Mag.* Apr. 809/2 We would not give being the author of one of Mr. Aldrich's beautiful sonnets to be the author of many 'Wyndham Towers', however skilfully architected. 1913 RALEIGH *Some Authors, Boccaccio* (1923) 3 He has come out of the prison-house of theological system, nobly and grimly architected. 1923 *Public Opinion* 29 June 622/3 A..vague notion that a building ought to be architected.

A·rch-stone. *U.S.* [ARCH *sb.* III.] *Arch-stone State*, the 'Keystone State', Pennsylvania.
1840 *Congr. Globe* 25 Jan., App. 263 In this severance and sectioning, what would Pennsylvania, that 'arch-stone' State, say?

Arc-lamp, -light, -lighting: see ARC 5.
1882 *Electric Light* 21/2 The wires for 'arc lights' to be insulated and protected in the same manner as the aforesaid main rods or wires. *Ibid.* 24/1 They are of opinion that 'arc lamps are well adapted for the illumination of very large areas'. 1890 *Electrical Engineer* 7 Feb. 102/2 Prices of Arc Lighting. 1897 *Daily News* 29 April 3/5 Repairs of the arc-lighting mains. 1906 *Daily Chron.* 30 Nov. 7/3 The arc-lamp standards were torn up and twisted like straw. 1911 *Encycl. Brit.* XVI. 659/2 F. P. E. Carré in France in 1876 began to manufacture arc lamp carbons of high quality from coke, lampblack and syrup.

Arcosolium (āɹkosǭu·liǝm). Pl. **-ia.** [med.L., f. *arcus* bow, arch + *solium* seat, throne.] An arched cell or niche, vaulted in semicircular form, serving as a tomb in the Roman catacombs.
1876 [see *table-tomb* s.v. TABLE *sb.* 22]. 1905 *19th Cent.* Nov. 785 Both the 'table-tomb' and the 'arcosolium' are as a rule confined to those many crypts..which opened out of the various galleries.

Arctalian (āɹktē·liăn), *a.* *Zoogeography.* [f. mod.L. *Arctalia* (f. Gr. ἄρκτος: cf. ARCTIC + ἅλς sea) + -AN.] Belonging to the marine region called *Arctalia*, comprising the seas of the northern hemisphere as far south as the isocryme of 44° Fahr.
1888 *Proc. Biol. Soc. Washington* II. 34 (Cass. Supp.) The fauna is very different from the Arctalian. *Ibid.* [see TROPICALIAN].

Arctic. **B.** Add:

Supplement, p. 3873; Corrigenda, p. 4092; Spurious words, p. 4093; Books quoted, p. 4094

2. *pl.* Thick waterproof over-shoes for winter wear. *U.S.*

1883 M. ARNOLD *Lett.* (1895) II. 239, I have bought a pair of *arctics*, the lined waterproof boots which everybody here [*sc.* in Boston] wears in winter. 1892 HOWELLS *Mercy* 38 He put on his overcoat and arctics.

Arctoid (ā·ɹktoid), *a.* (*sb.*) *Zool.* [f. mod.L. *Arctoidea* neut. pl., f. Gr. ἄρκτος bear: see -OID.] Resembling a bear; *spec.* Belonging to, or having the characters of, the division *Arctoidea* of Carnivora, comprising the bears and allied animals; as *sb.* an animal of this division. Also **Arctoi·dean** *a.*

1869 W. H. FLOWER in *Proc. Zool. Soc.* 14 Jan. 24 The reproductive organs [of the dogs] belong neither to the Arctoid nor to the Æluroid type. *Ibid.* 30 An arboreal, prehensile-tailed, omnivorous, Procyonine Arctoid. 1885 *Athenæum* 3 Jan. 20/3 The view that the Pinnipedia were evolved from some arctoid, probably ursine, form of land Carnivora. *Ibid.* 2 May 570/1 The arctoidean carnivorous mammals. 1923 J. A. THOMSON in *Glasgow Herald* 27 Mar. 6/2 The polecat..has nothing to do with any cat...It is Arctoid, not Feline.

Arcturian (aɹktiū·riăn), *a.* (*sb.*) *Astr.* [f. ARCTUR-US + -IAN.] Pertaining to or resembling Arcturus; applied to a class of stars having a spectrum like that of Arcturus; as *sb.* a star of this class.

1909 [see *ANTARIAN].

Ardeine (ā·ɹdi,əin), *a. Ornith.* [f. mod.L. *Ardeinæ* fem. pl., f. L. *ardea* heron: see -INE[1].] Belonging to, or having the characters of, the subfamily *Ardeinæ*, comprising the herons and their near allies.

1875 *Encycl. Brit.* III. 713/1 *note*, *Balæniceps* has the head of a Stork, but its body is largely Ardeine.

Ardri (ā·ɹd,ri). Also -righ. [Ir. *árd-* chief- + *ríog* king.] A head king. Hence **A·rdriship.**

1889 *Athenæum* 17 Aug. 215/2 The usurpation of the ard-righ-ship by Brian Boru. 1896 *Westm. Gaz.* 29 Dec. 3/1 To make the Ardri-ship (or head kingship) a reality. 1922 *Edin. Rev.* Apr. 243 Ireland will now welcome any native Government strong enough..to give her peace, whether Free State, or Republic, or an Ard-rí chosen from one of her royal races to rule once more from the hill of Tara.

Area. 2. b. Add quots. for *area sneak*, *sneaking*, and: **area-way** = AREA 2; also *U.S.* an area serving as a passage-way.

1812 J. H. VAUX *Flash Dict.*, *Area sneak, or *Area slum*, the practice of slipping unperceived down the areas of private houses, and robbing the lower apartments of plate or other articles. 1839 DICKENS *Nickleby* lix, Why wasn't I a thief, swindler, housebreaker, area-sneak, robber of pence out of the trays of blind men's dogs? 1906 *Daily Chron.* 14 May 6/3 To prevent burglary and *area-sneaking. 1903 *N. Y. Times* 30 Oct. 1 The body was concealed in the home until Monday night, when it was placed in the *area-way. 1907 *Chicago Even. Post* 4 May 3 The building is connected with the main hospital by a covered areaway. 1914 A. B. REEVE *Exploits of Elaine* v. 82 A sinister face appeared in a basement areaway nearby.

Areopagus. Add quots.:

a 1670 HACKET *Abp. Williams* II. § 159 (1693) 169 And therefore, my H. Lordships, here I have fixt my Areopagus, and dernier Resort, being not like to make any further Appeal. 1900 *Daily News* 28 Apr. 5/3 A permanent areopagus has been created, with fixed arbitrators, secretaries, &c. 1919 VON TIRPITZ *Mem.* I. xvi. 249 The European 'areopagus' (as Bethmann called it), proposed by Grey, ought not to have been refused. 1920 *Q. Rev.* Apr. 475 The Commission of Reparations, whose duty it should be to become a..Rhadamanthine Areopagus.

Aretalogy (ærètæ·lŏdʒi). [ad. Gr. ἀρεταλογία, f. ἀρετή excellence, wondrous deed, miracle: see -LOGY.] A narrative of the miracles performed by a god or semi-divine hero. So **Aretalogical** (ærètălǫ·dʒikăl) *a.*

1887 W. CORY *Lett. & Jrnls.* (1897) 525 The aretalogical succession is that traced back to the Scipio and Regulus of Cicero, Livy, and Horace. 1912 J. S. PHILLIMORE *Philostr. Apollon.* I. p. xiii, A life, or rather an edifying *Aretalogy*, of Pythagoras. 1925 W. R. HALLIDAY *Pagan Background* vi. 185 The aretalogy, which narrates the miraculous acts of some thaumaturge.

Argal (ā·ɹgăl), *sb.* Short form of ARGALI.

1928 V. G. CHILDE *Most Anc. East* ii. 44 The third variety of Old World sheep, the argal, lives to the east of the urial.

Argel (ā·ɹdʒel). *Med.* [a. Arab. حرجل *harjil* (Sharaf *Dict. Med.*).] The leaves of the African asclepiadaceous plant *Solenostemma Argel*, formerly used to adulterate senna.

1811 A. T. THOMSON *Lond. Disp.* (1818) 93 The leaf of argel is an inch or 14 lines long, while that of senna never exceeds nine lines. 1874 GARROD & BAXTER *Mat. Med.* (1880) 242 This addition to senna is important, as the argel is supposed to gripe and nauseate. 1920 H. G. GREENISH *Mat. Med.* (ed. 3) 34 Argel leaves, *Solenostemma Argel*, Hayne;..formerly regularly mixed with the senna but now of rare occurrence.

Argentine (ā·ɹdʒĕntəin), *a.*[2] and *sb.*[2] [ad. Sp. *Argentina*: see defn.]

A. *adj.* Of or belonging to Argentina, the federal republic (*Republica* or *Confederacion Argentina*) which occupies the greater part of the southern end of South America, and is named from the Rio de la Plata (Sp. *plata* silver).

1834 *Penny Cycl.* II. 308/2 Argentine republic. 1875 *Encycl. Brit.* II. 288/2 Along the Argentine slopes of the Andes. 1892 T. CHILD *Spanish-Amer. Republics* 280 The Argentine love of showy novelties. 1917 G. ROSS *Argentina & Uruguay* 46 According to Argentine Law, all children born on Argentine soil are *ipso facto* Argentines. 1920 *Cornh. Mag.* Sept. 334 No two Argentine horses are of the same mind for more than a few seconds at a time.

B. *sb.* 1. A native or inhabitant of Argentina. Also, a horse or pony of a breed peculiar to Argentina.

1860 *Chambers's Encycl.* I. 388/2 The Banda Oriental has been a bone of contention between the Brazilians and the Argentines. 1892 T. CHILD *Spanish-Amer. Republics* 275 In all that concerns civilization, the Argentines look up to the French. 1893 C. E. AKERS *Argentine Sketches* 42 In very rare cases is an Argentine found doing anything that requires severe physical exertion. 1903 KIPLING *Five Nations, M. I.*, Atop of a sore-backed Argentine.

2. *The Argentine*, Argentina.

1892 T. CHILD *Spanish-Amer. Republics* 276 *note*, In the Argentine and in Uruguay. *Ibid.* 279 The auctioneer..is a great personage in the Argentine.

Hence **Argentinian** (ādʒĕnti·niăn) *a.*, belonging to the Argentine; also *sb.* = **Argentino** (ādʒentī·no), a native of the Argentine.

1919 CHARLOTTE B. JORDAN tr. *Ibanez's Four Horsemen of the Apocalypse* I. i, I am an Argentinian citizen. *Ibid.*, She was speaking alone to the Argentinian. 1920 *Cornhill Mag.* Sept. 335 The work of the Texans was neat and expeditious, that of the Argentiños clumsy and slow.

Arghan (ā·ɹgæn). [Etym. unknown.] The fibre of a South American plant recently cultivated in Malaya, which can be spun into a strong fine yarn. Also *attrib.*

1922 *Conquest* Oct. 485 Arghan, the new British textile. 1924 J. S. M. WARD *Textile Fibres* 52-3. 1927 *Chambers's Jrnl.* 236 The Arghan plant is Sir Henry [Wickham's] second gift to the Inde.

Argive (ā·ɹgəiv), *a.* and *sb.* [ad. L. *Argīvus* (Gr. Ἀργεῖος) pertaining to Argos, Ἄργος.] A. *adj.* Of or belonging to the city of Argos or the territory of Argolis. Hence used in Homer and later classical writers as = Grecian, Greek.

1598 CHAPMAN *Iliad* I. Argt., Apollos Priest to th' Argiue Fleete doth bring Gifts for his daughter. *Ibid.* 2 Till in my Royall Argiue court, her bewties strow my bed. 1675 HOBBES *Iliad* I. (1686) 1 The two Atrides..Who of the Argive Army were the best. 1715 POPE *Iliad* II. 675 Next move to War the gen'rous Argive Train. 1716 *Ibid.* VII. 259 Thro' ev'ry Argive Heart new Transport ran. 1858 BIRCH *Anc. Pottery* II. 107 The Lacedæmonian, Teian, Chian, and Argive cups were also esteemed. 1875 MORRIS *Æneids* II. 254 And now the Argive host comes forth.

B. *sb.* A native of Argos or of Argolis; *gen.* a Greek.

1675 HOBBES *Iliad* XVII. (1686) 267 Just so Patroclus body tugged they, Trojans to Troy, and Argives to the Fleet. 1716 POPE *Iliad* VIII. 436 Long since had Hector stain'd these Fields with Gore, Stretch'd by some Argive on his native Shore. 1875 MORRIS *Æneids* I. 40 And Pallas, might not she Burn up the Argive fleet and sink the Argives in the sea..? 1922 JACKSON & LAKE *Beginnings Chr.* II. 12 The ivory or other material..supplied by the Elians, Athenians, or Argives.

A·rgle-ba·rgle, *sb.* [f. *argle-bargle* vb.: see ARGLE *v.*] Disputatious argument, bandying of words, wrangling.

a 1881 CARLYLE in W. Knight *Retrospects* Ser. I. (1904) 25, I have for a long time given up the argle-bargle of metaphysics. 1927 *Observer* 11 Dec. 15/2 Can they..stand up to a good and sufficient argle-bargle that lasts for the best part of three hours?

So **A·rgy-ba·rgy (argue-bargue)** *v.* and *sb.* (orig. Sc.).

1887 *Jamieson's Sc. Dict.* Suppl. s.v. *Argewe*, The terms *argie-bargie*, *argie*, and *bargie*, are applied to such contentions. 1888 BARRIE *Auld Licht Idylls* 35 I'se nae time to argy-bargy wi' ye. 1905 H. G. WELLS *Kipps* I. ii, An occasional argey-bargey that sprang up between Carshot and Buggins at dinner. 1906 W. DE MORGAN *Joseph Vance* xxiii, He argue-bargues with you like a winkle that won't come out of its shell. 1922 *Blackw. Mag.* July 65/1 Do not argy-bargy with such scoundrels.

Argon (ā·ɹgǫn). *Chem.* [mod.L., f. Gr. ἀργόν, neuter of ἀργός idle, inactive, f. ἀ- priv. + ἔργον work.] A colourless odourless gas occurring in very small quantity (less than 1 per cent.) in the air. First discovered in 1894 and named, as a new element, from its chemical inertness.

1895 (31 Jan.) LD. RAYLEIGH & W. RAMSAY in *Phil. Trans.* CLXXXVI. A. 187 Argon, a New Constituent of the Atmosphere. *Ibid.* 234 The gas deserves the name 'argon', for it is a most astonishingly indifferent body, inasmuch as it is unattacked by elements of very opposite character. 1913 *Bloxam's Chem.* (ed. 10) 293.

Argonaut. Add:

1. b. *transf.*

1807 W. IRVING *Salmagundi* (1824) 85 A celebrated Roman Knight..who..became a great favourite of Prince Madoc, and accompanied that famous argonaut in the voyage which ended in the discovery of this Continent. 1893 KATE SANBORN *S. California* 1 The *fin-de-siecle* Argonaut, in Pullman train, flees the cold and grip.

c. An adventurer who went to California in 1849; a forty-niner. *U.S.*

1873 *Overland Monthly* (S. Franc.) X. 434 Argonauts of '49. 1875 B. HARTE (*title*) Tales of the Argonauts.

Arguably (ā·ɹgiuăbli), *adv.* [f. ARGUABLE + -LY[2].] As may be shown by argument or made a matter of argument.

1890 *Sat. Rev.* 22 Feb. 216/2 His policy, if sometimes arguably mistaken, was almost always a..generous policy. 1920 *Q. Rev.* Apr. 404 The zeal for order and moral righteousness is arguably more purely Jewish in its origin than [etc.].

Argufier (ā·ɹgiufəiəɹ). [f. ARGUFY *v.*] One who argufies or is given to arguing.

1871 JOWETT *Plato* III. 494 We know that they are tremendous argufiers, and are able to impart their own skill to others. 1880 CLARK RUSSELL *Sailor's Sweetheart* i, I have noticed that your people who are pretty well agreed are always the fiercest argufiers.

Argy-bargy, etc.: see under *ARGLE-BARGLE.

Argyle, variant spelling of ARGYLL.

1906 H. C. MOFFATT *Old Oxf. Plate* 54 Two-handled Argyle with Cover. Silver. 1779. 1909 *Brasenose Coll. Quatercent. Monogr.* I. v. 42.

Argyrol (ā·ɹdʒirǫl). *Pharmacy.* [f. Gr. ἄργυρον silver + -OL.] Vitellin of silver, a dark brown powder of which the aqueous solution is used as a local antiseptic.

1910 *Practitioner* Mar. 397 The ducts..should be swabbed out on each of these days with a solution of argyrol.

Arhat (ā·ɹhæt). Also **Arahat** (æ·răhæt). [a. Skr. *arhat* adj. deserving. *Arahat* is the Pali form.] A Buddhist saint of the highest rank. Hence **A·r(a)hatship,** the state of an Arhat.

1875 R. C. CHILDERS *Pali Dict.*, *Arahâ*,..an Arhat... *Arahattam*, State of being an Arahâ, Arhatship. 1877 RHYS DAVIDS *Buddhism* 84 The Buddhist Arahats or saints. 1882 *Encycl. Brit.* XIV. 226/1 The central point of primitive Buddhism was the doctrine of 'Arahatship'. 1912 H. G. RAWLINSON *Bactria* vii. 111 The Siamese tradition of Menander's attainment to Arhatship.

-arian (ē·riăn) *suffix*, based on L. *-ārius* -ARY[1] with the addition of -AN, used to form adjs. or corresponding sbs. The earliest formations of a general character are *disciplinarian* (sb.) of the late-16th century, *agrarian*, *antiquarian* (sb.), *proletarian*, *corpuscularian*, and *veterinarian* (sb.) of the 17th century; of the numeral adjs. *quinquagenarian* (1569) and *septuagenarian* (1715) are the earliest recorded. The commonest use of the suffix is in terms denoting religious or moral tenets, as *Millenarian*, *Predestinarian*, *sectarian*, *Sublapsarian*, *Supralapsarian*, *Trinitarian*, *Unitarian* of the 17th century, *Tractarian* (1824), on the analogy of which were formed *necessitarian*, *utilitarian*, *humanitarian*, and the jocular *anythingarian* and *nothingarian* of the 18th century, and the nonce-word *strictarian* (after *sectarian*).

1799 SOUTHEY *Devil's Walk* xxix, My Utilitarians, My all sorts of -inians And all sorts of -arians My all sorts of -ists. 1867 F. H. LUDLOW *Fleeing to Tarshish* 125, I believe there are strictarians who think it too gay.

Aridly (æ·ridli), *adv.* [f. ARID *a.* + -LY[2].] In an arid manner, with aridity.

1883 MISS BROUGHTON *Belinda* II. iv. 228, 'I think', he says aridly, 'that..we had better keep to the subject in hand.' 1906 HARDY *Dynasts* II. II. vi. 201 Were I as coarse a wife As I am limned in English caricature..You could not speak more aridly.

Arimasp (æ·rimæsp). [ad. L. *Arimaspī* pl., Gr. Ἀριμασποί, said to mean in Scythian 'one-eyed'.] One of the Arimaspi, a mythical race of one-eyed men in northern Europe, occupied in endeavouring to wrest gold from the griffins (γρῦπες) who guarded it. They are sometimes figured in Greek vases, fighting with griffins.

1600 F. WALKER *Sp. Mandeville* 11 b, The Arimaspes, being a people with one eie. 1872 C. W. KING *Antique Gems & Rings* Index 472 Arimasp and Gryphon. 1889 *Cent. Dict.* s.v., Figures of Arimasps occur sometimes in Greek art, represented in Oriental dress and fighting griffins. 1905 H. B. WALTERS *Anc. Pottery* II. 148 In one instance an Arimasp woman is seen shooting at a Gryphon of curious type. 1913 E. H. MINNS *Scythians & Greeks* iv. 56 An Arimasp such as we find on the calathos from the Great Bliznitsa.

Arimaspian (ærimæ·spiăn). [f. L. *Arimaspi* (see prec.) + -IAN.] = prec.

1667 MILTON *P. L.* II. 945 As when a Gryfon through the Wilderness..Pursues the Arimaspian, who by stelth Had from his wakeful custody purloind The guarded Gold. 1775 J. BRYANT *Anc. Mythol.* I. 380 *note*, This may have been one reason..why the Cyclopians and Arimaspians are represented with one eye. 1827 *Blackw. Mag.* XXI. 780/1 Mermaid or salamander..miser or arimaspian. 1913 E. H. MINNS *Scythians & Greeks* v. 113 The representations of Arimaspians and griffins in art. *Ibid.* xi. 391 The centre group, in which there are two griffins to one Arimaspian.

Arise, *v.* 18. Add:

Arising out of: used, with loose construction, to introduce a circumstance, action, proposal, etc., arising out of an event, statement, etc.

1928 *Daily News* 8 Dec. 9/3 Arising out of the Goddard case, [a man] was summoned..for threatening..an ex-Constable.

Aristo (ări·sto). *colloq.* [Fr., shortened f. *aristocrate.*] An aristocrat.

1864 M. J. HIGGINS *Ess.* (1875) 172 In 1795, the aged Honorius died..in consequence of the..imprisonment to which he had been subjected as an *aristo*. 1888 LD. R. GOWER *Rec. & Remin.* (1903) 425 Charles Villiers..said how snubbed Dizzy used to be in old days by the aristos whom he got to serve him in his later life. *Ibid.* 133 Now that aristo-Liberals vote often with Conservatives.

Aristol (ări·stǫl). [f. Gr. ἄριστος best + -OL.] A brownish-red powder used as a deodorant antiseptic.

1891 *Medical Annual* 11 Aristol..is said to be formed, as a voluminous red-brown amorphous precipitate, when an aqueous solution of iodine in potassium iodide is treated with thymol in caustic soda solution. 1901 in DORLAND *Med. Dict.* (ed. 2).

Aristophanic (æ:ristofæ·nik), *a.* and *sb.* [ad. L. *Aristophanicus*, Gr. Ἀριστοφανικός.] A. *adj.* Of or pertaining to Aristophanes, the Athenian comic dramatist, or his plays; used by, occurring in, or characteristic of Aristophanes.

1827 CARLYLE *Germ. Rom.* II. *Tieck* 6 He had laughed with his whole heart, in a true Aristophanic vein. 1827 *Theatre of Greeks* (ed. 2) 109 *note*, The expressions which the Aristophanic Euripides employs in assailing Æschylus. 1835 T. MITCHELL *Acharn. of Aristoph.* 148 *note*, The word λαιω occurs in the Aristophanic writings. 1873 SYMONDS *Grk. Poets* viii. 245 If we are to seek for an approximation to Aristophanic humour, we shall find it perhaps in Rabelais.

B. *sb.* A logaœdic tripody beginning with a dactyl (—◡◡|—◡|—◡̄); a first Pherecratic.

1874 J. M. MARSHALL *Horati Op.* I. p. xxxiv, Sapphic (the greater). Alternately an Aristophanic and a greater Sapphic.

Aristotle's Lantern: see LANTERN 6 b.

Aristotype (ări·stotəip). *Photography.* [f. Gr. ἄριστος best + TYPE.] A printing process in which silver salts are used in collodion or gelatin; also, a print made with such a process. Also in shortened form **Ari·sto.**

1889 *Anthony's Photogr. Bull.* II. 15 Is there an opportunity for great depth, try an aristotype. 1894 *Amer. Ann. Photogr.* 68 When aristo papers were first introduced. *Ibid.* 274 Toning and fixing aristotype prints.

Ark, *sb.* 2. b. Add: Applied to something which protects or enshrines a precious possession.

1826 E. EVERETT *Address at Charlestown* 39 They [Adams and Jefferson] took up the ark of her [their country's] liberties with pure hands, and bore it through in triumph. 1888 BRYCE *Amer. Commw.* I. xxiii. 323 The functions which it [the Supreme Court] discharges in guarding the ark of the Constitution.

Ark, *v.* (Later U.S. example.)

1845 *St. Louis Reveille* 4 Aug. (Th.) I stood by while all the animals were arked.

Arka·nsan, *a.* and *sb.* [f. the name of the State.] a. *adj.* Of or pertaining to Arkansas. b. *sb.* A native or inhabitant of Arkansas.

1884 CABLE *Dr. Sevier* xv. (1885) 100 A tall Arkansan, with high-combed hair, ..and very broad, clean-shaven lower jaw.

Arkansas (ā·ɹkănsǫ, *also outside U.S.* aɹkæ·nzăs). [Name of a state of U.S.A.] A fine-grain variety of novaculite found in Arkansas, U.S.A. Also, a whetstone made of this. In full *Arkansas stone*, *hone* (see quot. 1910).

Arkansas toothpick: see TOOTHPICK.

1875 *Carpentry & Join.* 34 We often find it a good plan to rub down a tool on a bit of Arkansas of coarse quality. 1885 *Spons' Mechanics' Own Bk.* 242 Oilstones.—These are of several kinds, the best known being the Charnley Forest, Turkey, Arkansas, and Washita brands. 1910 *Encycl. Brit.* XIII. 653/1 Of Arkansas stones there are two varieties... The finer kind, known as Arkansas hone, is obtained in small pieces at the hot springs.

Arm, *sb.*[1] III. Add:

arm-guard, (*a*) in *Boxing*, defence with the arm; (*b*) a protecting covering for the arm; **arm-rest,** a device constructed for the arm to rest upon.

1889 MICHELL *Boxing* (Badm. Libr.) 148-9 Figure ix. Left *arm guard. *Ibid.* 156 Right arm guard. 1898 *Daily News* 25 Oct. 8/5 [They] seemed to depend more upon quick dodging than upon the armguard to avoid a blow. 1899 *Ibid.* 20 June 3/5 Two massive gold arm-guards, set with ..diamonds. 1905 *Daily Chron.* 11 Jan. 6/2 The girls wore arm-guards and masks. 1898 SLOANE *Stand. Elect. Dict.* App., *Arm rest, a device for lessening the fatigue of holding a telephone receiver to the ear. 1908 *Daily Chron.* 12 Mar. 5/6 The deceased's head was..over the mouth of the barrel, which was leaning against the arm-rest.

Arm, *sb.*[2] 9. Add to definition: air-service, now often called *the fourth arm*.

1914 *Engineering* 4 Sept. 312/2 Aircraft in Warfare: the Dawn of the Fourth Arm. By F. W. Lanchester.

Armageddon (āɹmăge·dǫn). [See Rev. xvi. 16 (A.V.). The Revised Version has *Harmagedon.*] The place of the last decisive battle at the Day of Judgement; hence used allusively for any final conflict on a great scale. Also *attrib.*

1811 SHELLEY *Let.* in Hogg *Life* (1858) I. 170 Faber, Rowland Hill, and several others of the Armageddon heroes. 1886 EARL SUFFOLK & W. G. CRAVEN *Racing* (Badm. Libr.) 247 As long as we have racing we shall have betting—that ceaseless war between layers and backers will still be waged. ..At present we see no sign of a final Armageddon. 1893 KIPLING *England's Answer* Poems 1919 I. 237 In the day of Armageddon, or the last great fight of all. 1910 *Encycl. Brit.* II. 561/1 From the application of the word Armageddon to the great battle of the End of Time comes the use of the phrase 'an Armageddon' to express any great slaughter or final conflict. 1914 *Brit. Chess Mag.* Sept. 339 The chess Megiddo has ever been a delightful seat of friendly antagonism, but to-day Armageddon is horrible to contemplate. 1928 W. DEEPING *Old Pybus* ii. § 2 Mr. Pybus had been able to speak of the war as Armageddon without cribbing an obvious bleat from the popular press.

Armagnac (aɹmæ·nyæk). A superior brandy made in the district formerly called Armagnac (department of Gers).

1910 *Encycl. Brit.* XI. 904/2 The remainder [of the wine produced in the department of Gers] is chiefly manufactured into brandy, known by the name of Armagnac, second only to Cognac in reputation. 1920 SAINTSBURY *Notes on Cellar-bk.* 119 You may drink Armagnac after Burgundy now and they won't quarrel.

Armamentarium (āɹmămentē·riǒm). [L., = arsenal, armoury.] The equipment of medicines, instruments, and appliances used by a medical man.

1874 [see ARMAMENTARY]. 1906 V. HORSLEY in S. Paget *Life* (1919) 236 A whole armamentarium of drugs.

Armature. Add:

8. *attrib.* and *Comb.*, as *armature bobbin*, *conductor*, *magnet*, *-winder*, *-winding*.

1884 HIGGS *Magn. & Dyn. Electr. Mach.* 34 The armature-bobbins revolve as near the magnetic poles as possible. *Ibid.* 247 The employment of only half as many inducing magnets as of armature magnets. 1901 *J. Black's Carp. & Build.*, *Scaffolding* 77 The winding of the armature conductors inside insulating tubes. 1902 *Encycl. Brit.* XXVII. 580/1 The separate small sections of the armature winding. 1908 *Daily Chron.* 24 Aug. 9/6 Armature winder wanted.

Arm-chair. Add:

Often used *attrib.* to express the attitude of persons who confine themselves or are addicted to home-made views or criticism of matters in which they take no active part; as *arm-chair critic*, *politician*.

1890 *Pall Mall Gaz.* 8 Sept. 2/2 The latter depends absolutely upon the vivifying force of emotion, the former condescends to nothing more violent than the gentle arm-chair titillation which can be developed over the pages of a history-book. 1894 *New Rev.* XI. 286 An essential difference between 'black' anarchists..and 'arm-chair' anarchists. 1896 W. H. S. AUBREY *Stock Exch. Investm.* i. 5 The arm-chair critic of politics, war, literature, or finance. 1899 *Geogr. Jrnl.* XIII. 153 Mr. Murray had convinced himself by experiments..that much of the objection to horizontal fishing had no greater weight than belongs to arm-chair disputations on the subject. 1902 *Lond. Q. Rev.* Jan. 70 Even to the armchair traveller the perusal of this Handbook would..suffice to attest the reality of the transformation of the..province. 1913 P. G. WODEHOUSE *Little Nugget* II. viii. § 3 The arm-chair critic, reviewing a situation calmly and at his ease. 1914 *Engl. Rev.* Sept. 259 Arm-chair strategists.

Armed, *ppl. a.*[1] 1. Add:

Armed camp, used esp. of Europe regarded as fully armed ready for war.

1898 *Daily News* 6 Oct. 5/7 The armed camp, which we call the continent.

Armeno-, used as comb. form of *Armenia* or *Armenian* (L. *Armenius*, Gr. Ἀρμένιος).

1898 P. GEDDES in *Ethical World* 12 Mar. 167/1 The Turcophobes and Turcophiles, the Hellenophobes and Hellenophiles, Armenophobes and Armenophiles of recent journalism. 1898 *Daily News* 25 Aug. 4/7 The Armenophile movement in England. 1905 *Westm. Gaz.* 15 Nov. 2/1 The Armenophobia of Russian officialdom.

Armistice. Add: 3. **Armistice Day,** the day, 11 Nov. 1918, on which the armistice was concluded which brought the war of 1914–18 to an end; also, any anniversary of that day.

Armorially (aɹmō·riăli), *adv.* [f. ARMORIAL *a.* + -LY[2].] In an armorial manner; in a way that pertains to arms or armour.

1861 *Temple Bar* Aug. 134 With big iron boots encasing their legs armorially. 1887 *N. & Q.* 7th Ser. IV. 54/2 Armorially speaking, I find no trace of Cornish Gunns in Burke's 'General Armory'.

Armour. II. Add:

armour-clad *a.*, protected by armour, as a vessel; also *sb.*, an armour-clad vessel; **armour-piercing** *a.* (of shot or shell, a gun) designed to pierce the armour-plating of ships; **armour-shelf,** a wide shelf extending below the water-line of an armoured ship, supporting the edge of the armour plating.

1863 *Armour-clad [see IRONCLAD *a.* 1 *note*]. 1869, 1882 [see ARMOUR-CLAD]. 1901 *Westm. Gaz.* 11 Apr. 10/2 Miolania, a large armour-clad aquatic tortoise. 1903 LYDEKKER *Mostly Mammals* 308 Armour-clad whales. 1897 *Daily News* 19 July 9/5 Their 12-inch *armour-piercing shot. 1922 *Encycl. Brit.* XXX. 122/1 Armour-piercing projectiles for maximum penetration. 1883 NARES *Constr. Ironclad* 7 The *armour shelf is fitted about six feet below the water line. 1890 W. J. GORDON *Foundry* 35 The next, in frame up to her armour-shelf, is an iron-clad of 10,000 tons, building for Her Majesty's Navy.

Armour-plated, *a.* Add:

fig. Insensitive to attack; callous.

1894 *Cassell's Fam. Mag.* Dec. 69/2 Hard armour-plated gambling. 1906 *Westm. Gaz.* 17 July 10/1 His armour-plated indifference. 1909 *Ibid.* 13 Aug. 3/1 His incisive humour, which got between the joints of his armour-plated victims.

Armpit, 1. *Up to the armpits*, in fig. use. *U.S.*

1869 *Congress. Globe* Apr. 549/1 The Company is steeped in fraud to the very armpits. 1878 *Congress. Rec.* Feb. 713/1 There certainly has been purgatory in the vicinity of his chamber, and I know that Colonel Polk has been in it up to his armpits.

Armure (ā·ɹmiuəɹ). [Fr.] A woollen or silk fabric, with a twilled or ribbed surface.

1880 WEBSTER Suppl. 1882 CAULFEILD & SAWARD *Dict. Needlework*, *Armure*, this is a silk textile; plain, striped, ribbed, or with a small design. Sometimes it is made of wool and silk. There is also Satin Armure and Armure Bosphore. 1894 *Daily News* 20 Jan. 5/7 Rich cream-coloured silk of the sort known as 'armure'.

Army. III. Add: **Army Service Corps** (abbrev. **A.S.C.**), that part of the army establishment which is concerned with commissariat and transport; previously called the Commissariat Staff Corps.

1871 *Hansard's Parl. Debates* CCVI. 961 The Army Service Corps is divided into three branches—supply, transport, and stores, with officers and men attached. 1916 BOYD CABLE *Action Front* 124 Army Service Corps supply points.

Arnaout (aɹnau·t). Also **Arnaut.** [See *ALBANIAN *a.*[2]] An Albanian, *spec.* one serving in the Turkish army. Also *attrib.*

1802 C. JAMES *Milit. Dict.*, *Arnauts*, Turkish light cavalry. 1833 *Penny Cycl.* I. 258/1 The population of Albania has always been of a warlike character...At present, under the denomination of Arnauts, they rank among the flower of the Ottoman army. 1863 PATON *Hist. Egypt. Revol.* II. xxiii. 256 Instances occurred of Arnaut soldiers getting richly dressed prostitutes, adorned with jewels, into their houses. 1910 *Encycl. Brit.* IX. 107/1 The Arnaut (or Albanian) soldiers in the service of Khosrev tumultuously demanded their pay. 1922 D. H. LOW *Ballads of Marko Kraljević* 129 A wild Arnaut woman bore me.

Aromal (ărōu·măl), *a.* [f. AROMA + -AL.] Of or pertaining to, concerned with or involving, aroma or aromas.

1848 *Tait's Mag.* XV. 704 Man, being in a proper state, *presto*, the aromal spherical bath will start forth and do its work. *Ibid.*, That the earth clogs the sun, in default of aromal discharges. *Ibid.*, Still, though dead, she has her use, that of 'mummy, or aromal loadstone'. 18.. WHITTIER *My Summer with Dr. Singletary* ii, Nature's healing ministrations came to me through all my senses. I felt the medicinal virtues of her sights, and sounds, and aromal breezes. 1867 T. L. HARRIS *Arcana of Christianity.* 1888 A. S. WILSON *Lyric of a Hopeless Love* I, Love is..an aromal fire That sweeps the spirit to dismiss All but its own desire.

Around, *adv.* Add: 5. a, b. (Earlier and additional U.S. examples.)

1828-32 WEBSTER, *Around*,..2. In a looser sense, at random; without any fixed direction; as, to travel around from town to town. 1834 *Deb. Congress* 6 Feb. 492 In looking around, the President had a right to select an officer who would honestly..discharge his duty. 1869 S. BOWLES *Our New West* viii. 170 We generally 'boarded around'. 1870 in Schele de Vere *Amer.* (1872) 435 She..is witty,..and must be pleasant to have around. 1873 J. H. BEADLE *Undevel. West* xxx. 651 It is told around for a fact that I could tell great confessions. 1887 F. FRANCIS Jr. *Saddle & Mocassin* 56 He said..he had promised his parents..'to sit around and reflect on Sunday mornings'. 1889 *Daily News* 14 Oct., Philip Schuyler was, all around, the greatest man ever born in the State of New York. 1916 J. BLACK *You Can't Win* iii. 16 When a new boy showed up, I was the one to show him around.

c. Going about; astir; out of bed. *U.S.*

1884 *Lisbon* (Dakota) *Star* 18 July, He is now able to be around, but has not yet fully recovered. 1887 F. FRANCIS Jr. *Saddle & Mocassin* 61 Mr. Maroney ain't long gone to bed...I guess he'll be around at midday. 1908 S. E. WHITE *Riverman* xvi. 142, I wasn't here until nine o'clock. I thought, of course, you'd be around.

B. *prep.* 4. b. Of time, amount, etc.: About, sometime near. *U.S.*

1888 *N. Y. Mercury* (Farmer) Presuming he was born around three o'clock in the afternoon, he is under Leo and the Sun. 1920 *Daily Tel.* 3 Apr. 10/6 (N.Y. Lett.), S. Motor Company shares, which usually sell around $100 each.

Arou·sement. [f. AROUSE *v.*] Arousing.

1904 *Springfield Weekly Republ.* 3 June 8 [A building] which the press bureau has lauded..to the arousement of the critical temper of the Haverhill Gazette.

Arpeggiated (aɹpe·dʒie̤ted), *ppl. a. Mus.* [f. ARPEGGIO + -ATE[2] + -ED.] Of a chord or series of chords: Played or sung in arpeggio.

1901 *Westm. Gaz.* 31 May 2/1 Arpeggiated accompaniments of a rather old-fashioned type. 1922 S. GREW *Art of Player-Piano* 96 The initial note preceded by an arpeggiated chord. 1924 P. A. SCHOLES *1st Bk. Gramophone Record* 21 A melody..smoother in motion, and hence well contrasted with the preceding, arpeggiated, theme.

Arpeggiation (āɹpedʒiē·ʃən). *Mus.* [f. ARPEGGIO + -ATION.] Playing or singing in arpeggio.

1889 in *Cent. Dict.*

Arrangeable (ărē·ndʒăb'l), *a.* [-ABLE.] That can be arranged. Hence **Arrangeabi·lity.**

a 1832 BENTHAM *Deontol.* (1834) I. I. vii. 88 Sanctions are arrangeable according to their nature, or according to their sources. 1858 CARLYLE *Fredk. Gt.* v. iii. (1873) II. 82 Let these be as in the Treaty of Utrecht; arrangeable in the lump. 1880 J. COOK *Boston Monday Lect.* 133 Disarrangedness in the soul implies its arrangeability.

Arra·nging, *ppl. a.* [f. ARRANGE *v.* + -ING[2].] Of a debtor: That makes an arrangement with his creditors.

1920 *Act* 10 & 11 *Geo. V*, c. 30 § 26 In the distribution of the property of a bankrupt or arranging debtor.

Arrayment. Delete ? *Obs.* and add to def.: Also, the act or fact of arraying or being arrayed.

1876 MORRIS *Æneids* II. 490 Other some..The nether doorways of the place in close arrayment hedge. *Ibid.* XII. 442 Then in arrayment close Antheus and Mnesthus rush to war. 1892 *Guardian* 11 May 706/2 Whose light arrayment is a mist of green. 1907 *Daily Chron.* 8 Nov. 4/6 The same arrayment of civic dignitaries in scarlet and fur.

Arrear, *sb.* 7. b. Add: *pl.* Used as a sing. *U.S.*

1902 *Rep. Librarian Congress* 30 They constitute a large arrears, which should be dealt with speedily.

Arrearage. 4. Add: In later use *U.S.*

1714 *Narragansett Hist. Reg.* III. 277 The committee chosen by the town to gather the arrearages of my sallary. 1781 *Baltimore Town Rec.* 42 All arrearages for Rent from the Butchers must be paid to the Clerk. 1817 in H. B. Fearon *Sk. Amer.* (1818) 231 When subscribers wish to discontinue, all arrearages must first be paid. 1827 J. F. COOPER *Prairie* v, So I left him, without calling in the paymaster to settle my arrearages.

Arrière-pensée (aryę̄r paṅse). [Fr., = behind-thought.] A concealed thought or intention.

1824 LADY MORGAN *Salvator Rosa* vi. 300 Such drear and fearful aspects of nature, mingled with such views of society, concealed an '*arrière pensée*'. 1884 *Engl. Illustr. Mag.* Dec. 246 He knew that I had guessed his *arrière-pensée*. 1900 H. B. FORMAN *Compl. Wks. Keats* I. 106 The meaning [of 'rest'] here is, probably merely inactivity, without the recuperative *arrière-pensée*.

Arriero (ari,ē·ro). [Sp.] A Spanish muleteer.

1826 HEAD *Rough Notes Pampas* 165 A mulish-looking sort of man who used to terrify all the arrieros and peons who passed. 1832 W. IRVING *Alhambra, The Journey* (1915) 9 Forwarding the most valuable part of our luggage a day or two in advance by the *arrieros*. 1923 *Blackw. Mag.* Sept. 339/2 We were probably reckoned as rather less than the *arriero* who owned two lean donkeys.

Arrival. 3. Add:

attrib. esp. in connexion with the place (platform) or time at which a railway train arrives at a station.

1838 F. W. SIMMS *Public Wks. Gt. Brit.* 2 On the opposite side an arrival stage or platform is erected. 1886 *Encycl. Brit.* XX. 235/2 The two general arrival platforms, one on each side of the cab road, are 721 feet long by 124 wide. 1897 *Westm. Gaz.* 31 Dec. 3/3 It is the arrival time, the departure being timed several minutes later. 1903 *Ibid.* 25 Mar. 6/3 A new wide roadway for carriages..will be used by arrival passengers.

Arrive, *v.* Add:

10. Of a person: To be successful, establish one's position or reputation. [After F. *arriver*.]

1892 *Daily News* 7 Apr. 5/2 M. Viaud may be said to have 'arrived' more quickly than any other French writer of the day. 1893 F. ADAMS *New Egypt* 197 He is a younger man, and has, in the large sense of the word, only arrived comparatively recently. 1893 *Daily Mail* 16 July 3 He has 'arrived' in the front rank of short-story writers.

Arrived, *ppl. a.* Also **arrivéd.** [ad. F. *arrivé.*] That has reached a position of success or distinction.

1896 *Godey's Mag.* Feb. 133/2 On the outskirts of the Monceau quarter, which is peopled with 'arrived' artists. 1899 *Westm. Gaz.* 3 July 3/1 Had Elizabeth come of that arrived race. 1907 *Daily Chron.* 4 Nov. 3/3 Mrs. Atherton is one of the arrived.

Arriviste (arivist). [Fr., f. *arriver* + *-iste* -IST.] One who is bent on 'arriving', *i.e.* on making a good position for himself in the world; a pushful person.

1912 *English Review* May 321 No amphibious *arriviste* here, half-gentleman, half-artist. 1924 *National Rev.* Dec. 479 The latter are still arrivistes who have so far failed to arrive. 1925 *Contemp. Rev.* Aug. 174 He [Canning] was an *arriviste*—an *arriviste* naked and unashamed.

Arrow, *sb.* II. Add:

Caustic arrow (Surg.): see quot. 1890.

1879 *St. George's Hosp. Rep.* IX. 384 A tumour around the anus was removed by the insertion of caustic arrows. 1890 BILLINGS *Nat. Med. Dict.*, *Caustic arrows*.., small, pointed cylinders or cones made of chloride-of-zinc paste or other caustics, intended for introduction into the substance of morbid growths.

III. **Broad arrow.** Add:

The figure of an arrow-head having the point upwards, with which the clothes of convicts are marked. Also *allusively*. Hence **Broad-arrowed** *a.*, marked with this.

1859 'OLINÉ KEESE' (*title*) The Broad Arrow, being passages from the history of Maida Gwynnham, a lifer. 1886 P. ROBINSON *Valley Teet. Trees* 50 The tiny double puncture which is the viper's broad-arrow of death. 1896 *Daily News* 29 July 7/4 Dr. Jameson..was..garbed in the prison shoes and broad-arrowed suit. 1901 *Daily Chron.* 17 June 5/6 His broad-arrow trousers. 1914 *N. & Q.* 11th Ser. IX. 482/2 The Prison Commissioners..wrote..that..the broad arrow..has been used in Convict Prisons and Hulks for more than 80 years, and was also used in Australia.

IV. 2. Add: **arrow-case** (modern U.S. examples); **arrow-point,** *fig.* a long slender point like that of an arrow; **arrow-weed,** a Mexican euphorbiaceous plant.

1846 SAGE *Scenes Rocky Mts.* (1859) 106 The Medicine Soldier..slung his 'arrow-case over his naked shoulders. 1867 *Amer. Naturalist* Aug. I. 287 After being turned right-side out, it makes an elegant arrow-case. 1887 *Harper's Mag.* Nov. 944/2 When I met him at the *arrow-point between Broadway and Fifth Avenue. 1876 *Field & Forest* II. 55 These Mexican jumping seeds, are derived from a plant called *arrow weed, or *Yerba de flecha*, and *Colliguaja* by the Mexicans.

Arrow, *v.* Add:

4. *intr.* To move swiftly through space, like an arrow in its flight; to dart. Also *to arrow one's way*.

1827 *Blackw. Mag.* XXII. 446 About an hour ago did we ..see that identical salmon..arrowing up the Tay. 1866 WHYTE MELVILLE *Cerise* xliv, Streams..where the otter lurked and vanished, where the noble salmon himself came arrowing up triumphant from the sea. 1905 HOLMAN HUNT *Pre-Raphaelitism* I. 71 Here the kingfisher arrowed his way. 1927 *Chambers's Jrnl.* 4/1 She [a filly] arrowed over her hurdles like the 'class' young lady that she was.

Arrow-leaf. *U.S.* = ARROW-HEAD 4.

1859 *Harper's Mag.* May 860/2 The yellow dock, white arrow-leaf, blue pickerel weed.

Arrow-wood. Add quots.:

1829-32 J. P. KENNEDY *Swallow B.* I. xv. 226 Morasses.. now over-grown with thickets of arrow-wood, nine-bark, and various other shrubs. 1873 J. H. BEADLE *Undevel. West* xv. 256 Dwarfish oak, and arrow-wood disappear.

Arroyo. (Earlier examples. The erron. form *arroya* also occurs.)

1847 E. BRYANT *What I saw in California* (1849) 269 An *arroyo*, or small rivulet fed by springs, runs through his rancho. *Ibid.* 277 The plain is watered by several *arroyos*.

Arsacetin (āɹsæ·se̤tin). [f. ARS(ENIC + ACET(YL + -IN.] (See quot. 1908.)

1908 *Practitioner* Nov. 760 Arsacetin, or sodium p-Acetylaminophenylarsinate-acetyl-arsanilate, is a white powder containing three or four molecules of water of crystallisation. 1920 *Discovery* Mar. 88/2 Specifics such as..soamin and arsacetin for sleeping sickness [are coal-tar products].

Arsenal. Add: 2. c. *transf.* A stock of weapons carried by a person.

a 1861 WINTHROP *John Brent* iv. (1862) 38 If he were but shaved and clipped..disarmed of his dangerous looking arsenal..seems to me I should know him.

Artefac. = next.

1906 CHAMBERLIN & SALISBURY *Geol.* III. 502 Following European precedent, the earlier students classed the rougher artefacs as paleolithic...The better fashioned artefacs were classed as neolithic. 1911 *Encycl. Brit.* XXI. 836/1 The difficulty of employing *artefacs* of stone as chronological indicators.

Artefact (ā·ɹtĭfækt), *sb.* and *a.* Also **arti-.** [f. L. *arte*, abl. of *ars* art + *factum*, neut. pa. pple. of *facere* to make. (Cf. Sp., Pg. *artefacto*, It. *artefatto*, adj. and sb.)] A. *sb.* Anything made by human art and workmanship; an artificial product. In *Archæol.* applied to the rude products of aboriginal art as distinguished from natural remains.

1821 COLERIDGE in *Blackw. Mag.* X. 256 The conception of all these, as realized in one and the same artéfact, may be fairly entitled, the Ideal of an ink-stand. a 1834 — *Lit. Rem.* (1838) III. 347 A lump of sugar of lead lies among other artefacts on the shelf of a collector. 1890 D. G. BRINTON *Races & Peoples* ii. 75 *note*, This is shown..by the presence of artefacts and shells from the Pacific in old graves on the Atlantic coast. 1922 *Class. Quarterly* XVI. 24 The shadows seem to be real till their originals are exposed as the paltry artefacts they are. 1925 *Times Lit. Suppl.* 13 Aug. 529/1 The distribution of artifacts. 1927 G. MURRAY *Class. Tradition* 243 Poetry..is an 'artifact'—I mean, it is a thing made.

B. *adj.* Made by human art and workmanship. *rare.*

1909 J. A. STEWART *Plato's Doctr. Ideas* 179 The rêverie-image of an object natural or artefact.

Artel (aɹte·l). [Russ. артель *artel'.*] An association or guild of workers in Russia. Also *attrib.* in *artel-man* [tr. Russ. *artel'shchik*].

1884 RAE *Contemp. Socialism* vii. 280 The *artel* of labourers' association and the commune. 1892 *Daily News* 22 Jan. 5/2 The only other kind of trade organization existing in the Empire is known as the 'Artel', and is peculiar to Russia. 1895 *Chambers's Jrnl.* 705/2 The authority of an artelman is unlimited. 1900 LOUISE MAUDE *Tolstoy's Resurrection* 226 We are all masons, and belong to the same *artel*. 1921 S. GRAHAM *Europe—Whither Bound?* vi. 89 An *artel* of Rostof engineers.

Arterial, *a.* 2. Add: Applied esp. to the construction of main roads or lines of transport or communication.

1865 *Chr. Misc. & Family Visitor* Ser. II. XI. 154/1 The termini of the different trunk or arterial railways. 1867 [in Dict.]. 1898 *Daily News* 17 Nov. 4/4 He urged that wide arterial improvements of the streets were needed. 1920 *Act* 10 & 11 *Geo. V*, c. 57 § 2 Land required for or in connection with the construction of any arterial road.

Arteriosclerosis (aɹtīə:rioskliərōu·sis). *Path.* [See ARTERIO- and SCLEROSIS.] Abnormal thickening and hardening of the walls of the arteries, occurring chiefly in old age.

1890 BILLINGS *Nat. Med. Dict.* 1901 *Practitioner* Mar. 315 The patient may be handicapped in his struggle with the fever by arterio-sclerosis.

Hence **Arte:rioscleroʹtic** *a.*

1894 GOULD *Dict. Med.* 1909 *Practitioner* Nov. 616 The arterio-sclerotic kidney.

Artesian, *a.* Add: By extension often applied to water obtainable by artesian boring.

1897 *Westm. Gaz.* 21 Apr. 8/2 A very large part of the interior of Western Australia is wholly unfitted for the purposes of human habitation. Its appearance may ultimately be changed by the discovery of artesian water.

Arthralgia (aɹþræ·ldʒiă). *Path.* [mod.L., f. Gr. ἄρθρον joint + ἄλγος pain.] Neuralgic pain in a joint. Hence **Arthra·lgic** *a.*

1848 DUNGLISON *Med. Lex.* (ed. 7), *Arthralgia*, arthrodynia, gout. 1878 *von Ziemssen's Cycl. Pract. Med.* XVII. 566 An attack of colic or arthralgia [in lead-poisoning]. 1890 BILLINGS *Nat. Med. Dict.*, *Arthralgic*.., pertaining to arthralgia.

Arthroplasty (ā·ɹþroplæsti). [f. ARTHRO- + -PLASTY.] The construction of an artificial joint. Hence **Arthropla·stic** *a.*

1890 BILLINGS *Nat. Med. Dict.*, *Arthroplasty*. 1913 DORLAND *Med. Dict.* (ed. 7), *Arthroplastic*. 1918 *Reveille* Aug. 67 There were very few stiff joints in which arthroplastic operations were urgently needed.

Arthurian (aɹþiū·riăn), *a.* [See -IAN.] Of or pertaining to the legendary British king Arthur, his court, and his knights. Also, resembling these or the romances in which they figure.

1853 BURTON *Hist. Scot.* I. 174 If any reality could be extracted from the Arthurian histories. 1869 STUART-GLENNIE *Arthurian Localities* 5 The Arthurian Cycle. 1875 A. W. WARD *Engl. Dram. Lit.* I. 121 The Arthurian legend. *Ibid.*, The Arthurian cycle of legend. 1899 A. NUTT *Celtic & Mediæval Romance* 14 The later works of the Charlemagne cycle are in detail, tone and spirit often as 'Arthurian' as any purely Breton romance. Huon and Ogier are Arthurian heroes who have strayed by accident to the Court of Charlemagne.

Articulable (ăɹti·kiulăb'l), *a.* [f. ARTICULATE *v.* + -ABLE.] That can be articulated.

1833 *Fraser's Mag.* VII. 706 Word-worshipping even the articulable clothing wherein the clear and ethereal harmony of Goethe is invested. 1916 F. VON HÜGEL *German Soul* 92 How impossible in practice is the maintenance of international obligations of any articulable kind.

Articular, *a.* 2. *Gram.* Add to def.: Having an article prefixed.

1906 MOULTON *Gram. N. T. Greek* I. 70 There is a very marked increase in the use of the articular nominative in address. 1926 PLATER & WHITE *Gram. Vulgate* 40 The Gerund with *in* is frequently used to render the Greek Articular Infinitive with preposition.

Articulated, *ppl. a.* 1. Add: Also *fig.*

1886 A. WEIR *Hist. Basis Mod. Europe* (1889) 122 The pettifogging lawyers who swarmed around the minutely articulated social structure.

Artifact: see *ARTEFACT.

Artificial. B. Add: Artificial manures.

1927 W. DEEPING *Doomsday* xix. § 2 Plenty of stock.. saved you from having to spend too much on artificials.

b. An artificial flower. *U.S.*

1846-52 MRS. WHITCHER *Widow Bedott Papers* xxi. 224 Her parasol and the artificials in her bunnit is jest as natral as life. *Ibid.* xxvi. 316 She had on a yaller bonnit with a great pink artificial in it. 1857 B. YOUNG *Jrnl. Discourses* V. 98 O dear, are there no ribbons coming? I want that artificial quick. 1872 E. EGGLESTON *End of World* xxxix. 246, I don't believe in all of Brother Goshorn's nonsense about wearing veils and artificials.

Artillery. 8. Add:

artillery wheel, a heavily-built dished wheel used on gun-carriages, and hence on motor-vehicles.

1900 RHYS JENKINS *Motor Cars* 210 The wheels [of the Daimler cars] are of wood, artillery pattern, fitted with pneumatic tyres. 1902 *Car* 15 Oct. 252/2 The Lanchester car was not strong enough to have artillery wheels, and so was fitted with wire suspension wheels. 1904 FILSON YOUNG *Complete Motorist* 203 The wheels [of the Baby Peugeot car] are of the artillery type.

A·rtisanship. [See -SHIP.] The work and activity of an artisan or of artisans collectively.

1827 CARLYLE *Germ. Rom.* IV. *Goethe* 24 Intellectual artisanship..is less desirable than intellectual manhood. 1831 CHALMERS in *Fraser's Mag.* III. 60 The toils of busy artisanship. 1832 CARLYLE *Ess.*, *Boswell's Johnson* (1840) IV. 102 Work out thy Artisanship in the spirit of an Artist! 1844 *N. Brit. Rev.* I. 139 Its artisanship and commerce [*sc.* of the Byzantine empire]. 1907 W. DE MORGAN *Alice-for-Short* xiv, The sudden substitution of inspiration for mere artisanship.

Arty (ā·ɹti), *a. colloq.* [f. ART *sb.* + -Y[1].] A jocular epithet for furniture, decoration, etc. of artistic pretensions; also applied to persons who wish to be regarded as artistic in taste, dress, etc.

1901 *Academy* 16 Mar. 221 The *Kensington* is its title; it is broad in the page, handsomely printed, and decidedly *Art-y*. 1910 *Daily Chron.* 5 Apr. 9/5 The house filled with badly made 'arty', not artistic, furniture. 1925 *Sat. Rev.* 7 Nov. 534/1, I do not like the long, rather 'arty' window on the front. 1927 *Daily Express* 30 Apr. 8/2 Artists and 'arty' persons—between the two there is a great gulf fixed.

Hence **A·rtiness.**

1901 *Academy* 12 Oct. 337 The infected age of artiness. 1907 *Daily Chron.* 17 Apr. 6/6 To go somewhat beyond the 'artiness' of the day. 1928 *Observer* 22 July 9/2 The same unambitious artiness recurs page after page.

Arty-and-crafty (ā·ɹti,ænd,krā·fti), *a. colloq.* [f. *arts and crafts* + -Y[1].] Characteristic of the work done by or under the auspices of the Arts and Crafts Exhibition Society founded in 1888; jocularly applied to works, esp. furniture, of specially artistic style but not conspicuously useful or comfortable; also, of their makers. (Cf. prec.)

1902 *Daily Chron.* 28 July 3/4 Canon Barnett..spoke of a coming Exhibition of Arts and Crafts, which, if not too 'Arty-and-Crafty', should be excellent. [1902 *Temple Bar* CXXVI. 63 The furniture is of the Artsy-Craftsy order. 1909 *Westm. Gaz.* 24 Dec. 2/2 An art and crafty tea-table.] 1925 *Sat. Rev.* 7 Nov. 524/1 The 'arty and crafty' furniture that is uncomfortable in use,..the model house in which no man can be at ease. 1927 *Observer* 18 Sept. 15/4 Country lore gathered chiefly from the works of arty-and-crafty peasants from Belsize Park.

Ary-, shortened form of ARYTENO-.

1879 *St. George's Hosp. Rep.* IX. 162 The right ary-epiglottidean fold. 1897 *Trans. Amer. Pediatric Soc.* IX. 180 A union of the aryepiglottic folds.

Aryanization (ē³riănaizē·ʃən). [f. ARYANIZE + -ATION.] The act of Aryanizing or fact of being Aryanized.

1889 I. TAYLOR *Aryans* iv. § 2. 212 The Aryanisation of Europe doubtless resembled that of India. 1904 *Athenæum* 24 Dec. 871/3 This Aryanization of inferior races.

Ascensional, *a.* Add:

2. b. *Ascensional screw*: a helical propeller to give a lifting motion to an airship or flying-machine.

1901 *Westm. Gaz.* 15 Aug. 6/1 With my ascensional screws ..I am indifferent to wind, because I can rise and descend in search of a suitable belt of air. 1903 *Daily Chron.* 27 Sept. 7/4 A new flying machine...It is the invention of Mr. H. A. Chubb, and it rises by means of ascensional screws or helices.

Ascensiontide (ăse·nʃəntəid). [f. ASCENSION 2 + TIDE *sb.* 6.] The period of ten days from Ascension Day to Whitsun Eve. Also *attrib.*

1871 (*title*) Ascensiontide. Thoughts on the Ascension Day Collect. 1898 *Westm. Gaz.* 19 May 10/3 The Ascensiontide feast. 1900 D. C. TOVEY *Lett. T. Gray* I. 90 *note*, These three spent the festival of Ascensiontide 1741, in Venice together.

Ascesis (ăsī·sis). Also **askesis** (æskī·sis). [ad. Gr. ἄσκησις exercise, training, f. ἀσκεῖν to exercise.] The practice of self-discipline.

1880 PATER *Greek Studies* (1904) 254 The sanity of soul and body..the perfecting of both by reasonable exercise or *ascêsis*. 1890 E. JOHNSON *Rise Christendom* 107 In the conduct of life they establish a strict ascesis..as a means of a closer communion with the Divine. 1922 *Q. Rev.* July 95 Complete possession of the self by this means is..the most perfect *ascesis* for all human beings. 1924 J. KELMAN *Prophets of Yesterday* i. 24 The Greek idea of *askesis* was but the habit of the athlete.

Ascetism (ăse·tiz'm). [f. Gr. ἀσκητής (see ASCETIC) + -ISM.] = ASCETICISM.

1870 *Contemp. Rev.* XIII. 391 The melodramatic ascetism upon which such great store was then set. 1889 *Macm. Mag.* Jan. 236/1 There is certainly not a tinge in Shakespeare of sympathy with Catholic ascetism.

Asciferous (ăsi·fĕrəs), *a.* [f. mod.L. ASCUS: see -FEROUS.] = ASCIGEROUS.

1882 *Encycl. Brit.* XIV. 557 There is a parallelism between the fructification of lichens and the asciferous section of fungi.

Asco- (æsko). Add:

Ascogenous (æskǫ·dʒĭnəs), *a.* [Gr. -γενής producing + -OUS], that produces asci; **Ascomycete** (æ:skomaisīt) [Gr. μυκητ-, μύκης mushroom], a fungus belonging to the *Ascomycetes*; **Ascophore** (æ·skofōəɹ), an ascophorous hypha or filament.

1882 VINES *Sachs's Bot.* 239 The ascogenous filaments and the asci which proceed from them. *Ibid.* 250 Reess considers..the yeast-fungus..to be an Ascomycete. 1877 BENNETT tr. *Thomé's Text-bk. Bot.* 282 The filaments which bear the asci (*ascophores*).

Ascription. Add:

4. b. *spec.* The formula used by a preacher at the end of a sermon in which he ascribes praise to God ('Now to God the Father..be ascribed all praise..').

1899 DEARMER *Parson's Handbk.* 201 It has become customary to conclude the sermon with an ascription.

-ase, *Chem.*, a suffix taken from the ending of DIASTASE, and used in naming ferments, as *casease*, *lactase*, *maltase*, *pectase*, *urase*, etc.

Asepsis (ăse·psis). [f. A- 14 + SEPSIS.] Absence of septic matter; freedom from sepsis or poisoning by the products of putrefaction.

1900 *Daily News* 7 May 3/2 The conditions as regards asepsis were by no means ideal. 1920 W. J. GRENFELL *Labrador Doctor* iv. 70 Removing a leg at the thigh..without any attempt at or idea of asepsis.

Aseptically (ăse·ptikăli), *adv.* [f. ASEPTIC: see -ICALLY.] So as to be free from sepsis.

1906 *Practitioner* Dec. 802 The ligature..if aseptically inserted..has done no other harm than the prick of the needle.

Asepticize (ăse·ptisaiz), *v.* [f. ASEPTIC + -IZE.] *trans.* To render aseptic, sterilize.

1907 *Practitioner* June 803 Bottles and forceps were asepticised by being dipped in carbolic lotion.

Ash, *sb.*[1] 5. Add: **ash(-leaf, -leaved) maple** *U.S.*, the box elder; **ash-swale, -swamp** *U.S.*, a swale or swamp in which the ash is the prevailing tree.

1865-6 *Trans. Ill. Agric. Soc.* VI. 390 The Box Elder of our river bottoms comes back to us under the name of.. *Ash Leaf maple. 1832 D. J. BROWNE *Sylva Amer.* 103 The *ash-leaved maple attains the height of 40 or 50 feet. 1846 — *Trees Amer.* 106 Ash-leaved Maple..[in] other parts of Anglo-America. 1834 *Southern Lit. Messenger* I. 98 On emerging from the wilderness, the customary variety of oak, *ash maple, and hickory presents itself. 1861 *Trans. Ill. Agric. Soc.* IV. 449 The Box Elder or Ash Maple is decidedly and distinctly a maple, as its name—*Acer negundo*—indicates. 1839 in *Trans. Mich. Agric. Soc.* (1856) VII. 368 It follows mainly the course of two brooks,..and embraces the intervening *ash swales. 1668 *Boston Town Rec.* VII. 42 The first tree..is..A chestnut by the *ash swampe. 1708-9 *Lancaster Rec.* 305 He hath one piece laid out..in an ash swamp. 1789 MORSE *Amer. Geog.* 143 The descriptive names of maple, ash, and cedar swamps.

Ash, *sb.*[2] Add:

1. d. The residue of wine when evaporated to dryness.

1875 *Encycl. Brit.* I. 173/2 The ash, or involatile constituents of wine, should range between 0·19 and 0·5 per cent.

e. *Ash(es) of roses*: a greyish-pink colour.

1893 *Daily News* 17 May 3/4 The soft greyish pink known as 'ashes of roses'. 1903 KIPLING *Five Nations* 113 Opal and ash-of-roses, Cinnamon, umber, and dun. 1927 *Daily Express* 14 Mar. 5 Pomegranate, mulberry red, mushroom, and ashes of roses, a colour that looks like blue ash with a touch of flame, are among the fashion reds.

4. b. *The ashes*: in *Cricket*, a term originating in a mock obituary notice published in the *Sporting Times* 2 Sept. 1882, after the sensational victory of Australia at the Oval on Aug. 29 of that year, announcing the cremation of the dead body of English Cricket and the taking of the ashes to Australia; hence, the losing or winning of the rubber in the series of test matches played periodically between the chosen representatives of English and Australian cricket is frequently described as the loss, or the recovery (if previously lost) or retaining (if previously held) of the ashes.

[1882 *Sporting Times* 2 Sept., In Affectionate Remembrance of English Cricket Which died at the Oval on 29th August, 1882. Deeply lamented by a large circle of sorrowing friends and acquaintances. R.I.P. N.B.—The body will be cremated and the ashes taken to Australia.] 1903 WARNER in *Westm. Gaz.* 8 Dec. 2/1 If we fail to bring home 'the ashes' it will certainly not be for want of trying. 1921 *Glasgow Herald* 21 Jan. 8 We must accept the transference of the 'Ashes' philosophically.

6. b. Ash-colour.

1876 *Field & Forest* II. 41 Admitting that *tephrocotis* 'has the least ash on the head', how can this fact be attributed to climatological influences?

8. b. **ash-barrel,** a barrel for holding ashes; **ash-boat** (see quot.); **ash-box,** a receptacle for ashes, (*a*) a pan beneath a fire-grate, (*b*) a dust-bin; **ash-hoist,** a hoist for removing ashes from the ash-pit of an engine house, the stokehold of a vessel, etc.; **ash-hopper** *U.S.*, a lye cask, resembling a hopper in a mill; **ash-house,** an outhouse for receiving ashes; **ash-man,** a collector and remover of ashes; **ash-pan,** also, earlier term for *ash-tray*; **ash-pone** *U.S.*, an ash-cake; **ash-riddling,** the northern custom of riddling ashes on the hearth on St. Mark's Eve as a method of divination; **ash-shoot,** a shaft through which the ashes are shot, or are raised from the stokehold to the deck of a ship; **ash-tray,** a small tray, pan-shaped or bowl-shaped, to receive the ashes of tobacco when smoked.

1871 EGGLESTON *Hoosier Schoolm.* 84 There..was Granny Sanders's log cabin..with..its *ash-barrel by the fence. 1872 HOWELLS *Wedding Journ.* (1892) 30 A long row of ash-barrels posted sentinel-like on the edge of the pavement. 1909 *Daily Chron.* 18 Aug. 7/4 Ships in harbour are not allowed to throw their ashes overboard, but must signal for the '*ash-boat'. 1833 LOUDON *Encycl. Archit.* § 605 The bottoms of these chambers should have an *ash-box fitted into them. 1920 *Blackw. Mag.* Sept. 303/2 The noise of the *ash-hoist greeted his ear. 1843 CARLTON *New Purchase* 51 Most time, man, you'll have to work your own *ash-hopper. 1885 'C. E. CRADDOCK' *Prophet Gt. Smoky Mts.* i. 13 Some fifteen or twenty hounds that suddenly materialized from the ash-hopper. 1807-8 W. IRVING *Salmag.* iv. 73 He once shook down the *ash-house, by an artificial earthquake. 1873 ALDRICH *Marj. Daw* etc. 142 He has fought the *ash-man's boy, the grocer's boy [etc.]. 1857 E. FITZGERALD *Lett.* (1901) I. 341 The last Cheroot he had tried lay three quarters smoked in its little China *Ash-pan. 1826 'A. SINGLETON' *Lett. fr. South & West* (1824) 78 What slaves I have seen have fared coarsely upon their hoe-cakes and *ash-pone. 1838 S. G. GOODRICH *Syst. Univ. Geog.* 260 Hoe-cake..and ash-pone, a coarse cake baked under the ashes, are in common use, as bread. 1825 BROCKETT *N. C. Words* s.v. *Ass*, *Ass-riddlin, the riddling or sifting of the ashes on the hearth, on the eve of St. Mark. The superstitious notion is, that, should any of the family die within the year, the shoe will be impressed on the ashes. 1893 KATH. SIMPSON *Yorksh. Stories* 240 Ash-riddling is an old custom which I like to keep up. 1889 *Century Dict.*, *Ash-shoot. 1898 KIPLING *Fleet in Being* 5, I heard Swinburne laying down the law to his juniors by the ash-shoot. 1920 *Blackw. Mag.* Sept. 303/2 He..watched the fireman unhook his first bucket of ashes from the hoist and carry them to the ash-shoot. 1890 KIPLING *Plain Tales fr. Hills*, *Germ-Destroyer* 116 He had tipped a bagful of his powder into the big silver *ash-tray. 1926 MAY SUTHERLAND *One o' the Herd* v, A lacquered Chinese table with .. a box of cigarettes and an ashtray upon it.

Ash-cake. *U.S.* [ASH *sb.*[2] 8 b.] A cake baked in or under the ashes of a fire.

1824 P. HORRY *Life Marion* (1833) 50 A rasher of fat bacon from the coals, with a good stout lump of an ash cake, is nice enough for me. 1834 *Congress. Globe* App. 631/3 At this dinner, a large ash-cake was baked containing about three bushels of corn meal. 1861 *Knickerbocker Mag.* June LVII. 624 Not even a guard being left to keep the ash-cakes from stray dogs. 1886 *Harper's Mag.* Oct. 697/2 She took the ash-cake out of the ashes. 1887 'C. E. CRADDOCK' *Keedon Bluffs* 25 Her father..deftly constructed an ash-cake.

Asherah (ăʃī·ră). Pl. **Asherahs, Asherim** (-rim). [Heb. אשרה *Ăshērāh*.] A wooden post, pillar, or trunk of a tree used as the symbol of the goddess Ashera, occurring near the altar in Canaanitish high places devoted to the worship of Baal. Also the goddess herself, associated with Baal in Syrian, Phœnician, and Hebrew heathen worship. (Cf. GROVE 3 a.)

1884 *Bible* (R.V.) Exod. xxxiv. 13 Ye shall cut down their Asherim. *Note.* Probably the wooden symbols of a goddess Asherah. — Deut. xvi. 21 Thou shalt not plant thee an Asherah of any kind of tree beside the altar of the Lord thy God. 1886 CONDER *Syrian Stone-Lore* v. 189 The 'hangings for the grove', or robe for the Asherah—the sacred tree erected even in the Jerusalem Temple in Josiah's time. 1912 H. F. HAMILTON *People of God* I. II. iv. 55 Poles, which served as substitutes for trees, called *asherim*. 1925 W. EWING *J. E. H. Thomson* xviii. 259 The altars, the pillars, and *Asherahs* were not destroyed.

Ashery. (Later U.S. example.)

1884 L. F. ALLEN *New Amer. Farm Bk.* 62 Spent lye of the asheries, is the liquid which remains after the combination of the lye and grease in manufacturing soap.

Ashkenazim (æʃkĕnā·zim), *sb. pl.* [mod. Heb., f. *Ashkenas*, the name of a son of Gomer (Gen. x. 3, 1 Chron. i. 6), son of Japheth, son of Noah, typifying a race of people identified with the Ascanians of Phrygia, and, in medieval times, with the Germans.] Jews of middle and northern Europe as distinguished from Sephardim or Jews of Spain and Portugal. Hence **Ashkena·zic** *a.*, of or belonging to the Ashkenazim.

1842 BONAR & M'CHEYNE *Narr. Mission Jews in 1839* iv. 330 There are no rabbies properly speaking among the Ashkenazim. 1892 ZANGWILL *Childr. Ghetto* I. 4 All the Ashkenazic tribes lived very much like a happy family. *Ibid.* 38 Spanish Jews look down on the later imported Ashkenazim, embracing both Poles and Dutchmen in their impartial contempt. 1914 *East & West* XII. 154 The true Zionists are mostly Ashkenazim Jews from all Europe.

Ashkoko (æʃkǭu·ko). [Abyssinian.] The Syrian hyrax or daman (*Hyrax Syriacus*).

1790 BRUCE *Trav. Nile* V. 139 Ashkoko. This curious animal is found in Ethiopia, in the caverns of the rocks. *Ibid.* 143 In Amhara this animal is called Ashkoko, which I apprehend is derived from the singularity of those herinacious hairs, which, like small thorns, grow about his back, and which in Amhara are called Ashok. 1884 *Cassell's Nat. Hist.* II. 292.

Ashlar (æ·ʃlăɹ), *v.* [f. ASHLAR *sb.*] *trans.* To cover with ashlar; cf. ASHLAR *sb.* 3.

1836 *Mirror* XXVIII. 147/1 It has been generally done by 'ashlering' them..with thin blocks or slabs of the same stone. 1895 HARDY *Jude the Obscure* v. vii, Sometimes setting the parapet of a town-hall, sometimes ashlaring an hotel at Sandbourne.

Ash-plant. [ASH *sb.*[1]] A sapling of the ash tree, used as a walking-stick, whip, goad, etc.

1850 'H. HIEOVER' *Pract. Horsemanship* 180 Sit tight, and lay your ash plant well into his ears. 1858 MUNDY *Our Antipodes* (1857) 189 He..trudges away..supported by his son on one hand and an ash-plant in the other. 1919 P. MACGILL *Glenmornan* vi. 140 He hit a bullock near him with his ash-plant.

Ashthroat. [ASH *sb.*[2] 8 a.] More fully **ash-throated flycatcher,** *Myiarchus cinerascens* of the western U.S.

1859 S. F. BAIRD *Catal. N. Amer. Birds* 132 Ash-throated Flycatcher. 1872 E. COUES *Key N. Amer. Birds* 171 Ash-throated Flycatcher. 1903 *Atlantic Monthly* July 31 Up in the oaks the ashthroat chuckles.

Asianic (ēiʃiæ·nik), *a.* [f. ASIAN *a.* + -IC.]

1. Of or pertaining to Asia Minor.

1883 I. TAYLOR *Alphabet* II. 116 A syllabic writing,.. which prevailed throughout the whole of Asia Minor, and which has been designated by Professor Sayce as the Asianic syllabary. 1927 SIR W. RAMSAY (*title*) Asianic Elements in Greek Civilization. 1928 C. DAWSON *Age of Gods* xiii. 289 The bulk of the population belonged to the native Asianic stock.

2. Pertaining to or characterized by the florid and inflated literary style of the Asiatic Greeks in the three centuries preceding the Christian era.

1920 *Q. Rev.* July 42 His elaborate Asianic style.

Asianize (ēi·ʃiănaiz), *v.* [f. ASIAN *a.* + -IZE.] *trans.* To make Asian in character, habits, customs, etc. Hence **A·sianized** *ppl. a.* So also **A:sianiza·tion,** the process of becoming Asian.

1893 F. ADAMS *New Egypt* 50 Europe has indeed annexed this outpost of Asianised Africa [Cairo]. 1921 *19th Century* May 884 A humanity asianised in sentiment. *Ibid.* 888 The Arab and Hindu..who have undergone asianisation in the continent of their adoption.

Asiatic, *a.* Add: *Asiatic cholera* (see CHOLERA 3).

1831 (*title*) Asiatic, or spasmodic cholera. 1832 *Deb. Congress* 30 June 3833 A deliverance from the impending judgement of the Asiatic cholera.

Aside, *adv.* 10. Add: *Aside from*: a. Apart from, even excluding. (Earlier example.)

1852 *Trans. Mich. Agric. Soc.* III. 184 Humanity, aside from interest, would direct such a system of treatment.

b. Besides, in addition to. *U.S.*

1869 *Amer. Naturalist* Mar. III. 4 Aside from the use of *Dentalium pretiosum* as money, I saw [etc.]. 1903 *Atlantic Monthly* July 6 Others aside from Mr. Edwin Markham might confess their great indebtedness. 1905 *Forum* Apr. 598 The city, aside from being a great industrial..centre, enjoys..a high moral record.

c. Except for. *U.S.*

1902 H. E. BOURNE *Teaching Hist. & Civics* 303 Aside from the wars in Europe..the history of the colonies..is uneventful. 1905 *Springfield Weekly Republ.* 25 June 14 Aside from a severe fright, Mr. Houghton was uninjured.

Asigmatic (ēisigmæ·tik), *a.* [f. A- 14 + SIGMATIC *a.*] Not sigmatic, formed without sigma.

1893 F. W. WALKER in *Classical Rev.* July 292/1 The one so called asigmatic tense that is not digammated is generally admitted to have dropped a sigma.

Asilid (æ·silid), *a. Ent.* [ad. mod.L. *Asilidæ*, f. *asilus*: see next and -ID[3].] Belonging to the family *Asilidæ* of dipterous insects, comprising the hornet-flies.

1904 *Athenæum* 24 Dec. 881/1 [Prof. E. B. Poulton] exhibited a photograph..showing the Xylocopid model and its Asilid mimic.

Asilus (ăsai·lǝs). *Ent.* [L. *asilus* gadfly.] A genus of flies belonging to the order *Diptera*, family *Asilidæ*; a fly of this genus, a hornet-fly, hawk-fly, or robber-fly.

1752 J. Hill *Hist. Anim.* 32 The great, smooth, black, and red Indian Asilus. 1866 Blackmore *Cradock Nowell* xxv, They discuss the asilus and the oestrum.

Ask, *sb.* Delete † *Obs.*, and add quots.:

1781 T. Twining in *Recreat. & Stud.* (1882) 108, I am not so unreasonable as to desire you to..answer all my asks. 1886 'Cavendish' *Whist* 127 When your three comes down in the next round, it is not an ask for trumps.

Ask, *v.* Add:

2. b. *To ask* (a horse) *the question*: to call upon him for a special effort.

1894 H. Custance *Riding Recoll.* vi. 88 Until the last ten strides, when I really asked 'King Lud' the question.

16. b. Phr. *To ask for it*: slang or colloq. substitute for *to ask for trouble* = to act in such a way as to bring trouble upon oneself, to give provocation.

1909 *Westm. Gaz.* 16 Sept. 12/2 There are vain-glorious players in this world who, to use a vulgarism, 'ask for it', and deserve it when they get it. 1916 Boyd Cable *Action Front* 165 Silly fools...What do they want to hoist that huge Red Cross flag up there for, where any airman can see it? Fairly asking for it, I call it. 1925 E. F. Norton *Fight for Everest 1924* 343 It is asking for trouble to give out any money except the daily ration allowance.

21. b. *To ask out*: to invite to parties or entertainments. *colloq.*

1888 McCarthy & Praed *Ladies' Gallery* I. xii. 289, I was asked out in a kind of way. 1890 Kipling *Plain Tales fr. Hills, Pride of Youth* 199 Now and again he was asked out to dinner.

Askar (æ·skāɹ). [Arabic عسكر *ᶜaskar* army.] A native Moroccan infantryman.

[1902 *Encycl. Brit.* XXX. 840/1 The infantry (Askária) are mostly rough, ill-trained levies.] 1918 Farrow *Dict. Mil. Terms*, *Askar*, in the Moroccan army, a native infantryman or foot soldier. 1925 *Blackw. Mag.* Nov. 619/1 An askar of the Riffi army. *Ibid.* 619/2 At our approach, bearded askar come to the salute.

Askari (æ·skārī), *sb. pl.* Also **-is**. [Arabic عسكري *ᶜaskarī* soldier.] Native soldiers of West Africa. Also as *sing.*

1906 *Macm. Mag.* Oct. 929 Before him stood a..native, who acted as interpreter and clerk of the court, and a dozen *askari* whose onerous duty it was to preserve order. 1910 Roosevelt *African Game Trails* i. 18 The askaris were uniformed, each in a red fez, a blue blouse, and white knickerbockers. 1927 *Chambers's Jrnl.* 694/2 An askari or native constable took it in turns with two others to guard the market.

Asked (askt), *ppl. a.* [pa. pple. of Ask *v.*] Mentioned as a request. Also *asked-for*.

1900 *Westm. Gaz.* 5 Feb. 2/2 The asked-for area. 1901 *Ibid.* 9 July 4/3 The asked price.

Askeletal (ēske·lĭtăl), *a.* [f. A- 14 + Skeletal *a.*] Having no skeleton.

1904 J. McCabe tr. *Haeckel's Wonders of Life* x. 288 The askeletal vermalia.

Askesis, var. *Ascesis.

A-smoke (ásmōᵘ·k), *adv. phr.* [f. A *prep.*[1] + Smoke.] Smoking.

1827 *Blackw. Mag.* XXII. 554 Cottages all a-smoke. 1876 Morris *Æneids* viii. 106 With yet warm blood the altars were a-smoke. 1904 B'ness von Hutten *Pam* 190 Its chimneys were all asmoke.

Asmonean, var. *Hasmonean.

Asocial (ēsōᵘ·ʃăl), *a.* [f. A- 14 + Social *a.*] Antagonistic to social order.

1883 Maudsley *Body & Will* III. i. 241 New products of an asocial or antisocial kind are formed in the retrograde metamorphosis of the human kind. 1920 W. H. R. Rivers *Instinct & the Unconscious* xix. 156 Some channel which leads in an asocial or antisocial direction.

Asparaginic (āspærădʒi·nik), *a.* *Chem.* Also **asparginic**. [f. Asparagine + -ic.] *Asparaginic acid* = Aspartic acid.

1885 Stirling tr. *Landois' Human Physiol.* I. 341 Asparaginic acid ($C_4H_7NO_4$).

Asparagus. 2. Add: **asparagus-bean** *U.S.*, a tropical American bean (*Dolichos sesquipedalis*).

1856 Cozzens *Sparrowgr. Papers* vii. 85 The asparagus bean, a sort of long-winded esculent, inclined to be prolific in strings.

Aspect, *sb.* **II.** Add:

Gram. In the Slavonic languages a verbal form of which the function is to express action or being in respect of its inception, duration, or completion; by extension applied to such forms in other languages.

The earlier term in Slavonic grammars was 'branch'.

1853 C. P. Reiff *Eng.-Russ. Gram.* I 86 The aspects have not all the same number of tenses; the imperfect aspect is used in all the three tenses; the perfect is employed in the preterit and future, while the iterative is met with only in the preterit. 1884 J. Nestor-Schnurmann *Russ. Man.* 97 The variations in form of the same action are expressed by what is called in Russian branches or aspects (ВИДЫ) of a verb...There are four branches, viz.: the Indefinite, the Perfect, the Semelfactive.., and the Iterative...A Fifth Aspect might be added, viz.: the Inchoative. 1889 Morfill *Gram. Russ. Lang.* 35 Verbs of this class [*sc.* perfective and imperfective] are said to be arranged according to their aspects. 1924 Jespersen *Philos. Gram.* xx. 286 It is generally assumed that our Aryan languages had at first no real forms in their verbs for tense-distinctions, but denoted various aspects, perfective, imperfective, punctual, durative, inceptive, or others.

5. b. (*a*) *Geom.* The position of a plane as determined by the direction of its normal. (*b*) *Mech.* A view of a plane from any given direction, esp. from above; the position in which a plane meets a current or a fluid through which it is passing.

Aspect ratio, the ratio of the long side to the short side of an aeroplane, or its wing.

Asperging (āspə̄·ɹdʒiŋ), *vbl. sb.* [f. Asperge *v.* + -ing[1].] The action of sprinkling (with holy water). Also *attrib.*

1865 Tylor *Early Hist. Mankind* ix. 258 The priest stands with an asperging-brush in his hand, with which he sprinkles them with holy water.

Aspersory (āspə̄·ɹsŏri), *sb.* [ad. med.L. Aspersorium.] A holy-water sprinkler; an aspersorium or aspergillum.

1881 F. E. Warren *Liturgy Celtic Ch.* 116 It rather resembles an aspersory than a pastoral staff. 1897 *Pall Mall Mag.* Mar. 367 A holy-water stoup with an aspersory stood at the feet [of a corpse].

Asphyxiant (æsfi·ksiănt), *a.* and *sb.* [f. Asphyxia + -ant.] **A.** *adj.* Causing asphyxia. **B.** *sb.* Any chemical substance that causes asphyxia.

1855 *Englishwoman in Russia* 302 Long-range guns and asphyxiant balls. 1888 *Chambers's Encycl.* I. 501 The term asphyxiants is applied to any gases having a suffocating.. effect on the human system. 1921 *19th Cent.* July 34 If in the Great War we had refused to use asphyxiant gas.

Aspidistra (æspidi·stră). [mod.L., f. Gr. ἀσπιδ-, ἀσπίς shield + *-istra*, after *tupistra*.] A genus of convallariaceous plants of China and Japan; a plant of this genus, esp. of the species *A. lurida*, or *A. lurida variegata*, a variety with striped yellow leaves, very commonly used as dwelling-room plants.

1822 *Bot. Register* 628 *Aspidistra lurida.* Dingy-flowered Aspidistra. 1852 G. W. Johnson *Cott. Gard. Dict.* s.v., The mushroom-shaped stigma by which Aspidistræ are characterised. 1920 'O. Douglas' *Penny Plain* iii, An aspidistra in a pot completed the table decorations. 1926 W. Deeping *Sorrell & Son* iv. i, Carrying out the aspidistras and washing them in the yard.

¶ Illiterate forms are frequent.

1895 *Daily News* 4 Dec. 6/7 The broad leaves of the aspidestria. 1899 *Westm. Gaz.*, They are just moderate-sized palms, ferns, and aspidestra.

Aspidosperma (æspidospə̄·ɹmă). [mod.L.] A genus of S. American trees, of which the species *A. Quebracho*, the white quebracho, is notable for its medicinal bark. Hence **A:spidosa·mine**, a basic principle obtained from quebracho-bark, used as an emetic. **A:spidospe·rmatine, A:spidospe·rmine**, alkaloids obtained from quebracho-bark.

1891 Martindale *Extra Pharmacop.* (ed. 6) 325 Quebracho contains six Alkaloids..Aspidospermine, Quebrachine, Quebrachamine, Aspidospermatine, Hypoquebrachine, and Aspidosamine.

Aspinall (æ·spinǫl), *v. trans.* To paint (articles of household furniture, esp. when old and shabby) with Aspinall's Enamel Paint. Hence **A·spinalling** *vbl. sb.*

1889 *Jrnl. Educ.* 1 Aug. 388/1 Three low wicker chairs 'Aspinalled' in dark green. 1891 M. E. Mann *Winter's Tale* II. i. xi. 25 The..stool, which Erica herself had aspinalled in a spare hour. 1891 (*title*) Guide to Aspinalling. By A Lady.

Aspirating (æ·spireⁱtiŋ), *ppl. a.* [f. Aspirate *v.* + -ing[2].] That operates by aspiration or suction.

1884 Knight *Dict. Mech., Suppl.*, *Aspirating Filter*, one in which the action is expedited by the withdrawal of air from beneath the filtering material. *Ibid.*, *Aspirating Winnowing Machine*, one which draws air through the grain instead of blowing it. 1895 *Catal. Surg. Instruments* (Arnold & Sons), Aspirating Syringe, Aspirating Guarded Needle. 1902 *Times* 25 Sept. 3/4 The operation was performed with an aspirating needle.

Aspiration. Add:

7. The action or process of drawing in, out, or through by suction; *esp.* the drawing out (of fluids, gases, etc.) by means of an aspirator.

1842 *Civil Engin. & Arch. Jrnl.* V. 203/2 The fluid was absorbed throughout all the pores of the [feiled] tree, by a process which is termed 'aspiration'. 1879 *Encycl. Brit.* IX. 344/1 Apparatus, in which the principle of aspiration, or drawing currents of air through the grain, is now extensively employed. 1881 *Trans. Obstetr. Soc. Lond.* XXII. 57 Aspiration was frequently resorted to, with the view of arresting the growth of the fœtus.

attrib. 1902 C. N. & A. M. Williamson *Lightning Conductor* 18 The 'aspiration pipe'..had worked loose.

Aspirational (æspireⁱ·ʃənăl), *a.* [f. Aspiration + -al.] Belonging to or characterized by aspiration.

1887 H. R. Haweis *Light of the Ages* iii. 83 Its sense of mystery feeble, and consequently its lift and aspirational power almost *nil.* 1919 A. M. Rihbany *Syrian Christ* ii. ii. 66 As pious in his imprecations and curses as he is in his aspirational prayer. *Ibid.* v. iv. 250 His infatuation is known as..pure, or aspirational love.

Aspirin (æ·spirin). *Chem.* [G. (Heinrich Dreser in *Pflüger's Archiv* 1899).] A white crystalline compound of acetyl and salicylic acid, used as a sedative drug; with *an* and *pl.*, a dose of this in tablet form. Also *attrib.*, as *aspirin tablet.*

1899 *Jrnl. Chem. Soc.* LXXVI. ii. 605 Physiological Action of Aspirin (Acetylsalicylic Acid). 1901 *Ibid.* LXXX. ii. 408 Aspirin (*o*-acetoxybenzoic acid) does not increase the flow of urine, but somewhat raises the total output of solids. 1922 *Blackw. Mag.* Apr. 460/1 He was always at hand with tea and brandy and aspirin. 1923 Mrs. A. Sidgwick *Nonegoby* xxix. 243, I think that frontal neuralgia is worse. You can give me an aspirin if you like. 1924 *Blackw. Mag.* June 801/2 Aspirin tablets.

Aspo·rtable, *a.* [f. Asport *v.*] Capable of being carried away.

1889 F. W. Maitland *Collected Papers* (1911) II. 173 The imaginary defendant is charged..with the asportation of all that is asportable.

Asportation. (Modern examples.)

1889 [see prec.]. 1890 *Harper's Mag.* Oct. 702/1 If the silver..could be deposited..in bars too heavy for asportation.

Asquithian (æskwi·þiăn), *a.* and *sb.* [f. the name of H. H. *Asquith* (afterwards Earl of Oxford and Asquith), prime minister of England 1908–15 + -ian.] **A.** *adj.* Of or supporting Asquith as leader of the Liberal party or, later, as leader of a group of the divided party. **B.** *sb.* A supporter of Asquith as leader of the Liberal party or a Liberal belonging to the group led by Asquith.

1910 *Spectator* 2 Apr. 530/1 The Asquithian Peers will, we venture to say, prove the most intractable of 'backwoodsmen'. 1928 *Daily Express* 24 Apr. 3/3 Montagu..belonged to the central Asquithian group in the Cabinet,..and as an Asquithian he preferred to support McKenna rather than Lloyd George.

Ass, *v.* **2.** Add: Now freq. in (orig. schoolboys') *slang*: To fool *about.*

1899 Kipling *Stalky* vii. 196 Don't mind learnin' my drill, but I'm not goin' to ass about the country with a toy Snider.

Assay, *v.* Add:

4. c. To show (a certain yield) by assay; to yield on assay. Also *absol.*

1882 *Rep. Prec. Metals U.S.* 305 Assay as high as $100 to the ton. 1892 *Graphic* 26 Mar. 387/1 A 'pocket'..which assays a good many ounces to the ton. 1927 *Sunday Times* 13 Feb. 2 Ore,..assaying as high as 7·3 dwts. (31s.).

Assemblage. Add: **2. b.** The fitting together of the parts of a machine.

1874 Knight *Dict. Mech.* I. 171/1 This system of interchangeability and assemblage..is one of the most beautiful triumphs of modern mechanism.

Assemble, *v.*[1] Add:

2. b. To put together (the separately manufactured parts of a composite machine or mechanical appliance); also with the machine as obj. Also **Asse·mbled** *ppl. a.*, **Asse·mbling** *vbl. sb.*; **Asse·mbler**, one who assembles a machine or its parts.

1865 *Mech. Mag.* 31 Mar. 200/2 When all these parts are assembled together. 1888 *Sun* 21 Mar. (Farmer), The steel forgings have been made and turned over to our ordnance officers to assemble into guns. 1894 *Harper's Mag.* July 252/1 The assembling, as the process of shrinking on the various parts which go to make up the modern cannon is called. *Ibid.* 256/2 The partly assembled gun. 1898 *Cricket & Football Field* 1 Oct. 3 'Assemblers'—men who buy [cycle] frames..then put in whatever fittings they or their customers may be inclined to use. 1907 *Westm. Gaz.* 9 Nov. 14/2 The vertically assembled differential case is being gradually superseded by the horizontally assembled case. 1908 *Daily Chron.* 21 Feb. 10/6 Arc lamp assemblers. 1909 *Ibid.* 21 Aug. 6/6 One cannot get such a cycle ready made, but a good assembler can build it up. 1909 *Westm. Gaz.* 28 Apr. 2/2 Structural steel is imported punched, riveted, and assembled to be set up. *Ibid.* 16 Sept. 5/1 If all the parts are not there when the time comes to assemble the chassis. 1923 *Ibid.* 15 Sept., Assembling and packing cycle bells.

Assembly. Add:

1. b. The assembling of troops; also *attrib.*, as *assembly-position, -trench.*

1920 *Q. Rev.* Jan. 108 The digging of assembly-trenches. *Ibid.*, Troops moving up to the assembly-positions.

c. The action or method of assembling a machine or its parts.

1897 [see *assembly-room below]. 1922 *Autocar* 10 Nov. 983 Arrol-Johnston gear assembly, showing how the whole can be removed without disturbing the box itself...Rear axle assembly.

IV. assembly-man (earlier U.S. example); **assembly-room**, (*b*) a room in a workshop where the parts of some composite article are assembled.

1836 Haliburton *Clockm.* Ser. i. xxxii. (1837) 347 He sot up for an Assembly-man. 1897 *Outing* (U.S.) XXX. 279/2 They are then polished, nickelplated,..and sent to the assembly-room to take their places in the wheel.

Assession. 2. Add: In the Duchy of Cornwall, the action of assessing or letting to rent the lord's demesnes, which was done at a court held for the purpose; also attrib. in *assession-court, -roll.* Hence **Asse·ssioning** *vbl. sb.* and *ppl. a.*; **Asse·ssionable** (ăse·ʃənăb'l) *a.* occas. **Asse·ssional** *a.*, applied to seventeen manors of the Duchy in which the lands were let by courts of assession.

1820 Sir J. Scarlett in G. Concanen *Rep. Rowe v. Brenton* (1830) App. 77 *note*, There is no custom stated for the free tenants to attend the assession-court, only the conventionaries. 1820 Brougham *Ibid.*, They have done enough to differ the present case, of tendering the assession-roll, from the circumstances under which it was tendered before. 1828 Barnewall & Cresswell *Rep.* VIII. 740 The seventeen manors hereafter mentioned as assessionable manors. *Ibid.* 750 A roll called an Assession Roll, which purported to be an account of the acts done by certain assessors in the 7 Edw. 3., under a commission to them by John Earl of Cornwall. 1830 G. Concanen *Rep. Rowe v. Brenton* (title), The right to minerals in the assessional lands of the duchy

of Cornwall. *Ibid.* Introd. 23 The mode of letting the lands of the assessional manors by the assessioning commissioners. *Ibid.*, The assessioning of the same manors occurred at intervals of less than seven years. *Ibid.* 36 The conventionary tenants of the seventeen assessionable manors of the Duchy. 1839 *Penny Cycl.* XIV. 389–390. 1848 *Act 11 & 12 Vict.* c. 83 (*title*) An Act to confirm the Awards of Assessionable Manors Commissioners.

Assignment. Add: **11. b.** A task assigned to one; a commission or appointment. *U.S.*

1897 *Scribner's Mag.* Aug. 232/2 The reporters..were waiting to be sent off on their first assignments before getting breakfast. 1903 J. Ralph *Making of Journalist* 126 The first 'assignment' I ever had as a New York Reporter was to go to Delaware to see a woman whipped. 1904 *N. Y. Even. Post* 11 May 9 He..went into the Presbyterian ministry receiving assignments in various parts of the mining camp West. 1910 Mulford *Hopalong Cassidy* xvii. 99 At first his assignment had pleased, but as hour after hour passed with growing weariness, he chafed more and more.

Assimilate, *v.* Add:

1. d. *Philol.* To render (a sound) accordant, or less discordant (*to* another sound in the same or a contiguous word).

1852 *Proc. Philol. Soc.* V. 200 In our own language..it is to be expected that some traces of the law of assimilated vowels should appear. 1879 Roby *Lat. Gram.* II. § 1829 Ad is usually assimilated to c and (written c) to q.

Assimilation. Add:

1. b. *Philol.* The action of assimilating or fact of being assimilated: see prec.

1849 *Proc. Philol. Soc.* IV. 89 The law for the assimilation of vowels..will account for the introduction of an *o* in *biodhmur*,..before the *u* of the final syllable. 1871 *Public Sch. Lat. Gram.* 18 Complete Assimilation occurs, when, of two meeting Consonants, the former becomes the same as the latter. 1885 Cook *Sievers' O. E. Gram.* § 86. 38 A partial assimilation of the basic vowel to the following sound.

Assist, *sb.* Delete † *Obs. rare*[−1] and add:

b. *Baseball.* (See quot. 1896.)

1891 N. Crane *Baseball* 79 *Assist*, the credit given by the scorer to a fielder who handles the ball in assisting to put out a player. 1896 Knowles & Morton *Baseball* 101 The fielder who handles the ball in sufficient time to aid in retiring a base-runner is credited with an assist. 1917 C. Mathewson *Sec. Base Sloan* xiv. 187 Five strike-outs, three assists and no errors was considered a fine record.

Assist, *v.* Add:

6. a. Frequently with adv. or advb. phr. denoting that in which the assistance is given.

1837 Howard *Old Commodore* I. v. 186 Assist the chaplain down the poop-ladder. 1843 Lever *Jack Hinton* xxv, He assisted me on with my great-coat. *Ibid.* xxvii, As I assisted her from the carriage, I could not but mark the flashing brilliancy of her eye. 1854 — *Sir Jasper Carew* xxix, He assisted me off with my coat. 1865 Mrs. Gaskell *Wives & Dau.* v, 'May I help you to potatoes?' or, as Mr. Wynne would persevere in saying, 'May I assist you to potatoes?' 1882 Mrs. J. H. Riddell *Senior Partner* I. vi. 116 The way in which he assisted the elder guest off with his coat..was a study. *Ibid.* II. xi. 228 'It's no use my trying to put in a friendly oar', said Mr. McCullagh, assisted perhaps to this last figure of speech by the sight of an outrigger spinning down the stream. 1924 Rose Macaulay *Orphan Island* xi, Miss Smith..was assisted from her hammock.

7. c. Of the dealer's partner in the game of euchre: To order the adoption of the suit of the card turned up as trump.

1878 *Encycl. Brit.* VIII. 654/2 If the first hand passes, the second may say 'I assist', which means that the dealer (his partner) is to take up the trump. *Ibid.* 655/1 A player can declare to play alone when he or his partner orders up, or when his partner assists.

Assistant, *a.* **3.** Add:

Assistant curate: see Curate 2. *Assistant master, mistress* (in a school).

1851 C. Cist *Cincinnati* 304 In September..he received the appointment of assistant professor of mathematics. 1872 *Schoolmaster* 6 Jan. 4/1 Wanted..an Assistant Master, Ex P. T., for Canal-street Wesleyan Schools, Derby. *Ibid.*, Wanted, in a Mixed School, an ex P.T., as Assistant-Mistress. 1902 A. C. Benson *Schoolm.* 29 As to corporal punishment, the doubtful privilege of dispensing it is, at my own School, not conceded to the assistant-masters.

Assize, *sb.* Add: **19.** *attrib.*: **assize sermon**, a sermon preached at the holding of assizes (sense 12).

1859 Reade *Love me Little* iii, Shall you go to the assize sermon?

Associate, *ppl. a.* **1.** Add examples of recent usage.

1891 D. C. Gilman *Johns Hopkins Univ.* 60 The persons below named have been appointed associate professors. 1900 *Daily News* 14 Nov. 6/3 Associate-editor of the 'Engineer'. 1904 *N. Y. Even. Post* 23 July 4 He is associate editor of the *Evening Wisconsin.* 1905 *Ibid.* 23 Dec., The additional class is that of associate professors. All assistant professors under the old order were made 'associate'. 1907 *Westm. Gaz.* 22 Feb. 1/3 Associate-editor of that oldest of the Australian dailies.

Associating, *ppl. a.* Add: *associating fibres* = *association fibres* (see next).

1885 *Harper's Mag.* Mar. 640/1 One set serves to connect the cells of different areas of the cortex (the 'associating fibres').

Association. Add:

7. b. Psychol. *Laws of association*, see quot. 1897. *Mediate association*, association by unconscious or unnoticed intermediaries. *Simultaneous, successive association*, forms of association of ideas in which the process of connexion is simultaneous or falls into two stages. Also *attrib.*, as *association test, theory, time.*

1897 tr. *Wundt's Outlines Psychol.* 13 Intellectualistic psychology has in the course of its development separated into two trends..The logical theory...The association-theory. *Ibid.* 225 The following forms were discriminated: association by similarity and contrast, and association by simultaneity and succession. These class-concepts gained by a logical dichotomic process were dignified with the name 'laws of associations'. 1924 tr. *Freud's Collected Papers* II. 13 Association test.

9. *Physiol.* Used attrib., as *association areas, centres, spheres*, those portions of the cortex of the brain which lie between the sense-spheres believed to be concerned with the function of ideation, etc.; *association fibres*, those which connect the various areas of the cortex, as distinguished from the commisural fibres.

1901 *Allchin's Man. Med.* III. Physiol. Introd. 31 A portion of the 'association' field of the cortex. 1902 *Encycl. Brit.* XXXI. 742/1 The areas of intervening cortex, arriving at structural completion later than the..sense-spheres, are called by some association-spheres. 1904 J. McCabe tr. *Haeckel's Wonders of Life* i. 13 In 1894 Flechsig showed that there are four central sense-regions..in the gray cortex of the brain, and four thought-centres ('association-centres', or phroneta).

10. A personal connexion or link; esp. *attrib.* in *association book, copy*, a volume showing some mark of personal connexion with the author or a former owner (of note).

1912 *Times* (Weekly ed.) 7 June 444 The collection is chiefly remarkable for what are termed in America 'association books'. 1914 *W. M. Murphy's Catal. Bks.* 19 Jan. 5 Association Copy..A most interesting 'Association book'. 1918 *Times* 21 Feb. 3/3 It is very rich..in what Americans call 'association books', such as the copy of 'Vanity Fair' which Thackeray sent to Charlotte Brontë. 1918 *Times Lit. Suppl.* 21 Nov. 567/2 There never was an 'association-book', as the Americans call it, more palpitating with reminiscence. 1928 *Bookseller's Catal.*, An association copy with an autograph inscription. 1928 *N. & Q.* 12 May 341/2 Presented by Sir Walter Scott to Lydia White...Double association of good interest.

11. Applied to the game of football played according to the rules of the Football Association formed in 1863, as distinguished from the Rugby game. (Cf. *soccer*, Socker.)

1874 *Elizabethan* I. No. 4. 25 Westminster and Charterhouse profess to play the strict Association game. 1879 *Encycl. Brit.* IX. 368/1 The intricacies of the Association game are far fewer [than those of the Rugby game]. 1885 Shearman & Vincent *Football* 45 Before the days of the Rugby Union and Association rules. *Ibid.* 53 The ball..is several ounces heavier than an Association ball. 1898 G. O. Smith *Football* 49 Association Football.

Associationist. Add: Also *attrib.* or as *adj.* = next.

1886 A. Weir *Hist. Basis Mod. Europe* (1889) 500 The associationist psychology.

Associationistic (ăsōᵘʃieⁱʃəni·stik), *a.* [f. Associationist + -ic.] Of or relating to associationism or associationists.

1901 W. James *Mem. & Stud.* vii. (1911) 148 All psychology, whether animistic or associationistic, was written on classic-academic lines.

Assortative (ăsǭ·ɹtătiv), *a.* [f. Assort *v.* + -ative.] That assorts. *Assortative mating*, sexual selection.

1900 K. Pearson *Gramm. Sci.* (ed. 2) 429 We are largely thrown back for our quantitative determinations of assortative mating on man. 1902 W. F. R. Weldon in *Encycl. Brit.* XXXIII. 637/1 Assortative mating exists when individuals which mate are not paired at random, but a definite correlation is established between the characters of one mate and those of the other. 1903 *Biometrika* Nov. 373 We could hardly want stronger evidence of the existence of assortative mating in man.

Asso·rter. *U.S.* [f. Assort *v.* + -er[1].] One who assorts.

1897 *Scribner's Mag.* Jan. 17/2 The assorter, who distributes the bundles [of goods] into lots to go to the different parts of the city.

Assuetude (æ·swĭtiud). Delete † *Obs. rare*[−1] and add quots.:

1830 Marryat *King's Own* xxxvi, To whose..beauty, from assuetude, he had..been blind. 1873 *Contemp. Rev.* XXII. 699 The petrified assuetudes and porcelain effeminacies of the Chinese. 1890 *Daily News* 15 Nov. 5/6 At the same time..the effect of assuetude may become apparent.

Assumingly (ăsiū·miŋli), *adv.* [f. Assuming *ppl. a.* + -ly[2].] In an assuming manner, presumptuously.

1839 J. P. Smith *Scripture & Geol.* 215 What I may, not assumingly, call the whole body of geologists. 1927 *Scots Observer* 12 Mar. 3/5, I ken him fine commented the other assumingly.

Assumptionist (ăsʌ·mᵖʃənist). [f. Assumption + -ist.]

1. One who bases his arguments on assumption.

1891 G. A. Denison *Let.* 9 Mar., in *Fifty Years at East Brent* (1902) 344 He is a remarkable assumptionist—he is no logician.

2. *R. C. Ch.* A member of the congregation entitled Augustinians of the Assumption, 'which had its origin in the College of the Assumption, established at Nîmes, in France, in 1843' (*Cath. Encycl.*).

1898 *Westm. Gaz.* 30 Sept. 6/2 An article in the *Croix* by its editor, the Assumptionist Father Bailly. 1901 *Daily News* 3 Jan. 4/7 The Assumptionists, who have played such an infamous part in French politics the last three years.

Assuring, *ppl. a.* Add:

2. That takes out a policy of assurance.

1891 Tebbutt in *Charity Organis. Rev.* VII. 262 Each assuring member secured a small payment at death.

Astatki (æstæ·tki). [Corruptly ad. Russ. остатокъ *ostatokŭ* remainder.] The waste product of the distillation of Russian petroleum atomized with steam and made combustible for use as fuel. Also *attrib.*

1898 B. Redwood *Rep. Schibaieff's Petrol. Refinery* 3 Storage is provided for..kerosene, astatki, and lubricating oils. 1902 *Encycl. Brit.* XXXI. 646/1 Large quantities of refuse were produced—known by the Russian name of *astatki.* *Ibid.* 646/2 Practically all the steam power in South Russia..is now raised from *astatki* fuel.

Aster. Add:

4. *Biol.* A star-shaped karyokinetic division-figure of a cell, esp. of one dividing by mitosis; also *attrib.*, as *aster rays*, the radiating fibres of this in certain organisms. Also, the group of chromosomes when forming a star-shaped figure during mitosis.

1881 Rolleston & Jackson *Anim. Life* p. xxv, A star or aster with a pronucleus as a centre. 1909 J. W. Jenkinson *Exper. Embryol.* 107 Each sperm forms its own aster, and these combine with one another to form various irregular miotic figures (triasters, tetrasters, and so on).

5. *Zool.* A star-shaped spicule.

1887 *Encycl. Brit.* XXII. 417 The rays of an aster as of other spicules may be spined. 1920 L. Doncaster *Introd. Study Cytology* iii. 31 The centrosome with its system of rays is called an *aster*, and the two asters with the sheaf of fibres connecting them are the achromatic or mitotic spindle.

Asterisked (æ·stĕriskt), *ppl. a.* [f. Asterisk *v.* or *sb.* + -ed.] Marked with an asterisk.

1897 *Westm. Gaz.* 20 July 2/2 An asterisked speech [in 'Hansard'].

Asteroid, *a.* and *sb.* Add:

A. *adj.* **2.** *Zool.* Of, belonging to, or characteristic of the Asteroidea.

1888 Rolleston & Jackson *Anim. Life* 5 The Asteroid larva closely resembles the Holothurioid. 1900 E. R. Lankester, etc. tr. *Bather's Echinoderma* 3 No sharp line can be drawn between Asteroid and Ophiuroid structure.

B. *sb.* **4.** *Zool.* A star-fish of the class Asteroidea.

1840 E. Forbes *Brit. Starfishes* i. 3 The Crinoids as analogues of the Polypes are lower than the Asteroids. 1888 Rolleston & Jackson *Anim. Life* 563 The apical system of plates is well defined in the young Asteroid. 1900 E. R. Lankester, etc. tr. *Bather's Echinoderma* 14 The Asteroids were probably the last group to branch off from the fixed Echinoderms. 1921 *Chambers's Jrnl.* 502/1 The mauve of these beautiful asteroids blends perfectly with the soft gray sands of the North Pacific.

Asthma. Add:

2. *attrib.* **asthma herb** *Austral.* (see quots.).

1887 Moloney *Forestry W. Afr.* 411 Australian Asthma-Herb (*Euphorbia pilulifera*, L.). 1889 J. H. Maiden *Useful Native Plants Australia* 183 Queensland Asthma Herb.

Astigmatism. Add:

b. *Optics.* A similar defect in a lens.

1859 Parkinson *Optics* (1866) 51 When a pencil of rays is reflected or refracted at the surface of a medium, the reflected or refracted rays will not, in general, pass accurately through one point. This peculiarity is sometimes called astigmatism. 1892 J. T. Taylor *Optics Photogr.* xxiii, Astigmatism is a serious fault for a lens to possess in any marked degree.

Astonish, *v.* **4.** Add: Also *absol.*

1904 L. T. Meade *Love Triumphant* III. i, There might come to you a knowledge which would astonish and terrify.

Astræan (æstrī·ăn), *a.* [f. mod. L. *Astræa* + -an.] Pertaining to or resembling *Astræa*, a genus of stone-corals, the type of the family *Astræidæ* or star-corals. So **Astræ·id** *a.* and *sb.*; **Astræ·iform** *a.*

1877 *Encycl. Brit.* VI. 383/2 *Holocystis* is also composite and astræiform. 1884–5 *Trans. R. Soc. Edin.* XXXII. 551 Astræid and brain corals. *Ibid.* 558 Imbedded in the base of this cliff of coral limestone were two dome-shaped masses of Astræan corals of different species. 1886 J. J. Quelch *Rep. Reef-Corals* 8 (Challenger Rep., Zool. XVI), *Moseleya latistellata*..is..undeniably Astræid in its characters.

Astrakhan. Add:

b. A kind of cloth (see quots.) used chiefly as an edging or trimming for garments.

1887 *Cassell's Fam. Mag.* Oct. 698/1 The curled cloths or woollen Astrachans used for trimmings and for entire jackets. 1904 *Tailor & Cutter* 4 Aug. 479 Astrachan: A cloth made of worsted material, with a long and closely-curled pile, in imitation of the fur of that name.

Astral, *a.* (and *sb.*). Add:

3. *Theosophy.* Pertaining to or consisting of a supersensible substance considered to be next above the sensible world in refinement and held to pervade all space. *Astral body*, the ethereal counterpart or shadow of a human or animal body.

1877 Helena P. Blavatsky *Isis Unveiled* in *Secr. Doctrine* (1888) II. 74 When those circulations—which Eliphas Levi calls 'currents of the astral light'—in the universal ether..take place in harmony with the divine spirit, our earth..enjoys a fertile period. 1880 Anna Kingsford in *Life* (1913) I. 401 In man the astral fluid becomes transformed into human life at the moment of conception. *Ibid.*, All they whose bodies have decomposed leave, or have left, their shadow in the astral space. 1881 Sinnett *Occult*

World 162 Even our astral bodies, pure ether, are but illusions of matter so long as they retain their terrestrial outline.

4. *Cytology.* Of or pertaining to an aster.

1901 Calkins *Protozoa* iii. 82 In others they [the rays] are focussed in a central or 'astral' granule (*Gymnosphæra, Actinophrys, Sphærastrum*, etc.), which in some cases has been seen to divide like a centrosome and to form an amphiaster. *Ibid.* viii. 278 In some cases this structure resembles the astral system of Metazoa.

B. *sb.* **2.** An astral body.

1880 Anna Kingsford in *Life* (1913) I. 400 The Astral is not an entity, for it cannot reproduce itself. It is an imprint only, a shadow, a reflect, an echo. 1888 Helena P. Blavatsky *Secr. Doctrine* (ed. 2) I. 639 Our more intimate astral, or inner man.

Astrally, *adv.* Add:

2. As an astral body.

1886 *Sat. Rev.* 4 Dec. 751 Whether the Thibetan Adepts go spooking astrally through the world.

Astream (ăstrī·m), *adv.* [f. A- 2 + Stream *sb.*] In line with the stream.

1906 *Daily Chron.* 29 Aug. 6/6 The swimmer commenced to lose ground,..the bearings showed him to be astream of the Varne buoy.

Astrographic (æstrogræ·fik), *a.* [f. Astrography + -ic, after *photographic.*] Of, pertaining to, used in, or produced by astrography.

1893 *Westm. Gaz.* 5 June 6/3 With the astrographic equatorial 722 photographic plates..were taken. 1895 *Athenæum* 8 June 743/1 The shutter of the astrographic dome was torn off and blown into the courtyard. 1903 H. H. Turner *Astrographic Chart* 13 The real work of the Astrographic Chart consists in measuring the positions of the stars, which will tell us ultimately their motions.

A:strophoto·graphy. [f. Astro- + Photography.] The application of photography to astronomy. So **A:strophotogra·phic, -gra·phical** *adjs.*, of, pertaining to, used in, or produced by astrophotography.

1889 Winterhalter (*title*) The International Astrophotographic Congress. 1892 *Pall Mall Gaz.* 9 Aug. 2/1 The astrophotographic telescope. *Ibid.*, The new astrophotographical telescope is..controlled by an electric current. 1903 Agnes M. Clerke *Problems in Astrophysics* 5 Astrophotography is an art, and has a technique of its own.

Astrophysics (æstrofi·ziks). [f. Astro- + Physics.] That branch of astronomy which treats of the physical and chemical composition of the heavenly bodies. Hence **Astrophy·sicist**, a student of astronomical physics.

1890 *Sat. Rev.* 9 Aug. 176/1 The new science of 'astrophysics'. 1902 Newcomb *Stars* 10 The astronomer, or astrophysicist as he now calls himself. 1906 *Westm. Gaz.* 1 June 12/1 That wonderful science of astrophysics which has enabled astronomers to see elements present in our own earth..in the absorbent vapours surrounding the..stars.

Astropyle (æ·stropəil). *Zool.* [f. Gr. ἄστρον star + πύλη gate.] A tubular aperture or funnel-like membranous projection found in some radiolarians (see quots.).

1888 Rolleston & Jackson *Anim. Life* 876 Or again there is a main oral aperture or astropyle...The astropyle consists of a tubular proboscis, rising from the centre of a radially striated disc or operculum. 1901 Calkins *Protozoa* iii. 70 The Cannopylea, in which the membrane around the pores is drawn out into funnel-like projections termed astropyles.

Astrosphere (æ·strosfīəɹ). *Cytology.* [f. Astro- + Sphere.] The central portion of the aster in the karyokinetic figure inclusive of the region in which the centrosome lies, but exclusive of the astral rays. **b.** The whole aster exclusive of the centrosome.

1901 Calkins *Protozoa* 278 This structure resembles the astral system of Metazoa, in consisting of an outer spherical mass with radiating processes (astrosphere).

A-swirl (ăswə̄·ɹl), *adv.* [f. A *prep.*[1] 11 + Swirl *v.*] In a swirl, swirling.

1909 H. G. Wells *Tono-Bungay* iv. iii, The water all a-swirl with the wash of shipping. 1915 C. C. Martindale *In God's Army, Commanders in Chief* 125 Despite the..mists that set the imagination a-swirl.

Asynergy (æsi·nəɹdʒi). *Path.* [f. A- 14 + Synergy.] Lack of co-ordination of parts or organs normally acting in harmony.

1901 Dorland *Med. Dict.* (ed. 2). 1907 *Practitioner* Dec. 851 The laryngitis of singers..is made evident..by muscular troubles (vocal asynergy).

At, *prep.* Add: **1. b.** Used with the cardinal points of the compass, as *at the Eastward* (later *East*), to indicate parts of the country. *U.S.*

1646 Winthrop *Lett.* (1869) 357 Some hurt was done here..much fish and salt lost at eastward. 1672 *Roxbury Rec.* 210 A great Eclipse of the Sun, which at the eastward was total. 1692 *Essex Inst. Hist. Coll.* XLII. 142 Marke How that is now dead, who dyed at the Eastward. 1697 *Ibid.* XI. 76 In going over a reaver [= river] at ye Southward. 1721 *Jrnls. Ho. Repr. Mass.* III. 94 Mr. Secretary brought down..Letters from several of the Inhabitants at the Eastward. 1782 *Essex Inst. Hist. Coll.* I. 13/2 My company being at the Sotherd, the money was drawn for them for 3 months. 1835 J. H. Ingraham *South-West* II. 213 The opinion, that their sons can be educated at the south by northern professors as well as at the north. 1851 Hawthorne *Ho. Seven Gables* xiii, A still unsettled claim to a very large extent of territory at the eastward. 1883 J. Quincy *Figures of Past* (1884) 343 Characteristic of slave-holders when upon their good behavior at the North.

c. *Naut.* Indicating the quarter of the wind.

1635 R. Mather *Jrnl.* 18 Afore noone the wind waxed strong at north. 1733 Franklin *Poor Rich. Alm.* 10 Clouds and winds at southwest. 1780 *Heath Papers* 93 The wind which now blows at east. 1848 J. F. Cooper *Oak Open.* II. xiv. 203 The wind stood at the westward.

d. Used superfluously after *where.* *U.S.*

1859 Bartlett *Dict. Amer.* (ed. 2), *At* is often used superfluously in the South and West, as in the question 'Where is he at?' 1898 A. Nicholas *Idyl of Wabash* etc. 34 Where does he live at? 1903 *N. Y. Sun* 8 Nov. 6 The business world wants rest. It wants to know where it is at. 1911 E. Ferber *Dawn O'Hara* xx. 294 This is where I get off at. 1914 G. Atherton *Perch of Devil* i. 8 She..disliked ..not knowing where she was at.

13. c. *esp.* with verbs of speaking, with implication of indirect attack.

1721 Preaching at [in Dict.]. 1836–7 Dickens *Sk. Boz, Tales* x. ii, Mrs. Parsons talked *to* Miss Lillerton and *at* her better half. 1837 [see Talk *v.* 3 d]. 1863 Cowden Clarke *Shaks. Char.* v. 133 The latter..always make her speak *at* her husband.

Ataman, var. Hetman.

1835 *Court Mag.* VI. 3‥/1 'We may not do this', replied one of the Cossacks, 'without the consent of our Ataman.' 1920 *Glasgow Herald* 18 Aug. 7 The Ataman of the Don Cossacks. 1924 *Blackw. Mag.* Feb. 171/2 The Ataman had been waiting a mile away..for the last of the attacking party to come in.

Atap, var. *Attap.

Atavistically (ætăvi·stikăli), *adv.* [f. Atavistic *a.*: see -ically.] In a manner exhibiting atavism.

1864 *N. Amer. Rev.* Sept. 253 The ancient types crop out atavistically. 1898 E. P. Evans *Evol. Ethics* i. 33 The lower classes..reflect atavistically the ideas and passions of primitive man.

Atelectatic (ætĭlektæ·tik), *a.* *Path.* [f. Atelectasis.] Characterized by atelectasis. Also **Atele·ctic** *a.*

1875 Gamgee tr. *Hermann's Human Physiol.* 159 The lungs left to themselves contain no air: they are *atalectic* [sic], like the lungs of the fœtus before it has 'breathed'. 1880 Flint *Princ. Med.* (ed. 5) 187 Occlusion of the bronchi immediately connected with the atelectatic spots can be demonstrated.

Ateleiosis, ateliosis (ătelai-, ătīliōᵘ·sis). [f. A- 14 + Teleiosis.] Defective or arrested development.

1903 *Med. Record* 18 July 96 (Cent. Dict. Suppl.). 1927 *Times* (Weekly ed.) 28 Apr. 475/2 The existence in an adult (a-teleiosis) of child characters (elves).

A tent. *U.S.* [f. the letter A, from its shape.] A tent with sides sloping downwards from a ridge pole.

1888 *Century Mag.* Jan. 447/2 Three wall tents..and twice as many 'A' or 'wedge' or common tents. 1904 Eliz. Robins *Magnetic North* xvi. 284 Down in the desolate hollow a ragged A tent sagged away from the prevailing wind.

Athematic (æ-, ēþīmæ·tik), *a.* *Gram.* [f. A- 14 + Thematic *a.*] Characterized by the formation of verb-forms by the immediate addition of suffixes to the verb-stem without a connecting (thematic) vowel.

1896 Lindsay *Short Latin Gram.* 86.

Athermic (æ-, ēþə̄·ɹmik), *a.* [ad. F. *athermique*, f. Gr. ἀ priv. (see A- *prefix* 14) + θέρμη heat + -ic.] **a.** That is not pervious to heat or heat-rays. Cf. Adiathermic *a.* **b.** Without fever or rise of temperature (Dorland 1901). **c.** (See quot. 1911.)

1862 *Catal. Internat. Exhib.* II. xiii. 16 Melloni's apparatus for illustrating the athermic and diathermic character of minerals. 1911 Webster, *Athermic*, heatless; as, an athermic motor.

Athetesis (æþĭtī·sis). [a. Gr. ἀθέτησις, f. ἀθετεῖν (see next).] The setting aside or rejection (of a passage) as spurious.

1887 J. S. Reid in *Classical Rev.* June 135/2 He is judiciously conservative and takes no notice of such extravagant *athetesis* as those put forward by Lütjohann in a paper on the *Cato Maior.* 1888 Leaf *Iliad* II. 435 Aristarchos' athetesis of 614–7 has been generally accepted, but..on inadequate grounds.

Athetize (æ·þĭtaiz), *v.* [f. Gr. ἄθετος set aside + -ize: formed to render Gr. ἀθετεῖν to set aside, reject as spurious.] *trans.* To set aside (a passage) as spurious. Hence **A·thetizer.**

1886 Jevons in *Jrnl. Hellenic Studies* VII. 306 The solution is to athetize B 35–41 [of the *Iliad*]. 1888 Leaf *Iliad* II. 435 The opening passage (1–30) contains an unusual number of lines which have been suspected on undeniably valid grounds since the time of Aristarchos, who athetized no less than fourteen. 1889 *Athenæum* 26 Oct. 553/1 Dr. Leaf..controverts with success the athetizers and abjudicators of Homeric verses.

Athetosis (æþĭtōᵘ·sis). *Path.* [f. Gr. ἄθετος without position or place + -osis.] An affection characterized by involuntary movements of the hands and feet, which cannot be retained by the patient in any position in which they are placed. Hence **Athetotic** (æþĭtǫ·tik) *a.*, characteristic of or resembling athetosis.

1871 W. A. Hammond *Treat. Dis. Nervous Syst.* 654 Under the name of athetosis..I propose to describe an affection which..is mainly characterized by an inability to retain the fingers and toes in any position. 1897 *Trans. Amer. Pediatric Soc.* IX. 158 In the analysis of 151 cases of cerebral paralysis in children..he found..athetosis six times. 1898 Dawson Williams *Med. Dis. Inf.* 560 The general character of athetotic movements.

Athleticize (æþle·tisaiz). [f. Athletic *a.* + -ize.] *trans.* To make athletic.

1896 *Godey's Mag.* Apr. 447/1 Are we to be so athleticized that we will disdain all fripperies? 1897 *Eclectic Mag.* Oct. 523 France, superficially, has become Anglicized, athleticised.

At home. Add:

A. 4. *Cribbage.* (See quot.)

1877 H. Jones in *Encycl. Brit.* VI. 577/1 (*Cribbage*) Each player ought to reckon slightly over six in hand and play and five in crib, or seventeen and a half in two deals to be *at home.* A player who scores more than the average and leaves his adversary six or seven points in arrear is *safe at home.* When at home it is best to play off; when the adversary is safe at home it is best to play on.

Ati·choo. A representation of the characteristic noises accompanying a sneeze.

1873 Miss Broughton *Nancy* iii, I sneeze loudly and irrepressibly. Atcha! Atcha! 1878 *Punch* 26 Jan. 36 A cough tears your lungs, but a sneeze tears you through—A'd—gooddess!—it's cubbi'g—a-tschoo—A-tischool [1828 *Hood's Comic Ann.* 54 I've got such a cold. Er-tchiou—er-tchiou!] 1892 Zangwill *Childr. Ghetto* I. 112 Ezekiel sneezed. It was a convulsive 'atichoo'. 1910 *Punch* 30 Nov. 383 There, that's all right. A-a-a-tishoo!

Atlantic, *a.* **1.** Add: *Atlantic states*, those of the United States situated on the Atlantic coast.

1829–32 J. P. Kennedy *Swallow B.* II. xiv. 233 Old Nick ..is falling into the sere and yellow leaf, especially in the Atlantic states.

Atmosphere, *sb.* Add: **4. b.** Characteristic environment; surroundings or setting of a character appropriate or peculiar to the thing in question.

1886 *Harper's Mag.* Nov. 831/2 The constituent parts of literary society..are obliged to house themselves transiently in the most incongruous spots, with little, if any, 'atmosphere' about them. 1916 Bower *Phantom Herd* i. 1 Such wanted several rehearsals of 'atmosphere' scenes before turning the camera on them. *Ibid.* v. 66 There's a lot of atmosphere you couldn't get, anyway.

Atmospherics (ætmǫsfe·riks), *sb. pl.* [pl. of Atmospheric, after *acoustics*, etc.] Atmospheric disturbances of electrical origin causing interference with aerial communication, esp. in wireless telegraphy. Also occas. *sing.*

1913 *Year-bk. Wireless Telegr.* 334 No signal nor atmospheric can put it out of action. 1915 *Wireless World* Apr. 55/1 To protect the condenser from strong 'atmospherics', a spark gap should be connected to the two plates of the condenser. 1919 R. Stanley *Text-bk. Wireless Telegr.* I. 173 Irregular noises are produced in the receiver telephones which seriously interfere with the reception of the regular signals; they are due to 'Atmospherics', or 'strays', or Xs. 1922 *19th Cent.* Apr. 619 It was possible, atmospherics or no atmospherics, to communicate daily both ways between England and Australia.

Atmosteon (ætmǫ·stiǫn). *Ornith.* [f. Gr. ἀτμός air + ὀστέον bone.] Any ossified tube by which air passes into the bones of a bird; an air-bone.

1884 Coues *Key N. Amer. Birds* (ed. 2) 168 The siphon-like tube..may ossify..resulting in a neat tubular 'air-bone' or *atmosteon.*

Atocha (ătōᵘ·tʃă). [Sp.] Esparto. Also *attrib.* as *atocha grass, plant.*

1868 *Rep. U.S. Commissioner Agric.* (1869) 262 There are two classes of this plant, the 'atocha', properly so called, and the coarse or 'bastard' atocha...The atocha grass, which is called esparto, is not cut like ordinary grass, but is pulled up from its socket. *Ibid.* 264 It is at about this elevation [*sc.* 3,500 feet] where the snow usually commences, that the atocha plant ceases to grow.

Atoke (æ·tōᵘk). [ad. Gr. ἄτοκος, f. ἀ- priv. (A- 14) + τόκος birth.] The sexless part of certain polychætous worms. Hence **Atokal** (æ·tŏkăl) [-al] *a.*, non-sexual.

1903 J. S. Kingsley tr. *Hertwig's Zool.* 311 The atoke..forms chains of dimorphic individuals which later separate. 1904 *Jrnl. R. Microsc. Soc.* Apr. 183 The total length [of the marine worm palolo] averages 400 mm., about one-fourth of which is in the anterior atokal part.

Atomize, *v.* Add:

2. b. To reduce (a liquid) to very small particles or to the condition of spray. Hence **A·tomised** *ppl. a.* (Cf. Atomizer.)

1865 Morell Mackenzie in *Lancet* 25 Feb. 202/2 (*heading*) On the treatment of chronic disease of the lungs by the inhalation of atomised liquids. *Ibid.* 203/1 The author observed that his own atomiser is very simple and can be used very easily. The liquid is driven from a fine glass pipe on to a projection in a bell-shaped tube, by the descent of a piston. 1865 Williams *Ibid.* 203/2 He believed that atomising the fluids was unnecessary, on the ground that they could be introduced in the simplest manner by ordinary inhalation. 1866 Beigel *On Inhalation* v. 49 The minuteness of atomization. 1871 Holmes *Syst. Surg.* (ed. 2) IV. 530 The inhalation of 'atomised fluids', or spray. 1902 *Encycl. Brit.* XXXI. 646/1 Utilising the waste product [of petroleum] as fuel by spraying or atomizing it with steam.

Atonal (ătōᵘ·năl), *a.* *Mus.* [f. A- 14 + Tonal.] Applied to a style of composition in which there is no conscious reference to any scale or tonic. So **Atonality** (ætonæ·lĭti).

1922 A. E. Hull in *Musical Opinion* Oct. 48/1, I have been working for two years at a system of non-tonal harmony, which I had long been unable to christen. Now, after visiting no less than seven foreign countries I not only find that the thing is widely known as Atonality, but [etc.]. *Ibid.* 48/3 Keyboard chord-writing as well as linear, tonal as well as Atonal. 1923 *Mus. Assoc. Proc.* 1922–3 67 We find the principle of polytonality or atonality superseding the old key system. 1923 *Observer* 11 Nov. 8/4 Modern music in Vienna. 'Atonal' and otherwise. 1928 *Ibid.* 18 Mar. 12/5 His music is distinguished by simplicity, melody, and genuine feeling. Despite the dicta of the 'atonal' composers, significantly enough, he reverts to fugues with marked effect.

Atoxyl (ătǫ·ksil). *Chem.* [a. F. *atoxyle*, f. A- 14 + Tox(ic + -yl.] A compound of arsenic with an aniline derivative used hypodermically in skin diseases.

1906 *Daily Chron.* 18 Sept. 3/4 The treatment of the patients was based on the simultaneous use of atoxyl and strychnine. *Ibid.* 21 Dec. 5/3 Professor Koch decided to employ atoxyl injections of half a gramme. 1911 *Allbutt's Syst. Med.* IX. 104 Optic atrophy caused by arsenical injections, in the form of atoxyl. 1920 J. M. H. Macleod *Diseases of Skin* 111 Arsacetin and orsudan have the advantage over atoxyl of being more stable and capable of being boiled without decomposition.

Atriopore (ē·triopōᵊɹ). *Zool.* [f. L. Atrium + Gr. πόρος passage, Pore *sb.*[1]] The posterior opening of the atrium or cavity in the body of the lancelet.

1892 *Athenæum* 13 Aug. 227/2 There are no buccal cirri, and, so far as can be made out, no atriopore [in a certain specimen of Amphioxus]. 1896 *Boas' Text Book Zool.* 355.

Atrioventricular (ē·trio,ventri·kiŭlăɹ), *a.* [f. *atrio-*, comb. f. Atrium + Ventricular *a.*] Of or belonging to the atrial and ventricular cavities of the heart.

1879 *St. George's Hosp. Rep.* IX. 93 The heart showed..very slight thickening of the atrio-ventricular valves.

Atrochal (æ·trokăl), *a.* *Zool.* [f. A- 14 + Trochal *a.*] Having no definite rings of cilia.

1880 F. M. Balfour *Comp. Embryol.* I. 274 The atrochal forms are to be regarded as larvæ which never pass beyond the primitive stage of uniform ciliation. *Ibid.*, The atrochal larvæ are not common.

Atrophying (æ·trŏfi,iŋ), *ppl. a.* [f. Atrophy *v.* + -ing[2].] That atrophies.

Atrophying cirrhosis, cirrhosis characterized by shrinkage and shrivelling of the organ.

1886 *Brit. Med. Jrnl.* 2 Oct. 650/2 Atrophying cirrhosis was diagnosed.

Atta (æ·tă). *Anglo-Ind.* [Punjabi *aṭṭa.*] Wheaten flour or meal.

1860 Russell *Diary India* II. 206 Each man with his *viaticum* of atta in skin-bags tied over his hips. 1920 *Blackw. Mag.* Oct. 445/2 Sacks of atta for the troops.

Attaboy (æ·tăboi), *int.* *U.S.* Also **ata boy.** [Careless pron. of *that's the boy!*] An exclamation expressive of encouragement or admiration.

1917 C. Mathewson *Sec. Base Sloan* xxii. 298 'Ata boy!' called the Damascus catcher. 1925 H. L. Foster *Trop. Tramp Tourists* 101 The marines rose from their chairs to encourage the new performer: 'Attaboy, soldier! Attaboy! Shake 'em doggies!' 1926 S. Leacock *Winnowed Wisdom* 79 Full of pep they all shouted, 'Attaboy, Lizzie!' 1927 *Blackw. Mag.* July 4/2 Cries, also, of 'Attaboy!' leave no doubt that the greeting is not entirely British.

attrib. 1926 S. Leacock *Winnowed Wisdom* 73 The new Attaboy language.

Attach, *v.* Add:

6. b. *Mil.* and *Naval.* To allocate for service *to* a particular unit: chiefly *pass.*

1802 C. James *Milit. Dict.* s.v., Officers and non-commissioned officers are said to be attached to the..army, regiment, [etc.]..with which they are appointed to act. 1909 *Regulations for Mobilization* 8 The equipment..which he would take with him when transferred or attached to another unit.

Attaché case (ătæ·ʃeⁱ keⁱs). A small rectangular case (such as attachés use) for carrying papers, documents, and the like, usually made of leather, and often fitted with writing materials.

1904 *Army & Navy Co-op. Soc. Price List*, 'Attaché' cases. Green and brown leather, double-action lock. 1918 H. Walpole *Green Mirror* II. i. 146 The two young men in perfect attire and attaché cases.

Attachment. Add:

10. *Mil.* The fact or condition of being attached to a particular unit.

1909 *Regulations for Mobilization* 18 Units which do not exist as such in peace are completed in officers by special appointments made at the War Office, and as regards other ranks by attachments or transfers from existing units, and by reservists. 1914 *Daily Express* 5 Oct. 5/1 Each man wearing an armlet indicating his attachment to these special siege batteries.

Attack, *sb.* Add:

2. b. Lacrosse. *The attack*: the 'attack fields' collectively. *Attack field*: see quot. 1892.

1892 *Outdoor Games* 507 The players stand all down the field, from goal-keeper to goal-keeper, a defence man watching one of the opposite attack. *Ibid.* 508 The three men nearest the opponents' goal (they are called the 'home', first, second, and third, first being nearest the goal) should practice throwing at goal...The two players next nearest are called the 'attack fields'. 1902 *Westm. Gaz.* 28 Apr. 7/3 His place in the attack field.

7. *Mus.* [after It. *attacca.*] The action or manner of beginning a piece, passage, or phrase, in respect of precision and clarity.

1880 *Grove's Dict. Mus.* I. 100 *Attack*, a technical expression for decision and spirit in beginning a phrase or passage. 1891 *Durham Univ. Jrnl.* 11 Nov. 216 There was a certain want of precision in the attack. 1905 *Westm. Gaz.* 12 Dec. 3/2 Mr. Runcie has fancy, verve, and what artists call 'attack'.

Attack, *v.* Add:

7. *Mus. intr.* and *trans.* (See quot. and cf. prec.)

1835 *Court Mag.* VI. 264/1 The instruments do not *attack* properly—that is to say, they do not come in simultaneously with sufficient precision to form a sharp, crisp chord, as if proceeding from a single instrument.

Attap (æ·tăp). Also **atap, adap.** [Native word.] The name used in Malayo-Javanese regions for any palm-fronds used in thatching, *esp.* those of the palm *Nipa fruticans*; hence, a thatch made of these. Also *attrib.*

[1672 Baldæus *Ceylon* 164 Het Huys is van Leem gemaakt, ende gedekt met *Atap*, ofte bladeren von Palmeer-boomen.] 1817 Raffles *Java* I. iv. 166 In the maritime districts *atap*, or thatch, is made almost exclusively from the leaves of the *nipa* or *bilyu.* *Ibid.*, The leaves of the *gébang*..are too large and brittle to form durable *atap.* 1886 *Jrnl. Anthrop. Inst.* Feb. 293 The roof is thatched with the common Brettam attaps in the same way as Malay houses. 1897 *Blackw. Mag.* Nov. 637/2 Overhead lizards ran in the attap thatch. 1923 *Ibid.* May 647/2 A shed..thatched with attap palm. 1924 *Chambers's Jrnl.* 72/1 The atap-thatched, pile-perched native hutches. 1928 *Daily Express* 13 Mar. 12/2 The coolie women of Bangkok, who cook their food..over an open fire in front of their 'atap' houses.

Attempt, *sb.* Add:

2. b. A concrete result of an attempt.

1871 L. W. M. Lockhart *Fair to See* xxiii, His first attempt [*sc.* a letter] ran thus.

Attention. Add:

3. b. More widely: The action of taking special notice of a person, whether favourable or unfavourable. Often *pl.* euphemistically.

1771 *Town & Country Mag.* Jan. 12/1 The particular attention paid to her by a certain northern potentate. 1882 Gunter *Mr. Potter* II. viii, To shield her from the attentions of the thoughtless or the vicious. 1920 Rose Macaulay *Potterism* v. § 4. 187 An egotistic craving for attention, even unfavourable attention. 1929 *Morn. Post* 26 Mar. 14/5 By submitting to the attentions of a Roman officer.

5. b. *To stand* (*at, to*) *attention*: to stand in the military attitude assumed at the word of command 'Attention!' Also *to draw oneself up, spring*, etc. *to attention.*

1860 Whyte Melville *Holmby House* xviii, He..stood gaunt and dripping at 'attention'. 1866 — *Cerise* i, Like a soldier who springs to 'attention'. 1879 H. Hartigan *Stray Leaves* Ser. II. 146 He drew himself up to attention, and performed the lance exercise. *Ibid.* 181 The old man was standing at attention. 1892 Kipling & Balestier *Naulahka* 259 A trooper..stood to attention at the horse's head. 1893 *St. Nicholas Mag.* Jan. 182/1 He..stood attention' respectfully. 1895 *Cornhill Mag.* Dec. 633 He..saluted, and stood at attention. 1896 Merriman *Sowers* ix, The..keepers..standing stiffly to attention. 1899 *Allbutt's Syst. Med.* VIII. 8 Make the patient 'stand attention'.

Attentional (ăte·nʃənăl), *a.* [f. Attention + -al.] Of or pertaining to attention.

1901 Titchener *Exper. Psychol.* I. ii. 206 The experiments on attentional time-displacement form one of the most interesting..chapters of experimental psychology.

Attenuity (ætĕniū·ĭti). [f. Attenuate after *tenuity.*] = Tenuity I.

1830 J. Wilson in *Blackw. Mag.* XXVIII. 387 Not so much as the taperest wine-glass wire-woven into almost invisible attenuity. 1861 *Temple Bar* III. 437 No cotton-yarn of such attenuity as this can be..woven. 1898 *Echo* 22 June 1/4 Drawing his thin willowy form..to its full attenuity.

Attest, *v.* **5.** Add:

To enrol for military service (see quot. 1812 in Dict.); used esp. in connexion with the 'Derby Scheme' of 1915. Also *intr.* to enrol oneself as ready for military service when called up. Hence **Attested** *ppl. a.*

1915 Ld. Derby in *Times* 20 Oct. 10/1 They would be medically examined, and, if found fit, attested there and then. 1917 J. H. Worrall *Tribunal Hand-bk.* 128 Police magistrates who..will not..see that the attested man before them is shorn of justice, because, unfortunately for him, he attested. 1922 *Encycl. Brit.* XXX. 212/2 In Oct. 1915 the 'Derby Scheme' or 'Group System' was initiated by Lord Derby,..Between Oct. 25 and the middle of Dec. 2,000,000 men were attested under this system.

Attic, *sb.*[2] Add:

4. *Anat.* The upper part of the tympanum of the ear.

1890 Billings *Nat. Med. Dict.* (citing *Leidy*). 1891 *Med. Ann.* 159 Pathological Changes in the External 'Attic' of the Tympanic Cavity. 1901 Dorland *Med. Dict.* (ed. 2), *Attic*, the part of the tympanum that is situated above the atrium.

Attid (æ·tid), *sb.* and *a.* *Zool.* [ad. mod.L. systematic name *Attidæ.*] Any one of the family *Attidæ* of short-legged spiders; a jumping spider. Also as *adj.*

1889 in *Cent. Dict.* 1925 E. F. Norton *Fight for Everest 1924* 287 We found little Attid spiders, immature, minute.

Attingent, *a.* Delete † *Obs.* and add:

1895 Story-Maskelyne *Crystallogr.* ii. § 15. 16 To each octant there will correspond three adjacent octants, which have each one axial plane in common with the original octant; three attingent octants, in contact with it only along an axis.

Attitude. Add:

2. c. *Aeronautics.* See quots.

1910 R. Ferris *How it Flies* 455 *Attitude*, the position of a plane as related to the line of its travel. 1914 *Roy. Engineers Jrnl.* Nov. 311 *Attitude*, an aeroplane's or wing's position relative to the direction of motion through the air.

Attraction. Add: **10. attraction sphere**, = *Centrosphere.

1896 E. B. Wilson *Cell in Developm. & Inher.* 36 The centrosome..lies outside, though near, the nucleus, in the cyto-reticulum, surrounded by a granular, reticular, or radiating area of the latter known as the *attraction-sphere* or *centrosphere.* *Ibid.* Gloss. 334 *Attraction-sphere*, the central mass of the aster from which the rays proceed.

Attributal (ætribiū·tăl), *a.* [f. Attribute *sb.* + -al.] Of the nature of an attribute.

1894 *Standard* 30 July 6/6 Why do not Welshmen take as surnames..the attributal adjectives by which they are known? William Thomas, distinguished by Tynawern (the house in the wood) would always be identified as William Tynawern. 1902 *Jrnl. Amer. Folk-lore* Jan.–Mar. 14 It is oftentimes difficult to discover their identities, since they bear many attributal or descriptive names.

Attributeless (æ·tribiutlės), *a.* [f. Attribute *sb.* + -less.] Without attributes.

1894 *Thinker Mag.* VI. 448 The Vedântin is more drawn by the fascination of that attributeless immensity. 1924 *Expositor* Feb. 107 Esoterically he holds that nothing is real but the attributeless Brahman.

Attuition (ætiu,i·ʃən). *Psychol.* [f. L. *ad* (see Ad- *prefix*) + Tuition.] A hypothetical apprehension higher in order than mere animal sensation and lower than human perception; animal consciousness. Hence **Attui·tional** *a.* So **Attuent** (ætiū·ent), *a.* [L. *tuēnt-*, pr. pple. of *tuērī* to look at], that has the function of, or is characterized by attuition. **Attuite** (ætiū·it) *v. trans.*, to become conscious of (an object) by attuition. **Attu·it**, something of which one becomes conscious by attuition. **Attu·itively** *adv.*, by attuition.

1884 S. S. Laurie *Metaph. Nova et Vetusta* 6 *note*, This word (Attuition) is here coined, in order to indicate that state of Consciousness which lies between Sensation-proper and Perception-proper. *Ibid.* 11, I may now define *Attuition* to be the reflex co-ordination of the elements or units of Sensation into an image or synopsis: it is a synthesis *in* and *for* the Conscious Subject. *Ibid.*, The range and character of attuitional intelligence. *Ibid.* 29 The Will then has now affirmed the attuited totality in perception as a one totality. *Ibid.* 49 The Attuent consciousness at the moment of receiving the 'impression' of Extension, locates it as outside itself. *Ibid.* 143 An animal is attuitively conscious of the *à posteriori* categories, but it cannot categorize, because it cannot affirm. They are present to it as sense-attuits. 1888 Martineau *Study Relig.* I. II. i. 180 In the higher quadrupeds..a state is reached which may be called Attuition, marked by discrimination of particular objects from each other in space..but without corresponding discrimination of them from the attuent subject. *Ibid.* 184 How I should feel if I were..reduced to the 'attuent' condition, I find it impossible to judge. 1902 *Encycl. Brit.* XXX. 677/2 Supposing..that a man, or a dog, through association 'attuites' sequence and invariableness of succession.

Attune, *v.* Add:

4. *Wireless Telegr.* To tune in. (Now *disused.*)

1900 R. Routledge *Discov. 19th C.* (ed. 13) 546 A Geissler tube, when its circuit is properly attuned, can be lighted up by the magneto-electric disturbances propagated without material contacts, and this itself would constitute a method of signalling to a distance. 1901 *Westm. Gaz.* 23 Dec. 5/1 The message..would reach every attuned recorder within that distance. 1902 *Ibid.* 30 Apr. 12/2 Inventions covering the attuning of transmitters and receivers.

Atypical (æ-, ēti·pikăl), *a.* [f. A- 14 + Typical *a.*] Not typical; not conformable to the ordinary type. Hence **Aty·pically** *adv.*, in an atypical manner.

1886 Fagge *Princ. Med.* I. 100 Carcinomata can be..distinguished from other epithelial growths by their being 'atypical'. 1916 *Times* 25 Oct. 7/3 The cases up to this time were mostly mild and atypical. 1918 *Saturday Westm. Gaz.* 13 Apr. 11/1 She,..something atypically for a woman, appears to be more interested in places than people.

Aubergine. Add:

b. A purple colour resembling that of the fruit. Also *attrib.* and as *adj.*

Aubergine purple, a shade of purple found in Oriental porcelain.

1895 *Windsor Mag.* I. 109/1 An aubergine silk lining. 1898 *Daily News* 29 Sept. 3/4 Cashmere in a tone of Burgundy that is sometimes called aubergine, from the deep reddish mauve of the vegetable. 1903 *Daily Chron.* 31 Oct. 8/4 Aubergine..is a tint with some claret and a touch of violet in it. 1909 *Ibid.* 29 Jan. 4/5 Aubergine coloured cloth. 1927 *Daily Tel.* 5 Apr. 13/3 Examples of the Ming dynasty..vases, jardinières, bowls,..an aubergine fish-bowl.

Aubrietia (ǭbri,ī·ʃiă). Also very freq. in erron. form **aubretia.** [mod. L., f. the name of Claude *Aubriet*, after whom it was named by Adanson in 1763: see -ia[1].] A genus of spring-flowering dwarf perennial plants belonging to the order *Cruciferæ*, of trailing habit, bearing flowers of various shades of purple, grown as a rock plant or garden edging; also, a plant of this genus.

1829 Loudon *Encycl. Plants* (1836) 544. 1883 F. M. Peard *Contrad.* I. 227 Lilac aubretias clamber up the meadows behind Titian's house. 1911 A. Marshall *Eldest Son* xxx, The station-master's arabis and aubrietia..were making a fine show.

Aubusson (obüsoñ). [Name of a manufacturing town, dept. Creuse, France.] Tapestry made at Aubusson, *esp.* a tapestry carpet made of this, more explicitly *Aubusson carpet.*

1851 *Illustr. Exhibitor* p. xxx. 1866 *Argosy* Jan. 142 The elegant Aubusson carpet. 1900 El. Glyn *Visits Elis.* (1906) 110 The room..is hung with aubusson. 1918 Vachell *Some Happenings* xii. 194 Throwing delicate shadows upon the Aubusson carpet. 1927 J. B. Priestley *Adam in Moonshine* vi. 101 Wasn't that the dreadful hairy, smelly one [a Russian conspirator] who spoilt your Aubusson?

Au courant (o kuraṅ). [Fr., = in the (regular) course (of events).] Acquainted with what is going on: const. *with* or *of.*

1849–50 THACKERAY *Pendennis* xv, Doctor Portman and Smirke were both cautious of informing the widow of the constant outbreak of calumny which was pursuing poor Pen, though Glanders, who was a friend of the house, kept him *au courant*. 1885 *Law Q. Rev.* Apr. 138 To keep themselves fairly *au courant* with what was being decided in the various Courts. 1928 *Daily Tel.* 23 Oct. 11/3 It would have been wiser if the United States had been kept au courant of the negotiations from the very outset.

Auction, *sb.* 5. Add: *auction-room, -sale*; **auction bridge, pool**: see *BRIDGE *sb.*[3], *POOL *sb.*
1779 SHERIDAN *Critic* I. i, Like the bidders in their own auction rooms. 1791 BOSWELL *Johnson* 8 Apr. 1775, [That] a certain celebrated actor was just fit to stand at the door of an auction-room with a long pole, and cry 'Pray gentlemen, walk in'. 1898 *Daily News* 3 Mar. 3/3 Auction sale of rights of patronage was absolutely prohibited.

Auctorial (ǫktō°riăl), *a.* [f. L. *auctor* AUTHOR: see -ORIAL.] Of or pertaining to an author. (Cf. AUTHORIAL.)
1821 *Examiner* 300/1 Pricked to it..by auctorial jealousy. 1868 *Blackw. Mag.* July 74/2 Miss Hannah More's auctorial merits excited Peter's critical ire. 1900 SPIELMANN *Ruskin* 65 What is his reflection on his own auctorial life? 1926 A. BRENT SMITH *Studies & Caprices* 153 Auctorial bias.

Audad, var. *AOUDAD.

Audile (ǭ·dəil), *a.* and *sb.* [Badly f. L. *audīre* to hear + -ILE.] **A.** *adj.* Pertaining to or received through the auditory nerves. Of a person: Capable of hearing.
1897 *19th Cent.* Aug. 229 The phenomena..may be dichotomised as (1) audile, (2) visual. The audile subdivide into (1) Footsteps. (2) Voices..(3) Raps..(4) and (5) Noises..(6) A detonating noise. 1909 *Daily Chron.* 22 Feb. 4/7 Unless you are a microcephalous idiot, you are either Audile, Motile, or Visile.

B. *sb.* A person in whom auditory images are predominant over motile and visual presentations.
1886 *Mind* July 415 M. Paulhan, an audile, declares..he can represent the auditory images of *i* and *u* while the motor presentation of *a* is being presented. 1917 J. ADAMS *Student's Guide* 23 Some prefer to learn through the eye, others like to learn through the ear, still others through the sense of touch. The first kind are called *visuals*, the second *audiles*, the third *tactiles*.

Audion (ǭ·diǫn). *Wireless Telegr.* [Coined in 1906 by C. D. Babcock, assistant to the inventor, Lee de Forest; f. L. *audīre* to hear + *-on*.] A trade name for a three-electrode thermionic valve, used as a detector and an amplifier.
1915 E. H. ARMSTRONG (*title*) Some Recent Developments in the Audion Receiver. 1916 *Chambers's Jrnl.* 63/1 The audion, or wireless lamp, which plays such a part in wireless telephony between Arlington, Hawaii, California, Paris and other distant parts. 1926 *Encycl. Brit.* New Suppl. I. 838/1 De Forest, Lee...The most important of his inventions was the Audion amplifier, which made possible long-distance telephony.

Audist (ǭ·dist). [Badly f. L. *audīre* to hear + -IST.] (See quot.) Cf. VISUALIST 1.
1895 *Pop. Sci. Monthly* Apr. 732 'Audists'—those whose memories were of things heard, whose auditory sense was paramount.

Audition. Add:
1. b. A trial by hearing of an applicant for employment as a vocalist or instrumentalist.
1908 *Evening News* 18 June 3/3 When she was nineteen she was given an 'audition' at the Santa Cecilia Conservatoire. 1926 *Westm. Gaz.* 30 Jan., The plaintiff gave auditions to several girl saxophonists to fill the vacancy.
c. *Chromatic* (or *coloured*) *audition*: the mental impression of a colour excited by sound.
1898 *Daily News* 6 May 4/7 'Coloured audition' is another mental phenomenon.

Auditize (ǭ·ditəiz), *v.* *Psychol.* [f. L. *audit-*, ppl. stem of *audīre* to hear + -IZE.] *trans.* To image or represent in sounds. Hence **Auditization** (ǭ:ditəizē¹·ʃən), the action or process of auditizing.
1900 *Amer. Jrnl. Psychol.* XII. 119 Particular parts of a context are often visualized as printed, or heard out separately ('auditized'). 1901 *Ibid.* 309 That in silent reading there is a similar phrase motorization (or auditization, or both as is most usual) following behind the eye.

Auditor. 4. Add: Also see quot.
1919 MOORE-ANDERSON *Sir Robert Anderson* i. 4 Of his University life [Trin. Coll., Dublin] he..cherished pleasant memories..associated with the College Historical Society, of which he became Auditor, a position corresponding to that of President of the Union at Oxford or Cambridge.

Augmentor (ǫgme·ntǫɹ). *Anat.* [f. AUGMENT *v.* + -OR.] Applied to the nerves by the stimulation of which the cardiac contractions are increased.
1902 *Nature* 6 Nov. 3 The anabolic inhibitory and the katabolic augmentor parts. 1907 *Practitioner* Nov. 692.

Augustal, *a.* Delete † *Obs.* and add: *Augustal Prefect* (L. *præfectus Augustalis*), the title of the prefect of Egypt.
1731 *Hist. Litteraria* II. 57 The great power that was lodged in the Augustal Praefect of Egypt. 1907 W. G. HOLMES *Age of Justinian & Theodora* vii. II. 475 The Augustal Praefect resigned the control of all Egypt for that of Alexandria and the adjacent country.

Augustanism (ǫgʊ·stăniz'm). [f. AUGUSTAN *a.* + -ISM.] The condition of being Augustan.
1903 T. WATTS-DUNTON in *Chambers's Cycl. Eng. Lit.* III. 5/1 [Gray's] chief poem, the famous elegy, furnishes a striking proof of the poet's slavery to Augustanism.

Aul, var. *AOUL.

Aularian, *a.* Add: Pertaining to or characteristic of a hall in a university, esp. in respect of its power of self-administration.
c 1849 *Stranger's Guide Oxford* 92 *note*, As the foundation of this establishment marks a new era in the academical annals of this University, it is not without reason,..that,..the name of *New College* should still attach to this erection. Before this period, however, the Aularian system was generally prevalent. 1895 RASHDALL *Universities Europe Mid. Ages* II. 624 Aularian Statutes at Oxford. *Ibid.* 626 Even these Oxford Statutes which had for their very object to assert the authority of the University and of the Principals contain traces of the old Aularian self-government.

Au naturel (o natyrɛ̄l). [Fr.] In the natural state; cooked plainly; uncooked; undressed.
1845 BREGION & MILLER *Pract. Cook* 40 *Au naturel.*—Plain done. 1862 THACKERAY *Philip* xvi, I..forget whether it was a cold dagger *au naturel*, or a dish of hot coals *à la Romaine*, of which they partook. 1905 MRS. H. WARD *Marriage W. Ashe* II. x, You would have preferred ankles *au naturel*? 1908 *Practitioner* Apr. 563 In Bulgaria, where milk..is never taken *au naturel*.

Aunt. Add: **1. c.** *U.S.* (See quots.)
1835 LONGSTREET *Georgia Scenes* 110 'There they are, Aunt Glory'. *Footnote*: 'Aunt' and 'Mauma'..are terms of respect commonly used by children to aged negroes. 1864 J. T. TROWBRIDGE *Cudjo's Cave* xxxiv. (1868) 160 'Where is Aunt Deb?'..'Here I is!'..It was the voice of the old negress, who had hid herself in the chambers. 1869 *Atlantic Monthly* Oct. 479/2 A pleasant, industrious 'Aunt Sally,' a mulatto. 1888 FARMER *Americanisms*, *Aunt*, a familiar name often given in the States and West Indies to negresses advancing in age. 1904 HARBEN *Georgians* 106 A negro woman, Aunt Amanda,..passed in and out.
5. *My* (*sainted*) *aunt!* a trivial exclamation.
1888 *Boy's Own Paper* Summer No. 35/2 'My aunt!' exclaimed Guy, with a start. 1888 KIPLING *Soldiers Three*, etc. (1889) 180 Prince Kraft a stable-boy—Oh, my Aunt! 1921 P. G. WODEHOUSE *Jill Reckless* 301 'My sainted aunt!' he said slowly.

Auntie. b. (Earlier U.S. examples.)
1835 J. H. INGRAHAM *South-West* II. 241 Nor are planters indifferent to the comfort of their gray-headed slaves..They always address them in a mild and pleasant manner as 'Uncle' or 'Aunty'. 1852 *Knickerbocker Mag.* Oct. XL. 326 So long as the race of good old colored 'aunties' do the cooking. 1865 G. W. NICHOLS *Story Gt. March* 132 [To negro-woman] 'What was it that struck you, aunty?'

Au pair (o pɛ̄r). [Fr., = on equality.] Applied to an arrangement between two parties by which mutual services are rendered without consideration of money payment.
1928 *Sunday Express* 22 July 15 To have a German lady on 'au pair' terms in my house to teach German to my children in return for education in English.

Aura. Add: A supposed subtle emanation from and enveloping living persons and things, viewed by mystics as consisting of the essence of the individual, serving as the medium for the operation of mesmeric and similar influences. So **Aural** *a.*[2]
1874 P. B. RANDOLPH *Seership* 77 Peculiar substances can be charged with the efflux or aura of the human being. *Ibid.* 78 The substances thus chargeable..can be filled with the aura of hadean lust and passion. 1903 BEATRICE HARRADEN *Kath. Frensham* 35 My aura does not match with Marianne's aura. 1918 VIOLET TWEEDALE *Veiled Woman* vii. 83 [His] personality happens to be very distasteful to me. Our auras don't blend. 1920 ROSE MACAULAY *Potterism* III. i, Unless..the immortal soul wraps itself about in some aural vapour that takes the form it wore on earth.

Aurantia (ǫræ·nʃiă). [L. *aurantia*: see ORANGE.] An orange-yellow dye colour.
1890 WOODBURY *Encycl. Photogr.*, *Aurantia*, a beautiful orange dye, the ammonia salt of an acid. It is used as a sensitiser in orthochromatic photography...To make an aurantia screen for orthochromatic photographic purposes. 1899 *Orthochromatic Phot.* (ed. Tennant) 281 Aurantia is an orange-yellow coal-tar dye much used in dyeing leathers.

Aureole (ǭ·riǭ³l), *v.* [f. AUREOLE *sb.*] *trans.* To encircle with or as with an aureole or halo. Chiefly in *pa. pple.*
1868 *Macm. Mag.* July 188 Their forms are intertwined with rainbows and aureoled with light. 1896 MARY COWDEN-CLARKE *My Long Life* 13 His seraph-like face,..aureoled by its golden hair. 1905 C. KERNAHAN *Visions* 240 The cloud-rack which aureoled the moon.

Aureus (ǭ·ri,ŏs). Pl. **aurei** (-əi). [L., subst. use (sc. *nummus*) of *aureus* golden, f. *aurum* gold.] An ancient Roman gold coin of the value of 25 denarii or 100 sestertii.
1609 HOLLAND *Amm. Marcell.* XX. iv. 149 He..promised unto them all throughout five *aurei* apeece. *a* 1700 EVELYN *Diary* 6 May an. 1645, As to Coins and Medails, 10 Asses make the Roman Denarius, 5 the Quinarius, 10 Denarii an Aureus. 1884 *Encycl. Brit.* XVII. 653/1 Augustus struck the aureus at 40 to the pound, equal to 25 denarii at 84 to the pound. 1895 G. ALLEN *The Woman who did* xv, His profile was clear-cut, like Trajan's on an aureus.

Au revoir (o rəvwā·r). [Fr., = lit. 'to the seeing again', i.e. in anticipation of seeing (meeting) you again.] An expression implying farewell for the present; hence as *sb.*, a farewell of this kind.
1694 N. H. *Ladies Dict.* 15/1 He must kiss his Landlady .., and so parting, says *a Revoir*, Madam, till I see you again. 1761 CHESTERF. *Lett. to his Son* 6 Dec., *Au revoir*, as Sir Fopling says, and God bless you. 1800 MAR. EDGEWORTH *Belinda* xv, Instead of adieu, I shall only say *au revoir*. 188. *Popular Song*. Say au revoir but not goodbye. 1905 *Daily Mail* 5 Aug. 6/1 The King and Queen, after an au revoir of ceremonious courtesy, left for their own yacht.

Auric (ǭ·rik), *a.*[2] [f. AURA + -IC.] Of or pertaining to an aura; aural.
1889 in *Cent. Dict.* 1910 *Westm. Gaz.* 13 Apr. 5/2 An auric veil. 1917 *14 Lessons in Yogi Philos.* 66 Providing he understands the language of the Auric colours.

Aurignacian (ǫrinyē¹·ʃăn), *a.* [f. the place-name *Aurignac* (France).] Of or pertaining to the Aurignac cave of the Pyrenees; belonging to the *Aurignac era* or *period*, that indicated by the remains and works of art found in the cave.
1920 J. RITCHIE *Influence Man Anim. Life Scot.* VI. iii. 344 The Aurignacian painting of two Reindeer fronting each other. 1920 *Q. Rev.* Oct. 377 The course of Art, from the Aurignacian era (circa 35,000 B.C.) till to-day. 1926 *Times Lit. Suppl.* 2 Sept., During the greater part of the upper palæolithic age the culture of Europe was what is termed Aurignacian.

Ausaba, var. *AUSUBO.

Auslaut (au·slaut). *Philol.* [G., f. *aus-* denoting termination + *laut* sound.] The final sound of a syllable or word.
1892 *Classical Rev.* Feb. 3/2 It is further probable that the form *-endus* for *-vendus* arose primarily in verbal roots with vocalic auslaut.

Ausonian (ǭsō³·niăn), *a.* and *sb.* [f. L. *Ausonia* Lower Italy, poet. Italy, Gr. Αὐσονία poet. Italy, f. Αὔσων, son of Ulysses, who was fabled to have settled there.] Of or pertaining to Ausonia or to the Ausonians, the primitive inhabitants of middle and lower Italy; hence, Italian. Also *sb.* a native of Ausonia, an Italian.
1667 MILTON *P. L.* I. 739 And in Ausonian land Men called him Mulciber. 1819 BYRON *Proph. Dante* II. 131 The Ausonian soil. 1827 K. DIGBY *Broadst. Hon.* (1848) III. 326 Ausonian skies. 1833 TENNYSON *Pal. Art* 111 Or..stay'd the Ausonian king to hear Of wisdom and of law. 1876 DISRAELI *Let. to Lady Chesterfield* 31 Mar. in *Life* (1920) V. xii. 472 The spring of Ausonian lands. 1882 *Encycl. Brit.* XIV. 344/2 The Auruncans, or Ausonians as they were termed by Greek writers.

Aussie (ǫ·si). [Hypocoristic f. *Australian*: see -IE.] An Australian; esp. in *pl.* the Australian troops which took part in the war of 1914–18.
1918 (*title*) Aussie. The Australian Soldiers' Magazine. *Ibid.* 2/1 A certain Aussie Unit. 1927 *Daily Express* 30 May 17/1 Aussies in Singapore. The match between the Australian cricket team and Singapore..ended on Saturday.

Austenian (ǫstī·niăn), *a.* and *sb.* **A.** *adj.* Of or pertaining to Jane Austen, novelist, 1775–1817, or her writings. **B.** *sb.* = *AUSTENITE[1]. So **Austenish** (ǭ·stěniʃ) *a.*, characteristic of Jane Austen's work. **Austenite**[1] (ǭ·stěnəit), an admirer of Jane Austen's writings.
1898 J. JACOBS *Jane Austen's Emma* Introd., If 'Emma' is not the most striking of Jane Austen's works, it is the most Austenish. 1901 *Westm. Gaz.* 11 Dec. 3/1 The Austenian topography seems to me tolerably complete. 1903 *Daily Chron.* 16 May 3/7 With Mr. Perugini Austenites will have a quarrel. 1928 *Observer* 22 Jan. 6 The claim that this unknown book is at least better than 'Sense and Sensibility' is calculated to prejudice Austenians against it from the outset.

Austenite[2] (ǭ·stěnəit). *Metallurgy.* [f. the name of Sir Roberts *Austen*.] = TROOSTITE 2. Hence **Austeni·tic** *a.*, of, pertaining to, or characteristic of austenite.
1902 [see TROOSTITE 2]. 1905 *Nature* 18 May 69/1 The polyhedral or 'austenitic' type of structure has never been obtained alone in a pure carbon steel...The austenitic structure appears to be that of the nose of the tool in actual use. 1927 *Observer* 11 Dec. 23 The so-called 'austenitic' varieties of corrosion-resisting steels.

Austinian (ǫsti·niăn), *a.* Of or pertaining to John Austin (1790–1859) and his theory of government. Hence **Austi·nianism.**
1882 *Encycl. Brit.* XIV. 359/1 So far as the mere size of the community is concerned, there is no difficulty in applying the Austinian theory. 1917 LASKI *Stud. Probl. Sovereignty* ii. 66 It goes back to that passionate Erastianism of Luther which was the only answer he could make to the Austinianism of Rome. 1921 *Contemp. Rev.* Dec. 858 The unified, mechanical, Austinian State.

Austral, *a.* Add: Of or pertaining to Australia or Australasia.
1823 WENTWORTH *Australasia* 21 Grant that yet an Austral Milton's song..flow deep and rich along;—An Austral Shakspeare rise. 1855 W. HOWITT *Two Years in Victoria* I. 43 Every servant in this Austral Utopia thinks himself a gentleman. 1898 E. E. MORRIS (*title*) Austral English. A Dictionary of Australian Words, Phrases, and Usages. 1904 *Westm. Gaz.* 30 Mar. 7/2 The Austral Club at 44, Queen's House, St. James' Court, Buckingham Gate. 1912 (*title*) The Austral Avian Record. A scientific journal devoted primarily to the study of the Australian avifauna.

Australasiatic (ǭstrălē¹ʃi,æ·tik), *a.* [f. *Australasia* (see AUSTRALASIAN) + ASIATIC *a.*] Consisting of or characterized by a mixture of Australian and Asiatic elements.
1819 *New Whig Guide* in *Blackw. Mag.* V. 96 Craf-callee, which is a kind of Australasiatic Delos. 1890 *Cornhill Mag.* July 98 It was neither Cockney nor Yankee, but a nasal blend of both..: in a word, it was Australasiatic of the worst description.

Australian, *a.* Add: **b.** *Australian ballot* (see quot. 1903).
1888 *Nation* (N.Y.) 2 Aug. 91/2 By introducing the secret 'Australian ballot' in Congressional elections..the use of bribery in the choice of Congressmen might be discouraged to some extent. 1889 *Boston Alderm. pamphlet* Title-p., The so-called Australian ballot law. 1903 A. B. HART *Actual Government* 74 The so-called Australian ballot

system, under which all the candidates appear upon one ballot, prepared and distributed by the state, and the voter indicates on the ballot his choice of candidates.

Australianism (ǫstrē¹·liăniz'm). [f. AUSTRALIAN + -ISM.] An idiom or mode of expression peculiar to Australian English. So **Australasianism.**
1891 *Daily News* 26 June 5/2 He appears to think that our speech is in danger of being invaded by Australianisms. 1891 *Harper's Mag.* July 215/1 The coming degradation of the English language by the invasion of Australasianisms. 1905 *Daily Chron.* 22 Nov. 6/7 There are 'Australianisms' enough to make a dictionary an essential for the proper understanding of an Antipodean journal.

Australianize (ǫstrē¹·liănəiz), *v.* [f. AUSTRALIAN + -IZE.] *trans.* To naturalize as an Australian; to make Australian in habits, customs, etc.
1883 *St. James's Gaz.* 10 May, Are the latter wronged..in having to become for instance, 'Australianized'? 1888 D. B. W. SLADEN *Australian Ballads* (ed. 2) 280 Even in his own particular line of 'Australianised Calverley'. 1908 SIR H. JONES in Hetherington *Life & Lett.* (1924) 213 She is, I think, the wife of an old Scot who has been Australianized.

Au·strianize, *v.* [f. AUSTRIAN *a.* + -IZE.] *trans.* To convert into an Austrian type; to affect with Austrian methods.
1860 LOWELL *Election Nov.* Pr. Wks. 1890 V. 39 Speech is no longer free, the post office is Austrianized.

Austro- (ǭ·strǫ), comb. form of *Austria*.
1851 *Fraser's Mag.* Feb. 141/2 The Austro-Russian ascendancy over Germany. 1866 *Macm. Mag.* XIV. 387 The state of public opinion which preceded the Austro-Prussian war. 1868 *Appleton's Amer. Cycl.* 57/2 The whole Austrian monarchy is now officially called the Austro-Hungarian empire. 1904 *Life of Hugh Price Hughes* x. (1905) 233 *note*, The Austro-Hungarian Club, whose evil practises were notorious even in Soho. 1910 *Westm. Gaz.* 9 Apr. 2/1 The links between Italy and her ally can hardly be strengthened without provoking a fresh outburst of Austrophobia in Italy, or weakened without making the Austrophobes rather more dangerous. 1918 *Current History* May p. vi, Our exaggerated Austrophilism. 1920 *Glasgow Herald* 6 Apr. 7 Austrophile inhabitants. 1920 *Q. Rev.* July 204 The endeavours of far-seeing Austro-German patriots. 1921 *Contemp. Rev.* Oct. 493 Carducci, the most prominent of Austrophobes.

Ausubo (ausū·bo). Also **ausaba.** [W. Indian native name.] The name, used in Porto Rico, of the mastic tree, *Sideroxylon fœtidissimum*; also, the timber obtained from this tree.
1900 *Engineering Mag.* XIX. 693 The wood may be one of several native varieties, probably ausaba—a hard, tough, and durable timber.

Authentic, *a.* 9. Add: Also, composed in an authentic mode. *Authentic cadence*: that form of perfect cadence in which the (major) chord of the dominant immediately precedes that of the tonic. Opp. to PLAGAL.
1806 CALLCOTT *Mus. Gram.* 160 The Dominant..derives its name from the ancient Church Tones, in which it was the Fifth in the Authentic, and the Octave in the Plagal Scales, but always a Fifth above the final or modern Tonic. 1873 [see Dict.]. 1880 *Grove's Dict. Mus.* I. 105/2 'Ein feste Burg' and 'Eisenach' are examples of 'authentic' melodies, and the Old 100th and Hanover of 'plagal' ones. *Ibid.* II. 18/1 When first employed in polyphonic music, the Authentic scale was usually transposed.

Authigenic (ǭþidʒe·nik), *a.* *Geol.* [f. Gr. αὐθιγενής born on the spot, native + -IC.] Originating where found.
1890 C. R. VAN HISE in *Bulletin Geol. Soc. Amer.* I. 231 It has been seen that much if not all of the mica is authigenic. 1893 GEIKIE *Text-bk. Geol.* (ed. 3) 65 *note*, Such crystals, which are obviously more ancient than those forming the general mass of the rock, have been called *allogenic*, while those which belong to the time of formation of the rock, or to some subsequent change within the rock, are known as *authigenic*.

Author, *sb.* 6. Add: Frequent in appos. use, as *author-actor, -artist, -manager*.
1835 *Court Mag.* VI. 51/1 His peculiarity as an author-actor. 1898 *Daily News* 21 May 2/2 My friend the author-statesman. 1903 *Book Lover* Sept. 4/1 The author-artist has been as successful with his pen as with his brush. 1905 *Daily Chron.* 16 Dec. 8/5 The brilliant young author-manager. 1909 *Westm. Gaz.* 15 Dec. 1/2 There was only one author-producer in his experience in whose judgment the actor could always trust implicitly.

Authoritarianism (ǭþǫritē°·riăniz'm). [f. AUTHORITARIAN + -ISM.] Authoritarian principles.
1914 STREETER *Restatement & Reunion* ii. 47 Logical arguments in defence of authoritarianism. 1927 W. R. SELBIE in *British Weekly* 30 June 285/3 A decided drift towards authoritarianism, whether Catholic or fundamentalist.

Autism (ǭ·tiz'm). *Psychol.* [ad. mod.L. *autismus* (also used), f. Gr. αὐτός self + -ISM.] Morbid admiration of oneself. Hence **Autistic** *a.*, characterized by this; also **Auti·stically** *adv.*
1912 BLEULER in *Amer. Jrnl. Insanity* LXIX. 874 When we look more closely we find amongst all normal people many and important instances where thought is divorced both from logic and from reality. I have called these forms of thinking *autistic*, corresponding to the idea of schizophrenic autismus. *Ibid.* 884 The unconscious can think logically or autistically. 1912 A. HOCH *Ibid.* 888 The chief traits which had existed before the mental breakdown were those which I at that time called the shut-in tendencies—tendencies to which Professor Bleuler has recently applied the term autism. 1923 tr. *Jung's Analytical Psychology* 203 Autism (Bleuler) = Auto-eroticism (Freud). For some time I have employed the concept of *introversion* for this condition. 1917 tr. *O. Pfister* in W. McDougall *Outline Abnormal Psychol.* (1926) 452 If an idea accompanied by strong emotion is repressed and fortified by its autistic gain of pleasure.

Auto (ǭ·to), *sb.*, abbreviation of AUTOMOBILE *sb.* after F. *auto*; also *attrib.* and *Comb.* See also *AUTO-[2].
1899 *Boston Herald* 9 July 6/3 The accident to Mr. W. K. Vanderbilt's 'auto'. 1902 *Aeronautical World* (U.S.) 1 Oct. 60/1 Cycles, autos and all other contrivances for rapid transit. 1909 *Westm. Gaz.* 12 Oct. 5/4 A mysterious automan. 1910 *Daily Chron.* 12 Mar. 6/4 The auto-manufacturing business. 1915 *Literary Digest* 4 Sept. 467/1 Busy autos and delivery wagons are about all the time. 1927 *Blackw. Mag.* Nov. 646/2 The auto-trip to Ixtlan del Rio. *Ibid.*, The auto stage man informed me that he would leave at eight in the morning. 1928 *Sunday Express* 24 June 8/2, I was raised in Canada sixty odd years ago, when..the country was not safe for slick auto-tourists.

Auto (ǭ·to), *v.* *U.S.* Shortened form of AUTOMOBILE *v.* Hence **Autoing** (ǭ·toiŋ), *vbl. sb.*
1909 *Cent. Dict.* Suppl., *Autoing*, the use of automobiles for business or pleasure traveling. 1919 MENCKEN *Amer. Lang.* 110 *Auto* is almost unknown [in England], and with it the verb *to auto*.

Auto-. Read **Auto-**[1] and add: In free composition as a prefix element, its chief meanings are: (*a*) of oneself, one's own; self-; (*b*) self-produced or -induced, (pathologically) within the body or organism; (*c*) spontaneous, self-acting, automatic (cf. esp. b below).

Autacanthid (ǭtăkæ·nþid), *a.* *Zool.* [Gr. ἄκανθα spine], of a starfish, having spines on special plates, as distinguished from 'typacanthid'. **Auto-a·bstract,** a speaker's own abstract of an address or speech prepared for publication. **Autocata·lysis** *Chem.*, catalysis of a substance by one of its own products; hence **Autocataly·tic** *a.* **Autoclastic** (-klæ·stik), *a.* *Geol.* [CLASTIC *a.*], of a rock, composed of its own fragments produced by crushing or granulation. **Autocytotoxin** (-səitotǫ·ksin) [CYTOTOXIN], a cytotoxin formed in the body. **Au:todiagno·sis,** diagnosis of one's own disease; hence **Au:todiagno·stic** *a.*, of or pertaining to diagnosis. **Au:todige·stion** = *AUTOLYSIS. **Au:tohypno·sis** [HYPNOSIS 2], **Autohy·pnotism,** a self-induced hypnotic condition. **Au:tohypnotiza·tion,** the inducing of hypnosis by auto-suggestion. **Auto-infe·ction,** infection from within the organism, self-infection; so **Auto-infe·ctive** *a.*, **Auto-infe·ctant** *sb.* **Auto-inocula·tion,** inoculation of a person with a virus from his own body. **Auto-into·xicant,** a toxic substance generated in the system. **Auto-intoxica·tion,** poisoning by or resulting from toxin produced within the body. Also *fig.* **Automorph** (ǭ·tomǫɹf), *Math.* [Gr. μορφή form], (see quot.). **Autopho·tograph** = *autoradiograph* (see below). **Autopoi·soning,** poisoning caused by a virus formed within the body. **Autopoi·sonous** *a.*, that is poisonous to the organism within which it is formed. **Autora·diograph,** a photograph or picture of a mineral or other object produced by the radio-action of the thing itself on a sensitive surface. **Au·toscript,** a communication received by a medium by means of the planchette. **Autosoteric** (-sote·rik), *a.* [Gr. σωτηρία salvation], relating to salvation by oneself; so **Autosoterism.** **Autotelic** (-te·lik), *a.* (see quot.). **Autotrophic** (-trǫ·fik), *a.* [Gr. -τροφός + -IC. Cf. Gr. τροφικός nursing, tending], of a plant, self-nourishing, as distinguished from parasitic and saprophytic. **Autotropism** (ǭtǫ·trǒpiz'm), *Bot.* [TROPISM], (see quot.).
1881 *Proc. Zool. Soc.* 502 The forms in which the spines thus rise from special plates may be distinguished as **autacanthid*. 1903 *Nature* 15 Jan. 253/2 It is pleasing to note that a considerable number of these are *auto-abstracts, for this method of summarising is the only one which ensures that the really essential points in the various investigations are brought forward. 1891 *Jrnl. Chem. Soc.* LX. *Abstracts* 1151 *Autocatalysis...The presence of a salt of the acid, for instance the sodium salt, in the solution, retards the formation of the lactone very considerably, and the amount of free acid in the solution, as determined alkalimetrically, remains constant for days together. 1913 DORLAND *Med. Dict.* (ed. 7), *Autocatalysis*.., catalysis, or alteration of the velocity of a reaction, produced by products formed during the course of the reaction. **Autocatalytic*.., pertaining to or producing autocatalysis. 1903 LAMPLUGH *Geol. Isle of Man* 70 The *autoclastic structure occurs where strata of different characters are in juxtaposition. 1902 *Science* 2 May 697 In a few instances *autocytotoxins for blood-cells have been produced. 1894 GOULD *Dict. Med.*, **Autodiagnosis*.., self-diagnosis; the morbid impression sometimes possessed by a patient that he is affected with some particular disease. 190. *Med. Record* LXIII. 169 (Cent. D. Suppl.) The same hand must not be used for *autodiagnostic purposes all the time. 1913 DORLAND *Med. Dict.* (ed. 7). 1890 BILLINGS *Med. Dict.*, **Autodigestion*, self-digestion of stomach by gastric juice. 1896 *Jrnl. Chem. Soc.* LXX. *Abstracts* 616 In autodigestion, xanthine-like substances are formed. 1903 *Cohen's Syst. Physiol. Therap.* VIII. 275 *Auto-hypnosis..relieves the cortex of the corrective restraint imposed in the waking condition by the contact of the senses with the outer world. 1913 DORLAND *Med. Dict.* (ed. 7), **Autohypnotic*..1. Pertaining to self-induced hypnotism. 2. One who can put himself into a hypnotic state. 1894 GOULD *Dict. Med.*, **Autohypnotism*.., mental stupor induced by dwelling intensely upon some all-absorbing delusion. 1902 *Encycl. Brit.* XXXII. 53/1 They [*sc.* our witch-burning ancestors] could scarcely have reasoned otherwise..in certain cases of hysteria and *autohypnotization. 1887 A. M. BROWN *Anim. Alkaloids* p. iii, Their action as *auto-infectants. 1876 T. BRYANT *Pract. Surg.* I. 135 *Auto-infection..is not seen equally in all the sorts of infectious tumours. 1877 A. M. BROWN *Anim. Alkaloids* 136 The body escapes disturbance and disintegration by processes purely *auto-infective. 1874 VAN BUREN & KEYES *Dis. Urin. Org.* 19 *Auto-inoculable. *Ibid.*, *Auto-inoculation is the proper test. 1901 DORLAND *Med. Dict.* (ed. 2), **Auto-intoxicant*, a poison generated within the system. 1909 *Nation* 29 Apr. 427/2 They have ceased to get very much excited since they have learned that selfishness and greed are auto-intoxicants. 1887 A. M. BROWN *Anim. Alkaloids* p. v, Lessons on *Auto-intoxication in Disease. 1893 SIR J. C. BROWNE in *Times* 3 Oct. 9 The practice of introspection not rarely results in autointoxication or the generation of doubts and perplexities that work like poison in the blood. 1901 H. H. FOSTER in *Amer. Jrnl. Psychol.* Jan. 160 The common starting point of auto-intoxication theories is the influence of certain products of decomposition of living substance upon the continuance of cell activity. 1902 W. JAMES *Memories & Studies* vii. (1911) 163 Slight organic alterations, intoxications, and auto-intoxications. 1928 GALSWORTHY *Swan Song* I. vii. 55 You suffer from auto-intoxication in that House [i.e. Parliament]. 1901 *Rep. Brit. Assoc. Advancem. Sci.* 552 Mere *automorphs of the same form, *i.e.*, products of the form by its unit-form..are not to be considered as distinct forms. 1904 *Nature* 25 Feb. 403 Thorium with less than a trace of actinium produces an *auto-photograph. 1924 *Chambers's Jrnl.* 773/2 Constipation is..responsible for more ultimate disease or *auto-poisoning than anything else. 190. *Buck's Handbk. Med. Sci.* IV. 184 (Cent. D. Suppl.) *Autopoisonous. 1903 *Dublin Rev.* July 170 *Auto-radiographs of thorium. 1909 *Review of Reviews* Feb. 121/1 *Autoscript from 'F. W. H. Myers'. 1909 *Daily Chron.* 19 Feb. 6/5 A friend of mine who has a remarkable faculty of automatic writing sends me the following autoscript which she received this morning. 1894 *Autosoteric [see *heterosoteric* s.v. HETERO-]. 1909 B. B. WARFIELD *Calvin as Theologian* iii. 31 The logic of Socinianism gave us..an auto-soteric religion. *Ibid.* ii. 18 There is nothing against which Calvinism set its face with more firmness than..*auto-soterism. 1902 BALDWIN *Dict. Philos. & Psychol.* I. 96/1 *Autotelic is suggested as serving, in the phrases autotelic function, process, &c., the meaning indicated by the German Selbstzweck. 1902 I. B. BALFOUR in *Rep. Brit. Assoc. Advancem. Sci.* 820 The root-difference between plants and animals is one of nutrition. Plants are *autotrophic, animals heterotrophic. 1898 *Nat. Science* June 387 By *autotropism is implied the inherent tendency of vegetable organs to grow in a straight line.

b. Used frequently in the names of self-acting mechanisms, machines, instruments, etc.; esp. **Auto-cohe·rer** *Electr.* [COHERER], a coherer that spontaneously recovers its resistance. **Auto-conve·rter** *Electr.* = *auto-transformer* (see below). **Auto-sta·rter** *Electr.*, an auto-transformer used for starting motors. **Auto-transfo·rmer** *Electr.*, a transformer or compensator in which a part of the primary coil is used as a secondary, or a part of the secondary as a primary coil. **Au·to-valve,** the valve that shuts off the supply in an automatic gas-meter.
1885 *Jrnl. Chem. Soc.* XLVIII. *Abstracts* 854 New Pile, or Auto-accumulator. 1895 S. P. THOMPSON *Polyphase Electric Currents* x. 186 The auto-transformer (or 'one-coil' transformer) merely consists of a coil of wire wound on an iron core, and connected across the mains. 1898 tr. *L. Lockert's Petroleum Motor-cars* 3 Such benefactors to the cause of auto-locomotion as Papin, Cugnot, Watt, [etc.]. 1898 *Daily News* 22 Jan. 3/2 A so-called auto-regulator, the object of which is to maintain the straight course of torpedoes. 1899 *Motor-Car World* Oct. 10/1 Electricity, which seems to be the ideal power for auto-locomotion. 1902 W. J. DIBDIN *Public Lighting* 176 The auto-valve, which is not affected by condensation or grit. 1903 *Daily Chron.* 25 Sept. 3/2 A novelty in cash registers is..the 'Auto-Check'. 1904 *Elect. Rev.* 17 Sept. 459 (Cent. D. Suppl.) An 'oil-break autostarter' switch. 1908 *Installation News* II. 162/2 Autotransformers converting the pressure to, say, 25 volts, will be employed. 1927 *Observer* 16 Oct. 11/4 Auto-electric advertising machines.

Auto-[2] (ǭ·to), abbreviation of AUTOMOBILE used as comb. form, chiefly in the names of vehicles. See also *AUTOBUS, *AUTOCAR, *AUTOCYCLE.
1897 *N.Y. Herald* 19 Sept. 2/1 The introduction of an efficient autocab service in the streets of Paris. 1899 *N.Y. Jrnl.* 17 June 5/2 The New York Auto-Truck Company. 1899 *Westm. Gaz.* 4 July 6/3 The auto-conveyances of members of Parliament. 1900 G. D. HISCOX *Horseless Vehicles* 212 The Canda auto-quadricycle. 1900 *Engineering Mag.* Aug. 733 The auto-waggon, which provides just that rapid and cheap form of independent direct transport [etc.]. 1904 *Westm. Gaz.* 23 Sept. 7/3 Mr. W. K. Vanderbilt, junior's auto-boat 'Mercédès the Sixth'. 1909 *Daily Chron.* 22 Nov. 9/1 The Wall auto-wheel, which offers a compromise between cycling pure and simple and the ordinarily accepted motor cycling. 1927 *South America* May 137/2 The autocoach is much needed to replace the horse-coach.

Autobiographist (ǭ:to,bəi,ǫ·grăfist). [f. *AUTO-[1] + BIOGRAPHIST.] = AUTOBIOGRAPHER.
1840 *Fraser's Mag.* XXII. 579 We must first describe this volunteer autobiographist. 1890 *Tait's Mag.* XVII. 525/2 Our autobiographist betakes himself to London. 1920 *Westm. Gaz.* 26 Nov. 8/2 Too indiscreet a candour in autobiography ..may..involve unfortunate consequences upon the autobiographist.

Autobus (ǭ·tobʊs). [f. *AUTO-[2] + BUS *sb.*[2]] An automobile omnibus, a motor bus.
1900 *Motor-Car World* Nov. 33/1.

Autocar (ǭ·tokāɹ). [f. *AUTO-[2] + CAR *sb.*] = MOTOR CAR. Also *attrib.*

1895 *Westm. Gaz.* 17 Dec. 3/1 We congratulate the police authorities..on having convicted the owner of an autocar for proceeding along a road at a pace exceeding three miles an hour. 1896 *Standard* 5 Feb. 3/6 An autocar..was treated as a locomotive, and the owners were summoned for not carrying in front the necessary flag of warning. 1927 *Chambers's Jrnl.* 375/2 You can..explore the French side.. from end to end by safe, strong, comfortable autocar.

Autochrome (ǭ·tokrǭ³m), *a.* and *sb.* *Photogr.* [f. Gr. αὐτο- (see *AUTO-[1]) + χρῶμα colour.]
A. *adj.* Defining a process and a plate used in colour-photography, invented by Messrs. Lumière of Lyons; also, a slide produced by this process.
1907 *Daily Chron.* 12 July 6/4 The new plates are called 'The Autochrome Plates'. 1907 *Brit. Jrnl. Photogr.* 2 Aug. 573/1 The Lumière 'Autochrome' Plates. 1920 *Glasgow Herald* 1 Mar. 13 A series of autochrome slides.
B. *sb.* A photograph produced by this process.
1907 *Brit. Jrnl. Photogr.* 2 Aug. 573/1 The reproduction of Lumière 'Autochromes' on 'Uto' paper. 1910 *Westm. Gaz.* 16 Apr. 11/2 An excellent collection of autochromes.

Autochthonously (ǫtǫ·kþŏnəsli), *adv.* [-LY[2].] As originating in or from that part of the body in which they occur.
1885 *Encycl. Brit.* XVIII. 361/2 The larger number of maladies do not arise autochthonously or 'under a whole skin', they are generated by certain morbific causes.

Autoclave. Add:
2. A vessel used for heating liquids under pressure.
1876 *Jrnl. Chem. Soc.* II. 451 Saponification of Neutral Fats in Autoclaves. 1886 *Ibid.* L. *Abstracts* 112 High Pressure Digesters (Autoclaves) for Chemical Laboratories. ..The apparatus consists of a cylindrical copper vessel, provided with a cover, which is firmly fastened down by a screw.

Autocopyist (ǭtokǫ·pi,ist). [f. *AUTO-[1] + COPYIST.] An apparatus for producing facsimile copies of written matter.
1888 *Encycl. Brit.* XXIV. 697/2 In principle the autocopyist is like the hektograph. 1907 *Daily Chron.* 21 Jan. 3/5 Sketch maps..have been reproduced by means of an autocopyist.

Autocracy. Add:
2. c. Autocrats collectively; the realm of autocrats.
1905 *Smart Set* Sept. 125 Of all the fish that swim or swish In ocean's deep autocracy There's none possess such haughtiness As the codfish aristocracy. 1928 *Manch. Guardian Weekly* 19 Oct. 301/2 She is credited with wiser views of Russian policy than were commonly found in the heads of that fated autocracy.

Autocratism (ǫtǫ·krătiz'm). [f. AUTOCRAT + -ISM.] The principles or practices of autocrats.
1848 *Fraser's Mag.* XXXVII. 96 To liberal sentiments he united the instincts of autocratism. 1926 SIR V. HORSLEY in S. Paget *Life* III. iii. (1919) 315 It is interesting to appreciate the sensation of an autocratism.

Autocritical (ǭtokri·tikăl), *a.* [f. *AUTO-[1] + CRITICAL *a.*] Critical of oneself or one's own work.
1642 *Fuller Answ. to Ferne* 14 Thats the peculiar Priviledge of Gods word to be autocritical, its own last judge. 1821 *Blackw. Mag.* X. 116 We differ..from the autocritical junto who are willing to dictate to us. 1850 L. HUNT *Autobiogr.* I. p. vi, Coleridge's *Literary Life* is professedly autocritical.

Autocycle (ǭ·tosəik'l). [f. *AUTO-[2] + CYCLE.] A cycle propelled by a motor, a motor cycle.
1905 *Daily Chron.* 21 July 5/5, 86 miles an hour. Wonderful Performance on an Autocycle. 1920 *Daily Mail* 29 Nov. 8 The Autocraft Board, which has an Auto-cycle section.

Autodidactic (ǭ:to,didæ·ktik), *a.* [f. AUTODIDACT + -IC.] Self-taught; acquired by teaching oneself.
1847 S. AUSTIN *Ranke's Hist. Ref.* III. 586 Autodidactic artisans. 1878 *Tinsley's Mag.* XXIII. 293 Autodidactic studies. 1886 *Contemp. Rev.* Feb. 293 He [*sc.* Menzel] was from the beginning an auto-didactic realist; he drew and painted as he saw.

Autœcious (ǫtī·ʃəs), *a.* *Bot.* Also **autecious, autoicous.** [f. Gr. αὐτός same + οἰκία house: see -IOUS.] **a.** Of parasitic fungi: Inhabiting the same host throughout their life. **b.** Having both sexual organs on the same plant, monœcious.
1882 VINES *Sachs' Bot.* 332 Such forms [of parasitic fungi] as these are said to be heterœcious (metœcious), to distinguish them from those..which inhabit the same host throughout their whole life (autœcious). 1900 B. D. JACKSON *Gloss. Bot. Terms*, *Autoicous*, in Bryophytes, the male and female inflorescences on the same plant.

Auto-erotic (ǭ:to,īrǫ·tik), *a.* [f. *AUTO-[1] + EROTIC *a.*] Pertaining to auto-erotism.
1898 HAVELOCK ELLIS in *Alienist & Neurol.* Apr. 260 Among auto-erotic phenomena..we must further include those religious sexual manifestations for an ideal object, of which we may find evidence in the lives of saints.

Auto-erotism (ǭ:to,e·rǒtiz'm). [f. *AUTO-[1] + EROTISM.] Spontaneous erotism, aroused without the presence or thought of another person.
1898 HAVELOCK ELLIS in *Alienist & Neurol.* Apr. 260 (title of paper), Auto-Erotism, a Psychological Study. *Ibid.*, By 'auto-erotism' I mean the phenomena of spontaneous sexual emotion generated in the absence of an external stimulus proceeding, directly or indirectly, from another person. 1910 — *Studies Psychol. Sex* (1923) I. 161 In a wide sense..auto-erotism may be said to include those transformations of repressed sexual activity which are a factor of some morbid conditions as well as of the normal manifestation of art and poetry. 1920 *Times Lit. Suppl.* 16 Sept. 603/3 The..well-considered treatment of autoerotism at schools.

Autogamous (ǫtǫ·găməs), *a.* *Bot.* [f. Gr. αὐτο- (see *AUTO-[1]) + γάμος marriage: see -OUS.] Characterized by self-fertilization.
1894 GOULD *Dict. Med.* 1925 *Glasgow Herald* 20 June 4 Distomum hepaticum is an autogamous bermaphrodite.

Autogamy. Add:
In *Biol.* The mating of like with like. **Autogamic** (ǭtogæ·mik) *a.* *Biol.*, of or pertaining to autogamy.
1900 K. PEARSON *Gram. Sci.* (ed. 2) 437 Is there any form of sexual selection such as autogamy, endogamy, apolegamy, or homogamy, using these terms in their broadest senses? *Ibid.* 501 Variations do not occur accidentally or in isolated instances; autogamic and assortative mating are realities.

Autogenesis (ǭtodʒe·nĕsis). [f. *AUTO-[1] + GENESIS.] Origination within the organism.
1890 BILLINGS *Med. Dict.*, *Autogenesis*.., spontaneous generation.

Au:togene·tic, *a.* [f. prec.; see GENETIC.]
1. *Med.* Developed by or due to autogenesis; produced within the organism. Hence **Au:togene·tically** *adv.*
1886 *Brit. Med. Jrnl.* 10 Apr. 694/1 Autogenetic puerperal fevers. Mental worry from illicit pregnancies and clandestine marriages was a common source of autogenetic empoisonment. *Ibid.*, Some septic poison, either from without or autogenetically, might cause the same series of symptoms.
2. *Phys. Geogr.* Of or pertaining to a system of drainage developed by erosion of the stream itself.
1902 in WEBSTER Suppl.

Autogenic, *a.* Add: = AUTOGENOUS in various senses (in quot. = self-induced).
1890 MERCIER *Sanity & Insanity* xiii. 343 The melancholy ..is a spontaneous and autogenic melancholy.

Autogiro (ǭ:to,dʒəi°·ro). Also **auto-gyro.** [f. *AUTO-[1] + It., Sp. *giro* GYRE.] A type of flying-machine supported by overhead windmill sails instead of wings.
1925 *Daily News* 23 Oct. 8/3 Senor de la Cierva; the inventor of the 'Autogiro'. 1927 *Observer* 17 Apr. 10/2 The wider range of control promised by such types as the 'autogyro'.

Au·tographed (-graft), *ppl. a.* [f. AUTOGRAPH *v.* + -ED[1].] On which the person's autograph is written; signed.
1901 *Daily Chron.* 10 July 3/5 Autographed photographs of celebrities. 1908 LD. ROSEBERY in Begbie *Life W. Booth* (1920) II. xxviii. 398 Send me your autographed photograph.

Autographic, *a.* Add:
2. *Path.* (See quot.)
1894 GOULD *Dict. Med.*, *Autographic..Skin*, a condition of vaso-motor paralysis, usually in hysterical patients, in which markings made upon the skin form quite persistent and intensely red traces. *A. woman*, one with an *Autographic Skin*.

Autographism (ǫtǫ·grăfiz'm). *Path.* [f. AUTOGRAPH + -ISM.] A condition of the skin in which tracings leave an elevated mark. Hence **Auto·graphist.**
1890 *Globe* 13 June 6 Autographism, as this phenomenon is called, is believed to be due to a nervous susceptibility which may exist for years in a patient. 1894 GOULD *Dict. Med.*, *Autographist*.., one who has an autographic skin.

Autogravure (ǭ:to,grăviū°·ɹ). [f. *AUTO-[1] + F. *gravure*, after *photogravure*.] A photo-mechanical modification of the etching process. Used *attrib.* in *autogravure process*. Also, a picture produced by this process.
1885 *Athenæum* 31 Jan. 156/3 Plates, produced by the autogravure process of the Autotype Company. 1888 *Chambers's Encycl.* I. 606 *Autogravure*, a peculiar process of photo-engraving patented by J. R. Sawyer, London, on November 12, 1884. 1889 *Guardian* 23 Jan. 137/1 An autogravure from Correggio.

Autoharp (ǭ·tohāɹp). [f. *AUTO-[1] + HARP *sb.*] A musical instrument of the zither type provided with dampers for the mechanical production of arpeggio effects.
1894 *Work* 23 June 365/2 An auto-harp can be bought from almost any dealer in musical instruments. 1897 MARY KINGSLEY *W. Africa* 82 Captain Heldt..produced an autoharp, an instrument upon which he was himself proficient.

Autoist (ǭ·to,ist). *U.S.* [f. AUTO *sb.* + -IST.] One who uses or drives an automobile; a motorist.
1903 *Sci. Amer.* 21 Feb. 134/1 Bills giving equal rights to autoists and the drivers of horses. 1904 *New York Globe* 29 Mar. 4 A protest against the young lawbreakers who stone autoists.

Autolithography (ǭ:toliþǫ·grăfi). [f. *AUTO-[1] + LITHOGRAPHY.] A form of lithographic printing in which the drawing, etc., is first made on transfer paper, then put on stone for printing. Hence **Au:tolithogra·phic** *a.*, of or belonging to autolithography. **Autoli·thograph** *sb.*, a picture or print produced by this process. **Autoli·thograph** *v.*, to produce by this process.
1874 (*title*) The Lenoir Collection of original French portraits at Stafford House. Auto-lithographed by Lord Ronald Gower. *Ibid.* Pref., This collection of portraits which I have attempted to reproduce in autolithography. *Ibid.*, Autolithographic copies aiding me in the production of these Autolithographs. 1895 *Daily News* 22 Nov. 6/3 An autolithograph by Mr. Whistler. 1905 *Edwards' Catal.* No. 270. 85 Ten Auto-Lithographs of the Lower Thames, by C. E. Holloway and T. R. Way, signed Artist's proofs.

Autolysis (ǫtǫ·lisis). [f. Gr. αὐτο- (see *AUTO-[1]) + λύσις a loosing.] **a.** Self-acting disintegration of tissue. **b.** The destruction of cells of the body by the action of its own serum. Hence **Autolytic** (ǭtoli·tik) *a.*, belonging to or of the nature of autolysis. **Autolyse** (ǭ·toləiz) *v.*, *intr.* and *trans.* (causative), to undergo or cause to undergo autolysis.
1902 *Jrnl. Chem. Soc.* LXXXII. *Abstracts* 35 After autolysis, the same organs yield solutions which hinder blood-clotting. 1902 *Science* 28 Nov. 858 Autolytic ferments. 1903 FLEXNER *Ibid.* 3 July 15 An acute lobar pneumonia in which the inflammatory exudate..failing to autolyze perfectly cannot absorb, and hence undergoes organisation. 1911 *Encycl. Brit.* XX. 922/1 Autolysis is a disintegration of dead tissues brought about by the action of their own ferments, while degeneration takes place in the still living cell. The study of autolytic phenomena..has thrown much light on these degenerative processes.

Automatic (ǭtomæ·tik), *sb.* Abbreviation of 'automatic pistol': see next.
1902 in WEBSTER Suppl. 1914 GERTRUDE ATHERTON *Perch of Devil* II. vii, I've even bought an automatic. I suppose.. I should call it a gun. 1915 R. H. DAVIS *With the Allies* 34 We were arrested by a smart..officer, who rode up to the side of the taxi and pointed an automatic at us. 1920 *Blackw. Mag.* Aug. 154/1 A German automatic hung at his side.

Automatic, *a.* Add:
2. b. Of a firearm: Furnished with mechanism for successively and continuously loading, firing, and ejecting a cartridge as long as ammunition is supplied.
1902 *Encycl. Brit.* XXX. 401/2 In the modern 'automatic' machine gun the loading, firing, extracting, and ejecting are all performed automatically by the gun itself. *Ibid.* XXXII. 649/2 No nation has yet armed her forces with an automatic rifle. *Ibid.* 658/2 The Colt Automatic Pistol, calibre ·38.
6. *Spiritism.* Of or pertaining to automatism; performed by unconscious or subconscious action.
1883 W. S. MOSES *Spirit-Teachings* Introd. 1 Automatic Writing is a well-known method of communication with the invisible world of what we loosely call Spirit. 1889 BARKWORTH in *Proc. Soc. Psychical Research* Dec. 85 It is only the execution and not the initiation of the movements which is automatic, the suggestion for them being external to the subject's own personality. MYERS *Ibid.* 189 Automatic writing occurs..under more forms than any single observer has yet noted. 1902 A. LANG in *Encycl. Brit.* XXXII. 52/2 The information nominally given by 'spirits' of the dead through the mouth or by the automatic writing of Mrs. Piper (Boston, U.S.) and other mediums.

Automatism. Add:
4. *Spiritism.* Any psychic phenomenon that appears spontaneously in consciousness; any action performed subconsciously or unconsciously, undirected by the mind or will of the normal personality; also, the mental state in which these phenomena occur.
1887 MYERS in *Proc. Soc. Psychical Research* 28 Jan. 209 The phenomena of automatism,—the indications given by unwilled or unconscious action of mental processes going on within us. 1889 BARKWORTH *Ibid.* Dec. 85 The actions of the hypnotic state..are largely characterised by what may be called automatism; that is to say, being started by suggestion they seem to be carried on without volition. *Ibid.*, We have..instances of complete automatism in the case of the sleep-walker who goes through a variety of complicated actions entirely self-suggested. 1902 A. LANG in *Encycl. Brit.* XXXII. 52/2 This leads us to the chief field of research in 'automatisms', or actions of the subconscious or 'subliminal' self. 1903 MYERS *Human Personality* I. Gloss. s.v., Sensory automatism will thus include visual and auditory hallucinations; motor automatism will include messages written without intention.

Automatist. Add:
2. *Spiritism.* One who experiences the phenomena of automatism.
1887 MYERS in *Proc. Soc. Psychical Research* 28 Jan. 212 Let us simply suppose..that the automatist can at any time.. induce insignificant messages, mainly resembling each other in handwriting and signed with the same name. 1889 *Ibid.* Dec. 189 M. Janet supposes that my automatist is partially anæsthetic...But he is not in any degree anæsthetic..; he has the full sensation of the movements. 1903 — *Human Personality* I. 28 The ordinary consciousness of the automatist appears to be suspended; he passes into a state of trance. 1914 TEIXEIRA tr. *Maeterlinck's Unknown Guest* iii. 5 Sometimes even the 'automatist' speaks or writes languages of which he is completely ignorant.

Automatization (ǫtǫmătəizē¹·ʃən). [f. AUTOMATIZE + -ATION.] The action of making or condition of being made automatic or an automaton.
1924 *Psyche* July 67 The pointing method in localization ..does not tend so readily toward automatization.

Automatograph (ǭtomæ·tǒgraf). [f. Gr. αὐτόματος acting of itself + -γραφος writing, writer, -GRAPH.] A scientific form of the planchette, used for recording the involuntary movements of the hand and arm. Hence **Automa·togram.**
1892 J. JASTROW in *Amer. Jrnl. Psychol.* Apr. 400 This apparatus enables us to record all movement in the horizontal plane, and, inasmuch as its chief purpose is to write slight involuntary movements, we have given it the name of the *automatograph* and may speak of such a record as an *automatogram*. 1901 TITCHENER *Exper. Psychol.* I. i. 95 Automatograph. This consists of a light but strong board, ..carrying at one end a small block of wood,..hollowed out to take the elbow, and pierced at the other end by a circular hole, through which the stylus passes.

Automnesia (ǭtomnī·ziă). *Psychol.* [f. Gr. αὐτο- (see *AUTO-[1]) + μνῆσις memory.] (See quot. 1903.)

1897 tr. *Ribot's Psychol. Emotions* 153 By some phenomenon of affective automnesia, this same event reproduced itself. 1903 MYERS *Human Personality* I. Gloss., *Automnesia*, spontaneous revival of memories of an earlier condition of life. *Ibid.* II. 139 Littré..described what he calls the 'affective automnesia'—or spontaneously arising flow of emotion.

Automobile (ǭtomǭ³·bil, ǭ:tomǒbī·l), *a.* and *sb.* [a. F. *automobile* (1876 in Littré Suppl.), f. Gr. αὐτός self + F. *mobile*: see *AUTO-[1] and MOBILE *a.*]
A. *adj.* That moves by means of mechanism and power within itself, esp. of a vehicle, self-propelling as distinguished from horse-drawn.
1886 *Harper's Mag.* June 25/2 These vessels..besides their equipment of auto-mobile torpedoes, are provided with powerful batteries. 1895 *Daily News* 15 Oct. 5/3 Signor Cleto Brena has arrived at Naples with his automobile carriage from Milan. 1902 *Encycl. Brit.* XXXI. 12/1 France has undoubtedly led in the development of the light automobile vehicle.
B. *sb.* An automobile or self-propelled vehicle; a motor vehicle. (Little used in Great Britain.)
1895 *Pall Mall Gaz.* 15 Oct. 2/3 Three miles an hour gives the automobile little chance of displaying the powers it doubtless enjoys. 1899 *Motor-Car World* 8/1 The theory and practice of automobiles. 1902 *Encycl. Brit.* XXXI. 11/1 On the Continent of Europe and in the United States the usual expression for these vehicles [motor-cars] is 'automobile'.
attrib. 1896 *Manchester Guardian* 24 Sept. 10/1 The Automobile Club of France. 1901 *Daily News* 16 Feb. 6/1 The French have shown themselves keenly interested in the subject of auto-mobile races.

Automobile (ǭtomǭ³·bil), *v.* [f. prec.] *intr.* To travel or ride in an automobile or motor car; to motor. Hence **Automo·biling** *vbl. sb.*, the action or practice of using an automobile: also *attrib.*
1898 *Cosmopolitan* Sept. 485/1 Mr. Tiffany assures the writer that he finds 'automobiling' more interesting than coaching. 1901 W. R. H. TROWBRIDGE *Lett. her Mother to Eliz.* xii. 54 Blanche spent the morning..automobiling with the Vicomte and the Marquise. 1902 C. N. & A. M. WILLIAMSON *Lightning Conductor* 51 While I was reflecting that automobiling, like fishing, is a pursuit whose followers are peculiarly ready to sacrifice truth on the altar of picturesqueness. 1903 *New York Times* 19 Dec. 9 Here is a hat for the skating girl and the automobiling woman. 1924 *Public Opinion* 24 Oct. 403/2, I have lately automobiled in Cornwall, Devonshire, Somerset and adjoining counties.

Automobilism (ǭtomǭ³·biliz'm). [f. AUTOMOBILE + -ISM after F. *automobilisme*.] The use of automobiles or motor vehicles.
1898 *Cosmopolitan* Sept. 483/2 As a sport, automobilism now occupies the foremost rank. 1899 *Motor-Car World* Oct. 8/1 Automobilism will be the method of locomotion of the future. 1901 *Pall Mall Mag.* Sept. 62/2 Automobilism was popular in France before it was practical.
So **Automobilist** (ǭtomǭ³·bilist), one who uses an automobile or motor vehicle, a motorist.
1897 *Daily News* 26 July 5/5 The hour's rest at St. Germain was improved by the automobilists to see that their machines were in order. 1902 C. N. & A. M. WILLIAMSON *Lightning Conductor* 114 The old peasant..exclaimed that if all automobilists were like us there would never be complaints. 1907 F. MILTOUN (*title*) The Automobilist Abroad.

Automobility (ǭ:tomobi·lĭti). [f. AUTOMOBILE + -ITY.]
1. The use of automobiles or motor vehicles as a mode of locomotion or travel.
1903 *Times Lit. Suppl.* 16 Oct. 295/3 To come..upon a book..packed with suggestions for the well-being of the walker is, in this year of grace and automobility, no small joy. 1926 *Daily News* 29 Oct. 6/7 The automobility of society.. has helped many Englishmen to discover England.
2. Mobility by means of automobile vehicles.
1909 *Westm. Gaz.* 18 Mar. 2/3 The interesting experiment of conveying troops by motor vehicles to Hastings..proves what may be called the automobility of a defensive force. 1926 *Blackw. Mag.* Mar. 309/2 The small expedition, being totally inadequate to its purpose, achieved nothing but automobility.

Automobilize (ǭtomǭ³·biləiz), *v.* [f. AUTOMOBILE + -IZE.] *intr.* To use an automobile as a means of locomotion; to ride in or drive a motor car; also *trans.*, to travel to or through (a place) by automobile; to visit by motor car; to supply with automobiles; to convert into an automobile.
1898 *Cosmopolitan* Sept. 480/1 It is scarcely an exaggeration to say that Paris is becoming 'automobilized'. 1902 *N.Y. Times* 26 Mar. (Cent. Dict. Suppl.). 1906 *Church Times* 12 Jan. 35/2 They have auto-mobilised their pulpits in order to preach at large those doctrines of party politics which have become..the religion of Dissent.

Automorphic, *a.* Add:
2. *Math.* Characterized by automorphism (sense 2 below).
1898 E. T. WHITTAKER in *Phil. Trans.* (1899) CXCII. 1 The only automorphic functions known hitherto which have been applied to uniformise forms whose genus is greater than unity, are those given by certain sub-groups of the modular group. 1902 — *Mod. Analysis* 339 Two classes of automorphic functions are known by which this uniformisation may be effected.
3. *Cryst.* = IDIOMORPHIC *a.* (Webster *Suppl.* 1902.)

Automorphism. Add:
2. *Math.* 'The property of remaining unchanged by all the substitutions of any group of linear transformations' (*Cent. Dict.* Suppl.).
1903 *Science* 5 June 904 Class of a group and degree of transitivity, automorphism, representation, index notation.
3. = ANTHROPOMORPHISM 1 b.
1894 H. M. STANLEY *Stud. Evol. Psychol. Feeling* 297 But when we come to interpret the psychoses of the lower animals in connection with sexuality we may still more easily slip into a doubtful automorphism.

Automotive (ǭtomǭ³·tiv), *a.* [f. *AUTO-[2] + MOTIVE *a.*] **a.** Of or pertaining to an automotor. **b.** Self-propelled, automobile.
1898 tr. *L. Lockert's Petroleum Motor-cars* p. ix, His work ..is read with satisfaction by all amateurs of automotive touring. 1901 [see *AUTOMOTOR]. 1922 *Public Opinion* 7 Sept. 222/1 He chugged up the street in an automotive contraption.

Automotor (ǭtomǭ³·tǫɹ, -əɹ). [f. *AUTO-[2] + MOTOR.] An automobile motor or motor vehicle.
1895 *Daily News* 30 Nov. 5/1 To apply the new principle of the 'auto-motor' to road-waggons, heavy drags, hunting-traps, and stage-coaches. 1896 (*title*) The Automotor Journal. 1897 *Westm. Gaz.* 4 Mar. 10/1 There is to be the automotor, and attached to it a couple of vans. 1901 (*title*) The Automotor and Horseless Vehicle Pocket-Book of Automotive Formulæ.

Autonomism (ǫtǫ·nŏmiz'm). [f. AUTONOMY + -ISM.]
1. The principle or system of autonomy or self-government.
1874 FISKE *Cosmic Philos.* II. 205 The two feelings known to the Greeks as Pan-Hellenism and Autonomism, represented respectively by Athens and by the Doric communities.
2. 'The theory that the forms into which animals and plants develop are determined by an inward agency' (*Cent. Dict.* Suppl.).

Autonomistic (ǭtǫnŏmi·stik), *a.* [-IC.]
1. Of or pertaining to autonomism or the principle of self-government.
a 1870 GEN. R. E. LEE in *Westm. Gaz.* (1898) 25 May 3/1 The Autonomistic Cabinet.
2. *Biol.* Of or pertaining to autonomism or the theory of self-determined development.
1904 *Biol. Bull.* (Mass.) Sept. 201 They [*sc.* changes] resemble in character certain of the phenomena which have led Driesch to assume the existence of an autonomistic principle or entelechy governing form.

Autonomously (ǫtǫ·nŏməsli), *adv.* [-LY[2].] In an autonomous position, as an autonomous state, etc.
1881 G. S. HALL *German Culture* 183 We must know and autonomously will to follow non-egoistic absolute ends as essentially our ends. 1897 GLADSTONE *Let. Dk. Westminster* 14 Why should not Crete be autonomously united with Greece, and yet not detached in theory from the body of the Ottoman Empire?

Autonym (ǭ·tŏnim). [f. Gr. αὐτο- self (*AUTO-[1]) + ὄνυμα, ὄνομα name.]
1. A real name or one's own name as distinguished from a pseudonym or anonym, esp. the real name of an author; also, a book published under the author's real name. Also *attrib.*
1867 O. HAMST *Mart. Bibliogr.*, *Autonym*, a book published under the author's real name. 1895 *Daily News* 23 Dec. 5/1 Autonym works, anonymous works, and special works.
2. The name by which a tribe calls itself as distinguished from that by which it is known to other tribes.
1895 in *Funk's Standard Dict.*
3. = HOMONYM 1 a.
1889 in *Cent. Dict.*

Autophone (ǭ·tofō³n), *sb.* Short for *automatic telephone* (cf. *AUTO-[1] b). Hence **Au·tophone** *v.* *intr.*, to use an automatic telephone.
1927 *Daily Express* 28 Oct. 3/1 Mysteries of the New Autophones...London's first automatic telephone exchange will be opened this year. 1928 *Ibid.* 25 Apr. 11/3 How to 'Autophone'.

Autopiano (ǭ:to,pi,æ·no). [f. *AUTO-[1] + PIANO.] A piano with a playing apparatus.
1906 *Strand Mag.* Jan., Advt. 1928 *Sunday News* 17 June 4/4 Their sale bargains including several auto-pianos.

Autoplast (ǭ·toplæst). [f. *AUTO-[1] + -PLAST.] **a.** *Embryol.* An autogenous cell as distinguished from a cleavage cell. **b.** *Physiol. Bot.* A chlorophyll granule.
1883 E. RAY LANKESTER in *Encycl. Brit.* XVI. 682/2 In addition to the layer of cleavage cells..additional cells are formed.., each cell having a separate origin, whence they are termed 'autoplasts'. 1885 [see *trophoplast* s.v. TROPHO-].

Autoplate (ǭ·toplē¹t). *U.S.* [f. *AUTO-[1] + PLATE *sb.*] A curved stereotype for newspaper printing, made by an autoplate machine; also, the machine itself. *Autoplate machine*, a machine for automatically casting, shaving, and bevelling stereotypes.
1902 *Westm. Gaz.* 22 May 9/1 The Autoplate, a wonderful revolution in stereotyping. 1902 *Census Bulletin* 28 June 51 (Cent. D. Suppl.) A device known as the autoplate was invented in 1900 by means of which the time required for casting plates was..reduced.

Auto-portrait. [*AUTO-[1]. Cf. G. *selbst-porträt*.] A portrait of an artist by himself. (Cf. quot. 1828 s.v. AUTO-.)
1922 *Glasgow Herald* 20 Apr. 6 The thirty or so British-born painters whose auto-portraits are in the Uffizi. 1928 *Observer* 15 Jan. 10 It is scarcely credible that the ill-constructed head of Mrs. Smith..and many another portrait come from the brush that shows such authority in the auto-portrait.

Autopsic (ǫtǫ·psik), *a.* [f. mod.L. *autopsia* AUTOPSY + -IC.] Of or pertaining to autopsy; based on personal observation; *spec.* in *Med.*, obtained by means of the post-mortem examination of a body. Also **Auto·psical** *a.* = prec.
1881 tr. *von Ziemssen's Cycl. Med.* Suppl. 561 Basing his opinion upon the autopsical examination of five patients. 1886 *Alienist & Neurol.* July 533 The autopsic and the combined ante-mortem testimony to his insanity was not more confirmatory. 1892 LEWINS in G. M. McCrie *Miss Naden's World-Scheme* 29 *note*, We are only self-inspecting (autopsic), even when seemingly occupied in apparently far other regions of thought.

Autopsy (ǭ·tǫpsi, ǭtǫ·psi), *v.* [f. AUTOPSY *sb.*] *trans.* To perform an autopsy on or make a post-mortem examination of (a body).
1900 *Jrnl. Exper. Med.* V. 257 One of the pigs was killed and autopsied, with the result that its organs..were found to be entirely free of lesions. 1919 SACHS in S. Paget *Sir V. Horsley* II. iv. 190 It was the first walrus that had been autopsied in London for many years.

Autoscope. Add:
2. (See quot. 1903.)
1900 *Daily News* 10 Apr. 6/2 The so-called Divining Rod ..is only one of many 'autoscopes,' which perhaps bring into observation what is passing in the mysterious entity styled 'the subconscious self.' 1903 MYERS *Human Personality* I. Gloss., *Autoscope*, any instrument which reveals a subliminal motor impulse or sensory impression; e.g. a divining rod, a tilting table, or a planchette.

Autosite (ǭ·tosəit). [f. Gr. αὐτόσιτος bringing one's own provisions (used jokingly of a 'parasite'), f. αὐτός self + σῖτος food.] The larger twin of a double monster, which supplies nourishment to the smaller (called the parasite); also, a single monster capable of independent life. Hence **Autosi·tic** *a.*, that is, or is of the nature of an autosite.
1848 DUNGLISON *Med. Lex.* (ed. 7), *Autosite*.., a single monster, capable of deriving nourishment from its own proper organs, in contradistinction to *Omphalosite*. 1894 GOULD *Dict. Med.*, Autosite. *Ibid.*, Autositic.

Au:to-sugge·stion. [*AUTO-[1].] Subconscious suggestion; *spec.* in *Psychol.*, the subconscious realization of an idea suggested to oneself for adoption. (Cf. SELF-SUGGESTION 2.)
1890 *Standard* 12 Apr. 5/5 The greatest criminals..may be the responsible victims of a 'suggestion', or even of an 'auto-suggestion'. 1896 *Academy* 21 Nov. 416/1 A man who had the power of auto-suggestion in a remarkable degree, and could persuade himself to believe anything. 1907 J. COATES (*title*) Self-Reliance: Practical Studies in Personal Magnetism, Will-power and Success, through Self-help or Auto-Suggestion. 1921 *Punch* CLX. 238/2 Though we cannot all of us be born at Newmarket, we can by auto-suggestion and psycho-analysis..persuade ourselves that we have been born there.
So **Auto-sugge·stionist; Auto-sugge·stive** *a.*, arising from or due to subconscious suggestion.
1908 S. MCCOMB *Relig. & Med.* 102 The auto-suggestionist must have the intellectual acquisitions in connection with the idea which he seeks to realize. 1910 *Athenæum* 5 Mar. 273/2 An hysterical girl under autosuggestive influences. 1926 *Spectator* 26 June 1074/1 No one..will care to deny that Mrs. Besant's auto-suggestive hallucinations are sincere.

Autotheistic (ǭtoþī,i·stik), *a.* [f. AUTOTHEIST + -IC.] Of or pertaining to the autotheists or to autotheism.
1854 *Fraser's Mag.* XLIX. 708 There is this boundless difference between the healthy and godly 'subjective' style, and the unhealthy autotheistic subjective style. 1868 *Contemp. Rev.* IX. 75 Emerson's doctrine, too, is..essentially autotheistic. 1872 A. M. FAIRBAIRN *Ibid.* XX. 49 In principle they [*sc.* the Hindu philosophies] might be Theistic, Auto-Theistic, Pantheistic or Atheistic.

Autotomy (ǫtǫ·tŏmi). [f. Gr. αὐτο- self + -τομος -cutting, -cutter: see *AUTO-[1] and -TOMY.] The casting off or ejection of some part or parts of the body as a reflex action peculiar to some animals when disturbed or in order to escape. Hence **Auto·tomous** *a.*, pertaining to or of the nature of autotomy. **Auto·tomize** *v.* *intr.*, to practise autotomy.
1897 *Proc. Zool. Soc.* 911 The autotomous break occurs between femur and coxa. *Ibid.*, The autotomy of the jumping-legs takes place at the femoro-trochanteric suture. 1899 *Q. Rev.* July 281 The self-mutilation (autotomy) met with in lizards. 1901 T. H. MORGAN *Regeneration* 153 In this way the arm may be autotomized, piece by piece, to its very base.

Autotoxæmia (ǭ:totǫksī·miă). Also **-toxemia.** [f. *AUTO-[1] + TOXÆMIA.] Toxæmia or poisoning by a virus generated within the body.
1890 BILLINGS *Med. Dict.* 1924 *Psyche* July 67 A form of blood poisoning due to the development of autotoxaemia from over indulgence in flesh foods.

Autotoxic (ǭtotǫ·ksik), *a.* [f. *AUTO-[1] + TOXIC *a.*] Causing or caused by an autotoxin. Hence **Autotoxication** (-tǫksikē¹·ʃən), poisoning by a virus generated within the body. **Autotoxin** (-tǫ·ksin), a poisonous substance formed in the body itself.
1894 GOULD *Dict. Med.*, *Autotoxin*.., any product of tissue-metamorphosis within the organism that has a toxic effect upon that organism. 1903 *Med. Record* 30 May 857 (Cent. D. Suppl.) We believe the excitant is a toxic or autotoxic agent. 1927 *Times Lit. Suppl.* 5 Dec. 371/3 Thus regarded, senility is an autotoxic phenomenon.

Autotypic (ǭtoti·pik), *a.* [f. AUTOTYPE + -IC.] **1.** Of, pertaining to, or reproduced by the autotype process.

1885 *Athenæum* 14 Mar. 351/3 The 'Little Devil's Bridge'..could hardly be surpassed in autotypic reproduction.

2. Of the nature of an autotype or reproduction of an original.

1904 G. S. HALL *Adolescence* I. 124 Man..is more autotypic than he knows, reproducing in his representation of the human form the type of his own race.

Autoxidize (ǭtǫ·ksidəiz), *v. Physiol. Chem.* [f. *AUTO-[1] + OXIDIZE *v.*] *intr.* To oxidize by direct combination with oxygen at ordinary temperatures. Hence **Autoxidi·zable** *a.*, capable of oxidizing by contact with the air. **Autoxid(iz)a·tion**, oxidation by direct combination with oxygen. **Auto·xidator**, a substance in an active cell, oxidizable by water, producing hydrogen dioxide.

1883 *Science* 30 Mar. 229/2 Autoxidation in living vegetable cells. *Ibid.*, Autoxidizable substances,..those bodies which, at a low temperature, and by the action of free, passive oxygen, can be oxidized. *Ibid.* 230/1 In every active cell, autoxidators are formed; that is, substances which, at a low temperature, and by the action of molecular oxygen, can be oxidized in the presence of water. 1903 *Amer. Chem. Jrnl.* Mar. 179 Where hydroperoxide has been observed among the products of autoxidation.

Autozooid (ǭtozōu·oid). *Zool.* [f. *AUTO-[1] + ZOOID.] The normal zooid in Alcyonarians, as distinguished from the siphonozooid.

1881 [see *siphonozooid* s.v. SIPHONO-]. 1888 *Athenæum* 3 Mar. 279/3 Dr. G. H. Fowler [read a paper] on a new Pennatula from the Bahamas, the most interesting feature of which was the presence of immature autozooids at the dorsal end of the leaves.

Auxanometer (ǭksǟnǫ·mĭtəɹ). [f. Gr. αὐξάνειν to increase + -OMETER.] An instrument for measuring growth in plants.

1878 MASTERS *Henfrey's Elem. Bot.* (ed. 3) 612 Where great accuracy and the measurement of minute spaces [in growth] are demanded, recourse must be had to special instruments called Auxanometers. 1887 BATESON & DARWIN in *Jrnl. Linn. Soc., Bot.* XXIV. 2 The increase in length was measured by means of an auxanometer-lever.

Auxetophone (ǭksĕ·tǒfōun). [f. Gr. αὐξητός that may be increased + φωνή sound.] A pneumatic recorder for a phonograph; also, a phonograph fitted with this recorder.

1904 *Daily Chron.* 9 June 4/6 The Hon. C. A. Parsons..has recently amused himself by devising a little valve called the auxetophone which promises..to advance the phonograph. 1907 *Ibid.* 6 Aug. 4/7 An instrument..known as the Auxetophone, gives..vocal and instrumental selections. 1911 *Musical Assoc. Proc.* 73 They will be required to sing their parts..into some reproducing medium of the phonograph order..(but with Parsons' auxetophones attached).

Auxochrome (ǭ·ksokrōum). [f. Gr. αὐξάνειν to increase + χρῶμα colour.] Any salt-forming atomic group that, when combined with a chromogen, produces a dyestuff. Hence **Auxochromic** (-krōu·mik), **Auxochromous** (-krōu·məs), *adjs.*, defining such groups.

1893 *Athenæum* 15 July 100/1 They [sc. chromogens] become true dyestuffs by the introduction of..what Witt terms auxochromes. 1895 *Bloxam's Chem.* (ed. 8) 662 An acid auxochrome will yield an acid dyestuff, capable of being fixed by a basic mordant (alumina, &c.). 1902 *Brit. Jrnl. Photogr.* 11 Apr. 299 Auxochromic groups. 1902 *Encycl. Brit.* XXVII. 564/2 Such compounds containing chromophorous groups are termed chromogens, because, although not dyestuffs themselves, they are capable of generating such by the further introduction of salt-forming atomic groups—*e.g.*, OH, NH_2. These Witt terms auxochromous groups.

Auxospore (ǭ·ksospōəɹ). *Bot.* [f. Gr. αὔξειν to grow + σπόρος SPORE.] A spore formed in diatoms by the union of two cells or by the excessive growth of an individual cell. Also, the resting-spore of the diatoms.

1884 MASTERS & BENNETT *Henfrey's Elem. Bot.* (ed. 4) 425 The individuals must..constantly diminish in size, until the original size is restored by the production of auxospores. 1888 *Encycl. Brit.* XXIV. 126/2 *Diatomaceæ*...Reproduction, vegetative by division or by means of asexually-produced spores (auxospores). 1904 G. S. WEST *Brit. Freshwater Algæ* 269 A normal auxospore can be regarded as one produced by the conjugation of two cells (or gametes), those produced without conjugation being parthenogenetic.

Avail, *sb.* **5.** (Earlier U.S. example.)

1812 A. STODDARD *Louisiana* (Bartlett) Expecting to subsist on the bounty of government, rather than on the avails of their own industry.

Avail, *v.* **5. a.** Add quots.:

1899 *Westm. Gaz.* 25 Aug. 4/1 It is now definitely settled that the Admiralty..will avail of the opportunity..for the renewal of the subsidies. 1927 *Daily Tel.* 30 Aug. 8/6 The wonderful system of drainage is being availed of.

Availability. 1. b. (Earlier U.S. example.)

1844 *Congress. Globe* 4 June 683 App. (Th.) The *Eastern Argus* describes the following as the traits of character which, in the estimation of the Whigs, constitute the *ne plus ultra* of 'availability'.

Available, *a.* Add:

3. b. *U.S. Politics.* That the party can avail itself of, for special reasons apart from statesmanship, as a candidate for election. (Cf. AVAILABILITY 1 b.)

1840 *Congressional Globe* 6 Mar. (Thornton) Goody Harrison, a gossiping old lady, and an available. 1842 H. MANN *Fourth July Orat.* (Boston) 66 If we would have better times, the available school teacher must be sought for, as anxiously as the available candidate for office. 1848 *N. Y. Tribune* May (Bartlett) Mr. Clay is a great man—able statesman—all of us prefer him to anybody else if he could be elected, but I'm afraid he isn't available. 1864 HOLLAND *Lett. to Joneses* 278 Occasionally a patriot has been 'available' for carrying out the purposes of politicians. But often imbecility and rascality have been found 'available'. 1888 BRYCE *Amer. Commw.* III. lxx. II. 550 The man fittest to be adopted as candidate..is the man most likely to win, the man who, to use the technical term, is most 'available'. 1906 *Westm. Gaz.* 11 Jan. 2/1 What the Americans would call an 'available' man—that is to say, a man of sufficient prestige and authority to be well in the front rank.

Availingly (ăvē^i·liŋli), *adv.* [f. AVAILING *ppl. a.* + -LY[2].] In an availing manner; so as to avail or profit.

1853 FABER *Ess. Lives of Saints* 116 Its intrinsic beauty pleads availingly with the man of letters. 1871 *Contemp. Rev.* XIX. 136 Neither the royal Placet,..nor the right to convene synods, could be availingly employed.

Aval (ē^i·văl), *a.* [f. L. *avus* grandfather + -AL.] Relating to grandparents.

1884 *Science* 21 Mar. 345/2 There is reason to believe that aval heredity is relatively more frequent than direct parental heredity.

Avalanche (æ·vălɑnʃ), *v.* [f. AVALANCHE *sb.*] *intr.* To descend in or like an avalanche; also *trans.*, to carry by or as by an avalanche.

1897 *Daily News* 31 Mar. 6/5 He was gently avalanched downstairs into the street. 1899 SOMERVILLE & ROSS *Irish R. M.* 244, I avalanched down the companion. 1923 *Daily Mail* 23 June 7 The boulders on the edge are continually avalanching down.

Avalanchy (æ·vălɑnʃi), *a.* [f. AVALANCHE *sb.* + -Y[1].] Liable to descend in or be swept by an avalanche.

1894 FENN *In Alpine Valley* I. vi. 117 Rather an avalanchy place, this. 1894 *Contemp. Rev.* Aug. 218 Snow-slopes, of which one was rotten and avalanchy.

Avalite (æ·vălait). *Min.* [ad. G. *avalit* (1884), f. *Avala*, name of a mountain near Belgrade, its locality + -ITE[1].] A green earthy mineral containing chromium oxide.

1889 in *Cent. Dict.* 1896 CHESTER *Dict. Min.*

Avar (ā·vaɹ). A member of an Ural-Altaic race, prominent in south-eastern Europe from the 6th to the 9th c. A.D. Hence **Avarian** (avā·riăn), *a.*, of or pertaining to the Avars.

1882 FREEMAN *Lect. Amer. Audiences* 339 The Empire which had beaten back the Persian and the Avar lost its provinces to the Saracen and the Bulgarian. 1902 *Encycl. Brit.* XXVII. 341/2 The Avarian is a sort of inter-tribal tongue. 1911 WEBSTER s.v., *Avarian rings*, vestiges of Avarian fortifications formed by stakes surrounding a settlement. 1920 H. G. WELLS *Outline of Hist.* VI. xxxi. § 1 The Avars and Slavs struck down from the Danube country towards the Adriatic.

Avenolith (ăvī·nolip). *Path.* [irreg. f. L. *avena* oats + Gr. λίθος stone, -LITH.] An intestinal calculus or concretion formed around a grain of oats.

1897 [see *oat-stone* s.v. OAT *sb.* 6 b].

Aventurine. Add:

4. aventurine sealing-wax, sealing-wax of a translucent brown colour speckled with gold.

1900 KIPLING in *Daily Express* 29 June 4/6 In one hand he held a stick of avanturine sealing-wax, and in the other a..seal.

Avenue, *sb.* **4.** (Examples of U.S. usage.)

1780 J. MASON Jr. in *Boston Orat.* (1785) 135 Till oppression stalked at noonday through every avenue in your cities. 1799–1801 *Deb. Congress* (1851) 1336 Four thousand five hundred of which lots shall be to the southwest of Massachusetts avenue. 1851 C. CIST *Cincinnati* 147 Only the leading avenues were marked out and graded. 1892 J. A. RIIS *How other half lives* 160 East of Second Avenue and west of Ninth Avenue as far up as the Park. 1901 *Munsey's Mag.* XXIV. 530/1 Somewhat wider streets, termed 'avenues'.

Avenued (æ·vĭniūd), *ppl. a.* [f. AVENUE *sb.* or *v.*] Furnished with or having an avenue or avenues.

1870 RUSKIN *Verona* § 31 One paradise of lovely pasture and avenued forest of chestnut and blossomed trees. 1899 *Daily News* 7 Nov. 3/5 An open, avenued, highly-cultivated plateau.

Average, *v.* Add:

4. *intr.* with *out*: To work out so as to produce an average. Also *trans.* in corresponding sense.

1910 SHAW *Misalliance* (1925) 41 Averages out the human race. Makes the nigger half an Englishman. Makes the Englishman half a nigger. 1922 *Times Lit. Suppl.* 28 Sept. 610/4 The particular obstacles will vary from time to time and from species to species, but on the whole will average out. 1928 *Britain's Industr. Future* (*Liberal Ind. Inquiry*) v. xxxi. § 5 446 Any attempt to average out burdens.

Aversant, *a.* Delete † *Obs. rare*[−1] and add: *Her.* Turned to show the back (said of a right hand).

1830 ROBSON *Brit. Herald* III. Gloss., *Aversant*, or *Dorsed*; as, a right hand *dorsed* or *aversant*, when turned to shew the back part. 1889 ELVIN *Dict. Her.*

Avertive (ăvɔ̄·ɹtiv), *a.* [f. AVERT *v.* + -IVE.] Designed to avert or ward off.

1889 *Cornhill Mag.* May 491 A series of avertive and violent sweeps of a table-napkin. 1895 *Q. Rev.* July 211 We are not convinced that the heraldic animals were originally 'avertive' amulets.

Avesta (ăve·stă). = ZEND-AVESTA, q.v. Hence **Ave·stan, Ave·stic** *adjs.*, of or belonging to the Avesta; *sbs.* the language of the Avesta.

1868 *Chambers's Encycl.* X. 344/1 Old sayings in the Avesta. 1881 OGILVIE (Annandale), Avestan. 1888 *Encycl. Brit.* XXIV. 775/2 Although the Avesta is a work of but moderate compass..there..exists no single MS. which gives it in its entirety. 1922 *Times Lit. Suppl.* 27 Apr. 279/2 Kurmanji is in consonance with Pahlevi and New Persian in many of its..developments from Avestic.

Aviate (ē^i·vieit), *v.* [Back-formation from AVIATION.] *intr.* To navigate the air in an aeroplane; to 'fly'.

1900 *Manch. Guard.* 4 Apr. 9/2 In the event of the sudden failure of the aviating mechanism. 1908 *Punch* 21 Oct. 305/2 'To aviate' is nauseous enough, and 'planing', in the atmospheric slang of country-house parties, is pretty bad; but we do draw the line at 'aerogation'.

Aviatik (aviatī·k). [G. (= aeronautics, flying), f. *aviat-* as in AVIATION.] A type of aeroplane made by the Aviatik und Automobil Aktien Gesellschaft of Leipzig (1910–1922).

1914 *Scotsman* 20 Oct. 3/3 A duel in the air..between two biplanes—a Voison (French) and an Aviatik (German). 1915 *Morning Post* 22 July 7/4 Three aviatiks were put to flight by our pursuing aeroplanes. 1920 *All the World's Aircraft* 175 a, Aviatik aircraft.

Aviation (ē^ivi,ē^i·ʃən). [ad. F. *aviation*, irreg. f. L. *avis* bird + -ATION.] Aerial navigation by means of an aeroplane (see *AEROPLANE 2); 'flying'.

1887 tr. *J. Verne's Clipper of Clouds* iv, Robur the conqueror had flown, as if some apparatus of aviation had borne him into the air. 1891 *Daily News* 27 Aug. 5/1 The frequency of the term 'aviation' as a synonym for aerial navigation. 1891 *Century Mag.* Oct. 829 *note*, The French, I believe, have agreed on the term 'aviation' in case they ever succeed in flying. 1910 R. FERRIS *How it Flies* 455 *Aviation*—Flying by means of power-propelled machines which are not buoyed up in the air, as with gas bags. 1911 *Daily Express* 13 June 1/3 The Home Secretary has issued an order prohibiting aviation in specified areas.

attrib. 1908 *Daily Report* 12 Sept. 4/4 Santos-Dumont..won the first aviation prize. 1909 *Westm. Gaz.* 9 Mar. 4/2 The Gordon-Bennett Aviation Cup. *Ibid.* 14 Sept. 7/4 A new aviation motor of 30-h.p. 1909 *Daily Chron.* 18 Mar. 1/5 The King..drove by motor-car to the aviation ground. 1909 *Ibid.* 18 Aug. 1/1 The great aviation week at Rheims. 1915 T. F. FARMAN in *Blackw. Mag.* Apr. 435/2 The ever-increasing number of avions and aviation pilots.

Aviator (ē^i·vieitəɹ). [ad. F. *aviateur*, f. L. *avis* bird + *-ateur* -ATOR.]

†1. A flying-machine (cf. *AEROPLANE 2). Also *attrib. Obs.*

1891 *Brooklyn Morning Jrnl.* 22 July 1/6 (Funk) Mr. Maxim's invention is called an Aviator. It is in form like a huge kite of silk, to which hangs a platform carrying the engines and the screw propellers. 1892 *Sci. Amer.* 13 Feb. 105 Mr. Trouvé considers his apparatus as the lightest aviator that it is..possible to construct. 1895 *Knowledge* 2 Dec. 276/1 Mr. Maxim represents gunnery and the aviator flying machine. *Ibid.* 276/2 It appears..impracticable..to suppose that aviators could be put to any other use, for purposes of war, than that of observing an enemy [etc.]. 1901 *Flying* Dec. 13 The non-rotative motor for use with wing-propelled aviators.

2. The pilot of an aeroplane.

In early use, as distinguished from an aeronaut.

1896 *Westm. Gaz.* 15 Sept. 1/3 Intending aviators and aeronauts. 1902 *Daily Chron.* 18 Sept. 3/3 Thus the aeronaut has so far accomplished more than the 'aviator'. 1908 *Westm. Gaz.* 13 Aug. 6/3 Mr. Wilbur Wright..made another ascent with his aeroplane...The aviator then decided on making a new experiment. 1909 *Ibid.* 26 Oct. 1/3 Other 'aviators'—the word has forced itself into the vocabulary, and it seems futile to resist it any longer—had other machines. 1911 *Yorksh. Post* 3 Aug. 9/6 At height of 1,000 metres an aviator can find a submarine.

Hence **A·viatress, -trice, -trix**, a female aviator.

1910 *Daily Chron.* 5 Jan. 1/7 The aviatrice made a bad turn. 1911 *Aero* June 74/2 Various articles on the subject of 'Aviatresses' which have appeared from time to time. 1919 *The Vote* 1 Aug. 275/2 A Famous Aviatress [Baroness de la Roche]. 1921 *Glasgow Herald* 15 Oct. 10 Miss Madeleine Davis, a well-known aviatrice in the States. 1921 *Blackw. Mag.* Dec. 716/1, I had been an aviatress. 1927 *Glasgow Herald* 29 Sept. 11 The English aviatrix, Miss Evelyn Spooner.

Avicennia (ăvisenĭ·ă). [Named after *Avicenna*, Arabian physician (980–1037).] A plant of the genus so named, esp. *A. tomentosa*, the White Mangrove.

1829 LOUDON *Encycl. Plants* (1836) 522. 1871 KINGSLEY *At Last* xiii, The statelier Avicennias, or white mangroves. 1883 *Encycl. Brit.* XV. 481/2 The 'white mangrove', *Avicennia*, a verbenaceous plant.

Avicolous (ăvi·kŏləs), *a.* [f. L. *avis* bird + *-colus* inhabiting + -OUS.] Living, as parasites, on birds.

1895 *Cambr. Nat. Hist.* V. 349 The greater portion of the avicolous species have two claws.

Aviculoid (ăvi·kiuloid), *a.* [f. mod.L. *Avicula*, dim. of *avis* bird + -OID.] Resembling (that of) bivalves of the genus *Avicula*, which have pearly shells.

1886 *Amer. Jrnl. Sci.* Ser. III. XXXI. 140 *Strophodonta planulata* (?) occurs in a blue stratum not far below the Oriskany, associated with an aviculoid shell probably *Megambonia aviculoidea*.

Aviculturist (ē^i·vikɒltiŭrist). [f. AVICULTURE + -IST.] One who practises aviculture; a bird-fancier.

1904 *Nature* 31 Mar. 507/2 His work forms an excellent history of these beautiful birds, and is alike interesting to the field naturalist and the aviculturist. 1923 *Glasgow Herald* 23 Oct. 6 Probably Mr Farrar thinks that only aviculturists will concern themselves with his writing.

Aviette (ăvie·t). [Fr., f. *avion* + -ETTE.] An engineless aeroplane or glider.

1912 *Daily News* 1 June 1/4 It is called an aviette competition, an aviette being a flying machine propelled by muscular force alone. 1923 *Westm. Gaz.* 7 Apr., The 'Aviette', as the new glider with an auxiliary motor threatens to call itself.

Aviform (ē^i·vifǫɹm), *a.* [f. L. *avis* bird + -FORM.] Bird-like in structure and form.

1876 HUXLEY *Lect. Evol.* in Essays (1893) IV. 110 These more or less avi-form reptiles of the Mesozoic epoch.

Avion (avyoṅ). [F. *avion*, f. *aviateur* AVIATOR, app. after *ballon* BALLOON.] A flying-machine, esp. a French aeroplane.

1898 *Sci. Amer.* 27 Aug. 137 The 'Avion' in its position of flight. 1915 T. F. FARMAN in *Blackw. Mag.* Apr. 435/1 How many avions the French and British military authorities possessed when war broke out. 1927 *Chambers's Jrnl.* 258/2 Less easy prey they may be for the avions.

Avoidance. Add:

7. b. *Anthropology.* The custom prevalent among many primitive tribes by which one member of a family is forbidden to meet and address another member.

[1865 TYLOR *Early Hist. Man.* x. 287 Their object seems to be in general the avoidance of intercourse or connexion between parents-in-law and children-in-law...But the reasons for this avoidance are not clear.] *a* 1903 J. J. ATKINSON *Primal Law* 269 Avoidance would arise at the same time between mother-in-law and son-in-law. 1903 *Lancet* 22 Aug. 532/2 The conditions in which he lived with the female members of his own family gave origin to the curious etiquette of 'avoidances' which is still to be found amongst some savage races.

Avro (æ·vro). [From the name of *A. V. Roe*, the designer.] The name of a type of aeroplane designed by A. V. Roe.

1909 *Bolton* (Lancs.) *Jrnl. & Guardian* 15 Oct., A breezy-natured young man of 31 or 32, he has named his flying machine the Avro-plane, the first three letters forming his own initials and, further, 'avro' being akin to the Latin words which relate to flying. 1920 *Glasgow Herald* 10 July 5 A baby Avro (which won the aerial Derby in 1919). 1922 RALEIGH *War in the Air* I. 355 An Avro, with an 80-horse-power Gnome engine.

Awakenedness (ăwē^i·k'ndnės). [f. AWAKENED *ppl. a.* + -NESS.] The condition of being awakened.

1869 J. M. CAMPBELL *Christ the Bread of Life* (ed. 2) 61 Some measure of awakenedness on the subject of religion. 1883 MEREDITH *Earth & Man* xxxiii, With awakenedness of glee To feel stern joy her origin.

Awakeningly (ăwē^i·k'niŋli), *adv.* [f. AWAKENING *ppl. a.* + -LY[2].] In an awakening manner; so as to awaken.

1865 MEREDITH *R. Fleming* xlii, 'Hoy, Gammon!' he sang out, awakeningly to ordinary ears. 1866 — *Vittoria* xx, The intentness sent that last falling..note travelling awakeningly through their minds.

Awareness (ăwē^ə·ɹnės). [f. AWARE *a.* + -NESS.] The condition of being aware (*of* something or *that* something is).

1828 MOIR *Mansie Wauch* xxii, My awareness of the danger of riding in such vehicles. 1880 [see Dict.]. 1885 *Sat. Rev.* 31 Oct. 590 The most pig-headed Englishman and the most stolid German have..an awareness (if we may be granted the word) of the existence and manners of foreign barbarians. 1892 *Monist* II. 239 The fall of a stone may be characterised as a blind motion without awareness. 1904 *Daily Chron.* 16 Sept. 3/4 He has the peculiar 'awareness' of a soundly cultured Catholic. 1915 C. C. MARTINDALE *In God's Army* 125 An ultimate awareness that right is right. 1925 *Punch* 20 May 559/1 And, since I own his charm of style, I can't be saddled with unfairness For wishing he had spared those vile New *clichés*, 'glimpsing' and 'awareness'.

A-wash, awash. Add: Also as attrib. adj.

1897 *Strand Mag.* Christmas No. 641/1 A coasting schooner had..come to grief on the just awash rocks. 1901 *Westm. Gaz.* 14 Mar. 8/2 The boat will be brought to an awash condition. 1903 *Motorist's Ann.* 281 Making, with her submersion tanks empty, an average speed of 8½ knots; in the 'awash' condition, 8 knots.

Away, *adv.* Add:

II. and **V.** In reference to games or matches played away from the home ground; so *away point*, one scored in such a match.

1893 *Abingdon Sch. Football Club Fixture Card*, Oct. 18, St. John's School, Away. 1902 *The Ousel* Christmas No., Only losing to Dulwich (away) by 19 runs. 1907 *Daily Chron.* 14 Jan. 9/1 Thirteen drawn games and three away wins. *Ibid.* 28 Oct. 9/4 Arsenal's 'away' point. *Ibid.* 16 Dec. 1/7 Chelsea won their first victory 'away'. 1923 *Daily Mail* 11 Jan. 9 West Ham have played so well in recent away games.

11. b. Used with intensive force, chiefly with advs., as *away back, down, up*, etc., = far. *U.S.*

1873 J. H. BEADLE *Western Wilds* xxix. 450 Tourists by the Pacific Railway think themselves away up when at Sherman. 1891 MARAH E. RYAN *Told in Hills* III. vii. 234, I allow that—a d—d good man..and a fighter from away back. 1903 W. F. JOHNSON *Century of Expansion* 81 He insisted upon this away back in the Revolution. 1903 *N. Y. Sun* 26 Nov. 5 Turkeys are away up in price. 1904 *N. Y. Tribune* 15 May 8 The next American port..is away down in the twenty-first place. 1906 *N. Y. Even. Post* 28 Apr., Manufacturers of all good cars are away behind in their deliveries. 1910 W. M. RAINE *B. O'Connor* 217 That..pony in front belongs to sheriff Forbes, or I'm away wrong.

c. *From away*, from a distance. *U.S.*

1888 *Boston Jrnl.* 6 Nov. 1/4 It is rumored that capitalists from away are making an effort to establish an industry in Rockland.

Awedly (ǭ·dli), *adv.* [f. AWED *ppl. a.* + -LY[2].] In an awed manner.

1927 *Chambers's Jrnl.* 301/1 'He's afraid!' the girl repeated—rather whisperingly, rather awedly.

Aweto (ăwē^i·to, ăwī·to). [Maori.] The vegetable caterpillar of New Zealand, consisting of a fungus which fastens upon caterpillars and mummifies them; dried and burnt it produces a pigment.

1889 [see *vegetable caterpillar*, VEGETABLE *a.* 7]. 1896 A. B. JONES in *Pearson's Mag.* Sept. 290 The dye..was a solution of burnt or powdered resin, or wood, or the aweto.

Awful, *a.* **4.** (Earlier U.S. examples.)

1814 J. LAMBERT *Trav. Canada & U.S.* (1816) II. 505 Every thing that creates surprise is *awful* with them; 'what an *awful* wind! *awful* hole! *awful* hill! *awful* mouth! *awful* nose! &c.' 1816 PICKERING *Vocab.* 42 *Awful*, Disagreeable, ugly. *New England.* In New England many people would call a disagreeable medicine, *awful*; an ugly woman, an awful looking woman...This word, however, is never used except in conversation, and is far from being so common in the sea-ports now, as it was some years ago.

b. As *adv.* = AWFULLY *adv.* 3.

1846–52 MRS. WHITCHER *Widow Bedott P.* ix. 89, I never thought *that* was so awful handsome as some folks does. 1848 BARTLETT *Dict. Amer.* s.v., It is even used in this sense adverbially...Thus we not unfrequently hear such expressions as 'an awful cold day'. 1876 'MARK TWAIN' *Tom Sawyer* ii. 17 You see, Aunt Polly's awful particular about this fence. 1891 MARY E. WILKINS *New England Nun* 123 I'm awful glad you've come. *Ibid.* 129, I did an awful mean thing marryin' you. 1921 R. D. PAINE *Comr. Rolling Ocean* iii. 39 A prairie town called Follansbee that looks awful good to me.

Awfully, *adv.* **3.** (Earlier U.S. example, in sense 'very badly'.)

1816 PICKERING *Vocab.* 42 A perverse, ill-natured child, that disobeys his parents, would be said to behave *awfully*.

Awheel (ăhwī·l), *adv.* [f. A *prep.*[1] + WHEEL *sb.*] On wheels, on a cycle, cycling. Cf. AWHEELS.

1888 PENNELL in *Pall Mall Gaz.* 25 Oct. 5, I have looked forward to my annual trips awheel..with..delight. 1890 *Pictorial World* 4 Dec. 706/2 The average cyclist will not perhaps be tempted awheel on a dirty day. 1903 ARTHUR JOSE (*title*) Two Awheel and some others afoot in Australia.

Awkward, *a.* Add:

7. c. Phr. *The awkward age*: the time of life when one is no longer a child and yet not properly grown up. (Cf. F. *l'âge ingrat.*)

1895 *Windsor Mag.* I. 705/1 She was..at what ladies call 'the awkward age'. 1928 *Daily Mirror* 7 Dec. 11/2 'How old are you, Bobbie?' 'I'm just at the awkward age.' 'What do you call the awkward age?' 'I'm too old to cry and too young to swear.'

Awn (ǭn), *v.*[3] [Back-formation from AWNING.] **a.** *intr.* To hang as or like an awning. **b.** *trans.* To cover or shelter with an awning. Said also of the awning itself. So **Aw·ning** *ppl. a.*

a 1839 GALT *Demon Destiny* VII. 48 The awning clouds were as a cavern's ceil. 1844 THACKERAY *May Gambols* Wks. 1900 XIII. 420 Trafalgar Square is to be awned in. 1890 *Longm. Mag.* Apr. 630 Trust Mrs. Robson for seeing that her guests were well awned on a night like this. 1904 *Daily Chron.* 8 July 7/3 The ball rested..on the canvas that goes to awn the first floor.

Axe, *sb.* Add:

The axe (fig.): the cutting down of expenditure in the public services; also, a body appointed to do this. Hence **Axe** *v. trans.*, to remove (officials, etc.) to save expenditure; to cut down (expenditure) by means of 'the axe'.

1922 *Glasgow Herald* 5 Oct. 7 Another class of military officers for some of whom assistance..may be needed are those who are the unhappy victims of the Geddes economy 'axe.' *Ibid.*, The 'axed' officer. 1923 LIEUT.-COL. W. GUINNESS *Sp. Ho. Comm.* 15 Mar., Under the Geddes recommendations fifteen hundred officers had been 'axed'. 1923 *Times* 16 Mar. 12/1 Army and the 'axe'. Limit of safety reached...No fewer than 1,500 officers had fallen before the Geddes axe. 1923 *Daily Mail* 28 June 10 Lord Inchcape, the chairman of the Committee which recently 'axed' the expenditure of the Services in India. 1926 *Encycl. Brit.* New Suppl. II. 160/2 Sir Eric [Geddes] himself was appointed in Aug. 1921 chairman of a small committee, later known as the 'Geddes Axe', to recommend public economies to the Government. 1926 *Times Lit. Suppl.* 21 Jan., The Inchcape Axe has not deprived students of the Memoirs issued by the Archæological Survey.

Ax(e)man. 1. *U.S.* (Earlier examples.)

1671 *Essex Inst. Hist. Coll.* XX. 145 The time of meeting for ax men is to be by the sun half an hour high. 1777 *Maryland Jrnl.* 18 Mar. (Th.) Five hundred good carpenters, with ax-men and sawyers in proportion. 1785 A. ELLICOTT in *Life & Lett.* (1908) 45 From a Hill where our Axe-men are now Encamped we have a most beautiful Prospect.

Axillant (æksi·lănt), *a. Bot.* [f. AXILLA + -ANT.] Of or growing from the axil.

1883 *Encycl. Brit.* XVI. 841/2 A bud with its axillant leaf. 1899 *Nature* 15 June 149/1 Buds are protected by means of developments of the axillant leaf.

Axite (æ·ksait). [f. *ax* in *bonax, primax*, names of sporting cartridges manufactured by Messrs. Kynoch (I.C.I. Metals Ltd.) + *-ite* of CORDITE.] A smokeless powder for sporting rifles, composed of strip cordite in which a little of the gun-cotton is replaced by potassium nitrate.

1904 *Trade Mark Jrnl.* 19 Oct. 1905 *Kynoch Jrnl.* Jan.–Mar. VI. 86 'Axite' Service cartridge. 1915 A. MARSHALL *Explosives* 239 Kynoch Ltd. in axite have replaced a portion of the gun-cotton by means of potassium nitrate or oxalates of potassium and barium. 1919 E. de B. BARNETT *Explosives* 78 Axite..is practically Cordite M.D. to which 2 per cent. of potassium nitrate has been added. 1921 *Blackw. Mag.* Dec. 802/2 A high-velocity axite charge.

Axminster (æ·ksminstəɹ). [The name of a town in Devonshire.] Used attrib. in *Axminster carpet* or *rug*, a seamless carpet formerly manufactured at Axminster, noted for its thick and soft pile resembling that of a Turkey carpet. Also used *absol.*

1818 *Public Ledger & Daily Advertiser* 1 Apr. 1/4 Capital Axminster, Turkey, Brussels, and Kidderminster carpets. 1845 DISRAELI *Sybil* II. i, The Axminster carpets [etc.] imparted even to this palatian chamber a lively and habitable air. 1853 URE *Dict. Arts* (ed. 4) I. 380 Fabrics with a cut pile, like the Axminster or Wilton rugs or carpets. 1876 *Encycl. Brit.* V. 131/1 Patent Axminster Carpets owe their origin to Mr James Templeton of Glasgow, who obtained a patent for his invention in 1839.

Axon (æ·ksǫn). *Anat.* Also **axone**, pl. **axones**. [ad. Gr. ἄξων axis.] **a.** The body axis. **b.** An axis cylinder process of a nerve cell.

1848 DUNGLISON *Med. Lex.* (ed. 7), *Axon*, axis. 1884 WILDER in *N. Y. Med. Jrnl.* 2 Aug. 113 *Axon*, the mesal, longitudinal, skeletal axis, represented in Branchiostoma and embryos by a membrano-gelatinous notochord. 1899 L. HILL *Human Physiol.* xxix. 337 Each [nerve-] fibre consists of a soft central strand of protoplasmic substance called the axon or axis cylinder. 1902 *Encycl. Brit.* XXV. 394/1 A neurone consists of three parts..(2) A single filament or axon, starting from the perikaryon.

Axoneme (æ·ksonīm). [f. Gr. ἄξων axis + νῆμα thread.] One of the threads or strands in the central portion of the contractile stalk of *Vorticellidæ*.

1901 G. N. CALKINS *Protozoa* 179 The strand has three threads which Entz calls *spasmoneme*, *spironeme*, and *axoneme*.

Azaleine (ăzē^i·li,in). *Chem.* Also **-in**. [f. AZALEA + -INE[5].] = ROSANILINE.

1894 GOULD *Dict. Med.*, *Azalein*.., same as *Rosanilin*. 1900 G. ILES *Flame, Electricity & Camera* 283 The dyes at present used in the preparation of orthochromatic plates are chiefly eosin,..azaleine, and croculein.

Azan (ăzā·n). [Arabic اذان *adān* invitation.] The Mohammedan call to public prayers, made by the crier from the minaret of the mosque.

1855 R. F. BURTON *El-Medinah* xvii. II. 142 Here he prayed, hearkening to the Azan, or devotion-call, from the roof. 1922 *Blackw. Mag.* Dec. 821/2, I was wakened by the sound of the Azan from the village mosque close by.

Azelaic (æzĭlē^i·ik), *a. Chem.* [f. AZO- + Gr. ἔλαιον oil + -IC.] In *Azelaic acid* = ANCHOIC *acid*.

1838 *British Annual for 1839* (ed. R. D. Thomson) 350 Azelaic acid. 1885 REMSEN *Org. Chem.* 142 Azelaic acid, $C_7H_{14}(CO_2H)_2$.

Azilian (ăzi·liăn), *a. Archæol.* [f. *Azil* in Mas d'Azil (dept. of Ariège, France), where discoveries were made by Ed. Piette of primitive civilization; cf. F. *époque asylienne*, etc. (f. med.L. *Asylum*: see *L'Anthropologie*, VI. (1895) 151).] Of or belonging to the transition period between the palæolithic and neolithic ages. Also *sb.*

1899 A. H. KEANE *Man: Past & Present* 30 M. Piette..states..that '13 out of 23 Phoenician characters were equally Azilian graphic signs.' 1920 J. RITCHIE *Infl. Man Anim. Life Scot.* 30 The shell-mounds of the Azilian or early Neolithic settlers in Oronsay. 1920 H. G. WELLS *Outline of Hist.* x. § 4 For a time there were in Southern Europe drifting communities of some little known people who are called the Azilians. *Ibid.*, These Azilian people have left behind them a multitude of pebbles, roughly daubed with markings.

Azo-. Add:

3. b. Azo-colours, -dyes, a group of coal-tar colours or dyes.

1879 WITT in *Jrnl. Chem. Soc.* XXXV. *Trans.* 181 The variety of azo-colours in the market, and the number of patents..are constantly increasing. 1884 *Ibid.* XLVI. *Abstracts* 237 The preparation of azo-dyes from the trisulphonic acids of β-naphthol. 1894 GOULD *Dict. Med.*, *Azo-dyes*, a well defined group of the coal-tar colors, all containing the diatomic group −N=N−, bound on either side to a benzene radical. 1902 *Encycl. Brit.* XXVII. 559/1 Azo colours which are developed..upon the fibre itself (usually cotton) by the successive application of their constituent elements.

Azoimide (æzo,i·maid). *Chem.* [f. AZO- + IMIDE.] Hydrazoic acid.

1891 *Athenæum* 24 Jan. 126/1 Prof. Curtius..has obtained the compound N_3H, to which he has given the name azoimide or hydrogen nitride. 1894 [see HYDRAZOIC *a.*].

Azolla (ăzǫ·lă). [mod.L.; said to be f. Gr. ἄζειν to dry + ὀλλύναι to slay.] A genus of small floating plants of the family *Salviniaceæ*; a plant of this genus.

1872 DOMETT *Ranolf* xiv. 221 Minute azolla-stains of ruddiest hue. 1877 tr. *F. von. Müller's Botanic Teachings* 130 Of Marsiliaceæ we have examples..in the *Azollas*.., which in large often purplish sheets float like duckweeds.

Azotea (aþotē^i·ă). [Sp.] The flat roof of a house, used as a place of resort in hot climates.

1921 *Chambers's Jrnl.* 257/2 Roses and carnations..trailing from every *azotea*. 1925 *Ibid.* 469/2 This space..to which he ascended in pleasant summer evenings was his azotea.

Azoted (æ·zoutėd), *a.* [f. AZOTE + -ED.] Nitrogenized, azotized.

1848 DUNGLISON *Med. Lex.* (ed. 7), *Azoted*, nitrogenized.

1872 AITKEN *Sci. & Pract. Med.* (ed. 6) II. 1061 In proportion as animals are fed on animal diet or on azoted substances, their urine becomes more and more loaded with lithic acid.

Azoxy (æ·zǫksi), *a.* [f. AZ(OTE + OXY(GEN.] Defining a compound containing the azoxy group of elements consisting of an azo-group into which an oxygen atom has been introduced.

1894 *Rep. Brit. Assoc. Advancem. Sci.* 245 Very interesting in point of fastness to light are the azoxy colours.

Aztec (æ·ztek), *sb.* and *a.* An Indian of the Nahuatian tribe, which founded the empire of Mexico. Also *attrib.* or as *adj.* = **A·ztecan.**

1787 CULLEN tr. *Clavigero's Hist. Mexico* I. II. 112 The Aztecas or Mexicans, who were the last people who settled in Anahuac. 1814 HELEN M. WILLIAMS tr. *Humboldt's Researches* I. 81 The Toltecks, the Cicimecks, the Alcolhuans, the Tlascaltecks, and the Aztecks, who, notwithstanding their political divisions, spoke the same language. *Ibid.* 83 Tezcatlipoca, the first of the Azteck divinities after Teotl. 1835 *Penny Cycl.* III. 208. 1886 *Science* 5 Nov. 403/2 Its circular ornamentation is not Artecan. 1920 *Edin. Rev.* Oct. 350 In the Aztec mind, stone was symbolic of the atonement of sin. 1922 W. R. INGE *Outspoken Essays* Ser. II. 74 The half-civilised Aztecs practised human sacrifice and cannibalism.

Azurine, *sb.* Add:

Dyeing. A base obtained from aniline black, giving a bluish black shade in printing; also the colour itself.

1878 *Jrnl. Chem. Soc.* XXXIV. *Abstracts* 572 Azurine is characterised by the blue fluorescence of its solutions. 1894 GOULD *Dict. Med.*, *Azurin*..Same as *Azulin*. 1902 *Encycl. Brit.* XXVII. 563/2 There are several oxidation products of aniline. The first..is..emeraldine..which by treatment with alkali yields a dark blue base called azurine.

Azygospore (ăzəi·gospōəɹ, ăzi·g-). *Bot.* [f. A- *prefix* 14 + ZYGOSPORE.] A spore not formed by conjugation but by direct conversion (see quot.).

1894 in GOULD *Dict. Med.*, etc. 1898 H. C. PORTER tr. *Strasburger's Bot.* 348 Although the conjugating hyphæ meet in pairs, no fusion takes place, and their terminal cells become converted directly into spores, which are termed azygospores.

B

B. III. Add: B. and S., brandy and soda; B.B.C., British Broadcasting Corporation (before 1927, Company).

a 1878 WHYTE-MELVILLE *Black but comely* xxvii. (1879) II. 112 Now for a B-and-S, one quiet cigar, and then bed. 1882 *Punch* 11 Feb. 69/1 He'll nothing drink but 'B. & S.' and big magnums of 'the Boy'. 1925 *Ibid.* 22 Apr. 440/1 The daily wireless programme of the B.B.C. 1926 *Encycl. Brit.* New Suppl. I. 454/2 The 'B.B.C.' is constituted as a limited company, the shareholders being wireless manufacturers and traders.

Baas (bās). [Du.: see BOSS *sb.*[6]] In S. Africa: A master, employer of labour. Often as a form of address.

In quot. 1625 used for a ship's captain.

1625 PURCHAS *Pilgrimes* I. II. 117 Our Baase (for so a Dutch Captaine is called). 1785 G. FORSTER tr. *Sparrman's Voy.* I. 55 The steward (or as they call him there, the *baas*) presented me with a glass of strong-bodied wine. 1801 *Damberger's Trav.* (Dublin) I. 26 The officers who do not serve in the regular military force, and called *bas* (or *bas-officiers*). 1850 R. G. CUMMING *Hunter's Life S. Afr.* i, At the door he is met by the baas, or master. *Ibid.* ix, The Hottentot replying, 'Like so, baas'. 1885 RIDER HAGGARD *K. Solomon's Mines* xx, Don't you know me, Baas? I'm Jim the hunter. 1920 *Chambers's Jrnl.* 25 Dec. 59/2 Jeri stated that he believed the *baas* to be bewitched.

Babelish, *a.* Delete † *Obs.* and add:

1825 *New Monthly Mag.* XIII. 406 He may know a Babelish confusion of languages. 1898 *Daily News* 24 Aug. 3/2 A perfectly Babelish commingling of tongues fell upon the ear.

Babi (bā·bī). Also **Babee**. [Pers., f. *Bab*-ed-Din (= 'gate of the faith'), the name assumed by Mirza Ali Mohammed ibn Radhik (1820–50).] The name of a pantheistic Persian sect, whose doctrine and practice combine Mohammedan, Christian, Jewish, and Parsee elements. Hence **Ba·bism**, the doctrine or practice of this sect; **Ba·bist**, an adherent of Babism, a Babi.

1869 *Contemp. Rev.* XII. 245 (*heading*) The Bab and Babeeism. *Ibid.* 246 He..learned the principles and substance of the Babee doctrines. *Ibid.* 266 Faithful Babees. 1877 M. DODS *Mohammed, Buddha, and Christ* 195 The martyrs of Babism. 1892 *Daily News* 5 Feb. 5/5 The two conflicting sects into which Babism is now divided. 1896 *Ibid.* 30 June 6/1 The Babis of Persia. 1904 *Daily Chron.* 6 Aug. 3/6 He..spoke with hope especially of the spread of the Babists.

Babiche (băbī·ʃ). *N. Amer.* [Canadian Fr., said to be ad. Micmac *ababich* string, cord.] Thongs or thread made of raw hide, sinew, etc.

1836 in *Life T. Simpson* (1845) x. 189 Babiche for snow-shoe lacing. 1899 O. T. MASON in *Rept. Smithsonian Inst.* 1897 732 Fine babiche or rawhide string for the webbing of the snowshoe.

Babul, babool (băbū·l, bā·bul). *Anglo-Ind.* [Hind. *babūl*, *babūr*, Pers. *babūl*.] A thorny mimosa, *Acacia arabica*, common in India.

1824 HEBER *Narrative* 12 Dec. (1828) I. 529 A formidable underwood of cactus and bâbool. 1861 BENTLEY *Man. Bot.* 531 The barks of *A[cacia] arabica* and *A. Catechu*..are used extensively in India under the name of Babool. 1886 KIPLING *Departm. Ditties, Moon of Other Days*, In place of Putney's golden gorse The sickly *babul* blooms. 1921 *Times Lit. Suppl.* 8 Sept. 574/3 Babul seeds.

Baby, *sb.* Add:

1. b. *fig.* Applied to a person's invention or achievement.

1890 *Jrnl. Soc. Arts* XLVIII. 65/1 Count Chardonnet..was then shewing his new-born baby, which he called *soie artificielle*.

c. *slang.* A girl.

1911 H. S. HARRISON *Queed* xiii. 167 Bad-eyed young men who congregate..to smirk at the working girls..'Where you goin', baby?' 1918 C. SANDBURG *Corn Huskers* 60 My baby's going to have a new dress. 1927 VACHELL *Dew of Sea* etc. 269 I'm beginning to think that baby is half vamp and half floosie.

8. *transf.* The youngest or most junior of a family or group of persons.

1897 P. WARUNG *Tales Old Régime* 243 Blake was twenty-five, Clyde was twenty-four, and Entworth forty-one...Short was the 'baby'. 1914 *Daily Express* 19 Sept. 5/1 The 'babies' of the Southern League, Croydon Common, will face Crystal Palace. *Ibid.* 20 Nov. 5/4 [He] was only eighteen years of age, and was known as 'the baby' of his company. 1926 DEEPING *Sorrell & Son* xxiv. § 2 There was one young Pentreath,—the baby.

b. In trivial expressions, chiefly of U.S. origin.

1927 *Daily Express* 8 July 6 Disclaiming responsibility for all the financial misfortunes of the country, he found himself confronted by Mr. Jack Jones, who told him that he was 'carrying the baby' anyhow. 1927 A. E. W. MASON *No Other Tiger* xxiii, He certainly has had the baby to hold all his life, hasn't he? 1927 *Observer* 31 July 6 In the course of the last month we have shown that, in the expressive American phrase, we do not intend to 'hold the baby'. That means the suspension of policy while China remains in the grip of animosity and chaos. 1928 *Daily Express* 14 Jan. 11/7 If other bidders enter into competition, they find themselves run up to a high figure, and are then left to 'hold the baby'. 1928 *Observer* 1 July 6/4 There is always, of course, when reactions are 'on', a risk of throwing out the baby with the bath.

B. 1. passing into *adj.* = young; small or diminutive of its kind.

1873 ALDRICH *Marj. Daw* etc. 120 Can you fancy a schoolmaster going about conjugating baby verbs out of a dratted little spelling book? 1877 *Design & Work* 1 Dec. 602/2 Gas bags..floating high over their heads, by means of baby screws..and the like. 1878 *Ibid.* 16 Feb. 199/3 He was surprised at the strength displayed by the baby iron rope. 1899 *Daily News* 17 Oct. 6/6 [He] decided that her baby-jib must be responsible for the Shamrock's poor pointing. 1901 *Daily Chron.* 27 Sept. 5/6 Both yachts then carried mainsails, big jackyard topsails, jibs, baby jibs, and staysails. 1908 FINDLATER *Crossriggs* iv. 28 She led him out of the nursery..'There's a babier baby than Mike,' she said. 1909 *Daily Chron.* 12 Oct. 4/4 Baby beef, which is grown so little in this country. 1917 W. PETT RIDGE *Amazing Years* vii, One attractive baby grand that Millwood picked up. 1926 *Daily Express* 30 July 9/5 Imported films for use in 'baby' cine-cameras. 1927 *Daily Tel.* 6 Dec. 9/2 The heaviest baby beeve among Red Polls. 1928 *Daily Express* 11 Oct. 1/1 Wonderful improvement in the 'baby car' of seven horse-power.

2. baby act *U.S.*, an act or statute for the protection of minors; *to plead the baby act*, to enter a plea that one is not legally responsible by reason of youth or inexperience; **baby-carriage, baby coach** *U.S.*, a perambulator or bassinette; **baby-house**, a doll's house (later U.S. examples); **baby jumper** (examples); **baby lace** (see quot.); **baby powder**, a skin powder for babies; **baby-ribbon**, narrow ribbon such as was used for babies' clothes; **baby walker**, a device for enabling babies to walk.

1873 *Congress. Globe* Feb., App. 191/1 [Mr. Bingham] did not plead ignorance or the *Baby act. 1888 *Congress. Rec.* Aug., App. 440/1 [Mr. S. S. Cox] admits the authorship..but pleads the baby act, and says he was a boy when he wrote it. 1901 *Forum* Jan. 592 One minute reading the riot act of manly independence, and the next pleading the baby-act of thoughtless irresponsibility. 1903 *N. Y. Sun* 3 Nov. 7 It gave a chance for a lot of jokes which were so distinctively British that a *baby carriage was called a 'perambulator'. 1909 EATON & UNDERHILL *Runaway Place* 155 To their astonished eyes, he seemed to slip directly through a baby carriage. 1903 *N. Y. Times* 1 Oct. 3 English *baby coaches...The carriages are a distinctly English idea—they dub them 'Perambulators'. 1843 CARLTON *New Purchase* I. ix. 60 As neat as a little girl's *baby-house. 1861 MRS. STOWE *Pearl Orr's Isl.* I. xii. 106 Mara and Sally..were revelling in apronsful of shells and seaweed, which they bustled into the other room to bestow in their spacious baby-house. 1855 *Trans. Mich. Agric. Soc.* (1856) VII. 81 Wm. Phelps..[exhibited] 1 baby walker, 1 *baby jumper. 1872 *N. Y. Times* 24 Apr. 8 Advt. (Hoppe) Cradle, Baby-Jumper and Nursery Chair Combined. 1882 CAULFEILD & SAWARD *Dict. Needlework*, *Baby Lace, an English pillow lace, formerly made in Bedfordshire and Buckinghamshire, and called English Lille...The name Baby Lace was given, as, on account of the narrow width of the lace, it was chiefly used for trimming babies' caps. 1914 G. ATHERTON *Perch of Devil* I. 63 She..rubbed the puff on her face. It was ordinary *'baby powder' for the bath. 1893 *Cassell's Fam. Mag.* Feb. 175/1 Various ways in which skilful fingers can utilise the *baby ribbons, for which there has been such a rage of late,..the width seldom exceeds a quarter of an inch. 1906 *Westm. Gaz.* 28 Apr. 14/1 Baby-ribbon velvet. 1909 *Daily Chron.* 1 June 7/5 A sandwich which was tied up with pink baby-ribbon. 1855 *Baby walker [see above].

Baby, *v.* Add:

2. *intr.* To act as if dealing with a baby.

1913 MRS. STRATTON-PORTER *Laddie* xi. (1917) 211 I'll wager a strong young girl like the Princess will laugh at you for babying over her.

Ba·by-farm. A place where the lodging and care of babies is undertaken for profit. Hence **Ba·by-fa:rming** *vbl. sb.*, the keeping of such a farm; also *ppl. a.*; **Ba·by-farmed** *ppl. a.*; **Ba·by-fa:rmer**, one who keeps a baby-farm.

1870 *Times* 16 June 12/4 Two children..alleged to have been brought from a baby-farming establishment. 1878 W. S. GILBERT *H.M.S. Pinafore* II, I practised baby-farming. 1880 *Encycl. Brit.* XIII. 4/2 The infamous relations between the lying-in houses and the baby-farming houses of London. 1880 WEBSTER Suppl., *Baby-farm*, a place where board, lodging, and attendance for babes are offered. *Baby-farming*, the business of keeping a baby-farm. 1881 OGILVIE (Annandale), *Baby-farmer*, a woman who receives infants, generally illegitimate, from their parents, on the pretext of bringing them up, the object being to have the child removed from sight; one who lives by baby-farming. 1896 *Daily News* 26 Apr. 2/3 The great ledger in which are kept their patiently accumulated records of the baby farmers. 1896 *Westm. Gaz.* 30 May 3/1 The baby-farmed child. 1899 *Ibid.* 28 Sept. 8/2 For keeping an unregistered baby-farm and neglecting five children under her care.

Babyless (bē^i·bilės), *a.* [f. BABY *sb.* + -LESS.] Having no babies, without a baby.

1871 CHRISTINA G. ROSSETTI *Sing-Song* 125 Motherless baby and babyless mother.

Bacca, clipped form of TOBACCO. (Cf. BACCO, BACCY.)

1858 *Tough Yarns, Greenwich Hospital* 7 He whips out his old quid, flings it into the fire, and we sported a fresh bit o' bacca.

Baccalaureate. 1. (Later examples.)

1849 *Cat. Wesleyan Univ.* 22 (Hall, College Words) The Seniors will be examined for the Baccalaureate, four weeks before Commencement. 1895 RASHDALL *Univ. Middle Ages* I. 210 *note*, The institution of the Baccalaureate or pupil-teachership. 1907 *Elem. Sch. Teacher* Mar. 372 All of these four baccalaureates extend practically the same privileges to those who have obtained them.

3. Add quot.:

1891 D. C. GILMAN *Johns Hopkins Univ.* 66 The manifold forms in which the baccalaurate [*sic*] degree is conferred.

Bacchiac (bækəi·æk), *a.* [ad. L. *bacchīacus*, Gr. βακχειακός.] Of the nature of a BACCHIUS; consisting of or characterized by bacchii.

1766 LOWTH *Larger Confut. Bp. Hare* 36 Bacchiac and Cretic Feet. 1857 PARRY *Terentii Comoed.* p. lix, Cretic and bacchiac measures. 1861 PALEY *Æschylus* (ed. 2) *Pers.* 671 *note*, The bacchiac metre also suggests τί ταῦτα for τι τάδε.

Bach (bætʃ), *sb. U.S. slang.* [Shortened f. BACHELOR 4.] A bachelor. Also phr. *to keep bach* for earlier *to keep bachelor's hall* = next.

1857 W. CHANDLESS *Visit Salt Lake* II. vi. 236 Mormons look upon a 'bach' with great suspicion..because they consider all men should marry. 1879 MISS BIRD *Lady's Life Rocky Mts.* (1885) 157 A cabin..where two brothers and 'a hired man' were 'keeping bach'. 1883 E. EGGLESTON *Hoosier School Boy* xvi. 106 Don't you know..any place where we could keep 'bach' together? 1904 HARBEN *Georgians* 188, I..thought now was the time fer me, old bach' that I am, to..show them ladies I'd been about.

Bach (bætʃ), *v. U.S. slang.* Also **batch**. [f. prec.] *intr.* Of a man: To live as a bachelor; to live alone and do his own cooking and housekeeping. Also with *it*.

1879 MISS BIRD *Lady's Life Rocky Mts.* (1885) 156 The men don't like 'baching', as it is called in the wilds—i.e. 'doing for themselves'. 1888 *Century Mag.* Jan. 412/2 He had always 'bached it' (lived as a bachelor). Next winter his nephew was coming to live with him. 1898 *Lett. fr. Canada* vii. in *Times* Nov., 'To batch' upon the prairies represents perhaps the *minimum* of pleasure in existence. 1900 H. LAWSON *Over Sliprails* 45, I hurried home to the tent—I was batching with a carpenter. 1927 P. H. PEARSON *Prairie Vikings* 13 For two years they 'bached' as huntsmen along the creek banks.

Bachelor. Add:

4. c. *transf.* One of the young male fur-seals which are kept away from the breeding-grounds by the adult bulls. (These are the seals which may legally be killed for their fur.)

1881 H. W. ELLIOTT *Seal-Isl. Alaska* 43 The 'holluschickie' or 'bachelor' seals. *Ibid.* 44 Sports and pastimes of the young 'bachelors'. 1897 D'ARCY THOMPSON in *Parl. Papers* CII. 442 We saw a body of about 200 bachelors, mostly young or old, those of intermediate 'killable' size being very few. 1898 D. S. JORDAN *Fur Seals* I. 50 The bachelor seals begin to arrive at about the same time as the bulls...The older bachelors come first.

6. bachelor girl, woman (orig. *U.S.*), an unmarried female who has her own income and lives independently, apart from her family or relatives; **bachelor('s) hall** *U.S.*, apartments for bachelors (see also *BACH *sb.*).

1833 H. BARNARD in *Maryland Hist. Mag.* XIII. 369 He keeps bachelor's Hall. 1835 INGRAHAM *South-West* II. 60 Here are congregated store-houses, boarding houses, and bachelor's halls. 1857 W. CHANDLESS *Visit Salt Lake* II. vi. 235 Several of them kept 'bachelors' hall' together in a small house. 1899 *Tit-Bits* 8 Sept. 452/3 A latch-key—that prized possession and mark of identity of the American bachelor girl. 1902 *Daily Chron.* 15 Sept. 3/6 The bachelor woman who earns from two guineas a week. 1906 *Queen* 10 Nov. 808/2 The term 'old maid' is now seldom or never heard; the expression 'bachelor girl' has taken its place. 1928 F. N. HART *Bellamy Trial* i. 25 He keeps bachelor hall in a small bungalow near the village.

Bachelorism. Add:

2. The condition of being a bachelor or unmarried man; the behaviour, conduct, or character characteristic of this. Also *old bachelorism.*

1834 *Blackw. Mag.* XXXV. 769 Bound in the triple steel of resolute bachelorism. 1838 *New Monthly Mag.* LIV. 442 This omission may be looked upon as by no means characteristic of old bachelorism. 1842 J. Aiton *Domest. Econ.* (1857) 83 A prim correct sort of bachelorism. 1884 *American* VIII. 236 The oddest theory of voluntary old bachelorism.

Bacillar (bǟsi·lăr), *a.* [ad. mod.L. *bacillāris*: see -ar[1].] Of, pertaining to, or of the nature of bacilli.

1884 E. Klein *Micro-organisms* 72 The bacillar growth.. is thus removed from the surface. 1884 Blackmore *Tommy Upmore* xxxiv, The great bacillar experiment. 1887 A. M. Brown *Anim. Alkaloids* 122 Bacterial and bacillar biologies.

Bacillary, *a.* Add:

Of, pertaining to, or caused by bacilli.

1894 *Lancet* 3 Nov. 1022/1 A further attempt on the part of the organism to protect itself against bacillary attack. *Ibid.* 1022/2 A drying process incompatible with bacillary life. 1908 R. T. Hewlett *Bacteriology* (ed. 3) 351 In one type of dysentery, the so-called epidemic or bacillary form.

Bacillicide (bǟsi·lisaid). [f. Bacillus + -cide[1].] An agent or substance that destroys bacilli. Also *attrib.* or *adj.* = **Bacillici·dal** *a.*

a 1889 *Disinfectants* 19 (Cent. D.) A combination of lime with chlorine, perhaps the best of all the bacillicides. 1890 Billings *Med. Dict.* 1894 *Lancet* 3 Nov. 1021/1 Antiseptic or bacillicide measures. *Ibid.* 1021/2 Bacillicide treatment. *Ibid.* 1022/2 Sunshine and pure air are the best bacillicides. 1894 Gould *Dict. Med.*, *Bacillicidal*.., destructive to bacilli.

Bacillus. Add: freq. in *fig.* use.

1905 Sir W. Lee-Warner in *Anti-Slavery Reporter* June–July 63 We must not allow this bacillus of slavery to take a more virulent form. 1907 *Jewish Chron.* 15 Mar. 19/1, I refer to the existence of anti-Semitic bacilli which poison the whole air of Russia. 1918 *The Crime* II. 145 They found a fostering soil..on which the bacillus of war could develop unhindered.

Back, *sb.*[1] Add:

3. b. Used *ellipt.* (quasi-*adj.* or *adv.*) in *one-, two-, three-pair back*, a room at the back of a house on the first, second, third floor. (Cf. Front *sb.* 11.)

1836 [see *two-pair*, Two IV. 2]. 1838, 1883 [see Three-pair]. 1873 J. H. Beadle *Undevel. West* xiii. 233 City pastorals, written in a third story back, by men reared in the city.

c. *To talk out of* or *through the back of one's neck*: to talk nonsense. *slang.*

1923 *Pall Mall Gaz.* 13 Apr. 3/3 Anybody who gets up in this House and talks about universal peace knows he is talking through the back of his neck.

23. g. *back-to-back*: advb. phr. used attrib.

1870 *Food Jrnl.* 5 Feb. 34 So long as back-to-back houses ..exist.

24. a. *To break the back of* (fig.): (*a*) to cripple; (*b*) to get over the worst or hardest part of.

1883 E. G. Holtham *Eight Years in Japan* vii. 151 That I had better stick to my onward route, at any rate till I had 'broken the back' of the journey overland to Kiyōto. 1891 Kipling *Life's Handicap* (1915) I. 48 Your flanks are unprotected for two miles. I think we've broken the back of this division. 1901 *Westm. Gaz.* 9 Mar. 4/1 The back of the fire was broken at noon. 1911 H. S. Harrison *Queed* iv. 40 The very next day, the back of the morning's mail being broken, [etc.].

h. *To put one's back into*, to employ the whole strength of one's back in (rowing, lifting, hauling, etc.). Also *fig.*

1882 Stevenson *New Arab. Nts.* (1884) 301 They put their back into their work, they sang loud and louder. 1885 Rider Haggard *K. Solomon's Mines* xviii, Tackle on, and put your back into it; you are as strong as two. 1889 Doyle *Micah Clarke* iv, Pull, Micah! Put your back into it!

Back, *a.* Add:

1. c. *Phonetics.* Of a sound: Formed by restriction of the oral passage at the back of the mouth; formed by the back or root of the tongue. Also *Comb.*, as *back-lateral*, *-round* adjs.

1867 A. M. Bell *Visible Sp.* 61 The 'shut' consonants are sufficiently distinguished.. by the four radical varieties 'Back', 'Front', 'Point', 'Lip'. *Ibid.* 72 The vowels..are divided into three classes of palato-lingual formations, according as the oral cavity is moulded mainly by the 'Back', the 'Front', or the 'Mixed' (Back and Front) attitudes of the tongue. The 'Back' vowels have the largest oral cavities. 1877 Sweet *Handbk. Phonetics* 11 'Back' (guttural) vowels, in which the tongue is retracted as much as possible. *Ibid.* 31 By place there are five main classes [of consonants]. (1) Back (guttural) formed by the root of the tongue and the soft palate..(2) Front (palatal)..(3) Point...(4) Teeth...(5) Lip. 1910 *Mod. Lang. Rev.* V. 91 A back-modified glide or murmur vowel develops between a long vowel and a back-lateral.

3. Of rent, taxes, etc. (Earlier U.S. examples.) *Back pay*, payment to cover a past period of time; also *back salary*, *wages*, etc.

1779 *Proc. Mass. Hist. Soc.* Ser. II. II. 460 [He] received 500 lashes, it being back allowance due to him. 1788 G. R. Minot *Insurrections in Mass.* (1810) 59 They completed an act providing for the payment of the back taxes in specifick articles (1786). 1811 *Boston Selectm.* 14 Aug. 23 Messrs. Crane & Sohier having given up their office in the Town house,—to be notified to settle their back rent with the Treasurer. 1874 'Mark Twain' *Sketches* Wks. XIX. 408 Nearly all the back pay members contemplate making the round trip with us. 1888 A. C. Gunter *Mr. Potter of Texas* xviii, He was paying him back wages. 1890 C. L. Norton *Pol. Americanisms* 98 The act..gave back-pay for the entire session to the very men who had the measure under consideration. 1905 *N. Y. Even. Post* 29 Nov. 10 Nearly two hundred claims for back pay have been left with the consulate. 1906 *Ibid.* 26 Dec. 8 It is a disgrace to the city that he should be compelled to sue for back salary.

3. b. Belonging to past time; see also *Back number.

1869 *Contemp. Rev.* XI. 342 It is the duty of the resident governess..to see that the knowledge of back work is carefully kept up. 1910 'Dehan' *Dop Doctor* xxxix, To its back-files I must refer those who seek a fuller account of the function.

Back, *v.* Add:

2. b. *Photography.* To coat the back of (a plate) with some substance which will absorb light and so prevent halation. Hence **Backed** *ppl. a.*; **Backing** *vbl. sb.*, often *concr.* = the coating applied to the plate.

1882 W. K. Burton *A. B. C. Mod. Phot.* 59 It is well to 'back' the plate; that is, to paint or otherwise cover it at the back with some substance which will absorb light. 1892 *Photogr. Ann.* II. 50 Back your plates with caramel, as there is no doubt it forms the most effectual backing. 1906 R. C. Bayley *Compl. Photogr.* 95 A thick coat of backing is quite unnecessary. *Ibid.* 320 If there be one purpose for which backed plates are more then ever necessary, it is in interiors.

c. *Bookbinding.* To force the backs of the sections of (an unbound book) outwards on each side so as to form grooves or ledges into which the edges of the binding boards will fit. The sheets are clamped in a press, after rounding, between two bevelled boards, and the backs struck with a hammer. Hence **Backing** *vbl. sb.*; also *attrib.* in *backing-board*, *-hammer*, *-machine*.

1738 Chambers *Cycl.* s.v. *Book-binding*, Then the back is turned with a hammer, the book being fixed in a press between boards, called backing-boards; in order to make a groove for fixing the paste-boards. 1818 *Art Bookbinding* 12 Place the backing-boards a little below the back on each side. *Ibid.* 13 The centre must only be well rubbed over with the face of the backing-hammer to make it smooth. 1846 Dodd *Brit. Manuf.* VI. 89 In the process of 'backing',.. the book is laid on a bench,..and hammered near the back edge, with such a peculiar movement of the left hand as causes the back to become rounded while the hammering proceeds. *Ibid.*, When the book is 'backed'. It is placed between two pieces of plank called 'backing-boards'. 1880 Zaehnsdorf *Bookbinding* 44 The boards required for backing, called backing boards, should always be the same length as the book. *Ibid.* 167 *Backing Machine.*—A small machine introduced for backing cheap work. 1901 D. Cockerell *Bookbinding* 118 Rounding and backing are best done after the glue has ceased to be tacky.

12. b. (Mod. U.S. examples.) Also *U.S.*, to address (a letter).

1859 Bartlett *Dict. Amer.* (ed. 2) s.v., To *back* a letter, is Western for to 'direct' it. 1889 Farmer *Americanisms* s.v., The frequently-heard commercial phrase of *to back*, in the sense of 'to endorse', literally, to write on the back of a letter, bill, or cheque. 1902 Clapin *Dict. Amer.* 30 *To back*, often heard, in parts of the West and the South, in sense of to address a letter.

15. b. *To back water* (earlier U.S. example).

1806 Ashe *Trav. Amer.* xxxvii. (1808) 303, I again took the helm, and ordered the men to back water with all their might.

16. b. *To back and fill* (see Fill *v.* 4 c, d), to recede and advance; to go backward and forward. Also *fig.* *U.S.* (Earlier s.v. *Backing *vbl. sb.* 4.)

1848 Durivage & Burnham *Stray Subj.* 174 (Th.) The steam was well up on both boats, which lay rolling, and backing and filling, from the action of the paddles, at the dock. 1854 *Congress. Globe* 11 Dec. 57 Men will be sent to Congress who will not 'back and fill', and be on one principle for one week..and upon another principle another week. 1869 'Mark Twain' *Innoc. Abr.* xxiii, How in the world he [the gondolier] can back and fill, shoot straight ahead,..is a problem to me. 1890 *Harper's Mag.* Sept. 598/2 Nimble stewards back and fill from galley to pantry. 1903 *N. Y. Even. Post* 24 Oct., The engine was backing and filling on a sidetrack.

17. Said of a railway train, etc.

1894 *Idler* July 609 Sometimes he would pull out when he could hear the express coming, and make her back down to the next station. 1901 Guy Boothby *Myst. Clasped Hands* iv, At last the train backed into the station.

19. *To back down.* Orig. *U.S.* (Earlier examples.)

1849 C. Lanman *Lett. Alleghany Mount.* xi. 90 When we got up about half way..they all three of 'em backed down and said I must not keep on. 1859 Bartlett *Dict. Amer.* (ed. 2) 17 *To back down*, to withdraw a charge, eat one's own words; as 'I asked Jenkins, before witnesses, if he had called me a cheat; and he backed right down.' 1879 Stockton *Rudder Grange* x. 113 We're not going to back down.

20. Of a building, etc.: To be so situated that the back abuts *on* a particular piece of land or property.

1891 Fenn *Mahme Nousie* II. xv. 257 This opening backed on to the forest and the escaping party passed in at once among the trees. 1921 *Edin. Rev.* Jan. 190 In St. James' Square, on which the club backs, the attack was more serious.

VII. 21. To carry on the back. *U.S.*

1840 R. H. Dana *Bef. Mast* xx, We started off every morning..and cut wood..and after dinner..carted and 'backed' it down until sunset. 1861 G. W. Wilder *MS. Diary* 24 Feb., All turned out and backed rails. 1895 *Outing* (U.S.) XXVII. 47/2 These hardy woodsmen backing packs of from eighty to one hundred pounds each.

Back, *adv.* **13.** *Back and forth.* (Illustrations of U.S. usage.)

1816 Pickering *Vocab.* s.v., *Back and Forth*, backwards and forwards. Ex. He was walking back and forth. This is a very common expression in New England; but it is used only in conversation. 1836 Dunlap *Mem. Water Drinker* (1837) I. 57, I am not one of your brook trout to be played back and forth with a hair line as her husband catches um. 1857 Hammond *Wild Northern Scenes* 138 (Th.) They would run here and there, back and forth, at full speed along the sands. 1872 *Congress. Rec.* Dec. 243/1 Various propositions were made [between the U.S. and France] back and forth. 1899 *Ibid.* Feb. 1743/1 Some of you..remember when at Vicksburg our boys got so close to the Confederates that they talked back and forth. 1907 U. Sinclair *Industrial Republic* xii, I would find myself comparing..the two eras, and transposing its leading figures back and forth.

14. *Back of.* (Earlier examples.)

1694 *Cal. Virginia St. Papers* I. 44 We Ranged on Ackoquane and so back of the Inhabitants and ye So[u]th. 1755 L. Evans *Geogr. Ess.* 15 If the French settle back of us, the English must either submit to them, or have their throats cut. *Ibid.* 16 If we secure the Country back of Carolina in time. 1776 *Essex Inst. Hist. Coll.* XXI. 231 Said Braish shall build a wharff back of the old wharff. 1779 E. Parkman *Diary* 119 The work of straightning the Road through my land back of the Meeting House. 1823 G. W. Ogden *Lett. fr. West* 76 The uplands back of the Oak Hills of the Ohio river. 1840 Dana *Bef. Mast* ix, The mission stands a little back of the town.

Back-action. [Back- 11.] Backward or reverse action. Also *attrib.* and *fig.*

1872 E. Eggleston *End of World* xvi. 111 She's told paytent [= patent] double-back-action lies that worked both ways. 1873 J. H. Beadle *Undevel. West* 800 That sort of detraction has an awkward back-action about it. 1874 Knight *Dict. Mech.* 205/2 Back-action Steam-engine.

So **Back-actioned** *a.*

1875 'Stonehenge' *Brit. Sports* I. I. xi. § 1 The back-actioned lock does not speak so well as the old bar-lock.

Backage (bæ·kėdʒ). [f. Back *sb.*[1], after Frontage.] The back part of a building or row of buildings; the line or outlook of buildings or plots of land on the rear side.

1887 Fenn *This Man's Wife* II. xviii, A high wall right and left to complete the blankness of the frontage. It ought to have been called the backage; for Sir Gordon Bourne's house was very pleasant on the other side. 1892 *Pall Mall Gaz.* 22 Mar. 2/3 Converting slummy 'backages' into handsome frontages. 1894 Du Maurier *Trilby* vi. II. 191 Tall trees, whose lightly-falling leaves yellowed the pavement for at least a hundred yards of frontage—or backage, rather; for this was but the rear of that stately palace.

Back bench. [Back *a.* 1, Back- A. 4.] Any one of the benches in the House of Commons or similar assembly occupied by members who are not entitled to a seat on the front benches on either side. Usu. *attrib.* (with hyphen). Hence **Ba·ck-be·ncher**, a member who occupies a seat on the back benches on either side of the house.

1902 T. W. H. Crosland *Outlook Odes* 2 You look embarassed, turn tail, retire to your back bench. 1905 *Daily Chron.* 13 July 6/1 Back-bench Members on the Ministerial side of the House. 1906 *Outlook* 7 Apr. 474/1 The Colonial Office is at present palpably at the mercy of any back-bench rhetorician who [etc.]. 1923 *Daily Mail* 23 May 6 Mr. Baldwin filled the modest rôle of a back-bencher in the House for many years. 1928 *Daily Tel.* 13 Mar. 9/3 The situation was obviously developing into general back-bench communal bickering.

Back blocks, *pl.* *Austral.* [Back *a.* 1, *Block *sb.* 14 d.] Land in the remote and sparsely-inhabited interior. Also, land distant or cut off from a river-front. Also **Back-block** *attrib.* or *adj.*; **Back-blocker,** a resident in the back blocks.

1872 *Glimpses of Life in Victoria* iii. 31 We were doomed to see the whole of our river-frontage selected and purchased by two gentlemen newly arrived in the colony. The back blocks which were left to us were insufficient for the support of our flocks, and deficient in permanent water-supply. 1890 E. W. Hornung *Bride fr. Bush* xix. 298 'Down in Vic' you can carry as many sheep to the acre as acres to the sheep up here in the 'back-blocks'. 1891 'R. Boldrewood' *Sydney-side Saxon* xii. 215 One of the back-block youngsters. 1892 E. W. Hornung *Under Two Skies* 21 Sitting on his heels over the fire in an attitude peculiar to back-blockers. 1893 Mary Gaunt in *Eng. Illustr. Mag.* Feb. 294/1 The back blocks are very effectual levellers.

Backbone. 2. Add: esp. *U.S.* of mountain ranges.

1816 U. Brown in *Maryland Hist. Mag.* X. 280 On the West Side of the Aleghany Mountain, the Back-Bone of America. *Ibid.* XI. 359 Baker informed us, that Fairfaxes Stone..lay between what was called the Back-bone and the Alleghany Mountain. 1835 *Southern Lit. Messenger* I. 615 In the distance, the 'back bone' of the Alleghany. 1885 'C. E. Craddock' *Prophet Gt. Smoky Mts.* xii. 234 'Over yander on the backbone', returned the guileless Jacob,.. pointing toward the base of the mountain. 1920 Hunter *Trail Drivers of Texas* 150 When we arrived on the divide or the backbone,..we passed along.

4. (Earlier U.S. examples.)

1857 *Republic* (Bartlett) Backbone is the material which is designed to make an upright man. 1859 Bartlett *Dict. Amer.* (ed. 2) 17 *Backbone*, moral stamina..a figurative expression recently much used in political writings.

Backboneless, *a.* Add quot.:

1903 *German Ambitions* 89 Backboneless submissiveness to Britain.

Back-cap. *U.S. slang.* *To give one a back-cap*, to disclose or state something to one's detriment; to run down. Also as *v. trans.*

1883 'Mark Twain' *Life Mississippi* iii. 462 Now I didn't fear no one giving me a back-cap (exposing his past life) and running me off the job. 1902 Clapin *Dict. Amer.* 31 *To back cap*, to speak evil of some one, so as to spoil his game.

Back-chat. *slang.* [? orig. soldiers' slang; cf. Back- A. 12 c.] Saucy or impertinent replies to a superior; abuse, insulting speech; altercation, heated talk. (Cf. 'to answer back' in Back *adv.* 8, and *Back-talk.)

1901 *Subaltern's Lett. Wife* 108 'That'll do, Sergeant Jones', I heard one of our colonial officers remark; 'I don't want any more of your back-chat'. 1922 Sir D. Maclean in *Daily Mail* 31 Oct. 9 It was very amusing to hear public men described as 'cabin boys' and 'kitchen staff'; it was what children described as 'calling names' and soldiers 'back-chat'. 1922 W. J. Locke *Tale of Triona* viii, 'Here you are, you blackmailing thief.' 'None of your back-chat..' said the taximan. 1924 E. Marsh *Fables La Fontaine* 85 Hammer and tongs the back-chat starts again.

Back-cloth. [Back *a.* 1, Back- A. 4.]

1. *Theatr.* The painted cloth hung across the back of the stage as the principal part of the scenery. Also *transf.* and *fig.*

1886 *Cornh. Mag.* Oct. 435 They gazed awestruck at the backcloth and the flies. 1926 *Spectator* 10 July 44/2 Thirty acres or so for a stage and the whole firmament of heaven for a back-cloth. 1927 *Observer* 6 Nov. 9 The background ..is not a carefully constructed scene, but only a flimsy and dim back-cloth.

2. *Calico-printing.* A cloth placed between the fabric that is being printed and the 'blanket', in order to keep the latter clean. Otherwise called *Back-grey.

1874 Knight *Dict. Mech.* 1897 C. F. S. Rothwell *Print. Textile Fabrics* 34 The back tenter's work is to guide the piece and back cloth into the machine. 1901 A. Sansone *Print. Cott. Fabrics* (ed. 2) 420 For keeping the blanket clean, the back cloth is allowed to go between the blanket and the printing cloth.

3. *Naut.* 'A triangular piece of canvas fastened in the middle of a topsail-yard to facilitate the stowing of the bunt of the topsail' (*Cent. Dict.* 1889).

Back country. Chiefly *U.S.* [Back *a.* 1.] The country lying towards or in the rear of a settled district.

1755 Washington *Lett. to R. Orme* 2 Apr., Writ. 1889 I. 145 I herewith send you a small map of the back country. 1784 A. Ellicott in *Life & Lett.* (1908) 20 The greatest consolation which I have in this Back Country. 1789 Morse *Amer. Geog.* 415 The mistletoe is common in the back country. 1817 S. R. Brown *Western Gaz.* 206 The back country for several miles is reported to be swampy. 1831 Peck *Guide for Emigrants* III. 292 It..has an abundance of excellent water, and a back country as range for stock. 1868 *Putnam's Mag.* Nov. II. 562 The hotel was a roomy log-house,..and commanded a view of the back country—a prairie stretching off into the western horizon. 1876 *Congress. Rec.* Jan. 668/2 West point for all practical purposes is an isolated place. There is no back country to speak of. 1902 *Westm. Gaz.* 6 Aug. 2/1 The unappropriated back-country of Tunis and Tripoli.

b. *attrib.*, as *back-country district*, *gentleman*, *Indian*, etc.

1787 in *Amer. Museum* (1789) II. Chron. 1/2 The back country people have killed three hundred Indians. 1806 *Deb. Congress* 15 Apr. (1852) 1043 Back-country gentlemen, who live inland all along from New Hampshire to Georgia. 1872 Eggleston *Hoosier Schoolm.* Pref. 5 Describing life in the back-country districts. 1887 *Harper's Mag.* Jan. 328/1 In a back-country town..there chanced to die one of the members of the community. 1895 *Century Mag.* July 323/1 To make this New Jersey holiday, assemble a thousand back-country vehicles, of all sorts. 1901 'Linesman' *Words by Eyewitness* (1902) 161 Imaginations so crude as those of the back-country Boers.

Hence **Back-countryman.**

1796 *Gaz. U. S.* 19 Nov., Advt. (Th.) A new Ballet Dance, called the Back Countryman, or the New Settlers. 1845 W. G. Simms *Wigwam & Cabin* 22 The boatman, who.. knew by his dialect and dress that he was a back countryman, came to his relief.

Back county. *U.S.* [Back *a.* 1.] A county lying in the inland part of a state. Also *attrib.*

1775 *Maryland Hist. Mag.* X. 317 Finding it difficult to go thro' the back County..he agreed to accept a Commission. 1788 *Massachusetts Spy* 11 Nov. (Th.) A back-county correspondent informs us that [etc.]. 1803 T. M. Harris *Jrnl. Tour* 6 June (1805) 59 In the back counties of Virginia. 1821 *Massachusetts Spy* 24 Oct. (Th.) [The cattle were] all purchased from back counties. 1904 W. H. Smith *Promoters* xx. 290 The little book agent..was working one of the brethren from some back county in great style.

Ba·ck-down. *colloq.* [f. Back *v.* 19.] A complete surrender of claims; a retreat from a position taken up or from a stand made.

1886 *Sat. Rev.* 25 Dec. 853 The present crisis, end as it may—in a general 'backdown' or a general war—is essentially a small business as compared with much that Europe has seen in its day.

Ba·ck-draw. *U.S.* = Drawback 4.

1883 *Century Mag.* Oct. 815/2 There are great back-draws to the bee business, the irregularities of the flowers being chief.

Backen, *v.* **2.** Delete † *Obs.* and add (U.S.):

1904 Eliz. Robins *Magnetic North* II. 181 Butts had backened a step behind the stove-pipe.

Back-fire, *sb.* [f. *Back-firing.]

1. A fire purposely lighted ahead of an advancing prairie-fire in order to deprive it of fuel and so extinguish it. *U.S.*

1905 *U.S. Forestry Bureau Bull. No. 61* s.v., The back fire is intended to burn only against the wind.

2. A premature ignition or explosion in a gas or oil engine, causing the piston to be driven in a direction reverse to that in which it should travel.

1897 G. D. Hiscox *Gas* etc. *Engines* 86 Misfire or back-fire explosives. 1902 A. C. Harmsworth, etc. *Motors* 169 These 'back fires' are the result of what is called 'premature ignition'. 1903 Macredy *Dict. Motoring* s.v., An explosion in the silencer is also called, but incorrectly, a back fire. 1904 Filson Young *Compl. Motorist* ix. 215 This is necessary in order to prevent a back-fire of the engine in starting it.

Back-fire, *v.* [Back-formation from *Back-firing.]

1. *intr.* To light a fire ahead of an advancing prairie-fire in order to deprive it of fuel. *U.S.*

1909 in *Cent. Dict.* Suppl.

2. Of an explosive-mixture burner or engine: To ignite or explode prematurely.

1906 *Westm. Gaz.* 23 Oct 4/2 Some engines are obstinate starters. Others have a nasty tendency to back-fire. 1909 *Ibid.* 13 Oct. 7/4, I think the gas had backfired. 1922 *Ibid.* 24 Nov., A mechanic started the engine on a car, which back-fired, setting the car ablaze.

fig. 1912 C. Mathewson *Pitching* xiii. 300 One of McGraw's schemes back-fired on him.

Back-firing, *vbl. sb.* [Back *adv.*, Back- A. 10.]

1. The lighting of a fire ahead of an advancing prairie-fire in order to deprive it of fuel. *U.S.*

1801 E. Eggleston *Faith Doctor* iv. 49 So, as he rose to go, like a prairie traveller protecting himself by back-firing, he said [etc.]. 1892 *Boston* (Mass.) *Jrnl.* 10 Oct. 9/3 By back-firing, the people of Hitchcock yesterday saved their town from being destroyed by the great prairie-fire then raging.

2. Premature ignition or explosion in a motor-engine or other mixed-combustion device.

1897 G. D. Hiscox *Gas* etc. *Engines* 86 Back-firings in the muffler and exhaust pipe. 1907 *Daily Chron.* 11 Nov. 7/4 The air enters the working cylinder in advance of the combustible mixture, thus preventing backfiring.

Backforemost, *a.* Perverse, wrong-headed.

1889 Stevenson *Master of Ballantrae* iv, Perhaps because he knew he was by nature inclining to the parsimonious, he took a backforemost pleasure in the recklessness with which he supplied his brother's exigence.

Back-formation. *Philol.* [Back *adv.*, Back- A. III. (Hence G. *rückbildung*.)] The formation of what looks like a root-word from an already existing word which might be (but is not) a derivative of the former.

1887 *N. E. D.*, *Burgle*..A back-formation from *Burglar*. 1907 *Athenæum* 5 Jan. 7/3 'Narration' is fifteenth century, 'narrative'..and 'narrator' as early as Bacon, so that, like many verbs of the same termination, it ['narrate'] may have been a back-formation.

Back-front. [Back *a.* 1, Back- A. 5.] The rear boundary line or elevation of a building.

c 1710 Celia Fiennes *Diary* (1888) 293 The back Front goes out into a Garden or Court. 1724–27 De Foe *Tour thro' Great Britain* ii. (1753) I. 116 On the Back-front of the House was to be a noble Range of Stoves for tender Exotic Plants. 1726 Leoni *Alberti's Archit.* I. 39/2 From the middle of the Fore-front of the Work I draw a Line quite thro' to the Back-front. 1800 *Hull Advertiser* 28 June 3/4 The workmen employed in modernising the backfront of the house. 1806 T. Thornton *Sporting Tour through France* II. 104 A Sporting palace..The back-front is decorated with a profusion of horns of stags, deer. 1852–61 *Archit. Publ. Soc. Dict.*, *Back front* (Fr. *face de derrière*).

transf. 1900 Kipling in *Times* 15 Mar. 8/1 The home Government..maintain intimate relations with all sides, with the front, and the far more important 'back-front' which begins at Pretoria.

Ba·ck-furrow, *v.* *U.S.* [Back *adv.*] *trans.* To plough (land) so that a second furrow-slice is laid against the face of the first by ploughing in the reverse direction. Also *back-furrowing* vbl. sb.

1861 *Trans. Ill. Agric. Soc.* IV. 113 Mr. K. K. Jones..had his land plowed deep, [and] back furrowed it in beds twenty-four feet wide. *Ibid.* 392 This mode of plowing (called 'back-furrowing') is always to be observed when the track of the road is plowed. 1873–4 *Rep. Vermont Board Agric.* II. 239, I plow and harrow again, and then in a few days back-furrow in ridges with a side hill plow.

Back-gate. [Back *a.* 1, Back- A. 5.] A gate at the back of, or leading to the rear part of, a house or other premises.

1442 *Extr. Aberd. Reg.* (1844) I. 9 Al man that has back yettes close thaim. 1709 [see Back- A. 5]. 1873 E. Eggleston *Myst. Metrop.* xxxvi. 307 When Mrs. Ferret came home from prayer-meeting she entered by the back gate. 1905 Jack London *War of the Classes* 274, I battered on the drag and slammed back gates with them, or shivered with them in box cars and city parks.

Back-grey. *Calico-printing.* [Back *a.* 1, Back- A. 4, Grey *sb.* 1 b.] = *Back-cloth 2.

1896 G. Duerr *Bleaching & Calico-print.* 22 Very often unbleached pieces of cloth (called back greys) are used for the purpose of keeping the blanket from getting dirty too soon;..the 'back greys' are run between the blanket and the pieces which are being printed. 1897 C. F. S. Rothwell *Print. Textile Fabrics* 34 These pieces, or *back-greys* as they are called, are afterwards bleached and printed with their own patterns.

Background, *sb.* Add: *attrib.* or as *adj.* (*colloq.*) = keeping in the background, retiring.

1896 *Westm. Gaz.* 9 Dec. 2/1 A reticent, background kind of lover. 1904 *Daily Chron.* 11 Feb. 8/6 'Cultivate a background manner,' is the advice of a lady..to governesses seeking situations.

Background, *v.* Add quots.

1768 S. Bentley *River Dove* 8 Far distant as Vision can go, High Weever back-grounds the gay Scene. 1891 C. James *Rom. Rigmarole* 75 The 'antique spires' of the College Chapel, backgrounded with crimson sunset. 1904 *Westm. Gaz.* 17 Nov. 4/2 Planted on to the material like a raised embroidery, and backgrounded with manipulations of tulle or chiffon. 1905 *Ibid.* 4 May 4/2 Hair..well dressed can background these [features] with such effect that the face..may become almost beauty.

Back-handed, *a.* **3. b.** (Earlier U.S. example.)

1800 *Deb. Congress* (1851) 832 In a back-handed way, and not in the fair regular manner.

Backing, *vbl. sb.* Add: **4.** *Backing and filling* (see *Back *v.* 16 b).

1777 *Essex Inst. Hist. Coll.* XLII. 315 He was then order'd.. to Stillwarter, then ordered from Stillwarter to Benington...This, in the Salers Frase is Backing & filling, [and] makes but poor way ahead. 1854 *N.Y. Herald* 15 June (Bartlett) There has been so much backing and filling, not only upon the Cuban question, but upon every other. 1869 Semmes *Service afloat* 255 The reader need no longer wonder at the backing and filling of the Iroquois around the little Sumter.

attrib. 1902 Clapin *Dict. Amer.* 31 A backing and filling policy is one which is shilly-shally, trifling, irresolute.

6. d. *Backing-out* (see Back *v.* 18).

1880 Tourgee *Invis. Empire* v. 413 In explanation of the backing-out process, he says it consisted simply in not going to any more meetings.

Back-load, back load. [Back- A. 3.] An amount that can be carried on the back.

1725 [see Back- A. 3]. 1823 *Massachusetts Spy* 3 Dec. (Th.) A black fellow was taken up on suspicion, with a back load of live turkeys. 1853 B. Young *Jrnl. Discourses* I. 255 You might go round exhibiting a back load of gold. 1856 *Ibid.* III. 323, I have myself seen them take back loads of wood. 1894 *Outing* (U.S.) XXIV. 88/1 She had brought us a large back-load of wood.

Back-mark, *v.* *Sporting slang.* [Cf. next.] *trans.* To put (a competitor) back at the start of a race. Hence, to leave far behind in a contest.

1890 Farmer *Slang* s.v., *To be backmarked*..(pedestrian), in handicapping to receive less start from 'scratch' than previously given—even to being put back to 'scratch'. 1895 *Field* 24 Aug. 315/3 Jersey men eagerly awaited the issue of the race between the amateur champion of the world and their own island champions, not that they ever expected them to back mark Tyers. 1928 *Sunday Express* 17 June 20/3, I venture the opinion that he would readily back-mark any man in Scotland over a mile course.

Back-marker. [f. *back mark* (Back *a.* 1, Mark *sb.*[1]) + -er[1].] One who starts 'scratch' in a game, match, or race.

1895 *Daily News* 5 Sept. 7/3 The back-markers were well up in the last lap. 1899 *Westm. Gaz.* 14 Mar. 10/1 One day there was an exhibition game of billiards.. Captain Johnson took 150 in 300 from Cook, and had been passed by the 'back-marker'. 1903 *Daily Chron.* 26 Dec. 5/3 The crowd favoured the back-markers.

Back number. [*Back *a.* 3 b, Number *sb.* 6.] A number of a magazine, periodical, etc., earlier than the current one; hence *colloq.* (orig. *U.S.*) one who or a thing which is behind the times or out of date.

1866 *Boy's Friend* III. 575/2 All the back numbers of the Boy's Friend are in print. 1888 *Nation* (N.Y.) 9 Aug. 115/3 He needs to be thrice armed who steps into the arena, as Mr. Lowell has done, laden with 'back numbers'. 1890 *Harper's Mag.* Feb. 439/2 Whereas if Galen should appear among us to-day, ..he would be told he was a back number. 1892 *Congress. Rec.* Apr. 2964/1 We have not many Indians left in Minnesota. The Indian is a back number there. 1893 *Advance* (Chicago) 21 Dec., It [Russia] is a back number by several centuries. 1896 Knowles & Morton *Baseball* 89 The season contained many surprises, and pitchers who were sarcastically referred to as 'back numbers' sprang up when least expected. 1907 *Westm. Gaz.* 4 Dec. 2/3 There are now so many competing forms of transport..that the steamboat seems to be doomed to be what is in current terminology called a 'back number'. 1924 Galsworthy *White Monkey* I. iv, Lady Alison..finding a certain poignancy in contact with the New Age, on Fleur's copper floor. On that floor she at least felt a back number.

attrib. 1911 H. Quick *Yellowstone N.* xi. 286 Let us say repugnant to some back-number criminal law.

Hence **Ba·ck-nu·mber** *v. trans.*, to treat as a 'back number', to set aside as useless.

1924 A. J. Small *Frozen Gold* vi. 140, I said, you lied when you told me Norvice was back numbered.

Back of (or **o'**) **beyond** (orig. *Sc.*): see Beyond C. b.

1816 Scott *Antiq.* ii, You..whirl'd them to the back-o-beyont, to look at the auld Roman camp. 1828 Moir *Mansie Wauch* vii, Like an auncient hermit far away among the hills, at the back of beyont. 1867 Smyth *Sailor's Word-bk.*, *Back-o'-beyond.* Said of an unknown distance. 1889 'R. Boldrewood' *Robbery under Arms* xvii, These far-out back-of-beyond places.

Ba·ck-out. *U.S.* [Back *v.* 18.] An act of backing out or withdrawing from a position; inclination to back out.

1832 Paulding *Westw. Ho* II. 136 He could whip his weight in wild cats, there being no back out in him or any of his breed. 1836 Crockett *Exploits & Adv. Texas* (1837) 4 Now that idea..was a sort of cornering in which there was no back out. 1855 Barnum *Life* 35 I'll do as I say, and there's no back-out to me. 1888 *Boston Weekly Globe* 28 Mar. (Farmer) Mr. Barker's back-out has not much surprised me.

Back-pedalling, *vbl. sb.* [Back *adv.* 5.] *Cycling.* The action of pressing down upon the pedal as it rises, in order to check the movement of the wheel. Also *attrib.* Hence (as a back-formation) **Back-pedal** *v. intr.* and *trans.*

1887 Bury & Hillier *Cycling* 377 This form of clutch.. does not admit of back-pedalling. 1891 *Ibid.* (ed. 2) 373 A break should always be used—it is absurd to do hard work back pedalling down-hill. 1897 *Encycl. Sport* I. 268/1 Do not back-pedal too suddenly, or you may break your chain. 1898 J. Pennell in *Fortn. Rev.* Jan. 60 The machine can be back-pedalled. *Ibid.* 63 An endless number of back-pedalling brakes have been brought out during the last year.

Ba·ck-rest. [Back- A. 3, 4.]

1. A contrivance to support or ease the back of a person when seated or engaged in manual work (e.g. at a lathe). Also, provision for such support.

1879 Holtzapffel *Turning* IV. 20 The turner using the pole lathe..requires the back rest to steady and support his body. 1909 *Daily Chron.* 13 Nov. 9/6 Neither does it mean that the passengers have their comfort curtailed in respect of insufficient back-rest.

2. A guide attached to the slide-rest of a turning-lathe and placed in contact with the work to steady it.

1907 O. E. Perrigo *Mod. Amer. Lathe Practice* 164 There are two classes of these rests which may in a general way be called 'center rests' and 'back rests'. The center rests usually have jaws bearing upon the work at three points spaced equally around the circle, while a back rest bears upon the work generally at the back and on top only.

3. *Weaving.* A bar over which the warp passes from the warp-beam.

1894 T. W. Fox *Mech. Weaving* 369 Each warp beam.. must be parallel with back rest, breast beam, and taking-up roller.

Ba·ck-scra·tching, *vbl. sb.* *vulgar colloq.* [f. Back *sb.*[1], Back- A. 1 + Scratching *vbl. sb.*, in allusion to the saying, 'You scratch my back, and I'll scratch yours'.] The performance of mutual services; always with the suggestion or doubt as to the legitimacy of the transactions. So **Ba·ck-scra·tcher.**

(See also *back-scratcher*, *-scratching* in Dict. s.v. Back- A. 1.)

1897 *Daily News* 9 Jan. 4/7 Does it not rather partake of the ethics of the back-scratcher and the log-roller?

Back seat. [Back *a.* 1, Back- A. 4.] A seat towards the back of a hall, etc., or at the back of a vehicle; hence *colloq.* a position of inferiority or comparative obscurity (orig. *U.S.* in phr. *to take a back seat*).

(*a*) 1860 Holland *Miss Gilbert's Career* xiii. 227 The double of Mrs. Gen. Cadwallader took the back seat to herself. 1873 Aldrich *Marj Daw* etc. 36 The colonel drove, with my father in front, Miss Daw and I on the back seat. 1898 H. S. Canfield *Maid of Frontier* 176 We took a back seat [in the meeting], me and my girl did.

(*b*) *a* 1863 *Southern Hist. Soc. Papers* IX. 133, I tell you, those able-bodied men who are sleeping in feather beds tonight,..must be content to take back seats when we get home. 1866 *Congress. Globe* May 2402/2 When [he]..was acting with the Union party, he proclaimed to the world 'that traitors should take a back seat'. 1885 *Society* 7 Feb. 9 (Farmer, Slang) This great batting achievement must, however, take a back seat. 1890 'R. Boldrewood' *Col. Reformer* (1891) 92 'Bouncing Bob' [was] relegated to a 'back seat' as wit and occasional bully of the camp. 1904 *Pittsburg Gaz.* 8 Aug. 4 This fad for the Pomeranian..has given the broken-nosed pugs a back seat.

Back-stone. *Lead Manuf.* [Back- A. 4.] The piece of cast iron at the back of an ore-hearth. (Cf. Pipe-stone 2, Work-*stone*, and *Fore-stone.)

1839 Ure *Dict. Arts* 756.

Back-talk. (orig. *dial.*) = *Back-chat; retort or reply which is regarded as superfluous or impertinent.

1858 *Dialogue* in *Ulster Jrnl. Archæol.* VI. 41 Oh, indeed 'twas yerself'at begun it, So A'll give ye back-talk till ye're tired. 1880 *Antrim & Down Gloss.*, *Back talk*, saucy replies from a child or an inferior. 1887 J. D. Billings *Hard Tack & Coffee* (1888) 150 Back talk,..which..means answering a superior officer insolently, was a prolific cause for punishments. 1888 *Harper's Mag.* Nov. 972/1 That'll do, my friend, I don't want no back talk. 1899 Kipling *Stalky* 204 I've heard more back-talk since this volunteerin' nonsense began than I've heard in a year in the service. 1903 G. H. Lorimer *Lett. Self-made Merchant* xiii. 177 That order for a car-load of Spotless Snow Leaf from old Shorter is the kind of back talk I like. 1921 G. O'Donovan *Vocations* viii, ''Twas enough to disturb any girl,' her mother said..' I'm off communion myself this morning, with all the back talk I had with your father over it last night.'

Back to the land. [Back *adv.* 5.] A catch-word applied to schemes for turning some of the dwellers in crowded cities into rural settlers. Hence **Back-to-the-lander,** a townsman thus converted into a rural worker.

1903 *Times Lit. Suppl.* 16 Oct. 296/2 The common instincts that our 'back-to-the-landers' strive to relearn with arduous art. 1904 *Daily Chron.* 16 July 4/7 This is the way the successful small holder sets about the business. But it is not the fumbling, ineffective way of the townsman Back-to-the-Lander. 1905 *Westm. Gaz.* 15 Aug. 3/2 Farmers, who are paying so much heavier rates than 'Back-to-the Landers'. 1905 *Spectator* 23 Dec. 1076/1 'Back-to-the-land!' is a cry full not only of pathos, but of cogency. 1906 G. Herring in *Times* 15 Feb. 15/6 By doing so you may make the catchwords [*sic*] 'Back to the Land' a reality.

Back track. *U.S.* [Back *a.*] A track lying or leading towards the rear; esp. in phr. *to take the back track*, to return or retreat; also *fig.*

1724 *Lancaster Rec.* 230 We kept scouts upon our back tracks to see if there would any pursue. 1802 *Balance* (Hudson, N. Y.) 6 Apr. 106 (Th.) I must have been taking the course which hunters would call the Back Track. 1829 *Massachusetts Spy* 14 Jan. (Th.) The dogs, although on a back track of the animal, were fortunately in hearing at the time. 1834 W. G. Simms *Guy Rivers* I. 88 You know the back track to my house. 1846 Sage *Scenes Rocky Mts.* (1859) 44 Two of our party..wisely resolved to take the back track, and accordingly left for home. 1869 *Congress. Globe* Feb. 1606/1 We all have occasionally to take the back track. None of us are so proud as never to confess that we are wrong. 1892 *Ibid.* June, App. 444/2 You are arresting progress and taking the back track on civilization.

Hence **Back-track** *v. intr.*, to return.

1904 Eliz. Robins *Magnetic North* II. 164 Now I'd advise you..to back-track home.

Back trail. *U.S.* [Back *a.*] = prec.

1869 C. L. Brace *New West* viii. 99 There's that darn'd mule on the back trail agin! 1891 Maran E. Ryan *Told in Hills* II. ix. 254 You can strike the back trail as soon as you've a mind to. 1908 Mulford *Orphan* xi. 132 One of his men..knelt behind a rock, his rifle covering the back trail.

Hence **Ba·ck-trail** *v. trans.*, to trace back.

1924 A. J. Small *Frozen Gold* i. 33 They back trailed him as far as Five Fingers and there the trail ended.

Back-turn. *Mus.* [Back- A. 11.] = *inverted turn*: see Turn *sb.* 5.

1876 Stainer & Barrett *Dict. Mus. Terms* s.v. *Turn*, The common turn..takes a higher note first in the change. ..The back-turn taking a lower note first in the change.

Ba·ckveld. [Back *a.* 1, Back- A. 4.] In S. Africa, the primitive or unprogressive rural districts lying away from the towns. Also *attrib.* Hence **Ba·ckvelder,** a dweller in the backveld.

1908 *Times* 4 Mar. 7/1 So far as their backveld followers are concerned, the general opinion is that Ministers have finally burned their boats. 1908 *Westm. Gaz.* 4 Mar. 2/3 The back-veldt members of Het Volk. 1911 *E. London Disp.* 28 Oct. 3 (Pettman) To present the rugged backvelder in his true colours. *Ibid.* 8 Nov. 6 (Pettman) A few visitors from the back veld. 1920 *Contemp. Rev.* Feb. 197 In the *dorps* and the *backveld*, society, business, religion, and politics are closely interwoven.

Backwater, *sb.* **2.** (Later U.S. examples.)

1816 U. Brown in *Maryland Hist. Mag.* XI. 49 [I] was obliged to pay..for ferry over on the back water forced into said gully by the River. 1857 Olmsted *Journ.* 213 At the last freshet, the whole roof of the mill..was covered by the back water of the river. 1878 J. H. Beadle *Western Wilds* xxv. 399 But the Columbia often rises so as to cause backwater, giving the Willamette a variation of thirty-two feet.

Ba·ckwater, *v.*

1. *intr.* = the phr. *back water*: see Back *v.* 15 b.

1828 *Examiner* 56/1 They won't backwater when he endeavours to give way. 1922 *Short Stories* Feb. 141/2 He backwatered so that the canoe paused at the foreman's feet.

2. *trans.* To bring into a backwater, away from the stream. In quot. *fig.*

1922 Galsworthy *Forsyte Saga* II. I. viii, What on earth did such a woman do with her life, backwatered like this?

Back-wind, *v.* To be taken, or cause to be taken, aback. Hence **Back-wind** *sb.*, a gust that lays a sail aback.

1899 *Daily News* 6 Oct. 7/3 At this stage both yachts were compelled to close haul to avoid back-winding. *Ibid.* 21 Oct. 3/4 The Columbia's [spinnaker]..behaved badly, back-winding the defender constantly. 1909 *Westm. Gaz.* 30 Jan. 9/1 A whaleboat..capsized,..the sail being caught by a back-wind, as the course was being changed.

Backwoods. (Earlier examples.)

1742 *Cal. Virginia St. Papers* I. 235 Severil of ous that were the first settlers of these back woods. 1768 *Boston Gaz.* 25 Jan. (Th.) The chain of forts through the back woods. 1775 *Pennsylv. Gaz.* 16 Aug. 3/2 Upwards of 130 Men from the Mountains and back Woods. 1807 *Repertory* (Boston) 15 Dec. (Th.) The members from the back woods seem to be the deepest skilled and most active men in Congress.

b. Also *backwoods peer* = next, b.

1927 J. A. Spender *Life, Journalism & Politics* I. 236 The backwoods peers said that if they had to submit they would rather go down fighting than have their privileges bartered away in secret.

Backwoodsman. (Earlier examples.)

a 1793 Freneau *Poems* (1809) II. 20 To Crispin O'Conner. A Back-woodsman. 1798 *Monthly Mag.* Mar. 185/1 The Back Woodsmen, as the whites all along the interior line of the states are termed, are almost gigantic. 1803 T. M. Harris *Jrnl. Tour* 6 June (1805) (Th.) Most of the 'Back-wood's men', as they are called, are emigrants.

b. In modern politics applied to the members of the House of Lords who rarely, if ever, attend meetings of that body, but are prepared on occasion to assert their political rights.

1909 *Daily Chron.* 11 Sept. 1/5 This speech will undoubtedly encourage the backwoodsmen in the House of Lords to take strong action. 1928 *Observer* 15 July 10/4 It has been saved by 'backwoodsmen' in the Lords from undergoing the indignity of being inspected..by county councillors.

Back yard, back-yard. [Back- 5.] A yard or enclosure at the back of a house.

1679 [see Back- 5]. 1837 *Southern Lit. Messenger* III. 224, I found myself on a little piazza, in a back yard. 1860 O. W. Holmes *Prof. Breakf.-t.* x. 311 A stone with a whitish band crossing it, belonging to the pavement of the back-yard. 1882 [see Back- 5].

Bacon. *sb.* **6.** Add: *bacon-curer*; bacon-hog, -rind (modern U.S. examples).

1867–9 *Trans. Ill. Agric. Soc.* VII. 432 Hogs for 'bacon-curers and city consumption. *Ibid.*, The weather became much warmer, thus lessening the demand for 'bacon hogs. 1873 J. H. Beadle *Undevel. West* xxiv. 492 He suggested 'bacon rind to mitigate thirst and..it proved quite efficacious.

Ba·con, *v.* *U.S.* [f. Bacon *sb.*] *trans.* To convert into bacon.

1890 *Congress. Rec.* Aug. 8887/1 We consumed or sold our own pork, and we baconed it ourselves.

Baconian, *a.* and *sb.* Add:

2. In recent times used with reference to the theory that Francis Bacon wrote the plays attributed to Shakspere. Also **Baco·nianism.**

1886 P. M. Wallace in *19th Cent.* May 697 What is known as the 'Baconian movement'. *Ibid.*, The 'Baconians' do not rely upon this Cipher for the unflinching belief which they accord to their theory. 1903 Garnett *Eng. Lit.* II. 201 Baconians talk as if Bacon had nothing to do but to write his play at his chambers and send it to his factotum, Shakespeare, at the other end of the town. 1904 *Daily Chron.* 14 Jan. 3/2 If Baconianism had no more cogent evidence to encounter, the game would be in its hands. Since Bacon, on the Baconian hypothesis, certainly broke all other records, why not this one as well? 1907 Doyle *Through Magic Door* viii. 165 Even Shakespeare may be jostled in his throne of honour by plausible Baconians. 1927 *Observer* 18 Sept. 15/4 'The Shrew' is a wonderful tester of mood. One can see it and love it, or come away convinced that Baconianism is no dubious theory but gospel truth.

Bacte·rially, *adv.* [f. Bacterial + -ly[2].] By, with, or in regard to bacteria.

1892 *Daily News* 16 Nov. 5/4 The Thames at Hampton was, both chemically and bacterially, in rather a bad condition, owing to the autumn decay of vegetation. 1908 *Daily Chron.* 24 July 5/5 Bacterially-infected food.

Bactericidally (bæktersisəi·dăli), *adv.* [f. Bactericidal + -ly[2].] So as to destroy bacteria.

1899 G. Newman *Bacteria* i. 24 The blue and violet rays acted most bactericidally.

Bactericide (bæktī·risəid). [f. Bacterium + -cide 1.] A substance that destroys bacteria.

1884 *Therapeutic Gaz.* 15 Dec. 561 [Permanganate of potash] is not a bactericide of great activity. 1894 *Athenæum* 11 Aug. 199/1 A solution of formaldehyde..appears to be a very powerful bactericide.

Bacteride (bæ·ktěrəid). [See definition.] A micro-organism of the genus *Bacteridium* or the family *Bacteridæ*.

[1886 E. Klein *Micro-organisms* (ed. 3) 144 Pollender [etc.] recognised in the blood of animals dead of malignant anthrax the presence of stiff short and long rods, which Davaine called *bactéridie du charbon*.] 1887 A. M. Brown *Anim. Alkaloids* 114 In the same way bacterides at a low temperature may remain in contact with albumen without exciting putrefaction.

Bacteriform (bæktī·rifǭm), *a.* [f. Bacterium + -form.] Resembling bacteria; rod-shaped.

1878 Parkes' *Pract. Hygiene* (ed. 5) 63 *note*, Bacteria, vibriones, or microzymes. [*Note*] Frequently spoken of as Bacteroids and smaller forms as Bacteriform puncta.

Bacterioid (bæktī·ri,oid), *a.* [f. Bacterium + -oid.] = Bacteroid *a.*

1889 in *Cent. Dict.* 1896 Henslow *Wild Flowers* 91 The nodules found on the roots of leguminous plants contain bacterioid fungi.

B. *sb.* An organism shaped like a bacterium; *spec.* the branched form of bacteria found in the root-nodules of leguminous plants.

1909 *Cent. Dict.* Suppl.

Bacteriolo·gic, *a.* = next.

1898 McFarland *Pathogenic Bacteria* (ed. 2) 164 The bacteriologic examination of the air. *Ibid.*, In our bacteriologic researches.

Bacteriological (bæktī·ri,ǫlǫ·dʒikăl), *a.* [f. Bacteriology: see -ical.] Pertaining to bacteriology.

1886 *Brit. Med. Jrnl.* 21 Aug. 383/2 A number of little bacteriological accessories. 1886 E. M. Crookshank *Bacteriology* 3 The apparatus commonly employed in a bacteriological laboratory. 1898 R. T. Hewlett *Bacteriology* 165 The bacteriological study of diphtheria.

Hence **Bacteriolo·gically** *adv.*

1892 A. C. Abbott *Bacteriology* 229 Typhoid fever is bacteriologically one of the most unsatisfactory of the infectious diseases.

Bacteriologist. Add quots.:

1891 G. S. Woodhead *Bacteria* 412 Another great stand-by of bacteriologists is fuchsin. 1898 McFarland *Pathogenic Bacteria* (ed. 2) 127 A very convenient simple apparatus used by bacteriologists.

Bacteriolysin (bæktī·ri,ǫ·lisin). Also *erron.* -ine. [Formed as next + -in[1].] A substance formed in the body during an infectious disease which has the property of destroying the specific bacterium of the disease.

1900 tr. P. Ehrlich *Immunity* in *Proc. R. Soc.* LXVI. 441 The specific bacteriolysines, which dissolve the bacteria. 1908 R. T. Hewlett *Bacteriology* (ed. 3) 157 The protection afforded by the anti-serum is therefore due to the destruction of the microbes by solution, the process being known as bacteriolysis, and the bodies which bring it about being termed bacteriolysins.

Bacteriolysis (bæktī·ri,ǫ·lisis). [f. *bacterio-*, combin. f. Bacterium + Gr. λύσις dissolution.]

1. A name proposed for: The artificial liquefaction of solid organic matter in sewage by means of certain bacteria.

1897 W. E. Adeney in *Trans. R. Dublin Soc.* Aug. 270 The two stages by which organic substances successively suffer aërobic fermentative change in waters...It has been suggested to me to employ the terms bacteriolysis or aërobiolysis for the first stage, and to restrict the use of the term nitrification to the second stage, of change. 1898 E. C. S. Moor *Sanitary Engineering* 474.

2. The destruction or dissolution of bacteria by an anti-bacterial serum ('lysin' or 'anti-serum').

1900 tr. P. Ehrlich *Immunity* in *Proc. R. Soc.* LXVI. 443 The Pfeiffer phenomenon of bacteriolysis. 1908 R. T. Hewlett *Bacteriology* (ed. 2) 138 The protection afforded by the anti-serum is therefore due to the destruction of the microbes by solution, the process being known as bacteriolysis. 1906 A. C. Abbott *Bacteriology* (ed. 7) 568 The endotoxins..are associated with the bacterial cells, and are only liberated through the solution of the bacteria—that is, through bacteriolysis.

Bacteriolytic (bæktī·ri,ǫli·tik), *a.* [Formed as prec. + λυτικός able to loose or dissolve.] Capable of causing the destruction of bacteria; pertaining to or of the nature of bacteriolysis.

1901 Dunglison *Med. Dict.* Suppl., *Bacteriolytic*, producing decomposition of bacteria. 1903 *Therapeutic Gaz.* 15 May 292 It was found that in nearly every case the bacteriolytic power of the blood was sufficient to destroy the typhoid bacillus. 1910 R. Muir in *Encycl. Brit.* III. 177/2 Lysogenic or bacteriolytic action. 1911 R. T. Hewlett *Bacteriology* (ed. 4) 207 Some anti-microbic sera, *e.g.* anthrax serum, are not bacteriolytic.

Bacterioscopic (bæktī·r,iosko·pik), *a.* [f. Bacterioscopy + -ic.] Pertaining to bacterioscopy. Hence **Bacterioscopically** *adv.*

1886 P. F. Frankland in *Phil. Trans.* CLXXVIII. B. 119 The bacterioscopic examination of air. 1896 E. Klein *Micro-organisms* (ed. 3) 67 Bacterioscopic Examination of Water. 1903 *Nature* 19 Feb. 370/2 The City Corporation has therefore caused a number of samples [of shell-fish] to be bacterioscopically examined by Dr. Klein.

Bacteriosis (bæktī·riōu·sis). [mod.L.: see -osis.] Any disease of plants ascribed to the action of bacteria.

1899 G. Massee *Plant Diseases* 338 Bacteriosis of tomatoes. *Ibid.* 339 Pink bacteriosis of wheat. 1900 M. C. Potter in *Proc. R. Soc.* LXVII. 456 Arthur ascribes the action of bacteria in the bacteriosis of carnations to an enzyme.

Bacteriotherapeutic (bæktī·ri,ǫþerăpiū·tik), *a.* [See next and Therapeutic *a.*] Of or pertaining to bacteriotherapy.

1886 *Medical News* 10 July 41 Dr. Ballagi has carefully followed the bacteriotherapeutic details advised by Cantani.

Bacteriotherapy (bæktī·ri,ǫþe·răpi). [Gr. θεραπεία medical treatment.] Treatment of disease by introducing bacteria into the system.

1886 *Medical News* 10 July (*heading*) Bacteriotherapy of Phthisis Pulmonalis.

Bacteriuria (bæktī·riyūə·riă). *Path.* Also **bacteruria.** [f. Bacterium + -uria.] The presence of bacteria in the urine.

1890 Billings *Med. Dict.*, Bacteruria. 1901 Dorland *Med. Dict.* (ed. 2), Bacteriuria. 1907 *Practitioner* Aug. 328 Septic bacteruria.

Bacteroid, *a.* Add:

B. *sb.* A micro-organism of bacterial character; *spec.* one found in the root-tubercles of leguminous plants.

1878 [see *Bacteriform]. 1887 H. M. Ward in *Phil. Trans.* CLXXVIII. B. 552 The gemmules or 'bacteroids' [in the Leguminosæ]. 1898 R. T. Hewlett *Bacteriology* 26 If the roots of a pea, bean, or vetch be examined, numerous little nodules will be found upon them; on examining these microscopically small irregular bodies are found to be present, which have been termed bacteroids. On inoculation into culture media the bacteroids give rise to a growth of organisms resembling bacteria; these 'fix' the atmospheric nitrogen.

Bactrian (bæ·ktriăn), *a.* (*sb.*) [ad. Gr. Βακτριανός, L. *Bactriānus*.] Of or belonging to Bactria, an ancient country of central Asia, lying between the Hindu-Kush and the Oxus. Also *sb.*, a native of this country.

Bactrian camel, the two-humped camel of central Asia.

1788 *Encycl. Brit.* (1797) II. 728/1 The Bactrians differed little in their manners from the Nomades. 1832 *Blackw. Mag.* XXXII. 207/2 The priests of Mithras..offered him.. their Bactrian dromedaries, if he chose to depart. 1908 *Animal Management* 276 The double-humped camel, also called the 'Bactrian,' is found in Turkestan, and throughout central Asia. 1912 H. G. Rawlinson *Bactria* i. 15 The Bactrians were famous for their pithy proverbial sayings. 1927 W. J. Turner *Aesthetes* 14 On a Bactrian Horse, T'ang period.

Bad, *a.* Add:

Used to indicate a decided or pronounced degree of a thing which is evil or undesirable in any case; as, a bad blunder, a bad headache. Also *colloq.* in phrases: *bad egg* (see Egg *sb.* 4), *bad form* (Form *sb.* 15 b), *bad hat* (Hat *sb.* 5 c). *Not bad, not so bad, not half bad*: used pred. of a state of things, the result of an effort, etc.: Less bad than it might be (or have been); hence, by meiosis, fairly good, deserving some praise or congratulation.

1835 *Naut. Mag.* IV. 689 The idea of a sailor's *chemise* is not bad. 1838 in Emily Eden *Up the Country* (1866) I. 129 These [letters] are five months old, but that is not so bad. 1839 *Mag. Dom. Econ.* May 332 Leaving out the cheese, the thing itself is not so very bad. 1860 *Englishwoman's Dom. Mag.* Oct. 26 'Not bad!' Bloomfield replied with a loud laugh. 1867 *Field* 6 Apr. 246/3 This is not half bad,..a fish a-piece, although we were clean till four o'clock. 1891 E. Roper *By Track & Trail* vi. 81, I asked..'How do you like it?' They said it was not so bad; some day it would be better. 1899 Kipling *Stalky & Co.*, *Last Term* 220 'Not half bad years, either,' said McTurk. 1900 Sir W. R. Kennedy *Hurrah Life Sailor* xii. (ed. 3) 180 We had bagged three bulls before breakfast, which was not so bad. 1926 W. Deeping *Sorrell & Son* xvii. § 3 'Did they make it rather beastly—for you?' 'O, not so bad, pater.'

6. b. Difficult, hard (const. inf.). *slang.*

1884 H. Smart *Post to Finish* xi, I have heard you say ..that..their very temper makes them bad to beat.

C. *adv.* Delete † *Obs.* and add U.S. examples.

1816 U. Brown in *Maryland Hist. Mag.* X. 273 Land of not much account, farm'd bad. 1845 J. J. Hooper *Adv. Simon Suggs* vii. 94 'Pshaw!' said Suggs, 'you aint bad hurt.' 1854 Susan Hale *Lett.* (1919) 7 The children..during that time act as bad as they can! 1859 Bartlett *Dict. Amer.* (ed. 2) s.v., I want to see him bad. 1870 *Trans. Ill. Agric. Soc.* VIII. 238 This speaks bad for our application of the art. 1888 *Daily Inter-Ocean* 9 Mar. (Farmer) As the case now stands, the defense want Myers, and want him bad. 1901 Marah E. Ryan *Montana* 3 There is one thing I want in this world, and want bad.

b. *Bad off*, badly off (Badly *adv.* 1).

1817 U. Brown in *Maryland Hist. Mag.* XI. 371 Land full of Lime Stone..bad off for Timber and Water. 1845 J. J. Hooper *Taking Census* i. 152 Yes, send for your marshall ..if you're bad off to. 1879 Tourgee *Fool's Err* xxix. 179, I told him how bad off I was.

Badger, *sb.*[2] Add:

2. (Earlier example.)

1833 Hoffman *Winter in West* (1835) I. 207 A keen eyed, leather-belted 'badger' from the mines of Ouisconsin.

4. b. *To draw the badger*: to entice (an opponent) to come into the open.

1890 *Daily Chron.* 29 Sept., The Parnellite taunts regarding Balfour's indifference have at last drawn the badger.

5. **badger plane** (see quot.); **Badger State** *U.S.*, the State of Wisconsin.

1874 Knight *Dict. Mech.*, *Badger Plane, a panel plane whose mouth is cut on the skew, and from side to side, so as to work up close to a corner in making a rabbet or sinking. 1871 Schele de Vere *Americanisms* (1872) 662 *Wisconsin*, abounding during early days in badgers, has ever since retained the name of *Badger State. 1904 *N. Y. Times* 26 July 3 The Speaker will make several speeches in the Badger State.

Badger, *sb.*[3] [f. Badge *sb.* + -er[1].] One who wears a badge (of a specified kind).

1890 Farmer *Slang*, *Badger*,..6. (Wellington School). A fellow who has got his 'badge' for play in the 2nd xv. at football. 1920 *John Bull* 28 Aug. 16/1 There are idle Badgers at Elmswell, where the job of Rate Collector was going the other day. 1925 *Glasgow Herald* 23 July 7 A Doggett badger is a man to be reckoned with in the rowing world.

Bad lands. *U.S.* [Bad *a.* 4.] (See quots.)

1868 W. F. Raynolds *Explor. Yellowstone* 8 The bluffs bordering the valley are throughout the much-dreaded and barren 'bad lands'. 1871 Schele de Vere *Americanisms* (1872) 180 It is different with the *Bad Lands*, which border the Missouri for about twenty miles, and were called by the first French settlers, *Mauvaises Terres*. 1885 Proctor in *Knowledge* 28 Aug. 171/2 *Bad lands*, waste lands unfit for any sort of agriculture, and hard to travel through. 1887 *Harper's Mag.* May 870/2 At four o'clock that afternoon, they entered the Bad Lands of the Little Missouri. 1895 C. King *Fort Frayne* ii. 20 Two Indian Scouts..had made their unerring way..through a labyrinth of Bad Lands.

Bad man. *U.S.* [Bad *a.* 5, after Sp. *malo hombre*.] A desperado. (See quots.)

1888 Roosevelt *Ranch Life Far West* in *Century Mag.* Feb. 504/1 The 'bad men', or professional fighters, and man-killers, are of a different stamp, quite a number of them being, according to their light, perfectly honest. 1891 E. S. Ellis *Check No 2134* ix. 59 It is much more pleasant to relate how such a young gentleman outwitted a 'bad man'. 1906 *N. Y. Even. Post* 9 Nov. 6 He even appointed a typical 'bad man'—that is, manslayer—to office as a proof of his fondness for Arizona. 1910 Mulford *Hopalong Cassidy* i. 9 They were good bad-men and bad bad-men, the killer by necessity and the wanton murderer.

Bael, bel (bēl). Also 7 beele, bille, 9 bhel, bĕl, bél. [Hindi *bel*, Mahr. *bail*:—Skr. *bilva*, *vilva*.] An Indian tree, *Aegle marmelos*, or its aromatic fruit; the Bengal quince. Also, the medicinal extract of the fruit.

1618 in Foster *Eng. Factories India* (1906) 10 Greene ginger, mirabilons, and beeles. 1619 *Ibid.* 76 Mirabilons and billes in conserves. 1854 Hooker *Himal. Jrnls.* I. 50 The Bhel fruit, lately introduced into English medical practice, as an astringent of great effect, in cases of diarrhœa and dysentery. 1874 Garrod & Baxter *Mat. Med.* (ed. 4) 219 Indian bael has obtained much reputation in India in the treatment of diarrhœa and dysentery. 1877 D. Wright *Hist. Nepāl* 33 Every Newār girl, while a child, is married to a bĕl-fruit, which after the ceremony is thrown into some sacred river. 1910 *Encycl. Brit.* III. 191/1 Bael fruit (*Aegle marmelos*).

Bætyl. Add:

Also in Gr.-L. form **baitylos, bætylos, -us**; also **bætylion** (pl. *-ia*) (Gr. βαιτύλιον). Hence **Bæty·lic** *a.*, of the nature of a bætyl.

1884 *Proc. Soc. Psychical Research* II. 117 Aerolites were scouted as a kind of fetish *in excelsis*—a transcendental bætyl—'the image which fell down from Jupiter.' 1889 W. R. Smith *Relig. Semites* 193 *note*, The use of baetylia, or small portable stones to which magical life was ascribed. 1901 A. J. Evans in *Jrnl. Hellen. Stud.* XXI. 106 The rough pyramidal pillars of the Bhuta Spirit,..and many other rude 'baetyls' of the same kind..are commonly set up beneath holy trees. *Ibid.* 113 An artificial pillar image of the divinity, it may be even the actual 'baetylos' of remote tradition. *Ibid.* 118 The sanctity of baetylic stones and pillars is due to a variety of causes. 1903 G. F. Moore in *Amer. Jrnl. Archæol.* VII. 200 He found the stone cooled off, and, recognizing that it was a baetyl, took it home with him. 1923 *Trans. Scott. Ecclesiol. Soc.* 97 The Clack or stone [at Clackmannan]..is a true Fetich or Baitylos.

Baff (bæf), *v.*[2] *Sc.* [Cf. Baff *sb.*] To beat, strike; *spec.* in Golf, to strike the ground with the sole of the club-head in making a stroke. Hence **Ba·ffing-spoon** = *Baffy.

1858 *Chambers's Jrnl.* X. 157/1 The names of the wooden-headed clubs principally used at St. Andrews..are as follows: the play-club, long-spoon, mid-spoon,..putter, and baffing-spoon. 1881 R. Forgan *Golfer's Handbk.* 10 The 'Baffing Spoon' is so called from the sound produced by it as it smites the ground in making the stroke. *Ibid.* 33 Baff. 1890 H. G. Hutchinson *Golf* 445 Baff.

Baffle, *v.* Add: **8. d.** In technical uses.

1883 Gresley *Gloss. Coal-m.*, *Baffle*, to brush out or mix fire-damp with air in order to render it non-explosive; a dangerous practice, and not now allowed. 1885 *Marine Engineer* 1 Apr. 3/2 The corrugations serve to break up the volume of steam, and also baffle the water passing through the condenser. 1911 Webster s.v., Plates are used for baffling the steam.

Baffle-plate. [Baffle *sb.*[1] 5.] A plate hindering or regulating the passage of fluid through an outlet or inlet, or the direction of sound. Hence **Baffle-plated** *a.*, having a baffle-plate. Similarly **Baffle-disc.**

1882 *Nature* XXV. 220 A kind of baffle plate hung at the back of the grate. 1906 *Daily Chron.* 3 Mar. 3/6 A system of tubes or baffle-plates which break up the hot gas. 1908 *Westm. Gaz.* 31 Dec. 5/1 In this Radiator the Baffle Plated Hood replaces the Frieze and Trivet. 1920 *Chambers's Jrnl.* Nov. 767/1 [Gas] is passed upwards through water dripping from a series of baffle-plates in chambers known as scrubbers. 1926 *Ibid.* Apr. 270/1 The oil rises through a series of perforated baffle discs to the top of the tank.

Baffy (bæ·fi). *Golf.* [f. Baff *sb.* or *v.[2]] A short wooden club used to hit the ball into the air. Also *baffy spoon*.

1888 *Daily News* 22 Sept. 5/1 The old 'Baffy, a funny little toy club, with a sloped face. 1890 H. G. Hutchinson *Golf* 59 The 'baffy', very short and stiff and with face very much laid back. *Ibid.* 335 To Allan was due..the introduction of irons and cleeks for the approach to the hole, these shots having been previously played with baffy spoons.

Bag, *sb.* Add: **II.** *U.S.* In baseball: (see quot. 1874).

1874 H. Chadwick *Base Ball Man.* 9 The other three bases are canvas bags, fastened to posts sunk in the ground on each corner of the square located to the left, the right, and the rear of the pitcher's position. 1917 Mathewson *Sec. Base Sloan* xiii. 177 Hunt was two yards from the bag when the ball reached third base.

9. *fig.* Add quots.:

1900 *Daily News* 9 June 5/5 Our bag was 4 engines and 84 trucks, with a quantity of coal. 1917 Gibbs *Battles of Somme* 105 'We took bags of 'em [*sc.* Germans],' said an officer.

16. *Bags* is now a common colloquialism for 'trousers'.

18. *To give* (a person) *the bag*: variant of phr. *to give the sack* (Sack *sb.*[1] 4). Similarly *to get the bag*, to be dismissed.

1870, etc. [see E. D. D.]. 1913 'Ian Hay' *Happy-go-lucky* i, 'Your fag, isn't he?' 'I gave him the bag two terms ago. ..Tiny has him now.'

Bag, *v.*[1] **1. b.** Add: Said esp. of trousers which become out of shape at the knees.

1913 Ascott R. Hope *Half and Half Tragedy* 32 (*Sent to Coventry* iv.) The Captain of the school has a pair of new breeches..; but they bag at the knees.

Ba·gaty, ba·ggety. *Sc.* The lump-fish.

1794 *Statist. Acc. Scotl.* XII. 521 (Dysart) The fish caught here are..mackerel, baggety, sand-eel [etc.]. 1838 Fleming *Hist. Brit. Anim.* 190 Lump-fish..Hush, Bagaty. 1867 Smyth *Sailor's Word-bk.*, *Lump*..the trivial name of the baggety..*Cyclopterus lumpus*.

Baggage. 1. (Earlier U.S. examples.)

1748 Washington *Diaries* I. 5 We sent our Baggage to Capt. Hites. 1753 C. Gist *Jrnls.* 80 He..lent us a canoe to carry our baggage to the forks. *Ibid.*, We met our baggage, and swimmed our horses over Allegheny. *a* 1793 Freneau *Poems* (1809) I. 52 My baggage was stow'd in a cart very snug. 1822 J. Russell in *Boston Gaz.* 23 Nov. (Th.) I shall set off as soon as I can obtain my baggage. 1842 J. S. Buckingham *Slave States* II. 173 The cart he was driving contained their baggage. 1852 Bristed *Upper Ten Thousand* 81 An American never uses the conversational term luggage, but always speaks of his impediments as baggage.

b. *ellipt.* A baggage-car on a train. *U.S.*

1926 J. Black *You Can't Win* vii. 82 It was a warm night, and riding the front end of the baggage was pleasant enough.

C. 2. (Earlier and additional U.S. examples.)

1871 Schele de Vere *Americanisms* (1872) 357 The stamped marks are entered into the 'baggage-agent's books. 1884 H. S. Cummings *Sk. Class 1863 Dartmouth Coll.* 45 From this position he was promoted to the responsible place of General Baggage Agent. 1835 J. H Ingraham *South-West* I. xvi. 172 A long train of 'baggage or cargo cars were on the rear of these. 1846 *Mass. Statutes* 16 Apr. c. 251. 176 For passenger and baggage cars. 1878 B. F. Taylor *Between Gates* 26 A Babel of trunks is surging towards the baggage-cars. 1842 J. S. Buckingham *Slave States* II. 173 A barouche..and a 'baggage-cart following with five trunks. 1888 *Harper's Mag.* Oct. 760/1 The detail that most impressed me was the racks and rows of 'baggage-checks. 1887 C. B. George *40 Yrs. on Rail* iv. 58, I..moved to Reading, Massachusetts, where I was 'baggageman on the Reading train. 1904 *Atlantic Monthly* Mar. 381 A baggageman..was making much ado over the single parcel left on the hot planks. 1849 D. Nason *Jrnl.* 112 The 'baggage master said he should charge for the tool-chest. 1860 Holland *Miss Gilbert's Career* xxv. 442 Moustache leaving the car..and coming back from certain interesting conferences with the baggage-master. 1862–3 E. E. Hale *If, Yes, & Perhaps* (1868) 25 Some pirate from the pier..had seized the waiting trunk..while the baggage-master's back was turned. 1872 J. S. Ingram *Centen. Expos.* 701 It contained..coat and 'baggage room. 1859 Bartlett *Dict. Amer.* (ed. 2), *Baggage-smasher, a man who transfers baggage to and from railroad cars, steam-boats, etc. 1871 G. A. Townsend *Mormon Trials* 9 [They] resembled a parcel of baggage smashers warming themselves in a railroad depot between trains. 1879 Stockton *Rudder Grange* vii. 75, I went up-stairs and got a *baggage tag. 1791 Washington *Diaries* IV. 149 My equipage and attendance consisted of a Chariot..a light *baggage Waggon and two horses. 1849 D. Nason *Jrnl.* 78 [I] got a ride in a baggage wagon, for which I paid 37½ cents.

Ba·ggageless, *a.* Having no baggage; having lost one's baggage.
1891 *Daily News* 28 Nov. 3/6 On Sunday he wandered about alone and baggageless. 1905 *Westm. Gaz.* 6 Dec. 9/1 Drenched, weary, and baggageless travellers.

Baggager. Add: A beast that carries baggage; a baggage horse, camel, etc.
1859 *Blackw. Mag.* Apr. 459/2 Whack goes the long whip, aimed at the rearmost baggager. The aggrieved horse flies out with a bounce. 1908 *Animal Management* 279 The ordinary pace [is] two and a half miles an hour for 'baggagers', and up to twelve miles for riding camels.

Baglet (bæ·glėt). [See -let.] A small bag.
1885 *Graphic* 3 Jan. 18/2 He has brought back in his baglet..a dozen new-laid eggs, some milk, and a loaf of bread. 1926 *Chambers's Jrnl.* 101/2 She opened a black baglet she carried—a silken affair with an amber hoop.

Bags I. [Bag *v.*[1] 6; cf. the vulgar 'says I'.] A formula used (orig. by children) to assert a claim to some article on the ground that one is the first to speak for it.
1866 A. Dobson *Bob Trevor & I* ii. in *Beeton's Ann.* 215 Deep in a hole..gleamed the clear water of a shallow well. 'Bags I first drink,' says Bob, according to the polite practice of schoolboys. 1886 *Cheshire Gloss.*, *Bags I*,..an expression used by boys in claiming the first place in a game; or in laying claim to any treasure trove. 1899 Kipling *Stalky* 35 There's a *Monte Cristo* in that lower shelf. I saw it. Bags I, next time we go to Aves! 1921 A. A. Milne *Second Plays* 7 Bags I all the presents.

Ba·g-worm. *U.S.* [Bag *sb.* 1.] The larva of American lepidoptera of the family *Psychidæ* (esp. *Thyridopteryx* and *Œceticus*), injurious to trees, which builds as a portable habitation a silken case or sac covered with little twigs and leaves. Called also *basket-worm*, *drop-worm*.
1862 *Congress. Globe* Jan. 232 On the avenue and in the parks you will find the evergreen trees..being destroyed by the bag-worm. 1870 Mrs. Stowe *Oldtown Fireside Stories* (1871) 158 The young Hokums was jest like bag-worms, the more they growed the more they eat. 1885 H. C. McCook *Tenants Old Farm* 384 Basket or bag-worms. 1897 J. H. Comstock *Insect Life* 204 The Bag-worms, family *Psychidæ*. 1899 D. Sharp *Insects* ii. 394 One of the North American basket- or bag-worms *Thyridopteryx ephemeraeformis*.

Bahadur (bāhǭ·dur). *Anglo-Ind.* Also 8 behauder, baha(u)door, bahawder. [Hindi *bahādur* hero, champion.] A great man, distinguished personage. Often affixed as a title to an officer's name.
'*Bahādur* and *Sirdār Bahādur* are also the official titles of members of the 2nd and 1st classes respectively of the Order of British India, established for native officers of the army in 1837' (Yule).
1781 J. Lindsay in Ld. Lindsay *Lives* (1849) III. 296 Sheikh Hussein..tells me that our army has beat the Behauder [*i.e.* Hyder Ali]. 1841 Thackeray *Major Gahagan* iv, The lips of the Bahawder are closed...Bobbachy Bahawder has seen the dreadful Feringhee. 1848 *Eerie Laird* x. 110 While he, a man of genius, must be content with the empty title of Bahadur (or knight). 1879 in T. H. S. Escott *Pillars Emp.* 275 There is nothing of the great *behawder* about him; he is easy of access, civil, and obliging to all who approach him. 1922 *Blackw. Mag.* Oct. 519/2 He was a Bahadur, which is Indian for 'hell of a fellow'.
Hence **Bahadur** *v. intr.*, to play the bahadur.
1860 W. H. Russell *Diary India* I. 272 They had been curvetting, prancing, and bahadooring with their swords in the air.

Bahai (bahā·ī). Also Beha'i. [Pers.] A follower of Baha-ullah (1817–92) and his son Abdul Baha (1844–1921), propagators of a religion based on *Babism. Also *attrib.* Hence **Baha·ism**, **Baha·ist**, **Baha·ite**.
1892 E. G. Browne in *Relig. Syst. World* 351 So for these Behá'is, as they are now called, the writings of the Báb became an old testament. 1903 M. H. Phelps *Abbas Effendi* p. xxix, The religion of Babism, or Beha'ism. *Ibid.* p. xxxiii, The Babis, who have since that time generally styled themselves..'Beha'is'. 1909 E. Hammond *Splendour of God* 10 Bahais..claim that Bahaism has..the Light of Love. 1909 H. Dreyfus *Bahaism* 26 The Bahai theology. *Ibid.* 72 When finally they left the neighbourhood of Baghdād,..the Babis had become Bahais. 1914 Cheyne *Reconcil. Races & Relig.* 132 The confinement of the Bahaites at Acre. 1924 *Expositor* Feb. 152 The Bahaists ..have been turning their attention to the Western world and its Christianity.

Baianism (bēi·yăniz'm). Also Baj-. [Cf. F. *baïanisme* (1738), *baïaniste* (1720).] The heretical teaching of the Louvain theologian Michel de Bay (Latinized as Baius), 1513–89, a forerunner of the Jansenists. So **Bai·anist**, a supporter of this teaching, a follower of Bay.
1733 J. Gordon *Mem.* (title-p.), Wherein..the History of Baianism, Jansenism, and the Constitution *Unigenitus*, [is] impartially related. *Ibid.* (1734) 33 The Bull..did not meet with the same Reception from the Secular Clergy, who for a considerable time openly oppos'd it, and who for that Reason were called Baianists. 1928 J. Brodrick *Card. Bellarmine* I. iv. 74 Heresies allied to Baianism.

Baily's beads: see Bead *sb.* 7.

Bairnhood. [Bairn.] Childhood. *Sc.* or *affected*.
a 1835 *Whistle-Binkie* (1890) II. 161 The broomy hill, Where we used to stray in bairnhood's day. 1894 R. Ford (*title*) Ballads of Bairnhood.

Baister, Baisting: var. ff. Baster[1], Basting *vbl. sb.*[1]
1881 *Instr. Census Clerks* (1885) 74 Braider,..Stitcher, Baister, Button-hole Maker. 1890 *Daily News* 2 Jan. 5/3 Baisting cotton. 1903 *Daily Chron.* 5 Mar. 10/5 Coat Machinists..wanted, baisters and finishers. 1906 *Ibid.* 23 May 11/7 Tailoresses wanted; must be good coat baisters.

Bait, bate (bēit), *sb.*[2] *slang.* [f. Bait *v.*[1]] A fit of bad temper; a rage, 'wax'. Hence **Bai·ty** *a.*
1857 [A. L. Mayhew in *Eng. Dial. Dict.* s.v. *Bate* sb.[3] 'He was in an awful bait' was common in the Clapham Grammar School, 1857]. 1882 'F. Anstey' *Vice Versâ* iii. (ed. 4) 48 It would put him in no end of a bait. 1899 Eden Phillpotts *Human Boy* 95 I've just left Milly, and she's in a frightful bate. 1921 Sylvia Thompson *Rough Crossing* ii. § 3 Jolly lucky the C.O. didn't notice it yesterday—he gets 'baity' on these occasions. 1925 *Chambers's Jrnl.* 838/1 Now I must be going, or else dad'll be baity with me.

Baitable (bēi·tăb'l), *a.* [f. Bait *v.*[1] + -able.] Serviceable as cattle fodder.
1890 W. Carruthers in *Jrnl. R. Agric. Soc.* 756 At Meldon not only was there clover, but also a considerable quantity of baitable grasses. *Ibid.* 759 Grasses which are rejected when the stock has a sufficient supply of baitable food to permit of a choice.

Baitless, *a.* Add:
2. Not furnished with bait (for fish); unbaited.
1854 *Tait's Mag.* XXI. 275/1 Holding in his hand the listless line, whose baitless hook, three fathoms down, has become a jest and a laughing-stock to..the finny tribe.

Baitylos: see *Bætyl.

Bake, *v.* 5. Of land. (Earlier U.S. examples.)
1868 *Rep. U. S. Commissioner Agric.* (1869) 357 When the proportions of clay and sand are such that the soil will not bake,..it may properly be called loam. 1873 J. H. Beadle *Undevel. West* xxxiii. 710 The land is never water-soaked, never 'bakes', and I never saw a clod as big as my fist.
7. (Earlier examples of *bake-kettle, -oven*. U.S.)
1812 *Massachusetts Spy* 2 Sept. 3/4 [He] threw it in the bake-oven, which had just before been heated..to bake bread. 1846 Sage *Scenes Rocky Mts.* (1859) 187 On one occasion they carried off a bake-kettle to a distance of several hundred yards. 1859 Bartlett *Dict. Amer.* (ed. 2) 19 *Bake-Oven*. This term is often used in the West for the simple word *oven* in a bakery. It is also applied to the iron bake pan.

Bake-apple. *U.S.* [Bake *v.* 7.] The (dried) fruit of the cloudberry. Also *baked-apple*.
1889 *Century Dict.* s.v. *Baked-apple*. 1895 *Outing* (U.S.) XXVII. 18/1 The outlying islands furnish the curlew-berry and bake-apple in profusion.

Bakelite (bēi·kĕləit). [ad. G. *bakelit* (Chem. Zentralblatt, 1909, 1478), f. the name of L. H. Baekeland its inventor + -ite[1].] A condensation of phenol or other phenolic bodies and formaldehyde used as a plastic and for insulating purposes.
1913 G. Martin *Ind. & Manuf. Chem.* 211 Bakelite (sp. gr. 1·25) is very hard, not elastic, and an excellent insulator of heat and electricity. 1913 *Jrnl. Soc. Chem. Ind.* 16 June 563/2 Bakelite varnish has been suggested for use as an antiseptic in hospitals. 1921 Thorpe *Dict. Applied Chem.* I. 501/1 There are..bakelite plants in Germany, France and England, and several factories where bakelite goods, such as buttons, are manufactured under licence.

Baker. Add:
1. b. A fruit or vegetable that bakes (well, etc.).
1852 De Quincey *California* Wks. 1871 XVI. 191 Not but the apples might have been 'good bakers'.
2. *U.S.* (Examples.)
1841 *Lowell (Mass.) Offering* I. 227 (Th.) A peep into the baker told that the potatoes were cooked. 1857 Thoreau *Maine W.* (1912) 320 Somebody had left..on a deserted log ..a loaf of bread baked in a Yankee-baker. 1897 *Outing* (U.S.) XXIX. 489/1 The cooking utensils consisting of three dripping pans, one patented baker and one large coffee-pot.

Bakhara, var. of *Buckayro.

Baking-powder (s.v. Baking *vbl. sb.* 3). Add quots.:
1863 Mrs. Beeton *Bk. Househ. Managem.* 856, 2 teaspoonfuls of baking-powder. 1878 E. B. Tuttle *Border Tales* 40 Flour biscuits, made up in a hurry, and quite light with 'baking powder' or soda. 1887 I. R. *Lady's Ranche Life Montana* 30 We have been living..on baking-powder bread, but everyone told us it was unwholesome. 1909 *Westm. Gaz.* 1 June 7/4 Baking-powder beer.

Baku (bā·ku). Also -ou. A fine kind of straw grown in the Philippines and woven in China.
1927 *Vogue* Mar. 40 Baku, a linen-like straw. 1928 *Ibid.* 4 Apr., Advt. 26 Natural Bakou Straw, trimmed with a feather cockade. 1929 *Ibid.* 20 Feb. 57 Toque of beige baku straw. 1929 *Chicago Tribune* 9 May, Bakus and balibuntals.

Balaclava. *Balaclava helmet*: a woollen covering for the head and shoulders worn esp. by soldiers on active service; named after Balaclava, the site of a battle fought in the Crimean war, 25 October 1854.
1892 C. T. Dent *Mountaineering* (Badm.) 48 A knitted woollen Balaclava (Templar) cap is useful for sleeping out. 1900 *Queen* 10 Feb. 222/1 Balaclava Helmet in crochet. 1914 *Scotsman* 17 Sept. 8/5 The articles which at the moment will be most useful to officers and men in ships afloat are Cardigan jackets..Balaclava helmets, mufflers. 1916 *Blackw. Mag.* Mar. 398/1 Baa's balaclava helmet and woolly muffler were flaked with white.

Balakhana (bælăkā·nă). Also -khaneh, -hané. [Pers. بالا خانه *bālā-khāna* upper room.] An upper room in a Persian house, in which travellers are lodged.
1840 J. B. Fraser *Trav. Koordistan* I. ii. 31 Desiring that this Khan should have such a suite of rooms..and another such a *dellān*, or *balakhaneh*. 1882 O'Donovan *Merv Oasis* I. xxii. 369 Above the arch was a square-topped room known as the *bala hané*, which served as quarters for the better class of travellers, as well as a kind of watch-tower and look-out station. 1921 *Blackw. Mag.* Dec. 825/2 Very soon our horses were tethered, and champing good dry lucerne under the bala-khaneh of a two-storied guest-house.

Balalaika (bælălai·kă). [Russ. балалайка.] A musical instrument of the guitar kind, with a triangular body, popular in Russia and other Slav countries.
1788 tr. *Stæhlin's Anecd. Peter Gt.* 319 In his youth he had never heard any [music] but that of drums, fifes, balalaikas, and bagpes. 1864 Engel *Mus. Anc. Nat.* 55 The Russian *balalaika*, an instrument said to be of high antiquity. 1885 A. J. C. Hare *Stud. Russia* i. 27 Formerly the peasants used to dance the Barina..accompanied by the Balalaika. 1913 H. H. Munro *When William Came* iii, The thrumming music of a balalaika orchestra coming up from the restaurant below.

Balance, *sb.* Add:
17. c. Phr. *On balance* (or *upon the balance*): taking everything into consideration.
1861 upon the balance [in Dict.]. 1928 *Britain's Industr. Future* (*Liberal Ind. Inquiry*) ii. vii. 89 We believe that these provisions would be, on balance, overwhelmingly in the interest of the investor.
20. a. *Balance in hand*, fig., 'something to spare.'
1876 *Coursing Calendar* 5 Wheatear..working with great smartness, won with a nice balance in hand.
21. Orig. *U.S.* (Earlier examples.)
1805 *Deb. Congress* (1852) 1043 The balance of the year [i.e. from 15th Oct.] is appropriated to hunting. 1817 S. R. Brown *Western Gaz.* 167 The inhabitants are more than half French; the balance consists of emigrants..from various parts of Europe and America. 1833 *Sketches & Eccentr. D. Crockett* (1834) 82 The balance of the dogs buckled in, and off they went right up a hollow. 1845 S. Judd *Margaret* I. xiii. 96 Deacon Hadlock himself, hearing Obed's entreaties, consented to remit the balance of the penalty.

Balancer.
4. Add: In technical use (see quots.).
1904 S. P. Thompson *Dynamo-Electric Mach.* (ed. 7) I. 775 Uses of Motor-Generator Combinations...Equalization of voltages in a 3-wire or 5-wire system of distribution; in which case, the apparatus is termed a Balancer. 1923 *Daily Mail* 17 Feb. 4 The Lanchester balancer incorporated with the five-bearing crankshaft...The balancer consists of two weighted drums driven by a helical gear wheel fixed to a web of the crankshaft. They revolve at twice the crankshaft's speed and ensure its perfect balance and harmony.

Balata (bæ·lătă). Also 9 ballata. [S. Amer. Sp., prob. ad. a native word. So Fr. (1777).]
1. The dried juice or gum of *Mimusops balata* and *M. globosa*, sapotaceous trees of Guiana, used as a substitute for gutta-percha. Also *attrib.* and *Comb.*
1860 *Jrnl. Soc. Arts* 24 Aug. 713/2 A few months ago it was announced in the French journals that M. Serres, Pharmacien, at Paris, had been so fortunate as to prepare gutta percha from the Balatas of the sapotaceous plants in Guiana and Central America. 1862 *Catal. Contrib. Br. Guiana to Internat. Exhib.* in R. Duff *Br. Guiana* (1866) 99 The leaves, branches, and trunk [of the bully tree] produce a whitish milk, forming the gum, now known as ballata. 1864 Sir W. Holmes in *Jrnl. Soc. Arts* 4 Mar. 245/2, I believe..that *Balata*,..will supply the great want of the day, as a good insulating medium for telegraphic purposes. 1866 Veness *El Dorado* ix. 94 The ballata-gatherer..may thus bleed a great many trees in a single day. 1900 W. T. Brannt *India Rubber*, etc. 371 The manufacture of balata belts is analogous to that of rubber belts. 1925 *Chambers's Jrnl.* 550/1 Wandering balata-bleeders from the lower forests.
2. Any of several sapotaceous trees of Guiana and the W. Indies, esp. *Mimusops balata*, *M. globosa*, and *Bumelia retusa*. Also *balata-tree*.
1858 De Verteuil *Trinidad* 101 Balata (*Mimusops*). The Balata, or Bullet-wood, is one of our best and most useful timbers. 1860 *Jrnl. Soc. Arts* 24 Aug. 713/2 It appears also that the *Sapota Mulleri*, the tree producing the gutta percha of Surinam, is called Balata in French Guiana, Les Antilles, and elsewhere. 1864 Grisebach *Flora Brit. W. Ind. Isl.* 781 Ballata tree (Dominica): *Bumelia retusa*. 1871 Kingsley *At Last* I. vi. 223 A huge dark-headed Balata [*note* Mimusops Balata]. *Ibid.* vii. 257 (*page-heading*) The Balata Tree.

Balayeuse (balĕyȫ·z). *Dress-making.* [Fr., fem. of *balayeur* sweeper.] (See quot. 1882.)
1882 Caulfeild & Saward *Dict. Needlework*, *Balayeuse, or Sweeper*.—A French term to signify the frilling of material or lace which lines the extreme edge of a dress skirt to keep the train clean as it sweeps along the floor. The balayeuse is allowed to project beyond the edge of the dress, so as to form a decorative as well as a useful trimming. 1894 *Daily News* 20 Jan. 5/7 Three flounces of pink, green and cream-coloured silk forming a richly-rustling balayeuse beneath the hem.

Bald, *sb.* [f. Bald *a.*]
1. A species of domestic pigeon; = Bald-head (quot. 1867).

1854 *Poultry Chron.* I. 21/2 For the best pair of Balds or Beards. 1876 Fulton *Illustr. Bk. Pigeons* (1883) 172 There are plenty of the pheasant-faced Balds which are all that could be desired in colour and marking. *Ibid.* 173 The Bald has so many white flights in each wing.
2. A mountain summit or region naturally bare of forest, esp. in the southern Appalachians. *U.S.*
[1840 C. Lanman *Lett. Alleghany Mount.* Add. 184 The sides of the Roan, the Black, the Bald, and others, are covered with a deep rich vegetable mould.] 1877 *Field & Forest* III. 40 These 'Balds' cover most of the summits of the mountains over 6000 feet in height..and are a marked feature of the Southern Appalachians. 1885 'C. E. Craddock' *Prophet Gt. Smoky Mts.* i. 2 She paused often, and looked idly.. at the great 'bald' of the mountain. 1887 — *Keedon Bluffs* 169 For they were in truth near the summit, not ascending the great bald, but in a gap between two peaks. 1890 *Buckskin Mose* xi. 163 Another signal had been kindled on a large bald or bare mountain on our left.

Bald, *a.* 4. a. and c. (Later examples.)
a. 1840 C. F. Hoffman *Greyslaer* I. x. 116 There's a ledge of bald rock to the left yonder. 1869 *Amer. Naturalist* II. 647 A few clumps of willows..are the only objects remaining..except the bald bluffs. 1872 E. Eggleston *End of World* xli. 257 A large bald hill overlooking the Ohio was to be the mount of ascension.
c. 1856 *Trans. Mich. Agric. Soc.* VII. 805 He..raises..the old-fashioned bald or bearded wheat.

Bald eagle, bald-eagle. *U.S.* [Bald *a.* 2.] The American eagle. (Cf. Eagle 1 b.)
1691 R. Frame *Descr. Pennsylv.* 27 The Turky-Buzzard and Bald-Eagle high, Wild Ducks, which in great Companyes do fly. 1705 Beverley *Virginia* ii. (1722) 133 The Bald-Eagle no sooner perceives a Hawk that has taken his Prey, but he immediately pursues. 1775 A. Burnaby *Trav. N. Amer.* 28 The bald eagle, which is generally upon the watch, instantly pursues. 1826 T. Flint *Recoll.* 6 The wolf, the bear, and the bald eagle, were the most frequent emblems on the tavern signs [among the Allegheny mountains]. 1868 *Amer. Naturalist* II. 194 So cautious is he lest the Bald-eagle (*Haliaetus leucocephalus*)..may approach. 1878 J. H. Beadle *Western Wilds* xxx. 483 Small is the pleasure one can take..in the sweep of the bald eagle, when the next occupation of that eagle may be in picking the meat from his bones.

Bald-face. *U.S.* [Bald *a.* 2.]
1. The widgeon (also called *bald-head, -pate*).
1709 J. Lawson *New Voy. Carolina* 151 The bald or white Faces are a good Fowl. *Marg.* Bald-Faces. 1768 Washington *Diaries* I. 253 Went a ducking between breakfast and dinner and killd 2 Mallards and 5 bald faces.
2. A variety of whisky.
1840 *Daily Pennant* (St. Louis) 28 Apr. (Th.) He called lustily for a horn of bald-face and molasses. 1848 *Knickerbocker Mag.* Nov. XXXII. 402 What is classically denominated 'bald-face', or old brown whiskey. 1871 Schele de Vere *Americanisms* (1872) 581 *Bald-face*, one of the many slang terms under which bad whiskey passes in the West.
3. *attrib.* (See quot.)
1876 *Fur, Fin & Feather* Sept. 142 Green Martin tells of a bear, rarely seen in the mountains which old hunters call the bald-face bear.

Ba·ld-faced, *a.* [Bald *a.*] Having a bald face.
1677 [see Bald *a.* III.]. 1861 *Trans. Ill. Agric. Soc.* IV. 341 The nest of our bald-faced hornet is occasionally suspended in a house to kill off the house-flies. 1885 *Century Mag.* Nov. 60/2 He jogged along on his bald-faced bay in the bleak untempered light.

Bald-headed, *a.* Add:
b. colloq. phr. (orig. *U.S.*) *To go bald-headed* (*for, at*), to dash or charge forward, without heeding danger or obstacles. Hence **Bald-hea·dedly** *adv.* (in similar sense).
1846–48 Lowell *Biglow P.* Ser. i. vi, 'Pious editor' x, I scent wich pays the best, an' then Go into it baldheaded. 1867 *Ibid.* Ser. ii. Introd., 'To go it bald-headed': in great haste, as where one rushes out without his hat. 1888 *Pall Mall Gaz.* 22 June 4/2 The Chicago Republicans, to use an Americanism, have gone 'baldheaded' for Protection. 1915 W. J. Gordon *Flags of World* 77 Warburg, where the colonel of the Blues, the Marquis of Granby, after a high trot of five miles led them hatless in the charge, 'going bald-headed for the enemy', and thus originated the well-known phrase. 1920 W. J. Locke *House of Baltazar* v. Quong Ho..tried zealously, then desperately, then bald-headedly, but never a wild blow could pass the easy guard of his smiling master. 1927 *Daily Express* 28 Feb. 7/3 It is the way of a woman to go bald-headed at her objectives.

Baldness. 2. Add earlier U.S. quot.:
1840 C. Lanman *Lett. Alleghany Mount.* ix. 72 The legend ..accounts for the baldness of the mountain.

Baldwin (bǭ·ldwin). *U.S.* [The personal name.] A common variety of eating apple.
1826 *Catal. Fruits in Gard. Hortic. Soc. Lond.* 108 (Apples) Baldwin's. 1842 *Ibid.* (ed. 3) 5 Apples...Baldwin. 1848 Lowell *Biglow P.* Ser. i. ix. end, Looking out through my study window, I see Mr. Biglow..busy in gathering his Baldwins. 1859 *Trans. Mich. Agric. Soc.* (1860) X. 254 Baldwin is a very popular market fruit in New England. 1861 *Trans. Ill. Agric. Soc.* IV. 468 Our farmers set in the early orchards of Wisconsin a large proportion of Roxbury Russets, Baldwins,..and Spitzenbergs. 1887 Mary E. Wilkins *Humble Romance* 238 On the right of the garden were two old apple-trees, a Baldwin and a Porter.

Bale, *sb.*[3] 3. Add: **bale-band, -hook, -sack, -sling** (see quots.). b. **bale-cloth** *U.S.*, cloth used for covering bales; **bale-rope** *U.S.*, rope used for securing bales.
1891 Patterson *Naut. Dict.*, *Bale-band*, a big shackle-shaped iron at the mast-head, supported by the cap-band, and to which the standing part of the flying jib-stay is bent on. 1862 *Trans. Ill. Agric. Soc.* (1865) V. 159 We have pressed the sirup from the sugar through fine *bale-cloth. 1824 *Deb. Congress* 16 Feb. (1856) 1542 But in selling cotton, the bagging and *balerope are all weighed and sold as cotton. 1837 *Mass. Statutes* 12 Apr., A corporation, by the name of the Goulding Patent Bale Rope Manufacturing Company, for the purpose of manufacturing bale rope. 1883 *Century Mag.* Oct. 817/2 This man flung them into an enormous *bale-sack, swinging wide-mouthed from a derrick. 1883 *Man. Seamanship for Boys* 93 There are several methods of slinging a cask, either with a pair of butt slings, *bale slings, or a bowline knot. 1891 Patterson *Naut. Dict.*, *Bale-sling*, a simple strap passed round a bale or bag, the two ends meeting on top, one dipping under the other.

Baled, *ppl. a.* Add: esp. *U.S.* in *baled hay, straw.*
1872 E. Eggleston *End of World* xxx. 197 [The steamer] took on a new cargo of baled hay and corn and flour. 1891 C. Roberts *Adrift Amer.* 135, I was fortunate enough to be able to stow myself away in a car that was partly filled with baled hay. 1918 *Nation* (N.Y.) 7 Feb. 168/1 The baled straw for the mattresses.

Baleen. 3. Add: **baleen whale**, a whalebone whale; any member of the *Mystacoceti*.
1878 J. Murie in *Cassell's Nat. Hist.* II. 257 Scammon says that three or four [killer-whales] do not hesitate to grapple with the largest Baleen Whales. 1883 *Encycl. Brit.* XV. 393/1 The Baleen Whales or *Mystacoceti*.

Balibuntal (bælibʊ·nt'l). Also balli-, bally-, -buntl(e (as one word or as two); also shortened to bal(l)i. [Short for *Baliuag buntal*, a weave of *Buntal originating from Baliuag in Bulacan, Philippine Islands.] A fine straw of a very close weave, used for hats. Also *attrib.*, and short for *balibuntal hat*.
[1911 C. B. Robinson in *Philippine Jrnl. Science* June 115 The Baliuag buntal hat is..more closely woven than that of Lucban, and is consequently stronger.] 1918 *N. Y. Times* 25 Apr. 5 (Advt.), Light as a feather and as flexible as a Panama, the Bally Buntle is one of the strictly new, extremely modish Hats. 1925 *Ibid.* 1 Mar. (Advt.), Hats of Horse Hair, Balli Buntle, Bankok. 1927 *Observer* 12 June 11/4 A bali-buntal in mauve. 1928 *N. Y. Times* 1 Apr. 7 (Advt.), Baku and Balibuntal are favorite straws for Easter Wear. *Ibid.* 11 Apr. (Advt.), This Untrimmed Baliibuntl Needs Little Adornment. *Ibid.* 15 Apr. (Advt.), Balibuntal hat with velvet petals.

Balisaur (bæ·lisǭɹ). [Native name.] A badger-like animal of India, *Arctonyx collaris*.
1881 in *Cassell's Encycl. Dict.*

Balisier (balizye). [Fr.] The West Indian musaceous plant *Heliconia bihai*, with very large leaves and brilliant orange flowers.
1858 De Verteuil *Trinidad* 95 Balizier (*Heliconia*). 1871 Kingsley *At Last* I. vi. 222 Under the shade of great Balisiers or wild plantains. [*note*] Heliconia. *Ibid.* vii. 266 Above these, again, the Balisiers bend their long leaves, eight or ten feet long apiece.

Balistic, -ics, var. ff. Ballistic, -ics.

Balk, *sb.* Add:
5. b. *U.S.* In baseball: (see quot.).
1867 H. Chadwick *Base Ball Player* 53 A balked Ball.—Should the pitcher move his foot in delivery—thereby making a 'balk'—and the Umpire call a 'balk' until the ball is returned to the pitcher, [etc.].
9. *attrib.* uses:
1839 [in Dict.]. 1896 W. Broadfoot *Billiards* ix. 283 (*heading*) Safety and baulk play. *Ibid.* ix. 285 A few examples of safety and baulk strokes. 1906 *Daily Chron.* 19 April 4/7 The 18.1 in. baulk-line champion.

Balk, *sb.*[2] [f. Balk *v.*[1] in the local sense of 'to leave unfinished'.] Of cloth: In the raw or unfinished state.
1847 R. W. Hamilton *Nugæ Lit.* 357 (Yorksh. Dial.) *Balk*,..cloth in an unfinished state. 1860 S. Jubb *Hist. Shoddy-Trade* 40 Short Ends were sold to the merchants.. in the grey raised (not balk state). 1876 Cudworth *Bradford* 519 These clothiers attended the Leeds White Cloth Market..selling their cloth in the 'balk', or raw state.

Balk, *v.*[1] 3. Add: Also *fig.* (*colloq.*) To 'shy' or 'jib' *at*.
1908 J. M. Dillon *Motor Days Eng.* xx. 241 It was the only time I ever saw Maud balk at gooseberries.

Balkan (bǭ·lkăn), *a.* Of or pertaining to the peninsula bounded by the Adriatic, Ægean, and Black Seas, or to the countries or peoples of this region; *spec.* with allusion to the relations (often characterized by threatened hostilities) of the Balkan states to each other or to the rest of Europe; so in the derivatives, **Balkanic** (bǫlkæ·nik) *a.*, **Ba·lkanism, Ba·lkanize** *v.*, **Ba·lkaniza·tion.**
1922 *Encycl. Brit.* XXX. 370/2 *Balkanic Italy (country of Gorizia E. of the Isonzo, W. Carniola, Istria, Trieste and Zara). 1925 *Contemp. Rev.* Apr. 476 Matters that, like everything Balkanic, lie very much on the knees of the gods. 1925 *Public Opinion* 23 Jan. 86/2 His swarthy face with its cunning Balkanic eyes. 1924 *Scribner's Mag.* Jan. 19/2 Patches of glaring 'Westernism'..merely emphasize Belgrade's fundamental '*Balkanism'. 1920 *Nineteenth Cent.* Mar. 536 Great Britain has been accused by French observers of pursuing a policy aimed at the *Balkanisation of the Baltic provinces. 1921 S. Graham *Europe—Whither Bound?* vii. 95 Hungary avers that a large stretch of Hungarian territory..is being *Balkanized. 1923 *Edin. Rev.* Jan. 170 It was preparing to play its part in Balkanising Europe at the Versailles Conference. 1925 *Contemp. Rev.* Sept. 353 We talk glibly about a Balkanised Europe.

Balked, *ppl. a.* Add: 4. *U.S.* In baseball: (see *Balk *sb.* 5 b).

Ba·lkiness. [f. Balky *a.*] The quality in a horse, etc., of being balky.
1894 *Outing* (U.S.) XXIV. 349/1 The mules were the very embodiment of balkiness. 1909 J. C. Lincoln *Keziah Coffin* x. 143, I, bein' a Hammond, with some of the Hammond balkiness in me, I set my foot down as hard as his.

Ball, *sb.*[1] Add:
1. b. *Ball and chain*, a heavy metal ball secured by a chain to the leg of a prisoner or convict, to prevent escape. (Cf. *Chain *sb.* 2.) *U.S.*
1873 J. H. Beadle *Undeveloped West* vii. 132 Those who had fined and imprisoned culprits, or sent them to work with ball and chain. 1902 Harben *Abner Daniel* 94 They put a ball an' chain to one of his ankles an' sent him out with the nigger gang. 1904 *Brooklyn Daily Eagle* 10 June 4 Tammany was..made work for him under ball and chain and in stripes. 1904 *Newark Even. News* 3 Aug. 6 Hammonton ..has resolved to see what the ball and chain gang system will do in the way of driving off the tramps and vagrants.
10. d. *Metallurgy.* A mass of puddled iron formed by the workman into a pasty lump, to be hammered and rolled when taken from the furnace.
1825 J. Nicholson *Oper. Mech.* 334 When the iron is deprived of the carbon..the furnaceman rolls it up into balls of one half or three quarters of a cwt. each. 1852 J. A. Phillips *Metallurgy* 285 It now only remains for the workman to form the iron into balls. 1855 W. Truran *Iron Manuf.* 134/1 After 8 or 9 minutes raking of the iron, now in the condition of pasty lumps,..the puddler commences the formation of the puddle balls. 1892 F. Joynson *Iron & Steel Maker* 69 The work of the puddler is..confined to..the production of the lumps or masses of metal technically called 'balls', and sometimes, though rarely in this country, 'blooms'.
21. *ball-field, -game, ground, play, player, playing, -stick, -team* (U.S. quotations).
1903 *N. Y. Times Sat. Rev.* 22 Aug., When he excels others fairly in schoolroom or on the *ball-field. 1849 C. Lanman *Lett. Alleghany Mount.* xiii. 100 Since my arrival here the Indians have had one of their *ball games. 1888 *N. Y. Life* 11 Aug. 18 You know it is the Sabbath day and you have been to the ball game. 1898 Susan Hale *Lett.* 335 These men were just like..Harvard men, after the ball game has gone right for us. 1903 Susan H. Ward *Life G. H. Hepworth* 19 The two friends did not join in ball games. 1904 *N. Y. Times* 2 May 9 Cheering like rooters at a ball game. 1845 J. J. Hooper *Adv. Simon Suggs* ix. 112 An Indian ball-play was announced to 'come off'..at the *ball ground near the river. 1829–32 J. P. Kennedy *Swallow B.* I. xviii. 186 The Indians pretended they were going to have a *ball play. 1892 J. L. Ford *Dr. Dodd's School* i. 18 Although, like most of his race, [Monsieur Valcour] was no *ball-player. 1849 C. Lanman *Lett. Alleghany Mount.* xiii. 100 The manly game of *ball-playing is still practiced after the ancient manner. 1845 J. J. Hooper *Adv. Simon Suggs* ix. 113 They..knock down their antagonists with their *ball-sticks. 1899 A. H. Quinn *Pennsylv. Stories* 37 Harvard had sent down its *ball team, with an enthusiastic crowd of rooters.
22. **ball-fringe**, a fringe used esp. for mantel-pieces; **ball-headed** *a.*; **ball-peen, -pome** (see Peen *sb.*, Pome *sb.* 3); **ball-race** (see Race *sb.*[1] 8 g); **ball-trap** (see Trap *sb.*[1] 8 and cf. *ball-valve*).
1909 H. G. Wells *Tono-Bungay* i. ii. § 4 Stuff with *ball fringe along the mantel. 1902 *How to make useful Things* 48/2 With a *ball-headed hammer strike the petals of the discs. 1874 Knight *Dict. Mech.*, *Ball-peen Hammer, a metal-worker's hammer with a spherical peen. 1884 *Ibid.* Suppl., *Ball-peen Hammer*, one whose peen is round, or ball-shaped. 1922 *Weekly Dispatch* 17 Dec. 15, 1-lb. *Ball-pome Hammer. 1907 *Westm. Gaz.* 18 Nov. 7/2 The *ball-races fitted between the springs and the axle on which the long semi-elliptical springs are carried. 1908 *Ibid.* 30 June 4/2 Of the three Ariels [one] had the misfortune to break a ball-race in the hub. 1873 Parkes *Pract. Hygiene* (ed. 4) 344 The *ball-trap is used in some special cases only; a ball is lifted up as the water rises, until it impinges on and closes an orifice.

Ball, *v.*[1] Add:
2. b. To clench (the fist) tightly. Also with *up*: To roll up in a ball-like lump or mass.
1823 *New Monthly Mag.* VII. 542 Ball'd up to a mass, in a moment unconll'd They rose, and again disappear'd in the dark. 1889 Clark Russell *Marooned* xvi, A spun-yarn winch was rattling on the forecastle; and the half-blood Charles..was balling up the stuff as it was manufactured. 1889 Baring-Gould *Arminell* vi, With teeth clenched, and fists balled in his breeches pocket. 1892 *Temple Bar* Jan. 120 He dropped his sword, balled his strong hands. 1925 *Chambers's Jrnl.* 581/1 No one had ever seen a balled-up swallow.
c. Metallurgy. *To ball up*: to form (molten iron) into 'balls' in the puddling furnace, for hammering or rolling. Also **Balling up** *vbl. sb.*
1855 W. Truran *Iron Manuf.* 134/1 The period for balling-up arrives. 1868 Joynson *Metals* 62 The metallic matter is..balled up and shingled. 1887 J. A. Phillips *Metallurgy* (ed. 2) 294 When the whole charge has been balled up. 1895 T. Turner *Metall. Iron & Steel* 291 *Balling up stage*, which occupies some twenty minutes.
4. b. (Earlier U.S. quot.)
1788 Washington *Diaries* III. 297 Apprehension of the Horses balling with the Snow.
5. Of bees: To surround (the queen) in a dense cluster, often with the result that she is suffocated or crushed to death.
1888 F. R. Cheshire *Bees* II. 426 If very many pass the guards [of a strange hive] unchallenged, they are likely to ball the queen, and possibly destroy her. 1919 T. W. Cowan *Bee-keepers Guide Bk* (ed. 23) 141 It is sometimes very difficult to introduce queens into hives having no young bees, as the old bees frequently 'ball' the queen and hug her to death unless she be released.
6. *To ball up* (U.S.): a. *intr.* To become clogged. (Cf. 4 b.) Also *fig.* (see quot. 1889).
1889 Farmer *Americanisms*, *Ball up* (College) at Middle-

bury College, to fail at recitation or examination—Hall's College Words and Customs. 1902 Clapin *Dict. Amer.* 35 It probably comes from the 'balling up' of a horse in soft, new fallen snow, when a snowball forms within each shoe.
b. *trans.* To bring into a state of entanglement or difficulty.
1887 *Harper's Mag.* Sept. 605/2 'You seem balled up about something.'..'Balled up!..I'm done for.' 1896 G. Ade *Artie* xi. 98 She had him balled up till he couldn't say a word. 1911 H. Quick *Yellowstone N.* ix. 238 Every time old Hen stepped, he balled things up worse. 1923 Watts *Luther Nichols* 280 They're always getting in the way of liberal government and balling things up.

Ballast, *sb.* 6. b. Add:
ballast-fin *U.S.*, a fin-shaped metal extension of the keel of a yacht serving to ballast her and to enable her to sail close to the wind.
1894 *Outing* (U.S.) XXIV. 194/2, I have not a word to say against the ballast-fin so far as racing is concerned.

Ba·llastless, *a.* [Ballast *sb.*] Without ballast; *fig.* unsteady.
1885 Wingfield *Barbara Philpot* III. ii. 34 She was unstable and ballastless, subject to delusions. 1886 *Bedford Times* 30 Oct. 5 They serve the purpose of ballast to a ballast-less leader.

Baller. Add: 1. *spec.* A workman who charges puddled bars into a balling or reheating furnace.
1881 *Instr. Census Clerks* (1885) 104 Baller (Tin Plate).
3. a. One who makes yarn, etc. into balls; one who attends to a balling machine. b. A balling machine.
1881 *Instr. Census Clerks* (1885) 104 Baller (Carpet). 1884 McLaren *Spinning* 216 The balling head and creel motion ranks along with Blamire's as the best...The sliver before going into the baller can be drawn off the doffer in two ways. *Ibid.* 220 This is a side-drawing system, and, on our former supposition of speeds, would have the same number of doublings per sliver as in the baller.

Ballet (bæ·lėt), *sb.*[3] *Hist.* [16–17th c. spelling of Ballad.] A form of madrigal in dance-rhythm.
1595 T. Morley (*title*) The first booke of balletts to fiue voyces. 1597 [see Ballad 1]. 1598 T. Weelkes (*title*) Balletts and madrigals to fiue voyces. 1879 Grove *Dict. Mus.* I. 132/2 *Ballets*, compositions of a light character, but somewhat in the madrigal style, frequently with a 'Fa la' burden which could be both sung and danced to. 1921 E. H. Fellowes *Eng. Madrigal Composers* 57 An essential feature of the Ballet..was the introduction, at the end of each section, of a florid and rhythmical passage vocalized to the syllables *Fa la la*.

Balling, *vbl. sb.*[1] Add:
1. *Spinning.* (Additional quots.)
1884 McLaren *Spinning* 116 Balling, or making into 'tops'. *Ibid.* 117 As this balling head moves from side to side quickly, the ball is made by the sliver constantly passing from side to side. *Ibid.* 221 With the Blamire and balling systems one card can run while the other is standing.
3. *Farriery.* The administration of medicine to a horse in the form of a ball (see Ball *sb.*[1] 11), which he is made to swallow. *Balling iron, pistol*, instruments sometimes used for this purpose.
1831 Youatt *Horse* 385 The balling iron, while it often wounds and permanently injures the bars, occasions the horse to struggle more than he otherwise would against the administration of the ball. 1884 M. H. Hayes *Veterin. Notes* (ed. 3) 456 The *balling iron* is an instrument for keeping the mouth open. *Ibid.* 457 A *balling pistol* is useful for giving balls to fractious animals. 1908 *Animal Management* 308 *Balling*.—Take the tongue in the left hand..and push the ball as far as possible over the root of the tongue.

Ballistic, *a.* Add:
c. *ballistic galvanometer*, one in which damping is minimized, used to measure transient currents.
1878 Ayrton & Perry in *Rep. Brit. Assoc.* 487 To obtain a galvanometric arrangement of sufficient sensibility to measure the small capacity of such an air condenser, and sufficiently ballistic that the air damping should be almost inappreciable. *Ibid.*, The arrangement of a ballistic galvanometer to fulfil the two conditions mentioned..was very troublesome. 1879 — in *Philos. Mag.* Apr. 287 There was always some slight damping even in our ballistic galvanometer. 1880 J. E. H. Gordon *Phys. Treat. Electr. & Magn.* I. 240 In order to diminish the resistance of the air as much as possible, a 'balistic galvanometer' has been used.

Balli·stically, *adv.* In relation to or in the way of ballistics.
1879 Ayrton & Perry in *Philos. Mag.* Apr. 284 But this arrangement [of the galvanometer]..had far too much damping for being used ballistically. 1889 J. A. Longridge *Internal Ballistics* 16 Although there is no positive evidence of 'Dissociation' in a gun, it may be well to examine what would be the effect ballistically, if it did take place.

Ballistics. Also balist-. Add:
Exterior ballistics, that branch of ballistics which deals with the flight of the projectile after leaving the gun. *Interior* (or *internal*) *ballistics*, that branch which deals with the propulsive effect of a charge and the action of the projectile in the bore of the gun.
1840 *Civil Eng. & Arch. Jrnl.* III. 21/2 They afford positive data, and the bases of experimental balistics, so necessary for artillery practice. 1873 F. Bashforth *Motion of Projectiles* Pref. p. viii, On the institution of the Advanced Class for Officers of the Royal Artillery in 1864, there was no satisfactory work on ballistics. 1886 J. M. Ingalls (*title*) Exterior Balistics in the plane of fire. 1889 J. A. Longridge (*title*) Internal Ballistics. 1893 *Arms & Explosives* Aug. 244/1 Interior ballistics, exterior ballistics, and the ballistics of penetration. 1917 W. H. Tschappat *Ordnance & Gunnery* iv. 108 Interior ballistics treats of the motion of the projectile while still in the bore of the gun. *Ibid.* ix. 424 Exterior Ballistics treats of the motion of a projectile after it has left the piece.

Ballistite (bæ·listəit). [f. Ballista + -ite[1].] A smokeless powder invented by A. Nobel, consisting of gun-cotton and nitroglycerine in about equal parts.
1892 *Arms & Explosives* Oct. 11/1 The new explosive 'Ballistite', which the Italian War Office has lately been experimenting with. 1895 O. Guttmann *Manuf. Explosives* II. 254 Nobel's ballistite, which has soluble gun-cotton as its base. 1896 P. G. Sanford *Nitro-Explosives* 171–2. 1912 J. M. Ingalls *Interior Ballistics* (ed. 3) 140 The ballistite.. was in the form of cubes 0·3 of an inch on a side.

Ballon d'essai (balon desę). [Fr., = trial balloon.] An experimental project or piece of policy put forward to test the feeling or attitude of a person or body of persons.
1883 *Standard* 24 Jan. 5 (Stanf.) The contents [of the letter] would make it appear a sort of *ballon d'essai*, designed to throw light on the prospects of an Orleanist Restoration in France. 1905 Mrs. H. Ward *Marriage W. Ashe* ii. xiii, In the early morning she had sent her note to Kitty—a *ballon d'essai*, dispatched in a horror of great fear. 1928 *Daily Tel.* 18 Sept. 11/5 The rumours about Mlle. Lenglen's future plans have recently died down. This one may be in the nature of a ballon d'essai.

Ballonnet, ballonet (bæ·lǫnet). Also ballon(n)ette. [ad. F. *ballonnet*, dim. of *ballon* Balloon.] A balloon inflated with air, placed inside a gas balloon to enable it to keep its shape if deflated.
1901 E. P. Lyle in *Smithsonian Rep.* 583 The ballonet fills with air automatically from a pump worked by the motor. 1903 *Daily Chron.* 21 Sept. 3/6 In the central compartment is an internal air balloon, or *ballonnette*. 1907 G. H. Bryan in *Cornh. Mag.* May 609 An internal balloon or 'ballonet'. 1917 C. C. Turner *Aircraft of To-Day* xiii. 203 All non-rigid and semi-rigid airships are provided with ballonnets.

Balloon, *sb.* Add:
7. b. A lofty hit or kick given to a cricket-ball, base-ball, or football. *colloq.*
1904 *Daily Chron.* 8 June 5/3 With his score at 45 Jackson was missed off a 'balloon' in the long field by Gooder. 1922 *Daily Mail* 8 Dec. 11 For the most part the ball was kicked anywhere—for choice high in the air. 'There's no one up there,' shouted an ironical spectator after one of many balloons.
10. b. **balloon sleeve** (earlier U.S. example); **balloon-tyre**, a pneumatic tyre used on a motor vehicle; also **balloon-tyred** *a.*; **balloon vine** *U.S.*, a handsome tropical American tree, which bears large balloon-like pods.
1837 *Southern Lit. Messenger* III. 3 Women come to the spring for water in great *balloon sleeves and prunella shoes. 1924 *Motor* 27 May 715/1 The low-pressure or *balloon tyre manufacturers in the United States have adopted the straight-sided type of rim exclusively. 1895 *Daily News* 7 June 3/1 The Princess Maud..here mounted on a *balloon-tired 'safety'. 1868 *Rep. U. S. Commissioner Agric.* (1869) 206 *Balloon vine (*Cardiospermum halicacabum*).

Balloon, *v.* Add: 3. b. *trans.* To puff out or cause to be inflated like a balloon; *spec.* to distend with air, gas, or water, as the abdomen in tympanites, or the rectum or vagina with specially constructed apparatus.
1889 [see *Ballooning *vbl. sb.* 2]. 1906 *Macm. Mag.* Dec. 119 The wind..ballooned his cassock and carried his hat into the ditch. 1909 *Practitioner* Dec. 807 Several equal lengths of rubber tubing..were obtained, and at about the centre of some of them aneurysms..were ballooned. 1926 W. Deeping *Sorrell & Son* ii. § 2 Sorrell saw the labouring of the ballooned waistcoat.
4. *trans.* To hit (a cricket-ball) or kick (a football) high in the air. *colloq.*
1904 *Daily Chron.* 20 July 7/2 As he did not quite get to the ball, he ballooned it to Garnett in the out-field, who brought off a well-judged catch. 1927 *Daily Tel.* 8 Feb. 16/3 As for the half-backs, they lacked method; it was not a light or flighty ball, but they were for ever ballooning it.

Balloonet (bălū·net). Also -ette. = *Ballonnet.
1902 *Westm. Gaz.* 11 Apr. 8/1 Within the main balloon there is to be a smaller balloon. This can be filled with air. If, therefore, the balloon becomes slack, it can immediately be made taut by pumping air into the balloonet. 1909 H. G. Wells *War in the Air* iii. § 5 A long internal balloonette of oiled and toughened silk canvass.

Ballooning, *vbl. sb.* Add:
2. Dilatation of the walls of a cavity of the body as a symptom or for therapeutic purposes.
1889 T. Bryant in *Lancet* 5 Jan. 8/1 On the diagnostic value of 'ballooning of the rectum' in cases of stricture of the bowel...The surgeon will often find..that he has entered a cavity, the walls of which are expanded or 'ballooned'... The extent of ballooning will be found to vary in every case. 1890 Billings *Med. Dict.*, *Ballooning, vaginal*, distension of vagina as by tampons, water- or air-bags, etc. 1893 A. S. Eccles *Sciatica* 3 In the remaining nine cases there was more or less ballooning of the rectum.
3. (See quot.)
1924 T. Lawson *Woollen Yarn Production* Introd. p. ix, *Ballooning*, extension of the arc of the axis of the spinning thread.

Ballot, *v.*[1] Add:
5. *trans.* To procure the vote by ballot of (a body of voters) on a specific motion.
1898 *Daily News* 25 June 6/6 The Llwynpia colliers to-day rejected a motion to ballot the men for or against a sliding scale. 1899 *Ibid.* 9 Jan. 7/3 If the textile unions are to be balloted on the question of raising the age.

Bally (bæ·li), *a.* and *adv. slang.* A euphemism for *bloody* (see Bloody *a.* 10), used as a vague intensive of general application; 'jolly', 'confounded'.
1887 S. Butler in H. F. Jones *Life* xxvi. (1919) II. 54 No one in those days gave him or herself any bally airs about it. 1889 Jerome *Three Men in Boat* ii, 'Ah, the bally idiot!' you hear him mutter to himself. 1898 Steevens *With Kitchener to Khartum* 112 I've been in this bally country five years. 1919 Christine Orr *The Glorious Thing* v. 56, I..talked gaily about the bally old war. 1922 H. Walpole *Cathedral* I. vi. 103 All the time behind you and them some force was insisting on places being taken, connections being formed. One was simply a bally pawn..a bally pawn.

Ballyhoo (bælihū·), *sb. U.S.* A 'barker's' speech; publicity in advance of a project; hence, blarney, 'eye-wash'.
1924 *Philad. Even. Post* 9 May, A live, little park full of side show tents..with..barkers spieling before the entrances and all the ballyhoos going at full blast. 1925 H. L. Foster *Trop. Tramp Tourists* 36 Above all, don't let them use a megaphone. It's too much like a ballyhoo. 1927 *Daily Express* 21 Sept. 1/2 Mr. Wiener, chairman of the Pennsylvania State Athletic Commission..calls Dempsey's letter 'mere ballyhoo'. 1928 *Ibid.* 3 Mar. 9/2 Mr. McAndrew characterised Mr. Thompson's charges as 'lies and ballyhoo'.
attrib. 1928 *Weekly Dispatch* 20 May 15 To make the season pay Sir Barry would have had to descend to ballyhoo standards.
Hence **Ballyhoo** *v. trans.*, to commend, urge, or the like, in the manner of a 'barker'.
1927 *Scots Observer* 28 May, Our people will not be bullied and bally-hoed into churchgoing or anything else. 1928 *Weekly Dispatch* 6 May 15/2 How the late P. T. Barnum would have enjoyed ballyhoo-ing this new Drury Lane spectacle!

Balm, *sb.* Add: 11. b. The balsam poplar (*Populus balsamifera*). *U.S.*
1784 Cutler in *Mem. Amer. Acad.* (1785) I. 491 *Populus* ..The Black Poplar, commonly called, in the northern states, the Balm of Gilead. 1861 *Trans. Ill. Agric. Soc.* IV. 448 The Balm of Gilead is hardy thousands of miles north of this. 1897 G. B. Sudworth *Nomencl. Arbor. Flora U.S.* 130.
c. The balsam fir (*Abies balsamea*). Also *attrib.*
1854 Shillaber *Mrs. Partington* 27 The balm-of-gilead buds and rum that occupied their position in the buffet, were not prepared for her. 1887 *Scribner's Mag.* Dec. 731/1 Just ..pick me a handful o' balm o' Gilead buds. I want to put 'em in a half a pint o' new rum. 1902 Clapin *Dict. Amer.* 35 The tree itself is also known as *Balm of Gilead*, in imitation of the Eastern terebinth.

Balmy (bā·mi), *a.* Add:
7. 'Soft', weak-minded, idiotic. Also as *sb.* (see quot. 1903). *slang.* See also *Barmy *a.*
1851 Mayhew *Lond. Labour* I. 217/2 (Street-patterers' slang) *Balmy*, insane. 1859 *Slang Dict.*, *Balmy*, insane. 1891 Farmer *Slang* II. 224/1 Balmy in one's crumpet. 1892 *Daily News* 17 Nov. 6/6 Regarding the old 'balmy' criminals, they are poor creatures, far more to be pitied than condemned. 1903 Ld. W. Nevill *Penal Servitude* 150 These are officially classed as 'W. M.'—that is, weak-minded—but are invariably known colloquially as 'balmies'. *Ibid.* 151 A man who appears to be playing 'balmy'. 1912 Masefield *Dauber* ii. in *English Rev.* Oct. 350 Painting's a balmy's job [*ed.* 1913, p. 21 a balmy job] not worth a nail.

Balneary. Add:
B. *adj.* Of or pertaining to the bath or bathing.
1883 H. James *Portr. Places* vii. 142 The French do not treat their beaches as we do ours—as..places animated simply during the balneary hours. 1924 *Weekly Westm. Gaz.* 29 Aug. 530/3 In fantasy I view and loathe each balneary station—I have been down at Pebbleton-on-Sea.

Balneologist (bælniǫ·lŏdʒist). [f. L. *balneum* bath + -ologist.] An expert in balneology.
1902 *Times* 22 Jan. 2/4 Applications are invited for the appointment of balneologist under the New Zealand Government in connexion with the Thermal Springs of the Colony. 1921 *Times Lit. Suppl.* 6 Oct. 646/3 Dr. Herbert..in 1902 was appointed as Government balneologist to advise on the development of the health resorts of New Zealand.

Ba:lneothe·rapy. Add quots. Hence **Ba:lneotherapeu·tic** *a.*
1881 tr. *von Ziemssen's Cycl. Med.* Suppl. 184 Balneotherapy, when there was no mercury used, has proved of no greater worth. 1906 *Practitioner* Dec. 764 The initiation of balneo-therapeutic measures. 1907 Sir H. & F. P. Weber (*title*) Climatotherapy and Balneotherapy.

Balsa. Add:
2. A bombaceous tree of tropical America, *Ochroma Lagopus*, with very light wood (corkwood).
1866 *Treas. Bot.* s.v. *Ochroma*, The very buoyant rafts or balsas, the unsinkable properties of which caused such surprise among the discoverers of America, are likewise made of it, whence the tree is called Balsa in some parts of America. 1924 *Contemp. Rev.* Jan. 95 The balsa tree, a wood which, from its extreme lightness, is specially suitable in the construction of aeroplanes.

Balsam, *sb.* Add: 7. **balsam fir, poplar** (earlier U.S. examples). Cf. *Balm *sb.* 11 b, c.
1807 P. Gass *Jrnl.* 138 The country is closely timbered with..what some call *balsam-fir. 1849 Willis *Rural Lett.* i. 18, I showed the first symptom..by ordering my breakfast under a balsam-fir. 1819 D. Thomas *Trav.* 93 The true *balsam poplar differs greatly in the leaf. 1832 D. J. Browne *Sylva Amer.* 254 This tree which is a genuine Balsam Poplar, is commonly seen growing before the houses.
8. *Balsam of Gilead* (see *Balm *sb.* 11 c).
1832 D. J. Browne *Sylva Amer.* 95 This species of spruce ..is called Silver Fir, Fir Balsam, and Balsam of Gilead.

Baltimore. (Earlier example.)
1709 J. Lawson *New Voy. Carolina* 145 The Baltimore-Bird, so call'd from the Lord Baltimore, Proprietor of all Maryland, in which Province many of them are found.

Baltimo·rean, *a.* [f. *Baltimore*, the capital of Maryland, U.S.A.] A resident or native of Baltimore.
1816 U. Brown in *Maryland Hist. Mag.* X. 280 Baltimoreans, look; Land selling in the middle of the Alleghany Mountains. 1830 *Deb. Congress* 25 Mar. 679/2 Last year the Legislature of Pennsylvania..refused to permit the patriotic Baltimoreans to make a railroad up into that State. 1876 D. C. Gilman *University Probl.* (1898) 38 A Baltimorean still living provides for the foundation of an astronomical observatory in Yale College.

Balto-Slavic (bǫ·ltoslæ·vik), *a.* and *sb.* Also -Slavo·nic. [f. *Balto-*, used as comb. form of *Baltic*.] The designation of the group of Indo-European languages which comprises the Baltic branch (Lithuanian, Lettish, and Old Prussian) and the Slavonic branch (Russian, Polish, Czech, Serbian, Bulgarian, etc.).
[1891 A. L. Mayhew *O. E. Phonol.* p. xii, Baltic-Slavonic, including Old Prussian, Lithuanian, Lettish, and Old Bulgarian.] 1902 O. F. Emerson *Brief Hist. Eng. Lang.* 8 The Balto-Slavic branch consists of two divisions. 1910 P. Giles in *Encycl. Brit.* XIV. 495/1 North of the Black Sea.. comes the great Balto-Slavonic group. *Ibid.* XVI. 246/1 The words *mentīri, rēs, ignis* have close equivalents in Balto-Slavonic.

Baluch (bălū·tʃ), **Baluchi** (bălū·tʃi). Also 7 Bolloch, Balloch, Buluch, Boloch, 8 Ballowch, 9 Belooch(e, -ee, Bloach, Bilochee, Baloochi. [Pers. *Balūchī*.] An inhabitant or native of Baluchistan, a country lying between the lower Indus and south-east Persia. b. The Iranian language of Baluchistan. Also *attrib.* or as *adj.*
1617 Purchas *Pilgrimage* (ed. 3) 550 The Persian Gulfe hath beene awed, and the Arabike or Red Sea tamed, in requitall of the Turkes and Buluches Trecheries. 1619 in Foster *Eng. Factories India* (1906) 84 [They blame the] Bolloches [for the disaster]. 1727 A. Hamilton *New Acc. E. Indies* I. 107 They were lodged in a Caravanseray, where the Ballowches came with about 300 to attack them. 1816 H. Pottinger *Trav. Beloochistan* 53 The Belooches, who form the great bulk, or perhaps, very strictly speaking, the whole of the population throughout Beloochistan, are a people whose origin is so obscure [etc.]. 1848 L. R. Stacy *Narr. Beloochistan & Affghanistan* 72 The Brahooe and Belooche tribes. 1875 *Encycl. Brit.* III. 300/1 (*Baluchistan*) The country derives its name from the Baluches, but the Brahoes are considered the dominant race. 1882 Floyer *Unexpl. Baluchistan* 158 One tribe of Balūchis will 'chapao,' or plunder, another tribe directly they get a chance. 1885 *Encycl. Brit.* XVIII. 655/2 Baluch, the language of Baluchistan..very closely akin to New Persian, but especially distinguished from it in that all the old spirants are changed into explosives. 1886 *Ibid.* XX. 109/2 Baluchi is spoken on the same frontier, farther south, adjacent to Baluchistan. 1920 *Blackw. Mag.* Aug. 185/2 He spoke only Baluchi and indifferent Persian. 1925 *Ibid.* Apr. 490/2 He knew exactly the line of conduct which would most effectively appeal to the Baluch nature.

Baluchitherium (bălūtʃiþī·riŏm). *Palæont.* [mod.L., f. prec. + Gr. θηρίον beast.] A gigantic extinct land mammal of which remains have been found in the upper oligocene deposits of the Bugti hills of Baluchistan.
1913 C. Forster-Cooper in *Ann. & Mag. Nat. Hist.* XII. [376 Thaumastotherium osborni, a new Genus of Perissodactyles from the Upper Oligocene Deposits of the Bugti Hills of Baluchistan...During an expedition to Baluchistan in 1911 I found..a mammalian atlas and dorsal vertebra remarkable for their unusually large size. *Ibid.* 377, I propose the generic and specific names *Thaumastotherium osborni*. *Ibid.*] 504, I learn that the generic name *Thaumastotherium* proposed..is preoccupied. The generic name *Baluchitherium* is therefore proposed as a substitute. 1925 *Chambers's Jrnl.* 217/2 It was a baluchitherium, the greatest of all varieties of rhinoceros. It stood thirteen feet at the shoulder, and its neck, relatively as long as a horse's, gave it an additional reach of four or five feet when it raised its great head.

Baluster. Add:
6. *attrib.* and *Comb.*: *baluster column* or *shaft* (see quot. 1853); *baluster-stem* (of a cup, chalice, etc.); *baluster-shaped* adj.
1844 baluster shaft [see Baluster 1 b]. 1853 *Archit. Publ. Soc. Dict.*, *Baluster column*, the name given to a pillar used in the so-called Saxon architecture of England for a divisional support in windows. 1871 Nesbitt *Catal. Slade Coll. Glass* 120 Goblet, with a..baluster stem. 1878 W. J. Cripps *O. Engl. Plate* x. 292 The foot is much like those of earlier cups, but the stem is different, being formed as acanthus or other leaves, the upper part of it baluster-shaped. 1912 *Eng. Hist. Rev.* Oct. 832 A rather early baluster-stem cup.

Bamboo, *sb.* Add:
2. Cane-coloured porcelain biscuit, invented by Wedgwood. Also *bamboo ware*.
1787 Jos. Wedgwood in L. Jewitt *The Wedgwoods* (1865) 310 *Bamboo*, or cane-coloured bisqué porcelain, of the same nature with the porcelain No. 3 [*i.e.* a fine white biscuit ware]. 1865 L. Jewitt *The Wedgwoods* 410 *note*, An open basket of bamboo. 1904 W. Burton *Hist. Eng. Earthenware* 162 The simple patterns of lines and foliage in blue and green enamel which he [*sc.* Elijah Mayer] used on his bamboo wares.
3. [= 2 in Dict.] **bamboo joint**, an internode of bamboo (with its nodes) cut and fashioned into a vessel for carrying water, cooking rice, etc.; **bamboo palm** (see quot.); **bamboo rat**, a rodent belonging to the genus *Rhizomys*, found in Malacca; **bamboo ware** (see 2 above).
1924 Mrs. Leslie Milne *Home of Eastern Clan* iii. 47 Water is carried in large *bamboo joints. These are pierced near the top, a string is passed through the holes, and the joints are hung on one end of a pole, which rests on the shoulders. 1891 *Kew Bulletin* Jan. 3 The '*Bamboo' palm, or *Raphia vinifera*, is perhaps the commonest tree in the swamps [of Lagos]. 1881 *Cassell's Encycl. Dict.*, *Bamboo-rat*, a rodent mammal belonging to Gray's genus Rhizomys. 1914 *Brit. Mus. Return* 135 An Ashy Bamboo Rat (*Rhizomys canescens*) from the Shan States.

Bamboo, *v.* Add:
2. *trans.* To furnish with bamboo or bamboo laths.
1925 *Blackw. Mag.* Apr. 537/2 The roof was bambooed and ready to be thatched.

Bamboos (bæmbū·s). *S. Afr.* Also -ous. [ad. Du. *bamboes* Bamboo.] A wooden vessel for milk, water, etc. (Cf. *Bamboo *sb.* 3.)
1822 J. Campbell *Trav. S. Africa* I. 46 (Pettman) They brought us three bamboeses...A bamboos is a deep wooden vessel..cut out of a block of wood. 1842 R. Moffat *Missionary Labours S. Africa* x. 144 A kind housewife would hang a bamboos, or wooden vessel filled with milk..near my head. 1844 J. Backhouse *Narr. Visit Mauritius & S. Afr.* 565 Bambouses..are a sort of jars made of willow-wood.

Ban (ban). [Fr.] (See quots.)
1900 *Daily News* 14 Aug. 8/2 On the falling of the curtain, however, when a 'ban' was called for, the ice was broken. The 'ban' is the characteristic ovation of the French student. 1906 *Daily Chron.* 20 Aug. 6/5 At the end it was 'Vive' everybody, and a perfect salvo of 'triple bans' was given.

Banagher (bæ·năgəɹ). [Name of a town in Ireland, which is said to have become proverbial as a 'rotten borough'.] Phr. *To beat* (or *bang*) *Banagher*: to surpass everything. (Cf. Bang *v.* 6.)
a 1845 Barham *Ingol. Leg.* Ser. iii. *House-warming*, Whose name..in the records of fame..beats Banagher. 1890 Farmer *Slang* s.v., *He beats Banagher*, an Irish saying of one who tells wonderful stories. 1928 *Weekly Disp.* 24 June 2 'You beat Banagher, Pat,' said Willie, admiringly, 'and Banagher beat the Divil'.

Banana. Add:
2. b. The yellow colour of a ripe banana. Also *banan* (= F. *banane*).
1923 *Daily Mail* 3 Apr. 10 In shades of..Banana and Cream. *Ibid.* 7 May 1 In Pale Jade, Banan, Tuscan.
3. **banana bird, banana oriole**, names given by early writers to some South American and West Indian species now included in the genus *Icterus*, containing the so-called American orioles; **banana fly** (see quot.); **banana liquid** (see quot.); **banana quit**, a name applied in Jamaica to any bird of the genus *Certhiola*, esp. *C. flaveola*, the black and yellow honey-creeper; **banana solution**, a solution, having the odour of bananas, used as a vehicle in applying bronze pigments.
1713 Sloane in Ray *Synopsis Avium* 187 *Passer coeruleo-fuscus*. The *Bonana Bird..Arbores Bonanas dictas frequentat, unde nomen. 1734 Albin *Nat. Hist. Birds* II. 37 The Banana Bird from Jamaica..of the Bigness of our English Starling. 1756 P. Browne *Jamaica* (1789) 477 *Icterus major*..The large Banana Bird. 1847 Gosse *Birds of Jamaica* 226 Banana-bird. *Icterus leucopteryx*...Fruit is his principal diet; a ripe banana, or orange. 1921 *Conquest* Sept. 493/2 The common *Banana Fly (*Drosophila ampelophila*). 1916 L. A. Flemming *Practical Tanning* (ed. 3) 474 Because of its characteristic odor the amyl acetate solution is frequently called *banana liquid. 1809 Shaw *Gen. Zool.* VII. 431 *Banana Oriole. 1847 Gosse *Birds of Jamaica* 84 Black and yellow creeper. *Banana Quit. 1894 Newton *Dict. Birds* 761 The Banana Quit is the Sugar-bird.

Bana·naland. [See quot. 1898.] A colloquial Australian name for Queensland. Hence **Bana·nalander.**
1898 Morris *Austral English*, *Banana-land*, slang name for Queensland, where bananas grow in abundance. *Bananalander*, slang for a Queenslander. 1900 *Daily News* 3 July 3/2 He's a brave Bananalander. 1901 *Westm. Gaz.* 2 Apr. 1/3 The Bananaland capital. 1901 *Daily Chron.* 4 Apr. 5/1 [He] was born in 'Bananaland'. *Ibid.* 18 Nov. 5/1 The Bananaland statesman.

Banausian (bănǭ·siăn), *a.* [f. as Banausic *a.* + -ian.] = Banausic *a.*
1901 Laurie *Training of Teachers* 235 The occupations which to the Greek sages were banausian, if not degrading.

Bancal (bankā·l). [Sp., f. *banco* bench.] A carpet or other decorative covering for a bench or seat. ? Misused in quot. 1891.
1891 Doyle *White Company* I. xi. 275 He caught a quick shimmer from the corner of a high-backed bancal in front of him. 1893 — *Refugees* i, It was the sort of window which was common in Paris about the end of the seventeenth century... Inside, the window was furnished with a broad bancal of brown stamped Spanish leather.

Banco: see *Bunco.

Band, *sb.*[2] III. Add:
band-brake, a brake consisting of a band operating on a spindle; **band-knife**, an 'endless' knife; **band-sawyer**, an operative who uses a band-saw.
1889 *Century Dict.*, *Band-brake. 1908 *Daily Chron.* 21 Nov. 9/4 A band-brake operates on the balance gear. 1926 *Glasgow Herald* 12 July 8 Following the sewing machine come the *band knife. 1909 *Daily Chron.* 25 Sept. 7/6 *Band Sawyer wanted.

Band, *sb.*[3] Add: 3. b. A herd or flock. *U.S.*
1859 Bartlett *Dict. Amer.* (ed. 2) s.v., A troop or herd of bisons is called, in prairie parlance, 'a band of buffalo'. *a* 1861 T. Winthrop *John Brent* ii. 13, I had come upon a band of horses feeding on the prairie. 1871 Schele de Vere *Americanisms* (1872) 210 California for instance, forms its vast flocks of sheep into *bands*, of about a thousand each. 1920 Hunter *Trail Drivers of Texas* 319 How many of the 'band' (meaning the herd) are gone?
4. b. Phrases. *When the band begins to play*, when matters become serious. *To beat the band*: lit. so as to drown the noise made by the band; hence, to exceed, surpass, or beat everything.
1892 Kipling *Barrack-r. Ballads* 6 It's 'Thank you, Mister Atkins', when the band begins to play. 1900 G. Bonner *Hard Pan* iii. 81 Doesn't that beat the band? 1910 W. M. Raine *B. O'Connor* 24 It's send for Bucky quick when the band begins to play. *Ibid.* 236 Eating together like brothers and laughing to beat the band.
7. *band-playing, -wagon* (U.S., freq. *fig.*).
1855 Barnum *Life* 205 At Vicksburg we sold all our land conveyances excepting four horses and the 'band wagon'. 1905 *N. Y. Sun* 13 Nov. 12 Advt., We're abreast the band wagon—plenty of our..suits have a brownish tinge. 1905 *N. Y. Even. Post* 21 Oct. 1 Jerome's band wagon began to move over the town to-day. 1915 *Lit. Digest* (N.Y.) 21 Aug. 337/2 There has been no howl about impending calamity, no call to arms, no band-playing or trumpets blowing.

Band, *v.*[1] 4. a. Add: Also, to form (cattle or sheep) into a herd or flock. *U.S.*
1878 B. F. Taylor *Between Gates* 266 O leave him to 'band' his sheep and herd his bees as he pleases.

Bandabust, var. *Bundobust.

Bandar (bʊ·ndăɹ). Also bunder. [Hind.] The Rhesus monkey, *Macacus rhesus*. Also in *Bandar-log* [Hind. *log* people], Kipling's nation of monkeys (see quot. 1895); hence *fig.*, any body of irresponsible chatterers.
1886 Kipling *Other Verses* (1899) 54 It was an artless *Bandar*, and he danced upon a pine. 1895 — *2nd Jungle Bk.* 63 Men are blood-brothers of the *Bandar-log*. 1917 'Ian Hay' *Carrying On* xiii. 313 That is just what the *Bandar Log* overlook, when they jabber about the dreadful industrial upheaval that is coming with peace. 1922 *Chambers's Jrnl.* June 393/1 He was too used to the wordy clatter of the *bunderlogue* to notice it. *Ibid.*, Their attentions the unhappy *bunder* would gladly dispense with.

Bandbox. Add: Also applied allusively to a fragile or flimsy structure or one in which the accommodation is restricted (cf. next).
1875 H. Lee *The Octopus* viii. 81 The vessel was lightly built—a mere bandbox of a craft.

Bandboxy (bæ·ndbǫksi), *a.* [f. Bandbox + -y[1].] Resembling a bandbox in the fragility of its structure or its restricted accommodation. (Cf. Bandboxical.)
1891 *Cornh. Mag.* Feb. 160 Houses,..light and small and bandboxy. 1896 C. Allen *Papier Mâché* 80 Sheds, and bandboxy houses all tilted up on stumps.

Bandeau (bæ·ndo). Add:
c. A strip of velvet or other material generally made up in a circular form to be stitched inside the lower part of the crown of a hat that is too large for the head.
1908 *Daily Chron.* 29 Jan. 4/7 With the right sort of 'bandeau'..you need not wear a hatpin at all.

Banded, *ppl. a.* Add: Also in specific names as *banded drum, sunfish*.
1848 Bartlett *Dict. Amer.* 165 *Grunter*, one of the popular names of the fish called by naturalists the *Banded Drum*. 1870 *Amer. Naturalist* IV. 102 The banded Sunfish (*Bryttus Chaetodon*).

Bandie (bæ·ndi). *Sc.* and *north.* Also bandy. [perh. derived from Banstickle.] The stickleback, *Gasterosteus aculeatus*.
1825 Jamieson. 1854 Miss Baker *Northampt. Gloss.* 1876 Smiles *Sc. Natur.* i. 14 'Mother,' said he, 'where are my crabs and bandies?' 1921 *Glasgow Herald* 25 Mar. 7/2 Little boys poking in their depths for bandies.

Banditism (bæ·nditiz'm). [f. Bandit + -ism. Cf. F. *banditisme* (Flaubert, 1853).] The practices of banditti.
1885 *Manch. Guard.* 25 May 8 In England they re-establish the fusillade, in Russia torture, in Germany banditism. 1921 *19th Cent.* Sept. 407 The resistance of the peasantry to the Communist system of food supply is one of the causes of the development of banditism.

Banditry (bæ·nditri). [f. Bandit + -ry.] The practices of banditti.
1922 *Q. Rev.* July 157 Already they have made short work of banditry. 1924 *Glasgow Herald* 29 Oct. 8 The ponderous banditry which the Chinese dignify by the name of war.

Bandobast, var. *Bundobust.

Bandolero (bændolē·ro). [Sp.] A highwayman or robber. Also *attrib.*
[*c* 1645 Howell *Lett.* I. xxiii. (1650) 38 These parts of the Pyreneys that border upon the Mediterranean, are never without Theeves by Land (call'd *Bandoleros*).] 1832 W. Irving *Alhambra* (1896) 9 The solitary *bandolero*, armed to the teeth..hovers about them. 1924 *Glasgow Herald* 2 Feb. 4 He confuses picadors with bandoleros. 1927 *Chambers's Jrnl.* 733/2, I was soon rigged out in the costume of a Spanish villager; that is, rope-soled shoes, white woollen stockings, bright yellow knickerbockers, a frilled shirt, and a bandolero hat.

Bandoliered (bændŏlī·ɹd), *ppl. a.* [f. Bandolier, -eer + -ed[2].] Wearing a bandolier.

1900 *Daily News* 29 Jan. 7/5 The dashing bandoliered invader. 1921 *Blackw. Mag.* Oct. 458/1 A bandoliered and sheep-skin cloaked policeman.

Bandyman (bæ·ndimăn). [f. BANDY *sb.*2 + MAN *sb.*1] The driver of a bandy (see BANDY *sb.*2).
a 1881 CALDWELL (Ogilvie) When also, as all over India, our white kinsmen speak of bandymen and bandies, the word thus anglicized is simply the old Tamilian one. 1922 *Other Lands* Apr. 76/2 The shout of 'Ho, Bandyman'.

Banesman (bēⁱ·nzmăn). *pseudo-arch.* Also **baneman.** [Rendering of ON. *banamaðr*, f. *bana*, gen. of *bani* BANE *sb.*1 + *maðr* MAN *sb.*1] A murderer.
1870 MAGNÚSSON & MORRIS tr. *Völsunga Saga* ii. (1888) 3 He had slain all his father's banesmen. 1926 *Trans. Scott. Ecclesiol. Soc.* 74 He prayed, not only for himself and his friends, but still more for 'his foes and banemen'.

Bang, *sb.*1 Add:
4. *colloq.* A 'thumping' lie, a banger. *Bang-words*: explosive epithets, 'swear' words.
1879 MEREDITH *Egoist* xxix, Every crack and bang in a boy's vocabulary. 1906 *Westm. Gaz.* 20 Jan. 2/1 When the recipient of a letter has to..go in for a comparative analysis of the different letters..he is justified in using bang words.

Bang, *v.* Add:
5. c. *Stock Exchange.* To depress (prices, the market). Cf. HAMMER *v.* 2 d (*b*).
1884 [see Dict.]. 1907 *Daily Chron.* 10 Dec. 5/4 What prompted the selling is unknown. It appears like an attempt to bang the price. 1927 *Sunday Times* 13 Feb. 2 Attempts to bang prices failed to induce much selling.
7. b. (Later U.S. example.)
1912 C. MATHEWSON *Pitching* xii. 261 Baker balanced by banging the home run into the right field bleachers in the ninth inning.
8. d. *humorous* (with allusion to 'bang goes saxpence' as in 8 c *Mod.*): To spend ('saxpence') all at once in a fit of extravagance. Hence **Ba·nging** *vbl. sb.*
1897 *Westm. Gaz.* 17 May 10/1 The desirability of avoiding any unnecessary banging of saxpences. 1901 *Daily Chron.* 11 Nov. 3/7 Our Northern friends look twice before they 'bang' their 'saxpences'.

Bang, *adv. dial.* and *U.S.* [See BANG *v.* 8, and cf. SLAM-BANG.] Thoroughly, completely; exactly.
1885 TENNYSON *Spinster's Sweet-arts* x, Steevie be right good manners bang thruf to the tip o' the taail. 1924 A. J. SMALL *Frozen Gold* i. 28 Here they were right bang on hand—and..they might as well be a thousand miles away.

Bangalow (bæ·ŋgălōᵘ). Also **-alo.** [Native name.] Either of the Australian palms, *Ptychosperma elegans* or *P. cunninghamii*, having feathery leaves. Also *attrib.*
1851 J. HENDERSON *Excurs. N. S. Wales* II. ix. 229 The Bangalo..is a palm, and a native of the brushes...Its bunch of large leaves, surmounting a fine, straight stem, has a very beautiful effect. 1878 W. R. GUILFOYLE *Austral. Bot.* 18 The Aborigines of New South Wales and Queensland..eat the young leaves of the cabbage and bangalow palms. 1886 KENDALL *Poems* 193 You see, he was bred in a bangalow wood, And bangalow pith was the principal food. 1905 *Westm. Gaz.* 27 Mar. 2/1 The forest of lofty gums and iron-barks, and clumps of graceful bangalow palms.

Banger. Add: A bludgeon. *U.S. slang* (at Yale).
1843 (*title*) The Yale Banger (Th.). 1856 *Yale Lit. Mag.* XXI. 282 (Th.) Brandishing a banger above my head, I came on to the stage with a yell. 1906 *Springfield Weekly Republ.* 10 May 1 He..has rescued from some museum of Yale antiquities..his old 'banger' of student days.

Banghy, var. *BANGY.

Bangkok (bæ·ŋkǫk). [Name of the capital of Siam.] A kind of woven straw for hats.
1924 *Sketch* 9 Apr. p. xii, Charming Hat in Chinese bangkok. 1927 *Observer* 28 Aug. 17/2 It matters little whether it [*sc.* a hat-shape] be carried out in felt or bangkok or manilla.

Bango (bæ·ŋgo). An East African reed.
1899 WERNER *Captain of Locusts* 15 His dug-out canoe..was found..among the *bango* in a sheltered backwater. *Ibid.* 66 Sleepy natives..were turning over on their *bango* mats. 1907 *Macm. Mag.* May 525 All the bango reed was dead and burnt.

Bangorian (bæŋgōᵊ·riăn), *a.* [f. *Bangor* + -IAN.] Of or pertaining to Bangor, N. Wales, in *Bangorian controversy*, a religious controversy raised by a sermon preached before the king in 1717 by Benjamin Hoadly, Bishop of Bangor, directed against the non-jurors.
1838 *Penny Cycl.* XII. 254/1 The celebrated Bangorian controversy.., one of the most remarkable in the history of the Protestant church of England. 1875 *Encycl. Brit.* III. 280/2 It was the year [1717] in which Bishop Hoadley preached that famous sermon on *The Kingdom of Christ*, which gave rise to the..theological war known as the 'Bangorian controversy'. 1881 *Ibid.* XII. 29/1 A war of pamphlets known as the Bangorian controversy.

Bang-up, *adj. phr.* and *sb.* Add: [Illustration of the orig. advb. phr. *bang up* = quite close up:
1858 LYTTON *What will he do with it?* I. i, Smart and sharp, bang up to the day. 1914 J. JOYCE *Dubliners, The Dead* (1926) 239 Drive bang up against Trinity College gates.]
(Later U.S. examples.)
1877 BARTLETT *Dict. Amer.* (ed. 4) 28 This cloth is bang-up. 1921 R. D. PAINE *Comr. Rolling Ocean* vii. 118 The salaries are bang-up nowadays.
B. *sb.* **a.** A man of fashion.
1811 *Lex. Balatronicum* Pref., We trust..that the whole tribe of second-rate Bang ups will feel grateful [etc.]. 1824 *Examiner* 613/1 Our Corinthians, *Routs* and Bang-ups. 1882 *Punch* 22 Apr. 185/1 The Trio turned into the Arcade, and saw a number of gay sparks and fair ones promenading. ..These then are the dandies, the fops, the goes, and the bang-ups, these the Corinthians of to-day.
b. A heavy overcoat (see quot. 1902). *U.S.*
1835 *Fraser's Mag.* XI. 293 Dames in bang-ups, Shawls swath'd round men. 1842 *Spirit of Times* (Philad.) 13 Jan. (Th.) A gentleman dressed in a dark coloured fashionable bang-up. 1843 LEVER *J. Hinton* xxi, A green coat..over which he wore..a white 'bang-up', as it was called. 1846 J. KEEGAN *Leg. & Poems* (1907) 396 His old grey frieze bang-up. 1853 *Public Ledger* (Philad.) 11 June (De Vere), He was attired in an old bang-up, black vest, grey pants, and straw hat. 1902 CLAPIN *Dict. Amer.* 36 *Bang-up*, an old word for a heavy overcoat, still surviving in some parts of the Union.

Bangy, banghy (ba·ngi). [Hind. *bahangī*, Marathi *bangī* (Skr. *vihaṃgika*).] A yoke for carrying loads; such a yoke with its pair of baskets or boxes; hence, parcel post.
1789 R. BROOME *Lett. Simpkin the Second* 21 I'll give them Two Thousand, with Bangies and Coolies. 1809 VISCT. VALENTIA *Voy. & Trav. India* I. 67 We take.., in six bangys, sufficient changes of linen. 1810 T. WILLIAMSON *E. India Vade-Mecum* I. 325 The bangy-wollah, that is, the bearer who carries the bangy. 1837 T. BACON *First Impr. Hindostan* II. vii. 218 A weighty banghi-load of provisions. 1841 *Narr. Three Months' March India* vii. 200 Hindoos carrying small baskets..in bangy-fashion. 1842 in Baron Colchester *Ind. Administr. Ld. Ellenb.* (1874) 221, I will forward with this, by bhangy dâk, a copy of [a book].

Bani(y)a, var. *BUNNIA.

Banjo. Add:
(Earlier U.S. examples of mod. form.)
1774 P. V. FITHIAN *Jrnl.* (1900) 103 In the School-Room, ..several Negroes & Ben & Harry are playing on a Banjo & dancing. 1801 *Port Folio* (Philad.) I. 270 (Th.) The sound of Banneker's banjo would be as tuneable as Gallatin's spoken French. 1836 *Southern Lit. Messenger* II. 162, I found a crowd of negroes..dancing..to the music of a banjo.
2. *transf.* Applied to contrivances of the shape of a banjo: see quots.
1867 SMYTH *Sailor's Word-bk.*, *Banjo*, the brass frame in which the screw-propeller of a steamer works, and is hung for hoisting the screw on deck...The banjo is essential to lifting the screw. 1902 *Encycl. Brit.* XXXII. 147/2 (*Railways*) The enclosed disc signal, commonly called a 'banjo', is a circular box..with a glass-covered opening, behind which a red disc is shown to indicate stop.
b. *attrib.*, with the meaning 'banjo-shaped', as *banjo axle*; **banjo-frame, -signal**: = *BANJO 2.
1888 *Lockwood's Dict. Mech. Engin.*, *Bow Connecting-Rod*..or *Banjo Frame*, a form of connecting-rod employed in steam pumps. 1922 *Autocar* 10 Nov. 962 A vertical banjo type of back axle. *Ibid.* 982 A neat banjo axle.

Banjolin (bæ·ndʒŏlin). [f. BANJO + *-lin* of MANDOLIN.] A musical instrument combining the characteristics of the banjo and mandolin, used in rag-time music.
1889 *Pall Mall Gaz.* 4 July 5/1 An instrument that appeared to be a cross between a banjo and a mandolin—dubbed on the spot a 'banjolin'. 1923 *Ashore & Afloat* Aug. (Advt.), Banjolins or Jazz Banjos.

Banjulele (bændʒŭlēⁱ·li). Also **banjo-.** [f. BANJO + *-ulele* of UKULELE.] A stringed musical instrument of a type between a banjo and a ukulele.
1925 *Glasgow Herald* 7 Apr. 8 A native band playing on banjoleles, a sort of zither, from which the tones are provided by gourds filled with varying amounts of water. 1926 *Bulletin* 27 Feb. 10 Alvin D. Keech, from Hawaii, has secured a British patent for his invention, the banjulele. 1926 *Westm. Gaz.* 1 July, A youth..strumming on a banjulele.

Bank, *sb.*1 Add:
12. *Aeronautics.* The lateral inclination of an aeroplane when turning or rounding a curve.
1913 C. MELLOR *Airman* vi. Illustration 29 A left-handed turn with plenty of bank. 1928 C. F. S. GAMBLE *Story N. Sea Air Station* xiii. 225 When turning with a heavy bank.
III. bank-bait, the may-fly; **bank-beaver** (see *BEAVER 1 1 b); **bank-engine**, also, a locomotive used to assist in taking a heavy load up a steep incline (cf. *BANKER 3 5).
1879 E. P. WRIGHT *Animal Life* (1885) 485 A great many [may-flies] fall into the water a prey to fishes...Hence the name *bank-bait. 1895 *Funk's Dict.*, *Bank-engine.

Bank, *sb.*2 Add:
7. b. *Optical bank*: an optical bench, a graduated bench, usually of steel, on which the holders of lenses, prisms, etc., may be set up in alinement.
1888 SIR O. LODGE in *Electrician* 21 Sept., To order expensive and highly polished optical banks and other apparatus from an instrument maker.

Bank, *sb.*3 Add: **8. a.** *bank-monger, -president, -robber, -snatcher.*
1814 JEFFERSON *Let. to J. Adams* 24 Jan., Writ. 1854 VI. 305, I was derided as a maniac by the tribe of *bank-mongers. 1902 MCFAUL *Ike Glidden* iii. 18 The *bank president was fully satisfied with the confidence he had placed in Ike. 1799 *Aurora* (Philad.) 15 Mar. (Th.) Groups of pickpockets, *bank-robbers, and hen-pecked dotards. 1890 *Harper's Mag.* Feb. 472 One of the most daring *bank snatchers in the city effected two robberies in the course of a single day.
b. bank paper (later U.S. examples); **bank roll** *U.S.*, a roll of bank-notes.
1816 U. BROWN in *Maryland Hist. Mag.* X. 356 This morning..receives in *Bank paper of him $25.00. 1836 *Southern Lit. Messenger* II. 461 A substitute for bank paper. 1916 BOWER *Phantom Herd* xx. 325 But, believe me, boys, she's shaping up like a *bank roll.

Bank, *v.*1 Add:
8. b. *spec.* To pile up (logs) at a landing, etc., for transport by water or rail. *U.S.* and *Canada.*
1856 *Trans. Mich. Agric. Soc.* VII. 828 There will be logs enough cut and 'banked' for 100,000,000 feet of lumber. We are informed that the amount now banked daily, will amount to 2,500,000 feet. 1888 *B. C. Moon* 21 Apr., Wright & Davis ..have purchased the logs banked at West Superior. *a* 1904 S. E. WHITE *Blazed Trail Stories* iii. 40 The firm agreed to pay..for all saw-logs banked at a rollway.
12. *trans.* **a.** To ascend (an inclined surface). **b.** To cause to travel an ascending track; also in *vbl. sb.* (attrib. in *banking engine* = *bank-engine*, *BANK *sb.*1 III).
1892 *Live Stock Jrnl. Alm.* 34 They ascended a steep hill, banking field after field to a flag-post at the top. 1908 *Model Engineer & Electr.* 11 June 570 Where banking engines are employed for assisting trains on inclines. *Ibid.*, Wherever banking assistance is taken. *Ibid.*, The practice of banking trains out of Euston, up the Camden incline.
13. *Aeronautics. trans.* To tilt (an aeroplane) sideways in turning. Also *intr.*, to incline inwards in turning. Also with *up*.
1911 GRAHAME-WHITE & HARPER *Aeroplane* 133 He 'banked' his biplane over too sharply. 1913 C. MELLOR *Airman* vi. 29 We swung round left-handed and the machine 'banked' up to the right. 1920 *Blackw. Mag.* July 72/2 Adam Smythe..then banked left-handed towards Delhi Fort.

Bank, *v.*2 Add: **4. c.** To 'put one's money' *upon*; to count or rely *upon* with confidence or assurance. Also const. *that.* orig. *U.S.*
1883 NYE *Baled Hay* 127 The man who ranks as a dignified snoozer, and banks on winning wealth and a deathless name. 1892 *Congress. Rec.* Apr., App. 249/2, I am not banking heavily on [him]..as an honest man. 1898 *N. Y. Sun* 14 Sept., The Democrats are banking upon this movement to help them out this fall. 1903 A. ADAMS *Log Cowboy* vi. 79, I was banking plenty strong, that next year..I'd take her home with me. 1910 W. M. RAINE *B. O'Connor* 58 The one friend you would have banked on to a finish.

Bankable, *a.* (U.S. examples.)
1828 WEBSTER, *Bankable*, receivable at a bank, as bills; or discountable, as notes. (Of recent origin.) 1832 *Congress. Deb.* 7 Mar. 204 A currency..perhaps not bankable at all places. *Ibid.*, Any broker..would make it bankable any where in the Union. 1848 BARTLETT *Dict. Amer.* 22 In New York, at auction sales, the auctioneer..invariably states, that the money must be bankable.

Bank-barn. *U.S.* [BANK *sb.*1 2 b.] (See quot. 1909.)
1894 *Congress. Rec.* Jan. 1036/1 On my father's farm, when I was a boy, there stood a big bank-barn. 1903 *Forest & Stream* 21 Feb., Advt. 1909 *Century Dict.* Suppl., *Bank-barn*, a barn built on a hillside or sloping ground, so that three sides of the lower story are surrounded by earth, the fourth being unbanked. (U.S.)

Banker1. Delete † *Obs.* and add: Now *arch.* or *dial.*
1870 BOTTRELL *Trad. W. Cornwall* 257 The cosy, old, panelled settle, but now without the bankers and dorsars, or the cushions, for the seats and back. 1890 W. MORRIS in *Eng. Illustr. Mag.* July 755 Some went to the chests and brought out the rich hangings, the goodly bankers and dorsars.

Banker2. Add:
4. A card game in which the banker divides the pack into a number of piles placed face downward, and each punter bets on the chance that the bottom card of the pile chosen by him is higher than the bottom card of the pile left to the banker.
1891 *Daily News* 3 Dec. 7/6 A boy..was charged with gambling with cards at 'banker'. 1903 *Daily Chron.* 14 Mar. 7/5 He got £150 during the voyage home on the troopship by playing 'banker' and 'the crown and anchor'.

Banker3. Add:
1. (Later U.S. example.)
1815 J. Q. ADAMS *Duplicate Lett.* (1822) 219 Those descriptions of vessels are not so valuable as the bankers, more particularly those that go from the District of Maine, Connecticut, and Rhode Island.
5. *Banker* (*engine*), a locomotive used to assist in taking a heavy load up a steep slope. (Cf. *bank-engine*, *BANK *sb.*1 III.)
1907 *Westm. Gaz.* 3 Dec. 7/2 A 'banker' engine had been fixed to the rear of the mineral train to help to take the load up a steep incline. After going some 300 yards the 'banker' was cast off.

Banker4. **b.** Add:
attrib. **banker-mark** (see quot. 1928).
1910 *Encycl. Brit.* III. 319/2 Banker-marks are..to be found on all old buildings of consequence, ecclesiastical or otherwise. 1928 G. G. COULTON *Art & Reformation* viii. 143 'Banker-marks', that is, the mason's sign-manual which he set on his finished stone before it left the banker, or working-bench.

Banket (bæ·ŋke·t). [ad. Du. *banket* banquet, also a confection resembling almond hardbake (see quot. 1887).] A gold-bearing conglomerate found in the Witwatersrand district of the Transvaal.
1887 *Chambers's Jrnl.* Apr. 284 The conglomerate..is a peculiar formation of almond-shaped pebbles, pressed into a solid mass in a bed of rock of an igneous nature, and is called 'Banket' on account of its resemblance to a favourite Dutch sweetmeat known in England as almond rock. The 'Banket' is also rich in gold. 1897 BRYCE *Impressions S. Africa* 217 In 1885 the conglomerate or *banket* beds of the Witwatersrand were discovered. 1900 *Times* 13 Feb. 13/3 The banket formation of the Witwatersrand.

Bank holiday. Add *attrib.*
1899 DOYLE *Duet* (1909) 9/2 If he had to travel all the way from Edinburgh with a Bank-holiday crowd.

Ba·nking, *ppl. a.*1 [f. BANK *v.*1 9.] Forming into banks.
c 1867 'MARK TWAIN' *Sketches* Wks. XIX. 372 A weird picture, that small company of frantic men fighting the banking snows.

Bank-note. Add: **b. bank-note detector**, table, a list of notes issued by the various banks, giving the current value of each. *U.S.*
1834 *Congress. Deb.* 23 Jan. 2523 Examine the bank note table which is almost daily furnished us in the public prints. 1894 *Congress. Rec.* 5 June 5790/2 One of the old bank-note detectors which have been so often referred to.

Banksian (bæ·ŋksiăn), *a.* [f. the name *Banks*: see below and -IAN.] Epithet of: (*a*) a Chinese species of climbing rose, bearing small white or yellow flowers in clusters, named after Lady Banks; (*b*) the Labrador, Grey, or Jack Pine, *Pinus Banksiana* or *P. divaricata*, named after Sir Joseph Banks.
1841 MRS. LOUDON *Ladies' Comp. Fl. Gard.* 252/1 The Banksian Roses..which are of two kinds. 1864 S. HIBBERD *Rose Bk.* 31 The Double White Banksian was introduced in 1807, and was so named in honour of Lady Banks. 1886 *Encycl. Brit.* XX. 851 The Banksian Rose is a Chinese climbing species, with small white or fawn-coloured flowers of great beauty. 1920 *19th Cent.* July 175 The little yellow Banksian is still incomparable.

Banner, *sb.*1 Add:
1. e. A flag awarded as a distinction. (See quot. 1840 and cf. *6 b.) *U.S.*
1840 *Log Cabin* (N. Y.) 5 Dec. 2/3 It is known that the Ladies of New Orleans early in the late contest offered a splendid Banner to the State which should give the largest relative majority for Harrison and Tyler in its popular vote for Presidential Electors. 1900 *Century Mag.* LIX. 636/1 Local authorities..united in the belief that..Ashtabula County might be accorded the banner.
3. b. (*a*) Each of the eight divisions, with distinguishing flags or banners, into which the Manchu army is divided. (*b*) A military subdivision of Mongolian tribes.
1848 S. W. WILLIAMS *Middle Kingd.* (1857) I. vii. § 6. 333 The Manchu army..was assisted by Mongols and Chinese, the three nations were divided into eight corps or 'banners'. 1880 J. ROSS *Manchus* xvi. 610 Up till 1613 the Manchus were divided into four banners—yellow, red, blue and white; but they had become so large an army, that for efficiency in manoeuvring they were sub-divided into as many more—bordered yellow, bordered red, bordered blue, and bordered white. *Ibid.* 611 In 1635, the Mongols were separated from the Manchu banners, under eight banners of their own. 1894 *New Review* Nov. 528 The Banner troops received donations from the Emperor. 1898 [see *BANNERMAN 2].
6. b. Entitled to a banner as a distinction (orig. in *banner state, county*); hence, pre-eminent, supreme. *U.S.*
1840 *Niles's Reg.* 5 Dec. 210/1 Which is the Banner State?—The Whigs..proposed to designate whichever state should give the Harrison ticket the largest majority, as the banner state. *Ibid.*, The banner county. Designation is claimed by Worcester, Massachusetts. 1866 *Congress. Globe* Jan. 241/3 [Mr. Price] came within a few votes of losing the banner county of his State. 1886 *Harper's Mag.* June 78/2 The Magnolia Plantation..which claims to be one of the banner plantations of the State. 1887 *Ibid.* July 237/2 She had the banner crop of tobacco in that county last year. 1890 *Congress. Globe* June 6522/1 One of the arguments.. is that Newcastle is the banner town of Crook County. 1903 *N. Y. Even. Post* 21 Sept., The earnings of all Vanderbilt lines had a banner month in August. 1911 S. E. WHITE *Bobby Orde* x. (1916) 128 On his banner day he brought down two fox-squirrels.

Bannerman. Add: **2.** A soldier belonging to any of the eight banners of the Manchu army.
1898 MRS. H. FRASER *Dipl. Wife in Japan* II. 133 Shin-no-Shiko nodded to his green bannermen to slay them. 1908 *Westm. Gaz.* 17 Dec. 7/3 The Manchu 'Bannermen' (soldiery) of Pekin.

Bantam. Add:
1. c. *Bantam weight* (Boxing): see quot. 1897.
1894 *Outing* (U.S.) XXIV. 71/2 An attempt to match the coxswains for a bantam-weight contest. 1897 *Encycl. Sport* May 139/2 Boxers are divided by the Amateur Boxing Association into five classes, according to their weights, as follows:—Bantam Weight, not exceeding 8 st. 4 lb.
d. Applied to battalions (etc.) of small-sized soldiers.
1914 *Daily Express* 20 Nov. 5/5 'Bigland's Bantams' will probably be the pet name of a battalion which is being raised of men who are just too short to enlist under the ordinary conditions...The Bantams Battalion has been recognised by the War Office. 1914 *Scotsman* 11 Dec. 7/4 The Edinburgh Rotary Club..has now completed arrangements for the raising of a 'Bantam Battalion'. 1927 *Observer* 30 Oct. 7 The 35th was a bantam division which went out to France very early in 1916.

Banteng, banting (bæ·nteŋ, bæ·ntiŋ). [Malay.] A species of wild ox; = TSINE.
1860 *Chambers's Encycl.* I. 674/2 *Banteng*..a native of Java and Borneo..black, with white legs. 1880 *Encycl. Brit.* XII. 742/2 The *tsine* or *banting* (*Bibos sondaicus*), found in Burmah. 1894 *Field* 9 June 815/3 Blood-curdling tales are told in Batavia of the ferocity of the rhinoceros and banteng.

Banter, *sb.* **4.** *U.S.* (Illustrations of usage.)
1835 LONGSTREET *Georgia Scenes* 26 No, said Peter, you made the banter, now make your pass. *a* 1861 WINTHROP *John Brent* ii. (1862) 20 I'm goan to make yer a fair banter. 1871 SCHELE DE VERE *Americanisms* (1872) 439 We had a fine banter, but the match was postponed till spring.

Banter, *v.* **6.** *U.S.* (Illustrations of usage.)
1834 CARRUTHERS *Kentuckian in N. Y.* I. 183, I was thinking of walking out into the country and bantering somebody for a footrace. 1836 *Col. Crockett in Texas* 83 The black-leg set to work with his thimble again, and bantered me to bet. 1860 *Knickerbocker Mag.* Aug. LVI. 221 The farmer again bantered him to buy his berries. 1872 E. EGGLESTON *End of World* xxvi. 177 The cards were put face down, and the company was bantered to bet the wine. 1902 HARBEN *Abner Daniel* 163 Colonel Barclay has..bantered me for a trade time an' again.

Banting, var. *BANTENG.

Bantu (bæ·ntu). [In certain Bantu dialects, pl. (also *abantu*, etc.) of *-ntu* man.] The name of an extensive group of negroid races inhabiting the equatorial and southern region of Africa, and of the languages spoken by them.
1862 BLEEK *Compar. Gram. S. Afr. Lang.* I. 4 The South African division of the Bâ-ntu family of languages consists of one large middle body, occupying almost the whole known territory between the tropic of Capricorn and the equator. *Ibid.* 11 The abandonment in the Bâ-ntu languages of such syllabic elements as are more difficult of pronunciation. 1880 *Encycl. Brit.* XIII. 820/2. 1884 *Ibid.* XVII. 319/1. 1926 *Contemp. Rev.* Mar. 298 The Bantu, or Native races, numbering 4,698,000.

Banya, var. *BUNNIA.

Banzai (bænzai·), *int.* [Jap., literally, ten thousand years.] A shout or cheer used by the Japanese in greeting the emperor or in battle.
1904 *Daily Chron.* 12 Feb. 5/5 The crowd sang national songs, and shouted 'Banzai' continuously. 1905 *Times* 7 Oct., Enthusiastic banzais were given for King Edward and the Emperor of Japan.

Baptism. Add:
2. b. *Baptism of fire*: after eccl. Gr. βάπτισμα πυρός (e. g. Macarius Ægyptius *Hom.* xxvii. 17; cf. *Matt.* iii. 11) (*a*) the grace of the Holy Spirit imparted through baptism, as distinguished from the sacrament or rite; (*b*) martyrdom, esp. by fire; (*c*) the undergoing of any severe ordeal or painful experience; (*d*) a soldier's first experience 'under fire' in battle (so F. *baptême de feu*). Cf. *fire-baptism* (Carlyle *Sartor Res.* II. viii.).
1857 LAWRENCE *Guy Liv.* xiii, It's only in their baptism of fire that the young ones shrink and start. 1881 *Cassell's Encycl. Dict.* s. v., When during the Franco-German war of 1870, Prince Louis Napoleon..was first exposed, by direction of his father, Napoleon III, and with his own consent, to the fire of the enemy at Saarbrück, the event was called a 'baptism of fire'.

Bar, *sb.*1 Add:
5. *Stars and Bars*: see STAR *sb.*1 6 b. *U.S.*
b. *Bar of Michael Angelo*, the superciliary ridge or prominence of the frontal bone at the base of the forehead, characteristic of the heads of Michael Angelo's statues.
1850 TENNYSON *In Mem.* lxxxvii, And over those ethereal eyes The bar of Michael Angelo.
9. b. *spec.* in *pl.* A set of wooden rails which may be withdrawn to afford an opening through a fence or wall. (Cf. DRAW-BAR.) *U.S.*
1660 *Rec. Providence, R.I.* II. 139 Provided that they Keepe a Sufficient inlett of Barres at Each End of the highway for A cart to passe through. 1670 *Charlestown Land Rec.* 156 From Deacon Stitson's to the Barres at Mr. Nowel's pasture in sixteene foot. 1703 *Rec. Providence, R.I.* V. 109 [He] shall set up a Gate, or inlet of Barrs in said fence. 1743 MACSPARRAN *Diary* 9 She sent Jack to open ye Gates and Bars. 1856 *Trans. Mich. Agric. Soc.* VII. 805 He..uses bars instead of gates between his inclosures. 1887 MARY E. WILKINS *Humble Romance* 315 The younger of the two old women let down the bars which separated the blooming field ..from the road, and they passed through.
25. b. The counsel retained in a particular case.
1891 E. KINGLAKE *Australian at Home* 36 He had as strong a Bar as could be retained on his side. 1892 *Daily News* 25 Mar. 5/2 There has rarely been such a Bar in any modern case, either for quantity or for quality. Sir Charles Russell, the Attorney-General, the Solicitor-General, Sir Henry James, Mr. Inderwick, and Mr. Tindal Atkinson were but a few of them.
30. bar-bell, a steel bar weighted with a ball of iron at each end, used as a dumb-bell; **bar-boat**, also, a boat adapted for carrying goods across the bar of a river; **bar-cutter**, a shearing-machine for cutting metallic bars into lengths; a workman who passes the metal through the machine; **bar-frame** (or **-framed**) *a.*, of a beehive: fitted with bars instead of sections; **bar-head**(**ed goose**, a goose found in India and Central Asia, *Anser indicus*; **bar-hive**, a bar-framed beehive; **bar-keel**, one composed of rectangular bars of iron or steel; **bar-keep**, a bar-keeper; **bar-soap**, soap made up into bars as distinguished from soap in cakes or tablets; also *attrib.*; **bar-super**, a super hive in which the honeycomb is hung from bars instead of stored in sections.
1887 *Hour Glass* I. 17 A complete set of dumb-bell, *bar-bell, marching and running exercises. 1895-6 *Cal. Univ. Nebraska* 252 The gymnasium..is well equipped with clubs, wands, bar bells, and dumb bells. 1883 MOLONEY *W. African Fisheries* 17 (Fish. Exhib. Publ.) *Bar-boats of seven to eight tons have been used at Lagos. 1897 MARY KINGSLEY *W. Africa* 625 [It is] too bad a bar for boats to cross; but a steamer on the Lagos bar boat plan might manage it. 1874 KNIGHT *Dict. Mech.*, *Bar-cutter* (Metal-working), a shearing-machine which cuts metallic bars into lengths. 1904 *Westm. Gaz.* 13 June 7/2 He gives bar-cutters an advance of a halfpenny per ton. 1881 *Gardening Illustr.* 7 May 123/3 There would be no difficulty whatever in putting swarms of bees into a *bar-frame hive, provided it has a movable top and floor-board. 1892 *Garden* 27 Aug. 168 Two and three-quarter supers from each bar frame hive have not been uncommon takes. 1906 *Daily Chron.* 18 June 6/6 Bar-frame beehives. *Ibid.* 1 Sept. 6/4 *Bar-framed hives. 1924 *Glasgow Herald* 29 July 3 The *barhead goose and the ruddy sheldrak collect in flocks on the Tibetan swamps. 1879 *Encycl. Brit.* X. 777/2 The *Bar-headed Goose (*Anser indicus*). 1884 PHIN *Dict. Apiculture* 70 *Bars*, strips of wood to which combs are attached, and from which they hang in *bar-hives. 1874 THEARLE *Naval Archit.* 69 The *Bar Keel..is generally of hammered iron, made in pieces as long as can be conveniently forged. 1918 H. A. VACHELL *Some Happenings* i. 2 Hobo listened attentively to the *bar-keep. 1926 B. CRONIN *Red Dawson* vii, There's no one with her but Lee Wing and the bar-keep. 1893 EARL DUNMORE *Pamirs* I. 64 Some common yellow *bar-soap. 1906 *Westm. Gaz.* 25 Oct. 7/2 Bar-soap sellers. 1884 PHIN *Dict. Apiculture* 70 A *bar super is simply a case or crate in which the honeycomb is hung from bars.

Bar, *sb.*5 *U.S.* [Of doubtful origin: cf. *BEAR *sb.*6] A mosquito net.
1835 J. H. INGRAHAM *South-West* II. 243 To suspend their 'bars'..that they may not be troubled with musquitoes. 1866 GREGG *Life in Army* xv. 140 Nothing can exceed the luxury of lying down inside your 'bars' of a midsummer night, and feeling secure from their voracious bills.

Bar (bāɹ), *sb.*6 *Meteorol.* [ad. Gr. βάρος weight.] A unit of barometric pressure equivalent to a pressure of 29·53 inches or 750·1 mm. of mercury at 32° F in latitude 45°.
1914 *Q. Jrnl. R. Meteorol. Soc.* Apr. 160, I [*sc.* Bjerknes] therefore coined the terms 'bar', 'decibar', 'centibar', and 'millibar', as names for the units of pressure...I employed these expressions for the first time in a paper published in 1906 [in *Beiträge zur Physik der freien Atmosphäre*, Strassburg]. *Ibid.* July 187 The bar, with its multiples the micro-bar, millibar, centibar, and decibar. 1918 *Meteorol. Gloss.* s. v., The meteorological bar is thus one million chemical bars, and what chemists call a *bar* we should call a *microbar*. One bar is 100 centibars or 1,000 millibars.

Bar, *v.* **9.** (Now frequent.)
1914 *Daily Express* 26 Sept. 3/3 Angry London crowd bar the enemy's goods.

Bar, *prep.* Add:
b. In *Betting.* *Bar one*: excluding one horse, in such phrases as *two to one bar one.*
1860 *Slang Dict.* (ed. 2), *Bar*,..in common use in the betting-ring; 'I bet against the field bar two'. 1874 *Ibid.* s. v., 'Two to one bar one', *i.e.*, two to one against any horse with the exception of one.

Baræsthesiometer (bæresþīsiǫ·mĭtəɹ). Also **bares-.** [f. Gr. βάρος weight + αἴσθησις perception + -OMETER.] An instrument for measuring the sense of pressure. Hence **Baræsthesiome·tric** *a.*
1876 tr. *von Ziemssen's Cycl. Med.* XI. 213 Eulenburg has materially facilitated the testing of the sense of pressure by constructing a baræsthesiometer..., on which, by varying pressure upon a string, different degrees of pressure may be read off on a dial. 1885 STIRLING tr. *Landois' Human Physiol.* 1092 In order to avoid the necessity of changing the weights, A. Eulenburg invented his baraesthesiometer, which is constructed on the same principle as a spiral spring paper-clip or balance.

Barasingha (barasi·ŋgă). Also **barasingh.** [Hind. *bārah singā* lit. twelve-horn.] The East Indian deer *Cervus wallichii*; also, *C. duvauceli*, the Swamp Deer.
1880 *Encycl. Brit.* XII. 742/2 The swamp deer or *barasingha*..which is common in Lower Bengal and Assam.. 1895 KIPLING *2nd Jungle Bk.* 37 The *barasingh*, that big deer which is like our red deer, but stronger. 1902 [see *swamp deer*, s. v. SWAMP *sb.* 3 b]. 1921 *Brit. Mus. Return* 98 A Kashmir Barasingha (*Cervus cashmiriensis*).

Barathea (bærăþī·ă). Also **barrathea.** [Origin unknown.] A cloth of a fine texture composed of a silk warp and woollen weft, also of cotton and wool and entirely of wool.
1862 *Catal. Internat. Exhib., Brit.* II. No 3958. Cobourg, paramatta, barathea, reps, cords, cloths. 1897 *Daily News* 30 Oct. 6/5 Venetian crape..has taken the place of the old baratheas, Balmorals, bombazines, &c.

Barb, *v.* Add:
6. To bend into hook form the points of wire teeth used in carding textile fibres.
1890 NASMITH *Mod. Cotton Spinning Mach.* 94 There are two evils to be guarded against—the barbing or hooking of the wire points and the striation of the sides of the teeth. *Ibid.* 95 Striated sides and barbed points are common in this series.

Barbadoes. Add: **Barbadoes gooseberry** (see quot.).
1875 *Encycl. Brit.* IV. 626/2 *Pereskia aculeata*, or Barbados Gooseberry, the *Cactus Pereskia* of Linnæus.

Barbarianess (barbēᵊ·riănes). [f. BARBARIAN + -ESS.] A female barbarian.
1868 M. ARNOLD *Lett.* (1895) I. 387 As a very charming Barbarianess, Lady Portsmouth, expresses a great desire to make my acquaintance, I daresay the race will bear no malice. 1885 F. HALL in *Nation* (N.Y.) 4 June 466 This perilous feat [*sc.* that of eating peas with a knife] he has, in person, contemplated as performed by a charming Viennese barbarianess.

Barbecue, *sb.* **4.** (Earlier examples.)
1769 WASHINGTON *Diaries* I. 326 Went up to Alexandria to a Barbecue and stayed all Night. 1773 *Ibid.* 124 Went to a barbicue of my own giving at Accatinck. 1774 P. V. FITHIAN *Jrnl.* (1900) 242, I was invited this morning by Captain Fibbs to a Barbecue:..instead of Fish the Dinner is roasted Pig, with the proper appendages, but the Diversion & exercise are the same at both.

Barbecue, *v.* **2.** (Later U.S. example.)
1920 HUNTER *Trail Drivers of Texas* 82 We killed and barbecued a beef.

Barbed, *ppl. a.*1 Add:
4. b. *Barbed wire*: see WIRE *sb.* 1 e.

Barber, *sb.* Add:
1. c. *transf.* In Canada, a storm accompanied by snow and spray which freezes upon the face; also, the vapour rising from the water on a frosty day, esp. *locally*, the haze which rises from the waters of Halifax Harbour.
c 1890 [Known in Halifax, Nova Scotia]. 1899 *Westm. Gaz.* 1 Mar. 10/1 Our searching east winds are nothing in comparison with the Canadian 'barber'.
2. *barber-shop* (earlier U.S. example).
1889 J. P. KENNEDY *Swallow B.* Introd. Ep. 8 A thorough going violin..in an illuminated barber shop.
3. *Barber's itch* or *rash*: a disease affecting the face and neck, caused by a fungoid organism resulting from the use of insanitary shaving apparatus.
1890 BILLINGS *Med. Dict.*, *Barber's itch*, tinea barbæ. 1906 *Daily Chron.* 2 Jan. 6/2 A skin complaint known as 'barber's rash'.

Barbiers (bā·ɹbiəɹz). [Fr. alteration of BERIBERI.] A form of paralysis frequent in India.
1698 FRYER *Acc. E. India & P.* 68 Whence follows Fluxes, Dropsy, Scurvy, Barbiers. 1768 LIND *Ess. Dis. Hot Climates* 260 The barbiers, a species of the palsy...Its attack is generally sudden, and entirely deprives the limbs of their motion. 1822 GOOD *Study Med.* (1829) IV. 493 Beribery. Barbiers. 1833 *Cycl. Pract. Med.* I. 243 Barbiers is generally a chronic disease.

Barbital (bā·ɹbităl). The equivalent in the U.S. Pharmacopœia of *BARBITONE.
1922 E. PHILLPOTTS *Grey Room* viii. 183 A woman, who had taken morphine and barbital, was found apparently dead. 1926 T. SOLLMANN *Man. Pharmacol.* (ed. 3) 757 Barbital (veronal; diethyl-barbituric acid). This was introduced by E. Fischer and Mering, 1903 and 1905...Barbital is used in nervous insomnia, mania and delirium.

Barbitone (bā·ɹbitoᵘn). [f. as next + -ONE.] A synonym of VERONAL.
1914 *Brit. Pharmacopœia* 62 Barbitonum. Barbitone. Synonyms—Diethyl-barbituric Acid: Malonurea: Diethyl-malonyl-urea..$C_8H_{12}N_2O_3$. 1918 *Nomencl. Dis.* (ed. 5), Chloral and other Hypnotic Drugs. Sulphonal, Trional, Tetronal, Barbitone, Proponal. 1923 *Brit. Pharmac. Codex* 175 Barbitone was introduced and first tested, pharmacologically and in clinical practice, under the trade-name Veronal. 1927 *Daily Express* 30 Dec. 7/7 The chemist ..supplied a bottle containing twenty-five tablets of barbitone, which was the equivalent of veronal.

Barbituric (baɹbitiūᵊ·rik), *a.* *Chem.* [ad. F. *barbiturique* (Ann. de Chimie et de Physique, 1865), f. G. *barbitur* in *barbitursäure* (Baeyer in Ann. d. Chemie und Pharm. 1863).] *Barbituric acid*, a crystalline compound obtained by heating alloxantin with sulphuric acid; malonyl urea.
1866 ODLING *Anim. Chem.* 128 Baeyer has increased the list of compounds by his discovery of..the violuric and barbituric acids. 1885 REMSEN *Org. Chem.* (1888) 204 Barbituric acid..is a product obtained from uric acid.

Barbizon (bā·ɹbizǫn), *a.* [The name of a village near the forest of Fontainebleau, France.] Epithet of a French school of painting of the middle of the 19th century associated with the village of Barbizon.
1891 D. C. THOMSON (*title*) The Barbizon School of Painters. 1896 *McClure's Mag.* VI. 471/2 Corot, Daubigny, Dupré, Troyon, Diaz, Jacque, and others who[m], with our mania for classification, we call the 'Barbizon school'.

Barbola (baɹbōᵘ·lă). In full *barbola work*, decorative work composed chiefly of flowers and fruit modelled in a plastic paste and coloured, used to embellish small articles of wood, glass, pulp, etc.
1927 *Daily Express* 26 Sept. 5/5 Tiny porcelain-looking flowers..for the newest buttonholes..which are really a form of barbola work, are arranged in small round posies. 1928 *Ibid.* 22 Feb. 5/3 The latest designs in barbola work mirrors. ..The barbola or other wood-carving decoration is sparingly used—just a cluster of the painted raised flowers.

Barbotine. Add:
b. *Barbotine ware*: pottery with ornamentation in barbotine or slip.
1888 *Atalanta* Sept. 692/2 'Barbotine' work is like very rough painting with thick *impasto*. 1891 *Mag. Art* 353/1 There is 'barbotine' for those who like it—rich in colour. 1914 *Oxf. Univ. Gaz.* 573/1 (Rep. Ashmolean Mus.) Fragments of barbotine ware, showing that this type of pottery was popular in Memphis as well as in the Sudan.

Barb wire: see WIRE *sb.* 1 e.

Barcelona. Add:
Used *attrib.* in *Barcelona nut* or as short for this.
1851 MAYHEW *Lond. Labour* I. 89/1 The 'Barcelonas' are from 4½*d.* to 6*d.* a quart to the street-sellers. 1880 *Encycl. Brit.* XI. 549/1 Hazel-nuts, under the name of Barcelona or Spanish nuts, are largely exported from France and Portugal, and especially Tarragona.

Barchan (baɹkā·n). Also **barkhan, barkan.** [Native name.] A crescent-shaped dune of shifting sand such as occur in the deserts of Turkestan.
1888 *Encycl. Brit.* XXIII. 511/2 Shifting sands blown into *barkhans*, or elongated hills, sometimes 50 and 60 feet in height. 1900 *Geog. Jrnl.* XV. 24 On the higher portions of the foreland, to leeward and further from the river barchans (or medanos) occur.

Bardolatry (baɹdǫ·lătri). [f. BARD *sb.*1 (sense 4) + -OLATRY.] Worship of the 'Bard of Avon', i.e. Shakspere; Shaksperolatry. So **Bardolater** (-ǫ·lătəɹ) [-OLATER], a worshipper of the Bard, a Shaksperolater.
1901 G. B. SHAW *Plays for Puritans* Pref. 31 So much for Bardolatry! 1903 — *Man & Superman* Ep. Ded. 30 Foolish Bardolaters make a virtue of this after their fashion. 1911 *Times Lit. Suppl.* 9 Nov. 440/3 Playing for the sympathy of the 'bardolaters'.

Bare, *sb.* Delete † *Obs.*, and add to 1:
1906 *Westm. Gaz.* 29 Dec. 16/1 The downtrodden slippers tied on with string, toes out, and hardly any sole: the child is walking 'on the bare', as the saying is.

Barefoot, *a.* Add: *U.S.* in fig. use (see quots. and cf. *BARE-FOOTED b).
1866 LOWELL *Biglow P.* Ser. II. Introd., 'I take my tea barfoot', said a backwoodsman when asked if he would have cream and sugar. 1888 *Chicago Herald* (Farmer) Never touch coffee unless you like it barefoot, that is, without sugar or milk.

Bare-footed, *a.* Add:
Of a horse: Having a shoeless foot. Hence **Barefoo·tedness.**
1756 TOLDERVY *Hist. 2 Orphans* I. 74 Many worthy gentlemen are become egregious sufferers, both by the barefootedness of their horses and the loss of their hares. 1891 *Athenæum* 28 Nov. 714/1 The barefootedness of the women and children. 1906 SOMERVILLE & ROSS *Some Irish Yesterdays* 88 'Ye're barefooted', he said. I found that I [my hunter] had indeed lost a foreshoe.
b. *U.S.* (See quots. and cf. *BAREFOOT.)
1847 PAULDING *Amer. Comedies* (Philad.) 194, I thought even a Yankee knew that 'stone fence barefooted' is the polite English for whisky uncontaminated,—pure, sir! 1878 J. H. BEADLE *Western Wilds* xii. 183 It was sod corn [*sc.* whiskey] barefooted.

Baren (ba·ren). [Jap.] A pad used in wood-block printing.
1916 F. M. FLETCHER *Wood-block Printing* ii. 12 Pressure is then applied to the back of the paper as it lies on the wet block. This is done by a round pad called the *baren* by the Japanese. It is made of a coil of cord covered by bamboo sheath. 1924 H. FURST *Mod. Woodcut* 94 The Japanese manner of designing in map-like spaces and printing from the plank by rubbing with the 'baren'..became general.

Bargain, *sb.*1 Add:
3. b. In certain coalfields in England, a piece of work let to the workmen making the lowest offer. Also Comb., as *bargain-letter, -man, -tacker, -taker, -work* (see quot. 1851 in sense 8 in Dict.).
1825 E. MACKENZIE *Hist. Northumb.* (ed. 2) I. 200 These bargains are taken in partnerships, consisting of from two to eight men. 1858 SIMMONDS *Dict. Trade*, Bargain-men. 1881 *Instr. Census Clerks* (1885) 84 Copper Miner...Bargain Man. 1897 *Daily News* 18 Mar. 3/4 They cannot take special bits of work, known as bargains, but must go to the bargain-takers and ask them for rock to cut up. 1897 *Westm. Gaz.* 1 Sept. 7/1 Bargain-letting recommenced to-day at Lord Penrhyn's Carnarvonshire slate quarries.
8. bargain-counter *U.S.*, a counter at which goods professedly marked down in price are offered as exceptionally good bargains; also *fig.* and *allusively*; **bargain-day** *U.S.*, the day in each week on which bargains are on sale at the bargain-counters; **bargain-hunter**, one who is on the look-out for bargains in shopping (cf. *bargain-hunting* in Dict.); **bargain-price**, a professedly marked-down price of an article, esp. at a sale; **bargain-sale** *U.S.*, a sale at which bargains are offered. Also *attrib.*
1888 *Scribner's Mag.* III. 65/2 All the finery that the '*bargain counters' of Fourteenth Street could furnish. 1890 *Congress. Rec.* 28 Aug. 9258/1 You may go into any of the large mercantile establishments..and you will find what they call a bargain-counter. 1900 *Ibid.* Feb., App. 77/2 Were the Spaniards right in their derisive epithets calling us 'pigs' and a 'bargain counter nation'? 1903 *N. Y. Times* 8 Sept., Men may sniff at the bargain counter and bargain counter habits. 1904 *Rochester Post Express* 22 July 4 The bargain counter rates for steerage traffic. 1898 C. A. BATES *Clothing Bk.* No. 1373 Instead of 'Dog Days' these twenty-four hours should be called '*bargain days'. 1868 *Great Unwashed* 214 'What will you take for these?' asked the *bargain-hunter. 1886 A. LANG in *Longm. Mag.* VII. 447 Last month was a lucky one for bargain-hunters. 1904 *Westm. Gaz.* 7 Jan. 8/1 Jewellery and chiffons and laces are there, going at *bargain prices. 1898 C. A. BATES *Clothing Bk.* No. 5211 Garments for which you pay the additional price at widely advertised '*bargain' sales. *a* 1906 'O. HENRY' *Trimmed Lamp*, etc. 115 'Have I ever chucked any bargain sale stuff at you, Moll?' asked the Kid, with calm dignity.

Barge, *sb.* Add: **6. b.** A large carriage. *U.S.*
1881 HOWELLS *Modern Instance* xxvii. 328 Marcia watched him drive off toward the station in the hotel barge. 1903 *Boston Herald* 19 Aug., The visitors were conveyed in barges to the crest of High Pole hill. 1907 *Springfield Weekly Republ.* 21 Feb. 16 [A sleigh-ride] which required every four-horse barge in the north half of the county.

Barge, *sb.*2 (See quot.)
1908 *Animal Management* 206 A piece of leather..running from the fore-wale beneath the after-wale [of a horse's collar] is known as the 'barge'.

Barge, *v.* Add:
3. *intr.* To bump heavily *into* (a person), to knock roughly *against*; to go roughly and heavily *through, into, along, about*, or *against* (a place, etc.); also with advs. *about, around*. Also *to barge one's way*.
1888 *Boy's Own Paper* Christmas No. 56/2 Dig your heels in, old chap,..and barge into the bank! 1890 FARMER *Slang* I. 124/1 *Barge*..(Uppingham School.)—To knock against a person; to come into collision with. 1899 *Daily News* 10 July 9/2 Defendant denied that the cocks were fighting. They were merely 'barging' as it was called in Lancashire. 1904 KIPLING *Traffics & Discov.* 318 You ought to have summoned me for trespass when I barged through your woods. 1904 — in *Windsor Mag.* Jan. 234/2, I remember..the dropped jaw of the midshipman in her whaler when we barged fairly into him. 1906 *Westm. Gaz.* 4 Oct. 4/2 Old Bubblyjock barges backwards and forwards through the midst of us. 1911 C. E. W. BEAN '*Dreadnought*' *of the Darling* xxxviii, A crowd of men came barging into the hut. 1919 CHRISTINE ORR *Glorious Thing* vi. 63 His first mishap was to barge into Isabel's fiancé, his second to be barged into by Isabel. 1924 *Chambers's Jrnl.* 294/2 Pattering donkeys barge their way through the crowded alleys. 1924 *Blackw. Mag.* June 751/2 The camel..is an awkward and troublesome creature on a narrow road, especially if he takes fright, barging about to the danger of everybody.
b. *transf.* and *fig.*
1923 *Chambers's Jrnl.* 718/2, I hadn't barged about the world then. 1928 *Observer* 11 Mar. 14/5 There is a sort of masterful way in which a theme is made to barge its way through its surroundings.
c. *trans.* To cause to move forcibly or heavily.
1923 *Public Opinion* 19 Jan. 61/2 Heaven knows I'm always trying to barge it at you. 1927 *Observer* 3 Apr. 27/6 Scotland bore down in a body, and Morton barged the ball past Brown.

Barge (bāɹdʒ), *v.*2 *slang.* ? *dial.* [? Back-formation f. BARGEE, as if 'to use the language of a bargee'.] *trans.* To abuse or 'slang' (a person).
a 1860 ALB. SMITH *Med. Student* (1861) 102 Whereupon they all began to barge the master at once; one saying 'his coffee was all snuff and chickweed.' 1881 KEENE *Six Months in Meccah* iv. 98 My informer..blaming those 'Shaitan' English, and barging them in choice Arabic.

Bargemaster. Add quots.:
1664-5 in C. Welch *Hist. Company of Pewterers* (1902) II. 132 The salary of Mr. Pike, barge master, was fixed on 16th March at 3*l.* yearly. 1892 W. C. HAZLITT *Livery Companies* 475 The duties of the Bargemaster, which, after the discontinuance of water-pageants, have been confined to the supervision of the swans on the Thames. 1898 *Daily News* 21 Apr. 2/2 The Fishmongers' Company's late Bargemaster. —The office of bargemaster is one of the most ancient in the annals of the City Companies.

Barge-pole. A long pole with which a barge is propelled (see also quot. 1890); frequent in colloq. phr. *I wouldn't touch him* (*it*) *with a barge-pole*, I refuse to have anything to do with him (it).
1877 [remembered in use at Harrow School]. 1890 FARMER *Slang* I. 124 *Barge-Pole.* (Winchester College.) A large stick or thick bough, of which there was one in each fagot. Also generally used for any large piece of wood. 1915 A. H. GIBBS *Persistent Lovers* ii, Hideous little beast! I wouldn't touch him with the end of a barge pole. 1918 MRS. H. WARD *War & Elizabeth* v, If he tries to leave me this funny old place..there are two can play at that game. I wouldn't touch it with a barge pole.

Barging (bā·ɹdʒiŋ), *vbl. sb.* [f. BARGE *sb.* + -ING1. Cf. BARGE *v.*] Transport by barge.
1904 *Daily Chron.* 29 Jan. 3/6 The barging is done by contract. 1905 *Westm. Gaz.* 9 Mar. 9/2 The cost of 'barging' and transport.

Barhal, variant of *BURREL.

Bark, *sb.*1 Add:
6. b. *With the bark on*, in a rough or unpolished form. *U.S.*
1872 'MARK TWAIN' *Roughing it* xv. 124 That is the word with the bark on it! 1903 *N. Y. Sun* 28 Nov. 7 Your Westerner with the bark on is fond of..picturesque figures of speech.
10. bark-beetle, any beetle of the family *Scolytidæ*, the members of which burrow beneath the bark of woody plants; **bark-borer** *U.S.*, a species of bark-beetle; **bark-hut**, a hut built with the bark of trees; also *attrib.*; **bark-peeler**, an implement for peeling bark (see quot.).
1862 T. W. HARRIS *Insects Injur. Veget.* 85 Though these cylindrical *bark-beetles are of small size, they multiply very fast. 1857-8 *Trans. Ill. Agric. Soc.* (1859) III. 345 Another species is that sometimes called the *bark borer, from its feeding exclusively upon the cambium immediately beneath the bark. 1843 R. CARLTON *New Purchase* i. 2 We..talked of *bark huts and bows and arrows. 1890 'R. BOLDREWOOD' *Miner's Right* vi. 61 Bark-huts, of which both sides, and sometimes doors are composed of sheets of the flattened eucalyptus bark. 1904 *Daily Chron.* 25 May 3/5 Nomad bark-hut settlements of the natives [during a Siberian journey]. 1902 *Encycl. Brit.* XXV. 376/1 All textile work [of American Indians] was done by hand; the only devices known were the *bark-peeler, the shredder [etc.].

Bark, *v.*1 Add:
2. *To bark up the wrong tree.* (Earlier examples.)
1833 *Sketches & Eccentr. D. Crockett* (1834) 58, I told him..that he reminded me of the meanest thing on God's earth, an old coon dog, barking up the wrong tree. 1833 J. HALL *Leg. West* 46 You are barking up the wrong tree, Johnson. 1841 *Congress. Globe* 25 Jan., App. 153 The stock-jobbers were barking up the wrong tree when they wrote those letters.
b. To call out or 'spiel' at the entrance of a cheap shop or show to attract customers. (Cf. *BARKER1 2 b.) *U.S.*
3. b. Of a fire-arm: To go off with a sharp report. (Cf. BARKER1 4.)
1907 S. E. WHITE *Arizona Nights* III. xiii. 342 The Colt's forty-five barked once, and then again.
5. Delete † *Obs.* and add quots.:
1881 CLARK *Vill. Minstr.* II. 33 The dog bark'd a welcome. 1864 TENNYSON *Boädicea* 13 Bark an answer, Britain's raven! 1916 BOYD CABLE *Action Front* 131 Both the muzzles tilted a little and barked off another flight of shells. 1922 *N. & Q.* 12th Ser. XI. 206/2 A stable secret which has leaked out and is common property is referred to as 'the dogs are barking it'.
6. To drive *away* or *back* by barking.
1829 MISS MITFORD in *The Gem* 195 Frisk's own doggish exploit in barking away a set of pilferers. 1891 MEREDITH *One of our Conq.* II. iii. 42 The Dog..would have barked the breathing intruder an hundredfold back to earth.

Bark canoe. *U.S.* [BARK *sb.*1 10.] A canoe made of birch-bark.
1725 *Lancaster Rec.* 232, 27 day we traveld down the river and found a bark cannow. 1755 L. EVANS *Anal. Map Colonies* 27 (1) Toby's Creek, is passable with Bark Canoes a good way up. 1817 S. R. BROWN *Western Gaz.* 253 This renders the communication impassable in summer, except with small bark canoes. 1848 J. F. COOPER *Oak Open.* I. i. 12 A score of respectable families patiently waited for the arrival of the capacious bark canoe. 1888 *Harper's Mag.* Mar. 537/1 But only a bark canoe now and then comes along from one of the thirteen rivers.

Ba·rken, *a.* [f. BARK *sb.*1 + -EN 4.] Made or consisting of bark.
1835 R. M. BIRD *Hawks of Hawk-h.* I. v. 61 Perhaps some tall and tawny hunter..may yet..urge his barken canoe over some cypress-fringed pool. 1890 *Harper's Mag.* Aug. 365 A sword-lunge of assailant thunder Slashed down thy barken mail.

Barker1. **2.** Add: One who 'barks' at a cheap shop or show: see *BARK *v.*1 2 b. Chiefly *U.S.*
a 1700 B. E. *Dict. Cant. Crew*, *Barker*, a Salesman's Servant that walks before the Shop, and cries, Cloaks, Coats, or Gowns, what d'ye lack, Sir. 1822 [see Dict.]. 1859 *Slang Dict.*, *Barker*, a man employed to cry at the doors of gaffs, shows, and puffing shops, to entice people inside. 1897 HOWELLS *Landlord at Lion's Head* 247 The barker began to fill the night with hoarse cries of 'Miss Lynde's carriage; carriage for Miss Lynde!' 1903 *N. Y. Times* 28 Aug., Conditions were so dull that barkers had to be enlisted to call the public's attention to the boats. 1910 H. A. FRANCK *Vagabond Journ.* 276 The secretary was a man..with the voice of a side-show barker.

Barking, *vbl. sb.*2 **2.** **Barking irons** (add quot.).
1845 S. JUDD *Margaret* I. iii. 12 Here were a draw-shave, a cross-cut saw..barking irons, a scythe.

Barking, *ppl. a.*1 **2. b.** Add:
barking deer, the Indian muntjac, *Cervulus muntjac*, found in India, Burma, and Tibet; so named from its call; **barking-iron** (earlier U.S. example); **barking-wolf** *U.S.* (see quot.).
1880 *Encycl. Brit.* XII. 742/2 The *barking deer or muntjac (*Cervulus vaginalis*). 1898 *Geog. Jrnl.* XI. 502 The small barking deer, called 'pause' by the natives. 1825 PAULDING *John Bull in Amer.* 56 Seeing the *barking iron [*sic*] shrunk back. 1867 *Amer. Naturalist* I. 289 The Prairie or *Barking Wolf (*Canis latrans*, Say), is by far the most abundant carnivorous animal in Arizona, as it is also in almost every part of the West.

Ba·rk-louse. *U.S.* [BARK *sb.*1 10.] Any one of a number of aphids infesting the bark of trees.
1852 *Trans. Mich. Agric. Soc.* III. 199 Bark lice and Caterpillar; wash them [apple trees] with lye. 1862 T. W. HARRIS *Insects Injur. Vegetation* (ed. 3) 248 Bark-lice (*Coccidæ*). 1884 *Rep. Commissioner Agric.* 352 The ordinary food-plant of this species of bark-louse is the Soft or Silver maple. 1867 *Amer. Naturalist* I. 223 Fruit-trees should be again washed and rubbed to kill off the young Bark-lice, of which the common apple Bark-louse..is a too familiar example.

Bark-mill. *U.S.* [BARK *sb.*1 9.] A mill in which tanning bark is ground.
1824 *Rouse's Point Harbinger* 17 Feb. 4/2 A Bark-house, and a good iron Bark mill. 1832 J. P. KENNEDY *Swallow Barn* I. xxi. 209 He..goes at it with the reluctance of an old horse in a bark-mill. 1831 *Louisville Publ. Adv.* 1 Sept., Bark Mills, Wind Mill Irons...A supply of the above article on hand. 1861 CLEMENS in O. J. Victor *Hist. Southern Reb.* I. 270 He must recede as submissively as a blind horse in a bark-mill. 1885 [see BARK *sb.*1 9 a].

Barkometer (baɹkǫ·mĭtəɹ). [f. BARK *sb.*1 + -OMETER.] A tanners' hydrometer for testing the strength of bark infusions.
1821 J. SWAN (*title*) Explanation of improved mode of Tanning;..intended to accompany the New Invented Barktrometer [*sic*]. *Ibid.* 40 Though you show us, by the assistance of your new Barktrometer that there is a something derived from the bark of which it shows the quantity. 1852 MORFIT *Tanning & Currying* (1853) 329 A barkometer..is specially adapted to testing the strength of bark lyes. 1882 [see *tan-liquor* s.v. TAN *sb.*1 C. 1].

Barlow knife. *U.S.* [From the name of the maker.] A large single-bladed pocket-knife.
1779 *New-Jersey Jrnl.* 12 Oct., Advt. in *N. J. Archives* Ser. II. III. 676 Barlow penknives. 1819 *Massachusetts Spy* 29 Dec. 3/2 A barlow knife, bloody, and another knife, rusty, lay along side of him. 1845 S. JUDD *Margaret* I. vi. 36 On the left were cuttoes, Barlow knives, iron candlesticks. *c* 1860 G. W. BAGLEY *Writ.* (1884) I. 185 A Barlow knife, which I always carry, because I am a Virginian. 1876 'MARK TWAIN' *Tom Sawyer* iv. 30 Mary gave him a brand-new 'Barlow' knife. 1896 J. C. HARRIS *Sister Jane* 229 There on the side of the pew were the letters W. W. which many years ago I had carved with my barlow knife.
ellipt. 1890 *Congress. Rec.* Aug. 8818/2 He did not want to carry a cheap and nasty knife, but the little fellow has to carry a ten cent Barlow.

Barminess (bā·ɹmines). [f. BARMY *a.* + -NESS.] Weakness of intellect.
1896 [see next]. 1908 E. V. LUCAS *Over Bemerton's* vi. 60, I heard what sounded like a sarcastic sniff deprecative of her uncle's barminess.

Barmy, *a.* Add:
2. b. = *BALMY (of which it is an altered form, after BARM *sb.*2). *slang.*
1896 *Westm. Gaz.* 30 May 8/1 Should not 'balmy' be 'barmy'? I have known a person of weak intellect called 'Barmy Billy'..The prisoner in the paragraph meant to simulate semi-idiocy, or 'barminess,' not 'balminess'. 1902 *Ibid.* 8 Nov. 2/1 All the boys think him barmy.

Barn, *sb.* Add: **1. c.** A stable or cattle-house. *U.S.*
1828 MRS. ROYALL *Black Bk.* II. 71 Every farmer has his small wooden barn, under which name they include stables. 1901 M. D. BABCOCK *Thoughts* 17 Locking a barn seems no longer commonplace when the horse is stolen. 1904 *N. Y. Even. Post* 28 Jan. 1 Cattle were found frozen stiff in the barns by farmers this morning.
2. barn-boss, a horsekeeper. *U.S.*
1902 S. E. WHITE *Blazed Trail* xxix, So Shearer had picked out a barn-boss of his own.

Barnbrack (bā·ɹnbræk). *Ir.* [f. Ir. *bairín* cake of bread + *breac* speckled.] A cake or loaf of bread containing currants.
1772 VALLANCEY *Ess. Antiq. Irish Lang.* 22 On St. Briget's Eve every Farmer's Wife in Ireland makes a Cake called bair-in-breac. 1867 P. KENNEDY *Banks of Boro* xiii. 349 Piles of hot griddle-baked wheaten cakes.., barn-bracks, and other varieties of the staff of life. 1901 G. B. SHAW *Plays for Puritans, Devil's Disciple* 1, Two green ware plates, on one of which she puts a barnbrack. 1928 *Universe* 3 Feb., A loaf of curious, very sweet currant bread is made and sold for All Souls Day. Even the poorest household manages to secure one of these Barn-bracks.

Ba·rn dance. orig. *U.S.* [BARN *sb.*] A dance danced in a barn; applied *spec.* to a kind of schottische in which the partners advance side by side for a few steps and then dance a waltz or schottische step.
1892 *Daily News* 28 Sept. 5/5 The now inevitable barn dance figured once on the programme. 1895 MRS. LILLY GROVE *Dancing* 424 (Badminton Libr.) 'Barn dance' is an American designation; but as many other dances take place in barns out West, it is difficult to see why the title is specially applied to this Scotch lilt and schottische hops.
allusively. 1898 KIPLING *Fleet in Being* 7 We of the light horse did barn-dances about the windy floors.

Ba·rn-yard. Chiefly *Sc.* and *U.S.* [BARN *sb.* 2.] The yard attached to the barn on a farm.
1473 *Acta Auditorum* (1839) 28/1 The wrangwiss occupacion of a berne..and a bernezarde. 1491 *Acta Dom. Conc.* (1839) 184/2 Awaytakin..out of his barne zarde and feilde ..of all the cornez. 1565 *Reg. Privy Council Scot.* I. 392 To collect and gadder the teind schaves..and place the samyn within the berne yaird. 1616 *Reg. Magni Sig. Scot.* 106/2 Cum horreo lie barneyaird eorundem. 1656 *Sutherland Charters* 198 Of victuall the excrescens of his Maynes in bairne and bairneyaird. 1683 *Connecticut Probate Rec.* I. 344, I give my Barn Yard equally to my sons. 1805 SCOTT *Last Minstrel* IV. vi, Barn-yard and dwelling, blazing bright, Served to guide me on my flight. 1838 H. COLMAN *Rep. Agric. Mass.* 67 All the washings of the barn-yard are received into the lower story or cellar. 1859 *Trans. Mich. Agric. Soc.* (1860) X. 552 What sites are usually selected for barn-yards?
attrib. 1840 J. BUEL *Farmer's Comp.* 196 A load of barn-yard manure. 1863 *Trans. Ill. Agric. Soc.* (1865) V. 867 *Panicum Crus-galli*, Barn-yard grass, is a coarse weed. 1897 KIPLING *Capt. Courageous* vi. 129 You barn-yard tramps go hoggin' the road on the high seas with no blame consideration fer your neighbours.

Barocco (bărǫ·ko), *a.* [It.] = *BAROQUE.
1877 SYMONDS *Renaiss. in Italy, Fine Arts* ii. (1882) 99 Palladio was followed by the violent reactionaries of the *barocco* mannerism. *Ibid.* x. 503 Stucco, fresco, and gilding in a style only just removed from the *barocco*. 1881 S. BUTLER *Alps & Sanct. Piedmont* 332 The architecture is late, and *barocco*, not to say *rococo*, reigns everywhere. *a* 1902 — *Note-Bks.* (1912) 260 The band played the barocco music on the barocco little piazza and we were all barocco together. 1923 L. PULLAN *Religion Since Reform.* vii. 221 Peter the Great..pronounced the name of his new capital as if it were Dutch, and his architects built it after the manner of the Dutch and German barocco cities.

Barocyclonometer (bærŏsaiklonǫ·mĭtəɹ). [f. Gr. βάρος weight + CYCLONE + -METER.] An aneroid barometer with diagrams and directions for detecting the existence of a storm at a distance of several hundred miles.
1906 *Month* Dec. 562 The ships that sail the seas of the Far East are equipped with the Barocyclonometer.

Baron. Add:
2. b. A great merchant in a certain commodity, defined by a qualifying word, as *beef baron, coal baron.* (Cf. *king, magnate.*) *U.S.*
1887 *Harper's Mag.* Apr. 822/1 When the great 'coal barons'..deliberately combine to put up the price of coal. 1888 *N. Y. Life* 18 Feb. 27/2 One of the 'several times' a millionaire lumber 'Barons of Michigan. 1895 J. L. FORD *Lit. Shop* iv. (1896) 46 Magazine barons. 1902 *Westm. Gaz.* 17 May 5/2 Nearly 150,000 coalminers are on strike in the anthracite region of Pennsylvania...The coal barons have built barricades and barbed wire fences around the shafts. 1904 'O. HENRY' *Cabbages & Kings* 4 A rubber prince, a sarsaparilla, indigo, and mahogany baron. 1907 *Westm. Gaz.* 20 Dec. 9/4 The American beef barons, Armour's, Swift's, and Morris, are..the greatest captains of commerce in any market.
c. *slang.* (See quot.)
1919 *Athenæum* 15 Aug. 759/1 Slang in War-time...Baron, army commander.

Baronetize (bæ·rŏnĕtaiz), *v.* [f. BARONET + -IZE.] *trans.* To confer a baronetcy on, make a baronet.
1861 MEREDITH *Evan Harrington* xiv, Third son! Don't commit yourself there. We dare not baronetise him. 1892 GORDON HAKE *Mem. 80 Years* lxv. 276 We have no 'Sir Barry' nowadays; premiers do not build houses, so that they do not baronetize architecture.

Baronian (bărōᵘ·niăn), *a.* [f. BARONY + -AN.] = BARONIAL *a.*
1656 PRYNNE *Fund. Rights of Eng. Freemen* 31 The particulars whereof would amount to many Baronian Tomes, if at large recorded. 1905 *Daily Chron.* 14 June 4/7 The castle is built of granite, in the Scotch Baronian style.

Baroque, *a.* Add:
Applied to a florid style of architectural decoration which arose in Italy in the late Renaissance and became prevalent in Europe during the 18th century. Also *transf.* in reference to other arts.
This term and *rococo* are not infrequently used without distinction for styles of ornament characterized by profusion, oddity of combinations, or abnormal features generally.
1869 *Baedeker's Central Italy & Rome* (1881) p. lix, The authors of the degenerated Renaissance known as Baroque were really Vignola (1507–73) and Fontana's nephew Carlo Maderna (1556–1639)...An undoubted vigour in the disposition of detail, a feeling for vastness and pomp, together with an internal decoration which spared neither colour nor costly material to secure an effect of dazzling splendour; such are the distinguishing attributes of the Baroque style. 1928 *Times Lit. Suppl.* 15 Mar., French-Canadian art..is being recognized..as a baroque style which is other than the European baroques.

Barotaxis (bærotæ·ksis). *Physiol.* [f. Gr. βάρος weight + τάξις turning.] 'Stimulation of living matter by change of the pressure relations under which it exists' (Dorland).
1901 CALKINS *Protozoa* 300 A general result of mechanical stimulation is a motor response followed by the tendency to turn away from the source, and the general reaction, whether positive or negative, since it deals with the question of pressure in some form or other, is called *barotaxis* (Verworn).

Barrack, *sb.* Add:
2. c. Also *attrib.*: **barrack school**, a disparaging term applied to a large district school for poor-law children.
1894 E. HART in *Brit. Med. Jrnl.* 21 Apr. 879/2 The system of pauper district schools organised on the 'barrack' principle should be mended or ended as soon as possible. *Ibid.* 28 Apr. 928 Poor Law Barrack Schools. 1902 *Encycl. Brit.* XXXI. 835/1 Adverse criticism..in 1874..has been directed against these large, or, as they are invidiously called, barrack schools.
d. *transf.* A large plain building or range of buildings, tenements, or flats in which a number of people are housed; also, any strikingly plain-looking building suggestive of a military barracks. Also *attrib.* as *barrack-flat*.
1886 *Contemp. Rev.* Sept. 329 The railway has come close under the walls of the *château*, while an ugly barrack has sprung up on the other side. 1909 *Westm. Gaz.* 20 Oct. 1/3 A feature of German housing which reformers desire to abolish: that is, of the many-storied barrack-flat system.

Barrack (bæ·răk), *v.*2 [orig. Australian; alteration of *BORAK, q. v.]
intr. To shout jocular or sarcastic remarks or words of advice as partisans *for* or *against* a person, esp. a person, or side collectively, engaged in a contest. (Said of a section of the crowd of spectators, orig. Australian.) Also *transf.* **b.** *trans.* To shout in this way at (a player). Hence **Ba·rracking** *vbl. sb.* and *ppl. a.*; also **Ba·rracker.**
1890 FARMER *Slang*, *Barracking* (Australian), banter, chaff. 1890 *Melbourne Punch* 14 Aug. 106/3 To use a football phrase, they all to a man 'barrack' for the British Lion. 1893 *The Age* 27 June 6/6 (Morris) People were afraid to go to them [*sc.* football matches] on account of the conduct of the crowd of 'barrackers'. *Ibid.*, The 'barracking' that was carried on at football matches. 1895 *Westm. Gaz.* 1 Mar. 5/1 A spontaneous burst of cheering and 'barracking,' with loud cries of 'Bravo, Stoddart!' were heard. 1900 H. LAWSON *On Track* 89, I was too shy to go in where there was a boy wanted and barrack for myself properly. 1901 *Westm. Gaz.* 19 Aug. 6/2 The crowd had absolutely no right..to 'barrack' the players by yelling in concert now and again, at a critical moment. 1904 WARNER *How we Recovered the Ashes* 73 Hayward and myself had to undergo some 'barracking' for playing slowly. *Ibid.* 167 They will grow up into the type of man who 'barracked' Crockett so disgracefully at Sydney. 1926 *Chambers's Jrnl.* 543/2 Only once..was a querulous barracking voice raised.

Barracoat, var. *barrow-coat*: see BARROW *sb.*4

Barrage (bæ·răʒ, -ĕdʒ, ‖ bară·ʒ). Add: In modern military use: A barrier of continuous artillery or machine-gun fire concentrated in a given area, used to prevent the advance or retreat of enemy troops, to protect troops advancing against the enemy, to repulse attacks by aircraft, and for destructive purposes. *Creeping* or *moving barrage*, a curtain of fire moving before and directed from behind advancing troops. More explicitly *barrage fire.*
1917 *Times* 11 July 5/5 The German barrage fire on the trenches, though it lasted so short a time, was of extreme severity. *Ibid.* 26 Sept. 7/6 The barrage was effective in keeping the raiders at a great height. 1918 BOYD CABLE *Air Men o' War* ix. 118 Next instant he plunged at, into, and through the barrage, his machine rocking and pitching and rolling in the turmoil of shell-torn air. 1922 *Encycl. Brit.* XXX. 230/1 This breakdown of communications..led to the general introduction of the 'creeping barrage' (French *barrage roulant*, German *Feuerwalze*). Briefly, it is a

screen of shells bursting on and close to the ground, which is moved forward across the country by short leaps according to a pre-determined time-table.

b. *transf.* and *fig.*

1918 *Daily Chron.* 20 Dec. (Weekley) Field-Marshal Sir Douglas Haig passed into London through a creeping barrage of cheers. 1920 W. J. Locke *House of Baltazar* xxiv, If the barrage of silence is maintained. 1921 *Spectator* 19 Mar. 360/2 It seems to me like firing both barrels simultaneously at a partridge; but if it should be regarded as putting up a barrage, then, of course, it would be better to fire both barrels.

Hence **Barrage** *v. trans.*, to put a barrage upon; *intr.* to put down a barrage.

1918 Boyd Cable *Air Men o' War* xvii. 230 The only bit of the whole line they managed to barrage properly. 1918 E. A. Mackintosh *War, the Liberator* 124 The artillery will barrage at x. 20.

Barrel, *sb.* Add:

5. d. A cylindrical button used in conjunction with a loop of braid as an ornamental fastening of a coat.

1898 *Daily News* 12 Nov. 6/3 Frogs and barrels are adapted to the otherwise plain red coats. 1900 *Ibid.* 29 Dec. 6/6 The fronts are fitted out with braided frogs and barrels.

11. **barrel cactus**, the genus *Echinocactus*; **barrel-fish**, the Black Rudder-fish, *Lirus perciformis*, found off the U.S. coast; **barrel house, barrel shop** *U.S.*, a low-class drinking-saloon.

1881 *Amer. Naturalist* XV. 984 The 'nigger-head' or '*barrel' cactus. 1884 Goode, etc. *Nat. Hist. Useful Aquatic Anim.* I. 334 This fish is also called by the fishermen 'Log-fish' and '*Barrel-fish'. 1884–5 *Stand. Nat. Hist.* (1888) III. 191 The fishermen call them barrel-fish, though the most usual name is rudder-fish. 1888 *Missouri Republican* 11 Feb. (Farmer) The West-side police are still arresting *barrel-house loafers. 1904 *Chicago Tribune* in *N. Y. Even. Post* 2 June 3 The tramp..could go his way in the morning to the barrel house or the beer saloon. 1904 *N. Y. Tribune* 12 Oct. 1 A poisonous substitute for whiskey sold in the low '*barrel shops' along Tenth Avenue.

Barrelage (bæ·rĕlĕdʒ). [f. Barrel *sb.* + -age.] The total amount of any commodity, especially beer, as measured by barrels in a specified period; output estimated in barrels.

1890 *Certificate of valuation of Breweries*, The barrelage for the same period was, for the year 1888/9..312,292 bls. 1893 *Star* 10 Jan. 3/5 The increase in barrelage since the company was formed in 1887 amounted to 42,400. 1917 *Times* 26 Feb. 9/6 It is..impossible for us to guarantee the food of this country without making a very much deeper cut into the barrelage of the country.

Barrel-organ. Add to def.: Also extended to similar instruments not of the organ type but producing the notes by means of metal tongues which are struck by pins fixed in the barrel. The tone resembles that of a piano; hence they are distinguished as 'piano organs'. Hence **Barrel-organ** *v. intr.*, to play a barrel-organ.

1871 Le Fanu *Checkmate* xxxiii, The guitarring, singing, barrel-organing,..all make a curious and merry Babel. 1928 *Times* 27 Dec. 15/7 Those who have barrel-organed in a hard December.

Barremian (bărē·miăn), *a. Geol.* [f. F. *Barrême*, canton in department of Basses-Alpes + -ian.] = Urgonian.

1903 Geikie *Text-bk. Geol.* (ed. 4) 1197 The abandonment of the term Urgonian and the adoption in its place of 'Barremien'. 1914 *Brit. Mus. Return* 210 The Barremian Beds of Sandown Bay, I. of Wight.

Barren, *a.* Add:

4. b. *Barren Grounds*, the district lying between Hudson Bay and Mackenzie River in Canada, used attrib. in *Barren-Ground Bear* (see quots.); *Barren-Ground Caribou*, any of the several varieties of reindeer found in the Barren Grounds and Greenland, esp. *Rangifer arcticus* and *R. grœnlandicus*.

1825 J. Richardson in *Parry's Jrnl. 2nd Voy.* App. 329 The *cetrariæ, corniculariæ*, and *cenomyces*, which clothe the barren-grounds like a carpet. *Footnote*, The Barren Grounds ('Hi lichene obsiti campi quos Terram Damnatam diceret peregrinus', Flor. Lapp., p. 374). 1829 — *Fauna Bor.-Amer.* I. 23, I have given this one the *ad interim* name of Barren-ground Bear, until its difference from, or identity with, the *Ursus arctos* of Linnæus be fully established. *Ibid.* 241 Cervus tarandus var. a., arctica. Barren Ground Caribou. 1877 *Encycl. Brit.* VII. 25/1 The Barren Ground Caribou, and the Woodland Caribou. 1897 Lydekker in *Proc. Zool. Soc. London* 425 *Ursus arctus Richardsoni*—Barren-Ground Bear...This Bear..differs from the Grizzly in the shorter skull.

B. *sb.* 3. b. *attrib.* as **barrens oak** (see quot.).

1832 D. J. Browne *Sylva Amer.* 269 In New Jersey and Pennsylvania it [the Black Jack Oak] is called Barrens Oak.

Barrette (bare·t). [a. F. *barrette*, dim. of *barre* Bar *sb.*1]

1. The crossbar of a fencing foil or the hilt of a rapier.

1909 *Cent. Dict.* Suppl.

2. A bar for supporting a woman's back hair; also, a hair-ornament.

1905 *Westm. Gaz.* 6 Apr. 4/2 The dog-collar of opals with diamond barettes. 1908 *Ibid.* 29 Feb. 13/2 The front part of the barette forms a bandeau. 1908 *Ladies' Field* 4 Apr. 197/1 The favourite [hair-ornament] seems to be Greek barrettes over hair combed low.

Barricading, *vbl. sb.* Add: b. *concr.* A barricade or the materials of a barricade.

1890 J. Watson *Conf. Poacher* (1893) 159 Quietly as we could, we undid the barricading. 1910 *Westm. Gaz.* 24 Jan. 8/1 Some of the barricading was thrown among the crowd.

Barristress (bæ·ristrĕs). [f. Barrister + -ess.] A woman barrister.

1898 *Fortn. Rev.* LXIV. 127 The modern barristress. 1899 *Westm. Gaz.* 8 June 1/2 Barristress-at-law.

Barsac (bā·rsæk). Also **barsack**. [a. F. (see below).] A white wine, sweetish, but with a bitter flavour, made in Barsac, department of Gironde, France.

1820 *Blackw. Mag.* VIII. 44 To lawyers I would give the sharp Bar-sac. 1827 *Mirror* II. 164/1 Elephants don't drink barsack. 1845 *Tait's Mag.* XII. 698 Barsac, champagne, hock, and claret. 1877 *Temple Bar* XLIX. 359 [He] drinks a mixture of barsac and quassia.

Ba·r-share, -shear. *U.S.* [f. Bar *sb.*1 1 + Share *sb.*1 1.] A plough having a bar extending backwards from the share. Usu. *attrib.* with *plough*.

1785 Washington *Diaries* II. 438 Tools and Implements. ..Bar Shear Plows, 9. 1786 *Ibid.* III. 80, I ordered..the Bar share plow to be used, till the common Corn was all crossed. 1857 *Trans. Ill. Agric. Soc.* II. 365 The shovel plow..was superceded by the bar-shear. 1862 *Ibid.* (1865) V. 507 The bar-share plow.

Bartender (bā·ɹtendəɹ). *dial.* and *U.S.* a. A keeper or manager of a refreshment bar. b. A bar-attendant or barman.

1864 G. A. Sala in *Daily Tel.* 21 Nov., The bar-tender is a person of great gravity of countenance. 1878 J. Hartley *Seets i' Lundun* (ed. 2) 53 (E.D.D.) Aw axed th' bartender if he'd onny. 1883 [see Tender *sb.*1 2].

Barterable (bā·ɹtərăb'l), *a.* [f. Barter *v.* + -able.] Capable of being bartered; suitable for trading by exchange.

1852 Mundy *Antipodes* (ed. 2) II. 234 They found it a barterable commodity. 1890 H. M. Stanley *Darkest Africa* I. vii. 155 Trifles..were easily barterable for sugar-cane.

Barukhzy (baru·kzi). [*Bārakzi*, name of an Afghan tribe.] The Afghan hound.

1895 *Daily News* 11 Dec. 2/1 An Afghan Barukhzy hound. 1927 *Daily Tel.* 17 May 15/6 Every sort of dog—from the barukhzy of Cabul..to my lady's Pekingese.

Barum = Barnstaple (Devon). Used *attrib.*

1899 *Westm. Gaz.* 6 Mar. 6/2 They presented to 'Barumites in London' one of the choicest production of the Royal Barum ware pottery.

Barysphere (bæ·risfiəɹ). [f. Gr. βαρύς heavy + σφαῖρα Sphere.] The internal substance of the earth enclosed by the lithosphere.

1901 *Science* 15 Nov. 747 It was argued by Posepny that the ores came from the barysphere. 1926 *Encycl. Brit.* New Suppl. II. 172 The bulk of the earth consists of a nickel-iron mass, the barysphere, which is enclosed by a rocky crust, the lithosphere.

Basally (bē·săli), *adv.* Add:

2. *Nat. Hist.* In a basal position, at the base.

190. *Buck's Handbk. Med. Sci.* V. 868 (Cent. D. Suppl.).

Bascology (baskǫ·lŏdʒi). Also **Bask-**. [f. *Basc-*, used as comb. f. Basque + -ology.] The study of the Basques and their language. So **Basco·logist**, a student of, or one versed in Bascology.

1896 *Academy* 18 July 52/2 This Bascologist is incorrect. 1901 E. S. Dodgson in *N. & Q.* 9th Ser. VIII. 377/2 The following complementary details concerning the book..will be of interest to Baskologists. 1903 *Ibid.* XI. 355/2 Mr. Hutchinson has done good service to Bascology.

Base, *sb.*1 Add:

15. c. esp. in *Baseball*, each of the four stations at the angles of the 'diamond', all of which the batsman has to touch in succession in order to score a run. *Base on balls*, a base allowed to the batsman when the pitcher has delivered four balls.

1869 Chadwick *Game Base Ball* 34 He has also to look sharp after a base runner, when he is trying to run to second base. 1874 — *Base Ball Manual* 92 The bases must be four in number, and they must be placed and securely fastened upon each corner of a square whose sides are respectively thirty yards...The first, second, and third bases shall be canvas bags, painted white, and filled with some soft material; the home base shall consist of white marble or stone. 1891 N. Crane *Baseball* x. 79 Base on balls. When a batsman is awarded first base by the umpire on 'four balls' called on the pitcher, the batsman is said to 'take his base on balls'.

19. In sense 16, *base camp, censor, port, ship.*

1898 *Daily News* 27 May 7/5 The boats will be used as base camps. 1900 *Blackw. Mag.* Sept. 442/1 If..the senior officer commanding the Channel Squadron..brings his fleet into one of its natural base-ports. 1915 *Daily Express* 12 Nov. 5/3 It had been resealed in the customary way with the printed label showing that it had been 'Examined by Base Censor'. 1928 *Ibid.* 13 June 1 It was sent by wireless to the expedition's baseship.

20. **base hospital** *Mil.*, a hospital at some place distant from the area of active operations; **base-line**, 'a line, as of frontier, sea-coast, or forts, taken as the base of operations of an army, that is, from which operations advance, supplies of food, ammunition, and men are sent to the front, and to which the army may retreat in case of disaster' (Ogilvie); **base rate** (see quot.).

1895 *Daily News* 29 Apr. 5/3 It was intended to divide the '*Base Hospital' among several of the larger stations within easy reach of the frontier. 1895 *Westm. Gaz.* 30 Dec. 5/1 There are no dangerous cases of illness at the base hospital. 1802 James *Milit. Dict.*, *Base-line, the line on which troops in column move, the first division that marches into the alignement forms the base line, which each successive division prolongs. 1805 *Ibid.* (1810), *Base-line* also signifies the line on which all the magazines and means of supply of an army are established, and from whence the lines of operation proceed. 1902 *Daily Chron.* 25 July 3/3 A definite base-line from which the future progress of Irish industry can be measured. 1923 J. D. Hackett *Labor Terms* in *Management Engineering* May, *Base Rate, the ordinary day rate of wages guaranteed, in scientific management, whether the standard task is accomplished or not.

b. In *Baseball*, as *base-player, -playing, -stealer, -stealing*; **base hit**, a hit from which the ball cannot be fielded in time to prevent the batsman from reaching his base; **base-line** (*a*) the line, three feet wide, marked on the turf from base to base of a baseball field; (*b*) the line at each end of a lawn-tennis court, also *attrib.*, as *base-line game, driver*; hence **base-liner**, one who drives from the base-line, also a base-line drive; **base-runner**, the player who, having made a fair hit or in other contingencies specified in the rules, is running the bases.

1874 Chadwick *Base Ball Manual* 83 All ordinary errors, such as dropped flyballs, bad muffs, wild throws, and failures on the part of base players to hold balls thrown to them—all count in preventing *base hits being made. *Ibid.* 26 When [the ball] is flying about inside the *base lines or from base to base. 1875 *Encycl. Brit.* III. 406/2 [Base ball] The position of the bases and base lines may be likened to a 90 feet square shaped diamond. 1875 'Stonehenge' *Brit. Rural Sports* 690/1 (*Lawn tennis*) The player who wins choice of courts serves; *i. e.* delivers the ball, standing with one foot outside the base line. 1878 *Laws of Lawn-tennis* 7 At each end of the Court, parallel with the net, and at a distance of 39 ft. from it, are drawn Base-Lines. 1905 *Westm. Gaz.* 29 June 5/2 Unsurpassed as a base-line driver. 1903 *Ibid.* 27 July 10/2 Ritchie displayed remarkable activity and resource in getting back most of his opponent's lightning '*base-liners'. 1869 Chadwick *Game Base Ball* 34 The first *base player has the least active fielding to do, and the second base player the most. *Ibid.*, We now come to *base playing, and we propose to show that each position has its peculiar points of play. *Ibid.*, *base runner [see 15 c above]. 1875 *Encycl. Brit.* III. 407/1 Directly a striker has fairly struck a fair ball he becomes a base-runner. 1917 Mathewson *Sec. Base Sloan* xi. 157 He..developed an almost uncanny ability to out-guess the base-runner. 1874 Chadwick *Base Ball Manual* 83 No runs can be earned by chances given for successful *base-running through fielding errors. 1886 Chadwick (*title*) The Art of Batting and *Base Running. 1888 *Outing* Aug. 407 It is only by..a lucky act of base-running..that a single run is obtained. 1912 Mathewson *Pitching in a Pinch* 272 Merkle..is a great *base stealer because he has acquired the knack of 'getting away'. 1917 — *Sec. Base Sloan* xi. 145 He got to first and gave a very pretty exhibition of *base-stealing a moment later.

Baseball. Add: b. *attrib.*, as *baseball field, game, player, practice, reporter.*

1857 in Chadwick *Base Ball Manual* (1874) 7 The National Association of Base Ball Players. 1860 (*title*) Beadle's Dime Base-ball player comprising [etc.]. 1867 Chadwick (*title*) The Base Ball Player's Book of Reference..By Henry Chadwick,..Base Ball Reporter of the Principal New York Weeklies. *Ibid.* 119 Base Ball Practice. 1874 — *Base Ball Manual* 9 A base ball field. 1911 H. Harrison *Queed* xviii. 225 On the following Saturday,..he took Miss Weyland to another base-ball game.

Hence **Ba·seballer, -ballist.**

1868 (*title*) New England Base Ballist. A weekly journal. 1886 *Congress. Rec.* 2 Apr. 3043/2 [He is well known] as a baseballist among constitutional lawyers, and a constitutional lawyer among baseballists. 1888 *Battle Creek Jrnl.* 12 Dec., Western Base Ballers. 1896 Knowles & Morton *Baseball* 79 He..at once became a London baseballer.

Base-burner. *U.S.* (See Base *sb.*1 20 and quots.)

1874 Knight *Dict. Mech.* I. 242/1. 1877 Bartlett *Dict. Amer.* (ed. 4) 32 *Base-burner*, a sheet-iron stove for burning anthracite coal, which is only fed at the top, while the fire is confined to the base, or lower part of the stove. 1893 'O. Thanet' *Stories Western Town* 34 We got to keep a fire in the base-burner good, all night, or the plants will freeze. 1908 S. E. White *Riverman* xxi. 188 When the very cold weather came and they had to light the base-burner stove. *Ibid.* 189 He shook down the base-burner vigorously. 1922 Titus *Timber* ii. 28 A gaunt man..was putting wood in the base burner.

So **Base-burning** *a.* (with *furnace* or *stove*).

1874 Knight *Dict. Mech.* I. 242/1.

Based (bēɪst), *pa. pple.* [f. Base *sb.*1 16 + -ed.] Established as a base.

1925 E. F. Norton *Fight for Everest 1924*, 57 No. 1 party was to..remain based there for the purpose of getting the next camp on to the North Col.

Baseman (bē·smĕn). [f. Base *sb.*1 (15 c) + Man *sb.*1] Each of the fielders who stand near the first, second, and third bases in baseball.

1874 Chadwick *Base Ball Manual* 13 The positions in the field are as follows:—Catcher, pitcher, first baseman, second baseman, third baseman, short-stop, left fielder, centre fielder, and right fielder. 1893 *Stories of the South* 54 He had been an excellent first 'base-man' at college. 1899 Tarkington *Gentl. Indiana* v. 64 Tom Meredith..the thin, red-headed third baseman. 1917 Mathewson *Sec. Base Sloan* xi. 145 A dexterous hook-slide that kept him far out of reach of the baseman's sweep.

Bash (bæʃ), *v.*3 *local.* 'To fill with rubbish the spaces from which the coal has been worked away' (Gresley *Gloss. Coal-m.* 1883). Hence **Ba·shing** *vbl. sb.*

1905 *Daily Chron.* 26 June 6/5 A 'bashing'—a barricade of coal and rubbish.

Bashaw. Add:

3. Local name for a very large catfish of the species *Leptops olivaris*. Also called *Bashaw cat*; the mud cat. *U.S.*

1888 G. B. Goode *Amer. Fishes* 378 *Leptops olivaris*, the 'Mud Cat', 'Yellow Cat', 'Goujon', or 'Bashaw' is found in all the large rivers of the West and South. 1923 *Public Opinion* 12 Oct. 357/3 A good-sized fish, itself Carnivorous, called a basha.

Bashed (bæʃt), *ppl. a.*2 [f. Bash *v.*2 + -ed 1.] Having the surface beaten or smashed in.

1830 J. Wilson *Noct. Ambr.* xxv. Wks. 1856 III. 16 Like a beap o' bashed and birzed paddocks. 1898 *Westm. Gaz.* 31 Mar. 7/2 A bashed mask.

Basher (bæ·ʃəɹ). [f. Bash *v.*2 + -er 1.] One who gives, or strikes with, a smashing blow; *spec.* a pugilist.

1882 *Daily Tel.* 16 Dec. 2/6 The professed 'basher'. 1886 *World* 11 Aug. 8 This bruiser of the police court, this basher of a little foreign Jew. 1927 *Daily Tel.* 11 Oct. 12/6 He fights as if he enjoys fighting; and there is much of a basher in him.

Bashing (bæ·ʃiŋ), *vbl. sb.* [f. Bash *v.*2 + -ing 1.]

1. The action of striking so as to dint, bruise, or crush; an instance of this.

1733 W. Ellis *Chiltern & Vale Farm.* 45 Its hard and crusty Surface, so made by the Weights and Bashings of the heavy Rains. 1921 *Public Opinion* 21 Jan. 62/2 One would have expected to find a studious cultivation of more scientific methods of bashing.

2. A flogging (with the cat-o'-nine-tails).

1877 *Five Years' Penal Servitude* iii. 157 There were the evidences of former floggings, or 'bashings', as the prisoners call them. 1898 *Daily News* 23 Feb. 3/5, I got a bashing as well.—What do you mean by that?—Oh, I had the 'cat'.

Bashlik (bæ·ʃlik). Also **beshlik, bashluik, bashlyk.** [Russian.] A kind of hood with long side-pieces worn by Russians in inclement weather as a protective covering for the head. Also *transf.* a light covering for the head, worn by women in the U.S. (*Cent. Dict.*).

1884 O'Donovan *Merv* ii. 20 Hanging between the shoulders, and knotted around the neck, is the *bashlik*, or hood, worn during bad weather. 1884 A. Forbes *Souvenirs of Some Continents* (1885) 330 The flames danced..on the sombre hoods of beshliks. 1904 *Daily Chron.* 28 Mar. 3/1 The bashluik, or hood, worn to protect the ears.

Basic, *a.* Add:

1. b. That is or constitutes a base or starting-point in a scale of remuneration or the like.

1922 *Encycl. Brit.* XXXI. 392/1 When trade unions fix the length of the working day, they mean the basic work-day, with a higher rate of pay for overtime. 1923 J. D. Hackett in *Management Engineering* May, *Basic Eight-Hour Day*, that period of time for which a specific wage rate is paid, beyond which a higher rate, generally 'time and a half,' is paid. *Mod.* The examiners in the School of English Language and Literature receive a basic sum of £50.

c. *Gram.* Of or belonging to the base or theme of a word. See Base *sb.*1 14.

1885 Cook *Sievers' O. E. Gram.* § 86. 38 The development of the basic vowel into a diphthong.

2. d. *Basic slag*, slag from the basic or Bessemer process of steel manufacture, used as a fertilizer when finely ground.

1888 *Chambers's Jrnl.* 28 July 478/2 The value of basic slag as a manure. 1920 *Conquest* Aug. 487/2 Owing to the cattle grazing..phosphates and lime are withdrawn from the soil, but a dressing of basic slag..replaces this loss.

Basically (bē·sikăli), *adv.* [f. Basic *a.*: see -ically.] As a basic or fundamental principle, condition, matter, etc.; essentially; fundamentally.

1903 *Academy* 11 Apr. 364/1 Accent..though usual, is not invariable, not basically indispensable. 1905 Chesterton *Heretics* 270 The basically democratic quality which belongs to a hereditary despotism. 1915 *Protectionist* (Boston) June 71/1 A protection tariff is basically correct. 1920 W. J. Locke *House of Baltazar* xvii, They were so much alike—from the feminine point of view, basically children. 1927 *Observer* 20 Mar. 17/7 The author's thesis that airship navigation is basically impracticable.

Basicity. Add:

2. (See quot.)

1888 *Lockwood's Dict. Terms Mech. Engin.*, Basicity. Refers to the proportion of metallic oxide present in, and the absence of silicon from a furnace lining, a cinder, flux, or slag. The fettling of a puddling furnace depends for its efficacy on its basic character.

Basilar, *a.* Add:

b. Of or belonging to a low moral nature or condition.

1884 H. W. Beecher in *Chr. World Pulpit* XXV. 235/2 Rousing men and lifting them out of the basilar into this higher spiritual condition. 1899 *Westm. Gaz.* 9 June 2/1 He makes evident the disgust of his own higher nature for the past excesses of his basilar passions.

Basilian (băzi·liăn), *a.* [f. L. *Basilius*, St. Basil the Great + -an.] Of or pertaining to St. Basil or to the order of monks and nuns following his monastic rule.

1756–9 A. Butler *Lives Saints* (1780) VII. 344 *note*, A..convent of Basilian monks. 1847 Manning *Pius IX* II. ii. 59 The Basilian nuns of Minsk. 1890 *Athenæum* 8 Feb. 182/2 The Basilian monk and savant Father Cozza. 1923 L. Pullan *Relig. since Reform.* App. 278 In it there were seven Greek Basilian monasteries in the fifteenth century.

Basin. Add:

15. *Hort.* The depression at the apex of a pomaceous fruit, in which is situated the calyx or eye.

1909 in *Cent. Dict.* Suppl.

Basion (bē·siǫn). *Anat.* [mod.L., f. Gr. βάσις Base *sb.*1] The riddle of the anterior border of the occipital foramen.

1878 Bartley tr. *Topinard's Anthrop.* 234.

Basis. III. Add: **basis wine**, a fermented liquor obtained chiefly from raisins or concentrated must and used as the basis or main constituent in the manufacture of various wines.

1905 A. Chamberlain *Sp. in Ho. Comm.* 10 Apr., Wine manufactured..partly from imported grape must, more largely from currants and raisins..known to the trade as basis wine. 1905 *Daily Chron.* 21 Dec. 6/3 Fraudulent wines, containing what was called 'basis' wine.

Baskerville (bæ·skəɹvil). The name of John *Baskerville* (1706–75), type-founder and printer, applied to types of his founding re-cut.

Basket, *sb.* Add: 2. *A basket of chips*, used in comparisons, esp. with reference to smiling. *U.S.*

1806 *Spirit of the Public Jrnls.* (Baltimore) 115 (Th.) She smiled like a basket of chips. 1819 Moore *Tom Crib's Mem. Congress* 25 On which the whole Populace flash'd the white grin Like a basket of chips. 1827 *Massachusetts Spy* 28 Nov. (Th.) The Yankee will say of a young lady. 'She is a real pretty girl, but she is as homely as a basket of chips.' 1878 Rose T. Cooke *Happy Dodd* xxvi. (Th.) They'll make up to-night, and she'll be as pleasant as a basket of chips. 1892 *Congress. Rec.* Mar. 2367/1 My ticket was handed to me at once and the seller looked as pleasant as a basket of chips.

B. 1. b. **basket-bodied** *a.*, having a wicker body.

1903 *Daily Chron.* 19 Oct. 3/2 The wax-headed basket-bodied lady in a draper's window. 1908 *Ibid.* 25 Aug. 7/3 The slender-wheeled basket-bodied chairs.

2. **basket chair**, one made of wickerwork, a wicker chair; **basket-clause** *U.S.*, a clause of a general or comprehensive nature; **basket coil, winding** *Wireless Telegr.* (see quots.); **basket dinner, lunch, picnic** *U.S.*, one for which the provisions are brought in a basket; **basket mat** (see *Mat *sb.*1); **basket-meeting** *U.S.* (see quots.); **basket-plant**, an orchid of the genus *Stanhopea*, grown in baskets through which the flowers protrude; **basket sugar, basket-worm** (see quots.).

a 1631 Donne *Elegies* i. 22 When he swolne, and pamper'd with great fare, Sits downe, and snorts, cag'd in his *basket chaire. 1783 E. Parkman *Diary* 298, 1 great chair 3/- Six lath basket chairs 24/-. 1896 Mrs. Caffyn *Quaker Grandmother* 20 He sank into a well-cushioned basket-chair. 1883 *Congress. Rec.* Feb. 2580/1 This *basket-clause seems to be a sort of Prophetic fine-comb with us. 1897 *Ibid.* Mar. 367/2 If we strike..[an item] from the dutiable list, we transfer it to the 'basket clause' at 25 per cent. 1923 *Daily Mail* 28 Apr. 5 Those compact multilayer coils called '*basket,' 'pancake,' or 'honeycomb' coils. 1904 *Charlotte Daily Observer* 21 Aug. 8 After the speech a *basket dinner will be enjoyed by the picnickers. 1905 *Springfield Weekly Republ.* 11 Aug. 14 At noon a bountiful *basket lunch was served under the trees in the park. 1859 Bartlett *Dict. Amer.* (ed. 2), *Basket-meeting, in the West, a sort of pic-nic, generally with some religious 'exercises'. 1871 Schele de Vere *Americanisms* 191 A corn-husking is announced..and the neighbors from far and near assemble, each bringing his provisions in a basket. From the latter feature these pic-nics derive their names of Basket-meetings. 1874 Eggleston *Circuit Rider* xxiii. 215 He had been to Jenkinsville t'other day to what the Methodis called a 'basket-meetin'. 1889 Farmer *Americanisms*, *Basket-meeting*,..It sometimes occurs in sparsely populated districts, that a clergyman's stipend is largely paid in kind, and the occasions upon which the obligation thus incurred is carried out, are called in the West *basket-meetings*. In the East they are *Donation-parties*. 1904 *Boston Herald* 22 Aug. 6 A long political speech in the open air..at a *basket picnic meeting in Ohio. 1862 *Trans. Ill. Agric. Soc.* (1865) V, The *stanhopea sigrina* (or *basket plant) is exceedingly rare and fragrant. 1902 *Encycl. Brit.* XXXIII. 45/1 In certain districts, notably in the Straits Settlements..it [syrup] is slowly boiled up in open double-bottom pans...The sugar thus produced..forms a species of small-grained concrete. It is called '*Basket Sugar'...In the Straits Settlements the 'Basket Sugar' factories are of considerable importance. 1910 H. M. Hobart *Dict. Electrical Engin.*, *Winding*, *Basket*, more often known as the chain type of winding..., in which the coils belonging to the three separate phases are laid out in two ranges, the centre of one coil or set of coils being occupied by the side or sides of the adjacent coil or coils on opposite sides. 1862 Harris *Insects Injur. Veget.* 415 A case or cocoon..covered with a few little sticks longitudinally arranged. It contained a female chrysalis, with the remains of the caterpillar. In Philadelphia.. these are..popularly called *drop-worms* and *basket-worms*.

Ba·sket-ba·ll. A game played indoors or out of doors with a large inflated rubber ball covered with leather, which is thrown from player to player, the object being to score by casting it into one's opponents' goal, a basket fixed ten feet above the ground at the end of the field of play.

1893 *Birkenhead News* 9 Dec. 7/5 Interesting Basket-Ball Match. 1898 *Daily News* 8 June 5/2 Vassar, Syracuse, Cornell, Wellesley, and Rosemary Hall have each their teams of girl basket-ball players. 1901 *Westm. Gaz.* 1 May 7/1 A game of 'basket ball,' played by ten over-heated and dishevelled ladies in—bloomers! 1926 *Encycl. Brit.* New Suppl. I. 337/2 Basketball has become the national indoor game of the United States...It was invented in 1892 by Dr. James Naismith, at the Y.M.C.A. Training School, Springfield, Mass.

Baskish, var. *Basquish.

Baskonize, *v. trans.* To turn into Basque.

1904 *N. & Q.* 10th Ser. I. 18/2 Castilian *voz* = voice would be baskonized by *bos*.

Basophil (bē·sŏfil), *a.* and *sb. Biol.* Also -phile (-fəil). [f. Gr. βάσις Base *sb.*1 + φίλος loving: see -phil, -phile.] A. *adj.* Applied to cells having an affinity for basic substances; that stains readily with a basic dye. B. *sb.* A cell of this nature. Hence **Basophi·lic, Baso·philous** *adjs.*

1890 Billings *Med. Dict.*, *Basophile*, staining well with basic aniline dyes. 1894 Gould *Dict. Med.*, *Basophilic*.., combining readily with bases; stainable by means of basic dyes. *Basophilous*.., stained by basis rather than by acid dyes (applied to certain cells and tissue-elements). 1898 *Allbutt's Syst. Med.* V. 402 The further division of the latter [the granular form of white blood-corpuscles] into basophil and oxyphil. 1908 *Notes on Books* X. 340/2 The cytogenesis or origin of various blood cells (neutrophil, eosinophil, basophil, and other forms of leucocyte..) in the marrow, is discussed.

Basqueless (ba·skles), *a.* [f. Basque *sb.* + -less.] Without a basque (Basque *sb.* 4).

1895 *Daily News* 3 Sept. 6/3 A tight-fitting coat.., basqueless in front and at the sides, but with a full one at the back. 1909 *Daily Chron.* 8 Dec. 9/2 A basqueless blouse.

Basquish, *a.* and *sb.* Delete †*Obs.* and add: (Also **Baskish.**)

1706 J. Stevens *Sp. & Eng. Dict.* Pref., This Basquish is so different from all the other European Languages. *Ibid.*, *Arriugurridca*, it signifies red Stones in the Basquish Language. 1910 E. S. Dodgson (*title*) The Leiçarragan Verb. From the Baskish New Testament of 1571. 1918 *Trans. Scott. Eccles. Soc.* 229 They..spoke a language probably akin to the Baskish.

Bass, *sb.*2 Add:

1. c. A fibre obtained from the leaf-bases or leaf-stalks of certain palms, used in the manufacture of brushes, ropes, etc.; also the palm from which this fibre is obtained. Also comb.: **bass-broom** (cf. *Bast *sb.*1 1 b).

1881 *Instr. Census Clerks* (1885) 79 Bass Broom Maker. 1883 *Cassell's Fam. Mag.* 222/1 The coarse familiar bass-brooms. 1891 *Kew Bulletin* Jan. 3 (*heading*) Extract of Minute by the Governor of Lagos on the Bass fibre of the Bamboo palm (*Raphia vinifera*). *Ibid.*, The 'African Bass' is..a stiff and wiry fibre, varying in colour from dark brown to light red. 1895 *Army & Navy Co-op. Soc. Price List* p. xx, Bass Brooms. *Ibid.* 182 Bass Heads... Handles for Bass, each extra, 0/2. 1902 Hannan *Textile Fibres Commerce* 145 Bass, Monkey, or Grass, Leopoldinia Piassava or Para Piassava. 1914 *Daily Express* 8 Dec. 4/5 The connection between the war and bass brooms seems at first sight somewhat obscure, but broom manufacturers..explain that the bass comes principally from Germany.

Bass (bæs), *sb.*6 [Proper name: see below.] Bass's ale or beer, the 'India Pale Ale' or 'Bitter Beer' manufactured by Messrs. Bass & Co. of Burton-on-Trent. Also with *a* and *pl.*, a bottle of Bass.

1849 *Illustr. Lond. News* 26 May 336 The consumption of Bass..is beyond belief. 1909 *Daily Chron.* 3 Feb. 4/6 The first signs of returning vitality given by the Prince was to ask feebly for a bottle of 'Bass'.

Bassalia (băsē·liă). *Zoogeogr.* [mod.L., f. late L. *bassus* deep, Base *a.* + Gr. ἁλία assembly, with allusion to ἅλς sea.] The region of the deep sea. Hence **Bassalian** (băsē·liăn), *a.*, of, pertaining to, or found in this region.

1884 T. Gill in *Rep. Nat. Acad. Sci. Washington* (1885) 6 On the Ichthyological Peculiarities of the Bassalian Realm. 1884 *Science* 23 May 621/1 A special realm, which has been called 'Bassalia' or the 'Bassalian realm'.

Bass-court, var. Base-court.

Basset, *sb.*1 Add: *attrib.* in *basset-hound.*

1928 *Morning Post* 20 Oct. 6/1 Basset Hounds—those wholly delightful miniatures of the classic Bloodhound.

Bassine (bæsī·n). [f. Bass *sb.*2 + -ine 4.] A fibre obtained from the leaf-bases of the palmyra *Borassus flabellifer*, used in the manufacture of brooms, ropes, etc. Also *attrib.*, as *bassine broom.*

1902 Hannan *Textile Fibres Commerce* 149 Bassine or Palmyra Fibre. 1923 *Daily Mail* 16 June 10 Best Hair broom, bassine broom (etc.).

Basso-profondo, usually **-profundo** (bæ·so,prǫfǫ·ndo). *Mus.* [It., = deep bass.] A deep bass voice, having a compass of about two octaves above D below the bass stave; also, a singer having a voice of this compass. Also *attrib.*

1860–3 Thackeray *Round. Papers* (1863) 34 (*On ribbons*) Why not a singing artist? Why not a basso-profondo? 1909 *Daily Chron.* 19 Jan. 4/4 The basso-profundo thunderer of the church choir. 1924 *N. & Q.* 22 Mar. 221/1, I heard a song sung by a *basso profundo*, once a professional.

Bass-wood. *U.S.* (Earlier examples.)

1670 *Rowley Rec.* 210 The Northwest Angle is a basswood tree. 1728 *Boston Town Rec.* 25 June VIII. 222 We are of Opinion That no..Black ash, Basswood, or Ceder Shall be Corded up. 1779 *Narrag. Hist. Reg.* I. 41 [I] made a hoe handle of bass wood. 1805 *Massachusetts Spy* 17 July 3/1 The main body [of birds]..appeared to be hovering round the top of an old bosswood [*sic*] tree. 1814 Pursh *Flora Amer. Septentr.* II. 362 *Tilia glabra*..Basswood; Spoonwood.

Bast, *sb.*1 Add: 1. b. **Bast-broom** (cf. *Bass *sb.*2 1 c).

1867 *Ure's Dict. Arts* (ed. 6) I. 282 Bass or *Bast*...The name is also used for the bark or tough fibres of the flax and hemp plants of which Bast brooms are made. 1877 *Design & Work* 11 Aug. 235/2, I have been making some bast brooms.

Bast, *sb.*4 [Persian.] Sanctuary, refuge, asylum. So **Ba·sti**, a refugee.

1894 Safar Nameh *Persian Pict.* 32 Across the gateways a chain is drawn, denoting that the garden is Bast—sanctuary—and into these the European may not go. 1923 *Blackw. Mag.* Jan. 49/1 In Persia the system of 'bast', or asylum, was the only means whereby the oppressed could do something to right..his grievances. *Ibid.* 49/2 The refusal of bast to any one with a legitimate grievance would be an affront to public opinion. *Ibid.* 56/1 The Bastis had not come to the Consulate by my invitation.

Bastard, *a.* Add: 5. f. **Bastard sugar** (cf. *sb.* 10). **Bastard trout**: see Trout *sb.*1 3.

1833 B. Silliman *Man. Sugar Cane* 93 The language of the sugar refiners appears to be tolerably uniform, in applying the term bastard sugar to that which is formed from the first dripping of the lump.

Bastardy. Add:

5. *attrib.*, as *bastardy law*; **bastardy order**, an order made by a magistrate for the support of an illegitimate child by the putative father.

1872 *Act* 35 & 36 *Vict.* c. 65 An Act to amend the Bastardy Laws. 1880 *Act* 43 & 44 *Vict.* c. 32 § 2 This Act may be cited as the Bastardy Orders Act, 1880. 1912 G. Stone *Quest. National Insur.* 100 Will the fact that the mother..is receiving maternity benefit make any difference to the amount of the bastardy order?

Bastnäsite (bæ·stnēsəit). *Min.* [f. F. *bastnaesite* (1841), f. the place-name *Bastnäs*, Sweden, its locality: see -ite 1 2 b.] A fluo-carbonate of cerium, occurring in small imbedded masses, with a greasy lustre and wax-yellow colour.

1872 Dana *Min.* App. I. 2. 1914 *Brit. Mus. Return* 229 Crystals of betafite, bastnäsite, columbite (etc.).

Bastose (bæ·stōus). *Chem.* [f. Bast *sb.*1 + -ose.] = Lignocellulose (see Ligno-). Also *attrib.*

1882 Cross & Bevan in *Jrnl. Chem. Soc.* XLI. 102 We propose to give the name of *Bastose* to this transition modification of cellulose, at the same time observing that as there are many celluloses, so there would be necessarily corresponding forms of bastose. 1902 Hannan *Textile Fibres* 17 The blending of the bastose and plumose fibres to make one complete yarn is not feasible to begin with.

Basuto (băsū·to). A member of a S. African tribe of the Bantu stock. Also *attrib.* or *adj.*

1876 *Encycl. Brit.* V. 47/1 The Basutos, sometimes called Mountain Bechwanas, the fragments of several broken tribes of the Bechwana Kaffres. 1892 Widdicombe *14 Yrs. Basutoland* ii. 20 The Basuto Christians in communion with the English Church are called *Machurche*. 1902 *Encycl. Brit.* XXVI. 166/1 The uplands form excellent grazing grounds for..horses (the hardy and sure-footed 'Basuto ponies'). 1926 *Blackw. Mag.* June 826/1 He is a Basuto.

Bat, *sb.*1 Add:

1. b. Phrase. *To have bats in the belfry*: to be crazy or eccentric. Similarly *to take the bats.*

1911 [see *Belfry 4 e]. 1927 A. E. W. Mason *No Other Tiger* xix, 'On this sort of expedition!' Phyllis Harmer exclaimed, looking at Strickland as if he was a natural. 'Dear man, you've got bats in the belfry.' 1927 *Chambers's Jrnl.* 740/2 Have you taken the 'bats' or what? 1928 *Blackw. Mag.* Jan. 17/2 The sahib had bats in his belfry, and must be humoured.

2. **bats-wing**, applied to that part of the human face which surrounds the eyes and nose.

1908 *Practitioner* Jan. 22 The bat's-wing area of the face.

Bat, *sb.*2 Add: 3. c. In baseball. Hence in fig. phrases, *at bat, hot off the bat. U.S.*

1883 Nye *Baled Hay* 52 An umpire..to decide who is at bat..in a conversation. 1888 *Outing* May 118/2 Ferguson won the toss, sent the Cincinnatis to the bat, and at three P.M... the contest began. *Ibid.* 119/2 The Reds went to the bat, got in two runs, and took the lead by 7 to 5. 1904 *Chicago Even. Post* 23 Aug. 2 The Democrats, of course, claim they were first at bat. 1910 W. M. Raine *B. O'Connor* 65 Turn loose your yarn at me hot off the bat.

V. **bat-willow**, a species of willow from which cricket bats are made.

1907 *Kew Bulletin* No. 8. 311 The supplies of the best 'Bat Willow' have become seriously limited. 1910 *Westm. Gaz.* 6 Apr. 4/2 The fast growing bat-willow..a first-cross between two common varieties of willow..appeared in Norfolk about 1700. It is still chiefly obtained from East Anglia.

Bat, *sb.*4 Also **batt.** *U.S. slang.* [Of obscure origin: cf. *Batter *sb.*4] A spree or frolic.

1848 Durivage & Burnham *Stray Subj.* 102 (Th.) Zenas had been on 'a bat' during the night previous. 1869 W. T. Washburne *Fair Harvard* 69 (Th.) I went to a 'bat' in S.'s room, and we smoked and drank till three. 1891 *Harper's Mag.* Oct. 778/1 He had been on a bat, and all on earth that ailed him was that spree. 1901 [P. L. Ford] *House Party* 188 We defied the Head and went off on the meekest and stupidest little bat you ever saw.

Bat (bæt), *sb.*5 [Hindi, = speech, language, word.] *The bat*: the colloquial speech of a foreign country; chiefly in phr. *to sling the bat.*

1892 Kipling *Barrack-r. Ballads, Route Marchin'* iv, An' ow they would admire for to hear us sling the *bat*. 1919 *Athenæum* 18 July 632/1 Native words picked up by the soldier in India who learned 'to sling the bat' ('bat' itself being another native word for 'the language'). 1919 *War Terms* in *Athenæum* 8 Aug. 729/1 A variant for 'sling the bat' (speak the lingo) is 'spin the bat.' 1924 *Glasgow Herald* 14 Apr. 10 He continued eagerly..'that in the bat of the Arab "Shmallock" and "Amenak" mean "left" and "right"'.

Batavia (bătē·viă). [Name of the capital of the Dutch East Indies.] A kind of shot silk material. Also *attrib.*

1907 *Daily Chron.* 10 June 8/1 A new shot silk, known as 'Batavia'...Smart little coats carried out in this Batavia silk look particularly well. 1909 *Cent. Dict.* Suppl. s.v. *Weave*, *Batavia weave*, a kind of twilled armure weave made on four harnesses.

Batch, *sb.*1 Add:

6. c. The quantity of stricks or bundles of jute laid out at one time for treatment. (Cf. *Batch *v.* 1.)

1880 *Encycl. Brit.* XIII. 803/1 These batches [of jute], which generally contained from 4 to 5 tons each, were allowed to lie from twenty-four to forty-eight hours. 1893 W. Leggatt *Jute Spinning* 21 The batch put down for ordinary hessian warps should be composed of six bales.

d. *Calico-printing* and *Dyeing*. The mass of material collected in 'batching' (cf. *Batch *v.* 2). Also *attrib.*

1911 Trotman & Thorp *Princ. Bleaching and Finishing Cotton* xxviii. 304 The chief use of the machine is to transfer cloth from the lap to the batch form. *Ibid.*, The bearings of the batch roller work in vertical slides under the pressure of springs or weights, and can be raised and held with a pawl to unroll a part of the batch for detailed inspection.

Batch (bætʃ), *v.* [f. Batch *sb.*1]

1. *trans.* To treat (bundles of raw fibre of jute, wool, etc.) in batches for various purposes. Hence **Ba·tching** *vbl. sb.*, the action or process by which this is done. Also *attrib.* Also **Ba·tcher**, an operative who does this.

1880 *Chemical News* XLII. 77/2 The fibres are matted together by a resinous constituent, and in order to fit them for the operations of combing they are subjected to the preliminary treatment of 'batching'. This consists in moistening the fibre with a mixture of oil, [etc.]. 1880 *Encycl. Brit.* XIII. 802/2 (Jute) Batching or Softening. 1881 *Instr. Census Clerks* (1885) 71 Jute preparing: Preparer. Batcher. 1882 P. Sharp *Flax, Tow, & Jute Spinning* 158 In this system the jute is batched in the same way as tow. 1893 W. Leggatt *Jute Spinning* 19 The batchers..break up the large streaks or heads into streaks of about two pounds each. *Ibid.*, The jute warehouse, which will be seen from a reference to the ground plan to adjoin the batching house. 1910 H. R. Carter *Flax, Hemp, & Jute Spinners' Catechism* 11 For common sacking wefts, a cheap batching mixture.. will serve the purpose. 1921 Mackinnon *Social & Industr. Hist. Scot.* II. 115 This is done in the 'batching room', where the raw material is sprinkled with oil and water. 1921 *Dict. Occupational Terms* (1927) § 398 Batcher (flax and hemp); (i) arranges different qualities of tow in layers to facilitate mixing of tow for carder; (ii) applies water and oil to opened out hemp, to soften fibre and to prevent it from 'licking up' during..carding.

2. *Calico-printing* and *Dyeing*. To collect into a 'batch' or mass. Hence **Ba·tching** *vbl. sb.* (also *attrib.*).

1876 *Encycl. Brit.* IV. 685/2 In printing, the white calico is batched at C, and the cloth D passes inwards over tension rails. 1911 H. R. Carter *Bleaching, Dyeing of Flax*, etc. 90 The cloth..is..'batched' on to a larger roller, upon which it is removed for subsequent processes—washing, drying, &c. 1911 Trotman & Thorp *Princ. Bleaching & Finishing Cotton* xxviii. 304 When wound up, the bearings of the batching roller are racked up and the roll unwound or removed. *Ibid.*, The winding-on frame, or canroy, is a frame with tensioning staves, rollers, and scrimp rails, and batching tackle.

Batch, variant of *Bach *v.*

Batea (bătī·ă). *U.S. mining.* [a. Sp. (also Pg.) *batéa* tray, trough.] A shallow wooden vessel used in the washing of ores in California and Mexico.

1859 Mowry *Arizona & Sonora* (1864) 44 In the rubbish which was thrown out of the old mine, a comfortable subsistence is gained by washing in bateas. 1874 Raymond *Sixth Rep. Mines* 315 In these they wash the gravel and earth, by means of wooden bowls or Bateas. 1897 *Engineering Mag.* XVI. 51 Wooden bateas about eighteen inches in diameter (probably used to carry the ore out of the mine).

Bateau. (See also *Batteau, *Battoe.) Add: 2. *attrib.*: *bateau (neck-) line*, in *Dressmaking*, a décolletage having a bow-shaped curve from shoulder to shoulder.

1923 *Daily Mail* 20 Feb. 14 The bateau neck-line...This décolletage still retains its popularity. *Ibid.* 1 Mar. 15 The bateau line is still seen on smart gowns.

Bateless, *a.* Add: 2. Unabating.

1886 P. H. Hayne in *Harper's Mag.* May 884 From heaven of heavens above God speaketh with bateless breath.

Bateleur (bæ·t'lōr). [F., = 'juggler', applied by Levaillant to this eagle.] (In full *bateleur eagle.*) A species of eagle found in South Africa characterized by the shortness of the tail feathers.

1872 C. J. Andersson *Notes Birds Damaraland* 10 Helotarsus ecaudatus..Rufous-backed Bateleur eagle. 1895 Lydekker *Roy. Nat. Hist.* IV. 211 The handsomely coloured bird known as the bateleur eagle..differs from the sea-eagles..by the extreme shortness of its tail. 1914 R. C. F. Maugham *Wild Game in Zambezia* 333 The bateleur eagle is easily identified as he soars aloft in the clear African sky.

Bath, *sb.*1 Add:

9. b. In the hydropathic treatment of disease, any yielding medium, as water (natural or medicated), mud, sand, etc., in which the body is bathed or immersed, or with which it is sprayed or showered: for examples see Douche-*bath*, Mud-*bath*, Needle-*bath*, Sand-bath 2, Shower-bath, Turkish-*bath*, etc.

11. b. *spec.*, *foot-bath*, a small metal bath of oval shape and about one foot deep used in bathing the feet; *hip-bath*, a metal bath with a back in which one may crouch or sit immersed to the hips; *sponge-bath*, a large shallow metal bath in which one may crouch or stand and pour water over the body with a sponge.

1822–34 Hip-bath [see Hip *sb.*1 4 b]. 1858 Foot-bath [see Foot *sb.* 35]. 1859 Sponge-bath [see Sponge *sb.*1 11].

16. b. *spec.* in *dung-bath*: see Dung *sb.* 5 c; *long bath*, a dilute bath in which chemical action is comparatively slow; *short bath*, a concentrated bath; *single bath*, one in which the whole operation is completed; *standing bath*, one that is used continuously; *white bath*: see White *a.* 11 e.

VI. *bath-bed, -brush, -gown, -mat, -robe*; **bath cubes, salts**, toilet preparations for softening or perfuming bath-water; **bath-vat** *poet.* = Bath *sb.*1 11.

1894 *Daily News* 8 Oct. 7/1 The appliances for treatment of special diseases, such as *bath beds for typhoid. 1900 H. Lawson *On Track* 72 In the other hand she carried her tooth-brush and *bath-brush, and soap. 1909 *Westm. Gaz.* 19 Aug. 5/3 The dressing- and *bath-gowns. 1895 *Army & Navy Co-op. Soc. Price List* 190 Felt *Bath Mats. 1905 *Smart Set* Sept. 155/2 A red eiderdown *bath-robe. 1924 Anne D. Sedgwick *Little French Girl* II. v, One undressed in one's room and ran out over the cliff-top in *espadrilles* and bath-robe. 1874 Swinburne *Bothwell* II. xviii. (1882) 216 A cover for his *bath-vat. 1887 Morris *Odyssey* VIII. 456 He gat him up out of the bath-vat.

Bath, *sb.*2 Add:

1. b. As a place of consignment for a person one does not wish to see again, in the phrase *to go to Bath*, chiefly used imperatively.

1837 Barham *Ingol. Leg.* Ser. I. *Grey Dolphin* (1905) 48 'Go to Bath!' said the Baron. 1859 Thackeray *Virgin.* xvi, She may go to Bath, or she may go to Jericho for me. 1908 *Daily Chron.* 27 Oct. 6/6 A later use of the expression was 'Go to Bath and get your head shaved'.

2. **Bath Oliver**, an unsweetened digestive biscuit said to have been invented by William Oliver (1695–1764), a physician of Bath; formerly simply *Oliver*. **Bath White** (*butterfly*), a rare butterfly of the species *Pieris daplidice*, having the under side of the lower wing of a greenish colour spotted with white.

1900 *M. A. P.* 19 May in Ware *Passing Engl.* s.v. 'Bobs' fights on '*Bath Olivers'. 1928 Compton Mackenzie *Extremes Meet* 123 We had a periscope scare about five hours out from Malta...This time it was a Bath Oliver biscuit tin. 1832 J. Rennie *Consp. Butterfl. & M.* Index, *Bath White B. 1885 Kane *European Butterflies* 9 *Pieris Daplidice* L. The Bath White.

Bathing, *vbl. sb.* Add:

1. b. The conditions under which bathing can be carried on at a watering-place, etc. (including the quality of the water, the character of the beach, accessibility, and the like).

1880 *Seaside Watering Places* 18 The bathing is good and safe. 1881 *Dict. Watering Places* 108 The sands and bathing [at Westward Ho] are good, machines and tents abundant.

2. *bathing-house, -robe.*

1816 U. Brown in *Maryland Hist. Mag.* X. 267 Bath or Bathing Houses for each Sex are provided. 1835 J. H. Ingraham *South-West* I. xvi. 174 The long white bathing-houses, which stretched along the south side of the pier. 1924 Anne D. Sedgwick *Little French Girl* II. ix, When they came to the rock where, with safety, the bathing-robes might be deposited.

Bathless (ba·þlĕs), *a.* [f. Bath *sb.*1 + -less.] Without a bath or baths; not taking or having taken a bath. **Ba·thlessness**, bathless condition.

1889 *Century Mag.* Aug. 503/2 A bathless, breakfastless Mexican smokes his cigarette. 1907 *Daily Chron.* 14 Oct. 4/4 A crowd who have worked for a hot week, bathless. 1909 H. G. Hutchinson in *Cornhill Mag.* Aug. 230 About the fact—of the bathlessness of the Pickwickians—we may infer that here is no doubt whatever. 1914 W. J. Locke *Jaffery* 286 With three days' bathlessness of my domestic staff upon my conscience. 1923 *Blackw. Mag.* May 605/1 We both regretted our bathless decision.

Bathmic (bæ·þmik), *a.* [f. Gr. βαθμός: see *Bathmism + -ic.] Of or pertaining to bathmism; exhibiting or caused by bathmism as a form of evolution.

1872 Cope *Origin of Fittest* i. (1887) 26 It is a nice point of phylogeny (or the science of genealogy) to ascertain whether adaptive or strictly 'bathmic' (or embryonic grade) characters came first in a time in a given group. 1879 *Ibid.* vi. (1887) 229, I compared the transmission of bathmic force to that of the phenomenon of combustion. 1905 G. A. Reid *Princ. Heredity* i. 12 The Bathmic [doctrine of racial change], which attributes it to an 'inherent adaptive growth-force'.

Bathmism (bæ·þmiz'm). [f. Gr. βαθμός step, threshold (f. root of βαίνειν to walk, step) + -ism.] A term invented by E. D. Cope to denote a form of chemical force which is active in the processes of growth.

1871 Cope *Origin of Fittest* v. (1887) 205 The Vital forces are (nerve-force) Neurism, (growth-force) Bathmism, and (thought-force) Phrenism.

Batholith (bæ·þolip). *Geol.* Also (now disused) **bathylith** (f. Gr. βαθύς deep). [f. Gr. βάθος depth: see -lith.] Each of a series of masses of granite or anorthosite in a mountain ranged in the direction of its axis, having been brought up from great depths. Hence **Batholi·thic** *a.*

1905 Chamberlin & Salisbury *Geol.* I. 477 Great masses of irregular or undetermined forms..are called *bathyliths*. 1906 *Ibid.* II. 131 The Archean batholiths. 1912 R. A. Daly *Geol. N. Amer. Cordillera* II. 726 The batholithic axes may have indefinite relations to axes of earlier and later crustal deformation.

Bathonian, *a.* Add:

2. *Geol.* Denoting a sub-division of the Jurassic, of which the formations at Bath are typical.

1857 *Q. Jrnl. Geol. Soc.* 17 June 100 The Oolitic rocks.. may be thus tabulated..Portland Oolite. Portlandian. ..Cornbrash, Forest Marble, Bradford Clay, Bathonian. 1903 Geikie *Text-bk. Geol.* (ed. 4) 1140 The Great Oolite (Bathonian), between Dorset and Somerset on the west and Oxfordshire on the east. 1914 *Brit. Mus. Return* 201 Ophiuroidea from..the Bathonian of Ardècke.

Bathy- (bæ·þi), comb. form of Gr. βαθύς deep, as in Bathymetric: **Ba·thyæsthe·sia**, muscle sensation produced by muscular movement (Dorland, *Med. Dict.* 1901). **Bathyco·lpian** *a.*, a more normal form of Bathukolpian (deep-bosomed). **Ba·thylimne·tic** *a.* [Gr. λίμνη pool], pertaining to or inhabiting the depths of freshwater lakes (Webster, Suppl. 1902). **Ba·thylite** [-lite], = *Batholith. **Ba·thyorogra·phically** *adv.*, so as to depict the variations of level in the depths of the sea.

1858 O. W. Holmes *Aut. Breakf.-t.* iv. (1859) 66 The *bathycolpian Herè..sent down Iris. 1902 *Encycl. Brit.* XXVI. 528/2 The Rocky Mountains..comprise, however, in their central parts..great masses of granite that have welled up as '*bathylites' along the axis of elevation. 1921 *Times Lit. Suppl.* 6 Oct. 646/3 This map of the Pacific, on Mollweide's homolographic projection, is *bathyorographically coloured in shades of blue and brown.

Bathybial (băþi·biăl), *a.* [f. Bathybius + -al.] Of or pertaining to bathybius or the depths at which it is found; belonging to or living in the deepest parts of the sea. So **Bathy·bian, Bathy·bic** *adjs.*

1876 *Encycl. Brit.* XXI. 774/2 [Sharks] known to belong to the bathybial fauna. 1881 *Arc. Cruise of Corwin* 14 (Cent. Dict.) The use of the dredge resulted in finding the usual bathybian forms. 1891 G. W. Field tr. *Haeckel's Planktonic Studies* in *Rep. U.S. Fish. Comm.* XVII. 582 The deepest part of this zonary fauna forms the bathybic plankton. 1898 *Athenæum* 4 June 729/3 Bathybial and pelagic life.

Batik (bæ·tik). Also **battik.** [Javanese *'mbatik* writing, drawing.]

1. The Javanese art and method (introduced into England by way of Holland) of executing designs on textiles by covering the material with wax in a pattern, dyeing the parts left exposed, and then removing the wax, the process being repeated when more than one dye is used. Also, a fabric dyed in this way; the kind of pattern, consisting of a medley of colours, characteristic of this art.

1880 *Encycl. Brit.* XIII. 604/2 Another mode is to cover with melted wax or damar the part of the cloth not intended to receive the dye...The 'battiks', as the cloths thus treated are called, are in request by the wealthier classes. 1906 *Daily Chron.* 26 Jan. 4/6 Java is the home of Batik, which is a kind of colour-printing on fabrics. 1922 *Daily Mail* 8 Aug. 3/3 Exact in detail, faultless in design, brilliant in colour, good batik is joy. 1924 *Times Lit. Suppl.* 20 Nov., 'Batik' is a Javanese word, and the art was originally practised in Java, whence the Dutch brought it to Europe over three hundred years ago.

2. *attrib.* passing into *adj.* Executed by the art or method of batik; of, or ornamented with, batik work; hence, loosely, characterized by a fantastic colour-pattern.

1914 *Studio* 14 Mar. 154/2 Examples of embroidery and batik work. *Ibid.* 155/1 Batik Shawl. 1920 *Brit. Museum Return* 64 A piece of batik cloth, dyed with Chinese designs, from Java. 1923 *Advt.* (Nonesuch Press) in *Times Lit. Suppl.* 27 Sept. 627 [Volumes] bound in quarter-vellum with batik sides. 1927 *Punch* 20 Apr. 424/3 He removed his horn-rims and began polishing them vigorously, producing for the purpose a large silk handkerchief of chaste design. There is nothing batik about Edward.

Hence **Ba·t(t)iking** *vbl. sb.*, the production of batik work.

1880 *Encycl. Brit.* XIII. 604/2 A more rapid process of battiking by means of hand stamps has begun to be employed both by native and Chinese workers.

Batoid (bæ·toid), *a.* and *sb.* [f. mod.L. *Batis*, genus of fishes (a. Gr. βατίς flat fish) + -oid.] A. *adj.* Of or belonging to the genus *Batis* or sub-order *Batoidei*. B. *sb.* A fish of this genus or sub-order.

1914 *Brit. Mus. Return* 199 A series of large specimens of Chimæroids and Batoid Selachians have been mounted.

Batologist (bătǫ·lŏdʒist). [f. Gr. βάτος bramble + *-ologist*: see -ology.] One who makes a botanical study of the genus *Rubus*, esp. the blackberry bramble. So **Bato·logy; Batolo·gical** *a.*

1889 *Cent. Dict.* 1897 G. C. Druce *Flora Berks.* 187 Boar's Hill, that very interesting locality to the batologist. 1899 Hanbury & Marshall *Flora of Kent* 109 Our leading English batologist.

Baton, *sb.* 2. Add: *attrib.* esp. in *baton charge*, a charge made by police constables with drawn truncheons.

1900 *Westm. Gaz.* 12 Nov. 5/1 There a large force of police was gathered, and, a baton charge taking place, several people were badly injured. 1906 *Daily Chron.* 2 Nov. 7/6 Bleeding..from stick and baton wounds. 1908 *Ibid.* 28 July 1/7 The police..first attempted to disperse the mob by a baton charge.

Batonless (bæ·tǫnlĕs), *a.* [f. Baton *sb.* + -less.] Without a baton.

1885 [in Dict. s.v. Baton *sb.* 6]. 1906 *Daily Chron.* 7 May 4/5 Batonless conductor. 1909 *Westm. Gaz.* 22 Oct. 5/2 M. Safonoff conducted, and the chorus-singers seemed a little bewildered by his batonless movements.

Bâtonné (batone). *Philately.* [Fr., pa. pple. of *bâtonner* to beat with a stick, f. *bâton* stick.] (See quot. 1897.)

1892 R. B. Earée *Album Weeds* (ed. 2) p. ix. 1897 O. Firth *Postage Stamps* 15 The thin laid paper commonly called 'foreign note' is known in the stamp world as *bâtonné*; if it be plain between the lines for writing on, it is known as 'wove *bâtonné*'; if filled with the usual lines, 'laid *bâtonné*'. *Ibid.* 16 The local Mexican stamps of Guadalajara..are to be found printed upon these *bâtonné* and *quadrillé* papers of various colours. 1928 *Stanley Gibbons' Catal. Stamps, Foreign Countries* 12.

Bâtonnier (batonye). [Fr., = 'staff-bearer', f. *bâton* staff.] The title of the doyen of the Bar of Paris and of Quebec.

1907 *Westm. Gaz.* 26 Nov. 10/1 It is from circumstances connected with St. Catherine's festivals that the 'bâtonnier' of the Paris Bar derives his curious designation. 1918 Sir E. Clarke *Story of my Life* xxviii. 368, I was entertained at dinner by the Quebec Bar; Mr. Donald MacMaster, the batonnier, presided. 1921 *Q. Rev.* Jan. 23 The riding in which he [*sc.* Sir W. Laurier] had practised as a lawyer; in which he achieved the only prize in his profession that ever fell to him—election as batonnier by the Bar of the county.

Batrachiate (bătrē·kiĕt), *sb.* and *a.* [f. Batrachia + -ate 2.] = Batrachian.

1902 *Encycl. Brit.* XXVIII. 139/2 In the batrachiate Amphibia, Héron Royer succeeded in 1883 in rearing..a few hybrids.

Batsman. Add: Also in baseball.

1874 Chadwick *Base Ball Manual* 9 The batsman's position is within a space of ground three feet by six feet.

Batsmanship (bæ·tsmænʃip). [f. Batsman + -ship.] The batsman's art; the art of batting at cricket; batting performance.

1907 *Westm. Gaz.* 30 May 10/1 The Rev. F. H. Gillingham ..has done splendid service for Essex by his vigorous batsmanship. 1912 C. B. Fry (*title*) Cricket: batsmanship.

Batteau, var. of Bateau. Also *attrib.*

1775 *Jrnls. Cont. Congress* III. 447 About one Regiment.. are still employed..as batteau-men on the lakes. 1776 *Ibid.* IV. 111. 1815 Drake *Cincinnati* i. 34. 1834 R. Carlton *New Purchase* viii. 43.

Batten, *sb.*1 1. Add: esp., a strip of wood carrying electric lamps; also attrib. *batten (lamp) holder*, a wall socket for an incandescent lamp-holder.

1899 *Army & Navy Auxiliary C. S. L. Catal.* 384 Batten lampholders. For use on low ceilings, such as lavatories, &c. 1902 *Daily Chron.* 19 July 6/1 That electric light 'battens' should be substituted for gas. 1926 *Electrical Educator* (ed. J. A. Fleming) I. 138/1 The Batten Holder..is just a simpler..form of backplate holder. 1926 *Sun Electrical Co. Catal. Electr. Supplies* 328 Angle Batten Lampholders for window and showcase lighting.

Batten, *v.*2 1. (Earlier U.S. example.)

1675 *Plymouth Rec.* 147 He is to batten the walles and to make a small paire of staires.

Ba·tter, *sb.*4 *slang.* [Of obscure origin: cf. *Bat *sb.*4] A spree.

1839 A. Rodger in *Whistle-Binkie* Ser. II. 17 My hat was smash'd..Ae night when on the batter. 1856 *Knickerbocker Mag.* Nov. XLVIII. 502 Ellis had..just returned from a prolonged batter in Paris. 1865 *N. & Q.* Ser. III. VIII. 369/2 It was among working-men that I first heard 'on the batter' employed as an equivalent for going 'on the spree'.

Batter, *v.*2 2. (U.S. example.)

1815 Drake *Cincinnati* iii. 138 To the height of 40 feet, the wall is battered, or drawn in.

Battery. Add: 4. c. In baseball, the pitcher and catcher. Also *attrib. U.S.*

1888 H. Chadwick in *Outing* May 117/1 The champion team..included Asa Brainard and Douglas Allison as the battery—pitcher and catcher. 1896 Knowles & Morton *Baseball* 101 *Battery*. The pitcher and catcher. The term has its origin in telegraphy, the pitcher being the transmitter, and the catcher the receiver. 1897 *Daily News* 29 July 9/2 So good was the fielding and battery work..that no scoring took place.

5. c. An oblong box or boat submerged to the brim, used in wild fowl shooting; = Sink *sb.*1 12 a. Also *attrib.*, as *battery-gunner, shooting. U.S.*

1859 Bartlett *Dict. Amer.* (ed. 2) 24 *Battery*, a sort of boat used for duck-shooting in the Chesapeake, in which the shooter lies below the surface of the water. 1859 [see Sink *sb.*1 12 a]. 1866 *Game Laws Va.* in *Fur, Fin & Feather* (1872) 144 Any person shooting or using a skiff, box or battery while hunting wild fowl. 1874 J. W. Long *Wild Fowl Shooting* 71, I shall describe that in reference to battery-shooting. 1875 *Fur, Fin & Feather* 120 But this is nothing to the numbers slain by the battery; and we have known one battery to kill over three hundred fowl in a tide. *Ibid.* 122 The battery gunner..has a great advantage over the fowler who shoots from the shore. 1885 *Forest & Stream* 1 Jan. 441 One of the commonest and most successful methods of killing fowl along the seaboard is from batteries. *Ibid.*, Some plan of action by which battery-shooting could be wholly done away with.

7. (Earlier U.S. examples.)

1861 Hittell *Mining in Pacific States* 160 In the Sierra Buttes mills two-thirds of the gold is caught in the batteries. 1872 'Mark Twain' *Roughing it* xxxvi. (1882) 195 These [six rods] rose and fell, one after the other,..in an iron box called a 'battery'...One of us stood by the battery all day long.

12. b. A set of pans used in sugar-boiling.

1833 B. Silliman *Man. Sugar Cane* 33 The largest [kettle] is called the *grande*..and the last the *battery*. 1886 *Harper's Mag.* June 80/2 These processes..are effected by what is known as a 'battery' of open pans or 'taches'.

Batting, *vbl. sb.* 1. b. Add: *attrib.*, as in *batting-glove.*

1910 *Westm. Gaz.* 14 Apr. 7/4 Cricketers will have to pay a trifle more for batting-gloves and bat handles.

Battle, *sb.* 13. Add: *battle fleet, front, battle-practice* (also attrib. in *battle-practice target*).

1898 Kipling *Fleet in Being* ii. 17 That a cruiser at 7.30 that morning had reported to the Battle Fleet..'Enemy to the Westward'. 1902 *Westm. Gaz.* 6 Jan. 4/3 So long as our battle-fleet is able to keep the seas. 1903 *Ibid.* 13 Aug. 6/2 Rear-Admiral Domvile himself cannot get a battle fleet ready until four a.m., twenty hours after Wilson has started. 1905 *Ibid.* 20 June 2/2 Battle-practice has for 1905 been ordered on more regular and practical lines than hitherto. 1909 *Ibid.* 9 Feb. 1/2 Mr. Solano, the inventor of the new system of battle-practice targets, which has received the approval of the War Office. 1914 *Scotsman* 6 Oct. 4/1 The latest news from the two great battle-fronts affords no ground for dissatisfaction.

Ba·ttle-crui·ser. An armoured cruiser or cruiser-battleship (see *Battleship b).

1911 *Times* 22 Nov., In order to distinguish the armoured cruisers of earlier dates from those of the 'Invincible' and later types the latter vessels are to be..classified as battle cruisers. 1914 *Daily Express* 9 Sept. 1/2 The Nuremberg, a German cruiser, is said to be flying from a British battle cruiser.

Ba·ttleplane. [f. Battle *sb.* + *Plane *sb.*3, after *battleship*.] An aeroplane designed for use in warfare, carrying a gun or guns, bombs, etc.; a fighting aeroplane.

[1915 *Daily Express* 15 Oct. 4/3 The French Government has now no objection to the world at large knowing that battle-aeroplanes of large size are being built in France.] *Ibid.* 16 Dec. 4/5 Genuine battleplanes were first heard of officially in the German communiqués. 1917 'Contact' *An Airman's Outings* 180 The Fokkers were satisfactorily dealt with by the de Haviland and the F. E. 'battleplane', as the newspapers of the period delighted to call it. 1917 *Observer* 11 Mar. 10/3 The effort of each side is bent on producing not giant battleplanes but faster and better climbing small craft.

Battleship (bæ·t'lʃip). [Shortening of *line-of-battle ship*: see below.] A warship of the largest and most heavily armoured class designed to meet the most powerful ships in battle.

[*Line-of-battle ship* (also irreg. *line of battle-ship*): a ship of war designed to fight in line of battle: see quot. 1867.

1705 *Admiralty Sec. in Lett.* 5249 (P. R. O.) The capital ships and line-of-battle ships are often laid up in the winter. 1745 *Observ. conc. Navy* 48 It would be of great use on board every Line of Battle Ship. 1800 Nelson in A. Duncan *Life* (1806) 121, I saw the Alexander in chase of a line of battle ship. 1829 Marryat *F. Mildmay* iii, One of the French line-of-battle ships. 1840 *Penny Cycl.* XVI. 118/2 The French force in serviceable line-of-battle ships in March, 1803, was 66. 18.. Adm. Ld. C. E. Paget *Autobiog.* vi. (1896) 193 [In 1859] I protested that the day of line-of-battle ships was past...I had given my evidence before the royal commission strongly urging the construction of ironclads. *Ibid.* 196 Our armour-clads were on the scantling of line-of-battle ships, but with the addition of considerable beam or width. 1861 *Sat. Rev.* 7 Dec. 582 We leave out of view entirely the sailing line-of-battle ships. 1867 Smyth *Sailor's Word-bk.*, *Line-of-battle ships*, formerly those of 74 guns and upwards; or in these iron days, any vessel capable of giving and taking the tremendous blows of the larger ordnance. 1894 *Times* (weekly ed.) 19 Jan. 50/1 A heavily armoured line-of-battleship. 1899 R. Routledge *Discov. & Invent. 19th Cent.* 167 Before the close of 1894, the British navy possessed no fewer than eight of the largest armoured line of battle-ships.]

1884 *Marine Engineer* 1 Apr. 4/2 The very heavily-armed battle-ship. 1886 *Harper's Mag.* June 24/1 Capable of contending on equal terms with the heaviest European battle ships. 1889 *Morning Post* 15 Apr., The new battle-ships. 1898 *Harper's Mag.* XCVI. 830 She has eight battle-ships built. 1902 *Encycl. Brit.* XXXI. 92/2 At that time [1901] British naval practice..was to put 9-inch armour on to the sides of battleships and 4-inch on to the sides of cruisers.

b. *Cruiser-battleship* or *battleship cruiser*: a battleship of the type designed for speed, less heavily armoured than a ship of the line.

1909 *Whitaker's Alm.* 681/2 Modern vessels of this class are no longer, save in official phraseology, 'armoured cruisers', but 'cruiser-battleships', or 'cruiser-Dreadnoughts'. 1909 *Westm. Gaz.* 18 Mar. 7/2 Armoured cruisers, or 'battleship cruisers,' as they have been popularly termed.

c. *attrib.*

1901 *Westm. Gaz.* 8 Aug. 6/1 To choose his own time and place for the battleship action. 1904 *Ibid.* 11 Feb. 8/2 The battleship strength of the Russians at Port Arthur. 1908 *Ibid.* 11 Feb. 3/3 When the Dreadnought appeared battleship building in foreign yards paused. 1908 *Daily Chron.* 21 Aug. 1/7 The American battleship fleet.

Battlesome, *a.*1 (Modern U.S. example.)

1888 *Harper's Mag.* Apr. 690 Of battlesome wit..the author has so much of his own that he has given some to all of his characters.

Battleworthy (bæ·t'lwɒ̄:ɹði), *a.* [f. Battle *sb.* + Worthy *a.*; after *seaworthy*.] Of a ship:

Supplement, p. 3873; Corrigenda, p. 4092; Spurious words, p. 4093; Books quoted, p. 4094

That is in a perfectly fit condition for fighting. Also *transf.* Hence **Ba·ttlewo:rthiness.**

1889 MUNDELLA *Sp. in Ho. Comm.* 22 Feb., A really good battleworthy sword. 1892 *Pall Mall G.* 13 Sept. 2/2 If the ship is not battle-worthy, the best thing is to sell her or break her up at once. 1904 *Times* (weekly ed.) 1 Jan. 7/1 Battle-worthiness—a..compendious term, including all the essential qualities required of a vessel intended to fight in line.

Battling, *vbl. sb.*⁴ Add: *battling-bench, -board, -stick.*

1845 J. J. HOOPER *Taking Census* II. 183 John Green's sister..goes to her battlin bench. 1851 — *Widow Rugby's Husb.* 96 What a devil of a paddlin' the old woman gin him with the battlin'-stick. 1887 *Harper's Mag.* July 272/1 The splay legged battling-boards fastened themselves into the earth under the blows of the bats.

Ba·ttoe, freq. obs. U.S. var. of BATEAU.

1758 *Essex Inst. Hist. Coll.* XII. 135, I went up ye River in a Battoe with the Baggage. 1770 WASHINGTON *Diaries* I. 381 Got the Battoe, and the two Boats round to the Mill with Stone. 1774 P. V. FITHIAN *Jrnl.* (1900) 209 It is a light neat Battoe elegantly painted and is rowed with four oars.

Hence **Battoe man** (cf. *batteau-man* s.v. *BATTEAU), **Battoeing** *vbl. sb.*

1760 *Essex Inst. Hist. Coll.* XX. 199 This Day ye Battoue men marched off. *Ibid.*, To Day there was a Draught out of our Company for battowing from fort Miller to fort Edward.

Batty (bæ·ti), *a. colloq.* or *slang.* [f. BAT *sb.*¹ + -Y¹.] 'Balmy', 'dotty'. (Cf. *BAT *sb.*¹ 1 b.)

1922 *Short Stories* Feb. 18/2, I must be getting batty as well as gray. 1926 *British Weekly* 25 Nov. 242/3 He's a bit batty every now and anon.

Bauera (bau·ərǎ). [mod.L., f. the name of Franz and Ferdinand *Bauer*, botanical draughtsmen.] The Tasmanian name for a shrub of the species *Bauera rubioides*, one of the three Australasian species of the genus, N.O. *Saxifragaceæ*. Also *attrib.*

1835 *Ross's Hobart Town Alm.* 70 *Bauera rubiæfolia.* Madder leaved Bauera. 1888 R. M. JOHNSTON *Geol. Tasmania* Introd. 6 The Bauera scrub..is a tiny, beautiful shrub. 1927 *Chambers's Jrnl.* May 345/1 An impenetrable thicket of bauera.

Bauhinia (bǫhi·niǎ). [mod.L. (Linnæus 1737), named after Jean (1541–1613) and Gaspard *Bauhin* (1560–1624).] A genus of plants (N.O. *Leguminosæ*) of which there are many tropical species. Also *attrib.*

1833 *Penny Cycl.* I. 447/1 (*America*) Bauhinias..cling round the trees like enormous cables. 1849 CAPT. C. STURT *Narr. Exped. C. Australia* I. 359 The Bauhinia here grew to the height of 16 to 20 feet. 1887 MOLONEY *Forestry W. Africa* 187 Plaintain and Bauhinia fibres. 1922 *Chambers's Jrnl.* Dec. 859/2 Trees..with a good deal of Bauhinia creeper all over.

Bauxite [F. *bauxite*, 1821], var. BEAUXITE.

1872 *Jrnl. Chem. Soc.* XXV. 467 Bauxite from the Wochein (Austria). 1883 *Ibid.* XLIV. *Abstracts* 397 The practical value of bauxite depends on the high amount of alumina in proportion to the silica. 1922 *Blackw. Mag.* July 18/2 A pink vein of bauxite ore.

Bavarian (bǎvēə·riǎn), *a.* [f. *Bavaria* + -AN.] Of or belonging to Bavaria; in special collocations (see quots.).

1880 WEBSTER Suppl. s.v. *Cream*, *Bavarian cream*, a preparation of gelatine, milk, cream, and eggs, flavored, and eaten cold. 1892 *Encycl. Cookery* (ed. T. F. Garrett) I. 9/2 Almond Bavaroise, or Bavarian Cream. *Ibid.* 87/2 *Bavarian beer*..The average beer brewed is not of a very high alcoholic character, and is said to obtain some of its characteristic flavour from the pitch used to line the casks. *Ibid.*, *Bavarian creams*, a great variety of these are to be found under the name of Bavaroises. 1893 *Ibid.* II. 385/2 Bavarian Sauce. 1893 KNECHT, RAWSON, & LOEWENTHAL *Man. Dyeing* 479 Diphenylamine-blue. $C_{37}H_{30}N_3$.Cl. Bavarian Blue..gives a finer blue shade than..any other blue.

Bawl, *v.* Add: **3. c.** With *out*: To reprove or reprimand loudly or severely. *U.S.*

1907 REX BEACH *Barrier* xvii. (1908) 270 If you'll go back on your word like this you'll 'bawl me out' before the priest. 1917 MATHEWSON *Sec. Base Sloan* xv. 203 You'll get bawled out when you pull a boner. *Ibid.* xviii. 239 Wayne thought that the manager's 'bawling out' that forenoon had done good. 1922 H. L. FOSTER *Adv. Trop. Tramp* ix. 119 In private Griffis bawled me out for my rashness.

Hence **Bawl-out** *sb.* a 'taking-down'. *U.S.*

1926 J. BLACK *You Can't Win* vi. 70, I..don't want to..give myself a bawl-out in front of the woman.

Bawley (bǭ·li). *local.* Also **bauley, baully.** [Of obscure origin.] A fishing smack peculiar to the coasts of Essex and Kent. Also *attrib.*, as *bawley-boat.*

1888 *Sat. Rev.* 24 Mar. 349 A little creek where barges and bawley-boats can ride. 1895 *E. Angl. Gloss.*, *Bauley Boats*, Harwich fishing-smacks. 1921 *Spectator* 7 May 589/1 Leigh-on-Sea is the producer of the bawley, a type of craft which has a loose-footed mainsail, but would otherwise be called a cutter.

Bay, *sb.*¹ **4.** Add: **bay-gall** *U.S.* (see quots.); **bay-rum** (earlier U.S. examples); **bay-swamp** *U.S.* = BAY *sb.*² 4 b.

1871 SCHELE DE VERE *Americanisms* (1872) 440 *Bay-Galls are large, gloomy, almost impenetrable swamps in Florida, full of deer, bear, and catamount. 1889 *Century Dict.*, *Bay-gall*, a watercourse covered with spongy earth, mixed with matted fibers, and impregnated with acids. 1902 WEBSTER Suppl., *Bay-gall* 1. (*Bot.*) The red bay (*Persea Borbonia*, syn. *P. Carolinensis*). 2. A tract of boggy land, esp. one overgrown with bay trees and gall-berry bushes (Southern U.S.). 1846 *U.S. Statutes* IX. 44 Ale, beer,..*bay rum. 1859 BARTLETT *Dict. Amer.* (ed. 2) 25 *Bay Rum*..is chiefly used for the purposes of the toilet. 1765 J. BARTRAM *Jrnl.* (1769) 7 Then savannahs and ponds,..together with the cypress and *bay-swamps. 1832 D. J. BROWNE *Sylva Amer.* 164 These spots are entirely covered with the loblolly bay, and are called Bay Swamps.

Bay, *sb.*² Add: **4. b.** (Earlier examples.)

1806 WEBSTER, *Bay*..land covered with the bay tree (Carol.). 1845 W. G. SIMMS *Wigwam & Cabin* 17 He wandered along the edges of a dense bay or swamp-bottom.

5. bay-bird *U.S.*, a shore-bird that frequents the bays and estuaries of the Atlantic coast; **bay-craft** *U.S.*, a vessel or vessels used in the navigation of bays; **bay-ice** (earlier example); **bay-snipe** *U.S.* = *bay-bird*; **Bay State** *U.S.* (earlier examples); **bay-vessel** *U.S.* = *bay-craft.*

1789 *Maryland Jrnl.* 2 Jan. Advt. (Th.) Within a Quarter of a Mile of Bear-creek, which is navigable for *Bay-craft to its head. 1835 LATROBE *Rambler in N. Amer.* (1836) II. 102 Many a settler loads his small bay-craft with planks and shingles in the spring of the year. 1818 SCORESBY in *Ann. Reg. 1817, Chron.* 534 This is termed *bay-ice. 1875 *Fur, Fin & Feather* 121 It is also a capital place for *bay-snipe shooting in summer. 1801 *Spirit of Farmer's Museum* 198 Down here in the *Bay State and all about the country. 1837 R. M. BIRD *Nick of Woods* I. 132 He was from the Down-East country; a representative of the Bay State. 1789 *Maryland Jrnl.* 24 Feb. (Th.) I will exchange a small *Bay Vessel for a large one, and give the difference.

Bay, *sb.*³ Add:

5. b. A section of a trench in which the line is modified in order to allow more space for passing.

1916 BOYD CABLE *Action Front* 73 The trenches..with bays and niches cut deep in the side to permit the passing of anyone meeting a line of pack-burdened men in the shoulder-wide alley-way. 1918 E. A. MACKINTOSH *War, the Liberator* 154 'Don't put it in so high up, boys,' he said. 'They'll see it and knock this bay to hell.'

6. A side or subordinate line of railway at a station; also *attrib.* in **bay-line**, a line at the side of, and terminating in, a railway station.

1906 *Westm. Gaz.* 20 Sept. 7/1 A bay line out of Grantham Station crosses some of the roads. 1907 *Ibid.* 10 June 9/1 The passenger station has not been interfered with, except in No. 1 bay-line. 1928 W. GILLETTE *Astound. Crime Torrington Rd.* 1. 7 Kept an eye on him through the station when we got in—South Station, not Back Bay.

Bay, *a.*¹ (and *sb.*). Add:

2. b. *The Bays*: see quots.

1837 *Hist. Records Brit. Army, Second Dragoon Guards* 64 About this period [1767] the regiment was mounted on Bay Horses; and as the other regiments of heavy cavalry were mounted on black horses (except the Scots Greys) the Queen's Dragoon Guards were commonly styled the Queen's Bays. 1878 R. TRIMEN *Regiments Brit. Army* 14 Second Dragoon Guards..Being mounted on bay horses about 1767 caused it to be called the 'Queen's Bays'...It is now commonly called 'the Bays'.

Bay, *v.*⁶ [f. BAY *sb.*²] *intr.* To spread *out* in a bay-like form.

1906 A. HOPE *Sophy of Kravonia* viii, The town was no more than one long street, which bayed out at the farther end into a market-place.

Bayadère. Add:

2. Any textile fabric having stripes running across the material. Also *attrib.* or as *adj.*, defining a material striped in this way.

1879 *Cassell's Fam. Mag.* Apr. 312/1 Pompadour silks with Bayadère stripes beneath the bunches of flowers are somewhat new.

Bayberry. 2. (Earlier examples.)

1687 *Manchester* (Mass.) *Rec.* 32 The sd. tree being near Vincsons baiberry medow. 1769 *Massachusetts Gaz.* 21 Dec., Advt. (Th.) Bayberry-wax candles. 1773 *Boston Gaz.* 19 July, Advt. (Th.) Mould, Dip, and Bayberry Candles. 1792 J. BELKNAP *New Hampsh.* III. 123 The bay berry (*myrica cerifera*), the leaves of which yield an agreeable perfume, and the fruit a delicate green wax, which is made into candles.

Bay-like (bē¹·ləik), *a.* [f. BAY *sb.*² + -LIKE.] Resembling a bay.

1874 DISRAELI in Buckle *Life* (1920) V. ix. 354 The waters glittering in the bay-like coast. 1897 MARY KINGSLEY *W. Africa* 130 The great forest sweeping away in a bay-like curve.

Bay-man, bayman¹. [BAY *sb.*² 5.]

1. A resident beside a bay (usu. some specific bay); one accustomed to navigating a bay. (In early use with reference to the mahogany-cutters of Honduras.)

1765 *Ann. Reg., Chron.* 101/1 Numbers of the baymen's slaves desert daily to the Spaniards. 1779 [see BAY *sb.*² 5]. 1812 *Ann. Reg. 1810*, 621 This is the bay-man's greatest evil, for the wood more particularly subject to this inconvenience is invariably the largest and of the finest quality. 18.. *Shore Birds* 43 (Cent.) When the birds are traveling with the wind, or as baymen call it, a 'free wind'. 1904 *N. Y. Even. Post* 11 June, Somers P'int, as the baymen call it, is one of several very attractive summer resorts that have grown up about the bay in recent years.

2. *U.S. Hist.* An inhabitant or native of Massachusetts Bay.

1773 W. GORDON *Hist. Amer. Rev.* (1788) I. 272 [These publications] suited the too levelling disposition of the Baymen. 1775 *Ibid.* II. 38 There is too great a nationality among the Bay-men.

Bayman². *U.S.* [BAY *sb.*³ 3.] A sick-bay nurse.

1888 CHURCHWARD *Blackbirding* 25, I stole a beautiful knife from the sick bayman's locker. 1891 H. PATTERSON *Naut. Dict.* 346 *Bayman*, a hospital nurse.

Bayonet, *sb.* Add: **5.** Also *bayonet plant.*

1823 W. FAUX *Memorable Days* 82 Hedges of bagonet plants and myrtles.

6. bayonet-capped *a.*, fitted with a cap for fastening in a socket as a bayonet joint; **bayonet catch**, the spring catch by which a bayonet is secured to a rifle.

1904 *Daily Chron.* 18 June 2/6 *Bayonet-capped [electric] lamps. 1901 'LINESMAN' *Words Eyewitness* (1902) 317 They have struck as true and hard as any, right up to the *bayonet-catch.

Bayou. Add: Also **byo, bayeau**, *pl.* **bayoux.** Earlier and later examples are:—

1806 ASHE *Trav. Amer.* xl. (1808) 323 Below the Red River, five miles, is one of the most dangerous bayeaus on the Mississippi. 1822 BRACKENRIDGE *Views Louisiana* (1814) 162 On some of these bayoux the land is sufficiently high to admit of settlements. 1834 CROCKETT *Narr. Life* vi. 53 A small byo, across which there was a log. 1872 *Amer. Naturalist* VI. 725 A peculiar feature of the bottom lands of the western and southern rivers, locally termed bayous. 1901 S. E. WHITE *Westerners* xiii. 93 In a word the broad sea of the wilderness has shrunken to bayous and bays.

attrib. 1886 *Harper's Mag.* Aug. 483/1 The following bayou version of one of the negro folk-lore stories.

Be, *v.* Add:

4. b. slang phr. (derived from the music halls) *Now we shan't be long!*: expression denoting satisfaction with an arrangement, state of affairs, etc.: often used sarcastically.

1897 MAUGHAM *Liza of Lambeth* v, 'Now we sha'n't be long!' she remarked, as she handed him back the pot. 1897 *Oxford Mag.* 27 Jan., By the time he's through the trembling bard has written half his song, While his tyrant watching grimly mutters 'Now we shan't be long'.

6. c. *Been and* (*gone and*) —: vulgar expletive amplification of the pa. pple. of a verb, used to express surprise or annoyance at the act specified.

1837 DICKENS *Pickw.* xxvi, Lauk, Mrs. Bardell,..see what you've been and done! 1848 THACKERAY *Van. Fair* xv, Sir Pitt has been and proposed for to marry Miss Sharp. 1891 *Temple Bar* Aug. 470 That I should actually have been and gone and told him so!

Beach, *sb.* **4.** Add:

beach crab, any crab of a species living on sea-beaches, esp. *Ocepoda arenaria*; **beach cusp**, a cusp of gravel or sand found at intervals of about 20 to 30 feet on a beach; **beach gown**, a bathing wrap; **beach-grass** (earlier U.S. example); **beach-man**, 'a person on the coast of Africa who acts as interpreter to ship-masters, and assists in conducting the trade' (Ogilvie 1881); **beach-plum** *U.S.* (see quot.); **beach-wagon** (U.S. quot.).

1900 J. C. BRANNER in *Jrnl. Geol.* VIII. 481 (*title*) The Origin of *Beach Cusps. 1900 *Geog. Jrnl.* Dec. 704 The author comes to the conclusion that beach cusps are produced by the interference of two sets of waves of translation on the beach. 1928 *Sunday Dispatch* 8 July 16 When getting a bathing suit, don't forget a *beach-gown, which is now worn with a monk's hood, on the shore. 1833 *Mass. Statutes* 21 Mar., An Act to prevent the Destruction of *Beach Grass in the towns of Provincetown and Truro. 1877 BARTLETT *Dict. Amer.* (ed. 4) 550 *Sand-Plum*,..a *beach-plum. A plum growing on plum-trees whose habitat is sandy beaches. 1868 MISS ALCOTT *Little Women* (1869) II. iii. 35, I shall hire a *beach-wagon.

Bea·ch-co:mbing, *vbl. sb.*

1. Living as, or following the occupation of, a beach-comber (see BEACH *sb.* 4).

1918 W. J. LOCKE *Rough Road* iv, An old hand who knew the whole thing backwards, from company promoting to beach combing.

2. *Mining.* Working the sands on a beach for gold, tin, or platinum.

1900 *Coal and Metal Miners' Pocketbk.* (ed. 6) Gloss.

Beach-la-mar (bītʃ la māɹ). (Also biche-.) [Alteration of Pg. *bicho do mar* *BÊCHE-DE-MER.] The jargon English used in the Western Pacific.

1910 in Bohun Lynch *Isles of Illusion* (1923) 61, I will omit the Biche-la-mar and give you the gist of his story. 1911 W. CHURCHILL (*title*) Beach-la-mar.

Bea·chward, -wards, *advs.* [see -WARD, -WARDS.] In the direction of or towards the beach.

1831 *Blackw. Mag.* XXIX. 883 A neap-tide comes flowing beachward. 1896 KIPLING *Seven Seas, Song of Banjo*, The grandam of my grandam was the Lyre..That the Stealer stooping beachward filled with fire. 1909 *Daily Chron.* 21 Sept. 7/4 He put the dinghey about and ran beachwards.

Beaconed, *a.* (Modern U.S. example.)

1890 *Harper's Mag.* Sept. 596/2 The beaconed ledges and buoyed reefs..slip helplessly into the Powder Fog.

Beaconite (bī·kənəit). [f. *beacon* in the title of I. Crewdson's *A beacon to the Society of Friends*, 1835 + -ITE¹.] In the history of the Quakers, one of a party who, following the lead of Isaac Crewdson, held that the current Quaker doctrines were contrary to Scripture and seceded in 1836.

1836 J. SOUTHALL in *Jrnl. Friends Hist. Soc.* (1920) XVII. 82 The Beaconites preach up charity so exclusively. *Ibid.* 83 A..man..labouring under disadvantage from Beaconite associations. 1921 R. M. JONES *Later Periods Quakerism* I. ix. 310 The position of the 'Beaconites'—*i.e.* the position of literalism and ultra-orthodoxy.

Bead, *sb.* Add: **5.** *spec.* of sweat, esp. on the face.

1888 A. C. GUNTER *Mr. Potter of Texas* v, [He] wipes the great beads of exhausted toil from his forehead. *Ibid.*, The beads of perspiration.

8. bead lightning (see quot.); cf. *beaded lightning*; **bead-plane**, a carpenter's plane for running a bead on moulding; **bead-stone**, also, see quot.

1899 *Rep. Smithsonian Inst.* (1901) 129 *Bead lightning..is a very beautiful luminous appearance, like a string of beads hung in a cloud. 1858 SIMMONDS *Dict. Trade*, *Bead-plane*, a moulding plane of semicylindrical contour. 1896 *Trans. Victoria Inst.* XXVIII. 206 *Bead-stone is also called St. Cuthbert's beads, Fairy beads..and St. Boniface's money. They are the ring-like transverse sections of the so-called Vertical Column of stalked Echinoderms.

Beaded, *ppl. a.* Add:

5. *Beaded-edge*, defining a kind of pneumatic tyre with bead or thickened edge that fits into the turned-over rim of the wheel. *Beaded lightning*, bead lightning (see *BEAD *sb.* 8).

1902 *Windsor Mag.* May (Advt.), Wired or *beaded edges optional. 1904 *Westm. Gaz.* 19 Sept. 9/1 The Bartlett beaded-edge—or, as it is more generally known, the Clincher—tyre. 1889 *Morning Post* 29 June 5/7 Photographs of lightning..arranged..according to their form—stream,..*beaded..lightning.

Beader (bī·dəɹ). [f. BEAD *sb.* or *v.* + -ER¹.]

1. a. One who sews beads on fancy work. **b.** One who puts a beading on an article.

1881 *Instr. Census Clerks* (1885) 105 Beader (Coach), Beader (Lace), Beader on Net. 1886 BESANT *Childr. Gibeon* II. iv, She was a beader she was that clever with her fingers she could do all kinds of things. 1921 *Dict. Occupational Terms* (1927) § 254 *Beader*..a press hand who places machine folded body of tin..on block of beading machine and operates lever to form a beaded edge. *Ibid.* 407 *Beader, bead trimmer, bead worker*,..sews beads, by hand, upon a fabric foundation. *Ibid.* 414 *Beader*..applies waxy mixture..round edge of sole [etc.].

2. A machine for cutting or stamping a bead or beading.

1884 KNIGHT *Dict. Mech.* Suppl.

b. A woodworker's tool resembling a spoke-shave, having a number of interchangeable irons for cutting various forms of beading.

1909 *Cent. Dict.* Suppl.

Beading, *vbl. sb.* **3.** Add:

spec. in *Arch.* and *Joinery*, a bead; also collectively, the beads of a moulding. Also *attrib.*, as *beading plane* = *bead-plane* (see *BEAD *sb.* 8).

1858 SIMMONDS *Dict. Trade.* 1875 *Carpentry and Join.* 27 The beading planes are made of various widths.

Beady, *a.* Add:

1. b. *Comb.*, as *beady-eyed* adj.

1873 M. F. MAHONY *Chron. Fermors* I. xiii. 249 That beady-eyed,..lanthorn-cheeked little lady. 1897 KIPLING in *Pearson's Mag.* Dec. 615/2 The 600 quick-footed, beady-eyed rank and file. 1904 *Daily Chron.* 15 Sept. 4/4 A beady-eyed inscrutable stare.

2. b. Of a garment, material, etc.

1892 *Longman's Mag.* May 76 Beady and buttony girls. 1897 *Daily News* 25 June 3/1 Cheap black, sheeny cloth, very beady, much trimmed.

Beagle. 3. *beagle-hound* (mod. U.S. example).

1902 S. E. WHITE *Blazed Trail* xxxi. 221 He left behind him four little long-eared, short-legged beagle-hounds.

Beagling (bī·gliŋ), *vbl. sb.* [f. BEAGLE *sb.* + -ING¹.] The sport of hunting with beagles. Hence **Bea·gle** *v. intr.*, to hunt with beagles; **Bea·gler.**

1889 *Pall Mall G.* 24 Oct. 7/1, I am in the habit of accompanying my brothers out shooting and beagling. 1895 *Daily News* 20 July 8/2 Coursing—which, with 'beagling' and 'harriers,' takes up a large part of the book. 1910 *Humanitarian* Mar. 21/1 Beaglers' manners. 1915 *Oxford Mag.* 5 Mar., He beagled and played cricket. 1923 J. O. PAGET *Beagles & Beagling* i. 15 The sport of beagling is every day becoming more popular.

Beak, *sb.*¹ Add:

1. c. *transf.* The long snout of a fish.

1889 in *Cent. Dict.* 1927 *Observer* 24 July 22 A 38-lb. cock-salmon...I was obliged to measure it, and I made it over 50 inches, from tail to beak.

Beak, *sb.*³ Add:

b. *transf.* (*Schoolboys' slang.*) A schoolmaster.

1888 *Pall Mall G.* 9 Feb. 5/1 One of the Eton masters, or 'beaks', if we may be allowed to use a schoolboy phrase. 1918 E. F. BENSON *David Blaize* ix, You can have your crib spread out..and he won't see it. He didn't ought to be a beak at all. 1926 *Spectator* 11 Sept. 383/1 This scholarly Irishman and Eton 'beak'.

Beak, *v.* Add:

4. *trans.* To ram (a vessel). Also *absol.* Hence **Bea·king** *vbl. sb.*

1898 KIPLING *Fleet in Being* 55 We could run in and beak 'em while it's thick. I believe in beaking...Oh, he'd beak like a shot, if he saw his chance.

Beaked, *ppl. a.* **2. c.** Add:

Beaked whale (see quot.).

1877 *Encycl. Brit.* VII. 280/2 The *Hyperoodontidæ*, or beaked-whales, are widely distributed in northern, southern, and tropical seas.

Beam, *sb.*¹ Add:

24. *Wireless Telegr.* In full *wireless beam*: Wireless waves sent as a beam, i.e. undispersed, from a special aerial system, part of which acts as a reflector; used *attrib.* in *beam* (*wireless*) *system*, *-station.*

[1899 MARCONI in *Jrnl. Inst. Electrical Engin.* XXVIII. 274 Should it be necessary to direct a beam of rays in one given direction I prefer to use an arrangement similar to a Righi oscillator placed in the focal line of a suitable cylindrical parabolic reflector.] 1924 (July 2) MARCONI in *Jrnl. R. Soc. Arts* 25 July 607/2 The transmission and reception of intelligible signals over a distance of 1½ miles of a beam system employing short waves and reflectors. 1924 *Westm. Gaz.* 24 July, Arrangements had been made for the erection of a beam station in Canada. 1924 *Daily News* 14 Nov. 7/4 Beam wireless. 1928 *Morning Post* 23 Mar. 14 Beam-cable fusion [*sc.* of the Eastern Exchange Cable Company and Marconi Company]...The beam system of telegraphy.

IV. beam-action, the action of a **beam-engine**, a steam engine having a vibrating beam through which the piston effort is transmitted to the crank.

1844 H. STEPHENS *Bk. Farm* II. 312 The *beam-engine of 6-horse power. 1874 KNIGHT *Dict. Mech.*, *Beam-engine*..., an engine with an oscillating beam, to whose respective ends the connecting-rod from the piston and the pitman from the crank are attached. 1896 *Daily News* 7 Jan. 6/5 The..beam-action locomotives of that extremely primitive line [Stockton and Darlington Railway]. *Ibid.*, A slow moving and dignified beam-engine.

Beam, *v.* Add:

3. b. Of a person: To smile radiantly.

1893 *Illustr. Sporting & Dram. News* 11 Mar. 28/2, I..tried to beam on a friend—albeit, a poor beamer at the best. 1900 ELINOR GLYN *Visits Eliz.* (1906) 14 He..jumped off his horse and beamed—just as if we had parted the best of friends.

III. *trans.* To transmit by the beam system of wireless telegraphy. (Cf. *BEAM *sb.*¹ 24.)

1927 *Daily Express* 5 July 3/3 The King's message..was almost instantaneously 'beamed' to the receiving station at Milnerton, seven miles from Capetown.

Beamage (bī·medʒ). [f. BEAM *sb.*¹ + -AGE.] A deduction for loss of weight by evaporation in cooling, made in weighing the dressed carcass of a beast.

1902 in WEBSTER Suppl.

Beaming, *vbl. sb.* **2.** Add:

Comb., as *beaming-tool*; **beaming machine** (*a*) a machine for beaming and working hides; (*b*) a machine for filling the beams of looms with yarn; also called *beaming mill.*

1874 KNIGHT *Dict. Mech.* 257/2 Beaming-machine. (Leather.) *Ibid.*, The beaming-tool *f* is brought in contact with the leather or raised therefrom by means of the eccentric-rods. 1878 *Sci. Amer. Suppl.* 1938 Self-stopping Beaming Machine. 1884 KNIGHT *Dict. Mech.* Suppl. 85/1 *Beaming Machine*, one for filling yarn beams of looms.

Bean. Add:

4. Queensland or **Leichhardt's bean**, Australian names for a tall climbing leguminous plant *Entada scandens*, bearing long scimitar-shaped pods, which are used to make match-boxes, snuff-boxes, etc.: the seed is also called *match-box bean* (see MATCH *sb.*² 5) and *scimitar-pod* (see SCIMITAR 3).

1889 J. H. MAIDEN *Useful Native Plants Australia* 175 *Entada scandens*..'Queensland Bean', 'Leichhardt Bean'.

5. b. The head. *U.S. slang.*

1921 R. D. PAINE *Comr. Rolling Ocean* x. 168 If these Dutchmen get nasty, bang their blighted beans together.

6. e. Slang phrases. *To know beans* (U.S.): to know something, to be well-informed; *not to care beans*, not to care at all. *A hill of beans* (U.S.): a thing of little value. *To spill the beans* (U.S.): to make a mess of things. *To be full of beans*: to be full of energy, and in high spirits (cf. BEANY *a.*). *To give* (a person) *beans*: to deal severely with, to punish heavily; so *to get beans.* *Old bean* (cf. OLD *a.* 8), a familiar form of address.

1855 *Yale Lit. Mag.* XX. 192 (Th.) Whatever he knows of Euclid and Greek, In Latin be don't know beans. 1857 *Knickerbocker Mag.* Feb. XLIX. 138 (Th.) I don't care beans for the railroad. 1863 'E. KIRKE' *My Southern Friends* v. 80, I..karn't take Preston's note—'taint wuth a hill o' beans. 1888 *Chicago Herald* (Farmer) One has to know beans to be successful in the latest Washington novelty for entertainment at luncheons. 1901 HARBEN *Westerfelt* 5 He didn't care a hill o' beans fer no gal. 1904 'O. HENRY' *Cabbages & Kings* xii. 216 He wasn't a hill of beans to her. 1919 T. K. HOLMES *Man fr. Tall Timber* xxviii. 355 'Mother certainly has spilled the beans!' thought Stafford in vast amusement. 1921 R. D. PAINE *Comr. Rolling Ocean* viii. 136 The beans are spilled, and that is what Maddigan guessed the moment he set eyes on you.

1881 EARL GRANVILLE in Fitzmaurice *Life* (1905) II. 237 'Full of beans', an 'ossy' phrase. 1911 GALSWORTHY *Patrician* I. x, Versatile, 'full of beans'. 1925 *Daily News* 20 Aug. 7/1 He does it—being full of grit, And also full of beans, sir! 1927 JOSEPHINE ELDER *Thomasina Toddy* xxiii. 226 We start off—oh, full of beans—and then we stop.

1892 *Punch* 24 Sept. 133 Bad enough if you 'ave to wolf one, but it fair gives yer beans when 'tis two. 1900 *Daily News* 5 June 3/4 We started shelling them in the open, and gave them beans. 1903 *Daily Chron.* 16 Oct. 5/6 Sir Henry..was invited to give 'Old Joe,' 'beans,' and 'beans' the Leader of the Opposition proceeded to administer to the ex-Colonial Secretary. 1914 *Evening News* 29 Sept. 2/2 We can't get them in the open, only on very rare occasions, and when we do, by gum, they don't half get beans!

1905 H. G. WELLS *Kipps* vi. § 4 When this here old Bean told me, you could have knocked me down with a feather. [Said of a character named 'Bean'.] 1918 *Blighty Christmas No.* 27 'What made you join the air service?' 'No earthly reason, old bean! Why did you go into the submarines?' 'Oh!—divers reasons, you know!' 1920 *Punch* 1 Sept. 168/1 The anxiety of the 'Bewildered Parent' who complains of the child of two and a-half years who addressed her learned parent as 'Old bean'. 1920 *Glasgow Herald* 29 Sept. 3 The story is..told..in the patois of Piccadilly of the 'old bean' and 'old thing' variety.

f. Formerly, a sovereign or a guinea; now only in phraseological use, a coin, a bit of money (*not a bean*, no money whatever, not a stiver). *slang.*

1811 *Lex. Balatr.*, *Bean*, a guinea. 1834 AINSWORTH *Rookwood* III. vi, As yellow as a bean. 1878 *Ibid.* ix, Offering a *bean to half a quid* (in other words, a guinea to a half-guinea). 1885 D. C. MURRAY *Rainbow Gold* v. vi, 'Here's some of the beans', he continued figuratively, as he drew five sovereigns from the same pocket. 1903 A. ADAMS *Log Cowboy* xii. 80 Flood, who had anteed up his last bean. 1928 GALSWORTHY *Swan Song* II. iv, They..never saved a bean, having no beans to save. 1928 D. L. SAYERS *Bellona Club* iii, None of the Fentimens ever had a bean, as I believe one says nowadays.

7. e. in the names of various machines for harvesting field beans and preparing them for use, as *bean-harvester, -mill, -sheller, -thresher.*

1858 SIMMONDS *Dict. Trade*, Bean-mill. 1874 KNIGHT *Dict. Mech.*, Bean-harvester..Bean-sheller.

8. bean cake, a material consisting of compressed beans, or some substitute, deprived of oil, used in China as a food and fertilizer; **bean curd, paste**, a thick jelly or paste made from beans, eaten in north China and adjacent countries; **bean-fed** *a.*, *fig.* living on the best of everything; **bean metal** *Salt-mining*, marl in the form of granules (cf. *beany metal*, s.v. *BEANY 2); **bean oil**, oil expressed from beans in the manufacture of bean cake, used as an illuminant; **bean-shooter** *U.S.*, a blow-gun used for shooting with beans.

1887 *Encycl. Brit.* XXII. 733/2 *Bean-cake..is also imported in large quantities from New-chwang, Chefoo [etc.]. 1889 KIPLING *From Sea to Sea* vi. Wks. 1900 I. 289 The *bean-fed, well-groomed subaltern with the light coat and fox-terrier. 1892 *Cornh. Mag.* Sept. 263 A shaft is sunk till the 'flag' or '*bean metal' has been pierced. 1908 *Westm. Gaz.* 15 Oct. 13/2 According to reports from Chefoo,..*Bean-oil is giving place to kerosene. 1904 R. J. FARRER *Garden of Asia* 146 Buns stuffed with the cloying mustiness of *bean-paste. 1890 *Congress. Rec.* Mar. 1920/1 Some boy, with a *bean-shooter..struck Mr. Benjamin.

Beanfeast. Add earlier quots. (also *beanfeast day*):

The earlier quots. give conclusive evidence of the origin of the word from BEAN.

1806 *Spirit Publ. Jrnls.* X. 248 A few days ago, a Gentleman Tailor, celebrated for his liberality, gave a rich treat to his men, at his occasional country residence. It was called a Bean Feast; but, exclusive of the beans, the table literally groaned with bacon [etc.]. 1875 W. T. VINCENT *Warlike Woolwich* 49 The holiday..on the second Saturday in July, which is a special and extra holiday, known as 'Bean-feast day', and is usually spent in excursions to some country place and a dinner, at which beans form an indispensable dish. 1897 *Daily News* 23 Sept. 8/5 A beanfeast party from Woolwich.

b. *fig.*

1908 W. J. LOCKE *Beloved Vagabond* iii, He..alluded to 'the regular beanfeast' they would have when they were married. 1922 MRS. A. SIDGWICK *Victorian* xxix, 'Won't life be a beanfeast?' she said. 'We shall enjoy ourselves.'

Beano (bī·no). *slang.* orig. Printers' abbreviation of BEANFEAST. Later, in gen. use, a festive entertainment frequently terminating in a noisy frolic or spree.

1888 JACOBI *Printers' Vocab.*, *Beano*, a slang abbreviation for 'beanfeast', which is, however, usually termed 'goose' or wayzgoose by compositors. 1897 *N. & Q.* 8th Ser. XII. 175/1, I can remember hearing a street song, some years ago, in which one of the lines ran something to the effect that We don't have a beano every day. 1914 *Evening News* 15 Oct. 4/6, I wish you could hear the men on their first morning in the hospitals...'Fighting's a beano with this sort of thing for dessert.' 1920 W. J. LOCKE *House of Baltazar* ii, I'll get hold of Dorothy, and you and I and she'll have a little beano at the Carlton. 1924 *Blackw. Mag.* Oct. 494/1 There had been one of those awful last-night-of-leave beanos in town.

Beany, *a.* Add: **2.** Salt-mining. *Beany marl* or *metal* = *bean metal* (*BEAN 8).

1886 *Cheshire Gloss.*, Beany marl. 1892 *Cornh. Mag.* Sept. 258 After a while what is locally termed 'beany metal' is reached.

Bear, *sb.*¹ Add:

2. *To play the bear with* (colloq.): to play the deuce with, inflict great damage upon.

1881 *Leics. Gloss.* s.v., The hail has played the bear with the apple-blossom. 1889 'R. BOLDREWOOD' *Robbery under Arms* xxiii, Chaps that have got something on their minds can't stand idleness, it plays the bear with them. 1891 J. M. DIXON *Dict. Idiom. Phr.* s.v., The last storm has played the bear with my crops.

10. bear animalcule, a microscopic animal of the group *Tardigrada*, a water-bear; **bear-fight** *v. intr.*, to behave rowdily; **bear-lead** *v. trans.*, to act as bear-leader or travelling tutor to (a youth); hence, to supervise the conduct of, arrange the affairs of; hence *bear-leading* ppl. adj.; **bear oak** *U.S.*, the black scrub-oak, *Quercus ilicifolia*; **bear-pit**, a sunk enclosure in which bears are kept for exhibition; **bear-sign** *U.S.*, the track of a bear, esp. as shown by its droppings; also *transf.* doughnuts; **Bear State** *U.S.*, the State of Arkansas; **bear-trap**, a trap set for bears, in which logs are propped up; **bear-wallow** *U.S.*, a hollow in the ground attributed to the wallowing of bears.

1889 *Cent. Dict.* s.v. *Arctisca*, *Bear-animalcules. 1892 *Daily News* 23 Feb. 4/8 Did she *bear-fight and play

practical jokes on the Lord Admiral? 1900 *Ibid.* 24 Oct. 10/2 A don called Bedmynster used to bearfight in hall. 1891 C. DUNSTAN *Quita* I. i, I do call it hard..to condemn me to *bear-lead a savage. 1898 *Daily News* 31 Aug. 5/5 It was he who bear-led Admiral Avellane and his officers. 1901 'LINESMAN' *Words Eyewitness* (1902) 289 A guard of honour, and a bear-leading general officer to see the creature safely and comfortably down to the sea. 1921 *Times Lit. Suppl.* 8 Sept. 576/3 For a space he [Mat. Prior] bearleads Lord Exeter's sons. 1928 *Daily Tel.* 7 Aug. 6/5 There are..more applicants for what used to be called 'bear-leading' than there are bears to be led. 1832 D. J. BROWNE *Sylva Amer.* 263 This diminutive species is known in the Northern and Middle States by the name of *Bear Oak. 1893 TORREY *Footpath-Way* 81 The rest of the vegetation was more or less familiar, I believe: bear oak; chinquapin. 1849 *Near Home, Berne* 297 In the city [Berne] there is a *bear pit with three fat lazy living bears. 1857 F. LOCKER *London Lyrics* (1862) 66 The Bear Pit at the Zoological Gardens. 1887 *Scribner's Mag.* Sept. 305/1 They reported any amount of *bear-sign on the slopes leading to the river. 1903 A. ADAMS *Log Cowboy* xviii. 280 She asked me to make the bear-sign, doughnuts she called them. 1859 BARTLETT *Dict. Amer.* (ed. 2) 26 *Bear State*, a name by which the State of Arkansas is known at the West. 1871 SCHELE DE VERE *Americanisms* (1872) 658 Arkansas is called the Bear State, although within its limits and throughout the West, the name is pronounced Bar State. 1835 R. M. BIRD *Hawks of Hawk-h.* I. xx. 269 You are in a *bear-trap, and the log will soon be on your back. 1849 C. LANMAN *Lett. Allegheny Mount.* xviii. 149 Having come to one of his bear-traps..he thoughtlessly..went under the trap to arrange his bait. 1859 BARTLETT *Dict. Amer.* (ed. 2), *Bear-Wallow. 1889 FARMER *Americanisms*, *Bear Wallows*..are, however, purely natural phenomena. 1891 MARAH E. RYAN *Pagan of Alleghanies* v. 62 He rode..on through the columns of white-oak, whose feet are caressed by feathers and fern in the long, desolate 'bear-wallow'.

Bear, *sb.*³ Add: **3.** *Bear-up* (U.S. colloq.): the act of 'following' a woman.

1900 H. LAWSON *On Track* 33 You don't expect I'd 'fox' a feller I see doing a bit of a bear-up to a girl, do you?

Bear, *sb.*⁶ *U.S.* Also **baire.** [Perh. the same as BEAR *sb.*⁴, but cf. *BAR *sb.*⁵] (See quot. 1775.)

1775 B. ROMANS *Florida* 228 *note*, Baires are a kind of tent made of a light coarse cloth, like canvas gauze, called by the French *villemontiers*. 1797 F. BAILEY *Jrnl. Tour* (1856) 309 Over the whole [bed] there is a large gauze net (called a *bear*), which is intended as a defence against the mosquitos. 1798 A. ELLICOTT in *Life & Lett.* (1908) 158 Our beds are all surrounded with a kind of thin curtains called bears to keep them off when we go to rest.

Bear, *v.*¹ Add: **11. b.** Of ice: To support the weight of a person, etc.

1768 WASHINGTON *Diaries* I. 246 Attempted to go into the Neck on the Ice, but it wd. not bear.

16. Delete †. Add *Obs.* exc. *arch.*

1874 SWINBURNE *Bothwell* II. i. (1882) 97 It may be you do well to bear me hard.

23. Add: Phr. *To bear date*: to be dated (as specified).

1446 in *Trevelyan Papers* (Camden) 27 Your letters..beryng date at Westm̄ the xx day of Juyl the xxv yere of your..regne. 1503–4 [in Dict.]. 1712, 1837 [see DATE *sb.*² 1]. 1875 *Encycl. Brit.* II. 593/2 Bearing date the 16th April 1871.

Bear, *v.*² Add: *transf.* and *fig.* Also, to affect (the market) in this way. Hence **Bea·ring** *vbl. sb.*, in quot. *attrib.*

1848 W. ARMSTRONG *Stocks* 19 This is perhaps the grand theatre for bulling and bearing stocks. 1861 *N. Y. Tribune* 29 Nov. (Bartlett) His Lordship is wholly guiltless of the charge which the 'Herald' in its anxiety to bear the market has brought against him. 1867–9 *Trans. Ill. Agric. Soc.* VII. 431 The strong influences which were used to 'bear' the hog market. 1887 *Pall Mall Gaz.* 26 Nov. 12 Bulling and Bearing Men's Lives. 1887 *Century Mag.* XXIII. 500 Even the best regulated thermometer will have its vagaries, and there is no protection against it when it does 'bear' the weather. 1897 *Daily News* 26 Apr. 5/4 'Bearing' influences are encouraged, and those whose interest is in forcing down prices are very active in that direction.

Beardedness (bīə·rdėdnės). [f. BEARDED *ppl. a.* + -NESS.] Bearded condition.

1888 *Times* 18 Aug. 9/1 The beardedness of the chief. 1917 W. J. LOCKE *Red Planet* xii, Their composite paunchiness, beardedness, scragginess,..impressed me unfavourably.

Beardie. Add:

2. A local Australian nickname applied to a body of Southcotians, followers of John Wroe, who called themselves Christian Israelites.

1875 *Melbourne Spectator* 21 Aug. 190/1 The Beardies or Christian Israelites of Ballarat. 1905 *Daily Chron.* 8 Mar. 4/7 There is only one founder of a religion buried in Australia—John Wroe, who started the 'Christian Israelites,' nicknamed the 'Beardies,' since they never cut their hair.

Bearer. Add:

1. f. *Bearer company, corps*, a medical division for military field service.

1878 (*title*) Stretcher-Bearers and Bearer-Companies. Manual of Exercises for, Horse Guards. 1899 *Daily News* 27 Nov. 5/3 More assistance will be necessary, both in skilled attention to wounded, and in carrying them from the field. This is provided for by 'bearer companies.' 1901 *Empire Rev.* I. 432 The work of the bearer company is intermittent, having to collect the sick and wounded after a fight, and to bring them to the field hospital. 1902 *Encycl. Brit.* XXV. 352/1 The bearer company..is composed of three officers, thirteen non-commissioned officers, and forty-eight privates of the Royal Army Medical Corps, with a detachment of the Army Service Corps for transport duties.

3. b. *Bearer security*, an unregistered security the title to which is vested in its possessor and is transferred by simple delivery. So *bearer bond, warrant.*

1897 *Westm. Gaz.* 5 Aug. 6/3 These bearer-warrants are, we venture to imagine, part of the £140,000 in fully-paid shares. 1906 *Ibid.* 12 July 9/2 All kinds of bearer securities.

IV. 12. *Geom.* A space of any sort which is the locus of a collection of geometrical objects of any sort; e.g. a straight line is the *bearer* of the set of all points on it.

1909 in *Cent. Dict.* Suppl.

Bear-grass. *U.S.* [BEAR *sb.*¹ 10.] One or other of several species of Yucca (esp. *Yucca filamentosa*), or of some similar plants.

1807 P. GASS *Jrnl.* 167 One of them had a hat made of the bark of white cedar and bear-grass. 1832 *Louisville Directory* 102 The commodious harbor presented by the bend of the river towards the mouth of Beargrass creek. 1859 BARTLETT *Dict. Amer.* (ed. 2), *Bear-Grass*, sometimes called Silk Grass, from the fibres which appear on the edges of the leaves. It is not a grass. 1909 *Century Dict.* Suppl., *Bear-grass* 2. a bunch-grass, *Stipa setigera*, ranging from the mountains of California, where it is considered valuable, to Oregon and Texas.

Bearing, *vbl. sb.* Add: **14. c.** *Line of bearing*: the direction in which a thing lies or moves.

1839 URE *Dict. Arts* 967 When the line of dip, and consequently the line of bearing which is at right angles to it, are unknown, they are sought for by making three bores. 1930 *Discovery* Nov. 330/1 Collingwood signalled to some of his ships to spread out.., the result being a partial resemblance to what is called a line of bearing.

Bearing, *ppl. a.*¹ **5.** Add: Also of years, etc.

1859 *Trans. Mich. Agric. Soc.* (1860) X. 614 Of fruits, although it was not a 'bearing year', the exhibition was very fine.

Bea·r-meat. *U.S.* Also bear's meat. [BEAR *sb.*¹] The flesh of the bear used as food.

1816 U. BROWN in *Maryland Hist. Mag.* XI. 47 Dined on Bears meet and Wild Turkey. 1836 *Southern Lit. Messenger* II. 597 Animal food, both of beef and pork, of venison and bear meat. 1856 [see BEAR *sb.*¹ 9]. 1890 MARAH E. RYAN *Told in Hills* 96 Jimmy brought out..some bits of salt meat—evidently bear-meat.

Bearskinned (bēə·ɹskind), *a.* [f. BEARSKIN + -ED².] Wearing a bearskin.

1694 S. S. *Loyal & Impartial Satirist* 14 When Bear-skin'd Men in Floating Castles land. 1909 *Daily Chron.* 1 Oct. 4/6 The bearskinned heroes.

Bea·rwood. *U.S.* [BEAR *sb.*¹] (See quot.)

1870 *Amer. Naturalist* III. 407 Oregon Bearwood (*Frangula Purshiana*).

Beast, *sb.* Add:

5. b. *fig.* applied to things; also in colloq. phr. *A beast of a*...: an abominable or disgusting..., a beastly...

1862 SUSAN HALE *Lett.* 13 [I'm always afraid about your poor eye...It seemed to act like a beast]. *Ibid.*, One thing shall I rejoice at,—my own bed,—for this husk thing we sleep on is a beast. 1878 W. S. GILBERT *Pinafore* I, It's a beast of a name. 1898 *Westm. Gaz.* 4 May 2/2 I've had a beast of a time.

IV. beastman, a cattleman.

1899 *Yorkshire Post* 26 Dec., Wanted, beastman,..on farm, near Hull. 1921 *Dict. Occupational Terms* (1927) § 22, *Cattleman*, beastman, byreman.

Beastly, *a.* **5.** Add: Also with weakened emphasis, as a mere expletive.

1888 A. C. GUNTER *Mr. Potter* xxiii, I..came to tell her that story of her father's flying to escape arrest is all beastly rot.

Beat, *sb.*¹ Add:

7. *In* or *out of beat, off the beat*: making a regular or irregular succession of strokes.

1883 BECKETT *Clocks, Watches, & Bells* (ed. 7) 79 When a clock with any kind of anchor escapement..sounds 'out of beat', it wants either one side lifting or the crutch bending. 1889 HASLUCK *Clock Jobber's Handybk.* v. 94 Put on the pendulum, and set the clock 'in beat'. The meaning of 'in beat' is, that the escape takes place at equal distances each side of the pendulum's centre of gravity...When 'in beat' the tick sounds regular, and nearly equal, differences of the drop making it slightly uneven.

8. b. *Wireless Telegr.* (See quots.)

1918 W. H. ECCLES *Wireless Telegr.* Gloss., *Beats* occur when two oscillations of differing frequencies occur simultaneously in the same system. The gradual change of phase difference causes the amplitudes to be opposed at one instant, and to concur at a later instant, with all the intermediate stages in the interval; the time between two successive oppositions, *i.e.* between two instants of minimum resultant amplitude, is called the time of a beat. The beat frequency is therefore equal to the difference between the frequencies of the two oscillations. *Ibid.*, *Beat Reception* (or Interference Reception) is the process of making high-frequency oscillations received by an antenna audibly evident by combining with them other oscillations of suitably different frequency. 1921 L. B. TURNER *Wireless Telegr.* 74 During a signal, the two oscillations are combined, with the interference or beat effect familiar in acoustics when two musical tones of slightly different pitch are mingled.

10. c. *U.S.* (See quot.)

1876 *Fur, Fin & Feather* Sept. 124 The bear goes to and from his den..by certain paths called 'beats'...A bear will use the same 'beat' for years.

d. 'In Alabama and Mississippi, the principal subdivision of a county; a voting-precinct' (*Cent. Dict.* 1889).

1893 *Congress. Rec.* Feb. 2298/1 The evidence shows that his tickets were brought to the polls by friends of Turpin, and peddled there by them. This is shown to have been the case at Steep Creek beat,..at Hopewell beat, in Loundes County. 1896 *Ibid.* Mar. 2788/1 Testimony was taken to show that fraud was committed in certain beats,—the River beat, Union, and one or two others.

14. The action or an act of beating in order to rouse game.

1897 *Encycl. Sport* I. 84/2 The Sloth Bear..except when driven out in the course of a beat..will not be observed during the day.

15. *U.S.* (chiefly *dial.*) **a.** That which surpasses, excels, or outdoes (something). Only in phr. *to see*, or *hear, the beat* (*of*).

1834 S. SMITH *Major Downing* 129, I never see the beat of it. 1846–52 MRS. WHITCHER *Widow Bedott P.* 112 But here's that silk, did ye ever see the beat on't? 1847 *Great Kalamazoo Hunt* (Philad.) 100 (Th.) You don't tell me so! Did I ever hear the beat o' that! 1878 MRS. STOWE *Poganuc P.* x. (1890) 110 That Bill is saassy enough to physic a horn-bug. I never see the beat of him. 1888 'C. E. CRADDOCK' *Broomsedge Cove* v. 80 Waal, sir, eatin' supper by a tallow dip—who ever hearn the beat! *a* 1906 'O. HENRY' *Trimmed Lamp*, etc. 212 Count Fernando Mazzini was his name. I never saw the beat of him for elegance.

b. *To get a beat on*: (see quot.).

1889 FARMER *Americanisms* s.v., *To get a beat on* is to get the advantage of..As used by thieves and their associates, *to get a beat on one*..also implies that the point has been scored by underhand, secret, or unlawful means.

c. A success scored against rivals by a reporter or newspaper; an item of news secured and published in advance of competitors.

1875 MRS. STOWE *We & our Neighbors* xxxi. 292 If any one of them gets a bit of news before another, its a victory—a beat. 1887 *Detroit Tribune* 27 June 3/2 They finally succeeded, and cheered lustily as the Ocean King steamed for New York with a big 'beat' for the Times. The office was safely reached, and the 'beat' appeared that morning. 1895 *St. Louis Star* 6 May 4 This was the largest price paid for a newspaper 'beat' up to that time. 1899 HOWELLS in *Literature* 1 July 691 Within the limits of fiction or of fact the highest achievement of a reporter is to make his story a beat.

16. [f. BEAT *ppl. a.*] An idle, worthless, or shiftless fellow. (Cf. DEAD-BEAT *sb.*²) *U.S.*

1877 J. D. BILLINGS *Hard Tack & Coffee* 95 (Th.) The original idea of a beat was that of a lazy man or a shirk who would by hook or by crook get rid of all military or fatigue duty that he could. 1881 A. A. HAYES *New Colorado* vi. 93 But he said that these beats, when they were at home, had old squirrel rifles..with flintlocks. 1887 *Harper's Mag.* Dec. 107/1 The inevitable squad of 'beats' with bleary eyes and wolfish faces infesting the doorways of the saloons. 1903 *Boston Herald* 19 Aug., He would not loan money to policemen or firemen, stating that they were the biggest beats in the country.

Beat, *v.*¹ Add:

3. b. *To beat one's way*: to travel, or make one's way, *spec.* by illicit means. *U.S.*

1887 M. ROBERTS *Western Avernus* 235, I could walk or 'beat my way' on the train. 1891 C. ROBERTS *Adrift Amer.* 53 To beat one's way, or to beat the conductor or the railroad, are equivalent phrases for travelling in the cars without paying any fare. *Ibid.* 195 There was nothing for it but to start out and beat my way there. 1904 *N. Y. Tribune* 8 May 10 [They should] stop trying to 'beat their way' by stealing a right of way that belongs to other people.

c. *To beat it*: to go away, to 'clear out'. *U.S.*

1908 A. RUHL *Other Americans* ii. 10 He'll be beatin' it for Paris pretty soon where the rest of 'em all went. 1917 MATHEWSON *Sec. Base Sloan* xiv. 193 You get your boss to let you off for that long, beat it over to Harrisville tomorrow night. *Ibid.* xxi. 283 Beat it! Get out of here. 1926 LEACOCK *Winnowed Wisd.* 79 'To your posts, all of you!' she cried, 'Beat it,' she honked.

10. d. To get the better of (one) by trickery; to cheat or defraud. *U.S.*

1886 *Century Mag.* Feb. 513/2 How do I know you ain't tryin to beat me? 1888 *Daily Inter-Ocean* 23 Mar. (Farmer) Two boys..were each fined twenty-five dollars...They have been beating boarding-houses all over the West Side. 1891 [see 3 b above]. 1904 *Columbus Even. Dispatch* 29 June 4 The..people who try to beat the street car conductors out of their fare.

e. To get ahead of. *To beat* (one) *to it*: to anticipate in doing something. *U.S.*

1898 H. S. CANFIELD *Maid of Frontier* i. 21 He's watching the rangers,..and will probably try to beat them here. 1911 H. QUICK *Yellowstone N.* xii. 321 She found that Reddy'd beat her to it. 1923 WATTS *Luther Nichols* 198 If the sheriff don't beat me to it.

f. slang phr. *To have* (a person) *beat*: to be sure of his defeat; hence *gen.* to have got the better of.

1916 BOYD CABLE *Action Front* 30 Why..you can't make your hands do what your tongue says 'as me beat.

40. f. To beat soundly, to thrash. *U.S.*

a 1906 'O. HENRY' *Trimmed Lamp*, etc. 159, I wouldn't have a man..that didn't beat me up at least once a week. 1912 MULFORD & CLAY *Buck Peters* i. 24, I found that I'd beat up a couple of policemen when I was drunk.

Beat, *ppl. a.* Add:

2. *Beat hand, knee, elbow*: injuries incident to miners caused by the jarring and friction of the pick.

1905 *Daily Chron.* 17 Mar. 5/6 Judge Greenwell decided that 'beat hand' could not be classed as an accident...He found similarly in a claim with respect to 'beat knee'. 1907 *Ibid.* 17 May 5/5 'Beat hand', 'beat knee', and 'beat elbow'.

Beatable, *a.* (Modern example.)

1892 *Atlantic Monthly* Mar. 331 A more beatable child than Samuel Taylor it would be hard to find.

Bea·temest, *a.* *U.S. dial.* Also **-omest, -in'est, -enes', -enest.** [app. f. *beat 'em* + -EST *superl. suffix*; later apprehended as f. *beating* ppl. adj.] Most excellent or splendid.

1833 J. NEAL *Down-Easters* I. 62 Old rugged-an'-tough they used to call his dad, famous wrastler he was too,..beatemest fellow ever you see for some things. 1838 B. DRAKE *Tales* 30 Your the beatomest shakes I ever seed. 1874

EGGLESTON *Circuit Rider* 147, I reckon I am the beatin'est man to ax questions in this neck of timber. 1889 *Harper's Mag.* Dec. 120/1 Thet thar rock house o' bis'n,..I 'low it's the beatenes' house in creation. 1908 ELIZA C. HALL *Aunt Jane of Kentucky* ii. 33 Of the preachers that ever I heard, he certainly is the beatenest.

Beater. Add:

2. b. *Paper-manuf.* A pulping machine. Also *attrib.* and *Comb.*, as *beater plate, roll*; **beater-man**, the operative who has charge of a pulping machine or beating-engine.

1825 J. NICHOLSON *Operat. Mech.* 368 (Paper manufacture) The only difference between the washing-engine and the beater is that the teeth of the latter are finer. 1880 J. DUNBAR *Pract. Papermaker* (1881) 44 Two chests should be used, the beaterman emptying into the one, and the machine-man working from the other. *Ibid.* 71 The beater roll and plate should..be in good order.

3. A person or thing that beats or excels others. *U.S. dial.*

1845 S. JUDD *Margaret* II. v. 283 Take it by and large..and she is the beater of all. 1886 *Harper's Mag.* Sept. 580/2 I've heerd news that beats the beater! *Ibid.* Nov. 835/1 Well, for getting sunthin outer northing, she's a beater!

Beating, *vbl. sb.* **6.** Add: **beating-engine**, a machine (*a*) for preparing the materials used in the manufacture of paper, strawboard, millboard, etc.; (*b*) for opening, beating, and cleaning cotton in cotton-manufacture; **beating frame** (see quot. 1915).

1825 J. NICHOLSON *Operat. Mechanic* 368 (Paper-manufacture) The beating-engines..are seldom provided with these waste-pipes. 1846 DODD *Brit. Manuf.* VI. 21 The rags are..conveyed to the washing-engine,..then let off into the beating-engine. 1880 J. DUNBAR *Pract. Papermaker* (1881) 61 Alum intended for the beating-engine should be perfectly pure. 1890 NASMITH *Mod. Cotton Spinning Mach.* 30 The cotton, which, as it is impelled by the stroke of the beating blade, will very readily roll past the projections. 1915 R. BEAUMONT *Woollen & Worsted* 631 'Beating'..is done on the beating frame, consisting of a roller, round which the piece is wrapped face downwards.

Beatitude. Add:

1. b. An honorific title (rendering Gr. μακαριότης) applied to ecclesiastics of the Eastern Church of patriarchal rank.

1658 J. BURBURY *Hist. Christina Q. Swedland* 127 When his Beatitude had declared four extraordinary Nuntii, to receive her on the confines of the Ecclesiastical State. 1751 CHAMBERS *Cycl.* s.v. *Holyness*, S. Gregory compliments some of his cotemporary bishops with, your beatitude, and your holyness. 1925 *Glasgow Herald* 7 Sept. 11 His Beatitude the Lord Photios, Patriarch and Pope of Alexandria.

Beau geste (bo ʒɛst). [F., = fine gesture.] A display of magnanimity.

1922 *Westm. Gaz.* 9 Dec., I think Germany can pay,..and Italy is too poor to make the *beau geste* of abandoning her claims. 1926 W. DEEPING *Sorrell & Son* xv. § 3 He gave in...He was not going to quarrel with a *beau geste.*

Beaujolais (boʒolɛ). [Name of an ancient district of France.] A light red Burgundy wine.

1863 T. G. SHAW *Wine* viii. 258 All common cheap French red wines seem now to have got the name of Beaujolais, as white have that of Chablis. 1879 STEVENSON *Trav. Cevennes*, *I have a Goad*, I uncorked my bottle of Beaujolais, and asked the host to join me.

Beaumontage (bōᵘmǫntā·g). Also **-montague.** [Said to be f. name of Élie de *Beaumont* (1798–1851), French geologist.] A composition (of various mixtures) used by cabinet-makers, pattern-makers, and iron-founders for the concealment of cracks and holes in wood or metal work. Also *fig.* (see quot. 1895).

1886 ELWORTHY *W. Somerset Word-bk.*, Boman teg. 1888 *Chambers's Encycl.* II. 3 Beaumontague is a composition..which is used to fill up cracks in an iron casting. 1895 BREWER *Dict. Phrase & Fable*, *Beaumontage* (pronounced *bo-mon-taig*), bad work, especially ill-fitting carpenter's work; literary padding; paste and scissors literature. 1899 HASLUCK *Wood Finishing* ix. 67 Beaumontage..is generally called 'stopping-out wax'.

Beaune (bōᵘn). [The name of a town in the department of Côte d'Or, France.] A red wine of Burgundy, produced in the district around Beaune.

1818 MOORE *Fudge Fam. Paris* iii. 51 Some glasses of *Beaune.* 1841 THACKERAY *Mem. Gormandising* Misc. Essays, &c. (1885) 386 Always drink red wine with beef-steaks..good Beaune, say. 1863 T. G. SHAW *Wine* viii. 255 Beaune, 1858, first growth, high flavour, much body, fine. 1875 *Ure's Dict. Arts* III. 1143 Haute-Burgogne..produces the most famous wines in Burgundy...Here grow the renowned *Volnay, Pomard, Beaune, Nuits.*

Beaut (biūt). *U.S. slang.* Also **bute.** [Abbrev. of BEAUTY 5.] Something fine or splendid.

1896 G. ADE *Artie* i. 5 They was beauts too. 1902 CLAPIN *Dict. Amer.* s.v. *Bute.* 1910 O. JOHNSON *Varmint* i. 16 The tin one was easier, but it's a beaut. *Ibid.* v. 67 Some of the fellows have perfect beauts. 1911 H. QUICK *Yellowstone N.* xii. 318 Verily, Aconite was a beaut.

Beautician (biūti·ʃən). *U.S.* [f. BEAUTY + -ICIAN.] A specialist in cosmetics.

1926 *Glasgow Herald* 12 June 8 The immense growth of 'beauty parlors' in the United States has added to the American language the word 'beautician'.

Beauty, *sb.* Add:

5. c. In various collectors' names of butterflies.

1832 J. RENNIE *Consp. Butterfl. & M.* 104 The Oak Beauty (*Biston prodromarius*, Leach). The Brindled Beauty (*Biston hirtarius*, Leach). 1921 *Conquest* Sept. 495/3 The Pale Brindled Beauty (*Phigalia pilosaria*)..has a particularly handsome black form.

6. b. *pl.* In the titles of collections of the beautiful or choice passages of a writer or speaker, or examples of art.

1752 W. DODD (*title*) The Beauties of Shakespear. 1767 (*title*) The Beauties of English Poesy. Selected by Oliver Goldsmith. 1786 (*title*) Beauties of the British Senate, from the Beginning of the Administration of Sir R. Walpole, to the Second Session of the Administration of W. Pitt. 1860 *Athenæum* 31 Mar. 442/1 It might have been fancied that the days of 'Beauties', 'Gems', 'Anthologies' were over. 1865 (*title*) Beauties of Poetry and Art.

III. b. beauty doctor, specialist, one who practises the art of applying cosmetics, face massage, etc.; **beauty parlour** *U.S.*, an establishment in which this trade is carried on; **beauty spot**, a locality conspicuous for its beauty.

1921 *Dict. Occupational Terms* (1927) § 920 Beauty specialist, *beauty doctor. 1926 *beauty parlor [see *BEAUTICIAN]. 1927 *Daily Tel.* 1 Nov. 9/7 'Slaves of Beauty'..enables..a large audience to play the rôle of Paul Pry in an American 'beauty parlour'. 1917 W. PETT RIDGE *Amazing Years* viii, There are *beauty specialists in Bond Street. 1919 *Times* (weekly ed.) 5 Sept. 864 A former Middlesex *beauty-spot—Hanworth Park.

Beautyhood (biū·tihud). Also **beautihood.** [f. BEAUTY *sb.* + -HOOD.] The period of a woman's 'reign' as a beauty; society of beauties, also beauties collectively.

1889 MRS. H. MARTIN *Common Clay* III. xv. 240 The short season of her beautihood in London. 1889 H. F. WOOD *Englishman Rue Cain* xvi, Initiation into the Fashionable Beauty-hood.

Beaver¹. Add:

1. b. *Bank beaver*, a beaver living in a burrow apart from the colony.

1903 *Windsor Mag.* Sept. 405/1 Some people who write stories for the papers say that what are called bank beavers are lazy old males that have been forced out of the house by the rest of the family.

c. *coll.* Beavers. *U.S.*

1770 WASHINGTON *Diaries* I. 441 Then Bever catch it in there way up. 1789 MORSE *Amer. Geog.* 198 In this country are..beaver, otters, sables. 1840 C. F. HOFFMAN *Greyslaer* I. v. 60, I had gone clean up to Racket Lake..hoping to get a few beaver. 1878 J. H. BEADLE *Western Wilds* xii. 188 Then Clear Creek, Colorado, was lively with beaver. 1890 L. C. D'OYLE *Notches* 66, I knew that beaver were plentiful.

d. Phr. *to work like a beaver*: to work hard. *U.S.*

a 1775 in J. T. Buckingham *Specim. Newsp. Lit.* (1850) I. 131 The very best Negro Woman..as brisk as a Bird, and will work like a Beaver. 1835 *Col. Crockett's Tour* 73 Ingham worked honestly, like a beaver. 1877 RAYMOND *Mines* 225 Mr. Baldwin..has worked like a beaver since he assumed the management of the mine. 1915 *Lit. Digest* (N. Y.) 21 Aug. 347/2 Every one knows what 'working like a beaver' means.

2. c. Beaver-pelts as an article of exchange or trade, or as a standard of value. *U.S.*

1630 *Rec. Mass. Bay* I. 76 It was ordered that those..who bought certayne cattle shall pay 9 l. of beaver. *a* 1649 WINTHROP *New Eng.* I. 165 They have a great trade of beaver,—about nine or ten thousand skins in a year. 1658 *Essex Inst. Hist. Coll.* II. 46/2 Beaver is exceedingly low at this time. 1686 SEWALL *Letter-Bk.* (1886) I. 32 A small trus of Bever in a box weighing sixteen pounds or better. 1902 S. E. WHITE *Conjuror's House* iii. 26 He too reported of the trade—so many 'beaver' of tobacco, of powder, of lead.

†d. A beaver's skin. *U.S. Obs.*

1677 *New Castle Court Rec.* 53 The Pl't. demands of the deft...the sume or quantity of fifty five Bevers or thirteen hundered and twenty Gilders. 1680 *Ibid.* 381 Twoo Bevers, makeing in all fourteen Bevers.

2. e. A shade of brown colour resembling that of the fur of a beaver; more explicitly *beaver-brown.*

1895 *Cassell's Fam. Mag.* Feb. 234/1 A picture hat..of beaver brown velvet. 1914 *Scotsman* 26 Oct. 12/2 The shades are Steel, Oxford and Parson Grey, Mole, Beaver, Fawn.

6. *beaver-canal, -meadow, -skin* (earlier examples); **beaver-eater** (see quot.); **beaver finish**, a finish giving a resemblance to beaver fur; hence, a finish in which the fibres are all laid in one direction; so **beaver-finished** *a.*; **beaver-sign** (= tracks); **beaver-tree**, *Magnolia glauca*, the Sweet or White Bay of the U.S.; **beaver-wood**, (*a*) the hackberry tree of the U.S., *Celtis occidentalis*; (*b*) the wood of the beaver-tree; **beaver-works** (see quot.).

1889 *Harper's Mag.* Jan. 234/2 It is not so easy to determine what is and what is not a *beaver canal. 1797 *Encycl. Brit.* (ed. 3) XVIII. 692/2 The *luscus*, or wolverine...In America it is called the *beaver-eater. 1904 *Technol. & Sci. Dict.* (ed. Goodchild & Tweney), *Beaver Finish. 1909 BEAUMONT *Finishing Textile Fabrics* 11 The lateral surfaces of the fibres mainly resist the friction in the *beaver-finished cloth. 1876 *Fur, Fin & Feather* Sept. 141 While walking through an old *beaver meadow..he was..that some large body was approaching him. *a* 1848 RUXTON *Life Far West* (1849) 28 Thar plans is plain to this child as *beaver sign. 1890 L. C. D'OYLE *Notches* 66, I had taken good stock of the beaver 'sign' and such things. 1616 CAPT. J. SMITH *Descr. New Eng.* (1865) 20 Wee got for trifles neer 1100 *Beuerskinnes. 1654 E. JOHNSON *Hist. New Eng.* xvii. 38 Having some small Trading with the Indians for Beaver-skins. 1678 *New Castle Court Rec.* 218 Mr. Tom..was debtor..ye sume of seven pound and one bever skin. 1859 BARTLETT *Dict. Amer.* (ed. 2), *Beaver-tree (*Magnolia glauca*). Called also Beaver-wood, and sometimes Castor-wood, probably from the preference shown by the beavers..is also known by the name of Beaver-tree, because the root is eaten by beavers. 1832 D. J. BROWNE *Sylva Amer.* 209 In Philadelphia and New York and in their vicinity, this tree is called Magnolia, which denomination has entirely superseded those of Swamp Sassafras and *Beaver Wood. 1841 RHIND *Hist. Veg. Kingd.* 452/1 The Small Magnolia...From its [wood] obtaining the name of 'beaver-wood', it is probable these animals at one time were inhabitants of the localities where it grows. 1880 *Encycl. Brit.* XI. 360/1 [The hackberry tree] is also known under the name of 'beaver-wood', and 'nettle tree'. 1889 *Harper's Mag.* Jan. 230/1 '*Beaver-works', as the trappers call the range of land and water occupied by a colony of beavers.

Bea·ver-dam. A dam made by beavers.

1664 *Plymouth Rec.* 75 A small brooke..called the beaver dam brooke. 1676 [see BEAVER¹ 6]. 1703 *Cal. Virginia St. Papers* I. 83 To three white oakes, by the East side of the Tuckahoe Bever Dam. 1849 PARKMAN *Oregon Trail* 293 The stream was clogged with old beaver-dams. 1878 J. H. BEADLE *Western Wilds* xii. 188 It was the good old time..when beaver dams adorned every stream in the mountains. 1903 S. E. WHITE *Forest* xvi. 231 He knows the beaver-dams, how many animals each harbors.

Beaverette (bīvəre·t). [f. BEAVER¹ + -ETTE.] An imitation beaver fur; also, cloth with a beaver finish (see *BEAVER¹ 6).

1922 *Daily Mail* 12 Dec. 1 Pelt in superb quality pulled Beaverette. 1923 *Ibid.* 16 Jan. 1 Beaverette stoles. *Ibid.* 29 Jan. 1 Rubber on strong Beaverette Cloth.

Bêche-de-mer. For etym. read: Quasi-Fr. of English origin, altered from *biche de mer*, a. Pg. *bicho do mar*, lit. sea-worm. And add: Also = *BEACH-LA-MAR.

1908 JACK LONDON *Cruise of Snark* xvi, Bêche de mer English was the product of conditions and circumstances.

Becquerel (be·krĕl). The name of a French physicist, Antoine Henri Becquerel (1852–1908), used *attrib.* in *Becquerel('s) rays* (see quots.).

1896 S. P. THOMPSON in *Philos. Mag.* July 105 While agreeing with the Röntgen rays in the property of penetrating aluminium [etc.], the Becquerel rays differ in the circumstance that they can be refracted and polarized. 1897 — *Light Visible & Invis.* 279 Becquerel's rays possess..the property of diselectrifying charged bodies. 1898 *Physical Rev.* Apr. 239 Becquerel rays, or uranium rays, as Becquerel himself called them.

Becuiba (bĭkwī·bǎ). [Tupi *bicuiba, bicuhyba.*] Used attrib. in **becuiba nut**, the fruit of the Brazilian tree *Myristica Bicuhyba*; **becuiba tallow** or **fat**, a balsamic product of the becuiba nut.

1884 *Encycl. Brit.* XVII. 744/2 Becuiba tallow. [Source] *Myristica Becuhyba.* [Principal use] medicine candles. 1889 *Cent. Dict.*, Becuiba-nut.

Bed, *sb.* Add: **12. f.** The body of a cart or wagon. *dial.* and *U.S.*

c 1700 KENNETT *MS. Lansd.* 1033, *Bedd* of a cart, the body of it. 1854 MISS BAKER *Northampt. Gloss.*, *Bed*...3. The body of a cart or waggon. 1873 J. H. BEADLE *Undevel. West* xxiv. 491 In this [bayou] we encountered dangerous whirls and jump-offs, the wagon often plunging in up to the bed. 1904 W. H. SMITH *Promoters* xviii. 270 Some of these beds will hold more than a hundred bushels.

19. bed-book, a book read in bed; **bed-cord** (modern examples); **bed-cover**, (*a*) a covering or case for a feather- or flock-bed, etc.; (*b*) a bed-quilt; **bed-plane** *Geol.*, the junction between two layers or strata; **bed-plate** (U.S. quot.); **bed-sitting-room**, an apartment serving both as a bedroom and sitting room; in University slang, **bed-sitter**; **bed-slip** = *bed-cover* (a); **bed table**, a small table or tray usually with a ledge at the back and sides, adapted for placing on or over the bed of an invalid person.

1928 *Publishers' Weekly* 9 June 2373 'Cranford' was one of the favorite *bed-books of the late A. C. Benson. 1874 J. W. LONG *Wild-Fowl Shooting* 107 All you need to carry besides your ordinary bed-clothes is a common *bed-cord. 1886 *Harper's Mag.* June 58/2 Traces are made of hickory or papaw, as also are bed-cords. 1837 *United Service Jrnl.* June 107 Those *bed-covers which our grandmamas were delighted to cobble together. 1924 *Sale Catal.*, 100 Bed-covers (or *Bed Slips as they are sometimes named). 1895 DANA *Manual of Geol.* (ed. 4) 111 *Bed-plane faults are still another kind in which the plane of displacement is that between two layers or strata. 1850 N. KINGSLEY *Diary* 107 Putting in timbers to set the *bed-plates to the Engines. 1911 H. S. HARRISON *Queed* x. 119 The *bed-sitting-room into which he now ushered his guests. 1926 W. DEEPING *Sorrell & Son* i. § 2 A bed-sitting-room for him and the boy. 1894 *Daily News* 28 June 6/3 In white enamelled wood are some *bed tables...They are for resting on the knees while sitting up in bed.

Bed, *v.* Add: **6. b.** *To bed down*, (of cattle) to be bedded for the night. *U.S.*

1903 A. ADAMS *Log Cowboy* viii. 110 Not a hoof would bed down. 1920 MULFORD *J. Nelson* xxvi. 267 After..the great herd had bedded down.

17. *refl.* and *intr.* Of eels (see quots.).

1758 *Binnell's Descr. Thames* 194 [They] get into the soft Earth or Mud..and bed themselves. 1883 G. C. DAVIES *Norfolk Broads* xxxi. (1884) 239 Big and little [eels], start on this singular voyage,..and 'bed' themselves. 1902 CORNISH *Naturalist Thames* 216 In winter the eels 'bed', *i.e.* bury themselves in the mud.

Bedazement (bĭdē¹·zmĕnt). [f. BEDAZE *v.* + -MENT.] Bedazed condition.

1887 M. ARNOLD *Ess. Crit.* Ser. II. ix. (1888) 311 This bedazement with the infinite. 1903 *Westm. Gaz.* 30 June 7/2 The Unionist Party is being caught in the Protectionist toils before it can recover from its bedazement. 1918 A. T.

BED-BUG

Quiller-Couch *Foe-Farrell* x. 175 He followed me .. in mere bedazement, speechless.

Bed-bug. [Bed *sb.*] = Bug *sb.*² 2 a.

Freq. in U.S., on account of the use of *bug* in the general sense of 'insect'.

1809 R. B. Thomas *Farmer's Almanac* (Boston) July 1 Ladies, for mercy's sake, see about the bed bugs. 1813 [see Bed *sb.* 18]. 1834 S. Smith *Maj. Downing* 139 [He has] gone back..to New York..with a bed bug in his ear. 1863 Boudrye *Fifth N. Y. Cavalry* (1868) 348 With wise discrimination he can trace The difference 'twixt the louse and bedbug race. 1883 Nye *Baled Hay* 58 It seems the house ..has a lot of bedbug tonic. 1909 *Century Dict.* Suppl., *Bedbug-hunter*, a reduviid bug,..which inhabits houses, where it preys upon bedbugs.

Bedder (be·dəɹ). *University slang.* [See *-er⁶.] A bedroom.

1897 *Westm. Gaz.* 2 Feb. 1/3 She'd want to come up to my bedder and give me Somebody's beastly food for infants.

Bedding, *vbl. sb.* III. Add:

bedding-ground *U.S.* = *Bed-ground; **bedding-plane** = *bed-plane* (*Bed *sb.* 19); **bedding-plate** = *bed-plate* (Bed *sb.* 19).

1884 W. Shepherd *Prairie Exper.* 199 For the *bedding-ground a bare open spot..away from damp. 1920 Hunter *Trail Drivers of Texas* 215 It looked like a 'round up' when turning them off of the bedding ground. 1908 *Daily Chron.* 15 Dec. 1/5 Originally..horizontal, the *bedding plane now dips gently to the south. 1920 L. V. Pirsson *Physical Geol.* (ed. 2) 271 The two layers will be separated by a distinct juncture plane..; this is stratification, and the juncture plane is called a bedding plane. 1879 *Man. Artill. Exerc.* 255 The racer is secured to the *bedding-plate by steel bolts with wrought-iron nuts.

Beddy (be·di), *a.* [f. Bed *sb.* + -y¹.] Of stone: Having natural cleavages, with liability to split.

1709 T. Robinson *Nat. Hist. Westmld. & Cumbld.* xiv. 79 Under this white Metal, comes in a beddy Free-stone, which is always of a grey Colour. 1829 *Glover's Hist. Derby* I. 88 The freestones,..often called building stone.. (in distinction from beddy stone, flags or paviers). 1887 Baring-Gould *R. Cable* xlii, He may discover, when he's half cut it [*sc.* granite], that it's beddy (liable to split). 1892 *Northumbld Gloss.* s.v., 'Beddy freestone' is thus distinguished from a compact, granular deposit.

Bed-ground. *U.S.* [Bed *sb.* or *v.*] Ground on which cattle are bedded for the night.

1920 Mulford *J. Nelson* xxvi. 267 The bed ground was well chosen and the night promised to be a good one. 1921 — *Bar-20 Three* xvii. 220 The best bed-ground on the ranch.

Bedlamer. Add: **2.** A seal-hunters' name for a hooded seal of one year old and a harp-seal of two years old.

1854 *Chambers's Jrnl.* I. 76 The bedlamer, or old hood [seal]. 1895 *Outing* (U.S.) XXVII. 22/1 The harp seals.. post a sentinel, usually a bedlamer or two-year-old harp, on one of the highest pinnacles of the floe. *Ibid.* 23/2 The 'Sculp'..of the harp and bedlamer will average one hundred and fifty pounds.

Bedlington (be·dliŋtən). [Named after *Bedlington* in Northumberland.] In full *Bedlington terrier*: A short-haired terrier characterized by a narrow head, short body, and longish legs.

1872 in Dalziel *Brit. Dogs* (1889) II. 322 Of the breed of dogs for which this locality is noted, none has caused so much controversy as the Bedlington Terrier. 1875 in V. Shaw *Illustr. Bk. Dog* xix. (1884–6) 144 The Bedlington Terrier should be bread in the nostril, with a flesh-coloured nose. 1884–6 *Ibid.* 143 The support of the public at large has not hitherto extended much beyond affording prizes for Bedlingtons.

Bed-post. Add: *Between you and me and the bed-post*: in all confidence or secrecy.

1830 Mrs. Royall *Lett. fr. Alabama* 136 Between you and I and the bed post, I begin to think it all a plot of the priests. 1832 Lytton *Eugene A.* iv. i, Ah, sir, all very well to say so; but, between you and me and the bedpost, young master's quarrelled with old master.

Bed-rock. orig. *U.S.* (See Bed *sb.* 19.)

1850 N. Kingsley *Diary* 154 We are in for seeing the bed rock all along the bottom. 1871 Schele de Vere *Americanisms* (1872) 171 The miner..hopes to reach bed-rock, where gold is found in quantities. 1873 [G. A. Lawrence] *Silverland* 181 The material invariably waxes greatly richer as the 'bed-rock' is neared. 1879 [see Bed *sb.* 19].

fig. 1869 S. Bowles *Our New West* v. 99 We came down to 'bed-rock' as the miners say, i.e. an extra flannel shirt and a pocket-comb. 1883 Nye *Baled Hay* 65 Whenever the dead-beat poet strikes bedrock. *a* 1909 'O. Henry' *Roads of Destiny* iii. 52 From general topics the conversation concentrated to the bed-rock of grim personalities.

Bedside. Add:

b. *attrib.*, as *bedside book, literature*; **bedside manner**, the deportment of a medical man at the bedside of a patient.

1869 Prentiss *Stepping Heavenward* xxv. (1870) 237 He was her 'pet-doctor', he had such 'sweet, bed-side manners'. 1884 *Punch* 15 Mar. 121 *Lady Visitor.* 'Oh that's your Doctor, is it? What sort of a doctor is he?' *Lady Resident.* 'Oh well, I don't know much about his ability; but he's got a very good bedside manner!' 1907 *Westm. Gaz.* 4 Dec. 2/3 Sir Ray Lankester [at inaugural dinner of The Royal Society of Medicine, Dec. 3] claimed that .. to-day .. even the 'bedside manner' was strictly guided by scientific knowledge. 1907 *Brit. Med. Jrnl.* 28 Dec. 1845/1 The ordinary notion is that a good bedside manner consists of suavity carried to the verge of civility. 1920 *Cornhill Mag.* July 63 Bedside Books. *Ibid.* 64 Bedside literature.

Bedspread (be·dspred). orig. *U.S.* [f. Bed *sb.* + Spread *sb.* 8 a; cf. Du. *bed(de)sprei.*] A light thinnish coverlet for a bed, usually removed when the bed is occupied.

1848 Bartlett *Dict. Amer.*, *Bed-spread*, in the interior parts of the country, the common name for a *bed*-quilt, or coverlet. 1887 *Queen* 29 Oct. 558/1 For bedspread and chair-seats in your pink room. 1888 *Missouri Republican* 24 Feb. (Farmer) Mattresses, pillows, bedspreads, etc. 1914 *Evening News* 15 Oct. 7/6 You will have a pretty, light, and warm bedspread at a cost of 1s. 7½d. 1926 *British Weekly* 24 June 250/5 Silk bedspreads in rich colourings, with shot effects.

Bee¹. Add: **4.** (Earlier example.)

1769 *Boston Gaz.* 16 Oct. (Th.) Last Thursday about twenty young Ladies met at the house of Mr. L. on purpose for a Spinning Match; (or what is called in the Country a Bee).

7. bee-balm, (*a*) the balm or balm-mint, *Melissa officinalis*; (*b*) *American bee-balm*, Oswego tea; **bee-gum, bee-line** (earlier U.S. examples); also *attrib.*; **bee-loud** *a.*, resonant with the hum of bees; **bee-louse**, an insect of the family *Braulidæ*, parasitic on bees, esp. *Braula cæca*; **bee-man**, a bee-keeper or bee-master; **bee-martin** *U.S.*, the king-bird (*Tyrannus tyrannus*); **bee-moth** *U.S.*, *Galleria mellonella*: = *wax-moth* (see Wax *sb.*¹ 12); **bee-range** *U.S.*, a row of bee-hives; **bee-smoker**, a bee-keeper's apparatus for driving smoke into a hive to stupefy the bees while the honeycomb is being removed; **bee-tree** (earlier U.S. examples); **bee-van**, a van fitted with the apparatus necessary for the use of an itinerant lecturer on bee-culture.

1904 Mary E. Waller *Wood-Carver* vi. 264 Stalks of the *bee-balm. 1848 *Major Jones's Sk. Trav.* (Philad.) 143 (Th.) A fisherman's house..lookin' 'bout as big as a *beegum agin the everlastin stone wall behind it. 1859 Bartlett *Dict. Amer.* (ed. 2), *Bee-gum*, in the South and West, a term originally applied to a species of the gum-tree from which bee-hives were made; and now to beehives made of any kind of boards. 1830 *Massachusetts Spy* 24 Nov. (Th.) The squirrel took a *bee line, and reached the ground six feet ahead. 1862 Lowell *Biglow P.* Ser. II. ii. 20 An' Concord Bridge, thet Davis, when he came, Found was the bee-line track to heaven an' fame. 1891 W. B. Yeats *Lake Isle of Innisfree* i, Poems (1901) 126, [I will] live alone in the *bee-loud glade. 1875 J. Hunter *Man. Bee-keeping* xxx. 198 On the Continent of Europe a small insect known as the *Bee-louse, *Braula Cæca*, often infects the Bees. 1861 *Trans. Ill. Agric. Soc.* IV. 82 Our best *bee men. 1928 *Daily Tel.* 11 May 19/5 Uncontrolled swarming..is not permitted by the experienced modern beeman. 1891 J. B. Grant *Our Common Birds* 81 The honey-bee affords a most highly-prized tidbit to the Kingbird, and the gratification of the bird's taste has earned for it the name, *Bee-martin. 1829 *Massachusetts Spy* 27 May (Th.) Instinct teaches the *bee-moth to secrete herself, during the day, in the corners of the hive. 1837 Colman *Rep. Agric. Mass.* (1838) 71 The bee moth is to be guarded against by making the crevices of the hive tight with putty or glue. 1862 Harris *Insects Injur. Veget.* (ed. 3) 489 The group called Crambidæ, or Crambians, among which the bee-moth or wax-moth is to be placed. 1845 S. Judd *Margaret* III. 402 In the garden is a large *Bee-range. 1897 *Westm. Gaz.* 7 Aug. 8/1 A *bee-smoker filled with tobacco and brown paper. 1817 J. Bradbury *Trav.* 33 The hunters..had found a *bee-tree, and were returning to the boat for a bucket, and a hatchet to cut it down. 1834 Brackenridge *Recoll.* xii. 129 A harmless fellow, who followed hunting bee trees on the mountains for a living. 1896 *Natural Science* Oct. 273 County Councils have already done good work in providing lecturers..by means of travelling *bee-vans to many rural districts.

Bee³. The name of the letter B. *Bee aitch* = B.H., abbreviation of 'bloody hell'.

1928 Galsworthy *Swan Song* I. vii, Mr. Blythe's continual remark: 'What the bee aitch are they all about?'

Beech. 4. Add:

beech disease, beech-wood (see quots.); **beech-drops** (earlier U.S. quot.).

1905 *Daily Chron.* 3 July 9/1 *Beech disease (*cryptococcus fagi*) is widely distributed throughout England. 1815 Drake *Cincinnati* ii. 86 *Beech drops. 1913 Dorland *Med. Dict.* 919/1 *Beechwood sugar, xylose.

Beef, *sb.* Add: **3. b.** Common in U.S.

1758 *Essex Inst. Hist. Coll.* XVIII. 93 Six men..put under Guard on suspicion of killing a young Beef and 2 Calves. 1828 *Richmond Inquirer* 29 Aug. 4/2 (Th.) So little was the faith of those who knew him, he could not be trusted for a beef. 1878 *Southern Hist. Soc. Papers* VI. 212 Behind these came a beef, driven by soldiers...The beef was immediately shot at and butchered. 1904 Claiborne *Seventy-five Yrs. Old Virginia* 289 A beef..was driven up and shot.

4. *beef animal, cattle* (examples).

1837 Colman *Rep. Agric. Mass.* (1838) 73 They agree to pay 32 cents. for the offal of every *beef animal there slaughtered. 1789 Washington *Diaries* IV. 21 Four droves of *Beef Cattle for the New York Market. 1801 in C. Cist *Cincinnati* (1841) 188 To kill beef cattle. 1831 Peck *Guide for Emigrants* 169 The amount of beef cattle that Illinois is capable of producing. 1890 L. C. D'Oyle *Notches* 58 As they go along they cut out, from among the 'beef-cattle', the beasts that they branded yesterday. 1899 *Scribner's Mag.* XXV. 116/2 We passed a herd of fine beef cattle on their way to Santiago.

5. beef essence (see quot. 1890); **beef extract**, an extract of the soluble fibrin of beef.

1857 Dunglison *Med. Lex.*, *Beef essence. 1890 Billings *Med. Dict.*, *Beef essence*, cooked juice of beef, prepared by introducing lean beef in small pieces into a bottle, and subjecting it to heat of a boiling water-bath for an hour. 1894 Gould *Dict. Med.*, **Beef-extract*, the soluble fibrin of lean meat partly desiccated.

Beef, *v.* Add: **2.** To put more muscle into, to drive harder. *U.S.* (College slang.)

1860 *Yale Lit. Mag.* XXVI. 37 (Th.) The first boat in is the winner of the race, so round they turn, and 'beef her' for the home stretch.

3. To slaughter (an ox, etc.) for beef. Also *transf.*, to knock down. *U.S.*

1889 Farmer *Americanisms* 487 *To beef*, to kill oxen and convert their flesh into beef. 1916 B. M. Bower *Phantom Herd* xvi. 268, I calc'late I'd better beef another critter. 1926 J. Black *You Can't Win* xiii. 185 When one of them got peeved..some hard-fisted miner beefed him like an ox.

Beefy, *a.* Add:

Formerly used colloq. in depreciatory sense of 'carrying an excess of flesh', now usually with favourable implication = heavy and muscular.

1860 *All Y. Round* No. 66. 367 There are no beefy boys at these schools. 1865 *Slang Dict.*, *Beefy*, unduly thick or fat, commonly said of women's ancles. 1889 *Cent. Dict.*, *Beefy*.. 2. Brawny; muscular; hardy.

Beega(h, var. ff. *Bigha.

Beehive. 3. Add: **beehive tomb**, a dome-shaped subterranean tomb of the Mycenæan age.

1887 Mahaffy *Rambles Greece* xv. (ed. 3) 417 A race.. who constructed great beehive tombs. 1922 *Encycl. Brit.* XXX. 181/1 At Tiryns .. a beehive tomb, perfectly preserved and used throughout the classical period.

Beer, *sb.*¹ 4. Add: **beer drink** *S. Afr.*, a Kaffir gathering for the purpose of drinking Kaffir beer.

1895 Scully *Kafir Stories* 182 Lukwazi rode..from beer-drink to beer-drink, and he was drunk most of his days. 1899 W. H. Brown *On S. Afr. Frontier* xv. 213 When the bride reaches her new home the event is celebrated with a big dance and a 'beer drink'.

Beerless (bī·ɹlės), *a.* [f. Beer *sb.*¹ + -less.] Without or unprovided with beer.

1846 Ford *Gather. Spain* xv. 169 This..tealess, beerless, beefless land. 1909 *Daily Chron.* 24 June 4/4 A beerless public-house, where sugary non-alcoholic beverages are sold.

Beestie: see Bheesty.

1922 *Blackw. Mag.* Sept. 408/2 A beestie .. splashed a little water from his mussack on his upturned face.

Beetle, *sb.*² 5. Add: **beetle-crusher, -squasher** *slang*, a boot or foot, esp. a big one; an infantry soldier (Farmer *Slang*); so **beetle-crushing** *a.*, wearing big boots; belonging to the infantry; **beetle-stone** = Septarium 2.

1869 W. B. Woodgate *The O.V.H.* xxi, The infliction which the *beetle-crusher of a recent arrival had just inflicted on his pet corn. 1870 Miss Broughton *Red as Rose* xxxv, What howible boots! Whoever could have had the atwocity to fwame such beetle-cwushers? 1897 *Punch* 30 Oct. 195/1 If you need a meal, you can boil your beetle-crushers. 1871 G. A. Lawrence *Anteros* xiv, The possibility .. of exchange into a sedate, *beetle-crushing corps. 1859 Page *Handbk. Geol. Terms* s.v. *Septarium*, Such ..nodules..when split up..exhibit very curiously marked sections; hence the names **beetle-stones, turtle-stones*.

Beeve (bīv). [sing. form derived from *beeves*, pl. of Beef.] An ox; = Beef *sb.* 3.

1847 Whittier *Drovers* 61 Each stately beeve bespeaks the hand That fed him unrepining. 1899 *Daily News* 4 Dec. 8/3 Herefords are a noble type in all the points that are expected in the modern beeve.

Before. Add: **A. 2.** (Later U.S. quot.)

1870 T. D. Price *MS. Diary* 24 Aug., Had Barney [*sc.* a horse] shod before [= on front feet].

E. 1. b. The prep. in comb. with a sb., used *attrib.*

1898 *Daily News* 28 Sept. 5/1 The 'before luncheon' rehearsal. 1902 Mabel Barnes-Grundy *Thames Camp* 83 These before-breakfast expeditions. 1906 B'ness von Hutten *What became of Pam* II. x, The obligatory before people bravery of good breeding. 1920 P. G. Wodehouse *Damsel in Distress* iv, A fellow with the appearance of a before using advertisement of an anti-fat medicine.

Beg, *sb.* [f. Beg *v.*] *Card-playing.* In Seven-up, an act of begging (see next).

1897 R. F. Foster *Complete Hoyle* 289 (*Seven-up*) No second beg is allowed, but when only two play, if either player is dissatisfied with the new trump he may propose to bunch the cards.

Beg, *v.* Add:

2. h. *Card-playing.* In Seven-up, to ask for a point, or three additional cards and a new trump (said of the eldest hand).

1890 Marah E. Ryan *Told in Hills* 255 Why, you are begging on a full hand, Mister. 1897 R. F. Foster *Complete Hoyle* 289 If the eldest hand is not satisfied, he says: I beg; and the dealer, after examining his own hand, has the option of giving him a point or running the cards. *Ibid.* 290 Begging is resorted to by a player who holds no trumps.

i. Said of a dog trained to sit up and hold up its fore paws when told to beg.

1837 Jas. Prior *Life Goldsmith* II. 33 Teaching a favourite dog to sit upright upon its haunches, or as is commonly said, to beg. 1854 Wood *Anim. Life* 98 Four cats .. had taught themselves the art of begging like a dog...They waited until they saw the dog sit up in the begging position, and immediately assumed the same attitude. 1884 *Century Mag.* Dec. 198/2 To squat back and raise his front legs from the ground, much in the position of a 'begging' poodle. 1907 E. V. Lucas *Stray Ess. Dogs* iv. 32 He begs even when there is no meal in progress.

3. b. ellipt. for *beg leave.*

1767 Wilkes *Corr.* (1805) III. 197, I shall very soon beg to call the public attention to some points of national importance. 1898 *Westm. Gaz.* 29 Oct. 7/3 You say, 'I beg to take exception', which, of course, is not English at all. You mean, 'I beg (leave) to take exception'.

7. To make (one's way) begging.

1840 Dickens *Old C. Shop* xliv, To-morrow we will beg our way to some quiet part of the country.

Bège, variant of *Beige.

Begin, *v.* Add: **1. e.** Usu. with preceding negative: To make any (or the least) approach to, to come anywhere near. *U.S. colloq.*

1840 *Wilmington* (N. C.) *Commercial* 5 Apr. 2/1 We can't begin to come up to the prospectus. 1852 J. Weir *Simon Kenton* (Philad.) 13 Bust my buskins .. if them ar' kind of tactics would begin to do with the redskins. 1865 *Congress. Globe* Feb. 664/1 New York does not begin to have sixty-nine thousand square miles. 1888 *Harper's Mag.* Sept. 545/2 He got Bret to take her picture,..and he said it didn't begin to do her justice. 1907 Howells *Through Eye of Needle* 43 Often there's a..dinner that you couldn't begin to get for the same price anywhere.

f. To compare in any degree *with*. *U.S.*

1897 'Mark Twain' *Following Equator* xxxviii. 347 Indeed, our working-women cannot begin with her as a road-decoration.

Beginner. Add: **4.** *Arch.* The lower part of a mullion worked on the stone forming the sill.

1886 Willis & Clark *Cambridge* II. 514 The mullions of the four-light window..do not correspond with the 'beginners' on the sill.

Begoniaceous (bǐgōniē·ʃəs), *a. Bot.* [f. mod.L. *Begoniaceæ*: see -aceous.] Of or belonging to the family *Begoniaceæ*.

1889 in *Cent. Dict.*

Begorra (bǐgǫ·rǎ), *int.* Also **begarra, begorrah.** Irish alteration of the expletive *By God* (see God *sb.*¹ 13, 14); cf. Begar, and dial. *begor(z.*

1839 Carleton *Fardorougha* xvi, Begarra, Captain dear, it seems that good people is scarce. 1842 Lever *J. Hinton* ii, 'Begorra, you're in it', was the answer. 1856 — *Martins of Cro' M.* x, Be gorra! when a man would give four hundred for a bull, there's no saying what he'd stop at. 1895 Jane Barlow *Strangers at Lisconnel* i, Fine company they'd be for anybody begorrah.

Begrudgingly (bǐgrʌ·dʒiŋli), *adv.* [f. *begrudging* ppl. adj. + -ly².] In a begrudging manner or spirit.

1853 *Fraser's Mag.* XLVIII. 159, I looked begrudgingly on them as they occupied the whole pool. 1878 Hardy *Ret. Native* vi. iv, The original owners..cackled begrudgingly at sight of such a quantity of their old clothes. 1890 *Illustr. Lond. News* 29 Nov. 686/1 It was a narrow little way begrudgingly left between these sullen hedges.

Behaviourism (bǐhēi·vyəriz'm). *Psychol.* [f. Behaviour + -ism.] A theory and method of psychological investigation based on the study and analysis of behaviour. Hence **Beha·viourist**, one who practises this method; also *attrib.* **Behaviouri·stic** *a.*, of or belonging to the behaviourists; characterized by behaviourism.

1913 J. B. Watson in *Psychol. Rev.* XX. 158 Psychology as the behaviorist views it is a purely objective experimental branch of natural science. Its theoretical goal is the prediction and control of behavior. *Ibid.* 166, I feel that *behaviorism* is the only consistent and logical functionalism. 1916 *Boston Even. Transcript* 26 July 116 A behavioristic psychology. 1921 *Edin. Rev.* Apr. 351 Psychologists are divided into several camps, one of which, the American 'Behaviourists', cares very little for the social aspects of the subject. 1922 *Times Lit. Suppl.* 20 July, The determinist is logically driven to 'behaviourism'. 1944 J. B. Watson in *Psyche* July 11 Behavioristic psychology.

Behind. Add:

A. 7. (Later U.S. quot.)

1873 T. D. Price *MS. Diary* 19 Nov., Had Barney [*sc.* a horse] shod behind [= on hind feet].

B. *prep.* **3. c.** To *be behind the times*: see Time *sb.* 5. Also *attrib.*

1905 *Daily Chron.* 14 Feb. 6/3 A slow-going, old-fashioned, behind-the-times country.

C. as *sb.* **2.** *Australian Football.* A point scored when the ball is kicked behind the goal-line, within a specified distance on either side of the goal.

1888 *Pall Mall G.* 23 July 6/2 The visitors won by five goals and ten behinds to four goals and eight behinds. 1890 *Melbourne Punch* 14 Aug. 107/2 South Melbourne 3 goals 10 behinds.

b. (See quot.)

1898 *Encycl. Sport* II. 143 (Eton football) Each side consists of the 'bully', outsides, and behinds, but all except the behinds are commonly spoken of as 'the bully'. *Ibid.*, The 'behinds' are 'short' and 'long behind' and 'goals'.

Behinder (bǐhəi·ndəɹ). [f. Behind *adv.* + -er¹.] An operative in certain trades, as a tin-plate worker whose work lies behind the rolling-mill; and the man who works at the back of a welding-furnace in a tube mill.

1881 *Instr. Census Clerks* (1885) 105 Behinder. Tin Plate Worker. 1906 *Westm. Gaz.* 10 June 2/1 Behinders [tinplate millmen].

Beige (bēʒ), *sb.* and *a.* Also formerly **bège.** [a. F. *beige* adj.] **A.** *sb.*

1. A fine woollen fabric used as a dress-material, originally left in its natural colour but now dyed in various colours. Also *beige cloth.*

1858 Simmonds *Dict. Trade*, *Beige*, a French coarse cloth. 1879 *Cassell's Fam. Mag.* Sept. 634/2 The young lady.. is in bège and silk. *Ibid.* Nov. 755/1 Her skirt is of silk and beige cloth. 1882 Caulfeild & Saward *Dict. Needlework* s.v. *Beige* or *Bège*, Beige is made of undyed wool, is an extremely soft textile, graceful in draping, and employed for morning and out-door wear...There is a description of this textile, called snowflake beige, of a neutral ground. 1890 Doyle *Sign of Four* ii, The dress was a sombre grayish beige, untrimmed and unbraided.

2. A shade of colour like that of undyed and unbleached wool; yellowish-gray. Also *beige colour*, whence *beige-coloured* adj.

1879 *Cassell's Fam. Mag.* Mar. 249/1 Beige shades go with moss-green. *Ibid.* 250/2 The hat..is of bège-coloured plush. 1896 *Daily News* 9 May 8/6 The colour of grass lawn is technically known as beige. 1899 *Ibid.* 19 Aug. 7/4 Beige is the coolest possible colour.

B. *adj.* Of wool or woollen fabric, etc.: Of a natural yellowish-gray colour.

1879 [implied in 2 above]. 1899 *Daily News* 20 Mar. 8/7 The creamy lace .. will be deep enough in tint to be beige. 1926 *British Weekly* 24 June 250/5 The dress of beige lace is very much liked just now.

Beignet (bɛnye). *Cookery.* [F.] A fritter.

1892 *Encycl. Pract. Cookery* (ed. T. F. Garrett) I. 132/1, II. 34/2. 1901 *Daily Chron.* 7 Sept. 8/4 Cheese beignets.

Beisa (bəi·sǎ). [Native name.] An African antelope, *Oryx beisa*.

1902 *Encycl. Brit.* XXV. 454/2 Widely different..is the African group of *Hippotraginæ*...Among these are..the straight-horned gemsbok and beisa (*Oryx*). 1921 *Edin. Rev.* July 105 Others..are driving ostriches, gemsbok, and beisa antelopes.

Bejuco (bɛhū·ko). [Sp.] A liana, esp. the vine of tropical America *Hippocratea scandens*.

1848 Whittier *Slaves of Martinique* 19 As the serpent-like bejuco winds his spiral fold on fold Round the tall and stately ceiba, till it withers in its hold.

Bekko(-ware). [Jap.] Tortoise-shell.

1889 Rein *Industries Japan* 421 Bekkô, tortoise-shell, comes principally from *Chelonia imbricata*, L., the genuine loggerhead turtle.

Bel: see *Bael.

Belar (bī·lāɹ). Also **beela, belah, beala, billa, beal.** [Native name.] The Australian name for the she-oak *Casuarina glauca*, which the Colonists name the bull-oak; also, the wood of this tree.

1862 H. C. Kendall *Poems, Kooroora* 14 A voice in the beela grows wild in its wail. 1868 J. A. B. '*Meta*' 19 Blazing fire of beal. 1874 Ranken *Dom. Australia* vi. 110 These scrubs .. sometimes crown the watersheds as 'belar'. 1911 C. E. W. Bean *The 'Dreadnought' of the Darling* xix. 188 Mulga trees, and belar.

Belatedly (bǐlē·tėdli), *adv.* [f. Belated *ppl. a.* + -ly².] In a belated manner.

1896 *Westm. Gaz.* 21 Sept. 3/3 A fact..which her allies.. appear now somewhat belatedly to recognise. 1910 H. G. Wells *Hist. Mr. Polly* ix. 240 He came belatedly in. 1917 Chesterton *Short Hist. Eng.* 219 Gladstone..rather belatedly realized that the freedom he loved in Greece and Italy had its rights nearer home.

Belatedness. Delete † *Obs.* and add:

1909 *Letter to F. J. Furnivall* 7 Feb. (MS.), So please forgive the belatedness—to coin a word—of my good wishes! 1922 *Glasgow Herald* 12 Oct. 9 Considerable comment is being aroused by the long delay.., but this belatedness is, I understand, unavoidable.

Belay (bǐlē·), *sb.* [f. Belay *v.*] A turn or fastening of a rope by belaying (see Belay *v.* 5).

1908 *Westm. Gaz.* 12 June 5/1 A special knowledge of knots and roping method and belays might be their [*sc.* mountaineers'] only salvation.

Bel canto (bɛl ka·nto). [It., = fine song.] Singing characterized by full, rich, and broad tone.

1908 *Daily Chron.* 9 May 4/4 In New York musical critics complain that audiences do not want Wagner,..and that the public flocks to the Italian bel canto. 1920 *Glasgow Herald* 14 May 8 For pure bel canto the English blackbird is hard to beat.

Belfry. Add: **4. e.** The head. See also *Bat *sb.*¹ 1 b. *slang.*

1911 H. S. Harrison *Queed* vii. 84 Something loose in his belfry. 1911 R. D. Saunders *Col. Todhunter* ix. 123 It's a case of bats in his belfry on that one subject.

Belga (be·lgǎ). [L., fem. of *Belgus* Belgian, sc. *pecunia* or *moneta.*] A Belgian unit of exchange equivalent to five francs of Belgian currency.

1926 *Times* 27 Oct. 21/3 Dealings began yesterday in the Foreign Exchange market in the new Belgian currency unit, the belga. 1927 *Sunday Times* 13 Mar. 14 When the Belgian Government stabilised their franc, they established, for the purposes of international exchange, a unit called the 'belga'...The belga was established at 35 to the pound (reckoning the pound as 4.86 2-3 dollars).

Belgravia (belgrē·viǎ). [f. *Belgrave*, a town in Leicestershire, ground landlord of the site + -ia.] A fashionable residential district in London, south of Knightsbridge. Hence **Belgra·vian** *a.* and *sb.*, pertaining to or characteristic of, a resident in, Belgravia.

1848 Thackeray *Van. F.* li, Ask the Reverend Mr. Thurifor if Belgravia is not a sounding brass, and Tyburnia a tinkling cymbal. *Ibid.*, Her [*sc.* Semele's] myth ought to be taken to heart amongst..the Belgravians. 1851 Knight *Cycl. Lond.* 758 Architecture..in the Belgravian style. 1851 Mayhew *Lond. Labour* (1861) II. 395/2 The patrician squares of what has been called Belgravia and Tyburnia. 1864 M. Arnold *Lett.* (1895) I. 232, I just get here, within reach of the Belgravian paradise. 1882 *Encycl. Brit.* XIV. 851/1 The fashionable Belgravia was built about 1825. 1891 *Athenæum* 27 June 824/2 That ineffable Belgravian, Lady Galbraith. *Ibid.*, The De Moleyns are excellent conventional Belgravians.

Believe, *v.* **5.** Add: *Believe me*, used to strengthen an assertion.

1807–35 Moore *Ir. Melodies, Believe me* 1 Believe me, if all those endearing young charms..Were to change by tomorrow Thou wouldst still be ador'd. 1918 C. Sandburg *Cornhuskers* 30 Pike's Peak is a big old stone, believe me.

Belittle, *v.* **1.** (Earlier U.S. example.)

1782 Jefferson *Notes Virginia* (1787) 107 So far the Count de Buffon has carried this new theory of the tendency of nature to belittle her productions on this side the Atlantic.

3. (Earlier U.S. examples.)

1836 Haliburton *Clockm.* Ser. I. xxii. (1837) 226 When.. they began to raise my dander, by belittling the Yankees. 1843 — *Attaché* xviii. II. 39, I won't stay here and see you belittle Uncle Sam, for nothin'.

Belittler (bǐli·t'ləɹ). [f. Belittle *v.* + -er¹.] One who belittles or depreciates.

1887 *Daily News* 27 Jan. 6/3 The belittlers more than half confirm the story they would be delighted to contradict. 1898 *Pop. Sci. Monthly* LIII. 396 His belittlers emphasize Gerarde's ignorance of the classic writers on botany. 1920 *Contemp. Rev.* Aug. 171, I protest against all the patriotic belittlers of their own nations.

Bell, *sb.*¹ Add:

7. c. *To ring the bell* (colloq.): to carry off the prize; to be the best of a lot: in allusion to the ringing the bell attached to a strength-testing machine.

1928 *Publishers' Weekly* 26 May 2094 This [book] liberally illustrated, with a great jacket, rings the bell.

12. bell-bottomed *a.*, of trousers, having a considerable increase in width from below the knee to the bottom of the leg, giving a bell-shaped appearance; also, of an individual, esp. of a class accustomed to wear such trousers; **bell-bottoms** *sb. pl.*, bell-bottomed trousers; **bell-crater** *Gr. Antiq.*, a bell-shaped bowl (see Crater 1); **bell-hop** *U.S.* and *Canada*, a hotel page-boy (cf. *Bell-boy); **bell instrument**, one for signalling by means of a bell; **bell-mouth** *v. trans.*, to furnish with a bell-mouth, to expand like the mouth of a bell; **bell-punch** (see quot. 1884); **bell-push**, the button that is pushed to ring an electric bell; also, a table bell to be rung in this way; **bell-shade**, a bell-shaped light-shade; **bell-signal**, a signal transmitted by the bell-telegraph; so *bell-signalling*; **bell-skirt**, a bell-shaped skirt of a garment; **bell-telegraph**, an instrument in which two bells are used to transmit a message, one indicating (by its tone) the movement of the needle to the right, the other, to the left; **bell-topper**, a 'topper', top-hat, or tall hat, esp. one of old-fashioned type with bell-shaped crown.

1891 *Argus* 5 Dec. 13/2 (Morris) The *bell-bottomed ballottee. 1904 *Daily Chron.* 6 June 4/5 The crews were not less smart in..blue jackets and white bell-bottomed ducks. 1910 *Westm. Gaz.* 20 Jan. 2/3 A navvy with a three weeks' beard and bell-bottomed trousers. 1929 *Daily News* 10 Apr. 7/3 An official [of the Admiralty] said:..'*Bell-bottoms are the Navy. Abolish them and you abolish the Navy.' 1921 *Brit. Mus. Return* 61 *Bell-crater, latered-figure style. 1922 *Short Stories* Feb. 21/1, I ran into a *bell-hop who was paging me. 1926 Anita Loos *Gentlemen Prefer Blondes* 83 The boy friend of ours who is the bell hop, waked me up at ten o'clock. 1907 *Westm. Gaz.* 29 Oct. 9/1 He used the *bell instrument for the Kilburn signal-box. 1880 *Encycl. Brit.* XII. 463/2 It is often desirable to *bellmouth the ends of pipes. 1883 Ogilvie Suppl., *Bell-punch. 1884 Knight *Dict. Mech.* Suppl., *Bell Punch*, a hand-punch, for perforating a ticket or trip slip. It secures the piece punched out, and rings a bell; in some instruments it also registers the fares collected. 1894 *Westm. Gaz.* 26 Sept. 2/2 Thanks to the bell-punch, the number of passengers carried can now be estimated with tolerable accuracy. 1887 *Cassell's Fam. Mag.* 703/2 An indicating disc, which by its vibrations tells the *bell push..of the person who has rung up. 1921 *Blackw. Mag.* June 739/2 Pressing the bell-push to call the steward. 1890 W. J. Gordon *Foundry* 140 At one chair here some large *bell-shades for lamps are being made. 1905 *Westm. Gaz.* 19 Apr. 8/1 He announced the fact.. by sending to him the block telegraph *bell-signal 'Vehicles running away on right line'. 1905 *Daily Chron.* 16 Nov. 7/3 *Bell-signalling between torpedo craft and submarines in night-time. 1916 'O. Henry' *Strictly Business* xx, The latest thing in suitings with side vents and *bell skirt. 1874 Knight *Dict. Mech.*, **Bell-telegraph*, .. invented by Sir Charles Bright. 1859 W. Kelly *Life Victoria* I. 268 *note*, *Bell-topper was the derisive name given by diggers to old style hat, supposed to indicate the dandy swell. *Ibid.*, Merchants ventured to the Chamber of Commerce in the regular British 'bell-topper', some of the nattier going the length of sporting kid gloves. 1871 Simpson *Recit.* 6 A bell-topper hat. 1888 Farjeon *Miser Farebrother* II. i. 3 On his head the shiniest of belltoppers.

Bell, *v.*⁵ Add: **2. b.** *intr.* with *out.* To spread *out* like the mouth of a bell.

1922 *Blackw. Mag.* June 731/2 The skirt belled out like an inverted campanula bloom.

Belladonna. **2.** Add *attrib.*

1869 G. Lawson *Dis. Eye* (1874) 148 A fold of lint..kept moist with..the belladonna lotion. 1885 *Buck's Handbk. Med. Sci.* I. 486/2 The clinical history of a case of belladonna poisoning. *Ibid.*, The patient..had eaten..about thirty belladonna berries. 1890 Billings *Med. Dict.*, Belladonna-leaves...B. plaster. 1896 *Daily News* 10 Sept. 2/6 Belladonna poisoning. *Ibid.*, The belladonna liniment.

Belladonnin, -ine (belǎdǫ·nin, -in). *Chem.* [f. Belladonna + -in(e.] An alkaloid obtained from belladonna.

1880 *Jrnl. Chem. Soc.* XXXVIII. 410 Commercial belladonnine appears to be a mixture of belladonnine and atropine.

Bell-bird. Add quotations:

1825 Waterton *Wand. S. Amer.* 117 The celebrated Campanero of the Spaniards, called .. bell-bird by the English. 1839 E. J. Wakefield *Adv. N. Zealand* (1845)

I. 23 The melodious chimes of the bell-bird were especially distinct. 1865 *Ibis* (N.S.) I. 90 The Costa-Rican Bell-bird (Chasmorhynchus tricarunculatus). 1882 W. L. Buller *Birds N. Z.* 11 Anthornis melanura. Bell-bird. Mocker. Korimako. Makomako. 1888 *Ibid.* (ed. 2) I. 92 Anthornis Melanocephala. (Chatham-Island Bell-Bird.) 1903 *Westm. Gaz.* 28 Oct. 12/2 The Banded Bell-Bird..(*Cotinga cincta*).

Bell-boy. *U.S.* [Bell *sb.*¹ 1.] A boy who answers the bell in a hotel.

1886 *Harper's Mag.* Dec. 147/2 Neither of them had observed the bell-boy's face as Beryl ordered her ice-water. 1893 Kate Sanborn *S. California* 10 Brought back by a passing bell-boy, I shall now keep a tighter rein. 1899 G. Ade *Doc. Horne* ii. 10 Lusk sent the bell-boy for a bottle of whiskey. 1903 *Smart Set* IX. 13/2 A bell-boy arranged the tray on the table.

Belleter (be·lėtəɹ). *Hist.* [= *bell-yetter* (Bell *sb.*¹ 12).] A bell-founder.

1891 *Athenæum* 12 Sept. 360/2 On the tenor at Great Bradley we recognize the time-honoured name of a belleter whom Mr. Stahlschmidt..restored to renown. 1898 *Ibid.* 16 July 103 The Van den Ghens, of Louvain and Malines, were belleters of renown.

Belletrist. Add: *attrib.* or as *adj.* = Belletristic. **Belletri·stical** *a.*, **Belletri·stically** *adv.*

1840 *Fraser's Mag.* XXI. 199 No historical, biographical, geographical, or *belle lettristical* book..would now have much chance. 1889 J. M. Robertson *Ess. Crit. Method* 40 The belletrist essays of Mr. Lowell have had a wide public. 1894 J. Davidson *Ballads & Songs* 38 Heed not bellethrist jargon. 1894 *Westm. Gaz.* 25 June 3/1 He trifles bellettristically around ghosts,..and the relation of ghosts to religion.

Belleville (be·lvil), in full **Belleville boiler**, a large-tube marine boiler, named after its designer. Hence **Be·lvilled, Belville-boilered** *adjs.*, having a Belville boiler.

1899 Bullen *Way Navy* 84 Our fitness is also a grand testimonial in favour of the circular boilers, just as the cruisers' deficiencies are the reverse for the Bellevilles. *Ibid.*, The many glaring defects of the Belleville boilers. 1901 *Daily Chron.* 27 June 3/7 In the latest Hyacinth (Belleville) and Minerva (cylindrical) trials the Bellevilled ship has been an all-round victor. 1902 *Encycl. Brit.* XXVI. 283/2 The large-tube type hitherto generally used is the 'Belleville' boiler (which, however, has been adversely criticized, and was reported against by the Admiralty Boiler Committee in 1901). 1903 *Westm. Gaz.* 18 Feb. 7/3 The Belleville-boilered 'Hyacinth' has..broken down. 1904 *Daily Chron.* 4 Aug. 3/3 The Committee experimented with cylindrical boilers in the Minerva and Saxonia, with Bellevilles in the Diadem and Hyacinth.

Bellite (be·ləit). [ad. Sw. *bellit.*] An explosive consisting of a mixture of ammonium nitrate and metadinitro-benzene, invented by Carl Lamm of Stockholm.

1889 *Daily News* 2 Feb. 6/7 Bellite was burnt in a fire, smashed by a heavy weight, dropped from a height of 18 feet, and placed beside blasting powder, which was fired, with no explosion of the bellite.

Bellum (be·lǝm). [a. Pers. *balam*; cf. *balaum* s.v. *Baloon* in Yule *Hobson-Jobson*, and see Balloon *sb.*²] A small boat or canoe used in ports along the shores of the Persian Gulf.

1901 *Wide World Mag.* VI. 464/1 Queenie was landed easily enough in a *bellum*. 1916 Sir V. Horsley in *Life* (1919) 319 The whole real traffic of the place is done..by 'bellums': these are exactly like dugouts.

Bellwort. (Earlier examples.)

1846–50 A. Wood *Class-bk. Bot.* 555 *Uvularia perfoliata*, Mealy Bellwort...*U. grandiflora*, Large-flowered Bellwort.

Belly, *sb.* Add: The sound-board of a piano. Also *Comb.*, as *belly-bar, -bridge*; **bellyman**, the workman who makes and fits the 'belly'.

1845 G. Dodd *Brit. Manuf.* IV. 155 The 'bellyman' or 'sounding-board maker'. 1905 Hasluck *Pianos* 21 Prick through the belly about every ¾ in. with a small bradawl; this will help in putting on the belly bridges. 1905 *Sci. Amer. Supp.* 6 May 24536 The sound-board..barred beneath with batons..technically 'belly-bars', which strengthen the belly. 1910 *Daily Chron.* 19 Jan. 12/7 Pianos. Bellyman and marker-off contractor wanted.

Belly, *v.* Add: **4.** To remove the wool on the belly of (a sheep) before shearing. *Australia.*

1911 in Webster.

Beloid (bī·loid), *a.* [f. Gr. βέλος arrow, dart + -oid.] Arrow-shaped; spec. in *Craniometry*, having a broad occiput and narrow frontal region.

1901 G. Sergi *Mediterranean Race* v. 110 These six photographs present one [skull] of beloid shape.

Belong, *v.* **4. b.** Substitute: With an adv. or advb. phr. (esp. *here, where* = to this or these, to which), also without const.: To be related or connected; to have a certain connexion indicated or implied in the context. orig. *U.S.*

1861 [in Dict.]. 1866 Augusta Wilson *St. Elmo* x, To replace it in the glass box where it belongs. 1889 Walt Whitman in *Century Mag.* (1911) 11 Jan. 256/2 He was not a closet man, belonged out-of-doors. 1897 *N.E.D.* s.v. *Fit v.*¹ 2 The first example given under..3 may belong here. 1902 E. Carpenter *Civilisation* ii. 58 The theories of Science generally belong under the second head. 1924 D. H. Lawrence *England* 232 He was still in the choir of Morley Chapel—not very regular. He belonged just because he had a tenor voice, and enjoyed singing. 1924 Anne D. Sedgwick *Little French Girl* I. x, I saw you took to each other. I saw you belonged with each other. *Ibid.* II. xiv, From the first moment I saw her I felt that she belonged.

Below, *adv.* **1.** Add: Phr. *Below there!* a warning addressed to persons to beware of a descending object.

1896 *Bow Bells* 6 Mar. 264/2 One man was tying a paint-pot to the rung of the ladder, the cord slipped, down came the pot, the man singing out 'Below there!'

3. (Earlier and later U.S. examples.)

1645 *Springfield Rec.* I. 154 The Brooke in the longe meddow..and the Brooke a little below on the other side. 1817 *Essex Inst. Hist. Coll.* VIII. 238 Mr. Lefavour of Salem, who was living below, had come up here on business. 1845 Simms *Wigwam & Cabin* Ser. I. 16 There's ne'er a house either above or below for a matter of fifteen miles.

5. = below zero (see B. 6 a).

1904 Mary E. Waller *Wood-Carver* ii. 82 [It was] twenty-seven below this morning.

Belt, *sb.*¹ Add: **1. e.** *To tighten* (etc.) one's *belt*: to stave off hunger for lack of a meal.

1841 Lever *C. O'Malley* xx, 'Perhaps not' lisped Melville, tightening his belt; 'but it's devilish convivial'. 1876 Besant & Rice *Golden Butterfly* Prol. i, This pilgrim has tightened his belt to stave off the gnawing at his stomach. 1885 Rider Haggard *K. Solomon's Mines* vi, Umbopa..with a leather belt strapped so tight round his stomach to 'make his hunger small', as he said. 1891 Kipling *Life's Handicap* 190, I also was once starved, and tightened my belt on the sharp belly-pinch. 1907 Mulford *Bar-20* v. 46 They's three things that's good for famine.. Yu can pull in your belt, yu can drink, an' yu can eat. 1927 *Observer* 24 Apr. 15/3 A travelling troupe who quoted Corneille while tightening their belts.

2. d. A zone or district. Usu. with defining term as *black, corn, cotton, wheat belt.* *U.S.*

1871 R. Somers *Southern States* xxxvii. 263 The 'Cotton Belt' of the Southern States. 1875– [see *Black belt]. 1891 *Harper's Mag.* Aug. 446/2 A fierce storm swept over the whole gold belt. 1903 A. B. Hart *Actual Govt.* 116 Illinois is divided into a wheat belt, a corn belt, and the city of Chicago.

3. b. In a machine gun, a length of woven fabric or of metal plates pinned together, fitted with cartridges and revolving on the feed-block.

1902 *Encycl. Brit.* XXX. 403/1 Figs. 7 and 8 show the feed-block and method of packing the cartridge belts. The greatest number usually carried in a belt is 250. *Ibid.* 406/1 A belt of cartridges..has been placed on the feed-wheel. 1914 *Scotsman* 26 Sept. 5/6 The belt of the gun [*sc.* a Maxim] was still charged.

6. b. belt-driven *a.*, *Mech.*, driven by means of a flexible endless belt; hence **belt drive**, driving mechanism of this type; **belt-knife**, (*a*) a knife carried in a belt for use as a weapon, hunting-knife, etc.; (*b*) *U.S.*, a revolving knife on the band-saw principle, used in splitting hides or skins; **belt line**, a railway or tram line that makes a complete circuit of a city; so *belt tram.*

1906 *Motor Cycles & how to manage them* (ed. 10) 89 Types of *Belt Drive. 1907 *Daily Chron.* 17 Oct. 8/2 A motor cycle..with belt drive. 1893 *Jrnl. Soc. Arts* 5 May 621/1 Seventeen dynamos, all *belt-driven. 1906 *Westm. Gaz.* 26 Mar. 10/2 The old belt-driven Benz [motor car] of a prehistoric past. 1908 *Ibid.* 30 Jan. 4/1 A belt-driven fan. 1892 Nasmith *Student's Cotton Spinning* Index 428 *Belt Driving. 1895 *Daily News* 21 Mar. 5/7 That they had not ..so much as a *belt knife. 1909 H. G. Bennett *Manuf. Leather* 279 There are three types of splitting machine, the 'union', the vibrating knife, and the band-knife (or belt-knife) machine. 1900 *Engineering Mag.* XIX. 698 The *belt-line railway, running largely in cuttings and underground. 1894 J. Dale *Round the World* 333 The *belt tram took us round the city, 8 miles.

Belt, *sb.*⁴ *colloq.* [f. Belt *v.* (sense 4).] A heavy blow or stroke.

1899 Somerville & Ross *Exper. Irish R.M.* 217 Will I give him [*sc.* a horse] a couple o' belts, your Honour? 1927 *Glasgow Herald* 26 Aug. 11 [He] took three mighty belts at the ball.

Belt, *v.* Add: **2.** *spec.* to girdle (a tree) by stripping off the bark. *U.S.*

1853 Strother *Blackwater Chron.* xiv. 216 One man,.. in a hundred days, would belt or deaden one hundred acres.

6. *trans.* To connect with a machine-driven belt. Also *absol.*

1902 J. S. Thompson *Mech. Linotype* xxiv. (1908) 169 The size of the pulley on the motor to which it is belted will decrease the speed. *Ibid.* 172 To drive the machine by belting directly to the intermediate shaft.

7. *intr.* To hurry, to bustle. *dial.* and *U.S.*

1890 *Gloucester Gloss.* (E. D. S.), *Belt v.* to racket or bustle about. 1894 *Outing* (U.S.) XXIV. 57/2, I belted along as fast as the waders and treacherous footing would allow.

Be·ltful. [f. Belt *sb.*¹ + -ful.] As many cartridges as are contained in a belt.

1916 Boyd Cable *Action Front* 131 The first [anti-aircraft] gun opened with a trial beltful.

Belting, *vbl. sb.* Add:

1. b. Beating, thrashing.

1854 Miss Baker *Northampt. Gloss.* s.v. *Belt*, 'He got a good belting'. 1896 A. Morrison *Child of Jago* 33 The belting was bad..very bad. 1907 *Westm. Gaz.* 16 Aug. 5/2 He is a very bad boy...After a 'belting' he seems worse.

2. (Add quotations.)

1884 A. Daniell *Princ. Phys.* 162 Belting.—There is a very interesting and familiar case in which friction serves as a means for the transmission of energy—that is, transmission by machine-belting. 1898 *Westm. Gaz.* 14 Jan. 9/3 Men mounted the belting of the ship. 1910 *Ibid.* 11 Jan. 5/2 The snapping of some of the steel belting.

Bematist (bī·mătist). [ad. Gr. βηματιστής, f. βηματίζειν to measure by paces, f. βῆμα pace, step.] An official road-measurer or surveyor in the time of Alexander the Great and the Ptolemies.

1875 *Encycl. Brit.* II. 748/2 The bematists or surveyors of Alexander and the Ptolemies. 1886 Sheldon tr. *Flaubert's Salammbô* x. 242 The bematists of Euergates, who measured the heaven by calculating the number of their paces.

Bemusedly (bǐmiū·zėdli), *adv.* [f. Bemused *ppl. a.* + -ly².] In a bemused or bewildered manner or condition.

1896 A. Morrison *Child of Jago* 141 'Lor', she said bemusedly. 1921 A. S. M. Hutchinson *If Winter Comes* III. ii. § 1 He spoke bemusedly. No need for caution that he could see.

Bemusement (bǐmiū·zmėnt). [f. Bemuse + -ment.] Bemused condition.

1907 Galsworthy *Country House* I. viii, The devilry, mockery, admiration, bemusement, had gone out of his face. 1921 A. S. M. Hutchinson *If Winter Comes* II. iv. § 9 She threw away the bemusement in which she had sat.

Benab (be·næb). Also **benaboo.** [Arawak (*u*)*bannabuhu.*] In Guiana, a shelter made of a framework of poles, covered with branches and leaves.

1899 Rodway *Guiana Wilds* 251 The benab was the property of the Mission, and had been put up for the accommodation of visitors. 1922 *Blackw. Mag.* July 10/1 There are Indian benabs, close by in the forest.

Benatura (benatū·ra). [app. alteration of *Bénitier on some wrong analogy.] A holy-water stoup, bénitier.

1868 J. Maclean *Hist. Trigg Minor* I. 508 On the eastern side of the south door is a fine Benatura,..well carved. 1891 *Athenæum* 28 Mar. 412/3 Dr. Fryer..reported the discovery of the site of an ancient Benatura in the south porch of St. Mary Redcliffe.

Bench, *sb.* Add:

7. (Illustrations of U.S. use.)

1811 *Deb. Congress* (1853) 2116 Towards the left flank this bench of high land widened considerably. 1846 E. Bryant *What I saw in California* (1849) 133 The mountains on both sides rise in benches one above another. 1873 J. H. Beadle *Undevel. West* xxiv. 481 We turn south-west, rising by successive 'benches' to a vast barren table land. 1892 *Harper's Mag.* June 100/2 The hills and upper benches, all covered with self-curing bunch grass, will still remain. 1920 Mulford *J. Nelson* xii. 129 Right on them benches on th' east end of th' mountain.

b. *Geol.* A natural terrace marking the outcrop of a harder seam or stratum.

1884 *Science* 13 June 729/1 On this rest argillaceous, splendent, siliceous talc schists..; and on these, three benches of conglomerates, tuffs, and argillaceous schists and lime-stones. 1898 *Westm. Gaz.* 20 May 9/1 The same feature will doubtless exist as each bench is worked.

c. The ledge or floor upon which the retorts stand in a retort-house; also, a set of retorts; also, the complete furnace or oven containing a set of retorts.

1841 *Civil Eng. & Arch. Jrnl.* IV. 100/2 The works are laid out in eight distinct sections of ten 'benches', or thirty retorts each. 1920 *Conquest* May 320/3 In a large retort-house the settings are built in benches containing as many as 150 'through' retorts.

9. bench-man, an operative who works at a bench, in various trades, as a joiner; also, a cabinet-maker who assists at bench-work, a labourer who works at a coke bench; **bench root** *Agric.*, 'an abnormal root development due to the presence of tough seed coats; the roots are often twisted together or badly formed' (Webster *Addenda* 1918); **bench-show** (U.S. quot.); **bench test**, a test of a motor engine carried out in a workshop before fitting it to a motor body; **bench-wagon** *U.S.*, an open carriage with seats across it; **bench-warrant** (mod. U.S. example).

1901 *Daily Chron.* 7 May 10/6 Boot trade.—Good *bench-man wanted for repairs. 1887 *Harper's Mag.* May 934/1 The American *bench shows furnish an opportunity to most readers to see the best mastiffs in the country. 1909 *Westm. Gaz.* 6 Apr. 4/2 Their .. 38 h.p. motors which recently underwent a 132 hours' continuous running *bench test at Coventry. 1885 Howells *Silas Lapham* (1891) I. 88 Lapham arrived..in his four-seated *bench-wagon. 1878 J. H. Beadle *Western Wilds* xxxii. 514 Another called for the immediate arrest of Brigham on a *bench warrant before he could fly the country.

Bench, *v.* Add:

3. c. *trans.* To put (a dog) on a show-bench for exhibition; to exhibit at a dog-show.

1891 *Times* 28 Oct. 11/5 Almost every breed of spaniel is benched. 1898 *Standard* 1 Dec. 2/6 Possibly the soundest coloured Chow ever benched. 1924 *Westm. Gaz.* 22 Oct., Among those benched at the Toy Dog Show..will be black-and-tan miniature dogs.

5. *trans.* To turn off, to discharge. *U.S. slang.*

1917 Mathewson *Sec. Base Sloan* xvi. 224 Some of you stuffed sausages will be benched mighty quick if you don't wake up.

Bench-land. *U.S.* [Bench *sb.* 7: see above.] Land situated in, or forming, a 'bench'.

1857 W. Chandless *Visit Salt Lake* II. x. 326 Bench-land fifty or hundred feet above the water-level. 1862 B. Young *Jrnl. Discourses* IX. 169 We can gather from this bench land—this gravelly soil—thirty bushels of wheat to the acre. 1868 *Life among Mormons* 71 The entire valley, with all the bench-lands and the mountains surrounding these. 1892 *Harper's Mag.* June 96/2 The bench lands form the bulk of what remains.

Bench-legged, *a. U.S.* [Bench *sb.* 1.] Having the fore-legs wide apart.

1866 C. H. Smith *Bill Arp* 159 Dodds says,..he'd have his soul transmigrated to a bench-leg'd fice [dog]. 1889 *Harper's Mag.* Aug. 485/2 Selling his little bench-legged mule to a travelling showman. 1903 A. Adams *Log Cowboy* xii. 79 The Indians' little bench-legged ponies were no match for them. *Ibid.* xv. 100 A long bench-legged black dog with a Dutch name.

Bench-table. *Hist.* [f. Bench *sb.* + Table *sb.* 8 c.] An official body of benchers of the Inner Temple: see quot. 1896.

1673 *Cal. Inner Temple Rec.* (1901) III. 92 Ordered at the bench table that Kenricke Eyton..and Ralph Sumner.. do by the beginning of Michaelmas term next write a court hand. 1692 Sherlock (*title*) A Sermon Preached at the Temple-Church, May 29. 1692. And Printed at the Desire of the Bench-Table of the Honourable Society of the Inner-Temple. 1896 *Cal. Inner Temple Rec.* I. Introd. p. xxxiii, The officers of the house..met together frequently..at what was and is known as the Bench Table, when orders were made for the governance of the Inn.

Bend, *sb.*⁴ Add:

2. b. *The bends*: a disease incident to those who work under high atmospheric pressure, characterized by paralytic and apoplectic symptoms. Also called *caisson-disease*.

1894 *Westm. Gaz.* 16 Oct. 3/2 The pressure..is quite enough to give the men a dose of the 'bend' [*sic*] as it is called. 1902 *Idler* July 485 That..terrible air-pressure disease known as the 'bends'. 1913 *Pembrey & Ritchie's Gen. Path.* 494 These pains [*sc.* in Caisson disease] pass off in a few hours, and are known to the workmen as 'bends', apparently because of the flexed positions which they induce.

5. b. The curve of a gun-stock, shaped to fit the arm of the person for whose use it is made.

1859 'Stonehenge' (J. H. Walsh) *Shot-gun & Sporting Rifle* iv. i. 229 In addition to the adaptation in length and bend of the stock, it is also..bent sideways. 1892 Greener *Breech Loader* 73 The distance from A to heel, and from B to comb. This is the bend.

c. A curved drain-pipe.

1884 Knight *Dict. Mech.* Suppl., *Bend*, a flexed pipe, changing the direction. 1908 *Animal Managem.* 53 Any change of direction being made by curved pipes or 'bends'.

d. In a carding machine, the semicircular frame which carries the brackets in which the rollers are borne; also, in a carding machine of the revolving flat type, the curved surface which sustains the chain of flats.

1882 *Spons' Encycl. Industr. Arts* V. 2073 As the periphery passes round to the cylinder, the teeth are then in the act of ascending (the bend being thus in the opposite direction), and presenting facilities for being stripped of the wool they have acquired. 1890 Nasmith *Mod. Cotton Spinn. Mach.* 64 The phrase 'bend' should only be applied to that portion of the mechanism upon which the flats actually travel. 1892 — *Student's Cotton Spinning* 101 The whole of the rollers are borne in brackets fixed to a semicircular frame bolted on the lower frame P, and known as the 'bend', the brackets having open bearings formed at their heads.

III. 10. Phrases. *On the bend*: by means that are not straightforward, 'crookedly'. *To go on the* (or *a*) *bend*: to go 'on the spree'; cf. *Bender 5 b. *slang.*

1863 Jeaffreson *Live it Down* xxviii, I'll order my executor to buy my coffin off the square. He shall get it on the bend, somehow or other. 1887 F. Francis Jr. *Saddle & Mocassin* 84 They do say as he was 'customed to go on a scoop—on a bend, occasionally, as it were. 1891 Kipling *City Dreadf. Nt.* 71 The gallant apprentice may be a wild youth with an earnest desire to go occasionally 'upon the bend'. 1891 — *Life's Handicap* (1915) I. 82, I went on the bend with a intimate friend.

b. *Above one's bend*: beyond one's powers. *U.S.*

1835 Crockett *Tour down East* 44, I shall not attempt to describe the curiosities here [at Peale's Museum]; it is above my bend. 1848 J. F. Cooper *Oak Open.* (De Vere) It would be above my bend to attempt telling you all we saw among the Redskins. 1871 Schele de Vere *Americanisms* (1872) 577 *Above one's bend* means, above one's power of bending all his strength to a certain purpose.

Bender. Add:

4. b. A leg. *U.S. slang.*

1849 Longf. *Kavanagh* xii, Young ladies are not allowed to cross their benders in school.

5. b. A bout of drinking, a spree; a riotous feast. *U.S.*

1827 *Newsp.* in Bartlett *Dict. Amer.* (1859), A couple of students of Williams College went over to North Adams on a bender. 1848 Lowell *Biglow P.* Ser. I. Introd., 'Two Gunners' 39 'I won't agree to no such bender,' Sez Isrel; 'keep it [the goose] tell it's tender.' 1862 *Ibid.* Ser. II. i. 272 To go off on benders..an' waste their time in foolin'. 1886 J. Hatton *Old Ho. Sandwich* I. II. iv. 82 The boss of Drummond's Gulch may be said to have begun his 'bender', as a bout of drunken dissipation was called in these regions. 1902 A. D. McFaul *Ike Glidden* xv. 177 Jim took the money, and started for the city on an old fashioned bender.

7. A big or good specimen of its kind; a 'whopper', 'bouncer', 'corker' (*s.w. dial.*).

1842 Daniel *Bride of Scio* 190 (E.D.D.) Ma vice [= fist] es wat I kal a bendur. 1891 *Hartland Gloss.* s.v., 'A proper bender, an' no mistake!' 1898 Kipling *Day's Work*, *William the Conqueror* 180 By Jove, it's a bender of a night.

Bending, *vbl. sb.*¹ Add:

2. b. *spec.* The curvature of a beam. *Bending moment*, the moment tending to produce curvature in a beam. *Bending stress*, pressure that causes curvature in a bar, beam, etc.

1858 Bending moment [see Moment *sb.* 8 b]. 1876 *Encycl. Brit.* IV. 290/1 The moment of this couple must be equal to the moment of the couple tending to bend the beam at this section, or to what is called the bending moment. 1887 *Ibid.* XXII. 601/1 The strain produced by bending stress in a bar or beam. 1888 *Lockwood's Dict. Terms Mech. Engin.*, *Bending*, or *Flexure*, the curvature of a beam about its axis or central plane.

7. The action or process of shaping wood, iron, or other material by pressure instead of by cutting or casting. Chiefly *attrib.* and *Comb.*: *bending machine, rolls*; **bending cradle** (see quot. 1874); **bending form**, a kind of bench anvil used in bending steam, gas, and water pipes; **bending slab**, an iron floor upon which ships' frames are bent.

1874 Thearle *Naval Archit.* 132 The 'bending cradle' is composed of a pair of stout iron vertical frames, between the bars of which transverse beams of iron, bent to the necessary curvature, are secured. 1884 Knight *Dict. Mech.* Suppl. 97/1 Bending and Straightening Machine. *Ibid.* 97/2 A French bending machine, for cart and wagon tires. 1888 *Lockwood's Dict. Terms Mech. Engin.*, *Bending Rolls*, heavy rollers of cast iron or steel set in strong standards, and used either for the straightening of crooked plates or for bending them into arcs of circles or into complete cylinders. *Ibid.*, *Straightening machine*,..a machine in which channel, angle, and bar iron are straightened or bent, in boiler and smiths' shops, by squeezing...Since it will bend as well as straighten it is also called a bending machine. 1890 W. J. Gordon *Foundry* 60 The 'bending-slab'—a pavement of square masses of iron,..large enough to take any frame required in the ship to be built.

8. *Horsemanship.* (See quot. 1891.)

1891 J. M. Brown *Polo* 323 The 'bending' course is a capital institution, of which I believe the Earl of Harrington was the originator about eight years ago. Two lines of sticks should be set up 20 yards apart and parallel to each other. The sticks should be about 7 feet high and 8 yards apart...Then begin by cantering your pony up one side and down the other zigzagging between the posts. *Ibid.*, I may here remark that this 'bending' competition is the most invaluable practical test of a really good polo pony. 1900 *Daily News* 16 Mar. 3/4 The bending competition, in which the considerations of pace, precision, riding, and 'make' [of a pony] are joined in equal importance. 1908 *Animal Managem.* 153 The 'bending' lessons of the riding school. 1922 *Times* 20 June 7/2 Both [polo ponies] being particularly handy at turning and bending.

Bendy (be·ndi). Also **bendee, bendi, bindy, banda.** [Hind. (Hindi) *bhiṇḍī.*] The plant *Hibiscus* (or *Abelmoschus*) *esculentus*, also the fruit of this plant. Also *attrib.* = Okro.

1812 Maria Graham *Jrnl. Resid. India* 24 The bendy, called in the West Indies *okree*, is a pretty plant resembling a holyhock. 1813 Jas. Forbes *Oriental Mem.* I. 32 The banda (hibiscus esculentus, Linn.) is a nutritious oriental vegetable. 1866 *Treas. Bot.* 1135/1 *Tetrameles*...This tree is the Jungle-bendy of India, and the Weenong of Java. 1927 *Blackw. Mag.* Nov. 678/2 Flanking the western slopes ..were the dense bendi scrubs.

Bendy-tree. (See quot.)

1886 Yule & Burnell *Hobson-Jobson*, *Bendy-tree*, this, according to Sir G. Birdwood, is the *Thespesia populnea*.

Benedictiness (benǐdi·ktinės). [f. Benedictine + -ess.] A nun of the Benedictine order.

1872 J. Morris *Condit. Cath. under Jas. I* p. ccvii. *note*, Father Gerard..took one [image] to Ghent, which he gave to the English Benedictinesses there. 1909 *Dublin Rev.* Jan. 61 We have Benedictinesses at East Bergholt [etc.].

Benedictional (benǐdi·kʃənăl), *a.* [f. Benediction + -al.] Of or pertaining to the pronouncing of a benediction.

1902 *Encycl. Brit.* XXVII. 238/2 Small benedictional crosses belong to each altar, and processional crosses are common [in the Coptic Church].

Benedictionally (benǐdi·kʃənăli), *adv.* [f. prec. + -ly².] In or by way of benediction.

1911 W. De Morgan *Likely Story* 208 The old lady..kissed her benedictionally.

Benefact (be·nǐfækt), *v.* [Back-formation f. Benefactor.] *trans.* To help or endow as a benefactor.

[1594 O. B. *Questions* 3 Whose benefacting .. extended chiefle to their supposed children and Paramoures.] 1898 E. W. B. Nicholson in *Westm. Gaz.* 10 June 2/3 Mr. Gladstone..offered to try to get one of the richest men in the world to benefact us. 1923 *Chamb. Jrnl.* Aug. 507/2 He did not want to benefact Hamborne in any kind of way. 1924 *Serena Blandish* vii, The benefactress was gone, and the benefacted remained alone to ponder her benefactions.

Benefactrix (be·nǐfæktriks). [mod. L., f. Benefactor after *lector, lectrix.*] A female benefactor.

1614 Day *Festivals* xi. (1615) 301 The Widowes that wept so much for the Death of Dorcas their Benefactrix. 1713 *Lond. Gaz.* No. 5124/4 The great Benefactrix unto the Nations of the Earth. 1775 Challoner in E. H. Burton *Life* (1909) II. xxviii. 116 God reward the good Lady, our benefactrix. 1907 W. De Morgan *Alice-for-Short* xxxii, The expedient of merging her personality in that of an imagined benefactrix.

Bénéficiaire (benefisyɛ̄r). [a. F. *bénéficiaire*, f. *bénéfice* benefit.] A player who is taking a benefit (Benefit *sb.* 4 a).

1905 *Daily Chron.* 13 July 3/5 Fifty baskets of flowers.. were brought on the stage and surrounded the bénéficiaire. 1927 *Daily Tel.* 23 Aug. 5/3 Sandham's Benefit Match... The beneficiaire was not destined to do well.

Benefit, *sb.* Add:

4. d. That which a person is entitled to in the way of pecuniary assistance, medical or other attendance, pension, and the like, under the National Insurance Act of 1911 or as a member of a benefit society; more explicitly *maternity, medical benefit.*

1911 *Act 1 & 2 Geo. V*, c. 55 § 8 Payment in the case of the confinement of the wife..of an insured person..of a sum of thirty shillings (in this Act called 'maternity benefit'). *Ibid.*, In the case of insured persons who have attained the age of seventy, the right to sickness benefit and disablement benefit shall cease. *Ibid.* § 10 His right to medical benefit, sanatorium benefit, and maternity benefit shall be suspended. 1927 Carr-Saunders & Jones *Soc. Struct. Eng. & Wales* 150 The applicant may at the discretion of the Ministry of Labour receive 'extended' benefit for the remainder of the benefit year.

e. Something beneficial or profitable; an agreeable occupation and the like; a fine time, a fine job: used ironically. *colloq.*

Benevolence. Add:

2. b. *Love of benevolence*, in religious use: see Love *sb.* 2.

Bengal. **2.** Add:

Bengal isinglass = *Agar-agar.

1863 [see *Agar-agar].

Bengalese (bengǫlī·z), *a.* and *sb.* [f. Bengal + -ese.] = Bengali *a.* and *sb.*

1778 Halhed *Gram. Bengal Lang.* p. xxi, The native Bengalese. 1871 Calverley *Fly Leaves* (1903) 91 A patient of Skey's, Who is prone to catch chills, like all old Bengalese.

Benignant, *a.* Add:

2. b. Of a disease: Not malignant or recurrent; = Benign *a.* 5 b.

1897 [see Siphoned *a.* 2]. 1901 Dorland *Med. Dict.*

Benish (bǐnī·ʃ). Also 8 **beniche,** 9 **beneesh.** [Turkish *binuš, bunuš* (properly = riding-habit), f. *binnek* to mount a horse.] An outer garment of cloth with very full sleeves.

1797 *Encycl. Brit.* VI. 405/2 [The Mamlouks] have an outer covering called the *beniche*, which is the cloak or robe of ceremony...Thus when the beniche and other accoutrements are on, the whole body appears like a long sack. 1836 Lane *Mod. Egypt.* I. 34 A *beneesh*, or *benish*; which is a robe of cloth, with long sleeves. 1840 J. B. Fraser *Koordistan* II. 404 The furred *kurks* and flowing *benishes* of former days.

Bénitier (benitye). [Fr., f. *bénit(e* blessed + -*ier* -er² 2.] A vessel to contain holy water.

1858 Simmonds *Dict. Trade*, *Benitier*, a holy-water pot or vessel, sometimes a large shell, used in Catholic countries. 1907 *Connoisseur* 1 Oct. 4/6 For benitiers—especially of the domestic type—Flanders will safely bear the palm. 1908 Beatrice Harraden *Interplay* II. i, A photographic series of bénitiers and drinking horns. 1913 *Blackw. Mag.* Aug. 156/2 Marie took it to the church and dipped it into the bénitier.

Benitoite (benī·toˌəit). *Min.* [f. San *Benito* County, California, where found: see -ite¹.] A sapphire-blue crystallized barium titanosilicate.

1912 *Brit. Museum Return* 196 Benitoite crystals.

Be·njamin³. The name of the patriarch Jacob's youngest son. Hence *allusively*, the youngest (and, consequently, favourite) son of a family. *Benjamin's mess*: the largest share or portion (with allusion to Gen. xliii. 34).

1852 H. W. Greville *Leaves fr. Diary* (1883) 417 Another person was chaffing Lady Colchester..upon the Government being designated 'Benjamin's Mess' (with allusion to Benjamin Disraeli). 1913 Ascott R. Hope *An Old Friend* viii. in *Half and Half Tragedy* 219 The new uncle being my granny's Benjamin. 1926 W. Deeping *Sorrell & Son* xviii. § 1 Kit was his Benjamin of pupils.

Benne (be·nǐ). Also **beni, bene, benni, benny.** [ad. Malay *bijen.*] Sesame, the East Indian plant *Sesamum indicum.* Chiefly *attrib.*, as *benne-seed, -oil.*

1874 Flückiger & Hanbury *Pharmacogr.* 425 Oleum Sesami. Sesamé Oil, Gingeli,..Til or Teel Oil, Benné Oil. 1885 *Buck's Handbk. Med. Sci.* I. 487/1 The Benné plant is a native of Africa, and probably also of Asia. *Ibid.* 487/2 The leaves of Benné are very mild and mucilaginous. 1887 Moloney *Forestry W. Afr.* 50 Beni-seed (*Sesamum indicum*).

Beno (bī·no). [Pseudo-phonetic representation of Sp. *vino* wine, with bilabial *v.*] In the Philippine Islands: = *Aguardiente. Also *attrib.*

1903 *Med. Record* 4 Apr. 547 (Cent. D. Suppl.) The vile whiskey and 'beno' selling dens.

Bent, *sb.*² 10. Add:

Building, Carpentry, etc.: A section of a framework or framed building.

1874 Knight *Dict. Mech.*, *Bent*, one section of the frame of a building, which is put together on the ground..and then raised. 1898 *Engineering Mag.* XVI. 91 The cradle is composed of forty-three inverted bents, twelve feet apart.

Bent, *ppl. a.* Add:

1. d. in the names of articles, work, etc. in which the materials are bent to shape, as **bent iron work**, the making of ornamental ironwork as a home occupation, by bending strips of iron to form the various parts of the design; also, the ornamental ironwork thus made; **bent-panel**, one that is bent to shape instead of framed, in quot. attrib.

1858 Simmonds *Dict. Trade*, *Bent-timber Manufacturer*, a shaper of timber by steam and pressure. 1902 P. N. Hasluck (*title*) Bent Iron Work. 1909 *Stratford-on-Avon Herald* 7 May 4/3 For sale, excellent Bent-panel dog cart.

Benthos (be·nþǫs). *Biol.* [a. Gr. βένθος depth of the sea.] Haeckel's name for the flora and fauna at or near the bottom of the sea. *Abyssal benthos*, plants and animals of the deep sea: *littoral benthos*, those of the sea near the coast. Hence **Be·nthic, Bentho·al, Bentho·nic** *adjs.*

1891 G. W. Field tr. *Haeckel's Planktonic Studies* in *Rep. U.S. Fish. Comm.* XVII. 582 The abyssal benthos. 1895 *Nat. Sci.* July 29 The greatest part of the..discoveries..concerns the Benthos. 1897 T. J. Parker & Haswell *Zool.* II. 600 Others [sc. marine animals]..are either permanently fixed, like Zoophytes and Stalked Crinoids, or move by creeping over the sea-bottom, like Starfishes, Holothurians, Chætopods, etc.; such forms constitute the *Benthos*, or 'bottom-fauna'. 1902 *Encycl. Brit.* XXXIII. 933 Each of the three benthic groups is well characterized by a special fauna. 1905 *Q. Jrnl. Geol. Soc.* LXI. Proc. p. lxxiv, The benthoal organisms existing in tracts where the physical conditions..vary rapidly, are limited as to their horizontal range by the distribution of those conditions which determine their station. 1921 *Discovery* Oct. 265/1 Marine organisms can be roughly divided into..*plankton* or drifters, the *nekton* or swimmers, and the *benthos* or fixed organisms. 1923 W. A. Herdman *Founders Oceanogr.* 327 The demersion upon which hordes of benthonic animals can browse.

Bentonite (be·ntənait). *Min.* [f. *Benton* (see below) + -ITE[1].] A clay found in the Fort Benton strata of the Cretaceous of Wyoming.

1898 *Engin. & Min. Jrnl.* 22 Oct. 491 (Cent. D. Suppl.).

Benturong, var. *BINTURONG.

Benzenoid (be·nzīnoid), *a.* [f. BENZENE + -OID.] Derived from or related to benzene.

1887 *Standard* 16 Sept. 3/3 Transition from tars of the paraffinoid to those of the benzenoid or ordinary gas tar varieties. 1900 *Rep. Brit. Assoc. Advancem. Sci.* 166 Like hexamethylene, tetrahydrobenzene shows no selective absorption. The examination of these two substances thus confirms the conclusion previously reached, that the banded spectrum is shown only by substances which possess the true benzenoid structure.

Benzine (be·nzīn), *sb. Chem.* Also -in. **a.** The name originally given to BENZENE. **b.** An inflammable liquid (petroleum ether) prepared by purifying, deodorizing, and distilling natural petroleum, and used as a solvent; it is a mixture of hydrocarbons of the paraffin series.

1885 *Buck's Handbk. Med. Sci.* I. 487/2 Benzin is not used in medicine, but is useful to the pharmacist for its solvent powers over fats, resins, volatile oils, and other bodies. 1887 J. W. Richards *Aluminium* 236 Mourey..recommends the employment of benzine in the melting of all the noble metals. 1895 *Bloxam's Chem.* (ed. 8) 515 Benzine (sp. gr. 0·74), a solvent which must not be confounded with benzene, the coal-tar product. 1908 *Chemist & Druggist* 25 July 144/2 Benzine..in U.S. means always petroleum benzin, while benzole is the name for the coal-tar product C_6H_6. 1913 G. Martin *Ind. Chem., Org.* 8 Coal-Tar Naphtha, Benzene or Benzol, C_6H_6, is quite a different product from benzine or petroleum naphtha, being obtained by distilling coal-tar. 1928 *Observer* 26 Aug. 6/4 Another fuel..called Steiger-Brennstoff..contains no benzin or benzol at all.

Benzine (benzī·n), *v.* [Formed on the sb.] *trans.* To clean with benzine. **Benzi·ned** *ppl. a.*

1886 W. J. Tucker *E. Europe* 371 Benzined dress-suit of well-to-do..relative re-benzined this morning.

Benzoline (benzǒlī·n), *v.* [f. BENZOLINE *sb.*] *trans.* To clean with benzoline.

1886 W. J. Tucker *E. Europe* 4 I'll send you the old dress-suit..which, thoroughly benzolined, will prove presentable.

Bepuzzled (bĭpʊ·z'ld), *ppl. a.* [f. BEPUZZLE *v.* + -ED[1].] Utterly or completely puzzled.

1826 *Examiner* 647/2 The bepuzzled scribblers. 1888 *Westm. Rev.* July 2 The bepuzzled claimant for a vote.

Ber (bēɹ). Also bher, bir. [Hindi.] The Chinese date or jujube, *Zizyphus jujuba.* Also *attrib.*, as *ber-fruit, -tree.*

1874 Stewart & Brandis *Forest Flora India* 87 All Bĕr trees of North and Central India. 1886 Yule & Burnell *Hobson-Jobson*, Bear-tree, Bair, &c. 1887 Moloney *Forestry W. Afr.* 299 Jujube or Ber Tree. 1895 Mrs. Croker *Village Tales* (1896) 22 The sahibs shall sit above in the old bher tree. 1908 *New Reformer* I. 414 The *Zezyphus Jujuba*, the Bir universally known in India. 1924 *Blackw. Mag.* Oct. 478/1 Thickets of *ber* and acacias. 1925 *Ibid.* Jan. 66/2 These [bears] had fallen out to-night over their supper of *ber*-fruit. 1925 *Countries of the World* No. 33. 3341/2 The almost universal scrub jungle on the low hills, as well as the bhér are all in evidence.

Berberine. Add: **berberine tree**, an African tree, *Xylopia polycarpa*, which yields a yellow dye containing berberine.

1861 Bentley *Man. Bot.* 440 The Berberine or Yellow-dye tree of Soudan.

Berberine[2] (bɜ̄ɹbərīn). [prop. pl. used as sing., f. BERBER + Arab. pl. suffix *-īn* (cf. *fellaheen*, pl. of FELLAH).] A Berber. Also **Be·rberin** *pl.*, Berbers; **Berberee·**, a Berber; **Be·rberize** *v. trans.*, to impart a Berber character to.

1875 *Encycl. Brit.* I. 260/2 The Barábra or Berberines are a people well known in Egypt. 1900 Conan Doyle *Green Flag, Three Corr.* 270 In front rode the three Berberee body-servants upon donkeys. 1906 *Daily Chron.* 22 Sept. 2/7 The municipality of Alexandria are now endeavouring to induce the surplus Berberin, &c., to return to their own country, on the upper reaches of the Nile. 1914 *Engl. Hist. Rev.* Oct. 786 Many Arabs..had settled down [in Tunisia, Algeria, and Morocco] and become in part Berberized. 1928 *Blackw. Mag.* Mar. 406/1 This..was given to me..by a grateful Berberine.

Beret. Add: **b.** A Basque cap, or one resembling it, worn by men and women, especially as part of a costume suitable for sports or holiday wear.

[1835 Fanny Kemble *Jrnl.* I. 68 Saw a woman riding to-day; but she has gotten a black velvet beret upon her head.—Only think of a beret on horse-back!] 1901 *Daily Chron.* 3 Aug. 10/3 The beret so specially becoming to a young face. *Ibid.* 7 Sept. 8/3 The beret shape is always modish on the moors. 1909 *Ibid.* 18 Jan. 7/5 A beret of sable. 1926 *Sketch* 7 July 6 Borotra, the active young Frenchman who always plays in a Basque béret.

Berg[2] (bɜ̄ɹk). *S. Afr.* [Du., = OE. *beorg*, etc. BARROW *sb.*[1]] A mountain or hill.

1902 De Wet *Three Years War* 25 As there was no water to be obtained nearer than a mile from the berg, we suffered greatly from thirst.

b. Comb.: *berg edge*; *berg-battered, -imprisoned* adjs.; **berg adder**, a S. African adder, *Bitis atropos*, found on high ground and the hillsides; **berg cypress**, a mountain shrub, *Widdringtonia cupressioides*, found growing from Cape Town to Natal; **berg winds**, the hot, arid winds prevalent in the neighbourhood of George, Cape Colony, towards the end of the winter.

1896 Kipling *Seven Seas, Story of Ung* 129 Men of the berg-battered beaches. *Ibid., Song Engl.* 5 Hear now the Song of the Dead—in the North by the torn berg-edges—They that look still to the Pole, asleep by their hide-stripped sledges. 1897 Sir J. D. Hooker in *Life* (1918) II. 364 The glacier-clothed and Berg-imprisoned mountain chain of South Victorian Land. 1905 *Westm. Gaz.* 9 Oct. 10/1 Patches of berg cypress..afford splendid cover for that magnificent antelope the eland. 1907 T. Sim *Forests Cape Gd. Hope* 38 The effect of berg winds cannot under ordinary conditions be considered beneficial to forest vegetation. 1912 Fitzsimons *Snakes S. Afr.* 242 The venomous Berg Adder (*Bitis atropos*) which inhabits the mountainous parts of South Africa. *Ibid.* 243 The Berg adder is as venomous as the Puff Adder.

Berghaan (bɛ·ɹχhān). *S. Afr.* [Du., f. *berg* (see prec.) + *haan* cock.] A South African eagle, esp. the black eagle, *Helotarsus ecaudatus.*

1867 Layard *Birds S. Afr.* 18 Helotarsus Ecaudatus..*Berghaan* (cock of the mountains) of the Colonists. 1889 H. A. Bryden *Kloof & Karroo* 273 Suddenly..comes..a great black mountain eagle. We know him at once for a berghaan. 1893 Newton *Dict. Birds, Berghaan* (Mountain-cock), the name given to some of the larger Eagles, and especially to the beautiful *Helotarsus ecaudatus*..by the Dutch colonists in South Africa. 1910 J. Buchan *Prester John* viii, A brace of white *berghaan* circled far up in the blue.

Bergschrund (bɛ·ɹkʃrunt). *Phys. Geogr.* [G., f. *berg* (see BARROW *sb.*[1]) + *schrund* cleft, crevice.] A crevasse or series of crevasses often found near the head of a mountain glacier.

1897 *Outing* (U.S.) XXIX. 339 Crevasses..varying in width from fissures that a child could easily step across, to yawning 'bergschrunds,' ten or twelve feet wide. 1902 *Encycl. Brit.* XXXI. 24/1 At the foot of a snow or ice slope is generally a big crevasse, called a bergschrund.

Bergsonian (bɔɹgsōu·niăn), *a.* [f. the name *Bergson* (see below) + -IAN.] Of, pertaining to, or characteristic of the French philosopher, Henri Bergson. So **Bergsonism** (bɜ̄·ɹgsŏniz'm), the philosophical doctrine of Bergson.

1919 H. Begbie *Wm. Booth* I. 146 Bergsonism has here a most admirable example of its thesis. 1924 *Contemp. Rev.* May 608 According to the Bergsonian doctrine, an animal..knows more of liberty than man does.

Beriberic (beribe·rik), *a.* [f. BERIBERI + -IC.] Infected by beriberi.

1898 P. Manson *Trop. Diseases* xiv. 242 A healthy, non-beriberic, high-lying locality.

Berkshire (bā·ɹkʃəɹ). Name of an English county, applied to a highly esteemed breed of pigs.

1842 D. Low *Dom. Anim. Brit. Isl.* I. *Hog* 27 The true Berkshires are of the larger races of Swine, though they fall short in size of some of the older breeds. *Ibid.*, The Berkshire breed has..been crossed and recrossed with the Chinese. 1856 Morton *Cycl. Agric.* II. 941 The Berkshire breed of pigs has probably been the best known, and had in the highest estimation of any of our British breeds. 1902 *Encycl. Brit.* XXV. 195/1 The Berkshire, though a black pig, usually has a white blaze or mark down the face, a white tip to the tail, and feet white up to the ankle joint.

Berlin. 4. Add: **Berlin spirit** (see quot.).

1878 *Chamb. Encycl., Berlin Spirit*, a coarse whisky made chiefly from beetroot, potatoes, &c.

Berlin[2] (bəɹli·n). Also -ine. [After F. *berline*; see BERLIN 1.] A limousine automobile having the driver's seat completely enclosed.

1912 H. J. Butler *Motor Bodies* 6 Limousines are sometimes built with a square, or D-front, when they are properly called a double, square, or D-fronted limousine, as the case may be. Windows may be arranged all round the upper part without any relief of panelling. Such a body is often referred to as a 'berline'.

Berm. Add:

3. A ledge or flat of land bordering either bank of the Nile and inundated when the river overflows.

1891 *Daily News* 31 Oct. 6/4 To raise the Nile at the apex of the Delta to a level sufficient to flood the islands and berms of the two branches in the Delta. 1900 *Westm. Gaz.* 10 July 2/2 The water level in the winter was some fifty centimètres below the general level of the berm.

Bermoney (bɜ̄·ɹmǒni). *Sc. local.* Also Beardmoney. (See quots.)

1856 in *Macqueen's Rep.* (1866) IV. 536 The mode of fishing by the use of Bermoney or Beardmoney boats, with fixed stakes, pins or anchors placed in the tidal bed of the river. 1863 *Ibid.* 554 That an individual having the right of fishing had no right to construct a permanent towing path in the river or a gangway in order to facilitate his operation of fishing, and they describe this Bermoney apparatus (as it is called) as being in reality a towing path or gangway. *Ibid.* 556 The Bermoney boat..was not introduced into the Tay before 1821.

Bermuda. Add:

Bermuda(s cedar, a species of juniper, *Juniperus virginiana*; Bermuda lily, a lily of the variety *Lilium longiflorum eximium*, known to florists as *Lilium harrisii*, originally obtained from Bermuda; Bermuda rig = *BERMUDIAN *rig.*

1829 Loudon *Encycl. Plants* 848 *Juniperus bermudiana*, *Bermudas Cedar. 1876 *Encycl. Brit.* V. 286 The Bermuda cedar..used in joinery and in the manufacture of pencils. 1911 *Sutton's Amateur's Guide in Hort.* 195 *Lilium Harrisii* (*Bermuda Lily). A large and elegant pure white Lily, adapted for forcing or growing in pots. 1853 R. Kipping *Masting Ships* ii. 5 Brig Forward, Common, and *Bermuda Rig.

Bermudan (bəɹmiū·dăn), *a.* [f. BERMUDA + -AN.] = *BERMUDIAN *a.*

1923 *Public Opinion* 24 Aug. 180/2 Her lofty Bermudan main-sail. 1928 *Daily Express* 20 July 10/2 The Astra and Cambria..carry the Bermudan-rig—a high tapering sail like the wing of a gigantic bird.

Bermudian (bəɹmiū·diăn), *a.* and *sb.* [f. BERMUDA + -IAN.] **A.** *adj.* Of or pertaining to the Bermudas or their inhabitants. **Bermudian rig**, a rig for a yacht, carrying a high tapering sail, called a *Bermudian mainsail*. So *Bermudian-rigged* adj., fitted with a rig and sail of this kind. **B.** *sb.* An inhabitant of the Bermudas; a Bermudian ship.

1781 *Essex Inst. Hist. Coll.* XIII. 228 Vessels now in port or Bermudians with salt. 1859 Bartlett *Dict. Amer.* s.v. *Chicken Grape*, The sterile vine is cultivated for its sweet-scented blossoms, and is then called Bermudian Vine. 1915 C. P. Lucas *Brit. Emp.* 163 The little Bermudian Assembly is..the oldest Parliamentary institution in the British Empire outside the United Kingdom. 1926 *Glasgow Herald* 20 Aug. 9 She is Bermudian rigged. 1926 *Blackw. Mag.* Nov. 698/1 By implicitly obeying the Bermudian, we escaped this danger. 1928 *Observer* 15 Apr. 29/5 The 12-metre yachts..with a Bermudian rig of moderate area, can be sailed efficiently with four paid hands. 1928 *Daily Tel.* 1 May 16/6 The Cambria will be Bermudian rigged, carrying a Bermudian mainsail.

Berrugate (berugē·t). [f. Sp. *verruga* wart.] A fish, *Lobotes pacificus*, found on the Pacific coast of Central America, used as a food.

1898 Jordan & Evermann *Fishes N. & Mid. Amer.* III. 2858 Abundant at Panama, where it is known as *Berrugate*.

Be·rrying, *ppl. a. U.S.* See BERRY *v.*[2], BERRYING *vbl. sb.*[2]

1890 Marah E. Ryan *Told in Hills* v. 58 A berrying crowd from the Kootenai tribe.

Berryless (be·rilès), *a.* [f. BERRY *sb.* + -LESS.] Without producing berries; not berried or furnished with berries.

1887 *Sat. Rev.* 30 Apr. 624 The female plant..berryless, may be said to have suffered a grass-widowhood of some eighty years. 1924 *Glasgow Herald* 3 Jan. 6 Berryless holly.

Berth, *sb.* **5. b.** (Earlier example.)

1745 *Maryland Hist. Mag.* VI. 220 When the old parson dies, w[hi]ch he will in a very little time, I hope he'll get the Birth.

Berth, *v.*[1] Add:

2. b. *intr.* To occupy a berth or berths.

1886 Stevenson *Kidnapped* vii. 61 The round-house, where he berthed and served. 1902 *Westm. Gaz.* 13 Sept. 6/2 The accommodation is very simple, consisting of berthing in two tiers in the women's ward, and feeding and living in a separate saloon.

Bertha. Add:

2. A small cape or wrap worn by women, usually crossed in front and open at the throat.

1895 in *Funk's Stand. Dict.*

Bertha[2] (bɜ̄·ɹþă). [Named after Frau Berta (or *Bertha*) Krupp von Bohlen und Halbach, head of the Krupp steel works in Germany.] A soldiers' name for a German gun of large bore, used in the war of 1914–18. *Big bertha*, a long-range gun, esp. one used to bombard Paris in 1918.

1914 *Scotsman* 30 Oct. 9/6 This mortar of 42 centimeters was made at the Krupp works, and for this reason the Germans have baptised it '*Bertha—die fleissige*' (Bertha, the Zealous), Bertha being the name of Madame Krupp von Bohlen. *Ibid.*, 'Bertha' is not the delicate plaything that it has sometimes been represented to be, and the maximum of 150 shells that they say can be fired from the gun is below the truth. 1925 E. Fraser & Gibbons *Soldier & Sailor Words* 22 Big Bertha.

Berthage. Add: Also, the dues payable for mooring a vessel.

1895 in *Funk's Stand. Dict.*

Berthing, *vbl. sb.*[1] Add:

1. b. The occupation of a berth or mooring position; also, mooring position.

1891 *Daily News* 15 July 5/8 There being a high wind from the north north-east..the berthing was very uncomfortable for the..launches. 1906 *Westm. Gaz.* 9 July 4/2 Berthing accommodation will be provided for about 300 boats. 1908 *Ibid.* 26 May 9/1 The..Railway Company's boats..have changed their berthing from North Wall to Carlisle Pier. 1909 *Daily Chron.* 6 Dec. 6/7 They..came up practically to the berthing which the Ellan Vannin used to occupy.

2. The arrangement of berths or the provision of sleeping accommodation; accommodation in berths.

1863 Luce *Seamanship* xvi. 297 Berthing requires the earliest attention, and the operation may be facilitated by having a plan of the decks. *a* 1871 C. F. Hall *Polar Exp.* (1876) 123 The special object of these [changes] was the economy of fuel, and the berthing of the whole crew below deck. 1890 *Allan Line Advt. Bk.* 7 Arrangements for the berthing of Steerage Passengers.

Bertillonage (bertiyonā·ʒ). [F., f. the name of the inventor (see below).] The system of identification of criminals by anthropometric measurements, finger-prints, etc., invented by Alphonse Bertillon, the French criminologist.

1892 F. Galton *Finger Prints* 156, 562 prisoners who gave false names in the year 1890 were recognised by *Bertillonage*. 1892 *Athenæum* 24 Dec. 893/3 An interesting part of the work is the criticism of Bertillonage. 1901 Henry *Finger Prints* (ed. 2) 63 The system suggested by Mr. Galton..failed to deal as effectively as Bertillonage with primary classification. 1920 *Discovery* Apr. 124/1 Extended examples are given of the possibilities of variation curves, variation 'steps', and 'gradation curves'; the combination of such data, constituting a quantitative diagnosis of a species, is defined as 'Bertillonage'.

Bertrandite (bɜ̄·ɹtrǎndəit). *Min.* [Named, 1883, after E. *Bertrand*, who first noticed it: see -ITE[1].] Hydrous silicate of glucinum.

1887 Dana *Man. Min. & Petrog.* (ed. 4) 275 Bertrandite is related to phenacite in composition. 1914 *Brit. Mus. Return* 222.

Berycoid (be·rikoid), *a.* and *sb. Ichthyol.* [f. mod.L. *Berycoidea*, f. *Beryc-*, *Beryx*, generic name: see -OID.] **A.** *adj.* Belonging to the superfamily *Berycoidea*. **B.** *sb.* A fish of this family.

1880 Günther *Fishes* 420 Fossil Berycoids show a still greater diversity of form than living. *Ibid.*, Berycoid fishes have a wide horizontal range. 1887 *Athenæum* 9 July 58/3 The genus had hitherto been erroneously associated with the percoids and berycoids.

Besiclometer (besik'lǫ·mǐtəɹ). [f. F. *besicles* spectacles + -OMETER.] (See quot.)

1921 *Dict. Brit. Sci. Instrum., Besiclometer*, an instrument which indicates the proper distance of spectacles between the hinges; that is the breadth of the forehead.

Besiegement. (Modern U.S. example.)

1885 U. S. Grant *Mem.* I. xxxiv. 495 It is not probable..that Pemberton would have permitted a close besiegement.

Bespeak, *sb.* Add:

2. An application made by a subscriber to a lending library for the loan of a book when it shall become available; also *attrib.*, as *bespeak system*.

1922 *Glasgow Herald* 28 Dec. 9 In the past year the number of 'bespeaks' was 4153, an increase of 650 on the previous year.

Bespell (bĭspe·l), *v.* [f. BE- 6 + SPELL *sb.*] *trans.* To cast a spell on; to bewitch literally and figuratively. Hence **Bespe·lled** *ppl. a.*

1894 Meredith *Ld. Ormont* iv, If his glory bespells her. 1897 A. Nutt in *Voy. Bran* II. 6 A bard..had threatened to bespell his land. 1902 — *Leg. Holy Grail* 58 The bespelled kinsman appears in a hideous guise. 1926 *Contemp. Rev.* Oct. 503 We were gazing, bespelled at the fair scene.

Bespoke (bĭspōu·k), *ppl. a.* [See BESPEAK *v.*] Of goods: Ordered to be made, as distinguished from READY-MADE. (Cf. BESPOKEN *ppl. a.* 2.) Also said of a tradesman who makes goods to order. Also *sb.*, a bespoke article.

1865 G. Measom *Illustr. Guide G. E. Railway* 69 The Bespoke or Order Department. 1866 *Chamb. Encycl.* VIII. 691/1 The shoemaking trade..is divided into two departments—the bespoke and the ready-made or sale business. 1907 W. De Morgan *Alice-for-Short* xlvii, His boots may have been 'bespokes' for anybody, except himself. 1908 *Daily Chron.* 13 June 4/7 A 'bespoke tailor'. 1928 *Punch* 30 May Advt. p. xv, Lotus Bespoke Model Shoes.

Besport (bĭspōə·ɹt), *v.* [Alteration of DISPORT *v.*, by exchange of prefix (BE- 1).] *refl.* To disport oneself. Also *intr.* (for *refl.*).

1855 *Chamb. Jrnl.* IV. 65 Living gems of light, besporting themselves on the bosom of the lake. 1906 W. J. Bryan in *Westm. Gaz.* 7 June 9/2 And surely Shylock never besported himself more ostentatiously. 1925 A. S. Alexander *Tramps across Watersheds* viii. 256 The famous golf course, where ladies and gentlemen besported in the glowing sun.

Bessemerize (be·sĭmərəiz), *v.* [f. BESSEMER + -IZE.] *trans.* To treat by the Bessemer process.

1901 *Prospectus Mond Nickel Co.*, Plant of the most modern type for Roasting, Smelting and Bessemerizing this ore.

Best, *a.* and *adv.* Add:

A. *adj.* **1. c.** *spec.* noting a certain grade of wrought iron; also *best best* adj., of a higher quality than the best; *best best best* adj., treble best.

1883 *Lockwood's Dict. Terms Mech. Engin., Best, or B.*—A brand of wrought-iron plate or bar equivalent to No. 3 quality, or that grade which is only just superior to the commonest..The 'best' plates of the first-class houses are, however, equal to the 'best, best' and 'treble best' of other firms. *Ibid., Best, Best, or B.B.*..obtained by piling, reheating, and rerolling 'best' or No. 3 bars. *Ibid., Best, Best, Best, or Treble Best, B.B.B.*

d. *spec.* in *best boat*, a racing boat on the Thames, as distinguished from the heavier types; esp. used attrib. in *best-boat race, racing, regatta, rowing*. Also *best-and-best boat, punt*: a boat of the lightest and narrowest construction, used for racing.

1890 *Lock to Lock Times* 23 Aug. 162/2 This year the amateur oarsmen have ungrudgingly given up their boats to the watermen, who have been rowing in the past regatta; wager, or 'best' boats, being in special demand by the fleet of scullers, who were attracted by the liberal programme. 1894 *Daily News* 5 May 6/5 The race will..be decided in best-and-best punts. 1897 *Ibid.* 30 Aug. 5/1 No best-boat racing will be attempted. 1900 *Ibid.* 25 Sept. 9/2 A sculling match, in best and best boats. 1902 *Daily Chron.* 19 July 8/6 Only three best-boat races are included. 1904 *Westm. Gaz.* 28 June 10/1 The best-boat regatta season. 1907 *Observer* 24 July 26/2 The best-boat rowing season..is all too short.

2. b. *Best girl* (GIRL *sb.* 2 c), favourite female companion. orig. *U.S.* Also *ellipt.* (U.S. slang) for *best girl*.

1904 *Democrat* (Celina, Ohio) in *Daily Chron.* 23 Feb. 5/2 Wm. Londen and best were at church Sunday evening. 1904 *Indicator* (Merriweather, Georgia) in *Daily Chron.* 21 May 4/5 Messrs. Bub Peary and Pierce Biggers called on their best girls last Sunday afternoon.

5. *To give* (a person or thing) *best*: to admit the superiority of, give way to.

1902 A. B. Paterson *Man from Snowy River* (1906) 71 My country joker, are you going to give it best? Are you frightened of the fences?

B. *adv.* **2. b.** *best-abused, -discussed, -hated.*

1864 *Blackw. Mag.* XCVI. 188 Daniel O'Connell used to say that he was the best abused man in Europe. 1869 *Church Times* 26 Feb., [Pusey] for years and years the best abused man in England. 1900 *Daily News* 16 Feb. 7/2 Englishmen are the best-hated people in the world. 1903 McNeill *Egregious Engl.* 100 The best-discussed and best-described man in England.

3. b. Best looker (*U.S.*), a very good-looking person; **Best seller** (orig. *U.S.*), one of the books having the largest sale of the year or the season; also, a writer of such books; also *attrib.* Hence **Best-selling** *a.*, that is a 'best seller'. Also **Best-sellership**, the position of a writer of best sellers.

1911 R. W. Chambers *Common Law* i. 10 There's always something wrong with the best lookers. 1912 — *Streets of Ascalon* vi. 143 His book had passed into the abhorred class of best sellers. 1913 — *Gay Rebellion* ii. 28 Go on with the dolly dialogue..you third-rate best seller. 1915 (*title*) The Baker & Taylor Co.'s Monthly Bulletin of the Latest and Best Selling Books. 1920 *Chamb. Jrnl.* 8 May 363/2 [He] promised to reach the doubtful altitude of best-sellership without difficulty. 1924 W. R. Inge *Lay Thoughts* (1926) 190 Best-selling novels. 1925 *Punch* 20 May 560/1 Fiction of best-seller quality. 1928 *Daily Express* 1 June 5/3 A house can be full of sweet scents..' writes one of our best-sellers, and he is perfectly right. 1928 *Ibid.* 16 July 8 A 'best-selling' biography.

Bet, *sb.* Add: **1. b.** In Card-games. *Heeled bet*: see *HEELED *ppl. a.*

1891 '*L. Hoffmann's*' *Cycl. Card Games* 202 If a player bets, or raises a bet, and no other player goes better, or calls him, he wins the pool. 1892 Florence *Gentl. Handbk. Poker* 59 When a player puts in only as much as has been put in by each player who has preceded him, that is called 'seeing' the bet. 1909 *Cent. Dict.* Suppl., *Bet*, in faro, a card which is a case, that is, the only one of that denomination remaining in the box: so called because the player cannot be split.

Bet, *v.* Add:

c. in various (orig. *U.S.*) slang asseverative phrases meaning: To stake everything or all one's resources (upon the truth of an assertion).

These expressions, as well as *You bet!* (see Dict.), have long ceased to be peculiarly *U.S.*

a 1868 Bret Harte *Poems* etc., *Tale of a Pony* 78 Smart! You bet your life 'twas that! 1868 *All Year Round* 31 Oct. 489/2 'You bet' or 'You bet yer life', or 'You bet yer bones', while to 'bet your boots' is confirmation strong as holy writ—in the mines, at least. 1888 *Daily Inter-Ocean* Mar. 7 (Farmer) Well, sir, it is the right kind of bravery: you may bet your bottom dollar on that.

Beta. Add:

2. e. *Beta rays* or *β-rays*, the second class of rays emitted by radioactive substances, having greater penetrating power and stronger photographic action than the alpha rays.

1899 Rutherford in *Phil. Mag.* Jan. 117 All the compounds of uranium examined gave out the two types of radiation, and the penetrating power of the radiation for both the α and β radiations is the same for all the compounds. 1904 Soddy *Radio-Activity* 12 The β-rays resemble ordinary X-rays in penetrating power, and pass with ease through thin metal foil, glass, etc. 1904 Rutherford *Radio-activity* 101 The β rays of uranium, thorium, and radium. 1908 Soddy *Interpr. Radium* 55 In ordinary circumstances radium appears to be expelling both α- and β-particles together.

Betacism (bĭ·tăsiz'm). [ad. mod.L. *betacismus*, f. *beta* (see BETA), after L. *iotacismus*, etc.] (See quot. 1926.)

[1885 *Amer. Jrnl. Philol.* VI. 501 Even these forms were threatened with destruction by the spread of Betacismus, whereby *amavit* was pronounced like *amabit* and vice versa.] *Ibid.*, In Africa, especially where betacism flourished, the need of new substitutes for the future made itself early felt. 1926 Plater & White *Gram. Vulgate* 43 *note*, What is called betacism (the interchange of *b* and *v*) causes great confusion in verbs of the first conjugation.

Betafite (bĭ·tăfəit). *Min.* [f. *Betafo* in Madagascar, one of its localities + -ITE[1].] A niobate and titanate of uranium, etc.

1912 *Jrnl. Chem. Soc.* CII. II. 567 Radioactive Uraniferous Columbotantalotitanites from Pegmatites of Madagascar..Betafite, D4. 17, is dark green, and shows rudimentary cubic faces. 1922 *British Museum Return* 153 Minerals from..Madagascar (chrysoberyl, betafite, columbite, etc.).

Betel. 2. Add:

Betel(nut) palm, the Areca palm, *Areca catechu*, from which the 'betel nut' or areca nut is obtained.

1861 Bentley *Man. Bot.* 684 The Catechu or Betel Nut Palm. 1875 *Encycl. Brit.* III. 616/2 The betel nut is the fruit of the Areca or betel palm, *Areca Catechu.*

Bête noire (bĕt nwaɹ, bǣt nwāɹ). [F. *bête noire* black beast; *fig.* insufferable person.] A person or thing that is the bane (of a person or his life); an insufferable person or thing; an object of aversion.

1850 *Household Wds.* 6 July 359/1 You or any one else's *bête noire* is apt to get polished off with a few extra touches of blacking. 1860 Russell *Diary India* I. 209 Jung Bahadoor, who is evidently the present *bête noir* of our General's life. 1866 Mrs. H. Wood *Elster's Folly* xiv, It was the bête noire of Clerk Gum's life. 1905 *Spectator, Lit. Suppl.* 28 Jan. 118/2 [His] *bête-noire* is the submission of military affairs to the control of 'political exigencies.'

Bethdin (bǣt dīn). [Heb. *bēth* house, *dīn* judgement.] A tribunal composed of the rabbi and two or more dayanim before which are brought cases in dispute among orthodox Jews.

1795 Sir W. Scott in J. Haggard *Rep. Cases Consist. Crt.* (1822) I. 244 The Answers of the Bethdin to the Questions proposed by the Court. 1897 *Daily News* 30 Jan. 3/3 Are you in competition with the Chief Rabbi in his Court the Beth Din?

Betol (bī·tǫl). *Med.* [f. BET(A + NAPHTH)OL.] A white powder, derivative of beta-naphthol, used as an intestinal antiseptic and antizymotic.

1891 *Medical Annual* 130 Betol, which divides into salicylic acid and betaphol. 1895 *Buck's Handbk. Med. Sci.* Suppl. 90/1 *Betol*, the beta-naphthol ether of salicylic acid, analogous to salol.

Betray, *v.* Add:

4. b. *esp.* To induce (a woman) to surrender her chastity by false promises; to seduce.

1891 Hardy *Tess* xvi, A conviction not so entirely unknown to the 'betrayed' as some amiable theorists would have us believe.

Better, *a.* Add:

1. c. *Comb.* with sbs. used attrib., as *better-class, -quality.*

1890 Sir W. F. Butler *Sir Chas. Napier* 7 Merchants or local better-class farmers. 1908 *Westm. Gaz.* 12 Aug. 11/3 Better-quality teas.

4. b. *You'd better believe*: you may be assured. *U.S. colloq.*

1856 *Yale Lit. Mag.* XXI. 171 (Th.) You'd better believe, I'll live in the clover. 1862 *Major Jack Downing* 26 May (1867) 70 You'd better believe we've been in an awful excitement here. 1872 O. W. Holmes *Poet Breakf.-t.* x, My old gentleman means to be Mayor or Governor or President..you'd better b'lieve.

(*b*) With *had* omitted. *U.S. colloq.*

1845 J. J. Hooper *Taking Census* i. 154 You better mind the holes in them ere rocks. 1910 Mulford *H. Cassidy* xi. 73, I reckon you better pull out—you ain't needed around here. 1911 R. D. Saunders *Col. Todhunter* iv. 54 You better mind your own business and let my affairs alone.

6. c. *For better, for worse*: see WORSE B. 3 a.

Betterment. Add:

2. b. Enhanced value (of real property) by reason of local improvements. *Betterment tax*, an assessment made on this.

1896 J. H. B. Browne & Allan *Compensation* 683 'Betterment' as a principle is only a proposal to tax the increment when it clearly and directly arises from an improvement carried out by a public authority and at the public expense. *Ibid.* 684 A betterment charge in respect of improvements affected by local authorities. 1902 *Encycl. Brit.* XXVII. 182/2 The principle of 'betterment', according to which promoters would be allowed to set off against an owner's claim for compensation any enhancement of the value of his land by the use of the land taken by the promoters. 1928 *Britain's Industr. Future* (*Liberal Ind. Inquiry*) IV. xxvii. 377 A share of the increased values given to these lands by such improvements should be obtained, by means of betterment taxes.

Better-to-do, *adj. phr.* [Comparative of WELL-TO-DO.] Above the well-to-do in social condition or worldly circumstances; more prosperous. Also *absol.*

1898 *Daily News* 6 Dec. 5/6 To the new L.C.C. buildings there had come many better-to-do workmen. 1905 *Daily Chron.* 1 Feb. 6/2 Children..of the better-to-do. 1905 *Westm. Gaz.* 31 Jan. 3/2 Better-to-do parents.

Betty Martin. In phr. (*All*) *my eye* (*and*) *Betty Martin*: (all) nonsense.

1785 Grose *Dict. Vulg. T.* s.v. *Betty Martin*, That's my eye betty martin. 1812 H. & J. Smith *Rej. Addr., Macbeth*, The knife that I thought that I saw Was nought but my eye, Betty Martin. 1819 Moore *Tom Crib's Mem. Congress* 2 All my eye, Betty. 1859 *Slang Dict.* 1 All my eye, answer of astonishment to an improbable story: All my eye and Betty Martin, a vulgar phrase with similar meaning.

Between, *prep.* and *adv.* Add:

B. *adv.* **4.** **between-lens shutter** *Photogr.*, a type of shutter that is fitted between the components of a double lens; **between-time** (delete † and add quot.); **between-times**, in the intervals of time: = BETWEEN-WHILES.

1909 *Westm. Gaz.* 20 Feb. 14/2 The popular *between-lens shutters. 1910 *Ibid.* 19 Mar. 14/2 The shutter is of the between-lens pattern. 1909 *Ibid.* 10 Aug. 6/3 There is no question of any *between-time. Immediately the day ends, the night's work begins. 1907 *Ibid.* 13 Sept. 2/1 The Fairy Queen sat *between-times, when she was aweary, beside the Fairy King.

C. 1. Also *pl.*, intermediate things or events.

1872 Eggleston *End of World* xxv. 167 A chapter of betweens.

Betwee·n-maid. A maid-servant who assists both the cook and the housemaid: = TWEENY. Also *between girl, servant*.

1890 *Daily News* 23 June 7/5 Between servant..to assist cook and housemaid. *Ibid.* 9 Dec. 7/6 Between-maid wanted. 1891 *Ibid.* 11 Nov. 8/4 Wanted..good Plain Cook, also Between Girl. 1903 J. M. Barrie *Admirable Crichton* I, A tweeny; that is to say, my lady, she is not at present, strictly speaking, anything; a between maid; she helps the vegetable maid. 1923 *Daily Mail* 25 Jan. 5 All of the general servant class masquerading as parlour-maids, cooks, between-maids, or others of experience.

Betweenness (bĭtwī·nnės). [f. BETWEEN + -NESS.] The condition or fact of being between; *spec.* in *Math.*, the ordinal quality possessed by one of every three points on a straight line, in virtue of which it may be said to lie between the other two points.

1892 *Monist* II. 243 In reality there are not two things and, in addition to them a betweenness of the two things. 1904 *Science* 11 Mar. 410 (Cent. D. Suppl.) Of Hilbert's betweenness assumptions, axioms of order, one of the five is redundant.

Bevel, *a.* and *sb.*[1] Add: **B.** *sb.* **4.** A piece of metal used by stereotypers to form the bevelled edge of a plate.

1874 Knight *Dict. Mech.*

C. **bevel hub**, a short connecting pipe bent to a bevel angle; **bevel jack**, an intermediate gearing consisting of a bevel wheel and pinion; **bevel plater**, a machine for rolling the bevelled circular plates used for shingling- and veneering-saws; **bevel protractor**, a protractor with a sliding arm, used for marking off bevel angles.

1884 Knight *Dict. Mech.* Suppl.

Beveller (be·vĕləɹ). [f. BEVEL *v.* + -ER[1].] An operative in various trades, esp. one who bevels the edges of plate glass or steel plates; one who cuts stereotype, electrotype, or process plates and bevels them; one who cuts, bevels, and (when necessary) gilds cards.

1881 *Instr. Census Clerks* (1885) 55 Plate and Looking Glass Silverer: Beveller, Dipper. *Ibid.* 83 Card, Pattern-card..Perforator, Beveller. 1890 W. J. Gordon *Foundry* 131 We may as well follow the plate to the bevellers, where the edges are again ground and smoothened. 1921 *Dict. Occupat. Terms* (1927) § 558 Card beveller..arranges a pile of cards so that edge of pile slopes at required bevel angle..and scrapes sloped edge with sharp knife.

Beveren (be·vĕrĕn). [Name of a town in Belgium.] A breed of rabbit.

1919 *Bazaar, Exchange & Mart* 18 Jan. Suppl. 14 Beverens for sale, bucks and does. 1920 *Ibid.* 19 Mar. Suppl. 24/2 Unique snow white Beverens, with sky blue eyes.

Bewrite, *v.* Delete † *Obs.* and add:

2. *trans.* To write about. In *pa. pple.*

1875 Swinburne in *Times Lit. Suppl.* (1909) 3 June 204/2, I have probably been more be-written and belied than any man since Byron. 1895 *Critic* 1 June 396/2 Tammany has been much be-written of late.

Beyond, *adv.* and *prep.* **D.** Add: **beyond man**, early synonym of SUPERMAN.

1896 A. Tille tr. *Nietzsche's Wks.* VIII. 5 Behold, I teach you beyond-man! Beyond-man is the significance of earth. Your will shall say: beyond-man shall be the significance of earth. *Ibid.* 129 Never yet beyond-man existed. I have seen them both naked, the greatest and the smallest man. 1896 T. Common tr. *Nietzsche's Twilight of Idols* Wks. XI. 198 To be set up..as a 'higher man', as a kind of beyond-man. 1908 *Athenæum* 13 June 729/1 The 'Super-tramp' is..the opposite of the 'oversoul' or 'beyond-man'.

Bhakti (bɒ·kti). *Hinduism.* [Skr.] Religious devotion, piety, or devoted faith, as a means of salvation.

1877 Monier-Williams *Hinduism* ix. 115 The doctrine of *bhakti*, or 'salvation by faith'. 1911 E. B. Havell *Ideals Ind. Art* 117 *Bhakti* is the moving spirit in all great religious art, in the West as in the East. 1915 N. Macnicol *Ind. Theism* 30 Those in India whose hearts are filled with *bhakti* or 'loving faith'. 1921 T. R. Glover *Jesus Exper. Men* iii. 41 Tuka and other mystics of India believed that from this a man might be saved by *Bhakti*, by self-annihilating devotion to a friendly god. *Karma* and *Bhakti* are the two poles of Indian religious thought.

Bhoosa (bū·să). *E. Ind.* Also bhoos. [Hindi *bhus, bhūsa.*] Husks and broken straw, used as food for cattle. Also *attrib.*

1819 Tod in *Annals* (1829) I. 700 *Bhoos* stacks are erected to provide provender for the cattle in scanty rainy seasons. 1904 *Daily Chron.* 28 Apr. 5/2 Two hundred and twenty-three maunds of bhoosa and 560 pounds barley. 1908 *Animal Managem.* 331 Tow, straw, bhoosa and sacking. 1920 *Blackw. Mag.* Oct. 449/2 Having to wait weary hours sitting on a bhoosa bale.

B'hoy. *U.S.* Also bo-hoy. [Irish pron. of BOY *sb.*[1]] A rough or rowdy.

1846 *Knickerbocker Mag.* May XXVII. 467 A smile on his lips peculiar to one of the bo-hoys. 1847 *Ibid.* Mar. XXIX. 204 [He] had lived too long in the 'wire-grass' region to misunderstand the character of that peculiar class of b'hoys who dwell there. 1852 Bristed *Upper Ten Thousand* 29 Of not-to-be-mistaken Bowery cut—veritable 'bhoys'. 1866 *Atlantic Monthly* Dec. 727 'I want', said the stranger, 'to see a b'hoy,—a real b'hoy.' 1868 *N.Y. Home Jrnl.* 17 Dec. (De Vere) The b'hoy is fast disappearing from among us, and the day is not far off, we apprehend, when the Bowery will know him no more.

Bias, *v.* Add; **4.** *trans.* To cut bias. *U.S.*

1883 *Century Mag.* XXVI. 960/1 You may baste, you may bias the Gore if you will.

Biaxial, *a.* Add:

2. *Geom.* (See quot.)

1889 Cayley *Math. Papers* (1897) XIII. 13 Each conic meets each axis in two points; and at each of these points the axis and the tangent to the conic form with the lines to I, J a harmonic pencil. The binodal quartic is in this case said to be biaxial.

Bib, *sb.*[1] **b.** *Best bib and tucker* (earlier quots.).

1793 [see TUCKER *sb.* 3]. 1822 *Massachusetts Spy* 27 Feb. (Th.) It is not in the evenings only that they are to be encountered in 'the best bib and tucker.' 1833 Crockett *Sk.* 37 Both girls and boys had on their best bib and tucker. 1855 *Sharpe's Lond. Mag.* V. 92/2 All-London..puts on its best bib and tucker.

Bi·bble-ba·bble, *v. intr.* [f. the sb.] To indulge in bibble-babble or idle talk.

1888 Doughty *Trav. Arabia Deserta* I. 256 They all love to bibble-babble their infirmities in the wholesome ears of the hakim. *Ibid.* 596 They sat out long hours bibble-babbling.

Bib-cock. [?f. BIB *sb.*[1]] A cock or tap with a turned-down nozzle, as distinguished from a stop-cock. So *bib-nozzle, -valve.*

1797 J. Curr *Coal Viewer* 63, 1 Piston cock (bib)..1 Air cock (bib) to fix in the sink pipe. 1853 *Dict. Archit., Bib-cock*, a term used..to distinguish a cock which delivers fluids out of a pipe, from a stop-cock which is placed in the length of a pipe. 1862 *Catal. Internat. Exhib., Brit.* II. II. x. 55 Bib cock. 1874 Knight *Dict. Mech.* s.v., *c* is a bib-valve, the closure being by a reciprocating slide.

Bibelot (biblo). [Fr.] A small curio or article of *virtù*.

1882 'Ouida' *Resurgo* vi. in *Belgravia* XLVI. 453 His soul never rises above brocades and *bibelots*! 1886 F. M. Crawford *Tale Lonely Parish* xviii, The spectacle of her pictures, her furniture and her bibelots. 1900 Harland *Cardinal's Snuff-box* xix, The table, with its books and bibelots.

Biberon[2] (bibroǹ). [Fr.] A drinking-vessel with elongated spout, for the use of travellers, invalids, and children.

1862 *Catal. Internat. Exhib., Brit.* II. II. xvii. 127 The Biberon, a new patent invention, adapted for a lady's travelling companion. 1905 *Westm. Gaz.* 27 May 15/3 The biberon is wrought in rock-crystal..and is in the form of a grotesque animal, of which the head is utilised as the spout.

Bibi, variant of BEEBEE.

1843 in Yule & Burnell *Hobson-Jobson* s.v. *Beebee*.

Bible. 1. Add: *The open Bible*: the Bible accessible to all in the vulgar tongue.

1837 *Ch. Eng. Mag.* 9 Dec. (*The Bible*), Bear witness, martyrs of the olden days, How your true hearts the open Bible priz'd. 1908 Tilby *Engl. People Overseas* I. 48 The persecution of Mary and the open Bible worked a change.

Bi·ble-back. *U.S.* and *dial.* [BIBLE III.] A hump-backed or round-shouldered person.

1890 *Buckskin Mose* x. 145 Pitching our camp..at La Due Very's, generally known as 'Old Bible-back'. 1896 *Warwickshire Word-Bk.* (E.D.S.), *Bible-back*, a person with broad, rounded shoulders. 'Here comes old bible-back!' 1903 (*Amer.*) *Dial. Notes* II. 349 *Bible-back*, Rockland Co. N. Y. Bergen Co. N. J.

So **Bible-backed** *a.*

1857 *Olympia* (W. T.) *Pioneer & Democrat* 11 Dec. (Th.) We might, in consequence, become somewhat round-shouldered and 'bible-backed.' 1873 *N. & Q.* Ser. IV. XII. 227 What kind of shoulders? Rather high. Anything else? He was humpy or bible-backed.

Biblioclast. Add quot. and **Bibliocla·stic** *a.*

1880 Blades *Enemies Bks.* 96 Such a wicked old biblioclast as John Bagford. 1887 *Longman's Mag.* Dec. 239 The biblioclastic dead.

Bibliope·gically, *adv.* [f. BIBLIOPEGIC: see -ICALLY.] As regards bookbinding. So **Biblio·pegism** = BIBLIOPEGY.

1817 Dibdin *Decam.* II. 513 The art and craft of bibliopegism. 1896 Gosse in *Contemp. Rev.* Jan. 98 His own library..was not conspicuous bibliopegically.

Bibliothecarial (bi:bliǫþikē·riăl), *a.* [-AL.] = BIBLIOTHECARIAN *a.* (under BIBLIOTHECARY).

1889 *Athenæum* 27 Apr. 539/2 Of the two sets of terms that are so constantly confounded, one may be said to be bibliographical or scientific, the other bibliothecarial or practical. 1893 F. Madan *Bks. in MS.* vii. 75 The one great bibliothecarial fact of antiquity is the Library of Alexandria. 1918 *Bodleian Q. Rec.* 31 Oct. 155 So little has happened in Bodley in this Long Vacation that it is lawful to extravagate a little in Oxonian (and not purely bibliothecarial) pastures.

Bibliothecary, *sb.* **2.** (Modern U.S. example.)

1887 O. W. Holmes *Hundred Days* vi. 218 These two experts in books, the bibliopole and the bibliothecary.

Bibliothetic (bi:bliǫþe·tik), *a.* [f. Gr. βιβλία books + θετικός concerned with placing or setting.] Relating to the placing and arrangement of books on the shelves of a library.

1901 E. C. Richardson *Classification* (1912) 46 The systems for classifying books on the shelves of a library, which if you need a technical name, may be called 'bibliothetic'.

Bibovine (bəibōu·vəin), *a. Zool.* [f. BI-[2] + BOVINE.] Designation of the group of bovine ruminants which includes the Oriental species, gaur, gayal, and banteng (forming the subgenus *Bibos*).

1889 Nicholson & Lydekker *Palæontol.* (ed. 3) II. 1351 The genus *Bos*..may be divided into the Bibovine and Taurine groups. In the former are included the wild Oxen of India and Burma. 1891 Flower & Lydekker *Mammals* 365 The Bibovine group.

Bibulo·sity. [See BIBULOUS *a.* and -OSITY.] Addictedness to tippling. So **Bi·bulousness** (cf. BIBULOUS *a.* 1, 2).

1844 *Jrnl. R. Agric. Soc.* V. I. 125 Their colour;..their bibulousness; all these properties conspire to the determination of the temperature of a given soil. 1901 Rashdall & Rait *New College* 207 The common-room which Spence occasionally adorned could not have been wholly given up to uncultivated bibulosity. 1928 *Daily Express* 2 Oct. 6 He caught the man under the arm and affected a slight bibulousness himself.

Bici·rcular, *a. Math.* [BI-[2] 1 and 2.]

1. Applied to a class of quartic curves each of which passes twice through each of the circular points at infinity, and thus resembles (analytically, and sometimes in form) a pair of circles.

1867 J. Casey *Bicircular Quartics* in *Trans. R. Ir. Acad.* XXIV. I. 458 A bicircular quartic; that is,..a quartic having the two circular points at infinity as double points. 1872 B. Williamson *Diff. Calc.* xi. 195 A curve of the fourth degree of the class called 'bicircular quartics'. 1879 G. Salmon *Higher Plane Curves* (ed. 3) 241 Quartics with two nodes, in the case where these are the circular points at infinity, have been extensively studied under the name of bicircular quartics.

2. Geom. *Bicircular coordinates*: coordinates formed by the intersection of a pair of circles meeting at a constant angle.

Bick. Short for *bick-iron*, the horn of an anvil. See BEAK-IRON, BICKERN.

1895 *Farriers' Price List* Suppl., Farriers' Anvils, with Steeled Bick.

Bicollateral (bəikǫlæ·tĕrăl), *a. Bot.* [BI-[2].] Of a fibro-vascular bundle: Having two masses of phloem on opposite sides of the xylem. (See COLLATERAL A. 1 e.) Hence **Bi:collatera·lity.**

1881 *Encycl. Brit.* XII. 18/1 In *Cucurbita*, *Solanum*, and others the bundles are 'bicollateral', there being an additional phloem portion inside the xylem. 1882 Vines *Sachs' Bot.* (ed. 2) 949 *Bicollateral bundles*, in which..there is a layer of phloem on the inner as well as on the outer side of the xylem. 1884 Bower & Scott tr. *De Bary's Phaner.* 319 A special subordinate form, to be called the double collateral or bicollateral, is distinguished from the usual one by the fact that two phloem groups lie on opposite sides of one xylem group. 1900 W. Wallace in *Ann. Bot.* Dec. 640 Most Cucurbitaceæ have bicollateral bundles. *Ibid.* 641 Weiss adopts this conception of bicollaterality.

Bicolour, -color (bəi·kɒləɹ), *a.* and *sb. Bot.* [ad. L. *bicolor* or F. *bicolore* adj.: see BI-[2].] **A.** *adj.* Having two colours. **B.** *sb.* A two-coloured blossom.

1898 [C'tess von Arnim] *Elizabeth & Germ. Gard.* 56 The Persian Yellows and Bicolors have been, as I predicted, a mistake among the teas.

Bico·nical, *a.* [f. BI-[2] + CONICAL.] Similar in shape to two cones placed base to base.

1875 *Encycl. Brit.* III. 775/1 Eggs of the Grebes..which also have both ends nearly alike but pointed, are so wide in the middle as to present a biconical appearance. 1928 V. G. Childe *Most Anc. East* viii. 191 Biconical faceted beads.

Bicursal (bəikɜ̄·ɹsăl), *a. Geom.* [f. BI-[2] + L. *cursus* course + -AL.] Of a curve: Having two paths.

1873 Cayley *Math. Papers* (1895) VIII. 181 A curve of deficiency 1 may be termed bicursal. 1876 *Ibid.* (1896) IX. 582 The bicursal sextic has in general 9 nodes.

Bicuspidal (bəikɒ·spidăl), *a. Geom.* [f. BI-[2] + CUSPIDAL.] Of a curve: Having two cusps.

1867 Cayley *Math. Papers* (1893) VI. 528 A bicuspidal or Cartesian curve. 1879 G. Salmon *Higher Plane Curves* (ed. 3) 241 Quartics having the two circular points as cusps have also been much studied under the name of Cartesians, the properties of which may similarly be generalized and stated as properties of bicuspidal quartics.

Bicyclette (bəisikle·t). [F., dim. of *bicycle.*] A low-wheeled or safety bicycle.

1895 *Columbus* (O.) *Dispatch* 17 Jan. 4/3 There were two-seated and four-seated vehicles and a petroleum bicyclette. 1895 *Blackw. Mag.* Nov. 646/2 If Nature..be more to you than bicyclettes and German bands.

Bid, *sb. fig.* Add: phr. *To make a bid for*: to make an attempt to secure, 'have a try' at getting.

1885 *Century Mag.* Dec. 179/2 He was a little ashamed of making such a bare-faced bid for her sympathy. 1893 *Cassell's Fam. Mag.* Apr. 357/2 The Colonel makes a good bid for the hole with the odd, and lies by the rim. 1895 *Geogr. Jrnl.* May 415 To make a bid himself for the throne.

Bidarka, -kee (bəidā·ɹka, -kī). Also bidarra. [Contamination of Russ. байдáкъ *baidák* and байдара *baidára*, names for kinds of canoes.] A portable boat of stretched skins, used by Eskimos.

1879 G. B. Goode *Catal. Anim. Resources U.S.* 144 Umiaks or bidarras. 1894 *Outing* (U.S.) XXIII. 389/1 A one-hatch *bidarka*, or hunting boat, of the Aleutian Islands. 1898 *Century Mag.* LV. 672 Their kayaks and bidarkees.

Biddy[1]. *U.S.* Add quots.

1858 O. W. Holmes *Aut. Breakf.-t.* xii. 363 Poor Bridget, or Biddy, our red-armed maid of all work! 1865–6 *Trans. Ill. Agric. Soc.* VI. 294 Two dollars a week would not tempt even the greenest Biddy to leave her Church.

Biddy-biddy. Also biddy-bid. [Corruption of Maori *piripiri*.] The New Zealand name for the troublesome bur of *Acæna ovina* or *A. Sanguisorba.*

1880 T. H. Potts *Out in the Open* in *New Zeal. Country Jrnl.* XII. 195 (Morris) Piri-piri (*acaena sanguisorbe*) by the settlers has been converted or corrupted into *biddy-biddy*. 1896 *Otago Witness* 23 Jan. II. 36 (Morris) Biddybids detract very materially from the value of the wool, and the plant should not be allowed to seed where sheep are depastured.

Bieberite (bī·bĕrəit). *Min.* [Named (G. *bieberit*, Haidinger 1845) from *Bieber*, near Hanau: see -ITE[1].] Sulphate of cobalt, found as a red crust on other minerals.

1854 Dana *Min.* (1868) 647. 1882 — *Mineral. & Lithol.* (ed. 4) 168 Bieberite or Cobalt Vitriol.

Bielid (bī·lid). *Astron.* [f. the name *Biela* (see below) + -ID[2], as in *Leonid*, etc.] An Andromede. So called because supposed to come from the remains of Biela's comet (named after the German astronomer, W. von Biela). Also *attrib.*

1899 *Edin. Rev.* Oct. 318 Displacements of the Bielid orbit are no abnormal events. 1899 *Sci. Amer.* 9 Dec. 379/3 A Shower of Bielids. A well-marked shower of Bielid meteors was observed at Princeton on the evening of November 24.

Bif, *int.* Exclamation uttered when something strikes an object: cf. next.

1905 H. G. Wells *Kipps* I. iv. § 1 When I go to turn, if I don't remember, Bif!—and I'm *in* to something. 1917 H. A. Vachell *Fishpingle* xi, Hamlin bowled straight and true for the middle stump. The youth smote and missed. 'Bif!' yelled Lionel.

Biff, *sb. slang.* [f. the vb.] A blow, whack. Also *fig.*

1889 Barrère & Leland *Dict. Slang, Biff* (Americanism), To give [one] a 'biff in the jaw.' 1902 Clapin *Dict. Amer.* 50 *Bif, Biff, Bift.* 1904 W. H. Smith *Promoters* x. 165 What an idiot a man can be when he gets a biff that takes his wind. 1926 *Blackw. Mag.* Feb. 224/1 Contusions on top of head..biff on the—bruise on inside of knee.

Biff, *v. slang.* [Imitative.] *trans.* To hit, strike.

1888 *Judy* 18 Jan. 27 He playfully biffed him with a brick. 1894 Kipling *Walking Delegate* in *Day's Work* 71 Ef we all biffed you now, these same men..'u'd call us off. 1902 Clapin *Dict. Amer.* 50 *Bif, Biff, Bift*, current in several parts of the States in sense of to strike, and especially to give a quick blow. 'He biffed him on the ear'. 1924 *Scribner's Mag.* Jan. 60/2, I gave Tim one between the eyes and I biffed his brother in the block.

Biflecnode (bəifle·knoud). *Math.* [f. BI-[2] + FLECNODE.] A point on a curve that is both a node and a point of inflexion for each branch passing through it. Hence **Biflecno·dal** *a.*

1874 G. Salmon *Analyt. Geom.* (ed. 3) p. xvii, Number of points at which two tangents are biflecnodal. *Ibid.* 521 Biflecnodal points. 1879 — *Higher Plane Curves* (ed. 3) 217 Such a node may be considered as the union of an ordinary node with (in the first case) a point of inflexion, and with (in the second case) two points of inflexion; and the node may be termed a flecnode or a biflecnode in the two cases respectively.

Bifo·cal, *a.* [BI-[2].] Having two foci. Used to designate spectacle-glasses with two segments of different focal lengths, the upper for distant, the lower for near, vision.

1894 Gould *Dict. Med.* 205/1 Bifocal lens. 1895 *Pop. Sci. Monthly* Aug. 470 Ordinary bifocal glasses.

Big, *a.* Add:

3. e. fig. phr. *Too big for one's boots* (*breeches, trousers*), inclined to swagger and play the great man among one's fellows.

[1879: see *BOOT *sb.*[3] 1 b.] 1905 H. G. Wells *Kipps* III. ii. § 1 He's getting too big for 'is britches. 1915 *Times* (weekly ed.) 11 June 523 For the first few weeks he was 'rather too big for his boots.'

7. In designations of operatives, denoting the chief or senior men; cf. *Big Four* in B.

1910 *Westm. Gaz.* 9 Mar. 4/1 There are over 40,000 male cotton-piecers who earn from 8s. 6d. to 13s. 6d. as little-piecers (youths), and from 13s. 6d. to 22s. 6d. as big-piecers (young men). 1921 *Dict. Occupational Terms* (1927) § 363 Big tenter. *Ibid.* 365 Big piecer..big spinner.

b. Of things: On a large or grand scale.

1928 *Morning Post* 4 Dec., Oxford's Big Rugby. 41 Points Against Edinburgh.

B. In collocations: **big bird, noise** (see the sbs.); **big dog** (earlier example); **big figure** *U.S.* (see quot. 1848); **big four** *U.S.*, a combination of four important things, persons, or companies; *spec.* the part of the New York Central Railway system connecting Cleveland, Cincinnati, Chicago, and St. Louis; similarly **big five**; **big gun**, a person of importance; †**Big Knife** *U.S.*, a white man, esp. a Virginian (so called by Indians); **big laurel** *U.S.*, species of magnolia and rhododendron; **big money**, orig. *U.S.* large sums of money, high wages or salary; **Big Muddy** *U.S.*, the Missouri river; **big pay** *U.S.*, high wages or salary; **big smoke**, (*a*) *Austral.*, aboriginal name for a town; (*b*) London (see SMOKE *sb.* 1 d); **big stick** *U.S.*, a display of force; hence *big-sticker, -stickism* (the currency of this is app. due to a speech by T. Roosevelt on 2 Sept. 1901); **big tree** *U.S.* (earlier examples).

1845 J. J. Hooper *Adv. Simon Suggs* x. 126 Pointing to the reverend gentleman who..was the '*big dog of the tan-yard'. 1836 Crockett *Exploits & Adv. Texas* (1837) 30 When a man sets about going the *big figure, halfway measures won't answer no how. 1844 [W. J. Thompson] *Major Jones's Courtship* (Bartlett) It's monstrous expensive..to do things on the big figure that's she's on now. 1848 Bartlett *Dict. Amer., Big figure.* To do things on the big figure, means to do them on a large scale. 1868 *Pickings fr. Picayune* 226 (De Vere) When I saw that, I thought I might as well go the big figure. 1886 *Outing* (U.S.) Nov. 156/1 The trial races proved beyond a doubt that the *Mayflower* was the queen of the '*big four'. 1890 *Congress. Rec.* May 4540/1 The monopolist who usurps and controls the markets, as the 'big four' have controlled the beef market of the country. 1894 *Ibid.* Aug., App. 1355/1 The conferees..went back and reconferred with the 'big four' of the Senate. 1896 R. G. Knowles & Morton *Baseball* 98 Spalding was engaged to serve the Chicago Club at his own terms, and this eventually led to the secession of the 'big four' of the period—under strict business rules—from the Boston to the Chicago Club. 1898 A. Nicholas *Idyl of Wabash* 208 Joe Little, brake-man on the Big Four railroad. 1908 *Westm. Gaz.* 13 June 2/1 In each State contingent the four 'delegates at large'—the 'Big Four', to give them their current title—are the men who really count. 1913 *N. Y. Even. Post* 1 May 1/6 A head-on collision between a Big Four passenger train and a freight train. 1927 Agatha Christie (*title*) The Big Four. 1865 Susan Hale *Lett.* 16 The *big guns of the parish. 1857, 1880 [see GUN *sb.* 7 b]. 1888 *Texas Siftings* 13 Oct. (Farmer, Slang) You don't consider that insignificant ink-slinger..a big gun, do you? 1750 C. Gist *Jrnls.* 36 Upon his understanding I came from Virginia, he called me the *Big Knife. 1786 *Massachusetts Gaz.* 17 Oct. (Th.) General Clarke of Virginia, whom the Indians dread, and stile the Big Knife. 1827 J. F. Cooper *Prairie* (1836) II. i. 6 It is farther to the towns of the Big-knives. 1832 D. J. Browne *Sylva Amer.* 210 At Charleston..this tree is commonly called *Large Magnolia*; but it is more generally known in the country by the name of *Big Laurel.* 1853 D. H. Strother *Blackwater Chron.* vii. 89 This dale is girt round..by a broad belt of the Rhododendron—commonly called the *big laurel* out here. 1888 *N. Y. Life* 28 Jan. 3/1 I'll bet my bottom dollar it would be worth 'big money to know what Alec just told Chauncey. 1907 *Westm. Gaz.* 16 Aug. 2/1 The skilled artisan has always been..well paid in Belfast. He makes what he calls 'big money.' 1857–8 *Trans. Ill. Agric. Soc.* (1859) III. 352 Most of the orchard trees north of the *Big Muddy. 1868 *Congress. Globe* June 2755/1 The train..comes back to Missouri with coal superior even to that of the Big-Muddy. 1915 *Lit. Digest* (N. Y.) 21 Aug. 362/1 Advt., Our course trains you to get and keep the *big pay jobs. 1848 H. W. Haygarth *Bush Life Australia* i. 6 As he gradually leaves behind him the '*big smoke' (as the aborigines picturesquely call the town). 1904 *Springfield Weekly Republ.* 26 Aug. 1 Happily the revolution in Paraguay is too far down in South America to arouse the '*big stick' in Washington. 1915 *Lit. Digest* (N. Y.) 21 Aug. 352/2 Mr. Joyce Kilmer, known as a poet and a critic,..on this occasion performs in the latter capacity with 'a big stick.' 1905 *Springfield Weekly Republ.* 9 June 1 A *big-sticker after Mr. Roosevelt's own heart. 1926 *Spectator* 2 Jan. 19/1 There is nothing in the British record to compare with Roosevelt's robust *big-stickism in the Alaska boundary case. 1869 C. L. Brace *New West* ii. 33 We can see the gigantic trunks of the superb 'Red Wood'..a near relative to the *Big Trees. 1875 *Field & Forest* I. 44 Equalling the largest known specimen of the 'big tree' proper.

b. In collocations used attrib.

1909 *Daily Chron.* 7 May 1/4 The big-fleet party in Vienna. 1909 *Westm. Gaz.* 27 Apr. 11/2 Big-print headlines in newspapers. *Ibid.* 29 Jan. 2/2 Whether we be 'big-Navy' men or 'little-Navy' men.

Bi·gamize, *v. U.S.* [f. BIGAMY.] *intr.* To commit bigamy.

a 1861 T. Winthrop *John Brent* vi. 61 When he came back the pretty girl had bigamized.

Big bug. orig. *U.S.* [See BUG *sb.*[1] 1 b.] A person of importance; a great man.

1830 Mrs. Royall *Lett. fr. Alabama* 42 One of them,..being asked rather peremptorily by one of the big bugs to rub down his horse, cursed him. 1835 W. G. Simms *Partisan* 323 Meant for great occasions when I am entertaining some of the big bugs in epaulettes. 1840 J. P. Kennedy *Quodlibet* 127 There are the mandarins, our big bugs, and I could name them to you. 1871 Schele de Vere *Americanisms* (1872) 392 Persons of great wealth and distinction are irreverently called Big Bugs, and 'I-street, in Washington', is thus said to 'be inhabited by the foreign ambassadors and other big bugs.' 1896 J. C. Harris *Sister Jane* 24 He don't belong to the big-bugs.

Bigeminous (bəidʒe·minəs), *a.* [f. L. *bigeminus* doubled (f. *bi-*, BI-[2] + *geminus* double): see -OUS.] Of a tooth: Imperfectly double; halfway between a single tooth and two teeth.

1894 W. Bateson *Study of Variation* 238 Since the bigeminous teeth are not completely divided, they must be reckoned as single teeth.

Bigenous (bəi·dʒĕnəs), *a.* [f. L. *bi-*, BI-[2] + *-genus* born: see -OUS. Cf. BIGENER.] Inherited from both parents.

1894 Körösi in *Phil. Trans.* Ser. B. CLXXXVI. 784 We may be allowed to introduce two denominations for the two species of natal probabilities, naming those which regard only one sex as *monogenous*, and those which take into consideration the age-combinations of both parents as *bigenous*. *Ibid.*, A complete bigenous table of natality.

Bigha (bī·gă). Also beega(h, begah, biggah. [Hindi.] A measure of land area in India varying locally from ⅓ acre to 1 acre.

1763 in Gleig *Mem. Hastings* (1841) I. 129, I never seized a boga [*sic*] or a beswa of the land belonging to Calcutta. 1823 Malcolm *Central India* II. 15 *note*, A Begah has been computed at one third of an acre, but its size differs in almost every province. The smallest Begah may perhaps be computed at one third, and the largest at two thirds of an acre. 1877 Meadows Taylor *My Life* xii. (1878) 251 It would be a noble sheet of water, and very profitable, as it would irrigate upwards of 10,000 *beegahs* of rice. 1895 Mrs. Croker *Village Tales* (1896) 167 Two biggahs of land, planted in rape and linseed. 1905 *Statesman* 22 Aug. 2/4 All that piece or parcel of vacant land containing by measurement one bigha fifteen cottahs more or less.

Big head, big-head. *U.S.* [BIG *a.* 3.]

1. A disease in cattle, characterized by a swelling of the head.

1805 *Lancaster* (Pa.) *Intelligencer* 3 Dec. Advt. (Th.) A Brown Steer, having 'what they call the Big Head.' 1867 *Rep. Iowa Agric. Soc.* (1868) 130, I have not lost but two of the bovine species..; one in 1861 had big head or jaw. 1889 in Farmer *Americanisms*.

2. *fig.* 'Swelled head'; arrogance, conceit.

1853 *Daily Morn. Herald* (St. Louis) 2 July (Th.) Mayor How's ungallant attack upon the little boys of our city is a weak emanation of a 'big head.' 1856 B. Young in *Jrnl. Discourses* IV. 69 They need to be careful, or they will have the 'big head,' and become as dead..as old pumpkins. 1896 *Congress. Rec.* Mar. 3030/2 [Such] men holding subordinate places in the government of the U.S. to-day..have got the 'big head' and got it bad. 1898 *Sat. Rev.* 2 Apr. 451 Suffering from an acute attack of what the Americans call big-head.

Big-horn, bighorn. *U.S.* [BIG *a.* B. 2.] A Rocky Mountain sheep.

1806 P. Gass *Jrnl.* (1807) 222 They saw a number..of the ibex or big-horn. 1837 W. Irving *Capt. Bonneville* iii. 68 Flocks of the ahsahta or bighorn, an animal which frequents these cliffs in great numbers. *a* 1861 Winthrop *John Brent* iv. (1862) 47 He turned butcher of buffalo, bears, and big-horn. 1879 Miss Bird *Rocky Mts.* 89 Here, in the early morning, deer, bighorn, and the stately elk, come down to feed. 1926 *Chambers's Jrnl.* July 449/1 It had been the regular route traversed by large droves of bighorn.

attrib. 1873 J. H. Beadle *Undevel. West* xxxi. 676 A day..will bring one to the range of larger game, such as cinnamon bears, mountain lions and bighorn sheep.

Big-side. (See quot. 1900.)

1845 *Rules Footb. Rugby School* § 21 Two big-side balls must always be in the Close during a match or big-side. 1848 *Recoll. Rugby* 133 'The Laws of Football', which were 'sanctioned by a Levee of Big Side', on the 7th of September, 1846. 1856 *Rugby School* 154 Allowing the blood to flow out freely in that most glorious channel—a Big-Side Match. *Ibid.* 157 The tuft of trees..bordering Big-side. 1892 F. Marshall's *Football* 16 Up to the year 1858 or thereabouts all the school who were not 'caps' had to stand in goal during Bigsides. 1895 *Athenæum* 30 Mar. 402/3 In..a big-side..in 1853..80 old Rugbeians played 120 of the school [at football]. 1900 J. S. Farmer *Public Sch. Word-bk.* 21 *Big-side* (Rugby and elsewhere). The combination of all the bigger fellows in the school in one and the same game or run. Also the ground specially used for the game so denominated.

Bijwoner, bywoner (bəi·wǫnəɹ). *S. African.* Also beiwoner, bywonner. [Du., f. *bijwonen* to be present at.] An authorized squatter on another man's farm (Pettman).

1889 H. A. Bryden *Kloof & Karroo* 253 A beiwoner (a sort of sub-farmer on the estate of a richer farmer, who is expected to perform certain duties for the privilege of running his stock). 1916 F. E. Mills Young (*title*) The Bywonner. 1916 *Times Lit. Suppl.* 24 Aug. 406 The 'poor-white' bywoner, who won't work for wages, and often uses a native's oxen.

Bike (bəik), *sb.*[2] Colloq. abbreviation of BICYCLE. Also **Bike** *v.*, **Bi·ker, Bi·king.**

1890 *Daily News* 19 Nov. 5/6 Washington has been called the Mecca of American wheelmen...'Bike' is the slang term in use there for bicycle. 1895 *Ibid.* 10 Sept. 7/1 Young girls..who are learning to 'bike'. 1895 *Westm. Gaz.* 14 Oct. 7/2 The 'biking' craze seems to grow...Lady Warwick..was one of the 'bikers'. 1896 R. S. S. Baden-Powell *Matabele Campaign* xix, The other..can use his revolver—which cannot be done by single bikers. 1901 W. R. H. Trowbridge *Lett. her Mother to Eliz.* vi. 25 Daisy biked over to Exeter this morning with Mr. Frame.

Bilabial, *a.* Add:

2. *Phonetics.* Of certain consonants (e.g. *p, b, m, v, w*): Produced by the juncture or apposition of both lips. Also *sb.*, a bilabial consonant.

1894 W. M. Lindsay *Lat. Lang.* 47 At some time before the fifth cent. A. D...initial *v*..seems to have passed from the bilabial spirant (Spanish *b*) to the labio-dental spirant (our *v*). 1898 W. Rippmann *Elem. Phonetics* (1910) 82 The labio-dentals and the bilabials. *Ibid.* 90 In general the lip stops are bilabial, *i.e.* formed by a closure of both lips. 1911 P. Giles in *Encycl. Brit.* XXVII. 830/1 The Latin V..was not a labio-dental spirant like the English *v*, but a bi-labial semivowel like the English *w*.

Bilge, *sb.* Add:

1. c. Nonsense, 'rubbish', 'rot'. *slang.*

1921 A. S. M. Hutchinson *If Winter Comes* II. vii. § 6 And they didn't talk any of this bilge about fighting us in England. 1925 P. G. Wodehouse in *Strand Mag.* Sept. 216/2 'Oh, I know he writes the most awful bilge,' said Anastatia.

Bilgy, *a.* Add U.S. quot.:

1890 *Harper's Mag.* Sept. 594/2 Living in quarters as crowded and bilgy as a slaver's hold.

Bilharzia (bilhā·ɹzia). [mod.L., named by T. S. Cobbold after Theodor *Bilharz*, a German physician who discovered the parasite in 1851.] A genus of trematode worms parasitic in the veins of the pelvic region and urinary organs of human beings, esp. in Egypt and other parts of Africa. Hence **Bilha·rzial, Bilha·rzic** *adjs.*; **Bilharzia·sis, -osis**, the disease produced by the presence of this worm in the bladder.

1864 T. S. Cobbold *Entozoa* 203 The blood..forms the proper habitat of the *Bilharzia*. 1877 Huxley *Anat. Inv. Anim.* 202 Diœcious Trematodes are very rare, the most important being the formidable *Bilharzia*. 1903 *Phil. Med. Jrnl.* 31 Jan. 208 (Cent. Suppl.) Bilharzic. 1903 F. C. Madden in *Jrnl. Trop. Med.* 1 Jan. (*title*) The presence of living adult bilharzia worms in bilharzial papillomata. 1906 *Lancet* 27 Oct. 1178/2 The liver proved to be a typical specimen of advanced bilharzial cirrhosis. *Ibid.*, A remarkable case of bilharriasis. 1907 F. C. Madden (*title*) Bilharziosis. 1913 A. R. Ferguson in *Glasgow Med. Jrnl.* Jan. 15 Egypt has well been termed the 'home of bilharziosis'.

Bilian (bi·liăn). Also billian. [Malay.] The ironwood of Borneo.

1882 De Windt *Equator* 63 Loading 'bilian' or iron wood. 1887 Daly *Digging S. Austr.* 272 Forests of bilian..in British North Borneo. 1906 *Macm. Mag.* Nov. 42 That wonderful wood *billian*, the Bornean iron-wood.

Bili·ngualism. [f. BILINGUAL + -ISM.] Ability

to speak two languages; the habitual use of two languages colloquially.

1897 A. J. Butler tr. *Ratzel's Hist. Mankind* II. 20 The bi-lingualism of the Carib tribes, whose women speak Arawak and the men Carib. 1926 *Encycl. Brit.* III. 114 The effects of bilingualism deserve attention, especially in those areas where permanent contact is established between two different families of speech, as in India. 1927 *British Weekly* 12 May 125/4 Welsh bilingualists [decreased] by more than two per cent.

Biliteral, *a.* Add:

2. Of an inscription: Written in two different scripts. Also *sb.*, a biliteral inscription.

1877 Skene *Celtic Scot.* II. 450 Several of those [*sc.* ogham inscriptions] in Wales being biliteral, and having a corresponding inscription in debased Roman characters. 1878 Stokes & Petrie *Christian Inscript.* II. 165 The biliteral inscriptions on our stone monuments. 1887 S. Ferguson *Ogham Inscript.* 114 Other biliterals of..mere British origin.

-bility [F. *-bilité*, L. *-bilitātem*], a termination forming abstract substantives from adjectives in -BLE.

Bilk, *sb.* 4. (Later U.S. examples.)

1869 A. K. McClure *Rocky Mts.* 211 A bilk is a man who never misses a meal and never pays a cent. 1873 J. H. Beadle *Undevel. West* iii. 78 Nineteen hotels and restaurants were in operation, and at every one of them 'bilks' abounded.

Bilker (bi·lkəɹ). *slang.* [f. Bilk *v.* + -er[1].] One who practises cheating; *esp.* one who evades payment of a cabman's fare.

1717 *Daily Courant* 27 Dec., A Dramatick Entertainment of Dancing, call'd, The Cheats, or, The Tavern Bilkers. 1887 *Tit-Bits* 25 June 172 Cab Bilkers. 1892 *Daily News* 6 May 6/5 Fares who tried to evade payment, known as 'bilkers'. 1898 *Ibid.* 8 Jan. 3/5 The London Cab Act, 59 and 60 Victoria, chapter 27, commonly known as the Bilkers' Act. 1909 H. G. Wells *Ann Veronica* xvi, Ann Veronica, you're a bilker!

Bill, *sb.*[3] Add:

5. e. At Harrow school, properly, the list of boys; hence, the calling-over of the list. Also *attrib.*

1814 W. C. Trevelyan *Diary* in G. T. Warner *Harrow in Pr. & Verse* (1914) 107 Locked up at 8 o'clock, placed at the 2 bill. 1815 *Ibid.* 113 Dr. B showed us a bill of Harrow School for 1770. 1818 N. Carlisle *Descr. Endowed Gram. Sch. Eng. & Wales* II. 148 The Absences for Bills..are regularly called every Two hours by The Head Master. 1880 Merivale *Autobiog.* (1898) 40 The writing of this Bill was entrusted to two of the most meritorious boys, who also wrote good hands. 1894 *Harrovian* 15 Nov. 103/2 From the Bill-yard to the Old Station. 1894 R. C. Welch *Harrow Sch. Reg.* 17 Our present Bill Books. 1898 *Howson & Warner's Harrow School* 275 The 4 bill in summer is double, part on the cricket-ground (cricket-bill)...At yard-bill the boys pass one by one in bill order before the bill-master of the week, answer their names, touch their hats, and walk on. *Ibid.*, For a master to get through bill in ten minutes is smart work,—there are well over 600 names to be called,—a quarter of an hour is the usual time.

8. c. *To fill the bill*: to fulfil the necessary requirements; to come up to the requisite standard. orig. *U.S.* (Cf. Fill *v.* 7 c.)

1860 *Trans. Ill. Agric. Soc.* (1861) IV. 471 Austin..Seedling, Dr. W. hopes well from because of its great vigor, but doubts if it fills the bill. 1881 A. A. Hayes *New Colorado* ii. 23 With this requirement in view does Colorado 'fill the Bill'? 1890 *Harper's Mag.* Feb. 441/1 They filled the bill according to their lights. 1902 Clapin *Dict. Amer.* 52 Some one 'fills the Bill' when he comes up to the description, or is able to accomplish what is undertaken. 1904 W. H. Smith *Promoters* i. 20, I don't think I ever saw a word used that..filled the bill quite so completely as this word 'experimentally' will do for us.

9. c. A bank-note. *U.S.*

1817 S. R. Brown *Western Gaz.* 112 The notes of this bank are in excellent credit, but bills from the neighbouring states..have a free and extensive circulation. 1852 Mrs. Stowe *Uncle Tom's C.* 438 She unlocked the desk, took from it a roll of bills, which she counted over rapidly. 1905 *N. Y. Even. Post* 1 Sept. 7 The coin..is certainly cleaner than the rumpled-up bills that prevail in the out-of-the-way places.

10. *Bill of costs* (see quot. 1911).

1826 *New Monthly Mag.* II. 109 [He] made the invitation an item in his bill of costs. 1869 *Yng. Men Gt. Brit.* 14 May 260/2 An attorney, about to furnish a bill of costs. 1911 *Encycl. Brit.* III. 932/2 A *Bill of Costs* is an account setting forth the charges and disbursements incurred by a solicitor in the conduct of his client's business. The delivery of a bill of costs is by statute a condition necessary before the solicitor can sue upon it.

11. (Sense 3) *bill-drafter, -drafting*; **bill-board** *U.S.*, a notice-board, a hoarding; **bill-book** *U.S.*, a pocket-book; **bill-clerk** *U.S.*, a clerk who makes out the bills at a hotel.

a 1877 in Bartlett *Dict. Amer.* (ed. 4) 44 People who fail to edit a *bill-board are firmly convinced that they could edit a newspaper. 1898 M. Deland *Old Chester Tales* 245 Well, I was advertised all round; you ought to have seen the bill-boards. 1904 *Atlantic Monthly* Mar. 295 An ordinance which demands that no billboard be erected on a residence street [etc.]. 1905 *N. Y. Times* 3 Feb. 3 In a *billbook in an inside pocket were many checks..on Plainfield banks. 1909 'O Henry' *Options* (1916) 77 Young New Yorkers who might be millionaires or *bill clerks. 1886 P. Robinson *Teetotum Trees* 65 The most experienced of *bill-draughters. 1894 *Westm. Gaz.* 6 Feb. 2/2 The kind of mistake for which even a Bill-drafter can hardly be expected to provide. 1895 *Ibid.* 8 Jan. 2/2 Ministers have led..a quiet, if busy and *Bill-drafting, existence.

Billabong (bi·läbǫŋ). *Austral.* Also billy-bonn, billi-bong. [Native name, f. *billa* river + *bung* dead.] A branch or effluent of a river, forming a blind channel or backwater or stagnant pool.

1862 W. Landsborough *Explor. Australia* vi. 31 In the south, such a creek as the Macadam is termed a *billy-bonn*. 1865 W. Howitt *Discov. Australia* I. 298 Their way on was intercepted..by..what the Major calls..anabranches of the river, but which the natives call billibongs, channels coming out of a stream and returning into it again. 1911 C. E. W. Bean '*Dreadnought' of Darling* xiv. 133 Australian rivers ..often have a long arm or two wandering off into the plain, and either coming back to the river again in the end or else straying off for perhaps a hundred miles and ending nowhere in particular. Those arms are what they call billabongs.

Billed (bild), *ppl. a.*[2] [f. Bill *v.*[3]]

1. Entered in a bill or list; *spec.* (see quot.).

1873 W. W. Knollys *Dict. Mil. Terms, Billed*, a term exclusively confined to the Foot Guards. It means that a man's name is placed in the list or bill of those who are to undergo drill and confinement to barracks. Hence a 'billed man'.

2. Announced or advertised by a bill. (See Bill *v.*[3] 4.)

1895 *Westm. Gaz.* 18 July 8/1 The..train reached Aberdeen at 6.46..or fourteen minutes before the billed time of arrival. 1897 *Daily News* 22 May 5/7 The establishment of a boldly billed enclosure for lost children.

Billet, *sb.*[1] Add:

4. b. A place in which a soldier is billeted; a soldier's lodging or quarters. Also *gen.*

1858 *Billets & Bivouacs* 246 Thou long-suffering reader,..tarry with me yet a moment in the last billet we shall ever share together—my dark abode on the dreary shores of Old Father Thames. 1875 *Encycl. Brit.* II. 571/2 The army lived in barracks, camps, or billets. 1920 Wodehouse *Damsel in Distress* vii, So George took up his abode..in the plainly-furnished but not uncomfortable cottage...He might have found a worse billet.

c. *transf.* An appointment, post, or 'berth'. app. orig. *U.S.* or *Colonial.*

1870 *Cassell's Mag.* II. 58/1 The private..doesn't see why ..he should give up his billet as pioneer or canteen waiter to do sentry, go. 1887 *Taken-in* 135 If you are out of work, or out of a situation, as we say, here [N. Zealand] it is called 'out of billet'. 1890 Hornung *Bride fr. Bush* xvii, If ever she went back to Australia, she'd remember my young man, and get him a good billet. 1891 Chas. King *Two Soldiers* (1892) 120 (Funk) A billet as clerk in the recruiting rendezvous.

Bi·lliardist. [f. Billiard-s + -ist.] A billiard-player.

1879 *N. Y. Even. Expr. Alman.* 371. 1888 *St. Louis Globe Democrat* 24 Jan. (Farmer) Each competitor has put up fifty dollars entrance money in Billiardist Daly's hands. 1901 *Daily Chron.* 3 Apr. 6/6 A player, like a billiardist, would require practice to be successful.

Billiards. 2. Add:

billiard-room (earlier U.S. example); **billiard-table**, used *attrib.* to describe a perfectly smooth road, green, etc.

1816 U. Brown in *Maryland Hist. Mag.* X. 265 Dined and fed at Jesse Brown's Hotel, an Inn kept in High Stile with Billiard Room. 1905 *Westm. Gaz.* 6 June 4/2 A land of billiard-table roads. 1907 *Ibid.* 12 Mar. 4/1 It is easy enough..to make a car that will successfully operate on the billiard-table roads of France and England. 1909 *Ibid.* 3 Mar. 12/2 The billiard-table smoothness of the putting green.

Billikin (bi·likin). *colloq.* [f. Billy[2] (1 c) + -kin, or alteration of *billy-can*.] A small 'billy' or tin can used as a kettle.

1926 *Spectator* 13 Feb. 267/2 They drank tea made in a billikin.

Billing, *vbl. sb.*[3] Add:

b. Announcing or advertising by bill or poster. Also *attrib.*, as *billing matter*.

1875 *Chambers's Jrnl.* 132/1 Advertisements, which most likely took the form of 'billing'. 1900 *Daily News* 4 Dec. 3/2 No billing is attempted in the City, and hence the urgent necessity for a thorough distribution of election literature. 1902 *Daily Chron.* 20 Mar. 7/4 If plaintiff did not send..particulars of her performance for billing purposes. 1905 *Ibid.* 28 June 6/2 The defence was that Mr. Elen did not send on 'billing matter' two weeks in advance of his engagement.

c. *Comm.* The act of making out or drafting a bill, invoice, etc. Also *comb.*, as *billing machine* (an automatic typewriter).

1908 *Westm. Gaz.* 26 Feb. 9/2 The billing machine..will produce half a dozen business documents at one operation, and will total up automatically the various items entered. *Ibid.* 29 Feb. 7/1 The special Oliver for Billing and Invoicing...Combined Billing and Adding Machines.

Billion. 2. (Earlier example.)

1840 *Congress. Globe* 6 Jan., App. 89/1 We may begin with the hundred and twelve millions, and then proceed..until we have bought and divided that billion of acres.

Billow, *v.* Add:

3. *trans.* To raise into billows or folds.

1885 Wingfield *Barbara Philpot* I. x. 290 The cold air rushing in billowed the curtains and extinguished the lights.

Bi·llowlet. [See -let.] A small billow.

1867 J. Macgregor *Rob Roy Baltic* 99 The dancing billowlets of the lake. 1892 *Temple Bar* Oct. 292 The bay..with its sheltered succession of crescent-shaped billowlets.

Billstead. *U.S.* (See quot.)

1832 J. F. Watson *Hist. Tales N. Y.* 164 (Th.) The general furniture [*c* 1780] was made of 'billstead', another name for maple.

Billy[2]. Add:

1. b. A policeman's baton. *U.S.*

a 1859 *N. Y. Herald* in Bartlett *Dict. Amer.* (ed. 2) 33 A poor German was taken to prison, and, on examining him, it was discovered that he was a victim to the billy. 1903 *N. Y. Times* 11 Sept., Eight men set upon a policeman this morning,..taking his revolver and billy away from him.

c. Also *billy-can*. (Cf. *Billikin.)

1885 Mrs. C. Praed *Head Stat.* xxiii, I lost the billy-can-lid.

d. = Billy-goat.

1928 *Daily Tel.* 9 Oct. 4/6 The Ministry of Agriculture, through the agency of its stud goat scheme, has now placed 103 'billies' at the disposal of smallholders.

Billy Fairplay or **Playfair.** *Coal-mining.* (See quot. 1883.)

1876 *Patent Specif.* No. 4387, Machines for weighing small coal known by the name of 'Billy fair play'. 1883 Gresley *Gloss. Coal Mining*, *Billy Boy* (South Wales), a lad who attends to the working of a Billy Playfair. *Billy Playfair* or *Fair-play*,..a mechanical contrivance for weighing coal, consisting of an iron trough with a sort of hopper bottom, into which all the small coal passing through the screen is conducted and weighed off and emptied from time to time. 1889 *Law Rep.* 14 App. Cases 281 The coal was shot down on a screen called Billy Fairplay.

Billy-o. *colloq.* Also -ho, -oh. Used in the intensive phr. *like billy-o* (see Like *adv.* 1 b). Cf. *like old Harry* = like the devil; see Harry *sb.*[2] 4.

1885 *Referee* 9 Aug. in Ware *Passing Engl.* s.v., Shure it'll rain like billy-ho! 1914 W. J. Locke *Fortunate Youth* iii, 'And they fight?' 'Like billy-o,' said Paul. 1927 *Observer* 11 Dec. 26 The Holy Rollers were going it like billy-oh to a tune which sounded like 'My old man's a fireman'.

Biloculine (bəilǫ·kiŭləin), *a.* *Zool.* [ad. mod. L. *Biloculīna*, f. *bi-* Bi-[2] + L. *loculus*, dim. of *locus* place: see -ine[1].] Having two chambers or compartments; characteristic of the foraminiferous genus *Biloculina*.

1898 Sedgwick *Zool.* I. 9 In the genus *Biloculina* (*Miliolidæ*), while the mode of growth of the megalospheric form is..on the biloculine plan from the first, that of the microspheric form is at first on the quinqueloculine plan, and it is not until many chambers have been formed that the biloculine plan, characteristic of the genus, is assumed.

Bilophodont (bəilǫ·fŏdǫnt), *a.* *Zool.* [f. Bi-[2] + *lophodont* (see Lopho-).] Of the molar teeth in certain ungulates: Having two transverse crests or ridges on the grinding surface.

1868 Owen *Anat. Vertebr.* III. 343 The 'bilophodont' sub-type becomes more marked in *Dinotherium*. *Ibid.* 358 Certain huge fossil bilophodont grinders, which seemed to indicate a gigantic Tapir. 1891 Flower & Lydekker *Mammals* 373 Molars brachydont and bilophodont.

Bim (bim). Also **Bimm.** Colloq. name for an inhabitant of Barbados.

1852 C. W. Day *Five Yrs. W. Indies* I. 15 The Barbadians are familarly known as 'Bimms'. 1860 Trollope *W. Indies* xiii. 207 One soon learns to know a —— Bim. That is the name in which they themselves delight, and therefore, though there is a sound of slang about it, I give it here. 1902 *Daily Chron.* 1 Feb. 5/1 Mr. Bosanquet's team of English cricketers, which has lately been playing in Barbados, and making but an indifferent show before the doughty 'Bims'.

Bimanual (bəimæ·niuăl), *a.* [f. Bi-[2] + Manual *a.*] Performed with both hands; in which both hands are employed. Hence **Bima·nually** *adv.*, by means of both hands.

1898 G. E. Herman *Dis. Women* 59 Bimanual examination. *Ibid.* 63 There are cases in which..you cannot bimanually feel the distinction. 1902 D. J. Cunningham *Anat.* 1233 By the bimanual examination the pelvic organs are steadied and pushed downwards towards the pelvic outlet by the pressure of the left hand applied in the hypogastric region.

Bimbashi (bimba·ʃi). Also **bimbashee**, **binbashi**. [Turk., lit. 'one who is head of a thousand' (*bīm* thousand, *bāsh* head; cf. Bashaw).] A Turkish military captain or commander. In Egypt, an English officer in the service of the Khedive.

1819 T. Hope *Anastasius* (1820) II. xv. 329 A Bimbashee [*note* Turkish colonel], with about eighteen hundred men. 1876 Gladstone *Bulgarian Horrors* 31 Their Bimbashis and their Yuzbachis, their Kaimakams and their Pashas. 1896 *Daily News* 28 Mar. 5/3 'Bimbashi' is the general name for the English officers attached to the Egyptian army. 1899 Kipling *Stalky* 197 He did not know that Wake..would be a bimbashi of the Egyptian Army ere his thirtieth year.

Bimbo. (Earlier U.S. example.)

1837 *Baltimore Commerc. Transcript* 5 Sept. 2/3 (Th.) The *U. S. Gazette* asks what is bimbo?..Bimbo is a rascally compound of brandy and sugar, flavoured with lemon peal [*sic*].

Bimeby (bəi·mbəi), *adv.* *U.S.* Reduced form of By and by A. 4. (Cf. *Bymeby.)

1824 *Nantucket Inquirer* 5 Jan. (Th.) Well, bimeby he took notion to hab my daughter... Well, bimeby I found em out. 1848 Lowell *Biglow P.* Ser. I. Courtin' 41 When Ma bimeby upon 'em slips, Huldy sot pale ez ashes. 1878 J. H. Beadle *Western Wilds* ii. 28 Bimeby one chap says: 'Oh, yes, I know Mr. Darnell.'

Bimetalli·stic, *a.* [f. Bimetallist + -ic.] Relating to, inclining to, bimetallism.

1889 in *Cent. Dict.* (citing *Contemp. Rev.*). 1897 *Daily News* 5 Feb. 10/5 The Agriculturists, with their..bimetallistic hankerings.

Bimolecular (bəimǫle·kiŭlăɹ), *a.* [Bi-[2].] Designating a chemical reaction in which two of the reacting substances are transformed.

1899 J. Walker *Introd. Phys. Chem.* 256 Saponification of ethereal salts by alkalies affords us an example of a bimolecular reaction. *Ibid.* 257 A bimolecular reaction, which is, strictly speaking, a balanced action, but proceeds very nearly to an end in aqueous solution, is the formation of urea from ammonium cyanate. 1904 J. W. Mellor *Chem. Stat. & Dynam.* 35 The hydrolysis of ethyl acetate by sodium hydroxide is a bimolecular reaction.

Bi-monthly, *a.* and *sb.* [Bi- *pref.*[2] 4, 4 b.] Occurring or produced every two months (every other month); *sb.* a bi-monthly periodical. Also used = occurring (etc.) twice a month (cf. *semi-monthly* s.v. Semi- 5 b).

1878 *Print. Trades Jrnl.* xxv. 4 A new Spanish bi-monthly journal. 1879 Gladstone in *Daily News* 1 Dec. 6/5 Annual as opposed to bi-monthly or tri-monthly budgets. 1891 (*title*) The Record of Technical and Secondary Education. A bi-monthly journal. 1906 *Daily Chron.* 11 Sept. 3/2 The slip-shod quarterly—bi-monthly, sometimes—productions that some of our novelists turn out. 1926 (*title*) Vogue Fashion Bi-Monthly.

Binary. A. f. Add: Of a quantic: Having two variables.

1858 Cayley *Math. Papers* (1889) II. 527 Certain binary quantics, viz. the quadric, the cubic, and the quartic.

Bind, *sb.* Add:

7. A bruise on a horse's foot caused by the pressure of a nail on the sensitive parts.

1908 *Animal Managem.* 239 'Pricks', wounds from nails driven into the fleshy part, and 'presses,' or 'binds,' from their being so close that they bruise them.

Bind, *v.* 17. b. Add: Also *absol.*

1917 *Oxford Jrnl. Illustr.* 17 Jan. 8/3 The prisoner was bound over for twelve months.

Binder. Add: **3.** (Additional examples.)

1880 *Plain Hints Needlework* 92 In plain-work, the linings [are] generally called 'binders,' e.g. the binders in a shirt, or night-dress, or shift. 1887 *Northern N. & Q.* Dec. 150 Small heart-shape brooches..fixed to the binders of babies to protect them from the witches and fairies.

7. b. In road-making (see quot.).

1911 *Encycl. Brit.* XXIII. 392/1 Upon the concrete foundation is first spread a layer of fine bituminous concrete called 'binder', 1½ in. thick, to unite the wearing surface to the concrete foundation. Upon the binder the asphalte is laid to a thickness of 2 in.

Bing-bang. *colloq.* An onomatopœic reduplication expressing a repeated heavy thump or a continued banging noise.

1914 W. J. Locke *Fortunate Youth* xiii, Lets 'em have it bing-bang in the eye. Don't he, Jane? 1926 *Glasgow Herald* 1 Mar. 10 Bing-bang, cling-clang clatter.

Binge (binʒ), *sb.* *slang* (orig. *dial.*: see *E.D.D.*). [Special use of dial. *binge* to soak (a wooden vessel).] A heavy drinking-bout; hence, a spree. So **Binge** *v. refl.* and *pass.*, to drink heavily, 'soak'; *trans.*, to raise the spirits of.

1854 Miss Baker *Northampt. Gloss.* s.v., A man goes to the alehouse to get a good binge, or to binge himself. 1889 Barrère & Leland *Dict. Slang*, *Binge* (Oxford), a big drinking bout. 1915 H. A. Vachell *Quinneys* xi. § 1, 155 It binges me up when I feel blue. 1922 *Chambers's Jrnl.* Sept. 569/1 This is only a binge—just a jolly old bachelor-party. 1925 *Sunday at Home* Dec. 146/1 One man was so binged in drink and so enchained by the craving for it. 1928 Wodehouse in *Strand Mag.* July 4 Eh? What about our Monte Carlo binge?

Biniou (bi·niŭ). [Breton, pl. of *benvek* tool, (musical) instrument.] The form of bagpipe used in Brittany.

1902 *Westm. Gaz.* 20 Mar. 10/1 A toast was followed by such music as the native biniou can produce. 1925 *Blackw. Mag.* Sept. 359/2 When Lommic took the biniou under his arm he made the pipes sing.

Binitarian (bəinitē·riăn), *a.* and *sb.* *Theol.* [f. L. *bīnī* (pl.) twofold, double, after Trinitarian. Cf. G. *binitarisch* (Loofs 1898).] **A.** *adj.* Of or belonging to a belief in a Godhead of two persons only. **B.** *sb.* A believer in this doctrine. Hence **Binita·rianism.**

1908 Sir W. R. Nicoll in *Life* (1925) 360 There are Trinitarians, Binitarians, Arians, and Unitarians. 1910 Sanday *Christologies Anc. & Mod.* i. 12 The same alternation of Trinitarian and Binitarian language (the conjunction of Father, Son, and Spirit by the side of Father and Son). 1928 K. E. Kirk in *Ess. Trin. & Incarn.* 207 The two strains of thought—the binitarian and the trinitarian. *Ibid.* 215 The binitarianism of Tertullian's earlier Catholic thought.

Binocular, *a.* 2. Add: In *Photogr.* = stereoscopic; also = binographic (see *Binograph).

1889 E. J. Wall *Dict. Photogr.* 18 *Binocular Camera*, another name for Stereoscopic Camera. 1901 *Amateur Photographer* 26 July 70/1 The binocular portraits of M. Fred. Boissonnas. *Ibid.*, Binocular photography. *Ibid.* 70/2 Binocular photographs.

Binodal (bəinōu·dăl), *a.* [f. Bi-[2] + Nodal *a.*]

1. *Bot.* Having two nodes or joints.

1848 Lindley *Introd. Bot.* (ed. 4) I. 324 The cyme of Dicotyledons is binodal, or multinodal.

2. *Geom.* Of a quartic curve: Having two nodes.

1872 Cayley *Math. Papers* (1895) VIII. 139 The binodal quartic curve. 1887 R. A. Roberts *Integr. Calc.* I. 244 The curve with two nodes..or binodal quartic, as it is called.

Binode (bəi·nōud). *Geom.* [Bi-[2].] A point on a surface at which there are two tangent planes.

1868 Cayley *Math. Papers* (1893) VI. 330 Conical and biplanar nodes, or, as I call them, cnicnodes and binodes. 1874 G. Salmon *Analyt. Geom.* (ed. 3) 457 The quadric cone may degenerate into a pair of planes. Such a node may be called a *binode*.

Binograph (bəi·nŏgraf). *Photogr.* [f. L. *bīnī* two each + -o- + -graph.] A photograph in which the two elements of a stereograph are united in one. Also **Binogra·phic** *a.*; **Bino·graphy**, the production of binographs.

1902 *Wall's Dict. Photogr.* (ed. 8) 81 Binocular Portraits or binographs. *Ibid.*, Binographic portraits. *Ibid.*, Binography.

Binturong (bi·ntiurǫŋ). Also **benturong.** [Malay.] A prehensile-tailed civet, *Arctictis* (formerly *Viverra*) *binturong*, also called *Ictides ater* (or *albifrons*), found in southern Asia.

1875 *Encycl. Brit.* II. 695/1 The benturong (*Arctictis*). 1883 *Ibid.* XV. 436/1 The Binturong, an inhabitant of southern Asia from Nepal through the Malay peninsula to the islands of Sumatra and Java.

Biny (bəi·ni), *a.* [f. Bine + -y[1].] Of hops: Abounding in bine, running much to bine.

1881 C. Whitehead *Hops* 36 It will be found in 'biny' years that many of the hops are light and 'white livered' from sheer lack of sunshine.

Bioce·ntral, *a.* = *Biocentric *a.*

1905 *Athenæum* 8 Apr. 436/2 The study of synthetical chemistry from the biocentral point of view.

Biocentric (bəiŏse·ntrik), *a.* [f. Bio- + Centric *a.*] Centring in life; regarding or treating life as a central fact. Hence **Bioce·ntrically** *adv.*, from a biocentric point of view.

1889 in *Century Dict.* 1899 R. Meldola in *Nature* 5 Jan. 217/1 In brief, there has arisen a set of ideas which are even broader than 'anthropocentric', and which might fairly be designated *biocentric*. 1904 — *Vital Products* I. 6 Organic Chemistry from the Biocentric Standpoint. 1913 L. J. Henderson *Fitness Environm.* 110 Water is the one fit substance for its place in the process of universal evolution, when we regard that process biocentrically. *Ibid.* 312 The biologist may now rightly regard the universe in its very essence as biocentric.

Biochemical (bəiŏke·mikăl), *a.* [f. Bio- + Chemical, after G. *biochemisch*.] Of or pertaining to biochemistry; chemicophysiological.

1867 R. E. Wallis tr. *Delitzsch's Bibl. Psychol.* 273 Without wishing to substitute for Scripture a knowledge of that bio-chemical process. 1897 A. B. Griffiths *Respir. Proteids* 107 The foundation of all life, the biochemical processes. 1902 *Encycl. Brit.* XXXI. 539/1 A constant constructive and destructive bio-chemical process occurs in the neurones of a healthy nervous system. 1904 R. Meldola *Vital Products* I. 5 It is doubtful whether this compound [furfural] is really a biochemical product.

Hence **Bioche·mically** *adv.*

1887 A. M. Brown *Anim. Alkaloids* 147 That which might seem *a priori* evident, is now bio-chemically proved to demonstration.

Biochemist (bəiŏke·mist). [After next.] One who is versed in biochemistry.

1913 [see *Biophysics]. 1922 *Encycl. Brit.* XXXII. 100/1 The problems of the biochemist.

Biochemistry (bəiŏke·mistri). [f. Bio- + Chemistry, after *Biochemical. Cf. G. *biochemie*.] The chemistry of living organisms; biological, physiological, or vital chemistry.

1902 *Nature* 14 Aug. 381/2 The chair of biochemistry recently founded in University College [Liverpool]. 1904 R. Meldola *Vital Products* I. p. v, I am not without hope that it may be found of service as a step towards the foundation of a more exact science of Biochemistry. 1916 A. P. Mathews *Physiol. Chem.* Pref., The science of physiological chemistry, or bio-chemistry. 1926 *Encycl. Brit.* Suppl. I. 373/2 Biochemistry may be defined as the study of the chemical or physico-chemical processes which play a part in the life phenomena of plants and animals.

Biogen (bəi·ŏdʒen). *Biol.* Also **-gene.** [See Bio- and -gen.]

1. (See under Bio-.)

2. [G. *biogen* (Max Verworn).] A hypothetical protoplasmic unit. (Cf. *Biophor.)

1909 *Westm. Gaz.* 23 Oct. 6/3 First, the biogene,..secondly, the cell, composed of a great number of biogenes. 1911 *Encycl. Brit.* XXI. 557/2 These combinations have been termed 'biogens'. 1915 W. M. Bayliss *Physiol.* 18 A certain theory, that of 'biogen molecules' has attracted many investigators (Verworn, 1903). 1916 A. P. Mathews *Physiol. Chem.* 261 A molecule which may be called a biogen. *Ibid.* 844 The biogenes or large molecules of the cell.

Bi:ogeo·graphy. [Bio-.] The science of the geographical distribution of living things, animal and vegetable. Hence **Biogeographic, -ical** *adjs.*

1899 H. R. Mill *Internat. Geogr.* 4 Living things possess the world, and the purpose of Biogeography is to trace out the reasons why particular species occupy the regions where they are now found. 1910 *Mill's Guide Geogr. Bks.* 110 This is also the aspect of biogeography usually dealt with in ordinary text-books.

Biograph, *sb.* Add:

2. An earlier form of cinematograph, introduced from the United States of America. (Cf. *Animatograph.) Also *attrib.*

1897 *Westm. Gaz.* 19 Mar. 3/3 The exhibition of the American biograph at the Palace Theatre..is another step towards the perfection of the animatograph. *Ibid.*, It cannot be claimed that the biograph is free from vibration, nor do the pictures rest as steadily on the screen as they might. 1898 *Brit. Jrnl. Photog. Alm.* 655 The exhibition of animated photographs on a larger scale than usual, by the biograph, the invention of an American, Mr. Casler. 1901 W. R. H. Trowbridge *Lett. her Mother to Eliz.* xviii. 89 The Palace [music-hall] in place of the ballet [at the Empire] has a Biograph, which wiggles and makes you feel cross-eyed. 1912 C. N. & A. M. Williamson *Heather Moon* II. iv, They're going to take photographs of a Gretna Green wedding..for a biograph show.

Hence **Bi·ograph** *v. trans.*, to make a biograph of.

1898 *Westm. Gaz.* 27 May 4/2 The finish of the Derby on Wednesday was 'biographed' for the Palace Theatre. 1901 *Ibid.* 14 Jan. 8/2 The experiment of biographing a battle is not absolutely new.

Bio·graphy, *v.* [f. the sb.] *trans.* To write the life of; to make the subject of a biography. Hence **Bio·graphied** *ppl. a.*, **Bio·graphying** *vbl. sb.*

1844 *Fraser's Mag.* XXX. 518/1 If..the biographied be of low birth. 1858 [see Biographying in Dict.]. 1887 *L'pool Merc.* 10 Mar. 4/5 Captain Burton is to be biographied. 1909 *Westm. Gaz.* 29 May 5/3 Diane de Poitiers, Lola Montez [etc.] are nearly all much-biographied ladies. 1908 *Fabian News* XIX. 22/2, I cannot help a sneaking regret that G. B. S. has mounted above us into the regions of the biographied.

Biologism (bəiǫ·lŏdʒiz'm). [f. Biology + -ism.] The interpretation of human life from a strictly biological point of view.

Motley's use of the word (see quot. 1852) is app. obs.

1852 Motley *Corr.* 18 May (1889) I. 143 Whenever a charlatan can't find any to believe in his tricks of mesmerism or biologism, or whatever may be the latest neologism. 1924 *Public Opinion* 25 Jan. 81/3 When we try to force all the facts of human society into frameworks of zoology we are guilty of a biologism. 1926 J. A. Thomson *Man in Light Evol.* 32 A biologism is an attempt to ignore the uniqueness of man by forcing his activities in their entirety into the framework of mammalian physiology...It is a biologism to picture an average man as the slave of his hormones.

Biolysis (bəiǫ·lisis). [f. Bio- + Gr. λύσις dissolution.] Chemical decomposition of organic matter brought about by bacteria, etc.

1897 Scott-Moncrieff in *Prof. Papers Roy. Engineers* XXIII. 213 (*heading*) Purification of Sewage by Biolysis.

Bi:omathema·tics, *sb. pl.* (See quot.)

1923 W. M. Feldman *Biomathem.* i. 1 Biomathematics is the science and art of rapid and accurate computation applied to the study and investigation of biological problems.

Biometric (bəiŏme·trik), *a.* and *sb.* [f. Bio- + Metric *a.*]

A. *adj.* Of or pertaining to biometry. So **Biome·trical** *a.*

1901 *Biometrika* I. 2 The collection of biometric data. *Ibid.* 6 Biometric workers. 1902 *Encycl. Brit.* XXVIII. 344/2 Biometric investigation. *Ibid.*, Biometrical inquiry. 1909 W. Bateson *Mendel's Princ. Hered.* 235 The misuse of statistical method so frequent in biological attempts to investigate heredity.

B. *sb. pl.* = *Biometry.

1902 *Encycl. Brit.* XXVIII. 344/1. 1923 W. M. Feldman *Biomathem.* xxi. 327 Biometrics is the application of modern statistical methods to the measurements of biological (variable) objects.

Biometrician (bəi:ŏmĕtri·ʃən). [f. *Biometric + -ian: cf. *metrician*.] One who is versed in biometry; one who applies statistics to the problems of biology, esp. that of variation. So **Biome·tricist.**

1901 F. Galton in *Biometrika* I. 10 Biology could soon be raised to the status of a more exact science.., if each of many biometricians would thoroughly work out his own particular plot. 1902 *Encycl. Brit.* XXVIII. 344/2 The biometricist demands statistics to show the range of the variations and the mode of their distribution. 1914 K. Pearson (*title*) Tables for Statisticians and Biometricians. 1922 W. R. Inge *Outspoken Ess.* Ser. II. 263 It seems to be established by the biometricians that children who are born after their fathers are fifty seldom attain distinction.

Biometry (bəiǫ·mĕtri). [See Bio- and -metry.] The science which deals with the quantitative measurement of biological facts, esp. with reference to the problems of variation.

1901 F. Galton in *Biometrika* I. 9 The primary object of Biometry is to afford material that shall be exact enough for the discovery of incipient changes in evolution which are too small to be otherwise apparent. 1927 Haldane & Huxley *Anim. Biol.* ii. 72 The science of biometry deals with studies of this sort.

Biomo·lecule. [Bio-.] (See quot.)

1901 J. G. McKendrick in *Rep. Brit. Assoc.* 810 The conception of a biomolecule, or living molecule, that is to say the smallest quantity of living matter that can exhibit some of the chemical phenomena of life.

Biomorph (bəi·ŏmǫɹf). [f. Bio- + Gr. μορφή form.] A decorative form representing a living object. Hence **Biomo·rphic** *a.*

1895 Haddon *Evol. Art* 126 The biomorph is the representation of anything living in contradistinction to the skeuomorph. *Ibid.* 188 Biomorphic Pottery.

Bionomic (bəiŏnǫ·mik), *a.* and *sb.* [f. Bio-, after Economic.] **A.** *adj.* Of or pertaining to the conditions under which an organism lives in its natural habitat; of or pertaining to bionomics (see B).

1899 J. A. Thomson in *Internat. Geogr.* 85 Bionomic Relations. 1919 F. A. Dixey *Addr. to Zool. Sect. Brit. Assoc.* 9 The formation of a great collection of butterflies—a most valuable asset for bionomic research.

B. *sb. pl.* The branch of biology which deals with the mode of life of organisms in their natural habitat, their adaptation to their surroundings, etc.; œcology.

1888 E. R. Lankester in *Encycl. Brit.* XXIV. 803/2 *Bionomics*..including thremmatology, or the science of breeding. 1895 *Naturalist* 337 The old out-door ornithologists are to-day's sportsmen, who study the bionomics of their quarry that they may outwit them. 1902 *Westm. Gaz.* 6 Dec. 8/1 The bionomics of the North Sea; in other words, the relationships of the various forms of life to one another and to their surroundings.

Biono·mical, *a.* Of or pertaining to bionomics (see prec. B); œcological.

1902 *Encycl. Brit.* XXVIII. 344/1 Bionomical investigators. 1909 *Athenæum* 17 July 72/1 The bionomical stores contained in its pages.

Biophor (bəi·ŏfǫɹ). *Biol.* Also **-phore.** [G. *biophor*, f. Gr. βίος life + -φορος -bearing.] In Weismann's theory of heredity: A supposed ultimate unit of living protoplasm.

1893 tr. *Weismann's Germ-Plasm* I. i. 40 We have to imagine that..protoplasm..consists of groups of molecules, each of which is composed of different kinds of chemical molecules. I shall call these units the 'bearers of vitality' ('Lebensträger') or 'biophors', because they are the smallest units which exhibit the primary vital forces, viz. assimilation and metabolism, growth, and multiplication by fission. 1894 *Nat. Sci.* Sept. 185 His [Weismann's] germ-plasm is made up of primary units, the biophores, which are built up into determinants, a determinant existing for each independently varying cell or group of cells in the adult organism.

Biophy·sics. The science which applies the laws of physics to explain the phenomena of biology. Hence **Biophy·sicist.**

1892 K. Pearson *Gramm. Sci.* 470 This branch of science which endeavours to show that the facts of Biology..constitute particular cases of general physical laws has been termed *Ætiology*. It would perhaps be better to call it *Bio-physics*. 1913 L. J. Henderson *Fitness Environm.* 310 While biophysicists like Professor Schäfer follow Spencer in assuming a gradual evolution of the organic from the inorganic, biochemists are more than ever unable to perceive how such a process is possible. 1926 *Encycl. Brit.* Suppl. II. 675/1 His main work is on the fundamental problem of biophysics—the stimulation of living matter.

Bioscope (bəi·ŏskōup). [See Bio- and -scope.]

†**1.** A view or survey of life. *Obs.*

1812 Granville Penn (*title*) The Bioscope, or Dial of Life, explained. 1824 [see under Bio- in Dict.].

2. An earlier form of cinematograph. (Cf. *Biograph 2.)

1897 *Wall's Dict. Photogr.* (ed. 7) 75 *Bioscope*. See *Zoetrope*. 1902 *Ibid.* (ed. 8) 81 *Bioscope*. See *Cinematograph*. 1901 *Daily Chron.* 27 Dec. 6/1 The Bioscope views are not so much incidents of the day as exciting adventures. 1925 *Public Opinion* 4 Sept. 234/3 No use to try and blame your poor digestion Nor yet the bioscope's unnerving scene.

Hence **Biosco·pic** *a.* (also *fig.*).

1903 *Athenæum* 12 Dec. 799/1 The utility of the bioscopic camera in zoological work. 1928 *Daily Tel.* 18 Sept. 6 It is excellent to have bioscopic presentations of the eminent, but Herr Ludwig's film is too long.

Biose (bəi·ōus). *Chem.* [f. Bi-[2] + -ose[2].] (See quots.)

1895 *Bloxam's Chem.* (ed. 8) 708 The Disaccharides.—The members of this class of sugars are characterised by being converted by hydrolysis into two molecules of glucoses (hence the synonym, *bioses*). 1903 *Jrnl. Chem. Soc.* LXXXIV. I. 713 By the action of alcoholic hydrogen chloride on bioses, hydrolysis occurred and glucosides of the monoses were formed. 1916 A. P. Mathews *Physiol. Chem.* 18 The monosaccharides are in their turn classified by the number of carbon atoms, or more properly by the aldehyde, ketone and alcohol groups they contain into bioses, trioses, tetroses, pentoses, hexoses, heptoses, octoses, nonoses, etc.

Biosphere (bəi·ŏsfĭəɹ). [f. Bio- + Sphere *sb.*, after *atmosphere*.] The totality of living things on the earth (see quots.).

1899 H. R. Mill *Internat. Geogr.* 4 Some geographers even bring in the layer of living matter to complete four parts of the physical globe—the lithosphere, hydrosphere, atmosphere and biosphere. 1909 H. B. C. Sollas tr. *Suess's Face of Earth* IV. 637 It brings with it the idea of a biosphere, which assigns to life a place above the lithosphere.

Biotechnics (bəiŏte·kniks), *sb. pl.* [f. Bio- + *technics*: see Technic B. 2 b.] (See quot.)

1925 Geddes & Thomson *Biol.* 245. 1926 *Encycl. Brit.* Suppl. I. 384/1 *Biotechnics*.—This term, proposed by Prof. Patrick Geddes, may be usefully applied to man's control of organisms for his own ends.

Biotron (bəi·ŏtrǫn). *Wireless Telegr.* [f. Bi- *pref.*[2] + *-otron* after *Pliotron.] (See quot.)

1926 S. O. Pearson *Dict. Wireless Techn. T.*, *Biotron*, a combination of two thermionic tubes connected in such a manner as to produce a particularly steep characteristic curve.

Bi·-pack. [Bi-[2].] In colour photography, a pack of two sensitive plates used to obtain colour separation.

1924 *Brit. Jrnl. Photogr.* Suppl., Sept. 35/2 The staining of the front member of a bi-pack with aniline orange.

Bipartite, *a.* Add:

1. d. *Math.* Of a curve (see quot. 1879).

1858 Cayley *Math. Papers* (1889) II. 527 Bipartite binary quantics. 1869 *Ibid.* (1893) VI. 464 The quantic is unipartite, bipartite, tripartite, &c., according as the number of sets is one, two, three, &c. 1879 G. Salmon *Higher Plane Curves* (ed. 3) 168 We shall then call the curve we have been considering a bipartite curve, as consisting of two distinct continuous series of points.

Bipa·rtizan, *a.* Representing, or composed of members of, two (political or other) parties.

1920 *Glasgow Herald* 13 Feb. 10 The 14 Republican reservations, as modified by the Bipartisan Conference.

Bi·-pa·rty. Used *attrib.* = consisting of, or representing, two (political or other) parties.

1898 *Westm. Gaz.* 17 Feb. 3/1 British institutions presuppose the British character, with..its faithful adherence to the bi-party system. 1900 *Ibid.* 2 July 3/1 Philosophers cling with the same pathetic insistence as members of Parliament to their traditional bi-party system. 1926 *Contemp. Rev.* Apr. 454 The bi-party system [in Canada].

Bipaschal (bəipa·skăl), *a.* *Hist.* [f. Bi-[2] + Paschal *a.*] Including two consecutive passover feasts.

Applied to the view that limits Christ's public ministry to a little over one year.

1883 Schaff *Hist. Ch., Apostol. Chr.* I. 131 The bipaschal scheme confines the public ministry to one year and a few weeks or months. 1893 Broadus *Harm. Gospels* (1903) 243 The Bi-paschal theory makes the time of the public life of Jesus one year, allowing only two Passovers to the Gospel of John.

Bipedal, *a.* Add:

4. Of a lizard: Running on the two hind feet. Hence **Bipe·dally** *adv.*

1896 Saville-Kent in *Nature* 27 Feb. 397/1 The absurdly grotesque appearances these lizards presented when progressing in this bipedal fashion. 1898 *Ibid.* 10 Feb. 341/1 The Mexican Iguanoid Lizard..also runs bipedally.

Bipe·rsonal, *a.* Of the godhead: Existing in two persons; also, relating to this system of belief, binitarian.

1928 K. E. Kirk in *Ess. Trin. & Incarn.* 162 *note*, 'Bipersonal', 'ditheistic', or 'dyarchian' are occasionally employed also as synonyms [of binitarian]. *Ibid.* 196 The cosmogony of *Poimandres* is fantastically pluralist..; its religion is strictly bipersonal.

Biplanar (bəi·plēinăɹ), *a.* (and *sb.*). [f. next + -ar[1]: cf. *planar*.] Lying or situated in two planes. Also *sb.*, a biplanar node or double point.

1862 Schläfli in *Phil. Trans.* CLIII. 207 Cubic surface of the ninth class with a biplanar node. 1862 G. Salmon *Analyt. Geom.* 380 A cubic then can have only three such biplanar double points. *Ibid.*, Each ordinary double point reducing the degree by two, and each biplanar by three.

Biplane (bəi·plēin). [f. Bi-[2] + Plane *sb.*[3]]

1. *Math.* (*pl.*) A pair of coincident planes (see quot.).

1868 Cayley *Math. Papers* (1893) VI. 335 The binode..is a biplanar node, where instead of the proper quadricone we have two planes; these may be called the biplanes, and their line of intersection, the edge of the binode. The biplanes form a plane-pair.

2. An aeroplane having two 'planes' or main supporting surfaces, one above the other.

[Cf. 1874 *aero-bi-plane* s.v. *Aero-.]

1908 *Westm. Gaz.* 14 Aug. 10/2 Mr. Wilbur Wright is busy experimenting with his greatly successful bi-plane. 1910 R. Ferris *How it Flies* 12 In March [1908], Delagrange flew in a Voisin biplane 453 feet. 1911 Grahame-White & Harper *Aeroplane* 17 He [Lilienthal] abandoned the monoplane type of glider in favour of a biplane. *Ibid.* 18 One of Chanute's biplane gliders was fitted with a stern rudder.

Biplate (bəi·plēit). *Optics.* [Bi-[2].] A combination of two glass plates used in polariscopic observations.

1890 T. Preston *Th. Light* 121 Bi-plates.—A beam of light may be subdivided by refraction through two plates, of the same nature and equal thickness, placed at an angle. 1904 A. Schuster *Th. Optics* (1909) 84 The 'bi-plate'..serves either to separate or to bring together two parallel beams of light. It consists of two plane parallel plates of glass cemented together at an angle.

Bi·prism. [Bi-[2].] A glass prism with a refracting angle of nearly 180 degrees, used in observing the interference of light.

1884 A. Daniell *Princ. Physics* 486 Such a beam may be divided in two parts..by refraction through a biprism. 1890 T. Preston *Th. Light* 119 Fresnel's Bi-prism...Let CDE represent a glass prism with a very obtuse angle E...The whole prism is as if made up of two prisms CE and DE of very small angle (at C and D) placed base to base at E, and hence the name bi-prism. 1904 A. Schuster *Th. Optics* 60 Fresnel's Biprism.

Bipunctual, *a.* Add:

2. Geom. *Bipunctual coordinates*, coordinates determining the position of a line, or of a point, by reference to two fixed points and a fixed direction.

Biquartz (bəi·kwǫɹts). *Optics.* [Bi-[2].] A double quartz plate used for detecting polarization.

1878 Lockyer *Stargazing* 452 There is also another instrument for detecting polarization which is perhaps more commonly used than the biquartz. 1884 A. Daniell *Princ. Physics* 510 A double-quartz plate, or Biquartz. 1890 T. Preston *Th. Light* 373 The biquartz..consists of two semicircular plates of quartz placed in juxtaposition. 1911 *Encycl. Brit.* XXI. 938/1 The chief features of Soleil's saccharimeter are the biquartz and the compensator.

Biquaternion (bəikwǫtǝ·ɹniǝn). *Math.* [Bi-[2].]

1. A quaternion with imaginary coefficients (Sir W. R. Hamilton).

1852 *Rep. Brit. Assoc.* (1853) Notices & Abstracts 2 On Biquaternions. By Sir William R. Hamilton. 1853 W. R. Hamilton *Lect. Quatern.* p. lxviii, A biquaternion may be considered generally as the sum of a biscalar and a bivector.

2. A combination of two quaternions (W. K. Clifford).

1873 W. K. Clifford *Math. Papers* (1882) 188 In this way the ratio $\frac{\gamma + \omega\delta}{\alpha + \omega\beta}$ is expressed in the form $q + \omega r$, which expression may conveniently be called a biquaternion. 1876 *Ibid.* 394 This combination of two quaternions I have called a Biquaternion.

Bi-ra·cial, *a.* [Bi-[2].] Containing or composed of two races.

1922 *Contemp. Rev.* Feb. 243 Belgium is bi-lingual and bi-racial.

Biramose (bəirēi·mōus), *a.* *Zool.* [f. Bi-[2] + Ramose.] = Biramous.

1877 H. Woodward in *Encycl. Brit.* VI. 652/1 Behind these are six pairs of powerful biramose natatory feet. 1888 Rolleston & Jackson *Anim. Life* 539 With a bivalve shell and large natatory biramose second antennæ.

Birational (bəiræ·ʃənăl), *a.* *Math.* [f. Bi-[2] + Rational.] Designating a transformation in which each of two sets of variables is expressed rationally in terms of the other. Hence **Bira·tionally** *adv.*

1902 in Webster Suppl. 1915 R. A. P. Rogers *Salmon's Analyt. Geom.* (ed. 5) II. 268 Such a correspondence is called birational. *Ibid.*, Any surface which can be birationally transformed into a unicursal surface is itself unicursal.

Birch, *sb.* 4. Add: **birch-builder** *U.S.*, a maker of birch-bark canoes; **birch canoe** *U.S.*, a canoe made of birch-bark; **birch-lands** *U.S.*, ground mainly covered with birch trees.

a 1861 T. Winthrop *Life in open Air* (1863) 49 These aborigines are the *birch-builders. 1697–8 S. Sewall *Diary* I. 475 Went to Hogg Island with Mr. John White in his *Birch canoe. 1758 *Essex Inst. Hist. Coll.* XVIII. 197 Major Rogers returned and brou't in two Burch Canoes. 1775 in *Proc. Mass. Hist. Soc.* Ser. II. II. 281 Here I found a fine Birch Canoe Carefully laid up. *a* 1861 T. Winthrop *Life in open Air* (1863) 48 A birch canoe is the right thing in the right place. 1875 Holland *Sevenoaks* xvi. 229 A birch canoe whose hiding-place Mike Conlin had revealed to him. 1789 Morse *Amer. Geog.* 143 One species generally predominating in each soil, has originated the descriptive names of..*birch, beach, and chestnut lands.

Birch, *v.* Add: **3.** *intr.* To voyage in a birch-bark canoe. *U.S.*

a 1861 T. Winthrop *Life in open Air* (1863) 50 He had birched it down to Lake Chesuncook in bygone summers.

Birch bark. *U.S.* [Birch *sb.* 4.]

1. The bark of the birch tree, employed esp. in the making of canoes.

1674 Josselyn *Two Voy. New Eng.* 27 An Indian-Pinnace.. made of Birch-bark. 1759 *Essex Inst. Hist. Coll.* XIX. 190 He found 5 Indians Connoes of burch Bark. 1789 Morse *Amer. Geog.* 224 He..provided several strips of birch-bark. 1837 *Southern Lit. Messenger* III. 733 Along the shore were Indian lodges, of a conical form, and covered with birch bark.

b. *attrib.* esp. with *canoe*.

a 1800 *Spirit of Farmer's Museum* (1801) 244 With panniers ..laden with birch bark boxes. *c* 1805 J. J. Henry *Camp. agst. Quebec* (1812) 29 The birch-bark canoe is the most ingenious piece of mechanism. 1843 Carlton *New Purchase* 175 To float in birch bark canoes on the swelling bosom of free waters! 1853 Mrs. Moodie *Life in Clearings* 16 The old bishop was crossing the Rice Lake in a birch bark canoe. 1903 S. E. White *Forest* x. 128 This birch-bark package contains maple sugar.

2. A birch-bark canoe.

1902 S. E. White *Conjuror's House* ii. 16 As the swift rush of the birch-barks brought them almost to their journey's end, they burst..into whoops of delight.

Bircher (bǝ·ɹtʃǝɹ). [f. Birch *v.* + -er[1].] One who administers a birch-rod; a flogger.

1888 *Ch. Times* 13 July 622 The renowned bircher [Dr. Keate]. 1908 *Daily Chron.* 18 June 4/7 The vicarious cane is considered by birchers of experience to be an unsatisfactory substitute for the birch rod itself.

Bi·rch tree. [Birch *sb.* 4.] A tree of one or other species of birch.

1578 Lyte *Dodoens* VI. lxxvii. 758 The Birche tree hath taglettes or Chattons for his blossom, lyke as the Hazell. 1654 *Rec. Providence* (R.I.) II. 78 On the South Corner a small Birch tree. 1725 *Rec. Providence* (R. I.) XVI. 399 A birch tree standing at the Edg of the hill. 1924 Miss C. Oman *Road Royal* xiv. § 2 She was made ready for bed and was all white as a moonlit birch tree.

Bird, *sb.* Add:

1. e. *jocularly.* A man, a 'cove'; esp. in *old bird*. Often in the punning collocation *downy bird*: see Downy *a.*[1] 5.

1853 'C. Bede' *Verdant Green* vi, I suppose the old bird was your governor. 1873 [see Downy *a.*[1] 5]. *a* 1885 'Hugh Conway' *Living or Dead* vii, After all, Philip,..your father must be a queer bird—excuse slang, mother. 1899 Kipling *Stalky* 131 The Head's a downy bird. 1928 Wodehouse *Money for Nothing* ii. 34 After they have been taking the treatment for a while, most of these birds would give their soul for a coffin-nail.

4. b. An exceptionally smart or accomplished person (freq. ironical); a first-rate animal or thing. *U.S. slang.*

1842 *Spirit of Times* (Philad.) 12 Feb. (Th.) Chippendale slept in the watch-house...Chippendale is certainly a bird. 1852 *Knickerbocker Mag.* Oct. XL. 320 Talking of fast men, that Williams is a bird. 1856 *Ibid.* Apr. XLVII. 429 A sleigh, drawn by a 'perfect bird' of a three-mile bay mare. 1907 S. E. White *Arizona Nights* I. vii. 129 A little place..in the Colorado mountains. Fellows, she was a bird. 1911 H. Quick *Yellowstone N.* ix. 230 He's got a disguise that's a bird.

5. b. *To get the* (*big*) *bird*: of an actor, to be hissed by the audience. (Cf. Goose *sb.* 1 g.) Hence *gen.* to be dismissed, get the sack. Similarly, *to give* (a person) *the bird*.

1865 *Slang Dict.* (ed. 2) s.v., 'To get the big-bird', *i.e.* to be hissed, as actors occasionally are by the 'gods'. 1884 *Age* Jan. in Ware *Passing Engl.* s.v., Professor Grant, Q.C., had both 'the bird' and 'the needle' at the Royal on Monday. 1886 *Graphic* 10 Apr. 399/2 To be 'goosed', or, as it is sometimes phrased, to 'get the big bird', is occasionally a compliment to the actor's power of representing villainy. 1895 *People* 6 Jan. (Ware), Three or four of the most prominent artistes..have been..threatened with 'the bird'. 1924 Galsworthy *White Monkey* 56 Mr. Danby had 'given him the bird'. *Ibid.* 255 When you were ill, I stole for you. I got the bird for it. 1928 Wodehouse *Money for Nothing* vii. 137 Would a Rudge audience have given me the bird a few years ago?

c. *Like a bird*: with swift and easy motion onwards; easily; without resistance, difficulty, or hesitation.

1873 W. S. Gilbert *Bab Ballads*, *Modest Couple* xvii, 'Miss Emily, I love you—Will you marry? Say the word!' And Emily said 'Certainly, Alphonso, like a bird!' 1879 *Cassell's Fam. Mag.* Mar. 197/2 Over he went like a bird, and, with his fair burthen yet in the saddle. 1890 'R. Boldrewood' *Col. Reformer* xi, [His horse] to use Jack Windsor's expression, 'went like a bird'. 1911 Shaw *Fanny's First Play* Induction, I told him Trotter would feel lonely without him; so he promised like a bird.

7. bird of Freedom *U.S.*, the American eagle.

1848 Lowell *Biglow P.* Ser. I. ii. (end), Yourn, Birdofredom Sawin. 1906 *Harper's Mag.* Mar. 638 The short story is peculiarly an American institution, and we are as proud of it as we are of the 'Bird of Freedom'.

9. bird-catching spider = **bird-spider*; **bird-glasses**, a field-glass for observing birds; **bird-land**, the land or realm of birds; so **bird-folk**, **bird-world**; **bird-louse**, any of the small wingless insects of the family *Mallophaga*, parasitic on birds and mammals; **bird sanctuary**, an enclosed piece of wooded land where birds are protected, and encouraged to build and breed; **bird-seed** (add quots.); **bird-spider**, a large hairy spider (*Mygale* or *Avicularia*) of tropical America, which kills small birds; also *bird-catching spider*; **bird-spider fly** (see quot.); **bird-tick**, a fly (*Olfersia*) parasitic upon birds (*Riverside Nat. Hist.* 1888 II. 433); **bird-watching**, the study of birds in their homes and haunts by a naturalist or bird-lover; also **bird-watcher**, one who thus observes the ways of birds; **bird-wittedness**, the condition of being bird-witted (see Dict.).

1805 Bingley *Anim. Biog.* III. 489 The *Bird-catching Spider. 1870 Kingsley *At Last* xvii, A live 'Tarantula', or bird-catching spider. 1901 F. T. Bullen *Sack of Shakings, The Orphan* 10 The hovering *bird-folk gathered in myriads. 1924 Anne D. Sedgwick *Little French Girl* I. vi, Yes, I can see him..And with his *bird-glasses. He would have been watching birds. 1924 Rose Macaulay *Orphan Island* iii, William..produced his bird-glasses and said no, it would, on the other hand, be a frigate-bird. 1900 O. G. Pike (*title*) In *Bird-Land with Field Glass and Camera. 1815 Kirby & Sp. *Entomol.* xii. (1818) I. 387 Some make their repast upon birds only, as the fly of the swallow, and other Ornithomyiæ, Latr., and the *bird-louse (*Ricinus*, De Geer). 1887 *Buck's Handbk. Med. Sci.* V. 751/1 *Mallophaga* (Bird-lice). Distinguished from the lice by possessing three- to five-jointed antennæ. [1909 *Compar. Legisl. Protect. Birds* 24 The formation of protected areas or sanctuaries in this country was initiated by the Wild Birds Protection Act of 1896.] 1922 (*title*) *Bird sanctuaries in Royal Parks. 1927 *Observer* 7 Aug. 3 Cannon Hill Common, Merton, Surrey,..is to have a bird sanctuary. 1865 G. Measom *Guide Gt. East. Railw.* Advts. 68 *Bird Seed, viz.—Canary, Hemp, Rape, Millet, &c. 1909 *Daily Chron.* 25 Sept. 5/3 A bird-seed company. 1826 Kirby & Sp. *Entomol.* III. xxviii. 40 In the class *Arachnida*, the *bird-spiders (*Mygale*) are amongst the principal giants. *Ibid.* xxxiv. 491 The enormous bird-spider (*Mygale avicularia*). 1885 *Riverside Nat. Hist.* (1888) II. 120 The large Bird spider of Surinam reaches a length of two inches. 1844 H. Stephens *Bk. Farm* III. 856 The smallest insect on the same cut is the *Bird-spider fly, *Ornithomyia avicularia*. 1905 E. Selous (*title*) The *Bird Watcher in the Shetlands. 1901 — (*title*) *Bird Watching. 1920 *Edin. Rev.* Jan. 63 Bird-Watching as a Hobby. 1928 E. W. Hendy (*title*) The Lure of Bird Watching. 1904 Raymont *Princ. Educ.* x. 231 The deliberate cultivation of mere irrelevance and *bird-wittedness. 1910 'Mark Rutherford' *Mr. Whittaker's Retirem.* in *More Pages fr. Jrnl.* 90 The birdwittedness, the absence of resistance and of difficulty, were intolerable. 1904 *Westm. Gaz.* 20 Aug. 2/3 In the *bird-world the lark has an exclusive and singular reputation for early rising. 1907 *Daily Chron.* 16 Feb. 6/7 The albinos—those freaks of nature in the bird-world.

Birdeen (bǝ̄ɹdī·n, bǝ̄·ɹdīn). [f. Bird *sb.* + *-een*, Ir. *-ín* dim. suffix: cf. *colleen*.] A young bird; also, a young girl (used as a playful form of address).

1895 'Fiona Macleod' *Mount. Lovers* 47 She was like a birdeen lured by the dancing sunrays. *Ibid.* 61, I am sure, birdeen. 1916 C. A. Renshaw *England's Boys* 58, I can bear your sleepy birdeens in their swaying moonlit nest. 1922 Isa J. Postgate (*title*) Robin in Khaki: A Book of Birdeens.

Birdie. Add: **2.** In golf: The fact of doing a hole in one under the par score. Chiefly *U.S.*

1921 *Glasgow Herald* 14 Sept. 10 Brown squared with a 'birdie' 3 at the second. 1923 *Daily Mail* 13 June 10 Then he went all out to 'shoot birdies'..the American colloquialism for aiming at doing holes in a stroke under the par scores.

Bi·rdman. *colloq.* (*temporary.*) An aviator, airman. So **Bi·rdwo:man.**

1909 *Daily Chron.* 27 Oct. 4/4, I shall say: 'I saw the first bird-men in England, my dears.' 1917 'Contact' *Airman's Outings* 244 Intrepid birdmen.

Bird-nesting. Add: Furring of a passage. (Cf. *Bird's-nest 5.)

1901 *Daily Mail* 26 Aug. 3/5 The cap ferrules of the Minerva's tubes were found to be partially choked from 'bird-nesting'.

Bird's-eyed, *a.* [f. Bird's-eye.] Of maple: Having small eye-like markings.

1855 *Trans. Mich. Agric. Soc.* VI. 528 Much of this maple timber is curled and some bird's-eyed.

Bird's-nest. Add: **5.** *Path.* (See quots.)

1879 *St. George's Hosp. Rep.* IX. 500 A tubular epithelioma..consisting of numerous tracks of epithelial cells (without any birds' nests). 1879 *Syd. Soc. Lex.*, *Bird's nest bodies*, a name given to a condition of arrangement of the scaly cells of epithelial cancer, in which they are placed in nest fashion around a circular central space, which contains amorphous colloid matter or degenerated cells. 1885 *Buck's Handbk. Med. Sci.* I. 771/1 Concentric formations known as 'birds' nests', which characterize the typical squamous epithelioma. 1894 Gould *Dict. Med.*, *Bird's-nest Bodies*, or *Cells*, the cells of certain forms of carcinoma, distinguished by the concentric arrangement of their cell-walls.

6. Bird's-nest spider = *bird-spider* (*Bird *sb.* 9).

1910 E. R. Lankester in *Encycl. Brit.* II. 307/1 The larger species of Bird's Nest Spiders (*Avicularia*)..undoubtedly attack young birds.

Bi·rd's-ne:ster. One who goes bird's-nesting.

c 1825 (*title*) Ben the Birdsnester. 1896 *Brit. Birds, Their Nests & Eggs* I. 35 A trick which..renders the birds-nester more satisfied that he is on the right scent.

Birefringence (bəirĭfri·ndʒĕns). *Optics.* [Cf. F. *biréfringence*, *-ent*.] = *double refraction* (see Refraction 2). Also **Birefri·ngent** *a.*

1889 *Cent. Dict.*, Birefringent. 1902 Webster Suppl., Birefringence. 1911 *Encycl. Brit.* Index, Birefringence: see Refraction, double.

Birl, *v.* Add: **3. b.** *spec.* Among lumbermen: To spin a log in the water while standing on it. Hence **Birler**; **Birling** *vbl. sb.* *U.S.*

1903 S. E. White *Forest* viii. 96 The birling matches, wherein two men on a single log try to throw each other into the river by treading, squirrel fashion, in faster and faster rotation. *a* 1904 — *Blazed Trail Stories* i. 7 Suddenly with one accord they commenced to birl the log from left to right. *Ibid.* 10 The indomitable Darrell still trod the quarter-deck as champion birler for the year.

Birman, var. *Burman.

Birotation (bəirŏtēi·ʃən). *Physical Chem.* [Bi-[2].] The power possessed by certain sugars of changing their rate of optical rotation according to the length of time they have been in solution. Now usually called *Mutarotation.

1889 in *Cent. Dict.* 1893 *Jrnl. Chem. Soc.* LXIV. I. 125 Birotation and Hydrazone Formation of some Sugars. 1896 *Ibid.* LXX. II. 139 The birotation phenomena of glucose. 1907 J. B. Cohen *Org. Chem.* 100 Freshly prepared solutions of certain sugars change in rotation on standing. The specific rotation of glucose sinks to one-half before becoming constant. The phenomenon was therefore termed *birotation*.

Birth, *sb.*[1] 13. Add:

birth control, the name given (by advocates of the system) to the artificial restriction of birth or the prevention of conception, recommended to be practised by married persons in ways that do not render them liable to criminal prosecution; hence **birth controller**; **birth-rate**, the ratio of the number of births to the population (usually calculated per thousand); **birth-root** (U.S. examples).

1914 Marg. Sanger in *The Woman Rebel* Apr., *Birth control. 1921 Ld. Dawson (*title*) Love—Marriage—Birth Control. 1923 Mai Edge *Artificial Birth Control* 15 Another reason the *Birth Controller gives in support of his theory is, that we are over-populated. 1927 *Daily Express* 10 Feb. 1 The pernicious doctrines and expedients of the birth controllers. 1868 J. Timbs *Notable Things* 192 (*heading*) *Birth And Death Rate Of The World. 1911 *Encycl. Brit.* XXII. 95/2 The crude birth-rate..is in general harmony with that of marriage. 1919 W. R. Inge *Outspoken Ess.* 69 In the Rhondda Valley the birth-rate is still about forty. 1920 G. U. Yule (*title*) The Fall of the Birth-rate. 1855 *Trans. Mich. Agric. Soc.* VI. 149 In the lower grounds are skunk cabbage, *birthroot, wild turnip. 1862 A. Gray *Man. Bot.* (1866) 464 *Trillium erectum*. Purple Trillium, Birthroot.

Birthday. 3. Add: **birthday honours**, the titles of honour conferred by the King on each anniversary of his birthday; so *birthday gazette*; **birthday suit**, (also) *slang*, a state of nature, nakedness; so *birthday attire*, *gear*.

1860 G. & P. Wharton *Wits & Beaux of Society* I. 127 In '*birthday attire'. 1731 Swift *Strephon & Chloe* 228 To see some radiant nymph appear In all her glitt'ring *birth-day gear. 1910 Beatrix Gatacre *General Gatacre* xvii. 262 On the 24th in the **Birthday Gazette*, his name appeared as a recipient of the Gold Medal of a New Order, the Kaiser-i-Hind. 1888 Kipling *Departm. Ditties* 8 Then the *Birthday Honours came. Sad to state and sad to see, Stood against the Rajah's name nothing more than C.I.E.! 1897 *Sat. Rev.* 5 June 626/2 In any list of Birthday honours or New Year honours one expects to see the name of at least one distinguished man. 1771 Smollett *Humphry Cl.*, *To Mary Jenkins* 7 Sept., We bathed in our *birth-day soot, after the fashion of the country. 1874 *Slang Dict.* 83 *Birthday Suit*, the suit in which Adam and Eve first saw each other, and 'were not ashamed'.

Biscuit. Add:

1. (Examples of U.S. sense.)

1828 Webster, *Biscuit*,..a composition of flour and butter, made and baked in private families. 1843 R. Carlton *New Purchase* v. 27 Hot rolls.., a novelty then, but much like biscuits in parts of the Far West.

b. *transf.* (*a*) (See quot.)

1881 *Encycl. Brit.* XII. 836 The flat rounded cakes of [South American] rubber made in this manner are known in the London market as 'biscuits'.

(*b*) *Military slang.* A square brown palliasse or mattress.

1917 *Times* 21 Nov. 11/4 Sleeping on the floor on army 'biscuits'—as they had already learned to call the military mattress. 1919 *Athenæum* 22 Aug. 791/2 'Biscuits.' These were the palliasses—square in form and brown as to colour—of which three went to each bed.

c. The characteristic light-brown colour of biscuits; biscuit colour; often *attrib.* = of this colour.

1884 biscuit colour, biscuit satin [see Dict. s.v. sense 3]. 1892 *Daily News* 16 Sept. 3/3 A biscuit straw hat. 1896 *Ibid.* 18 July 6/3 White, cream, and biscuit-fawn. 1897 *Ibid.* 15 Sept. 6/6 Biscuit-tinted lace insertion. 1923 *Daily Mail* 15 Jan. 6 Newest shades, including: Pale Pink.. Scarlet Fuchsia, Biscuit, Mauve.

3. biscuit root *U.S.*, the quamash (*Camassia esculenta*) of North America, or other esculent roots similar to this.

1837 W. Irving *Capt. Bonneville* (1895) II. 57 The cowish, also, or biscuit root, about the size of a walnut, which they reduce to a very palatable flour. 1845 De Smet *Oregon Missions* (1847) 116 The bitter root..grows in light dry, sandy soil as also the caious or biscuit root.

Bisensory (bəise·nsŏri), *a.* [Bi-[2].] Of an hallucination: Affecting two senses.

1894 *Proc. Soc. Psych. Research* X. xxvi. 194 In these 'bisensory' or 'trisensory' cases, the constructive imagination seems to have reached a higher point than in simple visual or auditory hallucinations. 1903 F. W. H. Myers *Hum. Pers.* I. 254 Visual, auditory, bisensory, and trisensory hallucinations.

Bishop, *sb.* 10. Add: **bishop('s) sleeve**, a sleeve in a woman's dress made full and gathered in at the wrist like the lawn sleeves of an Anglican bishop.

1829 *Mirror* 26 Sept. 205/2 The mistress..conceived the idea of bishops' sleeves, an article of dress which precludes all hope..of imitation in the kitchen. 1861 *Engl. Wom. Dom. Mag.* III. 69/1, 1. A bishop sleeve, with a narrow wristband. 2. A bishop sleeve, the fulness gathered in to a band the length of the arm, this band being shown on the upper part of the sleeve. 1894 *Daily News* 22 June 6/6 The bishop sleeves were gathered into a wide cuff.

Bi·shopless, *a.* [-less.] Lacking a bishop.

1909 G. T. S. Farquhar *Three Bishops of Dunkeld* I. xiii. 142 During this the darkest period of all there were no Ordinations for the Diocese. There was, however, one for Bishopless Edinburgh.

Bisontine (bəi·sǫntəin), *a.*[1] [ad. L. **bisontinus*, f. *bison*, *bisont-* Bison, after *elephantinus* Elephantine.] Pertaining to or resembling the bison.

1885 E. Balfour *Cycl. India* (ed. 3) III. 1104/1 The general aspect of the yak is distinctly bisontine. 1887 *Blackw. Mag.* CXLI. 795 The Bisontine group.

Bisontine (bəi·sǫntəin), *a.*[2] [ad. L. *Bisontīnus*, adj. of *Bisontium* Besançon.] Of or pertaining to Besançon.

1903 *Bookseller's Catal.*, Some pieces..touching bisontine society about 1550.

Bisque[2]. Add:

3. A light brown colour or tint. (Cf. *Biscuit 1 c.)

1922 *Glasgow Herald* 17 Aug. 6 A dress of pale bisque. 1923 *Daily Mail* 15 Jan. 1 In Navy, Bisque, Rust, Champagne, Orchid, Flesh, Silver, Nattier Blue, Black, Jade and Ivory.

Bit, *sb.*[1] Add:

8. d. *On the bit*: (of a horse) pulling at the bit. *Up to the bit*: up to the full speed allowed by the degree of restraint in which a horse is held by the bit. Also *transf.* (Cf. Bridle *sb.* 1.)

1928 *Daily Tel.* 16 Oct. 19/1 He was going so strongly and 'on the bit' that it took Dines nearly two furlongs to pull him up in his own time.

1859 *Art of Taming Horses* viii. 126 Your legs are to be used to force your horse forward up to the bit...Unless a horse rides up to the bit you have no control over him. 1875 Whyte Melville *Riding Recoll.* v. (1879) 92 Keeping the rebel up to his bit with legs and spurs if necessary. 1889 Lady C. Campbell *D. Blake* v. 95 'It's the only way to treat women', he thought; 'they will always come up to the bit if you show who is the master'. 1890 *Field* 6 Sept. 393 At the top of the hill we cast off our leader, the remaining four go in their collars and up to their bits.

e. *bit-chain.*

1902 *Daily Chron.* 26 Sept. 3/6 Something wrong with the bit-chain. 1908 *Westm. Gaz.* 5 June 10/1 Bombardier Mueller deposed that Thamme had struck him several times with his fist and bit-chains.

Bit, *sb.*[2] Add:

4. d. A short extract or 'cutting', such as forms the staple of certain popular periodicals. **Bi·tty** *a.*

1892 *Idler* May 483 Once on board ship, I tried a course of 'bits', pictorial, philosophical, scientific, conundrumistic, and otherwise. *Ibid.* 484 It is an awful thing to be shut up for a week with all the 'bitty' papers of the day. 1896 *Daily News* 4 Nov. 2/7 This is a weekly journal called 'Gems'. As its title suggests, the new paper will be of the 'bits' order.

e. *A bit*: a sum of money; money as 'I could do with a bit'. (Cf. 8 a.)

1894 A. Morrison *Mean Streets* 214 Bill had been 'left a bit', and 'a bit' means money, all the world over. 1909 Ware *Passing Engl.*, *Bit on, To have a* (Sporting), to have a bet on—a 'bit' of money on—a race. 1928 Galsworthy *Swan Song* II. iii. 124 He knew that everybody had 'a bit on' something now-a-days. For one person who ever went racing there were twenty..who didn't, and yet knew at least enough to lose their money.

f. Various colloq. and slang uses containing *a bit of* = a small amount or a small specimen of (see quots.). *A bit of blood*: a mettlesome horse. *A bit of cavalry*: a horse. *A bit of all right*: something highly satisfactory. *A bit of muslin* (see Muslin 2); similarly *a bit of fluff*, *a bit of mutton* (cf. Mutton 4). *To take a bit of doing*: to require all one's efforts, to be difficult to do. *Not a bit of it*: not at all, not so. Also *to do one's bit*, to take one's proper share

of work (in the war of 1914–18), to serve one's country either in the fighting forces or as a civilian.
1819 Moore *Tom Crib* (ed. 3) 11 A showy, but hot and unsound, *bit of blood*. 1821 Moncrieff *Tom & Jerry* I. vi, I shall here buy a bit of cavalry—that is a prad. 1823 [see Muslin 2]. 1844 Dickens *Mart. Chuz.* xxxvi, We rather put the bits of blood upon their mettle. 1853 C. R. Read *Austral. Gold Fields* 123 A good paddock, in which are a few *bits of blood*. 1853–4 Lever *Dodd Fam. Abr.* xxii, 'I'm sorry', said he, 'that the "bit of stiff"', meaning the bill, 'wasn't for five thousand francs.' 1874 *Slang Dict.*, *Bit-of-Stuff*, overdressed man; a man with full confidence in his appearance and abilities; a young woman, who is also called a *bit of muslin*. a 1889 J. Greenwood *Gaol Birds at Large* (Barrère & L.) Because the convicts to a man set such a high value on a bit of leaf. 1889 Barrère & Leland *Dict. Slang*, *Bit of blood*, a spirited horse that has some blood. *Bit of cavalry*, a saddle horse. *Bit of leaf* (prison), a small quantity of tobacco. *Bit of mutton* (common), a nice woman, generally in a questionable sense... *Bit of sticks* (sporting), a copse... *Bits of stiff* (popular), bank notes. 1905 H. G. Wells *Kipps* I. iv. § 1 That was a Fair Bit of All Right. 1910 — *Mr. Polly* ix, This beef is a Bit of All Right, Ma'm. 1919 C'tess von Arnim *Chris. & Col.* xxx. 394 Those cunning little bits of youngness, the Twinkler sisters.

Bitangent (bəitæ·ndʒĕnt), *a.* and *sb.* *Geom.* [Bi-². Cf. F. *bitangente*.] **A.** *adj.* Of a straight line or plane: Touching a curved line or surface at two different points. **B.** *sb.* A straight line which is tangent to a curve at two different points; a double tangent. Hence **Bitange·ntial** *a.*, designating a curve which passes through the points of contact of the double tangents of a given curve; also *sb.*, a bitangential curve.
1874 G. Salmon *Analyt. Geom.* (ed. 3) Index, Bitangent lines... Bitangent Planes. 1875 F. Purser in *Q. Jrnl. Math.* XIII. 338 On bitangents to the surface of centres of a quadric. 1879 G. Salmon *Higher Plane Curves* (ed. 3) 227 A non-singular quartic has 28 bitangents. *Ibid.* 351 The bitangential curve of a quintic. *Ibid.* 352 If the equation of this tangential curve were once formed, then, by forming the condition that the given tangent should touch this curve, we should immediately have the equation of the bitangential.

Bitch, *sb.*³ A primitive form of lamp used in Alaska.
1904 Eliz. Robins *Magnetic North* I. 233 'I'll light a piece of fat pine', shouted the Boy...'Where's your bitch?' said Dillon...'Haven't you got a condensed milk can with some bacon grease in it, and a rag wick?'

Bite, *v.* Add:
2. b. *To bite on* (fig.): to 'set one's teeth into', to take or get hold of (something substantial).
1904 W. H. Smith *Promoters* I. 20 They'll bite on anything that promises water west of either of those places. 1920 *Times Lit. Suppl.* 25 Nov. 770/2 These two writers are not ..'Academics'..and there is plenty to 'bite on' in their criticisms.
13. b. To exercise, excite, worry. *U.S. slang.*
1911 H. S. Harrison *Queed* vii. 84 Liberties—what's bitin' ye, man?
16. *To bite off more than one can chew*: to undertake too much, to be too ambitious. orig. *U.S.*
1878 J. H. Beadle *Western Wilds* ii. 42 Men, you've bit off more'n you can chaw. 1898 Hamblen *Gen. Manager's Story* 115 I'll tell you one thing,..you've bit off more'n you can chew this time. 1905 *Hartford Courant* 10 Feb. 8 Young Lawyer Comerford..bit off more than he could chew... He could not make good when called on for proof.
17. *To bite back*: to restrain (speech) by biting the lips.
1881 Mrs. Riddell *Senior Partner* xxv. II. 221 Hot and strong was the reply which rose to Robert's lips, but he bit it back. 1923 Joan Sutherland *Garland of Olive* xxv, Hunt bit back his sharply released breath.

Bi·tingness. [f. Biting *ppl. a.* + -ness.] Biting quality.
1894 *Contemp. Rev.* July 43 His article, by its very sharpness and bitingness, will help to wake our people up.

Bitten, *ppl. a.* Add:
5. Engraving. *Bitten-in*: see Bite *v.* 11 b.
1878 Abney *Treat. Photogr.* 183 The plate has to be..again heated to slightly melt the bitumen, so as to allow it to flow down the sides of the bitten-in lines.

Bitter, *sb.*¹ Add:
1. b. A bitter part.
1860 O. W. Holmes *Prof. Breakf.-t.* iv. 104 When you can get the bitter out of the partridge's thigh, you can make an enlightened commonwealth of Indians.
3. *colloq.* = *bitter beer*.
1856 'C. Bede' *Verdant Green* III. x, Mr. Verdant Green and Mr. Bouncer..turned into the coffee-room of 'The Mitre' to 'do bitters', as Mr. Bouncer phrased the act of drinking bitter beer. 1865 *Slang Dict.*, *Bitters*, 'to do bitters', to drink beer.—*Oxford*. 1874 *Ibid.* s.v., 'To do a bitter', to drink beer.—Originally Oxford, but now general. 1896 H. G. Wells *Wheels of Chance* ix, Every public-house..meant a lemonade and a dash of bitter. *Ibid.* xviii, 'A lemonade and bitter, please'. 1901 *Westm. Gaz.* 8 June 6/3 A bitter having been brought, he quaffed it to his second's health.

Bitter, *a.* **2. b.** *Bitter end* (early U.S. quots.).
1849 *Congress. Globe* 12 Dec. 23, I am unfortunately among those who voted for the gentleman from Indiana, even 'to the bitter end.' 1850 *Ibid.* 9 Apr., App. 434 Our defence is a just one, and will be maintained by us to the 'bitter end.'

Bitter, *v.* **2.** (Recent U.S. example.)
1911 J. C. Lincoln *Cap'n Warren's Wards* xv. 245, I managed to come out of it without lettin' it bitter my whole life.

Bitter-. 2. Add: **bitter-nut** (example); also *bitternut hickory*.
1832 D. J. Browne *Sylva Amer.* 170 This species is generally known in New Jersey by the name of Bitternut Hickory. *Ibid.*, The inhabitants of New Jersey give it the name of Bitternut, which..indicates one of the peculiar properties of the fruit.

Bi·tter-e·nder. *colloq.* [See Bitter *a.* 2 b and -er¹.] One who fights or holds out 'to the bitter end'; one who refuses to yield, give way, or compromise. Hence **Bitter-enderism** (Webster *Suppl.* 1924).
1850 *Congress. Globe* 12 Mar., App. 303 The disunionist looks forward to a southern confederacy; the bitter-ender to the triumph of his party. 1926 *Contemp. Rev.* June 687 The trade union world lies shattered and in ruins [after the General Strike]. There is fierce controversy between volunteers, 'scabs', 'hands-uppers', and 'bitter-enders'.

Bitterling (bi·tə̆ɹliŋ). [G., f. *bitter* Bitter *a.* (transl. L. *amarus*) + *-ling*, -ling¹.] A small carp-like freshwater fish, *Rhodeus amarus*, of Central Europe.
1880 Günther *Fishes* 601 The European species is known in Germany by the name of 'Bitterling'. 1911 *Encycl. Brit.* XX. 794/2 *Rhodeus amarus*, the bitterling,..injects its eggs into the mantle-cavity of pond-mussels, where the fry develop.

Bitters. Add: Also *fig.* (in sarcasm).
1812 in *Maryland Hist. Mag.* IX. 70 You might get your bitters in Baltimore Town.

Biune (bəi·yūn), *a. rare.* [f. Bi-² + L. *ūnus* one, after *triune*.] Two in one.
1897 F. Thompson *Orient Ode* in *New Poems* 34 Yea, biune in imploring dumb, Essential Heavens and corporal Earth await. 1900 G. W. Allen *Mission of Evil* 75 This Edenic Man was..male and female in one; that is, 'bi-une'.

Biurate (bəiyū·rĕt). *Chem.* [f. Bi-² + Urate.] An acid salt of uric acid.
1891 F. Taylor *Pract. Med.* (ed. 2) 702 They [*sc.* urates] are decomposed in the presence of water into free uric acid and biurates. 1908 *Practitioner* Apr. 517 The writer is doubtful that the cause of the pain, in gouty arthritis, is the result of the deposit of crystals of sodium biurate.

Biuret (bəi·yuret). *Chem.* [f. Bi-² + Urea: see quot. 1916.] A compound formed by heating urea. *Biuret base, reaction, test* (see quots.).
1874 *Jrnl. Chem. Soc.* XXVII. 683 Silver Compounds of Biuret. 1877 Roscoe & Schorlemmer *Chem.* I. 652 Biuret, $C_2O_2H_5N_3$. This compound, discovered by Wiedemann, is formed when urea is heated for some time to 150–160°. 1906 *Bio-Chem. Jrnl.* I. 391 Albumoses or peptone (biuret test). 1907 J. B. Cohen *Org. Chem.* 410 Triglycylglycine (biuret base). 1908 W. T. Hall tr. *Abderhalden's Physiol. Chem.* 163 The so-called 'Biuret-reaction'. If we freely add caustic soda or potash to an albumin solution, and then carefully, drop by drop, a dilute solution of copper sulphate, a blue to rose-violet coloration appears. 1916 A. P. Mathews *Physiol. Chem.* 145 Biuret, a substance..formed by the condensation of two molecules of urea (hence biurea or biuret) with the elimination of ammonia.

Bivalve, *a.* **1.** Delete † *Obs.* and add:
1875 Knight *Dict. Mech.* s.v. *Speculum*, Webber's magnifying bivalve ear-speculum. 1908 *Practitioner* Aug. 284 There was no appreciable difference obtained in the results by using a bivalve speculum in order to avoid contact with the external meatus.

Bivariant (bəivē·riănt), *a.* *Physical Chem.* [Bi-².] Having two degrees of freedom.
1902 J. E. Trevor in *Jrnl. Phys. Chem.* VI. 136, I would therefore suggest..that when the variance is successively zero, one, two, three, and more than two, the system be said to be in an Invariant, Univariant, Bivariant, Trivariant, Multivariant, state. 1904 A. Findlay *Phase Rule* ii. 16 We may also speak of the variability or variance of a system, and describe a system as being invariant, univariant, bivariant, multivariant, according as the number of degrees of freedom is nought, one, two, or more than two.

Bivoltin (bəivǫ·ltin), *a.* Also -ine. [a. F. *bivoltin*, f. *bi-*, Bi-² + It. *volta* time.] Of certain silkworms: Producing two broods per annum.
1887 Jas. Paton in *Encycl. Brit.* XXII. 58/1 The common silkworm produces as a rule only one generation during the year; but there are races in cultivation which are bivoltine, or two-generationed, and some are multivoltine. 1888 E. A. Butler *Silkworms* 69 Most of the other species produce two, three, four, six, or even eight broods per annum, and in the commercial world are..distinguished as 'bivoltins', 'trivoltins', 'quadrivoltins', etc.

Bivouacker (bi·vu̇ˌækəɹ). [-er¹.] One who bivouacs.
1908 Hardy *Dynasts* III. I. ii. 359 With the advance of day the snow resumes its fall, slowly burying the dead bivouackers.

Bivy, bivvy (bi·vi). *Army slang.* [Short f. Bivouac.] A temporary shelter for troops.
1920 *Blackw. Mag.* May 596/2 The Egyptian Camel Corps and Gurkhas arrived, bringing 'Bivies' and other luxuries. *Ibid.* 606/1 Tying his horse to my bivy-pole. 1925 *Glasgow Herald* 30 Mar. 10 That word was 'tambu', meaning a rough and ready shelter made of branches, planks, corrugated iron, a 'bivvy', in fact.

Biz (biz). Colloq. contraction, orig. *U.S.*, of Business.
1865 Artemus Ward *His Bk.* (1906) 141, I must forth to my Biz. 1873 Leland *Egypt. Sketch-Bk.* 35 No. IV. made it his 'biz' to fall upon the old hands. 1878 J. H. Beadle *Western Wilds* iii. 46 He had what he called a 'big biz' at each successive terminus town. 1889 Farmer *Americanisms* s.v., 'Good biz' is profitable business. 1890 *Harper's Mag.* Apr. 813/1 I'll go Down to the sale, if I can leave my biz. 1922 *Weekly Dispatch* 19 Nov. 9 'There is to be nothing of the limelight order in my conduct'...'I am out for real sober "biz"'.

Biza·rrely, *adv.* [f. Bizarre *a.* + -ly².] In a bizarre manner. So **Biza·rreness** (= Bizarrerie).
1884 Rider Haggard *Dawn* v, This woman so bizarrely beautiful. 1920 *Edin. Rev.* Oct. 255 Of his faults he was perfectly conscious—the over-intensities, the dualities, sometimes the bizarreness, which we have shadowed.

Black, *sb.* Add:
3. c. Deposit of dirt on the body. *dial.*
1753 Washington *Diaries* I. 49 You say this land belongs to you, but there is not the Black of my Nail yours. 1870 Robson *Evangeline* Introd. (E.D.D.) Aw ha'e wesht baith maw feet frae the black. 1889 *Yrks. Prov.* in *Eng. Dial. Dict.* s.v., He weant pairt wi' t'black afore his finger-nails.
7. d. A pigeon of a black variety. **e.** A black postage stamp.
1855 *Poultry Chron.* II. 515/2 A pen of short-faced bald head Tumblers, Blues, Blacks,..Almond, of rare quality. 1907 *Daily Chron.* 12 Dec. 6/6 A 12d. black of Canada, 1851.
8. *The Blacks.* In Italian history. **a.** The political faction of the Neri, composed of adherents of the Donati family, the opponents of the Bianchi (Whites). **b.** In Rome, the supporters of the Vatican as opponents of the Italian monarchy; the clericals.
[1680], 1849 [see White *sb.* 19]. 1877 *Encycl. Brit.* VI. 811/2 A quarrel had arisen in Pistoia between the two branches of the Cancellieri,—the Bianchi and Neri, the Whites and the Blacks. The quarrel spread to Florence, the Donati took the side of the Blacks, and Cerchi of the Whites. 1903 [see White *a.* 6 b]. 1909 *Daily Chron.* 29 Jan. 4/6 Most of the skaters are of the Vatican party...'Black' is the local name.
9. A black horse.
1845 J. J. Hooper *Taking Census* I. 153 Mounting our old black, we determined to give the old soul a parting fire. a 1861 T. Winthrop *John Brent* iii. 31 The black was within the corral, pawing the ground, neighing, and whinnying. 1873–4 *Rep. Vermont Board Agric.* II. 211 They are able to ride in grand carriages with their three minute blacks hitched thereto.
10. Short for Blackleg 3. (Cf. *Black *a.* 11 b.)
1866 *Sat. Rev.* 20 July 59 The lists of 'blacks', and the victims of the picket system.
11. *attrib.*, as *black-maker* (Black *sb.* 2); **black-tracker**, a native policeman employed chiefly in tracking down fugitive blacks and criminals.
1881 *Instr. Census Clerks* (1885) 58 Dye, Paint manufacture...*Black Maker. 1921 *Dict. Occupational Terms* (1927) § 158 *Black maker*, a colour mixer..preparing black pigments or paints from charcoal, graphite, calcined ivory or horn, carbon black, drop black, etc. 1867 *Australia as it is* 88–9 (Morris) The native police, or '*black trackers',..are a body of aborigines trained to act as policemen. 1870 *Argus* 26 Mar. 5/4 (Morris) The troopers, with the assistance of two black trackers, pursued the bushrangers. 1890 'R. Boldrewood' *Miner's Right* xvii, The sooner we get the black trackers on the trail, then the sooner we shall have a chance of seeing some of it back.

Black, *a.* Add: **6. b.** in the names of artificial flies used in fly-fishing.
1799 [see Midge 2]. 1837 Kirkbride *Northern Angler* 35 The Black Midge, or Gnat,..cannot be made too fine and small. *Ibid.* 51 The Black Palmer..is made with a body of black ostrich barle, ribbed with silver thread. *Ibid.* 57 The Black Spinner..has acquired a high reputation, both as a lake and a river-fly. 1923 *Daily Mail* 11 Aug. 7 The Lea should yield some good specimens of these fish to the black gnat.
11. b. Short for *Blackleg 3 b.
1927 *Daily Tel.* 22 Nov. 12/2 The Waterside Workers' Federation to-day declared as 'black' the steamer Kakakiri. 1928 *Daily Mail* 17 Apr. 12/4 The Maritime unions have threatened to declare 'black' all the Government liners.
14. b. *Black and Tans*: popular name for an armed force specially recruited to combat the Sinn-Feiners in 1921, so named from the mixture (black and khaki) of constabulary and military uniforms worn by them.
1921 *Times* 28 Jan. 7/5 'God Save the King' and 'God Bless the Black and Tans'. 1921 Ld. Braye *Sp.* 23 Mar. in *Fewness of my Days* (1927) 528, I rise to ask His Majesty's Government..whether they will..recall the Black-and-Tans.
15. c. Also *attrib.*, as in *black-and-white artist, drawing, sketch*.
1892 C. G. Harper *Engl. Pen Artists* 60 Such excellent black-and-white renderings of dog life. *Ibid.* 178 The arts of black-and-white drawing. *Ibid.*, Colourists or black-and-white artists. 1895 Pennell *Mod. Illustr.* Introd. 3 The amount of black-and-white work which he [*sc.* Dürer] produced. 1896 *Daily News* 29 Sept. 6/6 The well-known black-and-white artist, Mr. Fred Barnard.
18. *black-clothed, -draped, -spotted, -striped* (spec. of the perch), *-veiled* adjs.
1873 W. Cory *Lett. & Jrnls.* (1897) 322 Our parson bends his *black-clothed back in the sun. 1898 *Westm. Gaz.* 28 May 10/1 The bowed, *black-draped figure passing sadly from the shadows in the Abbey. 1904 *Daily Chron.* 8 Dec. 3/2 The black-draped scaffold at Whitehall. 1591 *Troub. Raigne K. John* I. iv, *Black-spotted Periure as he is. 1662 R. Smith (*title*) A Wonder of Wonders:..an Invective against Black-spotted Faces. 1783 Latham *Gen. Syn. Birds* II. II. 633 Black-spotted P[igeon]. 1901 *Westm. Gaz.* 27 June 3/2 Black-spotted white foulard. 1908 *Ibid.* 21 Nov. 16/2 The finest perch of the week (2½ lb.) also hails from this part, though some nice specimens of the *black-striped fish have been secured from the Thames. 1631 *blacke veyled [in Dict.]. 1906 *Westm. Gaz.* 18 Aug. 11/2 These black-veiled children of the East. 1906 B'ness von Hutten *What became of Pam* III. i, A black-veiled nursing-sister.

19. Black Army (see quot.); **Black Brigade** (see quot.); **black-buck**, a name used by sportsmen for the antelope proper (*Antilope cervicapra*); also, the South African *Hippotragus niger*; **Black Coats** *pl.* (*a*) German mercenaries of the 16th and 17th centuries (*Cent. Dict.* 1889); (*b*) see quot.; **black-coated** *a.*, spec. defining clerical or professional as distinguished from industrial or commercial occupations; hence, of or composed of persons engaged in such occupations; **black code** *U.S.*, a code or body of laws relating to negroes in some Southern States before the abolition of slavery; **black counties** *U.S.*, those counties in the Southern States in which negroes predominate; **black curlew** (see quot.); **black doctor** (see quot.); **black dress** *attrib.* (see quot.); **black-earth** *attrib.* in *black-earth country* = *Black belt; **black fast** *Eccl.*, a fast which includes abstinence from milk and eggs; **black fellow**, also *gen.* = *Black man; **black flesh** *U.S.*, negro slaves; **black frost**, a hard frost without snow or rime; **black gang**, a gang employed on such work as coaling, stoking, etc.; **black gown** *U.S.*, an Indian name for a Roman Catholic priest; **black growth** *U.S.* (see quot.); **Black Hand**, (*a*) defining a Spanish revolutionary society of anarchists; (*b*) defining a secret society of Italian immigrants in U.S., concerned chiefly in levying blackmail; hence **Black Hander**, a member of such a society; **black helmet**, a mollusc shell used in the making of shell-cameos; **black knot**, (*a*) a fast knot as distinguished from a running knot (Ogilvie, 1881); (*b*) any of certain kinds of fungus in the U.S.; **black larch** *U.S.*, an American variety of larch, the hackmetack; **black-lark** (see quot.); **black liquor**, acetate of iron used instead of green copperas as a mordant in dyeing (*Cent. Dict.* 1889); **black-plate** (see quot.); **black pope**, a nickname for the Superior-General of the Jesuits; **black print** *Photogr.* [Print *sb.* 13], a print giving black lines on a white ground; **black process** *Photogr.*, the process by which black prints are produced; also *attrib.* in *black process paper*, actinic paper used in this process; **black rubber vine**, an African plant producing a black juice which is used as rubber; **black saddler**, a workman who cuts out, blacks, and polishes leather for driving harness; **black scab** (see quot.); **black sheets** *pl.*, ungalvanized sheet iron; **black silk**, used *attrib.* to define a period of mourning during which black silk is worn instead of crape; **black spot**, a disease incident to rose trees when attacked by the fungus *Asteroma rosæ*, which causes the leaves to become spotted; **black spring** *Austral.* (see quot.); **black stripe**, a disease of the tomato-plant, produced by the fungus *Alternaria solani*; **black tongue**, a form of anthrax affecting horses and cattle; **black tooth** *U.S.*, a condition of pigs in which the teeth become black; **black trader factory**, a native African factory; **black wart** = *black scab*; **black widow** (see quot.); **black woman**, a black-skinned or coloured woman; **black work**, (*a*) blacksmith's work; also, forgings, rolled work, etc., that has not undergone a finishing process; (*b*) undertakers' work (cf. *Black man 3 and *Blackmaster).
1927 *Observer* 27 Mar. 18/3 The '*Black Army' (a secret force which was inaugurated to supplement the German Army after the Armistice). 1896 *Daily News* 18 July 5/1 The puny sacerdotalists, known in Parliament as the '*Black Brigade. 1888 W. T. Blandford *Mammalia* 521 *Antilope cervicapra*. The Indian Antilope or *black Buck. 1902 *Encycl. Brit.* XXV. 453/2 Antelope..properly denotes the Indian black buck, which alone constitutes the genus *Antilope*, with the title of *A. cervicapra*. 1927 *Daily Tel.* 26 Apr. 10/3 Gangs of '*Black Coats' or gunmen, who go before to prepare the way [for China's Nationalist Army]. 1893 *Jrnl. Soc. Arts* 14 Apr. 506/1 The young fellow who will devote himself to agriculture..in New Zealand..may do even better than the youth who wins his way to the *black-coated servitude of a bank. 1902 *Westm. Gaz.* 11 Aug. 7/3 A serried rank of the black-coated. 1928 *Observer* 17 June 20/5 The present system influences children in favour of the 'black-coated' occupations. 1928 *Britain's Industr. Future* III. xiv. § 6. 158 The workers are apt to be suspicious of 'black-coated' unions. 1866 Gregg *Life in Army* xxviii. 238, I will present a synoptical view of the pertinently named '*Black Code of Louisiana. 1876 *Congress. Rec.* Aug. 5347/1, I hold in my hand the laws of the Legislature of S. Carolina passed in the session of 1865–66...Among the very first acts that they passed was the act which is known all over this county and all over the world as the 'black code' of S.C., a code that should disgrace every one of its authors. 1879 Tourgee *Fool's Err.* xxi. 119 It was done in the very face of the 'Black Codes'. 1888 *Congress. Rec.* Sept. 8947/1 Justices of the peace in the *black counties..converted their offices into engines of oppression to both races. 1889 H. Saunders *Man. Brit. Birds* 379 The Glossy Ibis. *Plegadis falcinellus* (Linnæus)...was known to gunners and fishermen as the '*Black Curlew'. 1909 *Westm. Gaz.* 22 Oct. 4/2 When.. there is no possibility of catching a salmon except by that engine of death, the '*Black Doctor'—the three big hooks tied back to back and dragged along the floor of a pool. 1899 *Daily News* 3 July 5/6 The convict Billinge is what is known as a '*Black dress' man, being thus distinguished because of his bad conduct. 1905 *Athenæum* 5 Aug. 175/1 The *black-earth country of the south. 1577 R. Barnes in *Newcastle Tracts* (1847) 16 That no..superfluous faste be vsed as those called the Lady fast saint trinyons fast, the *black faste. 1738 F. Moore *Trav. Africa* 191 Natives, who had been got up together at the Persuasion of a *Black Fellow. 1828 *New Monthly Mag.* XXIII. 220 The fish are so abundant that a black fellow with a seine, can load a bullock-cart at one or two hauls. 1827 J. F. Cooper *Prairie* (1836) I. viii. 125 The newspapers of Kentuck have called you a dealer in *black flesh a hundred times, but little did they reckon that you drove the trade into white families. 1787 Washington *Diaries* III. 198 This Morning there was a small white frost and a *black one wch. was so severe as to stop brick laying. 1828– in *Eng. Dial. Dict.* 1851 [see Frost *sb.* 1]. 1921 R. D. Paine *Comr. Rolling Ocean* iii. 44 There wasn't a smarter man in the *black gang (=stokers). 1847 De Smet *Oregon Missions* 18 The savages assembled..to behold the **black gowns* of whom so much had been said. 1872 *Amer. Naturalist* VI. 94 Everywhere among the western Indians the Jesuits were known by the name of Blackgowns. 1851 S. Judd *Margaret* I. xvii. 137 Yet there are, what by a kind of provincial misnomer is called the *black growth, pines and firs. 1904 *N. Y. Tribune* 31 July 2 For months the *black hand society has been forcing Italians to contribute to its treasury with threats of death. 1905 *Westm. Gaz.* 5 Jan. 6/3 The notorious Italian blackmailing gang which has been given the name of the 'Black Hand Society'. 1906 *Ibid.* 2 June 9/3 *La Mano Negra*, the famous revolutionary Black Hand Society. 1923 L. J. Vance *Baroque* viii. 49 The Wop detective that used to play horse with the *Black Handers. 1861 *Chambers's Encycl.* s.v. *Cameo*, The *Black Helmet..has a dark onyx ground. 1876 *Encycl. Brit.* IV. 740 The black helmet (*Cassis tuberosa*) of the West Indian seas. 1856 *Trans. Mich. Agric. Soc.* VII. 714 In the eastern States the *black knot not only disfigures the trees but is sapping their vitality. 1884 Miller *Plant-n.* 252 *Sphæria mortosa*, 'Black knot' Fungus. 1908 *Board Agric. & Fisheries* (1919) No. 213 Gooseberry Black-knot (*Plowrightia ribesia*, Sacc.). The fungus..causing this disease is closely related to *Plowrightia morbosa*, Sacc., the widely distributed 'black knot' of plum and cherry trees in the United States and Canada. 1837 Colman *Rep. Agric. Mass.* (1838) 116 The Larch..there called the German Larch, is the common or White Larch (Larix Communis), and resembles our Hackmetack or *Black Larch (Larix Pendula) in the value of its timber and bark. 1907 *Westm. Gaz.* 11 Mar. 13/1 At the last meeting of the British Ornithologists' Club, three examples of the *black-lark (*Melanocorypha yeltoniensis*) were exhibited. 1858 Simmonds *Dict. Trade*, *Black Plates,..thin sheets of iron not coated with tin. 1877 O'Reilly *Life Pius IX* xiv. (1878) 168 Beneath the eyes of the Superior-General of the Jesuits, whom they were wont to designate as 'the *Black Pope'. 1880 *Encycl. Brit.* XIII. 648/2 The general [of the Society of Jesus] has usually stood towards the pope much as a powerful grand feudatory of the Middle Ages did towards a weak titular lord paramount..; and the shrewd Roman populace have long shown their recognition of this fact by styling these two great personages severally the 'White Pope' and the Black. 1888 *Lockwood's Dict. Terms Mech. Engin.*, *Black Print. 1902 [see *blue print*, *Blue *a.* 13]. 1887 Moloney *Forestry W. Afr.* 90 The *black-rubber vine, known to the natives as 'Duah Kurrie'. 1904 *Board Agric. & Fisheries* (1919) No. 105. 1 Wart Disease (*Black Scab) of Potatoes. (*Synchytrium endobioticum*.)...In recent years a variety of other names such as Black Wart and Potato Wart have been given to it. 1895 *Daily News* 18 Feb. 2/5 *Black sheets for galvanisers. 1894 *Ibid.* 22 Nov. 8/1 Deep crape and distinctive headgear have been dropped at the end of six months, the period known technically as '*black silk' then setting in. 1928 *Daily Express* 7 July 4/2 The blotch, or *black spot as it is sometimes called, appears on the upper side of the leaf, and the rose tree speedily loses its foliage. 1848 H. W. Haygarth *Bush Life Australia* ix. 98 A narrow rill, rising out of some rich dark soil, known in Australia as a '*black spring'. 1927 *Smallholder* 26 Mar. 104/2 If any [*sc.* tomato plants] have very finely cut, lace-like leaves, take them out... These plants have contracted *Black Stripe disease. 1853 C. Flint *Milch Cows*, etc. 281 Typhoid fever ..is sometimes followed by diseases known as 'black tongue, black leg, or quarter evil. 1877 *Rep. Vermont Dairym. Assoc.* VIII. 107 *Black tooth is a popular disease of swine. 1897 Mary Kingsley *W. Africa* 310 One of these *black trader factories is an exceedingly interesting place to stay at. 1861 *Trans. Ill. Agric. Soc.* IV. 454 It is sometimes affected by the *black wart. 1927 *Daily Express* 21 July 2/7 A small black spider known to entomologists as '*latrodectus mactans*', and commonly called the '*black widow' or 'shoe-button,' which has been introduced from Oriental ports into North America. 1788 A. Falconbridge *Acc. Slave Trade Africa* (ed. 2) 41 Observing with what..eagerness a *black woman seized some dirt from off an African yam. 1837 J. E. Alexander *Narr. Voy. Observ.* I. v. 110 The audience, principally black women. 1859 Sala *Gaslight & Daylight* xxvi, A florid man who.. sometimes takes a spell in the *black work, or undertaking line of business. 1874 Knight *Dict. Mech.*, *Black-work*, the work of the blacksmith in contradistinction to bright-work or the work of the silversmith. 1888 *Lockwood's Dict. Terms Mech. Engin.*, *Black Work*, work which has not been machined or polished. In some instances the term would apply to metal work which had been machined on a bearing section, but not elsewhere. And in other cases where no portion, working or otherwise, had been machined.
b. esp. in *Ceramics*.
1766 Wedgwood in L. Jewitt *The Wedgwoods* (1865) 187 Basaltes or black ware; a black porcelain biscuit. 1787 *Ibid.* 332 The black basaltes having the appearance of antique bronze..is excellently adapted for busts, sphynxes, small statues, etc. 1832 G. R. Porter *Porcelain & Gl.* 17 Basaltes, or black ware. 1865 [see *blue printing*, *Blue *a.* 13.] 1875 Metevard *Wedgwood Handbk.* 391 *Black Marble*. A crystalline terra-cotta body. The colour is black shaded. *Black painted*. Single stems and flowers painted on black glazed ware... *Black printed*. Cream-ware printed over or under the glaze with patterns in black. 1884 Knight *Dict. Mech.* Suppl., *Black-basalt Ware*. 1885 *Encycl. Brit.* XIX. 615/1 Etruscan Black Ware. *Ibid.* 618/2 Black Pottery is usually made from a very silicious or sandy clay. *Ibid.* 619/1 Roman black ware decorated with groups of dots in relief.

Black ash. *U.S.* [Black *a.* 6.] A North American species of ash (*Fraxinus nigra*), also called *basket-ash* and *hoop-ash*. Also *attrib.*
1673 *Essex Inst. Hist. Coll.* VI. 178/2 A forked Black ash which is also Osmund Trask his bound. 1765 J. Bartram *Jrnl.* (1769) 6 Here and near the river's bank grows the..elm and black-ash, with most of the South-Carolina plants. 1782 *Boston Town Rec.* VIII. 222 We are of Opinion That no Poplar,..Black ash, Basswood, or Cedar Shall be Corded up. 1832 D. J. Browne *Sylva Amer.* 157 The black ash requires a moister soil than the white ash. 1872 *Rep. Vermont Board Agric.* I. 154 An experiment had been tried by a Cornwall farmer, packing butter in spruce, oak and black ash tubs.

Black belt. *U.S.* [Black *a.* 1 c, *Belt *sb.* 2 d.] That portion of the southern United States (see quot. 1905) in which the coloured population is most numerous. Also *attrib.*
1875 *Congress. Rec.* Jan. 342/1 During this campaign I made a number of speeches in Georgia. I spoke in what is known as the 'Black Belt'. 1887 *Harper's Mag.* July 243/1 We will soon skirt the 'Black Belt', which is full of rich plantations. 1898 *Congress. Rec.* Feb. 1594/1 The Fourth Alabama Congressional district..was composed entirely of Black belt counties. 1905 *N. Y. Even. Post* 21 Nov. 3 The Black Belt has a curiously irregular shape. Extending from Virginia across North and South Carolina, Georgia, Alabama, to Mississippi and Southern Louisiana, it stretches a narrow arm across the river and up into southern and central Arkansas.

Blackberry (blæ·kberi), *v.* [f. the sb.] *intr.* To gather blackberries.
[1861–: see Blackberrying *vbl. sb.*] 1902 Mrs. Barnes-Grundy *Thames Camp* 152 Those golden September days on which we blackberried.

Black birch. *U.S.* [Black *a.* 6.] One or other of several North American species of birch, esp. *Betula lenta* and *B. occidentalis*.
1685 *Manchester* (Mass.) *Rec.* 20 From thence Esterly to a black burch near ye river. 1711 *Boston Town Rec.* VIII. 86 A blackburch on the Side of a Swamp. 1832 D. J. Browne *Sylva Amer.* 118 Wherever it grows in the United States, it is known by the name of Black Birch. *Ibid.* 119 The wood of the black birch, when freshly cut, is of a rosy hue, which deepens by exposure to the light. 1889 *Century Dict.* s.v. *Birch*, The black birch, *Betula occidentalis* of the Rocky Mountains and westward.

Black-bird. 1. (U.S. examples.)
1643 R. Williams *Key Lang. Amer.* xv. 89 Which mysticall Fowle follow the sowing of the Word..as these Black-birds follow the materiall seed. 1659 *Dedham* (Mass.) *Rec.* IV. 7 Killing blackbirds according to Towne order. 1697 *Portsmouth Rec.* 309 Every housholder..Shall kill twelve blackbirds. 1708 *Braintree Rec.* 68 Any person.. [who] shall..kill or destroy any old Black birds..shall be paid two pence pr. head. 1807 P. Gass *Jrnl.* 103 There is in the bottoms a great quantity of spear-mint... Also multitudes of blackbirds. 1836 *Southern Lit. Messenger* II. 358 They possess two qualities..in common with certain birds, such as rooks, crows, and blackbirds. 1868 J. Burroughs *Wake-robin* v. (1895) 137 Among the first birds that make their appearance in Washington is the crow blackbird. *Ibid.* 138 All parks and public grounds about the city are full of blackbirds.

Blackbirder (blæ·kbə̄ɹdəɹ). [f. Blackbirding + -er¹.] A man or a vessel engaged in Blackbirding or slave-traffic.
1888 Churchward *Blackbirding* 126 You see the harm those cussed blackbirders do in the islands. *Ibid.* 163 That chap whose throat I cut on board the blackbirder. 1928 *New Statesman* 28 July 507/2 Polynesians in their wild state..were..shipped to Australia by enterprising gentlemen called blackbirders.

Blackbirding, *vbl. sb.* Add quots.:
1888 Churchward (*title*) Blackbirding. 1898 W. C. Morrow *The Ape the Idiot, Faithful Amulet* 314 'Blackbirding' (which is kidnapping Gilbert Islanders and selling them to the coffee-planters of Central America). 1908 *Daily Chron.* 6 Nov. 4/6 'Blackbirding'..is not yet an entirely extinct industry [in the Pacific Islands].

Blackboard. Add: **b.** *attrib.*, as *blackboard clerk, drawing, lesson, rubber*.
1870 Medbery *Men & Myst. Wall St.* 21 The 'marker' or black-board clerk writes off the prices upon the tablet. 1880 *Plain Hints Needlework* 33 These three strips can be sewed..together, and thus form a dish-cloth or black-board rubber. 1890 Gordon *Foundry* 89 To see the service complete we should have been in the great hall, and heard the blackboard lesson. 1895 *Daily News* 26 Apr. 3/2 'Blackboard Drawing'..seemed to him to be useful..for..the student, the teacher, and the child. 1905 H. H. Stephens (*title*) Black-Board and Free-Arm Drawing.

Black-book, *v.* [f. Black book 4 b.] *trans.* To enter in a black book.
1828 Mrs. Royall *Black Bk.* II. 92 But I shall Black-book them all.

Black bottom. *U.S.*
1. [Black *a.* 1 c, Bottom *sb.* 5.] A low-lying area inhabited by a coloured population.
1915 *Lit. Digest* 4 Sept. 500/2 Uncle Mose aspired to the elective office of justice of the peace in the 'black bottom' part of town.
2. The name of a dance. Also as *vb.*
1927 *Observer* 6 Feb. 15/7 The accounts of the new dances are discouraging. There is the Black Bottom, the very name of which spoils a spring morning. 1927 *Daily Express* 25 May, Miss Bradhurst had black bottomed nineteen miles ..before she collapsed.

Blackboy (blæ·kboi).
1. An Australian grass-tree of the genus *Xanthorrhœa*, having a thick dark trunk and a head of grass-like leaves, esp. *Xanthorrhœa preissii*.

1839 *Hooker's Jrnl. Bot.* II. 344 One of the most striking plants to a stranger is our common Blackboy, a fine aborescent species of Xanthorrhœa. 1840 Pereira *Elem. Mat. Med.* II. 658 A red resin, probably from *X[anthorrœa] arborea*.., has been recently imported under the name of *black-boy gum*. 1846 Stokes *Discov. in Australia* II. 132 Black boy..gum on the spear—resin on the trunk. *Ibid.* 380 *note*, These trees, called Blackboys by the colonists, from the resemblance they bear, in the distance, to natives. 1870 W. H. Knight *W. Australia* 46 A resin got from the 'black-boy', or grass tree, (*xanthorrhea drummondii*).
2. (As two words.) A kind of black tobacco.
1898 *Daily News* 8 Oct. 3/3 She had been addicted to the use of the weed, in the specific shape of 'black boy,' for over forty years. 1908 *Daily Chron.* 10 Apr. 4/7 A black boy tobacco much in favour with mariners.

Black-browed, *a.* Add:
b. Black-browed Albatros (*Diomedea melanophrys*).
[1865 Gould *Birds Australia* II. 438 *Diomedea melanophrys*..Black-eyebrowed Albatros.] 1883 *Encycl. Brit.* XV. 334/2 All the rest of the plumage is white, except a dusky superciliary streak, whence its name of Black-browed Albatros.

Blackbu·rnian, *a.* *U.S.* [f. the name of Mrs. *Blackburn*.] *Blackburnian warbler*, a North American warbler (*Dendroica blackburniæ*). Also *ellipt.* as *sb.*
1783 Latham *Gen. Syn. Birds* II. II. 461 Blackburnian Warbler. 1868 *Amer. Naturalist* II. 179 The Blackburnian Warbler (*D. Blackburniæ*) is one of the most beautiful. 1893 Torrey *Footpath-Way* 6 We..soon were in the old forest listening to bay-breasted warblers, Blackburnians, black-polls, and so on. *Ibid.* 16 A Blackburnian warbler perched as usual, at the very top of a tall spruce.

Blackbutt (blæ·kbʊt). *Austral.* [Black *a.*, Butt *sb.*³ 2.] An Australian timber tree, *Eucalyptus pilularis*. Earlier, *black butted gum*.
1820 J. Oxley *Jrnls. Two Exped. N. S. W.* 331 The timber was chiefly black butted gum. 1847 Leichhardt *Jrnl.* ii. 49 The range..having, with the exception of the Blackbutt, all the trees..of Moreton Bay. 1901 *Daily Chron.* 3 Sept. 7/4 Fencing post of blackbutt, forty-five years in the ground.

Black-cap. Add: **5.** A variety of raspberry; the Black Raspberry, *Rubus occidentalis*. *U.S.*
1867–8 *Trans. Ill. Agric. Soc.* VII. 512 Home beds of raspberries, particularly the Purple Cane and Black Cap, have been full crops. 1871 *Ibid.* VIII. 173 The principal varieties that are cultivated in the West are the Black-caps. 1886 *Harper's Mag.* July 281/2 There is another American species of raspberry (*Rubus occidentalis*) that is almost as dear to memory as the wild strawberry—the thimble-berry, or black-cap.

Black-capped, *a.* [Cf. Black cap 3.] Of birds: Having the top of the head black.
a 1813 A. Wilson *Amer. Ornith.* (1831) II. 215 *Parus atricapillus*..Black-capt Titmouse. 1868 *Amer. Naturalist* II. 175 The Green Black-capped Warbler (*Myiodioctes pusillus*). 1870 *Ibid.* III. 74 The cries and habits of all these black-capped species. *Ibid.* IV. 543 In the depths of winter they and..the Black-capped Titmouse (*Parus Atricapillus*), enliven the woods.

Black currant. Add:
b. *Black currant mite*, an insect pest that attacks currant trees and gooseberry trees, but especially the black currant tree, living chiefly inside the buds and producing the disease known as 'big bud'.
1894 *Board Agric. & Fisheries* (1918) No. 1. 1 The disease known as 'big bud' in Black Currants, caused by the Black Currant Mite, was first recorded in these islands in the year 1869.

Blackee, var. of Blacky *sb.* 1.
1835 J. H. Ingraham *South-West* I. 102 The shining face of a blackee may be seen glistening from among his vegetables.

Black eye. Add: **2. b.** *fig.* A severe blow or rebuff. *U.S.*
1795 *Massachusetts Spy* 18 Feb. (Th.) Massachusetts beaten; and a black eye for Connecticut. 1876 *Congress. Rec.* Feb. 854/1 Some body was threatening to give a black eye to these bonds. 1888 *Battle Creek Jrnl.* 29 Feb., It is a subject for..congratulation that one gigantic monopoly was given a black eye, Thursday. 1900 *Congress. Rec.* Jan. 1004/2, I hope the Pension Committee will give a black eye to every bill of that kind. 1908 G. H. Lorimer *J. Spurlock* x. 257 It would give the [gambling-] house a black eye if it were known that there had been such a suspicion even.
3. The black-eyed pea. *U.S.*
1788 Washington *Diaries* III. 357 Finished planting of Pease here yesterday..two [lots]..were of the large and early black eye.

Black-eyed, *a.* [Black *a.* 18.]
1. Having black eyes. Cf. Black eye 1.
a 1667, 1775 [see Black eye 1].
b. Having a black eye; *spec.* of a variety of pea.
1786 Washington *Diaries* III. 56 They proceeded to sow the small black eyed pea. 1857 *Texas Almanac* 13 Plant Black-Eyed..Peas. 1862 *Chambers's Encycl.* s.v. *Dolichos*, *D. sphaerospermus* (Calavana or Black-eyed Pea), a native of the West Indies.
2. *Black-eyed Susan* (U.S.): **a.** (See quots.)
1889 *Century Dict.* s.v. *Thunbergia*, The hardy annual *T. alata*, known locally by the name *black-eyed Susan* from its buff, orange, or white flowers with a purplish-black center. 1906 H. D. Pittman *Belle of Blue Grass C.* xvi. 241, I found all of the waste places now covered with black-eyed susans. 1909 *Century Dict.* Suppl., *Blackeyed Susan*, one of several plants having flowers or heads with a dark center. One of these is *Flemingia alata*..; another, the flower-of-an-hour, *Hibiscus Trionum*; a third, *Rudbeckia hirta*.
b. *slang.* (See quot.)
1889 Farmer *Americanisms*, *Black-eyed Susan*.—Texan for a revolver.

Black fish. Add:
1. (U.S. examples.)
1859 Bartlett *Dict. Amer.* (ed. 2), *Tautaug* or *Tautog* (*Tautoga americana*), the name of the Blackfish caught in the waters of Rhode Island...In New York it is called Black Fish, from the color of its back and sides. 1888 Goode *Amer. Fishes* 39 The Sea Bass is also known south of Cape Hatteras as the 'Blackfish'. 1897 *Outing* (U.S.) XXX. 160/2 These fishermen, who think that God made blackfish for them exclusively.
4. The freshwater fish *Gadopsis marmoratus*, found all over Australia.
1850 Clutterbuck *Port Phillip* iii. 44 The Schnapper, blackfish and eel. 1885 McCoy *Zool. Victoria* I. 39 *Gadopsis gracilis*...The Yarra Blackfish. 1890 *Melbourne Argus* 9 Aug. 4/5 You could catch a few blackfish in the pools.

Black flag. Add quots., q.v.:
1720 De Foe *Capt. Singleton* xiii, We let them soon see who we were, for we hoisted a black flag, with two cross daggers on it. 1821 Scott *Pirate* xl, Up goes the Jolly Hodge, the old black flag, with the death's head and hour-glass. 1827 P. Cunningham *N. S. Wales* II. xiii. 302 Every effort ought to be made to impress..upon..the multitude the terrible nature of our punishments, without permitting them to be..spectators...The having..a black flag with emblems of death hung out [etc.]. 1870 Brewer *Dict. Phrase & Fable* (ed. 20) 301 *To unfurl the black flag*, to declare war. 1887 *Longm. Mag.* Nov. 105 In the New Princeton Review (Sept. 1887) Mr. Brander Matthews alleges that certain English publishers can also run up the 'Jolly Roger' on occasion, and sail under the Black Flag. *Correspondent*. Black flag hoisted as a signal of pestilence, as in London for cholera in 19th cent. I remember this in Golden Square in 1853.

Black fly. [Black *a.* 6.] **1.** (See quot. 1889.)
1845 S. Judd *Margaret* II. vii. 309, I recollect when we was in the Provinces down to Arcady, where the Black Flies come out as thick as birds arter a thunder storm. 1876 *Fur, Fin & Feather* Sept. 139 At Calais, Maine, last fall rugged grouse were as thick as black flies in August. 1889 *Century Dict.* s.v. *Fly*, *Black fly*, any one of the species of the genus *Simulium*, some of which are extraordinarily abundant in the northern woods of America, and cause great suffering by their bites.
2. A name given to various insects infesting plants, esp. to an insect of the species *Frankliniella robusta* (formerly *Thrips pisivora*) and *Aphis rumicis*: used *collect.* in *sing.* for thripses or aphides when infesting certain plants and giving a blackish appearance to the part affected, as the top of a bean-plant when infested with the Bean Aphis.
1837 *Annual Scrap-Bk.* 83. 1850 *Working Man's Friend* 13 July 55/1 To Remove the Aphides, or black fly. 1884 *Sutton's Cult. Veget. & Flowers* 269 The Blue and the Black Fly are common plagues of the Peach-house and the orchard. 1898 *Board Agric. & Fisheries* (1918) No. 48. 1 The small insects known as Thrips, Black Fly, or Thunder Fly. 1904 *Ibid.* (1919) No. 104. 2 The Bean Aphis, known variously as Black Fly, Collier, and Black Dolphin.

Black-grass. [Black *a.* 1.]
1. A species of foxtail grass, *Alopecurus agrestis*.
1798 W. Curtis *Flora Lond.* II. Plate 16 *note*, The Farmer also distinguishes the *Alopecurus agrestis*..by the name of Black Grass. 1832 *Scoreby Farm Rep.* 6 in *Husb.* (L.U.K.).
2. A species of rush (*Juncus Gerardi*) growing in salt-marshes. *U.S.*
1837 Colman *Rep. Agric. Mass.* (1838) 18 Black-grass (deemed the best product) grows on the higher parts of the marsh. 1871 Schele de Vere *Americanisms* (1872) 408 *Salt-Hay*, a very important product of salt-marshes, is of two principal sorts, called *salt-grass* and *black-grass*.

Blackguard, *v.* **2.** (Earlier example, in *ppl. a.*)
1789 in C. Cist *Cincinnati* (1841) 201 One answered, in a blackguarding manner.

Black gum. *U.S.* (Also hyphened and as one word.) [Black *a.* 6.]
1. A North American tree of the genus *Nyssa*.
1785 Washington *Diaries* II. 346 Planted all the..Blackgums in my Serpentine Walks. 1832 D. J. Browne *Sylva Amer.* 223 It is designated by the name of Black Gum, Yellow Gum and Sour Gum. 1835 J. H. Ingraham *South-West* II. 79 A fine though dusty road..bordered with noble forests of oak, black gum, etc. 1885 'C. E. Craddock' *Prophet Gt. Smoky Mts.* xv. 281 The hickory trees..were a lustrous contrast to the sombre pine..or the vivid crimson of the black-gum. 1901 C. Mohr *Plant Life Alabama* 32 Chestnut..and black gum (*Nyssa sylvatica*) are common. *Ibid.* 117 The deciduous black gum (*Nyssa biflora*).
attrib. 1785 Washington *Diaries* II. 392 The black Gum Trees..which put out leaf and looked well at first, are all dead. 1868 *Amer. Naturalist* II. 122 When mast is not plenty, they [*sc.* bears] lap black-gum berries. 1872 in Tourgee *Invisible Empire* viii. (1880) 444 One of them took a bundle of black gum switches.
2. The berries of the black-gum tree.
1868 *Amer. Naturalist* II. 122 Only severe hunger will force him to eat the meat of a bear that has lapped black-gum.

Black haw. *U.S.* [Black *a.* 6.]
1. a. A North American species of viburnum, esp. *V. prunifolium*. Also *attrib.* **b.** A species of hawthorn. **c.** One or other of two species of *Bumelia*.
1785 Washington *Diaries* II. 346 Planted..all the black haws, all the large berried thorns. 1817 S. R. Brown *Western Gaz.* 26 Spice wood, sassafras, black and white haws, are common to the best soils. 1857 *Trans. Ill. Agric. Soc.* II. 631 They are also very fond of the berries of the black-haw, (*Viburnum lentago*). 1872 Eggleston *End of World* xxi. 145 The black-haw bushes hung over the roadside. 1901 C. Mohr *Plant Life Alabama* 88 An undergrowth of dogwood, black haw, sourwood, and sumach.
2. The fruit of one or other of these.
1891 *Fur, Fin & Feather* Mar. 169 A bear likes wild plums and black haws.

Black-head. Add:
4. = Comedo. Also *attrib.*
[1847 Sir W. J. E. Wilson *Dis. Skin* 342 A little white cylinder..having the appearance of a small white maggot with a black head.] 1885 [see Comedo]. 1910 *Daily Chron.* 15 Jan. 9/1 Sometimes blackheads gather in the forehead lines,..they must be pressed out with the blackhead instrument, if steaming and massage fail to remove them.
5. *attrib.* = next.
1835 J. Martin *Gaz. Virginia* 483 A great variety of ducks as..the red head shoveler, the black head shoveler.

Bla·ck-hea·ded, *a.* Having a black head: used in the names of birds and beasts.
1774 [see Black *a.* 18]. 1783 Latham *Gen. Syn. Birds* II. I. 198 Black-headed B[unting]. *Emberiza melanocephala*. 1785 Pennant *Arct. Zool.* II. 398 Black-headed Warbler. a 1813 A. Wilson *Amer. Ornith.* (1831) II. 217 Having shot him..I found it to be the black-headed titmouse. 1870 *Amer. Naturalist* III. 75 The habits of the Black-headed grosbeak are quite different. *Ibid.* 234 The Black-headed Gull, a southern and somewhat rare species. 1880 *Encycl. Brit.* XI. 274/2 The Black-headed or 'Peewit' Gull, *Larus ridibundus*. 1902 *Ibid.* XXXII. 109/2 The Black-headed Rock Snake (*Aspidiotes*), one of the Pythons.

Black heart, black-heart (see quots. and Black *a.* 19).
1786 Washington *Diaries* III. 13 A black heart May cherry, grafted at the same time. 1833 H. Barnard in *Maryland Hist. Mag.* XIII. 377 Here were..numerous trees of ripe cherries, black hearts and red hearts. 1860 O. W. Holmes *Prof. Breakf.-t.* iii. 64 His eyes like black-heart cherries.

Black-hearted, *a.* [Black *a.* 18.] (See quot.)
1872 *Rep. Vermont Board Agric.* I. 94 The lower branches are suffered to grow until of such size that a dry, dead knot is left when they are cut off, which sometimes kills the center of the tree, making it 'black-hearted'.

Blacking, *vbl. sb.* Add:
1. b. *Blacking-out*: see Black *v.* 3 b.
1905 Miss Betham-Edwards in *Academy* 27 May 562/1 Maternal censorship is rigid, the Russian blacking-out system not more so.
3. c. Applied to boot-leather which is to be blacked as distinguished from patent leather.
1896 *Daily News* 2 July 8/7 High glacé boots have patent leather goloshes, and others have plain 'blacking' leather.

Black Jack. Add:
3. (Earlier examples.)
1782 Jefferson *Notes Virginia* (1787) 62 Black jack oak. Quercus aquatica. 1789 Morse *Amer. Geog.* 415 A species of oak grows in the moist, gravelly soil, called Black Jack. It seldom grows larger than 8 or 9 inches diameter. 1834 Carruthers *Kentuckian in N. Y.* I. 166, I never saw weeping pines and black-jacks (scrub oaks) before I came into South Carolina.
6. The black caterpillar of the turnip saw-fly, *Athalia centifolia* or *A. spinarum*.
1840 [see Nigger *sb.* 2].
7. A hooked seed of the South African plant *Bidens pilosa*.
1877 Lady Barker *Year's Housekeeping S. Africa* vii. 130 An innocent-looking plant..bearing a most aggravating tuft of little black spires, which lose no opportunity of sticking to one's petticoats in myriads. They are familiarly known as 'black jacks'.
8. = Black flag as the ensign of a pirate.
1867 Smyth *Sailor's Word-bk.*
9. Caramel or burnt sugar used for colouring spirits, vinegar, coffee, etc.
1858 Simmonds *Dict. Trade*.
10. A trade name for adulterated butter.
1858 Simmonds *Dict. Trade*.
11. A black portmanteau.
1885 in Ware *Passing Engl.* s.v., Burton also brought another second-hand portmanteau called in the trade 'Black Jack'.
12. (See quots.) *U.S.*
1863 'E. Kirke' *My Southern Friends* ix. 112 'Then be does pray better for a little whiskey?' 'Yes; a mug of "black jack" helps him amazingly.' 1877 Bartlett *Dict. Amer.* (ed. 4), *Black-Jack*..2. Rum sweetened with molasses. New England.
13. A weapon consisting of a heavy metal or weighted head and short pliable shaft or strip of leather used as a bludgeon. *U.S.*
1895 *Denver Times* 5 Mar. 8/5 During the scuffle Miss Alderfer, Knapp's niece, saw the 'black jack' up his sleeve, ..and as a result, swore out the concealed weapons charge. 1904 *N. Y. Even. Post* 10 Mar. 1 This position..was not such as the body would have taken had Newman been struck with a blackjack or other weapon.
Hence **Black-jack** *v.*, to strike with a blackjack.
1905 *N. Y. Even. Post* 2 Sept., 'I got a partner there' [in the penitentiary], Red said,..'blackjacked a man.'

Blacklead, *v.* Add:
b. In *Electrotyping*, to brush (the mould) over with blacklead. Hence **Blacklea·ding** *vbl. sb.*; *attrib.* in *blackleading machine*.
1888 *Encycl. Brit.* XXIII. 703/2 The mould, having been finished, has to be blackleaded...To facilitate this operation, a blackleading machine is used in large establishments...The process of depositing a copper solution upon the blackleaded surface of the mould is continued until a solid plate is formed.

Black-leg, blackleg. Add:
1. b. a. A potato disease (see quot. 1904). **b.** A disease that attacks cauliflowers.
1880 *Encycl. Brit.* XII. 281/1 To prevent the cauliflowers from getting the disease of 'black legs'. 1904 *Board Agric. & Fisheries* (1919) No. 117. 1 'Black-Leg' or Black Stem-Rot of Potatoes. (*Bacillus phytophthorus* or allied species.)
3. b. Used *attrib.* or as *adj.* to denote persons who are willing to work when others are on strike.
1890 *Daily News* 8 Sept. 6/1 There were hundreds of men ..being subjected to blackleg competition. 1894 *Ibid.* 31 May 7/5 There were two 'blackleg' cabs discovered on the rank. 1907 *Daily Chron.* 5 Sept. 1/7 The organisation of blackleg expeditions in this country to break up strikes abroad.

Blackleg (blæ·kleg), *v.* [f. Blackleg *sb.*]
a. *trans.* To take the place of (a worker who is on strike), thereby helping the employer to carry on his business and defeat the ends of the strike.
1897 *Daily News* 1 Sept. 2/4 They would be able to get many German engineers to 'blackleg' their English brethren. 1904 *Daily Chron.* 23 Apr. 5/7 The employers are permitted to persuade other workmen to 'blackleg' the men on strike.
fig. 1893 *Daily News* 10 July 5/2 Is it fair to 'blackleg' these industrious men, as it were,..and adapt their researches to the needs and purposes of romance? 1906 G. B. Shaw in *Fabian News* XVII. 2/2 One result is that the dead dramatist blacklegs the live one: Shakespeare can charge no royalty. 1927 *Daily Tel.* 6 Sept. 7/3 Mr. Wilson's record was a brilliant one, but he was now blacklegging the trade union movement.
b. *absol.* To act or work as a blackleg. *To blackleg it*: to return to work before a strike is settled (said of a trade-union workman).
1888 *Baltimore Her.* 6 May (Farmer) Knights of Labor who had determined to blackleg it, regardless of the jeers and threats of their companions. 1892 *Chambers's Jrnl.* 17 Feb. 98/1 Volunteers were also obliged..to satisfy the leaders that they never 'black-legged' in any Australian strike. 1907 *Daily Chron.* 9 Mar. 6/6 If the alternative is to 'blackleg' or to starve.
So **Blacklegging** *vbl. sb.* [partly from Blackleg *sb.*]
1839 Thackeray *Misc., Capt. Rook* (1856) II. 454 Blacklegging is as bad a trade as can be. 1909 H. G. Wells *Ann Veronica* x, It's a sort of blacklegging to want to have a life of one's own.

Black list, *sb.* Add:
1. (More recent examples, and of wider use.)
1788 Gibbon *Decl. & F.* xlviii, His memory was stored with a black list of enemies and rivals. 1841 *2nd Rep. Bookbinders' Consol. Union*. 1886 Ld. Walsingham, etc. *Shooting* (Badm. Libr.) xii. (1891) 274 Vermin...To begin with the first or 'black list'. 1913 'Ascott R. Hope' *An Old Friend* xi. in *Half & Half Tragedy* 261 Running into the arms of New Janie, who had me down on his black-list. 1920 *Nature* 27 May 392/2 A chapter is devoted to beasts which the author would place in a black list as having many undesirable proclivities.
b. *Naut.* A list of delinquents to whom extra duty is assigned as a punishment. Also, the punishment of being put on the black list.
1837 *United Service Jrnl.* II. 10 The cleaning, polishing, and black-list methods of wasting time. 1902 Sir W. Kennedy *Sport in Navy* 76 Ten days black list for the boat's crew for not giving way. 1914 Ld. Chas. Beresford *Mem.* I. 120 Such a process [*sc.* spit-and-polish system] involves perpetual extra bother and worry and black-list.
c. A list of persons convicted as habitual drunkards under the Licensing Act of 1902. Hence **Black-lister**, one who is put on the black list.
[Cf. 1902 *Act 2 Edw. VII* c. 28 § 6 [Habitual drunkards] Whether an order of detention is made or not, the court shall order that notice of the conviction, with such particulars as may be prescribed by a Secretary of State, be sent to the police authority (within the meaning of the Police Act, 1890) for the police area in which the court is situate.] 1903 *Daily Chron.* 7 Jan. 5/2 A..suitable word is wanted by magistrates..to denote a drunkard on the 'black list' under the new Act...The word 'blacklister' is one that readily occurs. 1903 *Ibid.* 19 Jan. 2/7 The first number of the 'Black List', issued under the new Licensing Act, was sent out from Scotland-yard on Saturday. 1904 *Ibid.* 16 Feb. 6/7 It was suggested that on the approach of a known 'black-lister' the police should give warning to the publican.
d. (*a*) An employers' list of trade-union workmen whom, as such, it is undesirable to employ. (*b*) A trade-union list of employers for whom their members are instructed not to work.
1888 *Atlantic Monthly* Nov. 611/2 He had got his name taken off from the black-list. 1888 *Encycl. Brit.* XXIII. 786/2 The..dreaded weapon known as the 'black list', by which combinations of employers..drove employees inclined to 'agitation' out of employment. 1923 J. D. Hackett *Labor Terms* in *Management Engineering* May, *Blacklist*, a list of union workmen circulated by employers to prevent such workers from being hired.

Black-list, *v.* Add quots. Also **Black-listing** *vbl. sb.*; also *attrib.* **Black-listed** *ppl. a.*
1888 *Atlantic Monthly* Nov. 608/1 The manufacturers.. had retaliated for some 'labor troubles'..by 'black-listing' about thirty men. *Ibid.*, Mr. H. informed us that he was a 'black-listed' man. *Ibid.* 608/2 The increase of evil in the world thus resulting from the black-listing scheme. 1892 *Pall Mall Gaz.* 29 Nov. 7/2 There are heavy penalties, too, for black-listing, or in any other way trying to induce persons to leave their employment [in Russia]. 1898 *Westm. Gaz.* 15 Nov. 7/3 They have black-listed me, and I will black-list them, unless they make it worth my while to keep quiet. 1899 *Daily News* 18 Jan. 4/5 The Plasterers' Union ..prohibiting their members from working for certain black-listed firms. 1902 *Encycl. Brit.* XXX. 105/2 There are, nevertheless, statutes aimed at..the prevention of intimidation, coercion, boycotting, and blacklisting. 1903 *Westm. Gaz.* 8 Jan. 7/2 A stoker in the Royal Navy, who has been black-listed for several weeks as a deserter. 1909 *Ibid.* 29 Jan. 9/1 Another of the black-listed M.P.'s..whose local association..withdrew its support from him owing to his Free Trade principles.

Blackly, *adv.* Add quots. for additional uses:
1876 Ruskin *Fors Clav.* lxix, A perfect example of the special type of youthful blackguard now developing generally in England; more or less blackly pulpous and swollen in all the features. 1894 H. Nisbet *Bush Girl's Rom.* 195 Mysterious ledges high up, which yawned blackly at the spectator below. 1898 H. S. Salt in *Dict. Nat. Biog.* LVI. 256/2 His writings are blackly pessimistic in the main. 1900 H. Lawson *Over Sliprails* 27 He went and stood before the fire..and looked blackly at a print against the wall before his face.

Blackmailed (blæ·kmēɪ·l'd), *ppl. a.* [f. Blackmail *v.* + -ed¹.] That is subjected to blackmail; also *absol.* (with *the*) the person on whom blackmail is levied.
1895 *Westm. Gaz.* 18 Feb. 2/1 There must be a distinct threat, a direct menace of the blackmailed by the blackmailer. 1898 *Ibid.* 10 June 6/1 The blackmailer naturally keeps his own counsel as well as the money, and the blackmailed submits in silence.

Black man.
1. A man having a black or very dark skin.
1591 [see Black *a.* 1 c]. 1738 F. Moore *Trav. Africa* 102 After which came on Shore the Captain, four Writers, one Apprentice,..and one Black Man. 1820 *Hist. N. Amer.* II. 10 Two slaves, the one a black man, a native of the place. 1894 F. A. Steel *Potter's Thumb* iv, He wondered ..what certain politicians at home would say to this candid distrust of the black man.
2. An evil spirit; also, the evil one, the devil; also, a fictitious spirit or bogey invoked in order to terrify children.
[1591 in Pitcairn *Crim. Trials Scotl.* (1833) I. 246 Þe Dewill start vp in þe pulpett, lyke ane mekill blak man, with ane blak baird stikand out lyke ane gettis baird.] 1658 tr. *Bergerac's Satyr. Char.* xii. 48, I send the Goblins..the nightbats,..the black men. 1851 *Fraser's Mag.* Feb. 240/2 'The foreigner', who is to the farmers what the black man and the sweep of nurse-maids are to children. 1861 G. Meredith *Evan Harrington* iii, Rich as Crœsus, and as wicked as the black man below! 1873 J. Ogg *Willie Waly* 123 (E.D.D.) Nor will the black man get ye. 1878 *Folk-Lore Rec.* I. 19 What nights of misery does that name, the black man, bring back to my memory! 1886 *W. Somerset Word-bk.*, *Black-man*, a terrible object; a bogy; a nursery terror. (Very com.) Now you be good chillern, else the black-man 'll come down the chimley arter ee.
3. A local equivalent of *Blackmaster.
1921 *Dict. Occupational Terms* (1927) § 925 Undertaker; blackman (Lancashire).

Black Maria.
1. A prison van for the conveyance of prisoners.
1874 *Slang Dict.* 1877 *Five Years' Penal Servitude* i. 60 The usual black Marias, some four or five of which were drawn up in the prison yard. 1880 G. R. Sims *Three Brass Balls* xvii. (1882) 103 Black Maria, the prison van, stands waiting at the door. 1924 *Punch* 17 Sept. 309 A Black Maria containing twelve prisoners.
2. A name used by soldiers in the war of 1914–18 for a German gun shell that on bursting emitted volumes of dense smoke, and for a German gun.
1914 *Scotsman* 12 Oct. 10/5 The 16-inch 'Black-Maria' shells of the heaviest German artillery. 1916 Ld. E. Hamilton *First 7 Div.* (1917) 139 The enemy were all this time steadily outranging our artillery with its big eleven-inch guns, popularly known as 'Black Marias'. 1919 *War-Slang* in *Athenæum* 11 July 583/2 For high or low velocity German shells, as substitutes for 'marmite', the British soldier came out with 'coalbox', 'Black Maria', 'Jack Johnson', 'heavy stuff'.

Black mass. [Mass *sb.*¹] A mass for the dead, at which the vestments and drapings are black. Also, a travesty of the rite used in the cult of Satanism.
1896 A. E. Waite *Devil-worship in France* 4 To say.. that Black Masses are celebrated..will not enhance the credibility or establish the intelligence of the speaker. 1904 Rolfe *Hadrian the Seventh* (1929) 61 My first Mass must be a black mass, Excellency.

Blackmaster (blæ·kmɑ̄stəɹ). [Black *sb.* 5.] A funeral furnisher, an undertaker.
1901 *Daily Chron.* 14 May 12/2 To Blackmasters and Undertakers. 1904 *Ibid.* 12 Nov. 6/7 'What is a blackmaster?'..'That's a well-known term in London', said the applicant, 'and means an undertaker'. 1905 *Ibid.* 11 Feb. 9/3 Goodwill of a Black Master's Business.

Black-neb. Add:
3. = *Blacknob.
1887 *Scott. Leader* 7 Oct. 4 Hundreds of men and women met the police and blacknebs.

Blacknob (blæ·knǫb). *Sc.* [prob. f. Black *a.* (after Black-leg 3) + Nob *sb.*⁶ Cf. Knobstick 2.] A blackleg.
a 1889 *Scotsman* (Cent. Dict.), Reports were submitted from the various works, which showed that all the men employed by the iron companies were on strike, with the exception of six black-nobs. 1890 Farmer *Slang*.

Black oak. *U.S.* [Black *a.* 6.] One or other of several North American species of oak having a dark foliage or bark. Also *attrib.*
1659 *Portsmouth* (R. I.) *Rec.* 377 Fortie fower acres of land..bounded..with a littel black Oake. 1671 *Rec. Providence* (R. I.) I. 25 So to range to a small black oake Tree, which is also marked. 1699 *Rec. Derby* (Conn.) 207 The est corner is a black oak buch upon a rock. 1723 *Rec. Providence* (R. I.) IX. 69 Thence south fifteene degrees East ten Rods to a black oake pole. 1817 S. R. Brown *Western Gaz.* 12 The trees post oak, white and black oak. 1829 J. F. Cooper *Wish-ton-wish* iii. 39 Walls that were wainscoted in the black-oak of the country. 1837 J. M. Peck *Gaz. Illinois* I. 18 Of oaks there are several species, as..black oak of several varieties. 1868 *Rep. U. S. Commissioner Agric.* (1869) 100 The larva of our native *Centronopus calcaratus* (Lec.) inhabits black-oak stumps. 1882 *Econ. Geol. Illinois* II. 105 Some regular post-oak flats..covered with post oak and black jack, and a few black-oak. 1884 W. Miller *Plant-n.* 238 *Quercus Robur*, Black Oak, Common Oak.

Black-poll. *U.S.* [Black *a.* 1.] A North American warbler (*Dendroica striata*), the male of which has a black head when in full plumage. In full, *black-poll warbler*.
1785 Pennant *Arct. Zool.* II. 401 Black-poll Warbler.. Inhabits during summer, Newfoundland and New York. 1868 *Amer. Naturalist* II. 180 It is very quick, scarcely less so than the black-poll. 1872 Coues *Key N. Amer. Birds* 100 Blackpoll Warbler..*Dendrœca striata*. 1893 Torrey *Footpath-Way* 6 We..were in the old forest listening to bay-breasted warblers, Blackburnians, black-polls and so on.

Black-pot. Delete † *Obs.* and add:
2. A black pudding. (Cf. Pot *sb.*¹ 8.) *local.*
1825 Jennings *Observ. Dial. W. Eng.*, *Black-pot*, black-pudding. 1880 Hardy *Trumpet-Major* xvi, Seventy rings of black-pot. 1891 — *Tess* I. i, I should like for supper,—well, lamb's fry if they can get it; and if they can't, black-pot. 1895 — *Jude* VI. viii, I shall have to make black-pot and sausages.
3. Coarse Danish crockery-ware exposed to dense smoke in baking as a substitute for glazing.
1889 *Cent. Dict.* 1902 in *Cassell's Suppl.*

Black rubric. An inaccurate term for the declaration explanatory of the rubric concerning kneeling at the reception of the Holy Communion, which was first inserted at the end of the Communion Office in the Book of Common Prayer of 1552 (omitted in 1559, and restored in 1662).
The term can have arisen only after the practice of printing the Prayer Book rubrics in red became current in the 19th century, when the Declaration on Kneeling was distinguished by being printed in black.
1866 J. H. Blunt *Annot. Bk. Com. Prayer* 199 They retained the protest against Transubstantiation, whilst they removed all risk of the Declaration, or 'Black rubric' as it was sometimes called. 1877 E. Daniel *Prayer-Book* 333 The Black Rubric explains the intention of the rubric, which prescribes that communicants should receive the Holy Communion kneeling. 1892 C. Whitaker *Stud. Aid Prayer Bk.* 94.

Blackshirt, Black Shirt. [tr. It. *camicia nera*.] A black shirt as the distinctive mark of the uniform of the Fascist army; hence *transf.* and *gen.* = *Fascist.
1923 Sir P. Phillips (*title*) The 'Red' Dragon and the Black Shirts. 1924 *Contemp. Rev.* Sept. 300 The Blackshirts were discounted as 'extremists' and 'reactionaries'. 1927 *Daily Express* 12 Aug. 7 You were in plain clothes and I took you for a Blackshirt.

Blacksmith. Add: **b.** *Blacksmith's* (U.S. *blacksmith*) *shop*, a smithy.
(*a*) 1781 in *Maryland Hist. Mag.* V. 130 They came on board, took out the prisoners and carrying them up to a blacksmith's shop, there had them put in irons. 1813 Paulding *J. Bull & Br. Jon.* xxiii. (ed. 2) 123 At the taverns, blacksmith's shops, and..at the church-doors. 1849 F. Douglas *Life* 94 Fred, go to the blacksmith's shop and get me a new punch. 1872 Eggleston *Hoosier Schoolm.* xxix. 195 He got to the blacksmith's shop. (*b*) 1816 U. Brown *Jrnl.* in *Maryland Hist. Mag.* XI. 151 This morning..carrys Cumberland to the Blacksmith Shop; Gets him shod. 1835 Paulding *Hist. Uncle Sam* 186 Then another chap..set up a blacksmith shop. 1877 Habberton *Jericho Road* xvi. 145 He walked so fast that the boys at the blacksmith shop stopped work to stare. 1889 *Harper's Mag.* Aug. 390/1 Perhaps he had better ride over to the blacksmith shop.

Blacksmithery (blæ·ksmiþəri). *U.S.* [f. Blacksmith + -ery.] Blacksmith's work.
1869 *Overland Monthly* III. 10 In North Carolina, as in the North, blacksmithery, wagon-making, coopery, and other sorts of hard-handed industry, were in noisy blast. 1889 *Advance* (Chicago) 21 Mar. 229 Carpentry, blacksmithery, wheel and carriage making are also chief industries for the Indian on the plain.

Black-snake. 2. *U.S.* (Earlier examples.)
1869 J. Ross Browne *Adv. Apache Country* 40 He would start up with a sudden yell of anguish, whirl his black-snake, and let fly at the mules. 1873 J. H. Beadle *Undevel. West* v. 98 The writer..wielding a big-bellied 'blacksnake' over the backs of six mules.
Hence **Blacksnake** *v. trans.*, to flog with a black-snake whip.
a 1875 'Mark Twain' *Sketches* Wks. XIX. 360, I lay I'll blacksnake you within an inch of your life.

Black-tail. Add: **3.** The black-tailed deer (see below). Also *attrib.* with *deer*, *buck*. *U.S.*
1871 Schele de Vere *Americanisms* (1872) 371 The variety found on the Pacific coast (*Cervus columbianus*) is more commonly designated as the Black-tail Deer, from the black tip to its tail. 1887 I. R. *Ranch Life Montana* 107 With the certainty of a good day's sport..and a possibility of white and black tail deer. 1890 L. C. D'Oyle *Notches* 66 It was the best place out for elk and 'black-tail'. 1895 *Outing* (U.S.) XXVII. 45/2 We..had two large black-tail bucks and a doe.

Black-tailed, *a.* [Black *a.* 18.] Having a black tail. *Black-tailed deer*, the Columbian deer (*Cervus columbianus*), or the mule-deer (*Cervus macrotis*) of North America. *Black-tailed godwit*: see Godwit.
1807 P. Gass *Jrnl.* 40 The black-tailed, or mule deer have much larger ears than the common deer and tails almost without hair, except at the end, where there is a bunch of black hair. 1837 W. Irving *Capt. Bonneville* (1895) I. 33

In these..elevated regions they began to see the black-tailed deer, a species larger than the ordinary kind. 1845 De Smet *Oregon Missions* (1847) 134 The black-tailed roe-buck, as well as its red-tailed relative. 1863 Black tailed godwit [see Godwit]. 1867 Wood *Illustr. Nat. Hist.* 693 The Black-tailed Godwit. 1879 *Encycl. Brit.* X. 780/2 The Black-tailed Godwit, *Limosa ægocephala*.

Black-throat. *U.S.* [Black *a.* 1.] A black-throated warbler. In full, *black-throat warbler*.

1785 Pennant *Arct. Zool.* II. 399 Black-throat Warbler. ..Inhabits, during summer, Canada and other parts of America, to the south. 1902 S. E. White *Blazed Trail* xiii. 296 Wilson's warblers..pine creepers, black-throats..passed silently or noisily.

Black-throated, *a.* [Black *a.* 18.] Of various birds: Having a black throat.

1785 Pennant *Arct. Zool.* II. 363 Black-throated Bunting. ..Inhabits New York. 1860 [see Black *a.* 18]. 1858 *Amer. Naturalist* II. 172 The Black-throated Blue Warbler (*Dendroica Canadensis*) arrives..in May. 1870 *Ibid.* III. 189 The only other bird of interest seen east of this was the pretty Black-throated Finch. 1893 Torrey *Footpath-Way* 16, I..saw and heard only 12 kinds of birds...Canada warblers (near the base), black-throated blues, black-throated greens [etc.].

Black-wash, *sb.* Add: **3.** The opposite of Whitewash *sb.* 3. Also **Bla·ck-wa:shing** *vbl. sb.*

1859 Kingsley *Misc.* II. 48 To remove..the modern layers of 'black-wash', and to let the man himself, fair or foul, be seen. 1877 *Chambers's Jrnl.* 28 Apr. 258/2 A skilful counsel..using as much whitewash as he can for the accused, and applying plentiful blackwash to the witnesses for the prosecution. 1890 *Literary World* XLI. 388/1 By giving Cromwell another plentiful coating of blackwash. 1905 Candler (*title*) The Black-washing of Dante.

Black water.

1. A stream stained brown by the peat of the mosses from which it flows.

1676 Walton & Cotton *Compl. Angler* II. ii. 14 This River [Trent] from its head for a Mile or two is a black water. *Ibid.* 16 The River Wye..a black water too at the Fountain... Derwent, a black water too.

2. A disease incident to sheep and cows.

1800 Tuke *Agric. N. Riding Yorks.* 272 There is another disorder to which lambs are liable in autumn; it is called the black-water. 1825 Loudon *Encycl. Agric.* § 6263 The black water is only the aggravated and latter stages of [red water]. 1879 J. Lucas in *Zoologist* Ser. III. III. 355 Many [sheep] die in cold nights, when they contract a disease known as 'blackwater'.

3. In full, *blackwater fever*, a tropical fever to which chiefly white people are subject, characterized by a brown or blue-black colour of the urine.

1884 J. F. Easmon (*title*) The nature and treatment of blackwater fever. 1897 Mary Kingsley *W. Africa* 645 Two extremely deadly forms of fever have come into notice here, malarial typhoid and blackwater. 1926 *Blackw. Mag.* Nov. 663/1 The doctor had died three weeks before of blackwater.

4. *attrib.* Producing water of a black colour.

1848 Buckley *Iliad* 151 Agamemnon arose, shedding tears like a black-water fountain.

Black-wood. Add: **b.** Evergreen trees collectively. (Cf. *black growth*, *Black *a.* 19.) *U.S.*

1871 Schele de Vere *Americanisms* (1872) 420 Black Wood is, in the Northern States, used as a generic term for the evergreens, hemlock, pine, spruce, and fir.

Bladder, *sb.* **10.** Add:

bladder lard, lard put up for sale in bladders, used spec. as the trade name for lard of the best quality; **bladder worm,** the larva of a tapeworm in its encysted state; a hydatid.

1872 *Eng. Mech.* 11 Oct. 82/3 The fourth [sample] (a bladder lard) contained 10 per cent. of water. 1877 Huxley *Anat. Inv. Anim.* iv. 211 A cystic worm, or bladder-worm. 1888 *Encycl. Brit.* XXIII. 49/2 The nurses develop from little round six-hooked embryos in a more or less complicated fashion as so-called 'bladder-worms'.

Blade, *sb.* **12.** Add:

blade-consonant *Phonetics*, a consonant formed with the blade of the tongue; also **blade-point** (see quot.); **blade-spring,** a form of spring used to hold piston rings in place; **blade work** *Oarsmanship*, work done with the blade of the oar.

1890 Sweet *Primer of Spoken Engl.* 8 The *blade-consonant *s* is formed with the 'blade' or flattened point of the tongue; if the tongue is retracted from this position, and the point raised, we get the *blade-point consonant *ʃ* in 'fish'. 1863 Campin *Mech. Engin.* 130 Four arms, which serve a double purpose, connecting the boss with the top and bottom of the piston, and carrying at their extremities the *blade-springs. 1905 *Daily Chron.* 30 Mar. 6/7 Their *blade work is not pretty, the finish not being clean, and the feather frequently under water.

Bladeless (blēⁱ·dlės), *a.* [f. Blade *sb.* + -less.] Without or lacking a blade.

1857 *Blackw. Mag.* Oct. 486/1 Only the bladeless [*i.e.* grassless] rocks rang hollow mocking replies to his despairing 'Allah!' 1896 J. A. Mitchell *Amos Judd* viii. 161 A bladeless jack-knife. 1927 *Glasgow Herald* 16 Apr. 9 A bladeless safety razor.

Blado (blā·do). *Typogr.* A fount of type named after Antonio *Blado*, of Asola, printer-publisher at Rome 1516–67.

1928 *Scholartis Press Catal.* July, The text being in 16 point Blado.

Blah (blā). *U.S.* [? Fanciful.] Pretentions talk or writing; blague. Also *blah-blah*.

1926 *N. Y. Times Book Rev.* 22 Aug. 4 There is usually a disgusting blah of important high-sounding words. 1927 in *Observer* 10 July 28/1 England isn't fooling anyone with so much 'blah' about the world's greatest tournament.

Blake, the name of the inventor of a sewing-machine, as in *Blake-sewn*, whence *Blake-sewer*, etc.

1895 *Daily News* 20 Mar. 6/7 A Levant goat quarter, whole satin golosh, blake sewn. 1921 *Dict. Occup. Terms* (1927) § 414 *Machine operator, Blake; Blake sewer, Blake sole sewer*, a sole attacher who stitches sole of boot or shoe on to insole..with a Blake sewing machine, i.e. heavy sewing machine worked by power.

Blame, *v.* Add: **7.** *dial.* and *U.S.* Used as an imprecation: **a.** In the imperative mood.

1835 Longstreet *Georgia Scenes* iii. 26 'Blame my buttons', said Blossom, 'if I like them eyes!' 1865 W. S. Banks *Wakefield Words* 8 'Blame it' is equivalent to 'confound it'. 1875 Parish *Sussex Gloss.* 19 Blame ye! ye be always at something. 1876 'Mark Twain' *Tom Sawyer* vii. 67 Blame it, I ain't going to stir him much. 1886 *Harper's Mag.* June 52/2 Blame me if them ain't the darnedest beans *I* ever seen!

b. In passive, in phr. (*I'm*) *blamed if* (etc.).

1867 R. Young *Robin Hill* 11 (E. D. D.) I'm bleamed if we beant in a mess. 1876 'Max Adeler' *Elbow Room* xv, Blamed if I haven't forgotten that word. 1883 S. K. Hocking *Dick's Fairy* ii. 11 Blamed if you're not a pretty little gal, anyhow. *c* 1904 H. R. Martin *Tillie* 322 I'm blamed if I dare advise you.

c. as *adv.* = *Blamed 2.

1843 R. Carlton *New Purchase* xvii. 134 'Blame close, stranger,' said the old hero. *a* 1861 T. Winthrop *John Brent* viii. 85 It's a free country, and I shall say what I blame please. 1876 'Mark Twain' *Tom Sawyer* vii. 67 He's my tick and I'll do what I blame please with him or die! 1904 C. H. Lorimer *Old Gorgon Graham* 160 You know blame well that I don't understand any French.

d. as *adj.* = *Blamed 1.

1886 J. C. Harris in *Century Mag.* Jan. 427/1, I got a dockyment here that 'll fetch you a blame sight quicker'n your dockyment 'll fetch me. *a* 1909 'O. Henry' *Roads of Destiny* xxi. 351 You're a blame Yankee, ain't you? 1911 R. O. Saunders *Col. Todhunter* i. 5 That's nobody's blame business but mine. 1913 Kipling *Diversity of Creatures* (1917) 263 The blame thing jarred off—spiteful as a rattler!

Blamed (blēⁱmd), *ppl. a.* and *adv. dial.* and *U.S.* [Cf. *Blame *v.* 7.]

1. *ppl. a.* Confounded.

1840 Haliburton *Clockm.* Ser. III. vi. 84 Yes, John Bull is a blamed blockhead. 186. Will Carleton *Farm Ballads* (1873) 6 And so that blamed cow-creature was always a-comin' up. 1876 'Mark Twain' *Tom Sawyer* ix, Drunk, same as usual, likely—blamed old rip! 1904 G. H. Lorimer *Old Gorgon Graham* 200 They've an ache or a pain in every blamed joint.

2. *adv.* Confoundedly, excessively.

1845 Mrs. Kirkland *Western Clearings* (1846) 70, I wasn't a goin' to let Dean know; because he'd ha' thought himself so blam'd cunning. *c* 1845 Paulding *Noble Exile* 139, I advised you not to answer that invitation..but you're so blamed fierce, you would do it. 1876 'Mark Twain' *Tom Sawyer* viii 79 Well, it's blamed mean—that's all. 1876 'Max Adeler' *Elbow Room* xv, The pistol looked so blamed dangerous when I cocked it that I changed my mind.

Blanch, *v.*¹ **1. c.** Add: *spec.* in coining money.

1883 *Encycl. Brit.* XVI. 489/2 The removal of a small portion of the alloying metal in this way constitutes 'blanching' or 'pickling' the coin.

Blanco (blæ·ŋko). [Trade name, f. F. *blanc* white.] A white preparation for whitening accoutrements. Also *khaki blanco*, applied to a similar preparation of khaki colour. Hence **Blanco** *v. trans.*, to treat with blanco.

1895 in *Army & Navy Co-op. Soc. Price-list.* 1906 *Daily Chron.* 30 Mar. 3/7 The sleeves get covered with 'blanco' off the belt. 1924 *Glasgow Herald* 3 Mar. 10, I was reminded of Army days and the power of a careful use of the blanco brush. 1912 E. Wallace *Pte. Selby* viii. 75 One unhappy mortal, 'warned' for guard..was lugubriously 'blancoing' his straps.

Blandander (blændæ·ndəɹ), *v. colloq.* [Jingling formation on the stem of Blandish *v.*] *trans.* To tempt by blandishment (*into*); to cajole.

1888 Kipling *Soldiers Three* (1895) 70 I've blandanthered thim through the night somehow. 1898 *Link* 3/1 When you bullied and blandandered me into learning how to ride. 1914 *Times Lit. Suppl.* 4 June 267/2 [European diplomacy] refused to be blandandered by King Nicholas.

Bla·ndishingly, *adv.* [f. Blandishing *ppl. a.* + -ly ².] With blandishment.

1861 Meredith *Evan Harrington* iv, Blandishingly she smiled on him.

Blanditude. Delete † *Obs.* and add:

1922 *Observer* 16 Apr. 10/5 Then Mr. Lloyd George rose ..in wise fun and paternal blanditude.

Blank, *sb.* Add:

5. c. *In blank* [after F. *en blanc*]: with blank spaces for the filling in of details.

1842 Stephen *Comm. Laws Eng.* II. II. v. 164 A bill, payable to order, is indorsed in *blank* by the payee. 1858 J. W. Smith *Law of Bills*, etc. 27 Another way in which the holder of a bill or note indorsed to him *in blank* may transfer it without incurring personal liability, is by writing over the indorser's signature the words, 'Pay A. B. or order'. 1882 Bithell *Counting-ho. Dict.* 45 Bills and Notes of this description are said to be drawn 'in Blank'.

6. Delete † and add: Now chiefly *U.S.*, freq. with defining term.

1805 D. McClure *Diary* (1899) 83 Dr. Wheelock..had given us blanks, for bills of Exchange, on the School's funds, in Scotland. 1845 J. J. Hooper *Taking Census* i. 151 Drawing our blanks from their case, we proceeded [etc.]. 1860 Holland *Miss Gilbert's Career* x. 181 You've had to write the whole of this. How long have we been out of blanks? 1904 P. H. Hanus *Mod. School* 128 By means of question blanks sent to the parents, much information..is secured by the teachers. 1904 *N. Y. Times* 24 Nov. 1 The messages were always on regular telegraph blanks. 1905 *Atlantic Monthly* Nov. 716, I wrote a story. It was returned with a printed blank that decapitated my hopes.

9. b. A sheet of glass upon which a subject is to be worked.

1899 *Daily News* 14 June 9/1 In the blowing of the opal glass surface of the 'blank' a blister or bubble may be caused.

13. A zero score in a game. *U.S.*

1888 *Outing* (U.S.) May 119/2 The tenth innings had seen both sides retire for blanks.

Blank, *a.* Add: *Cards.* In Sixty-six, a form of Bézique. (See quot.)

1895 Manson *Sporting Dict.*, *Blank*, a card in hand is said to be blank when there is no other card of the same suit in hand with it. The term is also applied to a king and queen of the same suit, in which case the twenty of that suit is blank.

4. c. Also const. *of*.

1924 A. E. W. Mason *House of Arrow* viii. 97 Hanaud's eyes..were blank of all expression.

Blank, *v.* Add: *Cards.* (Cf. *Blank *a.*)

1884 'Cavendish' *Whist* (ed. 14) 100 It is dangerous to unguard an honour, or to blank an ace.

Blank ¶.

1. Used as a verbal expression of the dash employed as substitute for a proper name, or for something which one is unable or unwilling to specify.

1773 Goldsm. *Stoops to Conq.* v. I, Anthony Lumpkin, Esquire, of blank place. 1818 Scott *Rob Roy* xi, A dispensation..to Diana Vernon to marry *Blank* Osbaldistone, Esq. 1837 Dickens *Pickw.* xxiv, Here's my authority. Blank Tupman, blank Pickwick—against the peace of our sufferin Lord the King. 1861 *Two Cosmos* v. ix. II. 83 She was married, though—blank—years younger than Miss Lambert. 1888 *Co-operative News* 24 Mar. 266 Our adjoining neighbours at blank—the place shall be nameless.

2. Used euphemistically as a verbal representation of a dash put instead of an oath or profane word. So (as adjs. or advs.) **Blankety** (blæ·ŋkėti), which represents an adj. derivative, such as *bloody*; less freq. **Blanky** (blæ·ŋki), rarely **Blanked** (blæŋkt).

1873 Reade *Simpleton* xxiii, Blank him! that is just like him. 1876 Bret Harte *Gabriel Conroy* vi. vi, Blank me, if she was inclined to show some attention to Colonel Starbottle. *Ibid.* vii, But what in blank are you waiting for? 1888 *Troy Daily Times* 3 Feb. (Farmer) He had known vessels to be hindered thirty days; yes, even three months, by that blankety blankety bar! 1888 *Owosso* (Mich.) *Press* Apr. (Farmer) 'I'm..Just as good as dead,' said he, 'or you wouldn't kick that dog in that way with safety. Not by a blankety blank blank sight.' 1889 *Liverpool Echo* 5 Aug. 3/2 The veteran lawyer who compared untruthful witnesses as liars, blanked liars, and experts. 1892 *Photogr. Ann.* II. 42 The blankety blankness that ensues when the tyro..finds that he has forgotten..his tripod top, &c.! 1896 *Daily News* 15 Feb. 5/1 He..is called 'a blanky capitalist'. 1900 H. Lawson *On Track* 31 And do you think I'd tell you a blanky lie? *Ibid.* 40 'What does he want to do that for?'. 'To get it blanky well analysed! You ass!' 1900 *Westm. Gaz.* 25 May 2/1 Then he lay back, swearing at the blankety blank young blanker. *a* 1904 S. E. White *Blazed Trail Stories* iii. 45 What's good enough fer th' boss is good enough fer any blank blanked scaler. 1908 Maud Diver *Great Amulet* xviii, Colonel Stanham Buckley..inquired picturesquely of a passing official when the blank this blankety blank train was supposed to start. 1914 Locke *Fortunate Youth* i, What cared he for the blankety little blanks who gibed at him?

Blank book, blank-book. *U.S.* [Blank *a.* 2.] A book of clean writing-paper in which to make entries, keep accounts, etc. Also *Comb.*

1768 in *Maryland Hist. Mag.* X. 132 To a Seven Quire Blank Book for a Register. 1779 *New-Jersey Jrnl.* 12 Oct., Advt. in *N. J. Archives* Ser. II. III. 676 Blank books. 1802 in C. Cist *Cincinnati* 193 For a blank-book to record ordinances. 1831 *Boston Directory* Advt. 18 Blank book manufacturers. 1841 in C. Cist *Cincinnati* Advt., Paper Ruler and blank book manufacturer. *Ibid.*, Every description of blank books, ruled to any pattern. 1886 S. W. Mitchell *R. Blake* ii. (1895) 14 He spent a few minutes more over the details of daily duty set out in a little blank-book.

Blanked: see *Blank ¶.

Blanket, *sb.* Add:

2. c. (See quot. 1859.) Hence *attrib.* = blanket-wearing. *U.S.*

1859 Bartlett *Dict. Amer.* (ed. 2), *Blanket*, a term used distinctively for the clothing of an Indian. To say of one's father or mother that they 'wore the blanket', implies that they were but half civilized Indians. Western. 1891 Marah E. Ryan *Told in Hills* III. iii. 166 You should hear her talking Chinook to a blanket brave. 1905 A. Adams *Outlet* 81 On our left was the reservation of three blanket tribes of Indians.

d. *attrib.*, with the meaning 'that wears a blanket', as *blanket Kaffir*; hence, by extension, *blanket vote* (S. Afr.), the Kaffir vote.

1892 Mitford *'Tween Snow & Fire* xxxvi, There were a few muttered jeers about..getting into the Assembly on the strength of 'blanket votes'. 1904 *Daily Chron.* 13 May 3/3 The 'compound' system is essentially degrading even for 'blanket' Kaffirs.

e. **Army blanket,** a coarse, stout, grey blanket made for use in the army. **Navy blanket,** a heavy, white, woollen blanket used in the navy.

1909 *Cent. Dict.* Suppl.

f. '*Com.* Any piece of cloth used as a sample by which to sell goods. *U.S.*'

1895 *Funk's Stand. Dict.*

7. *blanket-hidden, -tossed* adjs.; *blanket-tossing*; **blanket fish** *U.S.* (see quot.); **blanket flower,** popular name of the Gaillardia; **blanket pack,** a pedestrian traveller's kit with his blanket rolled about it; **blanket roll** *Mil.* (*U.S.*), a soldier's equipment of blanket and kit made into a roll for use on active service instead of the knapsack and blanket bag; **blanket shawl** *U.S.*, a thick woollen shawl; **blanket sheet** *U.S.*, a newspaper in folio form; also *attrib.*; **blanket stitch,** a buttonhole stitch worked on the edge of a blanket or other material too thick to be hemmed.

1870 *Amer. Naturalist* IV. 597 Large numbers of '*blanket fish' (a species of *Thymallus*) were to be seen ascending the small rivers. 1903 Kipling *Five Nations* 131 The funerals through the market (*Blanket-hidden bodies). 1920 *Chambers's Jrnl.* Apr. 220/1 Only one small tin of corned beef remained in his *blanket-pack. 1899 *Scribner's Mag.* XXV. 27/1 These men..were..making ready to disembark, carrying their *blanket-rolls and rifles with them. 1837 *Southern Lit. Messenger* III. 660 The *blanket shawls with their varied coloring looked pretty and comfortable. 1843 S. Marg. Fuller *Summer on Lakes* 41 England sat up all night wrapped in her blanket shawl. 1888 *Encycl. Brit.* XXIII. 765/2 The old '*blanket-sheet' newspaper, cumbrous to handle and slow in all its ways. 1889 *Cent. Dict.* (citing *Amer. Bookmaker*), *Blanket-sheet*, a large newspaper in folio form. 1882 Caulfeild & Saward *Dict. Needlework*, *Blanket Stitch, used in crewel work and other embroideries for edging woollen, linen, and silk materials, and for forming ornamental lines. It is a variety of button-hole worked wide apart in long loops. 1881 Duffield *Don Quixote* I. 374 The *blanket-tossed Squire. *Ibid.* 369 Never a word did he say of the *blanket tossing.

b. Used adjectivally in the sense of 'covering', 'inclusive'. *U.S.*

1896 *Congress Rec.* May 4783 Messrs. Morgan & Co. had given a blanket bid to cover the whole amount...Under the terms of the blanket bid, which covered all bids [etc.]. 1903 G. W. A. Luckey *Training Sec. Teachers* 254 There should be no blanket certificates issued. 1905 *N. Y. Even. Post* 12 May 5 The Bureau of Construction..has received a 'blanket' order to do everything which is absolutely necessary. 1910 *Outlook* 11 June 273 Should Congress pass a blanket law making all Porto Ricans citizens of the United States.

Blanket, *v.* Add:

1. (Examples of fig. use.)

1905 Holman Hunt *Pre-Raph.* I. 478 The heavy mist blanketing the uprising shore. 1895 Kipling *2nd Jungle Bk., Red Dog* 198 The face of the water was blanketed with wild bees buzzing sullenly and stinging all they found. 1897 — *Capt. Cour.* 106 Just before the fog blanketed the sea once again. 1910 Sir J. Simon in *Times* 11 Oct. 10/2 It was a free country, ..and he had no intention to blanket his opinion.

2. Also *fig.*

1903 *Weekly Dispatch* 1 Apr. 2 Lord Curzon's chief ambition has been to become Prime Minister, and he has been known to complain to his intimates that he has always been blanketed by Arthur Balfour, who was just a little ahead of him.

b. To interfere with (the gunfire of one's own fleet or squadron) by getting in or near their line of fire.

1909 in *Cent. Dict.* Suppl.

4. To supply with blankets; to furnish with blankets.

1874 *Contemp. Rev.* XXIII. 466 Schemes of clothing and blanketing whole districts. 1899 *Daily News* 21 July 8/6 The beds are amply blanketed hammocks.

5. *U.S. fig.* **a.** To include under one head or category.

1892 *N. Y. Law Jrnl.* in *Law Times* XCIII. 413/1 A bonâ fide immigrant..blanketed the aforesaid quarter-section with his own claim and the court held that the blanketer.. was *potior in jure*.

b. To suppress; to put in the shade.

1903 *N. Y. Sun* 6 Nov. 6 In this way the Republican campaign was blanketed. 1908 *Springfield Weekly Republ.* 17 Dec. 4 It so happened that Mr. Taft was completely blanketed by the San Francisco earthquake.

Blanket-coat. [Blanket *sb.* 2.] (See quot. 1871.) Also, one wearing a blanket-coat.

c 1805 J. J. Henry *Camp. agst. Quebec* (1812) 109 Having on a fine white blanket coat..made me, as it were, invisible in the snow. 1827 J. F. Cooper *Prairie* i, The buttons of his rude and soiled blanket-coat were of the glittering coinage of Mexico. 1837 R. M. Bird *Nick of Woods* I. 58 I'm for any man that insults me!..leather-breeches, green-shirt, or blanket-coat. 1871 Schele de Vere *Americanisms* (1872) 294 Mackinaw blankets..being very thick and well made,..served not only for beds but also for overcoats, which were called Blanket-Coats. 1888 T. Roosevelt in *Century Mag.* Oct. 834/2 A powerfully built trapper..who wore a gayly colored capote, or blanket-coat.

attrib. 1831 Mrs. Royall *Southern Tour* II. 125, I could not but admire the gallantry of..one of those blanket-coat stage drivers.

Blanketed, *ppl. a.* **1.** (Earlier U.S. example.)

1835 J. H. Ingraham *South-West* II. 176 His blanketed saddle is his cabriolet.

Blanket Indian. *U.S.* [Blanket *sb.* 2.] **a.** (See quot. 1859.) **b.** A semi-civilized Indian, who receives blankets and rations from government.

1859 Bartlett *Dict. Amer.* (ed. 2), *Blanket-Indian*, a wild Indian, whose principal article of dress is the blanket. 1875 *Congress. Rec.* Feb. 912/2 [This] argument applies to reservations made for what we call in the West 'blanket Indians'. 1886 *Ibid.* Mar. 2273/1 [The young Indians, leaving school] go back to barbarism, back to the tepee, back to the blanket Indians. What have you done to enable him to go back to anything but a blanket Indian? 1898 *Ibid.* Jan. 104/1 Even among Indians there are two parties. There is the 'hat' Indian and the 'blanket' Indian...The Indian who carries a bow and arrow and a tomahawk and wears a blanket is called a 'blanket' Indian. 1906 *Atlantic Monthly* Mar. 328/2 Only 26,000 blanket Indians are left in the United States.

Blanketing, *sb.* **1.** Add: Also, as a dress material.

1903 *Daily Chron.* 20 June 8/4 Wraps..made of fine cream blanketing with big sleeves brought into high cavalier cuffs. 1908 *Ibid.* 21 Sept. 7/2 The warm Witney blanketing..makes exceedingly cosy coats for girls.

5. The action of covering with, or as with, a blanket.

1896 *Pop. Sci. Monthly* L. 245 There's a blanketing of the earth's heat.

Blanketing (blæ·ŋkėtiŋ), *ppl. a.* [f. Blanket *v.* + -ing ².] That covers as with a blanket. Also *transf.*

1904 Farrer *Garden Asia* 244 The smoke descends densely upon the volcano in blanketing clouds. 1925 Joly *Surface-Hist. Earth* vi. 103 The blanketing effects of continental radioactivity.

Blanket(t)y, Blanky: see *Blank ¶.

Blast, *sb.* Add:

8. c. *Golf.* (Cf. *Blast *v.* 5 b.)

1927 *Daily Express* 29 Oct. 3/4, I described three kinds of shots which I employed from the sand: the blast, the chip, and..the cut shot.

10. **blast-lamp,** (*a*) see quot. 1884; (*b*) a lamp in which the flame is driven on to a surface by a current of air; a blow-lamp; **blast-pot** (see quot.).

1884 Knight *Dict. Mech.* Suppl., **Blast Lamp*, one with an artificially produced draft of air to aid combustion. 1902 Mrs. Barnes-Grundy *Thames Camp* 57 A benzoline blast lamp which would fetch off any varnish in the world. 1887 *Harper's Mag.* Apr. 670/2 Before the war only seven small furnaces—'blast-pots' they were called—having a total capacity of 20,000 tons, were in operation in all Tennessee.

Blast, *v.* Add:

5. b. *Golf. intr.* To hit a ball out of a bunker by an 'explosive' shot, causing it to jump up as if a mine had been exploded beneath it.

1927 *Daily Express* 29 Oct. 3/4 Here you are in a bunker.., the only thing you can do is blast.

10. freq. in imprecations in the imperative or optative form (for *God blast*...).

a 1634 Chapman *Revenge for Hon.* v, And thus I kiss'd my last breath. Blast you all. 1751 Fielding *Amelia* x. v, But, blast my reputation, if I had received such a letter, if I would not have searched the world to have found the writer. 1760–2 Goldsm. *Cit. W.* cv, 'Blast me!' cries Tibbs, 'if that be all, there is no need of paying for that.' 1824 Scott *St. Ronan's* viii, 'As I think, he laid hands on your body'... 'Hands,..no, blast him—not so bad as that neither.'

Blasted, *ppl. a.* **3.** Add: Also used adverbially.

1854 Mary J. Holmes *Tempest & Sunshine* xv. 204 Lord's sake be spry, for I'm blasted hungry. 1886 *Leslie's Pop. Monthly* Jan. XXI. 67/2 He's too blasted smart for an Indian.

Blasting, *vbl. sb.* Add:

6. **blasting cartridge,** a cartridge containing a blasting charge, usually exploded by electricity.

1889 *Cent. Dict.* 1899 *Westm. Gaz.* 1 June 4/1 Several cavalry horses have been injured by blasting cartridges exploded under their feet.

7. *Wireless Telegraphy.* (See quot. 1926.)

1926 S. O. Pearson *Dict. Wireless Techn. Terms*, *Blasting*, term used to denote the distortion which takes place in loud-speaker or telephone signals on extra loud notes, due to working beyond the straight portion of valve characteristic. 1928 *Observer* 29 Jan. 22/5 When the definite minimum level of sensitivity is given, so that the softer passages are not lost, heavy passages cause most distressing blasting.

Blastingly (bla·stiŋli), *adv.* [f. Blasting *ppl. a.* + -ly ².] In a shattering or withering manner.

1903 R. Langbridge *Flame & Flood* xvii, 'Really!' said Susette blastingly.

Blasto-. Add: **Blasto·phagine** *a.*, of or belonging to the *Blastophaga*, a genus of fig-insects; **Blasto·poral** *a.*, of or pertaining to the blastopore.

1921 *Brit. Mus. Return* 133 Notes on Fig Insects, including..a new *Blastophagine Genus. 1882 E. Ray Lankester in *Encycl. Brit.* XIV. 557 The ciliated 'planula'.. fixes itself, probably by the *blastoporal pole.

Blastogenesis (blæsto,dʒe·nėsis). *Biol.* [f. Blasto- + Genesis.]

1. Reproduction by gemmation or budding.

1889 in *Cent. Dict.*

2. The theory of the transmission of inherited characters by germ-plasm, as distinguished from 'pangenesis'.

1895 in *Funk's Standard Dict.*

Blastogenic (blæsto,dʒe·nik), *a. Biol.* [f. prec.: see *-genic.] Of or pertaining to blastogenesis; pertaining to origin from, or that originates in, the germ-cell or germ-plasm.

1889 Sir W. Turner in *Nature* 26 Sept. 531/1 Characters which are produced in the germ-plasm itself by natural selection, and all other characters which result from this latter cause, he names *blastogenic*. He further maintains that all blastogenic characters can be transmitted. 1893 tr. *A. Weismann's Germ-plasm* 174 The same is true as regards the formation of a new polype from a blastogenic cell and from an ovum. *Ibid.* 392 [I] contrast them [*sc.* 'somatogenic' characters] with the 'blastogenic' characters of an individual, or those which originate solely in the primary constituents of the germ.

Blastoid (blæ·stoid), *a.* and *sb.* [f. mod.L. *Blastoidea*, f. Gr. βλαστός sprout, germ + εἶδος form: see Blasto- and -oid.] **A.** *adj.* Of or belonging to the *Blastoidea*, a group of fossil echinoderms. **B.** *sb.* An echinoderm of this group.

1882 Geikie *Text-bk. Geol.* 722 The blastoids or pentremites, which now took the place in the Carboniferous waters that in Silurian times had been filled by the Cystideans. 1914 *Brit. Mus. Return* 202 Newly-described Blastoids from Somerset.

Blastula (blæ·stiŭlă). *Embryol.* [mod.L., f. Gr. βλαστός sprout + dim. suffix. Cf. Blastule.] An embryo, typically composed of cells arranged in a sphere enclosing the blastocœle. Also *attrib.*

1893 Tuckey *Amphioxus* 43 An equal segmentation leading to a blastula without any well-defined main axis.

Blat, *sb. U.S.* [f. next.] A bleating sound.

1904 M. E. Waller *Wood-carver* 71 Not a sound outside except..the thin blat of a sheep beneath the barn. 1911 H. Quick *Yellowstone N.* xii. 313 Every one swellin' the chorus o' blats.

Blat, *v. U.S.* [Imitative.] *intr.* To bleat, or make similar sounds. Also *fig.* to talk noisily.

1888 *San Francisco News Lett.* 4 Feb. (Farmer) One of these insects of an hour rears up and blatts. 1907 S. E. White *Arizona Nights* I. viii. 149 Perhaps the calf blatted a little as the heat scorched. 1926 B. M. Bower *Phantom Herd* ii. 24 The stockyards where a bunch of sheep blatted now in the thirst of mid-afternoon.

Blather (blæ·ðəɹ), *v.* orig. *dial.* [Variant of Blether.] *intr.* To talk foolishly, talk nonsense. Often in *ppl. a.*

1825 Brockett *N. C. Gloss.* 18 He blathers and talks, is a common phrase where much is said to little purpose. A person of this kind is..styled a *blathering hash*. 1891 Kipling *Light that Failed* iv. (1917) 50 If you were only a mass of blathering vanity,..I wouldn't mind. 1892 *Cassell's Fam. Mag.* Dec. 11/1 Hold your tongues, you blathering idiots. 1900 *Century Mag.* Feb. 504/1 Morland had a blathering contempt for nobility and society.

Blay (blēⁱ), *a.* Variant of Blae *a.*, esp. in sense 5 (= unbleached), frequent in Irish use.

1783 *Ann. Reg., Proj.* 85/1 When I mention white flax, I do it in opposition to that which..has the appellation of blay. 1860 O'Curry *MS. Materials* (1878) 38 Some with ..green or blay or white cloaks. 1913 'G. A. Birmingham' *Gen. John Regan* xvii, They draped it..in a large sheet of blay calico of a light yellowish colour.

Blaze, *sb.*¹ Add:

7. *Physiol.* An electric current passing along living tissue in response to mechanical stimulus. Also *attrib.* in *blaze current*. Hence *blaze reaction, response*, reaction or response so obtained.

1902 *Nature* 18 Sept. 491/2 The blaze reaction..requires short strong currents for its manifestation. 1903 *Ibid.* 9 July 238 This 'blaze' response is the algebraic sum of post-anodic and post-kathodic currents. 1903 *Jrnl. Roy. Microsc. Soc.* Oct. 599 A crystalline lens is a good object upon which to study the nature of blaze-currents.

8. In poker: (see quot.). *U.S.*

1889 Farmer *Americanisms*, *Blaze* (in Poker), a hand which consists of five court cards, and which, when played, beats two pairs.

Blaze, *sb.*² **2.** (Earlier example.) Also *attrib.* in *blaze-mark*.

1662 *Groton Rec.* 7 The meetinge house shall be set..by a small whit oak marked at the souwest side with two notches and a blaze. 1885 Mrs. C. Praed *Head Station* xlvi, Here were new blaze-marks; and here, upon a bottle-tree,—the bark unhealed—that old trace of Durnford's tomahawk.

Blaze, *v.*¹ Add:

1. *To blaze out*: fig. of an angry person.

1903 R. Langbridge *Flame & Flood* xii, 'I can't do it, man..,' she would blaze out.

9. *trans.* *To blaze* (*off*): to cause (the grease) to flash in the operation of tempering steel; also, of the grease, to flash; to temper (steel) by this process. Hence **Bla·zing** (*off*) *vbl. sb.*

1823 *New Monthly Mag.* IX. 121 The cast steel articles ..may be quenched in this composition, in order to harden them; and then be blazed off. 1854–67 *Tomlinson's Cycl. Useful Arts* II. 477/2 Each saw is heated over a coke fire until the grease inflames, an operation which is called blazing off. If the saws are to be rather hard, only a small portion of the grease is blazed off. *Ibid.*, Large saws..are..moved to and fro over the fire until the grease begins to blaze off. *Ibid.*, Moving them over a fire for the blazing-off. 1885 *Spons' Mech. Own Bk.* 66 They are then heated..till the grease inflames. This is called being 'blazed'.

Blaze, *v.*³ (Earlier example.)

1777 Anburey *Trav. Amer.* (1791) I. 263 For the more easy discovery of their way back again, their tomahawks are continually blazing the trees, which is cutting off a small piece of the bark.

b. freq. *fig.* in *to blaze the way* (*path, trail*, etc.); esp. *U.S.*

1902 L. Mead *Word-coinage* vi, Professor Bréal has blazed the way for future explorers in the wilderness of philology. 1910 G. H. Blakeslee in *Advoc. Peace* Dec. 263 Lord Morley..is following along the path which America has blazed in the Far East.

Blazed, *ppl. a.*³ **1.** (Later U.S. examples.)

1787 Washington *Diaries* III. 155 A sorrel mare, blazed face, off hind foot white. 1869 *Overland Monthly* III. 126, I had seen..an old gray mare, considerably flea-bitten, with a blazed face and a docked tail.

Blazer¹**.** Add:

2. Something that attracts attention. *U.S.*

1845 Mrs. Kirkland *Western Clearings* (1846) 127 T'other gal is likely enough, but the mother's a blazer! 1903 A. Adams *Log Cowboy* vi. 81 Are you sure you wasn't running a blazer yourself?..inquired Durham. 1906 *Springfield Weekly Republ.* 19 Apr. 1 The Kaiser's telegram..recalls some of his blazers in the past.

3. A small cooking apparatus. *U.S.*

1895 *Harper's Mag.* May 885/1 Delicacies which Tom prided himself on being able to prepare on a blazer.

4. A sheet of metal placed against the bars of a grate to create a draught and cause the fire to blaze; a blower. *north.*

1892 *Northumbld. Gloss.*, *Bleezer*, a hood to blow up a fire. 'Put the bleezer up, and let's hev a lowe.' 1922 T. Burt *Autobiogr.* (1924) 177 Women and children..armed with 'blazers' and tin-cans, which they used as cymbals.

Blazer³**.** [Blaze *v.*³] One who blazes trees.

1775 B. Romans *Florida* 105 These same two men serve as chain-bearers, and two as blazers.

Blazing, *vbl. sb.*³ (Earlier example.)

1799 *Aurora* (Philad.) 22 May (Th.) Gashing, notching, and blazing, are fallacious, futile, hurtful.

Blazing, *ppl. a.*¹ Add: Used as a substitute for a profane epithet.

1888 Kipling *Plain Tales fr. Hills, Thrown Away* (1890) 19 Once I said, 'What's the blazing hurry, Major?' 1916 Boyd Cable *Action Front* 66 You have the blazing cheek to keep me lying here in the filthy muck.

Bleach, *sb.*¹ **3.** Add: A bleaching process; also, a bleached condition.

1887 *Sci. Amer.* 16 Apr. 249/3 What is known as 'the three-quarter bleach' with flax. 1920 *Discovery* Mar. 86/2 A perfect bleach is almost impossible to secure.

5. A bleaching liquor or powder.

1898 *Daily News* 15 Dec. 6/5 A quantity of bleach escaped from a tank at one of the paper mills. 1910 *Daily Chron.* 23 Apr. 7/3 There are several good nail bleaches that are safe to use.

6. *collect.* Bleached goods.

1903 *Daily Chron.* 21 Nov. 7/3 Russia takes more British bleach than any other country except the United States.

Bleacher. Add: **3.** A plank-seat for spectators at baseball or football games, bleached by exposure to the sun; also, a bleachery (see below). Also *attrib.* *U.S.*

1892 *Alumni Weekly* (New Haven) 1 Mar., These Yale patrons..buy seats for the game..on bleacher & the grand stand close to the enemy's goal. 1900 A. F. West *Amer. College* 25 Or they are thronging to fill the 'bleachers' at a baseball or football game that is about to be played on the college grounds. 1904 *N. Y. American* 5 May 13 The bleachers of the club grounds have been so enlarged this season as to accommodate about 12000 persons...The largest of these open bleachers is about 325 feet long and 28 seats deep. 1917 Mathewson *Sec. Base Sloan* xviii. 237 The two boys settled themselves in their places on the bleachers. *Ibid.* 238 More than half of the bleacher seats were empty.

Hence **Blea·cherite,** a frequenter of bleachers. *U.S.* **Blea·chery,** an open-air stand for spectators. *U.S.*

1909 *Cent. Dict.* Suppl., Bleacherite. Bleachery. 1917 Mathewson *Sec. Base Sloan* xviii. 239 'Sailor' was a grand favourite with the bleacherites.

Bleachy (blī·tʃi), *a.*¹ *dial.* [f. Bleach *sb.*¹ or *v.*¹ + -y ¹.] Bleached, pale.

1821 Clare *Vill. Minstrel* II. 194 Nodding lands of wheat in bleachy brown. 1835 — *Rural Muse* 106 The mowers swept the bleachy corn.

Bleachy (blī·tʃi), *a.*² *dial.* Brackish.

1825 Jennings *Observ. Dial. W. Eng.* 1879 Hardy *Wessex T., Distracted Preacher* (1888) II. 148 It makes the stuff [*sc.* rum] taste bleachy.

Bleaty (blī·ti), *a.* [f. Bleat *sb.* + -y ¹.] Having a sound like the bleat of a beast.

1925 W. G. Whittaker *Class-Singing* 77 'A' (as in 'axe') is..apt to be 'bleaty'.

Bled, *ppl. a.* [f. Bleed *v.* 9.] Drained of blood or sap.

1894 *Pop. Sci. Monthly* June 284 A series of tests and examinations of bled and unbled timber has been carried on.

Bleed, *v.* Add: **2. b.** *transf.* Of a dye: To 'run' or become diffused when wetted.

1893 *E. Knecht's Man. Dyeing* 724 Fastness to washing and to bleeding or running should be determined with water alone and with soap. *Ibid.* 725 Most of the direct cotton colours bleed very much when dyed on cotton.

c. 'To leak; especially, to leak an iron-stained liquid, as the seams of a boiler' (*Funk's Standard Dict.* 1895). Hence **Blee·ding** *vbl. sb.* (see quot.).

1888 *Lockwood's Dict. Terms Mech. Engin.*, *Bleeding*, the red streaks of rust which weep through the scale adherent to the insides of boilers, and which reveal the presence of corrosion in the plates underneath.

3. (Modern example.)

1874 *Rep. Vermont Board Agric.* II. 189 If pruned later the trees will often 'bleed', though it is stated that a perfectly healthy tree will not bleed if pruned at any season.

10. (Recent example.)

1901 S. Merwin & H. K. Webster *Calumet K* xii. 224 Men will take every opportunity to bleed a corporation.

13. *Bookbinding.* To cut into the print of (a book) in trimming the margin. *Typogr.* (See quot.)

1874 Knight *Dict. Mech.* 1917 Gress *Typography* (ed. 2) 126 This plate can then be printed in color on gummed paper and the paper trimmed so as to 'bleed' the edges of the printed background.

14. To allow (liquid) to drain away or (gas) to escape through a cock or valve. So in **Bleeding** *vbl. sb.* (also *attrib.*, as *bleeding-valve*).

1895 *Funk's Standard Dict.*, Bleeding valve. 1928 *Daily Tel.* 17 Jan. 5 Where turbine 'bleeding' is resorted to for feed heating.

Bleeder. Add:

1. b. One who extorts money.

1894 *Columbus* (O.) *Dispatch* 5 Oct., It seems that the police of New York were not the only bleeders.

3. (See quot.) *low slang.*

1890 Farmer *Slang*, *Bleeder* (University), a duffer beyond compare; a superlative fool...A euphemism for 'bloody fool'.

Bleeding, *ppl. a.* Add:

5. **bleeding heart** (examples); **bleeding tooth,** a neritoid shell (*Nerita peloronta*) with a red mark on the columella tooth.

1825 Britton *Beauties of Wilts.* III. 371 *Bleeding-heart*, the wall-flower. 1897 *Outing* (U.S.) XXIX. 318/2 She held out a rose to Ferguson, but to Jonathan she gave a bleeding-heart. 1923 E. F. Wyatt *Invis. Gods* I. ii. 16 The sprays of bleeding heart.

6. A substitute for Bloody *a.* 10 (and *adv.* 2). *low slang.*

1858 Furnivall in *Athenæum* 24 July 118 Costermongers have lately substituted the participle 'bleeding' for the adjective ['bloody']. 'My bleeding barrow' is the latest phrase in vogue. 1876 Besant & Rice *Son of Vulcan* II. xxiii, When he isn't up to one dodge he is up to another. You make no bleeding error. 1896 A. Morrison *Child of Jago* i. 4 This is a bleed'n' unsocial sort o' evenin' party.

Blending, *vbl. sb.* Add:

b. *spec.* The action or process of mixing (materials used in woollen manufacture).

1884 W. S. B. McLaren *Spinning* ix. (ed. 2) 184 Blending ..is one of the most important operations in the whole manufacture...Blending may mean many things. It may be different colours of dyed wool, or wool and shoddy, mungo or flocks, or wool and cotton, or wool and silk, or all these together.

Blepharoplast (ble·fărŏplast). *Biol.* [f. Blepharo- + -plast.] **a.** A centrosome-like protoplasmic body found in the sperm-cells of certain plants. **b.** In protozoans, a minute granule at the base of each flagellum.

1897 H. J. Webber in *Bot. Gaz.* Oct. 233, I would..suggest the name *blepharoplast* to distinguish them from other organs of the cell. 1902 *Encycl. Brit.* XXVII. 339/1. 1908 *Practitioner* Feb. 227 Flagellated forms [possess] a nucleus and blepharoplast.

Blessing, *vbl. sb.* Add:

4. c. Phr. *A blessing in disguise*: said of a misfortune that works to the eventual good of the recipient.

1746 Hervey *Hymn*, '*Since all the downward Tracts of Time*', Ev'n Crosses from his sov'reign Hand Are Blessings in Disguise. 1873 *Cassell's Mag.* VI. 296/2 Like many similar disasters, this great calamity was in truth only a blessing in disguise. 1900 *Jrnl. Soc. Arts* 15 June 595 We find that the Pacific cable scheme has really been a blessing in disguise to those who dreaded it most. 1907 *Westm. Gaz.* 3 May 2/1 Religion would gain greatly if the clergy would make a more sparing use of the blessing-in-disguise argument.

Blethering, *ppl. a.* Add:

2. = *Blithering *ppl. a.* *colloq.* or *slang.*

1915 A. Kinross in *Times Red Cross Story Bk.* 148 If my boy ever gets married on the quiet and plays the fool, I'll break his blethering neck for him.

Bleu-de-roi (blö də rwa). *Ceramics.* Also -du-. [Fr., = king's blue.] The ultramarine blue of Sèvres porcelain; also called *bleu de Sèvres*. Also *attrib.*

1848 H. R. Forster *Stowe Catal.* 38 A coffee-cup and saucer—bleu du Roi. 1868 Sala *Notes & Sk. Paris Exhib.* xiii. 153 A Sèvres vase, *bleu-de-roi*. 1908 *Connoisseur* Jan. 70/1 Sèvres bleu du roi china.

Blow, variant of *Blue *v.*²

Blight, *sb.* **5.** Add:

blight-bird *Austral.*, a settlers' name for a bird belonging to the Australian genus *Zosterops*.

1882 T. H. Potts *Out in the Open* 130 (Morris) The white-eye or blight-bird..clears away multitudes of small insect pests. 1888 Newton in *Encycl. Brit.* XXIV. 824/1 In 1856 it was noticed..as occurring in the South Island of New Zealand, when it became known..to the English settlers as the 'Blight-bird'.

Blighted, *ppl. a.* Add: **b.** Used as a mild substitute for Blasted *ppl. a.* 3. *slang.*

1914–15 Locke *Jaffery* xxi. 271, I think he's a blighted malingerer.

Blighter. Add:

2. [After prec.] A contemptible person. Often merely an extravagant substitute for 'fellow'. *slang.*

1896 *Idler* Mar. 282/1 'Larry', says they, 'you ain't going to let that blighter throw you'. 1900 *Westm. Gaz.* 28 Mar. 9/3 Down with the dirty blighters who will not remove their hats. 1904 Kipling in *Windsor Mag.* Jan. 226/2 'There's an accommodatin' blighter for you!' said Pyecroft. 1920 Locke *House of Baltazar* xviii. 218 He could buy up this old blighter of a lord twice over. 1928 *Manchester Guardian Weekly* 5 Oct. 274/2 Why was the blighter [*sc.* the prosecuting counsel] allowed to make the witness say just what he wanted him to say?

Blighty (blai·ti), *sb. Army slang.* [Contracted form, originating in the Indian army, of Hind. *bilāyatī* = *wilāyatī* (ولايتى) foreign, and esp. European, f. *wilāyat* prop. Arabic, inhabited country, dominion, district, Vilayet, in Hind. esp. foreign country (cf. Arab. ولى *wālī* governor of a province, Vali, Wali).

Cf. '*Bilayutee pawnee, Bilātee panee.* The adject. *bilāyatī* is applied specifically to a variety of exotic articles,.. and most especially *bilāyatī pānī*, 'European water', the usual name of soda-water in Anglo-India (Yule & Burnell, *Hobson-Jobson*).]

England, home. (Used by soldiers on foreign service.)

1915 *Times* (weekly ed.) 8 Oct. 852 The only thing they looked forward to was getting back to 'Blighty' again. 1916 in *N. & Q.* 19 Feb. 151/1 One poem I have recently seen begins:—Oh, send me back to Blighty. 1917 P. MacGill *Gt. Push* xix. 238 I'll send out the money and fags when I go back to blighty.

b. *attrib.* or *adj.* 'Home', as distinguished from 'foreign'.

1918 *Aussie* Aug. 9/2 The C.O. endeavours to persuade Private Hardcase to accept Blighty Leave. 1926 *Morn. Post* 8 Dec., An Exhibition and Sale of Blighty Industries.

c. In the war of 1914–18 applied to a wound that secured return to England.

1916 *N. & Q.* 4 Mar. 194/2, I believe that 'B.B.' is the regular, though unofficial description of any non-fatal wound serious enough to send its victim back to a base hospital—Blighty Boy. 1916 *Daily Mail* 1 Nov. 4/4 So-and-so stopped some shrapnel and is back at the base in hospital,.. he wasn't lucky enough to get a blighty. 1918 Locke *Rough Road* xix, Mo says he's blistering glad you're out of it and safe in your perishing bed with a Blighty one. 1927 *Daily Express* 18 Oct. 1/1 Soldiers are visiting the battlefields.. in the hope of finding trenches, dug-outs, or the exact spot where they received their 'blighties'.

Blighty (blai·ti), *a.* [f. Blight *sb.* + -y ¹.] Affected with blight, blighted.

1900 *Standard* 9 Nov., The acorn crop is an abundant one, the fruit being rather blighty and undersized.

Blimey (blai·mi), *int.* Also **blymy.** Short for *Gorblimy (= God blind me!): a vulgar imprecation.

1889 Barrère & Leland *Dict. Slang.* 1894 *Punch* 27 Oct. 193/1 Blymy, you're a knockout! 1928 H. Fields *Hit the Deck*, Blimey, that ain't matey—you invited us and I'm hungry.

Blimp (blimp). [See quot. 1918.] A small non-rigid dirigible airship invented early in the war of 1914–18 and consisting orig. of the fuselage of a dismantled aeroplane supported by an elongated gas bag, used as a submarine scout.

1916 Rosher *In R.N.A.S.* 136 Visited the Blimps this afternoon at Capel. 1918 *Illustr. Lond. News* 27 July 96 Nobody in the R.N.A.S. ever called them anything but 'Blimps', an onomatopœic name invented by that genius for apposite nomenclature, the late Horace Shortt. 1928 Gamble *North Sea Air Station* x. 149 The Submarine Scout non-rigid type. The name was abbreviated to S.S. airships, but they were generally known as 'Blimps'.

Blind, *sb.* Add:

3. (Examples.)

1848 *Congress. Globe* 30 June, App. 820/1 [Mr. Polk] was worked into the Presidency with Oregon and Texas on either side, as a horse is worked with blinds. 1901 *Munsey's Mag.* XXV. 739/1 A halter has a soft leather covered bit, and is without blinds.

5. *spec.* A hiding-place in which a hunter conceals himself from the game. *U.S.*

1869 *Game Laws* (*Penn.*) in *Fur, Fin & Feather* (1872) 94 No person shall..build blinds for the purpose of killing.. any wild turkey. 1874 J. W. Long *Wild-Fowl Shooting* 45 Ingenuity in the providing of proper ambush, or blind, as all such hiding places are generally termed by wild-fowlers. 1887 *Nation* (N. Y.) 31 Mar. 271 Along the Atlantic coast, among the gunners who often hunt in parties stationed near together behind blinds, waiting for the flock of migratory birds. 1894 *Outing* (U.S.) XXIV. 73/2 A glance ..discloses the fact that no time should be wasted in getting started for the blinds.

8. **blind bridle** (earlier U.S. examples).

1861 *Trans. Ill. Agric. Soc.* IV. 376 A blind bridle may be tolerated on a blind horse. 1872 Eggleston *End of World* ix. 65 I'm dead sot in favor of charity,.. but I a'n't a-goin' to have her put a blind-bridle on to me.

9. In Poker, a stake put up by a player before seeing his cards (see quots.); cf. *Blind *a.* 1 h. Also *attrib.* in *blind-money*. Also *fig.*

1872 'Mark Twain' *Innoc. at Home* ii. (1882) 268 Now you talk! You see my blind and straddle it like a man. 1882 *Poker* 49 The straddle is nothing more than a double blind. *Ibid.* 91 It is an error on the part of the Age to fill the Blind simply because he has already invested the Blind-money. 1885 *Encycl. Brit.* XIX. 283/2 The next player [to the age] may *double the blind*, i.e., raise to double what the age staked; the next may *straddle the blind*, i.e. double again,..and so on. Only the age can start a blind. 1889 Farmer *Americanisms*, *Blind* (in poker), the ante deposited by the age previous to the deal...To make a blind good costs double the amount of the ante, and to make a straddle good costs four times the amount of the blind. 1894 *Congress. Rec.* May 4408/2 Put up your blind. It's my deal. 1898 *Hoyle's Games Modernized* (ed. Hoffmann) 221 [Draw Poker.] This stake [put up by the elder hand, the 'Age'], from the fact that it is made without seeing the cards, is known as a 'blind'.

10. Something mis-sorted or overlooked in sorting.

1898 *Daily News* 20 Dec. 3/3 Able to sort the whole 500 [addressed cards] in 30 minutes with not more than 30 'blinds' or mis-sorts, that is.

Blind, *a.* Add:

1. In comparisons, as *blind as a bat* or *brickbat*.

1850 Dickens *Dav. Copp.* xliii, The old Scholar..is as blind as a brickbat. 1926 W. Deeping *Sorrell & Son* xviii. § 2, I was blind as a bat. Pushed into a job by my people.

f. (See quot.)

1879 *Encycl. Brit.* IX. 292/2 The side [of a flat-fish] which is turned towards the bottom..is generally colourless, and called 'blind', from the absence of an eye on this side.

g. Short for *blind drunk* (see 15). Also as *sb.*, in *University slang*, a college 'wine'.

1622 J. Taylor (Water-P.) *Water-Cormorant* Wks. 1630 II. 5/1 For though he be as drunke as any Rat, He hath but catcht a Foxe, or Whipt the Cat. Or some say hee's bewitcht, or scratcht, or blinde, Which are the fittest tearmes that I can finde. 1845 Mrs. S. C. Hall *Whiteboy* v. 49 They'll be all *blind* by the time they get home from G. F.'s wedding. 1903 McNeill *Egreg. Engl.* 145 The artisan..improves the shining hours, by 'getting blind', to use his own elegant phrase.

h. In Poker, *To go blind*: to put up a blind (see *Blind *sb.* 9); hence *to go* (a specified stake) *blind*. Hence applied to forms of Poker in which this is done; so *blind hand*.

1871 [see i below]. 1882 *Poker* 88 For some reasons players never give the blind hand credit for a good or even an average hand. 1885 *Encycl. Brit.* XIX. 283/2 The age is sometimes allowed to *go blind*, i.e., to raise the ante before he sees his cards. 1885 B. L. Farjeon *Sacred Nugget* xvi, He put in [the pool] a bank-note, and said, 'Five pound blind'. Antonio..put in an I.O.U. for ten pounds, saying 'I straddle you'. *Ibid.*, Mike Patchett went ten pounds blind; he [*sc.* Antonio] straddled it with twenty.

i. fig. *To go it blind*: to act without previous investigation of the circumstances; to plunge without regard to the risks involved. Also *to go blind* (*on* —). Orig. in U.S. political use.

1846 *Congress. Globe* App. 120 All I ask of him is that he will not 'go it blind' upon Oregon. 1848 Lowell *Biglow P.* Ser. I. viii. 155 It gives a Party Platform, tu, jest level with the mind..Of..honest folks that mean to go it blind. 1862 *Ibid.* Ser. II. iv. 10 An' agin to impress on the poppylar mind The comfort an' wisdom o' goin' it blind. 1871 Schele de Vere *Americanisms* (1872) 328 Poker, when played by betting before looking at one's hand, is called *Blind Poker*, and this has given rise to the very common phrase, to *go it blind*, used whenever an enterprise is undertaken without previous enquiry. 1875 Gen. Sherman *Mem.* I. 342, I know that in Washington I am incomprehensible, because at the outset of the war I would not go it blind. 1888 *Chicago Ledger* 12 May (Farmer), I didn't go it blind, I employed a detective. 1909 *Daily Chron.* 8 Feb. 4/4 If that be true, shall we be quite wise to 'go blind' on Dreadnoughts alone?

7. b. (Earlier U.S. examples.)

1784 Washington *Diaries* II. 304 The path it is said is very blind and exceedingly grown with briers. 1796–1806 B. Hawkins *Lett.* 112 Continue on a blind tract thro' hilly.. land and down a stream.

d. *Bookbinding.* Ungilt; cf. *blind-blocking, -tooling* in 16 in Dict., *Blind *v.* 8.

1846 Dodd *Brit. Manuf.* VI. 105 The block..imprints the device; whether it be gilt or 'blind'.

10. c. Of an alphabetic letter: Written or printed with a closed loop: *spec.* in *Typogr.* defining the paragraph mark with a closed loop (also as *sb.*).

1888 Jacobi *Printers' Vocab.*, *Blind P*. A paragraph mark ¶ so called from the loop of the P being closed. 1905 F. H. Collins *Author & Printer* 34 Blind ¶. *Mod.* He invariably makes his *e*'s and *l*'s blind.

d. Of a baggage car on a train: (see quot. 1901). *U.S.*

1901 *Scribner's Mag.* XXIX. 429/1 The train's got a blind baggage-car on...That's a car that ain't got no door in the end that's next the engine. 1912 Mathewson *Pitching* xi. 249 He had come all the way either by side-door special or blind baggage. 1926 J. Black *You Can't Win* ix. 120 With much caution I made my way..till I got near enough to the depot to get aboard the blind end of a baggage car.

e. Of a photographic plate: Not sensitive to light. 1911 in Webster.

f. Of a shell: That fails to go off.

1916 Boyd Cable *Action Front* 182 The wail of the falling shell ended in a muffled thump that proclaimed the missile 'blind' or 'a dud'.

12. (Earlier U.S. example.)

1861 *Trans. Ill. Agric. Soc.* IV. 479 The blind eyes are the best for fruit.

16. **blind booking,** the booking of films without previous selection on their merits by cinema proprietors; **blind creek** (see quot.); **blind-eyed** *a.* (*lit.* and *fig.*); **blind hazard, hole** *Golf* (see quots.); **blind hookey** (earlier example); **blind ink, literature** (see quots.); **blind-pig** *U.S.*, a place where liquor is illicitly sold; hence *blind-pigger, -pigging*; **blind poker** *U.S.* (see *1 h); **blind spot,** also (b) *Cricket*, that spot of ground in front of a batsman where the ball being pitched by the bowler he is in doubt whether to play forward or back; (c) *Wireless Telegr.* (see quot. 1923); **blind staggers** (see Stagger *sb.*¹ 2); **blind stitch** *sb.*, a stitch taken on one side of the material so as to be invisible on the other; **blind-stitch** *v. trans.*, to sew or fasten with blind stitch; **blind tiger** *U.S.* = **blind-pig*.

1927 *Glasgow Herald* 20 Jan. 7 '*Blind-booking' was responsible for a very large percentage of the machine-made pictures which came from America to this country. 1927 *Daily Tel.* 15 Mar. 9/2 The Labour-Socialists..are in favour of the proposals for the abolition of blind booking and restrictions on advance booking. 1886 J. W. Anderson *Prospector's Handbk.* 115 *Blind Creek, a creek, dry, except during wet weather. 1887 Morris *Odyssey* x. 493 Tiresias.. The *blind-eyed, the foreseer, whose steadfast mind bides still. 1902 *Daily Chron.* 18 Feb. 3/2 Are we to suppose, then, that Goethe..was a blind-eyed fool? 1900 *Yng. Sportsman* (ed. A. E. T. Watson) 315 A *Blind hazard is also a hazard which is hidden from his view. *Ibid.*, A *Blind hole is one of which the putting-green is not visible to the player as he plays his shot. 1840 Haliburton *Clockm.* Ser. III. xi. 152 What do you say to a game at all-fours, *blind-hookey, odd or even,..just to pass time? 1884 Knight *Dict. Mech.* Suppl., **Blind Ink*. Invented by Edison. An ink which.. swells up into relief on the paper. 1921 *Post Office Guide* Aug. 25 '*Blind Literature'. Papers of any kind, periodicals, and books, impressed in 'Braille' or other special type for the use of the blind. 1903 *N. Y. Even. Post* 23 Sept., But a '*blind pig' is at best but a sordid institution. 1904 *Harper's Weekly* 20 Aug. 1272 Six non-commissioned officers have been reduced to the ranks for running what is technically known as a 'blind pig', or unlawful canteen. 1894 *Voice* (N. Y.) 6 Dec. 1/5 Headed by one of the *blind-piggers who was under arrest. 1918 Webster, Addenda, **Blind-pigging*, n. 1927 *Blackw. Mag.* June 833/1 Amongst the common herd two crimes ranked as serious—'blind-pigging' and 'high-grading'. 1891 Grace *Cricket* iii. 73 Too often would come a ball on the *blind spot. 1923 *Daily Mail* 13 Feb. 7 Wireless blind spots, where distant broadcasting is heard more clearly than that nearer at hand. 1838 H. Colman *Rep. Agric. Mass.* (1839) 75 Having no exercise, it tends to produce the *blind staggers. 1874 *Rep. Vermont Board Agric.* II. 431 The disease is frequently called 'blind staggers'. 1884 Knight *Dict. Mech.* Suppl., **Blind Stitch*. (Harness)...A stitch that is shown on one side only of the leather. 1909 *Daily Chron.* 14 Jan. 7/5 Facings should be *blind-stitched into place. 1903 *N. Y. Even. Post* 16 Sept., It will be interesting to note the effect [of the beer gardens] on the '*blind tigers', which have continued to flourish in spite of executive vigilance. 1926 D. L. Colvin *Prohibition in U. S.* 297 Some effort was made to suppress blind tigers which were then chiefly supplied by moonshine stills.

Blind, *v.* Add:

2. b. *intr.* To go blindly or heedlessly. *slang.*

1923 *Daily Mail* 21 June 12 Motor-cyclists who blind along the road. 1928 S. Kaye-Smith in *Daily Express* 19 May 10/6 By recreation I do not mean blinding along the Brighton road at fifty miles an hour.

3. (Additional quot.)

1859 Bartlett *Dict. Amer.* (ed. 2), *To Blind a trail*, to conceal a person's foot-prints, or to give them the appearance of going in a different direction; and, figuratively, to deceive a person by putting him on the wrong track.

8. *trans.* In *Bookbinding*, to stamp *in* (a pattern) without gilding.

1901 Cockerell *Bookbinding* 212 The pattern is blinded in through the leather.

9. To cover the surface of (a newly made road) with fine material. Cf. *Blinding *vbl. sb.* 4.

1812 Sir J. Sinclair *Syst. Husb. Scot.* I. 66 No large stones to be employed..nor sand, earth or other matter, on pretence of blinding [the road]. 1880 *Antrim & Down Gloss.* s.v., To 'blind a road' = to spread small stones or cinders so as to cover up the large stones, with which a new road has been 'pitched', and to fill the interstices.

Blind alley. An alley closed at one end (see Blind *a.* 11); a cul-de-sac; also *fig.*, a course of action that fails to effect its purpose or from which there is no resultant benefit.

1724 [see Blind *a.* 11]. 1854 Bayle St. John *Purple Tints Paris* II. 2 When..he..is compelled to become one of the blind-alleys of the species. 1882 P. H. Fitzgerald *Recreat. Literary Man* ii. (1883) 7 A familiarity with all the blind alleys..and passages of letters. 1898 Sir E. Grey in *Westm. Gaz.* 6 June 2/3 Many of Lord Salisbury's concessions were blind alleys which led to nowhere. 1926 W. Deeping *Sorrell & Son* iii. § 2 No blind alleys, or office stools.

b. attrib.: *blind alley employment, occupation*, etc., an employment, etc., that 'leads nowhere', i.e. offers no opportunities to young workers for the earning of an independent livelihood as adults.

1909 *Westm. Gaz.* 27 Oct. 2/1 'Blind alley' employments. 1910 *Ibid.* 6 Jan. 3/3 The number of lads between the age of fifteen and twenty who are engaged in what have come to be known as 'blind-alley occupations'. 1928 *Daily Express* 19 July 8/4 The girl who takes an easy, blind-alley, ill-paid job.

Blindfold, *a.* Add:

1. c. Of a match at chess: Conducted by a player without seeing the board but not necessarily blindfolded; hence *blindfold player*.

1850 Browning *Easter Day* vi. 50 Playing pawns at blindfold chess. 1869 *Yng. Men Gt. Brit.* 28 May 302/1 A blindfold match took place during the Congress,..between Mr. Blackburne and Herr Steinitz. 1900 *Westm. Gaz.* 31 May 2/1 In almost all these blindfold games I have the move... Occasionally I overlook something..in a blindfold match... The blindfold player..cannot see so far ahead as if he were looking at the board.

Blinding, *vbl. sb.* Add:

4. The process of covering the surface of a newly made road with fine material to fill up the spaces between the stones; also, the material used for this purpose. Cf. *Blind *v.* 9.

1843 *Civil Eng. & Arch. Jrnl.* VI. 274/1 The stoning and blinding is conducted in the same manner as in ordinary roads. 1874 Knight *Dict. Mech.* 1926 *United Free Ch. Miss. Rec.* May 224/1 The fierce wind tore the blinding from the hard clay roads.

Blinding, *ppl. a.* Add: **b.** *fig.* That dazzles the mind by excessive brilliancy.

18.. Andrew Lang, Only a man of the most blinding original genius could have written them.

Blindness. Add: **4.** Of a plant: Abortiveness.

1921 *Times Lit. Suppl.* 24 Feb. 130/3 The Frit Fly, which produces blindness in oats.

Blink, *sb.*² Add: **1. d.** *On the blink*: on the point of becoming extinguished; in a bad state. *U.S. slang.*

1904 'O. Henry' *Cabbages & Kings* iii. 51 This café looks on the blink, but I guess it can set out something wet. 1921 R. D. Paine *Comr. Rolling Ocean* xvi. 273 The engines had to be stopped and the first assistant reported that 'the condenser was finally and totally on the blink'.

2. b. The action or an act of blinking.

1924 Galsworthy *White Monkey* I. xii, He did not miss the shift and blink in the manager's eyes.

Blink, *sb.*³ *U.S.* A fisherman's name for the mackerel when about a year old.

1856 [see Tinker *sb.* 3].

Blink, *v.* Add:

2. b. *trans.* (*Coursing.*) To elude (the dogs) temporarily. (Cf. *Blinking *vbl. sb.* 3.)

1876 *Coursing Calendar* 197 The hare blinked Grace at the fence. *Ibid.* 252 Hylactor and Blue Sea ran very evenly for some distance, but, as puss blinked them in a hollow, Hylactor was so well placed that he made a few weak points before effecting the death.

4. d. *trans.* To send (tears) *away* by blinking.

1905 Elinor Glyn *Viciss. Evang.* 215 Tears kept rising in my eyes, and I did not even worry to blink them away. 1924 Rose Macaulay *Orphan Island* xxi. § 1 Rosamond blinked away tears, with the salt Pacific, from her eyes.

10. To look upon with the evil eye, to bewitch. *Sc.* and *Irish.*

1886 *Folk-Lore Jrnl.* IV. 255 Cattle can be fairy-struck or bewitched..the first is called 'sheetin' and the second 'blinked'. 1892 *Ballymena Observer* (E.D.D.), *Blink*, to bewitch cattle and cause them to have little or no milk and butter. 1926 *Blackw. Mag.* Apr. 479/1 Perhaps we are bewitched or blinked, as Shamus Byrne would say. 1927 *Scots Observer* 15 Oct. 2/5 Mrs. Hazelton..had indeed blinked William Blair's cows. *Ibid.*, He had set fire to the wisp of straw and had put it under a blinked cow's nose.

Blinker. Add:

4. A sporting dog that refuses to see and mark temporarily the position of game.

1845 Youatt *Dog* iii. 91 The chastisement..would make the setter disgusted..and leave him a mere *blinker*. 1848 W. N. Hutchinson *Dog Breaking* 94 Excess of punishment has made many a dog of good promise a confirmed blinker.

5. An intermittent flash-light.

1921 R. D. Paine *Comr. Rolling Ocean* xvi. 285 Take this bug-light [*sc.* an electric torch] and use it as a blinker. You learned the Morse code at Camp Stuart.

Blinkered (bli·ŋkəɹd), *ppl. a.* [f. Blinker *sb.* or *v.* + -ed.] Of a horse: Provided with blinkers. Also *fig.*, having a limited range of outlook.

1867 Hardy *Time's Laughing Stocks* '1967' 9 A century which..Will show..A scope above this blinkered time. 1897 *Daily News* 19 June 9/1 The colt..could not quite withstand the rush of the blinkered El Diablo. 1898 *Westm. Gaz.* 27 Aug. 1/3 The padded, blinkered life of her spinster sister. 1926 *Spectator* 20 Mar. 529/1 Our blinkered country takes a lot of beating.

Blinking, *vbl. sb.* Add:

3. The faulty action, in a sporting dog, of refusing to see and mark the position of game.

1848 W. N. Hutchinson *Dog Breaking* 10 The unreasonableness of not always giving initiatory Lessons. Causes Blinking. 1865 *Ibid.* (ed. 4) 202 Some argue that blinking arises from a defective nose, not from punishment. 1897 *H. Dalziel's Brit. Dogs* III. 336 Blinking..is caused..by undue severity or punishment administered for chasing game or poultry.

Blinking, *ppl. a.* Add: **4.** Used as a substitute for a strong expletive. *slang.*

1914 *Scotsman* 12 Oct. 7/5 One..Guardsman..declared.. that His Majesty seemed to carry the 'blinking Army List in his 'ead'. 1927 *Observer* 21 Aug. 17/5 The type of golfer who..hurls the bag of clubs after it, accompanied by the remark, 'Go on, have the blinking lot'.

Blister, *sb.* Add:

2. b. A disease incident to peach-trees, caused by the fungus *Exoascus deformans*, which produces a distortion of the leaves.

1889 *Cent. Dict.* 1904 *Board Agric. & Fisheries* (1919) No. 120 'Curl' or 'leaf blister' proves very injurious to peaches and nectarines during certain seasons.

4. **blister-fly** (earlier U.S. example); **blister furnace,** a furnace for the conversion of copper regulus or matte into blister-copper; **blister pearl,** a pearly excrescence of irregular shape found on the shell of a pearl oyster.

1836 Edward *Hist. Texas* 88 Next comes the Spanish or *blister fly. 1902 *Encycl. Brit.* XXVII. 237/1 The multiple system anodes are sometimes cast directly from the *blister furnace or the converter. 1885 *Ibid.* XVIII. 446/2 The mollusc..depositing nacreous matter.., thus forming a hollow body of irregular shape known as a '*blister pearl'. 1910 *Daily Chron.* 4 Apr. 4/5 Overdress of gauze encrusted with blister pearls.

Blister, *v.* Add:

5. Used as an imprecation.

1840 Cockton *Val. Vox* xxvi, Blister 'em! Where can the scoundrels be got to?

Blistered, *ppl. a.* Add:

1. b. (Earlier U.S. example of *blistered steel*.)

1770 *Carroll Papers* in *Maryland Hist. Mag.* XIII. 65 My Smiths say the Bristol or Blister'd steel sent to us is very bad.

c. Made of blister-copper or -steel.

1928 *Daily Express* 21 Nov. 1/1 The methods of defence employed by surface craft consist of anti-aircraft guns..; of reinforced or 'blistered' bottoms..; and of manœuvre.

Blistering, *ppl. a.* Add:

2. Used as a substitute for a strong expletive.

1900 *Daily News* 30 July 6/4 One blistering young woman actually unstraps her kodak and begins operations upon the great white mountain. 1918 Locke *Rough Road* xix, Mo says he's blistering glad you're out of it and safe in your perishing bed.

Blither (bli·ðəɹ), *sb.* [f. *Blither *v.*] Nonsense. Cf. Blether *sb.*

1901 *Daily Chron.* 10 Aug. 4/7 We have heard a lot of blither (and, perhaps, a little sense). 1911 E. Ferber *Dawn O'Hara* v. 68 'What utter blither!' I scoffed.

Blither (bli·ðəɹ), *v.* [var. Blether *v.*] *intr.* To talk nonsense; = Blether *v.* 1. Hence **Bli·thering** *vbl. sb.*

1868 Verney *Stone Edge* i, What did the imp come blitherin' and botherin' there for? 1903 J. K. Jerome *Tea-Table Talk* i. 20 If he was to blither, it was only fair that she should bleat back. 1921 *Blackw. Mag.* Oct. 455/1 The inevitable pasty-faced babu waddled up, blithering about the delay. 1925 *Public Opinion* 13 Mar. 258/2 He ignores all their blithering.

Blithering (bli·ðəriŋ), *ppl. a.* [f. *Blither *v.* + -ing [2].] Senselessly discursive or talkative, babbling; esp. of a person, used chiefly as an intensive adjective, with the meaning 'consummate' (freq. in *blithering idiot*); also more widely = despicable, contemptible.

1889 *Punch* 9 Feb. 65 I'll state pretty clearly that his son is a blithering idiot. 1895 *Ibid.* 30 Mar. 153, I had thought that you..would have had a soul above blithering detail. 1903 McNeill *Egreg. Engl.* 179 These songs..are of the most blithering and bathotic nature. 1923 *Blackw. Mag.* Jan. 70/2, I was cursing myself for the blitheringest ass that ever was born. 1925 G. Frankau *Masterson* xxix, I was a blithering idiot to get in—knowing you as well as I do. 1928 Rebecca West *Strange Necessity* 310 The blithering incompetence of English statesmen during the War of Independence.

Bli·thesomely, *adv.* [f. Blithesome *a.* + -ly [2].] In a blithesome manner; cheerily. So **Bli·thesomeness.**

1858 Whittier *Pipes at Lucknow* 62 Full tenderly and *blithesomely The pipes of rescue blew! 1888 Annie S. Swan *Doris Cheyne* xvii, 'I should scold you.., but I am so glad to see you that I have not the heart', she said blithesomely. 1886 *New Princeton Rev.* II. 78 A glad *blithesomeness belonged to her, potent to conquer even ill health and suffering.

Blizzard. *U.S.* [Etym. note. For 'Esherville, Ill.' read 'Esthersville, Iowa'.]

1. Alter def. to: A sharp blow or knock; a shot. Also *fig.*

1829 *Virginia Lit. Museum* 16 Dec., *Blizzard*, A violent blow. 1834 Crockett *Life* 152, I saw two more bucks, very large fellows too. I took a blizzard at one of them, and up he tumbled. 1856 *Sacramento City* (Cal.) *Item* (Th.) When some true archer, from the upper tier, Gave him a 'blizzard' on the nearest ear. 1871 Schele de Vere *Americanisms* (1872) 443 *Blizzard*..means in the West a stunning blow or an overwhelming argument.

2. (Earlier examples.)

1870 *North. Vindicator* 23 Apr., in *Amer. Speech* (1928) III. 201 Campbell has had too much experience with north-western 'blizards' to be caught in such a trap. *Ibid.* 30 Apr., ibid., The unfortunate victim of the March 'blizzard'..is rapidly improving. 1871 *Ibid.* 2 Dec., ibid. 207 Blizzards—Old Boreas during the past week has come down upon us like the 'wolf on the fold'. 1872 *Ibid.* 27 Jan., ibid., A Blizzard is raging as we go to press, with a prospect of continuing its regular season of three days. 1876 *Monthly Weather Rev.* Dec. 424, ibid. 212 The very severe storms known in local parlance as 'blizzards' were reported on the 8th as prevailing in Iowa and Wisconsin.

Hence **Bli·zzarded** *pa. pple.*, a more emphatic form of 'blowed' (Blow *v.*[1] 29); **Bli·zzardy** *a.* (fig.).

1891 Gunter *Miss Dividends* (1893) 67 Then he suddenly ejaculates 'Well I'm blizzarded!' 1888 *San Francisco News Letter* (Farmer), I should like to have seen the Colonel's face when he got that very cold blizzardy letter.

Bloat (blōut), *sb.* [f. Bloat *a.*[2]]

1. Bloatedness.

1880 G. B. Shaw *Irrational Knot* xi. (1909) 226 He..had noted with aversion a certain unhealthy bloat in her face.

2. One soaked in liquor; a drunkard. *U.S.*

a 1861 T. Winthrop *Life in Open Air* etc. (1863) 147 When I think..what a mean bloat I was, going to the stub-tail dogs with my hat over my eyes. 1871 *Congress. Globe* Feb., App. 129/1 Wife whippers, penitentiary birds, street vagabonds, beastly bloats, and convicted felons. 1889 Farmer *Americanisms*, *Bloat* (Cant). A drowned body; also a drunkard.

Bloat, *v.*[2] Add: 1. b. *fig.*

1896 J. A. Hobson *Probl. Unempl.* i Well-meaning..social reformers stretch the term ['unemployment'] and bloat it out to gigantic proportions.

Blob, *sb.* Add:

4. b. *Cricket. colloq.* A batsman's score of no runs, so called from the zero placed against his name in the score-sheet; = Duck's egg b. Also in fig. phr. *to make a blob*: to accomplish nothing.

1903 *Punch* 27 May 366 To come home and be treated as if I'd made a brace of blobs. 1912 J. B. Hobbs *Recov. Ashes* 19 Mr. Foster..taking the first wicket of the tour by bowling Mr. E. R. Mayne for a 'blob'.

Blob, *sb.*[2] *local.* A bait used in fishing for eels, consisting of a worm strung on a worsted thread. (Cf. Bob *sb.*[1] 7.)

1874 E. Peacock *J. Markenfield* vii, Along o' my runnin' away wi' her crewell ball, and makin' a blobb for eels wi' it. 1905 *Westm. Gaz.* 28 Apr. 3/1 Your plan is now, when the eel is thus grabbing the worm, to lift the 'blob' very gently.

Blobbing (blǫ·biŋ), *vbl. sb. local.* [f. prec.] The method of fishing with a bob for eels (cf. prec. and Bobbing *vbl. sb.* 3).

1877 *N. W. Linc. Gloss.*, *Blobbing*, a method of catching eels by means of worms strung on a worsted thread. 1905 *Westm. Gaz.* 28 Apr. 3/1 That is 'blobbing'.

Bloc (blǫk). [F., = Block *sb.*] In continental politics, a combination of divergent political parties which supports the government in power. Also *transf.*, a combination of groups, parties, or nations formed to foster a particular interest.

1905 *Spectator* 14 Jan. 38/1 It is more probable..that when the votes are open the members of the 'Bloc' will shrink from turning out M. Combes. 1907 *Westm. Gaz.* 5 Dec. 5/1 Prince Bülow..summoned the leaders of the 'bloc' parties to a meeting. 1908 *Daily Chron.* 20 Apr. 3/2 The support of the bloc policy by the Liberal party in the Reichstag. *Ibid.* 9 Oct. 4/6 Clémenceau, who was..the man of the Bloc, who had invented the name. 1923 *Daily Mail* 29 Mar. 6 France also can stand apart from Great Britain. She can join a Continental *bloc* with Italy and the Little Entente and Belgium.

Block, *sb.* Add:

6. e. A shaped piece of wood forming part of a shoeblack's equipment, on which a customer places his foot.

1872 *Cassell's Mag.* V. 84/1 The boys are provided with their uniforms, their block, blacking, and brushes by the society.

f. *Drapery.* A roll of material wound on a board: now called *piece*.

1905 H. G. Wells *Kipps* i. vi. § 4 Being subsequently engaged in serving cretonnes, and desiring to push a number of rejected blocks up the counter.

10. b. (Earlier and later U.S. examples.)

1870 Medbery *Men & Myst. Wall St.* 134 Block. A number of shares, say 5,000 or 10,000, massed together, and sold or bought in a lump. 1901 Merwin & Webster *Calumet K* iii. 40 A big block of treasury stock.

c. A number of sheets of paper glued together on the edges, presenting a top sheet for sketching or writing upon, which may be torn away after use. Also *attrib.* as in *block calendar*.

1874 Sketching-block [see Sketching *vbl. sb.* 2]. 1893 Sketch-block [see Sketch *sb.* 6]. 1908 Scribbling-block [see Scribbling *vbl. sb.*[1] 4]. 1910 *Brit. Empire Paper Trades' Jrnl.* Feb. 66/2 Blotting pads, books, etc., note books, note blocks, address books, etc. *Ibid.* May 186 Portrait and Figure Studies, with Daily Tear-off Block and Quotations for every day in the year. *Ibid.* 187/1 A new series of larger size shilling block calendars.

d. The carcass of a bullock; also *attrib.*, as *block test*, ascertainment of the dead weight of a beast when on the butcher's block for cutting up.

1893 *Westm. Gaz.* 8 Mar. 9/1 The 'block test'..used by Mr. M'Jannet, of Stirling...A set of tables by which, when the weight of the live bullock is ascertained, the weight of the 'block' as it hangs up in the flesher's shop for sale can be established within about a couple of pounds. 1902 *Encycl. Brit.* XXV. 188 In 1895 the Smithfield Club instituted a carcase competition...The cattle and sheep entered for this competition are shown alive on the first day, at the close of which they are slaughtered and the carcases hung up for exhibition, with details of live and dead weights. The competition constitutes what is termed a 'block test'.

12. c. *Arch.* A projecting division in an entablature; *transf.*, each of the squared pieces above and sometimes below the columns of a chimney-piece.

1777 Wedgwood in *Life* (1866) II. 373, I told Mr. G. we were making some metopes, tablets, oval bas reliefs for friezes, blocks &c. for wood chimney-pieces. 1875 Eliza Meteyard *Wedgwood Handbk.* Gloss. s.v., The more ordinary chimney-pieces had only a tablet and blocks...Occasionally the base of the columns had blocks also.

14. (Earlier U.S. examples.)

1796 *Aurora* (Philad.) 13 Dec. (Th.) The whole block of buildings included between that slip, Front Street, and the Fly Market. 1817 S. R. Brown *Western Gaz.* 101 Each block of lots has the advantage of two 16 feet alleys. 1837 *Knickerbocker Mag.* Jan. IX. 72 Paved thoroughfares and manufacturing or commercial blocks.

c. A fashionable promenade outside a particular block of buildings and shops in some Australian cities; hence *on the block*, on the promenade; *to do the block*, to lounge in the fashionable promenade.

1869 Marcus Clarke *Peripatetic Philosopher* 13 (Morris) If our Victorian youth showed their appreciation for domestic virtues, Victorian womanhood would 'do the Block' less frequently. 1872 'Resident' *Glimpses of Life in Victoria* 349 A certain portion of Collins Street, lined by the best drapers' and jewellers' shops..is known as 'The Block'. 1896 *Argus* 17 July 4/7 (Morris) Just as the busy man, who generally walks quickly, has to go slowly in the crowd on the Block. 1902 *Daily Chron.* 20 Oct. 5/2 Sundowners..who once enjoyed fat berths in Melbourne, 'doing the block' every afternoon in Collins-street.

d. Each of the large lots into which land for settlers is divided by the government. See also *Back blocks. *Austral.*

1858 Simmonds *Dict. Trade*, *Block*,..in colonial parlance a piece of land. 1866–7 *Acts S. Australia* 30 Vict. No. 21 § 6 No..lease shall be granted at a lower yearly rent than at the rate of Ten Shillings for every block or Section, and no such block or Section shall exceed one square mile of land therein comprised. 1872 *Ibid.* 35 & 36 Vict. No. 18 § 24 No person shall hold..more than three separate and detached blocks of land; and such area shall..be comprised in one block. 1909 B. R. Wise *Commw. Australia* 100 Some far-seeing men..would have set aside defined blocks for agricultural settlement. *Ibid.* 113, 27,000 acres, in forty-acre blocks. *Ibid.* 127 There has..been some 'dummying', but the majority of the block-holders are *bonâ-fide* occupiers.

e. *Mining* (Austral.). See quots.

1890 'R. Boldrewood' *Miner's Right* viii, The law said, if the ground was under a hundred feet deep it was no frontage, and must be worked on the block...The Liberator Lead was no frontage lead—but block, that is, ground to be worked in ordinary block claims. *Ibid.*, The ground will then be open for taking up claims in the block form.

f. A blockhouse. *U.S.*

1829 J. F. Cooper *Wish-ton-wish* vii. 108 He that is wise, however, will take but little of the latter, until his head be safely housed within some such building as yon block. 1845 W. G. Simms *Wigwam & Cabin* Ser. i. 57 As it was only a short mile and a half from the block, and we could hear of no Indians.

23. **block ball** *Baseball*, a ball, either hit or thrown, which is handled or stopped by a non-player; **block bond** *Bricklaying* (see quots. and Bond *sb.*[1] 13); **block capital**, a capital letter written in imitation of a printed capital; **block chain**, an endless chain composed of alternate blocks and links; **block coal**, coal that splits easily into blocks; *spec.* an American bituminous furnace coal; also, coal in large lumps; **block coefficient** *Naval Arch.* (see quot.); **block dwellings** *pl.*, dwellings consisting of sets of rooms for working-class families in large barrack-like buildings several stories high; hence *block dweller*; **block letter**, also = *block capital*; **block model** *Shipbuilding*, a model of a ship shaped from a block made up of flat pieces of wood fastened together, the lines of junction showing, on a reduced scale, the water-lines of the vessel to be built; **block plane** (see quot.); **block test** (see 10 d, above); **block train**, a railway train, the component parts of which form a complete train; **block working**, the working of railway traffic on the block system (see Block *sb.* 19 c).

1891 N. Crane *Baseball* 79 *Block ball, a batted or thrown ball handled by an outsider. 1864 Webster (1886) s.v. *Bond*, English or *block bond. 1901 Sturgis *Dict. Arch.* s.v. *Bond*, Block Bond. Same as Flemish Bond. 1902 *Combined Training* (War Office) 61 Names of places and persons will be written in *block capitals. 1924 *Contemp. Rev.* April 482, I published an article in the *Novoie Vremya* under the title 'Bread', which appeared in large block capitals. 1904 *Technol. & Sci. Dict.* (ed. Goodchild & Tweney), *Block Chain (*Cycles*). 1871 *Amer. Naturalist* V. 177 A visit will be made to the celebrated *Block-coal field (iron smelting coal). 1873 *Amer. Cycl.* (1881) IV. 726/2 The splint or block coal of north western Pennsylvania. 1883 Gresley *Gloss. Coal-m.* 1904 *Technol. & Sci. Dict.* (ed. Goodchild & Tweney). 1901 *Feilden's Mag.* IV. 421/1 In every case it is advisable also to calculate the value of the '*block coefficient' or so-called coefficient of fineness. 1902 *Encycl. Brit.* XXXII. 551/1 The block coefficient is the ratio of the volume of the immersed portion of the ship to the volume of the parallelopipedon. 1903 *Daily Chron.* 7 Jan. 3/3 No..dreams of impossible millennium will haunt the *block-dweller of the future. 1899 *Daily News* 17 Jan. 3/2 The slums are sickening,..and the *block dwellings often more like warehouses than homes. 1902 *Encycl. Brit.* XXXII. 673/2 Slum dwellings have been cleared under Cross's Acts 1875–82, and the Housing of the Working Classes Act, 1890; and..block dwellings have been erected. 1908 *Installation News* II. 115/2 The cost of current for a large *block-letter sign is frequently six or seven pounds a week. 1929 *Humorist* 5 Jan. 682 Name and address should be written here in plain block letters. 1901 *Feilden's Mag.* IV. 426/1 The angle of entrance..may either be measured from the *block-model or calculated. 1884 Knight *Dict. Mech.* Suppl., **Block Plane*, a plane, the bit of which is set at a very acute angle to the working surface, to enable it to plane across the grain of the wood. 1902 *Encycl. Brit.* XXXII. 154/2 In *block-trains, where the component coaches are permanently coupled together, one dynamo sometimes lights all the carriages. 1904 *Westm. Gaz.* 19 Jan. 10/2 With *block working, only about 25,000 miles..are at present worked in America on the block system.

24. *attrib.* and *Comb.*, with the meaning 'in a block or mass', 'inclusive', 'solid', etc., as *block rate, vote*, etc.; **block-booking** (see quot.); hence **block-booker**; **block closure**, the legislative closure of the clauses of a measure in a block or in blocks; **block grant**, a fixed inclusive parliamentary grant made to Board Schools under the New Education Code of 1900.

1927 *Daily Express* 25 July 6 The Wicked '*Block-booker'. 1925 *Weekly Westm.* 29 Aug. 444/3 *Block-booking is the system whereby American producers refuse to let the English exhibitors have one important film unless they take also a 'block' of others, which they may never have seen. 1926 *Manchester Guardian Weekly* Mar. 221/3 The Government are prepared to remove the block-booking grievance by legislation if necessary. 1901 *Daily Chron.* 14 Aug. 3/6 There was a *block closure to which the Government could resort. 1900 *Westm. Gaz.* 24 Mar. 2/2 Schools earning the very highest grants will suffer because their *block grant will be less than the old variable grant. 1902 *Encycl. Brit.* XXVII. 662/2 In place of a variable grant [there is to be] one block grant payable to all schools alike. 1909 *Westm. Gaz.* 1 Mar. 10/3 The insurance offices are reducing the *block rate of £1 per cent. that has been charged in the fire-zone of the City. 1901 *Daily Chron.* 15 July 7/3 Welsh miners, who, by the *block vote, were enabled to return a Welshman to the Victorian Parliament.

Block, *v.* Add: 3. c. *Draughts.* To force (one's opponent's men) into such a position that they cannot move without being captured.

1867 *Bohn's Handbk. Games* 408 The game is won by him who can first succeed in capturing, or blocking up, all his adversary's men. 1877 *Encycl. Brit.* VII. 445/2 The game [*sc.* draughts] proceeds until one of the players has all his men and kings taken, or has all those left on the board blocked.

d. *Cards.* (See quot. 1898.)

1885 'Cavendish' *Whist Devel.* Pref. p. x, All good players know that it is disadvantageous to block their partner's long suit. *Ibid.* 57 If the lead was from ace, queen, knave, ten only, B would block his own suit. 1898 Melrose *Scientific Whist* 24 The retaining of a high card against a partner's command is termed 'blocking' or 'obstructing' his suit.

4. (Earlier U.S. example.)

1844 G. W. Kendall *Santa Fé Exped.* II. xiii. 260 Soon after [he] ordered his own men to leave the gambling cot of the leper, and by this means 'blocked the game'.

b. *To block off*: to stop, to head off. *U.S. colloq.*

1893 W. K. Post *Harvard Stories* 86 The two opposing crowds..swept across the diamond 'blocking off the owners of the two dogs. 1899 A. H. Quinn *Pennsylv. Stories* 190, I tried to fix up two or three things with Miss Fitzgerald and she blocked me off each time, very nicely, it is true, but still she blocked me off.

9. (Additional U.S. examples of *block out*.)

1753 Washington *Diaries* I. 59 They..told 50 [canoes].. besides many others which were blocked-out, in Readiness to make. 1829 *Massachusetts Spy* 16 Dec. (Th.) There are portions [of the message] which bear the marks of having been 'blocked out' by General Jackson. 1879 F. R. Stockton *Rudder Grange* xvi. 194 I've blocked out the whole of the rest of it. 1911 H. S. Harrison *Queed* iv. 49, I wish you would block out a series of articles..designed to prepare the public mind for a thorough-going reform.

10. b. *Drapery.* To make into a block (*Block *sb.* 6 f).

1905 H. G. Wells *Kipps* i. iii. § 2 With hands much exercised in rolling and blocking. *Ibid.* iii. iii, One whole piece most exquisitely blocked of every possible width of tape.

11. b. To pave (a street) with blocks.

1891 *Argus* (Melbourne) 25 Nov. 7/8 Only those streets in which the most traffic takes place will be blocked.

12. *Sheep-shearing. To block out*: see quot.

1886 C. Scott *Sheep-farming* 171 The sheep should be.. shorn on the new wool. Blocking them out on the old wool is often done, but..any old wool left may disqualify a winner.

Blockade, *sb.* Add: 3. *spec.* in U.S., a stoppage or block on a railway by snow or some accident. (Cf. quots. 1881 in 3.) Also *attrib.*

1867–9 *Trans. Ill. Agric. Soc.* VII. 419 An effectual snow blockade around the city, and on nearly all our Western railroads. 1873 J. H. Beadle *Undevel. West* xix. 350 With the snow sheds since constructed, and other precautions, we may reasonably expect no more blockades. 1904 *N. Y. Times* 5 May 3 After it had become known that the system was paralysed 'blockade signs' were hung out at all the stations. 1910 *N. Y. Even. Post* 13 Dec. 3 When a drawbar on the middle car of a third Avenue elevated train broke..a long blockade began.

b. A barrier on a river. *U.S.*

1871 *Game Laws* (*N. C.*) in *Fur, Fin & Feather* (1872) 153 It shall not be lawful for any person to draw a seine.. between the blockade near Hill's Point..and the falls at Wm. S. Battle's factory.

Blockade, *v.* Add: 2. *spec.* in U.S., to block (a road or railway).

1872 *Rep. Vermont Board Agric.* I. 24 An exceedingly severe snow storm having completely blockaded many of the roads, many were prevented from attending the meetings.

Blocker. Add:

1. Also in *Hat-making* (cf. Block *sb.* 4 a, *v.* 8).

1894 *Daily News* 26 Apr. 2/5 A straw hat blocker. 1898 *Daily Chron.* 14 Oct. 10/5 Blocker..for felt and straw hats.

Blockhouse, *sb.* Add:

1. d. (Earlier U.S. example.)

1821 Z. Hawley *Tour* (Ohio) (1822) 52 (Th.) A block-house differs from a log one in this particular in the former the logs are hewn square, so that they are smooth within and without, and the latter are hewn, only within, having the bark on the outside.

3. **blockhouse system**, the system of separating the theatre of war by chains of blockhouses, devised by Lord Kitchener in the later stages of the South African war, 1899–1902.

1901 *Daily Chron.* 4 Sept. 5/3 The section of the line south of Pienaars River..is not yet fully protected by blockhouses, the blockhouse system having been first applied to those sections most requiring such protection.

Blockhouse (blǫ·khaus), *v.* [f. the sb.]

1. *trans.* To cut off from occupation or attack by a line of blockhouses under the *blockhouse system*, q.v.

1901 *Daily Chron.* 4 Sept. 5/3 Two thousand miles of railway are already 'blockhoused'. *Ibid.* 27 Dec. 4/5 General De Wet..is doing his best to prevent the 'blockhousing' of the north-eastern angle of the Orange River Colony.

2. To furnish with blockhouses.

1902 *Appleton's Ann. Cycl.* 629/1 All the 2300 miles of railroad were blockhoused.

Blocking, *vbl. sb.* Add:

1. b. Signalling by the 'block system' (see Block *sb.* 19 c). Also *attrib.*, as *blocking inspector*.

1903 *Westm. Gaz.* 26 Oct. 13/1 Blocking inspector between Eastwood and Bradford. 1908 Tratman *Railway Track* (ed. 3) 266 In some cases a third position [of the semaphore arm] is introduced for permissive blocking. 1908 W. G. Raymond *Railroad Engin.* 121 The foregoing description introduces no distant signals, and in early automatic blocking there were none. 1909 H. R. Wilson *Safety Brit. Railways* 59 The signalman must give what is known as the blocking-back signal.

c. *Bookbinding.* The impressing of book-covers with ornamental designs combined on one plate and impressed by machinery; also *attrib.*, as *blocking-machine, -press, -shop*.

1846 Dodd *Brit. Manuf.* VI. 103 This is..effected..by means of a small blocking-press. *Ibid.* 105 The punches or small devices..are fixed..to a metallic plate, and thus impressed on the book at one blow by a press. This is then called 'blocking'. In the 'blocking-shop' are [etc.]. 1902 *Encycl. Brit.* XXVI. 302/2 Blocking Machine...A blocking press is now, in consequence of the size of many of the blocks, a large and cumbersome machine.

d. *Hat-making.* The shaping of a hat on the block (see Block *sb.* 4 a); also *attrib.*, as *blocking-kettle, -machine* (hence *-machinist*).

1845 Dodd *Brit. Manuf.* V. 170 The shaping of hats, from the first rough 'blocking' to the production of a flat and smooth-edged brim. 1874 Knight *Dict. Mech.*, *Blocking-kettle*, a hot bath in which hats are softened in the process of manufacture, so as to be drawn over blocks. 1884 *Ibid.* Suppl., *Blocking Machine*, a machine in which the crude cone-shaped hat-body is brought to shape. 1921 *Dict. Occupational Terms* (1927) § 409 *Blocking machinist*; (i) (felt hats) pulls felt hood by hand on to block [etc.]; (ii) (straw hats) presses hat..in a gas-heated machine [etc.].

e. *Bootmaking.* (See quot. 1874.)

1874 Knight *Dict. Mech.*, *Blocking*,..the process of bending leather for boot-fronts to the required shapes. 1889 Shaw *Fabian Ess. Socialism* 67 A visitor to a shoe factory to-day will see the following machines..for blocking.

5. Blocks collectively.

1901 *Daily Chron.* 3 Sept. 7/4 Karri blocking.

Blockman [2] (blǫ·kmæ̆n). [f. Block *sb.*] A butcher's, fishmonger's, etc., shop assistant employed chiefly at the block in cutting up meat, filleting fish, etc.

1903 *Daily Chron.* 16 Sept. 8/5 Fishmongers.—Good blockman wanted.

Blocky (blǫ·ki), *a.* [f. Block *sb.* + -y [1].]

1. Of the nature of or resembling a block. *esp.* a. Of a person or animal: Of solid build, stocky. b. Defining a commercial grade of shellac.

1879 Miss Jackson *Shropsh. Word-bk.*, *Blocky*.., short and stout. 1895 *Daily News* 4 Sept. 7/5 Shellac...Ordinary to good second orange cakey and blocky 115s. to 119s. 1900 *Westm. Gaz.* 11 Dec. 7/3 A most shapely beast [*sc.* heifer], ..being grandly filled up, and of a most blocky type throughout. 1904 *N. Y. Tribune* 15 May, A blocky pair of forty-seven inch ponies.

2. *Photogr.* Having the appearance of being printed in blocks, from an unequal distribution of light and shade. 1889 *Cent. Dict.*

Blondinette (blǫndine·t). [f. Blond + -ine [2] + -ette.] A breed of oriental frilled pigeons.

1879 L. Wright *Pract. Pigeon Keeper* 177 Blondinettes ..are..peak-crested and plain-headed. 1881 J. C. Lyell *Fancy Pigeons* 234 The blondinette has been produced in recent years, according to Mr. Caridia...The blondinettes bear the same relation to the satinettes, in their several varieties, as the *schietti* or whole-coloured Triganicas do to the *gazzi* or pied ones. *Ibid.*, The blondinettes are grouse-legged and generally peak crested.

Blood, *sb.* Add:

1. f. Phrase. (*You cannot get*) *blood out of a stone* (fig.), i.e. pity or sympathy from the hard-hearted, or money from the avaricious.

1865 Dickens *Mut. Fr.* iv. xv, You can't get blood out of a stone, Riderhood. 1889 Stevenson & Osbourne *Wrong Box* 8 'You cannot get blood from a stone,' observed the lawyer. 1929 *Observer* 21 July 15 This Court has no machinery that I know of for extracting blood from stones.

3. d. *Blood and thunder*, bloodshed and violence; used attrib. in *blood-and-thunder book, tale*, etc., one describing the murderous exploits of desperadoes. (orig. *U.S.*) Also shortened to *blood* (esp. in *pl.*), as in *blood books*, (*penny*) *bloods*.

1870 F. Fern *Ginger-Snaps* 206 Some blood-and-thunder novel. 1875 *Congress. Rec.* Mar. 106/1 All the rest of these blood-and-thunder stories he does not profess to know. 1876 *Portland Transcript* May (Farmer) Beware of the cheap, trashy romances, the blood and thunder tales. 1881 A. A. Hayes *New Colorado* xi. 149 A hero for a juvenile 'blood-and-thunder' weekly. 1887 *Century Mag.* Dec. 194/2 I'm not likely to hold myself accountable to any blood-and-thunder reprobate who tries to influence my conduct. 1894 *Daily News* 29 May 6/4 'Blood and thunder books':.. 'blood books'—brief and brutal—is the expression in general use. 1897 Locke *Derelicts* iii, A writer of 'penny bloods.' 1927 *Observer* 11 Dec. 15/2 This play is a blood-and-thunder piece.

e. *Blood and iron* [G. *blut und eisen*], military force as distinguished from diplomacy, esp. in *the man of blood and iron*, Prince Bismarck, who advocated the use of this as his policy. Hence *Blood-and-ironness*.

1872 *New Dominion Monthly* Oct. 195/1 You will find him indeed a man of 'blood and iron'. 1877 *Gentl. Mag.* CCXL. 64 Sayings which, with Bismarck's signature affixed, have become..'winged words'. Some..like.. 'blood and iron'..he..repudiates. 1882 J. C. Morison *Macaulay* v. 158 Mr. Carlyle has been heard to say that Rhadamanthus would certainly give Macaulay four dozen lashes when he went to the Shades, for his treatment of Marlborough. This is quite in character for the Scotch apostle of 'blood and iron'. 1889 H. P. Hughes *Social Chr.* v. 74 'There', they are saying, 'nothing succeeds like a blood-and-iron policy.' 1891 *Sat. Rev.* 16 May 605/1 The blood-and-ironness of Bismarck. 1898 A. J. Butler tr. *Bismarck's Refl. & Remin.* I. 310 We should be unable to avoid a serious contest, a contest which could only be settled by blood and iron.

12. b. with a qualifying word.

1894 C. B. Lowe *Breeding Racehorses* 180 He will always do best with a strong return to his stout Blacklock, Birdcatcher, and Glencoe blood. 1902 *Encycl. Brit.* XXV. 190/2 When Shorthorn breeders of to-day talk of 'Booth blood', or of 'Bates blood', they refer to animals descended from the respective herds of Thomas Booth and Thomas Bates.

15. c. At public schools and universities applied to those who are regarded as setting the fashion in habits and dress; also, a youthful member of a party, etc.

1892 *Pall Mall Gaz.* 8 Mar. 7/1 The result was that the new party won by 127 to 103...A great triumph for the Bloods—as we are accustomed to call them—who mustered in great force to defeat Mr. Childers. 1893 *Granta* 9 June 374/2 A Committee, consisting of a blood, a Girtonian, and a resident married M.A., shall supervise all flirtations. 1896 *Ibid.* 16 May 310/1 Mifflin and 'is friends talked..an' said 'ow much better Cambridge'd be if there wasn't no 'bloods' to spoil things. 1901 *Wykehamist* 27 June (tr. Martial, Epigr. iii. 63) O Cotilus, you are a blood.

19. **blood-alley** [see Ally], a boy's white marble marked with red spiral lines; **blood-beet**, the red beet-root; **blood boat** (see quot. 1914), also *attrib.*; **blood cell**, a corpuscle of the blood, esp. an oval nucleated one; **blood count**, the action or process of counting the number of the corpuscles contained in a definite volume of blood; *differential blood count*, the determination of the relative numbers of the different varieties of white corpuscles; **blood culture** [Culture *sb.* 3 c] *Bacteriol.*, a culture made with blood serum as a medium; **blood disc**, a red blood-corpuscle; also, a *blood plaque*; **blood-drinker**, a primitive savage who killed and feasted on his 'kill'; *fig.* one who has a lust for blood; hence **blood-drinking** *ppl. a.*; **blood dust**, a collective name for the minute refractive bodies found floating free in the blood plasma; **blood-flow**, the flow of blood through the human system; **blood groove**, a groove cut in the head or the shaft of an arrow or spear, supposed to increase the flow of blood from the wound made by the weapon; **blood islands** *pl.*, reddish patches in the vascular area of the embryo, where blood vessels are forming (Billings 1890); **blood-lust**, lust for the shedding of blood; **blood orange**, a variety of orange having the pulp streaked with red; earlier *blood-red orange*; **blood pheasant**, a species of pheasant (see quot.) marked with red on the throat and breast; **blood plaque, plate, platelet**, a minute disc-shaped body found in large numbers in mammalian blood; **blood plasma**, the colourless fluid of the blood containing the blood corpuscles (Billings 1890); **blood-poisoning**, a morbid condition of the blood due to the introduction of poisonous matter from without; esp. toxæmia; **blood pressure**, abnormal pressure on the walls of the blood-vessels; **blood-pump**, (*a*) see quot. 1902; (*b*) *Pugilistic slang*, the heart; **blood-red orange** = **blood orange*; **blood revenge** = Vendetta; **blood spoor**, the trail of blood left by a wounded animal; **blood sports** *sb. pl.*, sports involving the killing of animals, esp. sports of the chase; **blood-stream**, the stream of blood circulating through the human system; **blood-striking**, a disease incident to cattle see Striking *vbl. sb.* 2 b; **blood sugar**, glucose contained in the blood; **blood-tax**, a derogatory term for military conscription.

1854 Anne E. Baker *Northampt. Gloss.* s.v. *Al*, *Blood alleys. 1881 *Leic. Gloss.* s.v. *Alley*, If streaked with red veins it is called a 'blood alley'. 1923 *Daily Mail* 29 Jan. 8 The most skilful English errand boys that ever shot a blood-alley. 1831 Peck *Guide for Emigrants* ii. 141 The *blood beet [is] less deeply colored. 1837 Colman *Rep. Agric. Mass.* (1838) 39 Other milk men speak of trials with the common blood-beet for the feed of milch cows with great advantage. 1889 Barrère & Leland *Dict. Slang*, **Blood boat* (naval). 1899 Bullen *Log Sea-waif* 230 Half the crew..looked as if all the ways of 'Western Ocean blood-boats' were familiar to them. 1914 Ld. Chas. Beresford *Mem.* I. 2 The 'blood-boat' (the jolly-boat bringing beef to the ship) midshipman of a man-of-war. 1866 Aitken *Pract. Med.* II. 57 Salts..in which the *blood-cells ultimately become deficient. 1878 Bell tr. *Gegenbaur's Comp. Anat.* 172 In many Nemertina the blood-cells have a red colour. 1901 Dorland *Med. Dict.*, *Blood-count. 1907 *Practitioner* Dec. 852 A blood-count, made two years ago, showed: Red cells, 5,000,000, [etc.]. 1925 Poulton, Symonds, & Barber *Taylor's Pract. Med.* (ed. 13) 87 *Blood culture gives a high proportion of positive results. 1845 Todd & Bowman *Phys. Anat.* I. 60 Certain particles, the *blood-discs, which float in it [*sc.* the blood] in great numbers. 1879 *Jrnl. Anat. & Physiol.* XIV. 295 All cells..from which red blood-discs may spring. 1898 Meredith *Odes Fr. Hist.* 16 The *blood-drinker's madness fast upon her. 1899 *Daily News* 28 June 8/4 The primitive 'food group' of hunters, who, like the beasts they killed, were 'blood-drinkers.' 1903 *Edin. Rev.* Oct. 307 *Blood-drinking savages. 1901 Dorland *Med. Dict.* s.v. *Blood*, *Blood-dust, or hemoconiæ. 1873 T. H. Green *Introd. Pathol.* 329 Thrombosis from Retardation of the *Blood-flow. 1875 Huxley & Martin *Elem. Biol.* (1883) 210 The blood-flow in the small arteries of the web. 1897 *Geogr. Jrnl.* (R.G.S.) X. 156 Arrowheads and spears, many of them curiously barbed and twisted, and some showing a knowledge of the value of the '*blood-groove'. 1896 *Daily News* 21 Jan. 5/4 The fiercest fighting I ever saw—the most envenomed *blood-lust. 1907 *Westm. Gaz.* 29 Aug. 7/3 It is a sort of blood-lust, and is well known to students of the psychology of crime. 1862 Hereman *Vine &*

Fruit Tree Cultiv. 43 Maltese *Blood Oranges. 1892 *Granta* 14 May 321/1 The piles of blood oranges were diminishing rapidly. 1864 Jerdon *Birds India* III. 572 *Ithaginis cruentus*,..the Green *Blood-Pheasant. 1884 *Encycl. Brit.* XVII. 341/2 Among the birds [of Nepal] are ..the blood pheasant (*Ithaginis cruentus*), etc. 1889 *Buck's Handbk. Med. Sci.* VIII. 626/2 *Blood-plaques, methods of studying. 1885 *Ibid.* I. 554/1 The *blood-plates are not products of the degeneration of white corpuscles. 1898 W. S. Lazarus-Barlow *Gen. Pathol.* 153 The number of *blood-platelets in normal blood has been variously estimated from 180,000 to 500,000 per cubic millimetre. 1882 (*title*) *Blood poisoning by water works filter beds. 1886 *Encycl. Brit.* XXI. 656/2 After a wound.. blood-poisoning may occur. 1874 Garrod *Mat. Med.* (ed. 4) 123 Small doses raise the *blood-pressure. 1888 *Encycl. Brit.* XXIV. 97/2 The blood-pressure gradually diminishes from the heart to the periphery. 1920 Wodehouse *Damsel in Distress* iv, His blood-pressure at a far higher figure than his doctor would have approved of. 1898 *Daily News* 15 Nov. 8/4 Ryan [a boxer] kept to work at his little target over the *blood-pump. 1902 *Encycl. Brit.* XXX. 379/1 For the purpose of his researches on the gases in the blood, he [C. F. W. Ludwig] designed the mercurial blood-pump. 1838 Loudon *Arbor. et Fruticetum Brit.* I. 396 The kinds are, the common, Seville, and *blood-red orange. 1855 Martineau tr. *Gregorovius's Corsica* i. x. 144 Many a case is known of one bandit having..slain another..for *blood-revenge. 1877 *Gentl. Mag.* Apr. 478 The vendetta or duty of blood-revenge. 1863 W. C. Baldwin *Afr. Hunting* v. 129 The *blood-spoor of one of the wounded koodoos. 1899 Rider Haggard *Swallow* iv, They started to follow the blood spoor up the kloof. 1895 *Humanity* Oct. 58 If a poll could be taken, we believe that *blood sports would be condemned by a larger number of persons than could be mustered on any other humanitarian issue. 1873 T. H. Green *Introd. Pathol.* (ed. 2) 109 The reproduction of the malignant growth in distant tissues is..owing to the entry of its elements into the *blood-stream. 1928 *Daily Express* 6 June 5/3 Alkaline citrates, which are changed into alkaline carbonates in the blood stream. 1861 *Blood-striking [see Striking *vbl. sb.* 2 b]. 1861 *Chamb. Encycl.* II. 135 Black Quarter,..Blood Striking...An apoplectic disease peculiar to cattle. 1927 Haldane & Huxley *Anim. Biol.* vii. 156 A dose of 100 grams will make the *blood-sugar rise above 0.17 per cent. 1890 H. P. Hughes *Philanthropy of God* v. 75 France is the mother of Conscription. What has she gained by that *blood-tax? 1901 Shee *Briton's 1st Duty* 250, I appeal to the working men of Great Britain.. not to be misled by catch-phrases about 'the liberty of the subject' and the ridiculous cant about a 'Blood Tax'!

Blood, *v.* Add:

5. To apply a coat of blood to (leather) in leather-colouring, in order to obtain a good black.

19.. *Mod. Amer. Tanning* 110 (Cent. Dict. Suppl.).

6. *intr.* with *it*: To play the 'blood'.

1922 Joad *Highbrows* v. 179 When I wasn't 'blooding' it with the second-year men..your scout..used to bring your lunch down into my rooms.

Blooded, *a.* 3. Add: Chiefly *U.S.* (Earlier examples.)

1778 *Maryland Jrnl.* 20 Jan., Advt. (Th.) Several blooded mares and fillies will also be sold. 1829 *Massachusetts Spy* 10 June (Th.) [He] presented Colonel Gardner Chandler with a fine blooded colt. 1836 *Southern Lit. Messenger* II. 161, I will get one of the blooded plough-horses, and he will make out as well as any.

Bloo·d-horse. Chiefly *U.S.* [Blood *sb.* 12 b.] A thoroughbred or pedigree horse.

1800 [see Blood *sb.* 12 c]. 1841 H. S. Foote *Texas & Texans* II. 383 They [*sc.* wild horses]..are ..inferior to the American blood-horse in volume of muscle. 1856 Mrs. Stowe *Dred* II. 145 The fleet blood-horse was whirling Harry and Lizette past bush and tree. 1860 O. W. Holmes *Prof. Breakf.-t.* iii. 65 Admiral Sir Isaac Coffin sent out two fine blood-horses.

Blood-money. Add:

c. 'A bonus paid to other workmen in a newspaper office for the privilege of setting fat copy' (*Funk's Standard Dict.* 1895). *Printers' slang.*

Blood-root. (Additional U.S. examples.)

1835 R. M. Bird *Hawks of Hawk-hollow* I. v. 62 There is such an array of azaleas below, with blood-roots, and wind-flowers. 1851 C. Cist *Cincinnati* 211 Jacobs Merrel ..prepares..extracts..such as..blood-root. 1898 B. Torrey in *Atlantic Monthly* Apr. 460/2 The sun's heat..melting the snow of the shad bushes and the blood root.

Bloodshot, *sb.* 1. (Later example.)

1801 in C. Cist *Cincinnati* (1841) 187 They..will so gorge themselves with the film, or bloodshots, that, in the morning, they will be discharged dead from the eye.

Bloodstock (blɒ·dstǫk). [f. Blood *sb.* (12 c) + Stock *sb.*[1] (54).] Thoroughbred or pedigree horses collectively. Also *attrib.*

1888 W. Day *Horse* 9 Those engaged in breeding blood-stock only. 1905 Ridgeway *Thoroughbred Horse* 216 The effect produced on Hittite horses by the blood stock imported through Solomon. 1909 *Westm. Gaz.* 15 July 12/2 Messrs. Tattersall's bloodstock sales at Newmarket. 1912 (*title*) The bloodstock breeder's review.

Blood-sucker. 1. Add:

spec. a. A lizard belonging to the species *Lacerta cristata*, the individuals of which change their colour, especially about the neck, from grey to dark red. b. A lizard of the genus *Amphibolurus* (*Grammatophora*), esp. of the species *A. muricata*.

a. 1819 J. Morton *Poet. Rem. Leyden* p. xc, A large lizard, termed a blood-sucker. 1882 *Encycl. Brit.* XIV. 736/2 *Calotes* is another genus of agamoids peculiar to the East Indies; it comprises numerous species well known in India by the name of 'blood-suckers.'

b. 1852 Mrs. C. Meredith *My Home in Tasmania* II. 37 Another description of lizard is here vulgarly called the 'blood-sucker'. 1886 F. McCoy *Zool. Victoria* (1890) II. xii. 47 Grammatophora muricata...The Blood-sucker.

Bloody, *a.* Add:

2. b. **bloody cardinal** = Cardinal-flower; **bloody chasm** *U.S.*, the estrangement between North and South caused by the Civil War; **bloody shirt** *U.S.*, the symbol of hostility between North and South; also in general use.

1852 D. G. Mitchell *Dream Life* 199 The *bloody cardinal of the swamp-lands. 1876 *Congress. Rec.* June 3791/1 This measure is one of conciliation. It reunites; it fills up the '*bloody chasm'. 1888 *Ibid.* Dec. 161/1, I hope I will be excused to-day from again shaking hands across the 'bloody chasm'. 1890 Farmer *Slang* s.v., To bridge the bloody chasm, a favourite expression with orators who, during the years immediately succeeding the Civil War, sought to obliterate the memory of the struggle. 1876 *Congress. Rec.* Apr. 2523/2 The '*bloody shirt' is freely used at one end of the Capitol, and here at this end is the bugaboo of State rights. 1887 *Nation* (N. Y.) 29 Dec. 514/1 It [the speech] was devoted to the waving of the bloody shirt. 1889 Farmer *Americanisms* s.v., To wave the bloody shirt..is a political phrase used in the States to signify the opening anew or keeping alive of factious strife on party questions. 1904 *Indianapolis News* 23 June 6 To those that remember campaigns a few years ago, this is very much like the 'bloody shirt', which did duty for so many years.

C. 2. **bloody-nosed beetle** (see quot.).

1880 *Encycl. Brit.* XIII. 150/1 *Timarcha* (the Bloody-nosed Beetle).

Bloom, *sb.*[1] Add:

4. d. (See quot.)

1908 *Animal Managem.* 134 In no case should..the work [be] so hard, that the colt's 'bloom,' *i.e.*, his round and glossy sleekness, disappears.

8. The perfume exhaled from wine, bouquet.

1888 *Encycl. Brit.* XXIV. 602/2 The smell common to all wines (which remains in an empty wine cask after the bloom proper has gone).

Bloomer [1]. Add:

3. [for *blooming letter*: see *Blooming *ppl. a.* 6.] A floriated initial letter of the alphabet.

1899 Mackail *W. Morris* II. 256 The large floriated initials, or 'bloomers', in the slang of the press. 1901 *Sunday Times* 21 Apr., This book will be in the new type, with a fresh set of 'bloomers' specially designed for it.

4. *slang.* [See quot. 1889.] A very great mistake: chiefly in phr. *to make a bloomer*.

1889 Barrère & Leland *Dict. Slang*, *Bloomer* (Australian), prison slang for a mistake. Abbreviated from the expression 'a blooming error'. 1902 *Westm. Gaz.* 25 Nov. 8/1 The defendant replied, 'You have made a bloomer, old chap; you never made a greater mistake in your life'. 1920 Wodehouse *Damsel in Distress* xv, I think you are making the bloomer of a lifetime over his hat-swatting chappie. 1928 *Daily Express* 19 Apr. 15 His mount, Clearmount, made a terrible bloomer at the last fence.

Bloomer [2]. Add: 1. (Earlier examples.)

1851 *Boston Transcript* 26 May 2/3 (Th.) The *Bee* says the daughter of Dr. Hanson, of this city, appeared in the Bloomer suit..last week. 1851 *Ibid.* 29 May 2/4 (Th.) The first 'Bloomer' made its appearance in our city yesterday. 1855 *Kansas Tribune* (Th.) Perhaps Lawrence [Kansas] is the only city in America where the majority of the ladies wear Bloomers.

b. Loose trousers reaching to the knee or knickerbockers worn by women for cycling, gymnasium practice, etc.; called also 'rational dress'.

1895 *Westm. Gaz.* 25 July 8/1 Female teachers who have been riding bicycles in male attire, commonly called bloomers. 1906 Galsworthy *Man of Property* iii. i. 289 She could tell you..what they were doing in Paris about wearing bloomers. 1909 *Daily Chron.* 5 Aug. 7/3 [The hockey girl] in her short skirts, bloomers, flannel blouse, and cloth cap.

2. (Earlier examples.)

1852 *Knickerbocker Mag.* Sept. XL. 241 The Bloomers once triumphant, so prophetic ken will be required to read their future tactics. 1854 *Congress. Globe* 20 May, App. 717 Bloomers wearing the apparel of men, and men wrapped in the apparel of women.

Hence **Bloo·mered** *a.*, wearing bloomer costume; **Bloo·merism** (earlier example); **Bloo·merize** *v. trans.* to dress in bloomers; also *fig.*

1900 *Daily News* 4 Dec. 6/5 In these days of Lady Wranglers and *bloomered 'sportswomen'. 1907 *Westm. Gaz.* 2 Oct. 1/3 The outer lines were marked by companies of ..bloomered Tirailleurs. 1852 *Knickerbocker Mag.* Sept. XL. 240 We consider *Bloomerism as the most dangerous of modern 'isms'. 1885 Mrs. Lynn Linton *Chr. Kirkland* III. i. 18 Doubtful whether they were girls *Bloomerized or boys in feminine tunics. 1897 *Daily News* 3 Feb. 6/4 The New Woman..has fairly bloomerised journalism in the United States.

Bloo·mful, *a.* [f. Bloom *sb.*[1]] Rich in bloom.

1890 *Lippincott's Mag.* Mar. 392 Bloomful maidens. 1913 Mrs. Stratton-Porter *Laddie* xv, Then she leant toward me all wavery, and shining eyed, and bloomful.

Bloominess (blū·minės). [f. Bloomy *a.*[1] + -ness.] The condition of being covered with bloom or having a bloom-like surface.

1889 'Theo Gift' *Not for the Night-time* 75 A canary-coloured gown, with a white bloominess on the edges of it. 1895 *Westm. Gaz.* 22 Apr. 3/1 In the lanes where the woodbine leaves are showing the brown bloominess on the backs of their unfolding leaves.

Blooming, *vbl. sb.*[2] *attrib.* Add: **blooming machine, blooming rolls** (see quots.).

1869 *Spons' Dict. Engin.* i. 367 The *blooming machine, invented by Jeremiah Brown..consists of three large eccentric rolls..placed horizontally in the strong holsters..,the centres of the rolls being arranged in a triangular position, and the bottom roll..being nearly central between the two top rolls. 1888 *Lockwood's Dict. Terms Mech. Engin.*, **Blooming Rolls*, see Puddling Rolls...*Puddling Rolls*, or *Forge Train*, the first set of rolls through which a shingled bloom is passed.

Blooming, *ppl. a.* Add:

6. *Blooming* (*initial*) *letter*: a floriated initial letter of the alphabet; = *Bloomer [1] 3.

1713 Jas. Watson *Hist. Printing* Pref. 9 Curiously cut Head-Pieces, Finis's, Blooming-Letters [etc.]. 1785 W. Herbert *Typogr. Antiq.* 527 The chronicle of each reign begins with a blooming letter. 1902 Sayle *Init. Lett. Early Eng. Printed Bks.* in *Trans. Bibliogr. Soc.* VII. 18 The bloomers or blooming initials as Herbert calls them.

Bloomsburian (blūmzbiū·riăn). [f. *Bloomsbury* (see below) + -an.] A dweller in Bloomsbury, London, formerly a fashionable residential district.

1902 *Daily Chron.* 24 Nov. 4/4 The flippant playwright who made one of his characters say that 'the Bloomsburians live mainly on a dish called "smoked 'addick."' 1927 *Weekly Dispatch* 23 Oct. 11/2 A horde of minor Bloomsburians.

Blossom, *sb.* Add: 1. b. Also said of grain, grass, etc.

1769 Washington *Diaries* I. 327 The head [of the wheat] was shot out, and in many places in Blossom. 1868 *Rep. U.S. Commissioner Agric.* (1869) 423 F. V. Stewart..states that his practice has been to commence cutting the grass when in the 'second blossom'.

3. a. (Example.)

1883 J. H. Beadle *Western Wilds* xxxiv. 560 We are certainly near the outcrop from which the 'blossom' was broken.

4. **blossom-rock** *U.S.* (see sense 3 a).

1878 J. H. Beadle *Western Wilds* xxx. 479 Men were let down from above to 'prospect', a crevice was found with blossom rock. 1881 A. A. Hayes *New Colorado* vi. 79 If he had only had a keen eye for 'blossom rock' and other indications,..how differently history might have read.

Blossom (blǫ·səm), *v.*[2] *dial.* [var. Blissom *v.*] *intr.* Of a ewe: To be desirous of coupling with a ram.

1808 *Compl. Grazier* (ed. 3) 47 Various expedients have been resorted to, in order to make the ewes *blossom*. 1823 E. Moor *Suffolk Words*.

Blossomry (blǫ·səmri). [f. Blossom *sb.* + -ry.] Blossoms collectively.

1901 Abp. Armagh in *Westm. Gaz.* 3 Jan. 8/2 Such souls predestined have not one high range, One climate's blossomry alone.

Blot, *sb.*[1] Add:

4. *Painting.* (See quot.)

1910 *Edin. Rev.* Apr. 371 Painters are accustomed to speak of the 'Blot' of a picture, meaning its immediate appearance as colour, line, massing, or flat space.

Blotch, *sb.* Add:

1. c. A disease of fruit or leaves, characterized by the formation of spots. *Sooty blotch*, a disease of the apple. 1909 *Cent. Dict.* Suppl.

Blotter. Add: 1. d. A 'brand-blotter'. *U.S.*

1920 Mulford *J. Nelson* xii. 126 There ain't no sense in totin' it by th' glass to a crowd of blotters. They'll hold more liquor than a gopher hole.

3. (Early U.S. examples.)

1769 *Carroll Papers* in *Maryland Hist. Mag.* XII. 284 In looking over the blotter I found your agrect with Rumsey to sell Deerhill for £50 Penn currency. 1770 *Ibid.* XIII. 61 Pray let me know the sum you charge in yr Blotter as paid you by me when I went downe.

4. A record of arrests and charges in a police office; a charge-sheet; also *gen.* a record-book or list. *U.S.*

1887 *Harper's Mag.* Mar. 500/2 Every item of police duty, and of civil or criminal occurrence, is inscribed on the 'blotter'. 1901 *Munsey's Mag.* XXIV. 540/2 It is a month of uncommon virtue when the blotter shows as few as a hundred arrests. 1906 *Atlantic Monthly* Feb. 264 It was necessary..to examine the day-book or blotter in the chief clerk's office [at the Patent Office]. 1910 *Washington Times* 14 Dec. 1 Three more additions were made yesterday to the hospital blotters.

Blotting, *vbl. sb.* Add:

4. *techn.* Material for blotting-paper; also, the finished article.

1872 *Eng. Mech.* 15 Nov. 228/3 [To] give to used..or dry ..blotting its original absorbent power. 1880 J. Dunbar *Pract. Papermaker* 72 For pink blottings furnish two thirds of white cottons and one third of turkey reds. *Ibid.*, In this way the author has made blotting which was considered a good article. 1920 *Printers' & Stat. Yr. Bk.* 13 Calf Papers, Blottings. Enamelled Blottings.

Blotting-paper. Add attrib. uses:

1894 H. Nisbet *Bush Girl's Rom.* 68 Acid with the soup, salt and warmth with the fish to intensify its brain-feeding and blotting-paper qualities. 1904 *Daily Chron.* 6 Feb. 9/1 Blotting-paper pink and turtle-dove drab. 1906 *Westm. Gaz.* 23 Apr. 4/2 A quaint touch of pale blotting-paper pink worsted embroidery upon stone-coloured muslin.

Blotto (blǫ·to), *a. slang.* [Obscurely f. Blot.] Fuddled with liquor; 'soaked'.

1919 *Winter's Pie* Pl. 17. 1921 *Blackw. Mag.* Feb. 157/1 The evening's potations left him, by bed-time, in a state somewhere between 'blotto' and 'blithero-blotto.' 1923 *Daily Mail* 13 June 12, I got properly 'blotto' and don't know what I did.

Blouse. Add:

4. A woman's loose-fitting dress-body worn tucked inside the skirt at the waist. Also called *blouse-bodice* (cf. *Blousée).

1870 *Yng. Ladies' Jrnl.* 1 Oct. 626/1 A costume for a young lady...A blouse, or tunic, of white and pink-striped silk. 1887 *Cassell's Fam. Mag.* Sept. 631/1 Frenchwomen show just the same favour to the blouse bodices as their sisters across the Channel. 1899 *Daily News* 24 Jan. 2/4 The fashionable blouse, or 'blouse-bodice.' 1909 *Westm. Gaz.* 15 Feb. 5/2 Blouses will be more in evidence this season than ever, for the mere strap that forms the bodice of the newest gowns, and the high waists, and bretelles, all demand the finishing touch of a blouse.

b. *attrib.* and *Comb.*, as *blouse-clad* adj., *-maker*, *-making* (also *attrib.*); **blouse coat**, a blouse with some of the characteristics of a coat, to be worn outside the skirt at the waist; **blouse length**, a piece of material sufficient for the making of a blouse, cut off for sale; **blouse slip** (see Slip *sb.*[3] 4 c); **blouse suit**, a blouse and skirt finished complete, and ready to wear.

1892 *Daily News* 2 July 6/7 A comparison between the *blouse-clad ladies and those who wear habit-bodices. 1898 *Westm. Gaz.* 16 June 3/2 Blouses and *blouse coats of Irish lace. 1910 *Ibid.* 29 Jan. 3/3 Who..would venture to buy a *blouse-length with the fate of the Budget hanging in the balance? 1905 *Daily Chron.* 18 Oct. 3/5 A wife who was employed at a *blouse-maker's. 1905 *Pearson's Mag.* July 105/1 The *blouse-making industry. 1908 *Westm. Gaz.* 21 Aug. 8/2 Working at blouse-making. 1907 *Ibid.* 21 Feb. 8/2 How to make a *Blouse-Slip. 1909 *Daily Chron.* 22 Feb. 7/5 With these cashmere gowns, blouse-slips of various kinds can be worn. 1905 *Ibid.* 20 Oct. 8/5 *Blouse-Suits in Velveteens, Silks, and Various Cloths.

Blousée (blū·ze), *a.* [f. Blouse + F. *-ée*.] In *blousée bodice* = *Blouse 4.

1899 *Westm. Gaz.* 24 Aug. 3/2 The simple blouse, or I might say *blousée* bodice, which will probably be the favourite for indoor wear. 1903 *Ibid.* 19 Feb. 4/2 The becoming *blousée* bodice for gowns.

Blow, *sb.*[1] Add:

1. c. A stroke of the shears in shearing sheep. *Austral.*

1890 *Melbourne Argus* 20 Sept. 13/7 The shearers must make their clip clean and thorough. If..a 'second blow' is needed, the fleece is hacked.

d. An outcrop of mineral. *Austral.*

1895 *Prospectus*, There are three large outcrops of quartz, locally termed 'Blows.' 1922 *Chambers's Jrnl.* Nov. 704/1 Silver-lead (galena) outcrops standing out in great 'blows.'

Blow, *sb.*[2] Add:

5. Secret information or warning. *slang.*

1928 *Sunday Dispatch* 2 Sept. 3/1 We've had the 'blow' that the 'Busies' are coming.

Blow, *sb.*[3] 1. Add quots.:

1866 M. Arnold *Thyrsis* 66 And stocks in fragrant blow. 1895 Meredith *Amazing Marr.* iv. (1904) 45 Purple crocuses in bud and blow.

Blow, *v.*[1] Add:

1. b. *Blow high, blow low*: whatever may happen.

1774 P. V. Fithian *Jrnl.* (1900) 235 Ben is in a wonderful Fluster lest he shall have no company to-morrow at the Dance—But blow high, blow low, he need not be afraid; Virginians..will dance or die! [1776 C. Dibdin *Song* 1 Blow high, blow low, let tempests tear The mainmast by the board.] *a* 1861 T. Winthrop *John Brent* vi. 63 I've booked Brother John fur Paradise; Brother Joseph's got a white robe fur him, blow high, blow low! 1921 R. D. Paine *Comr. Rolling Ocean* x. 171 There were three musketeers.. who were blithely resolved to stand by each other through thick and thin, blow high, blow low.

3. *spec.* of a deer.

1868 *Amer. Naturalist* II. 467 The hunter says he [*sc.* the buck deer] 'blows'; it may be a note of anger or defiance.

10. b. To lay out or get through (money) in a lavish manner; to squander. Cf. *Blue *v.*[2] *slang.* Also *refl.* (U.S. dial.): see quot. 1896.

1874 *Slang Dict.*, *Blew, or blow*,..to lose or spend money. 1892 *Daily News* 5 Sept. 6/3 Sometimes you'll blow a little money..but another week you may make a lot. 1896 (*Amer.*) *Dialect Notes* I. 412 'To blow oneself', to spend money freely. 1902 S. E. White *Blazed Trail* xxviii. 193 'Well, bub,' finally drawled a voice from the corner, 'blowed that stake you made out of Radway, yet?' 1904 W. H. Smith *Promoters* v. 100 The Church people in England were the folks that had the money to blow. 1921 R. D. Paine *Comr. Rolling Ocean* iv. 57 When I pick up easy money, I just naturally have to blow it.

c. *To blow in*: to spend, squander. Also *absol. U.S. slang.*

1887 F. Francis Jr. *Saddle & Mocassin* 144 'Sam went off on a bend.' 'To blow in?' Jake laughed assent. 1894 *Amer. Newspaper*, The third 'blows in' his money in a glorious drunk at the saloon. 1903 *Outlook* 7 Nov. 586 He had blown in all his earnings in a grand frolic. 1912 Thornton *Amer. Gloss.*, *Blow in*, to waste one's cash riotously. Modern slang.

12. b. (Later U.S. examples.)

1868 Susan Hale *Lett.* 42 She is a picturesque looking creature...Why she blows up and down the Nile year in and year out,..I dunno. 1903 E. C. Waltz *Pa Gladden* 61 The kitchen door opened and the wind-tossed farmer fairly blew in.

d. *To blow in*: to appear or turn up, unexpectedly; to drop in. orig. *U.S. colloq.*

1904 G. H. Lorimer *Old Gorgon Graham* 47 Yesterday our old college friend, Clarence, blew in from Monte Carlo. 1910 W. M. Raine *B. O'Connor* 97 Him and York Neil.. blew in last night from their mine. 1911 H. Quick *Yellowstone N.* ix. 241 A witness..from outside the jurisdiction had blowed in. 1924 Galsworthy *White Monkey* ii. iii, If anything blows in, I'll remember you.

13. b. To proclaim or praise boastfully. (Cf. 6.)

1878 J. H. Beadle *Western Wilds* viii. 126 This [State] the most loudly blowed and persistently advertised of the whole sisterhood, has been knocking for admission into the Union since 1849. *Ibid.* xiii. 194 In Kansas or Nebraska we should see..one or two live journals blowing the place as the 'future metropolis of the boundless West'.

17. c. Also *fig.*, to expire, die.

1845 W. G. Simms *Wigwam & Cabin* Ser. i. 58, I reckon I was clean gone, if it hadn't been that she blowed out before me.

19. b. *To blow on*: (*trans.*) to solder on by means of the blow lamp.

1893 *Spons' Mechanics' Own Bk.* (ed. 4) 641 Lead the pipe away to the main supply, and 'blow' it on by means of a union suited to the case.

c. *Electr.* (*intr.*) Of a fuse: To melt under an abnormally high-voltage electric current; to fuse. Also with *out*.

1902 in Webster Suppl. 1908 *Install. News* II. 86/1 A fuse has blown owing to a fault on the circuit.

24. c. *To blow from* (*the mouth of*) *a gun*, etc.: to execute summary justice on (a traitor, etc.) by binding him to the muzzle of a gun and firing the piece.

1857 *Blackw. Mag.* Sept. 389/1 That if there be 10,000 who refuse to use them, they are to be blown away from cannon. *Ibid.* Nov. 609 The mutineers..were all sentenced to be blown away from guns. 1885 *Century Mag.* Jan. 411/2 That Black Idol..Was..Blown hellward from the cannon's mouth. 1891 W. S. Gilbert *Rosencrantz & Guild.* ii, The Bench of Bishops seize you..And blow you from a gun.

d. *Sporting.* To shatter (a game bird) in shooting; more explicitly *to blow to pieces*. So (U.S. slang) *to blow apart*.

1892 Greener *Breech-Loader* 275, I defy any one, after a day's shooting, to point out a single bird that has been 'blown.' My experience has proved beyond doubt that the choke-bore does not blow pheasants or any other game to pieces at 20 yards. 1920 Mulford *J. Nelson* iv. 45 'Squint,' said his captor in a hard, level voice, 'if you give me th' least excuse I'll blow you apart'.

e. To remove by the force of an explosion; with advs. *away, back, off*.

1899 *Westm. Gaz.* 13 July 7/2 Cartridges in which the caps have been blown back when the rifle was discharged.

f. *To blow the lid off* (*fig.*): To expose (a state of affairs). *U.S.*

1928 *Daily Tel.* 1 May 9/5 He 'blew the lid' off a notorious national condition of affairs.

g. *To blow out*: (of a cock, valve, etc.) to be driven out by the expansive force of gas or vapour. 1911 in Webster.

h. To produce by blowing or shooting.

1891 C. Roberts *Adrift Amer.* 153 If you talk to me like that I'll blow a hole through you.

26. c. Said also of veins of metals; and *fig.*

1857 *Trans. Ill. Agric. Soc.* II. 364 Quantities of the public lands were entered to cover the supposed copper mines. It has all blown out. 1873 J. H. Beadle *Undevel. West* xviii. 333 The fluid turned aside to existing crevices, or 'blew out' through hollow chambers.

Blow-. Add: **blow-back** *a.* and *sb.* (cf. *Blow *v.*[1] 24 e); **blow lamp**, a lamp designed to give a condensed hot flame, directed by air-pressure or gas on the spot to be heated; used chiefly by plumbers, gas-fitters, and painters; **blow-off**, the action or operation of ridding a boiler of water or sediment by the force of steam; used *attrib.* in *blow-off apparatus, cock, pipe*; **blow-over** *Glass-making*, the surplus glass forced out of the mould in blowing (Knight *Dict. Mech.* 1874); **blow-room** = *blowing-room*: see *Blowing *vbl. sb.*[1] 5; **blow-through**, (*a*) the process of blowing steam through the cylinder of an engine, etc., to clear it of air; used *attrib.* in *blow-through cock, valve*; (*b*) defining a jet or lamp for the blowing of oxygen through a flame against lime or magnesium to produce a brilliant light; **blow torch** = *blow lamp*. See also *Blow-out, *Blow-up.

1899 *Westm. Gaz.* 13 July 7/2 Foul barrels were the cause of ineffectual shots and '*blow-back' caps. 1905 *Kynoch Jrnl.* Jan.–Mar. 10 The cracks..will at once develop into fissures when the cartridge is fired, cause 'blow-backs', and seriously reduce the velocity of the projectile. 1907 *Daily Chron.* 22 July 7/1 His cartridge being a defective one—what is called a 'blow back'. 1896 J. W. Hart *External Plumbing Wk.* 259 The tinning can be done best by means of a *blow-lamp of some kind. 1901 — *Hints to Plumbers* (ed. 3) 253 The solder is sweated in the joints by means of a blow-pipe, where gas is obtainable, otherwise a blow-lamp is used. 1909 *Westm. Gaz.* 27 Apr. 12/4 He was filling a blow lamp with motor spirit when it exploded. 1842 *Civil Eng. & Arch. Jrnl.* V. 367/2 *Blow-off cocks. 1859 Rankine *Steam Engine* § 305 The blow-off apparatus consists, in fresh-water boilers, simply of a large cock at the bottom of the boiler. 1874 Knight *Dict. Mech.*, Blow-off Pipe. 1899 *Daily News* 9 Mar. 5/3 The blow-off pipes into the sea being broken, the chief engineer..had to let the water run out of the boilers into the hold. 1908 *Daily Chron.* 5 Aug. 1/6 The card and *blow room hands. 1874 Knight *Dict. Mech.*, *Blow-through Valve. 1892 *Photogr. Ann.* II. 231 Blow-through jet. 1906 *Westm. Gaz.* 14 Nov. 14/2 A blow-through lamp. 1909 *Century Dict.* Suppl., *Blow-torch. 1921 R. D. Paine *Comr. Rolling Ocean* xvi. 274 Down to the engine-room went Briscoe and returned with..a blow-torch.

Blow-down. *U.S.* [Cf. Blow- 1.] A place encumbered with trees that have been blown down.

1895 *Outing* XXVI. 448/2 A line of blazes wanders erratically back and forth up the side of the mountain dodging 'blow-downs' and ledges. 1900 *Scribner's Mag.* Sept. 264/1 The horses picking their way carefully over blow-downs.

Blower [1]. Add:

3. b. *esp.* An apparatus for creating an artificial current of air by pressure, used as a ventilator, dryer, etc., and to produce a blast of air in a furnace, etc. *attrib.*, as *blower-engine, -fan, -pipe*.

1858 Simmonds *Dict. Trade*, *Blower*,..a fan used on board American river steam-boats, to increase the current of air. 1875 *Encycl. Brit.* III. 552/2 The rotary blower, invented by Messrs. Root of Connersville, Ind., is one which has of late years found extensive use both in America and Europe. 1900 *Everybody's Mag.* III. 528 The waves, breaking over the blower-pipes, poured through in such quantities as to dampen the belts of the blower-engine. 1903 *Daily Chron.* 9 Dec. 6/3 The air is first filtered...Afterwards it passes through a blower-fan.

c. A blowing-machine: (*a*) for cleansing and 'opening' the fibres of cotton or wool; (*b*) for cleansing and separating rabbit fur.

1867 *Chamb. Encycl.* IX. 46/2 The cotton or wool..is.. taken to the 'blower' or 'opener', and being put into a shaft, is there acted upon by a stream of air..which blows it forward, removes extraneous matters,[etc.]. 1874 Knight *Dict. Mech.*, *Blower*, a machine for separating the hair from the fur fibres [in hat-making].

Blow-hard, *a.* and *sb.* *U.S.* [Blow *v.*[1] 6.]

A. *adj.* Boastful, blustering.

1855 *Oregon Weekly Times* 21 July (Th.) The *Oregonian* ..has a blowhard article on the subject. 1921 R. D. Paine *Comr. Rolling Ocean* vi. 105 He don't get by with his blow-hard stuff, but I'll have to say he is entertaining.

B. *sb.* A blustering person; a braggart.

1889 Farmer *Americanisms*, *Blowhard*, a Western term of revilement, the precise meaning of which it would be difficult to explain. 1894 *Congress. Rec.* Jan. 1238/2 Anyone who will read the whole testimony will see that [this man] was a mere braggart, a pretender, a blow-hard. 1910 W. M. Raine *B. O'Connor* 48 He's the worst blowhard ever.

Blow-hole. 2. Delete †*Obs.* and add:

1878 *Ure's Dict. Arts* IV. 835 The following experiments were made in order to prepare solid steel without blow-holes by the crucible process. 1906 *Westm. Gaz.* 29 Aug. 2/1 The way to prevent steel rusting..is to have no blow-holes.

Blowing, *vbl. sb.*[1] Add:

1. b. *Cotton-manuf.* The cleansing of cotton.

1875 *Ure's Dict. Arts* I. 955 The willowing, scutching, or blowing, an operation which removes the seeds and dirt, and prepares the material in the form of a continuous lap.

c. The shattering (of a bird) in shooting. (Cf. *Blow *v.*[1] 24 d.)

1892 Greener *Breech-Loader* 271 No one could detect the 'blowing' of a single bird.

d. (See quot.)

1881 *Cassell's Dict.*, *Blowing of Firearms* (Gunnery), the art or operation of constructing firearms in such a way that the vent or touch-hole is run or 'gullied', and becomes wide, allowing the powder to blaze out.

e. *Blowing off*: the action or process of firing (a rifle) to cleanse the barrel.

1893 *Daily News* 2 Feb. 2/6 The ammunition..was issued in packets of ten, thus allowing for blowing off and for one compulsory sighting shot.

f. *fig.* Boasting, bragging. *dial.* and *Colonial.*

1873 A. Trollope *Australia & N. Z.* I. 387 A fine art much cultivated in the colonies, for which the colonial phrase of 'blowing' has been created. 1878 J. H. Beadle *Western Wilds* ix. 134 Its bright and saucy editorials excelled all specimens extant of Kansas blowing.

2. c. The formation of bubbles or blisters in the texture of a manufactured article.

1872 *Spons' Dict. Engin.* v. 1547 As the pressure is kept on the metal until it is well set and solid, such a thing as blowing will never, or very seldom take place.

5. **blowing-cone**, a volcanic cone by which vapours escape from a subterranean molten lake; **blowing-engine** (add quot.); **blowing-machine**, (*a*) any mechanical contrivance for producing a blast of air; (*b*) a machine for cleansing and separating fur in hat-manufacture; (*c*) an apparatus forming part of the machine for cleansing the cotton in cotton-manufacture; **blowing-pot**, a vessel containing clay paste which the workman 'throws' on (pottery) by blowing; **blowing-room**, a room in which the cleansing or separating of materials is done, esp. in a cotton factory; also *attrib.*, as (*card and*) *blowing-room hand, machinery, operative*.

1895 Dana *Man. Geol.* (ed. 4) 279 In cases, outside of the lava-lakes, where the bubbles are bursting beneath an opening in the bottom of the crater, the vapors and lava driblets escape from the aperture with a rush and a roar. The driblet-cone, thus made, is sometimes called a *blowing-cone. 1845 Dodd *Brit. Manuf.* V. 159 *Blowing-Engine. 1839 Ure *Dict. Arts* I. 345 Batting (*beating*), scutching, and *blowing machines. 1845 Dodd *Brit. Manuf.* V. 158 The 'blowing-machines'..act as follows. 1874 Knight *Dict. Mech.* 1875 *Ure's Dict. Arts* III. 622 Common earthenware is coloured by means of..the *blowing-pot. 1845 Dodd *Brit. Manuf.* V. 158 The fur..is conveyed to the *blowing-room, finally to effect the separation [of the coarse from the fine fur]. 1887 J. E. Holme *Cotton Spinning* Introd., The blowing-room machinery should be kept well oiled. 1892 *Daily News* 14 Apr. 3/4 The card and blowing-room hands. 1898 *Westm. Gaz.* 23 Dec. 7/3 The Card and Blowing-room Operatives Society.

b. With advs.: **blowing-off, -through** = *blow-off, -through* (see *Blow-).

1863 Atkinson *Ganot's Physics* vi. 328 Blowing off taps, for use when the pistons are in motion. 1874 Knight *Dict. Mech.*, Blowing-off...Blowing-through.

Blown, *ppl. a.*[1]

3. Delete † and add: (Of food) Stale or tainted from exposure.

1899 *Daily News* 16 Jan. 3/3 The sanitary inspector ex-

plained that the contents of a 'blown' tin would 'not taste so bad after the gas had come out'.

5. c. Filled with bubbles or the like. (Cf. prec. 2 c.)
1872 *Spons' Dict. Engin.* v. 1548 The..result is what moulders term a *blown* casting; that is, its surface becomes filled with bubbles of air, rendering its texture porous and weak.

6. a. *Plumbing.* Of a joint: Made with a blow-pipe. **b.** *Electr.* Of a fuse (see *Blow v. 19 c).
1904 *Technol. & Sci. Dict.* (ed. Goodchild & Tweney), Blown Joint. 1909 *Install. News* III. 137 We will allow 33⅓ per cent. of the nett price for all 'blown' cartridge fuses of our manufacture.

7. With advs. as *blown down, blown up.* For *blown in* and *out* see Blow v.^{1} 19.
1878 Morris in Mackail *Life* (1899) I. 360 The blown-down tree was a fine branchy tree. 1905 *Westm. Gaz.* 13 Sept. 6/3 The blown-up steamer.

Blow-out. [Blow- 1.]
1. An outbreak of anger; a quarrel, disturbance, row. *dial.* and *U.S.*
1826 [see Blow- 1]. 1838 J. C. Neal *Charcoal Sk.* (De Vere) He has a prompt alacrity at a blow-out, and has been skyed in a blow-up. 1842 *Spirit of Times* (Philad.) 15 Feb. (Th.) I've had five breezes, seven blow-outs, nine shindies, and a dozen ructions on this $1 Relief note.

2. A dinner, supper, or other entertainment for which an abundant supply of food and drink is provided or at which it is consumed; a 'feast' or 'feed'. *colloq.*
1824 Scott *St. Ronan's* xxxiii, 'She sent me a card for her blow-out,' said Mowbray, 'and so I am resolved to go.' 1837 Irving *Capt. Bonneville* (1895) I. 191 Captain Bonneville now gave the men what, in frontier phrase is termed 'a regular blow out!' 1840, 1856 [see Blow- 1]. 1913 Mulford *Coming of Cassidy* vii. 112 I'll clean you out an' have a real, genuine blow-out on your money.

3. a. *Mining.* A portion of a lode where the mineral appears to have been dislodged by some eruptive force. Also *fig. U.S.*
1873 J. H. Beadle *Undevel. West* xviii. 333 All the strange terms in mining parlance: 'true lodes,..blow-outs'. 1901 S. E. White *Westerners* xxiii. 214 He saw that..a third [claim]..gave indications of being nothing but a blow-out.

b. A butte, the top of which has been blown out by the wind until it resembles the crater of a volcano; a hollow in an area of shifting sand, caused by the action of the wind. *local U.S.*
1895 P. A. Rydberg in *U.S. Nat. Herb.* III. 135 It sometimes happens that settlers [in the sand-hill region] a few years after breaking their land find a field transformed into a big blowout. 1899 in use in western Nebraska and adjacent territory.

4. A burst in a pneumatic rubber tyre caused by air-pressure from the inside. Also *fig.*
1908 *Westm. Gaz.* 7 Jan. 4/1 Miraculum will not seal a blow-out. 1911 R. W. Chambers *Common Law* iv. 117 Your young man has me in the ditch with two blow-outs and the gas afire! 1915 *Lit. Digest* (N. Y.) 21 Aug. 387/1 The Goodyear Cord Tires, without a blow-out, took the car back to Detroit. *Ibid.* 4 Sept. 482/1 Advt., No domestic punctures or blow-outs—just easy running over smooth roads to Health and Happiness.

5. *Electr.* A device for suppressing an arc in an electric circuit, etc. Also *attrib.*
1902 *Encycl. Brit.* XXVIII. 97/2 A magnetic blow-out is simply a small magnet so arranged that the arc caused by breaking the circuit takes place in the magnetic field. 1916 *Standardisation Rules of Amer. Inst. Electr. Engin.* 28 June § 731 Fuses of the magnetic blow-out type.

6. *Electr.* The blowing of a fuse.
1928 *Daily Express* 25 June 12 Two of the municipal employees injured at the Johannesburg Power Station when a mouse caused a blow-out, have both died.

Blow-pipe. Add: **1. c.** (See quot.)
1894 E. L. Wilson *Cycl. Photogr.*, *Blow-Pipe*, used for the magic-lantern or for illuminating purposes by the use of the oxy-hydrogen light.

Blowser (blau·zəɹ). *local.* Also **blouser.** A landsman who assists in working the seine nets in pilchard-fishing time. Also **Blow·sing** *sb.*
1816 Paris *Mount's Bay* 91 It [sc. the net] is moored, or where the shore is sandy and shelving, as in Saint Ives Bay, drawn into shallow water, by a number of men, who are called *Blowsers*. 1877 *Fraser's Mag.* XV. 220 The whole is warped nearer to the shore by blousers, who are landsmen ..employed on land during the pilchard season for general purposes. 1879 *Encycl. Brit.* IX. 254/2 Landing and carrying the fish to the curing houses is done by men termed 'blowsers'. 1880 *W. Cornw. Gloss.*, *Blowsing*, working in seine boats.

Blow-up. Chiefly *U.S.* [Blow- 1.]
1. = *Blow-out 1.
1809 Sir W. Gell in *C. K. Sharpe's Lett.* (1888) I. 355 There won't be any quarrel, so you need not fear. The only chance is Keppel making a blow up when she abuses me. 1813, 1834 [see Blow- 1]. 1846 Sol. Smith *Theatrical Apprent.* 132 When we had got their jealousy and hatred excited to a proper pitch, it was agreed that a regular 'blow up' between the two should end the joke. *a* 1848 *Newsp.* in Bartlett *Dict. Amer.*, There was a regular blow-up at Tammany Hall,..which ended in a row, and broke up the meeting. 1900 H. Lawson *Over Sliprails* 46 Some others were making a night of it..as they'd been doing pretty often lately—and went on doing till there was a blow-up about it.

b. An explosion.
1867 M. Arnold *Lett.* (1895) I. 376 Every one is full of the Clerkenwell blow-up.

c. A scolding (cf. Blow v.^{1} 25 b).
1838 [see *Blow-out 1].

2. = *Blow-out 2.

1807–8 W. Irving *Salmagundi* xiii. 288 Our citizens did not refuse the invitation of the Society to the blow up.

8. *Sugar-manuf.* The place where the raw sugar is dissolved; also *attrib.* in *blow-up cistern, pan*, a vessel used in dissolving raw sugar by 'blowing' or forcing steam through it.
1833 B. Silliman *Man. Sugar Cane* 77 The vats, or blow-ups, as they are called, containing the sugar,..are heated by steam tubes passing through them. 1845 Dodd *Brit. Manuf.* V. 108 A steam-pipe, in communication with a boiler, is enclosed within the 'blow-up cistern' [for dissolving sugar]; and..steam is forced or 'blown' by its own pressure into the solution. 1874 Knight *Dict. Mech.*, Blow-up Pan. (*Sugar. Machinery.*) 1886 *Harper's Mag.* June 82/2 These 'mixers' or 'blow-ups' are really great stew-pans set in the ground.

Blowzily (blau·zili), *adv.* Also **blowsily.** [f. Blowzy + -ly^2.] In a blowzy way, coarsely. So **Blow·ziness.**
1866 Miss Braddon *Lady's Mile* xxii, She was a very handsome lady..in spite of a little blowsiness. 1905 *Daily Chron.* 5 Apr. 4/7 Daintiness would certainly pay better than the present blowziness [of the flower-seller]. 1914 Locke *Fortunate Youth* i, Once blowsily good-looking.

Blub (blʌb), *sb.* [f. Blub v.] A fit or spell of weeping.
1894 Du Maurier *Trilby* II. 255 It would do him good once more to have a good blub.

Blub, *v.* Add: **4.** Shortened form of Blubber v. in sense 3, to weep, cry.
1873 *Punch* 8 Mar. 97/1 The sentimental gentleman who blubs over bellowing garrotters. 1884 Blackmore *T. Upmere* vi, Keep up your spirits, young fellow, and don't blub. 1899 Kipling *Stalky* (1920) 48 Stalky..pretended to blub... Then I blubbed, too. 1928 Temple Thurston *Portrait of Spy, Paris* § 1 He was blubbing in her arms.

Bludgeon, *v.* Add:
b. *fig.* To strike heavily, as with a bludgeon. *To bludgeon in*: to drive in as with a bludgeon. Hence **Blu·dgeoning** *vbl. sb.* and *ppl. a.*
1892 Stevenson & Osbourne *Wrecker* xvii, Repentance bludgeoned me. 1894 *Athenæum* 14 July 55/1 It is not..the artful bludgeoning that gets the praise. 1906 R. Whiting *Ring in New* 238 The militant knifing and bludgeoning men. 1928 E. Blom *Limit. Music* 37 A truth that has no need of literal bludgeoning-in.

Blu·dgeoned, *ppl. a.* [f. Bludgeon v. + -ed^1.] Struck down or wounded with or as with a bludgeon.
1887 Stevenson *Misadv. J. Nicholson* vi, Next bludgeoned vanity raised its head again, with twenty mortal gashes.

Bludgeonist (blʌ·dʒənist). [f. Bludgeon sb. + -ist.] One who strikes with or as with a bludgeon.
1811 *Ann. Reg.* 1809 680 No hired bludgeonists astound him. 1903 *Daily Chron.* 25 May 3/3 Critic is a mild word to use. Bludgeonist would suit the case better.

Blue, *sb.* Add:
1. With qualification denoting a particular shade of the colour, as *Cambridge blue.*
1883 *Cassell's Fam. Mag.* Mar. 206/2 A huge wooden spoon, ornamented with bows of Cambridge blue. 1895 *Windsor Mag.* i. 403/2 A youth.., dressed in knickerbockers of dark blue velveteen trimmed with Cambridge blue.

b. *spec.* (See quot.)
1868 *Amer. Naturalist* II. 468 The fawn is similar in color, with two rows of white spots, and scattering ones on each side, which it retains often long after the winter-coat is assumed. This is called the blue. It is rather ashy-gray, or..slate-color.

2. c. A cake or ball of blue powder for laundry use: also *attrib.* in **blue bag**, a bag containing one of these for such use. See also Powder-blue 1, Stone-blue 1.
1836 *Mag. Dom. Econ.* I. 6 Make also a proper flannel 'blue-bag'. 1869 Mrs. Beeton *Bk. Househ. Management* 1098 To remove a Bee Sting, pull the sting out at once..wipe the place, suck it, and then apply the blue-bag. 1904 H. G. Wells *Food of Gods* i. ii. § 5 She 'athen't even got a Blue Bag, Thir. 1928 *Daily Express* 9 Aug. 3/3 The blue bag—that truly rural remedy for wasp stings.

3. esp. of blue uniform, e.g. of policemen, wounded soldiers in hospital, (*U.S.*) the Northern or Union soldiers (contrasted with the Southern or Confederate grey).
1831 *The Olio* June 341/2 A young off'sir—a likely youngster he would have been in blue, 'stead o' red. 1867 F. M. Finch in *Atlantic Monthly* XX. 369 (*title*) The Blue and the Grey. 1879 Tourgee *Fool's Err.* xxv. 153 He wore the blue. 1884 *Eng. Illustr. Mag.* Dec. 167 Answered the warder, 'He's in blue, so he's in his last year'. 1891 Marah E. Ryan *Told in Hills* iii. vi. 209 [The] petticoats..were of regular army blue, their only trimming belt and bands of 'yaller'. 1893 *Cassell's Fam. Mag.* Apr. 338/2 My little friend in blue [messenger boy]. 1895 C. King *Fort Frayne* xx. 290 Farrar was..just about the happiest fellow that wore the army blue. 1918 *Reveille* Aug. 94 The discharged men ..no longer cut the handsome gaudy figure of the man in blue.

b. *The men (gentlemen* or *boys) in blue*: (*a*) policemen; (*b*) sailors; (*c*) American Federal troops.
1851 F. Starr *Twenty Yrs. Trav. Life* xxxii. 317, I was not long managing my exit..whilst the 'gentleman in blue' was busy examining other tickets. 1857 Sir H. Lawrence in W. Brock *Biogr. Sk. Sir H. Havelock* viii. (1858) 125 The gentlemen in blue—the sailors. 1866 L. P. Brockett *Camp, Battle*, etc. ii. 264 Tread lightly, oh! loyal-hearted, the boys in blue are lying there. 1866 *Congress. Globe* 27 Jan. 460/1 The brave 'boys in blue' fought manfully and through their efforts the Union has been preserved. 1881 A. A. Hayes *New Colorado* iv. 60 Uncle Sam gave the soldiers in the Civil War the right to 160 acres each...Some of the boys in blue only took up portions. 1882 Besant *All Sorts* xliii, You must now begin to think seriously about handcuffs and prison, and men in blue.

4. (Quots. illustrating senses of: policeman, blue or blue-and-white china, etc.)
1844 Hood *University Feud* 122 Whether this here mobbing.. Will grow to such a riot that the Oxford Blues [*i.e.* policemen] must quell it. 1848 H. R. Forster *Stowe Catal.* 1 Twelve fruit dishes, of old blue and white. 1860 *Slang Dict.* (ed. 2), *Blue*, a policeman. 1877 *Five Years' Penal Servitude* iv. 257 'Bilking the blues,'—evading the police. 1898 Kipling *Fleet in Being* iii. 40 Next time you see the 'blue' ashore you do not stare unintelligently. 1903 Miss F. Simpson *Bk. Cat* xi. 126/2 As tiny kittens blues frequently exhibit tabby markings. 1928 *Sunday Express* 6 May 19 The two 'blues' took no notice of him. 1929 *Woman's Jrnl.* Feb. 70 The old Chinese blue-and-white porcelain which has been the delight of the collector of 'old blue'.

c. A blueberry or bilberry. *U.S.*
1709 J. Lawson *New Voy. Carolina* 104 The Hurts, Huckle-Berries, or Blues of this Country are four sorts... The first sort is the same Blue or Bilberry, that grows plentifully in the North of England.

d. A 'blue chip' in the game of poker. *U.S.*
a 1906 'O. Henry' *Trimmed Lamp* etc. 243 A good thing with a Van to his name threw me over with some other bills to buy a stack of blues. 1920 Mulford *J. Nelson* xxi. 228 'Two pairs...Well I'll see it an' add a blue.' 'Any time you raise a blue, you got two pairs, all right!'

Blue, *a.* Add:
1. b. *Magnetism.* Defining the south pole of a magnet (of a steel-blue colour) as distinguished from the north (red) pole; also, the magnetism of this pole.
1893 Sloane *Electr. Dict.* 345 A two-fluid theory of magnetism has been evolved... It assumes north fluid or 'red magnetism' and a south fluid or 'blue magnetism'.

f. See also Grey-blue, Powder-blue 2, *smalt-blue* (Smalt sb. 4), Stone-blue 2.

g. Defining a quality of sheep's wool (see quot.).
1888 *Encycl. Brit.* XXIV. 656/2 In the worsted trade the classification [of wool] goes..in descending series, from fine, blue, neat, brown, breech, downright, seconds, to abb... The greater proportion of good English long wool will be classified as blue, neat, and brown.

3. *Blue fear*, a variant of *blue funk.* Also *Blue-funk school*, a jocular perversion of 'blue-water school'.
1883 Stevenson in *Longm. Mag.* Apr. 683 The very name of Paris put her in a blue fear. 1908 *Daily Chron.* 24 Feb. 4/6 The identification by Mr. Harvey, M.P., of the 'blue-water school' with the 'blue funk school'. *Ibid.* 20 July 4/3 The Jingo..is a nobler being than the disciples of our 'blue-funk' school.

b. Of affairs, circumstances, prospects: Dismal, unpromising, depressing. Chiefly in *a blue look-out, to look blue.*
1833 *Mirror* 25 May 350 'Why it's a blue look out, Master,' said he. 1858 Trollope *Three Clerks* xxix, Charley replied that neither had he any money at home. 'That's blue', said the man. 1873 J. H. Beadle *Undevel. West* xxv. 528 The Agency employés had not been paid for a year, and as they have to buy their own provisions, things looked blue for them. 1878 — *Western Wilds* xi. 175 Night came on suddenly..and the situation looked blue. 1879 Hartigan & Walker *Stray Leaves* Ser. ii. xv. 257 If our present officers are like them ..it's a blue look-out for the Afghans! 1888 'R. Boldrewood' *Robbery under Arms* xxxv, It seemed a rather blue look-out.

8. *Blue murder*, used in intensive phrases; as *Like blue murder*, at a terrific pace, at top speed. *To cry blue murder*: see Murder sb. 3. *slang.*
1914 *Evening News* 1 Oct. 2/1 They were off down the road like blue murder.

12. a. Blue Albion (see quot.); **blue cat**, also (*a*) a North American species of cat-fish; (*b*) a blue Persian cat; **blue fly** *Sc.* and *U.S.*, a blue-bottle fly; **Blue Grey** (see quot.); **blue heron** *U.S.*, a North American species of heron.
1923 *Daily Mail* 12 June 10 An innovation in the cattle classes is the inclusion of 'Blue Albions, a Derbyshire breed. 1855 W. G. Simms *Forayers* (N. Y.) 275 In this [dug-out] sat a youth, fishing for *blue-cat and perch... The blue-cat of the Edisto is one of the nicest fish that swims. 1877 R. I. Dodge *Hunting Grounds Gt. West* 250 The blue cat is also common in all the plain streams, attaining sometimes a weight of fifteen to twenty-five pounds. 1903 *Daily Chron.* 28 Oct. 3/2 Blue cats. 1759 Goldsm. *Bee* No. 4 ℙ 30 A large *blue fly fell into the snare. 1856 Mrs. Stowe *Dred* 160 He just puts me in mind of one of these blue-flies. 1902 *Encycl. Brit.* XXV. 191/2 The cross between the Shorthorn and the Aberdeen-Angus [breed of cattle], known as the '*Blue Grey'. 1893 Torrey *Footpath Way* 198 Here let me say that the great *blue heron is..a big bird.

b. blue ash *U.S.*, a North American variety of ash; **blue spike**, a North American aquatic plant bearing a dense spike of blue flowers (see quot.); **blue star grass** (see quot.).
1819 D. Thomas *Trav.* 93 The *blue ash..is a fine stately tree of two or three feet diameter, generally of a straight grain, and may be easily split into rails. 1832 D. J. Browne *Sylva Amer.* 156 The Blue Ash is unknown to the Atlantic parts of the United States. 1784 Cutler in *Mem. Amer. Acad. Arts & Sci.* (1785) I. 433 *Pontederia*... Pickerelweed. *Blue Spike. 1886 *Encycl. Brit.* XX. 174/1 The *blue star [grass, of Queensland], *Chloris ventricosa.*

13. blue baby, an infant suffering from congenital cyanosis; **blue bag**, a barrister's (orig. a solicitor's) brief-bag of blue stuff; **blue band**, a band of glacier ice of a blue colour due to the absence of air-bubbles; **bluebeak**, a young bird; jocularly applied, in Army slang, to a young recruit; **Blue Blouses** *sb. pl.* (see quot.); **blue boys** *sb. pl.*, the police: alternative form of *boys in blue*, see *Blue sb. 3 b; **blue butter** = *blue ointment*; **blue earth** = *blue ground*; **Blue Flag movement, Blue Force, blue gas** (see quots.); **blue ground**, the dark soil, normally greyish-blue, in which diamonds are found; **blue measure** (see quot.); **blue Monday** (earlier U.S. example); **blue-mouldy** *a.* (*fig.*); **blue norther** *U.S.*, a north wind blowing in Texas; **blue oil** (see quot.); **blue ointment**, mercurial ointment (see Mercurial a. 5); **blue pencil**, a blue 'lead' pencil used chiefly in marking corrections, obliterations, and the like; **blue pencil** *v. trans.*, to mark, score through, or obliterate with a blue pencil; hence, to make 'cuts' in; to censor; hence **blue-pencilling** *vbl. sb.*; **blue pill** *U.S. slang*, a bullet; **blue print**, a photo-print composed of white lines on a blue ground or of blue lines on a white ground, used chiefly in copying plans, etc.; also, a blue-toned photograph; **blue-printing**, (*a*) the process of printing in blue beneath the glaze on china, as distinguished from 'black-printing'; (*b*) the action or method of making a 'blue print'; **blue process** (see quot.); **blue (process) paper**, a sensitized paper used for copying maps and plans, made by saturating the paper with potassium ferrocyanide; **blue streak** *U.S.*, a continuous stretch; **blue-washed** *a.*, (*a*) washed by the blue sea; (*b*) covered with a blue wash.
1837 Dickens *Pickw.* xxxiii, Mr. Pickwick..followed Mr. Perker and the *blue bag out of court. 1853 — *Bleak Ho.* i, A battery of blue bags is loaded with heavy charges of papers and carried off by clerks. 1902 [see *brief-bag*, *Brief sb. 11]. 1895 Dana *Man. Geol.* (ed. 4) 243 Lamellar or straticulate structure of glacier-ice modified by..the '*blue bands', or 'veined structure'. 1898 *Westm. Gaz.* 7 Apr. 4/1 He is very rude to '*bluebeaks,' as he terms recruits. 1927 *Observer* 16 Oct. 12 Soviet Russia's 'Living Newspaper'..appeared for the first time this week in Berlin. It was a small edition only, consisting of eight men and four women, grouped under the title of '*Blue Blouses'. 1883 Jas. Greenwood *Odd People in Odd Places* 68 The instrumental '*blue boys' belonging to several metropolitan divisions. 1912 A. S. M. Hutchinson *Happy Warrior* v. vii. § 2 The Blue Boys from the police-station..scoured the country. 1874 *Slang Dict.*, **Blue Butter*, mercurial ointment used for the destruction of parasites. 1897 *Westm. Gaz.* 22 May 3/2 The well-known '*blue earth' of the diamond mines. 1928 *Daily Express* 12 July 3/4 The *Blue Flag movement, an organisation for the purpose of getting people's minds off party politics. 1927 *Ibid.* 27 Dec. 1 The '*Blue Force,'—that is, the uniform branch of the police. 1902 *Encycl. Brit.* XXVIII. 602/1 Water gas in its original state is called '*blue gas', because it burns with a blue, non-luminous flame. 1886 J. Noble *Handbk. Cape Good Hope* 192 The '*blue ground' ..far from being barren of diamonds..yielded even better returns than the upper layers of 'yellow ground'. 1911 *Daily Chron.* 25 Mar. 3/2 Of very great rarity is a piece of 'blue ground' with a diamond embedded in it... The 'blue ground' ..is..not uncommonly black or brown. 1891 *Daily News* 27 Apr. 3/2 The '*Blue' Measure... A measure called the blue (which contained two-thirds of a pint, and was universally used in Wales). 1869 C. L. Brace *New West* xvii. 218 They never have, like the whites, a Sunday spree and a '*blue Monday'. 1900 *Daily News* 3 Apr. 2/5, I was '*blue-mouldy for want of a batin',' as they say in certain parts of the Empire. 1900 *Westm. Gaz.* 31 May 2/3 Bluemouldy from Ennui. 1871–3 *Texas Almanac* 98 There is evidently in these dry '*blue northers' (as they are called) a state of high electrical condition of the atmosphere. 1878 J. H. Beadle *Western Wilds* xxvii. 430 Warm, moist weather is generally followed very suddenly by a 'blue norther' that pinches one fearfully. 1885 *Encycl. Brit.* XVIII. 242/2 The oil from which hard and soft paraffin are separated..exhibits a blue fluorescence, and is hence called '*blue oil'. 1839 *R. Hooper's Lex. Med.* (ed. 7) 268/1 **Blue ointment*, the mercurial ointment. 1887 *Buck's Handbk. Med. Sci.* IV. 738/2. 1893 Kipling *Many Invent.*, *Matter of Fact* 167 The *blue pencil plunged remorselessly through the slips. 1899 *Daily News* 17 Feb., The actor will have a better chance after the blue pencil has eliminated the unnecessary verbiage in the dialogue. *a* 1904 S. E. White *Blazed Trail Stories* iii. 48 One log had not been *blue-pencilled across the end. *a* 1909 'O. Henry' *Roads of Destiny* xi. 273 Robbins was ..detecting..the envious *blue-pencilling his own stuff had received. 1914 G. Cannan *Old Mole* 39 He blue-pencilled false quantities in Latin verse. 1925 *Mus. Assoc. Proc.* 60 He would blue-pencil an unprepared chord of the seventh in a motet in the style of Palestrina. 1861 *N. Y. Tribune* 10 Nov. (Farmer, Slang) Between *blue pills, hatters, and the penitentiary we shall soon work off this element of rascaldom and horse-thieves. 1887 *U.S. Postal Laws & Reg.* § 364. 152 '*Blue prints' reproduced only as copies of the original. 1892 *Photogr. Ann.* II. 102 Blue Prints can be obtained on albumenised paper. 1902 *Encycl. Brit.* XXXI. 703/2 For architects and engineers, cyanotype and ferrogallic papers are prepared..for the direct reproduction of tracings and drawings, as blue or black prints by these methods. 1865 L. Jewitt *The Wedgwoods* 391 *Blue Printing was introduced at Etruria at an early date, and has, of course, with black, etc., been continued to the present day. 1889 *Century Dict.*, *Blue-printing*, a method of photo-printing [etc.]. 1884 Knight *Dict. Mech.* Suppl., **Blue Process for Copying*, a mode of copying tracings in lieu of re-tracing them. 1895 *Century Mag.* Sept. 676/1 He calmly lied to me a *blue streak, and he knew that I knew he was lying. 1895 Susan Hale *Lett.* 289, I..drove in her sort of..carryall..talking a blue streak two miles to her house. 1913 Mrs. Stratton-Porter *Laddie* ix. (1917) 178 He talked a blue streak about the money. 1905 *Westm. Gaz.* 18 Nov. 6/3 A small stone city, set round a *blue-washed bay. 1906 *Ibid.* 13 Jan. 4/3 Out in the blue-washed bay. *Ibid.* 14 Nov. 2/1 From the blue-washed wall an unshaped lamp shone brilliantly.

Blue (blū), *v.*^{2} *slang.* Also **blew.**
1. *trans.* To spend or get through (money) lavishly or extravagantly; = *Blow v.^{1} 10 b.
1859 *Slang Dict.* s.v. *Blewed*, 'I blewed all my blunt last night', I spent all my money. 1884 *Daily Tel.* 28 May 5/1 He took to horses, and blewed the blooming lot [£1,700] in eighteen months. 1887 *Punch* 10 Sept. 111/1, I never minds blueing the pieces purwided I gets a good spree. 1888 Farjeon *Miser Farebrother* III. i. 5 You brought down two thousand pounds with you, and you blued it. 1896 *Westm. Gaz.* 5 Dec. 10/1 A debtor who had some funds.., instead of paying his just debts, went to London and 'blued the lot'. 1916 Locke *Wonderful Year* ii, 'I'm going to blue twenty pounds,' she replied. 'I'll have a kummel glacé.'

2. To make a mess of, spoil, ruin.
1880 *Punch's Almanac* 2 This top coat would blue it.

Blueback (blū·bæk). [f. Blue a. + Back sb.^{1}]
1. Chiefly *pl.* Paper money issued by the Transvaal Government in 1865. *S. Afr.*
1876 Trollope *South Africa* II. 225 The blue-backs as they were called were printed. 1884 Martin *At Home in Transvaal* 501 (Pettman) They were not at all anxious to return to the time of blue-backs. 1900 *Daily News* 17 Sept. 5/2 President Kruger has deserted them, taking all the gold, and leaving them only 'blue-backs.'

2. A legal-tender note issued by the Confederacy during the Civil War. *U.S.*
1871 S. de Vere *Americanisms* (1872) 47 During the Civil War..the original Blue Backs of the Confederacy (so-called in opposition to the Green Backs of the Union) soon became known as Shucks.

3. A species of trout, salmon, or bird, having a bluish back. Also *attrib.*
1858 Simmonds *Dict. Trade*, *Blue-backs*, a name for the North American herring *Clupea elongata*. 1871 *Game Laws* in *Fur, Fin, & Feather* (1872) 158 This section shall not apply to the taking of blue back trout in Franklin and Oxford counties. 1881 *Amer. Naturalist* XV. 178 Of these species, the blue-back predominates in Frazer's river. *Ibid.* 180 Little blue-backs [sc. salmon] of every size down to six inches are also found in the Upper Columbia in the fall. 1883 [see Blue a. 12 a].

Blue bag: see *Blue sb. 2 c, and a. 13.

Blue·-bill. *U.S.* [Blue a. 12 a.] A North American species of wild duck.
1867 *Game Laws* (*Ohio*) in *Fur, Fin, & Feather* (1872) 58 It shall be unlawful for any person..to catch, kill or destroy ..any wild goose..blue-bill, or other wild duck. 1874 J. W. Long *Amer. Wild-fowl Shooting* Introd. 16, I shall treat of the..blue-bill or broad-bill. 1895 *Outing* (U.S.) XXVII. 211/2 Then through the willows came a flock of blue-bill. 1908 R. W. Chambers *Firing Line* x, The little blue-bill ducks came swimming in scores.
attrib. 1874 J. W. Long *Amer. Wild-fowl Shooting* xxvii. 273 Blue-bill shooting..is one of the prettiest of sports. 1894 *Outing* (U.S.) XXIV. 73 [A friend] had asked us to join him in a day's bluebill shooting.

Blue book. Add examples of general use:
1848 (*title*) The Blue Book of the British Manufacturers. 1909 B. Ward *Dawn Cath. Revival* I. i. 2 It is described in the Third Blue Book as follows. *Note*, The Blue Books were the official publications of the Catholic Committee. 1928 *Daily Tel.* 5 May 7/6 The 'Blue Book', the directory ..of the electrical engineering and allied trades.
Hence **Blue-booky** *a.*, **Blue-bookiness.**
1894 *Speaker* 9 June 649/1 A dry, blue-booky article. 1909 *Fabian News* XX. 76/1 His volume is..readable, notwithstanding the complete blue bookiness of its contents.

Blue buck. [ad. Du. *blaauwbok* Blauwbok.] The smallest of the S. African bucks, *Cephalophus monticola.*
1834 *Penny Cycl.* II. 88/2. 1835 Moodie *Ten Years S. Africa* II. 139 The woods also abound with..an elegant little antelope,..called the '*blaauw bock*' or blue buck. 1893 *J. Noble's Handbk. Cape & S. Afr.* 62 The diminutive blue-buck, not bigger than a rabbit.

Blue-cap. Add: **2. b.** A soldier belonging to the Dublin Fusiliers, which served under Havelock in the Indian Mutiny as the Madras Fusiliers, and were known as 'Havelock's Bluecaps'.
1897 *Daily News* 25 June 6/2 The author was..gazetted to the 1st Madras Fusiliers, subsequently known as Havelock's 'Bluecaps'.

Bluecoat. Add: **1. b.** A bluish colour of the coat in deer at a certain period.
1870 *Amer. Naturalist* IV. 190 The spike-horn was shot just as deer were attaining the 'blue coat'.

2. c. A soldier in the Federal army during the Civil War. *U.S.*
1865 G. W. Nichols *Story Gt. March* xxiii. 154 So we jogged on for awhile, and then..we descried a blue coat and a white-eared mule approaching. 1879 Tourgee *Fool's Err.* xxi. 122 But only wait until the States are restored and the 'Blue Coats' are out of the way. 1887 C. B. George *40 Yrs. on Rail* vi. 103 My train began to carry the 'blue coats'.

3. *blue-coat girl.*
1695 Pepys *Let. to Mrs. Steward* 20 Sept., Two wealthy citizens are lately dead, and left their estates, one to a Blue Coat boy, and the other to a Blue Coat girl, in Christ's Hospital. 1894 *Daily News* 30 Mar. 5/1 To many..the notion of a Bluecoat 'girl' will be somewhat strange. It appears, nevertheless, that the Hertford establishment now shelters no fewer than 112 scholars of that sex.

Blued (blūd), *ppl. a.* [f. Blue v. 1 + -ed^1.] Made blue; tempered to a blue colour.
1902 'O. Henry' *Rolling Stones* (1915) 67 The blued drills and punches of the finest temper.

Blue eye. Add: **d.** An Australian species of honey-eater (see quots.).
1848 J. Gould *Birds Australia* IV. pl. 68 *Entomyza cyanotis*, Swains. Blue-faced Entomyza. Blue-eye of the Colonists. 1861 *Chamb. Encycl.* II. 171/1 Blue-eye (*Entomyza cyanotis*), a beautiful little bird, abundant..in New South Wales.

Blue-eyed, *a.* (See Dict. s.v. Blue eye.) Add: *allusively*, innocent.
1920 *Star* 21 Aug. 15/4 The teacher's blue-eyed boy who can do no wrong!

Blue-fish. (Earlier examples.)
c 1622 Pory *Plymouth & New Eng.* (1918) 39 As concerning the blew fish, in delicacie it excelleth all kinds of fish that ever I tasted. 1639 *Plymouth Col. Rec.* XI. 34 To erect wares to take fish at Mortons hole, Blewfish River. 1672 Josselyn *New Eng. Rarities* 96 Blew Fish, or Horse. ..It is common in New-England and esteemed the best sort of Fish next to Rock Cod.
Hence **Bluefishing**, fishing for blue-fish.
1886 *Outing* (U.S.) IX. 73/2 From him we learned..that the best bluefishing was to be had right there.

Bluegrass, blue-grass. *U.S.* [Blue a. 12 b.]
1. A field-grass (*Poa compressa* or *pratensis*), characteristic especially of Kentucky and Virginia. (See also quot. 1902.)
1751 C. Gist *Jrnls.* 47 It is..full of beautiful natural Meadows covered with wild Rye, blue Grass and Clover. 1782 Jefferson *Notes Virginia* (1787) 63 The grasses are Lucerne, St. Foin,..greenswerd, blue grass, and crab grass. *c* 1805 J. J. Henry *Camp. agst. Quebec* (1812) 168 A basket-full of the ordinary blue-grass of our country. 1831 Peck *Guide for Emigrants* ii. 161 A species of blue grass is cultivated by some farmers for pastures. 1862 *Congress. Globe* Apr. 1692/1 Blue grass has..brought large profits to graziers. 1873 J. H. Beadle *Undevel. West* xxx. 656, I found good blue grass, which is very rare everywhere in the Rocky mountains. 1889 *Harper's Mag.* Jan. 259/1 The blue-grass ..blooms toward the middle of June in a bluish, almost a peacock blue, blossom, which gives to the fields an exquisite hue. 1902 Clapin *Dict. Amer.* 60 In Maryland the term *blue grass* is applied to a species of grass very injurious to wheat and clover, and hard to eradicate.

2. The region of the blue grass; *spec.* the State of Kentucky.
1871 Schele de Vere *Americanisms* (1872) 407 Both the region where it grows naturally, and the settlers there are known as Blue Grass simply, and hence the State of Kentucky especially is often thus designated. 1887 *Harper's Mag.* June 48/2 To that pleasant land of the Kentuckian, the 'Blue-grass'.

3. *attrib.*, as *blue-grass country, pasture, region, seed*; **Blue-grass State**, Kentucky.
1788 Washington *Diaries* III. 322, I sowed 3½ bushels of Blue Grass Seeds. 1831 Peck *Guide for Emigrants* ii. 161 Blue grass pastures may be kept green and fresh until late in autumn. 1871 *N. Y. Tribune* 6 Apr. (DeVere) It does not speak well for the condition of the Blue-Grass Region, that [etc.]. 1886 *Harper's Mag.* June 50/2 It is but a short distance from the blue-grass country to the eastern mountains. 1895 C. King *Fort Frayne* vii. 95 The blue-grass county she so fondly loved. 1907 *Springfield Weekly Republ.* 3 Oct. 3 Missouri, which adjoins the Blue Grass state along a stretch of the Mississippi river.

b. *ellipt.* as *adj.* Belonging to the blue-grass country.
1889 *Harper's Mag.* Aug. 459/2 Bud rode into the yard on Mollie...'Blue-grass all over. I wonder how he came by her.'

Blue Hen. *U.S.* The State of Delaware; chiefly in *Blue Hen's chickens* (see quot. 1840), *Blue Hen State.*
1830 Mrs. Royall *Lett. fr. Alabama* 69 He told one of our party he was 'One of the blue hen's chickens'. 1840 *Niles' Nat. Reg.* 9 May 154/3 In the revolutionary war ..Captain Caldwell [of Delaware] had a company called by the rest 'Caldwell's game cocks,' and the regiment after a time in Carolina was nicknamed from this 'the blue hen's chickens' and the 'blue chickens'... But after they had been distinguished in the south the name of the *Blue Hen* was applied to the state. 1864 *Congress. Globe* June 2968/2, I remember the early history of the Blue Hen's Chickens and it is a proud one. 1897 *Congress. Rec.* Mar., App. 68/2, [I thank] the gentleman from the 'Blue Hen State' for his suggestion. 1904 *N. Y. Even. Post* 10 Nov. 1 The most reliable information..from the Blue Hen State indicates [etc.].

Blue jay, blue-jay. *U.S.* [Blue a. 12 a.] A North American jay (*Cyanurus cristatus*).
1709 *Bristol Rec.* in *Narrag. Hist. Reg.* III. 211 The same order shall extend to the killing of blew Jawes [*sic*]. 1792 J. Belknap *Hist. New Hampsh.* III. 173 The blue jay, the wood pecker and the partridge..are then seen flying. 1807 *Repertory* (Boston) 2 Jan. (Th.) The blue jay, that is charmed by a black snake into its very jaws. 1838 [see Jay 1 b]. 1845 S. Judd *Margaret* i. ii. 8 She saw a blue-jay washing itself. 1886 *Harper's Mag.* Nov. 877/2 The bell note of the blue-jay comes up from some mysterious haunt. 1888 *Congress. Rec.* 4810/2 A day-school among the Comanches..would not be any better than having a school of blue-jays.

Blue-John. Add: **1. b.** (See quot.)
1869 *Overland Monthly* III. 129 North Carolinians call skimmilk 'blue John'.

Blue-joint. [Blue a. 1.] *Blue-joint grass*, a tall bluish-stemmed grass, *Calamagrostis canadensis*, or (in the Western states) *Agropyrum glaucum*; also *Andropogon furcatus* (cf. *Blue-stem).
1849 *Pres. Mess. Congress* ii. 427 A little meadow filled with tall bluejoint grass. 1870 *Amer. Naturalist* III. 162 The buffalo grass is replaced by others of a more vigorous growth, especially by the blue-joint grass. 1874 *Rep. Vermont Board Agric.* II. 548 The blue joint grass was already a foot high, and in September I cut a heavy crop of it. 1884 *Encycl. Brit.* XVII. 308/1 (Nebraska) Blue-joint (*Andropogon furcatus*, &c.) grasses.

Blue laws. *U.S.* (See Blue a. 13.)
1781 S. Peters *Hist. Connecticut* (1877) 44 Even the religious fanatics of Boston and the mad zealots of Hertford..christened them the 'Blue Laws'. *Ibid.* 61 They.. were very properly termed *Blue Laws*; i.e. *bloody Laws*; for they were all sanctified with..whippings, cutting off the ears, burning the tongue, and death. 1805 *Repertory* (Boston) 8 Jan. (Th.) The *Connecticut Courant* retaliated by publishing some of the obsolete enactments of the 'Old Dominion', under the heading of 'Blue Laws of Virginia'. 1818 Fessenden *Ladies' Monitor* 85 His blue laws never sanction'd by rewards, Seem form'd by Athens' sanguinary sage. 1829 L. Dow *Omnifarious Law Exempl.* 13 One of the blue laws of Conn. was, neither to give meat, drink, or lodging to a Quaker, or to tell him the road. 1860 S. S. Schmucker (*title*) Blue Laws of Connecticut,..with an introduction. 1871 Barnum *Struggles & Triumphs* 53 The following scene makes a chapter in the history of Connecticut, as the State was when 'blue-laws' were something more than a dead letter. 1906 *Springfield Weekly Republ.* 20 Dec. 5 He is not of those Puritans who bound the moral field by the Ten Commandments and the Blue Laws.
attrib. 1854 *Congress. Globe* 6 July 1618 (Th.), I know that Connecticut, in the olden time, was libeled by a Tory renegade..as the Blue Law State.

Blue light(s). [See Blue a. 13.] Employed allusively in U.S. politics.
The allusion was to the exhibition of blue lights, attributed to traitorous Federalists, on the heights above New London, Conn., as a signal to the British fleet in the war of 1812. An account of the incident is given in *Niles' Weekly Reg.* (1813) V. 280, 302.
1832 *Deb. Congress* 12 Mar. 2116 Mr. J[enifer] said he did not expect hereafter to hear any more in relation to the 'federalists', 'the Hartford convention', or 'blue lights', from that quarter. 1834 *Louisville Publ. Adv.* 13 Sept., Send us a blue light or two to examine them by. 1838 Drake *Tales fr. Queen City* 91 An adventurer from the land of 'blue lights' and Hartford Conventions. 1847 *Congress. Globe* 20 Jan., App. 252/1 Where, tell me where, have you buried the sins of these 'old blue lights' of New Hampshire? With what magic wand have you changed their Federalism into modern Democracy?
attrib. 1844 *Congress. Globe* 6 Mar., App. 309/2 [He was] as rank a blue-light federal whig as ever justified the Hartford Convention, or worshipped a coon. 1847 *Ibid.* 2 Mar. 418/2 The late war with Great Britain was unpopular with the blue-light Federalists.

Blueness. Add: **5.** A state of depression or melancholy.
1911 J. C. Lincoln *Cap'n Warren's Wards* ix. 147 Before evening his blueness had disappeared.

Blue-point. *U.S.* [The name of a headland near Great South Bay, Long Island.] Used *attrib.* or *ellipt.* to designate a small well-flavoured oyster from the south shore of Long Island; orig. one from a bed off Blue Point.
1832 J. F. Watson *Tales Olden Times* 165 The largest 'Blue-Point' oysters could be bought. 1897 *Daily News* 19 Nov. 5/2 The menu will include such national dishes as.. blue points, and pumpkin pie. *a* 1909 'O. Henry' *Roads of Destiny* xx. 343 He got along fine with the olives and celery and the bluepoints.

Blues (blūz). Orig. *U.S.* [A use of the pl. *blues* (see Blue sb. 12).] A melody of a mournful and haunting character, originated among the negroes of the Southern U.S.; hence, the name of certain dance tunes of this character and the dances themselves.
1921 *Outward Bound* May 58/2 These 'labour songs'... like the 'blues' of to-day, were rather humorous. 1923 *Daily Mail* 28 July 7 Noisy 'jazz' music..is being driven out..by the soft pulsing of muffled melody in new tunes known as 'Blues'. *Ibid.*, A special 'Blues Trot' has been devised for dancing with the tunes, which are slower than [those of] a fox-trot. 1927 *Daily Express* 11 Aug. 3/2 The Yale Blues. 1928 *Oxf. Mag.* 1 Nov. 84/2 The use of a blues for the slow movement is interesting.
Hence **Blues** *v.*, to dance a blues.
1928 *Sunday Express* 27 May 15 Shall she Charleston, Blues or Bridge that evening?

Blue-skin, blueskin. *U.S.* [Blue a. 2.] (See quot. 1848.)
1783 Freneau *Poems* (1809) II. 157 Let him stand where he is.. And he'll turn a true Blue-skin, or just what you will. 1830 Mrs. Royall *Southern Tour* I. 7 We laughed at my race from Betsy Chase and the Blueskins. 1846–52 Mrs. Whitcher *Widow Bedott P.* ix. 93 They call 'em 'Harrington blue-skins'. 1848 Bartlett *Dict. Amer.*, *Blue-skins*, a nickname applied to the Presbyterians, from their alleged grave deportment. 1871 Barnum *Struggles & Triumphs* 35 The congregation would sit and shiver till they really merited the title the profane gave them of 'blue-skins'.

Blue sky, blue-sky. *U.S.* [Blue a. 1; the allusion is supposed to be to one ready to sell the 'blue sky' to a credulous buyer.] Used *attrib.* to denote dealing in doubtful or worthless securities, or legislation relating to this.
1912 *N.Y. Even. Post* 13 Jan., Financ. Suppl. 3 The 'Blue Sky' law of Kansas prohibits the sale..of stock or bonds of any company chartered outside the State, unless [etc.]. 1919 *Detective Story Mag.* XXVIII. 59 That's where old Johnny McGrue had it on you blue-sky merchants. 1921 *Springfield Weekly Republ.* 3 Mar. 1 The origin of 'blue sky law'—legislation providing for State regulation of the sale of corporate securities—is middle western.

Blue-stem. *U.S.* [Blue a. 12 b.] A North American grass, esp. *Andropogon furcatus* and *Agropyrum glaucum.*
1888 *Harper's Mag.* Feb. 348/2 The beautiful carpet of natural grasses, buffalo, gramma, and blue stem. 1927 P. H. Pearson *Prairie Vikings* 24 On the high prairie..the settlers found queer little oases of rank blue-stem showing up in marked contrast against the buffalo grass.

Bluestone, blue stone.
1. A basalt used in Australasia for building and other industrial purposes.
1850 *Australasian* Oct. 138 A stone not unlike the trap or bluestone around Melbourne. 1883 J. Hector *Handbk. N. Z.* (1886) 58 Basalts, locally called 'bluestones', occur of a quality useful for road-metal, house-blocks, and ordinary rubble masonry. 1908 *Daily Chron.* 16 Nov. 4/7 He was a stonemason, and he continued to work at his trade after becoming an M.P. 'I hammer bluestone by day and the squatters by night' was one of his sayings.

2. 'A more or less argillaceous sandstone of bluish color, extensively quarried at various points along the Hudson river, and used for building purposes and for flagging' (*Cent. Dict.* 1889).
1895 Dana *Man. Geol.* (ed. 4) 593 The thicker layers [of flagstones] are called bluestone, from the bluish gray color. 1906 Chamberlin & Salisbury *Geol.* II. 559 Bluestone formation .. Purple shale and thin red sandstone, with calcareous beds.

3. Sulphate of copper.
1839 *R. Hooper's Lex. Med.* (ed. 7) 268/1. 1877 *Encycl. Brit.* VI. 351/2.

Blue tongue.
1. [Cape Du. *blaauwtong.*] A disease affecting horses and sheep, in which the tongue becomes swollen and blue. *S. Afr.*
1886 Rider Haggard *Jess* viii, It's a beautiful veldt.. no horse sickness, no blue-tongue. 1905 *Nature* 4 Sept. 502/2 Catarrhal Fever of Sheep: Blue Tongue.

2. An Australian lizard, *Cyclodus gigas* and *C. nigro-luteus.*
1883 F. McCoy *Zool. Victoria* (1885) I. viii. 15 These Lizards are very sluggish, so that the popular name 'Sleepy Lizard' as well as 'Blue-tongue' comes to be applied to both. 1904 *Daily Chron.* 28 Jan. 6/2 The 'Australian Blue-Tongue' is a..lizard, with a curious habit of thrusting forth a long tongue as bright as turquoise blue.
Hence **Blue-tongued** *a.*, having a blue tongue. *Blue-tongued lizard* = 2 above.
1883 F. McCoy *Zool. Victoria* (1885) I. viii. 13 Cyclodus Gigas... The Northern Blue-tongued Lizard. 1887 — *Nat. Hist. Victoria* II. 120 'Blue-tongued Lizard' or 'Sleepy Lizard'.

Bluette (blue·t). A breed of oriental frilled pigeons having a white body and blue or silver wings.
1879 L. Wright *Pigeon Keeper* 180 This is almost exactly the marking of the Bluette. 1891 R. Woods *Pigeon Culture* 138 Brunettes, Bluettes and Silverettes are..subvarieties of the Satinette, differing only in colour and markings.

Blue water.
1. The deep sea, the open sea.
1834 Marryat *Peter Simple* xxviii, We are not sorry when we once are fairly out of harbour, and find ourselves in *blue water.* 1886 *Encycl. Brit.* XXI. 603/1 *Blue water*, clear of the English Channel; at a distance from shore.

2. *attrib.* and *Comb.*: as *blue-water battle, torpedo-boat*; **blue-water school**, a collective term applied to politicians or political students who regard a strong navy and the command of the sea as essential to the security of the country, or as the chief or the only sufficient defence.
1905 *Daily Chron.* 13 May 4/3 It is quite likely that no such *blue-water battle..may take place. 1902 *Westm. Gaz.* 13 Jan. 3/2 Mr. Roosevelt is revealed..as convinced a member of the *blue-water school as Mr. Clowes in England. 1898 *Daily News* 29 Mar. 3/2 The *blue water torpedo-boats.

Blue-wing. [Blue a. 1.] A North American variety of teal. Also *attrib.*
1731 Catesby *Nat. Hist. Carolina* etc. (1754) I. 96 *Anas Americanus lato rostro.* The Blue-wing Shoveler. *Ibid.* 99 *Querquidula Americana fusca.* The Blue-Wing Teal. 1768 Washington *Diaries* I. 294 Went into the Neck and up the Creek after Blew Wings. 1874 J. W. Long *Amer. Wild-fowl Shooting* xv. 192 They are a trifle smaller than the blue-wings. 1895 *Outing* (U.S.) Oct. XXVII. 43/1 A bunch of blue-wing teal rose from the ice-pond.

Blue-winged, *a.* [Blue a. 11 b.] Having blue wings; *spec.* of certain species of birds.
1732 [see Shoveller^2 2]. 1789 Morse *Amer. Geog.* 59 The Blue winged teal. *Ibid.*, The Blue winged shoveller. 1874 Long *Wild-Fowl Shooting* 185 The flesh of the blue-winged teal is considered..to be superior. 1878 [see Blue a. 11 b].

Bluey, *a.* (*adv.*) Add quots.:
1889 *Pall Mall Gaz.* 1 May 3/1 An exquisite effect in bluey grey. 1900 *Daily News* 11 May 3/2 A bluey green colour.

Bluff, *sb.*^{1} Add: *attrib.* (see quots.)
1861–4 *Trans. Ill. Agric. Soc.* V. 628 The term loess is applied to a deposit which..has been sometimes called the 'bluff' deposit. 1880 Dana *Man. Geol.* (ed. 3) 549 The loess. ..In the Mississippi valley, it covers the 'Orange sand', forming with it the Bluff formation'—so called because standing in bluffs in Missouri. 1882 *Encycl. Brit.* XIV. 42/2 (Kentucky) A homogeneous buff-coloured silicious loam known as the 'bluff' or loess formation. 1884 *Ibid.* XVII. 309/2 (Nebraska) These so-called 'bluff lands', composed of loess materials.

2. *Canada.* (See quot.)
1895 *Times* 13 Sept. 12/3 [Manitoba.] Level or rolling prairie with scattered 'bluffs' (small patches of wood) in some districts.

Bluff, *sb.*^{2} Add: **3. b.** In fig. phrases, as *to call the bluff, to run a bluff on.*
1887 F. Francis Jr. *Saddle & Mocassin* 130 'You got the stock, though?' 'Oh,—yes! I run a bluff on 'em.' 1891 *Chambers's Jrnl.* 26 Sept. 618/2 A man may have a big name as a fighting man and yet not be able always to run a bluff on people so easily. 1910 *N. Y. Even. Post* 31 Mar. (Th.) The Canadians..regarded it as a bluff; and if they did not actually call the bluff, they came as near doing so as could be done.

c. *attrib.* as *bluff game.*
1845 J. J. Hooper *Adv. Simon Suggs* x. 129 'No!' said Simon..'the bluff game ain't played here!' 1888 *St. Louis Globe Democrat* 29 Apr. (Farmer) They..thought he could outnumber them. It was a bluff game, and he won.

4. A bluffer.
a 1904 S. E. White *Blazed Trail Stories* ii. 27 'You're a bluff!' said he, insultingly.

Bluff, *a.* Add:
1. e. Of other objects: see quots.
? 1637 *Trav. P. Mundy* (MS. Rawl. A. 315), Peeces of wood..bluffe or blunt att both ends. 1920 *Discovery* Mar. 78/1 The streamline form for a kite balloon is rather bluff.. and short compared with an airship.

Bluff, *v.*^{1} **2.** (Earlier example.)
a 1859 *N. Y. Spirit of Times* (Bartlett), 'I goes you five dollars this time,' says Jim,..'I..goes you ten better,' said Bill; 'you ain't agoin' to bluff dis child.'

3. *intr.* (Earlier example.)
1854 *Congress. Globe* 3 May 1070 We both know how that game [of brag] is played. I thought I would bluff back on him.

Bluffer. 2. (U.S. examples.)
1888 *Detroit Free Press* 5 May (Farmer) The American man-of-war..could be blown out of the water in five minutes by the guns of the Moors. Is Uncle Sam a bluffer? 1895 C. King *Fort Frayne* ii. 24 The Eleventh..had surrounded and disarmed Tall Bull's little band of ugly 'bluffers'.

Blu·ffing, *vbl. sb.* [f. Bluff v.^{1} 2.] The action of using bluff; also *attrib.*
1850 *Congress. Globe* 14 May, App. 606/1, I cannot look upon the effort of Texas in any other light than a bluffing, brow-beating game. 18.. *Southern Sketches* 137 (Bartlett 1859) Jim..tried the bluffing system; but Joe said he.. would put up with no more insults from his bullying neighbor.

Bluggy (blʌ·gi), *a.* Pretended infantile pronunciation of Bloody (see quot. 1877) used subsequently as a euphemistic pronunciation of 'bloody', esp. to define literature of the blood-and-thunder type. (See *Blood sb. 3 d.)
1877 J. Habberton *Helen's Babies* 68 Bliaff's head was all bluggy, an' David's sword was all bluggy—bluggy as everyfing. 1890 *Scott. Leader* 17 July 4 The shriek with which Mr. Hall Caine greeted Mr. Grant Allen's protest against bluggy novels. 1895 *Spectator* 12 Oct. 483/1 This very ugly word, which..was first used, we believe, as a mispronunciation of 'bloody' by one of 'Helen's Babies', is creeping into literature as a short expression for the fondness for blood which is displayed by some modern writers of fiction. 1921 *19th Cent.* May 770 East End ambuscades where the air is thick with the smell of fried fish and Yiddish and bluggy rhetoric.
Hence **Blu·gginess.**
1894 *Punch* 30 June 305 It is not poesy, culture, wisdom, wit,—That make the literary world go round.—Much 'blugginess' has more to do with it. 1901 *Academy* 2 Nov. 404 In the close it falls sheer into rant and 'blugginess'.

Blukar (blū·kaɹ). [Malay بلوكر.] A secondary jungle or forest in Malaya.
1906 *Macm. Mag.* Aug. 777 A tiger had taken up its abode in a patch of *bluker*, or secondary forest, behind the village. 1913 *Chambers's Jrnl.* Sept. 563/2, I took my gun and tramped through the blukar in the hope of putting up some game. 1926 *Blackw. Mag.* Apr. 505/1 Land previously cultivated by the native and left grows up into secondary jungle called 'Blukar'.

Blunder, *v.* Add:
7. b. *trans.* To bring or cause to fall *into* a state by clumsy or inept behaviour; to use blunderingly.
1901 *Westm. Gaz.* 27 June 4/3 They believe that Mr. Chamberlain has blundered the country into war. 1912 A. S. M. Hutchinson *Happy Warrior* v. x. § 1. 347 He.. hated to have blundered all his dullness on so rare and exquisite a thing.

Blunt, *a.* Add:
6. blunt head, a snake belonging to the family *Amblycephalidæ.*
1870 Gillmore tr. *Figuier's Reptiles & Birds* 51 The *Amblycephalidæ*, or Blunt Heads, comprise a few species of moderate or small size.

Blurb (blɜːɹb). Originally *U.S. slang.* [Of unknown origin.] A brief descriptive paragraph or note of the contents or character of a book, printed as a commendatory advertisement, on the 'jacket' or wrapper of a newly published book.
1924 *Spectator* 27 Sept. 426 The note of vanity is ominously accentuated by the publisher's blurb on the dust-cover, as silly and vulgar as the present writer has ever seen. 1924 Galsworthy *White Monkey* 214 What shall I do? It's so darned crude. 'Couldn't let you go, old man, without'—blurb! 1925 *Daily Sketch* 22 May 7/3 A book reviewer who probably neglects to read the publishers' blurbs on the jackets. 1926 *Times Lit. Suppl.* 21 Oct., The paragraph briefly setting forth the merits of the book (known in 'the trade' as a 'blurb').
Hence **Blurbed** *pa. pple.*, furnished with blurb.
1928 *Publishers' Weekly* 10 Nov. 1982 Only a fraction of books issued each year are worth while—Yet each is blurbed and ballyhooed as an authentic masterpiece.

Bluster, *v.* **4.** Delete † *Obs.* and add:
1891 C. Graves *Field of Tares* (N.Y.) 181 He blustered out another oath as he looked at her.

Blustery, *a.* **1.** (Earlier U.S. example.)
1774 P. V. Fithian *Jrnl.* (1900) 105 The day very blustry & cold.

Bo (bōᵘ). *U.S. slang.* Used vocatively to a male person.

a 1905 'O. Henry' *Heart of West* ix. (1912) 126 Why, say, Bo, I wish I had a dollar for every game of pinocle me and Heine has played on Sunday afternoons. 1916 *Lincoln Even. News* 1 Jan. in *Dialect Notes* IV. 272 The swaggerest rag you can put on, bo, is one of the non-skid, full-dress shirt bosoms. 1926 *Judge* (Ibid.), The man who tells the bootblack 'Keep the change, bo'.

Boagane (bōᵘ·gān). [Manx: cf. W. *bwgan*, Ir. *bocan* goblin.] A Manx goblin.
1887 Hall Caine *Deemster* ii, The men craythurs that hang up their hats over the straw to fright the boaganes.

Board, *sb.* Add:
I. In Colonial technical senses: see quots.
1890 *Chambers's Jrnl.* 17 May 310/2 Down each side [of the Australian wool-shed] is a clear space some ten feet in width, technically known as 'the board'. Here the shearers work. 1892 *Ibid.* 5 Mar. 159/1 (Prince Edward Island) The boat is carried out across the 'board' or standing ice some time previous to the arrival of the geese. 1893 *Herald* (Melbourne) 23 Dec. 6/1 (Morris) 'The board' is the technical name for the floor on which the sheep are shorn.

5. c. Also often *transf.* and *fig.*, to carry off all the stakes or prizes; hence, to carry off all the honours.
1882 H. Smart in *Liquor Christmas Ann.* ii. 7/1 We have swept the board so far [in racing]. 1884 *Live Stock Jrnl.* 25 July 83/3 Mr. Parry Thomas swept the board in Any Variety Sheep-dogs with his Sir Guy and Welsh Boy. 1905 Hornung *Thief in Night*, *Spoils of Sacrilege* (ed. Nelson) 289 The bloated Guillemard usually sweeps the board with his fancy flyers [sc. horses].

8. b. A committee. Also, the stock exchange (hence *board member*). *U.S.*
1905 *Daily Chron.* 28 Apr. 4/4 None of the 'board members'—as the Stock Exchange men are called—ever appears on the kerb... While fortunes are made and lost on the kerb, it does not seem so serious a business as 'on the board.' 1909 *Ibid.* 3 May 4/6 A 'board' appears to be a 'committee' in the United States, while their word committee is applied to what we should call a board.

12. e. *Board and board*: (sailing) by a succession of close tacks.
1926 Rex Clements *Stately Southerner* 156 She met with a severe hammering off the Horn, but clawed her way to windward, and, after a week of board and board, managed to slip round.

14. Hence *board-ship* used attrib. or as adj.
1852 *Life in Bombay* 216 The board-ship habit of taking brandy and water at night. 1894 Mrs. Dyan *Man's Keeping* (1899) 228 The liberal allowance of 'board-ship' flirtation. 1924 *Blackw. Mag.* June 743/2 In the curiously intimate routine of a board-ship life..we became very friendly.

18. board bill *U.S.*, the charge made for board; **board-work, -worker** (see quots.).
1890 *Harper's Mag.* May 908/1 All these brothers were earning their own *board bills. 1887 Creer (*title*) *Board work, or the Art of Wig making. *Ibid.* Introd., Board-work, in the fullest extent of its signification, means all that which is done by clever hairdressers and wig-makers in the workshop and at the work table. 1927 *Daily Express* 5 July 5/4 Students are taught the general principles of dressing hair and the technique of board-work, or preparation of hair for making transformations, wigs, and curls. 1921 *Dict. Occupational Terms* (1927) § 428 **Board worker*; hair-dresser's model maker, perruquier, postiche worker, posticheur, wig-maker; general terms for all workers engaged in..making wigs [etc.].

Board, *v.* Add: **7. d.** To treat (leather) with a graining-board.
1860 Ure *Dict. Arts* (ed. 5) 691 The stiffer parts being boarded both on the grain and flesh sides. 1882 *Encycl. Brit.* XIV. 387/1 When dry enough for the purpose, the skin is boarded,..the effect of which is to bring up the grain,..and also to make it supple.

8. b. To put up and feed (horses). *U.S.*
1905 *N. Y. Even. Post* 24 Feb. 1 The owner of a large stable..said that..he had recently had some seventy horses to board.

9. b. *To board round*: to board in succession in different houses. *U.S.*
1839 Mrs. Kirkland *New Home* xlv. 301 Mr. Cyrus Whicher,..a dignitary who had 'boarded round' till there was very little of him left. 1858 *Knickerbocker Mag.* Jan. LI. 31, I 'boarded round', a significant phrase, whose meaning every poor country schoolmaster learns, with all its variations. 1872 Eggleston *Hoosier Schoolm.* 15 It was as well for Ralph that he began to 'board round' by stopping at Mrs. Means's.

Boarded, *ppl. a.* Add: (to sense 1) boarded-up (see Board v. 7), (to sense 3) *boarded-out.*
1890 *Harper's Mag.* Dec. 102/2 It was not long before the dismal little, boarded-up, spidery coquina house was as clean as a whistle. 1896 *Daily News* 4 Apr. 3/1 Amongst boarded-out children ophthalmia is almost unknown. 1905 *Daily Chron.* 26 Jan. 5/1 The boarded-up shop fronts and broken windows.

Boarder. Add: **1. b.** A horse that is put up and fed at a livery-stable. *U.S.*
1903 *N. Y. Tribune* 20 Sept., Advt., Boarders wanted at Rochville Boarding Stable.

Board-fence. *U.S.* [Board sb. 17.] A close fence made with boards.
1725 *Manchester* (Mass.) *Rec.* 165 On ye esterly side by ye highway as the stone wall & board fence now stand. 1802 *Charleston Land Rec.* 252 From Col. David Wood's board fence over to Dea: John Larkin's wall is forty feet. 1820 *Boston Selectm.* 29 Mar., On condition they build a substantial board fence, lay a plank walk and leave the street thirty feet wide. 1860 O. W. Holmes *Prof. Breakf.-t.* xi. 331 When the boys used to make pictures of me with chalk on the board-fences. 1917 Mathewson *Sec. Base Sloan* xi. 143 It had a board fence around it.
So **Board-fencing.** *U.S.*
1871 *Trans. Ill. Agric. Soc.* VIII. 232 By means of hedging and movable board fencing keep up a great deal of pasturage.

Boarding, *vbl. sb.* **7.** Add: *boarding-knife*; **boarding-car** *U.S.*, a railway carriage fitted with sleeping, cooking, and dining accommodation; **boarding foreman, master, officer** (see quots.); **boarding-house** (earlier examples); **boarding-place** *U.S.*, a boarding-house; **boarding-stable** *U.S.*, a livery stable.
1891 C. Roberts *Adrift Amer.* 87 The *boarding cars had to be fitted up, the cooking appliances put in order, &c. 1921 *Dict. Occup. Terms* (1927) § 731 **Boarding foreman, boarding officer*, is responsible to harbour or dock authority for seeing that ship's papers, etc., are in order before allowing her to enter dock or harbour. 1789 *New Ann. Reg.* i. 126/1 They might as well..send him to one of those *boarding houses that take in unfortunate invalids. 1799 *Deb. Congress* 16 Feb. (1850) 2924 The gentleman from South Carolina.. had no information on this subject, except what he got from boarding-houses. 1807 *Maryland Hist. Mag.* V. 176 She proved to be a small Pilot Boat.., with 50 Muskets ready loaded, about 18 *Boarding knives, &c. 1904 *Daily Chron.* 31 Mar. 7/6 A Greek *boarding-master boarded a vessel in the Roath Dock with sailors. 1881 *Instr. Census Clerks* (1885) 36 *Boarding Officer. 1854 Mary J. Holmes *Tempest & Sunshine* iv. 52 Mr. Middleton set off for Frankfort to find 'as smart a *boarding-place for his gals as anybody had'. 1911 H. S. Harrison *Queed* iii. 28 She runs this boarding-place, and people of various kinds come to her. 1903 *Boarding stable [see *Boarder 1 b]. 1905 *N. Y. Even. Post* 27 Sept. 5 Many horses were suffocated..when fire destroyed the two-story boarding stable.

Board-nail. In later use *U.S.* [ME. *bordnail*, perh. alteration of *brodnail* (Brod sb.^{1}, Brad) by assimilation to *bord*, Board sb.] A nail of the brad type, or suitable for nailing boards. Also in phr. *to bite a board-nail off* or *in two* (see quots.).
1303–4 *Acc. Chamberl. Chester* (1910) 42 Bord-nail, schingelneil, latnail. 1334–5 *Ely Sacrist Rolls* (1907) II. 72 In v cent. de bordnayl empt. apud Bernewell prec. cent. xiiijd. 1422–3 *Abingdon Acc.* (Camden) 97 In lathnail et bordnail emptis iijs. 1530–1 *Durham Household Bk.* (Surtees) 72 Pro 1000 burdnayle. 1540 *Ludlow Churchw. Acc.* (Camden) 3 Borde nayle and lathe neale for the same cofer. 1770 *Massachusetts Gaz.* 29 Jan., Advt. (Th.) A Moses Boat, with the Larboard Gunwale broke, and mended with Board Nails amidships. 1833 Seba Smith *Major Jack Downing* (1860) 226 (Th.) Mr. Van Buren marched out of the room, looking as though he could bite a board nail off. 1854 — *Way Down East* 62 Then Father would look gritty enough to bite a board-nail off. 1867 Lowell *FitzAdam's Story* 417 He had been known to cut a fig in two, And change a board-nail for a shingle-nail.

Board-walk. *U.S.* [Board sb. 1.] A foot-way or walking-path constructed of boarding.
[1883 'Mark Twain' *Life Mississippi* xxx. 295 The board sidewalks on the ground level were loose and ruinous.] 1888 *Amer. Humorist* 1 Sept. (Farmer) Perhaps the greatest attraction of Asbury Park is the board-walk. It runs along the beach for over two miles. 1895 C. King *Fort Frayne* vii. 98 The back gate stood open..and the board walk leading from it to the rear door was visible for half its length. 1906 *Harper's Mag.* June 61 A few days later, on the board-walk at the sea-shore, she came face to face with Hugh Wilberding.
fig. 1909 'O. Henry' *Options* (1916) 61 That is a board-walk made of men like old Jerome.

Boardy (bōᵊ·ɹdi), *a.* [f. Board sb. + -y^1.]
1. (See quot.)
1893 Jacobi in *Trans. Bibliogr. Soc.* I. 197 Thickness has to be studied—a stout paper being clumsy, and handling very 'boardy'—an expression applied to cardboards.

2. Of the wire teeth of card-clothing when worn down: Stiff, not pliable.
1909 in *Cent. Dict.* Suppl.

Boast, *v.*^{2} Add form bost, and:
3. *Wood-carving.* To model roughly the details of (the design). Also with *in* or *out.* Also **Boa·sted** *ppl. a.*, **Boa·sting** *vbl. sb.*
1867 G. A. Rogers *Wood Carving* 11 When the stalk and leaves have been bosted into the agreeable curves they assume in nature. 1875 Sir T. Seaton *Fret Cutting* 36 Every piece of work of any importance must go through the three stages—blocked out, bosted, finished. *Ibid.* 97 The leaf having been bosted it must now be finished, so let my readers take pencil in hand, and..let them sketch on the bosted mass each leaflet, division, and part. 1890 C. G. Leland *Wood Carving* 50 The three stages of blocking out, bosting, and finishing. *Ibid.* 56 In commencing or bosting out this pattern. 1907 E. Rowe *Pract. Wood-Carving* vi. 68 The next step is to *bost in* the ornament.

Boast (bōᵘst), *v.*^{3}, *sb.*^{2} *Tennis* and *Rackets.* [? f. F. *bosse* the place where the ball hits the wall. (Cf. Boast v.^{2})] *trans.* To hit the ball not directly over the net but by striking it first against the side-wall; also to make (a stroke of this kind). Also *sb.* = the stroke. Also **Boa·sted** *ppl. a.*, **Boa·sting** *vbl. sb.*
1878 Jul. Marshall *Ann. Tennis* 156 This stroke is called *a boast*, or *boasted stroke.* *Ibid.* 176 What is called *boasting* the ball. *Ibid.*, We..call them all *boasts* or *boasted* balls indifferently, whether struck from one or the other side of the net. 1902 E. Miles *Racquets*, etc. 194 This is called 'boasting,' and it gives the ball a powerful twist. *Ibid.* 231 The Boasted Volley, the Volley hit direct onto the Side-wall.

Boat, *sb.* **3.** Add:
boat-bearer, a man or boy who carries the incense-boat, in attendance on the thurifer; **boat-bed**, a boat serving as a bed; **boat-boy**, (*a*) a boy engaged to help to manage a boat; (*b*) a boy who carries an incense-boat; **boat-car**, (*a*) a wheeled car used for launching or beaching a boat; (*b*) an air-ship-car built like a boat; **boat-hat** = *Boater; **boat-load** (add quots.); **boat-quarters**, the quarters taken up by members of crew detailed to man the boats; **boat-sponge**, a fine sponge of the Bahamas and Florida (see quot.); **boat-stretcher** = Stretcher 7.
1899 P. Dearmer *Parson's Handbk.* 128 The thurifer and *boat-bearer enter with the censer and boat. 1918 A. Fortescue *Cerem. Rom. Rite* 25 *note*, The boat-bearer will stand or kneel at the thurifer's left. 1897 *Outing* (U.S.) XXX. 257/1 As I looked over the gunwale of my *boat-bed. 1889 Gretton *Memory's Harkback* 78 One day I set out with a *boat-boy to sail and row to Ely. 1902 P. Dearmer *Parson's Handbk.* (ed. 4) 245 There is no English authority for a 'boat-boy' to accompany the thurifer. 1907 *Westm. Gaz.* 11 Sept. 8/3 A dozen soldiers hung on by the *boat-car..to keep it down. 1909 *Daily Chron.* 1 June 1/2 The two boat-cars which carry the engines. 1889 Gretton *Memory's Harkback* 310 The dandy of that time in Anglesea *boat hat, blue coat with brass buttons, high velvet collar, and swallow-tails. 1837 *Flemish Husb.* 21 in *Libr. Usef. Knowl.*, *Husb.* III, These tanks are generally filled by *boat-loads brought from the large towns. 1868 *Rep. U.S. Comm. Agric.* (1869) 321 Several boatloads of fish were brought ashore. 1888 *Daily News* 5 Nov. 6/1 A boatload, it appears, means thirty tons, or ten waggonloads. 1904 *Westm. Gaz.* 29 Dec. 8/2 The crew were kept at *boat-quarters in readiness for immediate launching. 1883 Saville Kent in *Fisheries Bahamas* 47 The so-called Velvet, Abacco-velvet, or *Boat-sponge (*Spongia equina*, var. *meandriniformis*). 1888 Churchward *Blackbirding* xii. 220 If they tried to shirk rowing, the chap in the bows or stern would fetch them a crack with the *boat-stretcher.

Boater. Add: A stiff straw hat with a flat crown and brim suitable to wear when boating. Also *boater straw.*
1896 *River* 8 Aug. 5/1 The news has gone forth from one end of Wood-street to the other that the Prince of Wales has purchased a 'boater,' and will wear it..for the rest of the summer. 1905 *Daily Chron.* 2 June 4/7 In a shop on Ludgate-hill, there are placards announcing 'straw boaters.' 1910 Wells *Mr. Polly* vii. 151 Boater straws, imitation Panamas, [etc.]. 1926 *Blackw. Mag.* June 735/1 That horrible and obsolete form of head gear..known as a 'boater'. 1927 *Daily Express* 23 Sept. 1 It will be remembered that the Prince led the post-war revival of shepherd's-plaid trousers, and in Canada recently adopted the straw boater fashion.

Boat-horn. *U.S.* [Boat sb. 1.]
1. A horn used for signalling by boatmen on the Mississippi.
1835 *Col. Crockett's Tour* (Philad.) 87 One fellow tried to sing, that was not half up to a Mississippi boat-horn. 1888 *Harper's Mag.* Dec. 48/1 The outline of his long boat-horn caught his eye, and picking it up he sounded its winding largo voice.

2. (See quot.)
1843 C. Mathews *Writ.* (1863) 71 A boat-horn..consists of the horn of an ox attached to the extremity of a wooden handle, and is used in sloops and other river craft to wet the sails.

Boating, *ppl. a.* (Earlier U.S. example.)
1870 Medbery *Men & Myst. Wall St.* 290 The start was what boating-men call a 'spurt'.

Boat-load. [Boat sb.] As much as a boat can carry.
1680 *New Castle Court Rec.* 442 Wee have sent away a boat load. 1745 MacSparran *Diary* 27 In the last Boatload ..I lost my dear Servant. 1777 *Essex Inst. Hist. Coll.* XLII. 209 [I] Brought three Boat Loads of Household Furniture Belongin to Mr. Tolman. 1789 Morse *Amer. Geog.* 49 The indigo planters carry them away in large boat loads. 1814 *Log of Chasseur* in *Maryland Hist. Mag.* I. 168 Received two Boatloads of water. 1847 C. Lanman *Summer in Wilderness* xxvi. 159 You may accuse me of telling a large story when I speak of boat-loads of trout.

Boatswain. 3. Add:
boatswain's chair, cradle, a board on which a sailor sits when at work aloft.
1902 Webster Suppl., Boatswain's chair. 1928 *Daily Express* 19 Nov. 11/7 When you have been sitting up in a bo'sun's cradle playing hell with a pneumatic riveter.

Bob, *sb.*^{1} Add:
2. c. A short sleigh-runner. *U.S.*
1889 Farmer *Americanisms*, *Bob* or *Bob Sled* or *Bob Sleigh*, a sleigh used in the West for conveying large timber, its special characteristic being two pairs of *bobs* or short runners. 1927 *Atlantic Monthly* Mar. 335 We sat on some boards nailed on the front bob of his old bobsled.

d. Abbrev. of Bob-sled, -sleigh. *U.S.*
1887 *Harper's Mag.* Dec. 113/2 The Captain's sleigh went townward toward evening, and the butcher's 'bob' tore an ugly groove along the lower edge. 1888 *Ibid.* May 973/1 Telling the little ones how they might have been mangled by one of the swift 'bobs'. 1906 *N. Y. Even. Post* 19 May 9 The same spruce and hemlock logs drawn on bobs.

e. In plural form = prec. *U.S.*
1911 S. E. White *Bobby Orde* xvii. (1916) 194 At last Bobby saw..a magnificent bobs that had not before appeared. *Ibid.* 195 If the bobs upset, or the horse went too fast.

f. Also *attrib.* in *bob-run.*
1927 *Observer* 18 Dec. 9/4 Long and well-made bob-runs.

7. *U.S.* (See quot.) Cf. *Bobbing vbl. sb. 3.
1883 *Century Mag.* July 383/1 The 'bob', which is formed by tying three books together, back to back, and covering their shanks with a portion of a deer's tail.

Bob, *sb.*^{7} Add: Short f. Bob-white.
1883 *Century Mag.* Aug. 483/2 The European partridge ..weighs twice as much as Bob White, but he has not Bob's

Supplement, p. 3873; Corrigenda, p. 4092; Spurious words, p. 4093; Books quoted, p. 4094

sturdy, rapid..flight. 1902 E. Sandys *Upland Game Birds* 9 Then brave, brown Bob..enters Love's fateful lists.

Bob, *v.*³ Add: **2. b.** To come or go *in, into, up*, etc.

1836–7 Dickens *Sk. Boz, Pass. Life Mr. Watkins Tottle* (1892) 415 'Please, Sir, missis has made tea', said a middle-aged female servant, bobbing into the room. 1924 Galsworthy *White Monkey* I. viii, Thanks, old man, awfully good of you—will you bob in, then? 1928 *Public Opinion* 19 Oct. 371/1 Everything but the kitchen stove, as our idiom has it, is likely to bob up for notice.

Bob (bɒb), *v.*⁵ [f. Bob *sb.*¹ (sense 5). Cf. Bob *a.* 1 and Bobbed *a.*]

1. To dock, cut short (a horse's tail, etc.). Also with *off*. ? *U.S.*

1822 J. Fowler *Jrnl.* 112 Two of them [sc. wild horses] must have been in Hands, as their tails were Bobed short. 1889 *Century Dict.*, Bob¹ v. 2. To cut short; dock: often with *off*: as, to *bob* or *bob off* a horse's tail.

2. To cut (the hair of a woman or girl) short and even all round the head.

1918 *Punch* 25 Sept. 193 Alarming spread of bobbing. 1919 *Home Notes* 8 Feb. 130, I went to a hairdresser's.. He bobbed my hair. 1920 Rose Macaulay *Potterism* I. i, When the time came to bob the hair, she bobbed it.

Bob (bɒb), *v.*⁶ [f. Bob *sb.*⁶] *trans.* To polish (metal) with a bob (see Bob *sb.*⁶).

1879 *Cassell's Techn. Educ.* IV. 414/1 Our spoons..will be first 'bobbed' with fine sand on an ordinary buff-covered polishing wheel.

Bob, *v.*⁷ [See *Bob *sb.*¹ 2 d.] **a.** *trans.* To carry on a bob-sleigh. **b.** *intr.* To ride on a bob-sleigh. Also **Bo·bbing** *vbl. sb.*

1904 *Windsor Mag.* Jan. 245/1 Bobbing can be practised on any high-road having a sufficient length of suitable slope. 1909 *Century Dict.* Suppl., *Bob*, v.t. To transport (a load, as of logs) on a bob or sled. 1928 *Even. Standard* 5 Jan. 6/2 Bobbing is carried out either on bobs (five passengers) or boblets (three passengers).

Bobachee (bɒ·bātʃī). *Anglo-Ind.* Also **babachy, bobarchee, bobba-, bobberjee.** [Corruption of Hindi *bāwarchī*.] A male cook.

1810 T. Williamson *E. Ind. Vade-Mecum* I. 238 It being in the power of the *babachy* to baste any part with great precision. 1863 G. O. Trevelyan *Dawk Bungalow* 18 And every night and morning The Bobarchee he shall kill The sempiternal Moorghye, And we'll all have a grill. 1881 E. H. Aitken *Tribes on Frontier* (1898) 35 He was only a *maistry*, or more vulgarly a *bobberjee*. 1920 *Outward Bound* Nov. 67/1 Here, you, bobbajee, khansammeh, send up a sack of potatoes.

Bobbed, *a.* Add later U.S. quots.

1768 Washington *Diaries* I. 256 Hunting again, and catchd a fox with a bobd Tail and cut Ears. 1894 *Outing* (U.S.) XXIV. 193/1 There is nothing more hideous than a bobbed jib. 1897 *Ibid.* XXIX. 464/2 Small boys strutting about in tail beavers with bobbed-off coats, looking..like tailless sparrows.

b. Of a woman's or girl's hair: Cut short and even all round. (See *Bob *v.*⁵ 2.)

1918 *Home Chat* 3 Aug. 106/1 There is quite a craze for 'bobbed' hair, for big and little girls alike. 1920 *Punch* 18 Aug. 135 Are your tresses luxuriant or 'bobbed'? 1924 Galsworthy *White Monkey* 63 Her bobbed black hair, crinkly towards the ends.

Bobber³ (bɒ·bəɹ). [f. *Bob *v.*⁶] One who polishes articles on a bob or polishing-disc.

1881 *Instr. Census Clerks* (1885) 53 Locksmith, Bellhanger, Bobber and Grinder. 1906 *Daily Chron.* 23 Apr. 10/6 Good emery bobber: must be used to cycle work. 1921 *Dict. Occup. Terms* (1927) § 237 Emery bobber (foundry). *Ibid.* 238 Bobber and polisher.

Bobber⁴ (bɒ·bəɹ). [f. *Bob *v.*⁷] One who rides on a bob-sleigh.

1904 *Windsor Mag.* Jan. 248/2 Thus spoiling many a race and importing many a risk to the bobber. 1906 *Tribune* 16 Jan. 3/7 Curlers and skaters have been enjoying themselves, but skiers and bobbers..are grumbling.

Bobbery (bɒ·bəri), *a.* *Anglo-Ind.* [? f. Bobbery *sb.*] Of a pack of hounds: Miscellaneous in breed or quality. Also more widely: Poor, of indifferent quality, 'scratch'.

1878 *Life in the Mofussil* I. 142 On the mornings when the 'bobberee' pack went out. 1894 Meg Dyan *Man's Keeping* i, The daily drills and the hunts with the bobbery packs. 1901 'Linesman' *Words by Eyewitness* (1902) 234 A mounted officer pushing forward here, another there trying to turn his 'bobbery' horse to get back.

Bobbing, *vbl. sb.*¹ **3.** Add: *U.S.* (see quot. and *Bob *sb.*¹ 7).

1883 *Century Mag.* July 383/1 Bobbing has been practiced in Florida for more than a century, and is a very simple but remarkably 'killing' method of fishing. 1888 Goode *Amer. Fishes* 62 Trolling with the rod, 'skittering', and 'bobbing' are other modes of local popularity.

Bo·bbing, *vbl. sb.*² [f. *Bob *sb.*¹ 2 d.] The pastime of riding on bob-sleighs. Also *attrib.*

1888 *Troy Daily Times* 31 Jan. (Farmer) All the village bobbing clubs will participate in the carnival at Albany tomorrow...There are seventy-eight entries for the bobbing parade. 1888 *Harper's Mag.* May 973/1 Ruby and Ned displeased their mother by joining a 'bobbing' party on a neighbouring 'hill' street.

Bobble (bɒ·b'l), *sb.*² [dimin. of Bob *sb.*¹: see -le 1.] A small woolly ball used as an ornament or trimming for ladies' dresses.

1923 *Daily Mail* 13 Feb. 1 Knitted Wool Jumpers, finished cord and bobbles. *Ibid.* 17 Apr. 1 Trimmed with bobbles of own material arranged in sets. 1927 Russell Thorndike *The Slype* vi, A black gaberdine with bobbles on it.

Bobble, *v.* Add quot. (in *Golf*). Also **Bo·bbling** *ppl. a.*

1892 *Daily News* 20 Sept. 6/4 If they must shoot something, let them pop away at bottles..in a bobbling sea. 1896 W. Park *Game of Golf* x. 202 It is absolutely essential that a putting-green be firm and smooth, and the turf close and short, so that the ball will roll on it and not 'bobble' or jump, as it certainly will if the turf be brushy and uneven.

Bobbly (bɒ·bli), *a. colloq.* [f. Bobble *v.* + -y ¹.] **a.** Jumpy, uneven. **b.** Loose and undulating.

1909 *Westm. Gaz.* 1 Feb. 12/2 The hard ground, the bobbly putting, and all the other horrors of golf in frosty weather. 1921 *Chambers's Jrnl.* Jan. 3/1 The fully-opened door revealed the white coat and bobbly trousers of a veritable bed-room steward.

Bobcat. *U.S.* [Bob *sb.*¹ 5, in allusion to the short tail.] The bay lynx, *Lynx rufus*. Also *transf.*

1888 Roosevelt in *Century Mag.* Mar. 656 We also keep hens, which, in spite of the damaging inroads of hawks, bobcats, and foxes, supply us with eggs. 1901 O. Wister *Members of Family* vii. (1911) 250, I came for a box of matches, y'u bawlin' bobcat. 1906 *Springfield Weekly Republ.* 20 June 2 The creation of this new commonwealth on virgin soil, where for centuries the wolves, bob-cats and Indians had leisurely roamed.

Bob-haired, *a.* [See Bob *a.* 1 and *Bob *v.*⁵ 2.] Of a woman or girl: Having the hair cut short round the head.

1923 Mrs. A. Sidgwick *None-Go-By* xvii, The bob-haired female gazed at him as if she wished to probe into his soul. 1925 *Daily News* 7 Sept. 5/4 A bob-haired brunette.

Bobolink. *U.S.* Add: Also **bob-a-link, bob-o'-linck, bob-a-linkum.**

1826 T. Flint *Recoll.* 243 Those merry and chattering birds, that we call bob-a-link, or French blackbird. 1840 C. F. Hoffman *Greyslaer* III. i. 104 There he goes..singing for all the world like a Bob-a-linkum on the wing. 1847 *Tom Pepper* I. 145 (Th.), I heard her voice, which was sweeter than a bob-o'-linck's.

Bob-sled, -sleigh. Add quots. Also **Bob-sleighing** *vbl. sb.*, the sport of riding on a bob-sleigh.

1889 [see *Bob *sb.*¹ 2 c]. 1892 *Eng. Illustr. Mag.* Sept. 882 The logs are loaded on bob-sleds and taken to the mills. 1894 H. Gibson *Tobogganing* 163 Bobsleighing is another amusing form of tobogganing which has become very popular during the last few years. *Ibid.*, A Bobsleigh consists of two machines..connected together endways by a board, upon which the crew sit or lie. *Ibid.*, The Bobsleigh, Bobsled, or double-ripper. 1907 *Ladies' Field* 19 Jan. 278/2 A bob-sleigh smartly turned out with a varnished and cushioned seat, a steering-wheel, brake, and motor-horn complete. 1910 *Daily Chron.* 12 Jan. 7/2 An English bob-sleigh team..dashed down the bobsleigh run and route above Grindelwald at a great speed.

Bob-tail. Add: **B.** *attrib.* **bobtail car** *U.S.* (see quot. 1889); **bobtail discharge** *U.S.* (see quot.).

1887 *Harper's Mag.* Sept. 646/1 In a New York *bobtail car. 1889 Farmer *Americanisms*, *Bobtail car*, the popular name for a small tram-car horsed by a single animal, and on which the only official is a driver, whose office it is to collect fares and generally perform the duties of conductor in addition to his own. 1886 *Outing* (U.S.) Dec. 227/2 Upon the expiration of his first enlistment, he was given what is called a '*bobtail* discharge, a discharge without character.

C. *sb.* **4.** Also *pl.* (cf. quot. 1785 in Dict.).

1926 J. Black *You Can't Win* xiii. 180 She poured liquor into the bums, beggars, ragtags and bobtails that hung around the saloons.

5. A four-card flush or straight in the game of poker. *U.S.* 1909 *Century Dict.* Suppl.

Bob-tailed, *a.* Add: Applied to vehicles. *Bobtailed car* = bobtail car (see above). *U.S.*

1889 *Century Dict.* 1901 S. E. White *Westerners* i. 4 He owned..a light, two-wheeled wagon of the bob-tailed type.

Bob-veal. *U.S.* [Bob *sb.*¹] Veal so immature as to be unfit for food.

1888 *San Francisco Weekly Exam.* 22 Mar. (Farmer) It is time this traffic in..bob-veal was stopped. 1911 *N.Y. Even. Post* 13 Oct. 1 A former butcher was sentenced..for..shipping..the carcasses of five bob veal calves to this city.

Bocconia (bɒkōᵘ·niă). [mod.L.; named after the Sicilian botanist, Paolo Boccone (1633–1704).] A tall herbaceous plant or shrub of the papaveraceous genus of the name, with large lobed leaves and panicles of flowers. The favourite species is *B. cordata*, with cream-coloured flowers growing on tall stems.

1902 W. P. Wright *Cassell's Dict. Gard.* I. 128 The herbaceous Bocconias like a rich, heavy soil.

Boche (bɒʃ). Also *erron.* **Bosch(e.** [Fr. slang. = rascal, German, said to be shortened from *caboche* head, or from *Alboche*, modification of *Allemand* German.] The French soldiers' name for a German. Also *attrib.* or *adj.* German.

[Cf. 1889 Barrère, *Boche*, rake, 'rip', 'molrower', or 'beard splitter'. *Tête de boche*,..a dull-witted person. Literally wooden head. Also a German.] 1914 *Daily Express* 30 Sept. 4/2 Monsieur had better come under cover. The 'Bosches' are still firing this way. 1915 *National Rev.* Mar. 21 Easter passed without the promised bonne-bouche for the Bosches. 1919 Boyd Cable *Old Contemptibles* viii. 130 A Boche..proceeded to drop bombs all over the place. 1920 *Punch* 20 Oct. 305/1 Bosch aeroplane observers.

Bock (bɒk). [Fr., a. G. *bock*, in full *bockbier*, shortened f. *Eimbockbier*, now *Einbecker bier*, f. *Einbeck*, *Eimbeck*, a town in Hanover.] A strong dark-coloured variety of German beer. With *a* and *pl.*, a glass of this or any other beer.

1867 Simmonds *Dict. Trade* Suppl., *Bock-beer*, a favourite Bavarian double strong malt beverage, of the best lager description. 1879 Sala *Paris Herself Again* I. 183 A 'bock', or glass of light and frothy beer. *Ibid.* 186 Allsopp at fifty centimes the 'bock'. 1882 *Standard* 2 Jan. 6 (Stanford) Those 'after hours' when briefless barristers and journalists out of work congregate over their coffee, their absinthe, or their *bocks*. 1921 *19th Cent.* May 924 You can drink bock at 75 centimes.

Bodach (bo·daχ). Also **-agh.** [Gaelic *bodach*, Ir. *bodagh*.] A peasant, churl.

1865 *Dublin Rev.* July 73 It admits of no doubt that the Gaelic is withering away...The coarse Bodach almost alone retains it as the language of common life. 1903 *Westm. Gaz.* 18 May 4/3 Father Dinneen's play 'The Enchanted Well' dealt with a rivalry in love between a rich 'bodach' and a poor poet.

Bodacious (bɒdē¹·ʃəs), *a.* *U.S. dial.* [Perh. a variant of Eng. dial. *boldacious*, a combination of *bold* and *audacious*.] Complete, thorough, arrant.

1887 'C. E. Craddock' *Keedon Bluffs* 153 Air ye turned a bodacious idjit, Skimp?

Boda·ciously, *adv.* *U.S. dial.* Also **bodyaciously.** [See prec.] Completely, thoroughly.

a. 1840 *Congress. Globe* 20 July 545 (Th.) [It has been proclaimed abroad] that the Administration is bodaciously used up. 1843 Carlton *New Purchase* 143 It was now snowing so bodaciously fast. 1878 J. H. Beadle *Western Wilds* viii. 118, I saw a man..who had been 'bodaciously chawed up,' to use his own language, by a grizzly bear. 1887 'C. E. Craddock' *Keedon Bluffs* 104 He drug two needles bodaciously out an spiled fower rows. 1904 Harben *Georgians* vii. 69 You was ruinin' yoreselves bodaciously.

β. 1833 J. Hall *Leg. West* 82 It seems like it would jist use me up bodyaciously. 1833 *Sk. D. Crockett* Pref. p. v, A constant repetition of the terms bodyaciously, teetotaciously, obflisticated, &c.

Bodegon (bɒdego·n). Pl. **-ones** (o·nes). [Sp., f. *bodega* Bodega.] Properly, a Spanish tavern-piece; hence, any Spanish picture representing still-life or a *genre* subject.

[1748 *Earthquake at Lima* (ed. 2) 317 Those who keep the Bodegones, (a Sort of Taverns, which are no better than a Chandler's-shop; for besides Wine, they sell Candles, Fish, Salt, Cheese and Bacon).] 1843 *Penny Cycl.* XXVI. 189/1 Beginning with subjects of still-life..such as meat, vegetables, and kitchen utensils: hence the generic name *Bodegones*, by which they are still known. 1848 W. Stirling *Artists of Spain* II. 580 These 'bodegones' of his early days are worthy of the best pencils of Flanders. 1896 W. Armstrong *Life Velazquez* 12 His earliest independent works were *bodegones*—kitchen and tavern scenes.

Bodoni (bɒdōᵘ·ni). A book produced by the celebrated Italian printer Giambattista Bodoni (1740–1813). Also *attrib.* in *Bodoni type*.

1880 A. Lang *Ballades in Blue China, Book-hunter*, In rich men's shelves they take their ease—Aldines, Bodonis, Elzevirs! 1922 D. B. Updike *Printing Types* II. 235 The 'Bodoni' type of commerce is a composite picture of many of Bodoni's fonts, rather than a reproduction of any one of them. 1928 *Scholartis Press Catal.* June, Printed by the Glasgow University Press in Bodoni type.

Bod-stick, variant of *bott-stick*: see *Bott 2.

1883 T. D. West *Amer. Foundry Pract.* (ed. 2) 331 The melter..runs the bod-stick without any clay on it into the running iron. 1900 [see *Bott 2].

Body, *sb.* Add:

7. The foundation of a felt or silk hat. Also Comb. *body-maker*.

1845 Dodd *Brit. Manuf.* V. 159 The 'body', or 'foundation', of a good beaver hat is..made of eight parts rabbits' fur [etc.]. 1880 *Encycl. Brit.* XI. 519/2 A silk hat consists of a light stiff body covered with a plush of silk. 1881 *Instr. Census Clerks* (1885) 74 Silk Hat Making: Body Maker. Finisher. Shaper. 1906 Watson Smith *Chem. Hat Manuf.* 65 The stiffening and proofing of hat forms or 'bodies'. 1921 *Dict. Occup. Terms* (1927) § 409 Body-maker [of hats].

8. b. (*a*) Further examples. (*b*) Used for the corresponding part in a motor-car and in an aeroplane. (*c*) *attrib.* and *Comb.*, as *body-strut, -work; body-builder, -maker, -mate; body-building, -making, -painting.*

(*a*) 1761, 1794 [see Carriage 28]. 1881 J. W. Burgess *Coach-building* 42 The body is a species of box, fitted with doors and windows, and lined and wadded for the purpose of comfort. 1897 J. Philipson *Coachbuilding* 2 The body is the most essential part of the carriage.

(*b*) 1896 *Horseless Age* May 20 Width of body [of motor-car] 32 inches; length of body 8 feet 6 inches. 1902 Lavergne & Hasluck *Automobile* 352 Before all else the body should be solid. 1906 *Motors* 52 The Tonneau body was till lately most popular. 1909 A. Berget *Conquest of Air* 166 The body..is the space designed to carry the motor, propeller, and the aviator. 1913 *Aeroplane* 13 Feb. 151/2 The pilots..are cosily placed in comfortable seats inside protective bodies. 1920 Jones & Frier *Aeroplane Design* 109 The main function of the body or fuselage is to provide accommodation for cargo, pilot, passengers, flying instruments, and a reliable bearing for the power unit.

(*c*) 1846 Dodd *Brit. Manuf.* VI. 113 'Body-makers' [are] employed principally on delicate framework and panelling. 1876 *Encycl. Brit.* V. 137/1 Body-makers, who build up the part in which persons sit. 1891 *Daily News* 29 Dec. 6/4 The body-making and harness departments. 1902 *Daily Chron.* 5 Mar. 10/3 Omnibus.—Good body mate, at once. 1908 *Westm. Gaz.* 19 Mar. 4/1 A large number of chassis..fitted with every class of bodywork. 1909 *Ibid.* 17 June 4/1 The body-painting, smithy, and upholstery shops. 1914 C. W. Terry *Motor Body-building* 58 Materials used by body-builders. 1920 Jones & Frier *Aeroplane Design* 99 The outer, inner, and body struts. 1922 *Autocar* 10 Nov. 948 The production of vehicles with slightly larger and more commodious bodywork.

21. b. *spec.* A mass or deposit of metalliferous ore.

1909 *Westm. Gaz.* 9 Feb. 11/4 The opening of an entirely

new body carrying on an average 3 per cent. copper and 15 ounces of silver to the ton. 1929 *Times* 25 Jan. 12/3 A number of areas [in Great Britain] are worth prospecting in the hope of discovering new ore bodies.

22. c. The paste or clay (of a particular kind) used in the manufacture of porcelain.

1839 Mortar body [see Mortar *sb.*¹ 5 b]. 1893 Bone body [see *Bone *sb.* 17].

30. body-box, a brood-box, brood-chamber; **body-building,** the feeding and strengthening of the human frame by diet and exercise; also *attrib.* or *adj.*; **body-cavity** *Zool.*, the cœlom; **body-face** = **body-type*; **body-line bowling,** fast bowling delivered persistently on the leg side, first so termed in Australia with reference to test-match cricket in Jan. 1933 (*Times* 19 Jan. 12/6); **body-mark, stroke,** *Printing*, the stem or 'thick-stroke' of the face of a type-letter; **body-rope** *Naut.* (see quots.); **body-type,** the type used for printing the body of a book; **body-wall** *Zool.*, the general envelope of an animal body; the cell-wall of a lower organism.

1881 T. W. Cowan *Bee-keeper's Guide Bk.* 37 A second hive, having eight frames the same size as those used in the *body-box, is provided for use on the top of the other. 1888 F. R. Cheshire *Bees & Bee-Keeping* II. 76 A body-box..arranged to take from ten to thirteen frames. 1895 *Modern Bee-Keeping* (ed. 8) 22 The body-box or brood-chamber. 1904 E. Sandow (*title*) *Body-building, or Man in the Making. 1910 *Daily Chron.* 5 Apr. 9/2 Rich in body-building or proteid elements. 1875 Huxley *Elem. Biol.* 100 The *body-cavity [in *Hydra*]. 1888 Rolleston & Jackson *Anim. Life* Introd. p. xxix, The cavity, or series of cavities, known as body cavities or coelome. 1901 Shipley & MacBride *Zool.* v. (1904) 83 Coelomic cavity or body cavity. 1927 Haldane & Huxley *Anim. Biol.* i. 10 The stomach and intestine lie in a space, the general body-cavity or coelom. 1898 J. Southward *Mod. Printing* I. 134 'Body or text faces. 1896 De Vinne *Moxon's Mech. Exerc., Printing* 414 Stem is the thick-stroke of a letter, sometimes called by type-founders the *body-mark. 1883 *Man. Seamanship Boys* 41 The ropes [for royals] are of two sizes only—viz., head rope, from earring to earring, and a *body rope on the foot and leeches. *Ibid.* 46 The largest or body rope..and the head rope. 1898 J. Southward *Mod. Printing* I. 140 The thick lines..are called the *body strokes. *Ibid.* 134 *Body or text types, used for plain paragraph matter. 1888 Rolleston & Jackson *Anim. Life* 357 The *body wall [in Vertebrata]. 1898 A. Sedgwick *Zool.* I. 542 The soft part of the body-wall [in Polyzoa], which consists of ectoderm and mesoderm. 1909 *Westm. Gaz.* 28 Aug. 13/2 A special series of muscles in the body-wall.

Boer. Add: **b.** Short for *Boer tobacco*, a brand of tobacco produced in Rustenburg, South Africa.

1900 *Westm. Gaz.* 14 July 8/1 A smoker may keep his pipe going from early morning till late at night if he uses good 'Boer'.

Bog, *sb.*¹ **4.** Add: **bog-garden,** a piece of ground laid out and irrigated to grow plants whose habitat is bog-land and a peaty soil; **bog ore** (later U.S. examples).

1883 W. Robinson *Engl. Flower Garden* p. lxiii/1 A more perfect *bog garden is made by forming a basin of brickwork and Portland cement, about one foot in depth. 1908 R. Farrer *Alpines & Bog-plants* 154 The prime..necessity of the bog-garden is the most perfect drainage. 1805 D. McClure *Diary* (1899) 131 The country abounds with sand or *bog oar. 1840 in *Trans. Mich. Agric. Soc.* (1855) VI. 278 Deposites of bog ore occur in limited quantities in many places.

Bog *v.*¹ **2.** (Modern examples. Also with *down* and *fig.*)

1900 Smithwick *Evol. State* 325 The animal had bogged in crossing the little creek. 1903 A. Adams *Log Cowboy* xii. 77 Bob Blades attempted to ride out of the river below the crossing, when his horse bogged down. 1928 *Saturday Even. Post* (N.Y.) 12 May 184/2 On a clean sheet of paper he wrote the words 'We know', and there he bogged down.

Bogey (bōᵘ·gi). *Golf.* Also **bogy, bogie.** [The following story reproduces the current account of the origin of the term:—

One popular song at least has left its permanent effect on the game of golf. That song is 'The Bogey Man'. In 1890 Dr. Thos. Browne, R.N., the hon. secretary of the Great Yarmouth Club, was playing against a Major Wellman, the match being against the 'ground score', which was the name given to the scratch value of each hole. The system of playing against the 'ground score' was new to Major Wellman, and he exclaimed, thinking of the song of the moment, that his mysterious and well-nigh invincible opponent was a regular 'bogey-man'. The name 'caught on' at Great Yarmouth, and to-day 'Bogey' is one of the most feared opponents on all the courses that acknowledge him (1908 *M.A.P.* 25 July 78/1).]

The number of strokes a good player may be reckoned to need for the course or for a hole. (Assigned to an imaginary partner 'Colonel Bogey'.)

1892 *Field* 2 Jan. 6/1 A novelty was introduced in shape of a Bogey tournament for a prize...Fourteen couples started, but the Bogey defeated all. 1893 H. Hutchinson *Golfing* 114 Bogey. Usually given the title of Colonel. 1903 *Westm. Gaz.* 21 Feb. 6/2 Jones, with a handicap of 17, receives an allowance against Bogey of 13 strokes. 1910 *Encycl. Brit.* XII. 221/2 There is also a species of competition called 'bogey' play, in which each man plays against a 'bogey' score—a score fixed for each hole in the round before starting.

Bogomil, -mile (bōᵘ·gǝmil, -mail). *Hist.* [ad. med. Gr. Βογόμιλος, of disputed origin; the first syllable may represent Russ. *Bog* God.] A member of a heretical Bulgarian sect which arose in the 10th or 11th century, whose main tenet was that God the Father had two sons, Satan and Christ. Hence **Bogomi·lian** *a.* and *sb.*, **Bo·gomilism, Bo·gomilist.**

[1574 R. Bristow *Motives Cath. Faith* To Rdr. ✱ iiij b, In the twelfth hundred [year after Christ], the Bogomili, the Petrobusians, the Apostolikes.] 1841 *Penny Cycl.* XX. 271/1 The sect of the *Bogomiles*, which was well known in the Greek empire. 1852 J. Torrey tr. *Neander's Ch. Hist.* VIII. 351 The sect of the Bogomiles. *Ibid.* 356 The Bogomilian view of the Trinity. *a* 1876 Finlay *Hist. Greece* (1877) III. 68 The Bogomilian heresy. *Ibid.* 69 A Bogomilian who was put to the torture by the imperial officers. 1887 M. Gaster *Greeko-Slavonic Lit.* 17 Bogomilism..ruled Bulgaria for not less than five centuries. *Ibid.* 20 Nikita, the bishop of the Bogomils of Constantinople. *Ibid.* 35, I will here give the version which comes nearest to the original Bogomilist form. 1920 *Q. Rev.* Jan. 71 He invited the Bogomile heretic, Basil, to a private colloquy.

Bogus, *sb.*¹ and *a.* Add: **1. b.** *Bogus press, machine* = sense 1 in Dict.

1844 *Spirit of the Times* (Philad.) 12 Oct. (Th.) A bogus press for making counterfeit money. 1850 *Frontier Guardian* (ed. O. Hyde) 23 Jan. (Th.) We employed that same Bill Hickman to ferret out a bogus press and a gang of counterfeiters...A part of the bogus machine has been found.

c. Counterfeit coin. Also *Comb.*

1844 *Nauvoo Neighbor* 12 June (Th.) To bolster up the interests of blacklegs and bogus-makers. 1848 W. E. Burton *Waggeries* (Philad.) 90 (Th.) No luggage, nor no nothing, but a roll of bogus. 1853 B. Young in *Jrnl. Discourses* I. 270 The Magicians of Egypt..produced a very good bogus, but it was not quite the true coin.

2. *adj.* (Earlier examples.)

1839 Mrs. Kirkland *New Home* xxxii. 212 The boxes..contained..half-dollars, 'principally bogus'. 1842 J. A. Clark *Glean. Way* 340 (Th.) Guilty of..cheating, selling bogus money (base coin).

Boh (bōᵘ). *Anglo-Ind.* [Burmese *bo.*] A chief or leader of dacoits.

1890 Kipling *Departm. Ditties, Grave of Hundred Head* (ed. 4) 82 Bohs that were brave departed. 1923 *Chambers's Jrnl.* Oct. 650/2 He would ask which was their Boh, or leader. 1926 *Ibid.* Feb. 85/2 A man, obviously the Boh, or Chief.

Bohairic (bohəi·ə·rik), *a.* and *sb.* Also **Bahiric.** [f. *Bohairah*, *Bahirah* (*Boheira*, *Beherah*), the Arabic name of Lower Egypt (Arab. بحير *buhair* lake).] The designation of the classical or standard form of Coptic spoken in Alexandria and the north-western Delta, and of the version of the Bible (the official version of the Coptic Church) written in this language. (= Memphitic.)

1830 H. Tattam *Gram. Egypt. Lang.* 135 The Coptic, or, as it has been called, the Bahiric, but more properly the Memphitic, was the Dialect of Lower Egypt. 1874 Lightfoot in Scrivener *Crit. N. T.* (ed. 2) 327 The Bahiric or Memphitic Version. 1898 (*title*) The Coptic Version of the New Testament in the Northern Dialect otherwise called Memphitic and Bohairic.

Bohemianize, *v.* Add: *trans.* To make bohemian in life and habits.

1899 Watts-Dunton *Aylwin* ii. 52 To run the risk of becoming bohemianised like Cyril Aylwin.

Bohereen, var. of Boreen.

1899 Somerville & Ross *Irish R.M.* 138, I thought you were a dead man when you faced him at the bohereen. 1920 *Cornhill Mag.* Oct. 494 A campaign among bogs and bohireens. 1921 *Blackw. Mag.* Jan. 11/1 The grass-grown bohereen leading over the crest of the hill.

Bohunk (bōᵘ·hɒŋk). *U.S. slang.* [Of obscure origin]. A Southern European of inferior class; hence, a low rough fellow.

A correspondent writes: 'In 1910, when the Grand Trunk Pacific Railway was being constructed out of Prince Rupert, B.C., it was a word in everyday use to describe the type of men (of foreign extraction) who passed along the right of way, presumably looking for work.'

1914 Gertr. Atherton *Perch of Devil* i. 58 The 'Bohunks', or 'dark men', an inferior class of Southern Europeans. 1921 *Chambers's Jrnl.* 848/2 To condemn his girl to a yellow bohunk like Milroy. 1927 *Daily Tel.* 24 May 17/6 A contractor for railroad ties employing hundreds of the roughest of bohunks to hew and carry them for him.

Boil, *sb.*² Add:

4. *U.S.* (See quots.)

1826 T. Flint *Recoll.* 87 The Mississippi..is full of singular boils, where the water rises with a strong circular motion. 1853 *Putnam's Monthly* Aug. 188/2 These 'boils', as the boatmen call them, are immense upheavings of the moving waters [of the Mississippi]. 1883 'Mark Twain' *Life Mississippi* ix. 120 Those tumbling 'boils' show a dissolving bar and a changing channel there.

5. *Angling.* A sudden bold rise of a fish at a fly.

1893 *Field* 17 June 894/3 A fish had made a boil at my fly. 1894 *Daily News* 22 Aug. 5/1 The only hopeful sign is when salmon now and then break the surface of the water with a 'boil,' a movement like the rise of a trout.

Boil, *v.* Add:

11. *Angling.* Of a fish: To rise boldly at a fly.

1898 J. A. Gibbs *Cotswold Village* viii. 164, I see one [*sc.* a trout] boil up just above that mess of weed.

Boiled, *ppl. a.* Add: **2.** Special comb. **boiled crow** (see Crow *sb.*¹ 3); **boiled dinner,** a dinner of meat and vegetables boiled together; **boiled shirt,** a white or dress shirt. *U.S.*

1878 *Harper's Mag.* LVII. 575 Slabs of fat..adding savour and strength to a 'b'iled dinner. 1897 Howells *Landlord Lion's Head* iii. (1908) 14 The woman brought in a good boiled dinner of corned beef, potatoes, turnips, and carrots. 1906 W. Churchill *Coniston* 120 He attacked the boiled dinner with a ferocity which should have been exercised against Jethro. 1869 A. K. McClure *Rocky Mts.* 412 In order to attend the Governor's reception, I borrowed a *boiled shirt. 1876 *Fur, Fin & Feather* Sept. 129 If a member puts on a 'boiled shirt' it signifies he is not going fishing again. 1903 *N. Y. Even. Post* 22 Sept., The fact is that Tammany Hall has merely progressed from shirtsleeves to the 'boiled shirt'.

Boiler. Add:

2. c. *To burst one's boiler* (fig.), to come, or bring, to grief. *U.S.*

1824 in Thornton *Amer. Gloss.* 1834 Carruthers *Kentuckian in N.Y.* I. 218 That'll make them think somebody's busted their biler. *c* 1845 Paulding *Madmen All* 189 May my boiler be eternally busted, if there isn't that are lady.

5. boiler-deck *U.S.*, the lower deck of a steamer, lying immediately above the boilers; **boiler plate** *U.S.*, stereotyped matter issued to the newspaper press.

1830 *Steamboat Disasters* (1846) 127 *Boiler-deck,—being that part of the upper deck situated immediately over the boilers. 1838 R. M. Bird *Peter Pilgrim* I. 86 He had followed his friend, the Kentuckian, to the boiler-deck. 1876 Habberton *Jericho Road* i. 10 The new hand reached the boiler-deck, and reported to the mate. 1893 *Congress. Rec.* Aug. 465/1 The country weeklies have been sent tons of '*boiler plates' accompanied by..letters asking the editors to use the matter as news. 1905 D. G. Phillips *Plum Tree* 190 He attended to the subsidizing of news agencies that supplied thousands of country papers with boiler-plate matter to fill their inside pages.

6. In the West Indies and Bermudas, a sunken coral reef into which the sea breaks with foam and spray. 1909 in *Cent. Dict.* Suppl.

Boiler (boi·ləɹ), *v. trans.* To furnish (a steamship) with its boiler or boilers. Also **Boi·lering** *vbl. sb.*

1890 *Whitby Times* 3 Jan. 4/4 The steamers built and launched at this port have to go elsewhere to be engined and boilered. 1897 *United Service Mag.* June 226 The special conditions which..govern the boilering of warships.

Boiling, *vbl. sb.* Add:

3. b. With *down*: The process of condensing or abridging literary matter; *concr.* a condensation or epitome. (See Boil *v.* 8.)

1898 *Daily News* 27 Jan. 8/4 The book is little more than a boiling-down of the vast literature on the subject. But the boiling-down is well done.

4. *fig.* (Earlier U.S. example.)

1786 *New Haven Gaz.* 13 Apr. 75/3 The d—l ran a hunting with the boiling of them.

Boiling, *ppl. a.* **4.** Add:

1893 W. K. Post *Harvard Stories* 118 The conflict was at its height, when dead Cæsar appeared, boiling drunk.

Boina (bo·ĭna). [Sp.] A flat cap worn in Spain.

1904 Gallichan *Fishing in Spain* 19 In his blue boina, a cap resembling the tam-o'-shanter, he looked like a 'braw Scot'. 1922 *Chambers's Jrnl.* 15 July 519/2 He wore a hat of soft black felt or else a *Boina* (the Biscayan bonnet).

Bois brûlé (bwa brüle). *U.S.* [Fr., 'burnt wood'.] An American Indian half-breed, esp. one of French and Indian extraction.

In popular use corrupted into *bob ruly*.

1840 C. F. Hoffman *Greyslaer* III. xiv. 260 Of Guisbert or Guise, as the 'Bois-brulé', or half-blood child was generally called, we have as yet been enabled to gather but few traditions. 1878 J. H. Beadle *Western Wilds* xxix. 380 Most of the drivers were of the pure Bois Brules stock. 1881 *Amer. Naturalist* XV. 123 Buffalo make good tractable work cattle when caught young, and the *Bois Brules* frequently use them as such.

Bois d'arc (bwa dark). *U.S.* Also **bow-dark, bodok.** [F., 'wood of bow'.] The wood of the osage orange, used by American Indians for making bows.

1805 [see *Bow-wood]. 1848 Bartlett *Dict. Amer.*, *Bow-dark tree* (Fr. *bois d'arc*), a western tree, the wood of which is used to make bows with. 1853 R. B. Marcy & McClellan *Expl. of Red River* 98 (Bartlett) The bows [of the Comanches] are made of the tough and elastic wood of the bois d'arc, or osage orange. 1858 *Texas Almanac* 69 The surface is rolling,..supplied with elm, ash..and especially *bois d'arc*. 1877 R. I. Dodge *Hunting Grounds Gt. West* 348 The best wood [for bows] is the Osage Orange (*bois d'arc* of the old French trappers, corrupted into 'bow dark' by plains Americans).

Boko (bōᵘ·ko). *slang.* Also **boco.** [?] The nose.

1874 *Slang Dict.*, *Boko*, the nose. Originally pugilistic slang, but now general. 1880 Besant & Rice *Seamy Side* i, 'Conk or boko', said Nicholas the vulgar. 'It's all the same'. 1903 *Daily Chron.* 19 Mar. 5/2 With his 'boko on the bolster he may find bliss in bed between the blankets.

Bola (bōᵘ·lă). [Cf. Sp. *bolado* cake of clarified sugar.]

1. A kind of sweetmeat.

1892 Zangwill *Childr. Ghetto* I. 14 The confectioners' shops, crammed with 'stuffed monkeys' and 'bolas'. *Ibid.* 18 Those who kneaded the toothsome bolas.

2. An iced 'cup' compounded of hock, soda-water, etc.

1905 Mrs. C. S. Peel *Still Room Cookery* 46.

Bold-face, -faced. Add: Used to designate type with a thick or 'fat' face, such as 'Clarendon' or 'antique'.

1902 T. L. De Vinne *Pract. Typogr.* 50 A bold-face with hair-lines and serifs too weak. *Ibid.* 331 A bold-faced clarendon with strong bracketed serifs. 1905 F. H. Collins *Authors' & Printers' Dict.*, *Bold-face type*..indicated in MS. by wavy underlining. 1911 H. S. Harrison *Queed* xviii. 228 Close beside this, lest the reader should fail to grasp the full meaning of the boldface, was a three-column cartoon.

Boldo (bɒ·ldo). *Med.* [Sp., a. the native Chilian

word.] The leaves and stem of *Peumus Boldus*, an evergreen shrub of Chili, used as a tonic. Hence **Bo·ldin, -ine** (also *boldoin*) [see -in ¹, -ine ⁵], a bitter alkaloid contained in boldo, used as a hypnotic.

1891 J. V. Shoemaker *Mat. Med.* II. 481 Boldo..Boldoin. 1892 Leonard & Christy *Dict. Mat. Med.* 64 Boldo..Boldine. 1908 *Practitioner* Aug. 339 Slight cholagogues, such as..boldo.

Bolero. Add:

2. A short jacket coming barely to the waist: **a.** worn by men in Spain.

1909 'O. Henry' *Roads of Destiny* ix. 151 He wore a suit of coarse brown ducking, the coat being a sort of rakish bolero. 1924 *Countries of World* 2495/2 Farmers and peasants..with wide-brimmed black felt hats, boleros, coloured sashes, and tight-fitting trousers.

b. worn as a fashionable garment by women, usually over a blouse or bodice.

1893 *Daily News* 1 Apr. 2/4 The Zouave is quite as popular as it was last year...Sometimes it is pure bolero. 1894 *Pall Mall Gaz.* 23 Oct. 4/3 Close-fitting boleros of sealskin. 1906 *Westm. Gaz.* 7 Apr. 18/2 Few fashions of our day have been so tenacious of life as the bolero.

Boll, *sb.*¹ **3.** (Earlier examples referring to cotton.)

1796–1806 B. Hawkins *Lett.* 301 The staple of the cotton good, tho' not so much as it would have been, had it been thined and toped. The bowls or pods would then have been larger. 1835 J. H. Ingraham *South-West* II. 284 The pericarp or boll of cotton..is generally matured in eight or ten weeks.

6. boll-weevil, a weevil (*Anthonomus grandis*) destructive to the cotton-plant; also *fig.*; **boll-worm** (examples).

1903 *Westm. Gaz.* 26 Nov. 12/1 The *boll weevil..has caused America a loss of £14,000,000. 1906 *Ibid.* 19 Dec. 13 The Mexican cotton boll-weevil. 1906 *Springfield Weekly Republ.* 19 July 16 The 'boll-weevil democrats' is the term of opprobrium which a southern paper applies to democrats who favour Hearst. 1928 *Manchester Guardian Weekly* 31 Aug. 180 Reports of boll weevil damage and crop deterioration. 1880 *Congress. Rec.* May 3216/1 If the producers of cotton were greatly suffering from the ravages of *boll-worms and caterpillars. 1888 *Ibid.* 12 May 4070 Then comes the 'army worm', and then the 'boll-worm'.

Bollock (bɒ·lək). *Naut.* [var. Ballock.] Either of two blocks fastened to the topsail-yard, for the topsail-ties to reeve through.

1889 *Cent. Dict.*, Bollock-block. 1898 Ansted *Dict. Sea Terms*, *Bollocks*, blocks secured to the middle of the topsail yards in large ships: the topsail ties pass through them, and thereby gain an increase of power in lifting the yards.

Bolo¹ (bōᵘ·lo). [Sp.] A kind of cutlass used in the Philippine Islands for agricultural and domestic work and as a fighting weapon. *Comb.*, *bolo-maker*; bolo-man, one armed with a bolo.

1901 *Westm. Gaz.* 1 Oct. 10/1, 400 bolomen attacked the garrison of seventy-two Americans. 1901 *Daily Chron.* 11 Oct. 5/7 Insurgents, who were armed only with bolos. 1905 Le Roy *Philippine Life* 85 The local blacksmith and bolo-maker, as he generally is (for the bolo is the chief working implement of the Filipino in the thicket or the field or about the house, as well as being, in another form, his principal weapon). 1906 *Macmillan's Mag.* Oct. 903 We had never visited the place before, and, for all we knew to the contrary, it was full of *bolo*-men.

Bolo² (bōᵘ·lo). **1.** One who pursues anti-patriotic 'underground' activities like those of Paul Bolo, a French adventurer shot for treason, April 17, 1918; one suspected of engaging in pacifist propaganda in favour of Germany during the war of 1914–18.

1917 *19th Cent.* Dec. 1265 The activity of those whom we might call the British and German Bolos, naturalised or not. *Ibid.* 1266 As far back as 1907 these Bolos were working under the guidance of German agents.

2. Misused for: A Bolshevik. Also *collect. sing.* = the Bolshevist enemy. Also *attrib.*

1919 *Blackw. Mag.* June 742/1 The Bolo was ignorant of the fate of our raft gun. *Ibid.* Nov. 722/1 A party of Bolo prisoners. 1920 *Ibid.* Mar. 396/1 The missing Bolos from Selmenga. 1924 *Ibid.* Sept. 387/2 Bolo and anti-Bolo propaganda.

Bologna. Add: Short for *Bologna sausage*. U.S.

1916 C. Sandburg *Chicago Poems* 24 The dago shovelman finishes the dry bread and bologna.

Bolograph (bōᵘ·lǝgraf). [See Bolometer and -graph.] An automatic record of the indications of a bolometer. Hence **Bologra·phic** *a.*, pertaining to this.

1903 S. P. Langley in *Astrophys. Jrnl.* Mar. 93 A study of the yearly variations of the selective absorption of the Earth's atmosphere by the aid of a long series of bolographs. 1903 Agnes M. Clerke *Probl. Astrophysics* 22 Using a 'bolographic' method, in which the camera registers what the bolometer *feels*.

Boloism (bōᵘ·lo,iz'm). [See *Bolo ².] Nefarious anti-patriotic activities resembling those of Paul Bolo; *esp.* the engineering of underground pacifist propaganda in favour of an enemy country. Also *erron.*, Bolshevism.

1917 Lloyd George *Sp.* 22 Oct., See what has happened in France..and look out for Boloism in all its forms. 1919 *War Slang* in *Athenæum* 11 July 582/2 In his [*sc.* the British soldier's] linguistic haziness he used 'Boloism' as a synonym for 'Bolshevism,' and found an etymology for both in 'Bolo,' a variant of 'diabolo,' the devil.

Bolshevik (bɒ·lʃĭvik), *sb.* and *a.* Also rarely **-ic.** [a. Russ. Большевикъ *bol'shévik*, f. большій *ból'shiy* (predicative больше *ból'she*). compar. of большой *bol'shoy* big. The Russ. pl. Большевики *bol'sheviki* has been used by some English writers.

The name was first applied to the section which favoured a maximum socialist programme (cf. *Maximalist) at the Second Congress of the Russian Social-Democratic Party, held in 1903. It was later interpreted as referring to the section which formed the majority. Cf. *Menshevik.]

A. *sb.* A member of the extreme wing of the Russian Socialist Party, which seized the supreme power in Russia after the revolution of March 1917. (Now called the Communist Party.)

1917 *19th Cent.* July 141 The Mensheviki or Minimalists (Moderate Socialists)...The Bolsheviki (Extreme Socialists). 1917 *New Europe* 6 Dec. 256 It was from this Conference [of Socialists at Stockholm, 1903] that the cleavage between Bolševiks and Menševiks dates, the former being those who held a 'majority' at the Conference, the latter a 'minority'. 1918 E. J. Dillon *Eclipse of Russia* 10 The Bolsheviks at once outbid the Cadets. *Ibid.* 33 After the triumph of the Bolsheviki. 1918 C. E. Russell *Unchained Russia* 253 The Bolshevic was in Russia the most natural fruitage.

b. *transf.* and *fig.* A person of subversive or revolutionary views; an out-and-out opponent of the existing social order or accepted codes.

1926 W. R. Inge *Lay Thoughts of a Dean* 29 The cliques of literary Bolsheviks, who seem to be inspired by a destructive hatred..of civilisation.

B. *adj.* = *Bolshevist *adj.*

1917 *New Europe* 8 Nov. 112 The Bolševik mentality. 1918 C. E. Russell *Unchained Russia* 261 The Bolshevic movement. 1919 J. Pollock *Bolshevik Adventure* p. xx, The part played by the Jews in Bolshevik Russia.

Hence **Bo·lshevikism** = *Bolshevism; **Bo·lshevikize** *v.* = *Bolshevize *v.*

1918 *Nation* (N.Y.) 7 Feb. 135/1 What Germany is resolved upon is that these lands shall not be Bolshevikized economically. 1919 H. S. King *Russia during War* 49 The rising tide of Bolshevikism.

Bolshevisia (bɒlʃĭvi·ziă). [f. Bolshevism + -ia ¹.] The land of Bolshevism; Russia under the rule of the Bolsheviks.

1919 J. Pollock *Bolshevik Adventure* 195 A producer [of stage-plays] in Bolshevisia. 1920 *Chambers's Jrnl.* 514/1 Life in Bolshevisia—such as it was in July 1918.

Bolshevism (bɒ·lʃĭviz'm). [f. *Bolshev(ik + -ism.] The doctrines and practices of the Bolsheviks; the communistic form of government adopted in Russia since the revolution of March, 1917.

1917 *New Europe* 8 Nov. 112 The good sense of Russian democracy threw off the yoke of Bolševism. 1919 J. Pollock *Bolshevik Adventure* 32 They would turn Bolshevism loose on Europe. 1926 W. R. Inge *Lay Thoughts of a Dean* 159 Bolshevism is no new thing there [*sc.* in Russia].

Bolshevist (bɒ·lʃĭvist). [f. *Bolshev(ik, by substituting the suffix -ist.] A Bolshevik; a supporter of Bolshevism. Also *transf.*, as a term of reproach for an out-and-out revolutionary. Also *attrib.* or *adj.*

1917 *19th Cent.* Dec. 1106 The reign of Bolshevists and Terrorists. 1920 *Edin. Rev.* July 33 The Government of Styria, which, having a large industrial population of its own, is particularly sensitive to the 'Bolshevist Peril'. 1920 *Chambers's Jrnl.* Aug. 513/1 Packing the meetings with Bolshevist agents.

Hence **Bolshevi·stic** *a.*, of, pertaining to, or characteristic of, the Bolshevists.

1920 *Glasgow Herald* 14 May 9 London has established the alarming precedent of applying such words as 'horrible' and 'Bolshevistic' to the well-intentioned proposals of certain pious Churchmen. 1920 *Punch* 13 Oct. 282/1 In these Bolshevistic days I should have preferred of course to have started off with 'Comrade' or 'Brother'.

Bolshevize (bɒ·lʃĭvaiz), *v.* [f. *Bolshev(ik + -ize.] *trans.* To make Bolshevist in character; to reduce (a country) to a Bolshevistic form of government.

1919 *Observer* 23 Mar. 10/5 Unless we want to bolshevise the Boche and the world. 1920 *19th Cent.* Mar. 536 Taking her chance that Germany will be Bolshevised before Russia is Germanised. 1920 *Contemp. Rev.* Aug. 268 Thereby preventing these people from being Bolshevized.

Hence **Bo·lshevized** *ppl. a.*; **Bo·lshevizing** *vbl. sb.* and *ppl. a.* Also **Bolsheviza·tion,** the process of making, or becoming, Bolshevist.

1920 *19th Cent.* Mar. 536 Great Britain has been accused ..of pursuing a policy aimed at the Balkanisation of the Baltic provinces. It may appear that we have only achieved their Bolshevisation. 1920 *Glasgow Herald* 15 Apr. 7/1 Syndicalists of a Bolshevik or Bolshevising hue. *Ibid.* 2 Oct. 7/2 The withdrawal of the Bolshevised troops from Asia Minor. 1921 *Ibid.* 6 Apr. 9/1 Western Bolsheviks or Bolshevisers. 1927 *Daily Tel.* 16 Aug. 11/5 With a view to the Bolshevising of the 400,000,000 of Chinese. *Ibid.*, A Bolshevised China would be the world's greatest peril.

Bolshevy (bɒ·lʃĭvi). [f. *Bolshev(ik, after *Muscovy*.] The land of the Bolshevists.

1921 *Times Lit. Suppl.* 18 Mar., Bolshevy from within. 1922 *Times* 18 Apr. 12/1 The Bondmaid of Bolshevy.

Bolshy, Bolshie (bɒ·lʃi). [-y ⁶.] A jocular and contemptuous name for a Bolshevik.

1920 *John Bull* 28 Aug. 1 We can quite understand the Bolshies' repugnance to labour—except with the jaw. 1920 *Punch* 10 Nov. 373/1 Mr. Stanton could think of no better retort than the stereotyped 'Bolshie!' 1921 Hichens *Spirit of the Time* xii, Those Russians..breed more princesses than we do..but they seem to be giving them toko over there—the Bolshies, I mean. 1923 D. H. Lawrence *Kangaroo* i. 1 A comical-looking bloke! Perhaps a Bolshy.

Bolson (bōᵘ·lsǝn, ‖bolsǝ·n). *U.S.* [Sp., augmentative of *bolsa* purse.] In the southwestern U.S. and Mexico, a basin-shaped depression surrounded by mountains. Also *bolson-plain*.

1838 'Texian' *Mexico v. Texas* 9 A desert known, in the maps [of Mexico], under the name of 'Bolson of Mapimi'. 1847 Ruxton *Adv. Mexico* xiii. 96 The sun was fast sinking behind the rugged crest of the 'Bolson', tinging the serrated ridge..with a golden flood of light. 1904 *Amer. Geol.* Sept. 164 The bolson plains may be considered as sections of an upraised peneplain surface in its earliest infancy, at a stage in which they are as yet untouched by stream-action.

Bolster, *sb.* Add:

4. d. An excrescence left on the stem of a plant by the fall of a leaf. 1895 in *Funk's Standard Dict.*

6. *attrib.* and *Comb.*: *bolster-shaped* adj.; **bolster collar,** a bolster-shaped collar of a woman's coat or cloak.

1900 *Westm. Gaz.* 16 May 2/1 The bolster-shaped kit bag. 1904 *Windsor Mag.* Jan. 238/2 Long bolster-shaped sweets. 1923 *Daily Mail* 19 June 1 New short coat..with smart finely pleated bolster collar.

Bolstered, *ppl. a.* Add: **2. b.** With *up* in sense of Bolster *v.* 4 b.

1901 *Westm. Gaz.* 17 Sept. 7/3 There is a fearful lot of over-trading and bolstered-up credit..in German industrials.

Bolt, *sb.*¹ Add: **10. b.** A block of wood from which smaller pieces are cut or split. *U.S.*

1639 *Portsmouth Rec.* 10 A shipp load of..pipe stauffes & clabboard boults. 1646 *Braintree Rec.* 4 In case any shall make sale of it [*sc.* timber]..either in boards or bolts. 1682 *Plymouth Rec.* 172 Making of shingles or bolts. 1853 *Trans. Mich. Agric. Soc.* IV. 156 This machine cuts, dresses, and joints a stave,..feeding itself from a bolt of wood.

Bolt, *sb.*³ Delete † *Obs.* and add:

2. A hypothetical law case propounded and argued for practice by students of the Inns of Court. (Cf. Bolting *vbl. sb.*¹ 2 b.)

1570 in R. J. Fletcher *Pension-bk. Gray's Inn* (1901) I. 4 Item it is ordered..that upon the other dayes not appointed for the moting it shalbe lawfull to the utter baristers to keepe bolts. 1593–4 in Douthwaite *Gray's Inn* (1886) 83 None shall be called to the barr but such as..have put Cases at Bolts in Term six times. 1598 Stow *Surv.* viii. 59 Young students..hauing performed the exercises of their owne houses (called Boltas [*read* Boltes], Mootes, and putting of cases)..proceed to..become students in some of these foure houses or Innes of Court. 1880 *Encycl. Brit.* XIII. 89/1 Bolts were of an analogous character, though deemed inferior to moots. Both had fallen into desuetude until lately.

Bolt, *v.*² Add:

2. c. *Hawking.* (See quot.)

1886 Salvin & Brodrick *Falconry Brit. Isles* Gloss. 149 *Bolt*, to fly straight from the fist at game, as Goshawks and Sparrow-Hawks do.

d. *Horticulture.* To 'run to seed' prematurely. 1889 in *Cent. Dict.*

3. a. *spec.* Of a rabbit, fox, etc.: To escape from its burrow or earth.

1576 Turberv. *Venerie* 179 Put in a Ferret close musseled, and she will make the Conies bolte out againe into your pursenets. *Ibid.*, It will make the Conies bolte out of the earth. 1851 [see *Bolt-hole 1]. 1900 *Young Sportsman* (ed. A. E. T. Watson) 234 A rabbit will bolt much sooner from a ferret that is free. *Ibid.*, A rabbit will sometimes decline to bolt, and will be killed in the burrow.

c. *U.S.* (Earlier examples.)

1833 *Louisville Daily Herald* 17 Oct., Does the Doctor apprehend that the editor is about to 'bolt'? 1854 *Knickerbocker Mag.* May XLIII. 522 Uncle R. was not much of a politician;..but he would often 'bolt' and carry the town with him. 1871 *St. Louis Democrat* 3 Apr. (De Vere) Several of our contemporaries have announced..that Carl Schurz has bolted from the Republican party.

4. b. *spec.* To cause (a fox, rabbit, otter, etc.) to retreat from its hole or burrow. Also *transf.* and *fig.*

1638 Guillim *Heraldry* iii. xiv. (ed. 2) 176 You shall say Bowlt the Conie. 1864 Atkinson *Stanton Grange* 201 He intended to dig at his leisure until he bolted him [*sc.* an otter]. 1892 Mrs. J. E. H. Gordon *Eunice Anscombe* 176 The terrier..was put into the hole to 'bolt' the otter. 1902 *Daily Chron.* 13 Mar. 8/2 A brace of foxes were next bolted from an artificial earth. 1914 R. Curle *Life is a Dream* 229 The dogs became wildly excited, pawing at the sand around the hole, bolting the crab, and then biting it. 1922 E. Phillpotts *Grey Room* vii. 172 He'll bolt it [*sc.* the evil spirit] yet,..like a ferret bolts a rat.

d. (*a*) *Archery.* To loose too soon after drawing the bow. 1909 in *Cent. Dict.* Suppl.

(*b*) *Golf.* To putt with so much force that the ball will go some distance past the hole if it fails to go into it. 1909 in *Cent. Dict.* Suppl.

7. *U.S.* (Earlier examples.)

1813 *Portsmouth* (N. H.) *Oracle* 20 Nov. 2/3 (Th.) Others, ..without sufficient courage to do their duty, bolted the question. 1847 *Congress. Globe* 4 Feb. 322/2 [I said] that I had never bolted a regular nomination of the Democratic party, from President to constable. 1867 *Ibid.* Apr. 847/1, I did not follow [Mr. Fessenden] in his leadership on that occasion. I have no recollection of ever having bolted my leader until that time, but then I did.

9. c. *absol.* or *intr.*

1847 Marryat *Childr. N. Forest* ii, We can bolt and bar.

d. *intr.* for *pass.*

1907 *Smart Set* Feb. 77/1 The door bolts on the inside.

Bolter². Add:

1. b. A fugitive from justice. Now *Austral.*

a 1700 B. E. *Dict. Cant. Crew*, *Bolter of White Friers*, one that Peeps out, but dares not venture abroad, as a Coney bolts out of the Hole in a Warren, and starts back again. 1737 Dyche *Dict.* (ed. 2), *Bolter*, a Cant Name for one who hides himself in his own House, or some priviledged Place, and dares only peep, but not go out of his Retreat. 1855 *Argus* (Melbourne) 19 Jan. 5/4 The arrest in London of a well-known bolter from Melbourne. 1897 P. Warung *Tales Old Régime* 160 One of the 'bolters', advertised by Mr. F. A. Hely, J.P., Principal Superintendent of Convicts, in the *Sydney Gazette*, in the year 1827.

2. (Earlier U.S. examples.)

1812 *Salem Gaz.* 10 July 4/1 (Th.) D. Tompkins would..send home the bolters by new prorogation. 1858 *N. Y. Tribune* 12 Jan. 2/3 (Th.) An attempt..to make the people go into the election and harmonize the bolters.

3. One who swallows (food) hastily or whole.

1825 *New Monthly Mag.* XVI. 178 Pettifogging strainers at gnats and bolters of camels. 1833 T. Hamilton *Men & Manners in Amer.* ii. (1843) 26 The most expeditious bolters of dinner.

Bolt-hole. [Bolt *v.*²]

1. A hole or burrow into which an animal bolts or runs for safety; *transf.* and *fig.* an avenue of escape. Also *attrib.*

1851 Sternberg *Dial. Northampt.*, *Bolt-hole*, the hole from which the rabbit makes its escape; or, in the phraseology of the craft, '*bolts*'. 1877 *N. W. Linc. Gloss.*, *Bolt-hole*, (1) the hole by which a rabbit makes its escape when the ferret pursues it. (2) Any unknown hole by which a person makes his way into or out of a house. 1887 Kipling *Lett. Marque* v. in *From Sea to Sea* (1900) 49 A figure in saffron came out of a dark arch into the sunlight, almost falling into the arms of one in pink...The pink and saffron figures..disappeared into separate bolt-holes. 1891 Major Grant in *Pall Mall Gaz.* 4 June 6/2 We left them no bolt-hole,..so every man fought till he was killed. 1893 Dk. Argyll *Unseen Found. Soc.* xi. 351 The bolt-hole postulate..out of which Ricardians seek to escape from the absurdity of the dogma. 1901 'Linesman' *Words by Eyewitness* (1902) 248 There are bolt-holes to north and east. 1924 E. Marsh *La Fontaine's Fables* 71 [The hare] heard a rustle, And took the hint to bustle Off to his bolt-hole.

2. *Coal-mining.* A short connecting heading or opening.

1839 Ure *Dict. Arts* 981 Two, three, or even four bolt-holes open into a side of a work, according to its extent. 1860 *Eng. & For. Mining Gloss.*, *Bolt hole*, a passage from a gate-road into a side of a work. 1877 *Encycl. Brit.* VI. 66/1 From the gate road a heading called a bolt-hole is opened.

Bolting (bōᵘ·ltiŋ), *ppl. a.* [f. Bolt *v.*² + -ing ².] That bolts or runs to cover.

1907 *Daily Chron.* 28 Nov. 8/1 Some of the bolting escort were returning. 1908 *Westm. Gaz.* 31 Jan. 4/2 The bolting rabbit.

Bo·ltless, *a.* [Bolt *sb.*¹] Without a bolt or bolts (in various senses).

1832 I. Taylor *Saturday Even.* xv. 248 The boltless thunders of the mere man of rhetoric. *c* 1877 Theodore Watts in *Westm. Gaz.* (1900) 15 Feb. 10/1 'Mid boltless thunder. 1902 'Monkshood' & Gamble *R. Kipling* 259 The boltless door. 1903 Kipling *Five Nations, Song of Wise Children* 75 We shall go back by boltless doors, To the life unaltered our childhood knew.

Bom (bɒm). The sound caused by the discharge of a gun, less deep and sonorous than a 'boom'.

1906 *Westm. Gaz.* 11 June 8/2 A faint distant Bom! and everybody murmurs with one accord, 'First Gun!'

Boma (bōᵘ·mă). [Swahili.] An enclosure or stockade used for herding beasts and for defensive purposes in Central Africa.

Now also, (*a*) a police post, (*b*) a district commissioner's or magistrate's office.

1878 Stanley *Dark Cont.* I. vi. 137 From the staked bomas..there rose to my hearing the bleating of young calves. 1898 *Geog. Jrnl.* (R.G.S.) XI. 389, I went out on a sandspit into the lake and camped, cutting down the bush and placing it across the shore end of the bank so as to form a boma. 1903 Stordy in *Jrnl. Soc. Arts* 10 July 691/2 The construction of the boma employed fifty hands for the space of nine weeks. 1920 *Blackw. Mag.* Jan. 59/1 It [*sc.* the fort] was a typical Boma, built of bricks and plaster.

Bomah (bōᵘ·mă). Also **boomah.** [Cf. Zulu *imboma* aloe-berry.] *Bomah nut*, the seed of a southern African shrub *Pycnocoma macrophylla*, used in tanning.

1866 *Treas. Bot.* 943/1 Boomah Nuts. 1887 Moloney *Forestry W. Africa* 417 The Bomah Nut..is extensively cultivated by the natives near the Victoria Falls.

Bomb, *sb.* **6.** Add:

bomb-maker; **bomb calorimeter** (see quot.); **bomb-carrier,** gear for carrying bombs in a bombing aeroplane; **bomb-carrying** *sb.*, the carrying of bombs (by an aeroplane); also *attrib.*, as *bomb-carrying gear*; **bomb-crater,** a cavity in the earth caused by the explosion of a bomb; **bomb-dropper,** an aeroplane equipped for dropping bombs; **bomb release,** an apparatus for releasing a bomb from an aeroplane; also *attrib.*, as *bomb-release gear, slip*; **bomb sight,** a device for sighting the target in bombing from an aeroplane; **bomb-thrower,** (*a*) one who throws a bomb as the weapon of an assassin, anarchist, or other anti-social fanatic, or as a weapon of war; (*b*) a mechanical device for throwing a bomb in warfare; **bomb-throwing,** (*a*) *sb.* the action of throwing bombs; (*b*) *adj.* that throws bombs.

1928 A. B. Callow *Food & Health* 29 The apparatus used for this laboratory oxidation is a small calorimeter which is known as the *bomb calorimeter, because the oxidation takes place inside a thick-walled vessel which in some ways resembles a bomb. 1928 Gamble *Story N. Sea Air Station* vii. 109 The only standard *bomb-carriers in service at this period were the single 16-lb bomb and the 20-lb gear for two Hale 20-lb bombs. *Ibid.*, Equipping all the machines with *bomb-carrying and release gear. 1920 *Blackw. Mag.* July 76/1 Ploughed up with *bomb-craters. 1928 Gamble *Story N. Sea Air Station* vii. 104 The last three machines were classified as 'Gun Machines' and '*Bomb Droppers'. 1905 *Westm. Gaz.* 19 June 5/1 The *bomb-makers..were inextricably trapped. 1928 Gamble *Story N. Sea Air Station* v. 87 Very little work had been done with *bomb releases. *Ibid.* vii. 110 Bomb-release gears. *Ibid.* xiii. 224 Bomb release-slips. *Ibid.* v. 87 Of the available *bomb sights, the most practical and successful were those invented by Lieutenant Scott, U.S.N., and Zeiss. 1891 *Pall Mall Gaz.* 14 Dec. 5/2 The *bomb-thrower, who lost his life in attempting that of Mr. Russell Sage. 1916 Boyd Cable *Action Front* 24 The bomb-thrower seized the missile quickly,..threw the bomb, and jumped back under cover. 1905 *Westm. Gaz.* 13 May 7/2 The workmen [of St. Petersburg] practised shooting and *bomb-throwing. 1908 *Daily Chron.* 14 Aug. 4/4 The attack from bomb-throwing airships is very little, if any, more alarming than from a gunboat.

Bomb, *v.* Add: **1. b.** To attack with an explosive bomb placed or thrown for the purpose of destruction; (of aircraft) to attack with bombs from the air; to drop a bomb or bombs upon. *To bomb one's way*: to advance by bombing. *To bomb out*: to clear by bombing.

1909 *Daily Chron.* 25 Feb. 1/6 Attempts had been made..to bomb trains known to contain Europeans. 1915 *Draconian* Apr. 1683/1 They bombed us periodically during the day and night. 1916 Boyd Cable *Action Front* 174 He himself had known a line bombed out. 1918 E. A. Mackintosh *War, the Liberator* 97 When we're bombing our way up the streets of Berlin. *Ibid.* 133 He turned to bomb the big dug-out.

Bombard, *sb.* Add: **4. b.** [Also in Fr. form.] A foot reed-stop of an organ.

1876 Stainer & Barrett *Dict. Mus. Terms.* 1884 *Encycl. Brit.* XVII. 833/1, 32 contra trombone, posaune, bombarde, sackbut (reed).

Bombard, *v.* Add:

4. 'To subject (a body) to the impingement of small particles or rays; also, to cause (small particles or rays) to impinge upon' (Webster, 1918). So **Bomba·rdment** (Cent. Dict. Suppl. 1909).

Bombay (bɒmbē¹·). The name of a western Presidency and its chief city, British India, used attrib. in: **Bombay chair** (cf. *Bombay furniture*); **Bombay duck** (see Duck *sb.*¹ 10); **Bombay furniture,** a style of furniture combining European forms with Indian ornamentation; **Bombay hemp** (see Hemp 5); **Bombay pearl** (see quot.); **Bombay shell,** the bull's-mouth shell, *Cassis rufa*, used for cutting shell cameos.

1896 *Pall Mall Mag.* Mar. 399 [They] succeeded in installing themselves in two immense *Bombay Chairs. 1885 *Encycl. Brit.* XVIII. 447/1 Most of the products of this fishery [*sc.* in the Persian Gulf] are known as '*Bombay pearls', from the fact that many of the best are sold there. 1858 Simmonds *Dict. Trade*, *Bombay Shells.

Bombe (boñb). *Cookery.* [Fr.: see Bomb *sb.*] A conical or cup-shaped item of a dish, confection, etc. Also *attrib.*

1892 *Encycl. Pract. Cookery* I. 40/2 Apricot Bombe with Maraschino...Set two freezing-pots and a bombe-mould in some pounded ice and bay-salt. 1902 *Daily Chron.* 24 May 5/4 Fish bombes are made with any kind of cooked white fish. *Ibid.*, Turn it out on a hot dish, place four little 'bombes' round it.

Bombed, *ppl. a.* Add: **b.** *spec.* in *Ethnol.*

1896 A. H. Keane *Ethnology* I. viii. 185 The small flat concave [nose] is usually correlated with high cheek-bones..; the short with wide nostrils and depressed root, with everted lips and bombed frontal bone (Negro).

Bomber (bɒ·məɹ). [f. Bomb *sb.* or *v.* + -er ¹.]

1. One who throws a bomb; *esp.* in military use, one of a bombing party.

1915 Buchan *Hist. War* V. 25 The bombers..seizing one of these rocket-like bombs from their belts..hurl them high above the parapet. 1927 *Daily Tel.* 8 Mar. 12/2 A fifth attempt to dynamite the Roman Catholic Church of S. Peter and Paul, San Francisco, ended yesterday in the killing of one bomber.

2. An aircraft equipped with bombs for bombing an enemy, his positions, territory, etc.

1923 Sir S. Hoare *Sp. Ho. Comm.* 14 Mar., Five service squadrons [of which] only one consisted of fighters and four were bombers. 1923 *Daily Mail* 19 Mar. 9 Goods-'planes—all capable of transformation into bombers.

Bombilla (bɒmbi·lʸă). [Sp., dim. of *bomba*.] A vessel from which maté is drunk in South America.

1921 *Glasgow Herald* 11 Feb. 9 A bombilla manufactured specially for the South American market. 1921 *Chambers's Jrnl.* June 382/1 Maté circulates in a small gourd-shaped vessel, each person taking a pull at the *bombilla*, a kind of spoon-strainer perforated to let the liquid pass.

Bombing, *vbl. sb.* Add: The action or operation of throwing or dropping bombs. Chiefly *attrib.*, as *bombing party* (Mil.), a party of infantry equipped with bombs for attacking an enemy; *bombing raid* (*a*) an air-raid for dropping bombs on an enemy, his position, territory, etc.; (*b*) a raid by a bombing party of infantry.

1915 *Morning Post* 29 May 8/1 A bombing party presents a weird sight...The men carry 5 or 6 grenades each. 1916 Boyd Cable *Action Front* 68 He only gave the..briefest account of his successful patrol and bombing work.

Bombolo (bɒ·mbǝlo). [ad. It. *bombola* pitcher.] A bomb-shaped flint glass vessel in which camphor is sublimed.

1851–4 *Tomlinson's Cycl. Arts* (1866) I. 286/2 This process [*sc.* the sublimation of camphor] is carried on in spheroidal vessels, called bomboloes.

Bomb-proof. Add: **A.** *adj.* **b.** *fig.* Not exposed to the dangers of war. (Cf. below.) *U.S.*

1868 *Putnam's Mag.* I. 715/1 During the late war the Simminses did their share of the fighting, for..none of them had influence to get 'bomb-proof' places, and keep in the rear. 1869 *Congress. Globe* Feb. 950/2 These sleek, bomb-proof patriots, who fight the battles of their country by strutting about the avenue here. 1895 *Congress. Rec.* Jan. 887/2 He asked to be relieved from a bombproof situation under the Govt., in order to join his regiment.

B. *sb.* **b.** In the Southern states, one who stayed away from the fighting-line during the Civil War. *U.S.*

1869 *Overland Monthly* III. 128 In the cis-Mississippi States they were generally dubbed 'bomb-proofs'. 1872 Schele de Vere *Americanisms* (1872) 281 Officials who were not expected to expose themselves to the fire of the enemy, like quartermasters, commissaries, etc. were nicknamed *bomb-proofs*. 1876 *Southern Hist. Soc. Papers* II. 229 While the war lasted, it was the delight of some of the stoutly built fellows to go home for a few days, and kick and cuff and tongue-lash the able-bodied bomb-proofs.

Bomb-shell. Add: Often *fig.* (or in fig. phr.). A shattering or devastating act, event, etc.

1926 May Sutherland *One o' the Herd* vii, Do you think it was kind to let her think she had plenty and then drop down on her like this? It's a regular bomb-shell. 1928 *Manchester Guardian Weekly* 26 Oct. 337/1 The letters do not drop any historical bombshells.

Bon, *a.* Add:

Bon enfant (bon añfañ). lit. 'Good child'; an agreeable or jolly companion.

1836 H. Greville *Leaves fr. Diary* (1883) 105 He is very merry and *bon enfant*, and quickly enters into conversation. 1848 Thackeray *Van. Fair* lxiv, Look, Madame Crawley, you were always *bon enfant*, and I have an interest in you, *parole d'honneur*. 1883 *Sat. Rev.* 6 Jan. 3/1 He was always and to every one *bon enfant*.

Bon jour (boñ ʒūr). lit. 'Good day'; a form of salutation on meeting in the daytime; hence, a civil greeting.

a 1577 Gascoigne *Fable of Ieronimi* Wks. (1587) 260 Who after theyr Boniure dyd all seeme to lament the sicknesse of Ferdinando. 1588 Shaks. *Tit. A.* i. i. 494 To morrow..With horne and Hound, Weele giue your Grace *Bon iour*. 1592 — *Rom. & Jul.* ii. iv. 46 Signior Romeo, *Bon iour*, there's a French salutation to your French slop. 1595 Goodwine *Blanchardine* K 2, After Sadony had royally presented himselfe to the veiw of all, giuing a princely boniure to the Lordes. 1823 Scott *Quentin D.* iii, The landlord entered,—answered Maitre Pierre's *bon jour* with a reverence. 1854 Thackeray *Newcomes* v. I. 50 The sea being recommended to him Mrs. Newcome..transferred him to his maternal aunt at Brighton. Then it was *bonjour*.

Bon viveur (boñ vivör). [F. *viveur* liver.] A pseudo-French substitute for Bon vivant.

1865 'Ouida' *Strathmore* xx. I. 297 A cosy bachelor-villa, that had been long inhabited by an old English *bon viveur*. 1888 *Athenæum* 11 Feb. 171/3 Mr. Rogers has said and eaten as many good things as those excellent *bons viveurs*.

Bon voyage: see Boon *a.* 2.

Bonanza. 1. (Earlier examples.)

1847 Ruxton *Adv. Mexico* xi. 79 The..famous black vein of Sombrerete yielded the greatest *bonanzas* of any mine on the continent of America. 1875 *Scribner's Mag.* July 272 But a bonanza with 'millions in it' is not struck every week.

Bon-bon. Add: **3.** In full *cracker bon-bon*: see Cracker 6 b. Also *attrib.*

1894 H. Nisbet *Bush Girl's Rom.* 287 Gilt paper and coloured bon-bon stuff. 1901 *Daily Chron.* 10 Aug. 10/3 Frieze suits in the loveliest bon-bon shades of blue and red.

Bond, *sb.*¹ Add:

11. Phr. *To go* (a person's) *bond*: to be or go surety for (him).

1922 J. A. Dunn *Man Trap* xiii, 'He knows who I am. He knows where to secure vouchers for me.' 'Would he go your bond?' It was the hotel detective who spoke.

13. d. *Electr.* A metallic connexion between conductors forming part of an electric circuit, as between the abutting or adjoining rails of an electric railway line.

1903 [see *Bonder¹ 3]. 1904 *Westm. Gaz.* 14 Dec. 10/2 To provide electric continuity [both] are connected together by flexible strips of copper called 'bonds'.

14. bond paper, a paper of superior manufacture used for bonds and other documents. (Also simply *bond* in some trade-names of writing-paper.)

1874 Knight *Dict. Mech.*, Bond-paper. 1909 *Buckeye Informer* IX. 214/2 A small quantity of Japan dryer added to heavy black inks will accelerate their drying on linen and bond papers.

Bond, *sb.*³ Add: See also *Africander. Also *attrib.* Hence **Bo·ndite,** a member or supporter of the Bond; **Bo·nd(s)man,** a member of the Bond.

1884 Bondsmen [in Dict.]. 1890 *Pall Mall Gaz.* 4 Feb. 2/2 Smith sits for Graaffreinet, is an extreme Bondsman, and cannot speak English. 1896 C. Garner ('S. Cumberland')

What I think of S. Africa xi. 150 The slave-owners of the Southern States, too, were angels of goodness as compared with the Boer bondsmen-holders. 1898 *Daily News* 22 Mar. 5/1 Two Progressives were elected, and one Bondman. 1900 *Ibid.* 23 July 5/7 Bondites are largely influenced in the adoption of obstructive tactics by the desire to obtain the maximum Parliamentary allowance.

Bond, *v.* Add:

6. *Electr.* To connect with an electrical bond. (See *Bond *sb.*[1] 13 d.)

1904 *Jrnl. Franklin Inst.* Apr. 287 My experience in bonding rails is that [etc.]. 1908 *Installation News* II. 103/2 Care should be taken to maintain the continuity of the run ..by means of bonding round the block with a piece of copper wire.

Bonder[1]. Add:

3. One who fixes or adjusts the metallic bonds of an electric circuit. (Cf. *Bond *sb.*[1] 13 d. and *v.* 6.)

1903 *Westm. Gaz.* 20 Jan. 9/2 The bonders being told off to attend to the copper bonds which make the electrical connexion between each of the three rails.

Bondite, Bond(s)man: see *Bond *sb.*[3]

Bo·ndmaid, -maiden. [Bond *a.*] A slave girl. So **Bo·ndservant, -service.**

1526 Tindale *Gal.* iv. 22 Abraham had two sonnes, the one by a bonde mayde, the other by a fre woman. 1535 Coverdale *Lev.* xxv. 44 Yf thou wylt haue bonde seruauntes and maydens. 1552 Abp. Hamilton *Catech.* (1884) 193 Behald the bound maidin of our Lord. 1591 Spenser *Virg. Gnat* 489 Th' one was rauisht of his owne bondmaide. 1596 Shaks. *Tam. Shr.* ii. i. 2 To make a bondmaide and a slaue of mee. 1611 *Bible* 1 Kings ix. 21 A tribute of bond-seruice. 1814 Scott *Lord of Isles* ii. xxv, Like a..bond-maid at her master's gate.

Bondon (bondon). [Fr., = bung.] A soft Neufchâtel cheese.

1902 *Encycl. Brit.* XXVII. 355/2. 1921 *Dict. Occup. Terms* (1927) § 448.

Bone, *sb.* Add:

2. Phrase (always with negative). *To* (*live to*) *make old bones*: to live to an old age.

1873 [in Dict.]. 1886 Miss Braddon *One Thing Needful* i, Lord Lashmar would never make old bones.

3. b. *To feel ... in one's bones*: to have a sure intuition of (something). *To be in one's bones*: to be felt as certain.

1844 in T. W. Barnes *Mem. Thurlow Weed* (1884) 123 It was in my bones all summer. 1875 Holland *Sevenoaks* xxiii. 315, I know the thing is coming. I can feel the thing in my bones. 1877 J. H. Beadle *Western Wilds* ii. 42, I felt in my bones no good could come of it. 1902 H. L. Wilson *Spenders* xxxviii. 466 It is a happy man who has divined the leisure of eternity, so he feels it, like what you say, 'in his bones'. 1912 Mulford & Clay *Buck Peters* iii. 57 Son, there's a big time due in these parts; I feel it in my bones. 1923 J. A. Spender in *Westm. Gaz.* 13 Oct., They know in their bones it is nonsense.

5. f. *Golf.* (See quot.)

1900 *Young Sportsman* (ed. A. E. T. Watson) 315 *Bone*, the piece of horn, vulcanite, or other material let into the sole of wooden clubs to protect the lower edge of the face.

12. b. The 'skeleton' of a novel, play, or other literary work; basis of literary style.

1888 *Sat. Rev.* 15 Dec. 714/2 There are 'the bones of' something like a novel of some merit in *The Jewel Reputation*. 1905 *Westm. Gaz.* 23 Mar. 7/3 Counsel did not allege that Mr. Tanner had copied plaintiff's dialogue, but the 'bone' was the same. 1928 *Publishers' Weekly* 9 June 2373 My own bed-book is Mrs. Gaskell's 'Cranford', and as I read it again that night I could find no bones in it at all.

c. A hardness of the ground due to frost.

1906 *Westm. Gaz.* 23 Feb. 5/1 The night's frost had left a great deal of 'bone' in the ground. 1927 *Observer* 18 Dec. 25/2 The ground had been protected by straw, but there seemed to be a good deal of bone in it.

17. bone-bleached *a.*, bleached to the whiteness of bone; **bone body**, a paste containing phosphate of lime used in the manufacture of certain kinds of pottery; **bone-boiler**, a workman who performs the operation of boiling or steaming bones used in the manufacture of glue, bone meal, etc.; **bone-cell, -corpuscle**, an osteoblast; **bone china**, china-ware made of clay mixed with bone-dust or phosphate of lime; **bone-digester**, a tank in which bones are boiled down in the manufacture of bone manure, etc.; **bone-dry** *a.*, dry as a weathered bone; now *U.S.* absolutely without intoxicating liquor; **bone-fat**, fatty matter extracted from fresh bones for use in the manufacture of soap; **bone-flour**, a flour obtained by sifting ground bones, used as a fertilizer; **bone-forceps**, a surgical forceps used for removing portions of bone; **bone-framework**, the bony framework of an animal body, the bones as distinguished from the muscles and flesh; **bone-head** *U.S.*, a blockhead; **bone-headed** *a. U.S. colloq.*, thick-headed, stupid; **bone-heap**, a heap of bones; *spec.* in *Archæol.*, a refuse pile of bones, etc., of a prehistoric village (*Funk's Standard Dict.* 1895); **bone-idle** *a.*, idle 'to the bone', downright idle (cf. Lazy-bones); **bone (manure) man**, an employee of a bone manure factory; **bone-marrow** = Marrow *sb.*[1] 1; **bone-meal**, the coarser siftings of ground bones, used as a fertilizer; **bone naphtha** (see quot.); **bone phosphate**, a commercial name for tricalcium phosphate, the phosphate that forms bone-tissue; **bone-pit** *U.S.* (see quot.); **bone porcelain** = *bone china*; **bone pot**, (*a*) an ancient funeral urn; (*b*) a pot used in making animal charcoal; **bone powder**, powdered bone, used as a fertilizer; **bone-saw**, a surgical saw for severing a limb; **bone-seed** (see quot.); **bone-tired** *a.*, excessively tired; **bone turquoise** (see Turquoise 4).

1896 Kipling *Seven Seas* 73 *Bone-bleached my decks. 1893 E. A. Barber *Pottery & Porcelain of U.S.* 127 The proportion of phosphate of lime..being..a very much smaller percentage than in the English *bone body. 1843 *Civil Eng. & Arch. Jrnl.* VI. 216/2 Any trade or business such as.. *bone-boiler. 1906 *Daily Chron.* 26 May 2/7 Bone boilers and tallow melters. 1839–47 *Todd's Cycl. Anat.* III. 856/1 The *bone-cells..form the outer layer of cells in the Haversian system. 1903 M. L. Solon *Brief Hist. Old Eng. Porcelain* 220 Josiah Spode..composed a new china body which..from the nature of its chief constituent..received the vulgar name of '*Bone China'. *Ibid.*, This evergreen 'bone china' has remained unaltered ever since the first pieces of it came out of Spode's oven. 1875 *Encycl. Brit.* I. 854/1 The lacunæ look like solid, black bodies, and..were erroneously called by the earlier observers *bone-corpuscles. 1898 *Westm. Gaz.* 31 Aug. 7/2 A large cylinder, technically called a '*bone digester'. 1847 Halliwell, **Bone-dry*, perfectly dry. 1865 J. Young *Homely Pict.* 128 (E.D.D.) An auld neebor hove in sight, Bane dry himsel' An spread abune me, drookit wicht His big umbrell'. 1919 Boyd Cable *Old Contemptibles* xvi. 268 They was like a good long drink to a bone-dry man. 1873 Spon *Workshop Rec.* Ser. i. 373/2 For purifying *bone fat, melt the fat and a small quantity of saltpetre together. 1887 *Jrnl. Soc. Chem. Industry* VI. 825/1 Loss of Nitrogen in the Manufacture of Bone-fat and the Analysis of Bone-fat. 1888 *Ibid.* VII. 81/2 The bones..are first broken up more or less finely, and go to produce what are known as—⅛ inch bones. ½ inch bones. Crushed bones. Bonedust. Bonemeal. *Boneflour. 1879 *St. George's Hosp. Rep.* IX. 259 One of these presented a bony growth..the end of which was cut off with *bone-forceps. 1902 *Westm. Gaz.* 11 Aug. 7/2 The horses were different, for their *bone-framework was no longer visible. 1913 Biggers *Seven Keys Baldpate* viii, Still that *bone-head from the woods sat there, his mouth open. 1924 A. J. Small *Frozen Gold* i. 36 Can't understand Norvice doing a fool thing like that...Norvice isn't a bonehead. 1903 *Smart Set* IX. 96 You talk like a *bone-headed fool! 1836 Carlyle *New Lett.* (1904) I. 8 For the last three weeks I have been going what you call *bone-idle*. 1891 Kipling *Light that Failed* (1900) 84 Bone-idle, is he? Careless, and touched in the temper? 1913 *Daily Mail* 18 June 8 They are bone-idle and pleasure-seeking. 1899 *Daily News* 21 July 5/2 Defendant gave instructions for the *bone man to take away the bad meat. 1908 W. E. C. Dickson (*title*) The *Bone-Marrow. 1927 Haldane & Huxley *Anim. Biol.* ix. 189 An extra production of red blood-corpuscles by the bone-marrow. 1868 *Rep. U.S. Commissioner Agric.* (1869) 401 *Bone-meal prepared by high-pressure steam contains not much less nitrogen than ordinary bone dust. 1884 *Encycl. Brit.* XVII. 175/1 *Bone naphtha, or bone oil, known also as Dippel's animal oil, is a most offensively smelling product of the distillation of bones in the preparation of animal charcoal. 1848 Craig, **Bone-phosphate*. 1869 Roscoe *Elem. Chem.* (1871) 219 Calcium phosphate, or bone phosphate. 1889 Farmer *Americanisms*, **Bone-pits*, Indian places of interment. These bone-pits are found scattered throughout the United States and Canada. 1884 Knight *Dict. Mech.* Suppl., **Bone Porcelain*, a ware into the composition of which enters phosphate of lime in the form of bone dust. 1889 *Century Dict.*, *Bone-pot. 1888 *Jrnl. Soc. Chem. Industry* VII. 133/1 The 'bone-powders' of commerce are not always products of manufacture solely derived from the grinding of bones. 1884 Knight *Dict. Mech.* Suppl., **Bone Saw*. 1898 *Daily News* 12 Apr. 5/5 And all because of her skill with the knife and the bone-saw. 1908 Hardy *Dynasts* iii. vii. v, A surgeon's horse..laden with bone-saws,..and other surgical instruments. 1866 *Treas. Bot.*, **Bone-seed*, the common name for *Osteospermum*. 1921 A. S. M. Hutchinson *Happy Warrior* i. i. § 3 Egbert was *bone-tired. 1928 *Daily Express* 7 Aug. 3/4, I returned.. bone tired, thoroughly weary.

Bone, *v.*[1] Add:

4. *intr.* To apply oneself diligently or determinedly. Also with *in*. *U.S.*

a 1861 T. Winthrop *Life in open Air* etc. (1863) 148 We was about sick of putty-heads and sneaks that..didn't dare to make us stand round and bone in. 1883 H. A. Beers in *Century Mag.* June 273/2 I'm going to bone right down to it.

b. *fig.* To bristle *up* or stiffen. *U.S.*

1888 Mrs. Custer *Tenting on Plains* ix. (1893) 181, I have known the General to 'bone up', as his West Point phrase expressed it, on the smallest details.

Boneen (bǫnī·n). *Irish.* [ad. Ir. *banabhín* sucking-pig, f. *banabh* + *-ín* dim. suffix.] A young pig.

1841 Lever *C. O'Malley* lxxxv, What's that you have dragging there behind you? A boneen, sir. 1852 Mundy *Antipodes* (1857) 195 The wretched shieling of poor Paddy, with his dudeen, his caubeen, his boneen. 1892 Emily Lawless *Grania* I. iv. 22 The relative number of cows, turkeys, feather-beds, boneens, black pots and the like.

Bone-fish. Chiefly *U.S.* [Bone *sb.*] A name applied to various fishes (see quots.).

1734, 1809 [see Bone *sb.* 17]. 1884 Goode, etc. *Nat. Hist. Aquatic Anim.* 279 The 'Bone-fish' of Key West, according to Stearns, belongs to this [sturgeon] family and genus. *Ibid.* 612 With us it [sc. *Albula vulpes*] is usually called the 'Lady-fish'; in the Bermudas the 'Bone-fish', or Grubber. *Ibid.* 674 In Southern New England this fish [sc. dogfish] is called the 'Bone-fish'. 1897 *Outing* (U.S.) XXIX. 331/1 The bone-fish somewhat resembles a whiting in shape, with the mouth of a sucker and no teeth.

Bonelessness (bōu·nlĕsnĕs). [f. Boneless *a.* + -ness.] Boneless condition. Also *transf.* and *fig.*

1885 *Spectator* 20 June 805 They weary of the besetting defect of modern English statesmen, bonelessness. 1895 *Athenæum* 2 Mar. 289/1 The partial bonelessness..is [perhaps] due to them. 1928 *Daily Express* 9 Nov. 15/1 The softness of this chair!..And its bonelessness and bendability!

Boneyard. *U.S.* [Bone *sb.*] A yard or place where the bones of dead animals are collected; also, a cemetery.

1872 'Mark Twain' *Innoc. at Home* ii. (1882) 270 When some roughs jumped the Catholic bone-yard, and started in to stake out town-lots in it. 1903 W. J. Long *Beasts of Field* 70, I have met men..who speak of 'bone yards' which they have discovered—places where they can go at any time and be sure of finding a good set of caribou antlers. 1903 *N. Y. Even. Post* 7 Oct. 7 A dilapidated horse saved from the bone-yard.

Bongo (bǫ·ngo). [Cf. Bangi *mbangani*, Lingala *mongu*.] (In full *Bongo antelope*.) An African bush-buck belonging to the genus *Boöcercus*, esp. the East African Bongo, *B. eurycerus* (*isaaci* or) *itraali*; also the West African Bongo, *B. eurycerus*.

1902 O. Thomas in *Ann. & Mag. Nat. Hist.* Ser. VII. X. 309 No evidence as yet exists as to whether the true western Bongo has horns in the female. 1910 *Westm. Gaz.* 15 Mar. 11/1 Next come nine white rhinoceroses and a couple of bongos, a specimen of the latter animal never before having fallen to the gun of a white man. 1911 Roosevelt in Charnwood *Life* (1923) 243 He had killed a bongo, a bull.

Bonhomous (bǫ·nǫməs), *a.* Also (*rare*) **bonhomm(i)ous.** [f. Bonhomie + -ous.] Full of bonhomie or good-fellowship. Hence **Bo·nhomously** *adv.*

1905 *Spectator* 18 Feb. 257/1 A delightful bonhomous person. 1917 R. Farrer *On Eaves of World* II. 301 Gentlemanly bonhomousness of outlook. 1927 *Observer* 10 July 6 The hearty and bonhomous J. D. Marstock. 1928 E. Waugh *Decline & Fall* x. 109 Lady C.'s hardly what you might call bonhommious.

Bonify, *v.* Add: **3.** To give a bonus to. [1876: cf. Bonification 2.] 1905 *Glasgow Herald* 3 Aug. 6/5 These preferences are given not to bonify one German trader competing with other German traders.

Bonism (bǫ·niz'm). [f. L. *bonus* good + -ism.] The doctrine that the world is good, but not the best possible. So **Bo·nist**, one who favours this doctrine; hence **Boni·stic** *a.*

1882 J. W. Barlow *Ultim. Pessimism* 5 So we say that Optimist and Pessimist are no longer suitable names, and the positive forms Bonist and Malist would certainly be more appropriate. 1893 Myers *Sci. & Future Life* 10 The view of the universe loosely styled optimism, but which some would term *bonism*, with no greater barbarism in the formation of the word, and more accuracy in its meaning. 1896 Tollemache *Jowett* 91 Jowett's optimism verges on pessimism, or, as I may say, his *bonism* verges on *malism*. *Ibid.* 95 After setting side by side the bonistic and malistic sayings of Jowett.

Bonnaz (bǫ·næz). [Name of J. Bonnaz of Lyons, inventor (1863) of a chainstitch embroidering machine.] A kind of machine-made embroidery.

1881 *Instr. Census Clerks* (1885) 75 Bonnaz Machinist. 1903 *Daily Chron.* Mar. 9/6 Bonnaz Machinists...Bonnaz Braiding Machines. 1921 *Dict. Occup. Terms* (1927) § 8 Bonnaz book maker.

Bonner (bǫ·nəɹ). *University slang.* [f. Bonfire + *-er[6].] A bonfire.

1898 *Oxford Mag.* 19 May, While the Bonner burns, we haste to pass The Revellers firework-scattered on the Grass. 1898 *Westm. Gaz.* 6 Dec. 10/1 The authorities of a certain college gave permission for the turf of the quadrangle to be taken up in order to make better provision for the 'bonner'. 1927 *Daily Tel.* 15 Mar. 10/4 We should be rightly apprehensive if we were to hear of no more 'rags' or 'bonners'.

Bonnet, *sb.* Add:

6. f. 'The hood over the platform of a railroad-car' (*Cent. Dict.* 1889).

g. The protecting hood over the machinery of a motor vehicle.

1902 Harmsworth *Motors & Motor-Driving* 181 If you have a flare-up,..take off bonnet to save the paint, and smother the flames. 1904 Young *Compl. Motorist* (ed. 2) 111 The engine, instead of being placed vertically under a bonnet in front of the car, lies horizontally immediately in front of the dash-board. 1915 'Bartimeus' *Crab Pots* iv. in *A Tall Ship* i. 31 The fragments of the shattered wind-screen tinkled down over the bonnet and footboard.

10. *bonnet-box* (earlier U.S. example).

1854 Mary J. Holmes *Tempest & Sunshine* xxv. 347 Upsetting the pile of bonnet boxes, which rolled promiscuously over the floor.

Bonnet, *v.* Add: **4.** To provide (a safety lamp) with an iron bonnet or shield.

1901 *Jrnl. Inst. Elect. Engin.* XXX. 834 In appearance it is a bonneted Mueseler lamp.

Bonsense (bǫ·nsĕns). [f. Bon *a.* + Sense *sb.*, after *nonsense*.] Good sense.

1713 Craig in R. Smith *Poems of Controversy* (1853) 11 As to thy Poetry its nonsense, and therein not a word of bonsense. 1900 H. Harland *Cardinal's Snuffbox* xxi, Nonsense or bonsense, that is the sober truth.

Bont tick. Also **bonte tick.** [f. Du. *bont* variegated + Tick *sb.*[1]] A South African tick, *Amblyomma hebræum*, parasitic on cattle, ostriches, and man.

1881 Douglass *Ostrich Farming* 17 (Pettman) The large Bonte tick that..produces terrible sores on all animals. 1900 C. P. Lounsbury in *Proc. Assoc. Econ. Ent.* 42 (Cent. Dict. Suppl.) The tick of greatest importance, because of its injuries to stock, is *Amblyomma hebræum* Koch, commonly known as the bont tick.

Bony, *sb. U.S. mining.* [Cf. Bone *sb.* 13.]

1874 Raymond *Statist. Mines & Mining* 39 It [sc. the coal] is interstratified with sand-rock and shale. In some of the mines the roof consists of a mixture of the two, called by the men 'bony'. *Ibid.* 41 The Black Diamond vein has for roof and floor shale, slate, and 'bony'.

Bony, *a.* **3.** Add: **bony-fish** *U.S.*, the menhaden or moss-bunker (*Brevoortia tyrannus*).

1848 Bartlett *Dict. Amer.*, *Menhaden*..is also known by the names of Bony-fish, White-fish, [etc.]. 1871 *Game Laws N. Y.* in *Fur, Fin & Feather* (1872) 21 Bony fish, or moss bunkers..are exempted from the operation of this section. 1884 L. F. Allen *New Amer. Farm Bk.* 80 The moss-bonker, or bony-fish [etc.]..are caught in seines, and sold to the farmers by the wagon load.

Bonzer (bǫ·nzəɹ), *a.* *Austral. slang.* [Perhaps from Bonanza.] Excellent, extremely good.

1915 C. J. Dennis *Sentimental Bloke* 18 An' on the air a sad, sweet music breaves A bonzer song. 1922 *Glasgow Herald* 8 Nov. 8, I have..heard Australians described as 'Bonzers,' probably owing to the way they have of over-working that strange compound. It is used in the various States in place of the adjectives good, great, and splendid, as, for example, 'Massenger is a bonzer player; he scored a bonzer try.' 1927 *Daily Express* 2 Apr. 2/2 'Oh! Ain't they both bonzer,' remarked one woman spectator, using a familiar Australian expression of appreciation.

Bonzo (bǫ·nzo). [Arbitrarily formed by Capt. Bruce S. Ingram, editor of 'The Sketch'.] The figure of a comically-shaped puppy which came into vogue through a series of drawings by G. E. Studdy (the first of which appeared in 'The Sketch' 8 Nov. 1922), and used in various forms, as toys, etc. Hence (*trivial*) **Bo·nzoid** *a.*

1927 *Bulletin* 11 Oct. 5/4 The craze for vanity bags in the form of Teddy Bears, Bonzos, and other zoological specimens. 1928 Galsworthy *Swan Song* ii. vi, You're 'for it', as they say in this Bonzoid age.

Bonzoline (bǫ·nzŏlīn). A composition used as a substitute for ivory in the manufacture of billiard balls.

1896 *Daily News* 18 Apr. 6/1 During the last two or three years the balls have been made of a new composition called bonzoline. 1899 *Westm. Gaz.* 10 Nov. 5/2 Bonzoline billiard balls.

Boo, *v.* Add: **2.** *trans.* To assail with cries of 'boo!' as an expression of dissatisfaction or disapproval; to condemn by booing. Hence **Boo·er.**

1893 *Daily News* 27 Jan. 5/1 It was not a booing that booed the piece to immediate perdition. 1904 *Daily Chron.* 19 Nov. 4/6 The 'booer,' she argues, does not make himself heard at the opening of all new hotels, banks, and public buildings. What indeed would be thought of the man who 'booed' his dinner at the Carlton because his appetite failed? 1923 *Daily Mail* 28 Sept. 6/3 Then..the booer will learn to give vent to his feelings in a more civilised way.

Boob (būb). *U.S. slang.* Shortened f. Booby.

1912 R. W. Chambers *Streets of Ascalon* i. 16 I'm talking like a writer, that's all. That's how you boobs talk, isn't it, Karl? 1920 *Chambers's Jrnl.* May 282/1 Of course war is wrong—any boob knows that. 1921 J. F. Fraser in *Glasgow Herald* 4 Apr. 8 The belief that the United States was made to appear a poor boob in the eyes of the world. 1922 J. A. Dunn *Man Trap* xiv, As for this boob, Royce, he's through with his star as far as this town is concerned.

Booby. 3. Add:

booby-hack = **booby-hut, -hutch** *U.S.* (earlier examples); **booby prize**, a prize (of no value) awarded in ridicule or fun to the player with the lowest score; **booby-trap** (see also quots.)

1888 *Boston Daily Globe* (Farmer) They collided with Crowley's *booby hack, knocking the horse down and demolishing the front of the vehicle. 1812 *Boston Gaz.* 28 Dec. (Th.) He has on hand, for sale, a number of *Booby-Huts and Carriages. 1846 G. Warburton *Hochelaga* II. vi. 146 A covered conveyance, enclosed partly with glass;..it is called a 'Booby-hut'. 1766 *Boston Gaz.* 29 Dec. (Th.) A very neat *Booby-hutch to be sold cheap for Cash. 1900 Ellen T. Fowler *Farringdons* iii, Your prize would have been no better than a *booby-prize. 1918 P. Gibbs *From Bapaume to Passchendaele* 4 The enemy left...'*booby-traps' to blow a man to bits or blind him for life if he touched a harmless-looking stick or opened the lid of a box. 1922 *Chambers's Jrnl.* 217/1 Every kind of booby-trap and delay-action mine.

Boodle[1]. Add: **1.** (Earlier U.S. examples.) Freq. *whole kit and boodle.*

1833 J. Neal *Down-Easters* I. 61, I know a feller 'twould whip the whool boodle of 'em an' give 'em six. 1847 D. P. Thompson *Locke Amsden* 76 [He] stumped all the rest to come on, one at a time, and there wasn't a soul of the whole boodle that dared do it.

2. [For def. read:] *U.S.* **a.** Counterfeit money.

1858 *Harper's Weekly* 3 Apr. (Th.) Boodle is a flash term used by counterfeiters...The leaders [of the gang] were the manufacturers and bankers of the boodle.

b. Money acquired or spent illegally or improperly, esp. in connexion with the obtaining or holding of public offices; the material means or gains of bribery and corruption.

1884 *Mag. Amer. Hist.* XII. 566 [Boodle] has come to mean a large roll of bills such as political managers are supposed to divide among their retainers. 1887 *Congress. Rec.* Jan. 1025/1 [In Rhode Island] the man who is bribed you could not punish, while the man who furnished the 'boodle' was liable to indictment. 1894 *Ibid.* Jan. 667/2 Republican conventions have always 'pointed with pride' to any channel that floated boodle their way.

attrib. 1887 *Nation* (N. Y.) 14 Apr. 307/3 New York is better known all over the..world for boodle Aldermen and municipal rings than for anything else. 1888 *Puck's Library* May 3 (Farmer, Slang) You're convinced..That be ponders of divorce, Or of boodle cases great.

Hence **Boo·dle** *v.*, to bribe; to practise bribery; **Boo·dleism**, bribery and corruption, embezzlement of public funds; **Boodlei·stic** *a.*, addicted to boodleism; **Boo·dleize** *v. trans.*, to bribe; **Boo·dler**, one who practises boodleism; **Boo·dlerism, Boo·dlery, Boo·dling** = *boodleism*.

1904 W. H. Smith *Promoters* iv. 86 If you're going to *boodle you've got to do it on a party basis. If I wanted to boodle an Illinois legislature, [etc.]. 1894 *Congress. Rec.* Aug.. App. 1229/1 What we call the government of the people..has become a government of boodlers, by the use of boodle for the benefit of *boodleism. 1904 *Minneapolis Times* 6 July 6 If they say he has been making war on boodleism for political effect, good citizens..reply [etc.]. 1898 *Congress. Rec.* Apr. 4385/1 The barking of this mangy Wall-street *boodleistic cur..reminds me of a lonely coyote baying the moon. 1886 *Ibid.* July 7266/1 There are no seven men in the state of Ohio, unless they were *boodleized, who would agree to any such proposition. 1887 *Nation* (N. Y.) 17 Nov. 386/3 It is suspected that '*boodlers' are at work undermining the enterprise, so far as public officials control it. 1888 *Omaha World* (Farmer) We have elections and campaigns, and political parties, and bosses, and ringsters, and boodlers. 1896 G. Ade *Artie* xii. 108 He turned out to be a boodler, eh? 1887 *Advance* (Chicago) 30 June 408 '*Boodlerism' in the management of our city and county and State affairs. 1887 J. C. Ambrose *Ibid.*, Let her not plead great conscience..but grant open licence to *boodlery. 1890 *School Board* Feb., Something akin to '*boodling' has been unearthed in the public educational system of New York city. 1903 *N. Y. Even. Post* 31 Aug., We fancy that the people of Missouri will conclude to diminish boodling rather by taking from than adding to the powers of the dominant machine.

Boojum (bū·dʒəm). [Invented by 'Lewis Carroll' (C. L. Dodgson) in *The Hunting of the Snark* (1876).] An imaginary animal, a particularly dangerous kind of 'snark'.

1904 B'ness von Hutten *Pam* iii. vi, We are both too obstinate...I am a boojum, and I know. 1922 *Edin. Rev.* Oct. 241 Both these beautiful abstractions are in reality boojums. 1925 *Blackw. Mag.* Mar. 345/1 A solitary Boojum-like person.

Book, *sb.* Add: **3. d.** *transf.* of things composed of 'leaves' or 'plates'.

1840 R. H. Dana *Bef. Mast* xxix. (1841) 85/1 A large 'book' was made of some twenty-five to fifty hides, doubled at the backs, and put into one another, like the leaves of a book. 1885 J. S. Kingsley in *Q. Jrnl. Microsc. Sci.* Oct. 538 The primary stigma formed by the insinking of the respiratory book is not the functional one of the adult. 1892 *Photogr. Ann.* II. 327 To put the book in camera, the camera is tilted front up. *Ibid.* 328 The book of plate-holders.

e. An angler's pocket-book for fishing-tackle.

1847 Stoddart *Angler's Comp.* 61 Angler's trouting book.

9. c. *West Africa.* (See quots.)

1863 *Fraser's Mag.* LXVII. 146/1 It was resolved..to renew his 'book'. 1897 Mary Kingsley *W. Africa* x. 203 In order to..simplify this goods traffic, a written piece of paper is employed—practically a cheque, which is called a 'bou' or 'book' and these 'bous' are cashed—i.e. gooded, at the store. *Ibid.* xii. 286, I would give the creditor a book on Hatton and Cookson for the coat.

11. b. The cards forming a complete set in 'Authors' and similar games.

1895 in *Funk's Standard Dict.*

15. *To suit* (a person's) *book*: to fall in with his plans or answer his requirements, be agreeable to.

Orig. a bookmaker's phr.: see sense 10. Cf. 1869 *Gentl. Mag.* July 231 He wins your money with a smile, will accommodate his book to suit what bets you may choose to make. 1851 Murchison in *Life of Prestwich* (1899) 83 Would it suit your book to make a run of a day or two to the other side of the Weald? 1852 F. E. Smedley *Lewis Arundel* vi, By which time he expects to be so hard up that he must marry somebody, and as there will be plenty of the needful she will suit his book as well as any other. 1895 *Cassell's Fam. Mag.* 462/2 It suits the owners' book that this steamboat should be lost. 1928 *Britain's Industr. Future* (Liberal Ind. Inquiry) 420 The actual results have probably been variable in any given year..to suit the book of the Chancellor of the Exchequer for the time being.

b. *Like a book*: see *Like *adv.*

18. book agent *U.S.*, one who pushes the sale of books; **book-boy**, a boy employed to fetch books for readers in a library; **book canvasser**, one who canvasses schools, public offices, etc., for the sale of books, esp. on the subscription system; **book-cloth**, a cloth manufactured for the bindings of books; **book-club**, delete (*obs.*) and add quot.; also, a society which produces books for its members, such as the Warton Club, the Roxburghe Club, the First Edition Club; **book concern** *U.S.*, an establishment engaged in the printing and sale of books; **book-edge gilder, marbler**, a bookbinder's workman who gilds or marbles the edges of books; **book ends** *sb. pl.*, a pair of (ornamental) book props (see below), used to keep a row of unshelved books in an upright position; **book-farmer**, one who farms with knowledge acquired from books; so **book-farming**; **book-folder**, (*a*) a printer's, bookbinder's, or stationer's employee who folds the paper sheets into page-size; (*b*) the paper wrapper of a newly-published book; **book-form**, in advb. phrase *in book form* (see sense 16); also *attrib.*; **book-gill**, the respiratory organ of the king-crab; **book hand**, the hand or writing used by the official transcribers of books before the invention of printing; **book hunt** *v. intr.*, to follow the pursuit of a book-hunter or searcher of old and rare volumes; **book-label**, a label bearing the title and author's name, the owner's name, etc., affixed to the cover of a book; **book-louse** (U.S. example); **book-lung**, the lamellate respiratory organs of a scorpion; **book mite** (see quot.); **book name**, a name of a plant or animal, other than the scientific name, used only in books; also *transf.*; **book-number**, 'in library-cataloguing, a particular number (or a number and a letter) designating the book in its proper sequence in the smallest division to which it belongs' (Cent. Dict. Suppl. 1909); **book piles**, a type of book-plate in which piles of books are used as the design; **book prop, support**, an angular support for the end of a row of books, esp. in a partly-filled shelf; **book-stamp**, a stamp for embossing the covers of books; **book-table**, a table intended solely or mainly for books; **book type** (see quot.); **book value** *Book-keeping*, the value of a commodity as shown by a firm's books, as distinguished from its market value; **book-world**, the world and the affairs of life as described in literature.

1848 *Philadelphia Almanac* Advt. 2 *Book canvassers and agents wanted. 1886 *Harper's Mag.* Dec. 162/1 They may both be glad to invoke the aid of the despised book agent, who carries literature from door to door. 1910 Mulford *Hopalong Cassidy* vii. 50 Was you ever an auctioneer..or a book agent? 1903 *Daily Chron.* 13 Feb. 5/1 His first situation was as *book-boy in the library of the Bristol Law Society. *Book canvasser [see *book-agent*, above]. 1921 *Dict. Occup. Terms* (1927) § 774 *Book canvasser*, canvasses schools, public offices, etc., for sale of technical or other books on subscription system. 1891 *Pall Mall Gaz.* 30 Nov. 7/1 Makers of *book-cloth. 1905 *Times* 20 Sept. 5/5 The privileges of *The Times* *Book Club are offered to those only who subscribe to *The Times* for a year. 1929 H. Williams (*title*) Book Clubs and Printing Societies of Great Britain and Ireland..published by the First Edition Club. *Ibid.* 7 The prototype of the book club, the Roxburghe. 1840 *Congress. Globe* 4 Jan. 170 This House has become the greatest '*book concern' in the Union. 1872 *Congress. Rec.* May 3909/3 Every book published by the Methodist Book Concern..is published on sized paper. 1900 *Ibid.* Mar. 3002/1 A little fellow who is attempting to establish a book concern in another place might be crushed. 1858 Simmonds *Dict. Trade*, **Book and card-edge gilder and marbler*, a workman who ornaments and finishes off the edges of books, etc. 1906 *Daily Chron.* 24 Sept. 10/6 Book-edge gilders wanted. 1921 *Dict. Occup. Terms* (1927) § 548 Book-edge marbler. 1855 *Trans. Mich. Agric. Soc.* VII. 806 A notorious *book farmer succeeded in making one of the best farms in the State of New York. 1859 *Ibid.* (1860) X. 573 Another man..primarily pronounces all *book farming a humbug. 1867 *Rep. Iowa Agric. Soc.* (1868) 125 The reason that so many take no particular pains to improve their stock is..they don't believe in book-farming. 1903 *Daily Chron.* 24 Feb. 8/5 *Bookfolder. Apply..Printing Dept. 1925 *Publishers' Weekly* 5 June 538/3 Blurbs, those interesting little paragraphs which appeared on bookfolders. 1893 *Photogr. Ann.* 337 Kodak camera, with..*book-form double dark slides. 1901 'Linesgood' & Gamble *Kipling* 161 This story passed from 'Lippincott's Magazine' to the pomp and pride of a book-form Edition. 1909 *Cent. Dict. Suppl.*, **Book-gill*. 1885 *Encycl. Brit.* XVIII. 143/2 Down to the time of the introduction of printing, writing ran in two lines—the set *book-hand and the cursive. 1893 E. M. Thompson *Handbk. Gk. & Lat. Palaeogr.* xix. 301 We find it convenient to treat the cursive or charter-hand as a separate branch of mediaeval English writing apart from the literary or book-hand. 1927 *Daily Tel.* 19 July 15/5 Lord Delamere sent a fifteenth century English manuscript..with others written in a very fine book-hand. 1880 Lang *Ballades in Blue China*, *Ballade of Bk.-hunter*, He *book-hunts, though December freeze. 1895 *Daily Chron.* 19 Dec. 6/2 An interesting copy of the works of Horace, having John Kemble's leather *book-label inside the covers. 1867 *Amer. Naturalist* I. 312 The little *book-louse (*Atropos*) scampering irreverently over the musty pages of his *Systema Naturæ*. 1897 Parker & Haswell *Zool.* I. 604 The organs of respiration are sometimes tracheæ, similar to those of Insects, sometimes *book-lungs or sacs containing numerous book-leaf-like lamellæ. 1883 *Encycl. Brit.* XVI. 528/2 *Cheyletidæ*, the so-called *book mites,..quite unconnected with books. 1886 Jamestown (Dakota) *Star* 27 Mar. 5 A Chinaman..gets a *book name when he goes to school. 1886 Britten & Holland *Dict. Engl. Plant-n.*, *Aconite*, a common book-name for *Aconitum Napellus*. 1902 *Encycl. Brit.* XXVI. 305/1 '*Book piles', exemplified by the *ex-libris* of W. Hewer (Samuel Pepys's secretary). 1895 *Funk's Standard Dict.*, *Book-stamp. 1909 Cyril Davenport (*title*) English Heraldic Bookstamps. 1895 G. Stikeman *Adjustable Book-support* 4 *Book supports, for partially filled shelves. 1903 *Daily Chron.* 23 May 4/6 A lovely inlaid *book-table. 1888 *Encycl. Brit.* XXIII. 699/1 Types are divided into two classes—*book type, including Roman and Italic, and job type. 1905 *Daily Chron.* 18 July 3/2 The whole book world is a commonwealth to which certain first, fixed principles apply. 1906 *Ibid.* 7 May 3/5 The book-world..is the edited reflection of life, brings the great facts of contrast into added prominence.

Book, *v.*

2. c. To enter orders in an order-book for goods to be supplied on credit.

1889 Swallow in *Co-operative News* 15 June 611 The pernicious system of *booking* has been allowed..to creep in.

d. To put (tackle) in a fishing-book.

1892 *Field* 18 June 921/3 We therefore book our cast, and wind up for the day.

3. b. To enter (the arrival or departure of an employee) in a book; so *to book in, out.*

intr. *to book off*, to sign an attendance book on going off duty.

1908 *Daily Chron.* 13 May 10/5 Baker's..Bookkeeper.—Young lady required, with good experience, to book men and keep books. *Ibid.*, Wanted young lady,..one able to book in. *Ibid.*, Shopwoman wanted, capable of booking out men. 1928 *Observer* 3 Feb. 12/7 To-night he drives his engine for the last time. To-morrow he 'books off'..and the Line knows him no more.

4. b. Also intr. *To book through*: to obtain a railway ticket to cover the whole journey.

1844 Dickens *Mart. Chuz.* li, The other [man], seating himself on the steps of the coach, remained in conversation with Slyme...'He's booked', observed the man. 'Through,' said Slyme. 1858 *Penny Cycl.* 2nd Suppl. 565/2 A man may now 'book through' from London to so many continental cities. 1884 [in Dict.].

Bookable (bu·kăb'l), *a.* [f. Book *v.* + -able.] That may be booked.

1903 *Daily Chron.* 30 Mar. 6/6, I think some [seats] should be bookable, and some should be unreserved. 1926 *Music & Letters* Apr. 102 The house..would be designed..to accommodate the largest possible audience..with all seats bookable.

Bookbindery. *U.S.* (Earlier examples.)

1817 S. R. Brown *Western Gaz.* 311 Zanesville..has a..post-office, book-bindery [and] two printing-offices. 1827 Drake & Mansfield *Cincinnati* viii. 64 Six Book Binderies.

Booked, *ppl. a.* Add:

4. Entered in an official book or list; scheduled.

1892 *Daily News* 3 June 5/4 That the Board of Trade shall have compulsory powers..to order a railway company to revise the booked time of the men. 1898 *Ibid.* 15 Dec. 7/4 Certain booked trains will be discontinued.

5. Having (a specified amount of) orders or engagements in one's book or books. Also with *up*; and in transf. sense: Having engagements, engaged (cf. 3).

1905 *Westm. Gaz.* 3 Oct. 9/1 The iron, steel, and allied trades are heavily booked. 1911 John Vincent in *Rep. Labour & Social Cond. Germany* III. Nos. vi and vii. 52 We found ..the trades were busy and well booked up with orders. *Mod.* I am booked up every night next week.

Bookful, *a.* Delete † *Obs.* and add:

2. Full or stored with books.

1896 *Literary World* 7 Aug. 115/2 Coleridge, in this bookful age, is..getting to be more and more *nominis umbra*. 1904 *Daily Chron.* 3 Oct. 3/4 In bookful loneliness.

Bookie (bu·ki). Also **booky.** Colloquial modification [see -y [6]] of Bookmaker 2.

1885 [see -y [6]]. 1887 *Pall Mall Gaz.* 15 Sept. 5/1 Both played their parts so well that they collared both the 'bookies' without any trouble at all.

Book-store. *U.S.* [Book *sb.* 17 a.] A book-shop.

1763 *Boston Even. Post* 3/3. 1785 A. Ellicott in *Life & Lett.* (1908) 51 Examined several Book stores. 1788 *Massachusetts Spy* 3 Apr. 4 Printed at Worcester (Massachusetts) by Isaiah Thomas, Printer, Bookseller and Stationer. Sold at his Bookstore. 1818 W. Darby *Tour to Detroit* (1819) 22 Bookstores afford..the best data from which can be calculated the state of public literary improvement. 1834 H. Brackenridge *Recoll.* viii. 80 This gentleman..had set up a book store and library in a wing of the house. 1860 Holland *Miss Gilbert's Career* xxiv. 430 There are none of his lame ducks here,..for bookstores are not abundant. 1888 *Harper's Mag.* Aug. 436/2 The town has at least one book-store of the first class. 1904 *Critic* May 434 One bookstore sold four hundred copies a month.

Booky, *a.* (Earlier U.S. example.)

1833 Paulding *Banks of Ohio* I. 194 (Th.) What! You're one of the booky fellers, that think on one thing while they are talking about another.

Boolian (bū·liăn), *a.* [f. the proper name *Boole* (see below) + -ian.] Of or pertaining to the theories of George Boole (1815–64), mathematician and logician.

1895 *Funk's Standard Dict.* s.v., Boolian algebra; Boolian notation in logic. 1902 *Encycl. Brit.* XXV. 312/2 Algebraic forms...The Boolian System.

Boom, *sb.*[2] Add:

3. b. *pl.* The floating timbers placed between portions of the lines of piles marking the regatta course at Henley-on-Thames, to prevent the encroachment of boats during a race.

1899 *Daily News* 5 July 4/7 It will be impossible to pronounce definitely on the success of the booms until the regatta is in full swing. 1902 *Encycl. Brit.* XXXII. 306/2.

4. b. *Fender, glancing*, or *sheer boom*, a boom erected to guide logs in the desired direction. *U.S.*

1896 *U.S. Monthly Weather Rev.* Nov. 407 (Cent. Dict. Suppl.) The driving of piles..to hold a sheer boom for the purpose of running the logs.

5. boom end *v. trans.*, to run out a boom or spar at the end of a yard so as to extend the foot of a sail; **boom mat** (cf. Mat *sb.*[1] 4); **boom net**, a fishing net connected with a boom.

1840 R. H. Dana *Bef. Mast* xxvii. 90 The studding-sail halyards were let go, and the yards *boom-ended. 1890 Clark Russell *Ocean Trag.* I. viii. 164 Then boom-ending her fore-topmast studdingsail she backed her main topsail. 1883 *Man. Seamanship for Boys* 182 In making a heavy *boom mat a fiddle is used instead of a loom. 1925 *Glasgow Herald* 25 Aug. 5 The relationships of the young year classes caught by *boom-net and seine-net to the mature herring in the drift-net fishery.

Boom, *sb.*[3] For *U.S.* read 'orig. *U.S.*', and add:

1. (Earlier example.)

1875 *Scribner's Mag.* July 277 in Farmer *Slang*, Another boom in prices is to be looked for.

3. A rush made by 'boomers' or settlers into a newly opened district or region of Indian land.

1891 *Daily News* 23 Sept. 5/1 The 'boom' of 1889 was the occupation of part of the above named district by settlers who were lucky enough to be first on the spot.

4. *attrib.* and *Comb.*, as *boom magic, -maker, price, time, value*, etc.; **boom city, town**, one that owes its origin, growth, or prosperity to a boom in a particular trade, mining, etc.

1886 *Leslie's Pop. Monthly* XXI. 306/1 Cities..whose inhabitants had yet to be gathered in from the four corners of the earth by boom magic. 1891 *Anthony's Photogr. Bull.* IV. 23 The old town of San Juan Capistrano I found had been divided in the 'boom' times. 1895 *Century Mag.* Aug. 6/8 2 The troop of boom-makers has actively given its perennial leisure to extravagant schemes of town-platting. 1897 *Daily News* 23 June 15/2 Supposing..that you had a boom time..and your trustees lent on the boom values. 1900 Smithwick *Evol. State* 19 Colonel De Witt was as enthusiastic as the real estate dealer in a *boom town* nowadays. 1902 *Daily Chron.* 24 Mar. 3/5 The boom prices did not come off. 1903 *Ibid.* 18 Dec. 5/3 Its rapid growth..resembles very closely a 'boom' mining town in America. 1904 *Philad. Public Ledger* 14 June 6 No 'boom city' of the West can boast such a record of amazing..growth. 1905 *Daily Chron.* 7 Nov. 4/5 Such..are the common incidents of a boom city. 1906 *N. Y. Even. Post* 4 Aug. 4 Quite as melancholy..are the frame-built 'boom' towns of the West, located where the railroad was once expected to go, but did not.

Boom, *v.*[2] Add:

2. *U.S.* (Earlier example.)

1798 *Boston Town Rec.* 45 [That] the Aqueduct Corporation be allowed the privilege of securing by booming their logs on such part of the beach at the foot of the Common.. as the Selection..may appoint.

b. To protect (a regatta course) from encroachment by pleasure boats during a race, by placing floating booms (*Boom *sb.*[2] 3 b) between the piles. Also with *off*. Hence **Boo·ming** *vbl. sb.*

1899 *Daily News* 29 Apr. 7/3 It is proposed to 'boom' the whole length of the course along the Bucks side and for some distance on the Berks side. 1900 *Ibid.* 6 July 7/4 Owing to the booming of the course, the expenses of the regatta are much heavier. 1902 *Encycl. Brit.* XXXII. 306/2 This proposal to boom off the [regatta] course was very severely criticized.

Boom, *v.*[3] For *U.S.* read 'orig. *U.S.*' and add:

1. (Earlier examples.)

1873 'Mark Twain' & C. D. Warner *Gilded Age* xxvii, There's $200,000 coming, and that will set things booming again. 1875 *Scribner's Mag.* July 272 Stocks may 'boom' to-day, but droop to-morrow.

Boom-boat. (Also **bomboat.**) [Boom *sb.*[2]] Any of the boats stowed in the booms of a vessel.

1867 Smyth *Sailor's Word-bk.* 1873 Bedford *Sailor's Pocket Bk.* vii. 271 By placing boats inside her present boom boats. 1893 *Daily News* 3 July 5/6 Seeing the critical condition of the Victoria,..boats were immediately prepared and boom boats got ready to be hoisted out.

Boomer[2]. Add:

2. A trappers' name for the North American rodent *Haplodon rufus.*

1890 *Chambers's Encycl.* V. 550 The trappers call it the 'Boomer' or 'Mountain Beaver'.

Boomer[3] (bū·məɹ). [f. Boom *sb.*[3] + -er [2].] A settler who takes part in a boom or rush to occupy a newly opened region.

1890 J. K. Bangs in *Harper's Mag.* Dec. 160/1 Donkey parties in the temporary canvass residences of the fashionable boomers had been held. 1891 *Daily News* 23 Sept. 5/1 A rush of 'boomers' into a newly-opened region of Indian land is one of the strangest..sights in the world.

Boomlet (bū·mlet). [f. Boom *sb.*[3] + -let.] A small boom on the Stock Exchange.

1897 (Dec. 10) H. Bottomley in Ware *Passing English* (1909) s.v., I may mention that during the recent West Australian boom—or, as some of my Stock Exchange friends prefer to call it, 'boomlet'—we succeeded in realising, etc. 1898 *Westm. Gaz.* 23 Apr. 9/2 A very favourable feature has been a recovery in Westralian stocks. Something like a boomlet prevailed at first. 1900 *London Stock Market Rep.* 18 Aug. 5 What may be called a Republican boomlet has been started in the Yankee corner. 1912 *Throne* 7 Aug. 238/2 The probability of a boom or a boomlet during the present month..appears to be very remote.

Boomslang (bū·mslæŋ). *S. Afr.* [Du. *boomslang*, f. *boom* tree + *slang* snake.] The Tree Snake, *Dispholidus typus.*

1849 Andrew Smith *Illustr. Zool. S. Afr.*, *Reptilia* Plate xiii, The natives of South Africa regard the *Boom-slange* as poisonous; but in their opinion we cannot concur. The *Boom-slange* [*Bucephalus capensis*] is generally found upon trees. 1912 Fitzsimons *Snakes S. Afr.* 136.

Boongary (bū·ŋgări). [Native name: *bangaray* in the Port Jackson dialect.] The tree-kangaroo of North Queensland, *Dendrolagus lumholtzii.*

1889 C. Lumholtz *Among Cannibals* xviii. 227 Upon the whole, the boongary is the most beautiful mammal I have seen in Australia.

Boorga, Boorka, var. *Burga, *Burka.

Boost, *sb.*[2] *U.S.* (Earlier examples.)

1825 J. Neal *Bro. Jonathan* II. 101 (Th.) Shall I give him a boost? or no? 1830 Seba Smith *Major Jack Downing* (1860) 114 (Th.), I got a pretty good boost in Boston, by the editors giving me recommendations.

Boost, *v.* Add:

1. Also, to assist over obstacles, to advance the progress of; to praise *up*, extol by puffing; also *absol.* orig. *U.S. colloq.* Hence **Boo·sting** *vbl. sb.*

1826 *Massachusetts Spy* 29 Nov. (Th.) The crooks, in danger of being boasted [*sic*], were compelled to knock under. 1834 Seba Smith *Major Jack Downing* 139 You..give me a lift into public life, and you've been a boosting me along ever since. 1845 *Yale Lit. Mag.* XI. 34 (Th.) There is one poor fellow getting his comrade to boost him, while he hangs to the skirts of the one above. 1887 F. Francis Jr. *Saddle & Mocassin* 121 If you think that I'm trying to boost the place up because it belongs to us. 1903 F. Norris *Respons. Novelist* 299 Considered at first as a fad, it has been at length boosted and foisted upon the public attention. 1907 *Westm. Gaz.* 26 Aug. 3/2 'They seem to give Nature a boost'; 'The man who boosts himself over a tough place' will jump into his regular place without 'any let-up';.. phrases such as these simply conceal the thought of the author. 1909 *Daily Chron.* 21 Oct. 3/5 In times like these, when trade and other factors are bad, it is the duty of the Press to 'boost' in the interests of the nation, for when trade is good it will 'boost' itself. 1910 *N. Y. Even. Post* 24 Feb. (Th.) Kindliness, optimism,..the national inclination to 'boost' and not to 'knock', are admirable virtues. 1920 *Chambers's Jrnl.* Aug. 557/2 These arrangements are supplemented by 'boosting' fans at intervals of about 2000 feet. 1925 Bennet Copplestone *Dead Men's Tales* ix, Though.. he dared not give her more than a reefed lug foresail, she was boosted along by continuous gales. 1926 *Publisher's Weekly* 16 Jan. 147 Perhaps advertising might help boost their sales. 1928 *Ibid.* 29 Sept. 375/2 Many important reviewers were boosting it as the more brilliant of the two books.

2. *Electr. trans.* To regulate (the electromotive force in an electric circuit).

1909 *Installation News* Jan. 1/2 With the result that the station man is seeking 'pastures new' whereby he may boost up his load. 1911 *Engineer* 10 Mar. 237/2 It is far more profitable to boost the pressure at the generating station.

Booster (bū·stəɹ). [f. Boost *v.* + -er [1].]

1. One who boosts. orig. and chiefly *U.S.*

1909 *Cent. Dict.* Suppl. 1920 *Glasgow Herald* 23 Aug. 7 It is not suggested that we should become 'blatant-boosters'. 1928 *Observer* 1 July 11/2 President Coolidge, a true 'booster' of his country.

2. *Electr.* A machine interposed in a circuit for the purpose of increasing (or decreasing) the electromotive force acting in the circuit.

1896 S. P. Thompson *Dynamo-Electric Mach.* (ed. 5) 726 A third service for which motor-dynamos are employed is to compensate the drop in voltage on long mains by inserting into the main at a distant point a series motor driving an armature placed as a shunt across the mains. Lahmeyer calls this device a 'far-leading' dynamo (Fernleitungs-dynamo). American electricians term it a 'booster'. 1902 *Encycl. Brit.* XXV. 34/1 Taking the current from the mains to the battery through a 'booster', that is, a dynamo arranged so that its E.M.F. is added to that of the mains. 1906 *Times, Engineering Suppl.* 22 Aug. 267/3 The use either of a large full-voltage battery for regulating purposes, a set of cells as back E.M.F.'s for the near feeders, or as a third alternative, the provision of extra boosters. 1911 *Engineer* 10 Mar. 237/3 A booster in use for boosting the pressure of an overhead conductor of an electric tramway system.

3. *attrib.* **Booster club** (*U.S.*).

1922 S. Lewis *Babbitt* i. § 4. 19 He stuck in his lapel the Boosters' Club button. 1923 *Glasgow Herald* 7 June 4 The deadening influences of a wife, a family, a motor car, and a Booster Club. 1929 *Daily Tel.* 8 Jan. 9/3 While other cities over the country are organising 'booster' clubs, New York [has] started a 'back to main street movement.'

Boosy. Add:

attrib. **boosey close**, the close in which the cow-sheds stand; **boosey** or **boosy pasture**, pasture land lying near the cow-sheds.

1794 T. Brown *Agric. Surv. Derbysh.* 45 A specified close, which the way-going tenant has for foddering his cattle in, under the name of a Boosey pasture. 1844 *Jrnl. R. Agric. Soc.* V. i. 86 Tenancy commences..on the 2nd of February as to all the other lands, except the boosey pasture. 1862 *Catal. Internat. Exhib.* II. x. 27 Boosey or manger bricks. 1905 *Oswestry & Border Counties Advertizer* (Advt.), 6 acres of Boozy Pasture. 1922 Weyman *Ovington's Bank* xxxvi, A countryman, whom the news had only just reached in his boosey-close or his rickyard.

Boot, *sb.*[1] **2.** Add: Later and U.S. examples are:

1811 A. Graydon *Mem.* (1846) 30 He picked up six or eight of my marbles, and throwing me down three or four times the number of his own, the amount of boot being apparently wholly unworthy of calculation, he decamped in a twinkling. 1831 Mrs. Royall *Southern Tour* II. 183, I asked no boot in the world. 1846–52 Mrs. Whitcher *Widow Bedott P.* xi. 115 I'll be darned if I wouldn't offer to swop for a small matter o' boot. 1888 'C. E. Craddock' *Broomsedge Cove* vi. 105 The horse-trade was complete, the exchange made, the boot paid.

Boot, *sb.*[3] Add:

1. b. *The boot is on the other leg* (delete † and add quots.). Also *the boot on the wrong leg* or *foot.*

1834 Carruthers *Kentuckian in N. Y.* I. 97 He's got the boot on the wrong leg. 1861 Mrs. Riddell *City & Suburb* 385 That's what I call putting the boot on the other leg with a vengeance. 1863 (*title*) The Boot on the Other Leg; or, Loyalty above Party. 1870 (*title*) The Boot on the Wrong Foot. 1899 [see Leg *sb.* 2 a].

c. (Additional phrases.)

1873 J. H. Beadle *Undevel. West* xxii. 435 It will be said in Western dialect, 'They died in their Boots.' 1879 Tourgee *Fool's Err.* xvi. 84 They are gittin so big in thar boots they can't rest [cf. *Big *a.* 3 e]. 1888 *Denver Republ.* 9 Apr. (Farmer, Slang) When in liquor he was quarrelsome and the prediction was commonly made that he would die with his boots on. 1890 *Adrian Times* 6 Mar., 'Gov. Luce,' he said, '..can beat Barnes out of his boots.'

d. *To give* (a person) *the boot* or *the order of the boot*: to 'kick out', dismiss, 'sack'. So *to get the boot.*

1888 Rider Haggard *Col. Quaritch* xii, There'll be the money to take over the Moat Farm and give that warmint the boot. 1904 *Minister's Gaz. Fashion* Dec. 219/2 Various accounts of 'padding the hoof', getting the 'boot', [etc.].

4. d. (Later examples.)

1858 *Life Among Mormons* 41 The mail is carried in the boots of stage-coaches. 1886 *Leslie's Pop. Monthly* XXI. [illegible] The great boot was securely strapped down over the baggage.

e. *U.S.* (See quots.)

1848–52 Webster, *Boot*, 3...An apron or leathern cover for a gig or chair, to defend persons from rain and mud. *This application is local and improper.* 1911 J. C. Lincoln *Cap'n Warren's Wards* i. 9 The 'boot' was a rubber curtain buttoned across the front of the buggy, extending from the dashboard to just below the level of the driver's eyes.

6. e. *Ornith.* An entire tarsal envelope characteristic of the legs of some birds.

1875 Coues *N. Amer. Birds* 71 Typical Thrushes. With the tarsus, in the adult, enveloped in one continuous plate, or 'boot'.

f. The feathered legs of some varieties of pigeons and poultry.

1895 *Poultry Chron.* III. 348/2 The boots, or as Shanghai fanciers would style it, the vulture hock, must be white. 1902 *Westm. Rev.* XXVI. 949 Instances..in which the feet of pigeons or fowls are abnormally feathered, or, as it is termed, furnished with 'boots'.

g. *Agric.* The uppermost leaf-sheath, just below the brush or head, of a broom-corn plant; also the lowest leaf-bearing internode on a stalk of wheat. *U.S.* 1909 *Cent. Dict.* Suppl.

7. *attrib.*, as *boot-upper*: = Upper *sb.* 1.

1879 [see *boot-crimp* in 8 below]. 1879 *Birmingham Daily Post* 21 June 5/3 Charged with..stealing a quantity of boot-uppers. 1906 *Times* 13 Dec. 4/2 The [stolen] boot uppers were found at the shop.

8. boot-clamp, -crimp (see quots.); **boot-grain**, a cowhide leather used for heavy boots; **boot-hole**, the place where boots are cleaned in a large establishment; **boot-hook** (U.S. example); **boot-jack**, also (*b*) a part of a railway line in which the boot of an unwary person is liable to become fixed between the rails; (*c*) *Theatr. slang*, an actor of utility parts; **boot machine operator, boot machinist**, any person engaged in any machine operation in the manufacture of boots; **bootman**, a dealer in boots and shoes; **boot powder**, a powder, as of soapstone, used for dusting the inside of a boot or shoe; **boot-strap**, the strap by which the skirt of a lady's riding habit is held down by the toe of the boot. See also *Boot-leg.

1875 Knight *Dict. Mech.*, **Boot-clamp*, a device for holding a boot while being sewed. *Ibid.*, **Boot-crimp*, a tool or machine for giving the shape to the pieces of leather designed for boot uppers. 1906 *Strand Mag.* June 683/1 If one of us gets returned they will put him into the *boot-hole, where he will have to clean the other members' boots! 1855 Q. K. Thompson *Doesticks* xxxiii. 297, I could forgive thee thy shae coats,..thy pantaloons so tight thou hadst to draw them on with *boot-hooks. 1890 T. M. Cooley, etc. *Railways Amer.* 222 At all places where two rails cross or approach each other..dangerous *boot-jacks are formed by the railroads. 1895 *Funk's Standard Dict.*, *Boot-jack*, a utility actor in a theater. 1898 *Engineering Mag.* XVI. 64/2 The 'Bootjack' Signals of the Lake Shore and Michigan Southern Ry. 1891 *Daily News* 30 Dec. 3/2 *Boot Powder. 1927 *Daily Express* 27 May 6/1 [Obtainable] from all *Bootmen. Fixing Extra. 1908 *Daily Chron.* 11 Sept. 5/5 He put her up, adjusted *boot-strap and skirt.

Boot, *v.*[3] Add:

4. To kick (a person) as a punishment or as a method of attack.

1883 D. C. Murray *By the Gate of the Sea* II. ix. 43, I have felt..an electric sensation in the right foot, indicative..of a desire to boot a noble swell or two who hover in her train. 1890 *Daily News* 11 Feb. 7/3 At him, lads! Boot and kick him! 1892 Stevenson *Wreckers* xii, I saw a big hulking beast of a Dutchman booting the ship's boy. 1913 'Ian Hay' *Happy-go-lucky* i, You will be booted for that ..., my lad.

b. To kick (a person *out of* a place).

1898 *Westm. Gaz.* 1 Oct. 7/2 Burgess literally booted him out of office.

c. *fig.* To 'kick out', get rid of, dismiss.

1893 *Westm. Gaz.* 13 Nov. 2/2 Who flocked together in the House of Lords..to 'boot' the Home Rule Bill. 1907 *Daily Chron.* 5 Nov. 10/4 That German scrub wants me to boot him.

5. To kick (the ball) with more than the usual vigour. *Football colloquialism.*

1914 *Morning Post* 2 Mar. 4/1 The ball was booted too hard and the defence got the touch down.

Boot-black. (See Boot *sb.*[3] 8.)

1817 *Essex Inst. Hist. Coll.* VIII. 246 They had a boot-black and barber. 1849 D. Nason *Jrnl.* 112 The bootblack came round very cautiously. 1855 Barnum *Life* 125 The boot-black asked us to remember him. 1869 S. Bowles *Our New West* xiv. 279 The boot-blacks and baths and barbers are of European standards. 1883 [see Boot *sb.*[3] 8].

Bootee. (U.S. examples.)

1799 *Aurora* (Philad.) 15 Nov. (Th.) For sale, 180 pairs of bootees. 1800 *Spirit of Farmer's Museum* (1801) 262 He is, literally, made up of marechal powder, cravat, and bootees. 1844 *Congress. Globe* 11 Mar. 361/3 Men's boots or bootees ..., women's boots or bootees,..children's boots, bootees, and shoes. 1848 Bartlett *Dict. Amer.*, *Bootee*, a half boot, a boot without a top, or a shoe made like a boot without a leg.

Boot-leg, bootleg (bū·tleg). *U.S.* [See Boot *sb.*[3] 7.] The leg of a tall boot, or the leather cut out for this.

1855 M. M. Thompson *Doesticks* xxi. 181 The man who would..hopefully essay the concoction of a satisfactory stew from jack-knife-handles and bootlegs. 1887 *Harper's Mag.* Dec. 78/2 Timothy..drew his 'shooting-iron' from his boot-leg, and cocked it with a metallic click. 1888 'C. E. Craddock' *Broomsedge Cove* iv. 65 He..paused only to slip into his long boot-leg a 'shootin' iron'.

b. *attrib.* with reference to illicit trading in liquor. Cf. *Boot-legger.

a 1889 *Omaha Herald* (Barrère & Leland) There is as much whisky consumed in Iowa now as there was before,..'for medical purposes only,' and on the boot-leg plan. 1921 W. D. Newton in *Chambers's Jrnl.* Mar. 154/2 Joe left him apparently sleeping the solid sleep of 'bootleg' whisky in his shack. 1922 C. Sandburg *Slabs of Sunburnt West* 25 Burnt like a shot of bootleg booze. 1929 *Morn. Post* 7 June 11/2 Alleged bootleg ring.

Hence **Boot-legger**, one who carries liquor in his boot-legs; hence, an illicit seller of liquor; **Boot-legging**, illicit trade in liquor; also *attrib.* and *ppl. a.*; whence **Boo·tleg** *v. trans.*, to traffic illicitly in (liquor); also *transf.*

1890 *Voice* (N. Y.) July 17 The 'bootlegger' is a grim spectre to the anti-Prohibitionist...He is a man who wears boots in whose tops are concealed a flask or two of liquor. 1904 *Topeka Daily Capital* 29 May 4 A United States marshall arrested a boot-legger at Osborne for selling whisky without a government licence...Bootlegging is a bad business. 1919 T. K. Holmes *Man fr. Tall Timber* vi. 59 Who's got the forty-rod, Steve?..There's a bootlegging place somewhere, I'll be bound. 1922 *Glasgow Herald* 16 Sept. 9 He denied that he had been engaged in 'bootlegging' along the American shore. 1927 'Sax Rohmer' *Moon of Madness* 14 A deck load of Dagos..that would have frightened a Chicago bootlegger. 1927 *Saturday Even. Post* (N.Y.) 24 Dec. 44/2 It would make me into a bootlegging grandfather. 1928 *Observer* 5 Feb. 18/2 Negroes who carried bootlegged liquor. *Ibid.*, The result is that books are bootlegged in Boston as liquor is bootlegged in other cities. 1928 *Saturday Even. Post* (N. Y.) 10 Mar. 169/1 Since 1924 an unknown number [of Mexicans] have been 'bootlegged' across the border.

Bootlick, *sb.* (bū·tlik). orig. *U.S.* [f. Boot *sb.*[3] + Lick *v.*] A toady. Also (in British use) **Boo·tlicker**, in same sense. So **Boo·tlick** *v. intr.* and *trans.* (orig. *U.S.*) to toady (to); also **Boo·tlicking** *vbl. sb.*

1845 J. J. Hooper *Adv. Simon Suggs* v. 58 A young man was inclined to boot-lick anybody suspected of having money. 1846–52 Mrs. Whitcher *Widow Bedott P.* xxvii. 331 Sweezer's very intimit with the squire's folks—a kind of 'boot-licker tew'em. 1860 Bartlett *Dict. Amer.* (ed. 3), *Boot-lick*, one who cringes to and flatters a superior for the purpose of obtaining favors; a lickspittle, a toady. 1890 Farmer *Slang*, *Bootlick*, *subs.* (American), a flunkey, hanger-on...In England such a one is called a 'bootlicker'. *Verb.* To toady; to hang on; to undertake 'dirty' work. 1891 *Pall Mall Gaz.* 12 Dec. 5/1 Debased boot-lickers. 1894 *Current Hist.* (Buffalo, N.Y.) IV. 472 Working his way by scheming and bootlicking into the good graces of..a young idiot of a lord. 1906 *Westm. Gaz.* 27 June 2/1 If boot-licking became permanently fashionable, we should in course of time have various grades of boot-lickers. 1915 *N. Y. Tribune* 24 Mar. 5/3 It..accused 'The Spectator's' staff of grafting and bootlicking their advertisers. 1924 B. J. Hendrick *Life of Walter H. Page* I. 19 That the recipient is either a humbug or a bootlicker.

Booze, *sb.* Add:

1. b. Alcoholic drink, chiefly beer; *U.S.* esp. spirits.

1859 *Slang Dict.* 1895 *Daily Tel.* 2 Dec. 5/1 She heard some men shout that they wanted some more booze. Mr. Justice Wright 'What?' Mr. Willis: 'Booze, my lord, drink'. Mr. Justice Wright: 'Ah!' 1896 *Voice* (N.Y.) 16 July 1/6 The Duckworth club..consumed large quantities of booze. 1900 *Daily News* 8 Dec. 6/2 On his way home he drops into a pub, and gets some 'booze'. 1904 *Omaha Daily Bee* 6 July 3 A large number of those who expected to celebrate the Fourth simply had to go without booze.

c. *attrib.* and *Comb.*

1896 G. Ade *Artie* xii. 110 He's..dug up the long green and he's puttin it out at the booze joints. 1916 C. Sandburg *Chicago Poems* 170 A bricklayer and a booze-fighter. 1922 H. L. Foster *Adv. Trop. Tramp* v. 60 After that the police had a private booze-party of their own on the proceeds. *Ibid.* ix. 127 Riotous booze-fights..were less in evidence.

2. b. Phrase. *To be on the booze*: to be having a spell of hard drinking.

1889 'R. Boldrewood' *Robbery under Arms* ii. (1890) 11 Poor old Mr. Howard wasn't always on the booze.

Bora[2] (borā·). Also **bor(r)ah.** [Hindi *bohrā*.] A Mohammedan trader. Also *attrib.*

1698 Fryer *Acc. E. India & P.* 93 Schisms they have made, as *Bilkim*, *Jemottee*, and the lowest of all is *Borrah*. 1822 Maria Graham *Jrnl. Res. India* 33 The inside of a Borah's box is like that of an English country shop. 1863 Badger *Introd. to Vartheme* (Hakl. Soc.) p. xlix, A considerable trade is still carried on, chiefly by Borah merchants of Guzerat and Cutch. 1876 *Encycl. Brit.* IV. 537/1 Borás, a class of commercial Mahometans.

Bora[3] (bō·rā). [Aboriginal Australian.] A rite amongst the aborigines of eastern Australia, constituting the admission of a young black to the rights of manhood.

1875 W. Ridley *Kamilaroi* 24 Girdle-bōr or būr. (Hence Bora, the ceremony of initiation into manhood, where the candidate is invested with the belt of manhood.) 1885 Mrs. C. Praed *Austr. Life* 24 The great mystery of the Blacks is the Bora—a ceremony at which the young men found worthy receive the rank of warriors. 1892 J. Fraser *Aborigines of New South Wales* 6.

Boraciferous (bōrăsi·fĕrəs), *a.* [f. *borac-*, Borax + -(i)ferous.] Containing or yielding borax.

1886 *Sci. Amer. Supp.* 27 Sept. 9093 The boraciferous basin of the Sultan Chair, near the Simaov River.

Borak (bǫ·rək). Also **-ack.** *Australian.* ['Aboriginal word of New South Wales' (Morris *Austral English*). See *Barrack *v.*] Gammon, chaff, banter; esp. in *to poke borak*, to make or poke fun.

1845 T. McCombie *Arabin or Adv. Colonist* 273 *Borack*, gammon, nonsense. 1898 in M. Davitt *Life & Progr. Australia* xxxv. 192 A jest is 'poking borac'. 1904 *Blackw. Mag.* June 832/1 One of the crowd was poking borak and said something pretty bad to him at the beginning.

Bo·rated, *a.* [f. Borate + -ed.] (See quot.)

1901 Dorland *Med. Dict.* (ed. 2), *Borated*, combined with or containing borax.

Borax. Add:

3. borax carmine (see quots.).

1887 *Amer. Naturalist* XXI. 596 For staining, borax-carmine was used. 1890 Billings *Nat. Med. Dict.*, *Borax carmine*, an aqueous solution of borax and carmine...A pure and intense nuclear stain if bleached with an acid.

Bordeaux. Add:

2. Any of several red azo-dyes derived from beta naphthol; the shade of red so produced.

1904 *Westm. Gaz.* 10 Mar. 4/2 Bordeaux-coloured straw. 1909 *Ibid.* 11 Jan. 5/2 The various shades of violet, blue, and what we have called Bordeaux.

3. *Bordeaux mixture*: a mixture composed of blue vitriol, lime, and water, used for the destruction of fungi.

1892 R. Veitch & Son *Prev. Potato Dis.* 4 The Bordeaux Mixture, or 'Bouillie Bordelaise'. 1921 *Discovery* May 130/1 Bordelaise, or Bordeaux mixture..was first used to cover grapes growing alongside paths and roads to prevent 'finger blight'.

Border, *sb.* **12.** Add: **border ruffian** *U.S.* (see sense 3 c and quots.); hence **border-ruffianism** (cf. 3 c); **border states** *U.S.* (*a*) the southern States bordering on the northern; (*b*) the northern States bordering on Canada.

1856 *Congress. Globe* 5 Mar. 585/3 The Missouri '*border ruffians', as they have been termed. 1857 J. Taylor in *Jrnl. Discourses* V. 116 A great majority of the people of the West, on the borders, may be emphatically termed 'Border ruffians'. The Eastern people call them by that name. 1864 *Congress. Globe* June 3234/2 We in Kansas have carried on a war for years against Indians, against border ruffians and against rebels. 1870 *Ibid.* Apr. 2391/1 While Senators were denying the existence of *border-ruffianism in Kansas, border ruffians were laying waste and murdering people. 1872 Eggleston *Hoosier Schoolm.* vi. 71 It is out of these materials that border ruffianism has grown. 1849 *Niles' Reg.* 14 Feb. 97/3 The *border States of the South. 1860 *Congress. Globe* 19 Dec. 139/3 It is an intimidation to the border States, alluding especially, I suppose, to Virginia, Maryland, Kentucky, and Missouri. They constitute the first tier of the border slave States. 1863 'Gail Hamilton' *Gala-Days* 92 For these Border State men..I have found a profound contempt. 1888 A. C. Gunter *Mr. Potter* viii, Miss Potter still keeps her Border-State accent and her Border-State manners. 1904 *Louisville Courier Jrnl.* 12 July 4 The Free Silver Fetish..drove us to close quarters in the Border States. 1916 *U.S. Weather Bureau* (Boston) Aug. 3 (Canadian frontier).

Borderland. Add:

b. Often in sense 'debatable ground'; the 'land between this world and the next.'

1894 F. Podmore *Apparitions & Thought-Transference* xi. 249 The voice in this case awoke the percipient,..but it was of the 'borderland' type. *Ibid.* 257 The hallucination should be classed as a 'borderland' case. 1898 *Daily News* 30 July 5/5 One thing about the deceased deputy may interest 'Borderland' readers. 1909 *Times Lit. Suppl.* 14 Jan. 9/1 It is a vague, borderland word.

3. *attrib.* = *Border-line 2.

1896 *Brit. Med. Jrnl.* 25 Jan. 61/1 Mental or Borderland case. 1904 E. G. Younger *Insanity in Every-Day Pract.* 99 Borderland states..are cases of nervous weakness which do not quite fit in with any of the recognised forms of insanity. *Ibid.* 101 Dr. Walsh has told me of a borderland case under his care which benefited greatly under his treatment. 1904 *Westm. Gaz.* 1 Dec. 6/3 He regarded the deceased's as a 'borderland' case.

Border-line.

1. The strip of land along the border between two countries or districts; a frontier-line; often *fig.*

1869 *Cassell's Mag.* Dec. 31/1 On the very border-line of the Black Country. 1892 Kipling *Barrack-r. Ball.*, *East & West* 80 Thou must harry thy father's hold for the peace of the Border-line.

2. *attrib.* or as *adj.* Occupying a border-line; esp. (*a*) Verging on the indecent or obscene; (*b*) Verging on insanity.

1907 F. J. Poynton in *Edin. Med. Jrnl.* Sept. 232 There are border-line cases which are well worthy of consideration by those who are interested in this form of arthritis. 1908 *Practitioner* Aug. 280 The so-called 'border-line' cases in which it is doubtful if the entire growth can be taken away. 1913 R. H. Cole *Mental Dis.* 223 Many come within the range of the so-called 'Border-line' cases. 1917 E. F. Ballard *Epit. Mental Dis.* 10 Therapeutic suggestive conversation with these early or border-line types of disorder is never wasted. 1927 *Observer* 30 Oct. 7 A highly interesting borderline subject between Law and Economics. 1928 *Sunday Express* 29 Apr. 3/4 Men are fond of 'thrillers'. Girls prefer rather shocking 'border-line' books. 1928 *Daily Tel.* 11 May 7 [He] described the cases..as border-line cases, and bound them over under probation for two years.

Bore, *v.* Add:

1. f. *intr.* 'To be pierced or penetrated by an instrument that turns; as, this timber does not bore well'.

1828–32 Webster.

Boree (bǫ·rī). [Aboriginal *booreah* fire.] A variety of myall, *Acacia pendula*, found in Eastern Australia.

1889 J. H. Maiden *Usef. Native Plants* 363 'Weeping', or 'True myall'...Called 'Boree' by aboriginals, and often 'Boree', or 'Silver-leaf Boree', by the colonists of Western New South Wales. 1890 'R. Boldrewood' *Squatter's Dream* iii. 30 Myall and boree belts of timber.

Borer. Add: 1. d. A bagman, drummer. *U.S.*

1836 *Philad. Public Ledger* 23 Aug. (Th.) [Drummers in Philadelphia] are called borers, probably from some resemblance in qualities to a worm that infests fruit trees. 1856 *Knickerbocker Mag.* Oct. XLVIII. 407 Felicien B. blessed the drummers and borers of New York.

Boresome (bōə·ɹsǒm), *a.* [f. Bore *sb.*[2] + -some.] Tending to be a bore, boring. Hence **Bo·resomeness.**

1868 Ld. R. Gower in *Rec. & Remin.* (1903) 150 So little real enjoyment to make up for so much loss of time and boresomeness. 1895 *Nineteenth Cent.* Sept. 474, I spent a boresome fortnight at Aden. 1905 Elinor Glyn *Viciss. Evangeline* 152 They were all casual and indifferent to their poor wives! and boresome, and bored!! 1925 P. A. Scholes *Second Bk. Gramophone Rec.* p. xii, There is..a degree of boresomeness in some of Beethoven's compositions.

Boring, *vbl. sb.*[1] Add: 1. b. *pl.* The chips or dust produced in boring; also called *boring-dust*.

1847 in Webster.

Boring, *ppl. a.*[1] 1. Add: **boring sponge,** a saltwater sponge of the genus *Cliona*, which bores shells.

1881 *Cassell's Encycl. Dict.* 1885 *Encycl. Brit.* XVIII. 107/2 *Cliona*, the boring sponge, destroys the shells and so injures the oyster.

Bo·ringness. [f. Boring *ppl. a.*[2] + -ness.] The quality of being boring or annoying.

1893 *Sketch* 316/2 His boringness is a quality inherent in him...Boringness springs, surely, in some measure from want of tact. 1927 *Observer* 28 Aug., Our priggishness and boringness.

Born, *pa. pple.* *Born and bred*: see Breed *v.* 11. *Born in the purple*: see Purple *sb.* 2 d.

Borné (borne), *a.* [Fr., pa. pple. of *borner* to limit.] Limited in scope, outlook, mental equipment, or the like.

1850 *Househ. Words* 3 Aug. 434/1 The Rockvilles remained high, proud, bigotted, and *borné*. 1852 W. R. Greg *Misc. Ess.* Ser. ii. (1884) 234 Lord Sidmouth—the shallowest, narrowest, most *borné*, and most benighted of the old Tory crew. 1883 *Macm. Mag.* Dec. 92/2 A mind so *borné* upon some sides of it.

Bornean (bǭ·ɹnɪ̆ăn), *a.* and *sb.* [f. *Borneo* (see below) + -an.] Of or pertaining to, a native of, Borneo, the largest island in the Malay Archipelago.

1876 *Encycl. Brit.* IV. 59/1 The Chinese..form..one of the most valuable elements in Bornean civilization. *Ibid.*, The former class [of Chinese] are called Kehs by the Borneans. 1920 *Q. Rev.* July 175 Their ancient Italian forefathers..were clearly once at much the same grade of social development as the Bornean tribes.

Bornite (bōə·ɹnəit). *Min.* [ad. G. *bornit* (1845), f. the name of Ignatius von *Born*, an Austrian mineralogist (1742–91): see -ite[1].] A brittle reddish-brown sulphide of copper and iron; also called *purple copper ore* or *erubescite*. Hence **Borni·tic** *a.*

1868 Dana *Min.* (ed. 5) 44. 1877 *Encycl. Brit.* VI. 347/2 Erubescite, bornite, or horseflesh ore is a sulphide of copper and iron much richer in copper than the ordinary pyrites. 1896 *Times* 21 Aug., The great bornite mine at Nelson (British Columbia). 1898 *Daily News* 8 Mar. 2/7 The immense rich bornite ore body.

Boronia (borōu·niă). [Named after Francesco *Borone*, an Italian botanist (1769–94).] A plant of the rutaceous genus so named, a sweet-scented Australian shrub.

1852 Mundy *Antipodes* I. 76 The Boronias shoot up their slender stems..towards the sun. 1896 *The Melburnian* 28 Aug. 53 (Morris) The scent of boronia and the odour of wattle-blossom greet us from baskets of the flower-girl.

Borough. Add:

3. d. An incorporated town or village; a town having a warden or chief burgess as its official head. *U.S.*

1828–32 Webster s.v., In Connecticut, this word, *borough*, is used for a town or a part of a town, or a village, incorporated with certain privileges, distinct from those of other towns and of cities; as the Borough of Bridgeport. 1841 *Stat. Connecticut* (1854) 329 The wardens and a majority of the burgesses of any such borough, may, in like manner, authorize such an alley to be kept at any place in any such city or borough. 1919 H. L. Mencken *Amer. Lang.* 296 This is now Allegany for the Maryland county..and Allegheny for the Pittsburg borough and the Pennsylvania county. 1925 G. P. Krapp *Eng. Lang. in Amer.* I. 178 Now that the word Manhattan has been legalized as the name of the Borough of Manhattan, it is possible it may become colorlessly official and lose some of its romantic glamour.

e. (*a*) In New Zealand, a village, township, or town having a special governing body called a borough council; (*b*) In New South Wales, a municipal corporation of not less than 1,000 inhabitants and not more than 9 square miles in area. In Victoria, such a municipality of not less than 300 inhabitants.

1865 *Baillière's Victorian Gazetteer* 59 Brunswick is a borough township,..in the..electoral district of E. Bourke boroughs. 1867 *Acts New Zealand* 31 Vict. No. 24 § 29 There shall be in and for each single borough a council consisting of nine councillors. 1874 *Silver's Handbk. Australia & New Z.* (ed. 2) 131 At the end of 1871 there were sixty-four corporate towns and boroughs, containing within their municipal limits about one-half the population. A borough must not have an area of more than nine square miles.

7. c. **borough court,** a court of limited jurisdiction held in a borough by special privilege; **borough sessions,** a court held by the recorder of a borough, usually quarterly, established under the Municipal Corporations Act of 1835.

1769 Blackstone *Comm.* Index, Borough courts. 1835 *Act 5 & 6 Will. IV* c. 76 § 110 *marg.*, Offenders committed to Borough Sessions whose Jurisdiction is taken away to be tried in the adjoining County.

Borrow, *v.*[1] Add:

1. d. *trans.* and *intr. Golf.* (See quots.)

1897 *Encycl. Sport* I. 472/1 *Borrow*, to play a ball up a hill or slope, instead of straight across it, so that the slope will cause the ball to return towards the hole. 1909 Vaile *Mod. Golf* 55 You allow for the slope..and the curve..will be the result if you have correctly estimated length and the amount you ought to 'borrow'...In golfing language, 'always borrow enough'. *Ibid.* 64 Both these cuts may be used when putting across a slope to hold the ball up against the natural tendency to run down a hill. If they are used it will obviously be unnecessary to 'borrow' so much in allowing for the slope.

e. *To borrow trouble*: to go out of one's way to meet trouble. *colloq.*

2. b. In organ-building: see next.

1894 T. Elliston *Organs & Tuning* 76 Borrowing from one stop to form part of another is undesirable; the wind coming sometimes from one source, and at other times from another, or from both sources at once, make it impossible for the note to be always in tune...The Pedal Organ is somewhat exempt from the faults of borrowing, inasmuch as usually only one note is used at a time. 1902 J. W. Hinton *Organ Constr.* (ed. 2) 64 *Borrowing*, arranging a certain number of pipes so as to be common to two or more stops. 1905 T. Casson *Pedal Organ* 24, I once tried the experiment of borrowing the Quint from a manual Bourdon. *Ibid.* 27 The borrowing must be economical; that is, it must cost less in room or money, or both, than actual independent pipes. 1927 Seth Bingham in *The Organ* VII. 75 While he was about it, the builder might have borrowed this 'creamy' bourdon into the pedal.

Borrowed, *ppl. a.* Add:

2. b. In organ-building, said of a pipe, a stop, or a set of them which is sounded at the expense of another or is incomplete of itself and is eked out by the use of pipes of another stop or set.

1840 in Grove *Dict. Mus.* (1880) II. 600/2 'Borrowed' Solo Organ. 1880 *Ibid.* 595/1 Choir Organ. 2 real stops; 4 borrowed...Borrowed by communication from the Great Organ. *Ibid.* 595/2 The extra department consisted of a complete borrowed organ of 13 stops derived from the Great Organ. *Ibid.*, Second Great Organ. 13 borrowed stops.

Bo·rrow-pit. [app. f. Borrow *v.*[1]] In civil engineering, an excavation formed by the removal of material to be used in filling or embanking. Also **Bo·rrow-hole.**

1898 Kipling *Day's Work* 2 The raw earth-ends were..alive with hundreds upon hundreds of tiny asses climbing out of the yawning borrow-pit below with sackfuls of stuff. 1901 Manson in *Practitioner* Mar. 258 'Borrow-holes' in railway embankments. 1907 *Notes on Books* June 267/2 An easily applied check on borrow-pit measurements.

Borsch (bǭɹʃ, ‖ borʃtʃ). Also borsh, bortsch, borscht. [Russian *borshch*.] A Russian ragout of several ingredients, coloured with red beet-juice.

1887 *Scott. Leader* 15 Sept. 5 Gentle reader, have you ever partaken of bo[r]sh? 1892 Zangwill *Childr. Ghetto* v, A favourite soup was *Borsch*, which was made with beetroot, fat taking the place of the more fashionable cream. 1927 *Blackw. Mag.* Sept. 294/1 Caviare, crimson bowls of bortsch, with thick seasoned cream. 1929 *Daily Tel.* 22 Jan. 7/6 The borscht is a delicious consommé of beef and duck, ham, beetroot.

Borsella (bǫɹse·lă). [Perversion of It. Procello.] In glass-making, an instrument for modifying the form of vessels.

[1699 tr. *H. Blancourt's Art of Glass* 31 The Instruments mark'd E. serve to finish the Work, which the Italians call *Ponteglo, Passage, Procello, Spici*, and also *Borsello*, whereof we want the Figure.] 1823 Crabb *Technol. Dict.*, *Borsella* (Mech.), an instrument with which glass makers contract or extend their glasses at pleasure. [In mod. Dicts.]

Borstal (bōə·ɹstăl). [Name of a town near Rochester in Kent.] Now in full *Borstal Institution*: A reformatory for 'juvenile adults', conducted according to the method put into practice at Borstal prison in 1902 and adopted afterwards elsewhere. So *Borstal prisoner, system*, etc.

1902 *Encycl. Brit.* XXXII. 8/2 More positive and more tangible results are hoped for from the less ambitious methods to be pursued at Borstal. 1907 *Daily Chron.* 6 June 5/4 The 'Borstal prisoner'. 1907 *Borstal System* 2 Every lad who is imprisoned in Dartmoor or Borstal passes into the care of the Borstal Association on his discharge. 1909 *Westm. Gaz.* 21 Jan. 1/3 When in 1895 the experiment of separating the juvenile from the adult criminals was made, Bedford Prison was the chosen theatre. Had it been continued there we should now be hearing of the Bedford instead of the Borstal system...In a year or two the experiment was transferred to Borstal, where the whole prison..was given up for the purpose. 1917 *Times* 7 Feb. 5/6 Four youths have escaped from the Borstal Institution, Rochester. 1920 *Glasgow Herald* 14 June 10 Reports are furnished by the Governors of Barlinnie Prison and Duke Street Prison, Glasgow, on the Borstal sections. 1921 *Ibid.* 15 Nov. 6 The Borstal boys have five meals a day at Portland.

Borussian (bouɹʊ·ʃăn), *sb.* and *a.* [f. med.L. *Borussi* pl. or *Borussia* (app. etymologizing perversion of stem *Prūs-*, as if f. Slavonic *po* by, alongside + *Russia*): see -ian.] = Prussian.

1882 *Encycl. Brit.* XIV. 702/1 The Lithuanian stem was divided into three main branches:—the Borussians or Prussians; the Letts..and the Lithuanians. *Ibid.*, The Borussians soon fell under the dominion of Germans. 1921 *Trans. Scott. Eccles. Soc.* 126 So far as they are free from Wendish or Borussian admixture. 1925 *Contemp. Rev.* Jan. 72 The country was occupied by aboriginal tribes of Finns, Letts, Lithuanians, Borussians, and Poles or kindred Slavs.

Borzoi (bǭ·ɹzoi). [Russian Борзой swift.] A breed of dog, also called the Russian or Siberian wolf-hound.

1892 *Pall Mall Gaz.* 11 Feb. 7/2 The Grand Duke owns seventy of these barzois [*sic*] or Russian wolfhounds. 1892 *Field* 5 Mar. 325/1 There seems to be a general feeling among owners of Borzois that the time has now arrived for the successful starting of a special club. 1895 *Westm. Gaz.* 9 Oct. 7/2 The Borzois Club is going to be remodelled, but I am glad to hear..that there is no immediate intention of altering the existing scale of Borzoi points.

Bosch(e, erron. ff. *Boche.

Bosh, *sb.*[4] *slang.* [ad. Romany *bosh-* to crow, fiddle, etc., a. Skr. *vāś-* to low, bellow.] A fiddle. *Comb.*: bosh-faker, boshman, one who plays a fiddle.

1859 *Slang Dict.*, *Bosh*, a fiddle. *Bosh-Faker*, a violin player. 1865 Nixon *Peter Perfume* 102 'Boshman' in the old-hand vernacular signifies a fiddler. 1876 Hindley *Cheap Jack* 231 Can you rocker Romanie, Can you fake a bosh?

Boshy (bǫ·ʃi), *a.* [f. Bosh *sb.*[3] + -y[1].] Of the nature of bosh; contemptible, trumpery.

1882 'F. Anstey' *Vice Versâ* iv, There was no dancing, only boshy games and a conjuror.

Bosniac (bǫ·zniæk). Also -ak. [ad. F. *Bosniaque*, or G. *Bosniake*, ad. Russ. Босніякъ.] = *Bosnian *sb.*

1836 *Penny Cycl.* V. 231/1 The inhabitants of Bosnia are composed of Bosniaks, a race of Sclavonian origin. 1861 *Chambers's Encycl.* II. 257/1 The Bosnians, or Bosniaks,..are partly Mohammedans..and partly of the Greek and Roman Catholic Churches. 1886 *Fortn. Rev.* Jan. 146 All this petty persecution has made Austrian rule odious among the Bosniacs. 1920 *Edin. Rev.* Oct. 218 The ruling race absorbed large numbers of Christians, Greeks, Slavs, and later on Albanians and Bosniacs.

Bosnian (bǫ·zniăn), *a.* and *sb.* [f. *Bosnia*: see -ian. Cf. F. *bosnien*.] A. *adj.* Of or pertaining to Bosnia, a province lying west of Serbia. B. *sb.* A native of Bosnia.

1836 *Penny Cycl.* V. 230/1 The Verbas, another Bosnian river, rises in the heart of the country. 1847 Mrs. A. Kerr tr. *Ranke's Hist. Servia* 167 He opposed to the great Bosnian army about 1500 men. 1924 *Contemp. Rev.* Nov. 620 'The Bosnians are never satisfied', we were told.

Bosom, *sb.* Add:

3. d. The front of a shirt. *U.S.*

1872 *N. Y. Times* 24 Apr. 8 Advt. (Hoppe) Shirts made to order, with beautifully embroidered Bosoms. 1903 *N. Y. Tribune* 27 Sept., The waiters did not wear..shirts with soiled bosoms. 1905 *N. Y. Even. Post* 26 May 12 Men's Unlaundered Shirts... Three-ply linen bosoms reinforced back and front.

9. **bosom-knee,** 'a knee secured to a vessel's side and the after side of a deck-beam; also called *lap-knee*' (Cent. Dict. Suppl. 1909).

Boss, *sb.*[1] Add:

3. g. A soft pad used in ceramics and glass-manufacture for smoothing and making uniform the colours applied with oil to a glass or porcelain surface, and for cleaning gilded surfaces.

1860 Ure *Dict. Arts* (ed. 5) III. 506 The 'boss' is made of soft leather. 1874 Knight *Dict. Mech.* s.v. *Bossing*, The bossing is laid on with a hair-pencil, and leveled with a boss of soft leather. 1879 E. C. Hancock *Amateur Pottery* 49 The boss consists of a lump of cotton wool, screwed up, as it were, in two or three thicknesses of fine soft linen.

h. (See quot.)

1874 Knight *Dict. Mech.*, *Boss*, a plate of cast-iron secured to the back of the hearth of a traveling-forge.

Boss, *sb.*[6] (Earlier examples.)

1806 W. Irving *Life & Lett.* (1862) I. 96, I had to return, make an awkward apology to boss, and look like a nincompoop. 1818 H. B. Fearon *Sk. Amer.* 59 My boss..ordered me to turn out every coloured man from the store right away.

c. (Earlier examples.)

1840 J. P. Kennedy *Quodlibet* 221 Charley Moggs, long known as the boss loafer of Bickerbray. 1848 W. E. Burton *Waggeries* (Philad.) 63 (Th.) 'How d'ye do, folks?'..'is the boss devil to hum?'

Boss, *sb.*[7] *U.S.* [app. the same word as Eng. dial. (south-western) *borse, boss, buss* six-months-old or half-grown calf (1790 Grose *Prov. Dict.*, etc.).] A word used in addressing a cow. (Cf. *Bossy *sb.*) Also, the American bison.

1848 Bartlett *Dict. Amer.*, *Boss*, among the hunters of the prairies, a name for the buffalo. 1874 *Rep. Vermont Board Agric.* II. 706 So-o-o boss! There, you've kicked it over—All that milk, now, I declare! *a* 1895 Trowbridge *Evening at Farm* iii. (Funk) When to her task the milkmaid goes, Soothingly calling, 'So, boss! so, boss! so! so! so!'

Boss, *v.*[1] Add:

2. b. In ceramics, to smooth a surface of boiled oil on pottery by means of a boss (*Boss *sb.*[1] 3 g).

1860 Ure *Dict. Arts* (ed. 5) III. 506 A coat of boiled oil adapted to the purpose being laid upon the ware with a pencil, and afterwards levelled, or as it is technically termed 'bossed', until the surface is perfectly uniform. 1879 [see *Bossing *vbl. sb.*[1] d]. 1881 [see Boss *v.*[1] 2, where this quot. is wrongly placed].

Boss (bǫs), *v.*[3] *dial.* and *slang.* [Cf. *Boss-eyed, *Boss-shot.] *trans.* To miss or bungle (a shot); *gen.* to bungle, make a mess of. Also *absol.*

1887 *N. & Q.* 7th Ser. III. 236/2 To boss is schoolboy slang for 'to miss'. 1889 Barrère & Leland *Dict. Slang* s.v., To *boss* anything, to make a mess of it, to spoil it. 1898 *Eng. Dial. Dict.* s.v., He had six shies at the cocoa-nuts, and he bossed every time. 1903 *Fluff-Hunters* 74 You're simply bossing up the whole show by philandering with a widow.

Hence **Boss** *sb.*[8] = *Boss-shot.

1898 *Eng. Dial. Dict.* s.v., He then tried to jump the ditch to the big stone, but in his hurry he made a boss and fell into the water.

Bossdom (bǫ·sdəm). [f. Boss *sb.*[6] + -dom.] The condition of being a boss, that which constitutes the sphere of influence of a political boss, the control of politics by bosses.

1888 Bryce *Amer. Commw.* lxiii. II. 462 The extinction of the Boss himself and of bossdom. 1893 *Black & White* 1 Apr. 383/1 He was going to make John Bull realise that his days of bossdom were over. 1894 *Citizen* (Albion, Mich.) 293 It is not healthy for a party, if the few are allowed to do all and say all. That way Rings and Bossdom lie.

Boss-eyed, *a. dial.* and *slang.* [Cf. *Boss *v.*[3], *Boss-shot.] Having only one good eye; squint-eyed, cross-eyed. Also *fig.* oblique, crooked, one-sided.

1860 *Slang Dict.* (ed. 2). 1882 Chamberlain *W. Worc. Gloss.*, *Boss-eyed*, squinting. 1890 [see *Boss-shot]. 1898 *Eng. Dial. Dict.* s.v., The horse shied and we ran up against the gate-post, and knocked the step of the cart all boss-eyed.

Bo·ssible, *a. U.S.* [f. Boss *v.*[2]] Capable of being bossed.

1926 D. L. Colvin *Prohibition in U.S.* 563 The liquor vote was the largest..bossible and corruptable vote which existed.

Bossing, *vbl. sb.*[1] Add:

d. In ceramics, the process of smoothing the surface of colour applied to pottery over a coating of boiled oil; also, the coating of oil used for this purpose.

1874 Knight *Dict. Mech.*, *Bossing*, ground-laying the surface of porcelain in an unfinished state, to form a basis of adherence for the color...The bossing is a coat of boiled oil, to hold the colour. 1879 E. C. Hancock *Amateur Pottery* 49 When the oil has become somewhat set, so as to be 'tacky' to the finger, it is ready for the second process, called 'bossing'.

Bossship (bǫ·sʃip). *U.S.* [f. Boss *sb.*[6]] The rule of a boss in politics.

1894 *Voice* (N.Y.) 6 Sept., It was thought to be an auspicious time to shake off the 'bossship' exercised by Mr. Platt for many years. 1904 *N. Y. Even. Post* 16 Dec. 6 [To] make the time ripe for a party to revolt against a hideous boss-ship.

Boss-shot. *dial.* and *slang.* [See *Boss *v.*[3]] A bad shot or aim; *fig.* an unsuccessful attempt.

1890 Farmer *Slang*, *Boss*, to miss one's aim; to make such a shot as a boss-eyed person would be expected to make. Boss-shot is a common phrase. 1898 *Eng. Dial. Dict.* s.v., A bad shot with a stone is called a boss-shot.

Bo·ssy, *sb. U.S.* [Eng. dial. (south-western), dim. of *boss*, *Boss *sb.*[7], used in the same way.] A call to a calf; a calf or cow. Also *bossy-calf.*

1844 'Jon. Slick' *High Life N. Y.* II. 181 Like a great bossy calf, I had to jine in agin [in crying]. 1848 Bartlett *Dict. Amer.*, *Bossy*, a familiar name applied to a calf. 1863 'Gail Hamilton' *Gala-Days* 95 Bossy starts from the post, tail up in a hand gallop. 1907 *N. Y. Even. Post* 25 Feb. 3 He..will go out to interview a bossy [= cow] who has eaten her last wisp of hay. 1911 H. Quick *Yellowstone N.* xii. 314 A notion o' what it means to incorporate the fruit of the nest [= eggs] with the bossy. 1912 Mulford & Clay *Buck Peters* xiv. 138 Domesticated 'bossies' in pasture.

Bost, variant of *Boast *v.*[2]

Bosthoon (bǫstū·n). *Irish English.* [Irish *bastun* whip made of green rods, soft or spiritless fellow.] An awkward fellow; a tactless, senseless person.

1830–2 Carleton *Traits* (1843) I. 348 Sure only for this, I say, you bosthoon..where 'ud the purty colleen be? 1841 S. C. Hall *Ireland* I. 75 Ye grate Bosthoon. 1902 *Daily Chron.* 30 July 7/1 If they had you in Tipperary they would duck you in a horsepond for the cowardly Saxon bosthoones you are.

Boston[2]. Add:

2. A variation of the waltz. (Found 1883 in Fr.)

1911 H. S. Harrison *Queed* ix. 108 Of her infinite poetry of motion it is only necessary to say that she could make even 'the Boston' look graceful. 1913 E. Scott *All about the Boston* 21 Mr. Henry Zay wrote: 'I have danced the "Boston" for twenty years (I am an American) and say emphatically that there is no set figure that can be called the "Boston". It is a series of steps or figures—such as the ordinary waltz-step, the "dip", the "run", the "reverse", etc. *Ibid.* 24 At the present time the term 'Boston' is applied to the kind of movement that in its best and most graceful form would be far more consistently described as Rectilineal or Diagonal waltzing.

†Bo·stoner. *U.S. Obs.* [f. *Boston*, Mass. + -er[1] 1.] A Bostonian.

1758 *Micmakis & Maricheets* 65 On condition of the Bostoners returning to Petitpas.

Bostonese (bǫstŏnī·z). *U.S.* [f. as prec. + -ese.] a. *coll.* Natives or inhabitants of Boston. b. (See quot. 1889.)

1888 *N. Y. Herald* 29 July (Farmer) There were a number of people present, principally Bostonese. 1889 Farmer *Americanisms*, *Bostonese*..is a method of speech or manners supposed to be specially affected by the residents of that city.

Bostonian (bǫstōu·niăn), *a.* and *sb.* [f. as prec.]

A. *adj.* Belonging or native to Boston.

1698 C. Mather (*title*) The Bostonian Ebenezer. 1781 S. Peters *Hist. Conn.* (1829) 202 The New York and Bostonian merchants. 1794 Humphreys *Industry* 15 Where Bostonian maids, with songs, prepare, The canvass wings to wanton wide in air O'er Seas unknown. 1920 *Chambers's Jrnl.* 15 May 374/1 His carefully nuanced Bostonian accent.

B. *sb.* A native or inhabitant of Boston.

1698 C. Mather *Bostonian Ebenezer* Title-p., The Bostonians. 1773 [J. Allen] (*title*) An oration upon the beauties of liberty;..by a British Bostonian. *c* 1845 Paulding *Noble Exile* 107 Nay..we Bostonians have the reputation of being Bostonians wherever we go. 1897 Flandrau *Harvard Episodes* 18 'When I say "a Bostonian"'..I mean of course a Bostonian that one knows.'

Hence **Bosto·nianism,** features or traits characteristic of Boston.

c 1845 Paulding *Noble Exile* 107 We do mingle a little Bostonianism in every style we assume.

Bosun, var. of Boatswain, representing the common pronunciation.

1869 W. S. Gilbert *Bab Ballads* 85 And a bo'sun tight, and a midshipmite, And the crew of the captain's gig. 1928 *Daily Express* 19 Mar. 3/2 Men swinging perilously in bosun's chairs.

Boswellia (bǫzwe·liă). *Bot.* [f. the name of Dr. John *Boswell* of Edinburgh: see -ia[1].] Any tree of the genus so named, native to northern and eastern Africa, Arabia, and India, distinguished by triangular winged seeds, esp. the frankincense-tree, *Boswellia carteri*, the incense-tree, *B. thurifera* (*glabra* or *serrata*), and the elemi-tree, *B. frereana*.

1852 in G. W. Johnson *Cottage Gard. Dict.* 144 The brittle resin of Boswellia.

Boswellian. Add:

B. *sb.* A student or admirer of Boswell. Also **Bo·swellize** *v. trans.*, to treat in the Boswellian style; **Bo:swellia·na,** the literary works of, or matters connected with, Boswell.

1908 *Daily Chron.* 11 Nov. 3/4 Their appearance in print was hailed with pleasure by Johnsonians and Boswellians. 1921 *Glasgow Herald* 29 Jan. 13 Johnsonians and Boswellians alike will therefore receive with joyful gratitude Dr. J. T. T. Brown's paper. 1921 *Spectator* 20 Aug. 239 The Queen's early Diaries wherein she Boswellized Lord Melbourne. 1927 *Glasgow Herald* 2 June 4 A Boswellised life of Carlyle. 1929 *Daily Tel.* 22 Jan. 6/5 The personal papers of James Boswell..are being published...Sixteen or eighteen volumes will eventually be needed to hold all the new Boswelliana.

Bot. 3. Add: *bot-worm*.

1877 *Rep. Vermont Dairym. Assoc.* VIII. 105 Grub-in-the-head is a bot-worm,..cousin to the bots in horses.

Botallackite (botæ·lăkəit). *Min.* [f. the *Botallack* mine, Cornwall: see -ite[1].] A name given by A. H. Church in 1865 to a variety of atacamite containing a large proportion of water.

1865 A. H. Church in *Jrnl. Chem. Soc.* Ser. II. III. 213. 1868 Dana *Min.* (ed. 5) 121 Botallackite occurs at the Botallack mine, Cornwall, in thin crusts of minute interlacing crystals, closely investing killas.

Botany. Add: 2. b. Short for *Botany wool*.

1884 W. S. B. McLaren *Spinning* (ed. 2) 116 When the material is very short Botany, the advantage is not so great...It is confined to commission combers and Botany spinners. 1900 *Daily News* 16 Oct. 2/6 In the botany trade it is difficult for spinners to obtain orders.

Both. 3. c. Add: *To have it both ways*: to have advantages from two opposed or contradictory positions; to make use of alternatives or contradictories according as it suits one; to 'eat one's cake and have it'.

1911 Shaw *Fanny's First Play* II, Then I suppose what I did was not evil; or else I was set free for evil as well as good. As father says, you cant have anything both ways at once.

Bothrodendron (bǫþrode·ndrǫn). *Bot.* [mod. L., f. Gr. βόθρος pit + δένδρον tree.] A genus of fossil plants, found in coal measures (cf. Lepidodendron); a plant of this genus.

1833–5 Lindley & Hutton *Fossil Flora Gt. Brit.* II. 97 Bothrodendron. Stem not furrowed, covered with dots. Scars of cones, obliquely oval. 1862 Burton *Bk. Hunter* I. 2 Your other hard names—your ichthyodorulite, trogontherium, lepidodendron, and bothrodendron. 1902 *Encycl. Brit.* XXXI. 413/2 The cuticles of a Bothrodendron.

Botryogen (bǫ·triǫdʒen). *Min.* [ad. G. *botryogen* (W. Haidinger, 1828), f. Gr. βότρυς a bunch of grapes + -gen.] A red or deep yellow mineral found at Falun, Sweden, composed of the hydrous sulphates of iron, magnesium, and calcium.

1865 Brande & Cox *Dict. Sci.* etc. 306.

Bott (bǫt). [? F. *botte*.]

1. The name given by lace-makers to the cushion on which lace is woven.

1849 in Craig.

2. In founding, a clay plug used to close a hole against molten iron (Cent. Dict. Suppl. 1909). Also *attrib.* Hence **Bo·tting** *vbl. sb.* (see quot. 1874).

1874 Knight *Dict. Mech.*, *Botting*, restopping the tapping-hole of a furnace after a part of its charge has been allowed to flow therefrom. 1888 *Lockwood's Dict. Mech. Engin.*, Bott Stick. 1900 J. Sharp *Mod. Foundry Pract.* 144 A round ball of this [loam] is placed on a disc of iron at the end of an iron rod, and is forced into the tap-hole..when it is wished to stop a tapping out with the bott or bod stick.

Bott-hammer (bǫ·t,hæ:məɹ). [ad. G. *botthammer*, f. *botten* to break flax + *hammer* Hammer *sb.*] A wooden hammer used to break the stalks of flax.

1858 Simmonds *Dict. Trade*, *Bott-hammer*, a wooden block with a long bent helve or handle, and having channels or flutings under its face used to beat flax. 1874 Knight *Dict. Mech.*, *Bott-hammer*, a wooden mallet with a fluted face, used in breaking flax upon the floor to remove the boon.

Bottle, *sb.*[2] 5. Add:

bottle-arsed *a. Printing* (see quots.); **bottle-baby,** a baby reared by means of a feeding-bottle; **bottle-end,** a round of glass resembling the bottom of a bottle, used in windows; **bottle-fed** *a.*, (of an infant) brought up on the bottle (see Bottle *sb.*[2] 1 e): cf. **breast-fed*; **bottle-grass** *U.S.*, a variety of fox-tail grass, esp. *Setaria viridis*; **bottle-imp,** also, a Cartesian devil, a hollow figure suspended in a bottle of water; **bottle-jack,** (*b*) applied to an escapement in a clock or watch resembling that of a bottle-jack; (*c*) a kind of lifting-jack (Knight *Dict. Mech.* 1874); **bottle-shaker,** an apparatus used in centrifugation; **bottle-shop,** a shop licensed to sell wines and spirits only in the bottle; **bottle-swallow,** an Australian bird, a species of martin; **bottle-washer** (earlier U.S. example); **bottle-windowed** *a.*, having windows made up with 'bottle-ends' (see above).

1770 Luckombe *Hist. Printing* 233 It [*sc.* the type] drives out, or gets in, either at the head, or the foot, and is, as Printers call it, **Bottle-arsed*. 1838 Timperley *Printers' Man.* 64. 1890 Farmer *Slang*, *Bottle-arsed*, type thicker at one end than the other—a result of wear and tear. 1893 *Daily News* 9 Mar. 2/7 Was it what you call a *bottle-baby? 1905 *Westm. Gaz.* 23 Oct. 4/1 Wanted, nurse for night duty only; one thoroughly accustomed to bottle babies. 1907 W. De Morgan *Alice-for-Short* ix, A..window..filled with what some called *bottle-ends, and others German rounds. 1907 *Westm. Gaz.* 10 Apr. 10/1 This might be one of the causes of..infantile mortality, especially amongst *bottle-fed children. 1909 *Ibid.* 23 Aug. 5/2 With bottle-fed infants it is highly important to get the quantities as well as the nature of the food right. 1863 *Trans. Ill. Agric. Soc.* (1865) V. 867 *Setaria viridis*, Green Fox-tail or *Bottle-grass, is from the South of Europe. 1862 *Catal. Internat. Exhib., Brit.* II. No. 5598 *Bottle imps. 1928 *Daily Tel.* 17 Jan. 10/6 He was seized with stage fright,..he was left to do as best he could with his 'bottle imp'. 1850 Denison *Clock & Watchm.* 50 The *bottle-jack or 'vertical' pallets. 1860 *Ibid.* (ed. 2) 35 The bottle-jack escapement is precisely the same as in De Vick's clock. 1913 *Oxford Univ. Gaz.* 4 June 943/2 Motor driven centrifuge and *bottle-shaker. 1929 *Times* 30 Jan. 9/7 These were what were known as '*bottle shops', and could not sell less than a bottle of spirits and a half-bottle of wine at any one time. 1898 Morris *Austral Engl.*, **Bottle-Swallow*, a popular name for the bird *Lagenoplastis ariel*, otherwise called the Fairy Martin...The name refers to the bird's peculiar retort-shaped nest. 1837 *Southern Lit. Messenger* III. 656 They have yet founded no city to themselves..but are willing to remain the boot-cleaners and the *bottle-washers of the whites. 1899 Kipling *Stalky* 224 A little *bottle-windowed, half-dairy, half-restaurant, a dark-browed, two-hundred-year-old house.

Bottle, *v.*[1] Add: 3. *intr.* with *up*. To become confined as in a bottle.

1881 A. A. Hayes *New Colorado* v. 70 If I had to live here, I'd just bottle up and die.

4. *Printing.* To make bottle-arsed.

1877 *Design & Work* 15 Sept. 341 The letters stand fair and square on the shank—that is, not 'bottled', as we say in the trade. 'Bottling' arises from the following cause—imperfect locking up, or lines badly spaced out...The risk of getting 'bottled' letter is, however, not very great...Amateurs are in..danger of 'bottling' their own letter.

Bottled, *ppl. a.* Add:

2. b. *transf.* and *fig.* Stored up, concentrated.

1872 W. W. Reade *Martyrdom of Man* 399 Life is bottled sunshine.

Bottle-neck (bǫ·t'l,nek). [f. Bottle *sb.*[2] + Neck *sb.*[1]]

1. A narrow entrance to or stretch in a road, compared to the neck of a bottle in shape; *gen.* a narrow or confined space where traffic may become congested. Also *attrib.*

1896 *Daily News* 26 Dec. 3/1 The widened portions at Holloway and elsewhere are rendered useless by narrow, bottle-neck approaches to Finsbury-park. 1907 *Westm. Gaz.* 21 Aug. 5/2 The bottle-neck, known as London-road, at the Elephant and Castle. 1914 W. J. Locke *Jaffery* x. 123 Through the bottle-neck of Brentford,..we crawled as fast as we were able. 1928 *Britain's Industr. Future* (*Liberal Ind. Inquiry*) IV. xxiii. 314 Any failure to maintain dock and harbour facilities..results in delays...Ports then become the 'bottle-necks' of ocean traffic and congestion results.

2. *fig.* Any narrow opening or avenue.

1928 *Observer* 15 July 10/3 It is hoped to make one side of the higher science forms of the school a bottle-neck through which boys of special intelligence..may pass.

3. *attrib.* and *Comb.* in general use.

1898 *Daily News* 19 Oct. 3/1 [He] called Old Jewry 'a bottle-neck-shaped street.' 1908 *Daily Graphic* 21 Mar. 13/3 Our desire at present is to look so feminine that bottle-neck shoulders are praised.

Bottle-tree (bǫ·t'l,trī). [f. Bottle *sb.*[2] + Tree *sb.*] An Australian tree of the sterculia family, either the Queensland tree *Sterculia rupestris* or the similar *Sterculia diversifolia* of Victoria, so called from the bottle-like shape of its trunk.

1846 C. P. Hodgson *Remin. Australia* 264 The sterculia or bottle-tree is a very singular curiosity. It generally varies in shape between a soda water and port wine bottle. 1885 Mrs. C. Praed *Head Stat.* 179 In dense scrub, where the bottle-trees rose weird and white. 1889 J. H. Maiden *Useful Native Plants* 60 A 'Kurrajong'. The 'Bottle-tree' of N.E. Australia, and also called 'Gouty-stem'. 1891 'Coo-ee' *Tales Austral. Life* 284 A great white bottle tree, its trunk perfectly bare.

Bottom, *sb.* Add: 4. b. Now esp. *U.S.* (with later examples). Also in pl. form.

1817 S. R. Brown *Western Gaz.* 12 Pea vine on the hill sides and in the bottoms. 1837 Peck *Gaz. Illinois* 1. 3 The term 'bottom' is used throughout the west to denote the alluvial soil on the margin of rivers, usually called 'intervals' in New England. 1851 C. Cist *Cincinnati* 18 Cincinnati itself is built on an ancient alluvial plain, lying in two levels called the 'upper and lower bottoms'. 1882 *Econ. Geol. Illinois* II. 59 These bottoms are mostly prairie, with narrow belts of timber skirting the streams. 1896 J. C. Harris *Sister Jane* 204 Some, who..went west, some to Alabama, and some to the rich Mississippi bottoms. 1907 Mulford *Bar-20* xx. 200 They crawled to the last line of brush and looked out over an extensive bottoms.

c. In gold-mining, the channel of an old river containing rich deposits of gold; also called the gutter. *Australia.*

1887 Hayter *Christmas Adv.* 5 We reached the bottom, but did not find gold.

5. d. *Mining.* Usually *pl.* The lowest workings in a mine. Also *attrib.*, as *bottom captain, coal, worker*.

1778 Pryce *Min. Cornub.* 174 The Bottom-Captains, whose business is to see that the common men perform due labour down in the mine. 1860 *Eng. & For. Mining Gloss.* (ed. 2) 5 *Bottoms*, the lowest workings either in a stope, level, or elsewhere. 1883 Gresley *Gloss. Coal-mining*, *Bottom*, the bottom of the shafts and roadways, &c., near the shafts. 1892 *Daily News* 26 Feb. 5/6 It comprises about 280,000 miners, of whom 200,000 are 'bottom workers.' 1900 *Daily Express* 28 June 7/3 There is an immense quantity of coal known locally as 'bottom coal' practically intact.

e. The part of a boot or shoe below the uppers; the sole, heel, and shank.

1841 *Penny Cycl.* XXI. 410/2 The employing master..prepares and sorts the sole or bottom-stuff for the maker. 1881 *Instr. Census Clerks* (1885) 76 Bottom Finisher. 1886 *Encycl. Brit.* XXI. 831/1 He then pares off inequalities and 'levels the bottoms'. 1911, 1921 [see *bottom-scourer* in 19].

10. c. The bed of calcined sand and ore in a copper-smelting ore-furnace.

1868 Joynson *Metals* 95 The calcined [copper] ore is placed on the 'bottom' of the hearth.

d. A dye used as a foundation for a subsequent dye.

1876 *Calvert's Dyeing & Calico-printing* 131 Sandal wood is employed, chiefly on the continent, to give a bottom to woollen cloth which is to be afterwards dyed with indigo.

e. The support upon which an article is placed in a scale to be weighed.

1884 Knight *Dict. Mech.* Suppl.

11. c. In fig. phrases. *The bottom falls out of*: there is a collapse of. *To knock the bottom out of*: see Knock *v.* 6 b.

1637 Rutherford *Lett.*, *To Earl Cassils* 9 Sept. (1671) 144 The bottom hath fallen out of both their wit and conscience at once. 1872 'Mark Twain' *Innoc. at Home* xiii. (1882) 341 Gould and Curry soared to six thousand three hundred dollars a foot! And then—all of a sudden out went the bottom, and everything..went to ruin and destruction! 1926 Ethel M. Dell *Black Knight* 1. x, 'I try to take things as they come.'..'And when the bottom falls out of everything—what do you do then?' 1928 *Manchester Guardian Weekly* 2 Nov. 350/3 Prince Max thought..that once this became an agreed point in British and German war aims the bottom would fall out of the British home front.

15. b. Delete † and add quot.

1868 *Rep. U.S. Commissioner Agric.* (1869) 288 The twisting or 'throwing' process is done by passing the thread of raw silk from an upright bottom through the eye of a craned wire flyer.

18. a. *bottom-discharge*; *bottom rock*, also *fig.*; *bottom-heavy* adj. b. *bottom-liver*.

1874 Knight *Dict. Mech.*, *Bottom-discharge Water-wheel*, a turbine from which the water is discharged at the bottom instead of at the sides. 1887 C. B. George *40 Yrs. on Rail* v. 93 About the time I had reached bottom rock in my financial troubles,..I met A. B. Pullman. 1900 *Daily News* 24 Oct. 7/7 Orders for 160 bottom-discharge trucks have been placed in America. 1927 Haldane & Huxley *Animal Biol.* xii. 302 They are all marine and essentially bottom-livers. 1927 *Sunday Times* 6 Mar. 7/3 The double basses are generally too plentiful at these concerts, and..they too often made the music sound bottom-heavy.

19. **bottom-bed,** the lowest stratum of a formation of rocks; **bottom-boards,** boards at the bottom of a boat serving to protect the outer planking; **bottom-boarding,** the bottom planks of a boat; **bottom dollar** *U.S.*, (one's) last dollar, usu. in allit. phrase with *bet*; **bottom facts** *U.S.*, the fundamental facts; **bottom fermentation,** that during which the yeast cells collect at the bottom of the liquid; also *attrib.*; **bottom-gear,** the lowest-speed gear (see Gear *sb.* 7) in a motor; **bottom-line,** the lower part of a fishing-line; **bottom-plate,** (*a*) an iron plate in a printing-press; (*b*) the set of knives forming the bed of a pulping machine in paper-making; **bottom-planks,** the outer planking of the bottom of a boat; **bottom prairie** *U.S.*, a prairie lying along the bank of a river; **bottom-scourer,** an operative who smooths the 'bottoms' of boots and shoes; **bottom side** = sense 1; **bottom timber** *U.S.*, timber growing in bottom-lands; **bottom-tool,** a tool used in wood-turning; **bottom wool** (see quot.); **bottom yeast** = *bottom fermentation* yeast.

1845 P. B. Brodie *Hist. Fossil Insects* 58 Hard blue limestone, ('*bottom bed') with Ostrea, Modiola minima, and other shells. 1883 *Man. Seamanship for Boys* 84 Q. What are *bottom boards? A. Long pieces of wood nailed together, which lay from the stern sheets to the bow. 1895 Kipling *2nd Jungle Bk.* 103 He would take a boat in the evenings and shuffle with his feet in the bottom-boards. 1900 G. Swift *Somerley* 110 At the risk of tearing out what was left of the *bottom-boarding, we hauled her on to the beach. 1866 *Congress. Globe* Mar. 1474/1 His opinion is that a State can go out of the Union and he is willing to bet his *bottom dollar on his judgment. 1888 *Inter-Ocean* 7 Mar. (Farmer) It is the right kind of bravery; you may bet your bottom dollar on that. 1904 Harben *Georgians* v. 43 You bet yore bottom dollar I'm open to criticism myself. 1877 *N. Y. Tribune* 17 Mar. (Bartlett) Curiosity has been on the tiptoe these many weeks to know the *bottom facts. 1883 'Mark Twain' *Life Mississippi* xlii. 393 Though there ain't only one or two ways when you come down to the bottom facts of it. 1905 J. L. Baker *Brewing Industry* 100 Brewers' yeast (*Saccharomyces cerevisiæ*) is divided into two classes, top fermentation and *bottom fermentation yeast. 1923 *Westm. Gaz.* 2 Feb., A stiff climb on *bottom gear brings Mosul..in sight. 1837 Kirkbride *Northern Angler* 91 The *bottom or casting-line must consist of three lengths of twisted gut. 1891 Kipling *Light that Failed* (1900) 23 The whale-boat..chose to hit a hidden rock and rip out half her *bottom-planks. 1874 Knight *Dict. Mech.*, **Bottom-plate* (printing), a plate of iron belonging to the mold of a printing-press, on which the carriage is fixed. 1884 *Ibid.* Suppl., *Bottom plate* (paper-making), the gang of knives forming the concave or bed beneath the cylinder of a rag-grinding machine or pulping engine. 1807 P. Gass *Jrnl.* 36 We..passed a handsome *bottom prairie. 1882 *Econ. Geol. Illinois* II. 73 The latter are the so-called 'ridge prairies', while the former are sometimes designated as 'bottom prairies'. 1911 Frederick Sellers in *Rep. Labour & Social Conditions in Germany* III. 95 *Bottom-scourers 24s. (Frankfurt per week). 12s. to 16s. (Leeds per week). 1921 *Dict. Occup. Terms* (1927) § 429 *Scourer*,..designated according to parts upon which he works, *e.g.* bottom or naumkeag scourer, heel scourer. 1856 Cozzens *Sparrowgr. Papers* vii. 88 It was vexatious enough to see our lawn *bottom-side up on a festive occasion. 1868 *Rep. U.S. Commissioner Agric.* (1869) 327 Put the box in a pan of water and turn it nearly bottom-side up. 1837 Peck *Gaz. Illinois* II. 125 The *bottom timber consists of oaks [etc.]. 1874 J. W. Long *Amer. Wild-fowl Shooting* ix. 150 How much better walking it is in this bottom-timber than in the woods of New England. 1874 Knight *Dict. Mech.*, **Bottom-tool*..., a turning-tool having a bent-over end, for cutting out the bottoms of cylindrical hollow work. 1848 H. W. Haygarth *Bush Life Australia* v. 47 The wool nearest the skin, or, as it is called, the '*bottom wool,' which is the hardest to cut, but the most weighty and valuable. 1910 J. L. Baker in *Encycl. Brit.* X. 278/1 It has not..been possible to transform a typical top yeast into a permanent typical *bottom yeast.

Bottom, *v.* Add: 1. b. To use a preliminary dye as a foundation for another.

188. *Fibre & Fabric* V. 16 (Cent. Dict.) They [*sc.* worsted goods] should be bottomed with indigo.

c. To underlie. *U.S.*

1877 Raymond *Statist. Mines & Mining* 56 The company is extending and straightening the bed-rock tunnel, so that it..will 'bottom' all the land on this end of the claim.

4. c. *fig.* Of prices, etc.: To fall to the lowest level.

1892 *Daily News* 17 Nov. 7/1 Discount rates appear to have bottomed for the time. 1920 *Glasgow Herald* 6 Sept. 9 Others with shallower purses are content to wait until prices have bottomed.

5. *trans.* In gold-mining, to reach the bottom of, to reach a point (in a mine) beyond which further mining is useless; also *absol.* to get down to the bed-rock or clay. b. *intr.* Said of a claim, etc.: To be worked to the bottom. *Australia.*

1858 McCombie *Hist. Victoria* xv. 219 In their anxiety to bottom their claims, they not seldom threw away the richest stuff. 1890 'R. Boldrewood' *Miner's Right* viii, As soon as the main body of block claims began to bottom, gold flowed in with almost fabulous profusion. *Ibid.* xiii, Though they had a week's start of us, we bottomed on the same day, and by nightfall the field was aware that Olivera's half-share men had bottomed another duffer. 1900 H. Lawson *On Track* 143 One day Peter..told us that his party expected to 'bottom' during the following week...Later came the news that 'McKenzie and party' had bottomed on payable gold.

6. *Mech. intr.* To strike or touch the bottom or far end (see quot.).

1874 Knight *Dict. Mech.* s.v., Cogs are said to bottom when their tops impinge upon the periphery of the co-acting wheel. A piston which strikes or touches the end of its cylinder is said to bottom.

Bottoming. Add:

1. d. *attrib.*, as **bottoming-hole,** the open mouth of a glass-making furnace; **bottoming-tap,** a square-edged tap for cutting an internal thread uniformly to the bottom of a hole.

1839 Ure *Dict. Arts* 582 This spheroid having become cool and somewhat stiff, is next carried to the bottoming hole. 1874 Knight *Dict. Mech.*, *Bottoming-hole*, the open mouth of a furnace at which a globe of crown glass is exposed during the progress of its manufacture, in order to soften it and allow it to assume an oblate form. 1884 *Ibid.* Suppl., *Bottoming tap*, one for carrying the thread of full size to the bottom of the hole.

2. The process of reaching bed-rock. *Australia.*

1890 'R. Boldrewood' *Miner's Right* viii, The bottoming of three or more shafts on the supposed line of lead shall be a sufficient test.

Bo·ttom-land, bo·ttomland. (Also as two words.) *U.S.* [Bottom *sb.* 4 b and 18.] A stretch of level land beside a river; an alluvial plain forming a river-bottom. Also *attrib.*

1785 A. Ellicott in *Life & Lett.* (1908) 40 The Bottom-lands on this stream are very good but they are narrow. 1817 S. R. Brown *Western Gaz.* 52 Its branches, upon which there is some of the best bottom lands in the western country. 1841 C. Cist *Cincinnati* 66 The larger streams are now found meandering through alluvial plains called 'bottom lands'. 1874 J. W. Long *Amer. Wild-fowl Shooting* xv. 193 If the sportsman is desirous of shooting them..he should visit the low overflowed bottom-lands. 1888 *Harper's Mag.* Feb. 399/2 The navigable part of Red River meanders through heavily timbered alluvial bottom-lands of the most prolific character. 1903 *N. Y. Even. Post* 12 Sept., The tract consists of a bottom land along the Ohio River, and a plateau elevated 300 feet above the bottom land. *Ibid.* 19 Sept., To complete the maturity of the bottomland crops.

Botuline (bǫ·tiuləin). *Med.* [f. L. *botulus* sausage: see -ine[5].] A poisonous ptomaine found in decaying meats and other foods. Hence **Botuli·nic** *a.* Also **Botulinus** (bǫtiuləi·nǒs) [mod. L.], specific name of the bacillus of botulin, used *attrib.*

1899 *Clinical Jrnl.* 7 June 112/2 An efficient antitoxin for the botulinic poison. 1901 Dorland *Med. Dict.* (ed. 2), *Botulin*, a poisonous ptomain sometimes found in preserved meats: it is produced by *Bacillus botulinus*. 1929 W. Bulloch in *Syst. Bacteriology* III. 380 In preserved vegetables..antigenic substances are formed capable of absorbing complement in the presence of ordinary botulinus antitoxin. *Ibid.* 386 Botulinus toxin is unaffected by peptic digestion. *Ibid.* 394 Botulism can hardly arise from the ingestion of botulinus spores. *Ibid.* 397 The botulinus serum should be a polyvalent one.

Botulism (bǫ·tiuliz'm). *Med.* [f. L. *botulus* sausage + -ism, after G. *botulismus*.] Poisoning caused by eating decomposed foods, esp. preserved meats, and due to *Bacillus botulinus* (discovered by Van Ermengen in 1896).

[1878 tr. *von Ziemssen's Cycl. Med.* XVII. 539 In the larger towns, botulismus occurs extremely seldom.] 1887 A. M. Brown *Anim. Alkaloids* 156 Intoxication by the alkaloids, that is to say, those cases in which hypothermia is present. In Germany it is known by the term *botulism*, a form of poisoning of the organism observed to result from the ingestion of putrefying meats. 1899 *Clinical Jrnl.* 7 June 112/1. 1922 *Times* 6 Sept. 7/3 He had no doubt the deaths in this case were due to botulism, for which disease antitoxins..had proved disappointing.

Bough, *v.*[1] Delete †*Obs.* and add: c. With *down* (see quot.). *U.S.*

a 1861 T. Winthrop *Life in Open Air* (1863) 89 Iglesias and I stripped off armfuls of boughs and twigs from the spruces to 'bough down' our camp. 'Boughing down' is shingling the floor elaborately with evergreen foliage.

Bought, *sb.*[1] 2. b. Delete †*Obs.* and substitute: Now *poet.* (revived by Tennyson).

1872 Tennyson *Gareth & Lynette* 229 The dragon-boughts and elvish emblemings Began to move, seethe, twine and curl. 1906 C. M. Doughty *Dawn in Britain* xv. IV. 148 Like as some serpent, which..in the sun, displays her glittering boughts.

Boughten, *ppl. a.* (Later U.S. examples.) See also Eng. Dial. Dict.

1844 'Jon. Slick' *High Life N. Y.* I. vii. 104 Fifty dollars, enough to rig out all the gals in Weatherfield with boughten finery. 1887 Mary E. Wilkins *Humble Rom.* 121 She could not think of such things as boughten trimming for her poor little wedding outfit. 1906 H. D. Pittman *Belle of Blue Grass C.* x. 146 To come in next week and get some boughten stuff for herself.

Bouillabaisse (buyabɛ̄·s, -bę·s). [Fr., ad. mod. Prov. *bouiabaisso*.] A dish of Provençal origin, composed of fish stewed in water or spiced white wine.

a 1863 Thackeray *Ball. & Tales* (1869) 46 This Bouillabaisse a noble dish is. 1902 *Westm. Gaz.* 9 July 2/1 Let it be noted that the greater variety of fish employed to fashion a *bouillabaisse*, the greater the grace and excellence of the same. 1911 R. W. Chambers *Common Law* x. 305 Only art is one delicious bouillabaisse to him.

Bouillon. Add: 1. b. A broth used as a medium for the culture of bacteria. Also *attrib.*

1901 Dorland *Med. Dict.* (ed. 2), *Bouillon*..used..as a bacteriologic culture-medium. 1903 *Daily Chron.* 21 Oct. 10/1 Five cubic centimetres of a highly poisonous bouillon culture of certain bacteria (streptococci) was injected under the skin of the ears of rabbits. 1909 *Practitioner* Nov. 591 Five decigrams of a bouillon culture of streptococcus of erysipelas.

Boulangism (bula·nʒiz'm). [ad. F. *Boulangisme*, f. the name of General Georges Ernest Jean Marie *Boulanger* (1831–91).] The principles and methods of Boulanger and his party who, from about 1886–1889, advocated a policy of militarism and revenge against Germany. Hence **Boula·ngist,** an advocate of Boulangism.

1888 *Times* 16 Mar. 5/4 Nothing proved that Boulangism had anything in common with Bonapartism. 1889 F. Turner *General Boulanger* 197 Another method invented by the Government to crush out Boulangism was the employment of numbers of police spies to watch the General, Count Dillon, and all the principal members of the National party. 1889 *St. James's Gaz.* 16 Jan. 10/2 The source of the Boulangist election expenditure is a burning question in France. *Ibid.* 3 Aug. 9/2 Fifteen telegraph clerks, reported to the Postmaster-General as Boulangists.

Boulder, *sb.*[1] 4. Add:

boulder-strewed, *-strewn* adjs.; **boulder-belt,** a belt of boulders deposited by a glacier on melting; **boulder-cracker,** a heavy iron rod used to break rock encountered in a deep boring for a well; **boulder-fans,** a series of boulder-trains with divergent lines of direction; **boulder-pavement,** a bed of boulders naturally arranged; **boulder-train,** boulders deposited by the melting of a glacier.

1894 J. Geikie *Gt. Ice Age* (ed. 3) 742 In some instances these '*boulder-belts are all the marginal morainic representatives that can be detected over considerable tracts. *Ibid.* 523 Here and there '*boulder-pavements' occur. 1897 *Outing* (U.S.) XXIX. 339/2 A wearisome tramp over the *boulder-strewed mountain side. 1897 *Daily News* 5 May 3/1 Arta Hill, bleak and *boulder strewn. 1899 *Westm. Gaz.* 11 Dec. 8/1 The precipitous boulder-strewn heights.

Bou·ldered, *a. U.S.* [f. Boulder *sb.*[1] 1.] Laid with cobblestones.

1873 J. H. Beadle *Undevel. West* xxxi. 682 There is not a foot of regular turnpike, a rod of bowldered street, or a mile of navigable canal in the entire Territory.

Boule[3] (bau·lī, bū·le). [a. Gr. βουλή senate.] A legislative council of ancient Greece, originally aristocratic and consisting of the heads of families, later consisting of representatives chosen by lot.

1846 Grote *Hist. Greece* I. xx. II. 89 The Boulê, or council of chiefs, and the Agora, or general assembly of freemen. 1905 *Spectator* 4 Mar. 318/2 The Boulé, which answers practically to the House of Commons.

Boule[4] (būl). [app. a use of F. *boule* Bowl *sb.*[2]] A game resembling roulette.

1927 *Daily Express* 31 Aug. 4 Boule, that anaemic variation of roulette. 1928 *Daily Tel.* 10 July 15/5 Rooms for boule and baccarat.

Bouleuterion (buliūtī·ə·riǫn). Pl. -ria. [a. Gr. βουλευτήριον, f. βουλεύειν to deliberate, f. βουλή counsel.] The house of assembly of the *Boule[3].

1862 E. Falkener *Ephesus* i. iv. 68 The bouleuterion of Elis was attached to the gymnasium.

Boulevard. Add: Now freq. in *U.S.* as a designation of wide and well laid-out main streets or roads.

1875 *Scribner's Monthly* Sept. 541/2 The boulevard which started from Lincoln Park, connects the Central and Douglas Parks, and then continuing [etc.]. 1888 *Harper's Mag.* May 874/1 These parks are all connected by broad boulevards. 1903 A. B. Hart *Actual Govt.* 328 Hence have grown up systems of boulevards, broad, winding, and well-surfaced, reaching from park to park and often from city to city.

Boulevarded (bu·lvārded), *ppl. a.* [f. Boulevard + -ed[2].] Provided with boulevards.

1891 *Pall Mall Gaz.* 21 Dec. 1/3 An ideal of a boulevarded London. 1897 *19th Cent.* June 931 It has no boulevarded, Parisianised streets.

Boulevardeer, var. of Boulevardier.

1916 H. L. Wilson *Somewhere in Red Gap* ix. 374 Roystering blades from Pittsburgh or boulevardeers from Bucyrus—not a New Yorker in sight.

Boulter (bōu·ltəɹ), *v.* [f. Boulter *sb.*] *intr.* To fish by means of the long fishing-line known as a boulter.

1907 *Daily Chron.* 9 Nov. 6/6 Many of them have begun bouttering for conger and whiting.

Boulton (bōu·ltən), *a.* [The name of a firm of glove-manufacturers.] Of the thumb of a glove: Cut with a shaped piece extending upwards into the palm.

1922 *Daily Mail* 12 Dec. 1 Real Kid Nappa Gauntlet Gloves,..boulton cut thumb. *Ibid.*, Mocha Gloves...Pique sewn, boulton thumb. 1929 *Penberthy's Sale Catal.* Mar. 24 An ideal Glove for hard service. Boulton cut. *Ibid.* 26 Men's English Tan Cape,..Boulton cut.

Bounce, *sb.*[1] Add: 3. b. An act of bouncing or ejecting. Also *fig.* *U.S.*

1877 Bartlett *Dict. Amer.* (ed. 4) Add., *Bounce*. To get the *grand bounce* is to be dismissed from service; particularly from an office under government. 1910 'O. Henry' *Rolling Stones* (1915) 122 'Had you ever thought' I asks,..'of giving her the bounce yourself?'

Bounce, *sb.*[3], short for Cherry-bounce.

1835 R. M. Bird *Hawks of Hawk-hollow* II. xv. 171 Here I've mixed you a brandy cock-tail, and you've spilled the bounce into it.

Bounce, *v.* Add: 8. b. To eject summarily. *U.S.*

1882 *Washington Republ.* 28 Jan. (Th.) (*heading*), Gibson bounced. A Blackmailer kicked out. 1891 C. Roberts *Adrift Amer.* 128 Here I jumped another train and got 'bounced' at Bernalillo. *a* 1906 'O. Henry' *Trimmed Lamp* etc. 48 A certain man named Adam, whom the cherubim bounced from the orchard.

c. To throw over (as a suitor). *U.S.*

1893 'O. Thanet' *Stories Western Town* 213 You don't suppose it would be any use to offer Esther a cool hundred thousand to promise to bounce this young fellow?

Bouncer. Add: 5. One engaged to eject undesirable or unruly persons from a saloon, ball-room, etc.; a 'chucker-out'. *U.S.*

1888 A. C. Gunter *Mr. Potter* xx, Several of the fighting brigade of the establishment, that in American slang would be termed 'bouncers'. 1903 A. Adams *Log Cowboy* xiii. 204 The bouncer of the dance hall of course had his eye on our crowd.

Bouncing, *vbl. sb.* Add:

5. *Firework-manuf.* (See quot.)

1888 W. H. Browne *Firework Making* 15 Furnishing the squib with its report is called bouncing. *Ibid.* 43 Bouncing, or giving to the saucisson its report.

Bouncy (bau·nsi), *a.* [f. Bounce *v.* + -y[1].]

1. That bounces; having a buoyant manner.

1921 *Chambers's Jrnl.* Jan. 1/2 The little, bouncy man waved his umbrella in excitement. 1928 *Sunday Dispatch* 2 Sept. 15 Once more George..forestalled the bouncy Irishman.

2. Resilient.

1926 *Sunday at Home* Jan. 220/2 This big, old house with the bouncy sofa and springy chairs.

Bound, *sb.*[1] Add:

2. c. *pl.* The limit or boundary beyond which soldiers, sailors, students, school children, etc., resident in a particular building, quarters, or area, may not pass. Now chiefly in *out of bounds*, outside or beyond this boundary.

1681 R. Knox *Hist. Ceylon* IV. ix. 156 Plain reason would tell him, that we being prisoners were without our bounds. 1720 De Foe *Capt. Singleton* xviii. (1839) 228 He would easily suspect they were out of their bounds, being captives. *c* 1805 *Regul. Sherborne School*, Every other part of the town is out of School bounds, except the Church-Yard. 1857 Hughes *Tom Brown* I. ix, The chief offenders..were flogged and kept in bounds. 1864 H. C. Adams *White Brunswickers* xii, He found out that old Giles's house was a hundred yards or so out of bounds. 1865 *Blackw. Mag.* Apr. 472/1 The reason of putting the river out of bounds was the danger incurred by boys who could not swim. 1890 Doyle *Firm of Girdlestone* v, A lad coming up to an English University..must be within bounds at a fixed time. 1893 Leland *Mem.* I. 91 Freedom from bad marks, and being ruled into bounds, and sent to bed at early hours. 1909 Douglas Sladen *Trag. Pyramids* xiii. 201 The decree of the General, which made the Considines out of bounds for the Army, like a Mohammedan festival.

5. **bound(s)-beater,** one who takes part in the ceremony of beating the bounds; **bound(s)-beating,** the ceremony of beating the bounds.

1909 *Essex Rev.* XVIII. 188 After the perambulation there was a dinner, jointly with the Little Leighs bounds-beaters, at the inn. 1927 *Sunday at Home* June 553/2 The religious part of the bounds-beating was prohibited.

Bound, *ppl. a.*[2] 7. b. Add: also (U.S.) *bound boy, girl.*

1846 *Congress. Globe* 6 Feb. 322/3 He has to stand by, as we say in the West, 'like a bound boy at a husking'. 1872 Eggleston *Hoosier Schoolm.* iv. 51 Ralph recognized Hannah, the bound girl at old Jack Means's. 1888 J. Kirkland *McVeys* 84 Hyer comes Widder Tansey's bound gal. 1891 *Congress. Rec.* Jan. 1890/1 [In the House of Commons] it rarely happens that more than two-thirds of the members are present, and when they are, all but 360 must stand round like 'bound boys', as that number exhausts the sitting space on the floor.

Boundary. Add:

1. b. *boundary line* (earlier U.S. examples).

1705 *Rhode Island Col. Rec.* III. 528 The boundary lines between this her Majesty's Collony..and her Majesty's Province of the Massachusetts Bay. 1784 A. Ellicott in *Life & Lett.* (1908) 19 We shall..begin to run the Boundary Line between Virginia and Pennsylvania. 1832 J. P. Kennedy *Swallow B.* II. ii. 67 Who but a man of genius could unravel the occult darkness of the boundary line?

2. *ellipt.* A boundary tree. *U.S.*

1772 *Carroll Papers* in *Maryland Hist. Mag.* XIV. 365 The Post placed in the roome of a White Oak & Hickory Boundaries of Kendalls Delight. *Ibid.*, At the White Oake a Boundary of Dryere & Dodderize.

3. *Cricket.* The bounds or limits of a match enclosure.

1889 *M.C.C. Laws of Cricket* (1892) Rule 44 [The umpires] shall pitch fair wickets, arrange boundaries where necessary, and the allowances to be made for them. 1899 W. G. Grace *Cricket. Remin.* ii. 23 There were no fixed boundaries at Lord's when I first played there. 1900 *Young Sportsman* (ed. A. E. T. Watson) 137 The boundaries and the times for stopping having been arranged, the captains..toss for the choice of innings. 1905 Vachell *The Hill* xii, [He] cut the sixth ball to the boundary.

b. A hit to the boundary; also, the number of runs allowed for the hit.

1896 *Westm. Gaz.* 24 July 5/2 His placing on the leg side, especially off Giffen, was extremely fine, and gave him several boundaries. 1900 Upward *Eben. Lobb* 74 The wicket simply got in the way of my bat, as I was preparing to hit a boundary. 1910 *Westm. Gaz.* 26 Feb. 16/2 A four boundary is often the result.

c. *attrib.*, as *boundary-hit, -play, -stroke.*

1896 *Westm. Gaz.* 7 Feb. 3/1 A splendid display of true cricket relieved by free 'boundary' play. 1900 *Young Sportsman* (ed. A. E. T. Watson) 137 Three runs should never be recognised for a boundary hit. 1905 *Westm. Gaz.* 15 June 7/1 It was not until the third over of the match that he opened the scoring with a boundary-stroke.

Bounder (bau·ndəɹ), *sb.*[2] *slang.* [f. Bound *v.*[2] + -er.[1]]

1. A four-wheeled cab or trap, so called from the bounding motion of the vehicle in passing over rough roads.

1842 *Hints to Freshman* (Slang Dict. 1865) The man who drives has a well-appointed 'bounder' of his own. 1859 *Slang Dict.*, *Bounder*, a four wheel cab. 1865 *Ibid.*, *Bounder*,..a University term for a trap.

2. A person who by his behaviour places himself outside the pale of well-bred society. Also in milder use as a term of playful abuse.

a 1889 in Barrère & Leland *Dict. Slang* s.v., If I ordered the particular hat I desired I should be taken for a bounder. 1889 *Ibid.*, *Bounder* (university), a student whose manners are despised by the *soi-disant élite*, or who is beyond the boundary of good fellowship...(society), a swell, a stylish fellow, but of a very vulgar type. 1890 Farmer *Slang* 307 *Bounder*,..2. A student whose manners are not acceptable; one whose companionship is not cared for...4. A vulgar though well-dressed man; a superior kind of ''Arry'; one whose dress and personal appearance are correct, but whose manners are of a questionable character. 1890 *Times* 2 May 13/5 To speak of a man as a bounder is to allude to him as an outsider or cad. 1899 W. Archer *Study & Stage* 48 That is an anti-social proceeding, the conduct of a 'bounder'. 1899 *Star* 11 Jan. 1/5 Bounder..a man with 'bounce' about him; an outsider, because he's outside the fringe of society and wants to be in the reserved enclosure. 1904 *Spectator* 31 Dec. 1089/1 His intimates are 'bounders' or Bohemians. 1917 J. Adams *Student's Guide* 27 A prig is one who has too much self-respect, a bounder one who has too little. 1920 Wodehouse *Damsel in Distress* vi, He had been marched up the Haymarket in the full sight of all London by a bounder of a policeman.

Bounderish (bau·ndəriʃ), *a.* [f. *Bounder *sb.*[2] 2 + -ish[1].] Having the character or characteristics of a bounder. Hence **Bou·nderishness.**

1899 E. Phillpotts *Human Boy* 35 With all his bounderishness, he was awfully clever. 1928 *Sunday Dispatch* 23 Dec. 12 An awfully bounderish and unbearable sort of young man.

Bounding, *ppl. a.*[2] Add: b. Of the pulse.

1879 *St. George's Hosp. Rep.* IX. 783 A very bad illness, marked by headache, bounding, hardly compressible pulse.

c. *fig.* Increasing by leaps and bounds.

1887 *Charity Organis. Rev.* III. 230 And yet, those..bounding vagrancy returns!

Boundless. Add:

B. *sb.* That which has no bounds, the illimitable.

1909 *Westm. Gaz.* 10 July 3/2 We, a handful of men, concerning ourselves deeply in small matters, are brought face to face with the boundless.

Bounty. Add:

5. e. *King's* or *Queen's bounty*: a sum of money given from the royal purse to a mother who has given birth to triplets.

1910 *Encycl. Brit.* IV. 324/2.

6. *bounty-jumping.*

1881 *Congress. Rec.* Feb. 1292/2 We had in some of our large cities men who were pursuing the very profitable industry of 'bounty jumping'.

Bouquet. Add: 1. b. *To throw bouquets*: to pay compliments. *U.S. colloq.*

1904 *Journalist* 28 May 89 We do not wish to say 'I told you so', or to 'throw any bouquets' in our own direction. 1905 A. Adams *Outlet* 230 Quince..threw bouquets at me regarding my ability always to find water.

Bouquetier (bukətīə·ɹ, ‖ buktye). Also erron. -ière. [Fr.: f. Bouquet.] A small holder for a bunch of flowers, esp. one carried in the hand.

1787 *Wedgwood's Catal.* (ed. 6) 61 Of root pots, as well for bulbous as other roots, and of flower pots or bouquetiers, there is a great variety. 1871 Nesbitt *Catal. Slade Coll. Glass* 80 Large Blue Bouquetière. 1875 Meteyard *Wedgwood Handbk.* 392 Bouquetier. A flower-pot,..often with a pierced cover for the insertion of the stems of flowers.

Bourbon. Add:

2. *U.S.* (Earlier examples.)

1859 *Olympia* (W. T.) *Pioneer & Democrat* 15 Apr. (Th.) The 'Bourbon' family have attempted to rule this territory from the earliest hour of its creation. 1877 *N. Y. Tribune* 15 June (Bartlett) Ex-governor Humphreys is an irredeemable Bourbon.

3. b. A class (*Rosa indica bourboniana*) of monthly roses, believed to have originated in a hybrid introduced from the Isle of Bourbon *c* 1825; also, a rose of this class. c. A rose, *Rosa borbonica*. (W. 1911.)

1829 Loudon *Encycl. Plants* 446 *Rosa centifolia*...Garden Varieties...Bourbon. 1841 *Penny Cycl.* XX. 158/1 Bourbon rose..is a natural hybrid between *R. Indica* and a variety called red four-seasons. This hybrid was found among a number of the latter plants in a hedge in the Isle of Bourbon. 1852 Miss Warner *Queechy* liv, The air was full of the sweetness of damask and Bourbon varieties. 1869 S. R. Hole *Book about Roses* 173 Of the Bourbons..there are several which are valuable additions to a general collection of Roses. *Ibid.* 174 Catherine Guillot, with Louise Odier,..are..two winsome maids of honour in waiting upon the Bourbon Queen.

d. *Bourbon tea*: see Tea *sb.* 6.

1861 Bentley *Man. Bot.* 667 *Angræcum fragrans*.—The dried leaves of this fragrant species are used as a kind of tea in the Mauritius. This is commonly known as *Faham* or *Bourbon tea*.

4. Whiskey of a kind originally made in Bourbon County, Kentucky. Also *attrib.* with *liquor, whiskey*. *U.S.*

1857 T. H. Gladstone *Englishman in Kansas* 40 When a barrel of Bourbon, or Monangahela, or Double Rectified was accessible, they forgot even in some instances to ask the politics of its possessor. 1862 *Congress. Globe* May 2288/3 One barrel of genuine Bourbon liquor. 1880 *Congress. Rec.* May 2938/2 [Every man who] makes deals in, or drinks Bourbon whisky knows very well that it requires nearly three years to produce a Bourbon whisky which is ready for consumption. 1886 *Harper's Mag.* June 55/1 A..discrimination between its effects and those of 'old

Bourbon'..after imbibing incontinently. 1891 C. ROBERTS *Adrift Amer.* 150 Taking an occasional overdose of Bourbon was his one particular failing.

Bou·rbonish, *a.* *U.S.* [f. BOURBON *sb.* 2.] Having the character of Bourbon democracy.

1906 *Springfield Weekly Republ.* 22 Nov. 8 On this matter that section is to-day more exclusive and bourbonish and reactionary than it was 30 years ago.

Bou·rbonized, *ppl. a.* *U.S.* [f. BOURBON *sb.* 2.] Converted to or affected by Bourbonism.

1906 *N. Y. Even. Post* 7 May 6 This difficulty in bringing 'Bourbonized' Republicans around to a successful advocacy of the old Democratic doctrines.

Bourdon³ (bū·ɹdǫn). The name of Louis *Bourdon* of Paris, designating his inventions: **Bourdon barometer**, a metallic barometer consisting of an elastic tube bent to a circular shape so that the ends of the tube separate as the atmospheric pressure decreases and approach as it increases; **Bourdon tube**, a coiled metallic tube which tends to straighten out when pressure is exerted within it.

1874 KNIGHT *Dict. Mech.* s.v. *Bourdon Barometer*, The Bourdon is commonly known as the metallic barometer. 1902 *Nature* 11 Dec. 140/2 The Hergesell instrument having a tube of German silver, instead of the Bourbon [*sic*] tube filled with alcohol.

Bourdonné (buəɹdǫ·ne), *a.* *Her.* [Fr.] Terminating in knobs or balls.

1612 PEACHAM *Gentl. Exerc.* 153 *Cosm.* Be there no more crosses then one borne in Armes? *Eud.* Yes...The most ordenary are these...Croiseè...Composeè...Bourdonneè. 1722 NISBET *Her.* I. 119 A Cross Bourdonee, as if it were made of Pilgrims Staves, which use to have a round Ball at the Top. 1780 EDMONDSON *Heraldry* II. Gloss. 1880 *Encycl. Brit.* XI. 696/1 Originally..the arms of the cross ended in knobs like the handles of a pilgrim's staff, thence called 'bourdonnée'.

Bourrée (bure·). [Fr.; see BOREE.] **a.** A lively dance, of either French or Spanish origin, in common time (two beats in a bar). **b.** A musical composition, written usually in duple rhythm and in two-measure phrases, in which the character of the lively dance so named is represented.

1776 HAWKINS *Hist. Music* IV. 390 The Bouree is supposed to come from Auvergne in France; it seldom occurs but in compositions of French masters. 1880 *Grove's Dict. Mus.* I. 264/1 The bourrée is often to be found in the older suites. ..In Bach's suites, a second bourrée frequently follows the first, in the same way as in a symphony or sonata, a trio follows a minuet, after which the first bourrée is repeated. 1891 *Queen* 3 Jan. 18/3 Minuet in D (No. 1) is fairly interesting, Bourrée in G (No. 2) is rather wild. 1891 *Leeds Merc.* 25 May 5/2 A charming minuet from 'Berenice', and a graceful bourrée from the Water Music.

Boursault (bū·ɹsǫlt). [The name of a Parisian rose-grower.] A species of climbing roses originating from the Alpine rose (*Rosa alpina*), introduced in 1683; also, a rose of this species.

1864 S. HIBBERD *Rose Bk.* 29 The Boursault roses...The Old Red Boursault..was the first double variety of *Rosa alpina*.

Bout, *sb.*² Add:

5. The inward curve of a rib in a violin or similar instrument, by which the waist is formed.

1889 *Cent. Dict.* 1893 *Fiddler's Handbk.* 4 Bouts,..the sides of the fiddle, divided into the lower, middle, and upper bouts. 1905 HAWEIS *Old Violins* 35 The curve of the bouts tilted, contracted, or elongated. *Ibid.* 38 Observe the improved purfling, the bouts and mitres cut with clear intention.

Bout (baut), *v.* [f. BOUT *sb.*² 1 b.] *trans.* To plough in such a manner as to make bouts. Hence **Bou·ted** *ppl. a.*, ploughed in this manner.

1733 W. ELLIS *Chiltern & Vale Farm.* 36 Bout it up at Allhollantide. *Ibid.* 37 In June harrow it down and bout it the same way; in July hack it overthwart, or bout it up across. 1844 *Jrnl. R. Agric. Soc.* V. I. 16 Two of these harrows cover a single ridge of four furrows; four cover an eight-furrow stretch, consisting of two ridges bouted into one. 1864 *Ibid.* XXV. II. 291 The fallows are broken up in the autumn.., ploughed back in spring, then twice across, and bouted in 27-inch ridges.

Boutade. Delete †*Obs.* and add:

1865 'OUIDA' *Strathmore* x. I. 164 One of those tantalising *boutades* that were her most cruel and certain witcheries. 1905 *Spectator* 28 Jan. 141/2 Miss Burney had the good fortune to see only the better side of the Doctor...She was seldom witness of his boutades. 1924 *Blackw. Mag.* June 783/2 A certain notoriety for boutades among my associates.

Bouting, *vbl. sb.* Add: also *attrib.*, as *bouting row*. (Cf. BOUT *v.* in Eng. Dial. Dict.)

1786 WASHINGTON *Diaries* III. 43 It should have been observed that the field intended for experiment at this Plantation is divided into 3 parts, by bouting Rows running crossways. 1788 *Ibid.* 440 Both Plows and Hoes were employed in breaking up the bouting Roes along the fence.

Bouton (buton). [Fr., = button.]

1. In *pearl bouton, bouton pearl*, anglicization of *perle bouton*, a round pearl with a flat back marking the place where it was attached to the shell.

1851 *Illustr. Catal. Gt. Exhib.* III. 689 Brilliant tiara, ornamented with fine oriental pearl drops and boutons. 1907 *Daily Chron.* 5 Apr. 4/5 An exquisite pearl and brilliant necklace, formed as fifteen graduated drops, each composed of one bouton pearl, one brilliant, and one pear-shaped pearl drop. 1927 *Daily Express* 9 May 5/3 If it is a round pearl, with a flat back showing, where it was attached to the shell, it will be called a 'bouton' pearl.

2. The button-like end of a honey-bee's tongue.

1886 CHESHIRE *Bees & Bee-Keeping* 95 The central and side ducts run down to that part of the tongue where the spoon, or bouton is placed.

Boutonnière (butonyę̄r). [Fr.]

1. A spray of flowers worn in the buttonhole.

*c*1867 B. HARTE *Story of a Mine* xi, She had distributed it to make *boutonnières* for other gentlemen. 1907 *Daily Chron.* 2 Sept. 2/7 The lapel of his coat was almost invariably ornamented with a boutonnière. 1919 *Hist. Amer. Lit.* II. 268 He had worn a high hat, cane, and boutonnière.

2. *Surg.* An incision made in the urethra in order to extract a calculus or remove a tumour.

1884 THOMPSON *Tumours of Bladder* 76 The high operation is a much more formidable and hazardous proceeding than the simple boutonnière. 1908 *Practitioner* Feb. 180.

Bouvardia (buvā·diā). *Bot.* [mod.L., f. the name of Dr. Charles *Bouvard*, superintendent of the Jardin du Roi, Paris: see -IA.] Any plant of the rubiaceous genus of this name, which was introduced from Mexico and Central America, bearing handsome red, yellow, or white flowers.

1846 LINDLEY *Veg. Kingd.* 764 The fragrance or beauty..of the Gardenias,..Bouvardias, Catesbæas, &c. is unsurpassed in the vegetable kingdom. 1872 MRS. WHITNEY *Other Girls* vi. 64 Scarlet bouvardias and snowy deutzias. 1907 *Westm. Gaz.* 9 Oct. 2/1 The garden, with odorous bouvardias all awake.

Boviander (bǭu·viændəɹ). [Etym. doubtful.] A name given in British Guiana to the people of mixed race who live on the river-banks.

1875 VENESS *Ten Yrs. Mission Life Brit. Guiana* 10 Some families of mixed race, called 'Bovianders', whose progenitors—of negro extraction—had intermarried with the Indians. 1882 *Timehri* June 145. 1895 *Sat. Rev.* 21 Dec. 828 The 'boviander' is almost amphibious...He may be a pure negro, a mulatto, or an indistinguishable compound of black, red, and white races, but, whatever his ancestry, he is always at home on or in the water. 1899 RODWAY *Guiana Wilds* 21 A boviander with whom he could chat about hunting and fishing on the rivers.

Bovinely (bǭu·vainli), *adv.* [f. BOVINE + -LY².] In a bovine, dull, or inert manner.

1900 CROCKETT *Joan of Sword Hand* xxxiv. 227 Seydelmann..simpered bovinely down upon the girls. 1902 *Daily Chron.* 7 Nov. 5/2 The slow-witted politician, bovinely chewing the cud of his correspondent's schemes. 1923 *Detective Mag.* Nov. 39 The bovinely expressionless face of the detective.

Bovrilize (bǫ·vrilaiz), *v.* [f. *Bovril* (f. L. *bōs, bovis* ox, cow), trade-name of a concentrated essence of beef, invented in 1889 by J. Lawson Johnston.] *trans.* To concentrate the essence of; to epitomize, condense. (Cf. TABLOID.)

1901 *Daily News* 11 Jan. 5/1 Here..is one of these 'bovrilised' announcements...: Wanted, Sit. as Comp. by Eng. lady, 35; good Fr.; good refs.; would trav. R.R., 100. 1902 *Daily Chron.* 22 Aug. 8/7 He must give us not life, but the essence of it—a bovrilised version, as it were. 1902 *Academy* 13 Dec. 655/2 His fondness for bovrilising thought ..into so small a compass of words that the sentences are really too 'meaty'. 1928 *Musical Times* Nov. 1003 The exercises..are short enough not to fatigue the attention, and they bovrilise the difficulties or virtues admirably.

Bow, *sb.*¹ Add:

4. e. *Cupid's bow*: see *CUPID.

11. d. A curved piece of metal used to make contact with an overhead wire in electric traction; = *bow trolley* (see 19 below). Also *attrib.*

1909 *Cent. Dict.* Suppl., *Bow-spring*, in electr. traction, the spring which keeps the bow spread out, when a bow is used to take current from a trolley-wire.

e. A leg of a pair of spectacles; also, the frame of either of the lenses. *U.S.*

1847 LONGF. *Evang.* I. iii. 4 Glasses with horn bows Sat astride on his nose. 1890 *Harper's Mag.* Oct. 720/1 A pair of ancient silver-rimmed spectacles from which the bows were lost.

19. bow-and-arrow *attrib.*, belonging to or characteristic of the period when the bow and arrow was the chief weapon of war; **bow-iron** (see quot.); **bow-key** *U.S.* = *bow-pin*; **bow-pin** (quot.); **bow-spring**, a bow-shaped spring; **bow-tie**, a tie made up into a bow; **bow trolley**, a device for collecting the current from an overhead wire in electric traction; **bow-whip** *U.S.* (see quot.).

1899 *Westm. Gaz.* 27 July 2/2 We may yet work back to the *bow-and-arrow period if modern inventions make war with their aid too grotesquely horrible and difficult. 1907 *Macm. Mag.* Oct. 935 Bow-and-arrow men. 1874 KNIGHT *Dict. Mech.*, **Bow-iron*, the staple on the side of a wagon-bed which receives the bows of the tilt or cover. 1857 J. YOUNG in *Jrnl. Discourses* VI. 230 You that have on such a yoke had better pull out the *bow-keys. 1857 F. D. RICHARDS *Ibid.* V. 47 You will not be so likely..to lose your *bow-pins, chains, or axe. 1840 *Civil Eng. & Arch. Jrnl.* III. 56/2 A vertebrated carriage..with *bow-spring bearers and buffers. 1910 *Westm. Gaz.* 24 Jan. 3/1 He wore a check suit..and a pink cotton *bow-tie. 1921 *19th Cent.* May 922 Two young Frenchmen in American jackets and bow-ties. 1901 *Trans. Amer. Inst. Elect. Engin.* 111 (Cent. Dict. *Suppl.* s.v. *Trolley*) *Bow trolley. 1902 *Encycl. Brit.* XXVIII. 98 On the continent of Europe considerable use has been made of bow trolleys, which consist of light metallic bow-shaped structures..running along on the under side of the wire against which they rub. 1890 *Harper's Mag.* Oct. 718/1 His whip was the fashionable '*bow whip' of the period, common enough now, to be sure, with a long lash, tapering down to a fine silk 'snapper' on the end.

Bow, *sb.*³ Add:

1. d. *Bow(s on*, with the bow of the vessel turned towards the object considered or in view.

[1858 T. WILLIAMS *Fiji & Fijians* I. vi. 205 The commander ordered it to be run with its bows on the shore.] 1877 *Design & Work* 218/2 To hit a craft coming bows on. 1893 KIPLING *Many Invent.*, *Finest Story* 104 A galley coming up bow-on. 1903 *Westm. Gaz.* 15 June 3/1 The 'standard type' has equal offensive strength in all directions—whether bows-on or broadside.

3. (Examples of some obvious combs.)

1877 W. H. WHITE *Man. Naval Archit.* 339 The armour and bow-plating. *Ibid.* 450 The position of the crest of the last wave in the train of waves that follow the bow wave, and lie along the side of the ship, exercises a very sensible effect on the resistance. *Ibid.* 457 Accelerations which lead to the production of the bow-wave. *Ibid.* 699 Of the auxiliary appliances fitted to increase the steering power of ships, the most important are bow rudders. 1904 *Westm. Gaz.* 14 Apr. 2/1 The bow-angles and lines of vessels. 1907 *Macm. Mag.* Feb. 316 The bow-wash broadened to a roaring water. 1908 *Westm. Gaz.* 16 July 4/3 The motor-boat, almost hidden in her bow spray. 1920 *Discovery* Nov. 328/1 Bow-fire was then limited to a couple of light guns.

Bow (bǭu), designating a make of china originally manufactured at the Bow China Manufactory at Stratford-le-Bow in Essex.

1879 E. C. HANCOCK *Amateur Pottery* 195 Bow china.. is often embossed and of quaint devices. 1898 BINNS *Story of Potter* 169 Advantage was taken..of the printing carried on at Liverpool to have the Bow ware so decorated. 1906 *Westm. Gaz.* 18 Apr. 3/1 An unusual..mark on Worcester is the Dresden 'crossed swords' on the saucer belonging to Dr. Crowe of Worcester, which appears with the Bow-marked Worcester among the illustrations.

Bow, *v.*¹ **7. c.** Add: Also with *oneself* as obj.

1888 RIDER HAGGARD *Col. Quaritch* xxxi, He..handed the squire a fully addressed brief envelope,..and adding that there was no answer, bowed himself out.

Bowel, *sb.* **6.** *bowel complaint* (examples).

1831 PECK *Guide for Emigrants* II. 84 The bowel complaint is more commonly fatal. 1850 N. KINGSLEY *Diary* 156 Indisposed by a bowel complaint.

Bower, *sb.*³ **2.** Delete †*Obs.* and add:

1921 *Dict. Occup. Terms* (1927) § 278 *Bower, fish hook bower*,..sets, feeds and operates small fly press which bends fish hooks and forms ring at end.

Bower, *sb.*⁸ (Earlier example.)

1858 *Congress. Globe* 28 May 2460/2 He uses terms which I do not understand: talking about the 'right bower', and 'ace', and all that sort of thing.

fig. 186. B. HARTE *Tennessee's Partner* Wks. (1872) 43 'What have you got there?—I call' said Tennessee quietly. 'Two bowers and an ace,' said the stranger, showing two revolvers and a bowie knife. 1870 *Congress. Globe* 27 Nov. (De Vere) As their Right Bower, General Butler, was absent, the stratagem would have succeeded.

Bowery, *sb.* *U.S.* Delete †*Obs.* and add:

b. *attrib.*

1862 O. W. NORTON *Army Lett.* 48 The Twenty-fifth New York is composed of New York Roughs, Bowery boys, 'Dead Rabbits', etc. 1909 [see *BOY *sb.*¹ 6 b].

2. (See quot. 1878.)

Both examples refer to Salt Lake City, Utah.

1869 S. BOWLES *Our New West* xii. 244 An audience of four or five thousands spread out under the 'Bowery' adjoining the Tabernacle where the summer meetings are held. 1878 J. H. BEADLE *Western Wilds* xxi. 341 At once the bretheren were called together in the bowery—an open shed where they usually worshiped.

Bow-head (bǭu·hed). [f. BOW *sb.*¹ + HEAD *sb.*] The Arctic right whale, *Balæna mysticetus*.

1887 *Pall Mall Gaz.* 8 Sept. 2/2 A bow-head whale preparing to 'sound'. 1888 *Encycl. Brit.* XXIV. 523/2 The 'bowhead' of the Okhotsk Sea and Behring Strait. 1896 KIPLING *Seven Seas* 129 Hath he..Spoke on the ice with the Bow-head—followed the Sabre-tooth home? 1908 *Westm. Gaz.* 28 Dec. 2/1 Nothing can possibly prevent the extermination of the bowhead whale..but the discovery of an adequate substitute for whalebone.

Bowie². *U.S.* (Earlier and later examples.)

1846 E. BRYANT *What I saw in California* xxxi. (1849) 327 A leathern girdle surrounds the waist, from which are suspended a bowie and a hunter's knife. 1853 J. G. BALDWIN *Flush Times Alabama* 190 Most men would have seized their gun, or Bowie, on such terrible aggravation. 1886 *Outing* (U.S.) Nov. 109/1 With bare arms I drove the 'bowie' deep into the grizzly's carcass.

Bowie-knife. (Earlier examples.)

1836 *Philad. Publ. Ledger* 12 Aug. (Th.) Our infamous Bowie knives, have made us a reproach to civilization. 1838 *Jeffersonian* (Albany, N.Y.) 8 Sept. (Th.) The *Louisville Journal* chronicles 'a challenge to fight with Bowie knives, toe to toe'.

Bow-knot. = BOW *sb.*¹ 16.

1547 SALESBURY *Welsh Dict.*, *Kwlwm dalen*, a bowe knot. 1671, 1768 [see BOW *sb.*¹ 16]. 1861 MRS. STOWE *Pearl Orr's Isl.* I. v. 30 When he had once seated himself in a double bow-knot at a neighbor's evening fireside. 1896 *Godey's Mag.* Apr. 446/2 A woman with her back doubled into a bow-knot.

Bowl, *sb.*² Add: **2. e.** A delivery of the ball in cricket: now usually *ball*.

1862 *Chambers's Encycl.* III. 320/1 At the end of every four bowls, the bowler, wicket-keeper, long-stop, and fielders, change places.

f. A turn or the delivery of a ball in the game of bowls.

1889 in *Cent. Dict.* 1893 E. T. AYERS *Bowls* (1894) 80 'Driver' on such occasions often comes in for reproach after an unsuccessful bowl.

Bowl, *v.*¹ Add:

5. d. To put on (a player) to bowl, at cricket.

1898 W. G. GRACE in *Daily News* 20 July 7/5 They never bowled the poor fellow again. 1901 *Field* 23 Feb. 251/3 That the committee unanimously indorse the action of the captain of the team..and the other captains..in agreeing not to bowl certain bowlers in 1901.

Bowless, *a.* Add quots.:

a 1847 ELIZA COOK *Hint to Lovers* xvi, The bowless blind boy [viz. Cupid]. 1861 *Temple Bar* I. 282 His bow-less

white neckcloth. 1905 *Daily Chron.* 25 Mar. 3/2 Her slippers were even bowless.

Bowman¹. **3.** Add U.S. quot.:

1815 D. DRAKE *Cincinnati* ii. 87 Bowman's root.

Bowsprit. Add: **3.** (Examples of obvious combs.)

1867 SMYTH *Sailor's Word-Bk.*, *Bowsprit-bitts* are strong upright timbers secured to the beams below the deck... *Bowsprit-cap*, the crance or cap on the outer end of the bowsprit...*Bowsprit-horses*, the ridge-ropes which extend from the bowsprit-cap to the knight-heads. *Bowsprit-ladder*, skids over the bowsprit from the beak-head in some ships, to enable men to run out upon the bowsprit. *Bowsprit-netting*, the netting placed just above a vessel's bowsprit, for stowing away the fore-topmast stay-sail...*Bowsprit-shrouds*, strong ropes or chains leading from nearly the outer end of the bowsprit to the luff of the bow, giving lateral support to that spar. 1883 *Man. Seamanship for Boys* 21 A bowsprit, made out of a single spar, has only two hoops on it,..one on the head..abaft the tenon or bowsprit-cap. *Ibid.* 32 Q. What are bowsprit shrouds? A. Ropes or chains leading from the outer end of the bowsprit to the bow giving lateral support to the bowsprit...Q. What are bowsprit collars? A. Strops round the bowsprit with thimbles for bowsprit shrouds, stays, and bobstays.

Bowstring, *v.* Add: In surgical use.

1907 *Practitioner* Nov. 633, A valve, or a vessel-leash, bow-stringing the ureter.

Bow-wood. *U.S.* (See quots. and BOW *sb.*¹ 19.)

1805 *Deb. Congress* 1806–7 (1852) 1138 One or two slips of the bois d'arc, bow wood, or yellow wood, from the Missouri. 1823 E. JAMES *Rocky Mt. Exped.* II. 344 The bow-wood, or, as it is sometimes called, the Osage Orange, is found upon the southerly tributaries of the Arkansa. 1847 DARLINGTON *Amer. Weeds* (1860) 297 *Maclura aurantiaca*, ..Osage-orange. Bow-wood.

Bow-wow. Add:

2. d. The dogmatic tone in speaking or writing; the stating of opinions in an arrogant manner. Also *attrib.*, as *bow-wow style*.

1889 GRETTON *Memory's Harkback* 207 Without any bow-wow or assumption of superiority, he would prove to demonstration that our fancied arguments were good for nothing.

e. *To go to the bow-wows*: to go to 'the dogs'. *jocular colloq.*

1838 DICKENS *Nich. Nick.* lxiv, It is all up with its handsome friend! He has gone to the demnition bow-wows. 1893 W. K. POST *Harvard Stories* 114 Everything was going to the bow-wows. 1897 *Advance* (Chicago) 9 Aug., Panmixia would..send society reeling and stumbling right back to the bow-wows. 1917 H. A. VACHELL *Fishpingle* xiii, He was going fast to the bowwows before I went to India.

Box, *sb.*¹ Add: **3. b. box briar**, a tropical American shrub, *Randia aculeata*, with fruits and leaves resembling those of the box; also called *inkberry, indigo-berry*; **box-edged** *a.*, having a border of box plants; **box-gum** *Austral.*, applied to various species of *Eucalyptus* (cf. c below).

1888 D. MACDONALD *Gum Boughs* 7 The clumps of box-gums clinging together for sympathy.

c. Applied to many Australasian species of *Eucalyptus* (see quots.), *Tristania conferta* (Bastard, Brisbane, Brush, Red, or White Box), and some other trees: see Morris *Austral English*.

1820 J. OXLEY *Jrnl. Two Exped. into N. S. Wales* 15 The timber, dwarf box, and gum trees (all eucalypti), with a few cypresses and camarinas. *Ibid.* 227 The country.. thickly timbered, chiefly with the species of eucalyptus called box. 1866 *Treas. Bot.*, *Box*..White, of Australia, *Eucalyptus albens*. Yellow, of Australia, *Eucalyptus melliodora*. 1889 J. H. MAIDEN *Usef. Native Pl. Australia* 121 Native box..is greedily eaten by sheep,..usually a small scrub, in congenial localities it developes into a small tree. *Ibid.* 468 *Eucalyptus hemiphloia*...This is a common 'Box' of New South Wales and Queensland.

Box, *sb.*² Add:

3. g. (See quot.)

1889 *Atalanta* June 597/1 For flower-painting never use what is technically termed 'box', viz.: the muddy colour.. that is left on the sides of the colour-box from former usage.

IV. Various uses (see quots.).

1825 J. NICHOLSON *Oper. Mech.* 390 The front rollers belonging to one division, or box, as it is commonly termed. 1839 URE *Dict. Arts* 1287 Iron plates, forming the bottoms of the shuttle-boxes...Small pegs or pins, planted in the posterior faces..of the boxes, round which the levers turn. 1849–50 WEALE *Dict. Terms*, *Box*, for mitring, a trough for cutting mitres...*Box*, of a rib-saw, two thin iron plates fixed to a handle, in one of which plates an opening is made for the reception of a wedge, by which it is fixed to the saw. 1874 KNIGHT *Dict. Mech.*, *Box*..., a drain with a rectangular section...(*Weaving*.) *a.* The pulley-case of a draw-loom on which rest the small rollers for conducting the tail-cords. *b.* The receptacle for the shuttle at the end of the shed. ..(*Vise*.) The hollow screw-socket of a bench-vise. 1892 *Lockwood's Dict. Terms Mech. Engin.* 373 *Three-part Box*, a moulding box or flask consisting of three parts, and used for moulding those patterns in which the middle section must be distinct from the top and bottom, as..in the case of a grooved pulley.

21. So *to be in the same box*: to be in a similar (unhappy) predicament.

1884 RIDER HAGGARD *Dawn* xlvii, Well, we are in the same box. 1911 H. WALPOLE *Mr. Perrin* v. i, He always told himself that all the members of the staff were in the same box.

24. box-bridge, an enclosed bridge; **box-cage**, a bird-cage which opens only in front; **box-camera**, (*a*) see quot. 1842; (*b*) a photographic hand camera of the form of a box, one portion of which slides telescopically into the other; **box-cañon** *U.S.*, a narrow cañon with flat bottom and nearly vertical walls; **box-cart** *U.S.*, a cart having a box-shaped body; **box-chisel**, a double-bladed chisel used for opening wooden boxes; **box-chuck**, a chuck resembling a vice, used by workers in brass in turning small flanged articles; **box-churn**, a churn resembling a box in shape; **box-cloth**, a thick coarse cloth material, usually of a buff colour, in which riding garments are made; also applied to the colour; **box-coil**, a heating apparatus consisting of a coil of straight tubes joined at the ends, and occupying a cubical space; **box-coloured** *a.*, coloured by immersion in a box or tray of dye; **box-cutter**, a person employed in cutting out the material for boxes; **box-desk**, a desk of a box-like shape; **box-dresser**, a person engaged in lining and trimming boxes; **box-fitter**, a worker in an iron and steel foundry who attaches fittings and adjusts the parts of the moulding boxes; **box-food**, food which is given to animals in a box; **box-frame**, the enclosed space in a window-frame for sash windows, in which the balance-weights are hung; **box-front**, a plain unfitted front of a garment; **box-gauge**, the usual form of gauge for measuring the tide, consisting of a vertical box with measuring apparatus; **box-gear**, a differential gear used in motors and in other machinery; **box-girder** (quots.); **box-grain**, a grain given to leather in which lines are crossed in rectangular fashion; **box-hand**, (*a*) a person engaged in the manufacture or packing of boxes; (*b*) the compositor who sets up the type for stop-press news; **box-hardening**, the process of case-hardening metal by cementation in a box; **box-head**, (*a*) an indented heading in a printed article; (*b*) the fresh-water squaw-fish, *Ptychocheilus oregonensis*; **box-honey**, honey stored by bees in boxes; **box-hook**, a hook used to handle, close, or raise boxes; **box-house** *U.S.*, a square-built house suggestive of a box; **box-key** = *box-spanner*; **box-kite**, (*a*) a toy kite having the form of a box; (*b*) a kite invented by Lawrence Hargrave, of Sydney, Australia, consisting of two light rectangular boxes secured together horizontally, much used in meteorological experiments; (*c*) = **box-kite aeroplane**, an early form of biplane in which the arrangement of the planes resembles a box-kite; **box-letters** *U.S.*, letters placed in a private box at the Post Office in place of being sent out and delivered to the addressee; **box-level**, a surveyor's level consisting of a glass-covered box instead of a level and tube; **box-loom**, a loom with more than one shuttle-box at either end of the lathe; **box-loop**, a long leather loop worked into a square form, used in harness; **box-mangle**, a mangle consisting of a rectangular wooden box, weighted with stones, which is run over the rollers on which the material to be mangled is placed; **box-master** *Sc.*, a treasurer; **box-meat**, meat packed in boxes for transport; **box-mill**, a modified form of box-tool; **box-motion**, the machinery for operating the shuttle-boxes of a loom; **box-nut**, a screw nut with a closed end; **box-office**, the office at which seats may be booked in advance for a theatrical performance (orig. for the hiring of a box); **box-oyster** *local U.S.*, a fine large oyster, formerly packed in boxes instead of barrels; **box-packing**, material such as cotton waste used for packing axle boxes; **box-piston**, a hollow piston; **box-relay**, a portable relay instrument; **box-rent** *U.S.*, the charge for a private post office box; **box-room**, (*a*) a room for storing boxes, trunks, etc.; (*b*) the dust-guard seat of a car-axle; **box-seat**, the driver's seat on the box of a coach (see sense 6); **box-set**, a theatrical scene closed in with walls and ceiling; **box-shutter**, a shutter that folds back into a box, also called boxing-shutter; **box-snuffers**, snuffers having a box-like receptacle for the cut-off wick; **box-spanner**, a spanner used to turn nuts and bolts which cannot be reached by an ordinary spanner; **box-square**, a metal-working tool used for marking parallel lines on round shafts; **box-stair** (see quot.); **box-staircase** *U.S.*, a closed staircase; **box-standard**, a hollow standard forming the main frame of a machine, combining strength with economy of material (Lockwood); **box-staple**, the staple on a door-post into which the bolt of a lock is shot, when the staple is so shaped that it covers the end of the bolt; **box-step**, in a car, a step or steps having closed-in sides; **box-stew** *U.S.*, a stew of box-oysters; **box-stone** *Geol.* (see quot.); **box-stoop** *U.S.*, a raised platform in front of a building, the steps of which are divided into two or more flights; **box-strap**, a flat bar bent at right angles to confine a square bolt or projection; **box-string**, a string-board of staircase in which the ends of the steps are entirely boxed in, also called *close string*; **box-swivel**, a swivel designed to prevent a fishing-line from tangling; **box-tail**, a box-shaped stabilizer of a biplane; **box-tappet**, a cam for working the shuttle-boxes of a loom; **box-tenon**, a tenon at an angle; **box-toe**, in boots and shoes, a toe with a stiff, strong lining; **box-tool(s**, an attachment to a lathe consisting of tools secured in a box-shaped holder (Lockwood); **box-trap**, a trap, shaped like a box, used for capturing animals; **box-trick**, a conjuring trick produced with the aid of a box; **box-tricycle**, a tricycle with a box in which articles can be carried; **box-tubular** *a.*, defining a tubular boiler in which the enveloping shell consists of flat surfaces designed to resist bulging; **box-valve**, a short rectangular section of a pipe, containing a valve; **box-van**, a van with a flat roof; **box-wagon**, (*a*) a closed van for the conveyance of goods on a railway; (*b*) an open wagon with a box-shaped body; **box-wrench**, a spanner with a socket-head to fit over the nut or bolt to be turned.

1842 FRANCIS *Dict. Arts* s.v. *Camera Obscura*, The *box camera is constructed as follows: procure a box, about 14 inches long E, having another box sliding in it F; the inner box having but one end, and in the centre of that end a double convex lens. 1902 *Encycl. Brit.* XXXI. 690/1 Single-magazine Box Camera. 1885 *Outing* (U.S.) Oct. 17/1 About noon of the 13th. we had descended into a small 'box cañon, where we were met by two white men. 1890 *Harper's Mag.* Apr. 725/1 Here the mountain torrents..pass for the most part through dark precipitous box cañons. *Ibid.* Mar. 569/2 Jim..returned with the *box-cart and horse. 1844 H. STEPHENS *Bk. Farm* II. 341 For a *box-churn, whether horizontal or vertical, the plunger should make about 60 revolutions per minute. 1853 *Jrnl. R. Agric. Soc.* XIV. I. 70 In the box-churn the whey often escapes through the spindle-hole. 1874 KNIGHT *Dict. Mech.* I. 550/1 Box churn ..has two dashers revolving at different speeds. 1894 *Daily News* 10 Sept. 6/5 Fawn and *boxcloth seemed to be the favourite colours. 1898 H. GRAVES, etc. *Cycling* 20 We are not aware of the existence of all-wool box-cloth. 1900 'LUCAS MALET' *Gateless Barrier* 115 Her purple, box-cloth coat and skirt. 1884 KNIGHT *Dict. Mech.* Suppl., **Box Coil*, a steam or hot-water coil of many members, occupying a cubical space comparable in its proportions to a box. 1903 L. A. FLEMMING *Pract. Tanning* 80 Sumac-tanned skins..are usually *box-colored, that is, dyed in trays or dye boxes. 1901 *Daily Chron.* 10 Sept. 10/7 *Box cutter..wanted, for box factory at Watford. 1905 *Ibid.* 21 Nov. 5/6 Two 'paltry pieces' of silk and a *box-desk were among the gifts. 1921 *Dict. Occup. Terms* (1927) § 949 **Box dresser*, lines wooden boxes with paper; labels box, and attaches lace paper edging. 1920 *Glasgow Herald* 18 Sept. 8 An agreement under which fitters, pattern-filers, and *box-fitters in the Glasgow area are to receive an advance of 5*s.* 6*d.* per week. 1886 C. SCOTT *Sheep-farming* 129 If it be intended to use *box food, the sheep require to be trained to eat from the boxes when hoggs. 1874 KNIGHT *Dict. Mech.*, **Box-frame*, a casing behind the window-jamb for counterbalance-weights. 1865 BRANDE & COX *Dict. Sci.*, etc., **Box Girder*, a form of girder resembling a box, made out of boiler plate, fastened together by means of angle irons, which are riveted respectively to the top and bottom plates. 1874 THEARLE *Naval Archit.* 73 The complex and varied systems of box-girder keels and keelsons. 1914 H. R. PROCTER *Making of Leather* 133 If the drawing down is repeated across the skin, a square or '*box' grain is formed. 1921 *Dict. Occup. Terms* (1927) § 449 **Box hand, box man*,..fills monorail bogies with *masse cuite*. *Ibid.* § 522 *Box hand, fudge box hand*, a compositor who sets up type, for 'latest news' or 'stop press,' which is put into a box and inserted in stereo cylinder. *Ibid.* § 554 *Box hand, box maker*,..turns up, to form box side, pieces of cardboard already cut to shape and creased. 1909 JACOBUS, etc. *Standard Bible Dict.* p. xxii, The larger articles [in the Standard Bible Dictionary] will be found to be divided into sections by *box-heads...This is done to facilitate easy cross-reference. 1884 KNIGHT *Dict. Mech.* Suppl., **Box Hook*. 1. A hook used in handling boxes; somewhat like a cotton-hook, which see. 2. A hook made on the plan of a cant-hook; used in closing boxes packed full of fish. 3. Hooks used in pairs in swinging boxes from a lifting-tackle. 1909 'O. HENRY' *Options* (1916) 239 There was a four-room, unpainted *box house in which the family lived. 1874 KNIGHT *Dict. Mech.*, **Box-key*, an upright key, used for turning the nuts of large bolts, or where the common spanner cannot be applied. 1908 *Westm. Gaz.* 11 May 4/1 The double *box-kite aeroplane with which Mr. Farman won the Archdeacon Prize in Paris recently. 1918 H. BARBER *Aeroplane Speaks* Pl. vi, In 1909 came the semi-Wright biplane...Then the first box-kite flown by Mr. Grace at Wolverhampton. *Ibid.* Pl. xii, The Curtiss biplanes..the box-kite type, 1909, on which Mr. Curtiss won the Gordon-Bennett Race at Reims. 1928 C. F. S. GAMBLE *North Sea Air Station* xx. 351 By means of a 5-foot linen box-kite and spare aerial with which I had been experimenting at Yarmouth we were able to get into and keep into [*sic*] constant wireless communication with Yarmouth. 1832 *U.S. Postal Regul.* 43 *Box-letters. 1909 *Century Dict.* Suppl., *Box-loom. 1884 KNIGHT *Dict. Mech.* Suppl., **Box Mangle*, one of which the weight is formed by a box containing stones or blocks. 1873 *Contemp. Rev.* XXI. 741 The treasurer of an ordinary Friendly Society, in Scotland, is sometimes its '*box-master.' 1885 D. BEVERIDGE *Culross* II. 155 The privilege of having a deacon and box master of their own. 1895 D. M. FORRESTER *At the Edge of Heather* ii. 23 The annual choice of a Box master (as the Session Treasurer is still called). 1906 *Daily Chron.* 7 June 5/4 The import of '*box' meat. 1909 *Cent. Dict.* Suppl. s.v. *Box-tool*, A modified form [of box-tool] carrying several cutters is called a *box-mill. 1894 T. W. FOX *Mech. Weaving* 393 The ever-increasing number of

different *box motions. 1888 *Lockwood's Dict. Mech. Engin.*, *Box Nut. 1812 *Examiner* 5 Oct. 631/2 Those who apply first for places at the *Box Office. 1907 *Daily Chron.* 16 May 3/5 The box-office value of every artist of prominence. 1884 KNIGHT *Dict. Mech.* Suppl., **Box Packing*, fibrous waste saturated with oil for the packing of axle boxes. *Ibid.*, **Box Relay* (Electricity), a portable relay instrument which is inclosed in a box. 1841 *Congress. Globe* 20 Feb., App. 343/2 [I proposed] to cure the abuse growing out of *box-rents. 1881 *Congress. Rec.* Mar. 2283/1 Postal funds are such funds as arise from box rents and from the sale of postage-stamps. 1849 DE QUINCEY *Eng. Mail Coach* Wks. 1862 IV. 294 The public took to bribing, giving fees to horse-keepers, etc., who held out their persons as warming-pans on the *box-seat. 1853 'C. BEDE' *Verdant Green* xii, Mr. Verdant Green tipped for the box-seat. 1888 *Lockwood's Dict. Mech. Engin.*, *Box Spanner. 1902 MARSHALL *Metal Tools* 18 A *box-square is an elongated form of square, the chief use of which is for marking parallel lines on round shafts or spindles. 1902 STURGIS *Dict. Arch.*, **Box Stair*, one made with two closed strings, so that it has a boxlike form of construction. 1907 M. H. NORRIS *The Veil* i. 5 Returning to the hall he opened the door of a *box stair-case, ascending unconsciously on tiptoe a broad flight of shallow stairs to an immense attic. 1874 KNIGHT *Dict. Mech.*, **Box-staple* (Carpentry), the box or keeper on a door-post, into which is shot the bolt of a lock. 1893 GEIKIE *Geol.* (ed. 3) 1009 Rounded pieces of brown sandstone, known as '*box-stones', evidently derived from the denudation of a single horizon, and enclosing casts of marine shells. 1874 KNIGHT *Dict. Mech.*, **Box-strap*, a flat bar, bent at the middle, to confine a square bolt or similar object. 1847 STODDART *Angler's Comp.* 138 The *box-swivel is a very necessary part of the minnow-tackle. 1856 'STONEHENGE' *Brit. Rural Sports* 235 Box-Swivels and Hook-Swivels. 1909 *Westm. Gaz.* 23 Oct. 9/1 His Voisin biplane,..with its *box-tail wagging high in the air. 1894 T. W. FOX *Mech. Weaving* 287 A lateral motion..is given to the shuttle-boxes by *box tappets and lever connections. 1911 WEBSTER, *Box toe. 1913 W. H. DOOLEY *Man. Shoemaking* 181 Box Toe, used to hold up the toe of the shoe so as to retain the shape. It is generally of sole leather, but often made of canvas or other material and stiffened with shellac or gum. 1876 J. BURROUGHS *Winter Sunshine* i. 22, I come upon their snares, dead-falls, and rude *box-traps. 1899 *Westm. Gaz.* 26 Dec. 2/2 The claimants of the £500 had, it was admitted, produced a *box trick which to the naked eye was exactly like Mr. Maskelyne's. 1896 *Daily News* 8 Oct. 9/2 The father of the deceased said his son was in the habit of riding a *box tricycle. 1884 KNIGHT *Dict. Mech.* Suppl., **Box Valve*, a box section in a pipe containing a valve, and having a cover for access. 1908 *Westm. Gaz.* 30 Mar. 5/2 A light *box-van. 1874 *Congress. Rec.* Apr. 3377/2 A small..covered carriage, sufficient to enable a Bureau officer to come to the Capitol.. upon a rainy day like this, and not be soaked in a '*box-wagon'. 1886 *Encycl. Brit.* XX. 247/1 Open or box waggon.

Box, *v.*¹ Add: **3. c.** *To box in* or *up*: To enclose in a box or casing.

1864 *Jrnl. R. Agric. Soc.* XXV. II. 354 Provision should be made, when practicable, to fence in or 'box up' the moving parts...It would be very easy to box up the gearing of a fixed thrasher...It would also be impossible to completely box-in a chaff-cutter. 1910 *Autocar Handbk.* (ed. 9) 129 In other cars the motor is boxed in nearly air-tight by a shield underneath and a closed bonnet above.

d. To mix up or allow to be mixed up (different flocks of sheep). Also *absol.* *Austral.*

1881 A. C. GRANT *Bush Life in Queensland* I. 253 All the mobs of different aged lambs which had been hitherto kept apart were boxed up together. *a* 1889 in Barrère & Leland *Dict. Slang* s.v., Now, mind yourselves, for if you box, You'll play the mischief with the flocks. 1890 'R. BOLDREWOOD' *Col. Reformer* ix, At nightfall the fifteen flocks of sheep were all brought in, and 'boxed', or mixed together.

e. *Printing.* To enclose within rules; to print with a border. Also with *in*.

1904 *Technol. & Sci. Dict.* (ed. Goodchild & Tweney), *Box In*, a term indicating that rules should be placed round as a border. 1924 W. M. RAINE *Troubled Waters* xxii, A leaded advertisement..boxed to draw more attention.

7. (Earlier U.S. example.)

1678 *Springfield Rec.* II. 75 Whatever Cart way..shal be stoped..by reason of any Persons boxing of Pine trees, the Improvers of yᵉ. Trees shal remove such nusances.

10. b. To provide with inside planking to prevent caving in, or 'to bring to a required shape, usually with *out, up*' (Webster). *U.S.*

1816 *Boston Selectm.* 18 Apr., To box the ground in making a well. 1821 *Ibid.* 7 Sept., Digging and boxing a cellar.

14. To make in or into the shape of a box.

1889 *Cent. Dict.*, *Box*, to form into a box or the shape of a box: as, to box the scenes on a stage. 1911 WEBSTER, *Box*, to make in the shape of a box; as, to box a cushion.

Box, *adv.* *Naut.* = *ABOX. (Cf. BOX-HAUL, BOX *v.*¹ 13, BOXING *vbl. sb.*¹ 3.)

1886 *Encycl. Brit.* XXI. 603/1 *Box*, or braced *abox*, the head-yards crossed the reverse way of the after-yards.

Box and Cox. The name of a farce written by J. M. Morton in 1847, in which two characters, John Box and James Cox, occupy the same apartment (the one by day and the other by night), etc.; hence applied allusively to an arrangement in which two persons take turns in sustaining a part, occupying a position, or the like.

1881 *Punch* 3 Sept. 100/1 This sort of Box and Cox life in a cabin. 1927 RAVEN *Creator Spirit* iii. 78 Representing mind and body as playing a perpetual game of Box and Cox.

Box-calf. [Named about 1890 by Edward L. White, of White Bros. & Co., Mass., U.S.A., after Joseph *Box*, bootmaker, of London. (The picture of a calf in a box was adopted as an advertising device.)] A calfskin tanned with chrome salts and having a grain of rectangularly crossed lines.

[1899 *Moniteur de la Cordonnerie* 437 (Bonnaffé *Dict.*).] 1904 P. N. HASLUCK *Leather Working* 15 Box Calf.—The grain side is the face of this leather. It is somewhat like firm ooze calf, only black. 1905 E. F. C. SWAYSLAND *Boot & Shoe Design* 87 A box calf skin measuring 13½ feet. 1906 *Boot & Shoe Trades Jrnl.* 26 Jan. 69 Box Calf..manufactured by White Brothers & Co., Boston, Mass., U.S.A., who originated both the name and the make. 1906 A. WATT *Leather Manuf.* 356 In box-calf it is usual to grain two ways only, once from the head to the tail, and then from belly to belly. 1908 TROTMAN *Leather Trades Chem.* 143 Ordinary chromed box-calf shavings containing 5·7 per cent. of chromic oxide.

Box-car. *U.S.* [BOX *sb.*² 24.] A large closed-in railway goods wagon. Also *attrib.*

1856 *Trans. Mich. Agric. Soc.* VII. 334 There are on the road..11 four-wheeled box cars. 1862 *Southern Hist. Soc. Papers* (1883) XI. 293, I made my bed on the top of a box-car, and slept soundly. 1888 *Harper's Mag.* Mar. 565/2 The construction train contained box cars two and three stories high. 1898 *Engineering Mag.* XVI. 69 The Illinois Central equipment was of the standard box-car type. 1917 MATHEWSON *Sec. Base Sloan* i. 3 An hour ago they had been rudely awakened from their sleep in a box car.

Boxed, *ppl. a.* Add: Applied esp. to eatables packed in boxes.

1900 KIPLING in *Times* 15 Mar. 8/1 The boxed machinery. 1905 *Westm. Gaz.* 29 Aug. 10/1 The reception and despatch of the boxed fruit. 1905 *Daily Chron.* 12 Dec. 8/4 Boxed figs are..commanding fairly high prices. 1926 *Chambers's Jrnl.* Apr. 224/1 Boxed luxuries for the good folk of Portree.

Box elder. *U.S.* Also **box alder.** (See BOX *sb.*¹ 3 b.)

1819 E. DANA *Geogr. Sk.* 171 The timber growth..consists principally of..boxelder. 1832 D. J. BROWNE *Sylva Amer.* 103 In the country west of the Alleghanies, where this tree is uncommon, it is called Box Elder. 1845 J. PALMER *Jrnl.* (1847) 30 The streams are lined with cottonwood, willow, and box-alder. 1878 J. H. BEADLE *Western Wilds* xxii. 351 About 10 P.M. three figures appeared in the shadow between the ward meeting-house and the line of box-elders beside it.

Boxer² (bǫ·ksəɹ). Add:

b. A member of a Chinese secret society organized about 1900, whose primary aim was to save the Chinese empire (and was consequently anti-dynastic); the movement ultimately became strongly anti-foreign. Also *attrib.*

The name represents Chinese *i ho chuan* or *chuen*, lit. righteous harmony boxers (fists).

1900 *Westm. Gaz.* 26 Apr. 8/4 A number of Boxers attacked a village where some Chinese Catholics live. *Ibid.* 25 May 5/2 The 'Boxer' menace in China continues to excite anxiety. *Ibid.* 7 June 5/7 A Boxer force was for several weeks drilling..within sight of the foreign concession. 1902 *Encycl. Brit.* XXIX. 228/2 The faith which he [*sc.* Sir Robert Hart] put in the Chinese made him turn a deaf ear to the warnings of the threatening Boxer movement in 1900.

Hence **Boxerism** (bǫ·ksəriz'm), the conduct and practices of the Boxers in China.

1901 *Westm. Gaz.* 11 Apr. 1/2 It is scarcely surprising.. that Boxerism is still lurking beneath the surface. 1907 *Daily Chron.* 28 Sept. 1/7 An outbreak of Boxerism has taken place in China.

Boxer³ (bǫ·ksəɹ). [f. BOX *sb.*¹ + -ER¹.] A box-wood peg-top.

1840 *Peter Parley's Ann.* 85 I'll give you my two pegs for your boxer. 1853 *N. & Q.* 1st Ser. VIII. 63/1. 1881 YOUNG *Ev. Man his own Mech.* § 577.

Bo·xer⁴. *Austral.* [?f. BOX *sb.*² + -ER¹.] A bowler or billycock hat.

1897 *Argus* 9 Jan. 14/2 (Morris) And will you wear a boxer that is in a battered state? 1904 *Westm. Gaz.* 9 June 12/1 In Melbourne..a..man in the ordinary Sunday suit of a worker, a boxer hat, and a blue shirt with a white collar.

Boxing, *vbl. sb.*¹ Add:

I. Various technical uses: see quots.

1874 KNIGHT *Dict. Mech.*, *Boxing*,..the fitting of the shoulder of a tenon in the surface of the timber, which is mortised for the reception of the tenon. 1884 *Ibid.* Suppl., *Boxing Machine*, a machine for boring out the boxes of hubs. 1900 *Coal & Metal Miners' Pocketbk.* 574 Boxing, a method of securing shafts solely by slabs and wooden pegs. 1903 *Daily Chron.* 10 Mar. 10/5 Wheeler..one used to riveting and boxing. 1913 W. H. DOOLEY *Man. Shoemaking* 180 *Boxing*, a term used to designate the stiffening material placed in the toe of a shoe to support it and retain the shape; such as leather, composition of leather and paper, wire net..etc.

4. b. A wooden casing, conduit, etc., constructed after the manner of a box; the lining of a well.

1865–6 *Trans. Ill. Agric. Soc.* VI. 319 A water pipe or boxing eighteen inches in the clear is laid under ground to the centre of the yard. 1907 M. H. NORRIS *The Veil* v. 44 Its [*i.e.* the well's] slimy, moss-covered stone boxing.

7. The words, figures, or signs written or printed above or at the sides of the columns of a table of statistics or the like, to indicate or explain the character of the contents. *U.S.* Cf. *box-head* (a) s. v. *BOX *sb.*² 24.

a 1889 *2nd Ann. Rep. Interstate Com. Commission* 271 (Cent. Dict. s.v. *Table*) The use of miscellaneous in the boxing of this table requires a word of explanation.

8. *pl.* Among millers, coarse flour separated in the process of bolting.

1860 in WORCESTER (citing BRANDE).

Box-tree. Add:

b. Applied to many Australasian species of *Eucalyptus*. Cf. *BOX *sb.*¹ 3 c.

1827 HELLYER in Bischoff *Van Diemen's Land* (1832) 168, I found the stump of a withered box tree. 1849 STURT *Narr. Exped. Central Australia* I. 116 The flats of the Darling..are..lightly wooded, having low and useless box-trees (the *Gobero* of Sir Thomas Mitchell), growing on them. 1883 KEIGHLEY *Who are you?* 43 Resting fast in a box-tree's fork. 1886 KENDALL *Poems* 19 Keen, fitful gusts,.. Fleet down by whistling box-tree butt.

Boxy (bǫ·ksi), *a.*² [f. BOX *sb.*² + -Y¹.]

1. Resembling a box in shape; comparable to a box.

a 1861 T. WINTHROP *John Brent* xxvi. 217 A frowsy county town, with a dusty public square, a boxy church, and a skittley court-house. 1883 SIR W. HARCOURT in A. G. Gardiner *Life* (1923) I. 492 A tall boxy house will not look well there. 1928 *Observer* 26 Feb. 20/2 A very covered and boxy effect.

2. Of the feet of a horse or mule: High and narrow.

1908 *Animal Managem.* 224 'Mule,' 'boxy,' 'narrow,' or 'club' feet are the opposite of 'flat'. *Ibid.* 271 The feet [of the mule] are narrow and boxy, as compared with the horse.

Boy, *sb.*¹ Add:

3. e. In S. Africa, a coloured labourer or servant of any age or race. *Cape boy*, a half-breed resulting from the union of a native black and a white settler.

1839 W. C. HARRIS *Wild Sports S. Afr.* 15 The..boisterous singing of a lame Irish cobbler, who was 'keeping it up'.. with two Hottentot 'boys', neither of whom was under fifty years of age. 1896 *Spectator* 2 May 629 A Cape 'boy' fighting at Bulawayo is..a coloured native enlisted and drilled within the Colony. 1900 *Daily News* 13 July 3/1 Admirable service has been done for the British troops by native dispatch-runners, several of the 'boys'..losing their lives.

6. b. A rough or rowdy (e.g. of the streets); esp. *pl.* in *the boys* = the thieves and swindlers that frequent race-courses. Cf. *B'HOY.

1843 *Punch* 29 Apr. 179/2 The comments and cheers of those very important members of street society, the boys. 1862 [see *BOWERY]. *a* 1889 in Barrère & Leland *Dict. Slang*, Cleansing the rings from..those criminal scoundrels known as the boys. 1890 FARMER *Slang* s.v. *Boys*, Bookmakers speak of their fellows..as the boys. 1909 *Cent. Dict.* Suppl. s.v., *Bowery Boy*, a young rowdy of a type once common in the Bowery, in New York city. 1922 *N. & Q.* 12th Ser. XI. 206/2 *Boys (the)*: *the 'legs'*, the three-card trick, pickpocket, dishonest Turf flotsam and jetsam.

c. *The boy*, champagne. *slang.*

It is said that at a banquet where champagne was handed by a boy, a lady, invited to choose her wine, said she would 'wait for the Boy!' (Cf. Farmer & Henley's *Slang* s.v.)

1882 *Punch* 11 Feb. 69/1 He'll nothing drink but 'B. & S.' and big magnums of 'the Boy'.

Boyam (boi·ăm). [Native name.] 'A native Australian name for the bulbous roots of certain orchids, esteemed for the viscid mucilage they contain' (Simmonds *Dict. Trade*).

1834 G. BENNETT *Wand. N.S.W.* I. 81 The little creatures would readily recognize their favourite '*boyams*' among the specimens I had collected.

Boyey (boi·i), *a.* [f. BOY *sb.*¹ + -Y¹.] Having the characteristic qualities of a boy (as contrasted, e.g. with a girl).

1885 MRS. MOLESWORTH *Carrots* i, He was a very boy-ey boy, very much inclined to look down upon girls in general. 1902 *Lond. Mag.* June 494/2 A delightfully boyey boy.

Boyla (boi·lă). [Native name.] An aboriginal Australian sorcerer.

1865 W. HOWITT *Discov. Australia* I. 386 A superstitious notion that by eating them he should subject himself to the absolute power of boylas, or evil sorcerers.

Boy Scout: see SCOUT *sb.*⁴ 2 c.

Bozeman (bǭu·zmăn). *Geol.* [Place-name in Montana.] A late Tertiary formation in Montana.

1906 CHAMBERLIN & SALISBURY *Geol.* III. 267 In Montana, the Miocene sediments (Bozeman formation) are described as lacustrine.

Brace, *sb.*² **20.** Add: **brace-rod**, a connecting rod used to support or give rigidity to any part of a structure; **brace-shot** *U.S.*, = *BRACKET *sb.* 5 b.

1844 H. STEPHENS *Bk. Farm* I. 428 In this plough..there is usually applied a brace-rod V. 1907 *Westm. Gaz.* 27 Dec. 4/2 On a special collar of the enclosed propeller-shaft are two brace-rods, extending triangular fashion to the sleeves of the live axle. 1915 R. H. DAVIS *With the Allies* 134 To find the range the artillery sends what in the American army are called brace shots.

Brace, *sb.*⁴ *U.S.* [f. BRACE *v.*¹ 5 b.] *To take a brace*: to brace oneself up.

1910 W. M. RAINE *B. O'Connor* 49 You want to take a brace and act like a man.

Brace, *a.* *U.S. slang.* [? attrib. use of BRACE *sb.*²] *Brace game*, a game in which there is concerted cheating. *Brace box*, a 'trained' box at faro.

1902 H. L. WILSON *Spenders* vii. 73 'Billy,' says he, 'cash in and come out; that's a brace game.' 1908 S. E. WHITE *Riverman* vi. 58, 'I tell you, you can't win!' cried Newmark disgustedly. 'It's a brace game pure and simple.' 1908 G. H. LORIMER *J. Spurlock* vi. 116 Life's not even a gamble in this age of commercialism, fo' Fo'tune deals from a brace box.

Brace, *v.*¹

5. Add quot.; also *pass.* (without *up*), to feel encouraged, to be 'bucked'.

1902 MRS. BARNES-GRUNDY *Thames Camp* 219 Zac and I are going to the seaside to be 'braced up'. 1915 ROSHER *In R.N.A.S.* (1916) 78 The C.O. was awfully braced.

b. Also freq. with *up*.

1887 MARIE CORELLI *Thelma* I. xvii, He paused—then suddenly bracing himself up, added [etc.]. 1891 HARDY *Group of Noble Dames* ix. 230 It gave him an opportunity to brace himself up. 1903 *25 Years in 17 Prisons by No. 7* xiii. 125 When I heard the words 'sad news',..I braced myself up, clenched my teeth..and prepared to bear the worst.

c. *intr.* *To brace up*: to brace oneself; to pull oneself together for an effort; also, to take a drink for this purpose. *U.S.*

1809 *Deb. Congress* 20 Jan. 1148 We have been..bracing up; we have had plenty of good wine. 1817 S. R. BROWN *Western Gaz.* 354 If the stomach be foul..take an emetic, and then brace up with bark. 1845 MRS. KIRKLAND *Western Clearings* 62 He braces up for the occasion. 1856 E. G. PARKER *4 July Orat.* (Boston) 7 We may brace up for one day. 1888 *Texas Siftings* 18 Aug. (Farmer) Let's go over to the saloon and brace up with a snifter. 1893 *Strand Mag.* VI. 216/1 At the end of the week she braced up again and soon got over her passion. 1896 G. ADE *Artie* x. 88 W'y, you big stiff, brace up and get through with it before you go daffy. 1898 'MARK TWAIN' *Myst. Stranger* (1916) 130 All that was needed..was that Wilhelm should brace up and do something that should cause favorable talk.

8. (See quot. 1889.) Also, to charge extortionately. *U.S. slang.*

1889 FARMER *Americanisms*, *Brace, To* (Cant.), to get credit by swagger. — *To brace it through*, to succeed by dint of sheer impudence. 1923 WATTS *Luther Nichols* 269, I haven't quite the cheek to brace you for board and lodging both.

Brace, *v.*² Delete †*Obs.* and add: **b.** *trans.* To assume a defiant attitude towards. *U.S.*

1922 ZANE GREY *To Last Man* vii. 165 He must have been crazy or drunk—to pop up there—an' brace us that way. *Ibid.* xii. 263 Ever since that cowman, Blue, braced us an' said he was King Fisher.

Bracelet. Add: **1. b.** *Palmistry.* A wrinkle crossing the wrist at its junction with the hand.

1883 FAITH & ALLEN *Chiromancy* 125 The Rascette or 'bracelets'..will be found in two or three distinctly marked lines underneath the hand. 1891 *Chamb. Encycl.* VII. 727 These last (the bracelets), if well marked, strengthen the effect of the line of life, each bracelet indicating thirty years of life.

c. A narrow band of hair left on the legs of an animal after it has been clipped.

1904 *Windsor Mag.* Jan. 290/1 The only sign of hair being on the ears and the 'bracelets' around the legs.

Bracer¹. Add: **3. b.** A drink taken to brace one up. *U.S.*

1829 *Savannah* (Ga.) *Mercury* 1 July (Th.) If I take..a cooler at nine, a bracer at ten, a whetter at eleven,..who has a right to complain? 1889 *Century Dict.*, *Bracer* 3...specifically, a drink taken early in the morning. (Colloq.) 1921 MULFORD *Bar-20 Three* vii. 87 Fisher..pushed through the thinning crowd to get a bracer at the bar.

Brachial. Add *sb.* **1.** One of the calcareous plates in the branches of a crinoid.

1888 ROLLESTON & JACKSON *Anim. Life* 572 The joints of the arms [in Crinoids] are termed *brachials*.

2. One of a series of bones in fishes to which the pectoral fins are attached.

1873 MIVART *Elem. Anat.* 162 The fourth or lowest of the four *brachials* which together may represent the humerus, and to which the fin-rays are attached.

Brachycephal (bræ·kisĕfæl). [Back-formation from BRACHYCEPHALIC.] A brachycephalic person. So **Brachycra·nial** *a.*

1907 *Practitioner* Aug. 318 Short-headed or brachycranial. 1928 V. G. CHILDE *Most Anc. East* x. 234 The European beakers were made and used by brachycephals.

Brachyodont (bræ·kiǫdǫnt), *a.* Also **brachydont.** [f. Gr. βραχύς short + ὀδούς (ὀδοντ-) tooth.] Designating teeth with short or low crowns and well-developed roots.

1883 W. H. FLOWER in *Encycl. Brit.* XV. 430/1 Modification of [the selenodont form] from a brachyodont to a hypsodont type. 1884 *Geol. Mag.* 548 Detached upper molars of a smaller form, with a brachydont..structure. *Ibid.*, Several lower molars and a fragment of a mandible from Hempstead indicate a brachydont anthracotheroid.

Bracket, *sb.* Add:

5. b. *transf.* The (specified) distance between a pair of shots fired, one beyond the target and one short of it, in order to find the range for artillery; chiefly in the phrase *to establish a bracket*.

1899 *Daily News* 6 Dec. 5/7 At first I fire at 3100 yards, and if I find that my shot is short I fire a second round, say at 3300, in order to go beyond the object. If I see that my shot does go over I am satisfied that I have established what is called 'a long bracket', that is to say, I have found two ranges, 300 yards apart, between which the object must lie. ..I..fire another shot to shorten the distance within which I can then know that the target must be. This we call, on the same principle as the other, 'a short bracket'. 1916 BOYD CABLE *Action Front* 42 The German gun had got its bracket. 1927 *Blackw. Mag.* Apr. 476/2 The shell passed over the ship, to be followed by a second one which fell short, establishing a 'bracket,' which..is all that a gunner desires.

6. *bracket bearings, principle*; **bracket fungus**, **mushroom**, any fungus which grows on trunks of trees forming a bracket-like projection; **bracket system**, in naval architecture (see quot. 1874).

1898 *Westm. Gaz.* 11 Nov. 1/2 Boring out the vessel's stern tubes and *bracket bearings. 1927 *Observer* 28 Aug. 18/1 The so-called *bracket mushrooms that chiefly flourish in rotting trunks have been platforms rather than brackets. 1907 *Westm. Gaz.* 21 May 6/3 The plans being based on the cantilever or *bracket principle. 1874 THEARLE *Naval Archit.* 86 The *Bracket System is the development..of the transverse and longitudinal systems combined, by which iron-clad ships have been built since their introduction. 1909 *Cent. Dict.* Suppl. s.v. *Bottom*, Cellular Double Bottom on the Bracket System of a War-ship.

Bracket, *v.* Add:

3. *intr.* To project like a bracket.

1855 FERGUSSON *Handbk. Archit.* IX. iv. 428 A number of small imitations of arches, bracketing one beyond the other.

4. In finding the range for artillery, to drop one shot beyond (the target) and one short of it. (The nautical term is *straddle*.) Hence **Bra·cketing** *vbl. sb.*

1919 *Athenæum* 23 May 360/1 For a well-known method

of range-finding the Army has the term 'bracketing'. 1926 J. J. CONNINGTON *Death at Swaythling Court* xvi, I took the liberty of bracketing the Lethal Ray machine..on Swaythling Court.

Bra·cketless, *a.* [-LESS.] Not having, or involving the use of, brackets (BRACKET *sb.* 2).

1926 *Glasgow Herald* 24 Mar. 13 The Bracketless Ship... The Bracketless System...A saving of about 5500 pieces would be effected—these pieces being brackets and their connecting angles. *Ibid.* 6 Aug. 8 The 'bracketless' ship, introduced by Sir Joseph Isherwood. *Ibid.* 14 Sept. 9 The British Inventor, the first 'bracketless' oil tanker to be built.

Braconid (bræ·kǫnid), *a.* and *sb.* [f. mod.L. *Bracon* + -ID³.] **A.** *adj.* Of or belonging to the *Braconidæ*, a family of small ichneumon flies. **B.** *sb.* A fly of this family.

1895 *Standard Dict.* 1913 *Oxf. Univ. Gaz.* 4 June 961/1 The Braconids *Cœlinius niger* and *Pezomachus fasciatus*.

Bradbury (bræ·dbəri). [The name of John Swanwick *Bradbury*, Secretary to the Treasury 1913–1919.] Colloquial name for a currency note of £1. (Cf. *FISHER.)

1917 *Punch* 22 Aug. 128 Parting with three Bradburys and three shillings. 1920 *Oxf. Tracts Econ. Subj.* xxvii. 4 The 'Bradbury', nominally a pound, and by statute legal tender for a pound of debt, has lost, from its abundance, a part of its purchasing power. 1920 *Q. Rev.* Apr. 430 Men and women, who had never dreamt of inquiring into the mysteries of the currency, are now eager to learn about the 'Bradbury', the franc or the mark. 1925 G. FRANKAU *Masterson* xvi, Cynthia had decided to 'risk a couple of Bradbury's each way'.

Bra·dded, *ppl. a.* [f. BRAD *sb.* + -ED².] Furnished with brads.

1897 *Westm. Gaz.* 26 Apr. 4/2 Various tips, and pelts, and bradded soles, all described as wear-resisting articles.

Bra·dding, *vbl. sb.* [f. BRAD *v.* + -ING¹.] Fastening with brads.

1901 *J. Black's Carp. & Build.*, *Home Handicrafts* 29 Some folks prefer to glue the mitres first, and this certainly renders the bradding more easy.

Bradoon (brădū·n). Modern form of BRIDOON.

1862 *Catal. Internat. Exhib., Brit.* II. No. 4693 Safety Springs, for riding and driving reins, to both bits, and one rein in hand, to act on the bradoon. 1889 *Catal. New Civil Service Co-operation* 271 Weymouth Bridle, with Stitched Noseband, Steel Bit, Curb and Bradoon.

Bradshaw (bræ·dʃǫ). Colloquial designation of 'Bradshaw's Railway Guide', a time-table of all railway trains running in Great Britain, the earliest form of which was first issued at Manchester in 1839 by George Bradshaw (1801–1853), printer and engraver.

1851 *Fraser's Mag.* Jan. 126/1 It is always dangerous to travel upon the faith of an old Bradshaw. 1855 TROLLOPE *Warden* xvi, He was at breakfast at nine, and for the twentieth time consulted his 'Bradshaw'. 1856 GEO. ELIOT *Ess.* (1884) 229 The word railways, for example, will probably call up, in the mind of a man who is not highly locomotive, the image either of a 'Bradshaw', or of the station with which he is most familiar. 1884 'EDNA LYALL' *We Two* xix, She went at once..for the *Bradshaw*. [1887 MRS. D. DALY *Digging & Squatting S. Australia* 253 Mr. Westgarth says: 'If the through route of Central Australia is some day to be Bradshawed'.] 1914 'BARTIMEUS' *Naval Occasions* xi. (1916) 77 The young Doctor looked up from the year-old 'Bradshaw' with which he was wont to enliven moments of depression by arranging mythical week-ends at friends' houses in various parts of England.

Bradycardia (brædikā·ɹdiă). *Path.* [mod.L., f. Gr. βραδύς slow + καρδία heart.] Slowness of the pulse.

1890 in BILLINGS *Med. Dict.* 1892 A. E. SANSOM *Dis. Heart* 137 Slow Pulse (Bradycardia). 1908 J. MACKENZIE *Dis. Heart* 133 True bradycardia..only occurs when all the chambers of the heart participate in the slow action.

Bradyphrasia (brædifrē¹·ziă). *Path.* [mod. L., f. Gr. βραδύς slow + φράσις speech.] Slowness of speech due to mental defect or disease.

1878 tr. *von Ziemssen's Cycl. Med.* XIV. 816 We find bradyphrasia and paraphrasia developed in a similar manner in conditions of morbid hebetude and intellectual weakness.

Bradyseism (bræ·disaiz'm). *Geol.* [f. Gr. βραδύς slow + SEISM.] A slow rise and fall of the earth's crust. Hence **Bradysei·smic, Bradysei·smical** *adjs.*, pertaining to such a movement.

1896 *Daily News* 11 Feb. 6/2 The slow movements, or bradyseisms..were those which had resulted in the formation of continents.

Brag, *sb.*¹ **6. b.** (Earlier U.S. example.)

1845 *Congress. Globe* 30 Dec. 112/2 [This] looked like playing the game of brag, while the negotiation was pending.

Brag, *a.* Add: **5.** Prime, first-rate, surpassingly good. *U.S.*

1836 *Jeffersonian* 5 May 96 (Th.) The Moselle was a new brag boat, and had made several quick trips. 1857 *Knickerbocker Mag.* Sept. L. 292 Isaac had once been the 'brag hand' of the plantation. 1893 *Outing* (U.S.) XXII. 92/1 His [*sc.* the pup's] sire was the brag runner of the country. 1904 HARBEN *Georgians* xvi. 160 A boy that blowed an army bugle come, an' the brag singer, a young man that sung 'Whar is my wanderin' boy to-night?'

Braga-beaker (brā·gă,bīkəɹ). [f. ON. *braga-* in *bragafull* the cup drunk at funeral feasts.] A cup from which a toast is drunk.

1854 W. B. JERROLD (*title*) A Brage-Beaker with the Swedes, or Notes from the North in 1852. 1921 *Public Opin.* 15 July 61/3 Wielding Thor's hammer and drinking from the braga-beaker in the hall.

Bragger. Add: **2.** *Card-playing.* In the game of brag, a nine or knave.

1807 W. IRVING *Salmag.* 31 Dec. 502 Presently one of them..exclaimed triumphantly, 'Two bullets and a bragger!' and swept all the money into his pocket.

Bragite (brǣ·gait). *Min.* [ad. Sw. *bragit* (1855), f. *Bragi*, a Scandinavian deity: see -ITE¹.] A variety of fergusonite found in Norway and Sweden.

1868 DANA *Min.* (ed. 5) 276, 525.

Braguette (brægĕ·t). Also **brayette.** [OFr.] A piece of armour of the fifteenth century corresponding to the cod-piece.

1867 W. MCDOWALL *Hist. Dumfries* xxvii. 349 His bulky dagger-proof coat of green velvet and scarlet braguette. 1895 *Oracle Encycl.* I. 160/1 Brayette and loin-guard.

Brahmi (brā·mī). [Skr.] The name of one of the oldest alphabets of India, perhaps of Semitic origin.

Cf. Bühler, *On the Origin of the Indian Brahma Alphabet*, 1898.

1902 *Encycl. Brit.* XXXIII. 901/2 The alphabets of India all spring from two sources: (*a*) the Kharosthī, (*b*) the Brāhmī alphabet. 1920 *Blackw. Mag.* May 621/2 A long inscription in Brahmi characters of about 150 B.C.

Brahmoism (brā·mǫiz'm). [f. *Brahmo* in *Brahmo Samāj* (Bengali) = society worshipping the supreme spirit (BRAHMA).] A reformed Hinduism of a theistic character founded by Ram Mohun Roy in 1830. So **Brah·moist**; also **Brah·mo** in same sense.

1857 DASS *Supreme Being of Brahmo Theol.* (Calcutta) 7 There is an impassable gulf which separates unitarian Christianity from Brahmoism. 1862 C. H. MANUEL *Destiny of Human Life* (Calcutta) 17 Brahmoism—pure Theism—is essentially anti-idolatrous. 1870 *Contemp. Rev.* XIII. 232 Which has raised Brahmoism from a small Hindoo sect into a comprehensive religion. *Ibid.* 239 A congregation of Brahmos. *Ibid.* XV. 131 The Brahmoists of both sections may already be numbered by thousands. 1884 RAM C. BOSE (*title*) Brahmoism, or history of Reformed Hinduism from its origin in 1830 to the present time.

Brailed, *ppl. a.* Add: **c.** Hauled (up, etc.) by means of brails. So **Brai·ling** *vbl. sb.* (also *fig.*).

1840 R. H. DANA *Bef. Mast* 226 These trades..blowing steadily on our starboard quarter..without our starting a brace, or even brailing down the skysails. 1849 CUPPLES *Green Hand* xiv. (1856) 138 The brailed foresail. 1902 CORNISH *Naturalist Thames* 8 A furling and brailing-up of the rain-clouds. 1921 *Spectator* 7 May 589/1 The brailing up of the loose-footed sail. 1924 *Weekly Westm. Gaz.* 13 Sept. 568/3 The brailed brown mainsail of a barge.

Braille (brē¹l). The name of Louis *Braille* (1809–1852) used to designate a system of embossed printing for the blind, perfected by him in 1834.

In this system the symbols for the letters are composed of raised dots arranged in different ways. It was adopted as the standard system in England by the British and Foreign Blind Association, 1869–70.

1871 T. R. ARMITAGE *Educ. Blind* i. 8 A modification of the Braille system has been suggested by Dr. Russ, of New York. *Ibid.* iii. 21 The reasons which have induced the Council to adhere to the original Braille, are briefly these:— 1st. The Braille type is very generally diffused [etc.]. 1892 *Daily News* 21 Feb. 5/4 The assistant transcribed her answers, written in Braille, into the ordinary characters.

Brain, *sb.* Add: **3. b.** *To have* (something) *on the brain.* (Early U.S. examples.)

1869 *Congress. Globe* Jan. 182/2 The Gazette seems to have the franking privilege 'on the brain'. 1870 *Ibid.* Mar. 1643/3 The somewhat notorious 'peace commission', who seem to have 'Indian on the brain'.

6. brain-axis = *brain-stem* (Dorland *Med. Dict.* 1901); **brain-ball**, the brain of an enemy slain in combat made into a ball by mixing it with lime and preserved as a trophy; **brain-dressed** *a.*, of skins, dressed with a liquor prepared by boiling deer brains; **brain-fag**, exhaustion of the brain by prolonged mental strain; **brain-fagged** *a.*, suffering from brain-fag; **brain-fever bird**, a bird having a persistent irritating cry; **brain-racking**, racking of the brain; also *ppl. a.*; **brain-sand**, minute particles of gritty substance found in the pineal gland; acervulus cerebri; **brain-stem**, the nerve fibres which connect the upper and front parts of the brain with the spinal cord; **brain-stone** (quots.); **brain-storm**, 'a succession of sudden and severe paroxysms of cerebral disturbance' (Dorland 1901); **brain-sugar** = *CEREBROSE; **brain-wave**, (*a*) a hypothetical telepathic vibration which conveys a thought from one mind to another without recourse to the usual methods of communication; (*b*) *colloq.* a sudden inspiration or bright thought.

1904 *Westm. Gaz.* 9 July 5/1 The old king, who sat with the *brain-ball in his head. 1907 *Folk-Lore* June 228 Mesgegra's brain-ball, an object that could be slung from a sling. 1887 *Harper's Mag.* June 61/2 These [deerskin leggings] were prepared of *brain-dressed skins that perfectly turned the rain and dew. 1857 DUNGLISON *Med. Lex.*, *Brain Fag. 1876 *Congress. Rec.* Aug. 5124/1 Prostrated by a protracted attack of 'brain-fag'. 1884 W. JAMES in *Mind* IX. 17 In states of extreme brain-fag the horizon is narrowed almost to the passing word. 1902 MCFAUL *Ike Glidden* ii. 13 He continued in this *brain-fagged and mentally-deranged condition for several weeks. 1903 *Daily Chron.* 20 Feb. 5/2 Nine weary brain-fagged City men were enjoying their pipes. 1885 in Dufferin *Viceregal Life in India* ii. (1890) 30 The '*brainfever' bird repeats his name over and over again until he nearly gives you the malady itself. 1902 *Badminton Mag.* Mar. 243 The ceaseless, irritating cry of the brain-fever bird. 1902 CROKER *Cat's-Paw* xiii, The 'coppersmith' and the 'brain-fever bird' were indefatigable. 1897 *Daily News* 30 Mar. 8/1 It is this that causes the English in South Africa so much *brain-racking. 1905 *Westm. Gaz.*

22 Mar. 1/3 It was a noisy..monster..and began its torturing, brain-racking persecution at eight in the morning. 1905 *Daily Chron.* 29 Sept. 3/3 Some less brain-racking railway guide. 1909 *Ibid.* 10 Mar. 9/2 A brain-racking problem. 1910 *Ibid.* 9 Feb. 6/5 An eternity of brain-racking dulness. 1873 T. H. Green *Introd. Pathol.* (ed. 2) 75 The corpora amylacea ..are very liable to become calcified, and they then constitute one form of '*brain sand'. 1890 Billings *Med. Dict.*, *Brain stem. 1927 Haldane & Huxley *Anim. Biol.* vi. 142 When we are 'doing nothing' the cortex is all the time inhibiting the postural centres in the brain-stem from producing rigidity. 1681 Grew *Musæum* II. v. i. 244 A flat Horney Shrub..Rooted in a kind of *Brain-stone. 1758 Borlase *Nat. Hist. Cornw.* 240 The fossil corals..such as brain stone. 1855 Kingsley *Glaucus* 34 A beautiful madrepore or brainstone on your mantelpiece, brought home from some Pacific coral-reef. 1870 — *At Last* i, Huge.. sea-urchins, huger brainstone corals. 1871 T. R. Jones *Anim. Kingd.* (ed. 4) 112 The beautiful structures known as *Meandrinæ*, or 'brain-stones'. 1907 *Daily Chron.* 13 Feb. 7/5 Ordeals of mind which formed a *brain-storm or mental explosion. 1907 *N. Y. Even. Post* 23 May 4 Referring to Mr. William's discussion,..[he] declares 'it is the result of a brain-storm'. 1908 *Westm. Gaz.* 8 Aug. 4/3 In the closing years of his active life, Ruskin had suffered from recurrent brain-storms. 1922 *Daily Mail* 2 May 5/4 If he were crossed he had brain storms which took the form of violent temper and depression. 1901 Dorland *Med. Dict.* (ed. 2), *Cerebrose*, *brain-sugar, $C_6H_{12}O_6$; a principle derivable from the brain-substance, and sometimes found in diabetic sugar. 1871 Anne Thackeray *Lett.* (1924) 147 You must have sent a *brain wave, for oddly enough we had all just read the book..when your letter came saying you too had been reading it. 1886 *Proc. Soc. Psych. Research* Oct. 178 Such expressions as 'brain-waves' (Knowles), 'mentiferous ether' (Maudsley)..testify to this natural, though premature, desire to ticket or identify a force which..cannot at present be correlated with nerve-force [etc.]. 1890 *Harper's Mag.* Apr. 744/1 Lucilla, with what she was fond of terming a brain wave, comprehended the situation. 1904 Sladen *Playing the Game* vii, There was a brain-wave between Rich and myself. 1916 *Blackw. Mag.* Aug. 264/1 Then the wirers got brain waves, saw the folly of their first orders,..and began to panic terribly. 1925 Mallory in E. F. Norton *Fight for Everest 1924* 219 I've had a brain-wave—no other word will describe the process by which I arrived at another plan for climbing the mountain.

Brainily (brē·nili), *adv.* [f. Brainy + -ly [2].] In a brainy fashion; with clever use of the wits. So **Brai·niness.**

1922 *Daily Mail* 21 Nov. 10 Lewis's tactics..were extremely bad. There was no suggestion of braininess. 1923 *Ibid.* 29 May 12 Against Lewis,..he certainly fought brainily.

Brake, *sb.*[3] 2. Add later quots. and: **brake-(break-)man, brakesman,** a man who operates a baker's kneading-machine **brake-staff** (see quots.).

1834-6 Barlow in *Encycl. Metrop.* (1845) VIII. 801/2 [The dough] is deposited on a strong wooden platform or table, called a *break*, to be operated upon by the breaksman, who seizes a strong lever called a *break-staff*, with which he presses down the dough. 1837 S. Graham *Bread* 93 The machine which the bakers call the break, used in making crackers and sea-bread. 1845 Dodd *Brit. Manuf.* V. 23 Ships' biscuits..made by hand...The dough was..taken from the trough and put on a wooden platform called the break. On this platform worked a roller, called the break-staff...One end..was loosely attached by a kind of staple to the wall, and the breakman, riding or sitting on the other end, worked the roller to and fro over the dough, by an uncouth jumping or shuffling movement. 1921 *Dict. Occup. Terms* (1927) § 433 *Brake operator, brakesman, breaksman*, ..is one of two men who operate brake machine for compressing, with rollers, kneaded paste into sheets, preparatory to biscuit stamping.

Brake, *sb.*[7] 3. Add: *brake-drum, -horse-power, lever*; **brake-cylinder** (cf. *brake-pipe*); **brake-gear,** the whole braking apparatus of a motor-car or train; **brake-handle,** a hand lever controlling a brake, taking the place of the usual brake-wheel; **brake-pipe,** the pipe of an automatic air-brake, which conveys compressed air to the cylinders operating the brakes of a railway train; **brake-strap,** a strap which surrounds the pulley of a brake worked by friction.

1874 Knight *Dict. Mech.* I. 356/2 The air-pipe under each car makes connection by a branch with..a..*brake-cylinder. 1896 *Cosmopolitan* XX. 420/1 A *brake-drum of peculiar construction placed under the seat. 1908 *Westm. Gaz.* 4 June 4/2 Inside the brake-drum..are four stout spiral springs. 1908 *Daily Chron.* 2 Jan. 6/4 It was far more important for a man to look to his *brake gear than to his speed gear. 1902 *Ibid.* 16 July 8/4 The woman climbed out at the back, using the *brake-handle as a step. 1908 *Westm. Gaz.* 16 July 4/2 For showing the *brake-horse-power actually developed at the road wheels. 1886 *Encycl. Brit.* XX. 249/1 The brake can be at once released by restoring the pressure in the *brake-pipe. 1835 Ure *Philos. Manuf.* 53 The frame..acts, of course, upon the slide-pieces..which hold the *brake-strap. 1897 *Outing* (U.S.) June 262/1 Right thumb on spool of reel, left thumb in leather brake-strap.

Brake, *v.*[5] Add: **b.** *intr.* To act as brakesman on a train. *U.S.*

1892 Gunter *Miss Dividends* 263, I'm braking on the Burlington again, and we're bound for Chicago.

2. To slow *up* by means of the brakes.

1891 E. S. Ellis *Check No. 2134* ii. 13 He felt the train braking up for the Station.

Brake(s)man. 2. *U.S.* (Earlier examples.)

1843 *Proc. Western Railroad Corp.* 48 Amount paid Brakemen on all the trains. 1848 W. Templeton *Locomot. Eng.* (ed. 2) 81 The amount of wages for breaksmen.

Bra·key. *U.S. colloq.* Also **brakie, breaky.** [f. Brakeman: see -y [6].] A brakesman on a train.

1887 M. Roberts *Western Avernus* 238 The brakie came down a step and made a kick at him. 1891 C. Roberts *Adrift Amer.* 92 Jumping on an east bound freight..I managed to..keep on it till I got to..Alameda, where I was spotted by an avaricious 'breaky'. 1911 H. Quick *Yellowstone N.* xii. 315 An' me ostrichized by the very brakey in the caboose.

Braking (brē·kiŋ), *vbl. sb.* [f. Brake *v.*[5] + -ing [1].] The action of applying a brake (to a wheel); also *attrib.*

1904 *Daily Chron.* 15 June 6/7 A clever braking arrangement secures a representation of the difficulties encountered in running on the metals. 1905 *Ibid.* 13 Feb. 3/7 Frictional braking is jarring, uncertain, difficult of gradual application, and most destructive to the parts concerned. 1909 *Westm. Gaz.* 16 Sept. 5/1 Fixed to these chains is a braking band.

Bramantesque (brāmănte·sk), *a.* [ad. It. *Bramantesco*, f. the name of *Bramante* d' Urbino (1444–1514), a celebrated Italian architect.] Designating the style of architecture now known as Renaissance.

1883 C. C. Perkins *Ital. Sculp.* 182 *note*, The artist who introduced Renaissance architecture, then called Bramantesque, into Lombardy. 1908 Mrs. E. Wharton *Hermit*, etc. 162 The Library cupola assumed a Bramantesque grace.

Bramling (bræ·mliŋ). *local.* Also Brambling. [The name of *Bramling* Farm, Ickham, Kent, where the first sets were raised.] A species of hop.

1899 *Westm. Gaz.* 15 Sept. 9/3 In many of the important parishes the Bramlings are all picked. 1902 *Times* 22 Sept. 11/6 Both the Bramlings and the Goldings have grown out fairly satisfactorily.

Bran, *sb.*[1] 3. Add:

bran-dance *U.S.* (see quot. 1833); **bran-drench,** a bath of bran and water in which leather is placed to remove the lime used in liming; **bran-duster** (early U.S. examples); **bran-pie** (see Pie *sb.*[2] 2); **bran-tub** = bran-pie.

1833 *Sk. D. Crockett* 148 This is the famous *bran-dance of the west, and derives its name from the fact that the ground is generally sprinkled with the husk of Indian meal. 1851 *Arkansas Doctor* (Philad.) 52 (Th.) There I stood, looking kin to a fool at a bran-dance. 1887 *Harper's Mag.* Dec. 61/2 It all kem about from that thar bran dance. 1883 Haldane *Workshop Rec.* Ser. II. 373 *Bran-drench..is prepared by soaking wheaten-bran in cold water..and straining the extract. 1853 *Trans. Mich. Agric. Soc.* IV. 35 E. R. Benton, Cleveland O. [exhibited a] *bran duster. 1859 Bartlett *Dict. Amer.* (ed. 2), *Bran-duster*, a sort of bolt in which the bran is freed from adhering flour. 1889 *Peel City Guardian* 28 Dec. 7/4 Sometimes what is termed a '*bran pie' is employed..for storing the presents in. 1904 *Daily Chron.* 27 Feb. 3/2 It is all very well to laugh over inept and tasteless fiction...But let the parents remember to be careful what toys they allow in the bran-pie. 1858 C. Parry in E. Parry *Mem.* vii. (1870) 173 It quite reminded me of the *bran-tub itself as I unpacked each separate article. 1909 *Westm. Gaz.* 22 Apr. 8/2 Sideshows will contain the ever-popular phrenologist's tent and bran-tub.

Branch, *sb.* Add: **2. b.** *U.S.* (Earlier and later examples.)

1674 in *Maryland Hist. Mag.* I. 10 Running north and by east fifty perches to a bounded oak by a small branch. 1699 *Cal. Virginia St. Papers* I. 64 We came to a broad Branch of about fifty or sixty yards wide. 1786 Washington *Diaries* III. 9 Found a Fox in the Branch within Mr. Thomson Mason's Field. 1796 B. Hawkins *Lett.* 25, I came to a branch covered with reeds. 1817 S. R. Brown *Western Gaz.* 12 Cane on the creeks and reed on branches. 1833 J. Hall *Leg. West* 27 He proceeded cautiously towards a rivulet, or in the vernacular of the country, a branch, that meandered along the foot of the hill. 1872 Eggleston *Hoosier Schoolm.* xxviii. 187 It was just by the brook, or as they say in Indiana, the 'branch'. 1887 'C. E. Craddock' *Keedon Bluffs* 109 He was the first fellow to fall into the briars and to flounder into the branch. 1917 Mathewson *Sec. Base Sloan* v. 67 An' there's a branch close by it too, mighty nice tastin water, Mas Wayne.

10. (Earlier U.S. example.)

1783 *Mass. Stat.* 11 July, To give to each of the said pilots branches or warrants for the due execution of the duties of their respective offices.

12. c. *branch bank* (early U.S. examples); **branch house,** an offshoot of a religious community, business firm, etc.

1796 *Boston Directory* ad fin., *Branch bank. State bank. 1832 *Deb. Congress* 8 Mar. 2073 Their great rival competitor, a branch of the Bank of the United States,..discounted at six per cent...Hence this branch bank was the great burden of their complaint. 1835 J. H. Ingraham *South-West* II. 165 It contains also a branch bank, court-house, gaol [etc.]. 1840 K. H. Digby *Mores Cath.* x. i. (1847) III. 229/1 Cisteaux, the mother house of the order, founded..in 1098...La Ferté was the first branch house. 1872 Geo. Eliot *Middlem.* lxi, There was a branch house at the west end.

13. branch-cut *Math.*, a line which may not intersect itself, which joins two branch-points or one branch-point to infinity; **branch-grass** *U.S.* (see quot.); **branch-island,** an island beside a river formed by an *Anabranch; **branch pilot** (earlier U.S. example); **branch-point** *Math.*, a fixed point upon a Riemann's surface round which two or more branches of an algebraic function of a complex variable move in such a way that the values of the function are interchanged; also called the point of ramification; **branch-water** *U.S.*, brook-water.

1837 Colman *Rep. Agric. Mass.* (1838) 18 **Branch Grass*, a short reedy grass, resembling much the fox grass..branches much and from this circumstance derives its name. 1834 Jackson in *Jrnl. R. Geog. Soc.* IV. 79 Thus, such branches of a river as after separation re-unite, I would term anastomosing-branches; or, if a word might be coined, ana-branches, and the islands they form, *branch-islands. 1783 *Mass. Stat.* 11 July, Every *branch pilot being commissioned and qualified as aforesaid. 1879 *Encycl. Brit.* IX. 823/2 *Branch-point (verzweigungspunkt). 1893 Forsyth *Th. Functions* vi. § 71. 111 All the singularities (and the branch-points, if any) lie on the discriminating circle. 1902 Clapin *Dict. Amer.* s.v., **Branch-water*, a Southern expression for stream-water, as distinguished from well-water. 1903 A. Adams *Log Cowboy* xiii. 200, I had scarcely drunk anything in three months but branch water.

Branchite (bræ·ŋkəit). *Min.* [ad. G. *branchit* (1842), f. the name of Professor J. *Branchi* of Pisa: see -ite [1].] A mineral resin found in fossil pine wood.

1862 Dana *Man. Min.* 97 *Branchite*, found with coal, especially brown coal, and resembling wax or tallow. 1883 *Encycl. Brit.* XVI. 429/1 Branchite,..is similar [to Scheererite].

Branchling (bra·nʃliŋ). [f. Branch *sb.* + -ling [1].] A small branch.

1910 Belloc *On Something* 272 The ovals of white where the branchlings had been cut away.

Brand, *sb.* 4. c. (Earlier U.S. example.)

1728 *Braintree Rec.* 126 It was also voted that the Brands of the Town for Shingles & Clapboards be a small [B].

d. *spec.*, a mark of ownership impressed on cattle or horses by branding. Also *attrib.* and *Comb.*: **brand blotter,** one who steals cattle and obliterates the ownership-marks. *U.S.*

1834 *Visit to Texas* vi. 59 As the brands on horses afford the only evidence of their identity,..the rules observed in respect to them are very strict. 1869 C. L. Brace *New West* xxii. 288 The brands, both of cattle and horses,..are controlled by law in California. 1888 Roosevelt in *Century Mag.* Apr. 860 A man must have natural gifts, as well as great experience, before he becomes a good brand-reader. 1889 Farmer *Americanisms*, *Brand*, a mark of proprietorship placed upon cattle, in the West especially...All brands [of cattle] are registered, and brand-readers are appointed as inspectors. *Ibid.*, *Brand-book*, a register of the multitudinous marks used in branding. *Ibid.*, *Brand-bunch*, a small herd of cattle. 1891 C. Roberts *Adrift Amer.* 193 There was some very shady business carried on, such as brand-altering. 1910 W. M. Raine *B. O'Connor* 107 You red-haided [= headed] son of a brand blotter.

5. (Earlier U.S. example.)

1692 *Connecticut Probate Rec.* I. 456, I..give unto my beloved son Samuel Halle..my two Horse Brands.

6. b. A steer or other animal bearing a particular brand-mark. *U.S.*

1903 A. Adams *Log Cowboy* vii. 90, I must have inspection papers before I can move a brand out of the county in which it is bred.

Brand, *v.* **2.** Add: *spec.* To mark cattle or horses in this way. orig. *U.S.*

1644 *Connecticut Public Rec.* I. 118 Owners..shall earemarke or brand all their Cattle and swyne that are aboue halfe a yeare old. 1669 *Springfield Rec.* II. 101 There are many horses to be branded. 1765 Washington *Diaries* I. 216, 22 Calves and Year[lin]gs branded on the Right Shoulder GW. 1772 *Carroll Papers* in *Maryland Hist. Mag.* XIV. 364 A darkish Grey Horse..Branded on the near Shoulder CC. 1834 *Visit to Texas* vi. 59 They are..purchased for three or four dollars, branded, hobbled [etc.]. 1869 C. L. Brace *New West* xxii. 288 Each owner..lassoed the cattle which were his, branding the calves and those whose marks were somewhat obliterated.

Brandenburg. Add: **b.** (also **brandebourg**). Ornamental trimmings (see quot. 1882) on a woman's dress in fashion from about 1880 to 1910.

1882 Caulfeild & Saward *Dict. Needlew.* 44/2 *Brandenbourgs.* Synonymous with 'Frogs.' A button formed somewhat in the shape of a long and narrow barrel, smaller at the ends than the middle, and made of silk on a wooden foundation. 1891 *Queen* 17 Jan. 103/1 Costumes of Hussar-blue cloth with black braid brandebourgs. 1902 *Daily Chron.* 8 Nov. 8/3 The fulness of the fronts is finished with brandebourgs of silk cords. 1909 *Westm. Gaz.* 17 July 15/1 It hangs rather full from the waist, is open in front, or caught with Brandenburgs of braid or tinsel.

Brandified. Add:

2. Mixed or treated with brandy.

1841 Thackeray *Mem. Gormandising* Wks. 1900 XIII. 576 A brandyfied liquor called sherry. 1877 Geo. Easton *Wine of Cana*, Brandified and whiskeyfied wines.

Branding, *vbl. sb.* **2.** Add: *branding-pen*; **branding-chute** *U.S.*, a gradually narrowing enclosure into which cattle are driven to be branded.

1895 *Funk's Stand. Dict.*, *Branding-chute. 1900 *Congress. Rec.* Jan., App. 22/1 Standing on a branding shute backed up against a sod corral out on the range. 1911 Mulford *Bar-20 Days* xx. 197 Johnny Nelson waited..on the platform of the branding chute. 1903 'O. Henry' *Rolling Stones* (1915) 88 He proved to be..as good..in the *branding pen as most of them.

Brandisite (bræ·ndisəit). *Min.* [ad. G. *brandisit* (1846), f. the title of Clement, Count of *Brandis*, after whom the mineral was named: see -ite [1].] A variety of seybertite.

1868 Dana *Min.* (ed. 5) 508. 1883 *Encycl. Brit.* XVI. 413/2 Brandisite is similar [to Clintonite].

Brandtite (bræ·ndtəit). *Min.* [ad. Sw. *brandtit* (1888), f. the name of Georg *Brandt*, Master of the Swedish Mint: see -ite [1].] Hydrated arsenate of calcium and manganese occurring in crystal form near Pajsberg in Sweden.

1896 Chester *Dict. Min.*

Brandy, *sb.* Add:

1. b. With *a* and *pl.* A drink of brandy. Similarly *brandy-and-soda*, pl. *brandies-and-sodas*.

1884 G. Moore *Mummer's Wife* (1887) 293 The brandies and sodas supped in the dressing room. 1900 Miss Glyn *Visits Elizabeth* (1906) 95 Charlie had two brandies-and-sodas instead of his usual glass of milk. 1903 *Daily Chron.* 11 Nov. 5/2 Took a brandy before going to kirk, lest I should smell of whisky in the house of the Lord!

2. brandy-smash *U.S.* (see quot. 1909 and Smash *sb.*[1] 5).

1855 M. Thompson *Doesticks* xxxii. 290 [A] man followed me in, and as I was taking a 'brandy-smash', he stepped up and asked me my name. 1869 'Mark Twain' *Innoc. Abr.* xv. 149 Our general said..'Give us a brandy smash!' 1909 *Century Dict.* Suppl., *Brandy-smash*, a drink made by mixing brandy with crushed ice and putting a few sprigs of mint in the glass.

Branner (bræ·nəɹ). [f. Bran *sb.*[1] + -er [1].]

1. An operative who cleans tinned plates with bran.

1881 *Instr. Census Clerks* (1885) 94 White Branner. 1921 *Dict. Occup. Terms* (1927) § 279 *Branner*, a tinman's helper attending branning machine,..sometimes specifically designated according to whether black or white plates are being cleaned, e.g., black branner, white branner.

2. A machine for removing the oil from tinned plates by means of bran and slaked lime.

1902 *Sci. American* 1 Nov. 290/2 As the plates leave the tin pot, they have upon them a thin coating of oil which has to be removed...They are put into a branner which is located conveniently at the side of the tinning machine.

Brash, *a.*[2] Add: (Illustrations of U.S. usage.)

1837 R. M. Bird *Nick of Woods* I. viii. 120 Strannger thar's as brash as a new hound in a b'ar fight. 1888 'C. E. Craddock' *Broomsedge Cove* ii. 27 Ye notice how turrible brash Josiah Preen be,—can't wait fur pa'son ter summons him.

b. Hard, harsh, rough. Also as *adv.* *U.S.*

1868 *Putnam's Mag.* Aug. (De Vere) See here, you are playing this a little too brash. 1871 Schele de Vere *Americanisms* (1872) 446. 1896 G. Ade *Artie* iii. 23, I swore I'd get next, no matter what kind of a brash play I had to make. 1901 *Munsey's Mag.* XXIV. 481/1 Ordinarily he had an impudent swagger, and was inclined to be 'brash' towards his fellow men.

2. Active, quick. Also as *adv.* *U.S.*

1887 'C. E. Craddock' *Keedon Bluffs* 63 'Whar's that buckeye tree ye war a-goin ter cut down fur me so brash?' 1891 Marah E. Ryan *Pagan of Alleghenies* viii. 118, I ain't so brash in the timber as I'd like to be.

Bra·shness. [f. Brash *a.*[1]] Brittleness.

1864 *Ret. Agric. Soc. Maine* 54 They [*sc.* sheep] become very fat in the summer, which increases the brashness of the wool. 1929 Nutman in *Ann. Appl. Biol.* XVI. 41 The term 'brashness' arose in America, and is now in common use in the timber trade of both this country and the U.S.A. In this paper its use will be restricted to that condition of timber.. which produces a peculiar 'carroty', short, fracture.

Brasque (brask), *v.* [f. Brasque *sb.*] *trans.* To line with brasque. Hence **Brasqued** *ppl. a.*

1880 *Encycl. Brit.* XIII. 319/2 The bed of this latter [*sc.* finery] is 'brasqued' or lined with charcoal powder moistened and rammed in. 1885 *Spons' Mechanics' Own Bk.* 17 If brass be heated in a brasqued crucible.

Brass, *sb.* Add:

5. b. Phr. *To come* (or *get*) *down to brass nails* or *tacks*: to come to facts or realities. orig. *U.S.*

1903 *N. Y. Sun* 28 Nov. 3 This bold sister was the first.. to get down to brass tacks in a discussion of the scandal. 1904 G. H. Lorimer *Old Gorgon Graham* 217, I cut it short there, and asked her to get down to brass tacks, as I was very busy. 1911 H. Quick *Yellowstone N.* xi. 288 When you come down to brass nails.

6. brass-helmeted *a.*, wearing a brass helmet.

1897 *Westm. Gaz.* 22 Nov. 9/1 The brass-helmeted firemen. 1904 *Ibid.* 26 April 5/1 At times the great masses of fire seemed to envelop the brass-helmeted men.

7. brass-blacking, a dead black surface given to brass ornaments by treatment with chemicals; **brass-bounder,** (*a*) see quot. 1890; (*b*) an apprentice on board ships of English companies, so called from the brass on his uniform; **brass-colour,** a preparation of oxidized brass used to stain glass to various tints of blue and green; **brass-hat** *slang*, an officer of high rank in the British army, so called on account of the gilt ornamentation of his cap; **brass-plater** *slang*, a man of the merchant class; **brass-powder,** a powder consisting of copper or one of its alloys used in varnish; **brass-rag,** in slang phr. *to part brass-rags*, to quarrel; **brass-rubbing** *a.*, that takes rubbings of old brasses; so **brass rubber, -rubbing** *vbl. sb.*

1884 Knight *Dict. Mech.* Suppl., **Brass-blacking*, a dead black color; used freely with French optical instruments. 1890 Farmer *Slang*, **Brass-Bounder* (nautical), a midshipman. 1927 *Blackw. Mag.* Sept. 374/2 There were none but sailors, brass-bounders, stewards. 1839 Ure *Dict. Arts* 169 *Brass Colour..is prepared by exposing for several days thin plates of brass upon tiles in the *leer* or annealing arch of the glass-house, till it be oxidized into a black powder. 1893 Kipling *Many Invent.*, *In the Rukh* 210, I tell you der big *brass-hat pizness does not make der trees grow. 1904 *Defence of Duffer's Drift* 16 Whether some 'brass hat' might not come round and inspect us next day. 1927 *Bulletin* 22 Sept. 5/2 A Rolls-Royce car containing two military 'brass-hats.' 1921 *Glasgow Herald* 9 Apr. 6 Steelworkers and bankers, ship-platers and '*brass-platers', 'workers' and 'parasites', we shall all have to take off our coats. 1927 *Scots Observer* 16 July 9/1 Brass-platers and fund-eaters are living spaciously in the southern counties of England. 1839 Ure *Dict. Arts* 169 Only so much of the *brass powder and varnish should be mixed at a time as is wanted for immediate use. 1904 Kipling *Traffics & Discov.* 49 Or you and me'll part *brass rags. 1916 *Punch* 15 Mar. 186/2 They had parted brass-rags' over Gallipoli, it was true. 1922 Mrs. A. Sidgwick *Victorian* vii, If you dare to use that word flapper in my hearing..we part brass rags. 1856 *Athenæum* 17 May 626 The quiet haunts of the *brass-rubber. 1893 *Girl's Own Paper* May (*heading*), Brasses and *Brass-rubbing. 1897 (*title*) Journal of the Oxford University Brass-Rubbing Society.

Brass, *sb.*[2] Modern form of Brace *sb.*[2] 2 (fathom).

1887 *Bombay Port Trust, Prince's Dock Extension Wks.* Progr. Rep. No. 28, 1,426 brass were built during the month, making a total of 46,528 brass since the commencement.

Brasserie (bræ·səri). [Fr., orig. = brewery, f. *brasser* to brew.] A beer-saloon, usually one in which food is served.

1882 *Ess. fr. Critic* (N.Y.) 124 (Stanf.) His comrades were singing in the brasserie. 1887 *Athenæum* 1 Jan. 10/3 [They] are delighted to earn a cheap reputation at the *café* or the *brasserie*. 1888 *Pall Mall Gaz.* 6 Mar. 4 The employment of girls in brasseries, which have so evil a name. 1899 *Westm. Gaz.* 21 Sept. 10/2 At last London has a *brasserie* worthy of the Metropolis. 1926 *Sunday at Home* June 536/1 You are impressed at once by the contrast of the innumerable *brasseries* and restaurants with our wretched public-houses.

Brassia (bræ·siă). [f. the name of *Brass*, a gardener who collected plants and seeds in Africa for Kew Gardens: see -ia [1].] An orchid of the genus so named, the species having yellow, brown, or purple flowers.

1899 Rodway *In Guiana Wilds* ii, Here also Allan found his first orchid, a Brassia.

Brassière (bræ·siēəɹ). [Fr.] A woman's underbodice worn to support the breasts.

1912 *Queen* 27 July 10 (Advt.) The Stylish Figure of To-Day requires a Brassiere.

Brassily (bra·sili), *adv.* [f. Brassy *a.* + -ly [2].]

1. With a brassy noise.

1898 Kipling *Day's Work* 94 Its band playing clashily and brassily a popular but impolite air.

2. With impudent or brazen confidence.

Brassy (bræ·si), *sb.*[2] *Golf.* Also **brassey, brassie.** [f. Brass *sb.* + -y [3].] A wooden club shod with brass.

1888 *Daily News* 2 July 5/1 The golfer will hunt for his 'brassey' in vain. 1895 Linskill *Golf* iii. (ed. 3) 20 A brassey is very similar to a wooden niblick, but..the sole of the head is shod with a plate of brass as a protection to the wood and bone.

b. *ellipt.* for *brassy shot.*

1906 *Daily Chron.* 22 May 9/5 He sliced his drive badly, but played a perfect brassey to within four yards of the pin. 1909 *Ibid.* 22 Apr. 8/4 His tee shots and brassies being of fine length and direction.

c. *attrib.*, as *brassy player, shot, stroke.*

1894 *Westm. Gaz.* 21 Dec. 7/2 To the third hole in, he got away a fine tee shot, which he followed by a good brassy stroke to the green. 1897 *Ibid.* 30 Dec. 7/3 Mr. Ramsay Islay..killed a seagull on the wing with a brassey shot. 1904 *Ibid.* 1 Jan. 3/1 He is a good brassy player.

Brassy, *a.* **3.** Add In medical use, describing a cough.

1880 Barwell *Aneurism* 91 Severe brassy cough. 1895 *Oracle Encycl.* II. 221/2 The patient..awakens..with a peculiar cough, called by physicians 'brassy'.

Bravaisite (brăvē·zəit). *Min.* [ad. F. *bravaisite* (1878), f. the name of Professor A. *Bravais*: see -ite [1].] A hydrous silicate of aluminium occurring in crystalline layers in the coal-measures of Noyant, Allier, France.

1883 *Encycl. Brit.* XVI. 425/1.

Brave, *v.* **7.** Delete †*Obs.* and add: Now in *to brave it out.*

1855 Tennyson *Maud* I. iv. v, However we brave it out, we men are a little breed.

Braveness. Delete ? *Obs.* and add:

1927 T. R. Glover in *Daily News* 14 May 4/3, I was much moved by the braveness and sincerity of the works I read.

Bray (brē), *sb.*[3] *Her.* Also **brey.** [a. OF. *braie, braye*, **breie*, now *broie*.]

1. A semicircular figure representing a barnacle or bit to restrain a restive horse.

1863 Boutell *Man. Her.* 45 *Breys*, barnacles for a horse's nose, used in breaking the animal. 1864 — *Her. Hist. & Pop.* xv. (ed. 3) 173 Three breys or barnacles in pale ar.

2. (Corresponding to F.) A tool used for breaking hemp, used as a bearing.

1882 Cussans *Handbk. Her.* 109 A Hemp-brey is really the same instrument as a Horse-brey, except that they were used for different purposes, and that the former is in Armory always represented as being upon a wooden stand.

Brazeless (brē·zlės), *a.* [f. Braze *v.*[2] + -less.] Without solder, unsoldered.

1897 *Westm. Gaz.* 6 Dec. 9/1 Among the other novelties are the brazeless but fixed joints shrunk together. 1898 *Ibid.* 16 Apr. 6/1 The other process, which is described as brazeless. *Ibid.* 21 May 6/3 Has your lordship heard of another company which intends to erect a brazeless jointing factory in London?

Breach, *sb.* Add: **3. c.** In colloq. and journalistic use, short for *breach of promise.*

1840 Dickens *Old Cur. Shop* viii, There's the chance of an action for breach. 1905 *Daily Chron.* 16 Aug. 6/7 'The breach action was not brought by her,' said Mr. Burnett, opening the present proceedings on behalf of the major. *Ibid.*, At the breach trial.

Breach, *v.* Add:

1. c. *intr.* To develop a breach, to become broken through.

1894 Sir C. Moncrieff in *Wkg. Men's Coll. Jrnl.* 153 If by any chance an embankment breached and a province was flooded.

Breachy, *a.*[2] (Earlier and later U.S. examples.)

1780 E. Parkman *Diary* 275 To my sorrow, my Oxen have been breachy at Mr. Isaac Parker's and let in Cattle with them into his Cornfield. 1846 Lowell *Biglow P.* Ser. I. vii. 61 Pledges air awfle breachy cattle. 1864 *Ret. Agric. Soc. Maine* 66 They [*sc.* sheep] become breachy and trespass upon neighbors. 1874 *Rep. Vermont Board Agric.* II. 378 The cows are unusually gentle...Never knew one to be breachy.

Bread, *sb.* Add:

3. b. In full *altar-bread*, chiefly pl.: A sacramental wafer.

1849 altar-breads [see Altar B. II]. 1877 J. D. Chambers *Div. Worship* 352 The Breads being now on the Corporal. 1899 W. J. S. Simpson *Mem. W. S. Simpson* 154 An iron instrument for stamping the altar breads.

5. b. *In good bread*: in a good living or position (? *obs.*). *In bad bread*: in a bad state, in difficulties; in disfavour *with* a person. *dial.* and *U.S.*

1763 *Essex Inst. Hist. Coll.* XLIX. 139 Mr. Barnard..is now in good bread, and seems loth to affront his people by telling them plainly of these public sins. 1778 *Ibid.* XLIII. 11 Old England I believe is got into Bad Bread. *Ibid.* 16 Hope it is the French Fleet, if not we shall be in Bad Bread, but we must see it out with them. 1825 Jamieson *Suppl.* s.v. *Bread*, *To be in bad bread*, to be in a dilemma, or in an evil taking. 1881 Sargisson *Joe Scoap* 139 (E. D. D.) That's hoo he gat inteh sec bad bread wih t'maister. 1895 P. H. Hunter *J. Inwick* xviii. 223, I saw fine I was gaun to be in bad breid wi' baith sides.

10. bread-line *U.S.*, a queue of poor people waiting to receive bread; also *fig.*

1900 *Lippincott's Mag.* LXV. 3 [Story by A. B. Paine entitled] The Bread Line. *Ibid.* 12 That's the bread line. They get a cup of coffee and a loaf of bread every night at twelve o'clock. 1904 *Charleston News* 5 Sept. 4 The 'bread-line' which nightly forms in front of Fleischmann's bakery in New York. 1909 H. N. Casson *Life C. H. McCormick* 12 This..republic could not develop beyond the struggle for food. It was chained to the bread-line.

Bread, *v.* **c.** (Earlier U.S. examples.)

1842 J. S. Buckingham *Slave States* II. 167 He always grows enough to *bread* his own people for a year at least, and sells the balance. 1857 H. C. Kimball in *B. Young's Jrnl. Discourses* V. 20/2 It now takes about one thousand bushels of wheat to bread my family one year.

Bread and butter. Add:

2. (Earlier examples of phrases.) Also *attrib.*

1732 Swift *Let. to Duchess Queensberry* 12 Aug., Your quarrelling with each other upon the subject of bread and butter is the most usual thing in the world. 1780 *Mirror* (Edinb.) No. 69. 4 Jan., How did she show superior sense by thus quarrelling with her bread and butter? 1809 *Deb. Congress* 20 Feb. 1467 Quarrelling with our bread and butter. 1820 Jefferson *Let. to Pinckney* 30 Sept., If they push it to that, they will have quarrelled with their bread and butter. 1929 *Publishers' Weekly* 30 Nov. 2588/1 The old stand-bys, the bread-and-butter books in every department.

4. bread-and-butter letter, a letter of thanks for hospitality written after a visit, a Collins.

1901 Howells *Pair of Patient Lovers* 82 His prompt bread-and-butter letter. 1927 *Scribner's Mag.* July 80/2 He was the solemn sort who always writes his bread-and-butter letters the day after he has finished a visit.

Bread-crumb, *v.* [f. the sb.] *trans.* To dip in bread-crumbs in preparation for cooking.

1846 Soyer *Cookery* 103 Egg and bread-crumb each piece. 1854 — *Shilling Cookery* 35 The heads when cooked may be egged and bread-crumbed over. 1897 *Westm. Gaz.* 16 Dec. 12/2 Bread-crumb the fillets and fry them in boiling fat.

Bread-kind (bre·d,kəind). [f. Bread *sb.* + Kind *sb.*] A West Indian name for yams, sweet potatoes, and other food-stuffs.

1697 Dampier *Voy.* 311 The Mindanao People live 3 or 4 months of the year on this food for their Bread kind. 1712 W. Rogers *Voy. Rd. World* 376 At which Allowance we have not above 12 Days at most, being all the Bread Kind we have in the Ship. 1891 Bunting in *Wesleyan Meth. Mag.* May 362 A brown woman..with a load of 'bread-kind' on her head. 1899 W. P. Livingstone *Black Jamaica* v, The principal food consisted of what is locally called 'bread-kind'; yams, sweet potatoes, cocos, plantains.

Breadth. Add:

2. b. (Earlier U.S. example of agricultural sense.)

1785 Washington *Diaries* II. 361, I sowed half a bushel of orchard grass seed..in a breadth through the Field.

4. b. Undue freedom or lack of decorum in dealing with indelicate matters; grossness or licence of expression. (Cf. Broad *a.* 6 c, Broadness 2.)

1873 W. C. Hazlitt *Feudal Period* Pref. p. ix, A few of them exhibit a breadth which is scarcely consonant with modern ideas of decorum.

Break, *sb.*[1] Add:

1. c. The breaking or grinding of grain; the coarse particles left when the flour has been removed.

1888 Powles tr. *Kick's Flour Manuf.* 223 The coarsest middlings are somewhat smaller than break, and thus only differ in size from first scalped. *Ibid.* 236 The break coming from the millstone passes into the separating cylinder s' (sizing reel), the meal falls through, that is, all the finer particles, the flour, dunst, the whole of the middlings, fine or coarse, whilst the scalped break falls out at the end of the reels.

d. *fig.* A break-away or break-down; a collapse or failure. *U.S.*

1827 J. Randolph *To Dr. Brockenbrough* 3 Mar. in *Life* (1851) II. 289, I am of opinion that (as we say in Virginia) we have made a 'great break'. In fact, the administration have succeeded in no one measure. 1888 Bryce *Amer.*

Commw. II. lxx. 568 One balloting follows another till what is called 'the break' comes...The break, when it comes, comes with fierce intensity.

4. b. A break-out; a rush. *U.S.*

1834 *Sk. & Eccentr. D. Crockett* 82 Just before I got there, the old bear made a break and got loose. 1845 J. J. Hooper *Adv. Simon Suggs* xii. (1928) 93, I made a brake on a bee line for Urwinton. 1878 E. B. Tuttle *Border Tales* 46 Finally, the leader [elk] will make a break in one direction or another...Having made one break..their wits are exhausted. 1889 Farmer *Americanisms* s.v. *Break*, [Bears] can smell a man a long way off, and as soon as they can do this they make a break for him. 1920 Mulford *J. Nelson* iv. 47 Oh, if you'll only make a break, or give me half an excuse to throw lead!

6. c. A continuous or unbroken run. *colloq.*

1898 *Daily News* 30 June 7/1 We understood that Waterloo and Exeter would be a '*break' accomplished by at least one of the South Western Company's West of England expresses. *Ibid.*, This is a 'break' of 130 miles at the speed of 53 miles an hour.

8. b. *spec.* of a racehorse, the act of breaking away from a level stride. (Cf. *Break *v.* 38 c.) *U.S.*

1868 H. Woodruff *Trotting Horse of Amer.* i. 41 The penalty of a break was such that the rider..would be afraid to push his horse up to the top of his speed. 1876 *Rep. Vermont Board Agric.* II. 143 His superior trotting motion.. is not disturbed by any attending circumstances into a break. 1890 *Harper's Mag.* June 50/2 But Lucifer was still ahead. There had not been a 'break' yet. 1902 McFaul *Ike Glidden* xxii. 200 When rounding into the home stretch his horse broke, and suddenly went to a wild swerving break that carried him to the complete outside of the track.

e. *A bad break*: a serious mistake. *U.S.*

1883 Nye *Baled Hay* 200 Possibly science may be wrong. We have known science to make bad little breaks. 1887 F. Francis Jr. *Saddle & Mocassin* 146 'Sam', he says, 'you've made one or two bad breaks since you've been in town'. 1897 *Congress. Rec.* Feb. 2364/1, I believe he made a bad break as a lawyer, but I believe him to be a good lawyer. 1911 S. E. White *Rules of Game* I. xvii, You made one bad break just now. 1926 Cosmo Hamilton in *Good Housekeeping* July 187/1, I wish you had told me how to address him before you went away. As it was I made a fearful break when he came to fetch me.

f. *Boxing.* The act of separating after the contestants have come to grips.

1928 *Daily Express* 2 Aug. 13/5 Lewis was disqualified for hitting on the break.

g. A short play-time between lessons in the middle of morning or afternoon school.

1921 Sylvia Thompson *Rough Crossing* ii. § 1, At 'break' Elizabeth met Lilian again. 1927 Josephine Elder *Thomasina Toddy* xvii, The next day the trio and Stella spent 'break' walking arm-in-arm round the garden together.

h. The angle between the brim and crown of a hat.

1882 in Ogilvie.

i. On the Stock Exchange, a sudden decline or falling off of prices. *U.S.*

1870 Medbery *Men & Myst. Wall St.* 203 To endure an occasional 'break' in stocks. 1902 Clapin *Dict. Amer.* s.v., *Break*,..a Wall Street term for a sudden decline in the value of stocks.

j. A freak or abnormal development from the parent stock.

1921 *Conquest* Sept. 491/3 These 'mutations', 'sports' or 'breaks', as they are variously called.

10. *spec.* a broken or disturbed portion on the surface of water. *U.S.*

1852 *Trans. Mich. Agric. Soc.* III. 231 They will make a break in the water near the shore with their tail. 1883 'Mark Twain' *Life Mississippi* xxx. 278 Beaver Dam Rock was out in the middle of the river now, and throwing a prodigious 'break'. 1890 *Harper's Mag.* Apr. 715/1, I run off once with my tackle, an' 'd jest throwed in my line an' seed a break, when mother calls out. 1897 'Mark Twain' *Following Equator* ix. 109 With..the 'break' spreading away from its head, and the wake following behind its tail.

c. The combination or junction of different styles or designs in the same building.

1889 in *Century Dict.*

d. *Fortif.* A brisure.

1874 Knight *Dict. Mech.*, *Break*, a change from the general direction of the curtain near its extremity in the construction with orillons and retired flanks.

e. *U.S.* (See quots. 1902.)

1895 C. King *Fort Frayne* ii. 27 And here, among the breaks of the Mini Pusa, Farrar had thrown his little command..square across the path of the foe. 1902 Clapin *Dict. Amer.* 74 *Break*, a rough, irregular piece of ground. (Neb.) 1902 Webster Suppl., *Break*..A line of cliffs, and associated spurs and small valleys, at the edge of a mesa. (*Western U.S.*)

11. b. *U.S.* (See quot.)

1859 Bartlett *Dict. Amer.* (ed. 2), *Break*, a regular sale of tobacco at the 'breaking' or opening of the hogsheads. Local in Virginia.

14. *An even break*: an equal chance. *U.S.*

1911 H. Quick *Yellowstone N.* v. 126 It's allus an even break whether they'll stan' and freeze in their tracks, or chase after some bunch of..natives. 1921 Mulford *Bar-20 Days* xxiii. 231 Now he wanted an 'even break' where once he would have called all his wits into play to avoid it. [1918 — *Man fr. Bar-20* xiii. 128 If th' stakes are high an' the breaks anywhere near equal, I'll risk my last dollar or my last breath.] 1923 Watts *Luther Nichols* 198 If I get an even break on it for five years, it's as much as I'm expecting.

b. *A fair break*: a fair chance. *U.S.*

1926 J. Black *You Can't Win* xxi. 331 After gathering every scrap of information available, I was sure I could 'take' the spot if I got a fair break on the luck.

15. A portion of a crop of turnips set aside for sheep to feed on. *local.*

1805 R. W. Dickson *Pract. Agric.* II. 672 Removing them [*sc.* sheep] to fresh portions or breaks every eight or ten days. 1886 C. Scott *Sheep-farming* 48 A certain breadth or portion of the turnips, called a 'break,' the extent of which is regulated by the number of sheep to be put on.

16. The quantity of hemp which is prepared in one year. *U.S.*

1796 *Mass. Mercury* 29 Apr. (Cent. D.) Best St. Petersburg clean Hemp of the break of the year 1796. 1907 *Daily Chron.* 7 Mar. 6/6 A 'break' of hemp, which in America means the quantity sold in a year.

17. In type-founding, a surplus piece of metal remaining on the shank of a newly cast type.

1683 Moxon *Mech. Exerc.*, *Printing* 370 *Break*,..the Mettle that is contiguous to the Shank of a New Cast Letter: This Break is formed in the Mouth-piece of the Letter-mould, and is called a Break, because it is always broke from the Shank of a Letter. 1843 Holtzapffel *Turning* I. 324 The breaks, or the runners, of the types are first broken off. 1874 Knight *Dict. Mech.*

18. *Electr.* The action of breaking contact in an electric circuit; the position in which contact is broken (in phr. *at break*). Cf. Make *sb.*[2] 9.

1875 Guthrie *Magn. & Electr* § 235 The automatic make and break. Fig. 181 shows the 'hammer break'. 1876 *Nature* XIV. 62/2 The increase of excitability was manifested towards make, and scarcely at all towards break.

19. *Electr.* and *Telegraphy.* A commutator or apparatus for interrupting or changing the direction of an electric current.

1854 *Tomlinson's Cycl. Useful Arts* I. 580/1 The other pole..communicates..with the little wheel, called the break, the circumference of which is partly of metal and partly of wood or ivory, so as to interrupt and renew, twice in each revolution, the metallic connexion. 1874 Knight *Dict. Mech.*

20. *attrib.*: **break-lathe,** a lathe having a portion of its bed open or removable so as to admit work of larger diameter; **break-line** *Typogr.*, the last line of a paragraph.

1883 *Encycl. Brit.* XV. 154/1 *Break lathes..were made by Mr. (now Sir Joseph) Whitworth as long ago as 1840. 1808 Stower *Printer's Gram.* 163 Part of a word, or a complete word in a *break line, if it contain no more than three or four letters, is improper. 1824 J. Johnson *Typogr.* II. 90 To take a comprehensive view of the copy,..to notice..the number of break lines. 1893 Hart *Rules for Compositors* 22 Breaklines should consist of more than five letters except in narrow measures.

Break, *sb.*[3] [var. Brake *sb.*[3] 2.] A bench on which dough is kneaded by machinery.

1834-6 Barlow in *Encycl. Metrop.* (1845) VIII. 801/2 It [*sc.* dough] is removed from the trough and deposited on a strong wooden platform or table, called a break. 1845 Dodd *Brit. Manuf.* V. 23. 1874 Knight *Dict. Mech.*, *Break*, a wooden bench on which dough is kneaded by means of a lever called a *break-staff*.

Break, *v.* Add: **2. e.** (U.S. example.)

1855 M. M. Thompson *Doesticks* vi. 44 'I had no further change', so was necessitated to get a bill broke.

i. In leather manufacture, to scrape a skin smooth and clean on the flesh side.

1842 *Penny Mag.* XI. 215/2 The lamb-skins having been steeped in water, 'broken' on the flesh side, and drained. 1845 Dodd *Brit. Manuf.* V. 187 The goat-skins are..soaked in water..to soften them, and then undergo the process of 'breaking'.

j. *To break the wicket* (Cricket): to dislodge a bail or the bails in stumping a batsman.

1901 *Strand Mag.* June 616/1 The ball was thrown in from the field, the bowler took it, and broke the wicket, so as to run the batsman out.

8. c. On the Stock Exchange, to decline suddenly in value. *U.S.*

1899 *Daily News* 15 May 2/6 Under the influence of Mr. Flower's death, what are known as Flower stocks broke in overwhelming volume.

9. *esp.* To defeat the object of (a strike) by engaging other workers.

1905 [implied in *strike-breaker*, Strike *sb.* 20]. 1914 *Round Table* Mar. 367 The farmers contributed the bulk of the power that..broke the strike.

b. To nullify or set aside (a will) by legal methods.

1891 *Melbourne Argus* 12 Dec. 11/8 [New York.] Under the law [she] would be entitled to one-half of the estate, should the will be broken.

15. f. *To break ship*: to fail to rejoin a ship on the expiration of leave.

1905 'Q' (Quiller-Couch) *Shining Ferry* III. xviii, I brought across a sailor-looking chap...Thinks I, 'You've broken ship, my friend'. 1907 *Daily Chron.* 3 Apr. 1/7 The serious offence of 'breaking ship.' 1909 *Ibid.* 28 June 8/7 In the afternoon he broke ship, but was undiscovered.

25. c. *Naut. trans.* To free and shake out (a flag or sail) which has been furled; also with *out.*

1889 *Times* 6 Aug. 8/3 The Royal Standard was broken on board the Victoria and Albert, and immediately H.M.S. Valorous..began to fire a salute. 1899 *Daily News* 9 Oct. 6/2 The Columbia broke out her spinnaker. 1901 *N. & Q.* 9th Ser. VII. 176/2 When a standard is 'broken' it is unfurled after being hoisted. 1902 *Daily Chron.* 26 Feb. 7/4 As the yacht slid gracefully into the water the American flag was broken out at the taffrail. 1914 *Times* 23 Dec. 7 After breaking a Union Jack at the head of a flagstaff. 1928 *Daily Tel.* 20 Mar. 13/7 The Afghan standard was broken from the Majestic's mainmast.

33. c. *To break the slate*: to refuse to allow one's name to stand as candidate for some office. (See Slate *sb.*[1] 2 c.) Also *transf.* *U.S.*

1888 Bryce *Amer. Commw.* III. lxiii. II. 458 The list so settled is now a Slate, unless some discontented magnate objects and threatens to withdraw. To do so is called 'breaking the slate'. 1888 A. C. Gunter *Mr. Potter* xxii, It's a desperate dodge, but I think it'll break the slate! [*Ibid.* xxiii, Her emissary had destroyed the document, though he'd left the wrapper whole, and so I tricked her and busted the slate!]

38. b. To make a dash; to set off at a run. *U.S.*

1834 Crockett *Narr. Life* ii. 11 Finding me rather too slow about starting, he gathered about a two year old hickory, and broke after me. 1883 'Mark Twain' *Life Mississippi* xxviii. 300 If your boat got away from you, on a black night, and broke for the woods, it was an anxious time with you. 1892 *Congress. Rec.* Jan. 655/2 When a man is working for wages in the hot harvest field there is nothing more delightful to him than a little fall of rain which will drive him in. So these harvesters broke for the barn.

c. Of a horse, esp. in racing: (see quot. 1908). *U.S.*

1868 H. Woodruff *Trotting Horse of Amer.* i. 42 When he breaks, he is to be immediately pulled to a trot. 1876 B. Harte *G. Conroy* vi. v, The springs creaked, the wheels rattled, the mare broke. 1890 *Harper's Mag.* June 51/1 Lucifer can do no more. He 'breaks'—breaks badly. 1902 McFaul *Ike Glidden* xxii. 198 They went along steadily.. until near the upper corner on the back stretch, when the colt broke and his head went up into the air. 1908 *Springfield Weekly Republ.* 8 Oct. 2 A trotter in a race breaks, that is, loses his level stride and reverts to an impossible kind of gallop which is not permitted by the rules of harness racing. *fig.* 1904 *N. Y. Even. Post* 17 May 1 Kane County deserted Yates...Will County broke also, and gave twenty-six votes for Lowden. 1908 *Springfield Weekly Republ.* 8 Oct. 2 The word 'break' applied to political campaigners has the same meaning [as in horse-racing].

44. e. *Boxing.* (See quot.)

1897 *Encycl. Sport* I. 139/1 *Break ground*, to take up a fresh position to the right or left.

49. Break away. d. Of the weather: To clear up. ? *Obs.*

1768 Washington *Diaries* I. 249 Very like to Snow but broke away abt. Sun Set. 1816 U. Brown *Jrnl.* in *Maryland Hist. Mag.* XI. 221 This morning rains very much, about Ten o'Clock breaks away.

e. *Boxing.* (See quot.)

1897 *Encycl. Sport* I. 139/1 *Break away*, to get away from an opponent.

50. Break down. d. Also of an engine, a machine, vehicle, or the like: To cease to function, esp. through the fracture or dislocation of a part.

1837 *United Service Jrnl.* May 112 One of her engines 'broke-down', as it is technically called.

52. Break in. g. In paper-manufacture, to subject (rags) to a process of washing and pulping.

1865 *Chambers's Encycl.* VII. 243 They are thoroughly washed and partly pulped; or, as it is technically called, *broken in.*

54. Break out. g. *trans.* To open up (a receptacle) and remove its contents. Also with the contents as obj.

[1833 Marryat *P. Simple* v, He was breaking Casks out of the hold.] 1849 N. Kingsley *Diary* 22 Broke out our chests to-day, found all our things in good order. *Ibid.* 73 They broke out the baggage room to-day to get iron for various purposes. 1877 *Fraser's Mag.* XV. 221 Afterwards the fish are *broken out* and washed, and then packed in wooden hogshead casks.

56. Break up. h. Of any kind of weather: To change.

1544 *Late Exped. Scot.* (1798) 10 And for asmoch as the myst yet contynued, and dyd not breake..we concluded, if the wether did not breake vp, to haue encamped our selues vpon the same ground. a 1586 Sidney *Arcadia* II. ix. (1912) 202 The weather breaking up, they were brought to the maine lande of Pontus.

Break-. Add:

I. 1. break-circuit, a device for opening and closing an electric circuit; **break-piece,** = *Break *sb.* 19; **break-wind,** a screen or protection against the wind.

1884 Knight *Dict. Mech.* Suppl., **Break-circuit*, an arrangement on an electro-magnetic or magneto-electric instrument, by which an operator can open or close the circuit at pleasure. 1842 Francis *Dict. Arts* Q 2 b/1 The fore part of the spindle is terminated by a wire, and a *break piece at the end of it. 1863 *Fraser's Mag.* Mar. 282/2 What the Australians call a '*breakwind', *i.e.*, a pent roof, looking like the falling flap of a large bird-trap. 1875 *Encycl. Brit.* II. 317/2 The Norway maple..is a hardy tree, used as a breakwind in exposed situations on the east coast. 1890 *Athenæum* 18 Oct. 516/1 [Tasmanians] were frequently content with a mere break-wind in lieu of any covered structure. 1900 H. Lawson *Over Sliprails* 135 Two sheets of bark had been raised as a break-wind.

2. break-front, having a front of which the line is broken by a curve or angle.

1928 *Daily Tel.* 24 July 12/2 A large break-front sideboard.

II. break-point, the point where an electric current is interrupted; **break-signal,** a signal used to separate distinct parts of a telegraphic message.

1879 G. Prescott *Sp. Telephone* 192 The *break-point, where the current is interrupted. 1876 Preece *Telegraphy* 287 These parts are separated from each other by a distinct signal, called the *break signal.

Breakable. Add: **B.** *sb. pl.* Things which are capable of being broken.

1880 Byron in *Engl. Stud.* (1898) XXV. 149 Mother Mocenigo will probably try a bill for breakables. 1904 H. G. Wells *Food of Gods* I. iv. 117 The child was born with good intentions. 'Padda be good, be good,' he used to say as the breakables flew before him. 1909 — *Tono-Bungay* I. ii. § 4 There was a plaster of Paris horse to indicate veterinary medicines among these breakables.

Breakage [1]. **1.** (Earlier U.S. examples.)

1775 *Essex Inst. Hist. Coll.* XIII. 189, I think it is probable all the muster did not end in Breakage alone. 1805 *Ibid.* XXXIX. 331 There is a violent brakage [*sic*] among the Democrats.

Break-away (brē·kăwē). Pl. **breaks-away.** [f. phr. *to break away*: see Break *v.* 49.]

1. The action of breaking away, severance.

1897 *Badminton Mag.* IV. 421 A big break-away occurs in the ranks [of flying rooks]. 1909 *Daily Chron.* 13 July 1/4 The owners report that there is no 'breakaway' from the agreement. 1923 *Glasgow Herald* 1 Feb. 6 A challenging breakaway from rhythm. 1923 *Daily Mail* 31 May 13 There is a natural breakaway of the water on one side into a bog. 1928 *Manchester Guardian Weekly* 7 Dec., Suppl. p. ix/2 But Mr. O'Neill's revolt from the familiar methods of presenting a modern prose play is an interesting accompaniment to Mr. O'Casey's break-away towards fantasy and symbolism.

2. A panic rush of animals, usually at the sight or smell of water, a stampede. *Australia.*

1891 'The Breakaway,' title of picture by Tom Roberts at Victorian Artists' Exhibition (Morris *Austral Eng.*).

b. An animal that leaves the herd. *Australia.*

1893 *Argus* 29 Apr. 4/4 (Morris) The smartest stock horse that ever brought his rider up within whip distance of a breakaway.

3. The or an act of breaking away or getting free.

a. *Athletics* (*Running*). A premature start. **b.** *Boxing.* The getting away from one's opponent or the separating of the combatants after a spell of in-fighting. **c.** *Football.* A sudden rush of players with the ball towards their opponents' goal, after a period of pressure.

1885 *Times* 4 June 10/3 After several breaks away the 12 competitors were despatched to an excellent start. 1906 *Daily Chron.* 7 Sept. 9/4 They scored from a breakaway. 1909 *Westm. Gaz.* 29 Nov. 12/2 The visitors fully deserved their win, for, save for a few spasmodic breaks-away by the home team, they were pressing continually.

Break-back, *a.* Add: **2.** Of a roof: having the lower portion at a different angle from the upper. Also *ellipt.* as *sb.* *U.S.*

1857 Goodrich *Recoll.* I. 78 The house..was a low edifice, two stories in front; the rear being called a break-back, that is sloping down to a height of ten feet. 1859 Bartlett *Dict. Amer.* (ed. 2), *Break-back*, a term applied to a peculiar roof, common in the country, where the rear portion is extended beyond the line of the opposite side, and at a different angle. The addition thus acquired is used as a wash-room, a store-house, or for farming implements.

Break-down. Add:

3. *attrib.*: **breakdown product,** a product resulting from the disintegration of a substance.

1929 *Birmingham Post* 22 Feb. 5/4 Maltose and cellobiose ..were to be regarded as definite breakdown products of the polysaccharides.

Breaker [1]. Add:

4. c. In paper-manufacture, a machine in which rags are washed and partly pulped. Also *attrib.*, as *breaker-plate.*

1880 J. Dunbar *Pract. Papermaker* 71 It may be mentioned that the breaker-plate ought to be sharp when starting to blottings. 1902 *Encycl. Brit.* XXXI. 456/1 The next step is that of washing and 'breaking in,' which takes place in an engine called the 'breaker'.

d. In anthracite mining, an apparatus for breaking, sizing, and cleaning coal for the market.

1885 *Encycl. Brit.* XVIII. 501/2 The 'breaker', an anthracite invention and a monster of destruction, is an edifice of wood and iron 100 feet high,..with rollers set with teeth to crush the larger lumps, with bolting screens to separate the sizes. 1900 *Coal & Metal Miners' Pocket-bk.* 574 *Breaker Boy*, a boy who works in a coal breaker.

e. In cheese-making, an implement for breaking the curd into small pieces.

1844 *Jrnl. R. Agric. Soc.* V. I. 88 The first process of breaking down the curd in the cheese-tub is..performed by a breaker or curd-cutter.

7. A horse that breaks (*Break *v.* 38 c). *U.S.*

1868 H. Woodruff *Trotting Horse in Amer.* xxiii. 201 Although a trotter of remarkably fine speed and power, he was such a bad breaker. *Ibid.* l. 388 Whether you shall suffer him to become a bad, losing breaker.

Breaking, *vbl. sb.* Add:

1. c. *Phonology.* [After G. *brechung*.] A sound-change consisting of the development of a diphthong from a single vowel due to the influence of certain following consonants; also called Fracture (5).

1883 March *A. S. Gram.* 20 Breaking is the change of one vowel to two by a consonant. 1885 Cook *Sievers' O.E. Gram.* § 77. 34 Breaking, according to Grimm, may be defined as the change of a short e to eo, and that of a short a to ea.

d. In woollen manufacture, the operation by which short combed slivers are combined and made into continuous lengths. Also *breaking-in.*

1843 *Penny Cycl.* XXVII. 554/1 The breaking being thus effected, the sliver of wool proceeds to a large bobbin or cylinder. 1915 R. Beaumont *Woollen & Worsted* 631 The piece, having been scoured, milled, dried, and tentered, is evenly damped, raised, or raised across before being passed on to the teazle machine. This is called 'breaking-in'.

5. *U.S.* (Earlier example.)

1867 *Putnam's Mag.* May (De Vere) Wide spaces of breaking showed the tender green of young wheat.

8. *breaking-plough, -strain*; **breaking-engine,** (*a*) in paper-manufacture, a machine for washing and pulping rags, a breaker; (*b*) in woollen-manufacture, a carding-machine; **breaking-off boy,** the boy who removes the piece of surplus metal from newly cast type; **breaking-rollers,** an apparatus for the mechanical kneading of dough.

1874 Knight *Dict. Mech.*, **Breaking-engine*, the first of a series of carding-machines, to receive and act on the lap from the lapper; it has usually coarser clothing than the finishing-cards. 1880 J. Dunbar *Pract. Papermaker* 71 When furnished in the breaking-engine, wash thoroughly before letting down the roll. 1839 Ure *Dict. Arts* 1261 From the *breaking-off boy the types are taken to the rubber. 1921 *Dict. Occup. Terms* (1927) § 279 *Breaker..., breaker-off, breaker-off boy* [also *breaking-off boy*], breaks off superfluous wedge-shaped piece of metal, which adheres to lower surface of type when type leaves casting machine, by pressing lower surface of type against table. 1891 C. Roberts *Adrift Amer.* 43 There had been an old *breaking plough left just outside the house. 1845 Dodd *Brit. Manuf.* V. 24 The dough is..placed under the *breaking-rollers..which perform the office of kneading. 1886 S. W. Mitchell *R. Blake* xix. (1895) 181 The engineer speaks of the *breaking-strain in materials; the breaking-strain in morals was near for Octopia. 1888 [see Strain *sb.*[2] 9].

Break-neck. A. Add:

b. *fig.* Blundering or lumbering headlong.

1887 Saintsbury *Hist. Elizab. Lit.* i. 6 Wyatt's awkwardness is not limited to the decasyllable, for some of his most breakneck work is in shorter lines.

Break-up. Add:

b. *attrib.*: **break-up price,** a price at which assets are sold upon the break-up of a concern.

1899 *Westm. Gaz.* 4 Dec. 10/2 A trade valuer was examined to show that he had advised the Grices to sell their business..at a break-up price. 1902 *Ibid.* 15 Nov. 7/1 At break-up values the assets of the company would pay 10s. in the pound to preference shareholders. 1909 *Ibid.* 19 May 2/2 Yesterday the plant of the Works Department of the London County Council was scattered at break-up price.

Bream, *sb.* Add: **2. b.** Applied to various species of sunfish, of the genera *Lepomis* and *Eupomotis.* *U.S.*

1791 W. Bartram *Trav. Carolina* 176 The golden bream or sun-fish, the red bellied bream,..also abound here. 1862 Lowell *Biglow P.* Ser. II. ii. Introd., The river's edge, Where I've sot mornin's lazy as the bream..(We call 'em punkin-seed). 1871 S. S. Haldeman in Schele de Vere *Americanisms* (1872) 382 To the name of Bream, used in New England, it has no title whatever. 1884 Goode *Nat. Hist. Aquatic Anim.* 406 The Blue Sun-fish—*Lepomis pallidus*..is known as the 'Blue Bream'.

Breast, *sb.* Add:

9. h. A large roller or cylinder in a carding-machine. Also *attrib.*, as *breast cylinder.*

18.. T. Lister in McLaren *Spinning* (1884) 229 A breast large enough to entitle it to the name of a cylinder. 1888 *Encycl. Brit.* XXIV. 659/1 Against the licker-in revolves the 'angle-stripper', the function of which is to remove the wool..and deliver it over to the great breast cylinder.

11. breast-fed *a.*, (of infants) fed at the mother's breast; so *breast-feeding* (opposed to *bottle-feeding*); occas. *breast-feed* vb.; **breast-shore,** each of a line of props supporting a vessel transversely in dry dock; **breast-stroke** *Swimming*, the stroke in which the breast is squarely opposed to the water; also as vb.; so **breast-swimming.**

1903 *Daily Chron.* 15 Jan. 5/2 That the death rate was thirty times as high in children fed on cow's milk as in those *breast-fed. 1904 *Fabian News* XIV. 25/1 The decline of breast-feeding. 1909 *Daily Chron.* 3 June 6/4 This figure including those breast-fed by the mothers. 1928 *Daily Express* 29 Feb. 3 Taken regularly—both before and after the birth—[it] enables nearly every mother to breast-feed her baby. 1894 W. H. White *Man. Naval Archit.* (ed. 3) 322 The shores under the bilges and bottom take part of the weight, and the '*breast shores' assist in maintaining form. 1867 C. Steedman *Man. Swimming* 93 There are four distinct kinds of motions for the arms, and the same number and kind for the legs, used in the common plain or *breast-stroke. 1904 Ralph Thomas *Swimming* (passim). 1922 E. Raymond *Tell England* II. vii. 237 Other flies fell into my tea, and did the breast-stroke for the side of the mug. 1928 *Daily Express* 18 Feb. 5/1 He..breast-stroked away toward the setting moon. 1867 C. Steedman *Man. Swimming* 106 Its superiority [*sc.* of side swimming] over *breast swimming.

Breast, *v.* Add: **7.** To excavate from the breast of a slope or mass.

1882 *Rep. Prec. Met. U. S.* 641 The gravel is..breasted out from that side of a block farthest from the main drift.

Breasting, *vbl. sb.* Add:

2. b. In paper-making, the curved trough, armed with knives, against which the cylinder of a rag engine works.

1874 Knight *Dict. Mech.*, *Breasting*,..the concave bed against which the wheel of a rag-engine works; between the two is the throat.

3. A method, used by deer-hunters, of riding abreast and shooting from the saddle. *U.S.*

a 1889 G. B. Grinnell *Gun & Rod* 152 (Cent. Dict.) Breasting is employed where the deer make their home in very high grass.

4. *attrib.* **breasting-knife,** a shoemaker's knife for cutting a clean face on the side of a boot- or shoe-heel next to the waist. *U.S.*

Breastwork. Add: **2.** (Earlier U.S. example.)

1747 *Maryland Hist. Mag.* IX. 52 [The Vestrymen] Ordered, That a Breast-Work be erected in the Chapel of this Parish, before the Clerk's seat.

3. The brickwork or masonry forming the breast of a fire-place.

1806 *Massachusetts Spy* 23 July (Th.) On the breastwork over the fireplace was the distinct impression of a bloody hand. 1833 Loudon *Encycl. Archit.* § 79 The fire-places to have each a strong iron chimney-bar (bar for supporting the breast-work, or front side of the flues).

Breath. Add:

5. c. *To take a person's breath* (*away*): to cause him to hold his breath owing to sudden emotion; hence, to dumbfound, flabbergast.

1898 'Mark Twain' *Myst. Stranger* (1916) 14 He said it placidly, but it took our breath for a moment and made our hearts beat. 1905 T. Dixon *Clansman* 351 The daring campaign these men were waging took his breath.

11. *breath-catching, -taking* (whence *-takingly* adv.) adjs.

1897 McConkey *Threefold Secret* iii. 112 What a far-reaching, heart-searching, breath-taking change this is. 1908 *Westm. Gaz.* 1 Apr. 7/3 This breath-taking assertion was made to a 'Westminster' representative. 1928 *Publishers' Weekly* 16 June 2442 The visit begins with a five-story trip on the elevator which transports you at once..to a breath-taking spectacle. 1928 *Daily Tel.* 6 Nov. 14/5 Green, Wood and Violet (who do some breath-catching tumbles). 1928 *Manchester Guardian Weekly* 31 Aug. 175/3 Breath-takingly beautiful.

Breather. Add:

3. b. In recent use, a short rest in which to recover breath, a breathing-space. (Cf. Breathe *v.* 13.)

1901 *Daily Chron.* 15 Oct. 5/4 But the horses have had their breather, and we must on. 1902 *Ibid.* 21 May 3/3 A field battery on the left had a hot time of it just at this moment, and drew out of action for a breather quite close to our guns. 1920 *Blackw. Mag.* Apr. 547/1 There they halted for a well-earned breather.

Breathing, *vbl. sb.* **10.** Add:

breathing mark *Mus.*, a mark to indicate the place where the singer may take breath.

1889 in *Century Dict.*

Breck. 2. Add quots. and *attrib.* uses.

1837 *Penny Cycl.* VIII. 282/1 The naked brecks (or undulating downs) of Norfolk. 1840 *Jrnl. R. Agric. Soc.* I. iv. 360 The first damside breck meadow on the plan. 1879 Lubbock *Fauna of Norfolk* Introd. p. viii, On the 'Breck' district the lordly Bustard roamed. 1897 W. Rye *Norfolk Songs* 124 Such cramped wild country, half rough breck land and half marsh.

Bredbergite (bre·dbəɹgəit). *Min.* [f. the name of B. G. *Bredberg*, who first described it: see -ite [1].] A name given by J. D. Dana in 1868 to an iron garnet found at Sala, Sweden, which contains a large amount of magnesium.

1868 Dana *Min.* 270 Lime-Magnesia Irongarnet; Bredbergite.

Bredi (brē·di). [Cape Du., from Malagasy.] A South African dish of meat and vegetables cooked together.

1815 Lichtenstein *Trav.* II. 82 *note*, Breedi signifies in the Madagascar tongue *Spinage*; the word is brought hither by the slaves, and at present, throughout the whole colony, every sort of vegetable which, like cabbage, spinage, or sorrel, is cut to pieces and dressed with Cayenne pepper, is included under the general term *Breedi.*

Breech, *sb.* **8.** Add:

breeches-boiler, a boiler in which two furnace tubes unite beyond the bridge (Webster 1911); **breeches-flue,** a flue composed of two conduits which unite and discharge into one stack (Funk's Stand. Dict. 1895); **breeches-pipe** (see quot.).

1888 *Lockwood's Dict. Mech. Engin.*, *Breeches Pipe*, a bend pipe having two legs or branches.

Breed, *sb.* Add:

2. e. A person of mixed descent, a half-breed.

1901 *Munsey's Mag.* XXV. 339/2 The breeds sullenly lying in their second line of defense. 1905 D. Wallace *Labrador Wild* iii. 47 Eskimos and 'breeds', the latter being a comprehensive name for persons whose origin is a mixture in various combinations and proportions of Eskimo, Indian, and European. *Ibid.* 48 Tom Blake, a breed, who had trapped at the upper or western end of Grand Lake.

4. breed-cup, breed-prize, a prize given to the best animal of its breed; **breed-society,** a society which is concerned with the production of a particular breed of animal.

1888 *Pall Mall Gaz.* 10 Dec. 8/2 There are seven silver *breed cups for the cattle classes. 1896 *Daily News* 8 Dec. 5/1 The Breed Cup for shorthorns was taken by the Earl of Rosebery's 'Proud Madam'. *Ibid.* 4 Mar. 8/6 Mr. G. Jackson, of Birmingham, has the *breed prize. 1892 *Ibid.* 14 Sept. 5/5 The future of stock fairs will be in some degree affected by the *breed-societies.

Breed, *v.* Add:

9. c. To put (a ram) *to* a ewe, etc., for breeding.

1886 C. Scott *Sheep-farming* 161 The ewes to which he is bred.

Breeze, *sb.*[2] **5.** Add: *breeze-swept* adj.

1872 Calverley *Fly Leaves* (1903) 4 Lingers on, till stars unnumber'd Tremble in the breeze-swept tarn. 1890 'R. Boldrewood' *Miner's Rt.* xxix, The breeze-swept ocean beach. 1894 Safar Namen *Persian Pict.* 48 On the threshold of his breeze-swept dwelling.

Breeze, *v.*[2] Add: **1. b.** To move or proceed briskly. *U.S.*

1907 *Chicago Even. Post* 4 May 9 He breezed through the Louvre at such a pace that he broke all the rapid sightseeing records. 1922 J. A. Dunn *Man Trap* ix. 129 If they show, breeze right along and forget me.

2. (Earlier U.S. examples.)

1752 Washington *Diaries* I. 31 At noon the Wind breezed up at So. and clouded. 1849 N. Kingsley *Diary* 10 Sun Easter day not much wind, quite pleasant, breezed up in the evening.

Breezy, *a.* 2. *fig.* Add: *esp.*, Characterized by brisk vigour or activity.

1896 Mrs. Caffyn *Quaker Grandmother* 112 A strong, vigorous, breezy, old woman. 1901 *Westm. Gaz.* 8 Mar. 4/2 A brawny, breezy-voiced man.

Breitschwanz (brai·tʃvants). Also **breitswan(t)z.** [G., = broad tail.] Imitation sable.

1923 *Daily Mail* 16 Apr. 15 The frilled coat had a sailor collar of dark blue breitschwanz. 1927 *Daily News* 26 Sept. 2/4 Especially good is the imitation or broadtail known as breitswanz. *Ibid.* 21 Nov. 2/3 Another black outfit was of face cloth and breitswanz. 1928 *Daily Express* 24 Jan. 5/4 Shaved lamb, breitschwantz, caracul, and astrakhan are seen in beige and light shades of golden brown.

Brekker (bre·kəɹ). *University slang.* [f. Breakfast + *-er 6.] Breakfast.

1889 Barrère & Leland *Dict. Slang.* 1900 G. Swift *Somerley* 66 Have you had any brekker? 1905 Vachell *The Hill* xiv, Scaife gave his farewell 'brekker' at the Creameries. 1908 *Daily Chron.* 20 Apr. 4/7 A young man who looked like an undergraduate wondered when his 'brekker' would be ready.

Brer. *U.S.* Negro pron. of Brother.

1880 J. C. Harris *Uncle Remus* i. (1881) 2 Arter Brer Fox bin doin' all dat he could fer ter ketch Brer Rabbit. 1890 'Mark Twain' in *Harper's Mag.* Feb. 440/1 If you read ..what this author says about Brer Albucasis.

Bretelle (brĕte·l). [Fr.] Each of the ornamental shoulder-straps extending from the waist-belt in front to the belt behind of a woman's dress. Chiefly *pl.* Also *attrib.*

1882 Caulfeild & Saward *Dict. Needlework, Bretelles*, a French term to signify an ornamental shoulder-strap. 1890 *Daily News* 21 Oct. 2/1 Bretelle-shaped lines of fine passementerie in green and gold. 1896 *Ibid.* 4 July 6/3 The bodice..has frills of black chiffon passing over the shoulders in bretelle fashion. 1908 *Daily Chron.* 25 Nov. 4/5 The Duchess of Portland..looked very beautiful in black velvet, with sables and bretelles of the gold-lace revived by the society. 1909 *Ibid.* 22 Feb. 7/5 These are arranged back and front bretelle-wise to fall over the deep, folded taffetas belt.

Breton (bre·tən), *sb.* and *a.* [ad. F. *Breton* (see Briton).] **A.** *sb.* A native of Brittany; the Celtic language of Brittany. **B.** *adj.* Belonging to or characteristic of Brittany, its inhabitants, or their language.

† *Breton tackle* (Naut.), app. the earlier form of Burton *tackle*.

1495 *Naval Acc. Hen. VII* (1896) 188 Brytton takles. *Ibid.* 198 Bretton takles. *Ibid.* 210 Breton takles. [1592 *Surv. or Topogr. Descr. France* 42 The other three dioceses do speake a mixed language, sometimes French sometimes Britton. *Ibid.* 44 The Brittains are generally tractable, but those that are neerer the sea coast are not so courteous as the rest. 1652 Heylin *Cosmogr.* i. 168/1 The Britains.. were questionless one of the first Nations that possessed any part of Gaul. See also Britain *sb.* 2, *a.* 3, Briton *sb.* 2.] 1797 *Encycl. Brit.* (ed. 3) VII. 421/2 Louis had driven the Bretons from the posts they occupied in Normandy before the duke of Burgundy could pass the Somme. 1818 Mrs. Stothard *Lett. Tour Normandy* (1820) 253 The Breton language appears to me..far more corrupted than the Welsh. *Ibid.* 254 The Bretons do not resemble in countenance either the Normans or French, nor have they much of the Welsh character. 1830 *Cambrian Q. Mag.* II. 192 The Breton-speaking Brittany. *Ibid.* 197 If the Welsh and Breton languages bear so near a resemblance to each other as is generally understood. 1855 Tennyson *Maud* ii. ii. iv, Here on the Breton strand! Breton, not Briton. 1861 *Chambers's Encycl.* II. 332/1 The Breton has generally a tinge of melancholy in his disposition. 1876 *Encycl. Brit.* IV. 334/2 A few seaport towns, which are rather French than Breton. 1913 J. Morris Jones *Welsh Gram.* Introd. 1 Keltic..The P division, consisting of Gaulish, and the British group, comprising Welsh, Cornish and Breton.

Breunnerite (broi·nərəit). *Min.* [f. the name of Count *Breunner* of Austria: see -ite¹.] A name given in 1825 to a carbonate of magnesia and iron found in the Tyrol.

1825 Haidinger tr. *Mohs' Treat. Min.* III. Index 293. 1862 Dana *Min.* 248.

Breviary. Add: **2. c.** fig. phr. *Matter of breviary* (= *matiere de breviaire*, Rabelais, Pantagruel iv. viii): a thing that admits of no question or doubt.

1889 *Sat. Rev.* 12 Jan. 29/1 It is matter of breviary with Gladstonians that Unionist journals are not to be trusted. 1894 *Ibid.* 27 Oct. 463 Is it not..rather matter of controversy than matter of breviary whether the distinction applies?

Brevicite (bre·visəit). *Min.* [Named *Brevicit* (1834) by P. Ström, f. *Brevig* in Norway: see -ite¹.] A hydrous silicate of aluminium and sodium.

1862 Dana *Min.* 167.

Brew (brū). Local variant of Brow *sb.*¹ 6 b.

1887 Hall Caine *Deemster* xxvii. 176 Nearer the cliff I found this, and this; and then down the brew itself..I saw this other one. 1891 L. Keith *Halletts* II. v. 107 He'll stand quiet enough:..it's the grass on the brew he's after. 1927 *Chambers's Jrnl.* Feb. 126/1 The brews of the ditches or hedge-bottoms.

Brey, variant of *Bray *sb.*³

Brick, *sb.*¹ Add:

2. Now extended to blocks or slabs made of sand and lime, concrete, and other materials.

1875– slag brick [see Slag *sb.* 5]. 1922 D. M. Liddell *Handbk. Chem. Engineering* II. 948 Common brick were formerly made of clay pressed into molds by hand or machinery and baked in kilns. At present bricks made from sand and lime are extensively used, while they have been used in Europe for 50 years.

4. b. *Brick couching*, in embroidery, couching in which the laid threads or cords are secured by cross stitches resembling, in their arrangement, the vertical joints of brickwork. Hence *in bricks*, in divisions resembling bricks.

1882 Caulfeild & Saward *Dict. Needlew.* 180/1 The chief varieties of Flat Couching are Brick, Broad, Burden, Diagonal, and Diamond. 1911 Alice Dryden *Church Embroid.* 112 The commonest form of stitching the gold is in bricks, each couching-stitch being in between the two stitches of the preceding line.

c. The colour of brick, brick-red.

1923 *Daily Mail* 16 Jan. 1 Blanket Cloth Magyar Wrap Coats..Cream, Beaver, Mole, Nigger, Brick. *Ibid.* 17 Apr. 13 Colours: Brick, Grey, Mauve, Nigger.

5. Also, *like a thousand* (occas. *hundred*) *of brick(s)*. orig. *U.S.*

1842 Mrs. Kirkland *Forest Life* I. xiii. 135 If folks is sassy, we walk right into 'em like a thousand o' brick. 1860 *New Orleans Picayune* 27 Apr. (De Vere) When we wanted to turn him out, he fell upon us like a thousand of bricks. 1867 *Congress. Globe* Feb. 1513/3, I had no expectation..of bringing down upon myself, 'like a thousand of brick' the torrent of his indignant eloquence. 1896 C. James *Yoke of Freedom* 161 Once let a man play me false, I'm down on him like a hundred of bricks.

b. *To have* (or *wear*) *a brick in one's hat*: to be under the influence of liquor. *U.S.*

1848 Durivage & Burnham *Stray Subj.* (Philad.) 61 (Th.) He wore a 'brick' within that hat. 1859 Bartlett *Dict. Amer.* (ed. 2) s.v., 'He has got a brick in his hat,' is an expression applied to an intoxicated person.

c. *To drop a brick*: to commit an indiscretion, make a 'bloomer'. *slang.*

1923 *Punch* 3 Oct. 334 It was hinted to me pretty plainly that I had dropped a brick, as you say. 1924 Galsworthy *White Monkey* iii. xii, I've got to keep my head shut, or I shall be dropping a brick. 1927 *Sunday Express* 16 Oct. 11/5 Might I suggest as an appendix to entries giving all the bricks we have dropped, that we add the names of the people who have helped us out of any difficulties. 1928 'Sapper' *Female of Species* xvii. 307 The stones of Stonehenge are little pebbles compared to the bricks you dropped, but I forgive you.

10. brick-bread, -loaf *U.S.* (early examples); **brick-pond** *U.S.*, a pond in a brickfield; **brick-stitch** = *brick couching* (see 4 b above).

1762 *Boston Selectm.* 29 Nov., A 4*d.* loaf of *brick bread is 3 oz. less than a 4*d.* white loaf. 1761 *Ibid.* 15 Apr., Four penny *brick loaf. 1811 *Massachusetts Spy* 9 Jan. 3/3 Two boys..were..drowned in a *brick pond in the vicinity of the city [Philadelphia]. 1850 *Wilmington* (N. C.) *Commercial* 5 Sept. 2/3 Water brought from the neighbouring brick-ponds [at Philadelphia] in buckets. 1882 Caulfeild & Saward *Dict. Needlework* s.v., *Brick stitch was largely used as back grounds in ancient embroideries. 1892 *Cassell's Fam. Mag.* May 345/2 What is known in modern canvas embroidery as 'brick'-stitch.

Brickbat. Add:

1892 Ranyard *Proctor's Old & New Astron.* 640 *note*, Clerk Maxwell used to describe the matter of the rings of Saturn] as a shower of brickbats, amongst which there would inevitably be continual collisions taking place. 1898 Agnes Clerke, etc. *Astron.* 340 It may be that collisions are infrequent in this conglomeration of 'brickbats'. 1926 Macpherson *Mod. Astron.* 78.

Bricking (bri·kiŋ). [f. Brick *sb.*¹ + -ing¹.]

1. Building with brick; brickwork. Also *attrib.*

1770 *Maryland Hist. Mag.* XII. 368 Pray defer yr Stable, Bricking in yr Garden or any other Jobs untill you have compleated the stone Wall. 1924 *Glasgow Herald* 20 Mar. 12 But between him and his coal, before ever he had sunk his bricking ring, intervened the war.

2. An imitation of brickwork, as on a plastered or stuccoed surface; in embroidery, brick-stitches collectively.

1874 Knight *Dict. Mech., Bricking*, the imitation of brick-work on a plastered or stuccoed surface. 1911 Alice Dryden *Church Embroid.* 112 For ordinary bricking use about ten stitches to the inch.

Brickish, *a.* Add:

2. Resembling brick in colour.

1900 Elinor Glyn *Visits Eliz.* (1906) 98 She has quite a different coloured chest to the top bit that shows above her pearl collar, which is brickish-red from hunting.

Brick wall, *sb.*¹ Add:

2. *fig.* as a type of something dense or an impasse, as in phr. *to talk to a brick wall, to be up against a brick wall.*

1898 *Westm. Gaz.* 19 July 1/2 We have been putting this dilemma to Liberals and Irish and the answers which we have obtained from both have brought us to what we have called the 'Irish brick-wall'. 1909 Jerome *They and I* vii, We mustn't have to tell 'em the same thing over and over again, like we was talking to brick walls.

Bricky, *a.* Add:

d. Like a 'brick' or good fellow.

1864 J. C. Atkinson *Stanton Grange* i, Old Milburn was the 'brickiest' master..at Elmdon.

Bridge, *sb.*¹ Add:

3. c. A causeway of logs, a corduroy road. *U.S.* (Cf. *Bridge *v.*¹ 2 b.)

1839 Mrs. Kirkland *New Home* ii. 19 The 'beautiful bridge', a newly-laid causeway of large round logs. *Ibid.* vii. 40 A marsh which we were crossing by the usual bridge of poles, or *corduroy* as it is here termed.

11. a. *bridge-builder; bridge-building.*

1772 C. Hutton *Bridges* 6 A Bridge-builder should be employed. 1873 'Mark Twain' *Gilded Age* xxiii, He wrote some papers..upon bridge-building.

b. bridge spectacles (see sense 6).

1832 J. F. Watson *Tales Olden Times* 154 In early years the only Spectacles ever used were called 'bridge spectacles'.

Bridge (bridʒ), *sb.*² Also 9 **biritch, britch.** [Etym. unascertained; prob. of Levantine origin, since some form of the game appears to have been long known in the Near East; the origin of the seemingly Russian forms *biritch, britch*, is unknown.] A card-game based upon whist. The dealer or his partner (dummy) names trumps, dummy's hand is exposed after the lead, and the odd tricks vary in value according to the suit named as trumps.

The game is said to have been played in Constantinople and the Near East about 1870. Formerly also called *bridge whist*. *Biritch* in quots. 1886 is applied to the call of 'no trumps'.

1886 *Biritch, or Russian Whist* 2 The one declaring may, instead of declaring trumps, say 'Biritch', which means that the hands shall be played *without trumps*. *Ibid.* 3 The odd tricks count as follows:—If 'Biritch' is declared each [odd trick counts] 10 points. *Ibid.* 4 There are four honours if 'Biritch' is declared, which are the four aces. 1894 (*title*) The Pocket Guide to Bridge..by 'Boaz'. 1898 *Nat. Rev.* Aug. 809 At a game of *wint* or *bridge*. 1901 'Slam' *Mod. Bridge* Introd., 'Bridge', known in Turkey as 'Britch'.

b. *Auction bridge*, a variety of the game which has superseded the original form. The right to name trumps and to play with the dummy goes, for each deal, to the player who undertakes to make the highest score. *Dummy bridge* (cf. Dummy *sb.* 2). See also *Contract *bridge*.

1903 O. Crawford in *Times* 16 Jan. 5/6 'Auction bridge' ..is more lively than dummy bridge. 1908 Dalton *Auction Bridge* p. iii, Auction Bridge is really a clever combination of the two games of Poker and Bridge. 1910—'*Saturday*' *Bridge* xvi. 227 Auction Bridge was invented in India as far back as 1902, but very little was known of it in England until it was taken up by the Bath Club somewhere about 1905. *Ibid.* 228 At Bridge the declaration is confined to the dealer and his partner. At Auction, every player in turn has the right of over-bidding the previous declaration. 1911 R. W. Chambers *Common Law* xviii. 528, I think I'll take Annan with me—just for company—or—dummy bridge on the way up.

c. *attrib.* and *Comb.*

1899 A. G. Hulme-Beaman *Pons Asinorum* 46 As in Bridge Whist everybody plays his own game. *Ibid.* 50 No amount of rule and precept will suffice to make a first-class Bridge player. 1905 *Daily Chron.* 27 Dec. 4/5 Are we, as they say at the bridge-table, 'content'? 1906 *Westm. Gaz.* 4 Aug. 15/1 Bridge hand No. VII. is another of those hands that look very simple but really are rather tricky. 1907 *Macm. Mag.* Sept. 805, I tried to slip away into the bridge-room. 1921 *Punch* 19 Jan. 49/1 The psychology of the Bridge partner. 1928 *Observer* 1 Apr. 11/2 The suburban wife who 'plays the exchanges' is present at every 'Bridge', as bridge parties are called in this country of short-cuts.

Hence **Bridge** *v.*² *intr.*, to play bridge; **Bri·dger** (cf. F. *bridgeur*, 1893), a bridge-player.

1907 Mrs. H. De La Pasture *Lonely Lady* xvi. 279 Miss de Courset, come and play billiard-fives,..unless you are a bridger. Are you a bridger? 1908 *Daily Chron.* 14 Nov. 6/4 We must dine and we must 'bridge'. 1928 *Sunday Express* 27 May 15 Shall she Charleston, Blues or Bridge that evening?

Bridge, *v.*¹ Add:

2. b. *spec.* in *U.S.* (See quot. Cf. *Bridge *sb.*¹ 3 c.)

1809 Kendall *Trav.* I. 235 But here, a sufficient, though not very agreeable road, is formed by causeys of logs; or, in the language of the country, it is bridged.

4. To join (a piece of land) *to* another by a bridge.

1904 Sladen *Playing the Game* i. ix, Islands..each bridged to each.

5. *intr.* To arch the recumbent body. *U.S.*

1913 Mulford *Coming of Cassidy* i. 21 The under man.. bridged so suddenly as to throw the hunter off him. *Ibid.* iii. 58 Trying in vain to bridge on his head and heels.

Bridgeable (bri·dʒăb'l), *a.* [f. Bridge *v.*¹ + -able.] That can be bridged or spanned by a bridge. *lit.* and *fig.*

1865 Carlyle *Fredk. Gt.* xviii. iii. (1873) VII. 135 Wadeable, bridgeable. 1890 *Advance* (Chicago) 13 Mar., Intervening islands break this distance [60 miles] into bridgeable lengths. 1898 *Daily News* 27 July 6/2 From the young officer to the preacher of non-resistance, there is a great gulf, but bridgable.

Bridgetin. Add the current forms: **Bridgettine, Bridgittine, Brigittine**; also the *attrib.* use.

1756–9 A. Butler *Lives of Saints* 6 Oct. *S. Bruno*, The Brigittin nuns of Sion. 1873 Blunt *Myr. Oure Ladye* p. xii, A Brigittine community of nuns. 1902 F. M. Steele *Convents Gt. Brit.* 62 The Bridgettine Rosary consists of seven *Paters* and sixty-three *Aves*.

Bri·dging, *ppl. a.* [f. Bridge *v.*¹ + -ing².]

1. Constructing or appointed to construct a bridge or bridges. (Perhaps orig. attrib. use of the vbl. sb.)

1891 *Daily News* 26 May 3/7 The bridging battalion of Royal Engineers. 1901 'Linesman' *Words by Eyewitness* (1902) 94 Losing eleven men of the bridging party, and having every pontoon and plank struck by the Boer marksmen.

2. bridging species *Bot.*, one of a series of plant-species on which a parasitic fungus may be trained or adapted to infect species otherwise immune. Also *bridging host.*

1903 H. M. Ward in *Phil. Trans.* B. CXCVI. 34 A certain species of grass (A) may be capable of infection by means of spores from two other host-plants (B and C), neither of which is predisposed to reciprocal infection, though both may be infected from such a 'bridging' species (A) as

is referred to above. 1922 *Encycl. Brit.* XXX. 478/2 'Bridging species'. *Ibid.*, 'Bridging hosts'.

Bridle, *sb.* Add: **5. g.** (See quot. 1906.)

1899 C. F. Marvin *Use of Kites* 211 The one-point attachment of bridle..is better suited to strong than light winds. 1906 A. F. Collins *Man. Wireless Telegr.* 209 *Bridle*, a cord attached to a kite that holds the latter at the proper angle in the wind; the kite-cord is attached to the bridle.

6. bridle stricture *Med.*, a stricture caused by a narrow band stretched across the urethra.

1894 Gould *Dict. Med.*

Bridle, *v.* Add: **4.** *intr.* of a horse: To rise to or answer the bridle.

1929 *Daily Express* 5 Jan. 7/5 Mr. Wroughton's horse never bridled well at the fence...It slipped and brushed through the fence, hardly rising.

5. *trans.* See *Bridle *sb.* 5 g.

1899 C. F. Marvin *Use of Kites* 210 Two methods of bridling the kite.

Bridle-path. (See Bridle *sb.* 6.)

1811 [s.v. Bridle *sb.* 6]. 1835 *Southern Lit. Messenger* I. 615 Our way, although little more than an indistinct bridle path, was more pleasant than that by which I had before crossed. 1840 C. F. Hoffman *Greyslaer* II. iii. 198 The road he was traversing could scarcely, indeed, be dignified with the title of a bridle-path. 1895 'C. E. Craddock' *Myst. Witch-Face Mt.* i. 30 Thar's a man..killed yestiddy in the bridle-path.

Bri·dle-wise, *a. U.S.* [Bridle *sb.* 1.] Of a horse, readily guided by a touch of the bridle.

1843 Carlton *New Purchase* 31 A spirited horse, scarcely broken, and certainly not bridle-wise. 1879 Tourgee *Fool's Err.* x. 42 Comfort had gone into town early with my little bridle-wise mare Jaca. 1895 *Century Mag.* Aug. 626/1 His bridle has one rein, his horse is bridle-wise. 1921 *Chambers's Jrnl.* Oct. 629/1 Quick-step..was the smartest and most bridle-wise pony that ever went on shoes.

Hence **Bri·dle-wisdom.**

1895 *Outing* (U.S.) XXVI. 477/1 Not that in the heat of play one relies upon this bridle-wisdom.

Brie (brī). A kind of soft cheese made in Brie, an agricultural district in the north of France.

1876 *Encycl. Brit.* V. 456 The principal kinds of cheese at present known in commerce...Camembert, Parmesan, Gruyère, Brie, Roquefort [etc.]. 1902 *Encycl. Brit.* XXVII. 355/2 The best known of the soft unpressed cheeses are Brie, Camembert, and Coulommiers. 1920 Tisdale & Jones *Butter & Cheese* 88 Soft Cheese (unpressed)..Brie, [etc.].

Brief, *sb.* Add:

7. Also *fig.*, as *to hold a brief for* (a person): to write like an advocate rather than an unbiassed and critical appraiser. Often colloq. in *to hold no brief for*: to be no advocate or supporter of.

1888 M. Arnold in *19th Cent.* Jan. 24 Professor Dowden holds a brief for Shelley; he pleads for Shelley as an advocate pleads for his client. 1918 R. A. Knox *Spiritual Aeneid* 215 When I was at Balliol, we used to adapt the phrase 'I hold no brief for So-and-so'.

11. brief-bag, the blue or red bag in which a barrister carries his briefs to and from court.

1865 G. Measom *Guide G.E.R.* Advt. 4 Brief Bags. 1895 *Cassell's Fam. Mag.* 323/2 Brief-bags carried by.. lawyers' clerks. 1910 *Encycl. Brit.* IV. 562/1 English brief-bags are now either blue or red. Blue bags are those with which barristers provide themselves when first called, and it is a breach of etiquette to let this bag be visible in court. The only brief-bag allowed to be placed on the desks is the red bag, which by English legal etiquette is given by a leading counsel to a junior who has been useful to him in some important case.

Brief, *v.*¹ Add: **2.** To relate briefly.

1904 Lynde *Grafters* vii, He briefed the story of House Bill Twenty-nine for her, pointing out the probabilities.

Brief, *v.*² **3.** Add: also *fig.*

1866 Lever *Sir B. Fossbrooke* xliv, They had not been well 'briefed', as lawyers say, or they had not mastered their instructions.

Brier, briar, *sb.*² Add: Also very freq. short for *briar-root, -wood*, which were formerly used = *briar-root* or *-wood pipe.*

1882 *Graphic* 16 Dec. 683/2 Nowadays, every third man you meet has a cigarette or a 'briar' in his mouth. 1885 Miss Braddon *Wyllard's Weird* i, He sat..lazily puffing at his black briarwood. 1891 L. Keith *The Halletts* xxviii, Pass me the brier-root. 1909 *Daily Chron.* 23 July 3/3 A briar being his constant companion while writing.

Brigade, *v.* **2.** Add mod. examples.

1908 *Daily Chron.* 17 June 7/7 You cannot brigade British industry. *Mod.* A man asked to do a certain part of an encyclopædia article will say 'they have brigaded me with so-and-so'.

Brigadier. **1.** Add: The rank of *brigadier general* was abolished after the war of 1914–18 and superseded by that of *colonel-commandant*. In 1928 this was superseded by *brigadier*.

1929 *Even. Standard* 13 May 13/2 Officers holding the new rank of Brigadier introduced in the Army last summer are still commonly known as 'Generals'.

Brigalow (bri·galo^u). *Austral.* Also **bricklow.** [ad. native name *būriagalah*.] Any one of several species of acacia, esp. *A. harpophylla.* Also *attrib.*

1847 Leichhardt *Jrnl.* i. 4 The Bricklow Acacia, which seems to be identical with the Rose-wood Acacia of Moreton Bay. 1862 Kendall *Poems* 79 Good-bye to the Barwan and brigalow scrubs. 1885 Mrs. C. Praed *Head Stat.* xvii, We are not fit for anything but store-cattle, we are all blady grass and brigalow scrub. 1901 F. Campbell *Love* 263 Long shafts of silvery moonlight creep in between the waving branches of blue gum and brigalow.

Brighamite (bri·gămǝit). *U.S.* A follower of Brigham Young; a Mormon. Also *attrib.*

1878 J. H. Beadle *Western Wilds* xxi. 342 The cannon and long range rifles of the Brighamite militia completely raked the interior of the camp.

Bright, *a.* Add: **1. e.** Also, hopeful, encouraging, cheering.

1860 *Merc. Marine Mag.* VII. 41 The look out..is not a very 'bright' one. 1917 C. Mathewson *Sec. Base Sloan* xiii. 174 Toonalta's chance to pull the game up high and dry looked bright.

10. bright-line, applied to a discontinuous spectrum consisting of bright lines resulting from radiation from an incandescent vapour or gas.

1890 G. F. Chambers *Handbk. Astron.* (ed. 4) II. 371 The spectra of bright-line stars. *Ibid.* 372 The meteorites in nebulæ giving a bright-line spectrum. 1901 *Nature* 12 Dec. 134/1 The bright-line stars and bright-line nebulæ.

Bright, *adv.* Add:

1. c. Jocular phr. *bright and early* (orig. U.S.).

1871 *Trans. Ill. Agric. Soc.* VIII. 79 Thursday morning, bright and early, we took a ride around the premises. 1887 Mary E. Wilkins *Humble Romance* 133 I'll speak to 'em bright and early. 1891 *Fur, Fin & Feather* Mar. 168 So I hitched up bright and early and started back. 1900 *Daily News* 18 July, Persons desirous of being present at this gathering should be there bright and early. 1920 P. G. Wodehouse *Damsel in Distress* vi, And this morning, bright and early, the beak parted him from ten quid. 1926 J. J. Connington *Death at Swaythling Court* xvi. 286 Next morning I got up bright and early.

Brilliantined (brilyăntī·nd), *a.* Dressed with Brilliantine.

1906 *Daily Chron.* 6 Apr. 9/5 Their adipose cheeks and brilliantined hair. 1926 *Chambers's Jrnl.* May 315/2 A sleek and pear-shaped gentleman heavily brilliantined and scented.

Brim, *sb.*⁵ *U.S.* [Var. of *Bream *sb.* 2 b.] The long-eared sunfish (*Lepomis auritus*).

1887 *Harper's Mag.* July 270/1 If they could slip away.., there would be a diminished number of 'brim' and 'goggle-eye,' in the ditch. 1894 *Outing* (U.S.) XXIII. 403/2 The brim, a small, red fish, which is excellent fried.

Brime (brəim), *v.* [See Briming (Cornwall).] *intr.* Of the sea: To be phosphorescent.

1893 Kipling *Many Invent.* 11 Dowse could see him of a clear night, when the sea brimed, climbing about the buoys with the sea-fire dripping off him.

Brimfulness. Add:

1891 Hardy *Tess* xxvii, The brimfulness of her nature breathed from her.

Brimmer, *sb.* **3.** Delete †*Obs.* and substitute: Now chiefly *local*; spec. a straw hat.

1888 Lowsley *Berkshire Gloss.*, *Brimmer*, a hat. 1893 *Wiltshire Gloss.*, *Brimmer*, a broad-brimmed hat. 1902 *Pall Mall Gaz.* 14 Apr. 2/3 The early brimmer marked a conspicuously daring spirit here and there against the crowd of silk hats.

Cf. *Local rhyme* (*Birmingham*). Straw brimmer, Ate the donkey's dinner.

Brimmy (bri·mi), *a.* [f. Brim *sb.*² + -y¹.] Having a wide brim; broad-brimmed.

1896 A. Morrison *Child of Jago* 112 The brimmy tall hat. 1908 *Westm. Gaz.* 28 Mar. 2/2 The cult flew..to big buttons on parachute-skirted coats,..to brimmy hats, brimmier hats, brimmiest hats, brimless hats. 1910 *Daily Chron.* 12 Mar. 4/4 He sported the brimmiest of hats.

Brimstone, *v.* [f. the sb.] *trans.* To smoke with brimstone.

1868 *Rep. U. S. Commissioner Agric.* (1869) 275 The yield is principally derived from hives that are 'brimstoned' in the fall, or from old combs that are unfit for use.

Brimstony, *a.* Add: *transf.* and *fig.* 'Sulphurous', 'fiery'.

1885 *Chambers's Jrnl.* Aug. 22 That brimstony old reprobate next door. 1924 Scholes *1st Bk. Gramophone Rec.* 93 The betrayer..came to a bad and brimstony end.

Brin (brin, as F. brɛ̃n). (See quots.)

1858 Simmonds *Dict. Trade, Brins*, a French name for coloured threads used in tapestry; the radiating sticks of a fan, which may be from 12 to 24 in number. 1908 Sir T. Wardle (*title*) An Examination into the Divisibility of the Brin or Ultimate Fibre of the Silk of Bombyx Mori. 1909 *Century Dict.* Suppl., *Brin*, one of the two circular fibers that issue from the silkworm. It consists of two parts, the inner of fibroin, or true silk, and the outer of sericin, or silk-glue. 1911 Webster, *Brin*, a kind of stout cloth of linen, sometimes partly cotton.

Bring, *v.* Add:

1. d. *To bring home the bacon* (fig.): to succeed in an undertaking; to achieve success. *slang.*

1924 P. G. Wodehouse *Ukridge* viii, It may be that my bit will turn out to be just the trifle that brings home the bacon. 1928 *Daily Express* 10 Aug. 3/5 If I fail to 'bring home the bacon' I will give £10 to any charity selected by your ladyship. 1929 *Publishers' Weekly* 30 Nov. 2590/1 There's a trio of names that will bring home the bacon... Jesus, Papini, and Dorothy Canfield.

18. j. Also *gen.*

1865 Meredith *Rhoda Fleming* xviii, He's mad...There ain't a doubt as t' what the doctors 'd bring him in...Lunatic's the word!

19. Bring off. d. To carry to a successful issue.

23. Bring round. c. To convert *to* an opinion.

1892 Mrs. H. Ward *D. Grieve* iv. (1901) 285/2 He talked to Lucy, and with great difficulty persuaded her in the matter of the hundred pounds...Ultimately, however, he brought his wife round. 1894 Bridges *Feast of Bacchus* iv. 1055 You've got..your father Brought nicely round: and all through my good management.

25. Bring to. f. To bring (land) into good condition. *U.S.*

1837 Colman *Rep. Agric. Mass.* (1838) 77 One of these gentlemen..has found this sort of land after it was thus 'brought to' extremely favorable to the growth of rye.

27. Bring up. a. Also, to cause (a person) to rise to his feet to answer a statement, etc.

m. To lead (troops, etc.) to the scene of action.

1885 U. S. Grant *Pers. Mem.* I. 415 The troops from Corinth were brought up in time to repel the threatened movement without a battle.

Bringing, *vbl. sb.* Add:

2. bringing up (*Naval*): see Bring *v.* 27 f.

1908 *Westm. Gaz.* 1 July 7/4 The 'Patrol' lost her anchor and cable in bringing up.

4. *attrib.* **bringing money,** money paid by a recruiting officer to a recruit on his joining the forces.

1892 *Rep. Comm. Terms & Cond. Service in Army* 63 The Committee have found a strong consensus of opinion that the reintroduction of bringing-money would probably give a great stimulus to recruiting.

Briny, *a.*¹ Add: **B.** *sb.* (colloq.) *The briny* = the ocean, the sea.

1865 *Slang Dict.*, *Briney*, the sea. 1880 H. Evans *Brighton Beach Loafer* (1888) 6 Tales of unutterable woe and adventures undergone on the 'briny'.

Briquet (bri·ke). *Her.* [Fr.] A steel for striking light from a flint; one of the ornaments used to form the collar of the order of the Golden Fleece.

1920 *Edin. Rev.* Oct. 314 The cross and briquet of Burgundy.

Briquettage (briketā·ʒ). [F. *briquetage.*] Objects fashioned of burnt clay.

1908 *Athenæum* 28 Mar. 391/2 The clay objects mentioned above, to which the Committee have provisionally given the non-committal name of 'briquettage'.

Briquette (brike·t), *v.* [f. the sb.] *trans.* To form (coal-dust, etc.) into briquettes. Also **Briquetting** *vbl. sb.*

1898 *Engl. Mechanic* 7 Oct. 194/1 Briquetting Sawdust. 1916 *Franke's Handbk. Briquetting* I. 621 Briquetting of Sawdust, and other Waste Wood. These materials can generally be briquetted fairly readily without a binding material. 1928 *Daily Tel.* 25 Sept. 11/5 The Yallourn briquetting plant of the State Electricity Commission of Victoria.

Brisance (brī·zaṅs). [f. F. *brisant*, pres. pple. of *briser* to break.] The shattering effect of such high explosives as nitroglycerine and gun-cotton.

1915 A. Marshall *Explosives* 390 It has been proposed by Bichel to use the expression $\frac{mv^2}{2}$ for the 'brisance' or violence of the blow given by an explosion, *m* being the mass of gas evolved and *v* the velocity of the detonation. *Ibid.* 320 For the brisance test quantities of 10 g. were used. *Ibid.* 407 *marg.*, Brisance meter.

Brisant (brī·zaṅ), *a.* [Fr.: see prec.] Of explosives: Shattering, smashing, breaking.

1905 Larsen tr. *Bichel's New Meth. Test. Explosives* 18 *note*, In this translation the word 'brisant' (explosives) has sometimes been used in preference to the rather inadequate expression 'high'. 1906 *Times* 14 Mar., Although these brisant substances belong directly to chemistry. 1918 Colver *High Explosives* 594 The genuine brisant explosives can only be detonated by means of the energy of a primary explosive.

Brisé (brī·ze), *a. Her.* [Fr.] Of a bearing: Broken, depicted as torn asunder. **b.** Bearing a mark of cadency or brisure.

[1780 Edmondson *Her.* II. Gloss., *Brisé*, in French armory, signifies broken...The English blazon it by the word *couped*; as thus, *a bend couped*.] 1828–40 Berry *Encycl. Her.* I.

Brise-bise (brī·zbīz). Also erron. **brise-à-bise, bris-à-bris**; colloq. **brisby.** [Fr., lit. 'break-wind'.] A curtain of net or lace for the lower part of a window.

1912 *Queen* 10 Aug. 266/1 Brise-bise curtains of striped net. 1923 *Advt.* in *Daily Mail* 14 Feb. 1 Cream Hemstitched Lace and Insertion Casements and Brise Bise. *Ibid.* 17 Apr. 14 Insertion Brise a bise. *Ibid.* 29 May 15 The *Brise-bise* Lace Curtain (familiarly called a 'Brisby'). *Ibid.* 14 Aug. 1/3 Cotton net..suitable for gowns, bris-à-bris.

Brisement (brī·zmaṅ). *Surgery.* [Fr.] A breaking asunder.

[1885 *Buck's Handbk. Med. Sci.* I. 201/1 Pyæmia and tearing of the nerves and vessels and soft parts about the joint were the not infrequent results of *brisement forcé*.] 1901 Dorland *Med. Dict.* (ed. 2), *Brisement*, the breaking up of anything, as of an ankylosis. (*Brisement forcé*, the breaking up of a bony ankylosis by force.)

Brisk, *v.* **2.** Add:

To brisk up: (also *gen.*) to become brisk, behave or move in a brisk manner.

1885 L. B. Walford *Nan* II. 76 After this adventure, we seemed..to brisk up afresh. 1903 R. Langbridge *Flame & Flood* xviii, Miss Lydia..brisked up suddenly and continued her narration. 1915 H. L. Wilson *Ruggles of Red Gap* iii. (1917) 40 As I brisked out of bed the following morning at half-after six. 1916 Boyd Cable *Action Front* 170 The rattle of rifle fire dwindled away at times to separate and scattered shots, brisked up again and rose to a long roll.

Brisken (bri·sk'n), *v.* [f. Brisk *a.* + -en⁵.]

1. *trans.* To make brisk or lively. Also with *up.*

1799 [A. Young] *Agric. Linc.* 451 Let your fuel be coke, which bears the bellows to brisken the fire, without raising a flame. 1838 *Eclectic Rev.* I. 551 Briskening the then dull tenor of periodical criticism. 1895 *Chambers's Jrnl.* XII. 667/2 Our movements were briskened painfully by the singing of bullets about our ears. 1901 *Daily Chron.* 27 Dec. 3/3 The Coronation, they think, may brisken up trade generally. 1905 E. F. Benson *Image in Sand* i. 8 Sir Henry briskened his pace a little.

2. *intr.* To become brisk, to speed up.

1876 W. Mathews *Getting on in the World* Ser. ii. iii. (1884) 68, I heartily wish that business may brisken a little. *a* 1911 *Scribner's Mag.* (Webster) Meanwhile our artillery fire briskened.

Hence **Bri·skening** *vbl. sb.*

1907 *Athenæum* 23 Mar. 364/1 This piece, with briskening of the action, will prove diverting. 1927 *Scots Observer* 4 June 17/2 A briskening of the air.

Brisky, *a.* Delete †*Obs. rare*⁻¹ and add:

1894 *Cornhill Mag.* Jan. 43 As we proceed, stopping regularly at every wayside public-house, many of the passengers betray symptoms of becoming 'brisky'. 1905 *Daily Chron.* 14 Mar. 6/7 The lamb soon got used to the new limb, and gambols about the farm in as brisky a manner as any of its companions.

Brisling (bri·sliŋ). Also **bristling.** [Norw. *brisling* sprat.] A small Norwegian fish of the herring family, resembling a sardine, which is cured and tinned for use as a table delicacy.

1902 Webster Suppl., Bristlings. 1913 *Times* (weekly ed.) 14 Nov., Mr. Charles Tate Regan, of the Fishery Department of the South Kensington Museum, gave evidence that 'Skipper Sardines' were bristling, or sprats. 1915 *Law Rep.* K. B. Div. III. 733 The Court of quarter sessions held, first, that the description 'Norwegian sardines' applied to the brisling packed in oil in the respondents' tins was a trade description as to the material of which the respondents' goods were composed. *Ibid.* 740 The Norwegian brisling were processed as sardines, labelled as Norwegian sardines, or smoked sardines, and put upon the English market in 1884. *Ibid.* 742 The brisling is the nearest approach to the sardine which the Norwegian seas provide. 1926 *Spectator* 2 Jan. 11/2 If the brisling fisheries fail the Stavanger Theatre shows a loss.

Brisque (brisk, brĭsk). [Fr.] In bézique and other card games, a privileged card, such as the aces and tens in bézique.

1870 'Cavendish' *Bézique* 8 Brisque (queen of spades and knave of diamonds, now called bésique), scored 40. Curiously enough, brisque did not exist in the game of *Brisque* itself. 1890 'Berkeley' *Bézique & Cribbage* 10 If the loser's score, with his brisques, is less than 1,000, he is said to be rubiconed.

Bristle, *sb.* **6.** Add:

bristle-bird, a name given to certain Australian reed-warblers; **bristle-rat,** another name for the hedgehog rat; **bristle-worm,** a chætopod.

1827 Vigors & Horsfield in *Trans. Linnæan Soc.* XV. 232 He [*sc.* Mr. Caley] calls it in his notes '*Bristle Bird*'. 1865 Gould *Birds Australia* I. 343 Sphenura longirostris... Long-billed Bristle-bird. 1911 A. H. S. Lucas & Le Souef *Birds Australia* 330 The Bristle-birds have a shy disposition, and live in reed-beds and thickets. 1908 *Westm. Gaz.* 8 Aug. 16/3 There is..a similarity in the eyes of the 'bristle-worm to those of the fly.

Bristletail. Add:

2. A name of the ruddy duck, *Erismatura rubida.*

1909 in *Cent. Dict.* Suppl.

Bristling, variant of Brisling.

Bristol. Add: **2. b.** In full *Bristol aeroplane*: a type of aeroplane constructed by the British and Colonial Aeroplane Co., Filton, Bristol.

1911 *Aero* May 52/1 In the new Bristol biplane all the supporting surfaces run in the slip-stream of the screw. 1913 A. E. Berriman *Aviation* xv. 148 The Bristol monoplane was similarly in the air in less than eighteen minutes. 1914 *Aeroplane* 22 Jan. 76/2 We already have machines which land fairly slowly—for example, the Avros and Sopwiths, and the latest Bristols. 1916 C. Winchester *Flying Men* 215 A Bristol scout. 1924 *Glasgow Herald* 30 June 11 Relay races were flown by Avros, Bristols and Snipes.

Brit, *sb.*³ Colloq. shortening of Briton.

1901 'Linesman' *Words by Eyewitness* (1902) 62 The Brit is at his old game. [1904 Sladen *Playing the Game* i. v, 'Imperial Government'! I call that too damned funny! Do you mean the Japs?' 'That word is most offensive to them. How would we like to be called Brits?']

Britain, *sb.* Add: *pl.* with reference to the several dominions and dependencies of Great Britain; cf. *Britt.* (*Omn.*) (= of (all) the Britains) in the legend on coins.

1897 Earl of Rosebery in *Daily News* 5 July 4/5 'Regina Britanniarum'—the Queen of the Britains...She is sovereign, not of one or two, but of numberless Britains, all self-supporting. 1901 *Westm. Gaz.* 11 Dec. 2/2 Lord Rosebery has succeeded with his cry of 'All the Britains', as the three letters 'Omn' on the new coins are to testify...Our King henceforth is to be King of All the Britains.

Britannia. **3.** Add: also *ellipt.* = Britannia metal.

1887 Mary E. Wilkins *Humble Romance* 107 Pouring the tea from the shiny britannia teapot into the best pink china cups.

Britannicize (britæ·nisəiz), *v.* [f. Britannic *a.* + -ize.] *trans.* To make Britannic or British in form or character.

[1811 *Ann. Reg.* 1809 Pref. p. iv, Such measures as may *Britannize*, as it were, all the other Grecian islands.] 1887 W. F. Rae *Miss Bayle's Romance* xvii, American gentlemen are 'britannicized Indians'. 1921 *Spectator* 16 Apr. 487/2 St. Paul did not fight a lifelong battle against judaising the Christian Church in order that we should britannicize it nowadays.

Britholite (bri·þolǝit). *Min.* [f. Gr. βριθος weight, in allusion to its high specific gravity, + -lite.] A rare silicate and phosphate of the cerium metals and calcium, found in southern Greenland.

1909 E. S. Dana & W. E. Ford *Sec. App. Dana's Syst. Min.* 19 Britholite...Orthorhombic. In pseudo-hexagonal prisms.

Briticism. (Earlier U.S. example.)

1868 R. G. White in *Galaxy* Mar. 335 This use of the word is a widespread Briticism.

British, *a.* Add:

2. Also *spec.* as connoting certain characteristics of true-born Britons, as in *British matron* (hence *British matronism*), *British workman.*

1889 *Standard* 18 July 3/7 An outbreak of some epidemic of British matronism.

b. British Empire. The empire consisting of Great Britain and the other British possessions, dominions, and dependencies.

1604 J. Dee *Pet. to King*, The Almightie and most mercifull God..make your Maiestie to be the most blessed and Triumphant Monarch, that euer this Brytish Empire enioyed. 1768 (*title*) The present state of the British Empire in Europe, America, Africa and Asia, containing a concise account of our possessions in every part of the globe, [etc.]. 1783 J. Galloway (*title*) Political reflections on the late colonial governments; in which their original constitutional defects are pointed out, and shewn to have naturally produced the rebellion, which has unfortunately terminated in the dismemberment of the British empire. 1784 (*title*) A view of the British Empire, or more especially Scotland. 1813 Hector Campbell (*title*) The Impending Ruin of the British Empire, its Cause and Remedy considered. 1876 *Encycl. Brit.* V. 336/2 In 1871 the first Imperial census of the British empire was taken.

attrib. 1902 *Encycl. Brit.* XXXIII. 303/1 The United Empire Trade League, the British Empire League, [etc.] endeavour to promote inter-Imperial trade.

5. British warm: see Warm *sb.*² 2.

Britishism (bri·tiʃiz'm). [f. British + -ism.] The characteristic qualities of the British; with *a* and *pl.* any of these; a British peculiarity, form of expression, or the like.

1894 *Harper's Mag.* Jan. 315 Doubtless he could use 'Britishisms' if he chose. *Ibid.*, Nor should we advise an American statesman to attempt a 'Britishism'. 1906 *Daily Chron.* 20 Oct. 4/4 Americanism yet Britishism, cosmopolitanism but Imperialism. 1915 Sanday *Meaning of War* 80 For the Englishman, *Britishism* (Britentum) and civilization, the idea of humanity, the peace of the world, and the idea of English world-predominance are one and the same. 1920 *Public Opinion* 23 Apr. 409/3 This sensibility and adaptability form..the chief distinguishing feature between Britishism and Prussianism. 1927 *Observer* 20 Nov. 11/1 These are a few of the concrete Britishisms which engage the vigilance of Chicago's mayor.

Britishly (bri·tiʃli), *adv.* [f. British *a.* + -ly².]

†**1.** In the ancient British tongue. *Obs. rare.*

1654 Vilvain *Enchir. Epigr.* vi. xxiii, Glassenbury, Brytishly cald Inis Avalon.

2. After the manner of the British, in British fashion.

1892 Stevenson & L. Osbourne *Wrecker* xxiii, Britishly chuckle-headed. 1892 Frances E. Trollope *That Wild Wheel* xiv, I shall come home..to grumble, Britishly, on my half-pay. 1900 *Daily News* 3 Mar. 6/1 As he took up his position, very Britishly in front of the fire. 1904 *Windsor Mag.* Jan. 294/1 A certain sedate and Britishly respectable old codger.

Britishness (bri·tiʃnės). [f. British *a.* + -ness.] †**a.** The conditions of the ancient Britons. **b.** The quality or character of the British.

1682 W. Richards *Wallogr.* 88 Primitive Brittishness was never acquainted with the habiliment of a Shirt. 1872 W. Clark Russell *Perplexity* xxvi, There were Frank's pure eyes, his clear-cut nose,..his manliness, his high-bred air, and, if I may coin a word, his thorough *Britishness*. 1904 *Daily Chron.* 9 Sept. 3/2 As Napoleon pulverised ancient kingdoms..so Hazlitt hurled himself courageously at the solid mass of complacent Britishness.

Brito- (bri·to), comb. form f. L. *Brit(t)o* Briton, used:

1. In sense 'belonging to the ancient Britons and..', as *Brito-Pictish, Brito-Roman* adjs.

1654 Vilvain (*title*) Enchiridium Epigrammatum Latino-Anglicum; an epitome of essais, Englished out of Latin... Containing six Classes or Centuries of 1. Theologicals. 2. Historicals. 3. Heterogeneals. 4. Bryto-Anglicals. 5. Miscellaneals. 6. Mutuatitials. 1860 *Chambers's Encycl.* I. 376/2 Of Roman or Brito-Roman manufacture. 1926 *Glasgow Herald* 25 Oct. 6 A long list of British or Brito-Pictish ministers.

2. In sense 'British and..', as *Brito-arctic, Brito-Japanese.* Also **Brito-centric** *a.*, having Britain as the centre.

1898 *Geogr. Jrnl.* XI. 134 It is evident, therefore, that the basalts of Cape Flora and Hooker island are similar to types widely distributed in the Brito-arctic volcanic province. 1905 *Westm. Gaz.* 11 Sept. 2/3 'Anglo-Japanese' certainly is an easier form than 'Brito-Japanese'. 1924 Rose Macaulay *Orphan Island* xvi. § 3 The world, as viewed from Orphan Island, wore a curious, Brito-Centric aspect.

Broach, *sb.* Add:

4. b. A shuttle used in weaving tapestry.

1783 *Encycl. Brit.* (ed. 2) X. 8536/1 They serve to keep the warp open for the passage of broaches wound with silks, woollens, or other matters used in the piece of tapestry. 1878 Mrs. Sketchley tr. *A. de Champeaux's Tapestry* 2 The material for the woof is wound on a wooden shuttle, called a 'broach' or 'flute'. 1888 *Encycl. Brit.* XXIII. 212/1 The design [of tapestry and pile carpets] is formed by short stitches knotted across the warp with a wooden needle called a broach.

III. as (sense 5) *broach-river; broach-splitting.*

1899 Rider Haggard in *Longman's Mag.* Mar. 410, I found ..Rough Jimmy..employed in splitting broaches to be used for thatching stacks. This is the process of broach-splitting. 1921 *Dict. Occup. Terms* (1927) § 499 *Broach river*; rives timber with a cleaver, and shapes the pieces of timber with a hand knife to form broaches, *i.e.* pointed implements used in thatching.

IV. In various technical senses: see quots.

1858 Simmonds *Dict. Trade, Broach*, a tool or fitting for an Argand gas burner. 1889 *Cent. Dict.*, *Broach*..14. That part of the stem of a key which projects beyond the bit or web, and enters a socket in the interior of the lock.

Broach (brō^utʃ), *sb.*² In 7 **baroche.** [Place-name.] A Surat cotton grown in the Broach district, Bombay Presidency, India.

1617 R. Cocks *Diary* (Hakl. Soc. 1883) I. 330 We gave our host..a peece of backar baroche to his children to make them 2 coates. 1877 *Encycl. Brit.* VI. 482/2 The principal sorts [of Surats] are Hingunghât, Oomrawuttee, Broach, Dhollera, and Dharwar.

Broach, *v.*¹ Add:

9. To enlarge and finish (a drilled hole) with a 'broach' or boring-bit. Also with adv. *out.*

1846 Holtzapffel *Turning* II. 572 Flutes and clarionets are first perforated with the nose-bit, and then broached with taper holes. 1879 *Ibid.* IV. 363 The work being removed from the chuck, the hole is broached out to size. 1889 Hasluck *Model Engin. Handybk.* (1900) 91 The hole in cross-head for piston-rod will have to be broached out.

Broacher. Add:

3. One who broaches holes.

1921 *Dict. Occup. Terms* (1927) § 200 *Broacher; broaching machinist*; a driller who enlarges or smooths out core hole, a hole previously drilled, using a broach or reamer in a drilling machine.

Broaching, *vbl. sb.* Add: **6.** The action or operation of enlarging and finishing a drilled hole. (Cf. *Broach *v.*¹ 9.) Also *attrib.*, as *broaching machine, machinist.*

1846 Holtzapffel *Turning* II. 575 For large works, broaching machines are employed. 1888 *Lockwood's Dict. Terms Mech. Engin.* s.v., Broaching is chiefly done in a drilling machine or a lathe. 1921 broaching machinist [see *Broacher 3].

Broad, *a.* Add:

1. e. Of bran: Consisting of large particles.

1908 *Animal Managem.* 98 Two varieties are distinguished as 'broad' or 'fine'; in 'broad' bran the wheat husk is more or less whole and gives the article a flaky appearance.

B. *sb.* **7.** *Turning.* A tool having a disc or angular end with a sharpened edge used for turning the insides and bottoms of cylinders.

1846 Holtzapffel *Turning* II. 515 The broad..requires to be held downwards or underhand.

D. 1. a. (sense 7) *broad-brogued, -tongued* adjs.

1889 Gretton *Memory's Harkback* 73 A broad-tongued North-countryman. 1900 *Daily News* 8 Oct. 6/6 One broad-brogued Irishman.

2. broad-banded *a.*, having broad bands of colour as a distinctive marking, esp. defining a species of armadillo; **broad-billed** *a.*, having a broad bill, esp. defining a species of sandpiper; **broadhead,** in full *grubber broadhead*, an anchovy of the species *Anchovia producta*; **broad-headedness** *Ethnol.*, brachycephaly; **broad jump** = long jump (see Jump *sb.*¹ 1 b); **broad-lace,** a woollen material about four inches wide, used as an ornamental border in carriage upholstery; **broad-leaf,** (also) a settlers' name for a New Zealand tree *Griselinia littoralis*; **broad stone** = Ashlar 1, Free-stone¹ 1.

1904 *Westm. Gaz.* 8 Sept. 10/1 The *broad-banded species (*Xenurus unicinctus*) is a rare creature [*sc.* armadillo] from Surinam. 1886 Newton in *Encycl. Brit.* XXI. 261/1 The *Broad-billed Sandpiper, *Tringa platyrhyncha*, of the Old World. 1890 Huxley in *19th Cent.* Nov. 758 In the extreme north..marked *broad-headedness is combined with low stature..in the Lapps. 1846 Dodd *Brit. Manuf.* VI. 132 The lace employed..is used as a binding or edging for various parts of the interior [of a coach]; the finest is called '*broad-lace'. 1879 W. N. Blair *Building Materials of Otago* 155 There are few trees in the bush so conspicuous, or so well known as the *broad-leaf. 1703 T. N. *City & C. Purchaser* 56 *Broad-stone..the same with Free-stone,..so called, because they are raised broad and thin out of the Quarries. 1842 Gwilt *Archit.* Gloss., *Broad Stone*, the same as free-stone.

Broad-acres. *The* (*land of the*) *Broad-acres*: Yorkshire. So **Broad-acred** *a.*, of or characteristic of Yorkshire.

1898 *Windsor Mag.* VII. 696/2 Yorkshire has in recent years..played its matches in various parts of the broad-acred shire. 1907 *Minister's Gaz. Fashion* Oct. 182/1 'There's a trip in fra' Leeds, my lad,' explained the man from broad acres. 1908 A. N. Cooper (*title*) Across the Broad Acres. 1928 *Sunday Dispatch* 8 July 22/3 The youth of the Broad-acres. 1928 *Sunday Express* 17 June 12/6 A red-faced..man of the broad-acred type.

Broad aisle. *U.S.* [Aisle 4 b.] The passage down the middle of a church or meeting-house.

1807 *Massachusetts Spy* 25 Mar. 4/1 [For sale:] Another Pew at the right hand of the broad aisle, esteemed the pleasantest in said house. 1809 *Repertory* (Boston) 16 June (Th.) For sale, a Pew in the broad Ile of the Chapel Church. 1845 S. Judd *Margaret* i. xiv. 108 She stood at the foot of the broad-aisle and looked in. 1887 *Harper's Mag.* Dec. 161/2 Miss Flint shall have pew No. 40 in the broad aisle. 1890 *Ibid.* Oct. 719/1 He then passed up the broad aisle in the wake of the procession.

Broad alley. *U.S.* [Alley 5.] = prec.

1763 *Essex Inst. Hist. Coll.* XLII. 139 With what face

can you require a young woman to stand in the broad alley and there confess fornication..? 1775 Trumbull *McFingal* i. 704 While, should you offer to repent, You'd need..more confessions than broad-alleys. 1806 *Intelligencer* (Lanc., Pa.) 21 Oct. (Th.) Mr. Deming was sitting in the Pew east of the broad Alley.

Broad-axe. (Earlier U.S. examples.)

1641 *Connecticut Publ. Rec.* I. 444 A broad axe, 2 narrow axes. 1678 *New Castle Court Rec.* 361, 4 axes, one broad-ax, one hatchett. 1777 *Essex Inst. Hist. Coll.* XLIX. 106 Sold..broad axes at 21s. 1779 *Maryland Jrnl.* 22 June, Advt. (Th.) A scar cut with the corner of a broad-axe. 1812 *Massachusetts Spy* 12 Dec. (ibid.) [She] had from the window observed the negro sharpening the broad axe upon the grindstone. 1836 Crockett *Exploits & Adv. Texas* vi. (1837) 52 A chap just about as rough hewn as if he had been cut out of a gum log with a broad axe.

Broad-bill, broadbill. [See Broad *a.* D. 2.]

1. The scaup-duck (*Fuligula marila*), or related species. *U.S.*

1848 Bartlett *Dict. Amer.*, Broadbill (*Anas marila*), the common name of a wild duck, which appears on our coast in large numbers in October. 1874 J. W. Long *Amer. Wild-fowl Shooting* Introd. 16, I shall treat of the red-head, blue-bill or broad-bill, tufted duck, and buffle-head or butter-ball.

2. A passerine bird of the family *Eurylæmidæ.*

1889 *Century Dict.* s.v., There are nine or ten species of broadbills peculiar to the Indian region.

Broad-brim. (Earlier U.S. example.)

1774 J. Adams *Diary* 20 Oct., Wks. 1850 II. 400 Two or three broad-brims over against me at table.

Broadcast. **C.** *sb.* Add: **2.** The action or an act of broadcasting by wireless telegraphy. Also *attrib.*, as *broadcast programme.*

1922 *Daily Mail* 8 Aug. 7/3 (heading) World Broadcast. 1924 *Wireless World* 3 Sept. 662/2 He was fined £2 for interfering with broadcast programmes. *Ibid.* 664/1 Broadcast Announcements in Two Languages. 1924 *Westm. Gaz.* 4 Dec., The Postmaster-General's power to include control over broadcast receivers. 1924 Reith (*title*) Broadcast over Britain. 1926 *Glasgow Herald* 16 Nov. 9 The ban on the broadcast of controversial topics.

Broadcast, *v.* Add:

3. To disseminate (a message, news, a musical performance, or any audible matter) from a wireless transmitting station to the receiving sets of listeners; said also of a speaker or performer. Also *absol.*

Inflected pa. t. *broadcasted*, pa. pple. *broadcast(ed.*

1921 *Discovery* Apr. 92/1 The [wireless] station at Poldhu is used partly for broadcasting Press and other messages to ships, that is, sending out messages without receiving replies. 1922 *Daily Mail* 8 Aug. 7/3 The largest and most powerful wireless station that can broadcast to the world. *Ibid.* 11 Nov. 7 Government arrangements for broadcasting. 1923 *Glasgow Herald* 3 Feb. 8 In cities the 'broadcasted' entertainment can never prove a serious rival to the theatre and concert hall. 1924 *Daily News* 13 Dec. 6/7 The speech broadcast to our homes to-day.

Broadcaster (brǭ·dkastəɹ). [f. Broadcast *v.* + -er¹.] A broadcasting company, station, or instrument; also, a person whose speech, performance, etc. is broadcasted.

1922 *Daily Mail* 30 Nov. 8 The Prince of Wales..made a great hit as a 'broadcaster'..when he delivered a message by wireless to the Boy Scouts. 1923 *Contemp. Rev.* Dec. 707 The universal 'broadcaster'..might effect a greater control over our thoughts and views than the most powerful newspaper proprietor. 1928 *Music Bulletin* May 131 Performers who have achieved very highly as recorders or broadcasters.

So **Broa·dcasting** *vbl. sb.*, the action of the verb; also *attrib.* or as *ppl. a.*, as *British Broadcasting Corporation* (abbrev. *B.B.C.*: see *B. III.).

1922 *Glasgow Herald* 21 Apr. 10 The 'broadcasting' of predetermined material of public interest from central stations. *Ibid.* 1 May 10 Whether the 'broadcasting' station itself shall be under or independent of official control. 1922 *Westm. Gaz.* 19 Oct., The British Broadcasting Company will broadcast news, information, concerts, lectures, educational matter, speeches, weather reports, and theatrical entertainments. 1926 *Encycl. Brit.* New Vol. III. 1046/2, Feb. 23 1920 saw the opening of the first wireless telephone broadcasting service in the world, when a programme of vocal and instrumental music..was transmitted.

Broaden, *v.* **1.** Add: also with *out.*

1888 Mrs. H. Ward *R. Elsmere* iii. I. 79 Her round comfortable face brightened and broadened out into a beaming smile. 1894 Beatrice Harraden *In Varying Moods* vii, The narrow, dull, everyday existence broadened out into many interesting possibilities.

Broa·d-horn, broa·dhorn. *U.S.* [Broad *a.* 1.]

1. A large flat-bottomed boat formerly used on the Mississippi and Ohio rivers. (See quot. 1820.)

1819 W. B. Dewees *Lett. fr. Texas* i. 11 The vessels upon this river consist in part of barges and keel boats; but mostly of upper country flat boats, (generally called broad-horns). 1820 J. Hall *Lett. West* (1828) 324 The flat-bottom boat is a mere raft...An immense oar is placed on the roof on each side, near the bow (which has given these boats the nickname of 'broad horns'). 1833 *Deb. Congress.* 20 Feb. 1764 It was too late to force his broadhorn against the current back into the main channel. 1843 Carlton *New Purchase* 34 The usual mode then of going down [the Ohio river] was in arks, broadhorns, keel boats. 1878 J. H. Beadle *Western Wilds* 27 He went off on a broadhorn. You don't know what a broadhorn is. No? Well, it's a flat-boat of the old rig. 1883 *Encycl. Amer.* I. 440/2 When the coal mines in the vicinity of Pittsburg began to ship coal to Southern markets, the 'broadhorn,' or 'coal-boat,' was invented.

2. The mountain-sheep or bighorn.

1847 *Knickerbocker Mag.* Aug. XXX. 141 He had wandered some distance up the [California] mountains in search of wild sheep or 'broad-horns.'

Broadland (brǭ·dlænd). [f. Broad *sb.* 5 + Land *sb.*] The district of the Broads; East Anglia, or a section of it. Also *attrib.* Hence **Broa·dlander.**

1889 (*title*) Summer in Broadland. 1899 *Daily News* 27 Dec. 6/4 The sluggish streams and low meadows of the Norfolk Broadland. 1902 N. Everitt (*title*) Broadland Sport. 1903 W. A. Dutt *Norfolk Broads* vi. 78 Among the characteristic Broadlanders..the wherrymen are the most numerous and conspicuous. 1926 *Daily Tel.* 6 Aug. 5/2 Broadland bream at this season are particularly partial to stewed wheat.

Broadmi·ndedness. [f. *broad-minded* (see Broad D. 1) + -ness.] The condition of being liberal or tolerant in thought or opinion.

1893 *Athenæum* 2 Dec. 770/3 There was a rare combination in him of bigotry and broad-mindedness. 1910 W. J. Locke *Simon the Jester* xv, Haven't I felt myself the same swelling pride in my broadmindedness?

Broadtail (brǭ·dte^il). In full *black broadtail* = *Breitschwanz.

1898 *Westm. Gaz.* 13 Jan. 3/2 A broadtail cycling suit is the latest whim in the Bois. *Ibid.* 3 Nov. 3/2, I can as strongly commend black broadtail. It is a fur very easy to manipulate. 1899 *Ibid.* 21 Sept. 3/2 The coat of black broadtail, or caracal, or Persian lamb or astrachan, all varieties of a species, is prophesied as the pet garment this winter. 1927 *Observer* 20 Nov. 21 Long waistcoats of ermine or squirrel or broad-tail.

Brocade, *sb.* **3.** Add:

brocade-matting, a floor matting of Japanese manufacture consisting of a texture of reeds and cotton yarn with a coloured design woven upon it.

1902 *Encycl. Brit.* XXIX. 696/2 The 'brocade-matting' industry of Okayama.

Brocadi·lla. [ad. Sp. *brocadillo.*] = Brocatello. Also *attrib.*

1872 *Rep. Vermont Board Agric.* 658 No other marble quarried in Rutland county resembling it except the brocatelle, known to the trade as 'brocadilla'. *Ibid.* 660 The 6th layer is of brocadilla marble, green and white varied.

Brocatelle. **2.** (Modern U.S. example.)

1872 *Rep. Vermont Board Agric.* 661 The presence of small particles of flint as in the brocatelle.

Broché (brō^u·ʃe, ‖broʃe), *a.* [Fr., pa. pple. of *brocher* to stitch.] Of a material, esp. silk: Woven with a pattern on the surface. Also *sb.*, a material of such a texture.

1874 Knight *Dict. Mech.*, *Broché-goods*, goods embroidered or embossed. 1882 Caulfeild & Saward *Dict. Needlework*, *Broché*, a French term denoting a velvet or silk textile, with a satin figure thrown up on the face. 1898 *Queen* 1 Jan. 31/2 Some silk crêpon gauzes, rich brochés, and fancy velveteen.

Brochette. Add:

2. A pin or bar used to fasten medals, orders, etc., to the coat or uniform of the wearer.

1849 Thackeray *Pendennis* xxv, He wore three little gold crosses in a brochette on the portly breast of his blue coat. 1896 *Daily News* 5 Mar. 7/5 M. Faure wore his brochette of Russian Orders.

Brodder (brǫ·dəɹ). *Sc.* and *north.* [f. Brod *v.* + -er¹.] One who brods or uses a brod. *Rug-brodder* (see quot. 1921).

1877 *Covenant Times* 200 This torture consisted in the free use of the 'brodder's' needles. 1885 W. Ross *Aberdour & Inchcolme* xi. 328 'Who', you say, 'was the Brodder?'..His office was to settle the question, whether those accused of being witches were so or not..by searching for the 'devil's mark' on their bodies, by 'brodding' or pricking it with a sharp needle. 1921 *Dict. Occup. Terms* (1927) § 398 *Rug brodder* (Yorks. term)..makes rugs, by hand, on a canvas ground, by piercing canvas with an awl and inserting cloth cuttings.

Broderie Anglaise (brodrī aṅglēz). [Fr., = English embroidery.] Open embroidery on white linen or cambric.

1852 *Illustr. Lond. News* 26 June 504/2 The *pardessus*,.. trimmed with *broderie Anglaise*. 1882 Caulfeild & Saward *Dict. Needlework* s.v., True broderie Anglaise patterns are outlines of various sized holes, arranged so as to make floral or geometrical devices. 1905 *Westm. Gaz.* 11 May 4/2, I am perfectly charmed with these embroidered lawn and Broderie Anglaise petticoats. The Broderie Anglaise muslins are simply everywhere. 1907 *Daily Chron.* 25 June 8/2 Coats in Broderie Anglaise...A plain full skirt..finished at the hem with a band of the broderie.

Brodrick (brǫ·drik). The name of the Secretary of State for War (1900–3), the Rt. Hon. W. St. J. *Brodrick*, afterwards Viscount Midleton, applied facetiously to: **a.** a soldier enlisted under the lower standard of physique introduced under his régime; more explicitly *little Brodrick*; **b.** an army cap invented and introduced by him.

1903 *Westm. Gaz.* 19 Mar. 8/1 'Brodricks' in South Africa. 1903 *Daily Chron.* 17 Sept. 7/2 There were comparatively few so-called 'Little Brodricks' in these sturdy line battalions of the 1st Army Corps. 1905 *Westm. Gaz.* 25 May 8/2 The other half in undress uniform, with..its fatigue jackets, its 'Brodrick' caps, and riding whips.

Brogan. *U.S.* (Later examples.)

1886 *Harper's Mag.* June 62/1 One may see them out in snow knee-deep clad in low brogans. 1887 *Ibid.* Mar. 618/2 Stout and rough-looking brogans enveloped the foot up to the ankle.

Bröggerite (brö·gərəit). *Min.* [Named 1884 (*Bröggerit*) after W. C. *Brögger*, Norwegian mineralogist, who discovered it: see -ite¹.] A mineral allied to uraninite.

1884 *Jrnl. Chem. Soc.* XLVI. 1102 The mineral, which has been named bröggerite by the author, is closely related to cleveite. 1901 *Ibid.* LXXX. ii. 306 The specimen of bröggerite..from which radioactive lead was obtained..had a hardness 5·5 and a sp. gr. 9·06 at 15°.

Brogue, *sb.*² Add:

1. b. In full *brogue shoe.* A strong shoe for country and sports wear.

1906 Hasluck *Boot & Shoe Pattern Cutting* 57 Brogue Shoes.—The gentleman's brogue is always a strong shoe for shooting, golf, fishing, etc. The wing of the vamp and cap are longer..than for a lady's brogue. 1917 *Mod. Boot & Shoe Maker* III. 234 Highland Brogue Shoe...The general design is similar to a very heavy golfing brogue. 1925 *Blackw. Mag.* Jan. 35/1 An enormous pair of unlaced black brogue shoes.

4. brogue heel, a low heel like that of a brogue shoe; **brogue vamp,** a stout vamp made like that of a brogue shoe.

1927 *Chambers's Jrnl.* XVII. 286/2 She'd only brogue heels on her feet; and her..shoulders were just about on a level with his. 1909 *Bootmaker's Price-list*, Gentleman's.. Lace Boot, brogue vamp.

Brogued, *a.* Add:

b. Of a boot: Made with a strong vamp like that of a brogue. Cf. *brogue vamp* (*Brogue *sb.*² 4.) Hence **Broguing** (brō^u·giŋ) *vbl. sb.*, the manufacture of brogued shoes or brogue vamps; the vamp itself.

1894 *Standard* 11 Apr. 3/1 Strong brogued walking boots. 1894 *Queen* 17 Nov. 870/1 White kid laid under the black broguing. 1906 Hasluck *Boot & Shoe Pattern Cutting* 22 In all cases where outside fittings are to be brogued.

Bro·guer². (See quot. and cf. Brog *sb.* and *v.*)

1921 *Dict. Occup. Terms* (1927) § 262 *Broguer*; a solderer who hermetically seals tins of meat after preserving process is complete, by soldering over brogue hole left for escape of air and steam while tins are in preserving retort.

Broguish (brō^u·giʃ), *a.* [f. Brogue *sb.*³ + -ish¹.] Inclined or tending to a brogue.

1899 *Echo* 6 July 1/5 A bright and intermittently brogueish Irishman. 1922 *Glasgow Herald* 25 Apr. 8 Fine big, broguish fellows, mostly from Ireland. 1928 *Daily Express* 11 Aug. 8/5 He has no ear at all and we all laughed at his broguish cacophonies.

Broil, bryle (broil, brəil). *Min.* (Cornwall.) Loose fragments, often of a metallic nature, found lying on the surface above a vein or lode.

1778 Pryce *Min. Cornub.* 125 Upon the top of most Tin Lodes..is that mineralized substance, which is called the Broil or Bryle of the Lode. 1818 W. Phillips *Geol.* 210 Loose fragments or portions of earthy or stony substances, having generally more or less of an ochreous tinge..called the 'bryle of the load'. 1839 De la Beche *Rep. Geol. Cornwall*, etc. xv. 528 *note*, The upper part of a lode is usually now termed the broil, or bryle. 1859 Forfar *Pentowan* v, Sometimes we do discover the lode by a broil.

Broiler¹. Add:

1. b. A gridiron or similar utensil used in broiling. Now *U.S.*

1632 Sherwood, A broiler, *gril.* 1828– Webster. *a* 1906 'O. Henry' *Trimmed Lamp* etc. 64 Two minutes longer on the broiler would have made this steak fit to be eaten by a gentleman, Francois.

2. (Earlier U.S. example.)

1876 *Rep. Vermont Board Agric.* III. 244 The cockerels should be sold for broilers when large enough.

3. An American railway carriage fitted with a grill-room. *U.S.*

1909 *Cent. Dict.* Suppl.

Broke, *ppl. a.* Add:

3. In predicative use: Ruined financially, bankrupt; (often less seriously) penniless; also *broke to the world.* (Cf. Broken *ppl. a.* 7.) *slang.* Often with qualifier, as *clean, dead broke* (Dead C. 2), *stone-broke* (Stone *sb.* 20), *stony broke* (Stony *a.* 6).

[Cf. the following, which are properly instances of Break *v.* 11, 11 b: 1665 Pepys *Diary* 6 July, It seems some of his creditors have taken notice of it, and he was like to be broke yesterday in his absence. 1668–9 *Ibid.* 12 Mar., Being newly broke by running in debt.]

1851 N. Kingsley *Diary* 173 To day men have come along 'dead broke' and have gone to work for 4 dollars pr. day. 1866 *Cincinnati Enquirer* 17 July (Schele de Vere) When he left the gambling-house, he was observed to turn toward a friend with the words, Dead-broke! 1886 H. Smart *Outsider* vii, Well, sir, I was broke—so broke as I hope I never shall be again—'dead stoney', barely expresses it. *a* 1889 in Barrère & Leland *Dict. Slang* s.v., Then came the *fiasco*, And Ben cried 'Carrasco! I'm bested, broke, busted—or partly!' 1889 *Pall Mall Gaz.* 14 Aug. (Farmer) I see that Sullivan made 21,000 dols. out of his fight, but as he was 'dead broke' before the battle, there won't be much of it left. 1890 *Buckskin Mose* i. 18 We were 'dead broke'. 1907 S. E. White *Arizona Nights* i. vii. 133 Well, it took me six weeks and two days to go broke. 1908 *Westm. Gaz.* 1 Feb., Ten and six for being manicured, and I'm absolutely broke. 1911 J. C. Lincoln *Cap'n Warren's Wards* xxi. 337 I'm flat broke. 1918 W. J. Locke *Rough Road* iii, I believe you good people think I've come back broke to the world. 1926 J. Black *You Can't Win* v. 53 [The landlady] wanted the rent. I told her I was broke. 1927 *Observer* 18 Sept. 8/5 The twins will not be completely 'broke' until they get to France.

4. Of animals: Broken to harness. *U.S.*

1833 Mary A. Holley *Texas* v. 97 This brutal process is repeated until the animal is thoroughly broke and rendered docile. 1850 W. Miles *Jrnl.* (1916) 12, 500 broke mules were to be in readiness. 1856 *Trans. Mich. Agric. Soc.* VII. 275 Oxen exhibited as working cattle, for their being the best broke, must be hitched to either a wagon or cart.

5. (See *BROKEN *ppl. a.* 1 h.)

Broken, *ppl. a.* Add:

1. c. broken letter *Typogr.*, distributed type.

1770 LUCKOMBE *Hist. Printing* 496 By broken Letter is.. meant..the breaking the orderly succession the Letters stood in..and mingling the Letters together.

e. *Phonetics.* (See quot. 1887.) = *FRACTURED.

1845 J. M. KEMBLE in *Proc. Philol. Soc.* II. 135 A tendency in the vowel to become dulled or broken when placed in particular positions. 1887 SKEAT *Princ. Etym.* 45 The symbol *ea* denotes that the vowel was, to speak technically, 'broken', i.e. was resolved into the diphthong *e-a*.

f. Of a bird: Shot down or killed in accordance with the rules, in trap-shooting.

1892 GREENER *Breech-Loader* 261 Judges..shall raise the red flag to indicate a 'broken' bird.

g. *Broken (over)*: in bookbinding, applied to the creasing down of a small part of an inserted print near the binding margin, for the purpose of giving support to the binding thread.

1880 ZAEHNSDORF *Art Book-binding* 169 Broken over. When plates are turned over or folded a short distance from the back edge, before they are placed in the volume, so as to facilitate their being turned easily or laid flat, they are said to be broken over. When a leaf has been turned down the paper is broken.

h. In paper-making, seriously damaged, denoting a quality of defective paper inferior to retree. (Also *broke*.)

1807 [see RETREE]. 1880 J. DUNBAR *Pract. Papermaker* 48 This method is a perfectly successful one, the author having had it in constant use when making thin papers. It saves broken [paper], and can be worked so near the edge that the impression is taken off at the cutter. 1888 C. F. CROSS & BEVAN *Paper-making* 104 'Broke' Paper.—Under this head may be included all the partially formed paper which is always obtained in greater or less degree when a paper-machine is started, or such portions as are occasionally unavoidably damaged in its passage over the drying cylinders. *Ibid.* 105 'Broke' paper may be advantageously disintegrated by means of an edge-runner. 1907 *Ibid.* (ed. 3) 150 Under the crushing and milling action of the stones, the fibres of the broken paper are not only separated, but are also further reduced and disintegrated.

12. e. *Hort.* Of a breeder tulip: That has developed into a striped or variegated flower. (See BREAK *v.* 32 c.)

1731 MILLER *Gard. Dict.* 8 D/1 If one of these Flowers [*sc.* of the tulip] is quite broken..it will never lose its Stripes. 1824 LOUDON *Encycl. Gard.* (ed. 2) 832 Save seed from these in preference to the finest of the variegated or broken sorts [of tulips].

f. *Broken time*, time lost from regular employment.

1895 *Westm. Gaz.* 8 Nov. 1/3 The formation of a new Union on the basis of payment for 'broken-time,' as it is called by courtesy. 1912 R. W. POULTON in *Life* (1919) 214 A carefully arranged payment for 'broken time' for men who are paid weekly or monthly for the hours they work. 1927 *Sunday Express* 27 Nov. 13/3 The resolutions passed at the recent Stadium Club meeting..on the question of 'broken time'.

17. broken-up (earlier American examples).

1637 *Cambridge Prop. Rec.* 42, 20 ac[res] of broken upp grounde..& 25 ac[res] unbroken upp lying by it. 1684 *Essex Inst. Hist. Coll.* IV. 68/2 He should have liberty to make use of part of the improved & broken up ground upon the said farme.

Brokeress. Delete † *Obs. rare*⁻¹ and add:

1827 CARLYLE *Germ. Rom.* I. 32 The talking brokeress.. was far from giving him a true disclosure of her blabbing. 1865 SWINBURNE *Chastelard* II. i, Yea, and she said, the Italian brokeress, She said such men were good for great queens' love. 1871 SCHELE DE VERE *Americanisms* (1872) 655 A couple of ladies having established their 'Exchange Office' in..Wall-street, they were at once spoken of in the New York papers as bankeresses or brokeresses.

Brolga (brǫ·lgă). [Native name.] The Australian Native Companion Crane, *Grus australasianus*.

1896 *Westm. Gaz.* 6 Oct. 2/1 The native companion crane, otherwise known as the brolga. 1911 BEAN '*Dreadnought' of Darling* xvii, Far up one of the Darling tributaries, the brolga (native companion) and crane and ibis seemed fairly thick.

Brolly (brǫ·li). *colloq.* Clipped and altered form of UMBRELLA.

1874 *Slang Dict.*, *Brolly*, an umbrella. Term used at both Oxford and Cambridge Universities. 1885 *Punch* 6 June 273 '2 Pair o' pattens and brolly are more in your line. 1899 KIPLING *Stalky* 209 What are you stealin' the gentleman's brolly for? 1925 *Sunday at Home* July 575/1 The lass was a clever thief who had hooked his brolly.

Brom- = BROMO-. Add:

1880 *Jrnl. Chem. Soc.* XXXVIII. 376 In both cases, bromamylene, C_5H_9Br, is the principal product. 1885 REMSEN *Org. Chem.* (1888) 131 Two brom-propionic acids. 1892 *Daily News* 29 Jan. 5/4 To be treated with large doses of brom-kalium to calm them. 1901 *Westm. Gaz.* 27 Nov. 8/1 The waters hold chlormagnesium, brommagnesium, and calisalt. 1913 *Jrnl. Chem. Soc.* CIV. I. 1023 Two Bromo-substituted Acidylcarbamides: Bromural and Adaline.

Bromelia (bromī·liă). [Named by Linnæus after Olaus *Bromel*, a Swede.] A plant of the genus *Bromelia*, or of the family *Bromeliaceæ*, consisting of plants indigenous to S. America and W. Indies, the species of which have short stems, and generally lance-shaped leaves with spiny margins.

1833 *Penny Cycl.* I. 447/1 Orchideous plants and bromelias overrun their limbs.

b. *attrib.*: **bromelia water**, water contained in the rosette of leaves of a Bromeliad.

1908 *Smithsonian Misc. Coll.* V. 73 The species was also bred from bromelia water near Tabernilla.

Bromeliad (bromī·liæd). *Bot.* [f. mod.L. *Bromeliaceæ*, f. *BROMELIA: see -AD.] Any plant belonging to the family *Bromeliaceæ*.

1866 *Treas. Bot.* 170/1 Some of the Bromeliads grow attached to the branches of trees, and are called Air-plants. 1902 *Encycl. Brit.* XXV. 438/1 In some aerophilous Bromeliads the rosette of leaves forms a cup in which water collects; into this débris both organic and inorganic falls, and produces a nutrient solution. 1927 *Glasgow Herald* 23 July 4 The 'vegetable horse hair' (Tillandsia Usneoides) is a rarely flowering Bromeliad that hangs in grey festoons from the branches of the trees.

Bromelin (brōᵘ·mĭlin). *Chem.* [f. *BROMELIA + -IN[1].] A digestive ferment obtained from the juice of the pineapple.

1894 *Jrnl. Chem. Soc.* LXVI. II. 63 Bromelin..appears to be associated with a peculiar proteose-like substance. 1901 *Ibid.* LXXX. I. 355 Bromelin..readily forms leucine, tyrosine, and tryptophan, even in acid media.

Bromide. Add:

2. A dose of bromide of potassium taken as a sedative.

1903 *Smart Set* IX. 24/1 I'll give you a bromide when you're ready for bed.

3. *fig.* A person whose thoughts and conversation are conventional and commonplace. Also, a commonplace saying, trite remark, conventionalism. orig. *U.S. slang.*

1906 G. BURGESS (*title*) Are you a Bromide? 1909 SIR W. RALEIGH *Lett.* (1926) II. 340 Bromides are dull partly because everyone pretends to understand them. 1924 HICHENS *After the Verdict* II. xvii, For once Mrs. Baratrie gave way to a bromide. She said: 'How good little Clive was!' 1925 *Contemp. Rev.* Oct. 469 There is the rise of slums which 'ought not to be in a new country', but which, in spite of this oft-quoted bromide, certainly existed in still earlier days. 1926 *Publishers' Weekly* 20 Feb. 563 The old bromide that poetry never sells is once again proved to be wrong. 1929 *Evening News* 4 Jan. 9/2 This is one of those self-evident propositions which used to be called *clichés* and are now referred to as 'bromides'.

4. *Photogr.* *Bromide emulsion*, a gelatine emulsion impregnated with a bromide, esp. silver bromide. *Bromide paper*, a paper coated with gelatino-bromide emulsion, used for contact printing and enlargements. *Bromide developer*, a developer suitable for bromide paper. Also *bromide print*, *printer*, *printing* (of or with reference to bromide paper).

1885 *Amateur Photographer* 27 Mar. 409 Britannia Bromide Paper, specially for enlargements. 1892 A. BROTHERS *Man. Photogr.* 73 Opal glass and paper are coated with silver bromide emulsion. *Ibid.*, Bromide-Printing Process. 1902 *Bromide Monthly* Jan. 10 One well-known Bromide printer we know of makes his exposures in contact printing to the light of an ordinary candle from preference. 1904 *Technol. & Sci. Dict.* (ed. Goodchild & Tweney), *Bromide Prints*..are developed and fixed like dry plates. 1923 S. E. SHEPPARD in *Photography* 165 Characteristic Curves for Bromide Papers.

Bromidia (bromi·diă). [f. BROMIDE + -IA[1].] A proprietary hypnotic and anodyne preparation.

1901 in DORLAND *Med. Dict.* (ed. 2). 1902 *Westm. Gaz.* 28 Apr. 5/2 Syncope brought on by an overdose of bromidia. 1903 *Daily Chron.* 29 Apr. 10/1 He..had suffered from sleeplessness for some years, and as a remedy had been in the habit of taking an American preparation called 'Bromidia'.

Bromidic (bromi·dik), *a. slang.* [f. *BROMIDE 3 + -IC.] Of the nature of a bromide; commonplace or conventional.

1906 G. BURGESS *Are you a Bromide?* 19 The Bromide can't possibly help being bromidic. 1911 H. S. HARRISON *Queed* xix, 'Did genius fail to burn?' he asked, employing a bromidic phrase. 1927 WILLEY *Early Ch. Portraits* 98 Athanasius did not desire the office of Bishop, in spite of the bromidic and venerable injunction of the Apostle.

Bromo-. Add:

1837 *Brit. Annual* (ed. R. D. Thomson) 345 Bromobenzoic acid. 1862 *Catal. Internat. Exhib., Brit.* II. No. 3150, Hardwich's bromo-iodized collodion. 1866 ODLING *Anim. Chem.* 137 Convertible by successive hydrogenation into bromobarbituric, and barbituric acid. 1878 ABNEY *Photogr.* xi. 83 With a bromo-iodised film more caution is required. 1878 *Jrnl. Chem. Soc.* XXXIV. 402 The action of baryta-water on bromomucic acid. 1881 *Ibid.* XL. 614 Bromocaffeine, $C_8H_9BrN_4O_2$. 1882 *Ibid.* XLII. 938 Bromochloral, Chlorobromal, Bromochloroform, and Chlorobromoform. *Ibid.*, Bromochloral and chlorobromal, like chloral, combine directly with amides. *Ibid.*, Bromochloroform, $CHBrCl_2$, is a colourless liquid..which gradually becomes yellow on exposure to light. 1885 *Ibid.* XLVII. 141 Action of Nitric Acid on Bromostrychnine. 1899 *Daily News* 30 May 4/6 Bromo-iodine baths. 1901 *Jrnl. Chem. Soc.* LXXX. II. 88 Velocity of Intramolecular Migration of Bromoamides under the Influence of an Alkali. 1901 DORLAND *Med. Dict.* (ed. 2), *Bromoseltzer*, a proprietary remedy for headache, etc. 1920 A. B. BAXTER *Parts Men Play* x. § 1 Lord Durwent read the *Morning Post* as a sort of 'prairie-oyster', or 'bromoseltzer'.

Bromoil (brōᵘ·moil). *Photogr.* [f. BROM- + OIL *sb.*] In full *bromoil print*, one obtained by bleaching a bromide print and restoring the image by applying pigment with a brush. *Bromoil transfer*, a picture in reverse taken from a freshly pigmented print.

1909 *Amateur Photographer* 3 Aug. 108/2 Most workers in the bromoil process not only use, but advocate, smooth, platino-matt. 1909 *Westm. Gaz.* 9 Jan. 14/2 How many.. camera-users ever attempt work in gum-bichromate or in bromoil? 1910 *Ibid.* 12 Mar. 14/2 When the photographer has grown tired of his silver-prints..Let him try platinum, carbon, bromoil. 1921 *Glasgow Herald* 13 July 7 A little knowledge of [art] may tend to convert a sound technical worker into a hopeless dabbler with bromoil or other media.

Brompton (brɒ·mptən). [Name of a former hamlet distant one mile from London, where the Brompton Park Nursery was founded in 1681.] In full *Brompton stock*, a biennial variety of the stock (see STOCK *sb.*[1] 43).

1731 MILLER *Gard. Dict.* Zzzz/2 The Brompton Stock-July-flower is by many People most valu'd, for the Largeness of its Flowers, and the Brightness of their Colour. 1796 C. MARSHALL *Gardening* xix. (1813) 352 Stock, Brompton, scarlet, blush, and white. 1852 G. W. JOHNSON *Cottage Gard. Dict.* 583 For the latter purpose [*sc.* spring-flowering] none [of the Stocks] beats the intermediate, Queens, Bromptons, and other biennials. 1880 *Encycl. Brit.* XII. 249/2 The Brompton Stock (Matthiola incana simplicicaulis) is a robust plant, growing 3 feet high, with a long central flower stem bearing very large flowers, which are crimson, purple, or white.

Bronc, bronch (brɒŋk). *U.S.* Also **bronk**. [Abbreviation of BRONCO.] A horse. Also *attrib.*

1901 S. E. WHITE *Westerners* i. 8 He's got a mighty good line of broncs. 1908 MULFORD *Orphan* v, Keep it up, bronchs! ..We'll win! 1910 W. M. RAINE *B. O'Connor* 72 You're going to..learn to stick to your saddle when the bronc and you disagree. 1911 H. QUICK *Yellowstone N.* x. 245 Old Jim Bridger was obliged to go up f'r three days on his bronk one time. 1918 MULFORD *Man fr. Bar-20* xiv. 137 A man on a bronc looks as big as a house. 1924 *Glasgow Herald* 12 June 9 The champion bronk riders, steer wrestlers, and trick horsewomen of America. *Ibid.* 4 July 9 The international bronk riding contest..took place yesterday afternoon at the Wembley Stadium.

Bronchitis. Add: **b.** *attrib.*: **bronchitis kettle**, a kettle with a long tube and a detachable medicator used for keeping the atmosphere of a room humid and for giving a medicated vapour inhalation to a patient in a case of bronchitis.

1888 MARCET in *Roy. Meteorological Soc.* May, On the measurement of the increase of Humidity in rooms by the emission of Steam from the so-called Bronchitis Kettle. 1896 *Lancet* 18 Apr. 1056/1 The unfortunate patient is kept in a room with the atmosphere saturated with moisture from a bronchitis kettle.

Broncho-. Add: **Broncho-cavernous** *a.* (see quot. 1890); **Broncho-constriction**, stricture of the bronchi; **Broncho-pneumonic** *a.*, pertaining to broncho-pneumonia or inflammation of the bronchi and the lungs; **Broncho-pulmonary** *a.*, pertaining to the bronchi and the lungs (cf. *bronchio-pulmonary*, s.v. BRONCHIO-); **Broncho-vesicular** *a.*, bronchial and vesicular.

1890 BILLINGS *Med. Dict.*, **Broncho-cavernous respiration*, sound heard from consolidated lung surrounding a cavity. 1922 in *F. W. Price's Textbk. Pract. Med.* 905 Broncho-cavernous breathing is incomplete cavernous breathing, inspiration being bronchial, while expiration is cavernous. 1910 *Practitioner* June 859 An amount of air may be sucked through the *broncho-constriction. 1883 G. S. WOODHEAD *Pract. Pathol.* 249 It [*sc.* capillary bronchitis] only occurs in connection with the *broncho-pneumonic process. 190. *Buck's Handbk. Med. Sci.* V. 848 (Cent. D. Suppl.) *Bronchopulmonary. 1916 OSLER & MACRAE *Princ. & Pract. Med.* (ed. 8) 636 Broncho-pulmonary hæmorrhage. 1887 *Buck's Handbk. Med. Sci.* V. 732/2 The *broncho-vesicular breathing..becomes..tubular in dyspnœa.

Bronchoscope (brɒ·ŋkoskōᵘp). [f. BRONCHO- + -SCOPE.] An instrument for inspecting the interior of the bronchi.

1899 *Westm. Gaz.* 20 Dec. 10/2 Kilian's (Berlin) bronchoscope was..introduced into the trachea. 1904 *Electr. World & Engin.* 16 Jan. 140 (Cent. D. Suppl.) A bronchoscope, which consists of a tube, the inner surface of which is highly polished to serve as a reflector, with an electric lamp arranged so as to throw a strong light on the tube.

So **Bronchoscopy** (brɒŋkɒ·skŏpi), the use of a bronchoscope.

1903 *Therapeutic Gaz.* Jan. 60 (Cent. D. Suppl.) Bronchoscopy allows the whole bronchial tree to be searched. 1927 *Daily Express* 6 July 9/2 The chair of bronchoscopy in the University of Pennsylvania.

Bronco, broncho. (Earlier examples.)

1869 S. BOWLES *Our New West* v. 101 A well-broken Indian pony or a 'broncho' (a California half breed horse) can be got. 1871 SCHELE DE VERE *Americanisms* (1872) 131 The horses, mules, and bronchos, as the packhorses are called. 1878 J. H. BEADLE *Western Wilds* 454 Our bronchos carried us with ease and safety.

b. *attrib.*, as *bronco-mule*, *-pony*, *-team*, *-type*; **bronco-grass**, a brome-grass of the Mediterranean region introduced into California (*Cent. Dict. Suppl.*).

1869 S. BOWLES *Our New West* v. 101 The mule and the Indian and 'broncho' ponies will live on the rich grasses of the country. 1881 A. A. HAYES *New Colorado* iii. 36 They are provided with swift and sure footed horses, generally, in these days, of the broncho type—a mixture of the American horse and the mustang. 1892 GUNTER *Miss Dividends* 163 You can drive down in a day with a good tough broncho-team. 1895 *Outing* (U.S.) XXVII. 244/2 Their pack train composed of hardy little broncho-mules.

c. *Comb.*: **bronco-buster**, a breaker-in of broncos; so *bronco-busting*.

1888 ROOSEVELT in *Century Mag.* Feb. 507 The flash riders, or horse-breakers, always called '*bronco busters', can perform really marvelous feats. 1897 *Westm. Gaz.* 8 Oct. 1/3 Those who saw Buffalo Bill's show will remember the riding of the broncho-busters. 1891 *Harper's Mag.* July 208/1 *Bronco busting is a distinct art. 1911 H. QUICK *Yellowstone N.* xii. 301, I had been asked to give a exhibition of broncho bustin.

2. As *adj.* Wild, uncontrollable.

1887 F. FRANCIS Jr. *Saddle & Mocassin* 146 Sam's too broncho: he gets all-fired mean sometimes when he's full.

Brontëana (brɒntiā·nă). [See -ANA *suffix*.] Literature connected with or bearing upon the Brontës.

1900 *Daily News* 17 Aug. 6/1 'Charlotte Brontë and her Circle' seems..to have finally exhausted the vast and well-explored mines of Brontëana. 1928 *Observer* 22 July 13/4 He wished the collection to be restored to Yorkshire after his widow..had taken any Brontëana for herself.

Bronto-, comb. form of Gr. βροντή thunder, as in **Brontogram** (brɒ·ntogræm), the record made by a brontometer or brontograph; **Bro·ntograph**, a recording brontometer; also, a chart of the phenomena recorded by that instrument; **Brontolo·gical** *a.*, pertaining to BRONTOLOGY; **Bronto·meter**, an instrument for recording the phenomena associated with thunderstorms; **Brontopho·bia**, intense dread of thunder and thunderstorms.

1888 *Symons' Monthly Meteorol. Mag.* June 71 Our German friends..were clearly the first as to thunderstorms, or rather *Brontological research. *Ibid.* May 50 Messrs. Richard Frères, of Paris, are constructing for Mr. Symons a very complicated apparatus (*Brontometer)..for recording the details of thunderstorms. 1905 W. G. HOLMES *Justinian & Theodora* I. iii. 298 *note*, He was affected with *brontophobia in his later years.

Brontosaurus (brɒntŏsǭ·rŏs). *Palæont.* [mod. L. (O. C. Marsh, Notice of New Jurassic Reptiles in *Amer. Jrnl. Sci. & Art* Ser. III. (1879) XVIII. 503), f. Gr. βροντή thunder + σαῦρος lizard.] An extinct genus of dinosaurian reptiles existing on all the continents during the Jurassic and Cretaceous periods; also, a reptile belonging to this genus.

1907 *Westm. Gaz.* 3 Apr. 8/1 A brontosaurus, or a chondrosteosaurus. 1924 *Public Opinion* 28 Mar. 300/3 [The Anglican Church] is going the way of the dinosaurus and the brontosaurus.

Bronze, *sb.* 7. Add:

bronze-backer *U.S.*, angler's name for the black bass; **bronze-founder**, one who founds or casts bronze, or fashions articles of bronze; so **bronze founding**; **bronze-winged** (also *bronzed-winged*) **pigeon** = *bronze-wing*.

1888 GOODE *Amer. Fishes* 56 '*Bronze-backer' is one of its pet names among the anglers. 1894 *Outing* (U.S.) XXIV. 452/1 This old bronze-backer [*sc.* small-mouth bass] weighed..six pounds and five ounces. 1839 URE *Dict. Arts* 333 The *bronze-founder should study to obtain a rapid fusion. 1885 *English Illustr. Mag.* Mar. 413/1 There are two methods of *bronze founding. 1897 *Daily News* 18 Jan. 6/4 Two works which Benvenuto Cellini wrote..on bronze founding. 1832 in Bischoff *Van Diemen's Land* ii. 31 The pigeons are by far the most beautiful birds in the island; they are called *bronze winged pigeons. 1852 MUNDY *Antipodes* xviii, I killed..a few bronzed-winged pigeons. 1897 *Daily News* 24 May 9/4 A pair of Smith's partridge bronze-winged pigeons (*Geophaps Smithi*) from Northern Queensland.

Bronzer (brɒ·nzəɹ). [f. BRONZE *v.* + -ER[1].] One who coats with, or colours like, bronze.

1865 *Congress. Globe* Feb. 682/1 The bronzer then [in the U.S. Treasury Department] puts the paper through his bronzing machine, and when it is all bronzed it is counted again by the man bronzing it.

Bronzing, *vbl. sb.* Add: **b.** (See quots.)

1868 LEA *Photography* 47 By this time the dark shadows ought to show the greenish, almost metallic look known as 'bronzing'. 1885 W. K. BURTON *Mod. Phot.* Index 127 Bronzing of prints. 1889 E. J. WALL *Dict. Photogr.* 23 *Bronzing*, a peculiar metallic lustre seen on looking at the shadows of some prints at a certain angle. 1903 H. R. PROCTER *Leather Manuf.* 404 'Bronzing', the dichroic effect produced by light reflected from the surface of many colouring matters, complementary to that transmitted by them.

(Examples of *bronzing machine*.)

1865 [see *BRONZER]. 1874 KNIGHT *Dict. Mech.*, *Bronzing-machine*, a machine for bronzing wall-papers or printed sheets. 1884 *Ibid.* Suppl. 1889 *Century Dict.*, *Bronzing machine*, a machine for decorating wall-papers, fabrics, labels, etc. with bronze-powder.

Brood, *sb.* Add:

1. f. Of bees and wasps: The larvæ while in the brood-cells. *Foul brood*: see FOUL *a.* 1 b.

1754 TEMPLEMAN *Remarks Physic* etc. (1755) II. 82 Till all the brood have sallied forth in the form of bees. 1806 tr. *Huber's Nat. Hist. Bees* (1808) 109 Another piece of comb, containing the brood of workers. 1869 *Good Words for Young* 1 Sept. 515/1 At length the first brood [of wasps] is hatched.

6. brood-box = *body-box* (*BODY *sb.* 30); **brood-cell**, (*a*) a cell in a honeycomb, made for the reception of a larva, as distinguished from a honey-cell; (*b*) *Bot.*, an asexually produced reproductive cell (Funk's Standard Dict. 1895); **brood-chamber**, (*a*) a chamber for holding the eggs or brood of an animal, etc.; (*b*) a chamber folded off from the uterus and closed around the embryo in some species of *Peripatus* (Cent. Dict. Suppl.); **brood-food**, a prepared food for young bees; a substance derived from pollen by digestion, and serving as a pap for a brood of bees; **brood-lamella**, 'in crustaceans, a part of an appendage modified to form a protective cover for the eggs or young' (Cent. Dict. Suppl.); **brood nest**, the space inside a hive occupied by the queen and brood; **brood-space** *Anat.*, a cavity in the body of an animal, in which eggs or young are received and remain for a time; **brood spot** (see quot.).

1888 F. R. CHESHIRE *Bees & Bee-Keeping* II. 99 The section-racks..are constructed on the general plan of the *brood-chambers..; their edges..abut accurately upon the *brood-boxes. 1901 SUTRO tr. *Maeterlinck's Life of the Bee* iii. § 60. 163 There were both *brood-cells and cells full of honey. 1875 *Encycl. Brit.* III. 494/1 In the early spring, if a clean empty piece of drone comb be put into the centre of the *brood nest, the queen will usually fill it with drone eggs. 1878 BELL tr. *Gegenbaur's Comp. Anat.* 268 An Egg in the *brood-space formed between the body and the mantle. 1896 tr. *Boas' Text Bk. Zool.* 450 Usually the sitting Bird is provided with *brood spots, regions from which the feathers have fallen off, so that the eggs may come into direct contact with the warm skin.

Brooder. Add:

2. A hen, etc., that broods or hatches eggs.

1599 T. M[OUFET] *Silkwormes* 26 Now what are seedes and egges of wormes or foule, But recrements of preexisting things..? Yea, from themselues corruption onely springs, Vnlesse by brooders heate..They changed be to belly, feete, or wings. 1854 *Poultry Chron.* I. 153 An anxious Brooder.

3. An apparatus for the artificial rearing of young chickens and other birds. *U.S.*

1880 H. TOMLINSON *Artificial Incubation* vii. 32 [Chickens] may..be transferred to an artificial mother, or *brooder* as the Yankees call it. 1896 J. RANKIN *Incubator & its Use* 58 The chicks..are then ready for the brooder and food. 1901 *Westm. Gaz.* 10 Oct. 4/1 The incubators and the accompanying 'brooders'.

Brooding, *vbl. sb.* Add:

1. d. The action of cherishing young under the wings.

1889 *Pall Mall Gaz.* 14 May 3 Ducklings..need no brooding.

Broodless (brū·dlės), *a.* [f. BROOD *sb.* + -LESS.] Without a brood or progeny.

1862 D. GRAY *Poems* 84 The broodless nest.

Broody, *a.* Add:

3. Brooding, meditative.

1900 H. LAWSON *Over Sliprails* 52 He..watched my brush for a while, as if he was thinking, in a broody sort of way, of..going in for house-painting. *Ibid.* 83 She took it all with broody cheerfulness.

B. *sb.* A broody hen.

1904 *Daily Chron.* 30 July 4/7 He would..defer putting the 'broody' on them [*sc.* the eggs] till dusk. 1923 *Daily Mail* 20 Jan. 11 Broodies of these highly developed strains are..unreliable sitters.

Brookless (bru·klės), *a.* [f. BROOK *sb.* + -LESS.] Having no brooks.

1903 KIPLING *Five Nations* 71 Our broad and brookless vales.

Broo·k-side. [BROOK *sb.*] The side or bank of a brook. Also *attrib.*

c 1403 CLANVOWE *Cuckoo & Night.* 60, I..held my way doun by a broke-syde. 1548 TURNER *Names Herbes* (E.D.S.) 61 It groweth in broke sydes. 1628 BURTON *Anat. Mel.* (ed. 3) *Abstr. Mel.* **2, When to my selfe I act and smile,.. By a brooke side or wood so greene. 1662 *Plymouth Rec.* 55 Att Manomett ponds att the brooke side. 1668 *Ibid.* 103 A great white oake tree standing by the brooke syde. 1863 ATKINSON *Stanton Grange* (1864) 17 In the course of their brook-side ramble. 1902 CORNISH *Nat. Thames* 177 These brookside jungles.

Broom, *sb.* 6. Add: **broom-croft**, a croft or field in which broom grows.

1870 KINGSLEY *At Last* x, Grand masses of colour..are supplied by a heather moor, a furze or broom-croft.

Broomstick. Add:

2. *transf. pl.* Applied to thin undersized limbs. *colloq.*

1896 'EDNA LYALL' *How the Children Raised the Wind* iii, 'Give it to me', said Fay, holding out her tiny arms, her 'broomsticks', as the boys irreverently called them.

Broom-straw. *U.S.* [BROOM *sb.* 3.] The straw of broom corn; also the plant itself. Also *attrib.*

1785 WASHINGTON *Diaries* II. 365 [I] had the Roots, shrubs (which had been grubbed) and tussics of broom straw..raked of[f] and burnt. 1837 *Southern Lit. Messenger* III. 217 In the centre of a large field of broom-straw..stood the house. 1840 BUEL *Farmer's Companion* 18 They still produce what we call hengrass, broom-straw, and, ever and anon, a starveling pine. 1845 J. J. HOOPER *Adv. Simon Suggs* iii. (1928) 30 In two hours more he wont be able to step over the butt cut of a broom straw. 1889 BRUCE *Plant. Negro* 220 A growth of briars or broomstraw. 1890 *Harper's Mag.* Dec. 111/1 All who are so lucky as to have first seen the light amid its broom-straw fields and ragged forests. 1895 *Outing* (U.S.) XXVII. 76/1 We dropped silently in a patch of broom-straw.

Broseley, the name of a town in Shropshire, used in *Broseley porcelain*, a soft-paste porcelain made by Thomas Turner (1749–1809) of Caughley, near Broseley, esp. the blue transfer-printed china of Oriental design, in which the *Broseley dragon* was extensively used.

1831-3 *Encycl. Metrop.* (1845) VIII. 464/2 The blue colours are supplied by the oxide of cobalt..Blue..Weak, (Broseley.) —Blue calc 20, flux 80. (Flint 70, nitre 9, borax 21;) or, calc 15, petuntse 85. 1878 L. JEWITT *Ceramic Art* I. 43 The white..is made of what is commonly called Brosely clay. *Ibid.* 268 The 'Broseley Blue Dragon' pattern.

Brosier, brozier (brōᵘ·ziəɹ, brōᵘ·ʒiəɹ), *sb.* **a.** A bankrupt. *dial.* **b.** A boy who has spent all his pocket-money. *Eton slang.* **c.** The custom of brosiering: see *BROSIER *v.* 2.

1826 WILBRAHAM *Gloss. Cheshire* (ed. 2), *Brosier*, a bankrupt. It is often used by boys at play, when one of them has nothing further to stake. 1850 *N. & Q.* 1st Ser. II. 44/1 A boy at Eton was a 'brosier', when he had spent all his pocket-money. 1907 *Daily Chron.* 17 Dec. 3/4 You have heard of the Eton custom of a 'brozier'? The attempt to eat out of house and home. 1926 *Glasgow Herald* 27 Dec. 6 It was reserved for Eton..to invent the..'brozier', where eating even to beyond repletion is indulged in to gratify a sense of injury.

Brosier, brozier (brōᵘ·ziəɹ, brōᵘ·ʒiəɹ), *v.* [f. prec.]

1. *pass.* To be bankrupt. *dial.*

1796 T. MORTON *Way to get Married* I. i, I am completely brozier'd, cut down to a sixpence, and have left town.

2. *trans.* In Eton College phraseology: To attempt to exhaust the supply of food at a meal, as an expression of dissatisfaction with the fare provided; esp. in the phrase *to brosier my dame* or *my tutor*.

1850 *N. & Q.* 1st Ser. II. 44/1, I well remember the phrase, 'brozier-my-dame', signifying to 'eat her out of house and home'. 1888 W. ROGERS *Remin.* 15, I joined a conspiracy to 'brozier' him. There were ten or twelve of us [at breakfast], and we devoured everything within reach. 1899 C. K. PAUL *Mem.* 111 If a tutor or a dame was suspected of being niggardly, it was determined to 'brosier' him or her.

Broth, *sb.* Add:

4. *Comb.*: **broth culture**, a broth prepared for the culture of bacteria.

1899 G. NEWMAN *Bacteria* ii. 65 A loopful of young typhoid broth culture. 1909 *Practitioner* Nov. 596 Over the surface of the agar..pour a two-days old broth culture of bacillus prodigiosus.

Brother Jonathan: see JONATHAN.

Brotherliwise (brɒ·ðəɹliwəiz), *adv.* [f. BROTHERLY *a.* + -WISE.] In brotherly fashion.

1891 KIPLING *Life's Handicap, Head Distr.* iv, Who brotherliwise had followed his kinsman's fortune.

Brotherly, *a.* Add: **1. c.** *City of Brotherly Love* (U.S.), the city of Philadelphia. (Cf. PHILADELPHIAN, PHILADELPHY.)

1799 *Aurora* (Philad.) 28 Sept. (Th.) A great wonder appeared in the city which is called Brotherly Love. 1832 *Deb. Congress* 12 June 348 During a short stay of mine in the city of brotherly love. 1887 *Harper's Mag.* Oct. 658/1 There arrived a dog..from the City of Brotherly Love.

Brougham. Add:

1. b. *Brougham-hansom*, a form of the hansom-cab in which the driver's seat is placed at the front, the entrance being at the rear.

1909 in *Cent. Dict.* Suppl.

2. a. A closed electric automobile with accommodation for four or five passengers. **b.** A petrol-driven automobile having a limousine body but without a roof over the driver's seat.

1903 A. H. BEAVAN *Tube, Train,* etc. xv. 213 The lemon-coloured electric broughams of a few years ago.

Brouillon (bruyoñ). [Fr.] A rough draught.

1678 SIR W. TEMPLE *Let. to Sir J. Williamson* 19 Aug., What was signed at first was rather a *brouillon* than any fair and formal draught. 1735 POPE *Let. to Ld. Oxford* 17 June, Your lordship has still in your custody the brouillons of verses. 1735 *Pope's Lett.* I. 37 *note*, The first Brouillon of those Verses, and the second Copy with Corrections. 1921 *Blackw. Mag.* Feb. 251/2 'Papa Crémieux' was called in to furnish *brouillons* for letters to duchesses and authors.

Brow, *sb.*[1] Add:

5. g. *Entom.* That part of the head of an insect which lies between the clypeus and the vertex.

1889 in *Cent. Dict.*

10. brow-ridges *pl.*, the supra-orbital ridges which overhang the eyes in the skulls of some monkeys; **brow-spot**, the interocular gland of a frog or toad.

1898 *Guide Mammalia Brit. Mus.* 15 Enormous *brow-ridges give them a ferocious and savage appearance. 1927 PEAKE & FLEURE *Hunters & Artists* 60 The great frontal torus or overgrown brow-ridges of Neanderthal Man. 1875 HUXLEY & MARTIN *Elem. Biol.* (1877) 195 The *browspot or inter-ocular gland.

Brow, *v.* 1. (Later U.S. example.)

1886 *Harper's Mag.* Nov. 868/2 Its crumbling walls are filled with trees and banked with weeds, its borders browed with lilacs.

Browallia (browǫ·liă). *Bot.* [Named by Linnæus after J. *Browall* (1707–55), Swedish botanist.] A plant of the genus of South American annual plants so named, bearing violet, blue, or white flowers.

1767 ABERCROMBIE *Ev. Man his own Gardener* (1782) 84 Tender Annual Flowers. The choicest kinds are..browallia, &c.

Browless, *a.* Add:

2. Without eyebrows.

1823 *New Monthly Mag.* VIII. 531 A composition which ..utterly destroyed the hair, and left him literally browless! 1905 EDEN PHILLPOTTS *Secret Woman* II. ix. 179 Browless eyes. 1906 B'NESS VON HUTTEN *What became of Pam* I. iv, The large..eyes,..so almost browless and lashless.

Brown, *sb.* Add:

3. c. Delete † and add:

1890 H. M. FIELD *Bright Skies* 147 In Jamaica..they are distinguished as the whites and blacks and *the browns*.

4. *The brown*: lit. the brown-coloured mass of a flock of game-birds; in phr. *to fire into the brown (of them)*: to fire into the midst of a covey instead of singling out a bird; also *transf.*, to fire, or launch a missile, indiscriminately into a mass.

1871 *Punch* 16 Dec. 256/2 Sportsmen, whose sport must mainly consist in 'firing into the brown'. 1885 *Ibid.* 31 Jan. 53 'Pop! Bang! Whose bird?' That's the French notion of a tag, as the husband looses off 'into the brown' of his wife's adorers. 1889 KIPLING *Phantom Rickshaw, Man who would be King* (ed. 3) 87 We three Martinis firing into the brown of the enemy. 1897 MARY KINGSLEY *W. Africa* xxiii. 545, I fired two..stools..into the brown of it, and the meeting broke up. 1899 *Daily News* 4 May 8/2 The sportsman..not firing into the brown, but taking careful aim at some particular bird. 1908 T. N. WALKER *Through the Mutiny* v. 90 Our officer..treated the General and his followers to some volleys fired right into the brown of them.

Brown, *a.* Add: **6.** *Comb.*: qualifying the name of another colour, as *brown-gold*.

1909 *Daily Chron.* 7 May 4/4 The sun..glittered on her brown-gold hair.

7. brown algæ, the algæ of seaweeds constituting the class *Phæophyceæ*, which contain a brown colouring matter in addition to chlorophyll; **brown-banded snake, brown-footed rat** (see quots.); **Brown Betty** *U.S.*, a preparation of apples; **brown house** *U.S.* = brown-stone house (see *BROWN-STONE); **brown moth**, an artificial fly used in angling by night; **brown-rot**, a disease of vegetables; also as *vb.*; **brown-tail (moth)** (see quots.); **brown top**, a species of Australian pasture grass (see quot.); **brown tubes** *pl.* (see quot.).

1902 *Encycl. Brit.* XXV. 272/1 A white efflorescence which appears on certain *Brown Algæ..when they are dried in the air. 1869 KREFFT *Snakes Australia* 55 The large-scaled snake..is confounded, in Victoria in particular, with the Tiger or *Brown-banded Snake (*Hoplocephalus curtus*). 1887 *Encycl. Brit.* XXII. 197/1 The Brown-banded Snake (*Hoplocephalus curtus*), with a similar distribution [throughout Australia], and also common in Tasmania, from 5 to 6 feet long. 1864 *Yale Lit. Mag.* XXIX. 187 (Th.) [In training,] tea, coffee, pies, and '*brown Betty' must next be sacrificed. 1911 S. E. WHITE *Bobby Orde* x. (1916) 126 It was the season of..apple-tapioca and Brown Betty. 1884 *Encycl. Brit.* XVII. 5/2 *Mus fuscipes*, Waterh., the *Brown-footed Rat of western and southern Australia. 1845 S. JUDD *Margaret* II. viii. 324 The Deacon's..was a small, one story *brown house. 1861 MRS. STOWE *Pearl Orr's Isl.* I. ii. 10 Down near the end of Orr's Island..stands a brown house. 1837 KIRKBRIDE *Northern Angler* 48 The *Brown Moth..is made with a feather from the wing of the dark-brown owl. 1899 G. NEWMAN *Bacteria* i. 37 Bacterial *brown-rot of potatoes and tomatoes is another plant disease probably due to a bacillus. *Ibid.*, The bacillus..brown-rots them from within. 1782 W. CURTIS *Brown-tail Moth* 10 The *Brown-tail Moth..is about two-thirds of the size of the Moth produced from the Silk-worm. 1815 KIRBY & SP. *Entomol.* vi. (1818) I. 207 The brown-tail moth (*Bombyx phæorhæa*, F.). 1832 J. RENNIE *Butterfl. & Moths* 42 The Brown Tail (*Porthesia Auriflua*, Stephens) appears in August. 1902 *Encycl. Brit.* XXXII. 108/2 Some [Queensland] stockholders consider that the 'Sugar grass' or '*Brown Top' (*Pollinia fulva*) surpasses them [i. e. the 'Mitchell grasses'] in its quickness of bursting into leaf. *Ibid.* 637/1 The excretory organs [of the Sipunculoidea].. serve as channels by which the reproductive cells leave the body, and they are sometimes spoken of as '*brown tubes'.

Brown, *v.* Add:

3. *trans.* (from *BROWN *sb.* 4). To fire indiscriminately at (a covey of birds or a mass of men).

1873 *Sat. Rev.* Sept. 310 We seldom did ourselves anything like justice until the coveys were out on the feed towards evening, when we were apt to brown them as they rose in little clouds. 1885 RIDER HAGGARD *K. Solomon's Mines* xiii, Good..began to fire,..industriously 'browning' the dense mass before him with a Winchester repeater. 1888 — *Col. Quaritch* xxii, I suppose..that the last covey twisted up and you browned them. 1921 *Blackw. Mag.* Jan. 122/2 He waited till the troop was some hundred and fifty yards away, and then he 'browned' it.

Brown-back. *U.S.* **a.** (In full *brown-back snipe*.) The red-breasted snipe, *Macrorhamphus griseus*. **b.** The great marbled godwit, *Limosa fedoa*.

1872 COUES *N. Amer. Birds* 252 *Macrorhamphus.* Red-breasted Snipe. Gray Snipe. Brown-back. 1893 *Outing* (U.S.) XXII. 96/2 'Brown-back' snipe.

Brownie [1]. Add:

2. A member of the junior section of the organization known as the 'Girl Guides'. Also *attrib.*

1916 *Home Chat* 30 Sept. 558 For the younger girls who are not eleven, and therefore not old enough to become Girl Guides, the Brownie movement has been started. 1918 BADEN-POWELL *Girl Guiding* 23 In the Brownie Pack every Brownie obeys the wishes of the leader. *Ibid.* 24 When a girl has passed her test as a recruit she is admitted into her Six as a Brownie. 1923 *Daily Mail* 12 Feb. 7, I must not cry, for I am a Brownie and Brownies do not cry.

Brownie [2], **browny** (brau·ni). [Subst. use of BROWNY *a.*]

1. Currant bread. *Austral.*

1890 E. D. CLELAND *White Kangaroo* 57 (Morris) Cake made of flour, fat and sugar, commonly known as 'Browny'. 1890 *Melbourne Argus* 20 Sept. 13/6 Tea and 'brownie' (a bread sweetened with sugar and currants). 1900 H. LAWSON *On Track* 129 Pile of 'brownie' on the bare black boards at the end of the table.

2. An angler's name for the trout.

1928 *Observer* 22 July 28/2 It is a difficult matter to creel a brace or so of brownies. The trout are there..but they stir not.

Browning (brau·niŋ). [The name of John M. *Browning* of Ogden, Utah, U.S.A.] In full *Browning revolver* or *pistol*, a form of automatic pistol; = *COLT *sb.*[2]

1905 *Daily Chron.* 9 Feb. 5/2 Hohental fired all the seven chambers of a Browning revolver at Herr Johnsson. 1906 *Ibid.* 6 Jan. 8/1 The party of freedom have to depend on revolvers, especially the 'Brownings'. 1906 *Westm. Gaz.* 6 Apr. 6/3 They were armed with Mauser pistols and Brownings.

Browningesque (brauninĕ·sk), *a.* [f. the surname *Browning* + -ESQUE.] Of, pertaining to, or characteristic of Robert Browning or his style.

1896 *Westm. Gaz.* 1 June 3/1 He can weave-in..the most ..far-fetched rhyme-words, and this without straying into the grotesque or the Browningesque. 1901 *Daily Chron.* 29 June 3/1 Monologues..which trace their lineage to *Lippo Lippi* and the rest of that most Browningesque series. 1910 H. WALKER *Lit. Vict. Era* 320 A Browningesque Touchstone, or Aguecheek,..is hardly conceivable.

So **Browningese** (brauniŋī·z), *a.* = prec.; *sb.* the language or style of Browning; **Brow·ningite**, an admirer of Browning; also *adj.* = *BROWNINGESQUE.

c 1882 BROWNING in W. Sharp *Life R. B.* (1890) 169, I am quite other than a Browningite. 1889 *Spectator* 14 Dec., [He] translated them all into Browningese forms. *Ibid.*, You never lose the Browningite manner of deliverance. 1910 H. WALKER *Lit. Vict. Era* 320 Thorold, Luria, Djabal, Valence, all speak Browningese.

Brow·n-stone, brow·nstone. *U.S.* (Also as two words.) [BROWN *a.* 2, 7.] One or other variety of dark-brown sandstone employed as a building material. Freq. in attrib. use.

1868 *Rep. U.S. Commissioner Agric.* (1869) 191 The material is pressed brick, with brownstone base, belts, trimmings, and cornices. 1871 SCHELE DE VERE *Americanisms* (1872) 447 In New York..a brown-stone front is apt to be looked upon as a sign of gentility. 1888 BRYCE *Amer. Commw.* III. lxii. II. 443 *note*, The so-called 'brown-stone districts' in New York City. 1902 CLAPIN *Dict. Amer.* 77 'Living in a brown stone house' is apt to be looked upon as a sign of gentility.

transf. 1909 *N. Y. Sun* 3 Nov. 6 The 'brownstone vote', as it is called, is cast as completely as is the vote of the most crowded tenement house districts.

Browny, *a.* Add:

2. *Comb.*: with the name of another colour, as *browny-green*, *-grey*.

1905 *Westm. Gaz.* 5 Aug. 10/2 It is a very becoming tone, that bronze browny green. 1906 *Daily Chron.* 10 Dec. 4/4 The browny-grey soldiers of Russia. 1907 *Ibid.* 12 Apr. 9/3 The browny-grey back of her sharply-pointed wings.

Browse, *v.* 3. (Later U.S. example.)

1876 *Rep. Vermont Board Agric.* III. 74 It was customary, in years past, when farmers were short of hay, to browse their cattle, as it was called.

Brozier, variant of *BROSIER.

Brugmansia (brugmæ·nziă). *Bot.* [mod.L., named after S. J. *Brugmans* (1763–1819), Dutch botanist: see -IA[1].]

1. A plant of the solanaceous genus so named, native to S. America (formerly included under the genus *Datura*), the species of which have white, orange, or red tubular blossoms.

1885 LADY BRASSEY *The Trades* 352 The garden contains some..pretty 'lily-trees', as they call them here; although I should describe them as a sort of datura or brugmansia.

2. A plant of a genus of parasitic plants of the family *Cytinaceæ*, found in the Malay islands, each plant of which consists of little more than a flower.

1885 *Encycl. Brit.* XVIII. 265/2 Raffelsia and Brugmansia consists one may say of a single flower.

Bruiser. Add:

5. A machine, tool, or other implement used for bruising or crushing; also, an operative who pulverizes materials.

In quot. 1828 applied to a tooth.

1828 FLEMING *Brit. Anim.* 9 In the lower jaw [of the badger], the bruiser is small, the chewer large. 1881 OGILVIE (Annandale), *Bruiser*..., the name of various machines for bruising grain, &c., for feeding cattle. 1921 *Dict. Occup. Terms* (1927) § 056 *Sample bruiser*; pulverises average sample of ore with flat-headed hammer, ready for sampler.

Brumby, brumbie (brɒ·mbi). *Austral.* Also **brumbee**. [Origin unknown.] A wild or unbroken horse.

1880 *Australasian* 4 Dec. 712/3 (Morris) These our guide pronounced to be 'brumbies', the bush name here [*sc.* Queensland] for wild horses. 1890 KIPLING *Plain Tales fr. Hills* 153 People who lost money on him called him a 'brumby'. 1895 *Chambers's Jrnl.* 702/1 The term 'with the Brumbies' is a common one throughout bush Australia to signify hopelessly lost. 1899 SEMON *In Austral. Bush* 95 When one of the brumbies begins to move all the herd follow. 1911 BEAN '*Dreadnought' of Darling* xxviii. 244, I had a brumby there at that time—a wild little horse dropped from a lot going through.

b. *attrib.*, as *brumby colt*, *horse*, *mob*, *trail*.

1895 *Chambers's Jrnl.* 702/1 The Brumbie Horse of Australia..is the descendant of runaways of imported stock. 1897 *Pall Mall Mag.* Feb. 190 And so to the unknown interior, past the points where sheep-tracks become brumby-trails. 1925 *Chambers's Jrnl.* 810/1 Wild or 'brumbie' mobs, which consisted of mares and one lord of the harem. 1926 *Brit. Weekly* 19 Aug. 412/5 An unbroken, raging devil of a brumby colt.

Brummellian (brɒme·liăn), *a.* [f. the proper name *Brummel* + -IAN.] Of, pertaining to, or characteristic of 'Beau Brummel' (G. R. Brummell, 1778–1840), leader of fashion in London. So **Bru·mmelism.**

1831 CARLYLE *Misc. Ess., Characteristics* (1872) IV. 26 Werterism, Byronism, even Brummelism, each has its day. 1832 *Ibid.*, *Boswell's Johnson* 127 Pharisaical Brummellean Politeness. 1908 'LEWIS MELVILLE' *Beaux of Regency* II. 70 The last three carried on the Brummellian traditions.

Brummer. *Brummer fly* (see quots.).

1913 PETTMAN *Africanderisms* 92 Brummer fly, *Cynomyia pictifacies*...An insect somewhat like the common house-fly, but considerably larger. It is useful in the destruction of locusts. 1924 *Chambers's Jrnl.* 314/2 The brummer fly (*Wolfahrtia brunis palpis*) lays its eggs in the neck of the locust.

Brunch (brɒnʃ). *University slang.* [A 'portmanteau' word f. BREAKFAST and LUNCH.] A single meal taken late in the morning and intended to combine breakfast with lunch.

1900 G. SWIFT *Somerley* 93 Brunches (*i.e.* breakfast-cum-lunch). 1900 *Westm. Gaz.* 19 Dec. 2/3 Perish Scrambling breakfast, formal lunch! Hardened night-birds fondly cherish All the subtle charms of 'brunch'. 1924 *Blackw. Mag.* Apr. 465/1 We proposed to have a substantial 'brunch' at eleven.

Brune (brün). [a. F. *brune*, fem. of *brun* brown.] A dark-complexioned girl or woman, a brunette.

1870 MISS BROUGHTON *Red as Rose is She* xiii, Priscilla, a beady-eyed, brisk brune. 1891 *Murray's Mag.* Oct. 565 Blondes and brunes. 1894 MEREDITH *Ld. Ormont* x, Brunes are exceptional in England.

Brunet (brune·t), *a.* and *sb.* [a. F. *brunet*, dim. of *brun* brown.] **A.** *adj.* Dark-complexioned. **B.** *sb.* A dark-complexioned person. Hence **Brune·tness.**

1888 DOLE tr. *Tolstoi's Russ. Proprietor* 247 But I should like to see what sort of a man this hussar is,—whether he is brunet or blondin. 1890 HUXLEY in *19th Cent.* Nov. 757 The brunet broad-heads now met with in central France. *Ibid.* 767 The present contrast of blonds and brunets existed among them. 1899 RIPLEY *Races Eur.* 147 Our map of the distribution of brunetness.

Brunette, *sb.* Add: **b.** A variety of the satinette pigeon.

1879 L. WRIGHT *Pract. Pigeon Keeper* 174 Brunettes are lighter Satinettes. 1891 R. WOODS *Pigeon Culture* 138.

Bruno (brū·no). In **St. Bruno's lily**, a bulbous plant of the species *Anthericum* (*Paradisea*) *liliastrum*, cultivated for its white sweet-scented flowers, which resemble small lilies.

1760 J. LEE *Introd. Bot.* App. 325 Saint Bruno's Lily, *Hemerocallis*. 1882 *Garden* 3 June 391/3 St. Bruno's Lily is beautiful in a glass by itself.

Brunsvigite (brɒ·nzvigəit). *Min.* [f. Da. *Brunsvig* Brunswick + -ITE[1].] A kind of chlorite occurring in gabbro in the Radauthal, Germany.

1914 *Brit. Mus. Return* 229.

Brunswick-black, *v. trans.* To varnish with Brunswick black; *fig.* to blacken.

1908 *Daily Chron.* 26 Mar. 3/3 Wide enough of eye to see how he Brunswick-blacked the greys of life.

Brush, *sb.*[1] Add: **2.** (U.S. examples.)

1801 *Massachusetts Spy* 23 Dec. 3/4 The imprudence of a person who set on fire a quantity of brush, &c. near Cambridge. 1817 S. R. BROWN *Western Gaz.* 58 Brush, and full grown trees. 1868 *Rep. U. S. Commissioner Agric.* (1869) 255 All trimming should be performed by striking..in the direction the brush leans. 1887 I. R. *Ranch Life Montana* 8 The bright red of the brush by the river-side.

4. *brush house*, *stable*, *tent*, *whisky*. *U.S.*

1853 B. YOUNG in *Jrnl. Discourses* I. 166 Families went there and lived in wagons and *brush houses. 1835 *Southern Lit. Messenger* I. 581 The pony..moves homeward with accelerated velocity, leaping every obstacle in his way to his *brush stable. 1878 J. H. BEADLE *Western Wilds* xix. 310 John A. Lee..had his wife living there in a sort of *brush tent. 1885 'C. E. CRADDOCK' *Prophet Gt. Smoky Mts.* xv. 275 The constable's heart was warmed by the *brush whiskey.

Brush, *sb.*[2] **12.** Add:

brush borer = **brush driller*; **brush-colour** (see quot.); **brush discharge** *Electr.* = BRUSH *sb.*[2] 6 a; **brush drawer**, an operative who puts in the bristles in 'drawn brushes'; **brush driller**, an operative who drills the holes in the stocks of brushes and brooms; **brush-grain**, a grain produced in painting woodwork by drawing the brush over a wet coat of paint so that the under-coat is seen through the brush-marks; **brush hand**, a house-painter; **brush-hat** (see quot.); **brush-holder** (see quot.); **brush-varnish** (see quot.); **brushware**, goods consisting of all kinds of brushes; **brush work**, painting, as distinguished from drawing; *spec.* the characteristic method (of a painter) of laying on the colours.

1921 *Dict. Occup. Terms* (1927) § 688 *Brush borer. 1845 G. DODD *Brit. Manuf.* IV. 130 Floor-cloth manufacture... A second coating of paint is laid on..wholly with a brush.. Hence it is called the '*brush-colour', to distinguish it from the first or 'trowel-colour'. 1849 NOAD *Electricity* (ed. 3) 42 The difference between the *brush discharge and the spark is, that in the former discharge begins at the root [etc.]. 1923 *Gloss. Radio Terms* in *Popular Wireless* 13 Oct. 11 *Brush discharge*, a discharge of high-tension electricity, which takes the form of a luminous glow. 1900 *Daily News* 6 Nov. 9/1 *Brush drawer. 1921 *Dict. Occup. Terms* (1927) § 688 *Brush driller. 1901 *N. & Q.* 9th Ser. VIII. 310/1 In the painting of woodwork, when the second coat, say of vermilion, is made to show through the third, say of brown, by passing the brush over it while the last coat is still wet, the result is spoken of as '*brush-grain'. 1900 H. LAWSON *Over Sliprails* 36, I did a deal of house-painting at one time; I was a pretty smart *brush hand. 1874 KNIGHT *Dict. Mech.*, **Brush-hat*, one in which the surface is continually brushed by a hand-brush, during the process of sizing. 1894 W. P. MAYCOCK *Electric Lighting* I. vi. § 114 (ed. 2) 179 Construction of..*Brush-holders. 1904 *Technol. & Sci. Dict.* (ed. Goodchild & Tweney), *Brush Holder*, the support or frame carrying the copper (or carbon) strips by which the current enters or leaves a motor or dynamo. 1875 SIR T. SEATON *Fret-Cutting* 31 Should you wish to varnish the work that has been fret cut or carved, you must do it with *brush-varnish, made with spirits of wine..laid on with a camel-hair brush. 1926 *Ironmonger* Suppl. 16 Jan. 52 British Made *Brushware. 1886 *Encycl. Brit.* XX. 218/2 Works.. wanting in the trenchant *brush-work..of subsequent productions. 1893 *Daily News* 8 Apr. 3/6 The brush work of this incomparable painter.

Brush, *sb.*[3] Add:

1. b. *At* or *after the first brush*: at or after the first encounter or meeting.

1815 SCOTT *Guy M.* lii, So you intend to give up this poor young fellow at the first brush? 1857 HUGHES *Tom Brown* II. ii, The people were..civil to you if you were civil to them, after the first brush.

c. A rapid run or race; a contest in speed. *dial.* and *U.S.*

1860 TROLLOPE *Framley P.* xiv, Mark..would enjoy a brush across the country quite as well as he himself. 1868 H. WOODRUFF *Trotting Horse of Amer.* ix. 105 He may have a couple of brushes of a quarter of a mile each. 1902 MCFAUL *Ike Glidden* iii. 20 He..'llowed his hoss ud beat mine 'n a half mile brush. 1903 *N. Y. Times* 7 Sept., Mr. Dodge..got into a brush with a passing horseman...His horse continued the brush for about ten yards. 1906 *N. Y. Even. Post* 16 June, Apart from the annual regatta, there are endless minor 'brushes' for the 'fresh-water sailormen'.

Brush, *v.*[1] Add: **2. b.** To force on (*fig.*); to drive hard. *U.S.*

1755 *Connecticut Gaz.* 29 Nov. (De Vere 275) As tending to beget ill will, and brushing a disunion in the several governments in America. 1827 J. F. COOPER *Prairie* x, I have at this moment a dog brushing a deer. 1868 H. WOODRUFF *Trotting Horse of Amer.* v. 70 Eight or ten days prior to the race..brush him a half mile. 1904 *N. Y. Times* 28 Nov. 5 The drivers..spent a couple of hours before dusk brushing their fast steppers on the upper stretch.

4. b. *To brush round*: to bestir oneself. *U.S. colloq.*

1875 HOLLAND *Sevenoaks* x. 127 If the feller that only had one talent had brushed round, he could 'a' made a spec on it. *Ibid.* xii. 156 You an' me has got to be brushin' round.

Brush, *v.*[2] Add:

1. e. To go over with a brush-harrow.

1857-8 *Trans. Ill. Agric. Soc.* III. 490 The ground should be fresh plowed, harrowed and rolled, or brushed.

2. b. *intr.* To make oneself more presentable or ready for action; to refresh one's memory. *U.S.*

1844 [W. T. THOMPSON] *Major Jones's Courtship* (Bartlett) When Miss Mary came, I brushed up, and was determined to have a rite serious talk with her. 1878 J. H. BEADLE *Western Wilds* xvi. 265 We here overhauled our kit, brushed up a little, and put on our best gear for a visit. 1903 *Dial* 1 Sept. Advt., If you wish to brush up on your English, you will find nothing better. 1904 *Hartford Courant* 5 Oct. 8 The ex-governor must brush up a bit on his ecclesiastical studies.

7. To trim (a hedge or tree, the sides of a ditch or path). *local.*

1513 [implied in BRUSHING *vbl. sb.* 1]. 1809 *Warehorne Highway-bk.* 29 June (E.D.D.) For brushing the footpath, 1s. od. 1845 *Jrnl. R. Agric. Soc.* VI. II. 479 They [*sc.* hedges] are carefully brushed, or clipped, twice a year. 1886 *Cheshire Gloss.*, *Brush*, to trim a hedge.

8. To beat (a covert). Also *intr.* in *vbl. sb.*

1876 *Coursing Cal.* 223 Our long dragging beats taking us..round the far side by Fliskoe Forest, in proximity to which the ranges were brushed, but with no good results. 1895 *E. Angl. Gloss.*, *Brush*, to beat a covert; 'a day's brushing with the governor'.

9. *Hunting.* To take the 'brush' from (a killed fox) as a trophy of the chase.

1879 *Tinsley's Mag.* XXIV. 334 As they then rode in the master 'brushed' him [*sc.* a fox], while the hounds were baying. 1893 *Field* 11 Feb. 191/3 Some twenty minutes later he had the satisfaction of brushing his fox.

10. Painting. *To brush (in)*: to put in with the brush, to paint in.

1897 *Daily News* 16 Jan. 6/3 For flesh painting, the torso ..is so firm, so luminous; the draperies, too, are decisively brushed in. 1901 *Ibid.* 7 Mar. 6/6 These are vivid, quickly brushed impressions by an artist who has an eye for.. Italian landscape.

Brushed (brɒʃt), *a.* *U.S.* [f. BRUSH *sb.*[1] + -ED[2].] Overgrown with brushwood.

1888 *Century Mag.* Jan. 453/1 A cañon, liberally wooded or 'brushed' with wild plums.

Brushing, *vbl. sb.* Add:

4. *Coal-mining.* The action of, or the work involved in, cutting or blasting down the roof, building supporting and blocking walls in a coal

mine. Also *attrib.* and *Comb.*, as *brushing contractor*; **brushing-bed** (see quot. 1883).

1883 GRESLEY *Gloss. Coal-m.*, *Brushers* (Scotland), men who brush the roof, build packs and stoppings, which work is called brushing. *Brushing-bed* (Scotland), the stratum brushed or ripped. 1923 *Glasgow Herald* 16 Oct. 9 The 'brushing' contractor.

5. Brush-work, as distinguished from drawing.

1896 *Daily News* 6 Apr. 6/5 No incompleteness of drawing, of brushing, or of line.

6. The action or process of applying the enamel in the manufacture of enamel-ware. Also *attrib.*

1893 *Daily News* 15 Dec. 5/4 The brushing department of enamelled plate works.

7. *Brushing-off*, the action or process of removing superfluous sugar from the base of a mould.

1845 DODD *Brit. Manuf.* V. 124 A man..scrapes the base ..of the sugar with a small instrument; a process which is called 'brushing-off'.

Brushing, *ppl. a.* 3. (See *BRUSH *sb.*[3] 1 c, *BRUSH *v.*[1] 2 b.) *U.S.*

1868 H. WOODRUFF *Trotting Horse of Amer.* xii. 124 Paul Pry was at no time a horse of brushing speed.

Brushlet (brɒ·ʃlĕt). [f. BRUSH *sb.*[2] + -LET.] A little brush; *spec.*, the stiff hairs on the legs of various hymenopters, as bees, used to cleanse the body (Westwood in *Cent. Dict.*).

Brushy, *a.*[1] (Earlier examples of U.S. use.)

1658 *Essex Inst. Hist. Coll.* IX. 221 A swampy brushy meadow in the great swampe near Wenham. 1693 *Mass. Prov. Acts* (1892) VII. 397 Though ye way [was] now most hideous, sometimes swampy, then stony and horibly Brushy, scarce passable for Horses. 1706 *Rec. of Derby, Conn.* 390 Bounded..east by a brushye hill side. 1785 A. ELLICOTT in *Life & Lett.* (1908) 47 The Hills extreme brushy, and no inhabitants within many miles.

Brut (brüt), *a.* [Fr.] Of wines: Unsweetened.

1891 *Longman's Mag.* Aug. 417 An especial brand of brut champagne. *Ibid.*, Brut wines. 1896 *Pall Mall Mag.* Mar. 399 Tell my man to bring me a quail, broiled, and a pint of Piper Heidsieck, *brut*.

Brutalitarian (brutælitē·riăn). [f. BRUTALITY, after *humanitarian*.] One who practises or advocates the practice of brutality.

1904 (*title*) The Brutalitarian, a Journal for the Sane and Strong. 1909 CHESTERTON *Tremendous Trifles* 215 It is only these two types, the sentimental humanitarian and the sentimental brutalitarian, whom one hears in the modern babel. 1910 — *Shaw* 83 And in this the brutalitarians hate him not because he is soft, but..because he is not to be softened by conventional excuses.

Brute. Add: **A.** *adj.* **4.** Crude, unrefined.

a 1861 T. WINTHROP *John Brent* i. 6 The precious metal was to the brute mineral in the proportion of perhaps a hundred pin-heads to the ton.

B. *sb.*[1] **1.** An animal, as an ox or cow. *U.S.*

1867-9 *Trans. Ill. Agric. Soc.* VII. 223, I..did not lose a brute until the past summer.

Brutedom (brū·tdəm). [f. BRUTE *sb.*[1] + -DOM.] Brutish nature.

1890 A. R. WALLACE in *Fortn. Rev.* Sept. 331 In proportion as men leave brutedom behind and enter into the fulness of their human heritage. 1904 *Westm. Gaz.* 29 June 2/1 The paths that lead to..the depths to which sheer brutedom may descend.

Bruting (brū·tiŋ), *vbl. sb.* [Rendering F. *brutage*, f. *brut* rough, unworked, unformed (cf. *BRUT *a.*, *BRUTE *a.* 4) as in *diamant brut*.] The roughing-out of a diamond (see quot.). Hence **Brute** *v.*, **Bru·ter.**

1903 L. J. SPENCER tr. *M. Bauer's Precious Stones* 82 Bruting..consists in rubbing together two diamonds, each being cemented at the end of a stick or holder, until the desired form is obtained. *Ibid.* 243 The stone to be bruted is fixed to a handle. *Ibid.* 244 The three operations..are entrusted to..skilled workmen, namely cleavers, bruters, and grinders or polishers. 1906 CLAREMONT *Gem-cutter's Craft* 41, 42.

Bryle, variant of *BROIL.

Bual (biū·ăl). A madeira made from a variety of grape so named.

1883 *Encycl. Brit.* XV. 178/1 (*Madeira*) Other high-class wines, known as Bual, Sercial and Malmsey. 1927 J. B. PRIESTLEY *Adam in Moonshine* vii. 134 'Old Madeira... Bual, they call it.' 'What!' cried the Baron...'An old Bual!'

Bub, *sb.*[5] *U.S. colloq.* [See BUBBY[2].] A form of familiar address to boys or men. (Cf. *BUD *sb.*[3])

1845 *St. Louis Reveille* 4 Aug. (Th.) Letters from a Baby, [signed] Bub. 1846-52 MRS. WHITCHER *Widow Bedott P.* xxiv. 287 Come here and see me, bub. 1872 'MARK TWAIN' *Roughing it* v. 51 Well, I shall have to tear myself away from you, bub. 1896 *McClure's Mag.* VI. 485/2 She always called him 'bub' when she wanted to vex him. 1902 S. E. WHITE *Blazed Trail* xxviii, 'Well, bub,'..'blowed that stake you made out of Radway, yet?'

Bubaline (biū·bălәin), *a.* [ad. mod. L. *būbalīnus*, f. *būbalus* BUBAL.] Belonging to the genus *Bubalis*.

1827 GRIFFITH tr. *Cuvier's Anim. Kingd.* IV. 378 The Bubaline Group. 1907 *Westm. Gaz.* 2 Jan. 10/2 The Bubaline antelope is uniformly coloured bright bay.

Bubble, *sb.* 6. Add: **bubble-foot**, an insect of the order *Thysanoptera* or *Physopoda*; **bubble-trier**, an instrument used for testing the accuracy of the tubes of spirit-levels; **bubble-tube**, the glass tube of a spirit-level containing spirit and enclosing an air-bubble; **bubble-weed**, a kind of seaweed.

1904 *Amer. Inventor* 1 June 244 (Cent. D. Suppl.) *Bubble-foot. 1874 KNIGHT *Dict. Mech.*, **Bubble-trier*, an instrument for testing the delicacy and accuracy of the tubes for holding the spirit in leveling-instruments. 1890 W. F. STANLEY *Surveying Instr.* 88 The Bubble Trier is a bar or bed 12 to 20 inches long, with two extended feet ending in points at one end, and a micrometer screw, the point of which forms a resting foot, at the other end, thereby forming a tripod. 1888 *Lockwood's Dict. Mech. Engin.*, **Bubble Tube*, or *Spirit Glass*, the tube of a spirit-level which contains the enclosed spirit. 1890 W. F. STANLEY *Surveying Instr.* 86 Level Tubes, or Bubble Tubes as they are technically termed, are used in nearly all important surveying instruments.

Bubblement (bɒ·b'lmĕnt). [f. BUBBLE *v.* + -MENT.] Effervescence (*lit.* and *fig.*).

1890 *Pall Mall Gaz.* 24 Mar. 1/2 Berlin is in a state of bubblement. 1893 *Field* 17 June 895/2 A flash, and swirl, a bubblement. 1902 J. H. SKRINE *Pastor Agnorum* 200 The wicked man..was an etymologist and knew that real means bubblement, effervescence.

Bubbly, *a.* Add: *Bubbly water* (slang), champagne; also *sb.* short for this.

1910 *Daily Chron.* 9 Apr. 9/3 'Too much bubbly water', so be explained, was responsible for the breach of the rules. 1920 *Chambers's Jrnl.* 346/2 It goes to the head like bubbly. 1927 *Blackw. Mag.* Feb. 231/2 [He] had finished up at dinner with some capital oysters and a bottle of bubbly.

Bubonic, *a.*[1] Add: Also as *sb.* short for *bubonic plague*.

1901 *Daily News* 11 Feb. 5/3 A native child died last night, and the post-mortem proved the existence of bubonic. 1907 KIPLING *Lett. Trav.* (1920) 121 A rot at what is called 'headquarters' may spread like bubonic, with every steamer.

Bubu(c)kled (biū·bɒk'ld), *a. pseudo-arch.* [f. BUBUKLE (only Shaks.) + -ED.] Covered with 'bubukles' or large pimples.

1822-9 *Good's Study Med.* (ed. 3) II. 357 A welky or bubukled-face. 1892 STEVENSON *Across the Plains* iv. 163 Poor bubuckled Commissary!

Bucchero (bukē·ro). *Archæol.* [It.] A type of pottery, characteristic of ancient Tuscany, of a uniform black, neither glazed nor painted, but decorated with figures in low relief, or, in later times, with figures moulded separately and applied to the pottery. Also *attrib.*

1889 in *Cent. Dict.* 1905 H. B. WALTERS *Anc. Pottery* II. 295 In the earlier chamber-tombs no *bucchero* is found. 1910 *Encycl. Brit.* V. 722/1 Bucchero ware—the national pottery of Etruria. 1922 *Edin. Rev.* July 54 Some goblets of finely modelled and burnished black bucchero.

Bucco- (bɒ·ko), used as comb. form (for the correct bucci-) of L. *bucca* cheek, with the meaning 'relating to the cheek (or mouth)', as *buccocervical*, *-facial*, *-labial*, *-lingual*, *-nasal*, *-pharyngeal* adjs. (see quots.).

1892 *Phil. Trans.* B. CLXXXIII. 98 Dastre and Morat find that the vaso-dilator fibres for the bucco-facial region of the Dog issue by the IInd., IIIrd., IVth., and Vth. thoracic nerves. 1903 DORLAND *Med. Dict.* (ed. 3), *Buccocervical*, pertaining to the neck and the buccal surface of a tooth. *Buccolabial*, pertaining to the cheek and lip. *Buccopharyngeal*, pertaining to the mouth and pharynx. 1907 *Practitioner* Dec. 813 The bucco-pharyngeal fascia. 1911 ST. CLAIR THOMSON *Dis. Nose & Throat* (1916) 121 The bucco-nasal membrane.

Buchan (bɒ·kăn). The name of a Scottish meteorologist, Alexander *Buchan* (1829–1907), used to designate certain specified periods of cold weather foretold by him as of annual occurrence.

1923 *Daily Mail* 11 May 7 The period from May 9 to 14 is known as 'Buchan's Winter'. Buchan, an old meteorologist,..50 years ago laid down six periods of which May 9–14 is the coldest. 1929 *Daily News* 17 Apr. 8/7 Is it not a fact that the proposal to fix the date of Easter will mean that this holiday will in future coincide with 'Buchan's Cold Spell' which we are at present enjoying?

Buchanite (bɒ·kănəit). *Hist.* [f. the name of Mrs. Elspeth *Buchan* (1738–91), commonly known as Lucky Buchan + -ITE[1].] A member of a sect which arose in 1783, in the Relief Congregation, Irvine, Ayrshire, Scotland, and became extinct in 1848 on the death of the only surviving member.

Mrs. Buchan believed herself to be the woman of Rev. xii.

1846 TRAIN (*title*) The Buchanites from First to Last. 1904 J. CAMERON (*title*) History of the Buchanite Delusion: 1783–1846.

Bucholzite (bɒ·kǫltsəit). *Min.* [ad. G. *bucholzit* (Brandes 1819), f. the name of C. F. *Bucholz*, a German chemist: see -ITE[1].] A variety of fibrolite.

1854 DANA *Syst. Min.* (ed. 4) 265 Bucholzite and fibrolite are generally fibrous massive, sometimes approaching distinct prisms.

Buck, *sb.*[1] Add: **1. a.** (Modern example.)

1869 C. L. BRACE *New West* xviii. 237 In the fall of 1861, W. Landrum obtained two bucks from a grower in the State of Georgia.

c. Also, the male of the ferret.

1904 *Westm. Gaz.* 11 Oct. 3/1 An old buck broken out of bounds is selfishly disposed.

d. A ram. Also *attrib.* *U.S.*

1851 *Trans. Mich. Agric. Soc.* (1852) III. 95 Sheep... Best buck over 2 years old. *Ibid.*, A lot consisting of 1 buck, 3 ewes. 1852 *Ibid.* 25 Best pen of 5 buck lambs. 1867-8 *Trans. Ill. Agric. Soc.* VII. 455 Our friend..crosses the fine wool buck with a coarse wool ewe. 1881 A. A. HAYES *New Colorado* iv. 60 His 'bucks' (say about three to each hundred ewes) will generally be merinos.

2. d. (Examples of senses, (*a*) aboriginal Indian of Guiana (cf. *BUCKEEN [3]), (*b*) negro, (*c*) North American Indian.) Chiefly *U.S.*

(*a*) 1806 PINCKARD *Notes West Indies* II. 405 The accuracy of the Bucks, in shooting with the long arrow, and in blowing the short poisoned one.

(b) 1842 *Philad. Spirit of Times* 18 Apr. (Th.) The most prominent object was a 'long nine' with a fierce looking buck of a colored fellow hanging to the end of it. 1880 *Congress.Rec.* June 4147/1, I told the boys that we wanted 20,000 'bucks', buck niggers, in Indiana this year. 1904 HARBEN *Georgians* 116 A big black buck, was a-leanin' over the side fence with a cigar in his mouth.

(c) 1860 J. C. ADAMS *Adv.* 109 (Th.) The bucks became lively and shouted, hallooed, and whooped, as if mad. 1882 *Congress. Rec.* July 5921/2 The cattle..are left by the bucks until the squaws can go to them. 1890 *Harper's Mag.* Apr. 726/1 So out he rode,..feeling pretty confident that..some young 'buck' would stab him in the back. 1903 A. ADAMS *Log Cowboy* x. 136 When the lead came within a few hundred yards of the Indians, one buck..rode forward a few rods.

3. *buck-fawn* (earlier example); *buck-Indian, -negro, -nigger, -warrior* (see 2 d above); *buck-ague, -fever* (see quot. 1871).

1844 G. W. KENDALL *Santa Fé Exped.* I. 172 There is a very common disease prevalent among young and inexperienced hunters in Texas, which is known as the '*buck ague'. 1871 SCHELE DE VERE *Americanisms* (1872) 208 The *buck*..makes him speak of *buck ague*, or *buck fever* when he wishes to describe the nervous agitation of the inexperienced sportsman. 1894 *Outing* (U.S.) XXIV. 344/1 My confusion..was the direct result of buck-ague. 1786 WASHINGTON *Diaries* III. 11 The largest of my *Buck fauns..came home after dinner with its left knee broke. 1857 S. H. HAMMOND *Wild North. Scenes* 127 Smith acknowledged to a severe attack of the *buck fever. 1895 *Outing* (U.S.) XXVI. 402/1, I had heard of the buck fever before but I never knew what it was until that moment. 1911 H. QUICK *Yellowstone N.* ix. 240 My mind was so full of curlicues..that I went into buck fever. 1840 C. F. HOFFMANN *Greyslaer* II. xii. 54 There they lay on the grass, six big *buck Injuns, likely fellows all. 1869 *Congress. Rec.* Feb. 1707/3 Chasing the fourteen year old buck Indians across the plains. 1882 *Ibid.* July 6540/1 A pound of striped candy for each buck Indian. 1860 *Richmond Enquirer* 30 Nov. 2/4 (Th.) He let drop from the canvas an unmistakable small, nappy-headed *buck negro. 1871 *Nashville Banner* 8 Jan. (De Vere) A big buck negro was found in a hollow, laying [*sic*] on his face, playing possum. 1863 'E. KIRKE' *My Southern Friends* iv. 66 Yer scented, bedevilled-up *buck niggers. 1876 *Congress. Rec.* June 3505/1 As soon as these *buck warriors smell the war-path.

4. *ellipt.* = BUCKSHOT. *U.S.*

1845 W. G. SIMMS *Wigwam & Cabin* Ser. II. 107 On using big buck, he numbered two sevens for a load; the small buck, three. 1876 *Fur, Fin & Feather* Sept. 135 The doctor soon drew a bird charge from his gun and loaded it with buck and fired. 1889 *Century Dict.*, *Buck-and-ball*, a cartridge for smooth-bore firearms containing a spherical bullet and three buckshot: now little used.

Buck, *sb.*4 Add: On the river Thames, a wooden framework at a weir, supporting eel-baskets. Cf. *eel-buck* (EEL 6). Also *buck gate*.

1694 *Act 6 & 7 Will. & Mary* c. 16 *Preamble*, For the..convenience of the Navigation [of the Thames and Isis] there..are diverse Lockes Weares Buckes Winches..and other Engines. 1791 *Rep. Committees Ho. Comm.* (1803) XIV. 263/2 (*Thames & Isis*) The difficulties made by the millers and fishermen, of drawing their bucks and sluices. 1791 R. MYLNE *2nd Rep. Thames Navig.* 12 Nuneham Wear..is now used as a Fishery only, having a Tumbling, solid Wear, and two sets of Buck Gates. 1902 *Thames Conserv. Bye-Laws Regul. Thames* 32 No person shall without the previous consent of the Conservators erect any new buck or weir.

Buck, *sb.*7 Add earlier example:

1839 C. F. BRIGGS *Harry Franco* II. i. 2 There were also wood sawyers sitting listlessly on their bucks.

Buck, *sb.*8 [Cf. BUCK *v.*3] = BUCK-JUMP.

1908 SOMERVILLE & ROSS *Further Exp. Irish R. M.* v, The white horse got over the ground in bucks like a rabbit.

Buck (bɒk), *sb.*9 *slang.* Also **bukh.** [a. Hind. *bak*, Hindi *buk buk.*] Talk, conversation; *spec.* boastful, bragging talk.

1805 MRS. CROKER *Village Tales* (1896) 20 Having a 'bukh' with the elders. 1912 A. NEIL LYONS *Clara* x. 99 We've 'ad enough of your old buck.

Buck (bɒk), *sb.*10 An earthenware pot found in parts of British Guiana. Also *buck-pot.*

1851 *Illustr. Catal. Gt. Exhib.* iv. i. 986/2 Buck pot, used in preparing pepper pot. 1898 KIRKE *25 Yrs. Brit. Guiana* App. 349/1 (Glossary of Creole Words).

Buck, *sb.*11 *U.S.* [f. BUCK *v.*3] An act of bucking; the power to buck.

1889 *Cent. Dict.* 1890 L. C. D'OYLE *Notches* 34 In two months from now the worst 'buckers' amongst them will not have a 'buck' left in them.

Buck, *sb.*12 *U.S.* [Origin obscure.] In the game of poker, any article placed in the pool with the chips. *To pass the buck to* (fig.): to make a scapegoat or dupe of (a person); to shift responsibility to (another).

1872 'MARK TWAIN' *Innoc. at Home* ii. (1882) 267 You ruther hold over me, pard. I reckon I can't call that hand. Ante and pass the buck. 1891 *Hoffmann's Cycl. Card & Table Games* 203 Straight Poker....To avoid dispute as to whose turn it may be, a pocket-knife, known as the 'buck', is passed round, resting with the player whose turn it is to 'chip' for the remainder. 1920 MULFORD *J. Nelson* vi. 60 Bein' a stranger down here I reckoned they'd pass th' buck to you. 1924 A. J. SMALL *Frozen Gold* iii. 92 Maybe you'll have time to get up to your location before they realize they've been presented with the buck.

Buck, *sb.*13 *U.S. slang.* [Obscure.] A dollar.

1896 G. ADE *Artie* xii. 106 Jimmy can afford to buy wine at four bucks a throw when he's only getting three a week out o' the job. 1903 *McClure's Mag.* Feb. 428 A man..passed around some gold watches....Twenty bucks they cost you over the counter. 1921 *Blackw. Mag.* Aug. 264/2, I wonder if I've done right forking out five bucks.

Buck, *v.*3 Add: Also *refl.*

1923 *Outward Bound* Mar. 408/2 Many ambitious young horses have bucked themselves to a finish without dislodging my cargo.

Buck, *v.*6 *U.S.* Add: (Later example.)

1878 J. H. BEADLE *Western Wilds* xxv. 402 On all rapids they [*sc.* salmon] are found 'bucking against the stream'.

2. *intr.* Of persons. Chiefly *fig.* with *against.*

1859 BARTLETT *Dict. Amer.* (ed. 2), *To Buck.* Used instead of *butt*,..metaphorically of players at football and such games, pugilists, etc. 1870 *San Antonio paper* (De Vere) You'll have to buck at it like a whole team, gentlemen, or you won't hear the whistle near your diggings for many a year. *a* 1889 *Arkansaw Traveller* (Barrère & L.) W'y how de work o' de Lawd gwine ter prosper when de white folks bucks ergin it dis way? 1900 G. BONNER *Hard Pan* ii. 41 There's no good bucking against bad luck. 1910 W. M. RAINE *B. O'Connor* 220 Some men..have to buck against so much in themselves.

b. *spec.* To play at a game of hazard.

1871 SCHELE DE VERE *Americanisms* (1872) 327 The fact that players at *Three-Card Monte*..are said to *buck* at monte, causes the familiar phrase of *bucking* at anything. 1876 B. HARTE *G. Conroy* iv. iv, I don't like your looks Jack, at all, I'd buck against any bank you ran, all night. 1890 L. C. D'OYLE *Notches* 164 Now and again he threw the dice;..he was inviting his friend to 'buck'. But, to use a local vulgarism, Woddell didn't buck worth a cent.

3. *trans.* To butt into or against. Freq. *fig.* to come up against, find oneself opposed to, oppose.

1891 C. ROBERTS *Adrift Amer.* 114 There was a snow plough with two engines to it 'bucking the snow' (as the expression goes here). 1904 G. H. LORIMER *Old Gorgon Graham* 307 There's no use bucking that idea. 1904 C. J. STEEDMAN *Bucking the Sagebush* ii. 14 If any convert..bucked the authority of the Church, he disappeared from his 'sphere of influence'. 1911 J. C. LINCOLN *Cap'n Warren's Wards* vii. 109 If this big-hearted, simple-minded countryman had come to New York to buck the stock market, it was time to sound a warning. 1918 MULFORD *Man fr. Bar-20* xii. 121, I ain't so harmless myself....An' now I know what I'm buckin'. 1922 J. A. DUNN *Man Trap* iii. 39 As I can't buck natural law, the inference is that if we are to meet and mate, we are. 1929 *Publishers' Weekly* 14 May 2456/2 It is wasted time and energy to try to buck any legitimate movement, and I think it is time and energy wasted for you men to attempt to buck the book clubs.

b. To push or thrust *in.*

1897 FLANDRAU *Harvard Episodes* 140 It was when everybody was tired of fighting that I bucked in McGaw.

4. *To buck the tiger*: to play against the bank at faro: see TIGER *sb.* 9 a.

1863 *Rocky Mt. News* 29 Jan. (Th.) At night [in Denver] you have a choice of..most anything, even to bucking the tiger, which we wouldn't advise any one to do. 1888 *Hotel Mail* (Farmer) He will find the sport most tame Compared with bucking the tiger At dear Long Branch. 1904 ELIZ. ROBINS *Magn. North* II. 124 You've got to a place where you can..go buckin' the tiger between whiles. 1910 W. M. RAINE *B. O'Connor* 96 Chinaman and cowpuncher,..tourist and tailor, bucked the tiger side by side. 1912 MULFORD & CLAY *Buck Peters* xiii. 127 Where in thunder was he? Maybe bucking the tiger at Little Nell's.

Buck, *v.*7 Add:

2. *To buck up.* **a.** *intr.* To cheer up, be encouraged. Also *trans.* in causal sense.

1889 BARRÈRE & LELAND *Dict. Slang* s.v., (Winchester College)..to 'buck up' is to be glad. 1890 FARMER *Slang*, *Buck up*,..(Winchester College), to be glad; pleased....The usual expression is 'Oh buck up', a phrase which at Westminster School would have a very different meaning, namely, 'exert yourself'. 1894 *Punch* 27 Oct. 193/1 Buck up, mate; you've no call to be yaller, nor a perminent bloo, heither! 1901 *Winchester Coll. Notions* 14 *Buck up*, Hurrah! The original meaning, which is still used. Hence later:—Cheer up, hurry up. 1906 B'NESS VON HUTTEN *What became of Pam* II. ix, Don't spoil it all by being weepy....Come, buck up, like a dear, and wish me joy. 1909 H. G. WELLS *Tono-Bungay* II. ii. § 1 Never saw her so larky. This has bucked her up something wonderful. 1910 W. J. LOCKE *Simon the Jester* xviii, Now and again one does help a lame dog over a stile which bucks one up, you know. 1922 INGE *Lay Thoughts of a Dean* (1926) 233, I asked the medical members ..in particular whether it was impossible that microbic diseases..might be benefited by 'bucking up' the patient.

b. *intr.* To make an effort, to 'brace up'; to hurry up.

1890 [see a]. 1909 H. G. WELLS *Tono-Bungay* I. i. § 8 It was equally impossible for him to either buck-up and beat me, or give in. 1910 W. J. LOCKE *Simon the Jester* ii, You must buck up a bit, Simon, and get your name better known about the country. 1913 'IAN HAY' *Happy-go-lucky* i, 'Hallo, you fellows—finished?' 'Yes, buck up!' commanded Rumbold.

Buck, *v.*8 *slang.* Also **bukh, bukk.** [Cf. *BUCK *sb.*9] *intr.* To swagger, talk big or bumptiously, brag.

1880 G. ABERIGH-MACKAY *Ali Baba* 164 He *bucks* with a quiet, stubborn determination that would fill an American editor..with despair. 1893 KIPLING *Many Invent.*, *Confer. of Powers* 27 You're ordered to *bukh*. 1895 MRS. CROKER *Village Tales* (1896) 157 Those who were wont to assemble..of an evening to smoke, argue, and bukh. 1899 *Daily News* 6 June 8/4 There is not much in this for Etonians to 'buck' about. 1908 MISS BROUGHTON *Mamma* xvii, 'You thought I *bucked* too much about it?' he answered in eager interruption. 1921 *Blackw. Mag.* Apr. 517/2 Arthur and I have 'bukked' till we're hoarse. 1925 *Chambers's Jrnl.* 464/2 I'd come back here and we'd 'bukk' about Palestine till it's time to go.

Buck-and-wing. *U.S.* [?f. BUCK *v.*3 + WING *v.*] A dance of a lively character, usually performed by a single person.

1907 MULFORD *Bar-20* x. 110 In the centre of the room was a large man dancing a fair buck-and-wing to the time so uproariously set by his companions. *Ibid.* 112 Up by the door Bigfoot Baker, elated at winning the buck-and-wing contest, was endeavouring to learn a new step. *a* 1910 'O. HENRY' *Rolling Stones* 231 He heard..the light stirring staccato of a buck-and-wing dance. 1926 J. BLACK *You Can't Win* v. 61 The two girls..that did the buck-and-wing dance.

Buckayro, buckaroo. *U.S.* Also **bakhara, buckhara; buckeroo.** [Corruption of VAQUERO.] A cowboy. Also *attrib.*

1889 W. B. DEWEES *Lett. fr. Texas* x. 66 These [rancheros] are surrounded by..peons and bakharas or herdsmen. 1889 *Century Dict.*, *Buckayro*...(Western U.S.). 1890 FARMER *Slang*, *Buckhara* (American), a name given in California to a cattle-driver or cowboy. 1904 *N. Y. Tribune* 17 July, He was herding a big bunch of cattle there with the help of half a dozen buckayros. 1910 JER. HART *Vigilante Girl* iv. 60, I can talk what they call 'buckayro' Spanish. 1916 H. L. WILSON *Somewhere in Red Gap* iv. 129 Nothing ever did worry that buckaroo as long as his fingers wasn't too cold to roll a cigarette. 1919 — *Ma Pettengill* i. 10 A mere scrub buckeroo named Sandy Sawtelle.

Bu·ckboard, *sb. U.S.* [See BUCK *sb.*5 3.]

1. A plank slung upon wheels, forming the body of a light vehicle.

1839 C. F. HOFFMAN *Wild Scenes* I. 10 Did he ever see a teamster riding upon a buckboard? a stout, springy plank, laid upon the bare bolsters of a waggon! 1885 [see BUCK *sb.*5 3].

2. A vehicle of this description. Also *Comb.*

1878 *Congress. Rec.* Mar. 1915/2 Upon the whole of that route there was only one mule and a buckboard. 1880 *Ibid.* Feb. 1165/2 The mail [in Kansas] is carried in buckboards drawn by one or two mules...Two horses or ponies in that country can draw a light buckboard twenty miles a day with perfect ease. 1886 *Outing* (U.S.) Oct. 57/2 For some reason or other, the buckboard driver, who usually brings us our mail, did not bring it yesterday. 1904 *N. Y. Even. Post* 18 June, When the mountain roads were in less perfect condition than they are to-day, the most comfortable vehicle was found to be the buckboard.

Hence **Bu·ckboard** *v. intr.*, to ride on a buckboard.

1904 F. LYNDE *Grafters* i. 2 Two men who buckboarded in ahead of the track-layers.

Bu·ck-brush. *U.S.* [BUCK *sb.*1] One or other variety of brush on which deer feed.

Differently applied in various parts of the U.S.

1874 J. W. LONG *Amer. Wild-fowl Shooting* ix. 152 Hang up your cartridge bag on a branch of the buck-brush. *Ibid.* xiii. 179 He may find good shooting..when the buck-brush is so close that the boat cannot be easily pushed through it. 1922 Z. GREY *To last Man* iv. 78 Through an opening in the fringe of buck brush she could plainly see the promontory.

Bucked (bɒkt), *ppl. a. slang.* [f. BUCK *v.*7 + -ED 1.] Cheered, encouraged, elated.

1907 *Varsity* 31 Jan. 194/3 We are very 'bucked' that he fitted in a visit this Term. 1909 SLADEN *Trag. Pyramids* i. (ed. 8) 39 So bucked at being with you again. 1922 A. A. MILNE *Red House Myst.* vii. 61 He was unusually bucked with himself this morning. 1928 *Punch* 23 May 561/2, I am so bucked that you have asked me what to wear when you are accompanying at the concert next month.

Buckeen 2 (bɒkī·n). [ad. Guiana Du. *bokin*, fem. of *bok* goat, buck (see BUCK *sb.*1 2 d).] A female aboriginal Indian in Guiana.

1806 PINCKARD *Notes West Indies* II. 405 The morning was..spent..in hearing M. Heynemann relate his adventures among the Indians; whom he termed Bucks and Buckeens. 1868 W. H. BRETT *Ind. Tribes Guiana* 34 *note*, The Indian men and women were called by the Dutch 'Bucks' and 'Buckeens'. 1899 RODWAY *Guiana Wilds* 39 They called her a 'buckeen'; how much prettier than the word squaw.

Bucket, *sb.*1 Add:

3. b. A scoop operated by power, used for hoisting coal, grain, etc., and in dredging and excavating.

1874 KNIGHT *Dict. Mech.*, *Bucket*, (3) The scoop of a dredging machine. 1884 [see GRAB *sb.*4]. 1902 *Encycl. Brit.* XXVII. 531/2 Grabs or buckets for dredging purposes.

5. bucket-door, the cover of an opening which gives access to the buckets of a pump; **bucket-(ladder) dredger** (see quots.); so **bucket-dredging** *vbl. sb.*; **bucket-pitch**, a circular line passing through the elbows of the buckets of an overshot water-wheel (*Cent. Dict.* 1889); **bucket-seat**, in a motor-car, a seat resembling a bucket in shape; **bucket-wheel**, also, an overshot or breast wheel operated by the impulse and weight of the water falling into the buckets or receptacles on its rim.

1797 J. CURR *Coal Viewer* 74 Cross Bars and Bolts for *Bucket and Clack Doors. 1902 *Encycl. Brit.* XXVII. 530/2 Where it is necessary to finish off the dredging work to a uniform flat bottom..*bucket dredgers are better adapted. 1909 *Westm. Gaz.* 5 Nov. 7/3 A twin-screw, self-propelling bucket dredger. 1898 *Engineering Mag.* XVI. 116/1 The *bucket-dredging-apparatus. 1877 *Encycl. Brit.* VII. 464/2 The main feature of the machine [*sc.* steam dredger] is the *bucket-ladder...Along this ladder a series of buckets traverse which cut into the bottom..and return loaded with the excavated material. 1885 *Marine Engineer* 1 Nov. 200/1 The bucket ladder dredges to a depth of 35 feet. 1902 *Encycl. Brit.* XXVII. 529/1 Bucket-Ladder Dredgers. 1908 *Westm. Gaz.* 29 Oct. 4/1 One is fitted with a luxurious body and the other left bare with two *bucket-seats. 1919 *Autocar Handbk.* (ed. 9) 229 Bucket or armchair seats are sometimes fitted. 1880 *Encycl. Brit.* XII. 523/1 When..the water supply is from 3 to 25 cubic feet per second, it is possible to construct a *bucket wheel on which the water acts chiefly by its weight.

Bucket, *sb.*3 *Rowing.* [f. BUCKET *v.* 5.] 'A plunge forward with the body when the stroke is concluded before the arms have been straightened out, and the hands at least passed the knees' (*Encycl. Sport*).

1898 ROWE, etc. *Rowing* (Badm. Libr.) 35 The swing forward should be kept as slow as is reasonably possible, and a 'bucket' avoided.

Bucket, *v.* Add:

4. b. To move irregularly or haphazardly from place to place. Also *intr.*, to be moved in such a way, to be jostled *along* or tossed *about.*

1879 WINGFIELD *My Lords of Strogue* iv, He..was painfully alive to the possibility of finding his daughter stolen one day,..to be bucketed about the country without a change of linen till his reluctant consent was wrung. 1904 *Westm. Gaz.* 13 Dec. 10/2 He..was bucketed about the garrisons from the Canadas and Cape Breton to the Mediterranean. 1911 BEAN '*Dreadnought' of Darling* i. 10 The coach bumped and bucketed over boulders. 1921 *Blackw. Mag.* Feb. 233/1 Poor preparation..for bucketing about the Baltic all the following day. 1922 *Chambers's Jrnl.* 437/2 The envious beggar..buckets his old boat along for nothing.

Bu·cketed, *a.* [f. BUCKET *sb.*1] Having the form of a bucket.

1886 B. HARTE *Snow-bound* 124 A vast niche or bucketed shelf in the hollow flank of the mountain.

Buck-eye. *U.S.* Add:

1. (Earlier and later examples.)

1784 J. FILSON *Kentucke* 23 Here also is the buck-eye, an exceeding soft wood, bearing a remarkable black fruit. 1807 P. GASS *Jrnl.* 18 On the north the land is level and well timbered, with..buck-eye, cotton wood and some other timber. 1878 B. F. TAYLOR *Between Gates* 214 Beneath avenues of line-oaks, among the junipers, the buckeyes and the buckthorns. 1886 B. HARTE *Snow-bound* 221 The trail was passable yesterday, for I went as far as the buckeyes.

attrib. 1871 EGGLESTON *Hoosier Schoolm.* 139 He didn't butt his brains out agin a buckeye-tree. 1878 B. HARTE *Man on Beach* 109 Looking down upon me through the buckeye bushes.

b. A chestnut from the buck-eye. Also *attrib.*

1785 WASHINGTON *Diaries* II. 360 Sowed..the following things: Box No. 1, partition No. 1, six buck eye nuts. 1884 'C. E. CRADDOCK' *In Tenn. Mts.* I. x. 60 Buck-eyes were falling. 1896 ELLA HIGGINSON *Fr. Land of Snow-pearls* (1897) 218, I kep' a buckeye in my pocket tell it wore a hole and fell out.

2. (Examples.)

c 1819 S. H. LONG *Exp. Rocky Mts.* (1823) I. 20 In allusion to this circumstance, the indigenous backwoodsman is sometimes called buck-eye. 1843 CARLTON *New Purchase* 45 We discovered on a bank, just about 'sunup' a full-grown male Buckeye..watching our progress. 1871 BARNUM *Struggles & Triumphs* 347 You may fool the New Orleans folks, but you can't come it over the Buckeyes. 1882 *Congress. Rec.* July 5811/1 The regenerated statesmanship of the modern Buckeye.

attrib. 1840 *Buffalo Commerc. Advertiser* 12 Sept. (Th.) Queer carryalls did these Buckeye boys construct. 1888 *Troy Daily Times* 8 Feb. (Farmer) A Buckeye damsel..decided she'd see about it. 1894 *Congress. Rec.* Jan., App. 79/1 The very author of the tariff plank in the Chicago platform was last fall buried beneath more than 80,000 votes in that grand old 'Buckeye' State.

3. A variety of potato.

1868 *Rep. U.S. Commissioner Agric.* (1869) 240.

4. A type of canoe or schooner. (See quots.)

1885 C. P. KUNHARDT *Small Yachts* 234 (Cent.) The buckeyes..are an exaggeration of the dugout canoe...The primitive builder bored two holes, one on each side of the stem, through which to pay out his cables. These were simply two round holes, bored with a large auger, and, when the boat was coming head on, resembled to the fancy of the negroes the eyes of a buck. 1889 *Century Dict.*, *Buckeye*... A flat-bottomed centerboard schooner of small size..decked over, and with a cabin aft, used in oyster-fishing in Chesapeake Bay. Also called *bugeye*.

5. An inferior oil-painting, made for the picture-trade or for auction-rooms. Also *attrib. slang.*

1881 *N. Y. Even. Post* 7 June (Th.). 1906 J. H. COLLINS in *Atlantic Monthly* Nov. 640 The despised 'buckeye' painter who paints for department stores and cheap picture shops.

Buck-horn. Add:

4. In full *buck-horn sight*: a branched form of sight of a rifle or sporting gun. *U.S.*

1877 R. I. DODGE *Hunting Grounds Gt. West* vii. 105 The very best sight, and the one almost universally in use by sportsmen and professional hunters on the plains, is the plain 'buckhorn'. *Ibid.*, Sportsmen who use the 'buckhorn' must learn to sight 'on the barrel'.

Buckish (bɒ·kiʃ), *a.* [f. BUCK *v.*3 + -ISH 1.] Inclined to buck; hence, high-spirited, in good fettle (*slang*, of persons).

1911 *Scott's Last Exped.* xiii. (1913) I. 392 The ponies are very buckish and can scarcely be held in.

Bucklandite (bɒ·klændait). *Min.* [f. the name of Dr. William *Buckland*: see -ITE 1.] A variety of allanite or the related mineral epidote.

1824 LEVY in *Ann. Philos.* Ser. II. VII. 134 At the suggestion of Mr. Heuland, I propose to give the name of Bucklandite (in honour of the celebrated Professor of Oxford), to a mineral substance, the crystallographical characters of which I find to differ from any hitherto described. 1854 DANA *Syst. Min.* (ed. 4) II. 208 Bucklandite is from Achmatowsk, Arendal, and Lake Laach. 1863 — *Man. Min.* 183 The mineral Bucklandite is an iron-epidote.

Buckle, *sb.* Add:

1. b. *To make buckle and tongue meet*: to make both ends meet. *U.S.*

1888 *Harper's Mag.* Apr. 703/1 Beginning without money, he had as much as he could do to make 'buckle and tongue meet', as the phrase goes.

d. An iron loop for fastening the blade to the frame of a wood-saw; a turn-buckle.

1846 HOLTZAPFFEL *Turning* II. 725 The chairmakers' saw is in general a diminutive of the ordinary pit saw, and has a central blade strained by buckles and wedges.

e. [app. f. BUCKLE *v.* 2 c.] A vigorous struggle or conflict.

1845 KEEGAN *Leg. & Poems* (1907) 268 Master Tom and the girls running out to..welcome me home, as if I was just returning from a buckle with the Terry Alts, or a rencontre with a scalping party of Huron Indians. 1876 *Coursing Cal.* 6 Wheatear and The Pet had a tremendous tight buckle for the lead. *Ibid.* 181 Liberator and Controversy made a tight buckle for pace.

Buckle, *v.* Add:

6. Also *fig.* in *pass.*

1921 *Contemp. Rev.* Mar. 291 It [*sc.* the ordinary Budget] may..for practical purposes, be considered to be 'buckled'.

c. *To buckle up*: to become warped and bent, to collapse. Also *fig.* (cf. 7).

1866 *Jrnl. R. Agric. Soc.* Ser. II. II. i. 140 Its expansion and contraction..rendering it [*sc.* plane iron] liable to 'buckle up'. 1927 *Daily Tel.* 1 Nov. 12/2 Such a man as Biquet is not given to buckling up.

Bucko (bɒ·ko). Pl. **buckoes.** *Nautical slang.* [f. BUCK *sb.*1 + -O.] **a.** A blustering, swaggering, or domineering fellow; sometimes used as a term of address. Also *attrib.* or as *adj.* = blustering, swaggering. **b.** Swagger, bluster.

1909 *Times Lit. Suppl.* 9 Sept. 325/2 Hudson was included among the victims because he was given to 'bucko' (to use a piece of sea slang). 1919 P. MACGILL *Glenmornan* ii. § 5 'Shake yer legs, me buckos!' Oiney shouted. 1924 *Times Lit. Suppl.* 6 Nov., Bucko skippers. 1926 *Spectator* 6 Feb. 229/2 A youngster who went to sea as apprentice and finished bucko mate of a Yankee packet. 1927 *Blackw. Mag.* Jan. 5/1 A great big bucko of a man.

Buckshee (bɒ·kʃi). *Army slang.* [Alteration of BAKSHEESH.] An allowance above the usual amount, as extra rations; hence *attrib.* or as *adj.*, and *adv.*, gratuitous(ly), free, gratis.

1916 *Daily Mail* 1 Nov. 4/4 'Buckshee' (probably derived from back-sheesh, meaning extra rations, or anything over after an issue has been made—buckshee loaf, buckshee 'fags', etc.). 1919 *War Terms* in *Athenæum* 1 Aug. 695/2 'Buckshee' deserves attention as probably, with 'scrounge', the most popular slang towards the end of the war. 1920 *Outward Bound* Nov. 66/2 The police help themselves freely to buckshee refreshments. 1921 *Glasgow Herald* 1 Nov. 5 To..give the goods almost buckshee to our cut-throat friends, the tribesmen of the N.-W. Frontier of India. 1927 *Ibid.* 27 Dec. 8 There is a curious relish in the action, for, of course, it is all 'buckshee' virtue.

Buck-shot. 2. Add: **buckshot soil** *U.S.* (see quot.); **buckshot war** *U.S.*, an outbreak in Pennsylvania in 1838, arising out of election disputes, so called because orders were issued to the troops to have cartridges loaded with 'buckshot and ball'.

1871 R. SOMERS *Southern States since War* 144 The soil is a dry deep red loam—what is called, in the language of the country [*sc.* the state of Mississippi], a '*buckshot soil', with a good deal of lime in it. 1842 *Congress. Globe* 16 June 609/1 Mr. Benton believed that was the phrase used in Pennsylvania, in time of the *buckshot war. 1871 SCHELE DE VERE *Americanisms* (1872) 279 A Whiskey War in Pennsylvania..followed by the so-called Buckshot War.

Buckskin. Add:

1. (Later U.S. example.)

1876 J. H. BEADLE *Western Wilds* xxxi. 510 They finally gave him some buckskins, and then began skinning the ox.

4. Also *attrib.*

1783 FRENEAU *Poems* (1809) II. 147 Teach me to take the true-born Buckskin side. 1835 R. M. BIRD *Hawks of Hawk-hollow* I. iii. 42 It was there sir, I first looked in the face of George Washington—a poor colonial Buckskin colonel then.

5. A horse of the colour of buckskin. *U.S.*

1889 *Century Dict.* 1891 H. C. BUNNER *Zadoc Pine* etc. 174 The man on the queer-looking buckskin..is McAlpine. 1894 *Outing* (U.S.) XXIV. 101/2 That Clip of hers (she's got him back now) is a pretty mustang. He's a bright buckskin with a dark stripe. 1910 W. M. RAINE *B. O'Connor* 40 The young man riding townward on a wiry buckskin.

6. A kind of strong twill cloth.

1894 *Tailoring* 3 Feb. 1/1 Coatings.—Black and Blue Serges, cut and covered in every size of twill,...Buckskins, 10s. 1895 *Oracle Encycl.* I. 518/2 *Buckskin*, a strong twilled woollen fabric for trouserings. The web is usually about 27 inches wide, and when finished the pile or nap is so shorn that the texture is seen through it.

7. As *adj.* Of the colour of buckskin, *spec.* of a horse. *U.S.*

1874 *Rep. Vermont Board Agric.* II. 402 The buckskin McClellan was a regular hollow or swayback. 1899 T. HALL *Tales* 263 'Buckskin Nell', they called her, because of the buckskin pony she rode with all the dash and skill of a cowboy. 1902 MCFAUL *Ike Glidden* iii. 23 Only thing he has against him's his color; says he can't bear buckskin.

Buckstick (bɒ·kstik). *Anglo-Ind.* [f. BUCK *sb.*9 or *v.*8 + STICK *sb.*1 12.] A braggart, boaster.

1924 *Blackw. Mag.* Apr. 451/2 He was..a bit of a self-conscious play-actor, of the order of 'bucksticks'.

Buck-tail. *U.S.* [BUCK *sb.*1 1.]

1. The tail of a buck.

1815 [implied in 2]. 1885 C. L. NORTON in *Mag. Amer. Hist.* XIII. 98 The members wore bucktails in their hats. 1889 *Harper's Mag.* May 977/2 The citizens who march and sing nonsense,..or wear a corn-skin or a buck-tail, are in deadly earnest.

2. A member of a political faction, originating in New York in 1815, the members of which wore buck-tails in their hats. Also *attrib.*

1820 B. F. BUTLER in W. L. Mackenzie *Lives Butler & Hoyt* (1845) 26 We have no Commissioner at our village (the men fit for it being chiefly Bucktails). *Ibid.* 27 Education, habit, inclination, and principle, all conspire to make me a Bucktail. 1842 J. D. HAMMOND *Hist. Polit. Parties* (1852) I. 451 The party opposed to the administration of Mr. Clinton were for a long time called the Bucktail Party. *Ibid.* 460 The New York Bucktails..formed an organized opposition. 1845 W. L. MACKENZIE *Lives Butler & Hoyt* 129 Walter [Bowne] was a delegate to the bucktail convention at Herkimer in 1828.

3. *pl.* A Pennsylvanian regiment which took part in the Civil War.

1863 O. J. VICTOR *Hist. Southern Rebell.* II. 470 (Th.) The Kentuckians first showed themselves, when the fiery Bucktails advanced upon them. 1876 *Southern Hist. Soc. Papers* I. 436 We awaited with beating hearts, the sure and steady approach of the 'Pennsylvania Bucktails'.

Buckwheat. Add: **1. b.** *attrib.* esp. *buckwheat cake* (U.S.); also *buckwheat meal, straw.*

1774 J. ADAMS *Diary* 21 Sept. (1850) II. 381 Mrs. Yard entertained us with muffins, *buckwheat cakes, and common toast. 1809 W. IRVING *Knickerb.* II. 187 To these..we are indebted for the invention of slap-jacks, or buckwheat cakes. 1831 PECK *Guide for Emigrants* II. 152 Pancakes..are a fine substitute for the buck-wheat cakes of New-Jersey. 1872 EGGLESTON *Hoosier Schoolm.* xxii. 156 Ralph was doing..justice to his Aunt Matilda's hot buckwheat cakes. 1787 WASHINGTON *Diaries* II. 230 That *Buck Wheat Meal made into a wash is most excellent to lay on fat upon hogs. *a* 1793 FRENEAU *Poems* (1809) II. 205 The horse..Not fed with oats, but filled with wind, And *buckwheat straw.

c. *ellipt.* = buckwheat cake.

1854 in Brewster *Life of J. T. Whitney* (1909) 141. 1859 S. S. COX *Eight Yrs. Congress* (1865) 114 Even our Quakers are willing to drink cheap damnation in their coffee-cups, and eat it on their buckwheats. 1904 G. H. LORIMER *Old Gorgon Graham* 227 A fellow'll load up with pie and buckwheats for breakfast, and go around wondering about his stomach-ache.

Bu·ckwood. *U.S.* [BUCK *sb.*1 1.] The Buckeye or American chestnut.

1797 MORSE *Amer. Gazetteer* (1810) s.v. *Ohio*, Hickory, cherry, buckwood or horse chesnut, [etc.].

Bucolicism (biuko·lisiz'm). [f. BUCOLIC + -ISM.] Bucolic qualities or characteristics; the bucolic style.

1879 M. PATTISON *Milton* iii. 41 This factitious bucolicism is pervaded by a pathos, which, like volcanic heat, has fused into a new compound the dilapidated débris of the Theocritean world. 1893 *Temple Bar* Jan. 63 Beer, brandy and bucolicism notwithstanding.

Bud, *sb.*1 Add: **3. d.** A girl who is just 'coming out'; a débutante. Also more fully *bud of promise. U.S.*

1881 [see 3 b]. 1888 *Charlestown Enterprise* (Farmer) The young, unmarried girl, in sport, is called a bud of promise. 1889 *Harper's Mag.* Sept. 571/1 As dashing a belle as there was in the rooms—not a bud—a belle of some six or seven years standing. 1894 *Outing* (U.S.) Apr. 43/1 [Picture of] A Chinese bud. 1903 *N. Y. Tribune* 4 Oct., Among the latter [*sc.* the debutantes] will be Miss Enid Shaw, the only bud of the Cabinet circle.

Bud, *sb.*3 *U.S.* [Childish or negro pron. of BROTHER. Cf. *BUB *sb.*5] Brother, used as a form of address.

1851 *Polly Peasblossom's Wedd.* 19 (Th.) 'An't you joking, bud?' asked Polly of her boy brother. 1889 *Harper's Mag.* Aug. 459/1 He said that his name was 'Bud' Lightwood...'It's *brother*', he said..'" bud" and "sis", you know.' 1896 J. C. HARRIS *Sister Jane* 99 Just tell Mandy that Bud wants to see her. 1920 MULFORD *J. Nelson* iv. 46 But, say, bud, we don't have to go to Highbank at all.

Also **Bu·ddy**, in the same sense.

1850 'PREMIUM' *Eight Years Brit. Guiana* 218 Buddy (brother) how you can fink me sha' talk so to you? 1897 *Scribner's Mag.* Dec. 727/1 Say, Buddy, you ain't a pedler, are you? 1920 MULFORD *J. Nelson* iv. 45 'I agree with you, buddy,' answered Johnny.

Budda (bɒ·dă). Also **buddah.** [Native name.] An Australian myoporaceous plant, *Pholidia mitchelli.*

1902 WEBSTER, *Suppl.* 1911 BEAN '*Dreadnought' of Darling* xv. 141 A feathery little bunch of light green..which we often saw along the Darling banks; the stumpy budda. 1923 *Chambers's Jrnl.* 24/2 The air was rich with the scent of sandalwood and buddah.

Buddawong, variant of *BURRAWANG.

Buddleia (bɒdlī·ă, bɒ·dliă). *Bot.* [mod.L., f. the name of Adam *Buddle* (died 1715), botanist; see -IA 1.] Any plant of the genus of shrubs and trees of this name, natives of America, Asia, and South Africa, introduced in 1774; esp. the orange ball tree *B. globosa*, an ornamental shrub bearing orange-coloured globose flowers.

1885 *Encycl. Brit.* XVIII. 673/2 The *Buddleia*..flourishes at a height of 12,000 feet round the shores of Lake Titicaca [Peru]. 1924 *Blackw. Mag.* Apr. 446/1 Red admirals in August sunning themselves on the buddleia. 1927 *Times* (weekly ed.) 22 Sept. 327/3 Purple buddleia.

Budgeree (bɒ·dʒəri). *Austral.* Also **budgery, boojery, boodjer-ree.** [Native word: cf. next.] Good, excellent.

1793 J. HUNTER *Port Jackson* viii. 213 They very frequently, at the conclusion of the dance, would apply to us..for marks of our approbation..which we never failed to give by often

repeating the word *boojery*, which signifies good; or *boojery caribberie*, a good dance. 1848 HAYGARTH *Bush Life in Australia* x. 112 A black..has at once declared it to be 'bale budgery' (no good). *Ibid.* xii. 134 'Budgery you' (clever fellow, you), said the black.

Budgerigar (bɒ·dʒərigāɹ). Also **betcherrygah, betshiregah, budgregore, budgery garr, budgeragar, budgereg(h)ar, bougirigard, (beauregard).** [Native Australian ('Port Jackson dialect', Morris *Austral English*), f. *budgeri, boodgeri* good + *gar* cockatoo.] The grass or zebra parakeet, *Melopsittacus undulatus.*

1847 LEICHHARDT *Overland Exped.* 297 The Betshiregah (Melopsittacus undulatus, *Gould*) were very numerous. 1848 HAYGARTH *Bush Life in Australia* xii. 139 A most brilliant little parrot..about the size of a bullfinch,..called the budgery garr. 1857 W. HOWITT *Tallangetta* ii. I. 48 Young paroquets, the green leeks, and the lovely speckled budgregores. 1857 HORT in *Life & Lett.* (1896) I. 388 A small green creature like a miniature cockatoo, called a Budgeragar. 1889 *Times* 16 Feb. 4/3 Crystal Palace Cagebird Show 1889...Two Australian budgerigars. 1922 E. V. LUCAS *Genevra's Money* xix. 132 Little foreign birds for the most part, avadavats, Java sparrows, budgerigars.

Budget, *sb.* Add:

2. d. A pouch or pocket used by carpenters and tilers for carrying nails.

1849–50 WEALE *Dict. Terms* 1874 KNIGHT *Dict. Mech.*

7. budget-trimmer, a man who prepares and fixes in position the leather fittings on coaches and carriages.

1881 *Instr. Census Clerks* (1885) 184. 1909 *Daily Chron.* 4 Mar. 4/7 Wanted..Budget Trimmers, accustomed to head work. 1921 *Dict. Occup. Terms* (1927) § 504.

Budget, *v.* Substitute for **b**:

intr. To draw up or prepare a budget (BUDGET *sb.* 4); esp. *for* a certain supply or establishment, or *for* a particular financial result.

1884 *Daily News* 9 Oct. 4/6 An army of 6,000 men and a force of 7,757 police were budgeted for in 1883. 1893 *Ibid.* 24 Mar. 5/6 Although the Government of India are most unwilling to budget for a deficit. 1900 *Westm. Gaz.* 23 Mar. 2/2 Every Chancellor of the Exchequer budgets with the fear of the Irish members before his [eyes]. 1901 *Ibid.* 4 June 2/2 When Sir Michael Hicks-Beach Budgeted for 1901–1902. 1922 G. A. GREENWOOD *England to-day* 28 There..is the inevitable wear and tear of the home to be budgeted for.

Add: **c.** To arrange for in a budget.

1890 *Sat. Rev.* 16 Aug. 191/1 General revenue, as budgeted for the years 1890–91, does not maintain the improvement of the previous year. 1909 *Westm. Gaz.* 10 Feb. 2/3 A budgeted decrease for the whole year of 2 millions. 1909 D. LLOYD GEORGE in *Daily Chron.* 23 Oct. 1/1 The increment duty, which I budgetted to yield £50,000 this year.

Budzat (bɒ·dzāt). *Anglo-Indian.* Also **budsart.** [a. Hindustani بدذات *badzāt* 'evil-race', low-born, f. Pers. *bad* evil + Arab. ذات *dāt* substance, nature.] A low fellow, scoundrel, blackguard.

1863 TREVELYAN *Compet. Wallah* (1866) 156, I had provided myself with one disparaging epithet, which seldom came amiss, 'Budzart'. *Ibid.* 248 The murders were perpetrated by the 'budzarts,' or black sheep, of the regiment. 1863 — *Dawk Bungalow* 1, Why the shaitan [devil] didn't you come before, you lary old budzart?

Buff, *sb.*2 Add:

5. b. In full *Buff Cochin*, a variety of the Cochin fowl, in which both cock and hen are of a uniform buff colour.

1855 *Poultry Chron.* III. 173 Our old friends, the Cochins, mustered pretty strong,..the buffs..were very good. 1872 L. WRIGHT *Bk. Poultry* 210 We have several shades in the Buff Cochin cock. *Ibid.* 213 The earliest and greatest breeders of Buff Cochins. 1899 NORRIS-ELYE *Brahmas & Cochins* 61 Evenness of colour is perhaps the greatest difficulty in breeding..buff Cochins.

6. (Royal assent was given to the restoration of buff facings to the East Kent Regiment on 19 August, 1890.)

Buff, *sb.*7 Short for *BUFFALO 1 e.

1879 *The Buffalo* 16 Jan. 3/3 The great scheme of a technical university now being taken up by the City companies, was first started by Buffs. 1897 *Buffalo World* Sept. 3/2 It should..be the aim of every loyal Buff..to show his desire to help on the cause for which we are fighting, viz. Progress and the Brotherhood of man. 1909 *Daily Chron.* 31 July 4/6 A..belief..that the 'Buffs,' as it is generally called, originated at the Harp Tavern, in Russell-street, Drury-lane, in 1822, where about this time a convivial club was held, with the somewhat appropriate title of the 'City of Lushington.'

Buff, *v.*3 Add: **2.** To impart a buff colour to.

1897 ROTHWELL *Textile Fabrics* 237 The pieces are to be 'buffed' or 'slop-padded' with substantive dyestuffs in solutions containing soap.

Buffalo, *sb.* Add:

1. c. (Earlier examples.)

1635 *Relat. Maryland* iii. 23 In the upper parts of the countrey there are Bufeloes, Elkes, Lions, Beares, Wolues, and Deare there are in great Store. 1743 CATESBY *Nat. Hist. Carolina* etc. (1754) II. App. p. xxvii, *Bison Americanus*, the Bufalo. 1770 WASHINGTON *Diaries* I. 424 On this Creek many Buffaloes use, according to the Indians acc[oun]t.

d. *collect.*

1770 WASHINGTON *Diaries* I. 427 This Country abounds in Buffalo and wild game of all kinds. 1817 S. R. BROWN *Western Gaz.* 30 The buffaloe..have lately disappeared. *a* 1861 T. WINTHROP *John Brent* xxvi. 275 We crowded through the buffalo. 1895 C. KING *Fort Frayne* xviii. 260 A deep cleft in the foothills through which the buffalo in bygone days had made their way.

e. A member of the Royal Antediluvian Order of Buffaloes, founded *c* 1875 for the purpose of promoting brotherhood among men. Hence **Bu·ffaloism.**

1879 *The Buffalo* 16 Jan. 3/3 Bro. Barrett, the Buffalo Bootmaker of Walworth. 1881 (*title*) The Buffalo Review and Lodge Reporter. 1897 *Daily News* 16 Mar. 8/3 A room in which certain 'Buffaloes' were holding a lodge meeting. 1897 *Buffalo World* Sept. 3/1 Buffaloism can boast an existence of 300 years at least.

f. A leather hamper used for carrying the bobbins used in cotton-manufacture.

1874 KNIGHT *Dict. Mech.*, *Buffalo*,..a hamper of buffalo-leather used in a factory to convey bobbins from the throstle.

3. (Earlier example.)

1840 *Knickerbocker Mag.* Apr. XV. 326 Don't forgit to Put in as many Seats as you can, and All your Buffaloes.

5. (Earlier and additional examples.)

Also *buffalo-bull, -calf, -cart, -cow, -hide, -horn, -hump, -hunt, -hunter, -hunting*, etc.

1805 T. M. HARRIS *State of Ohio* 179 There are found open cleared spots on the summit of hills, called '*Buffaloe beats' because supposed to be occasioned by the resort of those animals thither in fly time. 1827 J. F. COOPER *Prairie* ix, The man who denies that *buffalo beef is good should scorn to eat it. 1846 SAGE *Scenes Rocky Mts.* (1859) 69 A good supply of buffalo-beef. 1805 *Massachusetts Spy* 17 July 2/3 Scions of a new discovered berry, called the *buffaloe berry. 1846 SAGE *Scenes Rocky Mts.* (1859) 257 Buffalo-berry... This berry is about the size of and similar in shape to the common currant, there are three kinds, the white, yellow, and red. 1887 I. R. *Ranche Life Montana* 20 Two afternoons we spent in *buffalo-berrying and shooting combined. 1844 J. GREGG *Commerce on Prairies* I. 65 On some occasions caravans have been obliged to construct what is called a *buffalo boat, which is done by stretching the hides of these animals over a frame of poles, or, what is still more common, over an empty wagon-body. 1881 A. A. HAYES *New Colorado* x. 138 Men being sent ahead..to fabricate 'buffalo boats' of hides stretched over frames of poles and empty wagon bodies. 1841 CATLIN *N. Amer. Indians* I. 72 The *buffalo bushes, which are peculiar to these northern regions, lined the banks of the river. 1889 FARMER *Americanisms*, *Buffalo-bush*,..a shrub, the fruit of which is called the bull-berry. 1901 *Wide World Mag.* VIII. 206/2 The annexed photo. represents a Philippine *buffalo-cart, used for conveying women and children over the awful roads of the interior. 1846 E. BRYANT *What I saw in California* (1849) 84 Bacon broiled on a stick over a fire of *buffalo chips. 1903 S. E. WHITE *Forest* iv. 35, I once slept..before a fire of dried buffalo chips and mesquite. 1871 SCHELE DE VERE *Americanisms* (1872) 367 *Buffalo-cider is the ludicrous name given to the liquid in the stomach of the buffalo, which the thirsty hunter drinks, when he has killed his game at a great distance from water. 1785 WASHINGTON *Diaries* II. 426 Also sowed about a tablespoonful of the *Buffalo or Kentucke Clover. 1788 M. CUTLER in *Life, Jrnls. & Corr.* (1888) II. 285, I likewise wish particularly to know what you find the May-apple, Rich-weed, and Buffalo-clover to be. 1835 J. H. INGRAHAM *South-West* II. 88 The white clover of Kentucky, known by the name of Buffalo clover. 1860 HOLLAND *Miss Gilbert's Career* vii. 117 With whip in hand and *buffalo-coat still unbuttoned. 1922 ALICE BROWN *Old Crow* vii. 71 He saw Jerry Slate there..enveloped in the buffalo coat he had worn through the winter months. 1807–8 W. IRVING *Salmagundi* xii. 302 This spot was inhabited by a race of aborigines, who..danced *buffalo dances. 1841 CATLIN *N. Amer. Indians* I. 83 The head and horns of a buffalo..which he uses as a mask when called upon..to join in the buffalo dance. 1784 J. FILSON *Kentucke* 26 The fish common to the waters of the Ohio are the *buffalo-fish, of a large size, and the catfish. 1822 J. WOODS *English Prairie* 337 We had no *buffalo gnats. 1837 W. IRVING *Capt. Bonneville* (1895) I. 32 Excessively annoyed by musquitos and buffalo gnats. 1904 *Westm. Gaz.* 11 Aug. 8/1 The minute black fly of the Mississippi Valley, commonly known as the buffalo-gnat, from a fancied resemblance in outline to the buffalo. 1831 PECK *Guide for Emigrants* II. 103 Horses find..*buffalo grass..and other herbage for the summer range. 1845 FREMONT *Exped.* 209 The short sward of the buffalo grass which now prevailed everywhere. 1870 *Amer. Naturalist* III. 162 The Buffalo grass..does not grow more than three or four inches high. 1837 W. IRVING *Capt. Bonneville* (1895) I. 146 Their united force was not sufficient to venture on the *buffalo grounds. 1807 P. GASS *Jrnl.* 45 Their band of musick, or orchestra, was composed of about twelve persons beating on a *buffalo hide. 1895 *Century Mag.* Sept. 694/1 He..was required to procure a buffalo-hide from which the hair had been removed. 1841 CATLIN *N. Amer. Indians* I. 24 Mounted on his favorite *buffalo horse (i. e. the horse amongst his whole group which is best trained to run the buffalo). 1868 *Amer. Naturalist* II. 215 The Indians offer a big price (a large buffalo horse) for the dog. 1859 BARTLETT *Dict. Amer.* (ed. 2), *Buffalo nut (*Pyrularia oleifera*), oil nut. Western. 1806 T. ASHE *Trav. Amer.* xxxvii. (1808) 305 There was no possibility of ascending them..except through *buffalo-paths. 1846 SAGE *Scenes Rocky Mts.* (1859) 151 We continued our course by a winding buffalo-path. 1837 W. IRVING *Capt. Bonneville* (1895) I. 33 They had reached also a great *buffalo range. 1859 MARCY *Prairie Traveler* v. 161 It will be a wise precaution in passing through the buffalo range, to lay in a supply of jerked meat for future exigencies. 1750 T. WALKER *Jrnl. of Exploration* 3 Apr. (1888) 44 To the Eastward are many small Mountains, and a *Buffaloe Road between them and the Ridge. 1832 *Louisville Directory* 106 There would be found about a certain distance and course from a well known buffalo road a beech tree. 1849 PRITTS *Mirror Border Life* 434 It was about one hundred yards from a large buffalo road. 1806 PIKE *Sources Mississ.* 9 Feb. 68 The rider wraps himself up in a *buffalo robe..., having a cushion to lean his back against. 1845 FREMONT *Exped.* 145 It is only within a very recent period that they have received buffalo robes in trade. 1869 S. BOWLES *Our New West* v. 100 My bedding..consisted of two pairs of heavy blankets, a buffalo robe, a rubber blanket and a pillow. 1878 J. H. BEADLE *Western Wilds* ix. 131 The surface..is largely dotted with '*buffalo stamps'. These are said to have been caused by buffaloes..stamping and licking the ground. 1837 R. M. BIRD *Nick of Woods* I. 38 You've as..broad a trace before you as man and beast could make,..a *buffalo-street through the canes. 1832 *Louisville Directory* 106 The party..turned off the road some 300 yards about west of the *buffalo trace. 1887 *Harper's Mag.* June 48/1 A broad smooth turnpike that has replaced the ancient buffalo trace. 1841 CATLIN *N. Amer. Indians* II. 18 We will take that *buffalo trail, where the travelling herds have slashed down the high grass. 1878 J. H. BEADLE *Western Wilds* iv. 66 We descended through a side gorge into the canon of the Cimarron, winding along a buffalo trail. 1843 FREMONT *Exped.* 21 In the *buffalo..wallows, I remarked saline efflorescences. 1875 *Fur, Fin & Feather* 109 We made a little fire in an old buffalo wallow. 1901 S. E. WHITE *Westerners* vii. 46 Drinking muddy water from buffalo wallows which providential rains had filled. 1846 SAGE *Scenes Rocky Mts.* (1859) 79 The big white, or *buffalo wolf.

b. buffalo-bean, a milk vetch of the western United States (*Astragalus crassicarpus*); **buffalo-horn**, an African tree (*Zizyphus mucronata*).

1911 WEBSTER, *Buffalo bean*, the ground plum. 1922 *Chambers's Jrnl.* 219/1, I..became acquainted with a creeping plant that grows a bean...I have since heard it called buffalo-bean. 1887 MOLONEY *Forestry W. Afr.* 300 *Buffalo-Horn' (*Zizyphus mucronata*, Willd.).

Bu·ffalo, *v. U.S. slang.* [f. the sb.] *trans.* To overpower, overawe, or constrain by superior force or influence.

1904 *N. Y. Even. Post* 25 Oct. 10 All the rest [of the newspapers] were what we used to term in the Southwest 'buffaloed' by the McKinley myth—that is, silenced by the fear of incurring the resentment of a people taught to regard McKinley as a saint. 1910 W. M. RAINE *B. O'Connor* 77 O'Connor admitted that he was 'buffaloed' when he attempted an analysis of his unusual feeling. 1913 MULFORD *Coming of Cassidy* xiii. 214 It ain't his fault that Waffles buffaloed you fellers out of th' Hills, is it? 1920 BOK *Americanization of Ed. Bok* (1921) 321 That fellow Bok certainly has the women buffaloed for good.

Buffe (buf). [See BUFF *sb.*5] In ancient armour, a chin piece pierced with breathing-holes, worn with the burgonet.

1600 [see BUFF *sb.*5]. 1885 *Fairholt's Costume* (ed. 3) II. 102 A separate and distinct chin-piece called a *buffe* is so often associated with it [*sc.* the burgonet]. 1909 C. FFOULKES *Arm. & Weapons* iv. 83 The face-guard, when used with the burgonet, is called the Buffe. 1922 *Daily Tel.* 12 June 20/3 The 'Buffe' of French 16th century work, which belongs to the 'Colbert' casque.

Bu·ffel. *U.S.* [var. BUFFLE.] A small North American duck, *Charitonetta* (*Bucephala*) *albeola.* Also called *buffel duck*, *BUFFLEHEAD, etc.

1731 CATESBY *Nat. Hist. Carolina*, etc. (1754) I. 95 The Buffel's Head Duck. *Ibid.*, The length and looseness of these feathers make the head appear bigger than it is, which seems to have given it the name of Buffel's Head, that animal's head appearing very big by its being covered with very thick long hair. 1784–7 PENNANT *Arctic Zool.* (1792) II. 283 Buffel Duck. *a* 1813 A. WILSON & BONAP. *Amer. Ornith.* (1831) IV. 351 Red headed buffel duck.

Buffer 2. Add:

2. buffer-state, in international politics, a state lying between two others, owing allegiance to neither, and serving as a means of preventing hostile collision between them. So *buffer-duchy, -zone.*

[1876 B. FRERE in Worsfold *Life* (1923) 43 Using the Afghans as a 'buffer' to avoid immediate contact between our frontier and the Russian.] 1883 *Daily News* 27 July 5/1 The 'buffer' State—to borrow a simile from Indo-Afghan politics. 1897 *Daily News* 30 Dec. 5/5 Buffer States are of not the slightest real use. 1908 *Westm. Gaz.* 7 May 1/3 A 'buffer' zone, inhabited by independent tribes, lies between the boundaries of British India and Afghanistan. 1920 *Discovery* May 133/2 That treaty settlement of neutrality which regulated the status of Luxemburg as a buffer-duchy.

3. *buffer-bank, -salt*; **buffer-block**, (*a*) a framework of timber set up at the end of a railway line or siding; (*b*) a block on the end of a coach, which acts as a buffer; (*c*) the flat head of a buffer; **buffer-box, -case**, the case which encloses the buffer-rod and -spring; **buffer-knot**, an arrangement of two knots joining two parts of a fisherman's line in which the strain is taken by a piece of waxed silk which acts as a buffer; **buffer-plunger**, the portion of a buffer which slides in the buffer-case and carries the shock to the spring; **buffer-stop** = *buffer-block* (a).

1900 *Westm. Gaz.* 21 Aug. 6/1 The accident at Kent House Station, near Penge (in which a train ran into a *buffer-bank, injuring eleven people). 1889 *Century Dict.*, *Buffer-block. 1892 *Daily News* 14 Jan. 3/4 The effect was to cause the waggon furthest from the engine to mount the fixed buffer block. 1874 KNIGHT *Dict. Mech.* s.v. *Buffer*, The buffer bar or beam is attached to the framework of the car, and carries the *buffer-box, in which is the buffer-rod. 1880 *Engineering* XXX. 294 Projections h' on the *buffer case. 1885 TREHERNE in Pennell *Fishing* (Badm.) 41 Although I can lay no claim to be the inventor of the '*buffer knot', I can honestly say that I had never seen or heard of it before. 1895 BICKERDYKE *Sea Fishing* (Badm.) 69 The buffer knot is another good one;..I learnt the way of tying it, shown in the illustration, from an Irish friend, who has greatly improved on the old original buffer. 1880 *Engineering* XXX. 294 Tijou's mode of securing *buffer plungers. 1922 *Encycl. Brit.* XXXI. 59/1 Recent investigation suggests that death [after a long fast] will be due to acid poisoning, and it is stated that the administration of what are called '*buffer salts', for example acid phosphate of sodium, is instrumental in postponing the fatal issue. 1878 *Engineer* XLVI. 7 The standard *buffer stop on the London and South-Western Railway. 1906 *Westm. Gaz.* 30 July 7/3 The Reading train..ran into the buffer-stop with considerable force.

Buffer 3. Add:

d. A farrier's shoeing tool having a blunt chisel at one end to remove clinch nails and a point at the other to punch out nails embedded in the hoof.

1902 'VIOLET JACOB' *Sheep-stealers* xiv, A smith's buffer.

Buffer (bɒ·fəɹ), *v.* [f. BUFFER 2.] *trans.* To lessen the impact of, as by means of a buffer.

1894 *Speaker* 16 June 658/1 The crude..opinionativeness of the permanent official—which is used to being discounted and buffered by a lay chief.

Buffering (bɒ·fəriŋ), *vbl. sb.* [f. BUFFER 2 or *v.* + -ING 1.] The action of bringing the buffers into play; also, buffers collectively.

1898 *Times* 6 Jan. 7 The buffering up of the wagons caused one of them to tilt over. 1928 *Daily Express* 29 Dec. 9/4 The use of side buffering with screw couplings.

Buffing, *vbl. sb.*2 Add: **c.** The operation of reducing the thickness of a hide by shaving off the grain surface with a currier's knife or splitting-machine; also, the thin pieces of leather so removed. Also *Comb.*, as *buffing-machine, buffing-slicker.*

1884 KNIGHT *Dict. Mech.* Suppl., *Buffing* (leather), taking off thin shavings from the grain side with a buffing-slicker until the skin is very thin; the object being to make cowhide imitate calfskin. The operation is finished by whitening. 1885 C. T. DAVIS *Leather* (1897) 444 The buffings which are not required for japanning are sold in russet for making stained buffings. 1920 *Chambers's Jrnl.* Sept. 622/1 Leather buffings and shavings.

Buffish (bɒ·fiʃ), *a.* [f. BUFF *a.* + -ISH 1.] Somewhat buff, approaching buff in colour; also in comb. with other adjs. of colour.

1896 *Brit. Birds, Their Nests & Eggs* I. 3 The cheeks..are buffish white. 1900 ELINOR GLYN *Visits Eliz.* 38 Harvey announced 'Mrs. and the Misses Clarke,' and a thin, very high-nosed person, followed by two buffish girls, came forward. 1902 — *Refl. Ambrosine* 83 Terra-cotta and buffish brocade. 1910 *Westm. Gaz.* 29 Jan. 11/1 The white and buffish brown or ashy streaks..of his plumage.

Bufflehead. Add:

2. A species of wild duck. *U.S.* (See next.)

1870 *Amer. Naturalist* IV. 49 Buffel Head (*Bucephala albeola* Baird). 1874 J. W. LONG *Amer. Wild-fowl Shooting* Introd. 16 In the deep water varieties..I shall treat of the..buffle-head or butter-ball. *Ibid.* xxix. 281 Buffle-heads are exceedingly quick-motioned in all their action.

Buffle-headed, *a.* Add:

3. *U.S.* (See quots. and prec.)

a 1813 A. WILSON & BONAP. *Amer. Ornith.* (1831) III. 232 *Anas albeola*..Buffel-headed Duck. 1840 *Cuvier's Anim. Kingd.* 264 The little Buffel-headed Garrot (*Anas albeola* Lin.), common in North America, is nearly allied [to the Golden-eyed Garrot]. 1874 J. W. LONG *Amer. Wild-fowl Shooting* 279 Buffle-headed Duck (*Fuligula alveola*).

Buffum (bɒ·fŏm). [Origin obscure.] A mixture of inferior oils used to adulterate linseed oil.

1882 *Encycl. Brit.* XIV. 677/1.

Buffy (bɒ·fi), *a.*2 *slang.* [Origin obscure.] Intoxicated, squiffy.

1859 S. BROOKS *Story of Gordian Knot* viii, I must have conducted myself with extreme propriety, and not as you did at the Clissolds, when you came in buffy. 1866 YATES *Land at Last* I. vi, Flexor was fine and buffy when he came home last night. 1871 BESANT & RICE *Ready-money Mort.* xlii, When I feel a little buffy, in the morning. 1924 A. HUXLEY *Little Mexican* 225 She did like boasting about the amount of champagne she could put away without getting buffy.

Bug, *sb.*2 Add:

1. (Earlier U.S. example.)

1785 WASHINGTON *Diaries* II. 404 Indeed some kind of fly, or bug, had begun to prey upon the leaves before I left home.

b. A crazy idea; a craze. *U.S. slang.*

a 1909 'O. HENRY' *Roads of Destiny* xiii. 208 He's got bugs. Sitting on ice and calling his best friends pseudonyms. 1911 R. D. SAUNDERS *Col. Todhunter* ix. 123 He's perfectly harmless. He's got a bug on political celebrities, sir.

3. bug-hunter *colloq.*, one who engages in the collection of entomological specimens, an entomologist; more widely, a naturalist; so **bug-hunting; bug-juice** *U.S.*, bad whisky; **bug-trap** *Naut. slang* (see quot.).

1889 MARY E. BAMFORD *Up & down Brooks* 46 It seems sometimes to the *bug-hunter as though there would be but very few vacant rooms to rent in Nature's house. 1893 SIR J. D. HOOKER in *Bates' Nat. Amazon* Mem. p. xlviii, From Darwin to the merest bug-hunter. 1898 KIRKE *25 Yrs. Brit. Guiana* 171 A bug-hunter who visited the Demerara River had been assisted by Blunt. 1855 KINGSLEY *Glaucus* 7 The naturalist was looked on as a harmless enthusiast, who went '*bug-hunting', simply because he had not spirit to follow a fox. 1905 *Westm. Gaz.* 19 May 4/2 The pursuit that in schoolboy days of irreverence we used to call 'bug-hunting'. *a* 1877 *Osborne* (Kansas) *Farmer* (Bartlett) We have taken..*bug juice on subscriptions in our time. 1889 FARMER *Americanisms*, *Bug-juice*, the Schlechter whiskey of the Pennsylvania Dutch—a very inferior spirit. Also called *bug-poison*. These terms are now applied to bad whiskey of all kinds. 1897 KIPLING *Capt. Cour.* 140 A fifteen-gallon cask o' bug-juice. 1901 S. E. WHITE *Westerners* xxxiv. 313 'Plain case of bug-juice,' said one. 1895 *Boy's Own Paper* XVII. 427/1 Small vessels are..commonly called '*bug-traps', because they soon get filled up with cockroaches.

Bug, *v.*1 *U.S. colloq.* [f. BUG *sb.*2 1.] **a.** *intr.* (see quot. 1889). **b.** To clear (plants, etc.) of insects.

1877 *Rep. Vermont Board Agric.* IV. 113 This 'bugging the potatoes'..was the only effectual mode of combatting these insects. 1889 *Century Dict.*, *Bug*.., to hunt for bugs; collect or destroy insects: chiefly in the present participle: as, to go bugging. 1895 *Voice* (N. Y.) 8 Aug. 7/6 While 'bugging' potatoes this season I came across a number of beetles..that I have never seen any mention of.

Bug, *v.*2 *U.S. intr.* To bulge *out.*

1884 'MARK TWAIN' *Huck. Finn* xix, Jim's eyes bugged out, when he heard that; and I reckon mine did too. 1902 O. WISTER *Virginian* xxii. 408 Can't you tell a man what's making your eyes bug out so?

Bugaboo. Add: **c.** Loud talk, insolence.

1914 G. B. SHAW in *N. Y. Times Current Hist.* 12 Dec. 22 Smouldering revolt against swank and domineer, gaff and bugaboo.

Bugeye. *U.S.* [? f. BUG *sb.*2 1.] = *BUCK-EYE 4.

1889 [see *BUCK-EYE 4]. 1894 *Columbus* (O.) *Dispatch* 17 Oct., A small skiff..was coming to the wharf from the Bugeye..when a heavy sea caused it to capsize.

Buggy, *sb.*1 Add: **1. b.** *attrib.*, as *buggy-cushion, -harness, -horse, -ride, -sleigh, -trip.*

1842 E. E. HALE *If, Yes & Perhaps* (1868) 84 The dear girl..agreed to go to Mrs. Pollexfen's ball that evening ready to leave it with me in my buggy sleigh. 1862 *Catal. Internat. Exhib., Brit.* II. No. 4743 Gig, carriage, and American buggy harness. 1863 *Trans. Ill. Agric. Soc.* (1865) V. 255 The one on the gang plow would have a fine buggy ride. 1874 *Rep. Vermont Board Agric.* II. 401 He had no more training than we give our common buggy horses. 1881 *Amer. Naturalist* XV. 76 On a buggy trip from Statesville to Hickory. 1900 H. LAWSON *Over Sliprails* 29 She..returned with a buggy-cushion, which she slipped under his head.

Buggy, *sb.*2 [Elliptical use of BUGGY *a.*] *Tailoring.* In a coat, the piece of lining which covers the back of the shoulders.

Known in the trade from at least *c* 1880.

Buggy, *a.* (Earlier example.)

1669 S. SEWALL *Letter Bk.* 166 Her child had a Pea in the forhead, circumstanced as a Buggy Pea uses to be.

Bu·ghouse, *a. U.S. slang.* [Cf. *BUG *sb.*2 1 b.] Crazy.

1895 *Century Mag.* June 291/2 How's that for bein' bughouse, eh? 1896 G. ADE *Artie* xvii. 161 If I don't get mine inside of a week I'll go bug-house. 1904 *N. Y. Even. Post* 4 May 6 The soldiers out here [in the Philippines] are getting 'bughouse' drinking the native wine. 1917 DOYLE *His Last Bow* (1922) 292 It's enough to make a man bughouse.

Bugle, *v.* **a.** Add: Also, to make a sound like a bugle. Also **Bu·gling** *vbl. sb.* and *ppl. a.*

1847 *Infantry Man.* (1854) 93 Too much bugling..is to be avoided. 1881 W. WILKINS *Songs of Study* 76 The cheerful fields, the bugling winds, the azure-gleaming bays. 1891 MEREDITH *One of our Conq.* iv, He blinked, bugled in his throat,..and smiled. 1895 *Chambers's Jrnl.* XII. 648/2 The eternal bugling on the Canea walls still continued.

Bugler. Add: **b.** A Tasmanian name for the trumpet-fish, bellows-fish, or snipe-fish, *Centriscus scolopax.*

1889 *Century Dict.* 1898 MORRIS *Austral Engl.*

Bugology (bɒgǫ·lŏdʒi). *U.S. humorous.* [f. BUG *sb.*2 1.] The science of 'bugs' or insects; entomology. Also **Bugo·logist.**

1843 R. CARLTON *New Purchase* I. 171 Chemistry, botany, anatomy, conchology, bugology. 1888 *Grass Valley* (Cal.) *Tidings* (Farmer) Entomology, or bugology. 1898 *Congress. Rec.* Apr., App. 455/2 Those..acquainted with bugology know there is rather a disreputable bug that looks one way and rolls the other. 1901 G. S. HALL *Confess. Psychol.* 110 The 'Bugologist'..has long been the stalking horse or awful example of..narrowness.

Bugong (bū·gǫŋ). Also **bougong.** [Native name.] An Australian noctuid moth, *Danais limniace* or *Agrotis spina*, highly prized by the natives as an article of food.

1834 G. BENNETT *Wand. N.S.W.* I. 265 It is named the 'Bugong Mountain', from the circumstance of multitudes of small moths, called Bugong by the aborigines, congregating at certain months of the year about masses of granite on this and other parts of the range. 1859 H. KINGSLEY *G. Hamlyn* xxxix, To collect and feed on the great grey moths (Bougongs) which are found on the rocks. 1878 R. B. SMYTH *Aborig. Victoria* I. 207 The Bugong moths..are greedily devoured by the natives. 1906 *Daily Chron.* 5 Oct. 8/5 No European seems to have found the courage necessary to taste bugong cakes.

Buhr, var. of BURR *sb.*5 1.

1857 *Trans. Ill. Agric. Soc.* II. 360 Edgar's mill..was for the time, a fine flouring mill, with French buhrs.

Build, *v.* Add:

3. *Built like a castle*: said of a horse having a strong and sturdy frame.

1835 SIR G. STEPHEN *Adv. Search of Horse* i, He [*sc.* a cob] was, to use the accepted phrase, 'built like a castle!' 1882 *Illustr. Sporting & Dram. News* 4 Feb. 502/1 Miss Bell's colt is built like a castle, and full of massive strength from head to heels.

b. *To be built* (*that way*, etc.): to be (so) constituted or naturally disposed. *colloq.* orig. *U.S.*

1882 *Amer. Humorist* 12 May (Farmer) Even womankind is not built as she was a few brief years ago. 1888 *Missouri Republ.* 25 Jan. (Farmer) 'Why didn't you roll down?' 'I wasn't built that way.'

c. In card-playing: (see quot. 1901). *U.S.*

1901 *Munsey's Mag.* XXIV. 871/2 To build down..is to place a card upon one of the next higher denomination. To build up..is to do just the opposite—that is, to place an eight on a seven. 1903 A. ADAMS *Log Cowboy* vi. 76, I built right up to him.

Buildable (bi·ldăb'l), *a.* [f. BUILD *v.* + -ABLE.] Capable of being built.

1927 *Times* (weekly ed.) 10 Nov. 527/3 [A design] compact, orderly and simple—and eminently buildable.

Builder. Add:

b. *Builder's paper*, a strong paper sheeting used in building. *U.S.*

1917 MATHEWSON *Sec. Base Sloan* vii. 88 Red builder's paper superseded the boards across the window frames.

c. That part of a spinning-machine which regulates the yarn as it is wound on the bobbins.

1884 MCLAREN *Spinning* (ed. 2) 136 The lifter, or builder as it is called, moves more slowly as each layer is placed on the bobbin.

Building, *vbl. sb.* **4.** Add: *building-land, -lot, -material, -mover, -stone*; **building bee** *U.S.* (see BEE 1 4); **building berth** = *building-slip*; **building-block**, (*a*) one of the temporary supports for a ship's keel while the ship is being built (Knight *Dict. Mech.* 1874); (*b*) a block of building-material (*Ibid.* Suppl. 1884); (*c*) a child's 'brick'; **building-iron**, a tool for heating and applying wax in the preparation of an electrotype mould (Knight 1884); **building motion**, in *Cotton-spinning*, apparatus for winding and shaping uniformly the roving on the bobbins of a fly frame or the yarn of a cop on a mule; **building-slip**, an inclined plane on which vessels are built (= SLIP *sb.*3 1 b); **building-wax**, beeswax used to build up the blank spaces in an electrotype mould (Knight 1884).

1849 RUXTON *Life in Far West* 237 (De Vere) A *buildin' bee or a raisin' bee is, when they want to set up the frame or the logs of a house or barn. 1902 *Encycl. Brit.* XXXII. 594/1 A framework of wood is built up over the entire *building berth. 1905 *Westm. Gaz.* 12 May 7/1 The L.C.C. purchased squares at *building-land price. 1831 PECK *Guide for Emigrants* III. 295 *Building lots sell from twenty to one hundred dollars. 1851 C. CIST *Cincinnati* 152 An effort had already been made which secured $1500 toward a building lot on which to erect the necessary edifice. 1897 *Daily News* 29 Nov. 2/5 Messrs. J. Glover and Sons, *building material dealers. 1904 *Technol. & Sci. Dict.* (ed. Goodchild & Tweney), *Building Motion. 1874 KNIGHT *Dict. Mech.*, *Building-mover, a heavy truck on rollers or wide track-wheel, used in moving houses. 1846 DODD *Brit. Manuf.* VI. 147 Every ship-yard has got one or more '*building-slips'. 1837 PECK *Gaz. Illinois* II. 116 Coal, and *building stone, are abundant.

Built, *ppl. a.* Add:

1. *esp.* in built-up, constructed of parts, esp. of parts that are separately prepared and afterwards joined or welded together; also, erected; **built-up butt**, a raised as distinguished from a sunken shooting butt; **built-up gun**, a gun whose parts are constructed separately and united in such a way that the elastic quality of the metal is fully utilized; **built-up rope** (see quot. 1908).

1829 [see BUILT *ppl. a.* 1] A built-up lens. 1865 P. BARRY *Shoeburyness & the Guns* vi. 86 The built-up system demands the same care..as the Krupp blocks. 1887 *Cassell's Fam. Mag.* 509/1 A Built-up File. 1895 G. J. BURNS *Gloss. Techn. Terms*, *Built-up beam*, a large beam built up of several smaller pieces. 1896 *Daily News* 12 Dec. 6/6 Guns with barrels all in one piece, which would require..half the expense of a built-up gun of the same size. 1904 *Westm. Gaz.* 26 Aug. 3/1 A built-up butt. 1908 *Animal Managem.* (War Office) 143 The 'built-up' [picketing] rope, a portion of which is carried by each man.

b. The simple *built* is used in the same senses.

1860 [see BUILT *ppl. a.* 1] A built gun. 1874 KNIGHT *Dict. Mech.*, *Built-beam*..., a compound beam made up of a number of planks, or thin, deep beams, laid parallel and secured together. *Ibid.*, *Built-rib*..., an arched beam made of parallel plank laid edgewise and bolted together. 1908 *Westm. Gaz.* 14 Nov. 19/2 The built all-in-one frock of lace net. 1909 *Ibid.* 20 Mar. 8/3 Three-bladed propellers of the 'built' type.

Buisson (bwi·soṅ). *Hort.* [Fr.] A fruit-tree on a very low stem with the branches closely pruned.

1881 in OGILVIE (Annandale).

Bukh, Bukk, variants of *BUCK *sb.*9, *v.*8

Bulb, *sb.* Add:

4. In full *electric light bulb*, the glass bulb-shaped container of the incandescent filament used for producing electric light in a glow lamp.

1882 *Electric Light* 1 Sept. 70/1 Volatilized carbon being deposited on the inside of the bulb. 1883 *Electrical Engineer* 1 May 14/1 A vegetable fibre..mounted on platinum electrodes and sealed into the bulb. 1890 J. W. URQUHART *Electric Light Fitting* 170 It becomes a question whether it is economical to run such blackened bulbs longer after a certain percentage of light has been so cut off.

b. *Bulb of percussion*, the convex protuberance on the fractured surface of flints.

1895 in *Funk's Standard Dict.* 1902 SIR C. H. READ *Guide Antiq. Stone Age* (Brit. Mus.) 115 A 'bulb of percussion' is the characteristic mark of a worked flint. 1910 *Encycl. Brit.* II. 344 Even the one feature that is commonly held to determine human agency, the 'bulb of percussion', cannot be considered satisfactory without collateral evidence of some kind. 1923 *Discovery* Dec. 316/2 Even the bulb of percussion which arises when a flint is broken by a violent blow, owing to the elasticity of its substance, can be produced by [natural] forces.

5. bulb-fin, bulb-keel, a keel of a yacht having

Supplement, p. 3873; Corrigenda, p. 4092; Spurious words, p. 4093; Books quoted, p. 4094

a cigar-shaped attachment which in section presents a bulb-like appearance; also *ellipt.* a yacht having such an attachment.

1894 Sir E. Sullivan, etc. *Yachting* (Badm.) I. 91 She was very deficient in stability when the lead slab forming the keel was recast in the form of a bulb on the bottom of the plate, the completed design simply forming one of our modern bulb fin keels. 1895 *Outing* (U.S.) Sept. 481/1 The great bulb-fins *Jubilee* and *Pilgrim*. 1895 *Boy's Own Paper* XVII. 190/2 'A canoe-body and a bulb-keel', the sheer plan being not unlike a chopper.

Bulberry (bu·lbĕri). *U.S.* Also **bull-berry.** [f. Bull *sb.*[1]] The fruit of the buffalo-bush. Also *attrib.*

1880 *Libr. Univ. Knowl.* (N.Y.) X. 159 Bulberries, which resemble red currants, grow by the rivers [in Montana]. 1889 Farmer *Americanisms, Buffalo-bush*,..a shrub, the fruit of which is called the bull-berry. 1896 *Advance* (Chicago) 22 Oct. 541 The pretty growth of timber and bushes and the clumps of bulberry trees altogether made a landscape.

Bulbosity (bʊlbǫ·sĭti). [f. Bulbous: see -ity, -osity.] The condition or quality of being bulbous.

1901 'G. Douglas' *House w. Gr. Sh.* 209 He had..a body of such bulging bulbosity, that all the droppings of his spoon..were caught on his..waistcoat.

Bulgar (bʊ·lgaɹ), *sb.* (*a.*) [ad. med. L. *Bulgarus* (F. *Bulgare*, G. *Bulgar*), ad. OBulg. *Blŭgarinŭ* (Bulg. *Blŭgarin*, Russ. *Bolgarinŭ*, *Bulgarŭ*).] Any member of an ancient Finnish tribe who conquered the Slavs of Mœsia in the seventh century A.D. and settled what is now Bulgaria, becoming Slavonic in language; a native or inhabitant of Bulgaria. Also *attrib.* or as *adj.* = Bulgarian.

1759 *Mod. Part Universal Hist.* IV. iv. i. 498 Bulgars. 1886 *Encycl. Brit.* XXI. 78/2 The Bulgars, whose origin still remains doubtful. 1920 *Q. Rev.* Jan. 63 Basil II, whom the Greeks of to-day still admire as the 'Bulgar-slayer'. 1921 S. Graham *Europe—Whither Bound?* 27 The Bulgars have certainly hit on a novelty. *Ibid.* 33 Refugee Bulgars from the lost Bulgar territories.

Hence **Bu·lgarize** *v. trans.*, to make Bulgarian in character; so **Bu:lgariza·tion.**

1869 Tozer *Highl. Turkey* I. 183 They become denationalized and Bulgarized. *Ibid.*, The Bulgarians are endeavouring the ecclesiastical superiority over them, and..will bring about their Bulgarisation. 1903 *Daily Chron.* 9 Nov., The Bulgarisation of race-divided Macedonia. 1925 *Glasgow Herald* 2 Oct. 5 Fully Bulgarised Macedonians.

Bulgarian (bʊlgēə·riăn), *a.* and *sb.* [f. med.L. *Bulgaria*, f. *Bulgarus*: see prec. and -ian.] **A.** *adj.* Of or pertaining to the ancient Bulgars or to Bulgaria, a principality of the Balkans. **B.** *sb.* **a.** Any member of the Bulgarian race; a native of Bulgaria; a Bulgar. **b.** The language of Bulgaria. *Old Bulgarian*: the oldest extant form of the Slavonic group of languages, also called Old Slavonic, Church Slavic or Slavonic (G. *kirchslavisch*).

1555 Eden *Decades* (Arb.) 318 The Slauon tounge..vsed of..the Mysians, Seruians, Bulgarians. c 1789 *Encycl. Brit.* (1797) III. 769/1 The Bulgarians anciently inhabited the plains of Sarmatia that extended along the banks of the Wolga. *Ibid.*, Bulgarian Language, the same with the Sclavonic. 1845 *Encycl. Metrop.* XI. 413/2 A sudden..invasion of the Bulgarians..struck terror into the heart of Justinian. 1861 *Chambers's Encycl.* II. 418/2 The Bulgarian language is divided into two dialects—Old Bulgarian and New Bulgarian; the former, the richest and best of the Slavonic dialects. 1869 Tozer *Highl. Turkey* I. 182 Even the priest, a Bulgarian, did not know a word of Greek. *Ibid.* 190 Children are taught to read and write both Greek and Bulgarian. 1875 *Encycl. Brit.* I. 613/2 The old Bulgarian (commonly called the Ecclesiastical Sclavonic).

So **Bulgaric** (bʊlgæ·rik), *a.*, of or pertaining to the ancient Bulgars or their modern representatives; *sb.*, the language of the ancient Bulgars. **Bu·lgaro-**, comb. form of *Bulgar, *Bulgaria* or *Bulgarian, as in *Bulgaro-Wallachian* adj., **Bulgarophil(e, -philism, -phobe.**

1880 *Encycl. Brit.* XI. 119/1 The Bulgaro-Wallachian kingdom. 1888 *Ibid.* XXIV. 269/2 The Bulgaro-Vlach empire. 1917 *Observer* 15 Apr. 4/2 The war of 1912 made me Bulgarophil; the war of today makes us—with much better reason—Bulgarophobe. 1921 *Glasgow Herald* 30 Dec. 6 His passionate Bulgarophilism.

Bulge, *sb.* Add: **3. b.** A slight swell made on the surface by a fish moving through water as it feeds on flies, etc.

1877 C. Hallock *Sportsman's Gazetteer* (Cent. Dict.). 1889 F. M. Halford *Dry-fly Fishing* vi. 122 [The angler] knows only too well that the apparent rises are bulges. 1892 *Field* 16 July 104/2 The rises, splashes, and bulges of burly brown fish.

c. Usually with *the*: The advantage or upper hand, the superior position. *slang.* (orig. *U.S.*)

1860 *Richmond Enquirer* 30 Nov. 4/5 (Th.) It is in this respect [of field products] that the South has 'the bulge' on the North, and will always have it. 1872 'Mark Twain' *Innoc. at Home* ii. (1882) 267 Well, you've ruther got the bulge on me. Or maybe we've both got the bulge somehow. 1892 *Idler* I. 555 A master can call you an idiot, and you can't call him anything back again; so he has the bulge. 1893 *Columbus* (O.) *Dispatch* 28 Dec., The conductor kicked at what seemed a wholesale business, but the mother had the bulge on him. 1911 R. D. Saunders *Col. Todhunter* xxi. 306 They've got too big a bulge on us. Everything's fixed now to steal the..vote for old Steve Yancey, and that'll settle it.

d. *fig.* A rise in shares. *U.S.*

1908 G. H. Lorimer *J. Spurlock* xi. 272 The city house which the Bonsalls had occupied just before the big bulge in Southern Pacific landed them on top.

Bulge, *v.* Add: **3. b.** Of a fish: To make a bulge (see prec. 3 b). Hence **Bu·lger, Bu·lging** *vbl. sb.* and *ppl. a.*

1889 F. M. Halford *Dry-fly Fishing* vi. 116 A fish taking caddis, shrimp, or snails is said to be tailing, from its tail appearing at intervals above water,..when feeding on larvæ or nymphæ it is described as bulging, from its motion through the water. *Ibid.* 123 A bulging fish is feeding and looking out for food. *Ibid.* 124 At times trout bulge at shrimp, snail, and caddis. 1889 *Sat. Rev.* 18 May 612/2 Mr. Halford..mentions a short way with bulgers, which he condemns as unsportsmanlike. 1892 *Field* 4 June 838/2 The fish were smutting or bulging on the shallows. 1899 Sir E. Grey *Fly Fishing* 93 'Bulging' trout in particular are generally not shy, and will stand any amount of fair fishing without ceasing to feed. 1899 *19th Cent.* Jan. 120 A moderate performer with the rod..will..pick up..a bulger here, a tailer there. 1904 *Westm. Gaz.* 13 Dec. 4/2 The question of herrings 'bulging', as it is called.

5. *intr.* To rush *in*, make a rush *for*. Also *trans.* (causative). To cause to rush *off*. *U.S.*

1834 Crockett *Narr. Life* xiv. 96 My dogs..bulged in, and in an instant the bear followed them out. *Ibid.* xvi. 105 As soon as we struck, I bulged for my hatchway. 1868 H. Woodruff *Trotting Horse Amer.* xxii. 207 Brooks and Harry Jones bulged them [*sc.* the horses] off in the lead at such a rate I was forced to let them take the pole on the turn.

Bulger (bʊ·ldʒəɹ). [f. Bulge *v.* + -er[1].]

1. *Golf.* A wooden club with a convex face.

1889 *Sat. Rev.* 25 May 622/2 In golf there is little to note beyond the apparition of the Bulger. This club is the invention of a fresh and scientific mind. 1890 W. Park, jun. in *Golf* 17 Oct. 70/1, I know for a fact, which I can prove, that I invented the bulger..; and I am undoubtedly entitled to the honour of producing the first bulger cleek [*read* club]. 1907 *Westm. Gaz.* 15 Feb. 4/2 The 'bulger'..that club with the round face which was designed as an aid to straightness of hitting, but has now..been quite discarded.

2. (See *Bulge *v.* 3 b.)

Bulgily (bʊ·ldʒĭli), *adv.* [f. Bulgy *a.* + -ly[2].] In a bulgy manner.

1891 Cotes *Two Girls on a Barge* 156 Settling down bulgily, much as the robins do before they go to sleep.

Bulgingly (bʊ·ldʒiŋli), *adv.* [f. Bulging *ppl. a.* + -ly[2].] In a bulging manner; *fig.*, prominently.

1896 *Daily News* 25 Feb. 4/7 They only offend persons in whom the moral sense is so bulgingly hypertrophied as to prompt them to yell 'Plagiarist!'

Bulk, *sb.*[1] Add:

1. (Delete † *Obs.*) A pile of tobacco made up to undergo sweating. *U.S.*

1849 *Rep. U.S. Commiss. Patents* (1850) 322 Two rows or bundles are put in a bulk. 1863 *Ret. Agric. Soc. Maine* 163 Let the tobacco..be..laid straight in a bulk or pile. *Ibid.*, Taking more care to..make the bulk much wider. 1902 *U.S. Dept. Agric., Farmers' Bulletin* No. 60. 14 Before the sweat is completed the bulk is pulled down and built up eight or ten times.

attrib. 1693 *Cal. Virginia St. Papers* I. 48 An answer to a former message of yours relating to the Act of Ports & Bulke Tobacco.

c. (Earlier American example.)

1678 *New Castle Court Rec.* 253 Tobacco which was struck & Lay in bulke.

7. *attrib.* = in bulk, esp. with reference to the supply of electric power, as *bulk supply*; also, of transport (cf. *Bulk *v.*[1] 6).

1892 *Daily News* 13 May 5/8 The North of England Steamship Owners' Association..would prevent 'bulk transport' altogether, on the ground that bulk transport threatens 'danger to the security, safety, and freedom from interruption of the Suez Canal'. 1897 *Ibid.* 18 Nov. 2/2 A bulk sample of about 2 feet of the lode on the hanging wall. 1906 *Daily Chron.* 3 Mar. 4/4 Bulk power generation. *Ibid.* 13 June 4/6 A monopoly of the bulk supply [of electricity].

b. bulk barrel, a barrel of 36 gallons of wort or beer without regard to specific gravity (as distinguished from *standard barrel*); so *bulk gallon.*

1889 in G. Birch *Handbk. Gauging* (1894) 67 When the deduction for tenths reduces bulk gallons to less than those of next lower inch. 1905 *Daily Chron.* 29 July 4/5 The discrepancy between the number of 'standard' barrels of beer upon which duty is paid and the number of 'bulk' barrels actually brewed. 1909 *Ibid.* 12 May 1/4 The bulk barrel may be of any specific gravity. The average is, I should say, about 1·053.

Bulk, *v.*[1] Add:

4. To pile (tobacco) in the course of preparing it for use. *U.S.*

1849 *Rep. U.S. Commiss. Patents* (1850) 322 Stripping should never be done in drying..weather, unless the tobacco is bulked up almost as fast as it is stript. 1863 *Ret. Agric. Soc. Maine* 163 When the weather again becomes moist,..take it [*sc.* tobacco] down and carefully bulk it away as before directed. *Ibid.*, Care must be taken that the tobacco does not..get too high in case before it is bulked. 1902 *U.S. Dept. Agric., Farmers' Bulletin* No. 60. 17 These are tied up into hands and bulked down for a short time.

6. *trans.* To put together (two or more consignments of goods) for transport as one. Also *absol.*

1908 *Modern Business* Sept. 164/2 Had they been 'bulked'—*i.e.* sent as one consignment, from one consignee to an agent to deliver—the company would have had no alternative but to charge the lower rate. *Ibid.* 165/1 If a merchant can, by bulking several parcels, get them through at a much lower rate. 1928 Sir H. Walker in *Daily Express* 10 Mar. 9/4 Bulking means..that two or more consignments for different consignees in one town, forwarded at one and the same time, can be charged together as one lot.

Bulker[2]. Add: **2.** One who makes up tobacco into piles for curing. *U.S.*

1863 *Ret. Agric. Soc. Maine* 163 This [bulking] is done by lapping the bundles over each course..the bulker having his knees upon the bulk. *Ibid.*, Under the pressure of the bulker's knee.

Bull, *sb.*[1] Add:

1. c. *Like a bull at a* (*five-barred*) *gate*: with direct violence or impetuosity. So *bull-at-a-gate*, used attrib. to describe a direct and vigorous attack.

1896 *Westm. Gaz.* 14 Oct. 5/3 [He] cross-examined in his usual blusterous bull-at-a-gate sort of fashion. 1900 *Daily News* 22 May 3/1 They were accustomed to 'bull-at-a-gate' tactics, frontal attacks, and vigorous operations against almost impossible positions.

7. b. A locomotive engine. *U.S.*

a 1889 *On the Trail* (Barrère & Leland) Had just touched a bloke's leather as the bull bellowed for the last time. 1889 Farmer *Americanisms, Bull* (Cant), a locomotive; the word is sometimes lengthened into Bullgine.

c. A policeman. *U.S.*

1909 J. London in *Contemp. Rev.* June 699, I noticed the bull, a strapping policeman in a grey suit...I never dreamed that bull was after me. 1910 *N.Y. Even. Post* 7 Dec. 6 No sooner had the little knot of special police scattered..than there arose the cries that have warned gangs of the approach of a 'bull' for many a year.

8. b. bull-point *colloq.*, a point of advantage or superiority, a great 'score'.

1900 *Westm. Gaz.* 27 Sept. 9/3, I am afraid that Lord Lansdowne has proved anything but a bull point to the House. *Ibid.* 17 Nov. 11/1 The optimists make of the fact a bull-point. 1923 *Daily Mail* 12 Oct. 7/2 The great bull point of our manufactures is their reputation for quality.

10. a. *bull-charge, -meat, -team*; **b.** *bull-voice*; *bull-bodied, -brained, -bred, -mouthed, -throated* adjs.

1901 *Westm. Gaz.* 18 Apr. 2/1 He is a *bull-bodied, *bull-brained man of violent temper. 1896 *Daily News* 24 Nov. 5/1 English *bull-bred courage. 1899 *Westm. Gaz.* 18 July 6/3 Even the wildest lion is a coward when confronted with a *bull-charge. 1843 Fremont *Exped.* 24 Tough *bull meat without salt. 1846 Sage *Scenes Rocky Mts.* (1859) 64 Bull-meat at this time..is unprecedentedly tough, strong-tasted, and poor. 1896 Kipling *Seven Seas, Last Chantey* iv, When the *bull-mouthed breakers flee. 1881 A. A. Hayes *New Colorado* ii. 25, I wonder what they'd 'a said if they'd had to ride in a *bull team or drag a hand cart all the way. 1888 *San Francisco Weekly Exam.* 23 Feb. (Farmer), I gave instructions to the wagon boss, and the long bull-team moved away. 1890 Kipling *Departm. Ditties*, etc., *Ball. Fisher's Brdg.-Ho.* iv, Hans the blue-eyed Dane, *Bull-throated, bare of arm. 1928 *Daily Express* 12 Sept. 8 Bull-throated foremen bawled for more and yet more labour. 1892 *Daily News* 13 Feb. 5/6 A gigantic *bull-voice.

11. bull-ant = *bulldog ant* (Bull-dog 4 b); **bull-bat** (earlier example); **bull-beef, bull-fly** (later examples); **bull-hole** *U.S.*, a small pond or water-hole; **bull-net,** a large hoop-shaped fishing net; **bull-nose** = *bull's nose* (see 11 b in Dict.); also adj.; **bull-nosed** *a.* (see quots.); **bull-pine,** a pine, *Pinus ponderosa*, common in the western United States; **bull-puncher** *U.S.*, a cowboy, cow-puncher; so *bull-punching*; **bull-pusher** (see quot.); **bull-rope** (earlier example); **bull-strong** *a. U.S.*, strong enough to resist a bull.

1900 *Daily News* 26 May 3/5 As eager for fight as a *bull ant on a hot plate. 1908 *Westm. Gaz.* 10 Dec. 1/3 His first bite from an Australian 'bull-ant'. 1851 Mayne Reid *Scalp-hunters* xxxviii, The voice of the *bull-bat wails through the air. 1851 J. J. Hooper *Widow Rugby's Husb.* 23 You was feedin' us soap-tails on *bull-beef. 1853 J. G. Baldwin *Flush Times Alabama* 51 So scarce were provisions—bull-beef excepted,..that we were forced to eat green corn. 1781 S. Peters *Hist. Connecticut* (1829) 195 The *bull-fly is armed with a coat of mail, which it can move from one place to another. 1887 *Harper's Mag.* Feb. 350/1 These little ponds are called '*bull-holes'. The traveller is told that they are started in this watery soil by the pawing of bulls. 1884 Knight *Dict. Mech.* Suppl., **Bull Net* (Fishing), a large hoop-net, worked with ropes and blocks. 1858 *Skyring's Builders' Prices* 41 Circular styles to *bull-nose corners. 1884 Knight *Dict. Mech.* Suppl., *Bull-nose Rabbet Plane*, a plane with the bit at the end, in order to enable it to work up close into corners. 1895 *Funk's Stand. Dict.* s.v. *Locomotive*, Bull-nose or front coupler. *Ibid.* s.v. *Nose, Bull-nose*, a front coupler on a locomotive: named from its shape; a bull-nose coupler. 1904 *Technol. & Sci. Dict.* (ed. Goodchild & Tweney), **Bullnosed Bricks* (Build.), bricks having one angle on the end rounded off. *Bullnosed Step* (Carp. and Join.), a step with a rounded end. 1920 *Chambers's Jrnl.* Sept. 594/2 Immense *bull-pines. 1874 *Ibid.* 543/2 Commissariat beeves, guarded by the commissariat '*bull-punchers'. 1887 M. Roberts *Western Avernus* ii. 19 He followed the profession of a 'bull-puncher', that is, he went in charge of the cattle destined for slaughter and canning in the distant North, and made money at it. *Ibid.* 20, I found this *bull-punching a very wearisome and dangerous business. 1887 *Chambers's Jrnl.* 359/1 The cattleman..product of the Atlantic trade—the '*bull-pusher', as the sailor terms him. 1851 Mayne Reid *Scalp-hunters* xxx, Lamm him!..Warm his collops wi' the *bull-rope! 1878 J. H. Beadle *Western Wilds* i. 21 A fancy article [*sc.* fence] was made with six strands, which rendered it in local parlance 'horse-high, *bull-strong, and pig-tight'. 1879 Tourgee *Fool's Err.* xxx. 194 The split-board paling..was 'horse-high, hog-tight, and bull-strong'.

Bull, *sb.*[4] Add: **2. b.** *transf.* A bad blunder.

1904 *N.Y. Times* 4 July 3 They are going to nominate Parker, and they are going to make a bull by doing it.

Bull (bul), *sb.*[7] [Short for Bull's-eye.] The centre of a target; = Bull's-eye 7; also, a shot hitting the bull's-eye.

1900 *Westm. Gaz.* 13 June 5/2 Even suppose every adult citizen was able to hit a two-foot bull five times out of ten at 500 yards. 1916 Boyd Cable *Action Front* 41 'You see that target there, don't you?' 'See it a fair treat!' said Donovan..; 'I'll bet I plunk a bull in the first three shots'.

Bull (bul), *sb.*[8] [Origin obscure.] A game resembling quoits. Also *attrib.*

1863 Trevelyan *Compet. Wallah* 16 In search of sport these join the circle full That smokes and lounges round the game of 'Bull'. 1889 *Pall Mall Gaz.* 22 June 3/2 We tried to help on the dreary time with..a game called 'bull'—a kind of sea-quoits. 1928 *Blackw. Mag.* Mar. 418/2 Indifferent to the call of the 'Bull-board' or the deck-quoit.

Bull, ellipt. for Bull-dog.

1878 J. H. Beadle *Western Wilds* xii. 185 He went into the backyard and onloosed a regular old English bull. 1901 S. E. White *Westerners* xxii. 207 Your bull wouldn't be ace high. Look at the teeth on him.

Bull, *v.*[1] Add: **3.** *intr.* To advance in price; *fig.* to be in the ascendant.

1928 Vines *Humours Unrecon.* 252 Music was 'bulling' in Japan and the Conservatory crammed to bursting point.

Bull-. Add: **bull-nettle** *U.S.*, a pernicious weed (*Solanum carolinense*) of the night-shade family; **bull-nut, -thistle** *U.S.* (see quots.); **bull-weed** *U.S.*, the knapweed (*Centaurea nigra*).

1876 *Congress. Rec.* May 3166/2 [He] beat down the wild-brier and *bull-nettle,..felled the forest, and hewed out his humble home. 1871 Schele de Vere *Americanisms* (1872) 416 A larger kind of hickory-nut is known as *Bullnut. 1872 *Rep. Vermont Board Agric.* I. 282 Circium Lanceolatum, **Bull Thistle*, is a biennial of pastures and road sides everywhere. 1884 W. Miller *Plant-n.*, Bull Thistle, *Carduus lanceolatus.* 1597 *Bull weede [see Bull-]. 1888 'C. E. Craddock' *Broomsedge Cove* iii. 35 A tall bull weed, that swung, purple and burly, among the rocks was dry.

Bullamacow (bu·lămăkau). [Fiji combination of *bull* and *cow*.] **a.** Cattle. **b.** Tinned meat.

1887 W. B. Churchward *My Consulate in Samoa* xxiii. 277–8 'Bulli-ma-cou', applicable both to the meat and the animal...On the first animals being landed the natives..were told that the beasts they saw before them were a bull and a cow; so combining the two English words they made one of their own. 1902 *Westm. Gaz.* 30 July 2/1 Their supper of rice and bullmacow [*sic*]. 1925 *Chambers's Jrnl.* Feb. 87/2 If they wanted *bullamacow*..he would readily provide that food. 1927 *Observer* 6 Feb. 19/5 The Fijians had no words for bull or cow and now have only one portmanteau word, 'bulumacau'.

Bull-dog. Add: **4. a.** (Earlier example.)

1836 R. King *Narr. Journ. Arctic Ocean* I. 82 Horse-flies (significantly called 'bull-dogs').

9. *attrib.*: **bull-dog fly** = Bull-dog 4 a; **bull-dog pipe,** a short tobacco-pipe of brier-wood.

1895 H. S. Somerset *Land of Muskeg* 63 The mosquitoes and *bull-dog flies. 1895 *Army & Navy Co-op. Soc. Price List* 134 Pipes. '*Bull Dog.' Briar, Horn or Vulcanite Stem. 1899 W. C. Morrow *Bohemian Paris* 306 Three-days-in-Paris English tourists wearing knickerbockers and golf-caps, and always smoking bulldog pipes. 1901 *Westm. Gaz.* 5 Nov. 4/2 When he enters a room he is always stuffing a bull-dog pipe with tobacco.

Bull-dog, *v.* [f. Bull-dog *sb.*] *trans.* To attack like a bull-dog; to assail or treat roughly.

1842 *Congress. Globe* 29 Apr. 457/3 Mr. Stanly of N. Carolina said that Mr. Whitney had not been 'dogged' to the door of the committee-room, but, when inside, he had been 'bull-dogged' with a vengeance. *Ibid.* 478. 1883 Meredith *Lett.* (1912) II. 344 Greenwood..is bull-dogging France. 1897 *Daily News* 23 Sept. 3/3 For conspiring to injure, intimidate, blackmail, arrest, imprison, poison, and bull-dog me. 1921 Mulford *Bar-20 Three* iii. 35 Me an' you ain't goin' to bulldog that gang at all. *I* am.

Hence **Bu·ll-do:gging** *vbl. sb.*, wrestling with and throwing a steer or other animal. *U.S.* So **Bu·ll-do:gger.** *U.S.*

1907 S. E. White *Arizona Nights* I. viii. 148 The two 'bull-doggers' immediately pounced upon the victim. *Ibid.* 151 One of the men seized the tightened rope in one hand, reached well over the animal's [*sc.* a calf's] back to get a slack of the loose hide next the belly, lifted strongly, and tripped. This is called 'bull-dogging'. 1924 *Glasgow Herald* 17 Jan. 9 The Society's efforts to stop steer-roping and bull-dogging.

Bull-dogged (bu·ldǫgd), *a.* [f. Bull-dog *sb.*] Characteristic of or like that of a bull-dog.

1904 *Daily Chron.* 4 Jan. 9/1 The face has become pushed back, or 'bull-dogged'. 1921 Galsworthy *To Let* iii. ii. xi, All that was bull-dogged in Soames stared for a moment out of his grey eyes.

Buller (bu·ləɹ), *sb.*[3] *University slang.* [See *-er[6].] = Bull-dog 2.

1906 *'Varsity* 1 Feb. 165/3 There's a buller over there. Wonder if he's waiting to spot anyone. 1919 *Isis* 5 Nov. 7/2 The Proctor..on a motor-scooter, accompanied by a couple of attendant 'bullers' on a push-bike. 1923 *Weekly Dispatch* 4 Mar. 1 The 'Bullers' were reinforced and undergraduates were refused entry into the college.

Bullet, *sb.*[1] Add: **1. b.** A small nugget.

1889 K. Munroe *Golden Days* x. 112 In the clay he was..likely to strike 'bullets', lumps,..or pockets of pure gold.

3. b. *fig.* (See quots.) *Workmen's slang.*

1841 Savage *Dict. Art Printing* s.v., When a workman, at case or press, either for neglect, want of punctuality, or for gross misconduct, is discharged *instanter*, and the usual notice of 'a fortnight' is not given, it is said, *He has got the Bullet.* 1868 *Great Unwashed* 254 [One] who has..got 'the bullet', as the formal note intimating that, 'owing to a reduction of our establishment your services will no longer be required', is called among working men. 1874 *Slang Dict.* s.v., To shake the bullet at any one, is to threaten him with 'the sack', but not to give him actual notice to leave. 1887 *Punch* 17 Sept. 126/1, I have just got the 'bullet', Mate—sacked without notice.

c. A high-speed type of aeroplane, e.g. the small Bristol scout.

1916 Rosher *In R.N.A.S.* 136 *plate*, A Bristol Scout Biplane (or 'Bullet'). 1918 H. Barber *Aeroplane Speaks* pl. xvii, In 1912 came..Prevost's Gordon-Bennett 'Bullet'. 1928 C. F. S. Gamble *North Sea Air Station* x. 149 The Bristol 'Bullet' was a high-performance, single-seater, tractor machine.

8. *bullet-pouch*; *bullet-riddled, -swept* adjs.

1843 Carlton *New Purchase* 100 Otter skin *bullet-pouch with a tail gracefully pendent. 1849 Parkman *Oregon Trail* 20 His bullet-pouch and powder-horn hung at his side. 1905 *Daily Chron.* 10 Jan. 4/5 The head of the drum was so *bullet-riddled that it resembled a sieve. 1897 *Westm. Gaz.* 3 June 2/2 The *bullet-swept square. 1899 Sir R. Buller in *Daily News* 12 Sept. 5/3 A bullet-swept ground in front of them. 1901 'Linesman' *Words by Eyewitness* (1902) 33 The bullet-swept hills above Ladysmith.

Bulletin. Add: **2. b.** *attrib.* esp. in **bulletin-board** *U.S.*, a notice-board.

1873 Leland *Egypt. Sketch-Bk.* 265 Sometimes a notification to this effect is posted on the bulletin-board. 1886 *Harper's Mag.* July 192/1 The little crowd of daily reporters gathered in front of the bulletin-boards calls attention to their contents. 1897 'Mark Twain' *Following Equator* iv. 75 To-day per the bulletin-board at the head of the companionway, it is September 10. 1914 Gertrude Atherton *Perch of Devil* i. 188 A crowd had formed about a bulletin board to read the latest news.

Bullet-wood. [Cf. F. *bois de balle* and *boulet de canon*.] The wood of the bully tree (Bully *sb.*[4]).

1843 Holtzapffel *Turning* I. 77 Bullet-wood, from the Virgin Isles, West Indies. *Ibid.*, Bullet-wood, another species so called, is supposed to come from Berbice; its colour is hazel brown..; it is..well adapted to general and to eccentric turning. 1858 [see *Balata 2].

Bull-frog. (Earlier examples.)

1704 Petiver *Gazophyl.* iii. xxv, *Rana Caroliniana maxima, voce Taurino* [*sic*]. The American Bull-Frog. 1705 Beverley *Virginia* iv. (1722) 260 In the swamps and running Streams, they have Frogs of an incredible bigness, which are called Bull-frogs, from the roaring they make.

Bullhead. Add: **1. b.** An allied North American fish (*Amiurus nebulosus*); the bull-pout or horned pout. *U.S.*

1856 Cozzens *Sparrowgr. Papers* v. 62 Cat-fish, perch, bullhead and sucker, darted through the gap. 1871 Schele de Vere *Americanisms* (1872) 382 Its thick head, with its long feelers, has procured for it [*sc.* the catfish] the names of Bullhead and Horned Pout. 1886 *Leslie's Pop. Monthly* June XXI. 742/2 It is now a penal offence to place bullheads, perch or pickerel in waters where they do not exist. 1897 *Outing* (U.S.) XXIX. 574/1 Just then..the men appeared, bearing a string of bull-heads and one immense pickerel.

4. (Later U.S. example.)

1840 W. G. Simms *Border Beagles* 487 We've time enough to scud and run to-night, and to-morrow we can turn upon that bullhead, Rawling.

Bullhood (bu·lhud). [f. Bull *sb.*[1] + -hood.] The condition of being a bull.

1845 Ford *Hand-bk. Spain* I. 290 The priest..selected a bull and christened him;..but..on the morrow he relapsed into his former bullhood and brutality. 1885 *Fortnight in Waggonette* 92 He was destined never to reach the full maturity of bullhood.

Bullion[3]. Transfer †*Obs.* to 1 and 3, and add to 2:

1881 *Spons' Encycl. Industr. Arts* 1064 Pressing this lump upon an iron point, so as to give it the form of a little cup, he fits it, when thus shaped, on to the bullion-point, to which it soon becomes firmly attached. The lump thus formed is called the 'bull's-eye' or 'bullion' of the developed plate. 1885 *Spons' Mechanics' Own Bk.* 630 'Roundels' and 'bullions' are small discs of glass, some made with a knob in the centre, and used in fretwork with cathedral glass.

4. *Comb.*: **bullion-bar,** the bar on or against which the end of the sphere of glass is pressed in blowing crown glass; **bullion-point,** the point or end of a bulb that is being worked on a blow-pipe; also, the thick centre of a disk of blown glass, the bull's-eye; **bullion-rod** = *bullion-bar*.

1852–4 *Cycl. Usef. Arts* (ed. Tomlinson 1866) I. 773/2 In again blowing out the bulb, the man supports it on a horizontal smooth iron rod, called the *bullion-bar. 1881 *Bullion-point [see above]. 1884 Knight *Dict. Mech.* Suppl., *Bullion Point* (glass), the thick portion at the center of a disk of crown glass. 1890 W. J. Gordon *Foundry* 143 The globe is heated and again blown, and becomes a Florence flask, the 'bullion-point', the apex of the old cone, being still conspicuous. 1862 *Chambers's Encycl.* IV. 780/1 The workman..next ma[r]vers it, without, however, using the *bullion-rod.

Bullioned (bu·lyənd), *a.* [f. Bullion[4] 2 + -ed[2].] Ornamented with bullion.

1902 *Daily Chron.* 1 Feb. 8/3 Of clear white muslin..heavily bullioned up the centre breadth. 1905 *Westm. Gaz.* 13 July 5/1 The well-known ball dress of the British Navy, with its heavily bullioned epaulettes.

Bullishness (bu·lĭʃnės). *Stock Exchange.* [f. Bullish *a.*[1] + -ness.] The quality or condition of being bullish.

1895 *Daily News* 9 Feb. 8/4 'Bullishness' is a thing almost unknown. 1903 *Westm. Gaz.* 3 Jan. 7/1 The Kaffir Circus has come to a pause in its rakish career of bullishness. 1922 *Daily Mail* 1 Nov. 10 American Futures closed steady after recent bullishness.

Bulli soil. *Australian.* A kind of earth from Bulli, a town south of Sydney, New South Wales.

1904 *Westm. Gaz.* 18 Apr. 3/1 This Bulli soil is wonderful in its resistance to wet...The wet does not run through the Bulli; it runs off it on either side of the pitch, which is slightly higher than the rest of the ground. 1907 *Daily Chron.* 19 Dec. 4/7 The famous rain-resisting 'Bulli soil' of which the pitch on the Sydney Cricket Ground is composed...'Bulli soil' is of volcanic formation.

Bullock, *sb.* **6.** Add: *bullock-car, -carriage, -cart, -gear.*

1830 Moorsom *Lett. fr. Nova Scotia* 241 The Portuguese *bullock-car of Peninsular memory. 1903 *Daily Chron.* 11 Mar. 8/2 Mr. Chamberlain..subsequently proceeded to Mount Church, partly by municipal bullock-car. 1839 *Lett. fr. Madras* (1843) 299 All the poor widows, with their palanquins and *bullock-carriages covered with black cloth. 1828 *New Monthly Mag.* XXIII. 220 A black fellow with a seine, can load a *bullock-cart at one or two hauls. 1858 [in Dict.]. 1848 Haygarth *Bush Life Australia* ii. 19 Every sort of saddlery, *bullock-gear, and harness of every description.

Bullock, *v.* Transfer †*Obs.* to 1 and add:

2. *intr.* To work like a bullock, i.e. strenuously without intermission. *Austral.*

1888 'R. Boldrewood' *Robbery under Arms* vii, It would have paid us better if we'd read a little more and put the 'bullocking' on one side. 1900 H. Lawson *Over Sliprails* 12 You'll never make money, except by hard graft—hard, bullocking nigger-driving graft. *Ibid.* 19 We've..come down to have a bit of a holiday before going back to bullock for another six months or a year.

3. *To bullock one's way*: to make one's way with heavy violence.

1909 *Westm. Gaz.* 1 June 1/2 Sir William has frequently been referred to as 'bullocking' his way through Parliament. 1921 *Public Opinion* 10 June 538/2 To bullock his way through a British Amateur Championship.

Bullocker (bu·lǝkəɹ). [f. Bullock *sb.* or *v.* + -er[1].] **a.** A bullock-team driver. *Austral.* **b.** A ship used for carrying cattle between Madagascar and Zanzibar.

1889 Barrère & Leland *Dict. Slang* s.v. *Bullocky*, Bullockirs in Australia are as proverbial as bargees or Billingsgate fishwives in England for the forcibleness of their language.

Bullocky, *a.* Delete *nonce-wd.* and add:

2. Resembling (that of) a bullock in shape or build.

1890 *Temple Bar* Jan. 118 With more enthusiasm than persons of his bullocky conformation commonly exhibit. 1892 *Illustr. Sporting & Dram. News* 27 Aug. 862/3 Deer get bullocky if fed on ordinary cattle rations.

3. Having to do with driving bullocks or managing cattle. *Austral.*

a 1889 in Barrère & Leland *Dict. Slang* s.v., One of the sunburnt bullocky men. 1890 'R. Boldrewood' *Col. Reformer* xii. 121 By George, Jack, you're a regular bullocky boy.

B. *sb.* A bullock-team driver. *Austral.*

1889 Barrère & Leland *Dict. Slang.* 1900 H. Lawson *On Track* 49 The party had been increased by Jimmy Nowlett, the bullocky. 1911 Bean '*Dreadnought*' *of Darling* xxii. 208 There would be no love lost between the Afghan camel driver and this lonely bullocky. 1926 Kath. S. Prichard *Working Bullocks* i, Red Burke was the youngest bullocky in the Karri to own his team.

Bull-pen. *U.S.* [f. Bull *sb.*[1] + Pen *sb.*[1]]

1. A pen or enclosure for bulls; *spec.* a square enclosure made of logs, freq. used in early times as a place of confinement; hence, a lock-up or prison.

1844 P. Horry *Life of Marion* xxvii. (1833) 225 The tories were..confined together under a centinel in what was called a bull-pen made of pine trees. a 1845 W. G. Simms *Wigwam & Cabin* Ser. ii. 93 It is a common place of safe keeping in the absence of gaols and proper offices. It is called technically a 'bull pen', and consists of huge logs,..crossing at right angles, forming a hollow square [etc.]. 1879 *Congress. Rec.* May 1626/1 The cow-yards and the bull-pens. 1891 *Ibid.* Feb. 2693/2 [They] would coax these illiterate white men, weeks before election, and cage them in places called bull pens. a 1909 'O. Henry' *Roads of Destiny* x. 162 Unlock him at seven in the morning, and let him come to the bull-pen. 1922 *N.Y. Even. Post* 5 Sept. 2/5 Rioting convicts who broke out of 'bull pens' here are gathered in the prison yard, considering further steps.

2. A schoolboys' ball game, played by two groups, one group outlining the sides of a square enclosure, called the 'bull-pen', within which are the opposing players.

1872 Eggleston *Hoosier Schoolm.* iv. 48 He could not throw well enough to make his mark in that famous western game of bull-pen. 1883 — *Hoosier School-Boy* iii. 25 What did a boy that had lived on Wildcat Creek..know about playing bull-pen.

Bull's-eye. Add:

7. b. A shot that hits the bull's-eye of a target; *fig.* a 'shot' that hits the mark.

1904 Sladen *Playing the Game* ii. iii, 'You know you were just made to fool about in the open air, and spend money.' 'Bull's-eye!' he said.

13. A fish of New South Wales, *Priacanthus macracanthus*, excellent for the table.

1883 E. P. Ramsay *Food Fishes N.S.W.* 9 The 'bull's-eye', a beautiful salmon-red fish with small scales.

14. An old-fashioned type of watch, with the case partly enclosing the glass. Also *attrib.* *U.S.*

1858 O. W. Holmes *Aut. Breakf.-t.* ix. 221 With some trouble he dragged up an ancient looking, thick, silver bull's-eye watch. 1859 Bartlett *Dict. Amer.* (ed. 2), *Bull's-eye*, a small and thick old-fashioned watch.

Bu·ll-snake. *U.S.* [Bull *sb.*[1]] A large North American snake (*Pityophis melanoleucus*); the pine-snake.

1791 W. Bartram *Trav. Carolina* (1792) 272 The pine or bull snake is very large and inoffensive with respect to mankind. 1817 S. R. Brown *Western Gaz.* 357 Palmetto flatts, fit only for the present occupants, gouffres, salamanders, and bull snakes. 1878 J. H. Beadle *Western Wilds* ix. 133 The most formidable looking is the 'bull-snake', so called, an immense thing of four or five feet in length, which gets its name from its blunt head and thick clumsy body. 1891 C. Roberts *Adrift Amer.* 239 The bull snake is said to grow to an enormous size, and is a kind of North American python or boa. 1907 S. E. White *Arizona Nights* I. xvi. 219, I mind when they catched the great-grandaddy of all the bull-snakes.

Bu·ll-tongue, *sb.* *U.S.* [Bull *sb.*[1]] A simple form of plough. orig. *attrib.*

1857–8 *Trans. Ill. Agric. Soc.* (1859) III. 366 It will also serve to explain..why a bull-tongue or shovel plow..will raise more corn than a mouldboard plow. 1861 *Ibid.* IV. 204 It is planted..and covered with double shovel planes and 'bull tongues'. 1868 *Rep. U.S. Commissioner Agric.* (1869) 414 The field was plowed with a turning plow, followed in the same furrow with a long bull-tongue plow. 1885 'C. E. Craddock' *Prophet Gt. Smoky Mts.* i. 2 They [*sc.* the ploughs] are of the bull-tongue variety and are sometimes drawn by oxen. 1886 *Harper's Mag.* June 58/2 Ploughing is commonly done with a 'bull-tongue,' an implement hardly more than a sharpened stick with a metal rim.

Hence **Bu·ll-tongue** *v. trans.*, to go over (land or crops) with a bull-tongue plough.

1861 *Trans. Ill. Agric. Soc.* IV. 248 Whether hoeing the small corn or rolling or bull-tonguing or hilling-up.

Bu·ll-whack. *U.S.* [Bull *sb.*[1] 1.] (See quot.)

1885 C. L. Norton in *Mag. Amer. Hist.* XIII. 98 In Texas and western Louisiana the 'bull-whack' is a terrible whip with a long and very heavy lash and a short handle. It is used by drovers to intimidate refractory animals.

Bu·ll-wha:cker. *U.S.* [Bull *sb.*[1] Cf. prec.] **a.** A driver of cattle; a cowboy. **b.** = *Bull-whack.

1859 *Alta California* 17 Aug. (Th.) Gentile and Mormon, bull whacker and Pike's Peaker, all seem to mingle freely. 1883 Nye *Baled Hay* 48 The bullwhackers' straw hat of '79. 1887 Mrs. Custer *Tenting on Plains* (1889) 229 There is no sound like the snap of the lash of a 'bull-whacker'. 1903 A. Adams *Log Cowboy* ix. 129 'When I was boss bull-whacker,' he began, 'for a big army sutler at Fort Concho, I used to make two round trips a month with my train.'

Bully, *sb.*[2] Add:

2. *Hockey.* The procedure of putting the ball in play by two players, one on each side, who strike with their sticks, first the ground then their opponent's stick, three times alternately, after which the ball is in play. Also *bully-off*.

1886 *Rules of Game of Hockey* 11 After each goal and after half time, there shall be a bully in the centre of the ground. 1895 Battersby *Hockey* 92 From the bully off until his opponents' 'twenty-five' is invaded. 1897 *Encycl. Sport* I. 516/2 A penalty bully is given for deliberately unfair play by the defending side in their own circle. 1901 *Daily News* 28 Feb. 7/5 The Oxford centre-forward got away directly after the bully-off.

Bully, *a.*[1] **2.** Add: also *spec.* in the earlier *bully-boat*. *U.S.*

1844 *Scribblings & Sk.* 181 (Th.) A two days' race with bully-boats combines every sort of pleasing excitement. It were well to inform you that a bully-boat means a boat that beats everything on those [Mississippi] waters. 1846 W. T. Porter *Quarter Race Kentucky* 126 (Th.) Our 'bully' boat sped away like a bird.

Bully (bu·li), *v.*[2] [f. *Bully *sb.*[2] 2.] *Hockey.* *trans.* To put (the ball) in play by a bully. Also *intr.* with *off*, to start play in this manner.

1886 *Rules of Game of Hockey* 11 The game shall be started by one player of each side bullying the ball in the centre of the ground. 1909 *Westm. Gaz.* 30 Mar. 12/2 When two players are bullying-off they stand perfectly square.

Bult (bult). *S. Afr.* [a. Du. *bult* hump, hunch.] A hillock, ridge.

1868 Jas. Chapman *Trav.* II. 16 A succession of sandy bults or ridges. 1901 Turnbull *Tales from Natal* 149 Though hidden from view by a slight bult he was then ascending, he could tell it was approaching him. 1912 *South African Agric. Jrnl.* Aug. 236 (Pettman) Most of the vines are big and strong, especially on the bultjes, where they are simply splendid, and bear very heavily. 1926 *Blackw. Mag.* May 638/1, I was horrified to see what I took to be our herd of dairy cows grazing on a rise or 'bult' (as these are called locally) which I had sprayed on the previous day.

Bultong, var. of Biltong.

1883 Olive Schreiner *Afr. Farm* I. ii, Did not Tant' Sannie keep in the loft 'bultongs', and nice smoked sausages?

Bum, *sb.*[4] *U.S. colloq.* [Cf. Bum *sb.*[1] 2.]

1. A lazy and dissolute person; a habitual loafer or tramp; = Bummer[3].

1888 *Detroit Free Press* (Farmer) Twenty per cent. are chronic bums, who beg or steal the price of their lodgings. 1891 C. Roberts *Adrift Amer.* 68, I don't believe in feeding professional bums. *Ibid.* 139 Near to me came and sat down a couple of tramps, real bonâ fide 'bums'. 1912 Mulford & Clay *Buck Peters* i. 24, I found myself in a cell in a Philadelphia jail, along with bums and crooks.

2. A debauch or spree.

1890 *Home Missionary* (N.Y.) 531 A christian miner..kept his men at work on Sunday, thinking it preferable to the Sunday 'bum'. a 1909 'O. Henry' *Roads of Destiny* xvi. 271 All the heroes on the bum carry the little book.

b. *transf.* A state of disorder.

1896 G. Ade *Artie* iii. 28, I sized it up that the house was on the bum and she didn't want me to see it.

Bum, *a.* *U.S. colloq.* [Cf. prec.] Of poor, wretched, or miserable quality.

1888 *Nation* (N.Y.) 31 May 439/2 One of them..heard B. called a 'bum actor'. 1896 G. Ade *Artie* xii. 109 He didn't have a sou markee except what was tied up in a bum little grocery store. 1909 'O. Henry' *Options* (1916) 31 A manicure-painter could tell it was a bum picture in a minute. 1911 H. Quick *Yellowstone N.* vii. 190 A stranger that had seen better days and had a bum lung and was used to dressing for dinner. 1913 R. W. Chambers *Gay Rebellion* ii. 26 'A sharp crack is—'. 'Every bum novel begins that way.'

Bum, *v.*[6] *U.S. colloq.* [? back-formation from Bummer[3]. Cf. *Bum *sb.*[4], *Bum *a.*]

1. *intr.* To knock about; to wander *around*, loaf.

1883 C. S. Keene in Layard *Life & Lett.* (1892) 350 I've been bumming around all day..and haven't caught a darned fish. 1897 Kipling *Capt. Cour.* 72 You ought to hev more sense than to bum araound on deck this weather. 1904 Harben *Georgians* 218 The fust night I got to bed late, after bummin' round with a feller that I met on the train. 1920 Mulford *J. Nelson* xxiii. 256 A yearling bummed among them,..making life miserable for its elders as it..butted its erratic way.

b. (Also with *it*.) To go 'on the bum'; to act as a 'bum'; to sponge.

1889 *Century Dict.*, *Bum*, to sponge on others for a living; lead an idle or dissolute life. 1890 L. C. D'Oyle *Notches* 168 Qualifications which eminently fitted a man to 'bum it' on such a community. a 1906 'O. Henry' *Trimmed Lamp* etc. 47 Off every night playing pool and bumming with the boys instead of staying home with her.

c. *trans.* To sponge on (a person).

1923 H. L. Foster *Beachcomber in Orient* i. 2 Then he bummed me for the price of a 'square meal'.

2. *trans.* To travel on (a train) without a ticket.

1896 *Pop. Sci. Monthly* L. 254 Several of the 'lads' had been 'pulled' at the Rapids for 'bumming the freights'.

Bumble, *sb.*[1] Delete †*Obs.* exc. *dial.* and add:

2. c. An angler's artificial fly.

1889 F. M. Halford *Dry-Fly Fishing* vi. 123 An *orange bumble*, floated occasionally over the feeding fish, may be successful.

Bumble, *sb.*[2] Add:

3. A beadle; a member of a municipal corporation, parish council, or the like, to whom official pomposity and fussy stupidity are attributed; a consequential jack-in-office.

1856 [in Dict.]. 1865 *Slang Dict.* (ed. 2), *Bumble*, a beadle. 18.. *Punch* (Barrère & Leland) The apish antics of a bumble crew. 1890 Farmer *Slang* s.v., *Bumble-Crew*, a collective name for corporations, vestries, and other official bodies. 1895 Morris in Mackail *W. M.* (1899) II. 308, I hope we shall beat our Bumbles.

4. **bumble-foot,** (also) a disease of the feet of domestic fowls, etc.

1854 *Poultry Chron.* I. 105 Bumble-foot comes from the ball of the foot. 1886 J. W. Hill *Dis. Poultry* 87 Occasionally the sole of the foot becomes the seat of a thick corn-like growth, which ultimately festers and exposes a ragged ulcerated wound. Such a condition is commonly termed 'Bumble-Foot'.

Bumble, *v.*[1] Delete †*Obs.* and add to sense 1 later literary examples:

1916 'Ian Hay' *Right Stuff* 198 The bees were bumbling in the heather. 1925 C. Dodd *Farthing Spinster* 240 Grass-hoppers sang, bees bumbled.

Bumble, *v.*[2] Delete †*Obs.* and add:

1876 *Coursing Cal.* 212 Merry Girl beat Unknown in good style, the latter bumbling very much at his fences. 1886 Mrs. Lynn Linton *Paston Carew* ix, The rector's only son, a big bumbling young fellow. 1926 *Chambers's Jrnl.* 87/1 Ploughmen of thirty learning to hold a pen and 'bummel through the Single Carritch'.

Bu·mblepupper. [f. Bumble-puppy + -er[1].] One who plays unscientific whist. So **Bu·mble-puppist.**

1880 Pembridge *Whist*, etc. 2 The Bumblepuppist only admires his own eccentricities. 1891 *Daily News* 30 Sept. 5/1 The careless Bumblepupper dreads the expert.

Bumble-puppy. Add:

c. A game in which a ball slung to a post is struck with a racket by each player in opposite directions, the object being to wind the string entirely round the post.

1900 L. B. Walford *One of Ourselves* xiv, They had had a great game of 'bumble-puppy'. 1918 McCudden *Five Yrs. R.F.C.* 227.

Bumbo (bʊ·mbo). Also **bombo, bumboo, bungo.** [Native name.] A fabaceous tree, *Daniellia thurifera*, of Sierra Leone, yielding a fragrant resin; also *bumbo-*, or *bungo-tree*. Also, the gum or resin obtainable from this tree.

1874 *Treas. Bot.* Suppl. s.v. *Daniellia*.

Bum-bum. Echoic representation of the sound of monotonous music. (Cf. Tum-tum.)

1878 C. Tuttle *Border Tales* 67 The music seems to him..nothing but a bum-bum.

Bumby(e, *adv.* *U.S. dial.* [Var. of *Bimeby, *Bymeby.] By and by, presently.

1786 *Boston Exchange Advertiser* 19 Oct. (Th.) [Negro talk.] Oh! he say, land dear now, bumbye buy him five dollars nacre. 1862 Lowell *Biglow P.* Ser. ii. ii. 188 'You'll see nex' time!' an' 'Look out bumby!' *Ibid.* 216 She'll come out right bumby.

Bumf (bʊmf). *slang.* [Short for *bumfodder* 'anitergium' (see Bum *sb.*[1] 4).] Toilet paper; hence, paper (esp. with contemptuous implication), documents collectively.

1889 Barrère & Leland *Dict. Slang* s.v., A bumf-hunt is a paper-chase. 1890 in Farmer *Slang*.

Bummer[3]. (Earlier examples.)

1856 *San Francisco Call* 25 Dec. (Th.) Pon my word I'm no bummer. I never ate a lunch in all my life without taking a square drink. 1857 *Ibid.* 28 Apr. (ibid.) The irreclaimable town 'bummer' figured in the police court. 1861 *Maryland Hist. Mag.* V. 324 We have a fair sprinkling of bummers, but instead of demoralizing their betters by their presence, they are only laughed at.

Bummer[4] (bʊ·məɹ). (See quot.)

1905 *Terms Forestry & Logging* 32 *Bummer*, a small truck with two low wheels and a long pole, used in skidding logs. Syn.: drag cart, skidder.

Bu·mmerism. *U.S.* [f. Bummer[3].] Habits characteristic of a bummer. Also **Bu·mmery.**

1889 Farmer *Americanisms* s.v. *Bummer*, Also *Bummerism* to express habits of loafing and petty stealing. 1894 *Advance* (Chicago) 3 May, Petitions in Boots and Bummery. ..To some these straggling adventurers have been a sort of ..abnormal lesson in bummerism and vagabondage.

Bu·mming, *vbl. sb.* *U.S. colloq.* The action of *Bum *v.*[6]

1860 *Yale Lit. Mag.* XXV. 398 (Th.) Another great sham connected with our social life is that of spreeing or 'bumming'. 1891 C. Roberts *Adrift Amer.* 66 The idea of begging or 'bumming' as it is popularly called out there, went strongly against my stomach.

Bump, *sb.*[1] Add:

1. b. (See quots.)

1883 Gresley *Gloss. Coal-m.*, *Bump*, a very sudden breaking, sometimes accompanied by a settling down, or upheaval of, the strata, during the working away of the mineral, accompanied by a loud report or bumping noise heard in the mine. 1893 *Trans. Fed. Instit. Mining Eng.* V. 381 A bump (or earth explosion) occurred on November 5th, 1892. 1908 *Colliery Manager's Pocket Bk.* 89 Have you formed any opinion as to the cause of 'bumps' in the thick coal, and have you any suggestion to make as to prevention?

c. *Aviation.* A variation of air pressure, causing an irregularity in the motion of an aeroplane; formerly called *air-pocket*.

1914 Rosher *In R.N.A.S.* (1916) 15 While flying at 200 feet, the machine suddenly bumped [*Note*, Met an air-wave]...These bumps are due to the sun's action on the air and are called 'sun bumps'. 1918 E. M. Roberts *Flying Fighter* 279 When correcting bumps or small erratic air currents one has often to resort to his inclinometer. 1927 *Even. Standard* 12 Jan. 6/4 The Air Ministry acknowledges such words as 'bump', 'contact', and 'pancake'.

d. *Cricket.* The rise of a ball from the pitch to a greater height than is usual: see *Bump *v.*[1] 2 b.

5. The corner of the stock at the top of the heelplate of a gun (Knight *Dict. Mech.* Suppl. 1884).

III. bump-absorber, a contrivance for minimizing the impact of a flying-machine with the ground; **bump-ball** *Cricket*, a ball hit hard upon the ground close to the bat, coming with a long hop to the fieldsman, and having the specious appearance of a catch.

1908 *Westm. Gaz.* 3 Oct. 3/2 Pneumatic *bump-absorbers. 1897 *Encycl. Sport* I. 245/2 *Bump-ball.

Bump, *sb.*[3] Add attrib. uses of *bump-mill*.

1881 *Instr. Census Clerks* (1885) 68 Bump Mill Worker. 1921 *Dict. Occup. Terms* (1927) § 365 *Spinner, bump mill*..spins candle wick yarn from coarse cotton waste.

Bump, *v.*[1] Add:

1. b. *To bump off*: to remove by violence, to kill. *U.S. slang.*

1910 W. M. Raine *B. O'Connor* 117 I've got several good reasons why I don't aim to get bumped off just yet. 1918 C. Wells *Vicky Van* iv. 53 'A friend of hers named Somers has been bumped off.' 'What? Killed?' 'That's it.' 1927 *Cleveland Press* 29 Jan., Senator Thomas J. Heflin..informed his colleagues that a thug had threatened to 'bump him off'.

2. b. *Cricket.* *intr.* Of a ball: To rise abruptly to an unusual height. *trans.* Of a bowler: To cause (the ball) to bump.

1888 Grace in Steel & Lyttelton *Cricket* (Badm.) 310 Emmett was in his glory, his bowling bumping and kicking up as I have never seen it since. 1891 — *Cricket* 130 The first ball..bumped and hit him on the head. 1897 Ranjitsinhji *Jubilee Bk. Cricket* 122 He has three slips for Hareless, who dislikes a bumping ball. *Ibid.* 131 Throwing is bad, because it is dangerous owing to the terrific pace and bumping power it makes possible. 1899 Grace *Cricket Remin.* 21 The batsmen had to look out for shooters, and leave the bumping balls to look after themselves. 1929 *Times* 24 May 6/1 A pitch which, apart from the fact that two or three balls bumped in the afternoon, was beautifully easy.

c. *Aviation.* To move irregularly owing to an inequality of air pressure.

1914 [see *Bump *sb.*[1] 1 c].

8. b. To make a noise like that of an explosion; hence as in quots. (cf. *Bump *sb.*[1] 1 b).

1889 *Cent. Dict.*, *Bump*, in chem., to give off vapor intermittently and with almost explosive violence, as some heated solutions. 1925 Fraser & Gibbons *Soldier & Sailor Words*, *To Bump*, to shell, *e.g.*, 'The gunners are doing a lot of bumping to-day.' 'That village looks well bumped.'

c. *trans.* To explode (a mine or mine-field).

1915 'Bartimeus' *Tall Ship* ix. *Chummyships* 160 We haven't bumped a mine-field. *Ibid.* 168 It was the manœuvres ..all over again, with the chance of 'bumping a mine' thrown in. 1925 E. Fraser & Gibbons *Soldier & Sailor Words* 155 The mine bumping squadron. The name given to the Third Battle Squadron of the Grand Fleet.

Bumper, *sb.*[1] Add: **2.** esp. freq. in attrib. use = exceptionally abundant. Also *bumper game* (see quot. 1865).

1865 *Slang Dict.* s.v., A match at quoits, bowls, &c., may end in a 'Bumper game', if the play and score be all on one side. 1885 'bumper' crop [see Dict.]. 1898 *Westm. Gaz.* 18 Nov. 8/1 The past fortnight's bumper traffic. 1901 *Ibid.* 11 Feb. 9/1 A bumper increase of £7,721. 1908 *Daily Chron.* 8 Jan. 4/4 So far as the foreign trade of this country is concerned, 1907 was a bumper year.

5. b. (*a*) See quot.

1868 Fairley *Gloss. Terms Coal-m.* ii. 5 A massive piece of iron, so heavy that when the cage is at the bottom of the cut, it will draw it empty to the top, and when the cage at the top is laden, it will act as a balance as the cage descends: this piece of iron is called the bumper.

(*b*) A log, bar, etc. serving as a fender or shock-absorber. Also *attrib.*

1883 Gresley *Gloss. Coal-m.* 38, 45 *Bumpers...Catches*... Projecting blocks of wood attached to pump spears for preventing damage in case of a break down. 1889 *Century Dict.*, *Bumper-timber*, in some locomotives, a timber to which the cow-catcher or pilot is fastened, designed to receive the shock or blow of a collision. 1926 *Morris Owner* Feb. 1600/2 The front face of the bumper bar is attractively finished in bright nickel plate. 1928 *Daily Express* 21 Aug. 9/6 The new bumper consists of a specially prepared rubber bar, attached to the motor-car by movable steel arms.

6. One who or a thing that bumps; an operative employed in 'bumping'; *Cricket*, a bumping ball.

1881 *Instr. Census Clerks* (1885) 43 Rocker or Bumper. 1889 C. C. R. *Up for Season* 267 Up at Oxford by eights on the Isis, The gloom of bumpees and of bumpers the glow. 1904 *Westm. Gaz.* 24 May 3/2 That with the likelihood of..an occasional 'bumper' even such great batsmen as Mr. C. B. Fry and K. S. Ranjitsinhji might have failed. 1921 *Dict. Occup. Terms* (1927) § 279 *Bumper* (tin boxes, etc.), packs into bundles, scrap tinplate left from stamping or cutting, by shovelling it into iron box, ramming or bumping it into compact shape with long-handled iron ram. *Ibid.* § 409 *Bumper*, a planker who operates a bumping machine; places felt forms in a sort of trough, sets machine in motion, so that forms are bumped about against arms of machine.

7. A thing that administers a bump or blow. *U.S.*

1871 *Trans. Ill. Agric. Soc.* VIII. 247 He uses the wheel-barrow curculio bumper, his own invention.

Bu·mper, *sb.*[3] *colloq.* [*-er[6].] A bumping-race.

1920 *Rec. Rowing Club S. Philip & S. James', Oxf.* 13 Each of its two crews secured four bumps in the City 'Bumpers'.

Bumpety (bʊ·mpėti). Also **-ity.** Child's word for bump; *bumpety-bump*, with repeated bumps.

1874 Hardy *Far fr. Madding Crowd* lvii, Souls alive, what news! It makes my heart go quite bumpity-bump! 1894 B. Pain *Kindn. Celestial* 190 You could almost fancy that you heard the man going bumpety-bump down the stairs. 1902 W. de la Mare *Songs of Childh.* 10 A bumpity ride in a wagon of hay.

Bumping, *vbl. sb.* **3.** Add: **bumping-post, bumping-table** (see quots.).

1874 Knight *Dict. Mech.*, *Bumping-post* (Railway Engineering), a timber or set of timbers at the termination of a railroad track, to limit the motion of the train in that direction. 1889 P. Milford *Dict. Mining Terms* (ed. 2) 13 A bumping-table is an appliance used in a stamp-mill for treating tailings. It consists of an inclined table, which is given a bumping or jerking motion which serves to force upwards by each successive bump the mineral or heavier portion of the slimes, while the lighter portion is washed off the lower end of the table. 1902 *Encycl. Brit.* XXXI. 371/2 *Bumping Tables.*—Rittinger's table is a rectangular gently-sloping plane surface which by a bumping motion throws the heavy particles to one side while the current of water washes down the quartz to another.

Bumpo·logist. *humorous.* [f. Bump *sb.*[1] 4 + -ologist.] One who is learned in bumpology. So **Bumpolo·gically** *adv.*

1824 *Blackw. Mag.* XVI. 237 He you recollect is one, not of the Bumpologists, but of the Fistologists. 1837 *Southern Lit. Messenger* III. 107, I once had my head examined—bumpologically—in a regular way. 1899 *Westm. Gaz.* 3 Jan. 8/2 It is not only porters who patronise the bumpologist.

Bumpy, *a.* Add: **b.** Of a cricket ball: That rises abruptly from the pitch. **c.** In aviation, full of bumps or variations in air pressure.

1906 *Westm. Gaz.* 8 May 2/1 He delivers a very fast bumpy ball. 1911 H. R. P. Reynolds in Berriman *Aviation* (1913) 166, I scarcely moved my control lever until I got to Bletchley, where it [*sc.* the air] began to get rather 'bumpy'. 1918 H. Barber *Aeroplane Speaks* (ed. 6) 33 'Bit bumpy here under these clouds', is all the Pilot says as he heads for a gap between them.

Bun, *sb.*[2] Add:

1. b. *transf.* Hair coiled at the back of the head in a shape suggesting a bun. Also *attrib.*

1894 *Daily News* 26 May 6/4 The fashionable ladies to be seen in the Park with their bun-chignons. 1894 *Cassell's Fam. Mag.* Dec. 73/1 The days of the 'bun' coiffures are over. 1921 *Chambers's Jrnl.* Dec. 782/1 His chief glory was, however, his head, the hair of which was dressed in a large 'bun'. 1929 *Church Times* 19 Apr. 400/3 Victorian fashion, with hats perched on the head, permitted a free view of chignon, 'bun', or curls.

2. *bun-and-milk* attrib., *bun-shop*; **bun-struggle, -worry,** jocular expressions (orig. military) for a tea-party (cf. *tea-fight*).

1906 B'ness von Hutten *What became of Pam* i. v, The *bun-and-milk establishments. 1903 *Daily Chron.* 25 May 3/3 *Bun-shop waitress. 1906 *Westm. Gaz.* 18 Sept. 8/1 The proposed addition of 'bunshop' facilities to ordinary public-houses. 1889 Barrère & Leland *Dict. Slang*, **Bun-struggle* or **worry* (army), a tea meeting; an entertainment [for] soldiers in a garrison. 1911 W. De Morgan *Likely Story* 224 Madeline..had been going to a Bun-worry.

Bun, *sb.*[5] *Canadian.* A boat, resembling a punt, with flat bottom and square ends (*Cent. Dict.* 1889).

Bunch, *sb.*[1] Add:

1. (Delete †*Obs.*, and add later U.S. example.)

1874 *Rep. Vermont Board Agric.* II. 428 Their bite is poisonous to a certain extent, as bunches can be left around their bites.

2. b. A certain quantity fastened together for sale, as a bundle of flax, or of shingles (250).

1874 Knight *Dict. Mech.*, *Bunch*..(Flax-manufacture), three bundles, or 180,000 yards, of linen yarn. 1882 P. Sharp *Flax, Tow & Jute* 145 The bunch generally weighs about 40 lbs., the number of hanks depending on the size of the yarn.

4. Also, a company or band of persons. In later use esp. *U.S.*

1840 C. F. Hoffman *Greyslaer* I. v. 92 You'll find them pretty much here and there, in bunches, helping one another. 1889 *Kansas Times & Star* 11 Jan., A bunch of temporarily idle members of the Emma Abbott company. 1902 McFaul *Ike Glidden* xii. 91 He met a bunch of railroad laborers on their way to their tent. 1913 Mrs. Stratton-Porter *Laddie* viii. (1917) 148 But she said..with the bunch of us to educate yet, we'd need the money.

5. d. *Bunch of fives* (pugilists' slang): the fist clenched; also *gen.* the hand.

1825, 1863 [see Five *sb.* 3 b]. 1847 Lytton *Lucretia* ii. vii, Is this a h-arm, and this a bunch of fives? 1883 Sala in *Illustr. Lond. News* 27 Jan. 87/2 Glovers' 'bunches of fives'. 1895 *Cornh. Mag.* July 23 He did not find the bouquet of Tim Kelly's bunch-of-fives an agreeable perfume.

6. b. *Mining* and *Geol.* (See quot. 1849–50). Cf. *Bunch *v.*[2] 1 c.

1815 [see Dict.]. 1849–50 Weale *Dict. Terms*, *Bunch*, or *Squat*,..a quantity of ore, of small extent, more than a stone and not so much as a course. 1883 [see *Bunch *v.*[2] 1 c].

7. bunch bean *U.S.*, a dwarf kidney bean, also called *bush bean*; **bunch evergreen,** the ground pine, *Lycopodium obscurum*; **bunch flower,** a liliaceous plant of N. America, *Melanthium virginicum*; **bunch greens,** greens sold by the bunch; **bunch-knot,** a knot joining broken ends of yarn; **bunch-oyster,** a wild oyster which grows in clusters; **bunch pink,** a name for the Sweet-william.

1822 J. Woods *English Prairie* 304 There are some dwarf ones, called *bunch-beans. 1860 Darlington *Amer. Weeds* 107 The..Dwarf or Bunch Bean. 1884 Miller *Plant-n.*, *Bunch Flower. *Melanthium Virginicum.* 1899 T. W. Sanders *Encycl. Gardening* (ed. 3), *Melanthium* (American Bunch-flower). 1884 McLaren *Spinning* (ed. 2) 238 When one end of yarn breaks or runs out, the other must be broken too, and what is called a *bunch-knot tied. 1877 *Rep. Vermont Board Agric.* IV. 99 *Bunch pinks and candytufts coming from self-sown seeds.

Bunch, *v.*[2] Add:

1. c. *Mining.* Of a vein or lode of ore: To form an irregular mass. Cf. *Bunch *sb.*[1] 6 b.

1883 Baring-Gould *J. Herring* xlviii. III. 102 The vein 'bunched', and the bunch of nearly pure metal was before him. 1889 *Temple Bar* LXXXV. 26 The lode ran under Orleigh gardens and promised freely to 'bunch' under the mansion.

d. To crowd together in a body. Also with *up*. Chiefly *U.S.*

1887 F. Francis Jr. *Saddle & Mocassin* vii. 124, I knew at once that they had got scared, and had bunched up like a bevy of quail. 1888 *Century Mag.* Jan. 455 By the time the dumbfounded brutes had 'bunched',..we were right in among them. 1909 *Westm. Gaz.* 23 Dec. 12/3 The result..is to force the opposing defences back to their own goal and so bunch. 1924 Galsworthy *White Monkey* i. ii, The really big people don't talk—and don't bunch—they paddle their own canoes in what seem backwaters.

e. To push in among a number.

1902 H. L. Wilson *Spenders* ix. 86 They..came down the stairs and I bunched into the crowd and let myself ooze out with them.

2. (Earlier example.) Also *absol.* (See quot. 1887.)

1873 'Mark Twain' & Warner *Gilded Age* i. (1903) 16 The speaker bunched his thick lips together like the stem end of a tomato. 1887 *Overland Monthly* (Farmer) Two men often bunch on the march, *i.e.* unite their herds for convenience in driving.

b. In technical use (see quots.). Chiefly *U.S.*

1889 *Cent. Dict.* s.v., To bunch the hits in a game of base-ball. 1905 *Terms Forestry & Logging* 32 To *bunch load*, to encircle several logs with a chain and load them at once, by steam or horsepower. To *bunch logs*, to collect logs in one place for loading. 1911 Webster s.v., To bunch..shots (in target practice).

Bu·nch-berry. *U.S.* [Bunch *sb.*[1] 7.] A berry of the dwarf cornel (*Cornus canadensis*), of a bright-red colour when ripe; the shrub bearing this.

1845 S. Judd *Margaret* i. xiv. 106 She came to the shadows of the woods..where she got boxberry flowers and fruit, bunch-berry and star-of-Bethlehem flowers. 1887 *Harper's Mag.* July 303/1 The bunchberry made mounds of creamy bloom at the roots of ancient trees. 1895 *Century Mag.* July 328/2 A wild-wood garniture of 'bunch-berries' and moss.

Bunched, *ppl. a.* Add: **d.** *Bot.* Having convex protuberances. **e.** Clustered, gathered into bunches.

1776 J. Lee *Introd. Bot.* 378 *Fascicularis*, bunched. 1900 B. D. Jackson *Gloss. Bot. Terms*, *Bunched*, gibbous. 1904 Farrer *Garden Asia* 42 The ground is thick with the bunched stars of a wee blue gentian.

Buncher (bʊ·nʃəɹ). [f. Bunch *sb.*[1] or *v.*[2] + -er[1].] One who or that which bunches; *spec.* a machine for forming bunches or collecting things in bunches.

1881 *Instr. Census Clerks* (1885) 74 Straw Plait Buncher. 1911 Webster s.v., An asparagus buncher. 1921 *Dict. Occup. Terms* (1927) § 399 *Buncher, yarn buncher*; (i) ties several hanks of yarn into bunches, in readiness for succeeding processes, bleaching, etc.; (ii) [=] crofter.

Bu·nch-grass. *U.S.* [Bunch *sb.*[1] 7.] One or other of various grasses of western North America characterized by growing in clumps.

1837 W. Irving *Capt. Bonneville* (1895) I. 139 The upland bunch grass, which grew in great abundance, and, though dry, retained its nutritious properties instead of losing them like other grasses in the autumn. 1845 Fremont *Exped.* 160 A valuable nutritious grass, called bunch grass, from the form in which it grows, which has a second growth in the fall. 1872 *Congress. Globe* Jan. 660/2 The vegetation..is principally sage-brush, interspersed with bunch-grass. 1891 Marah E. Ryan *Told in Hills* ii. ii. 32 Where the 'bunch-grass' of the grazing levels bends even now under a chance wild stallion.

attrib. 1878 J. H. Beadle *Western Wilds* viii. 125 One may ride all day through good bunch-grass pasture and his horse be walking in sand all the time. 1899 *Scribner's Mag.* XXV. 114/1, I have never seen such luxuriant grass anywhere...It is of the bunch-grass variety.

Bunching, *vbl. sb.* **c.** Add technical examples.

1901 Waterhouse *Conduit Wiring* 51 The system of bunching which, with wood casing, is objectionable from a fire insurance point of view. 1906 Dewar *Faery Year* 27 Bunching up of the cress for local retail business.

Bunchy, *a.* Add:

1. b. *Mining.* (See quots.)

1778 Pryce *Min. Cornub.* 88 The Ore in this nidus is bunchy and uncertain. 1796 Kirwan *Elem. Min.* (ed. 2) II. 173 The surface often uneven and bunchy. 1849–50 Weale *Dict. Terms* s.v. *Bunch*, A mine that is sometimes rich and at other times poor, is said to be bunchy. 1867 *Ure's Dict. Arts* (ed. 6) 504 s.v. *Bunch*, A lode is said to be bunchy when the metalliferous ore is found in irregular and sparsely distributed masses.

Bu·nco, *sb.* *U.S. slang.* Also **banco, bunko.** [Said to be a. Sp. *banca*, a card-game similar to monte.] A swindle perpetrated by means of card-sharping or some form of confidence trick. Also *attrib.* (as *bunco-case, -game, -man*) or as *adj.*

1876 [see *Bunco-steerer]. 1883 [see Bunko]. 1888 *Daily Inter-Ocean* 2 Feb. (Farmer) The recent bunco game in which William Murdoch..was robbed of 10,000 dols. 1889 Farmer *Americanisms* s.v., From this we get such compounds as *bunco-case, bunco-game*, etc. *Ibid.*, The men who thus swindle, are termed bunco-men or bunco steerers. 1901 S. E. White *Westerners* xiii. 94 Bunco men can clean him out in a gambling joint. 1904 Harben *Georgians* 241, I jest axed you how much money you've turned over to this bunco shyster? 1906 *Springfield Weekly Republ.* 13 Dec. 1 The bunco nature of the British House of Lords is exposed..in Lord Lansdowne's speech.

Bu·nco, *v.* *U.S. slang.* [f. prec.] *trans.* To swindle or cheat.

1883 [see Bunko *v.*]. 1892 *Congress. Rec.* Mar. 2651/2 The farmer is always buncoed by the three-card monte, green-goods protection shouter. 1895 *Ibid.* Mar. 3215/1 If the old farmer goes to the city, and is buncoed once, I have considerable sympathy for him. If he is buncoed twice [etc.]. 1910 W. M. Raine *B. O'Connor* 214 Unless I can fix up a deal with him, Mr. Reilly's wise play buncoes us and himself out of thirty thousand dollars. 1926 J. Black *You Can't Win* xiii. 174 The way to sell a brass brick is to bunko yourself first into the belief that your brick is solid gold.

Hence **Bu·ncoer, Bu·ncoist,** = *Bunco-steerer.

1894 *Columbus* (O.) *Dispatch* 28 May, A noted buncoist, who attempted to turn a trick on Farmer Abel Comstock, of Wood County. 1904 E. Lefevre in *Bookman* Apr. 145 The great bankers became great buncoers and went into all manner of schemes during the boom.

Buncombe, bunkum. 1. a. (Earlier examples.)

1828 *Niles' Reg.* XXXV. 66/2 Now Mr. Huskisson did not know..that American Tobacco..was subject to a duty of three shillings per lb. on consumption in Great Britain, and was 'talking to Bunkum!' *Ibid.*, 'Talking to Bunkum!'—This is an old and common saying at Washington, when a member of Congress is making one of those..'long talks' which have lately become so fashionable.

Bu·nco-stee:rer. *U.S. slang.* Also **banco.** [f. *Bunco *sb.*] A swindler.

1876 Besant & Rice *Golden Butterfly* xxxi. III. 8 'Perhaps..you would explain what a Banco Steerer and a Roper are.'..'The Roper or the Banco Steerer, gentlemen, will strip you so clean that there won't be left the price of a four-cent paper.' 1886 *Leslie's Pop. Monthly* Apr. XXI. 423/2 The victims, like those of the 'bunco steerers' in our cities, are usually very loath to make their grievances known. 1890 *Congress. Rec.* Mar. 2378/2 Such a man would certainly become the victim of a bunco-steerer or a confidence swindler before he got out of town. 1920 O. Johnson *Varmint* iv. 55 Why, there's a bunch of young Stock jobbers around here that would make a Wall Street bunco-steerer take to raising chickens.

So **Bu·nco-stee:ring** *vbl. sb.* and *ppl. a.*

1889 Kipling *From Sea to Sea* (1904) I. xxiii. 481 Would you play a straight game..let me know something about bunco-steering. 1892 *Daily News* 1 Jan. 7/3 Obtaining a sum of money..in Albany, New York, by what at first appeared to be a variation of the confidence trick, locally known as 'bunco-steering'. 1929 *Atlantic Monthly* Sept. 378/2 I'm glad we got Aggie by a bunco-steering trick.

Bund (bunt), *sb.*[2] [G.; related to Band *sb.*[2], Bind *v.*] A league or confederacy; *spec.* the confederation of German states.

1851 *Fraser's Mag.* Feb. 144/2 The new 'Bund', with all the motley crew of his fifteen nationalities. 1903 *Forest & Stream* 24 Jan. 78 (Cent. D. Suppl.) The institution of revolver shooting is regarded likely to create much interest, as many members of the bunds favor this sort of work. 1905

Westm. Gaz. 4 July 4/1 After the massacre at Kischineff, after the bloodshed at Homel, the idea of self-defence took root..and the 'Bund' was organised. 1918 C. G. Robertson *Bismarck* ii. 81 German Liberalism called for the abolition of the Bund and the Diet.

Bund (bʊnd), *v.* [f. Bund *sb.*] *trans.* To embank.
1883 Day *Indian Fish* 41 Rivers which can be easily bunded. 1917 R. Dollar *Mem.* xiv. 141 The river front had been substantially *bunded*.

Bunder, var. *Bandar.

Bundesrat(h) (bu·ndəzrāt). [G., f. gen. of *bund* *Bund *sb.*[2] + *rat(h* council.] **a.** A federal council of 58 members appointed by the governments of 26 states of Germany. **b.** A federal council of 7 members in Switzerland.
1879 *Encycl. Brit.* IX. 62/1 Delegates of the various confederated Governments form the Bundesrath. *Ibid.* 62/2 The emperor..has power, with consent of the Bundesrath, to declare war in name of the empire. 1887 *Ibid.* XXII. 795/2 (Switzerland).

Bundle, *sb.* Add:
2. f. Two reams of printing or brown paper, a quantity fixed by statute.
1724 *Act 11 Geo. I* c. 7 p. 367/1 Brown Paper, the Bundle containing 40 Quire..3*s.* 4*d.*
g. *Bundle of ten*, a collection of articles consisting of a set of ten.
1925 Fraser & Gibbons *Soldier & Sailor Words, Bundle of ten*, a packet of ten cigarettes. The tens of various suits in a pack of cards. Also, Army blankets, always rolled in tens.
h. (See quot.)
1922 *N. & Q.* 12th Ser. XI. 206/2 *Packet, parcel* and *bundle*, a considerable sum of money. To say a person 'won a packet', &c., or 'had a parcel (or bundle) on a horse', infers that a considerable sum has been won or laid.
4. bundle-wood, fire-wood made up into bundles.
1879 *Good Words* 781/1 These great yards are the storage ground of the 'bundle' fire-wood trade. *Ibid.* 781/2 The bundle wood coming into his own household.

Bundle, *v.* Add:
6. *intr.* To bump heavily or barge *into* (a person).
1916 Hugh Walpole *Dark Forest* I. vi, An officer bundled into him, apologized, but quite obviously cursed him for being in the way.

Bundleman (bʊ·nd'lmæ̆n). *slang.* [f. Bundle *sb.* + Man *sb.*[1]] A married seaman: see quot. 1925.
1895 *United Service Mag.* 518 If one of the officers is on the sick list it is well to have a spare room in the bundle-man's house, where the invalid can be put up. 1925 Fraser & Gibbons *Soldier & Sailor Words, Bundle-man*, a Lower Deck phrase for a married man, apparently suggested by the small bundle tied up with a blue handkerchief which married seamen in a Home Port usually take ashore with them when going on leave. 1927 *Blackw. Mag.* June 712/1 Many of my messmates were 'bundle-men', and were busy arranging passages for their families to Malta.

Bundler. Add: **1.** (Examples of technical uses.)
1879 *Good Words* 781/2 Children, working shifts as half-timers, 'pile' for the bundler. 1881 *Instr. Census Clerks* (1885) 70 Flax, Linen Mill:..Drying and Bundling: Dryer. Bundler. 1921 *Dict. Occup. Terms* (1927) § 399 *Bundler, waste*, makes waste from various departments of mill up into bundles.
2. *U.S.* (Example.)
1774–5 [Janet Schaw] *Journ. Lady of Quality* (1923) 135 The Lady is a fair American... None of your bundlers a' faith for me.

Bundling, *vbl. sb. attrib.* Add:
1874 Knight *Dict. Mech.*, *Bundling-machine*, one for grasping a number of articles into a bundle ready for tying. 1879 *Good Words* 781/2 A chopper and chopping block, and a bundling machine. 1890 Jos. Nasmith *Mod. Cotton Spinning Mach.* 267 The hanks being reeled, they are, if cross reeled, dyed or bleached, and, if in leas, bundled. This operation is effected in a machine called a 'bundling press'. 1906 *Daily Chron.* 15 June 7/4 Princess Louise Augusta..sawed a huge chunk of wood, afterwards chopping it into firewood and working the bundling machine. 1909 *Cent. Dict.* Suppl., *Bundling-wire*, baling-wire; wire used for securing bundles or bales.

Bundobust, bandobast (bʊ·ndobʌst). *Anglo-Indian.* Also bundo-, bundoo-, bunder-, bunda-, banda-, bando-; -bustt, -bust, -bast. [Hind. (Pers.) *band-o-bast* tying and binding.] An arrangement, settlement.
1776 *Trial Jos. Fowke, Depositions* 17/2 In the year 1180..when the Bundobustt of the farms took place. 1813 *Gloss. 5th Rep. Sel. Comm. E. India* 10/1 Bundoobust...A settlement of the amount of revenue to be paid or collected. 1880 G. Aberigh-Mackay *Twenty-one Days India* 181 This unhappy creature whose mind is a perfect blank regarding *Faujdari* and *Bandobast*..will..actually presume to discuss Indian subjects with you. 1896 A. Forbes *Camps, Quarters* etc. 270 George Martell did not make quite so bad a *bandobast* after all. 1920 *Blackw. Mag.* Sept. 319/2 'Sahib, what *bundobast* for dinner?' asked Khuda Bux. 1925 E. F. Norton *Fight for Everest 1924* 163 [We] set off with a minimum bandobast to penetrate as far down into Nepal as we could. 1927 *Blackw. Mag.* Aug. 327/2 An Indian regiment whose water *bundobust* had somehow gone wrong.

Bundook (bʊ·ndūk). *Anglo-Indian.* [Hind. بندوق *bandūq*, a. Pers. *bundūq* filbert nut, musket or cannon ball, firearm, ad. Gr. Ποντικόν (sc. κάρυον hazel nut) Pontic *a.*[1]] A musket or matchlock.
1886 Yule & Burnell *Hobson-Jobson*. 1926 'Sapper' *Men, Women & Guns* (1917) 129, I had words with a sentry at the frontier, but I put it across him with his own bundook. 1923 *Blackw. Mag.* May 574/2 Those old *bundooks* were a source of perpetual nerves to us. 1926 *Ibid.* Nov. 664/2 Fortunately bundooks..do not shoot very straight.

Bung, *sb.*[1] Add:
3. b. A brewer, or landlord of a public house. Also, the brewing interest (as in politics); hence *attrib.* or as *adj.* favouring the brewers or their interests in politics.
1860 *Slang Dict.* (ed. 2), *Bung*, the landlord of a public-house. 1884 *Graphic* 23 Feb. 170/1 That Sir Wilfrid Lawson had turned 'Bung', and applied for a spirit licence. *a* 1889 *Truth* (Barrère & Leland) Within the last few years several bungs have been made Peers. 1891 *Pall Mall Gaz.* 31 Aug. 2/3 It is true that the temperance organizations rendered yeoman service, but as a consequence the 'bung' party put forth its full strength on the other side. 1910 *Daily Chron.* 1 Feb. 1/4 Since the power of 'Bung' has been so demonstrated in this constituency.
6. Various attrib. uses of sense 1.
1847 Webster, *Bung-drawer*, a wooden mallet..for taking the bung out of a cask (*Local*). 1874 Knight *Dict. Mech.*, *Bung-borer* (Coopering), a conical auger for reaming out a bung-hole. *Bung-cutter*, a machine for cutting bungs. ..*Bung-vent*, a passage for admitting air through the bung of a cask, to allow a free flow of liquid from the tap. 1876 *Catal. Sci. App. S. Kens. Mus.* § 10 For finding the bung diameter and diagonal of a cask. 1884 Knight *Dict. Mech.* Suppl., *Bung Bucket*, also known as a velinche, water thief, thief-tube, etc...*Bung Bush*, more correctly, bung-hole bush...*Bung Lathe*, a lathe for turning taper bungs.

Bung, *sb.*[3] *slang.* A lie, falsehood.
1882 M. Brookfield *Autob. Thomas Allen* I. v. 61 'And for having told a bung,' said Fisher. 'A beastly bung,' cried all the judges. 1913 M. Baring *Lost Diaries* (1927) 8 Mac reported him for telling bungs.

Bung, *a.*[2] *Austral. slang.* Also bong. [Native word.] **a.** Dead. **b.** Bankrupt. Also in phr. *to go bung*: (*a*) to die; (*b*) to fail, go bankrupt.
1882 A. J. Boyd *Old Colonials* 73 Just afore you hands 'im [*sc.* the horse] over and gets the money, he goes bong on you [i.e. he dies]. 1885 *Austral. Printers' Keepsake* 40 His musical talent had 'gone bung'. 1885 H. Finch-Hatton *Adv. Australia* x. 142 Directly me bung (die) me jump up white feller. 1893 *Argus* 15 Apr. 13/2 (Morris) All flesh is grass, says the preacher,.. And we gaze on a bank in the evening, and lo, in the morn 'tis bung. 1893 *Melbourne Herald* 25 Apr. 2/4 (Morris) One member of the mischief-making brotherhood wrote the words 'gone bung' under a notice on the Government Savings Bank.

Bung, *v.*[2] *slang.* (orig. *dial.*) [Echoic.] *trans.* To throw forcibly, 'plug'. Also *fig.* Also with *in*.
1825 Jamieson, *To bung*, to throw with violence, Aberd. 1898 *Eng. Dial. Dict.* 1903 *Daily Chron.* 8 Dec. 9/2 'We are police officers. What have you in that parcel?' Stevens replied, 'I don't know; I have just had it bunged on to me.' 1923 *Glasgow Herald* 29 Oct. 11 The cinema..can..take the skeletons of 'Macbeth,' [etc.] and make very entertaining films of them with..a good deal of photographed natural scenery bunged in. 1923 *Blackw. Mag.* Dec. 768/2 A spectator roused the boar..by bunging in a clod of mud through the window.

Bung, *adv.* [Cf. prec.] In or into the very midst of things; 'all of a heap'; straight, right.
1899 Kipling *Stalky & Co.* 132 They have babies and teething and measles and all that sort of thing right bung *in* the school. *Ibid.* 154, I used to go bung off to sleep on a form sometimes.

Bungaloid (bʊŋgăloid), *a.* [f. Bungalo(w + -oid after *fungoid*.] Having the appearance or style of a bungalow. Also *sb.* a bungaloid growth.
1927 Inge in *Daily Express* 22 Nov. 1/3 Hideous allotments and bungaloid growths make the approaches to any city repulsive. 1928 *Sunday Dispatch* 30 Sept. 11/2 Mr. Shaw designates our modern urban communities 'bungaloid promiscuities,' and refuses them the more dignified term of civilisations. 1929 *Morn. Post* 4 May 1/3 Will somebody..pay reasonable cash price for freehold and preserve its beauty from bungaloids.

Bungalow. Add: **b.** *attrib.* and *Comb.*
1903 *Arch. & Contr. Reporter* 24 Apr. 272/2 The buildings have been designed in a bungalow type. 1906 *Daily Chron.* 9 Mar. 8/3 The bungalow village. 1907 *Westm. Gaz.* 8 Apr. 9/1 At the meeting of bungalow-holders.

Bungarum (bʊŋgărŏm). Also bungarus, bungar, bongar. [Bengali (Skr., neut. sing. of *bhangura* bent, curled (sb. bend of a river), f. *bhanj* to break, bend).] Any of the venomous snakes of the genus *Bungarus*; esp., the krait of India.
1835 *Encycl. Metrop.* XXIII. 640/1 *P[seudoboa] Fasciata*, ..A native of India. In Bengal is called *Bungarum Pamah* and *Sackeenee*. 1870 Gillmore tr. *Figuier's Reptiles & Birds* ii. 71 According to Cantor, the Bungarums are capable of darting nearly the anterior half of the body. 1887 *Encycl. Brit.* XXII. 196/2 The fangs of the bungarums are shorter than those of the cobras.

Bungee: = Pungee.

Bu·nglesome, *a.* *U.S.* [f. Bungle *v.*] Awkward and troublesome.
1889 in *Century Dict.* 1897 *Congress. Rec.* Feb., App. 55/1 An inexcusable and bunglesome fraud or mistake on the part of some one handling [the ballots]. 1915 Mrs. Stratton-Porter *M. O'Halloran* xv. 337 But this sheet is going to be rather bunglesome. Ma, could you do anything about it?

Bungo[2]: see Bumbo.

Bu·ngtown. *U.S.* [app. a fictitious local name, associated with Rehoboth in Massachusetts (Schele de Vere *Americanisms* 587).] *Bungtown copper* or *cent*, a counterfeit English halfpenny or other spurious copper coin.
1787 *Newport Mercury* 13 Aug. in *Mag. Amer. Hist.* (1885) XIII. 206 We are informed that all Coppers by law, in New York, except Bungtowns, are fixed at 160 for a Dollar. 1840 *Knickerbocker Mag.* May XV. 385 [He took] a five cent piece and two bungtown coppers out of the till. 1845 S. Judd *Margaret* I. iv. 17 These flowers wouldn't fetch a bung-town copper. 1853 *Oregonian* 13 Aug. (Th.) What is the currency of the U.S.?—Coppers, bogus, Bungtown cents, pennies, fips, [etc.].

Bungy (bʊ·ŋgi), *sb.* *Anglo-Indian.* [Hind. *bhangī*.] In Bombay, a member of the low caste of sweepers.
1826 *Trans. Lit. Soc. Bombay* III. 362 The *Kalpa* or Skinner, and the *Bunghee* or Sweeper, are yet one step below the *Dher*. 1886 Yule & Burnell *Hobson-Jobson* s.v., The colloquial application of the term *bungy* to such servants is..peculiar to Bombay.

Bunk, *sb.*[1] Add: **1.** (Earlier examples.)
1780 *Heath Papers* 28 The bunks and lineing of the bomb proof were taken out. 1809 *Deb. Congress* 1810 (1853) 2448, 20 bunks at $3.50 each [among expenses in military hospital, New Orleans].
b. *attrib.*, as *bunk-car, -room*.
1855 M. M. Thompson *Doesticks* xii. 99 The black boy who sweeps out the bunk room. 1898 P. L. Ford *Hon. Peter Stirling* 236 By the light one of the superintendents found the bunk-cars gone. 1924 Mulford *Rustlers' Valley* vi, The cook was busy in the bunkroom.
2. (Example.)
1862 *Once a Week* 4 Jan. 51/1 One end of the stick is canted up with handspikes on to the 'bunk' of the sleigh.
3. A log car or truck. *U.S.*
1895 *Standard Dict.* 1905 *Terms Forestry & Logging* 32.
4. *Comb.*, as *bunk-chain, -hook, -load, -spike, -truss* (see quots.).
1895 *Funk's Standard Dict.*, *Bunk-truss*, an iron strap to strengthen the crosspiece on which lumber is loaded, as on a logging-car. 1905 *Terms Forestry & Logging* 32 *Bunk hook*, the hook attached to the end of the bunk on a logging car, which may be raised to hold the logs in place or lowered to release them. *Bunk load*, a load of logs not over one log deep; i.e., in which every log rests on the bunks. *Bunk spikes*, sharp spikes set upright in the bunks of a logging sled to hold the logs in place. *Ibid.* 51 *Toggle chain*,..bunk chain.

Bunk, *sb.*[3] [f. Bunk *v.*[2]] In slang phr. *To do a bunk*: to make an escape.
c 1870 *Broadside Ball.*, 'Peck's Bad Boy' (Farmer) The keeper tried to catch him, but the bad boy did a bunk. 1919 J. B. Morton *Barber of Putney* ix, 'All right, son,' said Curly. 'They [*sc.* Germans] done a bunk.' 1923 *Chambers's Jrnl.* Dec. 833/1 Now I'm spotted, I'll do a bunk.

Bunk, *sb.*[4] [Abbreviation of Bunkum.] Humbug, nonsense.
1918 in Webster Addenda. 1919 *Rebel Worker* (N.Y.) 1 Feb. 3/3 The usual bunk about 'disloyalty' is being employed to..blind them to their own interest. 1921 *Glasgow Herald* 3 May 3 As an American friend said..'Tell your people at home it is all bunk the United States intends to keep out of European affairs'.

Bunk, *v.*[1] Add: **1.** (Earlier examples.)
1840 R. H. Dana *Bef. Mast* viii, We turned in to bunk and mess with the crew forward. 1850 H. C. Watson *Camp-Fires Revol.* 250 It's about time for us to bunk.
2. *trans.* (See quot.)
1905 *Terms Forestry & Logging* 32 *Bunk*, to place upon the bunks, as to 'bunk a log'.

Bunked (bʊŋkt), *a.* [f. Bunk *sb.*[1] + -ed [2].] Furnished with or having a bunk or bunks.
1892 Stevenson & Osbourne *Wrecker* xiii, A double bunked division for the cook..and second mate.

Bunker, *sb.*[1] **3.** Delete (*Sc.*) in def., and add:
1921 *Dict. Occup. Terms* (1927) § 279 *Bunkerman*..tips wagons to discharge coal or iron into bunkers at ironworks.
b. *pl.* = *bunker coal* (see 5 below).
1883 Gresley *Gloss. Coal-m.*, *Bunkers*, steam coal consumed on board ship. 1898 *Daily News* 18 Apr. 11/5 More money has to be paid for steam, bunkers, and gas coals. 1905 *Spectator* 28 Jan. 132/1 The annual output has increased very largely since 1870,..and its rate of growth..has been 2½ per cent. per annum (and that of the exports, including bunkers, 4½ per cent. per annum).
c. = *bunker-man* (see 5 below).
1921 *Dict. Occup. Terms* (1927) § 744 *Bunker*, tips coal from baskets or trucks into coal bins or bunkers as they are lowered by hoist...*Collier*..includes bunker, trimmer, loader.
4. Now, an artificial sand-hole with a built-up face; also, any natural obstruction (as water, long grass, etc.) on a golf-course.
1893 H. G. Hutchinson *Golfing* 60 Sometimes you may be driven to invent hazards, by throwing up banks, cutting bunkers or planting bushes. 1897 *Encycl. Sport* I. 458/1 Between the teeing-ground and the putting-green should be found, whether they be natural or artificially formed, various 'hazards' in the shape of sand-pits or 'bunkers'. *Ibid.* 472/1 *Bunker*, originally a natural sand hole on the golf course. Now used also of artificially made hazards with built-up faces.
b. *fig.*
1905 *Westm. Gaz.* 28 Oct. 16/1 The Princess frock is a bunker not to be cleared by any economies or adaptations.
5. *attrib.* and *Comb.*, as (sense 3) *bunker-capacity, -hatch, -hold, -man, -plate, -room* (sense 4) *bunker-iron*; **bunker coal**, *spec.* steam coal; also, coal carried by a steamer for its own use and not as cargo.
1892 *Daily News* 28 July 6/7 That her *bunker capacity is 2,000 tons. 1885 *bunker coal (in Dict.). 1888 *Daily News* 10 July 5/2 The exports of 'bunker' coal..show an improvement. 1907 *Daily Chron.* 24 Jan. 6/4 The result of having a thing like this tangling our machinery is that we use an enormous quantity of bunker coal for very little speed. 1904 *Westm. Gaz.* 16 July 5/2 A low *bunker-hatch. 1890

Daily News 13 Oct. 3/6 The men at the *bunker hold of the Grecian. 1886 A. Lang in *Longman's Mag.* July 332 The iron head makes it more like a *bunker iron than a play club. 1921 *Dict. Occup. Terms* (1927) § 089 **Bunkerman*, in charge of bunkers at coke ovens where coal is stored. *Ibid.* § 279 *Bunkerman* (blast furnace)..tips wagons to discharge coal or iron into bunkers at ironworks. 1888 *Lockwood's Dict. Terms Mech. Engin.* 53 **Bunker Plate*, a plate of sheet iron which encloses the area utilised for the deposit of boiler fuel. 1894 *Daily News* 18 Dec. 5/4 *Bunker room for 1,500 tons of coal.

Bunker, *sb.*[2] *local U.S.* Short for *mossbunker*, the menhaden.
1888 Goode *Amer. Fishes* 386 New Jersey uses the New York name with its local variations, such as 'Bunker' and 'Marshbanker'.

Bu·nker, *v.* [f. Bunker *sb.*[1]]
1. *trans.* To fill the bunkers of (a steamer) with coal for its own consumption. Also with the coal as object.
1891 *Pall Mall Gaz.* 19 Jan. 4/1 Many..of the great steamship companies of Liverpool were simply begging for coal to either bunker or cargo their steamers. 1893 *Times* 11 July 3/6 The ordinary rate of bunkering coal by manual labour. 1925 *Blackw. Mag.* June 836/1 She was bunkered for the twenty-nine days' run to Batavia.
b. *intr.* To take in a supply of coal for consumption on a voyage.
1893 *Whitby Gaz.* 3 Feb. 2/6 The foreign coaling clause in the outward coal charter bound them to bunker with the agents of the charterers. 1895 *Ibid.* 11 Apr. 3/2 We bunkered at Malta at four o'clock in the morning. 1925 *Chambers's Jrnl.* Dec. 778/2 There was some delay at Durban, where she bunkered.
2. *Golf. pass.* **a.** Of the ball: To be hit into a bunker. Of a player: To have one's ball in a bunker.
1886 H. G. Hutchinson *Hints Game Golf* 40 Your adversary is badly bunkered. 1891 — *Famous Golf Links* v. 56 His ball lofted on Mr. Maitland's, knocked it out of the hazard, and lay bunkered in its place. 1903 *Punch* 22 Apr. 283 On ..the Golf Links..watching the Colonel, who has been bunkered for the last ten minutes.
b. To be furnished with a bunker or bunkers.
1907 *Daily Chron.* 17 Aug. 7/2 The point of controversy..is as to how such a hole should be bunkered, or rather as to whether it should be bunkered at all.
c. *fig.* (*colloq.*) To be placed in a situation from which it is difficult to extricate oneself.
1894 Baron Ribblesdale in *Westm. Gaz.* 6 Sept. 4/2 The Liberal peers were powerless. To use a golfing simile, they were bunkered. 1899 *Geog. Jrnl.* May 474 In the long narrow ice-bound valleys which lead up from the Hindu Kush to the Pamirs..we were once, to use a familiar term, fairly bunkered. 1905 *Westm. Gaz.* 27 Dec. 1/3 The truth is that Mr. Balfour is bunkered by his own record. 1913 Kipling *Diversity of Creatures* (1917) 293, I guess he was kinder bunkered for the minute. 1917 H. A. Vachell *Fishpingle* ix, 'Perhaps you regard golf as a sort of epitome of life?'..'I suppose I do.' 'If you found yourself "bunkered", you would not lose heart?'

Bunkering (bʊ·ŋkəriŋ), *vbl. sb.* [f. Bunker *v.*]
1. The action of filling a steamer's bunkers with coal. Also *attrib.*
1899 *Westm. Gaz.* 7 Nov. 9/3 It is thought that the North country coal will be used by transports for bunkering. 1920 *Act 10 & 11 Geo. V* c. 50 § 3 Regulating the export of coal and the supply of coal for the bunkering of vessels. 1922 *Daily Mail* 9 Nov. 3 A group of foreign bunkering depots.
2. The action of furnishing (a golf course) with bunkers.
1909 *Westm. Gaz.* 8 Mar. 12/2 The final bunkering of the course.

Bunkery (bʊ·ŋkəri), *a.* [f. Bunker *sb.*[1] + -y[1].] Full of or abounding in bunkers.
1890 *Sat. Rev.* 31 May 665/2 That mountainous range of bunkery sandhills. 1894 *Blackw. Mag.* Oct. 561 The sand was..strewed in a thick bunkery mattress over all the ladies' links.

Bu·nk-house. *U.S.* [Bunk *sb.*[1] or *v.*[1]] A house in which miners, lumbermen, or other workers are lodged.
1877 Raymond *Mines* 332 Outbuildings..Bunk-house. 1901 S. E. White *Claim Jumpers* xxii. 274 The old 'bunk house' now accomodated a good-sized gang of miners. 1913 Mulford *Coming of Cassidy* iii. 58 The Boss went in the bunkhouse, and soon returned.
attrib. 1928 E. W. Bradwin (*title*) The bunkhouse man; a study of work and pay in the camps of Canada 1903–1914.

Bunko, variant of *Bunco.

Bu·nky, bu·nkie. *U.S. colloq.* [f. Bunk *sb.*[1]] One who shares a bunk with another.
1858 Viele *Following the Drum* 218 Which triumph over paternal love I rewarded by giving him Jack for his 'bunkie'. 1903 *N. Y. Even. Post* 10 Oct., In a logging camp in Maine a lanky Yankee had been unburdening himself of his past life for the entertainment of his 'bunky'. 1920 W. M. Raine *B. O'Connor* 58 If it is certain that my old bunkie came to his death foully.

Bunnia (bʊ·nyă). *Anglo-Indian.* Also bunneya, bunia, -ar; bunneah, bunniah, bunnya; bania, -(i)ya. [Hind. *banyā*, a. Gujarati *vāṇiya* (see Banian).] A trader or merchant.
1793 Morse *Amer. Geog.* (1794) 687 The tribe of Beise, who are chiefly merchants, bankers, and banias or shop-keepers. 1829 *Encycl. Metrop.* XX. 33/2 Some of the Banyás are Awaks, or seceders from the Brahmanical faith. 1879 Mrs. A. E. James *Ind. Househ. Managem.* 77 The native *bunniahs*..do not give long credit. 1880 *Encycl. Brit.* XII. 760/1 In the interior of the Bombay Presidency, business is mainly divided between two classes, the Baniyas of Guzerat and the Marwaris from Rajputana. 1906 *Blackw. Mag.* Dec. 799/1 The Hindu Bunia in remote villages is still bullied by the wealthy zamindar of the neighbourhood.

Bu·nny-hu·g. [f. Bunny [2] 1 a + Hug *sb.*] An eccentric ragtime dance. So *bunnyhugging* vbl. sb.
1912 *Daily Mirror* 6 Jan. 7/1 Fashionable society in New York..is fighting upon the great question as to whether..'The Bunny Hug'..shall be..allowed. 1924 *Chambers's Jrnl.* May 310/2 The fox-trot or the bunny-hug of your London restaurants. 1928 Galsworthy *Swan Song* II. xiii, He had often..watched the dancing on deck—funny business nowadays, shimmying, bunnyhugging, didn't they call it?

Bunodont (biū·nŏdǫnt), *a.* and *sb.* [f. Gr. βουνός mound + ὀδοντ-, ὀδούς tooth.] **A.** *adj.* Designating molar teeth whose crowns are elevated into tubercles; having tuberculate molars. **B.** *sb.* A mammal with teeth of this pattern.
1883 Flower in *Encycl. Brit.* XV. 429/2 The grinding surfaces of the molar teeth either of a distinctly tubercular (bunodont) or of a crescentic ridged (selenodont) form. 1887 E. D. Cope *Orig. Fittest* 243 Bunodont type; crown supporting tubercles. *Ibid.* 244 The Bunodonts, except some Carnivora, are all of the former or isognathous type. 1902 *Nature* 25 Sept. 523 A series of six cheek-teeth, distinct and bunodont in type.

Bunow (bʊnou·). Also bunnow, banau. [a. Hind. (Hindi) *banāo* preparation, used in the sense of *banāwat* fabrication, invention, sham.] A fraud, sham.
1853 W. D. Arnold *Oakfield* II. 58 You will see within a week if this is anything more than a *banau*.

Bunt, *sb.*[3] Add: (Earlier U.S. example.)
1767 *Boston Gaz.* 19 Jan. (Th.) [The black ram] will sometimes come behind a great Weather..and give him a paultry Bunt at unawares.
b. *Baseball.* An act of stopping the ball with the bat without striking. Also *bunt-hit*.
1896 Knowles & Morton *Baseball* 114 A bunt hit is a deliberate attempt on the part of the batsmen to hit a ball slowly within the infield so that it cannot be fielded by any fielder in time to retire the batsman. 1902 *Encycl. Brit.* XXVI. 162/1 A batsman is put out..if he make three foul bunts (that is, attempts to block the ball with the bat). 1904 *Charlotte Observer* 20 June 4 Base hits or even successful bunts are not to be despised by the leaders. 1906 *Spalding's Base Ball Guide* 116 A 'bunt' hit is made when the batsman simply holds the bat up to meet the thrown ball, thereby allowing the ball to rebound from the bat to the ground. 1917 Mathewson *Sec. Base Sloan* ii. 169 Despaigne started out poorly enough, trickling a bunt to third.
c. *attrib.* **bunt-rush** *U.S.*, 'in foot-ball, a rush made by all the attacking side at once' (*Cent. Dict.* Suppl. 1909).

Bunt, *v.*[2] Add:
2. *Baseball.* To stop (the ball) with the bat without swinging the latter. Also *absol.* Hence **Bu·nted** *ppl. a.*, **Bu·nting** *vbl. sb.*
1906 *Spalding's Base Ball Guide* 116 The new rule thus describes a bunted ball. *Ibid.*, If the attempt to bunt result in a foul not legally caught, a strike shall be called by the umpire. 1912 Mathewson *Pitching* ii. 23 Doyle bunted and was safe, filling the bases. *Ibid.* xiii. 298 Once,..McGraw planned a bunting game against Overall.

Buntal (bʊ·ntāl). [Philippine name. See also *Balibuntal.] A straw prepared from the fibres of the petioles, or leaf-stems, of the talipot or buri palm (*Corypha umbraculifera*), used for the manufacture of hats in the Philippine Islands.
1910 Hugo H. Miller *Philippine Hats* 38 Very lately, buntal straw has been imported into Baliwag and there woven into very beautiful hats in the Baliwag weave. 1911 C. B. Robinson in *Philippine Jrnl. Science* June 114 Until the beginning of 1909, all buntal hats were made in one weave, that of Lucban, Tayabas. 1926 *Commerce & Industry Jrnl.* (Manila, P.I.) Nov. 11 The hat manufacturers of China..are making hats out of buntal fibers from the Philippines.

Bunter [4]. *U.S.* A buffer or fender of a railway carriage.
1884 Knight *Dict. Mech.* Suppl., *Bunter*, the bumper or buffer of a railway car. The bar on the front end of the car, which strikes against a similar bar on an adjacent car in coupling.

Bunting, *sb.*[1] Add:
1. b. Applied by extension to any bird of the finch family, and to similar birds of other families. *U.S.*
a 1813 A. Wilson *Amer. Ornith.* (1831) II. 242 Black-throated Bunting...In their shape and manners they very much resemble the yellow-hammer of Britain. *Ibid.* 245 *Fringilla Graminea*,..*Emberiza Graminea*..Bay-winged Bunting. 1893 Newton *Dict. Birds* 459 Indigo-bird,..a well-known North-American species,..American ornithologists give full accounts of the habits of this bird, together with those of..the still more gaudy Painted Bunting.
4. *attrib.*, esp. **bunting lark**, the common bunting; also *bunting-lark fly*, an angler's fly.
1802 Montagu *Ornith. Dict.* I, Bunting-lark. 1837 Kirkbride *Northern Angler* 25 The Bunting Lark Fly. 1876 Newton in *Encycl. Brit.* IV. 525/2 The true Bunting (or Corn-Bunting, or Bunting-Lark, as it is called in some districts). 1884 Coues *N. Amer. Birds* (ed. 2) 356 Bill very small and truly conic, well exhibiting 'emberizine' or 'bunting' characters.

Bunting, *sb.*[2] Add: *attrib.* **bunting-tosser** *Naval slang*, a signaller.
1905 *Daily Chron.* 23 Jan. 3/1 From which breathless catalogue it will be gathered that the path of the 'bunting-tosser' is not an easy one! 1909 Ware *Passing English*.

Bunting-iron, illiterate alteration of *punty-iron* (Punty 3), a glass-blower's tube.
1874 Knight *Dict. Mech.*, *Bunting-iron*.., the glass-blower's pipe.

Buntline. 2. Add:
1867 Smyth *Sailor's Word-bk.* s.v. *Buntlines*, To this buntline-toggle, the buntline attaches by an eye or loop. 1883 *Man. Seamanship for Boys* 38 The buntline patches, four in number, are placed at equal distances apart along the foot, extending from foot to middle or belly band. *Ibid.* 53 Q. What are buntline toggles? A. Toggles at the foot of the sail to which the buntlines are toggled. *Ibid.* 159 The buntline-whip is rove through the lower sheave of the buntline-block. 1909 *Cent. Dict.* Suppl., *Buntline-lizard*, a piece of rope having two legs, with thimbles spliced into the ends, through which the buntlines reeve.

Buntons (bʊ·ntənz). [orig. in sing. *bunting*, a piece of squared timber, of obscure etym.
1633 *Gateshead Church Bks.* in Heslop *Northumb. Words* s.v., It. pd for one bunting and two sparres to a yeat and the makeing it, 4*s.* 4*d.*]
Strong balks of timber placed crosswise in the shaft of a mine serving to divide it into compartments and to support the guides on which the cages run, etc. (Rarely *sing.*)
1839 Ure *Dict. Arts* 971 In quadrant shafts the buntons cross each other towards the middle of the pit. *Ibid.* 986 The compartment intended for the upcast is made air-tight at top, by placing strong buntons or beams across it. 1860 *Eng. & For. Mining Gloss.* (ed. 2) 51 *Buntons*, strong balks of timber. 1883 *Encycl. Brit.* XVI. 450/2 Pieces of timber parallel to the end-pieces (buntons or dividings) are fixed across the shaft, and serve to stay the wall-plates. 1888 Greenwell *Coal-trade Terms Northumb. & Durh.* (ed. 3) 81 A cistern which stands on a strong oak bunton.

Bunty, *a.* [f. Bunt *sb.*[2] + -y[1].] Of grain: Infected with bunt.
1855 Morton *Cycl. Agric.* I. 363/2 A year or two since, we saw a very bunty crop in the fields of a first rate farmer. 1896 *Chron.* 19 Dec. (E. D. D.) If he sowed bunty seed he should expect to reap bunty crop.

Bunya (bʊ·nyă). Also bunya-bunya. [Native name.] An Australian tree, *Araucaria bidwillii*, which bears a fir cone of great size yielding a pleasant and nutritious vegetable pulp. Also *attrib.*
1843 L. Leichhardt *Let.* in J. D. Lang *Cooksland* (1847) 82 The bunya-bunya tree is noble and gigantic. 1844 *Ibid.* 89 The kernel of the Bunya fruit. 1844 *Port Phillip Patriot* 25 July 4/4 The Bunya Bunya or *Araucaria* on the seeds of which numerous tribes of blacks are accustomed to feed. 1870 Braim *New Homes* vii. 348 The Bunya Bunya grows ..sometimes as high as 200 feet. 1875 *Encycl. Brit.* II. 310/2 The Bunya-Bunya pine, found on the mountains of Eastern Australia. 1885 Mrs. Praed *Australian Life* 22 The bunya is a handsome tree of the fir species. 1885 — *Head Station* 179 In dense scrub..where the stately bunya-branches drooped. 1887 J. Mathew in Curr *Austral. Race* III. 161 In laying up a store of bunyas, the Blacks exhibited an unusual foresight. *a* 1889 Hill in J. H. Maiden *Usef. Native Pl. Australia* 7 The bunya is remarkable as being the only hereditary property which any of the aborigines are known to possess, and it is therefore protected by law.

Bunyip (bʊ·nyip). Also bunyup.
1. The aboriginal name of a fabulous monster inhabiting the rushy swamps and lagoons in the interior of Australia.
1848 Westgarth *Australia Felix* 391 Certain large fossil bones..have been referred by the natives..to a huge animal of extraordinary appearance, called in some districts the Bunyup, in others the Kianpraty, which they assert to be still alive. 1888 *Athenæum* 14 Jan. 47/2 There are plenty of sea-gods, little better than salt-water kelpies or marine bunyips. 1888 Andrews *Temple Mystic* 1 In the forest dim, where the black bunyip creeps, roused from the dank morasses. 1891 'Coo-ee' *Tales Australian Life* 275 When a black fellow disappears, it is generally understood that the Bunyip has got hold of him. 1894 A. Robertson *Nuggets*, etc. 61 A weird boom, from bittern or bunyip, came from the swamp.
2. An impostor. Hence *attrib.*
1852 Mundy *Antipodes* ix. (1858) 215 Bunyip became, and remains a Sydney synonyme for *impostor, pretender, humbug*, and the like. 1853 W. C. Wentworth in Sir H. Parkes *Fifty Years Austral. Hist.* (1892) I. 41 A mushroom, a Brummagem, a bunyip aristocracy.

Buoy, *sb.* **3.** Add:
1870 *Chambers's Jrnl.* 15 Jan. 34/2 This 'buoy-shifting' is a duty which calls forth all the skill and energy of the officers and men. 1874 Knight *Dict. Mech.*, *Buoy-safe*, a metallic body divided into compartments, by which it is braced, and having water-tight doors opening to the inside. 1921 *Dict. Occup. Terms* (1927) § 731 Buoy master.

Buoyage. Add to def.: Also, buoys collectively, a series of buoys which mark out a channel.
1855 in Ogilvie Suppl.

Bur, burr, *sb.* Add:
5. b. An ornamental veneering wood or veneer, esp. of walnut, containing knots. Also *attrib.*, as *burr-walnut*. Cf. *Burl *sb.* 4 b.
1885 *Spons' Mechanics' Own Bk.* 357 Walnut burrs are best cut with scissors. 1901 *Tradesman's Catal.* 1 Bedroom Suite, in solid American Walnut and Burr. 1908 *Daily Report* 5 Sept. 8/2 A burr-walnut armoire. 1923 *Daily Mail* 23 Jan. 1 Sideboard in oak..with finely figured panels of burr walnut.

Buran (bū̆·rān). [Central Asian Turki.] In Central Asia, a snowstorm, esp. one accompanied by high winds; a blizzard.
1886 *Encycl. Brit.* XXI. 76 Gales with snow (*burans, myatels*), lasting from two to three days..are especially dangerous to man and beast. 1898 J. T. Bealby tr. *Sven Hedin's Through Asia* viii. I. 99 These burans or snow-hurricanes come on with startling suddenness.

Burano (burā·no). The name of an island near Venice, used attrib. in *Burano lace*, a needle-made lace having a net ground, resembling Alençon and Brussels lace.
1882 Caulfeild & Saward *Dict. Needlework* 56/1.

Burberry (bə̄·ɹbəri). The trade name distinctive of cloth or clothing made by the firm of Burberrys Ltd.
1903 *Burberry Yarn Proofs* 3 Burberry Yarn Proof Coatings. 1915 T. Cassels *Men Knotted Heart* iii. 37 Somebody presented to him once a Burberry. 1919 C. Orr *Glorious Thing* iii, She was clad in a drooping burberry coat.

Burble, *sb.*[1] Delete †*Obs.* and add:
3. A murmurous flow of words.
1898 G. W. Steevens *With Kitchener to Khartum* 33 An inarticulate burble more like the sound of a distant railway train than any known form of human speech. 1906 J. H. Skrine *Pastor Ovium* 140 What I listened to was a burble of platitudes in a honeyed voice. 1923 *Blackw. Mag.* Dec. 767/1 The low burble of petition-reading and the murmurous flow of false evidence were still proceeding.

Burble, *v.*[1] Add:
2. a. *intr.* To speak murmurously. **b.** *trans.* To say (something) murmurously.
1891 Kipling *Light that Failed* viii, You only burble and call me names. 1906 B'ness von Hutten *What became of Pam* III. iv, Miss Wantage..began to burble, and then to roar. 1920 Mulford *J. Nelson* vii. 67 'Forty feet of rope an' a sycamore tree.' burbled Smitty. 1921 *Blackw. Mag.* July 31/2 A sleepy dinner it was. We burbled a few plans for next day, and fell asleep by the fire. 1922 *Short Stories* Feb. 57/2 'Good old Uncle Alfred!' he burbled.
Hence **Bu·rbling** *vbl. sb.*
1920 *Blackw. Mag.* July 44/2 They..hold his answering burblings to be the divine voice of Kali.

Burbung (bə̄·ɹbʊŋ). Also burbong. [Native name.] The ceremony of initiation into the privileges of manhood practised by aboriginal natives of New South Wales.
1904 G. S. Hall *Adolescence* II. 240 Some Australian tribes have typical and elaborate initiation ceremonies, called Burbung or Bora, for their adolescents.

Burdekin (bə̄·ɹdəkin), the name of a river on the eastern seaboard of Queensland, Australia; used attrib. in *Burdekin plum*, an Australian timber tree (see quots.); *Burdekin vine*, an Australian vine, *Vitis* (*Cissus*) *opaca*, bearing large edible tubers, also called Round Yam.
1889 J. H. Maiden *Useful Native Pl. Australia* 67 *Vitis Opaca*, 'Burdekin Vine', 'Round Yam'. *Ibid.* 599 *Spondias pleiogyna*, 'Sweet Plum', or 'Burdekin Plum'. 1902 *Encycl. Brit.* XXXII. 108 Other orders..furnish equally serviceable, large-sized timber, particularly the following:—'Burdekin Plum' (*Pleiogynium Solandri*).

Burden, *sb.* Add:
2. phr. *The white man's burden*: a rhetorical expression for the responsibility of the white for the coloured races.
1899 Kipling *White Man's Burden* vi, Take up the White Man's burden—Ye dare not stoop to less. 1922 Joad *Common-Sense Theology* 135 Little nationalised Jingoes who are ready enough to adopt any parrot cry such as 'The White Man's Burden', or 'The Kultur of the Fatherland'.
VI. 13. *pl.* The floor boards of a rowing boat. *Side burdens*, the side seats in a rowing boat.
1857 P. Colquhoun *Comp. 'Oarsman's Guide'* 29 The flooring is termed *burthens*. *Ibid.* 31 *Side burthens* are extra thwarts laid in provisionally to carry sitters: *burthens* are the bottom boards. 1898 Ansted *Dict. Sea Terms* 37 In boats the burdens are the footwalings.

Burdensome, *a.* Add:
2. Capable of carrying a good burden. *U.S.*
1763 *Boston Even. Post* 9 May (Th.) A very good and burthensome Schooner for sale. 1834 M. Scott *Cruise Midge* xviii, 'Pull under the stern of that large ship'...'A fine burdensome craft that, sir.' 1835 Hoffman *Winter in West* II. 68 The burthensome steamboats from New-Orleans reach here at the lowest stage of the river.

Bure. Delete † *Obs.* and add:
2. (See quots.)
1909 *Westm. Gaz.* 4 Sept. 15/2 A favourite material with some of the best French designers is the coarse sacking of which nuns make their dresses...It is called bure; the finer makes of it are combined with velvet. *Ibid.* 9 Oct. 15/1 The fabric of the season is undoubtedly the coarse bure which takes its name from the stuff used for the costumes of monks in the Middle Ages.

Bureau. Add: **1. b.** A chest of drawers. *U.S.*
1819 *St. Louis Enquirer* 15 Sept. (Th.) Look in the bureaus and trunks of modern men of fashion and see the number of coats, waistcoats, pantaloons, &c. 1837 *Southern Lit. Messenger* III. 333 The only bureau and the only rocking-chair were in Charlotte's room. 1890 Mrs. Custer *Following Guidon* 253 Our *bureaus* were always called *bureaus*; but they were in fact packing boxes.
c. *attrib.*
1854 Mary J. Holmes *Tempest & Sunshine* xxiii. 328 Safely stowed away at the bottom of her bureau-drawer..was a big daguerreo-type. 1863 'Gail Hamilton' *Gala-Days* 201 They are lying..wrapped in oiled-silk in the upper bureau-drawer. 1866 Mrs. Whitney *L. Goldthwaite* i, Standing there with her hand upon the bureau-knob. *Ibid.* vi, Bits of most delicate ferns..filled a great shallow Indian china dish upon her bureau-top.

Bureaucrat. (Earlier example.)
1842 Motley *Corr.* 10 Jan. I. 94, I don't know whether I have ever described to you the great bureaucrat [Count Nesselrode] of the great autocrat [Emperor of Russia].

Bureaucratize (biuərǫ·krătəiz), *v.* [f. Bureaucratic + -ize.] *trans.* To govern by a bureaucratic administration or system. Hence **Bureau·cratizing** *vbl. sb.*: **Bureau:cratiza·tion.**
1892 Schäffle *Impossibility Soc. Democr.* 39, I do not by any means contemplate the bureaucratizing and nationalization of industry. 1920 *Times Lit. Suppl.* 2 Sept. 559/2 The centralization of power..was..accompanied by a progressive system of bureaucratization. 1920 *Contemp. Rev.* Dec. 882 It proved itself to be a mere bureaucratization of distribution.

Burette. Add:
3. A cruet used for the wine or the water at the Eucharist.
1856 J. C. Robinson *Invent. Objects Mus. Ornamental Art* 57 Plated Flagon or Burette. *Ibid.* App. 11 Pair of Sacramental Cruets, or 'Burettes'. 1872 O. Shipley's *Gloss. Eccl. Terms* 79/1.

Burg. Add:
2. A town or city. *U.S. colloq.*
1846 Sol. Smith *Theatrical Apprent.* 189 You will have the greatest congregation ever assembled in this burg. 1874 J. C. McCoy *Historic Sk.* 44 The business of the burg [Abilene in 1867] was conducted in two small rooms. *Ibid.* 64. 1888 *Battle Creek Weekly Jrnl.* 8 Feb., If successful, it will make a lively burg in the next few years. 1903 A. Adams *Log Cowboy* vi. 71 The wagon and a number of the boys went into the burg. *Ibid.* 264 We were less than five miles from the burg.

Burgh, var. of *Burg 2.
1901 Marah E. Ryan *Montana* viii. 114 Well, I think I'll rest my weary body in this 'burgh' for a few weeks to come.

Burga, boorga (bū̆·ɹgă). [app. dial. var. Russ. *purga*.] A storm of wind and sleet in Alaska.
1896 Kipling *Seven Seas* 71 Ever they wait the winter's hate as the thundering *boorga* calls.

Burgeon, *sb.* Add:
4. (Also burgen.) A boss used for the cover of a book, to prevent injury to the binding.
1889 *Cent. Dict.*

Burgher, *sb.* Add:
4. A citizen of the Transvaal Republic or of the Orange Free State before the South African War of 1899–1902. Also *attrib.*
1879 Bartle Frere, etc. *Speeches Cape Town* 24 To encourage the brave Burghers and Southey's Volunteers to do their best to put an end to the war on the northern border of the Colony. 1879 (*title*) Interview between..Sir Bartle Frere, and the Deputation from the Boer Committee, At the Burgher Camp, April, 1879. 1881 F. R. Statham *Blacks, Boers, & British* iii. 43 To save them from annihilation at the hands of the Free State burghers, the Basutos were, in 1868, taken under British protection. 1898 Kruger in *South Africa* 1 Jan. 11/1 Burghers and fellow-countrymen, the times are such that a wise and judicious development of our sources of aid requires the most earnest consideration. 1899 *Westm. Gaz.* 11 Dec. 6/2 Earl Grey, late Administrator of Rhodesia, deduces one lesson from the war—the immense value of the burgher principle, which found its counterpart in England in the Volunteer movement.

Burgheress (bə̄·ɹgəres). [f. Burgher *sb.* + -ess[1].] A female burgher.
1901 *Westm. Gaz.* 7 May 2/2 Stout German burgheresses patrolling the streets in whaleboned uniforms. 1912 Miss Broughton *Between two Stools* ix, A tender-hearted burgher-ess of Catterwell.

Burgherly (bə̄·ɹgəɹli), *a.* [f. Burgher *sb.* + -ly[1].] Of or belonging to a burgher.
1762 tr. *Busching's Syst. Geog.* IV. 445 The town consists of what are called free and burgherly houses, as also of free and burgherly inhabitants, and of the garrison. The free inhabitants are exempt from all burgherly burdens. *Ibid.* V. 381 Other villages, hamlets, and subjects,..over which it formerly enjoyed burgherly jurisdiction. 1906 *Daily Chron.* 19 Feb. 3 There met in Bruges..a princely and burgherly splendour.

Burglar (bə̄·ɹglăɹ), *v.* [f. the sb.] **a.** *trans.* To steal (goods) or rob (a place) as a burglar. **b.** *intr.* To commit a burglary. Cf. Burgle *v.* Hence **Bu·rglared, Bu·rglaring** *ppl. adjs.*
1890 Mrs. Hungerford *Born Coquette* II. xiii. 128 He certainly burglared Nan. He broke into the house..and stole her away. 1890 *Mercury* (Tasmania) 27 Dec., A news agency ..was burglared yesterday morning. 1909 *Daily Chron.* 31 Aug. 1/2 'Raffles' remains a more endeared and far more possible character than the burglaring 'Duke'. 1920 W. T. Grenfell *Labrador Doctor* iv. 76 He..got alarmed when busy burglaring. 1928 *Sunday Dispatch* 22 July 12/4 The burglared shop.

Burglarize, *v.* (Earlier examples.)
1871 *Southern Mag.* Apr. (De Vere) The Yankeeisms donated, collided, and burglarized, have been badly used up by an English magazine-writer. 1876 *Congress. Rec.* July 4419/2, I found that the house of a lady moving in good society had been burglarized.
Hence **Bu·rglarizing** *vbl. sb.*
1871 Schele de Vere *Americanisms* (1872) 655 In like manner the burglar's occupation has been designated as burglarizing.

Burgle (bə̄·ɹg'l), *sb.*[2] [f. Burgle *v.*] An act of burgling; a burglary.
1889 *Punch* 26 Jan. 37/2 The Burgle Song. 1898 *Tit-Bits* 26 Feb. 418/1 This afternoon we did a little burgle on our own account.

Burgoma·stership. [-ship.] The office of burgomaster.
1896 *Daily News* 28 Apr. 3/5 Dr. Lüger..proceeded to the Town Hall and communicated his renunciation of the Burgomastership. 1909 *Daily Chron.* 25 May 6/7 The burgomastership of Breslau.

Burgoo. Also burgout. Add:
2. *U.S.* A soup made with a variety of meat and vegetables, used especially at outdoor feasts in some Southern states.
1889 *Century Dict.* 1889 Farmer *Americanisms*. 1906 *Washington Post* 16 June 6 Who, excepting Kentuckians and their favored Southern friends and kinsmen, has ever really known the bliss of genuine burgoo? 1906 H. O. Pittman *Belle of Blue Grass C.* xix. 272 The old timers smacked their lips as they,..in fancy,..tasted the burgout.

Burgoyne (bə̄·ɹgoin). A jointed trenching tool used as a spade or an axe, with a perforated blade enabling it to be used as an extemporized mantelet.
1884 Knight *Dict. Mech.* Suppl. 147/2.

Burgundy. Add:
2. c. A red wine resembling the Burgundy of France, made in and imported from other wine-growing districts, esp. Australian and Californian 'Burgundy'.
1886 *Catal. Colonial & Ind. Exhibition, W. Australian Court* 53 One dozen Burgundy, vintage 1882. *Ibid.*, *S. Australian Court* 36/2 Number of gallons manufactured last vintage 18,000; of Burgundy type. 1888 *W. & A. Gilbey's Wine List* 11 Australian Wines—..Burgundy Red. 1894 C. F. Oldham *California Wines* 8 Of natural dry red wines, the Burgundy types are perhaps the best.
d. A shade of red of the colour of Burgundy wine.
1881 *Household Words* 9 July 215/2 New colours in gloves are steel and burgundy. 1891 *Daily News* 30 Dec. 2/2 Every tone of red, from brilliant military scarlet to the deep claret and burgundy tones. 1897 *Ibid.* 14 Dec. 8/7 The tint was a deep rich burgundy, with amethystine hues in the high lights.
6. *Burgundy mixture*, a preparation of soda and copper sulphate used for spraying potato-tops to destroy fungi.
1894 *Board of Agric. & Fisheries, Leaflet No.* 23 By the use of Bordeaux or Burgundy mixture, the spores of the fungus are prevented from germinating.

Burhel (bʊ·rēl). Also burrell, burrhel, barhal. [Hindi *bharal*.] The wild sheep of the Himalayas.
1838 *Proc. Zool. Soc.* 79 A skin of the Burrhal Sheep from the Himalaya Mountains. 1840 *Ibid.* 68 The Burrhel would seem to inhabit a much loftier region of the Himalaya than the Nahoor. 1880 *Encycl. Brit.* XII. 742 The *barhal*, or blue wild sheep. 1886 *Ibid.* XXI. 765/1 In Nepal and Little Tibet, is..the burrhel, *Ovis nahoor*. 1887 *Field* 19 Feb. 243/2, I had a shot at a small burrell and missed. 1924 H. Whistler *In High Himalayas* xiii. 165 We found the tracks of burhel on some bare soil.

Buri [1] (bū·ri). [Tagalog.] The talipot palm. Also *attrib.*
1899 J. Foreman *Philippine Isl.* 427 Tall *buri* palms. *Ibid.* 448 The canoe..was gaily decked out with festoons of *buri*. 1911 C. B. Robinson in *Philippine Jrnl. Science* June 106 Three different parts of the leaves of the buri palm are used for hats. 1926 *Commerce & Industry Jrnl.* (Manila, P. I.) Nov. 6 In the trade, 'buri hats' refer only to those made of the bleached buri leaf, as distinguished from those made from the unbleached leaves which are known as the 'Arayat hats'.

Buri [2] (bū·ri). [Native name.] An amygdalaceous tree, *Parinarium laurinum*, native to the Fiji Islands, producing a nut from which putty is made (*Cent. Dict.* 1889).

Burial. 5. Add: **burial-case** *U.S.* (examples); **burial permit** *U.S.*, a certificate authorizing the burial of a deceased person.
1851 C. Cist *Cincinnati* 191 Every possible variety in which iron can be cast, from a butt hinge to a *burial case. 1853 *Trans. Mich. Agric. Soc.* IV. 108 Stevens & Tug, Detroit, [exhibited] two metallic burial cases, a valuable improvement. *c* 1870 'Mark Twain' *Sketches* Wks. XIX. 259, I am talking about your high-toned, silver mounted burial-case. 1888 *St. Louis Globe Democrat* (Farmer) Yesterday's *Burial Permits. 1908 *Daily Chron.* 22 May 1/3 The case..has developed sensational features through the refusal of the authorities to grant a burial permit.

Buriat (bū·riăt). Also Buryat. A member of a race of Mongolians inhabiting the borders of Lake Baikal, Siberia. Also *attrib.* or *adj.* = **Buria·tic** *a.*, belonging to the Buriat race.
1836 *Penny Cycl.* VI. 29 The Buriates constitute one of the three great divisions of nations into which the Mongols are divided. 1895 *Westm. Gaz.* 23 Nov. 7/1 The thirty Mongolian Buriats who, on the Emperor's initiative, have been brought to St. Petersburg for their education. 1902 *Ibid.* 28 Feb. 2/1 Disguised as a Buryat, and accompanied by one Buryatic Cossack,..I set off. 1903 *Daily Chron.* 18 Nov. 3/2 He made the experiment..in disguise as a Buriat Lama. 1921 *19th Century* May 871 The bonbons of the new faith were cast indiscriminately amongst Circassians, Hindoos, Kirghizes,..Buryats and Negroes.

Burka [1] (bʊ̄·ɹkă). Also burqa, boorka, burko. [Hind. (from Arabic) برقع *burqaᶜ*.] A long veil worn in public places by Asiatic women to screen them from the view of men and strangers.
1905 Holman Hunt *Pre-Raphaelitism* I. 386 His pleadings to be allowed to satisfy his eyes as to the features hidden under the black *burko*. 1905 *Daily Chron.* 16 Nov. 5/4 The Begum was clothed in strictest purdah costume, and wore a burka. 1927 *Blackw. Mag.* May 755/1 A burka with netted eyeholes. 1929 *Daily Express* 15 Jan. 1/1 The Queen [of Afghanistan] is wearing the boorka—a heavy shapeless garment which effectually hides her beauty.

Burka [2] (bə̄·ɹkă). Also boorka, burqa. [Russ. Бурка.] A short round cloak of a coarse material worn by Russians, Poles, and Moldavians.

1916 J. Y. Simpson *Self-Discov. Russia* 138 Caucasian Cossack officers with..black burka sweeping behind them. 1924 *Blackw. Mag.* Feb. 180/2 The ample folds of the ankle-long burqa. 1927 *Ibid.* Sept. 299/1 Broad-built men, like giants in their hairy boorkas and astrakhan caps.

Burl, *sb.* Add: **4. b.** An overgrown knot or excrescence in walnut and other woods, used in veneering; also, a log or piece of timber containing such a knot; also, a veneer made with this wood. Cf. *Bur, burr, *sb.* 5 b.
1885 *Spons' Mechanics' Own Bk.* 356 French walnut burls. *Ibid.*, The ash burls..avoid the necessity of a stay log by having a sufficient part of the trunk on which the burl grew left to serve for this purpose.

Bu·rlap, *v.* [f. Burlap *sb.*] *trans.* To wrap round with burlap.
1927 *Ladies Home Jrnl.* Dec. 109/2 Evergreens should be balled and burlapped, if they are to be successfully transplanted. *Ibid.*, Insist on carefully balled and burlapped stock.

Burley [3] (bə̄·ɹli). *U.S.* [? personal name.] An American tobacco, of which there are two varieties, red and white.
1881 *Southern Planter* in B. W. Arnold *Tobacco Ind.* (1897) 35 The White Burley produced in the west has now thoroughly substituted our dark grades. 1900 in *Yearbk. U.S. Dept. Agric.* 435 The White Burley is entirely air cured, except in exceedingly damp weather, when wood fires may be used. 1909 *Westm. Gaz.* 10 Feb. 5/2 From the Blue Grass also comes most of what is called the Burley, another fine quality, which is made into chewing tobacco for the American and German.

Burman (bə̄·ɹmæ̆n), *a.* and *sb.* Also † Birman, Burmhan. [f. *Burma* + -an.] Of or belonging to, a native of, Burma; also, the Burman language.
1800 M. Symes *Embassy to Ava* 7 The Birmans..became masters of Ava. 1814 F. Carey *Gram. Burman Lang.* 1 The Burman alphabet consists of forty-five letters. *Ibid.* 39 This mark (:) is the only stop the Burmans have. 1821 Hiram Cox (*title*) Journal of a Residence in the Burmhan Empire. 1826 *Pop. Descr. Burma* 1 The vast region of Asia..comprehending the Birman empire, the kingdoms of Siam and Anam. *Ibid.* 10 The Birman, which is spoken in Ava and Arracan. 1835 *Penny Cycl.* IV. 439 Among the vegetable productions of the Birman forests the teak holds the first place. 1883 A. P. Phayre *Hist. Burma* 1 The Burman people..were formed into a nation by the union of Mongoloid tribes.

Burmese (bə̄ɹmī·z), *a.* and *sb.* Also † Birmese. [f. *Burma* + -ese.] **A.** *adj.* Of or belonging to Burma or the Burmans.
1823 A. Judson in F. Wayland *Mem.* (1853) I. 256 Translated from the Burmese original. 1827 H. G. Bell in *Constable's Misc.* IX. (*title*) A Narrative of the Late Military and Political Operations in the Birmese Empire. 1842 A. Judson *Burmese Lang.* 5 The Burmese alphabet consists of ten vowels..and thirty two consonants. 1876 *Encycl. Brit.* IV. 551 The Burmese empire with its present limits contains no maritime districts. 1920 *Blackw. Mag.* Oct. 519/2 Adorable Burmese babies.
b. in the specific names of minerals, fauna, etc., found in Burma, as *Burmese naphtha*. **Burmese squirrel**, a squirrel native to Burma and Tenasserim, closely allied to *Sciurus caniceps*. **Burmese worm**, a mulberry-feeding silkworm found domesticated in India.
1858 Fownes *Man. Chem.* (ed. 7) 655 The Burmese naphtha (Rangoon tar)..consists principally of liquid homologues of marsh gas, associated with small quantities of hydrocarbons of the benzol-series, [etc.]. 1887 *Encycl. Brit.* XXII. 60 *Bombyx arracanensis*, the Burmese worm. *Ibid.* 438 Burmese squirrel.
B. *sb.* **1.** Natives (also, a native) of Burma.
1824 in W. James *Naval Hist. Gt. Brit.* (1837) VI. 465 The Burmese jumping overboard to save themselves. 1842 A. Judson *Burmese Lang.* 9 The character °..is reckoned among the consonants, by the Burmese. 1876 *Encycl. Brit.* IV. 551 The sugar cane appears to have been long known to the Burmese. *Ibid.* 552 The Burmese in person have the Mongoloid characteristics. 1876 J. Bradley *Trav. & Sport* ii. 29 These people, like all other Burmese, were vivacious and noisy. 1885 G. C. Whitworth *Anglo-Ind. Dict.* 54/2 *Burman*, a native of Burma, a Burmese.
2. The language or literature of the natives of Burma.
1842 A. Judson *Burmese Lang.* 6 The pronunciation of the cerebrals and the dentals, though different in the Sungskrit, is the same in the Burmese. 1894 R. F. St. John *Burmese Reader* Pref., It is a great mistake to suppose that Burmese ..can be learnt properly from a phrase-book.

Burmite (bə̄·ɹməit). [f. *Burma* + -ite[1].] A variety of amber found in Burma, used by the Chinese in the manufacture of objects of art.
1909 in *Cent. Dict.* Suppl.

Burn, *sb.*[3] Add:
1. b. *spec.* An instance of burning the vegetation on land as a means of clearing it for cultivation. (Cf. Burning *vbl. sb.* 8 a.) **c.** A place where the trees or brush have been burned; a clearing in the woods made in this way. *U.S.*
1861 *Trans. Ill. Agric. Soc.* IV. 489, I considered two crops of small grain equal to a burn. 1868 *Amer. Naturalist* Oct. 468 They [*sc.* deer] resort always to a recent burn, when grass and weeds are just shooting again and are soft. 1872 *Rep. Vermont Board Agric.* 350 Mr. Hovey..spoke of the injury resulting from heavy burns in clearing land.
4. The quality of tobacco-leaf as indicated by its greater or less reduction to ash when smoked.
1901 *Yearbk. U.S. Dept. Agric.* 165 (Cent. D. Suppl.).
5. An injury to which tobacco-leaf is liable in the process of curing, as the result of excessive moisture in the air.
1909 in *Cent. Dict.* Suppl.

Burn, *v.*[1] Add:
8. d. To spend or use freely; esp. *to have* (money, etc.) *to burn*, to have in abundance or to spare. orig. *U.S.*
1897 *Congress. Rec.* Mar. 400/1 Mr. Simpson:—You have plenty of time. Mr. Payne:—No; I have not got time to burn. 1904 *Louisville Courier Jrnl.* 2 July 5 She has ..already had literary experience to burn. 1909 'O. Henry' *Options* (1916) 76 The gentleman of the family had owned plantations and had slaves to burn. 1910 W. M. Raine *B. O'Connor* 39 We'll keep an eye on the gambling bells and see who is burning up money. 1911 H. Quick *Yellowstone N.* ix. 240 The gall of my swearing against these big men that had money to burn. 1915 'Ian Hay' *First Hundred Thous.* xvi. (1916) 220 You will get baccy and cigarettes to burn out there. 1917 H. A. Vachell *Fishpingle* x, Why not? I have money to burn. 1928 *Sunday Express* 6 May 6 People in the States have 'money to burn'.
9. b. *To burn the earth* or *wind*: to go at full speed. *U.S.*
1903 A. Adams *Log Cowboy* iii. 37, I was half a mile in the lead burning the earth like a canned dog. 1910 W. M. Raine *B. O'Connor* 20 So burn the wind, and go through the car on the jump. *Ibid.* 57 When he finds out how the horse he's after is burning the wind, his suspicions grow stronger.
13. c. *To burn on*: to add (a part) to an injured or incomplete casting by running in a stream of molten metal.
1888 *Lockwood's Dict. Terms Mech. Engin.* 53 A sand mould of the portion to be burned on is made and placed in proper juxtaposition to the old casting in the bed of the foundry floor.
f. To vulcanize (india-rubber) by mixing it with sulphur or metallic sulphids and heating it.
1900 Sadtler *Handbk. Indust. Chem.* (ed. 3) 106 In vulcanizing by the first process, that of 'burning', as it is termed, the crude caoutchouc is mixed with varying amounts of sulphur.
14. f. To swindle. *U.S. slang.* ? *Obs.*
1844 *Philad. Spirit of Times* 19 Aug. (Th.) Two negro burners were arrested in the act of trying to burn two Pottsville boatmen with a plated chain worth about fifteen cents.
15. (Later examples.)
1851 C. Cist *Cincinnati* 250 Henry Albro, who was burnt out some months since, on Front street, has recently put up new veneer and saw mills. *a* 1861 T. Winthrop *John Brent* i. 7 They had been burnt out, they had been cleaned out, they had been drowned out.
18. *To burn out*: to fuse by means of an electric current. Cf. *burn-out* b, s.v. *Burn- 3.
1924 *Discovery* June 83/2 The Germans were using some objectionable form of frightfulness that burnt out the magnetos of French planes flying across German zones.

Burn-. Add:
3. With the verb + adv., as burn-out, (*a*) a complete destruction by fire; (*b*) *Electr.* the fusing of a wire or other electric conductor by excess of electric current; also *attrib.*, as *burn-out fuse, alloy*, one that melts at a comparatively low temperature and serves as a safeguard against damage by excess of current.
1903 *Daily Chron.* 29 June 7/5 It has been a burn-out of three floors and roof destroyed. 1907 *Installation News* Mar. 4/1 Incipient fires and burnouts, due to the earthing of high voltage systems on building fronts, etc.

Burner. Add:
1. c. A swindler. ? *Obs. U.S.* (Cf. *Burn *v.* 14 f.)
1838 *Lexington Observer & Reporter* 3 Nov., He pulls out his pocket book, it is seized by the burner who makes off with it. 1842 *Philad. Spirit of Times* 15 Jan. (Th.) The burners make better plots than most of our dramatists. 1845 *Congress. Globe* 6 Jan. App. 118/1 The Empire Club [of New York]..consisted of gamblers, pickpockets, droppers, burners, thimble-riggers and the like.
4. b. *Welsbach incandescent gas burner*, a burner devised by Auer von Welsbach for producing an incandescent light by means of a mantle (see Mantle *sb.* 5 g) and Bunsen burner. Also called the *Auer, incandescent*, or *Welsbach burner*.
1894 [see Incandescent *a.* 1 d]. 1902 *Encycl. Brit.* XXX. 260/2 Incandescent Burners. The invention of the Welsbach mantle places at the disposal of lighthouse authorities the means of producing a light of high intensity.
5. A blow-lamp for heating old paint to facilitate its removal (*Cent. Dict.* Suppl. 1909).

Burnet, *sb.*[2] Add:
3. In the names of species of moths belonging to the genus *Anthrocera*; cf. *burnet-moth* in 2.
1832 J. Rennie *Butterfl. & Moths* 22 The Melilot Burnet. ..The Trefoil Burnet...The Five Spot Burnet. 1921 *19th Cent.* Feb. 273 The Zygaenidae, or Burnets.

Burnham (bə̄·ɹnəm), name of Harry Lawson Webster Lawson, first Viscount *Burnham*, who was chairman of the Standing Joint Committee of Education Authorities and Teachers, set up on the 12th Sept., 1919; hence applied to the scale of salaries, etc. recommended by him.
1920 *Jrnl. Education* Jan. 18 The notable modesty of the proposals of the Burnham Committee on Salaries. 1921 *Ibid.* July 426 The Burnham scale of salaries.

Burning, *vbl. sb.* **8. b.** Add: Also, the quantity of bricks burnt at one operation.
1901 *Pall Mall Gaz.* 9 Dec. 8/2 No two burnings (a burning is a kiln full of bricks) have exactly the same shade of colour.

Burnsian (bə̄·ɹnziăn), *a.* and *sb.* [f. the name of Robert *Burns* (1759–96) + -ian.] **a.** *adj.* Of or relating to Burns, his works, or his style. **b.** *sb.* An admirer of Burns or his works. So also **Burnsia·na** [-ana], things connected with Burns. **Bu·rnsite** = *Burnsian *sb.*
1904 *Daily Chron.* 22 Aug. 3/1 The accumulating literature of Burnsian topography. 1905 *Westm. Gaz.* 13 Apr. 12/1 Collectors of Burnsiana. 1909 *Daily Chron.* 14 Aug. 3/1 All Burnsites—common or peculiar. *Ibid.*, Devotees of the Burnsian cult. 1920 *Glasgow Herald* 28 July 6 A representative gathering of Scottish Burnsians.

Burnsides (bə̄·ɹnsəidz), *sb. pl.* *U.S.* [f. the proper name: see below.] 'A style of beard such as that affected by General Burnside (1824–81), consisting of a mustache, whiskers, and a clean-shaven chin' (*Cent. Dict.* Suppl. 1909).
1930 *Publishers' Weekly* (N. Y.) 8 Feb. 679 In the days of copper-toed boots and burnsides..our grandfathers were buying this book.

Burnt, *ppl. a.* Add: **6. c.** (See quot.)
1909 *Daily Chron.* 23 Feb. 7/2 The buyer should beware of..burnt furs. Such furs have been over-dyed, and the hair will soon become rusty and fall out.
7. **burnt almond**, an almond enclosed in burnt sugar; hence, a fashion shade of brown; **burnt cork** *sb.* used attrib. in *burnt-cork artist*, a negro minstrel (see Negro 3); **burnt-cork** *v.*, to blacken (the face and hands) with burnt cork in imitation of the negro complexion; **burnt feed** *Austral.* (see quot.).
1850 *Family Friend* III. 327/1 Put a *burnt almond.. in the centre. 1892 *Encycl. Pract. Cookery* 14/2 Pound the Burnt Almonds..in a mortar. 1895 *Cassell's Fam. Mag.* June 554/1 [A bonnet] of burnt-almond straw. 1913 'Ascott R. Hope' *Half and Half Trag.* 121 Treating me to twopence worth of 'burned almonds'. 1873 — *Night Before Holidays* (1874) 98 We had one very fine false beard,..and there was plenty of *burned cork to be had. 1909 *Daily Chron.* 31 July 6/1 He was among the earliest of the 'Christy Minstrels', and..was in the front rank of burnt-cork artists. 1885 Jerome *On the Stage* 3 We..*burnt-corked our hands and faces. 1898 *Daily News* 6 May 2/6 For money-making it is necessary to wear masks or to burnt-cork the face. 1848 H. W. Haygarth *Bush Life Australia* vii. 73 A patch of '*burnt feed' (as the young herbage is called which springs up..where the old grass has been set on fire).
8. *Burnt* (*colour*), a deep shade of yellowish brown; hence *burnt, burnt-coloured* adjs.
1896 *Daily News* 2 July 8/7 Hats of 'burnt' straw, this being the technical name of a deep shade of yellowish brown. 1899 *Westm. Gaz.* 20 Apr. 3/3 Burnt-coloured straw. 1923 *Weekly Dispatch* 25 Feb. 14 Colours: Navy, ..Nut, Mastic and Burnt.
b. Of a colour or shade of colour: Having the appearance of loss of brightness by scorching rather than by fading.
1923 *Daily Mail* 19 Feb. 5 Coloured Shantung...In a full range of new colourings, including..Rose, Burnt Orange, Almond, [etc.]. *Ibid.* 19 Mar. 1 Burnt Gold.

Burnwood (bə̄·ɹnwud). A species of sumac, *Rhus Metopium*, found in the West Indies and southern Florida.
1874 *Treas. Bot.* Suppl., Burnwood of the West Indian negroes. *Rhus Metopium*.

Bur-oak, burr-oak. *U.S.* [Bur *sb.* 8.] A North American variety of oak (*Quercus macrocarpa*), so called from the appearance of the acorn; the overcup or mossycup oak.
a. 1815 D. Drake *Cincinnati* ii. 82 The most valuable timber trees are the..bur oaks. 1832 Peck *Guide for Emigrants* ii. 122 Several oaks—as, over cup bur oak, [etc.]. 1845 J. Gregg *Commerce of Prairies* II. 194 Large black and bur-oak. 1882 *Econ. Geol. Illinois* II. 3 The timber..consists principally of the swamps white oak, pin oak, bur oak, [etc.].
β. 1818 in *Trans. Ill. State Hist. Soc.* 1910, 157 The most Common timber is..Pin and Burrh Oak, Walnut, [etc.]. 1835 Hoffman *Winter in West* I. 218 A pile of burr-oak, which makes a capital fire, flames up the enormous wooden chimney before me. 1848 J. F. Cooper *Oak Open.* I. i. 10 The trees..were what is called the 'burr-oak', a small variety of a very extensive genus. 1861 *Trans. Ill. Agric. Soc.* IV. 452 Railroad men regard it as only second to the Burr Oak for railroad ties. 1873 *Congress. Rec.* Jan., App. 7/3 Large quantities of live-oak, white-oak, burr-oak. *attrib.* 1840 in *Trans. Mich. Agric. Soc.* (1855) VI. 275 Marl was examined..in a dry burr oak plain.

Burqa, var. *Burka [1].

Burr, *sb.*[3] Delete † *Obs.* and add quots.:
1856 P. Cartwright *Autob.* viii. (1858) 46, I struck a sudden blow in the burr of the ear and dropped him to the earth. 1928 S. French *In Valley* 121, I whammed him in the burr of the ear and piled him.

Burr, *sb.*[6] Add: **1. a.** (Earlier example.)
1652 *Dedham Rec.* 210 Things tendered to be sold..the mill itselfe,..the burre bought to make a new millstone, [etc.].
5. *burr millstone* (U.S.).
1829 S. Cummings *Western Pilot* 23 This..is famous for its quarries of stone; from which are manufactured burr mill stones. 1851 Cist *Cincinnati* 182 James Bradford & Co.. manufacture yearly seventy-five pairs burr millstones.

Burr (bə̄ɹ), *v.*[4] [f. Burr *sb.*[4]] **a.** *intr.* To use a burr. **b.** *trans.* To excavate (a tooth) with a burr. Hence **Bu·rring** *vbl. sb. attrib.*, as **burring-engine**, a dentist's machine for driving a burr-drill, etc.; **burring tool** (see Burr *sb.*[4] 2 b).
1875 *Dental Cosmos* XVII. 510 With the burring-engine I ground off enough of the cusp.

Burra Sahib (bʊ·rā,sā·ib). *Anglo-Ind.* [Hind. *barā* great, *çāhib* master (see Sahib).] A title of respect used by Indians in referring to the head of a family, the chief officer in a station, the head of a department, etc.

1863 Trevelyan *Dawk Bungalow* 1, Chota Sahib one rupee give. Burra Sahib two rupee. 1885 Lady Dufferin *Viceregal Life India* (1889) I. 57 The great lords and ladies (Burra Sahib and Burra Mem Sahib). 1922 *Blackw. Mag.* Sept. 283/2, I made my way to the burra Police Sahib. 1928 *Chambers's Jrnl.* Feb. 180/2 The Hindu..announced it to be the habitation of a very *burra* (high in station) sahib.

Burrass. (Earlier example.) Cf. Barras[1], and *barras* sb.[2] in Eng. Dial. Dict.

1770 *Carroll Papers* in *Maryland Hist. Mag.* XIII. 66 Pray write for 6 strong matrasses .. strongly Quilted & Covered with Burras or a Coarse strong Canvass.

Burrawang (bʊ·răwæŋ). *Australia.* Also **buddawong, burrowan, burwan.** [f. the name of Mt. *Budawang*, New South Wales.] An Australian tree, *Macrozamia spiralis*; the nut produced by this tree.

1827 P. Cunningham *N. S. Wales* I. 221 The burwan is a nut much relished by our natives. 1851 J. Henderson *Excurs. N. S. Wales* II. 238 The Burrowan, which grows in a sandy soil. 1877 Emily A. Heron *Balance Pain, Buddawong's Crown* i, A Buddawong seed-nut fell to earth. 1889 J. H. Maiden *Usef. Native Plants Australia* 41 'Burrawang Nut', so called because they used to be, and are to some extent now, very common about Burrawang, N. S. W.

Burred (bɔːd), *a.* [f. Bur *sb.* + -ed[2].] Rough and prickly like a bur.

1906 *Westm. Gaz.* 8 Sept. 2/3 He falls furiously on the ball..until it is hopelessly burred and gashed. 1924 *Glasgow Herald* 4 Apr. 8 The burred fruits are accounted for by their clinging to the feathers of birds.

Burrell, burrhel, var. *Burhel.

Burring, *vbl. sb.*[1] Add: **burring rollers** *pl.*, an apparatus for removing the burrs from wool in preparing it for carding.

1884 McLaren *Spinning* (ed. 2) 83 The burrs..lie along the fibres of wool...To clear them off, burring rollers are fixed on the top of two of the lickers-in. 1888 *Encycl. Brit.* XXIV. 658 The swift as it travels round is met by a series of three burring rollers rotating in an opposite direction.

Burring (bɔ̄·riŋ), *vbl. sb.*[2] [f. Burr *v.*[3] + -ing[1].] The pronunciation of *r* by uvular vibration.

1863 A. M. Bell *Princ. Speech* 190 The uvular vibration constitutes what is called burring.

Bu·rrite. *U.S. Hist.* [f. the name of Aaron *Burr* (1756–1836).] (See quot. 1885.)

1802 *Balance* (Hudson, N. Y.) 10 Aug. 250 (Th.) Burrites! Clintonians! Democrats! hear me or my family. 1841 Foote *Texas & Texans* I. 148 Blennerhasset's Journal.. asserts that they were both Burrites. 1885 C. L. Norton in *Mag. Amer. Hist.* XIII. 98 *Burrites*, an independent political party organized and led by Aaron Burr in 1797. Its existence was short-lived, terminating with Burr's overwhelming defeat at the polls the same year.

Burro. Add to def.: Now esp. *U.S.* (common in Western states).

1845 T. J. Green *Jrnl. Texian Exped.* xii. 166 The sick were permitted to ride upon 'burros' (jack-asses). 1882 *Rep. Prec. Met. U.S.* 569 With these attached a burro or horse runs the machine.

Burr-oak: see *Bur-oak.

Burrow, *sb.*[1] Add: **1. c.** *transf.*

1910 *Practitioner* June 838 In patients whose occupation necessitates frequent washing of the hands and arms, the typical burrows so usually found between the fingers and on the anterior aspects of the wrists may be entirely absent.

Bursati, bursautee (bɔɪsā·tī, bɔɪsǭ·tī). *Anglo-Indian.* Also **bursatti, -ee.** [Hindi *barsātī* adj., relating to rain, f. *barsāt* the rains.]

1. A disease incident to horses during the rains, characterized by pustular eruptions on the head and fore-parts of the body.

1886 Kipling *Departm. Ditties* (1888) 62 Blister we not for *bursati*?

2. A waterproof coat or rain coat.

1880 *Pioneer Mail* 8 July 12/1 The scenery has now been arranged for the second act of the Simla season..and the appropriate costume for both sexes is the decorous bursatti.

Bursiculate (bɔɪsi·kiŭlĕt), *a. Bot.* and *Anat.* [ad. mod. L. *bursiculatus*, f. *bursicula*, dim. of L. *bursa* purse.] Resembling a purse or pouch, bursiform.

1880 in Webster Suppl.

Bursitis (bɔɪsəi·tis). *Path.* [mod.L., f. Bursa + -itis.] Inflammation of a bursa.

1857 Dunglison *Med. Lex.*, *Synovitis*...When it affects the bursæ it is sometimes called Bursitis. 1908 *Practitioner* June 865 Myositis, phlebitis, bursitis.

Burst, *sb.* **7.** (Earlier example. See also Bust *sb.*[3])

1849 T. T. Johnson *Sights in Gold Region* xix. 183 Bill and Gus had come over from the Middle Fork for a particular, general and universal 'burst'.

Burst, *v.* Add:

2. d. With *up*. To become 'broken' or bankrupt.

1865 Dickens *Mut. Fr.* iii. xii, Then you think, Mrs. Lammle, that if Lammle got time, he wouldn't burst up?—To use an expression..which is adopted in the Money Market.

21. To spend (money) extravagantly; *esp.* to spend it 'on the burst' or 'on the spree'. *slang.*

1892 A. Murdoch *Yoshiwara Episode* 37 It sounds odd to be told that a fellow's conscientious scruples are lax enough to permit him to 'burst' $6 50c. on the very much off-chance of ever seeing a cent of his investment again. 1908 *Westm. Gaz.* 31 Mar. 10/3 Two natives..returned to visit their old relatives at home, and burst a little money on the spree.

22. In pin-pool billiards, to go beyond the score of 31. In ball-pool, to smash at the pyramid.

1890 C. C. Moore *Games of Pool* 71 Burst Players. If the player has knocked down pins whose aggregate number.. exceeds a total of thirty-one,..he is then 'burst', and must drop out of the game. *Ibid.* 72 When a player bursts and a privilege is taken, the player so bursting retains the original number in the order of its play.

Burst, *ppl. a.* **1.** Add: Also with advs., as *burst-out, burst-up.*

1900 *Engineering Mag.* XIX. 746/1 The burst-up condition of the decks..showing..the behaviour of the lyddite shells.

Bursted, *ppl. a.* Add: **b.** 'Cleaned out, broke.' *U.S. colloq.* (See also *Busted.)

1873 *Chicago Daily Tribune* 30 June (Farmer, Slang) Four lank and bursted frontiersmen.

Burster. Add: **3.** *Mining.* A blast-hole bored in coal not previously prepared for blasting (*Cent. Dict.* Suppl. 1909).

Bursting, *vbl. sb.* Add: **1. c.** *fig.* A financial break-down. *U.S.*

1834 H. Clay in *Congress. Deb.* 27 Feb. 747 You must lend us $300.000. to prevent a general bursting.

Burton[1] (bɔ̄·ɪt'n). Place-name (in full Burton-on-Trent) used attrib. in *Burton ale* = *Bass *sb.*[6]

1738 in *Westm. Gaz.* (1902) 24 Feb. 2/3 Genuine Burton Ale, Brew'd to the Greatest Perfection for Keeping by Sea and Land. 1846 Tizard *Brewing* (ed. 2) 114 The Burton ales principally owe their superior qualities and uniform permanency to the nature of the water there used. 1882 E. G. Hooper *Man. Brewing* (ed. 2) 118 The Burton beer has been long noted for its high character. 1884 *Glass of Pale Ale* 16 The Burton Ale diamond label was not issued until..1857. 1896 H. G. Wells *Wheels of Chance* vi, Burton and biscuit and cheese he had, which indeed, is Burton in its proper company.

Burton[2] (bɔ̄·ɪt'n). *Naut.* [Cf. Burton in Dict.] A term denoting the thwartship stowage of casks, bags, etc. Also **a-burton** (see quots. 1846, 1867).

1846 A. Young *Naut. Dict.* s.v. *A-burton*, Casks are said to be stowed a-burton, when placed athwartships in the hold. 1867 Smyth *Sailor's Word-bk.*, *A-burton*, the situation of casks when they are stowed in the hold athwart ship, or in a line with the beam. 1928 *Observer* 22 July 10/7 Terms as used by stevedores...'Burton' to describe the thwart-ship stowage of bags, as against the fore and aft method. *Ibid.* 29 July 7/3, I have..both stowed and worked out 'Burtons' many scores of times during the twenty-five years I spent along the East End waterside.

Burtonize (bɔ̄·ɪt'nəiz), *v.* [f. *Burton[1] + -ize.] *trans.* To harden (water for brewing) by treatment with gypsum, salt, and sulphate of magnesia.

1882 E. G. Hooper *Man. Brewing* (ed. 2) 120 Burtonising...A hardening mixture giving solids similar to those of the Burton water may be made as follows:—Four parts of gypsum [etc.]. 1892 H. E. Wright *Handy Bk. Brewers* 116 The presence of bicarbonates or carbonates may explain certain negative..results which sometimes attend the so-called 'Burtonising' of brewing water.

Hence **Burtonizer** (bɔ̄·ɪt'nəizəɪ): see quot.

1908 *Daily Chron.* 12 Nov. 1/2 Burtonisers..are chiefly sulphates and chlorides of calcium and magnesium.

Bury, *v.* **4. b.** Add: Of a vessel: To plunge the bows under water. *U.S.*

1886 *Outing* (U.S.) Nov. 117/1 It was asserted that she [*sc.* the keel schooner] was too fine forward,..that she would bury in driving hard.

Buryat: see *Buriat.

Bus, *sb.*[2] Add:

1. b. Phr. *To miss the bus* (fig.): to lose an opportunity; to fail in an undertaking. *slang.*

1915 C. J. Dennis *Sentimental Bloke* 118 The deeds and words of some un'appy bloke Who's missed the bus. 1922 *Daily Mail* 28 Oct. 8/3 The Prime Minister has 'missed the 'bus'...He has thrown away the greatest opportunity ever offered..to any statesman.

2. *colloq.* **a.** An aeroplane, esp. a heavy one. **b.** A motor car.

1913 *Aeroplane* 6 Feb. 124/2 The casual pilot calls the machine a ''bus'. 1916 C. Winchester *Flying Men* 213 We were about 2500 feet above the ''buses'. 1919 *Athenæum* 23 May 360/2 What may be called air-lingo comprises..such terms of affection as 'the old bus'. 1921 *Times Lit. Suppl.* 24 Feb. 113/4 Cadets..marching in their companies and battalions or gadgeting with 'buses on Port Meadow.

3. *attrib.* and *Comb.*: simple attrib., as *bus company, conductor* (Conductor 7); *bus-riding* adj.; **bus-bar, -conductor,** *Electr.*, a system of conductors in a generating station on which all the power of all the generators is collected for distribution or, in a receiving station, on which the power from the generating station is received for distribution; also *attrib.* (cf. Omnibus *a.* 2 c); **busman,** the driver of a bus; *a busman's holiday*, leisure time spent in occupations of the same nature as those in which one engages for a living; **bus-rod** = *bus-bar*; **bus-top,** the top of a bus, furnished with seats for outside passengers; also *attrib.*

1893 Sloane *Stand. Elect. Dict.*, *Bus Rod*...*Synonyms*—Omnibus Rod, Wire or Bar—*Bus Bar, or Wire. 1897 *Daily News* 9 Dec. 10/3 The currents of electricity generated at these dynamos are led to one common conductor called 'the bus-bar'. 1911 *Engineer* 10 Mar. 238/3 The busbar voltage suddenly dropped. 1905 *Times* 9 Mar. 13/4 The London and District Motor *Bus Company 1846 *Chambers's Jrnl.* V. 28/2 The only cry heard would be that of the *'bus-conductor for Paddington and Holloway. 1886 *Punch* 27 Nov. 254/1 Bus Conductor (shouting from the Foot-board). Wes'minister! 1902 Webster Suppl. s.v. *Bus*, Bus..conductor, etc. (*Elec.*). 1919 Barry Pain *Problem Club* x. 187 A more obliging set of men than the London bus-conductors couldn't be found. 1851, 1887 *busman [in Dict.]. 1921 *Times* (weekly ed.) 19 Aug., The proverbial 'busman's holiday' is nothing to that of the man who retires from business. 1927 *Observer* 21 Aug. 13/2 The U.S.A. Secretary for War..said..'No, I did not go to see the military manœuvres. Busmen's holidays do not give me any delight.' *Ibid.* 9 Oct. 16/6 A Foreign Secretary's holiday is in some degree a busman's holiday. 1898 *Daily News* 14 Apr. 7/2 The *'bus riding public. 1905 *Westm. Gaz.* 31 May 10/2 'The Delights of London', introducing various amusing 'imitations'—in a tea-shop, on a *'bus-top, and so forth. 1927 *Glasgow Herald* 18 Aug. 9 The most interesting 'bus-top ride which London can offer.

Bus, *v.* Add: Also without *it.*

1889 *Punch* 2 Mar. 107/1 'Bus'-ing on the cheap.

Busaun (bū·zaʊ·n). [G.] A soft reed stop on the organ.

1876 Stainer & Barrett *Dict. Mus. Terms* (1898) 65/2 Busaun. Busain. Buzain.

Buser (bɔ·səɪ). (Disused.) Also **busser.** [f. Bus *sb.*[2] + -er[1].] A bus horse.

1894 *Daily Tel.* 10 Nov. 10/5 [For sale] By order of the Star Omnibus Company, six useful busers. 1900 *Ibid.* 5 Sept. 7/2 The English 'bussers'..performed their part admirably as heavy artillery horses. 1901 *Morn. Post* 9 Apr. 8/1 Active short-legged bussers. All warranted quiet in harness.

Bush, *sb.*[1] Add: **1. d.** *U.S.* in *pl.* = sense 9.

1879 Tourgee *Fool's Err.* xxii. 130 That refuge of free thought at the South, the woods (or 'the bushes', as the scraggly growth is more generally termed). 1912 Mathewson *Pitching* x. 210 The youngsters, who have come from the bushes and realize that this is their..chance to make good.

6. b. A signalling instrument used in Cornish pilchard fishing. *local.*

1880 Miss M. A. Courtney *W. Cornw. Gloss.* 1892 *Graphic* 13 Aug. 194/1 The huers on land making signals to the boatmen with two instruments called 'bushes', which are hoops crossing each other, and covered with a white bag, and fastened to the end of short rods.

c. The cat-o'-nine-tails. *slang.*

1895 *Daily News* 13 Sept. 7/6 They might give him twenty years, and he should not care, so long as they did not order him the bush.

10. *bush-clad, -covered, -fringed* adjs.

1909 *Westm. Gaz.* 4 June 5/3 The *bush-clad plains of the North-Eastern Transvaal. 1901 'Linesman' *Words Eye-witness* (1902) 81 The rocky *bush-covered foot of Schwartz Kop. 1891 J. Evelyn *Baffled Vengeance* 47 The river between its *bush-fringed banks.

11. bush-baby, an African lemur of the species *Galago senegalensis* (or *G. moholi*); **bush-bean** (examples); **bush-beater,** (*a*) = Bushwhacker 1; (*b*) (cf. Bush *sb.*[1] 1 b, *fig.*); **bushboy,** a native Australian or South African bushman; **Bush Brotherhood,** a society of missionaries, clerical and lay, whose object is to evangelize the inhabitants of the Australian bush; **bush-car** (see quot. 1926); **bush-coral,** a bushy gorgonian, esp. *Acanella normani*, found in the North Atlantic (Funk's Standard Dict. 1895); **bush cow,** (*a*) a wild cow of the bush; (*b*) the tapir (see quot. 1851); **bushcraft,** skill in matters pertaining to life in the bush; **bush dassie,** a S. African cony, *Procavia arborea*; also *attrib.*; **bush deer,** in W. Africa, a gazelle; **bush dog,** (*a*) see quot.; (*b*) a lemur of the species *Perodicticus potto* (Cent. Dict.); **bush-dray** *Austral.* (see quot.); **bush-drive,** a drive of game in the South African bush; **bush eel** (see quot.); **bush flea,** a variety of *Pulex* so called in Natal; **bush-goat,** a S. African warbler (see quot.); **bush gourd,** the squash gourd, *Cucurbita Melopepo*; **bush-hawk** (see quot.); **bush-honeysuckle** (see Honeysuckle 3); also, any bushy species of *Lonicera*; **bush-hook** *U.S.* (earlier example); **bush-light** *U.S.* (see quot.); **bushloper** *U.S.*, one who tramps through the bush or wilderness, a pedlar; **bush-magpie,** a name given by Australian townsfolk to the crow-shrike of the bush, genus *Gymnorhina*, as distinguished from one tamed or domesticated; **bush-meeting** *U.S.* (see quot.); **bush partridge,** a S. African name of a species of francolin, *Francolinus subtorquatus*; **bush pea,** a leguminous plant of the genus *Thermopsis*, esp. *T. Montana*; **bush-pig,** a species of S. African swine, *Potamochœrus chœropotamus*; **bush poppy,** in *Californian* or *white bush poppy*, a papaveraceous plant of the species *Romneya coulteri*, a bushy plant bearing large poppy-like white flowers; **bush-quail,** (*a*) a Hemipod; (*b*) an Indian bird of the genus *Perdicula*, *Ophrysia*, or *Microperdix* (Stand. Dict. 1895); **bush-rat** *U.S.* (see quot.); **bush-scythe** (mod. U.S. examples); **bush-sheep** *U.S.* (see quot.); **bush-shrike,** a South American ant-eating bird of the subfamily *Thamnophilinæ*; **bush-sickness** (see quot.); **bush tea,** the leaves of certain shrubs, dried and used as tea in S. Africa, esp. those of a species of *Cyclopia*, used as tea and medicinally; **bush telegraph** *Austral.*, bushrangers' confederates who disseminate information as to the movements of the police; **bush-tick** (see quot. 1886); also *attrib.* in **bush-tick berry,** the fruit of *Osteospermum moniliferum*; **bush-tit,** a bird of the genus *Psaltriparus*; **bush-titmouse** *U.S.* (see quot.); **bush-warbler,** (*a*) a bird of any of the species belonging to the genus *Cettia*, found chiefly in Asia; (*b*) see quot.; **bush-water,** rain water that collects in the low-lying parts of tropical forests; **bush willow,** in S. Africa, a plant of either of the species *Combretum erythrophyllum* or *C. salicifolium*; **bushwoman,** a woman living in the Australian or African bush; **bush-wood,** Schimper's term (*buschwald*) for woodland in which the trees are so separated by shrubby growth that their crowns do not touch; **bush-wren,** the New Zealand colonists' name for a bird of the species *Xenicus longipes.*

1901 A. R. R. Turnbull *Tales fr. Natal* 81 The occasional cry of a *bush-baby alone broke the awful silence. 1928 *Daily Tel.* 15 May 14/3 Two bush babies, the pets of Baroness de Tuyll. 1862 *Trans. Ill. Agric. Soc.* (1865) V. 518 We usually plant *bush beans in garden drills. 1887 *Harper's Mag.* Jan. 307/2 Those who need much instruction in regard to bush-beans should remain in the city. 1809 W. Irving *Knickerb.* vi. iv, Such was the legion of sturdy *bush-beaters that poured in at the grand gate of New-Amsterdam. 1897 W. C. Hazlitt *Ourselves* v. 64 [Girls at bazaar] Many bush-beaters, one hare-catcher—the dear, good rector! *a* 1834 T. Pringle *Poet. Wks.* (1839) 8 Afar in the Desert I love to ride, With the silent *Bush-boy alone by my side. 1850 R. G. Cumming *Hunter's Life S. Afr.* (1902) 32/1, I found a funny little fellow in the shape of the Bushboy before alluded to, awaiting my arrival. 1899 Jas. Milne *Romance Proconsul* xiv. 149 He would..shoulder his rifle, and start off, with a couple of bush-boys for gillies. 1903 *Daily Chron.* 7 Nov. 5/5 Founding a *Bush Brotherhood under the direction of the Bishop. 1921 *United Free Ch. Mission Rec.* Apr. 116/1 She left at midday in a *bush-car. 1926 *Ibid.* May 227/1 The bush-car is an arm-chair placed high above one wheel, excellent for the narrow paths and high grass of Africa. 1851 W. H. Brett *Indian Missions Guiana* 37 The tapir or maipuri, called the *bush-cow by the settlers. 1897 Mary Kingsley *W. Africa* 734 The bush cow came on, and drove its horns through his thigh. 1897 *Westm. Gaz.* 22 July 4/2 Leichardt perished..because he lacked the rudiments of *bushcraft. 1911 Bean '*Dreadnought' of Darling* xxxvi. 324 Real scouting and bush-craft will always be part of the station life. 1911 *East London Dispatch* 20 Dec. 5 (Pettman) *Bush dassie flesh was the staple food for the Hottentots. 1897 Mary Kingsley *W. Africa* 734 He..put his net into the forest, and caught *bush deer (gazelles). 1883 *Encycl. Brit.* XV. 438/2 *Icticyon*, with one small species, *Canis venaticus*, the *Bush Dog, from Guiana and Brazil. 1848 Haygarth *Bush Life Australia* v. 48 The *bush-dray, the only vehicle used in New South Wales for the conveyance of wool and other produce, is open and low, more resembling a brewer's dray than any other description of dray known in England. 1899 *Proc. Zool. Soc. Lond.* 831 At the *bush-drives so common in the [Cape] Colony, Blue-buck are seldom turned out. 1828 Hone *Table-book* (1833) II. 224 At this season when persons, at inns in Lincolnshire, ask for 'eel pie', they are presently provided with '*bush eels'; namely snakes, caught for that purpose in the bushes. 1899 G. Russell *Old Durban* 503 The *Bush Flea..is quite content to share your camp blanket if you do not resent his liberty of action. 1908 Haagner & Ivy *Sk. S. Afr. Birds* 79 This Warbler is called the *Bush-goat on account of the plaintive goat-like call to which the bird gives utterance. 1842 *Bush gourd [see *squash-melon pumpkin* s.v. Squash *sb.*[3] 4]. 1882 *Encycl. Brit.* XIV. 54 No Kestrel is found in New Zealand, but an approach to the form is made by the very peculiar *Hieracidea* (or *Harpa*) *novæ-zelandiæ*.. the 'Sparrow-Hawk', 'Quail-Hawk', and '*Bush-Hawk' of the colonists. 1860 Holland *Miss Gilbert* iv. 55 The old man took down a *bush-hook that hung upon a post near the mill. 1838 Caroline Gilman *Recoll. Southern Matron* 82 A *bush-light was flaming near Jaque's habitation. [*Note*] A fire of light wood kindled on a small mound of earth. *a* 1909 E. Eggleston *Duffels* Pref. (Cent. D. Suppl.) *Bushloper. 1889 *Cassell's Picturesque Australasia* II. 235 The College precincts are sacred to the classic muse and the omnipresent *bush-magpie. 1889 Farmer *Americanisms*, **Bush meeting*, a gathering in the woods for the purpose of open-air preaching, and other religious exercises. 1909 *South African Field* 30 July 141 (Pettman) My companions called it (Coquifrancolin) the *bush partridge. 1844 J. Backhouse *Narr. Mauritius & S. Afr.* 213 The Bosch Vark, **Bush Pig*. 1910 John Buchan *Prester John* xiv, I was inclined to think him a very large bush-pig. 1899 T. W. Sanders *Encycl. Gard.* (ed. 3), *Romneya* (White *Bush Poppy). 1900 *Bk. Gardening* (ed. W. D. Drury) 281 Californian Bush Poppy. 1893 H. A. Bryden *Gun & Camera in S. Afr.* 158 Tiny *bush-quail (*Turnix lepurana*), dainty creatures, scarcely bigger than sparrows. 1867 *Amer. Naturalist* I. 399 The *Bush Rat (*Neotoma Mexicana*) is abundant throughout the territory [Arizona]. 1856 *Trans. Mich. Agric. Soc.* VII. 54 D. O. and W. S. Perry.. [exhibited] three *bush scythes. 1873–4 *Rep. Vermont Board Agric.* II. 194 It is possible to subdue them..by cutting them off near the ground with a bush-scythe. 1867–8 *Trans. Ill. Agric. Soc.* VII. 457 Sheep shipped in for sale because they 'didn't flourish' on prairie grass. These '*bush sheep', as they are called, have been in abundant supply. 1893 Newton *Dict. Birds* 21 The large genus *Thamnophilus*, containing upwards of 50 species, is one of the most important of the so-called '*Bush-Shrikes'. 1929 *Times* 1 July 15/6 Lack of minerals in pastures causes innumerable diseases, such as..'*bush-sickness'..in New Zealand. *Ibid.* 16/2 Able to..identify 'Nakuruitis' as similar to 'bush-sickness' in New Zealand. 1858 Simmonds *Dict. Trade*, **Bush Tea*, the leaflets of a species of *Cyclopia*, probably *C. latifolia*..supposed to possess expectorant and restorative properties. 1902 X. C. *Everyday Life in Cape Colony* ix. 122 In most of these Colonial stores 'bush' tea can be bought. 1878 *Australian* I. 507 (Morris) The police are baffled by..the number and activity of the *bush telegraphs. 1893 K. Mackay '*Out Back*' v, A hint dropped in this town set the bush telegraphs riding in all directions. 1865 Harvey & Sonder *Flora Capensis* III. 436 A large bush..the Colonial name is *Bush-tick Berry. 1886 *Pall Mall Gaz.* 22 July 4/1 The *carrapato*, or bush-tick..is a degenerate spider. 1893 Newton *Dict. Birds* 83 *note*, *Chamæa*...'*Bush-Tit' and 'Ground-Wren'. 1881 *Amer. Naturalist* XV. 213 That diminutive little bird, the least *bush titmouse (*Psaltriparus minimus*). 1898 Morris *Austral Engl.*, *Gerygone*...In New Zealand they are called *Bush-warblers. 1808 *Ann. Reg.* 1806 856 Some were cutting wood for firing—Some collecting *bush-water with a calabash. 1871 E. Jenkins *The Coolie* ix. 120 That strange ebonised 'bush-water', which..anon curls and eddies round us like the smiles on a Negro's face. 1891 *Eng. Illustr. Mag.* Feb. 383 The plantations..were surrounded by four dams or embankments;..one behind to exclude the 'bush water', the accumulated rain of the interior. 1863 Lyell *Antiq. Man* 484 The human brain here given..is that of an African *bushwoman. 1905 *Daily Chron.* 16 Dec. 4/7 Bushmen and bushwomen within a radius of forty or fifty miles ride to these functions. 1888 W. L. Buller *Birds N. Z.* I. 115 *Bush-wren [*Xenicus longipes*]..is generally met with singly or in pairs.

Bushed, *ppl. a.*[1] Add:

5. b. *transf.* and *fig.* Lost as in the bush. *Australian colloq.*

1885 Mrs. Praed *Australian Life* 29, I get quite bushed in these streets. 1898 *Westm. Gaz.* 29 Sept. 3/2 He tangled himself up and got 'bushed', and frantically implored.. everybody..to help him with his contract. 1900 H. Lawson *Over Sliprails* 1 The deeper you read..about things that end in ism..the more likely you are to get bushed.

Bushed (buʃt), *ppl. a.*[2] [f. Bush *v.*[3] + -ed[1].] Fitted with a bush or lining; lined.

1907 *Installation News* May 11/1 Bushed outlets. 1909 *Ibid.* III. 121 These..boxes are provided with bushed holes.

Bu·shel, *sb.*[3] *U.S.* [? Transferred use of *sb.*[1] or *sb.*[2]] A tailor's thimble. Hence **Bu·shel** *v. trans.* and *intr.*, to repair (garments); **Bu·shelman, -woman,** a man or woman employed in repair tailoring.

1889 *Century Dict.* 1909 'O. Henry' *Options* (1916) 92 You would say he had been brought up a bushelman in Essex Street.

Bush-fighting, *vbl. sb.* (Earlier U.S. examples.)

1758 *Essex Inst. Hist. Coll.* XVIII. 101 [I] improved this Day chiefly in yᵉ exercise of Bush Fiting. *Ibid.* 187 The Rangers exercise in Scout marches and Bush fighting.

Bush-harrow, *v.* (Earlier U.S. example.)

1788 Washington *Diaries* III. 328 He was sowing Seeds with intention to Bush harrow them in.

Bushido (bū·ʃidou). [Jap.: see quot. 1899.] In feudal Japan, the ethical code of the Samurai or military knighthood.

1899 I. Nitobé *Bushido* 3 Bu-shi-do means literally Military-knight-ways—the ways which fighting nobles should observe in their daily life as well as in their vocation. 1902 *Encycl. Brit.* XXIX. 709 It is essential to know something of the ethical code of the *samurai*, the *bushi-do* ('way of the warrior') as it was called. 1923 *19th Cent.* Jan. 133 The old samurai spirit of *bushido* will prove equal to stemming the tide of radicalism. 1928 *Present-day Japan, Coronation Number* 32 'Bushido', the hereditary noble spirit of chivalry which is in her blood.

Bushman. Add:

3. The language of the aboriginal bushmen of South Africa.

1869 Bleek *Bushman Lang.* in *Cape & its People* (ed. R. Noble) 277 Many nouns in Bushman vary in their terminations according to their position or use. *Ibid.* 278 The Bushman nouns do not appear to possess any representative parts. 1874 J. M. Orpen in *Folk-lore* (1919) XXX. 146 Then he sent another bird, the tinktinki..—qinqininyq in Bushman.

Bushveld (bu·ʃfelt, -velt). [a. Du. *boschveld*: see Bush *sb.*[1] and Veld.] **a.** Veld composed largely of bush. **b.** The 'Low Country' of the Transvaal.

1879 *Chambers's Jrnl.* 1 Mar. 134/2 For big game, the low country and Bushveld is that part of the Transvaal which the hunter must seek. 1887 *Atalanta* Nov. 80/1 The roar of a lion..in the solemn bush veldt. 1888 A. A. Anderson *Twenty-five Yrs. in Waggon* 153 The Notuane River, in what is termed the Bush Veldt. 1901 *Contemp. Rev.* Mar. 333 An efficient guide, whose knowledge of the dense bush-veld proved of great value. 1903 Kipling *Five Nations, Wilful-Missing* v, The Low Bush-veldt that sends men stragglin' unaware. 1903 'Indicus' *Labour S. Africa* 19 Their farm is of about 5,000 acres in extent, on the lower or Bush Veldt. 1907 Sir P. Fitzpatrick *Jock of the Bushveld* 14 Between the goldfields and the nearest port lay the Bushveld.

Bushwhacker. *U.S.* **1.** (Later example.)

1843 Carlton *New Purchase* II. xlii. 86 Do you think..all our eastern dignitaries combined could have compelled young bushwhackers to wear coats and shoes in recitation rooms?

Bushwhacking, *ppl. a.* (Earlier example.)

1813 *Massachusetts Spy* 27 Jan. (Th.) These bush-whacking Yankees won't do For me to be dwelling among.

Bushy (bu·ʃi), *sb. Austral.* [f. Bush *sb.*[1] + -y[6].] A dweller in the bush; a bushman as distinguished from a townsman.

1900 H. Lawson *Over Sliprails* 12 In the dress and character of busbies.

Bushy, *a.* Add:

3. c. *Ent.* Of antennæ: Covered with long, erect hairs (*Cent. Dict.* 1889).

6. *bushy-tailed* adj.

1868 *Amer. Naturalist* II. 535 It seems widely separated ..in habits from its nearest relative *Nycteris occidentalis*, or bushy-tailed Bat.

7. Concerned with the (Australian) bush.

1900 H. Lawson *On Track* 37 The foreman was a bushman; his sympathies were bushy. 1904 *Daily Chron.* 19 Apr. 3/5 Her stories are of the bush bushy.

Business. Add:

11. Phrase. *To make it one's business*: to undertake as a self-appointed task (*to* do something).

1642 [in Dict.]

13. c. *To mean business* (quots.).

1857 [in Dict.]. 1879 Spurgeon *Serm.* XXV. 359 The man who means business must sail whether it is dark or light. 1886 Lowell *Wks.* (1890) VI. 140 They look as if they meant business. 1897 *Daily News* 26 Oct. 5/2 'We mean business', said one of her Majesty's Ministers...He admitted that meaning business meant also some..increase in the Army Estimates.

d. (Later examples.)

1759 *Essex Inst. Hist. Coll.* XLIX. 21 They did the Business for him with an Iron Crow. 1773 Goldsm. *Stoops to Conq.* v. (Mrs. Hardcastle), Oh, Tony, I'm killed!..That last jolt, that laid us against the quickset hedge, has done my business. 1883 J. Greenwood *Odd People in Odd Places* 7 It was the bricks and mortar that did *his* business, poor chap. 1891 J. M. Dixon *Dict. Idiom. Engl. Phr.* 47 His last imprudent exposure of himself to the night air did the business for him.

15. d. *Letters of business*: a royal letter authorizing Convocation to transact business.

[1839 Cardwell *Doc. Ann. Ch. Eng.* II. 359 *note*, No business can be undertaken in convocation, unless it has been specially proposed to them by royal license. 1842 Lathbury *Hist. Convocation* 350 Parliament was summoned in February, 1713: and the convocation met on the 16th...On the 17th, the convocation was authorized, by a royal letter, to proceed to business.] 1873 Phillimore *Eccles. Law* 1934 In 1713, convocation had royal letters of business, and considered various subjects,—penance, excommunication, forms for the visitation of prisoners. 1906 *Convocations Cant. & York* in *Parlt. Papers* LXXXIV. 805 You may see your way to advise His Majesty the King to direct that Letters of Business be issued.

21. c. Action having a commercial basis or value.

1897 'Mark Twain' *Following Equator* iii. 53 He did a mighty thing for civilization,..but it was not 'business'.

d. *Bridge.* (See quots.)

1925 A. E. M. Foster *Auction Bridge* 46 The two players with the better cards are going to get the contract, or they are going to force the others into a bid when a real 'business' double for penalties can be made...A double of four or more is always a 'business' double. *Ibid.* 51 The Business Re-double is seldom sound business. 1926 Foster & Hervey *Auction Bridge* i. 13 In the early days of Auction Bridge the double was used simply and solely to defeat the opponent's contract and, by so doing, increase the penalties. This double..is now known as a *Business* Double to distinguish it from..the *Informatory* Double. *Ibid.* iv. 45 By passing, known as the Business Pass, B announces that the penalty to be obtained will, in his opinion, be worth more than can be got by a bid. 1927 *Observer* 6 Mar. 25 This Business Pass is one of the most formidable weapons. It converts the Informatory Double into a Business Double.

24. *business agent, centre, college, committee, proposition, suit, world*; **business doctor** *U.S.* (see quot.); **business man** (earlier examples); so *business woman*; **business manager,** a manager of the business or commercial side of an enterprise.

1849 C. Lanman *Alleghany Mts.* xi. 85 The 'guide' counsellor, and friend of the Indians, as well as their 'business agent. 1901 S. Merwin & H. K. Webster *Calumet 'K'* i. 15 All that remained was to wait until the business agent made the next move. 1851 C. Cist *Cincinnati* 278 'Business centre. 1888 J. Kirkland *McVeys* 4 In the 'business centre' one might see an occasional tall, narrow, straight-sided brick structure. 1902 McFaul *Ike Glidden* xvi. 124 He had just graduated from a 'business college, and claimed to know how to do business 'in a business like manner'. 1838 W. L. Garrison in *Life* (1885) II. 227 A 'business committee was then appointed. 1908 *Accountant* 8 Aug. 157/2 The methods of so-called ''business doctors'. 1909 *Modern Business* Jan. 606/1 In America..there exists a body of men who are known as 'Business Doctors', men who are called in to give advice upon the proper conduct of business. 1832 *Congress. Deb.* 30 Jan. 1511 Having been in the practice of the law..and somewhat conversant with 'business men. 1847 (*title*) The Business man's Assistant. 1860 O. W. Holmes *Prof. Breakf.-t.* i. 16 People of cultivation, of pure character,..shrewd business-men, men of science [etc.]. 1870 Ann S. Stephens *Married in Haste* lxiv. 324 I'm going to be the agent and 'business manager of this concern. 1906 B. Stoker *Pers. Remin. H. Irving* II. lxxiii. § 3. 319, I was Sir Henry Irving's business manager. 1907 *Daily Chron.* 9 Nov. 6/5, I would have suggested..the desirability of your becoming my business manager. 1901 S. E. White *Claim Jumpers* v. 70, I have a plain 'business proposition to make. You and I are going to be great friends. 1909 'O. Henry' *Options* (1916) 11 He had been used to having his business propositions heard of. 1904 'Alan Dale' *Wanted: A Cook* 66 That horrible garb known as a ''business suit', with a rude, short coat. 1863 'Gail Hamilton' *Gala-Days* 65 Some of these were, I suppose, what Winthrop calls ''business-women'. 1837 *Southern Lit. Messenger* III. 391 An extra-ordinary convulsion in the 'business-world prostrated his hopes.

Busker[2] (bɔ·skəɪ). [f. Busk *v.*[2] + -er[1].] An itinerant musician, etc.

1859 *Slang Dict.*, *Busker*, a man who sings or performs in a public house. *Scotch.* 1884 *Referee* 29 June (Cassell) The words and tune of which I remember hearing from the lips of a busker at Margate. 1901 *Westm. Gaz.* 19 Jan. 2/3 Anything

approaching a hint to tax the 'busker' has always raised a storm of protest from the patrons of the particular health resort involved. 1908 *Daily Chron.* 1 Sept. 7/4 'Buskers' ..can be counted as belonging to the most genuine of the professional vagrant fraternity.

Busser, var. *Buser, bus horse.

Bust, *sb.*[1] **4.** Add: *bust-costume, -improver.*

1910 *Maggs' Catal.* No. 255. 85 Etchings, Illustrating the Head-Dress and *Bust-Costume Worn by Ladies during the Early 17th Century. 1905 *Daily Chron.* 1 July 4/5 Many artificial aids have been devised, such as hip pads, *bust improvers.

Bust, *sb.*[3] Vulgar and U.S. pronunc. of Burst *sb.* Phr. *To go on the bust.*

1764 *Essex Inst. Hist. Coll.* XLIX. 284 Stray'd or stolen.. a Bay mare, with a cut main, and a Bust on the near Side of the Hind Flank. 1856 *Knickerbocker Mag.* Oct. XLVIII. 405 Mr. Carl Benson,..while reading one of my pieces, went off on a regular bust, and had his pocket picked of ninety-seven dollars. *a* 1860 [see Bust in Dict.]. 1890 'R. Boldrewood' *Col. Reformer* vii, There would be a slight probability of some of the party going 'on the bust' after three or four months' teetotalism. 1909 *Westm. Gaz.* 4 Sept. 2/3 We wish to go on the bust mildly.

Bust, *v.*[2] *Vulgar* and *U.S.* (= Burst *v.*) Add: (Examples.)

1839 Dickens *Nickleby* lvii, His genius would have busted all bonds. 1844 — *Mart. Chuz.* xvi, Keep cool, Jefferson. ..Don't bust! *Ibid.* xxxiv, If the biler of this vessel was toe bust, Sir. 1845 J. J. Hooper *Taking Census* i. 163 The furr a flyin'..like you'd a busted a feather bed open! 1854 Mary J. Holmes *Tempest & Sunshine* xv. 206, I was so feared Bill would bust his jacket open. 1920 P. G. Wodehouse *Damsel in Distress* iii, I shall infallibly bust you one on the jaw. *Ibid.*, The possibility of somebody someday busting you on the jaw.

b. *spec.* To break (a horse). Cf. *Buster 4.

1891 *Harper's Mag.* July 208/2 The whole secret of 'busting'..lies in completely exhausting the bronco at the first lesson. *Ibid.* 210/1 Two rides will usually bust a bronco so that the average cow-puncher can use him. 1903 *Wide World Mag.* Apr. 545 It is upon the cowboys that the task falls of breaking to the saddle, or busting, the almost intractable 'bronchos' that are raised..for the open market.

Bu·sted, *ppl. a. U.S. colloq.* [f. Bust *v.*[2] to burst.] Burst, broken; bankrupt or ruined. Also *busted-up.*

1881 A. A. Hayes *New Colorado* vi. 80 It was a regular amalgamation of busted people. 1889 *Century Dict.* s.v., A busted bank; a busted miner. *a* 1909 'O. Henry' *Roads of Destiny* xiii. 212 There was a buck coon..who had drifted down there from a busted-up colored colony. 1920 Mulford *J. Nelson* vi. 58 They took him over to th' SV to set Ol' Arnold's busted laig.

Buster. Add: **2. a.** (Earlier example.)

1845 J. J. Hooper *Taking Census* ii. 178 Seizing the opportunity..we kissed Miss Winny...'Ha!' exclaimed the old fellow..'Well 'twas a *buster* anyway.'

4. A horse-breaker. (Cf. *bronco-buster* s.v. *Bronco.) *U.S.*

1891 *Harper's Mag.* July 208/2 The buster must be careful to keep well away from sheds and timber. 1903 *Wide World Mag.* Apr. 545 On a large ranch which employs many cowboys, there is much rivalry among them as to whom is the best rider or buster.

Bustle, *sb.*[2] (Earlier U.S. example.)

1786 Abigail Adams *Lett.* 18 July (1848) 294 Pray, does the fashion of *merry thoughts, bustles*, and *protuberances* prevail with you? I really think the English more ridiculous than the French in this respect.

Bustle, *v.*[1] Add:

3. d. Of a place: To be full of activity or bustle; to be alive *with.*

1880 *All Year Round* 9 Oct. 514 Transports..bustling with sailors. 1905 Sir F. Treves *Other Side of Lantern* x. 85 Those who walk along its empty terraces..see it as it was when it bustled with men and women three centuries ago.

Bustler, obs. (or erroneous) var. of Bustle *sb.*[2]

The article cited appears to be the sole authority for the statement that the word originated in the visit to London in 1783 of the German duchess of Bustledorse (*sic*).

1787 *Newport* (R.I.) *Herald* in *Amer. Museum* (1789) II. 482, I hope that the fair of this town will follow the example of their sex in that large and polite city [London]—no longer disguise their beautiful forms with hoops or bustlers.

Bust-up (bɔ·st,ɒp). [See *Bust *sb.*[3]] = *burst-up* (see Burst *sb.* 2 b): an explosion (*lit.* and *fig.*); a flare-up; excitement.

1899 Kipling *Stalky & Co., Moral Reformers*, Then there's a big bust-up and a row that gets into the papers. 1908 W. De Morgan *Somehow Good* xi, There are hundreds of English equivalents for *éclaircissement*. There's bust-up. 1914 *English Rev.* Sept. 250 It [*sc.* this war] is the 'bust-up' of materialism.

Busy (bi·zi), *sb.*[2] *slang.* [f. Busy *a.*] A detective.

1904 *Daily Chron.* 17 Sept. 6/6 We had better slide; he looks like a 'busy'. 1928 *Sunday Dispatch* 2 Sept. 3/1 A porter..replied: 'Not to-night, sir...You see, we've had the "blow" that the "Busies" are coming'.

Busy, *a.* Add:

1. *To get busy*: to become active; to begin to act. *colloq.* orig. *U.S.*

1904 *Louisville Courier-Jrnl.* 27 Sept. 3 It was necessary to call upon the sergeant-at-arms...When that functionary got busy there came near being a riot. 1906 'O. Henry' *Four Million* 121 'Ikey,' said he,..'get busy with your ear. It's drugs for me if you've got the line I need'.

8. b. Of ornamentation: Full of detail.

1903 *Burlington Mag.* III. 86/1 The decoration, in dealers' language, being too 'busy' for broad effects.

Butalanine (biutæ·lănin, -in). *Chem.* [f. But(ane + Alanine.] Amidoisovaleric acid found chiefly in the pancreas of the ox.

1879 Watts *Dict. Chem.* VI. 372.

Butane (biū·tēn). *Chem.* [f. Butyl + -ane 2 b.] Butyl hydride, C_4H_{10}; = Tetrane.

1876 *Encycl. Brit.* V. 557 Butane or tetrane..can be written in two ways, and two isomerides are known. 1877 *Fownes' Chem.* (ed. 12) 47 Normal Butane, Diethyl, or Methyl-propyl. 1918 Colver *High Explosives* 60 The propane, butane, and pentane hydrocarbons in the form of gases and vapours which can only be condensed with difficulty.

Butcher, *sb.* Add:

3. b. A vender of sweets, fruit, etc., in a railway train. *U.S. colloq.*

a 1889 *Detroit Free Press* (Barrère & Leland) On a Michigan central train the other day as the butcher came into the car with a basket of oranges [etc.]. 1904 *Columbus Even. Dispatch* 16 Aug. 3 The days of the 'butchers' are numbered, and their privileges have been so restricted that they are able to do little, if any, business. 1924 W. M. Raine *Troubled Waters* vii. 70 From the train butcher he bought a magazine and settled himself for a long ride.

5. butcher-boots *pl.*, high boots without tops (see Top *sb.*[1] 10); **butcher-crow,** a crow-shrike (*Standard Dict.* 1895); **butcher's sleeves,** short sleeves covering the forearm from elbow to wrist, worn by butchers as a protection against soiling the sleeves of their ordinary wearing apparel.

1861 Whyte Melville *Market Harb.* v, My friend sharing with me a strong prejudice against what have been termed 'Butcher-boots'. 1886 *Engl. Illustr. Mag.* Mar. 414/1 A man in a round hat and butcher-boots is as out of place at a hunt as a man in a tweed suit at a ball. 1897 *Badminton Mag.* IV. 397 Men in cords and butcher boots, tweeds and gaiters. 18.. Dickens *Novels & Tales* I. 218 (Hoppe) After a long delay the doctor came in with scientific 'butcher's sleeves on his arms, and an apron tied round his waist.

Butcher, *v.* Add:

4. To cut up or divide (an animal or flesh) after the manner of a butcher; to cut *off* or *out* in this fashion. *U.S.*

1822 J. Fowler *Jrnl.* 121 The former killed two Elk, and left the latter to butcher them. 1843 Farnham *Trav. Gt. Western Prairies* I. 243 We butchered our meat, and.. loaded it upon our animals. *a* 1848 Ruxton *Life Far West* iv. (1849) 118 The..body of one of the Indian squaws, with a large portion of the flesh butchered from it. *Ibid.* 160 Bill ..called to him..to butcher off a piece of meat and put it in the pot. 1855 Mayne Reid *Hunters' Feast* xxxix, The fat cows only were 'butchered'. The bulls were left where they had fallen, to become the food of wolves.

5. *intr.* To do butchering. *U.S.*

1896 *Scribner's Mag.* VI. 484/1 'Don't butcher next week. Friday is Christmas day.'..'Well, we always butcher Christmas week, don't we?'

Butcherdom (bu·tʃəɪdəm). [f. Butcher *sb.* + -dom.] Butchers collectively or their trade.

1889 *Century Dict.* 1904 R. Harris *Remin. Sir H. Hawkins* II. 109 The butcher's slander was one that seemed to shake the very foundations of butcherdom throughout the world.

Butchering, *vbl. sb.* Add:

1. *The butchering*, the trade of a butcher. *colloq.*

1904 *Daily Chron.* 31 Dec. 4/7 You will always hear, 'I am in the butchering', or 'the tailoring'.

3. The slaughtering of cattle. Also *attrib.*, as *butchering cow.*

1900 *Daily News* 10 Apr. 8/6 Fat butchering cows.

Bu·tcher-knife. *U.S.* [Butcher *sb.* 5.] A large knife used by butchers.

1822 *Massachusetts Spy* 25 Dec. (Th.) Her foot slipt, and she fell upon a large butcher-knife which she had in her hand. 1845 Sage *Scenes Rocky Mts.* (1859) 38 A belt of leather, holding encased his butcher-knife and pistols. 1853 P. Paxton *Stray Yankee in Texas* 289 One of the hands of the dead man grasped a long butcher-knife. 1868 *Congress. Globe* Dec., App. 66/3 Butcher knives, cook's and shoe knives, and spatulas and palettes. 1878 J. H. Beadle *Western Wilds* xviii. 294 There we fell to with our tin-cups and butcher-knives and dug several holes.

Bute, variant spelling of *Braut. *U.S.*

1903 A. H. Lewis *The Boss* 272, I know that gang of card sharps,..an' they're a bunch of butes at that!

Butea (biū·tiă). [mod.L., named after John Stuart, Earl of *Bute* (1713–92).] A genus of East Indian leguminous plants yielding a valuable gum resin, esp. *B. frondosa* (or *monosperma*), the dak or palas of India. Also the gum (more fully *butea gum, kino*).

a 1815 W. Roxburgh *Flora Indica* (1874) 537 Here it [*sc.* the gum of *Pterocarpus santalinus*] differs from Butea gum. 1863 Watts *Dict. Chem.* (1879) I. 686 Butea gum. Bengal kino—The juice of *Butea frondosa*, Roxb., often sent into the market instead of genuine kino. 1866 *Treas. Bot.* 183 Butea kino or gum butea.

Butenyl (biū·tĭnil). *Chem.* [f. Butene + -yl.] The radical C_4H_7, of which butylene is the hydride.

1884 Roscoe & Schorlemmer *Treat. Chem.* iii. ii. 377 Butenyl Alcohol, $C_4H_7(OH)_3$.

Butic (biū·tik), *a. Chem.* [f. L. *but(yrum* Butter *sb.*[1] + -ic.] Derived from butine or from butter. *Butic acid*, a solid fatty acid obtained from butter (see quot.).

1857 Miller *Elem. Chem.*, *Org.* iv. § 1. (1862) 261 According to Heintz, the solid portion of butter contains..another acid, termed by him butic acid, HO, $C_{40}H_{39}O_3$.

Butine (biū·tin). *Chem.* [ad. G. *butin*, f. L. *butyrum* Butter *sb.*[1] + -ine[5].] The hydrocarbon C_4H_6.

1867 Bloxam *Chem.* 582 Butter..contains also *butine*, which yields glycerine and butic acid. 1895 Thomson & Bloxam *Bloxam's Chem.* (ed. 8) 524 The hydrocarbon C_4H_6 (*butine*) can exist in two forms.

Butlerish (bɔ·tləriʃ), *a.* [f. Butler *sb.* + -ish[1].] Belonging to or characteristic of a butler.

1923 Aldous Huxley *Antic Hay* iii. (1924) 45 He moved with a certain pomp, a butlerish gravity.

Butt, *sb.*[2] **3.** Add: **butt-howel,** a howeling-adze used by coopers (Knight *Dict. Mech.* 1874).

Butt, *sb.*[3] Add:

6. butt-adjuster, an appliance for squaring the butts of the sheaves in a self-binding harvester; **butt-cut** *Forestry* and *Logging*, (*a*) the first log above the stump; (*b*) the section of tanbark taken from the butt of a tree before felling it for further peeling (Terms Forestry & Logging 1905); **butt-hole,** a blind hole, a cul-de-sac; **butt men** *pl.*, *Mil.*, the men who handle the butt or foot of a scaling ladder.

1902 *Encycl. Brit.* XXV. 174 The butts are at the front of the machine and are evened up by a device called a 'butt adjuster, which is..given an elliptical movement..thus squaring the butt of the sheaf. 1905 *Westm. Gaz.* 3 Mar. 3/2 The old dog's got him [*sc.* the badger] in a *butt hole. 1884 *Instruct. Mil. Engin.* I. ii. 95 The 'butt men, when the ladder is turned over, pull the butt out 18 inches from the wall.

7. The piece of the inner margin of a single leaf of a book, which projects as a narrow strip beyond the sewing or other fastening when the book is bound.

1921 A. Esdaile in *Library* Dec. 185 The last leaf of B.. is a single leaf, whose butt is visible after B 1.

8. The fag-end of a cigar.

1847 *Paddiana* I. 235 Will yer honor give me the butt? 1886 Kipling *Departm. Ditties, Betrothed*, Like the Butt of a Dead Cigar.

9. The metal ring at the end of a hose-pipe, either of a half-coupling or that to which the nozzle is screwed. 1874 Knight *Dict. Mech.*

10. a. The surface of coal at a right angle to the face. **b.** A place where the stratum of the rock to be quarried is cut off by other rock.

1881 Raymond *Mining Gloss.*, *End of coal*,..sometimes called the butt. 1900 *Coal & Metal Miners' Pocket Bk.* (ed. 6) 576 The butt of a slate quarry is where the overlying rock comes in contact with an inclined stratum of slate rock.

Butt, *sb.*[4] Add:

1. (Later dial. and U.S. examples.)

1838 W. Holloway *Dict. Provinc.* 23 Butts and Bounds, the borders of a person's estate. *E. Sussex.* 1902 McFaul *Ike Glidden* vii. 44 Have you any documents for reference in order to fix the butts and bounds?

7. In grouse-shooting, a position either sunken or on the level ground, protected by a wall or bank of earth behind which the sportsman may stand and fire unobserved by the game.

1900 Marquis of Granby in *Encycl. Sport* I. 480/2 The butts, or batteries, as they are indifferently called. 1902 *Encycl. Brit.* XXXII. 604/1 Where possible, the 'butts' should always be placed in a hollow of the ground. 1904 *Westm. Gaz.* 26 Aug. 3/1 The depth of the butt will be such that a man of moderate height may fire comfortably over the heather topping the wall.

Butt, *sb.*[7] **2.** Add:

butt-chain (see quot.); **butt-joint** *v. trans.*, to join with a butt-joint; **butt-rivetting,** rivetting in which a butt-strap is used; **butt-strap** *sb.*, the metal strap that secures the abutting ends of rails and plates; *v. trans.*, to weld (two pieces of metal) so as to form a butting point (*Standard Dict.* 1895); **butt-strip** = butt-strap (*sb.*); **butt-weld** *sb.*, a butt-joint made by welding; *v. trans.*, to join with a butt-weld (Webster 1911); **butt-welded** *a.*, joined with a butt-weld.

1874 Knight *Dict. Mech.*, **Butt-chain* (Saddlery), a short chain which reaches from the leather tug to the single-tree, to each of which it is hooked. 1885 *Spons' Mechanics' Own Bk.* 361 There are 3 or 4 ways of *butt-jointing curbs. 1904 *Technol. & Sci. Dict.* (ed. Goodchild & Tweeney), **Butt Riveting*, a riveted joint where the plates touch at the edge only, and a strip overlaps and is riveted to both of them. 1898 Kipling *Day's Work* iii. (1904) 93 He started all his friends on the same *butt-strap, and the plates opened like a furnace door. 1904 *Technol. & Sci. Dict.* (ed. Goodchild & Tweeney), **Butt Strip*, the strip of plate used to cover a butt joint. 1864 Webster s.v. *Weld*, *Butt-weld, or jump-weld. 1927 *Glasgow Herald* 27 Aug. 12 *Butt-welded tubes.

Butt (bɒt), *sb.*[14] *dial.* Also **but.** A shoemakers' knife. Also *attrib.*, as *butt-knife.*

1847 Halliwell, *But*, a shoemaker's knife. *North.* 1905 *Daily Chron.* 7 Feb. 3/1 Butt-knives..of French and Swedish makes.

Butt, *v.*[1] Add:

1. d. *To butt in*: to thrust oneself into (an affair, discussion, etc.) unceremoniously and uninvited; to intrude, interfere without good reason. orig. *U.S.*

1904 *Philad. Even. Telegraph* 8 June 8 To the victors belong the spoils, and not to those who butted in when the smoke of the battle had cleared away. *a* 1905 'O. Henry' *Strictly Business* xvii. (1910) 179 Don't you butt in. 1909 — *Options* (1916) 29 Beg pardon..for butting into what's not my business. 1915 W. J. Locke *Jaffery* viii, If a man loves a woman..he ought to know what to do with the guy that butted in, without being told. 1920 Rose Macaulay *Potterism* iv. i. § 2 I've not gone there or written, or anything yet, because I didn't want to butt in.

Butt, *v.*[2] **1.** (Later U.S. examples.)

1816 U. Brown *Jrnl.* in *Maryland Hist. Mag.* X. 361 This [40,000 Acres] is butted and bounded and described directly as the grant is from the Commonwealth of Virginia. *Ibid.* 367 This John Hall..Butted and Bounded of the 2 first lines with our 70,000 Acre tract.

3. (Later U.S. example.)

1853 D. H. Strother *Blackwater Chron.* i. 6 A large spur —apparently the Backbone itself—keeps straight to the south, and butts down on the Cheat.

Butt, *v.*[3] **2.** *U.S.* (Earlier example.)

1850 S. Judd *R. Edney* 41 Richard took an axe and very neatly proceeded to 'butt' a log; that is, to cut the end of it square off.

b. To compete with in butting.

1884 E. Ingersoll *Country Cousins* i. (Cent. Suppl.), I had an uncle..who was a famous chopper...When he was past seventy, he had a man working for him..and my uncle offered to butt him.

Bu·tt-cut. *U.S.* [Butt *sb.*[3] 2.] The cut of a tree containing the butt-end. Also *fig.*

1830 *Northern Watchman* (Troy, N.Y.) 19 Oct. (Th.) [He] weighs little short of 450 lbs. and is familiarly known as the But-cut. 1840 J. P. Kennedy *Quodlibet* 172 Nebuchadnezzar couldn't beat him at a speech. He's the Butt cut of democracy. 1878 J. H. Beadle *Western Wilds* x. 143 The 'butt cut' of the tree lies as it fell, the top reached by means of a ladder.

Butt-end, *v.* Delete *nonce-wd.* and add: *trans.* To knock down or kill by striking with the butt-end of a gun or pistol.

1897 *Daily News* 18 June 8/6 They were shot, run through, or butt-ended. 1897 Kipling *Capt. Cour.* 131 You butt-ended *mucho bono*!

Bu·tt-ended, *a.* [f. Butt-end + -ed[2].] Having a blunt end; having ends that butt or come flat, the one against the other.

1898 *Cycling* 72 A hopeless single-tube tyre may be slit open at the valve and a butt-ended air-tube inserted.

Butter, *sb.*[1] Add:

3. c. A perfumed fat obtained by inflowering or maceration with a heated fat.

1885 *Encycl. Brit.* XVIII. 526 For the manufacture of perfumes for the handkerchief the greases now known as pomades, butters, or philocomes are treated with rectified spirit of wine..which practically completely abstracts the odour.

4. c. *attrib.*, similative, as *butter-smooth* adj.

1920 Galsworthy *In Chancery* ii. v, His grandfather's first gold hunter watch, butter-smooth with age.

5. butter-bush, an Australian tree, *Pittosporum phyllirœoides*, of which the wood is used for turnery and the leaves as fodder; **butter carrier,** a refrigerator for transporting butter; **butter cloth,** a thin loosely-woven cloth with a fine mesh used primarily as a wrapping for butter; **butter colour,** a preparation used to give a good colour to butter and butter substitutes; **butter cow** *U.S.*, a cow that yields rich cream; **butter-duck** *U.S.* (see quot.); **butter fat,** the essential fats of pure butter; **butter-knife** (U.S. examples); **butter letter,** a letter issued on ecclesiastical authority giving permission to eat butter in Lent; **butter muslin** = *butter cloth*; **butter oil,** that part of refined cotton-seed oil which is used in making oleomargarin; **butter paddle** = *butter spade*; **butter paper,** a semi-transparent waterproof wrapping paper for butter, cream cheese, etc.; **butter press,** a press for extracting cacao-butter from ground cacao in the manufacture of confectionery; **butter rations,** a special food given to cows to enrich their milk; **butter salt,** fine common salt in small crystals obtained by rapid evaporation of brine, used in salting butter; **butter scoop** (see quot.); **butter spade,** a wooden spatula used in cutting butter from a firkin or other vessel, or used (in pairs) for making up butter; **butter stamp** = Butter-print 1; **butter-stick,** a wooden implement used in working butter; **butter substitute,** a substance used as a substitute for butter in food, e.g. margarine; **butter tongs** (see quot.); **butter tower,** 'any of various church towers reputed to have been built from the proceeds of the sale of Lenten privileges, esp. that of using butter' (Webster 1911); **butter trier,** a segment of a tube used to pierce a firkin of butter for sample; **butter week,** a period of Lent during which relaxation from the fast is allowed; **butter-worker** (U.S. examples); **butter working,** the moulding of butter into rolls, prints, pats, etc., for sale; **butter yellow,** a coal-tar colour used for colouring butter, oils, etc.

1885 *Outing* (U.S.) Nov. 180/2 A thick hedge of *butter-bush. 1900 *Daily News* 16 Feb. 6/7 The veil should be..of..any of the bright colours as produced in *butter cloth. 1877 *Rep. Vermont Board Agric.* IV. 46 We..believe that the Jersey as a *butter cow has the advantage of at least the average life time of man. 1857 J. G. Swan *Northwest Coast* 357 The Colonel saw a '*butter-duck' in a shallow creek...These ducks are the black surf-duck (*Fuligula perspicillata*). 1899 *Daily News* 17 Feb. 8/3 The sample..afforded no evidence of the presence of fat other than *butter fat. 1906 *Macmillan's Mag.* June 612 If wanting in butter-fat, it [*sc.* milk] was not fit for the purpose for which it had been sold. 1856 *Trans. Mich. Agric. Soc.* VII. 268 Eleven *butter knives. 1870 F. Fern *Ginger-Snaps* 54 Some houses contain only silver soup-ladles, others a superabundance of butter-knives. 1893 *Westm. Gaz.* 25 Feb. 5/3 In Italy, butter is prohibited [in Lent]..The Northerners, however,..would have none of this, and special '*butter-letters' were consequently dispatched to them from the obliging Vatican. 1902 *Connoisseur* II. No. 8. p. xvii, Frilled *Butter Muslin. 1903 Walker-Tisdale & Robinson *Soft Cheesemaking* 34 Instead of paper, the cheese is done up in butter muslin. 1906 — *Butter-making* 55 Place a damp butter-muslin over the roller and butter-board. 1907 *Farm Butter-making* 5 Wrap a wet butter muslin round the roller of the worker. 1894 *Dairy Rev.* Aug. 46/2 Some makers used to prepare the annatto in *butter oil. 1884 *Cheshire Gloss.*, **Butter salt*, salt-making term. A fine boiled salt, not stoved, used specially for making up butter. 1892 *Cornhill Mag.* Sept. 264 The unmoulded salt—locally termed 'butter-salt'—is sent away in trucks. 1902 *Encycl. Brit.* XXVII. 358 The *butter-scoop is of wood, and is sometimes perforated; it is used for taking the butter out of the churn. 1881 Ogilvie, **Butter-stamp*, a piece of carved wood used to mark cakes of butter. 1836 *Southern Lit. Messenger* II. 480 To beat the collected ends of the fingers with an implement..made like a *butterstick. 1906 *Macmillan's Mag.* June 607 What are termed '*butter-substitutes',—in other words, fraudulent adulterants. 1908 *Westm. Gaz.* 5 Aug. 2/2 Vegetarians use very extensively a butter substitute derived from the fat of nuts. 1874 Knight *Dict. Mech.*, **Butter-tongs*, an implement for cutting and transferring pieces of butter. 1923 *Daily Mail* 3 Mar. 10 Maslenitza, or *Butter Week, as the Russians call the fortnight preceding Lent, is always celebrated with feasting and drinking in Russia. 1872 *Rep. Vermont Board Agric.* I. 152 Work [it] again in *butter-worker. 1882 *Rep. Maine Board Agric.* XXVI. 153 A good butter worker of some kind should be provided, and also a thermometer. 1906 *Daily Chron.* 25 Sept. 2/6 One is reluctantly obliged to conclude that *butter-working is a lost art amongst grocers' assistants.

Bu·tter-ball.

1. A ball of butter; butter moulded into a ball.

1892 J. C. Harris *Plantation Printer* 58 She wur a fine cow too, ez fat ez a butter-ball. 1902 Greenough & Kittredge *Words* 177 Thus we have butterball, a ball that consists of butter.

2. The buffle-head or buffle-headed duck, *Clangula albeola*, of North America, so called from its exceeding fatness in autumn. *U.S.*

1859 S. F. Baird *Catal. N. Amer. Birds* 595 Butter Ball. 1872 Coues *Key N. Amer. Birds* 290 Buffle-headed Duck. Butter-ball, Spirit Duck. 1874 J. W. Long *Amer. Wild-fowl Shooting* Introd. 16 In the deep water varieties..I shall treat of the..buffle-head or butter-ball. 1895 *Outing* (U.S.) XXVII. 212/1 Over me they went, so close that I could tell that they were butter balls. 1902 S. E. White *Blazed Trail* xiii. 85 He followed the trail by the river. Butterballs and scoters paddled up at his approach.

Bu·tter-bean. A variety of the bean, *Phaseolus lunatus*, of which the ripened seeds or the immature pods are used as a culinary vegetable. Also *attrib.*

1834 Miller *Plant-n.* s.v. *Bean*, Butter Bean, a tender-podded variety of *Phaseolus vulgaris*. 1899 *Daily News* 4 Nov. 7/6 Broad beans, haricots, butter beans, and delicious flageolets. 1904 *Daily Chron.* 28 Jan. 6/1, I asked for butter-beans; they offered me the little white haricot instead. 1906 *Macmillan's Mag.* July 676 Butter-beans somewhat resemble white fish in colour and the task of turning out a butter-bean fritter..to look like a fried sole would not be a difficult one.

Butter-box. Add: **1.** (U.S. example.)

1877 *Rep. Vermont Board Agric.* IV. 189 This gentleman has also invented a very neat butter box.

b. *transf.* (See quots.)

1840 Dana *Bef. Mast* ix, She was the *Loriotte*,..and was engaged in the hide and tallow trade. She was a lump of a thing, what the sailors call a butter-box. 1893 Clark Russell *List, ye Landsmen* ix, Why the deuce don't the shipwrights ease off when they come aft, instead of holding on with the square run of the butter-box to the very lap of the taffrail? 1909 *N. Y. Even. Post* 28 Jan. (Th.) What New York youngster ever heard of a butterbox? This is the name applied [in the country] to the spring wagons of farmer and grocer, divested of wheels and set up on runners for the winter season.

3. = *Butter-ball 2. *U.S.*

1817 *Ann. Reg.* Chron. 567 This is believed to be the same species of duck common to the Atlantic coast, and called the butter-box. 1874 J. W. Long *Amer. Wild-fowl Shooting* xxix. 281 Local names [of the buffle-headed duck]: butter-box, butter-ball, and little whistler.

Buttercupped (bɔ·təɪkɒpt), *a.* [f. Butter-cup + -ed[2].] Abounding in or covered with buttercups.

1872 Calverley *Fly Leaves* (1903) 89 Looking far over buttercupp'd leas. 1888 Mrs. H. Ward *R. Elsmere* xliv, A wavering rainy light played..over the buttercupped river meadows. 1924 *Public Opinion* 9 May 400/1 Banks all buttercup'd and burning.

So **Buttercuppy** (bɔ·təɪkɒpi), *a.*

1871 Morris in Mackail *Life* (1899) I. 237 The fields are all butter-cuppy.

Buttered, *ppl. a.* Add:

2. c. *Buttered eggs*: eggs beaten up and cooked with butter; now applied to the dish otherwise called *scrambled eggs.*

c 1410 *Master of Game* (MS. Digby 182) xii, Buttured egges doth hem moche goode. 1865 Mrs. Beeton *Dict. Everyday Cookery* 113/1 Buttered Eggs. Ingredients.—4 new-laid eggs, 2 oz. of butter.

Bu·tter-fish. Any of several fishes having a slippery coating of mucus, esp. the Gunnel, found in British waters; the Murray-Perch, *Oligorus mitchelli*, a fresh-water fish of Australia; the Kelp fish of New Zealand (see quot. 1880); the Dollar-fish, *Stromateus* or *Poronotus triacanthus*, a food-fish of the eastern U.S.; etc.

1674–1883 [see Butter *sb.*[1] 5]. 1850 J. B. Clutterbuck '*Port Phillip*' iii. 44 In the bay are large quantities of.. butter-fish. 1880 Günther *Fishes* 533 The 'butter-fish', or 'Kelp-fish' of the colonists of New Zealand (*C[oridodax] pullus*), is prized as food. 1883 E. P. Ramsay *Food Fishes N.S. Wales* 12 *H[aplodactylus] obscurus*,..known to our southern fishermen as the 'butterfish', is highly esteemed. 1888 G. B. Goode *Amer. Fishes* 221 The 'Butter-fish' of Massachusetts and New York, *Stromateus triacanthus*. *Ibid.* 232 [*Selene setipinnis*] is a frequent summer visitor all along the coast as far north as Woods Holl, Mass., where it [is called] the 'Hump-backed Butterfish'.

Butterfly, *sb.* Add:

2. c. Applied to persons whose periods of work or occupation of a place are transitory or seasonal.

1890 *Chambers's Jrnl.* 10 May 289/2 A '*butterfly' man rests for a moment to wipe his streaming brow, when the warder's stern voice bids him proceed with his work. 1891 *Daily News* 29 Dec. 6/4 The 'butterfly man', who is given cabs by the proprietors in the height of the season. 1894 *Labour Comm. Gloss.*, *Butterfly cabman*, cabdrivers whose actual cab-driving extends over about as many months of the year as the existence of a butterfly. 1895 *Westm. Gaz.* 8 Mar. 3/1 Those cabbies who come upon the streets in the fine days and disappear with the autumn leaves are called 'butterflies'. 1902 *Daily Chron.* 2 June 7/1 Chelsea will welcome the return of the truant 'butterfly' [*sc.* Mr. Whistler] to a region always to be associated with his artistic fame. 1912 *Standard* 15 Apr. 6/7 It was stated..that the word 'butterflies' was a 'technical term' for painters and decorators who worked upon bank holidays.

4. b. In full *butterfly bow*, a bow made-up or tied with the loop and end on each side spread apart like the expanded wings of a butterfly.

1870 *Young Ladies' Jrnl.* 1 Mar. 138/2 The butterfly bow..is of black or coloured velvet. 1888 *Cassell's Fam. Mag.* Feb. 182/1 A bonnet à la Folle, with a tricoloured butterfly bow at the top. 1920 *Punch* 4 Aug. 97/2 The wearing of a butterfly bow with a double event collar was a solecism past forgiveness.

5. Also *attrib.*, as *butterfly apparatus, catch.*

1887 *Daily News* 11 Jan. 2/7 The butterfly apparatus.. had acted, but..the bolts..were torn away. 1909 *Daily Chron.* 8 Jan. 5/3 When the winding rope was detached the safety 'butterfly' catches failed to act.

8. butterfly aeroplane (see quot.); **butterfly conch,** a Tasmanian mollusc, *Voluta papillosa* (Morris *Austral Eng.* 1898); **butterfly gurnard,** a gurnard of the species *Lepidotrigla vanessa*, found in Tasmanian and Australian seas; **butterfly kiss** (see quot.); **butterfly lily** = Mariposa lily; **butterfly lobster,** a marine crustacean, *Ibacus Peronii*, found in Tasmanian waters; **butterfly lupus,** lupus of the skin of the nose and cheeks; **butterfly nose,** a dog's nose when spotted or mottled; **butterfly-pea** (see Pea[1] 3); **butterfly ray,** a kind of sting-ray, *Pteroplatea maclura*, with very broad pectorals; **butterfly shell,** (*a*) a univalve of the genus *Voluta*; (*b*) = *butterfly snail*; **butterfly snail,** a mollusc of the sub-class *Pteropoda*, a sea-butterfly; **butterfly tulip** = Mariposa lily.

1909 *Daily Chron.* 10 Aug. 1/5 The Stewart-Brownell combination..have been preparing..what they call a '*butterfly aeroplane'. 1923 *Daily Mail* 14 Mar. 5 '*Butterfly kisses'...Do you know what they mean?—Yes, kisses with the eyelashes. 1880 Mrs. Meredith *Tasmanian Friends & Foes* 248 '*Butterfly lobsters'..the shell of the head and body..expands into something like wing-forms. 1913 Dorland *Med. Dict.* s.v. *Lupus*, *Butterfly lupus. 1890 *Chambers's Encycl.* V. 110/2 The yet more closely allied '*butterfly-snails' or Pteropods. 1899 T. W. Sanders *Encycl. Gardening* (ed. 3), *Calochortus* (*Butterfly Tulip).

Butterfly, *v.* Add:

b. *fig.* applied to flirting or philandering.

1893 *Chambers's Jrnl.* 12 Aug. 504/2 The young graduate was only butterflying after all. 1906 B'ness von Hutten *What became of Pam* iii. ix, 'What about Wantage?'.. 'He is still butterflying.'

Butterick (bɔ·tərik). [The name of a New York dealer in patterns for fashionable clothing.] (See quots.)

1901 J. L. Ford in *Munsey's Mag.* July 534 What is technically known as the 'butterick', a picture of two or more persons in conversational attire [*sic*], and usually amid the most luxurious surroundings. *a* 1910 'O. Henry' *Rolling Stones* (1917) 178 A buttonless flannel dressing sacque whose lines had been cut by no tape or butterick known to mortal woman.

Buttermilk. **c.** Add: Also quasi-*adj.* in *buttermilk land* U.S.

1843 R. Carlton *New Purchase* ix. 58 They had been sufficiently fortunate as to get a taste of 'buttermilk land'—'spouty land'.

Butter-nut. **3.** and **3. b.** (Earlier U.S. examples.)

1802 *Massachusetts Spy* 17 Nov. 3/1 The stockings were changed..to a brown, or what is commonly called a butter-nut color. 1810 *Ibid.* 21 Feb. (Th.) Two pair home-made pantaloons, the one dark-colored, the other light butternut.

Butter-print. Add:

3. The Indian mallow, *Abutilon Abutilon*, bearing a round seed-capsule marked with radiating furrows.

1909 in *Cent. Dict.* Suppl.

Butt-in. *U.S.* One who butts in (see *BUTT v.[1] 1 d); an intruder. So **Butt-iner.**

a 1910 'O. HENRY' *Rolling Stones* (1915) 194 Any of the Flat bush or Hackensack Meadow kind of butt-iners. 1911 J. C. LINCOLN *Cap'n Warren's Wards* viii. 124 If I had my way the old butt-in should understand exactly what I think of him.

Butting (bʊ·tiŋ), *vbl. sb.*[5] [f. BUTT v.[3] + -ING[1].]

1. The extraction of the butts or stumps of felled trees.

1928 *Daily Express* 3 Aug. 3/4 A man..gave me a job at 'butting'...He had some tree stumps that he wanted uprooted.

2. The action or process of trimming or squaring the ends or butts of timber; also comb.: **butting-machine**, a planing-machine for rounding and smoothing the ends of small timbers; **butting-saw**, a cross-cut saw for squaring the ends of logs in a saw-mill.

1874 KNIGHT *Dict. Mech.*

Buttle, *v.* Add:

b. To do a butler's work. *jocular.*

1918 MRS. H. WARD *War & Elizabeth* iii, The under-housemaid 'buttles' for him like a lamb. 1923 F. H. KITCHIN *Diversions of Dawson* 292 Nobody could buttle like James who had not been born in a pantry and taken pap out of silver spoons. 1929 W. J. LOCKE *Ancestor Jorico* xvi, Peters—the head steward—is a fat fool...Seems he buttled for decaying noble families.

Buttock, *sb.* Add:

8. *Coal-mining.* The portion of the working-face of coal to be broken out next. Hence **Buttocker,** a man who works at the buttock.

1884 GRESLEY *Gloss. Coal Mining.*

Button, *sb.* Add:

1. e. In phrases expressing weakness of intellect, as, *Not to have got all his buttons on, to be a button short.* Similarly *he has all his buttons* (*on*): he is sound in intellect, 'all there'.

1860 *Slang Dict.* (ed. 2) 109 *Not to have all one's buttons,* to be deficient in intellect. 1890 *Daily News* 21 May 6/3 He is 83 years of age, but as we say hereabouts, has all his buttons on. 1892 *Leeds Merc. Suppl.* 23 Jan. (E.D.D.) In Wilsden, one lacking full mental capacities has 'some of his buttons off'. 1893 MRS. A. KENNARD *Diogenes' Sandals* xi, They said..he had not 'got all his buttons', meaning that he was not 'all there'.

f. (*b*) *Button and eye*: a form of shackle for a horse.

1908 *Animal Managem.* 145 *Button and eye pattern.*—A loop of leather or webbing, one end of which is doubled into an eye, and the other gathered into a toggle or button.

h. A button of a particular colour, or bearing a distinctive design, worn as a party badge.

1908 *Westm. Gaz.* 3 Nov. 2/1 The donning of buttons is very far..from being either a modern or an American invention, for it may be believed to be traceable back to early Jacobite times; while 'Repeal buttons' were highly favoured in Ireland during the closing years of O'Connell's ascendency.

4. b. Phrase. *To press the button*: to push back the disc, pin, knob, or the like and thus produce the required result by completing an electric current, operating the shutter of a camera, etc. Often *fig.* in colloquial use, to perform an action that automatically brings about the required state of affairs.

1865 *Mech. Mag.* 10 Mar. 155/1 On pressing one of these buttons with the finger, the bell..is rung loudly. 1867 T. SPEIGHT *Brought to Light* I. iv. 97 To open the Secret Closet, press gently the fifth marble button from the top. 1893 *Cassell's Fam. Mag.* Mar. 318/1 Then he pressed the button of the camera. 1893 *Jrnl. Soc. Arts* XLI. 629/2 President Cleveland..pressed the button which started all the..machinery...The button..was of ivory. 1893 W. S. GILBERT *Utopia* I. 11 You only need a button press. 1905 *Minister's Gaz. Fashion* July 138/1 Pressing the Button. A Plea for Modern Methods...When the art of cutting will be reduced to a mechanical science. 1914 SIR E. GREY in *Europ. Crisis, Corr.* (Parlt. Papers Cl.) 46 Mediation was ready to come into operation..if only Germany would 'press the button' in the interests of peace. — SIR E. GOSCHEN *Ibid.* 59 The Chancellor told me last night that he was 'pressing the button' as hard as he could.

c. The leather projection on an oar, by which it is kept in position in the rowlock.

1902 *Encycl. Brit.* XXXII. 307/2 The only universal change in the pattern of oars has been the introduction of Messrs Ayling's patent button...Formerly the leather button where the oar rests in the rowlock was attached by two long nails.

d. In an organ, a round piece of leather that keeps the tracker from jumping out of place.

1876 STAINER & BARRETT *Dict. Mus. Terms* s.v. *Organ,* A tracker, a strip of light wood provided with a tap wire and leather button at the end. 1878 STAINER *Organ* 17 The little wire passing from the end of the tracker into the hole in the backfall is made like a screw,...so, where it appears below the backfall, a little leather button can be screwed on to it.

e. Each of the keys of an accordion.

1876 STAINER & BARRETT *Dict. Mus. Terms* s.v. *Accordion,* The first instruments had only four buttons, or keys, each of which acted on two reeds.

f. *Watchmaking.* The winding-knob of a keyless watch.

1904 *Technol. & Sci. Dict.* (ed. Goodchild & Tweney).

11. b. *Bagdad button*: a kind of boil, *furunculus orientalis,* endemic in Asia and Africa. So also *Aleppo, Biskra button.*

1897 *Daily News* 18 Sept. 6/2 They say in the East that if you visit Bagdad and escape the 'Bagdad button' (a painful species of boil), it will catch you in the world to come.

c. *Path.* Any small, rounded elevation on the cutaneous or mucous surface.

1900 *Jrnl. Exper. Med.* 15 Dec. 259 More characteristic lesions..are the so-called 'buttons'.

12. button balance, one for weighing assay buttons; **button blanket,** a blanket ornamented with pearls worn by British Columbia and Alaska Indians at festivals (*Cent. Dict.* Suppl. 1909); **button brass,** (*a*) see quot. 1884; (*b*) a strip of brass slipped under a metal button to shield the garment while the button is being cleaned; **button bud,** a bud resembling a button; **button cautery,** a cauterizing iron in the form of a disc; **button ear,** an ear, of a dog, that laps over and hides the inside; hence *button-eared* adj.; **button fastener,** (*a*) a spring loop, the free ends of which are passed through the shank of the button to keep it in place; (*b*) (see quot. 1884); **button-gall** (see quot.); **button-grass** (see quot. 1898); **button key** = *button fastener* (a); **button metal,** a metal used in the manufacture of buttons; **button-nosed** *a.*, (*a*) = *star-nosed* (see STAR *sb.*[1] 21); (*b*) having a small roundish nose; **button-quail** (see quot.); **button-scar,** a scar drawn up into button-shape, used for ornamentation of the body by African negroes; **button scurvy,** a skin disease characterized by button-like excrescences (Dorland *Med. Dict.* 1901); **button shell,** a small marine univalve of the genus *Rotella,* with a lenticular polished shell (*Stand. Dict.* 1895); **button-suture,** a modification of the twisted suture used in operations for hare-lip (*Stand. Dict.*); **button-tool,** (*a*) an instrument for cutting out leather 'buttons' (see quot.); (*b*) a tool for cutting out buttons or blanks for buttons (Knight *Dict. Mech.*); also, see quot.; **button-worm** (see quot.).

1900 *Coal & Metal Miners' Pocket Bk.* (ed. 6) 576 *Button Balance. 1884 LOCK *Workshop Rec.* Ser. III. 16/2 For *button brass, an alloy of 8 parts of copper and 5 of zinc is commonly used by the Birmingham makers, under the name of 'platin'. 1899 *Daily News* 27 Dec. 8/3 The 'button brass'...This little plate tucked under the button with its shank in the slit enables the button to be well rubbed without mischief. 1869 BLACKMORE *Lorna D.* xvii, The opening cones were struck with brown, in between the *button buds. 1890 BILLINGS *Med. Dict.*, *Button cautery. 1866 MRS. WHITNEY *L. Goldthwaite* x, She had hooks and eyes, and *button-fasteners, when these gave out. 1874 [see *button key*]. 1884 KNIGHT *Dict. Mech.* Suppl., *Button Fastener,* a clasp which hooks over the eye of a shoe button and is then clinched to the shoe. 1879 *Encycl. Brit.* X. 46 The '*button-galls' of *Neuroterus numismatis,* Oliv., are eaten by pheasants. 1898 MORRIS *Austral Eng.*, *Button-grass, *Schænus sphærocephalus,* Poiret, N.O. *Cyperaceæ*...So called from the round shaped flower (capitate inflorescence), on a thin stalk four or five feet long, like a button on the end of a foil. 1927 *Blackw. Mag.* Oct. 470/1 A steep razor-backed hill, covered with ragged clumps of button-grass and dwarfed ti-tree. 1874 KNIGHT *Dict. Mech.*, *Button Key *or* Fastener,* a spring loop..to..keep the button in place. 1884 LOCK *Workshop Rec.* Ser. III. 14 Cu+4Zn White *button metal. 1895 *Standard Dict.*, *Button-nosed,* star-nosed: said of the condylure. 1909 H. G. WELLS *Tono-Bungay* III. ii, Button-nosed, pink-and-white Aunt Susan. 1886 *Encycl. Brit.* XX. 147 There is another [group]..often termed Quails or *Button-Quails...This is that comprehended by the genus *Turnix,* or *Hemipodius* of some authors. 1897 A. J. BUTLER tr. *Ratzel's Hist. Mank.* II. 394 In the so-called '*button-scars', a row of button-shaped warty scars runs from the edge of the forehead to the tip of the nose; this is found both on the Congo and on the Zambesi. 1855 OGILVIE Suppl., **Button-tool,* an instrument used chiefly for cutting out the disks or buttons of leather, which serve as nuts for the screwed wires in the mechanism connected with the keys of the organ and pianoforte. 1847 STODDART *Angler's Comp.* 111 The Black-Head, or *Button-Worm..whose nature it is..to coil and knot itself up in the form of a ball or old-fashioned button.

Bu·tton-ball. *U.S.* [f. BUTTON *sb.*, from the form of the fruit.] The plane-tree or 'sycamore' of the United States; the button-wood.

1824 Z. THOMPSON *Gazetteer Vermont* 24 *Platanus occid.* Button ball tree. 1844 DE SMET *Oregon Missions* (1847) 82 In no part of this region have I met with a more luxuriant growth of pine, fir, elm, oak, buttonball, and yew trees. 1849 N. P. WILLIS *Rural Lett.* ii. 31 'Is it that big button-ball you'll have cut down, sir?' 'Call it a sycamore, Tom, and I'll come and see.' 1857 A. GRAY *First Less. Bot.* (1866) 80 A round or roundish cluster of flowers..as in the Button-ball, Button-bush..and Red clover. 1882 [see BUTTON *sb.* 12]. 1906 *Springfield Weekly Republ.* 22 Feb. 16 The large buttonball tree standing in front of the Field place at Northfield has recently been cut down.

Bu·tton-bush. *U.S.* (See BUTTON *sb.* 12.)

1784 CUTLER in *Mem. Amer. Acad.* (1785) I. 409 *Cephalanthus*...Globe-flower shrub. Pond Dogwood. Button Bush. 1845–50 MRS. LINCOLN *Lect. Bot.* 144 The Button-bush, (*Cephalanthus,*) of about five feet in height, affords a good example of this natural order. 1871 SCHELE DE VERE *Americanisms* (1872) 413 The Button-bush (*Cephalanthus occidentalis*) has its name from the resemblance of its globular catkins of flowers to round buttons. 1878 *Scribner's Mag.* XVI. 724/2 Bordered by willows and button-bushes. *Ibid.* 725/1 The button-bushes and the pickerel-weed are sere.

Button-hole, *sb.* Add:

1. c. spec. *The* or *one's buttonhole*: the button-hole in the lapel of a coat; also *colloq.* = *button-hole flower* (see 4 in Dict.).

1848 DICKENS *Dombey* xxxi, The Major..wears a whole geranium in his button-hole. 1863 [in Dict., sense 1]. 1876 MISS ALCOTT *Rose in Bloom* ix, Bending his head to kiss the hands that put a little white rose in his button-hole. 1879–1883 [in Dict., sense 3]. 1918 C. MACKENZIE *Sylvia Scarlett* vii, How nice you look, Arthur, in that buttonhole. 1928 EDINGTON *Studio Murder Myst.* xvii, The white gardenia in his buttonhole.

2. b. *Surg.* 'A small straight incision into a cavity or organ' (Dorland *Med. Dict.* 1913).

1907 *Practitioner* Oct. 526 Without making a 'button-hole' through the muco-perichondrium.

4. *button-hole cutter, hand, twist,* etc.; **button-hole globe, light,** an electric bulb to be fastened in one's button-hole as a reading light.

1868 *Rep. U.S. Commissioner Agric.* (1869) 289 Button-hole twist is the same, with a tighter twist. 1874 KNIGHT *Dict. Mech.*, Button-hole Cutter. 1890 *Daily News* 27 Jan. 3/1 The apparatus is about the same as that of the button-hole light, only that instead of a buttonhole globe at the end of a thread there is a fine, minute drill. 1908 *Daily Chron.* 12 June 9/6 Tailoring.—Wanted button-hole hand for coats and vests.

Button-hole, *v.* Add:

1. c. To make button-hole openings in.

1908 *Practitioner* Oct. 522 The hand is kept in that position ..by long strips of adhesive plaster..; these are button-holed over the knuckles to adapt themselves to them.

d. *Surg.* To make a button-hole incision in.

1907 *Practitioner* Oct. 530 It may seem impossible to strip off the muco-chondrium without buttonholing it.

3. *intr.* Of the texture of bread: To become full of holes suggesting button-holes.

1927 W. DEEPING *Doomsday* viii. § 1, Finding the loaf rather too new and the knife too blunt for the carving of slices of ideal thinness. The beastly things would button-hole!

Bu·tton-wood. *U.S.* [BUTTON *sb.*] The plane-tree or sycamore; the button-ball. Also *attrib.* with *tree.*

(*a*) 1680 *Conn. Hist. Soc. Coll.* XIV. 472 Two Button wood Trees one by each river. 1766 J. ADAMS *Diary* Wks. 1850 II. 194, I saw..a likely young button-wood tree, lately planted on the triangle made by the three roads. 1835 R. M. BIRD *Hawks of Hawk-hollow* II. xx. 255 His ride on the back of the buttonwood-tree. 1837, 1852 [see BUTTON *sb.* 12].

(*b*) 1691 PLUKENET *Phytogr.* Tab. lxxvii. Fig. 4 Arbor Americana triphylla .. Lignum fibularium (i.e.) *Button-wood* nostratibus dicta. 1778 J. CARVER *Trav. N. Amer.* 499 The Button wood is a tree of the largest size, and might be distinguished by its bark, which is quite smooth and mottled. 1831 PECK *Guide for Emigrants* II. 122 The sycamore is the button wood of New England. 1837 COLMAN *Rep. Agric. Mass.* (1838) 64, I think..that button wood (the Plane tree) and the white ash may be cultivated to as great profit on my land as any kind of forest trees whatever. 1858 O. W. HOLMES *Aut. Breakf.-t.* vii. 177 The button-wood throws off its bark in large flakes. 1906 *Harper's Mag.* Mar. 560 She watched him..come back,..walking very slowly under the mottled branches of the buttonwoods.

b. *attrib.* Built of button-wood timber.

1799 *Aurora* (Philad.) 21 May (Th.) The old button-wood meeting house in Philadelphia was made into a military riding-house.

Buttress, *sb.*[1] **6.** Add:

buttress thread, a screw-thread having one face at right angles to the axis of the bolt or shaft.

1887 LOW *Machine Draw.* (1892) 15 The Buttress thread..is designed to combine the advantages of the V and square threads.

Butty. Add:

4. A second barge or freight-boat in tow by the first. More explicitly *butty-boat.*

1909 'Q' *True Tilda* ix, With two horses hauling at the first [barge], and the second (which Sam called a butty-boat) towed astern. 1923 *Blackw. Mag.* Nov. 663/2, I overhauled two barges, the foremost with its little steam-engine towing the second or 'butty'.

Butyro-. Add: **Butyro-refractometer** [see REFRACTOMETER], a refractometer for testing the refractive power of butter-fat as a test of its purity.

c 1900 *Newspaper,* The Finance and Parliamentary Committee recommended that the Borough Analyst be empowered to obtain a Butyrorefractometer.

Butyrometer (biutirǫ·mitəɹ). [f. BUTYRO- + -METER.] An instrument for estimating the percentage of butter-fat in milk. Cf. *lactobutyrometer* s.v. LACTO-.

[1863 *Jrnl. R. Agric. Soc.* XXIV. II. 315 Marchand's lacto-butyrometer.] 1902 *Encycl. Brit.* XXVII. 360/1 The machines —often termed butyrometers—are commonly made to hold from two up to two dozen testers. *Ibid.*, The butyrometer is extremely useful, alike for measuring periodically the fat-producing capacity of individual cows in a herd, for rapidly ascertaining the percentage of fat in milk delivered to factories [etc.].

Buvette (büve·t). Add: Also, a refreshment bar or room. Cf. BUFFET *sb.*[3] 3.

1885 *Cornhill Mag.* June 597 We..went into the stove-stifling heat of the little buvette of the station to keep ourselves warm.

Buy (bəi), *sb.* orig. *U.S.* [f. BUY *v.*] A purchase; a bargain. *On the buy*: actively buying.

1890 VAN DYKE *Millionaires of a Day* 134 Biggest buy in town. 1911 H. QUICK *Yellowstone N.* vii. 191, I believe it's a good buy! 1929 *Star* 21 Aug. 18/2 His clients are 'on the buy'.

Buy, *v.* Add:

15. *To buy money*: (Racing slang) see quot. 1922.

1906 FOX-DAVIES *Dangerville Inheritance* vii. 99 The public had left off buying money, and the wagering had become slack. 1922 *N. & Q.* 12th Ser. XI. 206/2 *Buying money,* laying heavy odds on a favourite. 1928 *Daily Express* 12 July 12/2 Backers..had to buy money over On Avon and Rainbow Bridge.

Buying, *vbl. sb.* Add:

3. The purchasing of shares on the stock exchange. *Buying-in day,* the day on which, owing to non-delivery within the appointed time of shares bought, the buyer may purchase the shares on the market. *Buying-in rule,* the rule with regard to buying-in day.

1900 *Westm. Gaz.* 24 Mar. 7/1 'Buying-in Day.'..He immediately delivers the shares, usually on the day after the buying-in takes place. 1902 *Encycl. Brit.* XXXII. 865 The 'corner' in Northern Pacific common shares produced..the suspension for two or three weeks of the 'buying in' rule.

Buzz, *sb.*[1] Add:

1. b. *Phonetics.* A voiced hiss (see HISS *sb.* 1 b).

1877 SWEET *Handbk. Phonetics* 79 The voiced buzzes admit of more variety than the voiced stops. 1887 *Encycl. Brit.* XXII. 383 Glides to and from Hisses, Buzzes. *Ibid.*, A hiss (s), followed without a positional glide by the buzz (z). 1888 SWEET *Hist. Eng. Sounds* 24 Some consonants..are pronounced with..a complete absence of buzz. 1908 — *Sounds of English* 43 The English ~ is vowellike in sound, being quite free from buzz.

c. Phrase. *To go with a buzz* (fig.): to advance rapidly or 'swimmingly'.

1899 DOYLE *Duet, Two Solos,* By Jove, it simply went with a buzz from the word 'go'.

d. A round game in which each player in turn utters a number in numerical order, with the exception that 'buz' must be substituted for 7, multiples of 7, and numbers containing a 7, or pay a fine for its omission.

1865 *Slang Dict., Buz,* a well-known flash game. 1868 MISS ALCOTT *Little Women* iii, They..were in the midst of a quiet game of 'buzz'.

5. buzz-planer, a small wood-planing machine (Knight *Dict. Mech.* Suppl. 1884).

Buzz, *sb.*[2] **2. b.** Add: Also quasi-*adj.* of an artificial fly (see quot. 1877).

1877 HALLOCK *Sportsman's Gazetteer* 599 A fly is said to be buz when the hackle is wrapped on thick and it looks 'bushy' as we Americans would term it. 1889 F. M. HALFORD *Dry-Fly Fishing* ix. 205 Arguments in favour of dressing spinners hackle or buzz fashion.

Buzz, *v.*[1] Add:

6. b. *Phonetics.* To pronounce as or with a buzz.

1877 SWEET *Handbk. Phonetics* 37 (j) in N[orth] G[erman] is often distinctly buzzed. *Ibid.*, Buzzed (j) is the ordinary G. *g* in 'liegen', 'regen'.

9. To telephone or signal (a call or message) by the 'buzzer'. *To buzz off*: to ring off on the telephone. Also *intr.* of a message: To come *in* by the buzzer.

1914 *Pears' Christmas Ann.* 20/2 Are you the *Bainbridge*? Then buzz off!..You there—have you had a call from the *Bainbridge*? 1926 BOYD CABLE *Action Front* 173 The telephonists..'buzzed' even more monotonous strings of longs and shorts on the buzzer. *Ibid.*, The messages that had just 'buzzed' in over their wires. *Ibid.* 183 It's bad enough..to get all these messages through by voice. I haven't a dog's chance of doing it if I have to buzz each one.

b. To go *off* or *away* quickly. *slang.*

1925 ALDOUS HUXLEY *Those Barren Leaves, Journey* v. (1927) 313 So I buzzed after you till I saw old Ernest wiv ve car at ve side of ve road. 1930 *Diary Public Sch. Girl* 46 Buzz off, you idiot, or James 'll see you.

10. To cut (wood) with a buzz-saw. *U.S.*

1925 *British Weekly* 5 Mar. 554/5 His home-built contraption for 'buzzin'' wood.

12. To throw swiftly or forcibly. *colloq.*

1893 KIPLING *Many Invent.* ii. 35 Dennis buzzed his carbine after him, and it caught him on the back of his head. 1918 E. A. MACKINTOSH *War, the Liberator* 113 If we cannae throw a live We can aye buzz a dud.

Buzzard, *sb.*[1] Add:

1. b. (Later examples.)

1813 PAULDING *J. Bull & Br. Jonathan* xix. (1835) 87 He ..was between hawk and buzzard, as they say. 1832 J. P. KENNEDY *Swallow B.* (1860) 17, I entered Richmond between hawk and buzzard. 1895 *Brewer's Dict. Phr. & Fable* 193 *Between Hawk and buzzard.* Not quite a lady or gentleman, nor quite a servant. Applied to tutors in private houses [etc.].

c. The species of vulture more fully called *turkey-buzzard. U.S.*

1851 MAYNE REID *Scalp Hunters* xxx, 'Twur turkey-buzzart, then: that's what it wur. *Ibid.*, And when did ye eat the buzzard, old boy? 1871 SCHELE DE VERE *Americanisms* (1872) 373 Similar confusion prevails here about the name of Buzzard, which is commonly misapplied, being given to a vulture instead of a hawk. 1876 BURROUGHS *Winter Sunshine* i. (1892) 16 But the worst thing about the buzzard is his silence.

2. (Examples of recent U.S. use.)

1889 BARRÈRE & LELAND *Dict. Slang, Buzzard* (American), an oppressive, arrogant person, jealous of rivalry, and vindictive. 1918 MULFORD *Man fr. Bar-20* viii. 77 'Pop', he said, sharply, 'who is this buzzard?' *Ibid.* xi. 108 You two buzzards are about as cheerful an' pleasant as a rattler in August.

b. Applied to things: (see quot. 1871). *U.S.*

1871 *Lancaster Intelligencer* 6 May (De Vere) Said the venerable Mr. G. to one of his jours: Sir, I pronounce that job an unmitigated buzzard. 1871 SCHELE DE VERE *Americanisms* (1872) 587 *Buzzard* is the half-facetious half-contemptuous term applied in several mechanical professions to a badly-spoiled piece of work.

4. buzzard dollar *U.S. slang,* the silver dollar coined under the Bland bill of 1878, so called from having the figure of an eagle on the reverse; **buzzard lope** *U.S.* (see quot.).

a 1889 *Chicago Tribune* (Barrère & Leland), The waiters.. will take anything you give them, from a nickel up to a *buzzard dollar, and look happy. 1890 *Standard* 24 Apr., *Buzzard Lope—'the latest social institution of America'.. a dance taught to a Georgian negro by the turkey buzzard'.

Bu·zzardy, *a.* [f. BUZZARD *sb.*[1] + -Y[1].] Resembling a buzzard.

1885 'C. E. CRADDOCK' *Prophet Gt. Smoky Mts.* xiii. 242 An' I don't want ter stay in jail, an' be tried..an' mebbe hev them buzzardy lawyers fix suthin' on me ennyways.

Buzzer[1]. Add:

4. An electric mechanism for producing an intermittent current and a buzzing sound or series of sounds; used chiefly as a call or signal. Also *attrib.*

1884 KNIGHT *Dict. Mech.* Suppl., *Buzzer,* a telegraphic call in which a vibrating hammer strikes a sounding piece and gives out a buzzing sound, which, in certain cases, is preferable to a bell. 1901 'LINESMAN' *Words Eyewitness* (1902) 203 The little station, with its brave air of business, its stationmaster, and its electric 'buzzer'. 1916 BOYD CABLE *Action Front* 183 He could hear the morse signals on the buzzer plain enough. 1918 E. A. MACKINTOSH *War, the Liberator* 99 If..his bloody barrage-fire 's Broken all your buzzer wires Don't get flurried. 1920 *Conquest* June 404/1 There is a local buzzer-circuit in the call box. 1928 C. F. S. GAMBLE *Story of North Sea Air Station* Introd. 22 A buzzer worked off dry cells.

fig. 1926 H. NICOLSON *Swinburne* i. 11 Although, so to speak, this obstruction exists only on one line of communication, yet it acts as a buzzer which disturbs the rest.

5. *Electr.* The trembler of an induction coil.

1888 *Chambers's Jrnl.* 14 Jan. 25 It is called a 'buzzer'... It is a rapid current-breaker.

6. Applied to various machines that make a buzzing noise in operation. **a.** A polishing wheel. **b.** A circular saw.

1884 KNIGHT *Dict. Mech.* Suppl., *Buzzer,* a small, rapidly-revolving wheel, used in grinding or polishing small objects. 1925 *British Weekly* 5 Mar. 554/5 His 'buzzer,' as he calls it, is not 'boughten'.

Bu·zz-saw. *U.S.* [BUZZ *sb.*[1] 5.] A circular saw.

1860 HOLLAND *Miss Gilbert* xix. 350 If you'll take thunder and lightning and a steamboat and a buzz-saw and mix 'em up. 1882 *Congress. Rec.* June 5240/2 Gentlemen may commiserate the South..and wish they might hear the 'buzz-saw' humming and the spindle twirling there. 1883 NYE *Baled Hay* 24 We should learn from this never to lean on the buzz saw when it moveth itself aright. 1894 *Harper's Mag.* Apr. 807/2 A man..has got to..ride a race, or manage a buzz-saw, or be an expert farm hand.

attrib. 1897 'MARK TWAIN' *Following Equator* xxxiv. 313 One of those whizzing green Ballarat flies..with his stunning buzz-saw noise.

Hence **Bu·zz-saw** *v. trans.*, to cut with a buzz-saw. Also *fig.*

1883 LANDON *Wit & Humor* 118, I was buzz-sawed, sure.

Bwana (bwā·na). [Swahili.] A term of respectful address or reference used by the Swahili, equivalent to '(the) master', 'Mr.', or 'Sir'.

1878 H. M. STANLEY *Dark Cont.* iii. (1880) 38 Bwana, you see these scars. *Ibid.* 628 It is Bwana Stanley's expedition that has returned. 1886 E. C. DAWSON *James Hannington* (1887) 212 The cries of 'Run, bwana, run!' were accentuated by a double roar. 1921 *Blackw. Mag.* Jan. 119/1 He had not been able to tell his Bwana about the bustard. 1922 *Chambers's Jrnl.* Apr. 220/1 He might be called to account by the *bwana* at the Government camp.

By, *sb.*[1] Add: An instance of a place-name in *-by.*

1884 *Pall Mall Gaz.* 20 Feb. 5/1 Dr. Taylor..had already taught us to recognize the general tokens of Scandinavian settlement in the..*bys* where they [*sc.* the pirates] made their solitary..homesteads. 1908 W. G. COLLINGWOOD *Scandinavian Brit.* 113 'Thorpes' indicating villages as opposed to 'byes' or isolated farmsteads..are found.

By[2]**, bye,** *sb.* **3.** (Earlier U.S. example.)

1801 *Massachusetts Spy* 29 July 3/1 For fear of being drawn into a bye, he put to shore at a steep bank.

By, *prep.* Add: **26.** Phrase. *Do as you would be done by*: see DO *v.* 37.

29. Also with omission of the verb. *By the name of*: see NAME *sb.* 13.

1676– [see NAME *sb.* 13]. 1787 *Generous Attachment* III. 229. 1826 SYD. SMITH in Lady Holland *Mem.* (1855) II. 265 A very agreeable, clever woman, by the name of Quesnel. 1869 SIR J. T. COLERIDGE *Mem. Keble* 217 Dialogues, in which a mason by that name [*sc.* Richard Nelson] bears a principal part.

33. c. Used for: Written, painted, executed by (an author, painter, sculptor, etc.).

1570 (*title*) The Scholemaster..¶By Roger Ascham. 1595 (*title*) Colin Clovts Come home againe. By Ed. Spencer. 1673 (*title*) Poems, &c. upon Several Occasions. By Mr. John Milton: Both English and Latin, &c. Composed at several times. 1779 *Mirror* No. 24 Can the representations of moon-light, even by Homer, Milton, and Shakespeare, be more exquisitely finished? 1832 DISRAELI *Cont. Fleming* II. xiv, I must get 'Manstein' directly, if it be by young Moskoffsky. 1901 *Lincoln City & Cathedral* 154 The latter [window], by a Nuremburg executant, is poor and feeble.

d. Of a public house, etc.: Kept or managed by (as licencee).

1840 DICKENS *Old C. Shop* xxix, This is the Valiant Soldier, by James Groves. 1885 HENLEY & STEVENSON *Macaire* I. iii, *Auberge des Adrets,* by John Paul Dumont. 1919 MASEFIELD *Reynard the Fox* 2 The meet was at 'The Cock and Pye By Charles and Martha Enderby'.

34. b. From, after, according to (a model).

a 1650 E. NORGATE *Miniatura* (1919) 84 When the Italians have not the Life to draw by, they make use off Models. *Ibid.* 86 By these and such others they draw. 1654 VAUGHAN *Discourses* Wks. (ed. Martin) 260 Pictures that have not so much as an ayre of those faces they were drawn by.

B. *adv.* **5.** Over in duration, finished, at an end. Of time: Past, gone by. Also *by with. Sc.* and *north.*

1784 BURNS *Ep. Rankine* x, As soon 's the clocking-time is buy, And the wee pouts begun to cry. 1846 ALEX. LAING *Wayside Flowers* 20 Whan the buryin' was bye, an' relations a' gane. 1896 CROCKETT *Grey Man* xii, The days of curses are by with.

b. Of a person: Done for, ruined, dead: esp. in *to be by with it. Sc.* and *north.*

1890 SERVICE *Notandums* vi. 34 When the dykes are broken you're bye, ye ken,—ouay! fairly bye! 1892 STEVENSON *Catriona* xxx, You're by with it, James More. You can never show your face again. 1900 KIPLING in *Daily Express* 26 June 4/6 I'll not call it farmin'—up yonder, but ye're by with that even.

By-. Add:

2. b. by-child, -son, a bastard. *dial.*

Cf. BY-BLOW 3.

1894 HALL CAINE *Manxman* III. xvi, You'd be hearing of the 'by-child, it's like? 1887 A. E. BARR *Border Shepherdess* xii, 'That play-acting 'by-son o' the Graeme.' 'He was no by-son.'

3. a. *bye-spot.* **d.** *by-practice.*

1887 MABEL WETHERAL *Two N.-C. Maids* xxiv. 170 Gale Syke Tower is a bit lonesome, being what mother calls a 'bye-spot'. 1913 C. READ in *Eng. Hist. Rev.* Jan. 48 Walsingham believed that his [*sc.* Burghley's] by-practice through Hunsdon with Arran was influenced by these considerations.

4. *bye-betting, -wager*; *bye-election* in attrib. use.

1886 H. SMART *Outsider* II. i. 2 On no race of late years had there been so much bye-betting, that is to say, wagers in which one horse was backed against one other. *Ibid.*, Others..who had laid these heavy bye-wagers, looking upon the horse as having no possible chance, had never taken the trouble to secure themselves. 1897 *Daily News* 6 Jan. 4/5 Very actively engaged in by-election work. 1899 *Ibid.* 10 May 9/4 If the Executive through its bye-election Committee..decides not to help. 1908 *Westm. Gaz.* 29 Apr. 3/2 He attacked it [*sc.* the Bill] in the true by-election style.

5. *by-legislation, -point, -port*; **by-stake,** each of the short intermediate stakes used in basket-making; hence **by-stake** *v.*, to furnish with by-stakes.

1886 *Contemp. Rev.* Feb. 231 The Friendly Societies Act.. gives powers of *by-legislation on specified matters,..all which has only to be certified by a Crown registrar. 1577 W. BOURNE *Regiment for Sea* i. 8 Betweene euery one of these inferior poynts, and euery one of the head wynds there is a *bypoynt or winde. 1883 *Man. Seamanship for Boys* 98 By-Points. So called because they derive their names from the nearest cardinal or half-cardinal points they are near or by. 1887 *Pall Mall Gaz.* 3 Aug. 2/1 These nice little four or five thousand ton coasters take in and discharge more cargo at..these by-ports than any regular cargo boat ..flying [*sic*] from port to port.

By and by. Add:

B. 2. The name by which cannon are known to the natives of Natal.

1857 J. SHOOTER *Kafirs of Natal* 112 They believe that the fearful *by-and-bye* eats up everything. 1893 B. MITFORD *Gun-runner* xxiv, We laugh at their *bat-nbai*. What are guns, big or small, against the broad shields and devouring spears of the ever-conquering Amazulu? 1894 C. H. W. DONOVAN *With Wilson in Matabeleland* x. 234 They used to call common shells 'by-and-byes,' because they could see the smoke, and by and by a shell would explode in their midst.

By and large, *advb. phr.* orig. *U.S.* [Originally in nautical use: see BY *adv.* 1 d.] *To take.. by and large*: to take or regard in a general aspect, without entering into details. Also in later use without *take*; = on the whole.

1833 J. C. NEAL *Down-Easters* I. 23 A man who feels rather perplexed on the whole, take it by and large. 1845 S. JUDD *Margaret* II. v. 283 Take it by and large..and she is the beater of all. 1869 'MARK TWAIN' *Innoc. Abr.* v. (1897) 47 Taking it by and large, as the sailors say, we had a pleasant run. 1878 B. F. TAYLOR *Between Gates* 281 Those who sail over the old parallels of latitude by-and-large believe in fair play. 1890 *Congress. Rec.* May 4376/2 By and large all of us who live there..know the immense benefit that has been derived from it [*sc.* the prohibition law]. 1926 *Publishers' Weekly* 18 Dec. 2255 By and large the book-store in the South is a sorry institution.

By-bidder. (Earlier U.S. example.)

1848 BARTLETT *Dict. Amer., By-bidder,* a person employed at public auctions to bid on articles put up for sale, to obtain higher prices.

Bye, *sb.* Add:

1. d. esp. in *Cockfighting*: in full *bye-battle,* as distinguished from the 'main': see MAIN *sb.*[3] 3.

1716 *Lond. Gaz.* No. 5429/4 There will be By-Battles,.. And in the Afternoon will begin the main Match. 1859 LORD W. LENNOX *Pictures Sporting Life & Char.* I. 175 Eleven a-head on the main and byes seven. *Ibid.*, On the usual fighting night, Tuesday, at the same pit, for bye battles, there was very capital play. 1883 R. CALDECOTT *Graphic Pict.* 13 There were carpet-dances on off-nights by way of byes.

e. *Golf.* The hole or holes of the stipulated course that are unplayed when the match is finished.

1887 *Golfing* 92 *Bye.* Any hole or holes that remain to be played after the match is finished, are played for singly; unless the sides agree to make another match of them. 1890 *Sat. Rev.* 31 May 666/1 Prestwick golfers of to-day do not play for such stakes as a soul on the round and a nose on the bye.

3. = *BYWATER.

1928 J. R. SUTTON *Diamond* 34 Yellow Diamond...Fine White. White. First Cape...First Bye.

By-electoral (bəi,ĕle·ktŏrăl), *a.* [f. BY- 4 + ELECTORAL, after *by-election.*] Of, belonging to, or characteristic of a by-election.

1892 *Pall Mall Gaz.* 6 July 2/2 By this device the Liberals are deprived of their by-electoral successes altogether. 1905 *Westm. Gaz.* 10 Oct. 2/3 By-electoral oratory. 1928 *Daily Tel.* 25 Sept. 12/2 He was breaking the rule that..party leaders should not take part in by-electoral contests.

Byerite (bəi·ərəit). *Min.* [Named after W. N. *Byers*: see -ITE[1].] A mineral coal resembling albertite and torbanite, first found in Colorado, U.S.A.

1892 E. S. DANA *Dana's Syst. Min.* (ed. 6) 1024.

Bygone. Add:

B. *sb.* **1. d.** *sing.* A person or thing of the past.

1891 HARDY *Tess* xlv, Bygones would never be complete bygones till she was a bygone herself. 1891 *Daily News* 6 Mar. 5/3 That, however, is a byegone, and it is needless to go back upon it. 1897 *Westm. Gaz.* 24 July 4/2 We would let the bygone of the Rae Mine, whatever its case, be a bygone.

Bymeby, *adv. U.S. dial.* Also: **by'm by, bym by, by-am-by, bye'm by, byme-by.** [Reduced form of BY AND BY 4; the earlier stage *by'nd by* occurs in 1708 (*Deplor. State New Eng.* 35). See also *BIMEBY and *BUMBY(E).] By and by, presently.

1825 J. NEAL *Bro. Jonathan* I. 106 Bym by; naiteral enough; there they go. *Ibid.* 195 You'll believe what I say, by'm by. 1844 'JON. SLICK' *High Life N. Y.* I. vii. 101 They give all sich stranger-critters a name, and I s'pose you'll git one by-am-by, as well as the rest on 'em. *Ibid.* x. 152. 1848 J. F. COOPER *Oak Open.* I. iii. 41 Have yankee scalp, bye'm by. 1857 HOLLAND *Bay Path* (1864) 136 It's a thing that'll come round byme-by. *Ibid.* 334 Byme-by I looked up, and there stood the widow crying. 1873 'MARK TWAIN' *Gilded Age* ii. 32 But bymeby she roused up like, and looked around wild.

Bynedestin (binīde·stin). *Physiol. Chem.* [f. Gr. βύνη malt + *EDESTIN.] A typical globulin present in barley malt.

Bynin (bəi·nin). *Physiol. Chem.* [f. Gr. βύνη malt + -IN[1].] A proteid soluble in alcohol, contained in barley malt.

1890 *Review of Reviews* Nov. Advt. p. xvii/1 Liquid Bynin Malt. 1891 *Medical Annual* 540 Bynol,..another combination of bynin with cod-liver oil.

Byon (byō̆ⁿn). [Burmese *brun* refuse, as of grain, peas, etc., the matrix earth of rubies and the rejected stones; app. related to *prun, phrun* to be worn out or exhausted.] The ruby-bearing clay of the Ruby Mines district of Upper Burma.

1892 E. W. STREETER *Prec. Stones* (ed. 5) 153 A brown or yellowish clay, known locally as *Byon,* seems to be the typical Ruby-bearing earth. 1895 *Standard* 24 July, The valley byon beds of Mogok, Tagoungnandine, and Loodah. 1922 *Chambers's Jrnl.* July 447/1 Coolies will still..be required to take the 'byon' to the sluice.

By-pass (bəi·pas), *sb.* Also **bye-pass.** [f. BY- B. 3 b + PASS *sb.*[1]]

1. A secondary pipe issuing from the main or service pipe below a stop-tap or cock, allowing the free passage of a small supply of gas, steam, etc., when the main supply is shut off; *esp.* the small tube and pilot light of a gas-jet, which remains alight when the jet is turned off. Also *attrib.*

1848 E. ALBAN *Steam Engine* 264 It is a sort of by-pass to allow the steam to travel freely from the upper into the lower box. 1876 *Amer. Gas-L. Jrnl.* 3 July 20 (Knight 1884) Farmer's hydraulic main, with dip-pipe and bye-pass. 1888 *Morning Post* 12 Jan. 2/3 The only service from the stage supply that was open being one half inch bye-pass for the pilot light of auditorium sun burner. 1895 *Daily News* 10 Oct. 6/4 The innovation..consists of a little 'by-pass' arrangement by which a tiny flame is always kept going. 1902 *Daily Chron.* 29 Oct. 3/4 A by-pass is provided, so that if the pump creates a higher pressure than is desired the surplus oil merely passes back into the large supply tank.

2. A road diverging from and re-entering a main road, *esp.* a new road constructed as an alternative route to relieve congestion of traffic on the main road. Also *attrib.*

1922 *Daily Mail* 2 Dec. 5 New roads and by-passes, which should remove some of these danger spots. 1923 *Times* (weekly ed.) 25 Jan., The Kingston by-pass will begin at the Robin Hood gate. 1929 *Times* 13 Nov. 9/4 It was recommended that the proposal to make a by-pass road be dropped.

By-pass (bəi·pas), *v.* [f. *BY-PASS *sb.*]

1. *trans.* To furnish with a by-pass.

1886 *Sci. Amer. Supp.* 4 Dec. 9099/3, I next by-passed the outlet valve with a one inch pipe. 1928 *Even. Standard* 12 Mar. 6/2 King's Langley and Tring by passing Bushey and Watford. 1929 *Times* 28 May 17/4 Schemes are on foot for by-passing both Leatherhead and Dorking.

2. To conduct (liquid, gas, etc.) by means of a by-pass.

1909 *Cent. Dict.* Suppl. 1924 *Glasgow Herald* 6 Nov. 9 A small portion of the gas..is by-passed to a boiler.

Byronesque (bəirəne·sk), *a.* [f. the name of the poet Lord *Byron* + -ESQUE.] Having the characteristic style of Byron.

1888 *Temple Bar* Nov. 335 This eminently Byronesque epistle.

Bysmalith (bi·zmăliþ). *Geol.* [f. Gr. βύσμα plug + λίθος stone: see -LITH.] A large body of igneous rock which, when it was forced upward, lifted up the overlying rock.

1899 IDDINGS & WEED *Descr. Geol. Gallatin Mountains* 18 By this mode of intrusion the vertical dimension of the intruded mass becomes still greater as compared with the lateral dimensions, so that the shape is more that of a plug or core. Such an intruded plug of igneous rock may be termed a *bysmalith.* 1905 CHAMBERLIN & SALISBURY *Geol.* I. 477 Between the bysmalith and the laccolith there are various gradations.

Byssogenous (bisǫ·dʒĭnəs), *a.* [f. BYSS-US + -GEN 2 + -OUS.] That (normally) produces a byssus.

1895 *Camb. Nat. Hist.* III. 453 Foot with byssogenous slit, but no byssus.

By-the-way, *sb.* [f. phr. *by the way*: see BY *prep.* 12 b.] An incidental remark.

1896 *Punch* 1 Feb. 52/1, I think I may indulge myself with a short by-the-way on the subject of hampers. 1907 *Daily Chron.* 2 Oct. 3/3 Here are two 'by-the-ways' from her pages of observation.

Bywater (bəi·wǭtəɹ). [f. BY- B. 5 + WATER *sb.* (20).] Applied to a diamond of inferior water, yellowish in colour.

1895 *Westm. Gaz.* 1 Oct. 2/1, I..woke up to consider two fresh lots of treasure, 'whites' and 'by-waters,' so termed from their colour. 1916 F. B. WADE *Diamonds* 25 Yellows, or by-waters.

Bywoner: see *BIJWONER.

By your leave, *sb.* [f. phr. *by your leave*: see LEAVE *sb.* 1.] An expression of apology for not having asked permission.

1924 W. M. RAINE *Troubled Waters* i. 13 'With not even a by your leave. You're a claim jumper,' she said.

Byzantinist (bəi-, bizæ·ntinist). [f. BYZANTINE + -IST.] A student of or an expert in Byzantine matters.

1892 *Nation* (N.Y.) 21 Apr. 306/1 The collaboration of Greek, English, and Italian 'Byzantinists' is already pledged to support it. 1927 *Observer* 24 Apr. 20/3 The Congress of Byzantinists has concluded its work.

C

C. Add: **II. 1. b.** C 3: the lowest grade in the scale of physical fitness for military service employed in the classification of recruits conscripted under the Military Service Act, 1916; hence *fig.* of the lowest grade, of highly inferior status or quality.

1918 D. LLOYD GEORGE in *Times* 13 Sept. 8/2 You cannot maintain an A1 Empire with a C3 population. 1923 *Daily Mail* 1 Mar. 7 He would agree prisoner's left arm would be a C3 left arm. *Ibid.* 11 July 13 Sunshine all the way, no C3 affair but a magnificent blaze of light. 1924 GALSWORTHY *White Monkey* I. viii, Eight years her senior and C3 during the war!

III. 3. c. = cubic; as in c.cm. = cubic centimetre; C (American), $ 100; C.B., confined to barracks, as a punishment in the army; C.G.S. = centimetre-gramme-second; c.i., cast iron; C.I., Channel Islands, (Order of the) Crown of India; C.I.D., Committee of Imperial Defence, Criminal Investigation Department; C.I.E., Companion of the Order of the Indian Empire; C.I.F., c.i.f., Cost, Insurance, plus Freight; C.I.G.S., Chief of the Imperial General Staff; C. in C., Commander in Chief; C.Q.D., in wireless telegraphy, the signal formerly used by ships in distress, consisting of C.Q., the international sign for 'all stations', followed by D indicating 'urgent'; since 1908 superseded by S.O.S. See also C.O.D.

1890 KIPLING *Soldiers Three, God from Machine,* Now I put ut to you, Sorr, is ten days' C.B. a fit an' proper tratement for a man who has behaved as me? 1892 — *Barrack-room Ball., Cells* ii, O it's pack-drill for me and a fortnight's C.B. For 'drunk and resisting the Guard'! 1902 *Times* 7 July 3/3, 90 per cent. f.o.b. invoice on the basis of 52s. 6d. c.i.f. sawn pitch pine 35 cubic feet average Blaenavon. 1907 *Westm. Gaz.* 7 May 2/2 The United Kingdom figures are c.i.f. at the ports of arrival. 1909 *Daily Chron.* 17 Feb. 3/5 Among the ships responding to the 'C.Q.D.' message were the Lucania, [etc.]. 1914 W. CHURCHILL in *World Crisis* (1923) xii. 267 The situation .. is entirely different from those which have been discussed in the Invasion Committee of the C.I.D. 1919 *War Slang* in *Athenæum* 8 Aug. 727/2 When doing C.B.., he [*sc.* the soldier] was doing 'jankers' or 'Paddy Doyle'. 1928 *Manchester Guardian Weekly* 7 Dec. 450/3 That..when his ship took a list..[he] should have sent out a peremptory C.Q. call.

Caatinga (kā·tiŋgā). [Tupi, f. *caa* natural vegetation, forest + *tinga* white.] A forest consisting of thorny shrubs and stunted trees.

1846 G. GARDNER *Trav. Brazil* 166 Woods..consisting of low trees and shrubs..called by the inhabitants *Catingas.* 1869 BURTON *Explor. Highl. Brazil* I. 61 Low woods known in Brazil as Caatingas and Carrascos. 1927 KENDREW *Climates of Continents* 328 A region of caatinga or dry thornwood.

Cab, *sb.*[3] Add: **1.** Applied also to motor-driven vehicles (see TAXI-CAB).

1899 *Westm. Gaz.* 15 Nov. 4/3 The cab-without-a-horse.

3. *cab-body, -minder, -user, -washer.*

1908 *Westm. Gaz.* 30 Mar. 5/2 All Humber *cab-bodies are interchangeable. 1898 *Daily News* 16 Nov. 5/4 C. B... described as a *cab minder. 1894 *Westm. Gaz.* 22 May 5/3 The ins and outs of the matter are but imperfectly understood by the mass of *cab-users. 1897 *Daily News* 19 Oct. 2/3 The death of C. W...a *cabwasher.

Caballada (kæbălā·dă). *U.S.* [Sp., f. *caballo* horse. Cf. *CAVALLADA and CAVALLARD.] A train of horses.

1845 T. J. GREEN *Texian Exped.* vii. 75 Whether these gains be in the way of a caballada or baby-clothes. 1851 MAYNE REID *Scalp-hunters* xiii, I saw the camp and the caballada far above me on the bank. a 1861 WINTHROP *John Brent* iii. (1862) 31 The black..closed in with the caballada. *Ibid.* xii. 133 We shifted our little caballada to fresh grazing-spots sheltered by a brake. 1900 SMITHWICK *Evol. State* 22 He had his caballada driven in for us to choose from.

Caballero. (Earlier U.S. example.)

1848 E. BRYANT *California* xxiv. 314 In the rear were two caballeros, riding fine spirited horses.

Cabana. (Earlier U.S. example.)

1840 W. G. SIMMS *Border Beagles* 65 I'll go a quart and a dozen cabanas upon it.

Cabaret[1]. Add: **2.** Revived latterly to denote: A restaurant where an entertainment consisting mainly of song and dance is provided as an accompaniment to an expensive evening meal. Also short for *cabaret entertainment* or *show.*

1915 T. BURKE *London Nts., French Nt.* (1919) 188 Those melancholy places, the night clubs and cabarets, which had a boom a year or two ago. 1922 *Daily Mail* 13 Nov. 7 Cabaret, as exemplified by the Midnight Follies at the Hotel Metropole, also broke all records...This cabaret form of entertainment is very popular just now. *Ibid.* 25 Nov. 13 The new cabaret show which was to have been started on Tuesday has been rehearsed for a fortnight. 1923 *Westm. Gaz.* 22 May, There is to be a super cabaret at the Hotel Metropole on Friday evening. 1928 *Even. Standard* 2 Feb. 6/4 Cabaret..has..come to mean..a restaurant where a song-and-dance entertainment .. accompanies an expensive..supper.

3. A tea, coffee, etc., service, sometimes accompanied by a small table or tray.

1856 J. C. ROBINSON *Invent. Mus. Ornamental Art* 32 Old Sèvres porcelain...'Cabaret', rose du Barry ground.. the set consisting of four pieces. 1904 *Daily Chron.* 9 June 3/2 A cabaret, painted with flowers, fruit, and trophies..by Lene père.

Cabbage, *sb.*[1] Add:

5. *cabbage-bed, -seed*; **cabbage land** *U.S.*, land bearing the cabbage palm; **cabbage-palm, palm-tree** *Austral.* = CABBAGE-TREE 1 e; **cabbage-palmetto,** the West Indian cabbage-tree.

1840 *Cottager's Man.* 40 in *Libr. Usef. Knowl., Husb.* III, He will soon find out its value, if he diligently water his *cabbage-bed. 1837 WILLIAMS *Terr. of Florida* 54 A very crooked rise of *cabbage land. 1847 LEICHHARDT *Jrnl.* iii. 72 My companions suffered by eating too much of the *cabbage-palm. 1852 MUNDY *Antipodes* (1857) 194 The cabbage palm-tree..[is] becoming scarce. 1833 B. SILLIMAN *Man. Sugar Cane* 19 Large evergreen oaks..magnolia and *cabbage-palmetto. 1849 *Rep. Comm. Patents* (1850) 250 Adaptation of the branches of the *cabbage palmetto tree to the manufacture of brooms. 1840 *Cottager's Man.* 44 in *Libr. Usef. Knowl., Husb.* III, When the first *cabbage-seed is sown.

c. In the later years of the 19th century used to render F. *chou* (see *CHOU) in the description of large (orig. green) bows or knots of velvet, etc.

1888 *Daily News* 21 Sept. 5/6 A large 'cabbage' bow of surah in the same colour. 1895 *Ibid.* 19 Oct. 6/3 The toque worn with this had a large green velvet 'cabbage' at either side. 1896 *Ibid.* 14 Nov. 6/5 Folds of black satin, held down by 'cabbage' knots. 1899 *Ibid.* 3 June 8/3 The inevitable chou, or cabbage-bow, of black or dark green velvet.

Cabbage-tree. 1. a. (Later example.)

1835 R. M. BIRD *Hawks of Hawk-hollow* I. xv. 213 The cocoa-nut is, in every way, a much finer palm than the cabbage-tree.

Cabin, *sb.* **8.** Add: **cabin-ship,** a vessel carrying only one class of cabin passengers.

1928 *Saturday Even. Post* 4 Feb. 89/4 The George Washington, now the largest Cabin ship. 1929 *Even. News* 18 Nov. 5/5 The American ships..are to steam at 20 knots, an unusual speed for a cabin ship.

Cabinet, *sb.* Add: **13.** (Earlier U.S. examples.)

1806 *Deb. Congress* 5 Mar. (1852) 561 My answer was (and from a Cabinet Minister too) 'There is no longer any cabinet.' *Ibid.* 13 Mar. 765 The gentleman's [*sc.* Mirabeau's] fondness for Cabinet rank and Utopian glory. 1814 *Ibid.* 31 Oct. 1568 Occasional conversations..prior to the cabinet meeting on the first of July last. 1834 *Ibid.* 21 Feb. 631 If we were to ask, the Executive might tell us it was a cabinet secret.

14. cabinet finish *U.S.*, a superior style of finishing interior woodwork; **cabinet furniture** *U.S.*, furniture made by a cabinet-maker; **cabinet-pudding,** a pudding made of bread or cake, dried fruit, eggs and milk, usually served hot with a sauce; **cabinet shop** *U.S.*, a cabinet-maker's shop; **cabinet ware, work** *U.S.*, cabinet-makers' work.

1827 DRAKE & MANSFIELD *Cincinnati* viii. 59 Our Steam Engines, Castings, *Cabinet furniture..are sent to Kentucky, Alabama, Louisiana. 1822 KITCHINER *Cook's Oracle* (ed. 4) 451 Newcastle or *Cabinet Pudding. Butter a half melon mould, or quart basin, and stick all round with dried cherries, fine raisins, and fill up with bread and butter. 1823 UDE *French Cook* (ed. 7) 348 Cabinet Pudding or Chancellor's Pudding. 1817 S. R. BROWN *Western Gaz.* 93 There are.. five *cabinet shops. 1851 C. CIST *Cincinnati* 197 The ordinary *cabinet-ware coffins. *Ibid.* 200 Blending the chair business with what is called cabinet ware. 1874 *Rep. Vermont Board Agric.* II. 460 The consumption of valuable wood in large manufactories of fine cabinet ware. 1828 FEARON *Sk.* 24 Mahogany is used for cupboards, doors, and banisters, and for all kinds of *cabinet work.

Cabinetable (kæ·binetăb'l), *a. colloq.* [f. CABINET *sb.* + -ABLE.] That is fit to be a member of a political cabinet.

1896 *Daily News* 28 Nov. 4/7 The Prime Minister is.. chosen..practically by public opinion, and a small knot of what we may call 'Cabinetable' men. 1905 *Westm. Gaz.* 5 Dec. 4/3 There is rather an unusually strong reserve of 'Cabinet-able' men.

Cabine·tte. [CABIN *sb.* 2.] A small cabin.

1879 E. INGERSOLL in *Scribner's Monthly* Oct. 822 Can I ever forget that low-cowled cabinette,..up on the hill-side?

Ca·binless, *a.* [f. CABIN *sb.* 5 + -LESS.] Not furnished with a cabin.

1849 D. J. BROWNE *Amer. Poultry Yd.* (1855) 310 Small dirty, cabinless shallops, of a few tons burthen. 1890 *Harper's Mag.* Mar. 558/1 The *topi* .. are deckless and cabinless.

Cable, *sb.* Add: **1. c.** *ellipt.* A cable-car (see 7).

1892 SUSAN HALE *Lett.* 269 There are cables, and electrics. ..I mounted a cable, took a transfer [etc.].

6. (senses 1, 2) *cable-driving, ferry, -grip, gripper, -gripping, -hoist, -nipper, stopper, tramway*; (sense 3) *cable-cutting, -layer, -laying, -user.*

1897 T. E. HOLLAND *Lett. to Times* (1909) 138 The question as to the legitimacy of 'cable-cutting is covered by no precedent. 1897 *Daily News* 15 Jan. 7/4 Our fleet would deal with cable-cutting craft. 1887 J. B. SMITH *Cable Traction* 89 The *cable-driving drums are 12 ft. in diameter. 1900 *Daily News* 19 Jan. 5/3 Parties being sent across by the *cable ferry. 1887 J. B. SMITH *Cable Traction* 17 Elevated cable traction systems, for which he devised an ingenious *cable grip or catch. 1874 KNIGHT *Dict. Mech.*, **Cable-gripper,* a lever compressor over the cable-well, and by which the cable is stopped from running out. 1887 J. B. SMITH *Cable Traction* 30 The intermediate slot through which the cable gripper passed into the interior of the tube. *Ibid.* 16 An independent 'leading car' provided with a *cable-gripping apparatus fitted with vertically moving clamping jaws. 1900 *Daily News* 18 Jan. 5/3 A *cable hoist was..established up the slope, enabling ammunition to be brought up. 1908 *Daily Chron.* 25 Aug. 3/3 There is only room in the hearts..of men for..one *cable-layer. 1901 *Westm. Gaz.* 17 Aug. 3/2 The primary object of *cable-laying is to facilitate communications. 1874 KNIGHT *Dict. Mech.*, **Cable-nipper* (Nautical), a device serving to bind the messenger to the cable, and composed of a number of rope-yarns or small stuff marled together. *Ibid.*, **Cable-stopper*.., a device to stop the paying out of the cable. 1887 J. B. SMITH *Cable Traction* Introd. 2 A '*cable tramway,' or in other words a tramway on which the cars are drawn or hauled by means of a cable or rope receiving its motion from a stationary and distant source of power. 1888 *Encycl. Brit.* XXIII. 508/2 Cable tramways. Street tramways worked by means of a wire rope have been in successful operation in San Francisco since 1873..The motive power is transmitted from a stationary engine by a rope of steel wire. 1902 *Daily Chron.* 26 May 4/5 Melbourne and Brisbane merchants and other *cable users in Victoria.

7. cable-car, a tram-car moved by an endless chain or cable; **cable-carrier,** a tub or bucket slung from an overhead cable for the purpose of carrying heavy materials across a space; **cable-coating,** the material, such as gutta percha, rubber, or other insulating substance, used to encase submarine cables; **cable pattern** (see quot.); **cable railroad, -railway, -road,** one along which the carriages are drawn by an endless cable; **cable-rope** (later U.S. example); **cable screw** (see quots.); **cable-ship,** a ship used to lay a submarine cable; **cable-station,** a station from which a cable may be sent; **cable-stitch,** a kind of stitch in knitting and embroidery; **cable system,** a system of traction by cable or of telegraphy by submarine cables; **cable-tier** (earlier U.S. example); **cable-way,** (*a*) = *cable railroad*; (*b*) an overhead cable and apparatus for the transport of materials.

1887 J. B. SMITH *Cable Traction* 42 The excellent control of the *cable cars is..admirably demonstrated upon this line. 1888 SUSAN HALE *Lett.* 200 Two rival processions which encumbered the streets..almost prevented our getting there in the cable-car. 1891 C. ROBERTS *Adrift Amer.* 13 It was here that I first saw cable cars in operation. 1897 'MARK TWAIN' *Following Equator* xvi. 161 It has an elaborate system of cable car service. 1897 *Outing* (U.S.) XXX. 337/1 The actively inclined will enjoy cable-car athletics in hanging on to the slippery bilge of an egg-shell center-boarder. 1902 ELIZ. BANKS *Newspaper Girl* 254, I...took a cable car for Capitol Hill. 1884 KNIGHT *Dict. Mech.* Suppl., **Cable Carrier,* a means of transporting rough materials; stone, sand, lime, coal, earth, by a suspended bucket traveling on a wire cable. 1904 *Westm. Gaz.* 21 Nov. 8/2 Mr. Wall has discontinued the use of the overhead cable-carrier. 1902 *Ibid.* 22 July 9/1 African rubber is..useless for anything but *cable-coating. 1882 CAULFEILD & SAWARD *Dict. Needlework* 287/1 *Cable Pattern.—This is also known as Chain Stitch. 1887 J. B. SMITH *Cable Traction* 33 The Clay-street *cable railroad was opened for public traffic in August, 1873. *Ibid.* 15 The success that attended the working performances of early *cable railways. *Ibid.* 42 In January, 1882, the Union, Presidio, and Ferrie's *cable road commenced running. 1838 J. F. COOPER *Home as Found* xix. (1873) 316 You will confer an especial favor on me by not using such phrases as *cable-rope... No seaman uses them. 1884 KNIGHT *Dict. Mech.* Suppl., **Cable Screw,* a fastening for boot-soles; a wire in shape of a twisted cord. *Cable Screw Machine,* one for putting screw pegs into boot and shoe soles. It goes round the sole in 15 seconds, putting in 80 to 85 wire pegs. 1907 *Daily Chron.* 18 Jan. 7/4 The *cableship Henry Holmes left here for Jamaica yesterday... She goes..to repair the Colon cable. 1920 *Blackw. Mag.* Aug. 181/2 Chabbar was not a *cable-station. 1899 W. G. P. TOWNSEND *Embroidery* 95 *Cable-stitch...The first stitch of all is to make a small link. 1928 *Daily Express* 5 July 9 The white sweater of the season will be the favourite cable-

Supplement, p. 3873; Corrigenda, p. 4092; Spurious words, p. 4093; Books quoted, p. 4094

stitch. 1887 J. B. Smith *Cable Traction* Introd. 3 From the capabilities of the '*cable system,' it is now quite feasible to effect tramway communication in the most hilly districts. 1902 *Encycl. Brit.* XXXIII. 223/2 This spread of the cable system has naturally followed trade routes. 1778 *Essex Inst. Hist. Coll.* XXVI. 105 They drove us on board the frigate, and down in the *cable tier we must go. 1899 *Daily News* 11 Mar. 5/2 A *cableway right across the river. 1904 *Alpine Jrnl.* Nov. 336 The road which connects the Wetterhorn Hotel with the starting-point of the cable-way is finished. 1904 *Technol. & Sci. Dict.* (ed. Goodchild & Tweney), Cable Ways.

Cabler (kēi·b'ləɹ). [f. Cable *v.* + -er [1].] One who sends a cable message.

1890 *Daily News* 12 Dec. 6/3 The next I heard was that one of the cablers was among those who forced the offices. 1920 *Discovery* June 173/2 Those who held the view that the majority of cablers require speed without regard to cost were entirely mistaken.

Cabless, *a.* Add: also of railway engines.

1887 C. B. George *40 Yrs. on Rail* vii. 129 The cabless engines gave no shelter for engineer or fireman.

Cabling, *vbl. sb.* Add:

2. The transmitting of a message by electric cable.

1903 *Westm. Gaz.* 9 Mar. 10/2 Cable Chess: Great Britain v. America... The cabling will be done in the room.

3. *collect.* Lengths of cable.

1927 *Daily Tel.* 1 Nov. 10/7 The mechanical apparatus consists of a generator, an air-screw.., cabling, [etc.].

Caboclo (kabō·klo). [Brazilian Pg., derived by some from Tupi *caboculo* depilated.] A civilized Amerindian descended from aboriginals of Brazil. Also applied to various mixtures of the redskin with a negro or white race.

1816 Koster *Trav. Brazil* 387 Indians in a domesticated state, who are called generally Caboclos. 1825 Caldcleugh *Trav. S. Amer.* I. 80 Caboclos. *Note*, Mixture of the Indian races. 1874 R. F. Burton in *Captivity of H. Stade* (Hakl. Soc.) 45 *note*, Mamalucco, meaning the offspring of a white man by an 'Indian' woman, is obsolete in S. Paulo, where Caboclo..has taken its place. 1888 *Pall Mall Gaz.* 26 May 11/1 The Caboclo or aboriginal becoming thenceforth incorporated with the dominant Portuguese colonist. 1918 *Times Lit. Suppl.* 28 Mar. 146/4 The Portuguese-speaking natives [in Brazil]..Caboclos in the south or Mulattos further north.

Caboodle (kăbū·d'l). *slang.* (orig. *U.S.*) [Supposed to be a corruption of the phrase *kit and boodle* (see *Boodle [1] 1).] *The whole caboodle*: the whole lot (of persons or things).

a 1848 *Ohio State Jrnl.* (Bartlett, Add.) The whole caboodle will act upon the recommendation of the Ohio Sun. 1858 *New Orleans Picayune* 23 Feb. (De Vere) The whole caboodle came out and fell upon me. 1873 B. Harte *Fiddletown* 3 She had more soul than the whole caboodle of them put together. 1894 *Outing* (U.S.) XXIV. 102/2 How could I help bein' when she did so much better than the whole caboodle of them. 1904 *Daily Chron.* 6 May 8/4 'Give them a week's notice and start them.' 'What, the whole caboodle?' 1920 O. Johnson *Varmint* v. 71 This is the best thing in the whole caboodle. 1919 J. B. Morton *Barber of Putney* xvi. 259 If we know they're comin', you can bet your sweet life them as runs the 'ole caboodle [*sc.* war] knows it too. 1923 *Strand Mag.* Oct. 351 Actually, the whole caboodle, sold, not pawned, produced seventy, not fifty—hundred and twenty in all.

Cabook (kăbū·k). Also **kabook.** ['Perhaps the Port. *cabouco* or *cavouco* a quarry. It is not in Singh. Dictionaries' (Yule).] The name given in Ceylon to a reddish gneissoid building-stone, soft when quarried but hardening by exposure to the air; laterite.

1834 S. C. Chitty *Ceylon Gazetteer* 75 The houses are built of cabook, and neatly whitewashed with chunam. 1836 *Penny Cycl.* VI. 452/2 A reddish loam resulting from the decomposition of clay iron-stone called *cabook*. 1858 Simmonds *Dict. Trade*, Kabook. 1859 Sir J. E. Tennent *Ceylon* I. 17 Laterite, or, as the Singhalese call it, *cabook*, a product of disintegrated gneiss.

Caboose. Add: **1.** (Early U.S. examples.)

1747 *Essex Inst. Hist. Coll.* XLVI. 91 They shipp'd a sea which carried overboard..their boat and carpouse [*sic*]. *Ibid.*, Another [heavy sea] carried away their boat, cabbouze and one carriage gun. 1766 *Boston Even. Post* 10 Nov. (Th.) 'Twas imagined she took fire at sea, as her cabouse was burnt.

b. (Earlier U.S. examples.) Also *attrib.*

1779 in Almon *Remembrancer* VIII. 297, 2 cambouses. 1786 *Maryland Jrnl.* 23 June (Th.) For Sale, One elegant patent caboose. 1805 M. Lewis & Clarke *Trav.* (1817) I. 217 When the blacksmith cut up an old cambouse of sheet iron. 1837 C. F. Briggs *Harry Franco* II. vi. 71 A camboose factory.

2. (Earlier and later U.S. examples.)

1871 Schele de Vere *Americanisms* (1872) 343 The ship's caboose..has lent its mutilated name..to a small railroad-car, used for various special purposes, and not known on English railways. 1871 Barnum *Struggles & Triumphs* 679 If you can stand it to ride to Fort Wayne in the caboose of a freight train. 1901 S. Merwin & H. K. Webster *Calumet K* ii. 24 'Did you make the train?' 'Caught the caboose just as she was swinging out.' 1926 J. Black *You Can't Win* xvii. 234 The boy hid between box cars while I went to the top of the caboose.

attrib. 1862 *Ashcroft's Railway Directory* 76 No. of Caboose Cars [on the Central Railroad of New Jersey], 6. 1869 *Chicago Tribune* 10 Mar., A caboose car, hitched on to a freight train. 1903 *New York Even. Post* 25 Aug., The rest of the crew..saw from the caboose windows the bodies ..lying along the tracks.

3. A hut. *U.S.*

1839 *Congress. Globe* 15 Feb. App. 343/1 We have a postmaster in our village..and in his little caboose of a post office I found electioneering interferences. 1874 *Opelika* (Ala.) *Times* 30 Sept., [Such] a coloured man..should be preferred as tenant of our houses, cabooses on the farm, [etc.].

4. (See quot.)

1920 Hunter *Trail Drivers of Texas* 213 Under a camp wagon is usually suspended an old cowhide called the 'caboose', and in that we throw stray pieces of wood, [etc.].

Cabotinage (kăbotinā·ʒ). [Fr., f. *cabotin* strolling player, perh. ultimately f. *caboter* to coast, because of the resemblance between players who travel from town to town and coasting vessels.] The life or behaviour characteristic of low-class actors, with implication of 'playing to the gallery'.

1894 *Nation* (N. Y.) 22 Mar. 211 We can find the spirit of 'cabotinage'..even in the Church. 1895 *Daily News* 9 May 6/2 Dickens, yielding..to his native cabotinage, descended so low as to give readings from his own books! *Ibid.*, We cannot..blame the undeniable cabotinage of the great Napoleon. 1921 *Times Lit. Suppl.* 29 Sept. 626/2 In the narrow life of *cabotinage* there is little scope for originality.

Cabre (kēi·bəɹ), *v.* To fly or glide at an excessive angle of incidence; to tail down.

1917 H. Barber *Aeroplane Speaks* 135.

Cabriole (kæ·briōul). Transfer †*Obs.* to senses 1, 2, 3 and add:

4. A form of curved leg, frequent in Queen Anne and Chippendale furniture, so called from its resemblance to a quadruped's front leg making a leap or caper. Chiefly *attrib.* and *Comb.*

1781 *English Chron.* 27–30 Jan. 1/2 The..original Manufactory for all sorts of Cabriole Chairs. 1848 H. R. Forster *Stowe Catal.* Terminal Advt. 15 Cabriole Drawing Room Chairs. 1888 J. Marshall in *Catal. Exhib. Decor. Handiwork, Edin.* 59 Settees and chairs with their cabriole legs and lion-claw feet. 1902 L. V. Lockwood *Col. Furniture Amer.* 56 Walnut and Inlay Cabriole-legged Dressing-table. 1907 H. C. Candee *Decor. Styles* 202 The cabriole leg is the one great point of this decorative period with which collectors..must arm themselves. 1922 H. A. Tipping (*title*) English Furniture of the Cabriole Period.

Ca'canny (ka,kæ·ni). Also (after northern dialects) **-conny.** [See Call *v.* 15, Canny *a.* 10.] The practice of 'going slow' at work; a deliberate policy of limiting output of work. Often *attrib.*

1896 *Westm. Gaz.* 25 Mar. 1/3 He was the first English Labour leader to reduce to a fine art the 'ca'conny' policy so well known in Western America. 1896 *Seamen's Chron.* 24 Oct. in *Times* 18 Nov. (1901) 10/1 What is ca' canny? It is a simple and handy phrase which is used to describe a new instrument or policy which may be used by the workers in place of a strike. 1902 *Westm. Gaz.* 25 Apr. 8/1 A 'ca-canny' policy said to have been deliberately adopted by certain trade union officials. 1923 J. D. Hackett *Labor Terms in Managem. Engineering* May, Ca'Canny,..taking it easy at work as a protest against labor conditions or the general policy of the employer.

Hence **Ca'ca·nnyism,** ca'canny policy.

1921 *Glasgow Herald* 17 June 6 Mr Ramsay Macdonald recommends 'a magnificently organised system of passive resistance,' which, plainly interpreted by his followers, means Ca'-cannyism. 1926 W. S. Bruce *Salt & Sense* 186 To-day we have a new word for a novel disease, which began first on the Clyde. It is called 'Ca'cannyism'.

Cacao. Add:

4. *cacao-bush, -farm, -planter, -powder*; **cacao-bean**, the seed of the cacao-tree; **cacao-mother**, a tree used to protect the delicate cacao-tree.

1839 Ure *Dict. Arts* 292 The cacao-beans lie in a fruit somewhat like a cucumber. 1870 Kingsley *At Last* vii, Lombardy poplar[s]..the beauty of these 'Madres de Cacao', Cacao-mothers as they call them here because their shade is supposed to shelter the Cacao-trees. *Ibid.* xiii, The cacao-bush which produces chocolate. *Ibid.* xvi, Can nothing be done to increase the yield of the cacao-farms? 1908 H. H. Smith *Cacao Planting* 18 As long as cacao powder is so much in vogue. *Ibid.* 41 The Jamaica cacao planters.

Caccabine (kæ·kăbəin), *a.* [ad. mod. L. *Caccabinæ*, f. Gr. κακκαβίς partridge: see -ine [1].] Belonging to the subfamily *Caccabinæ* of gallinaceous birds which includes the partridges.

1894 Newton *Dict. Birds* 696 The groups of birds known as Francolins and Snow-partridges..probably belong to the Caccabine group.

Cache, *sb.* **1.** (Delete quot. 1595, which belongs to Cash *sb.*[1] 1.)

b. *U.S.* (Earlier example.)

1817 J. Bradbury *Trav.* 118 The Aricaras could not spare any provisions, as the excessive rains had penetrated into their caches, and spoiled the whole of their reserved stock.

Cache, *v.* orig. *U.S.* (Earlier examples. See also Cash *v.*)

1830 Mrs. Victor *River of West* (1870) 80 The manner of caching furs is this: a pit is dug [etc.]. 1843 Farnham *Trav. Gt. Western Prairies* I. 288 It was necessary to recover them [*sc.* horses], or cache, that is, bury in some secret place in the dry sand, their remaining property.

Hence **Cached** (kɒʃt) *ppl. a.*

1901 S. E. White *Westerners* vii. 47 Lone Wolf's band took up quarters within striking distance of the cached schooners. *a* 1906 'O. Henry' *Trimmed Lamp* etc. 234 The man from Nome, loyal to her who had resurrected his long cached heart..followed her.

Cache-peigne (kaʃpeɲ). [F. *cache-peigne*, f. *cacher* to hide + *peigne* comb.] A bow or hat ornament, usually worn under the brim at the back of a woman's hat.

1896 *Westm. Gaz.* 7 May 3/1 A pretty Parisian toque.. finished..with..a cache-peigne of peach-coloured roses. 1905 *Daily Chron.* 8 May 8/3 A very becoming..hat, which has a wreath of roses..finishing in the form of a cachepeigne at the back. 1906 *Ibid.* 9 Apr. 8/5 Hats..tilted up at the back by a cache-peigne of tulle.

Cachet. Add: **4.** A covering of paste, gelatine, or other digestible material, enclosing (nauseous) medicine; = Capsule 5.

1884 *Pharmac. Jrnl.* XV. 42/2 Cachets are..sheets of unleavened bread cut to a round or oval shape with a..concave towards the centre,..intended to receive the powder to be taken. 1898 Q. Hogg in Ethel M. Hogg *Biography* (1904) 349 My experience and cachets were of use to him. 1901 *Contemp. Rev.* Mar. 405 One cachet..to be taken with the midday meal and one in the evening.

Cachou. 2. Add quots.:

1880 in Webster Suppl. 1898 *Army & Navy Co-op. Soc. Price List*, Cachous, Atkinson's White Rose, Violet, Heliotrope, Citron..per box 0/8. 1909 *Daily Chron.* 23 Feb. 5/6 The tabloids might easily be taken for 'cachous.' 1922 *Glasgow Herald* 3 Apr. 4 He carried a little round, flat gilt box of Prince Albert cachous.

Cacique. Add:

2. In Spanish politics, a man who owes his ascendancy to his power or influence; a political 'boss'; *transf.* a political system in which the power is in the hands of such a man or men. Also *attrib.* Hence **Caci·qu(e)ism,** the cacique system.

1903 *Times* 3 June 3/5 Caciquism, the Spanish equivalent for the methods of Tammany. 1923 *Glasgow Herald* 23 Oct. 7 This decree,..of great importance for the destruction of 'caciquism', will be applied to about 500 towns. 1923 *Contemp. Rev.* Nov. 613 The cacique whether an employer of labour or a moneylender has the majority of the constituency under his thumb. 1923 *Glasgow Herald* 13 Dec. 12 The whole cacique system is..an immense satire on local authority in Spain.

Cacody·late. A salt of Cacodylic acid.

1908 *Practitioner* Aug. 338 Arseniate of soda is more brutal, as it were, than cacodylate, the action of which is prolonged and deliberate.

Cacogenic (kækodʒe·nik), *a.* [f. Caco- after *Eugenic.] The reverse of *eugenic*.

1929 R. R. Gates *Heredity in Man* 280 Out of 399 fertile marriages about 176 might be classed as eugenic matings and 223 as cacogenic.

Cactus. 3. Add: **cactus wren** *U.S.*, a North American wren of the genus *Campylorhynchus*, frequenting cactus plants.

1870 *Amer. Naturalist* III. 183 The Rock Wren and Cactus Wren..chirrup loudly from the tiled roof or dense thickets. 1881 *Ibid.* XV. 211 The cactus wren, so called from its habit of nesting in the cactus whenever available.

Cadaver. Add: **c.** A sculptured representation of a corpse on a monument.

1888 [communicated by correspondent]. 1921 F. H. Crossley *Engl. Ch. Monum.* 79 To place a shrouded figure or cadaver in the space beneath.

Caddy, *sb.*[1] Read 1⅓ for 1⅓ lb., and add: **caddy-spoon**, a spoon of a special shape used for measuring tea out of the caddy.

1927 *Daily Express* 31 Aug. 4 Old silver caddy-spoons that have survived from Georgian days.

Caddy, *v.* [f. *caddy*, var. Caddie *sb.*] *intr.* To act as caddy to golfers.

1908 *Daily Chron.* 26 Aug. 4/7 You've caddied for me before. 1928 *Daily Tel.* 29 May 9/4 The Prince had a local caddie named William Everett..who caddied for him once before. 1929 *Times* 6 Feb. 15/5 Does such a man do nothing but 'carry' for us? Of course, he does infinitely more. He 'caddies' for us, bless him.

Cadelle (kāde·l). [Fr., ad. Pr. *cadello*.] The larva or adult of a beetle (*Trogosita mauritanica*) very destructive to grain.

1861 *Chambers's Encycl.* II. 484/1 Cadelle (*Trogosita Mauritanica*..), an insect sometimes found in granaries in Britain.

Cadet. Add:

4. A boy in an ordinary school who receives military training with or without a view of entering the army. Also *attrib.*, as **cadet corps**, a company of schoolboys who receive such training.

1873 *Programme of Review at Charterhouse School* 6 Aug., The young gentlemen (or Charterhouse Cadets) will be drawn up in Line at Open Order on the Cricket Ground. 1901 *Public School Mag.* Mar. 215 The Cadet Corps paraded in front of the school and stood 'at rest' while the band played 'The Land o' the Leal'. 1901 W. H. Daniel *Milit. Forces Crown* 114 Every public school [in New Zealand] has its cadet corps.

Cadet[2] (kăde·t). [a. Russian *Kadet*, pl. *Kadeti*, representing the pronunciation of *K. Dti* (= K. D.'s), abbreviation of *Konstitutsionalnyie Demokrati* Constitutional Democrats.] In Russian politics, a member of the Constitutional Democratic (or Liberal) Party.

This party was formed about 1905 by a fusion of the group favouring autonomy for Poland and a federal constitution for the Russian empire with the (so-called) Independence Party formed by political exiles at Paris in 1903.

1906 *Daily Chron.* 22 May 7/5 The 'Cadets' (Constitutional Democrats)..have decided..to wait until the agrarian question comes on for discussion. *Ibid.* 10 Sept. 4/4 Professor Miliukoff..has been the leader of the Constitutional Democrats, or moderate party of reform, from the first... The 'Cadets', as his party was called for short, formed a large majority in the assembly. 1908 *Westm. Gaz.* 19 Aug. 2/1 The more brilliant Zemstvo Liberals, who did so much to found the Cadet (or Liberal) Party.

Cady (kēi·di). *local.* Also **cadey, -ie.** [Of unascertained etym.] A hat or cap.

1869 *N. & Q.* 4th Ser. III. 406 In Lancashire..a straw hat [is vulgarly called] a cady or straw cady. 1887 *Walford's Antiquarian Mag.* XI. 251 *note*, Cadey found its way into a music-hall song some years ago. The chorus was something like this:—..Sixpence I gave for my cadey, A penny I gave for my stick. 1887 *Jamieson's Scot. Dict.* Suppl., *Cadie*..2. A boy's cap; generally applied to a glengary. 1909 *Daily Chron.* 8 Dec. 6/7 The British navvy is never prouder than when he has, stuck in the ribbon of his best 'cady', a spray of the fateful [peacocks'] feathers.

Cænogenesis (sīnodʒe·nesis). More regular f. Kenogenesis (1879). So **Cænogene·tic** *a.*

1909 *Cent. Dict.* Suppl., Cænogenesis. 1930 G. R. de Beer *Embryol. & Evol.* i. 6 Haeckel concluded..that a new or caenogenetic stage had been intercalated in the ontogeny. *Ibid.* xv. 102 The appearance of characters in the early stages of development is caenogenesis, and these characters which loom so largely in neoteny and deviation are flies in the Haeckelian ointment of recapitulation.

Cæsar. Add: **2. c.** *To appeal to Cæsar* (with allusion to *Acts* xxv. 11): to appeal to the highest authority, esp. in politics, to appeal to the nation in a general election.

1894 T. B. Reed *Dog with Bad Name* xv. 156 'Can't she come, Father?' said Percy, adroitly appealing to Cæsar. 1903 J. Chamberlain in *Westm. Gaz.* 22 Oct. 5/1 If this policy..were not accepted as the policy of the Government ..I should feel it my duty to appeal to Cæsar.

Cæsareanist (sīzē·riănist). [f. Cæsarean + -ist.] One who advocates the use of the Cæsarean operation.

1888 *Buck's Handbk. Med. Sci.* VI. 700/2 The medical profession became divided into Symphysiotomists and Cæsareanists, each advocating the one plan of delivery to the disparaging of the other.

Cæsarianism (sīzē·riăniz'm). [f. Cæsarian + -ism.] = Cæsarism 1 a.

1866 W. P. Dickson tr. *Mommsen's Hist. Rome* v. xi. IV. 466 Construing our judgment respecting Cæsar into a judgment respecting what is called Cæsarianism.

Cæsaro-papism (sī·zăro,pē[i]·piz'm). [f. Cæsar + -o- + L. *pāpa* Pope [1] + -ism.] The supremacy of the civil power in the control of ecclesiastical affairs. So **Cæ·saro-pa·palism.**

1890 *Edin. Rev.* Apr. 349 Such a *régime* as the Cæsaropapism of Justinian. 1903 Fairbairn in *Cambr. Mod. Hist.* II. xvi. 567 A bill which went the full Henrican length in its Cæsaro-papalism and its severity. 1924 Foakes-Jackson *Studies in Life Early Ch.* 240 Another effect of the triumphant way in which Christianity won the respect and recognition of the Roman government was what is called Cæsaro-papalism. 1926 *Spectator* 15 May 849/2 The Church ..with all debasements into Caesaro-papism, was the salvation of mediaeval Europe from anarchy.

Café. Add:

2. *attrib.* and *Comb.*, as *café-habit, -haunting* adj.

1866 M. Arnold *Friendship's Garland* (1871) 167, I do not wish them [*sc.* my countrymen] to be the café-haunting, dominoes-playing Frenchmen. 1910 *Daily Chron.* 5 Mar. 4/4 Any slight modification in the national temperament which the café habit might..bring.

3. café chantant (ʃantaŋ), [lit. 'singing café'] a café in which the customers are entertained by singers or other music; **café noir** (nwār), lit. black coffee, i.e. coffee taken without milk.

1854 Bayle St. John *Purple Tints Paris* II. iii. 67 Go out to the Luxembourg, to a *café chantant*,..or to the country. 1896 Mrs. H. Ward *Sir G. Tressady* xvi, I suppose you don't go to *cafés chantants*? 1906 W. De Morgan *Joseph Vance* xliv. 447 We went into a café chantant to see some real life. 1909 *Westm. Gaz.* 25 Aug. 8/2 A café-chantant pianist. 1863 Mrs. Beeton *Bk. Househ. Managem.* 879 *Cafe noir. 1898 *Cornhill Mag.* Aug. 255 Never shall I forget the first occasion when the widow brought our *café noir* to us after dinner. 1914 *Daily Express* 29 Sept. 2/7 Men the colour of ebony, café noir, café au lait.

Café au lait (kæ·fe,olē[i]). [Fr., coffee with milk.] Coffee taken with (approximately) an equal quantity of hot milk; also, the colour of café au lait, a brownish cream colour.

1818 J. Griscom *Year in Europe* (1823) II. 32 We..refreshed ourselves..with an excellent cup of *caffè [*sic*] au lait. 1839 Ure *Dict. Arts* 420 Red with yellow, produces orange...To this shade may be referred flame colour,.. *café au lait*,..marigold. 1840 Thackeray *Paris Sketch Bk.* Wks. 1879 XVI. 10 Milk-women..selling the chief material of the Parisian *café-au-lait*. 1863 Mrs. Beeton *Bk. Househ. Managem.* 878 Cafe au lait. 1893 *Cassell's Fam. Mag.* Apr. 394/2 The faintest tinge of *café au lait* with a dash of yellow in it. 1899 *Daily News* 7 Oct. 8/5 Tones of nut-brown, cinnamon,..coffee, cigar and café-au-lait. 1907 *Westm. Gaz.* 13 Nov. 12/3 Café-au-lait brocade.

Cafeteria (kæfĕtĭə·riă). orig. *U.S.* [Sp. *cafetería* coffee-shop.] A restaurant in which the food is fetched from a counter by the customer.

1928 Webster Addenda. 1923 *Mod. Lang. Notes* Mar. 188 Every one knows by this time that a cafeteria is a 'help yourself' restaurant. 1925 *Glasgow Herald* 30 July, Cafeterias, although a commonplace in America, are just beginning to have a hold in Paris. 1926 *Public Opinion* 2 Apr. 345/1, I beheld over against the hotel a Cafeteria and I went thither.

Caffeism (kæ·fiiz'm). [f. Caffeine + -ism.] A morbid condition arising from the prolonged or excessive use of beverages containing caffeine. So **Ca·ffeinism.**

1886 *American* XII. 269 That class of diseases in which morphinism, caffeism and vanillism are found. 1889 *Cent. Dict.*, Caffeinism. 1906 *Westm. Gaz.* 27 Sept. 4/2 The beverage—I even hate its name: Guess it who can!—That makes the direful caffeism rage.

Cage, *sb.* **10.** Add: **cage aerial** (see quot.).

1926 S. O. Pearson *Dict. Wireless Techn.* T., Cage *Aerial*, an aerial in which a number of component wires are held in position round small star-shaped spreaders or round small hoops in such a manner as to form a 'cage'. This is done to reduce the high-frequency resistance of the aerial.

Cager (kēi·dʒəɹ). [f. Cage *v.* or *sb.* + -er [1].]

1. One who encloses in a cage. *rare.*

1889 Browning *Asolando, Which?* 5 Boy-Cupid's exemplary catcher and cager.

2. An operative who attends to a cage (in various trades).

1908 *Daily Chron.* 24 Apr. 7/5 The cager was..engaged in another part of the mine. 1921 *Dict. Occup. Terms* (1927) §§ 043, 056, 339, 399.

Cahier (kaye). Add:

2. *Hist.* The instructions prepared by each of the three representative bodies as a guide for their policy at the National Assembly of 1789 in France.

1847 C. Cocks tr. *Michelet's Hist. Fr. Rev.* 77 The uniformity of the memorials (*cahiers*) in which they recorded their complaints. 1879 *Encycl. Brit.* IX. 597/1 Early in 1789 all France was busy with the elections to the States-General, and in drawing up the *cahiers*, or papers of grievances. 1886 A. Weir *Hist. Basis Mod. Europe* (1889) 114 When justifying the acts of the National Assembly by comparing them with the demands of the cahiers, he cites more suggestions of..reform from those from the Tiers État. 1887 Leckie *Eng. in 18th Cent.* V. xx. 430 The cahiers of the clergy showed a frank willingness to surrender all privileges.

Cahoot. Add: Usually in *pl.*

1834 S. S. Prentiss in *Life* (1884) 239, I will splice the member from North Carolina to you, and for a short time will consider you in cahoot. 1862 G. K. Wilder *MS. Diary* 14 May, [He] wished me to go in cahoots in a store. 1892 *Congress. Rec.* 16 Mar. 2133/1 Let's go into cahoots and go a coon hunting. 1899 G. Ade *Doc Horne* xxv. 280, I have good reasons for thinking they were in cahoots.

attrib. 1845 J. J. Hooper *Adv. Simon Suggs* iii. 37 If..I could only get the township and range, I'd make a caboot business with old man Doublejoy.

2. A confederate.

1869 *Congress. Globe* 6 Apr. 538/3 Fisk and his 'cahoots' have got at cross purposes, and he has been put out of bed.

Cahoun (kă·hūn). Also **cahoon.** Frequent variant of Cohune.

1861 Bentley *Man. Bot.* 685 From the seeds of *A[ttalea] Cahouni*, the Cahoun Palm, a fatty oil may be obtained. 1867 Ure *Dict. Arts* 524 Cahoun Nuts. The fruits of *Attalea funifera*, the *Attalea cohune* of Martius. 1880 *Encycl. Brit.* XII. 133/2 The cahoon or coyol palm..producing clusters of nuts, from which is extracted a valuable oil.

Caid. Add: **kayed, kaid.** Hence **Cai·dship.**

1843 [see Kaid]. 1920 *Glasgow Herald* 23 Sept. 6 Kaid of Tangier. 1920 *Blackw. Mag.* Dec. 742/1 His half-brother was already nominated to the kaidship. 1925 *Ibid.* Nov. 622/2 Presently the Kayed will appear, walking with his chief villagers.

Cailcedra (kəil,se·drā). [Origin unknown.] A lofty tree of West Africa, *Khaya senegalensis*, of which the wood is specially adapted for joinery and the bark furnishes a bitter tonic.

1866 *Treas. Bot.*, *Cailcedra-wood*, the timber of *Flindersia australis*. 1886 *Encycl. Brit.* XXI. 662/1 The wood of the cailcedra..is used in joiner's work and inlaying. 1887 Moloney *Forestry W. Afr.* 297 Cail-cédra or Mahogany Tree of the Gambia.

Cain[2]. Add: **1. b.** *To raise Cain*: to make a disturbance. orig. *U.S.*

[1840 *Daily Pennant* (St. Louis) 2 May (Th.) Why have we every reason to believe that Adam and Eve were both rowdies? Because..they both raised Cain.] 1848 Dow Jr. *Patent Serm.* I. 247 (Th.) They will feel that they have been raising Cain and breaking things. 1869 Mrs. Stowe *Oldtown Folks* xx. 242, I expect Susy's boys'll be raising Cain round the house. 1901 R. D. Evans *Sailor's Log* 245 The Yorktown raised Cain, because she had a heavy following sea which made her roll very badly.

c. *What in Cain*: 'what on earth'. *U.S.*

1854 Mary J. Holmes *Tempest & Sunshine* xii. 172 It had been there two weeks, and he didn't know what in cain to do with it.

Cairene (kəiᵊrī·n), *a.* and *sb.* [f. *Cairo* (cf. F. *Caire*), ad. Arab. *El-Qāhirah* the Victorious (fem., scil. *Miçr* Egypt) + *-ene*, after *Nazarene*, etc.] **A.** *adj.* Of or pertaining to Cairo, the capital of Egypt. **B.** *sb.* A native or an inhabitant of Cairo.

1842 Sophia Poole *Englishwoman in Egypt* xi. (1844) 156 If we were conducted by a Caireen, no Turkish ladies were likely to address us. 1854 B. Taylor *Life fr. Egypt* xv. 205 A harem of Cairene ladies. 1855 R. F. Burton *El-Medinah* I. 270 The people of Suez are a finer and a fairer race than the Cairenes. 1892 S. Lane-Poole *Cairo* i. 26 The rose and oleander and the other favourites of Cairene horticulture. 1897 'Ouida' *Massarenes* v. Did our forefathers want Cairene winters? 1902 S. Lane-Poole *Story of Cairo* i. 14 The Cairene tucks his legs up under him on the divan. 1907 D. S. Margoliouth *Cairo* vi. 94 Some of the Cairene monuments date before Hasan's resumption of the sovereignty.

Cairn[2] (kēᵊrn). [Said to be so named from being used to hunt among cairns.] In full *Cairn terrier*, the smallest breed of terrier in Great Britain, somewhat long in the body and deep in the ribs, with short straight legs and a shaggy coat.

1910 *Kennel* Christmas No. 464/1 Cairn terriers promise to rank high in the near future, and already they are being bred to a fairly uniform standard. 1924 *Westm. Gaz.* 31 Oct., The handy little Sealyhams and Cairns. 1927 *Brit. Weekly* 27 Oct. 87/2 My small Cairn..makes a rush for the frog.

Cairngorm. Add: *attrib.* and *Comb.*

1871 Meredith *H. Richmond* I. 136 In satisfying Janet's wishes for riding-whips, knives, pencil-cases, Cairngorm buttons, and dogs. 1881 *Instr. Census Clerks* (1885) 91 Lapidary. Cairngorm, Cameo..Cutter, Worker. 1921 *Dict. Occup. Terms* (1927) § 638 Cairngorm grinder.

Cairo (kəiᵊ·rou). [The name of a town in Egypt.] A variety of the game of bridge, invented by F. Comber in Egypt in 1917.

1927 *Observer* 10 Apr. 25 Little coteries..play variations of Bridge, such as Contract, Cairo, Standard, and so forth. *Ibid.* 13 Nov. 25/2 This system of graduated penalties makes Cairo quite the fairest and soundest form of Bridge I have ever yet played.

Caisson. 4 Add: **caisson sickness** = *caisson disease*.

1911 *Engineer* 10 Mar. 243 Caisson Sickness and Compressed Air.

Hence **Caissonier** (kēⁱsəni·ɹ), one who works in a caisson; so **Cai·ssoning.**

1903 *Strand Mag.* Jan. 98/2 The lives of 'the men in the box', *i.e.* the caissoniers, are in the greatest danger. *Ibid.* 101/2 After all these terrors it is perhaps astonishing to be told..that caissoning would be sought by any considerable number of men.

Cajian, aphetic form of Acadian *a.*

1906 *Springfield Weekly Republ.* 28 June 11 Broussard is what is known in Louisiana as a 'Cajian'. That is, he is.. a descendant of the French Canadians who were driven out of Acadia.

Cake, *sb.* Add:

4. *spec.* in *Artificial Silk Manuf.* (see quot.).

1927 T. Woodhouse *Artificial Silk* 42 An annular package of yarn is gradually built up by the succeeding layers of yarn. This annular package is called a 'cake'.

7. *To take the cake* (earlier U.S. example).

1884 *Lisbon* (Dakota) *Star* 25 July, Sherriff Moore takes the cake for the first wheat-harvesting in Ransom county.

9. *cake-batter, -plate, -stand, -wagon, -woman.*

1890 *Harper's Mag.* Jan. 282/2 She sat on the door-step beating *cake batter in a deep pan. 1866 Mrs. Whitney *L. Goldthwaite* x, *Cake-plates were garnished with wreathed oak-leaves. 1851 J. J. Hooper *Widow Rugby's Husb.* 106 Here he went..clearing an old woman and her *cake-stand at a jump. 1866 Gregg *Life in Army* xv. 139 Farther on, you come in contact with candy shops, peanut stands, *cake wagons. 1836 *Southern Lit. Messenger* II. 303 Justices and jurymen,—counsellors and clients—.. constables and *cake women.

Cake, *v.* Add: **3.** *trans.* To entertain with cake. *U.S.*

1861 J. B. Jones *Rebel War Clerk's Diary* (1866) I. 33 [The ladies of Richmond] wine them and cake them—and they deserve it.

Cakelet (kēⁱ·klėt). [f. Cake *sb.* + -let.] A small cake.

1839 Ure *Dict. Arts* 458 These cakelets must be dried upon laths. 1914 Findlater *Crossriggs* xix, Bits of cake and stale cakelets. 1928 *Daily Express* 13 June 3/6 These elusive cakelets [*sc.* cookies] are evolved by mixing [etc.].

Cake-walk (kēⁱ·k,wǭk), *sb.* [f. Cake *sb.* + Walk *sb.*]

1. a. 'A walking competition among negroes, in which the couple who put on most style "take the cake"' (Thornton). **b.** A dance modelled on this.

It originated among the negroes of the southern United States.

1889 Farmer *Americanisms* s.v. *Cake*, In certain sections of the country, cake-walks are in vogue among the colored people. It is a walking contest, not in the matter of speed, but in style and elegance. 1894 Howells *Traveller fr. Altruria* 161 It is the man with the most money who now takes the prize in our national cake-walk. 1897 *Blackw. Mag.* Mar. 341/2 'Cake-walks' and frolics and preachings filled the cabins with sound and merriment. 1899 *Westm. Gaz.* 4 Feb. 8/2 Willie K. Vanderbilt recently gave a nigger cake-walk. 1902 Eliz. Banks *Newspaper Girl* 142 In the midst, doing an amateur 'cake-walk', was Dinah, hugging a blue tin can. 1902 Harben *Abner Daniel* 53, I was doing the cake-walk with that fat Howard girl from Rome.

attrib. 1901 *Westm. Gaz.* 3 June 3/1 Although there is a painful amount of cake-walk music. 1903 *Daily Chron.* 21 Apr. 7/3 The closing number in the bill will be a grand cake-walk promenade.

2. A form of entertainment consisting of a promenade moved by machinery on which people walk to the accompaniment of music.

1909 *Oxford Times* 11 Sept. 9/5 In dealing with the fair itself there were really no new features..except that of the Brooklyn cake-walk, an ingenious rocking platform which gave those who patronised it the sensation of a cake-walk dance... The novelty was in operation at the White City last year. 1914 *Ibid.* 12 Sept. 10/3 The absence of the popular joy-wheel, the cake-walk [etc.].

Hence **Ca·ke-walk** *v. intr.*, to walk or dance in this manner; **Ca·ke-walker.**

1898 *Westm. Gaz.* 3 Dec. 7/7 The cake walkers at Covent Garden. 1904 *Daily Chron.* 22 Mar. 4/7 The genuinely tip-top men were those who never cake-walked. 1905 *Westm. Gaz.* 17 Aug. 8/1 French singers, cake-walking coons, and fifth-rate English dancers. 1905 *Daily Chron.* 22 Sept. 2/6 A street male musician..'cake-walked with a whirling of skirts'. 1909 'O. Henry' *Roads of Destiny* xvii. 282 That's why you can see me cake-walking with the ex-rebs.

Calabar-bean. Add to def.: Used as a remedy in certain diseases.

Calabazilla (kalabaþī·lya). Also **calabicillo.** [Mexican Sp., f. *calabaza* Calabash.] A wild squash of California and Mexico.

1902 Webster Suppl. 1908 H. H. Smith *Cacao Planting* 39 Strong growing forastero or calabicillo, bearing the finest criollo beans.

Calaboose. *U.S.* (Earlier and later examples.)

1797 F. Baily *Jrnl. Tour* (1856) 289 [He threatened me] with the horrors of the Callibouse if I any longer disputed his authority. 1806 *Amer. St. Papers, Ind. Affairs* (1832) 727 Others..followed the merchants;..then the church and jail (callaboose), and now nothing of the old town is left. 1908 S. E. White *Riverman* iii. 32 I'll just get along and bail the boys out of the village calaboose. 1926 J. Black *You Can't Win* vii. 86 The big bum now led us out and to a near-by box car that served as a calaboose.

attrib. 1835 *Col. Crockett's Tour* 146 Sam he got off to the boat, but the Calaboos men got Joe.

Hence **Calaboose** *v. trans.*, to put in prison.

1857 *Cincinnati Commercial* (Bartlett) Col. Titus..was calaboosed for shooting at the porter of the Planters' House.

Calamarian (kælămēᵊ·riăn), *a.* [f. mod.L. *Calamariæ* or *-aria* + -an.]

1. Of or pertaining to plants of the family *Calamariæ*.

1894 *Naturalist* 237 The general character of the specimens must be attributed to some pathological development in a calamarian axis.

2. Of or pertaining to the genus *Calamaria* or family *Calamariidæ* of snakes (*Standard Dict.* 1895).

Calamistrum (kælămi·strəm). Pl. **-a.** [L., curling-iron.] A comb-line structure on the last joint but one of the hind legs of certain spiders, used to card and curl the silk as it issues from the spinnerets.

1866 Miss E. F. Staveley *Brit. Spiders* 14 These [spines] are called calamistra, and are used in the construction of the web. 1875 *Encycl. Brit.* II. 292 The function of the calamistrum has been proved..to be the carding, or teasing and curling, of a peculiar kind of silk, secreted and emitted from the fourth pair of spinners.

Calamitean (kælămai·tiăn), *a.* [f. Calamite 1 + -an.] Belonging or relating to calamites.

1895 *Naturalist* 237 The histology of calamitean leaves. 1904 *Amer. Nat.* Apr. 250 Thus such transitions are well known, though of a relatively simplified form in the structure of the calamitean stem.

Calamitously, *adv.* Add quot.:

1896 *Home Missionary* (N.Y.) July 145 Churches..brought suddenly and calamitously into missionary conditions.

Calamity. Add: **3.** *attrib.* and *Comb.*, as *calamity-howler, -howling, -prophet, -shouting* (U.S.).

1892 *Congress. Rec.* 2 Mar. 1654/1 We had some 'calamity howlers' here in Washington as well as in Kansas. *Ibid.* 17 Mar. 2160/2 Calamity-shouters whose occupation is gone unless they can prove that calamity stalks abroad. 1892 in *Rep. Camp. Text Bk.* (1894) 229 The calamity prophets of both parties. 1905 D. G. Phillips *Plum Tree* 264, I..sent Woodruff East to direct a campaign of calamity-howling in the eastern press. 1911 J. C. Lincoln *Cap'n Warren's Wards* i. 3 The pair of calamity prophets broke off their lament.

Calander. Add: Also in It. form **calandra.**

1906 *Westm. Gaz.* 19 Apr. 12/1 In Milan, and also in Florence,..he saw enormous masses of small birds..field and calandra larks, and robin-redbreasts. 1924 *Countries of the World* 1653/1 The most characteristic forms of bird-life, such as the little and great bustard, partridge, quail and the calandra.

Calcicolous (kælsi·kŏləs), *a.* [f. L. *calc(i)-* lime, Calx + *colĕre* to inhabit.] Growing upon limestone. So **Ca·lcicole** *a.*

1882 *Encycl. Brit.* XIV. 562/1 As to saxicole lichens..they may be divided into two sections, viz. *calcicole* and *calcifugous*. To the former belong such as are found on calcareous and cretaceous rocks. 1886 Bagnall *Handbk. Mosses* 33 Another very characteristic calcicolous moss is Eucladium verticillatum.

Calcicrete (kæ·lsikrīt). Also **calcrete.** [f. L. *calc(i)-* lime, Calx + Con)crete.] A calcareous mass formed on the sea-bottom by marine animals.

1902 *Irish Naturalist* Oct. 231 Over the Boulder-clay and the calcrete is a bed of limestone sand and gravel. 1903 *Geol. Mag.* Mar. 139 No one would be likely to quarrel with 'calcicrete' and 'silicicrete', of which one would be two, the other three, letters longer [than 'calcrete', 'silcrete']. 1903 *Nature* 22 Oct. 614/1 In the Gulf of Manaar, calcareous masses ('calcretes') of great extent are formed *in situ* on the sea-bottom by the cementing of sand and other loose material by calcareous incrusting Polyzoa.

Calcimine. Substitute for etym. and def.: Later modification of *Kalsomine, after L. *calci-*, *calx* lime. Hence as *vb.*, to distemper with calcimine.

1885 *Spons' Mechanics' Own Bk.* 612 The wash or calcimine can be used for ordinary purposes. 1903 *Westm. Gaz.* 23 Jan. 4/3 The old-gold calcimine..that covers the wall of the drawing-room. 1911 H. S. Harrison *Queed* xi. 134 Sharlee tapped the calcimine with her pointed finger-nails.

Calcrete: see *Calcicrete.

Calculate, *v.* **6.** (Earlier U.S. example.)

1802 in Maclean *Hist. Coll. N. Jersey* (1877) II. 38 We calculate on your taking the lead in promoting subscriptions.

7. *U.S.* (Earlier examples.)

1805 Pike *Sources Mississ.* II. 152 We had reason to calculate, that they had good guides. 1810 J. Lambert *Trav. Canada & U.S.* (1813) II. 506 The crops are progressing, says Nathan, though I calculate as how this is a propitious weedy soil. *a* 1818 J. Bernard *Retrosp. Amer.* (1887) 307 Capital, gentlemen, capital,..you are right humorsome, I calculate. What's to pay? 1822 J. Woods *Engl. Prairie* 345 Times are dull; I calculated to sell my creature there.

Calculating, *vbl. sb.* Add: **calculating machine**, any of various machines designed for the mechanical performance of mathematical operations.

1834 *Mechanics' Mag.* XXII. 192/1 Calculating Machine. ..A cabinet-maker is stated to have constructed a machine [etc.]. 1835 in *Babbage's Calcul. Engines* (1889) 5 A Letter from Mr. Babbage announces that he has for six months been engaged in making the drawings of a new calculating machine of far greater power than the first. 1855 *Ibid.* 264 Report of a Committee appointed by the Council to examine the Calculating Machine of M. Scheutz. 1889 Conan Doyle *Sign of Four* ii, You really are an automaton —a calculating machine. 1901 *Nature* 11 July 268/2 The advantages of the calculating machines..are so great, and they are in so many ways preferable to logarithms where they can be used.

Calculiform (kæ·lkiŭlifǭɹm), *a.* [f. L. *calculus* pebble + -(i)form.] Pebble-shaped.

1900 *Spectator* 24 Mar. 417/2 The people are still known as the Mayas, and the writing is called calculiform.

Calendarist. Delete †*Obs.*, and add quot.:

1875 O'Hanlon *Irish Saints* I. 379 All our calendarists agree in assigning St. Fechin's feast to the 20th of January.

Caliban. Add: *Comb.*, as *caliban-like* adj. So **Ca·libanish** *a.*

1909 *Lady's Realm* Feb. 465/2 He was a *Caliban-like creature, primitively ugly. 1921 *Chambers's Jrnl.* 22/2 A lunatic..indulges in Caliban-like gambols, unheeded. 1839 Kemble *Resid. in Georgia* (1863) 222 The Calibanish wonderment of all my visitors..is very droll. 1872 Du Chaillu *Country of Dwarfs* 62 The fiendish countenances of the living calibanish trio.

Calibrate, *v.* Add: Also in *Wireless telegraphy.* So **Calibra·tion.**

1930 *Daily Mail* 4 Jan. 7/1 To get the set to do its best it must be calibrated. *Ibid.*, With calibration you can tune in at will to any foreign programme that is within the receptive powers of the set.

Ca·librated, *ppl. a.* [f. Calibrate *v.* + -ed [1].] Tested and graduated with allowance for irregularities; standardized. So **Ca·librating** *vbl. sb.* (attrib.).

1897 *Westm. Gaz.* 14 Jan. 6/3 The tube was handed on to a calibrating machine, which accurately 'shaped' it. 1909 *Install. News* III. 95/1 A very accurately calibrated check meter. *Ibid.* 160 A complete Testing and Calibrating Plant.

Calibre. 1. b. (Later U.S. examples.)

1868 C. B. Norton & Valentine *Rep. Munitions War* 47 Mr. Burton's rifle is adapted for central-fire cartridges; calibre 0·577 inch. 1908 Mulford *Orphan* xiii. 169 My breech-loading Sharps, ·50 calibre. *Ibid.* 170 It heaves enough lead at one crack to sink a man-of-war, being a ·60 calibre. 1914 *Sunday Herald* (Boston) 23 Aug. 3/8 The rifle is ·30 calibre—that is the diameter of the bore is thirty one-hundredths of an inch.

Caliche (kalī·tʃe). *Min.* [Sp. *caliche* pebble in a brick, flake of lime.] Any of various mineral deposits (*spec.* native Chile saltpetre) containing from 50–75 % of sodium nitrate.

1858 Simmonds *Dict. Trade*, *Caliche*, a name for nitrate of soda found in Peru. 1883 R. Haldane *Workshop Rec.* Ser. II. 349/2 Iodine occurs in caliche or raw nitrate deposit, as iodate of sodium. 1892 *Dana's Syst. Min.* (ed. 6) 871 In the district of Tarapaca, northern Chili,..the dry pampa..is covered with beds of this salt (caliche) several feet in thickness.

Calico. Add: **3. b.** Coloured in a way suggestive of printed calico; variegated, piebald. Chiefly of horses. Also as *sb.*, a calico horse. *U.S.*

1807–8 W. Irving *Salmag.* xviii. 413 Bantering nature fairly out of countenance,—representing her tricked out in all the tawdry finery of copper skies, purple rivers, calico rocks, red grass, [etc.]. 1809 — *Knickerb.* vii. iii. (1820) 458 Behold..Van Corlear, mounted on a..calico mare. 1835 J. Martin *Gazetteer Virginia* 27 The carved or calico rock of Kanawha. *a* 1861 T. Winthrop *Canoe & Saddle* x. 203 A hundred horses, roans, calicos..blacks and whites. 1878 B. F. Taylor *Between Gates* 207 There would be scant room for the calico horses to canter. 1901 *Munsey's Mag.* XXIV. 508/2 Jim McCoy was riding a 'calico' mare—a fractious beast covered with white and brown blotches of hair.

4. calico-back *U.S.*, (*a*) the turnstone (*Arenaria interpres*); (*b*) the harlequin cabbage-beetle; **calico-bass** *U.S.*, a species of sun-fish; **calico-bush,** the American mountain laurel (*Kalmia latifolia*); **calico flower** *U.S.*, one or other species of *Kalmia*; **calico-tree** *U.S.* (see quot.).

1872 Coues *Key N. Amer. Birds* 246 *Strepsilas*...Turnstone. Brant Bird. *Calico-back. 1877 C. Hallock *Sportsman's Gazetteer* 164 [The name] Calico-back [has reference] to the curiously variegated plumage of the upper parts. 1895 Comstock *Man. Insects* (1923) 145 The Harlequin Cabbage-bug or Calico-back..is very destructive to cabbages, radishes, and turnips in the Southern States. 1884 Goode *Nat. Hist. Aquatic Anim.* 406 The *calico Bass. *Pomoxys sparoides.* 1829 Loudon *Encycl. Plants* 356 *Kalmia latifolia* *Calico-bush. 1870 *Amer. Naturalist* IV. 217 Mountain Laurel Calico-bush, Spoon-wood..is one of the most beautiful shrubs ever created. 1839 *Monthly Chron.* III. 513 The Kalmias are called by the Americans *Calico flowers, a name admirably adapted to express the peculiar appearance of the flower. 1832 D. J. Brown *Sylva Amer.* 191 The Mountain Laurel..indifferently bears the name of Mountain Laurel, Laurel, and *Calico Tree.

California (kælifǭ·rniă). The name of the State on the Pacific Coast of North America, used *attrib.*; esp. in names of various species of animals and plants. (Common in recent use.)

1840 R. H. Dana *Bef. Mast* xiv, A few hides were brought down, which we carried off in the California style. *Ibid.*, Telling us that it was 'California fashion' to carry two on the head at a time. 1846 in W. H. Emory *Notes Mil. Reconnoissance* (1848) 575 The California quail..differs from the quail of the United States. 1869 *Amer. Naturalist* III. 518 California Hawk. *Buteo Cooperii.* 1874 Coues *Birds of Northwest* 363 Ferrugineous Buzzard, or California Squirrel Hawk. 1881 *Appleton's Amer. Cycl.* XII. 312/2 *Ceanothus thyrsiflorus* is a small tree producing an abundance of light blue flowers, and known as the California lilac.

b. California fever *colloq.*, laziness; **California Jack**, a card-game ('a variety of seven-up for two players'); **California toothpick**, a bowie-knife; **California widow** (see quot.).

1840 R. H. Dana *Bef. Mast* xxi, If the '*California fever' (laziness) spares the first generation, it always attacks the second. 1921 Mulford *Bar-20 Three* iii. 39 For two hours they sat and played *California Jack in plain sight of the street. 1856 W. G. Simms *Eutaw* 142 A weapon only inferior in size and weight to the modern '*California toothpick'. 1889 Farmer *Americanisms*, *California widow*, a married woman whose husband is away from her for any extended period.

Hence **Califo·rniaized** *ppl. a.*

1873 J. H. Beadle *Undevel. West* ix. 156 Most of the business men were 'Californiaized Jews',—an improved variety of the race.

Californian (kælifǭ·rniăn), *a.* and *sb.* [f. prec.]

A. *adj.* Of or belonging to, native or peculiar to, California; esp. in the names of species of birds, beasts, and plants.

1801 Latham *Gen. Synop. Birds* 2nd Suppl. 281 Californian Quail. 1839 A. Forbes *California* 192 Many of the [Indian] baskets are ornamented with..the black crest feathers of the Californian partridge. *Ibid.* 251 The wheels of the Californian ox-cart..are of a most singular construction. 1841 Loudon *Encycl. Plants* Suppl. 1218 *Eschscholtzia californica* Californian Eschscholtzia. 1846 E. Bryant *What I saw in California* x. (1849) 121 Some four or five hundred Californian horses, which he intends to dispose of in the United States. *Ibid.* xxiv. 267, I tasted here, for the first time, *aguardiénte*, or brandy distilled from the Californian grape. *a* 1861 T. Winthrop *John Brent* iii. (1862) 31 'Mucho malicho!' cried Gerrian to Jose, not knowing that his Californian Spanish was interpreting Hamlet. 1869 *Amer. Naturalist* III. 477 My inquiries about the Californian opossum found along the Mexican boundary did not indicate its existence in this valley. 1873 *Ibid.* VII. 327 Next, we have the Californian Mocking-Thrush (*Harporhynchus redivivus*). 1874 Coues *Birds of Northwest* 634 Californian Gull. 1885 Lock *Workshop Rec.* Ser. IV. 93/2 The chain pump known as the Chinese or Californian pump..is in common use in alluvial gold diggings in America and Australia. 1900 *Bk. Gardening* (ed. W. D. Drury) 237 *Platystemon californicum* (Californian Poppy) is a beautiful plant on rockwork and in flower-borders.

B. *sb.* **a.** A native or inhabitant of California.

b. A red herring. *slang.*

1789 Morse *Amer. Geog.* (1792) 479 The characteristics of the Californian, are stupidity and insensibility. 1840 R. H. Dana *Bef. Mast* xiv, We saw three men..dressed partly like sailors and partly like Californians. 1870 *Amer. Naturalist* III. 354 A 'one-cow town' would certainly astonish the most stolid Californian. 1873 *Cassell's Mag.* VI. 245/2 About the time of the gold discoveries, some one applied the term Californian to these. The word was appropriate, and Californians such highly coloured herrings are called to this day.

Calina (kalī·na). [Sp.] (See quot. 1887.)

1887 *Encycl. Brit.* XXII. 296/2 In July and August the plains of New Castile..are sunburnt wastes;..the atmosphere is filled with a fine dust, producing a haze known as *calina*. 1927 Kendrew *Climates of Continents* 244.

Caliology (kæliǫ·lŏdʒi). [f. Gr. καλιά wooden dwelling, hut, nest + -ology.] That department of ornithology which is concerned with birds' nests. Hence **Caliolo·gical** *a.*

1875 Newton in *Encycl. Brit.* III. 772 *note*, There are not many works on nidification, for 'Caliology' or the study of nests has hardly been deemed a distinct branch of the science. 1884 Coues *N. Amer. Birds* 227 One of the most delightful departments of ornithology, called caliology. 1902 C. Dixon *Birds' Nests* Introd. 4 The late J. G. Woods' popular treatment of birds' nests..practically exhausts the special literature of caliology.

Calix. Add: *Gr. Antiq.* = Cylix.

1849 A. Rich *Dict. Rom. & Gr. Antiq.* 1912 H. B. Walters *Catal. Gr. Vases B. Mus.* I. ii. 228.

Call, *sb.* Add:

1. d. orig. the call 'Hallo!' made by the user of a telephone to the operator; so, *to put a call through* (said of the operator); hence *gen.* a conversation over the telephone. See also attrib. uses.

1879 Prescott *Speaking Telephone* i. 23 It being necessary to keep the vibratory bells at each station in circuits, in order that the calls may be heard. 1882 J. E. K. *The Telephone* 19 The number of calls made upon the Exchange clerks. 1884 *Routledge's Every Boy's Ann.* 199/1 Before we follow the series of operations forming a complete call, let us examine the system of telephones used in the Broadway Office. This..allows these batteries to be used for the calls to the subscribers by means of ordinary electric bells. 1899 *Post Office Guide* July 533 This deposit is refunded if the call is not extended. 1929 *Morning Post* 11 Jan. 13 The charge for a three-minute call between London and Warsaw will be 15s. 3d.

6. *Close call*: see *Close *a.* C. 3.

i. Also in poker, 'a demand for a show-down; the show-down itself' (*Cent. Dict.* 1891).

1853 J. G. Baldwin *Flush Times Alabama* 8 A negro *ante* and twenty on the call, was moderate playing.

15. call-book (also) a book in which calls are entered; **call-box**, a box or small enclosed erection containing a telephone for public use; **call-boy, call-man**, a boy or man who calls up the members of a staff or fire brigade for duty; also *transf.*; **call-button**, a push-button or other device for ringing a call-bell or alarm; **call disk**, a disk indicating the identity of a telephone call-signal; **call-loan** (earlier U.S. example); **call-meeting** *U.S.*, a meeting specially summoned; **call-office,** (*a*) a telephone office or central station where the call signals are received and where the connexions necessary to intercommunication are made; (*b*) = *call-box*; **call-over,** (also) in betting parlance, a calling over or reading aloud of a list of prices; **call-room,** (*a*) = *call-box*; (*b*) *U.S.*, the room in the Exchange where calls are announced; **call-sign,** the conventional sign used at the beginning of a wireless message to indicate the identity of the sender; e.g. 2LO = London; so **call-letter;** †**call signal,** (*a*) a signal for calling up on the telephone; (*b*) a call-sign; **call slip** *U.S.*, the slip on which a reader or borrower in a library enters the book or books required (*Cent. Dict.* Suppl. 1909); **call-station** = *call-office*.

1893–4 *Rept. Unemployed* 46 (Parl. Papers LXXXII) *Call books are kept at the lodge-house for members out of work to sign. 1893 *Cassell's Fam. Mag.* Apr. 338/2 Thus it was that I first became introduced to the *call-box system. 1895 *Daily News* 21 Nov. 9/5 The first calls received from call-box holders were from Messrs. Maple and Co. 1900 *Ibid.* 1 Aug. 7/1 A licence..which enabled them [*sc.* the District Messenger Company] to erect call boxes in the houses of their subscribers. 1927 *Observer* 16 Oct. 11/4 Auto-electric advertising machines are about to be placed in 2,500 public telephone call boxes in London. 1868 *Cassell's Mag.* 15 Aug. 256/1 Some of our great iron-clads have been furnished with electrical *call-boys. 1881 *Instr. Census Clerks* (1885) 29 Theatre and Opera...Call Boy. 1887 *16th Ann. Rep. Oxf. Volunteer Fire Brigade* 9 The improved method of calling by electric bells, instead of by call boys. 1921 *Dict. Occup. Terms* (1927) § 709 *Call boy, caller, caller-up*..must receive answering call from each man knocked up. 1882 J. E. K. *The Telephone* 19 The moment a subscriber presses his '*call button', the catch is drawn up by an electro-magnet. 1884 *Routledge's Every Boy's Ann.* 124/2 The circles in the figure are the little windows at which the *call-disc makes its appearance. 1913 *Year Bk. Wireless Telegraphy* 286 Combinations of '*call letters' which are in turn allotted to ship and land stations. *a* 1859 *N. Y. Herald* (Bartlett 1859) To speculate in fancy stocks on *call loans is simply to put your hand in the lion's mouth. 1905 *Westm. Gaz.* 19 Apr. 8/1 When instructions were sent to *call-man Hills to order out all the fogmen. 1904 Harben *Georgians* 31 That afternoon they held a *call meeting of Republicans in the parlor. 1895 *Daily News* 13 Sept. 5/3 The charge for conversations..within a distance of 25 kilometres from the *call-office..has so far been 5d. 1899 *Post Office Guide* July 533 The following additional charges.. also apply to conversations between call offices. 1927 *Daily Tel.* 8 Mar. 15/1 That all such bets transacted at the club's '*calls-over' would be free of tax to the backer. 1882 J. E. K. *Telephone* 33 *Call-rooms have been established in different parts of London, in which are placed telephones connected with the Exchanges. 1886 *Harper's Mag.* July 213/1 The Call Room daily presents an impressive spectacle of the traffic in grain. 1919 *Times* (weekly ed.) 17 Jan., She signalled the letters of her '*call-sign' and our wireless picked up her message. 1921 *Glasgow Herald* 4 Feb. 9 Shortly after two o'clock she was called, but did not answer her call-sign. 1884 *Routledge's Every Boy's Ann.* 120/2 This system can make a Bell telephone..speak loud enough to be heard throughout a room; and it comprises besides a *call-signal within itself. 1912 in *Year Bk. Wireless Telegr.* (1913) 52 The call signals must be differentiated from one another, and each one must consist of a group of three letters. 1907 *Lancet* 27 July 240/2 The telephone *call station.

Call, *v.* Add:

1. f. To make a telephone call.

1882 J. E. K. *The Telephone* 19 The means by which the Exchange operator knows which subscriber is calling is very ingenious and very simple. *Ibid.* 38 An anxious mother.. called through the Exchange for the doctor.

4. b. *fig.* To summon to another world.

1886 *Leslie's Pop. Monthly* May XXI. 611/2 All the doctors in Christendom..can't save him. He's called.

m. To transmit a wireless message to.

1921 [see *call-sign* above].

22. Call for. e. To claim the existence of.

1929 *R. Fletcher's Catal.* Sept. 16 Mr. Sadleir, in his Bibliography [of Wilkie Collins], calls for bright green cloth.

23. Call on or upon. c. (*b*) To require or urge (a horse, etc.) to exert itself further. Cf. *Ask *v.* 2 b.

1850 'H. Hieover' *Pract. Horsemanship* 163 In the last few strides [of a race], where sudden and increased exertion is called for, and the horse is, in technical phrase 'called upon'. 1886 Earl Suffolk, etc. *Racing* v. (Badm. 1889) 86 Romanus is seen to..lose his pace. Wood calls on him without mending matters. 1894 Custance *Riding Recoll.* xi. 162 When I called on the gallant animal for the final effort, he got up and won.

26. Call back. e. *intr.* To revert to type; = *throw back*, Throw *v.* 38 d.

1853 *Jrnl. R. Agric. Soc.* XIV. i. 112 Isolated individuals appear, which, in the phraseology of breeders, 'call back' to their more remote progenitors. 1855 *Ibid.* XVI. i. 22 The offspring are said..to call back to their grand parents.

27. Call down. e. To rate or reprove; to challenge sharply. *U.S. colloq.*

1899 G. Ade *Doc Horne* viii. 83 I'll call anybody down on them statements. 1904 F. Lynde *Grafters* v. 58 He..so far lost his temper as to get himself called down by the judge. *a* 1906 'O. Henry' *Trimmed Lamp* etc. 213 When Fernando wanted to give me several thousand dollars for my trousseau he called him down something awful. 1923 Watts *Luther Nichols* 65 No one should ever have the chance to call him down.

30. Call off. c. *trans.* To rescind (an engagement), draw back from (an undertaking); *intr.* to draw back, back out of an engagement, etc.

1888 Mrs. Oliphant *Second Son* v, Why, in the name of all that's idiotic, do you call off now, and disappoint her.. and defy me? 1902 *Daily Chron.* 17 Oct. 5/3 The delegates of the Miners' Convention must first pass a vote upon the question of calling off the strike. 1927 *Observer* 14 Aug. 6 That he would have been profoundly relieved if the whole expedition had been called off. 1928 *Weekly Disp.* 27 May 17/3 The American fly-weight champion, whose fight with ..the British champion has been called off.

32. Call out. b. *esp.* To summon to active or permanent service in a campaign or in a state of emergency.

1779 *Digest of Militia Laws* 112 Every such person, having served in the Militia when called out into actual service. 1798 *Lady's Mag.* Feb. 68 Before I have a regiment called out for the purpose of being reviewed. 1805 Gordon *Address Volunteer Corps* p. xvi, It is intended to advance to each Non-commissioned Officer, Drummer, Trumpeter, and Private so called out, in proportion to the Length of Time for which they may agree to assemble. 1849 Macaulay *Hist. Eng.* I. iii. 291 When the trainbands were called out against an enemy. 1853 Bunn *Old Eng.* II. 53 *note*, Shot by the military, who had been called out for the occasion. 1890 *Chambers's Jrnl.* 5 July 423/1 The fog-signalmen..are often called out for a night's 'fogging' just as they have finished a hard day's work. 1899 Atteridge *Wars of Nineties* 551 The 1st Reserve was called out to bring the active army up to war strength. 1921 *Act* 11 & 12 *Geo. V* c. 15 § 9 Where..a man of the Naval Reserves..is called into actual service or called out for permanent service ..on an occasion of great emergency.

35. Call up. f. To call to battle; *spec.* to summon to the colours according to military status or grade.

1830 Scott *Bonnie Dundee*, Come saddle the horses and call up the men. 1857 *Blackw. Mag.* LXXXII. 281/2 The landwehr of the first band are liable..in the event of war, to be called up. 1877 *Gentl. Mag.* Jan. 36 My driver..informed me that he belonged to the Mobiles, that he had not yet been called up. 1899 Atteridge *Wars of Nineties* 550/2 Thus Japan had an army of nearly 70,000 men on a peace footing, which by calling up the reserves could be expanded into a war force of more than a quarter of a million. 1914 *Engl. Rev.* Sept. 258 We saw young Belgians crowded in trains *en route* for the front, men who were 'called up' against the enemy.

g. To summon up (Summon *v.* 7).

1889 *Illustrations, a Pict. Rev.* 143 Calling up whatever remnants of valour were left to me,..I advanced.

h. To summon (a person) on the telephone; now more usually *ring up*.

1898 [implied in *caller-up*]. 1916 'O. Henry' *Strictly Business* ii, Kelly went to the nearest telephone booth and called up McCrary's café.

Calla. 1. (Examples.)

1829 Loudon *Encycl. Plants* 298 *Calla æthiopica*. Ethiopian Calla. 1845–50 A. Wood *Class-bk. Bot.* 520 *C. Palustris*. Northern Calla. 1869 C. L. Brace *New West* i. 18 The callas and exquisite water-flowers in the pools. 1885 *Outing* (U.S.) Nov. 178/2 An interesting plant is the wild Calla, growing in cold, wet places.

Callable (kǭ·lăb'l), *a.* [f. Call *v.* + -able.] That may be called (called in, called upon).

1826 *Examiner* 673/2 Judges called, or callable, rural. 1889 *Sat. Rev.* 16 Mar. 313/2 Without a cash reserve, or without callable loans with bill-brokers. 1892 *Ibid.* 11 June 678/2 As there is no callable capital, the shareholders cannot suffer more than the loss of the capital paid up.

Called, *ppl. a.* Add:

b. *Baseball.* See quot.

1874 H. Chadwick *Base Ball Man.* 49 A called ball is the penalty inflicted on the pitcher for sending a ball to the bat out of the striker's legitimate reach. *Ibid.* 85 No called balls can be justly charged as pitching errors unless they come under the head of 'wide balls'.

Callee (kǭlī·). [f. Call *v.* + -ee.] One who is called or called upon.

1872 Butler *Erewhon* xxi. 197 The callee would have been deaf to the caller. 1883 *Cambridge Staircase* v. 73 Our callee suggested that there were more comfortable seats.

Caller, *sb.* Add: **1. e.** One who makes a call on a telephone. Also *caller-up*.

1898 *Daily News* 6 June 6/2 The caller-up knowing whether he is through or not by the ringing or not ringing of his bell. 1899 *Post Office Guide* July 533 If a deposit has been made by the caller in the first instance to cover the fee for the second period of three minutes.

f. A man or boy employed to knock up for duty the members of a railway staff, usually at their homes. Also *caller-up*.

1921 *Dict. Occup. Terms* (1927) § 709.

Calliard (kæ·liăɹd). *local.* [Of doubtful origin; perh. connected with F. *caillou* pebble, and so ultimately with L. *calculus*. But cf. the later Galliard *sb.*[2]] A hard, smooth, flinty gritstone.

1781 J. Hutton *Tour to Caves* (ed. 2) Gloss. (E.D.S.) *Callierd*, an hard stone. 1833–4 J. Phillips *Geol.* in *Encycl. Metrop.* (1845) VI. 587/2 Some less regular sandstone beds, called 'Cankstone', approach very nearly to the nature of the ganister or calliard rocks of the coal strata. 1859 Page *Handbk. Geol. Terms* (1865), *Calliard*.., a local name for any hard siliceous stone; often applied by English miners and quarrymen to beds of cherty or siliceous limestone. 1876 Woodward *Geol. Eng. & Wales* 81 Some of the beds contain gritstone or greywacke, provincially called 'calliard'.

Callid, *a.* (Late U.S. example.)

1887 Lowell *Ep. to G. W. Curtis* Postscr. 4 Found lately, I have pieced it out, or tried, Since time for callid juncture was denied.

Calligraphy. Add: **1. b.** With reference to the use of the fine-hair brush by an artist for outlining. Hence **Calligra·phic** *a.*

1930 *Times Lit. Suppl.* 9 Jan. 25/3 Leonardo displays his extraordinary gift of enclosing a volume by a flowing and calligraphic line... The calligraphic beauty of line.

Calling, *vbl. sb.* Add:

8. With *up*.

1877 *Design & Work* III. 713/3 For calling-up purposes I have a bell in the bedroom of a very drowsy domestic. 1890 *Peel City Guardian* 12 July 6/1 The calling up of constables on probation. 1902 *Electr. & Magn.* xviii. 226 (Govt. Milit. Bk.) Calling-up may be done by means of an ordinary bell and battery. 1918 *Act 8 Geo. V* c. 5 § 4 (2) With a view to preventing..the calling up of himself..for any form of military service.

III. (Cf. Call *v.* 2, 2 b, 4 c.) **calling card** *U.S.*, a visiting-card; **calling list,** a visiting-list.

1890 Kipling *Plain Tales from Hills, Beyond the Pale* 163 [He] put on his calling-clothes and called on the ladies of the Station. 1893 *Westm. Gaz.* 19 Apr. 6/2 There will be four calling stations. 1902 *Ibid.* 13 Aug. 2/1 The dreamless sleep of the outdoor worker till calling-time next morning. 1905 *N. Y. Times* 7 Feb. 5 Advt., We'll execute calling cards to your order in conformity with the very latest requirements of fashion. 1908 *Westm. Gaz.* 27 Apr. 10/2 To ensure regularity in arriving at the various calling ports. 1908 *Daily Chron.* 24 Feb. 4/6 His seeing the Union Jack at every calling-port. 1909 *Ibid.* 16 Sept. 7/5 Constitutionally sleepy at calling-time. 1921 R. D. Paine *Comr. Rolling Ocean* viii. 129 And you decided to drop him from your calling list?

Callithump (kæ·liþɒmp), *sb.* and *v.* *U.S. colloq.* [App. back-formation from next.] (See quots.)

1871 Schele de Vere *Americanisms* (1872) 589 Callithump seems..to be of American origin. It represents the French *charivari*, the German *Katzenmusik*. 1889 Farmer *Americanisms*, *Callithump*, *To*, to caterwaul; to produce discordant 'musical' sounds by means of instruments, either incongruous in themselves or in conjunction—such as tin kettles, bells, rattles, etc.

Callithu·mpian, *sb.* and *a.* *U.S. colloq.* [Prob. a fanciful formation.] (See quot. 1848 and prec.)

1848 Bartlett *Dict. Amer.* s.v., It is a common practice in New York, as well as other parts of the country, on New Year's eve, for persons to assemble with tin horns, bells, rattles, and similar euphonious instruments, and parade the streets making all the noise and discord possible. This party is called the *Callithumpians* or the *Callithumpian Band*. 1886 *Harper's Mag.* July 213/2 The call [on the exchange] lasts ten or fifteen minutes, and occasionally has the accompaniment of callithumpian discord. 1904 *N. Y. Times* 25 May 1 The calithumpian band had kept up the music without interruption all night.

Callosal (kălō·săl), *a.* *Anat.* [f. L. *callōsus* + -al.] Of or belonging to the corpus callosum.

1889 in *Century Dict.* 1890 Sir W. Turner in *Jrnl. Anat.* XXV. 116 Marginal, callosal and hippocampal gyri are all differentiated.

Calloused, *ppl. a.* (Earlier U.S. example.)

1819 *Massachusetts Spy* 24 Mar. 2/1 One, more bold than the rest, with calloused sensibility, comes forth in the *Salem Register*..and with unparalleled effrontery boasts that the loaves and fishes of office are what some of his party seek.

Callousing (kæ·ləsiŋ), *ppl. a.* [f. Callous *a.* or *v.* + -ing [2].] That makes callous.

1921 *Sunday at Home* Jan. 214/1 My fellow-citizens are engaged on labour which is hard and callousing. 1928 *Sunday Express* 8 Jan. 9/1 The hardships and callousing brutalities of a mercenary force.

Callovian (kælō·viăn), *a.* *Geol.* Also *Kellovian. [mod.L. *Callovia*, ad. *Kelloways* in Wiltshire. So F. *callovien*.] Defining a subdivision of the Oxfordian division of the Jurassic system.

1882 Geikie *Text-bk. Geol.* 793 Oxfordian, divisible into two sections: (*a*) a lower zone of calcareous abundantly fossiliferous sandstone, known from a place in Wiltshire, as the Kellaways Rock (Callovian). 1903 *Ibid.* (ed. 4) II. 1157 Over the northern half of the country [*sc.* Russia] the various formations from the Callovian up into the Cretaceous system have been identified. 1914 *Brit. Mus. Return* 201 Crinoidea from..the Callovian of Ardèche and Neocomian of Isère.

Callus (kæ·lŏs), *v.* [f. Callus 3.] *intr.* To form a callus.

1864 Hibberd *Rose-bk.* 284 In all cases keep cuttings and eyes alive and fresh by sprinkling their tops frequently rather than making the soil they are in very wet, they will in fact callus quicker if the soil is nearly dry.

Calm, *sb.*[2] **2.** Delete † and add quots.:

1885 P. J. Davies *Pract. Standard Plumbing* 31 Put the sharpened end of the calme in between the cutters and turn the handle. 1885 *Spons' Mechanics' Own Bk.* 630 The use of lead 'calmes' for fixing window panes is of venerable antiquity. 1923 M. Drake *Doom Window* i. 15 Gleaming strips or 'calmes' of lead..shone like limp silver snakes.

Calm, *a.* Add: **1. e.** Quietly insolent; unabashed, impudent. *colloq.*

1888 *Atalanta* XI. 119/1 The critic on the hearth has the calm audacity to announce that [etc.].

Calmingly (kā·miŋli), *adv.* [f. Calming *ppl. a.* + -ly [2].] In a calming manner.

1908 A. Bennett *Buried Alive* viii, 'Of course you haven't', she said calmingly.

Calorie. Substitute for def.: (More fully *great* or *major calorie*) The amount of heat required to raise the temperature of 1 kilogramme (= 1 litre) of water one degree centigrade. In later use also (more fully *lesser calorie*), the amount of heat required to raise the temperature of 1 gramme (= 1 cubic centimetre) of water one degree centigrade.

1870, 1880 [in Dict.]. 1889 M. Foster *Text Bk. Physiol.* (ed. 5) II. 802 The following results expressed in calories, that is in gramme-degree units of heat. 1892 *Pall Mall Gaz.* 22 June 6/1 A pound of beefsteak contains..870 calories of energy. 1901 *Westm. Gaz.* 23 Dec. 2/3 The average energy-value of the food required by a..soldier must..be..more than..3,500 Calories. 1926 *Public Opinion* 13 Aug. 156/3 When the customary measure of calory value is applied to cake and bread, it is found that there is very little difference between these two staple foods.

Calotte. Add: **6.** *Geol.* An ice-cap or a glacier covering a large land area.

1894 J. W. Gregory in *Q. Jrnl. Geol. Soc.* L. 515 A 'calotte' or snow-cap, similar to those on Kibo..and Chimborazo.

Calpy (kæ·lpi), *a.* [f. Calp + -y [1].] Of the nature of calp.

1895 Wood-Martin *Pagan Irel.* 108 A floor..of calpy limestone flags.

Caltrop. Add:

4. In the nomenclature of the spicular elements of sponges, a tetraxial spicule with four equal arms radiating from a central point, so called from its resemblance to a caltrop (sense 2).

1887 Sollas in *Encycl. Brit.* XXII. 416/2 Tetraxon Quadriradiate Type (Calthrops). 1888 — in *Challenger Rep.* XXV. p. lxxii, The calthrops may have been derived from a triæne by shortening of the rhabdome, or from a microcalthrops by increased growth.

Calumet. Add: **b.** *attrib.* **calumet eagle** *U.S.*, an eagle with black and white tail-feathers.

1817 *Ann. Reg. 1816, Chron.* 564 With these feathers the natives decorate the stems of their sacred pipes or calumets, from whence the name the calumet eagle is derived. 1841 Catlin *N. Amer. Indians* I. 68.

Calve, *v.*[1] Add: *To calve down*: to breed from (a cow). Also *intr.* = *pass.*

1858 *Jrnl. R. Agric. Soc.* XIX. I. 27 These stock are generally calved down when little more than two years old, or else sold. *Ibid.* 28, I have myself known stock costing 6 *l.* per head worth at the end of the same year 13 *l.* or 14 *l.*, and the increase is just as great when they calve down.

Calycate (kæ·likeɪt), *a.* *Bot.* Also **calicate.** [ad. mod.L. *calycātus*, f. L. Calyx: see -ate [2].] Provided with a calyx.

1866 *Treas. Bot.*, *Calicate*, furnished with a calyx.

Calyx. 3. Add: **calyx-bursting**, bursting of the calyx, a defect in carnations; **calyx-crater** *Gr. Antiq.*, a crater or large bowl of the shape of a calyx.

1900 *Westm. Gaz.* 7 May 4/2 *Calyx-bursting is a fatal objection to many varieties otherwise superb. 1896 C. H. Smith *Catal. Gr. Vases B. Mus.* III. 280 *Calyx-form Craters. 1911–12 J. D. Beazley in *Ann. Brit. Sch. Athens* 225 The pattern No. 15 does not occur on any other rf. kalyx-krater. 1915 *Oxf. Univ. Gaz.* 3 Feb. 378/2 The other vases include two *hydriæ*,..two amphoræ,..and a calyx-crater. 1918 Beazley *Attic Red-figured Vases Amer. Mus.* xiv. 153 The painter of the Villa Giulia calyx-crater.

Cam, *sb.*[1] **b.** Add:

cam-box, a frame surrounding a cam and designed to compel the rod which the cam drives to follow the return motion of the projecting lobe; also, a casing enclosing the cam and its rollers in order that copious lubrication may be secured by having the cams revolve in a bath of oil (*Cent. Dict.* Suppl. 1909); **cam-cutter,** a machine-tool specially adapted for cutting and finishing cams; **cam-pump,** a pump in which the valve motion is given by a cam; **cam-yoke,** a frame attached to a valve stem or other reciprocating piece to which it gives intermittent straight-line motion from a cam on the face of a rotating disk; used in steam-engine valve-gears (*Standard Dict.* 1895).

1884 Knight *Dict. Mech.* Suppl. 156 *Cam Cutter. 1922 Jacobs *Cam Design* 74 The hand-made master cam is now placed in position on the cam cutter head spindle. 1884 Knight *Dict. Mech.* Suppl. 157 Drayton *Cam Pump.

Camaldolese (kămæ·ldǝlīz), *a.* and *sb.* Also **Camaldulese.** = Camaldolite, q. v.

1828 in B. Ward *Eve Cath. Emanc.* (1912) III. xlv. 198 Two have embraced the Order of Camaldolese Hermits. 1850 in *Ushaw Mag.* (1907) Mar. 62 In Rome the *Candela dell' Elevazione* is used by the Camaldolese only. 1873 Newman *Mission Bened. Order* (1908) 75 Monte Cassino excelled in *miniatura* and mosaic, the Camaldolese in painting, and the Olivetans in wood-inlaying. 1880 H. Collins *Heaven Opened* II. xix. 247 The Carthusians and Camaldulese have but one fixed recreation in the week. 1929 D. Gwynn *Cdl. Wiseman* i. 16 Clothed in his white robes as a Camaldolese monk.

Camaloté (kæ·mălōute). Also **camelote, -a.** [American Sp.] A water-lily.

1881 E. W. White *Cameos fr. Silver-Land* I. 243 When the river is high, it is no very uncommon circumstance to see the whole surface of this archipelago covered with the debris (*camelotas*) of these mud-formed islands, buoyed up by matted roots. 1882 *Ibid.* II. 3 Blue-flowered camalotes. 1905 R. B. Cunninghame Graham *Progress* 63 Camelotes brought down by the flood were wreathed about them like gigantic eels. *Note,* The camelote is a very thick-growing water-lily, which sometimes chokes small streams. 1918 W. H. Hudson *Far Away & Long Ago* xx. 261 The fourth lakelet..was..covered with a luxuriant growth of the floating *camalotê*, a plant which at a distance resembles the wild musk.

Caman (kæ·măn). Also **camman.** [Gaelic.] The stick or club used in shinty.

1891 *Daily News* 12 Oct. 5/6 The *camman* is the club..with which the Gaelic athletes play their favourite game. 1900 *19th Cent.* Aug. 307 Each man has a *caman* or hurley—a stick, about three feet long, with a bend or curve at the end. 1905 Sheehan *Glenanaar* i, The crack of the camans as they crossed in the air above or on the grass beneath.

Camanchaca (kamæ·ntʃākă). A heavy mist on the Peruvian coast.

1908 Enock *Andes & Amazon* (ed. 2) 5 The heavy mist upon the coast, known as *Camanchaca*. 1922 *Daily Mail* 17 Nov. 8 In the Northern rainless zone, the camanchacas, or heavy, overhanging mists, became much denser.

Camarage (kæ·mărĕdʒ). [ad. Sp. *camaraje*, f. *camara* storehouse:—L. *camara, camera* vault: see -age.] Rent paid for a granary.

1858 Simmonds *Dict. Trade.*

Camaron (kæmărō·n, kæ·mărǝn). Also **cammaron.** [ad. Sp. *camaron* shrimp, f. L. *cam(m)arus* sea-crab.] A freshwater shrimp or prawn resembling the crayfish.

1880 Huxley *Crayfish* 329 These fluviatile prawns (known in many places by the name of '*Cammarons*') are not unfrequently confounded with true crayfishes. 1920 *Glasgow Herald* 31 Dec. 11 Camarons are excellent when boiled.

Camata (kămātă, -ǝ·tă). [It.] The commercial name for the half-grown acorns of *Quercus Ægilops*, dried and used for tanning. Cf. next.

1858 Simmonds *Dict. Trade.* 1866 *Treas. Bot.* 950/1.

Camatina (kæmătī·nă, -ǝi·nă). [dim. of prec.] The commercial name for the incipient acorns of *Quercus Ægilops*.

1858 Simmonds *Dict. Trade.* 1866 *Treas. Bot.* 950/1. 1884 *Encycl. Brit.* XVII. 694/2 The valonia of commerce, one of the richest of tanning materials, is the acorn of *Q[uercus] Ægilops*...Immature acorns are sometimes exported under the name of camatina.

Camber, *sb.* Add: **1. b.** The arch of a road.

1905 *Westm. Gaz.* 13 Oct. 2/7 Another suggestion is that the 'camber' (i. e., the upward curve) of roadways should be lessened. 1907 *Ibid.* 30 July 8/1 The heavy camber of the sides..is the cause of very many mishaps. 1925 *Public Opinion* 11 Dec. 588/2 Hodge has always allowed his horse to take the top of the camber.

c. The curvature of the wings of an aeroplane.

1918 H. Barber *Aeroplane Speaks* (ed. 6) 5, I must have a certain chord to make it possible for my Camber (that's curvature) to be just right for the Angle of Incidence.

Cambered, *ppl. a.* Add recent quots.:

1909 *Flight* 20 Feb. 104/1 *Cambered*, this term denotes that the plane or wing has a curved transverse section. 1919 *Autocar Handbk.* (ed. 9) 223 When driving a car on a much-cambered or arched road. 1927 C. L. M. Brown *Conquest of the Air* 46 That a slightly concave or..'cambered' formation of the wing surface would obtain greater 'lift' from the air resistance than a perfectly flat plane surface.

Cambric. c. Add: *cambric needle*; **cambric tea** *U.S.*, a drink composed of hot milk and water, given to children in place of tea.

1869 Mrs. Stowe *Oldtown Folks* i. 2 Israel Cran's store, where everything was sold, from hoe-handles up to cambric needles. 1888 *Union Signal* (Chicago) 21 Jan. 3 [She] gave me a vast easy chair to sit in..and offered me tea, cambric tea to be sure, but in a beautiful cup.

Cambridge (kēɪ·mbridʒ), the name of a University town in England, used *attrib.*, as **Cambridge blue,** a light blue (see *Blue *sb.* 1); **Cambridge calf** (see quot. 1895); **Cambridge chimes,** the composition of Joseph Jowett and William Crotch, first employed in 1793 at the Church of St. Mary the Great, Cambridge; **Cambridge coprolite, greensand** *Geol.* (see quots. 1881, 1882).

1890 Denison *Clock & Watch-m.* 226 A clock made for a nobleman a few years ago, who intended to have the Cambridge chimes. 1881 *Spons' Encycl. Industr. Arts* IV. 1260 The most valuable beds of the mineral in this country are in the Upper Greensand formation, lying chiefly in Cambridgeshire, and merging into Buckinghamshire. These are known as 'Cambridge' coprolites. 1882 Geikie *Text-bk. Geol.* 809 The so-called 'Cambridge Greensand'—a bed about 1 foot thick lying at the base of the Chalk of Cambridge, and largely worked for phosphate of lime derived from coprolites and bones. 1883, 1895 Cambridge blue [see *Blue *sb.* 1]. 1895 Zaehnsdorf *Sh. Hist. Bookbinding* 20 Cambridge Calf.—Fine and dark sprinkled calf of two tints, a square panel being left in centre of sides. 1898 *Westm. Gaz.* 3 Mar. 9/2 The bulky little volume..in its Cambridge-blue cover. 1909 *Daily Chron.* 16 Feb. 4/6 As the 'Cambridge Chimes' at St. Stephen's strike 2 p.m. the King will arrive to open Parliament.

Cambridgeshire (kēɪ·mbridʒʃǝɪ). The name of the eastern county in which Newmarket (q. v.) is situated, used attrib. in *The Cambridgeshire Handicap* (*Stakes*) as the name of a horse-race originated in 1839 and run annually at Newmarket: usually abbrev. *The Cambridgeshire.*

1840 J. C. Whyte *Hist. Brit. Turf* II. 482 The Cambridgeshire stakes. 1856 'Stonehenge' (J. H. Walsh) *Brit. Sports* 373/1 Cambridgeshire Course..1 mile 240 yards. 1891 Sir G. Chetwynd *Racing Remin.* I. 10 The next day Vestminster won the Cambridgeshire.

Cambro- (kæ·mbro), mod.L. *Cambro-*, as in *Cambro-Britannicus* (1592), used as combining form in the sense 'pertaining to Cambria, Welsh'.

1712 P. Metcalf *Life S. Winefride* (1917) 69 Doctor John David Rhes, a Cambro-Britain. 1853 W. J. Rees (*title*) Lives of the Cambro British Saints. 1871 Lowell *Study Wind., Swinburne's Trag.* 164 Tennyson in the Cambro-Breton cyclus of Arthur. 1925 J. Joly *Surface-Hist. Earth* iii. 57 Almost complete submergence of North America in Cambro-Ordovician times.

Camel, *sb.* Add: **1. d.** The characteristic colour of a camel, a variety of fawn.

1922 *Daily Mail* 11 Dec. 14 Brushed Wool Scarf-wrap..Can be supplied..in plain colours—White,..Camel, Beige, Grey. 1923 *Ibid.* 26 Feb. 1 In good shades of Grey, Camel, Fawn. 1924 *Tourist* Winter Sports No. 20 Sports hats..of camel check Tweed with scarves to match.

2. b. A type of aeroplane (see quots.).

1918 McCudden *Five Yrs. R. F. C.* 278, I saw a derelict Sopwith 'Camel' which had apparently been shot down several weeks previous. *Ibid.* 310 On one of the Gotha raids I saw a Camel pilot firing at a Gotha at over half a mile range. 1925 Fraser & Gibbons *Soldier & Sailor Words, Camel, the*, the nickname of a type of Sopwith scout aeroplane carrying Vickers and Lewis guns. (From its distinctive appearance). 1928 C. F. S. Gamble *North Sea Air Station* xvi. 290 The Sopwith Camel—a single-seater fighter..derived its name from the hump which it carried on the forward top-side of its fuselage.

4. *camel-cart, -dung, -guide, -skin.*

1900 *Daily News* 25 Sept. 3/4 Our caravan..included..six *camel carts for the ladies and children. 1907 *Westm. Gaz.* 25 Nov. 2/1 The most striking..conveyance is a camel-cart. 1903 Clark Russell *Overdue* vi, Recollection reeks of the flavour of the *camel-dung cigarettes of Alexandria. *c* 1450 Capgrave *Life St. Aug.* 38 ȝe haue girdilis lich knytys; and þei with þongis of *chamel skynnys, as Hely and Ion, go girt in her lendes. 1497 Bp. Alcock *Mons Perfeccionis* E i b/1 Clothed in a camell skynne. 1903 *Month* Aug. 165 St. John in his camel-skin robe.

5. camel-gun, a gun, as a machine gun, made light and short so as to be transportable by camels; **camel-swallower, -swallowing** (see Camel *sb.* 1 c); **camel-trot, camel-walk,** a dance resembling the walk of a camel.

1891 Kipling *Light that Failed* (1900) 24 Aren't the *camel-guns ever going to begin? 1840 C. H. Townshend *Facts in Mesmerism* 332 The gnat-strainers and *camel-swallowers may be content to accept this story. 1858 Dickens *Lett.* (1880) II. 82 All manner of *camel-swallowing and of gnat-straining. 1923 *Weekly Dispatch* 8 Apr. 8 They call the modern dances *camel-trots. 1922 *Ibid.* 31 Dec. 9 The Chicago, *camel-walk,..and shimmy dances must cease.

Camelious (kămī·liǝs), *a.* [f. Camel *sb.* + -ious.] Jocular word invented by Kipling to describe the hump given to the lazy camel in *Just So Stories.* Hence *altusively* (to Hump *sb.* 3).

1902 Kipling *Just So Stories* 27 If we Kiddies and grown-ups too-oo-oo, haven't enough to do-oo-oo, We get the hump—Cameelious hump—The hump that is black and blue! 1909 'Ian Hay' *Man's Man* xvi, The men have both got camelious hump.

Camellia. Add: **camellia-red,** a bright red, the colour of red camellias.

1890 *Daily News* 21 Oct. 2/1 Camellia red felt.

Cameloid (kæ·mĕloid), *a.* and *sb.* [ad. mod.L. *Cameloidea*: see Camel *sb.* and -oid.] **A.** *adj.* Of or pertaining to the *Cameloidea* or camel family of ruminants. **B.** *sb.* An animal of this family.

1885 O. Schmidt *Mammalia* 156 The cameloid type of Ruminant. 1888 *Longman's Mag.* July 298 That the existing cameloids should be so strangely distributed. 1924 *Glasgow Herald* 8 Nov. 4 Herds of camels..trekked across..to Europe, leaving North America..with a glorious graveyard of cameloid progenitors.

Camelote, var. *Camaloté.

Camembert (kæ·manbēɹ). [Name of a village near Argentan, France.] In full *Camembert cheese*: a rich soft cheese made in the vicinity of Camembert; also, any cheese of the same type, wherever made.

1878 *Cassell's Fam. Mag.* IV. 535/1. 1890 J. Macdonald *Stephens's Bk. Farm* (ed. 4) IV. 518/1. 1908 *Westm. Gaz.* 5 Aug. 2/2 These foreign cheeses consist..of fancy varieties..Gruyère, Camembert, Roquefort, Gorgonzola, &c.—which please the epicure. 1909 *Ibid.* 9 Dec. 4/2 Roquefort, Gruyère, and Camembert are probably the three French cheeses best known in this country.

Cameo. Add:

b. Special Comb.: **cameo-embossing** (see quot.); **cameo glass,** an artistic glass consisting of layers of different colours, the outermost being cut away so as to leave the design or designs in relief, an example being the Portland vase; **cameo-incrustation,** the art of producing bas-relief casts within a coating of flint-glass; **cameo-type,** in photography, a name formerly given to a small daguerreotype which could be mounted in a jewelled setting; **cameo ware,** pottery with figures in relief on a background of a different colour, as in Wedgwood ware.

1878 *Encycl. Brit.* VIII. 160/2 In the second variety [of colour embossing]—called *cameo embossing—the colour is applied to the flat parts of the design by means of a small printing roller, and the letters or design in relief is left uncoloured. 1879 *Ibid.* X. 649/2 The first place among those processes in which one colour was superimposed on another may be given to that by which the *cameo glass was produced. 1910 *Ibid.* XII. 92/2 The carved or 'cameo' glass, introduced by Thomas Webb of Stourbridge in 1878. 1874 Knight *Dict. Mech.*, *Cameo-incrustation. *Ibid.*, *Cameotype, a fanciful name given to a small vignette daguerreotype for mounting in a jeweled frame like a cameo.

Camera. 3. b. Add: **camera booth** (see quot.); **camera-man,** a man provided with a camera to take snapshots or cinematographic photographs, esp. for the press.

1929 *Photoplay* Apr., *Camera booth, the movable sound-proof box with a glass front, in which cameras are enclosed in a talking picture studio in order that the sound of the camera may not intrude in the picture. 1908 *Westm. Gaz.* 21 Apr. 7/1 After both had posed to the inevitable *camera-men. 1920 *Q. Rev.* July 183 The camera-man will film you anything. 1928 S. Vines *Humours Unreconciled* xviii. 233 Swarms of little camera-men came down from Totsuka.

Camerata (kæmĕrā·tă). [mod.L., f. *camera* Chamber.] Each of the groups into which students of English theological colleges at Rome are divided.

1846 Newman in W. Ward *Life* (1912) I. iv. 132 The whole body of students is divided into eight classes or portions (cameratas?)—who are never allowed to speak to each other. If you and Christie and Penny went, they would of course put you into three separate cameratas. 1912 B. Ward *Eve Cath. Emanc.* III. xxxiv. 13 The students..likewise felt aggrieved at having to walk out in 'Camerata'.

Camerist [2] (kæ·mǝrist). Chiefly *U.S.* [f. Camera 3 b + -ist.] One who uses a camera, a photographer; a camera-man.

1890 *Anthony's Photogr. Bull.* III. 19 Theoretically, all camerists believe in a good negative. 1891 *Ibid.* IV. 85 A steady head is often needed to keep an enthusiastic camerist from being unduly depressed or exalted. 1900 *Boston Transcript* 23 Feb. (Cent. Suppl.) When a high wind is encountered, the cloth at one end can be buttoned..around the head or face of the camerist. 1906 *Westm. Gaz.* 15 May 12/3 Many of the pictures..are excellent examples of artistic photography..They have been taken by camerists..whose names are thoroughly well known. 1921 *Chambers's Jrnl.* Aug. 547/1 The camerist determines on some other makeshift foreground.

Camerlingo (kæmǝɹli·ŋgo). Also **camerlengo** [It. *camerlingo*: see Chamberlain.] **a.** The Pope's chamberlain and financial secretary; the highest officer in the papal household. **b.** The cardinals' chamberlain, the treasurer of the sacred college. Hence **Camerli·ngate,** the office of camerlingo.

1625 Purchas *Pilgrims* II. x. 1834 The Inhabitants are gouerned by a *Camarlingo*, in the behalfe of Venice. 1753 Chambers *Cycl. Supp.* s. v., The *camerlingo* is the most conspicuous officer in the court of Rome..The cardinals have also their *camerlingo*, or treasurer of their college. 1756–9 A. Butler *Lives Saints* (1845) XI. 77 St. Charles..absolutely refused the camerlingate, the second and most lucrative dignity in the Roman court. 1923 *Glasgow Herald* 10 May 9 He was all confused when taken to the presence of Her Majesty by a camerlengo.

Camerostome (kæ·mĕrostoum). *Zool.* [ad. mod.L. *camerostoma*, irreg. f. L. *camera* vault + Gr. στόμα mouth.] The anterior part of the body of arachnids which forms an arch over the mouth.

1880 Rolleston & Jackson *Anim. Life* 523 A well-developed chitinoid piece—the camerostome..overhangs the mouth anteriorly.

Cami- (kæ·mi), abbreviated form of *Camisole, used in *Comb.*, as **cami-bocker** [f. (*knicker*) *bocker*], an undergarment which combines camisole and knickers; also called **cami-knicker**; so **cami-petticoat,** etc.

1926 *Good Housekeeping* July 58 *Cami-bocker in cotton crêpon. 1915 *Home Chat* 30 Oct. 229 My new *cami-knickers. Quite a new pattern. 1923 *Daily Mail* 2 May 1 *Cami-petticoats made of..heavy Artificial Silk Stockinette.

Camion (kæ·miǝn). Delete *Obs.* and add quots.:

1865 Warren & Cleverly *Wand. Beetle* 102 The ponderous camion thundered over the uneven pitching of the streets. 1922 *Blackw. Mag.* Jan. 23/2 The French..had in their turn a splash of khaki on each of their *camions*. 1924 *Scribner's Mag.* July 40/2 We found that we were about one camion short to the company.

Camisole. Add: **2. b.** An underbodice, often embroidered and trimmed with lace.

1895 *Army & Navy Co-op. Soc. Price List* 1062 Tucked Camisoles. 1903 *Daily Chron.* 14 Mar. 8/4 There are many camisole patterns. 1906 *Ibid.* 7 May 11/6 Camisole machinists.

Ca·mman, var. *Caman.

Camote (kămōu·te). [Mexican Sp., ad. Nahuatl *camotli*.] A name in Mexico and other Spanish-speaking countries for any one of several tuber-bearing plants, e.g. the sweet potato and yam.

1885 *Encycl. Brit.* XVIII. 751/1 Sweet potatoes (camote)..are pretty generally grown [in the Philippines]. 1909 *Teachers' Assembly Herald* II. 44/2 [To] relieve the Igorot girls from their laborious toil in the camote patch.

Camoudie (kămū·di). Also **-di, camoodie, -oedi, -udi.** [Native name.] A boa constrictor.

1851 W. H. Brett *Ind. Missions in Guiana* 35 The reptile, a large camudi, sprang upon him. 1866 R. Duff *Brit. Guiana* 42 The camoedi was killed with a cutlass. 1887 *Timehri* Dec. 202 A very fine skin of a large Land-camoodie. 1898 H. Kirke *25 Yrs. Brit. Guiana* 90 A camoudie shot over him and wrapped itself round his body. 1899 Rodway *Guiana Wilds* 201 The passage of a real camoudi or boa-constrictor. 1904 W. H. Hudson *Green Mansions* ii, If dangerous creatures had existed there—tigers, or camoodis, or solitary murderous savages.

Camouflage (kæ·mufläʒ), *sb.* [Fr., f. *camouflet* (see Camouflet).] The disguising of any object used in war, such as camps, guns, ships, by means of paint, smoke-screens, shrubbery, etc., in such a way as to conceal it from the enemy; also, the disguise used in this way; freq. *attrib.* Also *fig.*, a means of putting one off the scent.

1917 *Daily Mail* 25 May 4/4 The act of hiding anything from your enemy is termed 'camouflage'. 1917 *Ibid.* 16 July 5/3 The King paid a visit to what is called a camouflage factory. 1919 *Athenæum* 23 May 360/1 'Camouflage', a word that..has met with more wear and tear in a few months than many receive in a century. 1920 Rose Macaulay *Potterism* I. iii, It's a very laudable object, and needs no camouflage.

Hence **Ca·mouflage** *v.*, to conceal by or as by camouflage.

1917 *Daily Mail* 16 July 5/3 The King saw all the latest Protean tricks for concealing or, as we all say now, for 'camouflaging' guns, snipers, observers. 1920 *Blackw. Mag.* Mar. 332/1 Number One, ensconced in the little camouflaged control. 1921 *Spectator* 23 Apr. 518/2 The house telephone..., its extremely ugly box 'camouflaged' with the pattern of the paper. 1922 W. J. Locke *Tale of Triona* ii. 21 These are real eggs, although they're camouflaged in a Chinese scramble. 1922 Inge *Outspoken Ess.* Ser. II. 99 The principate was from the first a carefully camouflaged autocracy. 1924 Galsworthy *White Monkey* II. xi, Queer how Nature camouflaged her schemes.

Camp, *sb.*[2] Add: **6. b.** A local division or lodge of a society or league. *U.S.*

1880 Tourgee *Invis. Empire* v. 413 Sometimes several 'camps' or 'dens' [of the Ku-Klux] would, independently of each other, direct a warning to be sent to the same individual. 1904 Harben *Georgians* 132 The general is invited to address nearly all the veteran camps over the State when the badges of honor are presented once a year.

VII. a. (Examples.)

a 1842 O. Russel *Jrnl.* xii. (1921) 55 The camp keeper's business in winter quarters is to guard the horses, cook and keep fires. 1861 O. W. Norton *Army Lett.* 21 Some say he expects to have us there on the fourth, but I think that's all camp talk. 1862 *Ibid.* 80, I..took my regular turn in all the work of the regiment except camp guard. *Ibid.* 110 The hardships of camp life. 1897 *Outing* (U.S.) XXX. 374/2 This style of camp-house has proved thoroughly useful. 1903 Kipling *Five Nations* 43 Heave the camp-kit over! 1921 *Spectator* 19 Mar. 356/2 We loaded our two pack-horses with camp-bedding. 1926 *Blackw. Mag.* Dec. 835/1 The camp-keeper for the day paddled us off.

b. camp-fever (later U.S. example); **camp-preacher** *U.S.*, a preacher at a camp-meeting.

1848 E. Bryant *California* ix. 128 The fatal febrile complaint known among them as '*camp-fever'. 1845 S. Judd *Margaret* I. xv. 152 In the midst of all..might be heard the voice of the *camp Preacher.

Camp, *v.*[1] Add:

2. c. *trans.* To excel or surpass in a contest. *Australian.*

1886 C. H. Kendall *Poems* 207 At punching oxen, you may guess There's nothing out can 'camp' him.

Camp, *v.*[2] Add:

1. b. With *down. lit.* and *fig.* *U.S.*

1781 T. Johnson in G. Powers *Hist. Sketches of Coos* (1841) 197 Camped down on the River Lamoille this night. 1868 Miss Alcott *Lit. Women* (1869) II. vii. 100 I'll be hanged if I camp down before her table afterward.

2. b. (Earlier U.S. examples.)

1748 in Washington *Writ.* (1889) I. 3 We camped out in ye field this night. 1803 L. Dow *Trav.* Wks. 1806 I. 229 Where I missed the trail, and was necessitated to camp out without any company. 1817 S. R. Brown *Western Gaz.* 28 Travellers are obliged to camp out two or three nights.

3. (Modern example.)

1920 Hunter *Trail Drivers of Texas* 63, I told the cook..to take the wagon and camp it up the river.

b. *intr.* To squat.

1908 *Animal Managem.* 267 The long periods camels are compelled to squat (camp) during rail or sea journeys.

Campaign, *sb.* **5. b.** (Earlier U.S. examples.)

1857 S. Bowles *Let. to H. L. Dawes* 16 Feb., We should get those amendments out of the way before we strike out for the summer campaign. 1871 Schele de Vere *Americanisms* (1872) 266 Whenever an election is to take place..a regular *campaign* is inaugurated.

attrib. 1871 *Congress. Rec.* 2 June 3543/1 It is said that we get all our campaign documents from the public printer. 1898 P. L. Ford *Hon. Peter Stirling* 281 They've flooded it [the ward] with campaign literature, which has served to light fires. 1900 *Congress. Rec.* 8 Mar. 2670/2 The wearing of a campaign button is a harmless sort of decoration. *a* 1909 'O. Henry' *Roads of Destiny* xviii. 301 New York has got the finest lot of campaign managers in the world.

Campaigned (kæmpē·nd), *ppl. a.* [f. Campaign *v.* + -ed [1].] Of estates in Ireland which came under the Plan of Campaign (see Campaign *sb.* 5 c).

1889 *Daily News* 24 July 3/3 Much light has been thrown on the grievous state of affairs..on the 'campaigned' estate of Mr. Leader in county Cork. 1892 *Sat. Rev.* 1 Oct. 381/2 Neither Mr. Dillon..nor Mr. Redmond..has as yet made it his business to stump the 'Campaigned' districts.

Campaigning, *vbl. sb.* Add: **b.** *transf.* The conducting of a political campaign.

1905 D. G. Phillips *Plum Tree* 273 A stickler for the etiquette of campaigning. *Ibid.* 276 The exigencies of campaigning, the necessity of rousing the party spirit.

Campan (kæ·mpæn, ‖ kaṅpaṅ). [Name of a town in the French Pyrenees.] A marble of which there are several varieties.

1796 Kirwan *Elem. Min.* (ed. 2) I. 115 The sp. gr. of green campan is 2,741. 1839 *Civil Eng. & Arch. Jrnl.* II. 452/2 Campan marble proper unites all these three varieties by very large stripes.

Campanularian (kæmpænīulē·riăn), *a.* and *sb.* *Zool.* [f. Campanularia + -an.] Pertaining to, a hydroid of, the genus *Campanularia.* So **Campanula·ridan.**

1883 *Science* I. 197/1 The Leptomedusæ..from the campanularian hydroids. 1888 Rolleston & Jackson *Anim. Life* 247 In addition to the possession of hydrothecae, a Campanularian differs from a Tubularian in three important respects. *Ibid.* 766 The destruction of Campanularidan colonies by parasitic Protophytes. 1898 *Naturalist* 218 The empty campanularian cups.

Campbellite. (Earlier U.S. examples. In def. for 'of Virginia' read 'in Pennsylvania'.)

1830 *Massachusetts Spy* 22 Dec. (Th.) Elder Rigdon, one of the early Mormons, is described as having been 'a Campbellite leader of some notoriety'. 1837 Peck *Gaz. Illinois* i. 73 The 'Reformers', or Campbellites as some term them. 1845 J. Palmer *Jrnl.* 23 A Campbellite preacher, named Foster, was reading a hymn.

2. *transf.* A sunfish of the Mississippi region.

1884 Goode *Nat. Hist. Aquatic Anim.* 407 The Crappie—*Pomoxys annularis*...Other names are..'New Light' and 'Campbellite' in Kentucky and Indiana.

Camper [2]. **3.** (Earlier U.S. example.)

1805 L. Dow *Trav.* Wks. 1806 II. 61 We held Quarterly-meeting on Clarke's creek; some supposed I would get no campers...This prepared the way for the Camp-meeting.

Camp-ground. *U.S.* [Camp *sb.*[2]] A camping-ground.

1805 L. Dow *Trav.* Wks. 1806 II. 94, I viewed the Camp-ground, and preparations making for the meeting. 1816 U. Brown *Jrnl.* in *Maryland Hist. Mag.* XI. 360 Their Pilot mist his way, and never could find their camp ground. 1856 Mrs. Stowe *Dred* 279 A fatted coon [was] to serve as the basis of a savory stew on the camp grounds. 1895 *Outing* Dec. 254/2 The soil of the camp-ground is light and sandy.

Camph-. Add: *ca·mphane, campha·nic acid, ca·mphate, ca·mphic acid, ca·mphoid, ca·mpholene, campho·lic acid, ca·mpholide, campholy·tic acid.*

1850 Fownes *Elem. Chem.* (ed. 3) 538 An acid body termed *campholic acid*, white, crystalline, and sparingly soluble in water, containing $C_{20}H_{17}O_3$,HO. By distillation with anhydrous phosphoric acid, this acid gives a volatile hydrocarbon, *campholene*. 1860 Watts tr. *Gmelin's Hand-bk. Chem.* XIV. 353 Camphate of potash is an uncrystallisable deliquescent syrup. *Ibid.*, Camphic acid is readily soluble in alcohol. 1872 *Jrnl. Chem. Soc.* XXV. 496 Camphic acid obtained by Berthelot's process (fusion of camphor with caustic potash)..is a syrupy liquid, which contains a feebly acid resin. *Ibid.*, The calcium salt furnishes on distillation, campholene, C_9H_{14}. *Ibid.* 821 Camphic acid is a resinous product of the action of potash on ordinary camphor. 1885 *Ibid.* XLVIII. I. 669 Camphanic acid can be most conveniently prepared by heating a mixture of 10 grams of camphoric acid with 12 grams of bromine in sealed tubes at 120°. 1896 *Ibid.* LXIX. I. 65 Pure camphanic acid melts at 201°. *Ibid.* LXX. I. 385 When an alcoholic solution of camphoric anhydride is reduced by means of sodium amalgam, the liquid being kept acid by addition of sulphuric acid, a small quantity of campholide, $C_{10}H_{16}O_2$, is obtained. 1900 *Ibid.* LXXVII. I. 251 If the saturated hydrocarbon, $C_{10}H_{18}$, of which camphor is a ketonic derivative, is spoken of as camphane. *Ibid.* 374 By the action of alkalis on the dibromide of campholytic acid, a bromohydrocarbon is produced. 1901 Dorland *Med. Dict.*, *Camphoid*, a thick paste of camphor, 20 parts, and pyroxylin, 1 part, dissolved in alcohol: used as a vehicle for the external application of medicines.

Camphor, *sb.* **3.** Add: **camphor-chest, -trunk** *U.S.*, a clothes-chest containing camphor as a protection against moths; **camphor ice** *U.S.*, a solid preparation of camphor.

1861 Mrs. Stowe *Pearl Orr's Isl.* I. viii. 59 That ar shawl your mother keeps in her *camfire chist. 1889 Mrs. Rose T. Cooke *Steadfast* v. 59 Mrs. Dennis was packing away blankets in the camphor chest upstairs. 1880 A. A. Hayes *New Colorado* xv. 197 In the alkali regions glycerine, or what is called '*camphor ice', should be used on face and hands. 1895 *Century Mag.* July 323/2 Cedar-chest and *camphor-trunk and flowered bandbox have been called upon to disgorge their treasures.

Campignian (kæmpi·nyăn), *a.* *Archæol.* Of or pertaining to *Le Campigny* (Seine Inférieure, France); characteristic of the palæolithic and neolithic remains discovered there, or the period to which these belong.

1927 Peake & Fleure *Hunters & Artists* 114 Campignian picks have been found in most parts of Europe except the extreme south. 1928 C. Dawson *Age of Gods* ix. 193 The Campignian flint-using culture of Northern France.

Campimeter (kæmpi·mĭtǝɹ). [f. L. *campus* field + -meter.] An apparatus designed to measure the field of vision, or the sensitivity of the retina to colour and space in indirect vision. Hence **Campi·metry,** the use of the campimeter, the measuring of retinal areas; **Campime·trical** *a.*

1889 *Buck's Handbk. Med. Sci.* VII. 660/1 The campimeter of De Wecker. 1901 Titchener *Exper. Psychol.* I. 9 The Distribution of Colour Sensitivity over the Retina: Campimetry. *Ibid.* 10 The campimeter must be set so high above the mixer that no shadow is cast by it upon the spot of colour seen through the circular opening. *Ibid.* 12 The experiment may be repeated with as many combinations of the colour discs as the time allotted to campimetrical work permits.

Campine (kæmpī·n). [The name of a district of Belgium.] A breed of domestic fowl, resembling the Hamburgs.

1892 Simmonds *Dict. Trade* Suppl., *Campine*, a Belgian breed of fowls. 1902 *Encycl. Brit.* XXXI. 876/1 The hardy Campine or Braekel, resembling the pencilled Hamburgh in plumage, but larger and with a single comb, and laying a large egg in great numbers. 1924 *Glasgow Herald* 26 Apr. 5 Few birds make a prettier show than the still uncommon Silver Campine, a gallant little Belgian.

Camping, *vbl. sb.* **2.** *camping-ground* (earlier U.S. examples).

1837 W. Irving *Capt. Bonneville* (1895) I. 319 Burnt patches of prairie, and deserted camping grounds. 1845 Fremont *Exped.* 261 They halted at the Archilette, one of the customary camping grounds.

Ca·mp-mee·ting. (U.S. examples.)

1803 L. Dow *Trav.* Wks. 1806 I. 220 A camp meeting, the first I ever attended, was held on Shoulder-bone-creek. 1856 Mrs. Stowe *Dred* 16 They'll all be taken with a very pious streak, to go to camp-meeting. 1878 B. F. Taylor *Between Gates* 281 In no state in the union is a camp-meeting..more exempt from interference than in California.

attrib. 1804 *Philadelphia Gaz.* 28 Sept. 3/2, 38 carts were counted on the camp-meeting ground on Sunday last. 1853 J. G. Baldwin *Flush Times Alabama* 108 His voice was..modulated according to the camp-meeting standard of elocution. 1872 Eggleston *End of World* xlii. 270 They had passed to an excited shouting of the old camp-meeting ditty.

Campo. Transfer †*Obs.* to sense 1 and add:

2. A field or plain; the Portuguese name for the grass plains of Brazil, which appear in the midst of the dense forests of the country.

1863 Bates *Nat. Amazons* (1864) 176 The country around Santarem is a *campo* region; a slightly elevated and undulating tract of land, wooded only in patches, or with single scattered trees.

Campo, var. *Campoi.

Campodean (kæmpōu·diăn), *a.* *Ent.* [f. mod.L. *Campodea*, f. Gr. κάμπη caterpillar + -φόης -formed: see -an.] Of or pertaining to the genus *Campodea* of insects.

1895 *Naturalist* 62 The rediscovery of the blind campodean *Lipura stillicidii*.

So **Campodeiform** (kæmpōudī·ifǭɹm) *a.*, resembling insects of the genus *Campodea*, used *spec.* of the larva, which resembles the adult insect of this genus.

1888 Rolleston & Jackson *Anim. Life* 150 There are two types of larval (or young) Insecta: one known as Campodeiform, from a more or less close resemblance to the genus *Campodea* among *Thysanura*; the other as eruciform, of which a caterpillar may be taken as a good example. 1895 *Nature* 19 Dec. 155 Lubbock's far bolder attempt to derive his Campodeiform larva from a Rotifer-like ancestor.

Campoi (kæmpoi·). Also **campo.** [Cantonese pronunc. of Chinese *kien* picked, selected + *pei* fire.] A fired variety of Congou tea.

1858 Simmonds *Dict. Trade, Campoi*, a kind of tea. 1860 *Ure's Dict. Arts* (ed. 5) III. 855 To the black tea belongs [*sic*] the varieties known as Bohea, Congou, Campoi, Souchong, Caper, and Pekoe.

Camp-out, *sb.* *U.S.* [f. Camp *v.*[2] 2 b.] An occasion of camping out.

1879 F. R. Stockton *Rudder Grange* xi. 190 If it gives you a good camp out, I don't mind.

Campshed (kæ·mpʃed). Also 6 **cambshide,** 6–7 **camshed(d, 7, 9 campshead.** Early variant (the second element = Shide *sb.*) of Camp-shot, whence Camp-shed *v.*, Camp-shedding (*campsheading*), q. v.

1531 *Lett. & Pap. Hen. VIII* V. 183, 2 sawiers strangers, sawing with the sawers of the ordinary waigis, as pedylles, byaders, anckers, camp shedes, grete postes, planckes, and other necesaries for the new frame of the est juttye. 1570 *Crt. Min. Surrey & Kent Sewers Comm.* (L.C.C. 1909) 85 To fill and to planke iiij roddes of the Cambshide againste the Thames. 1622 *Admir. Crt. Misc.* 1430, lf. 16 (MS.) The end of three piles at the topp of yt (*sc.* the wharf) are out of the campshead. 1632 in E. B. Jupp *Carpenters' Co.* (1887) 301 The making of Wharfes Camshedds Cranes and bridges of timber. 1841 *Civil Eng. & Arch. Jrnl.* IV. 106/1 These piles are placed from 3 to 4 feet apart from centre to centre, and have a capping or campshead 7 inches square. 1886 *Times* 26 Mar. 4 The starting boats were moored in mid-stream at Putney opposite the end of the campshed on the Fulham side.

Camptonite (kæ·mptǝnǝit). *Min.* [f. *Campton*, a town in New Hampshire, U.S.A. + -ite [1].] A name given by Rosenbusch in 1887 to certain porphyritic rocks, somewhat resembling basalt, which occur chiefly in dikes.

1895 Dana *Man. Geol.* (ed. 4) 87 Camptonyte.—Rock resembling diabase and dolerite. Consisting of hornblende (as an original mineral of the rock) and probably anorthite. 1901 *Nature* 19 Sept. 513/1 The sills of camptonite and felsite intrusive in the Cambrian rocks.

Campus (kæ·mpǝs). *U.S.* [L. *campus* field. First used at Princeton.] The grounds of a college or university; the open space between or around the buildings.

1774 in J. F. Hageman *Hist. Princeton* (1879) I. 102 Having made a fire in the Campus, we there burnt near a dozen pounds [of tea]. 1826 R. Mills *Statistics S. Carolina* 701 The whole disposed so as to form a hollow square containing about ten acres which is called the Campus. 1833 J. Finch *Trav. U.S. & Canada* 282 In front of the College is a fine campus ornamented with trees. 1879 H. J. Vandyke Jr. in *Princeton Bk.* 382 The central point of the Campus, the hub of the college world, is undoubtedly the big cannon. 1897 *Scribner's Mag.* July 23/1 Groups of men begin to thicken about the campus. 1904 H. N. Snyder in *Sewanee Rev.* Jan. 87, I am almost willing to shut my eyes to the excesses of the noisy strenuosity of the athletic mood if it bring into the campus life a warm, vital sense of college unity.

Can, *sb.*[1] Add:

1. c. A revolving cylinder open at the top to receive the sliver from a carding-machine. Also *attrib.* and *Comb.*

1825 J. Nicholson *Oper. Mech.* 382 The roving-frame..used..where mule-spinning is carried on..is termed the *can roving-frame*. 1844 G. Dodd *Textile Manuf.* i. 30 In the 'can-roving frame',..the cardings coming from two cans, and passing between the pairs of rollers, become elongated and fall into the can. 1853 *Ure's Dict. Arts* II. 697 The missing band or sliver was supplied out of a can, being the produce of a single carding-engine working into cans. 1882 *Spons' Encycl. Industr. Arts* V. 2091 The several drawings are passed into a coiling-can, by which they are loosely twisted into one. 1912 A. F. Barker & Priestley *Wool Carding* 201 A 'can' delivery apparatus. *Ibid.*, If the box is a 'can' box the sliver passes through a funnel and press rollers into a cylindrical can. *Ibid.* 228 The slivers are fed into the comb just as if they were fed out of the can-coiler from the carder.

4. can-opener *U.S.* (see quot.).

1874 Knight *Dict. Mech.*, *Can-opener*, a domestic implement for opening cans containing fruit, oysters, and what not.

Can, *v.*[1] Add:

A. 7. *Used to could*: a common phrase in certain dialects of England and in the United States for: used to be able to.

1827 J. F. Cooper *Prairie* II. xvi. 257 A small and trifling matter is it, to what I used-to-could offer in the way of bargains. 1848 Bartlett *Dict. Amer.* 372 *Used to could*, a vulgarism used in the Southern States for could formerly. 1848 A. B. Evans *Leicestersh. Words.* 1871 Schele de Vere *Americanisms* (1872) 646.

B. 6. b. To be allowed, to be given permission.

1894 T. B. Reed *Dog with Bad Name* xv. 156 Father says you can come. 1905 *Ch. Times* 3 Feb. 136/3 No one can play the organ during service time without the consent of the Vicar.

IV. *Can-doing*; *can't-doing*; *can't-eat*, *can't-work*: one who cannot eat, work, etc.

1842 J. Aiton *Dom. Econ.* (1857) 242 Let me have a first-rate goer, a good 'can do',—not that I mean in general to ride fast. 1900 *Westm. Gaz.* 15 Dec. 1/3 Achievement..is open to fewer persons than can't-doing. *Ibid.* 2/1 That the art of can't-doing has sprung from (1) the difficulty; (2) the barrenness of can-doing. *Ibid.*, Can't-eat, when applied, say, to lobster, is one thing; can't-eat, when relating to bread, is quite another. 1904 *Daily Chron.* 24 Feb. 6/5 We have then the 'Can't Works'. [1924 P. Vaux *Sea-Salt & Cordite* viii. 86 'You'll never get your intelligence away. You'll—' 'Can do!' interjected Torrington curtly.]

Can, *v.*[3] orig. *U.S.* (Earlier example.)

1861 *Trans. Ill. Agric. Soc.* IV. 511 Good fruit..is always marketable in large cities..and much will be dried, or canned, for export.

2. *slang.* To discharge from a situation: to expel from school or college; to 'cut out'. *U.S.*

1911 H. Quick *Yellowstone N.* ii. 37 Did you get canned for letting me in? 1914 Gertrude Atherton *Perch of Devil* ii. 269 They would merely be..canned—I beg pardon, fired. 1921 R. D. Paine *Comr. Rolling Ocean* vi. 99 He had a trouble in prep school and was canned, and he tutored for Princeton and flunked in Freshman year. 1926 *Ladies' Home Jrnl.* July 26 Can the bud stuff, Blank verse, old dear.

Caña (kæ·nyă). [Sp., = cane.] A spirit resembling rum made from the sugar cane.

1881 E. W. White *Cameos fr. Silver-Land* I. 40 Caña (White Rum). 1904 Gallichan *Fishing Spain* 211 A poor substitute for whisky is the spirit called caña. 1918 *Blackw. Mag.* Apr. 446/1 Supper and the tot of caña sacred to such occasions.

Canack, var. *Canuck.

Canada [1]. Add: **C. golden-rod,** *Solidago canadensis*; **C. jay,** *Perisoreus canadensis*; **C. thistle,** the creeping or corn-thistle, *Cnicus arvensis*; **C. violet,** *Viola canadensis.*

1902–9 F. S. Mathews *Field Bk. Amer. Wild Flowers* 482 *Canada golden-rod. *a* 1813 A. Wilson *Amer. Ornith.* (1831) I. 262 *Corvus canadensis*, Linnæus.—*Canada Jay. 1873 Tripp in Coues *Birds of Northwest* 222, I have never seen the Canada Jay below 9,000 feet, even in midsummer. 1901 S. E. White *Westerners* xvi. 126 Occasionally she threw a remnant to the few silent Canada jays. 1799 *Massachusetts Spy* 31 July (Th.) A torvous, stubborn, and vexatious weed, known by the name of the *Canada thistle. 1819 *Ibid.* 16 June (Th.) A labourer pointed out to me a piece of ground covered with the Canada thistle. 1860 *Congress. Globe* 23 May, App. 365/3, I should advise him to keep his Canada thistles at home. 1873 *Trans. Dep. Agric. Ill.* X. 208 'An act concerning Canada Thistles' approved and in force March 15, 1872. 1894 *Congress. Rec.* 17 July 7578/1 The Canada thistle..is said to be [as] destructive to agriculture as the Russian thistle is. 1856 A. Gray *Man. Bot.* (1860) 44 *V. Canadensis*, *Canada Violet. 1871 *Amer. Naturalist* V. 215 Pale Canada violets are blooming.

2. *ellipt.* **a.** A Canada goose. **b.** *pl.*, Shares of the Canadian Pacific Railway Company.

1894 *Outing* (U.S.) XXIV. 74/2 We see four old Canadas winging their way diagonally towards us. 1909 *Westm. Gaz.* 8 Sept. 10/3 Canadas steady.

Canader (kănē·dǝɹ). *University slang.* [f. Canad(ian + -er [6].] A Canadian canoe.

1893 H. W. Greene in *Oxford Mag.* 18 May, Beneath the Magdalen shadows, We'll drift in a 'Canader' When afternoons are warm. 1899 A. D. Godley *Lyra Frivola* 24 O it's Youth in a Canader with the willow boughs to shade her. 1919 R. B. Dawson *Light & Shade in Sarawak* iv. 33 'Get in carefully, old man', said he; 'it's like climbing into a Canader at Oxford.'

Canadian. Add in etym. [after F. *canadien*] and quots.:

1568 Hacket tr. *Thevet's New found World* lxxvi. 123 *marg.*, The amiable maners of these Canadiens. *Ibid.* 124 *marg.*, How these Canadians doe chase the dere & other wilde beastes. *c* 1789 *Encycl. Brit.* (1797) IV. 76/2 The commodities required by the Canadians from Europe are, wine, or rather rum;..linen; and wrought iron. *Ibid.* 77/2 The many specimens of profit to be made by the Canadian trade, at last induced the public to think favourably of it. 1836 *Penny Cycl.* VI. 215/1 The Canadians further urge that the province contains no aristocracy. 1855 Kingsley *Glaucus* 74 The Canadian Ledum. 1925 J. Joly *Surface-Hist. Earth* viii. 131 The mountains themselves have long ago been base-levelled by denudation to the existing peneplanes of the Canadian Shield, where they extend over an area of at least a million square miles.

b. C. golden-rod, violet (see *Canada [1]); **C. poplar,** the cotton-wood, *Populus canadensis.*

c 1816 Rees *Cycl.* s.v. *Solidago*, The Canadian golden-rod (Solidago canadensis). 1832 D. J. Browne *Sylva Amer.* 253 [Cotton wood] was probably introduced into France from Canada; such at least is its origin indicated by the name Canadian poplar. 1845–50 A. Wood *Class-bk. Bot.* 177 *V. Canadensis.* Canadian Violet.

B. *sb.*[2] A Canadian horse.

1876 *Rep. Vermont Board Agric.* III. 132 The result of the cross of the Morgan upon this Canadian has been a great improvement to the Canadian.

Canadianize (kănē·diănǝiz), *v.* [f. Canadian + -ize.] *trans.* To render Canadian in character. Hence **Cana:dianiza·tion. Cana·dianism,** the condition of being Canadianized; the spirit of the Canadians; a Canadian idiom.

1899 *Daily News* 17 Nov. 6/6 He declares that Afrikanderdom is the very opposite to Canadianism. 1902 *Monthly Rev.* Oct. 55 When he calls himself 'French-Canadian', he simply wants to differentiate his racial origin from that of his English, Scotch, or Irish fellow citizens, who, in his mind, are but partially *Canadianised*. 1906 *Westm. Gaz.* 20 May 12/1 It is quite likely that what is called Canadianism may grow more pronounced with the growth of population and the expansion of the country. 1925 *Contemp. Rev.* Nov. 605 They are in process of rapid 'Canadianisation'. 1926 *Brit. Weekly* 20 May 130/5 [He] had a flat in Charing Cross-road, London, from which he cultivated his virile Canadianism. 1928 *Daily Express* 4 Dec. 10/3 Perhaps one of the most descriptive Canadianisms is the word 'kick' instead of thrill.

Canaigre (kănē·gǝɹ). [Mexican Sp.] A species of dock, *Rumex hymenosepalus*, which is grown on sandy soils from Texas to Lower California, and whose roots are rich in tannin; also, the tannin obtained from this plant.

1884 *Encycl. Brit.* XVII. 401/2 The cañaigre has long been known to possess powerful tanning properties. 1901 *Westm. Gaz.* 21 Oct. 5/1 A plant indigenous to New Mexico, Arizona, and Lower California, known as Rumex hymenosepalus, or 'canaigre'. 1902 *Encycl. Brit.* XXV. 629/1 Considerable promise attends..the experiments upon canaigre as a source of tannin.

Canal, *sb.* Add:

1. b. *transf.* A passage or groove.

1891 *Daily News* 3 Feb. 7/3 One..had ploughed along the flesh, and made its exit again, the 'canal' of the wound being larger than the opening.

2. (See quots.)

1848 Dunglison *Med. Lex.* (ed. 7), *Canal, Hyaloid*, a cylindrical passage, described by M. J. Cloquet as formed by the reflection of the hyaloid membrane into the interior of the vitreous body around the nutritious artery of the lens. ..*Canal of Schlemm*, a minute circular canal..situate at the point of union of the cornea and sclerotica. 1890 Billings *Med. Dict.*, *Canal of Cloquet*, hyaloid canal. 1907 *Practitioner* Aug. 323 The lymph then passes into the canal of Cloquet, a tubular lymph space running from the posterior part of the lens capsule to the optic disc. *Ibid.*, The aqueous now filters through the corneo-iridic angle into the venous plexus, which forms the canal of Schlemm.

6. b. Any of the markings on the planet Mars, which are considered by some astronomers to be due to vegetation, which in turn presupposes the presence of water.

A misleading rendering of It. *canali* (Schiaparelli) = channels.

1888 *Edin. Rev.* Jan. 26 Indications derived as to the nature of the mysterious Martian canals. 1891 E. Dunkin *Midnight Sky* (new ed.) 253 Networks of dark lines, to which Schiaparelli has given the name of 'canals' [orig. It. *canali* channels], were noticed by him, in 1877 and 1882, to overspread the continents..of the planet.

10. canal incline, canal-lift, an incline or elevator used instead of a lock for transferring canal-boats from one level to another; **canal-moulding** (see quot.).

1882 L. F. Vernon-Harcourt *Rivers & Canals* I. 102 *Canal inclines are similar to inclines so common in mines. 1902 *Encycl. Brit.* XXVI. 555/1 Canal inclines were early adopted on canals where loss of water in lockage was of importance. 1858 Simmonds *Dict. Trade*, *Canal-lift. 1876 *Min. Proc. Instit. Civ. Eng.* XLV. 107 Hydraulic Canal Lift at Anderton, on the River Weaver. 1902 L. V. Lockwood *Col. Furniture Amer.* 56 The moulding..is formed by bordering an applied strip about half an inch wide with a bead-moulding. This is sometimes known as a *canal-moulding.

Canal, *v.* Add: *intr.* To make canals. *trans.* To make (a river) navigable by furnishing it with locks like a canal.

1828 *Deb. Congress* 9 Jan. 225 To canal across lofty mountains must be considered as a physical impossibility. 1905 *Daily Chron.* 29 July 9/2 The river..has now been canalled, and is controlled by fourteen locks.

Canalet (kænăle·t). [f. Canal *sb.* + -et. Cf. It. *canaletto.*] A small canal.

1892 *Q. Rev.* Jan. 394 Ship-timbered houses are a frequent evidence of former neighbouring canalets.

Canaliform (kănæ·lifǭɹm), *a.* [f. L. *canalis* Canal + -form.] Having the form of, or resembling, a canal.

1826 Kirby & Sp. *Entomol.* xlvi. IV. 340 *Canaliform*..when it [*sc.* the postscutellum] is a deepish elongate channel running from the postdorsolum to the abdomen. 1830 R. Knox *Béclard's Anat.* 132 The villosities do not appear conical, or cylindrical, or canaliform. 1903 *Westm. Gaz.* 16 Sept. 2/1 The 'canaliform illusion'. 1926 H. Macpherson *Mod. Astron.* 75 Canaliform appearances.

Canalization. Add:

3. *transf.* A furnishing with (underground) ducts or channels for the conveyance of cables, etc.

1889 *Daily News* 7 Oct. 3/1 This is what Mr. Crompton, borrowing a French expression, calls his system of undersurface 'canalization'.

Canalize. Add:

3. *transf.* To furnish with underground ducts or culverts for the conveyance of cables, etc.

1889 *Daily News* 7 Oct. 3/1 He has 'canalized' nearly the whole length of the principal streets in the South Kensington-Knightsbridge region.

4. *fig.* To lead in a desired direction, so as to control or regulate.

1922 J. R. Muir *Short Hist. Brit. Commw.* II. ix. v. 359 The development of means for 'canalising' the nation's unspent wealth. 1928 *Britain's Industrial Future* (*Liberal Ind. Inquiry*) II. Argt. 61 The stream of national investment..should be canalised by a Board of National Investment.

b. *intr.* To take a certain direction, to form a channel.

1927 *Observer* 13 Nov. 8/5 A latent crisis in civilisation, a crisis which should have canalised into a religious revolution.

Canalling, *vbl. sb.* (Earlier U.S. examples.)

1813 *N. Hampshire Gaz.* 1/4 The subject of Canalling is revived in Philadelphia. 1819 E. Dana *Geogr. Sketches* 20 The operation of canalling and locking the falls has lately been commenced. 1834 *Boston* (U.S.) *Post* 8 Aug. 2/3 Canalling Extraordinary.—..A small boat containing a family of 12 souls..passed through..on the Erie Canal.

Canapé (kæ·năpi). [Fr.] A piece of bread, fried in butter, on which anchovies, chicken, or mushrooms are served.

1890 Mrs. Beeton *Cookery Bk.* 4/1 Anchovy Canapés. 1908 *Daily Chron.* 10 Apr. 7/5 As an appetiser nothing is better than a canape of chicken.

Canard. Add:

2. A type of aeroplane in which the elevator, rudder, etc., are in front of the main lifting surface.

1918 H. Barber *Aeroplane Speaks* 137 *Canard*, literally 'duck', the name which was given to a type of aeroplane of which the longitudinal stabilizing surface was mounted in front of the main lifting surface. Sometimes termed 'tail-first' aeroplanes, but such term is erroneous. 1928 C. F. S. Gamble *North Sea Air Station* Introd. 11 These monoplanes were of the 'Canard' (or 'tail first') type.

3. A bright, deep blue, like the colour which is found on a duck's wing.

1902 *Daily Chron.* 13 Dec. 8/4 The peculiar bright, yet deep, blue known in Paris as 'canard'. 1908 *Westm. Gaz.* 22 Feb. 13/2 *Canard*—a new shade of blue inspired by the lovely patch of iridescent greeny blue that occurs on a duck's wing. 1923 *Daily Mail* 21 June 1 Over 40 shades including Ivory,..Apricot, Canard.

Canarese (kænărī·z), *a.* and *sb.* Also **kanarese.** [f. *Canara* (see below) + -ese.] **A.** *adj.* Of or pertaining to Canara in western India, or its people. **B.** *sb.* **1.** A native of Canara. **2.** The language of Canara, belonging to the Tamulic class of the Dravidian family, nearly allied to Telugu. Also called Karnata.

1875 *Encycl. Brit.* III. 513/2 Marâthi and Kanarese are both spoken. 1880 *Ibid.* XII. 428/2 In the different parts of the [Hyderabad] territory the Marathi, the Kanarese, and Telugu languages are spoken. 1920 *Public Opinion* 26 Nov. 521/2 Instruction in the following tongues, Hindustani, Kaffir, Kanarese. 1921 *Q. Rev.* Oct. 328 That Indian kings were deified after death is placed beyond doubt by a Kanarese inscription.

Canarian (kănē·riăn), *a.* and *sb.* [f. Canary *sb.* + -ian.] **A.** *adj.* Of or pertaining to the Canary Islands. **B.** *sb.* A Canary Islander.

1902 *Temple Bar* CXXVI. 86 The trend of the Canarian character. *Ibid.* 87 The lotos-eating Canarians. 1922 D. A. Bannerman *Canary Islands* i. 13 Carrying with him a number of the Canarians as captives. *Ibid.* iii. 57 The commoner forms of Canarian bird-life.

Canariensis (kănēri·e·nsis). [app. popular alteration of the specific name *canariense* in *Tropæolum canariense*, a former systematic name of *T. aduncum.* (*Canariensis* occurs as the specific name of canary seed, *Phalaris canariensis*, and canary wood, *Persea canariensis.*)] Canary-creeper, *Tropæolum aduncum.*

1901 'Lucas Malet' *Counsel of Perfection* iv, Vivid scarlet and orange flowers of climbing nasturtiums and canariensis. 1908 *Daily News* 21 Sept. 4/2 They frequently attack both the nasturtium..and the canariensis.

Canarine (kæ·nărin). *Chem.* [f. Canary + -ine [5].] A compound obtained by oxidizing potassium sulphocyanide with chlorate of potassium in the presence of hydrochloric and sulphuric acids, which is used to produce a fast yellow dye.

1884 *Jrnl. Chem. Soc.* XLVI. 797 Prochoroff of Moscow found that perthiocyanogen may be employed as a colouring matter, and has patented the preparation of this compound under the name of 'canarin'. 1893 *Athenæum* 15 July 100/2 Canarine, obtained from potassium thiocyanate, is employed in dyeing cotton yellow from an alkaline bath, when it serves as a mordant for basic colours.

Canary, *sb.* Add: **3. b.** At Eton College, a chorister.

1896 A. D. Coleridge *Eton in Forties* 194 The Colets and Lord Tenterdens who started in life as 'canaries'.

5. b. A gold coin, so called from its colour.

1890 *Pall Mall Gaz.* 8 May 6/2 'Canaries', or promissory notes, were returned for considerably over £2,000.

5. c. A convict. *Australian slang.*

1827 P. Cunningham *N. S. Wales* II. 117 Convicts of but recent migration are facetiously known by the name of *canaries*, by reason of the yellow plumage in which they are fledged at the period of landing. 1870 T. H. Braim *New Homes* ii. 72 The prisoners were dressed in yellow—hence called 'Canary Birds'. 1890 'R. Boldrewood' *Col. Reformer* vi. 49 Can't you get your canaries off the track here for about a quarter of an hour and let my mob of cattle pass?

7. canary-moss, canary-weed, a name for the lichens, *Roccella tinctoria*, etc., which yield litmus and archil.

1884 Miller *Plant-n.*, *Parmelia perlata*, Canary Moss.

Canary-bird. Add: **3.** *attrib.*: **canary-bird plant,** canary-creeper.

1864 Grindon *Brit. & Gard. Bot.* 153 The light and graceful Canary-bird plant, or *Tropæolum Canariense.*

Canaster. (Later example. See also Knaster.)

1879 F. R. Stockton *Rudder Grange* i. 17, I had..taken to a tall pipe and canaster tobacco.

Canaveg, variant of Candavaig.

1847 Stoddart *Angler's Comp.* 366 A variety of the salar, termed canavegs.

Cancel, *sb.* **3.** Add: Sense b (= *Cancellans) is now the prevailing use (as in quot. 1906–8 below); more explicitly *cancel-leaf.*

1906–8 Madan in *Trans. Bibliogr. Soc.* IX. 62 Cancels are newly-printed leaves intended to take the place of cancelled leaves. 1908 Pollard & Greg *Ibid.* 44 When we speak of a cancel nobody else ever knows whether we mean the leaf cut out and destroyed or the leaf inserted as a substitute. If we are careful we distinguish between a cancelled leaf and a cancel-leaf, but the person to whom we are speaking probably does not catch the subtle distinction. A change of terminology might be desirable. 1914 R. B. McKerrow *Ibid.* XII. 299 In one case the leaf has been simply cut out, but in all the others it is replaced by a cancel-leaf. 1924 R. W. Chapman in *Library* Ser. IV. V. 249 Notes on Cancel Leaves.

Cancel, *v.* Add: **2.** Also with *out.*

1924 Hichens *After the Verdict* II. xix, Her will, so it seemed to her, had been cancelled out by little Clive's death.

b. Delete † and add following quot.:

1925 *Wireless Weekly* July 449/1 There will be a position where the effects of the two field coils cancel out.

Cancellandum (kænsĕlæ·ndǝm). *Printing and Bibliography.* Also anglicized **ca·ncelland.** [neut. gerundive (sc. *folium* leaf) of L. *cancellare* Cancel *v.*] A leaf, or portion thereof, for which another is substituted. So **Ca·ncellans** [pres. pple.], the substituted leaf, etc.

1923 R. W. Chapman in *Library* Ser. IV. IV. 173 The function of a signature on a cancel is not to distinguish the *cancellans* from the *cancellandum*, but to tell the binder where the cancel is to be placed. 1927 McKerrow *Introd. Bibliogr.* 223 It is convenient to have a means of distinguishing clearly between the original sheet or portion of a sheet which is intended to be cancelled and what is intended to replace it. We may call the former the *cancellandum* or 'cancelland', the latter the *cancellans* or simply 'cancel'.

Cancrizans (kæ·ŋkrizænz). *Mus.* [med. L., pres. pple. of *cancrizare* to walk backwards, f. *cancr-, cancer* crab: see -ize.] A canon in which the theme or subject is repeated backward in the answer.

1880 Grove *Dict. Mus.* I. 302/2 Sometimes a canon is both cancrizans and by contrary motion. 1926 A. B. Smith *Studies & Caprices* 53 Inversions, diminutions, cancrizans exist only on paper.

Candidate, *v.*[2] *U.S.* (Examples of verb.)

1884 *Century Mag.* June 308/1 Let him put the question to some [choir-singers] who every spring have to candidate for a situation. 1909 *Springfield Weekly Republ.* 2 Sept. 14 Mr. Seccombe candidated in the Goschen church last spring.

Candidating, *vbl. sb.* *U.S.* (Earlier example.)

1848 Lowell *Biglow P.* Ser. I. viii. 122 The can'idatin' line, you know, 'ould suit me to a T...So I'll set up ez can'idate fer any kin' o' office.

Candle, *sb.* Add:

1. d. Also, with prefixed numeral, = *candle power* (see *7).

1880 J. W. Urquhart *Electr. Lt.* 279 A 2,000-candle light. *Ibid.* 282 A hundred-candle Sugg gas-burner.

e. An arrangement of carbons in an electric light.

1877 *Design & Work* III. 20 M. Paul Jablochkoff..has worked out his results in the form of an electric candle. 1882 *Dredge's Electr. Illum.* 530 When a candle is almost entirely burnt out, the voltaic arc and the incandescent portion of the carbons are brought into very close proximity to the strip.

5. i. *A lighted candle*: put symbolically for a place of social gathering or entertainment.

1928 Lady Walburga Paget *Linings of Life* I. 248 Lady G. Codrington's silver hair and dowagery face appeared under every lighted candle. 1928 *Correspondent.* Not long ago I heard a lady say of a man-about-town 'he went to every lighted candle'.

6. *candle-dish, -shade*; *candle-lit* adj.

1899 *Pall Mall Mag.* Jan. 77 Two silver *candledishes. 1890 *Pall Mall Gaz.* 22 Oct. 2/3 This *candlelit old hall. 1916 H. G. Wells *Mr. Britling* ii. § 9 Equally unexpected was the supper on a long candle-lit table without a cloth. 1780 *Hickey's Bengal Gaz.* 8 Apr. (Y.) Borrowed last Month by a Person or Persons unknown..a very elegant Pair of *Candle Shades. 1914 H. James *Middle Years* (1917) 76 Milford Cottage, with its innumerable red candles and candle-shades.

7. candle-balance, an instrument used in photometric research for measuring a burning candle's rate of consumption; **candle-bomb,** a sphere which explodes in the heat of a candle, giving out a brilliant light; **candle-bush,** a South African plant, *Sarcocaulon Burmanni*, so called from the readiness with which it burns; **candle-foot,** the intensity of light produced by a standard candle at the distance of one foot, a unit of illumination; **candle-metre,** the illumination of a standard candle at the distance of one metre; **candle power,** the illuminating power of an electric lamp, etc., reckoned in terms of the light of a standard candle.

1876 *American Gas-light Jrnl.* 3 July 6 (Knight, Suppl.) *Candle balance. 1868 *Model Steam Engine* 14 In *Candle Bombs the stem is long enough to admit of being fixed into the fat. 1890 Annie Martin *Home Life Ostrich Farm* 60 The *kerzbosch*, or *candle-bush, a stunted, thorny plant, if lighted at one end when in the green state, will burn steadily just like a wax candle. 1902 *Encycl. Brit.* XXVIII. 83/2 In order that street surfaces may be well lighted, the minimum illumination should not fall below 0·1 *candle-foot. 1928 *Sunday Dispatch* 30 Dec. 7/5 (L.C.C. Regulation) The lighting maintained in no part of the auditorium shall be less than ·025 candle-foot. 1877 *Engineering* XXIV. 333 In measuring the *candle power of the light produced by each machine. 1880 J. W. Urquhart *Electr. Lt.* 257 The rigid exclusion of all reflected or diffused light..will..account in a great degree for the lower candle power obtained in these experiments. *Ibid.* 278 Six electric lights of 480-candle power each. 1894 Salomons *Electr. Lt. Install.* (ed. 7) II. 248 The amount of energy required to incandesce the lamp determines its candle-power efficiency. 1908 *Westm. Gaz.* 27 Oct. 6/1 Employing the smaller candle-power lights upon circuits of high voltage.

Candleberry. (Earlier example.)

1731 Catesby *Nat. Hist. Carolina* (1754) I. 13 The broad-leaved Candle-berry Myrtle.

Candleless (kæ·nd'llès), *a.* [f. Candle *sb.* + -less.] Without a candle or candles.

1906 *Westm. Gaz.* 20 Jan. 5/1, I am left soapless, candleless, and forlorn. 1920 Santayana *Char. & Opin. U.S.* i. 6 Like those candlesticks, probably candleless, sometimes displayed as a seemly ornament in a room blazing with electric light.

Ca·ndle-li·ghting. (Later U.S. examples.)

1696 S. Sewall *Diary* I. 439 Just about Candle-lighting the news of it is brought to Town. 1784 *Maryland Jrnl.* 17 Sept. Advt. (Th.) Said School to begin at Candle-lighting, and continue till Nine o'Clock, P.M. 1835 Longf. *Pr. Wks.* (1857) 355 A short time after Candle-lighting. 1869 Mrs. Stowe *Oldtown Folks* xxxiv. 449 Designing to bring up at the red school-house..at 'early candle-lighting'. 1888 *Amer. Humorist* Aug. (Farmer) They were late, for the meeting was also appointed for early candle lighting.

Ca·ndler. [f. Candle *v.* 2.] One who tests eggs by the light of a candle or an electric bulb.

1906 *N. Y. Even. Post* 5 June 9 The candlers say ten hours' work on a stretch is harmful to their eyesight. 1921 *Dict. Occup. Terms* (1927) § 449 Egg candler.

Candle-wood. 1. *U.S.* (Earlier examples.)

1634 W. Wood *New Eng. Prosp.* (1865) 19 Out of these Pines is gotten the candlewood that is so much spoken of. 1645 *Springfield* (Mass.) *Rec.* I. 164 The bounds that is set for gathering candlewood into the woods. 1650 *Connecticut Publ. Rec.* I. 214 No particular person..shall buy of the Indians..any timber, candlewood, or trees of any sorte.

Candroy, variant of *Canroy.

Candy, *sb.*[1] **2.** Add: *candy-girl, -merchant, -shop, -stick*; **candy-pull** (earlier example); also as vb.; **candy-pulling** *U.S.* = *candy-pull.*

1855 M. M. Thompson *Doesticks* xxxiii. 299 With what an affectionate air couldst thou..box the ears of the little *candy-girl. 1863 Mrs. Whitney *Faith Gartney's Girlh.* xxxvi, The shivering little candy-girl, threading her way..among the throng. 1870 'Fanny Fern' *Ginger-Snaps* 61 To the delight of these youngsters and the *candy-merchants. 1873 Eliz. S. Phelps *Trotty's Wedding Tour* 139 'A *candy-pull', Rye suggested. *Ibid.* 181 Nuts too. Once I *candy-pulled some of my own. 1854 Shillaber *Mrs. Partington* 20 *Candy pullings, with their customary consequences to broad shirt-collars and cheeks sweeter than molasses. 1886 *Harper's Mag.* June 93/2 A considerable portion of the refined sugars find their way to the *candy shops. 1863 B. Taylor *H. Thurston* xviii. (1864) 234 Rows of glass jars full of *candy-sticks.

Candy, *v.* Add: **4. b.** To smear with candy.

a 1906 'O. Henry' *Trimmed Lamp* etc. 94 Sticky children tumbled, howling under his feet, candying his clothes.

Cane, *sb.*[1] Add: **1. c.** Canes collectively. *U.S.*

1836 J. Hall *Statistics of West* ii. 27 The inhabitants drive their cattle to the cane in the autumn. 1847 in D. Drake *Life Kentucky* i. 14 Their practice was..to..lodge separately among the cane, which flourished in great luxuriance. 1854 Bartlett *Pers. Narr. Texas*, etc. II. xxix. 187 The mules ate with avidity the cane which grew on the river's banks.

9. a. *cane-seat* (attrib. with *chair*); **b.** *cane-carrying.*

1852 Mundy *Antipodes* (1857) 27 They laughed at the *cane-carrying soldiers. 1924 *Glasgow Herald* 16 Apr. 10, I had not imagined..that cane-carrying was peculiar to some nations and not others. 1851 C. Cist *Cincinnati* 205 *Cane-seat and rocking chairs are made.

10. cane bottom *U.S.*, low ground abounding in canes; **cane-carrier** *U.S.* (see quot.); **cane colour,** the colour of cane as applied to pottery ware, or pottery of this colour; also as adj.; so **cane-coloured** *a.*; **cane-fruit,** a commercial name for such fruit as raspberries and blackberries which grow on canes; **cane grass** *U.S.*, the plant *Arundinaria macrosperma*, forming the cane-brakes of the southern United States; **cane knife** *U.S.*, a large knife used in cutting cane; **cane land** *U.S.*, land on which sugar-cane flourishes; **cane meadow** *U.S.* = *CANE-BRAKE; **cane-mill** *U.S.* (example); **cane-rat**, a South African rodent, *Thryonomys swinderenianus*; **cane-stab**, a puncture made by a cane-stem; **cane swamp** *U.S.*, a swamp overgrown with canes; **cane-telescope**, a small telescope attached to a walking-stick; **cane-top** *U.S.* (see quot.); **cane trash** (also, see quot.); **cane-work**, strips of cane interwoven and used to form the backs of chairs and other articles of furniture; **cane-worker**, one who makes articles of cane.

1819 E. DANA *Geogr. Sketches* 188 The river *cane bottom land. 1833 in *Life Benjamin Lundy* (1847) 37 The land here [on the Brazos River] is cane-bottom. 1833 B. SILLIMAN *Man. Sugar Cane* 31 The canes are brought up to the mill by means of a machine called the *Cane carrier. 1866 METEYARD *Jos. Wedgwood* II. p. xxiv, *Cane-colour Inkstand. 1875 — *Wedgwood Handbk.* Gloss. 393 *Cane-colour*, ware the colour of cane...Cane-colour was applied both to ornamental and to useful purposes. 1787 JOS. WEDGWOOD *Catalogue* 2 Bamboo, or *cane-coloured bisque porcelain. 1865 L. JEWITT *The Wedgwoods* 311 The 'bamboo, or cane-coloured' ware. 1845 W. G. SIMMS *Wigwam & Cabin* Ser. I. 15 Thickets of low stunted shrubbery, *cane grass, and dwarf willows. 1798 A. ELLICOTT in *Life & Lett.* (1908) 159 [The country] could only be explored by using the *cane knife and hatchet. 1887 *Harper's Mag.* July 272/1 The children..squabbling for the possession of one cane-knife to split kindlers. 1831 MRS. HOLLEY *Texas Lett.* (1833) 51 Hence when a colonist wishes to describe his land as first rate, he says it is all peach and *cane land. 1791 W. BARTRAM *Trav. Carolina* etc. (1792) 231 The most extensive Cane-break [*Footnote*: *Cane meadows, so called by the inhabitants of Carolina, &c.]. 1833 B. SILLIMAN *Man. Sugar Cane* 30 The *cane mill consists of three cast iron cylinders. 1876 H. BROOKS *Natal* 116 The *cane-rat or ground-rat, that feeds upon the sugar-canes, is properly more of a porcupine than a rat. 1849 PRITTS *Mirr. Border Life* 434, I got a *cane stab in my foot which occasioned my leg to swell. 1737 WESLEY *Jrnl.* 2 Dec., They are here of three sorts—cypress, river, and *cane swamps. 1817 S. R. BROWN *Western Gaz.* 11 The Alabama is margined with cane swamps. 1884 KNIGHT *Dict. Mech.* Suppl., **Cane Telescope*, an instrument with seats for the eye and object glasses upon a walking stick. 1833 B. SILLIMAN *Man. Sugar Cane* 12 But a part of the planting is done with *cane tops, or that portion of the Cane which is rejected in cutting it for the mill. 1790 CASTLES in *Phil. Trans.* LXXX. 349 Burning the *cane trash (or straw of the cane). 1858 TERESA VIELE *Following the Drum* 53 Divans of *cane-work. 1887 FORBES *Insulinde* 25 The backs of the open canework chairs. 1858 SIMMONDS *Dict. Trade*, **Cane-worker*, a maker of articles in rattans, Spanish and other canes; a basket-maker. 1901 *Daily Chron.* 24 Aug. 5/6 W.Y...cane-worker, pleaded guilty. 1921 *Dict. Occup. Terms* (1927) § 472 *Caner, cane worker*,..fills in framework of baskets, wicker furniture, and other basket ware by interweaving cane.

Ca·ne-brake. *U.S.* [f. CANE *sb.*[1] 1 + BRAKE *sb.*[2]] A tract of land thickly overgrown with canes (*Arundinaria macrosperma*).

1784 D. BOONE in C. B. Hartley *Life* (1865) 335 We lay in a thick cane-brake by a large fire. *Ibid.* 336, I..often reposed in thick canebrakes to avoid the savages. 1796 B. HAWKINS *Lett.* 15 Continued up 5 miles to a canebrake; here I encamped. 1817 S. R. BROWN *Western Gaz.* 125 The wild lands are finely timbered with pine,..willow, and occasionally impervious cane brakes. 1849 PRITTS *Mirr. Border Life* 545 While roving carelessly from canebrake to canebrake..they were alarmed by a party of Indians. 1885 *Outing* (U.S.) Oct. 64/2 A large track, which led into the canebrake,..was evidently made by some large animal.

attrib. 1869 *Overland Monthly* III. 129 When you see a man..get a cold boiled sweet potato..and a piece of cane-brake cheese..you may be certain he is a North Carolinian. 1909 *Century Dict.* Suppl., Cane-brake region. Cane-brake soil.

Caney, variant of CANY *a.*

Canezou (ka·nzū). *Hist.* [Fr., of unknown origin.] A woman's blouse-like garment of muslin or cambric.

1827 *Lady's Mag.* Sept. 510/2 A canezou spencer of embroidered muslin. *Ibid.* 511/1 Muslin canezous over high dresses. 1893 GEORGIANA HILL *Hist. Engl. Dress* II. 241 A cambric canezou..with sleeves full to the elbow. 1898 *Daily News* 26 Sept. 6/4 When the Restoration came in 1815,..Fleur-de-lys appeared on everything...The canezou replaced the hideous spencer.

Canfieldite (kæ·nfīldəit). *Min.* [f. the name of F. A. *Canfield*: see -ITE[1].] A rare sulphide of silver and tin.

1893 *Amer. Jrnl. Sci.* Ser. III. XLVI. 113 There can be no doubt that canfieldite and argyrodite have the same chemical composition.

Cangan (kæ·ngăn). Also **kangan**. A coarse cotton cloth woven in China.

1858 SIMMONDS *Dict. Trade*, *Cangan, Kangan*, a piece of coarse Chinese cloth, thinly woven, 19 inches broad, and 6 yards long, which has a fixed currency value.

Cango (ka·ngo). *S. Afr.* [Name of a district in South Africa.] A local name for a variety of Cape brandy.

1880 F. G. BROWNING *Fighting & Farming S.A.* 119 Two fellows had been drinking pretty freely (principally 'cango' and 'Cape smoke'). 1889 H. A. BRYDEN *Kloof & Karoo* 84 Cango..is the best kind of colonial-made brandy; it is of a rich yellow colour, is produced in the Oudtshoorn district, and when matured, is really a very reasonable substitute for the more expensive foreign liquors.

Canine, *a.* Add: **1. c.** *Canine letter* = DOG'S LETTER.

1890 HOWELLS *Shadow of Dream* 24 'Hermia' said Faulkner, sounding the canine letter in her name with a Western strength.

Canities (kăni·ʃiī). *Path.* [L.] Whiteness or greyness of the hair.

1848 DUNGLISON *Med. Lex.* (ed. 7). 1890 *Science* 3 Oct. 186/1 The sudden change in canities, when due to violent emotions.

Cank (kæŋk). *local.* The name in the Midland coalfields for a hard ferruginous sandstone. Also *cankstone.*

1833–4 J. PHILLIPS *Geol.* in *Encycl. Metrop.* (1845) VI. 587/2 Some less regular sandstone beds, called 'Cankstone', approach very nearly to the nature of the ganister or calliard rocks of the coal strata. 1860 *Engl. & For. Mining Gloss.* (ed. 2) 34 *Cank*, whinstone. 1877 [see GALLIARD *sb.*[2]].

Canned, *ppl. a.* Add: (Earlier U.S. example.)

1859 R. B. MARCY *Prairie Traveller* 31 Canned vegetables are very good for campaigning.

b. *fig.* Well-preserved. *U.S.*

1893 *Harper's Mag.* LXXXVI. 969/2 Many 'canned' reputations have been destroyed, and many maligned characters have been lifted to honour.

c. Intoxicated, 'tight'. *slang.*

1921 *Blackw. Mag.* Feb. 157/1 By the dinner hour he was pretty well 'canned'. 1926 J. J. CONNINGTON *Death at Swaythling Court* iv. 70 Being rather canned, he sticks the candle on the table, and forgets all about it. 1928 S. VINES *Humours Unreconciled* v. 71 'Good God!' Podler said to himself, 'the woman's canned!'

2. Having a can tied to the tail.

1903 A. ADAMS *Log Cowboy* iii. 37, I was half a mile in the lead, burning the earth like a canned dog.

Cannella, variant of CANELLA.

1836 J. M. GULLY *Magendie's Formul.* (ed. 2) 91 Cannella powder. 1887 A. M. BROWN *Anim. Alkaloids* 53 A precipitate of a cannella colour.

Cannelon (kanloṅ). *Cookery.* [Fr.] (See quots.)

1892 *Encycl. Pract. Cookery* (ed. T. F. Garrett) I. 281/1 Cannelons..are composed chiefly of nouille paste in the shape of small pipes about 3 in. long and ½ in. in diameter. They are generally made by rolling the paste out very thin, cutting into strips 3 in. by 2 in., and rolling up round small pieces of wood, which are removed after baking. *Ibid.* 281/2 Roll the Cannelons on the board to a cork shape. 1926 *Mrs. Marshall's Cookery Bk.* 542 Cannelon of Beef.

Canner. Add:

b. A beast fit only for canning. *U.S.*

1892 *Pall Mall Gaz.* 8 Dec. 2/1 'Canners', which is the designation of all animals collected at the Chicago and other markets, that are refused by the butchers as unfit for their trade. 1906 *Daily Chron.* 13 June 7/3 A 'canner'..is an animal with little, if any, fat on it, in fact often nothing more than skin and bone. 1911 H. QUICK *Yellowstone N.* xii. 303 A collection of skips an' culls an' canners that was sure a fraud on the Injuns.

c. A machine for canning food.

1928 *Daily Express* 6 July 5/5 Until now canning has been beyond me for want of a canner.

Cannery. Add: *attrib.*

1907 *Westm. Gaz.* 25 Sept. 10/3, 130 Oriental cannery hands. 1908 *Daily Chron.* 24 Sept. 8/4 The cannery ship.

Ca·nnibal[2]. [? Corruption of *Camdeboo*: see Pettman *Africanderisms* (1913).] *Cannibal stinkwood*, a South African name for *Celtis kraussiana.*

1859 R. J. MANN *Natal* 156 (Pettman) There is a variety of this wood known under the name of the Cannibal stinkwood. 1877 LADY BARKER *Yr.'s Housekpg. S.A.* 325 What rhyme or reason, what sense or satire can there be in such a name as 'Cannibal Stink-wood'?—applied..to a graceful, handsome tree whose bark gives out an aromatic..perfume.

Cannon, *sb.*[1] **7. b.** Substitute def.: *transf.* An act of cannoning (see CANNON *v.* 3 b); a collision between persons or animals (as in racing).

1806–7 [in Dict.]. 1876 *Coursing Cal.* 35 Bellini came best out of a cannon, and never let Hawkseye have a look in, except to kill.

9. Add: **cannon-fodder** [tr. G. *kanonenfutter*; cf. Shakespeare's *food for powder* (1 Hen. IV, IV. ii. 72)]: men regarded merely as material to be consumed in war.

1888 *N. E. D.* s.v. 1928 *Observer* 11 Mar. 12/4 Frederick's Ambassador, vetoing the sale of cannon-fodder under pain of civil war in Germany.

Cannon-ball. Add: *attrib.*

1920 TILDEN *Lawn Tennis* 146 A fast cannon-ball smash.

Canoe, *sb.* Add: **2.** See also PADDLE *v.* 2 b.

3. *canoe load*; *canoe-man* (earlier U.S. examples); **canoe-shell**, a shell shaped like a canoe, spec. *Scaphander lignarius.*

1691 *Annals of Albany* (1850) II. 115 Ye def't accused him of stealing 1/2 *canoe load of water millions. 1753 in Washington *Writ.* (1889) I. 15 They were sent from New-Orleans with..8 Canoe-Loads of Provisions. 1809 A. HENRY *Trav.* 63 Several canoe-loads of fish were exported. 1774 D. JONES *Jrnl.* (1865) 49 Our *canoe-men..made themselves half drunk. 1809 A. HENRY *Trav.* 109 The goods..would have been saved if the canoe-men had called them French property. *c* 1711 PETIVER *Gazophyl.* vi. Tab. liii, Small Indian *Canoe-shell...It's of an odd Shape, and sticks to larger Shells. 1850 MISS PRATT *Common Things Sea-side* 216 The Tufted Canoe-shell.

Canoeable (kănū·ăb'l), *a.* [f. CANOE *v.*] Capable of being navigated in a canoe.

1755 L. EVANS *Anal. Map Colonies* 28 'Tis canoable [*sic*] about twenty miles farther. 1756 J. MAURY in J. Winsor *Miss. Basin* (1895) 216 The navigable, or rather canoeable parts of the rivers.

Canon (kæ·nən), *v.* [f. CANON *sb.*[1] 7.] *trans.* To treat (a musical theme) in canon fashion. Also *absol.* or *intr.*

1894 DU MAURIER *Trilby* I. 41 They..fugued and canoned and counterpointed [that simple melody]..and exhausted all its possibilities of beauty. 1927 *Music & Lett.* July 347 The phrases [of bird singing] were more often alike and several times canoned one into the other in a most delightful way.

Cañon, *sb.* (Earlier U.S. examples.)

1834 A. PIKE *Sketches* 20 Two cañons ran up into the bosom of the ridge (by which word *cañon* the Spaniards express a deep, narrow hollow among the mountains). 1846 R. B. SAGE *Scenes Rocky Mts.* (1859) 151 The Platte forces its way through a barrier of table lands, forming one of those striking peculiarities incident to mountain streams, called a cañon.

b. **cañon-finch** (see quot.).

1881 *Amer. Naturalist* XV. 212 The canon finch (*Pipilo mesoleucus*).

Cañon (kæ·nyən), *v.* [f. CAÑON *sb.*]

1. *intr.* To form, or flow in, a cañon.

1851 MAYNE REID *Scalp-hunters* v, I soon came to a bend, where the stream, after running parallel to the ridge, swept round and cañoned through it. 1853 — *Rifle Rangers* xiv, We had struck the water at a point where the stream cañoned!

2. *trans.* To pierce with cañons.

1886 J. S. DILLER in *8th Ann. Rep. U.S. Geol. Surv.* 1886–87 I. 426 Deeply cañoned by numerous streams.

Cañoned, *a.* [f. CAÑON *sb.*] Formed into a cañon: intersected by a cañon or cañons.

1846 E. BRYANT *What I saw in California* (1849) 303 The shore is hilly, and *cañoned* in some places. 1846 in W. H. Emory *Notes Mil. Reconnoissance* (1848) 443 We reached the 'Ocate'; as it is *cañoned*, that is, is enclosed with high rocky walls, we were forced to go two miles up stream in order to reach the crossing.

Canonizable (kæ·nənəizăb'l), *a.* [f. CANONIZE *v.* + -ABLE.] Worthy of canonization.

1913 *Nation* (N.Y.) 16 Jan. 58 A fictitious Crispi—..wise, righteous, canonizable.

Canonry. Add:

2. An establishment of canons or canonesses.

1877 SKENE *Celtic Scot.* II. 243 Boys and youths who are educated in the canonry. 1925 C. S. DURRANT *Flem. Mystics* I. ix. 130 John Busch himself travelled across Germany with three nuns of Bronope to reform an Austin Canonry, that of Marienburg, near Hildesheim.

Canoodle (kănū·d'l), *v. slang.* (orig. *U.S.*) Also †**conoodle**. [Origin obscure.] *intr.* To indulge in caresses and fondling endearments. Also formerly *trans.* to persuade by endearments. Hence **Canoo·dler, Canoo·dling** *vbl. sb.*

1859 SALA *Tw. round Clock* 11 a.m., A sly kiss, and a squeeze, and a pressure of the foot or so, and a variety of harmless endearing blandishments, known to our American cousins..under the generic name of 'conoodling'. 1864 — in *Temple Bar* Dec. 40 He is an adept in that branch of persuasive dialectics known as 'conoodling'. He will 'conoodle' the ladies..into the acquisition of whole packages of gimcrack merchandise. 1879 *Punch* 15 Mar. 117/2 Then he and the Matchless one struggle, snuggle, and generally conoodle together rapturously. 1894 *Mexborough & Swinton Times* 2 Feb. 2/7 The money which he had lent in return for the privilege of canoodling his daughter. 1894 *Idler* Sept. 207 She is not to be overcome by courting or *canoodling*. 1903 'MARJORIBANKS' *Fluff-Hunters* 49 Though each couple occupied a skiff, they used it for purposes of canoodling. *Ibid.* 172 Two canoodlers tied up in knots and fastened with sealing-wax at the lips. 1921 H. WALPOLE *Young Enchanted* III. iii, She's in there. She'll be out in a minute. I'm off on some business of my own for an hour or two, so you can canoodle as much as you damned well please.

Canophilist (kănǫ·filist). [irreg. f. L. *canis* dog + -PHIL + -IST.] A lover of dogs.

1879 W. L. LINDSAY *Mind in Lower Animals* I. I. iii. 24 A distinguished author, well known as a canophilist. 1889 *Macm. Mag.* Apr. 463/1 A great comfort to those who devote themselves to canine pets, and to canophilists generally (a pretty new word).

Canopic. Add: *Canopic jar*, = Canopic vase.

1893 BUDGE *Mummy* 171 At each of the four corners or sides of the bier, is placed one of the so-called Canopic jars. 1898 *Nature* 17 Nov. 50/2 Sets of Canopic jars, in which the principal intestines of deceased were placed.

Canopy, *sb.* Add:

2. b. Also in phr. *under the* (or *God's*) *canopy*, used as an intensive = 'on earth'. *U.S.*

1862 *Congress. Globe* 23 May 2309/3, I do not suppose that any one under God's canopy would make any such decision. 1869 MRS. STOWE *Oldtown Folks* xi. 131 What under the canopy are you up to now, making such a litter on my kitchen floor? 1886 *Harper's Mag.* Sept. 581/2 But where under the canopy did you drop from?

4. A hood over a carriage or motor car. Also *attrib.*

1906 W. W. BEAUMONT *Motor Vehicles* II. 150 A..car with a closed tonneau body or limousine with canopy top and wind guard. 1907 *Westm. Gaz.* 19 Nov. 4/2 A 28-h.p. landau with canopy extension.

5. *Naut.* A light awning over a boat.

1867 SMYTH *Sailor's Word-bk.*, *Canopy*, a light awning over the stern-sheets of a boat.

Canroy (kæ·nroi). Also **candroy**. A machine, used in calico-printing establishments, through which cotton-cloth is passed before printing. Hence **Ca·nroyer**, one in charge of a canroy.

1836 *Penny Cycl.* VI. 151/2 If they are not calendered, they are run through a machine called in Lancashire the *candroy*, which spreads them smoothly in the act of rolling them upon a cylinder. 1896 DUERR *Bleaching & Calico-printing* 26 After being sewn, each batch is taken to the shearing and winding-on machines, generally called a 'canroy'. Sometimes the shearing machine and canroy are two separate machines. 1921 *Dict. Occup. Terms* (1927) § 384 *Canroyer*, a calenderer minding a canroy calender, having two iron rollers through which cloth is passed to break down stiffness after starching.

Cant, *sb.*[1] Add:

4. b. One segment of the rim of a wooden cog-wheel.

1874 KNIGHT *Dict. Mech.*

12. cant-board, also, a division in a shoot of a flour-bolt, which separates different grades of flour; **cant-chisel**, a strong chisel bevelled on one side only; **cant-file**, a file with cutting faces at an obtuse angle to each other; **cant-line**, a rope taken over the head of a lower mast in a sloping direction; **cant-rail**, a horizontal timber bevelled to fit the angle of the roof which supports the roof of a railway carriage; **cant-splice**, a splice made by cutting off a piece of rope and joining its ends to the body of the rope so as to make a loop.

1874 KNIGHT *Dict. Mech.*, **Cant-board*, a division in the conveyer-box of a flour-bolt, to separate grades of flour or offal. **Cant-chisel*, a long and strong chisel with the basil and a rib on one side. *Ibid.*, **Cant-file*, a file having the shape of an obtuse-angled triangle in its transverse section; used in filing the inner angles of spanners and wrenches for bolts with hexagonal and octagonal heads. 1867 SMYTH *Sailor's Word-bk.*, **Cant-line*, synonymous with *girt-line*, as to cant the top over the lowermast-head. 1871 *Saddl. Harn. & Carriage Builder's Gaz.* 1 Dec. 12/2 Levers and links, aided by springs, to throw open the '*cant rails' and 'uprights' of carriage heads by inside pressure. 1874 KNIGHT *Dict. Mech.* s.v. *Splice*, The *cut* or **cant* splice is made by cutting a piece from a rope and laying open the ends of the strands.

13. cant-fall, tackle connected with the cant-blocks of a whale-boat.

1867 SMYTH *Sailor's Word-bk.*, *Spike-tackle and cant-falls*, the ropes and blocks used in whalers to sling their prey to the side of the ship.

Cantabrian (kæntǣ·briăn), *a.* and *sb.* [f. L. *Cantabria*: see -IAN.] **A.** *adj.* Pertaining to the Cantabri, an ancient warlike tribe of northern Spain, or to Cantabria, the region formerly occupied by them. **B.** *sb.* **1.** One of the ancient Cantabri. **2.** The language of the Cantabrians.

1746 AKENSIDE *Hymn to Naiads* 144 The rough Cantabrian surge. 1797 *Encycl. Brit.* (ed. 3) IV. 122/1 The Cantabrians had waged war with the Romans for upwards of 200 years. *Ibid.* 122/2 The Cantabrian does not appear to have any affinity with any other known language. 1813 *Q. Rev.* Oct. 256 Classes and Families of Languages...Indo-european. ..Cantabrian. Sclavic. 1861 *Chambers's Encycl.* II. 572/1 Their bravery was evinced in the Cantabrian war, a six years' contest with the Romans. *Ibid.*, *Cantabrian mountains*, the general name of the several ranges of coast and boundary mountains. 1904 T. R. GLOVER *Virgil* vii. 145 In the course of the Cantabrian war he wrote to the poet from Spain letters full of playful entreaties.

Cantabrigian. Add: Also (one) belonging to Cambridge, Mass. *U.S.*

1887 *Harper's Mag.* Mar. 589/1 Mrs. Sainsbury was Boston-born, as well as Mrs. Pasmer, and was Cantabrigian by marriage. 1893 W. K. POST *Harvard Stories* 26 The New Haven men struggled to the Cantabrigian twenty-yard line.

Cantal (kæ·ntăl). [Name of a district in the south of France.] *Cantal cheese*, a hard cheese made chiefly in the Auvergne, France.

1890 J. MACDONALD *Stephens's Bk. Farm* (ed. 4) IV. 517/2 The Cantal cheese..is an extremely important one upon the Continent. 1902 *Encycl. Brit.* XXVII. 355/2 Cantal cheese ..is a product of the midland districts, and is made barrel-shape.

Cantaloup. Delete 'Chiefly *U.S.*' and add quots.:

1739 MILLER *Gard. Dict.* II. s.v. *Melo*, The Cantaleupt [*sic*] Melon:..the Flesh..is of a rich vinous Flavour. 1763 MILLS *Pract. Husb.* IV. 169 The Cantaleupe..is held in the greatest esteem by all the curious in Europe. 1777 COWPER *Let. to J. Hill* 23 Oct., The melon is a crimson Cantalupe. 1786, 1813 [see ROCK *sb.*[1] 9 e]. 1890 *Daily News* 18 Sept. 3/1 The very first item on the list is 'iced cantaloupes'. 1929 S. ELLIOTT NAPIER in *Times* 2 Aug. 14/1 Melon or bailer shells..are almost exactly the same shape, size and colour as rock melons, or canteloups.

Cantarist (kæ·ntărist). *Antiq.* [ad. med.L. *cantarista*, f. *cantaria* CHANTRY: see -IST.] A chantry priest.

1800 *Gentl. Mag.* Mar. 201 The almshouse..for one chaplain, or cantarist, and three almsmen. 1894 FISHWICK *Hist. Lanc.* ix. 213 Many of these cantarists, as they were called, were now pensioned off for life.

Cantate (kæntǣ·ti, kæntā·te). [a. L. *cantate* sing ye, the first word of the psalm.] The ninety-eighth psalm (ninety-seventh in the Vulgate) used as a canticle (e.g. as an alternative to Magnificat at Evening Prayer in the Church of England).

Cantate Sunday, the fourth Sunday after Easter, so called because the introit for that day is taken from this psalm.

c 1550 BALE *K. Johan* (Camden) 65 Now may we synge Cantate, And crowe Confitebor with a joyfull Jubilate. 1880 *Grove's Dict. Mus.* I. 305/2 The 17th canon of the council of Laodicea appointed lessons and psalms to be read alternately; and on this principle the 'Cantate' is to be considered as a 'responsory psalm' coming between the lessons. *Ibid.*, 'Cantate Services' are..rare.

Cant-dog. (Earlier U.S. example.)

1850 S. JUDD *R. Edney* 272 Leaning on a cant-dog, he could talk with Melicent and Barbara.

Canteen. Add:

1. b. In extended use.

1908 *Parish Councils* 13 At Limpsfield (Surrey) the school manager appointed by the parish council personally started a canteen, which fed 60 children who came from a distance.

3. b. A chest or case containing a set of table knives, forks, spoons, etc.

1895 *Army & Navy Co-op. Soc. Price List* 756 Canteens for wedding presents, yachting, college use, &c.

Canter, *sb.*[1] Add: **1. b.** In a sawmill, a machine placed over the carriage and used to cant or roll over the log on the carriage in making the first cuts; a canting-machine (*Cent. Dict.* Suppl. 1909).

Canthar (kæ·nþăı). [ad. L. *cantharus.*] = *CANTHARUS 1.

1873 LELAND *Egypt. Sketch-Bk.* 66 Old pateræ and canthars.

Cantharus, kantharos (kæ·nþărŏs, -ǫs). Pl. **canthari, kantharoi.** Also **cantharos.** [L. *cantharus*, Gr. κάνθαρος.]

1. *Classical Antiq.* A large, two-handled drinking cup.

1853 *Dict. Archit.*, *Cantharus*, the name of a peculiarly shaped drinking vessel particularly consecrated to the personifications of Bacchus. 1875 ELIZA METEYARD *Wedgwood Handbk.* 393 Cantharos. 1885 *Encycl. Brit.* XIX. 180/1 Silver Cantharus from Rhodes, with gold mounts.

2. A fountain or laver placed in the courtyard of an ancient church for the use of worshippers.

1842 GWILT *Archit.* Gloss. 943. 1902 *Encycl. Brit.* XXXII. 626/2 A court enclosed the whole; near the porch was a laver (*cantharus*) for the ablutions of intending worshippers.

Cant-hook. Add: **2. b.** 'A sling with hooks for raising and tilting casks, to empty them'. *U.S.*

1874 KNIGHT *Dict. Mech.* s.v.

Canting, *vbl. sb.*[1] Add: **d.** *attrib.*

1883 M. P. BALE *Saw-Mills* 9 Where the logs are few in number and light, they may be got into position with some good hand canting dogs. 1909 *Cent. Dict.* Suppl., *Canting-machine*, same as canter.

Cantino (kantī·no). [It.] The treble string upon a violin, the E string.

1876 STAINER & BARRETT *Dict. Mus. Terms.*

Cantle, *sb.* **5.** (Later U.S. examples.)

1903 A. ADAMS *Log Cowboy* ii. 15 The indispensable slicker [waterproof]..securely tied to our cantle strings. 1920 MULFORD *J. Nelson* xxv. 284 The cantle of the saddle, striking the barrel of the Winchester, tore the weapon from its owner's hands.

Ca·ntly, *adv.*[2] [CANT *sb.*[3] 4 c.] In canting phraseology; in slang.

1828 *Niles' Reg.* 27 Sept. XXXV. 66/2 This is cantly called 'talking to Bunkum'. 1890 *Field* 1 Nov. 655/2 They become open professionals, and 'go for the pieces', as it is cantly termed. 1906 CHESTERTON *Dickens* xii. 288 In attempting to decide whether an author will, as it is cantly expressed, live, it is necessary to have [etc.].

Canton, *sb.*[1] Add:

2. c. A corner of a building, emphasized by the presence of projecting quoins or pilasters.

Ca·nton, *sb.*[3] The name of the city in southern China used *attrib.* to denote various manufactured articles, as *Canton crape, flannel, matting.*

1860 *Texas Almanac* 244 Shirts, Carpets, Canton-Matting, shoes. 1889 *Century Dict.* s.v. *Matting*, Canton matting. Same as India matting. *Ibid.* s.v. *Crape*, Canton crape, China crape. 1889 *Anthony's Photogr. Bull.* II. 381 A good quality of canton flannel.

Cantonese (kæntŏnī·z), *a.* and *sb.* [f. *Canton*, China + -ESE.] **A.** *adj.* Of or pertaining to Canton or its inhabitants. **B.** *sb.* **a.** An inhabitant of Canton. **b.** The dialect of Canton.

1857 *Bombardment of Canton* 20 Between you and ourselves, the Cantonese, there have been relations of friendship. 1857 'ASIATIC' *China Question* 10 The Cantonese stir will be for the benefit of humanity. 1861 *Chambers's Encycl.* II. 575/2 The Cantonese are notorious for their turbulence and hatred of foreigners. 1877 EITEL (*title*) A Chinese dictionary in the Cantonese dialect. 1883 J. D. BALL (*title*) Cantonese made Easy. 1893 *Athenæum* 27 May 668/1 The book of English phrases compiled by a Cantonese for the use of those of his countrymen who aspire to become Hong Kong 'boys'. 1921 *Outward Bound* July 17/1 He converses freely in Hakka, Cantonese, Mandarin.

Cantoris (kæntō·ris). [L., genitive of *cantor* CANTOR.] Of or belonging to the cantor or precentor. *Cantoris side, stall*, the side occupied by the cantor, the north (exceptionally, the south) side. In *Music* used to indicate that side of the choir in antiphonal singing. (Correlative to DECANI.)

1724 CROFT *Thirty Select Anthems* 118. 1760 BOYCE *Cath. Mus.* I. 67. 1880 *Grove's Dict. Mus.* I. 306/1. 1894 [see DECANI].

Cantus (kæ·ntŏs). *Mus.* Pl. **cantus** (-ūs). [L.] A song or melody, especially ecclesiastical melody; also, the principal voice.

1590 WHYTHORNE (*title*) Cantus. (Bassus.) Of Duos, or Songs for two voices...Of the which, some be playne and easie to be sung, or played on Musicall Instruments. 1597 MORLEY *Introd. Mus.* 20 In this *Cantus* there is no difficultie if you sing your Semibreefes three Minyms a peece. 1666 J. FORBES (*title*) Cantus, Songs and Fancies, To Three, Four, or Five Parts, both apt for Voices or Viols, With a brief Introduction to Musick. 1887 *Athenæum* 25 June 842/1 The work is written for cantus, altus, and tenor—a rather unusual combination of voices.

Canuck (kănv·k). *U.S.* Also **Kanuck** (**K'nuck**), **Canack.** [App. f. the first syllable of *Canada.*]

1. A Canadian; *spec.* a French Canadian.

1855 *Knickerbocker Mag.* Apr. XLV. 341 [We gave] our donkey into the keeping of a lively Canuck. 1857 *Ibid.* Jan. XLIX. 40 My grandfather..got fifty [old French crowns] at once from a Kanuck in trading. 1884 *Harper's Mag.* June 125/1 A 'Kanuck' or French Canadian. 1895 *Century Mag.* Sept. 674/2 That would be convenient over the line among the Canucks. 1917 MATHEWSON *Sec. Base Sloan* 243 La Croix was a thick-set, hook-nosed Canuck.

2. A Canadian horse or pony. Also *attrib.*

1860 HOLLAND *Miss Gilbert's Career* ii. 29 I'll hang on the tail of it and try legs with that little Kanuck of his. 1862 *Congress. Globe* 29 Apr. 1867/3 They went..from St. Louis to Canada to buy the little Canuck ponies at $130 apiece.

Canvas, *sb.* **8.** Add: **canvas duck** *U.S.* = CANVAS-BACK 2; **canvas-top** *U.S.*, a wagon with a canvas tilt.

1813 PAULDING *Sc. Fiddle* v. (1814) 102 Twelve canvas ducks, at morning play, By that discharge all found their grave. 1901 S. E. WHITE *Westerners* xix. 174 Molly was by now..used to the narrow confines of her canvass-top.

Canvas-back. 2. (Earlier U.S. examples.)

1782 JEFFERSON *Notes Virginia* 130 Besides these [birds] we have..The Widgeon, Sheldrack, or Canvas back, Black head. 1809 W. IRVING *Knickerb.* II. 282 The gastronomical merits of..canvas-back ducks.

Canvass, *sb.* Add: **4. b.** A scrutiny of votes in an election. *U.S.*

1888 BRYCE *Amer. Commw.* II. App. 682 If all the returns have not been received, the canvass must be postponed... Upon the completion of said canvass and returns, the said Board shall immediately certify the same. 1903 *N. Y. Sun* 20 Nov. 5 The official canvass of the vote in the borough of Brooklyn was practically finished yesterday.

Canvass, *v.* **4. e.** Add: Also, in early use, to challenge or dispute (an election). Now *U.S.*

1791 *Massachusetts Mag.* Sept. 590/1 General Jackson is canvassing the election of General Wayne. 1792 JAY *Corr.* (1891) III. 428 Tiogo will most probably not be canvassed, as the box was delivered by a person deputed by a deputy. 1888 BRYCE *Amer. Commw.* II. App. 682 The officers..whose duty it is..to receive and canvass the returns from the several precincts of their respective counties..must then and there proceed to canvass the returns.

Canvasser. 1. d. (Recent U.S. example.)

1904 *Newark Even. News* 25 Nov. 5 Governor Murphy has appointed..as the State Board of Canvassers...The board will..officially determine the number of votes which were cast for the different candidates.

Canvassy (kæ·nvăsi), *a.* [f. CANVAS *sb.* + -Y[1].] Made of canvas, resembling canvas.

1892 *Dram. Opinions* 13 Jan. 1/1 The scenery..does not come up to the Lyceum standard, being more palpably *canvassy* than usual. 1903 *Westm. Gaz.* 12 Feb. 4/2 That nice crisp softness in the way they hang peculiar to things canvassy. 1923 *Blackw. Mag.* July 4/1, The material was quite loosely woven and canvassy.

Cany, *a.* **2.** (Earlier U.S. example.)

1831 MRS. HOLLEY *Texas Lett.* (1833) 57 Cane-break creek or Caney, as it is usually called, winds its way through this tract.

Canyon, *sb.* (Earlier example in form *kenyon.*)

1843 FARNHAM *Trav. Gt. Western Prairies* I. 267 About midway from the Great Gap and the Kenyon of the south Fork of the Platte. *Ibid.* 268 This Kenyon terminates thirty miles above the Gulf.

Ca·nyon, *v.* [f. the sb.] *trans.* To cut into canyons.

1879 MISS BIRD *Lady's Life in Rocky Mts.* (1885) 195 Rocks, cleft and canyoned by the river.

Caoine (kī·nə), Irish form of KEEN *sb.*

1916 STANFORD & FORSYTH *Hist. Music* (1925) 212 The principal styles [of Irish folk-music] are the songs, reels, jigs, caoines.

Caoline, var. of KAOLIN.

1895 BARING-GOULD *Noémi* x. 140 On the tops of the plateau..lies a film of caoline.

Cap, *sb.*[1] Add:

4. e. Also *spec.* the cap, of a special form or colour, denoting selection as member of a representative team, crew, etc.; hence, one who is awarded such a cap.

1892 [see *BIG-SIDE]. 1895 *Cassell's Family Mag.* June 518/2 He may possibly be one of the crew, and the vision of the Light Blue cap flits before his enraptured eyes. 1898 KIPLING *Day's Work, Brushwood Boy* (1904) 366 The 'new caps' of the team. 1902 *Football Who's Who 1901–2* 133 Cowan, James...Earned caps and medals galore. 1906 *A. Gibson & Pickford's Assoc. Football* IV. 28 He was eight seasons with the grand old club, and won his English cap. 1923 *W. J. A. Davies' Rugby Football* Pref. 16 In the season of 1911 he gained his Navy cap for the first time.

6. Delete †*Obs. slang* and add quots.:

1902 *Westm. Gaz.* 9 Dec. 3/2 Masters of Hounds are naturally averse to that method of enriching their treasuries which consists in taking a 'cap' from strangers. 1903 *Daily Chron.* 6 Mar. 5/2 The Cheshire Hunt..instituting a 'cap' of £1 from all non-subscribers (excepting landowners and farmers). 1928 *Daily Mail* 5 Nov. 12/3 If a visitor goes out with a pack like the Quorn he will have to pay a cap of £3 3s. per day.

10. d. *Ornith.* The pileum or top of a bird's head, especially when distinctively coloured.

1890 COUES *Ornith.* 142 'Top of the head' is a collective term for all the upper surface, from base of bill to nape, and laterally to about the level of the upper border of the eyes; this is the *pileum* or 'cap'..; it is divided into three portions.

e. The calyptra of mosses.

1864 OLIVER *Elem. Bot.* 281 The sporange is covered at first by a cap (*calyptra*). 1900 B. D. JACKSON *Gloss. Bot. Terms.*

11. c. (Also *blue cap.*) In coal-mining, a circle of bluish flame appearing above and around the wick of a safety lamp when a dangerous quantity of fire-damp is present.

1849 GREENWELL *Coal Tr. Gl.* (Eng. Dial. Dict.). 1877 *Encycl. Brit.* VI. 72/2 When a lighted candle is exposed in a non-explosive mixture of this gas [*sc.* fire-damp], the flame gradually elongates, forming a conical cap, floating above the wick. 1883 GRESLEY *Gloss. Coal-m.* s.v. *Blue Cap*, To carry on work in an atmosphere which shows a cap is unsafe. 1887 *Good Words* 99/1 The marsh gas is revealed..by the appearance of what is known as a 'cap' upon the flame. 1893 LUPTON *Mining* 284 If there is 2 per cent. of fire-damp in the atmosphere, a small blue-cap may be observed.

12 and 13. Various technical uses.

1884 KNIGHT *Dict. Mech.* Suppl., *Cap*, a short terminal section of a pipe, with a removable stopper called a plug. 1886 *Cassell's Fam. Mag.* 638/1 An outer cap protecting the point [of a fountain pen]. 1895 BURNS *Gloss. Techn. Terms* 18 *Cap and lining*, in gasfitters' work a joint used for connecting a composition pipe to an iron pipe. 1902 *Westm. Gaz.* 4 June 5/1 The effect of fitting shot or shell with a forged steel cap. 1905 *Kynoch Jrnl.* Jan.–Mar. 37 A bullet with a thick brass cap in front. 1906 *Life Story Waterman's Fountain Pen* 6 A..Waterman Ideal..consisting..of a barrel, cap, point section and feed. 1913 F. C. MORGAN *Artill. Matériel* (ed. 7) 105 Caps for A.P. shell are made of mild steel. The cap supports the point of the shell, and weakens the plate, thus reducing the work to be done by the undamaged point. 1919 *Conquest* I. 93/1 The reservoir, cap, [etc.] of a fountain pen. 1921 *Dict. Occup. Terms* (1927) § 254 *Cap maker* (electric lamps); a draw press hand making brass caps for electric lamps in a die press.

13. c. Mining. *In (the) cap*: see quots.

1884 KNIGHT *Dict. Mech.* Suppl. s.v., A vein is 'in the cap' when it is much contracted. 1889 P. MILFORD *Dict. Mining Terms* (ed. 2) 14 A mine when the vein matter is barren or when the vein is pinched, or contracted, is said to be 'in cap'.

14. b. The paper percussion cap of a toy pistol (formerly called *amorce*).

1877 *Design & Work* III. 521/3 Those small caps.. called French amorces. 1883 *B'ham Weekly Post* 15 Dec. 7/5 These toy pistol caps..were made of a very dangerous explosive. 1921 *Dict. Occup. Terms* (1927) § 149 *Snap cap maker*, tends machine which makes snap caps, for toy pistols.

18. a. *cap-border* (U.S. example).

1878 MRS. STOWE *Poganuc P.* xxii. 246 A thin old delicate face, with its aureole of white hair and its transparent cap-border.

19. cap-bar *Spinning*, an attachment to a drawing frame supporting the bearings of draft rolls; **cap-cell** *Bot.* (see quot.); **cap-chamber**, the chamber containing the percussion cap in cartridges; **cap-frame**, a type of spinning-frame in which the guide for the yarn takes the form of a cap; **cap-man**, a man who inspects the lamps attached to miners' caps; **cap-screw**, a screw with a cubical head.

1897 W. S. TAGGART *Cotton Spinning* II. 91 It was formerly the practice to make the *cap bars of cast-iron. 1898 *Ibid.* III. 241 The cap bar, for keeping the top rollers in position, is pivoted..so that it can readily be moved over out of the way when the rollers require attention. 1882 *cap-cell [in Dict.]. 1900 B. D. JACKSON *Gloss. Bot. Terms*, *Cap Cells*, the upper sister-cells of the embryo-sac in the ovule which are compressed as the embryo-sac develops and for a time figure as a cap on its apex. 1875 *Encycl. Brit.* I. 745/2 The cases [of cartridges] are made of sheet brass, with a thick base disc containing a *cap chamber, cap, and anvil. 1890 *Treat. Ammunition* 387 A brass cap chamber, pierced with a fire hole. 1884 W. S. B. MCLAREN *Spinning* (ed. 2) 160 For fine Botany yarns the *cap frame is always employed. 1921 *Dict. Occup. Terms* (1927) § 365 *Spinner, cap; cap frame tenter*; minds a spinning frame in which guide over spindle is in form of a cap. *Ibid.* § 947 **Capman*; a lampman who attends to lamps attached to miners' caps; used only in a non-fiery mine. 1884 KNIGHT *Dict. Mech.* Suppl., **Cap Screw*, a machine screw with a cubical head, used for screwing on the cylinder head.

Cap, *v.*[1] Add:

1. c. To award (a player) his cap (*CAP *sb.*[1] 4 e); to select a representative player *for* a country, etc.

1902 *Football Who's Who 1901–2* 131 He was first capped as far back as 1893 against Ireland. 1906 *A. Gibson & Pickford's Assoc. Football* II. 65 He was nine times 'capped' for England. 1925 *Glasgow Herald* 31 Mar. 6 No fewer than seven of the players are capped against Scotland for the first time.

4. c. (Earlier and later U.S. examples.)

1804 *Lancaster* (Pa.) *Intelligencer* 21 Feb. (Th.) Your correspondent caps the climax of Misrepresentation. 1891 *Fur, Fin & Feather* Mar. 158 A section of country..that caps the climax for quail, especially along the little creeks.

7. b. To free from husks.

1906 H. D. PITTMAN *Belle of Blue Grass C.* ix. 129 Close beside her sat a great basket of fresh strawberries which must be capped before she could set out for church.

10. To take cap-money (see CAP *sb.*[1] 19).

1843–54 R. S. SURTEES *Handley Cross* xxxiv. (1901) I. 372 Mr. Jorrocks allowed Pigg [his huntsman] to cap when they killed.

Capable. Add: **B.** *sb.* A capable person.

1902 *Contemp. Rev.* Mar. 410 A few hundred serious-minded capables.

Capacitance (kăpæ·sităns). *Electr.* [f. CAPACITY + -ANCE.] Electrostatic capacity.

1916 *Standardiz. Rules Amer. Inst. Electr. Engineers* 18 It is..recommended that..the term 'Capacitance' be used when referring to the electrostatic capacity of a device. *Ibid.* 53 Machinery of Low Capacitance.

Capacitive (kăpæ·sitiv), *a.* *Electr.* [f. CAPACITY + -IVE.] Pertaining to electrostatic capacity.

1916 *Standardiz. Rules Amer. Inst. Electr. Engineers* 97 Capacitive Coupler. An apparatus which, by electric fields, joins portions of two radio frequency circuits.

Capacity. Add:

1. d. The power of an apparatus to store static electricity, measured by the quantity of electricity which can be forced into the apparatus by the pressure of one volt; also, any apparatus which gives additional capacity, as *capacity cage, earth.*

1903 *Westm. Gaz.* 25 Feb. 5/1 The oscillatory circuit consists of a light wire cage, or 'capacity', suspended in the air at no great height, together with a condenser and two flat capacities near the ground, one of which may be the earth itself. 1906 A. F. COLLINS *Manual of Wireless Teleg.* 209 *Capacity cage*, a cylindrical cage made of wire and placed at the top of the aerial wire to give it additional capacity. 1913 *Daily Mail* 3 Mar. 5 If you are particularly bothered by the proximity of wires it is worth while to try the effect of substituting a 'capacity earth' for the ordinary earth connection. The capacity is a wire or wires stretched out below and parallel to the aerial above but insulated from the earth and connected to the 'earth' terminal of the receiver.

e. Ability to provide accommodation (for the discharge, transport, etc.) of a certain amount or volume; also *spec.* in *Phys. Geogr.*, ability to carry away detritus, measured by the quantity which passes a given point in a given time.

1885 *Engl. Illustr. Mag.* Sept. 813/2 The Nene does not discharge its waters so rapidly as it ought...Cut off the bends if you want a more efficient discharging capacity. 1892 *Jrnl. Soc. Arts* XLI. 96/2 The capacity of the present tunnel is sufficient to provide 100,000 horse-power applied to the turbines. 1900 *Ibid.* XLVIII. 835/1 The capacity of the larger canal would be over 20,000,000 tons a year. 1902 WEBSTER Suppl.

11. *attrib.* and *Comb.*, *capacity-catching.*

1904 *Westm. Gaz.* 17 Sept. 7/1 A certain groundwork of school knowledge, enough..to serve for what Professor Huxley called 'capacity catching'. 1905 *Daily Chron.* 31 Jan. 4/5 If you are out for what Mr. Sidney Webb would style 'capacity-catching'.

b. passing into *adj.* = That reaches or rises to the utmost capacity.

1920 *Times* (weekly ed.) 17 Sept., Profits are not unduly large in view of the fact that it is necessary to play almost to capacity business. 1925 *Times Lit. Suppl.* 27 Aug. 554/1 Both the play and film are now drawing capacity houses in London. 1926 *Westm. Gaz.* 11 Aug., Unless the play has a long run with 'capacity' houses. 1928 *Morning Post* 20 Oct. 10/6 A 'capacity' audience greeted the appearance of M. Ravel. 1929 *Ibid.* 28 Aug., Swimming baths, of course, attracted capacity crowds throughout the day.

Cap-box. [CAP *sb.*[1] 14.] A box for holding percussion caps.

1843 FARNHAM *Trav. Gt. Western Prairies* I. 2 Bullets were moulded; powder-horns and cap-boxes filled.

Cape, *sb.*[2] Add:

3. b. *Cape and sword* (also *cape and cloak*): phr. used to characterize romantic fiction or drama with a more or less historical background. Cf. *CLOAK *sb.* 6.

Cf. F. *roman de cape et d'épée.*

1898 *Westm. Gaz.* 3 Nov. 2/3 Plays of poetry and passion, Cape and cloak, are all the fashion. 1898 *Daily News* 4 Nov. 3/5 The drama of the 'Cape and Sword'. 1910 *Westm. Gaz.* 2 Feb. 6/4 The cape-and-sword romanticism of Anthony Hope.

c. *transf.* The short feathers on a fowl's back falling below the hackle.

1899 A. H. EVANS *Birds* 548 *Xanthomelus aureus*..has a ..black throat, tail, and part of wings and back, and a cape of hackled plumes falling over the last.

4. *cape-bonnet* (earlier example).

1838 C. GILMAN *Recoll. Southern Matron* 131 A young girl ..dressed in homespun, with a *cracker* or cape bonnet of the same material.

Cape, *sb.*[3] **4.** Add:

Cape blue asbestos, crocidolite occurring in Cape Colony; **Cape boy** (see *BOY *sb.*[1] 3 b); **Cape cart**, a two-wheeled horse-drawn vehicle peculiar to South Africa; **Cape doctor**, a common South African name for the strong south-east winds; **Cape Dutch**, (*a*) South Africans of Dutch extraction; (*b*) the Dutch spoken in South Africa, taal, Afrikaansch; **Cape jessamine**, (*a*) see quot. 1804; (*b*) = *Cape jasmine*; **Cape people**, South African natives of mixed descent; **Cape wagon** (see quot. 1850). (See also Pettman *Africanderisms* for many other specific names.)

1928 *Observer* 1 July 3 The history of the industry begins with the mining of crocidolite, commonly known as 'Cape Blue asbestos, in the Cape Province, in 1891. 1892 COUPER *Mixed Humanity* ii. 20 Cape carts, driven by Malays and 'Cape boys, rattled up and down the streets in numbers. 1896 F. C. SELOUS *Sunshine & Storm* 59 This force was, however, augmented by about 150 Cape boys, chiefly Amaxosa Kafirs and Zulus. 1877 LADY BARKER *Year's Housekeeping in S. Africa* i. (1894) 17 It was decided that I ought to take a drive in a *Cape cart. 1881 STATHAM *Blacks, Boers, & Brit.* 53 Do you know what a Cape cart is? It is a peculiar, but pleasant, institution—something like what was once in England called a 'Whitechapel'. 1910 BUCHAN *Prester John* vii, The half-caste who called him 'Sir' and drove his Cape-cart. 1878 *A. K. Johnston's Africa* xxiii. 382 With the 'south-easter' or '*Cape Doctor'..blowing most frequently from November to March. 1881 STATHAM *Blacks, Boers, & Brit.* 54 For it is here that the celebrated south-easter—the 'Cape Doctor', as Anglo-Indians were in olden days wont to call it—blows its strongest. And the 'Cape Doctor's' strongest is no joke. 1890 ANNIE MARTIN *Home Life on an Ostrich Farm* 15 That rough but benevolent south-east wind, which, owing to its kindly property of sweeping away the germs of disease, is called 'the Cape doctor'. 1826 *New Monthly Mag.* II. 488 The *Cape Dutch ..possess many estimable qualities. 1850 APPLEYARD *Kafir Lang.* 11 *note*, A grammar, [with] 'Proeve van Kaapsch Taaleigen', where the peculiarities of Cape-Dutch usage are exposed. 1852 *Punch* 3 July 19/1 They've christened me Zekoe—that's Cape Dutch for Sea-Cow! 1804 J. BARROW *Trav. Southern Africa 1797–8* II. 82 The *Gardenia Thunbergia*, or the wild *Cape Jessamine. 1858 TERESA VIELE *Following the Drum* 58 Cape jessamine hedges. 1900 RALPH *Towards Pretoria* i. 58 '*Cape people', who look like negroes, but are a mixture of Dutch, Hottentots, and Bushmen. 1798 LADY ANNE BARNARD *S. Africa a Century Ago* (1901) 157 Of course, it was a *Cape waggon; any other sort..is impossible..for such an excursion. 1837 J. E. ALEXANDER *Narr. Voy. Observ.* xiv. 348 It is quite astonishing to a stranger what severe work Cape wagons undergo without injury. 1850 R. G. CUMMING *Hunter's Life S. Afr.* (1851) I. ii. 22 The Cape waggon is a large and powerful, yet loosely-constructed vehicle, running on four wheels.

Capelet (kǣ·plėt). [f. CAPE *sb.*[2] + -LET.] A small cape.

1912 *Home Chat* 1 June 444/2 The new Puritan capelet of white lawn.

Capeline. 3. Add: In recent times, a hat for a girl or woman, having a wide brim often consisting of many folds of muslin, or the like.

1899 *Westm. Gaz.* 13 July 3/2 A girl..in a black muslin *capeline* with a band round the crown and a big front bow of vivid cerise. 1901 *Daily News* 11 Feb. 3/2 The black tulle capeline made with a brim of perhaps twenty to thirty double folds of tulle. 1928 *Observer* 12 Feb. 23 Later on, brims will widen, and capelines of a particularly picturesque type will accompany the dainty dresses worn in the afternoon.

Capellina (kapelʸī·nă). *U.S.* [Sp.] A name given in the western mining districts of the United States to the bell or cover under which mercury is separated from the amalgam by distillation.

a 1872 H. W. HALLECK (Cent. Dict.).

Capetian (kăpī·ʃăn), *a.* [ad. F. *Capétien.*] Pertaining to the third dynasty of French kings, founded by Hugh Capet in A.D. 987. Also as *sb.*

1836 *Penny Cycl.* VI. 264/1 The third, or,..Capetian dynasty of French princes. 1839 K. H. DIGBY *Mores Cath.* IX. xi. (1847) III. 161/2 The Capetians, whose title dates from Robert-le-fort. 1909 BELLOC *Joan of Arc* ii. 30 From him all the Kings were descended, and that Crown Capetian which was the centre and prop of the world and the eye of Christendom.

Capilotade. Delete †*Obs.* and add later quots.:

1892 *Encycl. Pract. Cookery* (ed. T. F. Garrett) I. 284/1 Capilotade..is literally the French term for a hash or ragoût, consisting usually of giblets and pieces of cold meat or poultry. 1926 *Mrs. Marshall's Cookery Bk.* 121 Capilotade of Sweetbread.

Capital, *a.* and *sb.*[2] Add: **A. 6. c.** Delete †*Obs.* and add quots.:

1652 in *Mariner's Mirror* (1926) XII. 399 They are between the I. of Wight and Portland with 45 sail, 12 of which are capital ships. 1679 PEPYS *Mem. Royal Navy* (1690) 8 A Force additional to all this of Thirty Capital Ships. 1793 LD. HOWE in Barrow *Life* (1838) 214 Under a repeated fire from three or four of their capital ships. 1805 D. MACPHERSON *Ann. Commerce* III. 250 They..took from our English East-India company their most important fort..; they also took one of that company's capital ships. 1909 *Hansard's Parl. Deb.* I. 1110/2 Mr. Robert Harcourt asked the First Lord of the Admiralty if he was prepared to give an official definition of the term capital ship? Mr. M'Kenna: The Board of Admiralty have never sanctioned the official use of the term, and they do not deem it expedient to do so. 1919 *Daily Tel.* 11 Aug. 9/6 The battle-fleet force became a vast assemblage of capital vessels, cruisers, light cruisers, destroyers and submarines. 1922 *19th Cent.* Jan. 20 There is no structure which employs so many trades in its building and equipment as a capital ship. 1928 *Britain's Industr. Future* (*Liberal Ind. Inquiry*) v. xxx. 426 A capital-ship base at Singapore.

B. 3. Also, the general body of capitalists or employers of labour, esp. with regard to its political interests and claims. (Cf. LABOUR *sb.* 2 b.)

1869 *Engl. Mechanic* 4 June 237/3 We might feel inclined to despair over the chances of Giant Capital and Dwarf Labour ever working harmoniously.

6. (attrib. use of 3.) *capital bonus*, a pro rata bonus distributed in shares; *capital goods*, commodities forming capital; *capital levy*, the confiscation by the state of a proportion of all property.

1895 *Min. Proc. Inst. Civil Eng.* CXXII. 224 When the North-Eastern Railway Company..includes the cost of between three and four hundred locomotives, which had presumably been charged to revenue, in the capital stock without any increase in capital account. *Ibid.* 234 The engine-miles run (excluding those by 'capital' engines) were 58,202,648. 1919 SIR D. MACLEAN in *Hansard's Parl. Debates* CXVI. 235, I do not see how you can have a capital levy under war conditions. 1920 R. MUIR *Liberalism & Industry* 178 If a capital levy can be proved the best way..out of our difficulties. 1928 *Britain's Industr. Future* (*Liberal Ind. Inquiry*) I. i. 11 The iron and steel and the engineering trades, which are largely concerned with providing capital goods. 1929 *Evening News* 18 Nov. 14/3 A capital bonus of 20 per cent. was distributed in 8 per cent. Second Preference shares.

Capitalistic, *a.* (Earlier U.S. example.)

1873 in *Doc. Hist. Amer. Industr. Soc.* (1910) IX. 371 The growth of capitalistic association and monetary institution.

Capitalistically (kæpităli·stikăli), *adv.* [f. CAPITALISTIC: see -ICALLY.] In a capitalistic manner.

1921 *Glasgow Herald* 24 June 9 When the concern was capitalistically owned. 1924 LEYS *Kenya* 360 Those tropical industries that are capitalistically conducted.

Capitalization. Add:

1. b. The sum or figure resulting from the action of converting into capital.

1906 *Daily Chron.* 13 Feb. 5/1 The companies have a capitalisation of 80,000,000 dols.

3. (Modern examples.)

1901 SAMPSON in *Milton's Lyr. & Dram. Poems* p. v, The text follows the first editions as closely as modern spelling, capitalization and punctuation permit. 1906 R. L. RAMSAY in *Skelton's Magnyf.* (E.E.T.S.) p. xx, The orthography is that of the original; punctuation and capitalization are modern.

Capitalize, *v.* Add:

1. b. To invest with capital. *U.S.*

1895 *Denver Times* 5 Mar. 8/4 The I.X.L. Candy company..is capitalized, and has 100 shares of stock. 1897 *Daily News* 13 Mar. 2/1 This Company is very moderately capitalised at £80,000 in Shares of £1 each.

c. To make capital out of, turn to account. Also *absol.* *U.S.*

1926 *Publishers' Weekly* 22 May 1701 The book-stores and the libraries can capitalize on that same interest. *Ibid.* 29 May 1795 The publishers..do not intend to capitalize the publicity.

3. (Earlier U.S. example.) Also in *vbl. sb.* = next.

1764 *Acc. Coll. New Jersey* 25 All these compositions.. are critically examined with respect to the..pointing, capitalizing, with other minutiae. 1809 W. CUNNINGHAM Jr. *Let. to J. Adams* 23 Sept., I capitalized the prophetic parts of the letter..and italicized the Latin.

Capitalling (kæ·pitălɪŋ), *vbl. sb.* [f. CAPITAL *sb.*[2] + -ING[1].] The furnishing of a word with a capital letter.

1683 MOXON *Mech. Exerc.*, *Printing* 261 The Correcter.. examines the Proof, and considers the Pointing, Italicking, Capitalling, or any error. 1770 LUCKOMBE *Hist. Printing* 249 Some [authors] give themselves no concern about capitaling. 1904 *Athenæum* 13 Feb. 210/2 The first variation, apart from detail of pointing and capitalling, is in line 17. 1905 *Ibid.* 14 Oct. 507/3 The 'copy' is marked by Shelley's usual peculiarities of spelling.., capitalling, and punctuation.

Capitao (kapitā·o). Also **capitow, capito.** [Pg., = CAPTAIN.] A head-man, leader of a gang, etc., in Africa.

1899 *Daily News* 21 Mar. 7/7 Parties of villagers who elect to work on the lines are in charge of the 'Capitows', or gang-leaders. 1925 *Chambers's Jrnl.* Oct. 655/2 Accompanied by my 'capitao', I reached the river bank. 1926 *Blackw. Mag.* Apr. 550/1 Our Safari consisted of A. and myself, two capitos (headmen), a few personal boys and gun-bearers, and forty-six porters.

Capitol. 2. *U.S.* (Earlier and later examples.)

1699 *Acts Assembly Virginia* (1727) I. 205 An Act directing the Building the Capitol and the City of Williamsburgh, &c. 1706 *Cal. Virginia St. Papers* I. 109 The main street..extending from the Capitol to ye utmost Limits of the City Westward. 1782 JEFFERSON *Notes Virginia* (1787) 254 The only public buildings worthy mention are the Capitol, the Palace,..all of them in Williamsburg...The Capitol is a light and airy structure. 1795 J. SCOTT *U. S. Gazetteer* s.v. *Washington* (D.C.), The capitol is now building and is situated upon a beautiful eminence. 1818 MELISH *Trav. U.S.* 144 Soon after this, the stage stopped, at Steele's hotel, nearly opposite the Capitol. 1878 J. H. BEADLE *Western Wilds* xxvi. 415 On the crest of the central one, which slopes evenly toward all the cardinal points, stands the capitol. 1888 *Harper's Mag.* June 50/1 The part of the Capitol which is completed (Senate Chamber, House of Representatives, Library, Historical Society, etc.).

attrib. 1835 J. MARTIN *Gazetteer of Virginia* 189 Beside the statue it is still in contemplation to erect a superb monument to the memory of Washington on the capitol square. 1869 S. BOWLES *Our New West* iv. 89 A quarter section just out there on the bluff..where the capitol buildings and the fine residences will all be located.

Capitoline, *a.* Add: Also, of the Capitol at Washington.

1906 *Nation* (N.Y.) 9 Aug. 120 The descent of that grave historian..upon the capitoline lobby.

Capitulum. Add:

3. b. *Bot.* In characeous plants, a head-cell borne by each manubrium.

1875 BENNETT & DYER tr. *Sachs' Bot.* 520. 1875 HUXLEY & MARTIN *Elem. Biol.* (1877) 45 At the free end of the manubrium is a rounded body, the *capitulum*, which bears six smaller, *secondary capitula*. 1898 tr. *Strasburger's Bot.* 339 Each manubrium terminates in a knob-like cell or capitulum, from which a large number of short cells grow out into the cavity of the antheridium.

Capless (kæ·plės), *a.* [f. CAP *sb.*[1] + -LESS.] Without a cap, having no cap.

1840 GALT *Demon Destiny* viii. 53 His hoary hair streamed capless. 1891 *Daily News* 30 July 2/7 He could not have a capless maid to answer the door. 1904 H. G. WELLS *Food of Gods* I. ii. 22 A very little old woman, capless, with dirty white hair.

Capo tasto (ka·po ta·sto). *Mus.* Also **capodastro.** [It., lit. 'head stop'.] A device consisting of a bar or moveable nut attached to the finger-board of a stringed instrument for the purpose of raising the pitch of all the strings at once.

1876 STAINER & BARRETT *Dict. Mus. Terms* 75 The capo tasto, or capodastro as it is sometimes called, is screwed over the strings on to the finger-board and forms a temporary nut. 1880 *Grove's Dict. Mus.* I. 306/2 The construction of a capo tasto varies according to the stringing and shape of the neck of the instrument it is to be applied to. 1897 *Army & Navy Co-op. Soc. Price List*, Capodastros.

Cappa (kæ·pă). *Eccl.* [It.: see CAPE *sb.*[1]] A cloak (cf. CAPA); a cloak forming part of a religious habit; a cope.

1859 J. MORRIS *S. Thomas Becket* vii. (1885) 79 (S. Thomas of Canterbury) put on a black cappa, which was closed all round and reached his feet...The black cappa with lambswool..was not the monastic habit of his monks of Christ Church. It was that of the Black Canons Regular, to which order Merton Abbey belonged. 1867 R. PALMER *Philip Howard* 15 In tropical climates where the cappa is less worn. 1909 *Westm. Gaz.* 14 July 7/2 The rich, flowing 'cappa' of the Archbishop.

Cappadocian (kæpădōᵘ·ʃiăn), *a.* and *sb.* [f. *Cappadocia*: see -AN.] Of or pertaining to, or an inhabitant or native of, Cappadocia, an ancient kingdom of Asia Minor, now a part of Asiatic Turkey.

c 1789 *Encycl. Brit.* (1797) IV. 139/2 The Cappadocians at first fancied themselves obliged to their new protector. *Ibid.* 141/1 We have now no system of the Cappadocian laws. 1836 *Penny Cycl.* VI. 272/1 The Cappadocians were very generally known during the Roman occupation of their country for their unprincipled and vicious character. 1845 *Encycl. Metrop.* XIV. 253/1 The Cappadocian horses have been the theme of much deserved panegyric from the pens of several historians. 1876 *Encycl. Brit.* V. 74/2 In the time of Herodotus, the Cappadocians occupied the whole region from the chain of Mount Taurus on the south to the shores of the Euxine. 1924 D. G. HOGARTH *Kings of Hittites* (1926) 7 Between their Cappadocian homeland and their south-Tauric client-states.

Capped. Add:

3. b. Of a projectile: Having a soft steel cap or nose to facilitate penetration.

1902 *Westm. Gaz.* 28 May 9/1 The superior penetrating power of capped shot. 1905 *Kynoch Jrnl.* July–Sept. 127 We have shown you that at 300 yds., if you want 'shock', what the Axite capped bullet will do.

4. (Example of *capped elbow.*)

1908 *Animal Managem.* 330 *Capped elbow* is the term applied to the swelling which results from a bruise to the skin at the point of the elbow from lying on hard ground, sharp stones, and in shod animals sometimes on the shoe.

Capper, *sb.*[1] Add:

4. One who or that which caps; in various technical senses.

1884 KNIGHT *Dict. Mech.* Suppl., *Capper*, a tool used in placing the priming cap on its seat in the rear end of the metallic shell. 1890 *Pall Mall Gaz.* 28 June 4/3 Employed by the prosecuting firm [of perfumers] as 'cappers'. 1921 *Dict. Occup. Terms* (1927) § 138 *Glass capper*, cuts off glass as it leaves tubes of glass blowing machine. *Ibid.* § 459 *Capper, bottle*,..fixes a small paper, tin, or lead foil cover over corks of bottles.

5. A confederate in a gambling game; a dummy bidder at an auction. *U.S. slang.*

1871 SCHELE DE VERE *Americanisms* (1872) 319 Cappers they ['strikers'] are called, when the game is the famous Three-Card Monte. 1878 J. H. BEADLE *Western Wilds* iii. 51 Crowd of..gamblers, 'cappers', and saloon-keepers. 1893 *Harper's Mag.* Apr. 712/2 Professional 'boomers' with a retinue of surveyors and cappers and strikers, invaded the State. 1913 MULFORD *Coming of Cassidy* vii. 109 He glanced around swiftly, trying to locate the cappers, but they were not to be seen.

Capping, *vbl. sb.* Add:

1. d. The practice of taking a definite sum of money for a day's hunting from a non-subscriber to the hunt. (See *CAP *sb.*[1] 6.)

1890 *Pall Mall Gaz.* 26 Feb. 3/1 The proceeds of the capping should go to a damage fund. 1897 *Daily News* 16 Jan. 7/6 It has just been decided by the Hunt Committee to introduce the 'capping' system into the Quorn country next season.

Ca·p-sheaf. [CAP *sb.*[1] 19.]

1. The top-sheaf of a shock or rick. Also *fig.*

1800 *Aurora* (Philad.) 8 Apr. (Th.) Goodrich a cap-sheaf, won't be led. 1805 R. W. DICKSON *Pract. Agric.* II. 793 These [hattocks]..are exposed to the action of the sun and air by taking off the hood, or cap-sheaves, in the day-time. 1844 W. BARNES *Poems Rur. Life* Gloss. 292 *Capsheaf*, a small sheaf of straw forming the tip of a thatched rick.

2. Something which is the climax or acme. Phr. *To put the cap-sheaf on.* *U.S.*

1815 *Massachusetts Spy* 31 May (Th.) This is the crowner, the cap-sheaf. 1834 *Georgian* (Savannah) 26 July 3/2 This is indeed the cap sheaf of outrage. 1840 J. P. KENNEDY *Quodlibet* 26 The commissioner came this way and put the cap-sheaf on Michael's worldly fortune. 1846–52 MRS. WHITCHER *Widow Bedott Papers* ix. 88 Of all the strains ever I heerd of I should think that was the cap sheef. 1871 MRS. STOWE *Sam Lawson* 185 That put the cap-sheaf on for Bill.

Capsian (kæ·psiăn), *a.* *Archæol.* [f. the place-name *Capsa*, old form of Gafsa, Tunis.] Of or belonging to the palæolithic period of culture following the Mousterian, as represented by the flint implements found at Gafsa in Tunis.

1921 R. A. S. MACALISTER *Textbk. European Archæol.* I. 537 To the Mousterian succeeds the stage to which de Morgan has given the name Captian or Capsian...The Capsian thus corresponds chronologically to the European Upper Palæolithic, and culturally to the Aurignacian stage. 1928 C. DAWSON *Age of the Gods* i. 17 The contemporary art of South-east Spain, the region of the Capsian culture.

Capsize, *v.* Add: **2. b.** Of wines (see quot.).

1888 *Encycl. Brit.* XXIV. 603/2 Sometimes a wine will 'capsize': the alcohol and the acid disappear and what was wine becomes an insipid undrinkable liquid.

Capstan. 2. Add: *capstan labourer, -man*; **capstan table**, a round table on a column, often with a revolving top.

1881 *Instr. Census Clerks* (1885) 94 *Capstan labourer. 1889 P. H. EMERSON *Engl. Idyls* 67 On deck, a countryman who had shipped as *capstan-man, was standing for'ard with the master. 1921 *Dict. Occup. Terms* (1927) § 706 *Capstan man*.., moves trucks in goods depôt by depressing foot lever actuating automatic capstan. *Ibid.* § 741 *Capstan man*, operates capstan,..allows capstan to revolve,..etc. 1921 *Glasgow Herald* 1 June 9 Cranemen, capstanmen, and others. 1927 *Daily Tel.* 31 May 4/1 An old English '*capstan' writing table.

Capsuli-, capsulo-. Add: **Capsulo·tomy**, the incision of the capsule of the eye, *spec.* in operations for cataract.

1907 *Practitioner* Dec. 778 The operation of capsulotomy for some cases of acute nephritis with threatened suppression of urine.

Capsulitis (kæpsiuləi·tis). *Path.* [f. CAPSULE + -ITIS.] Inflammation of a capsule (e.g. of the eyeball).

1848 DUNGLISON *Med. Lex.* (ed. 7). 1899 *W. F. Norris & C. A. Oliver's Dis. Eye* IV. 235 Aqueous capsulitis.

Captaincy. Add:

4. Captaincy-general = *CAPTAIN-GENERALCY.

1846 WORCESTER (citing Murray).

Captain-generalcy. The office or province of a captain-general. So **Captain-generalship.**

1846 WORCESTER (citing *Sat. Mag.*), Captain-generalcy. 1896 *Cosmopolitan* XX. 412/1 The captain-generalcy of Venezuela had then been under the Spanish crown two hundred and forty years. 1898 *Daily News* 28 Nov. 7/4 Before the colonies had secured their independence four of them were rated as Viceroyalties, and five as Captain-Generalships. *Ibid.* 10 Dec. 6/1 Promotion to the Captain-Generalship of Cuba. 1900 *Ibid.* 9 May 9/3 A headquarter [cyclist] corps in London, of which Mr. A. J. Balfour had accepted the Captain Generalcy.

Ca·ptaining, *vbl. sb.* [f. CAPTAIN *v.* + -ING[1].] Acting as the captain of a side.

1903 *Westm. Gaz.* 28 May 8/2 On fielding and on captaining. 1904 *Daily Chron.* 10 Aug. 7/3 Their captaining capacities.

Caption, *sb.* **2.** Delete †*Obs.* and add quot.:

1922 *Public Opinion* 14 July 36/1 Genius like hers stands above envy and caption.

4. Add earlier U.S. examples and examples of recent English use, now esp. associated with cinematographic productions.

1789 J. MADISON *Writ.* (1904) V. 355 You will see in the caption of the address that we have pruned the ordinary stile of the degrading appendages of Excellency, Esqrs. &c. 1821 *Massachusetts Spy* 24 Oct. (Th.) [The statute] is under the caption of 'Fees in the Secretary's office'. 1836 G. T. CHAPMAN *Serm.* 256 The result Mather gives us under this caption:—'Determination given by a late assembly' [etc.].

1920 *Glasgow Herald* 23 July 7 The Speaker said that this part of the bill—the caption, he believed was its proper title—was not submitted to the House. 1923 *Yorkshire Post* 17 Dec. 6/8 A continuous alternation of pictures and those pieces of text that are, one believes, known as captions.

Caption, *v.* [f. the sb.] *trans.* To provide with a caption, heading, or title; to entitle.

1901 *Science* 22 Nov. 808 An effective poem..captioned 'The Song of the Innuit'. 1922 JACK LONDON *Son of Sun* VII. ii, It means the feathers of the sun. Thus does this base interloper caption himself. 1927 *Observer* 27 Nov. 14/5 [His] article captioned 'Cecil Sharp'.

Captivate, *v.* **1.** (Later U.S. example.)

1840 C. F. HOFFMAN *Greyslaer* I. x. 114 We can captivate those chaps complete,..if they only move a little further down stream.

Captive, *a.* and *sb.* **A. 1. b.** Add quots. for *captive balloon* and the like. *Captive mirror, captive purse*, etc., fittings of a lady's hand-bag which are secured by means of chains.

1878 *Sci. Amer. Suppl.* VI. 2429 The great *captive balloon at Paris. 1885 *Sci. Amer.* 21 Nov. 328/3 The first captive balloon of Mr. Yon's make, provided with his hydrogen gas apparatus and windlass for ascents and descents. 1905 *Aëronautical Jrnl.* IX. 14 Captive Balloon Photography. 1898 *Army & Navy Co-op. Soc. Price List* No. 67. 971 *Captive Golf Ball. 1923 *Daily Mail* 12 June 7 Silk handbag...Fitted *captive mirror. 1923 *Weekly Dispatch* 13 May 14 Crocodile Calf handbag...Fitted *captive purse.

Capture, *sb.* Add:

1. b. *Physical Geog.* The process by which a stream by headwater erosion encroaches on the basin of a stream at a higher level, and diverts the upper waters of the latter into its own channel; also the point of such diversion; said also of a glacier.

1898 *Geogr. Jrnl.* (R.G.S.) XI. 441 M. Meunier explains the distribution of erratics in the neighbourhood of the Alps by the 'capture' of one glacier by another, the head of which has eaten back through the dividing wall, and thus tapped the ice-supply. 1908 J. LOMAS in *Nature Book* I. 165 Standing at the elbow of the capture of the Hodder, and looking seawards.

Capture, *v.* Add:

b. *Physical Geog.* Of a river or glacier: To divert by capture (see prec. 1 b).

1900 *Geogr. Jrnl.* (R.G.S.) XVI. 36 It may then have happened that whole basins, like that of Lake Mascardi, drained formerly towards Nahuelhuapi, have been captured towards the Pacific slopes. 1908 J. LOMAS in *Nature Book* I. 166 Along the Vale of York, where the rocks are softer than those of the Pennines or East Yorkshire, the Don sent up a tributary and successively captured the rivers to form what is now the Ouse.

Caput. 4. Add: *caput lupinum* (lit., wolf's head), an outlaw: see WOLF'S-HEAD 2.

[*c* 1789 *Encycl. Brit.* (1797) IV. 156/1 An outlawed felon was said to have *caput lupinum*.] 1841 MACAULAY *Ess.*, *W. Hastings* (1851) 602 Did it lie in their mouths to contend that a foreign settler who establishes an empire in India is a *caput lupinum*? **1888** *Guardian* 4 Apr. 488/2 The National League, if it did not formally decree the death of Fitzmaurice for disobedience to its orders, at least proclaimed him as a *Caput Lupinum*.

Car, *sb.*[1] Add:

1. e. = MOTOR CAR.

1896 D. FARMAN *Auto-cars* 132 The latter drove with a daring which may have been dangerous to himself, but which never affected his car. *Ibid.* 135 The three cars which came in next after Mr. Levassor's were all Peugeot cars. **1900** W. W. BEAUMONT *Motor Vehicles* I. 615 Hill-climbing trials alone would not of course be sufficient as a test of the wearing power or durability of a car. **1902** HARMSWORTH *Motors & Motor Driving* 23 The first car built by the Daimler Company at Coventry.

2. (Earlier example.)

1831 *Niles' Register* 10 Sept. XLI. 21 The cars now leave Schenectady at a little after 12 M.

b. *ellipt.* A car-load.

1867–8 *Trans. Ill. Agric. Soc.* VII. 446 A farmer had far better send..one car of good sheep in the twelve months, than six cars of each of bad breed.

4. b. The cage of an elevator. *U.S.*

1904 *N. Y. Even. Post* 2 Feb. 2 The elevator man seemed to lose control of the elevator at the fifth floor. The car made a sheer drop from the fourth story to the basement.

6. *car-construction, -drive, -owner.*

1907 *Westm. Gaz.* 28 Aug. 4/2 The whole lines of *car-construction are changing. **1924** GEIKIE *Long Life's Wk.* 220 We had long walks and still longer *car-drives. **1905** *Daily Chron.* 12 July 6/3 It is now proposed that all *car-owner members shall have commissions, and that motor-cycle members shall have the rank of sergeant.

b. *car-body, -door, -fare, -horse, -house, -line, -ride, -shed, -track, -wheel, -window.* (U.S. examples.)

1838 *Civil Eng. & Archit. Jrnl.* I. 390/1 The truck is guided by the *carbody with..mathematical precision. **1863** 'G. HAMILTON' *Gala-Days* 22 The heads of the two columns collide near the *car-door. **1870** 'FANNY FERN' *Ginger-Snaps* 182 What troubles me most is, whether I am to pay six cents for *car-fare. **1898** MARG. DELAND *Old Chester Tales* 243, I might not be able to get back in a hurry, I mightn't have my car-fare. **1900** (*Amer.*) *Dial. Notes* II. 26 A fish-scale..is the nickel with which a [Yale] student pays his car-fare. **1901** *Scribner's Mag.* XXIX. 423/1 If I should spend my savings in car-fare from place to place. **1907** M. H. NORRIS *Veil* v. 38 A *car-horse, sure-footed and generally weatherbeaten..completed this part of his purchase. **1839** *Boston Almanac* 72 From the *Car House in Boston to the Car House in Salem. **1859** BARTLETT *Dict. Amer.* (ed. 2), *Car-house*, a building in which railroad cars are kept. **1898** P. L. FORD *Hon. Peter Stirling* 365 All the *car lines took off their cars. Trucks disappeared from the streets. **1902** HARBEN *Abner Daniel* 25 Now I have a long *car-ride before me, and it's growing late. *Ibid.* 36 It was near the ancient-looking brick *car-shed under which the trains of two main lines ran. **1875** *Field & Forest* I. 36 One can hardly fail to notice the thrifty young trees..as they line each side of the *car tracks. **1882** *U.S. Rep. Prec. Met.* 639 The kind of car track employed can be allowed to control the grade within certain limits. **1887** C. B. GEORGE *40 Yrs. on Rail* iv. 67 Richard Norton Allen, the inventor of the famous paper *car-wheel called by his name. **1854** MARY J. HOLMES *Tempest & Sunshine* xvii. 239 From the *car windows Fanny watched the long blue line of hills. **1873** J. H. BEADLE *Undevel. West* ii. 53 From a car window one may note a curious though very gradual..change in soil and climate.

Car, *v.* Add: Also *intr.*: To go by car.

1907 *Daily Chron.* 23 Sept. 4/4 You just get out of your train, walk or 'car' to your hotel.

Carabideous (kærăbi·dĭəs), *a. Ent.* [f. CARABID + -EOUS.] Of or pertaining to the Carabidæ.

1835 J. DUNCAN *Beetles* (Nat. Lib.) 119 The majority of carabideous insects secrete an acrid and caustic fluid. **1835** [see SQUARE *a.* 1]. **1889** A. R. WALLACE *Darwinism* 44 The curious little carabideous beetles of the genus Notiophilus.

Caracul (kæ·răkŭl). Also **-cule, karacul.** [Russ.] A kind of fur, a variety of astrakhan; also a kind of cloth made in imitation of this. Also *attrib.*

1894 *Westm. Gaz.* 20 Sept. 3/3 Here is fashion's forecast for the winter season:—Blue the leading colour...Caracule the popular fur. *Ibid.* 4 Oct. 3/3 The most striking of this season's productions is caracule-cloth, which closely resembles the fur of that name. **1894** *Queen* 27 Oct. 735/3 A 'Caracule' plush, which simulates that fashionable fur. **1895** *Army & Navy Co-op. Soc. Price List* 1095 Astrachans, &c...Black Caracul. **1898** *Daily News* 15 Oct. 6/4 A tight-fitting caracul with revers of chinchilla. **1929** *Daily Express* 26 Jan. 5/3 The smarter coats are generally collared with a flat fur. These include astrachan, krimmna, and caracul, in black, beige, or grey.

Caramel, *sb.* Add:

d. The colour of caramel, brown.

1909 *Daily Mirror* 4 Oct. 10/3 Caramel is the name for various new shades of brown. **1927** *Daily Express* 12 Mar. 3/5 Caramel, a useful light brown, suitable for all kinds of walking costumes.

Caramel, *v.* Add: *intr.* To turn into caramel.

1887 *Century Mag.* Nov. 114/1 He seeks to keep the temperature down to 130°. If it is too high some of the sucrose will 'invert' or 'caramel' into glucose. **1897** *Yearbk. U.S. Dept. Agric.* 515 The sugar in the milk caramels in baking and browns the crust.

Carancha, variant of *CARRANCHA.

Carangoid (kăræ·ŋgoid), *a.* and *sb.* [f. mod.L. *Carangidæ*, a family of fishes + -OID.] Pertaining to or resembling, or one of the, Carangidæ.

1888 GOODE *Amer. Fishes* 226 The Cavally and other Carangoids.

Carapacial (kærăpē·ʃiăl), *a.* [f. CARAPACE + -IAL.] Of or pertaining to a carapace.

1880 HUXLEY *Crayfish* iv. 217 The lateral portions of the carapacial ridge.

So **Carapacic** (kærăpē·sik) *a.*

1903 *Ann. & Mag. Nat. Hist.* Ser. VII. XI. 442 The carapacic portion of the dorsal scute.

Carapato, variant of *CARRAPATO.

Caravan, *sb.* Add: **3. b.** A company of travellers, traders, or emigrants, with their wagons, mules, or packhorses, esp. in the Western States; a train (*of* wagons, etc.). *U.S.*

1791 W. BARTRAM *Trav. Carolina* etc. (1792) 376 Our caravan consisting of about twenty men and sixty horses, we made a formidable appearance. **1805** L. DOW *Trav. Wks.* 1806 II. 90 They, with their caravan, took the right-hand road to Pittsburgh, to go down the Ohio, to Natchez. **1817** S. R. BROWN *Western Gaz.* 77 General Harrison ..was accompanied in his march through the wilderness by a caravan of waggons. **1843** FARNHAM *Trav. Western Prairies* I. 24 He also divides the caravan into two parts, each of which forms a column when on march. **1871** SCHELE DE VERE *Americanisms* (1872) 105 The *caravan* is quite at home in New Mexico and Sonora, although frequently called there by its Spanish name, *conducta*. **1897** J. L. ALLEN *Choir Invisible* ii. (1918) 9 A company of travellers with pack-horses—one of the caravans across the desert of the Western woods.

attrib. **1846** SAGE *Scenes Rocky Mts.* (1859) 37 The caravan animals securely picketed..occupied an area of several acres. *a* **1861** WINTHROP *John Brent* xi. (1862) 120, I must wait for some artist..who can perceive the poetry of American caravan-life.

Caravan, *v.* [f. the sb.] *trans.* To convey by caravan.

1898 G. W. STEEVENS *With Kitchener to Khartum* 118 The Greek gets his stuff up everywhere:..he caravans it with a double-barrelled rifle on his shoulder.

Caravaneer. Add: **b.** One who lives or travels in a caravan.

1893 *Cornhill Mag.* Mar. 288 The joy of the caravaneer was ours.

Caravanner (kæ·rævænəɹ). Also **-aner.** [f. CARAVAN *sb.* + -ER [1].] **a.** One who lives and travels in a caravan (esp. on a pleasure tour). **b.** The conductor of a caravan in the East. (Cf. prec.)

1916 C'TESS VON ARNIM (*title*) The Caravaners. **1923** *Weekly Dispatch* 21 Jan. 5 Victor Maclaglen, who gives a magnificent performance as a gipsy king in the story, was urged to prolong his stay by the caravanners. **1929** *Daily Tel.* 22 Jan. 11/3 There is little doubt that information which caravanners gave me yesterday has now reached Kabul.

Carbide. Add: *spec.* Short for 'calcium carbide'.

1898 W. E. GIBBS *Lighting by Acetylene* 70 Water from an elevated reservoir enters T until the carbide is reached. **1904** A. B. F. YOUNG *Compl. Motorist* 257 Carbide lamps give a beautiful light when they are working properly.

Carbo-. Add: *carbo-hydrogen*; *-hydrous, -methylic* adjs.; **carbo-cyclic** *a.*, containing a ring of carbon atoms only; **carbo-dynamite**, a patented explosive, in which fine charcoal is used as the absorbent.

1899 *Jrnl. Chem. Soc.* LXXVI. I. 59 *Carbocyclic Compounds. **1904** *Nature* 11 Aug. 341/1 The stability of carbocyclic and heterocyclic chains. **1888** *Times* 2 Oct. 3/1 Some *carbo-dynamite, which had lain for eight months in water. **1866** ODLING *Anim. Chem.* 75 The *carbo-hydrogen of vegetable tissue. **1881** *Ann. Rep. Smithsonian Instit.* 393 The *carbohydrous material which is present in the plant. **1838** R. D. THOMSON in *British Annual* 323 *Carbo-methylic acid.

Carbohydrate. Add: Also *attrib.*

1888 *Jrnl. Chem. Soc.* LIV. 972 Acid in Healthy and Disordered Stomachs during a Carbo-hydrate Diet. **1900** *Westm. Gaz.* 21 Dec. 3/2 Concerning malt liquors, we are told that the large quantity of carbohydrate matter in them [etc.]. **1908** *Carnegie Trust Rep.* 22 The carbohydrate material and ferments of blood. **1910** *Practitioner* Jan. 129, I want to insist that pyorrhoea alveolaris is a local disease due to germ, or carbohydrate-germ.

Carbolic, *a.* Add: Also *ellipt.* for *c. acid.*

1907 M. C. HARRIS *Tents of Wickedness* I. iv. 58 The stone floors are so cold, and there is such a smell of carbolic.

Carbon, *sb.* Add:

1. b. A form of diamond, the black diamond or carbonado.

1869 *Engl. Mechanic* 20 Aug. 475/1 Diamond or carbon (the latter name is preferred) stands the severest tests for mechanical purposes without apparent wear. **1903** *Westm. Gaz.* 6 June 9/1 'Black diamonds'..technically known as 'carbons'.

c. Short for *carbon-paper. Hence attrib. *carbon copy.*

1895 COLLYNS *Typists' Man.* 55 Errors must not be erased while the carbons are in the machine. *Ibid.*, Carbon copies. **1913** E. P. SARGENT *Technique of Photoplay* 25 For carbon copies get the carbon second sheets. **1920** ROSE MACAULAY *Potterism* I. iv. 46 Jane extracted carbons from a drawer and fitted them to her paper.

3. a. carbon-bronze, an alloy used in journal-bearings to prevent friction; **carbon-paper**, (*a*) in photography, paper used in carbon-printing; (*b*) thin paper coated on one side with a preparation of lamp-black, used between two papers to make a duplicate copy of what is written on the upper sheet (earlier called *carbonic paper).

1884 KNIGHT *Dict. Mech.* Suppl., *Carbon bronze. **1878** *Jrnl. Chem. Soc.* XXXIV. 919 *Carbon-paper rendered Sensitive without a Chrome-Bath. **1895** COLLYNS *Typists' Man.* 55 In correcting the carbon copies, a narrow strip of carbon paper should be placed upon the ribbon to prevent the corrections being conspicuous.

Carbon, *v.* [f. the sb.] *intr.* or *pass.* Of the engine of a motor car: To become coated with carbon deposit. Const. with *up*.

1922 *Daily Mail* 28 Nov. 6 [A motor engine] longer to carbon up and easier to decarbonise than its rivals. **1925** *Morris Owner's Man.* 70 Thanks to good carburation, the Morris engine carbons up very slowly. **1928** *Daily Express* 3 Aug. 9 Even if the engine is carboned up, you get wonderful pulling.

Carbona (kaɹbō·nä). *Mining.* An irregular mass of ore, usually found in the vicinity of a lode.

1855 LEIFCHILD *Cornwall* 40 The formation of the tin ore in this mine is very singular, and is provincially termed *carbona*. **1875** J. H. COLLINS *Metal Mining* Gloss.

Carbonado (kāɹbonē·do), *sb.*[2] [Pg.] A dark, opaque variety of diamond, found near Bahia in Brazil, used in rock-drilling and stone-polishing.

1852 J. TENNANT *Gems & Prec. Stones* 94 A considerable quantity of a black substance was found, of specific gravity like the Diamond, but lamellar...It was termed 'Carbonado' by the discoverers from its charcoal like appearance. **1879** *Encycl. Brit.* IX. 345/1 The dressing and grooving of millstones is generally done by hand-picking, but sometimes black amorphous diamonds (carbonado) are used. **1895** *Bloxam's Chem.* (ed. 8) 71 A dark amorphous diamond (*Carbonado*) found at Bahia in the Brazils.

Carbonatation (kāɹbonətē·ʃən). [f. CARBONATE *v.*[1] + -ATION.] = CARBONATION.

1887 *American* XIV. 24 The process of carbonatation, or removing the excess of lime used in defecating the juice by carbonic acid gas. **1888** *Harper's Mag.* June 47 The best method of 'carbonatation' of the saccharine juice.

Carbonate, *sb.* Add:

2. More explicitly called *carbonate ore.*

1890 W. J. GORDON *Foundry* 96 The hæmatite,..unlike the carbonate ores,..requires no roasting. **1892** *Daily News* 29 Oct. 6/4 The new bodies of carbonate ore.

3. = *CARBON *sb.* 1 b.

1883 GRESLEY *Gloss. Coal-m.*, *Carbonates*, black imperfectly crystallised form of diamond used for rock boring; the abrasion of the diamond removes the rock in an annular form, producing cores.

Carbonator (kā·ɹbonētəɹ). [f. CARBONATE *v.*[1] + -OR.] One who carbonates.

1896 *Voice* (N.Y.) 21 May 4/5 (*title*) American Bottler and Carbonator. **1921** *Dict. Occup. Terms* (1927) § 459 *Carbonator*, is in charge of closed tanks into which beer is run in preparation for bottling.

Carbonic, *a.* Add: **1. c.** *Carbonic paper*, early name of *carbon-paper (*b*).

1876 PREECE & SIVEWRIGHT *Telegraphy* 289 The rest of the message..is transcribed on the public copy by carbonic paper. **1881** *Instr. Census Clerks* (1885) 82 Carbonic Paper Maker. **1884** LYND *Pract. Telegraphist* 26 The carbonic paper must be changed sufficiently often to admit of a clear and distinct impression being made. **1895** *Army & Navy Co-op. Soc. Price List* 548 Carbonic Paper. For Tracing and Transfers, Black both sides.

Carbonite (kā·ɹbonəit). [f. CARBON + -ITE [1].] A name for two different explosives (see quots. 1891, 1892).

1891 THORPE *Dict. Applied Chem.* II. 83/2 Carbonite is an explosive introduced by Hellhoff, of Berlin; stated to be composed of nitrobenzene, potassium nitrate, sulphur, and Kieselguhr. **1892** H. W. HUGHES *Coal-mining* 79 Carbonite is another explosive of late introduction. It is said to be composed of nitro-glycerine, sulphur, and nitro-benzol. **1910** *Encycl. Brit.* VIII. 764/1 Carbonite contains 25 % of nitro-glycerin. **1922** *Ibid.* XXX. 86/2 Bombs of a type known as 'Carbonite'.

Carbonizable (kā·ɹbonəizăb'l), *a.* [f. CARBONIZE *v.* + -ABLE.] That can be carbonized.

1883 J. W. SWAN *Provis. Specif. Patent* 31 Dec. (Pat. Off.) Carbonisable material in a plastic or semi-liquid state.

Carbonize, *v.* Add:

4. To destroy vegetable impurities in (wool, etc.) by treatment with an acid and heat, which reduces the vegetable matter to carbon dust. Hence **Ca·rbonizing** *vbl. sb.*, the action or process by which this is done. **Ca·rboniser**, an operative who performs or assists in the operation.

1909 *Cent. Dict.* Suppl. **1920** *Glasgow Herald* 6 July 7 Australian wool...There will be a considerable surplus of low and medium cross-breds and carbonising wool. **1921** *Dict. Occup. Terms* (1927) § 361 *Piece carboniser*; carbonises woollen fabrics in the piece.

Carbonizer (kā·ɹbonəizəɹ). [f. CARBONIZE *v.* + -ER [1].] One who or that which carbonizes. See also *CARBONIZE *v.* 4.

1908 *Daily Chron.* 24 Aug. 9/6 Foreman (Working) wanted for gas works; must be a good carboniser. **1913** *G. Martin's Industr. & Manuf. Chem., Org.* 302 Continuous carbonisers, such as Woodall-Duckham and Glover-West, have also been tried. **1921** *Dict. Occup. Terms* (1927) § 693 *Charger*,..*carboniser, carbonising man*; (i) general terms for men charging retorts and furnaces either by hand or machine.

Carbonizing, *vbl. sb.* and *ppl. a.* Add:

1898 *Westm. Gaz.* 17 Feb. 8/3 The company..pays 3s. 6d. per ton of coal for carbonising wages. **1898** *Ibid.* 7 Feb. 5/2 In 1888 the difference between the carbonising wages paid by the South Metropolitan and the other two companies per 1,000 ft. of gas sold was very slight. **1921** *Dict. Occup. Terms* (1927) § 693 Gas Stokers... *Charger, retort charger; carboniser, carbonising man*; general terms for men charging retorts and furnaces.

Carborundum (kāɹbŏrʊ·ndŏm). *Chem.* [f. CARBO(N + CO)RUNDUM.] A crystalline substance, SiC, consisting of carbon and silicon, used either as a powder or in blocks for polishing and scouring.

1893 *Amer. Jrnl. Sci.* Ser. III. XLVI. 472 While examining the hardness of 'carborundum', a carbide of silicon, made by Mr. Acheson of Pittsburg, it was found that it readily scratched red, blue, white, pink, and yellow corundum in the form of fine gems. **1895** *Bloxam's Chem.* (ed. 8) 127 Silicon carbide (carborundum)..is prepared by heating silicon or silica with carbon in the electric furnace. **1917** *Mod. Boot & Shoe Maker* III. 250 The rough scouring on the coarse sandpaper roll or the felt roller covered with carborundum. **1924** *Chambers's Jrnl.* 39/1 The cutting edge is bestowed by grinding on a carborundum wheel.

Carburant (kā·ɹbiurănt). [f. CARBUR(ET *v.* + -ANT [1].] A liquid or vapourized hydrocarbon used to carburet air or gas for the production of light or mechanical energy. Also **Ca·rburetant.**

1895 *Funk's Standard Dict.*, Carburetant. **1909** *Cent. Dict.* Suppl., Carburant. **1928** *Daily Tel.* 4 Sept. 9/3 To find a carburant less inflammable than petrol.

Carburation (kāɹbiurē·ʃən). [f. CARBUR(ET + -ATION.] The process of charging air with hydrocarbon in a finely divided liquid form, the resulting gas being burnt for the production of energy.

1896 B. DONKIN *Gas, Oil, & Air Engines* II. xxi. (ed. 2) 303 The carburation of the air takes place in the middle division. **1902** HARMSWORTH *Motors & Motor-Driving* 166 There may be a slight flare up, but this will assist the carburation. **1920** *Westm. Gaz.* 1 Apr. 4/2 Few improvements have been made to the various carburation systems.

Carburetted. Add: *Carburetted air*, air which has been impregnated with fine particles of hydrocarbon, and which provides the power by which motor vehicles are driven.

1896 B. DONKIN *Gas, Oil, & Air Engines* II. xxi. (ed. 2) 298 Inflammable petroleum essence..is perhaps best distinguished by the term usually applied to it abroad—'carburetted air'. **1898** tr. *L. Lockert's Petroleum Motor-cars* 143 The carburetted air inlet valve..must be shut off. **1899** *Motor-Car World* Oct. 9/1 A 'carburettor', the function of which is the production of a saturated mixture of spirit, vapour, and air, known as 'carburetted air'.

Carburettor. Add: (also **carburator**).

b. In motor vehicles the apparatus for the production of carburetted air (see prec.).

1896 *Jrnl. Soc. Arts* 27 Nov. 22/1 Where a vaporiser is employed, or a carburettor. **1898** tr. *L. Lockert's Petroleum Motor-cars* 145 The carburator, in which the petroleum essence..is vaporized. **1900** *Motor-Car World* Aug. 254 Supplemental exhaust tube for heating carburettor tank. **1902** HARMSWORTH *Motors & Motor-Driving* 166 Too rich a mixture may be caused by the presence of too much petrol in the carburator. **1912** *Motor Man.* 12 To obtain an explosive mixture of paraffin and air a special form of carburetter is required.

Carbyl (kā·ɹbil). *Chem.* [f. CARB(ON + -YL.] A name given by Magnus to the hydrocarbon ethylene when it forms a basic radical, as carbyl sulphate.

1844 FOWNES *Chem.* 395 Carbon, hydrogen, and the elements of sulphuric acid...Sulphate of carbyle. **1890** *Bloxam's Chem.* (ed. 7) 479 The compound formed by SO_3 with ethylene..is termed carbyl sulphate or ethionic anhydride.

Carbylamine (kāɹbilæ·məin). *Chem.* [f. CARB + -YL + AMINE.] A basic substance, consisting of a hydrocarbon radical, also called carbamine and isocyanide.

1872 WATTS *Dict. Chem.* VI. 522. **1887** A. M. BROWN *Anim. Alkaloids* 36 Heated with potash and chloroform, cadaverine does not give carbylamine. **1895** *Bloxam's Chem.* (ed. 8) 679 Isocyanides, or carbamines (carbylamines).

Carcajou. 1. *U.S.* (Earlier example.)

1744 A. DOBBS *Hudson's Bay* 40 The beavers have three enemies, man, otters, and the Carcajou [*sic*].

Carcass, *v.* Add: **b.** To make a carcass of.

1906 *Daily Chron.* 7 June 5/4 These animals realise only one-third as much as those fit for carcassing.

Carcel. Add: **2.** A French unit of illumination, equal to the light emitted by a standard carcel lamp burning 42 grams of colza-oil an hour and with a flame 40 millimetres in height.

1884 KNIGHT *Dict. Mech.* Suppl., *Carcel-bec*, the French unit of illumination. Given the preference over candle-power..at the Electrical Congress, in Paris, 1881. **1884** HIGGS *Magn. & Dyn.-Electr. Mach.* 119 The expenditure of work per second per Carcel-burner (7·4 candle power)...An illuminating power of 1·40 Carcels (10·36 candles). **1902** *Encycl. Brit.* XXX. 260/2 The values are expressed in carcels (9·5 candles) per square centimetre of the mean horizontal focal plane of the luminous source.

Carcharodont (kāɹkæ·rŏdŏnt), *a.* [f. Gr. καρχαρόδων, f. κάρχαρος sharp + ὀδούς (ὀδοντ-) tooth.] Having pointed teeth, having teeth resembling those of the extinct genus *Carcharodon.*

1886 *Encycl. Brit.* XX. 432/2 [Aristotle says] All Snakes are 'carcharodont'.

Carcinogenic (kāɹsinodʒe·nik), *a.* [f. *carcino-* in CARCINOMA + *-GENIC.] Cancer-producing.

1928 *Observer* 12 Feb. 22 The carcinogenic substance. **1928** *Daily Tel.* 19 July 9/1 Carcinogenic properties.

Card, *sb.*[2] Add: **2. b.** *To have a card up one's sleeve*: to have a plan in reserve.

1898 *Tit-Bits* 23 July 3289/3, I took the precaution of having what, I believe, you sporting men call a card up my sleeve. **1907** E. PHILLIPS OPPENHEIM *Secret* xxxvii. 231 If Guest has yet another card up his sleeve, he has kept it secret from me.

c. Also without adjective.

1911 ARNOLD BENNETT (*title*) The Card: a Story of Adventure in the Five Towns. **1929** W. DEEPING *Roper's Row* xxi, 'What the Midlanders call "a card"'. 'What's that?' 'An original, a person.'

d. *To play with* or *lay one's cards on the table*: to reveal all one's resources.

1907 E. PHILLIPS OPPENHEIM *Secret* viii. 55, I began to think that I had been rash to lay my cards upon the table. **1911** SHAW *Fanny's First Play* III, Tramps are often shameless; but theyre never sincere. Swells—if I may use that convenient name for the upper classes—play much more with their cards on the table. **1925** ALDOUS HUXLEY *Those Barren Leaves, Mrs. Aldwinkle* iii. (1927) 36 The cards are all on the table, nothing's left to fancy. All's above-board and consequently boring.'

5. b. A card held by a delegate of a trade union meeting or congress and representing a certain number of his constituents: cf. *card vote* in *14.

1902 *35th Ann. Rep. Trades Union Congress* 69 A vote by card was then demanded, and resulted in the Committee being supported by 796,000 to 375,000. *Ibid.* 85 The method of voting shall be by card, to be issued to the delegates of trade societies according to their membership, and paid for ..on the principle of one card for every 1,000 members or fractional part thereof represented.

c. *transf.* Anything having the form of a card. *U.S.*

1853 J. G. BALDWIN *Flush Times Alabama* 103 He distributed..a plug of tobacco there, or a card of *town* gingerbread to the little snow-balls. **1881** MRS. R. T. COOKE *Somebody's Neighbors* 393 Cards of yellow gingerbread. **1884** PHIN *Dict. Apiculture* 20 *Card*, a frame filled with honey comb. A sheet of honeycomb.

7. *U.S.* (Earlier examples.)

1769 *Boston News-Letter* 2 Feb. (Th.) A Card from the London and British Merchants to the American Merchants. **1788** *Gen. Even. Post* (London) 1–3 Jan. 2/3 A Card. Dr. Norris..desires to inform the public [etc.]. **1880** TOURGEE *Invis. Empire* xii. 512 Dr. P. J. McCormick..published a card declaring that Dixon was the leader of the mob which hung Patterson.

13. *card-dealer, -exchanging, -leaving, -plate.*

1902 O. WISTER *Virginian* iii. 31 Into my thoughts broke the voice of that *card-dealer. **1899** *Westm. Gaz.* 26 May 10/1 The Hague, in the opening days of the Peace Conference, was simply a mass of *card-exchanging foreigners. **1902** *Daily Chron.* 23 Apr. 3/3 Advice on such matters as *card-leaving. **1906** *Ibid.* 28 Aug. 4/4 Visits, servants, dress and card-leaving—all the minor courtesies of life come under notice. **1875** MRS. STOWE *We & Neighbors* v. 60, 'I see you have cards here for Mrs. Wat Sydney's reception this winter', said Aunt Maria, turning her attention to the *card plate.

14. card catalogue, a catalogue, esp. of a library, the items of which are entered on cards; **card-edge gilder**, a man who, or machine which, gilds the edges of cards; **card-index** *sb.*, an index recorded on separate cards; **card-index** *v.*, to make a card-index of; also *fig.*; so **card-indexing**; **card vote**, in trade union meetings, a method of voting by which the vote of each delegate counts for the number of his constituents.

1876 *Rep. Public Libr. U.S.A.* (Washington) 496 *Card Catalogue. The catalogue cards having received the shelf marks [etc.]. **1877** *Trans. & Proc. Confer. Libr. Lond.* (1878) 70 The importance of printed card-catalogues of old.. books. **1902** F. A. BATHER in *Museums Jrnl.* Apr. 291 The card-catalogue..is the form always used in America. **1917** FICKER *Industr. Cost-finding* 183 A card catalogue of all gauges in the factory should be kept. **1902** *Westm. Gaz.* 1 Jan. 1/7 Book *Card-edge Gilders. **1921** *Dict. Occup. Terms* (1927) § 538 *Card edge gilder*;..places cards in press after they are trimmed..; brushes them over with size, lays on gold leaf and allows it to dry; burnishes gold leaf by hand with agate or bloodstone burnishing tool. **1900** *Engineering Mag.* XIV. 767 Those who desire to clip the items for *card-index purposes. **1911** H. S. HARRISON *Queed* vi. 67 She had touched the spring of the automatic card-index system, known as his memory. **1927** *Daily Express* 31 Oct. 13 The film is an interesting example of the 'card-index' method of film construction. **1908** *Modern Business* Dec. 544/2 *Card indexing has become nowadays an essential requirement of modern business. **1917** TWYFORD *Purchasing & Storing* 16 Card indexing them [*sc.* specifications]..will make them available for rapid reference. **1920** ROSE MACAULAY *Potterism* I. iv, Jane, sitting in her father's outer office, card-indexing, opening and entering letters. **1929** *Sunday Dispatch* 13 Jan. 5 The little books have made it possible to 'card-index' my mind and systematise my memory. **1902** *35th Ann. Rep. Trades Union Congress* 74 Should a *card vote be demanded, it would of course be taken. **1924** H. G. WELLS in *Westm. Gaz.* 8 Mar., Should its [*sc.* the League of Nations'] members have a card vote after the pattern of a British Trade Union Congress?

Card, *v.*[2] Add: **4.** To affix by means of a card.

1844 POE *Oblong Box* Wks. III. 233, I observed that his name was carded upon *three* state-rooms.

Cardan (kā·ɹdăn). The name of *Cardan* (Geronimo Cardano, 1501–1576, an Italian mathematician), used attrib. in *cardan joint*, a universal joint, a joint permitting free motion of the different parts of the mechanism; *cardan shaft*, a shaft having a universal joint at one end or at both ends for transmitting motion from one shaft to another not in a direct line with it. Also *absol.*

1902 HARMSWORTH *Motors & Motor-Driving* 191 In order to permit of the free vertical movement of the wheels under the springs, two universal or 'Cardan' joints..are fitted within the length of the shaft. **1906** *Daily Chron.* 14 July 6/4 The cardan shaft, which connects the gear-box with the differential gear that works the driving wheel. **1906** *Westm. Gaz.* 2 Oct. 7/1 While oiling his motor as it was running, M. Santos-Dumont caught the sleeve of his leather jacket in the cardan. **1907** *Ibid.* 13 Nov. 9/2 The 15-h.p. is the only model having a cardan drive. **1908** *Ibid.* 16 Apr. 4/2 A very short cardan-jointed shaft. **1912** *Motor Man.* (ed. 14) 82 A 'cardan' shaft drive. **1922** *Autocar* 10 Nov. 974 The double brake fixed at the front end of the cardan-shaft.

Cardanic, *a.* Delete †*Obs.* and add: *Cardanic suspension*, a form of support in which an instrument is hung on gimbals, so as to allow free movement in all directions.

1892 *Review Rev.* (U.S.) July 718 (Funk) A highly sensitive vibrator, with cardanic suspension.

Cardboard. Add: *fig.* Unsubstantial, unreal, 'pasteboard'.

1893 *Jrnl. Soc. Arts* XLI. 476/1 When his cardboard empire of the East fell to pieces. **1928** (*title of play*) Her Cardboard Lover.

Carded. Add:

4. Entered on a programme card (CARD *sb.*[2] 6 e) or score-card.

1900 *Daily News* 18 Aug. 7/3 The next race carded was for the Rear-Commodore's Cup. **1927** *Daily Express* 19 Oct. 3/4 Nine times out of ten the carded distance is wrong.

Cardinal, *sb.* Add:

1. d. Either of two (Senior and Junior) of the minor canons of St. Paul's Cathedral.

1748 CHAMBERLAYNE *Pres. St. Gt. Brit.* II. III. 231, 12 Minor Canons [of St. Paul's Cathedral]...The Rev. Mr. William Rayner, Subdean, sen. The Rev. Mr. Dechair sen. Cardinal, The Rev. Mr. Hilman jun. Cardinal [etc.]. **1868** WALCOTT *Sacred Archæol.* 113 Cardinal. The word, when applied to an altar, means the high or principal altar, and from their attendance upon it two minor canons at St. Paul's are still called the senior and junior cardinals. **1877** J. D. CHAMBERS *Divine Worship* 90 At S. Paul's, London..there were four Vicars called Cardinals.

Cardinalize (kā·ɹdinăləiz), *v.* Transfer †*Obs.* to 2 and add to 1:

1921 S. LESLIE *Manning* xiii. 196 Meantime Cullen had been Cardinalised.

Carding, *vbl. sb.*[1] **3.** **carding-machine** (early example).

1789 WASHINGTON *Diaries* IV. 41 In this Manufactory they have the new Invented Carding and Spinning Machines.

Cardio-. Add: **Ca·rdio-diaphragma·tic** *a.*, pertaining to the heart and the diaphragm. **Ca·rdiogram**, the tracing made by a cardiograph. **Ca·rdiogra·phic** *a.*, of or pertaining to the cardiograph; hence **Ca·rdiogra·phically** *adv.* **Ca·rdio-inhi·bitory** *a.*, checking or arresting the heart's action. **Ca·rdiolo·gical** *a.*, of or pertaining to cardiology. **Cardio·logist**, one versed in cardiology. **Cardio·lysis**, resection of portions of the cardiac area. **Ca·rdiomo·tor** *a.*, pertaining to the action of the heart. **Ca·rdiopto·sis**, displacement of the heart downwards. **Ca·rdio-pu·lmonary** *a.*, pertaining to the heart and lungs. **Ca·rdio-re·nal** *a.*, pertaining to the heart and the kidneys. **Ca·rdio-respi·ratory** *a.*, relating to the action of both heart and lungs. **Ca·rdioscleros·is**, induration of the tissues of the heart. **Cardio·tomy**, dissection of the heart. **Ca·rdiova·scular** *a.*, relating to both the heart and the blood-vessels.

1907 *Practitioner* Apr. 528 A smaller movement of the right *cardio-diaphragmatic angle. **1888** *Buck's Handbk. Med. Sci.* VI. 95/2 The *Cardiogram.—A graphic record of the impulse of the heart against the chest-wall can be obtained by means of sphygmographs constructed on the principle of Marey's; or by modifications of the same for their better application to the thorax, as Galabin's cardiograph. **1892** A. E. SANSOM *Dis. Heart* 493 Dr. Hercules Macdonald obtained cardiograms from the posterior aspect of the heart. **1884** B. BRAMWELL *Dis. Heart* 751 *Cardiographic tracings are usually obtained from the pulsations of the left apex-beat. **1907** *Practitioner* Nov. 610 Both *cardiographically and clinically, its duration is well defined. **1884** BRAMWELL *Dis. Heart* 31 The *cardio-inhibitory centre in the medulla. **1907** *Practitioner* Nov. 693 The conservative influence of cardio-inhibitory action. **1922** *Encycl. Brit.* XXXI. 350/2 Another aspect of the *cardiological problem..is the so-called 'nervous or irritable heart'. **1927** *Daily Tel.* 21 June 15 The cardiological department contains an electrocardiograph. **1885** *Lancet* 26 Sept. 576/1 Being near the great *cardiologist, he thought he would hear what he had to say. **1903** *Ibid.* 18 July 188/2 Dr. Brauer performed an operation which has been called *cardiolysis and which consists in resecting some costal cartilages and a part of the sternum so that the heart would have more freedom of movement. **1918** F. W. PRICE *Dis. Heart* 346 The advisability of performing the operation of 'cardiolysis' in some cases of severe adhesions between the pericardium and the chest wall. **1924** R. W. G. HINGSTON in E. F. Norton *Fight for Everest, 1924* 250 The *cardiomotor mechanism of the vigorous man at a height of 16,000 feet closely resembles that of the physically inefficient person at sea-level. **1905** *Medical Annual* 185 Palpitations, attacks of vertigo, and occasionally inability to lie on the left side, are the principal symptoms... *Cardioptosis does not endanger life. **1918** F. W. PRICE *Dis. Heart* 24 The apex-beat ..may be displaced downwards in cardioptosis, emphysema, and pneumothorax. **1908** *Practitioner* Mar. 324 Such murmurs are louder during inspiration, and are literally *cardio-pulmonary, the pulmonary artery being compressed by the flattened chest-wall through the medium of the lung. **1913** *Jrnl. Chem. Soc.* CIV. I. 1022 Respiration and Metabolism in *Cardio-renal Disease. **1892** OSLER *Princ. Med.* 227 The so-called *cardio-respiratory murmur. **1908** J. MACKENZIE *Dis. Heart* 26 A cardio-respiratory reflex. **1894** GOULD *Dict. Med.*, *Cardio-sclerosis. **1908** J. MACKENZIE *Dis. Heart* p. xviii, The term cardio-sclerosis, unless qualified, will always refer to the group with arterial degeneration. **1922** *Encycl. Brit.* XXXI. 348/1 Doyen attempted *cardiotomy on a patient believed to be suffering from mitral stenosis. **1879** *St. George's Hosp. Rep.* IX. 798 *Cardio-vascular pulsation. **1909** *Practitioner* Nov. 617 The cardio-vascular hypertrophy. **1918** F. W. PRICE *Dis. Heart* 79 Those articles of food which especially stimulate the cardio-vascular system.

Cardol (kā·ɹdǫl, -ɔl). *Chem.* Also 9 **-ole.** [f. (ANA)CARD + -OL.] A vesicatory oil obtained from the pericarp of the cashew-nut.

1857 E. BALFOUR *Cycl. India*, Cardole. **1863** WATTS *Dict. Chem.* I. 803 Cardol. **1913** *Jrnl. Chem. Soc.* CIV. I. 885 Cardol can be distilled in superheated steam or under reduced pressure.

Care, *sb.*[1] Add:

4. *In care of* (U.S.): = *care of.*

1928 *N. & Q.* 4 Aug. 90 If owners of such letters will write to me in care of the Oxford University Press. **1929** *Science News-Letter* 20 Apr. 243 Mail the slip to the Secretary, Clarendon Press, Oxford..or in care of Science Service, Washington, D.C.

6. care committee, a committee which charges itself with the care of the poor.

1908 *Times* 3 Feb. 11/5 He had been told to devote the whole of his time to assisting the *Care Committee. **1909** M. FRERE *Children's Care Committees* 35 In 1900 the name [*sc.* Charitable Funds Committee] was changed to Children's Relief Committee, and finally, in 1908, to Children's Care Committee. **1914** PEPLER *Care Committee* Pref. p. iii, The 'after care' of children as they leave school is the most hopeful side of Care Committee work.

Cared (kēɹd), *ppl. a.* [f. CARE *v.* 3 + -ED [1].] In comb. with adv., as *cared-for*, attended to, looked after.

1911 *Rep. Labour & Social Condit. Germany* VI–VII. 190 The..cared for appearance of the children. **1924** ROSE MACAULAY *Orphan Island* xviii, He..had a cared-for looking white skin.

Careen, *v.* 4. Add: Also *transf.*; esp. (*U.S.*) of a motor car.

1883 G. MEREDITH *Poems, Lucifer in Starlight* 7 Now his huge bulk o'er Afric's sands careened. **1916** C. H. STAGG *High Speed* ix. (1920) 152 A hundred times their throats choked as the car careened on a bank. *Ibid.* xiv. 251 The car should have careened until it almost turtled. *Ibid.* xv. 272 A sickening skid,..a careening lurch that brought a cry from Dan.

Careenage. (Earlier U.S. example.)

1779 B. FRANKLIN *Wks.* (1889) VI. 432, I approve of the careenage for the Alliance as a thing necessary.

Careener (kărī·nəɹ). One who is employed to careen a ship.

1925 *Sunday at Home* Oct. 37/1 Along her barnacled keel gangs of careeners plied their slimy task.

Careerist (kărī·rist). [f. CAREER *sb.* + -IST.] One who though holding a public and responsible position is yet mainly intent on personal advancement.

[**1910** H. G. WELLS *Mr. Polly* vii. 165 He called him the 'chequered Careerist'.] **1917** *Times* 5 June 7/2 Half the present unpopularity of the 'lawyer-politician'..is due to the fact that he is too often a 'carpet-bagger' and a 'careerist'. **1929** G. B. SHAW in *Times* 6 Aug., There were already..members of it [*sc.* the labour party] who were 'careerists'—men who wanted to have a political career and joined the party they thought would give them the best prospects.

Carefree (kē·ɹfrī), *a.* [f. CARE *sb.*[1] + FREE *a.*] Free from care or anxiety. Hence **Ca·refreeness.**

1854 B. TAYLOR *Life & Landscapes fr. Egypt* vii. 96 We.. wander..as happy and care-free as two Adams in a Paradise without Eves. **1901** *Scribner's Mag.* XXIX. 426/2 Snatches of strange song fell from him..expressing his care-free mood. **1919** E. GRUBB *Relig. Exper.* xi. 133 This joyous, care-free, self-abandoning life. **1920** P. G. WODEHOUSE *Damsel in Distress* xx. 231 Nothing could have been more care-free and debonair than the demeanour of these men. **1924** *Public Opinion* 21 Mar. 292/2 It makes for joyous indolence and carefreeness of heart. **1928** G. COOKE *Theory of Music* 75 The apparently carefree joyousness of individual performance.

Caretake (kē·ɹtē̆k), *v.* [Back-formation f. CARE-TAKER.] *trans.* To take charge of, watch over, and keep in order (a house, estate, business premises, etc.) in the absence of the owner or customary occupants. Also *absol.*

1893 *Cornhill Mag.* Nov. 507 Martha caretakes a decrepit City warehouse. **1904** *Daily Chron.* 16 Apr. 9/5 House-keeper (Working)..occasionally to caretake. **1921** *Glasgow Herald* 6 Aug. 6 They have to be electrical and mechanical engineers, and to 'care-take' the whole establishment, as well as to operate.

Care-taking, *vbl. sb.* and *ppl. a.* Add later quots., esp. in the sense of taking charge of a house, etc.

1879 'E. GARRETT' *House by Works* I. 174 There will be none to send to market but that caretaking woman. **1883** 'ANNIE THOMAS' *Mod. Housewife* 139 To rely solely upon ..'trusty' servants, or care-taking models. **1895** *Atlantic Monthly* July 61 The feeding and care-taking inseparable from life in the nest.

Carf. 1. (Recent U.S. examples.)

1889 FARMER *Americanisms*, *Carf*, a 'blaze' or mark made on a tree destined to be felled. **1897** HOWELLS *Landlord Lion's Head* vii, He lifted his axe, and struck it into the carf on the tree.

Cargador (kārgadōɹ). [Sp.] In Spanish America: A porter.

1889 K. MUNROE *Golden Days* iv. 36 Nearly naked *cargadores*, or native porters [bent] beneath heavy burdens. **1904** CONRAD *Nostromo* viii. 81 A cargador would fly out head first and hands abroad. **1927** *Blackw. Mag.* Aug. 221/2 Toiling as a *cargador* on the *malecon*, he had seen the first Chilian squadron tossing in the bay. *Ibid.* Nov. 644/2, I gave the cargador the keys and asked him to put the baggage through whilst I bought a ticket.

Cargo, *sb.*[1] **3.** Add:

1834 M'CULLOCH *Dict. Commerce* 985 There is an immense variety in the qualities of rice. That which is principally exported from Bengal has received the name of cargo rice. **1907** *Motor Boat* 19 Sept. 190/2 A good, simple, and cheap cargo winch. **1920** *Blackw. Mag.* Mar. 316/2 The cargo-holds were refurbished. **1922** *Glasgow Herald* 14 June 12 A homeward bound cargoman. **1925** REX CLEMENTS *Gipsy of Horn* 151 Making the harpoon-line fast to the cargo-fall.

Ca·rgo, *v.* [f. CARGO *sb.*[1]] *trans.* To load.

1892 *Congress. Rec.* 18 Mar. 2188/1 Pelts and peltries, and anything else the teamster may be cargoed with. **1924** ROSE MACAULAY *Orphan Island* i, They were for leaving the island with the two boats, cargoed with fruit and cocoanuts.

Cariacine (kæriasəin), *a.* [f. *Cariacus* (see def.) + -INE[1].] Pertaining to a group of deer typified by *Cariacus virginianus*, the Virginian Deer.

1891 FLOWER & LYDEKKER *Mammals* 329 The typical Cariacine group, as represented by *C. virginianus.*

Cariama: see SERIEMA.

1889 *Daily News* 4 Dec. 2/7 A pair of cariamas..perambulate their cage in a dignified fashion. **1889** *Athenæum* 14 Dec. 826/2 Burmeister's cariama (*Chunga burmeisteri*).

Carian (kē̆·riăn), *a.* and *sb.* [f. L. *Caria*, Gr. Καρία + -AN.] **A.** *adj.* Of or belonging to Caria, an ancient province of Asia Minor. **B.** *sb.* A native or inhabitant of Caria.

1876 *Encycl. Brit.* V. 102/2 The Carians are spoken of by all ancient writers as a distinct nation from their neighbours. **1902** *Ibid.* XXXIII. 896/2 Symbols exactly like ϕ, χ, ψ.. are found in the Carian alphabet.

Caribe (karī·be, kæ·ribē). Also **cariba.** [Sp.: see CARIB.] A characinoid fish of the genus *Serrasalmo*, in the rivers of tropical S. America, noted for its voracity and sharp bite.

1880 GÜNTHER *Fishes* 613 The fish hooked is immediately attacked by the 'Caribe' (as these fishes are called). **1904** BOULENGER in *Cambr. Nat. Hist.* VII. 378 The 'Piranha' or 'Cariba' (*Serrasalmo*)..whose bite has been compared to the cut of a razor. **1926** *Chambers's Jrnl.* Aug. 509/2 The caribe is no more than three or four inches in length.

Caribou. (Earlier examples.)

1672 JOSSELYN *New Eng. Rarities* 20 The Maccarib, Caribo, or Pohano, a kind of Deer. **1703** tr. *La Hontan's Voy. N. Amer.* I. 59 Harts and Caribous are kill'd both in Summer and Winter. **1763** tr. *Charlevoix* in *Lett. to Dutchess of Les Diguieres* 66 Champlain speaks of..hunting ..caribous.

b. *attrib.*, as *caribou meat, shank, skin.*

1779 *Essex Inst. Hist. Coll.* XLIX. 112 Sold..82 caribou skins, at £6 10. o. **1887** *Harper's Mag.* Feb. 458/2 The hunter..covers his feet with..a pair of moose or caribou shanks, with the hair outside. **1902** S. E. WHITE *Conjuror's House* viii. 94 She felt..the hunger that yet could not stomach the..hairy, black caribou meat.

Caridea (kări·dĭă), *pl. Zool.* [mod.L. (neut. pl.), f. Gr. καρίς καριδ- shrimp.] A tribe of macrurous decapod crustaceans, containing the shrimps and prawns. Hence **Carid** (kæ·rid), a member of this tribe. **Cari·dean, Ca·ridid** *adjs.*, of or belonging to the Caridea. **Ca·ridoid** *a.*, resembling the Caridea.

1852 DANA *Crustacea* I. 528 In arranging the Caridea into groups, much stress is usually laid upon external form and length of beak. **1877** THOMSON *Voy. Challenger* II. iii. 193 Scarlet caridid and peneid shrimps. **1904** *Ann. & Mag. Nat. Hist.* Ser. VII. XIII. 147 This combination of characters [in Malacostraca] goes to make up what might be called the caridoid 'facies'. **1907** *Ibid.* XIX. 460 The absence [in the Penæidea] of the Caridean bend in the abdomen. *Ibid.* 461 The gill-series in the lower Reptantia are fuller than in either Penæids or Carids. **1909** G. SMITH *Crustacea* 158 Two of the Caridea, viz. the Shrimp..and the Prawn.

Carilloner (kāri·lyənəɹ), anglicization of CARILLONEUR.

1930 *Aberdeen Press & Jrnl.* 20 Jan. 6/6 Again and again the carilloner had to give encore pieces.

Caritative, *a.* Add:

2. *Gram.* Endearing, hypocoristic.

1906 DRIVER *Jeremiah* 368 It seems more probable that it has a diminutive, caritative force.

Carless (kā·ɹlės), *a.* [-LESS.] Not possessing, or unprovided with, a (motor) car.

1927 *Blackw. Mag.* Nov. 696/1 The transport problem —for of course I was carless—was solved by the arrival of Bosworth, one of whose cars I instantly seized.

Carlicue, var. of CURLICUE.

1840 C. F. HOFFMAN *Greyslaer* II. x. 27, I soon saw, by the way in which the white man's track doubled and doubled again..that the fellow could not be cutting such carlicues for nothing. **1848** BARTLETT *Dict. Amer.* Add., *Carlacue*, a caper or boyish trick. 'To cut up carlacues', is a common expression, equivalent to 'cutting up didoes'. Used in New York. **1898** *Literature* 17 Sept. 263/2 In Canada.. the English-speaking country people..often used the word ..to signify a trifle or a thing of little value.—e. g.' I don't care a carlicue.' 'It is not worth a carlicue.'

Ca·r-load. [CAR *sb.*[1]] A load carried or capable of being carried in a car.

1868 *Rep. U.S. Commissioner Agric.* (1869) 40 Loss six head, in two car-loads brought from Chicago. **1887** *Nation* (N.Y.) 29 Dec. 516/1 Several car-loads of flour..consigned to the Philadelphia Grain Elevator Company. **1898** *Daily News* 2 May 5/9, 30 carloads of provisions. **1902** HARBEN *Abner Daniel* 37 No parental objection, everything smooth, and a car-load of silverware. **1904** *Daily Chron.* 3 Feb. 6/5, 10 per cent. discount for carload lots. **1916** H. G. WELLS *Mr. Britling* II. §9 'Come to hockey!' shouted Mr. Britling to each departing car-load.

Carlowitz (kā·ɹlŏvits, -wits). [a. Ger. *karlowitzer*.] A red wine of Carlowitz on the Danube (above Belgrade).

1920 G. SAINTSBURY *Notes Cellar-bk.* 93 The commoner vintages were not intolerable; you *could* drink Carlowitz if you tried, and the Austrian Vöslauer was not to be despised.

Carmelite. Add: Belonging to, or a member of, an order of nuns organized on the model of the Carmelite or White Friars.

1739 GRAY *Lett.* 1 Apr. (1900) I. 17 We saw the chapel of Minims and the Carmelite Nuns. **1888** H. J. COLERIDGE *St. Teresa* III. 9 St. Mary Magdalene of Pazzi was a 'Mitigated' Carmelite. **1909** *Dublin Rev.* Jan. 61 We have.. Carmelites at Lanherne, Darlington, and Chichester.

Carmined (kā·ɹmind), *a.* [f. CARMINE *sb.* + -ED[2], after *rouged.*] Reddened with carmine.

1893 *Scribner's Mag.* June 702/2 These coarse carmined Delilahs. **1902** G. MEREDITH in *Westm. Gaz.* 4 Mar. 8/2 Warfare with carmined savages. **1920** *Chambers's Jrnl.* 344/1 Two parted, carmined lips.

Carminophilous (kāɹminǫ·filəs), *a. Biol.* [f. CARMINE *sb.* + Gr. φίλος loving + -OUS.] Epithet of those cytoplasmic granules which are readily stained by carmine.

1901 G. N. CALKINS *Protozoa* 143 Carminophilous granules ..are easily stained by carmine and many aniline colours. **1903** E. A. MINCHIN in *Lankester's Zool.* I. II. 182 The so-called carminophilous granules,..composed apparently of an albuminoid substance which is stained red by picro-carmine and acetocarmine.

Carmoot (kā·ɹmūt). Also **karmouth, harmoot.** [Ar. *garmūt.*] The native name for the cat-fish *Clarias lazera*, common in the Nile.

1880 GÜNTHER *Fishes* 563 *Clarias*...The vernacular name of the Nilotic species is 'Carmoot'. **1910** *Encycl. Brit.* V. 513/1 The common Nile species, the 'Harmoot' (*Clarias lazera*), occurs abundantly in the Lake of Galilee.

Carnalize, *v.* Add:

3. *intr.* To become carnal or unspiritual.

1873 W. R. GREG *Enigm. Life* Pref. p. ix, The Great Idea ..congeals and carnalises, the moment we endeavour to embody it, into something which is vulnerable at every point.

Carnary. Delete † *Obs.* and add: Still used at Norwich as the name of the crypt below the chapel of the cathedral grammar school, formerly one of the monastic buildings attached to the cathedral.

1911 *Encycl. Brit.* XIX. 820/1 The grammar school is a Decorated edifice, formerly a chapel of St. John, of *c.* 1316, with a 'carnary' or crypt below.

Carnival. Add: Hence **Ca·rnivaling, Ca·rnivalizing** *vbl. sbs.* Also **Ca·rnivalite, Ca·rnivaller**, one who takes part in the carnival.

1841 THACKERAY *Shrove Tuesday in Paris* Wks. 1900 XIII. 570 When they grow old, perhaps, they leave off gallantry and carnivalising. **1881** *Pop. Sci. Monthly* XIX. 151 All shouting and cheering, merry as carnivallers. **1893** *Westm. Gaz.* 25 Feb. 5/3 Feasting on wonderful and uncanny—but very dainty—dishes is another important part of carnivaling. **1896** *Daily News* 19 Feb. 3/4 These fashionable Shrove-tide carnivalites.

Carnotite (kā·ɹnŏtəit). *Min.* [Named after Adolphe *Carnot*, French mine-inspector general: see -ITE [1].] A yellow earthy vanadate of potassium and uranium, found in south-western Colorado, and worked as a source of vanadium, uranium, and radium. Also *attrib.*

1899 *Jrnl. Chem. Soc.* LXXVI. II. 434 Carnotite, a New Uranium Mineral. By Charles Friedel and E. Cumenge... A new mineral containing uranium and vanadium, to which the authors give the name *carnotite*, is found in yellow, friable masses, mixed with very variable quantities of silica, together with malachite and chessylite, in pockets at the surface of a grit in Montrose Co., Colorado. **1920** *Discovery* May 143/1 The carnotite beds on the borders of Utah and Colorado.

Carolean (kærŏlī·ăn), *a.* and *sb.* [f. L. *Carolus* Charles + -EAN.] **A.** *adj.* = CAROLINE *a.* 1 b. **B.** *sb.* One who lived in the reign of Charles I or II.

1911 *Chambers's Jrnl.* 15 July 513/1 The rapacity and meanness of the Ministers in the Carolean era. **1927** *Observer* 8 May 15/2 The spirit that animated the restored Caroleans in their exhumatory operations against the regicides. **1927** *Daily Tel.* 12 July 5/5 A Carolean Poet [Marvell].

Carolina. (Additional U.S. examples.)

a **1813** A. WILSON & BONAP. *Amer. Ornith.* (1831) III. 110 *Rallus carolinensis*,..Carolina Rail. **1821** MRS. ROYALL *Lett. fr. Alabama* xliv. (1830) 138 This is the region of the Carolina pink. **1848** BARTLETT *Dict. Amer.*, *Carolina potato*, the sweet potato..so called in the Eastern States. **1858** J. A. WARDER *Hedge Manual* II. 279 Carolina Laurel is a native evergreen found from Virginia to Louisiana. **1871** SCHELE DE VERE *Americanisms* (1872) 399 The Pink-root...is quite generally known as Carolina Pink also. **1881** *Amer. Naturalist* XV. 216 The Carolina dove (*Zenaidura carolinensis*) is very numerous. *Ibid.* 522 The Carolina waxwing, close cousin to that big Bohemian.

Carolinian, *a.* and *sb.* **b.** (Earlier examples.)

1705–6 PENN *Let. to Logan* 9 Dec. in *Corr.* (1872) II. 105 The Carolinian lords. **1707** J. ARCHDALE in *Narr. Early Carolina* (1911) 297 By the Encouragements of several Carolinians then in England, my Going was concluded on. **1832** D. J. BROWNE *Sylva Amer.* 251 The Carolinian poplar blooms in March or April.

Carotin, -ene (kæ·rŏtin, -īn). Also **carrotin.** [f. L. *carōta* CARROT: see -IN [1], -ENE.] A red crystalline compound contained in carrots and tomatoes. Hence **Carotinoid** *a.*

1863 WATTS *Dict. Chem.* I. 805. **1895** *Naturalist* 24 [Berries of mountain ash.] Their colouring matter is due to carotin. **1897** *Jrnl. Chem. Soc.* LXXII. II. 225 The author does not attempt to decide whether the crystals formed in this reaction are all xanthophyll or all carotin crystals, or whether these are identical or whether they consist in part of colouring matters nearly related to carotene. **1898** M. I. NEWBIGIN *Colour in Nature* 39 In plants the best known lipochrome is carotin. **1930** *Brit. Jrnl. Exper. Pathol.* Apr. 81 The relation between the carotenoid pigments and vitamin A.

Carp, *sb.*[1] **3.** Add: **carp-louse**, a name for various small crustaceans of the sub-order *Branchiura* or family *Argulidae*, parasitic on fishes (1889 in *Cent. Dict.*).

1909 LISTER in *Sedgwick's Zool.* III. 410, 413. **1911** W. T. CALMAN *Life of Crustacea* 41.

Carpathian (kaɹpē·þiăn), *a.* [f. *Carpathos*: see -IAN.] Of or pertaining to Carpathos, the ancient name of the island of Scarpanto in the Mediterranean.

1634 MILTON *Comus* 872 By hoary Nereus wrincled look, And the Carpathian wisards hook. *c* **1789** *Encycl. Brit.* (1797) IV. 179/1 The sea which, from this island, is called the Carpathian Sea. **1925** *Glasgow Herald* 30 July 6 In a spell of Carpathian silence.

Carpenter, *sb.* **5.** Add: **carpenter work**, carpentry. Also *fig.*

1553 *Respublica* (Brandl) v. vi. 59, I woulde ere long of yowe made suche carpenter weorke, That ye shoulde have saide Policie had been a clerke. **1720** in *Jrnl. Derbysh. Archæol. Soc.* (1905) XXVII. 216 Carpenter work 1 6 0. **1844** H. STEPHENS *Bk. Farm* I. 168 They embrace the particulars of mason-work, carpenter-work, slater-work,..smith-work. **1909** *Daily Chron.* 2 June 5/2 The play is at best a piece of very crude carpenter-work.

Carpenter, *v.* Add: *fig.* To cut to a certain shape, manipulate, or get up in a certain way.

1908 *Daily Chron.* 23 Oct. 6/1 The acting may be bad, the play cribbed and carpentered, but if people are genuinely moved the essence is there. **1909** MRS. STRATTON-PORTER *Girl of Limberlost* xi. 212 When I think of how you are carpentered, I'm adoring the result.

Carpet, *sb.* **5.** Add: **carpet shark**, a shark having spots on the back suggesting the pattern of a carpet; **carpet slipper**, a slipper the uppers of which are made of carpet-like material; also used *attrib.* to express a homely, fireside, easy-going, or slip-shod method of work.

1929 S. ELLIOTT NAPIER in *Times* 2 Aug. 14/1 The 'Leopard' or '*Carpet' shark. **1851** MAYHEW *Lond. Labour* I. 157/1 The large *carpet slippers that served her for shoes. **1902** *Chambers's Jrnl.* 10 May 353 Etymologists relieve the tedium of a hard day's work by a relapse into the carpet-slipper side of their science. *Ibid.*, The old monks were adepts at carpet-slipper derivation. **1905** H. A. VACHELL *The Hill* ii. (1923) 17 He slimes about in carpet slippers—the beast! **1907** *Daily Chron.* 6 Mar. 3/6 Her disgust at the carpet-slippers and the old aunt's bonnet. **1918** J. C. SNAITH *Mary Plantagenet* i, The miserable Joe took off his boots and put on a pair of carpet slippers.

Carpet-bag. (Earlier U.S. examples.)

1830 *Boston Directory* Advt. 28. **1840** *Ibid.* 11. **1843** CARLTON *New Purchase* I. ii. 5 The lower tier was composed of saddle-bags, valises, small trunks, and carpet-bags.

b. *U.S.* (Earlier examples.)

1857 *Herald of Freedom* (Lawrence, Kansas) 19 Sept. (Th.) Early in the spring several thousand excellent young men came to Kansas. This was jokingly called the carpet-bag emigration. **1870** in Tourgee *Invis. Empire* xii. (1880) 504 As to the carpet bag members of the Convention..they were thirteen in number.

Hence **Ca·rpet-bag** *v.* (Cf. CARPET-BAGGER.)

1889 *Century Dict.*, *Carpet-bag*, to act or live in the manner of a carpet-bagger. (U.S. slang.) **1890** *Congress. Rec.* 4 June 5598/2 It has been stated that Mr. McDuffie carpet bagged from somewhere down into Alabama...Now I will tell the House how Judge McDuffie happened to carpet-bag down into that district.

Carpet-bagging. *U.S.* Travelling with only a carpet-bag to contain one's effects; *spec.* the practice of carpet-baggery.

1869 *Atlantic Monthly* June 747 After three weeks' delightful Carpet-Bagging. **1888** BRYCE *Amer. Commw.* III. lxxv. II. 621 Negro suffrage produced, during the few years of 'carpet-bagging' and military government which followed the war, incredible mischief. **1904** *N. Y. Even. Post* 1 Feb. Let. to Editor, The infernal 'carpet-bagging' system at present in vogue should be done away with.

Carpet-baggism. *U.S.* (Earlier example.)

1872 *N.Y. Herald* 16 Dec. 5/1 Carpet-Bagism in Alabama.

Carpeting, *sb.* **2.** (Earlier U.S. examples.)

1758 B. FRANKLIN *Corr.* Wks. 1840 VII. 165 Some carpeting for a best room floor. **1784** *Indep. Chron.* (Boston) 13 May 3/3. **1790** *U.S. Stat. at Large* I. 181 Carpets and carpeting. **1794** *Ibid.* 391 [Duty of] Five per cent ad valorem...On carpets and carpeting.

Carpincho (kaɹpi·ntʃo). [Native name in Uruguay.] The capybara.

1839 DARWIN *Jrnl.* iii. 57 These great Rodents are generally called 'carpinchos'. **1879** *Cassell's Nat. Hist.* III. 145. **1904** *Westm. Gaz.* 6 Sept. 10/1 When alarmed the carpincho utters a kind of grunting cry.

Carrancha (kăræ·ntʃă). Also **carancha, caranco.** [Native name.] A South American caracara or carrion-hawk, *Polyborus tharus.*

1839 DARWIN *Jrnl.* iii. 64 *Polyborus Braziliensis*...is most numerous on the grassy savannahs of La Plata (where it goes by the name of Carrancha). **1889** SCLATER & HUDSON *Argent. Ornithol.* II. 81 *Polyborus tharus*...Carancho Carrion-Hawk. **1911** *Encycl. Brit.* XX. 901/1 The carrancha or carrion-hawk..is one of the characteristic features of a Patagonian landscape.

Carrapato (karăpā·to). Also **carapato**; and in Sp. form **garrapata.** [Pg.] A tick of the genus *Ixodes*. Also *attrib.*, as *carrapato disease* (quot. 1903).

1892 G. FLEMING *Neumann's Treat. Parasites* 103 These are popularly designated by such names as Ticks, Prickers, Garapattes, and Carapatos. **1903** *Jrnl. Tropical Med.* 2 Nov. 341/1 The carapato disease of the Zambesi basin is certainly produced by the bite of a tick—*Argas moubata*. **1906** F. C. GLASS *Through Heart Brasil* 20 The carrapato is a kind of minute tick.

Carrel(l (kæ·rəl). *Hist.* Variant of CAROL *sb.* 5 (a monk's study in a cloister) frequent in recent historical writers.

1890 J. W. CLARK *Cambr.* 274 They..retired thither for study after dinner, each sitting in his 'carrell' as it was called. **1893** F. MADAN *Bks. in MS.* 34 These carrels were fully open on one side of the cloister walk. **1899** *Trans. Bristol & Glouc. Archæol. Soc.* XXII. 262 The carrels were..in the inner wall of the cloister walk.

Carrel(l, early variants of CORRAL *sb.*

1845 JOEL PALMER *Jrnl.* (1847) 28 (Th.) On the eastern side of the fort is an additional wall, enclosing ground for stables and carrell. **1850** W. MILES *Jrnl.* (1916) 15 Our mules and cattle..might..be made secure within this carrel or yard.

Carretera (karetę̄·ra). [Sp.] A high road.

1900 *Engineering Mag.* XIX. 683 A *carretera*, or macadamized road is the 'best road' or route of the 'fast mail' in Porto Rico. **1923** *Blackw. Mag.* Aug. 178/1 The extreme provincialism of the Spanish *carretera*. **1924** *Ibid.* June 804/2 Very pretty they look sailing slowly along the dusty *carretara* to do the day's marketing.

Carriage. Add: **33.** (Earlier example.) Also *attrib.*

1744 A. DOBBS *Hudson's Bay* 34 The River..having about 30 Falls..where they must carry their Canoes. Two or three of them are Carriages of a League or two. **1775** J. MELVIN *Jrnl.* (1857) 10 The carriage-place is about a mile in length.

34. *carriage-hire, -maker, -window.*

1855 M. M. THOMPSON *Doesticks* xvi. 138 If there is any [money] left after paying expenses and the Committee don't spend it in *carriage-hire. **1875** MRS. STOWE *We & Neighbors* ii. 27 Carriage-hire costs money. **1848** E. BRYANT *California* vi. 77 With the aid of these, Mr. Eddy, a *carriage maker by trade, was soon busily at work. **1870** MRS. ANN S. STEPHENS *Married in Haste* xlix. 253 She looked steadily through the *carriage-window.

35. carriage cradle, a luggage rack; **carriage-house** (earlier U.S. example).

1866 *Chambers's Jrnl.* 28 July 466, I saw [him] clutch at the *carriage-cradle above his head, as though it would have relieved his mind to climb. **1858** TERESA VIELE *Following the Drum* 183 Arches..opened..into the *carriage-house, there stood the massive family coach.

Carrier. Add:

1. e. A case in which letters, etc. are enclosed for dispatch by pneumatic tube. Also, a small bag or case containing messages, attached to a homing pigeon.

1871–2 *Min. Proc. Inst. C. E.* XXXIII. 7 The carriers for the reception of telegrams, letters, or light parcels, consist of small cylinders made of gutta percha [etc.]. **1875–6** *Ibid.* XLIII. 60. **1892** *Pall Mall Gaz.* 18 Aug. 1/3 The actual form on which the message was written is put into a little cloth box, called a carrier, and blown through a tube to the central telegraph office. **1908** H. R. KEMPE *Engineer's Year-Bk.* 253 The carriers in which the messages are placed consist of a cylindrical tube of gutta-percha covered with felt. **1920** *Blackw. Mag.* Dec. 762/1 He took a message form, wrote a few words on it, and taking a pigeon from the basket, fixed a carrier to its leg.

f. A device for filling the magazine of a gun or rifle with a group of cartridges; a charger.

1885 *Marine Engineer* 1 July 95/2 The carrier which draws the cartridges out of the belt, and deposits them in the feed wheel. **1901** *Westm. Gaz.* 21 Mar. 4/3 By means of the carrier the cartridges are dropped into the magazine receptacle and the empty carrier thrown away. **1903** C. B. MAYNE *Infantry Weapon* 139 This..can only be done by rapidly loading the rifle by means of groups of cartridges temporarily held together by 'clips' or by 'carriers', also called 'chargers'. [*Note*] The 'carrier', or 'charger', is a strip of tin that grips the cartridges by their projecting bases only; the 'clip' is a tin framework that, more or less, grips the whole cartridge-case.

g. A box, metal plate, or other contrivance attached to a tricycle or bicycle for carrying parcels, luggage, or a pillion-rider.

1885 *Naturalist's World* Jan. 6 A 'carrier' can be fixed on to the rod supporting the seat. **1887** BURY & HILLIER *Cycling* 201 Luggage..should be carefully affixed [to the machine] by means of one or other of the carriers described elsewhere. *Ibid.* 429 The Carrier Cycle. **1911** C. S. LAKE *Motor Cyclist's Handbk.* 253 Luggage Carrier and Stand. It is common practice to make the carrier of tubular material. **1915** B. E. JONES *Motor Cycles* 137 A very light carrier can be fitted, as this machine is not strong..enough for passenger-carrier riding.

h. *gen.* A holder or receptacle for carrying articles in the hand or on one's person.

1904 *Windsor Mag.* Jan. 273/2 You can have breakfast, luncheon, tea, and dinner brought piping hot to your table in patent carrier trays. *Mod. Advt.* Pocket Carrier [for a patented drug in tablets].

i. A vessel which conveys fish from the fishing-ground to a port or market.

1883 R. F. WALSH *Irish Fisheries* 16 (Fish. Exhib. Publ.) Many plans of steam carriers have been devised and proposed... Amongst [them] is the vessel with false hold or bottom, which allows the water to pass through with a view to bringing the fish alive to market. **1896** *Daily News* 27 Feb. 8/7 The fish..arrived in eight carriers. **1907** *Westm. Gaz.* 25 Feb. 6/3 The 'Speedwell,' a steam carrier.

j. A person or animal that carries and disseminates disease-germs.

[**1899** *Leisure Hour* 176/2 Two-winged flies..act as carriers of disease.] **1906** *Medical Annual* 182 Carriers [of diphtheria] without symptoms or demonstrable contact. **1907** *Ibid.* 609 Prominence has been given during the year to the importance of what are known as 'carrier' cases of diphtheria. **1909** OSLER & M'CRAE *Syst. Med.* V. 818 Chronic Carriers.—In many cases the typhoid bacillus may be recovered from the gall-bladder years after an attack of typhoid fever. **1910** R. ROSS *Prevent. Malaria* 195 If the local carrier belongs to a species..which feeds almost entirely upon man. **1922** *Encycl. Brit.* XXXI. 896/1 Such arthropoda,..being specific 'nurses' or intermediary hosts of the parasite actually causing the disease, are known as 'carriers' or 'vectors'.

k. An insoluble substance (e.g. barytes, china clay, gypsum) used as a base to receive the colouring matter in the preparation of certain pigments.

1892 G. H. HURST *Colours* etc. 268 The base or carrier exerts a most important influence on the value of the lake as a pigment. **1915** J. C. SMITH *Manuf. Paint* 170 Many so-called lakes consist simply of a carrier..saturated with a soluble dye.

l. *Chem.* A catalytic by whose agency a transfer of some element or group is effected from one compound to another (Webster).

1892 BEDSON & WILLIAMS *Meyer's Theoret. Chem.* 214 Certain bodies act as carriers of chlorine in a similar way to the oxygen carriers. **1902** J. B. COHEN *Theoret. Org. Chem.* 368 If chlorine or bromine acts upon benzene in presence of a 'carrier', substitution occurs. **1910** N. V. SIDGWICK *Org. Chem. Nitrogen* 182 In neutral solution bromine has scarcely any action except in the presence of a carrier, such as iron wire. **1921** D. LL. HAMMICK *Org. Chem.* 156 [The iron] probably acts as a halogen 'carrier', ferric bromide being first formed, and then 'handing on' bromine to the benzene molecules.

m. *Telegraphy* and *Telephony.* A high frequency current, or each of a set of currents of varying frequency, used for multiplex transmission. In full *carrier current.* Also *attrib.*, as *carrier frequency, wave.*

1921 *Jrnl. Inst. Electr. Engin.* Apr. 402/2 The most valuable feature of the high-frequency carrier-wave system is its adaptability to multiplex telephony. **1921** COLPITTS & BLACKWELL *Ibid.* 412/2 Carrier-current Telephony and Telegraphy. **1922** *Encycl. Brit.* XXXII. 712/1 The high frequency current serves as a 'carrier' for the telephone current over the line. **1928** *Daily Mail* 25 July 8/3 The noise of London is..becoming more rhythmic. This enables certain sounds which are inaudible to act as carrier waves to others.

n. A small low detached cloud, betokening rain. *local.*

1844 H. STEPHENS *Bk. Farm* I. 251 The ominous scud is the usual harbinger of the rain-cloud, and is therefore commonly called 'messengers', 'carriers', or 'water-waggons'. **1884** *Upton-on-Severn Words.*

Carriole. 1. a. (Earlier U.S. example, in form *carriele*: cf. CARRY-ALL.)

1770 *Carroll Papers* in *Maryland Hist. Mag.* XIII. 55 Nothing is done to y^r Carriele, Because the wheelright is more usefully employed...The Carriele is kept on the Floor above the Dry well.

2. (Earlier example.)

1803 HARMON *Jrnl. Voy. N. Amer.* (1820) 109 Occasionally I visit our neighbours, drawn in a cariol by horses, if the snow is light, or by dogs, if it is deep.

Carrioling, *vbl. sb.* (Earlier example.)

1808 T. ASHE *Trav.* III. 30 In winter, carioling or sleying predominates.

Carrion. C. Add: **carrion-beetle**, any beetle of the family *Silphidæ*, which feed on carrion.

1815 KIRBY & SP. *Entomol.* viii. (1816) I. 228 A carrion-beetle (*Silpha lapponica*, L.). **1817** *Ibid.* xxi. II. 247 The carrion-beetles (*Silpha* and *Necrophorus*, F.),..defile us, if handled roughly, with brown fetid saliva.

Carro (kā·ro). [Pg.] In Madeira, a car or sledge on runners, drawn by bullocks.

1882 E. M. TAYLOR *Madeira* 198 Those Mount sledges, or *carros*, in which people are impelled down the steep Mount road at a very rapid rate. **1900** BIDDLE *Madeira Isl.* I. 118 The *carros* (bullock-cars mounted on runners).

Carrollese (kærəlī·z), **Carrolline** (kæ·rəlain), *adjs.* [See -ESE, -INE [1].] Resembling, or characteristic of, the style of C. L. Dodgson (1832–98), author of 'Alice's Adventures in Wonderland', who adopted the pseudonym of 'Lewis Carroll'.

1907 *Westm. Gaz.* 25 July 2/3 There is nothing Carrollese about the lines. **1927** *Observer* 3 Apr. 8 The book has the Gilbertian or, rather, Carrolline, title of 'Ships and Sealing Wax'.

Carrot, *sb.* **2.** Add: *To dangle a carrot* (before a donkey), a proverbial method of tempting the animal to move on; also *fig.* in allusion to this.

1895 *Westm. Gaz.* 24 Aug. 2/2 Among other carrots dangled before the electors last month was Bimetallism. [**1916** E. W. GREGORY *Furnit. Collector* 228 The spectacle of an otherwise intellectual individual engaged in trying to plumb the depths of duplicity to which dealers can descend in faking old furniture is like that of the donkey pressing eagerly forward after the dangling carrot. It would..be very pleasant to possess the carrot of complete knowledge, but the conditions render it impossible.]

2. b. (Later U.S. examples.)

1857 *Trans. Ill. Agric. Soc.* II. 360 The creoles manufactured the tobacco into carrots, as they were called. A carrot is a roll of tobacco twelve or fifteen inches long, and three or four inches in diameter at the middle of the roll, and tapered towards each end. **1890** *Congress. Rec.* 27 Aug. 9213/2, I have here some carots [*sic*] of Cuban tobacco.

Carrot (kæ·rət), *v.* [f. CARROT *sb.*, from the yellow colour imparted to the fur.] *trans.* To treat (fur) with nitrate of mercury (see quot. 1906). Hence **Ca·rroting** *vbl. sb.* and **Ca·rrotage** = SECRETAGE.

1879 *Encycl. Brit.* IX. 837/1 Furs..of the hare and the rabbit,..dressed, carroted, and cut from the skin. 1880 [see CARROTING in Dict.]. 1906 WATSON SMITH *Chem. Hat Manuf.* 17 The *sécretage* or 'carrotting' process..consists in a treatment with a solution of mercuric nitrate in nitric acid, in order to improve the felting qualities of the fur.

Carroty, *a.* For sense 'red-haired' add quots.:
1887 *Daily News* 9 Dec. 8/5 He was a tall, carroty man. 1912 C. N. & A. M. WILLIAMSON *Heather Moon* III. 297 The plainest, oldest, and carrotiest of the three red-headed maids.

Carry, *sb.* Add:
4. b. *Golf.* The distance between the spot from which a ball is driven and that where it first lands; also, the trajectory of the ball.
1887 SIR W. G. SIMPSON *Golf* 112 Getting both hands well under the club also produces a low carry. 1890 H. G. HUTCHINSON *Golf* (1892) 540 *Carry.*—The distance from the place where the ball is struck to the place where it pitches. Hence a *long carry*, and a *short carry*. 1896 W. PARK *Golf* 104 A well hit drive should be almost all carry; the ball should not run any distance after it falls. *Ibid.* 262 A long carry or a short carry are used to signify the distance a ball must be lofted usually over a hazard. 1899 *Golf Illustrated* 29 Dec. 319/2 The carry alone is estimated to have been close on two hundred and fifty yards.
5. *U.S.* (Earlier example.)
1857 *Knickerbocker Mag.* Nov. L. 494 From this place we were to walk over a 'carry'.

Carry, *v.* Add: **1. d.** *intr.* (for *pass.*) Of soil: To stick to the feet, or to horses' hoofs.
1892 *Field* 30 Jan. 153/2 The frost..caused the fallows and seeds to 'carry' a good deal, and they could only hunt very slowly. *Ibid.* 156/3 An expanse of ploughed soil which 'carries' considerably.
9. b. *Golf* and *Cricket.* Of the ball, or the player hitting it, or the bat, etc.: To cover (a distance) or pass (a point) at a single stroke. Also *absol.*
1875 *Golf* (ed. R. Clark) 213 The balls carried considerably higher than the weather-cock. 1887 SIR W. G. SIMPSON *Golf* 155 Many prefer it [*sc.* a dragging shot] to an ordinary loft at shortish distances, the latter being more difficult within, say, thirty yards than when the player has further to carry. *Ibid.* 184 His game is easily insulted by being made to go round, or play short of, a bunker, it ought to be allowed to try to carry. 1903 J. BRAID *Bk. Golf* 30 At a greater distance where the mashie will not carry I should very often use an iron. 1929 *Morning Post* 17 June 16/2 Off the next ball—a full-pitch—he only just failed to carry the ring.
16. c. To gain (a district, etc.) in an election. (Cf. 17.)
1905 D. G. PHILLIPS *Plum Tree* 122 We, our party, carried the state, as usual. Our legislative majority was increased by eleven.
26. d. Phr. *To carry one's life in one's hands*: to be exposed to fatal risks in the performance of one's regular duties or occupation.
1912 *Times Lit. Suppl.* 4 Jan. 2/2 The Transatlantic 'railway-man', whatever his rank,..must at times carry his life in his hands.
37. b. *To carry guns*: said of a ship, to be armed with (a specified number of) guns. Hence in fig. phrases *to carry too many guns for*; *to carry the biggest guns*: to be too well or best equipped with the means of attack or defence in argument, debate, etc.
1687 [see GUN *sb.* 1]. 1930 *Times* 25 Mar. 17/3 The Chancellor—whose..concern is to make the two ends of his Budget meet—necessarily carries the biggest guns.
38. c. *Comm.* To hold or keep on hand (securities, merchandise, a stock, etc.); to bear the charges or risk of holding (such property). Also, to keep (a customer) on one's books as a debtor. orig. *U.S.*
1848 W. ARMSTRONG *Stocks* 10 It is nominally considered that the stock is meanwhile 'carried' or possessed by the seller. 1869 J. H. BROWNE *Gt. Metrop.* iii. 48 (Funk) Operators can..carry such an amount of stocks as astounds the weaker ones of the street. 1870 MEDBERY *Men & Myst. Wall St.* 77 When a broker agrees to 'carry' stock, he says, Seven per cent, unless the market tightens. 1899 *Westm. Gaz.* 14 Nov. 11/3 They [*sc.* shops in Capetown] carry enormous stocks of goods from England, Germany, and America. 1905 *N. Y. Even. Post* 1 Sept. 7 One house in this city carries twelve hundred in picture post cards. 1917 TWYFORD *Purchasing & Storing* 325 It is not economical to carry in stock several variations of articles of a similar nature. 1917 ATWOOD *Exch. & Specul.* 51 In common parlance the customer trades on a 'margin'. Expressed in another way the broker 'carries' the customer for all except a small part of the cost. 1930 *Publishers' Weekly* 11 Jan. 214/1 Mr. Brady explained that he did not carry the book.
40. Also, to maintain (a population).
1905 *19th Cent.* Nov. 816 Mackay, with back country carrying about 15,000 people.
b. Of a journal: To print (an article) in its pages. *U.S.*
1890 (Remembered in use). 1926 *Publishers' Weekly* 22 May 1676/1 There are many towns in which the newspapers do not carry book reviews. 1927 *Ibid.* 12 Feb. 609 *Publishers' Weekly* of January 8th carried a letter signed by a committee of the American Booksellers' Association..which commented adversely on the Literary Guild.
43. b. To have (a specified dimension or weight). Also *pass.* with the same meaning.
1893 J. D. KENDALL *Iron Ores* 388 The same ore is mined by means of day levels, the headings being carried 9 feet wide. 1904 *Daily Chron.* 17 Aug. 4/7 The machine indicated that the Member for East Sydney 'carried' 18st. 4½lb. 1908 *Daily Report* 20 July 3/1 The 1,350-ft. level..is carrying 3½ ft. of quartz.
52. Carry on. d. Also, in military use, to continue as before, resume the former situation or occupation; to proceed to carry out instructions. Hence *gen.*, to 'keep going'; to make the best one can of abnormal conditions or difficult times.
1909 *Daily Chron.* 24 July 4/4 'Carry on!' is a word they have in the Navy. It is the 'great word' of the Service... To-morrow the workaday life of the Fleet begins again, and the word will be, 'Carry on!' 1915 'BARTIMEUS' *Tall Ship* i. 14 The ship..began to heel slowly over. The Captain..raised the megaphone to his mouth. 'Carry on!' he shouted. 'Every man for himself.' 1915 'IAN HAY' *First Hundred Thou.* xiv. 190 'Do you understand my order?' thundered the Colonel...'I do, sir,' replied Blaikie politely, 'but—' 'Then, for heaven's sake, carry on!' 1918 — *Last Million* vii. 97 I'm not one to ask for sympathy when there's others needs it more...Carry on—that's my motto! 1927 C. E. MONTAGUE *Right off the Map* 156 'We'll let the men carry on resting', said Willan.
e. (Earlier U.S. examples.) Also *spec.* To engage in flirtation, esp. of a dishonourable nature.
See also CARRYING *vbl. sb.* 3.
1828 MRS. ROYALL *Black Bk.* II. 27 They romped and squalled, and to use a Yankee phrase, 'carried on' at such a rate that he and Mrs. C. were greatly annoyed. 1834 S. SMITH *Sel. Lett. Major Downing* 18 These Legislaters have been carrying on so. 1856 [in Dict.]. 1876 BESANT & RICE *Golden Butterfly* xxxv, She and I carried on for a whole season. People talked. 1903 *Daily Chron.* 19 Feb. 7/5 Plaintiff accused him of 'carrying on' with another girl at the same time as he was engaged to her.
53. Carry out. c. *Cricket.* Also freq. with omission of *out.*
1884 *Boy's Own Paper* Summer No. 26 Keep your weather eye peeled, and just mind what you're at, And ev'ry man Jack of you'll carry his bat. 1888 R. H. LYTTELTON *Cricket* (Badm. Libr.) 336 His runs for seven innings came to a total of 61, or an average of 10 runs per innings, as once he carried his bat. 1895 *Westm. Gaz.* 18 May 7/1 Grace has carried his bat twenty-two times when scoring centuries.
54. Carry over. c. To transfer.
1889 E. CARPENTER *Civilis.* iv. 105 The ideal passion of that period..was that of comradeship, or male friendship carried over into the region of love.

Carry-all. *U.S.* (Earlier examples.)
1714 J. STODDARD *Jrnl.* in *N. E. Hist. & Gen. Reg.* V. 27 Mr. Longuille sent a carryall for us. 1775 in *Proc. Mass. Hist. Soc.* Ser. II. II. 288, I rode out in a Carry'al with my Landlord. *Ibid.*, I could not walk from the Carriall into the House without help. 1825 MOTLEY *Corr.* I. 3 We went to ride in a Nutshell, otherwise a monster of a carryall, with five seats in it.

Ca·rry-away. [f. *carry away*, CARRY *v.* 46 c.] In *Yachting*, the breakage of a spar, rope, etc.
1901 *Westm. Gaz.* 23 May 5/1 The 'carry-away'..was the most serious that could have happened. First bowsprit snapped, and topmast bent to leeward. 1928 *Daily Tel.* 11 Sept. 15/6 Mrs. Percy Sabel's Widgeon had a carry-away, and was forced to give up when well placed.

Carry-forward. *Comm.* [f. *carry forward*, CARRY *v.* 49.] The balance carried to the next account after declaration of dividend. (See CARRY *v.* 49.)
1898 *Westm. Gaz.* 17 May 8/1 The last carry-forward was £132. 1901 *Ibid.* 7 Aug. 7/1 This is one of the few companies which does not announce its carry forward with the dividend. 1929 *Evening News* 18 Nov. 15/2 After paying the Preference and Ordinary dividend the carry forward is £34,232 against £41,654 brought in.

Carrying, *vbl. sb.* Add: **2. carrying-over** = *CARRY-OVER.
1907 POLEY & GOULD *Stock Exch.* 168 The General Contango Day (these days are also known as Continuation or Carrying-over Days). *Ibid.* 175 Where the broker is himself the taker-in rendering a carrying-over note, he is not entitled to charge both commission and contango. 1910 H. WITHERS *Stocks & Shares* 277 If no charge is made for carrying over, a full commission is usually paid when the bargain is finally closed.
4. carrying chair, a chair in which a person is carried; **carrying charges,** the charges incident to holding goods for future sale (see *CARRY *v.* 38 c); **carrying-place** (earlier U.S. examples).
1894 *Outing* (U.S.) XXIV. 129/2 The Chinese mandarin..when seated proudly in his fancy *carrying-chair. 1905 *Westm. Gaz.* 25 Feb. 16/3 The carrying-chair used by Leo XIII. *c* 1707 in G. Sheldon *Hist. Deerfield* (1895) I. 361 At which time they got to the last *carrying place. 1721 *Jrnls. Ho. Repr., Mass.* III. 20 Fifty able Souldiers..constantly Scouting..the Rivers, Ponds, Carrying-places and Hunting Grounds. 1725 *Lancaster Rec.* 240 We..came to ye carrying-place, where ye Indians carry their conoes. 1753 WASHINGTON *Diaries* I. 55 It is 120 Miles to the carrying Place at the Fall of Lake Erie. 1759 *Essex Inst. Hist. Coll.* XIX. 148 The ginorals Borg [= barge] was..drawn a crost ye Carring Place and put into Lake Champlain.

Carrying, *ppl. a.* Add: **carrying comb** *Spinning* (see quots.); **carrying party** *Mil.*, a party detailed to carry or bring up supplies.
1868 *Patents, Abridgm. Specif. Spinning* II. 356 A pulley carried by a pillar placed within the main circle of *carrying combs. 1884 W. S. B. MCLAREN *Spinning* (ed. 2) 94 The carrying-comb carries off the wool from between its two plates. 1889 BURNLEY *Wool & Woolcombing* 269 The carrying comb advances in as near as possible a perpendicular position close to the nipper mouth and takes off the tuft of fibres. 1884 *Milit. Engin.* I. II. 109 A certain number..will be told off as *carrying party. They will be provided with bags of hay, shavings, wool, &c., boards, fascines. 1919 G. K. ROSE *2/4th Oxf. & Bucks Lt. Infty.* 72 When the evening's 'carrying parties' were finished.

Carry-over. [f. *carry over*, CARRY *v.* 54 b.] On the Stock Exchange: Postponement of payment of an account until the next settling-day; the amount so kept over. Also *attrib.*, as *carry-over day, price, rate.* Also *transf.* of other kinds of business.
1894 *Daily News* 29 Jan. 2/5 Grand Trunk stocks are from 2 to 4 per cent. higher than at the last 'carry over'. 1895 *Ibid.* 19 Oct. 2 The carry-over price was fixed at 2⅛. 1899 *Westm. Gaz.* 7 June 8/1 Monday is the carry-over day in mines.
transf. 1925 *London Teacher & Lond. School Rev.* 13 Nov. 393/2 The Board in 1921 announced suddenly that they would not pay grants on the full carry-over of the three Burnham scales. 1927 *Observer* 27 Nov. 21/2 A very heavy carry-over of work from the adjournment on December 21 is inevitable, as hundreds of cases are awaiting trial in the King's Bench Division. 1928 *Daily Express* 6 Jan. 6 Every session has its carry-overs, but there seems to be nothing this year to rival the importance of the Trades Disputes Bill.

Carstone (kā·ɹstoun). *Geol.* [app. = **carnstone*, for *quarn stone*, local form of QUERN-STONE.] A species of the Lower Greensand.
1815 W. SMITH *Mem. Map Strata Eng. & Wales* 43 Iron Sand, or Carstone. 1822 CONYBEARE & PHILLIPS *Outl. Geol. Eng. & Wales* 136 Iron Sand...We are able to trace and identify the present series throughout the island. In different counties it has received the name of Carstone and Quern stone. 1840 SPURDENS *Suppl. Forby's Voc. E. Anglia* (1858), *Car-stone*, a peculiar stone, found principally near Swaffham. 1876 WOODWARD *Geol. Eng. & Wales* 230 The hard beds, locally termed Carstone (or Quern stone), are worked for building-purposes. 1882 GEIKIE *Text-bk. Geol.* 820 The Upper Neocomian 'Car-stone'. 1885 *Ibid.* (ed. 2) 823 The Upper Neocomian sub-stage (Carstone) ranges into Norfolk.

Cart, *sb.* Add:
4. b. The carapace or upper shell of a crab. *colloq.* or *dial.*
1860 *Slang Dict.* (ed. 2) s.v. *Carts*, In Norfolk the carapace of a crab is called a *crab-cart*. 1887 *Girl's Own Paper* 16 July 661/2 Pick the meat from the cart, the breastplate, and the claws.
5. *In the cart*: (put or left) behind, in the rear, i.e. in a losing position. *slang.*
1889 *Evening Standard* 25 June (Farmer) It was alleged that in two races..Sir George Chetwynd—to use a vulgarism—had been put in the cart by his Jockey. 1908 *Punch* 12 Feb. 110 We were simply all over 'em, and had 'em in the cart in no time. *Ibid.* 4 Nov. 334 Something..tells me I am fairly in the cart. 1909 W. S. MAUGHAM *Smith* (1914) 13 Emily was left in the cart. 1911 W. J. LOCKE *Clementina Wing* xxi. 262 Lena Fontaine and Huckaby had put them in the cart. They were left, they were done, they were stung. 1924 J. B. HOBBS *Cricket Mem.* 158 We made 238, which was enough practically to put South Africa hopelessly in the cart.
6. cart-body (examples); **cart-road** (earlier U.S. example).
c 1325 *Gloss. W. de Bibbesw.* in Wright *Voc.* (1857) 167 *Le chartil*, the *carte body. 1407 in Kennett *Par. Antiq.* (1818) II. 213 Et pro sarratione et dolatione unius Cartbody..vj[d]. 1779 in *Narrag. Hist. Reg.* I. 93 Went to Tower hill for a cart body. 1834 W. G. SIMMS *Guy Rivers* 414 The conflagration..destroyed his cart-body and calicoes. 1700 *Cal. Virginia St. Papers* I. 72 From thence alonge yᵉ *Cart Roade until it comes..beyonde ye ffrench Ordinery.

Cart, *v.* Add:
1. *To cart off* or *away*: to carry off or away in a cart; hence *gen.* to carry off, take away, remove.
1881 *Punch* 8 Oct. 166/2 Napier and Havelock might be carted off to join the poor Duke of Kent at the top of Portland Place. 1891 FARMER *Slang.*
c. *Anglo-Indian.* (See quot.)
1837 T. BACON *First Impr. Hindustan* I. 137 Carting a girl, or riding out with her, is considered in India as a regular publication of the banns.
4. *trans.* To defeat easily in a game or match. *slang.* (Cf. prec. 5.) 1891 FARMER *Slang.*

Cartage. Add examples of attrib. use:
1901 *Daily News* 24 Jan. 9/1 The prisoner was doing some cartage work at Drayton Park. 1903 *Daily Chron.* 7 Jan. 8/1 A cartage contractor.

Cartel, *sb.* Add:
3. c. After G. *kartell* (a. F. *cartel* or It. *cartello*): In Germany and Austria, an agreement or association between two or more business houses for regulating output, fixing prices, etc.; also, the houses thus combined together; a trust or syndicate.
1902 *Daily Chron.* 24 May 6/3 He laid stress on the injury which would be done to the Indian industry if the country were flooded with 'Cartel' sugar. 1902 *Pol. Sci. Q.* XVII. 381 The cartel, or producers' syndicate. 1902 *Westm. Gaz.* 24 Nov. 10/1 The new cartel includes practically every important iron and steel interest in the Dual Monarchy. 1928 *Britain's Industrial Future* (*Liberal Ind. Inquiry*) II. viii. 93 Trusts, cartels, combinations.
d. *Hist.* The combination formed in 1887 between the Conservatives and the National Liberals in Germany to support each other's candidates, for the furtherance of Bismarck's military and imperial policy. Hence as a name for similar combinations in other countries.
1918 C. G. ROBERTSON *Bismarck* 453 The Chancellor's political cartel was complete; it consisted of the Conservatives, the old National Liberals, and the Centre; and the union gave him a decisive and obedient majority. 1918 A. W. WARD *Germany* III. 125 The entire *Cartel*, this time with the Centre, agreed to proceed with the loan. 1926 *Encycl. Brit.* II. 94/1 The Radicals, Radical-Socialists and Socialists formed a Cartel [France, 1924]. 1927 *Contemp. Rev.* Aug. 154 Hence an electoral cartel was inevitable, and to this the Transylvanians and Tsaranists consented. 1928 *Daily Tel.* 21 Aug. 8/3 The 'cartel' of Republican parties formed by him [*sc.* M. Venizelos].

Hence **Ca·rtel(l)ism,** the system of (political) cartels; **Ca·rtel(l)ist,** a member or supporter of a cartel; **Cartel(l)iza·tion,** the system of trade cartels; **Ca·rtel(l)ize** *v. trans.*, to combine into a cartel, bring under the control of a cartel.
1923 *Contemp. Rev.* June 716 Hitherto textiles were not regarded as favourable fields for cartelisation. 1925 *Glasgow Herald* 16 Apr. 9 Passionate Cartelist though he is. 1926 *Ibid.* 4 Jan. 7 The leading exponent of Cartellism. 1927 *R. Liefmann's Internat. Cartels* 98 Baron Tibbaut (Belgium) believed that cartellization spelled the death of 'protectionism'. *Ibid.* 101 In the face of a cartellized industry, strong organization of the consumers..was necessary. 1929 *Times* 5 June 15/3 In the late Council Anti-Cartellists and Cartellists were exactly balanced.

Cartel, cartle, var. ff. KARTEL, a hammock.
1880, 1885 [see KARTEL]. 1910 J. BUCHAN *Prester John* viii, [I] flung my kaross on the cartel which did duty as bed.

Carter[1]. Add:
4. In full **carter spider**: A spider of the family *Phalangiidæ*; = HARVESTMAN 2.
1665 HOOKE *Microgr.* 198 The Carter, Shepherd Spider, or long-legg'd Spider. 1746 B. MARTIN *Ess. Electricity* 22 That Sort [of spider] we call a Carter, or Father Long-legs.

Cartesian. Add: **Cartesian coordinate**: see COORDINATE *sb.* 2.

Carton[2] (kā·ɹtən). [ad. F. *carton*: see CARTON in Dict.] **a.** A box or case made of light pasteboard or cardboard, for holding goods. Hence **Cartoned** (kā·ɹtənd) *a.*, packed in a carton.
1906 *Daily Chron.* 24 Oct. 6/6 A pound carton [of soap]. 1921 C. C. MARTIN *Export Packing* 559 Sundry Cartoned Goods. 1924 *Public Opinion* 12 Sept. 258/3 Motorists' sandwich papers and cigarette cartons. 1926 *Spectator* 18 Sept. 412/1 The fish..are packed in specially designed cartons.
b. Light pasteboard or cardboard used for making boxes, etc. Also *attrib.*
1891 MAHAFFY *Flinders Petrie Papyri* 9 The coffins..were made of layers of papyrus,..stuck together so as to form a thick carton, painted within and without with designs and religious emblems. These carton-cases were made to fit the swathed body. 1908 J. H. JUDD (*title*) The 'A.L.' Carton Work. 1910 — Carton Designing for Juniors. 1913 *Bk. School Handwork* I. 183 Domestic Handicraft for Girls in Paper, Carton, Cardboard, and Woodwork. *Ibid.* 195 Paper folding and carton work..in the making of toys.

Cartonnage (kā·ɹtənédʒ). *Archæol.* Also **cartonage.** [Fr., f. *carton*: see prec. and -AGE.] An Egyptian mummy-case made of layers of linen or papyrus tightly pressed and glued together and fitting closely to the embalmed body; also, the material thus used. Also *attrib.*
1834 T. J. PETTIGREW *Egypt. Mummies* 116 The case I am describing is called by the French the 'Cartonage', from the resemblance of its composition to pasteboard. 1841 J. G. WILKINSON *Anc. Egyptians* Ser. II. II. 477 The innermost covering of the body..was the *cartonage*. This was a pasteboard case fitting exactly to its shape. 1881 RAWLINSON *Hist. Anc. Egypt.* I. 512 The swathed body was covered by a 'cartonnage', consisting of twenty or forty layers of linen tightly pressed and glued together, so as to form a sort of paste-board envelope, which then received a thin coating of stucco, and was painted in bright colours with hieroglyphics and figures of deities. 1889 PETRIE *Hawara*, etc. 15 Mummies with gilt cartonnage heads. 1891 EDWARDS *Pharaohs*, etc. 156 The material of the mummy-case is the usual 'cartonnage'...This cartonnage is impressed all over the arms, shoulders and head-dress, with a..pattern. 1894 TIRARD *Erman's Anc. Egypt* 315 The inner coffins, which were of wood or cartonnage. 1908 *Athenæum* 21 Mar. 360/3 The cartonnage mask which decorated the inner coffin.

Carton-pierre (karton pyɛ̄r). [Fr., = 'cardboard (of) stone'.] A kind of papier mâché made to imitate stone or bronze. Also called **Carton-pâte** (Cent. Dict. 1889).
1851 *Illustr. Catal. Gt. Exhib.* III. 747/1 Bracket-table, ..the figures supporting it of carton-pierre. 1858 SIMMONDS *Dict. Trade*, *Carton-pierre*..has been used for roofing, and is composed of the pulp of paper mixed with whiting and glue. 1862 *Catal. Internat. Exhib., Brit.* II. No. 5752, Ornamental furniture, in carton-pierre and papier-mâché. 1885 *Spons' Mechanics' Own Bk.* 608 Carton pierre is a species of papier-maché made with paper pulp, whiting, and size, pressed into plaster moulds.

Cartoon, *sb.* Add:
2. (The term is no longer restricted to full-page drawings: see quot. 1910.)
1843 *Punch* 24 June 258/2 *Punch* has the benevolence to announce, that in an early number of his ensuing Volume he will astonish the Parliamentary Committee by the publication of several exquisite designs, to be called Punch's Cartoons! *Ibid.* 15 July 22/2 Substance and Shadow. Cartoon No. I. 1910 *Daily Chron.* 1 Mar. 6/6 The cartoon nowadays..is merely party-political. You find a scratchy sketch in the corner of a paper devoted to the week-end football matches or the spring handicaps, or Mr. Asquith's breakfast with the King. 'Cartoon!'

Cartoonery (kaɹtū·nəri). [f. CARTOON *sb.*] The making of cartoons; cartoons in general.
1911 WEBSTER, *Cartoonery*,..act or art of cartooning. 1914 *N. Y. Herald* 16 June 10/7 Typical of a vast amount of cartoonery.

Cartoo·ning, *vbl. sb.* [f. CARTOON *v.* + -ING[1].] The drawing or execution of cartoons; representation in a cartoon.
1846 BROWNING *Lett.* 9 July (1899) II. 319 Then comes the rest from cartooning and exhibiting. 1927 *Sunday at Home* June 540/1 The cartooning of nature has been aided by some touching up from a tricksy human hand.

Cart-wheel, *sb.* **2.** (Earlier U.S. example.)
1855 BARNUM *Life* 21 Talk of 'cart wheels', there was never one half so large as that dollar looked to me.
4. A form of fire-work.
1840 R. H. DANA *Bef. Mast* xiii. 72 We had..everything..from Chinese fire-works to English cart-wheels.

Cart-wheel, *v. intr.* To move like a rotating wheel; esp. of an aeroplane which makes a bad landing on one wing-tip.
1920 *Blackw. Mag.* July 85/1 He cart-wheeled round right-handed to get behind her again. 1925 E. F. NORTON *Fight for Everest, 1924* 114 Somervell's axe slipped from his numb fingers and went cart-wheeling down the slopes below. 1928 *Daily Express* 24 Sept. 7/4 The machine continued to lose height, and suddenly cartwheeled vertically to the ground.

Cart-whip. (Later U.S. example.)
1869 MRS. STOWE *Oldtown Folks* xii. 136 He had helped himself to a long cart-whip which stood there.

Ca·rucated, *ppl. a. Hist.* Measured and assessed by carucates.
1908 W. G. COLLINGWOOD *Scandin. Britain* 111 Leicestershire..was a carucated district.

Carval (kā·ɹv'l). *Isle of Man.* Also **carvel.** [Manx *carval.*] A carol.
1887 HALL CAINE *Deemster* xxxiii, Sometimes he crooned a Manx carval. 1910 *Encycl. Brit.* V. 639/2 Most of the existing literature..consists of ballads and carols, locally called carvels.

Carver. Add: **3. c.** A carver's chair.
1927 *Daily Tel.* 3 May 3/3 A set of Hepplewhite chairs and carver upholstered in pigskin.

Carving, *vbl. sb.* **4.** Add: **carving horse** *U.S.* (see quot.)
1920 HUNTER *Trail Drivers of Texas* 297 The specially trained horses used [to cut out cattle]..are called 'carving horses'.

Caryo-: see KARYO-.

Casa (kā·sä). *U.S.* [Sp. *casa* house:—L. *căsa.*] A country-house in the Western States.
1870 B. HARTE *Notes Flood & Field* II, His 'casa''s built too high.

Casaque (kazak). [Fr.] A kind of jacket or jumper worn by females.
1894 *Daily News* 30 Oct. 6/6 The 'casaque', or Louis XVI. jacket, in brocade or very handsome fancy cloth, is another revival of this season. 1923 *Daily Mail* 19 Feb. Advt., Knitted Wool Casaques.

Casaquin (kazakæ̃n). [Fr.: see CASSAKIN.] A kind of bodice or jumper.
1922 *Daily Mail* 4 Dec. 15 The casaquin bodice was joined to a full ankle-length skirt. 1923 *Ibid.* 18 Jan. 11 Another frock from Paris has a casaquin..over a plain skirt. *Ibid.* 12 Feb. 15 The casaquin jumper of this three-piece suit.

Casca·ding, *ppl. a.* [f. CASCADE *v.* + -ING[2].] Falling in or as in a cascade.
1889 C. EDWARDES *Sardinia* 159 The cascading stream. 1916 BOYD CABLE *Action Front* 179 From overhead..there came..the clatter and rattle of cascading bricks and tiles. 1923 *Glasgow Herald* 9 May 11 Climbing and cascading plants.

Cascalho (kaska·lyo). Also -hao. [Pg.] In Brazil, a deposit of pebbles, gravel, and ferruginous sand, containing diamonds or gold.
1812 J. MAWE *Trav. Brazil* 77 The gold lies..in a stratum of rounded pebbles and gravel, called *cascalhão*. 1813 — *Diamonds* (1823) 35 In one part of the Diamond District the *cascalho* forms a solid breccia. 1867 C. W. KING *Precious Stones* (ed. 2) 59 The gravel—*cascalhao*—filling their beds is dug out. 1910 *Encycl. Brit.* VIII. 160/1 The diamond is found..in the gravels of the present rivers, embedded in a ferruginous clay-cemented conglomerate known as *cascalho*.

Cascara. Add:
2. *Med.* The bark of a Californian buckthorn, *Rhamnus purshiana*, used as a cathartic or laxative. Popularly pronounced (kaskā·rā). In full *Ca·scara Sagra·da*, 'sacred bark'.
1879 A. O'NEILL in *New Preparations* (Detroit) III. 140. 1885 *Brit. Pharmacopœia* 151 Extract of Cascara Sagrada. *Ibid.* 152 Mix the cascara with two pints of the spirit.

Case, *sb.*[1] Add:
3. b. *A case*: an instance of what may be expected under the circumstances. *slang.*
1924 J. B. HOBBS *Cricket Mem.* 30 A. E. Relf was batting. 'Razor' sent down an off-spinner, and appealed. It looked a case. 'Not out,' says Albert Trott.
4. b. *In the case of*: as regards (a specified thing or person). *In that case*: if that is true; if that should happen; that being so. Similarly, *in the first case*, etc. *In any case*: whatever may happen, whatever the fact is. (Cf. 13.) *In many cases*: in a number of instances. Similarly, *in some cases.*
1791 J. WALKER *Pron. Dict.* s.v. *Medicinal*, Poets..who have, and, perhaps, in some cases, ought to have, a language different from prose. 1881 *Spons' Encycl. Industr. Arts* IV. 1252 In many cases, flax-spinning establishments have weaving branches in connection with them. 1893 E. S. GUNN *Business Training Man.* (ed. 2) 55 In the case of liquids, should there be any appearance of leakage, if the receipt is signed without any remark, it is called a 'clean' receipt. 1894 SWEET *Anglo-Saxon Reader* (ed. 7) 227 The parts of speech are not marked in the case of adjectives, pronouns and weak verbs. 1894 THUDICHUM *Wines* 92 In the case of an excellent young Palatinate wine we found that the heating diminished the albumen from 0·3550 per cent. to 0·2448 per cent. *Ibid.* 136 When he comes to his vineyard he finds his crop either eaten by flies and other vermin, or rotten, or overripe, and in any case it yields him a lesser quantity or quality of wine. 1896 L. FLETCHER *Introd. Study Meteorites* 36 In some cases the chondrules consist wholly or in great part of glass. 1909 BEYNON *Drapery* 76 'And if I can show you cheaper lines than you are buying, you won't buy?' 'No, I will not buy even in that case.' 1912 C. N. & A. M. WILLIAMSON *Heather Moon* II. iii. 128 'It didn't seem to me there was anything romantic about Mr. Douglas, except his name.' 'In that case, you are a little flirt,' said he. 1916 E. W. GREGORY *Furnit. Collector* 227 But in any case worm-eaten furniture is not at all desirable. 1917 ATWOOD *Exchanges & Specul.* 66 In most cases the broker serves the banker gratuitously. 1921 A. L. SIMON *Wine* 59 In the first case, the wines are sent over here, as a rule two years after vintage. 1929 PINERO in *The Eighteen-Seventies* 133 The difficulties of great men are intensified in the case of little ones.
5. b. In U.S. *spec.* of tobacco.
1640 *Maryland Archives* I. 98 Bad Tobacco shall be judged..[what is] sooty, wett, or in too high Case. 1661 *Maryland Hist. Mag.* VIII. 7 [Two hogsheads] struck in too high case and in a rotting condition. 1800 W. TATHAM *Cult. & Com. Tobacco* 37 It must be stretched gently over the ends of the fingers and knuckles, and if it is in good case, *i.e.* plight, or condition, it will discover an elastic capacity. 1853 *Trans. Ill. Agric. Soc.* (1865) V. 667 The fires should be suffered to go out, and the tobacco be suffered to come in case, or get soft again. *Ibid.* 669.
8. d. *U.S.* In the game of faro, the fourth card of any denomination, when the other three have been taken from the dealing-box. *To keep cases*: to note the cards as they come from the box; hence *fig.* to keep watch. *To come down to cases*: to get down to the point.
1896 G. ADE *Artie* iii. 24, I could see that a Johnny-on-the-spot with a big badge marked 'Committee' was tryin' to keep cases on her. 1903 A. ADAMS *Log Cowboy* xiii. 199 We found Quince Forrest and Wyatt Roundtree playing the faro bank, the former keeping cases. 1918 MULFORD *Man fr. Bar-20* ii. 21 Comin' down to cases, you ain't really a cow-puncher. 1920 — *J. Nelson* xiv. 144 I'm keepin' cases on these cattle.
10. b. (*in case.*) Sometimes used brokenly without a following sentence, to indicate an unspecified apprehension of accident.
1898 KIPLING *Fleet in Being* 28 One leg over the edge of the bunk—in case.
14. case-keeper *U.S.*, one who 'keeps cases' in faro (see *8 d); the device used for this purpose.
1909 *Century Dict.* Suppl., *Case-keeper*, in *faro*, the player who marks the cards as they come from the dealing-box... Small buttons are pushed along wires for this purpose. 1913 MULFORD *Coming of Cassidy* vii. 115 Why weren't there cue-cards, so the players could keep their own tally of the cards instead of having to depend on the cue-box kept by the case-keeper?

Case, *v.*[2] **4.** (Later examples.)
1821 J. FOWLER *Jrnl.* 44 The Hunters killed two deer, [and] Cased the Skins for Baggs. 1900 SMITHWICK *Evol. State* 178 The vessels for carrying water were made of deer skins cased—stripped off whole—the legs and necks tied tightly with sinews.

Casease (kē·si,ēs). *Chem.* [f. CASEIN: see *-ASE.] A proteolytic ferment formed by certain bacteria, capable of decomposing the casein of milk and cheese.
1899 J. R. GREEN *Soluble Ferments* 218.

Caseate (kē·si,eɪt), *v. Pathol.* [f. L. *cāseus* cheese + -ATE[3].] *intr.* To undergo caseous degeneration. See CASEATION b.
1873 T. H. GREEN *Introd. Pathol.* (ed. 2) 79 In..fatty degeneration..subsequent changes invariably take place; the part either softening, caseating, or becoming the seat of calcification itself. 1907 *Practitioner* Dec. 737 If the appendix is subsequently removed, you may find a caseating centre near it. 1910 *Ibid.* June 743 Caseated glands.

Casement. Add: **1. b.** The matrix cut in stone to receive a monumental brass.
1454 in Dugdale *Antiq. Warwicksh.* (1656) 354/1 Either of the said long plates for writing shall be in bredth to fill justly the casements provided therefore. 1890 J. T. FOWLER in *Proc. Soc. Antiq.* XIII. 34 *note*, It has been proposed to revive 'casement', an equally good word at one time in use. 1891 W. H. ST. JOHN HOPE *Ibid.* 213 Beneath the figure is the casement of the inscription. 1903 *Yorks. Archæol. Jrnl.* 307 The top slab with the casement of the brass taken up and inserted in the north wall.
5. casement cloth, a cotton cloth used primarily for casement curtains, but also as a dress material, etc.; so **casement fabric,** which is of wider application; **casement curtain,** a curtain of the kind made to fit a *casement window* (see sense 2).
1908 *Home Chat* 6 June 572/2 Linen, or *casement cloth, employed as concluding note to a skirt of the same. 1830 TENNYSON *Mariana* ii, She drew her *casement-curtain by. 1910 *Daily Chron.* 5 Apr. 9/4 Our windows are furnished with casement curtains. 1912 *Queen* 27 July 180/2 Patterns of Sundour *casement fabrics and washing materials. 1920 *Home Chat* 4 Dec. 428 Casement Fabrics made to measure.

Cash, *sb.*[1] Add: **2. b.** *Cash on delivery*: applied to the forwarding of goods to order, payment being made to the carrier or postman when the goods are delivered. Abbreviated C.O.D.
1899 *Pitman's Office Routine* 2nd Stage 139. 1904 *Daily Chron.* 13 Apr. 6/3 The cash-on-delivery system of transmitting goods by parcel post.
f. *Cash down* (DOWN *adv.* 12): ready money.
1855 HALIBURTON *Nat. & Hum. Nat.* II. 111 What's the price..cash down on the nail?
3. *cash-article, girl*; **cash account** (earlier examples); **cash carrier, conveyer, railway,** a device employed in shops by which money is carried in a receptacle running on a line between the cash-

desk or counting-house and the several counters; **cash-price** (early example); **cash register,** orig. *U.S.*, a till furnished with an apparatus which visibly records the amounts put into it; **cash-sale** (examples); **cash-store,** orig. *U.S.*, a store in which credit is not given.
1770 *Carroll Papers* in *Maryland Hist. Mag.* XII. 295 Do not give yˢelf the Trouble of sending me an Extract of yʳ *Cash Acct. 1772 *Ibid.* XIV. 363, I have a Regular Cash Acct in an old Book Here. 1835 *Southern Lit. Messenger* I. 339 But a man was a *cash article there. 1889 *Century Dict.*, *Cash-carrier. 1902 *Bldgs. World's Columbian Expos.* 2/1 The Transportation exhibits..range..from a *cash conveyor to a balloon. *a* 1906 'O. HENRY' *Trimmed Lamp* etc. 78, I was a *cash-girl and a wrapper and then a shop girl. 1781 *Cal. Virginia St. Papers* I. 438 The articles were furnished at *cash prices. 1886 *Cassell's Family Mag.* 123/1 The *cash register which is represented in the woodcut is only twelve inches in height. 1911 H. S. HARRISON *Queed* viii. 102 He was as definite as an adding-machine, as practical as a cash register. 1816 U. BROWN *Jrnl.* in *Maryland Hist. Mag.* XI. 350 [He] advises me to sell the whole of Clement Brooks property for cash, or at a *Cash Sale. 1837 COLMAN *Rep. Agric. Mass.* (1838) 90 At the same time we are always sure of a cash sale. 1879 TOURGEE *Fool's Errand* viii. 36 The plantation would never have brought that price at a cash sale. 1911 R. D. SAUNDERS *Col. Todhunter* viii. 109 Quit settin' there lookin' like a poor man at a cash sale. 1830 PAULDING *Chron. Gotham* 156 The Honourable Peleg Peshell, *cash-store keeper at Peshellville. *Ibid.* 159 Passing a unanimous resolution, not to buy anything at his cash-store. 1849 WILLIS *Rural Lett.* xviii. 156 You do injustice to the 'cash stores' of Oswego.
b. Applied adjectively to (*a*) commodities purchasable for cash. (*b*) tradesmen or commercial houses doing business for ready money only. Cf. *cash article, -sale*, etc., above.
1898 *Daily News* 15 June 6/2 Mr. Armour to-day bought all Mr. Leiter's cash wheat in the north-west. 1903 *Daily Chron.* 7 Apr. 5/2 Cash Dispensing Chemists.

Cash (kæʃ), *sb.*[4] Anglicized f. CACHE *sb.*
1835 N. WYETH *Jrnl.* 236 Camped..just above the mouth of the Utalla where I have a cash of traps.

Cash, *v.*[2] Add:
2. *U.S.* **Cash in,** to settle accounts in the game of poker; hence in general use, to clear accounts; to close up a matter. (Sometimes *trans.* with *checks* as object.)
1889 *Kansas Times & Star* 20 Mar., The market value now is about $1,700 a front foot, and many members favor 'cashing in' at such a fancy price, and building elsewhere. 1891 [see below]. 1896 G. ADE *Artie* v. 46 If you're struck on him I'll cash in right here and drop out of the game. 1899 — *Doc Horne* xxi. 232, I lost back the $2,500 and cashed in. *a* 1904 S. E. WHITE *Blazed Trail Stories* xii. 224 By all the rules of the game, Peter should have failed long since, should have 'cashed in and quit' some five years back.
b. *fig.* To die. (Also without *in.*)
1891 FARMER *Slang*, *Cash* or *pass in one's Checks* verbal phr..to die. 1908 MULFORD *Orphan* xix. 250 The Orphan not only saved me but also some of them, for I'd a gotten some of them before I cashed. 1920 — *J. Nelson* xx. 220 He's been follerin' me around steady since Wolf cashed in.
c. To get in *with*; to stake money or capital *on*. *U.S.*
a 1904 S. E. WHITE *Blazed Trail Stories* viii. 146, I don't stack very high in the blue chips when it comes to cashin' in with th' gentle sex. 1927 *Daily Express* 12 Sept. 11 An enterprising American company..'cashed in' on Mr. Arlen by acquiring the screen-rights of one of his earliest stories. 1930 *Publishers' Weekly* 1 Mar. 1040 Cash in on this tremendous wave of interest and enthusiasm! A large national advertising campaign will start the novel toward a big sale!
d. *trans.* To pay *in* to a bank; to earn, gain.
a 1906 'O. HENRY' *Trimmed Lamp* etc. 233 With his gold dust cashed in to the merry air of a hundred thousand..the Man from Nome sighed to set foot again in Chilkoot. 1910 W. M. RAINE *B. O'Connor* 21, I know your kind—hell-bent to spend what you cash in.
3. To pay *over* or *up*. Now *U.S.*
1825 *New Monthly Mag.* XIV. 193 When it came to 'cashing-up', affairs assumed a soberer complexion. *Ibid.* 556 The call to 'cash up' is unheeded By holders of Mexican Scrip. 1831 *Examiner* 296/2 A certain Alderman..did not cash up to his supporters on the former election. 1842 BARHAM *Ingol. Leg.* Ser. II. *Merch. Venice*, He could not cash up, spite of all he could do. 1854 MARY J. HOLMES *Tempest & Sunshine* xxi. 227 Tempest is in a desput hurry to know whether I'm goin to cash over and send her to market in New Orleans. 1890 *Buckskin Mose* xvii. 246 He might run to Tom Long's, and inform him of our use of the contents of his cellar, without cashing up.

Cash (kæʃ), *v.*[3] Anglicized f. CACHE *v.*
1821 J. FOWLER *Jrnl.* 9 We this morning Berryed or Cashed, as the french call it, 32 Bever traps. 1842 M. CRAWFORD *Jrnl.* 14 Finished making packsaddles, cashed goods and preparing to start tomorrow. *Ibid.*, Stopped early for dinner, cashed liquor.

Cashable (kæ·ʃāb'l), *a.* [f. CASH *v.*[2] + -ABLE.] Capable of being cashed.
1891 *Pall Mall Gaz.* 21 Sept. 2/1 The money card would not be cashable. 1928 *Daily Express* 2 July 10/2 Cashable orders on retail or manufacturing firms.

Cashaw (kāʃǭ·). *U.S.* Also **cushaw, kershaw.** [Algonkin.] A variety of pumpkin.
1705 BEVERLY *Hist. Virginia* (1722) 124 Their *Cushaws* are a kind of Pompion, of a blueish green Colour, streak'd with White, when they are fit for Use. 1859 BARTLETT *Dict. Amer.* (ed. 2), *Cashaw*, sometimes spelt *kershaw*, a pumpkin. Western.

Casher-box (kæ·ʃəɹ bɒks). In crown glass manufacture, a table covered with coal cinders on which the globe of glass rests while the blowing tube is detached and the pontil attached to the flattened side of the globe.
1839 URE *Dict. Arts* 580 The flattened globe is removed from the fire, and its rod..rested on the casher box covered with coal cinders. 1879 *Encycl. Brit.* X. 660/1 When..the glass has been allowed to cool a little, it is rested on the 'casher box', and an iron rod, called a 'pontil'..is applied to the flattened side.

Cashless, *a.* (Earlier U.S. example.)
1833 *Niles' Register* 20 July XLIV. 347 They with rich land, and staple productions..are becoming poor and cashless.

Casinese, variant of *CASSINESE.

Casing, *vbl. sb.* **2. c.** *U.S. Mining.* (Earlier example.)
1872 'MARK TWAIN' *Roughing it* xl. (1882) 213 It's a blind lead..!—hanging wall—foot wall—clay casings—everything complete!
d. The framing round a door or window. *U.S.*
1873 J. H. BEADLE *Undevel. West* xxii. 449 Grasping the casing I got in at the door. 1887 TOURGEE *Button's Inn* 203 A hand touched the casing, and a footstep..fell upon the floor. 1910 *Atlantic Monthly* Jan. 36 Ellen leaned her head against the casing. 1913 MRS. STRATTON-PORTER *Laddie* ii. (1917) 38 All the casings were oiled wood, and the walls had just a little yellow. *Ibid.* xviii. 364 He carefully loaded his gun, and leaned it against the front casing.

Casing, *ppl. a.* Add: *casing rock* = CASING *vbl. sb.* 2 c.
1872 'MARK TWAIN' *Roughing it* xxix. (1882) 160 The wall or ledge of rock..was perfectly distinct from the casing rock on each side of it.

Cask, *sb.* **5.** Add: *cask-body, -head, -steamer, -washer.*
1874 *Spons' Dict. Engin.* VIII. 2919, Having thus far followed the shaping of the staves, and the conversion of the same into *cask bodies, it will be necessary to direct our attention to the formation of *cask-heads. 1905 *Daily Chron.* 10 Oct. 2/5 The old-fashioned cask-heads with the familiar legend of 'Fine old Port'. 1881 *Instr. Census Clerks* (1885) 61 *Cask Washer, Steamer. 1891 *Daily News* 12 Feb. 2/8 A cask-washer, employed at the Berkshire Brewery. 1921 *Dict. Occup. Terms* (1927) § 459 *Washer, barrel*; *cask washer*..(i) *cask steamer*; rolls barrels to feed end of washing machine..(ii) cleans barrels by pouring water and stone into them.

Casket, *sb.*[1] **3.** Add to def.: *spec.* one of a rectangular form.
1863 HAWTHORNE *Our Old Home, About Warwick* 102 'Caskets'! a vile modern phrase, which compels a person..to shrink..from the idea of being buried at all.
4. *Comb.*: **casket lens** (see quot. 1895).
1892 J. T. TAYLOR *Optics Photogr.* 88 Casket lenses are now being made by several manufacturers. 1895 J. A. HODGES *Photographic Lenses* xviii. 113 'Casket' lenses..are not usually 'combination' lenses,..the casket usually containing three or more doublet lenses...The casket system..provides the novice with several lenses of various focal lengths..so that different angles of view may be included upon the same plate.

Caslon (kæ·zlən). *Typography.* The name of William *Caslon*, father (1692–1766) and son (1720–1778), applied to the type foundry established by the father, and to the old-face type cut there, or (later) one cut in imitation of this. Also *Comb.*, as *Caslon-shaped* adj.
1825 T. C. HANSARD *Typographia* 353 The Caslon foundry is still upheld. 1836 *Gentl. Mag.* May 557/2 The printers, whose offices were generally stored with the Caslon founts. *Ibid.* 558/1 The true Caslon-shaped Elzevir types. 1877 *Caslon's Circular* July, William Caslon, Founder of the existing Caslon Letter Foundry in Chiswell Street. *Ibid.*, Early Caslon Lead Mould. 1898 J. SOUTHWARD *Mod. Printing* (1910) I. xxii. 136 The Elzevir types prevailed for a long time all over Europe; and the first William Caslon adopted them as his models—hence his types are known as Caslon Elzevirs. 1922 UPDIKE *Printing Types* II. 106 Caslon types are..beautiful in mass, and above all..legible. 1927 MCKERROW *Introd. Bibliogr.* 300 *note*, It may perhaps be well to warn the reader that 'Caslon' as applied to type has not an absolutely precise connotation. Though, for example, the founts of different sizes cut by Caslon himself are in the same general style, the forms of the letters do not correspond with mathematical exactness...When it is added that 'Caslon' founts have been repeatedly cut in modern times, it will be evident that we must be prepared for a certain range of variety. *Ibid.* 301 The Caslon italic retained something of the angularity of the current script. *Ibid.* 305 The thick strokes of 'old style' are on the whole thinner than in Caslon.

Cassab (kăsā·b). Also **cussab.** [Hind., a. Arab. قصاب *qassāb* butcher.] A seaman of Asiatic nationality employed in the merchant service.
1881 *Instr. Census Clerks* (1885) 35 Cussab or Cassab..in P. and O. Service. 1921 *Dict. Occup. Terms* (1927) § 735 *Cassab, cussab*; a member of Asiatic crew employed, either as lamp trimmer (on deck) or as storekeeper in steward's department. 1924 *Glasgow Herald* 17 May 4 There is usually an elder, not necessarily a Haji, who carries a copy of the Quran. On board ship he is, as a rule, the cassab.

Cas(s)alty, -elty, dial. ff. CASUALTY.
1886 *Cornhill Mag.* June 582 A Cas'alty Corner is a feature of every district of outcast London, is to be found wherever the poor of the great city most do congregate. *Ibid.*, Cas'alty labourers. 1892 TENNYSON *Church-w. & Curate* i, Nasty, casselty weather!

Cassandra (kăsæ·ndrā). [L. *Cassandra*, Gr. Κασ(σ)άνδρα.] A daughter of Priam, sought in love by Apollo, who gave her the gift of prophecy and when she deceived him ordained that no one should believe her prophecies, though true.
1670 LASSELS *Voy. Italy* Pref. a x, Other Governours (Cassandra like) telling their Pupils many excellent truths, are not believed by them. 1711 ADDISON *Spect.* No. 130 ¶ 2 A Cassandra of the [Gypsy] Crew..told me, That I loved a pretty Maid in a Corner. 1837 CARLYLE *Fr. Rev.* II. I. ii, A Cassandra-Marat cannot do it. 1874 W. R. GREG (*title*) Rocks ahead; or, the warnings of Cassandra. *Ibid.* 1 The part of Cassandra can never be a pleasant one for any man to play. It makes others uncomfortable and himself unpopular. 1901 *N. Amer. Rev.* Feb. 236 Far be from me the Cassandra task of attempting to persuade my countrymen that an army of any given size is a necessity for the Republic. 1926 CHESTERTON *Incredulity of Fr. Brown* v. 177 Lady Diana had recovered a little from her trance of Cassandra.
Hence **Cassa·ndrian** *a.*
a 1876 EADIE *Comm. Thess.* (1877) 347 Baxter..accused Grotius of a design to reconcile Papists and Protestants in a Cassandrian Popery. 1903 H. BEGBIE in *Daily Chron.* 28 May 3/7 Remembering the Cassandrian comparison which has been made between the Transvaal and Ireland.

Casse (kæs, ‖kas). [Fr., vbl. n. f. *casser* to break.] Incipient souring of certain wines, accompanied by loss of colour and a deposit of sediment.
1883 *J. Gardner's Brewer, Distiller*, etc. 226 If the breakage, or *casse*, as it is termed, has not exceeded 7 or 8 per cent. by the time August is reached, he..lets the wine remain. 1911 *Encycl. Brit.* XXVIII. 720/1 The disease known as *tourne* or *casse* is generally caused by the wine having been made..from grapes affected by mildew.

Cassel (kæ·sĕl). The name of Cassel (now Kassel), a town in Germany, used attrib. to designate various pigments, as **Cassel brown, Cassel earth,** a brown prepared from impure lignite, Vandyke brown; **Cassel green,** a green consisting chiefly of barium manganese; **Cassel yellow,** a patent yellow pigment.
1660 URE *Dict. Arts* (ed. 5) I. 805 Vandyke, Cappah, Rubens, Cassel, and Cologne Browns. 1875 SIR T. SEATON *Fret-Cutting* 105 The brown pigment is well known to artist's colourmen as Cassel earth. 1882 *Encycl. Brit.* XIV. 379/1 Another oxychloride, $PbCl_2 \cdot 7PbO$, known as 'Cassel yellow'. 1885 *Ibid.* XIX. 38/1 Cassel Green, called also Rosenstiehl's Green, is a fine innocuous pigment made by melting together sulphate of baryta and oxide of manganese...Vandyke brown and Cologne or Cassel brown, peaty ochres...Real Vandyke Brown..ought to be a kind of bituminous peaty earth..allied to which are Cologne and Cassel Earth.

Casserole. 1. Add: Also *à la casserole*, now usually *en casserole.* Also *attrib.*, as *casserole cookery, dish, pan.*
1870 M. DUBOIS *Cosmopol. Cookery* § 727 Capon of Caux, roasted 'à la casserole'...Braised or roasted in a stewpan. 1898 *Mrs. Roundell's Pract. Cookery Bk.* 264 Chicken à la Casserole. 1904 C. H. SENN (*title*) Chafing Dish and Casserole Cookery. 1905 A. KENNEY-HERBERT *Commonsense Cookery* 192 A *poulet*, or pheasant *à la casserole.* 1906 FILIPPINI *Internat. Cook Bk.* 378 Heat one tablespoon butter in an earthen casserole pan. *Ibid.* 565 Sweetbreads en Casserole. Blanch and trim six heart sweetbreads. Place in an earthen casserole dish [etc.].

Cassican (kæ·sikăn). [f. mod.L. *Cassicus* + -AN.] Any oriole of the tropical American genus *Cassicus.*
1840 *Cuvier's Anim. Kingd.* 202 The Cassicans (*Cassicus*, Cuv.). 1861 *Chambers's Encycl.* II. 654/1.

Cassie[2] (kæ·si). *U.S.* [Fr., ad. Pr. *cacio* acacia.] The flower-heads of *Acacia farnesiana.*
1905 *Yng. Woman* Apr. 230/1 Mignonette, and cassie.

Cassinese (kæsinī·z), *a.* and *sb.* Also **Casinese.** [ad. It. *Casinese*, f. Monte *Casino*, near which the earliest Benedictine monastery was founded: see -ESE.] **A.** *adj.* Of or pertaining to the Benedictines of Monte Casino. **B.** *sb.* A monk of the monastery founded near Monte Casino, or of any monastery connected therewith.
1881 B. WELDON *Chronol. Notes* Pref. p. x, The reigning Pope Julius II gave the name of the Cassinese Congregation to the whole body of the reformed Benedictines of Italy. 1884 ADDIS & ARNOLD *Cath. Dict.* (1897) 82/2 There is a monastery at Ramsgate belonging to the Cassinese branch of the order. 1910 HAILE *Life Pole* 127 The Benedictines of St. Giustina at Padua—who were beginning to call themselves Casinese to denote their union with Monte Casino.

Cassinette. (Earlier U.S. example.)
1817 S. R. BROWN *Western Gaz.* 94 The articles manufactured consist of..chambrays, cassinets, sattinets.

Cassiri (kæsī·rɪ). Also **kasiri, casiri(e, cassiree, casseri(e.** [a. Carib *cassiri*: see CASSAREEP (etym.).] An intoxicating liquor made in Guiana from sweet potatoes fermented.
1796 STEDMAN *Surinam* I. 392 Another drink called *cassiree* is also much used by these Indians. 1851 W. H. BRETT *Indian Missions Guiana* 103 There is another drink made in a more cleanly manner from potatoes, called Kasiri. 1855 H. G. DALTON *Hist. Brit. Guiana* I. 82 They have also another intoxicating beverage, called cassiri. 1879 BODDAM-WHETHAM *Roraima* 248 The favourite beverage among the inhabitants was a disagreeable-looking compound called cassiree. 1904 W. H. HUDSON *Green Mansions* i. 26 More cups of casserie followed this outburst.

Cassolette. Add:
3. A small casserole, an outer edging of rice of smaller size than the casserole.
1827 L. E. UDE *French Cook* 401 Mind that the cassolettes are to be quite cold before you take them out of the mould.

1898 *Mrs. Roundell's Pract. Cookery Bk.* 195 Scoop out the insides and fill them with mince and sauce, after heating the Cassolettes in the oven. 1905 A. KENNEY-HERBERT *Common-sense Cookery* 177 Potato cassolettes.

Cassone (kassō·ne). Pl. -ni (nī). [It., augmentative of *cassa* chest.] A large Italian coffer, esp. one made to hold the outfit of a bride, often elaborately carved and decorated.
1883 J. W. MOLLETT *Illustr. Dict. Art & Archæol.* 60 *Cassone*, an Italian chest, richly carved and gilt, and often decorated with paintings, which frequently held the *trousseau* of a bride. 1904 *Studio* Sept. 303/2 The collecting of wedding-coffers, or 'cassones' as they are sometimes called. 1922 *19th Cent.* May 803 The fourteenth century round-backed chair and the *cassone* attributed to Ammannati, which are shown in the same room.

Cast, *sb.* **42.** Add: **cast-net,** a net which is cast and drawn immediately, as distinguished from a net which is set and left.
1647 HEXHAM *Dutch Dict.* (1660) s.v. *Net*, A cast-net, *een werp net.* 1767 FAWKES *Theocritus* XXI. 13 The seine, the cast-net, and the wicker maze. 1883 DAY *Indian Fish* (Fish. Exhib. Publ.) 46 In some places several cast-nets are joined together, to stop up all passage of fish along a stream.

Cast, *v.* Add: **6. d.** To throw the line over (a piece of water). Hence **Ca·stable** *a.*
1892 *Field* 16 July 104/2 A fairly strong stream of only about 2 ft. in depth, and just a nice 'castable' width. *Ibid.* 1 Oct. 522/2, I therefore began to cast the lower portion of the pool. 1900 *Westm. Gaz.* 19 Jan. 3/1 On Nov. 30 they can cast the classic waters of the Tweed.
23. Of crops: To yield, bear fruit, produce. *dial.*
1890 GISSING *Village Hampden* vii, They tell me as the Lammas wheat be a-casting badly. 1893 *Field* 8 Apr. 530/1 A dry March..is of universally good omen for the coming corn crops. These never 'cast' so well as they do when a warm soil causes the under ground progress to be earlier and quicker than is that above the surface.
79. Cast off. j. *Printing.* To estimate how much printed matter will correspond to (a piece of MS. copy). Also *absol.* (Cf. *CAST-OFF *sb.*[1] 2.)
1683 MOXON *Mech. Exerc., Printing* xxii. ¶ 9 Casting off Copy..is to examine..how much..of Printed Copy will Come-in into any intended number of Sheets..; or how much Written Copy will make an intended number of Sheets..: Therefore if I shew you how the Compositer Casts off Written Copy, I do at the same time inform you how to Count off Printed Copy. 1784 B. FRANKLIN in *Ann. Reg.* (1817) *Chron.* 389 The compositors in your chapel do not cast off their copy well. 1808 STOWER *Printer's Gramm.* 135 To cast off manuscript with accuracy and precision, is an essential object. 1824 J. JOHNSON *Typogr.* II. 89 To cast off manuscript..is a task of a disagreeable nature. 1892 OLDFIELD *Man. Typogr.* xii. 97 Sometimes copy is so badly arranged that it is almost impossible to cast-off accurately...In casting-up allowance must be made for chapter-heads, &c.

Cast, *ppl. a.* **1.** Add: *Cast shadow*, in painting, a shadow cast by an object within the picture, and serving to bring it out against the objects behind it.
1849 J. D. HARDING *Less. Art* liii, In shading this Lesson care must be taken to make the cast shadow GHF darker at the points G and F, and also sharp on the edge. 1891 tr. *Adeline's Art Dict.* 362/1 The cast shadow is always darker than the shadow, properly so called, if the body casting the shadow and the surface receiving it are of the same tonality.

Castanite (kæ·stănəit). *Min.* [f. L. *castanea* chestnut + -ITE[1].] A hydrated ferric sulphate of chestnut-brown colour, found in Chile.
1892 DANA *Syst. Min.* (ed. 6) 964 Castanite...Monoclinic, with a prismatic angle of 82°.

Casteless (kā·stlĕs), *a.* [f. CASTE *sb.* + -LESS.] Having no caste or castes.
1886 [in Dict. s.v. CASTE *sb.*]. 1898 *Daily News* 15 Aug. 6/2 Reformed casteless Hindoos. 1906 *Macm. Mag.* July 714 While he [*sc.* the Maharajah of Travancore] journeyed over the black water to distant, and to them casteless and almost godless, Britain.

Castellated, *ppl. a.* Add:
1. c. *transf.* Of a nut or disc: Having grooves or recesses on its upper face.
1904 A. B. F. YOUNG *Complete Motorist* iv. (ed. 2) 73 Castellated nuts are used throughout, with split pins. 1922 *Times* 20 June 8/5 The wheel and consequently the castellated shaft will be rotated.

Caster. Add: **2. b.** (Earlier U.S. example.)
1793 *Ship Owner's Manual* (1795) 141 Many seamen, keelmen, casters.
c. One who takes or makes a model by running some liquid or forcing a plastic substance into a mould.
1921 *Dict. Occup. Terms* (1927) § 105 Potters; ware-makers, casters and finishers. *Ibid.* § 414 *Caster*, takes plaster cast of foot where any special form of boot is required, as in case of malformation, etc.
d. (See quot.)
1921 *Dict. Occup. Terms* (1927) § 049 *Caster*, examines coals sent from screens, and removes splints, *i.e.* slaty coal, in readiness for sale as house coal.

Castice (kæ·stis). Also **castize, castees, castess.** [ad. F. *castice* = Sp. *castizo*, a. Pg. *castiço*, f. *casta* CASTE.] An inhabitant of the East Indies born of Portuguese parents.
1662 J. DAVIES tr. *Mandelslo's Trav.* II. 103 (*Goa*) Those of the third Generation [of the Mestizes] are as black as the Inhabitants of the Country, which happens also in the fourth Generation of the Castizes. 1889 *Cent. Dict.*

Casting, *vbl. sb.* Add: **1.** esp. The action or process of founding (metal or glass).
c. *Casting of drapery*, the proper disposition of the folds of garments, in painting and sculpture. (Cf. CAST *sb.* 27, *v.* 47 b and F. *jet d'une draperie.*)
1842 FRANCIS *Dict. Arts*, Casting of Draperies. 190. R. STURGIS *Appreciation of Sculpture* 25 (Cent. Dict. Suppl.) Note, in the draped female statues, the casting of the drapery.
d. In sail-making, the calculated dimensions and shape of each cloth in a sail.
1886 *Encycl. Brit.* XXI. 154/2 There is got out what is technically termed a 'casting', which simply means the shape, length, &c., of each individual cloth in the sail.
d. In ploughing, the method and operation of turning all the furrow-slices of a ridge in one direction, and those of the adjoining ridge in the opposite direction.
1837 J. F. BURKE *Brit. Husb.* II. 46 (L.U.K.) It is sometimes desirable to throw two ridges into one...This operation is called casting. 1856 MORTON *Cycl. Agric.* II. 646/1 'The mysteries of 'gathering up', 'rown and furrow' ploughing, 'casting', 'yoking or coupling' ridges [etc.].
3. a. (Earlier U.S. examples.)
1817 S. R. BROWN *Western Gaz.* 112 They [*sc.* manufactures] consist of..castings, nails. 1831 PECK *Guide for Emigrants* III. 310 An iron foundry for castings, the only one in the State. 1841 C. CIST *Cincinnati* 131 Among the manufactures..were castings in brass and iron.
4. casting-ladle, an iron ladle used for conveying the molten metal into the mould in casting; **casting-machine,** (*a*) in a blast furnace a machine used in casting metal; (*b*) a machine for founding type; **casting-pit,** that part of a foundry where the moulds are placed and the castings made; **casting-plate** = *casting-table*; **casting-pot,** (*a*) a box in which a stereotype plate is cast; (*b*) a crucible; **casting-press,** an apparatus for subjecting metal to pressure during the process of casting; **casting-reel,** the reel of a casting-line; **casting sand,** black moulding sand that has been used for castings; **casting-shop,** the place where the operation of casting metal, etc., is carried out; **casting-slab, -table,** a table of polished metal with raised edges which serves as a mould for plate-glass.
1861 FAIRBAIRN *Iron* 157 No sooner is the mixture of the metals effected than the *casting-ladle is brought under the mouth of the vessel. 1880 *Encycl. Brit.* XIII. 343/1 The casting ladle into which the contents of the converters are emptied. 1899 *Chambers's Jrnl.* 25 Nov. 829/2 Pig-iron *casting-machines. 1908 *Census Bulletin* 216, 28 June 58 (Cent. Dict. Suppl.) The monotype..consists of two machines—a perforating device operated by a keyboard, and a casting-machine. 1921 *Dict. Occup. Terms* (1927) § 524 *Monotype caster attendant*..operates and adjusts casting machine. 1884 W. H. GREENWOOD *Steel & Iron* (ed. 2) 469 In the centre of the [Bessemer] *casting-pit is fixed a hydraulic crane. 1921 *Dict. Occup. Terms* (1927) § 279 *Moulder, casting pit*..shapes moulds in sand, in casting pit. 1881 *Spons' Encycl. Industr. Arts* III. 1061 The impressions are given by projections on the *casting-plate, which acts as a mould. 1846 DODD *Brit. Manuf.* VI. 60 The *casting-pot, with the mould,..is gradually forced down into the molten mass. 1881 *Instr. Census Clerks* (1885) 88 Casting Pot Maker. 1874 KNIGHT *Dict. Mech.*, **Casting-press*, one in which metal is cast under pressure, as in the car-wheel press. 1892 NIVEN *Brit. Angler's Lexicon* 192 The 'Malloch' *casting reel is used for spinning only. 1849 N. KINGSLEY *Diary* 30 Our sugar is black enough for *casting sand. 1871 *Daily News* 2 Jan. 3/5 He was carrying some lead from one part of the yard to the *casting shop. 1874 KNIGHT *Dict. Mech.*, *Casting-slab. 1728 CHAMBERS *Cycl.* s.v. *Glass*, When the first Annealing Furnace is full, the *Casting-table is to be carried to another. 1838 *Penny Cycl.* XI. 256/1 The cuvette is withdrawn from the furnace and taken to the casting-table.

Castle, *sb.* Add:
3. f. A heap of brushwood or sticks under which rabbits hide when being hunted.
1898 *Encycl. Sport* Mar. 175/1 The whole space is laid out in lines of some 20 to 30 yards in breadth, marked out by heaps of sticks or brushwood euphemistically termed 'castles'. *Ibid.* 175/2 When three or more residents turn out together from the same 'castle', and perchance bolt backwards, then complications ensue.
g. 'The principal village of an Indian tribe. *New York State*' (Webster).
1693 *Col. Rec. of Conn.* IV. 87 In possession of two of the neerest of the Maquas castles. 1779 *Mass. Hist. Soc.* Ser. II. II. 456 [We] cut of three Indian Castles at Onidauga. *Ibid.* 468 The Indian fields continued near 5 miles on our way from this Castle. 1794 S. WILLIAMS *Hist. Vermont* 142 The Indians..have no other fortification but an irregular kind of fortress, which they call a castle or fat.

Castlet. Delete †*Obs.* and add quots.:
1813 *Æditvus Metrical Remarks* 22 These walls so thick, ..With castlets by their sides, squat shapeless things. 1907 E. H. COLERIDGE *Christabel* 24 Triermain Castle must have been but a castlet compared with Naworth.

Cast-off, *sb.*[1] Add:
2. *Printing.* A calculation of the amount of space which will be required by a given amount of copy. (Cf. *CAST *v.* 79 j.)
1898 J. SOUTHWARD *Mod. Printing* I. xliii. 263 These two lines must be reckoned for in the cast off. 1917 F. S. HENRY *Printing for School & Shop* iii. 32 If the cast-off leaves but two or three lines on the last page, it is better to have the few previous pages each a line long.

Castor[1]. Add:
1. b. Among French Canadians, a member of the party which called itself the national party, the beaver being the national emblem of Canada.
1889 *Cent. Dict.*
6. Glove leather made from goat-skins; it is given a very soft finish of a gray colour.
1897 C. T. DAVIS *Manuf. Leather* (ed. 2) 519 When finished, [they] bear a close resemblance in texture and quality to deer-skin or castor. 1910 FLEMMING *Tanning* (ed. 2) 292 The tanner who wants to make mocha castor glove leather from kid and goat skins. 1923 *Daily Mail* 14 Feb. 11 Ladies' good quality Washable Castor Gloves.
7. A light drab colour.
1904 *Daily Chron.* 24 Oct. 8/4 Castor-coloured cloth (a soft beaver shade). 1923 *Daily Mail* 5 June 1 Colours: Nude, Fawn,..Mouse, Castor, Dark Tan.

Castor[2]. Add:
3. *attrib.* and *Comb.*, as *castor-stand*; **castor-sugar,** powdered sugar, so called from its suitability for use in a castor; **castor-wheel,** a small wheel which turns on its own and a vertical axis, used to support or steer an agricultural machine, or enable it to be turned short round.
1867 F. S. COZZENS *Sayings* iii. 13 The reflected sunshine from those cut bottles in the *castor-stand. 1885 *Catal. Cookery & Food Exhib.* 32 *Castor Sugar, specially prepared for the London trade. 1894 *Encycl. Pract. Cookery* (ed. T. F. Garrett) II. 533/1 White [sugar]..being sometimes sold in the form of a powder as 'caster Sugar'. 1899 E. E. MANN *L'pool Sch. Cookery Recipe Bk.* (1911) 87 Sift over with castor sugar to dry the surface. 1805 DICKSON *Pract. Agric.* I. Plate ix. to face p. 40 The profile of a six-shared horse-hoe on the principle of the pentagraph, improved by Mr. Amos by the addition of two *castor-wheels to regulate depth. 1874 KNIGHT *Dict. Mech.* s.v., The caster-wheel is used as a support to the front parts of machines, such as harvesters..and plowing machines, to enable them to be steered or to turn short around at the end of the row.

Castor[6] (ka·stəɹ). Applied to ancient British pottery made in the neighbourhood of Castor in Northamptonshire.
1868 C. R. SMITH *Collect. Antiqua* VI. 175 'Upchurch pottery' and 'Castor ware' are terms..denoting certain classes of fictile vessels made near Upchurch on the Medway, and at or near Castor on the Nen. 1924 COLLINGWOOD *Roman Britain* 73 The imported Samian ware..provoked the British manufacturer to..put on the market a style of pottery which resembled it in having ornament in relief and a highly glazed surface. Thus was produced what is known as Castor ware.

Ca·stor-bean. *U.S.* [See CASTOR OIL.] The castor-oil bean.
1835 J. MARTIN *Gazetteer Virginia* 250 There is here [*sc.* Northampton, Va.] an article of culture which is not much met with in other parts of the state—it is the palma christi, called castor bean. 1862 *Trans. Ill. Agric. Soc.* (1865) V. 508 The cotton plant in its habits of growth is similar to the castor bean. 1901 C. MOHR *Plant Life Alabama* 56.

Castorless (ka·stəɹlĕs), *a.* [f. CASTOR[2] 2 + -LESS.] Having no castors.
1883 [in Dict. s.v. CASTOR[2]]. 1891 MISS DOWIE *Girl in Karp.* 143 A castorless arm-chair. 1906 *Westm. Gaz.* 28 July 3/1 In the affectionate embrace of our stuffed arm-chair—how we love its scarred skin, its castorless immobility!

Castor oil. b. Add: **castor-oil bean,** the bean or seed from which the oil is obtained; also, the castor-oil plant.
1831 PECK *Guide for Emigrants* II. 158 The Palma christi, or castor oil bean, is produced [in Illinois]. 1846–50 A. WOOD *Class-bk. Bot.* 488. 1901 C. MOHR *Plant Life Alabama* 594 *Ricinus communis.* Castor Oil Bean.

Castor-pomace. 1877, 1878 [see POMACE 2 b].

Castrate, *sb.* Delete †*Obs.* and add:
1782 ELPHINSTON *Martial* I. iii. 3 No castrate or suborner shall there be: Erewhile the castrate was the debauchee. 1905 W. G. HOLMES *Justinian & Theod.* I. 134 *note*, The emperor cannot even uncover his head without the castrates closing round him to intercept the gaze of rude mankind.

Castrensic (kæstre·nzik), *a.* [f. L. *castrensis* (f. *castra* camp) + -IC.] Of or pertaining to a camp; military; = CASTRENSIAN.
1840 KEIGHTLEY *Rom. Emp.* III. iv. 348 The emperor distributed civic, naval, and castrensic crowns to those who had most distinguished themselves.

Castrum (kæ·strəm). Pl. **-a.** [L.] A Roman encampment or fortress.
1836 *Penny Cycl.* VI. 353/2 Roman Castra were probably sometimes formed on the sites of British works. 1850 C. R. SMITH *Antiq. Richborough* 31 The remains of the castrum at Richborough. 1886 *Athenæum* 13 Mar. 365/2 Another characteristic of a Roman castrum,..a huge wine cellar filled with thousands of amphoræ.

Cast-steel. [CAST *ppl. a.* 8.] A hard steel made from broken-up blistered steel melted in a crucible and run into ingot-moulds; crucible-steel. Also *attrib.*
1800 *Repertory of Arts* XIV. 177 The general principles of my process or processes are the fusion of malleable iron or of iron ore in such manner and by such means as immediately to convert them into cast-steel. 1812, 1858 [see STEEL *sb.*[1] 1 c]. 1824 [see CAST *ppl. a.* 8]. 1842 *Penny Cycl.* XXIII. 3/1 The celebrated wootz, or Indian steel, is cast-steel. 1851 WATTS tr. *Gmelin's Hand-bk. Chem.* V. 207 Specific gravity..of hardened cast-steel, 7·6578. 1868 *Jrnl. Chem. Soc.* XXI. 281 Cast-steel containing less than 0·3 per cent. of carbon is no longer capable of being hardened. 1880 *Encycl. Brit.* XIII. 356/2 Cast steel products.

Casual, *a.* (*sb.*) Add:
1. d. *Golf. Casual water*: see quot. 1899.
1899 *Rules of Golf, St. Andrews* 7 'Casual Water' shall mean any temporary accumulation of water (whether caused

by rainfall or otherwise) which is not one of the ordinary and recognised hazards of the course. 1908 *Encycl. Brit.* XXIX. 27/1 Standing as far behind the hazard or casual water as he may please.

6. b. Showing unconcern or lack of interest (real or assumed).

1916 BOYD CABLE *Action Front* 105 [She] answered Toffee, with an attempt to appear as off-handed and casual and at ease as his questioner. 1924 ROSE MACAULAY *Orphan Island* xvii. 230 She was casual and indifferent, but Rosamond.. stood up and said 'Yes'.

9. *Casual labour*: see quot. 1923. So *casual hand, labourer*.

1851 MAYHEW *Lond. Labour* II. 248/2 This mixture of constant and casual hands is..a necessary consequence of all trades which depend upon the seasons...Those who have paid attention to the subject of dock labour and the subject of casual labour in general. *Ibid.* 380/1 Greenwich may be looked upon as the first stage or halt for casual labourers, on their way to London. 1889 C. BOOTH *Life & Labour* I. 42 In East London the largest field for casual labour is at the Docks. 1905 *Daily Chron.* 25 July 5/4 He would not admit that the policy of the guardians had increased the casual labour system. 1908 H. W. CASLON *Letterpress Printing* 64 Casual labour is, and must be, a disturbing element in the costing of work. 1923 J. D. HACKETT *Labor Terms* in *Management Engineering* May, *Casual Labor*. 'Unskilled help, employed and discharged at frequent intervals, and dependent upon the varying demand of the labor market from day to day, without any prospect of continuous employment.' (*What's What in the Labor Movement*, Waldo R. Brown, p. 59.)

b. Of a soldier detached from his unit (so *c. camp, company*, etc., composed of such men). *U.S.*

1927 *Pocket Oxf. Dict.* (Amer. ed.).

B. *sb.* **3.** = *casual labourer*.

1851 MAYHEW *Lond. Labour* II. 246/1 The 'casuals' being mostly paid by the day. *Ibid.* 248/2 Of the scavagers proper there are..two distinct orders of workmen, 'the regulars and casuals' to adopt the trade terms. 1887 BEATRICE POTTER in *19th Cent.* Oct. 488 The true casual is seldom employed. 1889 C. BOOTH *Life & Labour* I. 202 The work of the casuals was a dead loss to the contractor.

Casualty. Add:

2. c. used of an individual killed, wounded, or injured.

1898 W. P. DRURY *Tadpole of Archangel* 173 A girls' school would shoot straighter...We haven't had a single casualty yet! 1900 W. S. CHURCHILL *London to Ladysmith* 393 In spite of more than a hundred casualties, the advance never checked for an instant. 1916 BOYD CABLE *Action Front* 144 Such casualties as could walk back walked. 1919 G. K. ROSE *2/4th Oxf. & Bucks Lt. Infty.* 86 Nearly 40 rank and file were casualties. 1925 E. F. NORTON *Fight for Everest, 1924* 87 With half a dozen porters to wait for our return in case there should be casualties to carry down the glacier.

6. Similarly *casualty hospital, nurse, sister*; **casualty insurance** (cf. *accident insurance*, *ACCIDENT *sb.* 10); **casualty list**, a list of the dead, wounded, etc. in an engagement or campaign; so *casualty returns*; **casualty man** = *CASUAL *sb.* 3.

1808 *Watering & Sea-bathing Places* 47 The Casualty Hospital is intended for such unfortunate persons as suffer by sudden accidents. 1846 *United Service Mag.* May 127 Casualty Return. 1864 *Standing Orders, Dress Regul. Artillery* 73 The casualty returns being the documents on which the correctness of Brigade Records mainly depends. *Ibid.* 173 (in List of Periodical Returns) Casualty list. 1887 BEATRICE POTTER in *19th Cent.* Oct. 489 A considerable number of men, possessing a preferred right to employment, act as an intermediate class between the permanent staff and the 'casualty' men. 1896 *Daily News* 17 June 8/3 The casualty nurse. 1901 *Punch* 4 Sept. 163/1 The casualty lists appear about as long as ever. 1902 *Encycl. Brit.* XXIX. 509/2 Another large class of casualty insurance applies to various forms of damage to property. 1902 *Westm. Gaz.* 10 June 10/2 Casualty insurance is yet in its infancy. 1907 *Ibid.* 3 Apr. 7/1 In view of the avowed determination of the fire offices to go into the casualty business. 1919 SHAW *Heartbreak House* (1927) p. xxii, The emotional strain, complicated by the offended economic sense, produced by the casualty lists. 1926 WARWICK DEEPING *Sorrell & Son* xxix. 294 He performed three minor operations, with the.. casualty-sister assisting him with critical and voiceless composure.

Casuistics (kæziu,i·stiks), *sb. pl.* [See CASUISTIC and -ICS.]

1. = CASUISTRY 1.

1882 *Pop. Sci. Monthly* Sept. 660 The question is raised in the casuistics of Mohammedan ritual, whether it is right to eat the flesh of the Nesnās.

2. = CASUISTRY 2.

1895 *Funk's Stand. Dict.* 1903 *Phil. Med. Jrnl.* 31 Jan. 203 (Cent. D. Suppl.) The casuistics of malignant growths of the abdominal cavity.

Casus belli (kē·sə̆s be·ləi). [f. L. *casus* CASE *sb.*[1] + *belli*, gen. of *bellum* war.] An occasion of war; an act justifying or regarded as a reason for war; *gen.* a ground of quarrel.

1853 H. GREVILLE *Diary* 22 June (1884) 60 He thought the Russians would soon occupy the principalities, which, however, the other Powers would not pronounce to be a *casus belli*. 1878 *Times* 2 Feb. 6/3 He did not say what was to be the *casus belli* or the *casus armandi*.

Casus fœderis (kē·sə̆s fī·dĕris). [f. L. *casus* CASE *sb.*[1] + *fœderis*, gen. of *fœdus* treaty.] A situation or occurrence covered by the provisions of a treaty or compact, and so requiring the action of the parties thereto.

1780 J. ADAMS *Let.* 31 Dec., Wks. 1852 VII. 348 These powers will not be duped by the artifice of the British Court, and adjudge this war not a *casus fœderis*. 1834 H. GREVILLE *Diary* 30 July (1883) 16 A quadripartite treaty, of which your person is the *casus fœderis*. 1882 *Standard* 20 Dec. 5/7 The Treaty of Alliance with the Austrian Empire, including those paragraphs..which define the special obligations of each contracting party under a casus fœderis.

Caswellite (kæ·zwĕləit). *Min.* [Named after John H. *Caswell* of New York: see -ITE[1].] A micaceous mineral of a copper-red colour, probably an altered form of biotite.

1894 A. H. CHESTER in *Trans. N.Y. Acad. Sci.* XIII. 49. 1896 *Jrnl. Chem. Soc.* LXX. II. 309 It is supposed that the caswellite has been derived by the local action of water containing manganese and calcium on this biotite.

Cat, *sb.*[1] Add:

4. b. (Earlier U.S. examples.)

1705 BEVERLY *Virginia* (1722) 129 Conger-Eels, Perch, and Cats. 1760 WASHINGTON *Diaries* I. 149 Hauld the Sein again, catched 2 or 3 White Fish..and a great Number of Cats. 1765 J. BARTRAM *Jrnl.* (1769) 6 'Tis full of large fish, as cats, garr, mullets. 1790 *Massachusetts Spy* 16 Sept. (Th.) Perch, pike, eel, and cats of a monstrous size.

11. b. *pl.* The salt which crystallizes round the edge of the pan or beneath the holes in the bottom of the trough in which salt is put to drain.

1886 *Cheshire Gloss.*, Cats, salt-making term. Masses of salt formed under a pan when it leaks. 1892 *Cornhill Mag.* Sept. 265 The 'cats', or salt that has become encrusted round the edges of the pan, is sent to the pottery works for glazing pipes and pitchers.

13. *To make a cat laugh*: said of something excruciatingly funny. *Not a cat's chance*: no chance whatever.

1902 CUTCLIFFE HYNE *Mr. Horrocks Purser* 100 Crutches by themselves wouldn't have stood a cat's chance. 1907 W. W. JACOBS *Short Cruises* 230 It would ha' made a cat laugh. 1909 *Punch* 14 July 26 It's enough to make a cat laugh. 1927 *Daily Express* 13 Dec. 16/6 There did not seem a cat's chance for Oxford on comparative form. 1928 *Ibid.* 6 Aug. 2/5 'Is there any likelihood of food prices being controlled by the Government?'..'By the record of the existing Government there is not a cat's chance.'

18 and 19. Cat-and-mouse Act, nickname for the Prisoners (Temporary Discharge for Ill-health) Act of 1913 to enable hunger-strikers to be released temporarily; **cat-berry**, the gooseberry; **cat-burglar**, a burglar who enters by extraordinarily skilful feats of climbing; **cat-castle** (see CAT *sb.*[1] 6 and quot. 1907); **cat chain** (see quot.); **cat-footed** *a.* (*a*) stealthy in movement; (*b*) (see quot. 1884); **cat-footedness**, sure-footedness; **cat's-head fern**, *Aspidium aculeatum*; **cat('s)-lick**, colloq. expression for a perfunctory manner of washing oneself; also as vb.; **cat-squirrel** (earlier examples); **cat('s) whisker**, a fine adjustable copper or gold wire in a crystal wireless receiver.

1913 *Punch* 23 July 81/1 Plural Residence, which will still be permitted after the abolition of Plural Voting, is being encouraged by the *Cat-and-Mouse Act. 1884 MILLER *Plant-n.*, *Cat-berries, *Ribes Grossularia*. 1886 BRITTEN & HOLLAND *Plant-n.* 91. 1907 *Daily Chron.* 18 Apr. 1/7 Owing to his skill in climbing he was known as 'the *cat burglar'. 1927 *Daily Express* 24 Mar. 2/6 A 'cat' burglar broke into the house..by climbing a stackpipe. 1861 *Chambers's Encycl.* II. 668/1 *Cat*, or **cat-castle*, in the military engineering of the middle ages, was a kind of movable tower to cover the sappers as they advanced to a besieged place. 1907 COLLINGWOOD in *Trans. Cumbld. & Westmld. Archæol. Soc.* (N.S.) VIII. 100 'Catcastle' in local [Kendal] dialect is the second figure in the game of Cat's-cradle. 1883 *Man. Seamanship Boys* 195 Q. What is a *cat chain? A. A chain which is rove through the cat block, and shackled on to the upper end of ground chain to bring the anchor to cat head. 1598 *Cat-footed [see CAT *sb.*[1] 17 in Dict.]. 1884 G. STABLES *Our Friend the Dog* vii. 59 *Cat-footed*—Having the toes well knuckled up, making the foot short and round. 1929 W. J. LOCKE *Jorico* 94 He had the peculiar, sure *cat-footedness of those who follow the sea. 1880 LOUISA A. MEREDITH *Tasm. Friends*, etc. 220 The *cat's-head fern..is full of beauty—the pinnules so exquisitely formed and indented [etc.]. 1859 GEO. ELIOT *A. Bede* xi, Th' men ne'er know whether tha floor's cleaned or *cat-licked. 1892 *Leeds Merc. Suppl.* 12 Mar. (E.D.D.) Thah's nobbut gien thisen a cat-lick asteead ov a reight wesh. 1898 *Eng. Dial. Dict.* s.v. *Cat* sb.[1], Yer may ev catlicked the flooer; yer hevn't weshed it. 1906 W. DE MORGAN *Joseph Vance* vii. 65 Anne..soaped me with a vigour far beyond any experience of washing I had had up to that date. My method had been Cat-licking, she said. 1834 MCMURTRIE *Cuvier's Anim. Kingd.* 80 The *Cat Squirrel (*Sciurus cinereus*, Lin.) of America is cinerous above, white beneath. 1855 MAYNE REID *Hunters' Feast* xix, The species found in these woods was the large 'cat-squirrel' (*Sciurus cinereus*), one of the noblest of its kind. 1915 A. F. COLLINS *Bk. of Wireless* 205 Adjust the wire until the pointed end presses on the crystal and you will have what is called a *cat-whisker detector. 1923 *Daily Mail* 28 June 13 A crystal called 'Radiocite'.. used with a 'cats-whisker' contact, and the pressure necessary is extremely light.

Cat, *sb.*[3], variant form of KAT.

1877 *Encycl. Brit.* VI. 110/2 In Arabia the beverage [*sc.* coffee]..only supplanted a preparation from the leaves of the cat, *Celastrus edulis*. 1904 *U.S. Consular Rep.* No. 285. 549 The cat is a plant containing a medicinal principle which acts as a tonic upon the muscles of the heart.

Cat, *v.*[1] Add:

1. Also *absol.*

1890 W. CLARK RUSSELL *Ocean Trag.* iii, They had catted, and were fishing the anchor forwards.

5. *intr.* To be deposited in the manner of salt, etc. round objects, in crevices, or the like. (Cf. *CAT *sb.*[1] 11 b.)

a 1909 *Buck's Handbk. Med. Sci.* VII. 901 (Cent. Dict. Suppl.) The material which cats here is in a state not capable of ready absorption, and must act locally.

Cat, *v.*[2] *U.S.* [f. CAT *sb.*[1] 4 b.] *intr.* To fish for cat-fish.

1834 CARRUTHERS *Kentuckian in N.Y.* II. 217 I'm jist now like I've been at times when I've been out catting. 1859 BARTLETT *Dict. Amer.* (ed. 2) s.v. *Catting*.

Cata-: see also KATA-.

Catabolic (kætăbǫ·lik), *a.* *Biol.* = KATABOLIC.

1887 *Athenæum* 7 May 611/3 The interpretation of all the phenomena of male and female sex as the outcome of katabolic and anabolic preponderance.

Catabolism (kătæ·bŏliz'm). *Biol.* = KATABOLISM.

1889 BURDON-SANDERSON in *Nature* 26 Sept. 525/1 The words in question, 'anabolism', which being interpreted means winding up, and 'catabolism', running down, are the creation of Dr. Gaskell. Prof. Hering's equivalents for these are 'assimilation', which, of course, means storage of oxygen and oxidizable material, and 'dissassimilation', discharge of these in the altered form of carbon dioxide and water.

Catabothron: see KATABOTHRON.

Cataclastic (kætăklæ·stik), *a.* *Geol.* [f. Gr. κατακλαστός, f. κατά down + κλαστός, f. κλᾶν to break.] Designating a structural character due to intense crushing.

1896 J. W. JUDD *The Student's Lyell* 560 Many metamorphic rocks exhibit a similar 'cataclastic' structure. 1903 GEIKIE *Text-bk. Geol.* (ed. 4) 421 When the temperature is 300° C. or 400° C. no cataclastic structure is observable.

Cataclysmically (kætăkli·zmikăli), *adv.* [f. CATACLYSMIC: see -ICALLY.] By a cataclysm.

1889 I. TAYLOR *Aryans* iii. 132 The civilization..was not introduced cataclysmically, by the immigration of a new race.

Cat-a-cornered, variant of *cater-cornered* (see CATER *adv.*).

1902 S. E. WHITE *Blazed Trail* vii. 53 When the log had been cat-a-cornered from its bed, the chain was fastened [etc.]. 1906 *Harper's Mag.* July 252 'You do leave things so catacornered,' Martha observed.

Cataded, -did, obs. ff. KATYDID.

1829 T. FLINT *George Mason* 11 The measured creaking of the crickets and catadeds. 1829–32 J. P. KENNEDY *Swallow B.* I. xxviii. 311 The little catadid pierced the air with his shrill music.

Catagenesis (kætădʒe·nĕsis). [See CATA- and GENESIS.] Retrogressive evolution.

1887 E. D. COPE *Orig. Fittest* 434 The process of creation by the retrograde metamorphosis of energy, or, what is the same thing, by the specialization of energy, may be called *catagenesis*. 1900 B. D. JACKSON *Gloss. Bot. Terms*.

Hence **Catagenetic** (kætădʒĕne·tik) *a.*, of the nature of retrogressive evolution.

1896 E. D. COPE *Prim. Factors Org. Evol.* 482 If the tendency of the catagenetic energies is away from vital phenomena.

Catalan. Add: so *Catalan furnace, hearth*, etc.

1861 FAIRBAIRN *Iron* 42 The disposition of the Catalan hearth during the process of reduction. 1867 BLOXAM *Chem.* 321 In the Pyrenees, where the Catalan process is employed. 1874 KNIGHT *Dict. Mech.*, *Catalan-furnace*, a blast-furnace for reducing iron ores, extensively used in the North of Spain.

Catalanist (kæ·tălænist). [f. CATALAN + -IST.] One who favours the independence of Catalonia; usually *attrib.* or as *adj.* So **Ca·talanism.**

1905 *Daily Chron.* 23 Sept. 5/3 The Catalanist Agitation. 1907 *Westm. Gaz.* 25 May 2/1 The 'Catalanist' Home Rulers. 1923 *Glasgow Herald* 8 Oct. 9 The suspension of ..more or less seditious Catalanist journals. 1930 S. DE MADARIAGA *Spain* xviii. 304 Catalanism is, above all, a Barcelona affair.

Catalase (kæ·tălēs). *Chem.* Also **katalase.** [f. CATAL(YSIS + *-ASE.] An enzyme capable of decomposing hydrogen peroxide by catalysis.

1901 *Jrnl. Chem. Soc.* LXXX. I. 435 Catalase occurs in an insoluble (α-catalase) and in a soluble form (β-catalase). 1904 *Brit. Med. Jrnl.* 20 Aug. 28 Yeast contains..nuclein, zymase, endotrypsin, and katalase.

Catalectic, *a.* Add: Often in postposition in imitation of L. **b.** *sb.* A catalectic line or verse.

1625 B. JONSON *Staple of News* IV. iv, Pentameters, Hexameters, Catalecticks. 1842 *Penny Cycl.* XXIV. 228/1. 1887 GOODWIN *Gk. Gram.* § 293 The tetrameter catalectic.

Catalecticant (kætăle·ktikănt). *Math.* (See quots. 1852, 1860.) So **Catale·ctic** *a.*, **Catale·ctically** *adv.*

1851 J. J. SYLVESTER *Canonical Forms* Coll. Math. Wks. 1904 I. 211 The theory of the catalectic forms of functions of the higher degrees of two variables. *Ibid.*, If, however, certain further relations obtain between the coefficients of *F*, the canonical form reappears catalectically, the function becoming in fact representable as a single cube. 1852 *Ibid.* 293, I shall hereafter refer to a determinant formed in this manner from the coefficients of *f* as its catalecticant. 1860 CAYLEY *Coll. Math. Papers* (1891) IV. 606 The name catalecticant denotes a certain invariant of a binary quantic of an even order.

Cataleptize (kætăle·ptəiz), *v.* [f. CATALEPTIC + -IZE.] *trans.* To throw into a cataleptic fit; to render cataleptic.

1887 *Fortn. Rev.* May 733 The corresponding side of the body is cataleptized. *Ibid.* 739 We read of priests being cataleptized..in the attitude of elevating the sacrament.

Catalexis (kætăle·ksis). [f. Gr. κατάληξις termination, f. καταλήγειν to leave off.]

1. Absence of a syllable in the last foot of a verse.

1830 SEAGER tr. *Hermann's Metres* II. xix. 46 Cretic verses are for the most part terminated by that same foot, and have no other catalexis. 1898 SAINTSBURY *Short Hist. Engl. Lit.* II. iii. (1900) 77 Halidon is told (by Minot) in octave eights admitting catalexis. 1921 *Edin. Rev.* Apr. 331 Introducing further variety by the frequent use of catalexis.

2. A catalectic verse or line.

1850 MURE *Lit. Greece* III. 55 The combination of a single short verse or 'catalexis' with one or more longer verses.

Catalo (kæ·tălo). *U.S.* Also **cattalo, cattelo.** [f. CAT(TLE + BUFF)ALO.] A cross between the male buffalo and the domesticated cow.

a 1889 C. J. JONES in H. Inman *Buffalo Jones' Forty Years of Adv.* 243 To these cross-breeds I have given the name, 'Catalo', from the first syllable of *cattle* and the last three letters of *buffalo*. 1889 *Kansas Times & Star* 20 May, Colonel [Charles] Goodnight was the first man to experiment with crossing buffalo and cattle. A big herd of the hybrids, called 'cattalo', is now on his Texas ranch. 1906 *Harper's Mag.* Apr. 798 [The buffaloes] sad captives sinking to slow extinction in the hybrid cattelo with his mongrel name. 1925 *Chambers's Jrnl.* 167/1 The resulting cattalo will populate the northern prairies.

Cataloguable (kæ·tălǫgăb'l), *a.* [f. CATALOGUE *v.* + -ABLE.] That can be catalogued.

1922 *Times Lit. Suppl.* 28 Dec. 866/3 There are no moral or immoral actions catalogued and cataloguable.

Catalogue, *sb.* Add: **3. a.** A list of college or university graduates, alumni, or teachers. **b.** A university or college calendar. *U.S.*

1682 J. BISHOP in *Mass. Hist. Coll.* Ser. IV. VIII. 311, I lately received..a Catalogue of Harvard's sons. 1712 J. LEVERETT *Diary* 43 The Catalogue of Graduate[s]. 1786 in J. Maclean *Hist. Coll. N.J.* (1877) I. 344 Ordered, That a complete catalogue of the graduates of this College be prepared and published at the expense of the present Senior class. 1812 (*title*) Catalogue of the Officers and Students [of Harvard]. 1823 (*title*) Catalogue of officers and students in Yale College November 1823. 1842 Z. THOMPSON *Hist. Vermont* II. 155 Middlebury College.. Catalogue of Alumni and Honorary Graduates. 1873 J. H. BEADLE *Undevel. West* xxxi. 686 The 'University of Deseret' puts forth a pretentious catalogue, with a lengthy list of professors. 1899 E. E. HALE *Lowell & Friends* 170 In 1856, the year when Lowell's name first appears as a professor in the Harvard catalogue.

4. Miscellaneous attrib. uses.

1892 *Photogr. Ann.* II 127 Each of the catalogue plates will have two exposures. 1894 *Daily News* 11 Apr. 6/4 Taking the breeds in catalogue order. 1899 *Ibid.* 29 Apr. 7/3 A Piccadilly firm have offered to buy at catalogue price the picture by Policeman Jones, of Leeds, accepted for the Royal Academy. 1909 *Daily Chron.* 5 May 1/2 The gross catalogue value of all extracts.

Catalogue raisonné (katalog rɛzone). Also formerly erron. **raisonnée.** [Fr., = carefully studied or methodical catalogue.] A descriptive catalogue arranged according to subjects, or branches of subjects; hence *gen.* or *loosely*, a classified or methodical list.

1791 C. SMITH *Desmond* (1792) III. 169 He had glided away on a descriptive tour to his own seat near Bath; and was giving a *catalogue raisonnée* of its conveniences. 1803 *Edin. Rev.* Oct. 79 A *catalogue raisonnée*, if executed with judgment and impartiality, would be a very useful appendage to every work. 1818 HAZLITT *Engl. Poets* viii. *Of the living poets* (1929) 252 There is no Gay in the present time to give a *Catalogue Raisonné* of the performances of the living undertaker of epics. 1835 *Penny Cycl.* IV. 380/2 The best specimen of a *Catalogue Raisonné* that we know of any of the more considerable collections of this country, is that of the library of the writers to the Signet in Edinburgh, published in one volume quarto in 1805. 1836 C. FORSTER *Jebb* I. ii. 135 Having written my list, which I have endeavoured to make a sort of catalogue raisonné.

Catalonian (kætălōu·niăn), *a.* and *sb.* [f. *Catalonia*: see -IAN.] = CATALAN. Also **Catalu·ñan** (-lū·nyăn) *a.* [Sp. *Cataluña*, Cat. *Catalunya*.].

1781 *Lett. Engl. Traveller in Spain 1778* v. 63 The Aragonians and Catalonians adopted the Castilian dialect. 1836 *Penny Cycl.* VI. 361/2 During the war of the Spanish succession, the Catalonians..took the part of the Archduke Charles of Austria against Philip of France. 1847 tr. *Bouterwek's Hist. Span. Lit.* 3 In the kingdom of Arragon, the language in general use was the Catalonian. 1875 *Encycl. Brit.* II. 433/2 This Catalonian work of the 14th and 15th centuries. 1876 *Ibid.* V. 217/2 The Catalonians are a frugal, sharp-witted and industrious people. 1899 *Daily News* 24 Nov. 4/6 The extreme Cataluñan party is clearly schismatic.

Catalpic (kătæ·lpik), *a.* [f. CATALPA + -IC.] *Catalpic acid*: an acid derived from trees of the genus *Catalpa*. Also **Cata·lpin**, a crystalline glucoside of similar origin.

1885 *Jrnl. Chem. Soc.* XLVIII. I. 272 The analyses of the acid and its barium and silver salts point to the formula $C_{14}H_{12}O_6$; it is proposed to call the substance catalpic acid. 1888 *Amer. Chem. Jrnl.* X. 329 Catalpin forms radial aggregates of white acicular or silky, slender, and often curved crystals.

Catalyse (kæ·tăləiz), *v.* Also **kata-, -lyze.** [f. CATALYSIS after *analyse, analysis*.] *trans.* To dissolve, break down, decompose. Hence **Ca·talysator, Ca·talyser,** a catalyst; also *fig.*

1890 *Nature* 13 Nov. 25/1 Every micro-organism produces, from the substances which it katalyzes..a material or materials, which, on accumulation, inhibit its growth. 1893 *Ann. Rep. Smithsonian Inst.* 237 Numberless specific catalysators exist which act only upon certain phenomena. 1904 *Jrnl. Phys. Chem.* May 373 Measurements were made of the effect of catalyzers on the formation of C_6H_5Cl and $C_6H_6Cl_6$ from benzene and chlorine. 1904 tr. *Haeckel's Wonders of Life* ii. 47 Many recent chemists and physiologists are of opinion that plasm is a colloid catalysator. 1926 *Spectator* 21 Aug. 280/1 [Advertising] is..the great mover of merchandise, the catalyser of commerce.

Catalyst (kæ·tălist). *Chem.* [f. CATALYSIS, on the analogy of *analyst*.] A catalytic agent; a catalyser.

1902 *Nature* 3 Apr. 523/1 No reactions are possible under the influence of catalysts that could not take place in their absence without a breach of one of the laws of energy. 1920 *Chambers's Jrnl.* 284/1 Nickel is used as a 'catalyst', or a carrier of hydrogen in the hydrogenation..of oils for use in the manufacture of margarine. 1927 HALDANE & HUXLEY *Anim. Biol.* viii. 169 We have begun to isolate many of the intermediate products of metabolism and the catalysts that govern the course of the reactions by which they are formed.

Catalytic, *a.* Add *sb.* (see quot.)

1885 *Buck's Handbk. Med. Sci.* I. 125/2 Alteratives. (Syn.: Catalytics, eutrophics.) The class of remedies thus designated are agents which, promoting nutrition, so alter the course of morbid processes as to lead to the elimination of disease and a return of the organism to a normal, healthy condition.

Catalytical (kætăli·tikăl), *a.* = CATALYTIC *a.*

1889 in *Cent. Dict.* 1923 *Glasgow Herald* 30 May 8 Catalitical salts.

Cataphoresis (kæ:tăfǒrī·sis). *Med.* Also kata-. [f. Gr. κατά down + φόρησις being carried.] The action of causing medicinal substances to pass through the skin into living tissue by the use of an electric current. Hence **Ca:taphore·tic** *a.* (Dorland *Med. Dict.* 1903).

1890 BILLINGS *Med. Dict.*, Kataphoresis. 1895 *Buck's Handbk. Med. Sci.* Suppl. 267/1 The use of iodine by cataphoresis has been attempted in cases of goitre. 1908 *Times* 9 Oct. 10/1 The possibility of using cataphoresis as a means of conveying foods and drugs to the system.

Cataphoric (kætăfǫ·rik), *a.* = KATAPHORIC.

1891 M. A. STARR in *Electricity in Daily Life* 271 The second action of a continuous galvanic current is to move along with it the fluids which lie in its path. This is called its cataphoric action. 1895 *Buck's Handbk. Med. Sci.* Suppl. 267/1 The cataphoric transfer of molecules of protoplasm and liquid from one cell to another.

Cataphractic, *a.* Add to def.: Covered with or as with armour.

1891 MEREDITH *One of our Conq.* I. v. 67 Not even the flower..would hold constant, as they, to the constantly unseen—a trebly cataphractic Invisible.

Catapophysis (kætăpǫ·fisis). *Anat.* [mod.L., f. Gr. κατά down + ἀπόφυσις outgrowth, process.] Any protuberance or process, usually of bone or of brain tissue, esp. one of a pair of processes developed on the sides of the ventral face of the cervical vertebræ in birds. Hence **Ca:tapophy·sial** *a.*, of or pertaining to catapophysis.

1899 *Proc. Zool. Soc. Lond.* 21 Mar. 406 Catapophyses of cervicals never meeting in mid-ventral line to form a canal. 1901 *Ibid.* 371 All Storks that I have examined, except *Anastomus* and *Dissura*, possess a catapophysial canal occupying a varying number of vertebræ.

Catapult, *sb.* Add:

3. Applied to mechanical contrivances by which objects are shot out at a great speed: cf. next.

1927 *Daily Express* 12 Dec. 11/4 Béarn, new aircraft carrier, will carry forty airplanes to be launched by a compressed air catapult at forty-seven miles per hour after a run of sixty-five feet along the deck. 1928 *Times* 28 Aug. 12/6 Catapult Air Mail.

b. catapult fruit (see quot.).

1900 B. D. JACKSON *Gloss. Bot. Terms*, *Catapult Fruit*, those fruits dispersing seeds or fruit segments by the elasticity of their peduncles.

Catapult, *v.* Add:

d. To discharge by means of a 'catapult' contrivance.

1928 *Daily Express* 29 Aug. 8/2 The Post Office has just announced that for a special fee it will accept British letters and postcards for the United States on the understanding that before arriving in New York they are to be catapulted from the ship by seaplane. 1928 *Scotsman* 30 Aug. 9/6 The aeroplane will be catapulted into the air on approaching the American coast.

Cataractal (kæ·tăræktăl), *a.* [f. CATARACT + -AL.] Of the nature of a cataract (*lit.* and *fig.*).

1888 W. CLARK RUSSELL *Death Ship* xxxviii, A cataractal roaring of water. 1891 *Illustr. Lond. News* 17 Jan. 74/2 The sea swept..with a cataractal fury. 1926 C. L. WARR *Principal Caird* 237 The outburst of popular indignation.. was simply terrific in its power of cataractal denunciation.

Catarrhed (kătā·ɹd), *ppl. a.* [f. CATARRH *sb.* + -ED[2].] Infected with catarrh.

1890 'R. BOLDREWOOD' *Col. Reformer* xxiv, A lot of catarrhed sheep.

Catatonic (kætătǫ·nik), *a.* Characterized by KATATONIA.

1908 *Practitioner* Jan. 12 There may be catatonic stupor, automatic obedience, and occasionally impulsive automatism.

Catavothron. = KATABOTHRON.

1869 TOZER *Highl. Turkey* I. 160 The Mediævals..had the idea of there being a *catavothra* from the lake. 1878 *Encycl. Brit.* VIII. 685/2 The subterranean course of the streams is frequently indicated by peculiar vents or pits caused by the subsidence of the soil; they are popularly known in Greece as *catavothra*.

Catawampous, *a.* *U.S.* (Earlier and later examples.)

1843 CARLTON *New Purchase* I. xxviii. 265 The tother one what got most sker'd is a sort of catawampus (spiteful). 1844 DICKENS *Mart. Chuz.* xxi, There air some catawampous chawers in the small way too, as graze upon a human pretty strong. 1885 'C. E. CRADDOCK' *Prophet Gt. Smoky Mts.* ix. 153 She got me plumb catawampus. 1888 — *Broomsedge Cove* iii. 44 But it's a powerful differ ter please this man an' not git that one set catawampus.

Catbird. Add:

b. The name given to several species of Australian birds whose cry resembles the mewing of a cat.

1848 J. GOULD *Birds Australia* IV. pl. 11 Ptilonorhynchus Smithii...Cat Bird. *Ibid.*, Situations suitable to the Regent and Satin Birds are equally adapted to the habits of the Cat Bird. 1888 D. MACDONALD *Gum Boughs* 36 One of the most peculiar of birds' eggs found about the Murray is that of the locally-termed 'cat-bird', the shell of which is very thickly with dark thin threads as though covered with a spider's web. 1889 C. LUMHOLTZ *Among Cannibals* vi. 96 The cat-bird (*Ælurædus maculosus*), which makes its appearance towards evening, and has a voice strikingly like the mewing of a cat. 1902 *Encycl. Brit.* XXXII. 109/2 A second characteristic [of Queensland] is the great development of that quaint company, the Bower Birds, among them the Regent Bird, Satin Bird, Cat Birds, &c., constructors of the elaborate playgrounds which have excited so much attention.

Cat-boat: see CAT *sb.*[2]

Catch, *sb.*[1] Add:

1. c. In Rugby football and baseball (see quots.).

1867 *Routledge's Handbk. Football* 47 A Fair Catch is a catch from a kick, or a knock on from the hand but not from the arm of the opposite side, or a throw on. 1896 R. G. KNOWLES & MORTON *Baseball* 14 He..must be proficient in making running catches as in bringing off standing ones. 1897 *Encycl. Sport* I. 431/1 If a player makes a fair catch he shall be awarded a free kick.

d. *Rowing.* The grip of the water taken with the oar at the beginning of a stroke.

1881 *Standard* 30 Mar. 3/7 The shallow waters of the Cam ..make it very difficult for a crew to imitate the catch at the beginning of the stroke. 1898 *Encycl. Sport* II. 273/2 The beginning must be caught with full power (it is a grip rather than a catch, certainly not a snatch). *Ibid.* 296/2 *Catch*, the instant application of the weight and muscles of legs and body to the oar at the moment it enters the water.

2. c. A crop (with reference to germination or rooting). *U.S.*

1872 *Rep. Vermont Board Agric.* I. 126 A moderately wet season is more favorable to a good 'catch' of grass than a dry one. 1898 *L. H. Bailey's Princ. Agric.* 81 On hard and poor lands, it is often difficult to secure a 'catch' of clover.

d. A stretch of water in which fish may be caught.

1891 *Field* 7 Mar. 342/1, I am standing by a charming catch on the noble Wye, which catch I have been thrashing for a good hour and a half.

e. A place where something is caught.

1920 HUNTER *Trail Drivers of Texas* 98 Our camp was the catch and cut-out for all the other bosses.

3. *Catch-and-bowl*, a catch made by the bowler.

1907 *Westm. Gaz.* 20 July 15/1 Hence the number of catches-and-bowls he used to bring off.

7. b. A hidden element (in a proposal, etc.) designed to take advantage of another person; something concealed with the intention of catching or tripping one up; hence, an unforeseen difficulty or awkwardness, a 'snag'.

1855 BARNUM *Life* 120 The old farmer, who was pretty 'cute, was sure that there was some 'catch' in this offer. 1913 *Punch* 18 June 474/1, I say, I'm a burglar. There is no catch in it. 1914 *Daily Express* 22 Dec. 2 It is not a trick or a 'catch', but a genuine game. 1916 H. L. WILSON *Somewhere in Red Gap* vi. 252 She says she knew there must be some catch about it [*sc.* a card-game]. 1919 WODEHOUSE *Damsel in Distress* x, There's nobody I think a more corking sportsman than Maud, if you know what I mean, but—this is where the catch comes in—I'm most frightfully in love with somebody else.

11. Similarly, *No catch*, a bad bargain, an unwelcome acquisition. *colloq.*

b. *colloq.* A person matrimonially desirable on account of wealth or position.

1837 MARRYAT *Snarleyyow* xx, She..fully proved to his satisfaction that, independent of her beauty, she would be a much greater catch than Frau Vandersloosh. 1842 *Comic Almanack* 333 (Farmer) Angelina Ampletin was one of the prettiest girls in Pimlico, and..very far from one of the worst catches. 1888 A. C. GUNTER *Mr. Potter* viii, Something in this catch-of-the-season's manner has set this young English barrister hoping for what rich dukes had hoped for in vain. 1917 H. A. VACHELL *Fishpingle* x, Matrimonially he was a great 'catch' for an heiress of quality.

Catch, *v.* Add:

12. b. *Rowing.* To grip the water with the oar at (the beginning of a stroke).

1886 *Encycl. Brit.* XXI. 32/1 The oar should be struck down firmly and decisively into the water.., and the weight of the body be thrown entirely upon it, by which the beginning of the stroke is caught. 1898 *Encycl. Sport* II. 273/2 The beginning must be caught with full power. 1902 *Encycl. Brit.* XXXII. 307/2 Swivel rowlocks..are considered unsuitable to eight-oared rowing, where the beginning of the stroke has to be firmly and smartly caught.

c. Of a crop: To germinate and grow. *U.S.* (Cf. *CATCH *sb.*[1] 2 c.)

1909 *Cent. Dict.* Suppl.

14. Also in wider application.

1924 G. L. MALLORY in E. F. Norton *Fight for Everest, 1924* 213 The wind and sun between them have fairly caught us all these last three days.

16. b. To fasten, attach (some object) *back* or *up*.

1895 *Funk's Stand. Dict.*, To *catch up*, to raise by attaching something; festoon; loop up; as, her dress was caught up with ribbons. 1898 *Daily News* 11 May 4/4 [Her] rose-tinted brocaded train was caught back at one side.

24. c. Also *caught and bowled* (abbrev. c. and b.), caught by the bowler.

1883 [in Dict.]. 1897 *Encycl. Sport* I. 245/2 *Caught and Bowled*, caught by the bowler who delivered the ball. 1924 J. B. HOBBS *Cricket Mem.* 169 Then Mr. Simms got rid of Woolley with a magnificent 'caught and bowled'.

d. *Baseball.*

1874 CHADWICK *Base Ball Man.* 88 There be was when Mills was caught out on the fly. 1896 R. G. KNOWLES & MORTON *Baseball* 39, I would have meant 'caught out'. 1902 *Encycl. Brit.* XXVI. 160/1 In base-ball if the ball is knocked in a certain direction it is called a foul, and the player who knocked it has not the privilege of making a run, but may be caught out.

e. *intr.* To act as catcher in the game of base-ball.

1890 WILL CARLETON *City Legends* 39 'An' will you pitch or catch?' Says I, 'I'll catch, if so desired'.

39. b. *Catch-as-catch-can*, the Lancashire style of wrestling. Also *attrib.*

1889 W. ARMSTRONG *Wrestling* Introd. p. xiv, In 1871, the late Mr. J. G. Chambers..some time editor of *Land and Water*, endeavoured to introduce and promote a new system of wrestling at the Lillie Bridge Grounds, West Brompton, which he denominated, 'The Catch-as-catch-can Style; first down to lose'. 1898 *Encycl. Sport* II. 548/2 The principal chips associated with catch as catch can wrestling are the double Nelson, the half Nelson, the heave [etc.]. *Ibid.* 549/2 Turkish wrestling is principally carried out in catch as catch can style. 1905 *Daily Chron.* 21 Dec. 9/5 A catch-as-catch-can wrestler needs to be wonderfully active.

49. Catch off. b. To get to sleep. *U.S.*

1927 *Pocket Oxf. Dict.* (Amer. ed.).

51. Catch out. c. *fig.* To catch in a mistake, catch napping or in the act.

1815 JANE AUSTEN *Emma* II. xiv. Wks. 1926 IV. 279 Ah! there I am—thinking of him directly. Always the first person to be thought of! How I catch myself out! 1881 MRS. LYNN LINTON *My Love* xvii, Randolph caught himself out in the vileness of wishing that she was just a trifle less superior.

53. Catch up. e. Also in non-physical senses, and *intr.* esp. in *to catch up on, to, with.*

1886 *Calcutta Englishman* in J. M. Dixon *Dict. Idiomatic Engl. Phrases* 58 He has not caught up (overtaken) his rival by the time earlier educational honours are distributed. 1925 E. F. NORTON *Fight for Everest, 1924* 114, I had to wait quite half an hour for him to catch up. 1925 *Times* (weekly ed.) 26 Nov., The police caught up on the men just as they entered a dark archway. 1926 *Ibid.* 5 Aug., Its sanitation can never catch up to its needs.

Catch-. Add:

1. catch-water, a vessel designed to catch water.

1888 *Lockwood's Dict. Terms Mech. Engin.*, *Interceptor*, a T-shaped cylindrical vessel employed in connection with marine engines to prevent particles of water from being carried over with the steam into the cylinders...Called also catch water. 1901 M. W. TRAVERS *Exper. Study Gases* 33 The water runs into a catch-water below the bulb, and is conducted away.

3. a. *catch-bar, -bolt, -boom, -pot, ratline* (see RATLIN(E 2), *-tank*; **catch-basin,** (*b*) a reservoir for catching and retaining surface-drainage over large areas; **catch-box,** a box-like clutch of a spinning machine; **catch-fake** (see quot.); **catch-feeder** (see quot.); **catch-motion** (see quot.); **catch-point,** a throw-off or derailing switch on a railway siding to prevent a train, truck, etc. from running on to the main line; **catch-wheel,** a wheel capable of motion in one direction only, a ratchet-wheel; **catch-work,** used attributively to define a system of irrigation in which the water drains into a feeder or feeders at a lower level.

1849 *Rep. U.S. Comm. Patents* (1850) 170 The second crank to slide the *catch bar. 1874 KNIGHT *Dict. Mech.*, *Catch-bar* (Knitting-machine), a bar employed to depress the jacks. 1884 *Science* III. 372/1 Whether any..system of *catch-basins or reservoirs, could..mitigate..such..floods. 1874 KNIGHT *Dict. Mech.*, **Catch-bolt*, a cupboard or door bolt which yields to the pressure in closing and then springs into the keeper in the jamb. Usually retracted by a small knob. 1905 *Terms Forestry & Logging* 33 **Catch boom*, a boom fastened across stream to catch and hold floating logs. 1825 J. NICHOLSON *Oper. Mech.* 426 When the *catch-box 14 is in contact with the sheeve *s*. 1892 NASMITH *Students' Cotton Spinning* 320 The wheel..is provided with a catch box..and by its means drives the shaft. 1867 SMYTH *Sailor's Word-bk.*, **Catch-fake*, an unseemly doubling in a badly coiled rope. 1874 KNIGHT *Dict. Mech.*, **Catch-Feeder* (Hydraulic Engineering), an irrigating ditch. *Ibid.*, **Catch-motion* (Machinery), a motion in a lathe by which speed is changed. 1895 *Daily News* 7 Dec. 7/7 That *catch points should be more clearly indicated. 1898 *Ibid.* 14 Mar. 5/2 It cut through the catch points and buffer stops. 1902 *Encycl. Brit.* XXXII. 144/2 A throw-off or derailing switch ('catch-points'). 1831–3 *Encycl. Metrop.* (1845) VIII. 619/1 This cylinder carries a *catch wheel..the teeth of which engage the click..attached to the wheel C by a screw. 1799 T. WRIGHT *Art Floating Meadows* 82, I have seen the common plan of *catch-work watering resorted to. 1805 R. W. DICKSON *Pract. Agric.* II. 930 There is another description of watering, usually denominated Catch-work. 1830 *Cumbld. Farm Rep.* 52 in *Libr. Usef. Knowl., Husb.* III, There are 18½ acres of water meadow on the ridge or bed system, and about 10½ on what is termed catch-work. 1844 H. STEPHENS *Bk. Farm* III. 1022 Catch-work irrigation.

b. *catch-cry*; **catch title,** an abbreviated title sufficiently expressive of the full title to identify the book.

1901 *Daily Chron.* 20 Nov. 4/5 Some very sound remarks ..on certain catch-cries of the day. 1911 WEBSTER, *Catch title*, a short expressive title used for abbreviated book lists, etc.

c. catch question, a question that catches one up or has a catch in it; also as vb.

a 1860 ALB. SMITH *Med. Student* (1861) 14 Legendary 'catch questions'. *Ibid.* 116 The inquisitors..are willing to help a student out of a scrape, rather than 'catch question' him into one. 1905 *Westm. Gaz.* 22 Apr. 3/1 The critics and commentators for centuries have been, like the philosophers, fooled by the catch-question of the Stuart King concerning the weight of a live fish in a bucket full of water.

d. That is or may be taken or 'caught' to one's advantage.

1905 *Spectator* 7 Jan. 3/2 To put the policy of development at the mercy of a catch vote. 1907 *Daily Chron.* 15 Aug. 7/5 There was a strong catch tide in favour of the swimmers.

4. catch-weight, also in *Boxing* and *Wrestling* (see quots.).

1863 *Punch* XLV. 86 The Archimandrite Nilos has offered to fight the Bishop of London for 20 pound a side, catch-weight. 1897 *Encycl. Sport* I. 139/1 *Catchweight* (*To box at*)—Boxing without restrictions as to weight. 1907 *Daily Chron.* 18 Oct. 9/3 To wrestle the best of three falls for £50 a side at catch-weight.

Ca·tch-all, *sb.* (*a.*) *U.S.* [CATCH- I.]

1. A general receptacle.

1838 *Congress. Globe* 16 Apr. App. 275/1 [The party includes] old Federalists,..Antimasons, and Abolitionists. They have, sir, been a kind of catch-all, or *omnium gatherum*. 1866 MRS. STOWE *Lit. Foxes* 27 The general catch-all and menagerie..for all the family litter. 1892 *Harper's Mag.* June 29/1 A shrewd spider..had spread his gossamer catch-all beneath the bramble. 1897 'MARK TWAIN' *Following Equator* xli. 383 It seemed to have been designed as a catch-all for every thing that can damage it. 1923 J. L. VANCE *Baroque* xiv. 86 The tenement yard was a simple black hole, for generations a common catch-all.

2. *Mech.* (See quot.)

1884 KNIGHT *Dict. Mech.* Suppl., *Catch-all*, a tool for withdrawing from drilled wells broken tools or bars which have fallen in.

B. *adj.* Serving as a general receptacle.

1875 HOWELLS *Foregone Concl.* xviii. (1882) 296 They hunted out Ferris's property from a catch-all closet in the studio of a sculptor with whom he had left them.

Catcher. Add:

2. c. In full *torpedo* or *torpedo-boat catcher*: a torpedo gun-boat for destroying enemy torpedo-boats.

1886 *Chambers's Jrnl.* 30 Jan. 77/2 The establishment of the torpedo system has necessitated the introduction of.. torpedo catchers. 1895 *Min. Proc. Inst. Civil Eng.* CXXII. 51 The..torpedo-boat catchers, as they were then [1886] called—the name has since been changed to torpedo gun-boat. *Ibid.* 79 They had been called torpedo-boat destroyers or catchers. 1902 *Daily Chron.* 18 Apr. 3/3 The various stages of the catchers, the destroyers, and the scouts. 1925 *Blackw. Mag.* Aug. 208/1 These catchers are most efficient little vessels, fast, handy, perfectly equipped.

Catch-hold. *Wrestling.* [f. phr. *to catch hold*: see CATCH *v.* 45.] (See quot. 1889.)

1883 *Encycl. Brit.* XXIV. 690/2 The 'catch hold, first down to lose' style of wrestling. 1889 W. ARMSTRONG *Wrestling* 34 The catch-hold fashion is a most rational style of wrestling, as the competitors are..at liberty to catch each other as they please..provided they do not hold by the legs or clothes. 1898 *Encycl. Sport* II. 546/1 A style on the 'catch hold' principle.

Ca·tchiness. [f. CATCHY *a.*] The quality of being catchy.

1898 *Century Mag.* Mar. 773 In spite of its dangerously instantaneous catchiness, it [*sc.* an étude] expresses just the sentiment of flattery in all its shades.

Catching, *vbl. sb.* Add: **c.** *attrib.*

1874 KNIGHT *Dict. Mech.*, **Catching-hook*, a crochet-hook. A crook or animal-catching hook. 1874 HARDY *Madding Crowd* xxii, In one angle a *catching-pen was formed, in which three or four sheep were continuously kept ready for the shearers to seize without loss of time. 1894 A. ROBERTSON *Nuggets*, etc. 4 He dashed into the catching pen, and seized the smaller of two sheep that remained. 1891 *Scribner's Mag.* X. 470 During the planting-time [for oysters] as well as in the *catching-season.

Catching, *ppl. a.* **3.** (Later U.S. example.)

1876 *Rep. Vermont Board Agric.* III. 481 The 'catching' rains of harvest time..will always fetch a lugubrious wail from any farmer.

Catchy, *a.* **2.** Add: Also, liable to 'trip one up', difficult to manage or execute.

1876 *Coursing Calendar* 285 Mr. Hedley, for the second time, pleased everyone with his judging; whilst Johnston, who slipped for the first time on such catchy ground, performed his duties well. 1882 *Cassell's Encycl. Dict.*, *Catchy*, ..difficult, not easy to learn or to execute. (*Colloquial.*)

Cat-claw. [CAT *sb.*[1]; cf. *cat's claw* (19 b).] A prickly shrub of the south-western United States.

1898 H. S. CANFIELD *Maid of Frontier* 204 The catclaw flowered into white after each infrequent rain.

Cat-cry. [CAT *sb.*[1]] = CAT-CALL *sb.* 2.

1898 MARG. DELAND *Old Chester Tales* 53 The audience came stamping and scuffing in,..and much loud, good-natured raillery, and some cat-cries.

Catdom (kæ·tdəm). [f. CAT *sb.*[1] + -DOM.] The condition or quality of cats; the world of cats.

1888 *Pall Mall Gaz.* 25 Oct. 3/1 A charming specimen of catdom in one 'Jimmy.' 1890 *Illustr. Lond. News* 10 May 599/3 The winning ways of 'catdom' and 'kittenhood.'

Catechol (kæ·tĭtʃǫl). *Chem.* [f. CATECHU + -OL.] = *pyro-catechin* (s.v. PYRO- 2 b).

1880 *Jrnl. Chem. Soc.* XXXVIII. 417 The author denies the presence of catechol in the leaves of *Ampelopsis hederacea*. 1892 *Photogr. Ann.* II. 87 Catechol in dilute solution develops slowly, but gives excellent detail and opacity.

Catechu. Add: Also *attrib.* or *Comb.*: **catechu brown,** a brown colour produced by the use of catechu as a dye.

1860 URE *Dict. Arts* (ed. 5) I. 805 Catechu Brown, rich and transparent. 1880 J. DUNBAR *Pract. Papermaker* 41 Catechu dyed papers. 1902 *Encycl. Brit.* XXVII. 564/1 Catechu browns are fast to a variety of influences.

Catechumenal (kætĭkiū·mĕnăl), *a.* [f. CATECHUMEN + -AL.] Catechumenical.

1883 C. C. PERKINS *Italian Sculpture* Introd. p. liv, He had laid aside his white catechumenal robes.

Catenist (kăti·nist). [f. CATENA + -IST.] A maker of a catena of authorities or evidence.

1880 SWETE *Theodore of Mopsuestia on St. Paul's Ep.* I. 240 Theodoret followed his master, without, however, condescending to the level of the mere catenist.

Catenoid (kæ·tĭnoid), *a.* and *sb.* [f. CATENA + -OID.] **A.** *adj.* Catenary, chain-like. **B.** *sb.* *Math.* The surface formed by the revolution of a catenary about its axis.

1876 *Encycl. Brit.* V. 68/2 This catenoid..is in stable equilibrium only when the portion considered is such that the tangents to the catenary at its extremities intersect before they reach the directrix. 1901 CALKINS *Protozoa* 156 Such pseudoconjugation frequently leads to the formation of catenoid colonies.

Cater (kē·təɹ), *sb.*[3] [f. CATER *v.*[1]] The act or habit of catering.

1888 *Voice* (N.Y.) 23 Feb. 3/2 One of the many steps in the long continued Republican cater to the beer-garden.

Cater, *adv.* Add: **Cater-cornered** (earlier example); also **Ca·ter-cornering** *a.* (See also *CATTY-CORNERED.)

1843 CARLTON *New Purchase* xxvii. 261 With directions how..to secure by two strings diagonally fastened, or as he better understood it—'katterkorner'd-like'. 1885 *Century Mag.* Nov. XXXI. 64/1 He just takes them records..and brings his side line down catercornerin'—that way. 1888 J. KIRKLAND *McVeys* 59 Now, suppose the railroad runs diagonally across a field, 'cater-cornering', as he says.

Catering (kē·təriŋ), *ppl. a.* [f. CATER *v.*[1] + -ING[2].] That caters.

1923 *Glasgow Herald* 21 Mar. 11 A large London catering firm.

Caterpillar. Add:

1. b. In full *caterpillar tractor*: A type of tractor which travels upon two endless steel bands, one on each side of the machine, each fitting over two cogged wheels, a device which enables the tractor to travel over very rough ground. Also *caterpillar car*, etc.

1915 *Lit. Digest* 4 Sept. 467/1 Government road-building throughout the interior has paved the way for automobiles, caterpillars and traction-engines. 1922 *Other Lands* July 119/1 It has caterpillars and motor-ploughs. 1923 *Contemp. Rev.* Oct. 487 The arrangement of 'caterpillar' traction, with which they were fitted. 1928 HAARDT & AUDOUIN-DUBREUIL *Black Journey* i, On the 28th of October, 1924, the eight caterpillar auto trucks left Colomb-Bechar.

5. b. caterpillar wheel, a wheel of a heavy vehicle having a broad tread divided into separate sections for use on rough or uneven ground; hence **caterpillar-wheeled** *a.*

1914 *Illustr. Lond. News* 5 Sept. 369 A 21-centimetre siege-mortar—with 'caterpillar' wheels. 1922 *Westm. Gaz.* 28 Dec., From In-Salah the caterpillar-wheeled cars will cross the plateau of Tidikelt.

Cat-fish. Add: Also applied to various species of fish in Australasia and S. Africa.

1851 J. HENDERSON *Excurs. N.S.W.* II. 207 The Cat-fish, which I have frequently caught in the McLeay, is a large and very ugly animal. 1871 *Cape Monthly Mag.* (N.S.) II. 135 A most horrible creature called a 'catfish', but which ought more properly to have been named 'a sea devil',..as it was all arms and legs, and huge goggle-eyed head. 1897 T. J. PARKER & HASWELL *Text-bk. Zool.* II. 212 The Cat-fishes (*Siluridæ*). 1900 H. A. BRYDEN *Anim. Africa* 196 When..African rivers dry up, there is nothing left for the Cat-fish but to burrow in the mud.

Ca·t-foot, *v.* *U.S.* [CAT *sb.*[1] + FOOT *sb.*] *intr.* To walk stealthily or noiselessly.

1916 H. L. WILSON *Somewhere in Red Gap* iii. 119 Mebbe it's a Blackhander's camp, I think; so I didn't yell any more. I cat-footed. And in a minute I was up close. 1928 *Collier's Mag.* 10 Nov. 42/2 Tichenor arose and nonchalantly cat-footed down the field for a deceitful touchdown.

Cathar (kæ·þăɹ). Also **-are.** [ad. med.L. *Cathari.*] = CATHARAN. Also *adj.*

1637 [see CATHARAN]. 1907 *Cath. Encycl.* I. 557/1 The Cathares and the Patarines. 1927 F. J. E. RABY *Hist. Chr. Lat. Poetry* xiii. 416 Based like the Cathar and Waldensian [religions], on poverty and renunciation.

Catharsis. Add: (also **katharsis**):

b. The purification of the emotions by vicarious experience, esp. through the drama (in reference to Aristotle's *Poetics* 6). Also more widely.

1904 DOWDEN *Browning* 289 Balaustion, stricken at heart, yet feels that this tragedy of Athens brings the tragic katharsis. 1924 L. COOPER *Aristotelian Theory Com.* 180 Aristotle..would recognize some sort of catharsis, and the resultant pleasure, to be the proper end of comedy. 1924 SELBIE *Psychol. Relig.* 159 There may..be cases where experiences of this kind produce a moral catharsis which has good results.

c. *Psychotherapy.* The process of relieving an abnormal excitement by re-establishing the association of the emotion with the memory or idea of the event which was the first cause of it, and of eliminating it by 'abreaction'. 1918 WEBSTER Addenda.

Ca·t-haul, *sb.* *U.S.* [CAT *sb.*[1] 17.] (See quot.) Also **Ca·t-haul** *v. trans.*, to subject to this punishment; *fig.* to examine stringently.

1816 'A. SINGLETON' *Lett. fr. South & West* (1824) 79 The cat-haul; that is, to fasten a slave down flatwise..and then to take a huge fierce tom-cat by the tail backward, and haul him down along the..bare back, with his claws clinging into the quick all the way. 1840 *Congress. Globe* 12 Jan., App. 99/2 White people of the South..hunting slaves with dogs and guns,—cat-hauling slaves, &c. 1881 *Congress. Rec.* 28 Feb. 2202/2 You begin to ransack and examine and cat-haul the whole navy, big and little.

Cathayan (kăþē·ăn), *a.* and *sb.* Also -aian. [f. med.L. *Cat(h)aya* + -AN. Cf. CATAIAN.] Chinese.

1667 MILTON *P.L.* X. 293 Mountains of Ice, that stop th' imagin'd way Beyond Petsora Eastward, to the rich Cathaian Coast. *Ibid.* XI. 388 Cambalu, seat of Cathaian Can. 1876 *Encycl. Brit.* V. 628/1 The identity of these Cathayans with the Seres of classic fame. 1928 *Blackw. Mag.* Jan. 1/1 To push back a Cathayan encroachment.

Cat-head, *sb.* Add: **3. c.** 'An attachment to a lathe to assist in supporting long bars when they are being turned' (*Cent. Dict.* Suppl. 1909).

4. *attrib.*, as *cat-head stopper* (see small-type Note ad fin.).

1829 *Patents* in *Ann. Reg.* 551/2 Improvements in the construction of cat-head stoppers. 1883 *Man. Seamanship for Boys* 10 For lifting the anchor from the water's edge to the cat head in order to pass the cat head stopper.

Cat-head, *v.* Add: (Earlier U.S. example.)

1840 R. H. DANA *Bef. Mast* xxv, Everything was sheeted home and hoisted up, the anchor tripped and cat-headed.

Cathedral, *sb.* **3.** Add: **cathedral glass,** coloured glass leaded after the fashion of the stained windows of churches, used (e.g.) in the panels of the vestibule doors of houses.

1858 SIMMONDS *Dict. Trade*, *Cathedral Glass*, stained or painted glass for church windows sold either in sheets or small squares. 1885 *Spons' Mechanics' Own Bk.* 630 'Roundels' and 'bullions' are small discs of glass..used in fretwork with cathedral glass. 1905 H. A. EVANS *Highways & Byways Oxf. & Cotswolds* 329 The exquisite pale green transparent glass of the windows,..displaced to make room for the vulgar abomination known as 'cathedral glass'.

Catherine wheel. Add:

1. b. In embroidery, a design resembling a wheel.

1882 CAULFEILD & SAWARD *Dict. Needlework* 62 *Catherine Wheel.*—This wheel is also known by the name of Spider Wheel or Spider Stitch, and is chiefly employed to fill up round holes in embroidery on muslin.

Catheterize, *v.* Add: *trans.* To employ a catheter to.

1908 *Practitioner* Jan. 44 A true stricture,..forming an irregular channel, through which urine passes with difficulty, and which it is almost impossible to catheterise.

Cathexis (kăþe·ksis). *Psychol.* [a. Gr. κάθεξις holding, retention; intended as a rendering of G. *besetzung* (Freud).] The concentration or accumulation of mental energy in a particular channel.

1922 STRACHEY tr. *Freud's Group Psychol.* 48 Dread in an individual is provoked either by the greatness of a danger or by the cessation of emotional ties (libidinal cathexes [orig. *Libidobesetzungen*]). 1923 E. JONES in *Internat. Jrnl. Psycho-Analysis* IV. 209 In hetero-suggestion..a hyper-cathexis of the idea of the operator is correlated with a hypo-cathexis of all ideas in conflict with his. *Ibid.* 302 The intense concentration of attention (which Abraham terms *Besetzung*, i.e. cathexis) or self-absorption..is exclusively concerned with the..conscious sexual phantasy.

Cathisma (kăþi·zmă). Pl. **cathismata.** [a. Gr. κάθισμα seat, f. κατά down + ἵζειν to sit.] In the Greek Church: A portion of the psalter, containing from three to eleven psalms. Also, a short hymn used as a response.

1850 J. M. NEALE *Holy Eastern Ch.* I. 844 The Greeks rarely sit in church: the cathismata are therefore pauses for rest; and are longer than the usual troparia. 1880 *Encycl. Brit.* XII. 580/1 In various parts of the services solitary troparia are sung, under various names, 'contacion', 'cecos', 'cathisma', &c.

Cathode. Add:

c. *attrib.* and *Comb.*: **cathode dark space,** in a vacuum tube traversed by an electric discharge, the dark space immediately surrounding the cathode and separating it from the negative glow; also called *cathodic dark space*, CROOKES *dark space*; **cathode photograph, photography,** = *CATHODOGRAPH, *CATHODOGRAPHY; **cathode rays,** rays issuing from the cathode of a vacuum tube having a very high vacuum when an electric discharge takes place, moving at very high velocities in straight lines unless deflected by a magnetic or electric field, and producing X rays by contact with an obstruction.

1920 *Discovery* July 217/1 The dark space around the negative pole, which has since been referred to as the Crookes or *Cathode Dark Space. 1896 *Daily News* 31 Jan. 7/2 Experiments in *Cathode photography. 1905 *Jrnl. Chem. Soc.* LXXXVIII. II. 224 With copper, nickel, gold, and bright platinum, the *cathode potential for a given current density goes on increasing for hours. *Ibid.*, *Cathode process and anode liquid are opposed to each other. 1897 *Nature* 25 Feb. 386/2 Lenard's famous researches on the *Kathode rays. 1900 *Jrnl. Chem. Soc.* LXXVIII. II. 587 Electrical Conductivity in Gases traversed by Cathode Rays. 1927 N. V. SIDGWICK *Electronic Th. Valency* 7 The wave-length of the X-rays given off by various elements when bombarded with cathode rays.

Cathodic. Add:

3. *Electr.* Of or pertaining to a cathode, as *cathodic dark space, cathodic rays* (see prec.).

1896 *Daily News* 18 Jan. 5/4 Taking photographs with cathodic rays. 1896 *Review Rev.* (U.S.) Mar. 303 Professor Roentgen provisionally designates his peculiar form of cathodic rays.

Cathodo- (kæ·þǫdo), used as combining form of CATHODE.

1909 *Physical Rev.* XXVIII. 349 With regard to the dependence of kathodo-luminescence upon discharge potential and current strength. 1914 *Ibid.* Ser. II. IV. 21 The brightness of the crests of the red and blue bands of the white and pink kunzite under kathodo-excitation. 1923 *Amer. Jrnl. Sci.* Oct. 373 The minimum energy required to excite cathodo-luminescence.

Cathodograph (kăþǫ·dograf). Also **cathodegraph, kathodograph.** [f. CATHODO- + -GRAPH.] A photograph of normally invisible objects taken by means of cathode rays, an X-ray photograph. Hence **Catho·dograph** *v. trans.*, to take an X-ray photograph of; **Cathodography** (kæþodǫ·grăfi), photography by cathode rays.

1896 *Century Mag.* May 120/1 No school or college has considered the day well spent in which..it has not taken 'cathodographs' of hands and coins. *Ibid.* 121/1 Key cathodographed through a book of 526 pages. *Ibid.* 126/2 A cathodograph picture. *Ibid.*, Cathodography of corked bottles would uncork them. 1897 *Daily News* 2 Feb. 5/2 Its transparent honesty was recognised by the 'cathodegraph' showing only the setting, the diamond being represented by a white space.

Cat-hole. Add: **2.** (Later U.S. example.)

1867 *Amer. Naturalist* July I. 255 She brushes against a lid which hangs from above, not unlike an old-fashioned swinging door of a cat-hole, as sometimes seen about barns or corn-cribs.

4. A bog-hole.

1857–8 *Trans. Mich. Agric. Soc.* IX. 578 The very important work of draining our swamps, marshes and cat holes, has been fairly commenced.

Catholic. Add:

A. *adj.* **11.** *Comb.*, as *Catholic-minded* adj.

1879 T. E. BRIDGETT in *Dublin Rev.* Jan. 95 The learned, irresolute, yet pious and Catholic-minded men at the head of whom was Fisher's friend, Cuthbert Tunstal.

B. 2. Examples of *English Catholic* = English Roman Catholic.

1584 in Foley *Rec. Eng. Prov. S.J.* VI. 740 Hesaid..that all English Catholics were bound to pray for the King of Spain. 1641 J. LOUTH in A. H. Matthew *Convers. Sir T. Matthew* (1904) 176 The innocency and loyalty of English Catholics towards others. 1715–6 in J. O. Payne *Eng. Cath. Nonjurors of 1715* (1885) 8, I, Henry Englefield, do declare that I am, by the grace of God, an English Catholic. 1800 C. BUTLER *Life Alban Butler* xvi, A person would deserve well of the English Catholics who should translate it into English. 1889 J. O. PAYNE (*title*) Records of the English Catholics of 1715.

b. *Old Catholic*, a term introduced after the secession of John Henry Newman and others to distinguish hereditary Roman Catholics in England from converts.

1847 A. ST. JOHN in W. Ward *Life Newman* (1912) I. v. 174 As to Dr. Griffiths or the old Catholics they are not.. in good odour here at all. 1857 NEWMAN *Let.* 19 Jan. in Gasquet *Ld. Acton* p. xxiii, Suddenly I find that there is a great split between old Catholics and converts. 1909 *Dublin Rev.* Jan. 56 The friction between converts and old Catholics ..was inevitable.

Catholicization (kăþǫlisəizē·ʃən). [f. CATHOLICIZE *v.* + -ATION.] The action of making Catholic.

1905 *Nation* (U.S.) 28 Dec. 522 The catholicization of France by Clovis.

Catholyte (kæ·þŏləit). [f. CATH(ODE + ELECTR)OLYTE.] That part of the electrolyte which adjoins the cathode.

1904 *Electrochem. Industry* Mar. 99 (Cent. D. Suppl.).

Catilinarian, *sb.* Add examples:

1889 SKRINE *Mem. Thring* 155 The senate which quelled the Catilinarians met in the Temple of Concord. 1925 *Glasgow Herald* 16 Apr. 9 He is still a sort of Catilinarian doomed to reckless experiments.

Catocalid (kætǫ·kălid), *a.* *Ent.* [f. mod.L. *Catocala*, f. Gr. κάτω below + κάλος beautiful: see -ID[3].] Belonging to the genus *Catocala* of beautiful noctuid moths.

1913 *Oxf. Univ. Gaz.* 4 June 960/2 A fine set of 28 Catocalid moths.

Catostomid (kătǫ·stŏmid), *a.* and *sb.* Also **catastomid.** [ad. mod.L. *Catostomidæ*, a family of fishes, f. *Catostomus*, the typical genus, f. Gr. κάτω down + στόμα mouth.] Pertaining to, a fish of, the family *Catostomidæ*, of which the American suckers and mullets are the chief representatives.

1908 *Smithsonian Misc. Coll.* V. 97 This character suggests a cyprinid or a Catostomid.

Catpiece (kæ·t,pīs). *U.S.* [f. CAT *sb.*[1] + PIECE *sb.*] In logging, a perforated bar of wood fitting on the tops of uprights in floating booms, so that the space between the booms may be narrowed when necessary.

1905 *Terms Forestry & Logging* 33.

Cat-rigged, *a.* See CAT *sb.*[2] and add U.S. quots.

1885 *Outing* (U.S.) Nov. 205/2 She..was an open centre-board boat, cat-rigged. 1886 *Ibid.* Apr. 58/1 All half-round yacht-built boats, cat-rigged or sloop-rigged.

Cat's-eye. 2. Add attrib. uses.

1874 *Jrnl. Chem. Soc.* XXVII. 355 The so-called Cat's-eye and Fibrous Quartz. 1899 T. M. ELLIS (*title*), The three Cat's-eye Rings. 1903 *Daily Mail* 8 Sept. 7/4 A..narrow edging of cat's-eye green.

Catskin. Add:

1. b. *Catskin earl*, each of the three senior earls in the House of Lords, viz. the Earls of Shrewsbury, Derby, and Huntingdon.

1869 HOOK *Lives Abps.* VIII. 264 *note*, The Earl of Huntingdon is one of the three catskin earls of the present day, one of the first three earls in the House of Lords.

Cat-stairs. *dial.* and *U.S.* Also **cat's-.** [CAT *sb.*[1] 19.] (See quots.)

1825 JAMIESON *Suppl.*, *Cat's-stairs*, a plaything for children, made of thread, small cord, or tape, which is so disposed by the hands as to fall down like steps of a stair. Dumfr., Gall. 1828 CARR *Craven Gloss.* (ed. 2) 64 *Cat-stairs*, Tape, &c. so twisted, that by its alternate hollows and projections, it resembles stairs. 1886 *Leslie's Pop. Monthly* Feb. XXI. 150/1 'Twere vain to tell what sylvan treasures accumulated in our back yard that summer. The flights of catstairs [etc.].

Cat-stick. (Modern U.S. examples.)

1859 BARTLETT *Dict. Amer.* (ed. 2), *Catstick*, a stick or cudgel used by New England boys in a game at ball..In Pennsylvania, Maryland, and further south, the term is applied to small wood for burning. 1867 LOWELL *Fitz Adam's Story* 466 And more to abate the price, his gimlet eye Would pierce to catsticks that none else could spy.

Cat-tail: see CAT'S TAIL 2 b.

1857 *Trans. Mich. Agric. Soc.* VIII. 649 Upon land which ..was originally a cat-tail swamp, we saw a field of corn. 1873 *Amer. Naturalist* VI. 77 The long strap-shaped leaves and the dark cylindrical spikes of *Typha latifolia* form the veritable cat-tail flag. 1891 *Scribner's Mag.* X. 470 A tangled growth of..cat-tails, elder and salt-grass.

Cattalo, variant of *CATALO.

Catted (kæ·tĕd), *ppl. a.* See CAT *v.* 1. So **Ca·tting** *vbl. sb.*

1867 SMYTH *Sailor's Word-bk.*, *Catting*, the act of heaving the anchor by the cat-tackle. 1883 *Man. Seamanship for Boys* 210 When stowing the anchor for sea after the second catting. 1901 *Daily Chron.* 12 June 7/2 The 'catted' port anchor of the schooner.

Cattimandoo (kætimæ·ndū). Also **cattamundoo, kattimandoo, kattimundoo, callemundoo.** [Telugu *kattimandu*, the name of the plant.] A resinous substance obtained from the milky juice of *Euphorbia cattimandoo* or other species of *Euphorbia*; used as a cement and as a cure for rheumatism. **b.** The plant from which the gum is obtained.

1858 SIMMONDS *Dict. Trade*, Cattemundoo, Callemundoo. 1866 *Treas. Bot.* 1880 *Encycl. Brit.* XI. 339/2 Many of the euphorbias yield milky juices...The chief among these are the cattimandoo..and the Indian spurge tree.

Ca·ttiness. [f. *CATTY *a.* + -NESS.] = *CATTISHNESS.

1920 *19th Cent.* Nov. 752 Her antagonism to her own sex.. known colloquially as 'cattiness'. 1928 *Sunday Express* 6 May 4 Manx folk are wonderfully good-natured, and.. cattiness, is practically non-existent.

Cattish. Add:

b. Of a sly or spiteful character. (Cf. CAT *sb.*[1] 2.)

1883 BLACK *Yolande* III. vii. 127 The cattish temper of the old woman. 1893 SALTUS *Madam Sapphira* 15 The stealthy air and cattish smile of the mother.

Hence **Ca·ttishly** *adv.*, in a cattish spirit; **Ca·ttishness,** the quality of being 'cattish', spitefulness.

1894 MEREDITH *Ld. Ormont* xxii, Thither he walked, prepared for cattishness. 1907 *Daily Chron.* 8 July 3/4 Thus..was Mrs. Steel's cattishness brought home to her. 1909 *Westm. Gaz.* 8 June 3/2 Elizabeth, we are afraid, is developing into a little 'cat,' as her female friends would probably say...That is where the 'cattishness' of Elizabeth shows itself. 1923 'M. ARLEN' *These Charming People* 189 'Society Hostess Robbed.' It's almost worth it for her, he thought cattishly, to be called a Society Hostess.

Cattle. Add:

8. a. *cattle-driving, -grower, -maiming, -minder, -raiding, -raiser, -raising, -rustler, -rustling, -thief.*

1834 *Visit to Texas* xiii. 121 He had had experience in *cattle-driving long before I had ever seen Texas or a wild ox. 1886 *Harper's Mag.* July 252/1 The English *cattle-grower views with indignation the incursions of American beef on the English market. 1907 *Westm. Gaz.* 6 Sept. 5/1 The renewed outbreak of *cattle-maiming in this parish [*sc.* Great Wyrley]. 1908 *Daily Chron.* 1 June 5/5 Eye Green, near Peterborough, is becoming as notorious as Great Wyrley for cattle-maiming outrages. 1846 in Claiborne *Life & Corr. J. A. Quitman* 284 A place for *cattle-minders and grazing herds. 1899 *Daily News* 13 Nov. 7/4 The real object of this *cattle-raiding expedition. 1870 MEDBERY *Men & Myst. Wall St.* 2 The heavy *cattle-raisers of Texas..are the veriest victims of circumstance. 1872 *San Francisco Weekly Bulletin* 27 May (Hoppe) It costs the Texas cattle-raisers $339,500 per annum to feed that one Mexican town. 1896 *Daily News* 16 Jan. 5/6 All the victims were well-known cattle-raisers. 1883 *Athenæum* 2 June 693 In Galicia *cattle-raising is rapidly superseding tillage. 1896 *Daily News* 16 Jan. 5/6 Horse-stealing and cattle-raising are unpardonable crimes in the eyes of the Slav peasantry. 1912 *Daily Mail* 15 Feb. 8 A great crisis has fallen upon the cattle-raising industry of this Republic. 1925 *Chambers's Jrnl.* 268/1 Regions in the plains, where cattle-raising ceased to be profitable. 1903 A. ADAMS *Log Cowboy* vii. 86 The stampede..was the work of *cattle rustlers. 1907 S. E. WHITE *Arizona Nights* I. iv. 81 There couldn't be much doubt that cattle rustlers was at work. *Ibid.* iii. 60 We..saw the beginning of the *cattle rustling. 1903 A. ADAMS *Log Cowboy*

vii. 101 The biggest *cattle-thief ever born in Medinah County.

b. *cattle-country, -path, -show, -track; cattle-boat, -ship.*

1860 Sala *Make your Game* 14 Not a *cattle-boat luckily, though, in some pens forward, there were a few sheep. 1889 C. Edwardes *Sardinia* 375 This Black Hole of a cattle-boat. 1902 *Westm. Gaz.* 28 Aug. 4/2 In the Canadian and American trade the loss [of cattle] works out fractionally at 0·2 or 0·1, so complete are the cattle-boat arrangements. 1907 S. E. White *Arizona Nights* I. vi. 110 The ponies stood where we left them, 'tied to the ground' in the *cattle-country fashion. 1887 *Outing* (U.S.) May X. 117/2 The bank was worn away on the other side by a *cattle-path just wide enough for one. 1891 *Scribner's Mag.* X. 610 The loading of *cattle-ships. 1838 Colman *Rep. Agric. Mass.* 92 A *cattle show and exhibition is annually held in some town of the county. 1871 Mrs. Stowe *Sam Lawson* 184 Each on 'em sent a bull to the cattle-show. 1858 Mrs. Viele *Following the Drum* 150 It was a beaten *cattle-track cut thru the chapparal.

9. cattle-bird *U.S.* (see quot.); **cattle-bush**, an Australian tree, *Atalaya hemiglauca*, used in periods of drought as fodder for cattle; **cattle chips** *U.S.*, dried cattle-dung used for fuel; **cattle-duffer**, an Australian term for a man who steals cattle by altering the brand; **cattle-egret**, a small Egyptian heron belonging to the genus *Bubulcus*; **cattle-fever** = Texas *fever*; **cattle-killer**, an instrument for slaughtering cattle, a 'humane killer'; **cattle king** *U.S.*, an owner or rearer of cattle on a large scale; **cattle lick** *U.S.*, a salt-lick for cattle; **cattle-puncher**, a 'cow-puncher'; **cattle-racket** (see quot.); **cattle-ranch, -ranching, -range** (examples); **cattle-road, -way**, a road made by man for the use of cattle.

1837 *Brit. Cycl. Nat. Hist.* II. 158 Cow-bunting or *Cattle-bird (*Molothrus pecoris* Swainson)...The American cattle-bird..is a small bird about the size of the European sky-lark. 1889 J. H. Maiden *Useful Native Plants* 116 *Cattle Bush...The leaves of this tree are eaten by stock, the tree being frequently felled for their use during seasons of drought. 1903 A. Adams *Log Cowboy* xiii. 210 We were frequently forced to resort to the old bed grounds..for *cattle chips. 1886 *Melbourne Punch* 15 July (Morris) *Cattle-duffers on a jury may be honest men enough, But they're bound to visit lightly sins in those who cattle duff. 1921 *Chambers's Jrnl.* 791/2 Chatting away about these infernal cattle-duffers. 1905 *Spectator* 14 Jan. 47/1 In Egypt the *cattle-egret, a small white heron, is pointed out by the dragoman, and accepted..as the true sacred ibis. 1909 *Westm. Gaz.* 6 Sept. 7/3 The *cattle-fever epidemic. 1907 *Daily Chron.* 3 Aug. 6/4 The woman picked up a patent *cattle killer and shot her husband in the back. 1886 *Harper's Mag.* Nov. 883/1 Hundreds of men who..went into the business with exceedingly limited means have become '*cattle kings'. 1888 Roosevelt in *Century Mag.* Feb. 500 Anything more foolish than the demagogic outcry against 'cattle-kings' it would be difficult to imagine. 1921 Mulford *Bar-20 Three* ix. 106 Soon a bundle of handbills was on its way to the office of the cattle king. 1887 *Harper's Mag.* Feb. 349/1 Large blocks of it [*sc.* salt] are sent to the Western Plains for '*cattle licks'. 1928 *Collier's Mag.* 18 Aug. 19/1 We wasn't horse breakers; we was *cattle punchers. 1847 [Alex. Harris] *Settlers & Convicts* 294 A *Cattle-racket. The term at the head of this chapter was originally applied in New South Wales to the agitation of society which took place when some wholesale system of plunder in cattle was brought to light. It is now commonly applied to any circumstance of this sort, whether greater or less, and whether really springing from a felonious intent or accidental. 1857 Olmsted *Journ. Texas* 160 Some live upon the produce of farms and *cattle-ranches owned in the neighborhood. 1879 Boddam-Whetham *Roraima* 114 Two boatmen who once rowed us over..to visit a cattle ranch, were both generals. *a* 1887 Mary E. Wilkins *Humble Romance* 228 He was reported to be running a cattle ranch in one of those distant territories. 1902 A. D. McFaul *Ike Glidden* v. 31 The estate of Jonathan Wiggins, consisting of immense mining properties and cattle ranches in the West. 1884 *Standard* 12 July Advt., By far the best results in *cattle ranching have been attained with the largest herds. 1888 Roosevelt in *Century Mag.* Feb. 500 Cattle-ranching can only be carried on in its present form while the population is scanty. 1640 *Essex Inst. Hist. Coll.* V. 1701 Ordered that none of the land within the *cattle range shall be granted..to any man. 1835 C. F. Hoffman *Winter West* II. 130 We entered at once upon a large and beautiful park or chase (*Note*, called a cattle-range, if I mistake not, in Kentucky). 1905 *Spectator* 18 Feb. 248/1 The important feature which the *cattle-roads make even to-day in modern embankments. 1905 A. & G. Hubbard *Neolithic Dew-Ponds & Cattle-Ways* 38 The length of the ascending *cattle-way is a quarter of a mile or more.

Cattleya (kæ·tliă). *Bot.* [mod. L., f. name of William *Cattley*, an English patron of botany: see -ia.] An epiphytal plant belonging to the orchidaceous genus *Cattleya*, native to Central America and Brazil, bearing handsome violet, rose-coloured, or yellow flowers.

1846 *Chambers's Jrnl.* 31 Oct. 282/2 Several of the superb tribe, the Cattleyas,..were in full beauty. 1864 Grindon *Brit. & Gard. Bot.* 668 Cattleyas, in their finest species, have prodigious blossoms of two or more shades of deep rich lilac and purple. 1927 *Times* (weekly ed.) 2 June 603/1 An absolutely clear yellow cattleya.

Catty (kæ·ti), *a.* [f. Cat *sb.*[1] + -y [1].] Of or pertaining to cats; concerned with the breeding or exhibiting of cats.

1903 F. Simpson *Bk. Cat* v. 84 The question of open judging at cat shows has frequently been discussed in catty circles.

b. = *Cattish b.

1886 Mrs. Argles *Lady Branksmere* ix, There is a sly, *catty* look about her. 1909 *Westm. Gaz.* 11 Dec. 16/2 A noted prelate..said recently in addressing a community composed of the fair sex that all such communities had the temptation to be catty'.

Catty-cornered, -cornering, varr. of Cater-cornered, -cornering.

1837 J. C. Neal *Charcoal Sk.* 196 One of that class..who, when compelled to share their bed with another, lie in that engrossing posture called 'catty-cornered'. *a* 1854 Dow Jr. *Patent Serm.* IV. 79 (Th.) All the cris-crossings, meanderings, trianglings, and catty-cornerings [of a dance]. 1882 Susan Hale *Lett.* 135 One, a big *salon* of a catty-cornered description, with windows looking all sorts of ways.

Cattyman (kæ·timæn). *U.S.* In logging, one who is expert in 'driving' or floating logs.

1905 *Terms Forestry & Logging* 33.

Catydid, var. Katydid.

1825 Paulding *J. Bull in Amer.* iii. 35 The frogs croaked, the caty-dids caty-didded it, the crickets chirped. 1838 E. Flagg *Far West* II. 214 Even until the morning dawned did a concert of whippoorwills and catydids keep up their infernal oratorio. 1859 Alice Cary *Pictures Country Life* iv. 92 The caty-dids..were noisily welcoming the early autumn.

Caucasic (kǫkæ·sik), *a.* [f. *Caucasus* + -ic.] Caucasian. So **Caucasoid** (kǭ·kăsoid) *a.*, resembling the Caucasian race.

1895 *Funk's Stand. Dict.*, Caucasic. 1898 *Q. Rev.* Apr. 418 That particular offset of the Caucasic stock. 1899 A. H. Keane *Man* xii. 449 Fresh accessions to the original and later (historical) Caucasic domains. 1902 *Encycl. Brit.* XXV. 372/2 There is lacking any biological evidence of Caucasoid or Negroid blood flowing in the veins of Americans before the invasions of historic times.

Cauchero (kautʃē·ro). [f. next + -*ero*.] A rubber-gatherer.

1898 Adamson in *Board of Trade Jrnl.* June 674 Many of the 'caucheros' (or rubber collectors) are working on Brazilian rivers. 1921 *Glasgow Herald* 3 May 3 The cauchero would laugh immoderately were it claimed for him that he is a civilising agent.

Caucho (kau·tʃo). [S. Amer. Sp., a. Peruvian *cahuchu*: see Caoutchouc.] A variety of rubber, esp. that prepared in the Amazon basin from species of *Castilloa*. Also *attrib.*

1899 *Board of Trade Jrnl.* June 673 The 'caucho' rubber of Peru. A despatch received at the Foreign Office from H. M. Consul at Pará states that the tree which produces the quality of india-rubber exported from Peru through Pará under the name of *caucho*, has recently been determined by M. Huber...The total shipments of *caucho* from Amazonian ports amount to about 2,000 tons annually. *Ibid.* 674 It would now..appear that the *caucho* tree of Peru is a *castilloa*. 1921 *Glasgow Herald* 3 May 10 The caucho trees are smaller than the shiringas.

Caucus, *sb.*

1. (Earlier U.S. example.)

1760 *Boston Gaz. Suppl.* 5 May, The new and grand Corcas...The old and true Corc.

3. (Early U.S. examples.)

1762 O. Thacher in *Proc. Mass. Hist. Soc.* (1884) XX. 48 The connections and discords of our politicians, corkusmen, plebeian tribunes, &c. 1809 *Deb. Congress* 7 Feb. 1421 We are to meet to-morrow here to attend the registering of the election of a caucus President. *Ibid.*, The caucus bulletin or general orders. 1824 *Niles' Reg.* 7 Feb. 353 The caucus-party have resolved to hold one [*sc.* a meeting]. *Ibid.* 20 Mar. 39/1 They would oppose the caucus nomination. 1842 H. Mann *Boston Orat.* 10 Our National Songs, our Fourth of July Orations and Caucus Speeches.

Caucus, *v.* (Earlier U.S. examples.)

1822 *Amer. Beacon* (Norfolk, Va.) 11 July 3/2 To Caucus and nominate candidates for the Presidency and Vice-Presidency. 1824 *Massachusetts Spy* 14 Jan. (Th.) A tavern is a little republic, where you may caucus and nominate, and vote for yourself without a dissenting voice. 1837 Whittier in *Life* (1894) I. 199 We have caucused in season and out of season.

Hence **Cau·cusing**, *vbl. sb.* (additional quot.). Also **Cau·cuser**. *U.S.*

1823 *Niles' Reg.* 18 Oct. 101 The choice would not come before the house, if caucussing had legitimate caucussing power. *Ibid.*, The danger of a choice..would not be dreaded, even by..the great caucussers of the day.

Cauda (kǭ·dă). *Anat.* and *Zool.* [L.] A tail-like appendage, as **cauda equina**, the bundle of nerves at the base of the spinal cord (= Mare's tail 3).

1848 *Quain's Anat.* (ed. 5) II. 820 The nerves of the cauda equina are vertical. 1892 Osler *Princ. Med.* 855 Cases of injury of the cauda equina.

Hence **Cau·dad** *a.* [*-ad], towards the tail, in the direction of the tail.

1889 *Buck's Handbk. Med. Sci.* VIII. 135/2 At the meson it is seen as a raised transverse band, but laterad, on account of its deflection caudad, it is divided obliquely. 1898 *Proc. Zool. Soc.* 973 At the level of the posterior border of the palatine instead of a little caudad of this.

Caudated. Add:

b. caudated rime = *tailed rime* (see Tailed [1] 1 d); **caudated sonnet**, a sonnet with an additional couplet.

1886 W. Sharp *Sonn. Century* 308 For all their structural drawbacks they [*sc.* stanzas in G. Meredith's 'Modern Love'] are in other things essentially 'caudated sonnets'. 1898 G. Wyndham *Poems Shaks.* 248 A caudated sonnet with two couplets instead of one after the third quatrain. 1907 E. K. Chambers *Early Engl. Lyrics* 286 A habit of translating the couplets of a caudated poem.

Caught (kǭt), ppl. adj. of Catch *v.*

1883 R. W. Dixon *Mano* I. xiii. 44 But she, like a caught adder, stood aghast.

Caul, *sb.*[4] (Earlier U.S. example.)

1851 C. Cist *Cincinnati* 206 The glue and cauls..are heated by steam.

Cauliflory (kǭ·liflōri). *Bot.* [f. L. *caulis* stem + *flōs, flōris* Flower.] The production of flowers directly from the trunk or branches.

1903 tr. *A. F. W. Schimper's Plant-Geog.* 336 In cauliflory the flowers appear sometimes only on main stems, sometimes only on branches, sometimes, and this is most usual, on both main stems and branches alike. *Ibid.*, In constantly humid tropic forests cauliflory, that is to say, the formation of flowers on old wood, is not rare. 1908 tr. *Strasburger's Text-bk. Bot.* (ed. 3) 625 The flowers are borne on the main stem or the older branches, and arise from dormant axillary buds (cauliflory).

Cauliflower. Add:

1. b. *transf.* A thing which resembles a cauliflower in shape.

1892 *Daily News* 31 May 2/3 A tiny fan of black lace with a 'cauliflower' of yellow baby ribbon. 1904 *Amer. Jrnl. Sci.* Jan. 34 The reddish dust 'cauliflowers' accumulated about every half-hour and rolled down the gorge of the Rivière Blanche from the cone.

2. *cauliflower-like* adj.; **cauliflower-bow**, a bow of ribbon resembling a cauliflower in shape; **cauliflower-cloud**, a cloud, esp. a volcanic cloud, which takes a massed shape.

1892 *Daily News* 31 May 2/3 A very small '*cauliflower' bow. 1903 Heilprin *Mont Pelée* xv. 223 The majestic *cauliflower clouds rose on all sides. 1873 Ralfe *Phys. Chem.* 8 The crystals..are arranged in *cauliflower-like groups consisting of oblique prisms.

Cauling (kǭ·liŋ). [f. Caul *sb.*[4] + -ing [1].] The action of applying a heated board in veneering.

1885 *Spons' Mechanics' Own Bk.* 361 Before cauling, raise the veneer and glue the ground well.

Caulker. 2. Delete †*Obs.* and add:

1899 *Daily News* 10 June 8/7 The pneumatic caulkers.

Caurus (kǭ·rŏs). [L., also *Corus*.] The stormy north-west wind, often personified.

c 1374 Chaucer *Boethius* I. met. iii. (1868) 9 A swifte wynde þat hyȝt chorus. 1696 Phillips *World of Words*, *Caurus*, a Western or Northwest Wind blowing commonly out of the British Sea. 1748 Thomson *Cast. Indol.* II. lxxviii, The ground, by piercing Caurus seared.

Causational (kǭzē·ʃənăl), *a.* [f. Causation + -al.] Belonging to the law or doctrine of causation.

1925 J. E. Turner *Theory of Direct Realism* 9 The causational aspects of perception. 1930 G. R. de Beer *Embryology & Evolution* i. 7 The causational idea that the succession of palingenetic stages in ontogeny is due to these stages having succeeded one another in phylogeny.

Cause célèbre (kōz selębr). [Fr.] A celebrated legal case; a law-suit that excites much interest.

1858 Trollope *Three Clerks* xli, Of course a *cause célèbre* such as this was not going to decide itself in one day. 1860 *Once a Week* 22 Sept. 363/2 Well-nigh all the great murders—the *causes célèbres* of blood in our day—have been most deliberately planned. 1882 *Standard* 16 Dec. 5/6 In the Criminal Court of Innsprück to-day proceedings were opened in a *cause célèbre* of a..most painful character.

Causerie (kōu·zəri, ‖kozri). [Fr., f. *causer* to talk, ad. L. *causārī* to plead, dispute, f. *causa* Cause *sb.*] Informal talk or discussion, esp. on literary topics; also, a chatty article or paragraph.

1827 *Edin. Rev.* Oct. 386 The volume which has been the innocent cause of all this *causerie*. 1841 C'tess Blessington *Idler in France* I. 269 The lively *causerie* of the *habitués de maison* supersedes the constraint of ceremony. 1892 Zangwill *Childr. Ghetto* I. xvi. 154 He was specially polite...There was an intimate, tender tone about these causeries.

Causeway, *v.* 2. (Earlier U.S. example.)

1702 *Proprietors' Rec. Cambridge* (Mass.) (1896) 230 Those Barrs yt lead into ye sd Meadow on ye easterly Side where it is Caswayed with Gravel & timber.

Causse (kōs). [Fr.] A limestone plateau.

1883 *Encycl. Brit.* XV. 8/2 By the Dordogne and Lot the surface is divided into a number of limestone plateaus known by the name of 'causses'. 1922 *Glasgow Herald* 5 Aug. 4 The weirdly sombre causses of the Cevennes.

Caustic, *a.* Add:

1. c. **caustic creeper**, an Australian name for *Euphorbia drummondii*, the milky juice of which is used by the natives as a remedy for various diseases, but which is poisonous to sheep; **caustic plant**, an Australian name for *Sarcostemma australis*, a plant poisonous to cattle and sheep.

1889 J. H. Maiden *Useful Native Plants* 127 Euphorbia Drummondii...Called 'Caustic Creeper' in Queensland. Called 'Milk Plant' and 'Pox Plant' about Bourke. This weed is unquestionably poisonous to sheep. 1898 Morris *Austral Engl.* 84 Caustic-Plant, or Caustic-Vine..Cattle and sheep are poisoned by eating it.

Caustic (kǫ·stik), *v.* [f. Caustic *sb.*] *trans.* To treat with a caustic.

1888 Mrs. H. Ward *R. Elsmere* xii, I causticked all the diphtheritic throats..with my own hand.

Cauterizing, *ppl. a.* Add: Also *fig.*

1903 R. Langbridge *Flame & Flood* xiv, There was a cauterising comfort in the cruel finality of that first sentence.

Cavalier. B. *adj.* 4. Add: **cavalier cuff**, a cuff of gauntlet shape.

1902 *Daily Chron.* 17 Aug. 8/3 The cavalier cuff of stiffened velvet. 1923 *Daily Mail* 1 Mar. 6 Sleeves that end in a flounce..—gowns with no sleeves at all—Cavalier cuffs—there is infinite variety.

Cavallada, var. of *Caballada. (Cf. next.)

1844 G. W. Kendall *Santa Fé Exped.* (1855) I. 97 Nothing can exceed the grandeur of the scene when a large cavallada, or drove of horses, takes a 'scare'. *Ibid.* II. 47 An arid and sandy plain..with but scanty picking for the large cavallada of horses, mules, and cattle.

Cavallard. Also **cavalyard**. (For 18.., read 1846.) Add:

1836 W. B. Dewees *Lett. fr. Texas* xx. 208 They..soon obtained a fine cavalyard of horses, which they drove into Arkansas for sale. 1846 Sage *Scenes in Rocky Mts.* 80 Stealing our whole cavallard, consisting of ten head of horses and mules. 1878 J. H. Beadle *Western Wilds* iv. 69 All hands sprang up only to witness our noble *cavallard* under full headway before a body of Mexican horsemen.

Cavalry. 4. Add: *cavalry officer*; **cavalry curate**, a curate who rides on horseback to perform his duties in an extensive and scattered parish.

1838 *Annual Scrap-Book* 19 The amount of a tailor's bill, on fitting out his son as a cavalry officer. 1854 Thackeray *Newcomes* vi, This distinguished cavalry officer swore very freely. 1855 E. B. Hamley *Story Sebastopol* vii. 49 Some luckless cavalry officer. 1894 G. H. Hamilton *Charge* 8 Mission Chapels—where the 'Cavalry Curates' ought to reside. 1898 *Westm. Gaz.* 14 Jan. 1/3 The immense extent of many parishes, into some of which 'Cavalry curates' have been introduced with advantage. 1903 *Ibid.* 5 Oct. 1/3, I bought him on the advice of two cavalry-officer friends who knew him.

Cavayado, var. of *Cavallada.

1901 in *Kansas Hist. Coll.* (1902) VII. 52, I was driving a cavayado...The Mexicans always drove their cavayado in front of their trains.

Cavayard, cavy-yard (kævă-, kæ·viyā̆d). *U.S.* Also **cavvi-, cavvie-yard, caviarde; cavvieyeh, caviya.** [Var. of Cavallard, with *y* for Sp. *ll*.] A drove of horses.

α. 1847 W. B. Dewees *Lett. fr. Texas* 3 Mar. 301 Two hundred dollars would be sufficient to purchase a cavayard of twenty [mares]. *a* 1848 Ruxton *Life in Far West* (1849) 12 But before we get to the fires, the Injuns were among the cavayard. 1851 Mayne Reid *Scalp-hunters* xxvi, How are 'ee gwine to get in with this cavayard 'ithout makin' sign? β. 1824 W. B. Dewees *Lett. fr. Texas* viii. 53 Coraseo..was driving a large cavyyard of horses and mules to Louisiana. 1836 Edward *Hist. Texas* 107 When this powerful tribe wishes to raise the wind as the saying is, they will cavy back a Mexican cavy-yard. 1843 Farnham *Trav. Western Prairies* I. 187 The Indians..make an annual levy upon the cavy-yard of the fortress. 1853 S. A. Hammett *Stray Yankee in Texas* 97 Two or three more [darkies] were mounted, and sent into the prairie in search of the 'caviarde' of horses—and we went in to dinner. 1874 J. C. McCoy *Hist. Sketches* 11 The extra horses not under the saddle are called the cavvie-yard, and are driven behind the camp wagon. 1901 *Munsey's Mag.* XXV. 404/2 Each man roped a fresh horse from the cavviyard. γ. 1908 Mulford *Orphan* ii. 24 He was soon able to count seven warriors who were driving another 'cavvieyeh' of horses. 1920 — *J. Nelson* xxiv. 267 The caviya of a hundred and thirty saddle horses.

Cave, *sb.*[1] 5. Add:

cave-dweller *fig.*, a person who exhibits the characteristics of a prehistoric cave-man; similarly **cave-man, -woman.**

1906 B'ness von Hutten *What became of Pam* II. xiii, You will always be a *cave-dweller,..for you always were a little savage. 1897 Mary Kingsley *W. Africa* x. 208 These pots have a *cave-man look about them; they are unglazed unlidded bowls. 1924 W. M. Raine *Troubled Waters* xxviii. 280 He was a throw-back to the cave man. 1926 *Westm. Gaz.* 7 Aug., The devotion of the modern girl to the 'cave man' of fiction. 1927 *Daily Express* 5 Sept. 8/3, I simply refuse to believe that every woman does admire a cave man. 1903 Ellen Thorneycroft Fowler *Place & Power* v, Miss St. Just..belonged to the *cave-woman species.

Cave, *sb.*[4] [f. Cave *v.*[3]] A fall of earth, a cave-in.

1876 B. Harte *G. Conroy* VI. viii, Gabriel was amazed to find that during the earthquake a 'cave' had taken place in the drift. 1877 Raymond *Statist. Mines & Mining* 319 A very serious cave occurred about 170 feet from the entrance of the drift. 1887 Farrell *How He Died* 164 A 'cave' had happened in a mine.

Cave, *v.*[3] Add: 1. (Earlier U.S. examples.)

1707 S. Sewall *Diary* (1879) II. 186 Grave was caved in. 1728 J. Comer *Diary* (1923) 57 This day a man..digging a well after he had dug 20 feet deep, it cav'd in upon him. 1764 *Boston Even. Post* 30 Jan. (Th.) The People found the Well caved in.

b. Without *in*.

1848 Thoreau in *Atlantic Monthly* (1892) LXIX. 744 His cellar..has caved and let one end of the house down. 1873 J. H. Beadle *Undevel. West* iii. 69 He had dug two wells,..but struck sand which 'caved so he could not curb'. 1882 *U. S. Rep. Prec. Met.* 639 Wherever the rock in the tunnel has a tendency to cave.

c. *transf.* To yield to outward pressure.

1898 Hamblen *Gen. Manager's Story* 32, I was caught between the corners of the cars..and heard my ribs cave in.

2. b. (Earlier U.S. examples.)

1858 *N. Y. Tribune* 1 May 4/2 One..of the six South American opponents of Lecompton caved; the others stood firm. 1860 Holland *Miss Gilbert's Career* xxii. 390, I tell you when a man gets in front of him Sunday, he catches it—no use dodging—might as well cave.

3. (Earlier U.S. examples.)

1857 *Knickerbocker Mag.* Mar. XLIX. 278 He would feel like caving my head in, if he knew. 1862 'Artemus Ward' *His Bk.* (1865) 45, I kin nevertheles kave in enny man's hed that calls me a obtoos.

b. *To cave down*: to bring down by an excavation caving in. *U.S.*

1851 C. Cist *Cincinnati* 244, I obtained permission to open a sand-pit, which had long been closed for fear of caving down a house, by further excavation.

c. *To cave in*: to cause to fall in.

1916 Boyd Cable *Action Front* 56 'If we can plant a bomb or two in the right spot, it will bottle up any Germans working inside!' 'Sure to!' said Ainsley. 'It will cave in the entrance completely.'

Hence **Caved** *ppl. a.*

1865 'Artemus Ward' *His Bk.* (1906) 57 A old kaved in hat. 1872 'Mark Twain' *Innoc. at Home* vii. (1882) 309 An Hour in the Caved Mines.

Cave (kē·vi), *int.* *School slang.* [L., imper. of *cavēre* to take care, beware.] Beware!: a signal of warning, e. g. of the approach of a master.

1868 *Cassell's Mag.* 17 Oct. 390/1 [Title of Poem] Cave! 1873 'Ascott R. Hope' *Night Before Holidays* (1874) 110 There was a heavy footstep sounding along the passage... 'Cave!' 'Canem,' responded Lessing, burying himself under the bedclothes again. 1883 Miss Braddon *Phant. Fort.* xxxvi, That indefinable air..which gives society as fair a warning as if the man wore a placard on his shoulder with the word *Cave*. 1922 *Blackw. Mag.* May 557/2 One of their number doing sentry-go gives the native equivalent for the schoolboy's 'Cave' on the reappearance of their employer.

Cavea (kē·viă). *Rom. Antiq.* Pl. -eæ. [L.] The auditorium of an ancient theatre, so called from its concave shape; also the whole theatre.

1860 Donaldson *Theatre of Greeks* (ed. 7) III. i. 222 The *cavea* of the theatre at Catana as seen from the stage. 1886 *Athenæum* 4 Dec. 751/2 The peculiarity of this theatre [at Laurium] is the strange form of the cavea, which sweeps inward in a loop to the right as viewed from the proscenium. 1889 Haigh *Attic Theatre* iii. 113.

Caveat, *sb.* Add:

1. b. *Caveat emptor* (lit., let the purchaser beware): let the purchaser examine the article he is buying before the bargain is completed, so that in case of disappointment after purchase he may not blame the seller.

1523-34 Fitzherb. *Husb.* § 118 He [*sc.* the horse] is noo chapmannes ware, if he be wylde; but if he be tame, and haue ben rydden vpon, than *Caueat emptor*, beware the byer. 1616 T. Adams *Pol. Hunting* Wks. (1629) 118 We compell none to buy our Ware; *Caueat emptor*. 1902 *Economic Jrnl.* XII. 12 *Caveat emptor*. It is the employer on whom the responsibility rests of testing the quality of the article he buys.

Cavernicolous (kævəmni·kŏləs), *a.* [f. L. *caverna* Cavern + -*colus* inhabiting.] Cave-dwelling.

1929 *Nature* 28 Dec. 1004 Two Reduviid bugs are recorded and a dozen beetles—none markedly modified for a cavernicolous habit.

Cavernous, *a.* Add: 3. b. *Path.* Applied to respiration marked by a prolonged hollow resonance. (Cf. *Broncho-cavernous.)

1853 W. O. Markham tr. *Skoda's Auscult.* 94 'By the term cavernous respiration,' says Laennec, 'I understand the murmur which occurs during inspiration and expiration in a cavity formed in pulmonary tissue.'

Caviare. Add:

2. *slang.* A passage blacked out by the Russian Press Censor by the use of a stamp which when inked and applied to the paper leaves a close network of white lines and black diamonds, resembling to some extent the appearance of caviare spread upon bread and butter. Hence **Caviare** *v. trans.*, to block out or censor in this way.

1890 *St. James's Gaz.* 25 Apr. 7/1 Every one of Mr. Kennan's articles in the *Century* has been 'caviared'. 1894 *Westm. Gaz.* 2 Nov. 1/2 The Czar..had..to seem as if he had blotted the assassin's menace out from his mind as completely as his own censors 'caviared' it out of the newspapers. 1899 Gissing *Crown of Life* xix, We call caviare the bits blacked out in our newspapers and periodicals. 1920 S. Colvin in *Times* 5 Nov. 13/4 Surely there would have been ample time to prevent its appearance in the book itself..either by cancelling the leaf on which it was printed ..or by the process called 'caviare'.

Cavil, variant of Kevel *sb.*[3]

1842 Gwilt *Archit.* Gloss. s.v. *Nidged Ashlar*, It is brought to the square by means of a cavil or hammer with a sharp point.

Cavil, *v.* 2. b. Delete † and add:

1863 Lytton *Caxtoniana* I. 91 Nurse, cherish, never cavil away, the wholesome horror of Debt.

Caving, *vbl. sb.*[2] (Earlier U.S. examples.)

1809 *Massachusetts Spy* 25 Oct. (Th.) Mr. Benanuel Bucklin was killed by the caving in of a fountain which he was stoning. 1852 *Congress. Globe* 17 May 1385/3 The result..will be a universal 'caving in' upon the part of Southern Whigs.

Caving, *ppl. a.* Add: Also **caving-in**.

1857 T. B. Gunn *N. Y. Boarding Houses* 98 (Th.) An especially uncomfortable chair with a caving-in seat and rickety back was assigned to me.

Cavitate (kæ·vitā̆t), *v.* [Back-formation from *Cavitation.] *intr.* To form cavities or spaces in a fluid by the rapid whirling motion of a propeller.

1909 *Westm. Gaz.* 7 Jan. 4/2 The..difficulty..of obtaining a suitable screw-propeller that will not cavitate at such speeds as one wishes to attain.

Cavitation (kævitā·ʃən). [f. Cavity: see -ation.]

1. The formation of cavities in a fluid by the rapid motion of a propeller, thus causing a loss of efficiency.

1895 *Min. Proc. Inst. Civ. Engineers* CXXII. 67 'Cavitation', as Mr. Froude has suggested to the Authors that the phenomenon should be called, appears to manifest itself when the mean negative pressure exceeds about 6¼lbs. per square inch. 1902 *Nature* 6 Nov. 24/1 The name cavitation is given to the phenomenon met with when a screw is driven in water at speeds above a certain limiting value. 1916 *Yorkshire Post* 18 Apr. 8/1 'Cavitation'..does not begin suddenly.

2. *Path.* The formation of phthisical cavities in the lungs.

1909 *Practitioner* Dec. 862 'Post-tussive suction'..is a very distinctive feature in advanced cavitation. 1913 Dorland *Med. Dict.* (ed. 7), *Cavitation*, the formation of cavities, as in pulmonary tuberculosis.

Cavort, *v.* *U.S.* Add: Also **covault**, and earlier examples.

1830 Mrs. Royall *Lett. fr. Alabama* 122 *Covault* is of Tennessee birth and not inaptly applied in the sense they use it. It signifies an unruly or ungovernable man; also an untame horse, or anything that cannot be controlled. 1834 W. G. Simms *Guy Rivers* 283 What became of that beautiful young girl from Carolina...You were then cavorting about her in great style. 1835 Longstreet *Georgia Scenes* (1871) 23 In short, he cavorted most magnanimously (a term which, in our tongue, expresses all I have described and a little more).

Hence **Cavo·rtish** *a.*

1835 Longstreet *Georgia Scenes* (1871) 30 Bullet became more and more cavortish, insomuch that, when the blanket came off, he had reached the kicking point in good earnest.

Cayenne. Add:

c. *Cayenne whist*, a variety of whist in which the dealer's side names the trumps and in which the suits have different values.

1887 Beatty-Kingston *Music & Manners* II. 253 As much 'cayenne' whist as their means will permit of their indulging in.

Cayeute, cayote, variants of Coyote.

1846 Sage *Scenes Rocky Mts.* (1859) 79 The cayeute, or medicine-wolf of the Indians. *a* 1848 Ruxton *Life Far West* (1849) 250 One may safely wager to see a dozen cayeutes or prairie wolves loping round. 1850 W. R. Ryan *Upper & Lower California* I. 250 Our horses..were set free by the cayotes—a species of animal something between a fox and a dog. 1884 W. Shepherd *Prairie Exper.* 42 The cayote will sneak in, and have his pickings on the offal.

Cayuse. *U.S.* Also **kiyuse**. (Earlier examples.)

1857 *Oregon Weekly Times* Jan. (Th.) All manner of wrought and cast work,..down to Shoeing a 'Cultus' Cayuse Horse. 1869 A. K. McClure *Rocky Mts.* 302 Twice our kiyuse broke nearly out of the harness...The kiyuse is never perfectly tamed. 1873 J. H. Beadle *Undevel. West* xxxv. 750, I mounted a *cayuse* and rode seven miles over the hills.

Caza (ka·za). [Turkish قضا *qaḍā*, related to قاضي *qāḍī* Cadi.] A district in Turkey subject to a judge's jurisdiction.

1903 *Westm. Gaz.* 20 Aug. 7/2 In the Caza of Lerin. 1920 *Glasgow Herald* 9 Aug. 7 The reincorporation with Lebanon of the four cazas of Baalbek, Bekkam, Rachaya, and Hasbaya. 1922 *Contemp. Rev.* Dec. 705 The local bishop, vicar or priest has been an ex-officio member of the governmental Council of the *vilayet, sanjak* or *caza* in which he resided.

Cease, *v.* Add: 6. d. To put a stop to, bring to an end, discontinue.

1894 *Westm. Gaz.* 3 May 5/1 He appealed to those present who had ceased their connexion with their Union to again join it. 1899 *Ibid.* 24 Apr. 3/2 This plan of ceasing the edition, after a certain number. 1907 *Ibid.* 24 Aug. 2/1 In the United States, where players begin and cease the game years earlier than they do here.

e. *Campanology.* To bring (a peal) to an end; to let (a bell) down.

1684 R. H. *School Recreation* (1696) 101 For Ceasing a Peal of Bells; let them fall gradually from a set Peal. 1753 *Campanalogia Impr.* 12 The learning to Raise and Cease a Bell in Peal. 1858 B. Thackrah *Art of Change-ringing* 8 The raising and ceasing (or settling) a bell in peal. 1904 Bulwer *Gloss. Techn. Terms Bells* 33 *Ceasing in order*, letting the bells down together, but in regular order of striking, as in ringing 'rounds' or some other sequence.

Ceased. Delete †*Obs.* and add:

1927 *Observer* 10 July 11/1 New stations..numbered 22,100, and ceased stations 13,044.

Cebian (sī·biăn), *a.* [f. Cebus + -ian.] = Cebine.

1893 *Athenæum* 18 Mar. 349/3 The pithecian and cebian monkeys.

Cecropia (sĭkrō·piă). [mod. L., f. *Cecrops*, early king of Attica.]

1. Any tree of the genus so called of moraceous trees of tropical America, yielding a milky juice which furnishes caoutchouc.

1833 *Penny Cycl.* I. 447/1 Among the airy foliage of the mimosa, the cecropia elevates its giant leaves and heavy candelabra-shaped branches. 1875 *Encycl. Brit.* II. 98/1 The *Cecropia*, or trumpet tree of Central America, is tenanted by ants.

2. A large silkworm moth of the eastern United States, *Samia (Attacus) cecropia*.

1868 *Amer. Naturalist* II. 313 It is not a soft, flossy cocoon, like that of *Cecropia*. 1884 *Ibid.* XVIII. 1046 Poison Glands in the skin of the Cecropia caterpillar. 1885 *Ibid.* XIX. 1142 The anatomy of the Cecropia moth. 1909 Mrs. Stratton-Porter *Girl of Limberlost* viii. 157 Big gray Cecropias come from this kind, brown Polyphemus from that.

Cedar. 4. Add: *cedar knob* U.S. (Knob *sb.* 2); **cedar bird** (earlier example); **cedar-chest** *U.S.*, a chest made of cedar-wood as a protection against moths; **cedar-closet** *U.S.*, a closet lined with cedar-wood; **cedar cooper** *U.S.* (see quot.); **cedar-lot** *U.S.*, a piece of land in a cedar-swamp; **cedar-root** *U.S.* (a plant-name); **cedar-wood**, also, cedar trees.

1791 W. Bartram *Trav. Carolina* etc. (1792) 288 Ampelis garrulus; crown bird or *cedar bird. 1891 'C. E. Craddock' in *Harper's Mag.* Jan. 219/1 The simple furnishings—a *cedar chest, a few garments. 1895 *Century Mag.* July 323/2 Cedar-chest and camphor-trunk and flowered band-box have been called upon to disgorge their treasures. 1866 E. E. Hale *If, Yes, & Perhaps* (1868) 256, I was up in the *cedar closet one day. 1832 D. J. Browne *Sylva Amer.* 148 The superior fitness of this wood [*sc.* white cedar] for various household utensils, has given rise, in Philadelphia, to a distinct class of mechanics called *cedar coopers. 1828 Drake *Tales & Sk.* 33 He was a full grown Kentuckian, born on the *cedar knobs of the Blue Licks. 1813 *Massachusetts Spy* 14 Apr. 4/4 To be sold..two *Cedar Lots, lying in the Great Cedar Swamp. 1805-9 J. J. Henry *Camp. agst. Quebec* 42 The *cedar root was in plenty under our feet. 1857 W. Chandless *Visit Salt Lake* I. v. 64 *Cedar-wood is sprinkled thinly over the bluffs.

Ce·dar-swamp. *U.S.* [Cedar 4.] A swamp in which the cedar is the prevailing tree.

1637 *Plymouth Col. Rec.* I. 51 A parcell of land..betweene the two cedar swamps at Iland Creeke Pond. 1775 *Coll. Mass. Hist. Soc.* Ser. II. I. 233 At 2 o'clock I crossed the 3d pond and encamped in a cedar swamp. 1840 in *Trans. Mich. Agric. Soc.* (1855) VI. 291 Sandy ridges, with intervening swales, and cedar swamps. 1871 Schele de Vere *Americanisms* (1872) 420 The Cedar Swamps..in the South are uniformly low grounds under water, and filled with cypresses. *a* 1904 S. E. White *Blazed Trail Stories* vi. 87 The high beech-ridge..ended in a narrow cedar-swamp.

Cedula. Delete *Obs.* and add:

1920 J. M. Keynes *Econ. Conseq. Peace* 164 Germany has also sold certain overseas securities, such as Argentine cedulas.

Ceil, *v.* Add:

5. *Aviation.* To climb to a great height.

1919 *Glasgow Herald* 19 Dec. 10 After a loftier cruise than usual he may admit that he was 'ceiling'.

Ceile (kyē·lə). *Irish.* Also **kyle**. [OIr. *céle*.] In ancient Irish society, a vassal.

1875 Maine *Early Hist. Instit.* 158 It is by taking stock that the free Irish tribesman becomes the Ceile or Kyle, the vassal or man of his Chief, owing him not only rent but service and homage.

Ceiling, *vbl. sb.* Add:

2. b. *Aviation.* The action of ascending to a great height, high flying; also, the maximum altitude above sea-level to which a given aeroplane can attain.

1917 *Jane's All the World's Aircraft* 9 a/4 The extreme height to which an aircraft will rise,..familiarly known as the 'ceiling' or 'roof' of that particular machine. 1919 *Parlt. Papers* X. 49 In a long flight it is most economical to climb an aeroplane in the attitude corresponding to the maximum value of the lift-drag ratio until it approaches its ceiling. 1919 Maj.-Gen. Trenchard in *Lond. Gaz.* 1 Jan. 136/2 Ceiling was of more importance than speed for long-distance day bombing work. 1928 *Fortn. Rev.* Dec. 764 Its ceiling when fully loaded was sometimes far under 10,000 feet.

7. **ceiling rose, rosette** (see quot. 1910).

1901 *Waterhouse Conduit Wiring* 36 The ceiling rose boxes would generally be in the run of the conduit. 1907 *Installation News* Jan. 16/1 Ceiling roses, switches, wall sockets, etc. 1910 N. Hawkins *Electr. Dict.*, *Ceiling rose*, or *Rosette*, an ornamental ceiling block for suspending an incandescent lamp.

Celanese (selănī·z). [Arbitrarily f. Cellulose.] A proprietary name for artificial silk twist and for a woven fabric of artificial silk made by British Celanese Ltd. (formerly British Cellulose and Chemical Manufacturing Company).

1923 *Daily Mail* 20 Feb. 1 Celanese Artificial Silk. *Ibid.* 27 Feb. 16 Like silk, 'Celanese' is lustrous, with an even more beautiful sheen. 1926 *Spectator* 24 Apr. 751/1 The other process is the Celanese, by which cotton is combined with acetic acid to alter its organic composition.

Celebrate, *v.* 3. Add: Also *absol.*

1929 *Randolph Enterprise* (Elkins, W.Va.) 26 Sept. 3/2 [He] came over..Sunday night to celebrate a little.

Celebratory (se·lĭbrētəri), *a.* [f. Celebrate *v.* + -ory [2].] Serving to celebrate, used in or designed for the celebration of an event, etc.

1926 *Glasgow Herald* 1 June 7 Without a celebratory or consolatory bite and sup. 1927 *Radio Times* 22 Apr. 153/1 Imperial March..Sullivan..This was Sullivan's celebratory piece for the opening by Queen Victoria of the Imperial Institute at South Kensington, in 1893.

Celebret (se·lĭbret). [L., = 'let him celebrate', 3 sing. pres. subj. of *celebrāre* to Celebrate.] A document, signed and sealed by the bishop, giving a priest permission to say mass in a certain parish.

1844 Ignatius Spencer in Fr. Pius *Life Fr. Ignatius* (1866) xiii. 282, I had forgotten to get credentials from Dr. Wiseman, and so he hesitated, but gave the *celebret*. 1907 G. Tyrrell in *Daily Chron.* 25 Sept. 4/6, I am told that the Pope will give me a celebret. 1908 *Cath. Encycl.* III. 477/1 The absence of the celebret does not suffice for the refusal of permission to say Mass, if persons worthy of belief bear positive testimony to the good standing of the priest. 1918 M. D. Petre *Modernism* 237 The subsequent refusal, on the part of his bishop, to grant him a *celebret*.

Celery. Add: **celery-leaved, -topped,** or **-top pine**, any Australasian tree of the genus *Phyllocladus*, in which the upper part of the branchlets resemble the foliage of the celery.

1883 [see Tanekaha]. 1889 T. Kirk *Forest Flora New Zealand* 9 The tanekaha is one of the remarkable 'celery-topped pines'. 1927 *Blackw. Mag.* Oct. 464/1 Graceful featherwoods and celery-top pines.

Celesta (sĭle·stă). [app. pseudo-latinization of F. *céleste* (cf. Celeste).] A keyboard instrument with piano-like action, having hammers that strike upon steel plates placed over wooden resonators, invented by Auguste Mustel of Paris in 1886.

1899 E. Prout *The Orchestra* II. 158 Only a few of the strings are employed to accompanying the *celesta*. 1927 *Grove's Dict. Mus.* (ed. 3) I. 591 The tone of the celesta itself is of exquisite purity.

Celestial, *sb.* 2. (Earlier U.S. example.)

1849 T. T. Johnson *Sights Gold Region* xxiv. 238 The Canton Cafe was kept by Chinamen, who were real celestials.

Cell, *sb.*[1] Add:

4. b. *pl.* Imprisonment in solitary confinement as a punishment for offences against military law.

1891 Kipling *Life's Handicap* 23 You 'ave been absent without leave an' you'll go into cells for that. 1928 W. J. Locke *Rough Road* xvii, At the worst they might give him cells when he recovered.

9. c. *Math.* See Peaucellier cell.

14. d. *fig.* A centre or nucleus of propaganda.

1930 *Observer* 4 May 13 Among the [Russian revolutionary] methods employed are attempts to create 'cells' within the [Indian] regiments by enlistment of seditionists.

15. *cell-debris, -degradation*, etc.; **cell-layer** = Germinal *layer*; **cell-spot**, a spot of colour occurring in the spaces between the nerves in the wings of certain lepidopterous insects.

1907 *Practitioner* Sept. 456 The histogenous wandering cells..are peculiarly active as regards other cells and *cell-debris. 1908 *Ibid.* Mar. 389 This indication of excessive *cell-degradation. 1907 *Ibid.* Aug. 195 The result of transplantations of *cell-grafts from Jensen's original tumour. 1908 *Ibid.* Jan. 19 The membranes and perivascular spaces showed some *cell-infiltration. 1893 Tuckey *Amphioxus* 55 All changes from the blastula onwards can be traced to these primitive *cell-layers. *a* 1909 *Buck's Handbk. Med. Sci.* II. 685 (Cent. D. Suppl.) *Cell-nesting. 1902 *Proc. Zool. Soc.* I. 49 The black *cell-spots on the primaries.

Cell, *v.* Transfer †*Obs.* to senses a and b and add: c. *trans.* To store in cells.

1820 Wiffen *Aonian Hours* (ed. 2) 75 Honey, which the bee Cells beneath briery boughs. 1927 *Chambers's Jrnl.* Feb. 90/1 Last autumn one of my stocks celled twelve pounds in twelve hours.

Cellar, *sb.* 6. **cellar-way** (earlier example).

1854 Shillaber *Mrs. Partington* 56 Avoid the coal-holes and cellar-ways that are open for your unwary feet.

Cellarless (se·lə̆lės), *a.* [f. Cellar *sb.* + -less.] Having no cellar.

1853 R. S. Surtees *Sponge's Sp. Tour* (1893) 12 Little cellarless wine-merchants. 1900 *Westm. Gaz.* 9 May 2/2 All this legislation is passed by the cellared population and not by the cellarless population.

Cellifugal (seli·fiŭgăl), *a.* [f. *celli-*, comb. f. L. *cella* Cell *sb.*[1] + *fugere* to flee: see -al.] Of the nerve-currents in a ganglion-cell: Passing from the body of a cell. So **Cellipetal** (seli·pĭtăl) *a.* [L. *petere* to seek], moving towards the body of a cell.

1904 Titchener tr. *Wundt's Physiol. Psychol.* I. 42 The dendrites are devoted exclusively to cellipetal, the neurites to cellifugal conduction.

'Cellist (tʃe·list). Shortened f. Violoncellist, after 'Cello. Also **'Celloist** (tʃe·loist).

1888 Mrs. H. Ward *R. Elsmere* v. xxxi, The 'cellist with the hair. 1897 *Daily News* 25 Mar. 9/2 The pianist came, but the 'celloist did not turn up at all.

Cellobiose (selobai·ous). *Chem.* [f. Cell(ulose + -o- + *Biose.] A biose, $C_{12}H_{22}O_{11}$, obtained from cellulose by the action of sulphuric acid and acetic anhydride followed by saponification.

1902 *Jrnl. Chem. Soc.* LXXXII. 135 The name cellobiose is now used for the substance previously termed cellose. 1929 *Birm. Post* 22 Feb. 5/4 Over 50 % of starch can be converted into maltose, and..cellulose can be transformed into the related disaccharide cellobiose.

Celloidin (seloi·din). [f. Celloid + -in [1].] A pure form of pyroxylin, soluble in ether, used in microscopy for embedding specimens of tissues so that sections may be prepared, and for a photographic film.

1886 *Jrnl. Royal Microsc. Soc.* Ser. II. VI. 350 The celloidin layers are slow in dehydrating. 1892 *Photogr. Ann.* II. 107 Making an enlarged transparency..on a rapid celloidin film. 1908 *Practitioner* Feb. 201 Three healthy foetuses..were hardened in formol, two of them being cut in celloidin.

Cellophane (se·lŏfēn). [f. Cell(ulose + -o- + -*phane*, as in *tryptophane*.] A proprietary name for a transparent material made of wood pulp and used as a wrapper for boxes of confectionery, etc.

1921 *Spectator* 23 Apr. 522/2 Ciré, raffia,..tinsels, cellophane, and other ornaments. 1929 *Publishers' Circular* 22 June 739/1 A..book jacketed in cellophane.

Cellose. An earlier name for *Cellobiose, q.v.

1901 *Jrnl. Chem. Soc.* LXX. 370 Cellose, a Biose from Cellulose.

Cellular. Add: 2. b. Of open texture, as *cellular linen*; also *sb.*, a material of open texture.

1888 *Cassell's Fam. Mag.* Dec. 60/1 Cellular Clothing. Under-clothing of every kind is now being made of a cellular cloth. 1889 *Pall Mall Gaz.* 5 Jan. 7/1 Cellular linen... Gentlemen have tennis-shirts of real silk cellular now.

Cellulase (se·liŭlēs). *Chem.* [f. Cellul(ose + *-ase.] A ferment which brings about the decomposition of cellulose.

1905 *Jrnl. Royal Microsc. Soc.* Feb. 98 He [*sc.* Van Itersen, jun.] finds that the destruction of cellulose by moulds is due to an enzyme, to which he gives the name of 'cellulase'.

Cellule. Add: 1. b. A small room or cell.

1894 A. Morrison *Tales Mean Streets* 222 The family should take a whole house..instead of the two rooms and a cellule upstairs now rented. 1908 *Westm. Gaz.* 12 June 8/1 'Each go into a cell and shut the door!' ordered a wardress, indicating a row of tiny cellules.

Cellulitic (seliŭli·tik), *a.* [f. Cellulitis + -ic.] Pertaining to cellulitis.

1906 Ferguson in *Trans. Edinb. Obstet. Soc.* XXXI. 127 Where there is no cellulitic abscess which can be evacuated.

Celluloid. Substitute for def.: A solid material, rigid when cold, and plastic when hot, consisting essentially of soluble cellulose nitrate and camphor. In the United States a trade name for the product of one manufacturer, in Europe a general designation.

Cellulose. Add: b. Now *esp.* as the basis of important commercial products. In popular use the word commonly designates compounds of cellulose, particularly cellulose acetate and cellulose nitrate, solutions of which form the 'cellulose' finishes used in varnishing metal, woodwork, etc. Also *attrib.*, as *cellulose dope, varnish*.

1898 *Daily News* 9 Nov. 4-6 A sawmill and a cellulose factory have just been set up at Mitrovitza. 1902 *Westm. Gaz.* 6 Jan. 2/1 The sulphite cellulose process is due to the labours in the laboratory of Al. Mitscherlich and Tilghmann. 1927 *Observer* 16 Oct. 27 Bodies finished in cellulose.

c. **cellulose acetate**, any of several compounds formed by the action of an acid on some form of cellulose, esp. cotton, used in the manufacture of artificial silk, electric insulators, varnish, etc.; **cellulose nitrate**, a compound formed by the action of nitric acid on a cellulose; nitrocellulose.

1884 Roscoe & Schorlemmer *Treat. Chem.* III. 581 Cellulose Dinitrate, $C_{12}H_{18}(NO_3)_2O_{10}$, is formed as the first product of the action of the hot dilute mixture of acids upon cotton-wool. 1895 Cross & Bevan *Cellulose* 35 The cellulose acetates about to be described are of undetermined molecular weight. *Ibid.* 39 Although gun cottons, or pyroxylines, are generally spoken of as nitro-celluloses, they are perhaps more correctly described as cellulose nitrates. 1909 Keane *Mod. Org. Chem.* 199 Conditions.. favourable to explosibility are present in gun-cotton, a mixture of cellulose nitrates, and in blasting gelatine.

Celosia (sĭlōu·siă, -ʃiă). *Bot.* [mod.L., f. Gr. κήλεος burning, κηλός dry, so called from the burnt appearance of the flowers of some species.] A plant of the amaranthaceous genus so named, esp. the cock's-comb, *Celosia cristata*.

1807 T. Martyn *Miller's Gard. & Bot. Dict.* I. 7 D/8 Celosias or Cock's-combs, are all herbaceous plants. 1899 *Westm. Gaz.* 16 Aug. 4/2 A very fine collection of celosias, a handsome feathery flower, in shades of gold and dark crimson.

Celsius (se·lsiŏs). The name of a Swedish astronomer, Anders *Celsius* (1701–44), the inventor, in 1742, of a thermometer, of which the scale runs downwards, the boiling-point being marked 0° and the freezing-point 100°. Also, and more commonly, applied to the centigrade thermometer, of which the scale runs upwards.

1797 *Encycl. Brit.* (ed. 3) XVIII. 497/2 Celsius's thermometer. 1850 Weale *Dict. Terms* 451/2 The Celsius, or Centigrade thermometer. 1863 E. Atkinson tr. *Ganot's Physics* § 235 On the continent..this division [into 100 parts] is called the centigrade or Celsius scale. *a* 1928 in Gamble *Story North Sea Air Station* 410 My altitude was..about 5,800 metres, the temperature 28° Celsius.

Celtdom (se·ltdəm). [f. Celt [1] + -dom.] Celtic peoples collectively; the Celtic spirit or genius.

1895 A. Nutt *Voyage Bran* 206 That natural magic which we seek in vain outside Celtdom. 1920 *Glasgow Herald* 25 Sept. 6 An Comunn Gaidhealach has done much to unveil the heart of Celtdom.

Celtiberian (seltibī·riăn), *a.* and *sb.* [f. L. *Celtiberia*: see Celt [1] and Iberian.] a. *adj.* Of or pertaining to Celtiberia, an ancient province of Spain lying between the Tagus and the Ebro, or to its inhabitants the Celtiberi, a union of Celts with Iberians. b. *sb.* An inhabitant of Celtiberia.

1622 Peacham *Compl. Gent.* 48 How Titus Sempronius Gracchus subdued the Celtiberian Spaniards. *c* 1789 *Encycl. Brit.* (1797) IV. 284/1 The Celtiberians were very cruel towards their enemies. 1845 *Encycl. Metrop.* XXV. 1345/1 The Celtiberian alphabet, of which there are several specimens in inscriptions and on coins, has not as yet been fully deciphered. 1924 *Glasgow Herald* 28 July 5 Numantia, the capital of the powerful Celtiberian tribe, the Arevaci.

Celtic. 2. Add: *Celtic fringe*, the Scots, Welsh, Cornish, and Irish, as occupying the fringe or outlying edge of the British Isles.

This phrase was coined by the 3rd Marquess of Salisbury.

1899 A. H. Keane *Man Past & Present* 523 The 'Keltic fringe', that is, the strips of territory on the skirts of the Teutonic and Neo-Latin domains in the extreme west. 1904 *Westm. Gaz.* 8 Jan. 9/2 They had welcomed him greedily—a free import from Wales and one of the chiefest ornaments of the Celtic fringe. 1907 A. S. T. Griffith-Boscawen *Fourteen Yrs. in Parlt.* ii. 11 Their majority [in 1892]..came entirely from Scotland, Wales, and Ireland, or, as Mr. Balfour aptly said, 'the Celtic fringe'. 1908 *Westm. Gaz.* 2 June 2/2 Apparently he has now got tired of his Celtic-fringe seat.

Celticist (se·ltisist). [f. Celtic.] = Celtist.

1912 *Irish World* 12 June 7/2 The celebrated philologist and Celticist.

Celtish (se·ltiʃ), *a.* [f. Celt [1].] = Celtic *a.*

1888 *N.E.D.* s.v. *Celt* [1]. 1906 *Daily Chron.* 6 Jan. 6/5 The Celtish melancholy and the Celtish gleam in his eyes. 1914 Rupert Brooke in Marsh *Mem.* (1918) 136 Where our huts are was an Iberian fort against the Celts—and Celtish against the Romans—and Roman against Saxons.

Celto-. Add: **Celtoma·nia**, excessive regard for or devotion to Celtic matters (cf. Celtomaniac). Similarly **Ce·ltophobe, -pho·bia**.

1848 A. Herbert in Todd *Irish Nennius* Notes p. xlii, Dr. Owen Pughe, under strong Celtomania, invented..the gloss [etc.].

Cembalo (tʃe·mbălo). *Mus.* [It.] A musical instrument, consisting of wire strings which are struck by hammers. b. A similar instrument operated by a key-board, the harpsichord: an abbreviation of *Clavicembalo. (Cf. Cembalist.)

1864 Webster. 1928 *Radio Times* 23 Nov. 520/1 A cembalo, the delicate-toned ancestor of the pianoforte.

Cembra (se·mbră). Also -o. [mod.L., f. G. dial. *zember, zimber*, var. of *zimmer* Timber.] In full *cembra pine*: The Swiss stone-pine, *Pinus Cembra*. Also *attrib.*, as *cembra nut*.

1796 W. Marshall *Planting* (ed. 2) II. 440 Pinus Cembra, Cembro Pine. 1807 T. Martyn *Miller's Gard. & Bot. Dict.* II. 8 G/1 The Cembra Pine grows higher up the Alps than any other Pine. 1848 Dunglison *Med. Lex.* (ed. 7) s.v. *Pinus Cembra*, The nuts, Cembro nuts, have an eatable kernel. *a* 1895 Symonds *In Black & White* IV. 2 (Funk) The deep wide walls with Cembra-plank and pine Are timbered. 1909 *Westm. Gaz.* 9 Oct. 14/2 Two bent and stunted cembras.

Cement, *sb.* Add:

5. b. See quot. (cf. *cement-gold*).

1874 Knight *Dict. Mech.*, *Cement*,..3...*a*. The brown deposit in the precipitation tank, wherein the soluble chloride of gold, obtained by the chlorination process, is deposited by the addition of sulphate of iron to the solution. *b*. The material in which the metal is imbedded in the cementing-furnace. 1889 [see next].

Cementation. Add: *attrib.*, as *cementation furnace, process*.

1884 W. H. Greenwood *Steel & Iron* (ed. 2) § 689 The Cementation process for the conversion of bar-iron into cementation or blister steel...The process is conducted in a converting or cementation furnace. 1887 D. A. Low *Machine Draw.* (1892) 79 In the cementation process, bars of wrought iron are imbedded in powdered charcoal in a fireclay trough. 1889 *Q. Rev.* July 137 This is known as the 'converting' or 'cementation' process, and the charcoal employed as the recarbonizing agent is termed 'cement'.

Cemented (sĭme·ntėd), *ppl. a.* [f. Cement *sb.* or *v.* + -ed.] Treated with cement; united with or as with cement.

1874 Knight *Dict. Mech.*, Cemented-back Carpet. 1903 *Daily Chron.* 16 June 7/4 To realise the fair dream of a cemented Empire. 1909 *Ibid.* 10 Apr. 3/4 Dry cemented roads. 1909 *Westm. Gaz.* 20 Sept. 4/1 Krupp cemented armour.

Cementer. Add quots. illustrating technical uses:

1903 *Daily Chron.* 24 Feb. 8/5 Envelope Cementers.. wanted. *Ibid.* 9 Dec. 9/6 Tortoiseshell Worker.—Good cementer, used to repairs. 1921 *Dict. Occup. Terms* (1927) § 429 *Solutioner* (boots); *cementer*; uses a rubber solution or cement, on lining of upper.

Cementite (sĭme·ntəit). [f. Cement *sb.* + -ite [1].] A hard and brittle carbide of iron.

1889 [see Pearlite].

Cementoma (simentō·mă). Also **cementome**. [f. L. *cementum* Cement *sb.* + *-oma.] (See quot. 1893.)

1893 J. B. Sutton *Tumours* 35 When the capsule of a tooth becomes enlarged,..and these thick capsules ossify, the tooth will become embedded in a mass of Cementum. To this form of odontome the name cementoma may be applied. *Ibid.*, The largest cementome from a horse known to me..weighs seventy ounces. 1910 *Practitioner* Jan. 124 The curious odontomata known as cementomata.

Cenacle. Add:

b. A place in which a group of people meet for the discussion of common interests; also, the group of people so meeting, *spec.* any of several literary cliques. [After F. *cénacle*.]

[1879 *Encycl. Brit.* IX. 676/1 The famous *cénacle* or clique in which Hugo was chief poet, Sainte-Beuve chief critic.] 1889 H. F. Wood *Englishman Rue Cain* xiii, The pundit of some cenacle in Garrick Street. 1899 Lyall *Asiatic Studies* Ser. II. 61 Within the philosophic cenacle I should entirely concur. 1926 *Contemp. Rev.* Jan. 85 In England and France schools and 'cénacles' of literature sprang up round the great writer of the moment.

Cenomanian (sĭnomē·niăn, sen-), *a.* *Geol.* [ad. F. *cénomanien*, f. med.L. *Cenomania*, now Le Mans, France, L. *Cenomani*, an ancient Gallic tribe of northern Italy: see -ian.] Designating a subdivision of the Upper Cretaceous period, corresponding to the Lower Chalk and Upper Greensand of British geologists; of flora, etc., belonging to or found in this strata.

1882 Geikie *Text-bk. Geol.* 820 The Cenomanian formation consists in Hanover of earthy limestones and marls. 1902 *Encycl. Brit.* XXXI. 434/2 The Cenomanian flora of central Europe. 1914 *Brit. Mus. Return* 206 The Cenomanian Chalk Marl of Cambridge.

Cenosite (se·nosəit). *Min.* Also **kainosite, cainosite**. [Named *kainosit* (Nordenskiold, 1886), f. Gr. καινός novel, in reference to its unusual composition, + -ite [1].] A hydrous silicate and carbonate of yttrium, erbium, and calcium, occurring in Norway and Sweden in the form of greasy, yellowish-brown, prismatic crystals.

1888 *Jrnl. Chem. Soc.* Abs. 234 Kainosite. 1892 E. S. Dana *Dana's Syst. Min.* (ed. 6) 698 Cenosite.

Cenotaph, *sb.* Add: *The Cenotaph*, the national monument erected in Whitehall, London, as a memorial to the British who fell in the war of 1914–18.

Cenotaph, *v.* [f. the sb.] *trans.* To honour or commemorate with a cenotaph.

1891 Kipling *Light that Failed* iv, The oblivion that is preceded by toleration and cenotaphed with contempt. *a* 1895 J. H. Boner *Poe's Cottage* vii. (Funk) And fate that then denied him, And envy that decried him, And malice that belied him, Have cenotaphed his fame.

Cenote (senō·te). [Yucatan Sp., f. Maya *conot*.] A natural underground reservoir of water, such as occur in the limestone of Yucatan.

1902 *Encycl. Brit.* XXV. 379/2 The cenotes or underground reservoirs were the important factors in locating the ruins of Northern Yucatan. 1902 *Amer. Anthropologist* IV. 128 Offerings..were cast into..the deep *cenotes*, or natural wells, to appease the gods believed to dwell therein.

Cense, *v.*[1] 2. Delete †*Obs.* (cf. Censing *vbl. sb.*[1]) and add:

1873 J. B. Dykes in Fowler *Life* (1897) 306 The prevalence of the practice of censing in the diocese.

Ce·nsing, *ppl. a.* [f. Cense *v.*[1] + -ing [2].] That censes or offers incense.

1893 *Athenæum* 26 Aug. 296/2 A censing adult angel.

Censor, *sb.* Add:

2. b. More explicitly *dramatic censor, film censor*.

1888 *Encycl. Brit.* XXIII. 227/2 The master of the revels appears to have been the dramatic censor from 1545 to 1624. 1930 G. B. Shaw in *Times* 17 Feb. 15/5 Mr. Edward Shortt, who lately succeeded the late T. P. O'Connor as Film Censor.

e. An official whose duty it is to censor private correspondence (as in time of war: cf. *Censor *v.*).

1914 (*Stamped on envelope of Soldier's Letter from the Front*) Passed by Censor. 1915 'Ian Hay' *First Hundred Thou.* xix. 290 These [*sc.* letters]..are stamped with the familiar red triangle and forwarded to the Base, where they are supposed to be scrutinised by the real Censor. 1918 B. Miall tr. *A. Hamon's Lessons of World-war* 146 In a letter written from England to a French non-commissioned officer, the censor cut out all that concerned the miners' strike in Wales! *Ibid.* 147 Correspondence from neutrals was examined and bore the paper band now well known in the United Kingdom: 'Opened by the censor'.

4. *Psycho-analysis.* A power within the soul which represses certain elements in the unconscious and prevents them from emerging into the conscious mind.

1913 Brill tr. *Freud's Interpretation of Dreams* vi. 287 We may state, as a second condition which the elements must satisfy in order to get into the dream, that they must be withdrawn from the censor of resistance. 1926 Coster *Psycho-Analysis* 200 The endopsychic censor, the judge within the soul.

attrib. 1920 B. Low *Psycho-Anal.* 63 This force of the Unconscious..at times so powerful that the Censor-barrier ..is swept aside.

Censor, *v.* Delete *rare* and add quots. having special reference to the control of news and the departmental supervision of naval and military private correspondence (as in time of war) or to the censorship of dramatic or cinematographic productions. Often in *ppl. a.*

1895 *Blackw. Mag.* Feb. 320/1 The severely censored columns of the Russian daily press. 1897 *Daily News* 13 Sept. 5/2 All news is being rigorously censored. 1899 *Westm. Gaz.* 9 Mar. 5/3 Everything read to him is carefully censored. *Ibid.* 22 Nov. 2/1 Finally the correspondent is handed back his censored despatch, probably reduced to a mere sequence of words conveying little intelligence. 1904 *Daily Chron.* 13 May 4/4 Censoring is very strict during the war. No news is allowed to be published which has anything to do with the movements of the army. 1907 *Westm. Gaz.* 21 Oct. 9/2 Ibsen's censored play entitled 'Ghosts'. 1915 R. Brooke *Coll. Poems* (1918) Mem. p. cxlviii, I must go and censor my platoon's letters.

Censorable (se·nsərăb'l), *a.* [f. Censor *v.* + -able.] Subject to censoring, in need of censoring.

1906 *Westm. Gaz.* 27 Jan. 2/2 To avoid Censorable references to prominent politicians. 1926 *Spectator* 30 Oct. 767/2 Mr. Gilhooley is not more censorable, and not less suitable for what used to be called family reading, than psycho-analytic text-books.

Censorial. 2. Delete †*Obs.* and add:

1866 Br. Gott *Lett.* (1917) 145 The very nature of a creed is personal, never censorial of others.

Censorship. Add:

2. b. (See *Censor *sb.* 2 b.)

1879 *Encycl. Brit.* IX. 143/1 A notable incident in the history of the stage, inasmuch as it led to the institution of the dramatic censorship. 1917 *New Europe* 13 Dec. 287 The *Berliner Tageblatt* (extremely popular: has come under ban of censorship for pacifist tendency). 1918 B. Miall tr. *A. Hamon's Lessons of World-war* 146 The censorship of all correspondence was a stupendous task. 1930 *Times* 17 Feb. 15/5 Mr. Shaw on Film Censorship.

3. *Psycho-analysis.* (See *Censor *sb.* 4.)

1924 W. B. Selbie *Psych. Relig.* 80 Unpleasant experiences..driven out of consciousness, and kept there by means of what Freud calls a censorship. *Ibid.* 90 The repressions and censorships of which Freud and others make so much are connected with changes in the nervous system.

Census, *sb.* Add: 3. (Earlier U.S. example of mod. use.)

1777 *N. Y. Constit.* § 5 A census of the electors and inhabitants of this state shall be taken, under the direction of the legislature.

b. *attrib.*, as *census-table, -taker*.

1831 Peck *Guide for Emigrants* 199 The *census table of last autumn. 1845 J. J. Hooper *Taking Census* i. 149 The popular impression..caused the *census-taker to be viewed in no better light than that of a tax-gatherer. 1890 *Harper's Mag.* Oct. 807/1 The writer met..a forlorn census-taker who had been six weeks in the saddle.

Cent[1]. 4. a. (Examples of depreciative use.)

1836 Haliburton *Clockm.* Ser. I. vii. (1837) 46 As for Latin and Greek, we don't valy it a cent. 1848 Lowell *Biglow P.* Ser. I. Introd. 'Gunners' 29 Sez Isrel, 'I don't care a cent.' 1887 Tourgee *Button's Inn* 131 Your dying wouldn't do her a cent's worth of good. 1902 Harben *Abner Daniel* 59 He'd cut her off without a cent. 1904 — *Georgians* 116, I don't care a red cent how many schools *you* build.

Centaurea (sentǭrī·ă, sentǭ·riă). [med.L. *centaurea*: see Centaury.] A plant of the genus so named.

1835-6 Maund *Botanic Garden* VI. No. 506 Chiron, the wise centaur, having been represented as using the original Centaurea in the cure of a wound. 1864 Oliver *Elem. Bot.* 190 Corn Centaurea, or Bluebottle. 1900 *Daily News* 5 May 4/5 The centaurea has for long been regarded as only half-hardy. 1907 *Westm. Gaz.* 18 July 6/3 An exceedingly fine show of roses and centaureas.

Centavo (sentā·vo, ‖þentā·vo). [Sp., f. L. *centum* a hundred.] A small coin of Spain and Portugal, and of Central and South America.

1883 *Encycl. Brit.* XVI. 733/1 Chili—100 Centavos = 1 Peso. 1896 *Westm. Gaz.* 18 Mar. 8/1 The 1-centavo stamp is orange-yellow,..the 20-centavos black. 1920 *Chambers's Jrnl.* 465/2 Two centavos to the escudo is the 'assistance' tax in hotels and restaurants.

Centering, *vbl. sb.* 4. Add: *centering cup*.

1849 *Rep. U.S. Comm. Patents* (1850) 346 We do not claim..a cup to intervene between the bail spindle and fixed centering cup.

Centesimal, *a.* 2. Add: *Centesimal anniversary*.

1807 in *Publications Col. Soc. Mass.* XXVI. 415 Report of the Proceedings of..the Second Centesimal Anniversary.

Centibar (se·ntibāɹ). *Meteorol.* One hundredth of a bar (see *Bar *sb.*[6]).

Centimetre. Add: *Centimetre-gramme-second*, used attrib. to designate a system of measurement introduced in 1874 in which the unit of length is the centimetre, the unit of mass the gramme, and the unit of time the mean solar second; commonly abbreviated C. G. S.

1875 J. D. Everett (*title*) Illustrations of the Centimetre-Gramme-Second System of Units. 1883 *Encycl. Brit.* XV. 699/1 In the Centimetre-Gramme-Second system of units, the absolute unit of force produces in one second, in a mass of one gramme, a velocity of one centimetre per second. 1884 Higgs *Magn. & Dyn.-Electr. Mach.* p. xiii, The absolute or C. G. S. (centimetre-gramme-second) units.

Centimo (þe·ntimo). [Sp.] A Spanish coin of the value of $\frac{1}{100}$ of a peseta.

1900 St. Barbe *Mod. Spain* 64 Countless five-centimo cigars. 1926 *British Weekly* 20 May 125/3 Dr. Irwin exhibited an indulgence which he bought for 70 centimos (7*d.*) in Madrid.

Centipede. Add:

c. A device consisting of a long piece of wood pierced with holes through which ropes are rove, used for suspending an awning. Also, a strong piece of rope running the length of the boom, with short cross-pieces used in stowing jibs.

1883 *Man. Seamanship for Boys* 138 A Centipede, or, as it is sometimes called, a Euphroe..is used as a crowfoot, fitted with a number of legs, for ridge ropes of awnings.

Central. Add:

1. *Central State*, the state of Kansas. *U.S.*

1888 *Harper's Mag.* June 39/1 The Central State. Its physical features and resources. *Ibid.*, When they think of.. her geographical situation, then Kansas is the 'Central State'.

4. *Central heating*, a system of heating a building by hot water or steam conveyed through pipes from a central source. *Central school* (see quot.).

1921 R. Hichens *Spirit of Time* iii, There was no *central heating on. 1919 A. W. Newton *Eng. Elementary School* 167 *Central schools..are intended to attract the best scholars from the upper classes of neighbouring schools, and to provide a higher course than the ordinary school can offer.

Centralism. (Earlier U.S. example.)

1831 *Deb. Congress* 2 Feb. 51 A system of centralism, hostile to the federative principle of our Union.

Centralist. (Earlier U.S. examples.)

1836 Edward *Hist. Texas* 125 The second faction of this party, called the Centralists, wish to..form a central government. 1849 *Tait's Mag.* XVI. 241/2 A federalist must in Texas be a welcome man, simply because General Santa Anna was a centralist.

Centre, *sb.* Add:

6. a. *spec.* A place forming a central point in a district or neighbourhood. *U.S.*

1843 J. Hayward *Gaz. U.S.* 48 Buxton Centre. *Ibid.* 49 Cumberland Centre. 1855 E. A. Charlton *New Hampshire* 295 At Meredith Centre are a meeting house..and three stores. 1889 Mrs. Rose T. Cooke *Steadfast* xxvii. 292 Tempy Hopkins had come down in the chaise with Parson Dyer from Pickering Centre.

11. d. In various games, a player on each side whose position is the middle of a line or field of players; esp. in association football and hockey = centre-forward (see *19); in other games, the player in the middle of the field.

1868 *Chambers's Encycl.* X. 597/1 La Crosse...In the arrangement of the men on each side..centre is in the centre of the field. 1892 *Young England* Sept. 442/1 The big 'centre', taking in the situation at a glance, slips round. 1897 *Encycl. Sport.* I. 411/2 [Rugby football.] Three Three-quarters.—The Centre—A centre is the correlative of the half-back. *Ibid.*, The centre will, of course, be on the look out for a drop at goal. 1922 *Daily Mail* 8 Dec. 12 M. A. Ap-Rhys Price, Marlborough's best centre, was unable to play.

e. A pass or kick from either of the wings towards the middle of the line of forwards.

1900 *Westm. Gaz.* 23 Apr. 8/3 The greatest fault of the forwards was that they were never where they should have been when centres..were put across. 1927 *Daily Express* 20 Apr. 13/2 H. met with his head a glorious centre by W.

19. centre-bully, a bully taken in the middle of the field at the start or re-start of play (see *Bully sb.² 2); **centre-fire,** *fig.* (see quot.); **centre-forward,** (*a*) a player in association football, hockey, and other games, who plays from a central position in the forward line; (*b*) the position occupied by that player; **centre-half, centre half-back,** (*a*) a player who plays from a central position among the half-backs; (*b*) the position of that player; **centre-line,** any line passing through a centre; *spec.*, in drawing, a line from which measurements are made, and in ship-building, a line passing lengthways through the hull and dividing it into two sections; **centre-piece** (earlier U.S. example); **centre-plate,** (*a*) each of the metal plates composing the bearing for a railway carriage or engine on the centre of the truck; (*b*) each of the metal plates used to hold a dowelled pattern while it is being turned in the lathe; (*c*) a metal centre-board; **centre-school** *U.S.*, a school serving a particular centre or neighbourhood; **centre-seated** *a.*, placed in the centre of the boat; **centre-square,** a straight-edge for finding the centre or arc of a circle.

1910 *Westm. Gaz.* 1 Mar. 16/2 From the *centre-bully Cambridge again pressed. 1907 S. E. White *Arizona Nights* III. iv. 288 A sidesaddle had arrived...It was '*centre fire', which is to say it had but the single horsehair cinch. 1891 *Peel City Guardian* IX. 7/3 The teams were as follows:...*centre forward [etc.]. 1897 *Encycl. Sport* I. 421/1 The centre-forward is in the middle of the other four; the two on each side of him form the wings. 1891 *Peel City Guardian* IX. 2/4 Our friend John at *centre-half. 1908 *Westm. Gaz.* 30 Nov. 14/4 If he were to stick to centre-half always. 1890 C. W. Alcock *Football* vii. 46 An inside man can give him a pass when he is clear from the *centre half-back. 1909 *Westm. Gaz.* 7 Aug. 2/2 Close inshore a fleet of racing dinghies..spun round like tops upon their *centre-keels. 1777 *Monthly Review* LV. 306 Section through the *center line of the Register Office, from North to South. 1874 Knight *Dict. Mech.*, *Center-line*, a central, longitudinal, vertical section of the hull. 1887 D. A. Low *Machine Draw.* 2 After drawing the centre line of any part the dimensions of that part must be marked off from the centre line. 1803 *Deb. Congress* 10 Jan. (1851) 345 An appropriate and characteristic equestrian statue..as a beautiful *centre piece for the entire plan. 1875 M. N. Forney *Catech. Locomotive* (1883) 316 The weight of the front end of the engine rests on a cast iron *centre-plate. 1884 Knight *Dict. Mech.* Suppl. 185/1 Center-plate. 1894 *Outing* (U.S.) XXIV. 194/2 The movable center-plate will always let you know when you get on a shoal. 1860 Holland *Miss Gilbert's Career* vii. 125 A fit person to take charge of the *centre school. *Ibid.* xi. 180 Dr. Gilbert ..knocked at the door of the centre school-house. 1906 *Westm. Gaz.* 13 Aug. 5/2 Their craft is fitted with *centre-seated slides and swivel rowlocks. 1875 Knight *Dict. Mech.* 2294/1 s.v. *Square*, The *center-square, for finding the center of a circle. 1886 [see Radius-finder].

Centre, *v.* Add:

4. Also, to occupy, distinguish, or mark the centre of; *fig.* to be the central point of.

1886 W. J. Tucker *E. Europe* 260 There is the eternal 'Kugelhupf' (a genuinely Austrian coffee-cake) centring the table. 1894 *Daily News* 2 July 3/4 When the scarlet liveries of Royalty are seen centreing the procession across the bridge. 1898 *Ibid.* 27 May 4/6 Centring the Hall was the dais. 1902 C. N. & A. M. Williamson *Lightning Conductor* 95 This châteaux country of the Loire..centreing as it did the old court life of France.

b. In association football and hockey, to kick or hit (a ball) towards the centre of the line of forwards. Also *absol.*

1890 C. W. Alcock *Football* vii. 47 When..the ball is centred..from the left wing. 1891 *Peel Chron.* 14 Mar. 5/4 Radcliffe neatly centred. 1897 *Daily News* 12 Feb. 8/6 The latter, as..the Cambridge back dashed at him, again centred the ball. 1904 *Daily Chron.* 15 Feb. 8/4 Wright ran smartly down on the left and centred.

¶ *To centre* or *to be centred round, around, about*: an illogical phrase, now very frequent = to have its centre in or on (cf. sense 6), to move or revolve round (something) as a centre.

1868 [in Dict., sense 2]. 1870 *Chambers's Jrnl.* 12 Nov. 731/1 The only man she had ever loved—around whom centred her most precious memories. 1878 *Harper's Mag.* 308/2 The real interest of the story centres about the lives of four personages. 1886 *Chambers's Jrnl.* 17 July 449/2 The assistant's chief hardships centre round the abnormal length of his working-day. 1893 H. B. Clarke *Spanish Lit.* 163 The plot invariably centres round the love intrigue of persons in the middle or upper classes of life. 1898 Kipling *Day's Work, Bridge-Builders* 7 The little cluster of huts where he and his gang lived centred round the tattered dwelling of a sea-priest. 1909 *Daily Chron.* 27 July 4/6 Its most enduring traditions centre round the ancient cathedral. 1929 *Times Lit. Suppl.* 3 Oct. 753/2 The group of gifted men and women who centred round Henry Adams.

Centre-board. (Earlier U.S. example.)

1849 *Rep. Commissioner of Patents* (U.S.) 221 What I claim..as my invention..is suspending in a jointed frame a centre board composed of one or more pieces capable of being turned with either their edges or sides to the bottom of the vessel.

Centre-boarder. [f. Centre-board.] A boat with a centre-board.

1886 *Outing* (U.S.) VIII. 58/1 The boats are necessarily of light draught and center-boarders. 1897 *Ibid.* XXX. 337/2 The slippery bilge of an eggshell centreboarder.

Centre-table. Chiefly *U.S.* [Centre sb. 6.] A table intended for the centre of a room, esp. a parlour or drawing-room, and commonly used for the display of books, albums, etc.

1835 *Southern Lit. Messenger* I. 298 You should have an elegant centre-table in your drawing-room. 1852 G. W. Curtis *Lotus-eating* 22 The choice centre-table and crimson-covered lounges. 1860 Holland *Miss Gilbert's Career* xiii. 240 The moment she retired he went to the centre-table [and] turned over the cards and billet-doux. 1868 [see Centre sb. 18]. 1872 Lowell *Among my Bks.* Ser. II. (1899) 276 A book..for the student, and..more likely to find its place on the library-shelf than the centre-table. 1896 J. C. Harris *Sister Jane* 64 [The Bible] sets right on the centre-table in my parlor.

Centriciput (sentri·sipɒt). *Anat.* [mod.L., f. L. *centrum* centre + *caput* head.] The middle part of the head, that part of the head which lies between the sinciput and the occiput. Hence **Centrici·pital** *a.*, pertaining to the centriciput.

a 1889 *Amer. Cycl.* XIII. 424 (Cent. Dict.) His [*sc.* Carus's] three principal cranial vertebræ correspond to the three cerebral masses, and are the occipital, centricipital, and sincipital.

Centrifugal. Add:

5. Obtained by the use of a centrifugal machine.

1880 *Army & Navy Co-op. Soc. Price List* 34 Sugars.. Centrifugal, or White Crystals. 1900 *Year-bk. U.S. Dept. Agric.* 613 (Cent. D. Suppl.) Fresh butter, made from sweet centrifugal cream.

6. As *sb.* A centrifugal machine.

1904 Brannt tr. *Bersch's Cellulose* ix. 221 The bleached skeins of silk are..dehydrated in a centrifugal.

Centrifugalization (sentri·fiugălaizē·ʃən). [f. Centrifugalize: see -ation.] The process of subjecting to centrifugal action.

1901 *Science* 29 Mar. 513 Juices, blood, etc., taken at various stages of the disease, with and without centrifugalization. 1908 *Practitioner* June 830 Sedimentation and centrifugalisation.

Centrifugalize, *v.* Add: To subject to a centrifugal process. Also *absol.*

1903 *Science* 6 Mar. 369 (Cent. D. Suppl.) The blood was.. centrifugalized to get rid of the stroma. 1910 *Practitioner* June 866 Hyaline casts may be found..if the urine be centrifugalised. 1925 C. H. Browning *Bacteriology* vi. 122 By..re-suspending the sediment in..sodium chloride solution and again centrifugalising, the corpuscles are freed from..the serum.

Centrifugate, *v.* Add: **b.** *trans.* To expel from the centre, *spec.* by centrifugal action.

1851 A. J. Davis in Pember *Earth's Earliest Ages* (1884) 353 She centrifugated it in a thousand forms of expression. *a* 1909 *Buck's Handbk. Med. Sci.* I. 564 (Cent. D. Suppl.) The fluid should be centrifugated, the sediment spread on cover slips.

Centrifuge (se·ntrifiūdʒ), *v.* [f. the sb.] = Centrifugalize. Also in *ppl. a.* and *vbl. sb.*

1903 *Nature* 3 Dec. 111/2 By mixing bacteria with the white cells of the blood obtained by centrifuging and adding blood serum. 1908 *Practitioner* Jan. 12 If the cerebro-spinal fluid withdrawn by this operation is centrifuged, and a deposit found,...we can certainly exclude neurasthenia. 1910 *Ibid.* Apr. 447 Centrifuged specimens. 1920 L. Doncaster *Introd. Cytology* 34 Owing to the centrifuging, the polar spindle of an egg is greatly elongated.

Centriole (se·ntriōl). *Cytology.* [ad. mod.L. *centriolum*, dim. of *centrum* centre.] A minute granule in the centre of the astrosphere, regarded by some scientists as identical with the centrosome and by others as contained within it.

1901 G. N. Calkins *Protozoa* 258 The centrosome (including the centriole).

Centripetalism (sentri·petăliz'm). [f. Centripetal + -ism.] Movement towards a centre.

1887 *Westm. Rev.* June 409 The plague of centripetalism is a curse which has come to us [*viz.* New Zealand] across the seas from older countries.

Centrist. Add quots. illustrating recent political situations. Also *attrib.*

1923 E. A. Ross *Russian Soviet Republ.* 22 To Lenin Trotsky wrote,...The 'Berliner Tageblatt' and the 'Vossiche Zeitung' demand an understanding with Russia by all means. The Centrists favor an agreement. 1928 *Illustr. Hist. Russ. Rev.* I. 135 *note*, In international Social Democracy 'Centrists' are those who swing to and fro between the Jingoes..and the Left such as:..MacDonald and Co. in England. 1928 *Manch. Guardian Weekly* 21 Sept. 224/1 The 'Temps' shows some uneasiness..at the attacks on Herr Müller in the Centrist and Populist press.

Centro-. Add: **Centroge·nesis,** evolution from the radiate or peripheral type of organism assumed by plants and some of the lower forms of the animal kingdom; hence **Centrogene·tic** *a.*; **Centrole·cithal** *a. Biol.*, having the food yolk in the centre of the ovum; **Centroso·ma, Ce·ntrosome** *Biol.*, one of two protoplasmic corpuscles in a fertilized ovum, supposed to have an important function in connection with its division; **Ce·ntrosphere** *Biol.*, a mass of cytoplasm surrounding the centrosome when present, from which the rays extend and which forms a karyokinetic spindle during the division of the cell; *Geol.* the nucleus or central portion of the earth; **Centro·tylote** *a.*, of a biradiate sponge-spicule, having a central swelling.

1896 L. H. Bailey *Survival of Unlike* i. 17 We may, therefore, contrast these two great lines of ascent which, with so many vicissitudes, have come up through the ages, as Dipleurogenesis and *Centrogenesis. *Ibid.* 19 With this development has come the perfection of *centrogenetic form. 1880 Balfour *Comp. Embryol.* I. iii. 90 The food-yolk is however placed, not at one pole, but at the centre of the ovum. This group of ova I propose to name *centrolecithal. 1888 Rolleston & Jackson *Anim. Life* p. xxvi, Centrolecithal ova are confined to Arthropoda. 1889 Geddes & Thomson *Evolution of Sex* xi. 146 Both Van Beneden and Boveri have recently agreed on the existence of two 'central corpuscles' (*centrosomata) in the protoplasm [of a fertilized ovum]. 1893 tr. *Weismann's Germ-Plasm* Introd. 23 We now know..that even in Phanerogams a small cell-body surrounds the nucleus [of the male cell in fertilization], and that a special structure, the '*centrosome',—which is absolutely essential for the commencement of development,—is contained within it. 1927 Haldane & Huxley *Anim. Biol.* ii. 53 A group of spermatids, produced at the close of the maturation divisions. Each has a nucleus and a centrosome. 1896 Wilson *The Cell* 232 The *centrosphere has a radiate structure, being traversed by rays which stretch between the centrosome and the peripheral microsome-circle. 1899 *Geog. Jrnl.* XIII. 228 The Earth consists of three parts: there is the vast unknown interior, or 'centrosphere' [etc.]. 1887 Sollas in *Encycl. Brit.* XXII. 417/2 A *centrotylote microxea. 1900 *Proc. Zool. Soc.* 131 The microstrongyles..are occasionally centrotylote.

Centrum. Add: **2.** *Geol.* The place from which an earthquake originates.

1887 *Nature* 31 Oct. 657 The determination of earthquake origins, the depth of 'centrums' [etc.].

Centuriate, *a.* Delete † *Obs.* and add: also in *centuriate comitia*; also, of, pertaining to, or divided into centuries or hundreds.

1901 F. F. Abbott *Hist. & Descr. Rom. Pol. Instit.* 27 The action of the centuriate *comitia* in electing magistrates, in passing laws, and in deciding appeals was of no great immediate value to the plebs. *Ibid.* 76 The reformed centuriate assembly was essentially democratic. 1918 Haverfield in *Eng. Hist. Rev.* XXXIII. 296 The boundaries of Roman centuriate land.

Centuriate, *v.* Transfer † *Obs.* to sense 1 and add: **2.** In Roman colonization, to divide and assign land (see next).

1918 Haverfield in *Eng. Hist. Rev.* XXXIII. 289 It would follow that the *territorium* of..a provincial *colonia*.. would be centuriated when first surveyed and laid out. *Ibid.* 296 The whole of northern Essex..would have been surveyed and centuriated on one general scheme.

Centuriation (sentiūəriē·ʃən). [ad. L. *centuriātiōnem*, n. of action f. *centuriāre* to Centuriate.] (See quot. 1869.)

1869 H. C. Coote in *Archæologia* XLII. 133 The territory having been thus appropriated to the colony, the next step was to divide and assign it..in *centuriæ*, or private estates, to and amongst the colonists. This *centuriation*, as it was called, was the legal and constitutional act which perfected the change from public land into private property. 1918 Haverfield in *Eng. Hist. Rev.* XXXIII. 291 Numerous attempts have been made to detect centuriation, or something like it, in Britain.

Centurion. Add:

3. *Sport.* A player who makes a hundred or more runs in an innings at cricket; one who has ridden, etc., a hundred miles in one journey. *Double centurion*, a player who makes a double century (see next).

1886 *Graphic* 31 July 107/2 Some other 'centurions' have been Chatterton (108) for M.C.C., A. Shuker (103 not out) for Trent. 1897 *Outing* (U.S.) XXX. 346/1 There are long-distance riders, too galore in the N.Y.A.C. and not a few centurions. 1900 *Westm. Gaz.* 18 July 2/3 This is the third time he has been a double centurion.

Century. Add:

3. b. *spec.* in *Cricket*, a hundred or more runs made by one player in the same innings. *Double century*, two centuries by the same player in the same cricket match. Also in *Bicycling*, etc., a hundred miles in a race or ride; *double century*, a cycling run of two hundred miles.

1883 *Graphic* 11 Aug. 138/2 His batting this year has been of the highest order, as witnesses among his many good performances that against the Players, when be marked his 'century'. 1897 *Outing* (U.S.) XXX. 343/1 The probability is that he will place to his credit on the [cycling] club records one or more double centuries. *Ibid.* 348/1 The more

enthusiastic indulge in century runs. 1909 *Daily Chron.* 15 May 8/5 Putting the new Humberto a test of a century run.

c. *Sporting slang.* A hundred pounds.

1864 *Derby Day* 131 (Farmer) I'll lay you an even century about Nimrod. 1883 *Echo* 1 Nov. 4/2 (ibid.) Golding..purchased Passaic from F. Archer for a century. 1888 F. W. J. Henning *Recoll. Prize Ring* 155 Having made up his mind that he was going to pocket the century.

9. century-plant (earlier examples).

1846–50 A. Wood *Class-bk. Bot.* 539 American Aloe. Century Plant...It is a popular notion that it flowers but once in a hundred years. 1857 A. Gray *First Lessons Bot.* (1866) 53 This takes place..very strikingly in the Aloe and in the Century-plant. 1869 C. L. Brace *New West* xxiii. 299 A beautiful product of the south of California—the Century Plant, or Agave Americana.

b. pl. (sense 5) in comb., as *centuries-old* adj.

1908 *Daily Chron.* 15 June 1/3 The centuries-old division which has separated man and woman. 1908 *Westm. Gaz.* 29 July 1/3 Giant centuries-old plane trees.

Cephal- (se·făl), combining form of Gr. κεφαλή head, as **Ce·phalhæmato·ma,** a bloody swelling or tumour beneath the pericranium; **Cephalhy·drocele,** a serous or watery tumour outside the cranium.

1908 *Practitioner* Apr. 467 *Cephalhaematoma situated beneath the periosteum usually takes some weeks to absorb. *Ibid.* 466 The conditions necessary for the formation of a *cephalhydrocele are a fracture with laceration of the dura.

Cephalad (se·fălæd), *adv.* [f. Gr. κεφαλή head + *-ad.] Towards the head.

1887 Wilder in *Amer. Nat.* June 545 In Ceratodus alone ..is there a prerima,—that is, a rima extending cephalad from the margin of the porta.

Cephaletron (sefălī·trɒn). Pl. **-tra.** [mod.L., f. Gr. κεφαλή head + ἦτρον abdomen.] Owen's name for the head or anterior division of the body of some of the crustaceans, as the king-crab.

1872 [see *thoracetron* s.v. Thoraco-].

Cephalin (se·fălin). *Zool.* [f. Gr. κεφαλή head + -in¹.] = *Cephalont.

1888 Rolleston & Jackson *Anim. Life* 858 A Polycystid possessing all three segments is known as a Cephalin or Cephalont.

Cephalization. Add:

b. A supposed correlation between an increase in the size of the brain and mental development.

1899 *Amer. Anthropologist* July 410 These changes represent a process of *cephalization*, discussed long ago by Dana as manifested chiefly by lower organisms, and more recently by Marsh as manifested chiefly by the higher vertebrates. 1908 *Westm. Gaz.* 8 July 2/2 What Dubois called 'the coefficient of cephalisation'.

Cephalize (se·fălaiz), *v.* [f. Gr. κεφαλή head + -ize.] *trans.* To develop the head of, to cause cephalization of or in.

1889 *Cent. Dict.* 1901 G. Gissing *Our Friend the Charlatan* ii, Evolution is engaged in *cephalizing* the political aggregate.

Cephalodiscus (se:fălodi·skɒs). [mod.L., f. Gr. κεφαλή head (see Cephalo-) + δίσκος Disk.] A deep-sea animal belonging to the genus of that name.

1882 M'Intosh in *Ann. & Mag. Nat. Hist.* X. 343 *Cephalodiscus* also diverges in regard to the thin postoral lamella. 1885 *Encycl. Brit.* XIX. 435/1 The dwelling of Cephalodiscus is a gelatinous, irregularly branched, and fimbriated mass. 1902 *Ibid.* XXIX. 251/1 Dorso-ventral section of an adult *Cephalodiscus*. 1915 E. R. Lankester *Divers. Naturalist* 8 One of the most interesting deep-sea creatures discovered by the 'Challenger'..received the name Cephalodiscus.

Cephalon (se·fălɒn). [mod.L., f. Gr. κεφαλή head: cf. Encephalon.] The region of the head in a crustacean.

1875 Huxley & Martin *Elem. Biol.* (1877) 128 An anterior division, which belongs to the head or cephalon.

Cephalont (se·fălɒnt). *Zool.* [f. Gr. κεφαλή head + ὤν, ὀντός being, pres. pple. of εἶναι to be.] That phase in the development of a septate gregarine in which an epimerite is attached to the anterior cyst.

1885 *Encycl. Brit.* XIX. 854/1 The epimerite serves to attach the parasite to its host.—The phase in which it is present is called a 'cephalont', the phase after it has broken off a 'sporont'. 1901 G. N. Calkins *Protozoa* 145.

Cephalophine (se·fălɒfain), *a.* [f. mod.L. *Cephalophinæ*, a subfamily of antelopes of the genus *Cephalophus*: see -ine¹.] Having the characteristics of the Indian and African antelopes of the subfamily *Cephalophinæ*.

1891 Flower & Lydekker *Mammals* 337 Cephalophine Section. Small or medium-sized African and Indian Antelopes.

Cephalotic (sefălɒ·tik), *a. Biol.* [f. Gr. κεφαλή head + οὖς, ὠτ- ear + -ic.] Characterized by the presence of the ears on the middle line of the head.

1894 W. Bateson *Study of Variation* 458 Dareste also declares that the cephalotic state is similarly first indicated by a premature union of the folds in the region of the medulla, taking place before this part of the brain has widened out.

Cepheid (se·fiid, sī·fiid), *a.* and *sb. Astr.* [f. L. *Cepheus*, Gr. Κηφεύς Cepheus, a mythical king whose name was given to a constellation, + -id², as in *Leonid*, etc.]

A. *adj.* Pertaining to or resembling the variable star δ Cephei. **B.** *sb.* **1.** A variable star of the type of δ Cephei. **2.** Any of a shower of meteors which appears to radiate from the constellation Cepheus.

1921 *Discovery* Feb. 38/1 To determine the absolute magnitude..of every Cepheid variable in the heavens. 1927 *Glasgow Herald* 7 Oct. 11/2 When a Cepheid's period was noted its brightness could be stated. 1927 A. S. Eddington *Stars & Atoms* 93 In 1924 Hubble discovered a number of Cepheid variables in the great Andromeda nebula.

Ceppo (tʃe·ppo). [It.] The cemented glacial gravels of northern Italy.

1881 J. Geikie *Prehistoric Europe* 316 Those wide-spread masses of conglomerate, which are called *Ceppo* by the Italian geologists. 1894 — *Gt. Ice Age* (ed. 3) 562 The highly denuded 'Ceppo' underlying the great terminal moraines of Ivræa, Como, etc.

Ceramicist (siræ·misist). [f. Ceramic + -ist.] = Ceramist.

1930 *Observer* 25 May 18/3 Many countries have great ceramicists capable of building up a great pottery industry.

Ceramidium (serămi·diɒm). *Bot.* [mod.L., f. Gr. κεραμίδιον, dim. of κεραμίς earthen vessel.] A cystocarp.

1882 *Cassell's Dict.* 1902 *Encycl. Brit.* XXV. 270/1 In *Rhodomelaceæ* there is a special urn-shaped envelope surrounding the sporogonous filaments. This is a ceramidium.

Cerastium (siræ·stiɒm). *Bot.* [mod.L., f. Gr. κεράστης horned.] A plant of the caryophyllaceous genus of that name, characterized by small leaves and white flowers with bifid petals, and comprising the mouse-ear chickweed and other weeds.

1829 Loudon *Encycl. Plants* 1059 Caryophylleæ...Many are common weeds, as most of the Cerastiums, Spergulas, and others. 1925 *Chambers's Jrnl.* Jan. 35/2 He had observed..what he knew to be a very rare cerastium.

Ceratioid (siræ·tioid), *a.* and *sb.* [f. *Ceratias*, a genus of fishes: see -oid.] **A.** *adj.* Of or pertaining to the family *Ceratiidæ* of fishes (or the genus *Ceratias*). **B.** *sb.* A fish of this family.

1889 *Cent. Dict.* 1925 *Glasgow Herald* 21 Mar. 4 The fishes..belong to the Ceratioid section of the Anglers.

Ceratodus (siræ·tŏdɒs). *Zool.* [mod.L., f. Gr. κέρας, κερατ- horn + ὀδούς tooth.] A fish of the genus of that name, belonging to the order *Dipnoi*.

1874 Darwin *Desc. Man* (ed. 2) 37/2 The opinion lately advanced by Dr. Günther on the paddle of Ceratodus. 1897 E. R. Lankester in *Times* 8 Feb. 10/6 The larval stages of the remarkable fish ceratodus of Queensland. 1899 *Daily News* 10 Apr. 8/2 The ceratodus, a fish with lungs, which, though its fossil remains are scattered over the world, is now confined to two rivers in the south of Queensland, the Mary and the Burnett.

Ceratosaurus (se:rătosǭ·rɒs). [mod.L., f. Gr. κέρας, κερατ- horn + σαῦρος lizard.] An extinct dinosaurian reptile such as those reconstructed from remains found in the Upper Jurassic rocks of Colorado.

1893 H. N. Hutchinson *Extinct Monsters* 84 Externally, also, the Ceratosaurus differs from other members of the Carnivorous group. 1927 Haldane & Huxley *Anim. Biol.* xi. 242.

Cereal, *sb.* Add: **b.** An article of diet (esp. a breakfast dish) made from some cereal. *U.S.*

1906 R. W. Chambers *Fighting Chance* 145 To breakfast all alone was delicious..to loiter over cream-jug and cereal.

Cerealist (sī·riălist). [f. Cereal sb. + -ist.]

1. One who advocates a cereal diet.

1905 *Daily Chron.* 7 Aug. 4/5 Cerealists preach absolute abstention from pheasant, turbot, and turtle.

2. One who makes a special study of cereals and the conditions necessary for their cultivation.

1907 L. H. Bailey *Cycl. Amer. Agric.* II. 663/2 Cerealists as well as practical producers of grains. 1920 *Glasgow Herald* 29 Sept. 9 The present year's wheat yield is nothing of which to boast, but it relieves the apprehensions of cerealists. 1924 *Ibid.* 13 Sept. 6 Dr. Saunders had been the Dominion cerealist.

Cerebello- (se·rĭbelo), used as comb. form of Cerebellum = pertaining to the cerebellum (and another part).

1901 Dorland *Med. Dict.* (ed. 2), *Cerebellospinal*, pertaining to the cerebellum and spinal cord. 1903 *Ibid.* (ed. 3), *Cerebello-olivary*, connecting the cerebellum and olivary body. 1907 *Practitioner* Apr. 584 The disturbing influence exerted by the tumour upon the cerebello-vestibular apparatus.

Cerebralize (se·rĭbrălaiz), *v.* [f. Cerebral + -ize.] *trans.* To pronounce as a cerebral letter. Hence **Ce:rebraliza·tion.**

1869 W. H. Ferrar *Compar. Gram.* I. 340 Cerebralisation is a phenomenon that has arisen within the limits of the Sanskrit language.

Cerebricity (serĭbri·siti). *rare.* [f. Cerebrum brain, after *electricity*.] Brain-cell power.

1890 O. W. Holmes *Over Teacups* i. 15 Your incident is a typical example of cerebral induction from a source containing stored cerebricity. I use this word, not to be found in my dictionaries, as expressing the brain-cell power corresponding to electricity. 1894 *Arena* IX. 336 Mere manifestations of psychic power, referable to the dark field of cerebricity and clairvoyance.

Cerebrize (se·rĭbraiz), *v.* [f. Cerebrum: see -ize.] = Cerebrate *v.*

1887 *Science* 2 Dec. 269/2 The normal process of 'cerebrising' consists of an ever-changing focusing on one set of impressions, then a diffusion of these. 1901 G. Gissing *Our Friend the Charlatan* xxi, 'Morality', he says, 'depends upon cerebral oxidation'...If I am not cerebrally oxidised, or oxidally cerebrized, in the right degree, it's all over with my hopes of leading a moral life.

Cerebro-spinal. Add: esp. in *cerebro-spinal meningitis* or *fever*, inflammation of the meninges of the brain and the spinal cord, otherwise called *spotted fever*.

1889 Osler *Cerebral Palsies* 18 Cerebro-spinal meningitis was stated to be the cause of the trouble. 1897 *Trans. Amer. Pediatric Soc.* IX. 189 Four ounces of turbid cerebro-spinal fluid were collected and measured. 1901 Osler *Princ. & Pract. Med.* (ed. 4) 101 Sporadic cerebro-spinal fever occurs in all the larger cities..of this continent.

Cered. Add: **2.** Equipped with a cere.

1872 Coues *N. Amer. Birds* 199 Birds with strongly hooked and truly cered bill.

Ceremoniarius (se:rĭmōuniē·riɒs). *Eccl.* [L., sb. use of adj. f. *cærimōnia* Ceremony.] An official who superintends the ceremonies and assists the ministers in a liturgical service.

1865 F. G. Lee *Direct. Anglicanum* 264 The ceremoniarius should be vested in cassock and cotta. 1898 *Westm. Gaz.* 10 Nov. 5/2 Before the prayer for the Church Militant the ceremon[i]arius..again said the requiem æternam.

Ceriman (se·rimæn). *Bot.* A West Indian climbing plant, *Monstera pertusa*; also a Mexican plant, *M. deliciosa*, yielding an edible fruit.

1871 Kingsley *At Last* vii, Up the next [stem] the Ceriman spreads its huge leaves, latticed and forked again and again.

Cerne, *sb.* Add: **2.** A method of hunting buffalo by surrounding a herd.

1839 C. A. Murray *Trav. N. Amer.* I. 336 A 'cerne' or 'surround', in this part of the wilderness, requires a great deal of arrangement to render it successful.

Cero (sī·ro). [Altered f. Sp. *sierra* saw, saw-fish.] A fish of the mackerel family, *Scomberomorus regalis* or *S. cavalla*, found in the West Indies.

1884 Goode *Nat. Hist. Aquat. Anim.* 307 The Spotted Cero, or King Cero, *Scomberomorus regalis*.

Ceroon. *U.S.* (Examples.)

1832 *Louisville Public Adv.* 3 Mar., 8 puncheons Jamaica rum; 2 ceroons indigo. *a* 1861 T. Winthrop *Isthmiana, Chitrés*, A young ragamuffin, who had come into town on a nag between two hide ceroons, full of mami apples.

Cert (sɜ̄ɹt), *sb. slang.* [Abbreviation of Certain or Certainty.] *gen.* A certainty (e.g. *a dead cert*); *spec.* in horse-racing, a horse that is considered certain to win.

1889 *Man of the World* 29 June (Farmer) I hear Pioneer is a cert. for the St. James's. 1894 *Westm. Gaz.* 10 Aug. 8/2 'Special snips,' 'paddock wires,' and other forms of what the advertisers, with unintentional humour, describe as 'certs.' 1899 T. M. Ellis *3 Cat's-eye Rings* 32 Tatwood, you know—the trainer—he tips me all the certs. 1921 A. Graham *Voyage Home* xxi, Honiton has admitted the whole thing to Miss Upton, so it's a cert. 1927 S. Kaye-Smith in *Sunday Express* 11 Sept. 9 They had guessed for a cert where he was.

Certain, *a.* Add: **7. e.** Also, (*a woman*) *of a certain description*, i.e. of the demi-monde; *in a certain condition*, pregnant.

1802 Lemaistre *Rough Sk. Mod. Paris* xiv. 122 Women, too, of a certain description, do not ply for custom. *Ibid.* xxviii. 232 When I first came here, I supposed that these ladies were of a certain description.

C. *adv.* **1.** (Later U.S. examples.)

1859 Bartlett *Dict. Amer.* (ed. 2), *Certain*, for certainly. 'He's dead certain'. 'I'll go to-morrow sure and certain'. Very common. 1871 Schele de Vere *Americanisms* (1872) 450 He's done it sure and certain.

Certifiably (sɜ̄ɹtifaiăbli), *adv.* [f. Certifiable + -ly².] In a certifiable degree; so as to admit of being certified.

1891 *Daily News* 12 Mar. 2/3 The evidence showed that as soon as Mrs. Stoney became certifiably insane the defendant took measures for her removal.

Certificate, *v.* Add:

2. b. *intr.* = Certify *v.* 4.

1907 W. De Morgan *Alice-for-Short* xxvi, Verrinder died of the chloroform, of course. But Fludyer will find enough fatty heart to certificate on.

Certify, *v.* Add: **2. c.** To transfer or convey (land) by formal certification.

1845 J. J. Hooper *Adv. Simon Suggs* vi. 71 Her father must 'certify' his land to him.

4. b. *Law.* To give a certificate for costs on a certain scale.

1887 J. E. Davis *Pract. County Crts.* (ed. 6) 122 Where a Judge certifies under sect. 5 of the County Courts (Costs and Salaries) Act, 1882, a minute of the certificate..shall be entered on the minutes of the Court. 1889 C. A. White *Archbold's County Crt. Pract.* 135 A judge has no power to allow costs on a higher scale unless he certify under the above section. 1910 *Encycl. Brit.* VII. 324/2 In every indictable case in which the committing justices or the court of trial certify for legal aid.

Ce·rtifying, *ppl. a.* [f. prec.] Giving certification.

1845 J. J. Hooper *Adv. Simon Suggs* vi. 71 The certifying agent saw a thousand silver dollars paid to the Indian.

Cerulignol (sīrūli·gnɒl). *Chem.* [f. L. *cæru(leus* dark blue + *lign(um* wood + -ol.] A colourless compound obtained from beech-tar oil.

1909 *Century Dict.* Suppl. 1923 *Nature* CXI. 763/1 The presence of cerulignol in these tars, giving a blue coloration in alcoholic solution with lime or baryta.

Cervicitis (sɜ̄ɹvisai·tis). *Path.* [mod.L., f. L. *cervix, cervic-* neck + -itis.] Inflammation of the neck of the uterus; trachelitis.

1901 Dorland *Med. Dict.* (ed. 2). 1910 *Practitioner* Mar. 395 Every cervical erosion, cervicitis, or irritating leucorrhoeal discharge.

Cervico-. Add *cervico-dorsal* adj.

1908 *Practitioner* Sept. 404 The cervico-dorsal spine.

Cesarewitch (sezē·revitʃ). [Named after the Russian prince who became Alexander II.] A long-distance handicap horse-race run at Newmarket, instituted in 1839.

1840 J. C. Whyte *Brit. Turf* II. xi. 481 Newmarket Second October Meeting...The Cesarewitch stakes. 1856 'Stonehenge' (J. H. Walsh) *Brit. Sports* 373/1 Cesarewitch Course...2 miles, 2 furlongs, 28 yards. 1891 Sir G. Chetwynd *Racing Remin.* I. 29 It was at Warwick, too, that the big Cesarewitch commissions usually made their first appearance in the market. *Ibid.* 31 At the next Newmarket meeting Cardinal York won the Cesarewitch by six lengths.

Ceteris paribus (se·tĕris pæ·ribɒs). [L.] Other things being equal, other conditions corresponding.

1604 T. Wright *Passions* Pref. A 4 b, Yet my meaning is alwayes, *cæteris paribus*, because [etc.]. 1659 Baxter *Key Cath.* II. iv. 445 General Councils of true Pastors *cæteris paribus*, are to be most reverenced by the Princes and people. 1751 Chesterf. *Lett.* (1774) II. 124 And *cæteris paribus*, a French minister will get the better of an English one, at any third court in Europe. 1887 W. J. Harris in *Nat. Rev.* Dec. 454 The wonder is that France is not in a far worse state than ourselves. *Cæteris paribus*, she ought to be, with her unsettled government [etc.]. 1907 W. De Morgan *Alice-for-Short* xxxvi, 'Would you guarantee her surviving the operation, Johnson?' 'No, I wouldn't! Nor your mother's either, *caeteris paribus*.'

Ceylon (silɒ·n). The name of an island in the Indian Ocean, used attrib. in **Ceylon moss** (see Moss sb.¹ 4); **Ceylon pumpkin,** a large pumpkin found originally in Ceylon; **Ceylon rose,** the Natal name for *Nerium Oleander*, the common oleander or rose-bay, a poisonous flowering shrub of the Levant.

1861 Bentley *Man. Bot.* 721 *Gracilaria lichenoides* or *Plocaria candida*, is our commercial *Ceylon Moss. 1875 *Encycl. Brit.* V. 508/2 *Gracilaria lichenoides*, under the name of Ceylon moss, is used for soups and jellies. 1913 Pettman *Africanderisms* 118 *Ceylon pumpkin*, a large, oval-shaped pumpkin with orange-coloured flesh. 1858 *Irons's Settler's Guide Cape G. Hope & Natal* 96 (Pettman) Lemon trees interspersed with acacia and oleander or the *Ceylon rose. 1868 Jas. Chapman *Trav. S. Africa* II. 15, I find that the Ceylon rose..is..the other poison with which the Damaras tip their arrows in war.

Ceylonese (silɒnī·z), *a.* (*sb.*). [f. Ceylon + -ese. (An earlier, now disused, form was *Ceylonian*.)] Of or pertaining to the island of Ceylon or its inhabitants, Cingalese. Also as *sb.*, an inhabitant or native of Ceylon.

This form is now in official use preferred to *Sinhalese* (*Singalese, Cingalese*).

c 1789 *Encycl. Brit.* (1797) IV. 310/2 The Ceylonese make use of boats hollowed out of the trunks of trees. *Ibid.* 311/1 The Ceylonese monarch was driven from his capital. 1836 *Penny Cycl.* VI. 457/2 The sailing of vessels at the Ceylonese ports.

Ch., abbreviation of *chapter, church*. Ch. B. = L. *Chirurgiæ Baccalaureus*, Bachelor of Surgery. Ch. Ch. = Christ Church (Oxford). Ch. D. = L. *Chirurgiæ Doctor*, Doctor of Surgery.

Chaack. [Imitative.] The cry of the jackdaw.

1906 *Westm. Gaz.* 9 June 13/2 With a little flutter of the wing and a cheery 'Chaack!' he hopped off one head on to another. 1907 *Ibid.* 19 Oct. 16/1 The cheering 'cha-ack' of the jackdaw is everywhere in the air.

Chabootra (tʃăbū·tra). *Anglo-Ind.* Also **cherbuter, chabootah, chebootura, chabootera, chapudra.** [Hind. *chabūtrā, chabūtara*.] 'A paved or plastered terrace or platform, often attached to a house, or in a garden' (Yule).

c 1810 Mrs. Sherwood in *Life* (1854) 369 We sat on the cherbuter till it was quite dark. 1827 Scott *Surg. Dau.* xiv, This splendid procession having entered the royal gardens, approached..a chaboatra, or platform of white marble..which occupied the centre. 1848 *The Eerie Laird* x. 111 The..*chabooteras* of Delhi. 1882 F. M. Crawford *Mr. Isaacs* x. 227 Some ryots had been called in to..raise a rough *chapudra* or terrace. 1895 Mrs. Croker *Village Tales* (1896) 154 He sat on his chabootra stolidly smoking his huka.

Chack-chack. [Imitative.] The cry of the fieldfare and wheatear. Also as *vb.*

1906 *Westm. Gaz.* 29 Dec. 16/3 The hoarse 'chack-chack' of the fieldfare. 1908 *Ibid.* 21 Mar. 14/1 Even if you only hear his [*sc.* the wheatear's] sharp note 'Chack-chack'. 1930 E. W. Hendy *Wild Exmoor* 236 Stonechats 'chack-chack' from the top of a spray.

Chackra: see *Chakra 1.

Chadband (tʃæ·dbænd). [A character, 'Rev. Mr. Chadband', in Dickens's *Bleak House* 1853.] A canting unctuous hypocrite. Hence **Chadba·ndian** *a.*, **Cha·dbandism.**

1908 *Daily Chron.* 4 Nov. 5/3 There is no Chadbandian caricaturing of the parson. 1923 A. G. Gardiner *Cadbury* 259 His dislike of narrowness of view and Chadbandism kept him free from censoriousness.

Chaddar (tʃɒ·dăɹ). *Anglo-Ind.* Also 7 **chader,** 7–9 **chadar,** 9 **chadder;** 7 **shuddero.** Variant of Chuddar.

1614 Chadar [see Chuddar]. 1622 R. Cocks *Diary* (1883) I. 109 Chaders, cambias, and buxshaws. 1634 Sir T. Herbert *Trav.* (1638) 53 He..clothes his naked body with a fine Shuddero or linnen reaching to his wast. 1876 *Cornhill Mag.* XXXIV. 335 Get a *chaddar* (cloak) to wrap round you. 1900 *Daily News* 16 Feb. 6/7 A Hindu woman actually needs but two garments, a skirt and a chadar, or veil.

Chæta (kī·tă). Pl. **chætæ** (kī·tī). [mod.L., ad. Gr. χαίτη long, loose, flowing hair.] = Seta.

1866 *Treas. Bot.*, *Chæta*, a bristle, the slender stalk of the spore-case of mosses; also called Seta. 1896 Benham in *Cambr. Nat. Hist.* II. 266 The chaetae or bristles are mainly used in locomotion. 1902 *Encycl. Brit.* XXV. 689/2 The Chætopoda are characterized by the possession of horny epidermic chætæ embedded in the integument and moved by muscles.

Chætigerous (kīti·dʒĕrəs), *a. Zool.* [f. Gr. χαίτη: see prec. and -gerous.] Setigerous.

1896 Benham in *Cambr. Nat. Hist.* II. 263 Chaetigerous segments. *Ibid.* 312 The peristomium is chaetigerous.

Chætognatha (kītɒ·gnăþă). *Zool.* [mod.L., neut. pl. of *chætognathus*, f. Gr. χαίτη *Chæta + γνάθος jaw.] A class of vermes, chiefly pelagic, occurring in all seas, the members of which have two rows of stout spines on the head and a single row of sickle-shaped setæ or jaws. Hence **Chætognath** (kī·tɒgnæþ) *a.* and *sb.*, belonging to, a member of, the Chætognatha; **Chætognathous** (kītɒ·gnăþəs) *a.*, pertaining to or having the characteristics of the Chætognatha.

1870 Rolleston *Anim. Life* Introd. 137 The *Chaetognatha*, an order of marine worms of small size. 1896 Shipley in *Cambr. Nat. Hist.* II. 191 *S[agitta] hexaptera* is the largest Chaetognath known.

Chætopodan (kītɒ·pŏdăn), *a.* [f. Chætopod + -an.] Belonging to or characteristic of the *Chætopoda*, an order of annelids.

1902 *Encycl. Brit.* XXV. 452 [Chætopoda, Echiuroidea, and Hirudinea] are generally admitted to have been derived from a common ancestor of marine habit and chætopodan type.

Chætotaxy (kī·totæksi). [f. Gr. χαίτη + τάξις: see *Chæta and -taxy.] The arrangement or plan of distribution of the bristles on the bodies of dipterous insects.

1893 E. A. Butler *Our Household Insects* 188 The plan of their distribution has been called by Osten-Sacken chætotaxy, i.e., bristle arrangement. 1903 *Entomol. News* 247 A careful exposition of the chaetotaxy of the Muscidæ.

Chaff, *sb.*¹ **7. b.** Add:

chaff-box, a chaff-cutter to be worked by hand; **chaff-halter,** a lady's bridle with double reins (Knight *Dict. Mech.* 1874); **chaff-scale** *Bot.* (see quots.).

1837 *Flemish Husb.* 89 in *Libr. Usef. Knowl., Husb.* III, The chaff-cutter is exactly like our common *chaff-box, where the work is done by the hand. 1908 *Essex Rev.* XVII. 24 A century or so ago, a handworked chaff-box was in almost daily use on every large farm. 1856 W. B. Carpenter *Microsc.* § 246 The hairs with which the *paleæ* (*chaff-scales) of most Grasses are furnished, are strengthened by the like siliceous deposit. 1888 *Encycl. Brit.* XXIV. 531 At the base of each spikelet [of wheat] are two empty boat-shaped glumes or 'chaff-scales'.

Chaff (tʃaf), *v.*³ *Bread making. trans.* To roll up (dough) into a rounded form in the moulding of a round loaf.

1892 R. Wells *Pract. Bread Baker* 44 How to mould a round loaf...Divide the dough into parts, having the right hand piece smaller than the left. Now chaff this into two round pieces. 1925 *Glasgow Herald* 9 Oct. 6 The loaf is shaped on the chaffing table.

Chaffy (tʃɑ·fi), *a.*² [f. Chaff sb.² + -y¹.] Given to chaff or chaffing.

1855 A. Macmillan in C. L. Graves *Life* (1910) 78 The comic 'chaffy' vein is very monstrous. 1875 Stedman *Vict. Poets* (1887) 24 The time is off-hand, chaffy, and must be taken in its mood. 1889 Mrs. M. L. Cameron *Lost Wife* v, He answered in the most 'chaffy' tone.

Chagigah (hăgī·gă). [Heb.] The voluntary sacrifices offered with the paschal lamb at the Jewish passover.

1846 tr. *D. F. Strauss' Life Jesus* III. 144 It [*sc.* the entering of a Gentile house in the morning] would have been such [*sc.* a disqualification] for the partaking of the Chagiga, which was eaten in the afternoon. 1891 Streane (*title*) A Translation of the Treatise Chagigah from the Babylonian Talmud.

Chain, *sb.* Add:

2. *Chain and ball*: see *Ball sb.¹ 1 b. Also *attrib.*

1872 E. B. Tuttle *Boy's Bk. Indians* (1882) 127 The fellow while in limbo sawed off the chain and ball from his leg and escaped. 1887 F. Francis Jr. *Saddle & Mocassin* 62 A chain-and-ball gang of convicts slowly advanced, sweeping the dusty road.

4. c. A number (of cigars or cigarettes) consumed in continuous succession. Cf. **chain-smoker* in 19.

1908 *Field* 19 Sept. 544/3 Mr. Travis smoked a chain of long black cigars during all his matches...Mr. Hilton used to smoke a chain of cigarettes.

5. e. *Chem.* The atoms of a compound assumed to be linked together by chemical force. *Closed chain*, a ring of linked atoms.

1881 Roscoe & Schorlemmer *Chem.* III. *Org.* I. 113 The atoms may thus be represented as forming a chain, one atom being linked on to the other, so that when one of them is removed without altering the position of the others, the chain is broken. 1913 J. B. Cohen *Org. Chem.* II. 137 The addition of hydrogen cyanide to aldehydes and ketones giving cyanhydrins afford an extremely useful method for the preparation of hydroxy acids containing an additional carbon atom in the chain. 1921 J. R. Partington *Inorg. Chem.* 391 Compounds containing chains of singly-linked oxygen atoms. 1928 Kingzett *Chem. Encycl.* (ed. 4) 131 Open chains are regarded as having terminal atoms not mutually in combination, by which, for example, aliphatic combinations, such as the olefines and paraffins, are characterized. *Ibid.* 132 In closed chains, the terminal atoms are regarded as mutually combined, forming a ring, as in benzene.

f. A series of branch businesses or stores controlled by one owner or firm. Cf. *chain grocery, chain store* in *19.

1906 S. E. Sparling *Introd. Business Organiz.* 205 A better illustration of the chain of stores operated by the manufacturer is the Douglas chain of shoe stores and the Lipton tea stores.

19. chain-bag, a woman's hand-bag made of fine metal chain-work; **chain-ball,** a projectile with a light body fastened to its posterior end to prevent its rotation (*Funk's Standard Dict.* 1895); **chain barrel,** a cylinder round which the chain of a hoist is wound; **chain-bearer** = *Chain-man; **chain-bit,** a horse's bit with a chain mouthpiece; **chain-brow way** *Coal-mining* (see quot.); **chain-carrier** = *Chain-man; so *chain-carrying*; **chain case,** the protective covering of the chain gear of a cycle, motor vehicle, etc.; **chain chest** *Naut.*, a locker in the channels for storage of wash-deck gear; **chain coral,** a kind of fossil coral, *Catenipora escharoides*; **chain dog,** (*a*) a dog controlled by a chain; (*b*) a chain having at each end a 'dog' or hook, which is driven into logs to fasten them together into a raft (*Funk's Standard Dict.* 1895); **chain-dotted** *a.*, (of a line) marked with alternate dot and dash; **chain drive, driving,** a method of transmitting power by means of a chain gear, esp. from the motor to the driving wheels of a cycle, motor vehicle, etc.; **chain-driven** *a.*, driven by means of chain gear; **chain driver,** a vehicle driven by this method; **chain fastening,** a sailor's bend or cable mooring (Knight *Dict. Mech.* 1874); **chain feed,** a 'feed' or feed-motion operated by chain gear; **chain gammoning** *Naut.*, gammoning consisting of a chain; **chain-gang** (earlier U.S. example); **chain gear, gearing,** a gear for transmitting motion by means of an endless chain; esp. one in which the chain transmits motion from one sprocket-wheel to another; **chain gemma** *Bot.* (see quot. 1900); **chain grate,** a device for feeding fuel to a furnace (*Cent. Dict.* 1889); **chain-grocery,** a grocery business of the chain-store kind; **chain horse,** a horse harnessed with chain traces, employed as an additional horse in drawing heavy loads, esp. up a hill; **chain inclinometer,** an instrument for indicating the inclination of a surveyor's chain; **chain knot** (see quot.); **chain letter,** a letter written with an invitation to the recipient to pass it on to another (or copies of it to others), these doing the same, and so on in a continuous chain until a certain total is reached; **chain messenger** *Naut.*, a messenger consisting of an endless chain; **chain pipe** *Naut.* (see quot.); **chain-pull** [Pull sb.² 6], a chain used as the device for operating an electric switch; **chain rivetting, road** (see quots.); **chain-smoker,** tr. G. *kettenraucher* (see quot. and sense *4 c); **chain-snake** (later U.S. examples); **chain-store** *U.S.*, one of a series of stores belonging to one firm and dealing in the same class of goods; **chain wire** *Paper-making* (see quot.); also in the names of various appliances of which a chain is an important part.

1902 *Westm. Gaz.* 29 Dec. 3/3 These glasses..can easily be carried in the modish silver or gold *chain-bag along with the handkerchief. 1888 *Lockwood's Dict. Terms Mech. Engin.*, *Chain Barrel. 1736 *Cal. Virginia St. Papers* I. 226 We do..appoint you James Thomas junr, Surveyor,.. To take three *Chain-bearers. 1798 *Deb. Congress 1807–8* (1852) 2741 You will see I have omitted taking those [depositions] of Mr. Gillespie and the chain-bearers. 1869 *Overland Monthly* III. 248 The chain-bearers signaling to those holding the ropes. 1883 Gresley *Gloss. Coal.-m.*, *Chain-brow Way*, an underground inclined plane worked by an endless chain. 1702–3 J. Logan *Let. to Penn* 3 Jan. *Corr.* (1870) I. 174 Neither surveyors nor *chain-carriers will go thither. 1798 *U.S. Statutes* I. 543 For compensation to the assistant surveyors, chain carriers, axe men and other persons. 1816 U. Brown in *Maryland Hist. Mag.* XI. 220 This afternoon hunts up Chain Carriers and an Axman or marksman. 1838 *Southern Lit. Mess.* IV. 307 The surveyor and two of his chain-carriers were killed. 1798 *Deb. Congress 1807–8* (1852) 2737 The surveying at present is done by Mr. Gillespie, the *chain-carrying by Mr. Ellicott and Mr. Walker. *a* 1909 'O. Henry' *Roads of Destiny* vi. 93 I'll..go back to chain-carrying for the county surveyor. 1907 *Westm. Gaz.* 9 Nov. 14/2 The Daimler Company..have designed their *chain-cases to act at the same time as radius-rods. 1909 *Ibid.* 17 Nov. 5/2 Detachable oil-bath chain-cases. 1884 Luce *Seamanship* (1898) 4 *Chain chest. 1808 J. Parkinson *Org. Rem. Former World* II. 20 The *chain coral (*Tubipora catenulata*, Linn.) composed of parallel tubes. 1842 Sedgwick in *Hudson's Guide Lakes* (1843) 223 The chain coral (*Catenipora*). 1871 Lyell *Student's Elem. Geol.* 449 The 'chain-coral', *Halysites catenularius*. 1895 K. Meyer tr. *Voy. Bran* I. 81 [She had] a large *chain-dog with her. 1878 Abney *Photogr.* 260 *Chain-dotted straight lines. 1903 *Daily Chron.* 20 Apr. 7/2 The *chain-drive is infinitely superior to the belt. 1907 *Ibid.* 17 Oct. 8/2 A 5 h.-p. twin-cylinder Roc, fitted with a Peugeot engine and chain drive. 1898 *Cycling* 59 We do not anticipate that for serious riding it will oust the *chain-driven safety. 1900 *Engineering Mag.* XIX. 740 Chain-driven heavy freight vehicles. 1909 *Daily Chron.* 22 Nov. 9/1 The new light Phelon and Moore is chain-driven. 1910 *Westm. Gaz.* 17 Feb. 5/1 The 65-h.p. and 75-h.p. six-cylinder *chain-drivers. 1888 *Lockwood's Dict. Terms Mech. Engin.*, *Chain Feed*, a mode of feeding balks of timber along to frame saws by means of an endless chain led around sheave wheels. 1883 *Man. Seamanship for Boys* 22 Gammoning Fish..are..nailed on the upper part of the bowsprit, in the wake of the *chain gammoning. 1841 C. Cist *Cincinnati* 261 The grandson of a general officer of the revolution..is a vagabond..on the *chain gang. 1874 Knight *Dict. Mech.*, *Chain-gear. 1902 *Daily Chron.* 5 Sept. 7/5 Another car stopped near Hickstead with a chain-gear mishap. 1897 *Daily News* 30 Oct. 5/2 A boy..got drawn into the *chain-gearing of the wheels. 1895 *Standard Dict.*, *Chain-gemma. 1900 B. D. Jackson *Gloss. Bot. Terms*, *Chain-gemma*, in Fungi, having the form of a septate confervoid filament, the segments of which are capable of growth; termed also sprout-gemma. 1928 *Saturday Even. Post* 12 May 59/2 Managing director of a big *chain-grocery concern. 1899 *Westm. Gaz.* 2 May 6/3 The great, strong, glossy *chain-horse, dragging the brewers', the carriers', the builders', the stonemasons', and other vans and vehicles. 1906 *Ibid.* 7 May 8/1 Now we have a request to establish a chain-horse on Surbiton-hill. 1874 Knight *Dict. Mech.*, *Chain-inclinometer*, a form of level in which the inclination of the surveyor's chain is indicated on a scale by the pointer on the end of the level. *Ibid.*, *Chain-knot. 1. A succession of loops on a cord, each loop in succession locking the one above it...2. A kind of knot used in splicing. 3. The loop-stitch in some sewing-machines. 1906 *Daily Chron.* 27 July 6/2 In 1896 Miss Audrey Griffin, of Hurstville, New South Wales, initiated a '*chain letter' with the object of obtaining 1,000,000 used postage stamps. 1928 *Publishers' Weekly* 10 Nov. 1982 The chain store idea and the chain letter are here being combined. 1883 *Man. Seamanship for Boys* 14 Parts of a Capstan, &c...An iron band fitted with teeth,..which enters the long links of the *chain messenger in weighing anchor. *Ibid.* 12 Q. What are *chain pipes? A. Apertures through which chain cables pass from the chain lockers to the deck above. 1911 *Chambers's Jrnl.* 17 June 475/1 Users of electric light..will be interested in a *chain-pull switch. 1888 *Lockwood's Dict. Terms Mech. Engin.*, *Chain Riveting*, rows of rivets placed in parallel lines, both in the longitudinal and transverse directions. 1895 G. J. Burns *Gloss. Techn. Terms*, *Chain riveting*, in this kind of riveting the rivets are placed in parallel rows in the direction of the stress, the rivets in adjacent rows being opposite each other. 1883 Gresley *Gloss. Coal.-m.*, *Chain Road*, an underground wagon-way worked upon the endless chain system of haulage. 1890 *Review of Reviews* I. 279/2 Bismarck is, or used to be, what the Germans call a *chain-smoker, that is to say, that he would smoke on and on an endless chain of cigars, lighting each from the ashes of its forerunner. 1789 Morse *Amer. Geog.* 61 Of the Snakes which infest the United States, are the following, viz... *Chain [snake]. 1875 *Field & Forest* I. 30, I observed..a reptile which proved to be the Chain, or Thunder snake (*Ophibolus getulus*). 1922 S. Lewis *Babbitt* iv. § 5 One of these cash-and-carry *chain-stores..cutting prices below cost. 1928 *Publishers' Weekly* 16 June 2449 Sales of five-and-ten cent chain stores..were larger. 1889 *Athenæum* 30 Mar. 409 There are stout wires, about an inch apart, called '*chain wires',..which run from top to bottom [of the mould].

Chain, *v.* **5.** (Modern U.S. example.)

1816 U. Brown in *Maryland Hist. Mag.* XI. 224 [But for the rain] I should Certainly have Caused this line on the river to have been Correctly run and Chain'd.

Chained, *ppl. a.* Add:

1. b. Of a book: Secured to its shelf, a desk, table, etc., by a chain in order to prevent its removal. Also *attrib.*

1846 *Wesleyan-Meth. Mag.* (Abr. ed.) Ser. IV. II. 255/2 What a hold he has of that great chained Bible! 1908 *Daily Chron.* 10 Jan. 6/7 The old chained-Bible table previously in the church of St. Mary Bourne..has been restored.

3. Also *transf.*

1871 Schele de Vere *Americanisms* (1872) 217 Chain-lightning..is generally..changed into *chained-lightning*. In both forms it is constantly applied to inferior whiskey.

Chainer (tʃē¹·nəɹ). [f. Chain sb. + -er¹.] **a.** One of a surveyor's party who carries the chain; a chain-carrier. **b.** One who twists material into a chain. **c.** One who tends the chain of a haulage system.

1849 Capt. C. Sturt *Narr. Exped. C. Australia* I. 323, I had sent Mr. Stuart and Mr. Piesse with a party of chainers, to measure along the line on which I intended to move. 1921 *Dict. Occup. Terms* (1927) §§ 03, 367, 399.

Chaining, *vbl. sb.* Add:

2. The action or process of forming a long cotton warp or chain into links for bleaching or dyeing. Also *Comb.*, as *chaining-machine*.

1909 *Cent. Dict.* Suppl., Chaining-machine.

Chainless, *a.* Add:

2. Of a machine, vehicle, etc.: Without chain gear or chain drive as a part of the mechanism. (Usually implying its former use.)

1905 *Daily Chron.* 17 June 9/2 Mr. Napier was the first constructor to use this chainless form of transmission for a powerful car.

Chai·n-li:ghtning. *U.S.* [Chain sb. 19.]

1. Lightning in the form of a continuous flash; forked lightning.

1830–33 Seba Smith *Major J. Downing* 37 I'm goin there like a streak of chain-lightning. 1852 E. Bennett *Mike Fink* v. 28/2 Or I'll jump right straight down yer throats, quicker nor a streak o' greased chain-lightning can down a nigger's!

1854 Shillaber *Mrs. Partington* 187 Chain-lightning alone could typify the glance. 1911 H. S. Harrison *Queed* xxiv. 311 A sensation closely resembling chain-lightning sprang up his arm.

fig. 1918 Mulford *Man fr. Bar-20* xiv. 141 I've told you he's dangerous, chain-lightnin' with his guns. 1922 — *Tex* viii. 111 A natural-born killer. They say he's chain lightnin' on th' draw.

2. A raw brand of whisky.

1843 Haliburton *Attaché* I. xv. 262 They hante no variety in them [*sc.* drinks] nother; no white-nose, apple-jack, stone-wall, chain-lightning, [etc.]. 1861 Lowell *Biglow P.* Ser. II. i. 64, I know ye ez I know the smell of ole chain-lightnin' whisky. 1871 Schele de Vere *Americanisms* (1872) 217 The worst of *lickers*..is called Chain-lightning, from its terrible strength and stunning effect. 1890 L. C. D'Oyle *Notches* 8 'Fine Old Rye Whisky', which was the well-sounding title which Old Hank was wont to affix to his bottles of 'chain-lightning'.

Chai·n-man. [Chain sb. 9.] One who carries the measuring-chain for a land-surveyor; a chain-bearer.

1717 *Jrnls. Ho. Repr. Mass.* I. 191 Praying, That he may have Liberty to take up, and lay out by a skilful Surveyor, and Chain-men under Oath, 150 Acres of Land. 1735 *Boston Town Rec.* XII. 124 Voted, That there be..laid out ..some Suitable Place..by a Surveyor and Chainmen. 1810 *Repertory* (Boston) 6 Apr. (Th.) Chadwick was acting as chainman. 1862 [see Chain sb. 19]. 1869 *Overland Monthly* III. 248 The only way for the chain-men to work along these cliffs..was by being suspended by ropes from above. 1921 *Dict. Occup. Terms* (1927) § 970.

Chair, *sb.*¹ Add:

1. c. A glass-blower's seat furnished with long arms upon which he rolls the pontil; hence, the gang of men consisting of the glass-blower and his assistants.

1845 G. Dodd *Brit. Manuf.* IV. 51 Another workman receives it and sits down in a chair having two flat parallel arms sloping downwards. 1890 W. J. Gordon *Foundry* 137 Every two crucibles supply one 'chair'. The glassworker's chair is practically his lathe. 1897 *Worc. County Express* 3 Apr., There were ten chairs at the works, each occupied by a glassmaker, servitor, and footmaker. 1902 *B'ham Daily Post* 2 Apr., Eighty is the limit number of strawstem wineglasses to be made in six hours by a 'chair', which consists of three men and a boy.

d. A chair in which a condemned criminal is placed when put to death by electricity: more explicitly *electric chair*. *U.S.*

1890 *Peel City Guardian* 9 Aug. 7/2 By half-past six o'clock..the electric chair and the foot-rest had been placed in position for the reception of the criminal. 1926 Cole *Blatchington Tangle* xiv. 102 The discovery of the murderer's handkerchief..was the means of bringing a most notorious criminal to the chair.

3. c. A chair occupied by a Welsh bard at an Eisteddfod, esp. one awarded as a trophy; also, a convention, now each of the four conventions, connected with the Welsh Eisteddfod.

1880 *Cambro-Briton* I. 36 He was placed, by the general voice, in the bardic chair, and invested with a blue ribbon. 1874 *Cassell's Mag.* IX. 431/1 The grand event of the whole Eisteddfod..—the giving of the Chair Prize. 1877 *Encycl. Brit.* VII. 791 The chair was a kind of convention where disciples were trained, and bardic matters discussed preparatory to the great Gorsedd... There are now existing four chairs in Wales. 1909 *The Eisteddfod* (ed. T. R. Roberts) 27 The earliest Eisteddfodau or 'Chairs' as they were then called,..were held under the patronages of the Princes of Wales at the beginning of the sixth century. *Ibid.* 36 The Gwyneddigion offered a silver chair to the bard who could write the best verses.

11. b. Also *attrib.*, as *chair-boy*.

1908 Chambers *Firing Line* ix, They went together in a double chair, spinning noiselessly over the shell road. *Ibid.* xiv, Their black chair-boy lay asleep under a thicket of Spanish bayonet.

15. *chair-factory*; **chair balance,** a weighing machine having a seat suspended from the spring balance; **chair-bard** [W. *cadeir fardd*], the successful competitor in the bardic competition held on 'chair day' of the Welsh National Eisteddfod; **chair binder** (see quot. 1921); **chair-car** *U.S.*, a railway carriage furnished with chairs (two on each side of the aisle) instead of the usual seats; also, a parlour car (see Parlour 6); **chair-carver** (see quot.); **chair day,** the chief day of the Welsh National Eisteddfod (see quot.); **chair-door** (see quot.); **chair drill** (see quot.); **chair frame maker, chair framer, chair matter** (see quots.); **chair-post** *U.S.*, one of the main uprights of a chair; **chair-rack** = chair-rail (*Cassell's Encycl. Dict.* 1882); **chair road,** a railroad having the rails fastened by chairs to the sleepers; **chair rusher, seater** = *chair matter*; **chair-table,** a table convertible into a chair or settle (Webster 1911); **chair turner,** a wood turner who specializes in chair legs, rails, etc.

1884 Knight *Dict. Mech.* Suppl., *Chair Balance. 1874 *Cassell's Mag.* IX. 431/1 The successful competitor will be installed as the *Chair Bard. 1895 *Daily News* 20 May 5/3 The chair-bard for this year of the Welsh National Eisteddfod. 1881 *Instr. Census Clerks* (1885) 53 *Chair.. Binder. 1921 *Dict. Occup. Terms* (1927) § 504 *Chair binder*, tacks hessian or other stuffing cover over padding of back and seat of chair and over webbing under seat. 1889 *Kansas Times & Star* 9 Oct., The Wabash railway..has added a new *chair car. 1901 *Westm. Gaz.* 11 July 6/1 A fire..partially destroyed a dining car and a chair-car. 1903 *Atlantic Monthly* Sept. 309 He had half slunk into a day coach, fearing to go into the chair car lest he should meet some one he knew. 1909 'O. Henry' *Options* (1916) 210 My chair-car was profitably well filled with people of the kind one usually sees on chair-cars. 1924 W. M. Raine *Troubled Waters* xxiii. 247 He..walked right through [the train] to the chair car. 1858 Simmonds *Dict. Trade*, *Chair-carver*, one employed in carving the upright posts and other parts of beds, arm-chairs, sofas, &c. 1921 *Dict. Occup. Terms* (1927) § 485. 1877 *Encycl. Brit.* VII. 792 The great day of the Eisteddfod is the '*chair' day—usually the third or last day—the grand event of the Eisteddfod being the adjudication on the chair subject and the chairing and investiture of the fortunate winner. 1906 Hardy *Dynasts* II. VI. vi, In addition to the grand entrance..there is a covert little '*chair-door'..for sedans only. 1908 *Daily Chron.* 5 Aug. 3/6 '*Chair drill', a novel form of exercise,..brought the programme to an end. 1827 Drake & Mansfield *Cincinnati* viii. 65 Six *Chair Factories, 38 hands. 1903 *Daily Chron.* 10 Mar. 10/4 Foreman required for large chair factory. 1897 *Daily News* 9 Mar. 2/6 *Chair frame maker. 1921 *Dict. Occup. Terms* (1927) § 473 *Chair frame maker*, **chair framer*, assembles parts of chair frames, prepared by woodworking machinist. *Ibid.* § 472 **Chair matter*; **chair rusher*; **chair seater*; weaves rushes, by hand, into chair seats or frames. 1788 *Amer. Museum* IV. 519 The snake was..about the thickness of a common *chair-post. 1872 *Congress. Globe* App. 578/2 They went out and got great big long brushes, as big as these chair posts. 1911 *Roxboro (N.C.) Courier* Nov., The snake was as large around as a chair post. 1895 *Westm. Gaz.* 12 July 2/1 In America the authorities assert that our *chair roads are not strong enough to stand their traffic. 1904 *Daily Chron.* 5 Jan. 2/7 He was a *chair turner by trade.

Chair, *v.* Add: **1. c.** To award the chair to (the successful competitor at the Welsh Eisteddfod). Also *ppl. a.* and *vbl. sb.*

1876 *Encycl. Brit.* V. 318 The chief of song was also called a chaired bard, because he was one of the fourteen entitled to a chair at court. *Ibid.* VII. 792 The chairing and investiture of the fortunate winner. 1890 *Pall Mall Gaz.* 11 Sept. 6/3 Tudno, the chaired bard at Bangor.

Chairman (tʃē·ɹmæn), *v.* [f. the sb.] *trans.* To preside over (a meeting) as chairman.

1888 *Pall Mall Gaz.* 11 Oct. 4/1 We refused to attend the meeting to be chairmanned by Sir William. 1897 *Westm. Gaz.* 29 Jan. 2/3 The firm Which is chairman'd by Masham at Manningham! 1904 F. Lynde *Grafters* xxiii. 293 It was late in the afternoon..that the Federative Council sent its committee, chairmanned by Engineer Scott, to interview the ex-general manager.

Chairoplane (tʃē·ɹoplein). Also **char-a-plane, chairplane.** [f. Chair sb., after *aeroplane, airplane*.] A roundabout with seats suspended by chains, the riders being swung round in a wide circle by the revolution of the machinery.

1922 *Westm. Gaz.* 3 Nov., 'Char-a-plane' victim. 1926 *Daily Express* 6 Aug. 3/2 'Chairplane' Tragedy. 1927 *Bulletin* 5 Dec. 7/2 A chairoplane erected on a fairground.

Chaitya (tʃəi·tyă). [Skr., relating to a funeral pile or mound (*citā*), sb. funeral monument, sacred tree, etc.] A Buddhist place or object of reverence or worship.

1875 *Encycl. Brit.* II. 394 Of the next two classes of Buddhist architecture, the temples (Chaityas) and monasteries (Viharas), no built examples exist in India. 1882 *Ibid.* XIV. 500 The peculiar Buddhist objects of adoration which we know as *dagobas* or *chaityas*. 1920 *Blackw. Mag.* May 622/1 Rows of pyramidical chaityas.

Chakra (tʃɒ·kra). [Skr. (cogn. with Wheel sb.).]

1. (Also **chackra.**) A discus or mystic circle placed in the hands of pictured Hindu gods.

1891 *Murray's Hand-Bk. India & Ceylon* 384/1 A small temple dedicated to the Chakrah, or discus, of Vishnu. 1903 E. Thurston *Anthropology, Marr. Cust. S. India* Bull. iv. 199 A few men are branded on both shoulders with chank and chakra.

2. A weapon used by a band of Sikhs who named themselves 'Akáli' or immortal: see quot.

1886 *Encycl. Brit.* XX. 111 The chakr or chakra is a thin knife-edged ring of flat steel, a severe missile in skilled hands, but not much used.

Chalan (tʃɒ·lən). *Anglo-Ind.* [Hind. *chalān*.] (See quot. 1858.)

1858 Simmonds *Dict. Trade*, *Chalan, Chillaum, Chulan*, a common Indian name for an invoice, pass, voucher, or way-bill. 1906 *Advice Note, Off. Supt. Govt. Printing, India* Voucher No. 5656 Payments should be made either by remittance transfer receipt or treasury chalan.

Chalazogamic (kælăzogæ·mik), *a. Bot.* [f. Gr. χάλαζα Chalaza + γάμος marriage + -ic. (Treub *Ann. Jardin Bot. de Buitenzorg*, 1891.)] Defining fertilization in which the pollen-tube penetrates the ovule by the chalaza. Hence **Cha·lazogam,** a plant characterized by this mode of fertilization. **Chalazo·gamy,** chalazogamic fertilization.

1894 *Times* 11 Aug. 11/3 Miss Benson read a paper upon the 'Chalazogamic Amentiferæ'..showing that..the pollen-tube forces its way through the chalaza in order to effect fertilization, and hence must be included among the group of chalazogams...Professor Vines..was inclined to regard chalazogamy as an adaptation. 1895 Oliver tr. *Kerner's Nat. Hist. Plants* II. 412 This type of fertilization has been termed *chalazogamic* in contradistinction to the more usual micropylar or *porogamic* method. 1898 tr. *E. Strasburger's Bot.* 492 According to recent investigations some undoubted *Amentaceæ* are also chalazogamic. 1902 *Encycl. Brit.* XXV. 436 The pollen-tube..may pierce the embryo-sac at the chalazal end or at the side (basigamy or chalazogamy).

Chalcid (kæ·lsid), *a.* and *sb. Ent.* [f. mod.L. *Chalcididæ*: see Chalcididan.] **a.** *adj.* Of, pertaining to, or characteristic of the family *Chalcididæ*. b. *sb.* A member of this family. So **Chalci·dian** *a.*^{2}, **Cha·lcidid** *a.*

1882 *Encycl. Brit.* XIV. 49 Parasitic hymenoptera of the chalcidian group. 1891 *Proc. U.S. Nat. Museum* XIV. 570, I know no case in which a chalcidid is a parasite of a proctotrypid. *Ibid.* 571 Chalcidid parasites of the Hemiptera-Heteroptera are very rare. 1893 ORMEROD *Injur. Insects* 16th Rep. 66 The little Chalcids were a species of Entedon. *Ibid.*, We should get no good by endeavouring to rear these Chalcid flies. 1895 *Cambr. Nat. Hist.* V. 545 In the cells of the same bee Newport discovered another curious parasitic Chalcid, *Anthophorabia retusa*.

Chalcidian (kælsi·diăn), *a.*^{3} and *sb.* [f. *Chalcis*, *Chalcid-* (Χαλκίς, Χαλκιδ-) + -IAN.] a. *adj.* Of or pertaining to Chalcis, the chief city of Eubœa. b. *sb.* A native or inhabitant of Chalcis. So **Chalci·dic** *a.* (L. *Chalcidicus*).

1649 OGILBY *Virg., Bucol.* x. (1684) 45 *note*, The Verses of Euphorion the Chalcidean. 1838 *Penny Cycl.* X. 60 While Alexander was absent in his Persian wars, the Chalcidians increased and improved their fortifications. 1880 *Encycl. Brit.* XI. 95 Naxos, founded by the Chalcidians of Eubœa (735 B.C.). *Ibid.*, The sharp distinction between Dorian and Ionian (or 'Chalcidic'). *Ibid.* XIII. 125 The alphabet used by the Romans is identical with that of the Chalcidian colonies in southern Italy and Sicily .. except the three aspirates θ, φ, χ.

Chalcolithic (kælkoli·þik), *a.* *Archæol.* [f. CHALCO- + Gr. λίθος stone + -IC.] Of or pertaining to a period of culture characterized by the concurrent use of stone and bronze implements. (Cf. *AENEOLITHIC.)

1902 *Nature* 6 Nov. Suppl. p. iii, The Neolithic vase-types ..merge insensibly into those of the earliest dynastic period, which was 'Chalcolithic' in character. 1912 J. L. MYRES *Dawn Hist.* x. 224 A long chalcolithic..phase, in which good cheap stone and bad expensive bronze were in use concurrently. 1928 V. G. CHILDE *Most Anc. East* iv. 98 All the elements that distinguish neolithic and chalcolithic culture..had been created in Egypt out of the common palæolithic heritage of south and north.

Chaldean, *sb.* Add: Also, = CHALDEE *sb.* b.

1897 J. H. BRIDGES *Life R. Bacon* iv. (1914) 74 Teachers for the three languages, Hebrew, Arabic, and Chaldæan.

Chalice. Add: **3. b.** A cup-shaped globe for diffusing artificial light.

1902 W. J. DIBDIN *Public Lighting* 406 Under them [*sc.* three arc lights] he put an opal chalice 12 ft. in diameter.

Chalicotheroid (kæ·likoþiə·roid), *a.* and *sb.* *Palæont.* [f. mod.L. *Chalicotherium* (f. Gr. χάλιξ, χάλικος gravel + θηρίον wild animal) + -OID.] a. *adj.* Of, belonging to, or characteristic of the *Chalicotherioidea*, a superfamily of ungulated mammals. b. *sb.* A mammal of this superfamily.

1889 NICHOLSON & LYDEKKER *Man. Palæont.* (ed. 3) 1373 The genus *Leptodon*, described on the evidence of a lower jaw with a Chalicotheroid dentition.

Chalk, *sb.* Add: **3.** *Black chalk*: see quot.

1886 J. W. ANDERSON *Prospector's Handbk.* 115 Black Chalk—a variety of clay containing carbon.

6. b. *To walk one's chalks* (earlier U.S. example).

1836 CROCKETT *Expl. & Adv. Texas* iii. (1837) 18 O! wake snakes and walk your chalks!

7. chalk-back day (see quots.); **chalk-mark** *sb.*, a mark, esp. a distinctive mark, made with chalk; *v. trans.*, to mark with chalk, esp. with a distinctive mark; to draw (a line) with chalk; hence *chalk-marked* adj.; **chalk period**, the cretaceous period (see CRETACEOUS 2); **chalk stream**, a stream flowing over chalk; **chalk talk** *U.S.*, a lecture or speech illustrated by chalk sketches made by the speaker; hence *chalk-talker*.

1851 *N. & Q.* 1st Ser. IV. 501/2 At Diss, Norfolk, it is customary for the juvenile populace, on the Thursday before the third Friday in September..to mark..each other's dress with white chalk, pleading a prescriptive right to be mischievous on '*chalk-back day'. 1906 *Westm. Gaz.* 27 Feb. 2/3 In Norfolk there used to be an annual 'Chalk-back Day', the servants hired at the September fair at Diss being marked with chalk on either jacket or dress to indicate that they were settled. 1860 3 THACKERAY *Round. Papers* (1879) 95 On the doorpost..is a little *chalk-mark. 1878 *Chambers's Jrnl.* 14 Dec. 791/2 The white chalk-mark on his [*sc.* a Brahmin's] forehead, which signifies his rank to the world. 1880 R. ROWE *Picked up in the Streets* 221 Rows of broken, dusty, *chalk-marked shutters. 1927 *Scots Observer* 11 June 2/2 A happy-go-lucky Customs officer chalk-marked my suit case. 1928 *Daily Tel.* 9 Oct. 8/2 He has to toe the line which I chalk-mark, otherwise out he goes. 1904 J. R. A. DAVIS *Nat. Hist. Animals* (1905) III. iii. 309 The toothless Pterosaurs (species of *Pteranodon*), which flourished during the *Chalk Period. 1829 ARNOLD in Stanley *Life & Corr.* (1890) 491 As gentle and as limpid as one of the clear rapid *chalk streams of the south of Hampshire. 1858 KINGSLEY *Prose Idylls* (1884) 50 In chalk streams the largest fish are found oftener in the mill-heads than in the mill-tails. 1904 E. F. BENSON *Challoners* xiv, The chalk-stream..was brimful from bank to bank of hurrying translucent water. 1906 *Macm. Mag.* Apr. 453 The chalk stream regions to-day are not fishing countries in the sense that Devon, Hereford, or Wales are. 1881 *Christian Miscell.* V. 40 His inimitable '*chalk-talk'.

b. In the names of butterflies and moths, as *chalk carpet*, *chalk hill blue*, *chalk pit* (see quots.).

1832 J. RENNIE *Butterfl. & Moths* 18 The Chalk Hill Blue (*Polyommatus Corydon*, Stephens). *Ibid.* 117 The Chalk Carpet (*Larentia bipunctaria*, Ochsenheimer). *Ibid.* 125 The Chalk Carpet (*Xerene procellata*, Ochsenheimer). *Ibid.* 230 The Chalk-pit Plume (*Pterophorus migadactylus*, Fabricius) 'frequents chalky districts'. 1927 *Daily Express* 14 July 5/5 The chalkhill and holly blues would make beauty spots among the yellow iris.

Chalk, *v.* Add: **2. c.** *To chalk* (a person's) *hat*, *to have one's hat chalked*: to allow, be allowed, free travel on a railway. *U.S.*

1823 QUITMAN *Let.* in *Life & Corr.* 78, I will 'chalk your hat' for the journey. 1881 A. A. HAYES *New Colorado* xi. 149 Twenty-five seedy, second-class ruffians, who proposed to travel, as they say in the West, 'with their hats chalked', or free. 1887 *Nation* (N.Y.) 21 Apr. 329/1 It would seem that all railway officers and most railway employees have their 'hats chalked' all over the U.S.

d. To put through (the customs) by making an official mark with chalk. *U.S.*

1892 'MARK TWAIN' *£1,000,000 Bank-note* etc. (1893) 258 In his first agitation he was going to try to bribe the postman to chalk it through.

3. b. To write *down*; to set down as a sum or estimate.

1835 R. M. BIRD *Hawks of Hawk-hollow* II. viii. 78 He chalked me down like a fool, me and Tom Staples; being old friends, or sort of. 1874 *Rep. Vermont Board Agric.* II. 618 The farmers on that committee were outwitted, for while they chalked from $25,000 to $30,000, others chalked from $150,000 to $200,000, a sum which nobody expected could be raised.

c. *intr.* To mount *up* in an account.

1878 MRS. STOWE *Poganuc People* iii. 36 But who's going to pay for it all? These 'ere sort of things chalk up.

Chalker. (Earlier U.S. example.)

1834 *Jack Downing's A. Jackson* 201 Mr. Blare..is one of the chalkers, and is nation cute at findin' out a false from a pretended friend. He markes in red all he suspects.

Chalk-line. a. (Of uncertain meaning.) b. A line drawn with chalk; see also quot. 1874.

a 1450 *Fysshynge wyth an Angle* (1883) 15 A good fyne lyne of þak thryde made yn maner of a chalke lyne. 1631 WINTHROP *New Eng.* I. 458 Store of shoe-makers' thread and hobnails; chalk and chalk-line. 1771 *Carroll Papers* in *Maryland Hist. Mag.* XIII. 173 Pray desier Mr Deards to send me by him two Drumlines... The Chalk lines are too weak & small. 1874 KNIGHT *Dict. Mech.*, *Chalk-line*, a cord rubbed with chalk or similar material, used by artificers for laying down straight lines on the material as a guide for a cutting instrument.

Challengeful (tʃæ·lendʒfŭl), *a.* [f. CHALLENGE *sb.* + -FUL.] Fraught with a challenge.

1903 HARDY *Dynasts* I. II. v. 52 And I only own—such is my challengeful character—that perhaps He [*sc.* Napoleon] do eat pagan infants when He's in the desert. 1927 *Chambers's Jrnl.* June 381/2 An interrogation..vital and challengeful.

Challengingly (tʃæ·lendʒiŋli), *adv.* [f. CHALLENGING *ppl. a.* + -LY^{2}.] In a challenging manner; so as to convey a challenge.

1907 A. BENNETT *Grim Smile Five Towns, Begin. New Year* i. 165 Toby gazed around, half challengingly and half nervously. 1921 A. S. M. HUTCHINSON *If Winter Comes* II. i. 67 His face seemed to say to the world challengingly, 'I am here!'

Chalmoogra: see *CHAULMOOGRA.

Chalukah: see *HALUKA.

Chalybeous (kăli·bĭəs), *a.* [f. L. *chalybēius* Chalybeian, of steel + -OUS.] Of a steel-blue colour; dark blue with a metallic lustre.

1826 KIRBY & SP. *Entomol.* xlvi. IV. 283 Chalybeous... The blue splendour of steel case-hardened, or of the mainspring of a watch.

Chamæ- (kæmi), combining form of Gr. χαμαί on the ground, low, used in anthropological terms, as **Chamæcephalic** (-sĭfæ·lik), **-cephalous** (-se·făləs), *adjs.*, characterized by or exhibiting chamæcephaly; **Chamæcephaly** (-se·făli) [Gr. κεφαλή head], a formation or development of the human skull, in which the cephalic index is 70 or less; **Chamæconchic** (-kǫ·ŋkik), **-conchous** (-kǫ·ŋkəs), *adjs.*, characterized by or exhibiting chamæconchy; **Chamæconchy** (-kǫ·ŋki) [Gr. κόγχη CONCH], the condition of having a low form of the orbits, showing an orbital index of 80 or less; **Chamæcranial** (-krē·niăl), *a.* [Gr. κρανίον skull], characterized by having a low skull, of a length-height index of 70 and less; **Chamæprosope** (-prǫ·sǫup) [Gr. πρόσωπον face], a human skull with a broad, low face; **Chamæprosopic** (-prǫsǭ·pik) *a.*, characterized by chamæprosopy; **Chamæprosopy** (-prǫsǭ·pi), the condition of having a low form of face with a facial index of 90 and less.

1902 *Biometrika* Aug. 462 Are the brachycephalic races hypsicephalic and the dolichocephalic races *chamaecephalic? *Ibid.* 460 In the male brachycephaly is associated with hypsiconchic, in the female with the *chamaeconchic character. *Ibid.*, A quite sensible association of platyrhiny with *chamaeconchy. *Ibid.* 462 Brachycranial, stenocranial, and *chamaecranial characters. 1900 DENIKER *Races of Man* 60 To separate skulls into brachy- or dolichofacial, or, as they are also called, *chamæprosopes and leptoprosopes. 190. *Buck's Handbk. Med. Sci.* VII. 231 (Cent. D. Suppl.) *Chamæprosopic. 1902 *Biometrika* Aug. 434 *Chamaeprosopy.

Chamærops. (Earlier U.S. example.)

1766 J. BARTRAM *Jrnl.* 40 The small palmetto or chamaerops.

Chamar (tʃămā·ɪ). Also **chumar.** [Hind., a. Hindi.] A member of a very low Indian caste whose occupation is leather working; a worker in leather, tanner, shoemaker. Also *attrib.*

1858 SIMMONDS *Dict. Trade.* 1899 C. W. DOYLE *Taming of Jungle* ii. 18 A wee little manikin of the chamar (tanner) caste. 1924 *Blackw. Mag.* Nov. 693/1 This little swine of a chŭmar.

Chamber, *sb.* Add:

4. e. *Chamber of Horrors*: see HORROR *sb.* 5.

9. c. *Lead chamber*, a seamless receptacle made of sheet lead, used in the manufacture of sulphuric acid. *Moist* or *wet chamber*, a circular glass dish with a glass cover for bacteriological cultures in a moist atmosphere.

1879 LUNGE *Sulphuric Acid* I. 261 That apparatus..in which now-a-days all sulphuric acid, except the Nordhausen oil of vitriol, is made, viz. the lead chamber.

13. chamber acid, sulphuric acid in the condition and of the strength at which it is removed from the lead chambers; **chamber arrest**, confinement in one's chamber under arrest; **chamber cantata**, a cantata suitable for performance in a private room; **chamber-closet**, a commode or night-chair for invalids and the infirm (Knight *Dict. Mech.* 1874); **chamber gage**, one used in verifying the size of a howitzer or mortar-chamber (ibid.); **chamber-gas**, the gas, or mixture of gases, contained in the large lead chambers used in the manufacture of sulphuric acid; **chamber kiln**, a kiln consisting of a series of chambers arranged in circular form, used for burning cement, bricks, and tiles; also *attrib.*; **chamber lad**, a bedroom attendant in chambers; **chamber man**, a man employed in or about a chamber, esp. to do the work connected with a manufacture by a chamber process; **chamber process**, a manufacturing process that is carried out by means of a closed or sealed chamber; **chamber-set**, a set of chamber ware; **chamber-work** (*b*) (earlier examples).

1872 tr. *Wagner's Chem. Technol.* 206 *Chamber Acid. As soon as the acid formed in the leaden chambers has acquired a sp. gr. of 1·5 = 50°B. = 140° Twaddle, it is run off into a reservoir. 1879 LUNGE *Sulphuric Acid* I. 296 At Oker each cubic metre of chamber-space yields 2·85 kilograms chamber-acid of 106° Tw. in the case of rich ores. 1903 *Daily Chron.* 19 Dec. 5/1 Frederick the Great, when Crown Prince, was not only condemned to *chamber-arrest, but actually flung into prison. 1905 E. J. DENT *Scarlatti* 9 The immense popularity of the *chamber-cantata during the whole of the seventeenth and the early part of the eighteenth century. 1892 GREENER *Breech-Loader* 137 Guns bored cylinder, and guns with sudden *chamber cones cause the shot to spread more irregularly than choke bores. 1879 LUNGE *Sulphuric Acid* I. 331 If..a straight tube is introduced..into the draught-pipe taking away the *chamber-gas. 1884 KNIGHT *Dict. Mech.* Suppl., **Chamber Kiln*, a brick or tile kiln in compartments; sometimes capable of being heated in succession. 1902 *Encycl. Brit.* XXVI. 630 The kilns most commonly employed nowadays [for burning Portland cement] are 'chamber kilns'. 1921 *Dict. Occup. Terms* (1927) § 092 *Chamber kiln man* (cement);..regulates supply of gas in chamber kilns. 1889 GRETTON *Memory's Harkback* 157 Sugden became *chamber lad to a conveyancer, where he picked up the foundation of his law knowledge. 1921 *Dict. Occup. Terms* (1927) § 148 '*Chamber man* (white lead); makes white lead by chamber process. 1879 LUNGE *Sulphuric Acid* I. 302 A very important assistance in judging of the *chamber-process is afforded by glass windows or sights. 1858 *Texas Almanac* Advt., Parlor and *Chamber sets. 1870 'FANNY FERN' *Ginger-Snaps* 20 Having done *chamber work or cooking, for such a number of years in New York. 1872 *Rep. Vermont Board Agric.* I. 311 Laundry, chamber work, &c., must be dealt with every day.

Chamber, *v.* Add: **4. c.** To contain or hold as in a chamber. Of a fire-arm: To receive in the chamber.

1835 N. WYETH *Jrnl.* 251 Building a canoe 60 feet long, wide and deep enough to chamber barrels, of which she will take 25. 1902 S. E. WHITE *Blazed Trail* xx. 141 Wallace's rifle chambered the ·38 Winchester cartridge. *a* 1904 — *Blazed Trail Stories* 163 Each was armed..with a brace of Colt's revolvers, chambering the same-sized cartridges as the rifle.

7. *intr.* Of a mining vein: To open up, expand. *U.S.*

1873 J. H. BEADLE *Undevel. West* xviii. 335 The miner starts with a vein a foot or more wide..then it suddenly 'chambers' to some size, then 'pinches' to the thickness of a knife-blade.

Chambering, *vbl. sb.* Add:

4. *Zool.* The formation of chambers or loculi. Cf. CAMERATION 2.

1885 *Encycl. Brit.* XIX. 846 The test has usually a chambered structure... The chambering of the test does not express a corresponding cell-segmentation of the protoplasm.

Chamberlainism (tʃē·mbərlĕniz'm). The policy or principles of the politician Joseph Chamberlain (1836–1914). So **Cha·mberlainic** *a.*, **Cha·mberlainite**, **Cha·mberlainize** *v.*, **Chamberlainiza·tion.**

1898 *Westm. Gaz.* 10 Nov. 3/2 Chamberlainic 'principles'. 1899 *Daily News* 20 June 7/2 There is a characteristic Chamberlainism in the last telegram published in the Transvaal Blue Book, dated May 24. 1900 SIR W. HARCOURT in *Westm. Gaz.* 11 Oct. 8/2 It was because the country had had a surfeit of Chamberlainism. 1904 *Spectator* 31 Dec. 1072/2 Though Mr. Balfour fills his Cabinet with Chamberlainites. 1905 *Daily Chron.* 12 Jan. 4/2 The Chamberlainising of the Conservative Party on Protectionist lines. 1906 *Ibid.* 20 Jan. 4/3 The Chamberlainisation of the party.

Chamberlet. Add: spec. in *Zool.*, a small chamber or division of the test of a foraminiferous animalcule. Hence **Cha·mberletted** *a.*

1862 W. B. CARPENTER *Microsc.* (ed. 3) 500 A ring of small chambers (or chamberlets) is formed around the primordial chamber. 1879 *Encycl. Brit.* IX. 376 *Fabularia*, a fossil.. in which the principal chambers are subdivided into 'chamberlets' as in *Orbiculina* and *Orbitolites*. 1884 *Amer. Jrnl. Sci.* Ser. III. XXVII. 328 The division of the chamber-segments of the body into chamberletted sub-segments.

Chamber-master. Add:

2. A furrier who obtains skins from the wholesale manufacturer and makes them up at home or on his own premises.

1901 *Daily Chron.* 4 Dec. 9/2 Chambermasters and cutters wanted for hare work.

Chambray (ʃe·mbrē). A kind of gingham with linen finish used for women's dresses.

1874 KNIGHT *Dict. Mech.* 1909 *Public Ledger Philadelphia* 24 June 5/7 Lawns, percales and chambrays.

Chameleon. Add:

6. c. chameleon moth, a S. African noctuid moth, *Actæa chamæleon*, of extreme variability in colour; **chameleon silk**, **tulle** (see quots.).

1848 *Chem. Rep. & Mem.* (ed. T. Graham) 230 The shot silk stuffs known as chameleon silks. 1896 *Daily News* 14 Nov. 6/5 One of the latest novelties in ball dresses is the chameleon tulle, composed of veils of different colours laid over each other.

Chamferer (tʃæ·mfərəɪ). Also **champherer.** [f. CHAMFER *v.* + -ER^{1}.] One who chamfers; *spec.* (see quot.).

1921 *Dict. Occup. Terms* (1927) § 200 *Barrel chamferer*; operates a chamfering lathe, to chamfer or bevel bottom edge or shield of metal bobbins [etc.]. *Ibid.*, *Chamferer, champherer*; a bolt facer or nut facer..who feeds and operates specially converted lathe on which bevel of nuts and round end of bolts are formed.

Chamfering, *vbl. sb.* **3.** Add: **chamfering-bit**, a boring-bit used with a brace to chamfer holes to receive the heads of screws; **chamfering lathe** (see quot.); **chamfering machine**, 'a machine for bevelling the ends of staves after being set in a cask' (Knight *Dict. Mech.* Suppl. 1884); **chamfering-tool**, a saddlers' tool for paring down the edges of leather.

1874 KNIGHT *Dict. Mech.*, Chamfering-bit, -tool. 1921 *Dict. Occup. Terms* (1927) § 200 A chamfering lathe, to chamfer or bevel bottom edge or shield of metal bobbins [etc.].

Chamisal (tʃæ·misæl). Also **chemisal.** [Mexican Sp., f. *chamiso.*] a. A dense growth or thicket of chamiso. b. = *CHAMISO.

1870 B. HARTE *Notes by Flood & Field* II, With my hand dipped listlessly over the thwarts, I detect the tops of chimisal, which shows the tide to have somewhat fallen. 1908 *Bureau Plant Industry* (U.S.) *Bull.* XII. 31 These chaparral areas..have become landmarks, the word chamisal, sometimes corrupted into chemisal,..being adopted as a local name.

Chamiso (tʃæ·miso). [Mexican Sp.] A Californian evergreen shrub, *Adenostoma fasciculatum*. Also *attrib.*

1889 *Century Dict.* 1904 *N. Y. Tribune* 17 July, One afternoon they located a grizzly, and ran him into a field of chamiso brush.

Chamois, *sb.* **3.** Add: The colour of chamois leather; hence *chamois-coloured* adj.

1882 [in Dict.]. 1898 *Daily News* 26 Sept., Chamois-coloured kerseymere. 1923 *Daily Mail* 26 Feb. 1 Gauntlet Gloves..in Chamois.

Chamotte (ʃamǫ·t). [Origin unknown.] Fragments of burnt fire-clay ground to powder and used with fresh fire-clay in making new vessels.

1890 THORPE *Dict. Appl. Chem.* I. 502 *Chamotte*, a mixture of fire-clay and burnt pottery used for making fire-bricks, crucibles, pipes, &c.

Champ, colloq. abbrev. of CHAMPION *sb.*^{1} 4.

1917 MATHEWSON *Sec. Base Sloan* xix. 262 We were the champs three years running. 1924 A. J. SMALL *Frozen Gold* vii. 159, I reared her myself from a couple of champs—last year's winners on the Yukon Championship Race.

Champa (tʃæ·mpa). = CHAMP *sb.*^{3} (q. v.), CHAMPAC.

1905 L. HOPE *Indian Love* 72 'Tis the scent of the champa's breath. 1908 *Westm. Gaz.* 23 Mar. 5/1 The chief perfumes are champa, cajuput oil, [etc.].

Champagne, *sb.* Add: Also *fig.* Something that exhilarates.

1896 *Godey's Mag.* Apr. 365/1 His candid devotion to 'small cold bottles' is unfailing champagne to the audience. 1897 *Westm. Gaz.* 23 June 2/2 You drink in the picture... This, you involuntarily cry, 'This is the champagne of the century!'

b. *champagne-coloured* adj.; **champagne-bottle**, a strong bottle of flawless glass with a long neck and sloping shoulders; also *allusively*; **champagne brandy**, a brandy most in repute of the cognac class; **champagne cup** (CUP *sb.* 11), a 'cup' of which champagne is the basis or chief ingredient; **champagne gas**, **-glass** (see quots.).

1858 SIMMONDS *Dict. Trade*, **Champagne bottle*, a strong and particular shaped bottle, which has the cork secured with wire, when holding champagne. 1901 *Westm. Gaz.* 2 May 3/2, I don't mean that champagne-bottle shoulders are in vogue again, but that the shoulder line is not at all square. *Ibid.* 24 May 3/2 A very handsome coat of *champagne-coloured cloth lined with silk. 1901 *Daily News* 4 Mar. 7/4 The refrigerant is to be carbonic anhydride, or *champagne gas. 1858 SIMMONDS *Dict. Trade*, **Champagne-glass*, a long, narrow glass, made for drinking effervescing wines from.

2. *attrib.* or quasi-*adj.* Of a colour: Like that of champagne (see quot. 1903). Of a material: Champagne-coloured.

1881 *Cassell's Family Mag.* 186/2 The colours..include.. the shade known as 'champagne'. 1893 *Ibid.* Apr. 304/2 The new coloured straw called 'Champagne'. 1903 *Daily Chron.* 21 Feb. 8/4 One of the colours with which women will be tempted..is champagne... It is a beautiful shade of pale straw, with a suggestion of pink about it. 1903 *Lady's Realm* Apr. 761/2 That pale biscuit colour which has been known..as the 'champagne' shade is now described as 'almond' colour. 1909 *Daily Chron.* 20 Jan. 6/3 A champagne dress.

Champagnize (ʃæmpē·naiz), *v.* [f. CHAMPAGNE + -IZE.] *trans.* To impart a champagne-like quality to.

1904 *Sci. Amer.* 31 Dec. 477/1 The apparatus is christened the 'Moussogène' ('froth-generator'), and is used by the inventor for champagnizing his wines.

Champion, *sb.*^{1} **5. c.** Add examples of extended use; also advb. (*dial.*).

1889 BARRÈRE & LELAND *Dict. Slang* s.v., An exemplary humbug is described as 'a champion fraud'. A noisy candidate for office was denounced by a Chicago newspaper as 'the champion gas-bag'. 1914 *Daily Mail* 1 June 3/6 'It was champion', he added. 1914 *Concise Oxf. Dict.* s.v., Champion idiot, blunder. 1923 *Daily Mail* 26 Mar. 9 'He cried champion', said a proud Yorkshireman.

Champlevé (ʃanlve, ʃæmplevē·), *sb.* and *a.* [Fr., f. *champ* field, *levé* raised.] Applied to enamel work in which the metal ground is engraved, cut out, or depressed, and the spaces filled with enamel pastes and fired.

1861 H. HAINES *Monumental Brasses* I. p. ix, These early enamels show the 'champ-levé', i.e. the copper is raised into ridges of partition between the colours. *Ibid.*, Like the field of a Limoges champ-levé enamel. 1874 H. H. COLE *Catal. Ind. Art S. Kens. Mus.* 144 Silver, inlaid with champlevé translucent enamel. 1877 tr. *C. Blanc's Orn. & Dress* 259 Champlevé enamels are sometimes called *taille d'epargne* enamels. 1880 *Encycl. Brit.* XIII. 679 In champlevé the enamelling substance is applied to the surface of the gold as ornamental details. 1906 *Daily Chron.* 3 Oct. 3/3 The chief seats of the champlevé work of the Middle Ages were the Rhenish provinces and Limoges.

Chance, *sb.* Add:

4. Often const. *of.* Also *pregnantly* = chance or opportunity of escape, acquittal, or the like.

1885 *Manch. Exam.* 6 May 5/1 A peace which is not cemented with blood has the best chance of permanency. 1888 BRYCE *Amer. Commw.* xciii. III. 296 In prosecutions for gambling or the sale of intoxicants a defendant had no chance before them [*sc.* a jury composed of women].

b. A quantity or number. Used with adjs., as *smart*. *U.S. dial.*

1819 D. THOMAS *Trav.* 230 (Th.) A considerable quantity is expressed by a smart chance; and our hostess at Madison said there was a smart chance of Yankees in that village. 1830 MRS. ROYALL *Lett. fr. Alabama* 121 There was..a powerful chance of apples and cyder. 1843 CARLTON *New Purchase* I. xiv. 107 She..pulled off what she called 'a right smart chance of rattles'. 1878 J. H. BEADLE *Western Wilds* xiv. 212 Fine chance o' corn planted, an' doin' well. 1888 'C. E. CRADDOCK' *Broomsedge Cove* xiv. 250 I've been huntin' guinea-hens' aigs...I fund a right smart chance of 'em.

c. A space of time. *U.S. dial.*

1845 W. G. SIMMS *Wigwam & Cabin* Ser. I. 45 Well, there I stood, a pretty considerable chance, looking and wondering and onoeknowing what to do.

d. *Cricket.* An opportunity of dismissing a batsman, given to a fieldsman by the batsman's faulty play, chiefly in phr. *to give a chance.*

1875 *Field* 8 May 458/3 The batsman..gave an easy chance to Mr. Grace off his own bowling. 1899 W. G. GRACE *Cricketing Remin.* 241 A matter of a few inches converts a chance into a boundary hit.

7. Also, *by any chance.*

1914 'IAN HAY' *Knight on Wheels* x, Are you engaged to be married, by any chance?

11. c. *To take chances*: to take risks.

1902 S. G. FISHER *True Hist. Amer. Rev.* 311 Washington thought himself justified in taking the chances rather than abandon New York without a blow. 1904 *N.Y. Even. Post* 24 Oct. 12 Passengers on stalled trains took chances with the third rail, and getting off walked to the nearest station. 1912 H. CROLY *Marcus Alonzo Hanna* 99 In the beginning he may have taken some long chances in order to accelerate the progress of the firm, but later his boldness was tempered with caution.

D. *chance-met* pa. pple. and ppl. adj.

1894 *Outing* (U.S.) XXIV. 418/2 A friend chance-met during a tour of the Pacific. 1907 *Westm. Gaz.* 13 Feb. 10/1 The pretty chance-met Scotch *ingénue*.

Chance, *v.* Add:

4. b. Colloq. or slang phrases. (*a*) *To chance one's arm*: to perform an action in the face of probable failure; to take one's chance of doing something successfully. Similarly *to chance one's mit.*

1889 BARRÈRE & LELAND *Dict. Slang*, *Chance your arm* (tailors), try, let it go, chance it. 1899 *Daily News* 13 Nov. 7/1 B. P. says 'to chance your arm' means to risk a court-martial which has the power to take all the pretty pretties off a man's sleeve. I first heard the phrase in 1886. 1919 *War Slang* in *Athenæum* 8 Aug. 728/1 'Chancing his mit' means risking a great deal, or playing a losing hazard. 1926 *Westm. Gaz.* 7 Jan., If such people as this defendant can chance their arm in this way, amateur sport is not going to be kept pure. 1927 *Daily Express* 10 June 9/3 Joanna [Southcott] seems to have chanced her arm, so to speak, in her prophecy of the end of the world, which she fixes as due to happen on June 31 next.

(*b*) *And chance the ducks* or *and chance it*: whatever the result or upshot may be; anyhow, anyway. *vulgar colloq.*

1886 *N. & Q.* 7th Ser. I. 108/1 I'll do it, an' chance th' ducks. 1924 B. GILBERT *Bly Market* 12 'Mackenzie Quick says the old man's breaking up.' 'He wasnt last Sunday week, and chance the ducks.'

Chanceless (tʃɑ·nslès), *a.* [f. CHANCE *sb.* + -LESS.] Without giving or receiving a chance. In *Cricket*, without giving the fieldsmen a chance (see *CHANCE *sb.* 4 d).

1903 *Daily Chron.* 27 May 5/4 A result made probable by the century of McGahey, a chanceless but hardly faultless innings. 1928 *Daily Tel.* 7 Aug. 12/7 The feature of the first day's play..was a chanceless century by I. Akers-Douglas, the Etonian.

Chancer, *v.* *U.S.* Delete *rare* and add earlier and later examples.

1684 *Rec. Crt. Assistants Mass.* (1901) 261 The plaintiff and defend[an]ts pleas as to the Chancering of the bond. 1692 *Acts & Res. Mass.* (1869) I. 75 The justices..are impowred to chancer the same [bond] unto the just debt and damages. 1709 *Rhode Isl. Col. Rec.* (1859) IV. 26 Judgement was given for the appellee, in that the bond should be chancer'd. 1761 *Connecticut Col. Rec.* XI. 547 Resolved.. that the bond..be chancer'd down to the sum of sixty-two pounds. 1903 *U.S. Reports* 466 The commissioner had a right, which he seems to have thought that he did not possess, to chancer the estimates.

Chancery, *v.* *U.S.* = prec.

1674 *Rec. Crt. Assistants Mass.* (1901) 21 The Court.. chanceried the damage additional to 40s. only. 1684 *Ibid.* 261 The plaintiff desired his bond might be chanceried. The Court..did chancery it to sixty-eight pounds.

Chancing (tʃɑ·nsiŋ), *ppl. a.* [f. CHANCE *v.* + -ING^{2}.] That chances. a. That comes or is present by chance. b. That relies upon chance.

1889 *Daily News* 7 Aug. 5/4 Mackerel are a chancing fish, and the abundance of them cannot always be relied on. 1896 W. WAKEFIELD in *Spectator* 31 Oct. 589/2 Each a chancing guest Unknown before, we tarried certain days. 1909 *Westm. Gaz.* 1 Apr. 8/2 'A chancing man.'..What is that?—He's a horse-dealer, and sells animals on chance as to whether they are good or bad.

Chancre. Add:

2. A disease incident to the tobacco-plant, said to be caused by *Bacillus æruginosus.*

1903 *Nature* 17 Sept. 492/2 On a bacterial disease of tobacco, 'chancre' or 'anthracnose', by M. G. Delacroix.

Chancy, *a.* Add: **4.** *Cricket.* Full of 'chances' (*CHANCE *sb.* 4 d).

1875 *Field* 8 May 458/1 Rumsey's long and very chancy innings.

Chandelier. 4. Add:

chandelier lily (also simply *chandelier*), a bulbous South African plant of the genus *Brunsvigia*; **chandelier plant**, a species of *Euphorbia.*

1818 LATROBE *Jrnl. Visit S. Afr.* 1815–16 165 We noticed here a gigantic species of a plant, from its singular form.. called the chandelier. 1837 *Scenes, etc., in Albany & Caffer-Land* 4 We..crossed a tract of land covered with aloes, called likewise the chandelier plant. 1871 *Cape Monthly Mag.* III. 122 (Pettman) A grand family of plants—the Amaryllidaceæ—of which our Chandelier lily (*Brunsvigia Josephinæ*) is an example.

Chang (tʃæŋ), *sb.*^{2} Also **chong.** [Tibetan *chaṅ.*] A beer or wine made chiefly from barley or rice.

1800 S. TURNER *Acc. Embassy Court of Teshoo Lama* I. ii, Chong is a slightly acid and spirituous liquor. 1887 *Field* 19 Feb. 243/1 The headman came out with jugs of 'chang' (a kind of beer made from grass). 1925 E. F. NORTON *Fight for Everest, 1924* 21 It was up to them..to take as many drinks of their chang as they could before setting out for Tibet.

Changa (tʃæ·ŋgā). A mole-cricket, *Scapteriscus didactylus*, native to Porto Rico, but found also in Georgia, U.S.A.

1901 *Yearbk. U.S. Dept. Agric.* 510 (Cent. D. Suppl.) The 'changa'..a kind of mole cricket, which has become very troublesome.

Change, *sb.* Add: **7. c.** So, *not to get any change out of*: to get no return or result from.

12. a. change gear, gearing by which changes may be made in the relative number of turns per minute for the driving or driven shafts of lathes and similar machines; **change key**, one adapted for opening only one set of locks, as distinguished from a master key; **change lever** = *change-speed lever*; **change pinion**, a pinion by which a change of speed is effected in a roving or spinning machine; **change point** *Kinematics*, 'a position of a mechanism in which a lack of constrainment causes the mechanism to transform itself into an entirely different, and usually simpler, mechanism, or into a pair of elements' (Webster 1911); **change-speed**, (*a*) mechanism for effecting a change of gear and thereby increasing or decreasing the speed of a cycle, motor car, or other machine; also *attrib.*, as *change-speed gear*, *lever*, etc.; (*b*) = *change gear*; **change valve**, 'a valve for admitting water under pressure into one or more cylinders of a hydraulic crane or lift, in order that the power used shall be proportional to the load' (*Cent. Dict.* Suppl. 1909).

1908 *Daily Chron.* 14 Nov. 8/6 This..gear is now equipped with a *change-lever. 1904 A. B. F. YOUNG *Compl. Motorist* iii. (ed. 2) 60 The *change-speed gear in its simplest and commonest form. 1907 *Daily Chron.* 17 Aug. 7/5 For the next [cycle] tour that I make in company I shall insist on all machines being fitted with the useful change-speed. *Ibid.* 11 Nov. 7/3 When the change-speed lever is pushed away from the driver, the jaw clutch engages the low gear wheels. 1922 *Times* 20 June 8/5 The change-speed lever provides four forward positions.., a neutral and a reverse.

b. *Baseball.*

1896 KNOWLES & MORTON *Baseball* 73 He..was attracted to the Baseball Park, where he was snapped up by the Fullers to play short-stop and change-pitcher.

Change, *v.* **8.** Delete †*rare* and add:

1842 LEVER *Jack Hinton* xxx, He changed all the splints and bandages to the sound leg.

Changelessly, *adv.* Add quots.:

1902 W. WATSON *Coron. K. Edw. VII* iii, And changelessly the river sends his sigh Down leagues of hope and fear. 1910 *Times* 21 Mar. 6 1 The axis round which the policy of the Austro-Hungarian monarchy changelessly revolves.

Change-over. The action or an act of changing over. a. Alteration from one working system to another. Also *attrib.* b. A reversal of the situation in affairs, of opinions, etc.

1907 *Westm. Gaz.* 26 Nov. 4/3 The fuel..will be paraffin, which will be used with Messrs. Thornycroft's patent change-over device from a preliminary start on petrol. 1920 H. G. WELLS *Outl. Hist.* 645/1 Now here was a change-over of quite primary importance in human affairs. 1927 *Glasgow Herald* 3 Dec. 11 A method of converting the station from the use of one wave to that of another within a far shorter time than at present occupied by the change-over. 1928 *Observer* 1 Jan. 10/2 Water engineers..said the change-over to river supplies must come about..in the next generation. 1928 *Daily Tel.* 6 Nov. 17/4 The change over on the Central Section of the Southern Railway from the overhead to the third rail system.

Changing, *vbl. sb.*^{1} **4.** Add: **changing note** *Mus.*, a note not essential to the harmony, as a PASSING NOTE, GRACE *note*, etc.

1876 STAINER & BARRETT *Dict. Mus. Terms*, *Changing notes*, passing notes or discords which occur on the accented parts of a bar.

Chank, *v.* Delete †*Obs.* and add recent U.S. examples.

1902 CLAPIN *Dict. Amer.* 105 *Chank*, to chew noisily. (N.Eng.) 1909 MRS. STRATTON-PORTER *Girl of Limberlost* xxi. 393 'Did they eat it?' demanded Wesley. 'They just chanked into it,' replied Billy. 1913 — *Laddie* iv. (1917) 75 The pigs..chanked up every peach that fell there.

Channel, *sb.*^{1} Add:

9. c. Short for *channel bar*: see *12.

1904 *Westm. Gaz.* 21 Aug. 5/1 Structural material, such as joists, channels, and other sectional bars.

12. channel bar, an iron bar or beam flanged to form a channel on one side; **channel bass**, the red-fish, *Sciæna ocellata*; **channel-board** *Organ-building* = *groove-board* (see GROOVE *sb.* 6); **channel cat** *U.S.*, a catfish of the genus *Ictalurus*; **Channel Fleet**, the portion of the British fleet detailed for service in the English Channel; **channel iron**, (*a*) = *channel bar*; also, the concave metal support of a rubber tyre; (*b*) a support for the guttering of a building (Knight *Dict. Mech.* 1874); **channel-leaved** *a.* *Bot.* (see quot.); **channel-section** = *channel-shaped section* (see next), in quot. *attrib.*; **channel-shaped** *a.*, shaped like the section of a channel bar; **channelward(s** *advs.*, in the direction of the Channel.

1904 G. P. NEELE *Railway Remin.* 219 Some *channel bars of iron on a down goods train..had gradually shifted. 1884 JORDAN in *Goode's Nat. Hist. Aquatic Anim.* 627 The common *Channel Cat—*Ictalurus punctatus*. *Ibid.* 628 The Channel Cat of the Potomac—*Ictalurus albidus*. 1888 *Boston* (Mass.) *Jrnl.* 17 People who like fish in Atlanta are eating..channel-cat and black bass. 1897 *Outing* (U.S.) XXX. 439/1 What the boys called 'channel-cats' were taken from midstream by long hand-lines. 1831 J. WATKINS *William the Fourth* I. ii. 36 The encounter of the *channel-fleet with the combined French and Spanish squadrons. 1904 *Admiralty Order* in *Times* 12 Dec. 4/1 The present so-called Home Fleet is henceforth to be known as the Channel Fleet. 1888 *Lockwood's Dict. Terms Mech. Engin.*, *Channel Iron*, rolled wrought iron bar, whose section is that of three sides of a parallelogram, used in bridge and girder work, and for structural purposes generally. 1895 G. J. BURNS *Gloss. Techn. Terms*, *Channel iron*, wrought iron of U-shaped section. 1860 WORCESTER (citing LOUDON) *Channel-leaved.., having leaves folded together so as to resemble a channel. 1910 *Westm. Gaz.* 22 Mar. 5/2 The motor..is mounted..on a *channel-section underframe suspended at three points. 1928 C. F. S. GAMBLE *North Sea Air Station* xxii. 392 These lighters..were built of steel... The general section was *channel-shaped. 1920 *Chambers's Jrnl.* 67/2, I waved my hand *Channelward. 1890 W. J. GORDON *Foundry* 96 The works grew..*Channelwards by the deposit of their own slag.

Channelization (tʃænĕlaizē·ʃən). *Neurol.* [f. CHANNEL *sb.* + -IZATION.] The formation of a channel of nervous conduction or discharge. (Cf. CANALIZATION 2.)

1902 *Amer. Jrnl. Psychol.* XIII. 405 The problem is how to give normal emotional channelization, the safety valve of this biological heredity.

Channeller^{2}, **channeler** (tʃæ·nĕləɪ). [f. CHANNEL *v.* + -ER^{1}.] A machine for cutting channels or grooves in rock in quarrying. Used chiefly with a qualifying word, as *bar-channeller*, one in which the cutters are attached to a bar or carriage; *rock-channeller*; *track-channeller* (TRACK *sb.* 13).

1897 *Review Rev.* Nov. 567 What are called channellers have been utilized.

Channelling, *vbl. sb.* Add:

1. b. A gutter to carry off rain water from a road or carriage-way; = CHANNEL *sb.* 3 a.

1892 *Times* 23 Mar. 3/2 There had always been a stone kerb and channelling across the so-called carriage way.

Chant(e)y (tʃɑ·nti). Frequent variants of SHANTY *sb.*^{2}

1883, etc. [see SHANTY *sb.*^{2}]. 1888 LAURA A. SMITH (*title*) The Music of the Waters, a Collection of the Sailor's Chanties, or Working Songs of the Sea of all Maritime Nations. 1896 *Westm. Gaz.* 17 Nov. 2/1 Their shining teeth and dusky faces,..their weird chanties. 1900 *Daily News* 9 Apr. 5/1 The British chantey, 'For he's a jolly good fellow'. 1906 *Temple Bar* Jan. 60 *The Chantyman*. The Crimee war is over now. *The Sailors.* Sebastopol is taken.

Chantlate (tʃɑ·ntlēt). *Arch.* [ad. F. *chanlatte*, f. *chant* narrow end + *latte* lath.] A piece of wood carrying and tilting the row of slates or tiles at the edge of a roof so as to throw rain water clear of the wall.

1895 in *Funk's Standard Dict.* 1901 STURGIS *Dict. Arch.*

Chanty: see *CHANTEY.

Chanukka·h (hænu·ka). Also **Chanukah**, **-cah**, **hanukkah**, **-cha.** [Heb. חנכה *ḥanukkāh* consecration.] A Jewish festival beginning on the 25th of Kisslew (November–December) and lasting eight days, held to commemorate the purification of the Temple at Jerusalem by Judas Maccabæus after its pollution by the Syrians.

1902 *Daily Chron.* 23 Dec. 5/1 The feast of 'Hanucha', or dedication, is celebrated by the Jews this year simultaneously with Christmas. 1902 *Jewish Encycl.* III. 665/2. 1904 *Ibid.* VI. 223/2. 1903 *Daily Chron.* 12 Dec. 5/2 The Chanucah Military Service is now an important annual feature of Jewish life in London. 1907 *Ibid.* 2 Dec. 4/6 As a military festival, Chanucah stands alone among Jewish celebrations.

Chapao, variant of CHAPPOW, a raid.

1894 MRS. DYAN *Man's Keeping* ix, He grew accustomed to the frequent chapoas [*sic*], or night attacks. 1902 *Nature* 28 Aug. 418/2 The 'chapaos' of the Baluchis have been checked.

Chaparejos (tʃæpărē·hǫs), *sb. pl.* *U.S.* Also **chaparajos**, **chaperajos.** [Mexican Sp.] Stout leather trousers worn by cowboys and others in the Western States as a protection against bushes and thorns. Freq. abbrev. as *CHAPS. Hence **Chapare·joed** *a.*, wearing chaparejos.

1861 TYLOR *Anahuac* 335 *Chaparreros*, over-trousers of goatskin with the hair on, used in riding. 1887 *Outing* (U.S.) X. 115/1 We had all discarded our *chaparajos*, and the horses were lightly blanketed. 1888 ROOSEVELT in *Century Mag.* Feb. 505/2 The broad hat, huge blunt spurs, and leather *chaperajos* of the rider. 1903 *Forest & Stream* 21 Feb. 147 A bit farther on we saw some cowpunchers, or what seemed such, for they sat in cow saddles and wore chaparejos. 1921 *Chambers's Jrnl.* May 321/1 The cowboy, lolling with his hands tucked under his chaparejos. *Ibid.* 322/1 A weird assortment of humanity filled the spacious room beyond—humanity bristling and *chaparejoed*, or *chaparejoed* and pomaded.

Chaparral. *U.S.* (Earlier example.)

1845 T. J. GREEN *Texian Exped.* vi. 59 Suddenly the head of the line was turned..into a dense and most difficult chaparral.

attrib. 1887 MRS. CUSTER *Tenting on Plains* (1889) 204 The chapparral bushes defeated us frequently, by making such good hiding-places for the hare. 1897 *Outing* (U.S.) XXX. 234/2 Sometimes the chapparral thickets made a wall of green on each side. 1920 HUNTER *Trail Drivers of Texas* 134, I walked all day with nothing to eat but chapparal berries.

b. **Chaparral cock** (earlier example).

1859 S. F. BAIRD *Catal. N. Amer. Birds* 68 *Geococcyx californianus*, Baird. Paisano; Chaparral Cock.

Chapati, variant of CHUPATTY.

1858 SIMMONDS *Dict. Trade*, *Chapata* (Hindustani), a thin unleavened cake of flour and water, toasted or baked over a fire. 1898 *Westm. Gaz.* 21 Feb. 4/3 All histories of the Mutiny relate that about the time of the outbreak mysterious 'chapatis' began to circulate among the people.

Chaperonless (ʃæ·pĕrǫnlès), *a.* Also **chapronless**, **chaperone-less.** [f. CHAPERON *sb.* + -LESS.] Without a chaperon.

1831 *Examiner* 5/2 Travelling and voyaging together, *solus cum sola*, chapronless. 1900 G. SWIFT *Somerley* 44 We see a girl, say, out boating, chaperonless, with a man. 1906 GALSWORTHY *Man of Property* II. ii, This evening .. was stolen, chaperone-less.

Chappprasser, **chapras(s)i**, var. ff. CHUPRASSY.

1858 SIMMONDS *Dict. Trade*, Chappprasser. 1879 MRS. A. E. JAMES *Indian Househ. Managem.* 44 The touts, or *chaprassies*, from the various hotels, will take your baggage. 1925 E. S. JONES *Christ of Indian Road* x. 210 They sent out the notices through government chaprasis, or runners.

Chaps (tʃæps), *sb. pl.* Short for *CHAPAREJOS.

1883 NYE *Baled Hay* 139 'Chaps', as they are vulgarly called,..are made of leather with fronts of dog-skin with the hair on,..the seat of the garment has been postponed *sine die*. 1885 *Harper's Mag.* July 190/1 His lower limbs clad in the heavy 'chaps'—or leather overalls. 1907 S. E. WHITE *Arizona Nights* I. vii. 126 His leather chaps were plain and worn. 1922 MULFORD *Tex* i. 2 His chaps of soft leather..have the look of long service.

Chaptalize (tʃæ·ptăləiz), *v.* [f. the name of the inventor of the process, J. A. *Chaptal* (1756–1832), French chemist + -IZE.] *trans.* To correct or improve the must, in wine-making, by neutralizing an excess of acid and adding sugar. So **Cha·ptaliza·tion**, this method or process.

1891 *Cycl. Temp. & Prohib.* (U.S.) 647/1 Chaptalization.., by which an excess of acidity is neutralized by adding marble dust, and the quantity and alcoholic strength is increased by means of cane or starch sugar. 1895 SADTLER *Hand-bk. Industr. Chem.* (ed. 2) 204 Chaptalization consists in neutralizing the excess of acidity in the must by the addition of marble-dust.

Chapter, *sb.* Add: **5. b.** A local branch of a college fraternity. *U.S.*

1882 *Alpha Delta Phi* p. xxv, This meeting [in 1836] after formally adopting the word 'Chapter' and disapproving of the words 'club' and 'branch', passed a series of resolutions. 1899 E. E. HALE *Lowell & Friends* 26 To this little circle somebody addressed himself who wanted to establish a chapter of Alpha Delta Phi in Cambridge in 1836.

Chapter-house. Add: **2.** 'The house or building which a chapter of a college fraternity uses as a club-house' (*Cent. Dict.* Suppl. 1909). *U.S.*

Chapterman (tʃæ·ptəɪmæn). [f. CHAPTER *sb.* 4 + MAN *sb.*^{1}] A member of the chapter of a monastic order.

1844 *Orthodox Jrnl.* 16 Mar. 175 The rev. deceased was a Chapterman. 1926 C. BUTLER *Life Bp. Ullathorne* I. v. 124 The General Chapter..conferring on him a titular office that made him a chapterman for life.

Chaqueta (tʃakē·ta). [Sp.] A jacket; *spec.* a leather jacket worn by Texan cowboys when travelling through the chaparral.

Char, *sb.*^{5} Short for CHARCOAL = bone-black.

1887 *Century Mag.* Nov. 113/2 The 'char' must be washed with hot water..and dried in a kiln. 1902 *Encycl. Brit.* XXXIII. 47 Vessels..of such diameter as to hold a given quantity of animal charcoal (also called 'bone-black' and 'char'). *Ibid.*, This..'sweet water' is sometimes..passed through the char filter.

Char (tʃāɪ), *sb.*^{6} *colloq.* Short for CHARWOMAN.

1906 *Daily Chron.* 7 June 3/4 We find him trying to gain a pension for 'Granny Deane', his ancient 'char'. 1919 C. ORR *Glorious Thing* viii. 89, I had to scrub the kitchen today, because the char couldn't come.

Char (tʃāɪ), *v.*^{5} [f. *CHAR *sb.*^{6}] *intr.* To do the work of a charwoman. Hence **Cha·rrer.**

1881 *Instr. Census Clerks* (1885) 114 Charrer..Charwoman. 1906 *Daily Chron.* 28 Aug. 8/5, I feel grateful to 'My Charwoman,' for it is certain she knows her business—she can char. 1925 *Contemp. Rev.* July 86 The scene where Lummox 'chars' in an immoral house.

Char-, the first element of CHARWOMAN, used in new formations, as **char-boy**, **charmaid**, **charman**; **char-lady**, a jocular substitute for CHARWOMAN.

1902 *Fortn. Rev.* June 1005 For wages..*char-boy £8. 1895 *Westm. Gaz.* 11 Aug. 8/1 She had a good post to offer to the *charlady. 1927 E. BRAMAH *Max Carrados Mysteries* 109 'The old party there'—a comprehensive nod in the direction of the absent charlady. 1882 *Cornhill Mag.* 337 Little *charmaids. 1888 *Pall Mall Gaz.* 10 Oct., The Guards' Memorial is now given over to the *charmen. 1895 *Macm. Mag.* July 201/1 The charmen (the men who sweep out the House of Commons).

Chara^{2} (ʃæ·rā). *vulgar colloq.* Short for CHAR-À-BANC. (Cf. *CHARRY.)

1927 F. E. BAILY *Golden Vanity* xv, I don't approve of them charas on the Kingswear Road.

Charabancer (ʃæ·răbæŋkəɪ). Also **-banker.** [f. CHAR-À-BANC + -ER^{1}.] An excursionist who travels by char-à-banc.

1920 *Punch* 11 Aug. 115/2 One of the hardiest 'charabankers' was recently prostrated in that village by a well-aimed epithet from the oldest inhabitant. 1927 *London Mercury* Sept. 451 One fine day perhaps the charabancers awake to the fact that what they came for is no longer there.

Character, *sb.* Add:

18. (Later example.)

1888 *Harper's Mag.* Oct. 678/1 Among the latter were many of the so-called 'characters' who..made for the West its popular reputation.

19. *character-building*, *-forming*, *-moulding*, *-training* sbs. and adjs.; **character sketch**, a brief description of a person's character; so *character-sketching.*

1888 *Springtime* Apr. 121/2 *Character-building is much similar. It is inward. 1897 *Westm. Gaz.* 30 Sept. 7/1 The present system of unregulated specialisation..ignores the paramount importance of character-building. 1900 J. CLIFFORD in *Daily News* 28 Nov. 4/4 Character-building literature. 1926 W. DEEPING *Sorrell & Son* vii. 69 They call it 'forming your mind'—character building. 1903 ABP. CANT. in *Westm. Gaz.* 22 Aug. 3/2, I want the fullest assurance I can get that one who is to help the children..regards the Book as..far superior in *character-forming power to the creeds of the Churches. 1910 *Daily Chron.* 25 Jan. 7/4 This..character-forming state can be keyed up by passion into an everlasting harmony. 1877 *New Dominion Monthly* I. 183 It is only *character-moulding,..for which we demand neither preparation nor a knowledge of the business. 1907 *Daily Chron.* 27 Aug. 3/3 The restricting and character-moulding nature of environment. 1885 *Engl. Illustr. Mag.* May 515 (*heading*) Wolseley: A *Character Sketch. 1897 LADY MARY LOYD & MISS F. SIMMONDS tr. *Gréard's Meissonier* 71 His charming character-sketch of this worthy is almost a water-colour. 1888 *Atalanta* I. 413/2 It is full of bits of *character-sketching. 1898 *Daily News* 27 June 4/7 The social side of *character-training is to be attempted.

Characterful (kæ·rĕktəɪfŭl), *a.* [f. CHARACTER *sb.* + -FUL.] Strongly expressive of character.

1901 S. DARK *Stage Silhouettes* 87 Archer..is a tallish man, with a military walk and bearing, and a strong, characterful face. 1905 W. J. LOCKE *Usurper* ii. 22 The writing was dainty, feminine, characterful.

Characterology (kæ·rĕktərǫ·lŏdʒi). *U.S.* [f. CHARACTER *sb.* + -OLOGY.] The science that deals with the study of character.

1903 *Amer. Jrnl. Psychol.* July–Oct. 356 An iconoclastic attitude towards all attempts at practical characterology. 1920 L. H. MCCORMICK (*title*) Characterology; an Exact Science.

Char-a-plane: see *CHAIROPLANE.

Charbon. Add:

3. A fungoid disease incident to the vine, and to orange and lemon trees.

1882 *Encycl. Brit.* XIV. 437/2 In damp valleys it [*sc.* the lemon] is liable to be attacked by a fungus called 'charbon' (*Dematium monophyllum*). 1888 *Ibid.* XXIV. 240/1 Anthracnose is the name usually given to a disease which was formerly known as 'charbon'.

Charcoal, *sb.* Add:

1. d. used attrib. in the names of foods or preparations containing wood-charcoal as an anti-fermentative, absorbent, or deodorizer.

1885 *Army & Navy Co-op. Soc. Price List* 759 Bragg's Charcoal Biscuits.

Charcoaling (tʃā·ɪkōʊliŋ), *vbl. sb.* [f. CHARCOAL *v.* + -ING^{1}.] Suffocation with the fumes of charcoal.

1888 *Buck's Handbk. Med. Sci.* VI. 679/2 An account of a 'wholesale charcoaling', in which a father, mother, and two children sought death in this way.

Charcutier (ʃarkütye). [Fr., f. †*char* (= *chair*) *cuite* cooked flesh.] A pork-butcher; a preparer or vendor of **Charcuterie** (ʃarkütri), pork, ham, sausages, black and white puddings, and the like.

1858 SIMMONDS *Dict. Trade*, *Charcuterie*...dressed hams, cold meats and fowls, tongues, sausages, etc. 1903 P. MCNEILL *Egregious Engl.* 152 Inferior cuts of butcher's meat with charcuterie and dried fish thrown in. 1906 *Daily Chron.* 10 Sept. 4/6 Charcutiers and preparers of cooked viands. 1921 *Dict. Occup. Terms* (1927) § 770 Butcher, pork; charcutier.

Chardonnet (ʃardo·ne). The name of the French inventor, Hilaire de *Chardonnet* (1839–1924), of a process for producing an artificial silk from a nitro-cellulose substance, used *attrib.* in *Chardonnet process*, *silk*.

1893 *Jrnl. Soc. Arts* 12 May 649/1 The Chardonnet process of making silk from wood-pulp. *Ibid.* 650/2 Reducing the inflammability of the Chardonnet silk. 1925 *Good Housekeeping* Apr. 142/2 Chardonnet silk, made from cotton treated much as in the making of gun-cotton. 1926 *Chambers's Jrnl.* 725/2 The nitro-cellulose or Chardonnet process.

Charge, *sb.* Add:

10. b. (Earlier U.S. example.)

1817 S. R. BROWN *Western Gaz.* 90 The taverns are well kept, and charges reasonable.

13. Also, *to take charge*: colloq. (of a thing) to get out of control and act automatically, esp. with disastrous or destructive effect.

1890 *Daily News* 16 June 3/8 A seven-inch steel breech-loading gun 'took charge' in firing, and both gun and carriage were blown off the platform. 1897 *Ibid.* 23 Feb. 7/6 A large party of men were pulling the tackle, when suddenly the spar 'took charge', and swung back.

20. *Comb.* (in sense 4), as *charge mixer*, *moulder*, *putter-up*; **charge account** *U.S.*, a credit account at a store; **charge book**, a book containing the statements of the charges brought against prisoners in a police court; **charge engineer**, the engineer in charge of the engines and machinery at an electric power station; **charge hand**, a workman, in various trades, who is in charge of the work under the general supervision of a foreman; **charge house**, (*a*) a building in which prisoners are detained on a certain charge; (*b*) a workshop in which explosive is loaded into shells, etc., in an explosive factory, also *attrib.*; **charge-man**, also, a workman who controls the supply of materials to a furnace, machine, etc. in a workshop or factory; **charge-room**, the room, at a police-station, in which the charge against an arrested person is made and entered in the charge book or sheet.

1909 'O. HENRY' *Options* (1916) 96 I've got more power here than..a charge of dynamite, and a *charge account at Tiffany's combined. 1890 *Daily News* 18 Sept. 2/5 Sir Andrew Lusk made an entry in the *charge-book of the prisoner's death. 1907 *Install. News* Sept. 16/2 Young gentleman.. desires engagement as *charge engineer of private plant. 1921 *Dict. Occup. Terms* (1927) § 591 *Painter's foreman*..; 'charge hand'; is in charge of painters on a job. *Ibid.* § 691 *Charge hand* (electricity supply); a turbine or engine driver who is directly responsible to charge engineer for operation of turbine plant, [etc.]. 1922 G. T. TURNER & WOOD *Man. Up-to-date Organisation* 171 Charge hand is an operator having supervision of a section. 1925 *Glasgow Herald* 21 Sept. 12 A charge hand at a piano factory. 1900 *Daily News* 14 Aug. 5/4 Three hundred and eighty suspected persons found themselves lodged in the fort. Another four hundred and fifty.. in the *charge-house. 1921 *Dict. Occup. Terms* (1927) § 140 *Charge house man* (gunpowder),..wheels bogies (small trucks) of raw materials..between stores and scattered workshops of explosive factory. *Ibid.* § 091 **Charge man*; (i) (patent fuel) is in charge of operations in manufacturing patent fuel; [etc.]; (ii) (salt works) is responsible for regulating supply of steam, brine, etc. *Ibid.* § 279 *Charge man* (copper smelting)..; charges blast furnace, or cupola,..under direction of cupola furnace-man. *Ibid.*, **Charge mixer* (zinc); weighs charges (blende, calamine, anthracite, salt, etc.) and loads into barrow; pushes barrow to bin of mixing machine and tips in contents. 1881 *Instr. Census Clerks* (1885) 59 Gun Cotton Manufacture:..*Charge..Moulder. 1921 *Dict. Occup. Terms* (1927) § 148 *Charge moulder* (explosive)..; feeds and attends a machine which expresses cordite paste..through holes in a cylindrical die, forming a cord, tape or stick. 1921 *Dict. Occup. Terms* (1927) § 279 **Charge putter-up*; piles up near heating furnace puddled bars ready to be rolled into finished bars. 1906 *Westm. Gaz.* 23 Oct. 5/1 She was taken back to the *charge-room.

Charge, *v.* Add:

15. d. *absol.* or *intr.* To bring a charge.

1891 *Spectator* 2 May, If she can but get the High Court of Justice to charge on her side. 1929 *Publishers' Weekly* (N.Y.) 19 Oct. 1935/2 Thompson charged that McAndrew was the 'king's stool pigeon'.

Chargé. (Earlier examples.)

1768 CHESTERF. *Lett. Son* 12 Apr., Keith is rather inclined to go to Turin, as *Chargé d'Affaires*. 1783 J. ADAMS *Wks.* (1853) VIII. 130 In conversation yesterday with M. d'Asp, the *chargé des affaires* in Sweden. 1819 *U.S. Statutes* III. 501 The chargé des affaires at London, the Hague, and Stockholm.

Charger^{2}. Add:

6. b. A device for loading the magazine of a rifle. Also *attrib.* and *Comb.*, as *charger-loading*, *system.*

1902 *Encycl. Brit.* XXXII. 651/2 The charger, used in the Mauser system,..is placed over the top of the magazine, and all the cartridges in it pushed by one motion into the magazine. 1904 *Westm. Gaz.* 9 Dec. 7/2 The charger system of loading was also recommended. 1909 in *Hansard's Parlt. Deb.* X. 339/1 The charger-loading rifle.

Charging, *vbl. sb.* Add:

b. *attrib.* and *Comb.* in the names of appliances connected with the charging of a furnace, gas retort, battery, blast-hole, etc., as *charging barrow*, *door*, *shop*, *spoon*, etc.

1884 KNIGHT *Dict. Mech.* Suppl., **Charging Barrow*, a double-wheel barrow, for use in iron furnaces for conveyance of coal, coke, limestone, and ore, to be dumped in at the tunnel-head of the blast furnace. 1908 *Westm. Gaz.* 6 Aug. 7/3 The *charging-door in the furnace. 1895 *Daily News* 25 July 3/5 In one of these erections, known as a *charging 'shop'..the explosion happened. 1894 C. LE N. FOSTER *Ore & Stone Mining* 161 The *charging-spoon is a hollow half-cylinder of copper or zinc, at the end of a copper or wooden rod, which is used for introducing loose gunpowder into holes which are more or less horizontal.

Chariot, *sb.* Add:

1. a. (Later U.S. example.)

1849 *Presid. Mess. Congress* II. 460 [The ore] is sent down on a chariot which runs upon a tram-road to the platform.

4. b. A rotating piece of mechanism in a Hughes type-printing telegraph (see quot.).

1876 PREECE & SIVEWRIGHT *Telegraphy* 90 When one of these keys is depressed a pin is raised, which just catches a 'chariot'..rotating with the type wheel, and thus sends a current to the distant station.

c. A part of the mechanism of a stage (see quot.).

1902 *Encycl. Brit.* XXXII. 823 Each section [of the stage] is equipped with what is termed a pair of chariots, to hold 'wing' lights placed on so-called wing ladders.

5. chariot plane, a small smoothing plane used for internal angles and small work.

1909 P. A. WELLS & HOOPER *Mod. Cabinet Work* ii. 9.

Chariotee. *U.S.* (Example.)

1867 T. LACKLAND *Homespun* I. 128 The grand family wagon,—a cross between a hay-cart and a chariotee.

Charisma (kări·zmă). *Theol.* Pl. **charismata** (kări·zmătă). [Gr. χάρισμα, pl. -ατα: see CHARISM.] = CHARISM.

a 1641, 1876 charismata [see CHARISM]. 1875 *Encycl. Brit.* III. 823 Schleiermacher was accustomed to say of Bleek that he possessed a special *charisma* for the science of 'Introduction'. 1885 *Ibid.* XIX. 675 As yet the church constitution was not determined by the idea of office alone, that of *charismata* (spiritual gifts) still having wide scope alongside of the other. 1920 J. A. ROBERTSON *Hidden Romance N. T.* v. 101 He himself had the *charisma*, or spiritual gift of utterance. 1921 *Glasgow Herald* 22 Jan. 4 Not that I mean to countenance for one moment the foolish notion that any art is a charisma that needs no discipline.

Charitarian. (Recent U.S. example.)

1930 *Time* (U.S.) 17 Mar. 38/2 He is not so lavish a charitarian as was Brother-in-Law Bok.

Chariva·ri, *v.* [f. the sb.] *trans.* To assail with a charivari.

1900 SMITHWICK *Evol. State* 72 The boys went..to charivari them.

Charka (tʃɜ̄·ɪkă). Also **churka.** [Hind. *charkhah*, *charkhā* spinning-wheel (Skr. *cakrá*-WHEEL).] A roller cotton gin formerly much used in India.

1880 MARKHAM *Peru* 122 A machine..very like the Indian *churka*. 1888 *Encycl. Brit.* XXIV. 730/2 Such was the first spinning wheel which, in the form of the 'charka', has long been known in the East Indies. 1925 *Spectator* 6 Feb. 214/2 Gandhi..bade India spin cotton on the *charka*.

Charlady: see *CHAR-.

Charleston (tʃā·ɪlztən). The capital city of Charleston county, S. Carolina, U.S., used as the name of a dance characterized by side kicks from the knee. Hence **Charleston** *v. intr.*, to dance the Charleston.

1926 *Glasgow Herald* 7 June 8 In these days of fox trots and Charlestons it is refreshing to watch such clean dancing. 1927 *Punch* 9 Feb. 168/1 Charlestoning nymphs. 1927 *Observer* 6 Mar. 13/5 The 'Standstill' Charleston. The new Charleston step is going to be very much in favour in the crowded club and restaurant ballrooms... I have seen it done with a straight foot, in the 'flat Charleston' way. 1928 GALSWORTHY *Swan Song* II. xii. 210 They found a Charleston in progress, seven couples wobbling weak knees at each other in various corners of the room.

Charley. Add:

4. *Army slang.* (See quot.)

1919 *War Terms* in *Athenæum* 1 Aug. 695/1 'Old Charlie', the pack—an Old Army phrase now dying out, I think. *Ibid.* 8 Aug. 727/2 The infantryman's pack was his 'Charlie', his haversack was a 'Young' or 'Little Charlie'.

Charleyhorse (tʃā·ɪlihǫɪs). *U.S. slang.* Stiffness of the arms and legs in baseball players.

1901 DORLAND *Med. Dict.* (ed. 2).

Charlton white. A house-painters' pigment consisting of barium and strontium sulphates with zinc sulphide.

1885 *Encycl. Brit.* XIX. 86 Under the name of Charlton White or silicate paints, Mr. J. B. Orr prepares a range of white paints which have come into extensive use.

Charm, *sb.*^{1} Add: **1. c.** *Like a charm*: wonderfully, perfectly. Also *to a charm.*

1845 *Niles' Reg.* 25 Oct. 128/1 The new rig works to a charm. 1882 *Philad. Press* 19 Mar. (Th.) The freezing-out process was applied by Mr. Bliss to Cook, and it worked like a charm.

Charmaid, **Charman**: see *CHAR-.

Charmante (ʃā·ɪmant). [Fr., fem. of *charmant*, prop. pres. pple. of *charmer* to CHARM.] A silk fabric with a satin face and a heavy crêpe back. Also *satin charmante.*

1922 *Westm. Gaz.* 27 Dec. (Advt.), Satin charmante... For Day and Evening wear. 1923 *Weekly Dispatch* 8 Apr. 12 Charmante... Rich Crepe back quality. In the newest Spring shades.

Charmelaine (ʃā·ɪmĕlēⁱn). Also **charmaline.** [f. F. *charme* CHARM *sb.*^{1} + *laine* wool.] A dress material of artificial silk and wool.

1923 *Daily Mail* 5 Feb. 1 Charmaline, a rich fabric of Artificial Silk and Wool, suitable for Day and Evening Dresses. 1923 *Weekly Dispatch* 8 Apr. 12 Crepe Charmaline. 1927 *Westm. Gaz.* 24 Jan., Charmelaine in thirty-eight shades.

Charmeuse (ʃā·ɪmöz). [Fr., fem. of *charmeur*, agent-n. of *charmer* to CHARM.] A soft smooth silk fabric, having a satin-like surface. Also *attrib.*

1907 *Daily Chron.* 25 Nov. 4/5 The bride is to wear a wonderful robe of soft white satin 'Charmeuse'. 1908 *Westm. Gaz.* 31 Oct. 15/3 The sleeves of the charmeuse frock may be carried out in chiffon or net. 1922 *Daily Mail* 17 Nov. 8 Princess Louise, Duchess of Argyll, wearing embroidered black charmeuse.

Charmlessly (tʃā·ɪmlèsli), *adv.* [f. CHARMLESS *a.* + -LY^{2}.] In a charmless manner, without charm. So **Cha·rmlessness**, charmless condition.

1889 J. M. ROBERTSON *Ess. towards Crit. Meth.* 74 The Pope school strikes charmlessly on our sense. 1908 *Daily Chron.* 10 Nov. 4/4 One wonders whether the historic associations of the Mansion House will counterbalance its gloom and charmlessness. 1926 *Glasgow Herald* 29 Apr. 4 The most charmlessly didactic story that ever was written by the author of 'War and Peace'.

Charrer: see *CHAR *v.*^{5}

Charry. *colloq.* Variant of *CHARA^{2}.

1926 *Brit. Weekly* 1 July 267/2 The motor-omnibus..is another formidable competitor to the 'charry'.

Chart, *sb.* **1. b.** Add: *attrib.* **chart-house**, **-room**, an apartment, in a ship, in which the charts, navigating instruments, etc., are kept.

1895 *Daily News* 18 July 6/1 When the signals were hoisted he was on the top of the fore *charthouse. 1907 *Daily Chron.* 10 Aug. 4/4 The chart-house door. 1877 W. THOMSON *Voy. Challenger* I. i. 11 The *Chart-room..with ranges of shelves stocked with charts and hydrographic, magnetic, and meteorological instruments. 1896 *Westm. Gaz.* 23 June 9/1 During the thick weather he had been having his meals in the chart-room forward.

Charter, *sb.*^{1} **5.** Add: **charter hand** = COURT-HAND.

1888 J. H. HESSELS in *Encycl. Brit.* XXIII. 682/1 The court or charter hand was used for charters, title-deeds, papal bulls, &c. 1893 E. M. THOMPSON *Handbk. Gk. & Lat. Palæogr.* xix. 301 The cursive or charter-hand.

Chartered, *ppl. a.* Add:

1. b. *Chartered accountant*, an accountant who is qualified under the rules of the Institute of Accountants, which received a royal charter in 1880.

Chartophylax (kāɪtǫ·fĭlæks). *Gr. Ch.* [Gr. χαρτοφύλαξ, f. χάρτα paper + φύλαξ guard.] An officer of the household of the Patriarch of Constantinople who has charge of the official documents and records.

1879 *Encycl. Brit.* X. 429 He held..the offices of 'Chartophylax', 'Scenophylax', and 'Referendarius' in the 'Great Church' (that of St Sophia) at Constantinople. 1884 ADDIS & ARNOLD *Cath. Dict.* 423/2 The Chartophylax, who superintends ecclesiastical causes. 1928 *Observer* 1 July 10 Manuel I. Gedeon, the learned Chartofylax of the Great Church.

Chartreuse. Add:

3. *Cookery.* a. See quot. 1806. Also attrib. *chartreuse scoop*, a utensil used in preparing the vegetables for a chartreuse. b. A dish consisting of a mould of rice containing game, etc. c. Fruits enclosed in blancmange, etc.

1806 J. Simpson *Cookery* (1816) 103 A Chartreuse. Line a plain mould with bacon, cut turnip and carrot..scoop the turnips and carrots with chartreuse scoops. 1891 *Encycl. Pract. Cookery* (ed. T. F. Garrett) I. 340/1 Chartreuse of Vegetables and Game.

4. A variety of the domestic cat. Also **Chartreux.**

1838 *Penny Cycl.* X. 223 Among the most noted are..the Chartreux, which is bluish, and the Angora cat. 1876 *Encycl. Brit.* V. 206 The Chartreuse, of a bluish-grey colour.

Char-work. [f. *char-* Chare *sb.*1] Ordinary mechanical work.

1888 F. J. Child *Eng. & Sc. Pop. Ballads* III. 42/2 A considerable part of the Robin Hood poetry looks like char-work done for the petty press.

Chase, *sb.*1 Add:

10. Short for Steeplechase, used *attrib.*

1894 M. H. Hayes *Among Men & Horses* i. 12 The professional..regarded gratuitous chase riding as an unwarrantable attempt to take the bread, or rather the whisky, out of their mouths. 1927 *Daily Express* 22 June 16 Seamark will seek consolation for chase misfortunes in the valuable Prix des Drags.

Chase, *sb.*3 Add:

7. The apex of a cop or bobbin of a spinning-wheel.

1902 Hannan *Textile Fibres of Commerce* 124 The shoulder acts as a good support to the chase of the cop in winding.

Chase, *v.*1 Add:

6. Also with *off* (after something).

1920 Rose Macaulay *Potterism* iv. i. 172 Aunt Cynthia chased off after another exciting subject, and that was all about Gideon.

7. c. *refl.* To betake (oneself), to go or run. *U.S. colloq.*

1921 R. D. Paine *Comr. Rolling Ocean* xii. 206 Let him rest, Kid. You chase yourself below and look things over.

Chaser1. Add:

5. A small portion of spirituous liquor taken after coffee, tobacco, etc. (cf. Chasse 2); also, a small quantity of water or other mild beverage taken after spirituous liquor, etc. *colloq. U.S.* Also *fig.*

1897 *Daily News* 30 Aug. 2/1 Everything was 50 cents. a drink, no mixed drinks, and no water for a chaser. 1905 *N. Y. Even. Post* 8 Sept. 7 Drinking whiskey from a bottle and refusing a 'chaser'. a 1906 'O. Henry' *Trimmed Lamp* etc. 169 Eagerly gulping down the strong black headlines to be followed as a chaser by the milder details of the smaller type. a 1909 — *Roads of Destiny* xxi. 359 He offers me this oath of allegiance to take without any kind of a chaser.

6. A small, light, usually single-seated military aeroplane of great speed and climbing power, used in repelling hostile aircraft.

1915 Grahame-White & Harper *Aircraft Gt. War* 33 British pilots, having in view the pursuit of slower-flying German craft, have called these little machines [*sc.* the 'bullets'] 'the chasers'. 1919 A. E. Illingworth *Fly Papers* 41 A chaser squadron of picked pilots.

7. (See quot.)

1922 G. T. Turner & Wood *Man. Up-to-date Organisation* 171 Chaser is a progress man responsible for the progress of a job through the factory.

Chaser2. **2.** (Earlier U.S. example.)

1846 *Rep. U.S. Comm. Patents* (1847) 58 My fifth improvement relates to the arrangement of the thread-cutter or chaser.

Chasidim (hæsi·dim). Also **Chassidim.** [Rabbinical Heb. חסידים *ḥasīdīm* pl., the pious.] A name applied to mystical sects of the Jews of various periods. (Cf. Assidæan.) Hence **Chas(s)idic** (hăsi·dik) *a.*, of or belonging to the Chasidim; **Chas(s)idism** (hæ·sidiz'm), the tenets of the Chasidim.

1834 *Penny Cycl.* II. 502 The Assidians, or Chasidim, of those days, found a leader in Mattathias. *Ibid.*, Later Jews called those persons Chasidim who secluded themselves from worldly occupations and pleasures to devote their life solely to religious exercises and bodily chastisements. 1894 *Daily News* 18 Sept. 6/3 The Jewish inhabitants..are all of the sect known as the Chassidim. 1918 Zangwill *Chosen Peoples* iv. 39 The comparatively modern Chassidism. *Ibid.* 42 A Chassidic Rabbi.

Chasm. Add: **5. b.** *Bloody chasm* (U.S.): see *Bloody *a.* 2 b. Also without epithet.

a 1909 'O. Henry' *Roads of Destiny* xxi. 352 Don't reopen the chasm, Doc. Any Yankeeness I may have is geographical.

Chasmogamy (kæzmǫ·gămi). *Bot.* [f. Gr. χάσμα Chasm + γάμος -gamy.] The opening of the perianth at the time of flowering, as distinguished from cleistogamy. Hence **Chasmogamic** (kæzmogæ·mik), **Chasmogamous** (kæzmǫ·gămǝs), *adjs.*

1900 B. D. Jackson *Gloss. Bot. Terms*, Chasmogamy..; chasmogamic. 1906 J. R. A. Davis tr. *Knuth's Handbk. Flower Pollination* I. 55 The otherwise normally opening chasmogamous flowers remain closed.

Chassé-croisé (ʃa·se krwa·ze). [Fr., = Chassé *sb.* + *croisé*, pa. pple. of *croiser* to cross.] A dance figure in which one of two partners chassés first to the right and then to the left, while the other chassés first to the left and then to the right. Hence *transf.* and *fig.* applied to actions or situations in which persons or things cross each other or change positions backwards and forwards.

1876 *Ball Room Guide* 90 Chassez croisez. Lady and gentleman *chassez* in opposite directions. 1883 *Sat. Rev.* 10 Nov. 595/1 His drama is a perpetual *chassé-croisé* at the edge of a precipice. 1886 *Athenæum* 17 Apr. 516/1 When he arrived alongside, the Espiègle and the galley were performing a sort of vertical *chassé-croisé*. 1903 *Westm. Gaz.* 27 Jan. 3/2 A *ménage à trois* and a kind of matrimonial chassé-croisé are discussed. 1928 *Observer* 8 Apr. 5/2 The metamorphoses of character, the *chassé-croisé* of incident.

Chasseur. Add:

2. b. *Comb.*: **chasseur-blue,** a shade of blue resembling that of the uniform of a French chasseur.

1900 *Daily News* 1 Jan. 5/3 Costumes..in blue and black-chasseur-blue. 1910 *Daily Chron.* 2 Mar. 3/3 From head to foot a woman can now..array herself in the new 'Chasseur blue.

Chassidim, var. *Chasidim.

Chassis. Add:

3. The base frame of a motor car, with its mechanism, as distinguished from the body or upper part; also, in an aeroplane.

1903 *Sci. Amer.* 20 June 472/1 The motor is placed in the center of the chassis and the boiler is now quite in the rear. 1904 A. B. F. Young *Compl. Motorist* v. (ed. 2) 149 The frame of the chassis is the ordinary pressed steel frame as generally used on a petrol car. 1909 A. Berget *Conquest of Air* v. 211 The whole apparatus rests upon a running chassis for launching, and to ensure descent without shock. 1924 *Motor* 21 Oct. 583/1 The baffling diversity in methods of chassis construction.

Chasteningly (tʃē·s'niŋli), *adv.* [f. Chastening *ppl. a.* + -ly 2.] In a chastening manner or tone.

1905 W. J. Locke *Usurper* xxiii. 275 'The ultimate evolution of swelled-head', he answered chasteningly.

Chastisable (tʃæstəi·zăb'l), *a.* In 7 chastice-, chastiseable. [f. Chastise *v.* + -able.] That may be chastised; deserving of chastisement.

1611 Cotgr., *Chastiable*, chasticeable; fit to be chastised. 1632 Sherwood, Chastiseable. 1924 *Blackw. Mag.* Aug. 241/1 A more pernicious or chastisable guild of touts it has never been my lot to encounter.

Chat, *sb.*5 Add: Also *pl.*, the tailings or waste product from the concentration of ore.

Chat, *v.*1 **4.** Delete †*Obs.* and add quot.

1888 Mrs. H. Ward *R. Elsmere* xliii, The other men stood chatting politics and the latest news.

Château. Add:

b. In the names of various wines made in the neighbourhood of certain châteaux.

1754 Chesterf. in *World* No. 91 P 2 The wine was the very same which they had all approved of the day before; and..was true Chateau Margoux. 1833 Redding *Wines* 148 In this commune is grown the famous first quality, Châteaux Margaux. *Ibid.* 150 Nearly all the Château Lafitte, and indeed most of the other growths of this commune, are consumed in England. It is lighter than Château Latour. a 1845 Barham *Ingol. Leg.* Ser. III. *Lord of Thoulouse*, Chambertin, Château Margaux, La Rose, and Lafitte. 1886 *Catal. Colonial & Ind. Exh., S. Australian Court* 34/2 Twenty cases and one quarter cask Chateau Beaumont wine. 1894 X. L. *Aut Diabolus aut Nihil* 20 'Chateau Margaux, M. l'Abbé?' murmured the butler in his ear.

c. *Châteaux in air, châteaux en Espagne, Spanish château* = castles, or a castle, in the air (see Castle *sb.* 11).

1793 [in Dict.]. 1845 Ford *Handbk. Spain* I. 291/1 The scheme ended in nothing, like so many other loans, &c.—*Chateaux en Espagne.* 1852 Lever *Daltons* xxi, It was, however, an Irish fortune, and, like a Spanish château, its loss is more a question of feeling than of fact. 1888 *Ch. Q. Rev.* (Dixon) Mere *châteaux en Espagne*, the creation of architectural fancy run mad.

Chatelaine. 1. Add: Also, the mistress of a household.

1900 *New Cent. Rev.* VII. 381 The chatelaine of 17, Hertford Street, was hereditarily qualified to preside over a home whose natural atmosphere was one of culture. 1903 *M. A. P.* XI. 143/2 The châtelaine of a house in Eaton Square.

Chaton (ʃatoṅ). Also 6 chatton. [Fr., ad. G. *kasten* (OHG., MHG. *kasto*).] The head or broadest part of a finger-ring, in which a stone or intaglio is set or upon which a device is engraved.

1578 *Inv. R. Wardr.* (1815) 265 A chatton without a stane. *Ibid.* 267 A chatton without ane emerauld. 1880 C. T. Newton *Art & Archæol.* 269 The intaglio on the oval chaton of the other gold ring presents an equally strange subject. 1884 Sayce *Schliemann's Troja* Pref. 20 The double-headed axe is..engraved on the famous chaton of the ring discovered by Dr. Schliemann at Mykenæ.

Chattel. 5. Add: **chattel mortgage** *U.S.*, the conveyance of chattels by mortgage as a security for a debt.

1889 *Kansas Times & Star* 27 May, Gus Behr's famous Elite saloon..was closed by the sheriff today on a chattel mortgage.

Chattelization. (Earlier U.S. example.)

1854 A. L. Stone *Boston Orat.* 4 July 25 A system of human chattelization.

Chatter, *sb.*1 **3.** Add:

chatter-mark, (*a*) a mark left on a piece of metal by a cutting tool that works intermittently and thus makes a chattering noise; (*b*) a mark made on a surface by a fragment of rock on the under-surface of glacier ice.

1905 Chamberlin & Salisbury *Geol.* I. 270 Glacial striæ and bruises. The block to the right shows two sets of striæ: that to the left shows the peculiar curved fractures known as Chatter Marks.

Chattering, *ppl. a.* Add: **chattering plover** = Killdee, killdeer.

1731 Catesby *Nat. Hist. Carolina* etc. (1754) I. 71 *Pluvialis vociferus.* The Chattering Plover...In Virginia they are called Kill-deers.

Chattermag (tʃæ·tǝɹmæg), *sb. colloq.* [f. Chatter *sb.*1 + Mag *sb.*1] **a.** Chatter. **b.** A chatterbox. Hence **Chattermag** *v. intr.*, to chatter.

1895 C. W. Scott *Apple Orchards* 25 Gossip and chattermag. 1904 *Daily Chron.* 6 May 4/6 Philosophers..have suggested various causes for woman being such a 'chattermag'. 1909 *Westm. Gaz.* 15 May 2/3 Too late to wait while you stand chatter-maggin' there. 1926 *Sunday at Home* 149/1 She..would have thoroughly enjoyed the gossip of the excited young chattermags.

Chattily (tʃæ·tili), *adv.* [f. Chatty *a.*1 + -ly 2.] In a chatty manner.

1920 P. G. Wodehouse *Damsel in Distress* vi. 86 'Why, when I was at Oxford in the year '87', he said chattily.

Chaucerianism (tʃǫsī·riăniz'm). [f. Chaucerian + -ism.] = Chaucerism.

1909 Mackail *Springs Helicon* 77 For all his Chaucerianism, he [*sc.* Spenser] is, as Chaucer in his time had been, a modern of the moderns.

Chaud-froid (ʃofrwa). [Fr.] A dish composed of fillets of poultry, or the like, cooked to be served cold in jelly or sauce.

1892 *Encycl. Pract. Cookery* (ed. T. F. Garrett) I. 341/1 *Chaudfroids.* Literally 'hot-colds', applied to certain methods of preparing birds. *Ibid.* 612/2 Chaudfroid of Fowl. 1905 E. F. Benson *Image in Sand* vii, Arnold took some chaudfroid.

Chauffeur (ʃōu·fǝɹ, ‖ ʃofö̆r). [Fr., agent-n. of *chauffer* to heat.]

†**1.** An automobilist. *Obs.*

1899 *Motor-Car World* Oct. 3/1 The French 'chauffeur', Béconnais. 1901 *Daily News* 16 Feb. 6/1 Whilst automobilists in Great Britain have perhaps been saved from the 'racing fever'.., the French chauffeur has in part been encouraged in his rashness. 1903 *Lady's Realm* Apr. 684/1 All the members of the Italian Royal Family are enthusiastic *chauffeurs.*

2. A professional or paid driver of an automobile.

1902 *Westm. Gaz.* 5 Aug. 1/3 As to the driver, 'chauffeur' seems at present to hold the field. 1905 C. N. & A. M. Williamson (*title*) My Friend the Chauffeur. 1906 (*title*) The Chauffeur's Blue Book.

Hence **Chau·ffeur** *v. trans.*, to drive as chauffeur. Also **Chauffeuse** (ʃōu·fǝz, ‖ ʃofö̆z), a female chauffeur.

1903 *Westm. Gaz.* 16 May 7/2. 1903 *Motor Ann.* 73 A skilful *chauffeuse*. 1907 *Daily Chron.* 18 May 4/7 The goggles of the chauffeuse with which our ladies blind themselves. 1921 R. D. Paine *Comr. Rolling Ocean* iii. 44, I can chauffeur anything with an engine in it.

Chaulmoogra (tʃǭlmū·gră). Also -mugra, -maugra, chalmoogra. [East Indian.] Used attrib. in *Chaulmoogra oil*, a vegetable fat obtained chiefly from the seeds of an East Indian tree *Gynocardia odorata*, used in the treatment of various cutaneous diseases. So *chaulmoogra tree.*

a 1815 Roxburgh *Flora Indica* (1832) III. 836 Chaulmoogra and Petarkura, are the names of this tree, and the drug, hereafter mentioned, which it furnishes...The seeds of this tree, called Chaulmoogree. 1876 *Encycl. Brit.* V. 675 Chálmugrá oil. 1884 *Ibid.* XVII. 744 Chaulmoogra oil. *Gynocardia odorata.* 1907 *Practitioner* Aug. 245 Chaulmoogra oil is generally considered to have the greatest beneficial effect on leprosy.

Chaulmoogric (tʃǭlmū·grik), *a. Chem.* Also -mugric. [f. *Chaulmoogra + -ic.] *Chaulmoogric acid*, an acid obtained from chaulmoogra oil expressed from the seeds of *Hydnocarpus kurzii.*

1909 *Cent. Dict.* Suppl., Chaulmugric acid. 1921 *Glasgow Herald* 6 June 7 The fatty acids of the chaulmoogric acid series.

Chautauqua (tʃǫtǭ·kwă). *U.S.* [The name of a county and lake in the southwestern part of the state of New York.]

1. Used *attrib.* to designate a system of home-study originating with summer schools held at Chautauqua, or the organization resulting from this, established by charter in 1871.

1875 A. W. Young *Hist. Chautauqua Co.* 663 The name of the corporation is 'The Chautauqua Lake Camp-Meeting Association'. 1886 J. H. Vincent *Chautauqua Movement* 40 Meetings of the Chautauqua type. *Ibid.*, The camp-meeting period of Chautauqua exercises. 1902 Webster Suppl., *Chautauqua system* (of education). 1910 *Springfield Weekly Republ.* 15 Dec. 9 The men cheered and the many women gave a Chautauqua salute. 1926 *Even. Standard* 12 July 3/2, I once spent part of a month addressing chautauqua gatherings in a part of New York State.

2. An educational meeting conducted on the lines of the summer schools at Chautauqua.

1903 *Boston Even. Transcript* 26 Sept., The Methodist camp-meeting is no longer an evangelistic force, but the chautauquas and summer conferences are multiplying.

Hence **Chautau·quan** *a.* and *sb.*

1878 in J. H. Vincent *Chautauqua Movement* (1886) 80 Let every Chautauquan..read Dr. Vincent's lecture. 1909 *Century Dict.* Suppl.

Chavel (tʃæ·vǝl), *v.* Transfer †*Obs.* to sense 1 and add to 2 *dial.*, also *absol.* and *transf.*

1877 E. Peacock *N.W. Linc. Gloss.*, *Chavle*, to chew badly. 'That herse chavles strangely, he wants his teeth filin'.' 1911 D. H. Lawrence *White Peacock* III. vii. § 6 The bracken lay sere under the trees, broken and chavelled by the restless wild winds of the long winter.

Chawed, *ppl. a.* **2.** (Later U.S. example.)

1843 R. Carlton *New Purchase* xxvii. 257 He emptied all the contents on the counter, viz.: two silver fips, three 'chaw'd bullits', a damaged rifle-wiper [etc.].

Chawl (tʃǭl). [East Indian.] An Indian native lodging-house.

1891 *Pall Mall Gaz.* 7 Dec. 7/2 The gaol-bird is..better off in every way in gaol than he would be in his chawl. 1898 *Jrnl. Soc. Arts* 25 Feb. 312/1 Some of the Bombay 'chawls' or tenements, containing from 500 to 1,000 inhabitants each. 1901 *Q. Rev.* Oct. 566 The so-called 'chawls', in which a large part of the native population lives.

Chay-ka: see *Cheka.

Chazzan (kăzā·n). Also chazan. [Heb. *ḥazzan* governor, prefect, overseer, minister.] A cantor or precentor in a Jewish synagogue.

1764 *Mem. G. Psalmanazar* 270 Conversing with the Jews themselves, going to their synagogues, and hearing the Scriptures read by their *chazans* or ministers. 1892 Zangwill *Childr. Ghetto* I. 7 Prayers were shouted rapidly by the congregation, and elaborately sung by the *Chazan.*

Cheap, *a.* Add:

1. Phr. *Cheap and nasty*: of low price and bad quality; inexpensive at the expense of being unsuitable to one's purposes. Hence *cheap-and-nastiness.*

1831 [in Dict.]. 1850 C. Kingsley ('Parson Lot') (*title*) Cheap Clothes and Nasty. 1867 Carlyle *Shooting Niagara* vii. Misc. Ess. (1872) VII. 226 'Cheap and nasty'; there is a pregnancy in that poor vulgar proverb, which I wish we better saw and valued! *Ibid.* 230 All these are *Cheap and Nasty* in another form. 1905 *Studio* Sept. 368/1 The cheap-and-nastiness of our suburban houses.

b. Also in *cheap fare, rate.*

1709–10 W. Salmon *Family Dict.* Pref., Poor People would be furnished..with Firing..at very cheap Rates. 1776 *Monthly Rev.* Aug. 162 It may..serve to convey information 'at a cheap rate'. 1867 *Cassell's Mag.* I. 438/2 Omnibuses..for many years..were running at a cheap rate. 1887 *Peel City Guardian* 28 May 5/1 To make special daily sailings from Liverpool to the Isle of Man and back at cheap fares.

4. b. In poor health; out of sorts. (Hence *cheapness.*) *slang.*

1891 Farmer *Slang* s.v., *To feel cheap*, to 'have a mouth on'; to be suffering from a night debauch. 1900 *Westm. Gaz.* 28 May 2/1 Putting down his weakness, lassitude, and general feeling of extreme cheapness to the climate.

5. c. Low, poor, disparaging.

1907 M. C. Harris *Tents of Wickedness* III. iii. 250 He has a pretty cheap opinion of me, and I don't blame him, considering the people I go with generally.

D. cheap fare, a fare at a lower rate than the ordinary fare; used *attrib.*; also *cheap rate.*

1901 *Daily Chron.* 12 Aug. 7/5 For trade and cheap-rate passengers. 1902 *Westm. Gaz.* 14 Feb. 6/2 The Council are engaged in negotiations for the sale of all the 'cheap-fare' vehicles. 1902 *Daily Chron.* 26 Apr. 5/7 This is not a workman's train, but what is called a cheap fare train.

Cheat, *sb.*1 **9.** (Examples.)

1784 J. Smyth *Tour U.S.* II. 121 My fields consisted entirely of fine healthful clean wheat, without a single head of darnel or cheat. 1786 Washington *Diaries* III. 71 The first [*sc.* wheat], besides having a small head generally, was mixed exceedingly with cheat. 1849 *Rep. U.S. Comm. Patents Agric.* (1850) 455 Cheat is nothing more nor less than degenerated wheat. 1856 P. Thompson *Hist. Boston* 701 *Cheat*, the wild oat. 1861 *Trans. Ill. Agric. Soc.* IV. 351 'Chess', or 'cheat' as it is sometimes called is a species of grass. 1863 *Ibid.* V. 865 *Bromus secalinus*, cheat, chess, is a foreign annual weed. 1866 Brogden *Prov. Words Lincs.* 39 The field is very full of cheats to-year.

Cheat, *v.* Add: **3. b.** To lead *into* (an action) by deception.

1856 De Quincey *Confess.* 264 *note*, He..could not but find..himself cheated into cordial admiration, by the splendour of the verses. 1888 Mrs. H. Ward *R. Elsmere* x, They had tried to cheat her into sleeping.

Chebacco. Delete etym. note except last line, and add quots.

1823 J. F. Cooper *Pilot* I. i. 13, I was born on board a chebacco-man. 1835 J. H. Ingraham *South-West* I. iii. 27 Those short stump-masted *non-de-scripts*..sometimes denominated fishing smacks, but oftener and more euphoniously 'Chebacco boats.' 1859 *Congress. Globe* 22 Feb. 1210/1, I recollect a little stream in the county of Essex, in Massachusetts, where, some fifty years ago, they used to manufacture a sort of little boat, called chebacco boat. 1886 *Leslie's Pop. Monthly* XXI. 223/1 Squam was in its ascendency in the days of the old pinkies and of the still earlier chebacco-boats.

Chechia (ʃe·ʃiă). Also checchia. [Berber *tashashit*, pl. *tishushai* skull-cap.] A cylindrical tufted cap or fez worn by Arabs and by French troops in Africa.

1909 W. J. Locke *Septimus* xiii, He [*sc.* a Zouave]..swaggered off, his chechia at the very back of his head. 1913 *Chambers's Jrnl.* 331/1 A small procession of natives in red *chechias.* 1924 Hichens *After the Verdict* III. i, An omnibus ..driven by a big Arab in European clothes and a chechia.

Check, *sb.*1 Add:

5. e. *Mining.* A slight fault or dislocation of the strata.

1883 Gresley *Gloss. Coal-m.*

10. e. A form of catch on a rein; *ellipt.* a check-rein.

1868 H. Woodruff *Trotting Horse Amer.* xxiii. 202 In order to prevent him from throwing down his head.., the well-known Kemble-Jackson check..was invented. 1887 Tourgee *Button's Inn* 122 Throw me that off rein, if you please...Just shift those inside checks, won't you?

14. b. (Early U.S. examples.)

1835 J. H. Ingraham *South-West* I. xxi. 223 A shouting of 'Your check, sir! your check!—Give me your check—Please give me your check!' [*sc.* for re-admission to a theatre]. 1850 *Wilmington* (N.C.) *Commercial* 28 Feb. 3/3 Porters will receive checks, take charge of the baggage, and convey it to the Hotel.

15. (Earlier examples.)

1845 J. J. Hooper *Adv. Simon Suggs* v. 57 He called for 'Twenty, five-dollar checks..'. The dealer handed him the red checks. 1869 *Overland Monthly* III. 31 Three or four miners and axemen sat whittling on the logs as the doctor came out, and Hy Fender asked: 'Well, now; has be passed in his checks?'

19. check-man, a man who checks tickets, etc.; spec. *U.S.*, a transfer-man; **check reel,** also, an angler's reel fitted with a check (see Check *sb.*1 10 c). See also *Check-.

1907 *Daily Chron.* 23 Sept. 4/4 As you are nearing your destination, a '*check-man' boards your car. 1892 Niven *British Angler's Lex.* 72 *Check reels..should be humoured so as not to be too stiff or too slack. 1904 Gallichan *Fishing Spain* 208 Two metal check-reels for trout fishing.

Check, *sb.*2 Add: **3.** *Agric.* Each of a series of squares made by cross-marking. *U.S.*

1787 Washington *Diaries* III. 194 In each of these checks or crosses, one root, when it was large and looked well was put, and two where they were small. 1857 *Trans. Ill. Agric. Soc.* III. 62, I lay off my ground with a corn-marker..into checks of three feet three inches square. 1861 *Ibid.* IV. 248 If he wishes to plant in checks so as to plow the corn both ways, he must have a boy to tend the check-set.

Check, *v.*1 Add:

16. c. To accept or hand over (articles) in return for a check; to send to a destination in this way. *U.S.*

1860 *Congress. Globe* 21 Dec. 177/2 It is a great convenience to the traveling public to be able to check baggage through. 1866 *Ibid.* 20 July 3972/3 The Baltimore road..will not check baggage from here to any point in the West. They..compel you to recheck your baggage. 1888 *Amer. Humorist* 21 July (Farmer) Turning to the man who checks umbrellas and canes. 1897 *Westm. Gaz.* 25 Feb. 10/2 (U.S.) Remove your hats during the performance. You can check them with the maid. 1905 [see *Check-room]. 1922 *Publishers' Circular* 21 Jan. 43/2 We began to require all persons ..to check these books at the coat-rooms.

d. *To check up*: to examine, compare, or count up, in detail. Also *absol. U.S.*

1889 *Kansas Times & Star* 15 Mar., He says Willis checked them up closely and discovered nearly 600 saloons here, and only 400 paying a license. 1911 H. S. Harrison *Queed* xxiv. 309 In five years the experiment might enable me to check up some of my own conclusions. 1912 *Amer. Hist. Review* 819 There is..more chance to check up legislative ideals by the dry observations of chroniclers. 1924 Mulford *Rustlers' Valley* xxvii. 291 He was trying to check up the defenders in the cabin. 1926 *Publishers' Weekly* (N.Y.) 19 June 1966/2 Nor do the parents think of checking up the reading matter [taken to camp].

absol. 1925 H. L. Foster *Trop. Tramp Tourists* 51 As the sailing hour approached, the staff and stewards were busy checking up. 1928 C. M. Fuess *Men of Andover* 13 Every effort has been made to check up on even the least important statements.

e. To note with, or indicate by, some mark.

1928 *Publishers' Weekly* (N.Y.) 12 May 1973 For the reasons checked below, we regret that we cannot undertake the publication of your proposed book. 1929 *Ibid.* 14 Sept. 1064 Check the titles you want and we will mail you the books at once.

f. *intr.* To agree upon comparison. *U.S.*

1928 *Publishers' Weekly* (N.Y.) 22 Dec. 2491/2 One of the sheets,..checked closely with fiction which was found in the Gottschalk store.

17. (Earlier U.S. example.)

1809 *Deb. Congress* 20 Feb. 416 The money..is deposited in the Treasury as in a bank..to be checked for, whenever that commerce..shall be again reopened.

18. *trans.* (*a*) *Carpentry.* To notch or halve (timbers) in making a cross joint. *Sc.* (*b*) *Masonry.* To notch (one stone) *into* (another); also *to check down.* (*c*) To join (two pieces) in this manner (*Cent. Dict.* Suppl. 1909).

1833 Loudon *Encycl. Cottage Archit.* § 1066 All plates to be in long lengths, and chacked. *Ibid.* 1072 The rafters to be..chacked and spiked together. *Ibid.* 1778 The stair to the cellars..to be droved; the steps to be checked down on (notched into) each other. 1885 *Spons' Mech. Own Bk.* 678 The other 2 stones..are to be half-checked into it, also half-checked into each other where they meet in the middle.

Check, *v.*2 Add: **1. b.** To mark for planting in checks. *U.S.*

1768 Washington *Diaries* I. 265 At the first and last of which [plantations I] just began to check Corn G[roun]d. 1871 *Trans. Ill. Agric. Soc.* VIII. 239 After the field has been thoroughly prepared..proceed to check it off from east to west with a three-rowed marker.

c. *intr.* To split or crack along crossing lines. *U.S.* (Cf. *Check* sb.1 and v.1 in E.D.D.)

1902 *Contrib. Econ. Geol., U.S. Geol. Survey* 277 The coal is not crushed, but can be obtained in large pieces which 'check' but do not break up readily on exposure to the air.

Check-. Add: **check-band,** a drag-device attached to a spinning mule to check the varying velocity of the spindle carriage; **check-bar** (see quot.); **check-chain,** a chain used to check the movement of mechanism, a vehicle, etc. (see quots.); **check-cord,** (*a*) a cord used to check action or movement, *lit.* and *fig.*, spec. a long cord attached to the collar of a hunting dog to bring him to a sudden stop; (*b*) = Check-string; **check-lock, -locking** (see quot.); **check meter,** an instrument used to test the accuracy of electricity meters; **check-off,** used attrib. in *check-off system* (see quot. and cf. Check *v.*1 9); **check-rail** = Guard-rail 2; **check-rein** (earlier U.S. example); **check rope,** a rope used to check the recoil of a gun; **check-set** *U.S.*, a device for setting out the checks for planting; **check-stand** *U.S.*, a stand in which 'checked' articles are placed; **check-strap** *U.S.*, a strap controlling the bit in a horse's mouth; also *fig.*; **check-stub** *U.S.*, a counterfoil in a cheque-book.

1892 Nasmith *Students' Cotton Spinning* 276 Two principal faults arising from an imperfect adjustment of the *check band. 1874 Knight *Dict. Mech.*, *Check-bar, a bar which limits the backward play of the jacks [in a piano-movement]. 1805 R. W. Dickson *Pract. Agric.* I. 8 The latter has generally a *check-chain, by which the wheel is pulled up, in order to be out of the way. 1884 Knight *Dict. Mech.* Suppl., *Check Chain*, a chain connecting the car body with its truck. 1896 *Strand Mag.* XII. 325/1 The sliding ways, cradle, and ship..glide down the appointed pathway..until retarded..and finally brought to rest by check-chains..connecting ship and shore. 1908 *Daily Report* 7 Feb. 1/4 When the competitors..combine to fleece their customers, the *check-cord on their power to run up prices is sometimes more difficult to apply. 1903 *Westm. Gaz.* 1 Oct. 10/3 The '*check-locking' arrangement..ensures that until the movement of a point or signal has been fully completed the lever in the signal-box..is checked...As soon as the signal or point movement..is properly completed, the '*check-lock' is electrically removed. 1909 *Check meter [see *Calibrated *ppl. a.*]. 1923 J. D. Hackett *Labor Terms in Management Engineering* May, *Check-Off System*, a system whereby initiation fees, fines, and dues of union employees are deducted from their wages by the employer and periodically remitted to the district union organization. 1876 J. W. Barry *Railway Appliances* (1881) 58 The extra rail, which is called a *check rail, relieves the sideways pressure of the wheels. 1904 *Daily Chron.* 29 June 4/7 The..railwayman whose foot was wedged in a check-rail in front of an approaching train. 1906 *Westm. Gaz.* 3 July 5/1 The check-rail..—a rail laid..to minimise the danger of the curve. 1849 Willis *Rural Lett.* vi. 61 We provided for a night's toilet..and, easing off the *check reins a couple of holes..we struck into the traveller's trot. 1918 Farrow *Dict. Mil. Terms*, *Check ropes*, strong ropes employed to diminish recoil by increasing the frictional resistances. 1861 *Trans. Ill. Agric. Soc.* (1862) IV. 248 He must have a boy to tend the *check-set of the corn-planter. 1904 F. Lynde *Grafters* ii. 31 The train was in, and the porter had fetched Loring's hand-bag from the *check-stand. 1887 *Scribner's Mag.* Oct. 508/1 'I'll put a *check-strap on him, if he won't do it!' a little chap exclaimed..using a phrase drawn from the training of horses. 1911 H. Quick *Yellowstone N.* ix. 234 Smythe made him admit that he had bought the tools, and had no *check stub of the payment.

Checker, *sb.*1 Add:

3. A person who or a thing which checks, impedes, or retards.

1845 *Jrnl. R. Agric. Soc.* VI. II. 548 Checkers or curers of the disease.

Checker, *sb.*2 Add: Also 8 checkerd, -ard.

2. (Earlier U.S. examples.)

1786 A. Ellicott in *Life & Lett.* (1908) 59 Our Amusements such as Cards, and Draughts, commonly called checkers. 1794 *Ibid.* 119 We amuse ourselves with playing checkerds, or what is an infinitely more intricate and noble game, chess.

Checker-berry. (Earlier U.S. example.)

1784 Cutler in *Mem. Amer. Acad.* (1785) I. 444 *Arbutus.* ..Foxberry. Checkerberry.

Checking, *vbl. sb.*1 Add:

3. *attrib.*, as *checking-book*; **checking account** *U.S.*, a current banking account; **checking-room,** a room in which goods, etc. are checked; spec. *U.S.* = *Check-room.

1926 *Springfield Weekly Republ.* 19 Aug. 10 She preferred the more generous way, and they had a joint *checking account. 1895 *Westm. Gaz.* 10 Oct. 3/1 Others..are content with inscribing their names on their *checking-book...The scene..in the *checking-room is by no means a quiet one, for nearly every jobber's clerk..is shouting his firm at the top of his voice. 1910 *N. Y. Even. Post* 13 Dec. 7 Mr. Spottford arrived at the station carrying a small grip, and asked Charles where the checking-room was.

Che·ck-list. *U.S.* [Check-.] A list of names, titles, etc., so arranged as to form a ready means of reference, comparison, or verification; *spec.* a list of qualified voters for use at an election.

1853 (*title*) Check list of periodical publications received in the reading-room of the Smithsonian Institution. 1873 J. Robinson (*title*) Check List of the Ferns of North America north of Mexico. 1888 Bryce *Amer. Commw.* II. xii. II. 443 The composition of a primary is determined by the roll or 'check-list', as it is called, of ward voters entitled to appear in it. 1926 *N. Y. Times Book Rev.* 15 Aug. 18 The catalogue ..is a merely utilitarian production..little more than a check list.

Che·ck-room. *U.S.* [Check-.] A cloak-room or baggage-room in a hotel or railway station.

1905 *Springfield Weekly Republ.* 8 Sept. 5 Making for an inclosure which had every appearance of being a check-room, I lifted my grip upon the counter, and asked the young man behind it to check it for me.

Check-row. *U.S.* [*Check *sb.*2 3.] Each of a series of rows (in planting) so arranged as to form a check-pattern. Also *attrib.*

1861 *Trans. Ill. Agric. Soc.* IV. 209 In spring it will be harrowed thoroughly, planted by hands in check rows three feet ten inches apart each way. *Ibid.* 312 Most of the corn is now planted with drills, or check row machines.

Hence **Che·ck-rowed** *a.*, planted in check-rows;

Check-rower, a corn-planter, or a device attached to one, dropping the seed-corn in check-rows.

1884 Knight *Dict. Mech.* Suppl., *Check-rower.* 1888 *Sci. Amer.* N.S. LVIII. 298/1 Particularly for use on growing check-rowed and listed corn.

Check-up, *sb.* orig. *U.S.* [f. *Check *v.*1 16 d.] A detailed examination, scrutiny, or comparison with a list.

1924 *Glasgow Herald* 18 Sept. 7 (U.S.) A check-up of the miners shows that the number entombed..was 47. 1927 *Hutchinson's Myst. Story Mag.* X. 106 In the usual check-up of the rooms at one-thirty, the clerk became suspicious.

Chedar (he·dəɹ). Also cheder; pl. **chedarim.** [Heb.] A Hebrew school for Jewish children.

1892 Zangwill *Childr. Ghetto* I. 143 His father could not afford to send him to a *Chedar.* 1899 *Daily News* 17 Jan. 4/7 The Chedarim, or religious schools. 1900 C. Russell & H. S. Lewis *Jew in Lond.* 125 The *cheder*, or private Hebrew school.

Cheddite (tʃe·dəit). [a. F. *cheddite*, f. *Chedde* (in Haute Savoie): see -ite 1.] A high explosive of which dinitrotoluene is a constituent.

1915 A. Marshall *Explosives* 298 The velocity of detonation of Cheddite varies considerably with the density to which it is compressed. 1918 Colver *High Explosives* 280 Cheddites are very durable, and even prolonged heating at 120°C. causes no decomposition. 1926 *Glasgow Herald* 8 Nov. 12 A canvas bag containing blocks of cheddite and dynamite.

Cheechako (tʃī·tʃākǝ). Also chechaco, cheechaker. A newly arrived immigrant in the mining districts of north-western North America.

1901 *Pall Mall Mag.* Jan. 56 'Nome is a good camp, but too many cheechakers', that is tender feet', new comers. 1920 Charlotte Cameron (*title*) A Cheechako in Alaska and Yukon. 1922 *Chambers's Jrnl.* 91/2 The Chechaco turns away with heart too full for words.

Cheek, *sb.* 15. Add:

cheek-bristles *pl.*, whiskers (of a cat); **cheek-down,** incipient whiskers (of a youth).

1900 A. Hill *Introd. Science* 30 When darkness approaches ..its *cheek-bristles..save it from contact with passive objects. 1887 Morris *Odyss.* xi. 319 Upon their faces the *cheek-down blossomed fair.

Cheela, var. Chela 2.

Cheer, *sb.*1 **9.** Add: **cheer-leader** *U.S.*, one who leads the cheering on special occasions.

1921 R. D. Paine *Comr. Rolling Ocean* i. 1 The appeals of the frenzied cheer leaders to back up the team. 1927 H. E. Fosdick *Pilgr. Palestine* 262 A shouting, singing mob surges into the church..carrying cheer-leaders on their shoulders.

Cheer (tʃīǝɹ), *sb.*2 Also chir. [Native name.] The Indian pheasant, *Phasianus wallichi.*

1826 *Trans. Linn. Soc.* (1827) XV. 166 The local [Nepal] name of this bird is *Cheer.* 1879 Hume & Marshall *Game Birds India* I. 170 The best places in which to find Cheer are the Dangs or precipitous places. *Ibid.* 173 The Cheer Pheasant feeds chiefly on roots. 1922 *Blackw. Mag.* Mar. 334/1 There are three other varieties of pheasant—the cheer, the white-crested kaleeg, and the koklass.

Cheerio (tʃīǝriōu·), *int.* Also (earlier) cheero, cheer o. [f. Cheer *v.* 10 b + O *int.*, influenced later by Cheery *a.*] A parting exclamation of encouragement. Also quasi-adj.: cheery.

1910 *Punch* 12 Jan. 23 [One loafer to another] Cheero, Charlie. 1915 in W. N. P. Barbellion *Enjoying Life* (1919) 53 We just go on calling out 'The Devil a bit! Cheero!' 1915 Rosher *In R.N.A.S.* (1916) 66 Heaps of love to all, and Cheer O! 1921 O. S. in *Punch* 5 Jan. 2/1, I envy not these strange delights Nor wish to join the jocund 'Cheerio!' 1922 Mrs. A. Sidgwick *Victorian* ix, He hates scent too, so put on plenty to-night because..I want him to get used to it. Cheerio! 1923 H. Jenkins *Mrs. Bindle* ii. 51 Never seen 'er so cheerio in all my puff. 1924 Galsworthy *White Monkey* I. xi, Cheerio, my dear, don't quarrel with bread and butter.

Cheer pine, variant of *Chir pine.

Cheese, *sb.*1 Add:

1. d. *The Cheeses*: a nickname applied to the First Life Guards (see quot. 1903).

1890 *Chambers's Jrnl.* 19 Apr. 251/2 The old school of officers..sneered at their successors as 'Cheesemongers'. From this circumstance the regiments acquired the cognomen of the 'Cheeses'. 1903 *Westm. Gaz.* 24 Nov. 1/3 More regimental nicknames. That of 'The Cheeses' was bestowed on the Life Guards...The old-fashioned officers protested that the regiments were no longer composed of gentlemen but of cheesemongers.

3. (Earlier U.S. examples.)

1835 Longstreet *Georgia Scenes* 167 They took their seats with precisely the motion with which the school girls in my younger days used to make 'cheeses' as they called them, with their frocks. 1844 'Jon. Slick' *High Life N. Y.* I. 85 He put one arm round her little waist..and then they begun to make cheeses on the carpet.

4. b. (See quot.)

1915 *Lit. Digest* (N.Y.) 4 Sept. 469/1 The mass of partly crusht grapes, known as 'must', goes into large kettles...From this mass of 'hot must' are made the 'cheeses' that go into the presses. These 'cheeses' consist of about two thousand gallons each of grape-must roughly enclosed in heavy cotton-cloth.

c. A conserve of fruit pressed into the consistency of cheese, as *damson cheese* (see Damson 4 b).

5. b. Applied to various objects shaped like a cheese: see quots.

1884 W. S. B. McLaren *Spinning* (ed. 2) 218 The slivers, however drawn off, are automatically wound on to wooden rollers...These balls, or cheeses, as they are generally called, are set in a rack. 1898 *Encycl. Sport* II. 381 Skittles...Pin and Bowl, or Cheese. 1919 S. Paget *Sir V. Horsley* I. 10 The boys played the nobler form of the game [of skittles], throwing the discus, the big wooden 'cheese'. 1921 [see *Cheeser].

7. *cheese ramekin*; **cheese basket,** a wooden box or bowl in which curd is placed to drain; **cheese-box,** a box for holding cheese; also *transf.*, *U.S.* = *Cheese-tub 2; **cheese-cutter,** also (*c*) a device for breaking the curd into small pieces, that the whey may more readily exude (Knight *Dict. Mech.* 1874); **cheese-fingers,** puff paste on which a cheese mixture is spread, the paste being then folded over, cut into strips, and browned; **cheese-head** (rivet, screw), one of which the head is of the form of a squat cylinder; **cheese-hoop** (U.S. example); **cheese-knife,** also, a spatula used to break down curd in cheese-making; **cheese ladder** (see Ladder *sb.* 3); **cheese-straws** *pl.*, grated cheese and flour, or other material, made into a paste, cut into thin strips, and baked crisp; **cheese-turner,** 'a shelf capable of being inverted, so as to turn over the cheeses laid upon it' (Knight 1874).

1855 *Knickerbocker Mag.* XLV. 14 A *cheese-box, used as a tanning-vat. 1866 E. A. Pollard *Southern Hist. War* I. 278 Here, there, and everywhere, was the black 'cheese-box'. 1871 Schele de Vere *Americanisms* (1872) 335 Irreverent Confederates called the hideous-looking vessels cheese-boxes. 1878 E. B. Tuttle *Border Tales* 17 One of the redskins having manufactured a drum by stretching a deer-skin over the rim of a cheesebox. 1891 *Encycl. Pract. Cookery* (ed. T. F. Garrett) I. 348/1 *Cheese Fingers..should only be lightly browned. 1888 *Lockwood's Dict. Terms Mech. Engin.*, *Cheese Head Rivet...*Cheese Head Screw. 1907 *Install. News* Oct. 10/2 A small cheese head screw and washer [is] used to bind it. 1908 *Ibid.* II. 110/1 The binding screws..have cheese heads which permit of a deep slot for screwing up. 1849 *Rep. U.S. Comm. Patents* (1850) 257 Improvement in Machines for cutting and slitting *Cheese Hoops. 1839 *Mag. Domestic Econ.* Feb. 240 The curd..is cut through with a double or triple bladed *cheese-knife. 1725 [*Bradley's*] *Fam. Dict.* s.v. *Ramequin's*, To make *Cheese-Ramequins, a Farce is to be prepar'd of the same sort as that describ'd for Cheese-Cakes. 1891 *Encycl. Pract. Cookery* (ed. T. F. Garrett) I. 349/1 Cheese Puffs or Ramekins. 1899 *Daily News* 30 Sept. 7/4 Little individual dishes of devilled macaroni,..cheese ramaquins, etc. 1874 *Young Ladies' Jrnl.* XI. 475/1 Three Receipts for Making *Cheese Straws. 1891 *Encycl. Pract. Cookery* (ed. T. F. Garrett) I. 350/2 Cheese Straws..bake for ten minutes in a quick oven.

Cheesemonger. Add:

b. (See quot. 1874.) Cf. *Cheese *sb.*1 1 d.

1874 *Slang Dict.*, *Cheesemongers*, once a popular name for the First Lifeguards. 1893 *Eng. Illustr. Mag.* 125/1 'Come on, you Cheesemongers!' the bantering cry of a commanding officer of a cavalry regiment of the Household Brigade at Waterloo.

Cheeser (tʃī·zǝɹ). [f. Cheese *sb.*1 (*5 b) + -er 1.] An operative who tends a cheesing frame (see *Cheesing) for winding wool or silk.

1921 *Dict. Occup. Terms* (1927) § 367 *Cheese winder*; *cheeser*,..operates winding frame which winds yarn..on to ..tubes,..known as cheeses.

Chee·se-tub. [Cheese *sb.*1 6.]

1. A tub in which cheese is moulded.

1794 Wedge *Agric. Chester* 50 This whey is..returned into the cheese-tub again. 1844 'Jon. Slick' *High Life N. Y.* II. 91 Besides all these, was tu great round silk cushions, as thick as mother's cheese tub. 1879 [see Cheese *sb.*1 6].

2. *transf.* A contemptuous name for a monitor vessel. (Cf. *cheese-box*, *Cheese *sb.*1 7.) *U.S.*

1867 J. T. Headley *Farragut & Nav. Commanders* 519 But all this time, Worden in his 'cheese-tub', as the rebels called her, was crowding all steam to overtake his powerful adversary.

Cheesewood (tʃī·zwud). [f. Cheese *sb.*1 + Wood *sb.*] A yellowish-white wood obtained from the Australian trees *Pittosporum bicolor* and *P. undulatum*; also, a tree of either species.

1862 in J. H. Maiden *Useful Native Plants* (1889) 588 'Cheesewood' is yellowish-white, very hard, and of uniform texture and colour.

Cheesing (tʃī·ziŋ), *vbl. sb.* [f. Cheese *sb.*1 (*5 b) + -ing 1.] The operation of winding yarn or silk on cheese-shaped bobbins. *Cheesing frame*, a frame or machine that performs this operation; also *attrib.* (See also under Cheese *v.*1)

1921 *Dict. Occup. Terms* (1927) § 371 Cheesing frame minder, cheesing frame tenter.

Cheetal, -ul: see *Chital.

Cheiloplasty, etc.: see *Chiloplasty, etc.

Cheiropodous (kəirǫ·pŏdǝs), *a. Zool.* Also chiro-. [-ous.] Of or belonging to the *Cheiropoda* (see Cheiropod); having feet like hands.

1889 *Century Dict.*

Cheka (tʃe·kă). Also che(-)ka, chay-ka, tcheka. [Russ., f. the names (*che ka*) of the initials ч к of чрезвычайная коммиссия *tshresvytshāinaya kommissiya* extraordinary commission.] An organization set up in 1917 under the Soviet régime in Russia for the secret investigation of counter-revolution activities (superseded in 1922 by the G.P.U. or *Ogpu). Hence **Che·kist,** a member of the Cheka.

The translation of the full description of the body is 'The All-Russian Extraordinary Commission attached to the Council of People's Commissaries for combating Counter-revolution, Speculation, and Sabotage'.

1921 *Glasgow Herald* 14 Oct. 9 The Che·ka..rallied round itself not only Communists, but criminals, both Russian and Internationalists. 1921 *Blackw. Mag.* Dec. 725/2 A nurse.. gained a reprieve through consenting to act as spy for the Chay-Ka. 1922 *Glasgow Herald* 10 Mar. 5 This Government announces the trial before the Special Revolutionary Tribunal, that is to say, the Tcheka, of a number of our old comrades of the Central Committee of our party for fictitious charges of attempts upon the lives of the Bolshevist leaders. *Ibid.* 15 Apr. 8 The Che-Ka, be tried to explain, was simply a modern edition of the Committee of Public Safety during the French Revolution. 1925 Popoff *Tcheka* 230 On.. December 21, 1917, the first meeting of the first Tcheka Council took place in the Smolny building. *Ibid.*, Of the first Tchekists only a small number were Communists. 1927 *Blackw. Mag.* June 849/1 The ingenious wickedness of the Tcheka goes beyond all the previous experience of history.

Chela 2. Add: (also **cheela**) One who occupies the position of disciple and servant.

1901 Kipling *Kim* i, When I was faint with hunger he begged for me, as would a *chela* for his teacher.

Cheliped (kī·liped). [f. mod.L. *chēla* (ad. Gr. χηλή) claw + L. *ped-*, *pēs* foot.] Each of the large prehensile claws of a crustacean.

1889 *Century Dict.* 1922 *Outward Bound* Nov. 141/1 The Fiddler Crab with his one cheliped..so vastly bigger than the other.

Chellean (ʃe·liăn). [f. the place-name *Chelles*, in the department of Seine-et-Marne, France.] Of or belonging to the earliest palæolithic period of Europe as represented by the flint implements found at Chelles.

1895 Dawson *Meeting-place of Geol. & Hist.* iv. (ed. 2) 41 Flint hache of the Ancient or Chellean type. 1927 H. Peake & Fleure *Apes & Men* 56 The fashioning of the early Palaeolithic, Chellean, flints betokens a high degree of purposeful skill and artistry.

Cheloidal (kīloi·dăl), *a.* [f. Cheloid + -al.] = Keloidal *a.*

1908 *Practitioner* Jan. 42 An incision, which..has become cheloidal, contracted, and puckered.

Chelsea (tʃe·lsī). Designating a kind of porcelain made at Chelsea in the 18th c.: used attrib. in *Chelsea porcelain, pottery, ware.*

1754 in Jewitt *Ceramic Art* (1878) I. 173 Chelsea porcelain toys. 1878 *Ibid.* 171 A complete service of Chelsea china. *Ibid.* 196 Porcelain made at Caughley, and intended to pass as 'Chelsea Derby'.

Cheltenham (tʃe·lt'nǝm). Name of a town in Gloucestershire used attrib. to designate: **a.** the chalybeate waters of the springs at Cheltenham, or the salts left by the evaporation of these waters.

1837 *Penny Cycl.* VII. 31/1 The persons most benefited by the Cheltenham waters are those who, after a long residence in hot climates, are affected with diseased liver. 1848 Dunglison *Med. Lex.* (ed. 7), *Cheltenham Salts*, these are sometimes made from the waters; at others, factitiously... Cheltenham Water, Artificial, may be made of Epsom salt, gr. xij, iron filings, gr. j: [etc.]. 1874 Garrod & Baxter *Mat. Med.* (1880) 142 The so-called Cheltenham salts consist chiefly of sulphate of soda.

b. The name of a fount of type.

1917 F. S. Henry *Printing for Schools & Shop* iii. 79 Cheltenham Oldstyle...A Capital R of Thirty-six-point Cheltenham. This paragraph has been set in Cheltenham to show the long ascenders so characteristic of the family group.

Chelydoid (ke·lidoid), *a.* and *sb.* [f. mod.L. *Chelydidæ*: see -oid.] **A.** *adj.* Of or pertaining to the *Chelydidæ*, a family of tortoises. **B.** *sb.* A tortoise belonging to this family.

1886 Günther in *Encycl. Brit.* XX. 471/2 It may be seen from this list that no Chelydoid passes northward beyond the Isthmus of Panama.

Chemic, *sb.* Add:

4. b. *attrib.*, as *chemic mixer.*

1921 *Dict. Occup. Terms* (1927) § 380 *Chemic mixer*;.. mixes bleaching powder with water, in readiness for use in kiers.

5. A dye consisting of a very acid solution of indigo in sulphuric acid. Also *attrib.*

1818 W. Tucker *Family Dyer & Scourer* I. (ed. 2) 7 There are some blues on silk, of a very light shade, that are dyed with chymic blue. *Ibid.* 35 Chymic for light blues, and greens on silk or woollen. *Ibid.* iii. 46 From your chymic bottle, one or two drops.

Chemical (ke·mikăl), *v.* [f. the sb.] *trans.* = next.

1884 *Harper's Mag.* LXIX. No. 3 Advt., Washing compounds and soap..are highly chemicaled.

Chemicalize (ke·mikălaiz), *v.* [f. Chemical *a.* + -ize.] *trans.* To treat with a chemical or chemicals. Hence **Che:micaliza·tion.**

1902 *Clarion* 17 Oct. 1 If this change is produced in milk by chemicalising it, in the case of chemicalised meats, also, a similar result must follow. *Ibid.*, Milk,..if consumed soon after chemicalisation, may produce a mild..attack of suffering. 1907 *Lancet* 25 May 1443/1 The Chemicalised Road [the calcium chloride treatment of roads].

Chemicker (ke·mikǝɹ). [f. Chemic *v.* + -er 1.] (See quot.)

1921 *Dict. Occup. Terms* (1927) § 381 *Chemicker*,..minds a kind of mangle, trough of which contains chemicking (bleaching) solution.

Chemico-. Add: *chemico-engineering, -physics*; *chemico-crystallographical, -mineralogical* adjs.; **Che:mico-bio·logy,** the chemistry of living matter; hence **Che:micobiolo·gic** *a.*; **Che:mico-dyna·mic** *a.*, transforming chemical energy into the energy of motion.

1903 *Lancet* 22 Aug. *Advt.* 3 The results of bacteriologic and of *chemicobiologic research as applied to the pathology of midwifery. 1908 *Carnegie Trust Rep.* 24 *Chemico-crystallographical researches on thallic sulphates. 1909 *Cent. Dict.* Suppl., *Chemicodynamic. 1928 *Daily Express* 12 Sept. 11/4 The original structure of these cells is a chemico-dynamic structure which requires oxygen..to preserve it. 1897 *Daily News* 2 June 7/4 Prof. Dewar's magnificent *chemico-engineering laboratory. 1903 Geikie *Text-bk. Geol.* (ed. 4) I. 201 In Professor Rosenbusch's scheme of classification the *chemico-mineralogical characters of the igneous rocks are chosen as the basis of the grouping. a 1909 *Buck's Handbk. Med. Sci.* VII. 758 (Cent. D. Suppl.) *Chemico-physics.

Chemigraphy (kemi·grăfi). [f. Gr. χημία Alchemy + -graphy.]

1. Any mechanical engraving process depending upon chemical action; *spec.* a process of zinc etching without the aid of photography.

2. A process of obtaining half-tones by printing, from the same plate, in two colours, or two shades of the same colour, one of which is slightly out of register. Hence **Chemigra·phic** *a.*, pertaining to or produced by chemigraphy. Also **Chemi·grapher,** one who prints by a half-tone photo-mechanical process. **Che·migraph,** a print obtained by chemigraphy.

1892 *Daily News* 23 Mar. 6/3 Mr. Leon Warnerke next gave some illustrations of 'Chemigraphic etching'. 1897 H. W. Singer & W. Strang *Etching*, etc. 25 Whatever niceties the chemigrapher or white-line woodcutter can manage to put upon his block will come out in the printing.

Chemin de fer (ʃəmæ̃n də fɛ̄r). [Fr., lit. 'road of iron', railway.] A form of baccarat.

1902 *Encycl. Brit.* XXVIII. 583 To add baccarat banque and *chemin de fer* to the list of unlawful games. 1902 *Daily Chron.* 13 May 10/2 He raided the club, and found..the defendants seated round large tables playing chemin de fer.

Chemio-: = *Chemo-.

Chemisal: see *Chamisal.

Chemmy (ʃe·mi). Familiar f. *chemin de fer.*

1923 P. G. Wodehouse *Inimit. Jeeves* xvi. 214 We went on from Ciro's to play chemmy with some fellows.

Chemo- (ke·mo), used as combining form = Chemic *a.*, in **Chemokinesis** (ke:mokəinī·sis) [Gr. κίνησις movement] *Biol.*, a condition of increased activity of an organism, induced by the presence of a chemical substance; hence **Che:mokine·tic** (-kəine·tik) *a.*; **Chemore·flex** *sb.*, a response to a chemical change in the environment by a motor reaction; *a.*, pertaining to or designating a reflex action resulting from a chemical stimulus; **Chemosynthesis** (kemosi·nþĭsis) [Gr. σύνθεσις composition], the formation of carbohydrates out of inorganic compounds by an organism in darkness or in the absence of sunlight, as distinguished from 'photosynthesis'; **Che:motherapeu·tic(al** *adjs.*, of or pertaining to **Che:motherapeu·tics** or **Chemothe·rapy,** the treatment of internal disease by chemical re-agents that have a toxic effect on the disease-micro-organisms.

1900 *Amer. Jrnl. Physiol.* Apr. 398 The organisms soon leave the area of operation of the chemical causing the reactions. This phenomenon Garry calls '*chemokinesis'. 1901 G. N. Calkins *Protozoa* 299 If an effect is produced which is not directive, it is said to be *chemokinetic. 1902 *Pop. Sci. Monthly* Mar. 463 [The] complicated activities of such highly developed organisms as ants and bees may be subsumed, with surprising completeness, under some such heading as the '*chemoreflex'. 1903 tr. *E. Strasburger's Text-bk. Bot.* 197 The necessary energy is here obtained not from photosynthesis but from the oxidation of ammonia into nitrous acid, and this into nitric acid (*chemosynthesis). 1904 tr. *Haeckel's Wonders of Life* 222 Pfeffer has called this carbon-assimilation, on account of its purely chemical nature, 'chemosynthesis,' in opposition to the ordinary photosynthesis by means of sun-light. 1908 R. J. H. Gibson *Biol.* vi. 48 In all probability the energy required is obtained by the oxidation of primary organic compounds, and possibly of protoplasm itself (chemosynthesis). 1927 *Daily Express* 12 July 9/7 A concentrated attack is being made on the problem from many different angles—pathological, biochemical,..and *chemo-therapeutical. 1922 *Encycl. Brit.* XXX. 154/2 *Chemotherapy. The ideal method of using an antiseptic is to introduce it into the circulation.

Chemotaxis (kemotæ·ksis). *Biol.* Also chemio-. [mod.L., f. *Chemo- + Gr. τάξις arrangement.] The disposition exhibited by certain living cells, or free-swimming organisms, of movement towards or away from certain chemical substances held in solution. Also called **Chemota·ctism.** Hence **Chem(i)ota·ctic, -ical, -ta·xic** *adjs.*

1893 Burdon-Sanderson in *Rep. Brit. Assoc.* (1894) 26 As a general designation of reactions of this kind Pfeffer devised the term Chemotaxis, or, as we in England prefer to call it, Chemiotaxis. *Ibid.* 27 Chemiotactic cells—that is, cells which act under the orders of chemical stimuli. 1897 *Nature* 16 Sept. 481/2 This remarkable attraction—chemical attraction, or '*chemotaxis*'—is a very general phenomenon. 1898 tr. *E. Strasburger's Text-bk. Bot.* 263 The chemotactic irritability of Bacteria. 1902 *Encycl. Brit.* XXXI. 518 The influence of the chemical substance is either that of attraction or repulsion, the one being known as positive, the other as negative chemotaxis. 1903 Snyder *New Conceptions in Sci.* 202 It is simply a chemical reaction between certain substances in..the fly and the meat, a case of chemotactism. 1903 *Med. Record* 7 Mar. 392 (Cent. D. Suppl.) Chemotaxic. 1908 Hans Driesch *Sci. & Philos. Organism* I. 152 Each mesenchyme-cell is specified..with regard to its chemotactical irritability. 1908 *Practitioner* Jan. 22 Some of which [cells] die, and thus set up a chemotactic action. *Ibid.* Mar. 392 A negative chemiotactic effect.

Chemotropism (kemǫ·trǫpiz'm). *Biol.* [f. Gr. χημία Alchemy + τρόπος a turning + -ism.] A condition of sensitiveness to a chemical substance in solution, exhibited by certain organisms, or parts of organisms, producing curvature towards the stimulus, termed *positive chemotropism*, or away from it, *negative chemotropism.* Hence **Chemotro·pic** *a.*

1897 *Nature* 16 Sept. 481/2 The cause of the bending [of the hyphæ of fungi] lies in a powerful 'chemotropic' action. 1898 tr. *E. Strasburger's Text-bk. Bot.* 263 Corresponding to the chemotactic irritability of Bacteria and spermatozoids, roots, fungus hyphæ, and pollen tubes exhibit positive and negative chemotropic curvatures. *Ibid.*, Rheotropism..and Aerotropism, a form of chemotropism, are additional phenomena,..which stand in direct relations to certain vital requirements of plants. 1901 J. Loeb *Compar. Physiol. Brain* 186 The orientation of an organism by diffusing molecules is termed chemotropism.

Chenopodium (kenǫpǭ·diǒm). *Bot.* [mod.L., f. Gr. χήν goose + ποδ-, πούς foot.] A plant of the genus so named; goose-foot. Also *attrib.*

1807 T. Martyn *Miller's Gard. & Bot. Dict.* s.v., It is whiter than most of the Chenopodiums; and varies exceedingly, both when young, and in its seeding state. 1915 *Jrnl. Chem. Soc.* CVIII. I. 195 The toxicity of chenopodium oil is increased in starvation. 1926 *Contemp. Rev.* Feb. 235 A list of such flowers includes chenopodiums, [etc.].

Cheque, *sb.* **4.** Add: *cheque clerk*; **cheque end,** an ornamental device on the perforated edge of a cheque, money order, etc., as a safeguard against fraud; **cheque guard** (see quot.).

1908 *Westm. Gaz.* 29 Sept. 8/2 He presented a cheque for £1,000 to the *cheque clerk, who examined the balance and initialled the cheque. 1884 Knight *Dict. Mech.* Suppl., *Check Guard*, a means of preventing tampering with bank checks, raising the figures, etc.

Cheque (tʃek), *v.* In *U.S.* check. [f. Cheque *sb.*] trans. *To cheque out*: to pay out by cheque. ¶ For the intr. use 'to draw a cheque', see Check *v.*1 17.

1908 *Westm. Gaz.* 29 Dec. 3/1 Banking credit..which I can draw out wholly in gold or bank-notes, or which I can cheque out in settlement of my debts.

Chequer, *sb.*1 **16.** Add: **chequer-board** = *checker-board* (Checker *sb.*2 2 c).

1870 'Fanny Fern' *Ginger-Snaps* 79 When some clerical big-gun is supposed to make a false move on the sacerdotal chequer-board.

Chequerer (tʃe·kǝrǝɹ). [f. Chequer *v.* + -er 1.] One who makes a chequered pattern.

1921 *Dict. Occup. Terms* (1927) § 498 *Chequerer* (small arms); cuts a criss-cross or chequered pattern on wooden fore-ends and butts of guns and rifles by hand.

Chequer-work. 2. (Later U.S. example.)

1878 B. F. Taylor *Between Gates* 263 [The water] coursing along the checker work of channels.

Cherem (he·rem). Also **herem.** [Heb. חרם *ḥerem*, f. *ḥāram* to devote, put under a curse.] Excommunication from the Synagogue.

1903 *Jewish Encycl.* V. 286/2 If..the excommunicated showed no sign of penitence or remorse, the niddui might be renewed.., and finally the 'herem', the most rigorous form of excommunication, might be pronounced. 1925 W. Ewing *J. E. H. Thomson* 158 For some comparatively trivial cause a *cherem*, or ban, would fall like a bolt from the blue. 1926 *Expository Times* Aug. 500/2 It discusses the taboo..and the herem or ban.

Chermany (tʃɜ·ɹmăni). *U.S.* [Of obscure origin.] A variety of baseball played in the southern States.

1889 *Century Dict.* 1904 M. D. Conway *Autob.* I. 35 Our recess games were chiefly chermany and bandy.

Cherokee (tʃerokī·), *a. U.S.* **1.** The name of a tribe of North American Indians, formerly occupying a large portion of the southern United States, used *attrib.* or as *adj.* Of or pertaining to the Cherokees, or the region inhabited by them.

1716 *N. Carolina Col. Rec.* II. 256 The officers who shall command the said soldiers in the said Cherokee expedition. 1756 *Ibid.* V. 635 Major Lewis is return'd from the Cherokee Country. 1765 H. Timberlake *Mem.* 75 A war carried into the heart of the Cherokee country. 1778 *Cal. Virginia St. Papers* I. 306 This deponent says, that he does not understand the Cherokee Tongue. 1834 W. G. Simms *Guy Rivers* (1882) 347 The reader has already heard something of the Cherokee pony...They are a small, but compactly made and hardy creature. 1849 C. Lanman *Alleghany Mts.* i. 12 After the State Legislature had divided the Cherokee Purchase into lots..everybody was on tiptoe with regard to its distribution. 1868 *Trans. Ill. Agric. Soc.* VII. 142 The long-horned or Cherokee cattle passing through North Carolina and Virginia on their way to the Northern markets. 1927 *Blackw. Mag.* July 59/2 Prince Charles might just as well have invaded England at the head of a band of Cherokee Indians.

2. a. *Cherokee plum*, the Chickasaw plum.

1786 Washington *Diaries* III. 32 Hoed the ground behind the garden again and planted therein, in three rows, 177 of the wild, or Cherokee plumb. *Ibid.* 81.

b. *Cherokee rose*, a wild rose of the southern United States, *Rosa lævigata.*

1838 Caroline Gilman *Recoll. Southern Matron* 227 The piercing thorn of the Cherokee rose renders it impenetrable by cattle. 1846 T. B. Thorpe *Myst. Backwoods* 158 A rough Virginia fence, over which the Cherokee rose had entwined itself. 1896 J. C. Harris *Sister Jane* 19 The Cherokee rose was rapidly covering the broken-down fences with its glistening green shield. 1901 C. Mohr *Plant Life Alabama* 54 The Cherokee rose..is said to have been found by the whites on their first arrival at the villages of the Cherokees and Creeks.

ellipt. 1838 Caroline Gilman *Recoll.* xiii. 89 The Cherokee hedge shut out the view. 1888 *Harper's Mag.* May 867/1 Their only exit lay at the end of the Cherokee hedge.

3. *Cherokee Strip*, a part of the State of Oklahoma inhabited by the Cherokees; also *fig.* (see quot.).

1889 *Kansas Times & Star* 13 June, Andy Snider..is said to have thousands of cattle down on the Cherokee strip. 1905 *Baltimore American* 7 Mar. 4 On the boundary of what is known as the 'Cherokee Strip', or, in other words, the section on the Democratic side occupied by Republican Senators who cannot find desks on the Republican side.

Cherokee·, *v.* [f. as prec.] *trans.* To arrange in the fashion of the Cherokees.

1771 *Massachusetts Spy* 21 Mar. (Th.) An old fashioned lady, with a foretop of hair Cherokeed to imitate the Indian dress.

Cherried, *ppl. a.* Add:

2. Adorned or trimmed with artificial cherries.

1923 *Chambers's Jrnl.* 771/1 The gay cherried hat and flower-sprigged dress of some youthful my lady or Miss.

Cherrup, var. of Chirrup *sb.*

1843 R. Carlton *New Purchase* xix. 162 All cherrups and get-ups and even old-rascals-you..all, all were in vain!

Cherry, *sb.* Add: **2. b.** Also *attrib.*

1889 Rose T. Cooke *Steadfast* i. 13 A small cherry table with two leaves.

9. *cherry-time* (later example).

1849 F. Douglas *Life* 1, I do not remember to have ever met a slave who could tell of his birthday. They seldom come nearer to it than..cherry-time, spring-time, harvest-time, or fall-time.

10. cherry-birch *U.S.* (see quot.); **Cherry-breeches** = *Cherry-pickers*; **cherry coffee,** the fruit containing the coffee berry; **cherry cordial** = Cherry-bounce 1; **cherry country,** the district in Kent, where the cherry is largely grown, in extensive cherry-orchards, for commercial purposes; **Cherry-pickers,** a jocular name for the 11th Light Dragoons, now the 11th Hussars; **cherry-wood** (earlier U.S. examples).

1832 D. J. Browne *Sylva Amer.* 118 Black Birch: its secondary denominations are Mountain Mahogany in Virginia, and Sweet Birch and *Cherry Birch in Connecticut, Massachusetts, and further north. 1871 Forbes *Exper. War Fr. & Germany* III. ii. II. 181 When he [*sc.* Lord Cardigan] commanded the '*cherry breeches'. 1858 Simmonds *Dict. Trade*, *Cherry-coffee*, the planters' name for the fruit of the coffee as picked from the tree, before it has undergone the operations of pulping, drying, &c., to prepare the berry for shipment. 1709–10 W. Salmon *Family Dict.* 71/2 *Cherry Cordial. Take Black Cherries, [etc.]. 1836 *Mag. Domestic Econ.* I. 7 Make also..cherry cordial. 1902 *Garden* 10 May 309/3 To get into the heart of the *Cherry country one can make Maidstone, Sittingbourne, or Faversham the starting point, and work through miles of orchards. 1882 *Spons' Encycl. Industr. Arts* v. 1638 '*Cherry-gum' is a term applied very indefinitely to the gummy exudations of cherry, plum, apricot, almond, and other trees, included in the genera *Prunus, Cerasus*, and *Amygdalus.* 1865 *Notes & Queries* 3rd Ser. VII. 49/1 11th Hussars—Cherubims and *Cherry Pickers. 1903 *Westm. Gaz.* 2 Dec. 1/3 The 11th [Hussars] got its name of 'the Cherry-Pickers' through some of its men having been taken prisoners in a fruit garden during the war in the Peninsula. 1928 *Daily Express* 27 Mar. 10/6 Those crimson overalls of the 'Cherry-pickers'..were really a kind of wedding present from the Prince Consort. 1829 J. F. Cooper *Wish-ton-wish* iii. 39 Candles of tallow, on a table of *cherry-wood. 1840 C. F. Hoffman *Greyslaer* v. i. III. 10 A small cherry-wood table and a few rush-bottomed chairs.

Cherry-brandy. (Earlier U.S. example.)

1686 J. Dunton *Lett. fr. N. England* (1867) 33 Preserv'd Damozins, Cherry-Brandy, and the like Knick-knacks.

Chervonetz (tʃǝ·ɹvǫnets). Also -ets. Pl. **chervontzi, -si.** [Russ.] A Soviet bank-note nominally equal to ten roubles gold currency.

1923 *British Weekly* 15 Nov. 164/4, I was struck with the remarkable success of the new currency—the chervonets—which has a gold backing. 1927 *Times* (weekly ed.) 3 June 694/3 The purchasing power of the chervonetz has slowly but persistently fallen. 1928 *Daily Tel.* 17 Jan. 12/2 They receive an allowance of five chervontsi for their personal expenses on the journey.

Chess-board. b. Add: *attrib.* or *adj.* Resembling a chess-board; like that of a chess-board.

1903 *Daily Chron.* 11 Dec. 7/1 Such chessboard cities as Melbourne and Adelaide. 1904 *Ibid.* 10 Feb. 7/5 If the Russians adopt chess-board rules of war the next event will be an attack by Russian torpedo craft. 1924 Collingwood *Roman Britain* 48 To go in for a town-planning scheme, to lay out a chess-board street-plan.

Hence **Che·ss-board** *v. trans.*, to divide (land) into more or less equal portions resembling the squares on a chess-board.

1891 *Daily News* 12 May 4/8 Mr. Morley protested the other day against 'chessboarding' Ireland. 1924 *Chambers's Jrnl.* 747/1 A tract of low-lying, cultivated land, chess-boarded into fields under various crops.

Supplement, p. 3873; Corrigenda, p. 4092; Spurious words, p. 4093; Books quoted, p. 4094

Chessdom (tʃe·sdəm). [f. CHESS sb.[1] + -DOM.] The 'realm' of chess and chess-players.

1875 *City of London Chess Mag.* June 142 There are plenty of courts in Chessdom only too ready to investigate these complaints.

Chesser (tʃe·səɹ). *U.S.* [f. CHESS sb.[1] + -ER[1].] A chess-player.

1875 *City of London Chess Mag.* May 105 English chessers, to use the American word,..ought certainly to subscribe to this capital monthly.

Chessy (tʃe·si), *a.*[2] *U.S.* [f. CHESS sb.[3] + -Y[1].] Full of chess grass.

1842 MRS. KIRKLAND *Forest Life* I. 194 My wheat was unaccountably chessy, though I turned water upon it, and kept it moist all summer.

Chest, *sb.*[1] Add:

9. c. Phr. *To get it off one's chest*: to relieve one's mind by making a statement or confession. *vulgar colloq.*

1902 *Daily Chron.* 27 Sept. 3/2 The desire is either to deliver a message to the world or to express the individual personality—to 'get it off your chest' is the horrid, vulgar phrase. 1910 W. J. LOCKE *Simon the Jester* xxi, 'I've got to get it off my chest,' said he..'I want to tell you that I've been every end of a silly ass.'

10. a. chest-bellows, the piston bellows (Knight *Dict. Mech.* 1874); **chest-lock**, a mortise lock for a chest or box (Ibid.); **b.** *chest girth, measure, measurement*; **chest-deep** *a.* (*adv.*), so deep as to reach to the height of one's chest; **chest-expander** (see quot. 1858 and EXPANDER); **chest-piece**, that part of a stethoscope which, when in use, is placed against the chest; **chest register**, the lower portion of the compass of the human voice; **chest-wall**, the external surface of the thorax or chest.

1889 C. EDWARDES *Sardinia & Sardes* 172 The stream was strong and *chest-deep. 1849 *Rep. U.S. Comm. Patents* (1850) 270 Having thus fully described..the operation of the shoulder brace and *chest expander. 1858 SIMMONDS *Dict. Trade*, *Chest-expander*, an application of fixed or pliable materials for keeping back the shoulders. 1904 *Daily Chron.* 29 Dec. 6/6 A noticeable increase of *chest girth of every boy in the school. 1889 *Cent. Dict.*, **Chest-measure*, the greatest girth of the chest. 1894 *Brit. Med. Jrnl.* 3 Nov. 991/1 The ear pieces are made of india-rubber,..and the *chest piece has an india-rubber air pad cover. 1909 *Practitioner* Dec. 862 The edge of the metal chest-piece might be conveniently rimmed with hard rubber. 1879 *St. George's Hosp. Rep.* IX. 285 A wound on *chest-wall. 1909 *Practitioner* Dec. 862 Many physicians prefer to use the unaided ear applied direct to the chest-wall.

Chesterfield. Add: **2.** A stuffed-over couch or sofa with a back and two ends, one of which is sometimes made adjustable.

1900 *Westm. Gaz.* 30 Jan. 10/2 The club room, charmingly furnished with chairs and Chesterfields upholstered with blue cretonnes. 1919 C. ORR *Glorious Thing* vi. 67 'Is that the book?' asked Nannie, drawing in the Chesterfield, and motioning to him to sit down beside her. 1927 *Chambers's Jrnl.* 641/1 Both were seated, Jimmy in the chair facing him, and Betty on the chesterfield.

Chestertonian (tʃestəɹtōu·niăn), *a.* [f. the surname *Chesterton* + -IAN.] Of, pertaining to, or characteristic of Gilbert Keith Chesterton (1874–), journalist and author, his writings, style, etc.

1905 *Daily Chron.* 21 June 3/1 Chestertonian. [Heading of a review of *Heretics*, by G. K. Chesterton.] 1909 *Ibid.* 3 Mar. 3/3 He is immune from the Chestertonian taint of straining after paradox and epigram. 1921 *Public Opinion* 29 July 102/1 The Lord Chancellor was almost lyrical or Chestertonian in his rhapsody.

Chestful (tʃe·stful). [-FUL.] The quantity (of articles) contained in a chest. (See CHEST sb.[1] 10a, quots. 1723, 1884 in Dict.)

Chestnut, *sb.* Add:

3. b. Cape (or **Wild**) **chestnut**, a tree, *Calodendron capense*, indigenous to South Africa, bearing pink blossoms. **Wild chestnut**, (*a*) = *Cape chestnut*; (*b*) the edible nut of *Brabeium stellatifolium*, a South African tree.

1868 J. CHAPMAN *Trav.* II. 450 The Wild Chestnut..well deserving its name for its exquisitely-pencilled delicate pink flowers. 1875 S. W. SILVER & Co. *Handbk. S. Africa* 138 The..Wild Chestnut is the fruit of *Calodendron Capense.* 1909 *East London Dispatch* 3 July 5 (Pettman) The beautiful lilac flowers of the wild chestnut. 1912 *Ibid.* 12 Apr. 7 (Ibid.) It is very seldom that the Cape chestnut and the Wild fig become altogether devoid of leaves.

C. chestnut-extract, an extract from chestnut wood, used in dyeing silk black; **chestnut oak** (examples); **chestnut-roaster**, a stove used by itinerant vendors of roasted chestnuts; also, the vendor.

1881 *Spons' Encycl. Industr. Arts* IV. 1226 Hemlock-extract is a deep-red syrupy extract of the bark of the hemlock pine of America. *Chestnut-extract is a similar product from the rasped wood of the Spanish chestnut. 1766 W. STORK *Acc. East Florida* 45 The *chestnut oak..is very common in Florida. 1816 U. BROWN *Jrnl.* in *Maryland Hist. Mag.* XI. 221 [We] found on our right..a Chestnut Oak marked and Owned by Jacob Beeson. 1834 *Southern Lit. Messenger* I. 97 There is little timber of large size, the growth being chiefly chestnut oak. 1885 'C. E. CRADDOCK' *Prophet Gt. Smoky Mts.* xi. 197 A branch, too, of the low-spreading Chestnut-oak..was visible. 1909 *Westm. Gaz.* 4 Sept. 2/2 The bowed old woman who sits hugging her *chestnut roaster at the end of the Pont Marguet. 1921 *Dict. Occup. Terms* (1927) § 777 Baked chestnut man; chestnut roaster. 1923 *Weekly Dispatch* 29 Apr. 2, I have never more than once come across a genuine old chestnut-roaster with a pierced box and lid.

Chestnut, *v.* [f. the sb.] *trans.* To make (a joke, etc.) stale by constant repetition.

1909 T. C. DE LEON *Belles, Beaux*, etc. 266 The over familiar retort, chestnutted by frequent misapplication.

Chestnutting, *vbl. sb.* (Earlier and later U.S. examples.)

1875 MRS. STOWE *We & Neighbors* xxxiii. 314 Reminiscences of..boys and girls going chestnutting and having good times. 1907 M. C. HARRIS *Tents of Wickedness* II. i. 113, I know I would apostatise for a chestnutting in Frost's woods on a mellow September afternoon.

Chestnutty (tʃe·snʌti), *a.* [f. CHESTNUT + -Y[1].] Resembling (that of) a chestnut. **a.** Of a colour. **b.** Of an oft-told tale or joke.

a. 1893 *Strand Mag.* Nov. 537/1 His [eyes] are chestnutty brown.

b. 1906 *Daily Chron.* 12 Nov. 4/4 The story, slightly chestnutty in its flavour, of the theatre manager. 1908 *Ibid.* 19 May 3/1 There are tales of Sydney Smith, mostly, it must be said, of a chestnutty flavour.

Chesty (tʃe·sti), *a.* [f. CHEST sb.[1] 9, from the idea of thrusting out the chest as a gesture of conceit.] **1.** Conceited and self-assertive. *U.S. slang.*

1901 H. MCHUGH *John Henry* 57 It isn't quite as chesty as 'David Harum', but there's more poetry in it. 1903 *N. Y. Sun* 29 Nov. 26 His school reputation..may have had the effect of enlarging his self-esteem. He may have been a bit chesty, as it is known in the vernacular of the campus. 1912 MATHEWSON *Pitching* iii. 69 The team had won the championship in 1900, and naturally they were all pretty chesty. 1929 S. ANDERSON in *Mercury Story Bk.* 231 Her father was not rich to make her chesty because she was his daughter.

2. Inclined to, marked by, or symptomatic of chest disease. *colloq.*

Hence **Che·stily** *adv.*; **Che·stiness.**

1908 G. H. LORIMER *J. Spurlock* iii. 59 So I explained rather chestily to Horton. 'Of course, I didn't send those notes; but it was done by one of my authorized agents.' 1910 O. JOHNSON *Varmint* xiii. 181 Why so much chestiness? ..I haven't sold anything to any of you, have I?

Chetel. (Later U.S. example.)

1634 *Trelawny Papers* (1884) 31 The Chimnay..is so large that we can place our Chittle within the Clavell piece.

Chetel: see *CHITAL.

Chetive (ʃetiv), *a.* [Fr. *chétive*, fem. of *chétif*.] Frail, small and thin.

1908 LADY GROVE in *Daily Chron.* 30 Oct. 4/4 Her tall, strapping girl is usually accompanied in the streets by a chétive, but rather pretty little maid. 1921 *Blackw. Mag.* Feb. 250/1 Upon this small coterie..there burst..this insignificant *chétive* child.

Chetty (tʃe·ti). Also 8 Chitty, 9 Chettie. [Malayalam *chetti*, Tamil *shetti*.] An individual of any of the South-Indian trading castes so named. Also *attrib.*

1773 IVES *Voy.* 25 Chitties are a particular kind of merchants of Madrass, and are generally very rich, but rank with the left hand cast. 1880 *Encycl. Brit.* XII. 760/1 Along the eastern sea-board [of India] the predominating classes of traders are those named Chetties and Komatis. 1908 CAROLINE CORNER *Ceylon* xxix. 270 Very exclusive indeed is the Chettie socially. *Ibid.* 273 The host..a Chettie in chettie costume. 1912 *Times* 1 Oct. 6/6 A chetty gave as a treat to 173 persons a bushel of rice each. 1922 *Blackw. Mag.* Nov. 685/1 You will doubtless meet Chetty and even Brahman ladies from the hot plains of Tanjore.

Chevalet. Add:

c. *Glass-manuf.* A stand or bench upon which a cylinder of glass is laid before it is spread out.

1890 W. J. GORDON *Foundry* 147 The cylinder—some six feet long—is then laid on the wooden 'chevalet' or stand.

Chew, *v.* Add:

3. g. *To chew oakum* (Naut.): (of a ship) to grind the oakum out of its seams by the working of its timbers.

1867 SMYTH *Sailor's Word-bk.*, Chewing of Oakum or Pitch.

9. *To chew the rag* or *fat* (Army slang): to discuss a matter complainingly or grousingly; to reiterate an old grievance, dispute, etc.

1885 J. B. PATTERSON *Life in Ranks* ix. 77 Persisting to argue the point, or 'chew the rag,' as it is termed in rank and file phraseology, with some extra intelligent non-commissioned officer. *Ibid.* xv. 124 The various diversions of whistling, singing, arguing the point, chewing the rag, or fat. 1891 J. M. DIXON *Dict. Idiom. Eng. Phr.* s.v., He was chewing the rag at me the whole afternoon. 1919 *War Slang* in *Athenæum* 8 Aug. 727/2 If anyone starts fault-finding or 'chewing the fat' he is immediately 'ticked off'. 1928 *Daily Express* 2 Mar. 5/2 We 'chew the rag,' as our husbands would call it, over happenings of weeks and even months ago.

Chewing, *vbl. sb.* **3. chewing-gum** (earlier U.S. example); **chewing tobacco.**

1864 *Yale Lit. Mag.* XXIX. 293 (Th.) Burgundy pitch, two chaws for a cent, *Chewing gum, cent a stick. 1835 J. MARTIN *Gazetteer Virginia* 175 A dark greyish soil.. which produces the best *chewing tobacco in the state.

Chew-stick. Add: Also, in Sierra Leone, the root of the cola, *Bichea* (or *Cola*) *acuminata* and *Vernonia amygdalina* (see quots.).

1887 MOLONEY *Forestry W. Afr.* 287 The roots [of the cola], called 'chew-stick,' are used in Sierra Leone for cleaning the teeth and sweetening the breath. *Ibid.* 371 Chew-stick of Ewuro (*Vernonia amygdalina*, Del.).—Shrub..used in Sierra Leone as a bitter.

Chi (kəi). The name of χ, the 22nd letter of the Greek alphabet; used *attrib.* in the name of a moth having a marking of the form of this letter.

1832 J. RENNIE *Butterfl. & Moths* 77 The July Chi (*Polia Chi*). 1869 E. NEWMAN *Brit. Moths* 394 The grey chi. 1927 *Contemp. Rev.* July 97 The chi moth is wonderfully concealed when it rests on a grey stone wall.

Chianti (kiæ·nti). [Named from the *Chianti* Mountains, Tuscany, the region of its production.] In full *Chianti wine*: A dry red wine of Tuscany.

1833 REDDING *Wines* ix. 245 The wine of Chianti comes principally from a creeping species of vine, *vite bassa*. ..Chianti wine was formerly imported into Great Britain before that of Oporto had nearly excluded the other species, and the red wine of Florence continued to arrive after the importation of Chianti had ceased. 1887 *Athenæum* 12 Nov. 635/3 He lived in Florence..when a *fiasco* of good Chianti could be had for a paul.

Chiaster (kəi·æstəɹ). *Zool.* [f. Gr. χιαστός marked with a χ (*CHI) + ἀστήρ star (see *ASTER 5).] A star-shaped sponge-spicule with slender cylindrical rays.

1888 SOLLAS in *Challenger Rep.* XXV. p. lxiv. 1900 *Proc. Zool. Soc.* 20 Feb. 133 Somal chiasters.

Chic. Add:

A. *sb.* **b.** In the fine arts: Originality of conception employed in the production of a work of art, as distinguished from working with a model.

1883 *Century Mag.* XXV. 575/2 To use *chic*, in artistic parlance is to produce effects by means of the imagination and by means of analogy. 1891 [see the verb below].

c. 'A talent for rapid and effective art-work; facility and cleverness in execution, as distinguished from talent' (*Standard Dict.* 1895). *U.S.*

1889 HOWELLS *Hazard of New Fortunes* I. II. iv. 169 Where a girl doesn't seem very strong..no amount of *chic* is going to help.

B. *adj.* **2.** Chivalrous. *U.S.*

1892 *New York Tribune* 13 Mar. 16/6 It was very chic.. for him to have preferred to resign the chief magistracy of the Republic..rather than to affix his signature.

Hence **Chic** *v.*, in painting (see quot.).

1891 FARMER *Slang* s.v., Among English painters, *to chic up a picture*, or *to do a thing from chic* = to work without models and out of one's own head.

Chicane, *sb.* Add:

3. In the game of bridge, the condition of holding no trumps. *Double chicane*, chicane of both partners.

1886 *Biritch or Russian Whist* 4 If one hand has no trumps ..this is called 'chicane'. 1895 'BOAZ' *Laws of Bridge* 3 Chicane is thus reckoned:—If a player holds no trump, he and his partner score for Chicane twice the value of the trump suit trick. 1900 'J. DOE' *Bridge Man.* 8 Double Chicane is scored if neither of two partnered players has a card of the Trump suit...Double Chicane [counts] four by honours.

Chicaric (tʃi·kărik). *U.S.* [Echoic.] A name for the turnstone, *Strepsilas interpres.*

1877 HALLOCK *Sportsman's Gazetteer* 164 The names Chicaric and Chickling have reference to their rasping notes.

Chick, *sb.*[4] Add:

2. The call-note (of a bird). Also *chick-chick*. (Cf. CHACK *sb.*[3], *CHACK-CHACK.)

1859 H. KINGSLEY *G. Hamlyn* v, The chick-chick of the stonechat. 1894 R. B. SHARPE *Handbk. Birds Gt. Brit.* (1896) I. 105 They never uttered more than a whispered call-note, 'chick'. 1922 ZANE GREY *To Last Man* iv. 84 A hoarse-voiced old turkey gobbler was booming his chug-a-lug ..., and the softer chick of hen turkeys answered him.

Chickaleary (tʃi·kăliəri), *a.* (*sb.*) *Costers' slang.* [f. CHICK *sb.*[1] + LEERY *a.*[2]] Artful, downy. Also *sb.*, a 'downy cove'.

c 1869 VANCE *Ballad, Chick-a-leary Cove* (Farmer) I'm a chickaleary cove..; Whitechapel was the village I was born in. 1908 *Daily Chron.* 3 Aug. 4/4 It's the chickalearies and their donahs that are responsible.

Chickara: see *CHINKARA.

Chickaree. *U.S.* (Earlier example. See also *CHIPAREE.)

1829 J. RICHARDSON *Fauna Bor.-Amer.* I. 187 *Sciurus Hudsonius* (Pennant). The Chickaree.

Chickasaw (tʃi·kăsō), *a. U.S.* [The name of a tribe of North American Indians (also written *Chickesaw, Chicasa*), chiefly occupying the state of Mississippi.]

1. *Chickasaw rose*, the Cherokee rose.

1835 J. H. INGRAHAM *South-West* II. 108 The 'chickasaw rose', which is a beautiful hedge thorn, grows..luxuriantly [in Mississippi]. 1887 *Harper's Mag.* Feb. 350/1 Along one side of his home..runs a superb hedge of Chickasaw roses.

2. *Chickasaw plum*, a wild plum of the Mississippi region (*Prunus angustifolia*).

1821 T. NUTTALL *Trav. Arkansa* vii. 137 The abundance of Chickasaw plum bushes forming a grove. 1846–50 A. WOOD *Class-bk. Bot.* 241 *Prunus Chicăsa.* Chickasaw Plum...A fine fruit-shrub, native of Arkansas, etc., often cultivated. 1854 MARCY & MCCLELLAN *Explor. Red River* 19 The plums also grow upon small bushes from two to six feet high..they are the Chickasaw plum (*Prunus chicasa*). 1865–6 *Trans. Ill. Agric. Soc.* VI. 390 Our beautiful foliaged Chickasaw Plum.

3. Applied to a variety of grape.

1861 *Trans. Ill. Agric. Soc.* IV. 97 A new seedling which is called the Chickasaw, which is a very delicious grape.

Chicken[1]. Add:

1. d. *dial.* or *colloq.* as coll. sing. for fowls of any age; also individually (*U.S.*).

1829 SOUTHEY *Pilgr. Compostella* iv, The chicken were her delight. 1859 *Knickerbocker Mag.* Mar. LIII. 317 Tell Sal to knock over a chicken or two. 1864 in *Southern Hist. Soc. Papers* (1876) I. 379, I sent him off to cook a chicken and some biscuits. 1887 *Scribner's Mag.* May 621/1 The farm people had all retired with the chickens long before.

e. The prairie chicken or pinnated grouse; also, the sharp-tailed grouse. *U.S.*

1875 *Fur, Fin & Feather* Sept. 95 You can always find good chicken dogs wherever there are chickens. 1895 *Outing* (U.S.) XXVII. 42/1 Quickly the heavy sound of chickens' wings notified us that game had been found. 1901 S. E. WHITE *Westerners* xx. 189 The careful attention necessary for the destruction of the wily 'chicken' or experienced squirrel.

3. c. (See quot.)

1890 *Congress. Rec.* 21 Apr. 3637/1 The affection which a sailor will lavish on a ship's boy to whom he takes a fancy, and makes his 'chicken', as the phrase is.

7 and **8.** *chicken farm, -run* (RUN *sb.*[1] 21 b); *chicken-brooding, -raising, -rearer*; **chicken-corn** *U.S.*, the common sorghum growing out of cultivation; **chicken-eater**, N. American name for the peregrine falcon; **chicken farming** *U.S.*, poultry farming; **chicken-feed** *U.S.*, food for poultry; **chicken-fixings** *local U.S.*, fried chicken; also *fig.*; **chicken-grape** *U.S.* (earlier examples); **chicken gumbo** (see GUMBO 1 b); **chicken-hawk** *U.S.* = HEN-HAWK; **chicken-pie** *U.S.*, a pie made from the flesh of poultry; also *fig.*; **chicken-skin**, a surface resembling the skin of a chicken, as having pin-point markings; **chicken-snake** (earlier example); **chicken-thief** *U.S.* (see quot.).

1902 *Westm. Gaz.* 8 Oct. 8/2 Incubators, *chicken-brooding houses, and 'accessories' innumerable. 1856 *Congress. Globe* 17 Apr. 960/2 Chinese sugar cane is nothing more than what we call *chicken corn down in Georgia. 1901 C. MOHR *Plant Life Alabama* 339 *Sorghum vulgare*,..Chicken Corn, Durrha. Sugar-Corn... Escaped from cultivation, becoming a pernicious weed in many parts of the Southern States. 1870 GILLMORE tr. *Figuier's Reptiles & Birds* 578 The Peregrine Falcon..inhabits North America, where it is frequently called the *Chicken-eater. 1895 *Outing* (U.S.) XXVI. 452/1 Wilson ..owned a prosperous *chicken farm. 1887 I. R. *Ranche Life Montana* 56 The worst of *chicken farming here is, that in summer there is a glut of eggs, about 6d a dozen. 1879 F. R. STOCKTON *Rudder Grange* xiv. 173 The houses scattered a long ways apart, like stingy *chicken-feed. 1838 E. FLAGG *Far West* II. 72 Wheat-bread and *chicken fixens, or corn-bread and common doins? 1854 MARY J. HOLMES *Tempest & Sunshine* v. 70 We don't have any of your Chicken Fixins nor little three-cornered handkerchiefs laid out at each plate. 1874 EGGLESTON *Circuit Rider* ii. 20 The strife had given them vigorous relish for Mrs. Lumsden's 'chicken-fixin's'. 1886 PROCTOR in *Knowledge* 1 Apr. 179/1 *Chicken fixings*, originally a chicken fricassee, now applied sometimes to any particularly fine arrangements, as distinguished from 'common doings'. 1814 PURSH *Flora Amer. Septentr.* I. 169 *Vitus cordifolia*..commonly called Winter-grape or *chicken-grape. 1830 MRS. HOLLEY *Texas Lett.* v. 87 Almost every variety of grape is native in Texas from the large fox-grape down to what is called the chicken-grape. 1871 SCHELE DE VERE *Americanisms* (1872) 412 The Bermuda Vine (*Vitis riparia*) is the Chicken Grape of Southern States, famous for its fragrant blossoms, but bearing no fruit. 1884 PHILLIPPS-WOLLEY *Trottings of Tenderfoot* 5 A *menu*..including such hitherto unheard-of luxuries as *chicken gumbo..and mush. 1908 G. H. LORIMER *J. Spurlock* ix. 207 First there was a chicken gumbo soup, and then cold boiled Virginia ham. 1925 J. GREGORY *Bab of the Backwoods* ii, I never saw a buzzard and a sparrow nesting together. ..Nor a *chicken-hawk and a linnet. 1845 MRS. KIRKLAND *Western Clearings* 132 A huge *chicken-pie [was] distributed. 1857–8 *Trans. Mich. Agric. Soc.* IX. 307 The show of Poultry was not such as..the wants of the country call for in the form of 'Fresh Eggs' and 'Chicken Pie' at all seasons of the year. 1871 SCHELE DE VERE *Americanisms* (1872) 264 A curious term has, of late, sprung up in the South, to designate the necessary expenses for purchasing legislative votes and newspaper influence...These are called *Chicken-pie*. 1891 *Pall Mall Gaz.* 1 Apr. 3/3 Another industry that could be well pushed into greater prominence is *chicken raising. 1895 *Daily News* 9 Oct. 6/7 Silver medals were accorded.. for the *chicken rearer..and..a wheel-barrow fowl house. 1906 *Westm. Gaz.* 13 Oct. 16/3 Should it..miss the lizard that crawls out into the open space of the *chicken-run and pick up a young chicken instead—well, you can hardly blame it. 1901 *Lady's Realm* X. 652/2 The *chicken-skin [design]—namely, a sort of groundwork with tiny pin-points all over it, which shows up the flowers to perfection. 1908 *Daily Chron.* 19 July 8/3 Fans..composed of delicate lace inset with net or chicken-skin medallions. 1903 *Westm. Gaz.* 18 Mar. 5/2 The [fan] leaves of chicken-skin, vellum,.. or paper are painted with historical..scenes. 1904 *Daily Chron.* 31 May 3/1 Subtle effects of colour which [china] collectors prize under such names as 'egg-shell', 'chicken-skin', and especially 'flambé'. 1791 W. BARTRAM *Trav. Carolina* etc. (1792) 271 The *chicken snake is a large, strong and swift serpent...They are apt to disturb hen roosts and prey upon chickens. 1808 T. ASHE *Trav.* xxviii. 243 We called the following [snakes] to our recollection:..striped snake, chicken snake. 1828 T. FLINT *Geog. Mississippi Valley* I. 237 The..singular looking Spanish and French trading retail boats commonly called *chicken thieves.

Chicken [2] (tʃi·ken). *Anglo-Ind.* Also chickan, -un. [Hind., a. Pers. چکن *chakin, chikin* needle-work.] Embroidery. Also *attrib.*

1886 *Offic. Catal. Col. & Ind. Exhib.* 16 At Calcutta embroidered muslin is called *chikan* (needle work). *Ibid.* 43 The large collection of *chikan* work from Calcutta. 1886 YULE & BURNELL *Anglo-Ind. Gloss.*, *Chicken-walla*, an itinerant dealer in embroidered handkerchiefs, petticoats, and such like.

Chicle (tʃi·k'l, tʃi·klɛ), *sb.* Also chickle. [Amer. Sp., a. Mexican *tzictli*.] A gum-like substance obtained from the bully tree (*Mimusops globosa*), and from the sapodilla (*Sapota zapotilla*), largely used in the United States in the manufacture of chewing-gum; hence, chewing-gum. Also *attrib.*, as *chicle-gum*. Hence **Chicle** *v. intr.*, to chew gum.

1902 WEBSTER Suppl., *Chicle*. 1907 WISTER *Simple Spelling-Bee* 18 Fifty per cent of our population chickles. *Ibid.* 36 He again removed his chickle and placed it on the window-sill. 1925 *Countries of the World* XXVII. 2752/1 The collecting of chiclegum and the cultivation of rubber are notable.

Chicoried (tʃi·kŏrid), *a.* [f. CHICORY *sb.* + -ED.] Flavoured with chicory.

1879 SALA *Paris Herself Again* I. xi. 168 A cup of chicoried coffee.

Chicote (tʃikō·te). Also chicotte. [Sp., = rope's end.] A long whip of leather or hide, having a wooden handle, used in the Congo and Portuguese South Africa.

1903 *Daily Chron.* 10 July 6/5 The fearful whip made of hippopotamus hide, and called the chicotte, and with which the natives in all parts of the Congo are so familiar. 1906 NEVINSON *Mod. Slavery* iii. 55 Her back scored all over with the cut of the *chicote*. 1928 *Daily Express* 28 Nov. 9 Corporal punishment, or 'chicotte', now exists only in the Congo army.

Chide, *v.* Add modern instances of inflected forms:

1885 MRS. CAMPBELL PRAED *Head Station* xxiii, Mrs. Clephane..chided Jinks. 1889 MEREDITH *Rhoda Fleming* x, The farmer chidded her. 1897 *Daily News* 15 Apr. 6/3 We ..notice with interest that Mr. Meredith, after vacillating in former editions between 'chid' and 'chidded', has now resolved that the past tense of 'to chide' is 'chided'. 1925 C. S. DURANT *Flem. Mystics & Eng. Martyrs* I. x. 146 Margaret..quietly chode her elder.

Chief, *sb.* **13.** Add: **chief hare** *U.S.*, the cony or calling hare of western N. America.

1875 *Amer. Naturalist* IX. 150 A day's march..from the rocky haunts of the little chief hare (*Lagomys princeps*).

Chiefess. (Earlier U.S. example.)

1778 J. CARVER *Trav. N. Amer.* 41 This heroine was ever after treated by her nation as their deliverer, and was made a chiefess in her own right.

Chieflet. Delete *nonce-wd.* and add quots.

1883 BARING-GOULD *John Herring* xxxvi, A chieflet of indifferent character. 1890 *Pall Mall Gaz.* 16 June 1/3 The five young chieflets had remained behind in sunny Biskra.

Chiefling (tʃī·fliŋ). [f. CHIEF *sb.* + -LING.] A petty chief.

1891 STEVENSON *Vailima Lett.* (1895) 8 Henry is a chiefling from Savaii. 1926 *Brit. Weekly* 11 Mar. 566/5 A native chiefling..appeared in plus fours, a tall hat, a frock coat and patent-leather boots.

Chiefship. Add:

2. A state ruled by a chief.

1894 *Daily News* 18 May 6/2 The ordinary Briton never gives these native kingdoms, principalities, and chiefships a thought. 1899 *Ibid.* 17 Nov. 9/4 The native State—Sarawak—..became a model for the chiefships of the Archipelago.

Chiff-chaff. Add:

2. The note of the chiff-chaff, or sounds resembling this.

1908 *Westm. Gaz.* 21 Mar. 14/1 They..make their presence known by their cheery reiteration of 'Chiff-chaff, chiff-chaff'. 1909 *Daily Chron.* 31 May 4/4 The sounds (quite important barks and chiff-chaffs and gurgles and bubbles) that make the emphasis of conversation. 1916 *Westm. Gaz.* 19 Mar. 14/2 His cheery, oft-repeated note, 'Chiff-chaff, cheef, cheef, chaff'.

Chiffing (tʃi·fiŋ), *vbl. sb.* [Echoic.] A sound which may be represented by *chiff*.

1879 *Organ Voicing* 17 A scraping or chiffing noise.

Chiffon. Add:

2. (ʃi·fɒn). A diaphanous silky muslin used in dressmaking.

1890 *Pall Mall Gaz.* 4 Feb. 3/2 The..tea-gown was a combination of white chiffon and yellow silk. 1905 *Westm. Gaz.* 20 Apr. 4/2 Chiffon-like muslin.

Hence **Chiffony** (ʃi·fōni) *a.*, of the nature of or resembling chiffon.

1902 *Daily Chron.* 9 July 8/2 Billowy ruffles and chiffony hats. 1904 *Westm. Gaz.* 23 June 4/2 Taffeta and silk muslins, as we call these chiffony soft stuffs.

Chigger (tʃi·gəɹ). *U.S.* Also chigre. [var. of CHIGOE.] = JIGGER *sb.*[2] 2.

1871 SCHELE DE VERE *Americanisms* (1872) 394 The Seed-tick is, in all probability, the same insect as the hated Jigger or Chigre, of Kentucky. 1915 *U.S. Dept. Agric., Farmer's Bulletin* 671 Harvest mites, or chiggers.

Chi-hike (tʃəi·ˌhəi·k), *sb. slang.* Also chi-ike, chy-ack, chi-ak. The shouting of 'chi-hike' as a salute; hence, a noisy demonstration.

1859 *Slang Dict.*, *Chi-ike*, a hurrah, a good word, or hearty praise. *c* 1869 VANCE *Ballad, Chick-a-leary Cove* (Farmer) Now join in a chyike, the 'jolly' we all like. 1894 CHEVALIER *Coster's Serenade* ii, Folks with a 'chy-ike' shouted, 'Ain't they smart?' 1910 *Daily Chron.* 22 Apr. 7/7 The audience ..was out for a gigantic 'chi-hike', and it enjoyed itself to the full.

Hence **Chi-hike** *v. trans.*, to salute with the cry 'chi-hike'; also *absol.* or *intr.*, to make a noisy demonstration.

1874 *Slang Dict.*, *Chi-ike*, to hail in a rough though friendly manner; to support by means of vociferation. 1874 G. WALCH *Adamanta* II. ii. 27 (Morris) I've learnt to chi-ike peelers. 1878 *Australian* I. 742 (Ibid.) The circle of frivolous youths who were yelping at and chy-acking him. 1886 *Sporting Times* 17 July 7/2 There was no charge for admission. Enough. They came, they saw, and they chi-iked. 1894 E. W. HORNUNG *Boss of Taroomba* i, It's our way up here, you know, to chi-ak each other and our visitors too. 1906 WHITEING *Ring in New* 122 His 'chihiking' of members, popular and unpopular.

Chikara: see *CHINKARA.

Chikhor, chikor (tʃi·kɒɹ). *Anglo-Ind.* Also chichore, chikore, chuckoor, chukore, chukor, -ar. [Hind. *chakor*.] A sportsman's name for various game birds of India, esp. the red-legged partridge (*Caccabis chukar*).

1815 ELPHINSTONE *Acc. Caubul* 144 A bird which is called ..the hill Chichore by the Indians. *a* 1851 MRS. SHERWOOD *Life* (1854) 467 One day..he found a hill partridge...This bird is called the chuckoor, and is said to eat fire. 1879 HUME & MARSHALL *Game Birds India* II. 35 October is the best month..for Chukor-shooting. *Ibid.* 39 The inhabitants of Scio..keep tame Chukor Partridges. 1893 *Baily's Mag.* May 263/1 We also came across some chikhor (mountain partridge). 1909 *Times Lit. Suppl.* 1 Apr. 124/2 He has taken teal, chukor, stone-plover, and grouse. 1920 *Blackw. Mag.* May 664/2 Some of the officers went out one day to shoot *chikhor*. 1923 *Ibid.* Apr. 493/1 A dozen chikor or a haunch of venison.

Child, *sb.* Add:

21. e. passing into adj., with the meaning child's', or 'childish', as *child-brain, -face* (hence *-faced* adj.), *-mind, -voice.*

1904 *Daily Chron.* 21 May 4/5 My *child-brain, clear and natural, could not swallow the impossibilities administered to me as facts. 1909 *Westm. Gaz.* 23 Dec. 2/1 A *child-face glowing with more radiant happiness we have never seen. 1906 *Macm. Mag.* Oct. 942 The curly-headed, thick-lipped, *child-faced, gay, unlucky negro. 1906 *Daily Chron.* 8 Sept. 3/2 In order to interest the *child-mind, the subject is treated so as to focus attention on the marvellous intricacies of Nature. 1898 WATTS-DUNTON *Aylwin* i. § 2 Into my very being that *child-voice passed.

22. child-life, the lives of the children of a nation or community; also *attrib.*; **child-study**, the systematic physiological and psychological study of a child and its ways; so **child-psychology**, whence **child-psychologist**; **child welfare** [WELFARE 4], the betterment of the conditions of life of the children of the lower class population as a social work.

1884 *child-life [in Dict. s.v. 21]. 1885 M. I. BRYSON (*title*) Child Life in Chinese Homes. 1907 *Westm. Gaz.* 6 July 16/3 Aspects of Child Life and Education. 1909 *Daily Chron.* 17 May 3/3 Other aspects of the child-life problem were suggested by different exhibits. 1924 R. M. OGDEN tr. *Koffka's Growth of Mind* 3 The *child-psychologist can follow the growth of a human being. *Ibid.*, Principles of *child-psychology. 1899 *Daily News* 9 June 3/4 'Child-Study and Mental Training. 1908 H. G. WELLS *New Worlds for Old* xiii. 305 There is the need and opportunity of organizing..*child welfare. 1915 A. L. STRONG (*title*) Child Welfare Exhibits. 1920 N. MILNES *Child Welfare* 25 Those who wish to help in the Child Welfare movement should study Economics. 1930 *British American* 19 Apr. 6/1 Mrs. J. S. Inglis, Kilrymont, St. Andrews, who took a leading part in the child welfare movement and coined the term 'child welfare'.

Chili, Chile (tʃi·lɪ). The name of the South American republic used attrib. in names of products, as **Chili copper** (see quot. 1888); **Chili nettle**, any plant of the family *Loasaceæ*; **Chili pine**, the South American conifer *Araucaria imbricata*, cultivated as an ornamental tree, popularly known as the 'monkey-puzzle'; **Chili saltpetre** (see quot. 1880).

1801 LATHAM *Gen. Synop. Birds* 2nd Suppl. 140 Chili Woodpecker. This bird is scarcely as large as a Blackbird: it has a red-crested crown, and the body is banded with blue and white. 1849 BALFOUR *Man. Bot.* § 870 Loasaceæ, the Chili-Nettle Family...They are..chiefly distinguished for their stinging qualities, and hence the name of Chili-Nettle. 1852 G. W. JOHNSON *Cottage Gard. Dict.* 70 *Araucaria imbricata* (imbricated, or Chili pine). 1872 *Jrnl. Chem. Soc.* XXV. 1131 The Chili Saltpetre and Iodine Industry of Tarapaca. 1875 *Encycl. Brit.* II. 310/1 *Araucaria imbricata*, the imbricate-leaved pine, or the Chili pine, was introduced into Britain in 1796. 1880 *Ibid.* XI. 319 The nitrate of soda, called 'cubical nitre' or Chili salt-petre, which is found abundantly in South America. 1888 *Lockwood's Dict. Terms Mech. Engin.*, *Chili Copper*, black oxide of copper obtained in Chili.

Chilian, Chilean (tʃi·liăn), *a.* and *sb.* [f. prec. + -AN.] Of or pertaining to, an inhabitant or native of, Chili, a republic of South America. Formerly also †**Chilesian.**

1748 *Anson's Voy.* II. xiv. 282 The Arraucos, and the rest of the Chilian Indians. *c* 1789 *Encycl. Brit.* (1797) IV. 648/2 No defeats..could dispirit the Chilesians. 1818 *Deb. in Congress* (1854) 2038 The restoration of the banished Chilians to their families. 1837 *Penny Cycl.* XXXVII. 61/2 The Chilian Andes. 1876 *Encycl. Brit.* V. 618/2 In April 1811 the first blood was spilt in the cause of Chilian independence. 1898 *Jrnl. Sch. Geog.* (U.S.) Oct. 304 Punta Arenas..began its existence as a Chilean convict settlement. 1922 *Contemp. Rev.* Mar. 336 The Chileans seem to me to aim at being the aristocracy of the other hemisphere. 1924 *Public Opinion* 21 Mar. 278/2 The Chilian houseboy took us a short cut.

Chill, *sb.* Add:

5. (Earlier U.S. example.)

1849 *Rep. U.S. Comm. Patents* (1850) 153 All injury to the chill of the wheel is avoided.

c. The condition of being chilled or hardened by rapid cooling; also, the method or process of producing this condition.

1880 WEBSTER Suppl. 1928 *Daily Tel.* 6 Nov. 3 Glengarnock foundry pig-iron...This grade, while having a minimum of shrinkage, is free from chill.

Chill, *v.* Add:

6. b. To subject (meat) to a low temperature in a chill-room or in cold-storage. (Cf. *CHILLED *ppl. a.* 2 b, *CHILLING *vbl. sb.* c.)

Chill-. 2. Add: **chill casting** (see quot.).

1879 *Encycl. Brit.* IX. 481/2 In 'chill casting' a portion of the surface of the whole or a part of the mould is made of cast iron, so that the metal brought in contact with it is rapidly cooled.

Chilled, *ppl. a.* Add:

2. b. Of meat, esp. beef: Kept at a moderately low temperature in cold-storage, as distinguished from frozen meat.

1894 *Daily News* 23 Jan. 5/1 The newest thing is chilled beef, as distinct from frozen. 1895 *Austr. Pastoralist Rev.* 15 Aug. 303 When there is anything like a scarcity of chilled hind-quarters there will always be a good opening for defrosted.

Chiller. Add quot.:

1921 *Dict. Occup. Terms* (1927) § 279 *Chiller*; sprays moulds with water after use, to cool them, and sometimes whilst in use in order to hasten cooling of steel ingot.

Chilling, *vbl. sb.* Add:

c. The action or process of chilling meat. In quot. *attrib.*

1902 *Westm. Gaz.* 26 Nov. 10/3 The great River Plate exporters having adopted the 'chilling' process.

Chillsome (tʃi·lsŏm), *a.* [f. CHILL *sb.* or *v.* + -SOME.] Chilling, chilly.

1927 WHITHAM tr. *Latude & Linguet's Mem. Bastille* Introd. 40 Her mistress, who, chillsome in blood..dreaded that she might cease to be agreeable to her lusty sovereign. 1928 *Observer* 17 June 1/7 [Buxton] being built on rock... It means you can get utterly away from chillsome damps.

Chiloplasty (kəi·loplæsti). *Surg.* Also cheilo-. [f. Gr. χεῖλος lip: see -PLASTY.] Treatment of the lip by a plastic operation. Hence **Chiloplastic** *a.*

1854 R. DRUITT *Surgeon's Vade Mecum* (ed. 6) 413 Cheiloplastic Operations, by which are signified operations for the restoration of the lip. 1864 *T. Holmes's Syst. Surg.* IV. 1057 Cheiloplasty. 1902 tr. *Tillmanns' Text-bk. Surg.* II. 230.

Chilostome (kəi·lostoum), *a.* and *sb. Zool.* Also cheilo-. [ad. mod.L. *chilostomata*: see CHILOSTOMATOUS *a.*] **A.** *adj.* Of, pertaining to, or resembling the *Chilostomata*, an order of marine Polyzoa. **B.** *sb.* A member of this order.

1896 HARMER in *Cambr. Nat. Hist.* II. 481 The operculum is usually..a conspicuous feature of the Cheilostome zooecium. *Ibid.* 486 Some marine Cheilostomes may be saved from attacks..owing to the existence of their armoury of avicularia and vibracula. 1912 *Brit. Museum Return* 173 The collection of Cretaceous Cheilostome Polyzoa from France.

Chimney, *sb.* Add:

9. (Examples.)

1873 J. H. BEADLE *Undevel. West* xviii. 334 It may be a 'chimney' from some lode ten thousand feet away through solid rock. 1876 'JOAQUIN' MILLER *Unwritten Hist.* xvii. 256 A pouch in the rock—a little 'chimney' that nurses a few thousand dollars worth of dust about the flue.

11. chimney-bar, an iron bar supporting the masonry above a fireplace; **chimney cap**, (*a*) the top of a chimney, either as an ornament or cover; (*b*) = COWL *sb.*[1] 4; **chimney-cleaner, -cleanser**, a chimney-sweeper; **chimney-jack**, (*b*) = *steeple jack* (see STEEPLE *sb.*[1] 6); **chimney jamb** (mod. U.S. example); **chimney neck**, the shaft of a chimney; **chimney rock**, (*a*) *Geol.*, a chimney-shaped body of rock; (*b*) in Florida, a porous phosphate rock used in building; **chimney-stack**, (*b*) = *chimney-stalk* (b); **chimney-swallow, -swift** *U.S.*, a species of swift, *Chætura pelagica* (or *pelasgica*).

1833 LOUDON *Encycl. Archit.* § 79 The fire-places to have each a strong iron *chimney-bar. 1846 *Rep. U.S. Comm. Patents* (1847) 221 What I claim, therefore, as my invention ..is a ventilator or *chimney cap. 1910 BERESFORD PITE, etc. *Building Construction* I. 160 Chimney caps are so usual that the advisability of avoiding heaviness in their arrangement and design may be pointed out. 1906 *Daily Chron.* 20 July 4/6 Mechanical *chimney-cleaner. 1921 *Dict. Occup. Terms* (1927) § 924 Sweep, chimney sweep; chimney cleaner. 1905 *Daily Chron.* 11 Jan. 4/7 John Smith or so, '*chimney-cleanser'. 1907 *Westm. Gaz.* 16 Mar. 10/1 A competent *chimney-jack was despatched up a rope to work upon the crack. 1887 TOURGEE *Button's Inn* 253 'I don't know, sir,' she responded, setting the spider in its place by the *chimney-jamb. 1833 LOUDON *Encycl. Archit.* § 983 Deal sarking..to be laid on each side of the roof and *chimney necks (shafts). 1848 E. BRYANT *What I saw in California* vii. 99 The atmosphere this morning being clear, we saw distinctly the '*Chimney Rock'. 1883 M. P. BALE *Saw-Mills* 75 An important factor in the economical working of boilers is the correct arrangement of the *chimney stack. 1903 MCNEILL *Egregious English* 48 The top of the factory chimney-stack. 1794 S. WILLIAMS *Hist. Vermont* (1809) I. 140 The species called the house or *chimney swallow, has been found during the winter, in hollow trees. 1911 NEWTON in *Encycl. Brit.* XXVI. 231/1 *Chætura pelagica*, the 'chimney-swallow' of the United States. 1898 *Atlantic Monthly* Apr. 456/1 *Chimney-swifts were shooting hither and thither athwart the sky.

Chimneyed, *ppl. a.* Add:

b. Of rock: Having a vertical cleft. (Cf. CHIMNEY *sb.* 8.)

1897 *Outing* (U.S.) XXIX. 553/1 Troops of chimneyed rocks stepping out boldly into the wrinkled shoals.

Chimney-pot. 2. Add: Also simply *chimney-pot*. Now *rare*.

1851 *Expositor* 4 Jan. 145/1 The absurdity of the 'Chimney-pot' and 'Coal-scuttle' covering for the head at present in use. 1874 LISLE CARR *J. Gwynne* I. i. 33 So off went that penitential chimney-pot leaving such a great red line round his forehead. 1899 GODLEY *Lyra Frivola* 39 My Chimney-pot, farewell!

Chimney-sweeper. Add: **4.** (See quot.) *U.S.*

1849 *Rep. U.S. Comm. Patents, Agric.* (1850) 393 The sooty powder on the flowering parts of corn-plants, called smut, chimney-sweepers, and dust-brand, is formed of the spores of another uredo.

Chimonanthus (kəimonæ·nþŏs). [mod.L., f. Gr. χειμών winter + ἄνθος flower.] Japan allspice, a plant of the species *Butneria præcox.*

1829 LOUDON *Encycl. Plants* 454. 1858 W. BAIRD *Cycl. Nat. Sci.* s.v. *Calycanthaceæ*, The *Chimonanthus* is a native of Japan, and contains only one species. 1904 FARRER *Garden of Asia* 18 There are cherries, plums, chimonanthus, magnolia.

Chimp. Short for CHIMPANZEE.

1928 *Daily Tel.* 29 May 6 The 'chimps' behave almost perfectly at table.

Chin, *sb.*[1] **2.** Add: **chin-music** *U.S.* (earlier example); **chin stuff** *U.S.*, talk; **chin-wag** *v. slang*, to talk, chatter.

1844 'JON. SLICK' *High Life N.Y.* II. 108, I thought it wouldn't do no harm to give 'em a short specimen of Weathersfield *chin music. 1919 *Detective Story Mag.* XXVIII. 60 You always were there with the *chin stuff. 1920 *Blackw. Mag.* Feb. 182/2, I didn't waste any time *chin-wagging.

Chin, *sb.*[2] *U.S. slang.* [f. CHIN *v.* 3.] A talk. Also, reduplicated, *chin-chin.*

1914 GERTRUDE ATHERTON *Perch of Devil* I. xxiv. 148 There's a guy..come out to have a chin with you. 1918 E. M. ROBERTS *Flying Fighter* 189, I went back and resumed the 'chin-chin' with Kerr and the other boys. 1926 BERNARD CRONIN *Red Dawson* xiii, Duke kept coming over for a chin with our folks. 1928 T. GANN *Discov. & Adv. Central Amer.* 106 Whenever three or four of them came together for a 'chin'.

Chin, *v.* Add:

3. b. *trans.* To talk to, to address, esp. boldly or impudently. *U.S.*

1871 'MARK TWAIN' *Screamers* 77 It seemed hardly me that could have 'chinned' its towers ten minutes before. 1892 GUNTER *Miss Dividends* 247, I heard one of them call another 'Constable' and the other chinned him as 'Sheriff!' 1898 H. S. CANFIELD *Maid of Frontier* i. 7 He chinned the barkeep mos' to death. 1911 H. S. HARRISON *Queed* vii. 85 [I have] been up chinning your sporting editor.

4. *To chin the bar*: in gymnastics, to draw up the body until the chin is brought over the horizontal bar; also *absol.*

1906 'O. HENRY' *Four Million, Coming-out of Maggie* 85 He..could chin the bar twice with one hand.

China[1]. Add:

2. b. China-berry *U.S.*, (*a*) the wild China or soapberry (*Sapindus marginatus*), of the southern U.S.; (*b*) the China-tree, the Asiatic meliaceous tree, *Melia azedarach*; **China hog**, a breed of swine; also *ellipt.*; **China-tree** (earlier examples).

1890 SARAH O. JEWETT in *Harper's Mag.* Dec. 106/2 The high gray towers..were crowned with ornaments like the berries of the *chinaberry trees. 1908 R. W. CHAMBERS *Firing Line* xxix, A subtler scent..came to him on the sea-wind;..—the lilac perfume of china-berry in bloom. 1838 H. COLMAN *Rep. Agric. Mass.* 74 A cross with some of our small boned breed, such as the Byfield or the *China [hog]. 1851 C. CIST *Cincinnati* 279 The hogs raised for this market, are generally a cross of Irish Grazier Byfield..and China. 1872 EGGLESTON *Hoosier Schoolm.* xxvi. 180 You can't make nothin else out of him, no more nor you can make a china hog into a Berkshire. 1819 E. EVANS *Pedestrious Tour* 315 Here grew the *China tree, of a beautiful appearance, and bearing fruit of an inviting aspect. 1831 PECK *Guide for Emigrants* II. 48 The china-tree, catalpa, fig, pomgranate, banana, and orange..charm..the beholder. 1833 H BARNARD in *Maryland Hist. Mag.* XIII. 355 The streets of A. are planted with the China tree, which has a very bright green leaf.

4. c. china mark, a collectors' name for any moth of the genus *Hydrocampa* and allied genera; **china money** (see quot. and cf. **china token*); **china-shell**, a collectors' name of the *Ovulum ovum*, given in allusion to the white porcelain-like surface of the shell; **china token**, a token of porcelain or earthenware used in porcelain and pottery works; **china wedding** *U.S.* (see quot.).

1832 J. RENNIE *Consp. Butterfl. & Moths* 150 Hydrocampa...The Lettered *China-mark (*H. literalis*). 1902 W. F. KIRBY *Butterflies & Moths* 112 China Marks...are moths rarely exceeding an inch in expanse. 1868 L. JEWITT in *Art Jrnl.* 282/1 The issuing of 'chainé money', *i.e.*, tokens representing different values of money, made of china...They were called 'Mr. Cokes' coin', or 'chainé money' (*china money), in the provincialism of the locality. 1886 GRAY & WOODWARD *Sea-Weeds, Shells* 47 The *Cypræidæ*, or Cowries...With these is classed the '*China-shell' (*Ovulum*). 1878 JEWITT *Ceramic Art* II. 141 One peculiarity connected with the Pinxton China Works..is the issuing of *china tokens, *i.e.*, tokens representing different values of money, made of china, and payable as money among the workpeople and others, including shopkeepers. 1888 *Girl's Own Paper* 24 Mar. 407/2 In America..is the 'crystal-wedding', which is kept after fifteen years of married life...Then, too, there is the '*china-wedding', which is observed five years later.

5. Short for *China rose* (*a*): see 2 b in Dict.

1841 MRS. LOUDON *Ladies' Comp. Fl. Gard.* (1846) 340 *Rosa indica* (the common China); *Rosa semperflorens* (the monthly China).

Chinadom. (Earlier U.S. example.)

1872 'MARK TWAIN' *Innoc. at Home* xviii. (1882) 374 The combined stenches of Chinadom and Brannan Street slaughter-houses.

Chinar, var. CHENAR, the Oriental plane-tree; also, timber from this.

1889 *Cent. Dict.* 1917 *Blackw. Mag.* Sept. 414 The folds of the door are of solid steps of chinar. 1925 *Chambers's Jrnl.* 79/2 The tall Chinar trees stood up dreamily.

Chinatown (tʃəi·nătaun). A section of a large town, especially a sea-port, in England and U.S., in which Chinese live as a colony and to a great extent follow their own customs.

1880 IZA D. HARDY in *Belgravia* XLIII. 217 Within a stone's-throw of that fashionable thoroughfare [*sc.* Kearney Street, San Francisco] lie..the main arteries of China Town. 1889 *Chambers's Jrnl.* 19 Jan. 39/2 For filth and wretchedness you must go to Chinatown [San Francisco] by night. 1892 DOUGLAS B. W. SLADEN *Japs at Home* ii. (1895) 18 Separated from the Settlement and Chinatown..is the native town. 1903 *Living Lond.* III. 86 The Limehouse Chinatown.

Chi·nawo:man. [f. CHINA[1] 1, after CHINAMAN.] A Chinese woman.

1872 'MARK TWAIN' *Innoc. at Home* ix. (1882) 318 There are few white servants and no Chinawomen so employed.

Chincapin. Add: Also, the nut of this tree.

1893 LELAND *Mem.* II. 110 Rebeldom, where a Union man's life was worth about a chinquapin.

Chinch, *sb.*[1] **2.** *Chinch-bug* (earlier example. See also *CHINTZ-BUG).

1786 WASHINGTON *Diaries* III. 97 Examined the..corn in several parts of this field and discovered more or less of the Chinch bug on every stalk.

Chinche (tʃi·ntʃe). Also cinche, chincha. [Sp.] The S. American skunk, *Mephitis mephitica.*

1889 *Century Dict.*

Chinchilla. Add: **3.** (In full *Chinchilla rabbit*.) A variety of rabbit bred for its fur; also, the fur obtained from this animal.

1904 J. R. A. DAVIS *Nat. Hist. Animals* (1905) IV. lxvii. 243 Some of the races, especially Chinchillas and Angoras, are valued on account of their fur. 1920 *Bazaar, Exch. & Mart* 16 July, Suppl. 74/3 The Havana (that beautiful brown rabbit), and..the Chinchilla. 1921 H. A. DAY *Up-to-Date Rabbit-Keeping* 13 The Chinchilla-Coney..is a new French breed that deserves attention. 1927 *Smallholder* 26 Mar. 123/1 In Beverens and Chinchillas many specimens only moult twice in the year.

Chiné (ʃine·), *a.* and *sb.* [Fr., pa. pple. of *chiner*, f. *Chine* China.] **A.** *adj.* Of silk: Dyed or woven with a mottled or indistinct pattern after an actual or supposed Chinese fashion. **B.** *sb.* Chiné fabric.

1858 SIMMONDS *Dict. Trade*, *Chiné*, goods of worsted, cotton, silk, and linen, with printed warps. 1862 *Catal. Internat. Exhib., Brit.* II. No. 3901, Plain and figured chinés. 1862 SUSAN HALE *Lett.* 23 Sheer white muslin, most elaborately trimmed with brilliant rose and Chine ribbon, round the bottom of the skirt. 1896 *Daily News* 9 May 8/6 The chiné ribbon is in pink flowers, with a green border. 1900 *Ibid.* 8 Sept. 6/3 The coats are lined with chiné silks.

Chinee: see CHINESE B. 1 b.

1873 [G. A. LAWRENCE] *Silverland* 142 In extremes of cold or wet, the 'Chinee' is apt to shrivel up and wax flaccid.

Chinese, *a.* **2.** Add: **Chinese boxes**, a nest of boxes: see NEST *sb.* 6.

1829 R. C. SANDS *Writings* II. 57 Some of the members.. thus compacted like Chinese boxes.

Chinesery (tʃəini·zəri). [ad. F. CHINOISERIE (q. v.), f. *chinois* CHINESE + -*erie* -ERY.] *pl.* Practices, behaviour, objects, etc. of a fashion or form resembling those of the Chinese or of China, e.g. complicated formality.

1890 *Sat. Rev.* 15 Feb. 191/2 The Treasury..goes on with its old Chineseries. As for this particular Chinesery, it seems to us neither better nor worse than a round dozen of others we have seen. 1907 *Westm. Gaz.* 1 Oct. 2/1 The 1820 romanticalities of Wörlitz, and the dapper blue-and-yellow chineseries of Oranienbaum.

Chink, *sb.*[5] orig. *U.S. slang.* [Irreg. f. CHINA[1].] A Chinaman. Also *attrib.*

1901 *Munsey's Mag.* XXIV. 536 The leader suggested the 'chink', and to the one Chinese laundry..the little band departed. 1910 W. M. RAINE *B. O'Connor* iv. 41 Chinks, greasers, and several other kinds of citizens driftin' that way. 1915 H. L. WILSON *Ruggles of Red Gap* xvi. (1917) 282, I had the chink take him up about a gallon of strong tea. 1923 *Chambers's Jrnl.* 38/2 It was embarrassing..to find a dozen Chinks gathered round one's camp-stool. 1926 *Ibid.* 552/1 The towns, small or large, possessed from one to hundreds of 'Chink' laundries.

Chink, *sb.*[6] (See quots.)

1914 *Star* 14 Nov. 4/4 The 'iron chink' cuts off the heads, tails, and fins, dresses the fish at the rate of 3,000 per hour. 1924 *Chambers's Jrnl.* 325/2 They are beheaded and tailed, cleaned, cut up into even pieces by the great 'iron chink'.

Chinkara (tʃi·ŋkāra). Also **chi(e)kara.** [Hindi *cikārā*, Hind. (Skr. *chikkara*).] The ravine-deer, *Gazella bennettii.*

1860 *Chambers's Encycl.* I. 287/2 The Chikara and some other Indian species are distinguished by two additional rudimentary horns in front of the ordinary horns. 1897 *Encycl. Sport* (1911) I. 411 The Chickara, Chinkara, Ravine Deer, or Indian Gazelle (*G. bennettii*), is found throughout the plains of India. 1924 *Blackw. Mag.* Aug. 242/1 Neither I nor the Kumar had yet stalked black buck or chinkara in the flaming dāk jungle.

Chinked, *ppl. a.* Add: **2.** Filled up, made weather-tight. *U.S.*

1880 P. H. BURNETT *Recoll. Old Pioneer* 29 A log cabin about eighteen by twenty feet, with chinked cracks, clapboard roof, and puncheon floor.

Chinkeri(n)chee (tʃi·ŋkəri(n)tʃī·). Also **chinkering ching.** The South African plant *Ornithogalum thyrsoides.*

[1795 tr. *Thunberg's Trav.* 1770–9 I. 153 *Tintirintics* is a name given to a species of *Ornithogalum*, with a white flower, from the sound it produced, when two stalks of it were rubbed against each other.] 1904 *Cape G. Hope Agric. Jrnl.* July 6 (Pettman) The *Chinkerinchee, Chincher-and-ching*, 'Viooltjes', as that beautiful white flowering bulb, the *Ornithogalum thyrsoides*, is variously called in South Africa. 1923 *Daily Mail* 3 Dec., The South African flower the chinkerichee.

Chinkie, Chinkey (tʃi·ŋki). [f. *CHINK *sb.*[5] + -IE, -Y[6].] = *CHINK *sb.*[5]

1882 A. J. BOYD *Old Colonials* 233 The pleasant traits of character in our colonialised 'Chinkie', as he is vulgarly termed. 1899 BOXALL *Austral. Bushrangers* 241 They rode straight to the Chinese camp at Wombat, 'to give the Chinkies a lesson'. 1905 *Westm. Gaz.* 26 Sept. 6/1 The farmers getting a reward of £1 for each 'Chinkey' they turn over to the police.

Chinking, *vbl. sb.*[1] **3.** *U.S.* (Earlier example.)

1837 *Knickerbocker Mag.* X. 415 Venturing to peep through an opening where the chinking had fallen out.

Chinkle (tʃi·ŋk'l), *sb. Naut.* ? *U.S.* [f. CHINK *sb.*[4] + -LE. Cf. KINKLE *sb.*[1]] A turn or kink in a rope (*Cent. Dict.* Suppl. 1909).

Chinny, *a.* Add:

2. Marked by a conspicuous chin.

1920 GALSWORTHY *In Chancery* I. i, A face concave and long, with a jaw which divested of flesh would have seemed extravagant: altogether a chinny face, though not at all ill-looking.

Chino-[1] (tʃəi·no), used as combining form = Chinese. *Chino-Japanese* adj., Chinese and Japanese; sb., the Chinese language as spoken in Japan.

1888 *N. E. D.* s.v. *Chino* 2, Chino-Japanese. 1893 *Graphic* 11 Mar. 260/1 The tribes on the Indo and Chino-Burmese frontiers. 1895 H. NORMAN *Far East* 604 Chino-French relations at Monkay. 1904 *Daily Chron.* 8 Apr. 4/5 The Chino-Japanese war. 1904 *Westm. Gaz.* 14 Oct. 8/2 The Chino-Japanese and Australian service at Vancouver.

Chino-[2] (ki·no), variant (after G. *chino-*; cf. CHINA[3]) of *quino-*, as in *chinopyrin, chinosol, chinotoxin.*

1901 DORLAND *Med. Dict.* (ed. 2). 1904 *Westm. Gaz.* 24 Nov. 7/3 The razors..are sterilised in a solution..of chinosol. 1906 *Practitioner* Nov. 674 Sponging with a ·1 per cent. chinosol, or corrosive sublimate, lotion.

Chinook, *sb.* Add: **b.** *Chinook salmon*, the quinnat or California salmon (*Oncorhynchus chouicha*).

1881 *Amer. Naturalist* XV. 177 Quinnat—..Chinnook salmon, Columbia River salmon, Sacramento Salmon. 1884 GOODE *Nat. Hist. Aquatic Anim.* 479 On the Columbia River the name 'Chinnook Salmon' is in universal use. 1896 JORDAN & EVERMANN *Fishes N. Amer.* I. 479 Oncorhynchus Tschawytscha..Chinook Salmon. *Ibid.* 482 This species [*sc.* the redfish] enters the Columbia River with the spring run of the Chinook Salmon. 1897 *Portland Oregonian* in *Congress. Rec.* 16 Dec. 221/2 The number of fat Chinook salmon coming into the Columbia would be greatly increased. 1912 F. J. HASKIN *Amer. Govt.* 151 The bureau of fisheries ..has tried to establish the chinook salmon in Atlantic coast waters.

Chinoo·k, *v. U.S.* [f. the sb.] *intr.* To blow with the Chinook wind.

1914 GERTRUDE ATHERTON *Perch of Devil* III. 373 It's chinooking certainly...I hope that means we've had the last of winter.

Chinquepin, var. of CHINCAPIN.

1807 *Norfolk* (Va.) *Gaz.* 13 Nov. 4/3 For Sale, 2000 Cedar and Chinquepin Posts.

Chinse, *v.* **1.** (Earlier U.S. examples.)

1770 G. CARTWRIGHT *Jrnl. Labrador* (1792) I. 24 Fogarty chinsed the storehouse with moss. *Ibid.* 65, I ordered some of the workmen to gather moss, and chinse the store. 1792 *Ibid.* Gloss. p. x, *Chinsing* filling with moss the vacancies between the studs of houses, to keep out the wind and frost.

Chintz-bug, var. *chinch-bug*, CHINCH *sb.*[1] 2.

1786 WASHINGTON *Diaries* III. 96 An Overseer of mine (at the ferry) informed that the chintz bug was discovered in his Corn. 1816 [see CHINCH *sb.*[1] 2]. 1873 J. H. BEADLE *Undevel. West* xiii. 225 The fly is a little troublesome to wheat, but its principal enemy is the chintz bug, so called here.

Chionodoxa (kəiŏnodǫ·ksă). [mod.L., f. Gr. χιών snow + δόξα glory.] A genus of liliaceous plants indigenous to Crete and Asia Minor; any cultivated plant of this genus, bearing blue flowers, valued by horticulturists for its early-blooming habit, and popularly known as 'glory of the snow'.

1880 *Encycl. Brit.* XII. 251/1. 1893 *Daily News* 28 Mar. 2/2 Scillas and Chionodoxas now in full glory.

Chip, *sb.*[1] Add:

1. b. *spec.* in gem-cutting, a cleavage which weighs less than three-fourths of a carat (*Cent. Dict.* Suppl. 1909).

2. b. Also *pl.* Thin slices of potato fried crisp.

1886 *Chambers's Jrnl.* 18 Dec. 808/2 The hand of Zacharias was betrayed in potato chips and cunning sauces. 1895 *Standard Dict.* s.v. *Chip*[1], *Saratoga chips*, potatoes sliced very thin while raw, and fried crisp. 1899 W. C. MORROW *Bohemian Paris* 224 Here are..fried-potato women, serving crisp brown chips. 1906 *Daily Chron.* 13 Oct. 5/7 The chop and chips business. 1923 *Aerbut Paeshs of Baernegum* 15 'Ere, 'ave yo got any fish and chips?

2. c. (Earlier example.)

1840 R. H. DANA *Bef. Mast* xxxiii. (1873) 338 Had it not been for the sea from aft which sent the chip home, and threw her continually off her course, the log would have shown her to have been going somewhat faster.

d. *pl.* Money. Also, a piece of money. *To buy chips*: to invest. *colloq.*

a 1851 BOUVIER *Law Dict. U.S.A.* (1856) s.v. *Faro*, Sometimes instead of money, chips or small pieces of ivory or other substance are used. 1859 *Slang Dict.*, *Chips*, money. 1903 A. H. LEWIS *The Boss* 205 There was a saw-boness here, ..pawin' me over for a life-insurance game that I thought I'd buy chips in. 1905 *Daily Chron.* 11 Sept. 2/6 It is.. quite a commonplace remark to hear young men boast of the time when 'the old man turns up his toes', and they can 'collar the chips'. 1925 *Chambers's Jrnl.* 424/2 I'll give you ten chips myself.

e. *To pass in one's chips*: to die. *U.S. slang.* (Cf. CHECK *sb.*[1] 15.)

1890 *Harper's Mag.* Feb. 351/2 Ye kin bet yer life I ain't afeard o' passin in my chips. 1907 MULFORD *Bar-20* xi. 130 He passed in his chips last night.

4. b. Also for making baskets. Hence, short for *chip basket* (see 9 below).

1922 J. JOYCE in *Q. Rev.* Oct. 230 Chips of strawberries. 1923 *Westm. Gaz.* 15 Jan. 8/5 4lb. chips of apples. 1928 *Daily Express* 28 May 5/3 In Hampshire..these baskets contain two to four pounds, and are termed 'chips'.

5. c. A dried piece of buffalo- or cattle-dung. *U.S.* (Cf. *buffalo-chips* s.v. BUFFALO 5.)

1857 W. CHANDLESS *Visit Salt Lake* I. iv. 61 Buffalo were looked for; a solitary 'chip'—so the buffalo droppings are called—found one evening caused quite an excitement in our camp. 1903 A. ADAMS *Log Cowboy* xiv. 209 We had begun to feel the scarcity of wood for cooking purposes... These chips were a poor substitute.

8. *A chip on one's shoulder*, carried as a challenge to others (see earlier quots.); hence, a display of defiance or ill-humour. *U.S.*

1840 *Daily Pennant* (St. Louis) 9 May (Th.) Jonathan's blood is 'pretty considerable riz' anyhow, and it wouldn't take so much as knocking a chip off a boy's shoulder to make it a darnation sight riz-er. 1855 *Weekly Oregonian* 17 Mar. (Th.) Leland, in his last issue, struts out with a chip on his shoulder, and dares Bush to knock it off. 1887 *Harper's Mag.* Oct. 658/1 The way that dog went about with a chip on his shoulder..was enough to spoil the sweetest temper. 1903 *N. Y. Sun* 1 Nov., Who, they say, wears a chip on his shoulder because he didn't get the Republican nomination for City Treasurer. 1905 *Amer. Illustr. Mag.* Nov. 88 Each boy had a sort of chip-on-the-shoulder air.

9. chip bark, chips and broken pieces of cinchona bark, as distinguished from druggist's bark (*Cent. Dict.* Suppl. 1909); **chip basket**, a basket made of strips of thin wood roughly interwoven or joined, used chiefly for packing fruit for the market; also *attrib.*; **chip bonnet** (examples); **chip-carving**, wood carving in which the patterns are produced by chipping out the wood; so **chip-carver**; **chip potatoes**, sliced potatoes fried crisp; **chip-shot** *Golf*, a short lofted approach-shot on to the putting-green; **chip straw** (cf. CHIP *sb.*[1] 4); **chip-yard** *U.S.*, a wood-cutting yard.

1921 *Dict. Occup. Terms* (1927) § 472 **Chip basket maker*; ..plaits together..narrow strips of shavings of thin wood to make..chip baskets. 1820 S. BRECK in *Recoll.* (1877) App. iv. 298 She has gone on..bedecking herself in merino shawls, *chip bonnets, etc. 1845 M. M. NOAH *Gleanings* 65 On her little head she wore a good sized chip bonnet, decorated with artificial flowers. 1892 ELEANOR ROWE *Chip-Carving* 47 Instructions to the *chip-carver. 1888 *Queen* 29 Sept., Suppl., *Chip-Carving. 1902 *Westm. Gaz.* 26 Apr. 7/3 Examples of bent-iron work, and wood and chip carving. 1916 *Home Chat* 9 Sept. 432 Dinner 2. Salmis of Game. Potato Chips. Greengage Tart...The *Chip Potatoes. Fry these as usual, [etc.]. 1909 *Westm. Gaz.* 10 June 12/4 *Chip shots which he laid within two feet of the pin. 1920 P. G. WODEHOUSE *Damsel in Distress* iii, 'Not at all,' said George, trying a sort of vocal chip-shot out of the corner of his mouth. 1898 *Westm. Gaz.* 28 Apr. 3/2 *Chip straw is again to the fore, indeed, forms the foundation of some of the most exclusive hats. 1863 MRS. WHITNEY *Faith Gartney's Girlh.* xiv, The spicy smell of the *chip-yard round the corner where the scraps of pine lay..under the summer sun. 1865 — *Gayworthys* i. 11 The strawberry picker took up her pail and departed across the chip-yard. 1869 *Overland Monthly* III. 10 A rail-fence..banishes the chip-yard into the road. 1891 MARAH E. RYAN *Pagan of Alleghenies* xix. 232 Two men.. halted out at the chip-yard.

b. *Golf.* Short for *chip-shot*.

1909 *Westm. Gaz.* 9 June 14/3 He was short with his chip on to the green at the fourth. 1922 *Daily Mail* 12 Dec. 6 The first hole will measure 250 yards—a drive and a chip.

Chip, *v.*[1] Add:

3. e. *intr.* To make chipping strokes.

1908 A. BENNETT *Buried Alive* x. 248 Muscular, hairy males..were chipping and paring at huge blocks of stone.

8. Also *trans.*

1903 A. H. LEWIS *The Boss* 271 Madam, let me chip in a word.

b. To put in or stake chips (*intr.* and *trans.*).

1892 FLORENCE *Handbk. Poker* 89 *To chip in*, to put counters on the table. Equivalent to entering into the game. *Ibid.* 158 Every time my callow friend won a pot he put the silver and bills in his pocket and would chip in the stuff as he needed it. 1898 'L. HOFFMANN' *Card & Table Games* (ed. 2) 203 Each person puts up an agreed amount by way of ante...To avoid dispute as to whose turn it may be, a pocket-knife, known as the 'buck', is passed round, resting with the player whose turn it is to 'chip' for the remainder.

c. To contribute; to make a contribution. *U.S.*

1878 J. H. BEADLE *Western Wilds* ii. 41 At Angell's Camp, we chipped in together and hired regular guards. 1886 *Harper's Mag.* Dec. 36 'Here a dollar!' 'Here's another!' And they all chipped in their share. 1888 *Amer. Mag.* Sept. (Farmer) A man who won't chip in to charity is always an object of suspicion. 1903 *N. Y. Sun* 15 Nov., Nevertheless they all chipped in for the benefit of Simpson's widow and little child next day. 1908 S. E. WHITE *Riverman* ix. 80 Why, there isn't a man on that river who doesn't chip in five or ten dollars when a man is hurt or killed.

9. *To chip at*: also, to poke fun at. Hence *trans.* (by omission of *at*), to make (a person) the object of a joke, to chaff, banter.

1896 *Westm. Gaz.* 13 Jan. 6/2 The friends of the contending teams each 'chipped' and jeered at the other. 1898 *Daily News* 20 Aug. 5/4, I chipped them a little on their plump, well-fed condition. 1915 *Even. News* 24 Nov. 3/4 People have been telling me I'm a German and chipping me, and I wish to get it over. 1928 *Daily Express* 23 Feb. 6 Letitia Pilkington..was a sportswoman. She even chipped her confessor on her deathbed.

10. *Golf. intr.* To play a chip-shot.

1923 *Daily Mail* 8 May 12 He chipped to within eighteen inches of the hole.

Chiparee, earlier form of CHICKAREE.

1804 *Maryland Hist. Mag.* IV. 9 These squirrels are exceedingly active and the mountaineers call them the Chiparee squirrel.

Chip-bird. *U.S.* [CHIP *v.*[1]] = *Chipping-bird*, CHIPPING *ppl. a.* 2.

1824 *Massachusetts Yeoman* 28 Apr. (Th.) The destruction of a robin, chip, blue, or black bird is not all. 1869 LOWELL *Study Wind.* (1871) 15 The only bird I have ever heard sing in the night has been the chip-bird. 1872 COUES *Key N. Amer. Birds* 142 Chipping Sparrow, Chipbird or Chippy. Hairbird.

Chip hat. Chiefly *U.S.* [CHIP *sb.*[1] 4.] A hat made of thin strips of wood.

1771, 1859 [see CHIP *sb.*[1] 9]. 1845 M. M. NOAH *Gleanings* 11 If we agree to call a plain chip hat and a muslin gown *fashionable*. 1873 J. H. BEADLE *Undevel. West* ix. 156 The Chinese, with..their chip hats, rice feed, and cheap labor. 1889 ROSE T. COOKE *Steadfast* xviii. 194 A little white chip hat pinned on the high puffs of hair.

Chipped, *ppl. a.* Add: **2. b.** Of beef: Cut into thin pieces and dried. *U.S.*

1819 *Massachusetts Spy* 18 Aug. 4/2 No vapid tea, or cold toast, and greasy butter, and chipped meat. 1859 *Knickerbocker Mag.* Oct. LIV. 406 Such waffles, chipped beef, sweet-meats, melon.

3. b. *Chipped glass* (see quot.).

1903 *Chambers's Jrnl.* VI. 685/1 The material is known technically as chipped glass, for the pattern is actually chipped out of the surface.

Chipper, *sb.*[1] Add:

1. c. With advs.

1901 *Daily Chron.* 4 Dec. 9/3 Pianoforte.—Fitters-up and chipper-up and tuner wanted. 1921 *Dict. Occup. Terms* (1927) § 279 *Chipper-in* (rolling mill); a chipper *q.v.* chipping rough ends on rails with hammer and chisel. *Ibid.* § 643 *Chipper-up*; carries out first stage of tuning strings of pianos when partly finished.

Chipper, *v.* Add:

1. (Earlier U.S. examples.)

1712 S. SEWALL *Diary* (1879) II. 343, I saw Six Swallows together flying and chippering very rapturously. 1716 *Ibid.* (1882) III. 78 This day I first saw the Swallows; I think I had heard some Chiper before.

2. b. *intr.* To brighten *up*.

1886 *Harper's Mag.* Sept. 583/1 She'd chipper up and fix up what she could. 1904 G. H. LORIMER *Old Gorgon Graham* 129 'Young man, I've decided to help you out of this hole', he began. Percy chippered right up.

Chipping, *ppl. a.* **2.** Add: **chipping-bird** (earlier examples); **chipping-sparrow**, the chipping-bird.

1791 W. BARTRAM *Trav. Carolina* etc. (1792) 289 Passer domesticus; the little house sparrow or chipping bird. *a* 1813 A. WILSON *Amer. Ornith.* (1831) II. 255 *Fringilla socialis*, Wilson.—Chipping Sparrow. 1861 MRS. STOWE *Pearl Orr's Isl.* I. viii. 58 I've seen 'em big as chippin-birds' eggs. 1867 *Amer. Naturalist* I. 402 Simultaneously with the Bluebird the Chipping Sparrow awakes, and is soon heard chanting his simple cricket-like song from the garden and lawn. 1904 MARY E. WALLER *Wood-carver* iii. 144, I bethought me of the little chipping-sparrow's nest in a spruce tree.

Chi·ppy, *sb. U.S.* (Also *chippy bird, sparrow.*) = *Chipping-bird*, CHIPPING *ppl. a.* 2.

1872 COUES *Key N. Amer. Birds* 142. 1898 SUSAN HALE *Lett.* 338, I must tell you of our little chippy sparrows that had their nest in the trellis. 1900 *Congress. Rec.* 30 Apr. 4872/2 The ground chippy darted under the fences. 1913 MRS. STRATTON-PORTER *Laddie* iii. (1917) 56 In the hollow of a rotten rail a little chippy bird always built a hair nest.

Chippy, *a.* Add:

3. b. Also *gen.* 'off colour', 'cheap'.

1877 *Belgravia* XXXII. 235 After too copious libations of the above [*sc.* brandy and soda] a man is apt to feel 'chippy' next morning. 1884 HAWLEY SMART *From Post to Finish* xxi, A dozen cigars a day make one feel dreadfully 'chippy', in the morning. 1899 CONAN DOYLE *Duet* 74 'I feel a little chippy to-day.' 'That's the worst of these cheap champagnes.'

Chiprassi, var. CHUPRASSY.

Chipre, var. *CHYPRE.

Chip-sparrow. *U.S.* = *Chipping-sparrow*, *CHIPPING *ppl. a.* 2.

1852 Mrs. Stowe *Uncle Tom's C.* xvi. 191 Then she sat on his knee like a chip sparrow, still laughing.

Chip-squirrel. *U.S.* (Earlier examples.)
1844 'Jon. Slick' *High Life N. Y.* II. 220, I could feel the leetle hand a movin..like a chip squirrel in its nest. 1875 Mrs. Stowe *Deacon Pitkin's Farm* i. 35 The very chip squirrels in the stone-walls..were rushing about with chops incredibly distended.

Chiragh (tʃirā·g). [Hind., a. Pers. چراغ *chirāgh* lamp, light.] A primitive oil lamp used by natives in India.
1899 *Westm. Gaz.* 15 Aug. 1/3, I took the oil from my chirag and anointed my back therewith. 1920 *Chambers's Jrnl.* Dec. 863/2 To-night we'll light tiny, weenie *chiraghs*.

Chiral (kəi·răl), *a.* [f. Gr. χείρ hand + -al.] Of a crystal, etc.: Possessed of **Chirality** (kəi·ræ·liti) [-ity], the power of certain crystals and optically active substances of turning the plane of polarization of light to the right or left hand. Hence **Chiroid** (kəi·roid): see quot. 1903.
1893 Ld. Kelvin *Boyle Lect.* in *Jrnl. Oxf. Univ. Jun. Sci. Club* (1894) 25 May 25 *note*, I call any geometrical figure, or group of points, *chiral*, and say that it has *chirality*, if its image in a plane mirror, ideally realized, cannot be brought to coincide with itself. 1903 — *Baltimore Lect.* (1904) 439 For brevity I now call a molecule which has chirality, a chiroid.

Chi-rho (kəi rōu). The first two letters of Gr. ΧΡΙϹΤΟϹ Christ, often joined in a monogram ☧ and used to symbolize the name.
1611 Florio s.v. *Labaro*, The letter Chi and Rhò, which signifieth Christ. 1868 *Jrnl. British Archæol. Assoc.* XXIV. 132 The *chirho* also occurs on a doorstep. 1880 Smith & Cheetham *Dict. Chr. Antiq.* II. 1312/1 The upright cross being first added to the Chi-rho so as to form a kind of star. 1889 J. Romilly Allen *Monumental Hist. Brit. Ch.* 30 The Chi-Rho monogram. 1900 *Daily News* 8 Oct. 6/3 The monument consists of a simple monolithic block...Upon one side is incised a simple Chi-Rho enclosed in a circle. 1924 Collingwood *Roman Britain* 95 Engraved on a silver cup of foreign manufacture..we find the Chi-Rho monogram.

Chirimoya, var. Cherimoya.

Chirk, *a.* (Earlier examples.)
1789 Webster *Diss. Engl. Lang.* 387 This word is wholly lost except in New England. It is there used for *comfortably, bravely, cheerful*, as when one inquires about a sick person, it is said, he is chirk. 1816 Pickering *Vocab.* 59 It should be remarked, that the adjective *chirk* is used only in the *interior* of New England; and even there, I think, only by the illiterate. It is never heard in the sea-port towns.

Chirk, *v. U.S.* [f. Chirk *a.*] *intr.* and *trans.* To cheer *up*; to become or make cheerful.
(*a*) 1844 'Jon. Slick' *High Life N. Y.* I. 231 All I could do she wouldn't chirk up. 1886 Roe *Fell in Love* xiii. 117 Don't you worry now; chirk up and you'll come out all right. 1887 Mary E. Wilkins *Humble Romance* 17 P'rhaps nothin' awful's goin' to happen...Chirk up an' give us a kiss. (*b*) 1843 *Yale Lit. Mag.* Feb. I. 26 (Th.) All our folks appear more chirkier than they usually feel, in order to chirk her up. 1878 Rose T. Cooke *Happy Dodd* xii. 122 Ef there's a mortal thing I can do to help ye, or chirk ye up, I want to do it right off. 1911 E. Ferber *Dawn O'Hara* xvi. 238, I donned a becoming gown to chirk up my courage.

Chirognomically (kəiroɡnǫ·mikăli), *adv.* [f. Chirognomy + -ically.] As a matter of chirognomy.
1891 *Chambers's Encycl.* VII. 727 The thumb is generally regarded as chirognomically the most important part of the hand.

Chiromance (kəi·romæns), *v.* [f. Chiromancy.] **a.** *trans.* To divine by chiromancy. **b.** *intr.* To practise chiromancy. So **Chiro·mancist** = Chiromancer.
1873 Leland *Egypt. Sketch-Bk.* 235 The hands must be washed ere I can chiromance anything. 1882 — *Gypsies* vii. 181, I had chiromanced to the Romany clan. 1889 *Pall Mall Gaz.* 8 Mar. 3/1 The chiromancists or fortune-tellers.

Chiromantist. Delete † and add quot.:
1904 E. F. Benson *Challoners* vi, If I had been told by a chiromantist that I should shortly be writing the words *Sunday Magazine*.

Chironomid (kəirǫ·nǒmid), *a.* and *sb.* [ad. mod.L. *Chironomidæ*, f. *chironomus*, a. Gr. χειρονόμος: see Chironomy and -id³.] **A.** *adj.* Of or belonging to the *Chironomidæ*, a family of dipterous insects typified by the midge. **B.** *sb.* Any of these.
1895 *Standard Dict.* 1924 *Chambers's Jrnl.* 750/2 Chironomid gnats and moth flies (*Psychodidæ*) inhabit the tanks. 1925 R. W. G. Hingston in E. F. Norton *Fight for Everest, 1924* 288 Fragile Chironomids, delicate as mosquitoes, skated on the surface of the water.

Chiropractic (kəiropræ·ktik), *sb.* and *a.* [f. Gr. χειρο- + πρακτικός: see Chiro- and Practic *a.*] **A.** *sb.* Manipulation of the spinal column as a method of curing disease.
1908 *U. S. Congress* Apr. 6 A bill to regulate the practice of chiropractic, to license chiropractic physicians, [etc.]. 1913 B. J. Palmer (*title*) The science of chiropractic, containing a series of lectures..and used as a textbook at the Palmer School of Chiropractic. 1926 J. H. Jones *Healing by Manip.* 35 Chiropractic or bone-setting differs from most other methods of combating disease. 1928 *Sunday Express* 16 Dec. 2/3 Chiropractics..was born in America about 1894, and Mr. B. J. Palmer, the son of the founder, runs a chiropractic school at Davenport, Iowa.
B. *adj.* That practises or is concerned with this method.
1908 [see A. above]. 1919 S. J. Burich (*title*) A text book of chiropractic chemistry. 1920 *Chambers's Jrnl.* 348/2 The country is overrun with..chiropractic and osteopathic doctors. 1926 J. H. Jones *Healing by Manip.* 64 Biologists, once they become aware of the chiropractic principle..will probably do useful service.

Chiropractor (kəi·ropræ·ktəɹ). [f. *Chiropractic + -or.] One who practises chiropractic.
1913 Dorland *Med. Dict.* (ed. 7). 1926 J. H. Jones *Healing by Manip.* 14 There are more than eight thousand chiropractors in the United States and Canada. 1926 *Spectator* 24 July 148/1 Chiropractors have trebled their numbers in a very few years.

Chirp, *a. U.S.* [f. Chirp *v.*] Chirpy.
1863 'Gail Hamilton' *Gala-Days* 233 We walk away as 'chirp as a cricket'.

Chirp, *v.* **3. b.** Add: Also with *up. U.S.*
1897 R. M. Stuart *Simpkinsville* 35 Mis' Meredith is chirpin' up a' ready.

Chirpily (tʃɔ̄·ɹpili), *adv.* [f. Chirpy *a.* + -ly ².] In a chirpy or lively manner.
1923 *Daily Mail* 21 Feb. 8 Calthorpe veterans [*sc.* motor vehicles] 'still running' as chirpily as any highly-tuned racer. 1927 'Q' in *Blackw. Mag.* Aug. 156/2 Defendant (turning chirpily on his accuser).

Chir pine (tʃiə·ɹ,pəin). Also **cheer.** [Hindi *chīr.*] (See quot. 1885.) Also *attrib.*
1885 *Encycl. Brit.* XIX. 105 *Pinus longifolia*, a Nepal species...It is known in India as the 'Cheer-pine';..the tree is common on the foot-hills of the Himalayas. 1921 R. S. Troup *Sylvicult. Indian Trees* III. 1036 Long-leaved pine, chir pine. 1924 *Blackw. Mag.* Oct. 478/1 Our road ran through chir-pine forest and grassy glades.

Chirrupy, *a.* (Earlier U.S. example.)
a 1861 T. Winthrop *John Brent* xxvi. (1862) 280 He's one er them chirrupy, smilin' niggers.

Chisel, *sb.*¹ **5.** Add: **chisel end, head**, an end or head shaped or sharpened like a chisel; **chisel-mouth**, a cyprinoid fish, *Acrocheilus alutaceus*, of the Columbia river, having a large, straight-edged, horny plate in each jaw; also called *chiselmouth jack, hardmouth*, and *squaremouth*.
1876 Preece & Sivewright *Telegraphy* 194 The *chisel end of the punner bar. 1908 *Animal Managem.* 241 The 'chisel' head or sharp portion [of the frost nail] to remain above the [horse-] shoe. 1896 Jordan & Evermann *Fishes N. Amer.* I. 207 Acrocheilus, Agassiz. (*Chisel-mouths.)

Chit, *sb.*⁵ Add attrib. uses.
1845 Chit-system [in Dict.]. 1892 A. Murdoch *Yoshiwara Episode* 21 Billiard tables in the hotels galore (the 'chit' system was in vogue in running them too). 1892 *Daily News* 24 Mar. 5/4 The 'Chit system'..is the very general practice of putting the name on a piece of paper for every article that is purchased instead of paying cash down. 1924 *Blackw. Mag.* Aug. 264/2 For days the chit-coolies bore confidential messages.

Chit, *v.*¹ Add:
2. *trans.* To allow to sprout; to remove the sprouts of (potato tubers) for planting as sets.
1904 *Daily Chron.* 8 Apr. 6/4 Having chitted them [*sc.* 'Eldorado' potatoes] three times already, he has made between £7,000 and £8,000 out of his original purchase.

Chital (tʃī·tăl). Also **cheetul, -al, chetel.** [Hindi.] The Indian spotted deer, *Cervus axis*.
1880 *Encycl. Brit.* XII. 742 The *chitál* or spotted deer..is ..admitted to be the most beautiful inhabitant of the Indian jungles. 1923 *Blackw. Mag.* Sept. 381/2 He..had been after cheetul here and had come on a tiger. 1925 *Punch* 20 May 546/2 The best of his bag was a *chital* stag.

Chit-chatty (tʃi·t,tʃæti). [f. Chit-chat + -y ¹.] Of the nature of chit-chat or light chat; gossipy.
1889 J. Masterman *Scotts of Bestminster* III. xvii. 153 Long communications, chit-chatty, amusing.

Chitinogenous (kəitinǫ·dʒĭnəs), *a.* [f. Chitin + -(o)genous.] Consisting of or producing chitin.
1888 Rolleston & Jackson *Anim. Life* 227 *T*[*aenia*] *serrata*...In the 'embryonic mass' there are..flattened cells placed laterally and containing..nucleolated nuclei. These cells constitute a 'chitinogenous layer'.

Chitinoid (kəi·tinoid), *a.* [f. Chitin + -oid.] Resembling chitin.
1888 Rolleston & Jackson *Anim. Life* 429 The egg-shell in oviparous *Elasmobranchii* is chitinoid.

Chitosan (kəi·tosæn). *Physiol. Chem.* [f. Chitin + -ose + -an.] A substance obtained from chitin, formed by the action of alkali at a high temperature.
1895 *Jrnl. Chem. Soc.* LXVIII. I. 167 The conversion of chitin into chitosan and acetic acid by fusion with potash.

Chitra (tʃi·tra). Also **chittra.** [Hind.] = *Chital.
1843 J. E. Gray *List Mammals Brit. Mus.* 212 Axis Maculata. The Axis or Chittra.

Chittack (tʃi·tæk). [Bengali *chhaṭak.*]
1. An Indian weight about equal to 1 ounce, 17 pennyweights, 12 grains troy.
1889 Kipling *From Sea to Sea, Opium Factory* (1900) III. 230 The cake-maker..receives a lump of opium, weighed out, of one seer seven chittacks and a half.
2. A measure of land in Bengal.
1905 *Statesman* 22 Aug. 2/4 A..dwelling house containing by estimation 7 cottahs 7 chittacks 2 square feet.

Chittagong (tʃi·tăgǫŋ). [Name of a district of Bengal, British India.] A variety of a domestic fowl of the Malayan type.
1830 'B. Moubray' *Dom. Poultry* (ed. 6) 17 The Chittagong or Malay, another Indian variety. 1855 *Poultry Chron.* III. 201 Last spring I had a Chittagong and a black Spanish rooster.

Chitter, *v.* **1.** (Later U.S. example.)
1904 Mary E. Waller *Wood-carver* vii. 309 A chipmunk chittered along the stone wall.

Chitter-chatter. Delete *rare* and add:
1877 Disraeli in Buckle *Life* (1920) VI. 116 He did not want anything: only chitter-chatter. 1895 Kipling *2nd Jungle Bk., Red Dog* 193 Mowgli..imitated perfectly the sharp chitter-chatter of Chikai, the leaping rat of the Dekkan. 1908 *Daily Chron.* 3 Aug. 3/1 What is the use of smart women's chitter-chatter without their dresses? 1928 *Observer* 19 Feb. 10/1 The empty, drawing-room chitter-chatter plays.
b. Also as vb.
1928 *Hearst's International* Aug. 43/1 He never tired of the Esperanto of the ticker tape..chittering chattering fortune or disaster.

Chiv(e)y, chivvy, the more usual forms of Chevy.
1872 F. W. Robinson *Wrayford's Ward*, etc. III. 209, I thought that it was a very odd name,..and that the boys would be very severe upon it presently in the play-ground, and 'chivey' him. 1921 Shane Leslie *Manning* 442 By covering his views with refining words he escaped and chivied the partisan. 1924 *Glasgow Herald* 11 Mar. 7 For nearly an hour Mr Tom Shaw was teased and chivvied. 1927 *Blackw. Mag.* Aug. 169/1 Then would ensue the most delightful chivvy all round the upper deck. 1927 *British Weekly* 27 Oct. 85/2 Into this melee Mr. Sheppard proposes joyously to launch another fifteen, and chivy the ball in yet a third direction.

Chlamydospore (klæ·mido,spōəɹ). [f. Gr. χλαμυδ-, χλαμύς cloak + Spore.] **a.** *Bot.* A thick-walled resting spore produced by various fungi. **b.** *Zool.* A spore with protective chitinous covering, as distinguished from *gymnospore*.
1884 Henfrey *Bot.* (ed. 4) 160 Chlamydospores, when fully formed, are still enclosed within their parent cells. 1910 G. N. Calkins *Protozoöl.* 183 The covered spores or chlamydospores, of the sexual generation. 1910 *Encycl. Brit.* IX. 388/1 The chlamydospores, or true spores, occur in *Sarcocystis tenella* of sheep. *Ibid.* XI. 338/1 Some Mucorini show a peculiar mode of vegetative reproduction by means of gemmae or chlamydospores—*i. e.* short segments of the hyphae become stored with fatty reserves and act as spores.

Chloræmia (klōrī·miă). *Path.* Also **-emia.** [mod.L., f. Gr. χλωρός green, pale + αἷμα blood.] (See quot. 1890.)
1890 *Brit. Med. Jrnl.* 31 May 1239/1 Chloremia...A blood disorder, either idiopathic or associated with other ailments, consisting essentially of a greatly diminished percentage of hæmoglobin, and of a variable decrease in that of the red corpuscles. 1907 *Practitioner* June 826 To the greater part ..of the symptom complex of nephritis, he [*sc.* Widal] gives the name chloraemia.

Chloralamide (klōrălæ·məid). [f. Chloral + Amide.] A sedative formed by compounding chloral and ammonia.
1889 *Lancet* 7 Dec. 1192/1 Dr. Langaard of Berlin reviews in the *Therapeutische Monatsschrift* the present state of our knowledge of the action of chloralamide. 1897 *Trans. Amer. Pediatric Soc.* IX. 168 The treatment consisted of the administration of nervous sedatives, at first chloralamide, to which later was added hyoscine. 1909 Allbutt & Rolleston *Syst. Med.* VI. 490, I now use chloralamide which, I am told, is safer than chloral; it acts nearly as well.

Chloranthaceous (klōrænþē·ʃĭəs), *a. Bot.* Belonging to the family *Chloranthaceæ*.
1882 Sir J. D. Hooker in *Life & Lett.* (1918) II. 248 He has since published it as *Circaeaster agrestis*..and adopted an idea of Oliver's which I hardly share, that it is Chloranthaceous.

Chlorenchyma (klore·ŋkimă). *Bot.* [f. Gr. χλωρός green + ἔγχυμα infusion.] Green tissue consisting of cells containing chlorophyll, esp. in leafless branches having the function of leaves.
1894 Oliver tr. *Kerner's Nat. Hist. Plants* (1902) I. 278 In flowering plants the transpiring cells are situated as a rule in the interior of the green leaves, and also in the green cortex of leafless branches, forming a part of that green tissue which has been termed *chlorenchyma*, or when in the leaves, *mesophyll*.

Chloretone (klō·rĭtōun). *Chem.* [f. Chlor- ², with the termination of *acetone*.] A white crystalline substance, $(CH_3)_2C(OH)CCl_3$, tasting like camphor, used as a local anæsthetic.
1900 *Jrnl. Chem. Soc.* LXXVIII. II. 358 Pharmacology of Chloretone (Acetonechloroform). 1907 *Practitioner* Aug. 291 In this case, chloretone, dusted lightly on, will be found useful, as it is anesthetic and antiseptic. 1908 *Ibid.* Feb. 253 Chloretone Ointment.

Chlorider (klō·rəidəɹ). [f. Chloride + -er¹.] One who mines for ores containing chloride of silver.
1874 Raymond *Statist. Mines & Mining* 229 'Chloriders' have been at work during the past summer, and have shipped a few tons of ore to Eureka.

Chloridizing (klō·ridəiziŋ), *vbl. sb.* [f. Chloridize *v.* + -ing ¹.] Conversion into chloride. Also *attrib.* So **Chlo:ridiza·tion.**
1877 Raymond *Statist. Mines & Mining* 195 Where the natural chloridization is complete. 1882 *Rep. Ho. Repr. Prec. Met. U.S.* 176 A chloridizing furnace, for the purpose of working the rich auriferous sulphuret with which the ore abounds. *Ibid.* 183 Two silver mills..will next year reduce the ores of the Saw Tooth district, the method employed being chloridizing.

Chloroma (klorōu·mă). *Path.* [mod.L., f. Gr. χλωρός green + *-oma.] (See quot. 1886.)
1886 *Buck's Handbk. Med. Sci.* III. 402/1 *Chloroma*, a very rare tumor, agrees in structure with the round-cell sarcoma, and contains in its cells a bright green pigment. 1906 *Jrnl. Chem. Soc.* XC. II. 566 Acute and chronic lymphatic leucæmia and chloroma are all essentially the same. 1908 *Practitioner* Feb. 245 Most cases of chloroma are characterised by the presence of a lymphocythaemia.

Chlorophy·lloid, *a.* [See -oid.] Resembling chlorophyll.
1892 A. B. Griffiths *Physiol. Invertebrata* 236 *Flustra foliacea* also contains a chlorophylloid pigment.

Chloroplast (klō·rŏplæst). *Biol.* [f. Chloro-¹ + -plast.] A plastid containing chlorophyll. Also **Chloropla·stid.**
1888 *Jrnl. Chem. Soc.* LIV. 983. 1902 H. Wager in *Encycl. Brit.* XXVII. 333/1 As the cell grows they [*sc.* the chromatophores] may become converted into leucoplasts (starch-formers), chloroplasts (chlorophyll-bodies), or chromoplasts (colour-bodies). 1906 *Cambr. Nat. Hist.* I. 86 The cell [*Zooxanthella*] contains two chloroplastids, or plates coloured with the vegetal pigment 'diatomin'. 1908 R. J. Harvey-Gibson *Biol.* vi. 43 The chloroplasts are minute ovoid bodies, occurring singly or in large numbers in the cells...Each consists of a basis of protoplasm permeated by an oily matter in which the chlorophyll, or pigment proper, is dissolved.

Choana (kōu·ănă). *Anat.* Pl. **-næ** (-nī). [mod. L., a. Gr. χοάνη funnel.] A funnel-like opening; applied to the posterior nasal orifices.
1876 Macalister *Syst. Zool.* 13 The pair of maxillary lobes usually unite in the middle line, leaving behind them openings into the nasal cavities (*choanæ*). 1895 tr. *Wiedersheim's Struct. Man* 61 The choanæ of the Veddah's skull are.. half a centimetre lower than in the European.

Choano- (kōu·ăno), combining form of Gr. χοάνη funnel, as in **Cho·anocyte**, a 'collar cell' in sponges; hence **Cho:anocy·tal** *a.*; **Cho:anofla·gellate** *a.*, belonging to the order *Choanoflagellata* of Infusoria (see quots.); *sb.*, a member of this order; **Cho·anosome**, the inner part of a sponge, containing the choanocytes; hence **Cho:anoso·mal** *a.*
1888 W. J. Sollas *Tetractinellida* p. xiv, The endoderm is partly composed of flagellated collared cells (choanocytes), and partly of pinacocytes. *Ibid.* p. xv, This investing skin may be distinguished as the ectosome, the rest of the sponge as the choanosome, the latter name framed in allusion to its being the region to which the choanocytes lining the flagellated chambers are restricted. *Ibid.* p. xvi, Dividing the sponge..into a choanosomal and ectosomal portion. *Ibid.* p. xxxviii, A contraction of the choanocytal wall. 1900 E. A. Minchin *Porifera* 27 Each cell bears at its upper free extremity a single vibratile flagellum.., which springs from the centre of an area enclosed by a delicate cup or collar of protoplasm. On account of the latter peculiarity these cells have been termed collar cells or choanocytes. *Ibid.* 53 Each collar cell resembles..a single choanoflagellate monad. 1906 *Cambr. Nat. Hist.* I. 121 The Craspedomonadidae (often called Choanoflagellates). 1927 Haldane & Huxley *Anim. Biol.* xii. 264 The Choanoflagellates, a group of Flagellates in which a transparent collar of protoplasm surrounds the flagellum.

Choate (kōu·ĕt), *a.* An erroneous word, framed to mean 'finished', 'complete', as if the *in-* of *inchoate* were the L. negative.
1902 Sir W. B. Richmond in *Saint George* V. 288 He [*sc.* Ruskin] seemed to be under the spell of a vision which he would make choate. 1929 Winston Churchill in *Times* 13 Feb. 16/1 How could the peoples know?..What choate and integral conviction could they form?

Chock, *sb.*¹ Add:
4. b. *chock and log* (*fence*), a fence raised by placing layers of logs on 'chocks' or short wooden blocks placed transversely to the line of the fence. *Austral.*
1872 G. S. Baden-Powell *New Homes for Old Country* 207 Another fence, known as 'chock and log', is composed of long logs resting on piles of chocks, or short blocks of wood. 1890 *Melbourne Argus* 20 Sept. 13/5 A herd of kangaroos..bounding over the wire and 'chock-and-log' fences.

Chock, *v.*¹ Add:
1. b. *absol.* To fill *in* as packing. *U.S.*
1868 *Putnam's Mag.* June 668/2, I found afterward she had all her clothes and mine [in the truck] and then she'd chock'd in all around with maple sugar.

Chock, *v.*² (Modern U.S. examples.)
1888 *St. Paul & Minneapolis Pioneer Press* 22 July (Farmer) That duffer chocked up after going six furlongs. 1889 Farmer *Americanisms, Chock-up*,..used in the sense of to collapse; or to 'go to pieces'.

Chock, *v.*³ *U.S.* [See Shock *v.*²] *intr.* To enter with a slight shock or knock.
1913 Mulford *Coming of Cassidy* ii. 31 Skinny's smoking gun chocked into its holster. *Ibid.* xiii. 218 Towne's gun chocked back in the scabbard as its owner..went down.

Chock, *adv.* Add:
1. (Earlier example, replacing quot. 1860.)
1829–32 J. P. Kennedy *Swallow B.* I. xiv. 150 It's only the big wheel stopped as chock as a tombstone.
c. Chock-a-block: also of a place or person, crammed *with*, chock-full *of*.
1889 *Pall Mall Gaz.* 30 Sept. 6/2 You will find the place chock-a-block. 1894 *Idler* Sept. 132 We'll see..if that there foundered ship ain't a-going to work out this traverse the same as if she was chock-a-block with bullion. 1903 *Smart Set* IX. 9/1 Good-for-nothings in shop 22, who were full, chock-a-block, of socialism.

Chocker (tʃǫ·kəɹ), *v.* [? f. Chock *sb.*¹ + -er ¹.] In the game of Patience: To block (a card, or the player).
1887 Miss Whitmore Jones *Games of Patience* 9 If the cards come out unfavourably, you often have to put high upon low ones, at the imminent peril of chockering. *Ibid.* 20 Care and judgment are required here, not to place a card which will chocker the one below it. *Ibid.* 47 You are, in Patience parlance, 'chockered'. 1892 'L. Hoffmann' *Patience Games* Introd. 5 When the player reaches a point at which he can make no further progress, he is said to be 'blocked', or, less elegantly, 'chockered'.

Chocolate. Add:
2. esp. (more explicitly *eating chocolate*) a sweetmeat in the form of cakes, bars, or drops, often with a qualifying word (see quot. 1925). Also with *a* and *pl.*, a sweetmeat made entirely of or coated with chocolate.
1883 [see *chocolate drop* in *5]. 1887 *Army & Navy Co-op. Soc. Price List* 38 Chocolates in Boxes..per box 1/9. 1925 B. Beetham in E. F. Norton *Fight for Everest, 1924* 368 Chocolate..plain, nut, milk, nut-milk, Bitro, vanilla, coffee, etc.
4. b. in U.S. *spec.* of certain soils.
1821 T. Nuttall *Jrnl. Trav. Arkansa* vi. 99 The chocolate or reddish-brown clay of the salt formation. 1858 *Texas Almanac* 56 The soil is chocolate loam. 1869 *Overland Monthly* III. 130 Texas is notable for the number of its soils...There is the 'chocolate' prairie and the 'mulatto' and the 'mezquite' [etc.].
5. *chocolate-coloured* adj. (earlier U.S. example); **chocolate cream**, a sweetmeat consisting of a sweet and flavoured creamy paste coated with chocolate; **chocolate drop**, a small round sweetmeat made of chocolate.
1819 E. Dana *Geogr. Sk.* 188 An extensive body of level rich land, of fine black or *chocolate coloured soil. 1885 *Army & Navy Co-op. Soc. Price List* 30 *Chocolate Creams ..per box..1/8. 1891 *Encycl. Pract. Cookery* (ed. T. F. Garrett) I. 376/1 Fill up the moulds with melted cream, prepared as for Chocolate Creams. 1898 *Westm. Gaz.* 27 Apr. 2/2, I cease to ask whether the chocolate cream soldier is true to life. 1906 *Daily Chron.* 25 July 6/4 A shop-worn chocolate-cream bar. 1883 R. Haldane *Workshop Rec.* Ser. II. 160 *Chocolate Drops with Nonpareils.

Choctaw (tʃǫ·ktǭ). *Skating.* [The name of a tribe of N. American Indians.] A step from either edge on one foot to the opposite edge on the other foot, in an opposite direction. (Cf. Mohawk 4.)
1892 J. M. Heathcote, etc. *Skating* 81 Starting as before from the outside forward, it is possible to put the other foot down not on the outside but on the inside back. This step it is proposed to call a 'Choctaw'. 1892 Monier-Williams, etc. *Figure-skating* 61 A Choctaw is simply a step or stroke from any edge in one direction, to the opposite edge on the other foot, in an opposite direction. 1908 E. F. Benson *Engl. Fig. Skating* 119 Mohawks and Choctaws, to attempt a definition, are a cross between edges and turns...In Mohawks the same edge (outside or inside) as has been laid down by the first foot is taken up by the second; in Choctaws the opposite edge.

Chog. A dial. variant of Chock *sb.*¹
1926 *Blackw. Mag.* July 92/1 The port lifeboats tumbled out of their chogs.

Choga (tʃōu·gă). *Anglo-Ind.* [Turki *choghā.*] A loose garment with long sleeves like a dressing-gown, worn by Afghans.
1869 Watson & Kaye *People of India* IV. No. 209 A richly embroidered robe or choga of Cashmere cloth. 1883 *Q. Rev.* Apr. 303 We believe his favourite dishabille was an Afghan *choga*. 1891 Kipling *City Dreadf. Nt.* 20 The black frock-coat rises to explain his friend's amendment... The black *choga*..speaks again. 1905 *Westm. Gaz.* 2 Nov. 3/1 Mussulman Gentlemen. Black broadcloth or silk jubba, jama, choga or other robe worn over a saya.

Choical (kōu·ikăl), *a.* [f. Gr. χοϊκός earthy (f. χοῦς dust) + -al.] A Gnostic term for: Earthy.
1708 H. Dodwell *Explication* 6 He supposes them [*sc.* human souls]..to be Hylical and Choical, not Cælestial. 1914 R. M. Jones *Spiritual Reformers* Introd. p. xiii, There was in man..a visible body..believed to be composed, according to many of the Gnostics, of a subtle element.. which they named the *hylic* body, and a sheath of gross earthly matter which they called the *choical* body.

Choice, *a.* **3. b.** (Earlier U.S. example.)
1775 A. Adams in *Familiar Lett.* (1876) 128, I received.. the other articles you sent,..I shall be very choice of them.

Choice, *sb.* Add:
5. c. A place chosen by a settler for occupation. *U.S.*
1678 in *Maryland Hist. Mag.* XIX. 344 Benjamins Choice. 1688 *Ibid.* 365 Simsons Choice. 1698 *Ibid.* 367 Parkers Choice. 1707 *Ibid.* I. 7 That..a town should be erected on a tract on the same River..called Taylor's Choice. 1834 H. Brackenridge *Recoll.* ii. 19 In ten days we reached the encampment of General Wayne, at a place called Hopson's choice, now a part of the city of Cincinnati.

Choir, *sb.* **7.** Add: **choir nun** or **sister**, a member of a female religious society who is professed for the choir (i. e. to perform the choir offices), distinguished from *lay sister*; **choir offices**, the divine service which is said or sung in choir (i. e. the canonical hours, morning and evening prayer of the Book of Common Prayer); **choir practice**, the trial or performance of set pieces of music by a church choir, under the instruction of the choir-master, in preparation for the service in church.
1788–9 in *Cath. Rec. Soc. Publ.* (1910) VIII. 187 The Number of Religious at this time are 13 *choir Nuns 3 lay sisters & 3 novices. 1876 *St. Cross, Holywell, Parish Mag.* 277 The choral cope worn on ferias in large churches by all the clergy at the *choir offices. 1898 *Daily News* 26 Aug. 5/1 The canons are..free in all acts outside those of the choir offices. 1865 F. Helmore *Ch. Choirs* 65 In *Choir Practice ..let the Choir-master..insist on constant attention to the movements of his 'baton'. 1904 E. F. Benson *Challoners* vi, This afternoon..she would have to take choir-practice in the Room. 1889 Devine *Convent Life* (1890) 298 A Lay-Sister cannot be transferred to the state of a *Choir-Sister without the authority of the Holy See.

Choke, *sb.*¹ **4.** Add: In a firearm = Choke-bore (both senses).
1875 in Greener *Choke-bore Guns* (1877) 97 After firing upwards of 2,500 shots from each of the three guns to be tested, no falling off of any kind could be discovered, nor did the measurement by callipers vary even to the thousandth of an inch from the original diameter of the choke. 1877 *Ibid.* 149 A modified choke can be made to give a fair spread at 20 yards, and yet shoot well up to 50 yards. 1884 F. F. R. Burgess *Sporting Fire-arms* 4 The sketches..show the ordinary choke and the tulip choke respectively. 1892 Greener *Breech-Loader* 146 With a twelve bore gun, standard load distance and conditions, the ordinary full choke will make an average pattern of 215 pellets; The half-choke 185 pellets; The quarter-choke 160 pellets. 1895 *Q. Rev.* Jan. 105 In 1800..the safety-bolt, the inside hammer, and (in principle, at all events) the choke, had been known for some years.
6. *Electr.* (Also *choke-coil.*) = **choking-coil*. *Choke control* (in wireless telegraphy), modulation of the carrier-wave by means of a choke.
1913 *Year-bk. Wireless Telegr.* 331 The transformer secondaries..are protected..by air core chokes. 1915 tr. *Zenneck's Wireless Telegr.* 323 To block the path of the oscillations into the circuits of the auxiliary apparatus where a part of their energy would be wasted, by means of choke coils. *Ibid.*, *note*, Systems or methods of connection in which no choke coils are needed. 1923 Hawkhead & Dowsett *Techn. Instr. Wireless Telegr.* 156 A third method known as 'anode' or 'choke' control. *Ibid.* 184 The Choke Coils (Air Core). *Ibid.* 200 Air Core Choke. 1928 *Morn. Post* 9 July, When chokes having a winding of thick wire are used the voltage lost is quite small. 1928 *Times* 26 Nov. 11/3 R.W.C. ..was charged..with selling high frequency chokes, to which a false trade description..had been applied.
attrib. 1927 *Observer* 6 Mar. 25 Two stages of choke-capacity note magnification.

Choke, *v.* Add:
21. Choke in, up. *intr.* To refrain from speaking, to hold one's tongue. *U.S. colloq.*
1844 'Jon. Slick' *High Life N. Y.* I. 29, I wanted to tell Captain Doolittle about it. But, sez I to myself, I'll choke in to-day. *Ibid.* 259 She owed for her board, and so choked in. 1907 Mulford *Bar-20* ix. 105 'Why, about eight years ago I had business—' 'Choke up', interposed Red.

Choke-berry. *U.S.* [Choke- 1 b.] The fruit of the shrub *Aronia arbutifolia* or *A. sanguinea*; the shrub itself.
1778 J. Carver *Trav. N. Amer.* 511 The Choak berry. The shrub thus termed by the natives..bears a berry about the size of a sloe, [etc.]. 1836 D. B. Edward *Hist. Texas* iv. 66 The Cranberry and the choakberry. 1845–50 Mrs. Lincoln *Lect. Bot.* App. 76/2 *Aronia arbutifolia*..Red Choke-berry. *Ibid.*, *A. sanguinea*, bloody choke-berry. 1871 Schele de Vere *Americanisms* (1872) 403 Very different is the so-called choke-berry, in reality the fruit of a low apple-tree (*Pyrus arbutifolia*). 1898 *Atlantic Monthly* LXXXII. 497/2 With the huckleberry, was chokeberry, another New England acquaintance. 1901 C. Mohr *Plant Life Alabama* 71 The chokeberry, which is here of arborescent habit, presents a beautiful sight when loaded with its bright scarlet fruit.

Choke-cherry. *U.S.* (Earlier example.)
1784 Cutler in *Mem. Amer. Acad.* (1785) I. 449 The Black Choke Cherry...The Red Choke Cherry.

Choke-pear. 1. Delete † and add:
1840 J. Buel *Farmer's Comp.* 269 It is as easy to cultivate the vergalen as it is the choke pear. 1872 *Rep. Vermont Board Agric.* I. 107 Man, by his industry, skill and perseverance applied to the wild choke pear of our fields,.. has transformed it.

Choker. Add:
4. *Electr.* = **choking coil.*
1902 *Encycl. Brit.* XXXIII. 233/1 Choking or impedance coils..called 'chokers'.

Chokiness (tʃōu·kinės). [f. Choky *a.* + -ness.] The condition of being choky or inclined to choke.
1844 Hewlett *Parsons & Widows* vi, I felt a short, unpleasant kind of chokiness.

Choking, *vbl. sb.* or *ppl. a.* Add: **choking coil** *Electr.*, a coil of low resistance inserted in an alternating-current circuit to impede and cut down the current or to change its phase. Called also *impedance* or *reactance coil*.
1893 R. M. Walmsley *Wormell's Electricity in Service of Man* 644 An extremely pretty device known as a 'choking' coil. 1902 W. G. Rhodes *Altern. Currents* 83 Impedance coils, or choking coils, as they are often called, are simply coils having low ohmic resistance and high self-induction.

Chokra (tʃōu·kră). *Anglo-Ind.* [Hind. *chhokrā.*] A boy, youngster; esp. one employed as servant in a household or in a regiment.
1875 A. Wilson *Abode of Snow* 136 He was dubbed 'the Chokra', or simply 'boy'. 1895 Mrs. Croker *Village Tales* (1896) 51 The two natives—the open-mouthed, gaping chokra, the respectfully exultant bearer. 1926 *Blackw. Mag.* Oct. 499/2 In his absence the *chokra* was to look after me.

Choky, *a.* **3.** (Later U.S. example.)
1908 G. H. Lorimer *J. Spurlock* iii. 60, I felt a little choky, and wanted to get out.

Chol-. Add: **Cholangitis** (kǫlændʒəi·tis) [see Angio-], inflammation of a bile-duct.
1886 *Buck's Handbk. Med. Sci.* III. 290/1 The cases.. presented nearly all the anatomical appearances that occur in cholangitis and cholecystitis. 1907 *Practitioner* Oct. 571 Catarrhal cholangitis.

Chole-. Add: **Cholelithiasis** (-liþəi·ăsis), formation or presence of biliary calculi.
1887 *Buck's Handbk. Med. Sci.* IV. 560/1 Cholelithiasis, or gall-stone formation. 1906 *Practitioner* Dec. 809 Both in cholelithiasis and in nephrolithiasis.

Cholecyst. Add: **Cholecystendysis** (-e·ndisis) [Gr. ἔνδυσις an entering in] = *cholecystotomy*; **Cholecystenterostomy** (-enterǫ·stŏmi) [Gr. ἔντερον gut, intestine, στόμα mouth], the operation of establishing a passage between the gall-bladder and the intestine by incision and suture; **Cholecystorrhaphy** (-ǫ·răfi) [Gr. ῥαφή sewing, suture], suture of the gall-bladder after an incision; **Cholecystostomy** (-ǫ·stŏmi) [Gr. στόμα mouth], the operation of establishing an opening into the gall-bladder.
1904 *Westm. Gaz.* 6 May 6/3 The 'Matin' states that the operation performed on the ex-Premier was that of cholecystenterostomy. 1908 *Practitioner* Sept. 452 The removal of biliary calculi..either by cholecystostomy or cholecystenterostomy. 1910 *Ibid.* Mar. 377 The indications for cholecystendysis, as formulated by its chief exponents. *Ibid.*, As a general rule the operation of cholecystectomy shows a higher mortality than cholecystostomy. *Ibid.* 381 When the gall-bladder is found to be wounded, the question arises as to whether it should be treated by gauze packing, cholecystectomy, or cholecystorrhaphy.

Choledoch. Add: **Cho:ledocho·tomy** [see -tomy], incision of the gall-duct (to remove gall-stones).
1894 Gould *Dict. Med.* 1908 Allbutt & Rolleston *Syst. Med.* IV. I. 233 Out of 150 choledochotomies that I ..performed the mortality was under 4 per cent. 1908 *Practitioner* Dec. 829 Choledochotomy after cholecystectomy.

Cholera. Add:
2. *English cholera*, cholera morbus. *Cholera infantum*, a common and often fatal diarrhœa of young children prevailing in summer months.
1886 *Buck's Handbk. Med. Sci.* II. 135/1 The line of demarcation between cholera infantum and the ordinary summer diarrhœa, entero-colitis, cannot always be sharply drawn. 1886 Fagge *Princ. Med.* I. 307 No case of so-called 'English cholera'..has been admitted into Guy's Hospital since 1870. 1894 *Daily News* 19 Sept. 7/1 The certificate showed that death resulted from English cholera. 1895 *Outing* (U.S.) XXVI. 405/2 You are forced to wish that cholera-infantum had been more prevalent sixty years ago.
5. cholera belt, a waistband of flannel or silk worn as a preventive against stomachic ailments.
1892 Dent, etc. *Mountaineering* (ed. 2) 47 The ordinary flannel cholera belt, such as is commonly used in tropical climates.

Choleric, *a.* **5.** Add: *sb.* A person suffering from cholera.
1885 *U.S. Consular Rep.* No. lv. 680 The commission tried to make the autopsy of a choleric whom I saw in the penal establishment of San Miguel.

Cholesterol (kǒle·sterǫl). *Chem.* The name which has superseded Cholesterin (see -ol).
1894 *Jrnl. Chem. Soc.* LXVI. I. 486 A great number of analytical results obtained by the authors with cholesterol and its derivatives, seem to show that the composition of cholesterol is expressed by the formula $C_{27}H_{44}O$. 1923 T. R. Parsons *Bio-Chem.* 107–8. 1928 Kingzett *Chem. Encycl.* (ed. 4) 150 *Cholesterol* (Cholesterine)—Variously formulated as $C_{27}H_{46}O$, $C_{26}H_{44}O$, and $C_{27}H_{45}O$.

Cholla (tʃōu·lyă). *U.S.* [Mexican.] One or other of several species of *Opuntia*, native to the south-western United States and Mexico.
1891 *Century Mag.* Mar. 659 Their knees were full of the thorns of the cholla cactus. 1907 S. E. White *Arizona Nights* I. xii. 186 The hill I had to climb was steep and covered with *chollas*. *Ibid.*, I .. slipped down the bluff getting pretty well stuck up with the *cholla* spines.

Cholo (tʃōu·lo). [Sp., from *Chololllán*, now *Cholula*, a district of Mexico.] In Bolivia and Peru, an original Guichua Indian of the uplands, sometimes having an admixture of Spanish blood. The female is **Cho·la.**
1862 C. R. Markham *Trav. Peru & India* 80 The Cholos or Indians of Arequipa have long been notorious for their turbulence. 1877 E. G. Squier *Peru* 115 One of them [*sc.* Chinamen] had married a native *Chola*. 1908 C. R. Enock *Andes & Amazon* (ed. 2) 19 A Chola girl had entered my room to sell me a *cui*, or guinea-pig. 1909 *N.Y. Even. Post* 19 Jan. 6/3 The Westerner must then equally persecute the 'cholos' who have been pouring into his State from below the Rio Grande.

Chondrenchyma (kǫndre·ŋkimă). *Zool.* Also anglicized **Chondrenchyme** (kǫndre·ŋkəim, -kim). [f. Gr. χόνδρος (see Chondro-) + ἔγχυμα infusion, filling.] A cartilage-like tissue in certain sponges. Hence **Chondrenchymatous** (kǫ:ndreŋki·mătəs) *a.*, consisting of, of the nature of, chondrenchyma.
1888 W. J. Sollas *Tetractinellida* p. xcviii, The mesogloea..is in some very few of the Chondrospongiæ a chondrenchyme. *Ibid.* p. cli, The mesoderm is in part sarcenchymatous, in part chondrenchymatous. 1900 E. A. Minchin *Porifera* 52 Chondrenchyma. *Ibid.* 147 With dense sarcenchymatous choanosome and tough chondrenchymatous ectosome.

Chondriosome (kǫ·ndriosōum). *Biol.* [ad. mod.L. (through Ger.) *chondriosoma*, f. Gr. χονδρίον, dim. of χόνδρος cartilage + σῶμα body.] A protoplasm cell-particle, supposed to function in morphogenesis and heredity. So **Cho·ndriocont** (-kont) [Gr. κοντός pole]: see quots.
1910 C. E. Walker *Hered. Char.* 35 He [*sc.* Meves] suggests that certain cytoplasmic structures, 'chondriosomes', divide with the cell, and are handed on individually from generation to generation. 1911 *Jrnl. Morphology* XXII. 777 There are..no filamentous mitochondria (chondriokonts) in the spermatogonia. 1920 L. Doncaster *Introd. Cytology* 21 The structures grouped together under the general name of mitochondria, known also as chondriosomes, or when rod-shaped, as chondrioconts.

Chondrite. Add: **2.** *Min.* A meteorite containing chondrules.
1912 J. W. Gregory *Making of Earth* I. ii. 35 The meteorites with rounded grains (chondrites) have been regarded as due to the fusion of many separate granules into a large mass.

Chondritic (kǫndri·tik), *a. Min.* [f. prec. + -ic, after G. *chondritisch.*] Characterized by granular structure; of or pertaining to chondrites.
1896 L. Fletcher *Introd. Study Meteorites* 35 The stony part of the siderolites and aerolites is almost entirely crystalline, and in most cases presents a peculiar 'chondritic' or granular structure, the loosely coherent grains being composed of minerals similar to those which enclose them. *Ibid.* 36 About eleven out of every twelve of the stony meteorites belong to a division to which Rose has given the name of Chondritic. 1914 *Brit. Mus. Return* 223 Chondritic meteorites. 1922 *Chambers's Jrnl.* 226/2 The 'stones'..have a structure called 'chondritic', utterly unknown among terrestrial substances.

Chondro-. Add: **Chondrocra·nium**, the primitive brain-pan, composed of cartilage; **Chondro·meter** (quot.); **Cho:ndrosarco·ma**, a cartilaginous sarcoma.
1875 Huxley in *Encycl. Brit.* I. 753/1 The primordial skull or **chondro-cranium*. 1910 *Encycl. Brit.* XIV. 258/2 In front of the vertebral column lies the cartilaginous trough, the chondrocranium, which protects the brain. 1919 J. G. Kerr *Embryol.* II. 306 The skull consists in its simplest form primarily of a chondrocranium—a trough of cartilage, the cavity of which is occupied by the brain. 1897 Chaney *Weights & Measures* 130 In estimating the quality of corn a little instrument called a '*chondrometer' is sometimes used. 1894 Gould *Dict. Med.*, *Chondrosarcoma. 1906 *Practitioner* Nov. 663 Similar new growths have been labelled by different observers carcinoma, adeno-sarcoma, chondro-sarcoma, myxosarcoma.

Chondroma (kǫndrōu·mă). *Path.* [mod.L., f. Gr. χόνδρος cartilage + *-oma.] A cartilaginous tumour. Hence **Chondro·matous** *a.*
1886 *Buck's Handbk. Med. Sci.* II. 810/2 Chondromatous tissue is found somewhat more frequently (chondro-sarcoma). 1908 *Practitioner* Oct. 535 Excessive and exuberant callus, chondroma, sarcoma, etc., at the site of fractures are comparable with keloid, sarcoma, epithelioma, etc., arising in scars of soft parts.

Chondrosin (kǫ·ndrousin). *Chem.* [f. mod.L. *Chondrosia* (f. Gr. χόνδρος cartilage) + -in ¹.] (See quot.)
1886 *Jrnl. Chem. Soc.* L. 481 Chondrosine is a hyalogen obtained from the sponge *Chondrosia reniformis*. 1925 P. A. Levene *Hexosamines & Mucoproteins* Index.

Chondrule (kǫ·ndrūl). *Min.* [Formed as Chondrite + -ule.] A small spherical grain of mineral embedded in varying numbers in the matrix of chondritic meteorites. Also **Cho·ndrulite, Chondruli·tic** *a.* (see quot. 1928).
1896 L. Fletcher *Introd. Study Meteorites* 36 Through this paste are disseminated round chondrules of various sizes and with the same mineral composition as the matrix; in some cases the chondrules consist wholly or in great part of glass. 1906 Iddings *Rock Min.* 294 Enstatite..occurs in meteorites in radiating aggregates called chondrules. 1928 T. C. Chamberlin *Two Solar Families* 254 'Chondrulites' is merely a more general term here used to include not only chondrules but their débris and all such quasi-chondrulitic material as cannot be called chondrules. It is here used for the primitive chondrulitic accretions, whether they develop into chondrules or not.

Chone (kōun). [ad. Gr. χώνη, contr. f. χοάνη *Choana.] In sponges, a cortical dome-like structure communicating with the subdermal cavity. Hence **Chonal** (kōu·năl) *a.*, pertaining to this.
1887 Sollas in *Encycl. Brit.* XXII. 415/1 In many sponges..the cortical domes are constricted near their communication with the subdermal cavity by a transverse muscular sphincter, which defines an outer division or ectochone from an inner or endochone.., the whole structure being a chone. 1888 — *Tetractinellida* p. xxiii, The chonal sphincter. 1906 *Cambr. Nat. Hist.* I. 214.

Chong: see *Chang ².

Choola (tʃū·la). Also **choolah.** [Hind. *chūlhā*, *chūlhī* fireplace (Skr. *chulli*).] An extemporized or portable Indian fireplace or cooking-place.
1813 J. Forbes *Oriental Mem.* III. 120 A marble corridore filled up with *Choolas*, or cooking-places, composed of mud, cow-dung, and unburnt bricks. 1864 J. A. Grant *Walk across Africa* 51, I observed a portable Indian 'choolah' or fireplace inside the hut.

Choom (tʃūm). [Russ. чумъ.] A hut or tent made by the Samoyedes of fir poles covered with birch bark.
[1599 Hakluyt *Voy.* I. 284 Their tents are rounde and are called *Chome* in their language.] 1889 V. Morier in *Murray's Mag.* Aug. 175 A little encampment of Samoyede summer 'chooms', *i. e.* birch-bark tents. 1895 F. G. Jackson *Gt. Frozen Land* 82 Of the choom which forms the Samoyad's home there are two kinds, one for summer and another for winter.

Chop, *sb.*¹ Add:
2. d. Material, esp. fodder, which has been chopped up. Also *chop-feed*.
1852 *Trans. Mich. Agric. Soc.* III. 151 Chop feed is good for them in small quantities, say half a pint to a sheep. 1889 J. Wrightson *Fallow & Fodder Crops* 199 [He] is accustomed to cut rye and straw together and throw the 'chop' back into a barn. 1908 *Animal Managem.* 121 Chaff ('Chop').
4. d. *Cricket.* A stroke made by bringing down the butt of the bat sharply, edgeways, on the ball. **e.** *Lawn Tennis.* An undercut ground-stroke. Also *chop-stroke, -lob*.
1888 R. H. Lyttelton in *Cricket* (Badm.) ii. 62 If the ball..keeps a bit low after the pitch, it is a most effective stroke to come heavily down on it; if the force is put on the ball at the right moment it will go very hard, and may be called a 'chop'. 1920 Tilden *Lawn Tennis* Introd. p. x, An undercut ground stroke is the general definition of a chop. *Ibid.* 35 The chop lob, a heavily under-cut spin that hangs in the air. *Ibid.* 82 Tilden is a chop-stroke player.
6. b. *Metal-forging.* An indentation made in the surface of the metal.
1885 *Spons' Mechanics' Own Bk.* '84 If the hammer leaves indentations, or what are technically called 'chops'.

Chop, *sb.*² **6.** Add: **chop-jawed** *a.*, having heavy jaws.
1919 W. De Morgan *Old Madhouse* 133 The chop-jawed senior wrangler.

Chop, *sb.*⁵ **4.** Add: *no chop*, 'no class'.
1888 'R. Boldrewood' *Robbery under Arms* ii, There's good and bad of every sort, and I've met plenty that were no chop of all churches.

Chop, *sb.*⁸ *W. African colloq.* [Cf. *Chop *v.*⁶] Food. Also *attrib.*, as *chop-day, -money*; *chop-box*, a food-box.
1870 *Food Jrnl.* I. 154 In those days,..every chief of any consideration had what was called his chop-day, or feast-day. 1897 Mary Kingsley *W. Africa* 313 The unfortunate white men..are expected..to live on native chop. 1902 *Daily Chron.* 10 July 3/5 2s. a week 'chop' money or maintenance. 1920 *Blackw. Mag.* June 844/2 Evans went in to the chop-room. 1921 *Chambers's Jrnl.* 782/1 A chop-box (*Anglice*, food-box) did duty for a seat.

Chop, *v.*¹ Add:
7. d. *Cricket.* *intr.* To bring down the butt of the bat quickly and heavily, edgeways, in making a stroke; *trans.*, to strike (the ball) in this way. **e.** *Lawn Tennis.* (Cf. *Chop *sb.*¹ 4 d, e.)
1887 *Leisure Hour* 544/1 Jupp and Humphry..blocked and chopped in a style that was simply maddening. 1898 *Field* 18 June 911/3 Little could be done but to chop Lockwood's off balls for singles. 1920 *Westm. Gaz.* 16 June 10/1 This drive is alternated with a cut-stroke, and sometimes with a heavily chopped return. 1930 *Morning Post* 17 June 16/3 Slater chopped a ball on to his stumps.

Chop, *v.*³ **1.** For *Obs.* read *Obs.* exc. *U.S.*
1920 Hunter *Trail Drivers* 129 The cattle were poor and hungry, so went to chopping that grass as though they were paid.

Chop, *v.*⁶ *W. African colloq.* [See *Chop *sb.*⁸] To eat.
1896 *Westm. Gaz.* 18 Mar. 5/3 The natives have sent word ..that if the Consul interfered with them they would make a raid on the trading factories and 'chop' (a native expression for 'eat') the white traders there. 1920 *Blackw. Mag.* June 845/2 You're both chopping with me to-night, so we can talk things over.

Chopa (tʃōu·pă). [Sp.] A rudder-fish of various species of the genus *Kyphosus*, found in the tropical Atlantic and Pacific.
1883 Moloney *W. Afr. Fisheries* 57 'Chopa', a sea-bream which represented their bait for the large fish.

Chopper ¹. 1. (Additional U.S. quots.)
1765 A. Ellicott in *Life & Lett.* (1908) 44 My Brother Joseph at Present runs the guide Line for the Choppers. 1860 Holland *Miss Gilbert's Career* ix. 146 In the yards of the quiet dwellings the sturdy chopper's axe was swung. 1875 — *Sevenoaks* i. 4 Seven huge oaks which the chopper's axe, for some reason or other had spared.

Choppiness (tʃǫ·pinės). [f. Choppy *a.*¹ + -ness.] The quality or condition of being choppy.
1881 A. Elwes tr. *Pinto's How I Crossed Africa* I. 142 The water was..made perilous..by the excessive 'choppiness' of the surface caused by the proximity of the falls.

Chopping, *vbl. sb.*¹ **4.** Add: **chopping-bee** *U.S.*, a 'bee' for the cutting down of timber; **chopping-block** *colloq.*, also, applied to a boxer who sustains steady punishment; **chopping-horse**, **-note** (see quots.).
1809 *Massachusetts Spy* 12 July (Th.) At Bristol (Ver.), June 7, at a *chopping-bee, a limb of one of the falling trees struck one of the men. 1868 *Western Mag.* Jan. (De Vere) The inhabitants within a radius of ten miles were invited to a chopping-bee. 1928 *Daily Express* 10 Aug. 15/6 The New Zealander was outclassed by the champion, and in the last three rounds was only a *chopping block, but game to the last. 1920 Hunter *Trail Drivers* 297 The specially trained horses used [to cut out cattle] are called..*chopping horses. 1886 *Appleton's Ann. Cycl.* 87 The *chopping-note [of the nightingale] is a low-pitched and abrupt note, sounding like 'chop, chop', uttered several times in quick succession.

Cho·pping, *vbl. sb.*³ [? f. Chop *v.*³] The loud barking of a dog.
1897 *Outing* (U.S.) XXX. 127 Of a sudden the character of the baying changed from the noisy yapping of a lot of playful puppies to the persistent chopping of the driving hound—the fox was up.

Choppy, *a.*¹ Add:
3. Suggestive of chopping.
1922 Alice Brown *Old Crow* i. 4 He certainly was not the sort of hero his dramatic poems described with a choppy vigor of detail.

Chop-suey (tʃǫpsū·i). Also **-sooy.** [Chinese, = mixed bits.] A dish served in Chinese restaurants, consisting of meat or chicken, rice, onions, etc. fried in sesame-oil.
1904 *Rochester Post-Express* 8 June 12 One of the Chinese merchants of New York..explained that chop suey is really an American dish, not known in China, but believed by Americans to be the one great national dish of the Celestials. *a* 1906 'O. Henry' *Trimmed Lamp* etc. 184, I'd marry the Empress of China for one bowl of chop suey.
fig. 1906 'O. Henry' *Four Million, Sisters of Golden Circle* 218 The stations of which [*sc.* the Rialto] uniformed men sat and made chop suey of your tickets. 1910 — *Whirligigs, Calloway's Code* (1916) 51 The censor has put the screws on, or he wouldn't have cabled in a lot of chop suey like this.

Choral, *sb.* Add: **b.** A choral hymn, esp. as sung by the negroes of the South. *U.S.*
1875 E. King *Southern St. N. Amer.* 613 Listening to the singing of 'Dust an' Ashes', one of the sweetest and sublimest chorals ever improvised.

Choralism (kōə·răliz'm). [f. Choral *a.*¹ + -ism.] Choral composition; choral rendering and technique.
1927 *Observer* 29 May 9/3 From the cloisters of Magdalen College, Oxford, are to be sung at 9.15 two magnificent examples of choralism, Palestrina's motet 'Exultate Deo' and Byrd's anthem 'Sing Joyfully to God'. *Ibid.* 16 Oct. 5 The Sheffield Choir is noted for good, sound, clean choralism.

Chorasmian (koræ·zmiăn), *a.* [f. Gr. Χοράσμιοι (pl.) a tribe of Sogdiana + -an.] Belonging to the Chorasmii. *Chorasmian waste* (poet.), the desert land south of the Sea of Aral and about the lower course of the Oxus; also *allusively*.
1815 Shelley *Alastor* 272 At length upon the lone Chorasmian shore He paused. 1853 M. Arnold *Sohrab & Rustum* 878 The majestic river .. moved, Rejoicing, through the hush'd Chorasmian waste. 1890 'R. Boldrewood' *Col. Reformer* xix, In this lone Chorasmian waste, Mr. Neuchamp contrived to spend his time.

Chord, *sb.*¹ Add:
5. *Engin.* Each of the two principal members, usually horizontal, of a truss.
1875 Knight *Dict. Mech.* III. 2638/2 Rider's [truss-bridge] ..is composed of an upper and a lower chord,—the former of cast, and the latter of wrought, iron.
6. In an aeroplane, a straight line touching the lower surface of an aerofoil section at two points; hence, the dimension of an aerofoil from the leading edge to the trailing edge (the width of the wings as distinguished from 'span' or lateral spread).
[1909 A. Berget *Conquest of Air* iv. 188 When the apparatus is in flight, the 'chord' of the arc formed by the profile of the wings makes an angle varying from 6 to 8 degrees with the horizon.] 1920 *All the World's Aircraft* 123 a, Specification of the Westland 'Limousine'. Length overall, 28 ft. 6 in.; Span, 38 ft. 2 in.; Chord, 6 ft. 3 in. 1923 *Glazebrook's Dict. Applied Physics* V. 19/2 The ratio of the span to the chord gives the Aspect Ratio of the wing. 1928 V. W. Page *Mod. Aircraft* 143.

Chorda (kǭ·ɹdă). *Anat.* Pl. **chordæ** (kǭ·ɹdī). [L.: see Chord *sb.*¹] A name for certain string-like structures in the animal body; with defining L. adj., as **chorda dorsa·lis** the notochord; **chordæ tendi·neæ** *pl.*, fine tendinous cords attached to the auriculo-ventricular valves and the papillary muscles of the heart.
1873 G. Fleming tr. *Chauveau's Comp. Anat.* 905 There appear in the middle lamina of the blastoderm the *chorda dorsalis*, the *vertebral laminæ*, and the *lateral laminæ*. 1885 *Buck's Handbk. Med. Sci.* I. 562 Long, fibrous chords, called chordæ tendineæ, that arise from pyramidal muscles. 1886 *Ibid.* II. 328/2 A branch, named from its peculiar course, the chorda tympani. 1887 *Ibid.* V. 248/2 The inner chorda sheath is lost. 1927 Haldane & Huxley *Animal Biol.* iv. 97 One of the papillary muscles, attached by chordae tendineae to..the tricuspid valve between right auricle and right ventricle.

Chordata (kǫɹdē·tă), *sb. pl. Zool.* [mod.L., f. L. *chorda* Chord *sb.*¹, with termination as in Vertebrata, etc.] A sub-kingdom of animals having a more or less well-developed notochord.
1880 F. M. Balfour *Treat. Compar. Embryol.* I. 4 The larva of the Tunicata has the characters of a simple type of the Chordata. 1893 Tuckey *Amphioxus* 109 The Amphioxus is distinguished from all vertebrates and also from the Ascidians, thus from the whole race of the Chordata, by means of the notochord, which reaches right into the anterior end. 1906 Chamberlin & Salisbury *Geol.* II. 484 While perhaps they should remain under the broad mantle of the term *Chordata*, they must apparently be removed from the true vertebrates to a new class.

Chordate (kǭ·ɹdeɪt), *a.* and *sb. Zool.* [ad. prec.] Belonging to, having the characters of, or a member of the Chordata.
1897 [see *hemichordate* def., s.v. Hemi-]. 1927 Haldane & Huxley *Animal Biol.* ii. 79 They are therefore all classed as Vertebrates (or Chordates, with reference to the notochord).

Chore, *sb.*² Add:
1. (Earlier U.S. examples.)
1758 J. Adams *Wks.* (1850) II. 37 Chores, chat, tobacco, tea, steal away time. 1780 Eb. Parkman *Diary* 285 He must tend my Cattle, & cut wood, needful chores, go on Errands &c. 1789 Webster *Diss. Engl. Lang.* 112 *Chore*..is an English word..but in America, it is perhaps confined to New England. It signifies small domestic jobs of work, and its place cannot be supplied by any other single word in the language.
2. chore-boy *U.S.*, a boy employed in doing odd jobs.
1848 *Knickerbocker Mag.* Sept. XXXII. 230, I afterwards saw Petty,..laughing with the gardener and 'chore-boy'. 1856 *Ibid.* Jan. XLVII. 102 He entered the employ of the Chief Justice of the Province, Lewall, as a chore-boy. 1901 *Westm. Gaz.* 18 July 10/1 The Secretary of the Treasury began life as a bank clerk,..the Secretary of the Navy as a 'chore-boy' on a farm. 1902 S. E. White *Blazed Trail* xxviii. 187 You would have to be chore-boy in a lumber camp.

Chore, *v.* (Earlier U.S. examples.)
1788 J. May *Jrnl. & Lett.* (1873) 88 Two [hands] playing the whipsaw, and the rest choring in the woods. 1839 Mrs. Kirkland *New Home* xiv. 87, I was obliged to employ Mrs. Jennings to 'chore round', to borrow her own expression.

Choregus: see Choragus. Here used *fig.* (sense 3).
1901 *Fortn. Rev.* Sept. 403 Professor Haeckel, who is denounced in some quarters as the very choregus of materialism.

Choreo·graphist = Choreographer.
1927 *Observer* 24 July 13/2 The principals were excellent, but the corps-de-ballet achieved only a rough sketch of the choreographist's design. 1928 *Ibid.* 17 June 15/4 It is now to be heard..as the accompaniment of a ballet. This time Dolin is the choreographist.

Choreutes (kǫriū·tīz). *Antiq.* [Gr. χορευτής, f. χορεύειν to dance, f. χόρος Chorus.] A member of the chorus of Greek drama. Hence **Choreu·tic** *a.* [Gr. χορευτικός], of or pertaining to choral song and dance.
1861 Paley *Æschylus* (ed. 2) *Agam.* 1315 *note*, The first choreutes speaks [line] 1315. 1926 *Spectator* 5 June 948/1, I rather doubt if the musical and choreutic material from which the organizers drew could justify so extensive an enterprise.

Choriambize (kǫriæ·mbəiz), *v.* [See -ize.] *trans.* To make choriambic; to turn (a foot) into a choriambus.
1922 S. Grew *Player-Piano* 180 The choriambising of measures establishes two weak syllables between the initial syllable and the next strong one.

Chorioid, Chorioidal, variant forms of Choroid, -al.
1894 Gould *Dict. Med.* 1902 D. J. Cunningham *Anat.* 685 The chorioid (chorioidea) intervenes between the sclera and the retina. *Ibid.* 699 The chorioidal fissure.

Chorionic (kōəriǫ·nik), *a. Embryol.* [See -ic.] Of or relating to the chorion.
1892 E. L. Mark *Hertwig's Embryol.* 261 The double-layered chorionic epithelium is already distinctly present in eggs four weeks old. 1902 D. J. Cunningham *Anat.* 23 The placental area.., together with the blastoderm over the rest of the ovum, forms the chorionic area. *Ibid.* 50 The chorionic villi.

Chorister. 1. a. Add: Also, a choir-leader. *U.S.*
1769 *Plymouth Church Records* (1920) I. 332 To choose one or more persons (since our dear Brother John May is taken from us by death who was our former Chorister) to lead in singing in the publick Worship. 1777 *Ibid.* 353 Deacon Crombie, our former Chorister, had left ye usual Singer's Seat. 1832 Webster. 1889 *Century Dict.*

Choristid (kori·stid), *sb.* and *a.* [ad. mod.L. *Choristida* (see def.), f. Gr. χωριστός separate.] **A.** *sb.* A member of the group *Choristida* of sponges. **B.** *adj.* Belonging to this group. Also (in the same senses) **Chori·stidan** *a.* and *sb.*
1888 W. J. Sollas *Tetractinellida* p. xi, Recent Choristids. *Ibid.* xcix, The Choristid Sponges. 1900 E. A. Minchin *Porifera* 163 A corticate Choristid.

Chorizema (kōərizī·mă). [mod.L., f. Gr. χωρίζειν to separate.] A shrub of the Australian fabaceous genus so named.
1891 *Daily News* 11 Mar. 2/8 A fine group of cyclamen, acacias, chorizemas.

Chorizo (tʃorī·zo). [Sp.] A sausage of which the chief ingredient is pork.
1918 *Chambers's Jrnl.* 33 The red chorizos and pimentisco from Estremadura. 1927 *Daily Express* 13 Sept. 5/5 Chorizos is a Spanish sausage, made of lean beef and lean pork, resembling German Frankfurt sausages, but more highly spiced and seasoned.

Choroido-, used as combining form of Choroid in mod. Latin terms, as **Choroi:do-iri·tis**, inflammation of the choroid and the iris; **Choroi:do-retini·tis**, inflammation of the choroid and the retina.
1869 G. Lawson *Dis. Eye* (1874) 161 It is, however, generally succeeded by a low form of choroido-iritis or choroido-retinitis. 1879 *St. George's Hosp. Rep.* IX. 532, 2 cases of choroido-retinitis. 1894 Gould *Dict. Med.* 1908 *Practitioner* Apr. 542 Syphilitic choroido-retinitis.

Chorten (tʃǭ·ɹten). [Tibetan.] = *Chaitya.
1891 Rockhill *Land of Lamas* 63 *note*, Pilgrims, when journeying to a shrine, perform prostrations before each *ch'ürten* met on the way thither. 1893 E. F. Knight *Where three Empires meet* viii. (1897) 124 Gigantic *chortens*, or sarcophagi. 1894 Rockhill *Diary Journ. Mongolia & Tibet* 271 A small village of stone houses near which were several large *ch'örtens*. 1898 A. H. S. Landor *In Forbidden Land* II. 72 When a saintly Lama dies..either parts of the flesh, or, if cremation has been applied, some of his ashes, are preserved and placed in a Chokden erected for the purpose. 1902 *Chambers's Jrnl.* 444 The *gompa*..close to several *chortens* containing the bones of sainted lamas. 1905 P. Landon *Lhasa* I. List Illustr. p. xviii, A chorten of silver.

Chortle, *v.* Add: Also *trans.*, to utter or sing with a 'chortling' intonation. Also *sb.*, an act of 'chortling'.
1886 *Referee* 18 Aug. (Ware) Mr. Wilford Morgan has been engaged to chortle the famous song, 'Here's to the maiden of bashful fifteen'. 1889 *Ibid.* 29 Dec., Many present on Boxing Night fully expected that when he appeared he would chortle a chansonette or two. 1903 McNeill *Egreg. Engl.* 28 He would tell you..that he attributed his success ..(5) to marrying Mrs. Business-Man—this last, of course, with a chortle.

Chorus, *sb.* **7.** Add: *chorus-singing*; **chorus-girl**, a girl who sings or dances in the chorus of an opera, musical comedy, or revue.
1883 G. A. Sala *Living London* 84 There is really excellent character-drawing in..Nellie Millsom, the *débutante*; and in the retired 'chorus-lady', Mrs. Barker, her aunt. 1903 Annie W. Patterson *Schumann* 66 The chorus-singing had been excellent. 1905 F. Hopkinson Smith *At Close Range* 42 A Special loaded with chorus girls and props. 1907 *Daily Chron.* 21 Oct. 3/2 Elizabeth's two thoroughly vulgar chorus-girl friends.

Chose, *sb.* Add:
4. *Chose jugée* (ʒüʒe) [Fr.], a matter which has been formally adjudicated and decided and which it is therefore idle or presumptuous to discuss.
1898 *Daily News* 22 Mar. 6/1 The new doctrine of the sacredness of the 'chose jugée'.

Chota (tʃōu·tă). *Anglo-Indian.* [Hindi *chhoṭa.*] Small; younger, junior; *spec.* applied to a 'peg' of whiskey.
1853 Mrs. Colin Mackenzie *Life in the Mission* viii. (1857) 112 A horseman..asked for William as the 'Chota Pádre'. 1915 *Blackw. Mag.* Dec. 817/1, I was sipping a 'chota' whiskey. 1927 *Chambers's Jrnl.* 603/1 He..waited till the chota pegs had been served.

Chota hazri (tʃōu·tă hā·zrī). *Anglo-Indian.* Also **chotah**; **hazry, hazree, haziree, hazaree.** [Hindi *chhoṭa* or *chhoṭī hāz(i)rī* little breakfast.] A light early breakfast.
1863 Trevelyan *Dawk Bungalow* ii, Are you ready for some chota hazaree? 1866 E. J. Waring *Trop. Resid.* 171 There is one small meal..commonly known in India by the Hindústani name of *Chota-hasiri*, and in our English colonies as '*Early Tea*'. 1883 Mrs. Croker *Pretty Miss Neville* II. 23 At eight o'clock we had chotah-hazree under a big tree in the compound; it consisted of tea, toast, seed-cake, and fruit...We breakfasted at ten o'clock. 1907 — *Company's Servant* xviii, Chotah Hazree, 8 annas. Tiffin, 1 rupee, 8 annas. 1928 *Cornhill Mag.* Oct. 470 We sat down to a very early 'chota hazaree' that was laid outside in the moonlight.

Chou (ʃū). Pl. **choux** (ʃū). [Fr., = cabbage.]
1. A knot of ribbon, chiffon, etc., as an ornament to a woman's hat or dress. (Cf. *Cabbage 5 c.)
1883 *Peel City Guardian* 19 May 7/5 The tunic is draped high and wide on the right side, under a chou bow. 1891 *Queen* 7 Feb. 217/3 A new front drapery, which hooked on to the back beneath a 'choux'—namely, an oblong rosette. 1894 *Ibid.* 13 Oct. 637/2 A blouse bodice,..fastened with three large choux. 1894 *Paris Mode* I. 31/2 Sleeves are frequently caught in by a *chou* of ribbon.
2. A small round cake of pastry filled with cream or jelly.
1892 *Encycl. Pract. Cookery* (ed. T. F. Garrett) I. 382/1 Choux with Coffee Icing. *Ibid.*, Glazed Chou.
3. *Chou*(*x*) *paste* (F. *pâte à choux*): see quots.
1892 *Encycl. Pract. Cookery* (ed. T. F. Garrett) I. 382/1 Butter a baking-sheet, with a fork drop on it pieces of Choux paste about the size of fowls' eggs. 1892 Mrs. Beeton *Househ. Managem.* 830 Chou Paste. Ingredients.—½ lb. of flour, ½ lb. of butter, 8 eggs, ½ oz. of pounded sugar, 1 pint of water.

Chouette (ʃue·t). [Fr. (cf. phr. *faire la chouette* to sustain the attack of several persons at once).] A 'lone hand' at bezique or piquet.
1887 'Cavendish' *Rubicon Bézique* 39 Chouette Bézique. A player, who is willing to take all stakes, may declare to play *à la chouette*,—that is that he will play single-handed against all comers. .. If the *chouette* wins, one of his opponents takes the loser's place, and so on with the other opponents in rotation. 1927 *Sunday Express* 6 Nov. 2, I remember once this man taking a chouette at piquet against Mr. Ashmead Bartlett and myself. 1929 W. J. Locke *Ancestor Jorico* xi, When he was with us we played a chouette (three players) of Rubicon Bézique for hours together.

Chouse, *v.* Add: **2.** *U.S.* (See quot.)
1920 Hunter *Trail Drivers Texas* 313 The round-up boss would let no one ride through the herd and 'chouse' or unnecessarily disturb them.

Chow (tʃau), *sb.* [Shortened f. Chow-chow.]
1. A dog of Chinese breed, something like a Pomeranian, usually black or brown, with a black tongue. Also *chow-dog*. (See also *Chow-chow 4.)
1889 *Pall Mall Gaz.* 18 June 2/1 One half the pack ran into an unlucky chow-dog. 1897 *Westm. Gaz.* 18 May 2/1 The very chow-pup at his lady's feet looked impudent defiance. 1900 C. H. Lane *All about Dogs* 303 The Chow, ..with a short thick head and rather blunt prick ears.
2. *Pidgin-English.* Food of any kind. Also *spec.* = Chow-chow 1. Also *attrib.*
This sense is supposed to be due to the use of the chow ('the edible dog of China') as food by poor Chinese.
1886 Yule & Burnell *Hobson-Jobson* 164/2 *Chow* is in 'pigeon' applied to food of any kind. 1892 Douglas Sladen *Japs at Home* iv. (1895) 37 More chow..had been laid at our feet...This time it was..a sort of custard soup containing chicken [etc.]. 1897 *Outing* (U.S.) XXX. 209/1 The 'chow' served at the wayside tea-houses. 1926 *Chambers's Jrnl.* 213/2 Here were pots of boiling oil, chow, and mushrooms. 1926 M. Leinster *Dew on Leaf* 149 She took her chow-bowl into the kitchen.
3. A Chinaman.
1916 C. J. Dennis *Ginger Mick* 17 Noiseless Chows a-glidin' round wiv plates uv duck and fowl. 1921 *Chambers's Jrnl.* 690/1 The pearling-crews can get from Japs and Chows all the drink they want. *Ibid.* 718/1 Always have a Chow for your cook in these parts of the world.

Chow-chow. Add: **3.** = *Chow *sb.* 3.

Supplement, p. 3873; Corrigenda, p. 4092; Spurious words, p. 4093; Books quoted, p. 4094

1869 E. Howe *Boy in the Bush* 215 The Jerry's Town youngsters were pelting the Chinaman,..meanwhile shouting out 'Chow-chow!'

4. A Chinese domestic dog; = *Chow *sb.* 1.

1886 *Kennel Club Cal.* 397 Chow Chow. 1892 *Field* 5 Mar. 325/1, I should be glad to hear if any of your readers has ever seen grey Chow-Chow dogs. 1896 *Daily News* 9 Dec. 5 The chow-chow..came originally from China. 1900 C. H. Lane *All about Dogs* Illustr.

Chowder, *sb.* Add: **1.** (Earlier U.S. example.)

1751 *Boston Even. Post* 23 Sept., Directions for making a chouder.

b. A chowder party. *U.S.*

1884 *Century Mag.* XXVIII. 555 A chowder was given a few nights ago at the head of our little bay. 1906 *N. Y. Even. Post* 6 Nov. 8 The Bowery...went about the business ..with as much good nature as if it were 'Big Tim's' annual 'chowder'.

3. *attrib.*, as *chowder-builder*; **chowder excursion, party,** a picnic, esp. at the sea-side, at which chowder is the principal dish.

1840 *Knickerbocker Mag.* July XVI. 26 (Th.) The *chowder-builder and the poet must alike be born. 1889 Farmer *Americanisms*, **Chowder excursion*—No picnic by the sea would be complete without this almost national dish, [etc.]. 1848 *Yale Lit. Mag.* XVI. 380 (Th.) We hate *chowder-parties, we do. 1853 J. G. Baldwin *Flush Times Alabama* 80 In the science of getting up..a picnic or chowder party, or fish fry, the Virginian..was first.

Chowder, *v.* Add: **b.** *trans.* To convert into chowder. Hence **Chow·dering** *ppl. a.*

1884 *Century Mag.* XXVIII. 555 But it has been such a picnicing and chowdering place. 1889 *Century Dict.* s. v., To chowder fish.

Chowk (tʃauk). *Anglo-Indian.* Also 9 **choke.** [Hindi *chauk.*] An open place in the middle of a city where the market is held.

1833 T. Skinner *Excurs. India* I. 49 The Chandy Choke, in Delhi,..is perhaps the broadest street in any city in the East. 1895 Mrs. Croker *Village Tales* (1896) 20 One evening we all gathered round the big fire in the village 'chowk'. 1924 *Blackw. Mag.* Nov. 700/1 In the Chowk or Square of A., one of the most sacred cities of Hinduism. *Ibid.* 700/2 Padre Armstrong had been lent a pulpit in a corner of the Chowk.

Chowkidar, var. f. Chokidar.

1895 Mrs. Croker *Village Tales* (1896) 15 After some parley we were admitted by the chowkidar (or watchman). 1908 *Westm. Gaz.* 4 May 5/1 The 'chowkidar' of each village receives a Government salary of three rupees a month.

Chowrie, var. Chowry.

1864 J. A. Grant *Walk across Africa* 146 A small boy.. carried his chowrie, or fly-flapper.

Chrismon (kri·zmɒn). [med.L., f. *Chris(tus* + *mon(ogramma.*] The sacred monogram ☧.

1872 J. D. Champlin in *Appleton's Jrnl.* 28 Dec. 723 (Funk) The *chrismon*..is found on Christian tombs of the beginning of the second century.

Christ. 4. Add: *The Christ-child* (after G. *Christkind, -kindchen*), Christ as a child.

1842 W. Howitt *Rural & Dom. Life Germany* xii. 167 The Christ-kindschen is no other than the Christ of the old legends—Christ in his boyhood...This is exactly the Christ-child of Germany. 1857 *National Mag.* I. Christmas No., Suppl. 1 The Christ-child (bringer, according to German legend, of Christmas gifts and blessings to children). 1888 F. E. Weatherley *The Christ-Child* x, They fold their hands, and whisper, 'The Christ-Child has been here'. 1899 A. De Burgh *Eliz., Empr. Austria* 296 The benevolent Christ-child has already visited me. 1903 *Daily Chron.* 9 Dec. 3/3 The Christ-child of many painters.

Christianable (kri·styănăb'l), *a. colloq.* [Irregularly formed: see -able.] Fit for or befitting a Christian. (See Christian *a.* 5.)

1920 *Blackw. Mag.* June 774/2 The dug-outs more Christianable than manny. 1926 *Punch* 23 June 675/1 Whether the theme be dogs or tinkers' wives, Or country doctors' 'christianable' lives.

Christiania (kristiā·niă). [The name of the capital of Norway (changed back, in 1925, to Oslo).] A 'swing' in skiing, used to stop short.

1924 *Ski Terms* in *Tourist* Winter Sports No. 12/1 *Christiania.* Open, closed and jerked. Different forms of one of the best swings. 1929 *Daily Express* 16 Jan. 8/3 Finishing out in the crisp snow with a dead-stop Christiania'.

Chri·stianish, *a.* [f. Christian *a.* + -ish [1].] Somewhat Christian in character.

1882 H. W. Beecher in *Chr. World Pulpit* XXI. 285 A man whose brain is weakened cannot be a perfect christian though he may be christianish.

Christian Science. A theory of the nature of disease, and a system of therapeutic practice, founded on principles formulated by Mrs. Mary Baker Glover Eddy, of Concord, New Hampshire, U.S.A. *Christian Scientist,* one who holds and practises this; a member of the sect founded by Mrs. Eddy.

The principal tenet of this theory is that matter is an illusion, and that therefore what is supposed to be bodily disease is an error of the mind, which may be cured by leading the patient to apprehend the truth as revealed in the teaching and healing of Jesus Christ. The churches of Christian Scientists are called 'First (Second, etc.) Church of Christ, Scientist'.

1863 [cited as used by Quimby, in Georgine Milmine *Life M. B. G. Eddy* v. (1909) 87]. 1875 Mrs. Eddy *Sci. & Health* 456 Future years will..restore at length the fair proportions and radical claims of Christian Science. 1881 *Ibid.* xi. (ed. 3) II. 192 Platform of Christian Scientists. 1883 Mrs. Eddy in letter to the *Boston Post* 7 Mar., My discovery, in 1866, of the Science of Mind-healing, since named Christian Science. 1888 F. Lord (*title*) Christian Science Healing: Its Principles and Practice. 1891 Mrs. Eddy *Science & Health* Pref. p. xi, The first school of Christian Science Mind-healing was begun by the author in Lynn, Massachusetts, about the year 1867, with only one student. 1900 M. Benson *Rev. Chr. Sci.* 15 All the evidence given by Christian Scientists in support of the unlimited claim they make for the action of the mind, is not sufficient to prove as much as is already established and known about the effect of mind on body.

¶ Note the earlier occurrence of the phrase in a different sense.

1850 W. Adams (*title*) The Elements of Christian Science, a treatise upon moral philosophy and practice. 1854 Tulloch *Theol. Tendencies of the Age* 12 The element of traditional authority..is to be regarded as in itself wholly invaluable for the interests of Christian Science. *Ibid.* 24 The final arbiter of Christian Science, in short, is not the Bible, but the prevailing Christian sentiment.

Christmas, *sb.* 4. Add: **Christmas bush,** (*a*) an Australian shrub, *Ceratopetalum gummiferum,* used in Christmas decorations; (*b*) a Bermuda shrub, *Cassia bicapsularis,* used for hedges; **Christmas fern** *U.S.* (see quots.); **Christmas flower** (examples); **Christmas shield-fern** *U.S.* = *Christmas fern.*

1888 Mrs. M'Cann *Poet. Wks.* 226 Gorgeous tints adorn the *Christmas bush with a crimson blush. 1889 *Century Dict.*, *Christmas fern, *Aspidium acrostichoides,* a fern having simply pinnate fronds of firm texture, which remain green through the winter. 1911 Webster, *Christmas fern,* a North American evergreen polypodiaceous fern (*Polystichum acrostichoides*), the fronds of which are much used for decoration in winter. 1688 Holme *Armoury* II. 104/1 Hellebor, or *Christmas Flower. 1888 'C. E. Craddock' *Broomsedge Cove* xix, He stopped to pick a spray of the lilac 'Christmas flower'. 1884 W. Miller *Plant-n.* 164 *Aspidium acrostichoides,* *Christmas Shield-Fern, of N. America.

Christmassy, *a.* The more usual spelling of Christmasy: see Dict. and following quots.:

1894 *Pall Mall Gaz.* 20 Dec. 8/3 Oxford, with the undergraduates out of the way and a foot or two of snow in the streets, would look very Christmassy. 1901 G. Bourne *Bettesworth Bk.* 156, I saw that he looked pale and gently sick. 'Feel a bit Christmassy?' I said.

Christo-. Add: **Christoce·ntrism,** Christocentric doctrine; **Christo·cracy,** the rule or government of Christ; **Christocra·tic** *a.,* constituted under the rule of Christ; **Christolo·gic** *a.* = Christological.

1912 Von Hügel *Eternal Life* 198 Schleiermacher..insists ..upon so intense a *Christocentrism, as to prepare acute collisions with Biblical Criticism. 1925 *Brit. Weekly* 1 Oct. 5/4 Therefore, he preferred a *Christocracy to a democracy. 1907 *19th Cent.* Dec. 877 Her [*sc.* the Church's] powers are thus derived from Christ and His Apostles, and her constitution in the matter of teaching, ministry, and government is necessarily *Christocratic and Apostolic. 1920 J. R. Harris *Testimonies* II. vii. 66 The first Christian teaching had two sides—the polemic and the evangelic: the anti-Judaic and the *Christologic.

Chroma (krōᵘ·mă). [a. Gr. χρῶμα.] Purity or intensity as a colour quality.

1889 *Century Dict.* 1909 Titchener *Text-Bk. Psychol.* 54 Colour-depth or chroma.

Chromaffin (kromæ·fin), *a. Zool.* Also -ine. [a. G. *chromaffine,* f. *chrom-,* Chromo- 1 + L. *affinis* akin.] Designating certain pigmented cells in the medulla of the suprarenal glands. Hence **Chromaffi·nic** *a.*

1903 Swale Vincent in *Jrnl. Anat. & Phys.* XXXVIII. 41 The chromaffin cells of the suprarenal medulla. *Ibid.* 43 The chromaffin bodies in Petromyzon. 1909 *Jrnl. Chem. Soc.* XCVI. II. 686 A change in the adrenaline content, or the coloration of the chromaffine tissue. 1913 A. Keith *Human Embryol.* (ed. 3) 390 Coccygeal Body is a small mass of chromaffinic tissue.

Chromato-. Add:

Chro·matochyme *Biol.* [Chyme], an aggregate of pigment-cells; **Chro·matocyte** *Biol.* [-cyte], a pigment-cell; **Chromato·lysis,** the solution and disintegration of the chromatin of cell nuclei; **Chro·matoplasm** *Biol.* [-plasm], the coloured portions of protoplasm; the pigment substance of cells; **Chromato·psia,** L. form of Chromatopsy.

1888 W. J. Sollas *Tetractinellida* p. xl, *Chromatocytes or Pigment-Cells...Occasionally by repeated multiplication they form cellular aggregates, or *chromatochyme. 1908 *Practitioner* Jan. 19 A peri-nuclear *chromatolysis of the large psychomotor Betz cells. 1902 E. B. Wilson *The Cell* (ed. 2) 439 **Chromatoplasm*.., the substance of the chromoplastids and other plastids. 1894 Gould *Dict. Med.*, **Chromatopsia,* abnormal sensation of color. 1911 *Encycl. Brit.* XXIV. 195/2 Even small doses of santonin cause disturbances of vision, usually yellow vision or perhaps green (xanthopsia or chromatopsia).

Chromatoid (krōᵘ·mătoid), *a. Biol.* [f. Chromato- + -oid.] Capable of receiving a stain: said of certain grains or granules.

1901 G. N. Calkins *Protozoa* 144 The so-called chromatoid granules. 1912 E. A. Minchin *Protozoa* 289 Many trypanosomes contain granules in their cytoplasm which stain similarly to chromatin, so-called 'chromatoid grains'.

Chromatophore. Add:

2. *Bot.* A layer or granule of chlorophyll or other colouring matter occurring in the protoplasm of a cell.

1895 Oliver tr. *Kerner's Nat. Hist. Plants* II. 629 This chlorophyll-layer or chromatophore. 1902 *Encycl. Brit.* XXV. 407/2 A coloured protoplasmic body, called a chromatophore, the pigment of which in the pure green forms is chlorophyll, and which may then be called a chloroplast.

Hence **Chro:matopho·ric** *a.,* pertaining to or containing chromatophores.

1895 *Pop. Sci. Monthly* Jan. 389 The theory that light acts directly on the chromatophoric cells has been proved to be incorrect. 1904 *Philos. Trans. Roy. Soc.* Ser. B 392 The groups which make up the primary chromatophoric system.

Chrome, *sb.* Add:

2. b. Potassium bichromate used in dyeing.

1876 *Textile Colourist* II. 210 Caustic chrome, i.e. a mixture of bichromate of potash and lime. 1893 Knecht, Rawson, & Loewenthal *Man. Dyeing* 771 Potassium bichromate, $K_2Cr_2O_7$, known to the trade also as 'bichrome' or 'chrome'. 1906 *Dyer* 20 Jan. 10/1 The dyestuffs are fixed with chrome, and the printing colors are best prepared with the addition of acetate of chrome.

3. chrome-black, a colour produced by dyeing goods in a black dye and setting the colours by the use of potassium bichromate and copper sulphate; **chrome-blue,** a mordant coal-tar dye used chiefly in cotton-printing; **chrome brick,** a brick made from chrome iron ore; **chrome furnace,** a furnace in which chrome ores are converted into bichromates; **chrome garnet,** a pigment prepared from basic chromate of lead; **chrome handler,** one who tans leather by treating it with a solution of chromium salts; **chrome hole,** a hole made in the flesh by the caustic action of potassium bichromate; **chrome ink,** an ink made from logwood and sodic carbonate; **chrome leather,** chrome-tanned leather; **chrome maker,** one who makes chrome yellow pigments; **chrome-nickel steel,** an alloy of chromium, nickel, and steel; **chrome-spinel,** picotite; **chrome steel,** a hard fine-grained alloy of chromium and steel; **chrome-tanning,** the tanning of leather by treating it with an acid solution of potassium bichromate and afterwards with a reducing agent, so that chromic oxide combines with the fibre of the leather, rendering it tough and waterproof; hence *chrome-tanned leather.*

1874 Crookes *Dyeing* 544 *Chrome-blacks are cheap. 1876 *Encycl. Brit.* IV. 690/2 Chrome Black is an oxidation colour produced by printing with logwood liquor and passing the goods through a bath of bichromate of potash. 1892 *Dyer* 20 Jan. 3/1 *Chrome Blue is sold in the form of a paste of a blue-black color. Its special characteristic is that with chrome mordants it gives very bright blues. 1921 *Dict. Occup. Terms* (1927) § 102 *Chrome brick maker. 1885 *Census Clerks* (1885) 58 *Chrome Furnace Man. 1899 *Daily News* 20 June 5/5 To make a trial of stopping the chrome furnaces. 1876 *Encycl. Brit.* V. 705/1 Ouvarovite, or *chrome garnet, $Si_3CaCr_2O_{12}$. 1921 *Dict. Occup. Terms* (1927) § 333 **Chrome handler*; immerses hides and skins in chrome tanning pits, under direction of tanyard foreman. 1908 *Practitioner* Dec. 838 The dust of potassium bichromate, acting as a caustic, produces the '*chrome holes' of those engaged in its manufacture. 1880 *Encycl. Brit.* XIII. 80/1 Under the name of *chrome ink a black ink, discovered and prepared by the chemist Runge. 1881 *Ibid.* XIV. 390/1 The stuffing with fat or paraffin of *chrome leather. 1909 *Westm. Gaz.* 16 Nov. 6/2 A band of specially treated chrome leather. 1921 *Dict. Occup. Terms* (1927) § 143 **Chrome maker*; makes chrome yellow pigments by precipitating lead bichromate from a solution of potassium bichromate by running into it a solution of lead acetate. 1908 *Westm. Gaz.* 28 Apr. 4/3 Vanadium and *chrome-nickel steels—the most expensive materials—are considered to be the most suitable. 1892 Dana *Min.* (ed. 6) 221 Picotite or *chrome-spinel. 1878 *Jrnl. Chem. Soc.* XXXIV. 772 The history of the discovery of chrome steel and ferrochrome by Berthier in 1821. 1882 *Encycl. Brit.* XIV. 389/2 Heinzerling's *Chrome-tanned leather. *Ibid.* 390/1 Sheep skins in *chrome-tanning. 1903 Flemming *Pract. Tanning* 213 The following process of chrome tanning produces leather that possesses the good qualities of both alum and chrome leather. 1907 *Jrnl. Chem. Soc.* XCII. 54 Chrome-tanning Liquors. 1892 *Dyer* 20 Jan. 3/1 Chrome Violet .. gives a fine red shade of violet, which is equally as fast to soaping as the Chrome Blue.

Chrome (krōᵘm), *v. Dyeing.* [f. prec.] *trans.* To treat with a solution of potassium bichromate. Chiefly in *ppl. a.* and *gerund* or *vbl. sb.*

1876 *Textile Colourist* II. 35 Dark Brown for Stoving and Chroming. *Ibid.* 318 Chromed logwood colours have a tendency to become green. 1892 *Dyer* 20 Jan. 3/1 Chrome Violet may be used in wool dyeing on a chromed wool. 1893 Knecht, Rawson, & Loewenthal *Man. Dyeing* 536 The principal reason that tartar and tartaric acid have not been universally adopted in chroming is the expense. 1896 *Dyer* 20 Feb. 25/1 On chromed material it yields considerably darker shades.

Chromicize (krōᵘ·misəiz), *v.* [f. Chromic *a.* + -ize.] *trans.* To treat or impregnate with chromic acid or a chromate. Chiefly in *ppl. a.*

1907 *Practitioner* Sept. 428 The employment of the chromicised gut is better than the use of raw material, as it is a little stronger and more lasting. 1911 R. A. Freeman *Red Thumb Mark* xvi. 214 A plate of gelatine which has been treated with potassium bichromate,..chromicized gelatine, as it is called.

Chromidium (kromi·diŏm). Pl. **-idia** (-i·diă). *Biol.* [f. Gr. χρῶμα Chrome + L. dim. termination *-idium.*] An extranuclear granule of chromatin in the cell-body. Hence **Chromi·dial** *a.*; **Chromidio·gamy** (see quots. 1912, 1920); **Chromi·diosome** (quot. 1912).

1906 *Cambr. Nat. Hist.* I. 30 In many Sarcodina and some Sporozoa the nucleus gives off small fragments into the cytoplasm or is resolved into them; they have been termed 'chromidia' by R. Hertwig. *Ibid.* 52 The nucleus..often gives off 'chromidial' fragments. 1912 E. A. Minchin *Protozoa* 65 *note,* It is proposed in this work to use the term *chromidiosome* to denote the smallest chromatin-particles of which the chromidial mass is made up.. The term 'chromidiosome' must therefore be applied to the ultimate, individual grain or particle of chromatin, alike whether it be lodged inside or outside a nucleus. *Ibid.* 126 The chromatin that undergoes syngamic union may be in the form either of chromidia or of nuclei; in the former case the process is termed *chromidiogamy,* in the second *karyogamy.* 1920 W. E. Agar *Cytol.* 208 Fusion or mingling of chromidia (chromidiogamy, Swarczewsky).

Chromiole (krōᵘ·miōᵘl). *Biol.* [f. Gr. χρῶμα colour + *-ole.] A name for the minute chromatin-granules which by their aggregation are supposed to form the chromomeres.

1902 E. B. Wilson *The Cell* (ed. 2) 302 *note,* Eisen ('99) finds that the chromosomes of the spermatogonia of *Batrachoseps* always consist of six 'chromomeres', each of which consists of three smaller granules or 'chromioles'. 1920 W. E. Agar *Cytol.* 18 By many cytologists chromatin is believed to be composed of very minute granules, or chromioles.

Chromo, *v.* = Chromolithograph *v.*

1877 B. Harte *Story of a Mine* ix. 111 Something that could be afterwards lithographed, or chromoed.

Chromo-. 2. Add:

Chromoco·llotype, -co·llotypy, collotypy in colour; **Chromo·metry,** the measurement of colour intensity; **Chromopho·ric, Chromo·phorous** *adjs.,* colour-bearing or -producing, of the nature of a chromophore.

1891 *Pall Mall Gaz.* 30 Sept. 1/2 The process of *chromo-collotype is treading upon the heels of lithography for reproductive work of the cheaper class. 1896 *Brit. Jrnl. Photog. Alm.* 572 *Chromo-collotypy and allied processes. 1871 *Jrnl. Chem. Soc.* XXIV. 183 On the Constant Colour and Intensity of the Light from Clouds, for *Chromometry. 1893 *Athenæum* 15 July 100/2 The dyestuffs..are classed according to the particular *chromophoric groups they contain. 1893 Knecht, Rawson, & Loewenthal *Man. Dyeing* 404 A colour-bearing (*chromophorous) group or chromophor. 1902 *Encycl. Brit.* XXVII. 564/2 Such compounds containing chromophorous groups are termed chromogens.

Chromogen. Add: *spec.* in *Dyeing,* an acid colour used to dye brown. (Cf. quot. 1879 in Dict.)

1892 *Dyer* 20 June 92/2 Chromogen may even be used with other dyestuffs to obtain a variety of useful shades of brown. 1910 *Encycl. Brit.* VIII. 746/1 Other acid colours, e.g. Chromotrope, Chrome Brown, Chromogen, Alizarin Yellow, &c.

Chromogram (krōᵘ·mŏgræm). [f. Chromo- 2 + -gram.] A combination of three photographs taken by a special process, which being superposed produce an image in the natural colours of the object. (Cf. Heliochrome.)

1893 *Jrnl. Soc. Arts* 19 May 663 The heliochromoscope and its triple photograph, or chromogram. 1893 *Daily News* 18 May 6/7 It was necessary..to provide a special optical lantern for superposing on the screen the three images of the chromogram. 1894 *Amer. Ann. Photogr.* 208 The word chromogram designates the combination or the ensemble of three diapositives made from negatives representing the action of the blues, yellows, and greens respectively of the original.

Chromoleucite (krōᵘmoliū·səit). *Bot.* [See Leucite.] A protoplasmic colour granule.

1885 G. L. Goodale *Physiol. Bot.* 41 Chromoplastids, or chromoleucites. 1895 *Naturalist* 25 The colour of the petals is due to chromoleucites tinctured by carotin.

Chromomere (krōᵘ·mŏmiᵊɹ). *Biol.* [f. Chromo- 2 + Gr. μέρος part.] A name for the chromatin-granules which make up a chromosome; the Id of Weismann.

1902 E. B. Wilson *The Cell* (ed. 2) 301 The chromatin-thread consists of a series of granules (chromomeres) embedded in ..the linin-substance. 1920 W. E. Agar *Cytol.* 134 [The chromosomes in prophase] are often markedly moniliform, *i. e.* consisting of a row of bead-like swellings of chromatin, called chromomeres, joined to each other by a thinner linin thread.

Chromophil (krōᵘ·mŏfil), *a. Zool.* Also **chroma-, -phile.** [Gr. φίλος loving, dear.] = *Chromaffin *a.* Also **Chromo·philous** *a.*

1909 *Practitioner* Feb. 195 Chromophile cells, very similar to the cells in the medulla of the supra-renals. 1910 *Ibid.* Jan. 35 Chromophil granules. 1915 *Cunningham's Anat.* (ed. 4) 1341 The chromaphil system is composed of a number of discrete masses of tissue which produce and discharge adrenin. 1919 J. G. Kerr *Embryol.* II. 283 The medullary substance in mammals and what corresponds with it in other Vertebrates..takes on a deep yellow or brown colour when treated with salts of chromic acid. Hence it is convenient..to apply to it a name expressive of this reaction—such as Chromophile (Stilling), Chromaffine (Kohn) or Phaeochrome (Poll).

Chromoplast (krōᵘ·mŏplæst). *Bot.* [f. Chromo- + -plast.] A plastid or protoplasmic granule containing red or yellow pigments. Also *attrib.* So **Chromopla·stid.**

1885 G. L. Goodale *Physiol. Bot.* 41 Those [granules] which have some color other than green—Chromoplastids, or chromoleucites. 1902 E. B. Wilson *The Cell* (ed. 2) 52 The chromatophores or chromoplastids. 1910 R. C. Punnett *Mendelism* (ed. 2) 37 The tint of the flower being due to the presence of yellow-colouring matter in the small bodies known as chromoplasts. 1913 W. H. Bateson *Mendel's Princ. Heredity* 40 *Polemonium*...It may be inferred that the yellow of *flavum* is a chromoplast colour.

Chromoplastic (krōᵘmoplæ·stik). [f. Chromo- 2 + Plastic *sb.*[1]] Modelling in colours.

1902 *Encycl. Brit.* XXX. 788/2 The method of *moulage* or chromoplastic yields excellent impressions of living organisms.

Chromosome (krōᵘ·mŏsōᵘm). *Biol.* [ad. G. *chromosom* (Waldeyer, in Arch. f. Mikrosk. Anat., 1888, p. 27), f. Chromo- 2 + Gr. σῶμα body.] Each of the rods or threads into which the chromatin of the cell-nucleus is transformed just before the mitotic division of the cell.

1890 Sir W. Turner *Cell Theory, Past & Present* 29 The primary chromatin fibres, or *chromosome* as Waldeyer calls them, form a complex coil. 1892 E. L. Mark *Hertwig's Embryol.* 52 The chromatin..has assumed the form of small individual granules or chromosomes, which correspond in number with the spindle-fibres. 1907 C. E. Walker *Cytol.* 99 It has been held that every hereditary character is represented by a chromosome. 1922 R. C. Punnett *Mendelism* 100 Chromosomes..owe their name to the fact that they stain more deeply with various dyes than the rest of the cell protoplasm.

Chromosphe·rical, *a.* = Chromospheric.

1883 *World's Cycl. Science* (N.Y.) V. 8 Mr. Swift..[at] Denver, saw two of these prominences, which he describes as being near the chromospherical crescent.

Chromotrope (krōᵘ·mŏtrōᵘp). Also **-trop.** [a. G. *chromotrop,* f. Chromo- 2 + Gr. -τροπος turning.] An acid colour used in dyeing. Also *attrib.*

1893 Knecht, Rawson, & Loewenthal *Man. Dyeing* 536 A (new) dioxynaphthalene disulphonic acid (so-called chromotrop acid). *Ibid.* 537 The chromotrops do not dye evenly on previously mordanted wool. *Ibid.* 539 The chromotrop-blacks. 1902 *Encycl. Brit.* XXVII. 562/2 Chromotrope..is an Acid Colour which is applied to wool in an acid bath in the usual manner. 1906 *Dyer* 20 Jan. 15/1 Lactic acid is used in chromotrope dyeing.

Chromotrope, var. Chromatrope.

Chromotropic (krōᵘmotrɒ·pik), *a. Chem.* [f. *Chromotrope + -ic.] Having the property of varying its colour. Hence **Chromotro·pism.**

1899 *Jrnl. Chem. Soc.* LXXVI. I. 63 Phenylazochromotropic acid (chromotropic acid..), which the dye-works' chemists regard as a 2-azo-compound. 1908 H. Driesch *Sci. & Philos. Organism* II. 24 *note,* The crab *Maia* may change the quality—not the 'sense'—of its 'chromotropism', ..according to the colour of the ground it lives upon, and another crab, *Hippolyte,* changes its colour and its chromotropism correspondingly. 1918 A. W. Stewart *Rec. Adv. Org. Chem.* (ed. 3) 32 If a salt changes colour, it is said to be 'chromotropic' or 'variochromic'.

Chronic, *a.* **3.** Add:

Used vulgarly as a vague expression of disapproval = bad, intense, severe, objectionable. Also *something chronic* adv. phr. = severely, badly.

[1896 in Ware *Passing Engl.* (1909), *Chronic*..Ceaseless, persistent. 'Oh! Joe's chronic.' 'Charley's Aunt's chronic', —said of a piece that ran perpetually.] 1909 *Ibid.*, 'Oh, that theatre's chronic'—means that never is a good piece seen there. 1910 H. G. Wells *Mr. Polly* ii. 41 It's made my eyes water something chronic. 1915 *Scotsman* 26 Jan. 5/3 'The weather is chronic', says a Seaforth Highlander. 1926 J. J. Connington *Death at Swaythling Court* ix. 164 He puts a dash of whisky into the paraldehyde to disguise the taste, which is a chronic one, I can tell you.

Chronicle, *sb.* **4.** Add:

In *chronicle drama,* etc., used in imitation of †*chronicle history,* an Elizabethan descriptive title for plays based on historical matter such as is found in Edward Hall and Ralph Holinshed; **chronicle song** *U.S.,* a ballad of a historical nature.

1600 (*title*) The Cronicle History of Henry the fift. 1608 (*title*) M. William Shak-speare: His True Chronicle Historie of the life and death of King Lear and his three daughters. 1634 Ford (*title*) The Chronicle Historie of Perkin Warbeck. [1886 F. G. Fleay (*title*) A Chronicle History of the Life and Work of William Shakespeare.] 1902 F. E. Schelling *The English Chronicle Play* 30 The English *Chronicle Drama falls naturally into two groups. 1903 Hardy *Dynasts* Pref. p. ix, In devising this *chronicle-piece no attempt has been made to create that completely organic structure of action, and closely-webbed development of character and motive, which are demanded in a drama strictly self-contained. 1927 *Observer* 12 June 15/2 'Martha Washington' is a chronicle piece, after the manner of 'Abraham Lincoln,' but there is no drama in it from start to finish. 1853 J. G. Baldwin *Flush Times Alabama* 149 He was the merriest..feller..and can sing more *chronicle songs than one of these show fellers.

Chronophotography (krɒnofotɒ·grăfi). [f. Gr. χρόνος time.] An early term for cinematic photography. Hence **Chro:nophotogra·phic** *a.*

1899 Horwood *Living Pictures* 43 Chrono-photography and the practical development of the living picture. 1901 *Rep. Smithsonian Inst.* 309 The writer has pushed the improvement of his chronophotographic apparatus. *Ibid.*, Chronophotographic gun with a film ribbon.

Chronoscope. b. Add: Recently, used for measuring the time of reaction in psychophysical experiments.

1923 *Chambers's Jrnl.* 603/2 When the examiner speaks the chronoscope revolves; when the subject speaks, it stops. ..The hiatus [between question and answer] is duly recorded by the chronoscope.

Chrysanthemine (krisæ·nþĭmin). *Chem.* [See -ine [5].] A deliquescent alkaloid, $C_{14}H_{28}O_2N_2$, found in the flowers of *Chrysanthemum cinerariæfolium.*

1891 *Jrnl. Chem. Soc.* LX. I. 334 The alkaloid, named *chrysanthemine* by the author [*sc.* F. Marino Zuco], is readily soluble in water. 1918 A. W. Stewart *Rec. Adv. Org. Chem.* (ed. 3) 210 The anthocyanin of the winter aster is chrysanthemin, derived from dextrose and cyanidin.

Chrysid (krai·sid). *Ent.* [ad. mod.L. *Chrysididæ* (see definition), f. Gr. χρυσίς (-ιδ-) gold vessel, gold-broidered dress.] A member of the family *Chrysididæ* of hymenopterous metallic-coloured insects (ruby-wasps, cuckoo-flies). Also as *adj.*

1884 *Riverside Nat. Hist.* (1888) II. 524 In mode of life the Chrysids are either parasites or inquilines. 1910 *Encycl. Brit.* XIV. 180/2 The eggs are laid in the nests of various bees and wasps, the chrysid larva living as a 'cuckoo' parasite. 1913 *Oxf. Univ. Gaz.* 4 June 959/1 Dr. Longstaff's fine set of Sûdan Hymenoptera..included..40 Chrysids.

Chub. Add: **2. c.** A Texan. *U.S. colloq.*

1869 *Overland Monthly* III. 129 For the Texan soubriquet 'Chub' I know of no explanation, unless it be found in the size of the Eastern Texans.

Chu·bbily, *adv.* [-ly [2].] In the manner which befits one who is chubby.

1909 H. G. Wells *Tono-Bungay* II. iii. 152 'True,' said my uncle, chubbily and with a dreamy sense of mysticism.

Chubby, *a.* **1.** (U.S. example.)

1872 *Rep. Vermont Board Agric.* I. 207 A small sized, chubby, rugged little horse.

Chuck, *sb.*[3] Add: **3. b.** Dismissal, 'turning down'. Similarly **Chu·ck-o·ver** (cf. *chuck over,* Chuck *v.*[2] 2 b). *slang.*

1894 'J. S. Winter' *Red Coats* 135 'Yes, it was the clearest case of chuck-over I ever knew.' 'And who was the girl?' 1930 *Argosy* Apr. 15/1 When they gave me the chuck, you married me out of hand.

Chuck, *sb.*[4] **2.** (Earlier examples.)

1798 *Ann. Agric.* XXX. 314 in J. Britten *Old Country Words* (1880) 97 Bladebones chuck. Somerset. 1844 H. Stephens *Bk. Farm* II. 171 In the fore quarter, the fore rib, middle rib, and chuck-rib, are all roasting pieces [of beef]. 1865–6 *Trans. Ill. Agric. Soc.* VI. 642 No 2 [is the] Leather Chuck [of a pig]. No 3, Chuck.

Chuck, *sb.*[5] *slang* or *dial.* Now chiefly *U.S.* [perh. the same as Chuck *sb.*[4]]

1. Food, 'grub'. (In early use *spec.* bread or ship-biscuit.)

1850 *Lloyd's Newsp.* 6 Oct. (Farmer) The prisoner, upon coming to his cottage door had tried hard to get some chuck out of him, but had failed. 1860 *Slang Dict.* (ed. 2), *Chuck,* food, provision for an entertainment.—Norwich. 1864 *Standard* 13 Dec. (Farmer) Of naval slang Mr. Hotten has missed the words Chuck, used by sailors for biscuit, and Barge, the box or cask in which the chuck is kept by the messes on the lower deck. 1877 *Five Yrs.' Penal Servitude* i. 4 Two large slices of bread,..the allowance given out to some prisoner who..had forgotten to eat what in prison slang is called his 'toke' or 'chuck'. 1926 J. Black *You Can't Win* vi. 67 It's you kind of cats that make it tough on us, buying chuck.

attrib. 1905 A. Adams *Outlet* 16 A carpenter then at work building chuck-boxes for each of the six commissaries. 1926 J. Black *You Can't Win* iv. 39 New arrivals, who had not yet acquired the 'chuck horrors', that awful animal craving for food that comes after missing half a dozen meals.

2. The act of taking food.

1901 Marah E. Ryan *Montana* i. 25 After 'chuck' we'll go over and give you a nearer view of the tribe on the other shore. 1907 S. E. White *Arizona Nights* I. vi. 112 When the last man had returned from chuck, Homer made the dispositions for the cut.

Chuck, *v.*[2] Add:

2. b. *To chuck out*: to expel, discharge (from a public meeting, a theatre, a prison, a position or post). Also without *out.* Cf. *chucker-out,* Chucker [1] 3. *To chuck (up)*: to abandon, throw over; to dismiss; also *pass.* to be acquitted or released. *To chuck it*: to stop (doing something).

1865 *Slang Dict.*, *Chuck up,* to surrender, give in—from the custom of throwing up the sponge at a prize fight in token of yielding. 1878 *Chambers's Jrnl.* 333/2 A stalwart navvy,..after crossing the Danube several times at Alexandra Park, declared he must 'chuck it up' if he could not be a Turk. *c* 1879 *Broadside Ballad* (Farmer) Whatever may happen I get all the blame, Wherever I go, it is always the same—Jolly well chucked again! 1883 Hawley Smart *Hard Lines* xxvi, If you mean business, take my advice and chuck that corps. 1883 Miss Braddon *Phantom Fortune* xxv, Look how easily she chucked you up because she did not think you good enough. 1885 *Daily News* 27 Nov. 2 The town artisan is ready enough to chuck out an obstructor. 1887 Horsley *Jottings from Jail* 24 Kit, from 7 dials.. expects to get fulled or else chucked. 1889 *Times* 4 Nov. 3/6 Some of them have got chucked out, your Worship, excuse the language. 1890 *Daily News* 5 Dec. 7/1 'He's sure to get chucked'—a slang expression for discharged. 1893 *National Observer* 23 Sept. 483/1 That is a reason for living hopefully, not for 'chucking it up' in despair. 1908 E. W. Walters *Nipper* ii, 'Chuck it!' snapped the ill-nourished boy. 1922 *N. & Q.* 12th Ser. XI. 206/2 If at some stage in a race a horse is seen to 'shut up', and refuse to gallop his best, it is said to 'chuck it'. 1924 D. H. Lawrence *England, my England* 240 'Serve you right if she chucks you now' said Tinny.

c. *Chuck-and-chance-it*: a derisive phrase used *attrib.* to describe wet-fly fishing.

1899 *Westm. Gaz.* 12 May 3/2 A large proportion of anglers ..regard with unmerited contempt that which they are pleased to miscall the 'Chuck-and-chance-it system'. 1907 *Ibid.* 29 Nov. 3/1 Agreeing to scoff at every wet-fly angler as a mere chuck-and-chance-it angler.

Chu·ck-a-lu:ck. *U.S.* Also **chuck-luck, chuckle luck.** [Chuck *v.*[2] 5.] A gambling game played with dice.

1853 J. G. Baldwin *Flush Times Alabama* 124 Games of hazard, such as push-pin, marbles, chuck-a-luck, heads and tails, and other like boyish pastimes. 1856 *Liberator* 12 Jan. XXVI. 12 Leper and Doolin got into a quarrel over a game called 'chuckle luck'. 1879 *Southern Hist. Soc. Papers* VII. 489 Cards, monte, roulette, keno, faro, chuck-a-luck, and in fact every game of chance known. 1907 S. E. White *Arizona Nights* I. x. 165 And a man's so sick of himself by the time he gets this far that he'd play chuck-a-luck.

attrib. 1845 J. J. Hooper *Adv. Simon Suggs* ix. 111 The occasional exhibition of a chuck-a-luck table, at which the Captain himself presided. 1873 J. H. Beadle *Undevel. West* iv. 94 We walk down to the 'chuck-a-luck' board. 1925 Mulford *Cottonwood Gulch* iv. 57 Chuck-a-luck gamblers.

Chucker[1]. **1.** (Later U.S. example.)

1811 A. Graydon *Mem.* (1846) 55, I never could boast my winning at marbles or chuckers.

b. *U.S.* (See quot.)

1833 J. F. Watson *Hist. Tales Philad.* 153 (Th.) They pitched 'chuckers', a kind of pewter pennies cast by the boys themselves.

4. *Cricket. colloq.* A bowler whose delivery of the ball is considered to be a throw.

1882 Pardon *Australians in England* 158 Do not people tell you openly they think so and so a 'chucker'?

Chuck-full, *a.* Add later U.S. and dial. examples (see Chock-full 8).

1868 *Putnam's Mag.* Dec. (De Vere) These prairies are nature's banks, stuffed chuckfull of cash. 1888 'Q' (Quiller-Couch) *Troy Town* x, You niver seed a bull yet as wasn' chuck-full o' conviction, an' didn' act up to hes rights. 1893 W. K. Post *Harvard Stories* 31 The public wards are chuck-full. 1929 *Minnesota Alumni Weekly* 1 June 619 She sent us a letter just chuck full of interesting news items.

Chu·ck-hole. *U.S.* [Chuck *v.*[2] 5. Cf. *chock-hole,* Chock *sb.*[1] 7.] A deep hole in a road or track.

1869 S. Bowles *Our New West* xiv. 276 The jolting of the rocks and the 'chuck holes' of the road..kept us in a somewhat perpetual..motion. 1887 J. Kirkland *Zury* 2 'Chuck-holes' is the expressive Western name for the short, sharp depressions which use makes in unworked country roads. 1907 S. E. White *Arizona Nights* I. ii. 30 Every once in a while they'd stick in a chuck-hole.

Chu·cking, *vbl. sb.*[3] *Turning.* [f. Chuck *v.*[3]] The act of fixing in, or by means of, a chuck.

1889 Hasluck *Model Engin. Handybk.* (1900) 49 The flanges [should be] turned and faced up at one chucking. 1906 Cassal (*title*) Chucks and Chucking, for Metal and Wood.

Chu·ck-wa:g(g)on. *U.S.* [*Chuck *sb.*[5]] The wagon carrying the provisions of an 'outfit'.

1890 D'Oyle *Notches* 26 The sun blistered the paint upon the 'mess-box' behind the 'chuck-waggon'. 1910 Mulford *Hopalong Cassidy* iii. 25 A group of blanket-swathed figures lay about a fire near the chuck wagon. 1920 Hunter *Trail Drivers* 44 We drowned a horse hitched to the chuck wagon.

Chuck-will's-widow. (Earlier examples.)

1791 W. Bartram *Carolina* 154 *note,* Caprimulgus rufus called chuck-will's-widow, from a fancied resemblance of his note to these words. 1823 E. James *Rocky Mt. Exped.* I. 49 The yellow breasted chat, chuck-wills-widow, .. and numerous other birds occurred.

Chu·cky-chu·cky. *Austral.* Also **chuckie-, -chuck.** [Native name.] The fruit of *Gaultheria hispida.*

1885 Mrs. C. Praed *Australian Life* 146 To gather chucky-chuckies—as the blacks name that most delicious of native berries. 1885 — *Head Station* xxxv, Mollie Clephane had filled one of the saddle-bags with wild plums, chuckie-chuckies, and the scrub-turkey's eggs.

Chudleigh (tʃɒ·dli). A kind of tea-cake, named after Chudleigh, Devon.

1928 *Daily Express* 7 Mar. 5/4 Sally Lunn's tea cakes.. were light and spongy, rather resembling Cornish splits and Devonshire chudleighs.

Chuff (tʃɒf), *v.* [Onomatopœic.] *intr.* Of an engine or machine: To work with a hoarse, gasping sound. Also *sb.* Similarly **Chuff-chuff** *sb.* and *v.*

1921 D. H. Lawrence *Sea & Sardinia* 31 Slowly, with two engines, we grunt and chuff and twist to get over the break-neck heights. 1923 *Blackw. Mag.* Dec. 797/2 The chuff-chuff of the exhaust from the generating plant that supplied the house with electricity. 1928 D. H. Lawrence *Rainbow* xv. 426 The far-off windy chuff of a shunting train. 1929 J. B. Priestley *Good Companions* 612 The train.. slowly chuff-chuffed into the gloom.

Chug (tʃɒg), *sb.* orig. *U.S.* An onomatopœia framed to imitate a plunging or explosive sound.

1897 *Outing* (U.S.) XXX. 175/1, I accidentally cast myself into the pool with a sounding chug. 1904 Edith Rickert *Reaper* 335 No sound about him except the chug and splash of his own oars. 1923 *Outward Bound* Mar. 420/1 The chug of the engine still filled our ears.

Similarly **Chug-chug** *sb.* Also **Chug-drug.**

1894 *Outing* (U.S.) XXIV. 56/2 One weapon after another struck [the water] 'chug—chug—chug—chug,' while a flying furrow on the surface told of a swift shape speeding unharmed below it. 1895 Kipling *2nd Jungle Bk.* 219 He would hear.. the *chug-drug* of a boar sharpening his tusks on a bole. 1920 *Blackw. Mag.* May 649/1 The chug, chug of the dripping paddle floats. 1925 *Chambers's Jrnl.* 250/1 The 'chug-chug' of an oil-engine could be faintly heard.

Chug (tʃɒg), *v.* [Onomatopœic. See prec.] *intr.* To make an intermittent explosive sound as of the escape of exhaust gases from an engine cylinder; to move with a sound characteristic of a steam-engine or electric motor at work. Also adv., as *off, on, along, out.* Also quasi-*trans.*

1915 Will Irwin *Men, Women & War* 52 The grey motor cycles and automobiles streaked past, their mufflers cut out, chugging the message of death. 1916 *Church Army Rev.* June 4 Now she [*sc.* the tender] came chugging across and slid alongside. 1917 'Contact' *Airman's Outings* 114 Slowly ..our train chugged northward. 1919 *Detective Story Mag.* 25 Nov. XXVIII. 25 A distant chugging testified that the Duke's taxicab was approaching. 1923 *Challenge* 23 Mar. 523/1 The long-waisted fish-carriers which some two or three times a week chug their way through the crowded traffic of the Pool.

Similarly **Chug-chug** *v.*

1907 *Daily Chron.* 13 June 4/4 A big motor-car tooting and chug-chugging. 1928 *Daily Express* 11 Aug. 3/1 We chug-chugged comfortably down Southampton Water.

Chukar, -or, variants of *Chikhor.

Chukker (tʃɒ·kəɹ). *Polo.* Also **chucker.** [Hind. *chakar, chakkar,* = Skr. *cakra* circle, Wheel.] Each of the 'periods' into which the game is divided.

1900 *Overland Mail* 13 Aug. (Y.) In the opening chukker Capt. — carried the ball in. 1905 T. F. Dale *Polo* 339 The period of actual play at polo, known in India as a 'chukker', has altered considerably. 1906 T. B. Drybrough *Polo* (ed. 2) 283 The 'period' does not end—except in the case of the last chukker—till the ball goes out of play. 1923 *Daily Mail* 22 May 3 Four goals to one team in one chukker is very unusual in first-class polo.

Chulo (tʃū·lo). [Sp.] A bullfighter's assistant.

1926 *Blackw. Mag.* Sept. 290/2 When a horse ridden by a picador is badly hurt in the ring he is killed by a chulo.

Chum (tʃɒm), *sb.*[2] *U.S.* [Origin obscure.]

a. Refuse fish, esp. that remaining after expressing oil. **b.** Chopped fish, lobsters, etc., thrown overboard to attract fish, as in trolling. Hence **Chum** *v.,* (*a*) *intr.* to fish with chum; (*b*) *trans.* to bait with chum. **Chu·mmer,** one who is in charge of the bait and baiting.

1857 *Agric. Maine* II. 69 The fish known as menhaden, and often called..'poggies', are..pressed..to extract an oil ..; what remains after extracting the oil, is called 'poggy chum'. 1859 *Ibid.* IV. 182 Pogies will be caught for the chum and not for the oil. 1872 T. Lyman *Sixth Ann. Rep. (Mass.) Comm. Inland Fisheries* 25 The younger ones [*sc.* mackerel]..were laboriously chopped up with a hatchet and thrown over as 'chum'. 1876 *Fur, Fin & Feather* Sept. 131/1 The chummer cuts up the bait—menhaden or lobster—and thus manufactures the chum. *Ibid.* 131/2 He carries ..a 'chum-thrower' which may be described as a shovel with all the edges turned up. 1882 *Forest & Stream* XIX. 363 Chumming is much more sport, the fish then being captured with rod and reel. 1897 *Outing* (U.S.) XXX. 258/1 Some bait we had, but it was salt; here was the chance for an unlimited quantity, at any rate for 'chumming.' *Ibid.* 259/1 The doctor and myself, with Harry Elms to chum for us. *Ibid.*, His object now was to chum or draw the fish around us. *Ibid.* 261/1 The place had been so thoroughly chummed that fish must be there.

Chum, *sb.*[3] The dog salmon, *Oncorhynchus keta.*

1920 *Glasgow Herald* 2 Jan. 9 The salmon pack of British Columbia for 1919 was..about 400,000 cases less than put up last year, when a large quantity of 'chums' were canned.

Chum, *sb.*[4] *Ceramics.* (See quots.)

1887 *Leisure Hour* 705/1 If a cup is to be made, [he] fixes ..what is called a brass chum, a receptacle into which he drops a plaster-of-paris mould. In this he places the roughly formed cup, and..makes it perfectly smooth. *Ibid.* 705/2 In hollow-ware pressing the clay, when batted out sufficiently, is placed over a chum to bend it somewhat into the desired shape.

Chum, *v.* Add:

3. *intr.* To become intimate, be on friendly terms *with* (some one). Also with *in, up.*

1884 *Cheshire Gloss.*, *Chum,* to associate with. 1888 J. M'Carthy & Mrs. C. Praed *Ladies' Gallery* I. vi. 146 It's odd how Australians chum in together. 1889 Earl of Desart *Little Chatelaine* II. xxiii. 107 They will chum well with a child brought up by you. *a* 1891 in J. M. Dixon *Dict. Idiom. Phrases* s.v., Kenny tried to chum up with the new comer.

4. *trans.* To make a chum of (some one).

1880 *Eagle Mag.* (St. John's Coll. Camb.) XI. 1 He's an aristocrat,..and so our 'Old English Baron' chums him.

Chumar: see *Chamar.

Chummy, *a.* Add: **b.** Applied to a type of motor body intended to give comfortable accommodation for a small party (e. g. three or four). Also *absol.* or as *sb.*

1922 *Autocar* 10 Nov. 963/2 The 'chummy' body has been laid out with the idea of providing comfortable seating accommodation for three adults, or two adults and two children. 1924 *Morris Owner* Apr. 143 A 'chummy' model. Carry self, wife, one boy—say 375 lbs. *Ibid.* Sept. 683 This 'Chummy' carries a very heavy luggage load on its travels.

Chunga (tʃɒ·ŋgă). Also **chuña.** [mod.L., f. the native name.] An Argentine bird, *Chunga burmeisteri,* closely related to the seriema.

1881 E. W. White *Cameos fr. Silver-Land* I. 33 The two remarkable species of the Chuña, together with innumerable parrots and parakeets, make Santiago their home. 1882 *Ibid.* II. 209 As the Chuña was so dreadfully shy, my barrels slew other birds.

Chunk, *sb.*[1] Add: **1.** *fig.* (Earlier and later examples.)

1833 J. Hall *Leg. West* 50 (Th.) If a man got into a chunk of a fight with his neighbour, a lawyer would clear him for half a dozen muskrat skins. 1894 *Congress. Rec.* 13 July 7445/1 Just one moment, my friend. You are a lawyer... Yes, a chunk of a lawyer.

b. A block or log of wood.

1781 Witherspoon *Druid* No. vii, *Chunks,* that is brands, half burnt wood. This is customary in the middle Colonies. 1816 Pickering *Vocab.* 60 *Chunk*..is also used in the Northern States, to signify a thick, short block or bit of wood. 1821 Z. Hawley *Tour* 21 Jan. (1822) 44 (Th.) In the room of andirons, many families make use of what are here called chunks, which are the two brands of a large forestick, or billets of wood cut on purpose for this use. 1856 *Knickerbocker Mag.* June XLVII. 634 [In the factory at Nyack] The tub is placed over a 'chunk,' and turned off outside in a few moments, and hooped. It is next placed in a hollow chunk and turned out perfectly smooth inside. 1885 Jefferies *Open Air* 170 The pile of 'chunks'..formed a wall of wood at my back.

c. A fair- or large-sized specimen *of* an animal or person. *U.S.*

1822 J. Woods *Two Yrs.' Resid. Engl. Prairie* 285 A hog of two hundred lbs. weight is here called a fine chunk of a fellow. 1841 C. Cist *Cincinnati* 180 For sale—a good chunk of a plough horse. *a* 1861 T. Winthrop *Canoe & Saddle* (1862) 66, I chose first for my pack animal a strawberry roan cob, 'a chunk of a horse'. 1871 Schele de Vere *Americanisms* (1872) 454 'A tolerable chunk of a pony', means, in Southern and Western parlance, a cob. 1887 C. B. George *40 Yrs. on Rail* i. 22 You're a pretty good chunk of a boy to be riding for half [fare].

d. A stoutly-built horse or pony; *spec.* a heavy draught-horse. *U.S.*

1829 T. Flint *G. Mason* 108 (Th.) There were to be merry races of asses and 'chunks', by persons who volunteered as the Merry-Andrews of the meeting. 1887 *Boston Herald* 12 Aug. (Cent.) For sale, 4 Morgan chunks. 1906 *Springfield Daily Republ.* 7 Feb. 2 Advt., Pair gray farm chunks, 9 years, 2350 lbs.

e. A short, thickset person (Webster 1911).

2. chunk-bottle *U.S.,* a stout square-shaped bottle.

1845 W. G. Simms *Wigwam & Cabin* Ser. II. 146 Returning towards nightfall to the camp, Mingo brought with him a 'chunk-bottle' of whiskey.

Chunk, *v.*[1] *U.S. colloq.* [f. Chunk *sb.*[1]]

1. *trans.* To hit, or throw at, with a heavy missile.

1835 W. G. Simms *Partisan* 112 Well, doctor, get down and chunk it, if its worth having, its worth killing. *Ibid.* 425 His dog stole my bacon..and when I chunked the varmint, the nigger gin me sass. 1859 Bartlett *Dict. Amer.* (ed. 2), To *Chunk,* to throw sticks or chips at one. Southern and Western. 1871 Schele de Vere *Americanisms* (1872) 188 In the South..they say: 'I'll chunk him', meaning that they will throw a clod of earth or a stick of wood at some animal. 1886 J. C. Harris *Free Joe* 115 Ef you want to chunk anybody, chunk me...An' ef you don't want to chunk me, chunk your mammy. *a* 1910 'O. Henry' *Sixes & Sevens* xiii. 137 The crowd kept on chunkin' her till she run clear out of town.

2. To knock *out* with something hard or heavy.

1857 D. H. Strother *Virginia Illustr.* 204 (Th.) She handed her entrapped escort a stone. 'Here, Sammy, chunk your foot out with this.'

b. *To chunk up*: to replenish (a fire) with fuel; to collect materials for burning.

1850 L. H. Garrard *Wah-To-Yah* iv. (1927) 65 Smith kept the squaws of the lodge 'chunking' up the fire. 1905 *Terms Forestry & Logging* 33 *To chunk up,* to collect and pile for burning the slash left after logging.

c. *Logging.* (See quot.)

1905 *Terms Forestry & Logging* 33 *Chunk,* to clear the ground, with engine or horses, of obstructions which can not be removed by hand.

Chunk, *v.*[2] [Onomatopœic.] *intr.* To move with a plunging or explosive sound. Also *trans.* Hence *vbl. sb.* and *ppl. a.* Similarly **Chunk-chunk** *sb.* and *v.*

1892 Kipling *Barrack-room Ballads* 50 Can't you 'ear their paddles chunkin' from Rangoon to Mandalay? 1898 *Daily News* 20 Jan. 5/4 We heard the chunk-chunking sound of the Maxims. 1902 Edith Rickert *Cypress Swamp* 2 There was a chunking sound, followed by another. 1907 Tatlock *Devel. & Chronol. Chaucer's Wks.* 138 Amid the cluttering and chunking of one hundred and twenty-eight hoofs. 1908 *Daily Chron.* 29 Aug. 4/4 She makes a cheerful chunk-chunk with her paddles. 1924 *Scribner's Mag.* Feb. 206/2 The Chindwin's paddles chunked a song now. 1925 *Blackw. Mag.* Oct. 560/2 A Thames steamer chunking her way up the Tigris. 1926 'Lucas Malet' *Dogs of Want* iv. 103 A..paddle-steamer chunk-chunking across to St. Gingolph.

Chunky, *a.* (Earlier examples.)

1751 *Pennsylv. Gaz.* in *N. Jersey Archives* (1897) XIX. 95 A short, chunky, well set fellow. 1757 *Pennsylv. Gaz.* 29 Sept. 3/3 A short thick chunky Girl. 1787 *Maryland Jrnl.* 21 Dec. (Th.) Ran away,..Negro Jupiter,..thick and chunky made. 1816 Pickering *Vocab.* 60 The vulgar in this country also..say *junk* and *chunk*; and from this last substantive they have formed the adjective *chunky,* which they often apply to the stature of a person; as, he is a short, *chunky* man. 1840 W. G. Simms *Border Beagles* 303 The stranger was a chunky little imp, not more than four feet high. 1845 Mrs. Kirkland *Western Clearings* (1846) 126 Brumblebank's account of the two new belles was not very fascinating. 'The chunky one', said he, 'is fixed off like a poppy-show.'

b. Of things.

1899 A. T. Slosson in *Harper's Mag.* Dec. 146/2 Pely's little chunky, leather cover Bible. 1918 Mulford *Man fr. Bar-20* ix. 93 [The panther] raised its chunky head and neck.

2. Consisting of large lumps.

1886 *Harper's Mag.* Sept. 531/2, I have seen beds destroyed by too heavy a covering of chunky, rank manure.

Church, *sb.* **18.** Add: **Church Assembly,** short title of the National Assembly of the Church of England, a body established by statute in 1919 (the Church of England Assembly (Powers) Act); **Church Congress,** an annual (autumnal) meeting of members of the Church of England, lay and clerical, to discuss matters religious, moral, or social, under the presidency of the bishop of the diocese where the meeting is held; **church-fair** *U.S.,* a bazaar held in connexion with a church; **Church parade,** (*a*) divine service performed as part of the routine of military duty; (*b*) a turn-out of fashionable church-goers after the Sunday

morning service; (*c*) the attendance of the members of a society, etc., in a body at divine service; hence *Church-parader, -parading*; **church-people,** people belonging to the Church of England.

1919 *Act 9 & 10 Geo. V,* c. 76 § 1 'The National Assembly of the Church of England' (hereinafter called 'the *Church Assembly'). 1861 *Rep. Ch. Congress* (1862) p. v, A circular addressed to eminent Churchmen of all parties requesting their attendance at a *Church Congress in Cambridge. 1862 (*title*) Report of the proceedings of the Church Congress held in the Hall of King's College, Cambridge: November 27th, 28th, and 29th, 1861. 1876 *Church fair [see Fair *sb.* 1 c]. 1890 *Congress. Rec.* 8 May 4343/2 Certain entertainments and church fairs, which I have attended, when the admission was free. 1907 Mulford *Bar-20* vi. 63 All kinds of excitement except revival meetings and church fairs. 1869 *Porcupine* 13 Nov. 317/3 There will be a *Church Parade [of Volunteers] on Sunday next. 1883 *Peel City Guardian* 29 Sept. 3/2 The friendly societies.. have had their first public church parade. 1887 *Ibid.* 5 Mar. 7/1 The Church parade organised by the Social Democratic Federation, which was held at St. Paul's Cathedral. 1891 *Ibid.* 30 May 6/1 The Sunday before the Derby is..looked forward to as the best 'Church parade' of the season in Hyde-park. 1907 Adderley *Behold the days come* 18 The *Church-paraders whom he takes to be typical Christians. 1907 *Trollope's Three Clerks* Introd. p. v, *Church-parading to and fro beneath the trees. 1842 W. Palmer *Lett. Prot.-Cath.* 53 They are *Church people like ourselves at heart. 1928 *Daily Tel.* 15 May 13/2 Church-people throughout the dioceses.

Church, *v.* Add:

1. d. To call to account in church. *U.S.*

1901 Harben *Westerfelt* x. 136 He..said some'n about folks bein' churched in his settlement fer the mistreatment o' widows. 1902 H. L. Wilson *Spenders* xii. 132 Only I hope the First M.E. Church of Montana City never hears of her outrageous cuttin's-up...They'd have her up and church her, sure.

e. To marry in church.

1910 J. Jeffery Farnol *Broad Highway* II. xiii, If folk ..shake their heads over ye—w'y, let 'em, only don't—don't go a-spilin' things by gettin' 'churched'. *Ibid.*, Don't go spilin' things by lettin' this young cove go a-marryin' and a-churchin' ye.

Church-officer. (Earlier American example.)

1654 E. Johnson *Wonder-W. Prov.* vii. 211 The people gathered into a Church some..time before they could attain any Church-Officer to administer the Seals unto them.

Churchwarden. 1. *attrib.* Add: **churchwarden Gothic,** the sham Gothic affected in church building or restoration in the early nineteenth century. So *churchwarden window,* etc. Hence **Churchwardenise** *v. trans.,* to treat (a church) in 'churchwarden' style.

1831, 1863 [see Churchwardenize in Dict.]. 1840 Manning in Purcell *Life* (1896) I. 177 To survey and codify the laws of Churchwarden Gothic, beginning from the hat-pegs and wooden mullions at Bexhill. 1894 *Murray's Handbk. Oxfordsh.* 138 Aston Rowant... The windows throughout the church were despoiled of their tracery, and churchwarden windows inserted. *Ibid.* 172 Tadmarton..with a small Dec. church terribly churchwardenized. 1902 *Handbk. Berksh.* 120 The chancel windows have been..churchwardenised. 1912 Cranage *Churches Shropsh.* II. 895 The style is a peculiarly hideous variety of 'churchwarden Gothic', the original windows..having cast-iron tracery.

Churchy, *a.* **1.** (Earlier U.S. example.)

1843 Haliburton *Attaché* I. xii. 218 Preacher there don't preach morals, because that's churchy.

Churinga (tʃŏri·ŋgă). *Anthrop.* [Native Australian word.] A sacred object, an amulet.

1899 Spencer & Gillen *Native Tribes Central Australia* 123 The sacred stones, which are called by the Arunta natives Churinga. [*Note*] This Churinga is the equivalent of the bull-roarer or whirler of other authors. 1925 A. S. Alexander *Tramps across Watersheds* 101 The similarly marked shells and stones of Dumbuck are found to-day in the corresponding marks upon the sacred stone or stick, 'churinga', of the Australians. 1926 *Contemp. Rev.* Apr. 531 An individual entrusted with the *Churinga.*

Churn, *sb.* Add:

2. An instrument used in artificial silk manufacture.

1927 T. Woodhouse *Artificial Silk* 54 The contents of the maturing tins are placed into a sulphide kneader or churner. .. After the churn is charged with crumbs, the lid of the churn is securely fixed.

5. churn-dasher (examples).

1845 Mrs. Kirkland *Western Clearings* 101 Their hands had handled the churn-dasher too often to be very satiny in the palm. 1846–52 Mrs. Whitcher *Widow Bedott P.* xxiv. 291 Here the churn-dasher come down with such a vengeance.

Churnable (tʃɒ·ɹnăb'l), *a. Dairying.* [f. Churn *v.* + -able.] Ready to form butter in churning. Hence **Churnabi·lity.**

1896 *Agric. Gaz.* 18 May 467/1 The percentage of water a butter contains not only determines its quality, but is also a necessary factor in accurately estimating the churnability of the fat in milk. 1906 Walker-Tisdale & T. R. Robinson *Buttermaking* (ed. 2) 61 Sweet cream yields a smaller proportion of butter, as the fat is not so 'churnable' as after it has been subjected to the ripening process. 1911 *Farm Butter Making* (Intern. Corr. Schools, Scranton, Pa., Instr. Paper) 50 The quantity of fat in cream is another important factor influencing its churnability. *Ibid.* 51 The speed of operating the churn also affects the churnability of the cream.

Churner (under Churn *v.*). Add: Also, a churning-machine.

1894 *Westm. Gaz.* 25 Apr. 2/1 A big Bradford churner.. and..a Danish 'separating' machine. 1927 [see *Churn *sb.* 2].

Churrigueresque (tʃŏrigəre·sk), *a.* [See quot. 1853 and -esque.] Characteristic of the Spanish architect José Churriguera (died 1725), who overloaded building with florid ornament. As *sb.* = the architectural style of Churriguera. Also **Chu·rriguerism, -ist, -i·stic** *adj.*

1853 *Dict. Archit.* I. 91/2 Churrigueresque Style. (Sp. *stilo churrigueresco, el churriguresmo.*) The architects above named..exercised so important an influence on art in Spain, as to give their name to a style, for following which themselves and their imitators were called *gerigoncistas* or jargonists, *tramoyistas* or scene-painters, and *churrigueristas.* 1908 H. Havelock Ellis *Soul of Spain* 309 Christian plateresque work is sometimes almost as delicate as Moorish work, Christian churrigueresque almost as fantastic. 1913 C. Gasquoine Hartley *Cathedrals S. Spain* 87 The *coro*..is in the bad Churrigueresque style. *Ibid.* 124 It is easy to understand how the Plateresque..was transformed into the Churrigueresque. *Ibid.* 163 The worst change..is the Churrigueresque alteration of the clerestory.

Churus, var. Churrus.

1905 L. Hope *Indian Love* 7 Churus and Opium failed.

Chute, *sb.* Add: **1.** *U.S.* (Earlier examples.)

1805 *Amer. St. Papers, Ind. Affairs* (1832) IV. 736 (Stanf.) By..lightening the boat, they passed the chutes this evening. 1806 *Ibid.* V. 736 About four miles below the 'chutes' (falls) they, from a good observation, found the latitude. 1835 in J. Hall *Stat. West* (1836) ii. 40 The bars..are composed of fine gravel..and occur..at the lower junction of the chutes formed by the islands.

2. b. A fish-way. *U.S.*

1871 *Game Laws Ohio* in *Fur, Fin & Feather* (1872) 61 An act to provide for the erection and maintenance of 'chutes' for the passage of fish over the dams.

3. (Earlier examples.) Also *transf.*

1869 'Mark Twain' *Innoc. Abr.* lviii. 626 They dragged us up a long inclined chute...This chute..was walled, roofed and floored with solid blocks of Egyptian granite. 1872 — *Roughing it* lii. 380 Under the bins are rows of waggons loading from chutes and trap-doors in the bins.

b. A narrow passage or enclosure for cattle. (Cf. *branding-chute,* *Branding *vbl. sb.* 2.)

1916 B. M. Bower *Phantom Herd* xix. 307 The big four year old steer prodded up the Chutes into shipping cars. 1920 Mulford *J. Nelson* xxv. 259 You can build a chute that'll hold eight head [of cattle].

attrib. 1911 Mulford *Bar-20 Days* xx. 197 Chute-branding robbed them of the excitement..which they always took from open or corral branding.

Chute, *v.* Add:

1. *To chute the chute(s*: to slide in a car or boat down an inclined plane that terminates in a pool of water.

1908 *Daily Chron.* 5 June 5/4 The grand finale..of the show is the chuting of the chute by big elephants.

2. To drive into or pen up in a chute. *U.S.*

1920 Mulford *J. Nelson* xxi. 234 Anybody knows that chutin' em [*sc.* cattle], and stampin' on th' brand is easier.

Chy-ike, variant of *Chi-hike.

Chypre (ʃipr). Also **chipre.** [Fr., = Cyprus.] A perfume from Cyprus.

1898 *Westm. Gaz.* 13 July 1/3 An air befogged with Chypre. 1901 *Ibid.* 2 Dec. 2/1 No woman who uses *chypre* has any sense of proportion. 1901 C. Holland *Mousmé* 82 With a cobwebby lace handkerchief which emitted a faint odour of chipre.

Cibarian, *a.* Add:

2. *Ent.* Of, pertaining to, or characterized by the structure of the mouth-parts; usually in *cibarian system,* a system of classification attributed to Fabricius, according to which the Arthropoda were arranged with reference to the character of the trophi. Also (less freq.) **Ciba·rial** *a.*

1839 Westwood *Introd. Mod. Classif. Insects* I. 21 The partial success with which the employment of the variation of the mouth was attended, probably induced Fabricius to construct his Cibarian system, founded upon the characters of the Trophi alone. 1880 *Encycl. Brit.* XIII. 147/2 The 'cibarian' (or mouth-system, originating with, or at any rate elaborated by, Fabricius).

Cicad (si·kæd). Anglicized form of Cicada.

1855 Singleton *Virgil* I. 164 With their chirp The plaintful cicads shall the vine-trees rend. 1887 Forbes *Insulinde* 23 The song of the cicads. 1920 *Edin. Rev.* Oct. 338 The homopterous hosts are leaf-hoppers and other small insects (allied to cicads).

Cicada. Add: **cicada-killer,** a large American digger-wasp, *Sphecius speciosus,* which kills the annual cicada and stores it as food.

1895 Comstock *Study Insects* 653.

Cicatricose, *a.* Add: **2.** *Ent.* (See quot.)

1826 Kirby & Sp. *Entomol.* xlvi. IV. 272 *Cicatricose,*.. having elevated spots of a different colour from the rest of the surface, resembling scars.

Cicero·nianist. [f. Ciceronian + -ist.] One who practises Ciceronianism.

1882 *Encycl. Brit.* XIV. 342/1 That elaborate polishing of periods which had been the delight of the Ciceronianists.

Cichlid (si·klid), *sb.* [ad. mod.L. *Cichlidæ,* f. Gr. κίχλη a fish, 'labrus'.] A fish of the family *Cichlidæ.* Also *adj.* So **Ci·chloid.**

1884 Goode *Nat. Hist. Aquatic Anim.* 275 The Demoiselle and the Cichlid families. 1889 *Cent. Dict.*, Cichloid *a.* and *sb.* 1914 *Brit. Museum Return* 150 Five new Cichlid Fishes from Africa. 1926 *Sunday at Home* July 591/1 Some of the cichlids are remarkable for their breeding habits.

Cichlomorphous (siklomǭ·ɹfəs), *a.* [f. mod.L. *Cichlomorphæ* (f. Gr. κίχλη a bird resembling the thrush + μορφή form) + -ous.] Of or belonging to the *Cichlomorphæ.*

1883 *Catal. Birds Brit. Mus.* VIII. Introd. p. vii, A Catalogue of Cichlomorphous genera.

Cicinal (sisi·năl), *a.* = Cincinnal.

1875 Bennett & Dyer tr. *Sachs' Text-bk. Bot.* 157 A Scorpioid (cicinal) Dichotomy. *Ibid.* 522 The Unilateral Cicinal (Scorpioid) Cyme. 1876 *Encycl. Brit.* IV. 125/1 Scorpioidal or cicinal cyme of Forget-me-not.

Cicindelid (sisi·ndĕlid), *a.* and *sb.* [f. mod.L. *Cicindela* or *Cicindelidæ,* f. L. *cicindela* a glow-worm, reduplication of *candela* candle.] Pertaining to, a member of, the genus *Cicindela* or family *Cicindelidæ* (tiger-beetles). Also **Cicindeli·deous, Cici·ndelous** *adjs.*

1839 Westwood *Introd. Mod. Classif. Ins.* I. 74 The numerical majority of the Carabideous over the Cicindelideous insects. 1872 Packard *Study Ins.* (ed. 3) 567 The Cicindelous genus Tricondyla. 1899 D. Sharp *Insects* II. 202 Péringuey found a breeding-ground of *M[anticora] tuberculata* near Kimberley; the larvae were living in the usual Cicindelid manner. 1914 Stebbing *Indian Forest Insects* 94 *C[icindela] sexpunctata* is a common little cicindelid found in the rice fields.

Ciconian (sikōᵘ·niăn), *a.* [f. L. *cicōnia* stork + -an.] Of or belonging to storks.

1725 Pope *Odyss.* IX. 68 But when his evening wheels o'erhung the main, Then conquest crown'd the fierce Ciconian train.

Ciconiiform (sikōᵘni,ifɔɹm), *a.* [ad. mod.L. *ciconiiformis,* f. *ciconia* stork: see -form.] Of or pertaining to the structure of the *Ciconiidæ* or stork family.

1882 W. A. Forbes in *Rep. Voy. H.M.S. Challenger* XI. 62 *note,* No views regarding the affinities of the Petrels other than that to the Laridæ..and that to the Ciconiiform birds have..been..advanced.

Ciconiine (sikōᵘ·ni,əin), *a.* [f. L. *cicōnia* stork + -ine [1].] Belonging to or having the characteristics of the *Ciconiinæ.* So **Cico·nioid,** a bird of the family *Ciconiidæ.*

1874 A. H. Garrod in *Proc. Zool. Soc.* 119 The Cathartidæ possess the ambiens, which, in conjunction with many other Ciconiine characters, leaves no doubt about their position. 1889 Nicholson & Lydekker *Palæont.* 1238 An undetermined Ciconioid from the Pikermi beds of Attica. 1893 Newton *Dict. Birds* 147 The Old-World Vultures..exhibit striking Ciconiine similarities.

Cidarid (si·dărid). [f. mod.L. *Cidaris* (Gr. κίδαρις royal tiara) + -id [2].] A sea urchin of the genus *Cidaris.* Also *attrib.* or *adj.*

1909 F. A. Bather in *Ann. & Mag. Nat. Hist.* Ser. VIII. III. 48 The truly Cidarid nature of the species. *Ibid.* 49 He.. pointed out that *C[idaris] keyserlingi* was a true Cidarid.

Cidaris. Add: A head-dress used by the Jewish high-priests; a low-crowned mitre.

c 1790 *Encycl. Brit.* V. 8/1. 1877 F. G. Lee *Gloss. Liturg. & Eccl. Terms* 86.

Cider. 2. Add:

cider brandy *U.S.* (examples); **cider cart** *U.S.* (see quot.); **cider cheese** = Cheese *sb.*[1] 4; **cider oil** (see quot.); **cider press** (U.S. examples); **cider royal** *U.S.* (see quots.); **cider vinegar,** a vinegar produced by the acetification of cider.

1813 Paulding *J. Bull & Br. Jon.* xix. (ed. 2) 97 These people are also very ingenious in making tin ware, brooms, *cider-brandy,..and tallow candles. 1845 S. Judd *Margaret* I. vii. 42 Distilleries for the manufacture of cider-brandy. 1859 Bartlett *Dict. Amer.* (ed. 2), *Apple Brandy,* a liquor distilled from fermented apple-juice; also called Cider Brandy. 1877 *Southern Hist. Soc. Papers* III. 17 The passage of a *cider-cart (a barrel on wheels) was a rare and exciting occurrence. 1849 N. Kingsley *Diary* 30 A cask of peaches..did not look any more like peaches than an old *cider cheese. 1859 Bartlett *Dict. Amer.* (ed. 2), **Cider Oil,* cider concentrated by boiling, to which honey is subsequently added. 1846 *Rep. U.S. Comm. Patents* (1847) 335 What I claim as my invention..is constructing the *cider press as herein described. 1856 Alice Cary *Married* 389 Fruits were ripe, cider-presses busy. 1811 *Niles' Register* 7 Sept. 10/2 [There] passed the falls of Ohio, from October 1, 1810, to May 5, 1811,..*Cider-royal, barrels 1350. 1828 T. Flint *Geog. Mississippi Valley* I. 235 What is called 'cider royal' or cider, that has been strengthened by boiling, or freezing. 1836 *Southern Lit. Messenger* II. 161 The chariot horses Mass Charles sent to the court house with a barrel of cider royal to Capt. R. 1858 Simmonds *Dict. Trade*, **Cider-vinegar,* vinegar made in Devonshire and America from refuse cider. 1917 *Jrnl. Chem. Soc.* CXII. I. 313 The volatile reducing substances in cider vinegar consist largely, if not wholly, of acetylmethylcarbinol, which is shown to be a normal constituent of this vinegar.

Ciel (sīl). [Fr., sky.] Sky-blue: a fashion shade.

1910 *Daily Chron.* 26 Feb. 4/5 [She] was in ciel blue with a blue velvet train and gold trimmings. 1923 *Daily Mail* 23 Apr. 7 Shades..of Saxe, Ciel, Jade.

Cig, colloq. abbrev. of Cigar, Cigarette, or *Cigarillo.

a 1889 *Broadside* (Barrère & L.) Dancing the jig, Every fellow with a cig, And a cig of confounded bad tobacco. 1919 C. Orr *Glorious Thing* xxiii, Have a cig. Go on! They're only Nannie's.

Cigar. Add: **1. b.** The pod of the catalpa tree; the Indian bean. *U.S.*

1876 *Field & Forest* II. 51, I verily believe that some boys..took their first lessons, in smoking, by using the 'beans' or 'cigars' of the Catalpa.

c. The brown colour of a cigar. Also *attrib.*

1923 *Daily Mail* 16 Apr. 1 Grey, Mole, Cigar, Champagne, Light Tan. *Ibid.* 15 Oct. 15/4 This season there is a vogue for brown fur, and ermine, caracul, and squirrel are dyed to provide lovely shades of cigar, dead gold or mahogany.

2. *cigar-box* (example; also *fig.*), *-maker* (examples); **cigar-butt**, the waste end of a cigar; **cigar-case** (earlier U.S. example); **cigar-fish**, a small cigar-shaped West Indian fish, *Decapterus punctatus*; **cigar leaf**, tobacco suitable for cigars; **cigar-plant**, a Mexican plant, *Cuphea platycentra*, having a scarlet tubular corolla tipped with black and white; **cigar-tree** *U.S.*, the catalpa.

1854 MARY J. HOLMES *Tempest & Sunshine* xx. 273 She.. saw him take from the *cigar-box a much soiled yellowish-looking letter. 1878 B. F. TAYLOR *Between Gates* 252 We have been circling about that cigar-box of a town. 1907 tr. *Hanausek's Microsc. Techn. Prod.* 219 *Cedrela odorata* L., Spanish Cedar, Cigar-box Wood. 1893 W. K. POST *Harvard Stories* 225 He hurled his *cigar butt into the fireplace. 1902 *Daily Chron.* 5 Apr. 5/1 London's gutters now annually receive in cigar-butts and cigarette-ends tobacco to the value of £200,000. 1846 *Boston* (Mass.) *Almanac* 163/1 *Cigar Cases; Wallets; Pocket Books. 1884 GOODE *Nat. Hist. Aquatic Anim.* 325 The Round Robin—*Decapterus punctatus*..or, as it is called at Pensacola, the '*Cigar-fish'. 1863 *Trans. Ill. Agric. Soc.* (1865) V. 669 Tobacco of this description should be..prized lightly in the casks so as to admit of a free and open leaf, such being mostly required for *cigar leaf. 1888 *Buck's Handbk. Med. Sci.* VI. 36/2 *Cigarmakers' cramp must be an exceedingly rare affection. I can find reports upon it by only two observers. 1902 *Encycl. Brit.* XXXIII. 411/2 The Cigar-Makers' National Union dates from 1864. 1872 *Amer. Naturalist* VI. 727 The beautiful catalpa, or '*cigar-tree' (*Catalpa bignonioides*), grew as a common species among the underwoods. 1897 G. B. SUDWORTH *Nomencl. Arbor. Flora U.S.* 335.

Cigarette. 2. Add:
cigarette-box, catcher, -end, habit, -holder (example), *-maker, -merchant, smoking*; *cigarette-laden* adj.; **cigarette beetle** (see quots.); **cigarette card**, a picture card inserted by the makers in a packet or box of cigarettes; so *cigarette picture*; **cigarette heart**, a condition of the heart induced by excessive smoking of cigarettes; **cigarette lighter**, a pocket mechanical apparatus for lighting a cigarette; **cigarette machine**, a machine for the manufacture of cigarettes; **cigarette paper**, paper or a paper in which cigarettes or a cigarette is rolled; **cigarette tobacco**, tobacco specially adapted for cigarette making.

1895 COMSTOCK *Study Insects* 553 The *Cigarette Beetle, *Lasioderma serricorne*..is a serious pest in tobacco manufactories, infesting the dried tobacco-leaves and the manufactured products. 1896 J. B. SMITH *Econ. Entom.* 193 The *Lasioderma serricorne*, popularly known as the 'tobacco-' or 'cigarette-beetle'. 1890 *Peel City Guardian* 11 Jan. 3/5 The smoker's set of cigar and *cigarette box. 1916 *Punch* 11 Oct. 272 Please, Sir, have you got any *cigarette cards? 1921 *Dict. Occup. Terms* (1927) § 469 **Cigarette catcher*; *cigarette machine receiver*; gathers finished cigarettes from cigarette machine. 1893 *Graphic* 4 Feb. 110/2 The..dearth of..*cigarette-ends did not seem to depress him at all. 1902 *Westm. Gaz.* 24 Sept. 10/2 Someone dropped a lighted cigarette-end in the hay. 1914 *Evening News* 10 Oct. 2/7 Our officers..brought the *cigarette habit back with them from the Crimea, where they learned it from the Russians. 1908 *Daily Chron.* 29 Jan. 7/2 Witness examined his heart and found no organic disease; it was a '*cigarette heart'. 1879 MRS. HUNGERFORD *Airy Fairy Lilian* xv, Enough meerschaum pipes, and *cigarette holders, and tobacco stands to stock a small shop. 1905 *Daily Chron.* 17 July 8/6 The *cigarette-laden air of the sensuous room. 1915 *Scotsman* 26 Jan. 5/3 Colonel Thompson, of the Black Watch, asks for tinder *cigarette lighters. 1929 M. DE LA ROCHE *Whiteoaks* ix. 135 'The very thing for him!' she exclaimed to Alayne, energetically snapping her cigarette-lighter. *a* 1884 *Sci. Amer.* XXXVIII. 344 (Knight) French *cigarette machine. 1890 F. M. CRAWFORD (*title*) A *Cigarette Maker's Romance. 1894 *Daily News* 1 Oct. 5/3 The cigarette-makers' cramp, so well-known in the tobacco manufactories of Spain. 1897 *Lippincott's Med. Dict.*, Cigar-makers' cramp or Cigarette-makers' cramp. Painful contraction of the flexors of the fingers, sometimes seen in cigar- and cigarette-makers. 1901 *Brit. Med. Jrnl.* 13 July 100/1 For the purpose of selling ..any cigarettes, *cigarette paper, or any substitute for the same. 1912 EDGAR WALLACE *Private Selby* viii, What you ought to do..is to collect *cigarette pictures. 1906 *Westm. Gaz.* 10 Sept. 1/2 *Cigarette-smoking was then [*sc.* 1856] habitual in St. Petersburg. 1905 in *Daily Chron.* 10 Oct. 6/2 The..manufacture of cigarettes or *cigarette tobacco.

Cigarillo (sigari·lo͝u, ‖þigarī·lyo). [Sp., dim. of *cigarro* CIGAR.] A small cigar.

1832 W. IRVING *Alhambra, Local Trad.* (1875) 77 Your muleteer..will suspend the smoking of his cigarillo to tell some tale of Moslem gold buried. 1896 *Act* 59 & 60 *Vict.* c. 28 § 5 (3) The expression 'tobacco' in this section includes cigars, cigarillos, cigarettes, and snuff. 1909 *Daily Chron.* Summer No. 2/2 His accursed cigarillo, carelessly flung down, had reduced the seat of learning to ashes.

Cigarito. *U.S.* Also -ita. (Earlier examples.)

1844 G. W. KENDALL *Sante Fé Exped.* II. 131 The prettiest senora..can be seen at almost any time with a cigarrito in her mouth. 1848 E. BRYANT *California* xxv. 329 The cigarita is freely used by the senoras and senoritas.

Cilia, *sb. pl.* Add:
2. b. *Ornith.* The barbicels of a feather.

1893 NEWTON *Dict. Birds* 240 The *cilia* or barbicels with their *hamuli* or hooks are outgrowths of the radii.

Ciliation. Add: *concr.* An assemblage of cilia, the fine hairs of a fringed margin.

1852 DANA *Crustacea* I. 302 The ciliation of the front is quite as long as the front margin of either lobe.

Ciliato- (sili͡ēi·to), used as comb. form of CILIATE, as in *ciliato-dentate, -serrate* adjs., having ciliated teeth or serrations.

1871 W. A. LEIGHTON *Lichen-Flora* 32 Margins ciliato-dentate. *Ibid.* 33 Thallus..ciliato-dissected.

Cilician (sili·ʃiăn), *a.* and *sb.* [f. *Cilicia* + -AN.] Of or belonging to, a native of, Cilicia, a country of Asia Minor.

1594 J. KING *On Jonas* xxvi. (1597) 345 Hee had a purpose..to goe no further then to..the Cilician sea...But Ionas is borne from the Cilician to the Ægean. 1768 TUCKER *Lt. Nat.* II. I. xxiii. 258 The last who staid was the Cilician of Tarsus. *Ibid.* 263 The Cilician doctrines interpreted by philosophers. 1837 *Penny Cycl.* VII. 163/1 The annual tribute of the Cilicians to Darius consisted of 360 white horses and 500 talents of silver. 1845 *Encycl. Metrop.* XXV. 383/2 Mount Amanus..was anciently the boundary between Cilicia and Syria, the narrow pass on the beach being closed by strong walls and well-protected gates, called the Amanic or Cilician gates. 1883 *Encycl. Brit.* XVI. 531/1 The worship of Mithras became known to the Romans through the Cilician pirates captured by Pompey about 70 B.C. 1902 *Ibid.* XXVII. 94/1 The Cilicians appear to have belonged to that great family of non-Aryan tribes which included the Syro-Cappadocians, or Hittites, and the Proto-Armenians. 1920 *Glasgow Herald* 22 Nov. 12 The Committees of Finance and Foreign Affairs, which are sitting on the subjects of the Syrian and Cilician credits.

Ci:lio-re·tinal, *a.* Relating to the ciliary region of the retina.

1890 BILLINGS *Med. Dict.* I. 280/2 *Cilioretinal vessels*, vessels sometimes seen passing from posterior ciliary system to retina at optic nerve entrance. 1907 *Practitioner* June Plate foll. 814 Fundus Oculi showing large Cilio-Retinal Artery supplying Macular Region.

Cimarron (simarō͝u·n). Also **cimmaron.** [Sp., properly adj. = wild, untamed.] A Spanish-American name of the Rocky Mountain sheep, *Ovis montana*.

1854 MAYNE REID *Hunters' Feast* xxvi. 226 The grizzly bears..had reached the cliff in chase of the cimmaron.

Cimbia (si·mbiă). [It.]
1. *Arch.* A fillet or ring round the shaft of a column; an apophyge.

1613–39 I. JONES in Leoni *Palladio's Archit.* (1742) I. 38 A small Boultel or Torus B, under the Cimbia. 1664 EVELYN tr. *Freart's Archit.* 127 The Cimbia beneath the Astragal immediately above the Contraction. 1842 GWILT *Archit.* Gloss. 950.

2. *Anat.* A slender white band crossing the ventral surface of the crus cerebri (Century Dict. 1889).

Cimblin. *U.S.* Variant of SIMLIN.

1814 J. TAYLOR *Arator* 124 Cimblins or pumpkins.

Cimbrian (si·mbriăn), *a.* and *sb.* [f. *Cimbri* + -AN.] **A.** *adj.* Of or pertaining to the Cimbri, an ancient people of central Europe of unknown affinities. *Cimbric Chersonese* or *Peninsula*, Jutland. **B.** *sb.* One of the Cimbri. So **Cimbric** (si·mbrik) = above adj.; *sb.* the language of the Cimbri.

1781 GIBBON *Decl. & F.* xxxvi. (1787) III. 499 The broken trophies of Cimbric and Armenian victories. 1844 LONGF. *Arsenal at Springfield* 14 Through Cimbric forest roars the Norseman's song. 1853 LYELL *Princ. Geol.* (ed. 9) xx. 331 This event, commonly called the 'Cimbrian Deluge', is supposed to have happened about three centuries before the Christian era. 1862 *Chambers's Encycl.* III. 35/1 The extremity of the peninsula called from them the Cimbric Chersonese, now Jütland. 1876 *Encycl. Brit.* V. 780/1 Cimbri, or Cimbrians,..one of the most formidable enemies of the Roman power. 1879 *Ibid.* X. 7/1 All the modern sections of the Cimbrian Celts. 1902 *Ibid.* XXVII. 408/1 Denmark, in the strictest geographical sense, comprises the northern portion of the Cimbric Peninsula called Jutland (Jylland) and the Danish Islands.

Cimelia (simī·liă). Delete *Obs.* and add:

a 1889 *Art Jrnl.* VII. 210 (Cent. Dict.) The monsters of porcelain which compose the cimelia of the days of the Duchess of Portland.

Ciminite (si·minəit). *Min.* [f. *Cimini*, the name of mountains in the neighbourhood of Viterbo, Italy + -ITE¹.] A name for a type of trachytic lavas (see quot.).

1908 HARKER *Petrol. for Stud.* (ed. 4) 188 In examples from Bolsena in Italy the phenocrysts are of alkali-felspar, anorthite, augite, and biotite... One from the Viterbo district has labradorite in place of anorthite. A somewhat more basic type, from the Mti Cimini in the latter district, is styled ciminite.

Cimlin *U.S.*: see SIMLIN I and SIMNEL 2.

Cimmaron, var. f. *CIMARRON.

Cimmerian. Add: *sb.* **a.** One of the Cimmerii. **b.** One of a nomadic people of antiquity, the earliest known inhabitants of the Crimea who were expelled and overran Asia Minor in the 7th century B.C. Also *adj.*, of or pertaining to these.

1588 SHAKS. *Tit. A.* II. iii. 72 Your swarth Cymerion. *c* 1790 *Encycl. Brit.* (1797) V. 9/1 [The Cimbri] are said to have been descended from the Asiatic Cimmerians. 1862 *Chambers's Encycl.* III. 35/1 The Cimmerian Bosporus (Strait of Yenikale). 1871 BRYANT *Odyss.* xi, There the people dwell, Of the Cimmerians, in eternal cloud And darkness. 1886 *Encycl. Brit.* XXI. 577/1 The Cimmerians reached Asia Minor through Thrace. *Ibid.*, The Dniester was the grave of the Cimmerian kings. 1902 *Ibid.* XXV. 720/1 The Phrygian power was broken in the 9th or 8th century B.C. by the Cimmerians, who entered Asia Minor through Armenia.

Cinch, *sb.* Add (See also SINCH, SYNCH):
2. *fig.* A firm or secure hold; a sure, safe, or easy thing; a dead certainty.

1888 *N. Y. World* 22 July (Farmer) The racehorse owner, who has a cinch bottled up for a particular race. 1893 *Sun* (N.Y.) 10 Mar. 1/1 (Funk) Up to within two weeks Keene has proceeded upon the theory that he had a cinch. 1904 G. H. LORIMER *Old Gorgon Graham* 8 A man's son is entitled to a chance in the business, but not a cinch. *a* 1909 'O. HENRY' *Trimmed Lamp* etc. 211 'It's tough to be alone in New York—that's a cinch,' said Mr. Donovan. *Ibid.* 256 The devil seems to have a cinch on all the business in New York. 1911 H. QUICK *Yellowstone N.* iii. 69 The recent progress in bacteriological science..seemed to make the diagnosis a cinch. 1921 R. D. PAINE *Comr. Rolling Ocean* iv. 73 Going to sea was a perfect cinch with just enough to do to keep a fellow healthy.

3. A variety of all-fours, also called *double pedro* and *high five*.

1895 MANSON *Sporting Dict.*

Cinch (sinʃ), *v.* *U.S.* [f. CINCH *sb.*]
1. (Also with *up*.) *trans.* To fix (a saddle, etc.) securely by means of a girth; to fix (a girth).

1873 J. H. BEADLE *Undevel. West* xv. 273 With all set and everything tightly 'cinched', we took the start. 1897 *Outing* (U.S.) XXIX. 457/1 As the moment for the start approaches, the saddles are cinched tighter. 1905 A. ADAMS *Outlet* 310 Saddles were..cinched on waiting horses. 1912 JEB. HART *Vigilante Girl* x. 143 Each mule would carefully blow himself up to prevent his girth being cinched too tightly. 1912 MULFORD & CLAY *Buck Peters* iv. 58 Buck cinched up his saddle on Allday and led him out of the stable.

b. *intr.* To fix a saddle-girth.

1887 *St. Nicholas* XIV. 732 At Giles's ranch, on the divide, the party halted to cinch up. 1913 MULFORD *Coming of Cassidy* ii. 35 Cinching deftly, [he] slung himself up by the stirrup.

2. *fig.* To get (a person) into a tight place; to secure a hold upon. (See also quot. 1875.)

1875 *Scribner's Monthly* July X. 277/1 [At San Francisco] a man who is hurt in a mining transaction is 'cinched'. 1881 *N. Y. Times* 18 Dec. in *N. & Q.* Ser. VI. V. 65/1 It is unfairly said that the Northern Pacific Company intends to 'cinch' the settlers by exacting large prices for its lands. 1904 F. LYNDE *Grafters* ix. 125, I have it on pretty good authority that the ring is cinching the other companies right and left. 1910 ROOSEVELT in *Outlook* 3 Sept. 2/1 If the rich man strives to use his wealth to destroy others, I will cinch him if I can. 1916 H. L. WILSON *Somewhere in Red Gap* vii. 292 I'm cinched for hell, anyway, and don't have to make it tighter by torturing poor dumb brutes.

3. In the game of cinch, to protect (a trick) by playing a higher trump than the five (Webster 1911).

4. To finish properly.

1903 A. H. LEWIS *Boss* 315 Melting Moses..goes after him to cinch the play. I tell you one thing; he cinches it.

Cinch- (siŋk), f. *CINCHO- used before vowels, as in *cinchamidine, cinchene, cincholine* (see quots.).

1881 *Jrnl. Chem. Soc.* XL. 1045 Cinchamidine, $C_{20}H_{26}N_2O$, a new alkaloid found in the aqueous mother-liquors from the purification of homocinchonidine sulphate, is obtained by the addition of ammonia to this liquid. 1882 *Ibid.* XLII. 225 Nitrous acid has no action on cinchene. *Ibid.* 1114 Cincholine is prepared from the first mother-liquor obtained in the manufacture of quinine sulphate. *Ibid.* Cincholine is a pale-yellow oil, lighter than water. 1890 BILLINGS *Med. Dict.* I. 281/1 *Cinchene*, $C_{19}H_{20}N_2$, a crystallizable, volatile base obtained by partial decomposition of cinchonine. 1906 *Watts' Dict. Chem.* II. 178/2 Cinchamidine ..occurs in the mother-liquors from homocinchonidine.

Cincher (si·nʃəɹ). [app. f. *CINCH *v.* + -ER¹.] (See quots.)

1921 *Dict. Occup. Terms* (1927) § 399 *Plaiter-down*; *cincher, dodger*; folds wet cloth, in rope state for bleaching. *Ibid.* § 943 Plaiter, plaiter-down; cincher, cloth folder.

Cincho- (si·ŋko). *Chem.* Combining form of CINCHONA, as in *cinchocerotic, -cerotin, -meronic, -tannic, -toxin, -vatin* (f. the species *Cinchona ovata*): see quots.

1857 MILLER *Elem. Chem., Org.* 276 Aricine or cinchovatine. 1875 *Jrnl. Chem. Soc.* XXVIII. 89 Cinchomeronic acid crystallises anhydrous; its calcium salt is $(C_{11}H_5NO_8)_2Ca_3 . 10H_2O$. 1878 *Ibid.* XXXIV. 157 This base is oxidised by permanganate to formic acid and cinchotenine—$C_{19}N_{22}N_2O + O_4 = C_{18}H_{20}N_2O_3 + CH_2O_2$. 1884 *Ibid.* XLVI. 332 Cinchocerotic acid, $C_{24}H_{22}O_2$. *Ibid.*, Cinchocerotin..had been deposited in copper tubes through which hot alcohol was passed after having exhausted a mixture of calcium hydroxide and South American calisaya bark. 1886 *Encycl. Brit.* XX. 184/2 The alkaloids appear to exist in cinchona bark chiefly in combination with cinchotannic and quinic acids. 1907 *Jrnl. Chem. Soc.* XCII. I. 63 Nitrosoquinotoxine and the sulphonamide of cinchotoxine are not decomposed by sodium ethoxide and nitrobenzene.

Cinchol (si·ŋkǫl). *Chem.* [f. CINCH- + -OL.] An alcohol, resembling cholesterol, found in all true cinchona barks.

1885 *Jrnl. Chem. Soc.* XLVIII. II. 1076 Cinchol, $C_{20}H_{34}O + H_2O$, occurs in all true cinchona barks, but is not found in *China cuprea*. *Ibid.*, Cinchol is identical with Liebermann's oxyquinoterpene. 1906 *Watts' Dict. Chem.* II. 175/1.

Cinchon- (siŋkǫn), in names of alkaloids derived from cinchona.

1879 *Jrnl. Chem. Soc.* XXXVI. 169 Cinchonichine. 1888 *Ibid.* LIV. 380 Cinchonibine is insoluble in ether but crystallises from boiling alcohol in prismatic needles. *Ibid.*, Cinchonifine is insoluble in ether. 1893 THORPE *Dict. Applied Chem.* III. 914/1 Cinchonibine $C_{19}H_{22}N_2O$ is one of ten bases formed when cinchonine sulphate is heated with sulphuric acid.

Cinchono- (siŋkō͝u·no), comb. form of CINCHONA.

1886 *Encycl. Brit.* XX. 184/2 A red-colouring matter, known as cinchono-fulvic acid or cinchona red.

Cincinnatian (sinsinæ·tiăn), *a.*² [f. *Cincinnati* + -AN.] Of or belonging to Cincinnati in Ohio; *spec.* in *Geol.* designating a group of formations of late Lower Silurian age (see quots.).

1899 *Science* X. 876 Probably in no other region is the succession of these [Lorraine and Richmond] faunas so complete as about Cincinnati, and this fact justifies the recognition of the term Cincinnatian. 1906 CHAMBERLIN & SALISBURY *Geol.* II. 310 Cincinnatian (Neo-Champlainic): Richmond beds, Lorraine beds, Utica shales.

Cinctoplanula (siŋktoplæ·niŭlă). *Zool.* [irreg. f. L. *cinctus* girt + PLANULA.] A girdled planula; the collared embryo of sponges.

1884 HYATT in *Proc. Boston Soc. Nat. Hist.* (1888) XXIII. 81 The gastrula [of certain sponges] evidently occupies a stage between that of the amphiblastula, or the parenchymula when that is present and the cinctoplanula or girdled planula. *Ibid.* 89 A stage of the cinctoplanula in which the collar is completed.

Cinder, *sb.* 7. Add: *cinder-burner, -fire*; **cinder-cone**, a cone formed round the mouth of a volcano by debris cast up during eruption; **cinder track** = *cinder-path*; also *attrib.*

1881 *Instr. Census Clerks* (1885) 92 Wrought Iron Manufacture:..*Cinder Burner. 1887 P. MCNEILL *Blawearie* 165 Lyle the cinder-burner has been advised to shift from the Howe Colliery to Warlock Hill. 1921 *Dict. Occup. Terms* (1927) § 278 *Cinder burner,.. slag burner*; roasts tap cinder from puddling or blast furnace to make bulldog. 1850 DANA *Geol. U.S. Exploring Exped.* 354 *Cinder cones in the parts of the Pacific under examination are of various heights, to two thousand feet. 1885 GEIKIE *Geol.* (ed. 2) 227 Tuff-Cones, Cinder-Cones. Successive eruptions of fine dust and stones. 1905 CHAMBERLIN & SALISBURY *Geol.* I. 580 The larger portion of the lava blown into the air by the expanding gas-bubbles falls back in the immediate vicinity of the vent and builds up a cinder-cone. 1868 JOYNSON *Metals* 111 Cast-iron, which may require to be annealed in too large a quantity to render the expense of charcoal very agreeable, may be heated in a *cinder fire. 1887 SHEARMAN *Athletics & Football* (Badm. Libr.) 182 Nearly all the regular paths are '*cinder tracks'. 1893 *Outing* (U.S.) Nov. XXI. 135/2 There is a sharp line dividing cinder-track athletes from cross-country runners. 1917 MATHEWSON *Sec. Base Sloan* xi. 143 It had..a cinder track one-eight mile in circumference.

Cinderella. Add: *fig.* A neglected or despised member, partner, or the like.

[1846 D. JERROLD *Mrs. Caudle* ii. 4 It's enough for a wife to sit like a Cinderella by the ashes.] 1896 *Daily News* 25 July 8/3 For many years the Manchester, Sheffield, and Lincolnshire has been a cinderella among railways. 1914 *Scotsman* 14 Oct. 10/1 Their [*sc.* the Gaelic-speaking peoples of Scotland] language did not deserve to be the Cinderella of all the languages of the British Empire. 1925 *Morris Owner* Jan. 1185 Essex has been the Cinderella of the Home Counties ever since the advent of the motor car.

Cine (si·nĭ), colloq. or commercial abbrev. of *CINEMA used in comb., as *cine-art, -camera, -film, -goer, -matinée, -negative, -photography, -projector*; **cine-vari·ety**, a variety entertainment including a cinematographic show. Cf. F. *ciné* (1917).

1928 *Daily Express* 9 July 9 *Cine-art consists of adding smoothness to the appeal made to eye, mind, and emotion. 1920 V. STEER *Secrets Cinema* 25 Crowds of ebullient amateurs all so eager to 'strut their little hour' in front of the *cine camera. 1897 C. M. HEPWORTH *Animated Photogr.* 83 Hints and Cautions: Care of *Cinefilms, etc. 1921 *Oxford Times* 4 Mar. 4 One of the oldest and most accomplished favourites of the *Cine-goer. 1929 *Sunday Dispatch* 13 Jan. 16 When these films..are exhibited to the vast crowd of ciné-goers. 1908 *Westm. Gaz.* 6 Oct. 12/2 '*Cine-matinee' at the Pavilion. 1911 WEBSTER, **Cine-negative*, a continuous film of chronophotograph negatives taken in a cinematograph. 1920 V. STEER *Secr. Cinema* 108 Aerial *cinephotography. 1929 WHEELER *Amateur Cinematog.* 87 A *ciné-projector works on the same principle as a ciné-camera. 1928 *Daily Express* 20 Jan. 1, I am still looking for sites for new *cine-variety theatres. 1928 *Daily News* 7 Nov. 6/5 He agrees with Mr. Arnold Bennett in condemning talking pictures; but in favouring cine-variety he is opposed to Mr. Bennett.

Cinema (si·nĭmă). (See also *KINEMA.) [Abbreviation of *CINEMATOGRAPH, after F. *cinéma*.] A popular abbreviation of *CINEMATOGRAPH, q.v.; hence (short for *cinema hall*, etc.), a building in which cinematographic films are exhibited.

[1899 H. V. HOPWOOD *Living Pictures* 184 The Dom-Martin Cinéma is said to possess a spring-escapement mechanism.] 1910 *Daily Chron.* 7 Mar. 6/7 'Cinematograph' —which has just been cut down in a glaring advertisement to 'cinema'. 1913 V. STEER *Romance Cinema* 11 The so-called 'comic' films from France which one sees on the cinema. 1913 *Punch* 19 Feb. 147 Our Village Cinema. 1914 *Scotsman* 17 Sept. 1/5 Princes Cinema. 131 Princes Street. 1920 *Punch* 22 Sept. 234/1 How odd it is that our Papas Keep taking us to cinemas.

b. *attrib.*, as *cinema film, -goer, hall, play, rights* (pl.), *show, star, theatre.*

1912 *Field* 14 Sept. 548/2 A *cinema film of myself boxing a round or two. 1921 *Dict. Occup. Terms* (1927) § 882 Cinema film producer. 1920 *Q. Rev.* July 182 Young *cinema-goers. 1928 *Observer* 18 Mar. 15/7 As for chocolates, the cinema-goer's appetite is probably larger than the theatre-goer's. 1913 V. STEER *Romance Cinema* 124 The *cinema hall will become the social club of the future. 1920 *Q. Rev.* July 177 Prospectuses of new producing companies and cinema halls. 1913 V. STEER *Romance Cinema* 28 The first *cinema play produced in England was, I believe, 'The Soldier's Courtship'. 1920 — *Secrets Cinema* 49 £1500 is a fairly common figure to pay for the *cinema rights of a book. 1913 — *Romance Cinema* 112 First and foremost the *cinema show is a means of amusement. *Ibid.* 43 To become a *cinema 'star' is not an easy matter. *Ibid.* 29 Provincial *cinema theatres. 1915 'BARTIMEUS' *Tall Ship* iv. 69 The advertisement of a cinema theatre occupied a boarding near the landing place.

Cinematic (sinĭmæ·tik), *a.* [f. *CINEMA, after *cinematograph*: see -IC.] Of or pertaining to the cinematograph.

1927 *Daily Express* 10 Oct. 13/3 A masterpiece of cinematic treatment. 1929 *Evening News* 9 Jan. 6/6 The cunning lighting and grouping of the scenes make 'Thou Shalt Not' a piece of real cinematic art.

Cinematize (si·nĭmătəiz), *v.* [f. as prec. + -IZE.] *trans.* To adapt (a play, story) to the cinematograph; to make a 'film' of.

1919 *Book Monthly* June 457/2 Authors who have the good fortune to have stories cinematized. 1928 *Musical Times* 1 Aug. 735 In the cinematizing of a novel only the story is taken.

Cinematograph (sinĭmæ·tǒgraf), *sb.* [ad. F. *cinématographe*, f. Gr. κίνημα, κινηματο- movement + -GRAPH. Cf. KINEMATOGRAPH.] A device (and the necessary apparatus) by which a series of instantaneous photographs of moving objects taken in rapid succession are projected on a screen in similarly rapid and intermittent succession so as to produce the illusion of a single moving scene. Also (= *cinematograph camera*), a camera used for taking such pictures; (= *cinematograph picture* or *show*), an exhibition or show of such pictures; a moving picture, 'the pictures' (cf. *CINEMA).

[1896 (Feb. 21) Cinématographe: see KINEMATOGRAPH.] 1896 *Times* 22 Feb. 15/3 The Cinematograph..is a contrivance belonging to the same family as Edison's kinetoscope..but in a rather higher stage of development. 1896 (Mar. 26) Cinématographe [see *ANIMATOGRAPH]. 1896 O. WINTER in *New Rev.* May 513 The Cinematograph is but realism reduced to other terms, less fallible and more amusing. 1902 *Encycl. Brit.* XXVII. 95 The cinematograph, invented by Edison in 1894, is the result of the introduction of the flexible film into photography in place of glass. 1902 MRS. E. COTES *Those Delightful Amer.* v, We have had a cinematograph down from London for the children's school treat. 1920 *Q. Rev.* July 183 On the more ambitious side of the cinematograph we have the 'picturisation' of novels and plays. *fig.* 1901 *Academy* 5 Oct. 290/2 *Kim*..is a kinematograph of a people. 1905 *Westm. Gaz.* 18 May 2/1 The moving cinematograph of London traffic. 1906 *Daily Chron.* 30 June 6/2 Handwriting was a cinematograph of the heart.

b. *attrib.* and *Comb.*, as *cinematograph actor, actress, camera, entertainment, exhibition, film, outfit, picture, show, theatre.*

1914 *Scotsman* 8 Oct. 3/3 The adventures, observations, and experiences of a *cinematograph actress in West African forests. 1897 C. M. HEPWORTH *Animated Photogr.* 90 You have a *cinematograph camera. 1907 *Daily Chron.* 8 Nov. 3/5 Promiscuous *cinematograph entertainments. 1898 *Daily News* 24 Aug. 3/5 The show..consisted of a *cinematographe exhibition, and had been attracting large audiences. 1897 C. M. HEPWORTH *Animated Photogr.* 99 *Cinematograph films are usually manipulated in the dark-room. 1907 C. URBAN *Cinematograph* 17 Cinematograph film subjects of present-day events. 1925 E. F. NORTON *Fight for Everest, 1924* 57 Mules laden with *cinematograph outfit. 1897 C. M. HEPWORTH *Animated Photogr.* 6 *Cinematograph Pictures. 1907 C. URBAN *Cinematograph* 14 On the foundation of cinematograph pictures, imagination builds to right and left. 1912 *Home Chat* 24 Feb. 393/1 A few theatres and *cinematograph shows. 1913 V. STEER *Romance Cinema* 112 Chairman of two of the biggest circuits of *cinematograph theatres.

Cinema·tograph, *v.* [f. prec.] *trans.* To make a cinematographic record of.

1897 *Westm. Gaz.* 10 Dec. 10/3 Cinematographing the sun's eclipse. 1898 *Sci. Amer.* Suppl. 26 Feb. 18481 M. Camille Flammarion has undertaken to cinematograph the sky. He takes 3,000 photographs a night when it is clear. 1900 *Westm. Gaz.* 17 Sept. 4/2 The enchanting spectacle which cinematographed itself for us as we ascended. 1907 C. URBAN *Cinematograph* 20 The difficulties of cinematographing interiors.

Cinematographer (si:nĭmătǫ·grăfəɹ). [f. as prec. + -ER¹.] One who takes cinematographic pictures.

1897 C. M. HEPWORTH *Animated Photogr.* 97 A band-camera man chooses a time when such figures are not in the way: the cinematographer can do the same, but a hundred people may surge in front of his instrument before the exposure is finished. 1909 J. H. SKRINE *Pastor Ovium* 220 If our cinematographers had the instruments which could look into the dark backward and abysm of time. 1926 *Glasgow Herald* 1 Apr. 4 On his latest expedition he started from Kano, in Nigeria, with his cinematographer.

Cinematographic (sinĭmætogræ·fik), *a.* [f. *CINEMATOGRAPH *sb.* + -IC.] Of, pertaining to, concerned with the cinematograph or cinematography.

1897 C. M. HEPWORTH *Animated Photogr.* 90 The shutter is an important detail in the cinematographic camera. *Ibid.* 92 The lens which is best suited for cinematographic projection. 1898 *Westm. Gaz.* 3 May 5/2 Cinematographic experts. 1928 *Observer* 15 July 13/1 A skilled photographer, he is making a cinematographic record of his tour.

So **Ci:nematogra·phical** *a.*, **Ci:nematogra·phically** *adv.*

1898 *Westm. Gaz.* 21 May 6/3 The photograph was produced, and others, and his lordship, passing them before the interviewer's eyes cinematographically, clearly illustrated the process. 1912 F. S. CAREY *G. Goodwill's Elem. Mech.* (1913) Pref. 5 The cinematographical pictures by which the motion of balls moving under gravity is exhibited. 1923 *Contemp. Rev.* Jan. 71 The most striking analogy of Bergson was to speak of the intellect as cinematographical. 1928 *Daily Express* 12 Dec. 19 The almost cinematographically spectacular speed of his dash to his father's sick-bed.

Cinematographist (sinĭmătǫ·grăfist). = *CINEMATOGRAPHER.

1898 *Advt.*, Up-to-date Cinematography... Cinematographist, Mr. G. H. Philp. 1903 *Daily Chron.* 3 Nov. 5/1 The 'Bradford Argus'. At the Diamond Jubilee of 1897 it sent its cinematographist to London.

Cinematography (sinĭmătǫ·grăfi). [f. *CINEMATOGRAPH *sb.*: see -GRAPHY.] The use of the cinematograph; the art of taking and reproducing 'moving pictures'.

1897 C. M. HEPWORTH *Animated Photogr.* 7 The fact that the Edison pictures were far too dense to be satisfactorily projected was recognised in the very early days of cinematography. 1903 *Photo-Miniature* July 174 An expert in photography and cinematography (or biographic) methods of photography. 1907 C. URBAN *Cinematograph* 29 Dr. Doyen (Paris) has for the past ten years applied cinematography to record rare and difficult surgical operations. 1920 V. STEER *Secr. Cinema* 115 Home cinematography holds out many alluring possibilities.

Cinematoscope (sinĭmæ·tǒskoup). [f. Gr. κίνημα, κινηματο- motion + -SCOPE.] A form of cinematograph.

A machine was patented under the name *kinematoscope* in the United States in 1861.

1899 H. V. HOPWOOD *Living Pictures* 98 The inventor [*sc.* Birt Acres] found, to his surprise, that the programmes issued under Royal auspices referred to his invention as the 'Cinematoscope'. 1908 E. V. LUCAS *Over Bemerton's* xii. 120 That curious modern extension of the illustrated newspaper—the cinematoscope.

Cinene (sinī·n). Also **cyn-**. *Chem.* [f. next + -ENE.] A terpene derived from cineol. Hence **Cine·nic** *a.*

1884 *Jrnl. Chem. Soc.* XLVI. 1364 On dry distillation it [*sc.* cynene dihydrochloride] is decomposed into cynene and hydrochloric acid. 1885 *Ibid.* XLVIII. I. 172 Pure cynene is best prepared by warming a mixture of the iodide, $C_{10}H_{18}I_2$ (3 parts), with aniline (4 parts), and distilling the product in a current of steam. 1905 *Ibid.* LXXXVIII. I. 409 Cinenic acid. *Ibid.* 414 Cinene yields white needles..of an additive compound with hydrogen bromide in acetic acid solution.

Cineol (si·nĭǫl). *Chem.* [f. mod.L. *oleum cinæ* (reversed) oil of wormwood + -OL.] A volatile compound, $C_{10}H_{18}O$, occurring in oil of cajeput, oil of rosemary, and other oils. Hence **Cineo·lic** *a.*

1885 *Jrnl. Chem. Soc.* XLVIII. I. 172 Cyneol diiodide is formed when iodide acts on cyneol diluted with light petroleum. 1888 *Ibid.* LIV. 1205 Cineolic acid, $C_{10}H_{16}O_5$, is prepared by oxidising cineol with potassium permanganate. 1889 *Ibid.* LVI. 1072 The lower boiling fraction of oil of sage contains pinene and cineole. 1895 *Bloxam's Chem.* (ed. 8) 542 Cineol, $C_{10}H_{18}O$, is the chief constituent of eucalyptus oil.

Cinephone (si·nĭfo͝un). [f. *CINE + *-PHONE.] A former name for an apparatus designed for the production of a talking film.

1913 *Kelso Chron.* 15 Aug. 2/4 The Cinephone, which will enable the actor without any restriction to play his part and to have his voice and action recorded in absolute union. 1921 *Observer* 13 Mar. 14/2 These two men claim that their 'Cinephone', as they call it, makes the talking film a commercial possibility.

Cinerascent, erron. for CINERESCENT.

1816 STEPHENS in Shaw's *Gen. Zool.* IX. II. 540 The breast and rump cinerascent. 1887 W. PHILLIPS *Brit. Discomycetes* 272 White or yellowish-white, or cinerascent.

Cinerea (sinĭ͡ə·rĭă). *Anat.* [mod.L., fem. sing. (sc. *cortex*) of *cinereus* CINEREOUS.] Grey or cellular nerve-tissue; the grey substance of the brain and spinal cord. Hence **Cinere·al** *a.*

1889 *Buck's Handbk. Med. Sci.* VIII. 120/1 The boundaries of the cinerea (cortex, etc.) and alba (medulla) were ascertained by comparing the similarly exposed surface of a fresh brain. *Ibid.* 120/2 The cinereal margins of the cerebellum.

Cingular (si·ŋgiŭlăɹ), *a.* [f. CINGULUM + -AR¹.] Of or belonging to the cingulum or ridge of enamel round the base of a tooth.

1904 *Amer. Jrnl. Sci.* Mar. 204 The development of a distinct cingular cuspule internal to the main antero-internal cusp.

Cingulate (si·ŋgiŭlĕt), *a.* [ad. mod.L. *cingulatus*, f. CINGULUM.] Having a ring or rings (e.g. of different colours).

1826 KIRBY & SP. *Entomol.* IV. xlvi. 291 *Cingulate*,.. when the abdomen or the trunk is wholly surrounded by one or more belts of a different colour. 1916 *H. Gray's Anat.* (ed. 19) 800 The cingulate gyrus is an arch-shaped convolution, lying in close relation to the superficial surface of the corpus callosum.

Cingulum. Add: **f.** *Bot.* (See quot. 1845.) **g.** *Anat.* A bundle of nerve fibres connecting the callosal and hippocampal convolutions of the brain.

1845 *Florist's Jrnl.* (1846) VI. 227 Cingulum, that portion of a plant immediately between the stem and the roots, the neck. 1894 D. J. CUNNINGHAM *Man. Pract. Anat.* II. 529 If the deep surface of the callosal convolution which has been torn away be examined, a large bundle of longitudinally directed fibres will be noticed embedded in its substance. This is the cingulum. 1902 *D. J. Cunningham's Anat.* 548 The cingulum..lies under cover of the callosal gyrus.

Cinnamo·meously, *adv. rare.* [f. CINNAMOMEOUS + -LY².] In a cinnamomeous manner.

1887 HOOKER *Flora Brit. India* V. 273 Leaves..cinnamomeously tomentose.

Cinnamon. Add:
4. *cinnamon-blackish, -hued* adjs.; **cinnamon dove** (see quots.); **cinnamon fern**, a large N. American fern (*Osmunda cinnamomea*) with cinnamon-coloured fronds; **cinnamon rose** (mod. examples).

1887 W. PHILLIPS *Brit. Discomycetes* 337 Hymenium *cinnamon-blackish. 1895 LYDEKKER *Royal Nat. Hist.* IV. 380

The South African *cinnamon-dove (*Haplopelia larvata*) may be taken as a well-known representative of another subfamily of ground-doves (*Geotrygoninæ*). 1908 HAAGNER & IVY *Sk. S. Afr. Bird Life* 114 The Cinnamon Dove..is an inhabitant of the forests of the Cape, ranging from Knysna to Natal, and the Transvaal. 1868 *Amer. Naturalist* II. 522 The *Cinnamon Fern, and the Interrupted leaved Fern, well known to young botanists in the spring. 1899 *Daily News* 18 Dec. 6/6 Bound in *cinnamon-hued cloth. 1834 *Southern Lit. Messenger* I. 98 Clusters of..large double damask and *cinnamon roses. 1845–50 MRS. LINCOLN *Lect. Bot.* App. 157 *Rosa cinnamonea*, cinnamon rose..Stem brown, cinnamon-color. 1893 TORREY *Footpath-Way* 32, I wished also to say something of sundry minor enjoyments; of the cinnamon roses, for example.

5. *ellipt.* = *CINNAMON BEAR.

1855 F. S. MARRYAT *Mts. & Molehills* 253 The cinnamon's weight was quoted at 400 lbs. 1878 E. B. TUTTLE *Border Tales* 52 Lassooing a cinnamon. 1891 *Fur, Fin & Feather* Mar. 170 They were a big party of cinnamons harvesting their way back towards the mountains. 1903 A. ADAMS *Log Cowboy* xxiii. 366 Those of us who had fastened on to the old cinnamon.

6. A descriptive name for certain domestic birds (poultry, canaries).

1854 *Poultry Chron.* I. 197 Buff and silver cinnamon, early hatched Cochin chickens. *Ibid.* 270 Their buffs, cinnamons, and grouse with pea combs. 1909 *Westm. Gaz.* 3 Mar. 2/1 When an ordinary canary is hatched the eyes look black, but in the case of the cinnamons they look pink.

7. Yellowish brown, the colour characteristic of cinnamon quills.

1923 *Daily Mail* 15 Jan. 6 Newest shades, including: Pale Pink,..Rust, Beige, Antelope, Cinnamon. 1924 ANNE D. SEDGWICK *Little French Girl* III. iv. (1927) 250 The buffs and cinnamons and mole colours of the fields.

Ci·nnamon bear. *U.S.* [CINNAMON 4.] A cinnamon-coloured variety of the common black bear of North America.

1829 J. RICHARDSON *Fauna Bor.-Amer.* I. 15 The Cinnamon Bear of the Fur Traders is considered by the Indians to be an accidental variety of this species [*Ursus Americanus*]. 1855 F. S. MARRYAT *Mts. & Molehills* 253 A long-expected fight had come off between a grizzly bear and a cinnamon bear. 1877 R. I. DODGE *Hunting Grounds Gt. West* 216 The Cinnamon Bear..is the compeer of the grizzly in ferocity..and in everything but size. 1878 B. F. TAYLOR *Between Gates* 38 Those huge but rather amiable and aromatic brutes the cinnamon bears. 1891 C. ROBERTS *Adrift America* 112 Such a dangerous customer as a wounded cinnamon bear to deal with. *a* 1909 'O. HENRY' *Roads of Destiny* xviii. 309 He was dancing like a cinnamon bear.

Cinnet, var. SINNET.

1884 TURNER *Samoa* 165 Everything is fastened in their ancient style, with cinnet plaited from the fibre of the cocoanut husk. Cinnet is likely long to prevail in native canoe and boat-building.

Cinnoline (si·nǒlin). *Chem.* [An alteration of QUINOLINE.] A poisonous base, $C_8H_6N_2$.

1883 *Jrnl. Chem. Soc.* XLIV. 1105 Cinnoline-derivatives. By V. v. Richter. *Ibid.*, This base may be looked upon as quinoline in which one CH-group has been replaced by N, and the author therefore proposes the name cinnoline for it. 1929 *Encycl. Brit.* V. 386/2 The fusion of pyridazine with benzene may result in either cinnoline or phthalazine.

Cinq-trous (sæ̃ŋktru). [Fr., = five holes.] A form of mesh in certain French makes of lace in which openings are set alternately in quincunx form.

1882 CAULFEILD & SAWARD *Dict. Needlework* 80. 1902 *Mrs. Bury Palliser's Hist. Lace* 213 The fillings introduced into the flowers and other ornaments in Chantilly lace are mesh grounds of old date, which, according to the district where they were made, are called vitré, mariage, and cinq trous. 1908 N. H. MOORE *Lace Book* 155.

Cinquedea (tʃiŋkwĭdē·a). [(Venetian) It., f. *cinque* five + *dea* = *dita* fingers, pl. of *dito*:—L. *digitu-s* DIGIT.] A broad-bladed dagger or short sword of which the blade has the breadth of five fingers (whence the name).

1897 *Daily News* 1 Feb. 6/2 A cinquedea, the hilt composed of plaques of faceted ivory, Italian 15th century, in a finely decorated scabbard. 1911 *Archæol. Jrnl.* LXVIII. 159 The majority of these cinquedeas are about four and a half inches wide at the base of the blade. 1920 LAKING *European Armour* III. 61 The gorgeous enrichments of the various cinquedea-like daggers. *Ibid.* 70 Cinquedea sword daggers of late XVth and early XVIth century date.

Ciota, variant of COYOTE.

1849 N. KINGSLEY *Diary* 91 Plenty of Ciotas or praira wolves barking around us.

Cipher, *sb.* 1. b. *U.S.* Add:

1815 D. DRAKE *Cincinnati* ii. 94 From nine years observations, at Cincinnati, it appears that the thermometer falls below cypher twice every winter.

Cipher, *v.*
1. b. (Earlier U.S. examples.)

1825 J. NEAL *Bro. Jonathan* I. 172 Let each man take a slate and cipher it out. 1853 J. G. BALDWIN *Flush Times Alabama* 91 A sum ciphered out through a long column.

Cipherer. Add:
2. One who writes or is skilled in writing in cipher.

1885 C. LOWE *Bismarck* I. 526 A devoted band of privy-councillors, secretaries, cipherers, newspaper-hacks.

So **Ci·pherist.**

1902 *Academy* 1 Mar. 210/1 Lord Bacon was a literary man using a cypher, and not a cypherist blundering into immortal composition.

Circa. Add: Also, an instance of this.

1898 SAINTSBURY *Short Hist. Engl. Lit.* 314 All the more careful..accounts..mark the earliest play-dates..with a tell-tale *circa*.

Circassian (səɹkæ·siăn), *a.* and *sb.* Also 7 **sarcassen, -cashen, -cashian.** [f. *Circassia*, f. *Tcherkess*, the Russian name for the tribe called by themselves Adighe: see -IAN.] **A.** *adj.* Of or pertaining to, relating to or connected with, a group of tribes of Caucasian race but non-Indo-European in language, remarkable for their physical beauty. **B.** *sb.* An individual of any of these tribes; also, their language.

1555 EDEN *Decades* (Arb.) 318 The Slauon tounge..vsed of..the Circasians and Quinquemontanians. 1634 SIR T. HERBERT *Trav.* 66 Some captiue Sarcassens and Georgians. *Ibid.* 72 [The King of Georgia's] Wife, a Sarcashen. 1638 *Ibid.* 290 Scander,..King of Georgia..by a Sarcashian Lady had 3 hopefull sonnes. 1639 PAGITT *Relat. Christians* 47 Of the Greeke Communion are the..Georgians, Circassians, Mengrelians and Melchites. 1854 L. LOEWE *Dict. Circassian Lang.* Pref. 5 The Circassians call themselves the people of Addee-ghey (which word I take to signify 'Mountaineer', or 'Highlander', from the Circassian 'Attaghagh'). 1876 *Encycl. Brit.* V. 787/2 The Circassians, as a nation, may be regarded as extinct. *Ibid.* 788/2 The greatest stain upon the Circassian character was the custom of selling their children. 1920 *Blackw. Mag.* Aug. 153/2 A troop of some thirty Circassian horsemen.

Circinal, *a.* Add:
2. *Ent.* Rolled spirally backward and inward like the proboscis of a butterfly.

1889 *Century Dict.*

Ci·rcinately, *adv.* *Bot.* [f. CIRCINATE *a.* + -LY².] In a circinate manner or arrangement.

1866 J. SMITH *Ferns Brit. & For.* 73 Fronds circinately unfolding, uniform and leafy. 1872 H. C. WOOD *Fresh-w. Algæ* 40 Circinately or fasciately convolute.

Circiter (sō͡ə·ɹsitəɹ). [L.] = CIRCA.

1888 *Athenæum* 14 Jan. 49/1 The actual pedigree begins with William 'Pepis', of Cottenham,..living *circiter* 1500.

Circle, *sb.* 25. Add:
circle-cutter, circle-reading (see quots.); **circle-rider** *U.S.*, a cowboy engaged in circle-riding; **circle-riding** *U.S.*, a method of gathering in cattle (see quot.).

1884 KNIGHT *Dict. Mech.* Suppl. 197/1 **Circle cutter*, an optician's tool with a diamond on the arm, for cutting circles in thin glass for covers for objects on slides. 1921 *Dict. Occup. Terms* (1927) § 254 *Circle cutter*;..a cutter..pressing out circular shapes from sheet metal for lids, trays, etc. 1878 NEWCOMB *Pop. Astron.* 156 The mean of the results from the four microscopes is called the *circle-reading. 1888 ROOSEVELT in *Century Mag.* Apr. 860/1 As soon as..the last *circle-riders have come in..we begin to work the herd. *Ibid.* 857/2 This morning work is called *circle riding... As the band goes out, the leader from time to time detaches one or two men to ride.., making the shorter, or what are called inside, circles, while he keeps on; and finally..makes the longest or outside circle himself.

Circled, *ppl. a.* Add: 2. b. *spec.* Girdled.

1848 J. F. COOPER *Bee-hunter* II. viii. 223 That aspect of a rough beginning, including stubs, stumps, and circled trees.

Circling, *vbl. sb.* Add:
2. b. *spec.* (See quot.)

1878 J. H. BEADLE *Western Wilds* xxxiii. 536 The savages attacked in the manner known as 'circling'—that is, riding round and round the whites, hanging on the opposite side of their horses so as to be shielded.

Circs (sɔ̄ɹks), colloq. abbrev. of pl. of CIRCUMSTANCE.

1883 in Ware *Passing English* (1909) s.v., Under the circs I am disposed to exclaim, 'What extravagance!' 1897 W. J. LOCKE *Derelicts* vi. 75, I ain't going to give you away—don't you fear. It's only pleasant to meet old pals again—in better circs. Ain't it?

Circuit, *sb.* Add:
5. b. A number of theatres, music-halls, or cinemas under the control of one manager.

1889 in *Cent. Dict.* 1908 *Daily Chron.* 31 Oct. 1/4 The De Frece circuit of music-halls. 1913 [see *CINEMATOGRAPH *sb.* b. fin.].

10. **circuit-binding** (see quot.) = YAPP; **circuit-court, -judge** (U.S. examples); **circuit (fore) edge**, a flexible projection to the binding of a book; **circuit-preacher, -rider** *U.S.*, an itinerant preacher serving a circuit (sense 6).

1911 WEBSTER, **Circuit binding*, a style of binding for books having flexible projections of the covers, called *circuit edges, that fold and meet so as to close in the edges of the book. 1789 *Act of Congress* c. 21 § 1 All writs and processes issuing from a supreme or a *circuit court. 1831 *Amer. Almanac* 141 The Circuit Courts of the United States have original cognizance..of all suits of a civil nature. 1905 *Westm. Gaz.* 4 Apr. 12/2 In vellum binding with *circuit fore-edge. 1801 *Deb. Congress* 9 Jan. (1851) 902 His travelling expenses were trifling compared with those of the *Circuit Judges. 1831 *Amer. Almanac* 197 The eight circuit judges [of New York state] are vice-chancellors for their respective circuits. 1837 PECK *Gaz. Illinois* I. 73 The Illinois Conference [of the Methodist Episcopal Church] had 61 *circuit preachers. 1872 EGGLESTON *End of World* xxxix. 245 Then he stepped to the door and called in the circuit preacher. 1838 E. FLAGG *Far West* II. 61 A little, portly, red-faced man..announced himself a Baptist *circuit-rider. 1864 *Congress. Globe* 17 May 2317/3 As peripatetic as a tin-peddler's cart or a Methodist circuit-rider. 1894 HELEN H. GARDENER *Unofficial Patriot* 17 He intended to enter the ministry as a circuit rider. 1909 *N. Y. Even. Post* (semi-weekly ed.) 23 Sept. 5 A last survival was he of the old circuit rider of early Methodism.

Circuit, *v.* Add:
3. *trans.* To form (an electric wire) into a circuit. Hence **Ci·rcuited** *ppl. a.*

1895 *Pop. Sci. Monthly* Apr. 758 A circuited instead of a simple overhead wire.

Circular, *a.* Add:
10. *Circular saw* (earlier U.S. example).

1821 *Massachusetts Spy* 26 Sept. (Th.) The circular saw is a recent invention. The Shakers, at their village in Watervliet, near Albany, have this in very excellent use and great perfection.

B. *sb.* 3. A circular saw.

1909 S. E. WHITE *Rules of Game* I. iv, We cut with 'circulars' instead of band-saws. *Ibid.* vii, Band saws. No circulars here.

Circulariza·tion. *U.S.* [f. CIRCULARIZE *v.* 2.] The sending out of circulars.

1928 *Publishers' Weekly* 16 June 2450 If..the Guild advertising or circularization should be considered contrary to the spirit of this agreement.

Circulate, *v.* Add:
6. b. To travel or walk about. *U.S.*

a 1848 in Bartlett *Dict. Amer.* s.v., Arriving in Maryland, a slave State, he circulates at a cost of from three to five cents a mile. 1907 MULFORD *Bar-20* viii. 83 Shore, go home. I'll just circulate around some for exercise.

Circum-. 2. Add: *circumdental, -nuclear* adjs.

1910 *Practitioner* Jan. 115 The path of infection should be first examined. The obvious path is the circumdental sulcus. *Ibid.* July 102 The opacity of the circum-nuclear zone.

Circumambulator. (Earlier U.S. example.)

1787 JEFFERSON *Corr.* (1829) II. 162 He was determined to obtain the palm of being the first circumambulator of the earth.

Circumductory (sɜ̄ɹkǒmdɒ·ktəri), *a.* [f. CIRCUMDUCT + -ORY².] Pertaining to or characterized by circumduction (see CIRCUMDUCTION 2).

1872 HUMPHRY *Myology* 143 In the case of the proximal joint of the limb—that of the first cartilage or bone with the girdle—the movement is..circumductory or in any direction.

Circumlocutionize (sɜ̄ɹkǒmlǒkiū·ʃənəiz), *v.* [f. CIRCUMLOCUTION + -IZE.] *trans.* and *intr.* To speak of, or speak, in circumlocution.

1822 COBBETT *Weekly Reg.* 27 Apr. 249 To mention names, in such a case, is wholly out of the question...Circumlocutionize the profligate..and insolent crew. 1886 *N. & Q.* 7th Ser. I. 450/1 If we want to say, 'It was clearly meant as an insult, but he didn't choose to *relever* it', we must circumlocutionize with four extra words—'to take any notice of it', or at least with two—'to take it up'.

Circumpolar. Add: Also *sb.* A star situated within a few degrees of either the north or south pole of the heavens.

1889 C. A. YOUNG *Text Bk. Gen. Astron.* iv. 70 Determination of Latitude... By Circumpolars. 1910 G. L. HOSMER *Text-Bk. Pract. Astron.* 30 If the observer travels north until he is beyond the arctic circle, latitude 66° 33' north, then the sun becomes a circumpolar at the time of the summer solstice.

Circumstance, *sb.* Add:
7. c. With negatives: A fact or thing of importance or capable of being compared. *U.S.*

1836 *Crockett's Yaller Flower Almanac* 19 Orson, the wild man of the woods, is nothing to him—not a circumstance. 1845 S. JUDD *Margaret* II. v. 284, O, it an't a circumstance to what it used to be. 1901 HARBEN *Westerfelt* xvi. 219 'Mother told me he often drove you out home.' 'Oh, la, that ain't a circumstance, Harriet! He used to come out home mighty nigh every day or night.' 1903 *Nation* (N.Y.) 1 Oct. 258 Undigested securities are not a circumstance to undigested political principles.

Circumta·bular, *a.* [f. CIRCUM- 2 + TABULAR.] That sits round a table; round-table.

1919 N. HILL *Story Scott. Ch.* vii. 149 Circum-tabular oligarchies. 1920 *Glasgow Herald* 27 July 6 [They] had in view only a circumtabular gathering of the States engaged in mutual self-destruction. 1926 *British Weekly* 28 Oct. 86/4 All circumtabular dominant groups.

Circus. Add: 2. c. A disturbance or uproar; a display of rowdy sport. Also, an 'exhibition', a 'show'. orig. *U.S. colloq.*

1885 W. L. ALDEN *Adv. Jimmy Brown* 88 Mr. Martin.. sprang up, and nearly upset the table, and fell over his chair backward, and wasn't there a circus in that dining-room! 1887 *Harper's Mag.* May 944/1 The night grew rougher... 'I guess it's going to be a regular circus.' 1895 SCULLY *Kaffir Stories* 147, I guess we must see this circus out. If you have to shoot, aim low. 1895 C. KING *Fort Frayne* v. 69 We'll have a circus with him. 1897 *Westm. Gaz.* 6 Jan. 4/3 This manœuvre was successfully carried out by about 3.30 p.m., when our force prepared to retire; and then the circus commenced. 1900 *Daily News* 29 Aug. 3/1 Something has gone gravely wrong with the lieutenant, otherwise he would not be making a circus of himself in this fantastic fashion.

d. *Kaffir Circus*: in Stock Exchange slang, the South African mining share market.

e. (*a*) A travelling raiding party. (*b*) A squadron of aeroplanes. *Army slang.*

1918 C. G. GREY in *M. F. von Richthofen's Red Air Fighter* Pref. 19 Von Richthofen's chaser squadron—or Jägdstaffel, as the Germans call these formations—was the first to be known as a 'circus'. 1919 G. K. ROSE *2/4th Oxf. & Bucks Lt. Infty.* 58 The ugly Germans are members of a 'travelling circus'...They are a professional raiding party, with two successful raids at Loos, one at Ypres, and one near Hébuterne to their credit. *Ibid.*, Two 8-inch howitzers and several batteries of 5·9s and 4·2s belonging to the 'circus'.

Circussy (sɜ̄·ɹkǒsi), *a.* Also **-ussy.** [f. CIRCUS + -Y¹.] Resembling or characteristic of a circus.

1876 MEREDITH *Beauch. Career* iv, Here are lots of circussy heroes coming home to rest after their fatigues. 1894 — *Ld. Ormont* i, He accused Murat of carelessness of his horses, ingratitude to his benefactor, circussy style. 1928 *Sunday Dispatch* 2 Sept. 4/5 Circusy-looking horses.

Ciré (si·re), *a.* [Fr., = waxed.] Having a smooth polished surface. Also short for *ciré silk*, etc.

1921 *Spectator* 23 Apr. 522/2 Trades dealing in..ribbons,.. wool, ciré, raffia. 1922 *Glasgow Herald* 21 May 4 A chapeau of ciré silk or straw. 1922 *Daily Mail* 5 Dec. 14 Belted coatees of cire leather. 1923 *Ibid.* 18 Jan. 11 A casaquin covered entirely in ciré braid.

Cire perdue (sīr pęrdü). [Fr., = lost wax.] A method of casting bronze by making a model with a wax surface, enclosing it in a mould, melting the wax out, and running in the metal between the core and mould.

1876 *Encycl. Brit.* IV. 367/1 In the old method of bronze-casting, known as the *cire perdue*, wax is first used for the thickness of the statue..and is melted and run off before the metal is poured in. 1885 *Ibid.* XIX. 183/2 Casting (by the 'cire perdue' process). 1900 J. SHARP *Mod. Foundry Practice* 655 The cire-perdu process required great care, and could only be carried out effectively by the sculptor or modeller himself.

Cirrate (si·rĕt), *a.* *Ent.* [ad. L. *cirrātus.*] = CIRRATED.

1826 KIRBY & SP. *Entomol.* xlvi. IV. 321.

Cirro-. Add: **cirro-macula, -velum.**

1894 W. C. LEY *Cloudland* vi. § 106. 128 It is difficult perhaps to understand how threads of Cirro-filum can become twisted together and interwoven so as to form Cirro-velum. *Ibid.* § 113. 132 The festoons or 'pocks' of Cirro-velum Mammatum appear much smoother and more regular than those of lower clouds of Reversed Interfret. *Ibid.* § 116. 134 Cirro-macula always consists of ice, and nearly always is combined with a few threads of ice-particles.

Cirrolite: see CIRRHOLITE.

Cis-. Add:
1. **Cis-Atla·ntic** (earlier U.S. examples); **Cis-Atla·ntically** *adv.*, on this side of the Atlantic; **Cis-bo·rder** *a.*, on this side of the border; **Cisca·spian** *a.*, on this side of the Caspian; **Cis-Danu·bian** *a.*, on this side of the Danube; **Cis-I·ndus** *a.*, on this side of the Indus; **Cis-Ura·lian** *a.*, on this side of the Urals.

1782 JEFFERSON *Notes Virginia* (1787) 68, I only mean to suggest a doubt..whether nature has enlisted herself as a *Cis- or Trans-Atlantic partisan. 1806 FESSENDEN *Democracy Unv.* I. 112 *note*, Our poetical and rhetorical flourishes from Cis-Atlantic sources. 1909 *Daily Chron.* 23 June 3/2 In any case, it is not *cis-Atlantically true. 1901 *19th Cent.* Apr. 711 Raised in fixed proportion from the transborder and *cisborder clans. 1888 *Encycl. Brit.* XXIV. 5/2 The *Ciscaspian steppes. 1832–4 DE QUINCEY *Cæsars* Wks. 1887 V. 168 Homes had been found by Trans-Danubian barbarians upon the *Cis-Danubian territory of Rome. 1907 *New Reformer* Dec. 325 The..*Cis-Indus Aryan world. 1886 *Encycl. Brit.* XXI. 79/2 The Permians, or *Cis-Uralian Finns.

3. *Chem.*, designating (in contrast with *trans-* or *cis-trans-*) a compound in which two atoms or groups are supposed to be situated on the same side of some plane of symmetry passing through the compound.

1907 J. B. COHEN *Org. Chem.* 110 It exhibits lateral symmetry, and is known as the plane-symmetric, or, more commonly, as the cis or malenoid form.

Cisalpine, *a.* and *sb.* Add quots. for the specific application to the Gallican Church movement.

1792 R. BANISTER *Let.* 30 Apr. in *Ushaw Mag.* (1904) June 138 A new club..at London of 14 lay gentlemen..: it takes a new name and is to be called the Cisalpine club. 1793 in B. Ward *Dawn Cath. Revival* (1909) II. xxi. 46 He has given himself to the Cisalpines. *Ibid.* xxiv. 98, I should recommend the erection of a good Grammar School, such as would supersede the necessity of a Cisalpine one. 1830 MILNER *Suppl. Mem. Eng. Cath.* 109 A fresh contest arose between the Senior V. A. and certain powerful Cisalpines. 1825 C. BUTLER *Bk. Rom. Cath. Ch.* x. 123 The Cisalpines affirm, that in spirituals the pope is subject, in doctrine and discipline, to the church. 1909 B. WARD in *Dublin Rev.* Jan. 65 The Cisalpine party went to great lengths in their anti-episcopal—and even anti-Papal—declamations.

Cisco. *U.S.* Add:
The name is given to several species, esp. the larger lake-herring (*Coregonus* or *Argyrosomus artedii*) and the small moon-eye (*C.* or *A. hoyi*).

1848 BARTLETT *Dict. Amer.* 1872 *Fur, Fin & Feather* 200 Ciscoes are caught mostly on shore, although many take them..from boats. 1880 [see SISCOE]. 1884 D. S. JORDAN in Goode *Nat. Hist. Aquatic Anim.* 541 The Moon-eye or 'Cisco' of Lake Michigan,..is the smallest of our white-fish, rarely weighing over half a pound. 1903 *N. Y. Sun* 1 Nov., In the same warehouse are trout, ciscoes, bluefish, weakfish, porgies, and so on.

attrib. 1872 in *Fur, Fin & Feather* 200 Cisco fishing at Geneva Lake, Wis. *Ibid.*, Their coming is heralded by the Cisco-fly.

Hence **Ci·scoist**, one who fishes for cisco.

1872 *Fur, Fin & Feather* 200 The lucky ciscoist is he (or she) who brings to this classic shore a sixteen-foot rod.

Ciscoette, Ciscovet, varr. of SISCOWET.

1847 C. LANMAN *Summer in Wildern.* 159 A fish called ciscovet, is unquestionably of the trout genus, but much more delicious. *Ibid.* 161 The white-fish, ciscovet, and lake trout. 1854 — *Adv. Wilds N. Amer.* xxxiv. 253 We cannot leave Mackinaw without making a passing allusion to the fish whose Indian name is *ciscovet*. It is a handsome fish, unquestionably of the trout family. 1902 *Jrnl. Amer. Folk-lore* 243 Ciscoette. A name of the lake herring. Apparently a derivative, with French diminutive suffix, from *Cisco* (q.v.), but rather a corruption of *Siskowit*.

Ciseleur (sizlör). [Fr., f. *ciseler* to carve, chase.] One who carves metals, a chaser.

1862 *Catal. Spec. Exhib. S. Kens.* No. 826 The famous ciseleur Poutière.

Cissing (si·siŋ), *vbl. sb.* **a.** The preliminary operation in graining of moistening the wood with beer and rubbing it over with whiting in order that the colour may adhere. **b.** (See quots. 1877, 1885, and 1904.)

1875 E. A. DAVIDSON *House-Painting* 106 In order that the graining colours which are mixed with beer may adhere to the ground which has been painted in oil, it is necessary that the surface should be prepared. This is done by passing over it with a sponge moistened with beer and rubbed with whiting; when this is dry, the distemper colour will work freely over the oil, and will adhere to it. This process is called *cissing*. 1877 *Paperhanger, Painter, Grainer*, etc. 111 Vandyke Brown used in beer must be rubbed on with a tool..till there is no 'cissing', or curdling of the colour. 1885 *Spons' Mechanics' Own Bk.* 432 To prevent a graining coat from 'cissing' at a water-colour overgraining coat, that is repelling the water by antagonism of the oil. 1904 *Technol. & Sci. Dict.* (ed. Goodchild & Tweney), *Cissing*, a fault in a varnished surface in which small dull spots appear. Usually caused either by minute holes or grease spots.

Cissy (si·si). *U.S. slang.* [Variant of SISSY: see SISS *sb.*¹] An effeminate person. Also *attrib.*

1915 *Lett. from Front* (1920) I. 19 Ready to look down upon the Britisher as a good-for-nothing lady-like cissy. 1930 L. C. DOUTHWAITE in *Chambers's Jrnl.* Apr. 228 It takes more than a cissy Englishman who couldn't find the hole in a doughnut to break trail across 'the Barrens'.

Cist. 3. Add: *cist-grave.*

1902 *Encycl. Brit.* XXXI. 55/2 The wide range of the peculiar cist-grave strengthens the belief that late Stone Age culture in the Aegean was not of sporadic development.

Cistella (siste·lă). *Bot.* [mod.L., dim. of *cista* box.] = CISTULA 3.

1839 LINDLEY *Introd. Bot.* (ed. 3) 271. 1856 HENSLOW *Dict. Bot. Terms* 38.

Cistercianism (sistɜ̄·ɹʃăniz'm). [f. CISTERCIAN + -ISM.] The religious system of the Cistercians; the Cistercian spirit.

1895 *Athenæum* 6 Apr. 440/1 Welsh Cistercianism. 1898 S. EVANS *Holy Graal* 11 The predominance of what may be called Cistercianism in the Church.

Cistern. Add: 6. *Glass-making.* = CUVETTE 3.

1874 KNIGHT *Dict. Mech.*

7. **cistern bottoms** *U.S.* (see quot.); **cistern water** *U.S.*, rain-water collected in cisterns, in contrast to spring- or well-water.

1833 B. SILLIMAN *Man. Sugar Cane* 41 On draining off molasses cisterns, a greater or less deposit of sugar, called *cistern bottoms, is found in these vessels. 1858 *Texas Almanac* 82 *Cistern water is used for culinary purposes. 1863 'E. KIRKE' *My Southern Friends* 49 New England rum, and cistern water.

Cistophorus (sistǫ·fōrǒs). [L., a. Gr. κιστοφόρος, f. κίστη CHEST *sb.*¹ + -φορος bearing, -PHOROUS.] A Greek coin bearing the impress of a sacred *cista* or chest. Hence **Cistophoric** (sistofǫ·rik) *a.*, of or pertaining to this.

1848 AKERMAN *Introd. Study Anc. & Mod. Coins* ii. 33 The time of the first issue of cistophori is not known; but they were in circulation in the year of Rome 564 (B.C. 190). 1887 B. V. HEAD *Hist. Numorum* Introd. p. lxii, In Asia Minor the chief silver coinage consisted of the famous Cistophori. *Ibid.* 446 Cistophori with ΑΔΡΑ in monogram and autonomous drachms (45 grs.) of the cistophoric standard. *Ibid.* 587 Many of these tetradrachms are countermarked with a bow and bow-case crossed, accompanied by the names, for the most part, of cistophoric mints.

Cit. Add:
2. *pl.* Civilian clothes; 'civvies'. *U.S.*

1895 C. KING *Fort Frayne* vi. 86 Will was..vaguely longing to get out and air his new 'cits'. 1907 *Chicago Tribune* 8 May 2 They were in full dress uniform. Later they were joined by Maj. Judson of the engineers in 'cits'.

Citadeled (si·tădəld), *a.* [f. CITADEL.] Placed as in a citadel.

1892 STEDMAN in *Century Mag.* Apr. 826 Chartered to convey them all to the inward sight, the spiritual bearing of the citadeled soul.

Citation. Add: 5. Mention in an official dispatch. *U.S.*

1918 E. S. FARROW *Dict. Mil. Terms.* 1930 *Publishers' Weekly* 5 July 11 [He] holds the Congressional Medal of Honor, nine citations and the highest decorations of the Allied Governments.

Citified, var. of *cityfied*: see CITYFY *v.*

1855 M. M. THOMPSON *Doesticks* xvi. 132 Being so far citified in my habits that I desired to combine amusement with charity. 1862 *Temple Bar* VI. 190 The country population is..becoming citified. 1876 'MARK TWAIN' *Tom Sawyer* I. 7 He had a citified air about him that ate into Tom's vitals. 1889 FARMER *Americanisms*, *Citified*, a New England expression for pertaining to city life. 1916 D. GRAYSON *Adv. in Contentment* ii, I was 'citified', Horace said; and 'citified' with us here in the country is nearly the limit of invective. 1919 W. HUTCHINSON *Doctor in War* i. 4 The highly citified and alleged 'neurotic' Cockney.

Ci·tizendom. [f. CITIZEN + -DOM.] Citizens collectively.

1888 BRYCE *Amer. Commw.* II. xxxix. 73 The collective citizendom of the State.

Ci·tizening, *vbl. sb.* *U.S.* [Cf. CITIZEN *v.*] Admission to citizenhood.

1890 *Home Missionary* (N.Y.) Apr. 528 The citizening of the five tribes [in Indian Territory, U.S.] and statehood are inevitable.

Citizenly (si·tizĕnli), *a.* [f. CITIZEN *sb.* + -LY¹.] Pertaining to or characteristic of a citizen.

1899 *Remin. King of Roumania* 111 The citizenly virtues which appertain to such a quasi-republican form of State. 1905 *Academy* 16 Sept. 944/1 That the negroes' welcome be in the measure of their citizenly quality.

Citrange (si·trăndʒ). [f. CITR(US + OR)ANGE.] A hybrid fruit produced by crossing the hardy trifoliate orange, *Citrus trifoliata*, with the common sweet orange.

1904 H. J. WEBBER in *Yearbk. U.S. Dept. Agric.* 227 The Citrange, a new group of Citrus plants... It..becomes necessary to refer these hybrids to a new group of citrus fruits, and it is proposed to call them 'citranges'.

Citrated (si·treɪtĕd), *ppl. a.* [f. CITRATE + -ED.] Treated with sodium citrate.

1908 *Practitioner* Apr. 462 Citrated horse's blood. 1920 *Discovery* Apr. 105/1 It was found the citrated blood could be kept unchanged for twenty-four hours or more.

Citrazinic (sitrăzi·nik), *a.* *Chem.* [f. CITR- + AZ)OTE + -INE⁵ + -IC.] Designating a crystalline hydroxy acid, formed by condensation from an amide of citric acid.

1885 *Jrnl. Chem. Soc.* XLVIII. I. 139 Citrazinic acid, $C_6H_5NO_4$: citramide is treated with 4–5 parts of sulphuric acid (70–75 per cent). *Ibid.*, Citrazinic acid is very sparingly soluble even in boiling water. 1887 *Ibid.* LI. 406 Citrazinamide, like citrazinic acid, is a very stable compound.

Citrometer (sitrǫ·mĭtəɹ). [f. CITRO- + -METER.] An instrument used for determining the specific gravity of lemon juice in the preparation of citric acid.

1875 *Jrnl. Chem. Soc.* XXVIII. 930 Lemon-juice..is boiled down in copper vessels over an open fire till it is supposed to mark when cold 60° on the citrometer. 1879 *Spons' Encycl. Industr. Arts* 49.

Citron. Add:
3. Also as *adj.* = citron-coloured.

1924 ANNE D. SEDGWICK *Little French Girl* I. v, The old tapestry, grey and green and citron. *Ibid.* II. x, The drawing-room..so pale in its citrons, whites and dim jade-greens.

5. b. The citron melon. *U.S.*

1889 *Century Dict.*

7. **citron melon** *U.S.*, a variety of water-melon, having a small round fruit with qualities like those of the citron.

1857–8 *Trans. Ill. Agric. Soc.* III. 506 The citron melon is alone valuable for preserving. Its flesh is white, solid, and seeds red.

Citronella (sitrǒne·lă). [mod.L.] A fragrant grass, *Andropogon Nardus*, which yields an oil much used in perfumery; also, the oil itself.

1858 SIMMONDS *Dict. Trade*, *Citronella*, an essential oil obtained from the grass *Andropogon Citratum*, and chiefly imported from Ceylon. 1864 *Jrnl. Chem. Soc.* XVII. 8 *Citronella*.—This is produced from the leaves of the *Andropogon Schœnanthus*. 1884 *Encycl. Brit.* XVII. 749/1. 1887 BENTLEY *Man. Bot.* (ed. 5) 735 Citronella Oil or Oil of Citronelle. 1903 *Westm. Gaz.* 30 Nov. 2/1 One and a half million pounds of citronella oil are yearly exported. 1911 *Jrnl. Chem. Soc.* C. I. 476 The citronella grasses of Ceylon are of four kinds.

Hence **Citrone·llic** *a.*; **Citrone·llal**, a substance found in citronella, eucalyptus, and lemon oils; **Citrone·llol**, an alcohol found in rose, pelargonium, and geranium oils.

1872 *Jrnl. Chem. Soc.* XXV. 8 The refraction equivalent of citronellol is..79·3 or 79·8, instead of the theoretical 73·7. 1890 *Ibid.* LVIII. I. 231 The author names it *citronellic aldehyde*, and considers it to be β-methyl-δ-isobutylallylacetaldehyde. 1891 *Ibid.* LX. I. 285 Citronellic aldehyde must be regarded as a homologue of acraldehyde. 1893 *Ibid.* LXX. I. 382 Compounds of the Citronellal Series. 1906 *Ibid.* XC. I. 442 The citronella oil..contained 32·7 per cent. of geraniol and 55·3 per cent. of citronellal.

Citronelle (sitrǒne·l). [ad. mod.L. *citronella*.] = *CITRONELLA; also, a beverage made from this.

1861 BENTLEY *Man. Bot.* 699 Cetronelle or Citronelle oil, is the produce of this or of an allied species of *Andropogon*. 1899 *Scribner's Mag.* XXV. 50/1 As gay with flowers as a girl's hat, and as fragrant of sweet-olive, citronelle, and heliotrope as her garments. 1921 *Chambers's Jrnl.* Sept. 604/2, I tasted a new drink called 'citronelle', a kind of tea made from a grass which the French cultivate in their gardens.

Citrous (si·trəs), *a.* [f. CITRUS + -OUS.] Of or belonging to the genus *Citrus*.

1901 *Westm. Gaz.* 13 June 2/3 Citrous fruits. 1911 C. E. W. BEAN '*Dreadnought' of Darling* xl. 355 Land..which suits vegetables, lucerne, dairying, citrous fruits. 1924 *Glasgow Herald* 9 July 5 The citrous fruit industry.

Citrus. 1. Add: *attrib.*

1825 *Greenhouse Comp.* I. 81 The Citrus tribe is also propagated by cuttings and layers. 1904 *Westm. Gaz.* 18 Nov. 2/3 'Forbidden Fruit'—this name is sometimes loosely given to this whole group of citrus varieties. 1906 *Macm. Mag.* Aug. 794 Fruit-trees, especially the citrus and stone varieties.

City. 9. Add:
city editor (example); also *U.S.* (see quot. 1889); **city-lot** *U.S.*, a piece of ground lying within city-bounds; **city-man**, a man engaged (*a*) in 'the city', (*b*) in mercantile pursuits; **city-state**, a city which is also an independent sovereign state.

1858 SIMMONDS *Dict. Trade*, **City Editor*, the employee of a daily or weekly London journal, whose special duty it is to report upon the prices of public securities, the state of the money market, and other matters of commerce and finance. 1889 *Century Dict.*, *City editor*,..in the United States, the editor who superintends the collection and classification of local news. 1898 *Scribner's Mag.* May 580/1 White, the city editor, would soon be going home, and Stone, the night city editor, would take the desk. 1902 ELIZ.

Banks Autob. Newsp. Girl ii. 9 You might try it on the city editor; but, mind you, I can't promise that he'll print it. 1683 W. Penn Wks. (1782) IV. 316 The *city-lot [is conveniently posted] for a dock. 1829 R. C. Sands Writings II. 169 The latter sat pensive and silent, while Miss Violet discoursed..about western lands and city lots. 1844 Lee & Frost Oregon vi. 79 The..gentleman..was selling off small city lots at one hundred dollars a piece. 1857-8 Trans. Ill. Agric. Soc. III. (1859) 348 A thousand feet of city lot. a1861 T. Winthrop John Brent i. (1862) 7 They had been speculating in..city lots. 1836-9 *City man [see City 7]. 1875 T. W. Higginson Engl. Statesm. 350 (Cent. D.) He had made his mark in the mercantile world as a thoroughly representative City-man. 1893 W. Warde Fowler (title) The *City-State of the Greeks and Romans. 1906 Daily Chron. 25 Nov. 2/5 Athens, a city-state that could always give rise to great men. 1928 C. Dawson Age of the Gods vi. 113 The Diffusion of the City State in the Near East.

Cityfication (si:tifikēi·ʃən). [f. Cityfy: see -fication.] The process of being cityfied.
1906 Saleeby in Daily Chron. 23 Oct. 4/4 Keen observers are assured that civilisation is well named—it means cityfication. 1923 Glasgow Herald 26 May 4 American rural life has little tradition... Its citification is no great surprise.

Cityward. b. Add quots.:
1873 J. H. Beadle Undevel. West 804 The cityward bluff of the Colorado rises almost perpendicular for thirty feet or more from the water's edge. 1898 Daily News 28 Mar. 8/7 The cityward and homeward lines of traffic. 1900 Westm. Gaz. 25 July 2/3 Blocks in cityward traffic.

Citywards. Add: attrib. or adj.
1908 Daily Chron. 9 Jan. 3/2 We quite expect that..we shall meet him in the City-wards train.

Civaistic (sīvā,i·stik), a. Variant of Sivaistic.
1886 Encycl. Brit. XX. 360 Civaistic sects.

Civil, a. and sb. Add: **B. 5.** The civil: the civil thing (see quot. 1840 in A. 12).
1857 G. Lawrence Guy Liv. ix, Parndon was doing the civil to the 'great men in Israel', his heaviest subscribers. 1858 Trollope Doctor Thorne xxviii, I haven't exactly popped to her yet; but I have been doing the civil. 1877 Reade Woman-Hater II. xix. 150 He would go to the station and telegraph him; and by that means would do the civil and meet Miss Gale.

D. civil-spoke(n (see Spoken ppl. a. note).
1842 Lover Handy Andy xiv, He was a very 'close' man, as well as a 'civil-spoken'. 1880 E. H. Dering Freville Chase xi, There never was a kinder or civiller spoken gentleman nowhere. 1910 Farnol Broad Highway II. ii. 202 'What might you be wanting with a peaceable, civil-spoke cove like me?' he inquired.

Civilize, v. Add: **6. b.** To spruce up in dress.
1920 Hunter Trail Drivers of Texas 442 We would civilize up a bit when we went to a dance, that is, we would take off our spurs and tie a clean red handkerchief around our neck.

Civilizee. (Earlier U.S. example.)
a 1848 N. Y. Observer in Bartlett Dict. Amer., The barbarian likes his seraglio; the civilizee admires the institution of marriage. The barbarian likes a roving, wandering life; the civilizee likes his home and fireside.

Civvies (si·viz), sb. pl. colloq. Civilian clothes. Also attrib. in sing. form (civvy). Cf. next.
1889 Barrère & Leland Dict. Slang. 1915 'Bartimeus' Tall Ship v. 100 Nosey wore a rusty suit of 'civvies'. Ibid. 101 He still wore his 'civvy' suit. 1924 Glasgow Herald 18 Aug. 8 Field Marshals go about in the most inconspicuous 'civvies' that tailors can supply.

Civvy (si·vi). Short for Civilian.
1919 Punch 15 Jan. 38 'And I suppose you will be demobilised..?' 'Oh, no, Mum. You see, I was a soldier in civvy life.' 1927 E. Thompson These Men thy Friends 82 They are sure that any civvy who has had the honour of being associated with them and survives will lie awake the rest of his life saying..'I was an officer in the Loamshires'.

Clabber, v. (Later U.S. example.)
1920 R. L. Alsaker Eating for Health 47 Clabbered milk and buttermilk are easily digested.

Clack, sb. 10. Add: **clack valve** (earlier U.S. example).
1850 N. Kingsley Diary 112 Tried the pumps by takeing out the clack valve.

Clack, v.[1] B. (Later U.S. example.)
1835 R. M. Bird Hawks of Hawk-hollow II. xi. 115 It's just like sticking three bricks on an end; if you kick one, why down goes the second, and clack goes t'other.

Clack-clack, sb. [Imitative.] A repeated clacking noise. Also **Clack-clacking.**
c 1870 'Mark Twain' Sketches Wks. XIX. 250 Presently up the street I heard a bony clack-clacking. Ibid. 252, I heard another one coming—for I recognized his clack-clack. 1916 Boyd Cable Action Front 249 The clack-clack-clack of a machine-gun at close range.

Clacker (klæ·kəɹ), v. dial. and U.S. [Cf. Clack v.[1]] intr. and trans. = Clack v.[1] 1, 2.
1851 S. Judd Margaret III. (ed. 2) 345 Mounting a rock she harangued the people, or, rather, clackered her own merit. 1896 Chanter Witch of Withyford ii, She heard them all come clacking into the yard.

Clacket (klæ·kėt), v. Delete †Obs. and add:
1904 Gallichan Fishing Spain 144 Felicia stalked out, her wooden shoes clacketing upon the road.

Cladome (klæ·doum). [f. Gr. κλάδος branch + *-ome.] The branching arms of a rhabdus sponge spicule collectively. Hence **Cladomic** a.
1887 Sollas in Encycl. Brit. XXII. 417/1 The secondary rays are the arms or cladi, collectively the head or cladome of the spicule. 1888 — in Challenger Rep. XXV. p. lvi, The 'cladome' which consists of the three cladi (rays, teeth, arms).

Cladus (klǣ·dŏs). [mod.L., a. Gr. κλάδος branch.] One of the secondary arms or branches of a ramose sponge spicule. Hence **Cla·dal, Cla·dose** adjs.
1887 Sollas in Encycl. Brit. XXII. 416/2 The spicular rays..usually pointed (oxeate) at the ends..are also frequently..branched (cladose). 1888 — in Challenger Rep. XXV. p. lvi, The proximal or undivided part of a cladus is ..distinguished as the protocladus, the distal division, in the case of a dichotomous cladus as the deuterocladus. Ibid., A straight line drawn from the cladal origin to the end of a cladus is taken as its length.

Claim, sb. Add **3.** (Earlier examples.) To jump a claim: see Jump v. 9 b.
1817 S. R. Brown Western Gaz. 13 The eastern boundary of the Creek claims is pine land. 1846 E. H. Smith Hist. Black Hawk (Farmer) When I hunted claims, I went far and near. 1855 F. S. Marryat Mts. & Molehills 240 It is customary to leave your mining tools in your claim, to indicate to all new comers that it is occupied.

5. In the language of Christian Science, the imaginary disturbance which 'claims' to be an ailment.
1898 Westm. Gaz. 26 Mar. 3/1 Ailments were referred to as 'claims'. For instance, the other night this lady's eldest daughter came to her with the information that her sister had got a 'claim' of swollen glands..Soon after this, the mother herself was attacked by a claim of influenza. 1907 'Mark Twain' Chr. Sci. 57 The second witness testifies that the Science banished 'an old organic trouble', which the doctor and the surgeon had been nursing with drugs and the knife for seven years. He calls it his 'claim'.

6. attrib. and Comb., as (sense 1) claims adjuster, clerk, inspector (see Dict. Occup. Terms, 1921); (sense 3) claim-agent, -holder, -holding, -notice, -pegging, -shack, -shanty, -stake; **claim acreage,** acreage consisting of miners' claims.
1903 Daily Chron. 1 July 7/6 Ten times larger than the Kimberley mine in *claim acreage. 1888 Nation (N.Y.) 29 Apr. 311/2 The *claim agents..must be chuckling. 1903 N. Y. Even. Post 6 Oct. 6 Our pension policy has furnished an enormous incentive to claims agents and Congressman. 1890 'R. Boldrewood' Miner's Right xiv, All the *claim holders had closed round as far as could be seen in every direction. 1906 Westm. Gaz. 15 June 2/1 With the result ..of 'freezing out' the average claim-holder and obtaining his claims on their own terms. 1902 Ibid. 26 Nov. 11/3 Their total *claim-holding having been increased. 1889 Century Dict., *Claim-notice,..a notification posted by a miner or other settler upon a piece of public land [etc.]. 1892 Pall Mall Gaz. 23 Feb. 7/2 *Claim-pegging in the Transvaal. 1916 B. M. Bower Phantom Herd ix. 149 We learned our little lessons when we were building *claim shacks for ourselves. 1873 Eggleston Myst. Metrop. ii. 23 Here and there Charlton noticed the little *claim-shanties. 1888 Harper's Mag. Mar. 568/1 The country is now taken up and dotted with claim shanties. 1901 S. E. White Claim Jumpers iii. 37 In her hand was the missing *claim stake.

Claim, v. Add:
2. c. (Examples.)
1876 Troy Morning Whig 27 May, The man accused his wife of being intoxicated, which she denied and claimed that he was in that condition himself. 1887 Troy Daily Times 8 Jan., John Weatherwax..procured a peace warrant for the arrest of his son..who he claims has threatened to kill him. 1904 Providence Jrnl. 1 Aug. 4 Neighbors claim to have seen two men about the place. 1922 R. Dunn in World's Work July 119/2 Refet Bey..was hopping mad at an attempt which he claimed that the British had made to kidnap him.

8. b. To occupy land in virtue of a claim.
1786 Maryland Hist. Mag. XIX. 262 One Fleming who lived and claimed under Mr. Carroll..resided in a clap board house.

Clai·m-ju:mper. U.S. [See Claim sb. 3 and Jump v. 9 b.] One who appropriates a claim already taken by another. So **Clai·m-ju:mping** vbl. sb. and ppl. a.
1859 Bartlett Dict. Amer. (ed. 2). 1888 Critic 14 Apr. (Farmer) The claim-jumper laughed as though he enjoyed it hugely. 1909 Greely Handbk. Alaska (1925) 29 Thus ended claim-jumping by mass meeting. 1910 Jer. Hart Vigilante Girl xiv. 186 He has no sentimental prejudices about claim-jumping miners. 1922 Mulford Tex xvii. 237 An' he needs us to keep our eyes on them blasted claim jumpers.

Claimless, a. Add: **b.** Without a claim (see Claim sb. 3).
1927 Blackw. Mag. Oct. 460/1, I found myself claimless, and not likely to obtain another piece of ground. Ibid. 461/2 Many negroes claimless 'diggers'.

Clairce (klē·ɪs). [Fr., f. claircer to clarify, irreg. f. clair Clear a.] A syrup made from pure sugar, used in the process of sugar refining, for washing away impurities.
1902 Encycl. Brit. XXXIII. 48/1 This washing being supplemented by the injection of pure syrup of high density or 'clairce', when very white sugar is required.

Clair-de-lune (klęr də lün). [Fr., = moonlight.] The colour of moonlight, a soft white or pale blue-grey, the shade which appears in the glaze of certain Chinese porcelains.
1877 Young Ladies' Jrnl. XIV. 842/3 Bonnets embroidered with clare [sic] de lune beads. 1906 R. L. Hobson Porcelain 15 Lovely blue glazes, ranging from deep sky-blue to the palest clair de lune.

Clam, sb.[2] Add:
1. e. phr. As happy as a clam, etc. (see quots.). U.S.
1838 Knickerbocker Mag. XI. 208 'Happy as a clam', is an old adage. 1848 Bartlett Dict. Amer. s.v., 'As happy as a clam at high water', is a very common expression in those parts of the coast of New England where clams are found. 1873 J. H. Beadle Undevel. West 799 A thousand or more negroes thronged the streets 'happy as clams at high tide'. 1882 Howells Mod. Instance xxviii. II. 125 'And you're happy.' 'Perfect clam', said Bartley.

4. clam-digger (examples), -digging, -fishery; **clam-bait** U.S., clams used as bait; **clam-bank,** a bank where clams are found; **clam-chowder,** also, a picnic or feast at which this is the principal dish; **clam-cracker** (see quot.); **clam-fry,** a meal of fried clams; **clam-tongs,** tongs used for taking clams.
1838 Mass. Stat. ch. cxxiv, An Act to regulate the Inspection of *Clam Bait. 1871 Schele de Vere Americanisms (1872) 69 When salted for the fisheries it takes the name of clam-bait. 1634 W. Wood New Eng. Prosp. I. ix. 35 A man running over these *Clamm bankes will presently be made all wet. 1641 Dorchester (Mass.) Town Rec. 1 Jan., If there be any [hogs] Livinge neare unto any Clam bankes. 1871 Schele de Vere Americanisms (1872) 69 The clam of Boston is the Mya arenaria of the clam-banks. 1898 Hamblen Gen. Manager's Story 131 The engineers had a *clam chowder. 1911 Webster, *Clamcracker, a stingray (Dasyatis centrura) of the Atlantic coast. It feeds largely on shellfish. 1881 Amer. Naturalist XV. 364 The ancient *clam-diggers whose kitchen-middens are met with in many places on the Alameda. 1903 Atlantic Monthly Sept. 327 He became far and away the best among the clam-diggers. 1838 Knickerbocker Mag. XI. 207 Sam's trade was *clam-digging. 1860 Susan Warner Say & Seal xvi. 146 Faith..was certainly 'spry' in getting ready for the clam-digging. 1825 Mass. Stat. 15 Feb., An act to prevent the destruction of the Lobster and *Clam Fishery in the town of Truro. 1905 N. Y. Even. Post 10 June 6 'Fish dinners' and *clam fries are to be had at any number of eating-houses at the river's mouth. 1883 Goode Fish. Industries U.S. 52 *Clam-tongs are occasionally employed for catching crabs.

Clam, v.[4] U.S. Add: (Earlier American example).
1716 B. Church Hist. Philip's War (1865) I. 96 Some catching Eels and Flat-fish in the water, some Clamming.
2. To shut up, be silent. slang.
1916 H. L. Wilson Somewhere in Red Gap vi. 237 When I ask for details he just clams up. 1926 J. Black You Can't Win viii. 97 Smiler had continually drummed it into me never to answer any questions in case we were arrested. 'Just clam up, kid.'

Clamatorial (klæmătō·riăl), a. [f. mod. L. Clamatores, a suborder of passerine birds and also of gallinaceous birds: see -ial.] Of or pertaining to the Clamatores.
1875 Cope Check-list N. Amer. Batrachia 56 Struthious, Pullastrine, and Clamatorial Birds. 1884 Coues N. Amer. Birds (ed. 2) 239 The mesomyodian or clamatorial type of syrinx.

Clamatory (klæ·mătəri), a. [ad. L. clāmātōrius: see -ory [2].] Clamorous.
1900 H. G. Wells Love & Mr. Lewisham i. 11 A rousing day, a clamatory, insistent day, a veritable herald of summer.

Clamb, variant of Clam sb.[1] (sense 2).
1898 Daily Chron. 14 Oct. 10/7 Stitchers (Female leather) wanted, used to the clambs. 1909 Ibid. 2 June 9/5 Stitchers, female, leather, used to clambs.

Clammer [3]. A workman employed in any of several occupations involving the use of a clam or clamming-machine; also, a clamper.
1921 Dict. Occup. Terms (1927) § 278 Clammer, clamper (roller engraving); raises and etches mill (design in relief) on annealed steel roller from hardened steel die.

Clamming, vbl. sb.[1] Add: **b.** attrib., as **clamming-machine,** a press in which a design in intaglio is transferred in relievo from one roller to another for engraving the copper cylinder used in calico-printing.
1860 Ure Dict. Arts (ed. 5) I. 505 In the clamming machine the die revolving in contact with the mill repeats its surface so many times on the surface of the mill. 1874 Knight Dict. Mech.

Cla·mming, vbl. sb.[3] [f. Clam v.[4]] The gathering of clams. Also attrib.
1636 Dorchester (Mass.) Town Rec. 5 July, Provided they leave stiles and gates for persons and cattle, when persons are disposed to travell or drive Cattle or swine that way to Clamming. 1806 Webster, Clamming, the taking of clams. 1838 Knickerbocker Mag. XI. 207 Sam evidently looked upon clamming as an important and mysterious thing. 1883 Goode Fish. Industries U. S. 46 All along the southern shore of the sound are prolific clamming grounds. 1895 Outing (U.S.) XXVI. 408/2 Swimming, diving, driving, clamming, fishing,..they are equally at home in or out of the water.

Clamp, v.[1] Add:
1. b. transf. To seize or press firmly.
1904 F. Lynde Grafters xxiv. 305 In one motion he clamped the weapon and turned it aside. 1924 Mulford Rustlers' Valley vi. 66 Matt..clamped his own left arm down on the other's right.

Clamper, sb.[2] Add:
4. One who clamps, one who adjusts the clamps in machinery.
1881 Instr. Census Clerks (1885) 43. 1921 Dict. Occup. Terms (1927) § 384.

Cla·m-shell. [Clam sb.[2]]
1. The shell of a clam.
1500–1540 [see Clam sb.[2] 4]. 1765 H. Timberlake Mem. 50 Wampum, which are beads cut out of clam shells. 1862 [see Clam sb.[2] 4].
b. attrib. and transf. (See quots.)
1859 Bartlett Dict. Amer. (ed. 2) s.v., The padlock now used on the United States mail-bags is called the 'Clam-shell padlock'. 1861 Mrs. Stowe Pearl Orr's Isl. II. xv. 128 A pattern [for a quilt] commonly denominated in those parts clam-shell. Ibid. 130 She stuck a decisive needle into the first clam-shell pattern. 1861 O. W. Norton Army Lett. 18 A good many of them [sc. boys] are making Clam-shell rings. 1874 Knight Dict. Mech. 746/1 The 'clam-shell' dredge..consists of a pair of scoops which are hinged to an axis and close upon the load. 1877 Encycl. Brit. VII. 465/1 Dredging in Canada and the United States is done by what are called Dipper and Clam-shell dredges.

2. a. The head. **b.** The mouth; pl. the jaws or lips. slang.
1834 S. Smith Sel. Lett. Downing 104 Shut up your clack, or I'll knock your clam-shells together pretty quick. 1850 H. C. Watson Camp-Fires Revol. 159 If you will only shut up your eternal clam-shells. 1860 Holland Miss Gilbert's Career vi. 95 All those opposed will shut their clam-shells. 1861 Lowell Biglow P. Ser. II. i. 112 You don't feel much like speakin', when, ef you let your clamshells gape, a quart of tar will leak in.

Clang, sb. 3. Add: Also, in modern psychology, with reference to the acoustic sensation of musical sounds and their analysis.
1918 M. D. Eder tr. C. G. Jung's Word-Association 470 The 'clang' associations..in our experiment..were in the form of rhymes. Jung and Riklin consider that clangs appear when there is a decline of attention. 1924 R. M. Ogden tr. K. Koffka's Growth of Mind iv. 226 So-called clang-analysis, or hearing out the partial tones of a clang, has often been advanced as a striking demonstration of the existence of unnoticed sensations.

Clanism. Delete nonce-wd., and add: Also clannism, and the following quots.:
1831 Examiner 187/1 A report, that the Chancellor intends to select all his new judges in Bankruptcy from the King's Bench Bar, and principally from the Northern Circuit. This we do not believe..; we expect to see him..free from the clanism which is implied in this rumour. 1924 Blackw. Mag. Dec. 785/1 The clannism of the villager.

Clankety (klæ·ŋkėti). Onomatopœic extension of Clank as in clankety-clank (cf. clickety-clack s.v. Click sb.[1] 8).
1905 Daily Chron. 13 Apr. 4/4 The pumps still utter their mournful clankety-clank-clank. 1907 Ibid. 8 Nov. 4/7 A traction engine..with the clankety-clank and the earth-shaking passage that suggests an earthquake.

Clankingly (klæ·ŋkiŋli), adv. [f. Clanking ppl. a. + -ly [2].] With a clanking sound. So **Cla·nkingness.**
1891 Engl. Illustr. Mag. July 703 The clankingness that only the telegraph boy puts into the bell. 1894 Cornhill Mag. May 485 The road was strewn with new stones, and the quadruped trotted clankingly.

Clans-, = clan's, genitive of Clan sb., as in Clansman; so clansfolk, clanswoman.
1896 Giddings Princ. Sociol. 173 All clansmen and clanswomen had the right to vote in electing or deposing the officers of the clan. 1908 Daily Chron. 27 Sept. 5/1 The clansfolk were defeated at the Pass of Brander.

Cla·pboard, v. U.S. (Earlier examples.)
1637 Plymouth Col. Rec. XII. 26 The house to be..clap boarded within..and a partition to be made of clap board. 1642 Boston Town Rec. 6 Aug., The walls claboarded tight from the injury of rayne and snow. 1705 Charlestown Land Records 172 [To] board or clabboard the outside of said house. 1721 Harvard College Rec. (1925) II. 457 Voted, That..the sd College be clap-boarded on the East Side. 1740 Boston Town Records XII. 273 For Clapboarding the Backside and other Repairs. 1746 Harvard College Rec. (1925) II. 757 This Corporation will consent to..clapboard the upper part of the Front of the Meeting-house. 1787 W. Bentley Diary 6 June (1905) I. 66 The meeting house.. is finished but is but partly clapboarded without. 1810 J. Lambert Trav. Canada & U.S. (1813) I. 152 The neat wooden farm-houses..are generally clapboarded over the rough logs.

Cla·pboarding, sb. U.S. [f. Clapboard.] A series of clapboards on a building.
1637 Dedham Rec. (1892) III. 32 It is agreed concerning Clapboarding of houses yt it shalbe at liberty vntill midsomer day next. 1651 Watertown Rec. 29 About the scoolehouse ..Clapbording and shingling. 1767 Boston Even. Post 15 June (Th.) The lightning fell in a perpendicular direction, ripping the clapboarding and plaistering as it fell. 1769 in F. Chase Hist. Dartmouth Coll. (1891) I. 122 Materials ..such as glass, putty,..shingling, clapboarding,..etc. 1872 Rep. Vermont Board Agric. I. 300 Paper..can be advantageously used between floors and between boarding and clapboarding on the walls. 1905 H. Garland Tyranny of Dark 59 The paint was blistering and peeling from the clap-boarding on the sunny side of the main building.

Clapham Sect: see Sect sb.[1] 4 b.

Clapmatch. (Later example.)
1874 C. M. Scammon Marine Mammals 130 (Cent.) The younger of both sexes [of sea-lions], together with the clapmatches, croak hoarsely.

Clapper, sb.[1] Add:
3. c. A name given to Crotalaria burkeana from the rattling noise made by its seed-pods. S. Afr.
1911 S. Afr. Jrnl. Sci. Apr. 269 Crotalaria burkeana.. has for many years been recognised by farmers as the cause of a disease of stock known as Stytziekte...It is..called 'Klappers' from the character of the somewhat horny pods, in which the seeds rattle about.

9. clapper-bill, a name for the open-bill stork, Anastomus lamelligerus; **clapper-bolt,** the bolt by which the clapper is attached to a bell; **clapper rail** U.S., a species of rail or marsh-hen; **clapper-stay,** a detent for the clapper of a bell, used in silent practice-ringing; **clapper-valve,** a clack-valve.
1906 tr. C. G. Schilling's With Flashlight & Rifle I. 75 Now flit past a number of those very remarkable birds aptly termed *clapper-bills. 1904 Bulwer Gloss. Techn. Terms Bells 2 The modern practice is to insert, subsequently to casting, a bolt having a hinge joint, in which the 'clapper' is secured. This bolt is called the '*clapper-bolt'. 1835 Audubon Ornith. Biog. III. 33 The *Clapper Rail, or Salt-water Marsh-hen. 1870 Amer. Naturalist III. 48, I found the nest of a Clapper-rail (Rallus Crepitans) built in a bush. 1884 Knight Dict. Mech. Suppl., *Clapper Stay, a detent for the clapper in a bell. 1874 Knight Dict. Mech., *Clapper-valve.

Clapper, sb.[3] S. Afr. [a. Du. klapper coconut.] The fruit of Strychnos pungens and S. spinosa.
1863 W. C. Baldwin Afr. Hunting 198 Some wild fruit, about three times the size of an orange, called a clapper.

Clapper (klæ·pəɹ), sb.[4] local. [? Clapper sb.[2]] In full clapper bridge: A rough bridge or raised path of stones or planks.
1793 Polwhele Hist. Dev. II. 277 note, Clapper-bridge, partly in Honiton and partly in Combe-Raleigh, is chiefly built of flint stone. 1852 N. & Q. 1st Ser. VI. 542 We have here [at Edburton, Sussex] a lane called Clappers, so named from its 'clapper', i.e. a raised footpath at side, to keep foot-passengers out of the water. 1887 W. D. Parish & Shaw Kentish Dial. 1889 J. L. W. Page Explor. Dartmoor iii. 53 Piers of undressed granite blocks support two or more superincumbent slabs, of width sufficient for the passage of a vehicle..and varying in length according to the breadth of the river. A specimen easily accessible is that which spans the East Dart at Postbridge... Other specimens of these 'clapper' bridges..exist on the Moor. 1908 W. Johnson Folk Memory 67 Certain 'clapper' bridges, crossing the streams of Exmoor and Dartmoor, are often assigned to the Bronze Age, but they are more probably relics of pack-horse days.

Clapper, v. Add: **2.** (Earlier example.)
1845 S. Judd Margaret I. xvii. 163 The house jarred and creaked,..loose boards on the roof clappered and rattled.
Hence **Cla·ppering** vbl. sb., the action of the verb, a noise like that made by the clapper of a bell.
1874 Sir E. Beckett Clocks & Watches (ed. 6) 365 The lazy and pernicious practice of 'clappering', i.e. tying the bell-rope to the clapper, and pulling it instead of the bell. 1891 Pall Mall Gaz. 7 Dec. 6/1 He chatters in imitation of the 'clappering' of a stork. 1904 C. L. Marson Folk Songs Somerset Introd. p. xi, The clapperings of the steam-binder.

Clare. In def. insert 'Franciscan' before 'order', and add quots.:
1608 in Cath. Rec. Soc. Publ. (1914) XIV. 31 This Convent of Nazareth of the poor Clares erected in the Town of Graveling. a 1660 in J. Morris Troubles Cath. Forefathers (1872) Ser. I. VI. 277 The Rich Clares and Annunciates were their near neighbours. 1756–9 A. Butler Lives Saints (1779) III. 108 A new nunnery of Poor Clares being founded at Bologna. 1894 A. M. Clarke Life St. Francis Borgia viii. 141 His youngest daughter had become a Poor Clare.

Clarification. Add:
1. b. of ideas, thought, opinion.
a 1866 Whewell (Webster) The clarification of men's ideas. 1888 Bryce Amer. Commw. lxxxiii. III. 115 The maturing and clarification of political opinion. 1909 Times 20 Jan. 10/4 Clarification of thought within the party on the fiscal question.

Clarion, sb. Add:
5. c. Comb. in clarion-voiced adj. (parasynthetic f. clarion voice: see quot. 184. in 5 b).
1907 Daily Chron. 16 Sept. 3/4 Good old clarion-voiced Sir Oliver. 1910 Ibid. 6 Jan. 9/5 His clarion-voiced question.

Clarisse (klari·s). [Fr.] **a.** The French name for a Poor Clare. **b.** A nun belonging to that branch of the order of St. Clare which follows the original rule, as distinguished from the Urbanists who follow the mitigated rule approved by Pope Urban IV in 1264. (Also occas. **Clarist** and **Clarissine.**)
1693 tr. Emilianne's Hist. Monast. Orders 253 Clara.. withdrew herself..to the Church of St. Damian, and there gave beginning to the poor Maids, called from her name Clarisses. 1840 K. H. Digby Mores Cath. x. xiii. (1847) III. 419/1 His wife desired to enter a convent of Clarists. 1879 Encycl. Brit. IX. 153/1 One of the only two nunneries of the Clarisses in Scotland existed at Aberdour. 1883 Ibid. XVI. 711/1 The Poor Clares..have also divided into Clarissines and Urbanists.

Clarkia (klā·ɹkiă). Bot. [f. the name of Captain Clark, who accompanied Captain Lewis on the first U.S. government expedition across the Rocky Mountains in 1804: see -ia [1].] A plant belonging to the genus of that name, consisting of annuals bearing white, rose, lake, and purple flowers, natives of North America.
1864 Grindon Brit. & Gard. Bot. 484 In many of the willow-herbs, the Clarkias and Œnotheras, they [sc. the stigmas] are four in number. 1900 Daily News 5 May 4/5 Shirley poppies, nemophilas, clarkia, and mignonette should be got in upon the first warm showery day.

Claro (klā·ro). [Sp., = light, Clear.] The trade designation of the lightest-coloured cigars.
1891 Cigar & Tobacco World 12 Nov. 522/2 The lightest are called 'Claro'; the next darker 'Colorado Claro'.

Clash, v. Add: **4. c.** Of colours: To go badly together, to kill each other.
1894 [see *Clashing ppl. a. d].

Clashing, ppl. a. Add: **d.** Of colours: Disagreeing, going badly together.
1894 Daily News 4 June 9/1 The Royal ladies' dresses were not of clashing hues.

Clasp, sb. Add:
1. e. A frame for holding the loose ends of cotton, flax, etc. together during the process of spinning.
1839 Ure Dict. Arts 1318 The carding is conducted through between these two bars...When this bar is again let down, it pinches the spongy carding fast; whence this mechanism is called the clasp. 1844 G. Dodd Textile Manuf. v. 160 These clasps are long frames capable of admitting the handfuls of flax, which they hold tightly at one end. 1874 Knight Dict. Mech., Clasp, a device consisting of two horizontal beams, the upper one being pressed upon the lower one, or lifted, for drawing out the thread of cotton or wool.

Class, sb. Add:
3. b. U.S. (Earlier examples.)
1684 Harvard College Rec. (1925) I. 77 Mr. Samuel Mitchell was..desired to undertake ye charge of ye class of ye Sophimores untill further order. 1702 C. Mather Magnalia II. (1820) 9 The Fellows resident on the place, became Tutors, to the several classes. 1766 Clap Ann. Yale-Coll. 14 The Senior Class were removed to Milford. ..The rest of the Students were removed to Saybrook. 1778 Stiles Lit. Diary (1901) II. 278 Admitted Cooke..into the Sophimore Class:—he was of the Senior Class in Providence College. 1805 D. McClure Diary (1899) 9 My class recited to the president.

5. b. Distinction, high quality. No class, of no worth; of low quality, inferior. Also attrib. slang or vulgar colloq.
1874 Slang Dict., Class, the highest quality or combination of highest qualities among athletes. 'He's not class enough', i.e., not good enough. 'There's a deal of class about him', i.e., a deal of quality. 1884 Referee 23 Mar. 1/3 (Farmer) The elasticity necessary for anything like class at sprinting departs comparatively early. 1897 Daily Tel. June (Ware) Soldiers! Why, soldiers ain't no class. 1924 Selincourt Cricket Match II. iii. (1928) 26 If he'd had coaching, he'd be a class bowler.

9. class-conflict, -hatred, -war; **class-conscious** a., conscious of belonging to a particular social class and of being identified with its interests, often with implication of sharp differentiation from or hostility to other classes; so **class-consciousness; class-marriage,** marriage within a class.
1919 J. L. Garvin Econ. Foundations of Peace 106 Our whole future depends upon securing..better relations between Capital and Labour instead of *Class-conflict. 1906 Daily Chron. 18 Apr. 4/5 A *class-conscious political party. 1907 Fabian News XIX. 94/1 The middle classes are more class-conscious than the workers. 1922 Times Lit. Suppl. 16 Nov., The class-conscious Socialist. 1887 Moore & Aveling tr. Karl Marx's Capital I. Pref. p. xxiv, The German proletariat had attained a much more clear *class-consciousness than the German bourgeoisie. 1922 Westm. Gaz. 18 Dec., The belief that what was called class consciousness was necessary to social progress. 1908 Daily Chron. 29 June 4/4 From top to bottom of the social or economic scale of class-consciousness or *class-hatreds. 1928 Britain's Industr. Future v. xxx. 432 The evil passions and subversive dangers of class-hatred. 1899 Keane Man Past & Present 153 Here it is necessary to distinguish carefully between *class-marriages and the so-called 'communal' or 'group' marriages; the former having for their sole object, not, as is commonly supposed, the prevention of close consanguineous unions but the proper disposal of the stock of available food. 1920 19th Cent. July 15 Without class-consciousness the neophyte cannot begin to appreciate the glories of the *class-war.

10. class-attender, -holder; **class-book** U.S. (see quot.); **class-mark, class-number,** a mark or number indicating the class or subject of a book in a library and often its position on the library shelves. (Also earlier examples of U.S. terms, in senses 3 b and 7 b.)
1897 B'ham Inst. Mag. Nov. 214 Pity her sadness, ye happy lecture-goers and *class-attenders. 1851 [B. H. Hall] College Words 44 Every graduating class [at Harvard] procures a..substantial folio of many hundred pages, called the *Class Book, and lettered with the year of the graduation of the class. 1833 F. A. Whitney in Harvard Bk. (1875) II. 165 Our *Class Day, glorious summer weather. 1851 [B. H. Hall] College Words 47 An account of Class Day, near the close of the last century, may not be uninteresting. 1887 Harper's Mag. Feb. 395/1 In front of this yellow pine wall, with its ranks of benches, stood the Class Day Tree. 1892 Eleanor Rowe Chip-Carving 54 My experiences as a *class-holder in one of the evening classes of a London Board School. 1894 Daily News 28 June 6/3 Miss Nödel, the class holder, shows some excellent work in lacquered leather. 1838 Caroline Gilman Recoll. Southern Matron 269 note, It is the office of a *class-leader to assemble those under his charge..and instruct them in their Christian duties. 1849 F. Douglas Life 54 He was soon made a class leader and exhorter. 1871 Eggleston Duffels viii. (1893) 167 The..class leader, and the old ladies..were interceding with the Father of all for him. 1886 Willis & Clark Cambridge III. 429 When a book was given to a medieval library it was necessary..to write the name and *classmark across the fore-edge. 1790 Laws of Harvard College 35 Occasions which render it convenient that there should be *Class-meetings. 1837 Stat. & Laws Harvard Univ. 26 Being present at any class-meeting without special license from the President. 1849 F. Douglas Life 44 My mistress used to go to class meeting at the Wilk St. Meeting house. 1872 Eggleston End of World vii. 79 It was so wicked to enjoy one's self out of class-meeting! 1871 — Duffels viii. (1893) 165 The class meeting that followed..impressed him still more. 1855 Knickerbocker Mag. XLV. 194 He sends us an original '*class-song',..written by Oliver Wendell Holmes. 1892 Eleanor Rowe Chip-Carving 59 The important point in *class-teaching is to keep your students together.

Classer [2] (klɑ·səɹ). [f. Class sb. + -er [1].] In compounds, a member of a (specified) class, as big-classer, double-classer.
1897 P. Warung Tales Old Régime 146 Double-classer: A ship conveying both male and female transports. 1909 Public Ledger (Philad.) 24 June 12/6 Shamrock and White Heather, the only two big classers sailing in this year's regattas.

Classhood (klɑ·shud). [f. Class sb. 2.] Distinction of class.

1878 Congress. Rec. 7 Mar. 1551/2 [Free labor in America] eliminated classhood in society, and made opportunities for advancement socially, politically, and financially equal among men.

Classic, a. and sb. Add:
A. 5. The Classic City, Boston. U.S.
1871 Schele de Vere Americanisms (1872) 662 Boston.. is called the Classic City, in appreciation of the high culture of her inhabitants.
B. 5. Short for classic race (see A. 6 b).
1905 Daily Chron. 3 May 7/4 To witness the race for the first 'classic' of the season.

Classified (klɑ·sifəid), ppl. a. [f. Classify v.] Arranged in classes.
1903 A. B. Hart Actual Govt. 290 The act provides for the classification of clerks and other officers into four groups, according to their compensation; and hence the persons subject to competitive examination are said to be in the 'classified service'.
b. With reference to a social class system.
1901 Nation (N.Y.) 19 Sept. 230 The natural ease of manner among all degrees [in China] is something which the 'classified' British mind cannot even conceive.

Classify, v. Add to def.: Also, to assign to a class already existing.
1854 Bayle St. John Purple Tints of Paris II. vii. 153 When your husband..buys books, or classifies shells. 1929 Times 31 Oct. 16/1 Finland may minimize her own risks to avoid being classified as 'East European'.

Classis. 2. b. U.S. (Examples.)
1643 New Eng. First Fruits 14 That they studiously.. observe..the speciall houres for their owne Classis. Ibid. 16 The Students of the first Classis. 1673 Harvard College Rec. (1925) I. 56 Mr. Daniell Gookin..is forthwith to take upon him the charge of a classis. 1723 Ibid. 483 After his taking the Care of the Classis to the End of this year.
3. (Later U.S. example.)
1832 R. C. Sands Writings II. 316 Last year the classis met, and recommended to the congregation to build a new church.

Classism (klɑ·siz'm). [f. Class sb. 2.] Distinction of class.
1911 H. S. Harrison Queed xx, 'The Chronicle has won its great fight', so it nervily said, 'against classism in Blaines College'.

Classmate. (Earlier U.S. examples.)
All the earliest instances so far noted refer to Harvard College.
1713 S. Sewall Diary 5 June, He has spoken for my Classmate Capt. Saml. Phipps to the Gov[erno]r. 1727 Ibid. 22 Dec., I have now been at the Interment of 4 of my class-mates. 1752 J. Macsparran Amer. Dissected (1753) 12 Mr. Dinwoody, my Class-Mate at the College of Glasgow. 1776 A. R. Robbins Jrnl. (1850) 27 Came..to Lanesborough at night, cordially received by my dear classmate [at Yale], Mr. Collins. 1805 D. McClure Diary (1899) 18 Returned to Yale College with classmate D. Avery. 1806 in Proc. Mass. Hist. Soc. (1890) Ser. II. V. 171 Saw only two of my classmates... Seven of the class have departed to the world of spirits. 1833 H. Barnard in Maryland Hist. Mag. XIII. 271, I found myself very pleasantly situated among some class mates there. 1851 O. W. Holmes Song of 'Twenty-nine' 68 We'll say, before he's spoken—'Old Classmate, don't you cry!'

Cla·ssmating, sb. [f. Classmate.] The practice of cultivating the acquaintance of classmates.
1774 J. Adams in Familiar Lett. (1876) 10 You know I never get or save anything by cozening or classmating.

Classy (klɑ·si), a. slang or colloq. [f. Class sb. + -y [1].] Of high or superior class, stylish, smart.
1891 Duncan Amer. Girl in London 228 Why didn't one of you go? Not classy enough, eh? 1892 Temple Bar Nov. 393 Her successor is the 'smart' young married woman,.. who is chic and 'classy'. 1899 E. Phillpotts Human Boy 174 He said a man who sold pills and toothbrushes..could not be considered a classy chemist. 1903 'Marjoribanks' Fluff-hunters 94 Was she classy, well turned out, and all that sort of thing? 1920 C. Sandburg Smoke & Steel 225 It's a knockout, a classy knockout. 1929 Daily Express 2 Jan. 4/2 An assemblage as sophisticated and classy as ever gathered under one roof.

Clatter, v. Add: **2.** Also with off.
1916 Boyd Cable Action Front 187 The maxim clattered off belt after belt of cartridges.
2. c. trans. To make up hurriedly and noisily.
1907 M. C. Harris Tents of Wickedness II. i. 113 They'll clatter their clothes up in a sewing machine when their mothers won't do it for them any longer.

Cla·tting, vbl. sb. [f. Clat sb.[1] 1.] (See quots.)
1844 H. Stephens Bk. Farm II. 600 In preparing ewes for lambing..the looker..removes with the shears the wool on their tail, udders, and inside of their thighs... This treatment [is] called clatting. 1884 Allen New Amer. Farm Bk. 436 Tagging or clatting is the removal of such wool as is liable to get fouled when the sheep are turned on to the fresh pastures.

Clauber, variant of Clabber.
1890 Service Notandums 114 Whaur it was a' clauber yesterday, it's as hard as a horn the day. 1892 Yeats C'tess Kathleen i. 16 The dead leaves and clauber of four forests Cling to my foot-sole. 1921 G. O'Donovan Vocations v. 83 Good people..that wouldn't throw a lump of soft clauber at a cat.

Claudian (klǭ·diăn), a. [ad. L. Claudianus.] Of or pertaining to any of several distinguished Romans of the name of Claudius or the gens to which they belonged, esp. pertaining to or connected with the emperors Tiberius, Caligula, Claudius, and Nero (A.D. 14–68), or their epoch.
1826 K. H. Digby Broad Stone of Hon., Godefridus (1829) 236 The Claudian family..produced the sad Tiberius, then the monstrous Caligula. 1842 Macaulay Lay of Virginia 215 The face of Appius Claudius wore the Claudian scowl and sneer. 1876 Encycl. Brit. V. 817/1 The Claudian aqueduct and the harbour of Ostia. 1882 Ibid. XIV. 337/2 The epic poets of the Flavian age present a striking contrast to the writers of the Claudian period.

Claudication (klǭdikēi·ʃən). Delete †Obs. and add: **b.** Path.
1909 Practitioner Nov. 666 Angina pectoris, which is nothing else than intermittent claudication of the heart.

Clausal (klǭ·zăl), a. [f. Clause: see -al.] Of or pertaining to a clause or clauses.
1904 C. T. Onions Engl. Syntax § 300 A few broad principles have been enunciated, which, although they cover considerable ground, will not explain every kind of clausal combination which can be met with. 1905 Westm. Gaz. 25 Mar. 2/2 Would they have gagged and bound their country's hands In Saccharine Convention's clausal bonds?

Clause, v. [f. Clause sb. 1.] intr. To construct clauses.
1895 Proc. 14th Conv. Am. Instruct. Deaf 124, I have endeavored to make my pupils read and speak like hearing people, teaching them to phrase and clause.
So **Clau·sing** vbl. sb.
1908 Daily Chron. 3 Feb. 3/5 The clausing of the Bill..is not..as effectual as it might be.

Claustrophobia (klǭstrŏfōu·biă). Path. [mod. L., f. L. claustrum confined space, Cloister + -phobia.] A morbid dread of confined places.
1879 Brit. Med. Jrnl. 6 Sept. 371/1 On Claustrophobia. By B. Ball, M.D. (Paris). 1886 Buck's Handbk. Med. Sci. III. 51/1 Well-marked cases of anthropophobia,.. claustrophobia, and what might be called pyrophobia. 1906 Westm. Gaz. 18 Apr. 2/1 Others of us who have felt..an inexplicable horror of remaining within four walls..now know that we are sufferers from Claustrophobia. 1924 Galsworthy White Monkey I. v, Having a sort of mental claustrophobia, a dread of being hemmed-in by people.

Claustrum (klǭ·strŏm). Anat. Pl. **claustra.** [L.] A thin layer of grey matter in each cerebral hemisphere between the external capsule and the island of Reil.
1848 Quain's Elem. Anat. (ed. 5) 739 Beneath the white matter of those gyri, a thin layer of grey substance is met with, which has been named the claustrum (Burdach). 1889 Buck's Handbk. Med. Sci. VIII. 135 The lenticula.—Between the caudatum and the cortex the greatly thickened hemicerebral wall presents..(b) next the cortex, a sub-circular disk of cinerea, the claustrum.

Clavately (klǣ·vėtli), adv. [f. Clavate + -ly [2].] In club-shaped form.
1872 H. C. Wood Fresh-w. Algæ 176 Clavately swollen.

Clavel. Add: **2. clavel piece.** (Earlier American example.)
1634 Trelawny Papers (1884) 31 The Chimnay..is so large that we Can place our Chittle [sc. kettle] within the Clavell pece.

Clavicembalo (klævi,tʃe·mbălo). Mus. [It.] The harpsichord.
1858 Simmonds Dict. Trade. 1880 Grove Dict. Mus. I. 330/1 The dulcimer, or cembalo, with keys added, became the clavicembalo.

Clavula (klæ·viulă). Pl. -æ. [mod.L. Cf. Clavule.]
1. One of the knobbed ciliated setæ or bristles found on the exterior of spatangoid sea-urchins.
1884 tr. Claus' Zool., Protozoa to Insecta 296 The fascioles or semitæ..upon which..knobbed bristles with active cilia (clavulæ) are distributed. 1888 Rolleston & Jackson Anim. Life 558 Clavulæ, found only in Spatangidæ.
2. A spicule occurring in certain hexactinellid sponges in the shape of a toothed rod pointed at one end and thickened or knobbed at the other.
1887 Encycl. Brit. XXII. 417/2 The clavula, a tylotate form with a toothed margin to the head.

Claw, sb. Add:
5. Part of the mechanism of a lock.
1874 Knight Dict. Mech., Claw, a spur or talon projecting from a bolt or tumbler.
8. claw-mark, -scratch, -wound; claw-tipped; **claw-and-ball,** applied to furniture characterized by the representation of a claw clasping a ball; **claw-balk** U.S., a beam fitted with a claw, used in bridge-building; **claw-foot,** a disease causing distortion of the foot; a foot thus affected; **claw-hammer** (later example); also ellipt. for claw-hammer coat; **claw-lever,** a lever which divides into two claws in such a way that it can grip both sides of an article; **claw-wrench,** a wrench with a loose jaw which bites against a relatively fixed one.
1902 Connoisseur Jan. 55/1 It [sc. a wine cistern] is supported by four *claw-and-ball feet. 1906 Westm. Gaz. 23 Jan. 2/1 Perfect specimens of claw-and-ball furniture. 1884 Century Mag. XXIX. 280 Each two men carrying a *claw-balk, or timbers fitted with a claw, one of which held the gunwhale of the boat, the other the shore abutment. 1901 Dorland Med. Dict. (ed. 2), *Claw-foot, atrophy and distortion of the foot. 1920 Glasgow Herald 8 July 4 Foot-drop, corns and contracted toes, claw-foot. 1878 B. F. Taylor Between Gates 27 A youthful descendant of Ham, with a heel like a *claw-hammer. 1888 N.Y. Sun 29 Sept. (Farmer) Don't..call a dress-coat a swallow-tail, or a claw-hammer. 1895 Outing (U.S.) XXVI. 434/2 I'd..sow the dark woods with fragments of claw-hammer and patent leathers. 1892 Nasmith Students' Cotton Spinning 266 On the same arbor..is a *claw lever engaging with the ring groove. 1828 P. Cunningham N.S. Wales (ed. 3) II. 36 On the *claw-marks being discerned, they climb up by successive notches in the bank. 1920 Chambers's Jrnl. 89/2 Two parallel lines of claw-marks. 1897 P. Warung Tales Old Régime 190 A feline *claw-scratch. 1894 Outing (U.S.) XXIV. 417/1 His.. *claw-tipped fore-paws. 1891 Pall Mall Gaz. 22 June 7/1 Two *claw wounds on her chest. 1874 Knight Dict. Mech., *Claw-wrench, a wrench having a loose, pivoted jaw which binds of itself.

Claw, v. 7. Naut. (Later examples.)
1883 'Mark Twain' Life Mississippi vi. 81, I..began to claw the boat away from the danger. 1921 R. D. Paine Comr. Rolling Ocean xii. 202 An inch at a time, as you might say, she [sc. the ship] was clawing off a lee shore.

Clay, sb. 9. Add:
clay-bird, a piece of baked clay or other material, representing a bird, which serves as a target in trap-shooting; **clay-eater** U.S. (earlier example); **clay-field,** a tract of country where clay is found and worked; **clay hole,** a water-hole in a clay-bed; **clay-miner,** a workman whose occupation is the digging of clay; **clay-modeller,** one who makes models of clay; **clay-modelling,** the art or practice of modelling in clay; **clay-pan,** (a) a layer of clay in the soil U.S.; (b) a slight depression or shallow hole in the surface of the ground, having a bottom of clay or silt Austral.; **clay-pigeon** = *clay-bird; **clay-shale, -slip** (see quots.); **clay-works,** works in which clay is prepared for use; so clay-worker, clay-working.
1909 Westm. Gaz. 22 Mar. 10/1 The Stock Exchange *clay-bird shooting competition. 1841 W. G. Simms Scout (1882) 153 He was..a jaundiced..'*clay-eater' from the Wassamasaw country. 1909 Daily Chron. 11 June 5/5 The working of the extensive *clayfield. 1843 S. Marg. Fuller Summer on Lakes 215 He drowned himself.. in a broad and shallow *clay hole. 1881 Instr. Census Clerks (1885) 81 *Clay Miner. 1909 Westm. Gaz. 10 Feb. 7/2 The clay-miners entombed by a fall of silver-sand at Morden clay-pits, near Corfe Castle. 1881 Instr. Census Clerks (1885) 55 *Clay, Ornamental Modeller. 1898 Westm. Gaz. 5 Jan. 2/3 *Clay-modelling talent. 1837 Colman Rep. Agric. Mass. (1838) 78 This drain is four feet wide at the top, and goes down some small depth into the *clay pan. 1890 Melbourne Argus 2 Aug. 13/3 The baked surface of the claypan. 1889 Kansas Times & Star 4 Dec., One of the finest *clay pigeon or trapshooters hereabouts. 1893 W. K. Post Harvard Stories 16 He was to shoot a clay-pigeon match. 1895 Army & Navy Co-op. Soc. Price List 15 Sept. 958 The Anglo-American Ligowsky Clay Pigeon Traps. 1882 Econ. Geol. Illinois II. 10 It is underlaid by fire-clay, or *clay shale, twenty inches thick. Ibid. 18 This coal-seam is subject to some irregularities, such as '*clay slips' or 'horse-hacks' sometimes called 'faults' by the miners. 1909 Daily Chron. 11 June 5/5 Showing them over the *clayworks. 1902 Ibid. 21 May 6/3 The British Institute of *Clayworkers. 1900 Engineering Mag. XIX. 793/1 The *Clay-Working Industry of the Pacific Coast.

Clay-bank. U.S. [Clay sb. 9.] **a.** attrib. and Comb. in the sense of 'having the colour of a bank of yellowish clay', esp. clay-bank horse.
1851 [see Clay sb. 9]. 1855 Putnam's Mag. Feb. 188, I mounted a claybank colored nag and rode to the hunt. 1869 Overland Monthly III. 126, I met a man..who was mounted on a clay-bank horse. Ibid., 'Clay-bank' is a yellowish dun. 1874 Eggleston Circuit Rider viii. 79 Captain Lumsden himself galloping after them on his sleek, 'clay-bank' saddle horse. 1884 'C. E. Craddock' In Tenn. Mts. 101 A yoke of oxen, a clay-bank filly, ten hogs. 1887 F. Francis Jr. Saddle & Mocassin ix. 158 She..dropped it [sc. the noose] over the head of the 'clay-bank' nag that I was endeavouring to catch. 1906 'O. Henry' Rolling Stones (1915) 30 An elegant gentleman of a slightly claybank complexion. a 1909 — Roads of Destiny v. 81 Fergus was at the other end of the room trying to break away from two maroons and a claybank girl.
b. A horse of this colour.
1858 Kansas Hist. Colls. (1896) V. 540 Stolen..one yearling, a claybank with white and flaxen mane and tail. 1885 'C. E. Craddock' Prophet Gt. Smoky Mts. v. 108 The mountain colt, a clay-bank..reared violently under the surprise of the lash. 1886 Outing (U.S.) IX. 104/2 The 'clay-banks' were put to their speed.

Clayeyness (klē·inės). [f. Clayey + -ness.] Clayey nature or quality.
1888 Lowell Lett. (1899) II. 400 Slippery from clayeyness of soil.

Clayness (klē·nės). [f. Clay sb. + -ness.] = prec.
1849 Rep. U.S. Comm. Patents Agric. (1850) 115 The soil ..is one of medium clayness.

Clay-slate. (Earlier U.S. examples.)
1815 D. Drake Cincinnati ii. 65 Strata [of limestone] which alternate with layers of clay-slate. 1822 J. Woods Two Yrs.' Resid. Eng. Prairie 273 First, a vegetable mould, next loamy clay, then sand-stone, and lastly clay-slate.

Clean, a. Add:
1. e. Of a vessel: Clear of advance commission, dispatch money, and other charges, which may constitute deductions from the freight.
1890 Whitby Gaz. 17 Jan. 2/7 Thomas Turnbull, Cardiff to Cape Verde, 9s. 6d., clean. 1891 Ibid. 18 Sept. 3/2 Stakesby, Cardiff to Gibraltar, 6s. 6d., clean and nett.
3. c. spec. in clean proof, clean sheet, one in which the printer's final corrections have been made.
1858 Simmonds Dict. Trade, Clean Proof, a slip or sheet of printed matter sent to an author from a printer.
e. Of deer or their horns: That have shed their velvet.
1838 W. Scrope Art Deer-Stalking i. 6 When they have shaken off this skin, which is called the velvet, and which disappears in the months of August and September, they are said to have clean horns. 1897 J. G. Millais British Deer 95 Park stags are clean sometimes as early as 20th July.

1926 Hannan Isle of Mull 173 The stags were not 'clean' any earlier than usual.
4. c. In phr. the clean thing: Honest, straightforward. U.S.
1835 D. Crockett Tour 193 (Bartlett), I don't like it. It isn't the clean thing. 1855 Haliburton Nat. & Hum. Nat. I. 200 Hang me if he can be the clean thing anyhow he can fix it. 1871 Washington Patriot 3 Apr. (De Vere) It would have been the clean thing to say at once that no debate would be allowed.
d. Clean ticket (see quots.). U.S.
1859 Bartlett Dict. Amer. (ed. 2), Clean Ticket, the entire regularly nominated ticket at an election; a ticket without any erasures. 'He went the clean ticket on the Whig Nominations.' 1871 Schele de Vere Americanisms (1872) 269 Only when a man adopts the whole list as made up by his party, is it called a clean or straight ticket.
e. Of an author, his writings, etc.: Free from indelicate treatment of sexual matters.
1908 Westm. Gaz. 26 Oct. 1/2 M. René Bazin..has.. become known on this side of the Channel as the 'cleanest' of contemporary French novelists. 1911 E. J. Muddle's Picture Plays 10 The public..demands good, clean, wholesome pictures, to which it can take every member of its household, from the youngest upwards. 1929 Priestley Good Comp. II. i. 249 He's one of the best comedians going in Concert Party work—clever, and keeps it clean.

Clean, v. Add:
1. e. slang. = 4 b.
1926 J. Black You Can't Win iv. 27, I soon came to know the poker players..and dice sharks who brought their victims into the back room to 'clean' them.
3. To clean up: also, To obtain by cleaning, to acquire as gain or profit; also, to deal with effectively, to get the better of. (Cf. *Clean-up.)
1905 Rex Beach Pardners i. (1912) 25 When the river broke we cleaned up one hundred and eighty-seven dollars' worth of lovely, yellow dust. 1908 S. E. White Riverman xxxi. 254 We ought to clean up five dollars a thousand on our mill. 1922 H. L. Foster Adv. Trop. Tramp xii. 184, I haven't seen Red since..that night we cleaned up the police force.
b. To make a clean sweep of.
1903 Westm. Gaz. 31 Jan. 8/1 The seals clean up the seas much as the rabbits clean up the grass in Australia and the locusts clean up the crops in Africa.
c. To clear (a place) of undesirable people. U.S. Cf. *4 d.
1929 Times 15 Feb., More than 3,000 persons were arrested ..by the Chicago police in a new effort to 'clean up' the city.
4. To clean out. **b.** (Later U.S. examples.)
a 1861 T. Winthrop John Brent i. 7 They had been burnt out, they had been cleaned out, they had been drowned out. 1901 S. E. White Westerners xiii. 94 Bunco men can clean him out in a gambling joint.
c. To deal effectively with (a person); to eject from a place. U.S.
1866 Congress. Globe 19 Dec. 205/2, I hope my colleague will be allowed to proceed, and that I may be allowed to clean him out. 1867 J. M. Crawford Mosby & his Men xiv. 144 Our style of fighting being to pitch in, and 'clean' the enemy out, or be 'cleaned out'. 1871 Congress. Globe 5 Jan. 316/1 The enemy did take possession of the house one day. They were 'cleaned out' as we say; they were compelled to leave the house. 1892 J. L. Ford Dr. Dodd's School i. 10 He could lick the whole crowd of them with one hand tied behind his back. Do you remember how he cleaned out the townies that Saturday afternoon? 1908 S. E. White Riverman xxii. 197, I don't bet those Saginaw river-pigs are any more two-fisted than the boys on this river. I'd go up and clean 'em out.
d. To clear (a place) of the persons occupying it. U.S.
1858 Kansas Hist. Colls. (1896) V. 567 These same men attacked Barnesville..and literally cleaned it out, both of inhabitants and property. 187. B. Harte Society Stanislaus 20 On several occasions he had cleaned out the town. 1901 Marah E. Ryan Montana vii. 97 They..would proceed to 'clean out' any establishment where their own peculiar set was ignored. 1902 S. E. White Blazed Trail vi. 48 Nothing pleases him better than..to embark on an earnest effort to 'clean out' a rival town.
5. To clean off. (Later U.S. example.)
1910 O. Johnson Varmint iv. 58 You know you said you were going to clean off the whole slate with Al.

Clean-. Add: **2. clean-run,** defining a well-fed, bright-looking salmon newly returned to fresh water from the sea; also fig. of a young person.
1881 [see Run ppl. a. 4]. 1926 W. J. Locke Old Bridge I. i. 13 He was a clean-run, brown-haired, blue-eyed youth. 1929 — Jorico 64 They're very clean-run young women.

Cleaner. a. Add: Also cleaner up.
1908 Daily Chron. 24 Aug. 9/6 Pianos.—Fitters up; also a cleaner up. 1921 Dict. Occup. Terms (1927) § 499 Cleaner, cleaner-up (pianos); scrapes (mucks off) and rubs veneered parts of piano with sandpaper or glasspaper, preparatory to polishing. Ibid. (passim).

Cleaning, ppl. a. **Cleaning crop,** a crop serving to clear land in cultivation from weeds.
a 1909 T. Shaw Forage Crops 173 (Cent. Dict. Suppl. s.v. Crop) [Rye] becomes in a sense a 'cleaning' crop when another crop immediately follows the depasturing. 1921 Discovery Feb. 48/2 The farmer..tries periodically and systematically to rid his fields of [weeds], and takes what he calls a cleaning crop.

Clean-up. (See Clean sb.; additional U.S. examples.)
1866 Congress. Globe 18 June 3231/1 When what they technically call in mining the clean up comes, very often the clean-up exhibits the lofty sum of nothing, while thousands have been expended in the effort. 1876 'Joaquin' Miller Unwritten Hist. vi. 91 We will be ready for a big clean up by the time the snow flies. 1904 Topeka Daily Capital 8 June 4 The authentic story comes along of a clean-up somewhere along the line by the Japanese army or navy. 1908 G. H. Lorimer J. Spurlock i. 6 His clean-up in Consolidated Groceries was so big that [etc.]. 1910 Jer. Hart Vigilante Girl ii. 28 Where he made his biggest clean-up was in buying some mud-flats.

Clear, a. Add:
25. U.S. (Earlier example of clear grit.)
1825 J. Neal Bro. Jonathan xiv. II. 14 A chap, who was clear grit for a tussle, any time—any where.
b. In technical or trade use.
1822 J. Woods Two Yrs.' Resid. Eng. Prairie 211 A hundred middling ears of corn will yield a bushel of clear corn. 1851 C. Cist Cincinnati 214 Pig-iron, and one thousand tons Tennessee clear blooms. Ibid. 281 The inspection laws require that clear pork shall be put up of the sides, with the ribs out. 1865–6 Trans. Ill. Agric. Soc. VI. 645 Clear flooring, rejected on account of thickness, shall be classed with common flooring. 1874 Knight Dict. Mech. 564/1 Clear-stuff, boards free from knots, wane, wind-shakes, ring-hearts, dote, sap. 1889 Century Dict., Clear, without admixture, adulteration, or dilution; as, a fabric of clear silk; clear brandy; clear tea. 1908 Practitioner Dec. 841 To carbon-monoxide poisoning are exposed blast-furnace men, coal miners, and mechanics, when engaged in repairing exhausters or examining disused cylinders. The furnace men may be affected..by an escape of gas at some defective joint. It is known as 'clear gas'. 1917 F. S. Henry Printing for School & Shop vi. 80 Such an attempt [sc. to produce a letter of maximum legibility] on the part of L. B. Benton and his son Morris has resulted in the production of the type face known as Clearface... The general effect of Clearface is that it presents a uniform amount of white throughout the line. 1930 San Antonio (Texas) Light 31 Jan., Clear Sides Salt Bacon.
B. adv. **4. b.** clear-away: entirely, completely.
1883 Stevenson Treasure Isl. xxxii, And come to think on it, it was like Flint's voice, I grant you, but not just so clear-away like it, after all.
5. (Later U.S. examples.)
1835 Longstreet Georgia Scenes 270 Well I'm clear put out. 1845 Mrs. Kirkland Western Clearings 78 I'm clear tuckered out with these young 'uns.
C. sb. **5.** (Earlier American example.)
1674 Maryland Archives (1884) 405 The State house to be ..with a porch in front sixteene foote long and twelve foote broad in the Clear on the Inside.
6. b. With up, the action of clearing up, spec. the settlement of accounts (see Clear v. 27 g). Also attrib.
1901 Westm. Gaz. 24 May 7/1 The clear-up will have to come sooner or later. 1928 (From a Stockbroker's form) 29 May, Paid..in respect of the clear-up Dividend.
D. 3. clear-skin Austral., an unbranded beast (cf. clean-skin); **clear-way,** (a) a path or passage-way; (b) see quot. 1884.
1884 'R. Boldrewood' Melb. Mem. xv. 109 Calves and *clear-skins. 1888 — Robbery under Arms ii, I hadn't lived all my life on Rocky Creek..without knowing what 'clearskins' and 'cross' beasts meant. 1900 H. Lawson Over Sliprails 135 'Carn't you see it's a clear skin?' ..The idea of a '"clear skin" steer' would have amused her at any other time. 1884 Knight Dict. Mech. Suppl., *Clear Way. Said of a valve, hydrant, etc. One which lifts its valve entirely out of the way of obstructing the flow; not compelling the water to flow around it. Also called full-way. 1927 Observer 14 Aug. 18/1 All this clear-way in the grass is treated with cement or weed-killer.

Clear, v. Add: **10. b.** (b) (Earlier American examples.)
1634 W. Wood New Eng. Prospect (1865) 40 This place is called Massachusetts fields where the greatest Sagamore in the countrey lived, before the Plague, who caused it to be cleared for himselfe. 1640 Boston Rec. (1877) II. 53 Nathan Willis is spared from Cleareing half an acre of his ground.. in regard his servant did scald his legg.
13. (Early U.S. example.)
1839 Mrs. Kirkland New Home xv. 92 [He] stated boldly that Mr. Mazard had absconded; or in Western language 'cleared'.
25. Clear off. b. Also in wider sense (= 26 d), to take oneself off. (Earlier U.S. example.)
1816 U. Brown Jrnl. in Maryland Hist. Mag. XI. 365 [I] called to her [sc. a mare] and flattered her to come back; she would not; clear'd off and left me.
26. Clear out. d. (Earlier U.S. example.)
1816 U. Brown Jrnl. in Maryland Hist. Mag. XI. 231, I had got my horse ready to mount and clear out for Baltimore.

Clearable (klī·răb'l), a. [f. Clear v. + -able.] Capable of being cleared, able to be put in order.
1889 Westgarth Austral. Progr. 90 Stacking up for fire-wood all the clearable refuse.

Clearance. Add: **3.** Also attrib. **clearance sale,** a sale of goods at reduced prices to effect a clearance of superfluous stock.
1890 Jackson's Oxford Jrnl. 12 July 1/1 Harry Neville Prior's Great Clearance Sale. 1925 B. Beetham in E. F. Norton Fight for Everest, 1924 184 We decided to hold an autumn clearance sale of..general equipment.
6. Also attrib.
1902 P. Marshall Metal Tools 36 The widest part of a chisel should be at its cutting edge, behind which point a clearance taper..should be given. 1906 Westm. Gaz. 10 Aug. 4/1 As for building our 'buses lower down, we will do that as soon as the Commissioner of Police reduces the 10-in. clearance regulation.

Cleared, ppl. a. (American examples.)
1642 Virginia Stat. (1823) I. 244 Be it also enacted..That ev'rie planter shall make a sufficient fence about his cleared ground. 1838 Caroline Gilman Recoll. Southern Matron i. 10 The moon rises over the cleared fields, showing an amphitheatre of distant woods. 1843 Yale Lit. Mag. IX. 15 The new comers had purchased a piece of cleared land somewhere off among the mountains.

Clearer. Add:
1. b. One who transacts the business of passing cheques and bills, etc., through a clearing-house; a clearing-banker. Cf. In-clearer.
1884 Howarth Clearing System iv. 51 The men who transact the clearing business for the various banks are called 'the clearers'. 1892 Chambers's Jrnl. 613/2 The clearer we will say represents the London and County Banking Company.
2. d. pl. Spectacles that clear the vision.
1921 Public Opinion 23 Dec. 627/3 When their time comes to wear 'clearers'.

Clearing, vbl. sb. Add:
1. c. The clearance between the working parts of a machine.
1874 Knight Dict. Mech., Clearing, the amount of play between the meshing-teeth of cog-wheels, to avoid jam.
3. (Earlier U.S. examples.)
1821 M. Birkbeck Letter 150 The enormous expence of time and labour in clearing, which has been bestowed on every acre between this and the Atlantic. 1845 W. G. Simms Wigwam & Cabin 101 As free-spoken..as if they had been intimate from the first day of clearing in that country.
b. The removing of imperfections from silk fibre or yarn.
1874 Knight Dict. Mech., Clearing, the process of removing irregularities from silk filaments before spinning, by passing them beneath a scraper, or between steel rollers.
c. The washing of calico to remove excess dye.
1839 Ure Dict. Arts I. 164 Bran..is advantageously employed by the calico printers, in the clearing process. 1874 Knight Dict. Mech., Clearing.., washing the dye solution from the unmordanted portion of the cloth, in the 'madder style' of printing. 1876 Encycl. Brit. IV. 688/1 The operations of clearing are necessary to remove all the dye-stuff which is loosely attached to the whites, and to develop and brighten the tints of dyed pattern.
4. U.S. (Earlier examples.)
1817 M. Birkbeck Journ. Amer. 140, I could judge of the extent of the clearing, if I saw the people. 1830 J. Hall Lett. fr. West (1828) 191 Immediately below us is a clearing which seems to have been made some years ago.
8. clearing frame, knife, machine, room (sense *3 b); **clearing-hospital,** a hospital for the temporary reception and treatment of sick and wounded; **clearing-screw** (see quot.); **clearing-stone,** a fine stone used for sharpening curriers' knives.
1916 Boyd Cable Action Front 4 In *clearing-hospitals, ammunition parks, and Army Service Corps supply points. 1921 Dict. Occup. Terms (1927) § 371 Cleaner, clearer..; winds raw silk from bobbins, through cleaning or *clearing knives, on to fresh bobbins, to remove dirt, lumps, etc. 1875 Knight Dict. Mech. s.v. Silk-manuf., The *clearing-machine, where it is wound upon other bobbins. 1881 Instr. Census Clerks (1885) 68 Cotton and Flax...*Clearing Room: Clearer. 1874 Knight Dict. Mech., *Clearing-screw, in some fire-arms, a screw at right angles to the nipple, affording a communication with the chamber. 1860 Ure Dict. Arts (ed. 5) II. 687 [The currier's knife] is..rubbed on a fine Scotch or Welsh stone called a *clearing-stone.

Clearing, ppl. a. Add: Also clearing-up.
a 1862 Thoreau Maine Woods (1912) 229 It had rained a little in the forenoon, and we trusted that this would be the clearing-up shower, which it proved.

Clearing-house. Add: Also fig.
1903 Daily Chron. 10 Dec. 6/7 What is wanted is first a human clearing house, or, in other words, compulsory examination of all immigrants. 1906 Westm. Gaz. 17 Dec. 2/1 Washington is in one sense the clearing-house for the humanity of the entire continent.

Clear-starch, v. (Mod. U.S. example.)
1898 A. Nicholas Idyl of Wabash 6 I'd like to clear starch 'em all once.

Clear-up: see *Clear C. 6 b.

Clea·rweed. U.S. [Clear a. 3.] A North American plant (Adicea pumila) of the nettle family.
1862 A. Gray Man. Bot. (1866) 399 Pilea pumila. Richweed. Clearweed... Stems smooth and shining, pellucid. 1871 Schele de Vere Americanisms (1872) 406 A nettle with succulent, semi-transparent stems is called Clearweed (Pilea pumila). 1901 C. Mohr Plant Life Alabama 478.

Cleavage. Add:
1. e. Biol. Cell-division, segmentation.
1879 tr. Haeckel's Evol. Man I. 185 The parent-cell, which arose from the fertilized egg-cell, separates, by repeated cleavage, into a large number of simple cells. 1896 E. B. Wilson Cell 143 During the early anaphase of the first cleavage each centrosome divides into two. 1902 Encycl. Brit. XXVIII. 140/1 Segmentation or cleavage of the ovum.
3. cleavage-cavity = Blastocœle; **cleavage-cell, -globule** = Blastomere; **cleavage-mass,** (a) a mass of rock formed by cleavage; (b) = Blastomere; **cleavage-nucleus,** the nucleus of the fertilized egg resulting from the union of male and female pronuclei; **cleavage-spindle,** the karyokinetic spindle of the dividing blastomere.
1879 tr. Haeckel's Evol. Man I. 189 The inner cavity of the ball, which is filled with clear liquid or jelly, is called the *cleavage-cavity (cavum segmentarium), or the germ-cavity (blastocœloma). 1887 Encycl. Brit. XXII. 425/2 In this stage thin sections show that the cleavage cavity is obliterated. 1879 tr. Haeckel's Evol. Man I. 186 *Cleavage-cells or *Cleavage-globules (segmentella). 1871 Huxley Anat. Vert. 10 The *cleavage-masses eventually become very small, and are called embryo-cells. 1912 Brit. Museum Return 196 Enargite, large cleavage masses from Red Mtn.,

Colorado. 1896 E. B. WILSON *Cell* 156 The first *cleavage-nucleus. *Ibid.* 157 The centrosomes of the *cleavage-spindle.

Cleek, *sb.* Add: **1. b.** *Golf.* An iron-headed club with a straight, narrow face and a long shaft.

1829 J. S. BLACKIE *Let.* 11 Dec. in *Lett. to Wife* (1909) 42 As if the golfers at St. Andrews should go down to the links ..with an immense array of all sorts of clubs, and then, after having swung their drivers and cleques most scientifically in the air, should come back again without playing a single game. 1883 *Standard* 16 Nov. 5/2 He..is ready with..the cleek. 1891 H. G. HUTCHINSON *Golf* (ed. 6) 29 It is a stroke which is mostly used with the brassy, cleek or iron, when in a bad lie. 1893 — *Golfing* (ed. 2) 19 We cannot be far wrong in advising the golfer to choose his cleek-heads thick. 1909 P. A. VAILE *Mod. Golf* 107 The ordinary cleek shot.

Cleistocarp (klai·stokāɹp). *Bot.* Also **clistocarp.** [f. Gr. κλειστός closed + καρπός fruit.] In mosses and fungi an ascogonium whose asci and spores develop within a completely closed capsule, from which the spores escape by the rupture of the sack. Hence **Cleistoca·rpous** *a.*, having a closed capsule, having a capsule without an operculum.

1884 *Encycl. Brit.* XVII. 73/2 The *Phascaceæ* are termed 'cleistocarpous' in contradistinction to the 'stegocarpous' Mosses. 1887 tr. *Strasburger's Bot.* 261 The section of cleistocarpous Ascomycetes.

Clement, *a.* **2.** (Recent U.S. example.)

1916 H. L. WILSON *Somewhere in Red Gap* v. 174 A clement Sabbath would have seen her 'resting', as she would put it.

Clerestory. Add: **1. c.** A row of small windows above the main roof of a railway carriage.

1884 KNIGHT *Dict. Mech.* Suppl. 1903 *Westm. Gaz.* 15 July 6/3 G.W.R. eight-wheeled bogy coaches of the 'clerestory' pattern.

Clergy. Add: **1. f.** *Regular clergy, secular clergy*: see REGULAR A. 1, SECULAR A. 1.

Clergywoman. Add:

3. A woman acting as pastor of a congregation or as a minister of religion.

1871 *Chicago Tribune* 17 Feb. (De Vere) Mrs. E. Tupper Wilkes, the Minnesota clergywoman, has a salary of $2000 a year. 1904 *Westm. Gaz.* 25 Feb. 10/1 The Clergywoman in America.

Clerid (kle·rid), *a.* and *sb.* *Ent.* [ad. mod.L. *Cleridæ*, a family of beetles.] **A.** *adj.* Of or pertaining to the *Cleridæ*. **B.** *sb.* A beetle of this family (Cent. Dict. 1889).

1913 *Oxford Univ. Gaz.* 4 June 955/2, 1 ♀ Mutillid and 1 Clerid beetle mimicking it in a very remarkable manner.

Clerk, *sb.* Add: **1. a.** *Regular clerk, secular clerk*: see REGULAR A. 1, SECULAR A. 1.

6. c. *Clerk of the weather* (for earlier example, of 1835, see WEATHER *sb.* 2 h; cf. also **weather office*).

1831 B. HALL *Fragm. Voy. & Trav.* III. 206 Owing to their interest with the clerk of the weather office. 1843 J. F. MURRAY *World of London* II. 29 If the clerk of the weather office is determined to put a damper on the festivities.

d. A shop-assistant. *U.S.*

1840 *Knickerbocker Mag.* 507 The clerk [in the store].. came down directly. 1844 'JON. SLICK' *High Life N.Y.* I. 63, I..went to the tailor's store...'Have you got any first rate superfine broadcloth coats and trousers to sell here?' sez I...'Yes,' sez one of the clerks. 1889 *Century Dict.*, *Clerk* 6. In the United States, an assistant in business, whether or not a keeper of accounts; especially, a retail salesman. 1903 W. E. CURTIS *True Abraham Lincoln* 33 He ..became a clerk in the store..measuring calico, weighing sugar and nails.

Clerkess (klā·ɹkės). [f. CLERK *sb.* + -ESS.] A female clerk.

1923 *Glasgow Herald* 21 Mar. 10 A clerkess in a Glasgow firm's counting-room.

Clerodendron (klīərode·ndrɒn). *Bot.* Also **clerodendrum.** [mod.L., f. Gr. κλῆρος lot + δένδρον tree.] A climbing shrub of the verbenaceous genus of that name, composed of many species bearing white, crimson, and scarlet campanulate flowers, natives of Asia, tropical Africa, and America.

1829 LOUDON *Encycl. Plants* 1079 Some of the Vitexes and Clerodendrums are handsome shrubs. 1851 *B'ham & Midl. Gardeners' Mag.* Apr. 42 Pot the Clerodendrons in the pots which they are intended to bloom in. 1924 *Blackw. Mag.* Apr. 464/1 A tangle of rank undergrowth,.. convolvulus, smilax, and the scarlet clerodendron.

Clethra (klī·þrā, kle·þrā). *Bot.* [mod.L., f. Gr. κλήθρα alder, which it resembles in foliage.] A shrub of the ericaceous genus of that name, native of North and South America, bearing alternate serrate leaves and fragrant flowers usually white in colour.

1829 LOUDON *Encycl. Plants* 362. 1846 LINDLEY *Veget. Kingd.* 454 The genus Saurauja among Dilleniads, has very much the structure of a Clethra. 1895 *Outing* (U.S.) XXVI. 33/2 The white spiked Clethra flower.

Clever, *a.* Add: **2.** (U.S. example.)

1907 *Springfield Republ.* 13 May 2 Advt., For sale, one bay horse, weight 1200, good chunk, true, clever in harness.

4. b. (U.S. examples.)

1775 *Essex Inst. Hist. Coll.* XIII. 196 Father was very clever last Saturday P.M. 1815 *Massachusetts Spy* 14 June (Th.), I somehow did not feel quite clever, but hoped for the best.

8. b. (Later U.S. examples.)

c 1857 in *Lower Norfolk Co.* (Va.) *Antiquary* I. 110 John Savage..promised to do something clever for them. 1858 *Kansas Hist. Colls.* (1896) V. 567 On the night before last these same men attacked Barnesville quite a clever town, on the military road.

c. (Earlier and later U.S. examples.)

1758 *Essex Inst. Hist. Coll.* XII. 148 This afternoon secured a place to have ye Small Pox in, with a very clever family. 1768 *Boston Post-boy* 20 June, Or else how does it come to pass..That Young and Old, the Cross and Clever, Join hands, and live so well together? 1781 WITHERSPOON in *Pennsylv. Jrnl.* 9 May, He is a very *clever* man. She is quite a *clever* woman...In these cases Americans generally mean by *clever*, only goodness of disposition, worthiness, integrity, without the least regard to capacity. 1872 MARIETTA HOLLEY *My Opinions* (1891) 260 Josiah was awful clever to me, I guess it is natural for all men to conduct themselves cleverer when they are about to lose their pardners for a spell. 1883 EGGLESTON *Hoosier School-Boy* xviii. 119, I wanted to say that you fellows have always ..been 'clever' to me, and I don't want to see no harm done you. 1891 *Harper's Mag.* July 220/2 It is an Americanism to call him *clever* whom we deem good-natured only.

Cleverly, *adv.* **7.** *U.S.* (Earlier examples.)

1784 A. ADAMS *Lett.* (1848) 212 She is cleverly now, although she had a severe turn for a week. 1816 PICKERING *Vocab.* 63.

Clianthus (klai,æ·nþɒs). *Bot.* [mod.L., app. f. Gr. κλει-, by-form of stem of κλέος glory + ἄνθος flower.] An Australasian shrub belonging to the leguminous genus of that name, bearing handsome flowers in racemes.

1853 HOOKER *Bot. Antarctic Voyage* II. p. xxxi, Of *Clianthus*..there are but two known species, one in Australia, and the other in New Zealand and Norfolk Island. 1909 *Daily Chron.* 15 Apr. 7/2 The verbena and the clianthus grow rankly in the mild air.

Cliché. Add:

1. b. *fig.* A stereotyped expression, a commonplace phrase.

1892 A. LANG in *Longman's Mag.* Dec. 217 They have the hatred of *clichés* and commonplace, of the outworn phrase, of clashing consonants. 1902 GOSSE in *Encycl. Brit.* XXVIII. 261/1 All but the obvious motives tend to express themselves no longer as thoughts but as clichés. 1909 O. JENNINGS *Morphia Habit* vi. 72 The above description of morphinism has been repeated by one compiler after another, until it has become a *cliché*. 1922 JOAD *Highbrows* vi. § 7 'Must a woman spend all her life beating out her soul against the scullery sink?'—a favourite cliché this of old Peabody's which had never failed to move even the most hostile meeting.

Click, *sb.*[1] Add: **2.** (Later U.S. example.)

1849 *Rep. U.S. Comm. Patents* (1850) 234 We are aware that a rack and click or dog has long been used for trusses.

7. click reel, a reel of a fishing-rod having a click or detent.

1883 *Fisheries Exhib. Lit.* XII. 212 Leonard Click reel. 1888 GOODE *Amer. Fishes* 62 A more flexible rod..with a click-reel.

8. Add other examples of imitative formations: *click-clicking, click-clock; clickety* adj.; *click-clack, clickety-click* vbs.

1896 *Humanitarian* June 432 Click-clicking with a typewriter all day long. 1901 *Ibid.* 3 Sept. 1/3 The click-clock of passing iron shoes. 1914 W. DE MORGAN *When Ghost meets Ghost* II. xiv. 613 The up-express..dragged her train over oily lines and clicketty lines. 1920 *Chambers's Jrnl.* 67/1 The steady click-clock of his hoofs. 1926 *Glasgow Herald* 17 July 4 The omnibus train clickety-clicked.

Click, *v.*[1] Add:

1. d. *fig. intr.* To meet or fall in *with* fortunately or at the right moment; to come to an agreement or understanding; to come in *for* something; *spec.* to get killed. Also *trans.*, to get (something that comes or happens to one).

1915 T. BURKE *London Nts., Domestic Nt.* (1919) 80 The bright boys..saunter..up and down that parade until they 'click' with one of the 'birds'...They have 'clicked'. They have 'got off'. 1917 EMPEY *From Fire Step* 39 Shut your blinkin' mouth, you bloomin' idiot; do you want us to click it from the Boches? *Ibid.* 65 Trench mortars started dropping 'Minnies' in our front line. We clicked several casualties. *Ibid.* 81 No. 1 Section had clicked for another blinking digging party. 1919 *Athenæum* 11 July 582/2 A more interesting specimen is the verb 'click,' an active that has developed some passive meanings, such as to get killed. It appears to have signified first to get what one wants. *Ibid.* 8 Aug. 729/1 To 'click for fatigue' is to 'come in for' a fatigue duty at the psychological moment...'We've clicked' for 'we're all right' is, I believe, the later use. 1922 P. G. WODEHOUSE (*title*) The Clicking of Cuthbert. 1930 *Times* 29 Mar. 10/4 The objects are arranged but not composed..so that they remind you a little of people assembled harmoniously but lacking some common emotion. They don't 'click'.

4. *Printers' slang.* (See quot. and next, d.)

1860 RUSE & STRAKER *Printing* 121 A work is said to be 'clicked' when each man works on his lines, and keeps an account thereof.

Clicking, *vbl. sb.* Add: **c.** The process of cutting out the leather for boots and shoes. (See CLICKER[2] 2.)

1916 *Yorkshire Post* 15 Feb. 5/5 Women have not yet been put to clicking.

d. *Printing.* (See quot. and cf. CLICKER[2] 3.)

1860 RUSE & STRAKER *Printing* 121 *Clicking.* This is a term applied to the mode pursued in London of getting out work by the formation of a companionship, or selected number of men, who are appointed to go on with a certain work or works.

Cliff. Add:

3. b. The face of a bunker.

1891 H. G. HUTCHINSON *Golf* 33 The exact distance will depend on the height and nearness of the cliff of the bunker, and the consistency of the sand. 1904 *Westm. Gaz.* 21 Oct. 4/2 To get over the bunker's cliff.

Cliffless (kli·flės), *a.* [f. CLIFF + -LESS.] Without cliffs.

1897 *Naturalist* 224 In treeless and cliffless districts. 1898 *Speaker* 5 Mar. 297/1 The cliffless Downs.

Clift, *sb.*[2] (Later U.S. example.)

1888 C. D. FERGUSON *Exp. Forty-niner* ix. 127 The Armstrongs used to bring up cattle..and herd them down by a little bend..perfectly hemmed in by high clifts of rocks.

Cliftonite (kli·ftənait). *Min.* [Named after Robert Bellamy *Clifton* (1836–1921), an English physicist: see -ITE[1].] Carbon occurring as small cubic crystals in meteoric iron.

1887 *Mineralogical Mag.* July 130. 1910 *Encycl. Brit.* VIII. 162/2 Graphitic carbon in cubic form (cliftonite).

Climate, *v.* Add:

2. *trans.* To acclimatize. *U.S.*

1849 N. KINGSLEY *Diary* 92 Relinquishing the idea of going to the diggings this winter [to] get ourselves climated ready for spring.

Climatize, *v.* (Earlier U.S. example.)

1826 in Peck *Guide for Emigrants* (1831) 210 That some who have been born, or who have been climatized, in places, which to a stranger prove unhealthy—are generally free from disease..proves little.

Hence **Cli·matized** *ppl. a.*, **Cli·matizing** *vbl. sb.*

1828 P. CUNNINGHAM *N. S. Wales* 8 Our colonial climatised females mincing it past these undraperied *beaux*. *Ibid.* 48 It may possibly be ascribed to the climatising process.

Climatotherapy (klai:mătoþe·rāpi). *Med.* [f. CLIMATE + -O- + THERAPY.] The treatment of disease by a favourable climate. Also **Cli:matotherapeu·tic** *a.* and *sb. pl.*

1887 *Buck's Handbk. Med. Sci.* V. 32/1 Dr. Weber's article on climato-therapy. 1901 F. P. WEBER *Climatology* II. 245 Climatotherapeutics. *Ibid.* 300 This classification is convenient from a climatotherapeutic point of view.

Climaxing (klai·mæksiŋ), *ppl. a.* [f. CLIMAX *v.*] Reaching a climax; culminating.

1892 'MARK TWAIN' *£1,000,000 Bank-note* (1893) 17 Then came the climaxing stroke—..'Punch' caricatured me!

Climb, *v.* **5. a.** Add: Also *spec.* (see quots.), and in causative sense.

1874 J. W. LONG *Wild-Fowl Shooting* 245 They..can 'climb' out of gun-shot (as the hunters term their flying upwards when frightened at the appearance of danger beneath them) faster than most wild-fowl. 1919 *Parl. Papers* X. 49 It is most economical to climb an aeroplane in the attitude corresponding to the maximum value of the lift-drag ratio.

Climber. 1. Add:

fig. esp. one who seeks continually to advance himself. So **Cli·mbing** *vbl. sb.*

1833 *Knickerbocker Mag.* I. 179 But with all her meanness as a climber what a glorious leader of fashion she'd make. 1911 H. S. HARRISON *Queed* xxiv. 301 He was of the climber type, a self-made man in the earlier and less inspiring stages of the making. 1929 *Times Lit. Suppl.* 27 June 511 A windbag and a 'climber'..a man incapable of neglecting on any occasion his interest and his advancement. *Ibid.* 18 July 568/4 The 'events' of the season one cannot afford to miss, the 'right' charities to assist—in fact, the whole art of climbing.

Clinch, *sb.*[1] Add:

4. b. Grip or hold (of plaster on a wall).

1897 MOORE *How to Build* ii. 16 The lath should be furred out from the sheathing so as to secure a good 'clinch' or 'key' to the plaster.

5. Also (earlier) *clinch-fight.*

1840 C. LANMAN *Alleghany Mts.* vi. 50 On reaching the bottom, he found the wolf alive, when a 'clinch fight' ensued, and the hunter's knife completely severed the heart of the animal.

b. *spec.* in *Boxing.* Grappling at close quarters after an exchange of blows.

1899 *Life of Bob Fitzsimmons* 14 In a clinch Jeffries showed his great strength by pushing Fitz off with ease. 1901 FITZSIMMONS *Phys. Culture* 152 Corbett seemed to think clinches were his best time for a knock-out blow. 1923 TOSSWILL *Boxing Up-to-date* 58 The best thing to do is to fall into a clinch, dropping forward with your hands resting on your opponent's arms, while your ribs and stomach are protected by your elbows.

8. clinch plate, a plate on the inside of clinch-work.

1889 P. B. DU CHAILLU *Viking Age* I. xii. 219 The boat is clinch-built; that is, the planks are held together by large iron bolts with round heads outside, and clinch plates on the inside, at a distance of 5½ inches from each other.

Clinch, *v.*[1] Add:

2. e. *spec.* in *Boxing.* To fall into a clinch (see prec. 5 b). Also *trans.* with person as obj.

1860 [see 2 d]. 1893 DORAN *Sci. Self-Defense* 84 You can also take this hold as your opponent endeavours to clinch you. 1899 *Life of Bob Fitzsimmons* 6 In the sixth round the men clinched. *Ibid.* 14 The clinching was of the hottest kind. 1910 J. J. CORBETT *My Life & Fights* 26, I clinched with Kilrain. 1923 TOSSWILL *Boxing Up-to-date* 58 In competitions held under the auspices of the Royal Navy and Army..the command 'Break away' is given by the referee the moment the boxers clinch.

Clincher. 4. (Earlier and later U.S. examples.)

1784 *Belknap Papers* (1877) I. 403 The last stroke was a clincher. 1836 HALIBURTON *Clockm.* Ser. I. xxiv. (1837) 253 Have you ever seen this here book on the 'Elder Controversy'..? This author's friends say it's a clincher. 1873 J. H. BEADLE *Undevel. West* v. 102 This [argument] struck me as the nearest to a 'clincher' of all I had heard.

Cling, *sb.*[1] Add:

5. Short for CLINGSTONE. Also *attrib.* in *cling peach.*

1845 A. J. DOWNING *Fruits Amer.* 494 The Catherine cling is a very fine, old English variety. 1867–8 *Trans. Ill. Agric. Soc.* VII. 510 We have a late, large peach which we call the Allman Cling. *Ibid.*, It is sometimes called the Heath Cling, which it resembles. 1872 *San Francisco Weekly Bulletin* 27 Sept. (Hoppe) Cling peaches are moderately plentiful. 1913 MRS. STRATTON-PORTER *Laddie* iii. (1917) 55 One [peach] was a white cling, and one was yellow. *Ibid.* iv. 75, I led her straight to our best cling peach tree.

Cling (kliŋ), *sb.*[2] Delete †*Obs.* and add:

1886 W. J. TUCKER *E. Europe* 182 With martial strides, and a cling, cling, cling of spurs.

Cling, in *cling hold*, etc. (see quots.), stem of CLING *v.*[1] or CLING *sb.*[1] used in comb.

1920 G. W. YOUNG *Mountain Craft* iv. 162 The ordinary cling holds, when the fingers cling over an edge or knob and hold the weight in suspense. *Ibid.*, A cling 'over'-hold.. pulls us inward. *Ibid.*, A cling 'under'-hold keeps body and eyes free at the length of our arms, bent or straight.

Cling-fish. [f. CLING *v.*[1]] A small carnivorous gobiesocoid fish possessing a sucker on the under side of its body by which it is enabled to cling to any object.

1895 in *Funk's Standard Dict.* 1904 G. A. BOULENGER in *Cambr. Nat. Hist.* VII. 708 Cling-Fishes..can live a long time out of water. 1929 *Encycl. Brit.* IX. 326/1 The cling-fishes..of tropical and temperate seas, living near the coasts, adhering to stones or shells, and feeding on small invertebrates.

Clinginess (kli·ŋinės). [f. CLINGY + -NESS.] The quality of being clingy or adhesive.

1778 [W. MARSHALL] *Min. Agric.* 16 Jan. 1775, The clingyness of the soil. 1794 T. DAVIS *Agric. Wilts* 91 The 'clinginess' of the Wiltshire white lands. 1899 *Daily News* 28 Jan. 6/4 The tightness and clinginess of ultra-fashionable dresses.

Clingstone. (Earlier U.S. example.)

1705 BEVERLEY *Virginia* (1722) 279 The best sort cling to the Stone, and will not come off clear, which they call Plum-Nectarines, and Plum-Peaches, or Cling-Stones.

Clinic, *sb.*[2] Add:

2. [After F. *clinique*, G. *klinik.*] **a.** A private hospital or medical institution to which patients are recommended by individual doctors. **b.** An institution attached to a hospital or medical college, at which patients receive treatment free of cost or at reduced fees.

1892 *Cosmopolitan* XIII. 766/1 Clinics that are held by the professors of diseases of the eye. 1895 *Daily News* 18 June 6/2 The Council of State in St. Petersburg is busy with the project of a medical institute for women...After completing their studies the students will have to practice for one to three years in women's clinics or similar hospitals. 1908 *Daily Chron.* 13 Apr. 1/5 The establishment in Berlin of a clinic conducted entirely by female doctors. 1909 *Westm. Gaz.* 14 July 2/1 The clinic opens at nine on every school-day and also on Saturday with examination of cases.

Clinician. Add: **b.** A doctor in charge of a clinic (see prec.).

1897 *Trans. Amer. Pediatric Soc.* IX. 112 Clinician to Children's Clinic, Medical College of Ohio, Cincinnati, O. 1929 *Times* 2 July 19/4 At the Radcliffe Infirmary the assistant medical officer of health is assistant clinician.

Clink, *sb.*[2] Add: Now used generally for: prison, cells.

1906 *Daily Chron.* 28 Aug. 4/7 Escorting erring defaulters of his own creation to clink. 1919 *War Slang* in *Athenæum* 25 July 664/2 'Clink', punishment cells.

Clink-clank, *v. intr.* To make a clink-clank sound.

1921 H. WALPOLE *Young Enchanted* III. iii, The ships clink-clank against the side of the pier.

Clinker, *sb.*[3] Add:

2. b. A 'clinking' good thing: applied to persons and things of first-rate quality. *slang* (orig. *Sporting*; cf. CLINKING *ppl. a.* 2).

1869 *Daily Tel.* 5 Apr. (Farmer) Despite the indifferent manner in which Vagabond cut up at the finish of the Metropolitan, quite sufficient was seen of him to prove that at a mile and a half he is a clinker. 1871 *Daily News* 17 Apr. 2/1 (Ibid.) Ripponden and Cheesewring performed so indifferently as to strengthen the doubts whether they are really clinkers. *a* 1889 *Ward or Wife* (Barrère & L.) The yellow-haired girl at the bar. A clinker, ain't she? 1889 'R. BOLDREWOOD' *Robbery under Arms* vi, By George! how fond I am of a good horse—a real well-bred clinker. 1902 A. D. MCFAUL *Ike Glidden* iii. 19 That colt's a clinker an' I oughten ter let him go, but then I can't help it.

Clinker, *v.*[2] Add: **b.** To remove clinkers from (a furnace). Hence **Cli·nkerer**; **Cli·nkering** *vbl. sb.*

1901 *Feilden's Mag.* IV. 437/1 Long iron bars or clinkering tools. *Ibid.* 439/1 So that no rush of cold air may take place through the flues while clinkering is going on. *Ibid.* 439/2 The labour of stoking and clinkering the furnaces. 1921 *Dict. Occup. Terms* (1927) § 699 *Clinker man* (gas works), *water gas clinkerer*; removes clinker and ashes from producer gas furnace with long iron bar. 1926 *Spectator* 29 May 901/1 At the end of the journey it was found that no clinkering had taken place.

Clinkery (kli·ŋkəri), *a.*[2] [f. CLINKER *sb.*[1] + -Y[1].] Resembling clinkers.

1885 *Lyell's Student's Elem. Geol.* xxix. 463 The lava in cooling assumes a clinkery appearance.

Clinkety (kli·ŋkėti). Onomatopœic extension of CLINK as in *clinkety-clank, -clink* (cf. *CLANKETY).

1901 F. T. BULLEN *Sack of Shakings* 164 Clinkety-clank, bang, bang went the pumps. 1927 *Observer* 5 June 7/5 The clinkety-clink of metal on metal.

Clinure (klai·niūɹ, kliniū·ɹ). *Math.* [f. Gr. κλίνειν to slope + -URE.] Direction in space, or inclination, as of a vector, relative to some set of coordinates. Hence **Clinu·ral** *a.*

1884 JAS. THOMSON *Coll. Papers* (1912) 380 There is..a real distinction..between absolute rotation (or absolute clinural motion) and absolute freedom from rotation (or absolute clinural rest). *Note*, The word *clinural* is to be understood as introduced for conveying precisely one out of the various conflicting meanings of the word directional. All straight lines which are mutually parallel are, in this amended mode of nomenclature, said to be in one same *clinure*.

Clip, *sb.*[1] Add:

2. d. A receptacle containing several cartridges held together at the base for insertion bodily into the magazine of a repeating fire-arm.

1901 'LINESMAN' *Words by Eyewitness* vii. (1902) 146 *note*, The clip containing the cartridges for the Mauser rifle holds five rounds. 1902 *Encycl. Brit.* XXXII. 651/2 The clip, employed in the Mannlicher system, is used with a magazine with parallel walls. *Ibid.* 654/1 The loading by clip. 1905 *Kynoch Jrnl.* Jan.–Mar. 19 This ammunition is put up in clips, each containing five rounds.

3. clip-chair, a chair used on some railways to secure the rail to a metallic sleeper; **clip-loader**, a clip-loading fire-arm; **clip-loading**, the loading of a repeating fire-arm with cartridges in a clip (see *2 d).

1884 KNIGHT *Dict. Mech.* Suppl., The *clip chair is of horse-shoe shape, one side forming a hook about 2¼" wide, and the other side is like one jaw of an ordinary railway chair for taking a wooden railway key. 1901 *Chambers's Jrnl.* Apr. 285/1 The most perfect *clip-loader so far produced. 1901 *Westm. Gaz.* 23 Dec. 4/3 The weapon to be adopted in the immediate future for the British Army..must positively admit of *clip loading. 1902 *Encycl. Brit.* XXXII. 654/2 A clip-loading repeating rifle.

Clip, *sb.*[2] Add:

4. (Later U.S. examples. Also *fig.*)

1869 MRS. STOWE *Oldtown Folks* xx. 243 When you didn't mind, I hit you a good clip. 1886 J. C. HARRIS in *Century Mag.* Jan. XXXI. 426/1 I'm a great mind to hit him a clip jest to show you how he can go on. 1902 A. D. MCFAUL *Ike Glidden* iii. 20 My hoss..jist riz the dasher off'n my wagon the fust clip. 1913 MRS. STRATTON-PORTER *Laddie* xvii. (1917) 352 Robert wasn't a smidgin behind, for every clip he had the answer ready.

6. A rate of speed; a rapid pace or motion. *U.S. colloq.*

1868 H. WOODRUFF *Trotting Horse* vi. 79 It is believed that he can go a four-minute clip. 1876 *Rep. Vermont Board Agric.* III. 160 He would point out to me a horse with the remark..'can take a forty clip or better any day in the week'. 1893 *Outing* (U.S.) XXI. 457/2 Lastly, the bicyclists rode from six to ten miles daily at a stiff clip. 1893 *Field* 25 Feb. 295/3 In three days I could drive him any 'clip' I chose by just talking to him. 1899 A. H. QUINN *Pennsylv. Stories* 207 The Yale runner at once started at a fast clip. 1901 *Westm. Gaz.* 31 Aug. 6/3 As *Shamrock* returned the wind increased and the challenger with a magnificent burst of speed travelled at a 12-knot clip. 1911 H. S. HARRISON *Queed* vii. 90 You'll never finish your book at all at the clip you're hitting now. 1929 *Minnesota Alumni Weekly* 1 June 615 The infield was functioning at an improved clip during this second game.

7. An impertinent or forward girl. *dial.* and *U.S.*

1880 *Antrim & Down Gloss.* 21 *Clip*,..a mischievous young girl. 1901 MARAH E. RYAN *Montana* xi. 139 She is a clip, and I know it, but I think she only meant that game as a bit of a joke.

Clip, *v.*[1] Add:

3. b. To fasten with a clip or clips.

1902 ELIZ. L. BANKS *Newspaper Girl* 244 Page after page passed from under her pen. Then, clipping a dozen sheets together, she read them over. 1908 *Daily Chron.* 21 Nov. 9/4 Permanently fixed instead of clipped-on fittings. 1916 BOYD CABLE *Action Front* 220 He turned to the man, who was clipping a tiny mirror on to his bayonet.

Clip, *v.*[2] Add:

7. *U.S.* (Later examples.)

1886 *Harper's Mag.* Nov. 835/2 All that he could do was to take to his heels and clip down the steps and into the pung. 1897 SUSAN HALE *Lett.* 317 Though he had to row at first, the wind soon sprang up and we were clipping along. 1924 MULFORD *Rustlers' Valley* xxvi. 283 Now and then searching bullets clipped and sung below him.

8. *trans.* To hit smartly. *dial.* and *U.S.*

1871 SCHELE DE VERE *Americanisms* (1872) 453 *Clip*, to, in the sense of to give a blow; and the noun, a *clip*, meaning a blow, must be looked upon as Americanisms. 1880 *E. Cornwall Gloss.* 90 *Klip*, to strike or cuff. 'I klipped 'en under the ear.'

Clippable (kli·păb'l), *a.* [f. CLIP *v.*[2] + -ABLE.] Capable of being clipped, ready to be clipped.

1889 *Voice* (N.Y.) 29 Aug., A half column of short paragraphs wherein we can find nothing clippable. 1893 G. D. LESLIE *Lett. to Marco* i. 5 The yew hedges which I planted are fast becoming clippable.

Clipper[1]. Add:

4. a. (Earlier U.S. example.)

1836 HALIBURTON *Clockm.* Ser. I. xv. (1837) 130 A four year old colt,..a genuine clipper, could gallop like the wind.

b. (Earlier U.S. example.)

1824 W. N. BLANE *Excursion* 33 At this port [*sc.* Baltimore] are built those long sharp schooners celebrated under the name of the Baltimore Clippers.

c. (Earlier U.S. example.)

1836 HALIBURTON *Clockm.* Ser. I. xx. (1837) 198 She was a real handsum looking gall;..a real clipper, and as full of fun and frolic as a kitten.

Clipping, *ppl. a.*[2] **c.** Of pace: Fast, 'rattling'. *colloq.*

1845 *Punch* Sept. 122/1 When we do walk in our slumbers, we walk a clipping pace. 1896 *B'ham Daily Gaz.* 2 Sept. (E.D.D.) [The fox] ran at a clipping pace.

Clique. Add:

2. A business 'ring'. *U.S.*

1877 BARTLETT *Dict. Amer.* (ed. 4), *Clique*, a combination of stock-brokers or capitalists, for the purpose of increasing or diminishing the price of stocks, in order to break down the market. 1901 S. MERWIN & WEBSTER *Calumet 'K'* xv. 285 The clique of speculators who held the floor were buying, buying, buying.

Cliquy, *a.* Add earlier U.S. quot.

1863 'G. HAMILTON' *Gala-Days* 115 The priests are clique-y.

Hence **Cliquiness** (klī·kinės), cliquy character.

1927 BELLOC *Hist. Eng.* II. 282 The capriciousness with which the thing was done, and the cliquiness of it.

Clish-clash.

1. (Modern U.S. example.)

1872 H. W. BEECHER in *Chr. World Pulpit* II. 343 Everything goes clish-clash, clish-clash. We are tossed about in the world like a skiff on the waves of the sea.

Clitellar (klaite·lāɹ), *a.* [f. CLITELLUM + -AR[1].] Of or pertaining to the clitellum of earthworms.

1888 ROLLESTON & JACKSON *Forms Anim. Life* 198 Capillaries penetrate between the clitellar glands, and are very numerous in the common Earthworm.

Clithridiate (klaiþri·dieɪt), *a.* *Zool.* [f. Gr. κλειθρίδιον, dim. of κλειθρία keyhole + -ATE[2].] Shaped like a keyhole.

1884 G. BUSK in *Challenger Rep., Zool.* X. 184 Orifice (primary) broadly clithridiate or sinuate.

Clitoridectomy (klai:toride·ktŏmi). [f. Gr. κλιτορίδ-, CLITORIS + Gr. ἐκτομή excision.] Excision of the clitoris.

1890 BILLINGS *Med. Dict.* 1908 SIR H. JOHNSTON *Grenfell & Congo* II. xxv. 666 Circumcision in the males or clitoridectomy in the females.

Clivia (klai·viă). Also **clivea.** [Named in honour of Lady *Clive*, the wife of the third Duke of Northumberland (died 1847).] A plant of the genus of that name of African Amaryllids with beautiful orange flowers.

1866 *Treas. Bot.* 300/1 The *Clivias* consist of herbs with fasciculate fleshy roots. 1891 *Daily News* 11 Feb. 6/6 Messrs. Laing, of Forest Hill, received a vote of thanks for their stand of clivias.

Cloak, *sb.* **6.** Add:

cloak and dagger, cloak and sword [= F. *de cape et d'épée*, after Sp. *de capa y espada*], designating dramas or stories of intrigue and of manners in which the principal characters are taken from that class of society which formerly wore cloak and dagger or sword.

1806 LD. HOLLAND *Lope* (1817) I. 149 Comedias de Capa y Espada, Comedies of the Cloak and Sword. 1840 LONGF. in *Life* (1886) I. 353 In the afternoon read *La Dama Duende* of Calderon—a very good comedy of 'cloak and sword'. 1876 *Encycl. Brit.* IV. 660/2 Calderon's comedies of intrigue, the so-called 'comedies of cloak and sword'. 1893 H. B. CLARKE *Spanish Lit.* 163 The play of the 'cloak and sword' may almost be said to be his [*sc.* Lope's] own invention. *Ibid.* 220 The stock characters, the *galán* and *dama*, the *gracioso* and *barba* of their 'sword and cloak' plays. 1905 *Academy* 10 June 603/2 Thousands of cloak-and-dagger stories. 1907 *Daily Chron.* 14 Mar. 3/3 Fighting and brawling,..intrigues of love and politics, and all the elements of cloak-and-dagger fiction. 1921 H. WALPOLE *Young Enchanted* 42 The Cloak and Sword Romances.

Cloak, *v.* Add: **1. b.** *intr.* for *refl.* To put on a cloak, cloak oneself.

1865 CARLYLE *Fredk. Gt.* XXI. v. VI. 542 It rained hard the whole time we were out and as his Majesty did not cloak, we were all heartily wet. 1906 HARDY *Dynasts* II. II. iii. 184 All three cloak And veil as when you came.

Clo·bber, *sb.*[2] *slang.* Clothes.

1879 J. W. HORSLEY *Jottings from Jail* (1887) 10 Having a new suit of clobber on me. *Ibid.* 18, I..went home to change my clobber and put on the old clobber to work with the kipsy. 1908 *Daily Chron.* 3 Aug. 4/4 All just the common sort, in their new summer clobber.

Hence **Clobber** *v.*[2] *trans.*, to dress or 'tog' *up.*

1879 J. W. HORSLEY *Jottings from Jail* (1887) 9, I used to clobber myself up and go to the concert-rooms. 1889 E. SAMPSON *Tales of Fancy* 14, I must go there decently clobbered...I want you to go with me..to buy a check suit.

Clobber, *v.* Add: **b.** To add enamelled decoration to (porcelain, esp. blue-and-white). Hence **Clo·bbered** *ppl. a.*; **Clo·bberer.**

1889 in *Cent. Dict.* 1906 R. L. HOBSON *Porcelain* 63 The spurious ornament of this 'klobbered' ware may be easily recognized. 1910 — *Worcester Porcelain* 61 Clobbering was freely practised in Holland first and England afterwards from the early part of the 18th century. 1915 — *Chinese Pottery* II. 261 The clobberer became an established institution, and he was at work in London in the last century. 1922 *R. Drane's Coll. Old Worc. Porcelain* 32 Clobbered pieces. 471 An Oriental Tea Jar...When this was brought to Europe it was a plain blue and white object.

Cloche. Add:

2. In full *cloche hat*: A woman's close-fitting hat of a bell shape.

1907 *Daily Chron.* 25 June 8/3 The very latest 'cloche' shape. 1907 *Westm. Gaz.* 24 Aug. 13/1 The mondaine's big cloche hat. 1908 *Ibid.* 29 Feb. 13/2 So popular is the cloche or mushroom hat with the Parisienne. 1923 *Daily Mail* 3 Aug. 11 The narrow-brimmed, high-crowned cloche.

3. A bell-shaped part of the control lever in certain types of aeroplanes.

1916 BARBER *Aeroplane Speaks* 135. 1917 *All the World's Aircraft* 8a.

Clock, *sb.*[1] **11.** Add:

clock-bird, the Australian kingfisher, *Dacelo gigas*, so called from the regularity with which it announces sunrise and sunset; **clock-calm** (American example); **clock-golf**, a game in which each player in turn puts a ball, in as few strokes as possible, into a hole placed anywhere within a circle, except at its centre, from each in turn of twelve figures numbered and arranged in imitation of the dial of a clock; **clock-jack**, a figure on a clock tower, which gives warning, chimes, or tells the hour by striking a bell (cf. JACK *sb.*[1] 6, QUARTER-JACK 1); **clock-spring**, a coil spring which drives the train mechanism of a clock; **clock-train**, the mechanism of the going part of a clock; **clock-weight**, a weight (and cord) used instead of a pendulum or spring to give impulse to the movement of a clock.

1880 NUTT *Palace of Industry* 15 Where *clock-bird laughed and sweet wild flowers throve. 1777 J. ADAMS in *Fam. Lett.* (1876) 267 There is a *clock calm at this time in the political and military hemispheres. 1906 *Westm. Gaz.* 3 Nov. 3/1 To visit the putting hole of the *clock-golf. 1915 P. G. WODEHOUSE *Something Fresh* vii, [They] console themselves for the absence of a links..with the exhilarating pastime of clock-golf. 1926 *Glasgow Herald* 23 July 6 The fantastic little *clock-jacks of Norwich Cathedral. 1874 KNIGHT *Dict. Mech.*, **Clock-spring*, a coiled steel spring in the going-barrel or the striking-barrel of a clock which impels the train or strikes the hours, as the case may be. 1850 DENISON *Clock & Watch-m.* p. v, Common *clock train. 1868 *Chambers's Encycl.* X. 82/1 There is one more wheel and pinion in the watch-train than in the clock-train. 1877 *Encycl. Brit.* VI. 19/2 [A clock] must vary with the force of the clock train, due to different states of the oil. 1925 C. FOX *Educational Psychol.* 33 The running down of a *clock-weight.

Clock, *v.*[1] Add:

1. b. (*a*) with *in, off, on, out*: To register one's entry or exit by means of an automatic clock; also *refl.* in same sense. (*b*) To put *in* (so many hours) *at* a piece of work. Hence **Clocking-in**, etc. (also *attrib.*).

1924 H. H. EMSLEY *Factory Costing* 5 The 'job cards', on which the workers enter their time and particulars of the work they are engaged upon, depend upon the method in use for 'clocking on'. 1924 *Glasgow Herald* 14 Aug. 5 That any men could resume work provided they would clock out in accordance with the system which had been in operation since the works started. *Ibid.* 18 Aug. 9 An allowance of two minutes for 'clocking off'. 1926 *Spectator* 27 Feb. 359/2 He clocks himself in on an automatic timekeeper. *Ibid.* 360/1 He clocks off again and proceeds home. 1927 A. BENNETT *Woman who Stole Everything, Time to Think* i. 216 Both brother and sister had had to 'clock in' of a morning and 'clock out' of an evening for years. 1928 *Daily Tel.* 24 July 15/2 He..described the 'clocking-in' apparatus as an 'infernal machine, insulting to the integrity, honour, and dignity of the profession'.

Clock, *v.*[4] Also **clox.** [f. CLOCK *sb.*[2]] *trans.* To embroider clocks on. Hence **Clo·cker**, one who embroiders clocks.

1880 in Webster *Suppl.* 1921 *Dict. Occup. Terms* (1927) § 407 *Clocker*;..sometimes further designated according to thread used, *e.g.*, silk clocker. 1928 *Glasgow Herald* 9 Oct. 3 You must learn to clox your own stockings.

Clod, *v.* Add:

3. (Mod. U.S. example.)

1873 J. H. BEADLE *Undevel. West* iii. 74 The soil pulverizes finely in summer. It is never water soaked, consequently never 'bakes' or clods.

5. Also, to knock or drive by pelting (as with clods of earth). *dial.* and *U.S.*

1867 T. BLACKAH *Songs & Poems* 38 We'd to clod 'em [*sc.* sheep] away. 1904 'MARK TWAIN' *Adam's Diary* 15 Trying to clod apples out of that forbidden tree. *Ibid.* 29 She has been climbing that tree again. Clodded her out of it.

Clodder, *sb.* (Later American example.)

1752 *Boston News Letter* 23 Nov. 2/1 Large Clodders of Blood settled in and about the Brain.

Cloddiness. (Earlier U.S. example.)

1787 WASHINGTON *Diaries* III. 199 The barrow was ordered to precede it..as many times as the ground, from the cloddiness or grassiness of it, should appear to need it.

Clod-hopping, *a.* (Earlier U.S. example.)

1828 PAULDING *New Mirror* 28, I threw away my clod-hopping shoes and learned to dance.

Clogged, *ppl. a.* Add: **2.** *Photogr.* Of shadows in a print or negative: Composed of one heavy tone.

1918 *Photo-Miniature* Mar. 1919 *Brit. Jrnl. Photogr. Almanac* 247.

Cloisonless (kloi·z'nlės), *a.* [f. CLOISON + -LESS.] Without cloisons, having no visible cloisons.

1902 *Encycl. Brit.* XXIX. 730/1 The so-called 'cloisonless enamels'.

Clone (klǭn). Also **clon.** [ad. Gr. κλών twig, slip.] A group of cultivated plants the individuals of which are transplanted parts of one original seedling or stock, the propagation having been carried out by the use of grafts, cuttings, bulbs, etc.

b. Any group of individuals produced asexually from a single sexually produced ancestor. Hence **Clo·nal** *a.*, pertaining to or having the characteristics of a clone.

1903 *Science* 16 Oct. 502 (Cent. D. Suppl.) The differentiating clonal characters of chrysanthemums are mainly in the form and colour of the flowers. *Ibid.* 503 (Ibid.) The clons of apples, pears, strawberries, etc., do not propagate true to seed, while this is one of the most important characters of races of wheat and corn. 1928 *Times* 20 July 20/3 In a tapping test of buddings now being carried out by the institute, the highest-yielding clone has latex vessels of much smaller bore than the lowest-yielding clone...(Note.—Clone is the term given to all bud grafts taken from a particular parent tree.) 1929 A. D. HALL *Bk. Tulip* 23.

Clonus (klǭ·nɒs). *Med.* [L., a. Gr. κλόνος turmoil.] A spasm or series of spasms of alternate muscular contraction and relaxation.

1817 GOOD *Nosol.* 339. 1891 TAYLOR *Man. Pract. Med.* (ed. 2) 148 In some cases a *clonus* can be obtained at the knee. 1906 *Practitioner* Dec. 825 The patient has exaggerated tendon reflexes and sometimes a little clonus.

Clop (klɒp). A word imitative of a sharp sound, such as is made by feet or hoofs; used as *sb.* or *adv.* Also reduplicated *clop-clop.*

1903 A. SYMONS *Plays, Acting, & Music* 165 The clop-clop of uneven legs. 1912 MASEFIELD *Dauber* III. xxvi, His boots went clop along the stony ground. 1922 *Q. Rev.* Oct. 265 The clop and clink of hoofs. 1924 *Glasgow Herald* 29 Nov. 4 The clop of horses' feet.

Close, *a.* and *adv.* Add: **A. 20.** Also, having parties or votes nearly equal in number. *U.S.*

1870 *Congress. Rec.* 30 Jan. 1042/1 St. Helena is a very close parish. In 1870 it gave 30 democratic majority. It is considered a very close parish. 1887 *Ibid.* 20 Jan. App. 50/1 What do you mean by 'doubtful' counties?..Close counties, like some of those in the State of..Virginia. 1904 H. L. WEST in *Forum* July 17 In the last Congressional election there were comparatively few close districts.

21. Of the price of stocks, shares, etc.: Near the face value.

1914 *Scotsman* 17 Dec. 3/1 The last-named stock is the easiest in which to deal,..and usually a closer price than in other cases can be obtained.

B. 1. b. With *in.*

1872 [see IN *adv.* 3]. 1930 *San Anton.* (*Texas*) *Light* 31 Jan. 14/8 Furnished apartment; close-in.

C. 1 and **2.** *close-growing, -guarded, -hung, -lipped, -set* adjs.

1897 *Daily News* 16 Jan. 6/3 The abundance of the *close-growing hair. 1907 *B'ham Inst. Mag.* Mar. 126 The close-growing pines shut all from our view. 1898 W. GRAHAM *Last Links* 105 The *close-guarded secret. 1903 *Westm. Gaz.* 28 Jan. 2/3 Your door with its close-guarded wicket. 1904 *Daily Chron.* 22 Sept. 8/5 Where the waters narrow between *close-hung woods. 1905 *Westm. Gaz.* 20 May 3/3 That great sky close-hung with stars. 1853 M. ARNOLD *Scholar Gipsy* xx, With *close-lipp'd Patience for our only friend. 1905 *Daily Chron.* 10 Oct. 2/7 A thin close-lipped mouth. 1866 OWEN *Anat. Vert.* I. 379 Teeth..arranged..in alternate and pretty *close-set series. 1909 *Westm. Gaz.* 10 Apr. 15/1 A mass of close-set braiding.

3. close call, orig. *U.S. colloq.*, a near thing; something almost fatal; **close-communion** *attrib.*; **close out** *U.S.*, a near or short cut to a place; **close-herd** *v.* *U.S.* (see quots.); **close-lagged** *a.*, closely covered with lagging (see LAG *v.*[4], LAGGING *vbl. sb.*[3]); **close-reach**, a reach sailed close to the wind; also as vb., to sail on a close-reach.

1887 *Harper's Mag.* June 160/1 A sudden swoop..saved the occasion; but it was a *close call' for Sunday. 1904 F. LYNDE *Grafters* xxiii. 284 Though he escaped with his life and his job, it was a close call. 1924 MULFORD *Rustler's Valley* xiii. 160 'Milt had a close call, didn't he?' 'I hope he never has another as close.' 1834 CARRUTHERS *Kentuckian in N.Y.* I. 182, I thought that you were aware of my partiality for the *close communion Baptist. 1845 W. G. SIMMS *Wigwam & Cabin* Ser. II. 79, I was..mounting my good steed 'Priam' to find my way by a *close cut. 1887 *Scribner's Mag.* Oct. 508/2 A friend..has heard a sheriff talk of '*close-herding' several prisoners in his charge. On the plains it means the difficult art of keeping cattle in a compact body, close together. 1911 WEBSTER, *Close-herd v.* to herd (cattle) in a close group. *West. U.S.* 1923 B. M. BOWER *Parowan Bonanza* xxii. 264 He..told Tommy that he wouldn't be needed close herding any body. 1925 MULFORD *Cottonwood Gulch* xii. 148 We've got to round-up, loose herd durin' the day, an' close herd nights. 1883 *Specif. Alnwick & Cornhill Rlwy.* 4 The centres are to be *close-lagged to the satisfaction of the Engineer. 1899 *Daily News* 20 Oct. 5/7 The yachts *close-reached for home.

Close, *v.* Add:

16. Close down. Also *fig.*, to exercise repression.

1869 'MARK TWAIN' *Innoc. Abr.* xxiv. 254 They have set a gun-boat to watch the vessel night and day, with orders to close down on any revolutionary movement in a twinkling.

17. Close in. e. (Earlier U.S. example.)

1829 W. IRVING *Granada* (1850) 88 As the night closed in, they reached the chain of little valleys and hamlets.

19. Close out. b. To clear out (a stock of goods); to wind up (a business); to finish off. *U.S.*

1883 NYE *Baled Hay* 101 It will be closed out very cheap. 1888 *St. Paul Globe* 22 Jan. Advt., I shall also close out absolutely my Instruments of all kinds. 1909 S. E. WHITE *Rules of Game* III. x, I should advise closing out the business by killing the fowl.

absol. 1898 C. A. BATES *Clothing Bk.* No. 2502 There is no excuse for this with summer clothing at the prices at which we are closing out. 1903 A. ADAMS *Log Cowboy* vi. 80 About the time we closed out and were again ready to go home, there was a cattleman's ball given.

fig. 1907 *Smart Set* June 55/2 This must be ended; it must be closed out of our lives with all the rest.

Closed. Add: **b.** Confined to a few people, limited by certain conditions. (Cf. CLOSE *a.* 9 and quot. 1887 s.v. CLOSED in Dict.)

1923 J. D. HACKETT *Labor Terms* in *Management Engineering* May, *Closed Shop*, a plant in which only union men, or prospective union men are hired. 1927 CARR-SAUNDERS & JONES *Soc. Struct. Eng. & Wales* 82 There are a number of professions which are 'closed'. Complete closure exists when, as among dentists, certain functions and certain titles are legally reserved to persons whose names appear upon a statutory register.

Close-down (klǭ·z,daun). *U.S.* [CLOSE *v.* 16.] A stoppage of work by the closing of a factory, etc.

1889 *Voice* (N.Y.) Sept. 5 [To] interfere with the unrestricted manufacturing interests of our country by forced close-downs, lockouts, &c.

Closen, *v.* Add: **2.** *intr.* To close, close up.

1908 HARDY *Dynasts* III. III. iii, The retreating-way, Along which wambling waggons..Have crept in closening file. 1919 *Edin. Rev.* Oct. 241 The sudden closening of intercourse.

Close-up (klǭ·s,ɒp). [f. CLOSE *adv.* 1 b + UP *adv.*[2]] (In full *close-up picture.*) Part of a cinema film taken at short range in order to magnify detail. Also *fig.*, a detailed or intimate view.

1913 E. P. SARGENT *Technique of Photoplay* 16 A bust is a portrait showing the head and shoulders only, but bust is more definite than close up, which is sometimes used. 1916 *Ibid.* (ed. 3) 391 A continuous scene broken by close-ups of Hester. 1917 *The Cinema* 113 The 'close up' pictures of.. a man with a wound bleeding in his head. 1923 A. L. BENSON *New Henry Ford* 323 A 'Close-up' of Ford. 1924 GALSWORTHY *White Monkey* II. ix, The world was full of wonderful secrets which everybody kept to themselves without captions or close-ups to give them away! 1926 JOAD *Babbitt Warren* 103 It comes of seeing life as a series of 'close ups'. 1927 *Atlantic Monthly* Mar. 309 We have the spectacle of at least one great industry which affords us a close up of ruthless sabotage of invention.

Closh, *sb.*[3] [Origin unknown.] An upright piece of wood fixed in the deck of a whaling vessel, on which the blubber of the whale is spiked to be cut up. Also *attrib.*, as *closh-hook.*

1820 SCORESBY *Acc. Arctic Reg.* II. 308 Each of these officers, provided with a blubber-knife or a strand-knife, places himself by the side of a 'closh'..fixed in the deck. 1836 *Uncle Philip's Convers. Whale Fishery* 98 The blubber is put on the spikes of the closh, and the harpooner slices off the skin. 1886 *Good Words* 83 The harpoons of various designs, the closh, and the broken krenging hook.

Closing, *vbl. sb.* **1. b.** Add: *closing-out* (see *CLOSE *v.* 19 b). *U.S.*

1887 *Atlantic Monthly* Oct. 433/1 Bought..at the closing-out sale of an old house in Boylston Place.

Closish (klǭ·siʃ), *a.* [f. CLOSE *a.* + -ISH[1].] Rather close.

c 1830 GLADSTONE in *Daily News* (1898) 23 June 6/2 We forget the figures, but think it was a closish thing. 1859 'GEO. ELIOT' *Adam Bede* xxxvi, If you doant mind lyin' a bit closish a-top o' the wool-packs. 1901 H. SUTCLIFFE *Willowdene Will* ii. 40 Should they be closish behind.. 'twould fare ill with thee.

Clot, *sb.* **7.** Add: **clot-moulder** (see quot. 1921).

1843 *Civil Eng. & Arch. Jrnl.* VI. 349/1 The clot moulders were dispensed with. 1921 *Dict. Occup. Terms* (1927) § 119 *Clot moulder*;..prepares table and moulds for brick maker; works and forms lumps of clay ('clot') for his use.

Cloth, *sb.* Add: **10. b.** (*Cut* or *made*) *out of whole cloth*: see WHOLE CLOTH b.

19. *cloth-faced, -sided* adjs.; **cloth-board** (see BOARD *sb.* 4); **cloth-bound** (see BOUND *ppl. a.*[2] 8); **cloth-looker**, one who examines cloth in order to detect faults arising in manufacture; **cloth-plate**, the metal plate in a sewing-machine on which the work rests (Knight); **cloth-press**, a press used in the manufacture of woollen cloth (ibid.); **cloth-tenter** (see TENTER *sb.*[1] 1); **cloth-wheel**, (*a*) a polishing wheel consisting of cloth charged with some abrasive material; (*b*) a serrated feed wheel projecting through the cloth-plate in some sewing-machines (ibid.).

1832 *Cloth boards [see BOARD *sb.* 4]. 1845 *Penny Cycl. Suppl.* I. 220/1 Most persons who purchase books are aware that, if in 'boards' or 'cloth-boards', the top edges of the sheets, although placed level, are uncut. 1846 DODD *Brit. Manuf.* VI. 93 If a book is put into 'cloth boards'. 1870 *Gentl. Mag.* Oct. 642 A *cloth-bound, well-printed volume of 170 pages. 1904 *Westm. Gaz.* 15 July 12/2 The published price..will be..1s. net cloth-bound. 1884 T. C. HEPWORTH *Photogr. for Amateurs* 58 The *cloth-faced back is then inserted. 1881 *Instr. Census Clerks* (1885) 68 *Cloth Looker. 1927 *Sunday Express* 12 June 3 The clothlooker ..usually reports any faults he may find. 1925 MALLORY in E. F. NORTON *Fight for Everest, 1924* 233 My *cloth-sided shoes. 1849 C. BRONTË *Shirley* ii, To add to his possessions ..space for his *cloth-tenters.

Clothe, *v.* Add: **1. d.** To invest with a religious habit: cf. *CLOTHING *vbl. sb.* 1 c.

1628 in *Cath. Rec. Soc. Publ.* (1905) I. 98 She was cloathed in the new monastery at Gand the 25 of November 1626. *a* 1700 *Ibid.* VIII. 11 Mrs Elizabeth Poulton was cloathed with her for a lay sister.

Clothes, *sb. pl.* **4.** Add: **clothes-bag** (earlier U.S. examples); **clothes-pole** *U.S.*, a clothes-prop; **clothes-wringer** (U.S. example).

1834 *Knickerbocker Mag.* III. 81 The crew were disposed in various groups about the deck,..some with their *clothes-bags beside them. 1838 CAROLINE GILMAN *Recoll.* xxviii. 197, I manufactured for him a new sack, resembling more a clothesbag than a satchel. 1866 MRS. WHITNEY *L. Goldthwaite* iv, She..lifted her elbows, like *clothes-poles, to raise her draperies. 1872 *Rep. Vermont Board Agric.* I. 57 Untie these stripes, run them through a *clothes-wringer.

Clothing, *vbl. sb.* Add:

1. c. Investiture with a religious habit.

1628 in *Cath. Rec. Soc. Publ.* (1905) I. 98 Neece M. S. cloathing and profession. 1691 N. N. *Life Lady Warner of Parham* II. i. (1696) 73 My Lady took at her Cloathing the Name of Sister Teresa Clare. *Ibid.*, Father Martha, a Famous Preacher..of the Society of Iesus, made her Cloathing Sermon. 1701 in *Cath. Rec. Soc. Publ.* (1905) VII. 92 We were at ye cloathing of 2 Lay Sisters at ye Austines. 1884 [see Dict. s.v. 1].

5. a. *clothing-store* U.S., a draper's shop.

1837 PECK *Gaz. Illinois* III. 306 There are in the town two printing offices..one clothing store [etc.]. 1878 B. F. TAYLOR *Between Gates* 281 The dear old fathers of the Eastern churches would have..looked for an asbestos clothing-store.

Clotted. Add: **1. c.** Phr. *Clotted nonsense.*

1674 DRYDEN *Notes & Obs. Empress of Morocco* 23 Sure the Poet wrote these two Lines aboard some smack in a storm, and being Sea-sick spued up a good Lump of clotted Nonsense at once. 1834 *Sun* 1 Apr. (in Carlyle *Sart. Res.* (1871) 212) *Sartor Resartus* is what old Dennis used to call 'a heap of clotted nonsense'. 1909 *Westm. Gaz.* 8 Apr. 2/2 This is the kind of talk which has been admirably described as 'clotted nonsense'.

Clou (klū). [Fr., = nail, peg.] That which holds the attention; the chief attraction, point of greatest interest, or central idea.

1883 *Daily News* 4 Aug. (Ware) The degree of copyright in the central idea, or '*clou*', as it is called in France, of a drama or romance. 1885 *Ibid.* 24 Jan. (ibid.) The *clou* or mainspring of his play. 1904 *Amer. Inventor* 1 Aug. 337 (Cent. D. Suppl.) The displays of finished goods, each containing some '*clou*', such as a $5,000 blanket in the blanket section. 1907 *Westm. Gaz.* 9 Nov. 14/3 The new 30-h.p. six-cylinder Napier chassis..is, of course, the *clou* of the Napier exhibit. 1918 QUILLER-COUCH *Studies Lit.* iii. 67 This epigrammatic *clou*, of all things, Milton wished to avoid. 1927 *Observer* 25 Sept. 18 The 'clou' of the evening, a new string quartet by Arnold Schönberg.

Cloud, *sb.* **12.** Add: **cloud-attack** (*Mil.*), an attack preceded by the discharge of poison gas; **cloud negative**, a negative produced in photographing clouds or the sky.

1919 W. HUTCHINSON *Doctor in War* xiv. 185 The *cloud-attack method of using poison-gas. 1892 *Photogr. Ann.* II. 60 In the *cloud negative the lighting must be in the opposite direction to what it is in the view.

Cloud, *v.* **7.** (Earlier U.S. examples of *cloud over, up.*)

1807 P. GASS *Jrnl.* 171 In the evening it clouded over and rained again. 1834 CROCKETT *Narr. Life* iv. 28 While I was out it clouded up, and I began to get scared.

Clou·d-burst. orig. *U.S.* [f. CLOUD *sb.* 3 + BURST *sb.*] A torrential fall of rain.

[Cf. 1821 T. DWIGHT *Trav.* III. 249 This deluge, which they call the bursting of a cloud, took place in Oct., 1784.] 1872 *Amer. Naturalist* VI. 71 In the mountains there are 'cloud bursts', when the rains fall in a cataract, and filling the gulches sweep every thing before them. 1881 [see CLOUD *sb.* 12]. 1891 G. F. X. GRIFFITH tr. *Fouard's Christ* I. 308 Caught in one of these furious cloud-bursts, the little vessels were scattered far and wide. 1899 *Westm. Gaz.* 27 Mar. 5/2 A cloud-burst broke over Sidi-Naour, in Tunis, yesterday. 1904 *Scott. Hist. Rev.* Oct. 89 The cloudburst and flood of a dozen years ago.

Cloud-cuckoo-town. (Also **-land.**) [tr. of Gr. Νεφελοκοκκυγία (f. νεφέλη cloud + κόκκυξ cuckoo), the name of the town in Aristophanes' *Birds* (819) built by the birds to separate the gods from mankind.] Used vaguely for: A fanciful or ideal realm or domain.

1903 *Daily Chron.* 25 Sept. 3/7 Our new school of economists (sort of cloud-cuckoo-town). 1908 *Times Lit. Suppl.* 10 Dec. 458/3 His ideal state is a true Cloud-Cuckoo-Town. 1920 A. S. PRINGLE-PATTISON *Idea of God* 252 A cloud-cuckoo-land of subjective fancy. 1925 CABELL *Beyond Life* 30 Wycherley had the saving grace to present his men and women as trammelled by the social restrictions of Cloud-Cuckoo-Land alone. 1925 N. MITCHISON (*title*) Cloud Cuckoo Land. A tale of Sparta.

Cloué (klue), *a.* *Her.* [Fr.] Studded with nails.

1869 CUSSANS *Handbk. Her.* 116 *Cloué*, studded with nails. A Portcullis, or a Gate, is sometimes thus described.

Clove, *sb.*[2] **6.** Add: **clove-brown**, the colour of cloves, a medium shade of brown.

1796 KIRWAN *Elem. Min.* (ed. 2) I. 273 Its colour is clove brown. 1887 W. PHILLIPS *Brit. Discomycetes* 346 Scattered, erumpent, clove-brown, shortly stipitate.

Cloven, *ppl. a.* Add:

3. As *sb.* The cloven part; the cleft. *U.S.*

1903 A. ADAMS *Log Cowboy* xi. 161 They could pass a small rope around the pastern above the cloof, or better yet through the cloven in the hoof.

Clover, *sb.* **4.** Add:

clover-field, -hay (examples); **clover-eater** *U.S.* (see quot.); **clover-fern** *Austral.*, nardoo; **clover-huller** (examples); **clover-leaf sight** (see quot.); **clover-sick** *a.* (examples); **clover sickness**, inability of land to grow clover (cf. *clover-sick* adj., in Dict.); **clover summer**, *fig.* an exceptional time; **clover tea** (see quot.); **clover-tree**, a Tasmanian tree, *Goodenia latifolia.*

1869 *Overland Monthly* III. 129 For no particular reason that I am aware of, a Virginian is styled a '*Clover-eater'. 1878 R. B. SMYTH *Abor. Victoria* I. 209 They seem to have been unacquainted, generally, with the use, as a food, of the *clover-fern, *Nardoo.* *c* 1830 *Glouc. Farm Rep.* 16 in *Libr. Usef. Knowl., Husb.* III, They are..put to run in a fallow-field, if there is not a pasture or *clover-field. 1870 'FANNY FERN' *Ginger-Snaps* 257, I shall shortly find a clover field where I intend to bury my disgusted nose until October. *c* 1830 *Glouc. Farm Rep.* 18 in *Libr. Usef. Knowl., Husb.* III, Good rye-grass and *clover-hay is best for them. 1843 CARLTON *New Purchase* 26 The tea was a perfect imitation of clover hay. 1841 in C. Cist *Cincinnati* Advt., Agricultural Machinery,..including *Clover Hullers. 1853 *Trans. Mich. Agric. Soc.* IV. 35 A. O. Holmes,..clover huller. 1884 KNIGHT *Dict. Mech.* Suppl., **Clover Leaf Sight*, a rear gun-sight having side lobes, which slightly resemble two foils of the clover leaf. 1849 H. STEPHENS *Bk. Farm* (1851) I. 619 Such soils as are termed '*clover-sick*.' 1872 *Rep. Vermont Board Agric.* 408 The land was what they call 'clover-sick'. 1907 *Daily Chron.* 15 Feb. 4/6 It was intended to make a grant of £300 to Berkhamsted for the investigation of *clover sickness. 1866 MRS. WHITNEY *L. Goldthwaite* xi, It was a '*clover summer' for the Josselyns...They must make the most of it. 1799 in C. Cist *Cincinnati* (1841) 166 *Clover tea, under the name of Pouchong. 1898 MORRIS *Austral Engl.* 90 *Clover-Tree.

Clover, *v.* (Mod. U.S. example.)

1853 *Trans. Mich. Agric. Soc.* IV. 405 The best mode I have found of improving my farm, is by deep plowing and clovering.

Clown, *v.* Add: **1. b.** *trans.* To play the clown in (a part); to render comic or farcical.

1891 *Harper's Mag.* Sept. 500/2 A Benedick who makes faces and 'clowns' the part..leaves a distinct and horrible stain on the memory. 1930 *Spectator* 18 Jan. 83 Mr. Marshall was too intent on making his 'asides', and there were frequent episodes in which he definitely clowned the situation.

Clownage. Transfer †*Obs.* to 2 and add to 1:

1903 *Times* 23 Apr. 10/2 The outside circle was the marriage of Theseus and Hippolyta, then came the clownage of the play.

Clox, commercial spelling of pl. of CLOCK *sb.*[2] Cf. *CLOCK *v.*[4]

1923 *Daily Mail* 26 May 1 Silk Stockings (with lace clox). 1928 *Daily Tel.* 20 Mar. 14/6 The latest stockings, instead of having clox or embroidery to draw attention to ankles, are ornamented with hand-painted roses or with clox on the knee.

Cloyingly (kloi·iŋli), *adv.* [f. CLOYING *ppl. a.* + -LY[2].] In a cloying manner or degree.

1928 *Observer* 25 Mar. 15/4 This cloyingly sweet criticism.

Cloysome, *a.* Delete *rare* and add quots.:

1861 *Macm. Mag.* IV. 209/2 Cloysome contrasts are too frequently indulged in. 1902 G. C. WILLIAMSON *Holman Hunt* 18 The pictures of the day in their cloysome richness.

Club, *sb.* Add: **2. b.** (See quot.)

1889 *Century Dict.*, *Club*, a small spar to which the head of a gaff-topsail or the clue of a staysail or jib is bent to make the sail set to the best advantage.

5. Also, a clump (of trees). *U.S.*

1836 EDWARD *Hist. Texas* 36 We find..one solid prairie.. intersected..with variegated clubs of timber.

18. (sense 2) *club-face, -head, -maker, -shaft*; (sense 14) *club button, necktie, tie.*

1894 *To-day* 17 Mar. 182/2 Yachting suits of blue cheviot with *club buttons. 1928 *Daily Mail* 25 July 15/4 Much has been heard in recent years of the 'shut' and 'open' *club-faces. 1891 H. G. HUTCHINSON *Golf* 20 The *club-head will, so, describe the arc not of a circle but an ellipse. 1903 *Westm. Gaz.* 17 July 3/2 To bring the club-head down on the back of the ball and between it and the rim of the cup. 1891 H. G. HUTCHINSON *Golf* 54 The *club-maker whom you honour with your patronage. 1909 *Westm. Gaz.* 11 Jan. 12/2 Besides being a very fine player, Stephenson is a first-class club-maker. 1927 A. BENNETT *Woman who stole, The Umbrella* 152 He..wore..a *club necktie carelessly knotted. 1906 *Westm. Gaz.* 12 Oct. 3/1 A little twist in the hand, with the *club-shaft.

20. club-fungus, a fungus belonging to the family *Clavariaceæ*; **club-tail** (*local U.S.*), also, the common shad; **club-topsail**, a large topsail extended beyond the gaff by means of a small spar or 'club'; **club-wheat** (earlier examples).

a 1909 C. MACMILLAN *Minn. Plant Life* viii. (Cent. D. Suppl.) Not all of the *club-fungi are unbranched. 1848 BARTLETT *Dict. Amer.*, **Clubtail.* The common shad, the fatter portion of which have the tail swollen, and on the coast of Carolina, where they are taken, are called *club-tails.* 1886 *Outing* (U.S.) IX. 19/1 The Mohawk was lying..with all after canvas set, even to her enormous *club top-sail. 1849 *Rep. U.S. Comm. Patents, Agric.* (1850) 181 The *club wheat, which has a remarkably stiff straw. 1861 *Trans. Ill. Agric. Soc.* IV. 317 A neighbour tried shrunk club wheat for seed.

Clubby, *a.* *U.S.* Delete *nonce-wd.* and add:

1905 *Smart Set* Sept. 128/1 Our black coffee stories have become clubby to an extent that embarrasses a butler. *Ibid.* 129/1 She is not a creature to set to music—the clubby girl, the feminine good-fellow. 1928 F. N. HART *Bellamy Trial* i. 14 Charles Stuyvesant's the only one that won't have a good clubby time of it.

Clubmanly (klɒ·bmænli), *a.* [-LY[1].] Characteristic of a clubman.

1918 *Nation* (N.Y.) 26 Sept. 286 That clubmanly air which is so irresistible to the general public.

Clu·b-woman. [CLUB *sb.* 13–15.] A woman who is a member or habituée of a club or clubs.

1895 SUSAN HALE *Lett.* 294 She..is a 'club-woman',—and she early secured me to 'attend a meeting' of her club.

Clucker (klɒ·kəɹ). [f. CLUCK *v.* + -ER[1].] One who clucks or talks endlessly and aimlessly.

1891 KIPLING *Light that Failed* viii, What a one-idead clucker it is! 1921 *Chambers's Jrnl.* 355/2 People were mistaken who took Gilbert for an eternal clucker, for he could be stern enough.

Clump, *sb.* Add:

1. b. A clump-built ship. *U.S.*

1830 S. BRECK *Recoll.* iii. (1877) 139 But our brig was a *clump*, and made but small way.

2. b. Of people.

1896 *Harper's Mag.* XCII. 772/1 Clumps of Frenchmen were smashed to pieces, one on top of the other.

c. (*a*) A mass of bacteria which have come together through the action of agglutinins. (*b*) A mass of fibrin precipitated from the liquid plasma of the blood.

1899 G. NEWMAN *Bacteria* App. 343 The clumps of bacilli having fallen owing to gravity. 1902 *Encycl. Brit.* XXVI. 68/2 The aggregation into clumps of the bacteria uniformly distributed in an indifferent fluid. *Ibid.*, The clumps soon settle in the fluid and ultimately form a sediment. 1910 *Ibid.* IV. 81/2 The tendency the corpuscles have to run into clumps.

d. *Printing.* (See quot.)

1898 J. SOUTHWARD *Mod. Printing* (1910) I. xii. 87 *Clumps* are thick pieces of type metal, ranging in width from pearl to double pica, and of the height of leads. They are used in whiting out, also as footlines at the bottoms of columns and pages.

4. b. A blow, knock. **c.** A stick. *colloq.* or *dial.*

1858 *Farmer & the King* in *N. & Q.* 4th Ser. II. 152 He knocked and thump'd wi' his oaken clump. 1889 JEROME *Three Men in Boat* i. 7 They didn't give me pills; they gave me clumps on the side of the head. 1894 BLACKMORE *Perlycross* xxxvi, He dropped on the flags with a clump in his ear.

6. clump-foot = CLUB-FOOT. (Cf. †*clumped foot* s.v. CLUMPED *ppl. a.* 1.)

1922 *Chambers's Jrnl.* 863/2 He had a clump-foot.

Clump (klɒmp), *a.* *U.S.* [f. CLUMP *sb.*] = *clump-built* (s.v. CLUMP *sb.* 9).

1808 *Columbian Centinel* 17 Feb. 3/1 A clump black looking brig, ashore, with her foremast gone.

Clump, *v.* Add:

1. b. To move heavily or clumsily.

1903 CONRAD & HUEFFER *Romance* III. vi, The clumping staff of my heavy crucifix drew hollow echoes from the flagstones.

c. *trans.* To strike, punch, or beat. *colloq.* or *dial.*

1864 *Derby Day* 52, I want to clump them. It will spoil sport to call in the bobbies. 1874 *Slang Dict.*, *Clump*, to strike, to beat.—*Prov.* 1896 A. MORRISON *Child Jago* 162 Dicky 'clumped' Bobby Roper whenever he could get hold of him. 1903 *Daily Chron.* 10 Mar. 9/7 When I woke up I found my boy's hand in my pocket, and I clumped him, as a father should. 1924 *Blackw. Mag.* Feb. 145/1 [He] impartially..clumped the ears of each youth in turn.

2. b. *intr.* and *trans.* To form a clump or clumps (*CLUMP *sb.* 2 c). Hence **Clu·mping** *vbl. sb.*

1903 *Med. Rec.* Feb. 358 (Cent. D. Suppl.) The Seal Harbor bacillus refused absolutely to clump in any dilution above 1–10. 1904 *Jrnl. Med. Research* Oct. 321 (Ibid.) The table showing..no flagellar clumping. 1907 C. URBAN *Cinematograph* 42 The 'clumping' of Typhoid bacilli. 1908 *Practitioner* June 838,·1 per cent. saline solution, in which the organisms lose to a large extent their natural property of clumping. 1910 *Encycl. Brit.* IV. 81 Horse's blood offers one of the best instances of the clumping of red corpuscles.

Clumpy, *a.* Add:

1. b. Consisting of or growing in clumps.

1889 J. S. NICHOLSON *Dreamer of Dreams* II. vii. 100 The pastures were thick with heavy, clumpy grass.

Cluster, *sb.* Add:

3. c. A group of small stars forming a relatively dense mass, appearing as a nebula to the naked eye; a star-cluster. Also *attrib.*, as *cluster system, variable.*

1833 HERSCHEL *Astron.* (1859) 634 In the sword-handle of Perseus, also, is another such spot, crowded with stars, which requires rather a better telescope to resolve into individuals separated from each other. These are called clusters of stars. *Ibid.* 637 Nebulæ..have been separated by him [*sc.* Sir W. Herschel] into—1st, Clusters of stars, in which the stars are clearly distinguishable; and these, again, into globular and irregular clusters. 1854 [in Dict. s.v. 3]. 1902 *Encycl. Brit.* XXV. 753/1 In all 509 variable stars were found among 19,050 examined in twenty-three clusters...Perhaps the most interesting questions suggested by these cluster systems is that of their stability. 1926 H. MACPHERSON *Mod. Astron.* 121 In 1895 another sub-class was added by Professor Bailey of Harvard, who detected in that year the 'cluster variables', a type closely akin to the Cepheids and Geminids. 1928 JEANS *Astron. & Cosmog.* 26 It is not altogether clear to what extent the globular clusters and the moving clusters form distinct formations.

4. cluster-cherry (examples); **cluster-pin, -ring**, a breast-pin or ring set with a cluster of stones; **cluster-pore**, each of a number of small pores or orifices forming part of the system of mucous canals opening on the surface in *Chimæra.*

1731 P. MILLER *Gard. Dict.* s.v. *Cerasus*, The Flanders *Cluster-Cherry. 1765 J. BARTRAM *Jrnl.* (1769) 5 Chinquapines and cluster-cherry all of an uncommon size. *Footnote.* There is an evergreen sort of this Bird or Cluster cherry, which grows about 30 feet high in S. Carolina. 1873 'MARK TWAIN' & C. D. WARNER *Gilded Age* xxxiii. 301 He wore a diamond *cluster-pin and he parted his hair behind. 1895 *Proc. Zool. Soc. London* 880 There is also an absence of primitive pores, and the *cluster-pores are very few in number. *a* 1906 'O. HENRY' *Trimmed Lamp* etc. 173 She wore a *cluster ring of huge imitation rubies.

Clutch, *sb.*¹ **6. a.** Add: *spec.* in motor vehicles, a piece of mechanism by which power is transmitted from the engine to the wheels. Also *attrib.*

1899 *Motor-Car World* Oct. 10/1 The advantage of transmission by gearing is its positiveness, while its disadvantages are noise, cost of renewal when worn, and the necessity of using clutches. 1902 A. C. Harmsworth *Motors & Motor-Driving* x. 191 The forward end of the arbor shaft is connected to the engine shaft by a clutch. *Ibid.* 208 The motor and the main clutch shaft must be truly in line. 1904 A. B. F. Young *Complete Motorist* ix. 216 The car will now travel forward so long as the clutch pedal is not depressed. 1906 *Westm. Gaz.* 14 Nov. 9/2 A flexible joint on the driving shaft just at the rear of the clutch-sleeve. 1912 *Motor Manual* v. 162 To ensure a gradual 'take up' of the drive from the engine, the clutch should be let in very gently. 1928 Galsworthy *Swan Song* III. iv. 246 'This is where I put in my clutch', she said, 'as they say in the "bloods!"' And through Epsom and Leatherhead they travelled in silence.

Clutchy (klʌ·tʃi), *a.* [f. Clutch *v.*¹ + -y¹.] Inclined to clutch.

1876 A. S. Palmer *Leaves from Word-hunter's Notebk.* x. 246 Upon sins the devil is 'ready-to-take-hold', or, if we might forge a term for the occasion, is 'clutchy'. 1922 A. S. M. Hutchinson *This Freedom* II. iii. 96 Grotesque ideas,..masterfully shaping the child mind wherein they germinated; burrowing in clutchy roots.

Clutter, *sb.* Add: **2.** (Later U.S. example.)

1891 *Harper's Mag.* Nov. 881/2 A tiny clutter of frame houses and tents.

3. esp. in phr. *in a clutter.*

1890 *Blackw. Mag.* CXLVIII. 463/2 Up spring the partridges;..all in a clutter they are, one over the other.

Clutter, *v.* Add:

6. (Illustration of recent extended currency.)

1908 *Daily Chron.* 25 Feb. 4/4 The floor also was cluttered with papers and books of every kind. 1910 *Westm. Gaz.* 6 Apr. 2/1 The Second Chamber is now cluttered up with a brute mass of undistinguished bipeds. 1914 H. H. Fyfe *Real Mexico* 92 The lines here are all cluttered up with troop-trains. 1923 *Times Lit. Suppl.* 18 Jan. 36/2 The book is cluttered up with details of the number of troops present and tables of the exceedingly minute casualties.

Cluttered, *ppl. a.* **2.** Delete *U.S.* and add: Also with *up.*

1867–8 *Trans. Ill. Agric. Soc.* VII. 573 The slovenly, cluttered up appearance that characterizes Western habitations. *a* 1887 Jefferies *Field & Hedgerow* (1889) 189 'Cluttered up' means in a litter, surrounded with too many things to do at once. 1897 Kipling *Capt. Cour.* 53 The cluttered decks of a seventy-ton schooner. 1898 — in *Morn. Post* 8 Nov. 5/2 Cluttered-up boxes of machinery and bags of tricks. 1910 *Daily Chron.* 9 Mar. 7/3 To pick up débris from a cluttered room.

Cluttery (klʌ·təri), *a.* *U.S.* [f. Clutter *sb.* 2 b.] Somewhat cluttered.

1904 Susan Hale *Lett.* 388 At Bowbridge we rested the horses in a cluttery little town.

Clydesdale (klai·dzdēl), *a.* (*sb.*) Designating a breed of heavy draft horses originally bred round about the Clyde in Scotland.

1831 Youatt *Horse* 39 The Clydesdale is a good kind of draught-horse, and particularly for farming business and in a hilly country. *Ibid.* 40 The Clydesdale horse owes its origin to one of the Dukes of Hamilton, who crossed some of the best Lanark mares with stallions which he had brought over from Flanders. 1862 Morton *Farmer's Cal.* (ed. 2) 574 The Clydesdale is one of our best farm horses. 1884 *Times* 27 Feb. 7/6 The high-standing quick-stepping Clydesdales.

Clydesider (klai·dsaidəɹ). [f. *Clyde side* (Side *sb.*¹ 7 a) + -er.¹] A dweller on a bank of the river Clyde in Scotland; *spec.* applied to that group of the Labour party whose leaders are associated with Glasgow and the neighbouring industrial area.

1922 *Glasgow Herald* 7 Apr. 7 There does not appear to be much to interest the Clydesider in the news that the Norwegian four-masted barque Svartskog is long overdue. 1926 *Ibid.* 2 Apr. 9 Even the versatile loquacity of half a dozen of the more combative Clydesiders failed to spin things out till the hour appointed for dispersal. 1930 *Times Lit. Suppl.* 20 Feb., In that valley the Clydesiders were born with memories of the martyrs Muir and Palmer.

Cnicnode (nai·knōud). *Math.* [f. L. *cnicus, cnēcus* safflower = Gr. κνῆκος a plant of the thistle kind + L. *nodus* knot, node.] A conical point, a point where tangents form a cone of the second order. Also **Cni·ctrope** (see Trope), the reciprocal of a cnicnode.

1869 Cayley *Math. Papers* (1893) VI. 330, I take account of conical and biplanar nodes, or, as I call them, cnicnodes, and binodes. *Ibid.* 334 Consider a surface having the cnicnode $C = 1$, and the reciprocal surface having the cnictrope $C' = 1$. 1870 *Ibid.* (1894) VII. 246 There may be on the nodal curve points which, in the classification of the surfaces, must be counted as cnicnodes. 1887 *Encycl. Brit.* XXII. 669/1 As regards isolated singularities, it will be sufficient to mention the point singularity of the conical point (or cnicnode) and the corresponding plane singularity of the conic of contact (or cnictrope).

Cnida. Add: **Cni·docyst,** a nematocyst. **Cnido·genous** *a.*, producing or containing nematocysts. **Cni·dosac,** the dilated middle part of a tentillum in certain *Siphonophora.*

1898 Sedgwick *Text-bk. Zool.* I. 146 The swelling of the cnidosac is due to a rich development of nematocysts of various kinds, forming the battery. 1902 *Encycl. Brit.* XXX. 797/1 The hepatic cæca in the dorsal papillæ of Eolidoida actually communicate with the cnidogenous sacs at their extremity; cnidocysts are absent from Eolis glaucoides.

Co.³ Add: **1. b.** *colloq.* In phrases: *and Co.*, and the rest of that set; *in Co.* (*with*), in company (with). Chiefly *U.S.*

1816 U. Brown *Jrnl.* in *Maryland Hist. Mag.* XI. 147 This morning..in Co: with Doctor William Lee Brook, traverses Janesville..and pastes up our hand bills. 1836 'Texian' *Mexico v. Texas* 11 Two foreign physicians, the one a Frenchman, the other an American, exercised the healing art *in Co.* 1888 *Nation* (N.Y.) 5 July 3/2 In the case of Newfoundland Messrs. Frye, Tugalls & Co. consider the claim presumptuous.

Coacervate, *a.* Delete †*Obs.* and add: *Bot.* Clustered.

1845 *Florist's Jrnl.* (1846) VI. 246 Coacervate, growing together, clustered. 1866 *Treas. Bot.*

Coach, *sb.* Add:

1. d. (See also quots. below.)

1884 Knight *Dict. Mech.* Suppl., *Coach*, a first class passenger car, as distinguished from a drawing room car, or second class. 1911 Webster, *Coach*,..a first-class passenger car, as distinguished from a drawing-room car, sleeping car, etc.; sometimes, loosely, any passenger car.

3. c. A tame bullock or horse used as a decoy in catching wild cattle or horses. *Austral.*

1874 Ranken *Australia* vi. 110 To get them [*sc.* wild cattle], a party of stockmen take a small herd of quiet cattle, 'coaches'.

6. coach-built *a.*, of a motor body, built of wood throughout by craftsmen, or on a wood framework with metal panels; also sometimes designating merely such a framework; **coach-house,** also *Naut.* (see quot.); **coach-lace,** an ornamental woven band used as a trimming for carriages; **coach-lock,** a kind of spring latch; **coach screw,** a large screw with a square head, which is turned with a spanner; hence **coach-screw** *v.*; **coach-smith** (see quots.); **coach-work,** the woodwork of a motor-car body.

1904 *Daily Chron.* 19 Nov. 6/6 The new car, with a *coach-built seat at the rear in place of a tool-box. 1928 *Daily Express* 13 June 3 The coachbuilt bodies are beautifully finished. 1838 J. F. Cooper *Homeward Bound* I. 12 Mr. Effingham led his daughter into the hurricane-house or, as the packet-men quaintly term it, the *coach-house. 1853 *Jrnl. Soc. Arts* 11 Nov. 618/1 The object is to weave in *coach lace numbers and letters, so as to form words. 1921 *Dict. Occup. Terms* (1927) § 370 Coach lace weaver. 1884 Knight *Dict. Mech.* Suppl., **Coach Lock*, a spring latch operated either by a cross-bar handle on the exterior, or by a lever from within side the carriage. 1874 Thearle *Naval Archit.* 60 Very frequently *coach screws are placed between the bolts. *Ibid.* 48 Angle-irons being fitted in the corners, riveted to the beams, and *coach-screwed to the carlings. 1846 G. Dodd *Brit. Manuf.* VI. 122 A *coach-smith..has to work large and heavy bars of iron into forms containing several unequal curves, and varying greatly in thickness. 1921 *Dict. Occup. Terms* (1927) § 190 *Coach-smith*;..a smith who forges by hand or under power hammer..iron work used in building railway or tramway coaches, motor vans, carts, etc. 1906 *Daily Chron.* 20 Oct. 2/7 Special carburettors, governors, ignition gear, gear-boxes, *coachwork. 1907 *Westm. Gaz.* 11 Nov. 6/3 The best examples of high-class coach-work. 1922 *Autocar* 10 Nov. 1013 The advantage of this type of coachwork over the ordinary two-seater and dickey.

Coach, *v.* Add:

3. c. To decoy wild cattle or horses with tame animals. *Austral.*

1874 Ranken *Australia* vi. 121 [The wild horse] may be got by 'coaching' like wild cattle.

Coachee¹. **2.** *U.S.* (Earlier and later examples.)

1794 *U.S. Stat.* I. 374 For and upon every phaeton and coachee [a duty of] six dollars. 1796 *Mass. Stat.* c. 32. § 1 Any Coach, Chariot, Coachee or other Carriage. 1819 *Rees' Cycl.* s.v. *Philadelphia*, The coachee is a carriage thought to be peculiar to America. 1832 *Act Penn.* in *U.S. Stat.* (1856) IV. 554 [Toll] for every chariot, coach, coachee, stage, wagon,..with two horses and four wheels, twelve cents.

Coachman. Add:

1. d. The coach-whip bird. *Austral.*

1827 P. Cunningham *N. S. W.* II. 158 Our native *coachman*..whistling and cracking out his whiplike notes as he hops sprucely from branch to branch. 1888 Jas. Thomas in *Austral. Poets 1788–1888* 552 While the crested coachman bird Midst the underwood is heard.

Coach-whip. Add:

1. b. *ellipt.* The coach-whip bird. *Austral.*

1793 Tench *Port Jackson* 175 To one [of the smaller birds], not bigger than a tom-tit, we have given the name of coach-whip, from its note exactly resembling the smack of a whip. 1827 *Trans. Linn. Soc.* XV. 330. 1848 Haygarth *Bush Life in Australia* i. 7 The 'coach-whip,' with his peculiar jerking cry.

c. *ellipt.* The coach-whip snake. *U.S.*

1835 W. G. Simms *Partisan* 255 The skin of a monstrous coachwhip which..he had been successful enough..to kill without bruising. 1887 *Sci. Amer.* (N. S.) LVII. 7 A 'coach-whip', a snake much like the common black snakes in form, but in color a very dark brown some two thirds of its length.

Coachwood (kōu·tʃwud). [f. Coach *sb.* + Wood *sb.*¹] Either of two Australian trees, *Ceratopetalum apetalum*, yielding an aromatic close-grained wood suitable for cabinet making, or *Schizomeria ovata*; also, the wood of these trees.

1886 *Encycl. Brit.* XX. 174/1 Names are found oddly given by colonists. Their red cedar is the *Cedrela Goona*; ..coachwood, the *Ceratopetalum.*

Coact, *v.* **5.** (Modern U.S. example.)

1874 Knight *Dict. Mech.*, *Die* (Forging), a device consisting of two parts which coact to give to the piece swaged between them the desired form.

Coagulation. Add:

4. *attrib.*: **coagulation necrosis,** that form of necrosis in which dead tissue forms into a mass in the midst of tissue in which the blood continues to circulate. Also called *coagulative necrosis.*

1890 Billings *Med. Dict.*, *Coagulation necrosis*, necrosis with coagulation of dead tissues (Weigert). 1895 *Buck's Handbk. Med. Sci.* Suppl. 351/1 Coagulative necrosis, a condition confounded by some with gangrene, was given its name by Cohnheim.

Coagulin (koˌæ·giulin). *Biol. Chem.* [f. Coagul(ate *v.*: see -in¹.] An adaptation-product causing coagulation of an introduced substance.

1913 Dorland *Med. Dict.* (ed. 7). 1929 *Encycl. Brit.* III. 898/1 [Jules Bordet] has thrown light on the process of the formation of coagulin, showing that it includes two elements; the first, albuminoidal and peculiar to the liquid blood, and the other, lipoidal in nature, originating in the cells of the blood or tissues.

Coagulometer (koˌægiulǫ·mĭtəɹ). [f. *coagul-* in Coagulate, Coagulum, etc. + -(o)meter.] An instrument for examining the coagulability of blood.

1901 Dorland *Med. Dict.* (ed. 2). 1908 *Jrnl. Chem. Soc.* XCIV. II. 766 A modification of Buckmaster's coagulometer is described. 1910 *Practitioner* Apr. 428 The coagulation time of the blood, which was taken on several occasions by Wright's coagulometer.

Coal, *sb.* Add: **15.** *coal-carrying, -fed* adjs.

1892 *Daily News* 8 June 2/3 A most important *coal-carrying line. 1905 *Daily Chron.* 6 Jan. 5/5 The Berrington has been engaged in coal-carrying between the Tyne and the Continent for nearly forty years. 1890 *Pall Mall Gaz.* 2 June 3/3 The *coal-fed furnace. 1899 Mrs. H. Fraser *Diplom. Wife in Japan* I. 6 Our great coal-fed, screw-driven liner.

16. coal-ball, also, a round mass, usually of calcite or pyrite, found in or near a coal-seam; **coal-bank** *U.S.*, a bank from which coal is obtained; **coal baron** *U.S.* (see *Baron 2 b); **coal-bunker,** a place for storing coal, *spec.* in a ship; **coal-car** *U.S.*, a coal-wagon; **coal-face,** the surface of a seam exposed by mining; **coal-fired** *a.*, heated or driven by coal; **coal lumper,** one who loads coal into vessels; **coal-salt,** a fine salt (generally discoloured by soot) obtained from brine by surface-evaporation; **coal-tip,** an apparatus from which coal is tipped into a receptacle; **coal-washer,** a man or machine employed in washing impurities from coal; **coal-yard** (U.S. example).

1902 *Rep. Brit. Assoc. Adv. Sci.* 811 On the Occurrence of the Nodular Concretions (*Coal Balls) in the Lower Coal Measures. 1921 *Brit. Museum Return* 151 Two Coal-balls from the Coal Measures, Romsée, near Liége. 1816 U. Brown *Jrnl.* in *Maryland Hist. Mag.* XI. 142 Thence on said River 4 Miles to a *Coal Bank. 1837 Peck *Gaz. Illinois* II. 135 Extensive coal banks exist in the county. 1886 *Harper's Mag.* June 62/2 A gentleman who wanted a coal bank opened engaged for the work a man passing along the road. 1887 *Ibid.* Apr. 822/1 When the great '*coal barons'.. deliberately combine to put up the price of coal. 1840 *Monthly Chron.* (Boston) July 240 The engines, boilers, and *coal-bunkers [of S.S. 'Britania'] occupy a space of 70 feet, the width of the vessel. 1874 Knight *Dict. Mech.*, *Coal-bunker*, the closed room around the boiler and engine-room of a steam vessel for keeping the fuel. 1886 *Harper's Mag.* June 4/2 The capacity of her coal-bunkers is 630 tons. 1895 *Army & Navy Co-op. Soc. Price List* 15 Sept. 266 Coal Bunker. To hold 2 cwt., 18 by 16 by 36 in. high. 1903 *Westm. Gaz.* 30 Nov. 2/1 The saved coal-bunker space is.. available for additional cargo. 1858 *Penn. Rail Road Annual Rep.* 14 The rolling stock..consisted..of..92 Four-wheeled *Coal Cars. 1874 Knight *Dict. Mech.*, *Coal-car*, a freight-car designed especially for coal, having facilities for dumping. 1908 *Westm. Gaz.* 8 Jan. 10/1 At least 1,000 coal-cars were added to the rolling-stock. 1872 *Good Words for Young* 89/2 They hang their lamps above their heads, and then swinging their picks, make a ledge in the *coal face. 1883 Gresley *Gloss. Coal-m.* 55 *Coal Face*, the working face or wall of a stall, composed wholly of coal. 1929 *Daily Express* 7 Nov. 2/3 Two Lancashire Socialist members who recently worked at the coal face and were returned to Parliament for the first time in May. 1909 *Daily Chron.* 17 Apr. 4/7 Baked fifty-five minutes in *coal-fired oven. 1911 Harbord & Hall *Metall. Steel* (ed. 4) 538 The ordinary coal-fired furnace. 1908 *Daily Chron.* 29 Aug. 1/6 *Coal Lumpers Refuse to Work on American Hospital Ship. 1880 G. Lunge *Sulphuric Acid* II. 131 The very fine 'butter salt', or '*coal salt', obtained by top heat according to Pohl's process. 1906 Cornford *Defenceless Islands* 34 The frame-work with the rising platform is called a *coal-tip. 1874 Knight *Dict. Mech.*, **Coal-washer*, a machine in which coal which has been broken and assorted is finally washed to deprive it of the dust and dirt adhering. 1921 *Dict. Occup. Terms* (1927) § 049 *Coal washer*;..works at machine for washing coal in washery to remove impurities. 1851 A. O. Hall *Manhattaner in New Orleans* 6 The much talked of flat boats, mere floating granaries and coal-yards, secure in their timber fragility.

Coal-box. Add: **b.** A low-velocity German shell emitting black smoke, a Black Maria. *Army slang.*

1914 *Illustr. Lond. News* 3 Oct. 489 One of the German siege-guns—nicknamed..'coal-box'. 1914 *Scotsman* 13 Nov. 7/2 All you could hear was whizz, whizz! and then a deafening bang as a coal box would burst. 1916 Boyd Cable *Action Front* 15 'Coal-box', said Courtenay hurriedly. 'Come on. They're apt to drop some more about the same spot.'

Coaler. Add: **3.** A railway employed in transporting coal from coal-mining districts. **b.** *pl.* Stocks or shares of coal-carrying railway companies. *U.S.*

1892 *Daily News* 16 Feb. 6/6 Readings and other stocks reacted under realizations, but 'coalers' then gradually lost

their prominence. 1897 *Ibid.* 21 May 7/6 The feature of to-day's stock market was the remarkable weakness of Coalers. 1909 *Daily Chron.* 17 Apr. 2/1 Coalers were again the best stocks in the Yankee market.

Coalescence. 3. Add: *Psychol.* (See quots.)

1890 W. James *Text-bk. Psychol.* 339 Coalescence of Different Sensations into the Same 'Thing'.—When two senses are impressed simultaneously we tend to identify their objects as *one thing*...In this *coalescence in a 'thing'*, one of the coalescing sensations is held to *be* the thing, the other sensations are taken for its more or less accidental *properties*, or modes of appearance. 1896 G. F. Stout *Anal. Psychol.* I. 285 Suppose the components of the one combination are *a b c*, and of the other *a b x*; *c* may be so favored from the outset that it simply displaces *x* without any feeling of discrepancy arising, and without any attention to the difference. This process I call overlapping or coalescence. *Ibid.* 287 The gradual transformation undergone by a story as it passes from one person to another is in part at least to be accounted for by coalescence.

Coal-hole. 3. (U.S. example.)

1854 Shillaber *Mrs. Partington* 56 When you look up.. avoid the coal-holes and cellar-ways that are open for your unwary feet.

Coalitionism (kōuăli·ʃəniz'm). [See under Coalition.] The principles or advocacy of government by coalition. So **Coali·tionalism, Coali·tionalist** *attrib.* or as *adj.*

1922 J. M. Erskine in *Daily Mail* 6 Nov. 10 Untainted by the poison of Coalitionism. 1925 *Contemp. Rev.* May 648 A political crisis in which the whole philosophy of coalitionalism was killed. *Ibid.*, His late Coalitionalist Conservative colleagues. 1928 *Manchester Guardian Weekly* 17 Aug. 129/2 By coalitionism you sell half your soul to get the other half.

Coal-man. 2. Delete *nonce-use* and add:

1612 in *Court & Times Jas. I* (1849) I. 200 About fifty sail ..known to be cast away, especially about Yarmouth, great numbers of fishermen and coalmen.

Coa·l-oil. *U.S.* [Coal *sb.* 16.] Shale-oil, petroleum. Also *attrib.*

1858 *U.S. Patent* 25 May, Coal oil and other lamps. 1865 *Ibid.* 17 Jan., Coal oil stove. 1875, 1883 [see Coal *sb.* 16]. 1897 Beatrice Harraden *Hilda Strafford* vi. 94 Empty coal-oil tins and preserved pine-apples are not very fattening, are they? 1926 J. Black *You Can't Win* xv. 197 He sat in state on a coal-oil can by the fire.

Hence **Coal-oil** *v. trans.*, to smear with coal-oil.

1894 *Congress. Rec.* 5 Feb. 1862/1 The colored people are tortured; they are mutilated; they are coal-oiled and burned.

Coarse, *a.* **7. c.** Add: **coarse fish,** any fresh-water fish except the *Salmonidæ* (or game-fish). (In the 14th century the term was synonymous with *stock-fish.*)

1895 C. J. Cornish *Wild England of To-day* 178 Autumn and winter are the proper seasons in which to take coarse fish. 1897 *Encycl. Sport* I. 16/1 The taking of spinning-baits by grayling, and by the minor coarse fish. *Ibid.* 29/2. 1898 *Daily News* 9 Mar. 5/1 The coarse-fish men who aspire to baskets of pike, perch, and roach.

Coassine (koæ·səin, -in), *a.* [f. mod.L. *Coassus*, a genus of deer, f. Guarani *guazú* deer: see -ine¹.] Of, pertaining to, or designating a group of small American spike-horned deer.

1891 Flower & Lydekker *Mamm.* 330 The South American Coassine group comprises the small forms known as Brockets, in which the antlers form simple spikes not exceeding half the length of the head.

Coast, *sb.* Add:

4. c. Also, the West Coast of Africa, the Pacific Coast of N. America.

1888 Powles *Land of Pink Pearl* 280 He was then for a time 'on the coast', as it is called, a polite form of saying a man has been in the slave trade on the West Coast of Africa. 1930 *Publishers' Weekly* 8 Feb. 708/1, I like the Coast because it comprises California, Oregon, Washington and the contiguous States.

d. *spec.* One or other bank of the Mississippi near its mouth.

1812 Brackenridge *Views Louisiana* (1814) 174 The Coast may be said to begin at Pointe Coupée. From this to La Fourche, two thirds of the banks are perfectly cleared. 1835 J. H. Ingraham *South-West* II. 24 *note*, The banks of the Mississippi are termed 'the coast' as far up the river as Baton Rouge. 1868 *Putnam's Mag.* May 594/2 The left bank, or 'coast', of the river, as it is called in Louisiana.

13. *coast-defender, -survey, -trade, -trader.*

1883 *Whitaker's Alm.* 445/2 China.—3 ironclads. Two of them are double-turreted *coast-defenders of the first class. 1832 *Deb. Congress* 30 May 3187 The *coast survey..will not be completed..under sixty years. 1851 C. Cist *Cincinnati* 282 Flat-boats..take down more or less bacon for the *coast trade. 1864 J. A. Grant *Walk across Africa* 161 Jumah, a *coast-trader.

14. coast-defence, the protection of the coast of a country from attack by sea, either by forts or sea-vessels; **coast-fever,** a fever occurring in coastal regions; *spec.*, a disease, *Piroplasma parvum*, transmitted by ticks, which attacks cattle on the East Coast of Africa; **coast fox** *U.S.*, a fox of the Californian coast; **coast-liner,** a surveyor whose work is to map a coast-line; so *coast-lining*; **coast-man** (modern examples); **coast-partridge, -pheasant,** a Natal name for *Francolinus natalensis*; **coast-watcher, -watching** (see quots.).

1854 *Chambers's Jrnl.* 172/1 A plan for *coast defence. 1869 *Ibid.* 710/1 A low-speed coast-defence vessel. 1883 *Whitaker's Alm.* 445/2 Norway.—Has only 4 coast-defence monitors. 1886 *Harper's Mag.* June 23/1 Another type of ships, which are styled 'coast-defence vessels'. 1904 *Westm. Gaz.* 28 Dec. 2/1 Our coast-defence artillery. 1840 R. H. Dana *Bef. Mast* xxiii. (1862) 248 Keeping him hard at work while ill of the *coast fever. 1904 *Daily Chron.* 4 July 7/7 Coast fever. 1904 Dr. Theiler *Rep. S. A. A. A. S.* 211 (Pettman) East coast fever being a piroplasma disease, led investigators to believe that it must be carried by ticks. 1905 *Science in S. Afr.* 339 (ibid.) They clearly recognized and described the small and characteristic organisms of African Coast Fever. 1870 *Amer. Naturalist* III. 186 The *Coast Fox (*Vulpes littoralis*), if really distinct from the gray, does not occur northward. 1902 *Encycl. Brit.* XXXIII. 101/2 It is with the high-water line that the *coast-liner is concerned, delineating its character according to the Admiralty symbols. *Ibid.* 102/1 *Coast-lining.* In a detailed survey the coast is sketched in by walking along it, fixing by theodolite or sextant angles. 1927 *Blackw. Mag.* Apr. 516/2, I was..peacefully engaged in coast-lining with a sextant and theodolite. 1841 Poe *Tales Myst. & Imag.*, *Desc. Maelström*, Among the whole of the Lofoden *coastmen, we three were the only ones who made a regular business of going out to the islands. 1864 J. A. Grant *Walk across Africa* 161 They refused to allow any coast-men into their kingdom. 1911 Gilchrist *S. Afr. Zool.* 255 (Pettman) *Francolinus natalensis* is the *Coast partridge of Natal or 'Namaqua pheasant' of the Transvaal. 1916 *War Illustrated* IV. 604/2 They dont call us coastguards, mind you, but *Coast Watchers. 1928 *Daily Express* 23 Mar. 1/3 The small force of coast-watchers who have taken the place of the old coastguards. 1925 *Act 15 & 16 Geo. V.* c. 88 § 1 A *coast-watching force for the performance of the duties hitherto performed by the coast-guard.

Coast, *v.* Add: **13.** *U.S.* (Earlier examples.)

1836 *Boston Pearl* 9 Jan. (Th.) Skate, if you like; 'coast', if you are boy enough. 1854 *Springfield Republ.* (Th.) Adown thy hills, when I's a boy, O how I used to coast.

b. Also of a motor vehicle.

1925 *Morris Owner's Manual* 11 Do not 'coast' down hill with the clutch out. 1928 *Daily Mail* 25 July 7/5 Top gear in the Willys-Knight feels like free coasting in other cars.

c. To glide swiftly through the air, as a bird or aeroplane.

1904 *Sci. Amer. Suppl.* 11 June 23778 (Cent. D. Suppl.) The birds exhibiting no trace of fatigue even after 'coasting' long distances.

14. To loaf *about* from station to station. *Austral. slang.*

1890 'R. Boldrewood' *Squatter's Dream* xxv. 295, I ain't like you, Towney, able to coast about without a job of work from shearin' to shearin'.

Coastal, *a.* Add: **B.** *sb.* A coast-defence ship.

1912 Jane *Brit. Battle Fleet* 350 'Coastals' for local duties. 1919 *Daily Tel.* 9 Aug. 10/2 Of these airships and, afterwards, of the coastals, we had several subsequently.

Coaster. Add:

3. b. An animal of the ox-kind reared on the coast. *U.S.*

1902 *Rep. Kansas State Board Agric.* 1901–2, 154 Horns of the old Texas coaster.

7. c. A rest for the foot in coasting on a bicycle.

1897 *Outing* (U.S.) Feb. 463/2 Having gleefully perched my feet up on the coasters, I..shot forward like an arrow.

8. A loafer, sundowner. *Austral. slang.*

1890 'R. Boldrewood' *Squatter's Dream* viii. 75 A voluble, good-for-nothing, loafing impostor, a regular 'coaster'.

Coasting, *vbl. sb.* Add:

4. *U.S.* (Earlier examples.) Also *attrib.*

1775 J. Eliot in *Belknap Papers* III. 77 There is a declivity..which in the winter season the boys make use of as a coasting-place. *Ibid.*, The General at first did not understand what they meant by the term coasting. 1832 S. G. Goodrich *Syst. Univ. Geog.* 201 *Coasting* is another winter pastime, in which..the labor seems to be at least equal to the pleasure.

Coastwise, *a.* (Earlier U.S. example.)

1821 *Deb. Congress* App. 1726 Forts..to cover the coastwise and interior navigation.

Coat, *sb.* **14.** Add:

coat-collar, -cuff (example); **coat and skirt,** a two-piece costume; also *attrib.* (with hyphens); **coat-facing,** material of a kind different from the cloth of the coat used as a facing; **coat-hanger,** a piece of wood or metal on which a coat or dress may be hung, curved so as to fit the shoulders of the garment and having a hook by which it may be suspended in a wardrobe or elsewhere.

1895 *Army & Navy Co-op. Soc. Price List* 1234 Costumes. ..Plain Serge *Coat and Skirt. 1906 *Daily Chron.* 24 Sept. 8/1 Those useful coat-and-skirt costumes. 1913 Ian Hay *Right Stuff* II. xi. 212 I'm afraid she found my clothes rather overpowering, though I'd only a coat and skirt on. 1930 *Times* 11 Sept. 13/6 A coat and skirt in brown velveteen. 1837 Dickens *Pickw.* xxxi, The marks of hair-powder on his *coat-collar. 1860 Holland *Miss Gilbert's Career* viii. 132 A young man that..keeps the dander all off his coat-collar. *a* 1909 'O. Henry' *Roads of Destiny* ii. 38 Mr. Robert..turned his coat collar up about his neck and ears. 1845 J. J. Hooper *Adv. Simon Suggs* iv. 42 Note..the snowy spotlessness of the linen exposed by the turn up of his *coat-cuff. 1900 *Westm. Gaz.* 9 Sept. 3/2 Velvet is conspicuous as a *coat facing in some of the newest models. 1908 *Daily Chron.* 26 Feb. 8/5 Most women have six or seven *coat-hangers in their closets.

Coated. 3. (Additional mod. examples. *Coated paper*: see quot. 1902.)

1878 Abney *Treat. Photogr.* 124 The rapid evaporation of the solvents from the coated plate. 1879 *St. George's Hosp. Rep.* IX. 341 The tongue was white, coated, and moist. 1892 *Daily News* 13 Apr. 2/8 Coated pills. 1902 *Daily Chron.* 21 Feb. 3/2 We might have had the 'coated' paper which would have done justice to the 'Lilacs in Winter' picture. 1902 *Encycl. Brit.* XXXII. 17/1 'Coated' paper..is paper which, after manufacture, is passed through a bath of a preparation of china clay.

Coatie (kōu·ti). Also -ee. [f. Coat *sb.* + -ie.] A small coat.

1898 *Westm. Gaz.* 12 May 3/2 The day costume..is the black silk coatie and black and white checked skirt. 1906 *Ibid.* 19 Sept. 16/1 A pretty little design..for a fur coatie with a cloth skirt.

Coa·t-tailed, *a.* [f. Coat-tail + -ed².] Having coat-tails.

1902 *Westm. Gaz.* 20 Feb. 3/1 The bolero and blouse coat with their coat-tailed and basqued variations. *Ibid.* 25 Sept. 3/2 A coat-tailed bolero.

Coax, *v.* Add: **3. d.** To urge (a thing) by gentle means.

1841 S. Warren *Ten Thou. a Year* I. vii, After coaxing up the fire, I will proceed to tell you. 1866 Meredith *Vittoria* xxiv, Angelo knelt and coaxed the fire.

Cob, *sb.*¹ **IV.** Add: **cob-meal** *U.S.*, corn-cobs ground down; **cob-mill** (see quot.).

1837 Colman *Rep. Agric. Mass.* (1838) 83 Beef animals fattening..on boiled potatoes, apples, and *cob meal. 1868 *Rep. U.S. Comm. Agric.* (1869) 439 Poor pastures, poor meadows, hay, and a few shorts or cob-meal. 1859 Bartlett *Dict. Amer.* (ed. 2), *Corn and *cob mill*, a mill for grinding the entire ear of Indian corn.

Cobber¹ (kǫ·bəɹ). [f. Cob *v.*¹ or *sb.*¹ + -er¹.] (See quots.)

1778 Pryce *Min. Cornub.* 234 The picked Ore..is put to a number of girls called Cobbers, who break it..to the size of a chestnut and less. 1921 *Dict. Occup. Terms* (1927) § 056 *Cobber*; breaks ore into small pieces with small hammer, and sorts it according to value. *Ibid.* § 334 *Cobber*; in fellmongery trims shanks and neck portions of sheepskins free of hair and offal after wool has been removed, and cuts them off.

Cobber² (kǫ·bəɹ). *Austral. slang.* Companion, mate.

1916 *Anzac Book* 22/2 'Ow er yer orf fer socks, cobber?

Cobble, *sb.*¹ **4.** Add: *cobble-paved, -streeted* adjs.

1891 *Pall Mall Gaz.* 30 Nov. 3/1 The *cobble-paved road, bordered by endless crucifixes. 1910 W. J. Locke *Simon the Jester* xii, We crossed the cobble-paved courtyard. 1909 Margaret B. Saunders *Litany Lane* III. xxv, Little *cobble-streeted shady French towns.

Cobbler. Add:

1. b. The last sheep to be sheared, in punning allusion to the cobbler's last. *Austral. slang.*

1893 *Herald* (Melbourne) 23 Dec. 6/1 (Morris) Every one might not know what a 'cobbler' is. It is the last sheep in a catching pen, and consequently a bad one to shear, as the easy ones are picked first...In the harvest field English rustics used to say, when picking up the last sheaf, 'This is what the cobbler threw at his wife'. 'What?' 'The last.' 1894 A. Robertson *Nuggets* 4 The 'cobbler', a grizzled, wiry-haired old patriarch that every one had shunned.

c. A spinous fish of New South Wales, *Pentaroge marmorata*, belonging to the family *Scorpænidæ. Austral.*

1898 Morris *Austral Engl.*

3. *U.S.* (Later examples.)

1852 G. W. Curtis *Lotus-eating* 105 Various other select parties are..watching the sails and sipping cobblers. 1862 E. McDermott *Pop. Guide Internat. Exhib.* 185 There is an American bar, where visitors may indulge in 'juleps', 'cock-tails', 'cobblers', 'rattle-snakes', [etc.].

Cobbly (kǫ·bli), *a.* [f. Cobble *sb.*¹ + -y¹.] Paved with cobble-stones. Also *fig.*

In earlier dial. use in sense 'full of lumps'.

1891 *Bicycling News* 4 Apr. 197 Our rough cobbly roads. 1894 *Westm. Gaz.* Dec., We want to put, if possible, a bit of the 'light at eventide' on the cobbly path of the old women.

Cobb paper.

1880 Zaehnsdorf *Art Bookbinding* 28. 1911 Coutts & Stephen *Libr. Bookbinding* 226 Cobb Paper.—A self-coloured paper, obtainable in various shades, largely used by binders as end-papers and for the sides of books. It derives its name from its inventor, or the binder who first used it.

Cobbra (kǫ·bră). *Austral.* Also **cobra.** [Native word, of Malay origin.] The head, skull.

1881 A. C. Grant *Bush-Life in Queensland* iii. (1882) 23 The black fellow who lives in the bush bestows but small attention on his 'cobra', as the head is usually called in the pigeon-English which they employ. 1890 'R. Boldrewood' *Col. Reformer* xiii, Having an empty cobbra, as the blacks say.

Cobby. Add:

3. b. Shortish and thickset, 'stocky'.

1884 G. Stables *Our Friend the Dog* vii, *Cobby*—Nicely ribbed up, compact in form like a cob-horse. 1891 *New Review* June 545 The cobby man of 5 ft. 5 in. 1909 *Daily Chron.* 26 June 8/5 Pony (Welsh), cobby-built.

Cobdenism (kǫ·bdəniz'm). [f. the name of Richard *Cobden* (1804–1865).] A policy advocating free trade, peace, and international co-operation. So **Co·bdenite** *sb.*, a supporter of Cobdenism; *a.*, of or pertaining to Cobdenism; **Co·bdenic, Co·bdenitish** *adjs.*

1853 A. Somerville (*title*) Cobdenic Policy the Internal Enemy of England. 1887 W. J. Harris in *Nat. Rev.* Nov. 311 Cobdenites point to the agricultural population as too small a part of the total number to be considered in the arguments of Protection versus Free Trade. *Ibid.*, I am simply striving to escape the natural conclusion to which Cobdenism is driving me. 1929 *Daily Tel.* 8 Jan. 7/2, I met a Cobdenite the other day, and, like a true Cobdenite, he said he was in favour of letting the miners starve.

Co·b-house. *U.S.* (See Cob *sb.*¹ IV.)

1774 J. Belknap in *Life* (1847) 68 They have a neat poultry

house, built of sawed strips of wood, in the form of a cob-house. 1818 Birkbeck *Lett. Illinois* 116 In this country they build 'cob-houses';..with these cobs..structures are raised by the little half-Indian brats, very much like our houses of cards. 1834 *Deb. Congress* 26 Feb. 736 With the first shock in the commerce or credit of the country the whole cob-house fabric must tumble. 1858 E. E. Hale *If, Yes & Perhaps* (1868) 120 The child had been building cob-houses out of lucifer-matches in a paper warehouse. 1860 Susan Warner *Say & Seal* xxix. 264 This hard work being diversified.. with the continual additions he made to a cob-house on the hearth. 1881 [see Cob *sb.*¹ IV].

Co·b-pipe. *U.S.* [Cob *sb.*¹ II.] A tobacco-pipe made from a corn-cob.

1847 in D. Drake *Pioneer Life Kentucky* iii. 63 Quietly smoking a cob pipe in the corner. 1854 Mary J. Holmes *Tempest & Sunshine* xv. 94 Mr. Middleton puffed away at his old cob pipe. 1857 *Knickerbocker Mag.* Nov. 440 My taciturn host..took a cob-pipe down from a shelf over the fire-place. 1884 'C. E. Craddock' *In Tenn. Mts.* i. 16 She sat down..and pulled deliberately at her long cob-pipe. 1897 J. L. Allen *Choir Invis.* viii. (1918) 70 Taking a short cob pipe out of his mouth.

Cobra. Add: *cobra-hooded* adj.; *cobra-wise* adv.; **cobra-lily,** a name for the flower *Arum campanulatum*, so called from its resemblance to a cobra with raised head.

1887 A. M. Brown *Anim. Alkaloids* 102 The *cobra-hooded snake. 1886 Yule & Burnell *Hobson-Jobson*, **Cobra Lily*, the flower *Arum campanulatum*, which stands on its curving stem exactly like a cobra with reared head. 1905 Kernahan *Visions* 234 Crushing religion, *cobra-wise, in her folds.

Coburger. *U.S.* An army or navy officer who obtains a good appointment by underhand influence with the Government.

1886 *Pall Mall Gaz.* 15 June 14/1 There are quite a number of naval officers in Washington, comprehensively classed as Coburgers.

Cocainist (kokē¹·nist). [f. Cocaine + -ist.] One addicted to the use of cocaine.

1904 *Daily Chron.* 22 Aug. 7/5 The cocainist influences. 1908 *Westm. Gaz.* 17 Jan. 7/4 The cocainist..experienced singular elation.

Coccal (kǫ·kăl), *a.* [f. Coccus: see -al.] Of, pertaining to, or resembling a coccus; spherical or nearly spherical in form.

1928 *Lancet* 8 Dec. 1193/1 A blood culture was taken.., the organism grown being coccal in character.

Coccid (kǫ·ksid), *a.* and *sb.* *Ent.* [f. mod.L. *Coccidæ*, a family of insects.] **A.** *adj.* Of or pertaining to the *Coccidæ* or scale-insects. **B.** *sb.* A scale-insect.

1892 W. L. Distant *Naturalist in Transvaal* 88 The Coccid, or so-called 'Australian Bug' (*Icerya purchasi*). 1894 *Athenæum* 16 June 778/1 Male specimens of a coccid (*Lecanium prunastri*), bred from scales attached to shoots of blackthorn. 1913 *Oxf. Univ. Gaz.* 4 June 948/2 The Coccid food of the larva of *Spalgis lemolea.* 1920 Jas. Ritchie *Anim. Life Scot.* 474 A Coccid on oranges.

Hence **Coccido·logy,** the scientific study of scale-insects.

1904 *Science* 25 Mar. 501 (Cent. D. Suppl.) In the present state of coccidology.

Coccidiosis (kǫksidiōu·sis). [f. mod.L. *coccidium* + -osis.] A disease caused by the presence of coccidia.

1901 Dorland *Med. Dict.* (ed. 2). 1930 *Times* 17 Mar. 18/3 Coccidiosis, bacillary white diarrhœa, and other chicken diseases.

Coccinella (kǫksine·lă). *Ent.* [mod.L., f. L. *coccineus* scarlet.] A beetle of the genus so named or its family *Coccinellidæ*; a lady-bird. So **Coccine·llid** *a.* and *sb.*

1887 E. A. Ormerod *Australian Bug* 29 The grubs of a Coccinellid or Ladybird. 1913 *Oxf. Univ. Gaz.* 4 June 955/2, 2 Coccinellid beetles of the genus *Epilachna.* 1917 Sir J. D. Hooker in *Life & Lett.* I. 4 Seeing a Coccinella on a post.

Coccus. Add:

3. Any individual bacterium of a group including the genus *Micrococcus*, etc.

1886 *Encycl. Brit.* XXI. 404/2 The filaments separate first into shorter filaments, then into rodlets, and finally into 'cocci'. 1908 *Practitioner* Jan. 137 A mixture of cocci belonging to different groups.

Cochin (kōu·tʃin). Short for Cochin-China.

1853 [see Shanghai 1]. 1854 *Poultry Chron.* I. 34 Prize Buff Cochins. 1885 *Encycl. Brit.* XIX. 645/1.

Cochlearia (kǫkliˌē·riă). *Bot.* [mod.L., f. L. *cochleare* a spoon, so called from the shape of the leaves.] A plant of the cruciferous genus of this name.

1891 *Athenæum* 23 May 671/2 Specimens of a cochlearia from Ben More.

Cock, *sb.*¹ Add:

2. c. (Earlier U.S. example.)

1836 Crockett *Exploits & Adv. Texas* 99 The captain of the boat..went ashore in the hope of persuading them to refund—but that cock wouldn't fight.

10. *Cock of the plains*, a North American species of grouse; the sage-cock. *Cock of the Rock*, a South American bird belonging to the genus *Rupicola*, esp. *R. crocea*, the type of the genus.

1837 Swainson *Classif. Birds* II. 76 *Rupicola*, or rock manakin of Cayenne. The familiar name of cock of the rock, long bestowed on this bird, is very characteristic. 1838 Audubon *Ornith. Biog.* IV. 503 Cock of the Plains. 1877 R. I. Dodge *Hunting Grounds Gt. West* 224 'Cock of the plains.' *Tetrao (centrocercus) urophasianus.* 1883 *Encycl. Brit.* XV. 455/1 *note*, The beautiful orange-coloured birds well known as the 'Cocks of the Rock'. 1886 *Stand. Nat. Hist.* (1888) IV. 209 The sage-cock, or cock-of-the-plains, *Centrocercus urophasianus*, is the largest grouse found in America.

22. b. *Cock ship.*

1909 *Daily Chron.* 2 Aug. 1/6 The opinion that Natal was 'cock ship' among a crowd of extraordinarily efficient battleships and cruisers. 1926 *Spectator* 11 Sept. 375/2 She carried the golden cock at her masthead as cock ship of the Mediterranean Fleet.

23. cock-and-hen, applied *attrib.* to anything which admits or includes both sexes; **cock-schnapper,** a small schnapper (see Snapper *sb.*¹ 6).

1874 *Slang Dict.*, **Cock-and-hen-club*, a free and easy gathering, or 'sing-song', where females are admitted as well as males. 1922 Mrs. A. Sidgwick *Victorian* vii, 'Do you like a club better than a hotel?' 'Yes. I do.' 'Then you'd better join a cock and hen one as quick as you can.' 1926 Warwick Deeping *Sorrell & Son* xxiii, It was a cock and hen affair, but more hen than cock. 1882 Tenison-Woods *Fish N. S. W.* 41 The schnapper or count-fish, the school-fish, and squire...Juveniles rank the smallest of the fry, not over an inch or two in length, as the '*cock-schnapper'.

Cockade. Add: Also *transf.*

1890–3 E. M. Tabor *Stowe Notes, Lett. & Verses* 34 The sumach cockades off which I noticed them feeding.

Cockamaroo (kǫ·kămărū·). A variety of bagatelle.

1867 *Bohn's Hand-bk. Games* 613 Russian Bagatelle, or Cockamaroo Table. 1875 *Encycl. Brit.* III. 230/2 *Cockamaroo*, or Russian Bagatelle, is played on a table prepared with a number of pins, holes, arches, and bells, up to and through which the ball is played from the baulk end of the table. It is a childish amusement, requiring little skill. 1893 *Sat. Rev.* LXXVI. 561 Like a glass marble in the good old game of Cockamaroo.

Cock-and-bull. 3. (Earlier U.S. example.)

1795 *Gazette of U.S.* (Philad.) 2 Mar. (Th.) A long cock-and-a-bull story about the Columbianum [a proposed national college].

Cockatoo. Add:

3. *attrib.* and *Comb.*, with reference to the cockatoo's habit of sitting with others in a row on a fence; **cockatoo fence,** a rough fence of logs and saplings of the kind built by small farmers; so *cockatoo squatter, stockman.* Hence **Cockatoo** *v. Austral. intr.*, to sit on a fence, as the bird does; to farm in a small way.

1828 P. Cunningham *N. S. Wales* (ed. 3) II. 288 All the others [*sc.* convicts] divert themselves, or go to sleep. Such are known here by the name of 'cockatoo-gangs'. 1881 Cockatoo farmer [see sense 2 in Dict.]. 1884 'R. Boldrewood' *Melb. Mem.* xxii. 155 There would be roads and cockatoo fences,..in short, all the hostile emblems of agricultural settlement. 1890 — *Miner's Rt.* xliii. 377 The governor is a bigoted agriculturist; he has contracted the cockatoo complaint, I'm afraid. 1890 — *Col. Reformer* xviii, The correct thing, on first arriving at a drafting yard, is to 'cockatoo', or sit on the rails. *Ibid.*, The cockatoo stockmen, who are doing the 'reviewing', safely on the fence. 1890 — *Squatter's Dream* xx. 245 Fancy three hundred acres in Oxfordshire, with a score or two of bullocks, and twice as many black-faced Down sheep —Regular cockatooing. 1893 *Argus* (Melbourne) 17 June 13/4 (Morris) Hire yourself out to a dairyman, take a contract with a rail-splitter, sign articles with a cockatoo selector; but don't touch land without knowing something about it. 1895 *Funk's Stand. Dict.*, *Cockatoo squatter*, the owner of a limited right of pasturage on land granted by the government, who raises only a small amount of wool or cattle annually: used mostly in contempt.

Cock-bead. *Arch.* A quirked bead. (Cf. Cock-bead-plane.) Hence **Cock-beaded** *a.*

1805 *Edinb. Bk. Prices* p. vii, Cock-beaded..cockbeads. 1876 *Encycl. Brit.* IV. 487/2 If there be a deep sinking under a bead it is called a quirked or cock bead.

Cocked, *ppl. a.*¹ Add: **b.** (See quot.)

1889 F. M. Halford *Dry-Fly Fishing* ii. 36 A floating fly ..cocked, or, in other words, floating with the wings up. *Ibid.* 43 Floating a cocked fly over a likely place.

Cocked hat. 1. b. A note folded in a form of a cocked hat.

1865 Dickens *Mut. Fr.* I. x, Twemlow..received a highly-perfumed cocked-hat and monogram from Mrs. Veneering. 1886 Rhoda Broughton *Dr. Cupid* I. viii. 93 One of Lady Roupell's almost daily cocked-hat notes.

4. (Earlier U.S. examples.)

1833 Paulding *Banks of Ohio* I. 217, I told Tom..I'd knock him into a cocked-hat, if he said another word. 1848 Lowell *Lett.* I. 146 If he had riled me, I might have knocked him into a cocked hat in my satire. 1866 E. A. Pollard *Lost Cause* (De Vere) Although it took little more to knock Fort Sumter into a cocked hat, yet [etc.].

Cocked, *ppl. a.*² Add: **1. b.** *fig.*

1832 *Deb. Congress* 3 May 2795 We would say $20,000 is necessary. He would then be cocked and primed for his report.

Cocker, *sb.*⁵ [The name of Edward Cocker (1631–75), arithmetician, reputed author of a popular *Arithmetick.*] *According to Cocker*: by or in accordance with strict rule or calculation; exactly; strictly.

1825 *Mechanics' Mag.* 11 June 149/2 A short Table,..which, I think, will be found to be according to 'Cocker'. 1861 Hughes *Tom Brown at Oxf.* xxxii, 'So you ought to be, according to Cocker, spending all your time in sick rooms.' 'According to who?' 'According to Cocker.' 'Who is Cocker?' 'Oh, I don't know; some old fellow who wrote the rules of arithmetic, I believe; it's only a bit of slang.' 1883 G. A. Sala in *Illustr. Lond. News* 24 Nov. 499/2 The average American may not know what we mean by 'according to Cocker'; while the average Englishman may be unaware of the meaning of 'according to Gunter'. 1888 G. Allen *This Mortal Coil* ii, According to Cocker, nought and nought make nothing. 1893 E. F. Knight *Where Three Empires Meet* xxiv. (1897) 395 So, despite Cocker, at this short range..the guns opened on the fort.

Cock-eye¹. Add: **B.** *adj.* Cock-eyed, crooked. *colloq.*

1899 Kipling *Stalky* 229 Don't see how you can make Latin prose much more cock-eye than it is, but we'll try, said Beetle, transposing an *aliud* and *Asia* from two sentences. 1928 *Sunday Express* 16 Dec. 2/1 The world is all going cock-eye.

Cock-eye².

1. The loop at the end of a trace by which it is attached to the swingle-tree, etc.

1849 *Rep. Comm. Patents* (1850) 266 The combination of the loop of the trace with a sectional cross piece (B), and a Cockeye (A), whereby the trace is secured to a swivel cockeye. 1874 Knight *Dict. Mech.*, *Cock-eye*,..an iron loop on the end of a trace, adapted to catch over the pin on the end of a single-tree. Originally *woodcock eye.*

2. (See quot.)

1874 Knight *Dict. Mech.*, *Cock-eye*, (*Milling*), a cavity on the under-side of the balance-rynd to receive the point of the spindle.

Cock-horse. Add:

6. An additional horse for helping a coach uphill.

1891 *Field* 25 July 134/1 With no further use for the cock horse, we cast him off at the top of the hill. 1909 *Daily Chron.* 7 June 6/3 The Venture Challenge Cup attracted eleven road teams...One, with an attendant cock horse, [etc.]. 1928 *Times* 3 Sept. 16 The Old Berkeley passing the Five Alls on Dashwood Hill, with a pair of cock-horses to help the team over the Chilterns.

Cocking, *vbl. sb.*² **b.** Add: *cocking-dog, -handle, -lifter, -piece, -rod, -swivel.*

1892 Greener *Breech-Loader* 26 There is in this no cocking-dog, but the forward ends of the tumblers are turned in, and engage with..a cocking-swivel. *Ibid.* 28 When the tumbler is down, the cocking-rod is freed. *Ibid.* 111 The cocking-lifters of hammerless guns. 1902 *Encycl. Brit.* XXXII. 650/2 When released, the striker can be cocked by pulling out the cocking-piece by hand. 1905 *Kynoch Jrnl.* July–Sept. 141 The scear and cocking piece are on the right side of the action. 1917 *Blackw. Mag.* Mar. 382/2, I applied immediate action, pulled back the cocking-handle and pressed the trigger again.

Cockle, *sb.*⁸ Short for Cockle-bur.

1867 T. Lackland *Homespun* III. 328 Burs get worked into his hair, and cockles stick all over his clothes.

Co·ckle-bur. *U.S.* Also *dial.* **cuckle-.** (See Cockle *sb.*¹ 4.)

1815 D. Drake *Cincinnati* ii. 119 The wide alluvial vallies of these rivers..abound in..cockle burr (*Xanthium strumarium* L.). 1845 J. J. Hooper *Daddy Bigg's Scrape* 106 They was as thick all round me, as cuckle-burrs in a Colt's tail. 1871 *Trans. Ill. Agric. Soc.* VIII. 241 The cockle-burr and rag-weeds are great enemies to the farmers. 1874 J. W. Long *Wild-Fowl Shooting* xvi. 197 Smart-weed, cockle burr, and wild oats never grow there. 1911 R. D. Saunders *Col. Todhunter* ix. 118 A wall-eyed plow-horse with his tail full o' cuckle-burs.

Cockney, *sb.* **3.** (Delete †*Obs.* and add modern U.S. example.)

1904 *N. Y. Tribune* 17 July 8 Now even many rural districts are as dependent on the beef packer, the vegetable canner,..as the veriest cockney.

Cockneyess. (See under Cockney *sb.*; earlier U.S. example.)

1839 Fr. A. Kemble *Resid. Georgia* (1863) 132 There is one privilege which I enjoy here which I think few cockneyesses have ever had experience of.

Cockneyfication. (U.S. example.)

1877 H. James *Portr. Places* (1883) 248 With regard to most romantic sites in England, there is a sort of average cockneyfication with which you must make your account.

Cockpit. Add:

2. (U.S. example.)

1870 Medbery *Men & Myst. Wall St.* 30 The roar from the cock-pit rolls up denser and denser.

3. c. *Aviation.* In the fuselage of an aeroplane, hydroplane, or flying-machine, the enclosed space occupied by a pilot, observer, or a passenger.

1915 *Chambers's Jrnl.* 1 July, Advt., Pilot and passenger in separate cockpits arranged tandem fashion. 1917 *Blackw. Mag.* Mar. 383/1 Several bullets ventilated the fuselage quite close to my cockpit. 1918 McCudden *Five Years R.F.C.* 227 The observer disappeared into the cockpit apparently disabled.

Cocktail. Add: **3.** (Earlier U.S. example.)

1806 *Balance* (Hudson, N.Y.) 13 May 146 (Th.) Cocktail is a stimulating liquor, composed of spirits of any kind, sugar, water, and bitters.

B. 2. Also *Comb.*, as *cocktail-mixer, -shaker.*

1905 *Daily Chron.* 22 Dec. 4/5 The *cocktail habit. 1904 'O. Henry' *Cabbages & Kings* iii. 47 A bullet-headed man Smith was, with an oblique, dead eye and the moustache of a *cocktail-mixer. 1928 *Observer* 17 June 15/4 A grimacing waiter tilts his *cocktail-shaker.

Cock-throttled. = Cock-throppled.

1882 *Cassell's Dict.* 1908 *Animal Managem.* 24 A 'Cock-throttled' or 'swan-necked' horse is one which has a neck like a fowl.

Co·ck-winged, *a.* Defining an artificial fly used by anglers.

1897 *Encycl. Sport* I. 20/1 Small bottle of odourless paraffin for the anointment of the cock-winged flies. 1904 Gallichan *Fishing Spain* 207 Cock-winged, beautifully constructed dry flies.

Coco, cocoa. Add:

1. b. *slang* = 4 c. *U.S.*

1837 J. C. Neal *Charcoal Sk.* (1838) 37 Your cocoa is very near a sledge-hammer. If it isn't hard, it may get cracked.

3. coco-matting = coco-nut matting (4 d).

1883 *Peel City Guardian* 7 Apr., Advt., Cocoa Mattings.

4. Coco(a)-nut. c. (Earlier U.S. examples.)

1840 Haliburton *Clockm.* Ser. III. iii. 30 Who should I meet on the road but the Major a-pokin' along with his cocoanut down, a-studyin' over somethin' or another quite deep. 1854 *Knickerbocker Mag.* Apr. XLIII. 432 Do you remember breaking an ear of corn one night..over the old 'cocoa-nut' of that 'cross-patch', old J.

d. *coco-nut fibre, matting, oil* (quots.); **coco-nut shy,** an item of amusement in a pleasure fair, which consists in throwing balls at coco-nuts; **coco-nut water, whey,** applied to early stages of the milk of the coco-nut.

1851 *Illustrated Exhibitor* p. xxxix/3 Mats of *cocoa-nut fibre. 1862 *Cassell's Illustr. Family Paper Exhib.* 20 Sept. 143/2 Much might be written in commendation of *cocoa-nut matting. 1870 Kingsley *Madam How & Lady Why* ix. 216 He lines them with a quantity of cocoa-nut fibre, picked out clean and fine, just as if he was going to make cocoa-nut matting of it. 1854 *Toulmison's Cycl. Usef. Arts* I. 404/2 The lines are rubbed over with *coco-nut oil. 1903 McNeill *Egreg. Engl.* 175 Merry-go-rounds and *cocoanut-shies. 1924 D. H. Lawrence *England, my England* 55 In the cocoanut shies there were no cocoanuts. 1834 *West India Sketch Bk.* II. xviii. 26 Indolence or inactivity should be satisfied with *coco-nut water. 1883 *Chambers's Jrnl.* XX. 155/2 Cocoa-nut water, found in the green pod before the fibrous husk and nut as we know them here are formed. 1838 *Mag. Dom. Econ.* Feb. 254 The inhabitants give *cocoa-nut whey to their cattle.

Cocoa. = *Cocoa-grass. *U.S.*

1897 R. M. Stuart *Simpkinsville* 43 The blades of bright green cocoa spears.

4. Cocoa Press, a familiar term for a section of Liberal newspapers supposed to be controlled by certain important (Quaker) manufacturers of cocoa; so *Cocoa Quaker.*

1910 *Referee* 16 Jan., 'Modern Slavery', a pamphlet issued by the *World*,..speaks its mind frankly on..the Pro-Boer campaign conducted largely by the Free Trade Cocoa Press. 1915 *National Rev.* Jan. 689 The glory of the Cocoa Press has departed. *Ibid.* 712 According to the Imperial Chancellor Wilhelm II was a Cocoa Quaker.

Co·coa-grass. Also coco-. *U.S.* [Of obscure origin.] A plant of the sedge-family (*Cyperus rotundus*) prevalent in some of the southern states.

1853 J. G. Baldwin *Flush Times Alabama* 72 It is a sort of cocoa grass that has got into the soil. 1859 Bartlett *Dict. Amer.* (ed. 2), *Coco grass*, an insidious grass or weed much dreaded by Southern planters, as it will speedily overrun and ruin any field in which it takes root. 1894 *Congress. Rec.* 31 July 8049/1 That extraordinary grass known as cocoa grass, which has spread over large areas in the States of Louisiana and Mississippi.

Cocodette (kokode·t). [Fr.] A French prostitute of the fashionable world.

1867 in Ware *Passing Engl.* (1909) 82 In the circle of cocottes, and cocodettes, by which the French Court has during the last fifteen years managed to surround itself, fast American women have furnished no inconsiderable contribution. 1885 *Pall Mall Gaz.* 19 June 2/2 The cocodettes, or fine ladies, are no better than the cocottes.

Co-co·nscious, *a.* and *sb.* *Psychol.* [See Co-.] **a.** *adj.* Pertaining to the conjunction of experiences within a single consciousness; also applied to the knowledge which the Divine mind has of the conscious acts or states of all other beings. **b.** *sb.* A division of the subconscious. Hence **Co-co·nsciously** *adv.*, in a co-conscious manner; **Co-co·nsciousness,** the state of being co-conscious.

1904 W. James in *Jrnl. Philos. Psychol.* 536 (Cent. D. Suppl.) The conjunctive relation that has given most trouble to philosophy is the co-conscious transition, so to call it, by which one experience passes into another when both belong to the same self. 1906 G. T. Ladd *Philos. Relig.* II. 141 Is there consciousness, or self-consciousness, anywhere in the wide world of things and selves..? In this consciousness, or self-consciousness, God is co-conscious. *Ibid.*, The conception of the Divine Omniscience as a species of cognitive activity which is at one and the same time 'Self-consciousness', and 'Other-consciousness', in the form of an all-embracing co-consciousness, meets with its supreme psychological objection when it is applied to God's knowledge of the future. 1909 W. James in *Westm. Gaz.* 15 May 4/2 Some form of superhuman life with which we may, unknown to ourselves, be co-conscious. 1914 M. Prince *Unconscious* I. 1 *note*, I divide the Subconscious into two parts, namely the Unconscious and the Coconscious. 1920 *Discovery* Nov. 338/2 The possibilities of co-consciousness, i.e. the coexistence of two or more such fragments [of the conscious] in the mind. 1921 Sidis *Symtom. Psychopathic Dis.* 77 Hypnoid states are co-existent, 'co-conscious' states and may develop into co-existent, 'co-conscious' personalities. 1926 W. McDougall *Outline Abnormal Psychol.* 308 Prince adduces very strong evidence in support of the view that..the bodily changes express an emotional train of thinking or recollection that goes on concurrently or co-consciously with the conscious activity of the subject.

Cocoonery. *U.S.* (Earlier examples.)

1839 Fr. A. Kemble *Resid. Georgia* (1863) 186 Vineyards and olive orchards and cocooneries are part of the agricultural wealth here. 1847 *Rep. U.S. Comm. Patents* (1848) 178 Moisture in the cocooneries increases the chance of infection.

Cocorite (kōu·kŏrəit). Also 8 **cocareeta,** 9 **coucourite, cokarito, cokerite.** [Brazilian.] A small Brazilian palm, *Maximiliana insignis.*

1796 Stedman *Surinam* I. 246 A kind of low or dwarf palm-tree, called the *cocareeta.* 1825 Waterton *Wand. S. Amer.* i. 59 The arrow..is made out of the leaf of a species of palm-tree, called Coucourite. 1851 W. H. Brett *Ind. Miss. Guiana* 31 Numerous species of palms are also seen... Among them are the cokarito. 1871 Kingsley *At Last* v, Some,..like the Cocorite, almost stemless, rising in a huge ostrich plume. 1883 E. F. im Thurn *Among Indians Guiana* 267 The cokerite (*Maximiliana regia*). 1899 Rodway *Guiana Wilds* 36 Fine cocorite palms.

Cocotte (kokǫ·t). [Fr.] A prostitute; one of a class of the demi-monde of Paris.

1867, 1885 [see *Cocodette]. 1913 Caradoc *City of Plain* ii, I do wish you would not talk of ladies as if they were *cocottes.* 1920 S. McKenna *Lady Lilith* ii. 45 Nobody thought the worse of us, if we appeared at the theatre with a notorious cocotte. 1923 *Contemp. Rev.* Mar. 339 The platform at Wiesbaden swarmed with smart Parisian *cocottes.*

Cocum² (kōu·kŏm). *slang.* Also **cokum, koocum.** [ad. G. (Jews' cant) *kochem.*] Used without precise grammatical reference for that which is (*a*) advantageous, lucky, (*b*) proper, correct, or right.

1846 Snowden *Magistrate's Assist.* 343 To be cunning, wary, or sly—Fight cocum. 1851 Mayhew *Lond. Labour* I. 259/2 It's about 6d. a night to me for singing and patter in the tap-room. That's my cokum (advantage). 1861 H. Earle *Ups & Downs* 224 No one was allowed to get drunk; the governor said as how it wasn't cokum. *c* 1886 *Broadside Ballad* 'The Flippity Flop Young Man' (Farmer) I once was a Member-for-Slocum young man,..A know-pretty-well-what-is-kocum young man.

Cod, *sb.*³ **4.** Add: **cod-hook, cod-line** (earlier U.S. examples).

1686 S. Sewall *Letter Bk.* 34 Please to send 20 Doz. of middling *cod hooks. 1707 *Essex Inst. Hist. Coll.* VIII. 20 To 7 gross of Cod Hucks. 1838 J. F. Cooper *Homeward Bound* xxviii. 422 Small balls of marline to the end of each of which was attached a cod-hook. 1654 E. Johnson *Wonder-working Provid.* xiv. 31 They being provided with *Cod-line and Hooke hale up some store of fish. 1686 S. Sewall *Letter Bk.* 34, 20 Doz. of English cod Lines sound and strong.

C. O. D. (sī·ōudī·). orig. *U.S.* The initials of 'cash (costs, or collect) on delivery'. Also *attrib.*

1863 *Rocky Mt. News* (Denver) 12 Mar., When does your creditor consider you fishy? When he puts C.O.D. on your bill. 1871 'Mark Twain' *Screamers* 143 The..'agent'.. promised to divorce everybody who wished his services, and to send them new wives—C.O.D. 1892 *Congress. Rec.* 25 July 6722/2 It was a transaction payable on sight,—a C.O.D. transaction, so to speak—payable on the very day. 1904 *Daily Chron.* 8 Jan. 6/5 The great objection, I suppose, to the recipients of C.O.D. parcels opening them before paying would be the waste of the postman's time? 1908 *Letterpress Printing* 97 (*heading*) No. 18. C.O.D. It occasionally happens that costs are wanted with the goods, when the Form No. 18 should be used. *Ibid.* 174 They do not require..the C.O.D. Slip. 1908 *World's Work* Sept. 430/1 By Post C.O.D. 1913 Morley Roberts *Salt of the Sea* 42, I shot him last night and cut him up and pickled him in a cask...And I've shipped him to the British Ambassador at Washington, C.O.D.

Coda. Add: Also *fig.*

1889 Mrs. Lynn Linton *Thro' Long Night* I. i, The chapter of accidents has a long coda.

Codamine (kōu·dəmain). *Chem.* [f. Cod(eia + Amine.] A crystalline alkaloid contained in the aqueous extract of opium.

1872 Watts *Dict. Chem.* VI. 480 Codamine. $C^{20}H^{25}NO^4$. —A base recently obtained, together with others, by Hesse (*Ann. Ch. Pharm.* cliii. 47), from the aqueous extract of opium. 1874 Garrod & Baxter *Mat. Med.* 193.

Coddam (kǫ·dəm). Also **coddom.** [? = *cod 'em*: Cod *v.*³] Another name for Tip-it.

1865 *Slang Dict.* 1884 J. Greenwood *7 Yrs. Penal Serv.* (Farmer) A gambling game called coddom. 1894 *Sporting Life* 28 Feb. 7/5 A coddam match, for a wager and a fish supper. 1897 *Daily News* 11 May 5/3 When he wearied of skittles he took to coddam.

Code, *v.* Add: **b.** To prepare (a message) for transmission by putting it into code words. Hence **Co·ding** *vbl. sb.*

1898 *Westm. Gaz.* 20 Apr. 3/2 However inaccurately the message may be coded. 1903 Hardy *Dynasts* I. v. iii. 91 Now that the fume has lessened, code my biddance Upon our only mast. 1909 *Westm. Gaz.* 7 June 7/3 Coding had been really reduced to a fine art, and by its aid the cost of a cablegram was often reduced not merely to a penny per word, but to a farthing.

Co·dfish. [Cod *sb.*³ 1 b.] Add: Used fig. in *codfish aristocracy*, etc., to designate those who have become wealthy by trade. *U.S.* ? *Obs.*

1846–52 Mrs. Whitcher *Widow Bedott P.* xxv. 305 I've noticed that yer codfish gentility always dew. 1850 *Congress. Globe* 9 July, App. 1248 We should regard it as somewhat strange if we should require a codfish aristocracy to keep us in order. 1853 Poyes *Peep into Past* 37 James removed to Boston, to help on that of the Cod-fish aristocracy. 1865 [see Cod *sb.*³ 1 b *attrib.*].

Co·d-fi·shery. (See Cod *sb.*³ 4.) Add quots.:

1735 *Boston Town Rec.* XII. 120 Our Cod Fishery.. remains under such discouragement, that it's much to be feared that there will not be the Year ensuing, near Two Thirds of the Fishery kept up. 1753 [see Cod *sb.*³ 4]. 1837 *Southern Lit. Messenger* III. 414 Mr. Hardin..is represented in the reports of the discussion to have 'hit at cod-fishery, wooden nutmegs and tin-peddling'. 1857 *Mass. Acts & Res.* 657 Resolves concerning the proposed repeal of the Cod Fishery Bounty.

So **Cod-fisherman, Cod-fishing.**

1881 *Amer. Naturalist* XV. 367, I had the opportunity of spending three months on a cod fishing schooner. 1883 Shea *Newfoundland Fisheries* 12 (Fish. Exhib. Publ.) The fishing is attended to by the cod-fishermen as an adjunct to 'the fishery', as the cod-fishing alone is termed. 1907 *Daily Chron.* 16 July 3/2 Jack Ellison, a cod-fisherman. 1921 *Dict. Occup. Terms* (1927) § 000.

Co-dire·ctor. [Co- 3 c.] A joint director.

1869 *Porcupine* 24 July 153/1, I very much doubt if we shall ever again see the names..coupled together as co-directors. 1874 *Leisure Hour* 23 May 332/2 He was entirely at the mercy of his co-directors, who made use of his honest name. 1922 Sir H. E. Avory in *Daily Mail* 6 Dec. 12 Leaving your partners and co-directors to bear the burden of the disgrace.

Codling². **4.** Add: **codling-grub,** the larva of the codling-moth; **codling-moth** (earlier U.S. examples).

1900 Kipling in *Daily Mail* 2 May 4/4 Many apples sent to convalescents were full of *codlin-grub. 1861 *Rep. Mass. Board Agric.* II. 91 The apple worm, or *coddling moth (*Carpocapsa pomonella*). 1876 *Rep. Vermont Board Agric.* III. 582 Probably the most destructive..in Vermont, if not everywhere else, is the codling moth, *Carpocapsa pomonella.*

Cod's-head. 1. Add: *cod's head and mackerel-tail shape* (see quot.).

1891 *Scribner's Mag.* X. 5 Those forms of ships adopted for centuries by some European nations, and known to mariners as 'cod's-head and mackerel-tail' shape.

Co-ed. *U.S. colloq.* [abbrev. of Co-educational *a.*] A girl or woman student at a co-educational institution.

1904 *N. Y. Times* 16 Mar. 1 The Tufts College 'co-eds' proclaimed their independence to-night by giving a big dance and shutting the men out completely. 1908 A. Ruhl *Other Americans* vi. 79 She and two or three of her sister co-eds sat in a roomful of dark-eyed young men. 1910 E. A. Walcott *Open Door* ix. 107 'Tommy, did I ever deceive you?' 'Once—'twas about that black eyed co-ed'. 1928 *Morning Post* 20 Oct. 8/3 In some of the ultra-modern American Universities, where 'co-eds' abound. 1929 *Impressions of Los Angeles* in *Daily Tel.* 8 Jan. 15 'The co-eds' are fighting the 'football game' over again.

Co-e·ducate, *v.* [Back-formation from Co-education.] *trans.* To educate (persons of both sexes) together, or (one of either sex) with those of the other under a co-educational system. Also *transf.* Hence **Co-e·ducator.**

1894 *Forum* July 582 Will the Co-Educated Co-Educate their Children? 1897 *Educat. Rev.* XIII. 62 Sight, hearing and touch all have to be developed and trained and co-educated, taught to act together. 1909 H. G. Wells *Ann Veronica* i. 8 He had one son, who had been co-educated. 1923 T. P. Nunn *Education Data* 208 Co-educators aim.. at purifying and strengthening the bases of family life by teaching boys and girls to know one another.

Co-education. (Earlier U.S. example.)

1867 *Trans. Ill. Agric. Soc.* VII. 511 Co-Education of the Sexes...*Resolved*, That it is the sense of this Society, that in the admission of students to the Industrial University, both sexes be placed upon an equal footing.

Co·educa·tionalism. [f. Co-educational + -ism.] The system or principles of co-education.

1928 *Manch. Guardian Weekly* 10 Aug. 115/4 If this..is coeducationalism we are all for the monastic regimen.

Cœlenteron (sīle·ntĕrǫn). *Zool.* [mod.L., f. Gr. κοῖλος hollow + ἔντερον intestine.] The digestive cavity of a cœlenterate.

1893 Shipley *Zool. Invert.* 78 In the Acoelomata there is a common cavity, the Coelenteron, which is lined by endoderm cells, and which pervades various parts of the body. 1927 Haldane & Huxley *Anim. Biol.* xii. 268 The mouth leads into a cavity called the coelenteron.

Coelho (koˌē·lyo). [Pg.] A large food-fish resembling a mackerel, *Promethichthys prometheus*, found in the tropical Atlantic.

Cœlia (sī·liă). *Anat.* Pl. -iæ. Also **celia.** [mod.L., ad. Gr. κοιλία a hollow, cavity.] Any cavity of the body; *esp.* a ventricle or cavity of the brain.

1882 [see Procœlia].

Cœliotomy (sīliǫ·tŏmi). *Surg.* [f. Cœlio- + -tomy.] The operation of cutting into the abdominal cavity.

1881 *Trans. Obstet. Soc. Lond.* XXII. 128 If a new word was needed to supersede 'gastrotomy' perhaps 'cœliotomy' would do. 1908 *Practitioner* Oct. 608 Anterior and posterior vaginal coeliotomy.

Cœloblast (sī·loblɑst). *Embryol.* [f. Cœlo-¹ + -blast.] The endoderm of an insect, or part of the endoblast as distinguished from the myoblast.

1895 *Cambr. Nat. Hist.* V. 149 The blastoderm differentiates into Ectoblast and Endoblast; this latter undergoing a further differentiation into Coeloblast and Myoblast.

Cœlomo- (sīlōu·mo), used as combining form of Gr. κοίλωμα Cœlome, as in **Cœlo·moduct** [Duct *sb.* 6], **Cœlo·mostome** [Gr. στόμα mouth] (see quots.).

1902 *Encycl. Brit.* XXV. 691/1 The fifth [kind of merome is constituted] by the cœlomic pouches and their ducts and external apertures (cœlomo-ducts). *Ibid.* XXXIII. 882/2 The reproductive cells [of Polychæte worms] are developed from the cœlomic epithelium, ripen in the cœlom, and are carried to the exterior at maturity by special genital ducts (cœlomostomes). 1927 Haldane & Huxley *Anim. Biol.* Gloss. 338 Mesoderm...From it are derived..the coelom, the ..coelomoduct excretory organs (e.g. vertebrate kidneys).

Cœlostat (sī·lostæt). *Astr.* [f. Cœlo-² + -stat.] An instrument consisting of a mirror turned by clockwork on an axis parallel to itself and to the axis of the earth, by means of which the celestial bodies may be observed and photographed as in a stationary position.

1898 *Standard* 24 Jan. (Cassell's Dict. Suppl.) The present phenomenon [*sc.* the total solar eclipse of January 22, 1898] will be remembered as the first in which the instrument called the cœlostat was used. 1900 H. H. Turner in *Monthly Rev.* Sept. 108 A special arrangement..called a 'cœlostat', which reduces the whole sky virtually to rest in a most convenient manner. It was invented long ago by a Frenchman, but practically forgotten.

Coexcitation (kōu,eksitēi·ʃən). *Physiol.* [f. Co- 3 a + Excitation.] Simultaneous or collateral excitation.

1901 *Amer. Jrnl. Psychol.* Jan. 264 Training is by co-excitation, *i.e.*, by modifications of external conditions or fear—whereby the *sürs instincts* are readapted.

Coffee. Add:

1. c. A shade or tint of the colour of coffee (cf. 5 a below).

1815 J. Smith *Panorama Sci. & Art* II. 553 Coffee, damascene, and similar shades. 1818 W. Tucker *Family Dyer & Scourer* iii. (ed. 2) 83 For chocolate, coffee, &c. yellow is omitted.

5. a. *coffee-tinted* adj.; also quasi-*adj.* with the meaning 'coffee-coloured', as *coffee morocco.*

1899 *Daily News* 28 Jan. 6/4 Coffee-tinted chiffon. 1900 *Westm. Gaz.* 13 June 4/3 Armchairs, upholstered in 'coffee' morocco.

b. coffee bar, barrow, a bar or barrow at which coffee is sold as a beverage; **coffee-bean, -berry,** also *U.S.*, the Kentucky coffee-tree; **coffee-bore** = *coffee-borer*; **coffee cake,** a breakfast cake made with flour, butter, eggs, sugar, milk, and yeast, baked usually in a twisted or braided round cake, and glazed with melted sugar; also, a dark loaf cake containing coffee and fruit (Webster 1911); **coffee coat** = **coffee jacket*; **coffee-cooler** *U.S.*, a contemptuous name applied to inactive soldiers; **coffee cream,** a sugar cream fondant flavoured with coffee essence, sometimes coated with chocolate; also *attrib.*; **coffee disease** = **coffee-leaf disease*; **coffee-ground vomit,** a dark coloured vomit containing broken-down blood; **coffee jacket,** a jacket worn by women when taking coffee (cf. *tea-jacket*, *Tea *sb.* 9 c); **coffee-leaf disease,** a disease affecting the coffee plant, caused by a rust-fungus, *Hemileia vastatrix*; **coffee-mill** (later U.S. quots.; see also quot. 1887); **coffee palace, parlour** (see Palace *sb.*[1] 4, Parlour 4); **coffee rot,** a disease of the coffee plant, caused by the fungus *Pellicularia kolerota*; **coffee-set,** a set of ware used in serving coffee; **coffee stall,** a movable structure in which coffee, as a beverage, and other light refreshments are sold; also *attrib.*

1905 *Daily Chron.* 11 July 3/2 *Coffee-bar and grocery stall keepers. 1881 Mrs. Ewing *We & the World* xv, So you live in the docks with your *coffee-barrow? 1821 T. Nuttall *Trav. Arkansas* iii. 72 We still..observe the *coffee-bean (*Gymnocladus canadensis*),..the seeds of which ..produce a substitute for coffee greatly inferior to the cichorium. 1822 J. Woods *Two Yrs.' Resid. Eng. Prairie* 306 The woods..contain a great variety of trees;..On the creek bottoms, *coffee-berry, poplar, pecon, white walnut, &c. 1887 Moloney *Forestry W. Afr.* 107 The *coffee-bore, of which there are two species. 1923 Marg. Wilson *Able McLaughlins* xii, The German led her into the shanty, and set before her..coffee and *coffee-cake. 1905 *Daily Chron.* 29 May 8/5 *Coffee-coats have been banished to the limbo of forgotten things. 1890 *Congress. Rec.* 30 Apr., App. 106 Those who..delight in characterizing the old soldiers as '*coffee coolers', 'bounty jumpers', and 'bummers'. 1895 *Ibid.* 28 Jan. 1129/2, I am opposed to giving pensions to deserters, and 'coffee-coolers', and bounty jumpers, and camp followers. 1893 *Coffee cream [introduced by W. B. Fuller]. 1900 Elinor Glyn *Visits Eliz.* (1906) 88, I don't know how we should have got through tea if the coffee-cream cakes had not been so good. 1907 *Practitioner* Apr. 546 [It] leads to haemorrhage and to the clinically characteristic '*coffee-ground' vomit. 1901 *Daily Chron.* 3 Aug. 10/3 The newest tea jackets have changed their names to *coffee jackets. 1877 *Encycl. Brit.* VI. 112/2 The..*coffee-leaf disease appeared in Ceylon in 1869, and in Mysore a year later. 1887 Moloney *Forestry W. Afr.* 107 The coffee-leaf disease..is not likely to infect the coffee-trees in this part. 1848 E. Bryant *California* ii. 21 Jacob..could not make the *coffee-mill perform its appropriate duty. 1864 B. Taylor *H. Thurston* xxvi. 340 Then he heard..a stirring in the kitchen under him and presently the noise of the coffee-mill. 1887 H. L. Williams '*Buffalo Bill*' 10 One of the old-pattern Colts, with the barrels revolving, the ancient 'coffee-mill' or 'pepper-box', laughed at all over the West in the present day. 1879 *Postmaster General's Rept.* 54 Some of the '*Coffee Palaces' recently established in London and elsewhere. 1894 *Coffee parlour [see Palace *sb.*[1] 4]. 1877 *Encycl. Brit.* VI. 112/2 The *coffee-rot..works great havoc in the Mysore plantations. 1856 Mrs. Stowe *Dred* 18 A table, which displayed an antique *coffee-set of silver. 1858 Simmonds *Dict. Trade*, *Coffee-stall. 1909 *Daily Chron.* 13 Nov. 4/7 The coffee-stall keeper, after occupying the same 'pitch' for years, regards himself as possessing a 'goodwill' in the site.

Co·ffee, *v.* [f. the sb.]

1. *intr.* To take coffee.

1851 G. W. Curtis *Nile Notes* xiii. 100 He coffeed and smoked,..gave us all the last news [etc.]. 1885 W. T. Hornaday *2 Yrs. in Jungle* xxiii. 277 Rose very early, coffeed in haste, and..set out.

2. *trans.* To entertain at coffee.

1868 Susan Hale *Lett.* 48 The Colonel, who coffeed us the day before.

Coffee-house, *v.* *Sporting slang. intr.* To indulge in gossip while waiting for the hounds to draw a covert, etc., during a fox-hunt. Also *transf.* Hence **Coffee-housing** *vbl. sb.*, also *attrib.* Also **Coffee-houser,** one who indulges in the practice.

1883 Mrs. E. Kennard *Right Sort* xxiii, She found the hounds still engaged in drawing a large wood.., and people were standing about in clusters of twos and threes coffee-housing. 1892 *Field* 6 Feb. 188/2 The field are 'coffee-housing' around when 'Tally-ho!' and they are away. 1897 *Westm. Gaz.* 25 Oct. 2/1 'Coffee-housing'—to wit, chatting about runs past and future, and discoursing upon.. hounds and horses. 1907 *Ibid.* 5 Nov. 12/1 The term 'coffee-housers' is used by a certain quaint old M.F.H. to reproach those loud talkers who hinder the serious business..by the chatter of irresponsible frivolity. 1909 *Daily Chron.* 7 June 5/1 You, gentlemen, come here on no coffee-housing tour.

Coffee-nut. *U.S.*

1. (See Coffee 5 b.)

1817 S. R. Brown *Western Gaz.* 25 Sugar maple,..Coffee-nut tree, and Sycamore, are found in their congenial soils. 1883 Eggleston *Hoosier School-Boy* ix. 65 It might be coffee-nuts which would explode harmlessly.

2. The coffee-tree, *Gymnocladus canadensis.*

1815 D. Drake *Cincinnati* ii. 82 The most valuable timber trees are the..coffee nut and beech. 1827 Drake & Mansfield *Cincinnati* i. 9 Among the forest trees, may be enumerated the..coffee nut. 1876 *Field & Forest* II. 27 The Coffee-Nut and Buckeye are both scarcer and more local.

Coffee-tree. [Coffee 1.]

1. The tree or shrub from which coffee is obtained.

1741– [see Coffee 5 a].

2. The North American tree *Gymnocladus canadensis*; the coffee-nut. *U.S.*

1785 Washington *Diaries* II. 360 Eight Nuts from a tree called the Kentucke Coffee tree. 1796 Morse *Amer. Geog.* I. 636 The coffee-tree resembles the black oak, and bears a pod which encloses a seed, of which a drink is made not unlike coffee. 1832 D. J. Browne *Sylva Amer.* 166 The French of Canada call this tree *Chicot*,..and the inhabitants of the Western States, *Coffee Tree*. 1865–6 *Trans. Ill. Agric. Soc.* VI. 390 The Coffee Tree famed for its similitude to the fruit that adds to our morning meal. 1900 H. L. Keeler *Native Trees* (1902) 109 Kentucky coffee tree, stump tree, *gymnocladus dioicus.*

Coffin, *sb.* Add:

3. f. *Horticulture.* A long flower bed the sides of which are not parallel.

1912 Eva Lathbury *Shoe Pinches* vii. 124 Flower-beds, cut into quaint devices, stars and hearts and coffins.

13. coffin-nail, also, *slang*, a cheap cigarette.

1901 A. G. Robinson *The Philippines* 263 For a package containing thirty 'coffin-nails' the price was three and a half cents, American money. 1928 P. G. Wodehouse *Money for Nothing* ii. 34 Most of these birds [*sc.* invalids in a sanatorium] would give their soul for a coffin-nail.

Coffle, *v.* [f. Coffle *sb.*] *trans.* To fasten together *with* another slave.

1859 in J. Doy *Narr.* (1860) 128 Berkeley was afterwards sold for jail fees...He was coffled with a huge $1200 chattel.

Co-fo·rmulator. [Co- 3 b.] A formulator together with another or others.

1902 *Daily Chron.* 22 Sept. 3/3 The term proposed by Prof. Baldwin and his co-formulators for the theory. 1905 *Ibid.* 16 Oct. 3/1 Dr. Wallace,..the co-formulator of the theory of 'natural selection'.

Cog, *sb.*[2] Add:

1. c. Phr. *To slip a cog*: to make a single unsuspected mistake in one's work or calculations.

1909 *Cent. Dict.* Suppl.

6. cogman = Cogger[1] 2; **cog-rail** (example).

1921 *Dict. Occup. Terms* (1927) § 047 *Cogman. 1884 *Science* III. 415/2 The rack or *cog-rail in the middle of the track is made of two angle-irons which have between them cogs of one and a quarter inch iron.

Cogged (kǫgd), *ppl. a.*[3] *Carpentry.* [f. Cog *sb.*[3] or *v.*[2]] Composed of or secured by means of a cog (see Cog *sb.*[3] and *v.*[2]).

1904 *Technol. & Sci. Dict.* (ed. Goodchild & Tweney).

Cogging (kǫ·giŋ), *vbl. sb.*[3] [f. Cog *v.*[1] + -ing[1].] The action or process of rolling steel blooms from ingots. Also *Comb.*, as *cogging engine, mill, rolls* (hence *roller*).

1881 *Instr. Census Clerks* (1885) 92 Cogging Roller. 1888 *Lockwood's Dict. Terms Mech. Engin.*, *Cogging Engine*, an ordinary rail-mill engine used for driving the cogging mill. *Cogging Mill*, a rolling mill in which steel blooms are rolled out. 1921 *Dict. Occup. Terms* (1927) § 279 Oiler; ..cogging mill oiler. 1923 *Glasgow Herald* 31 Oct. 10 One of the cogging mills would also be put in operation.

Coggle, *sb.*[1] Add: In ceramics, a wheel of wood or iron, usually grooved, used to run indentations round the edges of plates.

Cogitatingly (kǫ·dʒitēitiŋli), *adv.* [f. pres. pple. of Cogitate *v.* + -ly[2].] In cogitation; cogitatively.

1928 'Van Dine' *Greene Murder Case* ii, 'There isn't much to tell.' Heath chewed on his cigar cogitatingly.

Cognac. 2. a. Delete † and 'Formerly', and add quot.

1909 *Westm. Gaz.* 8 Mar. 8/2 Mons. E. Martell gave evidence concerning Cognac brandy.

Cognate, *sb.* Add:

1. c. *Hindu Law.* A relative of a deceased person through the mother.

1902 *Encycl. Brit.* XXIX. 281/2.

Cognitum (kǫ·gnitǒm). [L., neut. of *cognitus*, pa. pple. of *cognoscere* to know.] An object of cognition.

1890 Martineau *Seat Author. Relig.* iv. ii. 403 All the particular cognitions are unified in the single cognitum.

Cogrediency (ko,grī·diĕnsi). *Math.* [f. Cogredient *a.*: see -ency.] The relation of cogredient sets of variables.

1889 *Cent. Dict.* 1902 *Encycl. Brit.* Index.

Cog-wheel. Add: **b.** *Cog-wheel railway, system*: a mountain-railway system in which the steeper grades are operated by means of a cog-wheel on the engine engaging with a rack between the rails; a rack railway.

1904 *Westm. Gaz.* 4 May 10/1 Lines up the mountains and over the passes worked on the cog-wheel system. 1907 *Ibid.* 24 July 1/3 The circuitous cog-wheel railway connecting Csorba with Csorba-tó.

Cohere, *v.*

6. Delete †*Obs.* and add quot.

1911 Mair *Engl. Lit.: Mod.* 100 His *Essays*..were in their origin merely jottings gradually cohered and enlarged into the series we know.

7. *trans.* To cause to cohere or hold together.

1875 Brash *Eccl. Archit. Irel.* 152 No cements were used to cohere the material.

Coherer (kohīə·rəɹ). *Electr.* [f. Cohere *v.* + -er[1].] A device used as a detector of electric waves by means of metal filings, wires, or springs in loose contact, used chiefly in wireless telegraphy; orig., the name given by Sir Oliver Lodge to the detector in the form of a glass cylinder containing metal filings, which cohere when struck by an electric wave.

1894 O. Lodge in *Proc. Roy. Inst.* XIV. 336 This arrangement, which I call a coherer, is the most astonishingly sensitive detector of Hertz waves. 1898 Sir W. Crookes *Addr. Brit. Assoc.* 19 Oliver Lodge..produced the vacuum filing-tube coherers with automatic tapper-back. 1913 'Ian Hay' *Happy-go-lucky* xiii, One could almost feel the Marconigrams radiating from Lady Adela. But apparently The Freak's coherer was out of order.

Coho (kohōu·). Also **cohoe.** [See quot. 1889.] A species of salmon, *Oncorhynchus kisutch*, found in the northern Pacific waters.

1889 *Cent. Dict.*, *Cohoes*, a name given to the salmon by the half-breeds of British Columbia. 1902 *Encycl. Brit.* XXVI. 390/1 The silver salmon or cohoe arrives [in British Columbia waters] a little later than the sockeye. *a* 1909 *Bulletin U.S. Fish Com.* XVIII. 6 (Cent. D. Suppl.) In the opinions of the canners..the coho should rank next after the king salmon in food value.

Cohog, var. Quahaug.

1788 M. Cutler in *Life, Jrnls., & Corr.* (1888) I. 426 Went into the water; found a great number of clam cohog shells. 1871 Schele de Vere *Americanisms* (1872) 29 The more costly beads [in wampum] came from the largest shells of the Quahaug or Cohog.

Cohue (koü). [Fr.] An unruly crowd; a mob.

a 1881 Carlyle in *Q. Rev.* (1903) July 134 It was in this way that I as good as missed Mallet du Pan, confounding him with the general cohue. 1901 'Linesman' *Words Eyewitness* (1902) 314 The *cohue* seethes and roars around the farm.

Coiffeuse (kwaföz). [Fr., fem. of Coiffeur.] A woman hair-dresser, esp. one skilled in designing and arranging the coiffures of women.

1927 *Daily Express* 5 July 5/5 In big West End saloons the highly skilled coiffeuse and beauty specialist can command £500 a year.

Coiffure (koi·fiūɹ, ‖kwafür), *v.* [f. Coiffure *sb.*] *trans.* To dress (a woman's hair).

1906 *Daily Chron.* 8 Nov. 6/1 She has a profusion of brown hair, beautifully coiffured. 1928 *Daily Tel.* 1 May 15/3 Her hair was elaborately coiffured every morning.

Coi·ffured, *a.* [f. Coiffure *sb.* or *v.*] Wearing a coiffure. Of head-dress or hair: Arranged in a coiffure.

1907 *Macm. Mag.* Jan. 5/1 Queen Elizabeth in full-dress, ruffled, coiffured, and corsetted. 1928 *Daily Tel.* 5 May 16/5 The feather-curl..can be worn close to the ears, as is sometimes expressed in the real coiffured coil.

Coign, *sb.* Add:

4. *Geol.* An original angular elevation of land around which continental growth has taken place.

1899 J. W. Gregory in *Geogr. Jrnl.* (R.G.S.) XIII. 245 South of the Scandinavian coign are the transverse east and western chains of the Alps and the Atlas. *Note*, The suggestion of the word 'coign' for 'corner' I owe to Mr. L. Fletcher...The term is suitable, as it is used for a printer's wedge as well as for the corner-stone of a house.

Coil, *v.*[3] Add:

1. b. To lay *down* in a coil or coils.

1915 'Bartimeus' *A Tall Ship* i. 27 A younger man..was busy coiling down something in the bows.

Coiler[1]. Add:

1. b. *spec.* A workman who coils or attends a machine that winds finished products in coils or on bobbins, drums, etc.

1881 *Instr. Census Clerks* (1885) 49 Ordnance manufacturer. Forge:..Coiler. 1921 *Dict. Occup. Terms* (1927) §§ 149, etc.

2. *Cotton-spinning.* An apparatus for coiling the sliver by feeding it into the coiler-cans. Also *attrib.*

1873 Leigh *Sci. Mod. Cotton Spinning* (ed. 2) 187 Shortly after the invention of the coiler Messrs. Tatham and Cheetham conceived the idea of adapting it as a slubbing frame. 1884 Marsden *Cotton Spinning* 141 The waste.. passes into a coiler at the end of the machine. 1890 Nasmith *Mod. Cotton Spinning Mach.* 55 A plate free to revolve and borne in the lower part of the coiler frame. 1892 — *Cotton Spinning* 127 The coiler can is 9 in. diameter. 1902 Thornley *Cotton Combing Machines* 235 The rule for total draft will serve here, substituting the block roller for the coiler roller.

Coiling, *vbl. sb.*[1] Add: **c.** *attrib.*, as **coiling motion** = prec. 2.

1873 Leigh *Sci. Mod. Cotton Spinning* (ed. 2) 168 This very ingenious contrivance is the celebrated 'coiling motion' patented about thirty years ago by Messrs. Tatham and Cheetham.

Coin, *sb.* **8.** Add: **coin-catcher,** a surgical instrument for extracting a swallowed coin.

1895 *Arnold & Sons' Catal. Surg. Instr.* 288 Probang, Œsophageal, with coin-catcher. 1903 *Daily Chron.* 27 Nov. 8/6 The doctor..passed the coin-catcher down his throat, but the child struggled so that the catcher broke, and was also swallowed.

Co-insu·rance. [Co- 3 c.] A form of insurance in which responsibility for loss is shared by two or more parties; also, insurance in which the insured, under certain conditions, is jointly responsible with the insurance company.

1889 *Cent. Dict.* s.v. *Insurance.* 1902 *Encycl. Brit.* XXIX. 512/2 The direction in which fire insurance..calls most pressingly for improvement is the extension of the principle of co-insurance.

Coiny (koi·ni), *a. colloq.* [f. Coin *sb.* + -y[1].] That has abundance of coin; rich. Hence **Coi·niness,** wealth.

1891 *Chambers's Jrnl.* 7 Feb. 83/2 He paints for amusement merely. He seems to be coiny. 1903 *Blackw. Mag.* Sept. 312/1 A fellow must be a coiny bird to bank with the Bank of England. *Ibid.* 313/2 Howell dying with over £4000, though he had considerably impaired the 'coininess' of other people.

Coke, *sb.* **2.** Add: *coke barrow, bogey, dust, fork*; **coke-breeze** (see Breeze *sb.*[3]); **coke-oil** (see quot.); **coke-oven,** an oven, furnace, kiln, or retort in which coke is produced by the expulsion of gas from bituminous coal.

1884 Knight *Dict. Mech.* Suppl., **Coke Barrow*, a large semi-cylindrical sheet-iron two-wheeled barrow used about coke ovens and furnaces. 1921 *Dict. Occup. Terms* (1927) § 609 *Coke man*..fills *coke bogeys with coke fork from stack, [etc.]. 1877 *Encycl. Brit.* VI. 118/1 The outside of the heap [of coal, in coking] is covered with a coating of wet *coke dust. 1909 *Cent. Dict.* Suppl., *Coke-dust*, powdered coke; used for blacking foundry molds. 1874 Knight *Dict. Mech.*, **Coke Fork*, a ten-tined fork for shoveling coke. 1862 *Chambers's Encycl.* IV. 645/1 There remains..a large residue of pitch, which is again distilled.., giving off an oil called *coke-oil. 1839 Ure *Dict. Arts* 997 A front elevation of two..*coke-ovens. 1861 J. Percy *Metallurgy* 157 In its simplest form a coke-oven is a chamber of fire-brick or some other refractory material, having an arched roof in which is a hole and an entrance below.

Coke, abbrev. of Cocaine. *slang.*

1914 E. B. Lowry *Himself* 179 A few years ago 'coke' fiends in a certain locality in Chicago made a regular practice of buying '——'s Catarrh Cure'.

Coked (kōukt), *ppl. a.* [f. Coke *v.* + -ed[1].] Reduced to coke.

1763 W. Lewis *Comm. Phil.-Techn.* 284 A Fire of coaked pitcoal. 1894 *Sat. Rev.* 25 Aug. 221 Coal-dust..in a coked and cindered condition.

Co·keman, co·ke-man. [Coke *sb.*] A workman employed in loading or unloading coke, charging a furnace, etc. with coke; or discharging coke from a furnace, etc.

1852 F. S. Williams *Our Iron Roads* 251 He in return signs the coke-man's book for the amount. 1892 *Daily News* 11 Mar. 5/8 The cokemen, the mechanics, and the miners in the Durham Miners' Federation. 1920 *Glasgow Herald* 1 Sept. 7 Cokemen employed on by-product plants at collieries. 1921 *Dict. Occup. Terms* (1927) § 049 *Cokeman*..works at box or bunker where 'breeze'..is collected after screening.

Coker (kōu·kəɹ). [f. Coke *sb.* or *v.* + -er[1].] One who superintends the coking of coal; also, a workman employed in handling coal in or about a coke-oven, etc.

1793 in Bogle *Founding Carron Wks.* (1898) 32 John Heggie, a fireman coaker. 1881 *Instr. Census Clerks* (1885) 93 Steel Melting:..Coker. 1921 *Dict. Occup. Terms* (1927) § 081, etc.

Cokerite: see *Cocorite.

Cokery (kōu·kəri). [f. Coke *sb.* + -ery.] A coke-furnace.

1923 *Glasgow Herald* 27 Mar. 9 The three cokeries already being exploited by the French. 1923 *Times* 3 May 11/2 Dozens of cokeries are said to be cold.

Coky (kōu·ki), *a.* [f. Coke *sb.* + -y[1].] Resembling coke.

1900 Sadtler *Handbk. Indust. Org. Chem.* (ed. 3) 359 Non-coking Coals..do not possess the property of fusing into a compact 'coky' mass.

Col. Add:

2. *Meteorol.* A region of lower pressure between two anticyclones, analogous to the 'col' or depression between two mountains.

1887 Abercromby *Weather* 26 Between every two anticyclones we find a furrow, neck or 'col' of low pressure. 1923 Sir Napier Shaw *Forecasting Weather* v. 117 A *col*, the saddle-shaped region between two lows and two highs. 1927 Kendrew *Climates of Continents* 354 The col is essentially an anticyclonic formation.

Colberter (kǫ·lbəɹtəɹ). [See Colbertine.] In *lace colberter*, a machine-hand who scollops and makes a fast edge to lace curtains.

1921 *Dict. Occup. Terms* (1927) § 385.

Cold, *sb.* **5. c.** Add: **cold struck** (see quot.).

1908 *Animal Managem.* 319 Where the days are very hot and the nights equally cold, these animals [*sc.* horses and camels] are often observed to be 'cold struck', stiff all over.

Cold, *a.* Add: **1. c.** Used also to denote the effect on a person of a severe blow or shock. *U.S.*

1905 Rex Beach *Pardners* v. (1912) 127 Some Polack.. laid out the quartermaster cold. 1928 F. N. Hart *Bellamy Trial* iii. 98 'What did you do?' 'Do? I don't know what I did. It knocked me cold.'

e. *To get* (a person) *cold*, earlier *to get it on* (him) *cold*: to have at one's mercy; to have captured completely.

1908 S. E. White *Riverman* xlvii. 353 I'll put Heinzman in the pen too. I've got it on him, cold. 1924 Mulford *Rustlers' Valley* xix. 213 What you doin'? I got you cold. 1927 F. E. Baily *Golden Vanity* xix, Cynthia's lapping like an angel. You've got London cold.

7. e. Phr. *It leaves me cold*: it fails to interest me or excite me to enthusiasm.

Cf. G. *Das lässt mich kalt.*

1888 H. Sweet *Coll. Papers* 250 His enthusiasm..leaves us cold. 1927 Aldous Huxley *Proper Studies* 173, I..am left cold by ritual, the corybantic emotionalism of revivals.

10. b. In advb. use: Without any mitigation; absolutely. *U.S. slang.*

1889 *Kansas Times & Star* 24 June, A. D. Taylor..trailed a variety actress..with whom he was infatuated...She shook him cold yesterday. 1905 Rex Beach *Pardners* iii. (1912) 79 We were liable to get turned down cold if we didn't have some story. 1916 H. L. Wilson *Somewhere in Red Gap* vi. 265 This game where you play cards with yourself and mebbe win a thousand dollars cold. 1918 Mulford *Man fr. Bar-20* xiv. 149 If I'd knowed he was a friend of yourn I'd 'a' stopped him cold down south of Hastings.

12. (Later U.S. examples.)

1773 Washington *Diaries* II. 100 Touched now and then upon a Cold Scent till we came into Colo. Fairfax's Neck. 1874 in S. Sidney *Bk. Horse* (1875) 398 When running a cold scent the music [of the hounds] is extremely fine. 1875 *Ibid.* 476 Where hounds run from grass to plough, it is often found that they decline from racing breast-high to cold hunting. 1877 Hallock *Sportsman's Gaz.* 440 (Cent.) The object is to obtain a fine nose [in a dog], so as to hunt a cold scent.

18. cold-drawn, also *fig.*, unaffected by the emotions, cool, calculated; *cold-rolled, -shut*; *cold riveting, rolling, sawing, soldering, stoking, tinning.*

1892 Stevenson & Osbourne *Wrecker* ix, The little beast means *cold-drawn biz. 1898 Kipling in *Morn. Post* 11 Nov. 5/1 Out of all manner of tight places that require dexterity and a cheek of cold-drawn brass. 1906 Cornford *Defenceless Isl.* 99 Cotton is the subject of much cold-drawn gambling. 1906 *Daily Chron.* 10 Feb. 7/1 A detective-sergeant, by relating cold-drawn facts..showed the prisoner to be an unprincipled scoundrel. 1888 *Lockwood's Dict. Terms Mech. Engin.*, **Cold Riveting*, small rivets in thin plates are hammered up without being heated in the fire. 1878 *Engineering* 1 Nov. 347 By comparing hot-rolled and *cold-rolled iron of the same kind, under physical stress. 1888 *Lockwood's Dict. Terms Mech. Engin.*, *Cold Rolled*, Bars and plates rolled without being previously heated. 1897 *Daily News* 8 Mar. 2/5 Steel..cold-rolled sheets. 1878 *Engineering* 1 Nov. 347 The *cold rolling is effected by means of a powerful train of the ordinary type. 1888 *Lockwood's Dict. Terms Mech. Engin.*, **Cold Sawing*, the sawing of iron while cold with a cold iron saw. 1882 *Cassell's Encycl. Dict.*, **Cold-shut*, closed cold without welding. 1873 Spon *Workshop Rec.* Ser. I. (1885) 337/2 Block tin dissolved in muriatic acid with a little mercury forms a very good amalgam for *cold tinning.

19. cold cook *slang*, an undertaker; **cold douche,** a stream of cold water directed against some part of the body as a remedial treatment; hence **cold-douching,** the application of the cold douche; in quot. *fig.*; **cold feet,** (*a*) in colloq. phr. *to get* (or *have*) *cold feet*, to be in a 'funk', become discouraged; hence = fear, 'funk'; (*b*) in horticulture (see quot. 1909); **cold-footer** *U.S. slang*, a timid person; **cold frame** *Hort.*, a frame in which small plants are grown and protected without artificial heat (see Frame *sb.* 13 c); **cold house** *Hort.*, a glass house in which plants are grown without artificial heat; also *transf.*; **cold kiss** (see quot.); **cold-pack,** a wet pack (see Pack *sb.*[1] 11) prepared with cold water; **cold point** = **cold spot*; **cold pole,** in high latitudes, the place of lowest temperature; **cold room** *Hort.*, a store room kept at a very low temperature for the retardation of bulbs and roots; **cold saw,** one for cutting cold metals (*Cent. Dict.* Suppl. 1909); **cold shot,** small globules of iron found in chilled portions of a casting (Knight *Dict. Mech.* Suppl. 1884); **cold soldering,** soldering without heat with the aid of mercury; **cold spot** *Physiol.*, a spot upon the skin which is sensitive to cold, but insensitive to warmth, pain, or pressure; **cold storage** (see Storage 2 b); hence **cold store,** a refrigerating chamber for the cold storage of meat; **cold sweating** *Tanning*, the process of soaking hides in cold water to facilitate the removal of the epidermis and hair.

1729 *Universal Spect.* 4 Oct. (N. & Q. 5 Oct. 1929, 236/2) He further directs, that no Undertaker, *alias* *Cold Cook, or Upholder shall have the Management thereof. 1860 *Slang Dict.* (ed. 2). 1835 *Cold douche [s.v. Douche in Dict.]. 1904 *St. George* VII. 168 He would have to be an uncommonly sturdy Simon Zelotes whose zeal survived the *cold-douching of schoolboy chaff. 1896 G. Ade *Artie* xii. 108 He's one o' them boys that never has *cold feet. 1904 Eliz. Robins *Magn. North* I. 8 But instead of 'getting cold feet' as the phrase for discouragement ran, and turning back, they determined [etc.]. 1907 Rex Beach *Barrier* xviii. (1908) 286 I've got some new clothes now...I bought 'em off a tenderfoot with cold feet. 1909 Webster, *Cold feet*,..the condition of plants due to excessive watering without proper drainage. 1914 Rosher *In R.N.A.S.* (1916) 40, I get awfully cold feet...That puts the fear of God into you. 1915 'Ian Hay' *First Hundred Thou.* xxi. 329 It seems that the enemy have evacuated Fosse Alley again. Nobody quite knows why: a sudden attack of cold feet, probably. 1920 Hunter *Trail Drivers of Texas* 429 Two of my men stayed with me, and the third, a '*cold-footer', crossed on the bridge. 1857–8 *Trans. Ill. Agric. Soc.* III. 503 The seed for early summer cabbages can be planted in a *cold frame early in September. 1877 *Field & Forest* II. 164 These insects had all gathered along the Northern and Eastern margin [inside] of a 'cold frame', in his garden. 1841 Mrs. Loudon *Ladies' Comp. Fl. Gard.* (1846) 65 *Cold Houses for Plants are not generally in use, though it is a common practice with gardeners to remove plants from hot-houses into the back sheds, in order to retard their blossoming. 1904 *Daily Chron.* 28 Jan. 6/1 It is the cold-house that has smiled upon them, in the shape of the refrigerated holds of the South African steamers. 1920 *Chambers's Jrnl.* 384/1 The 'forced' and 'cold-house' tomato is Guernsey's speciality. 1927 *Observer* 7 Aug. 8/6 The '*cold kiss' [in Berlin] is an ice-cream, flattened between two wafers. 1909 *Practitioner* Dec. 866 The *cold-pack is used for from 10 to 15 minutes every hour. 1909 *Cent. Dict.* Suppl.. s.v. *Pole*[2], Pole of cold or *cold pole. 1927 Kendrew *Climates of Continents* 167 In Eastern Siberia is situated the 'cold pole' of the earth. 1904 *Westm. Gaz.* 12 Jan. 4/2 In some of the largest nurseries..there exist *cold-rooms or stores, pitch-dark and packed full of lily-of-the-valley crowns, lilies, and other bulbs and plants. 1877 *Design & Work* 16 June 43/2 (*heading*) *Cold Soldering. 1895 tr. *Külpe's Outl. Psychol.* 94 Blix and Goldscheider..speak of heat and *cold spots, and regard them as the peculiar terminal organs of the temperature sense, and as independent of the pressure spots. 1901 E. B. Titchener *Exper. Psychol.* I. i. 57 To ascertain how these organs (warm spots or cold spots) respond to a stimulation. 1895 *Daily News* 29 May 8/4 Extensive *cold-store accommodation had been provided.

Cold deck. *U.S.* [Cold *a.* + Deck *sb.*] In poker-playing, a pack of cards in which the cards have been arranged beforehand.

1868 *All Year Round* 31 Oct. 490/1 He's got everything all set to ring a 'cold deck'. *a* 1875 'Mark Twain' *Sketches* Wks. XIX. 360, I never have gambled from that day to this..without a 'cold deck' in my pocket. 1887 F. Francis Jr. *Saddle & Mocassin* 225 Between them they put up a cold deck in a faro-box.

Hence **Co·ld-deck** *v.*; **Co·ld-de·cker.**

1902 H. L. Wilson *Spenders* xi. 123 A man wakes up to find that his natural promptin's has cold-decked him. 1920 Mulford *J. Nelson* xv. 163 I've had all th' visitin' I want with a bunch of cold-deckers. *Ibid.* xxv. 281 He's cold-decked, Ma'am; beat clean when he'd reckoned he'd won.

Cold meat.

1. Cooked meat that has become cold; hence used to connote inferior fare.

1814–15 Jane Austen *Emma* xlii, When you are tired of eating strawberries in the garden, there shall be cold meat in the house. 1894 *Daily News* 15 Sept. 3/2 It is hard to be treated like 'cold meat company'. 1909 *Daily Chron.* 24 Aug. 1/5 There is a run on cold-meat shops.

2. A corpse. Chiefly *attrib.*, as *cold-meat box* (coffin), *-cart* (hearse), *-train* (funeral train). Originally *pugilistic slang.*

1819 Moore *Tom Crib's Mem.* 25 In the Twelfth and Last Round Sandy fetch'd him a downer, That left him all's one as cold meat for the Crowner. 1820 J. H. Reynolds *Fancy* (1906) 38 He's for the cold meat cart, and so am I. 1837 Dickens *Pickw.* xix, You mustn't handle your piece in that ere way..or I'm damned if you won't make cold meat of some on us. [1876 R. M. Jephson *Girl He Left Behind Him* xi, The train by which Dorrien journeyed to Aldershot was that one known as the 'Cold Meat', which.. is dismally supposed..to convey corpses to Woking Cemetery...It carries nothing more dreadful than a portion of the beef and mutton for the morning's issue to the troops.] 1889 *Sporting Times* 3 Aug. 1/3, I should just come in where you were lying in the cold-meat box.

Cold-slaw. *U.S.* = Cole-slaw.

1794 *Massachusetts Spy* 12 Nov. (Th.) A piece of sliced cabbage, by Dutchmen ycleped cold slaw. 1821 J. F. Cooper *Spy* xiii. (1831) 156 Potatoes, onions, beets, cold slaw, rice, and all the other minutiæ of a goodly dinner. 1871 *Lippincott's Mag.* Feb. (De Vere) Coldslaw apparently cut with a harrow. 1886 [see Cole-slaw].

Cold snap. orig. *U.S.* [See Snap *sb.* 7 b.] A sudden spell of cold weather.

1839 *Knickerbocker Mag.* XIII. 509 We had a cold snap, last night. 1844 J. C. Neal *Charcoal Sk.* 143 (Th.) A warm spell which succeeded a 'cold snap'. 1861 *Trans. Ill. Agric. Soc.* IV. 118 The sun was shining upon them during a cold snap, after a thaw. 1875 *Field & Forest* I. 56 The 'cold snap' that occurred early in December. 1885 'C. E. Craddock' *Prophet Gt. Smoky Mts.* xv. 289 One might easily judge how few of the mountaineers had ventured out since the beginning of the 'cold snap'. 1894 T. B. Aldrich *Two Bites* etc. 92 The cold snap, with its freaks among water-pipes and window-glass.

Coldstreamers (kōu·ldstrīməɹz), *sb. pl.* [So named from *Coldstream* (on the Tweed), where the original regiment was assembled by General Monck.] The Coldstream Guards.

1671 Gumble *Life Gen. Monck* 15 Sir James Smith, now Lieutenant Colonell to the Cold Streamers. *Ibid.* 189 These Coldstreamers were..men of Might. 1902 *Daily Chron.* 14 Aug. 5/3 The massed bands of the Irish Guards and the Coldstreamers. 1908 Hardy *Dynasts* III. vi. iv. 470 The Fusileer-guards now (They pass)..Now the Coldstreamers.

Cold water. **c.** Add: Similarly, *to pour cold water upon.*

1893 *Times* 26 Apr. 9/4 He was obliged to pour cold water very plentifully upon the zeal of his Irish friends.

Colea (kōu·liă). [f. the name of Sir Lowry *Coles*, a former Governor of Mauritius + -a.] A tropical plant belonging to the bignoniaceous genus so named.

1927 *Blackw. Mag.* Apr. 508/2 A semi-wild garden of coleas, crotons, and dracænas.

Coleridgian (kōulri·dʒiăn), *a.* Also **-ean.** [f. the proper name *Coleridge*: see below and -ian, -an.] Of or pertaining to Samuel Taylor Coleridge (1772–1834) the poet, or to his writings, opinions, etc.

1851 Carlyle *Sterling* I. xv, By some Coleridgean legerdemain. 1893 Martineau in Ld. Tennyson *Tennyson* (1897) II. 171 The Coleridgian acceptation of these words was not less congenial to the Poet than to the Divine. 1910 H. Walker *Lit. Vict. Era* ii. 28 The importance of the Coleridgean influence is amply attested.

Coli- (kōu·ləi). Shortened form of *bacillus coli*, used as a combining form in various scientific terms, as *coli-group* (see quot.); *coli-like* adj., resembling *bacillus coli*; *coli-typhoid* adj., (a group) composed of *bacillus coli* and typhoid bacillus. Also *coli-bacilluria*, the presence of *bacillus coli* in the urine.

1910 *Practitioner* Apr. 449 Urotropin..appears to be of comparatively little use in the case of *coli-bacilluria. 1913 Dorland *Med. Dict.* (ed. 7), **Coli-group*, a group of bacteria, including the *Bacillus coli*, the paracolon bacillus, typhoid bacillus, paratyphoid bacillus, and the bacillus of psittacosis. 1902 *Daily Chron.* 5 Aug. 5/2 Bacillus coli, or other *coli-like microbes. 1908 *Practitioner* Aug. 261 Organisms of the *coli-typhoid group.

Coliform (kōu·lifǫɹm), *a.*[2] [f. *Coli- + -form.] Of the nature of or resembling a bacillus of the coli-group of bacteria.

1907 *Practitioner* Nov. 646 A coliform organism, which was not B. typhosus, nor the ordinary type of B. coli.

Colliplication, var. *Coloplication.

Collæmia (kǫlī·miă). *Path.* Also **-emia.** [f. Gr. κόλλα glue, αἷμα blood: see -ia.] A glutinous condition of the blood.

1901 Dorland *Med. Dict.* (ed. 2). 1910 *Brit. Health Rev.* Feb. 63 Defective circulation..has only two causes: (1) collæmia, and (2) weak heart.

Collapse, *v.* Add:

3. *trans.* To cause to break down, fall in, or contract. *lit.* and *fig.* Also *U.S.* to shut (a telescope).

1891 W. C. Sydney *Eng. 18th Cent.* II. 162 Which culminated in the battle of Culloden Moor, and collapsed the Jacobite cause. 1902 S. G. Fisher *True Hist. Amer. Revolution* 200 Such complete destruction and devastation of the country as would collapse the patriot party. 1904 *Daily Chron.* 8 June 5/3 Kent..,given a pinch of luck, might have collapsed Yorkshire! 1908 *Practitioner* Jan. 54 The urethra is alternately ballooned and collapsed. 1909 *Westm. Gaz.* 22 Apr. 4/2 The wind bringing its whole force to bear on the broadside and collapsing the structure. 1921 Mulford *Bar-20 Three* xviii. 229 Far back..a Mexican collapsed his telescope.

Collapsibility (kǫlæpsibi·liti). [f. Collapsible + -ity.] The quality of being collapsible. *lit.* and *fig.*

1890 *Pall Mall Gaz.* 24 June 6/1 Some spoke bitterly of the collapsibility of their leaders. 1892 *Pictorial World* 2 Apr. 664/1 He has pricked a little hole..to test its collapsibility.

Collar, *sb.* Add:

18. c. The area of junction between the stem and root of a tree.

1857–8 *Trans. Ill. Agric. Soc.* III. 344 The ravages of this insect may be prevented by surrounding the collar of the trees, early in June with leached ashes. *Ibid.* 465 Care should be taken not to set the trees too deep. It is better that the collar should be considerably above, rather than below the level of the lawn. 1887 Hardy *Woodlanders* xix, With a small bill-hook he carefully freed the collar of the tree from twigs and patches of moss.

21. collar-band, also, the band to which the collar is attached; the band forming the collar of a woman's dress; **collar bearing,** a bearing on a shaft, adapted for taking the end thrust of the shaft; **collar-bound** *a.*, of machinery, impeded by being clogged or cramped between collars; **collar box,** a square cardboard box in which collars are sold; also, a box, usually round, of leather, metal, etc., in which collars are kept for personal use; also *attrib.*; **collar facing** (see Facing *vbl. sb.* 4); **collar gage** (see quot.); **collar machinist** (*a*) a laundry-worker who irons starched collars by machinery; (*b*) one who stitches together the parts of a horse collar by machine; **collar-maker,** one who makes shirt collars; a saddler who makes horse and dog collars; **collar palm,** a tool used by horse collar makers for shaping a collar; **collar pore** *Zool.*, a tube or pore connecting the cavity of the collar of *Balanoglossus* with the first gill-slit; **collar-stamper,** a worker who stamps the size and other marks inside shirt collars; **collar stud,** a stud used to fasten a detachable collar to a shirt; **collar swage** (see quot.).

1884 *Myra's Jrnl. Dress & Fashion* 1 Aug. 367/2 The plain *collar band is of velvet. 1907 *Daily Chron.* 21 Jan. 8/1 The yoke and high collar-band in the gown..are fashioned of ermine. 1887 D. A. Low *Machine Draw.* (1892) 121 The weight of the shaft is supported by a *collar bearing. 1881 *Instr. Census Clerks* (1885) 83 *Collar Box Maker. 1899 *Westm. Gaz.* 27 July 3/1 A *collar facing of white silk. 1888 *Lockwood's Dict. Terms Mech. Engin.*, *Cylindrical Gauge*, a gauge composed of two pieces.., the plug gauge being inserted into a bored hole and the *collar gage being slid over the spindle. 1895 *Westm. Gaz.* 26 Apr. 3/2 Nor will there be an eager competition for the place of the *collar machinist at 1s. 4d. a day. 1858 Simmonds *Dict. Trade*, *Collar-maker. 1897 T. J. Parker & Haswell *Text-bk. Zool.* II. 2 The collar cavity communicates with the exterior by a pair of *collar pores—ciliated tubes leading into the first gill-slit or first gill-pouch. 1908 *Westm. Gaz.* 21 Aug. 8/3 A *collar stamper. 1885 *Chambers's Jrnl.* II. 320/1, I suppose he has lost his *collar-stud again. 1906 *Daily Chron.* 28 May 6/4 My collar-stud ran away and hid itself with great success. 1884 Knight *Dict. Mech.* Suppl., **Collar Swage* (Blacksmithing), a swage..used in swaging a collar on to a rod.

Collarer (kǫ·lărəɹ). [f. Collar *sb.* + -er[1].] An operative who fixes the caps on electric bulbs.

1921 *Dict. Occup. Terms* (1927) § 318 Cap fixer, capper (electric lamps); collarer, stud fixer.

Collargol (kǫlā·ɹgǫl). [f. Gr. κόλλα glue + ἄργ(υρος silver + -ol.] Colloidal silver used as a germicide and antiseptic. Hence **Collargo·lic** (*acid*).

1903 *Nature* 26 Mar. 503/2 Collargol is the soluble salt of an acid, collargolic acid, which is sufficiently strong to displace carbonic acid from carbonates. 1907 *Practitioner* Apr. 574 Collargol, used as an ointment, has always been satisfactory.

Collateral, *sb.*

6. *U.S.* (Earlier and later examples.)

1847 *Tom Pepper* I. 143 (Th.) I must have a thousand dollars. Here, take the collateral, and give me the money. 1869 *Congress. Globe* 25 Mar. 273/2 When we want money to move our wheat, we understand we can go down there and borrow it. If we have got the collaterals to put up, we get it. 1875 Holland *Sevenoaks* xxv. 359 He had already used these as collaterals, in the borrowing of small sums at short time. *a* 1909 'O. Henry' *Roads of Destiny* viii. 141 I'm no judge of collateral in bunches.

Colla·teral, *v. U.S.* [f. prec.] *trans.* To provide collateral security for.

1907 *Sun* (N.Y.) 18 Dec. 4/1 Using the stock of the last purchase to collateral a loan with which to buy the new.

Collect, *sb.* **4.** Delete †*Obs.* and add:

1885 E. C. Stedman *Poets of Amer.* 137 (Cent.) Yet anything that others can write of him is poor indeed beside a collect of his own golden sayings.

5. A place where something collects or is collected.

1839 in *Trans. Mich. Agric. Soc.* (1856) VII. 386 These sinks derive their name from the fact of their being collects for the waters of the surrounding region.

Collect, *v.* Add:

1. b. (*absol.*)

1889 Farmer *Americanisms*, *To Collect*, a contraction for 'to collect payments'. 1893 Kate D. Wiggin *Polly Oliver* xv. (1894) 165 In an hour another message, marked 'Collect', followed the first one. 1913 *U.S. Postal Laws & Reg.* 489 Collect-on-delivery service...A collect-on-delivery parcel. 1922 H. L. Foster *Adv. Trop. Tramp* xii. 186 He sends it [*sc.* telegram] to us 'collect'.

6. *colloq.* To 'pick up' from a place of deposit.

1875 C. James *Yoke of Freedom* 53 Jack went down the great marble staircase..collected his hat and cloak, [etc.]. 1895 *Nebraska State Jrnl.* 23 June 5/5 To 'collect' an old ram requires good lungs, good legs, good judgment, and good shooting. 1928 F. N. Hart *Bellamy Trial* ii. 30, I was to collect the keys under the doormat at the gardener's cottage.

Collectar (kǫ·lektəɹ). = Collectarium.

1904 Wordsw. & Littlehales *Old Service-Bks.* 210 Sequences are found..in Leofric's Collectar and Hymnary.

Collecting, *vbl. sb.* Add: *attrib.* and *Comb.*: **collecting box,** (*a*) a box in which scientific specimens collected in the field are temporarily placed; (*b*) a box for the collection of contributions of money; **collecting-cane,** a cane-gun used by naturalists for collecting specimens (*Cent. Dict.* 1889); **collecting station** (see quot.).

1863 *Collecting box [see Collecting *vbl. sb.*, *attrib.*, in Dict.]. 1899 *Westm. Gaz.* 28 Aug. 7/1 'Jack's' collecting-box was once again strapped on his back. 1908 *Ibid.* 16 Nov. 2/3 The penny..was taken from a collecting-box which the woman had obtained from Chelsea Hospital. 1900 *Ibid.* 2 Jan. 3/2 At the *collecting station..the wounded are collected as brought in by the stretcher-bearers, and are sent to the 'dressing station' in ambulances. 1915 *Daily Express* 5 July 6/3 He was received at a collecting station, obtained first aid for his wound, and was forwarded to the field hospital.

Collection. 2. Add: Also *attrib.*

1889 Gretton *Memory's Harkback* 212 He was astonished to see a sovereign on the collection-plate. 1904 *Daily Chron.* 19 Mar. 9/1 Collection-box robberies. 1905 *Westm. Gaz.* 16 May 2/1 The net result will be an addition of eight per cent. to the collection income.

Collective, *a.* (*sb.*) Add:

A. 2. c. *Collective bargain, bargaining, piece-work* (see quots. 1923, 1928).

1891 Beatrice Webb *Cooperative Movement* 217 Individualist exchange must follow individualist production, and give place to collective bargaining. *Ibid.*, To gain a clear conception of the collective bargain. 1897 S. & B. Webb *Industrial Democracy* I. 174 The Method of Collective Bargaining. 1900 *Daily News* 24 Dec. 5/6 The contracts should take the form of collective-bargains in which every man of the same class would share equally. 1923 J. D. Hackett *Labor Terms in Management Engineering* May, *Collective Bargaining*, a mode of fixing the terms of employment by means of bargaining power between an organized body of employees and an employer, or association of employers. 1928 *Britain's Industr. Future* (*Liberal Ind. Inquiry*) III. xvi. 195 'Collective piece-work', whereby a group of workers..are guaranteed their regular time-rates but are promised, over and above these, an agreed share of the costs they may save.

3. d. *Psychol.* (See quot.)

1926 W. McDougall *Outl. Abnormal Psych.* 190 It may ..be said that Jung's Unconscious comprises, in addition to the individually acquired and repressed complexes, all the innate structure of the mind, and that this, 'the Collective Unconscious', is very rich and complex.

Collectively, *adv.* Add:

2. By collective action or arrangement.

1902 *Daily Chron.* 17 Oct. 3/3 The collectively-agreed rate of a shilling per hour. 1908 *Ibid.* 28 Mar. 6/7 Collectively-owned property.

Collectivistic (kǫlektivi·stik), *a.* [f. Collectivist + -ic.] Based on collectivism.

1894 *Athenæum* 7 July 24/1 The ideal collectivistic state.

Collectivize (kǫle·ktivəiz), *v.* [f. Collective + -ize.] *trans.* To establish or organize in accordance with the principles of collectivism. Hence **Colle:ctiviza·tion.**

1890 *Good Words* Dec. 822/1 The collectivisation of capital is, from the socialistic point of view, a far more thorough and consistent scheme. 1892 *Ibid.* Sept. 621/2 This measure of expropriation, collectivisation, or spoliation, must be a revolutionary measure. 1894 *Speaker* 5 May 503/1 It cuts off the old hopes of 'bettering oneself', of rising above one's class. It collectivises even hope.

College, *sb.* Add:

1. b. *Electoral college*: see also Electoral *a.*

9. *college cook, library, yard* (esp. at Harvard), *-yell* (U.S.).

1684–5 *Sewall's Diary* I. 67 He had been *College Cook a long time. 1693 *Letter Book of S. Sewall* 139 Bestow the Skeleton in *Colledg Library. 1697–8 *Sewall's Diary* I. 475, I sent to the college Library my *Phaenomena*. 1639 *Harvard College Recs.* (1925) I. 172 The frame in the *Colledge yard. 1708 S. Sewall *Diary* 14 Oct., in *Collect. Mass. Hist. Soc.* Ser. v. V. 67 Goe with the Gov[r] about 2 p.m. Dine; into the College yard. Goe up into Library [etc.]. 1734 in B. Peirce *Hist. Harvard Univ.* (1833) App. 131 If any scholar shall go beyond the College yards or fences, without coat, cloak, or gown. 1807 in *Proc. Mass. Hist. Soc.* (1890) Ser. II. V. 172 The students..also resolved to..take away all the provisions and strew them over the college yard. 1837 *Knickerbocker Mag.* IX. 157 We entered the college yard [at Yale] a little after nine. 1923 E. F. Wyatt *Invis. Gods* II. iii. 62 Will Halliday seemed more and more the zenith of manly perfection..in *college yells.

Colleger. Add: **d.** A member of or student at a college. *U.S.*

1827 *Harvard Reg.* (1828) 214 If we get fore-handed enough we'll send him to be a Colledger, and make a Parson of him.

Collegiate. B. 1. (Later U.S. example.)

1854 Mary J. Holmes *Tempest & Sunshine* viii. 49 Miss Warner keeping a watchful eye upon her pupils, lest some lawless collegiate should relieve her from the trouble of seeing them safely home.

Collem (kǫ·lem), short for next.

1924 *Chambers's Jrnl.* 717/2 A great many 'Collems' live on the surface of water.

Collembola (kǫle·mbǒlă). *Ent.* [mod L., f. Gr. κόλλα glue + ἔμβολον peg, stopper, wedge.] An insect belonging to the sub-order of that name, characterized by the protrusile sucker in the basal segment of its abdomen.

1914 *Brit. Mus. Return* 197 Collembola and Psocids in drinking water. 1918 W. Beebe *Jungle Peace* x. (1919) 258 Simple insects, which we shall have to call collembolas, were difficult to capture.

Collet, *sb.*[1] Add: **2. b.** *spec.* A piece of ivory inserted between the upper and lower part of the handle of a metal teapot, etc., to intercept the heat.

1899 *Bill of Reid & Sons, Newcastle on Tyne*, An ivory collet supplied, 1s.

Collet, *sb.*[2] Add: **b.** *attrib.* **collet-side,** the under side.

1881 Watt *Mech. Industr.* I. 121 On the collet-side [of the diamond] are formed four irregular pentagons.

Colletocystophore (kǫlītosi·stǒfōəɹ). *Zool.* [f. Gr. κολλητής one who glues or fastens + *Cystophore.] A marginal body characteristic of lucernarian hydrozoans. Hence **Colle:tocysto·pho·ric** *a.* So **Colle·tocyst.**

1878 H. J. Clark *Lucernariæ* 111 Histology of the Colletocystophores (Anchors). *Ibid.*, The fully grown colletocystophore is divided into three distinct regions, viz., the pedicle, the nematocystophore, and the colletocystophoric mass. *Ibid.* 112 It is true that the colletocysts appear as soon as a change commences on the tentaculoid shaft, but [etc.].

Collins (kǫ·linz). [The name of a character, William *Collins*, in Jane Austen's *Pride & Prejudice* (ch. xxii).] A letter of thanks for entertainment or hospitality, sent by a departed guest.

1904 *Chambers's Jrnl.* 27 Aug. 611/2 When we do not call a letter of thanks for a visit 'a board and lodging', we call it a 'Collins'. 1905 Lucy M. Soulsby *Brondesbury Papers* iii. *Rules of the Road* 6 Write your 'Collins' after every visit (if only for a night) next morning at latest. 1907 Lady Grove *Social Fetich* 74 The 'Collins' letter I had dutifully bored my hostess with. 1921 Sir W. Raleigh *Lett.* (1926) 375 This is only a Collins, and a Collins should not wade into deep places. It should be loving but neat. 1928 Bridges *Mem. H. Bradley* 19 Wherever I can I shall let him speak for himself, and..group the quotations from his letters under subjects...This first Collins will serve to prelude them.

Collision. 4. Add: **collision door,** on board ship, a door to be closed after a collision, in order to cut off the inflowing water; **collision net,** a steel net used to support a damaged boat while it is being brought into port; **collision-proof** *a.*, of a railway carriage or train, capable of withstanding the shock of collision; **collision quarters, stations,** positions to be taken up by the passengers and crew of a ship in the event of collision.

1895 *Daily News* 7 Jan. 8/1 Finding the water penetrating, ..the chief engineer at once ordered the *collision doors to be closed. 1897 *Ibid.* 27 Apr. 7/6 The gunboat..was kept afloat by means of *collision nets and brought into harbour. 1906 *Daily Chron.* 18 Aug. 2/6 *Collision-proof railway cars. 1909 *Ibid.* 21 June 1/1 The call to '*collision quarters' was ..quickly..performed. 1908 *Westm. Gaz.* 31 July 2/1 Drills ..such as Fire and *Collision stations.

Co·llodio-bro·mide. *Photogr.* An emulsion of collodion with bromide of silver used for collodion dry plates.

1873 Spon *Workshop Rec.* 266 Collodio-Bromide Process. 1892 *Photogr. Ann.* II. 61 A Collodio-bromide Emulsion. 1899 *Westm. Gaz.* 20 May 4/3 Mr. William Blanshard Bolton..worked out and published the collodio-bromide process of photography. In 1874 his process was perfected, and became the universal method of working collodion dry-plates.

Collograph (kǫ·lǒgraf). [f. Gr. κόλλα glue: see -graph.] **a.** A manifold copying apparatus. **b.** A photomechanical print made by **Collography** (kǫlǫ·grăfi), the process or art of printing from a film of gelatine, esp. by the heliotype or collotype process. Hence **Collographic** (kǫlǒgræ·fik) *a.*

1871 *Nature* III. 188/1 Edwards's collographic method. 1882 *Spons' Encycl. Industr. Arts* v. 1609 Pumphrey's 'collograph' depends on the fact that when a film of moist bichromated gelatine is brought into contact with ferrous salts..the gelatine is so far altered as to acquire the property of attracting a fatty ink. 1891 *Anthony's Photogr. Bull.* IV. 296 A demonstration..of collography. *Ibid.* 417 Numerous collographic printing experiments have been made with parchment paper watered with bichromatized gelatine.

Collophore (kǫ·lǒfōəɹ). *Ent.* [f. Gr. κόλλα glue + -φορος bearing, -phore.] The ventral tube of the *Collembola.*

1903 *Knowledge* Nov. 260/2 Ventral view of *P[odura] aquatica*, showing the mouth, the collophore, and the 'spring' in its normal position.

Colloquian (kǫlōu·kwiăn). *U.S.* [f. Colloquy *sb.* 1.] (See quot.)

1871 G. R. Cutting *Student Life at Amherst Coll.* 40 For the Exhibition..the colloquians of each society unite in the composition of an original 'colloquy'.

Collotyped (kǫ·lǒtəipt), *ppl. a.* [f. Collotype + -ed.] Made by the collotype process.

1893 *Athenæum* 3 June 702/3 The collotyped reproduction of the ancient Yasna MS...is in the binder's hands.

Collotypist (kǫ·lǒtəipist). [f. Collotype + -ist.] A maker of collotypes.

1890 C. T. Chesterman in *Year Bk. Photogr.* 146, I presume that collotypists use stripped collodion or film negatives.

Collotypy (kǫ·lǒtəipi). [f. Collotype + -y[3].] The collotype process.

1896 [cf. *chromo-collotypy* s.v. *Chromo-]. 1911 Webster.

Collywobbles (kǫ·liwǫb'lz). [Fantastic formation on Colic and Wobble.] A disordered state of the stomach characterized by rumbling in the intestines; diarrhœa with stomach-ache; hence *gen.* indisposition. (In quot. 1853 used nonsensically.)

1841 Alb. Smith in *Punch* 9 Oct. 154/1 To..keep him from getting the collywobbles in his pandenoodles. 1853 'C. Bede' *Verdant Green* I. viii, A touch of the mulligrubs in your collywobbles? 1901 F. T. Bullen *Sack of Shakings* 308 He laughingly excused himself on the ground that his songs were calculated to give a white man collywobbles.

Colo- (kōu·lo), combining form of L. *colon* or Gr. κόλον, see Colon[1], used in scientific terms, as **colo-colic** *a.*, relating to two portions of the colon; **colo-enteritis,** inflammation of the small intestine and colon (Dorland), etc. See also *Colopexy, *Coloplasty, *Coloplication.

1903 *Therapeutic Gaz.* 15 Feb. 102 (Cent. D. Suppl.) An anastomosis is indicated, either colo-colic or ileo-sigmoid.

Colobus (kǫ·lǒbǒs). [mod.L., ad. Gr. κολοβός docked.] A genus of African monkeys, the members of which have short but distinct thumbs; also, a monkey of this genus, more explicitly *colobus monkey.*

1885 Hartmann *Anthrop. Apes* 286 Fossil remains of the African stumpy ape (*Colobus*) have also been found at Steinheim. 1889 Sir J. C. Willoughby *East Africa & its Big Game* 175 The beautiful black and white Colobus monkeys. 1898 *Daily News* 8 Sept. 5/1 Colobus..having only rudimentary cheek pouches. 1899 *Westm. Gaz.* 1 Apr. 2/1 The Colobus resembles a black judge with a white wig and a mantle of flowing hair of the same hue. 1904 *Ibid.* 1 Dec. 4/2 Beards as white as the beard of a colobus monkey.

Colometric (kōulǒme·trik), *a.* [f. Colometry + -ic.] **1.** Characterized by colometry. So **Colome·trically** *adv.*

1901 F. G. Kenyon *Handbk. Text. Crit. N.T.* viii. 308 The δ-text..exists quite definitely in the Graeco-Latin group of uncials.., all of which have been traced..to a common ancestor, written colometrically. 1907 A. H. M'Neile *Introd. N.T.* 143 *note*, The colometric arrangement in D suddenly ceases at xvi. 23.

2. *Astr.* *Colometric scale* (see quot.).

1928 J. H. Jeans *Astron. & Cosmog.* 42 A..scale of stellar magnitudes must be mentioned, namely, the Colometric scale, which measures the total radiation emitted by a star.

Colonel, *sb.* Add:

1. c. *The Colonel* = *Colonel Bogey* (see *Bogey).

1900 *Westm. Gaz.* 3 July 3/2 It [*sc.* the Royal and Ancient] leaves competitions against the 'Colonel' severely alone.

Colonial, *a.* Add:

1. (Earlier U.S. examples.)

1776 (Feb. 20) in *Remembrancer* (1777) III. 226 Their endeavours to preserve their colonial constitution. 1776 *Boston Town Rec.* 26 Aug., How many Persons belonging to this Family are now in the Service? Is it Continental, or Colonial? *Ibid.*, Any military Commission in the Continental or Colonial Army.

b. Belonging to, or characteristic of, the period of the colonies, esp. of architecture or furniture. *U.S.*

1886 *Harper's Mag.* Oct. 668/1 The building has rather a colonial character with its long corridors and pillared piazzas.

c. Dealing in produce of colonial origin.

1895 *Home & Colonial Stores Ltd. Prospectus*, The well-known business of The Home and Colonial Stores, which has experienced an uninterrupted and highly successful development since its establishment in 1888. 1928 *Daily Mail* 25 July 18/1 Colonial Merchants.

B. *sb.* **3.** *U.S.*

1900 H. Lawson *Over Sliprails* 70 'Wal, I reckon you can build me your national drink. I guess I'll try it.' A long colonial was drawn for him.

4. A member of a labour colony: see quot.

1906 *Westm. Gaz.* 20 July 3/1 It was a case of once a 'colonial' always 'a colonial,' as the man employed on relief works is called.

C. *attrib.* and *Comb.*, and special collocations, as *colonial-born, -manufactured* adjs.; **colonial experience man,** etc. (Australia), a man sent out from England to Australia to gain colonial experience; **colonial goose** (see quot.).

1900 *Daily News* 7 Mar. 5/5 *Colonial-born men led the rebels. 1890 'R. Boldrewood' *Col. Reformer* x, You're the first '*colonial experience' young fellow that it ever occurred to. 1891 *Argus* (Melbourne) 7 Nov. 13/5 They were colonial experience men. 1898 Morris *Austral Eng.*, **Colonial Goose*, a boned leg of mutton stuffed with sage and onions. 1906 *Westm. Gaz.* 15 Jan. 15/3 *Colonial-manufactured furniture is merely put together in Capetown.

Colonic (kōulǫ·nik), *a.* [f. Colon[1] + -ic.] Of or pertaining to the colon; affecting the colon; colic.

1906 *Practitioner* Dec. 812 The colonic distension and tympanites, associated with the colic. 1929 Doolin in *Irish Jrnl. Med. Sci.* Apr. 184 Colonic necrosis following the administration of avertin.

Colonist. Add:

3. A voter placed in a certain locality for the purposes of an election. *U.S. politics.* Cf. *Colonization 2, *Colonize *v.* 4.

1909 *Daily Chron.* 3 Nov. 1/6 It is more than likely that thousands of their 'colonists' have voted in some of the districts.

4. A member of a labour colony.

1896 J. A. Hobson *Probl. Unempl.* 137 About one half of the colonists seek temporary relief, the rest loaf round from colony to colony. 1904 *Daily Chron.* 5 Oct. 4/5 The colonist at Merxplas may earn from 1d. to 3d. a day.

Colonization. Add:

2. The action of placing political supporters where their votes will be important. *U.S. politics.*

1842 *Congress. Globe* 31 May, App. 471/1 Among these [*sc.* modern phrases describing political knavery] 'colonization' and 'pipe-laying' were the most significant.

Coloniza·tionism. *U.S.* [f. Colonization + -ism.] The principles of colonizationists.

1831 *Liberator* 29 Oct. I. 174 Some fair and able..advocate of Colonization-ism. 1832 in *Life W. L. Garrison* (1885) I. 327 Here I am now in the hot-bed of Colonizationism.

Colonizationist. *U.S.* (Earlier examples.)

1831 W. L. Garrison in *Life* (1885) I. 261, I am truly rejoiced to learn that you are no colonizationist. 1834 *Southern Lit. Messenger* I. 87 Tappan has two brothers in Boston, both ardent colonizationists.

Colonize, *v.* Add:

1. b. To occupy (land) as a bona-fide settler. *U.S.*

1909 S. E. White *Rules of Game* v. xix, It appears as though the lands were 'colonized'. *Ibid.* xxiv, They believe that we did actually colonize the lands.

4. *U.S. politics.* (See quot. 1889.)

1842 *Congress. Globe* 31 May, App. 471/1 So far as he was informed, the practice of colonizing had its origin, as connected with the elections of the people in our country in the city of New York. 1889 *Century Dict.*, *Colonize* v. 4 To place or settle for the time being in a voting-precinct so as to be able to vote at an election: as to colonize voters. 1903 *N.Y. Tribune* 13 Sept., The attempt to colonize in the Third Ward by a faction of the Democratic party was frustrated to-day.

Colonizer. Add: (Earlier U.S. example.)

1781 S. Peters *Hist. Connecticut* 25, I have given the Reader some idea of the first colonizers of Connecticut.

2. One who colonizes voters. *U.S. politics.*

1904 *N.Y. Even. Post* 7 Nov. 1 The superintendent of elections is authority for the statement that there are gangs of colonizers and repeaters in the city.

Colonoscope (kōu·lǫnǒskoup). [f. Colon[1] + -scope.] A speculum for the surgical examination of the colon.

1884 C. B. Kelsey *Dis. Rectum & Anus* iii. 76 Colonoscope of Bodenhamer.

Colony, *sb.* Add:

5. c. An establishment in which persons are engaged to work who are otherwise unemployed or unemployable, or are trained for some occupation or trade.

1888 *Charity Organ. Rev.* Jan. 43 The Council would gladly see an experiment made in the form of a Labour Colony, to which unemployed townspeople might be sent for a time, and where they would be employed with a view to undertaking labouring work in a colony. 1896 J. A. Hobson *Probl. Unempl.* 131 The proposals for the establishment of farm colonies and other labour colonies. Various colonies of different types where the labour is chiefly employed in cultivation of the land exist already in England or on the continent. *Ibid.*, Several penal colonies for convicted beggars and loafers exist in Belgium and Holland. 1897 *Encycl. Soc. Reform* 785 The experiment of the Home Colonization Society, in Westmoreland, is the most direct attempt to establish in England a labor colony by voluntary effort on similar lines to those adopted in Holland. The object of the society is to provide work in English 'industrial villages' for the able-bodied poor.

9. (Earlier and later Amer. examples.)

1637 T. Morton *New English Canaan* (1883) 342 Like the Colony servant in Virginia. 1661 *Providence Rec.* (1893) II. 138 Colony prison. 1733 *Connect. Col. Rec.* VII. 461 Colony treasurer. 1857 E. Stone *Life Howland* i. 33 Repairs of bridges on the great colony road. *Ibid.*, The distinction of colony roads and town roads should cease.

Colopexy (kōu·lǒpeksi, kōulǒpe·ksi). *Surg.* [ad. mod.L. *colopexia*, f. Gr. κόλον Colon[1] + πῆξις a fixing.] The operation of fixing the sigmoid flexure to the abdominal wall.

1908 *Practitioner* Sept. 459 Colopexy or colostomy may lead to a cure.

Colophon. Add: **3.** = Imprint *sb.* 3. *U.S.*

1930 *Publishers' Weekly* 19 Apr. 2113/1 The publishers must cut their lists and have their colophons stand for a particular quality which, in time, the bookseller will recognize and consider in his buying.

Coloplasty (kōu·lǒplæsti). *Surg.* [f. *Colo- + Gr. πλαστός moulded, formed: see -plasty.] A plastic operation on the colon.

1908 *Practitioner* Sept. 461 Neither coliplication nor coloplasty is likely to produce much permanent benefit.

Coloplication (kou:lǒplikēi·ʃən). *Surg.* Also **coli-.** [f. *Colo- + Plication.] 'The operation of unfolding or taking a reef in the colon in cases of dilatation' (Dorland).

1908 *Practitioner* Sept. 461 Entero-anastomosis and coliplication had proved failures.

Colorado. (Earlier U.S. example.)

1871 *Trans. Ill. Agric. Soc.* VIII. 174 The same remedy that answers for destroying the Colorado Potato beetle (Paris Green) would probably destroy the Currant worm.

Colorative (kǫ·l-, kv·lǒrĕtiv), *a.* [f. L. *colōrāt-*, ppl. stem of *colōrāre* to colour, give colour to: see -ative.] Depending upon coloration.

1905 *Westm. Gaz.* 11 Mar. 4/2 The dingy greyness of its coat affords it a good colorative protection. 1922 *Glasgow Herald* 21 Jan. 7 Its exquisite colorative distinction.

Coloratura (koloratū·ra). [It., f. L. *colōrāt-*, *colōrāre* to Colour; see -ure. Cf. Colorature.] 'Divisions, runs, trills, cadenzas, and other florid passages in vocal music' (Stainer & Barrett, 1876). Also *attrib.*

1902 *Westm. Gaz.* 30 Oct. 2/3 Rivalling a Melba in the ease and certainty of his coloratura. 1920 *Ibid.* 21 June 6/1 A famous American coloratura soprano. 1930 *Punch* 2 Apr. 387/1, I now know..that every Polish lady..was mistress of the purest *coloratura*, and could release it at a moment's notice or less without so much as a glance at any conductor.

Colossal, *a.* Add: **c.** Stupendous, 'immense'. *colloq.* (Cf. F. *colossal*, G. *kolossal*.)

1897 Mary Kingsley *W. Africa* 89 Being such a colossal ass as to come fooling about in mangrove swamps.

Colostomy (kou̇lǫ·stǒmi). *Surg.* [f. Gr. κόλον Colon[1] + στόμα mouth + -y[3].] The operation of making an artificial opening in the colon.

1903 *Med. Record* 11 July 71 (Cent. D. Suppl.). 1908 *Practitioner* Sept. 460 Colotomy was performed in one case and colostomy in another, both were followed by death.

Colour, *sb.* Add:

2. c. (Earlier U.S. example.)

1788 *Mass. Centinel* 30 July 155/3 'It is a very dark night', says Cato, to one of his brethren of colour.

3. c. See Off colour.

4. c. *Typogr.* The (relative) blackness of printed type.

1808 Stower *Printer's Grammar* vii. 211 It is a rule with careful pressmen, not to give proofs a high colour. 1888 J. Southward in *Encycl. Brit.* XXIII. 710/1 Comparing the old face and the modern characters, the latter are more regular in size, lining, setting, and colour. 1898 — *Mod. Printing* (1910) I. xxii. 141 The proportion of the thick to the thin strokes constitutes what typefounders call the colour of the letter.

6. c. *pl.* The distinctive colours of a school, college, club, etc., team, crew, or the like, as conferred to denote selection as a representative member; esp. in *to get* or *give* one's *colours*.

1896 *Westm. Gaz.* 11 May 4/1 Since the reduction..of the number and variety of colours to be given, interest in games ..has deteriorated...'To get his colours' is an ambition which every boy should look forward to.

7. e. *spec.* *U.S.* (See quot.)

1891 H. Patterson *Illustr. Naut. Dict.* 352 Colors, the national ensign. In port colors are made at 8 a.m. and

hauled down at sunset. When at sea colors are shown upon falling in with another vessel.

f. *pl.* A salute to the flag. *U.S.*

1921 WEBSTER, *Color* 8. pl. *U.S. Navy.* A salute to the flag accompanied by music at 8 A.M. and sunset, at hoisting and lowering it.

8. b. *Glass-painting.* (See quot.)

1914 *Jrnl. Royal Soc. Arts* May 568 The composition of the vitreous 'enamel brown', or 'colour', as it is termed by glass-painters, with which the outlines, tones, and shadows in a glass-painting are produced.

18. colour book, a book with illustrations in colour; **colour-cell**, a cell in animal tissue containing colouring matter, a pigment-cell; **colour-change**, the change in the colour of its coat, skin, etc. to be in accord with its surroundings, made by a beast, bird, etc., by protective instinct; **colour disk**, a disk with a series of colours arranged in sectors; also each of the disks of a separate colour used with a colour-mixer; **colour doctor** *Calico-printing* (see quots.); **colour dusting**, the application of finely ground colours to ware by means of a wad of cotton-wool; hence **colour duster**, a worker who performs this operation; **colour-fast** *a.*, dyed in unfadable colours; **colour-filter** *Photogr.*, a filter consisting of tinted gelatine or collodion on glass, or tinted water between two sheets of glass, adapted to prevent the passage of certain coloured rays and allow the passage of others; **colour-index** (*a*) *Path.*, the relative amount of colouring matter contained in a red blood-corpuscle; (*b*) *Astron.* (see quot. 1921); **colour-mixer**, any instrument of the revolving disk type used for combining colours in experimental psychophysics; **colour organ** (see quots.); **colour pan**, a pan in which a colour and its thickener are mixed and incorporated in calico-printing; **colour-photography**, the art of producing photographs in natural colours; **colour-roller** *Calico-printing*, a roller that revolves in the colour-box and carries the colour to the printing-roller, against which it presses; **colour scheme**, (*a*) an arrangement of colours following a thought-out design, e.g. in furnishing or decorating an apartment or in planting a flower garden; (*b*) a scheme of protective coloration (of animals or birds); **colour screen**, a plate of coloured glass or the like used as a screen to absorb certain rays of light while allowing others to pass; **colour-sensitive** *a.*, of photographic emulsion, plates, etc., sensitized for photographing in colours; hence *colour-sensitiveness*; **colour service** *Mil.*, service 'with the colours' as distinguished from 'on the reserve'; **colour-tone**, (*a*) a tone of colour; (*b*) *Art*, gradation and harmony of colour; (*c*) *Psychol.*, the colour quality of a coloured impression; chroma or hue as distinguished from brightness and saturation (*Cent. Dict.* Suppl. 1909); **colour value**, value with reference to a colour scheme; also *transf.*; **colour-wash**, coloured distemper (see DISTEMPER *sb.*[2] 2); **colour-wash** *v.*, to wash with coloured distemper; **colour-weak** *a.*, unable to distinguish colours at a low degree of intensity; hence *colour-weakness*; **colour-wheel** = **colour-mixer.*

1904 *Daily Chron.* 20 Apr. 3/5 A *colour book, as the term has now become, about the Channel Islands, is appearing. 1874 GARROD & BAXTER *Mat. Med.* 398 Those of the true sac exhibit distinct, regular *colour-cells. 1904 *Westm. Gaz.* 21 Sept. 10/1 The *colour-change [of the stoat] is fairly frequent in the Northern counties. 1873 E. ATKINSON tr. *Helmholtz's Pop. Lect. Sci. Subjects* Ser. I. vi. 244 It is in fact the same [series of colours] which we described as arranged around the circumference of the *colour-disc. 1839 URE *Dict. Arts* 217 A sharp-edged ruler of gun-metal or steel, called the *colour doctor. 1876 *Encycl. Brit.* IV. 685/1 The colour doctor..fits closely to the surface of the roller, and removes all colour except that which fills the engraved portions. 1900 *Daily News* 22 Feb. 7/4 [A] *colour duster. *Ibid.*, The magistrate remarked on the undesirability of permitting *colour dusting to be carried on in the printing shop. 1928 *Observer* 1 Apr. 13 Shrinkproof, stretchproof and *colourfast. 1900 *Jrnl. Soc. Arts* 7 Sept. 774/1 The permanency of a dye on a cotton fabric is of little use as an indication of its permanence in a sealed *colour filter. 1902 *Encycl. Brit.* XXXII. 16/2 Different makes of plates demand different colour-filters. 1908 *Practitioner* Aug. 323 Generally the fewer the red corpuscles, the higher is the *colour index. 1921 *Discovery* Feb. 38/1 The difference between the photographic and the visual magnitude of a star is therefore due to the colour of the star, and is called the colour-index. 1881 *Cassell's Fam. Mag.* 690/2 The different colours of the spectrum form a scale of light which has often been compared to the musical scale, and the idea has recently taken shape in what has been termed a *colour-organ. 1895 *Oracle Encycl.* II. 119 s.v. *Colour*, A 'Colour Organ' has been invented, which casts combinations of colour upon a screen somewhat on the same principle as a musical organ discharges sounds. 1860 *Ure's Dict. Arts* (ed. 5) I. 519 Down one side [of the colour-house] is fixed a range of *colour-pans. 1876 *Encycl. Brit.* IV. 685/2 The mordant..and its appropriate thickeners are placed in a range of colour pans, in which the materials are thoroughly incorporated. 1872 *Jrnl. Chem. Soc.* XXV. 30 The colours obtained in so-called *colour-photography. 1885 *Encycl. Brit.* XVIII. 834/2 In 1841..Robert Hunt published some results of colour-photography by means of fluoride of silver. 1890 W. J. GORDON *Foundry* 168 Between the *colour-roller and the calico is a thin strip of steel which scrapes the printing-roller free of cotton. 1921 GERTRUDE JEKYLL (*title*) *Colour Schemes for the Flower Garden. 1925 R. W. G. HINGSTON in E. F. Norton *Fight for Everest, 1924* 265 They are well able to defend themselves and thus have no need of a special *colour scheme. 1925 WARWICK DEEPING *Sorrell & Son* viii, The various colour schemes were of Roland's own planning. 1890 WOODBURY *Encycl. Photogr.* 479 To use a *colour screen of yellow glass behind the lens. *Ibid.* 163 *Colour-sensitive Plates. 1907 *Westm. Gaz.* 20 Sept. 4/3 Photographic colour-sensitive emulsion. 1909 *Ibid.* 17 Apr. 14/2 Colour-sensitive plates. 1888 ABNEY *Instruction Photogr.* (ed. 8) 233 That *colour sensitiveness can be given to a gelatine plate by coating it with either varnish or collodion in which various sensitive dyes are dissolved. 1909 C. E. K. MEES *Photogr. Col. Obj.* (1916) 37 The correcting action of such weak filters increases with the colour-sensitiveness of the plate, while the more colour-sensitive the plate the lower the multiplying factor of the filter. 1892 *Pall Mall Gaz.* 25 Feb. 6/2 Men..who have been transferred to the Reserve..should be allowed..to return to complete twelve years' *Colour service. 1875 tr. *Vogel's Chem. Light* vii. 60 The small number of *colour-tones compared with the large number of musical tones. 1896 *Westm. Gaz.* 18 Nov. 7/3 New designs produced in three styles of colour-tone, and black and white. 1904 *Burlington Mag.* V. 52/2 'The most important part of colour-tone atmosphere', Millet was fond of saying, 'can be perfectly rendered in black and white'. 1907 *Westm. Gaz.* 13 Sept. 2/1 Scarlet hips..a flaming colour-tone in the grey-green of the fading hedgerow. 1900 W. ROBINSON *Eng. Flower Garden* 196 The Carnation..has a fine *colour-value of foliage in winter. 1930 *Time & Tide* 7 June 744 Music is now moving towards a phase in which 'colour values' will be the principal means of expression. 1887 *Daily News* 29 June 5/8 *Colour-washed in several shades of pale grey and chocolate. 1905 HOLMAN HUNT *Pre-Raphaelitism* I. 114 The white-washing and colour-washing still not being completed. 1925 *Contemp. Rev.* Oct. 461 The bridegroom..glazes the windows and colour-washes the walls. 1925 R. M. OGDEN tr. *Koffka's Growth of Mind* 268 Being '*colour-weak', I see red and green only under favourable conditions. 1909 *Cent. Dict.* Suppl., *Color-weakness. 1895 *Funk's Standard Dict.*, *Color-wheel. 1925 R. M. OGDEN tr. *Koffka's Growth of Mind* 62 Rotating disk, or colour-wheel, half white and half black.

Colourant, var. form of COLORANT.

1916 F. B. WADE *Diamonds* 3 Iron as a colourant commonly produces yellow or brown in minerals.

Colouration: see COLORATION.

Colourful, *a.* Delete *rare* and add earlier and later examples of lit. and fig. uses.

1889 HISSEY *Tour in a Phaeton* 273 The distance then is delightfully distinct and colourful. 1905 *Century Mag.* Aug. 493/2 The English background lacks the gay and colorful beauty of our panoramic regattas. 1908 D. W. M. READ *Highways Hampshire* Pref., Hampshire, to me, is a bundle of memories, all colourful. 1908 *Daily Chron.* 23 Oct. 4/4 The gay, colourful city. 1911 J. LONDON *Adventure* viii, It is colourful life, to say the least. 1922 ZANE GREY *To the Last Man* x. 220 The morning was..colourful, and her mood was pensive, wistful, dreamy.

Hence **Co·lourfully** *adv.*, **-fulness.**

1921 J. F. PORTE *Elgar* 90 The opening theme appears vigorously in the trombones, the whole being colourfully treated. 1921 *Chambers's Jrnl.* 819/1 The play of Kismet, so colourfully produced. 1921 *Glasgow Herald* 7 Mar. 10 The imposing colourfulness of the mise-en-scène. 1928 *Observer* 24 June 8 So..movingly and colourfully does he tell his tale.

Colouring, *vbl. sb.* Add: **1. d.** *spec.* (See quot.)

1886 C. SCOTT *Sheep-farming* 172 Colouring is the art of painting the wool on the sheep's back.

4. *attrib.*: **colouring-wheel** *Tanning*, a revolving machine containing a colouring liquid in which skins are coloured.

1903 FLEMMING *Pract. Tanning* 179 The hides are put into clean cold water..and then into a coloring wheel, with a liquor of about twenty per cent. cutch or catechu.

Co·lourizer. [f. COLO(U)RIZE *v.* + -ER[1].] A colouring agent.

1880 *Libr. Univ. Knowl.* (N.Y.) VII. 430 The hematine not being able to perform the functions of a colorizer and oxygen-carrier alone.

Colourtype, colortype (kʌ·ləɹtəip). [f. COLOUR *sb.* + TYPE *sb.*] *Colourtype process*, a process for the reproduction of works of art in colour by the use of three-colour blocks. Also called the *three-colour process.*

1899 *Daily News* 24 Apr. 4/2 The three-colour process, called 'colortype'. 1900 *Westm. Gaz.* 27 Sept. 10/2 The Carl Hentschel Colortype process. 1904 *Ibid.* 24 Sept. 13/1 Illustrations faultlessly reproduced by the interesting Hentschel's colourtype process.

Coloury, *a.* **2.** Add: Also applied to a grade of tobacco. *U.S.*

1900 WHITNEY & FLOYD in *Yearbk. U.S. Dept. Agric.* 435 These tobaccos are used exclusively for pipe-smoking and cigarettes, the following grades being made by the packers: Fine yellow, medium bright, good ordinary 'colory', fine red.

Colpo- (kǫlpo), also *colp-* before a vowel, comb. form of Gr. κόλπος womb, used = vagina in terms of *Path.*, *Surg.*, and *Anat.*; as *colpalgia, -perinæorrhaphy, -rrhaphy, -stenosis, -tomy.*

1908 *Practitioner* Dec. 807 He subsequently performs a posterior *colpo-perinæorrhaphy. 1902 *Brit. Med. Jrnl.* 11 Oct. 1147/1, I now prefer bilateral *colporrhaphy to anterior and posterior colporrhaphy. 1905 *Brit. Gyn. Jrnl.* XXI. 75 Value of *Colpotomy in the Thrombotic Form of Puerperal Fever.

Colport (kǫlpōᵊɹt), *v.* [Back-formation from COLPORTEUR.] *intr.* To work as a colporteur. Also *trans.*

1888 *Centen. Confer. Missions* II. 337 Grants [of books] for distribution to those who want to colport. 1889 STEVENSON & OSBOURNE *Wrong Box* xvi, You don't mean to insinuate that thing I..colported with my own hands, was the body of a total stranger?

Colt, *sb.*[2] [The name of the inventor, Samuel *Colt* (1814–1862).] *Colt's revolver*, a type of repeating pistol invented and manufactured by Colt (patented 1835). Also *ellipt.*, as *Colt* or *Colt's.*

1852 E. G. SQUIER *Nicaragua* II. 92, I made a mental resolve..to appeal to my 'Colt', before admitting any too familiar approaches. 1854 J. R. BARTLETT *Personal Narrative* I. ii. 19 All were provided with rifles or carbines, and many of the cavalry with Colt's revolvers. 1855 *Knickerbocker Mag.* XLV. 190 John just then handing me my 'Colt's'..I dashed over the picket. 1881 A. A. HAYES *New Colorado* xiii. 177 'What kind of shooting-iron have you?' he asked. 'Navy Colt?' 1907 GREENER *Gun* (ed. 8) 517 The automatic Colt or 'Browning' pistol, is made in five different models..The magazine capacity is seven shots, and after its insertion in the handle the slide is drawn once to the rear by hand. 1908 MULFORD *Orphan* xi. 137 'That's enough, Sheriff', said Tex, moving cautiously forward behind his levelled Colt. 1911 J. LONDON *Adventure* v. 65 A woman qualified to wear a Baden-Powell and a long-barrelled Colt's. 1912 *Field* 28 Sept. 655/1 The Colt Automatic ·450 Pistol.

Coltskin (kōᵘ·ltskin). [f. COLT *sb.*[1] + SKIN *sb.*] Leather made from the skin of a colt.

1903 FLEMMING *Pract. Tanning* 397 Horsehides and coltskins are soaked..and washed in the usual manner.

Colt's tail. Add: **3.** *U.S.* (See quot.)

1829 *Massachusetts Spy* 13 May (Th.) It has been the uniform custom, at our courts, to break in the new members of every Grand Jury, by requiring them to pay what is called a colt's tail—or in other words a treat.

Colulus (kǫ·liŭlǒs). *Ent.* [mod.L., dim. of *colus* distaff.] A sclerite at the base of and between the front spinnerets in many spiders.

1904 *Ann. & Mag. Nat. Hist.* Jan. 65 The well-developed colulus, front spinnerets close together [etc.] show them to belong to M. Simon's group Cybæeæ. 1912 COMSTOCK *Spider Bk.* 136.

Columban (kǫlʌ·mbăn), *a.* and *sb.* [f. *Columba* + -AN.] **A.** *adj.* Of, pertaining to, or characteristic of St. Columba and his followers. **B.** *sb.* A disciple of St. Columba.

1879 *Dublin Rev.* Oct. 271 The Columban monastic bodies. *Ibid.* 273 The expulsion of the Columbans from Pictish territory. 1920 in H. F. Henderson *Relig. in Scot.* iii. 76 Hither resorted the young men..to..study the discipline of the Columban Church.

Columbian, *a.* and *sb.* **A.** *adj.* (Earlier and later U.S. examples.)

1784 FRENEAU *Poems* (1809) II. 197 Who would be sad, to leave a sultry clime, Where true Columbian virtue is a crime. 1809 FESSENDEN *Pills Poetical* 1 A State Physician most profound That ever trod Columbian ground.

B. *sb.* An American.

a 1793 FRENEAU *Poems* (1809) I. 256, Where Irish and English, Columbians and Dutch Had agreed to lie down, without quarrels or feuds. 1797 *Spirit of Farmers' Museum* (1801) 75 Bid each Columbian's mind, First love its country, then embrace mankind. 1806 FESSENDEN *Democracy Unveiled* II. 158 Let each Columbian hide his face And blush to own his native place.

Column, *sb.* Add:

8. esp. with qualifying phrase.

1885 *Encycl. Brit.* XIX. 34/2 This is termed the 'posterior vesicular column', or 'Clarke's column', after the late Mr. Lockhart Clarke, who did much to unravel the intricate anatomy of the nerve-centres. 1906 *Practitioner* Dec. 844 The columns of Morgagni are permanent vertical folds of the mucous membrane of the anal canal. 1907 *Ibid.* June 859 The postero-lateral column of Burdach. *Ibid.*, The postero-mesial column of Goll.

10. Phr. *To dodge the column* (see quot.).

1919 *War Terms* in *Athenæum* 1 Aug. 695/2 'To dodge the column' is to shirk one's duty.

b. *Column of route*: see ROUTE *sb.* 3 c.

c. *transf.* A body or party.

1906 *Forum* Apr. 448 The resulting dissatisfaction would be sufficient to throw Michigan..and possibly one or two other States into the Democratic column.

12. column man (*a*) see quot. 1899; (*b*) *pl.*, troops marching in column.

1898 *Daily News* 1 Aug. 5/6 He bade the column-men give him space to pass. 1899 *Ibid.* 6 Mar. 8/5 Sir Edward Grey sprang, upon the Fashoda crisis, into 'a column man', otherwise he is a 200-word speaker.

Columnal (kǫlʌ·mnăl), *sb.* [subst. use of COLUMNAL *a.*] A segment or joint of the stem of a crinoid.

1892 F. A. BATHER in *Ann. & Mag. Nat. Hist.* Ser. VI. IX. 212 Columnals rather low and alternating in thickness and height. 1914 *Brit. Mus. Return* 212 Two fragments of the 'shell-bed' with Crinoid columnals from the Lower Coal Measures.

Columnist (kǫ·ləmist, kǫ·liŭmist). *U.S.* [f. COLUMN *sb.* 4.] A writer for the newspaper press.

1920 *Blackw. Mag.* Aug. 146/1 The 'colyumist' of a New York paper. 1925 *Lit. Digest* (N.Y.) 27 June 27/2 Here is a Vashti leading the oppressed columnist into the promised land of intellectual liberty. 1926 *Spectator* 24 Apr. 770/1 One of the best known 'columnists' of the American press. 1930 *Publishers' Weekly* 1 Mar. 1063 Dorothy Herzog is a Hollywood columnist.

Colymbiform (kǫli·mbifǫɹm), *a.* *Ornith.* [f. Gr. κολυμβίς, -ιδ- diver (bird) + -FORM.] Having the characteristics of or resembling the *Colymbidæ*, or a member of this family.

1894 NEWTON *Dict. Birds* 651 Probably more or less closely allied to this genus [*sc. Hesperornis*] was the much smaller Colymbiform bird from the Cambridge Greensand.

Comacine (kōᵘ·măsəin), *a.* and *sb.* [ad. It. *comacino*, app. ult. f. *Como* in Italy (see quot. 1899).] **A.** *adj.* *Comacine masters* [It. *maestri comacini*], a mediæval guild of Italian masons. **B.** *sb.* A mason or builder belonging to this guild.

1899 'L. SCOTT' *Cathedral Builders* 5 The origin of the name *Comacine Masters* has caused a great deal of argument amongst Italian writers new and old. Some think it merely a place-name referring to the island of Comacina, in Lake Lario or Como; others take a wider significance, and say it means not only the city of Como, but all the province, which was once a Roman colony of great extension. Others again, among whom is Grotius, suggest that it is not a place-name at all, but comes from the Teutonic word *Gemachin* or house-builders. As the Longobards afterwards called them in Italian *Maestri Casarii*, which means the same thing, there is perhaps something to be said for this hypothesis. *Ibid.* 9 Rome is..full of remains of what is now styled Comacine architecture. *Ibid.* 17 There is no certain proof that the Comacines were the veritable stock from which the pseudo-Freemasonry of the present day sprang. 1900 *Monthly Rev.* I. 103 The Comacine masters have their existence sufficiently proved by..the edict of Rotharis (dated 653). *Ibid.* 104 The collegiate and Comacine constitutions.

Comb, *sb.*[1] Add:

1. d. *fig.* The action or process of 'combing out' (see next, 6 b).

1916 *Even. News* 8 Nov. 1/4 The comb which is being applied at the moment to the police appears once again to have begun at the wrong end.

3. e. A cluster of banana or plantain fruits.

1852–93 *Judson's Burmese-Eng. Dict.* 358 A stalk or bunch of plantain fruit containing several combs.

6. e. (Earlier U.S. example.)

1845 J. J. HOOPER *Taking Census* i. 161 They'd come and set on the comb of the house.

9. comb-bar (see quot.); **comb-case** (later U.S. example); **comb escalator**, an *ESCALATOR in which the treads of the steps are fitted with ribs or ridges laid in the direction of travel, which ribs mesh with and pass below similar projections beneath the hoods which form the take-off and landing at top and bottom of the flight; **comb-foundation**, a thin sheet of beeswax, made to resemble the middle wall of honeycomb, placed in a hive for bees to build their comb upon; **comb-fringe** (see quot.); **comb-jelly**, a ctenophoran jelly-fish belonging to the genus *Cydippe.*

1904 *Technol. & Sci. Dict.* (ed. Goodchild & Tweney), *Comb-bar (Lace Manufac.), a very accurately shaped and finished bar of iron..upon which the 'comb leads' are screwed side by side. 1838 INGRAHAM *Burton* II. xii. 194 An oilcloth-covered *combcase..in keeping with the pin and needle cushion. 1882 *N. Y. Tribune* 16 Aug., *Comb foundation is one of the great aids in apiculture. 1884 W. GORDON STABLES *Our Friend the Dog* vii. 59 *Comb-fringe—The hair that droops or bangs down from the tail of a Setter. 1903 J. R. A. DAVIS *Nat. Hist. Animals* (1905) II. xiv. 155 A common British *Comb-Jelly, Cydippe,..which is rowed through the water by eight longitudinal rows of little paddles, which suggest by their appearance the teeth of a comb.

Comb, *v.*[1] Add:

4. b. To search or examine minutely. orig. *U.S. colloq.*

1904 'O. HENRY' *Cabbages & Kings* iv. 80 In Coralia Senor Goodwin himself led the searching party which combed that town as carefully as a woman combs her hair. 1913 MULFORD *Coming of Cassidy* ix. 138 Then, sweeping north, they combed the range to the northern line [for cattle]. 1927 *Daily Express* 23 July 10/6 Search for missing scientist. Plans for 'combing' a ten-mile radius. 1927 *Morn. Post* 19 Aug. 7 (N. Y. Corresp.) The Pacific Ocean between San Francisco and Hawaii is being combed to-day by aircraft and shipping for signs of the two 'planes.

6. Comb out. a. *trans.* To disentangle or arrange (the hair) with a comb; hence *fig.*, to separate or sort out.

1854 SURTEES *Handley Cr.* lv. (1901) II. 112 Forthwith the dandified Horatio began to comb out his words, and string altogether his sentences. 1855 [see 1 in Dict.]. 1888 BURGON *Lives 12 Gd. Men* II. v. 33 It was as if he had combed out his cares.

b. To clear out (men) for military service from civil employments.

1916 *Daily Mail* 1 Nov. 5/6 'Comb out the contractors' useless men,' said a farmer delegate. 1918 MRS. H. WARD *War & Elizabeth* vii, My two brothers are dead in France. I shall be 'combed' out directly. 1923 G. D. H. COLE *Workshop Organiz.* 28 The successive 'combings-out' of the munition works for further 'man-power' for the fighting forces.

c. = *4 b.

1917 'IAN HAY' *Carrying On* viii. 212 Fighting in the Redoubt itself had almost ceased, though a humorous sergeant, followed by acolytes bearing bombs, was still 'combing out' certain residential districts in the centre of the maze.

Combativity (kǫmbăti·vĭti, kǫm-). [-ITY. Probably coined to avoid the phrenological association of *combativeness.*] The quality or character of being combative.

1905 *Westm. Gaz.* 28 Jan. 8/3 He has less..uncompromising combativity than his predecessor. 1925 *Spectator* 5 Dec. 1019/2 The innate and eternal combativity of the human race.

Combies (kǫ·mbiz), *sb. pl.* Colloq. (nursery) abbrev. of *combinations* (COMBINATION 9).

1923 UNA L. SILBERRAD *Lett. Jean Armiter* iv. 81 I'm not wet to the combies; as you would seem to be. 1923 KATH. MANSFIELD *Doves' Nest, Mr. & Mrs. Williams*, Long-sleeved woven combies.

Combinability (kǫmbəinăbi·lĭti). The quality of being COMBINABLE.

1900 G. ILES *Flame, Electr. & Camera* 255 Chemical combinability.

Combination. Add:

9. = *combination lock* (see below).

a 1909 'O. HENRY' *Roads of Destiny* x. 170 She had then shot the bolts and turned the knob of the combination as she had seen Mr. Adams do. 1910 — *Rolling Stones* (1915) 113 The clerks in Bell's..whirled the combination of the safe..and left for their homes. 1924 MULFORD *Rustlers' Valley* iii. 25 Counting money and manipulating his combinations were two things the banker could do automatically...Glenn slowly closed the safe, automatically spun the combination knob.

b. (In full *motor-cycle combination.*) A motor-cycle with a side-car attached for the conveyance of a passenger or goods.

1914 *Motor Cycling* 12 May p. v, Both Chater Lea combinations ran perfectly throughout. 1919 *Bazaar, Exch. & Mart* 28 June Suppl. 11/1 Wanted, motor cycle combination. 1920 *Motor Cycle* 2 Dec., Advt. 33 The Calthorpe 2-Stroke Combination. 1928 *Even. News* 24 July 1/1 Here two foot police were standing on the bridge and two others were on a motor-cycle combination.

10. combination bolt, lock, one which can be opened only after a certain combination of movements has been performed; **combination car** *U.S.*, a railroad car designed to be used for more than one purpose; **combination suit** = *combination garment.*

1851 C. CIST *Cincinnati* 215 *Combination and detector bank lock. 1884 KNIGHT *Dict. Mech.* Suppl., *Combination lock.* 1. A bank or safe lock,..operated by two graduated dials, whereby one bolt, common to both, is controlled by either of the two independent dials. 2. A permutation lock. 1902 HARBEN *Abner Daniel* 272 Wilson..then reluctantly turned to the big iron safe against the wall...With his fat, pink hand on the silver-plated combination-bolt he turned to Miller again. 1903 C. T. BRADY *Bishop* xv. 277 We were the only passengers in the *combination-car—half-baggage, half-passenger. 1893 A. S. ECCLES *Sciatica* 38 The safest garments for the use of female patients is what is known as a '*combination suit'.

Combinative, *a.* Add:

3. *Phonology.* Applied to sound-changes which are effected through a combination of influences: opposed to *isolative.*

1888 SWEET *Hist. Engl. Sounds* 17.

Combing, *vbl. sb.* **3.** Add: **combing plate** (see quots.); **combing skin**, a long-woolled skin; a skin bearing long wool suitable for combing.

1886 *Encycl. Brit.* XX. 521/1 Fig. 1...Grinding surface of a..molar of Rhinoceros..12, crochet (posterior *combing plate). *Ibid.* 521/2 The middle sinus is often intersected by vertical laminæ ('combing plates') projecting into it. 1895 *Daily News* 10 May 9/3 Good *combing skins show ½d. to ¾d. per lb. advance; short-woolled skins rule about on a par with..last auction values.

Comble, *sb.* Delete †*Obs.* and add:

2. The 'crown' or culmination. [A gallicism.]

1903 FALKNER *Nebuly Coat* viii He added the comble to all his graces and courtesies by shaking her hand. 1908 *Daily Chron.* 1 May 4/7 The disgust of those who believe that there is an art of acting which is marred..by such..interruptions reaches its comble.

Comboloio (kǫmbǫlǒᵘ·yo). [mod.Gr. κομβολόγιον rosary.] A Mohammedan rosary of ninety-nine beads.

1813 BYRON *Br. Abydos* II. v, And by her comboloio lies A Koran of illumined dyes. 1830 GALT *Byron* xii. (ed. 3) 83 In his left hand he held a string of small coral beads, a comboloio which he twisted backwards and forwards.

Comb-out. [f. phr. *comb out*: see *COMB *v.*[1] 6.] An act of combing or clearing out.

1919 *Cassell's New Eng. Dict.* Suppl., *Comb-out* (slang), a thorough clearing out or clean sweep of men of military age in an office, works, etc. 1928 *News of the World* 29 Jan. 1/1 Chief-insp. Berrett, of Scotland Yard,..supervised a comb-out of all the motor-bandits.

Combretum (kǫmbrī·tǒm). [See COMBRETACEOUS.] Any shrub of the genus so named.

1929 F. W. H. MIGEOD in *Times* 19 Dec. 15/6 This same land [in Tanganyika Territory], risen 700 ft. above the sea, now bears only grass with small trees, included among which are combretums, acacias, euphorbias, [etc.].

Combustibly (kǫmbʌ·stibli), *adv.* Delete *Obs.* and add:

1852 MUNDY *Antipodes* (1857) 209 Which despatch fell like a bomb-shell among the combustibly-disposed public.

Combustion. Add: **2.** *Internal combustion engine*, etc.: see *INTERNAL.

6. combustion chamber, (*a*) a space behind a furnace in which the hot gases from a boiler-grate become consumed; (*b*) in an internal combustion engine, the space in or above the cylinder where the charge is compressed and ignited; also *attrib.*

1854 *English Mechanic* LXI. 271/1 The combustion chamber allows of the mixture of the gaseous products of the two fires. 1888 *Lockwood's Dict. Terms Mech. Engin.* 1908 *Westm. Gaz.* 1 Oct. 4/2 Carbon deposits from the piston or combustion-chamber walls.

Come, *v.* Add:

1. c. Phr. *Let 'em all come*: a formula expressing cheerful acceptance of the inevitable.

1896 in Ware *Passing Engl.* (1909). 1912 KIPLING *Diversity of Creatures* (1917) 40 'The rest will be coming along to-morrow.' 'Let 'em all come!' said Vincent.

2. d. Phr. *To have come to stay*: to be permanent.

1909 R. A. KNOX in *Isis* 18 Jan. 5/1 Milton has had his day; Darwin has come to stay. 1916 H. M. BANNISTER *Missale Gothicum* (1917) p. x, Misleading..titles..are very hard to abolish; they have come to stay and die hard. 1928 EARL OF CAVAN *Sp. in Ho. Lords* 28 Feb., I think it is quite obvious that mechanisation has come to stay.

9. b. In pres. pple., due or properly accruing *to* one; deservedly falling or happening. *U.S. colloq.*

1888 *Detroit Free Press* 5 May (Farmer) A half-dollar was coming to me in change. 1896 G. ADE *Artie* v. 45 You kind o' feel there's a crack comin' to him. *a* 1904 S. E. WHITE *Blazed Trail Stories* i. 16 Dicky Darrell's got it coming. 1911 R. D. SAUNDERS *Col. Todhunter* v. 77 Don't you worry about their not getting what's coming to them. 1914 GERTRUDE ATHERTON *Perch of Devil* i. 91, I do believe in a woman..gettin' all the admiration that's comin' to her. 1916 H. L. WILSON *Somewhere in Red Gap* ix. 375, I got the long night's rest that was coming to me and started out early.

13. b. Of utterance: To issue from the mouth or the pen.

1735 POPE *Prol. Sat.* 128, I lisp'd in numbers, for the numbers came. 1887 MORRIS *Odyss.* x. 246 But though for speech he was striving yet never a word would come.

c. To take (a required) shape.

1877 MRS. OLIPHANT *Young Musgrave* x, Mrs. Pennithorne..failed entirely with Mary's frock. It would not 'come' as she wanted it to come. 1896 *Daily News* 5 Nov. 7/1 The Venus was..too stunted, and when..the painter attempted to drape her, the result would not 'come' well.

14. b. Of seeds: To germinate when sown; hence, to grow.

1892 *Field* 7 May 665/3 The barley had come remarkably well, and had shot about an inch high.

19. b. *Come day, go day*: applied to the conduct or character of one who is content to let time pass by without effort or trouble. orig. *dial.*

1854 ANNE E. BAKER *Northampton. Gloss.* I. 175 It's come day, go day, with him. 1865 [see COME *v.* 26 d]. 1876 *Whitby Gloss.*, *Come day, Gan day, God send Sunday.* The saying put into the mouths of indolent workers, who care not how the days come and go, provided they have little to do; and with a wish towards Sunday, when there is the least to do of all. 1903 MCNEILL *Egregious Engl.* 174 The come-day, go-day Englishman. 1928 *Manch. Guardian Weekly* 22 June 494/2 Young Joe carried on in his come-a-day go-a-day God-send-Sunday manner.

24. d. colloq. fig. phr. *To come undone, unput, unstuck*: to become disintegrated, 'fall to pieces', meet with disaster.

1915 C. G. GREY *Tales Flying Services* 35 One of them [*sc.* seaplanes]..had just alighted astern, and was 'taxying' along to pick up her own boom when somehow the last remaining bomb 'came unput'—as one who was present said—and fell into the water. 1922 *N. & Q.* 9 Sept. 207/2 When a fancied horse, thought to be 'a good thing' fails to realize expectations, it is said to be 'a good thing come undone'. 1925 *Glasgow Herald* 3 Feb. 6 It has become, to use a modern expression, 'unstuck'. 1928 *Sunday Express* 3 June 11/3 Soon after this I came unstuck over a horse which the Prince of Wales, later King Edward, had very kindly given me. 1928 *Observer* 29 July 19/2 But with freak distributions of cards which justify high bidding, doubles that look sound often come 'unstuck'. 1928 *Daily Express* 12 Nov. 12, I thought my theory had come unstuck.

29. (Earlier U.S. examples.)

1846–52 MRS. WHITCHER *Widow Bedott P.* xxiv. 285 It takes you to come it, Aunt Lucy. 1849 C. LANMAN *Alleghany Mts.* xi. 89 The fellers laughed at me and said I couldn't come it. 1866 J. C. GREGG *Life in Army* xv. 141 Feeling secure from their voracious bills, as they hum around your room, and try to 'come it', but find an abatis in their way.

39*. Come for—. To attack. Cf. 'come at' (COME *v.* 38 d), 'go for' (GO *v.* 58 e).

1890 *Blackw. Mag.* CXLVIII. 460/2 With a rush the hawk comes for him and misses.

41*. Come off—. *To come off it*: to desist from what one is doing. orig. *U.S. slang.* (Cf. *61 c.)

1912 A. NEIL LYONS *Clara* xxvi. 283 Mrs. de Courcy Allendale requested me to 'come off it'.

43. Come over—. h. To get the better of. *dial.* or *slang.*

1889 MRS. LYNN LINTON *Thro' Long Night* I. I. ix. 144, I doubt if ye'd come over me, if we set to!

53. Come away. c. Add quot.

1881 A. LANG *Library* ii. 41 Three jets of gas..made the backs of books come away in his hand.

54. Come back. a. Also, to return to consciousness (cf. quot. 1850 in Dict.).

1924 D. H. LAWRENCE *England, my England* 213 He worked a little longer. He could feel her live beneath his hands; she was coming back.

c. To retort or retaliate. *U.S.*

1896 G. ADE *Artie* vi. 54 Did you ever get the worst of it in such a way that you couldn't come back at the time? 1905 TARKINGTON *In Arena* 182 'Hello, Ben! I hear you're not *for* me!' he said cordially. 'How are you running?' I came back at him, laughing. 'Oh, we're going to beat you', he answered. 1916 H. L. WILSON *Somewhere in Red Gap* vi. 267 'And what a sweet little home you'll build for the Wales family!' I says...But he wouldn't come back; so I left him surrounded by the wreck of his former smartness and went home. 1928 F. N. HART *Bellamy Trial* i. 12 Just as I was thinking of something really bright to come back with, a nice soft little voice in the back of the ball said [etc.].

d. Of an athlete: To return to form.

1922 *Daily Mail* 22 Nov. 11 Since that time he has 'come back' with such certainty..that he must of necessity be regarded as on a level with all the other big men. 1928 *Daily Express* 12 July 12/7 Duncan remains a master of the art of 'coming back'.

e. To return to his or its former state of popularity or vogue.

1929 *Times Lit. Suppl.* 9 May 374/4 The way in which the tulip has 'come back' as a garden flower. *Mod.* Swinburne is coming back.

f. Of a guinea-fowl: To utter its cry (resembling 'come back'). Cf. COME-BACK *sb.*[1]

1892 *Leisure Hour* Dec. 143/1 His turkeys gobbled all day, his guinea-fowls 'come-backed'.

56. Come down. a. Also of fog: To 'settle'.

1891 *Longman's Mag.* July 238 The fog has come down as black as pitch.

i. To be removed from its position, esp. (of a tree) to be felled, (of a building) to be demolished.

1844 *Jrnl. R. Agric. Soc.* V. I. 109 Large numbers of oaks have recently been felled, and many more are marked to come down.

j. To become ill. *U.S. colloq.*

1911 J. C. LINCOLN *Cap'n Warren's Wards* ix. 147 The housekeeper felt sure he was 'coming-down' with some disease or other.

59. Come in. b. Also, to enter as a partner (in a company or *on* an enterprise).

1844 DICKENS *Mart. Chuz.* xxvii, Ha, Ha! Join us. You shall come in cheap. 1923 P. G. WODEHOUSE *Inimitable Jeeves* xiv, I came..to ask if you would care to come in on another little flutter.

d. Also, to be in the last stage of a run. (Cf. *COME-IN *sb.*)

1857 HUGHES *Tom Brown* vii, The whole hunt is out of ear-shot, and all hope of coming in is over.

k. Also of a person: To intervene *between.*

1915 E. B. HOLT *Freudian Wish* 9 She likes a certain young girl of my own age and always tries to come in between us and keep us apart.

q. Of a cow or mare: To calve or foal. *dial.* and *U.S.*

1857 [see *COMING *vbl. sb.* 7 d]. 1873–4 *Rep. Vermont Board Agric.* II. 93 He..has his cows come in usually in April. 1882 *Rep. Maine Board Agric.* XXVI. 22 The best cows we ever buy are those which happen to come in..the late fall or early winter. 1896 T. D. PRICE *MS. Diary* 27 Nov., Spotted Mahulm cow came in.

61. Come off. c. Also, to 'give over'; to stop talking. (Cf. 41* above.) *U.S. slang.*

1889 *Century Dict.*, *Come off*, to cease (fooling, flattering, chaffing or humbugging); desist: chiefly in the imperative: as, oh, come off! (Recent slang, U.S.) 1892 *N. Y. Mercury* Feb. (Ware) 'How much does yer ax for this book?' 'Six dollars,' replied the smiling clerk. 'Six dollars! Oh, come off!' 1904 S. E. WHITE *Silent Places* xiii. 139 Now you treat her decent and you treat me decent. It's time you came off. 1904 W. H. SMITH *Promoters* xx. 293 '[It] makes one conscious of his own superiority to call some one else down.' 'Oh, come off!' Goldsby replied.

m. To have (a certain) success; and *absol.* to be successful; to result in success.

1875 *All Year Round* XIII. 473/2 These latter often found the experiment 'come off' in a literal and aggravating manner. 1883 *Graphic* 11 Aug. 138/2 Batting is his forte, though he does not always 'come off'. 1896 *Daily News* 8 June 11/1 G. L. Jessop coming off both as batsman and bowler. 1904 *Daily Chron.* 11 July 3/2 Atmosphere is here; knowledge is here; graphic style is here. But..it does not in the telling language of the studio 'come off'. 1929 *Times Lit. Suppl.* 2 May 360/1 As a theologian he comes off no better, for against a stanza in which the Virgin responds to the Annunciation of Gabriel is placed the side-note 'The Immaculate Conception'!

67*. Come through. To succeed, attain an end; *spec.* to attain conversion. *U.S.*

1886 ANNIE EDWARDS *Playwright's Dau.* xvi, You will do as I tell you, and, please God, shall come through without a singe. 1912 MATHEWSON *Pitching* ii. 33, I have been told that Clarke was the most relieved man in seven counties when O'Toole came through with that victory in Boston. 1913 MRS. STRATTON-PORTER *Laddie* xii. (1917) 220 Leon said our house reminded him of the mourners' bench before anyone had 'come through'. *Ibid.* xv. 305 Pretty soon it began to look like she was going to come through as Amos Hurd did when he was redeemed.

69. Come up. a. *spec.* To present oneself before a judge or tribunal *for*, rarely *to*, judgement.

1888 FLOR. WARDEN *Woman's Face* II. xvii. 171 He felt as if he himself had come up to judgment before a stern and unbending judge. 1890 *Sat. Rev.* 20 Dec. 698/1 The order to come up for judgment if required.

b. Also phr. *To come up to* (*the*) *scratch, come up smiling.* orig. *Pugilistic slang*; also *transf.* and *fig.*

1821 [see SCRATCH *sb.*[1] 5]. 1886 MCCARTHY & PRAED *Right Hon'ble* II. xv. 47 One comes up smiling and ready for the next round. 1928 *Daily Tel.* 13 Mar. 16/3 His car..can be rubbed down dry,..and, as the phrase goes, it will come up smiling.

o. Also *fig.* in phr. *to come up with*: to get even with, get the better of.

1869 MRS. STOWE *Oldtown Fireside Stories* (1871) 180 He thought he must have his say with Miry, but he got pretty well come up with. *Ibid.*, The way he got come-up-with by Miry was too funny for anything. 1873 SUSAN HALE *Lett.* 123 She gets come up with occasionally, and then I'm delighted. 1901 S. E. WHITE *Westerners* xi. 78 Revenge with him seemed to lie..in the victim's realization that he was being come up with.

Come, *pa. pple.* Add: **b.** = *ARRIVED.

1896 C. JAMES *Yoke of Freedom* 21 A coming man in every sense of the words, if not, indeed, a come man, securely established.

Come-again, *sb.* Delete †*Obs.* and add:

2. A person who is told to 'come again'.

1909 *Westm. Gaz.* 20 Sept. 5/4 'Geography!' ejaculated another of the unfortunate 'come agains.' 'Why, I never heard of it until I wanted to become a taxi-driver.'

3. *attrib.* or as *adj.* Of recovery or renascence.

1868 H. WOODRUFF *Trotting Horse Amer.* xxxvi. 299 People forget the wonderful constitution and come-again qualities of Flora.

Come-and-go (kʌmənᵈgōᵘ·). [f. phr. *come and go* (see COME *v.* V), partly after F. *va-et-vient.*] Passing backwards and forwards.

1924 D. H. LAWRENCE *England, my England* 95 There was plenty of life in the little goods-yard: three porter youths, a continual come and go of farm wagons bringing hay.

Co·me-back, *sb.*[2] [COME *v.* 54.]

1. a. An act of retaliation. *U.S.*

1896 G. ADE *Artie* vi. 59, I never will be able to give him the right kind of a hot come-back for what he done to me. 1912 MATHEWSON *Pitching* ii. 34 Then I knew he was all right. He was there with the 'come-back!' 1920 MULFORD *J. Nelson* xvii. 186 No cussed man can spy on me without riskin' a comeback. 1928 *Sunday Express* 10 June 13/1 A Reuter message from New York says:—A snappy come-back by a British Government at our Governments.

b. A verbal retort; a reply. *U.S.*

1889 *Kansas Times & Star* 9 Nov., He shouldn't thus invite a sarcastic 'come-back'. 1908 MULFORD *Orphan* xiii. 168 He didn't have no come-back to that, but just looked sort of funny. 1926 *Ladies' Home Jrnl.* May 19 He hadn't no comeback to that, Cap.

2. A return; a recovery.

1922 A. S. M. HUTCHINSON *This Freedom* II. viii. 148 For a woman there is no come-back. They don't issue return tickets to women. 1924 A. J. SMALL *Frozen Gold* iii. 90 It looks as though I'm in time to congratulate you on a real come-back.

3. A return to one's former position; a reinstatement in a position of authority or power.

1928 *Daily Chron.* 8 Nov. 4/7 After Poincaré Poincaré! France expecting a come-back. 1929 *Times Lit. Suppl.* 18 July 566 3 He [*sc.* MacDonald] is compared with Lenin in that he inspires reverence and love in thousands of unknown hearts, which is the reason for his 'come-back' and not anything he has said or done.

4. A sheep that is a reversion: see quot. 1891. Also, the skin or fleece of a sheep of this type. *Austral.*

1891 R. WALLACE *Rural Econ. Austral.* etc. 360 When a pure Merino ram is put to a cross ewe the produce is termed a 'come-back' or 'quarter-back'. 1928 *Daily Tel.* 28 Aug. 3/6 Greasy merino realised up to 26d, comebacks 21½d.

Co·me-betwee·n, *sb.* One who or a thing which intervenes.

1893 *Black & White* 15 Apr. 448/2 Popery..and Independency..have each their vindication, but not the miserable make-shifts and come-betweens that find so much..favour nowadays. 1919 W. DE MORGAN *Old Madhouse* 125 That most respectable couple were good as come-betweens.

Comedial (kǫmī·diăl), *a.* [f. L. *cōmœdia* COMEDY + -AL.] Of or pertaining to comedy.

1908 WALLACE *Children Chapel* 168 Or did he simply find good comedial material here ready for further development?

Comedic, *a.* Delete *rare* and add quots.

1639 R. BAILLIE *Lett. & Jrnls.* (1841) I. 223 This might be the comedick catastrophe of our verie fearfull-like Episcopall tragedie. 1840 G. DARLEY *Introd. Beaum. & Fl.* (Rtldg.) p. xxv, Such a definition..would have the singular luck of excluding our very best comedic dramas from the list of comedies. 1897 *Sat. Rev.* 27 Mar. 314 Speaking of the masters of the comedic spirit (if I call it, as he does, the Comic Spirit, this darkened generation will suppose me to refer to the animal spirits of tomfools and merryandrews). 1905 *Pall Mall Gaz.* 24 Apr. 3/2 Miss Ethel Irving has conquered the musical comedy public, and that by comedic rather than by musical means. 1920 M. BEERBOHM *And Even Now* 316 Falstaff is a triumph of comedic creation.

Hence **Come·dically** *adv.*

1930 *Punch* 30 Apr. 498 The acceleration of the pace..leaves some of the conspirators realistically rather than comedically breathless.

Come-down, *sb.* Add: **1.** Now esp., a fall or drop in social or official position or status.

1887 H. H. JACKSON *Between Whiles* i. 18 It was a sad come-down from his old air-castles for her and for himself. 1891 *Cornhill Mag.* May 485 They regarded [it] as somewhat of a 'come down' in the world. 1919 BOYD CABLE *Old Contemptibles* xviii. 291 He joined the Volunteers, of course. It was a sad come-down.

Comedy[1]. Add:

5. *comedy-opera, -tragedy.*

1906 *Daily Chron.* 29 Oct. 3/5 In 'The Duchess of Dantzic'..he produced a '*comedy-opera'—such is the new word!—which was a genuine and delightful work of art. 1897 *Westm. Gaz.* 15 Mar. 3/1 There were no such things as Treaty Acts with their *comedy-tragedy of gorgeously bedizened Presidents.

Co·me-from. *sb. dial.* A place of abode.

1877 *Holderness Gloss.* s.v. *Cum-fra*, 'I ha'nt a cum-fra', I have no settled abiding-place. 1897 RHOSCOMYL *White Rose Arno* 291 This individual, one of no particular kin or come-fro', jumped at the chance of helping to hunt down a rebel.

Co·me-in, *sb.* The last stage of a run or race. Cf. *run-in*, RUN *sb.*[1] 8.

1870 *Chambers's Jrnl.* 401/2 How many eager crowds have gathered to watch at that come-in! 1892 *Sat. Rev.* 26 Nov. 621/1 For the last mile or so, which was called the 'come-in', every one went at the pace that pleased him.

Come-off, *sb.* **4.** (Earlier U.S. examples.)

1800 *Aurora* (Philad.) 19 May (Th.) He replied that he was not at liberty to say—we had a sedition law—which will soon be done away—then I can explain. [?]A very good come-off this! 1845 W. G. SIMMS *Wigwam & Cabin* Ser. I. 93, I began to think that what he said was only a sort of come-off.

Co·me-on, *sb.* *U.S. slang.* [COME *v.* 62.] A swindler. Also *attrib.* = swindling.

1905 *N. Y. Even. Post* 28 Jan. 2 The general appearance of the man caused the officer to become suspicious, and he soon learned that Dates was a 'come-on'. 1905 *N. Y. Times* 24 Feb. 1 Detectives yesterday arrested two men on a charge of participating in a clever 'come-on' game. 1908 G. H. LORIMER *J. Spurlock* viii. 174 Or wouldn't the come-on take the package of green goods? 1909 S. E. WHITE *Rules of Game* II. i, Great country! If you listen to all the come-on stuff you may be disappointed—at first. 1924 W. M. RAINE *Troubled Waters* xvi. 167, I reckon this confession talk is come-on stuff.

Come-outer, *sb.* *U.S.* (Earlier example.)

1840 *Boston Courier* Nov. (Th.) The come-outers are a sect recently sprung up in Cape Cod.

Hence **Come-outerism.**

1847 W. L. GARRISON in *Life* (1889) III. 202 A good deal of prejudice is cherished against me on account of my 'infidelity' and 'come-outerism'.

Comephorus (kome·fŏrǒs). [mod.L., f. Gr. κόμη hair + -φόρος: see -PHOROUS.] A fish belonging to the only known species of the genus *Comephorus* found only in Lake Baikal, Siberia.

1896 WENYON *Across Siberia* 159 Baikal abounds in fish of many kinds...One curious fish, the comephorus, is found only in this lake. It is of small size, and of the codfish family, but has never been caught, and never even seen alive. 1924 *Glasgow Herald* 9 Aug. 8 The comephorus..belongs to the cod family, and has never been caught or seen alive.

Comer. Add:

3. An animal that is coming on or shows promise. *U.S.*

1901–2 *Rep. Kansas State Board Agric.* 202 He..still shows that remarkable looseness and elasticity of hide that indicates a 'comer' when he is put next to the feed-box.

Comet. 4. Add: **comet claret**, claret made in a comet-year (cf. *comet vintage, wine*).

1864 MEREDITH *Emilia in England* xxxiii, There's seven bottles of my poort, and there's eleven of champagne and some comut clar't.

Come-uppance, -uppings. *English* and *U.S. dial.* [COME *v.* 69.] Enough to serve one (by way of retaliation or check); one's deserts.

Come-up-with is used in the same sense.

1880 *Gloss. Cornwall, W.Cornw.*, *Come-upping*, a flogging. 'I'll gi' 'ee a sound come-upping.' 1882 JAGO *Anc. Lang. Cornw.* 141. 1884 HOWELLS *Silas Lapham* (1891) II. 134 Rogers is a rascal..But I guess he'll find he's got his come-uppance. 1896 ELLA HIGGINSON *Tales Puget Sound* 155, I can give him his come-up-'ans if he goes to foolin' around. 1897 HOWELLS *Landlord Lion's Head* xxi. 153 Well, I did get my come-uppings that time. 1913 'B. M. BOWER' *Parowan Bonanza* vi. 70 'An' that's where he got 'is come-uppance', he gloated.

Comfort, *sb.* **8.** *U.S.* (Earlier and later examples.)

1834 *Southern Lit. Messenger* I. 168 A lady of our party..aptly compared it to a Yankee *comfort*. 1913 MRS. STRATTON-PORTER *Laddie* xi. (1917) 211 Laddie had..hung up a comfort at four o'clock to keep the Princess warm.

Comfortable, *a.* Add:

1. b. *The Comfortable Words*: in the Anglican Liturgy, the four scriptural passages following the Absolution in the Communion Office, prefaced by 'Hear what comfortable words' [etc.].

1855 PROCTER *Bk. Comm. Prayer* 324 The Comfortable Words that follow are the scriptural statements upon which the absolution is grounded.

B. 1. (Later Amer. example.)

1786 M. CUTLER in *Life, Jrnls. & Corr.* (1888) II. 247 He..proposes to provide well in comfortables for the journey.

2. c. *U.S.* (Earlier examples.)

1844 *Rep. Comm. Patents* (1847) 35 [Cotton] has already been employed in what are variously called 'comforts' and 'comfortables'. 1855 SARA T. L. ROBINSON *Kansas* (1856) 28, I..slept on comfortables and buffalo-robes on the floor in the attic.

Comforter. Add:

6. b. *U.S.* (Earlier examples.)

1832 S. G. GOODRICH *Syst. Univ. Geog.* 107 Padding or quilting bed coverings or comforters. 1840 *Boston Almanac* 126 Theodore Baker..has for sale..Quilts, Counterpanes, Comforters, Bockings, Crumb Cloths.

7. An india-rubber teat put into a baby's mouth to quieten it.

1898 *Daily News* 11 Mar. 3/1 Sucking air from a comforter (that is an indiarubber teat), which led, alas! to no bottle. 1912 A. NEIL LYONS *Clara* x. 99, I shall take you to a copper and give you up for stealin' the baby's comforter.

Comfy (kʌ·mfi), *a.* Infantile alteration of COMFORTABLE, with the hypocoristic suffix -Y[6]. Hence **Co·mfily** *adv.*

1829 *Hist. Little Louisa* 82, I am saving up my money to buy them two blankets, and then they will be much more *comfy*. 1888 KIPLING *Plain Tales fr. Hills* (1890) 252 Put to bed on some rolled-up carpets, all comfy. 1902 *Westm. Gaz.* 27 Nov. 3/2 A 'comfy' paletot for a little girl. 1905 ELINOR GLYN *Viciss. Evang.* 50 We might sit in that comfy window-seat and talk. 1915 ROSHER *In R.N.A.S.* (1916) 57, I arrived here safely in excellent time after quite a comfy journey. 1917 MAY SINCLAIR *Tree of Heaven* xvi, Not insanely happy..but quietly, comfily happy. *Ibid.* xx, You can't expect us to fight so comfy, and to be killed so comfy, if we know our womenkind are being pounded to bits in the ground we've just cleared. 1928 E. WALLACE *Again the Three Just Men* ii. 33, I am in London, which is delightfully capitalistic and comfy.

Comic, *sb.* **1. b.** Delete †*Obs.* and add quots.

1917 E. THOMPSON *These Men thy Friends* 93 That Grimes, he *is* a comic! 1927 *Cleveland Press* 31 Jan., [They] are highly amusing as dancers and knock-about comics.

2. Also, a comic valentine.

1889 *Kansas Times & Star* 13 Feb., St. Valentine's day should be generously observed...Only dolts will resort to 'comics'.

Coming, *vbl. sb.*[1] Add:

7. Coming in. d. Calving. *dial.* and *U.S.*

1857 *Trans. Ill. Agric. Soc.* II. 381 The coming in of the cows should be regulated to occur in early spring.

Coming, *ppl. a.* **3.** (Later U.S. example.)

1853 J. G. BALDWIN *Flush Times Alabama* 3 He lied with a coming appetite, growing with what it fed on.

5. Rising into prominence; likely to attain distinction.

1868 H. WOODRUFF *Trotting Horse Amer.* xxxiv. 282 Many thought then Lancet was the 'coming horse'. 1869 S. BOWLES *Our New West* xiii. 261, I can discover no successor to Brigham Young. He has men of ability..but I see no 'coming man' for his place. 1896 (see *COME *pa. pple.* b).

Comintern (kǫ·mintəɹn). Also **Kom-**. [Russ. коминтерн, f. the first elements of the Russ. forms of COM(MUNIST and INTERN(ATIONAL.] The Communist International party the headquarters of which are at Moscow.

1925 *Glasgow Herald* 22 Oct. 9 The international relations of the S.S.S.R. and the problems of the Komintern in connection with it. 1926 *Spectator* 10 July 43/2 As far as the Commintern was concerned they [*sc.* the Soviet Government] would be only too delighted to see it transferred to London. 1929 *Encycl. Brit.* XII. 513/1 The Communist International (abbrev. *Komintern*) is the international organization of the Communist party of all nations, founded in 1919. It is also called the Third International. 1929 *Times* 10 July 12/3 The Comintern. Relations with Soviet Government.

Comitadji (kǫmitæ·dʒi). Also **Kom-, -aji, -aggi.** [A Common Balkan form = Turk. *komita*, a. F. *comité* committee + -.. ; lit. member of a (revolutionary) committee.] In the Balkans, a band of irregular soldiers.

1903 *Times* 5 Sept. 7 The Komitajis and the Turks have made a desert of the disturbed vilayets between them. 1908 *Daily Chron.* 30 Oct. 4/6 Lately they had to resist the ferocity of the comitajis. 1909 *Westm. Gaz.* 15 Feb. 1/3 A band of 'Comittaggis' or Macedonian freebooters. 1920 *Glasgow Herald* 18 Mar. 9 The Montenegrin comitadjes..are gradually giving in. 1923 *Daily Mail* 16 Feb. 8 The Bulgarian Comitadjis.

Comitative, *a.*[2] Add: **b.** *sb.* A comitative prefix.

1903 *Amer. Anthropologist* Jan.–Mar. 13 Besides these, comitatives, similatives, partitives, and suffixes expressing similar ideas, are found.

Command, *sb.* Add: **7. b.** (*a*) *The higher command*: the general staffs collectively of the British Army; more particularly, the commander-in-chief.

1916 *Times* 15 Dec. 10/5 It was with great pain that he had heard the criticism upon the higher command. If there was one man in France who was trusted by every one from the highest to the lowest,..it was Sir Douglas Haig. *Ibid.* 16 Dec. 10/4 The hon. member's attack on the generals in the higher command. 1927 E. THOMPSON *These Men thy Friends* 30 And as for the Higher Command! How many generals do you suppose we've got rid of, up to date?

(*b*) *The high command*: rendering of foreign expressions, e.g. G. *hochbefehl.*

1917 *Times* 23 June 6/3 The High Command [of the Russian army]..is only too anxious to stand loyally by the Allies. 1918 *Ibid.* 7 June 6/1 The German High Command chose yesterday to issue its claims as to booty captured by the 'Army Group of the German Crown Prince'. 1919 MAURICE *Last 4 Months* 177 The High Command insists on the immediate issue of a peace offer to our enemies. 1928 *Illustr. Hist. Russ. Rev.* I. 137 The Army, which rose almost unanimously against its High Command.

8. (Later U.S. examples.)

1854 J. R. BARTLETT *Personal Narr.* II. xxxi. 259 Lieutenant Paige..set out on his return to the Colorado this morning, with his command. 1891 *Century Mag.* Mar. 645 The march began at sundown..the command halting only to tighten cinches.

10. command aeroplane (see quot.); **command allowance**, the additional allowance attached to a command; so **command pay**; **command paper** (abbreviated Cd or Cmd with register number, as Cd 5723), a paper laid before Parliament, etc. by command of the Crown; **command performance**, a theatrical, musical, etc. performance given by royal command.

1918 FARROW *Dict. Mil. Terms*, **Command Aeroplanes.*—Aeroplanes which observe the general progress of the combat and all that occurs on the side of the enemy. 1904 KIPLING in *Windsor Mag.* Jan. 228/1 'Is nephew wants two bottles [of rum] *command-allowance. 1922 *Westm. Gaz.* 1 Dec., There was issued as a *command paper yesterday the text of a supplementary extradition convention. 1928 *Daily Express* 4 July 2/4 Command Paper 7,419 of 1914. 1929 G. F. M. CAMPION *Proced. Ho. Comm.* 69 Command Papers cover all the more important documents which the Government and the departments wish to publish on their own initiative. 1875 *Encycl. Brit.* II. 576/1 Lieutenant-colonels of regiments, and other officers holding commands of wings, batteries, or depôts, receive '*command pay' of from 3s. to 1s. 6d. daily. 1876 VOYLE & STEVENSON *Milit. Dict.* (ed. 3) s.v. *Command*, A certain 'command pay' attached, in addition to the regimental pay. 1922 *Westm. Gaz.* 29 Dec., She was a favourite at *Command performances.

Commandant. Add: Revived in the war of 1914–18 as the title of an officer holding a special command, as of a place, depot, or the like, or of a particular force.

1915 P. GIBBS *Soul of War* 342 The Base Commandant's office was the sorting-house of the Expeditionary Force. 1915 GRAHAME-WHITE & HARPER *Aircraft Gt. War* 236 The commandant of the air corps. 1919 G. K. ROSE *2/4th Oxf. & Bucks Lt. Infty.* 145 A Brigade school, with Bennett as its commandant.

b. *S. Africa.* [= Du. *kommandant.*] The leader of a commando in the Boer army. Also **Commanda·nt-Ge·neral, -Ge·neralship.**

1898 *Westm. Gaz.* 4 Jan. 5/2 If Mr. Schalk Burger is returned he will resign his Commandant-Generalship. 1899 *Ibid.* 11 Nov. 8/1 Commandos, in which the burghers are under command of Field-Cornets and Commandants. *Ibid.*, The Commandant-General..is chosen by the whole force. 1902 *Encycl. Brit.* XXXIII. 438/2 Each district was furnished with a commandant, who had under him field-cornets and assistant field-cornets. 1914 *Times* 20 Nov. 7/5 Commandant S. P. Du Toit..to-day captured another of Beyers's rebel officers.

Commandeer (kǫmăndīᵊ·ɹ), *sb.* [f. the vb.] The action of commandeering.

1901 in J. Ralph *War's Brighter Side* 136 'So here's my bloomin' health', says he; 'I'm on the commandeer'. And without another word he commandeered it.

Commandeer, *v.* Add: **c.** *fig.* and *gen.* To take arbitrary possession of.

1900 KIPLING in *War's Brighter Side* (1901) 135 We never use such words as steal, or 'collar', 'pinch', or 'shake': The fashion is to say he 'commandeers' it. 1900 CONAN DOYLE *Great Boer War* 208 The naive claims put forward by the Boers to some special Providence—a process which a friendly German critic described as 'commandeering the Almighty'. 1902 *Westm. Gaz.* 3 Apr. 3/1 The sleeve commandeers to itself a share of attention..out of proportion to its place. 1928 *Punch* 6 June 620 The porter..came to the hotel long after the Merry Party had commandeered it for week-ends. 1929 *Daily Express* 12 Dec. 1/3, I commandeered passing lorries and any other vehicles which happened to be going down the road.

Hence **Commandee·red** *ppl. a.*, taken for military service or use; **Commandee·ring** *vbl. sb.*

1894 *Westm. Gaz.* 23 June 6/1 A number of commandeered settlers. 1894 *Athenæum* 28 July 125/2 The commandeering of British subjects in the Transvaal. 1899 *Daily News* 13 June 4/2 Each commandeered burgher.

Commander. Add:

2. b. *Lieutenant Commander*, a naval officer ranking next below a commander and above a lieutenant. In the Royal Air Force: *Wing Commander*, an officer corresponding in rank to a Commander in the Navy. *Squadron Commander, Flight Commander*, the two ranks next below this.

1914 *Navy List* Oct. 109 List of Officers on the Active List of Royal Navy...Commanders...Temporary Commanders...Lieutenant-Commanders. 1914 *Times* 19 Nov. 13/4 Royal Naval Air Service. Flight Lieuts...reappointed as Acting Flight Commanders. *Ibid.* 22 Dec. 4/3 Royal Flying Corps...Wing Commander.—Brev. Maj. H. R. M. Brooke-Popham, Oxf. and Bucks L.I. 1915 ROSHER *In R.N.A.S.* (1916) 131, I am to be 1st Lieut., good for me, but fear they may yet put in a Flight Commander. 1915 C. G. GREY *Tales Flying Services* 67 Detachments under five Squadron-Commanders. 1928 C. F. S. GAMBLE *North Sea Air Station* iv. 75–6 Wing Commander (relative rank of Commander, R.N.) Squadron Commander (relative rank of Lieutenant Commander, R.N.) Flight Commander (relative rank of Lieutenant, R.N.).

c. An overseer on a plantation. *U.S.*

1842 *McDonogh Papers* 65, I was in the habit of never retiring to rest at night until seeing my commander.

Commanding, *ppl. a.* **3.** Add:

1898 *Daily News* 14 July 6/1 His voice has a somewhat military tone...It is a so-called 'commanding' voice, but capable of great modulation.

Commando. Add: **b.** Phr. *On commando*, on militia service in the Boer army.

1824 BURCHELL *Trav.* II. 111 The master himself was at this time absent on the *Commando*, or militia-service, against the Caffres in the Zuureveld. 1879 *Chambers's Jrnl.* 344/1 All the men capable of bearing arms were then *on commando.* 1899 *Daily News* 30 Sept. 5/3 Burghers refusing to go on commando. 1900 KIPLING in J. Ralph *War's Brighter Side* (1901) 136 We sailed upon commando To vierneuk our Brother Boer.

2. In the South African War (1899–1902), a unit of the Boer army composed of the militia of an electoral district. Also *attrib.*

1899 *Westm. Gaz.* 11 Nov. 8/1 The President..has the right of declaring war and calling up one or more commandos. 1900 KIPLING in *Daily Express* 13 June 4/5 We kept our commando-horses ready for six months. 1902 *Encycl. Brit.* XXXIII. 438/2 Each field-cornet..was responsible for the arms, equipment and attendance of his commando—the commando being the tactical as well as the administrative unit. 1902 *Daily Chron.* 16 June 5/5 Burghers..all thronging into the commando trains.

Comme il faut (kǫm il fōᵘ, ‖kom il fo), *adj. phr.* [Fr., = as it is necessary.] 'As it should be'; according to etiquette; correct in deportment or behaviour; proper.

1756 WALPOLE *Lett.* (1857) III. 8 True critics..maintain that we are not dead *comme il faut*. 1818 LADY MORGAN *Fl. Macarthy* (1819) III. 158, I would not present in my own exclusive circle one who was not in all points *comme il faut*. 1824 L. M. HAWKINS *Annaline* I. 96 It would have been more comme il faut for me to have taken that step. *a* 1845 BARHAM *Ingol. Leg.* Ser. III. *Ld. Thoulouse*, Everything there they found quite *comme il faut*. 1857 MACAULAY in Trevelyan *Life* (1878) II. xiv. 459, I make large allowance for the difference of manners; but it never can have been *comme il faut* in any age or nation for a man of note..to be constantly asking for money. 1876 GEO. ELIOT *Dan. Der.* I. i, 'Who are these Langens? Does anybody know them?' 'They are quite *comme il faut*.'

Commencing, *vbl. sb.* Add: *attrib.*, as **commencing credit**, credit given to those who are starting a career.

1928 *Britain's Industr. Future* (*Liberal Ind. Inquiry*) IV. xxiv. 330 Commencing Credit, to enable new farmers..to stock and equip their holdings.

Commend, *v.* Add: **2. e.** *refl.*

1886 'MAXWELL GRAY' *Silence of Dean Maitland* I. x, [The gray suit] had commended itself to Everard from the sense of cleanliness that light colours always afforded him. 1888 MRS. H. WARD *R. Elsmere* xix, I am sorry for it if his methods do not commend themselves to you.

Comment, *v.* **2.** (Recent U.S. example.)

1904 *Nation* (N.Y.) 7 Apr. 272 Tennyson's In Memoriam, commented by L. Morel.

Commentary, *v.* **2.** (Modern U.S. example.)

1904 *Churchman* (U.S.) 4 June 705 A Bible commentaried to suit the fancies of human imaginings.

Commerce, *sb.* **7.** Add: **commerce-destroyer**, a fast cruiser designed to destroy the merchant vessels of an enemy; so *commerce-destroying*; similarly *commerce-raider, -raiding.*

1886 *Harper's Mag.* June 20/1 She could also be of service as a commerce destroyer. 1889 MAHAN *Influence Sea Power* 31 That form of warfare which has lately received the name of commerce-destroying. 1892 *Daily News* 28 July 6/7 The New United States Commerce Destroyer. 1898 *Westm. Gaz.* 23 May 6/3 Arming several more of their steamers as auxiliary cruisers and commerce destroyers. 1906 CORNFORD *Defenceless Isl.* 71 A commerce-raiding squadron. *Ibid.* 82 The Sumter had been gaily commerce-destroying for more than four months. 1927 *Observer* 29 May 20/4 The commerce-raider's career.

Commercial, *a.* **6.** Add: *Commercial agency* (U.S.), an organization which furnishes its clients with information as to the standing of commercial firms. *Commercial agent* (U.S.), an agent stationed abroad to attend to commercial interests. *Commercial college, school, university*, a college, school, university for instruction in commercial subjects. *Commercial paper* (see quot.). *Commercial sheep*, a sheep reared for selling and not for breeding purposes.

1897 *Bouvier's Law Dict.* I. 357/2 *Commercial Agency. 1902 *Encycl. Brit.* XXX. 634/1 Mercantile, or commercial, agencies in America. 1877 *Ibid.* VI. 317/1 The United States *commercial agents, although appointed by the president, receive no exequatur. They..are distinct from the consular agents. 1888 WORMELL in *Jrnl. Educ.* 1 Feb. 117/1 The advisability of having a separate council or body of trustees for the *Commercial College. 1908 W. H. DAWSON *Evol. Mod. Germany* 101 A Leipzig institution of recent origin, the Commercial College, founded in 1898 by the Chamber of Commerce of that town. 1897 *Bouvier's Law Dict.*, **Commercial Paper*, negotiable paper given in due course of business, whether the element of negotiability be given it by the law merchant or by statute. 1889 *Sonnenschein's Cycl. Educ.* (ed. A. E. Fletcher) 440/2 The training of the *commercial school will not make a boy a clever buyer and seller. 1892 *R. Gambaro's Less. Commerce* p. v, Lecturer on the English Language at the Royal High Commercial School at Genoa. 1901 F. HOOPER & JAS. GRAHAM *Comm. Educ.* 13 State-supported Technical and Commercial Schools and Institutions. 1914 *Scotsman* 10 Sept. 9/6 A big, strong *commercial sheep. 1853 *Scott. Educ. & Lit. Jrnl.* July 438 A movement..for the establishment of a *Commercial University.

Commercialese (kǫmɜ̄ɹʃălī·z). [f. COMMERCIAL + -ESE.] The diction of the commercial world.

1910 C. HEADLAM *Mem. W. Headlam* 44 This [*sc.* the language in which scholia and glosses were written] was a language by itself, like our Commercialese.

Commish., colloq. abbreviation of COMMISSION.

1914 D. O. BARNETT *Lett.* (1915) 15 Am taking commish. in regulars!

Commissar[2] (kǫmisā·ɹ). Also in F. form **-aire.** [Russ. коммиссаръ *kommissár'*, ad. F. *commissaire.*] The head of a government department of the United Socialist Soviet Republics.

1918 tr. *Lenin's Less. Revolution* (title-p.), By Vladimir Oulianow (N. Lenin) President of the Council of People's Commissars...Published by the Bureau of International Revolutionary Propaganda attached to the Commissariat for Foreign Affairs. 1920 *19th Cent.* Aug. 216 Some artists protected by commissars are well paid. 1920 HARD *Raymond Robins' Own Story* 121 It was headed: 'Suggested communication to the Commissaire for Foreign Affairs'. 1921 *Chambers's Jrnl.* 151/1 The Bolsheviks retreated in a panic, killing their own commissars as they fled.

Commissariat. Add: (= Russ. комиссариат.) A department of the Soviet Republic civil service.

1918 [see *COMMISSAR[2]]. 1919 C. E. B. *Facts about Bolsheviks* 7 [The] Central Executive Committee..elects and works with the 'People's Commissaries' in a score of 'Commissariats' or Ministries. 1920 GOODE *Bolshevism at Work* 28 He..is at the head of a very important Commissariat, that dealing with industries. 1921 *Q. Rev.* Jan. 173 Lenin had to complain that 'the departments of the Soviets are turning in many places into organs which gradually merge with the commissariats', i.e. the civil service. 1929 tr. *Larsons'*

COMMISSARY

Expert Service Soviet 135 The Narkomindel (the Commissariat of Foreign Affairs).

Commissary.[1] Add:

4. b. *ellipt.* A commissariat wagon or stores.

1905 A. Adams *Outlet* 245 A wagon-way could be easily cut in the bank and the commissaries lowered to the river's edge with a rope to the rear axle. 1929 A. C. & C. Edington *Studio Murder Myst.* xiv, Will you go with me to the commissary and have a drink?

c. = Commissariat 4.

1883 *Century Mag.* Sept. 672 This enforced idleness reduced our commissary to an alarming minimum.

7. *attrib.* (Earlier examples.)

1862 O. W. Norton *Army Lett.* 116 Artillery is being loaded up every night, commissary stores are going. 1887 *Harper's Mag.* Dec. 112/1 Commissary and butcher bills were still unpaid.

Commissary[2] (kǫ·misări). [ad. Russ. *kommissár'*.] **a.** A deputy, delegate. **b.** = *Commissar[2].

1917 *Times* 22 Mar. 7/2 The Commissaries of the Duma were arriving. *Ibid.* 11 Apr. 6/3 The department of international relations attached to the committee of workmen's and soldiers' delegates has the right to be represented by a commissary at the office of the Petrograd Telegraph Agency. 1920 Goode *Bolshevism at Work* 18 The Council of People's Commissaries. 1923 Leacock *Over the Footlights* 161 She goes out stealthily to denounce her husband and Hootch to the commissaries of the police. 1929 tr. *Larsons' Expert Service Soviet* 133 The Commissary for Finance, Sokolnikoff.

Commissaryship. (Later U.S. example.)

1811 J. Adams *Wks.* (1854) IX. 633 All applications..for commissions,..commissaryships, quartermasterships, &c.

Commission, *sb.*[1] Add: **3. e.** The period of active service of a warship (see 5 c).

1882 Sir W. H. White *Man. Naval Archit.* (ed. 2) 231 The commanding officer of one of these ships has stated 'that they may go through a commission and never heel or roll more than one or two degrees'.

5. c. Also *transf.*

1907 M. C. Harris *Tents of Wickedness* iv. ii. 342 From those [houses]..there came little light, there was..a general look of being out of commission.

13. commission note, a written promise to pay commission to an agent; **commission rank,** the rank of a commissioned officer.

1899 *Westm. Gaz.* 13 May 7/2 She did not know when or where she signed the *commission note. 1908 *Daily Chron.* 15 Jan. 7/2 [He] signed the commission notes on the assumption that he did belong to the senior branch. 1898 *Westm. Gaz.* 8 Jan. 7/2 Facilities for promotion to *commission rank in the Royal Marines.

Commission, *v.* **1. c.** Add: Also *intr.* Of a ship: To commence active service, to be put in commission.

1913 in C. F. S. Gamble *N. Sea Air Station* i. (1928) 38 [In the Admiralty announcement..it was stated that the Hermes was to] commission on the 7th May as parent ship of the Naval Air Services. 1915 'Bartimeus' *Tall Ship* i. 17 There's a super-Dreadnought commissioning soon.

Commissionary (kǫmi·ʃənări), *sb.*[2] = *Commissar[2].

1920 Hard *Raymond Robins' Own Story* 75 The Council of People's Commissionaries.

Commitment. Add: **6.** (Earlier U.S. quot.)

1789 Washington *Diaries* IV. 17 If Mr. Gouv'r Morris was employed in this business, it would be a commitment for his appointment as Minister.

b. Also, liability; *pl.* pecuniary obligations.

1892 *Pall Mall Gaz.* 2 Mar. 7/3 The Murrieta commitments are enormous. 1897 *Daily News* 24 Apr. 9/4 'Bear' commitments have been largely closed during the past few days. 1927 *Daily Tel.* 5 Apr. 11/5 The Peterel will be an additional commitment.

Committal, *sb.* Add: **7.** The action of committing the body to the grave at burial; esp. *attrib.*, as *committal prayer, sentences, service.*

1854 *Chambers's Jrnl.* I. 207/1 The committal to the grave..did not complete the funeral obsequies. 1892 *Daily News* 15 Nov. 3/4 The lesson was read by the Rev. A. Majendie, and the committal sentences by the Rev. Dr. Yule. 1898 *Ibid.* 24 Jan. 5/2 The committal portion of the service was taken by the Dean of Christ Church. *Ibid.* 7 Apr. 2/1 The committal prayers were read, though few in the dense crowd could hear them. 1927 *Observer* 28 Aug. 15 The Bishop of Aberdeen and Orkney conducted the committal service.

Common, *a.* Add: **6. c.** *Common lodging* or *lodging-house*, a lodging-house in which beds may be obtained for the night (see quot. 1860).

1851 *Act 14 & 15 Vict.* c. 28 (*title*) An Act for the well ordering of Common Lodging Houses. 1860 *Act 23 Vict.* c. 26 § 3 The Term 'Common Lodging House' shall mean a House in which Persons are harboured or lodged for Hire for a single Night, or for less than a Week at a Time, or any Part of which is let for any Term less than a Week. 1902 *Encycl. Brit.* XXX. 316/1 The keepers of common lodging-houses are required to limewash their walls and ceilings in the months of April and October. *Ibid.* XXXII. 680/2 The class found in casual wards, shelters and common lodgings.

13. *Common or garden*: see Garden *sb.* 5 c.

18. c. Psychol. *Common feeling*: = Cœnæsthesis.

1836–7 Sir W. Hamilton *Metaph.* xxvii. (1877) II. 157 The Vital sense receiving from various authors various synonyms, as coenaesthesis, common feeling, vital feeling, etc. 1897 tr. *W. Wundt's Outl. Psychol.* 161 The common feeling is always the immediate expression of our sensible comfort and discomfort.

19. *Common turn*: see Turn *sb.* 5.

21. *Common form*: (*a*) a form of probate in which the grant is made by the executor's own oath without opposition; (*b*) a customary form of words used in the pleadings in actions at common law; (*c*) a form of words common to documents of the same species; hence *colloq.*, a formula or the like of general application.

1766 Blackstone *Comm.* II. 508 The executor..must prove the will of the deceased: which is done either in *common form*, which is only upon his own oath before the ordinary, or his surrogate; or *per testes*, in more solemn form of law, in case the validity of the will be disputed. 1797 Tomlins *Jacob's Law-Dict.* s.v. *Pleading* i. 2 Special Pleas..always advance some new fact not mentioned in the declaration; and then they must be [*ed. Granger* (1835) they formerly must have been] averred to be true, in the common form:—'and this he is ready to verify.' 1820 in Barnewell & Alderson *Rep. Cases K.B.* III. 451 If the argument on the part of the plaintiff prevail, the common form of pleading not guilty of the grievances is bad upon special demurrer. 1857 *Act 20 & 21 Vict.* c. 77 § 2 'Common Form Business' shall mean the Business of obtaining Probate and Administration where there is no Contention as to the Right thereto, [etc.]. 1888 *Encycl. Brit.* XXIV. 572/2 Probate is confined as a rule to wills of personalty or of mixed personalty or realty, and is either in common form, where no opposition to the grant is made, or in solemn form, generally after opposition, when the witnesses appear in court. 1905 *Spectator* 18 Feb. 242 The article is what lawyers know as 'common form', and means simply that the nation..leaves it to its Executive to settle the details.

B. *adv.* (Modern U.S. example.)

1901 Harben *Westerfelt* iv. 41 'Oh, I reckon I'm all right,..How's Luke?' 'As well as common.'

Commonage. Add: *S. Afr.*

1893 *Westm. Gaz.* 23 May 6/1 A farm adjoining the Kimberley commonage. 1900 *Daily News* 24 Apr. 5/4 Two young Dutchmen acting as spies..were found hidden in a Kaffir hut on Barkly Commonage.

Commoner. Add:

3. *First Commoner*, the Speaker.

1885 *Peel City Guardian* 23 May 6/1 The 'First Commoner' who now occupies the chair. 1908 tr. *Redlich's Proc. Ho. Comm.* 137 As 'first commoner' in the realm his place is immediately after the peers.

Co·mmonership. [f. Commoner + -ship.] The position of being a commoner.

c 1907 F. Thompson *Life St. Ignatius* (1909) xiv. 288 He was unmolested in the heavenly commonership he had chosen. 1918 *Oxf. Univ. Gaz.* 6 Nov. 108 Accepted for a Commonership March, 1914.

Commonize, *v.* **2.** Delete (*U.S.*) and add:

1895 *Westm. Gaz.* 13 Mar. 5/2 The reproduction of copyright pictures in this way was obviously calculated to do injury by 'commonising' the artist's design. 1918 Galsworthy *Apple Tree* § 7 (1920) 152 Suppose..they commonised her, as Sunday clothes always commonised village folk!

Co·mmonplacely, *adv.* [f. Commonplace *a.* + -ly[2].] In a commonplace manner.

1892 'G. Travers' *Mona Maclean* vi, Humanity will all be uniformly, hideously, commonplacely yellow!

Commons. 2 c. Delete 'formerly' and add quot.:

1918 *Act 8 Geo. V.* c. 3 § 1 (3) Incapable of..sitting or voting as a member of the Commons House of Parliament.

Common school. *U.S.* (See Common *a.* 21.)

1795 in T. Boese *Public Educ. N. York* (1869) 21 The establishment of Common Schools throughout the state. 1818 in *Educ. Docs. Connecticut* (1853) 147 To the support ..of the public or common schools throughout the State. 1831 Peck *Guide for Emigrants* 243 Common schools are usually taught some part of the year in most of the settlements. 1856 Mrs. Stowe *Dred* 107 He was guiltless of all knowledge of common-school learning. 1887 *Harper's Mag.* Mar. 637/2 The common-school system has become a part of Southern life.

Commonwealth. Add:

4. b. The title of the federated states of Australia.

1891 *Proc. & Deb. Nat. Australas. Convention* Mar.–Apr. p. cxxix, Draft of a bill to constitute the Commonwealth of Australia. *Ibid.* p. cxxx, The name 'The Commonwealth of Australia' or 'The Commonwealth' shall be taken to mean the Commonwealth of Australia as constituted under this Act. 1900 *Act 63 & 64 Vict.* c. 12 § 3 The people of New South Wales, Victoria, South Australia, Queensland, and Tasmania, and also, if Her Majesty is satisfied that the people of Western Australia have agreed thereto, of Western Australia, shall be united in a Federal Commonwealth under the name of the Commonwealth of Australia. 1902 *Encycl. Brit.* XXV. 807/1 The bill of 1898..proposed to establish, under the Crown, a federal union of the Australasian colonies, to be designated the Commonwealth of Australia.

Communal, *a.* Add: **4.** *Communal kitchen*, a public kitchen under official management. *Communal land(s)*, land held by a community; also *attrib.*, as *communal land system, tenure.*

1917 *Times* 29 Mar. 9/3 The possibility of setting up *communal kitchens in the East-end of London. *Ibid.* 5 Apr. 8/6 Three communal kitchens were opened in East London yesterday. 1886 *Encycl. Brit.* XXI. 108 Prof. Michael Kovalevski, of the University of Moscow, is now publishing an excellent work on *Communal Land Tenure. 1899 *Daily News* 15 Apr. 8/2 Our Government is, as fast as it can, abolishing the dole and the communal lands systems.

Communality (kǫmiunæ·lĭti). [f. Communal + -ity.] Communal state or condition.

1901 *Smithsonian Rep.* 76 In such manner as to strengthen sentiments of communality and to keep alive the sense of community in interests.

Communicating, *ppl. a.* (see under Communicate *v.*) Add: In *communicating trench* = *Communication *trench.*

1914 D. O. Barnett *Lett.* (1915) 19 We couldn't go up the communicating trench to the firing line because it was full of water. 1918 Farrow *Dict. Mil. Terms.*

Communication. Add:

6. c. *Line(s) of communication(s)*: = *communication lines* (see below).

1888 *Encycl. Brit.* XXIV. 346/1 A system..by which along a regular chain of posts, or 'line of communications', an army received its supplies of food, [etc.]. 1899 *Westm. Gaz.* 16 Nov. 5/2 Inspector-General of Lines of Communication. 1900 Conan Doyle *Great Boer War* 201 One dashing raid carried out by a detachment from Methuen's line of communications. 1925 Mottram *Sixty-Four, Ninety-Four!* 228 Some lines-of-communication Head-quarters.

12. communication lines, lines by which a field army maintains communication with its base and along which all reinforcements and supplies are sent; **communication-plate,** a perforated portion of the wall between adjoining cells of a polyzoan colony; **communication-room,** a room in a warship containing apparatus which provides the means of communicating with different parts of the ship (*Cent. Dict.* Suppl. 1909); **communication sap** (Sap *sb.*[3] 2); **communication trench,** a trench forming a means of communication between two different positions.

1898 *Daily News* 17 Jan. 7/3 With 750 miles of *communication lines to protect. 1889 Nicholson & Lydekker *Palæont.* 607 Contiguous cells are commonly placed in direct communication with one another by what have been called '*communication-plates' or 'rosette-plates'. These are portions of the cell-wall pierced by one or more minute pores. 1929 E. Partridge in *Three Pers. Rec. War* 335 On leaving Sausage Gully, they entered a main *communication-sap. 1914 *Illustr. Lond. News* 24 Oct. 571 At all points subject to shell-fire access to the firing-line from behind is provided by *communication-trenches. 1914 *Times* 10 Dec. 6/1 Leading away from the firing line are what we call communication trenches, up which come our rations from the rear. 1925 Mottram *Sixty-Four, Ninety-Four!* 101 The two bays by the crump-hole at the mouth of the communication trench were always empty.

Communiqué (kǫmiū·nikē, ‖komünike). [Fr.; pa. pple. of *communiquer* to communicate, used subst.] An official intimation or report.

1852 *Illustr. London News* 12 June 458/3 [When the *Moniteur* was charged, in an article headed 'Communiqué', to state, that the French Government was not responsible for statements..unless the word *communiqué* was placed above them]. *Ibid.*, The *Moniteur* and its *communiqué* did not disavow the policy. 1882 Besant *All Sorts* xlv, The result appeared in a long *communiqué* which attracted general and immediate interest. 1904 *Spectator* 31 Dec. 1069/2 An official *communiqué* administering a severe rebuke to the leaders of the Zemstvo movement. 1914 *Aeroplane* 2 Apr. 404/1 The War Office, March 20th, 1914. The following communiqué has been received:—Royal Flying Corps (Military Wing).—Diary of work for week ending March 20th, 1914. 1927 E. Thompson *These Men thy Friends* 120 They brooded over their own Western Front communiqués—those announcements that went on endlessly.

Communitary (kǫmiū·nitări), *a.* *U.S.* [f. Community: see -ary 2.] Belonging to a community. Hence **Commu·nitariness.**

1895 *Advance* (Chicago) 14 Mar. 846/1 The societies in which they [*sc.* Harvard and Yale] were placed were characterized by a communitariness of blood, belief, interest and character. *Ibid.*, No communitary instinct pervades and unifies society [in the Western States, U.S.]. 1904 Branford in *Ideals of Sci. & Faith* 105 Adjustments and re-adjustments between group-interests and communitary interests.

Community. Add:

11. *attrib.*, as *community kitchen, dining room* U.S.; **community singing,** organized singing in chorus by large groups or gatherings of people; so *community chorus, song,* etc.

1929 *Encycl. Brit.* VI. 139/1 The *community chorus movement in the United States was launched in Rochester, N.Y., in 912 by Harry Barnhart. *Ibid.* 138/2 With the growth [in U.S. since 1910] of the *community kitchen and its corollary the *community dining room. 1919 M. Shaw *Brit. Hymn Festival Bk.* Pref., *Community hymn singing is very much in evidence to-day. 1922 S. Lewis *Babbitt* vi. 74 Ryland wore spats, he wrote long letters about City Planning and Community Singing. 1923 *Sackbut* Nov. IV. 115 The Town Hall, where the weekly Community Singing was advertised to be held. 1927 M. Shaw in *Sign* Sept. 115/1 Quite recently monster Community Singing gatherings have been held at the Albert Hall. 1927 (*title*) Labour *Community Song Book.

Communize, *v.* Add: **b.** To make communistic, give a communistic form to.

1920 *Glasgow Herald* 20 Mar. 6 To Socialise, Communise, Bolshevise,..any of the institutions on which our trade and commerce depend. 1921 *Public Opinion* 26 Aug. 202/2 To communise the teaching profession the Soviet Government resorted to abolition of all standards of education for teachers.

Commutate (kǫ·miuteit), *v.* Delete †*Obs. rare* and add:

b. *Electr.* = *Commute *v.* 6. Hence **Co·mmutated** *ppl. a.*, **Co·mmutating** *ppl. a.* and *vbl. sb.*

1893 Maycock *Electric Lighting* ii. vii. (1894) 228 There is a similarity in the methods of commutating the currents. 1896 D. C. & J. P. Jackson *Altern. Curr.* II. 261 When the commutating point is reached during the rotation of the commutator, the trailing brushes move on to intermediate segments. *Ibid.* 624 Commutated Armature. The armature may be wound with the coils so arranged that their conductors are in series when starting and in parallel when running. 1916 *Standardization Rules Amer. Inst. Electr. Eng.* 22 Commutating Machines.

Commutation. 8. Add: **commutation passenger** *U.S.*, a season-ticket holder on a railway; **commutation ticket** *U.S.* (earlier examples).

1887 C. B. George *40 Yrs. on Rail* v. 89 You have had a great deal of experience in carrying *commutation passengers in Boston. 1849 *Pathfinder* (Boston) 50 *Commutation tickets. 1885 *Good Words* July 450/1 A single 'Commutation' ticket is given, numbered and dated on the day on which it was issued. At each journey the conductor punches the ticket.

Commutative, *a.* **1.** Delete † and add: *Commutative contract*, a contract (e.g. a sale) in which each of the contracting parties gives and receives an equivalent.

1856 Bouvier *Law Dict.* I. 254.

Commutator. Add: **b.** *Electr.* An attachment, usually consisting of a ring of copper segments separated by insulating strips, connected with the armature of a dynamo, which, by revolving in contact with the brushes, directs and makes continuous the current produced in the armature coils of the machine. Also *attrib.*

1880 J. W. Urquhart *Electr. Lt.* 58 He placed the magnet vertically and revolved the coils about a horizontal axis, and added a commutator to make the currents flow in one direction. 1884 S. P. Thompson *Dyn.-Electr. Mach.* 133 The only other dynamo in which a commutator at all resembling that of the Brush machine is used is Newton's dynamo. 1896 *Ibid.* (ed. 5) 395 One of these commutator coils. 1902 *Encycl. Brit.* XXVII. 579/2 The levelling process may evidently be carried still further by the insertion of more coils and more corresponding sectors in the commutator, until the whole armature is covered with winding. ..A ring and a drum armature, each with eight coils and eight commutator sectors. 1909 *Installation News* III. 62/1 High speed tends to undue friction and wear of the commutator surface. 1916 *Standardization Rules Amer. Inst. Electr. Eng.* 47 Brush Friction of Commutator and Collector Rings.

2. A device effecting the automatic exposure of photographic plates at given intervals during a total eclipse of the sun.

1897 D. P. Todd in *Astrophys. Jrnl.* V. 323 The basis of the commutator is an old chronograph with a ten-inch cylinder. 1900 — in *Rep. Brit. Assoc. Adv. Sci.* 674 The commutator regulated the exposures and recorded their times as well.

Commute, *v.* Add: **6.** *Electr. trans.* To regulate (the direction of an electric current), *esp.* so that the direction of the current is made continuous.

1896 S. P. Thompson *Dyn.-Electr. Mach.* (ed. 5) 438 The commutator has 54 segments, and there are 54 'commuting coils'. 1902 *Encycl. Brit.* XXVII. 578/1 The current may be commuted. *Ibid.* 579/2 To commute its direction in any coil as it passes through the interpolar gap.

Compact, *sb.*[2] Delete †*Obs.* and add:

e. Compact powder or rouge, or the case containing this.

1930 *Woman's Life* 12 July 9/2 If you cannot buy a compact to fit your powder case, try this recipe.

Compagnon de voyage (kompan'on də vwayāʒ). [Fr.] A travelling companion.

1768 Sterne *Sent. Journ.* I. 97 Do not one half of our gentry go with a hum-drum *compagnon du voiage* the same round. 1840 Thackeray *Misc., Shabby Genteel Story* (1857) IV. 294 Her fair *compagnon de voyage*, whose name was Miss Runt. 1883 Ld. Saltoun *Scraps* II. iv. 118 Colonel Martin, my *compagnon de voyage* from Southampton to Malta.

Companion, *sb.*[1] Add:

1. d. *Astr.* The less brilliant member of a double star system or pair of stars.

1902 *Encycl. Brit.* XXV. 752/1 Partial eclipses caused by the interposition of a dark companion moving around them [*sc.* stars of the Algol type]. 1928 W. M. Smart *Sun, Stars & Universe* xiv. 215 The faint companion of Sirius.

10. companion cell *Bot.*, a cell that accompanies another cell, as each of the cells associated with the sieve tubes; **companion cropping,** a system of cultivation by which two or more kinds of crops are grown together on the same piece of land.

1887 tr. *Strasburger's Bot.* 146 Sieve-tubes, whose *companion-cells are the cells with narrower cavities, which follow towards the exterior. 1902 *Encycl. Brit.* XXV. 417/1 The proteid cells of the phloem are here always sister-cells of the leptoids and are known as companion-cells.

Companionate (kǫmpæ·nyəneit), *a.* Delete †*Obs.* and add: **2.** Phr. *Companionate marriage*, marriage with legalized birth-control and provision for divorce by mutual consent. Also *ellipt.*

1927 *Weekly Disp.* 26 June 1 There has arisen a group within the Church in America which sanctions an 'open mind' on the subject of relations between the sexes without marriage, provided birth control is exercised. This group employs the high-sounding phrase of 'companionate marriage'. 1928 B. B. Lindsey & W. Evans *Companionate Marr.* p. v, Birth control has brought the Companionate into existence.

Company, *sb.* **10.** Add: (sense 7) *company promoter*; **company sergeant major,** senior warrant officer of a company.

1893 W. S. Gilbert *Utopia* i, A *Company promoter this. 1913 *Army Order* 323 § 5 In each company there will be eventually a *company serjeant-major and a company quartermaster-serjeant. For the present the duties of these appointments will be carried out by the existing colour-serjeants. 1919 G. K. Rose *2/4th Oxf. & Bucks Lt. Infty.* 125 Moberly, Company Sergeant-Major Cairns, and Guest ..greatly distinguished themselves in the task of maintaining this exposed position.

Comparatival (kǫmpærătəi·văl), *a.* [f. Comparative *a.* 2, *sb.* 1.] Belonging to the comparative degree.

1900 F. Hall in *Nation* (N.Y.) 22 Mar. 220 Though its termination is comparatival, yet, primarily,..it denoted addition.

Comparison, *sb.* Add:

9. *attrib.* and *Comb.*, as **comparison plate,** each of the photographic plates of a planet, etc., taken at different stations and used for comparison in astronomical research; **comparison spectrum,** a spectrum formed for comparison wave-length by wave-length with the spectrum under observation.

1905 *Westm. Gaz.* 12 Oct. 12/1 The probable absence of good *comparison plates from other places—whereby the planet could be identified..—is very disappointing. 1890 G. F. Chambers *Handbk. Descr. & Pract. Astron.* viii. iv. (ed. 4) II. 372 The light from the terrestrial substance which gives the *comparison spectrum. 1897 *Daily News* 18 June 8/3 When the problem had to be solved of a satisfactory introduction of light for the comparison spectrum.

Compartment. Add:

5. b. Also of other vehicles (cf. *8).

d. *Forestry.* (See quot.) *U.S.*

1905 *Terms Forestry & Logging* 7 The unit of area treated in the working plan. The size and the shape of compartments are determined mainly by topographic features. *Ibid.* 23 *Stand method*, that method of conservative lumbering in which reproduction is secured from self-sown seed by means of successive cuttings...Syn.: compartment system.

6. b. Used (esp. *attrib.*) of methods of dealing with business in sections, as of the parliamentary rule to facilitate the passing of a bill by dealing with it in separate portions and allotting a limit of time for the discussion and closure of each.

1893 *Westm. Gaz.* 5 July 2/2 At the close of each compartment he [*sc.* the Chairman] simply becomes the instrument of the House in recording its decision...Closure by compartment must be supplemented with closure by clause. 1896 *Daily News* 25 Feb. 5/6 The necessity of having the compartment principle engrafted on the rule.

8. (sense 5 b) *compartment car, train, vehicle*; (sense 5 c) *compartment built* adj.; **compartment boat,** a boat built with watertight compartments.

1894 *Daily News* 1 Sept. 6/7 The *compartment boats sinking in Goole Docks. 1892 *Ibid.* 4 July 7/3 She is *compartment built,..and this has saved her from an immediate catastrophe. 1928 *Manch. Guardian Weekly* 26 Oct. 335/1 They live in *compartment cars, which are more or less like the European wagonlit. 1907 *Daily Chron.* 6 Sept. 7/6 The inconvenience on the car trains is certainly not so great as on the *compartment trains. 1908 *Westm. Gaz.* 17 Dec. 10/1 Single-decked *compartment vehicles.

Compass, *sb.*[1] **D.** Add: **compass course,** a course steered by compass; spec. *Naut.* and *Aeronaut.*, the line of direction indicated by the compass but not actually taken by a boat or airship, allowance having been made for deviation caused by wind, currents, etc.

1851 *Family Friend* IV. 294/1 Compass, which registers upon paper the compass course which a vessel has been steered in for twenty-four hours. 1880 C. R. Markham *Peruv. Bark* 201 To shape a direct compass-course over the cordilleras from Sandia to Vilque. 1900 *Westm. Gaz.* 13 Jan. 3/2 It is not a simple matter to keep a given compass course at night. 1916 Barber *Aeroplane Speaks* 39 Our compass course will then be in the direction A-E. *Ibid.* 41 A very simple way of calculating the compass course.

Compass-plant. *U.S.* (See Compass *sb.*[1] D., s.v. *compass-flower.*)

1848 A. Gray *Man. Bot.* (1857) 216 Lower leaves..on the wide open prairies, said to present their edges uniformly north and south, and hence called Compass-Plant. 1857 *Trans. Ill. Agric. Soc.* II. 671 The large fleshy root of the rasin-weed, or compass-plant (*Silphinium laciniatum*) appeared to have been eaten very freely in Autumn at least. 1870 *Amer. Naturalist* IV. 580 The plant popularly known as the compass plant.

Compel, *v.* Add: **1. d.** *absol.* Also **Compe·lling** *ppl. a.*

1903 R. Langbridge *Flame & Flood* vi, A voice that..asked like a child,..coerced like a man, compelled like the bidding of the Cosmos. 1904 Lillie T. Meade *Love Triumphant* iii. i, 'I have powerful hands', was his answer, 'hands that compel'. 1908 *Daily Chron.* 30 Sept. 3/4 The book is said to be very realistic and powerful, sincere and compelling.

Compensate, *v.* Add:

4. b. *Electr.* esp. in ppl. adjs. with reference to **Compensa·tion,** or the neutralization of one magnetomotive or electromotive force by another.

1896 D. C. & J. P. Jackson *Altern. Curr.* II. 316 The Westinghouse, so-called, 'compensated voltmeter'. 1896 S. P. Thompson *Dyn.-Electr. Mach.* (ed. 5) 392 An iron structure, slotted..to receive the compensating conductors. *Ibid.* 395 Sayers' compensating winding with commutator coils. *Ibid.* 800 Compensated armatures. 1906 A. Russell *Altern. Curr.* II. 40 Let n'C' be the compensating ampere-turns on each field magnet. 1909 C. F. Smith *Pract. Altern. Currents* (ed. 4) 415 Compensation for Armature Reaction. *Ibid.* 416 The compensating winding employed in a series motor consists of an additional winding on the stator placed with its axis midway between the main poles, and connected either in series with the main circuit or short-circuited on itself. *Ibid.* 427 A compensated motor will start from rest with a low power-factor.

Compère (koñpęr). Delete *Obs.* and add:

2. The organizer or general director of a musical or vaudeville entertainment.

1928 *Weekly Dispatch* 24 June 15 The genial Davy Burnaby seems to be quite content as a cabaret compère. He has got together a company for the underground grill of the Piccadilly.

Compilatory, *a.* Delete *rare* and add quots.

1894 *Temple Bar* Mar. 441 Journalistic, compilatory, biographical work. 1906 *Daily Chron.* 2 Aug. 3/3 There is far more of the compilatory than of the confessional element in his volume.

Complainant, *a.* Delete †*Obs.* and add:

1897 *Daily News* 23 July 4/5 The conference between the Postmaster-General and the complainant sections of the Post Office servants.

Complainee. (Earlier Amer. example.)

1779 J. Adams *Wks.* (1854) IX. 479 These might have determined whether the complainers or complainees have most to boast of.

Complected, *ppl. a.*[2] *U.S.* (Earlier and later examples.)

1822 *Amer. Beacon* (Norfolk, Va.) 8 Jan. 3/3 Advt., He is well made, light complected. 1834 H. Brackenridge *Recoll.* xix. 224 The next morning..poor Greares's face..became sallow complected and as spotted as a flounder. 1883 'Mark Twain' *Life Mississippi* lix, Monstrous bluffs on both sides of the river—ragged, rugged, dark complected. *a* 1906 'O. Henry' *Trimmed Lamp* etc. 66 A heavy-set man, sandy complected, about twenty-nine.

Complement, *sb.* Add:

5. i. *Biol. Chem.* In Ehrlich's theory of immunization, a substance of the nature of a ferment, which acts in conjunction with an amboceptor; also called *addiment, alexin,* or *cytase.*

1900 tr. *Ehrlich's Immunity* in *Proc. R. Soc.* LXVI. 443 Solutions containing either only the 'immune body' or only the 'complement' were brought in contact with suitable blood corpuscles. 1901–5 *Jrnl. Exper. Med.* VI. 282 Two principles are concerned in lysis...One..is the product of immunization. ..The other is normally present in the body juices...The latter principle, on account of the complemental nature of its action, they [*sc.* Ehrlich and Morgenroth] propose to call the 'complement'...This body is called 'alexin' by Bordet and probably agrees in part with the body of the same name described by Buchner. Metchnikoff calls it 'cytase'. 1903 *Med. Record* 14 Feb. 249 (Cent. Dict. Suppl.) [Bordet and Ehrlich] recognize the importance of an association of the amboceptor as a condition for the effective action of the complement (cytase). 1903 [see *Addiment].

Complementary, *a.* Add: **1. d.** (See quots.)

1891 W. Smart tr. *Böhm-Bawerk's Positive Theory Capital* ix. 170 Thus, for instance, paper, pen and ink, needle and thread, cart and horse, bow and arrow,..and so on, are complementary goods. *Ibid.* 175 Almost every product is the result of the co-operation of a group of complementary goods consisting of uses of ground, labour, fixed and floating capital. 1892 *Palgrave's Dict. Pol. Econ.* 380/1 *Complementary goods*, this expression is used by the Austrian economist Menger..who describes goods as of first, second, or higher rank in order of production...This conception becomes of special interest when the value of the complementary goods is considered for each separately.

Compleme·ntophil(e, *a.* *Biol. Chem.* [f. *Complement *sb.* 5 i + -phil.] Having affinity for or uniting with, the complement.

1903 *Lancet* 4 Apr. 943 The amboceptor will unite with the bacterium by its haptophore group, the complement will then fit into the complementophile group of the amboceptor and the bacterium will be destroyed.

Complex, *sb.* Add:

3. *Psycho-analysis.* A group of ideas of a spontaneous and emotional character associated by the individual with a particular subject, often indicating a kind of mental abnormality arising from repressed instincts or the like. Hence *colloq.* in vague use, a fixed mental tendency or obsession, esp. in phr. *inferiority complex.*

The use of the term was established by C. G. Jung, of Zürich, in 1907 (*Ueber die Psychologie der Dementia Praecox*), but it originated with Neisser in 1906 (*Individualität und Psychose*).

1910 E. Jones (*title*) The Œdipus-Complex as an Explanation of Hamlet's Mystery. 1911 Mitchell *Trans. Psycho-Med. Soc.* in Sidis *Diagnosis Psychopathic Dis.* 418 The delay in our response to the stimulus is due to the inhibition exercised by the manifold of associated complexes that have been aroused to function. 1913 Jung in *Trans. Internat. Congress Med.* xii. 67 The unconscious existence of manifold phantasies, which have their final root in the infantile past and turn around the so-called 'Kern-complex', or nucleus complex, which may be qualified in male individuals as the Œdipus-complex and in females as the Electra-complex. 1919 *Athenæum* 23 May 360/2 Without the adjective ['mental'], 'a complex' is now a polite euphemism for a bee in one's bonnet. 1920 B. Low *Psycho-Analysis* 87 Freud's theory of the Complex is inevitably bound up with that of Repression. 1921 *Punch* 5 Jan. 2/2 The distressing complex developed by his ordeal shows no signs of subsidence. 1924 N. P. Williams *Ideas of Fall & Orig. Sin* (1927) p. xxiv, We therefore identify the 'inherited infirmity' of theology with 'inherited weakness of herd-complex'. 1924 Leacock *Garden of Folly* 47 The man is rushed off to a rest-house to have his complex removed. 1926 McDougall *Introd. Soc. Psychol.* 403 The psycho-analysts use the term 'complex' to cover both the normal sentiments and the morbidly repressed sentiments. I have urged that by restricting the term 'complex' to the latter, and using the term 'sentiment' for the former, we usefully differentiate our terminology. 1926 — *Outline Abnormal Psychol.* xxvii. 433 The inferiority complex is an important factor in some neurotics. 1926 Arnold Bennett *Woman who Stole Everything, Umbrella* iii. 165 'Muriel's losing her sex-complex.' 'What on earth do you mean, boy?' 'She's getting herself tangled up with some man.' *Ibid.*, *Death*, etc. iv. 301 She raised herself on her elbows and kissed him; she had no forbidding complex. 1928 *Punch* 8 Feb. 157 A fond aunt with a commiseration complex.

Complicant (kǫ·mplikănt), *a.* *Ent.* [ad. L. *complicāntem*, pr. pple. of *complicāre* to fold together: see Complicate.] Of elytra: Overlapping.

1826 Kirby & Sp. *Entomol.* IV. xlvi. 334.

Complication. Add: **4. c.** *Psychol.* The simultaneous association of the perceptions or ideas received through different senses.

1894 tr. *W. Wundt's Hum. & Anim. Psychol.* 285 These connections of ideas of disparate senses which are referred to the same objects, and so belong closely together, we may term with Herbart *complications*. 1898 G. F. Stout *Man. Psychol.* I. 91 The process is called *complication*, because the result is merely a change in the constitution of *A*, and for the most part an increase in its complexity.

Complimentarily, *adv.* (Earlier U.S. example.)

1809 A. Henry *Travels* 297 These amusements were given to us complimentarily, by the chief.

Component. B. *sb.* **2.** Add: Applied *spec.* to the separate parts of motor cars and bicycles. Hence *attrib.* and *Comb.*, as *component maker*; *component-built* adj.

1896 *Daily News* 2 July 2/5 Manufacturers of cycle and cycle components. 1897 *Ibid.* 29 Mar. 8/7 Cycle tube and component makers. 1907 *Daily Chron.* 18 Jan. 9/2 A component-built machine. 1925 *Morris Owner's Man.* 95 The replacing of any worn component by a new one.

Comport, *sb.*[2] [The earlier evidence now available shows that *compote* in this sense (see *Compote 3 below) is later than *comport.*]

1771 in J. E. Nightingale *Contrib. E. E. Porcelain* (1881) 26 Four shell pattern comports, enamel'd in flowers. 1783 *Ibid.* p. lxxxii, A capital desert service of Worcester,..containing 18 comports of various shapes. 1811 in Jewitt *Ceramic Art Gt. Brit.* (1878) II. 107, 4 Comports of Landscapes, 6 Comports of plants. 1862 *Catal. Internat. Exhib., Brit.* II. No. 6769 Dessert service of flint glass,..consisting of decanters, carafes, finger basins, ice plates, elevated comports, jugs,..and other glasses. 1924 H. Barnard *Chats on Wedgwood Ware* 91 Dessert baskets, comports, compotiers, custard stands and cups, and candlesticks..in plain glazed cream colour.

Comportier, comporteer, var. ff. *Compotier.

1764 *Felix Farley's Jrnl.* 22 Dec. in Pountney *Old Bristol Potteries* (1920) 225 Matchless pieces of the fine Chelsea in Figures, Dishes, Plates, Comportiers. 1822 *Auction Catal. Fonthill Abbey* 31 Two old Derby montephs...Nine comportiers of the same. *Ibid.* 66, 2 rich Japan comportiers. *c* 1832 in E. A. Barber *Pottery & Porcelain U.S.* (1893) 150 Gravy boats..square comforts..high comporteers..cake stands. 1862 *Catal. Internat. Exhib., Brit.* II. No. 6897, Dessert comportiers, with parian supports.

Compositional, *a.* Delete *rare* and add:

1922 *Daily Mail* 8 Nov. 13 The compositional lines are so obvious that if the left half of the picture were covered up it would be..easy to fill in mentally the hidden part. 1927 *Observer* 10 July 14/2 This defiance of compositional rules. 1928 *Ibid.* 17 June 14/3 All the artists so far mentioned are mainly concerned with compositional problems.

Compote. Add:

1. b. A dish consisting of fruit salad or (mixed) stewed fruit.

1863 Mrs. Beeton *Bk. Househ. Managem.* § 1541 Take out the lemon peel, pour the syrup over the figs, and the compôte, when cold, will be ready for table. 1925 F. B. Jack *Gd. Househ. Cook. Bk.* 193 If the compote is not being used for children a little red wine may be added to the syrup when stewing the pears.

3. (In full *compote-dish.*) = Comport *sb.*[2] orig. *U.S.*

a 1904 in A. Hayden *Chats Engl. China* 160 Dessert service ..consisting of one tall compôte, seven oval dishes [etc.]. 1926 *Tribune* (Chicago) 11 June, Compotes...These may also be used as mayonnaise or bonbon dishes.

Compoted (kǫ·mpotĕd), *a.* [f. Compote 1 + -ed[2].] Forming compotes, made into compotes.

1920 C. Ranhofer *Epicurean* 11 Compoted dried fruits. 1928 *Daily Express* 4 June 5/3 [Strawberries] jellied and compoted.

Compotier (koñpotye). [ad. F. *compotier*, f. Compote.] = Comport *sb.*[2]; also, a dish for stewed fruit.

1755 in W. King *Chelsea Porcelain* (1922) 71 One oval scollop'd compotier, 2 large scollop'd ditto, 2 heart-shaped ditto, and 4 nurl'd. 1776 *Pennsylvania Ledger* 20 Apr., Joseph Stansbury..is selling off..his baking dishes, compotiers, pudding dishes [etc.]. 1851 *Offic. Descr. & Illustr. Catal. Gt. Exhib.* II. 720/1 Centre pieces, compotiers, dessert plates, &c., chased, painted, and gilt. 1856 J. C. Robinson *Invent. Objects Mus. Ornamental Art* 36 Oval-shaped 'Compotiere'. 1862 *Record Internat. Exhib.* 419 b, The introduction of parian for decorative purposes in centre-pieces, compotieres, &c., is Messrs. Minton's forte. 1885 A. H. Church *Engl. Porcelain* 51 One of the most popular of all the ornamental pieces made in English china factories during the last century is the 'shell centre-piece', or *compotier*, for the dessert table. It consisted of from one to five tiers of scallops.

Compound, *sb.*[2] Add:

2. In S. Africa, an enclosure designed to prevent the smuggling of diamonds, within which the labourers in the Kimberley diamond mines live and remain during their term of employment (see quot. 1893) and have no communication with the outside, all necessaries being supplied by shops, etc. within the compound. *attrib.*, as *compound manager, system.*

1893 T. Cook *Mission Tour* 25 The men sign articles to remain in these compounds for a certain period, usually six months, and are not allowed to leave for any cause until the time has expired. 1897 *Empire* 11 Dec., The Compound system saved the mines from the clutches of the illicit diamond buyers. 1901 *Contemp. Rev.* Mar. 320 How does he [*sc.* the native] get into the Kimberley compounds? He goes there of his own accord. 1906 *Westm. Gaz.* 19 June 2/2 A riot at the Nourse Mine..in which 400 Chinese wrecked the house of the compound manager.

Compound, *a.* **2. e.** Add: *compound-winding*; *-wound* adj.

1884 S. P. Thompson *Dyn.-Electr. Mach.* 96 Compound windings may be arranged in several different ways. If wound on the same core the shunt coils are sometimes wound outside the series coils: less frequently the series coils are outside the shunt. *Ibid.* 98 The compound-wound or self-regulating dynamos. 1902 *Encycl. Brit.* XXVII. 587/2 Compound-winding..was first used by S. A. Varley and by Brush.

Compound, *v.* Add:

2. f. *Electr. trans.* To wind the field magnets of (a dynamo) so that it will be excited by a current flowing through both a shunt and a series coil.

1884 Higgs *Magn. & Dyn.-Electr. Mach.* 253 The Gülcher machine..has been 'compounded,' or made self-regulating, by winding the field-magnets, so as to secure a constant potential at the terminals. 1902 *Encycl. Brit.* XXVII. 588/1 If the series-turns are still further increased, the voltage may be made to rise with an increasing load, and the machine is 'over-compounded'.

16. *Racing slang.* Of an animal: To fail to maintain its speed or strength, give out, fail.

1876 *Coursing Cal.* 126 It is difficult to say whether the best of the dog puppies came off successful, as they were all beginning to compound to-day. 1928 *Observer* 17 June 28/6 Once in the line for home, Goose Kiss did not remain at the head of affairs, for he compounded rapidly.

Compounded, *ppl. a.* Add: **4.** *Compounded tenancy*, tenancy by which the tenant's rates are included in his rent, and paid by the landlord.

1905 *Daily Chron.* 18 May 3/4 The owners of 'flats' and other 'compounded' tenancies get off with so much abatement.

Compounder. Add:

1. b. *Compounder of medicine*, an apothecary attached to the army medical corps.

1894 Campbell-Bannerman in *Hansard's Parl. Deb.* Ser. iv. XXVI. 830 With regard to the apothecaries, he was glad to say they were an expiring body, and as they ceased their places were taken by a class of non-commissioned officers who were called compounders of medicine. 1899 *Daily News* 21 Dec. 3/1 Royal Army Medical Corps. Compounders of medicine are urgently required for service in South Africa.

Compresence (kǫmpre·zĕns). Delete †*Obs.* and add mod. examples.

1920 A. S. Pringle-Pattison *Idea of God* 354 The compresence of all these moments in a single experience. 1924 Hetherington *Life & Lett. Sir H. Jones* 163 'There are minds and there are things.'..'They interact. During their interaction there is knowing.' But their interaction is not.. the casual outcome of their 'compresence' or co-existence.

Compress, *sb.* **2.** Add: Also, an establishment in which cotton bales are compressed. *U.S. colloq.*

1907 *Westm. Gaz.* 23 Sept. 6/3 [Mississippi.] The Gulf Compress Company.

Compress, *v.* Add: **2. c.** To subject to compression in an air-lock. Cf. *Decompress *v.*

Compression. Add: **1. d.** The reduction in volume of the explosive charge of gas and air drawn into the cylinder of an engine using this power.

1887 *Encycl. Brit.* XXII. 523/1 Compression did not in his case increase what may be called the theoretical thermodynamic efficiency. 1908 *Westm. Gaz.* 20 Aug. 4/2 It has been aptly stated that the carburetter is the lungs of the internal-combustion engine, and in a similar way the compression may be said to represent the muscle. 1912 *Motor Manual* 227 No engine ever pulled well with feeble compression.

e. The resistance of the steam left in an engine cylinder after the exhaust is closed.

1871 *English Mechanic* 7 July 377 The relative ratios of compression and of expansion during the exhaust and steam strokes. 1883 M. N. Forney *Catechism of Locomotive* 44 The steam-port is also closed to the exhaust, or compression, as it is called. 1886 *Sci. Amer.* (N.S.) LIV. 56/2 'Compression' [in a steam-engine] is confinement of steam by closing the exhaust opening before the return stroke is ended, thus causing a rise in pressure.

f. The process of subjecting to compressed air in an air-lock.

1906 [see *Decompress *v.*].

5. *compression gauge, spring*; **compression rib** (see quot.); **compression stroke,** the stroke of the piston effecting the compression of the gas and air in the cylinder of an engine.

1912 *Motor Man.* 234 Each cylinder fails to show a high reading on a *compression gauge. 1918 Farrow *Dict. Mil. Terms*, **Compression Rib*, in an aëroplane, a rib that acts as an ordinary rib, besides bearing the stress of compression produced by the tension of the internal bracing wires. 1904 Young *Compl. Motorist* (ed. 2) 82 The steering on the car is of an exceedingly strong character...Very strong and stiff *compression springs effectually prevent any possibility of 'backlash'. 1893 B. Donkin *Gas, Oil, & Air Engines* vii. (1896) 89 The *compression stroke forces this residuum and part of the fresh charge up the narrow passage leading to the hot tube, and causes ignition. 1908 *Westm. Gaz.* 22 Oct. 4/3 The compression-stroke, in which the piston, by its upward motion compresses the charge of gas into the head of the cylinder. 1912 *Motor Man.* 237 The power is developed during a complete cycle of four strokes..one occurring at each half revolution or every stroke of the piston; thus (1) suction stroke, (2) compression stroke [etc.].

Compressor. Add: **2.** One who compresses, *spec.* the attendant or operator of a compressing machine. Also *compressor man.*

1920 *Glasgow Herald* 3 July 8 John K. Robertson, compressor,..allowed three gallons of oil to escape from a compressed-air engine. 1921 *Dict. Occup. Terms* (1927) § 088 *Compressor man*;..operates, by hand, machine which compresses charge of partially dried coal into a solid cake [etc.]. *Ibid.* § 148 Compressor, carbonic acid gas.

Comprimaria (kǫmprimā·ria). [It., fem. of *comprimario*, f. *com* = Con- + *primo*, *-a* (as in Prima donna) + *-ario, -a,* -ary[1].] A singer who ranks with a prima donna.

1900 *Daily News* 2 Feb. 6/6 Tagliafico..playing..only a small part, while his wife..enacted the equally useful role of comprimaria.

Compromise, *sb.* Add:

7. Used *attrib.* in sense 5, esp. to define a thing intermediate between two others or possessing an accommodating combination of characteristics.

1893 *Westm. Gaz.* 17 Oct. 7/3 It is said that a compromise amendment will be laid before the Senate to-morrow. 1894 *Outing* (U.S.) XXIV. 477/1 In 1876 he designed *Petrel*, a compromise cutter. 1898 *Engineering Mag.* XV. 102 Better practice requires that the exhaust or low-pressure steam should be used, supplemented by high-pressure steam from the boilers, the combination giving the desired temperature. There are several similar compromise points, which need not be mentioned. 1904 *Daily Chron.* 21 Oct. 5/6 The House of Deputies subsequently adopted by a great majority a compromise resolution. 1906 *Ibid.* 24 Oct. 6/6 Wellington is a compromise capital. Auckland, the original capital, was too far north to suit the southern folks, and Dunedin..was too far south to be tolerated by the northerners.

Comptometer (kǫmᵖtǫ·mĭtəɹ). [app. f. F. *compte* Count *sb.*[1] + -ometer.] A calculating-machine.

1894 *Work* 24 Mar. 151 Burroughs' accountant and comptometer. 1904 *Engin. Mag.* July 612 The Comptometer is a key-operated machine for performing the four basic mathematical operations. 1921 *Dict. Occup. Terms* (1927) § 939 Comptometer operator. 1929 *B'ham Post* 17 Aug. 3/6 (Advt.) Comptometer operators...Comptometer school.

Compulsionist. Delete *nonce-wd.* and add: *spec.* an advocate of compulsory military service.

1906 *Westm. Gaz.* 13 Mar. 4/2 That we must protect ourselves against the Conscriptionists and Compulsionists. 1915 Earl of Oxf. & Asquith *Mem. & Refl.* (1928) II. 109 Two vital matters..which it seems to me the compulsionists have never thought out.

Comrade. Add: **f.** Used by socialists and communists as a prefix to the surname, to avoid such titles as 'Mr.' Hence used appellatively for a fellow socialist or communist.

1884 *Justice* 13 Sept. 7/1 A meeting was held..on Sunday last by Comrades Kelly and Maguire...Comrade Maguire spoke at some length on the 'Aims of Socialism'. 1885 *Ibid.* 25 July 3/2 Our comrade pointed out how the land was one of the means by which the labour of the workers was exploited by an idle class. 1887 *Commonweal* 12 Feb. 56/1 We held an outdoor meeting on Sunday morning on Mitcham Fair Green. Comrade Kitz and other Merton comrades assisted. 1920 Hard *Raymond Robins' Own Story* 58 'Yes' said Trotzky, 'I'll make the order'. He made it. It began: To Comrades Podvoisky, Krylenko and Elizarov. 1928 *Illustr. Hist. Russian Rev.* I. 189 Two comrades, Lashevitch and Kurayev, spoke to the soldiers.

Co·mradeless, *a.* [f. Comrade + -less.] Without a comrade or comrades.

1891 H. C. Halliday *Someone Must Suffer* III. xvi. 264 Alone and comradeless in the battle of life. 1913 R. Brooke *Clouds* Poems (1918) 31 Some pause in their grave wandering comradeless.

Comstockery (kǫ·mstǫkəri). [f. the name of Anthony *Comstock*, an American who attacked the nude in art.] Opposition to the realistic in art or literature. So **Co·mstockism**; **Co·mstocker,** one who advocates or practises Comstockery; **Co·mstockish** *a.*

1905 G. B. Shaw in *N. York Times* 26 Sept. 1/7 Comstockery is the world's standing joke at the expense of the United States. *Ibid.* 2/1 The good intentions of the leaders of the Comstockers. *Ibid.*, Socialism may become the..Puritanism of the Comstocker. 1906 *Westm. Gaz.* 27 Nov. 4/2 Played by American ladies one can only say, discreetly, that it is Comstockish. 1909 Ware *Passing English*, *Comstockism* (Amer.-Eng., 1885 on), opposition to the nude in art. 1919 J. B. Cabell *Jurgen* (1921) Foreword p. xvi, She is the Mrs. Grundy of the Leshy; she is Comstockery: and her shadow is common-sense. 1923 Aldous Huxley *On the Margin, Pleasures* 45 Such minor menaces as Prohibition, Lord Northcliffe, Mr. Bryan, Comstockery. 1927 *Observer* 27 Mar. 15/1 The apostles of Comstockery—sour-faced persons who think only in terms of suppression.

Con. Add: **b.** At Harrow School, abbrev. of Construe *sb.*

1905 Vachell *The Hill* iii, We must mug up our 'cons' well enough to scrape along without 'puns' and extra school. 1906 *Westm. Gaz.* 17 Dec. 11/1 He 'skewed' his 'cons' and 'reps'.

c. Abbrev. of Confidence. Used *attrib.* in *con game, man, talk*, etc. (Also *ellipt.*) *U.S.*

1896 G. Ade *Artie* i. 5 He was..puttin' up the large juicy con talk. *Ibid.* 8 Not that I'm strong on the con talk. 1903 *N. Y. Sun* 30 Nov. 7 Two sailors say he worked the 'con' game on them. 1911 H. Quick *Yellowstone N.* xii. 318 The cinnersure of the eye of every sure-thing or con-man on South Halsted street. 1928 F. N. Hart *Bellamy Trial* iii. 87 The stuff of which con men and race-track touts..are made.

Hence **Con** *v. trans.*, to swindle, dupe.

1896 G. Ade *Artie* iv. 35 Don't try to con me with no such talk. 1908 G. H. Lorimer *J. Spurlock* v. 103 The detective began to get a little angry. 'You've been conned, Miss Grey. ..He's all to the bad'. 1917 Mathewson *Sec. Base Sloan* xiv. 196 Don't let anyone con you into signing a contract.

Conalbumin (kǫnælbiū·min). *Chem.* [Con-.] The second albumin in egg white.

1911 J. A. Mandel tr. *Hammarsten's Physiol. Chem.* 602 The ovalbumin, like the conalbumin, has the properties of the albumins in general. 1925 A. P. Matthews *Physiol. Chem.* (ed. 4) 326.

Conant (konæ·nt). Name of Charles A. *Conant*, an American financier, designating the silver currency introduced into the Philippine Islands in 1903 by the United States of America. Also *sb.*, a Conant coin, esp. the peso.

1906 Mrs. C. Dauncey *Englishw. in Philippines* iii. 20 The money here is a dollar currency called Conant, which is worth 2s. 1d.—half the American dollar. *Ibid.* iv. 27 The Mexican dollar, which is only about two-thirds of the Conant unit.

Conation. Add: **3.** *Sociology.* Social effort, esp. of a community to improve its environment.

1903 L. F. Ward *Pure Sociol.* ii. xi. 247 We are now prepared to consider the third dynamic principle, which I call conation. *Ibid.*, Conation or social effort could not be understood without a clear conception of the true nature of a dynamic action.

Concaver (kǫ·nkēɪvəɹ). [f. Concave *sb.* + -er[1].] One who hollows out the sides of a boot last.

1921 *Dict. Occup. Terms* (1927) § 486 *Concaver, last concaver*..hollows out sides of boot last by holding wood against shaped power-driven cutter.

Co·ncaving, *ppl. a.* [f. Concave *v.* + -ing[2].] Curving inwards.

1871 Nesbitt *Catal. Slade Coll. Glass* 77 A very broad concaving neck.

Concede, *v.* Add: Examples of usage regarded as characteristic of U.S.A.

1905 *Westm. Gaz.* 15 Nov. 2/2 The Norwegian Referendum returns are not quite complete, but the Republicans 'concede' (as they say in the United States) that the country desires..to offer the vacant throne to Prince Charles of Denmark. 1908 *Westm. Gaz.* 21 Feb. 2/2 If we 'concede', as the Americans say, West Worcester, our opponents, on their part, 'concede' West Carmarthen. 1908 *Daily Chron.* 3 Nov. 4/6 He hid in terror, and contrived to have a telegram dispatched to Mr. Cleveland 'conceding' his election.

Conceivability. Add:

2. A conceivable circumstance or event.

1893 H. Spencer in *Pop. Sci. Monthly* XLIII. 23 Let us consider closely these several conceivabilities.

Concentrado (kǫnsentrā·do). [Sp., properly pa. pple. of *concentrar* to Concentrate.] A concentration camp.

1898 *Daily News* 7 Mar. 5/4 The distressed concentrados in Cuba. 1901 *Westm. Gaz.* 24 June 1/3 Such matters as farm-burning and the 'concentrado' policy.

Co·ncentratedly, *adv.* [f. Concentrated *ppl. a.* + -ly[2].] In a concentrated manner.

1891 *New Rev.* June 499 Mr. Irving worked more concentratedly than all the other actors put together. 1928 *Daily Express* 11 June 3/7 The body..will not be so concentratedly engaged in assimilating 'big' meals.

Concentration. Add:

6. *attrib.*: **concentration camp,** a camp where non-combatants of a district are accommodated, such as those instituted by Lord Kitchener during the South African War of 1899–1902; **concentration cell** *Electr.*, a cell whose difference of potential is due to the difference of concentration of the solutions in which the electrodes are immersed.

1901 J. Ellis *Sp. in Ho. Comm.* 1 Mar., The policy of placing the women and children confined in the *concentration camps in South Africa, whose husbands and fathers are in the field, on reduced rations. 1901 *Contemp. Rev.* Oct. 528 Considerable controversy has taken place concerning the Concentration Camps. 1900 *Amer. Jrnl. Phys. Chem.* IV. 413 The electromotive force of some *concentration cells and of cells with zinc and copper electrodes in organic solvents. 1916 W. C. McLewis *Phys. Chem.* II. 194 Concentration Cells with Single Selections.

Concentrator. 1. (Earlier U.S. example.)

1833 B. Silliman *Man. Sugar Cane* 66 Without running any risk of burning the sugar, the contents of the concentrator are emptied into the cooler.

Concentric, *a.* Add:

2. g. Electr. *Concentric cable*, a cable of several conductors, consisting of a central wire surrounded by insulated tubes arranged concentrically. So *concentric main.*

1892 J. A. Fleming *Altern. Curr. Transf.* II. 151 Simple straight-joint coupling in Siemens and Halske concentric cable. *Ibid.* 316 Mr. Ferranti designed for the London Electric Supply Corporation a form of concentric main, intended for extra high-pressure service.

h. Photogr. *Concentric lens*, a symmetrical doublet lens of two combinations, the surfaces of which are spherical and concentric.

1892 *Brit. Jrnl. Photogr.* 29 Apr. 273/1 We have on previous occasions spoken of a patent new 'concentric' lens. 1902 *Encycl. Brit.* XXXI. 695/1 The first lens made with the new glasses was Dr. Schroeder's 'Concentric'.

Concept, *sb.* Add: **2. b.** *attrib.*

1894 Creighton & Titchener tr. *Wundt's Hum. & Anim. Psychol.* xxi. 310 They serve to invest the concept-idea with the consciousness of its vicarious significance, and with the resultant concept-feeling. 1901 J. M. Baldwin *Dict. Philos. & Psychol.* I. 208/1 The concept triangle comprehends an indefinite multiplicity of actual or possible triangles.

Conception. Add: **1. d.** *attrib.*, as *conception-control* (cf. *birth-control*).

1930 *Lambeth Conf. Encycl. Lit.* 44 The Conference records its strong condemnation of the use of any methods of conception-control from motives of selfishness, luxury, or mere convenience.

Conce·ptively, *adv.* [f. Conceptive *a.* + -ly[2].] In a conceptive manner.

1865 J. H. Stirling *Sir W. Hamilton* 73 Conceptively he accepts them: perceptively, he..knows them not.

Conceptualize (kǫnse·ptiuăləiz), *v.* [f. Conceptual + -ize.] *trans.* To form a concept or idea of.

1912 Von Hügel *Eternal Life* x. 293 The reality which intuition grasps, and which is thus to be conceptualized, contains some permanence. 1927 *Brit. Weekly* 3 Feb. 462/1 Jesus is lost in the attempt to conceptualise Him.

Hence **Conce:ptualiza·tion** (see quot.).

1929 *Times Lit. Suppl.* 12 Dec. 1046 Perennial Philosophy. It is in virtue of this exception, or reservation, that the nature of the transition to, or combination with, the formally colder conceptualization of the 'Philebus' naturally suggests itself.

Conceptually (kǫnse·ptiuăli), *adv.* [f. Conceptual + -ly[2].] As a concept.

1902 *Nature* 18 Sept. 501/2 A substance is neither actually nor conceptually the sum of its radicals.

Concern, *sb.*

5. b. (Modern U.S. example.)

1875 Mrs. Stowe *We & Neighbors* xv. 172 If your friend Sibyl should have a 'concern' laid on her for your Mr. St. John, she would tell him some wholesome truths.

11. (Later U.S. examples.)

1873 J. H. Beadle *Undevel. West* xxix. 636 The two old men..with their butcher knives hacked out two concerns, which might serve in a rude fashion for oars. 1888 'C. E. Craddock' *Broomsedge Cove* xii. 224 The old doctor, ez seems to be a good, useful kind o' consarn.

Concern, *v.*

7. (Earlier U.S. examples, in form *consarn.*)

1829–32 J. P. Kennedy *Swallow B.* II. xvii. 222 'Consarn his pictur!' said Jeff. 1844 'Jon. Slick' *High Life N. Y.* I. 107 Somehow that tarnal Count, consarn him, put me all out on my natural reckoning. 1846–52 Mrs. Whitcher *Widow Bedott P.* i. 24 He only said, says he, 'Consarn it'.

Concerned, *ppl. a.*

3. *U.S.* (Earlier and later examples.)

1834 Seba Smith *Sel. Lett. Downing* Pref. p. vi, The vetoe, which is a consarnt good thing. 1846–52 Mrs. Whitcher *Widow Bedott P.* ii. 26 But that's the consarndest lie that ever was told. 1851 *Southern Lit. Messenger* Mar. (De Vere) That's a concerned ugly fix, and how we'll ever get out of it is more than I know. 1887 Mary E. Wilkins *Humble Romance* 405 I've always heard tell that there was two kinds of old maids—old maids an' consarned old maids.

Concert, *sb.* Add:

1. d. Phr. *The Concert of Europe.*

1879 Gladstone *Sp. Midlothian* (1880) 89 My third sound principle is to take care to cultivate and maintain to the utmost the concert of Europe, to keep the Powers of Europe together. 1897 Balfour in *Times* 17 Feb. 8/3 It is absolutely impossible that you should keep the Concert of Europe going for some purposes connected with the Ottoman Empire, and not going for all purposes. 1897 Marquis of Salisbury *ibid.* 20 Mar. 8/1, I feel it is our duty to sustain the federated action of Europe. I think it has suffered by the somewhat absurd name which has been given to it—the concert of Europe. 1901 in *Hansard's Parl. Deb.* Ser. iv. XCII. 184 He attributes all our misfortunes to the Concert of Europe. Sir, the Concert is not perfect as an international instrument.

5. *concert-bill, -goer, -hall, -recital*; **concert-master** (G. *concertmeister*), the first violin, leader of the orchestra.

1893 *Chambers's Jrnl.* 16 Dec. 795/1 An amusing *concert bill of the time of Queen Anne. 1927 *Daily Express* 4 Oct. 3/2 Among the songs which have made Mr. Weatherly's name known to millions of *concert goers all over the world are 'The Midshipmite' [etc.]. 1746 *Ipswich Jrnl.* 27 Dec. in *Chambers's Jrnl.* (1875) 800/1 The grand *Concert-hall of vocal and instrumental music. 1905 *19th Cent.* Oct. 567 One central concert hall would be utterly inadequate for the requirements of London. 1889 *Cent. Dict.*, **Concert-master*, the first violinist of an orchestra; the leader. [1915 *Scotsman* 22 May 14/8 Mr. Conn..was..at the date of internment concert-meister in a municipal orchestra in Germany.]

Concert, *v.* **2. c.** Delete ? *Obs.* and add: To act in harmony *with.*

1897 Marquis of Salisbury in *Hansard's Parl. Deb.* Ser. iv. XLVI. 370 Our naval officers have received instructions to take no isolated action, but to concert with the naval officers of the other Powers.

Concerted, *ppl. a.* Add:

3. United in action or intention.

1897 Marquis of Salisbury in *Times* 16 Feb. 8/1 The concerted sympathy of the Powers remains complete. 1897 *Daily News* 25 May 8/1 Europe unfortunately, concerted or otherwise, is pretty well case-hardened to suffering.

Concertina, *sb.* Add:

2. *War slang.* (See quot.)

1919 *War Terms* in *Athenæum* 15 Aug. 759/1 *Concertina*, collapsible wire entanglement.

3. *attrib.*: **concertina fish,** a South African fish of the genus *Drepane*, so named from the peculiar formation of its mouth.

1905 *Natal Pictorial Merc.* 141 (Pettman) The fish portrayed this week is locally known as the Concertina fish. 1906 *East London Disp.* 26 June (ibid.), I think it likely 'John Dory' has discovered a fish new to science in the Concertina fish.

Concerti·na, *v.* [f. the sb.] *trans.* and *intr.* To shut up like a concertina.

1906 *Daily Chron.* 11 June 7/3 Another blow from a stick on the right 'concertinaed' my hat. 1908 Kipling *Diversity of Creatures* (1917) 251 Then Beetle, concertinaing his books, observed to Winton, 'When King's really on tap he's an interestin' dog'. 1908 W. J. Locke *Beloved Vagabond* ix, 'It makes one talk unmentionable imbecility.' He just missed concertinaing the last two words. 1928 *Daily Express* 1 June 5/2 When closed the trellis work 'concertinas' into a very small space.

Hence **Concerti·naed** *ppl. a.*, closed or folded in a manner resembling a concertina.

1905 *Westm. Gaz.* 4 July 6/3 A concertinaed opera-hat. 1916 H. G. Wells *Mr. Britling* iii. § 4 Fold after fold of concertina-ed flannel gathered about his ankles.

Concertino. Add:

1. (Examples.)

1876 Stainer & Barrett *Dict. Mus. Terms* 104/1 *Concertino*..the diminutive of concerto. 1905 W. H. Hadow *Oxf. Hist. Mus.* VI. 228 The interesting Concertino in E minor for horn.

2. The group of solo instruments in a concerto.

1902 Fuller Maitland *Oxf. Hist. Mus.* IV. 162 In those [concertos] which have a definite 'concertino' the instruments forming it vary. 1902 *Grove's Dict. Mus.* IV. 596/1 Handel's six 'Hautboy Concertos' are Concerti grossi, written for a Concertino consisting of two Solo Violins, two Violoncellos, two Hautboys, two Flutes, and two Bassoons.

Conch. Add: **7.** *U.S.* (Examples.)

1861 *N. Y. Tribune* 27 Nov. (Bartlett 1877) A Negro on this Key..is a more successful cultivator of the soil than all the rebel concks together. 1875 *Circular No. 8, War Dept.* 1 May 144 The white Americans form a comparatively small proportion of the population of Key West, the remainder being Bahama negroes, Cuban refugees, and white natives of the Bahamas and their descendants, classified here under the general title of Conchs. 1877 Bartlett *Dict. Amer.* (ed. 4), *Konck* or *Conks*, wreckers are so called, familiarly at Key West; and the place they inhabit is called Koncktown. 1888 Powles *Land of Pink Pearl* 115 If it wasn't for the soldiers, we would cut the throats of every white Conch in Nassau.

9. A shell-shaped part of a concher-machine, used in making chocolate.

1921 *Dict. Occup. Terms* (1927) § 448.

Concher (kǫ·nkəɹ). [f. Conch + -er[1].] One who ladles out chocolate into a concher-machine. **b. Concher-machine,** a machine having shell-like appliances which work the chocolate and keep it plastic.

1921 *Dict. Occup. Terms* (1927) § 448.

Conchifragous (kǫŋki·frăgəs), *a.* [f. L. Concha + *-fragus* breaking.] Shell-breaking.

1904 *Amer. Jrnl. Sci.* Sept. 192 Cranium. Agreeing in most characters with the existing Cheloninæ, but specialized for a conchifragous habit.

Conchite[2] (kǫ·ŋkəit). *Chem.* [f. Conch + -ite[1].] A form of calcium carbonate, identical with aragonite, found in the shells of molluscs.

1900 *Min. Mag.* XII. 366 Conchite resembles aragonite and ktypeite.

Conchitis (kǫŋkəi·tis). *Path.* [f. Conch 6, Concha 4 a + -itis.] Inflammation of the concha or external ear.

1901 Dorland *Med. Dict.* (ed. 2) 170/2.

Conchoi·dally, *adv.* [f. Conchoidal + -ly[2].] In a conchoidal form.

1899 *Pop. Sci. Monthly* LIV. 64 The sandstone of this formation has the peculiarity of fracturing conchoidally.

Conchotome (kǫ·ŋkotoᵘm). *Surg.* [f. Concha 4 c + -tome.] An instrument for dividing or removing the turbinated bones in the nose.

1901 Dorland *Med. Dict.* (ed. 2) 171/1.

Conchy (kǫ·nʃi). *War slang.* Also **conshy.** Abbrev. for '*conscie*ntious objector' (viz. to military service): see *Conscientious 1 b.

1917 *Daily Mail* 9 Oct. 2/3 The assembly of eleven hundred 'conscientious' objectors at one spot, Princetown, on Dartmoor, where they are known as 'conchies'. 1917 *Blackw. Mag.* Nov. 698/1 So the Conchys, as the Bishop of Exeter calls them, live in a golden age. 1918 'Ian Hay' *Last Million* vii. 93 What are yours [*sc.* sons] in? The Circumloosion Office, or the Conchie's Battalion? 1928 Galsworthy *Swan Song* ii. xi. 105 Conshies and Communists and Profiteers—I'd have had 'em all against a wall.

Conciliation. Add:

4. c. The means by which employer and employee attempt to settle disputes failing the working of a trade agreement (see quot. 1902).

1902 *Encycl. Brit.* XXV. 550/1 The term 'conciliation' is ordinarily used to cover a large number of methods of settlement, shading off in the one direction into 'arbitration' and in the other into ordinary direct negotiation between the parties. 1909 *Parlt. Debates* 23 Mar. 1627 The conciliation scheme arranged in November, 1907, between representative railway companies and the railway workers. 1923 J. D. Hackett *Labor Terms* in *Management Engineering* May.

7. *attrib.*, as *conciliation act, board*; **conciliation grade,** that particular grade in an industry which can attempt a settlement of disputes by conciliation.

[1867 *Acts 30 & 31 Vict.* c. 105 § 18 In citing this Act for any Purpose whatever it shall be sufficient to use the Expression 'The Councils of *Conciliation Act, 1867'.] 1902 *Encycl. Brit.* XXV. 552/2 The Conciliation Act passed in 1896. *Ibid.* 550/1 The *conciliation boards established under the New Zealand Arbitration Act of 1894. 1909 Winston Churchill in *Parlt. Debates* 23 Mar. 1628 A conciliation board has been established for the Great Northern and City Railway. 1928 *Britain's Industr. Future* (*Liberal Ind. Inquiry*) iii. xvii. 216 The '*conciliation grades' on the railways.

Conciliatorily (kǫnsi·liătərili), *adv.* [f. Conciliatory + -ly[2].] In a conciliatory manner.

1903 *Daily Chron.* 23 June 7/1, 'I gave a vote you don't approve yesterday', said his Royal Highness most conciliatorily. 1907 W. De Morgan *Alice-for-Short* xxiii, 'Very likely,' said Peggy, conciliatorily, 'but it doesn't the least matter.'

Conck (kǫŋk). Also **conk.** The cry of the wild goose. Cf. Cank.

1904 *Westm. Gaz.* 10 Sept. 11/2 A joyful chorus of metallic notes—'conck-conck'. 1908 *Ibid.* 14 Nov. 8/3 The wild 'conk-conk' chorus of the bands as they fly in from the sea.

Concomitant, *a.* Add:
2. *Bot.* Occurring side by side, unseparated.
1900 B. D. Jackson *Gloss. Bot. Terms, Concomitant,* used of vascular bundles which run side by side without being separated by other bundles.

Co·ncord, *sb.*[2] *U.S.* [The name of the capital of New Hampshire, and of a village in Middlesex County, Massachusetts.]
1. *attrib.* in *Concord coach* or *wagon*, a type of vehicle originally made at Concord, N.H.
According to the *Randolph Enterprise*, this came out in 1827.
(*a*) 1855 F. S. Marryat *Mtns. & Molehills* 249 The stage coach was of American manufacture, and of the class known as 'Concord' coaches. 1873 J. H. Beadle *Undevel. West* xv. 255 From noon till 5 p.m. we endure the thumping of a concord coach over the Sierra spurs. 1887 *Harper's Mag.* May 871/2 Concord coaches with inviting outside seats stood about. 1909 C. H. Sternberg *Life Fossil Hunter* 144, I entered a Concord coach drawn by a team of eight horses. (*b*) 1860 Holland *Miss Gilbert's Career* xxiii. 399 Strings of rustic lovers in Concord wagons make pilgrimages to the shrines of learning. 1870 *Congress. Globe* 30 Mar., App. 264/2 Building the famous Concord wagons, found in all parts of the country. 1903 C. B. Loomis *Cheerful Americans* 3, I climbed into the Concord wagon, and had driven a mile on my way when [etc.].
b. *ellipt.* A Concord coach.
1908 Mulford *Orphan* iv. 38 Bill Howland emerged from the..office..and strolled down the street to where his Concord stood. 1925 — *Cottonwood Gulch* xiv. 172 Along the road came a dusty Concord,..drawn by six horses.
2. *Concord grape*, a variety of grape originating at Concord, Mass. Also *ellipt.*
Developed from a wild grape by E. W. Bull in 1840, and put on the market in 1854.
1858 *Trans. Mich. Agric. Soc.* X. 217 Mr. Prince thought it a better grape than the Concord. 1864 *Rep. Maine Board Agric.* IX. 35 Years after the introduction of the Isabella came the Diana, Concord, and some others. 1871 R. Somers *Southern States since War* 128 *note*, The 'Concord' grape is almost black, of rather thick skin, but juicy and sweet. 1902 *Fortn. Rev.* June 1007, I miss the California grapes and the Concords with their clusters of deep blue berries. 1911 S. E. White *Bobby Orde* x. (1916) 125 The satiny 'Concords'.., however, were better dipped in cool water.

Concordantial, *a.* (Later U.S. example.)
1900 *Nation* (N.Y.) 29 Mar. 246/2 The almost concordantial completeness of the text-critical apparatus.

Concordatory (kǫnkǭ·ɹdătəri), *a.* [f. Concordat + -ory, after F. *concordataire*.] Of or pertaining to a concordat, esp. that between church and state in France.
1896 *Edin. Rev.* July 212 The concordatory organisation, with all its diocesan and parochial ramifications, continues to exist. 1898 J. E. C. Bodley *France* III. iv. 201 The relations of Church and State also were organized by the same master-hand in the concordatory arrangement, which survives regimes most antagonistic in matters ecclesiastic. 1906 *Daily Chron.* 10 Dec. 4/6 On Tuesday next Article IV. of the Law of Separation will come into force in France. This marks the final exit of the Concordatory Church.

Concourse. Add:
8. a. The central or main hall of a building. *U.S.* b. In some railway stations in England, a large open space between the station buildings and the platforms.
1905 *Daily Chron.* 12 Jan. 8/3 Altogether, the station will be the most complete in America... The central hall, or 'concourse', as it is called, of the present station, is a beautiful building. 1908 *Ibid.* 22 June 4/4 The decorations of the foyer (or 'concourse', to use a new American term). 1909 *Westm. Gaz.* 20 Mar. 3/1 (Birmingham, Alabama) A thick brass rod running across the main hall, or 'concourse'. 1911 *Engineer* 6 Oct. 363 A feature of the new building [*sc.* Baker Street Railway Station] will be a..concourse 80 ft. × 50 ft.

Concrescence. Add:
1. c. *Embryol.* The formation of the vertebrate embryo by the growing together of two parts.
1890 C. S. Minot in *Amer. Naturalist* XXIV. 501 The Concrescence Theory of the Vertebrate Embryo. *Ibid.* 503 Concrescence in Bony Fishes. 1913 J. W. Jenkinson *Vert. Embryol.* i. 13 Concrescence of layers, as in the union of the embryonic plate with the trophoblast in some Mammals, where the layers unite by their margins, or as in the union of the medullary folds, or of the stomodaeum with the gut, where the concrescence is by the surfaces. 1917 Arey *Prentiss' Textbk. Embryol.* (ed. 2) 31 The primitive streak becomes highly significant when interpreted in the light of the theory of concrescence, a theory of general application in vertebrate development.
d. *Bot.* The union of cell-walls by a cementing substance; cementation.
1900 B. D. Jackson *Gloss. Bot. Terms.*

Concrescent (kǫnkre·sĕnt), *a.* *Bot.* [ad. L. *concrescent-, -ens*, pres. pple. of *concrescere*.] Growing together.
1902 *Encycl. Brit.* XXIX. 101/1 A single male flower consists of an axis enclosed at the base by an inconspicuous perianth formed of two concrescent leaves and terminating in two.

Concrete, *sb.* Add: 3. *Armoured* or *reinforced concrete*, concrete strengthened by the addition of iron or steel bars, wire, netting, etc., embedded in it. Also *Comb.*: **concrete mixer.**
1906 *Concrete* Mar. 13 The varied uses to which reinforced concrete has been applied. *Ibid.* p. ii, Armoured Concrete Constructions. 1906 *Daily Chron.* 13 Dec. 4/7 The magnitude of this building..will bring the use of reinforced concrete into greater prominence. 1907 *Daily Mail* 22 Oct., Armoured concrete, reinforced concrete, concrete-steel, or ferro-concrete. 1929 W. Heyliger *Builder of Dam* 33 A one-bag power concrete mixer.
b. Paving made of concrete.
1911 E. Ferber *Dawn O'Hara* ii. 13 No tramping of restless feet on the concrete all through the long, noisy hours.

Concrete, *v.* Add:
3. Delete *rare*. Also *refl.*
1864 *Good Words* 231/1 The effect produced by these sketchy portraits..was great in concreting the idea of them. 1884 G. Allen *Philistia* II. xxii. 249 Don't be so abstract, Ernest; concrete yourself a little. 1897 *Westm. Gaz.* 4 Mar. 2/3 It is quite right that a bachelor of thirty should stand *in loco penitentiae*, but to concrete this by putting him into a penitentiary is a little too violent. 1902 *Ibid.* 19 July 2/3 There are few French towns which do not concrete the memory of their distinguished natives by statues.
4. c. *trans.* To overlay or pave with concrete.
1875 *Boston Audit* 129 Concreting side and cross-walks $2170. 1888 *Harper's Mag.* Nov. 870/1 The first proposition to concrete the sidewalks of this village.

Concubitancy (kǫnkiū·bitănsi). [f. L. *concubitus* copulation + -ancy.] In Fiji, the custom by which the marriage of first cousins is obligatory.
1895 B. H. Thomson in *Jrnl. Anthropol. Inst.* May 372 Until..a better term is found to indicate the practice I shall speak of the relationship in which the marriage is obligatory as 'concubitancy'. 1908 B. Thomson *Fijians* 187, I have always been assured by the natives that the practice of concubitancy has greatly decreased since the introduction of Christianity and settled government. 1908 *Times Lit. Suppl.* 3 Dec. 443/2 The strange custom of concubitancy, by which the young Fijian is from his birth regarded as the natural husband of the daughters of his father's sister and of his mother's brother.
So **Concu·bitant,** one whose marriage is subject to the custom of concubitancy; also *adj.*; so **Concu·bitous** *a.*
1895 B. H. Thomson in *Jrnl. Anthropol. Inst.* May 373 The girls can exercise no choice. They were born the property of their male concubitant if he desire to take them. *Ibid.* 374 G. and H. being the children of tabu relations are concubitous. *Ibid.* 375 It must not be understood from the use of the word 'obligatory' that a woman who was concubitant with several males practised polyandry. *Ibid.* 380 It is..possible that concubitous marriage is a relaxation of the stricter prohibition in force among the Polynesians. 1908 *Practitioner* Oct. 596 He found that, as to both fecundity and vitality of offspring, the marriages between concubitants are greatly superior to those between relations (not concubitants). 1908 B. Thomson *Fijians* 187 The concubitant relationship might include third or even fifth cousins. 1908 *Times Lit. Suppl.* 3 Dec. 443/2 Even now 30 per cent. still marry their concubitants.

Concusconine (kǫnkɒ·skǭnin). *Chem.* [f. Con- + Cusconine.] One of the cinchona bases, found in the bark of *Remigia Purdeeana*.
1883 *Jrnl. Chem. Soc.* XLIV. 602 This concusconine.. bears the same relation to cusconine that quinidine does to quinine. 1885 *Ibid.* XLVIII. I. 66 Concusconine dissolves readily in acetic anhydride.

Condemn, *v.* Add:
7. b. To pronounce judicially as converted or convertible to public use. *U.S.*
1876 *Congress. Rec.* 2 Aug. 5079/1 If the Government has the right to make this improvement, and the State of Oregon does not furnish the land..the Government has a right to condemn it for that purpose.

Condemnation. Add:
5. Judicial assignation to public purposes. *U.S.*
1889 *Century Dict.* s.v., The condemnation of private lands for a highway, a railroad, a public park, etc.

Condemnator (kǫndemnēi·tǫɹ). *Sc. Law.* [L. *condemnātor* 'let him (her) be condemned', 3rd pers. sing. imperative pass. of *condemnāre* to Condemn.] A decree of the court in favour of the pursuer.
1557 *Acts Parlt. Scot., Mary* (1814) II. 502/2 The Lordis ordanis condempnatour or absoluitour of expensis to be maid at the decisioun of euerilk cause. 1609, 1838 [see *Absolvitor].

Condemned, *ppl. a.* Add:
1. b. Confounded, damned. *colloq.*
1921 R. D. Paine *Comr. Rolling Ocean* viii. 140 Bless my soul, what sort of a condemned rumshop have I stumbled into?

Condensance (kǫnde·nsăns). *Electr.* [f. Condens(er + -ance.] (See quot.)
1910 *Dict. Electr. Engineering* II. 425/2 Reactance is usually composed of one or both of two elements, viz. inductive or magnetic reactance, sometimes called inductance, and capacity reactance or condensance.

Condensation. Add: 6. *Organic Chem.* (See quot. 1886.)
1886 E. F. Smith tr. *V. von Richter's Org. Chem.* 155 Such a union of two or more molecules by the linking of carbon atoms..and the formation of complicated carbon chains is ordinarily termed condensation. 1907 Haskins & MacLeod *Org. Chem.* 104 Aldehyde molecules can be made to fuse together, forming a 'condensation' product, *aldol*. *Ibid.* 212 An aldose isomeric with dextrose and galactose can be made by condensation of two molecules of the triose, glyceric aldehyde.
7. *Psycho-analysis.* The process by which images characterized by a common affect are grouped so as to form a single composite or a new image.
1913 A. A. Brill tr. *Freud's Interpr. of Dreams* vi. 262 An abundant condensation of psychic material has taken place in the formation of dreams. 1913 E. Jones *Papers Psycho-Analysis* 27 *Condensation.*—Every element in the manifest content represents the fusion of several in the latent thoughts, and *vice versa*. 1922 J. Riviere tr. *Freud's Introd. Lect. Psychoanal.* 144 The first achievement of the dream-work is Condensation. 1922 E. & C. Paul *Baudouin's Stud. Psychoanalysis* Transl. Pref. 10 Now one of the most notable of Baudouin's contributions to analytical science, and a matter upon which he differs from the Freudian school, is his careful study of condensation..in its bearings upon representation by symbols.

Condensa·tional, *a.* [f. Condensation + -al.] Of or belonging to condensation.
1903 *Nature* 3 Dec. 104 Why may one attribute to ionised air different condensational properties, according as positive or as negative ions are in question? 1923 J. Joly *Lect.* 2 May in *Surf. Hist. Earth* (1925) 177 A layer which consists of a uniform homogeneous substance which can transmit both condensational and distortional waves.

Conde·nsely, *adv.* [f. Condense *a.* + -ly [2].] In a condensed manner or form; = Condensedly.
1832 I. Taylor *Sat. Evening* 232 It is condensely expressed in the second member of our apostolic canon. 1894 S. Brooke *Tennyson* 377 Their doings and sayings are so condensely given.

Condenser. Add:
10. *attrib.* and *Comb.*: *condenser plate*; **condenser current** *Electr.* (see quot.); **condenser door,** the plate the end of a surface condenser; **condenser house** *Electr.* (see Condenser 6); **condenser tubes,** tubes in which steam is condensed in a surface condenser (Lockwood, 1888).
1902 *Encycl. Brit.* XXVIII. 78/1 If the cable is open-circuited at the far end, a current will still be found flowing through the armature of an alternator connected to it. This is called the *condenser current or capacity current of the cable. 1888 *Lockwood's Dict. Terms Mech. Engin.*, *Condenser Door, the rectangular or round-ended cast-iron plate which closes the end of a surface condenser near the ends of the tubes. 1897 *Daily News* 1 Jan. 3/2 The condenser doors were also open. 1907 *Daily Chron.* 18 Oct. 5/1 Corrugated iron *condenser house. 1924 *Times, Trade & Engin. Suppl.* 29 Nov. 242/3 Wireless requisites, such as earphones, *condenser plates, and aluminium stampings.

Condigned (kǫndəi·nd), *ppl. a.* *U.S. slang.* = *Condemned *ppl. a.* 1 b.
1902 S. E. White *Blazed Trail* xiv. 95 And now this condigned jobber ties us up for a million and a half [of timber].

Condition, *sb.* Add: 8. *U.S.* (Earlier examples.)
1832 in *Atlantic Monthly* (1887) Oct. 434/1 She straightway got a tutor, and prodded Ralph night and day to make up the conditions. 1833 *Ibid.* 443/2 Ralph is..actually gone back to Cambridge to make up his conditions.
9. e. *In a certain, delicate,* or *interesting condition* (see the adjectives): pregnant.
14. a. *attrib.*
1849 *Rep. U.S. Comm. Patents, Agric.* (1850) 323 If it was conditioned properly, it will not change a particle while in the condition bulk.

Condition, *v.* Add: 8. *U.S.* (Examples.)
1832 in *Atlantic Monthly* (1887) Oct. 434/1 Well, on his examination at Cambridge last fall, he was heavily conditioned. 1849 *Let.* in B. H. Hall *College Words* (1856) 124 (Th.) [A young man] shall be examined and 'conditioned' in everything. *a* 1862 in *Harvard Mem. Biog.* (1866) II. 240, I was conditioned in Greek Grammar and prose reading, but soon rubbed the conditions off.
9. To bring to a desired state or condition; to make fit or in good condition.
1849 *Rep. U.S. Comm. Patents, Agric.* (1850) 322 The next process in this troublesome but beautiful crop is to 'condition' it for 'packing'. 1892 *Field* 14 May 730/2 Our friends across the water do not appear to know how to condition a dog. 1901 Jas. Donaldson *Roller Mill* 152 The most modern and effective system of conditioning wheat is by the use of air heated from 180 to 220 degrees Fahrenheit. 1908 *Westm. Gaz.* 1 Apr. 8/3 When my hunters were being conditioned in the autumn of 1906.

Conditionalism (kǫndi·ʃənăliz'm). [f. Conditional *a.* + -ism.] The doctrine of conditional survival after death. Hence **Condi·tionalist,** one who holds such doctrine (also *attrib.*).
1895 Salmond *Chr. Doctr. Immort.* vi. ii. 615 The literalists of the various forms of Annihilationism or Conditionalism. *Ibid.* 622 The Conditionalist doctrine involves conceptions both of man's nature and of Christ's work which are inadequate and unreasonable. 1918 J. H. Leckie *World to Come* 134 He affirms that Titus declared to his soldiers that those who died in battle secured for their souls a future life, while those who perished by natural decay or sickness passed utterly out of existence—which reads very like an excellent military version of Conditionalism. *Ibid.* 219 Conditionalism is formidable in this respect, that it, more than any other eschatological speculation, influences the entire theology of those who adopt it. *Ibid.* 223 This Conditionalist strain in early Christian thought attained to definite dogmatic expression in Arnobius.

Conditioned, *ppl. a.* Add:
7. b. *Conditioned reflexes*, reflexes or reflex actions which depend upon certain conditions. So *conditioned inhibition, stimulus*.
1915 W. H. Howell *Physiol.* (ed. 6) 189 A class of reflexes obtained through the cortex of the cerebrum which he [*sc.* Pawlow] calls conditioned reflexes, because they may be elaborated under certain conditions. 1925 E. P. Poulton *Taylor's Pract. Med.* (ed. 13) 892 Such associations are usually lost with further experience in the same way as the simpler conditioned reflexes established in animals can be broken down by further training. 1927 Anrep tr. *Pavlov's Lect. Conditioned Reflexes* ii. 25, I have termed this new group of reflexes conditioned reflexes to distinguish them from the inborn or unconditioned reflexes. *Ibid.* 26 Conditioned reflexes are phenomena of common and widespread occurrence... We recognize them in ourselves and in other people or animals under such names as 'education', 'habits', and 'training'. *Ibid.* 27 It is..necessary that the conditioned stimulus should begin to operate before the unconditioned stimulus comes into action.

Conditioner. Add:
3. One who tests the condition of yarn, etc.
1921 *Dict. Occup. Terms* (1927) § 398 *Conditioner, yarn conditioner, cop conditioner*;..dries and weighs samples of yarn, and calculates regain of moisture.
4. A machine used to bring grain into condition.
1909 *Cent. Dict.* Suppl.

Conditioning, *vbl. sb.* Add: 3. The act of bringing an animal, etc., into good condition.
1861 F. Taylor *Recoll. Horse Dealer* xvi. 258 Another very important matter in the conditioning of horses, is water. 1892 *Field* 19 Mar. 414/3 These horses are of necessity sent up with glossy coat, unduly fattened—indeed, in 'show' condition; this, too, at the very time of year when such 'conditioning' would be likely to be most injurious. 1904 *Daily Chron.* 8 Oct. 4/5 Prior to actual racing, the conditioning and training of the pigeons is an absorbing occupation. 1908 *Animal Managem.* 266 Conditioning for such horses must be gradual.
4. (See Condition *v.* 8.)
1897 *Educ. Rev.* XIII. 8 Who..get through by much coaching and conditioning.

Condolence. Add: 2. c. *Comb.*: **condolence council** *U.S.*, a tribal council of the Iroquois held after the death of a sachem.
1890 *Ann. Rep. Smithsonian Inst.* 49 The chants and speeches used in the condolence council of the league.

Condominium. Add mod. examples relating to contemporary politics.
1892 *Daily News* 11 Jan. 5/7 The abandonment of the condominium carried by the majority which made Tonquin. 1904 *Westm. Gaz.* 20 Jan. 7/1 To create a sort of Russo-Japanese Condominium in Korea. *Ibid.*, A mild revision of the Condominium Protocol. 1908 *Daily Chron.* 22 June 1/3 A condominium of men and women in public affairs.

Condrusian (kǫndrū·siăn), *a.* and *sb.* *Geol.* [ad. F. *condrusien*, f. L. *Condrūsi*, tribal name (Cæsar *B.G.* I. v), whence *Condreux* or *Condroz*, name of a district in Belgium.] The name given to the upper division of the Devonian rocks of Belgium and Northern France.
[1853 *Q. Jrnl. Geol. Soc.* IX. 22 The *Système Condrusien* corresponds to our *Carboniferous Series*. 1893 Geikie *Text-bk. Geol.* (ed. 3) 786 In the Belgian and Eifelian tracts they have been subdivided as under.—..Psammites du Condros (Condrusien), in which six zones are distinguished.]

Conducing, *ppl. a.* Add: In *conduct conducing*. Also **Conducive** *a.* in same sense.
1907 *Westm. Gaz.* 4 June 5/1 His lordship..referred to the charges of connivance and conduct conducive. *Ibid.*, The suggestion was that they (the jury) might find adultery which she said she never committed, and that in no sense had there been conduct conducing or connivance on the part of Mr. B.

Conduct, *sb.*[1] 12. Add: **conduct-book** *U.S.* (example); so **conduct-sheet.**
1856 Cozzens *Sparrowgr. Papers* xiii. 185 A *conduct-book! There was G. for good boy, and R. for reading and S. for spelling and so on. 1927 *Daily Express* 11 Oct. 3/4, I have known real bad lots suddenly reform, fellows whose *conduct sheets ran into three editions.

Conductance (kǫndɒ·ktăns). *Electr.* [f. Conduct *v.* + -ance.] (See quots.) Also *transf.*
1885 Heaviside *Electr. Papers* (1892) II. 24 'Permeability' ..does not admit of such easy adaptation to different circumstances as conductivity. Permeability referring to the unit volume, the word permeance is suggested for a mass, analogous to conductance. 1892 *Ibid.* I. 399 Let a cable be constructed according to the following simple specification:— Its electrostatic capacity to vary in simple proportion to the distance from one end O. Its conductance to vary in simple proportion to the distance from O. *Note*, 'Conductance' is here substituted for 'conductivity'. It means the reciprocal of the resistance. 1893 T. O'C. Sloane *Stand. Electr. Dict.* 144 *Conductance*, the conducting power of a given mass of specified material of specified shape and connections. ..Conductance is an attribute of any specified conductor, and refers to its shape, length and other factors. Conductivity is an attribute of any specified material without direct reference to its shape or other factors. 1903 N. H. Schneider *Man. Electr. Plants* 1 The power of conducting is generally conductance, or conductivity. 1926 Hawk & Bergeim *Physiol. Chem.* (ed. 9) 38 The blood and bile of most mammals..possess considerably higher conductances than milk and saliva.

Conducting, *ppl. a.* Add: c. *Bot.* in *conducting bundles, cells, sheath, tissue*.
1873 Frances H. Hooker tr. *Le Maout & Decaisne's Bot.* 70 A moist and loose parenchyma, named conducting tissue. 1875 Bennett & Dyer tr. *Sachs' Bot.* 499 The 'conducting-tissue', down which the pollen-tubes grow till they reach the cavity of the ovary. 1877 Bennett tr. *Thomé's Bot.* 48 In many Vascular Cryptogams, Gymnosperms and Monocotyledons, as well as in a few Dicotyledons, rows of vascular cells are found in places where, from the analogy of other plants, one would expect to find vessels, the partition-walls not having become absorbed. Such structures compose what is called a *conducting tissue*; and the separate cells are not called vascular, but *conducting cells*. 1880 Bessey *Bot.* 89 There may be a boundary tissue, a supporting tissue, and a conducting tissue, lying in the mass of less differentiated ground tissue. 1900 B. D. Jackson *Gloss. Bot. Terms* 60/2 *Conducting Bundles*, strands of elongated cells in leaves and even the stems of Mosses, simulating a vascular bundle. *Ibid.*, *Conducting Sheath*, elongated parenchymatous cells in the inner cortex of the stem, continued into the leaves as an investiture of the vascular bundle.

Conductor. Add: 7. *U.S.* (Earlier example.)
1839 *Eastern Argus* (Portland, Me.) 24 Sept. 2/4 (Th.) One of the conductors of the Baltimore and Ohio railroad.
12. c. (Earlier U.S. example.)
1764 in N. F. Moore *Hist. Sk. Columbia Coll.* (1846) 49 Ordered, that a conductor be fixed to the cupola of the college, as a security against lightning.
d. *Conductor rail*, in electric traction, the metallic rail through which the current transmits motive power to the moving car.
1900 *Daily News* 21 May 10/3 The electric contact obtained by a conductor-rail on either of the outward sides of the track. 1903 *Westm. Gaz.* 30 Mar. 6/2 The new motor-cars on the Central London Railway are dependent on the current supplied to them by the conductor rail.

Conduit, *sb.* Add:
1. b. *Electr.* A tube or trough for receiving and protecting electric wires; a length or stretch of this. Also *attrib.*, esp. in connexion with the **conduit system,** a system of electric traction in which the current conductor is installed in an underground conduit.
1884 *Cassell's Fam. Mag.* Jan. 127/1 Conduits for holding electric wires laid along the streets. 1894 *Daily News* 2 June 5/4 At Buda-Pesth, where the conduit electrical system is in such successful operation. 1894 *Cassier's Mag.* Sept. 385/1 A trial of the conduit on a commercial basis at Washington. *Ibid.*, Various conduit methods. *Ibid.* 385/2 The open slot conduit with a continuous, bare trolley wire. *Ibid.* 386/2 The contact or working conductors could readily be placed in a slotted conduit, or trough. *Ibid.*, The road at Blackpool, England,—an open conduit road. *Ibid.* 387/1 The Love conduit system. 1896 *Daily News* 17 Dec. 5/2 The electric power is conveyed from the conduit rail to the car by means of a small peculiarly-shaped conductor. 1899 *Ibid.* 9 Jan. 3/6 New York will soon have 150 miles of conduit. 1903 *Daily Chron.* 18 Nov. 3/5 A conduit line from Vauxhall Bridge to the Clapham-road. 1908 *Installation News* II. 47/2 Three parallel lengths of ⅝ in. Simplex conduit hung a few inches below the ceiling and seven feet apart.

Condurangin (kǫndiuræ·ndʒin). *Chem.* [f. *condurango*, Cundurango + -in [1].] Either of two glucosides found in cundurango bark.
1892 *Jrnl. Chem. Soc.* LXII. II. 1352 Condurangin is a glucoside, first obtained by Vulpius, from the bark of *Gonolobus condurango*. 1909 *Ibid.* XCVI. I. 40 Condurangin was isolated by extraction of the bark with alcohol.

Condylarthra (kǫndilā·ɹþrā). [mod.L. neut. pl. (sc. *animalia*), f. Gr. κόνδυλος knuckle, Condyle + ἄρθρον joint.] A group of extinct mammals of the eocene formation of North America. Hence **Co·ndylarth,** any of these; **Condyla·rthran** *a.* and *sb.*; **Condyla·rthrous** *a.*
1884 *Amer. Naturalist* XVIII. 793 Its Condylarthrous character. 1885 *Pop. Sci. Monthly* XXVII. 610 (Cent. D.) The Condylarthra with three tubercles are probably..the ancestors of the carnivorous orders. 1897 *Nat. Sci.* May 311 The Condylarthra cannot be considered as ancestral to the Lemuroidea. *Ibid.*, The difference in structure between the lemurs and condylarths. *Ibid.*, The view..that the lemurs were descended from condylarthrous ancestors. 1906 Chamberlin & Salisbury *Geol.* III. 229 The present great groups of herbivores were foreshadowed by the *Condylarthra*. 1927 Haldane & Huxley *Anim. Biol.* xi. 243 Eocene mammal of generalized type (Condylarthran). 1928 De Beer *Vertebr. Zoöl.* 456 Very early, a branch diverged from the Condylarthran stock and gave rise to the Amblypoda.

Condylarthrosis (kǫndilaɹþrōu·sis). *Anat.* [f. Condyle + Arthrosis.] A condyloid articulation: see quots. So **Co:ndylarthro·dial** *a.*, having the character of a condylarthrosis.
1848 Dunglison *Med. Lex.*, Condylarthrosis. 1889 A. Macalister *Hum. Anat.* 44 Condylarthrosis, when the convex articular head is ellipsoidal in outline, with a socket of corresponding shape, as in the metatarso-phalangeal joints, rotation is restricted or impossible, and the joint becomes practically biaxial. Most condylarthrodial joints are laterally double. 1902 *Encycl. Brit.* XV. 484/1 Condyloid joints (Condylarthrosis), allowing flexion and extension as well as lateral movement, but no rotation. 1907 T. Dwight, etc. *Hum. Anat.* 113 Condylarthrosis, an egg-shaped joint permitting angular motions more freely on the long axis than on the short one.

Condy's fluid. [Name of Henry Bollmann *Condy*, English physician.] A disinfecting fluid made of an aqueous solution of manganate or permanganate of potash. Also (*colloq.*) **Condy.**
1859 *Lancet* 1 Jan. 8/2 Condy's fluid was commenced on the fourth day, with immediate relief to the pain. 1866 *Chem. News* 17 Aug. 84 Put half an ounce of Condy's red fluid into every water receptacle that is made of wood. *Ibid.*, In the use of Condy's fluid for purifying water-butts, enough should be used. *Ibid.*, The addition of one or more drops of 'Condy'..will speedily remove that smell and taste. *Ibid.*, The microscopic animalcules.., if not destroyed by the Condy, would die of starvation. 1878 C. M. Tidy *Handbk. Mod. Chem.* 270 'Condy's green disinfecting fluid'..turns red (a permanganate being formed) on the addition of an acid. 1894 C. H. W. Donaldson *With Wilson in Matabeleland* iv. 67 We..syringed his deep wounds with Condy's Fluid.

Cone, *sb.*[1] Add: 1. d. *Physical Geog.* The fan-shaped alluvial deposit formed by a stream at the mouth of a ravine.
1864 Haast *Rep. Formation of Canterbury Plains* 19 Dr. Hector and myself, in drawing up a synopsis of the geological formations of New Zealand, have adopted for the formation of those subaerial accumulations the expression 'Fan', for those of regular water-courses; and of 'Half-cone', for those of intermittent mountain torrents. 1890 Gilbert in *U.S. Geol. Survey* 81 *note*, The 'alluvial fan' of Drew is the 'alluvial cone' of American Geologists.
15. **cone-anchor,** a conical drag employed by vessels in rough weather; **cone-cheese,** a wooden bobbin in the form of a cone on which yarn is spun; **cone-clutch,** a friction clutch with a conical contact surface; **cone drawing,** a method of drawing cotton (see Cone *sb.*[1] 8 b); **cone-in-cone** (see quots.).
1902 *Nature* 4 Sept. 447 M. Heureux dropped his *cone-anchor and waited until a tug-boat..threw a rope to the car, by which the balloon was tugged easily. 1927 T. Woodhouse *Artif. Silk* 100 The bottle bobbins or *cone cheeses.. containing the yarn are suitably supported on a stand near the top of the machine. 1874 Knight *Mech. Dict.* 578/2 The *cone-clutch consists of a tapered cylindrical plug sliding on a fast feather in one shaft, [etc.]. 1908 *Westm. Gaz.* 5 Mar. 4/2 The drive from engine to gear-box is through a leather-faced, self-contained cone-clutch. 1909 *Ibid.* 23 Feb. 4/2 The positive dogs being withdrawn before the leather cone-clutch is disengaged. 1884 W. S. B. McLaren *Spinning* (ed. 2) 136 In *cone drawing..all these defects are avoided. 1877 *Encycl. Brit.* VI. 45/2 Coal is perfectly amorphous, the nearest approach to any thing like crystalline structure being a compound fibrous grouping resembling that of gypsum or arragonite, which occurs in some of the steam coals of S. Wales, and is locally known as '*cone in cone'. 1882 Geikie *Text-bk. Geol.* 313 That the more complex structure known as 'Cone in cone' may be due to the action of pressure upon concretions in the course of formation. 1883 Gresley *Gloss. Coal-m.* 61 Steam or anthracite coal exhibiting a peculiar fibrous structure passing into a singular toothed arrangement of the particles called cone-in-cone coal or crystallised coal. 1921 *Brit. Mus. Return* 156 Cone-in-cone structure from Barf Hill, Keswick.

Conestoga (kǫnĕstōu·gă). *U.S.* Also 8 **Canastoe.** [The name of a tribe of North American Indians formerly inhabiting parts of Pennsylvania and Maryland.]
1. *Conestoga wagon*, a large travelling-wagon formerly in use. Also *ellipt.*
1783 W. Gordon *Hist. Amer. Rev.* (1788) IV. 306 A small dirty room in the Philadelphia tavern called the Canastoe-waggon. 1808 *Balance* (Hudson, N.Y.) 16 Feb. 28 (Th.) The throng of Pittsburg and Conestoga waggons. 1844 G. W. Kendall *Santa Fé Exped.* II. iii. 59 Her travelling carriage was nothing more or less than a huge Pennsylvania or Conestoga wagon, drawn by four yokes of oxen. 1851 C. Cist *Cincinnati* 308 The stage coach and ponderous Conestoga wagon rolling over the scientifically built turnpike. 1901 W. Churchill *Crisis* 356 Open waggons and conestogas, carryalls and buggies. 1912 H. Croly *Hanna* 3 In 1802 Robert Hanna, his wife and six surviving children migrated in a 'connestoga' wagon to the township of Fairfield.
2. Used to designate a heavy breed of horses. Also *ellipt.*, a horse of this breed.
1834 Seba Smith *Lett. J. Downing* (1835) 144 The best kind of horses—rale Conestogas. 1844 *Congress. Globe* App. 748/2 Mr. Buchanan..could come upon the turf successfully with his celebrated breed of Conestoga dray horses. 1857 H. W. Herbert *Horse & Horsemanship* II. 59, I am inclined to suspect, the Conestoga-horse is descended from a mixture of the Flemish cart-horse with the English breed. 1860 R. Jennings *Horse* 61 The vast, white-topped wagons, drawn by superb teams of the stately Conestogas. 1875 *Congress. Rec.* 22 Mar. 132/1 The Conestogas respond promptly to the whip.
3. A large coarse boot or shoe. (Cf. Stogy.)
1896 (*Amer.*) *Dialect Notes* I. 229. 1902 Clapin *Dict. Amer.* s.v.

Confab, *v.* (Modern U.S. example.)
1898 H. S. Canfield *Maid of Frontier* i. 19 What, Charlie, was you an' Lem confabbin about?

Confection, *v.* 3. (Earlier U.S. example.)
1839 Fr. A. Kemble *Resid. in Georgia* (1863) 134, I have ..spent considerable time in what the French call 'confectioning' baby bundles.

Confed. *U.S.* Short for Confederate (see A.3).
1865 Boudrye *Hist. Rec. Fifth N.Y. Cavalry* 259 For one dollar greenbacks, we can get from five to ten dollars Confed.

Confederal, *a.* (Earlier examples.)
1782 *Independent Ledger* 4 Feb. 3/2 Washington and the confederal forces. *Ibid.*, The confederal armies.

Conferee. 1. *U.S.* (Earlier examples.)
1771 J. Boucher *Causes Amer. Revol.* (1797) 238 By some logic of their own, their conferees have found out [etc.]. 1779 *Life Jos. Reed* (1847) II. 52 The Conferees of Congress gave this committee very ample assurances of the disposition of Congress to preserve the most perfect harmony. 1815 in Fearon *Sk.* (1818) 144 We enclose you the Democratic ticket which is recommended by the delegates and conferees fairly chosen, after public notice.

Conference. Add: 4. d. In modern legal practice, a meeting for professional advice at which only one counsel is present: distinguished from *consultation*.
1906 *Ann. Practice* II. 211 No fees are allowed for conferences in addition to the counsel's fees for drawing..any pleadings,..deeds, or other proceedings.

Confession. 9. Add: **confession album, book,** a book of personal questions to be answered on personal likes and dislikes.
1906 *Daily Chron.* 27 Sept. 4/7 'If not yourself, who would you rather be?' was a favourite question of the confession album of the seventies.

Confessor. Add: In sense 3 often pronounced (kǫ·nfesǫɹ).
1818 Byron *Don Juan* I. xlix, For half his days were pass'd at church, the other Between his tutors, confessor, and mother.

Confetti (kǫnfe·ti), *sb. pl.* Also sing. **confetto.** [Italian *confetti*, pl. of *confetto* Comfit.] Bonbons, or plaster or paper imitations of these, thrown during carnival in Italy; in England, *esp.* little discs of coloured paper thrown at the bride and bridegroom at weddings.
1860 *Once a Week* 24 Mar. 284 (Stanford) In the centre of their carriage stands a huge basket of *confetti*. 1883 Brinsley-Richards *7 Yrs. at Eton* i. 5 The *confetti* which are flung from the balconies of Roman houses at Carnival time. 1895 *Daily News* 27 Feb. 5/4 People young and old carry bags full of these confetti and fling them by handfuls in each other's faces and stuff them down their necks. *Ibid.* 26 Apr. 3/2 Visitors to the Riviera..were assured..that the confetti to be used at Eastbourne would be the small parti-coloured paper discs which are known in France, and which are taking the place of the time-honoured rice at English wedding festivities. 1897 *Ibid.* 3 Mar. 7/3 A real shower of rain put a stop to confetti-flinging. 1906 *Westm. Gaz.* 7 Nov. 7/1 A wild carnival of confetti-throwing and other forms of horseplay.

Confidante. Add: 2. (Also -ente.). The name given by the English designer Hepplewhite to a species of settee (see quot. 1925).
1794 Hepplewhite *Cabinet-Maker & Upholst. Guide* (ed. 3) Title-p., A great variety of patterns for Chairs Stools Sofas Confidante Duchesse Side Boards [etc.]. 1925 J. Penderel-Brodhurst & Layton *Gloss. Eng. Furniture, Confidente*, an upholstered settee with somewhat triangular seats beyond the arms at each end.

Confide, *v.* Add: 4. b. intr. *To confide in*: to take (a person) into one's confidence, talk confidentially to.
1888 Mrs. H. Ward *R. Elsmere* i, Mrs. Leyburn wanted to confide in her about a new cap. 1904 Lillie T. Meade *Love Triumphant* II. ix, I must confide in you, but you seem..so terribly restless that you have not patience to hear me out.

Confidence. 10. orig. *U.S.* (Earlier and later examples.)
1866 E. A. Pollard *Southern Hist. War* II. 477 President Davis..was surrounded by adventurers and 'confidence-men'. 1867 *Congress. Globe* 26 Nov. 801/2 A man playing a 'confidence game' of the meanest description. 1873 *Ibid.* 18 Jan. 692/1 Like a 'confidence-man' as he is, endeavouring to hoist himself into respectability. 1886 *Century Mag.* Feb. 512/2 [They are] Confidence sharps, young feller. 1887 *Harper's Mag.* Mar. 514/1 Bertha Heymann, 'Queen of the confidence women'. 1909 *Daily Chron.* 13 Nov. 4/4 Confidence-tricksters would rather meet a fly-flat than the most learned of Oxford dons; and that is also why the smart Yankee is their most common victim. 1911 *N. Y. Even. Post* 12 Sept. 1 S. A. Potter was arrested to-day on a charge of operating a confidence game.
Hence **Co·nfidence** *v. trans.*, to swindle by the confidence trick.
1888 *Missouri Republ.* 15 Feb. (Farmer) Detectives.. arrested Lawrence Stanley..on a charge of confidencing Henry Mueller.

Configuration. Add:
5. *Organic Chem.* The structure of compounds, esp. with reference to the special relations of the atoms in molecules.
1894 tr. *Bernthsen's Org. Chem.* (ed. 2) 22 It is the development of the above assumptions with respect to the special configuration of the carbon compounds which has led to a conception of the cause of such cases of fine isomerism. This latter is to be sought for in the relative special arrangement of the individual atoms within the molecule, *i.e.* in the configuration of the molecule. 1907 J. B. Cohen *Org. Chem.* 110 The methods..used for determining the configuration of the geometrical isomers. *Ibid.* 148 The behaviour of carbanilide compounds of the aldoximes can also be employed for determining configuration.

Conflagrated, *ppl. a.* (Earlier U.S. example.)
1814 J. C. Calhoun *Wks.* (1856) II. 102 Rebellion, civil war, prostrated liberty, and conflagrated towns.

Conflate, *v.* 3. Add: Also used *actively*.
1927 A. H. McNeile *Introd. N. T.* 61 The custom of the former [*sc.* Matthew] was to conflate the language of his sources when they overlapped.

Confocal, *a.* Add: B. *sb.* A figure having the same focus as another.
1902 *Rep. Brit. Assoc. Adv. Sci.* 506 A theorem which of course includes the corresponding proposition for confocals in plano.

Conformal, *a.* Delete †*Obs. rare* and add:
2. *Math.* Conserving the size and shape of all angles in the representation of one surface on another. Hence **Confo·rmally** *adv.*
1893 *Athenæum* 22 Apr. 509/3 'On a Problem of Conformal Representation', by Prof. W. Burnside. 1893 Hardcastle tr. *F. Klein on Riemann's The.* 57 Hitherto, two surfaces were only held to be equivalent when one could be derived from the other by a conformal representation with a uniform correspondence of points. Now there is no longer any reason for retaining the conformal character of the representation. 1898 Holgate tr. *Reye's Geom. Position* 210 In order, then, to depict a sphere *k* conformally upon a plane *s*, choose as centre of inversion *M* one of the two points of *k* whose tangent planes are parallel to *s*. 1913 J. W. Strutt *Sci. Papers* (1920) VI. 153 In what is called conformal representation the coordinates of one point x, y in a plane are connected with those of the corresponding point ξ, η by the relation $x + iy = f(\xi + i\eta)$..(1) where *f* denotes an arbitrary function.

Confound, *v.* Add: 2. b. *trans.* To say 'confound' with regard to (something).
1879 F. R. Stockton *Rudder Grange* ii. 22 Again and again I confounded—as far as mental ejaculations could do it—his suggestions.

Confrater. Delete *Obs.* and add:
1898 Taunton *Engl. Black Monks* I. 61 He was then received to the kiss of peace by all the convent, and was entered in the chart as a *confrater*. 1900 Gasquet *Eve Reform.* 28 Sir Thomas More, no doubt through his father's connection with the monastery of Christchurch, Canterbury, of which house he was a 'confrater', became a student at the monks' college at Oxford.

Confrontment. 2. (Modern U.S. example.)
1875 Stedman *Victorian Poets* 157 In youth feeling.. responds divinely to every sensuous confrontment with the presence of beauty.

Confusticated (kǫnfɒ·stikēⁱtĕd), *ppl. a.* Fantastic alteration of Confounded 2.
[1891 Farmer *Slang, Confusticate*, verb (American).—To confuse.] 1926 C. L. Graves *Hubert Parry* II. 113 He would at once begin to talk in schoolboy slang..interlarding his remarks with such words as 'awfully', 'confusticated'.

Congealability (kǫndʒīlăbi·lĭti). The quality or condition of being congealable.
1929 *Morn. Post* 9 Oct., Another constituent of snake venom is a substance which affects the congealability of the blood, and as far back as 1908 it was demonstrated..that epileptic patients had an abnormal congealability or clotting rate of their blood.

Conge·nial, *sb.* *U.S.* [subst. use of Congenial *a.*] A congenial person.
1908 S. E. White *Riverman* xxi. 185 A small coterie, among whom Carroll soon found two or three congenials.

Congery (kǫ·ndʒəri). (Also **congerie.**) [A false singular evolved from Congeries by the treatment of the final *s* as pl. inflexion.] = Congeries.
1897 F. J. Burgoyne *Libr. Construction* 293 The French National Library is contained in a congerie of buildings. 1920 *Blackw. Mag.* Aug. 210/1 He traces his way through the congery of squalid streets between the Cathedral and the Castle. 1928 Galsworthy *Swan Song* II. vi. 161 To the extent of pulling down a congery of old houses.

Congest (kǫ·ndʒest), *sb.*[2] [Back-formation f. Congested (see next).] In Ireland, a tenant living on land of which the resources do not adequately support him.
1902 *Daily Chron.* 15 Oct. 5/2 On market day the 'congests' of the district crowd the streets with their little carts and panier-bearing asses. 1920 *Contemp. Rev.* Sept. 310 Insisting in many cases on sale (often partial, not total) of ranches to 'congests' or landless men. 1927 *Sunday Times* 13 Mar. 11 A large farmer..whose lands would..be divided up among adjoining congests.

Congested, *ppl. a.* Add:
2. c. *Congested district, estate*: in Ireland and Scotland, an area of land of which the resources are inadequate to support its population. (Cf. prec.)
1883 *Peel City Guardian* 4 Apr. 3/1 The chronic distress prevailing in certain congested parts of Ireland. 1893 *Graphic* 14 Jan. 30/2 The Congested Districts Board. 1897 *Daily News* 30 June 3/4 Congested Districts (Scotland) Bill. 1902 *Daily Chron.* 26 Mar. 6/1 The definition of a congested estate is one in which one-half of the area is in holdings not exceeding ten acres, or one in which half of the area is bog land or mountain.

Congestion. Add:
3. b. A condition of insufficiency of resources in a district to support its population: see prec.
1906 *Westm. Gaz.* 7 Nov. 7/2 Congestion, as the word was used in Ireland, might be defined as the insufficiency of the arable and pastoral land..in a district for the support of the people.

Congo. Add: 1. (Earlier U.S. examples of the dance.)
1835 Longstreet *Georgia Scenes* 128 The minuet,..and the congo, which was only to chase away the solemnities of the minuet. 1856 S. Mordecai *Virginia* iii. (1860) 47 Minuets, reels and congoes.
·3. Any of a group of benzidine dyes (azo-compounds of benzidine or tolidine), so called after *Congo red*, the first of the direct cotton colours to be discovered (in 1884). Also *Kongo*.
1886 *Jrnl. Chem. Soc.* L. 889 Congo-red..when reduced in ammoniacal solution with zinc-dust, yields benzidine and a colourless..acid. 1915 *Ibid.* CVIII. I. 321 Blue and Red Congo Dyes. *Ibid.* 322 Isomeric Congo-acids have been isolated. 1919 *Ibid.* CXVI. II. 271 Dyes, such as..benzo-orange R, Congo-corinth G, and Congo-corinth B. 1920 *Ibid.* CXVIII. II. 171 Colour Change of Congo-rubin. 1902 *Encycl. Brit.* XXVII. 558/2. 1924 Kingzett *Chem. Encycl.* 177.

Congoese (kǫŋgoᵘī·z), *a.* and *sb.* Also **Kongoese.** [f. *Congo, Kongo*, a state and river of West Africa.] A. *adj.* Of or pertaining to the Congo (the Belgian Congo, Congo Free State) or its inhabitants. B. *sb.* Natives, or a native, of the Congo; the language of the Congo.
c 1790 *Encycl. Brit.* (1797) V. 321/1 A great number of the states that were under the Congoese monarchs..having withdrawn their allegiance. *Ibid.* 323/1 The Congoese are superstitious to the last degree. 1877 *Ibid.* (ed. 9) VI. 267/2 The religion..of the Congoese is a gross fetishism. 1902 *Ibid.* (ed. 10) XXV. 140/1 Kongoese..possesses the qualities of precision, flexibility, and subtlety of expression to such an extent that 'its daily use is in itself an education' (Rev. W. H. Bentley).

Congolese (kǫŋgolī·z), *a.* and *sb.* [ad. F. *congolais*, f. *Congo*: see prec. and -ese.] = prec.
1900 *N. & Q.* 9th Ser. V. 413/1 'Goober' and 'Pindar'.. are synonyms for the ground-nut or 'pea-nut...'Goober' is Angolan, and 'pindar' Congolese. 1904 *Daily Chron.* 15 Feb. 7/3 The Congolese are, indeed, worse off than slaves. 1905 *Westm. Gaz.* 10 Oct. 2/1 The Congolese 'groups' of Antwerp and Brussels found most of the capital.

Congregant. Add: Applied only to members of Jewish congregations (as in the quots. in Dict.).
1903 *Daily Chron.* 30 July 5/2 The congregants are seated on the ground; the service is chanted in a low and mournful way. The 'Book of Lamentations' is read. 1907 *Ibid.* 20 Sept. 6/7 At the Brondesbury Synagogue on the Day of Atonement, a congregant made an offering of two guineas in honour of the King.

Congress, *sb.* 9. Add: **Congress boot** (examples); **Congress gaiter** = *Congress boot*; **Congress land,** public land under the control of Congress; **Congress price,** a price fixed by Act of Congress.
1851 C. Cist *Cincinnati* 178 Men's dress boots, *congress boots, and fine shoes. 1865 A. Lewis & J. R. Newhall *Hist. Lynn* 417 The congress boot began to be manufactured at this time (1846). Its peculiarity consisted mainly in the substitution of an elastic gore for the old lacing. 1923 Kate D. Wiggin *Gard. Memory* 46 A Congress boot, with the triangle of elastic on the side which characterized that creation of the late sixties. 1885 *Good Words* July 454/1 Why boots with elastic sides should be called '*Congress gaiters' passes my comprehension. 1926 M. Sullivan *Our Times* 407 As late as the 1920's there were still customers for the type of footwear known as congress gaiters. 1817 S. R. Brown *Western Gaz.* 68 *Congress lands, after the auction sales are closed, sell invariably for $2 an acre. 1837 Peck *Gaz. Illinois* III. 278 The land office for the sale of Congress lands..is at this place. 1872 Eggleston *Hoosier Schoolm.* iii. 28 You see this ere bottom was all Congress land in them there days. 1776 A. Adams *Fam. Lett.* (1876) 183, I am determined not to be a purchaser [of tea] unless I can have it at *Congress price. 1831 Peck *Guide for Emigrants* 247 Land..can be purchased for the Institution at congress price.

Congressional, *a.* 2. (Earlier examples.)
1775 E. Quincy in *New Engl. Hist. Reg.* (1857) XI. 168 A happy effect..of the First American Congressional Appointment of the kind. 1783 Jefferson *Let.* Writ. 1894 III. 333 My hopes of the success of the Congressional propositions here have lessened exceedingly. 1785 *Ibid.* IV. 33 Give me fully always the Congressional news.

Congressman. *U.S.* (Earlier examples.)
1780 *The American Times* iii. 28 Ye coxcomb Congressmen, declaimers keen. 1788 J. Smith in *Mass. Conv.* 25 Jan. 133 [He] won't think I expect to be a Congress-man, and swallow up the liberties of the people. 1806 Fisher Ames *Wks.* (1854) I. 349 And I consider too, how unreasonable it is to expect a Congressman can fill letter after letter with important matter.

Conidium. Add: Also in bacteria.
1925 C. H. Browning *Bacteriology* iv. 67 The higher bacteria, like the fungi, develop special structures known as 'conidia', and these conidia then grow into the bacterial forms.

Coning (kōᵘ·niŋ), *vbl. sb.* [f. Cone *sb.*[1] or *v.*[1] + -ing [1].] The making of a cone-shaped tread (of a wheel); the condition of being coned (see Coned *ppl. a.* 2).
1837 W. B. Adams *Carriages* 297 The coning of the wheels must also act like a wedge... This, together with the coning of the wheels, would make a nearly perfect railway carriage. 1906 *Times Engin. Suppl.* 12 Sept. 291/2 The coning of the wheels and the slight inward cant of the rails.

Conjuration. 1. Delete †*Obs* and add quots.:
1891 *Scottish Leader* 29 June 4 Another secret society of criminals has been broken up by the Italian police. A most ferocious conjuration it would seem to be. 1907 W. G. Holmes *Justinian & Theodora* II. viii. 519 Communication and conjuration between the first two sections was established at Carthage.

Conk. Add: 2. A fungus which grows on the wood of trees, esp. *Trametes pini*; also, the disease produced by this fungus. *U.S. colloq.*
1851 J. S. Springer *Forest Life* (N. Y.) 99 (Th.) There is a cancerous disease peculiar to the Pine-tree, to which lumbermen give the original name of 'Conk' or 'Konkus'. 1902 *Bureau of Forestry, Bulletin* 33, 15 The 'conk' or bracket seen on affected trees is the fruiting organ... Conk spores never enter through the bark, but usually through the scars of broken branches.
Hence **Co·nky** *a.*, affected by this fungus.
1905 *Terms Forestry & Logging* 33.

Conk, *v. colloq.* [Of obscure origin.] *intr.* To break down, give out, fail, or show signs of failing. Also with *out*.
1918 E. M. Roberts *Flying Fighter* 334 *Conked*, a new word which is taken from the Russian language and which means stopped or killed. 1921 *Blackw. Mag.* June 788/2 My engine began to conk a bit. 1929 *Daily Mail* 9 Sept. 7 The old boat 'conked out' miles from anywhere.

Conker [2] (kǫ·ŋkəɹ). Also **conquer.** [f. dial. *conker* snail-shell (presumably f. Conch), later associated with Conquer *v.*] a. *pl.* A boys' game, played originally with snail-shells (see quot. 1877); now chiefly, a game played with horse-chestnuts, in which each boy has a chestnut on a string which he alternately strikes against that of his opponent and holds to be struck until one of the two is broken. b. A horse-chestnut on a string, used in the game; hence *gen.* a horse-chestnut.
1877 *Holderness Gloss.*, *Conkers*,..small snail-shells. In the boy's game of *conkers* the apexes of two shells are pressed together until one is broken, the owner of the other being the victor. [1879 Dowden *Southey* i. 9 One school-boy sport—that of 'conquering' with snail-shells—seems to have been the special invention of Corston. The snail-shells, not tenantless, were pressed point against point until one was broken in.] 1903 *Little Frolic* 78 'Please may I pick up the conquers?' 'What?' said Bessie. Bessie did not know that the boys call the pretty brown chestnuts 'conquers'. 1915 *Even. News* 15 May 1/7 The rich folk hereabouts calls it Motor Sunday, the general public calls it Conker Sunday [= Chestnut Sunday]. 1921 *Spectator* 2 July 8/1 There is a season for hoops and another for whip-tops,..to say nothing of the 'conkers' fashion. 1928 Cole *Man from River* xxxiii. 246 'What's this?' 'A chestnut on a string,' said Michael, picking it up. 'Not much good to us, is it? They're hardly likely to have been playing conkers here.'

Connecter, -or. Add: 3. attrib. use in *Anat.*
1920 T. P. Nunn *Education* 165 The nervous current conveyed through a receptor neurone passes, by way of its dendron and dendrites, into one or more 'connector neurones' that lie entirely within the spinal cord. *Ibid.* 166 The connector-neurones of the brain and cord. *Ibid.*, Connector-axons which make their way to effector-neurones entirely outside the cord.

Connexion. Add:
1. c. *Electr.* The linking up of electric current by contact; an apparatus or device for effecting this.
1832 *Natural Philos.* II. viii. 46 (Libr. Usef. Knowl.) When a connexion is made with the battery..so as to direct an electric current through the wire. 1898 *Westm. Gaz.* 9 June 5/1 The bombardment destroyed the French cable connexion house. 1907 *Installation News* Sept. 12/2 Heavy brass connection terminals.

Conniption. *U.S.* Add: also (and earlier) in the comb. *conniption-fit*.
1833 Seba Smith *Major J. Downing* 209 Ant Keziah fell down in a conniption fit. 1844 'Jon. Slick' *High Life N. Y.* II. 171 By Golly! it was enough to drive any human critter into a conniption-fit! 1872 Eggleston *End of World* xix. 130 It's only one of the old woman's conniption fits. 1911 H. Quick *Yellowstone N.* xi. 290 One of the lawyers.. threw a conniption fit every block.

Conquer, *v.* Add:
6. b. *Mountaineering.* To climb successfully.
1892 C. T. Dent, etc. *Mountaineering* 367 Most of the principal peaks had been conquered. 1902 *Daily Chron.* 5 Nov. 7/3 The same mountain was 'conquered'..by an Englishwoman. 1903 *Ibid.* 29 Oct. 3/1 Three of the more important peaks had been conquered.

Conquian: see *Coon-can.

Conscientious, *a.* Add: 1. b. *Conscientious objector*, one who refuses to conform to the requirements of a public enactment on the plea of conscientious scruple; *esp.* such an objector to military service (cf. *Conchy).
1899 [see Objector]. 1903 *Punch* 19 Aug. 117/2. 1910 *Blackw. Mag.* Mar. 424/1 Having quite properly insisted that vaccination should be universal and compulsory, it presently admits 'the conscientious objector'.

Conscious, *a.* Add: 6. f. *absol.* with *the*: The conscious mind.
1919 M. K. Bradby *Psycho-analysis* (1920) 34 They figure in her dreams in forms which imply moral condemnation in the unconscious as well as in the conscious, as demons or brutal people.

Conscript, *v.* (Earlier U.S. examples.)
1813 *Connecticut Courant* 23 Nov. 3/5 State troops..had been conscripted under the orders of the former Captain General. 1814 *Columbian Centinel* 21 Dec. 2/5 The bill for drafting, or Conscripting, the Militia, has passed both Houses of Congress.

Conscriptionist (kǫnskri·pʃənist). [f. Conscription + -ist.] An advocate of conscription. Also *attrib.* or as *adj.*
1901 *Daily News* 14 Mar. 7/1 Colonel Dooner is not a conscriptionist. 1907 *Westm. Gaz.* 6 June 2/2 Not of the Conscriptionist school. 1920 *Edin. Rev.* July 105 Conscriptionist Liberals. 1928 Visct. Cecil in *Daily Tel.* 23 Oct. 11/3 Technical difficulties in the way of limiting trained reserves in a conscriptionist country are very great indeed.

Conscriptive (kǫnskri·ptiv), *a.* [f. Conscript *a.* + -ive.] Involving conscription.
1915 *Morn. Post* 9 Feb. 4/4 It was possible to make a fair computation of the armies under a conscriptive system.

Consent, *sb.* 8. Add: **consent brief,** a brief where all parties agree in an application to a court, and the barrister's duty is merely formal.
1896 C. F. Keary *Herbert Vanlennert* xxviii. 253 Immediately he received two briefs—that was through the old firm of family solicitors... They were only consent briefs, that is true.

Consequent, *a.* Add: 8. *Geol.* (See quot. 1905.)
1895 *Geogr. Jrnl.* V. 127 The terms, consequent, subsequent, and obsequent, have been applied to rivers by Professor W. M. Davis. 1905 Chamberlin & Salisbury *Geol.* I. 74 Streams and valleys, the courses of which are determined by the original slope of the land, are said to be *consequent*. 1930 Peach & Horne *Geol. Scotl.* 10 Consequent valleys.

Conservative, *a.* Add: 3. b. Characterized by caution or moderation; (esp. of an estimate) purposely or deliberately low or 'on the right side'. orig. *U.S.*
1900 *Daily News* 28 Apr. 5/6 This is a conservative estimate of the loss caused by yesterday's fire here and at Hull. 1903 *N. Y. Tribune* 6 Sept., The visitors were spending on the island the enormous total of $1,500,000 a day..and this is a conservative estimate. 1916 *Times* 15 Nov. 8/3 A conservative estimate makes the figure today at least half a million. 1921 Lansing *Peace Negot.* 155 It is conservative to say that between two and three months were spent in the drafting of a document which in the end was rejected by the Senate. 1928 *Daily Tel.* 25 Sept. 15/3 The distances quoted are conservative.

Conservatively, *adv.* Add later examples illustrating wider usage.
1887 *Philad. Ledger* 30 Dec. (Cent.) It is very conservatively English to make concession at the eleventh hour and fifty-ninth minute; but the clock is fast in Ireland. 1906 *Daily Chron.* 8 Nov. 5/3 Modification of the tariff and public ownership inaugurated, but both should be done cautiously and conservatively. 1907 *Westm. Gaz.* 28 Aug. 2/3 'A Conservatively Cooked Green Vegetable'..is one more example of the growing fashion, largely owing to American usage, and not least that of Wall Street, of employing the word 'conservative' in many relations to which politicians are..unaccustomed.
2. On a 'conservative' estimate. orig. *U.S.*
1904 *San Francisco Chron.* 12 July 7 Wearing a diamond pin, conservatively valued at $75. 1928 F. N. Hart *Bellamy Trial* i. 2 There were, conservatively, about three thousand crowding the corridors and walking the streets.

Conse·rvativeness. = Conservatism.
1838 H. Winslow *Boston Orat.* 4 July 19 That the comparative silence of those who stand upon the side of conservativeness, implies a gradual concession. 1928 *Daily Express* 12 Dec. 3 A method of doing business which, in spite of the conservativeness to which he refers, is rapidly gaining ground.

Conservativism (kǫnsɜ̄·ɹvătiviz'm). = Conservatism.
1840 Carlyle *New Lett.* (1904) I. 183 Most of them seem to accuse me of a leaning to 'Conservativism'. 1895 W. J. Locke *At the Gate of Samaria* xviii. 210 The broader Conservativism of our day, between which and modern Liberalism he failed to appreciate the distinction. 1921 *Public Opinion* 28 Jan. 76/1 The enemies of Liberalism have confidently predicted its smash between the collision of Communism and Conservativism.

Conservatress. *U.S.* = Conservatrix.
1841 Foote *Texas & Texans* I. 17 That high moral grandeur..appertained to Rome as the genial mother and bounteous conservatress of Science and the Arts.

Conservatrix. (Later U.S. example.)
1798 J. Allen *Hist. Vermont* 279 The art, which is the conservatrix of all others, printing.

Conshy, var. of *Conchy.

Considerable, *a.* Add:
6. b. Freq. *absol.* followed by *of*. (Cf. B. 2 below.) *U.S.*
1716 B. Church *Hist. Philip's War* (1867) II. 112 Found considerable of their goods, and but few people. 1766 M. Cutler in *Life, Jrnls. & Corr.* (1888) I. 10 This morning.. considerable of a shock of an earthquake was felt. 1779 in *Coll. New Hampsh. Hist. Soc.* (1850) VI. 326 This is considerable of a village. 1816 [see 6]. 1835 *Southern Lit. Messenger* I. 422 [It is] considerable of a place. 1842 M. Crawford *Jrnl.* 21 We find considerable of sage yet in places. 1856 *Trans. Mich. Agric. Soc.* VII. 652 Considerable of the crop was, however, injured in quality by the frequent wettings it received. 1878 J. H. Beadle *Western Wilds* xix. 302 In two days intercourse we had learned considerable of each other's views and experiences. 1904 *N. Y. Even. Post* 26 Mar., Considerable of the moisture for which farmers have been eagerly watching has fallen this past week over the wheat belt.
7. *adv.* (Later U.S. examples.)
1849 N. Kingsley *Diary* 54 The sea is considerable rough. 1862 O. W. Norton *Army Lett.* 48, I presume I do have considerable more time for writing than you do. 1884 'Mark Twain' *Huck. Finn* i, By-and-by she let it out that Moses had been dead a considerable long time.
B. *sb.* 2. A fair amount, quantity, etc., *of* something. (Cf. 6 b above.) *U.S.*
1745 *Essex Inst. Hist. Coll.* XLVIII. 300 A Considerable of Cannon shot [was] hove at them. 1780 *Heath Papers* 5 A considerable of a trade carried on. 1838 Haliburton *Clockm.* Ser. II. ii. 10 I've been a considerable of a traveller in my day. *Ibid.* vii. 102 It's a considerable of a long story too. *c* 1845 Paulding *Noble Exile* 141, I shouldn't wonder if I could make a pretty considerable of a sharp guess.
b. A good deal.
1850 N. Kingsley *Diary* 110 They had been detained a considerable on the passage. 1858 Teresa Viele *Following the Drum* 30 'The bargain was closed', to the inexpressible delight of the shrewd..Noble Lovely, who realized quite a little considerable in consequence.

Consigne. Also in anglicized form **consign.**
1923 *Chambers's Jrnl.* Dec. 798/2 The sentry..let me pass without any consign.

Consociation. 4. c. *U.S.* (Later examples.)
1855 Barnum *Life* iii. 45 He overtook a brother clergyman ..who was wending his way to the Consociation. 1869 Mrs. Stowe *Oldtown Folks* xxxiv. 451 The Consociation was another meeting of the clergy but embracing also with each minister a lay delegate.

Consolation. 3. b. Add: *consolation prize* (see Prize *sb.*[1] 1); now usually, a prize given to a competitor who has not won one of the stipulated prizes. *Dutch consolation*: see Dutch *a.* 4.
1886 *Wesleyan-Meth. Mag.* Jan. 58 Only sixty-one can be successful, while nine others are granted the consolation prize of a half-degree. 1899 [see Prize *sb.*[1] 1]. 1928 *Manch. Guardian Weekly* 2 Nov. 352/2 The thousand-pound prize gives help to one (perhaps there are some consolation prizes) who..is quite good enough to look after himself.

Consolement. (Modern U.S. example.)
1904 Gertrude Atherton *Rulers of Kings* 25 Mr. Abbott had brought him a fishing-rod, which appeared to afford immediate consolement.

Consolidated, *ppl. a.* Add:
2. *spec.* (see quot. and *Consolidation 6).
1887 *Sci. Amer.* (N.S.) LVI. 3/2 The locomotive was one of the heaviest kind known as a consolidated engine, having four drive-wheels on a side, and weighing 106,000 pounds.

Consolidation. Add:
5. A company formed by combining several. *U.S.*
1882 *Rep. Prec. Met. U.S.* 74 The consolidation owns about 35 miles of ditches.
6. *U.S.* (See quot. 1884 and *Consolidated 2.)
1884 Knight *Dict. Mech.* Suppl., *Consolidation* (Locomotive), a type of freight locomotive, the name of the engine, the first of its class, built in 1866, at the Baldwin locomotive works. 1898 *Engineering Mag.* XVI. 160/1 Consolidation Locomotive for the Chesapeake & Ohio.

Consolidationist. *U.S.* (Earlier examples.)
1833 Webster *Sp.* Wks. 1860 I. 295 For one, I repel all such imputations. I am no consolidationist. 1835 P. H. Nicklin *Virginia Springs* 29 From the east you have consolidationists, tariffites and philanthropists.

Consommé. Add: Now esp. applied to clear soup. Also *fig.*
1815 Simond *Jrnl. Tour & Resid. Gt. Brit.* I. 45 The soup is always a *consommé*, succulent, and high-seasoned. 1831 *Athenæum* 22 Jan. 53/1 Quacks in literature..subtilize into essence, or reduce into consommé. 1842 Thackeray *Fitz-Boodle Papers* Wks. 1879 XVII. 209 Refreshments of a nature more substantial than mere tea—punch, both milk and rum, hot wine, *consommé*. 1846 Soyer *Cookery* 53 Consommé, or clear Soup. 1891 *Encycl. Pract. Cookery* (ed. T. F. Garrett) I. 429/2 Several futile attempts have been made by gastronomers to classify Consommés. 1909 *Westm. Gaz.* 1 Feb. 2/1 Friends have..supplied brandy, Marsala, *consommé*, and strong coffee; which have made an immense difference to the patients. 1920 *Blackw. Mag.* Aug. 139/1 In the smaller restaurants, cocktails were served in *consommé* cups.

Consonant, *sb.* 4. Add: **consonant shift** (transl. G. *lautverschiebung*), *Philology*, the change in consonantal sounds which took place (1) in the development of the Germanic languages, as set forth in the formula known as Grimm's Law, (2) in the later development of High German from Common West Germanic.
1888 Sweet *Hist. Engl. Sounds* 93 The second, or High German, consonant-shift. 1905 Jespersen *Growth Engl. Lang.* 23 The consonant-shift is important to the modern philologist.

Consonanted (kǫ·nsǭnăntĕd), *a.* [f. Consonant *sb.* + -ed [2].] With qualifier: Having consonants (of a certain kind).
1893 *Athenæum* 14 Jan. 49/3 The girl meets..her fate, in the shape of a kind of cosmopolitan painter, with a toughly consonanted name. 1895 *Ibid.* 13 July 57/3 The rhythm soon becomes graver, the lines charged with a more heavily consonanted burden of sound. 1893 *Nat. Observer* 7 Jan. 190/2 She rejects the many consonanted name.

Consorter. Add mod. example:
1924 *Blackw. Mag.* Jan. 42/2 Sir William Courteen was a man of power..and a consorter with the great.

Conspiracy. 2. Add: phr. *conspiracy of silence*.
1885 *Pall Mall Gaz.* 6 July 1 No longer will good men be able with easy conscience to join in that indignant 'Hush!' by which the evil-doers have hitherto silenced every attempt to make articulate the smothered wail that rises unceasing from the woeful under-world. There is now an end to that conspiracy of silence. *Ibid.* 10 July 1/1 The absurd conspiracy of silence which is making our contemporaries so supremely ludicrous. 1885 *Church Reformer* July 146/1 When such work as the *Pall Mall* has done is treated by the ordinary press with a conspiracy of silence, then it becomes our duty..to thank that paper for its outspoken boldness.

Conspirative (kǫnspi·rătiv), *a.* Transfer †*Obs. rare* to present sense, and add: 2. Engaged in, involving, or characterized by conspiracy.
1887 *Century Mag.* XXXV. 295 Who shall take part in collective and conspirative insurrection. 1921 *Contemp. Rev.* Jan. 29 Spies and active conspirative agents of the foreign and domestic enemy. 1922 *Chambers's Jrnl.* 289/2 The departure itself was arranged in almost a conspirative manner. 1927 *Observer* 11 Dec. 21/2 The Opposition.. continued to maintain..its conspirative organisation.

Conspiratorially (kǫnspirătǭᵊ·riăli), *adv.* [f. Conspiratorial + -ly [2].] In the manner of a conspirator.
1912 Chesterton *Manalive* II. iii, 'They said it was England,' said my imbecile, conspirator[i]ally. 1927 *Scots Observer* 22 Jan. 16/4, I came tiptoeing conspiratorially across the dread threshold of the studio.

Conspirer. (Modern U.S. example.)
1896 *Voice* (U.S.) 30 July 4/5 Those who want to fight the great conspirer against human life should get out their battle-axes and go for the rum fiend.

Constituted, *ppl. a.* (Earlier U.S. examples of mod. use.)
1807 J. Marshall *Washington* V. 354 Neither could he [*sc.* Jefferson] perceive danger to liberty except from the constituted authorities, and especially from the executive. 1816 Pickering *Vocab.* 69 *Constituted authorities*, the officers of government collectively, in a kingdom, city, town, &c. This expression has been adopted by some of our writers from the vocabulary of the French Revolution.

Constitutionalist. 2. (Earlier U.S. example.)
1782 J. Adams *Wks.* III. 353 Vaughan has a brother in Philadelphia, who has written him a long letter about the Constitutionalists and the Rupublicans.

Constitutionality. (Earlier U.S. examples.)
1787 A. Hamilton *Wks.* (1886) VII. 9, I pass now to an examination of the constitutionality of the measure. 1791 Washington *Writ.* XII. 18 The constitutionality of it [*sc.* an act] is objected to.

Construct (kǫ·nstrɒkt), *sb.* [f. Construct *v.*]
1. *Psychol.* A mental image called up by certain associations.
1890–1 C. L. Morgan *Anim. Life & Intell.* 312 At the bidding of certain stimuli from without we construct that mental product which we call the object of sense. It is of these mental constructions—'*constructs*' I will call them for convenience—that I have now to speak. *Ibid.* 317 What we call objects are human constructs.
2. *Math.* A configuration, outline, or surface.
1902 *Encycl. Brit.* XXVIII. 541/1 A monogenic algebraic construct (or configuration, or surface)... The notion of monogenic construct is wider than that of a monogenic function.

Construction. Add:
4. b. A mechanical structure used in a stage setting, or forming the setting itself.
1924 H. Carter *New Theatre Soviet Russia* 71 Instead of painted planes he [*sc.* Meierhold] uses constructions in volumes made of wood, iron and other suitable material.

Ibid. 72 Construction as it is now understood as an aid to acting and nothing more..arrived in April, 1922. 1929 — *New Spirit Russ. Theatre* 221 The bridge of Life and Death that forms the chief construction on the Japanese stage. 1929 *Encycl. Brit.* XXII. 34/2 High platforms, skeletonized structures, inclined planes, all manner of bare, unsentimentalized construction provide the footing as well as the background for the actors.

10. *construction camp, car*; **construction train,** a train conveying materials for the construction or repair of railways.

1869 C. L. Brace *New West* xiv. 184 Every stick of fuel, every railroad tie, and beam for trestle-work, must be carried on construction trains from these mountains. 1873 J. H. Beadle *Undevel. West* xxi. 397 Hitherto construction cars had been shoved across singly by hand. 1891 *Harper's Mag.* Nov. 887/1 It was Dunn's headquarters—the construction camp. 1900 *Daily News* 8 Mar. 3/2 The armoured train and construction trains can now go beyond Crocodile Pools almost to Ramutsa.

Constructional, *a.* Add: **1. b.** *spec.* Pertaining to or engaged in the manufacture of structural iron or steel.

1894 *Daily News* 5 Mar. 2/7 Most of the steel-works are well engaged, more particularly on constructional work. *Ibid.* 24 Sept. 2/7 The recent distribution of large railway orders in the district has caused constructional iron to be in good request. 1897 *Ibid.* 14 June 7/2 The constructional engineers. 1900 *Ibid.* 3 Dec. 2/7 Ironfounders and constructional engineers.

4. In theatrical scenery, characterized by 'construction'.

1924 H. Carter *New Theatre Soviet Russia* 73 A development of the constructional scenery appeared in the next production.

Constructionism (kǫnstrʊ·kʃəniz'm). [f. Construction + -ism.] Artistic expression by means of mechanical structures.

1924 H. Carter *New Theatre Soviet Russia* 187 They are being initiated into the 'mysteries' of constructionism, bio-mechanics, and other systems of brain and body discipline. 1929 — *New Spirit Russ. Theatre* 225 From expressionism ..to constructionism..has been the path of the Moscow Kamerny theatre.

Constructionist. Add: **3.** One who follows the principles of constructionism.

1924 H. Carter *New Theatre Soviet Russia* 70 The æstheticist, painter, sculptor, poet or any other is dead; the constructionist takes his place. 1928 *Daily Tel.* 12 June 12/6 International Federation of Expressionists, Futurists, Cubists, and Constructionists.

Constructive, *a.* Add: **5.** = *Constructional 4.

1924 H. Carter *New Theatre Soviet Russia* 71 By constructive scenery Meierhold understands essential scenery adapted to the realisation of man's free acting in space, and not photography or decoration. *Ibid.* 72 The scenery was simple, essential and constructive. 1929 *Encycl. Brit.* XXII. plate 111 (facing 24) Expressionistic, constructive and abstract settings.

Constructivism (kǫnstrʊ·ktiviz'm). [f. Constructive *a.* + -ism.] = *Constructionism. Hence **Constru·ctivist** *a.*

1924 H. Carter *New Theatre Soviet Russia* 71 Constructivism was also influenced by futurism. 1929 *Times Lit. Suppl.* 31 Jan. 74/4 The cubism and surrealism of Paris, the futurism of Italy, the constructivism of Moscow. 1929 H. Carter *New Spirit Russ. Theatre* 225 There are two methods by which an artist may express an idea: (1) Constructivism, or symbols and emblems of the world without us; and (2) Expressionism, or symbols and emblems of the world within us. 1929 *Observer* 1 Dec. 15/2 Constructivism was simply to be the theatrical parallel to industrial technique, demanding the exclusion of all useless decoration and the precise functional organization of the stage. 1930 *Ibid.* 26 Jan. 10 Some of the settings suggest the influence of constructivist architecture.

Consultation. 2. b. Add: In present legal usage confined to meetings where more than one counsel are present.

1906 *Ann. Practice* II. 211 The following fees are allowed to counsel's clerks...On consultations, senior's clerk..0 5 0 On consultations, junior's clerk..0 2 6.

Consulting, *vbl. sb.* Add: **consulting room,** a room in which a consultation takes place; esp. the room in which a physician examines his patients.

1869 *Porcupine* 12 June 100/1 A medical friend one morning, sitting in his consulting-room, was thus addressed. 1883 L. Browne & Behnke *Voice, Song, & Speech* 248 Our consulting-room, class-room, and the theatre. 1892 Conan Doyle in *Strand Mag.* Mar. 276/2 Two men had come from Paddington, and were waiting in the consulting room. 1894 — *Round the Red Lamp* 48 If you will wait here in the consulting-room I have no doubt that I shall be able to send the doctor in to you. 1900 Upward *Eben. Lobb* 118 He slowly grasped the fact that the greatest mind of this or any other age was present in his lowly consulting-room. 1923 Sir F. Treves *Elephant Man* vii. 123 A long building with many windows that I recognize as my old hospital, a consulting room with familiar furniture, [etc.].

Consultor. Add: **1. b.** *R. C. Ch.* (See quots.)

1896 *Westm. Gaz.* 24 Sept. 1/3 Consultor-General of the Chapter of the Pallottine Fathers, in Rome. 1901 *Daily Chron.* 24 Dec. 5/7 A Consultor of the Roman Congregation of Indulgences and Relics. 1907 *Cath. Encycl.* II. 71/1 The Auditors of the Rota..are generally also attached as Consultors to various Roman Congregations. 1908 *Ibid.* IV. 323/1 *Consultors, Diocesan,* a certain number of priests in each diocese of the United States who act as official advisers of the bishop in certain matters pertaining to the administration of the diocese. As a body they take the place of the cathedral chapter as established elsewhere...Their appointment was recommended [etc.]. 1912 *Ibid.* XIII. 137/2 The Holy Office ..has a number of consultors, chosen from among the most esteemed and learned prelates and religious. Some are ex officio consultors by virtue of a right anciently granted.

Consumer. Add: **2. b.** Pol. Econ. *Consumers' credit,* credit given to the consumer while he is in possession and use of an article for which he is paying by instalments. *Consumers' goods, rent, surplus* (see quots.).

1890 A. Marshall *Princ. Econ.* I. 109 Goods may be divided into goods of the first order, which satisfy wants directly, such as food, clothes, etc.; goods of the second order..Goods of the first order are sometimes described as consumption or consumers' goods. *Ibid.* 175 The excess of the price which he would be willing to pay rather than go without it, over that which he actually does pay is the economic measure of this surplus pleasure: and..may be called Consumers' Rent. *Ibid.* 446 We may now consider the effects which a change in the conditions of supply may exert on Consumers' Surplus or Rent. 1927 Seligman *Econ. Instalment Selling* I. 141 Consumers' credit would denote credit granted to consumers. *Ibid.* 143 It may be as well to study the institution of consumers' credit as a step in the granting of credit in a wider sense.

Consumptible (kǫnsʊ·mptib'l), *a.* Add: **B.** *sb.* Any object that is capable of being consumed as by wear, decay, etc., in the course of use.

1892 *Athenæum* 3 Sept. 318/3 The loan of a 'consumptible,' such as money. 1894 *Palgrave's Dict. Pol. Econ.* s.v. *Consumptibles,* The loaf which is eaten on the day of baking, the Suez Canal which will last, it is hoped, for centuries, are both consumptibles.

Consumption. 9. Add: *consumption credit* (= **consumers' credit*), *market, tax*; **consumption goods** = **consumers' goods*; **consumption test, trial,** the test of a motor vehicle with regard to its economical consumption of petrol.

1890 [see *Consumer 2 b]. 1894 *Palgrave's Dict. Pol. Econ.,* *Consumers' Goods* (or *Consumption Goods*) include all those desirable things which directly satisfy human needs and desires, *e.g.* food and clothing. 1895 *Daily News* 6 June 7/3 The chief Chinese consumption markets. 1902 A. R. Colquhoun in *Westm. Gaz.* 10 Nov. 6/3 The treaty provided for a 'consumption tax' on native produce. 1903 *Motor Ann.* 148 Hill-climbing and consumption trials. *Ibid.* 155 The consumption test was to determine which cycle would travel the greatest distance on a pint of petrol, at a minimum pace of 15 m.p.h. 1909 *Westm. Gaz.* 24 Aug. 4/2 In the consumption trial of the Liverpool Motor Club a 10-12 Humber car ..carried off the first prize. 1927 Seligman *Econ. Instalment Selling* I. 141 Consumption credit would denote credit utilized for the purposes of consumption. *Ibid.* 174 Consumption credit is in itself quite as legitimate as production credit.

Contact, *sb.* Add: **1. c.** *Electr.* The touching or uniting of points or surfaces of conductors to permit the flow of electric current; also, a device for effecting this.

1915 'Bartimeus' *Tall Ship* i. 30 'I suppose you tested the contacts?' he asked. 1917 *Blackw. Mag.* Mar. 381/2 The order, 'Start up!' passed down the long line of machines. 'Contact, Sir!' said the flight-commander's mechanic.

d. Exposure to contagious disease; hence, a person who has been exposed to infection by contact with a person suffering from a contagious disease.

1901 *Standard* 4 Mar., A large number of contacts and suspects have been placed in quarantine. 1902 *Encycl. Brit.* XXXI. 792/1 (Plague) 'Contacts' should be kept under observation. 1907 *Practitioner* Dec. 837 The infection of scarlet fever is not carried..in the clothes of mere contacts.

e. *Psychol.* A light pressure upon the skin or the sensation of this. Also *contact sensation.*

1901 Baldwin *Dict. Philos. & Psychol., Contact Sensation.* ..A sensation made up probably (Dessoir) of Touch Sensation and Pressure Sensation. 1903 Royce *Outl. Psychol.* 133 Still other points on the skin, very wealthily interspersed amongst the others, give us, if excited in isolation, sensations of contact or of pressure.

6. **contact bed,** a tank containing porous material through which sewage is filtered in order that contact with the bacterial organisms and atmospheric oxygen in the pores of the material may chemically destroy the noxious organic matter in the sewage; **contact block, brush, piece,** etc. *Electr.,* devices for the passage, conduction, or transmission of electric current by contact (see *1 c); **contact printing** *Photogr.,* the making of prints by placing sensitized paper, glass, or film in contact with a negative; so *contact plate, print, slide.*

1902 *Westm. Gaz.* 18 Aug. 2/1 The *contact bed treatment differs from the intermittent filtration method in that the sewage is rapidly run into a bed of cinders,..or the like, and after a few hours is as quickly run out. 1911 Kershaw *Sewage Purification* 226 Treatment of sewage in contact beds. 1901 Waterhouse *Conduit Wiring* 32 The *contact block of the ceiling-rose. 1884 Higgs *Magn. & Dyn.-electric Mach.* 264 The iron core is magnetised by the electric current flowing through the windings of the rotating helix from the one *contact-brush to the other. 1876 Preece & Sivewright *Telegraphy* 37 The zinc plate, fitted with a brass *contact piece. 1892 *Pall Mall Gaz.* 20 May 7/1 The engine is provided with a contact piece, and as soon as it touches the insulated bar electrical connection with the signal-box is established. 1892 Abney *Instruct. Photogr.* (ed. 9) 253 Transparencies by *Contact Plates. *Ibid.* 255 Transparencies by *Contact Printing. 1892 *Photogr. Ann.* II. 58 There is something in a slide by reduction which a *contact slide lacks, and no doubt this is due to the fact that the former is made by the agency of daylight.

b. Applied to operations (or units engaged therein) which have the object of maintaining contact between aircraft and advancing forces of infantry; e.g. *contact control, machine, patrol, work.*

1917 *Blackw. Mag.* Mar. 380/1 Machines would be detailed for contact work with our infantry. *Ibid.* Aug. 144/2 The low-flying contact machines..play their part of mothering the infantry. *Ibid.* 147/1 The new system of contact patrols was found (in 1916) to be useful in dealing with Boche movements directly behind the front line. 1918 E. M. Roberts *Flying Fighter* 131 Contact Control, the purpose of which is to keep in touch with advancing infantry, tabulate its progress, and then report to headquarters.

Contact, *v.* Add: **3.** *trans.* To get into contact or touch with (persons). *U.S.*

1929 L. F. Carr *America Challenged* 61 Mr. Dickey contacted every family in three representative agricultural counties.

Contain, *v.* Add: **11. c.** *Mil.* To keep (a superior enemy force) in position, by engaging its attention so that it cannot undertake any offensive action elsewhere. Freq. in ppl. adj. (*containing force*).

1899 *Westm. Gaz.* 21 Nov. 5/3 The opinion is now generally entertained in Sir George White's camp that only a containing force has been left outside Ladysmith, and that the bulk of the Boer commandos have moved south. *Ibid.* 23 Nov. 5/1 It is obviously impossible for Joubert to be able to contain White at Ladysmith, Hildyard at Estcourt, and Clery at Maritzburg. 1899 *Daily News* 27 Nov. 5/2 Not the besiegers of our several garrisons, but the garrisons themselves, have been playing most effectively the part of 'containing' forces in the military sense. 1900 H. A. Gwynne in *War's Brighter Side* (1901) 174 Infantry will be used for two purposes—to contain the opposing infantry, and to hold positions seized by the mobile portion of the force. 1904 *Westm. Gaz.* 11 Aug. 7/2 The Japanese, having left a containing force at An-shan-shan, are advancing with their principal force to the east.

Container. Add: In recent use applied esp. to vessels designed to contain or store certain articles.

1925 N. E. Odell in E. F. Norton *Fight for Everest, 1924* 331 Certain modifications had..been deemed advisable, especially in the cylinder containers. 1928 *Daily Mail* 25 July 4/3 This practical japanned metal container for soiled linen.

Contaminate, *v.* Add: **b.** *Palæography. pass.* To suffer contamination (see next, *c*).

1913 F. W. Hall *Comp. Class. Texts* 128 Contaminated texts existed in very ancient times.

Contamination. Add: **1. c.** (*a*) The blending of two or more stories, plots, or the like into one.

1877 *Encycl. Brit.* VII. 411/2 The Roman versions were probably terser than their originals, which they often altered by the process called contamination. 1909 *Nation* (N.Y.) 22 Apr. 407/2 In 'All Fools,' for example, we have a 'contamination,' to use the technical term, of the 'Heautontimoroumenos' and the 'Adelphi,' plus a sub-plot of Chapman's own invention.

(*b*) *Philology.* The blending of forms, words, or phrases of similar meaning or use so as to produce a form, word, or phrase of a new type.

1888 Strong tr. *Paul's Princ. Lang.* 160 By 'contamination' I understand the process by which synonymous forms of expression force themselves simultaneously into consciousness, so that neither of the two makes its influence felt simply and purely: a new form arises in which elements of the one mingle with elements of the other. *Ibid.,* Contamination manifests itself partly in the phonetic form of single words, partly in their syntactical combination. 1891 Strong, Logeman & Wheeler *Hist. Lang.* 142 We may lay it down that for analogy we must demand a sufficient number of examples on which to base a rule; while for contamination, a single form or construction may suffice. 1901 Oertel *Lect. Study Lang.* 174 The structure of grammatical paradigms does not escape contamination.

(*c*) *Palæography.* A blending of manuscripts resulting in the occurrence in a manuscript or group of manuscripts of readings belonging to different lines of tradition.

1913 F. W. Hall *Comp. Class. Texts* 130 The problem of relationship [of MSS.] is often rendered exceedingly complex by the tendency which is variously described as 'contamination', 'mixture', or 'eclectic fusion' of the different groups.

Contango, *sb.* Add quots.:

1893 W. G. Cordingley *Guide Stock Exchange* 44 The first day of the Settlement is called 'Contango Day'. 1898 *Westm. Gaz.* 20 Oct. 8/1 Monday, October 31, will be contango day in Watney-Combe securities. 1903 *Ibid.* 6 Feb. 9/1 Monday..is the official mining contango-day.

Conta·ngo, *v.* [f. the sb.] *trans.* To pay contango on (stocks or shares); also *absol.* to obtain deferment of payment of the purchase price of stocks in consideration of a contango.

1900 *Westm. Gaz.* 30 Apr. 9/1 In Chili they should have earned at least 8 per cent., on deposit here 3 per cent., and if used in 'contangoing' stocks, as in the case of the Bank of Tarapaca, considerably more. 1922 *Weekly Westm. Gaz.* 20 May 31/1 Probably at first many of the opponents of the measure may refuse to Contangoe at all. 1928 *Morning Post* 19 Nov., The broker will, as a rule, endeavour to carry over, give on, or contango—the words all mean the same thing—the 50 Gramophone shares.

Conte (kont). [Fr. (see Count *sb.*[1]).] A short story (as a form of literary composition).

1891 Lang *Essays in Little* 205 Few men have succeeded both in the *conte* and the novel. 1908 *Daily Chron.* 26 Feb. 3/3 There is no demand for the conte in England. 1929 *Encycl. Brit.* VI. 328/1 The most perfect modern writer of *contes* is Guy de Maupassant.

Contemporarily (kǫnte·mpŏrărĭli), *adv.* [f. Contemporary + -ly [2].] Contemporaneously.

1844 E. B. Elliott *Horæ Apocalypticæ* (1862) IV. 23 Some ominous derangement of the natural atmosphere may furnish a literal groundwork for the figure, nearly contemporarily. 1928 C. F. S. Gamble *North Sea Air Station* ix. 124 Contemporarily with this.

Contemporariness. (Mod. U.S. example.)

a 1889 *American* VIII. 252 (Cent. Dict.) Contemporariness with Columbus.

Contemptible, *a.* Add: **4.** as *sb.* *The Old Contemptibles*; a popular name given to the British army of regulars and special reserve which made up the expeditionary force sent to France in the autumn of 1914, in ironical allusion to the German Emperor's alleged exhortation to his soldiers to 'walk over General French's contemptible little army' (published in an annexe to B.E.F. Routine Orders of 24 Sept. 1914).

[1915 P. Gibbs *Soul of War* 107 A smashing blow against the army of Paris and the 'contemptible' British.] 1916 Boyd Cable *Action Front* 111 The Old Contemptibles. *Ibid.* 208 So it was that our New Armies had a glimpse of what the old 'Contemptible Little Army' has seen..so often.] 1917 *Blackw. Mag.* Aug. 140/1 The Royal Flying Corps.. sent whatever machines it could lay hands on to join the old contemptibles in France. 1919 Boyd Cable *Old Contempt.* Forew. p. viii, I was one o' French's bloomin' old original Contemptibles.

Content, *sb.*[1] Add: **1. c.** *sing.* The amount (of a specified substance or material) contained; the amount or quantity yielded.

1901 *Chemist & Druggist* LVIII. 18 Jeancard and Satie.. conclude that altitude has no influence upon the ester content of lavender oil. 1901 *Yearbk. U.S. Dept. Agric.* 41 (Cent. D. Suppl.) The director of the Arizona Experiment Station reported that the sugar content in pounds per acre..ranged from 1,491 to 3,361 pounds.

d. *Psychol.* (tr. G. *inhalt*): see quots.

1901 *Baldwin's Dict. Philos. & Psychol., Content,*..(2) A constituent of any kind of presented whole. (3) An object meant or intended by the subject...See *Intent* for this meaning. *Ibid.,* We may distinguish conveniently the presented content (argued about) and the process (the arguing). 1902 *Amer. Jrnl. Psychol.* Apr. 279 Funded or consolidated contents, are..such contents as are produced by bringing together, in a very intimate way, various part-contents. 1913 E. Jones *Papers Psycho-Analysis* 26 Freud..contrasts the 'manifest content', which is the dream as directly related, with the 'latent content', which is the group of thoughts reached by psycho-analysis of the dream. 1916 tr. *Jung's Coll. Papers Anal. Psych.* 14 A definite presentation-content [*Vorstellungsinhalt*] can even create a stereotyped repetition in the individual crisis. *Ibid.* 76 The hallucinatory content and loud speaking is also met with in persons with hallucinations in lethargy.

Content, *a.* Add: **3. d.** *To cry content with*: to be satisfied with.

Cf. Shaks. *3 Hen. VI,* III. ii. 183, I can..cry, Content, to that which grieues my Heart.

1923 *Daily Mail* 1 Feb. 9 It is notable that most of the old hands in turf strategy have cried content with their various horses...Mr. Sol Joel has cried content with Pondoland and Evander in the Jubilee.

Contestation. Add: **1. b.** In the Gallican liturgy, the prayer immediately preceding the Canon of the Mass.

1870 Procter *Hist. Bk. Com. Prayer* iii. § 3 (ed. 9) 354 *note,* The Roman Church possessed a rich store of these Illations, or, as they have been variously called, Prefaces, Contestations, or Prayers of the Triumphal Hymn. 1880 Scudamore in *Dict. Chr. Ant.* II. 1197/2 The Contestation invariably ended with the *Sanctus.* *Ibid.* 1695/1 The Roman words of contestation are, 'Vere dignum et justum est' [etc.].

Contestee (kǫntesti·). *U.S.* [f. Contest *v.*] A candidate for election who is in the position of having his seat contested by another.

1870 *Congress. Globe* 16 Feb. 1349/3 So many voted for the contestant and so many for the contestee in that ward. 1887 *U.S. Stat. at Large* XXIV. 445 Upon receipt of the contestee's brief the clerk shall forward two copies thereof to the contestant.

Continent, *sb.* **6.** *U.S.* (Earlier examples.)

1760 *New Jersey Archives* XX. 514 Every well disposed Person, either on the Continent, or in the West India Islands. 1765 *Boston Town Rec.* 18 Sept., The Representative of most of the other Collonies on the Continent.

Continental, *a.* *U.S.* Add: **3. b.** Used as a depreciatory epithet (orig. with reference to currency).

1841 W. G. Simms *Kinsmen* vii. (1882) 91, I wouldn't give a continental copper for the safety of your skin. 1874 Eggleston *Circuit Rider* (1903) 148, I tole him as how I didn't keer three continental derns fer his whole band. 1879 Tourgee *Fool's Err.* xxxvii. 259 These carpet-baggers don't care a continental cuss how many niggers your ancestors had.

B. *sb.* **2. a.** (Earlier examples.)

1779 in *Loyal Verses* (1860) 53 You Continentals, line th' Augusta road. 1781 W. Gordon *Hist. Amer. Rev.* (1788) IV. 58 Beef in quarters was found,..on which the hungry continentals fed greedily. 1783 *Lond. Chron.* 16–19 Aug. 170/1 The yesterday's paper mentions, that 1500 Continentals of the Eastern troops..had taken post near Philadelphia. 1806 Fessenden *Orig. Poems* 24 High bucks and ladies ..Make finer show than troops of continentals.

b. (Early examples.) Also *not to care a continental.*

1821 J. F. Cooper *Spy* xvi. (1850) 150 If it's silver or goold ..., it's but little I have, though I've a trifling bit of the continental. 1825 J. Neal *Bro. Jonathan* I. 159 'I outs with a handfull o' the right stuff; old continental'—paper money issued by the colonies. 1835 R. M. Bird *Hawks of Hawk-hollow* I. xix. 246 Were I a rebel, you would have found naught but a roll of beggarly continentals. 1842 in T. H. Benton *Thirty Years View* (1856) II. 392 Within you have a few continentals or promises to pay in gold or silver, which may now be servicable to the Treasury. 1897 *Daily News* 16 June 7/6 'Excuse me, Mr. Barnato'...' But I think you will admit I ought to know what I did.' 'I don't care a continental what you know', Barney replied. 1907 *Daily Chron.* 5 Nov. 6/6 The 'New York American'..incidentally isn't caring a continental what London thinks.

Continentaler. *U.S.* (Earlier example.)

1850 H. C. Watson *Camp Fires Revol.* 41 The continentallers..were ordered to march to Bunker Hill.

Continentality (kǫntinentæ·lĭti). [f. Continental *a.* + -ity.] The condition of being continental as distinguished from oceanic; *spec.* in *Meteorol.,* the qualities possessed by or typical of a continental climate.

1922 *Nature* CIX. 512/2 He lays stress on the distribution of land and water within the zones; climate is greatly affected by 'continentality' and 'oceanity'.

Continuation. 11. Add: *continuation class, course, education, schooling, study* (after G. *fortbildung*).

1887 *Peel City Guardian* 11 June 2/1 Evening continuation schools and classes. 1900 *Westm. Gaz.* 20 Dec. 3/2 Drill ought to form part of the continuation education. 1901 Rowntree *Poverty* 74 Attendance at the continuation classes..cannot make up for the loss resulting from the early age at which the children leave school to go to work. 1907 *Westm. Gaz.* 25 Sept. 2/1 Curtailing the period of the continuation courses from eighteen to eleven days. 1928 *Britain's Industr. Future* (*Lib. Ind. Inq.*) IV. Argt. 266 Part-time day continuation schooling up to sixteen years.

Continuity. Add: **6.** *attrib.*: **continuity clerk, writer,** a writer of continuation matter in a series of film captions.

1927 *Sunday Express* 29 May 10 Promising to let her be a continuity clerk if she did not get ahead as an actress. 1928 *Ibid.* 18 Mar. 4/3 The necessity for such titles as 'Time went on, and brought changes in the circus' would bring most continuity writers into disgrace.

Continuo (kǫnti·niu,o). *Mus.* = Basso *continuo.*

1876 Stainer & Barrett *Dict. Mus. Terms.* 1880 *Grove's Dict. Mus.* I. 151/2 In the score of the 'Matthäus Passion' of Bach..in the recitative a single line and figures is given for the 'continuo' alone.

Continuous, *a.* **3.** Add: *Continuous voyage,* a voyage which, though interrupted by stoppages at ports or otherwise, is regarded as a single voyage in reference to the purpose with which it was undertaken (e. g. the consignment of goods or materials).

1806 C. Robinson *Rep. Cases Crt. Admir.* V. 365 *marg.,* Continuous voyage in the colonial trade of the enemy. 1808 *Ibid.* VI. App. note ii, That branch of the colonial principle which relates to continuous voyages...It was in the first instance adopted as a rule of equitable construction in favour of neutral trade, in protection of that part of a cargo, which had gone from Hamburgh to Bourdeaux, and was afterwards captured on the ulterior part of the voyage to St. Domingo. Those goods..were excepted..by the interpretation which the Court adopted, that the touching at Bourdeaux, accompanied with an entry, and the forms of exportation, did not create such an incorporation into the commerce of France, as could render the destination of the continuous voyage liable to be considered, as between French ports only. 1892 Pitt Cobbett *Leading Cases Internat. Law* III. (ed. 2) 334 The doctrine of Continuous Voyages as applied in connection with the rule of War of 1756. 1902 *Encycl. Brit.* XXXI. 130/2 If the ultimate destination of goods, though shipped first to a neutral port, is enemy's territory, then, according to the 'doctrine of continuous voyages', the goods may be treated as if they had been shipped to the enemy's territory direct. 1914 *Round Table* Mar. 330 The decision..that the 'continuous journey' regulation was *ultra vires.*

Contortion. Add: **1. b.** In technical use.

1869 M. T. Masters *Veg. Terat.* 316 Contortion.—An irregular twisting or bending of the stem or branches is by no means of uncommon occurrence, the inducing causes being often some restriction to growth in certain directions, or the undue or disproportionate growth in one direction, as contrasted with that in another. 1882 Geikie *Text-bk. Geol.* 480 Among the sands and clays of the glacial deposits local examples of contortion occur.

Hence **Conto·rtional** *a.* = Contortive *a.*; **Conto·rtionate** *a.,* twisting, tortuous; **Conto·rtioned** *a.,* twisted.

1911 C. E. W. Bean '*Dreadnought*' *of Darling* xii, Its more particularly contortionate bends [*sc.* of the Darling River]. 1918 W. J. Locke *Rough Road* vi. 64 Such and such back-breaking and contortional performances in his bathroom. 1922 *Glasgow Herald* 25 Sept. 13 A pitiable, dazed, contortioned figure. 1928 Galsworthy *Swan Song* II. v. 145 They had so much soul, and that so contortionate, that she could not even keep her attention on them long enough to discover why they were not alive.

Contour, *sb.* **4.** Add: **contour chasing,** flying close to the ground and following the contours of the landscape.

1918 McCudden *Five Yrs. R.F.C.* 18 We got the old Blériot..out and went 'contour chasing' over the Plain.

Contour, *v.* Add: **3.** To follow the contour of.

1924 G. L. Mallory in E. F. Norton *Fight for Everest, 1924* 209 Contouring the hill until we could drop into this valley 6 miles below the bungalow.

Contrabandist. (Earlier U.S. example.)

1813 *Columbian Centinel* 28 Aug. 2/3 An expedition has been fitted out below to destroy the nest of French and creole Contrabandists and Pirates.

Contra-bassoon. A double bassoon.

1928 J. P. Sousa *Marching Along* xiv. 276 The additions [to the classic orchestra] to-day used by the moderns are piccolos, English horns, contra-bassoons, becklephone, [etc.].

Contraception (kǫntrăse·pʃən). [irreg. f. Contra- 2 + *-ception* in Conception.] The prevention of uterine conception. Hence **Contrace·ptionist,** one who practises or advocates contraception.

1917 *Boston Pilot* 14 Apr. 4/5 The contraceptionist would take from the Almighty all power over life and dispose matters after his own whim and liking. 1923 Stopes *Contraception* 23 Wholesome contraception is a valuable tool in the hands of those who work toward elevating our sex knowledge in the way urged by Professor Bayliss. *Ibid.* 213 Since 1920..contraception has been made criminal in France.

Contraceptive (kǫntrăse·ptiv), *a.* and *sb.* [f. Contra- 2 and Conceptive *a.,* after prec.] **A.** *adj.* Pertaining to or procuring contraception. **B.** *sb.* A means of procuring contraception. Hence **Contrace·ptively** *adv.,* by contraception.

1897 J. McCabe in *Literary Guide* 1 Oct. 145/2 Every Catholic knows that the Church has forbidden the use of contraceptives under 'the pain of mortal sin'. 1921 *Brit. Med. Jrnl.* 20 Aug. 302/1 A knowledge of contraceptive methods. 1922 *Ibid.* 8 July 69/2 A session to discuss contraceptive technique. 1923 Stopes *Contraception* 5 The result [of present economic conditions] too often is the use of harmful contraceptives. *Ibid.* 233 The Church however has already yielded the principle of the use of contraceptive means. 1927 *Scots Observer* 7 May 4/4 The people who advocate contraceptive methods. 1928 F. E. Williams *Orokaiva Magic* 211 Abortifacient and contraceptive drugs. 1928 *Devon & Exeter Gaz.* 21 Nov., The indiscriminate and constant sale of contraceptives, not only in the towns but in quite small villages. 1929 E. V. Lindsay *Birth Control* 67 Would they accept physical union made contraceptively sterile?

Contract, *sb.*[1] Add: **1. e.** An undertaking. *colloq.* orig. *U.S.*

1881 A. A. Hayes *New Colorado* vi. 87 A person should carefully study his temperament..before he takes a contract to go into a deep shaft. *Ibid.* xi. 159 Here, too was Armigo to have annihilated General Kearny, but for the unfortunate circumstance of his troops declining, as they say in the West, 'to take the contract'. 1891 E. S. Ellis *Check No. 2134* vii. 50 Any person might well shrink from the contract of corraling a couple [of such men].

f. A season railway-ticket. Also *Comb.*

1899 *Westm. Gaz.* 17 July 4/2 The justice of the peace.. decided that the company had no right to expect its contract-holders to carry business advertisements about for its benefit. 1904 *Notice* in *L'pool Exchange Station,* Passengers must show their Tickets (Contract or Ordinary) before passing through these Gates.

g. In the game of Bridge, an undertaking to make so many tricks; hence *contract bridge,* also simply *Contract,* a form of auction bridge.

1908 *Westm. Gaz.* 24 Dec. 14/2 Suppose the contract is two in hearts, and four by cards are made, the contracting side score 32 below the line, and game. If the contract had failed, and say two by cards had been lost, the adversaries would score 200 in their honour column. 1927 *Observer* 10 Apr. 25 Little coteries and sets play variations of Bridge, such as Contract, Cairo, Standard, and so forth. 1929 *Punch* 10 Apr. 420 'Contract bridge', which is superseding auction bridge on the Continent and in America, has taken a strong hold in Britain. 1929 *Observer* 24 Nov., Contract has been 'boomed' in a way that Auction never was.

Contract, *v.* Add: **2. d.** intr. *To contract out*: to make an arrangement or agreement not to come under certain conditions. Conversely, *to contract in.*

1894 *Times* 29 Jan. 11/4 With the exception of those men who now have contracting-out mutual insurance societies, the opinion of the working men..is..against permission to contract out on any terms. 1906 *Daily Chron.* 23 June 4/3 'The parents of at least twenty children' may appeal to the Board of Education, which, if it sees fit, may allow the school to contract-out...They do not contemplate ..any large amount of contracting-out. 1908 *Westm. Gaz.* 7 Dec. 2/2 The local education authorities would have insisted on getting the same State grant for each Council child as was paid to denominational associations for each contracted-out child. 1920 S. & B. Webb *Hist. Trade Un.* 366 *note,* By 'contracting out' was meant an arrangement between employer and employed by which the latter relinquish the rights conferred upon them by the Act, and often also their rights under the Common Law. 1927 *Daily Express* 24 Mar. 1 The Trade Union Bill will provide that members of a trade union wishing to contribute to political funds shall contract in.

e. *trans.* To arrange for by contract (Contract *sb.*[1] 1 b); to let by contract.

1897 *Daily News* 13 Sept. 7/5 Do you contract your work of construction, or do it by direct employment of labour? 1902 *Daily Chron.* 16 Aug. 6/2 We are forbidden to contract a 'boy' away from the country for more than a year.

Contractionist. *U.S.* (Earlier example.)

1875 *Nation* (N.Y.) 19 Aug. 112/2 As regards the Republican party, its own desire is to please everybody—both contractionist and inflationist, the solvent and insolvent, the creditor and the debtor.

Contractually (kǫntræ·ktiu,ăli), *adv.* [f. Contractual + -ly [2].] In contractual terms.

1920 Keynes *Econ. Conseq. Peace* 56 Too vague and general to be interpreted contractually.

Contra·cture, *v.* [f. the sb.] *intr.* To exhibit contracture.

1907 *Practitioner* Oct. 542 Dr. Charles L. Dana..would preserve the title of progressive muscular atrophy, and would limit the use of 'amyotrophic lateral scleroses' to those cases which show, only from the beginning and dominantly, the spastic and contracturing types of progressive muscular atrophy.

Contradeciduate (kǫntrădĭsi·diu,ĕt), *a.* [f. Contra- + Deciduate *a.*] Denoting that condition in which the placenta remains in the uterus after birth and is broken up and absorbed.

1897 Parker & Haswell *Text-bk. Zool.* II. 562 In the Mole and the Bandicoot not only is there no decidua thrown off, but the fœtal placenta with the distal portion of the allantois does not pass out after the fœtus, but remains, and is broken up or absorbed in the uterus. Such a condition has been termed contra-deciduate.

Co·ntra-indi·cative, *a.* [f. Contra-indicate *v.*] Of the nature of a contra-indication.

1906 *Practitioner* Nov. 629 When a condition contra-indicative of the treatment was in evidence.

Contranatant (kǫntrănē¹·tănt), *a.* [f. Contra- + Natant *a.*] Of the migrations of fish: Against the current. Hence **Contranata·tion.**

1915 A. Meek in *Nature* 29 Apr. 231 To define these and other migrations which are intimately associated with currents it is necessary..to introduce two terms which will serve to indicate movement against the current and with the current. My colleague Professor J. Wight Duff recommends a Latin root, *natare.* The words suggested therefore are *contranatant,* swimming against the current, and *denatant,* swimming or drifting with the current. The words *contranatation* and *denatation* are also available to indicate the act or habit of migration against or with the current. 1920 *Rep. Dove Mar. Lab.* 40 Evidence to support the theory of contranatation.

Contrapposto (kǫntrăppǫ·sto). [It., = contraposition.] In painting and sculpture, the crossing of limbs and contrasting of masses characteristic of the works of Michelangelo.

1903 *Burlington Mag.* III. 20/2 In the figure of the soldan he gives a superb instance of almost Michel-angelesque *contrapposto.*

Contraption. (Earlier U.S. and later English examples.)

1834 'J. Downing' *A. Jackson* iii. 24 The gineral oney intended to see what he would do, and then by a lettle contrapshion have him secur'd. *Ibid.* iv. 26 He had the nack of contrapshion tu a miracle. 1842 Mrs. Kirkland *Forest Life* I. 97 It's my vote that we turn these contraptions.. right out into the shed. 1895 *Westm. Gaz.* 23 Aug. 5/1 Their train consisting solely (and in the order given) of:— 1, the engine; 2, guard's van; 3, ordinary 'coach'; 4, ordinary 'coach'...The result can scarcely be called a train so much as a contraption. 1898 Kipling in *Morn. Post* 9 Nov. 5/1 Had I seen the new fore and aft bridge that we had managed to screw out of the Dockyard? A great contraption. 1925 Rex Clements *Gipsy of Horn* 207 The men temporarily lashed the crazy contraption to the lower mast.

Contrary, *a.* **3. b.** Add: Also in educated use.

1920 Rose Macaulay *Potterism* I. i. § 4 They were like that; conceited and contrary.

Contrary, *v.* Add: **1.** (Modern U.S. example.)

1903 *Nation* (N. Y.) 14 May 392/2 His [*sc.* Napoleon's] clannish instincts were somewhat contraried by the.. passionate sentiment which he felt for his wife Josephine.

c. To annoy by opposition. *U.S.*

1900 *Scribner's Mag.* Sept. 377/1 It did not matter what you said or did that contraried him.

Contrast, *sb.* Add: **5.** *Psychol.* The intensification of a sensation by the juxtaposition of an opposite.

1897 tr. *Wundt's Outl. Psychol.* 324 The law of psychical contrasts is, in turn, supplementary to the law of relations. *Ibid.* 325 The law of contrast has its origin in the attributes of the subjective contents of experience, but is secondarily applied to the ideas and their elements also. 1902 Brinton *Basis Social Relations* 42 The third law, that of Contrast, applies to the ethnic mind the curious fact in mental life that a prolonged devotion to one idea leads to a reaction in which the opposite of that idea becomes dominant.

b. The reciprocal induction of colours and brightnesses when brought into juxtaposition. *Contrast colour,* a colour assumed as the result of the environment of an inducing colour. *Contrast disk,* one used with a colour-mixer to exhibit the phenomena of brightness and colour contrast.

1901 Titchener *Exper. Psychol.* I. i. 19 The contrast disc, with an extra 30° of white or black in its ring, is set up before its appropriate background. The contrast colour is matched upon the second mixer as before. Note that the same grey background must be retained for the second mixer, in order that the contrast relations may remain the same on both discs.

Contrasty (kǫ·ntrɑ·sti), *a.* [f. Contrast *sb.* + -y [1].] Marked by or exhibiting (strong) contrasts; esp. of photographic negatives, having very marked contrast of light and shade.

1891 *Anthony's Photogr. Bull.* IV. 117 It is often advisable to print from contrasty negatives on unfumed paper. 1920 *Wall's Dict. Photogr.* 173 Should the negative be over-exposed and over-developed..the transparency should have the minimum exposure so that a prolonged development can be given..with a strong developer...If the negative is a contrasty one, exactly the reverse is done. 1929 A. J. S[heldon] in *B'ham Post* 30 Mar. 14/2 We were forced to make sudden adjustments of the listening faculty to a very contrasty scheme of tonal values.

Contribution. 5. *contribution box* (earlier U.S. example).

1845 'O. Optic' *In Doors & Out* (1876) 50 It is only two months since you refused to put anything in the contribution box for the missions.

Control, *sb.* Add: **4. b.** *Spiritualism.* The spirit who is alleged to enter the medium's body and control his words and actions.

1877 *Leisure Hour* 3 Nov. 694/1 The ghosts of old, if ghastly, were at least respectable, which is more than can be said of the 'controls' of a modern *séance.* 1895 J. N. Maskelyne in *Daily Chron.* 29 Oct. 3/4 We were particularly desired to..do all we could to encourage the medium and her 'control', who was known by the name of 'John'. 1902 O. Lodge in *Proc. Soc. Psych. Research* June 65 Everything known to the normal Mrs. Thompson must be considered equally known to the ostensible 'control' speaking with Mrs. Thompson's mouth.

c. The apparatus by means of which a machine in operation is controlled, as an aeroplane or motor vehicle; also, any of the mechanisms of a control apparatus or in *pl.* collectively for the complete apparatus. Also *attrib.,* as *control cable,* etc.; *control surface,* a movable airfoil for changing the attitude of an aeroplane or airship. Also, in an aeroplane, the vertical lever controlling the elevator and ailerons, more explicitly *control column, lever, stick.*

1908 H. G. Wells *War in Air* iii, The engine..was worked by electric controls from this forepart. 1912 Curtiss & Post *Curtiss Aviation Bk.* 285 One day when I was up in the air pretty high I seemed to forget..how to operate the controls. 1913 *Aeroplane* 13 Feb. 176/2 The control is dual; all moving gear is made of non-magnetic material, and all control wires are duplicated. 1916 Barber *Aeroplane Speaks* 28 Sometimes when the Aeroplane is on the ground the control lever or 'joy-stick' is lashed fast. *Ibid.* 39 All the control cables in perfect condition and tension. 1917 'Theta' *War Flying* 37 A dual-control machine. 1917 *All the World's Aircraft* 8a The control surfaces. 1918 E. M. Roberts *Flying Fighter* 303 My feet had been forced off the rudder control. 1925 *Morris Owner's Man.* 97 Slow running control not adjusted properly...Carburetter control improperly set. 1927 *Even. Standard* 12 Jan. 6/4 The 'joy stick' loses a certain liveliness in the new official term of 'control column'.

d. In automobile racing, a section of the road, usually through a town or village, over which speed is controlled; also, a section of the road or track where officials are stationed and contesting machines are halted for examination and repairs; similarly a station in aeroplane racing. Also *attrib.,* as *control timekeeper.*

1900 *Daily News* 2 May 7/2 These automobile fellows.. give you a programme with day runs full of 'Controls' and eight miles an hour slowings-up through towns. 1903 *Westm. Gaz.* 1 July 7/3 Some time must necessarily elapse before the control timekeepers can hand in their final reports. 1904 A. B. F. Young *Complete Motorist* xvi. 320 At a control established in some wayside village..stands a little group of officials with their paraphernalia of papers, stop-watches, reports, and time-sheets. 1912 André Beaumont *My 3 Big Flights* 86 On arriving at any control the pilot had to show two of the stamped parts both on the aeroplane and motor. 1928 *Daily Tel.* 17 July 7/7 At each of the 'controls' a compulsory halt of a certain duration will be made.

Controllability (kǫntrōᵘlăbi·lĭti). [f. Controllable + -ity.] The quality or condition of being (easily) controllable.

1905 *Westm. Gaz.* 20 June 4/2 The vastly superior controllability of the machine-driven vehicle. 1920 *Conquest* June 402/3 The enormously wide range of the acetylene explosive mixture..combined with the controllability that would result from its admixture with alcohol.

Controlled, *ppl. a.* Add: **2.** Of a house: Subject to government control with regard to restriction of rent, as enacted by the Increase of Rent and Mortgage Interest Restriction Acts of 1915, 1919, and 1920.

1930 *Daily Express* 8 Sept. 7/4 If it is a controlled house you are protected.

Controller. Add: **4. d.** *Electr.* An arrangement of switches, contacts, rheostats, and electromagnets, manipulated by a handle or handles, by means of which the current of an electric motor may be controlled.

1901 *Daily News* 3 Jan. 6/4 The controller, the main handle of which regulates the four motors going either ahead or astern. 1902 *Encycl. Brit.* XXVIII. 97/2 There is a reversing lever on the controllers separate from the controller handle. 1904 *Electr. Investm.* 7 Dec. 769/2 The controller goes automatically to the 'off' position on being released.

Conular (kǫ·niŭlăɹ), *a.* [f. mod.L. *conulus,* dim. of *conus* Cone *sb.*[1] + -ar.] Cone-shaped.

1904 *Science* 8 Apr. 585 (Cent. D. Suppl.) The passage of the molar teeth of the Proboscidea from the conular type of the mastodons to that of the elephants.

Conure (kǫ·niuəɹ). *Ornith.* [ad. mod.L. *Conurus,* f. Gr. κῶνος Cone *sb.*[1] + οὐρά tail.] A bird of the genus *Conurus* of American parrots or parakeets, distinguished by their cuneate tail.

1883 *List Anim. Zool. Soc.* (ed. 8) 341 Large Patagonian Conure. 1895 *Lydekker's Royal Nat. Hist.* IV. 116 In the typical conures..the fourth primary feather of the wing is attenuated, and the nostrils are exposed. 1897 *Daily News* 23 Apr. 6/5 The rich greens and flame colour and orange in those golden-headed Conures.

Conus (kōᵘ·nŏs). [L. *conus* Cone *sb.*[1]] **1.** *Anat.* A conical structure or organ, e. g. in the heart, the rounded anterior portion of the striatum. *Conus arteriosus,* the upper and anterior angle of the right ventricle of the heart.

1888 Rolleston & Jackson *Anim. Life* 76 The conus is separated from the ventricle by three valves. 1897 C. F. Cooper *Parker & Haswell's Textbk. Zool.* 84 A fourth chamber, the *conus arteriosus,* is added in front of the ventricle. 1907 *Practitioner* Oct. 466 The pulsation of the conus arteriosus is visible in the second or third interspaces.

2. A patch of atrophied choroid near the optic papilla in myopia.

1887 *Buck's Handbk. Med. Sci.* V. 89/2 The most common change seen in myopic eyes is the *crescent* or *conus* surrounding the optic papilla. This appears in the form of a crescentic white figure hugging the optic disk.

Convallariaceous (kǫnvălĕ·riē¹·ʃəs), *a. Bot.* [f. *Convallariaceæ*: see -aceous.] Of or pertaining to the *Convallariaceæ,* a family of liliaceous plants.

1909 Webster.

Convectional (kǫnve·kʃənăl), *a.* [f. Convection + -al.] Of or pertaining to convection; induced by convection.

1892 *Nation* (N.Y.) 1 Sept. 166 He concludes that the convectional origin of summer thunder-storms implies a like origin for such storms in winter. 1904 *U.S. Monthly Weather Rev.* Feb. 77 (Cent. D. Suppl.) The convectional currents. 1927 Kendrew *Clim. Continents* 223 The ground is heated by the strong sunshine, and convectional overturnings take place between the layers of air resting on it and those above.

Convector (kǫnve·ktǫɹ). *Electr.* [f. Convection: see -or.] An electrical heater that warms a room by convection.

1907 *Install. News* Dec. 21/2 The heating appliances cover several useful types of convectors. 1909 *Ibid.* III. 163 In use the convector body attains a temperature of about 220° F.

Convention. Add: **8. c.** *Cards.* The observance of the unwritten rules of play, as, in bridge, leading a heart when the pone doubles a no-trumper, or scoring spades without playing when the make is not doubled and the score is below 20.

1864 'Cavendish' *Whist* 52 The aggregation of the recognised rules of play, including the established conventions, constitutes what in practice is called the conversation of the game of whist. 1908 *Daily Chron.* 14 Sept. 7/3 Gray rose in disgust when she ignored the heart-convention and led him an unlovely spade. 1929 *Observer* 24 Nov., The introduction of conventions makes Contract an artificial game rather than an intellectual one.

10. b. A conventional style or treatment.

1926 Rutter *Evolution Mod. Art* 132 Henry Lamb had shown in a picture..that a flat, decorative convention could be combined with an unsurpassable intensity of emotion.

11. *convention hall*; **convention city,** a city in which conventions are commonly held.

1887 C. B. George *50 Yrs. on Rail* v. 92 Chicago..is the greatest railroad center on the globe, [and] is the chief *convention city in America. 1908 *Westm. Gaz.* 29 May 12/1 The total cost of 'transportation' will be about 100dols. a head, and, according to the more moderate estimate, another 50dols. per man will be needed for expenses in the convention city. 1889 *Kansas Times & Star* 6 June, The project of a big *convention hall was again fully discussed.

Conventional, *a.* Add **2. d.** *Cards.* Applied to any method of play which is not based on the principles of the game, but is used solely to convey information, such as the trump signal.

1864 Clay *Treat. Short Whist* iii. 97 This method of play being as old as whist itself, it was certain, sooner or later, to be reduced to the conventional sign,—good in the lowest cards as well as in the highest—of which I now treat. 1864 'Cavendish' *Whist* 51 The instructed player frequently selects one card in preference to another with the sole object of affording information. When the principle is carried thus far the play becomes purely conventional. 1884 *Ibid.* (ed. 14) 105 The system of returning the higher of two losing cards when they are both small cards, is purely conventional.

Conventionalist. Add: **1. b.** One who takes part in a convention. *U.S.*

1844 W. N. Blane *Excursion* 171 On their success in getting the votes of two-thirds of the legislature, the Conventionalists assembled at two or three public dinners.

Conventionist. 1. (Earlier U.S. example.)

1815 *Niles' Weekly Register* 25 Mar. VIII. 56/2 (heading) Hartford Conventionists.

Convergence. Add: **5.** *Biol.* The tendency in diverse or allied animals or plants to assume similar characteristics under like conditions of environment.

1866 Darwin *Orig. Spec.* (ed. 4) iv. 150 A distinguished botanist, Mr. H. C. Watson, believes that I have overrated the importance of the principle of divergence of character.., and that convergence of character, as it may be called, has likewise played a part. 1902 *Encycl. Brit.* XXVIII. 343/2 Multiradial apocentricities lie at the root of many of the phenomena that have been grouped under the designation *Convergence.* 1927 Haldane & Huxley *Anim. Biol.* xi. 223 Convergence, where a similar mode of life produces similar effects on quite unrelated animals.

6. *attrib.*: **convergence frequency,** in a spectrum series of lines, the limiting frequency toward which the higher members of the series converge as asymptotes.

1903 Agnes M. Clerke *Probl. Astrophysics* 53 This limit, known as the 'convergence frequency' is a distinctive feature of spectral series.

Convergent, *a.* Add: **1. d.** *Biol.* Due to or characterized by convergence; of similar structure but of different origin.

1897 Parker & Haswell *Zool.* II. 416 A convergent or polyphyletic group, owing its distinctive characters..to the independent acquisition of similar characters under the influence of like surroundings.

Conversation. Add: **6. b.** *Whist.* (See quot. 1864 s.v. *Convention 8 c.)

7. c. *To make conversation*: to converse for the sake of conversing, engage in small talk.

1921 Hichens *Spirit of Time* v, He simply could not 'make conversation' to her.

11. conversation lozenge, a lozenge with an inscribed motto.

1908 Findlater *Crossriggs* vi, [To] confine my speech solely within the limits of the conversation lozenge.

Convert. Add: **11. f.** *Rugby Football.* To kick a goal from (a try). Also *absol.*

1896 *Field* 12 Dec. 957/2 Bell, with a very fine place kick, converted the try. 1900 *Ibid.* 17 Nov. 772/2 Douglass.. gained a try, Franks converting. 1919 E. B. Poulton *Ronald Poulton* 179 Ronald gained two tries, both converted by Turner.

Converter. Add: **3. b.** Also a retort used for Bessemerizing copper ores.

1897 *Daily News* 4 Jan. 2/1 18,300 ounces of gold, contained in either converter bars, cast and refined copper, or bullion. 1906 *Westm. Gaz.* 22 Aug. 9/1 The works, which consist of three blast furnaces and two converters, are capable of treating 10,000 tons of ore per month.

Conveyer. 4. b. (Earlier U.S. example.)

1813 *Niles' Register* Addenda III. 15/2 The conveyor,.. while it cooled the flour, passed it on to the place where the elevator caught it.

Convicted, *ppl. a.* Add: **3.** Convinced of sin. (Cf. Convict *v.* 4.) *U.S.*

1845 J. J. Hooper *Adv. Simon Suggs* x. 124 By this time it had come to be generally known that the 'convicted' old man was Captain Simon Suggs the very 'chief of Sinners' in all that region.

Convolutionary (kǫnvŏl¹ū·ʃənări), *a.* [f. Convolution + -ary [1].] Of or pertaining to a convolution or convolutions, esp. of the brain.

1903 *Nature* 5 Nov. 8/1 Every detail of the convolutionary pattern.

Convoyer. Add mod. examples:

1892 *Monthly Packet* May 589 He commits him to twin fleet convoyers..who bear him swiftly to his own home. 1927 *Daily Express* 30 May 3/4 A sharp signal from [the] chief convoyer, a frenzied cutting of the seals on the baskets,.. and ten thousand birds..swept aloft.

Convulsedly (kǫnvʊ·lsėdli), *adv.* [f. Convulsed + -ly [2].] With convulsed action.

1903 Conrad & Hueffer *Romance* III. vi, He had been sobbing convulsedly.

Convulsibility (kǫnvʊlsibi·lĭti). [f. Convulsible: see -ity.] A tendency to convulsion.

1886 *Buck's Handbk. Med. Sci.* II. 287/2 Convulsibility is acquired..by infectious fevers.

Cony, coney, *sb.* Add: **2. b.** A hat made of rabbit-fur (in place of beaver).

1855 Barnum *Life* 99 If a 'pedler' wanted to trade with us for a box of beaver hats,..he was sure to obtain a box of 'coneys'.

7. b. (Example.)

1884 Goode *Nat. Hist. Aquat. Anim.* 412 The Coney, *Epinephelus apua,* of Key West, the Hind of Bermuda, is an important food-fish which occurs throughout the West Indies.

Coo (kū), *int.* A vulgar exclamation expressing surprise or incredulity.

1911 *Punch* 5 July 8/1 'My dear Bobby,' I said, 'I know everything about everything.' 'Coo—I bet you don't.' 1927 C. Mackenzie *Vestal Fire* III. ii, Coo! they don't mind bumping into you, do they? 1929 Raymond *Family that was* I. iv, 'Coo!' exclaimed Joyce. 'O Mummy, may he?'

Coobah, var. *Coubah.

Cooja (kū·dʒă). *Anglo-Ind.* [Hind. (Pers.) *kūza.*] A wide-mouthed earthenware water-vessel.

1883 E. H. Aitken *Tribes on my Frontier* 118 They [*sc.* tree-frogs] would perch pleasantly on the edge of the water *cooja* or on the rim of a tumbler.

Cook, *sb.* Add: **1. d.** *Chess.* A second solution that spoils a problem, position, etc.

1875 S. H. Thomas in *Westm. Papers* VII. 243, I almost imagined the author's solution a 'cook'. 1876 W. Nash *ibid.* IX. 53 If this is not a cook the problem is much under the composer's usually high standard. 1894 *Daily News* 30 July 6/7 The latest delinquent is the composer of problem No. 55, whose intention was to mate by 1 Q-Kt 4, overlooking the easy cook by 1 Q x Kt.

3. cook-book *U.S.* (earlier examples); **cook-camp** *U.S.,* the part of a camp in which the cooking is done; a building serving as kitchen and eating-room; **cook-general,** a domestic servant who does all the work of a house including the cooking; **cook-kettle** *U.S.,* a cook-pot; **cook-wagon** *U.S.,* a wagon with a cooking outfit.

1865 Mrs. Stowe *House & Home Papers* 258 A good roasted potatoe is a delicacy worth a dozen compositions of the *cook-book. 1873 'Mark Twain' & C. D. Warner *Gilded Age* xxxvi. 330 He said with cold dignity that cook-books were somewhat out of their line. 1882 Mrs. F. E. Owens (*title*) Cook Book, and useful Hints for the Household. 1895 *Outing* (U.S.) XXVI. 393/2 'Yer supper's ready' said Payson, emerging from the *cook-camp. *a* 1904 S. E. White *Blazed Trail Stories* iii. 44 The camp consisted..of three buildings ..a cook-camp, a sleeping-camp, and a stable. 1896 *Daily News* 30 Oct. 10/4 *Cook-general and Young Housemaid wanted. 1863 'E. Kirke' *Southern Friends* xxi. 215 A large iron pot..serving for both washtub and *cook-kettle. *a* 1904 S. E. White *Blazed Trail Stories* x. 178 The ponies, and the *cook-wagon, and the cook..had done the alkali for three days. 1907 Mulford *Bar-20* xi. 119 Two cook wagons were stalled a short distance from the corral.

Cook, *v.*[1] Add: **3. d.** *Chess.* In early use, to improve upon (a solution); now, to prove unsound.

1851 *Chess Player* 16 Aug. 40 Mr. Alexander's collection of two thousand problems contains many faulty positions, and we shall now and then cook some of them, which may amuse you and many of our readers.

Cookable, *a.* (Earlier U.S. example.)

1843 R. Carlton *New Purchase* viii. 47 Next came a resolution that the ladies should prepare the cookables— i. e. stuff the chicken with filling—beat eggs for puddings, and the like.

Cooked, *ppl. a.* Add: **2. b.** *Cooked goose*: see Cook *v.*[1] 4 b.

1861 Trollope *Framley Parsonage* xlii, Chaldicotes..is a cooked goose, as far as Sowerby is concerned.

Cookee (ku·kī). *U.S.* [f. Cook *sb.* 1.] An assistant to the cook in a lumberers' camp.

1889 *Century Dict.* 1891 *Harper's Mag.* Nov. 890/2 The rule is to have one cook and two 'cookees' to each sixty men. 1901 S. E. White *Westerners* xxvii. 250 The move necessitated a cook and 'cookee', and the weekly purchase of provisions. 1911 — *Bobby Orde* i. (1916) 17 Beyond, Bobby could hear the cook and his helpers, called cookees.

Cookie. Add: Also *S. Afr.*

1852 Barter *Dorp & Veld* 107 Cookies, or unleavened cakes of coarse meal, baked on the grid-iron. 1897 E. Glanville *Tales from Veld* 51 Raking the 'cookie' from the fire-place, whence it came baking hot.

Cookless (ku·klės), *a.* [f. Cook *sb.* + -less.] Without a cook. Hence **Coo·klessness.**

1898 *Cornhill Mag.* Aug. 255 The good old school-room days when one's dear mother used sometimes to admit that she 'had been cookless for six weeks'. 1904 'Alan Dale' *Wanted: A Cook* Ded., To Jennie Shalek: housewife, who, in my hour of drab and dreary cooklessness, when my heart fainted, and tragedy impended, sent her four fair daughters to my aid. 1908 Mrs. E. Wharton *Hermit* 271 There were no squalid cookless hiatuses between intervals of showy hospitality. 1928 *Sunday Express* 6 May 15 Catherine Ives...'When the Cook is Away.'..In coming to the rescue of the cookless—from whatever cause—the author has collected also an attractive assortment of recipes.

Cook-room. Add: In later use *U.S.*

1874 *Rep. Vermont Board Agric.* II. 509 The cook room, which is one of the utmost importance, should be one of great convenience. 1880 Tourgee *Invis. Empire* x. 467 There were four rooms,..a cook-room, dining room [etc.]. 1896 J. C. Harris *Sister Jane* 54, I made haste to go to the cook-room, intending to start the fire.

Cook-stove. *U.S.* A cooking-stove.

1837 Colman *Rep. Agric. Mass.* (1838) 80 The wood when cut fit for a cook stove is worth $4 a cord. 1868 *Putnam's Mag.* Jan. I. 40/2 If you call it warm,..what do you think it is, shut up in here with this cook-stove? 1885 *Century Mag.* Nov. 29/1 The cook-stove was there in the inclosed corner. 1913 Mrs. Stratton-Porter *Laddie* i. (1917) 4 They went to bring wood for the cookstove.

attrib. 1889 *Anthony's Photogr. Bull.* II. 220 A kitchen with a cook-stove attachment.

Cool, *a.* **8.** Add: *cool-burning* adj.; **cool chamber,** a chamber in which perishable goods may be preserved by the use of ice.

1907 *Practitioner* June 864 Arhovin..is a yellowish liquid of aromatic odour and slightly *cool-burning taste. 1887 *Col. & Indian Exhib., Rep. Col. Sect.* 140 The enterprise of Messrs. S. & Sons in fitting up one of their steamers with a *cool-chamber. 1901 *Daily Chron.* 1 June 8/6 Provided sufficient 'cool chamber' accommodation could be procured on the steamers trading between Australia and England.

Coolabah (kū·lăbā). *Austral.* Also **coolibah, -bar, -ybah.** [Native name.] Any of several Australian gum trees, such as *Eucalyptus microtheca.*

1889 J. H. Maiden *Useful Native Pl. Australia* 25 *Eucalyptus microtheca,* ('Bastard Box' or 'Coolibah'). *Ibid.* 495 'Coolybah' or 'Coolibar'. 1911 C. E. W. Bean '*Dreadnought*' *of Darling* xv, I found the whole place covered with coolabah. 1930 Groom *Merry Christmas* v. 37 They halted beneath a great spreading coolabah tree.

Coolaman, variant of *Cooliman.

Coolan, variant of *Coolung.

Cooler. Add: **2. b.** A vessel into which syrup is poured to crystallize into sugar, a crystallizer.

1819 Brande *Chem.* 355 The fire is instantly damped, and the boiling sugar carried off in basins to the coolers. 1853 Ure *Dict. Arts* (ed. 4) II. 766 From the...cooler, the syrup is transferred into wooden chests or boxes,..also called coolers, but which are more properly crystallizers or granulators. 1887 *Encycl. Brit.* XXII. 626/1 From the striking teach the concentrated juice is removed to shallow coolers, in which the crystals form. 1921 *Dict. Occup. Terms* (1927) § 449 *Heater man* (sugar refining); *cooler hand, cooler man*..., adds water to beaters, receivers, coolers or crystallisers.

c. A water-cooler. *U.S.*

1905 F. Hopkinson Smith *At Close Range* 250 'I'll go to the cooler and wash up what I can..' she said.

Cooley, var. Coulée.

1881 *N. Y. Times* 18 Dec. in *N. & Q.* 6th Ser. V. 65/1 Every ravine short of an inhabitable valley is called a 'cooley'. 1884 [see Coulée 2]. 1890 *Harper's Mag.* Aug. 383/1 Reno came quickly to a shallow 'cooley' (frontierism for gully), that led down..to the stream.

Coolidge (kū·lidʒ). The name of William David *Coolidge* (b. 1873), an American physical chemist noted for his development of X-ray devices, e.g. *Coolidge tube.*

1915 *Nature* 15 Apr. 195/2 The Coolidge tube is based on the discharge of independent electrons. 1929 *Encycl. Brit.* XXIII. 844/2 The target of the Coolidge tube is of massive tungsten.

Coolieism. *U.S.* (Earlier example.)

1870 *Congress. Globe* 21 Jan. 654/1 [To seek to encourage manufactures] by reductions on labor alone..is to depress labor, not to protect it. To seek it by Chinese immigration in the form of coolieism is still worse.

Cooliman (kū·limăn). *Austral.* Also **coolaman, kooliman.** [Native name.] A cup or vessel for carrying water, made of wood or bark.

1847 Leichhardt *Overland Exped.* 269 Three Koolimans (vessels of stringy bark) were full of honey water. 1863 Beveridge *Gatherings* 37 The beautiful Lubrina Fetched a Cooliman of water. 1885 Mrs. C. Praed *Australian Life* 76 *note,* Cooliman: a vessel for carrying water, made out of the bark which covers an excrescence peculiar to a kind of gum-tree. 1890 'R. Boldrewood' *Col. Reformer* xvii, The fire-barks [were] carried in the coolimans to prevent the tell-tale fall of ashes.

Cooling, *vbl. sb.* **2.** Add: **cooling-board** *U.S.* (see quot. 1859).

1859 Bartlett *Dict. Amer.* (ed. 2), *Cooling-board,* the board on which a dead body is laid out. Pennsylvania and Maryland. 1896 J. C. Harris *Sister Jane* 19, I don't want to be put on my cooling-board.

Coolth. For *rare* exc. *dial.* substitute: In sense 1 now chiefly *colloq.* (jocular).

1890 Kipling *Plain Tales fr. Hills* (ed. 3) 127 He kept on steadily and tried to think how pleasant the coolth was.

Coolung (kū·lʊŋ). *Anglo-Ind.* Also 7 **colum,** 9 **coolan, -en, cullum, kullum.** [Hind. *kulang.* a. Pers. *kulank.*] The great grey crane, *Grus cinerea*; also *erron.* the demoiselle crane, *Anthropoides virgo.*

1698 Fryer *Acc. E. India & P.* 111 A *Colum* may be hunted with a Greyhound, as we do Bustards, being a great Fowl and long in Rising. 1813 J. Forbes *Oriental Mem.* II. 29 Two stately birds, called the sahras and cullum. 1838 *R. M. Martin's Eastern India* III. 579 Large flocks of a crane called Kolong..frequent this district in winter. 1883 Aitken *Tribes on my Frontier* 160 Not being so green as I was, I let the tempting herd of antelopes pass, but the *kullum* I cannot resist. 1901 'Linesman' *Words of Eyewitness* (1902) 303 A trio of coolan flapped over his roof.

Coon, *sb.* *U.S.* Add: **2. b.** (Earlier examples.)

1840 Haliburton *Clockm.* Ser. III. xi. 153 Come, are you ready, my old coon? 1843 — *Attaché* xviii. II. 37 A knowin' old coon, bred and born to London, might, but you couldn't.

c. A negro. *colloq.*

1887 *Weekly Detroit Free Press* 23 July (Hoppe) The flasks are filled from the same barrel, but labeled variously to please the palate of the 'coon' or 'crackers'. 1892 *Congress. Rec.* 4 Feb. 856/1 Instead of seating one colored Representative, they seated two,—two coons in place of the elected Representatives of the people. 1903 *Westm. Gaz.* 18 May 3/2 The former represented a lively..jovial coon— possibly 'coon' is not the right word, which, however, is accepted here as modern slang for a nigger.

3. (Earlier examples of *a gone coon, a coon's age.*)

1840 C. F. Hoffman *Greyslaer* vi. iii. III. 221, I was afeared you were a gone coon, and was on the point of shoving off without you. 1845 J. J. Hooper *Taking Census* i. 155 We had not seen the amount of cash mentioned as lost, in a 'coon's age'.

4. *coon-band, -hunt, -hunting*; **coon-dog,** a dog good at hunting the racoon; **coon-oyster** (example); **coon song,** a negro or plantation song; 'a popular song, such as is common among the negroes of the southern United States: so called because originally associated with coon-hunting' (*Cent. Dict.* Suppl. 1909).

1928 E. Wallace *Kate, plus Ten* 77 The noisy *coon band kept up its rhythmic pandemonium in one corner of the room. 1855 Mayne Reid *Hunters' Feast* xiii. 97 Uncle Abe's dog—a stout terrier—was esteemed the 'smartest' *'coon-dog' in a circle of twenty miles. 1872 Eggleston *End of World* xi. 77 Like the man who warranted his dog to be a good coon-dog, bekase he warn't good for nothin' else. 1878 J. H. Beadle *Western Wilds* xi. 173 It..on the Hoosier's 'Coon-dog principle', ought to be rich in mines. 1855 Mayne Reid *Hunters' Feast* xii. 96 The *'coon-hunt is a nocturnal sport. 1887 'C. E. Craddock' *Keedon Bluffs* 98 All the boys of Tanglefoot Cove and the mountain slopes had gathered for a coon-hunt. 1855 Mayne Reid *Hunters' Feast* xii. 96 *'Coon-hunting is peculiarly a negro sport. 1862, 1890 [in Dict.]. 1870 *Amer. Naturalist* III. 460 The small oysters..are not generally eaten except by the racoons, hence the common name for them of *coon oysters. 1902 G. H. Lorimer *Lett. Self-made Merchant* xii. 167 The Doctor..sung *coon songs and imitated a saw going through a board very creditably. 1904 'O. Henry' *Cabbages & Kings* vi. 95 From that celebrated centre of molasses and dis-franchised coon songs we took a steamer for South America. 1904 *N. Y. Sun* 7 Aug. 18 'Coon songs', whether of the old plantation variety or the modern ragtime kind.

Coon, *v.* (Earlier examples.)

1834 A. Pike *Sk.* 77 (Th.) Irwin was obliged to straddle the log, and, as they quaintly call it in the west, 'coon it across'. 1835 W. G. Simms *Partisan* 320 That curious sort of locomotion which, in the South and west, is happily styled 'cooning the log'. 1845 J. J. Hooper *Daddy Biggs Scrape* 193 He must a'..cooned it on the top o' the limb.

Coon-can (kū·nkæn). Also **cooncan**; **conquian** (kǫ·nkiăn). [ad. Sp. *con quien* with whom?] A game of cards, originating in Mexico, the main object of which is to secure sequences.

Each player receives ten cards, and the aim is to form sequences of the same suit or sets of three or four cards of the same denomination. One card is placed face upwards and the rest of the cards face downwards, each player in turn taking either the exposed card or the top card of the pack, afterwards discarding any card in his hand. The player gets rid of his cards by declaring them when he has made a complete set or sets, and the winner is the one who first gets rid of all his cards.

1905 *Hoyle's Games* 203 The art in Coon Can, like in Cribbage, lies in the discard and in putting the cards, whether threes, fours, or sequences, at the proper time on the table. 1907 *Ibid.* 192 Conquian. 'With whom?' Or Coon Can. 1912 *Bath Club Rules for 'Cooncan',* Cooncan..may be

played by any number not exceeding five players. 1913 Kipling *Diversity of Creatures* (1917) 282 [They] played the rag-time tunes..till there was talk of coon-can. 1913 W. Dalton *Coon-Can* Introd. 13 We have no record as to when, or by whom, Coon-Can was first introduced into England. It made its first bow to the public at the Bath Club in Dover Street.

Cooning (kū·niŋ), *gerund* and *vbl. sb.* *U.S.* [f. Coon *sb.* + -ing¹]. Hunting racoons. Also *attrib.* or as *ppl. a.*

1876 J. Burroughs *Winter Sunshine* iii. 85 Cooning in the remote interior is a favorite pastime. *Ibid.* 86 A pell-mell rush of the cooning party up the hill.

Coo·n-skin, coo·nskin. *U.S.* (See Coon *sb.* 4.)

1818 Mrs. Royall *Lett. fr. Alabama* xxxvi. (1830) 103 He..axed marchant if he didn't want to trade for some coonskins. 1836 Crockett *Exploits & Adv. Texas* (1837) 5, I threw down the coon skin upon the counter, and called for a quart. 1840 W. G. Simms *Border Beagles* 305 A coon-skin cap..completed this parody on man. 1874 Eggleston *Circuit Rider* v. 53 His picturesque coon-skin cap gives him the look of a hunter. 1895 *Outing* (U.S.) XXVII. 72/2 We saw coon-skin hats, coon-skin waist-coats, while on the trees around the shingle camp were nailed scores of coon skins.

Coontah, coontie. *U.S.* (Earlier examples.) Also *attrib.*

1791 W. Bartram *Trav. Carolina* etc. (1792) 239 A very agreeable, cooling sort of jelly, which they call conte. 1819 *Pennsylvania Gaz.* 22 June 2/3 [The Seminoles] use a root called coonty, as a substitute [for corn]. 1823 G. A. McCall *Lett. fr. Frontiers* (1868) 60 To-day I found him digging coonta-root. 1837 J. L. Williams *Territory of Florida* 33 The inhabitants [live] principally on fish, turtle, and coonti; the last they bring from the main [land].

Co-op (kou·ǫp). [colloq. abbreviation of Co-operative *sb.* 2.] A co-operative store (in full *co-op store*) or co-operative society. *On the co-op*: on the co-operative principle.

1873 J. H. Beadle *Undevel. West* xviii. 339 The co-op store bought a thousand muskets at the Government sale. 1884 Cudworth *Yorks. Sk.* 20 Mary Umpleby said it 'bet t' Co-op. doo into fits'. 1894 *Warty Rhymes* 29 Neaw th' 'Co-ops' are th' bigg'st shops i' th' place. 1904 Steedman *Bucking the Sagebrush* 17 All trading was done at the 'co-op' stores. *Ibid.* 221 There was the 'co-op' store, which showed the presence of the Mormon. 1913 'Q' *News fr. Duchy* (1929) 13 Doin' it on the co-op, instead of an afternoon treat for each.

Cooper, *sb.*¹ **5.** Add: *cooper-shop* (delete † and add later U.S. examples), *-stuff.*

1801 in C. Cist *Cincinnati* (1841) 183 Charles Faran advertises for cooper-stuff. 1827 B. Drake & Mansfield *Cincinnati* viii. 65 Eleven cooper shops 48 men. 1894 H. Frederic *Copperhead* etc. 55 He had been a well-to-do man ..with a big cooper-shop.

Co-operativeness. (Modern U.S. example.)

1857 F. L. Olmsted in T. H. Gladstone *Englishman in Kansas* p. xxxiv, That peculiar political coöperativeness and efficiency which we see in the people of the South.

Co-optive (kou·ǫptiv), *a.* [f. Co-opt + -ive.] = Co-optative.

1894 *Tablet* in *Westm. Gaz.* 3 Dec. 2/2 Whenever a member [*sc.* of the School Board] retires or is removed, his place will be filled up upon the co-optive principle administered by the majority. 1922 G. M. Trevelyan *Brit. Hist.* i. 13 The House of Commons had, in effect, become a co-optive body.

Coorongite (kū·rǫŋgəit). *Min.* [f. *Coorong*, a district of South Australia: see -ite¹.] A mineral caoutchouc found in the district of Coorong.

1895 Groves & Thorp *Chem. Technol.* II. 129 The solid form of petroleum is represented by ozokerite, by asphaltum,..and, perhaps, by the 'coorongite' of South Australia.

Coot, *sb.*¹ **4.** (Earlier U.S. examples.)

1794 *Gazette of U.S.* (Philad.) 17 Jan. (Th.) But Satan was not such a coot To sell Judea for a goat. 1846–52 Mrs. Whitcher *Widow Bedott P.* ix. 92 He's an amazin' ignorant old coot.

Cooter. *U.S.* (Earlier examples.)

1827 *Massachusetts Spy* 22 Aug. (Th.) A few jolly topers, who wallowed in the sand, 'as drunk as a cooter'. 1835 W. G. Simms *Partisan* 308 You're turned now..on the flat of your back like a yellow-belly cooter.

Cootie (kū·ti), *sb.*² *Army slang.* A body louse.

1917 Empey *From Fire Step* 24 'Does the straw bother you, mate? It's worked through my uniform and I can't sleep.' In a sleepy voice he answered, 'That ain't straw, them's cooties'. 1918 in F. A. Pottle *Stretchers* (1930) 199, I could soon fall asleep thinking how absurd to worry over lice and cooties when a man was at war. 1918 E. M. Roberts *Flying Fighter* 106, I made the acquaintance of a new sport while with the battery. A saucer serves for an arena. Into this one puts a kootie and a flea.

Cop, *sb.*² **8.** Add: *cop-changing* adj.; **cop reel**, a machine which receives the yarn from the cops and winds it into hanks; so **cop reeler**; **cop warp**, warp-yarn spun on to cops; **cop winder**, one who winds yarn into the form of cops or winds yarn from the cops on to bobbins.

1927 T. Woodhouse *Artificial Silk* 131 One type of.. *cop-changing automatic loom. 1890 Nasmith *Mod. Cotton Spinning Mach.* xiii. 262 It depends upon whether it is employed to wind the yarn from cops or bobbins whether it is known as a '*cop' or 'bobbin' reel...Ordinarily one swift only is used in a cop reel, and two in a bobbin reel. 1881 *Instr. Census Clerks* (1885) 68 *Cop Reeler...*Cop Winder. 1862 *Catal. Internat. Exhib., Brit.* II. No. 3653, Cotton yarns, *cop warp, doubled yarns. 1907 *Daily Chron.* 11 Feb. 4/6 The reelers, hank makers, cop-winders, gassers, and doublers. 1921 *Dict. Occup. Terms* (1927) § 367 *Cop Winder*; (i) winds yarn from cops, short cylindrical paper tubes, on to bobbins; (ii) winds weft yarn from spinning frame bobbins, or from hanks, into form of cops.

Cop, *sb.*⁷ *slang.* [f. Cop *v.*³]

1. Capture; used chiefly in phr. *a fair cop.*

1889 *Standard* 9 Oct. 3/7 (E.D.D.) Prisoner remarked it was 'a fair cop'. 1891 *Daily News* 24 Oct. 5/2 'It's a fair cop', said the thief. 1895 *Argus* (Melbourne) 22 Nov., *Witness.* That was a fair cop. *Mr. Justice Hodges.* A fair what? *Witness.* A fair cop, your Honour, means a fair 'have'. 1898 *Daily News* 13 Apr. 8/7 It's a fair cop; you have got me all right and no mistake. 1901 W. W. Jacobs *Light Freights, An Odd Freak,* 'Fair cop', ses Ginger, who was still rubbing his leg.

2. Catch, acquisition. With negative, *no cop, not much cop*: of no or little value or use, worthless.

1919 J. B. Morton *Barber of Putney* xviii, 'Once upon a time..this 'eap o' bricks was a first-class billet.' 'Doesn't look much cop now', said Tim. 1929 Raymond *Family that was* ii. ii, A month or two in service, which was no cop —no cop at all.

Cop, *v.*³ Add: **b.** *To cop it*: to 'catch' it, to be punished, get into trouble; also, to die. So *to cop out. dial.* and *slang.*

1886 *Cheshire Gloss.*, *Cop*, to catch, both in the sense of capturing, and in the semi-slang sense of being scolded. 1905 *Daily Chron.* 19 Sept. 4/7 Though it tarry, it shall surely come; and when it does—as an errand boy would say—'somebody 'll cop out'! 1909 *Ibid.* 9 Apr. 6/6 When arrested he remarked, 'I suppose I shall "cop" it for this.' 1915 Cable *Between Lines* 194 By the way 'is 'ands jerked up an' 'is 'ead jerked back when I fired, I fancy 'e copped it right enough. 1927 *Blackw. Mag.* July 83/1 Half of the beggars had copped it for good and all.

Copal. 1. Add: Also *gum copal.*

1712 tr. *Pomet's Hist. Drugs* I. 201 The Gum Copal, which we call Oriental Copal. 1777 Robertson *Hist. Amer.* I. iii. 242 The people perfumed them as they landed with incense of gum copal. 1878 H. M. Stanley *Dark Cont.* II. xiii. 387 Another valuable article of commerce besides the bees-wax and india-rubber found here was gum copal. 1887 Moloney *Forestry W. Africa* 134 It is said by the natives that no trees grow on or near the places where the gum copal is found.

Copalm. (Earlier examples.)

1775 B. Romans *Florida* 336 Live oak abound here, intermixed with copalm and other timber. 1832 D. J. Browne *Sylva Amer.* 200 This tree is universally called Sweet Gum, and by the French of Louisiana Copalm.

Coparcener. (Later U.S. example.)

1900 *Nation* (N.Y.) 22 Nov. 400/3 'Ask Platt', said Croker ..; and that he and all his coparceners say now.

Cope, *sb.*¹ **11.** Add:

cope bead (see quot.); **cope-box**, a box for holding copes, a cope-chest; **cope-chisel** (see quot.); **cope ring**, a metal ring with handles used in carrying the sand and loam which forms the upper portion of a loam mould.

1885 *Spons' Mechanics' Own Bk.* 374 The other drawers.. receive a ½-in. mahogany beading all round. This is called a '*cope bead'. 1893 Fowler *Hist. C. C. C.* (O.H.S.) 246 A *Cope-box purchased for the College. 1874 Knight *Dict. Mech.*, **Cope-Chisel*, a chisel adapted for cutting grooves. 1888 *Lockwood's Dict. Terms Mech. Engineering*, **Cope Ring*, the ring which carries the bricks and loam forming the cope of a loam mould.

Copec (kōu·pek). A word made up from the initials of *Co*nference *o*n Christian *P*olitics, *E*conomics, and *C*itizenship.

1924 *Public Opinion* 29 Feb. 201/1 That remarkable movement which is described by the cryptic word Copec. 1924 *Brit. Weekly* 20 Mar. 560/4 Copec has entered into the heritage of the 'Christian Socialists', of Westcott and Dale, of the Christian Social Union and the rest. 1927 *Observer* 6 Nov. 13/2 His devotion to the Workers' Educational Association and his leadership of the 'Copec' movement.

Coperta (kopɛ̄·rtă). [It., = covering, f. *coprire* to cover.] A film of glaze given as a final coating to later Italian majolica ware.

1885 *Encycl. Brit.* XIX. 625/1 The glaze, 'coperta', an ordinary glass, made more fusible by the presence of lead, consisted of oxide of lead 17 parts, silica (sand) 20, alkali 12, and common salt 8 parts. 1903 Solon *Hist. O. Fr. Faïence* 186.

Co·-pi·lot. [Co- 3 b.] A fellow pilot of an aeroplane.

1927 *Glasgow Herald* 4 June 9 It is understood that Clarence Chamberlain..will be pilot. It has not yet been announced who will accompany Mr. Chamberlain as co-pilot. 1928 *Daily Express* 16 June 11/5 Mr. Alliott (the co-pilot) and myself are working like slaves, dismantling parts in a scorching sun.

Copper, *sb.*¹ Add:

1. c. *pl.* Shares in a copper-mining company.

1907 *Daily Chron.* 26 Oct. 1/7 Mines, including coppers, showed a general recovery. 1908 *Ibid.* 31 Aug. 2/2 Coppers were much quieter in sympathy with Yankees. 1909 *Westm. Gaz.* 10 June 10/4 Listless Coppers.

11. copper bolt (see quot.); **copper-bound** *a.*, ornamented with copper lace; **copper loss**, the loss of energy in the copper conductors of a dynamo or motor; **copper-skinned** *a.*, having a copper-coloured skin; **copper-tail** *Austral slang*, a person belonging to the lower classes of society; so **copper-tailed** *a.*; **copper-top** *dial.* and *slang*, a red head of hair; a red-headed person; so **copper-topped** *a.*

1884 Knight *Dict. Mech.* Suppl., **Copper Bolt*, a copper bit; a soldering tool. 1809 W. Irving *Knickerb.* vi. ii, The *copper-bound cocked hat. 1916 *Standardization Rules Amer. Inst. Electr. Eng.* 48 The no-load *copper loss. 1873 M. F. Mahony *Chron. Fermors* I. xiii, There was no room for personal rivalry with that beady-eyed, *copper-skinned.. little lady. 1907 *Q. Rev.* July 188 The lank-haired, copper-skinned Jakuns. 1890 Vogan *Black Police* 116 Those upper circles..termed in Australian parlance 'silver-tailed', in distinction to the '*copper-tailed' democratic classes. 1916 C. J. Dennis *Ginger Mick* 28 'E chews it over...Workin' 'is *copper-top a double shift. 1892 Heslop *Northumbld. Gloss.*, **Copper-topt*, red haired.

Copper, *v.* Add:

1. b. To furnish with copper coins.

1832 T. Hamilton *Men & Manners Amer.* II. 387 One member of Congress..was charged with selling franks at twopence apiece, and thus coppering his pocket at the expense of the public.

c. To colour by the use of a salt of copper.

1895 *Daily News* 7 Feb. 5/2 The defendant assured the Bench..that the public 'would not have them [*sc.* peas] without they were coppered'. 1900 *Westm. Gaz.* 8 Sept. 2/3 The prohibition of the sale of 'coppered' vegetables. 1902 *Encycl. Brit.* XXV. 92/1 Vendors of coppered peas.

2. *U.S.* (Earlier examples.)

1878 J. H. Beadle *Western Wilds* iii. 46 He..scarcely ate or slept till the tail of his last mule was 'coppered on the jack'.

absol. 1913 Mulford *Coming of Cassidy* vii. 108 He had played to win when he should have coppered, coppered when he should have played to win.

fig. 1883 'Mark Twain' *Life Mississippi* xxviii. 268, I reckon the safe way, where a man can afford it, is to *copper* the operation. 1904 *N. Y. Even. Post* 6 May 2 For some time, local politicians have 'coppered' with success Platt's predictions. 1924 Mulford *Rustler's Valley* ix, [Bud] likewise told me to go east for a job; but..I coppered Bud an' come here.

Copper-belly. *U.S.* (Examples.)

1842 Holbrook *N. Amer. Herpet.* IV. 33 *Tropidonotus erythrogaster*—Shaw...Copperbelly, *Vulgo.* 1871 Schele de Vere *Americanisms* (1872) 387 The Copperhead (Trigonocephalus contortrix)..is known as Copperbelly and Chunkhead.

Copper-bottomed, *a.* Add: Also *fig.* Thoroughly sound.

1890 Farmer *Slang* s.v. A 1, In mercantile circles, the expression has become popularly current, in a figurative sense, to signify the highest commercial credit; and..first-class; first-rate. The form varies, being rendered by..A 1 copper-bottomed, [etc.]. 1894 Stevenson & Osbourne *Ebb-Tide* ii. vii, The real, first-rate, copper-bottomed aristocrat.

Copperhead. 1. (Earlier examples.)

1788 M. Cutler in *Life, Jrnls. & Corr.* (1888) I. 415 Edmund Moulton bit by a copperhead this morning. 1817 S. R. Brown *Western Gaz.* 31 The only venomous serpents, are the common and prairie rattlesnakes, and copper-heads.

b. In full *copperhead snake.*

1788 J. May *Jrnl. & Lett.* (1873) 70 One of Colonel Stacey's men bit by a copperhead snake. 1822 *Massachusetts Spy* 31 July (Th.) A woman in Salisbury township.. discovered a copperhead snake on her dresser. 1866 Gregg *Life in Army* i. 18 There were also to be found great dens of the Copperhead Snake, and this species were considered the most poisonous, deceptive, dangerous and mean of all the snake family.

3. *U.S.* †**a.** A descendant of the Dutch settlers of New York. *Obs.*

1809 W. Irving *Knickerb.* vi. iv. (1825) 245 These were the men who vegetated in the mud.., being of the race of genuine copperheads. 1828 Paulding *New Mirr. Travellers* (1868) 208 (Th.) Death has sometimes had his match with some of these tough old copperheads.

b. (See quot.)

1831 Mrs. Royall *Southern Tour* II. 63, I forgive him for his bold and manly stand against the copper-heads, as the Presbyterians are often called.

c. An American Indian.

1853 C. W. Webber *Shot in Eye* etc. (1855) 132 He had a hatred for the 'yaller bellies', and 'copper heads', as he called the Mexicans and Indians, which was refreshingly orthodox. *a* 1861 T. Winthrop *Canoe & Saddle* x. (1883) 145 Five foul copper heads..lurked among the plunder of that noisome spot. *Ibid.* 149 Meanwhile those five copperheads watched me.

Copper-headed, *a.* *U.S.* [Cf. prec.] **a.** Having a copper-coloured head. **b.** Belonging to the Copperheads.

1806 Ashe *Trav. Amer.* (1808) II. 287 Copper Headed Snake. 1847 in D. Drake *Pion. Life Kentucky* ii. 25 The copper-colored man, and the copper-headed snake [were] then extremely common. *a* 1861 T. Winthrop *Canoe & Saddle* xii. 248 The copper-headed, snaky beguiler. 1863 *Congress. Globe* 936/2 The seat of rebellion..is among the copper-headed traitors of the North.

Copper Maori (kǫ·pəɪ ma·ŏri, mauə·ri). *New Zealand.* Also **Kopa Maori, Kapura Maori.** [Maori *kopa* oven, *kāpura* fire.] A native oven.

1888 *Trans. New Zeal. Inst.* XXI. 417 So they set to work and they dug holes in this flat,..each hole about 2 ft. across and about 1½ ft. deep, and shaped something like a 'kopa maori'. 1889 *Ibid.* XXII. 204 A number of *kapura Maori*, or native ovens.

Co·pperskin. *U.S.* [Copper *sb.*¹ 11.] An American Indian; a redskin.

1840 C. F. Hoffman *Greyslaer* ii. x. 26 'Go on, go on, Kit, d'ye say a dozen Injuns?' 'Yes, uncle, not a Copperskin less.' *a* 1861 T. Winthrop *Canoe & Saddle* x. (1883) 146 The five copperskins 'first eyed me over' with lazy thoroughness. They noted my arms and equipment. 1904 S. E. White *Silent Places* viii. 72 What the hell do we care for a lot of copper-skins from Rupert's House!

Coppery, *a.* Add:

1. c. *Coppery whipsnake* (see quot.). *U.S.*

1870 *Amer. Naturalist* III. 187 A few of the former [reptiles] are not known northward, viz...the Coppery Whipsnake (*Drymobius testaceus*).

2. *transf.* Biased in favour of the Copperheads.

1906 *N. Y. Even. Post* 24 Mar., The Rev. Ambrose Converse, a Northern man with Southern principles, made his pro-slavery Philadelphia *Christian Observer* so 'coppery' during the civil war that Seward suppressed it.

Coppicing. Add: **b.** The treating of wood as coppice; the cutting down of trees periodically so that new shoots may grow from the stumps. Also *attrib.*

1880 C. R. Markham *Peruv. Bark* 329 The coppicing system consists in cutting down the trees near the ground, and allowing one or more of the crops of shoots, which rise from the stumps, to grow. *Ibid.* 395 Uprooting, coppicing, and thinning. 1922 Schlich *Man. Forestry* (ed. 4) I. 236 Methods of thinning, coppicing, &c.

Coppled, *a.* **2.** (Later U.S. example.)

1813 *National Intelligencer* 9 Nov. 4/1 Again the coppled hills Shall greet the beamy sun.

Copy, *sb.* **C.** Add:

copy boy, a boy who takes copy from the writer to the printer; **copy-maker**, a copy-writer; **copy-paper**, paper on which copy is written for the press; **copy-press** *U.S.*, a copying press; **copy-reader**, one who reads and edits copy for a newspaper; so **copy-reading** *vbl. sb.*; **copy-slip** (earlier U.S. example); **copy-writer**, a writer of copy for the press.

1928 *Boston Even. Transcript* 30 Mar. 15/6 As I wrote, a '*copy boy' would take away every sheet of my manuscript as fast as it was completed. 1908 *Daily Chron.* 21 Sept. 4/6 The Telephone Company now maintains a special Directory Department where twenty expert *copy-makers are constantly employed. 1902 Eliz. L. Banks *Newsp. Girl* 259 The great pads of *copy paper supplied by the telegraph office for newspaper correspondents. 1911 L. V. Vance *Cynthia* 46 The lines of typewritten words, blurred and befogged with purple by the *copy-press. 1903 E. L. Shuman *Pract. Journalism* 18 Each of these departments has a force of *copy-readers, whose duty it is to edit the matter written by the reporters. *Ibid.* 25 In the first ten years the young journalist masters reporting, *copy-reading, and the rest of the routine work. 1838 Caroline Gilman *Recollections* xxviii. 194 One set of *copy-slips was to be substituted for another. 1921 *Dict. Occup. Terms* (1927) § 789 **Copywriter* (advertising); composes or writes the descriptive matter (copy) for advertisements. 1929 *Let. to Editor from U.S. Corresp.* 20 May, The word 'tubbable' has been used by copywriters for, I should say, at least ten years.

Co·pyable, *a.* In *copyable pencil*, an early name of *copying pencil* (see below).

1883 *Stationer & Bookseller* 8 May 35 'Automatic' Copyable Pencils.

Copybook. Add: **2.** phr. *To blot one's copy-book*: to commit a fault or misdemeanour which spoils one's record. *Colloq.*

b. More widely applied to action or conduct of an exemplary kind.

1927 *Times* 3 May 7/2 Twice in succession he drove Mr. Cameron to the boundary past mid-off with copybook strokes.

Copygram (kǫ·pigræm). [f. Copy *sb.* + -gram.] = *Copygraph.

1884 Knight *Dict. Mech.* Suppl. s.v. *Copy-graph.*

Copygraph (kǫ·pigraf), *sb.* [f. Copy *sb.* + -graph.] An apparatus for or the process of duplicating and multiplying copies of writing by means of a gelatine slab and aniline or similar ink.

1884 Knight *Dict. Mech.* Suppl.

Hence **Co·pygraph** *v. trans.*, to reproduce by means of the copygraph.

1900 H. G. Wells *Love & Mr. Lewisham* i. 10 Copygraphed sheets of instructions from his remote correspondence tutors.

Copyhold. (By Part V of the Law of Property Act 1922, all copyhold land was enfranchised.)

Copyholder². Add: A proof-reader's assistant who reads the copy aloud to the proof-reader.

1888 *Encycl. Brit.* XXIII. 701/2 This proof is read through and compared with the copy by the proof reader or corrector of the press and an assistant, the copy-holder or reading boy. 1888 *Congress. Rec.* 24 Jan. 666/1 Persons employed in the Printing Office under the names of proof-readers and copyholders. 1897 *Daily News* 2 June 12/6 Copyholder (expd.) seeks Grass or Permanency. 1906 *Daily Chron.* 14 June 5/5 A copyholder and assistant reader on a London morning-paper.

Copying, *vbl. sb.* **2.** Add: **copying (ink) pencil**, a lead, or a pencil containing a lead, composed of graphite, aniline blue, and kaolin or gum arabic, and used for indelible writing, and duplicating in a copying press; **copying machine, press** (early examples).

1885 *Army & Navy Co-op. Soc. Price List* 465 *Copying Ink Pencils. Automatic action. 1803 A. Ellicott in *Life & Lett.* (1908) 209, I have enclosed a copy of this letter taken in 15 seconds, by which you will see the value of a *copying machine. 1883 R. Haldane *Workshop Rec.* Ser. ii. 175/2 Copying...The subject may be divided into chemical..and mechanical methods, *copying pencils, and transferring. 1928 E. Blunden *Undertones of War* ii. 18 The censoring of the letters scrawled in copying pencil by our home-yearning stalwarts. 1786 Jefferson *Let.* Writ. 1894 IV. 325 Dilly's first parcel of books and the first *copying press are arrived at Rouen.

Copyright, *sb.* Add: **2.** (Earlier U.S. example.)

1870 *U.S. Stat. at Large* XVI. 213 [To] deposit in the mail two copies of such copyright book or other article.

3. *copyright act, law.*

1831 *Deb. Congress* 6 Jan. 424 His colleague..had described the copyright act as simply a remedy for the abuse of that right. 1835 *Knickerbocker Mag.* VI. 289 The passage of an international copy-right law betwixt America and Great Britain.

Co·pyrightable, *a.* [f. Copyright *v.* + -able.] Capable of being copyrighted.

1903 S. S. Elder in *Nation* (N.Y.) 30 Apr. 349/3 It is no longer possible to summarize it in a few sections covering every thing copyrightable.

Copyrighted, *ppl. a.* (Earlier U.S. example.)

1806 Webster *Compend. Dict.*, *Copyrighted*, as the sole right being secured.

Coque, *sb.* Add: **2.** (Example.)

1835 *Court Mag.* VI. p. xiv/2 A succession of *coques* rising one above another, in front of the crown.

b. pronounced (kōuk). Applied to feathers used in trimming.

1903 *Westm. Gaz.* 11 May 4/2 Those soft coq feathers are very much used too. 1905 *Daily Chron.* 13 May 4/7 Ostrich and coque boas. 1923 *Daily Mail* 26 Mar. 6 Clipped Coque Feather Stole.' 1928 *Daily Express* 7 May 5/2 Coque feathers applied closely on to the crown of the hat.

Coquina. (Earlier U.S. examples.)

1837 J. L. Williams *Territory of Florida* 44 The quarries of Coquina stone. *Ibid.* 52 This river being choked up by the Coquina formation.

Coraciiform (koræsi·ifǭım), *a.* *Ornith.* [f. mod.L. *Coraciæ*: see -form.] Having the characteristics of the *Coraciæ*, a sub-order of birds of the family *Coraciidæ*, of which the genus *Coracias*, consisting of the rollers, is the type.

1901 P. Chalmers Mitchell in *Trans. Linn. Soc., Zool.* VIII. 249 The Rollers and other simple short-gutted Coraciiform birds.

Coracoidal (kǫrăkoi·dăl), *a.* [f. Coracoid *sb.* + -al.] Of or pertaining to the coracoid.

1893 Lydekker in *Proc. Zool. Soc.* 14 Feb. 172 The coracoidal element forms a small moiety of the glenoid cavity.

Coral, *sb.*¹ Add: **5. a.** Also of crabs.

1895 *Funk's Standard Dict.*

9. coral-fern *Austral.*, the parasol fern, *Gleichenia circinata*; **coral-gall**, an excrescence produced on coral by the action of barnacles and parasitic animals of various species; **coral-limestone**, coralline limestone; **coral-pea** = *coral-creeper*; **coral-thrombus**, a red clot formed by the enclosing of red corpuscles by coagulating fibrin.

1898 Morris *Austral English*, *Coral-Fern. 1903 *Nature* 10 Sept. 457/1 These *coral galls may be found on the Milleporas and Madreporas of a certain portion of a reef and be absent from all the other genera of neighbouring corals. 1831 Lyell *Princ. Geol.* II. 287 The increase of *coral limestone..may vary greatly according to the sites of mineral springs. 1839 G. A. Mantell *Wond. Geol.* II. 563 In reference to the formation of coral limestones,..some beds..consist of a pure calcareous mud. 1878 *Jrnl. Chem. Soc.* XXXIV. 120 Formerly pyroclasite was supposed to be the result of volcanic action upon the coral-limestone. 1896 *The Melburnian* 28 Aug. 53 (Morris) The trailing scarlet kennedyas, aptly called the 'bleeding-heart' or '*coral pea'. 1900 *Jrnl. Exper. Med.* 25 Oct. 157 In the larger vessels considerable fibrin and a homogeneous material resembling *coral-thrombi are seen.

Cord, *v.*¹ Add:

2. b. *Bookbinding.* To tie (a book) between two boards to keep the cover smooth while drying.

1876 *Encycl. Brit.* IV. 43/2 As a last operation in forwarding, but one now frequently omitted, the book is 'corded', that is, firmly tied between two boards until it is dry, so as to insure perfect smoothness in the cover.

Cordelle, *sb.* **2.** *U.S.* (Earlier examples; also cordale.)

1811 Brackenridge *Jrnl.* in *Views Louisiana* (1814) 214 Continued until eleven, with *cordelle*, or towing line—the banks being favorable. 1816 H. Ker *Travels* 36 This is a great object to the bargemen in using their cordale.

Cordelle, *v.* *U.S.* (Earlier examples; also cordale.) Hence **Co·rdelling** *vbl. sb.*

1816 H. Ker *Travels* 36 After getting above their cordaling ground, in swift water they make use of their warp. 1826 T. Flint *Recoll.* 96 In two instances the boatmen.., when cordelling the boat directly at the base of these rocks, disengaged snakes from their retreats. 1832 Paulding *Westward Ho!* ix. I. 83 A rope was taken ashore, and fastened to a rock, or stump, or sapling, and by this the boat was drugged along. This process is called cordelleing.

Corder. Add: **1. b.** One who makes up wood into cords. *U.S.*

1654–5 *Boston Rec.* II. 123 Att a meething this Day..was Chosen..for Corders of Wood, Tho. Leader, Rich, Tayler. 1671 *Boston Rec.* (1881) VII. 59 It is ordered that the Select men shall haue powre to apoynt corders of wood for this towne. 1733 *Minutes Comm. Council Philad.* (1847) 326 Peter Cahoun, one of the present Corders of wood.

Cording, *vbl. sb.*¹ Add: **1. c.** The action of making up wood into cords. *U.S.*

1655 *Mass. Col. Rec.* (1854) III. 375 Considering the abuse that is in cordinge of wood and measuring of boards. 1671 *Boston Rec.* (1881) VII. 59 For preuenting of fraude..in cordinge of wood.

4. Formation resembling a cord.

a 1909 *Buck's Handbk. Med. Sci.* III. 658 (Cent. D. Suppl.) From obstruction of the jugular there are often cording of the vein..and cellulitis of the neck.

Cordon, *v.* Transfer †*Obs. rare* to senses 1 and 2, and add: **3.** To enclose or cut *off* with a cordon.

1891 *Cosmopolitan* XII. 61/1 Chicago is fairly cordoned by a great chain of mammoth manufacturing plants. 1905 *Westm. Gaz.* 1 July 11/2 The city blocks are rigorously cordoned by troops. *Ibid.*, Within the precincts of the cordoned quarantine harbour section. 1920 *Glasgow Herald* 15 Mar., The Wilhelmstrasse was at first cordoned off. 1927 *Daily Express* 11 Feb. 1/3 The building was promptly cordoned off until reinforcements arrived.

Corduroy, *sb.* and *a.* **B.** *adj.* **3.** *U.S.* (Earlier examples.)

1822 J. Woods *Engl. Prairie* 219 From this town..along a rough road with many log-bridges; but some of my fellow passengers, from the state of Kentucky, called them corderoy. 1824 W. N. Blane *Excursion* 147 A Corderoy Road consists of small trees, stripped of their boughs, and laid touching one another, without any covering of earth.

Corduroy, *v.* Add: Also *absol.*

1894 C. H. W. Donaldson *With Wilson in Matabeleland* x. 226 Scarping away the banks there, and 'corduroying' with bush where the ground was soft and boggy.

2. To make irregular lines or spots on the flesh side of (a hide) in splitting. Also *intr.*

1897 C. T. Davis *Manuf. Leather* (ed. 2) 203 The gears.. not only make a great deal of noise..but also tend to corduroy the leather. *Ibid.*, The knife..is more apt to leave an uneven surface, which tends to corduroy.

Cordwaining (kǭ·ɹdwēɪniŋ), *vbl. sb.* [f. Cordwain(er + -ing¹.] The art or craft of the cordwainer; cordwainery.

1812 *Sporting Mag.* XL. 13, I entertain the most exalted ideas of the ingenious 'art and craft of cordwaining'. 1900 *Daily News* 17 Oct. 6/2 He was initiated at his father's house of business..into the mysteries of cordwaining. 1905 W. J. Locke *Usurper* xv, I think I shall learn to make boots. Have you any professors of cordwaining at Greybrooke, Alicia?

Core, *sb.*¹ Add:

15. (sense 8) *core board, -drying, -iron*; **core-casting**, casting with a core to make a cavity in metal; **core-drilling**, a method of drilling in which an annular drill is used, so that a core remains as a specimen of the strata pierced; **core implement** *Archæol.*, an implement formed by chipping flakes off a block of flint; **core-loss**, the loss of energy due to hysteresis and to eddy-currents in the core of electric machinery; **core-wall**, a wall of solid masonry forming the core of a dike or dam consisting mostly of earth or sand; **core-wheel**, a mortise wheel in which the recesses for cogs are made by placing cores in the mould in which it is cast.

1888 *Lockwood's Dict. Terms Mech. Engin.*, **Core Board*, the board against whose edge a core is struck up on a revolving bar. It is commonly termed a loam board. 1928 V. G. Childe *Most Anc. East* v. 133 The process of *core-casting and the invention of the shaft-hole axe. 1903 *Sci. Amer.* 18 July 44/1 *Core drilling is indispensable in a great variety of engineering and mining enterprises, affording, as it does, a means for drilling out a sample core or column of rock. 1901 *Daily Chron.* 3 Dec. 2/1 For making steel, heating iron, *core-drying. 1927 Peake & Fleure *Hunters & Artists* 42 The earliest palaeolithic implements ..were mostly *core implements. 1917 *Standard. Rules Amer. Inst. Electr. Eng.* 44 *note*, Increased *core losses due to increased excitation for compensating internal drop under load. 1909 H. M. Wilson *Irrigation Engin.* (ed. 6) 366 The foundations for a masonry *core-wall should always rest only on firm homogeneous rock. 1884 Knight *Dict. Mech.* Suppl., **Core Wheel*, a wheel with recesses which answer as the interspaces of cogs, or into which wooden cogs may be driven.

Core, *v.* **3.** Add: *To core out*: to hollow out by using a core.

1888 Hasluck *Model Engin. Handybk.* (1900) 108 The barrel of the pump may be cored out in the casting. 1902 *Westm. Gaz.* 4 June 5/1 Its bottom is cored out to fit over the nose of the projectile itself.

Corean: see Korean.

Cored (kōəɹd), *ppl. a.* [f. Core *sb.*¹ or *v.* + -ed.]

1. Deprived of the core.

1912 *Daily Chron.* 11 Mar., Peaches and cored apples from California.

2. Cast with a hollow body by means of a core.

1918 Farrow *Dict. Mil. Terms*, *Cored Shot*, an elongated projectile having a cavity in the body of it for the purpose of throwing the center of gravity towards the front end of the projectile, thus insuring greater steadiness of flight.

Corfiote (kǭ·ɹfiǫ̈t), *a.* and *sb.* Also Corfiot, Corfute. [f. *Corfu*, after *Cypriote.*] Of or pertaining to, a native or inhabitant of, the island of Corfu.

1877 *Encycl. Brit.* VI. 396/1 The Corfiot peasantry are reputed the idlest of all the Ionians. 1923 *Contemp. Rev.* Oct. 412 Corfiote neutrality during the Greco-Turkish war. *Ibid.* 413 No Corfiote could be induced to get her off the rocks.

Corgi (kǭ·ɹgi). Also **corgy.** [W., f. *corr* dwarf + *ci* dog.] A small Welsh dog.

1926 *Bulletin* 25 Nov. 9/4 One little dog about a foot high ..a brown Welsh corgi. 1930 *Observer* 5 Oct. 13/2 What can one say of the Welsh corgis,..with their truncated legs, prick ears, foxy heads, and longish bodies?

Corial (koriā·l). Also 8 **corialla,** 9 **curial, corrial.** [Sp. *corial*, app. perversion of Arawak *kuljara.*] In Guiana, a dugout canoe with pointed ends.

1796 Stedman *Surinam* I. 240 A corialla or small canoe, composed of one single piece of timber. 1825 Waterton *Wand. S. Amer.* 223 We met the Indians going a fishing. I saw, by the way their things were packed in the curial, that they did not intend to return for some days. 1833 *Evangelical Mag.* Mar. 124/2 We set out in a *corial*, or small canoe, to visit the new station. 1852 C. W. Day *Five Yrs. West Indies* II. 18 We hailed a ferryman, who came over in a most ticklish *corrial.* 1922 *Blackw. Mag.* Apr. 525/2 People coming off..in bateaux and corials.

Coriandrol (kǫriæ·ndrǫl). [f. Coriander + -ol.] A colourless liquid obtained from oil of coriander.

1891 *Pharmaceutical Jrnl.* XXI. 940/1 Coriandrol is the name given by Semmler to the principal constituent of coriander oil. 1929 *Encycl. Brit.* VI. 431/1 Coriander..is used in medicine as an aromatic and carminative, the active principle of its volatile oil (*Coriandrol*) being isomeric with Borneo camphor.

Cork, *sb.*¹ **11. d.** Add: **cork carpet**, a kind of floor-cloth composed of ground cork, india-rubber, and gutta-percha; **cork-elm**, (*a*) the rock elm, *Ulmus racemosa*; (*b*) the winged elm, *Ulmus alata*; **cork linoleum** (or **lino**), linoleum made from canvas backed with a mixture of linseed oil and ground cork.

1813 H. Muhlenberg *Catal. Plants* 29 *Cork elm. *Ulmus alata.* 1884 Miller *Plant-n.* 259 *Ulmus racemosa*, American Cork Elm. 1909 *Daily Chron.* 11 June 7/2 '*Cork Linoleum' has to most people meant merely, or chiefly, a kind of trade mark.

Cork, *sb.*⁵, erron. spelling of Calk *sb.*

1806 Webster *Compend. Dict.*, *Cork*, a sharp point on a horse shoe. 1902 S. E. White *Blazed Trail* xxvii. 187 His face and flesh were ripped and torn everywhere by the 'corks' on the boots. 1922 Titus *Timber* ix. 82 He.. sharpened the corks, handling the foot gear with an odd excitement.

Cork, *v.*¹ Add: **2. b.** Also with *down.*

1860 F. W. Robinson *Grandmother's Money* vi. viii, If you will only listen to your lord and husband's conversation with these good gentlemen, and cork the sentimental down, we shall soon be Darby and Joan again. 1894 *Outing* (U.S.) XXIV. 220/1 The descriptions of the lion usually corked down in the 'animal books'.

Cork, *v.*⁴, erron. spelling of Calk *v.*

1776 *New Jersey Archives* Ser. ii. I. 166 A chestnut sorrel mare,..shod before, shoes are steel corked. 1806 Webster *Compend. Dict.*, *Cork*, *v.t.*,..to form sharp points or shoe with points. *a* 1817 T. Dwight *Trav. New Eng.* (1821) II. 217 The clay..., unless a horse is corked, is dangerous both to him and to the rider.

Corker. Add: **1. b.** One who corks; one who provides a bottle with a cork.

1881 *Instr. Census Clerks* (1885) 58 Blacking Manufacture: Liquid: Bottlers...Cooper. Corker. 1921 *Dict. Occup. Terms* (1927) § 459 *Corker*; *cork fitter*; drives corks into bottles filled with beer, mineral waters, etc., by hand, or by machine which he feeds with corks.

2. b. A person or thing of surpassing size or excellence; a stunner. *slang* and *dial.*

1877 *N.W. Linc. Gloss.*, *Cauker*, anything very big, especially a heavy blow or a great lie. 1882 *Cornhill Mag.* 325 We look over our boat-side and see the big 'corkers' rising up out of the marl and sand in which their roots lie buried. 1887 D. C. Murray *Nov. Note Bk.* v, My first job in this here line was just a corker...I *was* hed that time. *a* 1889 in Barrère & Leland *Dict. Slang* s.v., Jake Kilrain is a corker, and ought to have the championship of the world. 1903 *Westm. Gaz.* 7 Sept. 2/3 The chairman,..in proposing his health, is reported to have said, 'Sir Thomas, you're a corker'. 1909 H. G. Wells *Tono-Bungay* i. iii. 75 Had her cry, of course...But now—buoyant again!..She's a Corker.

Corking, *vbl. sb.* (see under Cork *v.*¹). Add: Of wines: The action or process of becoming corked (see Corked *ppl. a.* 4).

1904 *Lancet* 18 June 1758/2 'Corking' in wines or other fluids.

Corking (kǭ·ɹkiŋ), *ppl. a.* Chiefly *U.S.* [After *Corker 2 b.] Unusually fine, large, or excellent; stunning. Also *advb.*

1895 *Outing* (U.S.) XXVII. 193/2 Corking great fences the Vale doubles are. 1897 Flandrau *Harvard Episodes* 192 He had a corking big oak table. 1902 *Munsey's Mag.* Mar. 816 A good show...and a corking good show at that. 1909 *Daily Chron.* 4 Mar. 4/4 In a phrase that is already classic, but not yet classical, he [*sc.* Mr. Roosevelt] announced not long ago that he had had 'a perfectly corking time'. 1910 E. A. Walcott *Open Door* xv. 188 'It was a corking good story, Captain', responded Tommy cheerfully. 1918 'A. Hope' *Yng. Man's Year* xxiv, Arthur's approval was fortified and grew with contemplation. 'It's corking!' he declared. 1926 *Ladies' Home Jrnl.* Dec. 36 He..engaged me, at a corking fee, to come up and take this case.

Corks (kǭɹks), *int.* Deformation of *cock's*, as in *cock's squint*, vulgar substitute for *cock's body*, etc. (see Cock *sb.*⁸).

1926 'Berta Ruck' *Her Pirate Partner* xiii. § 3 Mrs. Llewelyn in stark agony had gasped out the word 'Corks!' 1927 *Daily Express* 8 July 8/7 Another frequent expression was 'Corks!'

Corkscrew, *sb.* **2.** Add: **corkscrew grass**, a kind of grass having a twisted seed with long awn.

1890 *Melbourne Argus* 26 Sept. 13/5 To get the fleeces off before the grass seeds ripen, those of the corkscrew grass especially. 1898 *Nature* 27 Jan. 311 Spear or corkscrew-grass (*Stipa setacea*).

Corkscrew, *v.* Add: **1.** Also, to twist spirally.

1851 H. Melville *Moby Dick* cxxxiv, Caught and twisted, corkscrewed in the mazes of the line, loose harpoons..came flashing.

2. b. To become twisted.

1909 *Chambers's Jrnl.* July 423/2 As in the case of the bayonets which 'corkscrewed' in the Soudan.

3. b. *intr.* To work *away at* as with a corkscrew.

1920 J. Gregory *Man to Man* iv, Trying to pump me and corkscrewing away at dad when he was full of whisky.

Corliss (kǭ·ɹlis). The name of G. H. Corliss of Providence, Rhode Island, U.S., used *attrib.* to designate (*a*) the valve gear invented by him in 1849 or a modification of it, (*b*) an engine equipped with such a valve gear.

1874 Knight *Dict. Mech.*, *Corliss-engine*, a form of steam-engine having a variable and automatic cut-off of peculiar character. 1876 *Engineering* XXII. 12 The great Corliss beam engine. 1887 *Encycl. Brit.* XXII. 507/2 Corliss Valve-Gear, Spencer Inglis form. 1888 *Lockwood's Dict. Terms Mech. Engin.*, Corliss Valve.

Corn, *sb.*¹ Add:

5. *U.S.* (Earlier examples.)

1608 J. Smith *Wks.* (1884) 9 It pleased God..to moue the Indians to bring vs Corne, ere it was halfe ripe. 1634 *Rel. Ld. Baltimore's Plantation* (1865) 17 Their ordinary diet is Poane and Omine, both made of Corne.

b. *ellipt.* Corn-whiskey. *U.S.*

1845 J. J. Hooper *Adv. Simon Suggs* v. 54 Let me git one o' these book-larnt fellers over a bottle of 'old corn'.

7. *To acknowledge* (*admit, confess*) *the corn.* Bring here def. and quots. from Corn *sb.*² 2. Schele de Vere (*Americanisms* 47) gives two accounts of the origin of the phrase.

1840 *Daily Pennant* (St. Louis) 14 July (Th.) David Johnson acknowledged the corn, and said that he was drunk. 1842 *Spirit of Times* (Philad.) 16 Mar. (Th.) Your honor, I confesses the corn. I was royally drunk. 1854 Shillaber *Mrs. Partington* 152 The old Sherry admitted the corn, turned over and slept on it. 1891 C. Roberts *Adrift Amer.* 54, I acknowledge 'the corn' myself, as they say across the Atlantic. 1902 Harben *Abner Daniel* 136 When anybody teaches me any tricks, I acknowledge the corn an' take off my hat.

9. *corn-barn, -basket, -colour, -coloured* (earlier examples), *-coverer, -planting, -plough, -row, -sampler, -shock* (modern example), *-top.*

1864 T. L. Nichols *Amer. Life* I. 22 At a little distance was..a *corn-barn for storing Indian corn. 1648 *Connecticut Public Records* I. 487, 1 spade..a *corne baskitt. 1809 W. Irving *Knickerb.* iii. iv, The contents filled a couple of corn-baskets. 1860 Susan Warner *Say & Seal* xxix. 264 In one corner of the hearth sat Mr. Skip,..a full corn basket beside him, an empty one in front. 1873 J. H. Beadle *Undevel. West* xix. 357 Rich dresses were numerous at church, particularly of *corn-color silk. 1854 Mary J. Holmes *Tempest & Sunshine* vii. 103 If I catch you here again dickerin' after Fanny, I'll pull every *corn-colored har out of your head. 1874 Knight *Dict. Mech.*, **Corn-coverer*, a plow or pair of plows to run alongside a row of dropped corn and throw earth upon the seed. 1831 Peck *Guide for Emigrants* 165 *Corn-planting was over. 1849 Pritts *Mirr. Border Life* 460, I remained in that situation till corn planting time. 1874 Knight *Dict. Mech.*, **Corn-plow*, a shovel-plow, double-shovel, or other form of plow for tending crops planted in hills. 1769 Washington *Diaries* I. 347 That part of it which the *Corn rows run through received no other plowing. 1879 Tourgee *Fool's Err.* xxviii. 173 My wife..took the children along the corn-rows to the woods. 1898 *Westm. Gaz.* 29 Dec. 5/2, A *corn-sampler,..living in Bermondsey. 1921 *Dict. Occup. Terms* (1927) § 789. 1857 *Trans. Ill. Agric. Soc.* II. 665 During winter they may be tracked..to the neighboring *corn-shocks, which they have visited for food. 1814 J. Taylor *Arator* 93 Some loss will accrue from the evaporation of a cover, whether composed of straw or *corn tops.

11. corn-ball *U.S.* (examples); **corn belt**, the area in which 'corn' is grown; **corn-blade** *U.S.* (earlier examples); **corn-broom** *U.S.* (examples); **corn-festival** *U.S.* (see quot.); **corn-fodder** *U.S.* (examples); **corn-fritter** *U.S.* (example); **corn-grinder**, (*a*) = Metate; (*b*) one who grinds corn; so *corn-grinding*; **corn-high** *a.* *U.S.*, as tall as a stalk of corn; **corn-hill** *U.S.* (earlier examples); **corn-knife** *U.S.* (example); **corn-moth** *U.S.* (example); **corn-muller**, a pestle used for pounding corn; **corn-oyster** *U.S.* (example); **corn-pit**, (*b*) *S. Afr.*, a deep hole made by Kaffirs for storing their maize and corn; **corn-popper** *U.S.* (examples); **corn-sheller** *U.S.* (earlier examples); **corn-shelling**, the process of detaching the grains of maize from the cob; **corn-silk** *U.S.*, the styles of maize; **corn-silker**, a machine for removing the corn-silk; **corn-spurrey**, a small weed, *Spergula arvensis*, bearing white flowers and whorled leaves; **corn states** *U.S.*, those States in which maize is the principal crop; **corn-weevil**, a weevil that infests corn; **corn-whiskey** *U.S.*, a spirit distilled from maize.

1843 Carlton *New Purchase* ix. 64 Nanny remained near the dutch oven to keep us supplied with red-hot pones or *corn-balls. 1873 E. Phelps *Trotty's Wedding Tour* 3 They were eating a corn ball at recess. 1922 Titus *Timber* i. 12 Didn't Michigan Pine build th' *corn belt? 1775 *Essex Inst. Hist. Coll.* XIII. 160 The Western shore their feed is *Corn-Blades & Oats. 1806 Webster *Compend. Dict.*, *Cornblades*, leaves of maiz. (S. States). 1843 Carlton *New Purchase* vi. 34 The driver..crowded the stage body even above the seats with corn-blades. 1823 J. Farmer & J. B. Moore *Gaz. New-Hampsh.* 127 Wooden ware, whips, *corn brooms,. are manufactured by them. 1845 F. Douglas *Life* 74 Making corn-brooms, mats, horse-collars and baskets. 1904 *Brooklyn Eagle* 31 Aug. 4 They are having *corn festivals in Kansas. Corn festivals in Kansas are public celebrations in recognition of good crops. 1772 *Carroll Papers* in *Maryland Hist. Mag.* XIV. 288 We shall get in all our *Corn Fother by the middle of next week. 1837 Colman *Rep. Agric. Mass.* (1838) 24 Farmers..estimate the corn fodder or stover upon an acre as equal to three fourths of a ton of English hay. 1904 Mary E. Waller *Wood-carver* ii, I can look..up the slope of the mountain, across the stony corn-fodder patch. 1862 Mrs. Stowe in *Independent* 13 Feb. (Bartlett) A very minute account which Mrs. Kittridge was giving of the way to make *corn-fritters which should taste exactly like oysters. 1841 *Knickerbocker Mag.* XVII. 234 Improved..*corn-grinders. 1854 Bartlett *Explor. Texas*, etc. II. 245 Several broken metates, or corn-grinders, lie about the pile. 1907 *Daily Chron.* 14 Nov. 6/2 Disguised as corn-grinders. 1921 *Dict. Occup. Terms* (1927) § 432 Rollerman,..corn grinder. 1905 *Westm. Gaz.* 30 Nov. 8/2 That they shall revert to *corn-grinding. 1927 Peake & Fleure *Peasants & Potters* 48 The discovery of corn-grinding stones. 1892 Gunter *Miss Dividends* (1893) 52, I was born in Chicago..and railroaded ever since I was *corn high. 1751 *Virginia Gazette* 17 Oct., A new Tobacco-House being built, and about 35,000 *Corn-Hills cleared. 1765 J. Bartram *Jrnl.* 28 Dec. (1766) 11 These are..the common planting grounds of the former Florida Indians, as is proved by..the vestigies of the corn hills still remaining. 1785 Washington *Diaries* II. 363 The Wheat ground..being..too much baked for the roller to make a proper impression, the Corn hills yielded but little to its weight. 1838 H. Colman *Rep. Agric. Mass.* (1839) 31 The corn hills were split with the common harrow. 1856 *Trans. Mich. Agric. Soc.* VII. 54 Six *corn knives. 1868 *Rep. U.S. Comm. Agric.* (1869) 315 The clothes-moth and *corn-moth are representatives of the family. 1881 *Rep. Smithsonian Inst.* (1883) 612 The stone with a hole in the center..is called a *corn-muller. ? 1862 Mrs. Stowe in *Independent* (Bartlett) In this secret direction about the mace lay the whole mystery of *corn-oysters. 1883 J. Edwards *Remin.* (1886) 83 In the '*corn pits' were..to be seen scores of human skulls. 1877 Bartlett *Dict. Amer.* (ed. 4) Add., **Corn-popper*, an instrument the top of which is like a sieve, in which corn is held over a fire to roast or 'pop'. 1878 B. F. Taylor *Between Gates* 57 Boulders dance about it [*sc.* a stream of water] like kernels in a corn-popper. 1909 S. E. White *Rules of Game* v. iii, One of you boys go rummage the store-room for the corn popper. 1825 *Boston Monthly Mag.* I. 25 A patent *corn-sheller..may be of more service to the community, than all the poems of Byron or the novels of Scott. 1851 C. Cist *Cincinnati* 169 Corn-shellers, to shell twenty to fifty bushels per hour. 1851 *Fredericksburg* (Va.) *News* 21 Mar., Corn Shellers—Both Hand and Horse Power. *a* 1848 Ruxton *Life Far West* (1849) 62 Better for him had he minded his *corn-shelling alone. 1876 Habberton *Jericho Road* xiii. 120 The pork-packin' and corn-shellin' seasons nearly on us. 1878 B. F. Taylor *Between Gates* 258 Let the fellow's hair turn the color of *corn-silk in the sun. 1902 S. E. White *Blazed Trail* xxxix. 279 His eyes desired to follow the soft white curve of her cheek to dance with the light of her corn-silk hair. 1902 *Encycl. Brit.* XXVI. 558/1 Among the devices in common use are..corn cutters, *corn silkers, pea briners, [etc.]. 1771 *Ibid.* III. 621/1 *Spergula.. arvensis*, or *corn-spurrey. 1846 J. Baxter *Libr. Pract. Agric.* (ed. 4) II. 294 Corn spurry..is found most frequently in soils rather moist. 1899 G. Ade *Doc Horne* xxvii. 292 The book-agent..was managing his wife's lecture tour throughout the *corn states. 1849 *Rep. Comm. Patents Agric.* (1850) 335 The other species of *corn-weevil alluded to,..the granary weevil, is more common in this country. 1843 Carlton *New Purchase* 172 Candidates..making licentious speeches, treating to *corn whiskey, violating the sabbath. 1857 Strother *Virginia Illustr.* II. 149 The room..reeked with fumes of tobacco and corn whiskey. 1873 'Mark Twain' & Warner *Gilded Age* xiii. 130 A bottle of apparently corn-whiskey.

Corn, *sb.*² **3.** Add: **corn-cure**, a remedy for corns.

1906 R. Whiteing *Ring in New* 158 The methods of a puff for corn-cure.

Corn, *v.* **8.** *U.S.* (Modern example.)

1886 *U.S. Consular Rep.* No. ix. 40 Those hundreds of thousands of acres of once valuable Southern lands, corned to death, and now lying to waste in worthless sage grass.

Corn-bread. *U.S.* [Corn *sb.*¹ 5.] Bread made of corn-meal.

1823 Long *Exped.* I. 68 They purchased a ham, and a loaf of corn bread of Mr. Kennedy. 1831 Peck *Guide for Emigrants* ii. 156 Pones of corn bread, smoking hot, are brought forward. 1843 Carlton *New Purchase* ix. 63 Corn-bread takes its own time to bake. 1865 T. W. Knox *Camp-fire & Cotton-field* 336 Corn-bread, bacon, and potatoes were the only articles set before us. 1876 Habberton *Jericho Road* xii. 111 A Dutch-oven, from which came an odor of corn-bread. 1913 Mrs. Stratton-Porter *Laddie* xii, There wasn't a crumb there except cornbread, and she didn't want that.

Corn-cake. *U.S.* (Earlier and later examples.)

1791 W. Bartram *Trav. Carolina* 38 It is..an ingredient in most of their cookery, especially homony and corn cakes. 1833 *Louisville Daily Herald* 18 Oct., Hence the corn cake and dodger cake, a species which Mrs. Trollope had the honor of inventing, for it was never heard of in Cincinnati before. 1864 B. Taylor *H. Thurston* xxvi. 337 The old Melinda alone remained in the Kitchen, to prepare her incomparable corn-cake. 1903 *N.Y. Sun* 1 Nov., Corn cakes as a substitute for bread are popular in the South.

Corn-cob. *U.S.* (Earlier examples.)

1797 Morse *Amer. Gaz.* s.v. *South Carolina*, Another tree, which bears an ear like a corn-cob. 1813 J. Lambert *Trav. Canada & U.S.* I. 132 They [*sc.* Canadians] are extravagantly fond of the corn cobs boiled or roasted and rubbed over with a little butter and salt.

b. Short for *corn-cob pipe.*

1923 *Blackw. Mag.* Dec. 727/1 Mr. Quigg puffing away at a corn-cob.

c. *attrib.* (Examples.)

1801 *Spirit of Farmer's Museum* 236 Jotham, get the great case bottle, Your teeth can pull its corn cob stopple. 1829–32 J. P. Kennedy *Swallow B.* II. xix. 246 He stood in the group, with his corncob pipe, puffing the smoke from his bolster-lips. 1856 *Yale Lit. Mag.* XXI. 145 (Th.) He was employed in whittling a corn cob bowl into a pipe. 1888 'C. E. Craddock' *Broomsedge Cove* iv. 53 An aroma lingered about its corn-cob stopper. 1911 *Springfield Weekly Republ.* 12 Jan. 1 Speaker Cannon gave Washington a shock Thursday by appearing in one of the Capitol lobbies smoking a corncob pipe.

d. *Comb.*, as *corn-cob crusher.*

1853 *Trans. Mich. Agric. Soc.* IV. 83 Best corn-cob crusher by horse power.

Corn-cracker. *U.S.* **2.** (Example.)

1884 Goode *Nat. Hist. Aquat. Anim.* 666 'Whipparee' or 'Corn-cracker' of the South (*Rhinoptera quadriloba*).

3. An apparatus for cracking corn.

1844 Lee & Frost *Oregon* xii. 134 At the mission we had a small cast-iron corncracker, in which we ground wheat after a fashion. 1900 Smithwick *Evol. State* 76 There was a sawmill with a corn cracker attached.

Corn-crake. 3. Add: **corn-crake fly**, an anglers' fly, the wings of which are made from a quill-feather of the corn-crake.

1898 *Westm. Gaz.* 25 June 7/2 The 'corncrake' fly was the successful lure.

Corn-crib. *U.S.* (Earlier examples.)

1716 B. Church *Hist. Philip's War* i. (1865) 56 A sort of Hovel that was build with Poles, after the manner of a corn crib. 1751 *Virginia Gazette* 7 Nov., A Stable and Corn-Cribb. 1809 *Massachusetts Spy* 6 Sept. (Th.) If they will establish a non-intercourse with my corn-crib, they will find their account in it. 1820 J. Woods *Two Years' Resid. Eng. Prairie* (1822) 177 There are no granaries or store-houses except corn-cribs. 1831 Peck *Guide for Emigrants* ii. 120 The more thrifty sprouts shoot forth and in ten years are large enough for corn-cribs and stables.

Corn dance. *U.S.* [Corn *sb.*¹ 5.] A dance, among Indians and negroes, connected with the sowing or harvesting of corn.

1836 *Knickerbocker Mag.* VIII. 154 Remaining away until the corn dances take place. 1837 *Southern Lit. Messenger* III. 391 The celebrated *corn dance* of the Seminoles is said to be connected with their religion. 1840 C. F. Hoffman *Greyslaer* III. viii. 185 De boys—..has gone to de village to hold corn-dance for seedtime. 1903 S. E. White *Forest* x. 128 Belts of beadwork, yellow and green, for the Corn Dance.

Corn-dodger. *U.S.* (Earlier example.)

1834 H. C. Kimball *Jrnl.* in *Prophet* (N.Y.) (1845) 15 Mar. (Th.) We sometimes had to live mostly on johnny-cake and corn-dodgers.

Cornely (kǫme·li, -ī·li). Also **cornelly.** Name of Émile *Cornely*, engineer, the first maker of the chain-stitch embroidery machine with universal feed invented by J. Bonnaz (cf. *Bonnaz): used to designate the machine, the machinist using it, and the embroidery made. Hence **Corne·lling**, the making of embroidery with this machine.

1903 *Daily Chron.* 27 Feb. 10/5 Bonnaz.—Few good Cornely hands..wanted. 1921 *Dict. Occup. Terms* (1927) § 407 By hand or by cornely appliqué machine. *Ibid.*, By cornely, singer or other machine. *Ibid.*, Machinist, cornely or cornelly; cornelling machinist; cornely hand.

Corner, *sb.*¹ Add: **3. b.** The angular projections (or projection) on each side of a violin or other similar stringed instrument. Also *corner-block.*

1888 *Encycl. Brit.* XXIV. 243/1 The Viol has..Square or obtuse corners...The Violin has..Acute corners. 1902 *Grove's Dict. Mus.* IV. 275/1 These corners mark the position of triangular 'blocks' inside, to which the ribs..are glued... Corner-blocks..first appear in the 15th century.

4. b. The triangular piece cut from the ham or hind-end (the gammon) of a side of bacon.

1891 *Encycl. Cookery* (ed. T. F. Garrett) I. 63/2 Gammon with Corner, 14 lb. *Ibid.*, Corner of Gammon, 4 lb. 1917 G. J. Nicholls *Bacon & Hams* 59 The gammon may also be cut into two pieces—a large corner and a large gammon hock. 1923 R. E. Davies *Pigs & Bacon Curing* 29 The side may be cut into three parts, comprising the fore end, the middle, and the gammon with corner.

5. c. *Tight corner*: see Tight *a.* 9.

12. *U.S.* (Earlier examples.)

1770 Washington *Diaries* I. 428, I marked two Maples, an Elm, and Hoopwood Tree as a Corner of the Soldiers Ld. 1816 U. Brown *Jrnl.* in *Maryland Hist. Mag.* XI. 221 If the old original white oak Corner cannot be found establish a Corner there in lieu and in place of said White Oak. 1832 *Louisville Directory* 107 A knot of valuable surveys depended on one corner; Sodowsky, who had marked the survey, was called upon in court to identify the corner.

13. b. *Poker.* (See quots.)

1876 Joaquin Miller *Unwritten Hist.* iv. 64 For the benefit of ladies..I may state that four aces in a game of poker make a 'corner' that cannot be broken. *Ibid.* xii. 180 They fell into an exciting game of poker, at ten dollars a corner.

d. *Hockey.* (In full *corner-hit.*) A free penalty hit against the defending side made by one of the attacking side from the corner flag.

1897 *Encycl. Sport* I. 518/2 A good goalkeeper..should never hesitate to concede a corner when he can see no other opening. 1907 *Hockey* 22 Nov. 22/1 Just before half-time, Mid-Surrey broke away, and, forcing a corner, Nash put in an excellent shot from the corner hit. *Ibid.*, Before the end Simmonds scored from a penalty corner.

14. *Comm.* orig. *U.S.* (Earlier example.)

1853 *Captain Priest* 249 (Th.) He is the greatest of all men for a 'corner'.

15. *corner-cupboard* (earlier quot.), *-seat, -shelf.*

1809 W. Irving *Knickerb.* ii. vii. (1887) I. 109 A fleet of boats..were piled up with all kinds of household articles,.. quaint *corner cupboards. 1852 *Illustr. Lond. News* 17 Jan. 51/3 The two *corner seats at the top of the interior [of an omnibus]. 1866 Mrs. Whitney *L. Goldthwaite* v, Mrs. Linceford got inside the vehicle at once, securing comfortable back corner-seats. 1894 J. T. Taylor *Veil Lifted* 31 His thoughts had been..concentrated upon..securing a corner seat in a smoking carriage. 1888 'C. E. Craddock' *Broomsedge Cove* xxii. 395 The quilts..were piled high on the '*corner shelf' which they had burdened of yore.

16. corner block (see *3 b); **corner-boy** *U.S.* (earlier example); **corner cutter**, a machine for cutting the corners of books, cards, etc.; **corner flag**, a flag marking each corner of the playing area of a hockey or football field; **corner-grocery** *U.S.* (see quot. 1859); **corner hit** (see *13 d); **corner-mark** *U.S.*, a boundary-mark at a corner of the land; so **corner-post, -stake.**

1855 D. G. Mitchell *Fudge Doings* (N.Y.) II. 47 (Th.) Presently the *corner-boy, Jerry, comes in. He is a short-haired, half-Irish boy, [etc.]. 1884 Knight *Dict. Mech.* Suppl., **Corner cutter.* 1. A machine for cutting the corners off cards or books...2. A machine for cutting out notches from blanks of cardboard, intended to be bent up to form boxes. 1898 *Encycl. Sport* I. 420/2 The ball must be placed a yard from the *corner-flag. 1859 Bartlett *Dict. Amer.* (ed. 2), **Corner-grocery*, a grocer's shop on the corner of two streets, a favorite location for such establishments in American towns. 1862 *Congress. Globe* 7 July 3159/1 Without subjecting themselves to the charge of disloyalty by every corner-grocery politician in the land. 1870 'Fanny Fern' *Ginger-Snaps* 106 Tea to the working-girl, taken in this way, is like the 'corner-grocery-drink' to the working-man. 1890 *Buckskin Mose* i. 11 Carrying out teas and sugar..with other such necessaries and luxuries, from a corner-grocery. 1868 *Rep. U.S. Comm. Agric.* (1869) 343 These fragile *corner-marks are strictly respected by the neighbors, and a case of trespass rarely occurs. 1648 *Charlestown Land Rec.* 110 A parcell of land lying within and between the upper *corner post of the house. 1785 A. Ellicott in *Life & Lett.* (1908) 41 Joseph went with some Hands to enlarge the Pile of Stones about the Corner Post. 1873 Eggleston *Myst. Metrop.* xi. 97 They sought first to guess out the line of a railroad; they examined *corner-stakes.

Corner, *v.* Add: **3. b.** *U.S.* (Earlier example.)

1824 *Massachusetts Spy* 21 Apr. (Th.) Cornered up so unexpectedly, she candidly confessed.

4. *Comm.* orig. *U.S.* (Earlier examples.)

1836 *Knickerbocker Mag.* VII. 42 He has been cornered by the brokers on the — stock and has lost all his fortune. 1841 *Week in Wall St.* 83 A squad of Bull-backers had been secretly..getting control of a certain stock, intending to 'corner' some one with it.

6. *intr.* *U.S.* (Earlier example.)

1821 *Boston* (Mass.) *Rec.* (1909) XXXIX. 189 A point where said fence and his other fence join cornering on said streets.

Cornerer. Add:

2. One who cuts the corners off or notches materials used in the manufacture of various articles.

1921 *Dict. Occup. Terms* (1927) § 279.

Cornering, *vbl. sb.* **2.** (Earlier examples.)

1841 *Week in Wall St.* 27 No cornering, I hope. 1845 C. Mathews *Writ.* I. 135 (Th.) They would no doubt have reached a high standing in the practice of what is called cornering.

3. The action of taking a corner on a course.

1928 *Times* 2 July 6/7 Kaye Don got ahead thanks to brilliant cornering.

4. The action of cutting off corners. Also *attrib.*

1884 Knight *Dict. Mech.* Suppl., *Cornering Machine*, a machine for rounding off the corners of stuff; especially used in implement and carriage work.

Corner lot. *U.S.* (See Corner *sb.*¹ 16.)

1702 Logan in *Corr. Penn & Logan* (1870) I. 129, I have sold the corner lot next the Meeting-House for £115. 1816 *Boston Selectmen* 29 July, The corner lot of the new street. 1863 *Congress. Globe* 28 Feb., App. 139/1 These early pioneers [in Colorado]..commenced laying off 'corner lots', and holding elections. 1873 J. H. Beadle *Undevel. West* iii. 65 Every man..is hopeful as a millionaire if he have a few corner lots, and ten dollars in his pocket. 1888 [see Corner *sb.*¹ 16].

attrib. 1868 *Putnam's Mag.* Jan. I. 24 No corner-lot banditti, Or brokers from the city.

Corner-man. Add: **4.** *Logging.* (See quot.) *U.S.*

1905 *Terms Forestry & Logging* 34 *Corner man*, in building a camp or barn of logs, one who notches the logs so that they will fit closely and make a square corner.

Corner tree. *U.S.* (See Corner *sb.*¹ 16.)

1661 *Portsmouth Rec.* 108 That the lotters are to run the line..from Corner tree to Corner tree. 1786 Washington *Diaries* III. 55 Not having Hough's field Notes, and no Corner trees being noted in His Plat, I did not attempt to look for lines. 1843 Carlton *New Purchase* xii. 87 We began to look through the legal blazes to espy a corner tree cut and notched in a peculiar way. 1859 Bartlett *Dict. Amer.*, *Corner-trees.* See *Witness-trees.*

Cornery, *a.* Delete †*Obs.*? and add quot. and fig. use.

1887 'Theo Gift' *Victims* xiv, A good fellow enough, but odd, you know, cornery. 1905 C. Jarrott in *Westm. Gaz.* 11 July 4/2 Undoubtedly it [*sc.* a course] is very 'cornery,' and if proper caution is not exercised serious accidents will doubtless result.

Cornet, *sb.*¹ Add:

2. c. A conical wafer filled with ice-cream.

1926 *Amer. Speech* Jan. 146 In England an ice-cream cone is called a *cornet*. 1927 *Glasgow Herald* 9 Aug. 7 A halfpenny 'cornet'.

Corneum (kǭ·ɹnĭǫ̆m). *Anat.* [L., neut. sing. of *corneus* horny.] Short for *stratum corneum*, the horny layer of the skin.

1911 T. L. Stedman *Med. Dict.*, *Corneum*, the horny layer of the skin.

Corn-fed, *a.* Add: **b.** Fed on maize. *U.S.*

1809 W. Irving *Knickerb.* iii. vi. (1825) 122 They grew up a ..hardy race of..strapping corn-fed wenches. 1835 R. M. Bird *Hawks of Hawk-hollow* II. xix. 223 While you was lying snorting here like a corn-fed pig, we was knocking the tories on the head at the yard-gate. 1862 'Artemus Ward' *His Bk.* (1865) 154 The corn fed gals of Ohio and Injianny. 1889 [see Dict.].

Cornfield. Add: **b.** A field in which maize is grown. *U.S.*

1634 *Cambridge Prop. Rec.* 1 The Constable shall make a Surveyinge of the Houses, backsids, Corne ffeilds,..and other lands. 1688 *Conn. Hist. Soc. Coll.* VI. 223 A Regulation ffor Cattle Corne ffields & ffences. 1752 W. Trent *Jrnl.* (1871) 86 French and Indians..surprised the Indians in the cornfields. 1772 *Carroll Papers* in *Maryland Hist. Mag.* XIV. 150 Our Cornfields are in very good order. 1809 W. Irving *Knickerb.* iii. vii. (1825) 123 He..clears away a corn field and potatoe patch. 1837 Peck *Gaz. Illinois* i. 25 The ..squirrels often do mischief in the corn fields. 1872 Eggleston *Hoosier Schoolm.* xi. 94 Ralph strolled through the Squire's cornfield.

attrib. 1871 Schele de Vere *Americanisms* (1872) 48 So-called self-made men are to this day fond of boasting that they never received any other education but in an *old cornfield school*. 1895 'C. E. Craddock' *Myst. Witch-Face Mt.* x. 157, I wouldn't hev trested him with a handful o' cornfield peas.

Corn-flour. (Earlier U.S. example.)

1791 W. Bartram *Trav. Carolina* 456 A meagre gruel, made of a little corn-flour and water.

Corn-flower. Add: **e.** The blue colour of the corn-flower: a fashion shade.

1923 *Weekly Dispatch* 4 Feb. 15. 1923 *Daily Mail* 28 May 1.

Corn-ground. (Later example.)

1760 Washington *Diaries* I. 160 [I] find..not half a crop, especially of Corn Ground, prepared.

Corn-house. 2. *U.S.* (Examples.)

1745 *Virginia Gazette* 19 Dec., Two Dwelling-houses, Milk-house, Corn-house. 1773 *Carroll Papers* in *Maryland Hist. Mag.* XV. 281 They may goe to the Island to get the scantlings for the Corn House, Sibthorp shall Carry with him the dimensions of my new Corn House. 1796–1806 B. Hawkins *Lett.* 54 Saying..he had not entered 3 of the Indian houses...He went to their doors..or sat under their corn house. 1836 *Southern Lit. Messenger* II. 157 That unlimited control which the said horse exercises over the corn in his corn-house. 1845 W. G. Simms *Wigwam & Cabin* 369 Considering that the Corn-House aint oberfull.

Corn-husker, -husking. *U.S.* (Earlier examples.)

1821 T. Nuttall *Trav. Arkansa* ii. 58 We took up our lodging where there happened to be a corn-husking. 1834 Crockett *Narr. Life* x. 71 He made a great corn husking, and a great frolic, and gave a general treat. 1871 *Amer. Naturalist* V. 317 Several Indian Stone implements..which are said to bear a striking resemblance to iron corn huskers now in use in the West. 1876 *Rep. Vermont Board Agric.* III. 609 The corn harvest may now be greatly accelerated by the use of the corn husker driven by horse power.

Cornish. Add: *Cornish cream.*

1906 A. L. Salmon *Lit. Rambles West of Eng.* 214 Ready to indulge eagerly in Cornish cream and saffron-cake. 1912 'Q' *Hocken & Hunken* vi, A delectable junket with Cornish cream.

Cornland. Add: **b.** Land suitable for growing maize. *U.S.*

1838 H. W. Ellsworth *Valley N. Wabash* iv. 39 The lands, that we call first rate corn-lands, are generally alluvial bottom lands.

c. *attrib.*: **cornland crow**, the Natal name of *Heterocorax capensis.*

1867 Layard *Birds S. A.* 168 *Corvus Segetum*... Korenland Kraai of Colonists, lit. Cornland-Crow. 1899 Woodward *Birds of Natal* 1 (Pettman) As this bird is very partial to cultivated ground it is often called the Cornland crow.

Corn-meal. (Earlier U.S. examples.)

1831 Peck *Guide Emigr.* III. 324 Flat boats..loaded with cornmeal, etc. 1849 F. Douglas *Life* 52 We were allowed less than half a bushel of corn-meal per week.

Co·rn-pla·nter. *U.S.* [Corn *sb.*¹ 5.]

1. One who plants Indian corn. Also *attrib.*

1832 *Deb. Congress* 9 Feb. 339 The corn planter and wheat grower understand their interests. 1833 *Ibid.* 29 Jan. 1444 Let the corn planter ask himself if he is not willing to pay a higher duty on broad-cloth than on coffee, for a few years. 1834 H. Brackenridge *Recoll.* vii. 74 The arrival of Corn-planter Indians, on the bank of the Alleghany. 1845 W. G. Simms *Wigwam & Cabin* Ser. ii. 104 One of a tribe [*sc.* the Crows], of which the corn-planter has an aversion.

2. A drill for planting corn.

1840 J. Buel *Farmer's Comp.* 151 Some of them, under the name of corn-planters, are employed in planting Indian Corn. 1856 [see Corn *sb.*¹ 11]. 1861 *Trans. Ill. Agric. Soc.* IV. 24 A petition, praying the Executive Committee to make a second trial of Cornplanters.

Corn-shuck. *U.S.* (Earlier example.)

1845 W. G. Simms *Wigwam & Cabin* 353 The wizard had rubbed down the back and shoulders of his patient with corn-shucks.

Corn-shucking. *U.S.* (Earlier examples.)

1819 W. Faux *Memorable Days* (1823) 211 A large party ..assembled to effect a corn shucking, something like an English hawkey, or harvest home...Corn shucking means plucking the ears of Indian corn from the stalk, and then housing it in cribs..for winter use. 1855 *Putnam's Monthly* V. 76 The annual corn-shucking season has its own peculiar class of songs, never heard but upon that festival.

Corn-stalk. Add:

1. (Earlier and later U.S. examples.)

1697 *Maryland Hist. Mag.* XV. 116 [The Indian] comes on the Back of his Plantation, gathers his Green Corn, cutts up his Corn stalks, and gathers his herbage. 1743 J. MacSparran *Diary* 31 Aug. (1899) 10 My men are going to help Jo: Mumford to cut Corn Stalks. 1768 Washington *Diaries* I. 262 Finishd cutting down Corn Stocks at all my Plantations. 1779 *Narrag. Hist. Reg.* I. 94 Cut corn storks for cousin Hagard. 1779 T. Smith *Jrnl.* 31 Aug. (1821) 147 Cut our corn stalks. Never was the corn so forward. 1807 *Deb. Congress* 3 Dec. (1852) 1023 The militia were but partly armed; and when drawn out to muster might be seen exercising with corn-stalks or walking canes. 1847 *Rep. Comm. Patents* (1848) 182 The manufacture of beet or corn stalk sugar. 1852 *Trans. Mich. Agric. Soc.* III. 101 Best corn stalk cutter. 1875 Mrs. Stowe *Deacon Pitkin's Farm* ii. 41 Through the glimmer of the yellow twilight might be seen the stacks of dry corn-stalks. 1896 Roosevelt *Winning of West* IV. 245 Such musters

were often called, in derision, cornstalk drills, because many of the men either having no guns or neglecting to bring them, drilled with stalks instead.

fig. 1898 *Congress. Rec.* 23 Apr. 4216/1, I was a tin soldier—a kind of cornstalk captain—but I had..[some] experience.

b. *Comb.*: **corn-stalk disease**, a disease of cattle caused by the eating of dry corn-stalks.

1900 *Yearbk. U.S. Dept. Agric.* 307 (Cent. D. Suppl.) The cornstalk disease..is a..little-understood malady of cattle.

2. (Earlier and allusive quots.)

1827 CUNNINGHAM *Two Yrs. N.S.W.* II. 116 We have, as I said before, first, the sterling and currency, or English and Colonial born, the latter bearing also the name of corn stalks (Indian corn), from the way in which they shoot up. 1848 H. W. HAYGARTH *Bush Life in Australia* xi. 123 The average height of the Australians is probably more than that of the English, but when they exceed a certain standard they are apt to become loose made and weedy, thereby justifying their appellation of 'cornstalks'. 1852 MUNDY *Antipodes* (1857) 6 There are probably more gleaners of the profits; not..a thinner crop of 'cornstalks' for the harvest,—some of them as long in the ear as could be wished.

Co·rn-stea·ler. *U.S. slang.* [CORN *sb.*[1] 5.] A hand.

1827 *Massachusetts Spy* 24 Oct. (Th.) Give us a shake of your corn-stealer; why, you look out in sorts, Dorcas. 1840 HALIBURTON *Clockm.* Ser. III. x. 134 And he squeezed his cornstealers till the old gineral began to dance like a bear on red hot iron. 1880 *Congress. Rec.* 22 Jan. 488/1 His phalanges or metacarpus, or rather Corn-stealers, are bigger than those of any other member [of the House].

Cornu- (kǭ·rniu), used as combining form of *Cornubian* Cornish, as in **Cornu-Bri·tish**, the British of Cornwall.

1769 BORLASE (*title*) Antiquities..of the County of Cornwall,..with a Vocabulary of the Cornu-British Language. 1897 E. PHILPOTTS *Lying Prophets* xii, The Cornu-British bishops.

Cornual. Add: b. Pertaining to cornua or a cornu.

1897 T. J. PARKER & HASWELL *Text-bk. Zool.* II. 118 A small cornual cartilage. 1907 *Practitioner* Sept. 357 As regards the relative strength of the cornual attachments, the posterior horns of both cartilages are firmly bound down to the tibia. *Ibid.* 401 In cornual pregnancy, the round ligament is attached on the outer side of the gestation sac.

Cornule (kǭ·rniul). *Zool.* [ad. mod.L. *cornulum*, dim. of L. *cornu* horn.] A small horny plate with the function of a tooth.

1889 NICHOLSON & LYDEKKER *Man. Palæont.* (ed. 3) 1265 Teeth are present in the young [*sc.* of Ornithorhynchus], and are succeeded by horny plates or cornules.

Cornus (kǭ·rnʊs). *Bot.* [L., = dogwood, f. *cornu* horn.] A shrub or small tree of the cornel or dogwood family.

1846 LINDLEY *Veget. Kingd.* 782 The Cornus of the ancients was the present Cornelian Cherry. 1920 *Blackw. Mag.* Nov. 621/1 A Cornus of some kind, bearing great clusters of scarlet fruit.

Corn-worm. Add: b. *U.S.* (See quot. 1889.)

1849 *Rep. Comm. Patents Agric.* (1850) 333 They are, I believe, called 'White corn-worms'. 1889 *Century Dict.*, *Heliothis*, a genus of noctuid moths...The larva, known as the boll-worm and corn-worm,..is especially injurious to the fruit of cotton, maize, and the tomato.

Corocoro (kǭ·rokǭ·ro). Also 7 **curricurro**, **-curre**, 8 **corrocorro**, **corracorra**, **caracore**, 9 **kora-kora**, **corocore**. [Malay *kurakura*. Cf. F. *caracore*, Sp. *caracora*, from which the English forms are mainly derived.] A boat used in the Malay Archipelago.

1634 SIR T. HERBERT *Trav.* 193 The shape of their Boates or Curricurroes have this representation. *Ibid.* 194 A Curricurre or boat. 1779 FORREST *Voy. N. Guinea* 23 A corocoro is a vessel generally fitted with out-riggers, with a high arched stem and stern, like the point of a half moon. They are used by the inhabitants of the Molucca islands chiefly. *Ibid.* 65 Got our stores, &c. very expeditiously on board, in a small new corocoro. 1798 in *Naval Chron.* (1799) II. 135 A *Corrocorro* is a vessel fitted with outriggers, having an high arched stem and stern. 1800 *Asiat. Ann. Reg.* 210/1 This expedition was formerly performed in large corracorras, or vessels like yachts. 1869 A. R. WALLACE *Malay Archip.* II. xxiv. 69 The boat was one of the kind called Kora-kora, quite open, very low, and about four tons burthen. It had outriggers of bamboo about five feet off each side, which supported a bamboo platform extending the whole length of the vessel.

Corolliform (kǫrǫ·lifǭɹm), *a.* [f. COROLLA + -(I)FORM.] Of the form or appearance of a corolla.

1889 *Cent. Dict.*

Corollula (kǫrǫ·liŭlă). *Bot.* [mod.L.: see -ULE.] A small or minute corolla.

1856 HENSLOW *Dict. Bot. Terms* 46. 1900 B. D. JACKSON *Gloss. Bot. Terms.*

Coromandel: see CALAMANDER.

1845 G. DODD *Brit. Manuf.* IV. 199 The coromandel-wood.

Corona. Add:

6. Also, the trochal disk of a rotifer; etc.

1898 A. SEDGWICK *Text-bk. Zool.* I. 299 *Phylum Rotifera.* ..It will be useful to use the word corona for the discoidal anterior end of the body. 1902 *Amer. Nat.* Dec. 932 In Melo and some other genera the spines project upwards and are generally unclosed on the apertural side. This produces the spiral 'corona', so striking a feature in some shells. 1906 *Cambr. Nat. Hist.* I. 539 Echinidae in which the plates of the corona dovetail into each other. 1929 *Encycl. Brit.* XIX. 575/1 Numerous cilia crowded upon a particular area of delicate skin close to or encircling the mouth...The whole area, including the mouth itself, as seen when the cilia are active, is called the corona.

9. *Electr.* The luminous discharge from a conductor (see quots.). Also *attrib.*

1906 ALEX. RUSSELL *Altern. Currents* II. 475 When the potential difference between the mains is very high, each main is seen surrounded by a faintly luminous enveloping cloud of a bluish colour, which apparently does not touch the conductor it envelopes. This cloud is called the corona. *Ibid.*, When coronae make their appearance it is found that the capacity between the mains and the loss of energy in distribution are increased. 1913 H. B. DWIGHT *Transmission Line Formulas* 6 A current in phase with the voltage will flow between the conductors, but it is only noticeable at very high voltages. Part of it is a leakage current flowing over the insulators, and part is a discharge through the air, and produces the glow called corona, on high-voltage conductors. 1918 *Jrnl. Chem. Soc.* CXIV. II. 42 The corona discharge. 1926 *Encycl. Brit.* and Suppl. I. 949/1 In the case of high voltage aerial lines there is a notable loss of power due to the ionisation of the air. This is called the corona effect since it makes the lines appear luminous in the dark.

Corona[2] (kǒrōᵘ·nă). [From the proprietary name *La Corona* (Sp.) the crown.] A well-known brand of Havana cigar.

1887 *Army & Navy Co-op. Soc. Price List* 127 Havana Cigars..'La Corona'..Aguilas Imperiales Corona. 1912 W. J. LOCKE *Advent. Aristide Pujol* viii, He found him smoking a large corona. 1915 *Morn. Post* 16 Mar. 4, I..bought a thousand Corona Coronas an hour ago. 1921 *19th Cent.* May 767 The fur-coated Corona-puffing multi-millionaire. 1926 M. WALSH *Key above Door* viii, I was in the middle of a long corona when Lady Clunas rose to go.

Coronadite (kǫrǫnă·dəit). *Min.* (See quot.)

1905 *Jrnl. Chem. Soc.* LXXXVIII. II. 96 Coronadite, a black metallic mineral, not unlike psilomelane in general appearance, and intimately intermixed with quartz, is found in fairly large amount in the Coronado vein.

Coronamen (kǫrǫnē·men). [mod.L., f. CORONA.] The coronet of the hoof. 1842 BRANDE *Dict. Sci.*, etc.

Coronary, *a.* Add:

3. d. *ellipt.* = coronary artery, etc.

1893 in H. MORRIS *Hum. Anat.* 972 [The right coronary artery] divides into its two main branches, one of which..anastomoses with the left coronary. 1907 *Practitioner* Oct. 491 The blood-pressure will rise, and the heart itself will be more fully flushed with blood through the coronaries. 1928 C. F. COOPER *Parker & Haswell's Zool.* (ed. 4) II. 310 The coronary..forms the upwardly directed coronoid process immediately behind the last tooth.

Coronation. 3. Add: **coronation bracelet, rolls** (see quots.).

1883 W. JONES *Crowns & Coron.* 284 The coronation rolls contain the commission and proceedings of the commissioners appointed to hear and declare claims of service to be performed at coronations, as well as the oaths taken by the king or queen when crowned. 1886 *Encycl. Brit.* XX. 340/1 The armillæ or coronation bracelets.

Coroner. Add: **2.** The chief officer or sheriff of a sheading in the Isle of Man.

1577 in M. A. MILLS *Stat. Laws I. of Man* (1821) 58 All Coroners shall make a generall Search four Times in the Yeare for my Lord his Proffitt,..every Coroner within his own Sheading. 1653 CHALONER *I. of Man* (1656) 17, 6 Coroners or Sheriffs of the 6 Sheadings. 1883 *Encycl. Brit.* XV. 452/2 The coroner of the sheading, who is appointed annually by the governor, is a kind of sheriff. 1894 HALL CAINE *Manxman* v. xi, The Coroner of the premier sheading began to recite the same titles in Manx.

Coronet, *sb.* Add: **1. c.** *transf.* A terminal or crowning circlet of spines, hairs, or other small objects.

1826 KIRBY & SP. *Entomol.* xxxiii. III. 385 *Coronula*..,a coronet or semicoronet of fixed spines observable at the apex of the posterior *Tibia* in *Fulgora candelaria*, etc.

5. b. The bur or ring of bone on the head of a deer, at the base of an antler.

1898 LYDEKKER *Deer of all Lands* 6 Towards the completion of its [*sc.* the antler's] growth a more or less prominent ring of bone, termed the burr or coronet, is deposited at its base just above the junction with the pedicle.

Coronet, *v.* Add quots.:

1900 *Daily News* 1 May 2/4 The circle of Westmoreland and Cumberland hills..still coroneted with snow. 1908 *Westm. Gaz.* 11 Aug. 10/1 The moment the crown was on the head of the Queen the peeresses all coroneted themselves.

Coronid (kǫ·rǒnid). *Astr.* [f. CORONA + *-ID[2].] Any of a group of meteors having their radiant in the constellation *Corona borealis*.

1899 R. H. ALLEN *Star-Names* 179 The radiant point of the Coronids, the meteor shower visible from the 12th of April to the 30th of June.

Coronillin (kǫrǒni·lin). *Chem.* [f. *Coronilla* + -IN[1].] A bitter, yellow glucoside contained in the seeds of species of *Coronilla*, esp. *C. scorpioides*, used as a heart stimulant.

1897 *Jrnl. Chem. Soc.* LXXII. I. 433 Coronillin is obtained by digesting the powdered seed..with six times its weight of water at 100°.

Coronitis (kǫrǒnəi·tis). [f. CORON(ARY + -ITIS.] Inflammation of the coronary substance of the hoof of a horse. 1890 BILLINGS *Med. Dict.*

Coronoid, *a.* Add: *sb.* One of the component bones of the jaw.

1893 in H. MORRIS *Hum. Anat.* 1122 On the inner side of the coronoid, between it and the tuberosity of the upper jaw, is a recess where a temporal abscess will point. 1903 *Proc. Zool. Soc.* 17 Mar. 267 In *Eudynamys*, *Cuculus*, and *Guira* the rami are pierced by a long lateral vacuity, which is partly closed by a long and slender coronoid.

Coroplast (kǭ·rǒplæst). [ad. Gr. κοροπλάστης, f. κόρη girl, doll: see -PLAST. Cf. F. *coroplaste.*] One who makes terra-cotta figures.

1885 *Nation* (N.Y.) 1 Oct. 286/3 The Myrinæan *coroplasts*, or manufacturers of terra-cottas, were certainly influenced by the models of their brethren in Tanagra. [1886 tr. *M. Collignon's Gk. Archæol.* 239 The art of the *coroplastes*, or modeller of figurines.]

Corporal, *sb.*[2] Add:

4. a. The head man of a cattle party. *U.S.*

1920 HUNTER *Trail Drivers of Texas* 229 Billy Henson was our corporal or boss.

b. (See quot.)

1921 *Dict. Occup. Terms* (1927) § 1041 *Corporal*; in Midlands, superintends haulage workers underground and controls pony drivers.

5. A cyprinoid fresh-water fish, *Semotilus corporalis.* *U.S.*

1888 GOODE *Amer. Fishes* 427 The name Corporal seems to have been derived from the Dutch or German settlers of the Middle States.

Corporation. 7. Add: *corporation carter, clerk, dinner, law, lawyer, limits, line, stock, stop, tax.* (Chiefly U.S.)

1771 *Carroll Papers* in *Maryland Hist. Mag.* XIV. 137 Does not the Corporation Law require Broader tred than 6 inches? 1809 W. IRVING *Knickerb.* III. ii. (1825) 92 It being their duty to..hunt the markets for delicacies for corporation dinners. 1841 C. CIST *Cincinnati* 29 Between Main street and the corporation line. 1847 C. LANMAN *Summer in Wild* iv. 30 When this city was in its glory..the corporation limits were uncommonly extensive. 1875 *Mass. Ho. Repr.* Doc. 15 (on Taxation) 122 The general corporation tax. 1881 *Instr. Census Clerks* (1885) 22 Corporation Clerk. *Ibid.* 34 Corporation Carter. *Ibid.* 87 Corporation Labourer. 1889 *Cent. Dict.*, *Corporation-stop*, a stop in a gas- or water-main for the use of the gas- or water-company only. (U.S.) 1893 'O. THANET' *Stories Western Town* 215 He went away for an interview with the corporation lawyer. 1901 W. G. CORDINGLEY *Dict. Stock Exch. Terms* 29 Corporation Stocks refer to the Stocks, Loans and Debentures of the Corporations of the various towns and boroughs in the United Kingdom. 1911 *Amer. Yr. Bk. 1910* 326 The President's suggestion was followed, and the corporation tax became law. 1920 *Act 10 & 11 Geo. V.* c. 18 § 52 There shall be charged..a duty (in this Act referred to as 'corporation profits tax') of..five per cent. of those profits.

Corporative, *a.* Add: **b.** Based upon corporate action or movement.

It. *stato corporativo* occurs 21 Apr. 1927 in *Carta del lavoro* § 7.

1927 *Times* 18 Aug. 11/6 The Corporative State offers..greater opportunities than the Liberal State. 1929 *Times Lit. Suppl.* 11 July 547/2 The Fascist Corporative State. 1929 *Encycl. Brit.* X. 563/2 The industrial unit..is at present being worked into the fabric of the Italian state which will become the 'corporative State' when, in the judgment of its present leaders, the revolutionary stage has been passed.

Corporealism. Delete †*Obs.* and add:

1894 *Classical Rev.* VIII. 463/2 Professor Windelband fully admits the naive corporealism of the earliest Greek philosophy. 1924 W. J. LOCKE *Coming of Amos* vii, I ought to have..taken him to London..and generally given him all the advantages, within my command, of the Higher Thought and the Lower Corporealism.

Corps. Add: **3. d.** A students' society in a German University. Also *attrib.*

1874 J. M. HART *German Univ.* i. (Cent. D.) A corps has no existence outside of its own university; it has no affiliations, no 'chapters'. 1904 *Daily Chron.* 29 Dec. 4/6, I hope that, as long as there are German corps-students, the spirit which is fostered in their corps..will be preserved. 1905 *Westm. Gaz.* 29 Apr. 14/1 As a corps-student the Crown Prince never felt at ease.

Corpse, *sb.* Add:

2. f. A horse not intended to win in a race. *slang.*

1863 *Baily's Mag.* Apr. 154 The circumstance of so many 'corpses' being led away after each race produced no sensation in the Ring. *Ibid.* May 208 The horse did all that could be expected of him, and was never the 'corpse' his opponents expected to have found him.

Co·rpulently, *adv.* [f. CORPULENT *a.* + -LY[2].] In a corpulent manner. 1847 WEBSTER.

Corpuscle. Add:

2. c. *Electr.* J. J. Thomson's name for what was subsequently called *ELECTRON. So **Corpu·scular** *a.*

1898 J. J. THOMSON *Discharge Electr. through Gases* 190 We shall call this theory of the cathode rays the 'corpuscular theory'. *Ibid.* 199 The carriers of the electricity are the 'corpuscles'. 1902 *Encycl. Brit.* XXX. 452/2 These particles, which were termed by their discoverer *corpuscles*, are more commonly spoken of as *electrons*, the particle thus being identified with the charge which it carries. 1904 J. J. THOMSON *Electr. & Matter* v. 98 We shall, for the sake of brevity, speak of this kinetic energy of the corpuscles within the atom as the *corpuscular temperature* of the atom.

Corrack, variant of CURRACH.

Corrade, *v.* Transfer †*Obs.* to sense 1 and add U.S. examples to sense 2:

1847 WEBSTER, *Corrade*, to rub off. 1877 G. K. GILBERT *Geol. Henry Mts.* 101 Streams of clear water corrade their beds by solution.

Corral, *v.* *U.S.* Add: **1.** (Earlier example.)

1846 E. BRYANT *California* iii. (1849) 19 The wagons, in forming the encampment, were what is called *corraled*, an anglicised Spanish word, the significance of which, in our use of the term, is, that they were formed in a circle.

b. *absol.* To draw up the wagons in a circle.

a 1848 RUXTON *Life Far West* (1849) 12 It was pretty nigh upon sundown, and Bill had just sung out to 'corral'. 1875 *Fur, Fin & Feather* 108 At midnight the rear drivers joyously see the little fires flashing up far ahead here and there upon the prairie, telling them that the head of the train has begun to corral. 1894 *Kansas Hist. Coll.* (1896) V. 93 Several trains were compelled to corral and 'stand them [*sc.* Indians] off' until relieved by the dragoons.

3. (Earlier examples.)

1860 *Knickerbocker Mag.* Jan. 100, I want to 'corel' you for a little chat. *c* 1866 'MARK TWAIN' *Sketches* Wks. XIX. 392 That sort of man would corral their sympathies.

Corrasion. Transfer † *Obs. rare* to 1 and add:

2. *Geol.* The wearing away of stones, etc. by mutual friction or by running water.

1877 G. K. GILBERT *Geol. Henry Mts.* 101 In corrasion the agents of disintegration are solution and mechanical wear. 1895 DANA *Man. Geol.* (ed. 4) 168 This corrasion tends to reduce the material to that fine impalpable state in which even slow-moving waters will transport them. 1905 CHAMBERLIN & SALISBURY *Geol.* I. 108 The more active and tangible processes by which surface rocks are broken up, such as wave wear, river wear and glacier wear, are processes of corrasion.

Correcting, *ppl. a.* Add: **b.** *spec.* in *correcting compass*, *magnet*.

1881 *Kaleidoscope* 13 Feb. 262/2 Perhaps this correcting compass might be applied in the round top, if there be not too much iron in that quarter. 1899 *Pract. Rules Deviations Compass* (Admiralty Publ.) 10 Alteration in position of Correcting Magnets. 1918 W. G. MCMINNIES *Practical Flying* vi. 91 Holes for the accommodation of correcting magnets.

Correctitude (kǫre·ktitiud). [f. CORRECT *a.* + -ITUDE, after *rectitude.*] Correctness of conduct or behaviour.

1893 *National Observer* 13 May 650/2 The high correctitude of his youth. 1897 *Westm. Gaz.* 20 Feb. 3/1 Dr. Jameson stepping in maintains order where disorder existed, and stepping in with the Colonial Secretary's orders, would have done so with perfect—if not 'unctuous—correctitude'. 1906 F. S. OLIVER *Alexander Hamilton* 316 Jefferson was overflowing with kindness—a contrast to the calm correctitude of his chief. 1922 G. A. GREENWOOD *England To-Day* ii. 72 The correctitude of attending eleven o'clock service.

Correlation. Add: **1. c.** In statistics, the relation of two or more variable quantities.

1899 R. MAYO-SMITH *Statistics & Econ.* 10 The third step in statistical method is correlation: *i.e.* to compare different phenomena with each other, in order to establish relations of co-existence or of sequence. 1901 A. L. BOWLEY *Elem. Statistics* 316 Correlation is a quantity which can be measured numerically; and its measurement has been the subject of much recent mathematical investigation. 1909 W. & E. ELDERTON *Primer Statistics* 57 In such cases there is no relationship, therefore, between length and breadth, and we say that the 'coefficient of correlation' is zero.

Correlationist (kǫrǐlē·ʃənist). [f. CORRELATION + -IST.] One who holds the doctrine of correlation of forces.

1872 *Jrnl. Spec. Philos.* Oct. 289 Do the correlationists believe in self-movement?

Correlativism (kǫre·lătiviz'm). [f. CORRELATIVE *a.* + -ISM.] A system of doctrine based upon the correlative nature of ideas.

1902 *Encycl. Brit.* XXX. 665/2 The universal relativism or correlativism of Laas.

Correspondence. Add:

1. b. *Math.* Relation of certain *a* members of one aggregate with each corresponding member of a second, and of certain *a′* members of the second with each corresponding member of the first.

Where *a* and *a′* are both 1, it is called a *one-to-one correspondence.*

1867 CAYLEY *Math. Papers* (1897) VI. 264 If two points of a unicursal curve have an (*a*, *a′*) correspondence, the number of united points is $= a + a'$. 1882 SYLVESTER *Coll. Math. Papers* (1912) IV. 24 The theorem of one-to-one and class-to-class correspondence between partitions of *n* into uneven and its partitions into unequal parts. *Ibid.* 38 There is thus a one-to-one correspondence, and consequently equality of content between the two systems of partitions. 1898 *Proc. Lond. Math. Soc.* XXIX. I. 71 These quantities vanish respectively when the ray *OP* is in the first or second plane of correspondence through *O*. 1906 *Trans. Amer. Math. Soc.* VII. 393 We thus establish a correspondence between points in the space *y*, and planes in the space *x*.

7. *attrib.*: (sense 6) **correspondence class, course**, a class or course conducted by correspondence; **correspondence clerk**, a clerk who deals with the correspondence of a business house; **correspondence school**, a school which instructs by means of correspondence.

1878 *Chambers's Jrnl.* 30 Nov. 768/1 The Glasgow *Correspondence Classes. 1885 *Ibid.* 610/1 The Correspondence Class is intended for the extension of skilled teaching to any woman within reach of the post. 1906 DICKSEE & BLAIN *Office Organis.* 8 *Correspondence clerks should have a good knowledge of shorthand. 1925 S. LEWIS *Martin Arrowsmith* xxii. § 1, The editor of the magazine which told clerks how to become Goethes and Stonewall Jacksons by studying *correspondence-courses. 1929 *Encycl. Brit.* VI. 468/1 In 1921 the U.S. department of war established 342 correspondence courses in military tactics for reserve officers. 1921 *Dict. Occup. Terms* (1927) § 789 **Correspondence school representative* (or business training college); calls at the homes of prospective students making preliminary enquiries to discuss course desired. 1929 *Encycl. Brit.* VI. 468/2 The correspondence school movement is rapidly reaching a recognized stage of permanency.

Correspondent, *sb.* Add:

4. c. *Foreign correspondent*, a clerk who deals with the foreign correspondence of a business house.

1881 *Instr. Census Clerks* (1885) 33 Commercial Clerk...Foreign Correspondent (Merchant's).

Corresponding, *ppl. a.* Add:

1. b. *Corresponding points*, those points on the two retinas which produce a single visual impression.

1906 MURLIN tr. *Tigerstedt's Hum. Physiol.* 555 Those points of the retinæ upon which the same parts of the two images fall are called corresponding points. 1907 W. H. HOWELL *Physiol.* (ed. 2) 350 Corresponding or identical points in the two retinas.

Corrida (korī·da). [Short for Sp. *corrida de toros* 'course of bulls'.] A bull-fight, bull-fighting.

1898 *Daily News* 12 July 5/6 The hotels were thronged with tourists from all parts attracted by the corridas. 1921 *Chambers's Jrnl.* Feb. 194/2 Those who think of this country as still sleeping, 'decadent', given up to the *corrida*. 1924 *Glasgow Herald* 11 Oct. 4 The cruelties perpetrated in the course of a 'corrida'.

Corridor. Add:

4. b. A similar passage in a railway carriage, upon which all the compartments open.

1899 *Railway Engineer* Jan. 26 The ceiling of the corridor, as will be seen from the drawing, is a complete arch made up in a similar way to that of the compartments.

c. A strip of the territory of a state running through another territory and so contrived as to give access to a certain part, e.g. the sea.

1919 *Economist* 5 July 6/2 The German connections across the Polish 'corridor' to the sea. 1920 H. SPENDER *Prime Minister* 310 When matters seemed at a deadlock—on the Saar Valley, the Polish Corridor, or even the perplexing question of Fiume. 1921 *Hist. Peace Confer. Paris* (ed. H. W. V. Temperley) IV. 273 The Czecho-Slovaks advanced a claim for territorial contiguity with the Yugo-slavs, to be attained by the creation of a corridor running from the Danube to the Drave. *Note*, The chief arguments for the 'Corridor' are given in *De Prague à l'Adriatique* by Arthur Chervin (Paris, 1919), who claims to be the author of both phrase and ideal. 1921 *Times* 4 Jan. 12/1 The Danzig corridor is bound to be the subject of dispute for long to come. 1922 *Westm. Gaz.* 23 Nov., Sig. Mussolini..has agreed to support the Bulgarian claim to Dedeagatch, and also to a corridor giving access to it.

5. corridor carriage, a carriage of a corridor train; **corridor train**, a railway train through the length of which a corridor or passage extends.

1892 Corridor train [in Dict.]. 1893 *Daily News* 22 June 2/3 First and third class 'corridor' carriages...The 'corridor' carriages will have an enclosed passage running along the side. 1894 *Strand Mag.* VIII. 170/1 The 2 p.m. from London to Crewe—the 'Corridor' train. 1896 *Daily News* 5 Aug. 5/1 The Board asks for information as to corridor trains, corridor cars, and carriages with open compartments. 1903 A. H. BEAVAN *Tube, Train, Tram, & Car* v. 59 The cars will be of the corridor type, seven to a full train. 1907 *Westm. Gaz.* 5 Sept. 10/1 The *Great Western Railway Magazine* for September claims for that company the credit of producing the first complete corridor-train, combining the privacy of separate compartments with the advantages of through communication from end to end and access to toilet rooms. It was 'built' in April 1892.

Corridored (kǫ·ridǫɹd), *ppl. a.* [f. CORRIDOR + -ED[2].] Furnished with a corridor.

1904 *Westm. Gaz.* 8 Jan. 1/3 The monastery of Rila, and ..its corridored balconies.

Corrie. Add: **b.** *attrib.*

1894 J. GEIKIE *Gt. Ice Age* (ed. 3) 254 No corrie-basin dates its origin to this stage. *Ibid.*, We have only to contrast the drainage-area of Glen Avon with that of Glen Derry or Glen Beg to see why it is that in the latter only high-level corrie-lakes occur. 1894 J. W. GREGORY in *Q. Jrnl. Geol. Soc.* L. 515 The 'corrie' or 'hanging glaciers'. 1904 *Nature* 7 Apr. 549/1 The phase of corrie-glaciers, when the glacial detritus was borne for no great distance from the local centres of dispersion.

Corrigan (kǫ·rigăn). The name of a Dublin physician, Sir Dominic John Corrigan (1802–80), in *Corrigan's button*, *cirrhosis*, etc. (see quots.).

1886 *Buck's Handbk. Med. Sci.* II. 86/1 The arteries seem to swell and elongate, and then suddenly shorten again. This is the so-called Corrigan's or piston pulse. 1887 *Ibid.* V. 196/2 Corrigan's pulse, the peculiar 'jerking', 'splashing', 'collapsing', or 'water-hammer' pulse of aortic regurgitation. *Ibid.*, Corrigan's button, a firing-iron consisting of a button of iron..fastened in a wooden handle by a rod two inches long. 1890 BILLINGS *Med. Dict.*, *Corrigan's cautery*, button cautery. *Corrigan's disease*, insufficiency of aortic valves. 1906 *Practitioner* Dec. 730 The bronchial tubes become dilated, until at length the whole of one lung consists of dilated tubes and fibroid tissue, in other words, Corrigan's cirrhosis. 1927 *Osler's Mod. Med.* (ed. 3) IV. 537 The Corrigan pulse is more marked when the radial artery is felt with the arm held vertical.

Corrigens (kǫ·ridʒenz). *Med.* [pres. pple. of L. *corrigĕre* to CORRECT.] A corrective.

1925 *Public Opinion* 20 Mar. 288/3 In the old medical prescriptions there was always a corrigens. You gave a man a particular drug and then you corrected it by an addition of something else.

Corrigent, *sb.* Delete †*Obs.* and add:

1841 E. SCUDAMORE *Dict. Arts & Sci.* 1874 GARROD & BAXTER *Mat. Med.* 341 The oil may be employed..as a corrigent to purgatives. 1901 DORLAND *Med. Dict.* (ed. 3), *Corrigent*...2. Any agent which favorably modifies the action of a drug which is too powerful or harsh.

Corroboree, *sb.* Add: **b.** A song or chant made for the occasion of such a dance.

1847 LEICHHARDT *Overland Exped.* 323 He sang most lamentable corroborries. 1881 A. C. GRANT *Bush Life in Queensland* (1882) 51 They send runners to the neighbouring tribes, inviting them to come over..and listen to the new corroboree. 1889 ZILLMANN *Austral. Life* 132 The story..became, no doubt, the theme for a 'corroboree'.

Corroboree, *v.* [f. the sb.] *intr.* To take part in a corroboree. Also *transf.* To 'dance'; hence, of a pot, to boil.

1830 R. DAWSON *Pres. State Australia* 61 They began to corrobery, or dance. 1846 C. P. HODGSON *Remin. Australia* 257 The mosquitoes from the swamps corroboreed with unmitigated ardour. 1881 A. C. GRANT *Bush Life in Queensland* (1882) 34 They had almost finished their meal before the new quart corroboreed. 1885 MRS. C. PRAED *Austral. Life* 22 A scene of feasting and corroboreeing.

Corrosion. Add:

1. d. *Geol.* The solution of a mass of rock or mineral by water; the eating away by fusion and absorption of a mineral in its magma. *Corrosion zone*, the intermediate composition thus formed.

1897 *Geog. Jrnl.* (R.G.S.) X. 502 Erosion, corrosion, and hydrostatic pressure have..formed a real sponge of stone. 1903 GEIKIE *Text-bk. Geol.* (ed. 4) 141 The ferro-magnesian minerals of earlier consolidation among basalts and andesites are sometimes surrounded with a dark shell called the corrosion-zone.

Corroval (kǫ·rovăl, kǫrōᵘ·văl). A South American arrow-poison, a variety of curare, which induces paralysis of the heart.

1859 W. A. HAMMOND in *Amer. Jrnl. Med. Sci.* N.S. XXXVIII. 13 Experimental researches relative to corroval and vao—two new varieties of woorara.

So **Co·rrovaline**, a poisonous alkaloid derived from corroval (Dorland 1901).

Corrugated, *ppl. a.* **2. b.** Add: Also *corrugated paper*, *strawboard*, etc., a packing material designed to give elasticity.

1897 *Chemist & Druggist* L. 746 Among the minor conveniences..is the article known as corrugated paper. 1912 *World's Work* Apr. 508/2 Corrugated packing material for packing bottles. Corrugated strawboard is generally considered the best medium.

Corrugator. Add:

3. One who superintends a corrugating machine.

1881 *Instr. Census Clerks* (1885) 91. 1921 *Dict. Occup. Terms* (1927) § 278 Zinc corrugator (galvanised sheet). *Ibid.* § 559 Corrugator, corrugated packing maker.

Corsage. Add:

3. (Earlier U.S. example.)

1856 MRS. HAWTHORNE in *N. Hawthorne's Wife* (1885) II. 88, I wore that violet brocade..with a corsage of low neck and short sleeves.

b. A bouquet worn on the bodice. *U.S.*

1911 H. S. HARRISON *Queed* ix. 105 On her rounded breast ..a splendid corsage of orchid and lily-of-the-valley.

Corsair. Add: **4. a.** A scorpænoid fish of the Californian coast. *U.S.*

1884 GOODE *Nat. Hist. Aquatic Anim.* 265 Corsair (*Sebastichthys rosaceus*)..is known to the Portuguese fishermen at Monterey by the name of 'Corsair'. *Ibid.*, Spotted Corsair (*Sebastichthys constellatus*).

b. A reduviid predatory bug.

1909 *Century Dict.* Suppl.

Corset. 4. Add:

1845 M. M. NOAH *Gleanings* 116 [The young lady] drew out a piece of long black iron or steel...It is my corset bone, whispered she.

Corsetier, Corsetière (kǭ·ɹsĕtye, -tyēr). [F., f. *corset* + *-ier* masc., *-ière* fem.] A corset-maker (male and female).

1848 THACKERAY *Van. Fair* xxix, She found fault with her friend's dress..and vowed that she must send her *corsetière* the next morning. 1899 *Westm. Gaz.* 18 July 3/3.

Corset(t)ing (kǭ·ɹsĕtiŋ), *vbl. sb.* [f. CORSET + -ING[1].] The fitting with a corset.

1845 M. M. NOAH *Gleanings* 15 Then commences the herculean task of corsetting, racking, bracing and bending. 1898 *Westm. Gaz.* 3 Mar. 3/1 That careful corseting..the French woman understands so much better than we. 1903 *Ibid.* 29 Oct. 8/2 Intelligent physical exercises and better corseting can do wonders. 1904 SLADEN *Playing the Game* I. v, A plumpness..kept within the bounds of beauty by admirable corsetting.

Co·rsetless, *a.* [f. CORSET + -LESS.] Without corsets or a corset.

1896 *Westm. Gaz.* 15 Apr. 8/1 The ladies of Tristan d'Acunha will for the present have to go corsetless. 1923 *Glasgow Herald* 21 Mar. 8 A..warfare against the corsetless and rationally corsetted figure.

Corsetry (kǭ·ɹsĕtri). [f. CORSET + -RY.] Corset-making or -fitting.

1923 *Daily Mail* 22 Feb. 1 Natural elegance subtly idealised by skilful Corsetry. 1924 (*title*) The Book of Corsetry.

Corsican (kǭ·ɹsikăn), *a.* and *sb.* [f. *Corsica*: see -AN.]

1. a. *adj.* Of, belonging to, or characteristic of Corsica or its inhabitants. **b.** *sb.* A native or inhabitant of Corsica; the Corsican dialect of Italian.

The Corsican (*the Corsican ogre*, *robber*, etc.), Napoleon Bonaparte, who was born in Corsica.

1768 BOSWELL *Acc. Corsica* 15 In general the Corsicans breathe a pure atmosphere. *Ibid.* 29 The Corsican villages are frequently built upon the very summits of their mountains. 1803 S. HOOLE *Anecd. J. Hoole* 1 The barbarities perpetrated by the Corsican Robber. 1814 SOUTHEY *Ode* ii, If that perfidious Corsican maintain Still his detested reign. 1841 THACKERAY *Chron. Drum* Misc. 1855 I. 16 Good Lord, how he doth plume himself, Because we beat the Corsican! 1855 R. MARTINEAU tr. *Gregorovius' Corsica* IV. vii. 283 That pantomimic dance of lament is called in Corsican the *ballata*. 1861 M. ARNOLD *Pop. Educ. France* 162 *note*, Corsican vengeance is proverbial. 1862 *Chambers's Encycl.* III. 258/2 The Corsicans under General Paoli made themselves in great part independent. 1880 *Ibid.* XIII. 494/2 In Southern Corsican *dr* for *ll* is conspicuous. 1882 *Gentl. Mag.* Jan. 1 The Iron Duke had thrashed the Corsican Ogre. 1897 *Fortn. Rev.* June 887 To remove the false impression of the Corsican bandit so dear to the transpontine stage. *Ibid.* 890, I could speak no Corsican. 1922

Chambers's Jrnl. 21 Jan. 113/2 Make up your mind to charm the Corsican.

2. Corsican cock, a variety of the domestic fowl; **Corsican granite**, a mixture of feldspar, hornblende, and quartz; **Corsican moss**, *Plocaria Helminthocorton*, a mixture of dried seaweeds, formerly used as a vermifuge; **Corsican pine**, a pine of the species *Pinus laricio*.

1854 *Poultry Chron.* I. 423 Chitteprat or *Corsican Cock. 1855 *Ibid.* III. 518 Chitteprat or Corsican. 1857 J. B. JUKES *Man. Geol.* 73 Globular Diorite, Orbicular Greenstone, *Corsican Granite. 1849 BALFOUR *Man. Bot.* § 1130 *Plocaria* (*Gigartina*) *Helminthocorton*, under the name of *Corsican Moss, was formerly used as a vermifuge. 1887 *Buck's Handbk. Med. Sci.* V. 26/1 As a medicine Corsican moss is of the past. 1879 *Encycl. Brit.* IX. 402/1 The ridges of the Crimea are clothed with *Corsican pine.

Corsite (kǭ·ɹsəit). *Min.* [Named by F. Zirkel (*Lehrbuch der Petrographie* 1866); f. F. *Corse* Corsica: see -ITE[1].] A mixture of anorthite, hornblende, and quartz, a typical occurrence of which is in Corsica. (Partly synonymous with *napoleonite*, *orbicular diorite*.)

1876 A. H. GREEN *Geol.* 65 Corsite or Napoleonite..is a granular mixture of Anorthite, Hornblende, and a little quartz. The most noticeable variety occurs in Corsica: the rock there is made up of balls from one to three inches in diameter. 1882 GEIKIE *Text-bk. Geol.* 143. 1888 TEALL *Brit. Petrogr.* 134.

Corticene, var. CORTICINE.

1897 F. J. BURGOYNE *Library Construction* 25 The most suitable covering for a wood floor is cork carpet or corticene. 1915 'BARTIMEUS' *A Tall Ship* vii. 118 Varnish..wherewith to beautify the corticene on the aft-deck.

Corticifugal (kǭɹtisi·fiŭgăl), *a.* [f. L. *cortic-*, CORTEX + *fugĕre* to flee + -AL.] Originating in and running from the cortex or outer layer of the cerebellum.

1898 *Phil. Trans.* 10 There was no clear evidence of corticifugal fibres passing from the angular gyrus to the basal ganglia. 1901 DORLAND *Med. Dict.* (ed. 2) 178/2.

Corticipetal (kǭɹtisi·pĭtăl), *a.* [f. L. *cortici-*, CORTEX + *petĕre* to seek + -AL.] Originating outside of and running into the cerebral cortex.

1898 *Phil. Trans.* 11 A corticipetal system, passing from the external geniculate body and pulvinar thalami to the cortex of the occipito-angular region.

Cortico-, used as combining form of CORTEX in various medical terms with reference to the cortex of the brain, as **Co·rtico-spi·nal** *a.*, relating to the cortex and the spine.

1901 DORLAND *Med. Dict.* (ed. 2) 178/2 Cortico-afferent. Cortico-efferent. Corticofugal. Corticopeduncular. Corticospinal. 1908 *Practitioner* Oct. 557 A purely spinal reflex, which appears in earliest infancy before the cortico-spinal paths are fully developed.

Cortina (kǭɹtəi·nă). *Bot.* [mod.L. use of L. *cortina* curtain.] The membrane which, in certain fungi, breaks away from the stipe and adheres in shreds to the margin of the pileus (cf. CURTAIN *sb.*[1] 5 a).

1832 LINDLEY *Introd. Bot.* I. iii. 208. 1866 *Treas. Bot.*, *Cortina*, the filamentous ring of certain agarics.

Cortlandtite (kǭ·ɹtlăntəit). *Min.* [f. the name of *Cortlandt* township, New York: see -ITE[1].] A coarse-grained rock composed chiefly of hornblende and olivine; a variety of peridotite.

1895 *Funk's Stand. Dict.* 1903 GEIKIE *Text-bk. Geol.* (ed. 4) 241 Cortlandtite..so named from its occurrence in the 'Cortlandt series' of eruptive rocks on the Hudson River. 1909 F. H. HATCH *Text-Bk. Petrol.* 243 Cortlandtite = olivine + hornblende + hypersthene...Name suggested by G. H. Williams.

Corton (korton). [f. Aloxe-*Corton*, near Beaune in France.] A red Burgundy wine made in the neighbourhood of Beaune, Côte-d'Or.

1833 REDDING *Wines* v. 98 In the commune of Aloxe, a wine called Corton is grown. 1889 W. GUTHRIE *Claret, Burgundy & Champagne* 21 In the Côte de Beaune are found the Corton, Volnay, Pomard, and many other well-known names. 1900 CHRISTIE, etc. *Catal. Wines, C. Boyle* 8 Three Dozens of Corton.

Corundellite (korʊ·ndĕləit). *Min.* [f. CORUNDUM + -ELLE + -ITE[1].] = MARGARITE[2].

1849 *Amer. Jrnl. Sci. & Art* Ser. II. VIII. 383. 1877 DANA *Min.* 336.

Corver[2]. Delete †*Obs.* and add quots.:

1858 SIMMONDS *Dict. Trade*, *Corver*, a man who makes and repairs corves or coal baskets. 1881 *Instr. Census Clerks* (1885) 84. 1921 *Dict. Occup. Terms* (1927) § 652.

Corvina (kǫrvi·nă). Also **cur(u)vina.** [Sp., Pg. *corvina*, f. L. *corvinus*, f. *corvus* raven: said to be so named from its black fins.] A fish of southern California, *Cynoscion parvipinnis*, related to the weakfish. Also applied to many other fishes of the family *Sciænidæ*.

1787 CULLEN tr. *Clavigero's Hist. Mexico* I. 65 The Curvina is about a foot and a half long, of a slender, round shape, and of a blackish purple colour. 1869 R. F. BURTON *Explor. Highl. Brazil* II. 303 The fish leaped and splashed in all directions...In a few minutes we had enough for a day's food. The worst was the Curuvina. *a* 1884 JORDAN in Goode *Nat. Hist. Aquatic Anim.* 379 *Cynoscion parvipinnis*..is usually known as the 'Corvina', or 'Caravina'. ..It is found from San Pedro southward to the Gulf of California.

Corvine, *a.* Add: *sb.* A member of the crow family.

1926 *Chambers's Jrnl.* 60/1 During migration time, of course, hawks and corvines feed well.

Cory- (kǫri), abbreviation of *Corydalis* (see CORYDALINE) in names of alkaloids obtainable from the roots of certain species, as **Corybu·lbine**, **Coryca·vine**, **Corytu·berine** (from *C. cava*, *C. tuberosa*).

1893 *Jrnl. Chem. Soc.* LXIV. I. 486 Corytuberine. *Ibid.* 492 A base (? Corycavine), which crystallizes in small, matted needles and melts at 218°. 1894 *Ibid.* LXVI. I. 100 Corybulbine is the name given..to a base isolated from commercial corydaline. 1902 *Ibid.* LXXXII. I. 307 There were obtained in the following order, beginning with the weakest base,..corydaline, corybulbine,..corycavine, corydine.

Corycian (kŏri·ʃiăn), *a.* Also 6 Coritian. [f. L. *Cōrycius*, a. Gr. Κωρύκιος, f. Κώρυκος Corycus or Κωρυκία Corycia (see def.): see -IAN.] Of or pertaining to the mountain cave of Corycus at the foot of Parnassus, sacred to the Muses, or to the nymph Corycia, daughter of Apollo; chiefly in *Corycian cave*, *Corycian nymphs* (the Muses).

1567 TURBERV. *Ovid's Ep.* xx. Tij, The famous Ile (where the Coritian Nymphes Did lodge of yore). 1621 G. SANDYS *Ovid's Met.* I. (1626) 230 Corycian Nymphs, and Hill-gods he adores. 1636 SALTONSTALL *Ovid's Heroic. Ep.* I. xix. 139 Cæa where Corycian Nymphs have, In Parnassus hill an old famous Cave. 1746 AKENSIDE *Hymn to Naiads* 319 To the cave Corycian, or the Delphic mount. 1877 *Encycl. Brit.* VII. 53/1 The famous Corycian cave, a large grotto in the limestone rock, which afforded the people of Delphi a refuge during the Persian invasion. 1883 R. WHITELAW tr. *Sophocles' Antigone* 1127 With nymphs Corycian in thy train. 1885 *Encycl. Brit.* XVIII. 318/1 Parnassus was..hallowed by the worship of Apollo, of the Muses, and of the Corycian nymphs.

Corydalic (kǫridæ·lik), *a.* *Chem.* [f. CORYDALINE: see -IC.] In *corydalic acid*, a name given to the acid ammonium salt obtained from corydaline by oxidation.

1894 *Jrnl. Chem. Soc.* LXV. 63 Corydalic acid dissolves readily in water and in alcohol.

Coryfin (kǫ·rifin). *Chem.* [Proprietary term.] The ethylglycollic ester of menthol, used as an anæsthetic and an analgesic.

1908 *Practitioner* Sept. 488. 1913 DORLAND *Med. Dict.* (ed. 7).

Coryl (kǫ·ril). *Chem.* [Named by G. Joubert.] A mixture of ethyl and methyl chlorides, used as a local anæsthetic.

1901 HALE WHITE *Pharmacol.* 86 Chlorides of methyl and ethyl..produce the best effects when mixed, as in 'coryl' and 'anestile'. 1908 P. W. SQUIRE *Comp. Brit. Pharmacopæia* (ed. 18) 111 Anæsthyl and Coryl are stated to be mixtures of Ethyl and Methyl Chlorides.

Corylaceous (kǫrilē·ʃəs), *a.* *Bot.* [f. *Corylaceæ*, f. *corylus* hazel.] Of or pertaining to the *Corylaceæ*.

Corylin (kǫ·rilin). *Chem.* [f. L. *corylus* hazel + -IN[1].] A proteid occurring in the walnut and the hazel.

1896 *Jrnl. Chem. Soc.* LXX. I. 716.

Corynactid (kǫrinæ·ktid). [f. mod.L. *Corynactis*: see -ID[3].] A sea-anemone belonging to the genus *Corynactis*.

1915 E. R. LANKESTER *Diversions of Naturalist* xi. 88 The most beautifully coloured of all sea-anemones are the little Corynactids.

Corynocarpine (kǫrinokā·ɹpin). *Chem.* [f. *Corynocarpus*, a genus of trees: see -INE[5].] An alkaloid found in the fruit of the karaka tree.

1903 *Proc. Chem. Soc.* 191. 1929 H. G. GREENISH *Mat. Med.* (ed. 5) 46.

Coryphodon (kǫri·fodǫn). [f. Gr. κορυφή top, summit + ὀδών, Ionic f. ὀδούς, ὀδόντος tooth.] A fossil mammal of the genus of this name: so called because the cusps of their teeth are developed into points.

Coryphodon bed, the lower division of the Lower Eocene in the Rocky mountain and Plateau region, in which coryphodon remains are found.

1846 R. OWEN *Brit. Fossil Mamm.* 304 The Tapir, which is the nearest existing analogue of the Coryphodon. 1848 *Q. Jrnl. Geol. Soc.* 3 Nov. 126 The swelling of the Coryphodon's jaw. 1884 *Amer. Naturalist* XVIII. 791 The foot structure of Coryphodon. 1895 DANA *Man. Geol.* (ed. 4) 886 Coryphodon beds of Marsh. *Ibid.* 907 The Coryphodons of the Wasatch. 1927 HALDANE & HUXLEY *Anim. Biol.* xiii. 324.

So **Cory·phodont.**

1880 DANA *Man. Geol.* (ed. 3) 503 The Coryphodonts are of special interest, because of their prototype characters. 1895 *Ibid.* (ed. 4) 928 Species of large, short-footed Ungulates, the Coryphodonts.

Coscoroba (kǫskǒrōᵘ·bă). [mod.L., f. native name in Chile and the Argentine.] A large swan-like duck of southern South America, having pure white feathers except for the black tips of its primaries.

1887 NEWTON in *Encycl. Brit.* XXII. 732/1 South America produces..the Black-necked Swan and that which is called Cascaroba or Coscaroba.

Cosh (kǫʃ), *sb.*[3] *slang.* Also **kosh**. A stout stick or truncheon; a school cane (*local*); a length of metal used as a life-preserver. Also *comb.* **cosh-carrier**, a prostitute's bully; so **cosh-carrying.** Hence **Cosh** *v. trans.*, to strike with a cosh.

1874 *Slang Dict.*, *Cosh*, a neddy, a life-preserver; any short, loaded bludgeon. *a* 1889 *Evening News* in Barrère & Leland *Dict. Slang* s.v., The officer..sought to give the finishing *coup de grace* with his cosh. 1893 *Nott. Express* 7 Mar. 6 (E.D.D.), 'I shall be a cosh-carrier the next trade I start.' That seemed to be a term to describe a man who looked after a common woman and lived on her prostitution. 1896 A. MORRISON *Child Jago* i, The cosh was a foot length of iron rod, with a knob at one end, and a hook (or a ring) at the other. *Ibid.*, His wife..brought in a well drunken stranger: when, with a sudden blow behind the head, the stranger was happily coshed. *Ibid.*, The coshed subject..felt the colder air, and moved a leg. *Ibid.*, Cosh-carrying was near to being the major industry of the Jago. *Ibid.* v, She neither fought nor kept a cosh-carrier. 1904 *Daily Chron.* 29 Sept. 4/5 'Coshes'—pieces of lead pipe, known to the police as life-preservers. 1927 *Weekly Dispatch* 23 Oct. 4 A truncheon, or, in prison vernacular, 'kosh'. 1927 E. WALLACE *Squeaker* xxvii, He pulled the life-preserver from his pocket and thrust it into Leslie's hand. 'Go and cosh him!'

Cosh (kǫs ĕtʃ). *Math.* Abbreviation for *hyperbolic cosine.*

Cosingular (kosi·ŋgiŭlăɹ), *a.* *Geom.* [f. Co-.] Having the same singular surface or lines.

1902 *Encycl. Brit.* XXVIII. 662/1 The theory of cosingular complexes is thus brought into line with that of confocal surfaces in four dimensions, and guided by these principles the existence of cosingular quadratic complexes can easily be established...Of cosingular complexes of higher degree nothing is known. *Ibid.* 662/2.

Coslettize (kǫ·zlĕtəiz), *v.* [f. proper name *Coslett* + -IZE.] *trans.* To treat (a bicycle frame or any steel article) with a special rust-preventing process. Hence **Co·slettizer.**

1908 *Daily Chron.* 21 Nov. 9/3 The treatment of frames to a special rust-preventing process known as Coslettising. 1921 *Dict. Occup. Terms* (1927) § 278 *Browner*; *coslettiser*; prepares bath of distilled water, phosphoric acid and iron filings; boils steel articles, e.g. parts of small arms, cycles, in bath. 1927 *Daily Express* 21 June 6 Frame coslettized, making it absolutely rust and weather proof.

Cosmatesque (kǫzmăte·sk), *a.* *Arch.* [f. the name of the *Cosmati*, a family of architects, sculptors, and mosaicists, who lived in Rome in the thirteenth century: see -ESQUE.] Designating a style of decoration characterized by the use of mosaics; also called *Cosmati* or *Cosmato work*.

1883 PERKINS *Ital. Sculpture* p. lvii, More Cosmatesque work of the first period is to be seen in the church of San Pietro d'Alba at Alba Fucense. 1927 H. GARDNER *Art through the Ages* 196 Cosmati work..consists of surrounding colored marble slabs with borders, frequently interlacing, made up of small pieces of marble and glass cut into various shapes.

Cosmic, *a.* Add: **3. c.** Applied to cloud or fog pervading certain groups of stars.

1903 A. M. CLERKE *Probl. Astrophysics* II. iii. 189 The entire Orion region..is pervaded with cosmic fog. 1927 EDDINGTON *Stars & Atoms* 67 This..demonstrates the existence of a cosmic cloud pervading the stellar system.

d. *Cosmic rays*, radiations having a shorter wave length and greater penetrative power than any previously investigated: so called because their source appears to be in interstellar spaces. So *cosmic radiation.*

1925 MILLIKAN in *Nature* 5 Dec. 824/2 We obtained good evidence that these cosmic rays shot through space in all directions. 1926 MILLIKAN & BOWEN in *Physical Rev.* Apr. 355 A crucial test as to whether there is such a cosmic radiation as the Hess-Kolhörster data seemed to require. 1926 MILLIKAN & OTIS *Ibid.* June 658 If cosmic rays exist at all..they must be more penetrating than any one had as yet suggested. 1928 *Nature* Suppl. 7 Jan. 19/1 The cosmic radiation is defined as that small portion of the 'penetrating radiation' which is of cosmic origin. *Ibid.* 21/2 All this [*sc.* the experiments of Millikan and Cameron] constitutes pretty unambiguous evidence that the high altitude rays do not originate in our atmosphere, very certainly not in the lower nineteenths of it, and justifies the designation 'cosmic rays'.

Cosmo-. Add: **Cosmoce·ntric** *a.*, centred in the cosmos; **Cosmorga·nic** *a.*, of or belonging to a hypothetical organic cosmos.

1907 INGE *Pers. Idealism* 103 Constructing our universe on a Christocentric or *cosmocentric basis, not a self-centred one. 1913 A. J. HUBBARD *Fate of Empires* II. vii. 167 The Chinese [people] must be classed as one profoundly moved by the sense of cosmocentric duty. 1878 *Encycl. Brit.* VIII. 768/1 We must suppose that the original source of the material world is an organism, namely, a primitive '*cosmorganic' condition of our earth. *Ibid.*, Consciousness was breathed into the cosmorganic matter by the Creator. 1902 *Ibid.* XXX. 662/1 A 'cosmorganic' evolution from a 'cosmorganic' or original condition of the world as a living organism into the inorganic.

Cosmopolis (kǫzmǫ·pǒlis). [f. Gr. κοσμός + πόλις, after COSMOPOLITE; see COSMO- and -POLIS.] The city of the world; a cosmopolitan city.

1892 *Daily News* 20 Dec. 5/5 'Paris', says the 'Patrie', 'has become the great cosmopolis.' 1928 ALEX. GRAY tr. *The Crime* II. 391 They would not at any price have their Fatherland a Cosmopolis. 1922 *Contemp. Rev.* Sept. 365 The well of English untainted by the infiltrations of cosmopolis [*sc.* London].

Cosmopo·litanly, *adv.* [f. COSMOPOLITAN + -LY[2].] In a cosmopolitan manner.

1896 KIPLING *Seven Seas*, *An Amer.* iii. 139 Where, cosmopolitanly planned, He guards the Redskin's dry reserve. 1926 *Spectator* 16 Oct. 618/1 Italians are far more cosmopolitanly minded than we.

Cosmoramic, *a.* (Earlier U.S. example.)

1827 B. DRAKE & MANSFIELD *Cincinnati* 45 Cosmoramic, optic, and prismoramic views of American scenery and buildings.

Cosmos[3] (kǫ·zmǫs). [mod.L. (replacing earlier *Cosmea*), a. Gr. κόσμος ornament, so named from its elegant foliage.] A plant of the composite genus so named, native to tropical America, species of which, bearing rose, scarlet, and purple single dahlia-like blossoms, are cultivated as hardy annuals and perennials.

1910 C. HARRIS *Eve's Husband* 295, I wore a muslin with faded lavender-colored cosmos blossoms in it. 1920 *United Free Ch. Miss. Rec.* Dec. 226/2 Patches of white and magenta flowers called Cosmos. 1922 *Glasgow Herald* 25 Jan. 8 The pale delicacy of great beds of cosmos. 1929 *Encycl. Brit.* VI. 493/1 The common cosmos..has a smoothish stem bearing much-cut, narrowly-lobed leaves and flower-heads with a yellow centre.

Cosne (kōᵘn). [f. *Cosne*, an arrondissement of Nièvre, France.] A red wine resembling Bordeaux, grown in the department of Nièvre in France.

1889 in *Cent. Dict.*

Cossack. Add: Also as adj., as in *Cossack horse*, *pony* (also *absol.*).

1816 J. SCOTT *Vis. Paris in 1814* xiii. (ed. 5) 210 The driver ..told me that his horse was a Cossack. 1831 YOUATT *Horse* 18 The most celebrated Cossack horses from the Don, the Black Sea, and the Ural. 1926 *Blackw. Mag.* Sept. 310/1 Our ponies nearly all of them came from England, but some people played Cossacks. I had a capital Cossack pony.

b. *Cossack post* (Mil.): an outpost of a few mounted men under a non-commissioned officer or senior soldier.

1853 L. OLIPHANT *Russian Shores Black Sea* 141 My importations from Don Cossack post-huts were considerable. 1860 T. W. ATKINSON *Trav. Amoor* 9, I had visited..all the Cossack posts on my way to the Altin-Kool. 1873 W. F. AINSWORTH *All Round World, Steppes of Russia* v. 732/2 The Cossack post of Schukovaia. *Ibid.*, They had to put up at a Cossack post-house, a mere hut. 1900 BADEN-POWELL *Aids to Scouting* 131 Each force will form a line of outposts, consisting of two Cossack posts, and scouts for reconnoitring patrols.

Cossaite (kǫ·să,əit). *Min.* [Named 1874, after Professor Luigi *Cossa* of Pavia: see -ITE[1].] A variety of paragonite.

1879 DANA *Min.* 314.

Co·sseting, *vbl. sb.* [-ING[1].] The action of the verb COSSET.

1880 LOUISA PARR *Adam & Eve* I. v. 128 With all his kissin' and cossetin' of her. 1901 *Westm. Gaz.* 22 May 3/1 In the other picture there is a sort of fond cosseting of colour and design. 1926 *Harper's Mag.* Feb. 352/2 The asthma and kindred ills born of their cruel cosseting.

Cossette (kǫse·t). Also -et. [Fr., dim. of *cosse* pod, husk.] A slice of a root, cut up during processes of manufacture; *spec.* a piece of sugar beet prepared for the extraction of juice, or of chicory prepared for drying and roasting.

1858 SIMMONDS *Dict. Trade*, *Cossets*, a name on the Continent for slices of beet-root, from which spirit has been distilled. 1902 *U.S. Dept. Agric.* Rep. No. 74. 39 (Cent. D. Suppl.) The raw beet is simply cut into long slender grooved slices. In the factory these slices are known as cossettes.

Cost, *sb.*[2] Add:

1. d. That which a thing originally cost. (Cf. *prime cost* in 1.) *At cost*: at the initial cost.

1873 *Rep. Vermont Board Agric.* II. 216 If they get cost in the spring for their sheep, throwing in their labor, they think the profits ample. 1898 C. A. BATES *Clothing Bk.* No. 2506 We sell..durable clothing very close to cost.

e. *Cost of living.*

1897 C. BOOTH *Life & Labour* IX. 421 The cost of living and money earned by boys and young men. 1913 KOLTHAMMER *Incidence Taxation* 3 The Ratan Tata Foundation ..conducts inquiries into wages and the cost of living. 1922 *Encycl. Brit.* XXX. 755/1 Till recent years the phrase 'Cost of Living' was only used loosely by economists when the balance between movements of wages and prices was in question...In popular parlance it has since become a recognized economic problem. *Ibid.* 755/2 The structure of the index numbers of the cost of living is shown most clearly by algebraic symbols. 1927 BOWLEY & STAMP *Nat. Income 1924* 31 Average earnings of all wage-earners for a full working-week are estimated to have increased 94 per cent. between 1914 and 1924, while the Cost of Living Index rose 75 per cent.

2. Also *attrib.*, as *costs clerk.*

1921 *Dict. Occup. Terms* (1927) § 939 *Costs clerk*..has special knowledge of costs and disbursements which solicitors are entitled to charge for their services..; draws bills of costs against client for services rendered.

5. b. *At all costs* [= F. *à tout prix*]: whatever the cost may be; in spite of all losses.

a 1919 in Boyd Cable *Old Contemptibles* vi. 90 To hold the position at all costs until relieved. 1926 ALDOUS HUXLEY *Two or Three Graces*, etc. 150 At all costs, no frankness!

6. cost account, an account kept of the cost of production of articles or works; so **cost accounting**, **cost bookkeeping**; **cost accountant**, **cost clerk**, **cost keeper**, one who keeps a record of wages, rents, and rates, cost of heating, etc., and other overhead expenses, in a business house; so **cost keeping.**

1896 *Daily News* 17 Nov. 2/2 The accounts are *cost accounts, and are designed to show the actual cost..of every work..executed by the Works Department. 1905 *Westm. Gaz.* 12 Oct. 12/1 To go through cost accounts with an eye to stopping small items of unnecessary expenditure. 1920 *Act 10 Geo. V* Sched. II. 11 Such cost accounts, trading accounts, and balance sheets..as the Controller may require. 1921 *Dict. Occup. Terms* (1927) § 933 *Cost accountant, costing accountant, costing clerk, costs clerk. 1913 MOXEY *Princ. Factory Cost Keeping* 8 All factory *cost accounting is based directly on the principles of double-entry bookkeeping. 1924 H. R. J. HOLMES *Farm Costing* 107 The whole object of cost accounting is the elimination of waste. 1928 *Britain's Industr. Future* (*Lib. Ind. Inq.*) I. i. § 4. 9 Cost accounting was taught to and imposed upon firms both great and small. 1924 H. R. J. HOLMES *Farm Costing* 19 *Cost Book-keeping begins essentially with an allocation of horses and manual labour to the separate departments for which a closing or working account is kept. 1898 *Engineering Mag.* XVI. 42 This forms the *cost clerk's authority for labor value in prime costs. 1902 *Daily Chron.* 5 Nov. 9/6 Timekeeper and Cost Clerk in engineering works [wanted]. 1898 *Engineering Mag.* XVI. 48 All of the *cost keeping is done by one *cost-keeper, one assistant, and a typewriter.

Co·-State. [Co-. Cf. G. pl. *mitstaaten.*] A State allied with another.

1795 *Ann. Reg.* 227/1 Declaration of the King of Prussia, to his Most High Colleagues, Co-States of the German Empire, and Members of the Germanic Leagues. *c* 1798 JEFFERSON *Resol. Alien & Sedition Laws* Wks. 1853 IX. 471 This commonwealth does therefore call on its co-States for an expression of their sentiments...The rights and liberties of their co-States will be exposed to no dangers. 1857 T. H. BENTON *30 Years' View* 349 Virginia exercises the right that pertains to a State in declaring her views, and inviting the like action of her co-States.

Cost-book. (Earlier U.S. example.)

1837 *Southern Lit. Messenger* III. 26 Men whose feelings are divided between their pleadings and their cost books.

Costean, costeen (kǫstī·n), *sb.* *Cornish Mining.* [See COSTEAN *v.*] In full *costean pit*: A pit sunk down to the rock.

1778 Costean pit [in Dict.]. 1895 *Daily News* 22 Oct. 2/1 No. 3 Reef, Eldorado, has been proved by costean pits for a length of 450 ft. 1896 *Westm. Gaz.* 20 Apr. 8/1 A costeen has exposed the cap of a reef 4 ft. wide of solid quartz. 1897 *Daily News* 19 Jan. 2/2 Recently two separate reefs have been struck in separate costeens. *Ibid.* 16 Feb. 8/1 A costeen over 100 feet in length has cut a strong reef 3 feet wide. 1920 *Glasgow Herald* 31 Mar. 11 The White Hope..has been opened up all along the line of lode by costeens.

Costerdom (kǫ·stəɹdəm). [f. COSTER 2 + -DOM.] Costers collectively; the realm of costers.

1893 *National Observer* 1 Apr. 488/2 The donas of costerdom. 1895 *Athenæum* 28 Dec. 897/1 The apotheosized costerdom of Mr. Albert Chevalier. 1903 *Westm. Gaz.* 19 May 8/1 The course was one huge sea of howling, jostling, struggling costerdom.

Costi- (kǫsti), combining form of COSTA (cf. COSTO-) as in **Costica·rtilage**, the cartilage of a rib (Dorland 1901); so **Co·sticartila·ginous** *a.*; **Costice·rvical** *a.*, pertaining to the ribs and neck (Dorland 1913); **Costispi·nal** *a.*, pertaining to the ribs and spinal column.

[1882 WILDER & GAGE *Anat. Technol.* Cat 167 Costicartilago—Costal cartilage.] *a* 1889 COUES (Cent. Dict.) Costispinal.

Co·sting, *vbl. sb.* [f. COST *v.* + -ING[1].] **a.** Estimation of the cost of production of an article, etc. **b.** The costs of production or working. Also *pl.*

1884– [see Dict. s.v. COST *v.* 4]. 1908 L. C. HEADLY (*title*) Boot and Shoe Costings. 1917 DICKSEE *Fundamentals Manuf. Costs* 7 They drop all attempt at accurate costing. 1922 G. T. TURNER & WOOD *Man. Up-to-date Organisation* 171 Costing is the collecting, calculating, and allocating of the cost of material, labour and the correct proportion of Overhead charges involved in a production or utility. 1924 H. R. J. HOLMES (*title*) A short System of Farm Costing. *Ibid.* 105 The application of this simple costings scheme to an actual farm account. 1929 *Times* 7 Feb. 9/3 So that he could compare the costings of the foreign manufactures with the costings of the corresponding English article.

Costus (kǫ·stʊs). [L., a. Gr. κόστος.] In full *costus root*: The root of the plant *Theodorea Costus* or *Saussurea Lappa.*

1812 J. SMYTH *Pract. Customs* (1821) 70 Costus. There are two sorts of this article, the sweet and the bitter. 1889 *Cent. Dict.*, Costus-root. 1915 *Jrnl. Chem. Soc.* CVIII. I. 275 Costus root oil. 1922 SCHLICH *Man. Forestry* (ed. 4) I. 133 *Saussurea Lappa* yields the valuable costus oil.

Cosy, *a.* Add: **3.** Of a job: = *CUSHY *a.*

1915 D. O. BARNETT *Letters* 198 That's a particularly cosy job, as he lives at brigade H.Q. and does nothing.

Cot, *sb.*[4] **5.** *cot-bed*, *-bedstead* (U.S. examples).

1838 J. H. INGRAHAM *Burton* II. xi. 175 A narrow *cott bed, with a military cloak thrown over it, constituted the sole furniture of the warrior's abode. 1856 ALICE CARY *Married* 416 The cot-bed whereon the miserable invalid lay. 1873 HOWELLS *Chance Acquaintance* iv, I've no fancy for a cot-bed in the hotel parlour. 1849 *Rep. U.S. Comm. Patents* (1850) 289 A folding *cot bed-stead.

Cot, *v.*[2] (Earlier U.S. example. See also COTTED *ppl. a.*)

1876 *Rep. Vermont Board Agric.* III. 213 A fleece..so destitute of oil that the ordinary exposure of the county would cause it to 'cot' on the sheep's back.

Cotarnone (kotā·ɹnoᵘn). *Chem.* [f. COTARNINE + -ONE.] A compound obtained indirectly from cotarnine.

1889 *Jrnl. Chem. Soc.* LVI. I. 418 Cotarnone dissolves freely in alcohol, ether, and acetic acid.

Coteau (koto). *U.S.* and *Canada.* [Fr., = hill, hill-side.] A broad flat-topped ridge; an upland.

1883 CHAMBERLIN in *3rd Ann. Rep. U.S. Geol. Survey* 19 The moraines of this region, as far north as the head of the *coteau*, together with the general character of the associated deposits of the adjacent territory.

Côte-rôtie (kotrǒti). A red wine produced in the vineyards of this name near Lyons.

1833 REDDING *Wines* v. 118 Côte Rôtie is remarkable for the excellence of its colour. 1898 CHRISTIE, etc. *Catal. Wines, T. Holden* 5 Four Dozen and Eight Bottles of Burgundy (Côte Rotie). 1908 E. & A. VIZETELLY *Wines of France* 136 The remarkable quality of Côte-Rôtie wine is attributable..to the extremely friable nature of the soil. *Ibid.* 137 Côte-Rôtie may be a little heady.

Cotham (kǫ·təm), the name of a village near Bristol, designating an argillaceous limestone having dendritic markings, also called *landscape marble* or *stone*.

1822 CONYBEARE & PHILLIPS *Outl. Geol. Eng. & Wales* I. 264 The lias..occasionally exhibits..dendritical appearances (Cottam stone or marble). 1845 P. B. BRODIE *Hist. Fossil Insects* 91 In most parts of the southern sections there is a band of stone locally termed 'Landscape stone', or 'Cotham marble'. 1883 *Encycl. Brit.* XV. 529/1 The well-known landscape marble or Cotham stone.

Coti·llion, coti·llon, *v.* [f. the sb.] *intr.* To dance cotillions.

1833 *Deb. Congress* 26 Jan. 1402 Daughters of very indulgent fathers enter the ball room, and waltz, and cotillon, ornamented with several hundred bales of cotton. 1900 *Daily News* 28 June 4/7 We dance, and cotillon, and listen to music.

Hence **Cotillonneur** (kotil^yonǒr), a dancer of the cotillion.

1898 *Daily News* 4 June 3/3 One of the best cotillonneurs going.

Cotinine (kōᵘ·tinīn). *Chem.* [Metathetic alteration of NICOTINE.] An alkaloid indirectly obtained from nicotine.

1893 *Jrnl. Chem. Soc.* LXIV. I. 287.

Cotnar (kǫ·tnaɹ). [Place-name.] A sweet white wine produced near Cotnar in Moldavia.

1833 REDDING *Wines* x. 256. 1845 BROWNING *Flight of Duchess* iii, A cup of our own Moldavia fine, Cotnar, for instance.

Cottage. Add:

4. c. A house which has only one story. *Austral.*

1898 MORRIS *Austral Engl.* 1904 D. SLADEN *Playing the Game* I. ix. 85 What rich Melbourne people call a cottage—a cottage with a ball-room and billiard-room, and enough bedrooms to take a good slice out of an acre. 1913 W. K. HARRIS *Outback in Australia* xxiii. 157 About a score of cottages for the blacks.

6. cottage right, 'in the early history of Massachusetts, an inferior right of commonage granted by certain towns to inhabitants not included in the original body of proprietors' (Cent. Dict.).

Cottagey (kǫ·tĕdʒi), *a.* [f. COTTAGE + -Y[1].] Resembling or characteristic of a cottage.

1883 SIR W. HARCOURT in A. G. Gardiner *Life* (1923) I. xxi. 492 We must have more of a cottagey building. 1923 A. G. GARDINER *Ibid.*, The house, Queen Anne in style, and 'cottagey' in feeling. 1923 UNA L. SILBERRAD *Lett. Jean Armiter* ii. 48 Perhaps not very cottagey with regard to furniture.

Cotterite (kǫ·tərəit). *Min.* [Named 1878, after Miss *Cotter*, who discovered it: see -ITE[1].] A name given by Professor Harkness to a pearly white laminated quartz.

1878 *Min. Mag.* July 82. 1892 E. DANA *Dana's Min.* 192.

Cottolene (kǫ·tǒlīn). [f. COTTO(N + L. *oleum* oil (see -OL) + -ENE.] A substitute for lard made of cotton seed and suet.

1895 in *Funk's Stand. Dict.* 1901 *Daily Chron.* 13 Sept. 7/6 The catalogue said '"Cottolene" has become recognised as the "Hall mark of butter"'. 1924 *Chambers's Jrnl.* 535/2 The various lard mixtures, such as cottolene.

Cotton, *sb.*[1] Add: **9. a.** *cotton bed*, *country*, *-hoe*; *cotton-field*, *-growing*, *-plantation*, *-planter*, *-planting* (earlier examples).

1833 B. SILLIMAN *Man. Sugar Cane* 20 If the field has been planted the previous year in cotton, the *cotton beds are shoved down into the alleys. 1858 J. A. WARDER *Hedges & Evergr.* I. ii. 34 Break up the soil deeply..., and throw up the dirt in the same manner as if preparing a cotton-bed. 1809 *Deb. Congress* 7 June 2171 Baling linen sufficient for the consumption of the greater part of the *cotton country. 1793 MORSE *Amer. Univ. Geog.* I. 616 *Cotton-field. 1834 *Southern Lit. Messenger* I. 122 The cotton field and garden ..lay on the one hand. 1821 *Amer. St. Papers, Finance* (1834) III. 598 There is scarcely a currency left, except in the *cotton growing States. 1844 *Rep. U.S. Comm. Patents* (1847) 35 We of the cotton-growing region..are determined to sustain you. 1869 *Overland Monthly* III. 11 Seventy huge, clumsy *cotton-hoes rose and fell in thoughtless machine-work. 1819 E. DANA *Geogr. Sk. West. Country* 174 Spacious *cotton plantations. 1808 *Deb. Congress* 2 Dec. (1853) 658 What say the *cotton planters, than whom none are more interested in foreign commerce? 1837 *Southern Lit. Messenger* III. 678 Our negroes are almost as valuable to our modern novelists as to our cotton planter. 1811 WEEMS *Lett.* III. 47 The busiest season of all the year, *Cotton planting.

b. *cotton-bale* (earlier U.S. example, also *transf.*), *-broker* (examples), *factor*, *factory*, *manufactory* (earlier examples), *market.*

1840 *Knickerbocker Mag.* XVI. 112, I could..lie down on the ground, or a *cotton-bale, or a bench, and repose. 1894 *Amer. Ann. Photog.* 24 The cloud well known as 'cotton-bales', or 'thunder-heads' we term cumulus. 1811 *London P.O. Direct.* 164 *Cotton broker. 1850 A. O. HALL *Manhattaner* 31 Yonder is the cotton broker, with the fluctuations of the market for a ten years past all penciled

Supplement, p. 3873; Corrigenda, p. 4092; Spurious words, p. 4093; Books quoted, p. 4094

on his face. 1857 *Texas Almanac* Advt., *Cotton Factors and Commission Merchants. 1870 Medbery *Men & Myst. Wall St.* 336 All our great grain-merchants, cotton-factors ..do the same. 1827 B. Drake & Mansfield *Cincinnati* viii. 65 Two Woolen and *Cotton Factories. 1834 *Southern Lit. Messenger* I. 157 The greater part..are attached to a cotton factory, but recently erected. 1849 Chamberlain *Indiana Gazetteer* 339 One *cotton manufactory employing about 100 hands. 1808 *Deb. Congress* Nov. 106 The operations in our *cotton market during the whole of last month have been immense. 1877 Phelps *Story of Avis* 224 What is it..that has happened to the cotton-market?

10. cotton bat, batting *U.S.* (see quots.); **cotton belt** *U.S.*, the area in which cotton is grown; **cotton-bush**, a name given to two Australian plants, *Kochia villosa* and *Bassia bicornis*, on account of their downy nature; **cotton-drill**, a coarse cotton fabric; **cotton flannel** (earlier example); **cotton gin**, (also) a building in which cotton is ginned; **cotton hook** *U.S.*, a hook with a cross-handle, used in handling bales of cotton; **cotton-leaf tea**, an infusion made from the leaves of a species of *Gossypium*, the cotton plant; **cotton-man**, one who trades in cotton; **cotton-press** (earlier example); **cotton rep**, a strong cotton material used for linings; **cotton-roving**, a rove of cotton; **cotton State** (earlier examples); **cotton-worm** *U.S.* (earlier example).

1844 *Rep. U.S. Comm. Patents* (1847) 35 These are nothing more than a thick layer of cotton, carded into what are called at the north '*cotton bats'. 1846 *Ibid.* 67 *Cotton batting.—One patent has been granted this year for improvements in the manufacture of this fabric. 1849 *Rep. U.S. Comm. Patents Agric.* (1850) 188 We have put down both the Isabella and the Clinton [grapes] in cotton-batting, and kept them fresh until February. 1883 [see Batting *vbl. sb.* 2]. 1871 R. Somers *Southern States since War* 257 In many other parts of the '*Cotton Belt'. 1891 M. Townsend *U.S.* 66 The central state of the Cotton Belt. 1897 *Lippincott's Mag.* May 688 The Cotton Belt embracing the heart of the Southern country. 1876 J. A. Giles in W. Harcus *South Australia* 126 A fine open hilly district..with plenty of herbage and *cotton-bush. 1899 *Daily News* 16 Oct. 6/6 The drab, *cotton-drill khaki. 1845 *Mass. Stat.* 21 Mar., Number of yards of *cotton flannel manufactured. Value of cotton flannel. 1866 Mrs. Whitney *L. Goldthwaite* ix, She came back, bringing some two or three pairs of cotton-flannel drawers. 1807 *Deb. Congress* (1852) 460, I went into the *cotton gin that was near the house. 1855 *Knickerbocker Mag.* XLVI. 542 Draymen threw their whips at him, laborers their *cotton-hooks. 1881 *Trans. Obstet. Soc. Lond.* XXII. 31 She said that she had brought down the milk by drinking '*cotton leaf tea'. 1906 *Daily Chron.* 26 Jan. 4/5 The *Cottonmen,..with an average protection of about 30 per cent., are asking for more. 1835 J. H. Ingraham *South-West* I. xviii. 190 The '*cotton press' a short distance below, on the left, fronting the river. 1882 Caulfeild & Saward *Dict. Needlew.* 89/2 *Cotton reps..are chiefly employed for the linings of crêtonne curtains. 1835 Ure *Philos. Manuf.* 317 The one [*sc.* spindle] which is advancing draws out the *cotton-roving from the range of bobbins at the back. 1845 *Whig Almanac* (N.Y.) 16/1 *Cotton States. 1851 Quitman in *Life & Corr.* (1860) II. xvi. 125 In the cotton states such sentiments prevail and are growing. 1847 *Rep. U.S. Comm. Patents* (1848) 170 There has been some complaint respecting the *cotton worm in the early part of the season.

Cotton, *v.*[1] **6.** Add: Also with *on* (*to* —).
1914 D. H. Lawrence *England, my England* 99 'Oh..I didn't want to'..'Didn't want to—didn't cotton on, like'. 1929 Pett Ridge *Affect. Regards* 137, I was one of the few that didn't cotton on to it.

Cottonade. (Earlier U.S. examples.)
1803 in *Deb. in Congress* 1804–5 (1852) 1524 The Acadians [in Louisiana] manufacture a little cotton into quilts and cottonades. 1835 J. H. Ingraham *South-West* I. xviii. 188 The gentleman..wears pantaloons of blue cottonade, coarse and unsightly in its appearance.

Cottondom. *U.S.* (Earlier examples.)
1861 A. Gray *Lett.* (1893) 466 But Cottondom will not have peace and union. 1862 'E. Kirke' *Among Pines* iii. 55 The sun..left us enveloped in a thick fog, which shut from view all of Cottondom. 1863 *Congress. Globe* 6 Jan. 203/3 There is not a foot of grazing land in the Southern confederacy when you cut those States off from cottondom. 1877 Bartlett *Dict. Amer.* (ed. 4), *Cottondom*, the States in which cotton is produced; generally at the South.

Cottonian (kǫtōu·niăn), *a.* Pertaining to Sir Robert Bruce *Cotton* (1570–1631) or the collection of books made by him, and deposited in the British Museum in 1753.
[1696 (*title*) Catalogus Librorum Manuscriptorum Bibliothecæ Cottonianæ.] 1700–1 *Act* 12 & 13 *Will. III* c. 7, That the said Library should be kept and preserved by the Name of the Cottonian Library for Publick Use and Advantage. 1756–9 Butler *Lives Saints* (1780) XI. 71 *note*, In her Cottonian life by an allusion to her name she is styled.. *Candida Wenefreda*. 1824 Ellis *Orig. Lett.* Ser. 1. I. p. xx, The Signature of King Richard the Second..occurs once in the Cottonian Library. 1866 Larwood & Hotten *Hist. Signboards* 174 A MS. in the Cottonian Library relating the journey of Margaret of England to Scotland. 1882 *Encycl. Brit.* XIV. 515/1 The Cottonian MSS., acquired by the country in 1700.

Co·tton-mouth. *U.S.* (See Cotton *sb.*[1] 10.)
1832 G. A. McCall *Lett. from Frontiers* (1868) 259, I found a large moccasin or cotton-mouth snake writhing on the ground. 1842 Holbrook *N. Amer. Herpet.* III. 33 *Trigonocephalus piscivorus*...Water Moccasin, Vulgo Cotton Mouth, in the western country. 1860– [see Cotton *sb.*[1] 10]. 1885 *Outing* (U.S.) VII. 67/2 The slimy moccasin and the deadly cotton-mouth lie in their coils ready to strike. 1907 Mulford *Bar-20* xix. 194 Every time I sees a cotton-mouth I feels like I had just sit down on one.

Co·tton-patch. *U.S.* [Cotton *sb.*[1]] A piece of ground in which cotton is grown; a cotton-field.
1760 Washington *Diaries* I. 134 The Pocoson at Cotton Patch Point. 1817 J. Bradbury *Trav.* 295 Almost all grow some flax, and south of latitude 39° they have what they call a cotton patch. 1818 Melish *Trav. U.S.* 371 Where we saw a very handsome field of cotton, called here a cotton patch. 1862 *Trans. Ill. Agric. Soc.* (1865) V. 517 In selecting a 'cotton patch', we should avoid a wet, cold, springy soil. 1901 Harben *Westerfelt* xxi. 289 I'm a-goin' home by the path through the cotton-patch.

Cotton-picker. *U.S.* **a.** (Example.)
1857 Olmsted *Journ. Texas* 52 A slate hung in the piazza, with the names of all the cotton-pickers.
b. (Earlier example.)
1833 *Deb. Congress* 26 Jan. 1363 To save this cost [*i.e.* of picking cotton by hand], a cotton picker has been invented.

Cotton-tree. Add: **3.** An Australian malvaceous tree, *Hibiscus tiliaceus*.
1876 *Harcus's South Australia* 178 One or two cotton trees in the grounds of the Government Resident have yielded excellent-looking staple. 1889 J. H. Maiden *Useful Native Pl. Australia* 624 'Cotton Tree'. 'Talwalpin' of the aboriginals.

Cottonwood. Add: (Earlier and later examples.)
1787 M. Cutler in *Life, Jrnls. & Corr.* (1888) I. 214 The tallest..cotton-wood trees I ever saw. 1807 P. Gass *Jrnl.* 83 The cotton wood leaves are as large as dollars. 1808 Pike *Sources Missis.* 1. (1810) App. 41 Timber generally hackberry, cottonwood, and ash. 1817 J. Bradbury *Trav.* 258 The alluvion of the river contains a greater variety of which the principal are—Cottonwood, sycamore, overcup oak, [etc.]. 1875 *Amer. Naturalist* IX. 391 Besides the maples and oaks some of the largest trees found in Illinois are the cottonwood. 1910 Jer. Hart *Vigilante Girl* xxv. 350 A scattered grove of cottonwoods grew about the water-hole.
2. An Australian asteraceous tree, *Bedfordia salicina*, so called from the abundance of down on its leaves.
1889 J. H. Maiden *Useful Native Pl. Australia* 386 The 'Cotton-wood' of Southern New South Wales.

Cotton-wool, *sb.* **2.** (Earlier U.S. example.)
1857 *Quinland* I. i. 23 He found a large silver cup, which had been carefully packed away in cotton-wool.

Cotton-wool, *v.* Add:
2. *trans.* To wrap in co·tton-wool; to coddle.
1905 Vaizey *How Like the King* i, He had to be fussed over, and cotton-wooled.

Cotype (kōu·taip). *Zool.* [f. Co- + Type *sb.*[1]] One of two or more specimens upon which the description of a species is based.
1893 Oldfield Thomas in *Proc. Zool. Soc.* 241 A Co-type is one of two or more specimens together forming the basis of a species, no type having been selected. 1898 *Smithsonian Rep.* 33 A number of valuable types and cotypes of fishes have also been transmitted by the Commission.

Couac (kuæ·k). [Fr.] A harsh sound produced by a clarinet when out of order or when unskilfully played.
1877 tr. *Offenbach's Amer. & Americans* 81 My two clarionettes made couacs every instant.

Couba (kū·bă). *Austral.* Also **coobah, coubah.** [Native name.] A variety of acacia, *Acacia salicina*.
1890 'R. Boldrewood' *Squatter's Dream* v. 46 A deep reach of the river, shaded by couba trees. 1890 — *Col. Reformer* xxviii, The willowy coubah.

Coucourite: see *Cocorite.

Couéism (kū·e͜i͜iz'm). [f. the name of Émile *Coué*, French psychologist + -ism.] Systematic auto-suggestion usually of a sanguine kind. Also **Cou·é** *v.*, to produce or bring into a certain state by Couéism; **Cou·éist**, one who practises Couéism, a follower of Coué.
1922 *Punch* 21 June 501 An echo of the heat-wave. *Ardent Couéist*. 'Quite cool, quite cool. Cool as blazes, cool as blazes.' 1923 *Daily Mail* 30 Apr. 7 Couéism is auto-suggestion. It is the power of making people heal themselves through their subconscious self. 1926 *Public Opinion* 9 July 30/3 Large numbers of sufferers..were cured by Couéism. 1928 *Daily Express* 27 July 10/2 He has Coué'd himself into a yearly fit of depression and lassitude. 1928 *Sunday Dispatch* 2 Sept. 17/1 An imaginary kink. A kink that is 'Coué'd'. *Ibid.* 23 Dec. 9/2 'We have had the course translated into seven languages', said one of the Couéists.

Cough, *sb.* **3.** Add:
cough-drop, also (*vulgar*), a person or thing of a pungent quality; a 'cure'; a 'caution'; **cough-mixture**, a medicinal concoction for the alleviation of a cough, specially manufactured or prescribed.
c 1895 *Comic Song*, She looks as if she could curl your hair, Oh you've got a nice little *cough drop there. 1908 *Daily Chron.* 3 June 1/6 Strike me lucky, it was a corf-drop, it was, an' no mistike! *Ibid.* 10 Aug. 7/4 Didn't I tell you, sir, that she was a cough-drop? 1917 *Strand Mag.* Dec. 620/2 One o' the lightermen said I was a 'wonder', and the other said I was a 'fair cough-drop.' Me! 1929 J. B. Priestley *Good Companions* II. i. 267 'Yond'sa coughdrop', he announced to the room at large. 1856 *Enquire Within* p. xii, *Cough Mixture for Children.

Cough, *v.* Add: **1. b.** *trans.* To bring into a specified condition by coughing.
1837 E. Howard *Old Commodore* ix. I. 293, I think I am the first naval officer who ever coughed himself into a commission. 1888 Mrs. H. Ward *R. Elsmere* xxi, One of them ..was sitting up..and coughing its little life away. 1904 Lillie T. Meade *Love Triumphant* Prol. ii, He kept.. coughing as though he would cough his life away.

3. b. Also (with *up*) in mod. slang use. orig. *U.S.*
1896 G. Ade *Artie* xi. 95 And I cough up to you because I know that you're a good fellow. 1904 W. H. Smith *Promoters* iv. 84 Don't you ever fear that I coughed up anything that would put him on to the true inwardness of what we're working now. 1929 Pett Ridge *Affect. Regards, On Solitude* 119 What started the notion, eh? Cough it up!
c. To utter or express with a cough.
1837 E. Howard *Old Commodore* ix. I. 293, I coughed out my gratitude.
d. To bring out, produce. *slang*. orig. *U.S.*
1904 W. H. Smith *Promoters* vii. 122 I'll cough up the stock and bonds all right. *a* 1909 'O. Henry' *Roads of Destiny* xix. 324 Everybody cough up what matches he's got.

Coulée. 2. *U.S.* (Later examples of this form, and of *coulie*.)
α. 1871 Schele de Vere *Americanisms* (1872) 98 The word *Coulee*, used in Oregon for a rocky valley with sloping sides (not precipitous as in a cañon) has not yet made its way beyond the new state. 1875 *Amer. Naturalist* IX. 75 In various parts of Montana, where there were..no breaks in the prairie excepting the 'coulés' (ravines). 1885 *Harper's Mag.* July 190/1 The little 'coulees' and mound-shaped buttes at the base of the hills. 1910 Mulford *Hopalong Cassidy* xii. 78 He rode through the coulee without seeing a single cow.
β. 1886 *Outing* (U.S.) VIII. 259/1 The bushy coulies and the heads of the ravines are its favorite resorts. 1888 Roosevelt in *Century Mag.* June 201 Coming to a wide, long coulie, filled with tall trees and brushwood, we as usual separated. 1902 — *Deer Family* 55 The other buck had disappeared, but there was blood on his trail, and I found him lying down in the next coulie, and finished him.

Couleur. Add: **2.** In rouge-et-noir: see quot.
1909 *Hoyle's Games Modernized* 465 The other chance, the *Couleur* and *Inverse*, is decided by the colour of the first card turned up. If the colour of this card corresponds with the colour of the winning row, then *Couleur* wins; if it is of the opposite colour, then *Inverse* wins.

Coultered, *a.* Add:
1847 in D. Drake *Pioneer Life Kentucky* iii. (1870) 45 After a first 'breaking up' with the coultered plow, the shovel plow was in general use.

Council. Add: **9.** In recent use with reference to the Russian soviets and similar bodies.
1922 *Encycl. Brit.* XXXII. 319/2 (Russia) The mob, led by the Council of Workmen and Soldiers. 1925 A. J. Toynbee *Surv. Internat. Affairs 1920–23* 89 Others, who joined the revolutionary movement for a time, formed a dangerous element and appeared in the Soldiers' Councils or Soviets.
17. council-fire *U.S.* (earlier example); **council-lodge** *U.S.*, an Indian lodge used for holding councils; **council room** (earlier U.S. example); **council school**, a school supported by a town or county council.
1753 Washington *Diaries* I. 57 At this Place a *Council Fire was kindled, where all their Business with these People was to be transacted. 1817 J. Bradbury *Trav.* 117 The news was carried through the village by heralds, who stood at the door of the *council-lodge. 1809 A. Henry *Trav.* 48 After our entering the *council-room, and taking our seats, one of the chiefs commenced an address. 1836 *Knickerbocker Mag.* VII. 385 The iron encasement of apparent apathy..is laid aside in the council-room. 1908 E. M. Sneyd-Kynnersley *H.M.I.* xxviii. 331 Other schools, both Board (or *Council) schools. 1911 *What an Education Committee can do* 3 (Fabian Tract No. 156) Some London council schools provide for five hundred and sixty pupils. 1926 W. Deeping *Sorrell & Son* i. i, The boy had had to go to a Council school.

Council-house. Add: **c.** A house used by North American Indians when in council.
1823 Long *Exped.* I. 112 It [*sc.* the lodge] serves as a council-house for the nation.
2. A dwelling-house erected by a town or district council.
1923 *Oxf. Times* 14 Sept. 16/5 When the time came for plumbers to get on with the Council houses. 1929 *Times* 29 Jan. 8/1 The Reigate Rural District Council are now insisting on building a street of council houses along one of the most beautiful lanes in Surrey.

Councilling, *vbl. sb.* (Earlier examples.)
1770 Washington *Diaries* I. 423 After much Councelling the overnight they all came to my fire the next Morning. *Ibid.* 424 The tedious ceremony which the Indians observe in their Councellings and speeches.

Councilmanic, *a.* *U.S.* (Earlier and later examples.)
1861 *N.Y. Tribune* Nov. (Bartlett) Fifth Councilmanic District. Delegates nominated. 1904 *Philad. Press* 1 June 4 Upon arriving at St. Louis the councilmanic party from this city will be taken to luncheon. 1911 H. S. Harrison *Queed* xvi. 197 He..read history..councilmanic proceedings.

Count, *sb.*[1] Add:
1. c. *Boxing.* In full *count-out*. The counting of ten seconds, the limit of time allowed to a fallen boxer to rise and resume the contest or accept defeat; esp. in *to take the count*.
1913 *Chums* 15 Mar. 498/2 The count was being shouted. ..Roy leaped to the centre of the ring before the count was finished. *Ibid.* 24 May 667/2 'I nearly took the count that time, old fellow', he said. 1917 Jeffery Farnol *Definite Object* xxi, I—I was knocked out t'night—I took th' count! 1923 Soutar *Battling Barker* ii. 28 He feinted with the left, and bringing the right over sharply, dropped Jud for the full count. 1927 Corri *Gloves & the Man* 214 Neither of them was knocked down until the eleventh round, when Sharkey took the count.
2. b. Also, the standard of fineness of yarn.
1927 T. Woodhouse *Artificial Silk* 35 The threads have to conform to well-established methods and rules of distinguishing the relation between the length and weight of

different yarns, or, briefly, to spin to fixed 'counts' or 'numbers' termed deniers.
c. A number, which is the sum of the wires across a card sheet, used to designate the fineness of pitch of the wire teeth used in carding operations.
1884 McLaren *Spinning* (ed. 2) 211 Cards are not ordered by the number of the wire but by counts and crowns.
d. *U.S.* (See quot.)
1883 Goode *Fish. Industr. U.S.* 47 'Count' Clams, the largest size,..sell for $3 per barrel, wholesale. It takes 800 'counts' to make a barrel.
9. count-fish *Austral.*, a full-grown schnapper (see quots.); **count-muster** *Austral.*, a gathering, *spec.* of cattle, for purposes of counting them.
1874 in Tenison-Woods *Fishes N.S.W.* (1882) 41 The ordinary schnapper, or *count-fish, implies that all of a certain size are to count as twelve to the dozen, the shoal or school-fish, eighteen or twenty-four to the dozen. *Ibid.*, The usual method of estimating quantity for sale by the fisherman is, as the schnapper or count-fish, the school-fish, and squire. 1891 'R. Boldrewood' *Sydney-side Saxon* Introd., The old man's having a regular *count-muster of his sons and daughters, and their children and off-side relatives.

'Count (in *no 'count*), dial. aphetic f. Account *sb.*
1854 Mary J. Holmes *Tempest & Sunshine* xxi. 302 He ..had come to the conclusion that 'they were of no 'count any how'. 1856 Mrs. Stowe *Dred* I. 116 It's no 'count talking to him! 1879 Tourgee *Fool's Err.* xxvii. 169, I would jes be makin' trouble fer myself to no 'count.

Count, *v.* Add: **2.** Also with *in*.
1857 *Knickerbocker Mag.* Feb. 185, 'I propose that we all just empty our pockets and show what we've got.' 'Good', says Hiram, 'count me in.' 1859 *Ibid.* Nov. 559 In these days of daring 'Balloonry', the Knickerbocker is to be 'counted in'.
15. Count out (see also 1 c in Dict.). **a.** To leave out of count or consideration; to reckon as not to be counted or depended upon. orig. *U.S.*
1854 *Knickerbocker Mag.* June 643 When it comes to hunting grizzlies on a pony, jist 'count me out'. 1863 *Congress. Globe* 23 Feb. 1227/3 If that is the gentleman's idea, I beg him to count me out. 1890 *Ibid.* 3 June 5545/1 The Democratic party..habitually count out the negro vote. 1906 *Churchman* (U.S.) 17 Nov. 743 We are ignored and counted out in the efforts of the common people to secure a fair chance.
b. To adjudge (a pugilist, etc.) to be the loser by a count-out (see *Count *sb.*[1] 1 c); freq. *pass.*
1808 *Repertory* (Boston) 2 Aug. (Th.) The judges were proceeding to 'count out' his antagonist [*sc.* a fighting cock]. 1903 *Science Siftings* XXIV. 79/1 He falls, and is counted out. 1923 Soutar *Battling Barker* xx. 282 He is down on the canvas and the referee is shouting in his ear. He is being counted out.
c. In children's games, to count the players with the words of a formula, the last at each turn being reckoned out of the game. Hence *counting-out rhyme, song*.
1842 Halliwell *Nursery Rhymes* 123 Children stand round, and are counted out one by one by means of this rhyme. 1888 H. C. Bolton *Counting-out Rhymes* 2 The leader then counts out once more, and the child not set free by the magic word is declared to be 'it'. 1900 E. V. & E. Lucas *What shall we do now?* 99 To decide who is to begin a game there are various counting-out rhymes. All the players stand in a circle, surrounding the one who counts. At each pause in the rhyme..this one touches the players in turn until the end is reached. The player to whom the last number comes is to begin. 1923 Kipling *Land & Sea Tales* 279 (*title*) A Counting-Out Song.
d. *intr.* To turn *out* on being counted. *U.S.*
1903 A. Adams *Log Cowboy* ii. 13 Just so the herd don't count out shy on the day of delivery.

Counter, *sb.*[3] **8.** Add: (sense 4) *counter-hand, -top*; **counter-pump**, a pump under a counter, for drawing liquids from barrels kept in a cellar.
1884 Knight *Dict. Mech.* Suppl., Counter Pump. 1897 Mary Kingsley *W. Africa* 17 Some brutal tradesmen.. affix tremendous nails..to the fronts of their counter tops, in order to keep their visitors at a respectful distance. 1908 *Westm. Gaz.* 11 Sept. 2/1 A child whose lint-white head scarcely reaches the counter-top. 1921 *Dict. Occup. Terms* (1927) § 929 *Counter hand*; sells light refreshments..to customers at counter of bar or buffet. 1927 *Daily Express* 17 Feb. 5/3 She..had been both a counter-hand and a mannequin before she was promoted to chief saleswoman.

Counter, *sb.*[4] Add:
5. The depressed part of the face of a printing type, coin, or medal.
1883 *Encycl. Brit.* XXIII. 698/1 The spaces at *h* and *k* are the counters, which regulate the distances apart of the stems in a line of type. 1892 A. Oldfield *Man. Typog.* xxii. 163 The stems should be of a good depth down to the shoulder and counter. 1896 De Vinne *Moxon's Mech. Exerc., Printing* 405 The deep cut or counter recommended for punches.
b. = *Counter-punch.
1895 *Funk's Standard Dict.*, Counter..8. A depressed or perforated block opposing a die or punch. 1917 F. S. Henry *Printing for School & Shop* xiv. 242 The next step is the making of the counter.
6. *Skating.* A turn in which the body is revolved in a direction opposite to that in which it was revolved in the previous turns. Called also *counter-rocker, counter-rocking turn*.
1892 T. M. Witham *Skating* (Badm. Libr.) 107 In the rockers and counters (which figures used to be designated rocking turns and counter-rocking turns), although there is a change of direction the nature of the edge is preserved. *Ibid.* 111 A counter may..be regarded as half a bracket plus half a three. 1898 *Encycl. Sport* II. 366/2 The four counter-rocking turns. Counter-rocking turns or counters are turns in which one edge of the skate only is used, the body being revolved in an opposite or counter direction to that in which it is revolved in the corresponding 'three' turns. 1902 *Encycl. Brit.* XXXII. 642/2 The 'star', consisting of four crosses (forward rocker, back loop, back counter). 1908 E. F. Benson *Engl. Figure Skating* 244 'Once counter back' is forward counter and inside back. 1928 *Daily Express* 19 Dec. 15/4 Her pirouettes, toe-spins, and counter-rockers.

Counter, *v.*[1] **3.** Add: Also *absol.* or *intr.*
1928 *Manch. Guardian Weekly* 22 June 494/4 When I quoted, rather aptly, I may say, from Jeremiah..he countered very weakly with a saying of Dean Inge.

Cou·nter-attack, *v.* [f. *counter-attack* sb. (Counter- 3).] *intr.* and *trans.* To make a counter-attack (upon).
1916 Boyd Cable *Action Front* 23 After the last of the counter-attacking party had swarmed out. *Ibid.* 193 The Germans..had been counter-attacked and partly driven back.

Cou·nter-fire. [ad. F. *contre-feu*: see Counter- 3.] A fire purposely lighted in order to combat a heath or forest fire: cf. *Back-fire *sb.* 1.
1905 *Terms Forestry & Logging* 6 Back fire...Counter fire. 1927 *Observer* 11 Sept. 9/2 There are many men in the local peasantry who well understand the principle of counter-fires.
Hence **Counter-fire** *v. intr.*, to use a counter-fire.
1895 W. R. Fisher *Forest Protection* 554 It may be necessary to counterfire from a road, stream, ride, or fire-trace.

Cou·nter-glow. *Astron.* [tr. G. *gegenschein*: Counter- 6 b.] A patch of very faint nebulous light occurring in the ecliptic opposite the sun.
1888 C. A. Young *Gen. Astron.* 347 There is said to be in it [*sc.* the zodiacal light] at the point exactly opposite to the sun a patch a few degrees in diameter of slightly brighter luminosity, called the 'Gegenschein' or 'counter-glow'. 1927 Macpherson *Mod. Astron.* 87.

Counter-jumper. (Earlier U.S. example.)
1831 *Finn's Amer. Comic Ann.* (Boston) 218 The folks said i mought take to be a counter jumper, but i had an idee my genus didn't take to dry goods.

Countermarch, *v.* Add:
4. To traverse in marching back.
1855 Barnum *Life* 13, I..had..a distance of three miles, which I marched and countermarched six times per week.

Counter-move, *v.* Add quot.
1890 *Harper's Mag.* June 49/2 The counter-moving streams on either side of the street.

Cou·nter-punch, *sb.* Add: *Typography.* [= F. *contrepoinçon*, G. *gegenpunzen*.] A die used in making the counter or open space (*Counter *sb.*[4] 5) of a type to be engraved on a punch. Hence **Counter-punch** *v. trans.*, to form by means of a counter-punch.
1683 Moxon *Mech. Exerc., Printing* xiii. ⁋ 1 Striking the Counter-Punch into the Face of the Punch. *Ibid.*, If the Letter be wholly to be Cut, and not Counter-Punch'd. 1898 J. Southward *Mod. Printing* I. 142 The counter is the open space in the face of letters..It is so called because the part corresponding to it in the original punch is not cut by hand, like the rest of the letter, but is hollowed out by a counter punch. 1902 De Vinne *Typogr.* (ed. 2) 15 When the proportions of the letters have been determined, the punch-cutter begins his work by making a counter-punch of steel. The illustration adjoining shows the form of a counter-punch for the letter H of the size of double english. It is an engraving in high relief of the counter or hollow part of the type, that is, of that part which appears white in the printed letter.

Countersinker. Add: **b.** One who operates a countersinking machine.
1881 *Instr. Census Clerks* (1885) 97. 1921 *Dict. Occup. Terms* (1927) § 200.

Cou·nter-stain, *sb.* [Counter- 3.] A dye used in staining the parts of a specimen left uncoloured after the application of a dye of another colour. Hence as *v. trans.*, to treat with a counter-stain, to stain (a tissue or specimen) with a contrasting colour.
1901 Dorland *Med. Dict.* (ed. 2), *Counter-stain*, a stain applied to render the effects of another stain more discernible. 1901 *Jrnl. Exper. Med.* V. 559.

Country. Add:
2. b. *God's (own) country*, the United States, or some special part of this. *U.S.* Also, more generally, an 'earthly paradise'.
1890 *Buckskin Mose* xv. 218 The memory of the little woman I had left behind me in the East, or 'God's country'. 1904 'O. Henry' *Cabbages & Kings* xvii. 298 A man had better be in God's country living on free lunch than there. 1906 H. D. Pittman *Belle of Blue Grass C.* i. 1, I entered 'God's Country', as the natives call that portion of Kentucky which lies within a radius of thirty miles of Lexington. 1914 Gertr. Atherton *Perch of Devil* i. 43 They always come home..talkin about..God's Own Country, and the Big Western Heart.
5. b. Used predicatively without article = rural, countrified.
1890 Susan Hale *Lett.* 235 It is far more country here than they are.
II. *Fortif.* 'The region outside of a fort down to which the glacis slopes' (Knight *Dict. Mech.*).
III. 16. country club, orig. *U.S.*, a club having its quarters out in the country for the sake of outdoor sports; **country-damaged** *a.*, damaged in the country, before shipment; **country-jake, -jay** *U.S.*, a rustic; **country mill-stone** *U.S.*, local rock suitable for mill-stones; **country sugar** *U.S.*, maple sugar; **country-wide** *a.*, as wide as the country, extending throughout the country.
1897 *Outing* (U.S.) XXX. 91/2 The team will play their.. games on the grounds of the *Country Club, at Bay Ridge, L.I. 1906 *Springfield Republ.* 19 July, It is to the game of golf that the country club is chiefly due, although golf is by no means the only sport which the well-developed country club now provides for. 1896 Taggart *Cotton Spinning* I. 43 Unless the bales have been lying in wet or mud before having been shipped on the railways or steamships, and have become what is known to the trade as '*country damaged', the quality of the article does not deteriorate. 1900 *Daily News* 12 Oct. 2/6 Coffee.—Ecuador country-damaged. 1911 R. D. Saunders *Col. Todhunter* ix. 128 Didn't I tell you beforehand that they'd shorely size me up as a *country-jake from the very beginning? 1899 Quinn *Pennsylv. Stories* 45 Well, you all know what a *country jay Dutch was when he came to college. 1834 *Southern Lit. Messenger* I. 97 Loose rocks..of the species of agglomerated quartz familiar to the west under the name of '*country mill-stone. 1872 Eggleston *End of World* xvi. 110 A feller don't like to eat up all his *country sugar to wunst. 1922 *Daily Tel.* 12 June 2/4 *Country-wide strikes in the United States. 1927 *Observer* 17 Apr. 18 A really representative country-wide association. 1928 *Daily Express* 8 Aug. 3/4, I have been astounded at the country-wide interest which my recent tramp has aroused.

Country road. [Country 5.] †**a.** A public road made and maintained by the country or province. *Obs.* **b.** A road leading through a rural district.
1669 *Essex Inst. Hist. Coll.* VI. 175/2 The highe way..to range up streight to the Country Roade. 1673 *Col. Rec. Conn.* II. 202 Where the country roade crosseth the s^d Riuer. 1710 *Rec. Providence, R.I.* XVII. 271 The laying out a Countrey Road thro' your Township. 1732 *Waterbury Prop. Rec.* 143 Up to the Common fence and so to the Cuntry Road to Tuds Meadow. 1873 E. Eggleston *Myst. Metrop.* 12 A country road where the dog-fennel blooms almost undisturbed by comers and goers.

Country-rock. *U.S.* (Examples.)
1873 J. H. Beadle *Undevel. West* xxv. 521 For the ninety miles..the 'country rock' is entirely of sandstone. 1883 — *Western Wilds* xxxv. 582 The enclosing rocks, known in reference to the vein as 'wall rock', and 'country rock', are somewhat more simple in construction. 1901 S. E. White *Claim Jumpers* ii. 24 Bennington did not even know what country-rock was. 1914 Gertr. Atherton *Perch of Devil* i. 66 They found nothing but low grade ore, which..roused about as much enthusiasm as country rock.

County[1]. **8.** Add: *county commissioner* (b), *house, rate* (earlier examples); **county cricket**, cricket, esp. of inter-county matches, played by the regularly organized and qualified elevens of the county clubs. So *county cricketer*.
1668 *Mass. Rec.* (1845) IV. II. 364 For *county commissioner, this Court doe nominate..Capt(ain) Hopestill Foster. 1671–2 *Boston Town Rec.* 4 Jan., To carry the votes of the freemen of this towne to the Countie Commissioners for the nomination of..a Countie Treasurer. 1887 *Field* 10 Sept. 411/2 *County cricket quite holds its place in the public estimation. 1899 *Daily News* 2 Aug. 8/2 It was at the end of the sixties that county cricket began to attract general attention. 1872 *Congress. Globe* 18 Apr., App. 269/1 Any one who would recommend him for any office ought to go to the *county-house. 1665 *Dorchester (Mass.) Town Rec.* 129 The Cuntry and *County Rate for this yeare is..80. 1680 *Boston Town Rec.* 17 Dec., To the Constable of Rumny Marsh for said Countie rate, £5. 0s. 9d.

County clerk. *U.S.* (See County[1] 8 a.)
1773 *Carroll Papers* in *Maryland Hist. Mag.* XV. 285 How unqualified are most of our County Clerks. 1821 J. F. Cooper *Spy* xviii. (1850) 165 I'll bet my spurs against a rusty nail, that you get to be a county clerk at least. 1827 — *Prairie* vii. (1879) 81 Is this the quality of land a man would choose who never troubles the county clerk with title deeds? 1866 in *Rep. Vermont Board Agric.* II. 498 The county clerk shall..cause warrants to be issued upon the county treasurer..which order shall be received by the treasurer in payment of all county taxes. 1879 F. R. Stockton *Rudder Grange* xviii. 225 He's a-goin to bring the county clerk up here to-morrow. 1909 S. E. White *Rules of Game* v. i, I didn't hire out for any such work. My father's county clerk down below.
Hence **County clerkship.**
1773 *Carroll Papers* in *Maryland Hist. Mag.* XV. 285 The County Clerkships in Virginia are filled by young Gent^n who Serve an Apprenticeship in the Secretaries Office.

County council. Add: *attrib.* **county council school** (see *Council 17).
1917 W. Pett Ridge *Amazing Years* iv, I ought to have remembered that a boy leaves the County Council schools when he reaches the age of fourteen.

County court. (American examples.)
1639 *Maryland Archives* 47 An Act For the Erecting of a County Court. 1656 *Jrnl. House Burg. Virginia* 101 It is ordered that the comissioners the next county court make enquirie of the desires of the inhabitants. 1685 Sewall *Diary* I. 85 After the County Court is over, is a Conference at his Honours. 1705 *Cal. Virginia St. Papers* I. 97 It is proposed that at every County Court..the sherif..shall attend and account with the people for all their publick dues. 1827 B. Drake & Mansfield *Cincinnati* vi. 50 The Supreme and County Courts are held in the Court House at the intersection of Main and Court Streets. 1836 *Southern Lit. Messenger* II. 433 County courts are attended by functionaries, litigants, and very near neighbors.
b. *attrib.* with *day*.
1837 *Southern Lit. Messenger* III. 223 Let us embody them in part of a speech..we may suppose to have been made by a member of Congress on County-Court-day. 1889 *Harper's Mag.* Aug. 386/2 All through the first quarter of the century..county court day in Kentucky was ..the occasion for holding athletic games.

County seat. *U.S.* (See County[1] 8 b.)
1815 D. Drake *Cincinnati* i. 44 Being made the county seat,

it began to prosper. 1833 [see *Court week]. 1877 Raymond *Statist. Mines* 344 The county-seat is located at the town of Florence. 1906 *N.Y. Even. Post* 9 Nov. 7 The county seat of Richmond County will be removed as soon as possible from Richmond Village to New Brighton.
attrib. 1872 Eggleston *Hoosier Schoolm.* x. 85 The county-seat village of Lewisburg. 1887 *Harper's Mag.* May 843 Much of his time was passed at county-seat taverns.

County town. (See County[1] 8 b.)
1700 *Col. Rec. Conn.* IV. 331 At the four countie townes of this Colonie. 1711 [see County[1] 8 b]. 1733 *Boston Town Rec.* XII. 50 The inhabitants..have not far to travel to their County Town. 1791 Washington *Diaries* IV. 186 Salisbury is but a small place, altho' it is the County town, and the District Court is held in it. 1835 R. M. Bird *Hawks of Hawk-hollow* I. i. 4 The village dignified with the title of County-town. 1848 [see County[1] 8 b]. 1853 F. W. Thomas *J. Randolph*, etc. 136 It was and is a county town, and court was regularly held there.

Coupé, *sb.* Add:
2. c. coupé lit, a coupé (sense 2 b) in which the seats can be extended to form a couch or bed.
1882 De Windt *Equator* 10 A sound sleep in a comfortable *coupé lit*. 1896 *Daily News* 28 Oct. 3/7 A coupé-lits-toilette and first-class carriage will run through to Ventimille by the 2.13 p.m. train from Boulogne. 1898 *Ibid.* 18 Oct. 2/2 A coupe-lit compartment at the Nord Station.
d. A closed motor car, usually a two-seater. *Coupé cabriolet*, one with a head adapted to fold down entirely.
1912 *Motor* 23 July 1104/2 The ordinary coupé or doctor's car. 1915 *Scotsman* 3 Apr. 12/1 Wanted, 2-Seat Car, with Coupé Body preferred. 1924 *Morris Owner* Sept. 653 The coupé is the ideal car for..the business man who has to motor in all weathers. 1926 *Spectator* 3 July 11/2 Father has his limousine. Mother has her coupé. Brother has his play-boy. 1930 *Motor Body Building* May 105 Coupé cabriolet.

Coupélet (kū·pelet). Also **coupélette.** [f. Coupé + -let.] **a.** A carriage with a coupé body and hood, a cabriolet (*Cent. D.* Suppl. 1909). **b.** A coupé motor car with a head adapted to fold down partially.
1918 Webster Addenda, Coupelet. 1930 *Motor Body Building* May 105 Coupélette.

Couper[2]. (See quot.)
1874 Knight *Dict. Mech.*, *Couper*, a lever on the upper part of a loom to raise the harness.

Coupler. Add:
2. c. *Zool.* A plate joining two opposite swimming appendages of a crustacean.
1897 T. J. Parker & Haswell *Zool.* I. 530 The first four thoracic appendages bear biramous swimming feet.., those of the right and left sides being connected by transverse plates or couplers.

Coupling, *vbl. sb.* **5.** Read: A transverse timber connecting a pair of rafters.
1814 J. Taylor *Arator* 122 No joists or loft [in the houses] but to be lathed on the rafters and their couplings, nearly to the top of the roof.
6. b. (Earlier U.S. example.)
1846 *Rep. Comm. Patents* (1847) 82 One patent has been granted for improved couplings for cars.
8. coupling-pole (example).
1852 *Florida Plant. Rec.* 64, I notice that they [= there] is noe way to alter the cupling Pole.

Coupon. Add:
c. A form used by an advertiser of an article or commodity to be filled up by an intending user or purchaser, and forwarded to the advertiser in exchange or part exchange for goods.
1906 *Westm. Gaz.* 19 Sept. 4/3, I mean to forbid the use of all coupon goods at my house. 1909 *Daily Chron.* 26 Feb. 4/4 Amending them [*sc.* the Lottery Laws] with a view..to checking coupon-competitions in newspapers. 1914 *John Bull* 5 Dec. p. ii, By sending this Coupon with P.O. for 2/6..the holder is entitled to receive a..Gold Nibbed Fountain Pen. 1915 *Daily Express* 27 Jan. 6 In addition, a Profit-Sharing Coupon and a Composite Flag of the Allies are enclosed in every packet [of cigarettes]. 1918 *Methodist Times* 5 Dec. 9/1 The amendment of the Gambling Laws, particularly in relation to football coupons, press competitions, foreign prize coupons and sweepstakes ..is long overdue. *Ibid.*, Will you advocate the suppression of professional and coupon betting? 1928 *Sunday Express* 19 Aug. 1/4 Newsagents as well as advertisers are perturbed by the menace of the multiple coupon. *Ibid.*, In Manchester many agents cut out the coupons for their customers and sell the couponless copies in bulk to waste-paper merchants.
d. In the war of 1914–18, one of a series of tickets entitling the holder to a certain ration of food.
1918 *Times* 25 Feb. 9/5 You must not tear off meat coupons yourself. This duty rests with the retailer. *Ibid.*, Only three coupons each week of a meat card can be used for butcher's meat. The fourth or any of the coupons can be used to buy bacon, tinned meats, poultry, and game. *Ibid.* 26 Feb. 7/6 A whole coupon [at the Express Dairy] entitled one to have stewed steak and carrots, two sausages, or cold ham and tongue. 1918 *Ministry of Food, National Rationing* 4 July, § 6 If you hold sugar coupons and not a sugar ticket, you may choose the retailer with whom you wish to register for sugar...§ 7 Lard will be rationed separately by means of the brown set of coupons.
e. A recommendation given by a party leader to a parliamentary candidate in recognition of a pledge given. Also *attrib.*, as *coupon candidate, majority*.
1918 *Methodist Times* 5 Dec. 7/2 Men whose tongues are tied by a pledge before they get their 'ticket-of-leave', or 'coupon', as it is contemptuously called, are being chosen for this English Reichstag by a secret cabal sitting in darkness. 'Half-coupon men' is the name bestowed on those who have not got the blessing, but are piteously bleating for it. 1919 *National Rev.* Feb. 690 Mr. Lloyd George and his principal colleagues were finally 'gingered up' into giving the required pledges, which were infinitely more useful to Coalition candidates than Coalition 'coupons'. 1919 Shaw *Heartbreak House* (1927) p. xxxii, Provided the leader will make their seats safe for them by the process which was called, in derisive reference to the war rationing system, 'giving them the coupon'. *Ibid.*, The electorate.. cast out all the coupon candidates at the earliest bye-elections by equally silly majorities. 1920 H. Storey *Case agst. Lloyd George Coalition* 8 The Government..issued recommendations (it may be remembered that they were called 'coupons') to all candidates who accepted its pledge. 1925 F. W. Hirst *From Adam Smith to Snowden* 64 The Coalition continued with a huge 'coupon' majority ready to extend protective measures.
f. *attrib.* and *Comb.*
1860 *Ann. Treas. Rep.* (U.S.) 480 Such coupon stock..may be assigned and transferred by the delivery of the certificates. 1861 *U.S. Stat.* XII. 259 The Secretary of the Treasury..is authorized to issue coupon bonds, or registered bonds, or treasury notes. 1887 C. B. George *40 Yrs. on Rail* xii. 253 It was to General Ticket Agent Marshall, of the Lake Shore Railroad, that the idea of coupon tickets..first occurred. 1887 *Nation* (N.Y.) 2 June 460/3 The select few of the coupon-clippers may escape it [*i.e.* being in debt].

Couponned, *ppl. a.* Add: Divided into coupons.
1915 *Lit. Digest* 4 Sept. 484/2 Advt., Couponed Pages..—Six coupons to a page. Put each note on a separate coupon —tear it out when it ceases to be of value.

Coupstick (kū·stik). [f. Coup *sb.*[3] 4 + Stick *sb.*[1]] A stick used by North American Indians in making a coup.
1911 Webster. 1921 *Glasgow Herald* 12 Nov. 7 Chief Plenty Coos laid his coupstick (symbol of tribal authority) and his war bonnet on the tomb.

Coureur de bois (kurör də bwa). Now *Hist.* [Fr., = wood-runner.] A wandering hunter and trader in the early French settlements in Canada.
1700 in *New York Col. Doc.* IV. 749 Severall of the French Coureurs de bois or hunters are there at this time. 1755 W. Douglass *Summary* II. 45 The French, consisting of 500 Coureur des bois (in New England they are called Swampiers), with as many Indians or savages. 1773–8 in T. Hutchins *Top. Descr. Virginia* 51 An Expedition undertaken by Himself [*sc.* P. Kennedy] and several Coureurs de Bois in the year 1773.

Courge (kūəʒ). [Fr., = gourd.] A basket, towed behind a fishing-boat, for holding live bait.
1865 J. C. Wilcocks *Sea-Fisherman* 45 Manufacture of 'cou[r]ges' or Sand Eel baskets. 1898 *Encycl. Sport* II. 321/2 The 'courge,' a torpedo-shaped basket into which the baits are introduced by an aperture that is closed with a bung. *Ibid.* 322/2 The orthodox Channel Islands 'courge'. 1900 *Cornhill Mag.* Nov. 626 We have lively sand-eels towing in the courge.

Courida (kūridă). *Bot.* Also **courada.** [Native name.] The common name in British Guiana for the black mangrove, *Avicennia nitida*, a verbenaceous shrub which grows on muddy flats along the sea-shore in the tropics; also, the timber from this.
1825 C. Waterton *Wand. S. Amer.* i. 10 The pelicans.. return at sundown to the courada trees. 1840 R. H. Schomburgk *Descr. Brit. Guiana* 7 A fringe of low ground, which is soon covered with..Courida Bushes. 1851 *Illustr. Catal. Gt. Exhib.* IV. 1. 984/1 Courida, transverse and vertical sections, from Plantation Woodlands, River Mahaica. 1866 *Treas. Bot.* s.v. *Avicennia*. 1912 Rodway *Guiana* 26 The coast is generally an alluvial flat..fringed with courida.

Couril (kū·ril). [Breton.] In Brittany, a small fairy, supposed to frequent druidical remains.
1889 *Cent. Dict.* 1924 *Chambers's Jrnl.* 770/2 The great circle was built by the Courils in a single night.

Course, *sb.* Add:
29. h. *Tobacco-manufacture.* (See quot.)
1849 *Rep. U.S. Comm. Patents, Agric.* (1850) 323 In putting the tobacco in the hogshead for packing, a man gets inside, shoes off...A single row of bundles is then laid all around the edge on the heads of the last circle, then across the hogshead in parallel rows...This is called a course and these courses are continued until the hogshead be filled.
39. course-clearer, one who clears the course for a race; **course-dinner**, a dinner consisting of several courses; **course-indicator**, an apparatus for determining the course of a ship.
1897 *Westm. Gaz.* 15 July 7/1 The *course-clearers ring, and the enthusiasts yell. 1895 *Outing* (U.S.) XXVI. 462/2 A *course-dinner followed by the enjoyment of Ada Rehan's *Rosalind* and Lewis's *Touchstone*. 1899 *Westm. Gaz.* 16 Mar. 10/2 Mr. Kipling was able to sit up in bed last evening, and to partake of a course dinner. 1900 *Ibid.* 14 Feb. 10/2 An absolutely correct magnetic *course indicator. 1904 *Ibid.* 18 Aug. 1/3 A holophote course-indicator for preventing collisions at sea.

Course, colloq. abbrev. of *of course*.
1901 S. Merwin & Webster *Calumet K* i. 13 Have you tried to get any of it here in Chicago? Course not. It's all ordered and cut out up to Ledyard. 1904 Mrs. Stratton-Porter *Freckles* xvi, 'I bet you it's a marked tree!' 'Course it is!' cried the Angel.

Court, *sb.*[1] Add:
12. c. *Out of court*: in extended fig. use, of any thing or person that has no claim to be regarded or considered.
1907 J. R. Illingworth *Doct. Trinity* iii. 47 When Christian apologists with..mistaken courtesy allow the Fourth Gospel to be put out of court. 1927 *Observer* 20 Nov. 26 If he is using a horn type loud-speaker, he is out of court at once. 1928 *Ibid.* 5 Feb. 15/1 Both American and British opinion is laughing out of court those who monger their scares about the United States Navy.
18. *court-chamberlain, -dressmaker*.
1895 K. Grahame *Golden Age* 158 Courtesies, welcomes, and other *court-chamberlain kind of business. 1896 *Westm. Gaz.* 29 Oct. 2/3, I have heard of *Court dressmakers.
19. court-bouillon, (*a*) a rich soup containing wine; (*b*) a stock for boiling fish, made from water and herbs; **court-metre**, the *dróttkvætt* metre used in the old Icelandic *drápa* or heroic laudatory poem, which was recited before the king and his retinue (*drótt*); **court-resident**, one who lives in a court (sense 3); **court tennis** *U.S.* = Tennis *sb.* 1; **court-train**, the train of a woman's court-dress; also *transf.*
1845 Bregion & Miller *Pract. Cook* 146 If the *court-bouillon is *gras*, put in some good stock, boil and use it. 1904 *Daily Chron.* 6 June 8/5 To make anguilles aux crevettes, first prepare the Court-bouillon. 1883 Vigfusson & Powell *Corpus Poet. Bor.* I. 432 The reason why the court-poets counted by the half-line..is manifest. The *court-metre was their standard. 1896 *Scot. Rev.* XXVIII. 334 *Drótt-kvætt*..was thus the commonest metre for the *drápa*, or laudatory poem...The name of 'court-metre' is thus appropriate enough. 1899 *Westm. Gaz.* 3 May 5/3 The..*court-resident in the East. 1930 *Times Lit. Suppl.* 1 May 375/2 Tennis—in America known as *court tennis. 1909 W. De Morgan *It never can happen again* xxxvii, A table-cloth of huge bulk, with a *court-train at each corner.

Court-craft. Add: **2.** Craft or skill in the movements required on a tennis-court, as distinguished from the strokes.
1923 *Daily Mail* 28 Mar. 9 She lacks courtcraft, and is frequently out of position. 1928 *Observer* 17 June 6 The learner will find most of the teachers agreeing about grip, position, swing, follow-through, balance, court-craft, [etc.].

Court-day. 1. (Later U.S. examples.)
1812 Weems *Lett.* III. 71 On the days immediately succeeding the Court days. 1836 *Southern Lit. Messenger* II. 432/1 To a northern traveller in the southern states, there is scarcely any thing more novel or entertaining than a *Court day*. 1849 C. Lanman *Alleghany Mts.* xviii. 148 The hermit said he would attend to it on the next court-day, and his word was accepted.

Court-house. Add: **1. b.** Common in U.S. (cf. 3).
1667 *Mass. Col. Recs.* (1854) IV. II. 351 For the necessary ..repaire of the Toune or Court House in Boston. 1683 *Maryland Hist. Mag.* I. 5 Ordered that Mr. Miles Gibson ..have power and authority to employ carpenters for repairing the Court house. 1776 [see 1]. 1815 D. Drake *Cincinnati* i. 38 It's only public building of note is a stone court house. 1856 J. G. Baldwin *Flush Times Alabama* 159 A lawyer's office..was as public a place as the court-house. 1884 'C. E. Craddock' *Tenn. Mts.* I. 59 A flag floated from the roof of the courthouse.
attrib. 1836 *Southern Lit. Messenger* II. 434/1 The moveable and excitable throng of a court-house-green. 1855 M. Thompson *Doesticks* v. 35 [I] took a last look at its town-pump, its grocery, and its court-house square. 1884 'C. E. Craddock' *Tenn. Mts.* II. 117 To the court-house fence were hitched several lean, forlorn horses. 1899 Tarkington *Gentl. Indiana* i. 2 Here stood the old red-brick court-house, loosely fenced in a shady grove of maple and elm..called the 'Court-House Yard'.

Courting, *vbl. sb.* **3.** Add: *courting flute, horse, play, room*.
1843 Marg. Fuller *Summer on Lakes* vi. 163 When the strain proper to the Winnebago courting flute was played to me on another instrument. 1855 *Knickerbocker Mag.* XLVI. 217 Observe how naturally the 'courtin'-room and its accessories are described. 1887 *Harper's Mag.* Feb. 354/1, I have read that the gallants train their little horses to prance and curvet and rear and fidget about, and that these are called 'courtin' horses', and are used when a young man goes courting, to impress his mistress with his manly horsemanship. 1904 *Good Words* Apr. 244/1 'The Winnebago courting flute,' says an old writer, 'is made of the bone of a turkey's leg, and is pierced with sundry holes, giving a mellifluous tone.' 1911 Thomson *Biol. Seasons* II. 220 Anything that might be interpreted as love-play or courting-play.

Court-room. (Earlier Amer. example.)
1677 *New Castle Court Rec.* 143 For ye making up of ye Court Roome in ye forte fitt for ye Court te sitt in.

Cou·rt week. *U.S.* [Court *sb.*[1] 11.] The week in which the county court meets.
1817 S. R. Brown *Western Gaz.* 99 It was court week, and the day very hot and sultry, when I arrived here from Cincinnati. 1833 H. Barnard in *Maryland Hist. Mag.* XIII. 350 It is Court week, when all the people..assemble in the county seat.

Coûte que coûte (kūt kə kūt). Also erron. *coûte qui coûte, coûte qu'il coûte*. [Fr.] Cost what it may, at all costs.
1715 Ld. Bolingbroke *Let.* in P. M. Thornton *Stuart Dynasty* (1890) 397, I could heartily wish ye Campion might be come back to ye coast of Britanny, before your Maj^ty sail'd, which he will attempt *coute qu'il coute!* 1841 C'tess Blessington *Idler in France* II. 170, I determined, *coute qui coute*, to pay a visit to my friend Madame Craufurd. 1863 Reade *Hard Cash* I. vii. 173 All the mother was in arms to secure her daughter's happiness coûte que coûte!

Couturière (kutüryę̄r). [Fr.] A dressmaker, modiste. So **Couturier** (masculine).
1818 Moore *Fudge Fam. Paris* xii. 88 That enchanting *couturière*, Madame le Roi. 1842 Thackeray *Fitz-Boodle Papers, Confess.*, Actresses, couturières, opera-dancers. 1929 *Daily Tel.* 15 Jan. 7/7 The famous couturier, M. Worth. 1929 *Daily Express* 26 Jan. 5 Couturières are doing strange, subtle things in the way of drapery.

Couvre-pied (kuvrəpye). [Fr., lit. 'cover foot', f. *couvrir* to cover, *pied* foot.] A rug to cover the feet.
1818 Lady Morgan *Fl. Macarthy* (1819) I. iii. 154 Will you just inquire for a couvre-pied, that is lying loose somewhere in the carriage? 1879 Mrs. Oliphant *Within the Precincts* xli, A wadded *couvre-pied*. 1905 Mrs. H. Ward *Marr. W. Ashe* II. xii. 228 He returned to his armchair and his books, but soon drew Kitty's *couvre-pied* over him and went to sleep.

Cove, *sb.*[1] **5.** (Earlier U.S. examples.)
1768 C. Beatty *Jrnl.* 22 Preached in the settlement of the great Cove. 1791 W. Bartram *Carolina* 203 We next passed over a level green lawn, a cove of the savanna.

Cove, *v.* **1.** (Later example.)
1708 E. Cook *Sot-weed Factor* (1865) 2 Weighing soon, we plough'd the Bay, To cove it in Piscato-way.

Cover, *sb.*[1] Add: **1. c.** *Calico-printing.* A design that is printed over another design in resist-work. Also *cover pattern*.
1874 Crookes *Dyeing* 564 The rest is taken up with the fine cover pattern. 1884 *J. Gardner's Bleaching, Dyeing,* etc. 101 Mordants, Discharges, Reserves, Covers, &c.
d. *Cricket.* = Cover-point 1.
1851 Pycroft *Cricket Field* x. (1854) 221 Cover is the place for brilliant fielding. 1897 Ranjitsinhji *Jubilee Bk. Cricket* 48 A fine exhibition of fielding at cover. *Ibid.* 49 Like third-man, cover must be ever on the alert to dash in any direction. 1903 *Cricket* (ed. H. G. Hutchinson) 130 When assisted by an extra mid-off, 'cover' should place himself much squarer with the wickets. 1922 F. B. Wilson *Sporting Pie* 74 The next ball he hit very hard to cover and called me for a run.
e. *Lawn Tennis.* (Cf. *Cover *v.*[1] 13 b.)
1907 Vaile *Mod. Lawn Tennis* 123 You must remember ..that he cannot do it [*sc.* drive down the side line] every time with sufficient accuracy to pass in the small margin over 'cover' which you will allow him.
2. f. The outer covering of a pneumatic tyre.
1898 *Science Siftings* 5 Nov. 46/2 All tendency to cracking of the outer covers is obviated. 1902 A. C. Harmsworth *Motors & Motor-Driving* 237 Even the covers of the driving wheels were quite smooth and unimpaired. 1904 A. B. F. Young *Compl. Motorist* 248 Two spare tubes should always be carried and one spare cover. *Ibid.* 251 When the tyre has been replaced and slightly inflated, the Continental 'cover plaster', a kind of long band or puttie, is wound round the tyre.
8. (sense 2 c) *cover-design*; (sense 5) *cover-money*; **cover crop**, a leguminous crop sown, after the main crop, chiefly in orchards, to protect the soil from weeds and excessive wet and to enrich the soil by being ploughed under in spring; **cover-day**, a day on which the covers are shot over for game; **cover-tread**, the tread of a tyre cover.
1909 *Cent. Dict.* Suppl. s.v. *Crop*, *Cover crop. 1926 *Contemp. Rev.* Dec. 765 The humble covercrops of purple vetch and millelotus clover. 1902 *Daily Chron.* 22 Aug. 9/6 Only outlying birds are shot before the big '*cover days' of November, December, and January. 1928 *S. J. Looker's Book-lover's Catal.* Jan. 8 A Pomander of Verse, by E. Nesbit, with a *cover-design..by Laurence Housman. 1909 *Daily Chron.* 14 Oct. 7/4 The *cover money required is temptingly small. 1908 *Westm. Gaz.* 16 Nov. 5/3 The metal studs are vulcanised into the *cover-tread.

Cover (kǫ·vəɹ), *sb.*[3] *Cornwall.* [f. Cove *sb.*[1] + -er[1].] One who lives in a cove.
1905 *Westm. Gaz.* 13 Apr. 8/3 This action has been deeply resented by the 'Covers', who a short time since removed these obstructions. 1913 'Q' *News fr. Duchy* (1929) 72 The 'Covers', or native fishermen.

Cover, *v.*[1] Add:
2. g. *Calico-printing.* To print over with a pattern, etc. (Cf. *Cover *sb.*[1] 1 c.)
1874 Crookes *Dyeing* 564 The piece is then printed over —technically called 'covered'—with a fine pattern, in purple or light chocolate, and dyed up with madder. *Ibid.* 578 The pieces are then 'covered' with iron liquor..to produce the small design in dark purple.
h. To affix the covering of cloth, leather, or other material on the boards of (a book) in binding.
1837 Hebert *Engin. & Mech. Encycl.* I. 226 The book is then ready for covering, with leather, if to be whole bound. 1876 *Encycl. Brit.* IV. 43/2 The materials used for covering are very various; but for the greater part of modern books calf-skin dyed of various colours is employed.
i. To put a temporary cover of paper or other material on (a book) in order to protect it.
1888 Mrs. H. Ward *R. Elsmere* xx, Rose..covering a parish library book the while in a way which made Catherine's finger itch to take it from her.
5. d. (Earlier U.S. examples.)
1762 in J. Hancock *His Book* (1898) 13 This is chiefly to cover you the Inclos'd Letter from Mr. Willm Bowes. 1776 A. Adams in *Fam. Lett.* (1876) 179, I wrote you two letters ..which were both covered together.
13. b *Lawn Tennis.* To defend by or be within the scope of one's play.
1897 Wilberforce *Lawn Tennis* xi. 35 The man at the net covers far more of the court. 1907 Vaile *Mod. Lawn Tennis* 111 You cannot cover the whole court, and you must go where you have the best chance of meeting the ball. 1920 Tilden *Lawn Tennis* 44 Your position should always strive to be such that you can cover the greatest possible area of court without sacrificing safety, since the straight shot is the surest, most dangerous, and must be covered.
14. c. To report (a meeting, etc.). *U.S.*
1898 *Scribner's Mag.* May 572/1 One day a cub reporter was sent to cover a meeting of an East Side literary club. *Ibid.* 581/1 'There's good humorous stuff in it', he said.. 'just your line. Do you care to cover it?' 1898 *Westm. Gaz.* 3 June 8/1 There was a licensed victuallers' dinner at Aston, and one of the reporting staff was sent to cover it. 1906 *N.Y. Even. Post* 20 Nov. 8 The Frankfurter Zeitung published a special from Berlin, covering the inaugural lecture of the Roosevelt professor. 1911 E. Ferber *Dawn O'Hara* vi. 79, I was sent to cover a Socialist meeting in New York.
c. *To cover the water* (see quot.).
1898 *Encycl. Sport* II. 296/2 A crew is said to cover or clear its water, when stroke dips his oar into the river at a point nearer the winning post than the eddy which was created by No. 2's oar in the previous stroke.
17. b. (Earlier U.S. example.)
1870 Medbery *Men & Myst. Wall Street* 227 (Bartlett) On dividing the assets it was discovered that the Treasurer had used up all the funds in a frantic effort to cover.
d. *U.S.* (Earlier example.)
1868 *Congress. Globe* 17 Feb. 1211/3 These covering warrants are drawn in this way, and receipted by the Treasurer. And this is technically called covering money into the Treasury.

Coverage (kʊ·vərédʒ). *U.S.* [f. Cover *v.* + -age.] The sum of advantages covered by a contract, *spec.* of the risks covered by an insurance policy.
1918 in Webster Addenda. 1930 *Prospectus Press Clipping Service* (*N.Y.*), This superb coverage costs you no more than the average press clipping service.

Cover-all (kʊ·vərǭl). [f. Cover *v.*[1] + All.] Something that covers entirely, esp. a full-length outer garment. Also *attrib.*
1830 J. Stewart *Killarney Poor Scholar* i. 2 All ready, your honours...Beauty has baskets, hampers, and coveralls galliore (*sic*) safe stowed. 1895 *Daily News* 12 Oct. 9/2 His left fore hoof enveloped in a cover-all shoe. 1901 *Daily Chron.* 27 July 10/3 A coat of full-length cover-all dimensions...Many women prefer to have their cover-all rendered storm-proof by a patent process.

Covered, *ppl. a.* Add:
4. b. *Covered wagon*, (*a*) a wagon with a tilt, used in travelling; (*b*) an aeroplane in which the pilot and passengers are covered in. *U.S.*
1842 M. Crawford *Jrnl.* 5 Rode all night in a covered wagon. 1846 Sage *Scenes Rocky Mts.* (1859) 319 A singular natural elevation in the form of a covered waggon. 1864 T. L. Nichols *Amer. Life* I. 108 Great covered waggons—such as are called vans in England—went about the country collecting the rosy maidens. 1928 *Daily Mail* 7 May 6/4 Covered Wagons.—Applied to the first cabin aeroplanes and used for any 'planes in which pilot or passengers are sheltered.

Coverer. Add:
1. c. One who shields from legal penalties, *spec.* a qualified medical man who is employed by an unqualified man. (See Cover *v.*[1] 10 b.)
1892 *Pall Mall Gaz.* 23 Nov. 5/2 The removal from the register of the person who acts as 'coverer', which is the term applied to the qualified man.

Covering, *vbl. sb.*[1] **3.** Add: (sense 17 of vb.) *covering purchase*.
1928 *Daily Mail* 25 July 13/4 Movements during the early part of the afternoon reflected local covering purchases.

Covering, *ppl. a.* Add: **covering-colour** (see *Cover *sb.*[1] 1 c, *Cover *v.*[1] 2 g).
1874 Crookes *Dyeing* 581 Where the reserve has been applied, the original shade—or white spaces—will remain untouched by the subsequent or covering-colour...Among the covering shades are..Drab..Olive [etc.].

Co-vo·lume. *Physics.* [Co-.] The part of the volume of a body which is not occupied by the molecules, as the volume of the interspaces between the molecules in a gas.
1901 Jas. Walker *Phys. Chem.* (ed. 2) 196 The molecular volume of a liquid is constituted of the sum of the atomic volumes of the atoms contained in it, but (and herein consists the peculiarity of Traube's method) there is always to be added to the sum of the atomic volumes a constant magnitude termed the molecular co-volume. *Ibid.*, The co-volume..having the constant value of 25·9 cc. for each molecular quantity in grams.

Cow, *sb.*[1] Add: **1. c.** *pl.* Cattle. *U.S.*
1869 *Overland Monthly* III. 127 The 'cow-whip'..is used only in driving the herd, which is often called 'the cows'.
3. b. (Earlier U.S. examples.)
1751 C. Gist *Jrnls.* 56 At night I killed a fine barren Cow-buffaloe. 1817 S. R. Brown *Western Gaz.* 198 The cow buffaloe was equal to any meat I ever saw. 1839 *Knickerbocker Mag.* XIII. 386 An enormous cow-whale rose close beside her wounded offspring.
4. c. Used as a term of abuse. *Australian slang*.
1916 *Anzac Bk.* 31/2 'Ee's a fair cow, 'e is.
7. *cow-country, -county, -creature, -driver* (examples), *-feed, stable* (later example), *-thief, -track, -trail, -whip, -yard* (earlier examples).
U.S., with *cow-* in the sense of cattle.
1904 *Collier's* 9 Jan. 9 How many communities, even in mining camp and '*cow-country', elect men to office while out on bail for a prison offence? 1878 J. H. Beadle *Western Wilds* vii. 113 Hence their leading industry—expressed in the local phrase—'the *cow counties'. 1873 Carleton *Farm Ballads* 18 That blamed *cow-critter was always coming up. 1889 Rose T. Cooke *Steadfast* xxi. 224, I had bought a cow-crittur of Minadab Sparks. 1772 *Carroll Papers* in *Maryland Hist. Mag.* XIV. 136, I have order'd Squires to go downe tomorrow with the *Cow driver. 1851 J. J. Hooper *Widow Rugby's Husb.* 102 The 'Colonel' being what in his region and times was called a cow-driver. 1885 Royce *Relig. Aspects Philos.* 202 To a cow all is either *cow feed or not cow feed. 1876 'Mark Twain' *Tom Sawyer* iii. 21 A muddy alley that led up the back of his aunt's *cow-stable. 1903 A. Adams *Log Cowboy* vii. 95, I think you're common *cow thieves. 1857 Olmsted *Journ. Texas* (1861) 93 Our road was little better than a *cow-track. 1920 Hunter *Trail Drivers Texas* 151 All the Texas outfit..took the 'cow trail for Texas. 1869 *Overland Monthly* III. 127 The '*cow-whip' is a very long lash with a very short stock, and is used only in driving the herd. 1637 *Cambridge Prop. Rec.* 42 My dwelling howse.. with the yardes cowhouse *cowyarde & my parte in the oxmarsh. 1755 *Essex Hist. Coll.* LII. 79 The wife enraged carey'd it out & Laid in a Cow y^d.
8. cow-barton, a cow-yard; **cow-gun** *colloq.*, a heavy naval gun; **cow-hitch** *Naut. slang*, a badly tied knot; **cow-horse** *U.S.*, a horse used in herding or driving cattle; **cow-man** (earlier and later examples); **cow-picker** = *ox-pecker* (Ox 6); **cow-pilot** (example); **cow sense** *U.S.*, intelligence in the care of cattle; **cow-shot** *Cricket slang*, a pull made by leaning forward on one knee and hitting across the ball; **cow work**, work connected with the tending of cattle.
1888 Hardy *Wessex Tales* I. 71 The dairyman..with manly kindliness always kept the gossip in the *cow-barton from annoying Rhoda. 1929 Masefield *Hawbucks* 34 He went out to the cow-barton to see the farm-men. 1902 J. H. M. Abbott *Tommy Cornstalk* 136 His two great '*cow-guns'—six-inch naval giants drawn by thirty-two bullocks apiece, and having another thirty-two to each timber. 1909 *Daily Chron.* 24 Sept. 4/4 Its motor machine-guns, its heavy 'cow-guns', and howitzers. 1911 Kipling *Diversity of Creatures* (1917) 317 The slow but well-directed fire of my cow-guns. 1867 Smyth *Sailor's Word-bk.*, *Cow-hitch, a slippery or lubberly hitch. 1907 S. E. White *Arizona Nights* III. ii. 277 He jingled loosely along on his *cow-horse. 1920 Mulford *J. Nelson* xxiii. 253 The speedy dash of the trained cow-horse headed them off. 1677 *Topsfield Rec.* 20 That popeler is his bound corner tree next to the *Coweman. 1924 W. M. Raine *Troubled Waters* xi. 115 Sam Yerby was an old cowman from Texas. 1915 E. R. Lankester *Divers. Naturalist* 20 Such useful birds as the vultures, secretary bird, owls and the *cow-pickers (Buphagus). 1884 Goode *Nat. Hist. Aquatic Anim.* 275 The 'Serjeant Major',..called in Bermuda the '*Cow-pilot', from an alleged habit of being always found in the society of the 'Cow-fish', or *Ostracion*. 1903 A. Adams *Log Cowboy* xx. 309 The wisdom of mounting us well..reflected the good *cow sense of our employer. 1920 Hunter *Trail Drivers Texas* 299 When a cowboy says that a man has good 'cow sense' he means to pay him a high compliment. 1922 G. Jessop *Cricketer's Log* vii. 198 My propensity for the '*cow shot'. 1928 *Times* 2 July 5/5 R. S. Walker made a glorious half '*cow-shot' to mid-wicket which was only a yard short of a 6. 1907 S. E. White *Arizona Nights* I. iii. 53 He kept his own mount of horses, took care of them, hunted, and took part in the *cow work.

Cowal ([illegible]). *local Austral.* [Native name.] A swampy depression or channel, similar to a billabong but not necessarily connected with a river.
1911 C. E. W. Bean '*Dreadnought' of Darling* i, The only place where the road was made was where it happened to cross a 'cowal'—a swamp left in a depression.

Co-wa·lker. [Co- 3 b.] In folk-lore, a double or apparition of a person, capable of acting independently of the physical body.
1902 *Encycl. Brit.* XXXII. 52/1 A is on his way to X, or is dreaming that he is on his way, and is seen at X by P, or by P, Q, and R, as may happen. These cases are common, and were explained, in Celtic philosophy, by the theory of the 'Co-Walker', a kind of 'astral body'.

Coward. A. 3. Add: **coward-tree**, a tree under which men who show fear in battle are killed, in accordance with the custom of some Zulu tribes.
1904 G. S. Hall *Adolescence* II. 720 Such chiefs as Chaka, who united many tribes, had a coward-tree where all who manifested fear were slain after every battle.

Cow-boy. 3. (Earlier example.)
1877 R. E. Strahorn *Hand-bk. Wyoming* 35 Part of the cow-boys hold the mass while others ride through it.

Cow-camp. *U.S.* [*Cow *sb.*[1] 1 c.] A camp of cow-boys.
1885 *Outing* (U.S.) VII. 52/2 It is only twenty miles to the ranches on one side, and fifteen to the 'cow-camp' on the other. 1899 *Scribner's Mag.* XXV. 11/2 Having left their lonely hunter's cabins and shifting cow-camps to seek new..adventures. 1905 A. Adams *Outlet* 40 Although in cow-camps a soldier's introduction is usually sufficient, the cook inquired the stranger's name.
attrib. 1920 Hunter *Trail Drivers Texas* 482 The boys immediately started to show him how they did things in high cow-camp society.

Cow-fish. 3. (Earlier example.)
1870 *Amer. Naturalist* III. 467 The odd-looking trigonal Trunk-fish (*Lactophrys camelinus* De Kay), sometimes called Cow-fish, a profile view of the head much resembling that of a cow.

Cow-hand. *U.S.* [*Cow *sb.*[1] 1 c.] One engaged in the tending of cattle.
1886 *Outing* (U.S.) VIII. 3/1 Though a first rate cow hand he very shortly proved himself to be wholly incapable of acting as head. 1903 A. Adams *Log Cowboy* i. 7 By the time I was twenty there was no better cow-hand in the entire country. 1919 Roosevelt *Maine my State* 21 Bill ..and I and only one or two cow hands worked hard.

Cow-hide, *sb.* **3.** *U.S.* (Earlier examples.)
1818 M. Birkbeck *Lett. fr. Illinois* 90 The enraged barrister, with a hand-whip, or cow-hide, as they are called ..actually cut his jacket to ribbons. 1825 Paulding *J. Bull in Amer.* ii. 14 The cow-hide, as it is called, that is, a hard ox skin, twisted in the shape of a whip.
4. (Earlier example.)
1819 W. Faux *Memorable Days Amer.* (1823) 305 One man then bound him to a tree and lashed him with a cow-hide whip.

Cow-hide, *v.* (Earlier U.S. example.)
1820 W. Faux *Mem. Days Amer.* (1823) 387 A fashionable, beautiful female,..yet able to cow-hide her negroes.

Cow-hunt, *sb.* *U.S.* [*Cow *sb.*[1] 1 c.] A search for strayed cattle. Also **Cow-hunt** *v.*, **-hunter, -hunting** *ppl. a.*

1898 H. S. Canfield *Maid of Frontier* 132 The ordinary immense Texas affair, intended only for cow-hunting males. 1920 Hunter *Trail Drivers Texas* 104 Soon the settlers began to organize cow hunts. *Ibid.* 175 Those old time ranchmen were content to simply cow hunt twice a year and brand their calves. *Ibid.*, I remember the many times that cowhunters rode up to my father's house.

Cowing (kau·iŋ), *ppl. a.* [Cow *v.*[1]] Overawing, intimidating.

1830 T. Wilson *Pitman's Pay* etc. (1843) 24 It was, ne doubt, a cooen seet [i.e. cowing sight]. 1888 Mrs. H. Ward *R. Elsmere* x, Her sharp tongue had sometimes a cowing effect on his curious nonchalance.

Cow-keeper. (Earlier American examples.)

1638 *Boston Town Rec.* XI. 33 William Hudson shall be the cowkeeper. 1665 *Ibid.* VII. 25 Edward Dauis is appointed to be Cow keper & pounder.

Cow-keeping, *sb.* (Earlier Amer. example.)

1656 *Essex Inst. Hist. Coll.* IX. 193 Upon the request of Giles Corey to be taken of from Cow keeping.

Cowling (kau·liŋ). [f. Cowl *sb.*[1] + -ing[1].] The removable covering over or round the engine of an aeroplane.

1917 *Blackw. Mag.* June 925/2 While attempting to fasten a small door in the cowling round the engine. 1928 C. F. S. Gamble *North Sea Air Station* ii. 55 A piece of tin in the inside of the engine cowling had come adrift.

Cow·-path. *U.S.* [Cow *sb.*[1] 1.] A path on which cows go to and fro.

1828 Mrs. Royall *Black Bk.* II. 25 Had it not been for those enterprising people New Nedderlands would have been..nothing but straggling cow-paths. 1847 C. Lanman *Summer in Wilderness* xxviii. 179, I had entered upon a cow-path and..forgot myself. 1864 J. T. Trowbridge *Cudjo's Cave* xxiii. 202 The cow-paths, which had been easy to follow at first, disappeared among the thickets. 1865, 1891 [see Cow *sb.*[1] 8]. 1885 'C. E. Craddock' *Prophet Gt. Smoky Mts.* xii. 233 Mirandy Jane wanted to tote him in the cow-path 'mongst the briers.

Cow-pen, *sb.* b. *U.S.* (Earlier examples.)

1731 Catesby *Nat. Hist. Carolina* etc. (1754) I. 34 *Passer fuscus.* The Cowpen Bird... They delight much to feed in the Pens of Cattle, which has given them their name... They inhabit Virginia and Carolina. 1791 W. Bartram *Trav. Carolina* etc. (1792) 289 Sturnus stercorarius: the cowpen bird.

Cow-pen, *v. U.S.* (Later examples.)

1786 Washington *Diaries* III. 131 [I] plowed a poor ½ acre to Cowpen on. *Ibid.* 183 About an acre was sown in my meadow, part of which had been cowpenned. 1832 [R. Baird] *Valley Mississippi* xxiv. (1834) 304 It grows well on marsh..and even pine barrens when they are well trodden, or cowpenned, as it is termed. 1871–3 *Texas Almanac* 12 Cow-penning, in successive lots..is a good plan for manuring.

Cowper-Temple. Name of William Francis Cowper, afterwards *Cowper-Temple* (1811–1888), used *attrib.* to designate religious teaching of an undenominational character in public elementary schools such as was proposed by him and provided for in a clause of the Education Act of 1870. Hence **Cowper-Te·mpleism,** the belief in undenominational religious teaching.

[1902 *Encycl. Brit.* XXVII. 661/1 Clause 14 of that Act [*sc.* Education Act of 1870], generally known as the Cowper-Temple Clause, enacts that 'in any school provided by a School Board, no religious catechism, or religious formulary which is distinctive of any particular denomination, shall be taught'. 1908 *Daily Chron.* 25 Feb. 5/7 In all these schools there may be Cowper-Temple religious teaching.] 1906 *Daily Chron.* 24 May 7/7 Rather than secularism, Mr. Balfour would prefer universal Cowper-Templeism 'with all its illogicality and its unfairness'. 1906 *Westm. Gaz.* 25 June 3/1 Our attitude towards the Bible has changed since the invention of Cowper-Templeism. That compromise is impossible and unreasonable to-day.

Cow·-po·ny. *U.S.* [*Cow *sb.*[1] 1 c.] A pony used in tending cattle.

1877 Bartlett *Dict. Amer.* (ed. 4) 156 [In Texas] the cowboy is the cattle-herder and drover. A cow-pony the mustang he trains and uses. 1884 W. Shepherd *Prairie Exper.* 35 The origin of the cow-ponies is the bronco. 1902 O. Wister *Virginian* i. 1 They were cow ponies in a corral, and one of them would not be caught, no matter who threw the rope. 1909 *Westm. Gaz.* 29 May 5/3 Racing a cow-pony against a train on the first railway made in Colorado near Denver. 1910 Mulford *Hopalong Cassidy* iii. 27 The cow-ponies, trained in the art of punching cows.

Cow·-pu·ncher. *U.S.* (See Cow *sb.*[1] 8.)

1879 *Tinsley's Mag.* XXIV. 354 Some of our men—'cowpunchers', we call them—are devoted to cards. 1889 [see Cow *sb.*[1] 8]. 1903 *Forest & Stream* 21 Feb. 147 (Cent. D. Suppl.) A bit further on we saw some cowpunchers, or what seemed such. 1916 B. M. Bower *Phantom Herd* ii. 36 A cow-puncher comes a long way from a ranger.

Cow·-pu·nching, *pres. pple.* and *ppl. a.* (See Cow *sb.*[1] 8.)

1884 W. Shepherd *Prairie Exper.* 35 Each boy, when out cow-punching, rides from six to ten horses, using them in turns. 1903 *N. Y. Times Sat. Rev.* 26 Sept. 652 The stories are concerned with the gun-firing, cow-punching West of the plains.

Cow-skin. 1. (Earlier example.)

1780 *Narrag. Hist. Reg.* I. 101 Carried the cow skin to tann by George Wilson. *attrib.* 1809 *Repertory* (Boston) 6 Oct. (Th.) A green or untanned cowskin whip. 1887 *Outing* (U.S.) X. 119/1 If I only had that cow-skin horse now what I used ter own back in old Missouri.

3. *U.S.* (Earlier example.)

1789 *Amer. Museum* V. 92 They will work on your fields, and if they are negligent, you will give them the cowskin.

Cow-skin, *v. U.S.* (Earlier examples.)

1799 *Aurora* (Philad.) 20 May (Th.), I am a constable, and may therefore kick, cuff, beat, bruise, cowskin, or kill any man I please. 1836 Crockett *Exploits & Adv. Texas* (1837) 78 The devil himself might, the next time, undertake to cowskin such a..scoundrel for him.

Cowslipping (kau·slipiŋ), *gerund.* [f. Cowslip + -ing[1].] Gathering cowslips.

1901 C'tess Arnim *Eliz. & German Garden* 29 We have been cowslipping to-day. 1928 *Daily Express* 7 Mar. 5/5 We go 'cowslipping' to the same..place year after year.

Cow-tail. Transfer †*Obs.* to 1 and add:

2. The coarsest grade of wool, sheared from the sheep's hind legs.

1884 W. S. B. McLaren *Spinning* 16 The coarsest part of the [sheep's] wool is known as breach, or britch, and even when very strong, as cow-tail.

Cow·-town. *U.S.* [*Cow *sb.*[1] 1 c.] A town forming a local centre in a stock-raising district.

1888 Roosevelt in *Century Mag.* Feb. 500 A true 'cowtown' is worth seeing. 1903 A. Adams *Log Cowboy* viii. 101 This cow town had the reputation of setting a pace that left the wayfarer purseless and breathless. 1907 Mulford *Bar-20* xxii. 212 Then [followed] a rollicking tale of the cow-towns and men.

Cow-tree. 2. Add: In New Zealand, the karaka, *Corynocarpus lævigata.*

1860 G. Bennett *Gatherings Naturalist* 346 The Karaka-tree of New Zealand.., also called *Kopi* by the natives, and Cow-tree by Europeans (from that animal being partial to its leaves).

Cowy (kau·i), *a.* Also cowey. [f. Cow *sb.*[1] + -y[1].] Of or pertaining to a cow or cows.

1893 *Field* 11 Mar. 363/3 We have tasted several samples of this Australian butter... The same 'cowey' flavour was discoverable. 1903 *Graphic* 3 Oct. 443 The occasional whiff from a cowy place. 1924 *Blackw. Mag.* Apr. 458/2 The cowy-smelling Himalayan road.

Coxswain (kɒ·kswein, kɒ·ks'n), *v.* [f. the sb.] *trans.* To cox (a boat). Hence **Co·xswained** *ppl. a.*, steered by a coxswain.

1928 *Daily Express* 22 May 3/4 He..resumed the task of coxswaining the Brighton lifeboat. *Ibid.* 7 Aug. 12/6 In Heat 1 of the second round of the coxswained pairs.

Coyish, *a.* (Modern U.S. example.)

1833 H. Barnard in *Maryland Hist. Mag.* XIII. 322 A lovely grand-daughter..was present, and was pleased not to be very coyish.

Coyote. Add: (Earlier U.S. examples.)

See also *Cayeute, cayote, Chiota, Kiota.

1834 A. Pike *Sketches* (Boston) 14 (Th.) The little gray collotes [*sic*] or prairie wolves, who are as rapacious and as noisy as their bigger brethren. 1846 E. Bryant *California* xix. (1849) 219 A species of jackal called here the *coyote*, frequently approached within a few rods of us.

b. coyote hole *U.S.* (see quot.).

1906 *N. Y. Even. Post* 12 Sept. 7 Drilling coyote holes is the name applied by railroad contractors to drilling blast holes in grade running cuts through hills.

2. a. *fig.* A scoundrel.

a 1909 'O. Henry' *Roads of Destiny* xvi. 266 She's married to Benton Sharp, a coyote and a murderer. 1910 W. M. Raine *B. O'Connor* 243 I'll not be such a coyote any more. 1920 Mulford *J. Nelson* xii. 128 Lookit my hat!.. Some coyote shot at me from up on Pine Mountain an' plumb ruined it!

b. *transf.* A horse of the colour of a coyote.

1903 A. Adams *Log of Cowboy* ii. 14 It was my good fortune to get a good mount of horses..three sorrels, two grays, two coyotes, a black, a brown, and a grulla.

Crab, *sb.*[1] 11. Add: crab-canon *Mus.* = *Cancrizans; **crab-eating** *ppl. a.*, that feeds on crabs (sometimes rendering L. *cancrivorus*); **crabwise** *adv.*, (moving) sideways or backwards like a crab; also *attrib.*

1908 *Strand Mag.* Jan. 30/2 Canons, so constructed that they would read the same backwards or forwards. For this reason they were called *Crab Canons. 1900 *Daily News* 28 Nov. 7/2 A *crab-eating racoon from South America. 1905 *Westm. Gaz.* 27 Dec. 10/2 A crab-eating opossum. 1910 *Encycl. Brit.* V. 375/1 *Lobodon carcinophagus*, the crab-eating seal. 1904 *Daily Chron.* 6 May 8/1 There are barges in the way, and these have to be coaxed aside before the Adler can approach *crabwise to the wharf. 1926 *Chambers's Jrnl.* 163/1 She went crabwise about the loch. *Ibid.* 224/1 A crabwise gait. 1927 R. A. Freeman *Certain Dr. Thorndyke* i. iii, He began to advance, crabwise, across the deck in the manner of a wrestler attacking.

Crab, *sb.*[4] *colloq.* [f. Crab *v.*[2] 2.] The action of crabbing or finding fault; an instance of this; an adverse criticism or objection.

1893 *Field* 11 Mar. 347/1 It will be said I am dreadfully 'on the crab', but I believe what I have written is only the simple truth. 1922 *Autocar* 10 Nov. 956 My only crab to them at present is that [etc.]. 1924 J. Buchan *Three Hostages* 25 The crab of the place was its neighbours. 1927 *Observer* 10 July 11 The only 'crab' we have against this is that cavalry of old effected most of their success by charging infantry.

Crab, *v.*[2] Add: 2. Also *absol.*

1891 'F. W. Carew' *No. 747; Autobiog. of a Gipsy* xx, Shice..alternately 'crabbed' and 'chy-iked' as the case might require. 1906 *Westm. Gaz.* 11 Aug. 1/2 The difference between us and you, said an American who had watched Mr. Chamberlain's Fiscal campaign, is that 'we boom, and you crab'.

b. To interfere with or obstruct the working, progress, or success of.

Cf. quots. 1812, 1890 in Dict.

1901 *N. Y. Independent* 12 Dec. (Cent. D. Suppl.) The use of foreign tires of course crabbed the deal. 1920 *Glasgow Herald* 18 Aug. 7 Posen contains a large German Irredentist minority, which might crab the Polish military defence. 1922 C. Sandburg *Slabs of Sunburnt West* 66 You're trying to crab my act.

Crab, *v.*[3] Add: 3. b. *Aeronautics.* To put (an aeroplane) in a position diverging from the straight course. Also **Crab** *sb.*[5], a divergent position.

1929 A. C. McKinley *Appl. Aerial Photogr.* 13 So that ..the necessary amount of crab can be obtained at which the airplane must fly. *Ibid.* 36 Adjusting the Camera for Crab.—On approaching the starting point of each strip the pilot will crab the airplane in order to make allowances for the wind.

Cra·bber [2]. [f. Crab *v.*[2]] One who finds fault or criticizes adversely.

1909 *Daily Chron.* 14 June 6/4 They wore the determined look of the born 'crabber'. They were there to discover something wrong. *Ibid.* 27 July 4/4 We have fallen from the frying-pan of the boomers into the fire of the crabbers.

Crab-grass. 3. *U.S.* (Earlier examples.)

1782 Jefferson *Notes Virginia* 69 Our grasses are Lucerne,..greensward, blue grass, and crab grass. 1833 B. Silliman *Man. Sugar Cane* 13 The Crab Grass (*Digitaria sanguinalis*) which comes up abundantly on new land, is cut up with hoes. 1857 Olmsted *Journ. Texas* (1861) 140 The crops..contrasted favorably with the patches of corn-stubble, overgrown with crab-grass.

Crack, *sb.* Add:

2. b. The break (*of* day). *dial.* and *U.S.*

1887 *Outing* (U.S.) X. 7/1 At 'crack of day' as the sergeant of the guard expressed it, the stir of camp was started by waking up the cook. 1899 *Cumbld. Gloss.*, *Crack o' day*, the first dawning before sunrise. 1922 Mulford *Black Buttes* ii. 27 You boys git what sleep you can. We'll round 'em up at the crack of dawn.

5. Also *fig.*, a sharp or cutting remark. *U.S.*

1903 A. H. Lewis *The Boss* 120 This is exec'tive session, an' that crack about bein' a taxpayer is more of a public utterance. 1921 R. D. Paine *Comr. Rolling Ocean* viii. 129 Do you remember the day before that when he made that crack at you in front of Miss Crozier? 1924 W. M. Raine *Troubled Waters* xviii. 197 Make another crack like that and there'll be trouble right here in Cell Fifteen.

7. c. *spec.* An opening between flooring-boards or in a floor; esp. in phr. *to walk a* (or *the*) *crack. U.S.*

1825 Paulding *J. Bull in Amer.* vii. 81 When I had qualified myself by being able to walk a crack after swallowing half a gallon of whiskey. 1875 Mrs. Stowe *We & Neighbors* ix. 100 They don't come it round Jim. Any boy that don't toe the crack gets it. 1902 Harben *Abner Daniel* 73 He could walk a crack with a gallon sloshin' about in 'im.

fig. 1869 Mrs. Stowe *Oldtown Folks* xxxvii. 483 Your minister sartin doos slant a leetle towards the Arminians; he don't quite walk the crack. 1878 — *Poganuc People* ix. 101, 'I bet you Reason can't walk a crack now', he said.

d. A slight opening between a door and the door-post; similarly of a window.

1898 Marg. Deland *Old Chester Tales* 237, I always think the door was open a little crack, and you could see out. 1911 Saunders *Col. Todhunter* xi. 161 Then the front door was opened on the crack. *Mod.* Open the window a crack.

Crack, *v.* Add: 1. b. (Earlier U.S. example.)

1835 J. H. Ingraham *South-West* I. xix. 202 He would reload..,cock his beaver, take aim, and crack again.

8. (Earlier U.S. examples.) Also, to repute.

1829 *Kentuckian* 28 May, He is not the thing he is cracked up for. 1835 Crockett *Van Buren* 175 Great men ..are not the things they are cracked up for. 1836 *Knickerbocker Mag.* VIII. 51 New-Orleans is not..half so bad a place as it is 'cracked up to be'.

15. Also freq. with *up.*

1922 *Daily Mail* 17 Nov. 11 She..looked all over the winner.., but when the pinch came she cracked up with dramatic suddenness.

16. b. *fig.* Of dawn: To break. *U.S.*

1845 Mrs. Kirkland *Western Clearings* (1846) 123 'When did you get home?' pursued the inquirer. 'Just as the east was cracking for daylight.'

21. (Later U.S. examples.)

1883 'Mark Twain' *Life Mississippi* xi. 140 When the shoalest water was struck, he cracked on the steam. *Ibid.* xxxix. 413 France and Italy..cracked on such a rattling impost that cotton-seed olive oil couldn't stand the raise. 1912 Mathewson *Pitching* vii. 145 The batter cracked out a base hit. *Ibid.* xi. 243 He cracked his now famous home run into the right-field bleachers.

22. (Earlier U.S. example.)

1824 P. Horry *Life F. Marion* xvii. (1833) 143 He would make nothing, at a hundred yards, to stop you a buck, at full tilt through the woods, as hard as he could crack it.

23. *trans.* To decompose (petroleum or similar oils) by the application of heat and pressure so as to produce lighter hydrocarbons (e.g. petrol, gasolene). Hence **Cracked** *ppl. a.*, **Cra·cking** *vbl. sb.*

1868 B. Silliman in *Chem. News* 10 Apr. 171/1 By the process called 'cracking', heavy oils unfit for illumination are broken up into bodies of less density, from light naphtha to the heavier illuminating and lubricating oils. 1868 in *Amer. Jrnl. Sci.* (1869) Ser. ii. XLVII. 13 Rapid distillation 'cracks' the oil, because it necessitates increased temperature to force the vapors from the still. 1882 S. F. Peckham *Petroleum* 179 The standard and prime oils, consisting largely of 'cracked' oils. 1896 B. Redwood *Petroleum* I. 317 The 'cracking process', whereby a considerable quantity of the oil which is intermediate between kerosene and lubricating oil is converted into hydrocarbons of lower density and boiling point, suitable for illuminating purposes. 1922 *Encycl. Brit.* XXXII. 80/1 Modern cracking dates back to the patent obtained in 1889 by the late Sir Boverton Redwood and Prof. Dewar. *Ibid.* 80/2 Cracked gasoline.

Crackajack, var. of *Crackerjack.

Cracked, *ppl. a.* Add: 2. b. *Cracked heel* (esp. in horses): see Scratch *sb.*[1] 2 a, Grease *sb.* 3.

1861 H. Beasley *Druggist's Gen. Receipt Book* 98 Ointments for..cracked heels. 1886 G. Fleming *Pract. Horse Keeper* 96 A predisposition to cracked heels is engendered by clipping the legs and pasterns in winter. 1898 F. T. Barton *Our Friend the Horse* 193 Cracked Heels...The result of irritation through sand, wet, etc.

8. (See *Crack *v.* 23.)

Cra·ckedness. [See Cracked *ppl. a.* 5.] Unsoundness of mind, craziness.

1910 W. J. Locke *Simon the Jester* xiv, This was sheer crackedness of brain... When people begin to talk that way they are not allowed to go about loose.

Cracker. Add: 4. *U.S.* (Earlier examples.)

The origin suggested in quot. 1887 in Dict. is supported by earlier statements from 1838 onwards.

1767 *N. Y. Mercury* 21 Sept., in *Mag. Amer. Hist.* (1878) II. 250 A number of people called Crackers, who live above Augusta, in the province of Georgia, had gone in a hostile manner to..Okonee. 1772 J. Habersham *Lett.* (1904) 204 Persons who..live by hunting and plundering the industrious Setlers... The people I refer to are really what you and I understand by Crackers.

b. *attrib.*, as *cracker funeral, life, man, planter, woman; the Cracker State*, Georgia. *U.S.*

1808 *Balance* (Hudson, N. Y.) 6 Sept. 144 (Th.) [Verses by] A cracker planter. 1838 Caroline Gilman *Recoll. Southern Matron* xix. 130 The servant told us that a *cracker* man and woman were in the drawing-room. 1856 Mrs. Stowe *Dred* xii. (1884) 131, I was amused..with Old Hundred's indignation at having to get out the carriage and horses to go over to what he called a cracker funeral. 1871 Schele de Vere *Americanisms* (1872) 659 Georgia..little deserves the name of Cracker State, by which it is occasionally designated. 1887 *Harper's Mag.* May 843/1 Numbers of lawyers would gather together and relate their observations of Cracker life. 1910 *Washington Herald* 27 Nov. 9 Through November the 'Cracker State' has occupied the center of motordom's stage just on account of this proclivity [to race].

6. b. *attrib.*, as *cracker motto, -paper, poetry*, etc.

1869 W. S. Gilbert *Bab Ballads, Ferd. & Elvira*, Only find out who it is that writes those lovely cracker mottoes! 1906 *Westm. Gaz.* 8 Sept. 2/2 A tragedy in rhymed verse not up to the standard of cracker poetry. 1907 *Ibid.* 25 Apr. 2/1 The gaily tinted scraps of cracker-paper that children love.

c. An attachment to the end of a whip-lash by which a cracking sound can be produced. *U.S.* and *Colonial.*

1835 Monett in J. H. Ingraham *South-West* II. 288 To the end of the lash is attached a soft, dry, buckskin cracker. ..So soft is the cracker, that a person who has not the sleight of using the whip could scarcely hurt a child with it. 1881 A. A. Hayes *New Colorado* x. 140 Each wagoner must tie a brand-new 'cracker' to the lash of his whip. 1890 'R. Boldrewood' *Col. Reformer* xviii, Stockwhips garnished with resplendent crackers.

9. *U.S.* (Earlier examples.)

1739 in *New Engl. Hist. & Gen. Register* (1868) XII. 296 Wee haue..sent a box of Crakers to you. 1773 *Newport Mercury* 20 Dec., Advt. (Th.) Said Johnson bakes the very best sort of crackers. 1775 in *Mag. Amer. Hist.* (1879) III. 516 Crackers for the use of the officers.

b. *attrib.* and *Comb.*, as *cracker-bag, -peddler*; **cracker-hash**, a sailors' hash of biscuits and meat; so **cracker-stew.**

1878 E. B. Tuttle *Border Tales* 27 One of the Indians had discovered that a comrade was dead, and lying on the *cracker-bags! 1897 Kipling *Capt. Cour.* v. 127 On his return the cocoa-tins and cracker-bags were counted out by the Frenchman's wheel. 1904 *Daily Chron.* 4 May 10/2 *Cracker hash, a savoury mixture of salt meat and biscuit. 1925 Rex Clements *Gipsy of the Horn* 38 Sea-biscuits broken into pieces and baked with small morsels of beef or pork and called 'cracker-hash'. 1928 *Sunday Express* 8 Jan. 4 Memories that go back to the days of 'cracker-hash', 'lobscouse', and hard-case. 1860 Holland *Miss Gilbert's Career* v. 76 'I'm going to be a *cracker-peddler', said Fred. 1909 *Daily Chron.* 14 Apr. 5/2 This is better.. than *cracker stew.

Cra·cker-box. *U.S.* [Cracker 9.] A biscuit-box. Also *attrib.*

1868 Mrs. Carrington *Absaraka* 101 Our attention was called to two small pieces of cracker-box planted by the road-side. 1873 Aldrich *Marj. Daw* etc. 116 The rest of the boys were scribbling away for dear life, with drum-heads and knapsacks and cracker-boxes for writing desks. 1890 *Harper's Mag.* June 142/1 A mouldy cheese.., some cracker boxes, and a case with a glass top. 1902 S. E. White *Blazed Trail* xxxv. 237 Entering, he would nod briefly and seat himself on a cracker-box. 1912 H. S. Harrison *Queed* xviii. 230 Republican cracker-box orators were trying somehow to make capital of the thing.

Cra·ckerjack, *sb.* and *a. U.S. slang.* Also **crackajack.** [A fanciful formation upon Crack *v.* or Cracker.] A. *sb.* 1. Something that is exceptionally fine or splendid. Also, a person who is exceptionally skilful or expert.

1897 *Outing* (U.S.) XXIX. 481/1 The old-fashioned dogs were heavier and slower than the latter-day crack-a-jack. 1897 *Boston Globe* 2 Nov. 2/7 [Applied to a fire-engine]. 1898 *Ibid.* 16 Aug. 7/3 This regiment is a crackerjack. 1902 J. London *Dau. Snows* i. 15 'Well, you're a—a—a cracker-jack!' he exploded with a final squeeze. 'Sure!' 1909 'O. Henry' *Road of Destiny* iii. 51 If the story was a cracker-jack he had Mesrour, the executioner, whack off his head. 1927 Vachell *Dew of Sea* etc. 262 The McCullough who was out with Prince Charlie in '45 challenged attention. 'Looks a crackerjack,' said Miss Angell.

2. A sweetmeat composed of pop-corn and syrup.

1905 Rex Beach *Pardners* i. (1912) 31, I bought a dollar's worth of everything, from cracker-jack to cantaloupe.

B. *adj.* Exceptionally fine or good; of marked excellence or ability.

1910 O. Johnson *Varmint* iii. 43 Say, by the way, look out—he's a crackerjack boxer. 1911 R. D. Saunders *Col. Todhunter* ix. 123 You've given me a cracker-jack talk on Missouri politics. 1916 H. L. Wilson *Somewhere in Red Gap* iv. 135 Ellabelle was a crackajack housekeeper. 1920 C. H. Stagg *High Speed* vi, It was a crackajack piece of work for a chauffeur.

Crackey, crackee, *int. U.S.* (Examples.)

1854 Mary J. Holmes *Tempest & Sunshine* xii. 74 He gave vent to his joy by uttering aloud, 'Crackee, this is jest the thing!' 1913 Mrs. Stratton-Porter *Laddie* ii. (1917) 30 'Whose money do you suppose that is?' 'Oh crackey! You can depend on a girl to see everything,' groaned Leon.

Cracking, *vbl. sb.* 4. Add: Financial breakdown.

1833 H. Barnard in *Maryland Hist. Mag.* XIII. 299 He said that if protection should be destroyed, there w'd be a tremendous cracking among sugar planters.

6. (See *Crack *v.* 23.)

Cracking, *ppl. a.* 3. *U.S.* (Earlier example.) Also as *adv.*

1830–3 S. Smith *Major Downing* 17 If you don't hear of cracking work down there, that will make 'em stare, I'm mistaken. 1903 *N. Y. Sun* 29 Nov. 11 The Hunters Champion Steeplechase resulted in a cracking good race.

Crackle, *sb.* Add:

4. = Crackling *vbl. sb.* 3 b. *U.S.*

1835 J. F. Cooper *Monikins* vi. (1860) 92 Exposure had tanned the skin of his face to the color of the crackle of a roasted pig.

Crackled, *ppl. a.* a. Add quot. (as used in *Ceramics*: cf. Crackle *sb.* 3).

1922 *Edin. Rev.* Apr. 322 We may describe specimens of intentionally crackled ware of the Sung Ch'uan type as Ka-ware.

Crackling, *vbl. sb.* 3. b. (U.S. examples.)

1834 D. Crockett *Life* xvi. 106, I looked like a pretty cracklin ever to get to Congress! 1835 Longstreet *Georgia Scenes* (1843) 24, I am perhaps..the best man at a horse swap that ever stole cracklins out of his mammy's fat gourd. 1845 J. J. Hooper *Adv. Simon Suggs* x. 133 'Ef them fellers aint done to a cracklin', he muttered. 1853 J. G. Baldwin *Flush Times Alabama* 160 Scarcely eating anything,..a light condiment of 'cracklin bread', and a half pint of hog-brains.

Crackly, *a.* Add: *transf.*

1923 Kipling *Land & Sea Tales* 15 There was a roar of rather crackly laughter.

Crack-voiced, *a.* [Crack- 2.] Having a cracked or broken voice.

1874 T. Hardy *Far fr. Mad. Crowd* vi, The crack-voiced cock-pheasants' 'cu-uck, cuck'.

Cradle, *sb.* Add: 14. (Earlier U.S. example.)

1833 H. Barnard in *Maryland Hist. Mag.* XIII. 347 The gravel is washed, by being thrown into what is called a rocker, or cradle.

17. cradle-books = Incunabula 2; **cradle-cannon** *Billiards*, a series of cannons with the two object-balls close on either side of a corner-pocket; **cradle-gate**, a kissing-gate; **cradle-hill** U.S. (example); **cradle-rocker**, (*a*) = Rocker[1] 2 b; (*b*) one who rocks a child's cradle; similarly **cradle-rocking.**

1902 *Daily Chron.* 7 Nov. 3/3 The whole of this second volume is devoted to *Incunabula*—the '*Cradle books'—the first fruits of the early presses. 1927 *Publishers' Weekly* 31 Dec. 2315/1 Black letter books and cradle books. 1907 *Westm. Gaz.* 6 Mar. 10/1 The '*cradle-cannon' has been responsible for another extraordinary break. 1910 *Encycl. Brit.* III. 936/2 The 'cradle-double-kiss' or 'anchor' cannon. 1903 *Standard* 26 Nov. 5/6 A *cradle gate for foot passengers and a larger gate for vehicular traffic. 1855 Haliburton *Nat. & Hum. Nat.* II. 374 The bye-road was so full of stumps and *cradle-hills, it was impossible to drive in it. 1891 Hardy *Tess* iii, The *cradle-rockers had done hard duty for so many years, under the weight of so many children, on that flagstone floor, that they were worn nearly flat. 1907 *Daily Chron.* 28 Aug. 6/7 How many of the cradle-rockers would gladly help to emancipate their sisters, but cannot. 1891 Hardy *Tess* iii, The *cradle-rocking and the song would cease simultaneously for a moment.

Cradle, *v.* 7. Add: With *out*: To extract by cradling.

1902 *Daily Chron.* 10 Sept. 5/2 The hand of the old fossicker who 'cradled' out the first few grains of gold among the Californian sierras in '47.

Cradler. b. (Earlier U.S. examples.)

1766 Washington *Diaries* I. 227 Let into it with my whole force and two cradlers hired. *Ibid.* 276, I rid to the Cradlers (cutting my Wheat at the Mill). 1827 J. F. Cooper *Prairie* xi, Show me..a cradler that knows better how to lead a gang of hands through a field of wheat.

Cradling, *vbl. sb.* Add: 3. *Med.* A form of hydropathic treatment (see quot.).

1908 *Practitioner* Apr. 434 Cradling is..very efficacious. The patient is stripped..; a cradle is put over extending from the chin to the feet, and over this is laid a single sheet, and, if necessary, ice-bags may be hung inside.

Craft, *sb.* 11. Add: Short for 'art and craft' (see *Art-and-crafty), as *craft-bowl, -work.* Also **craft-union**, a trade-union of men of the same skilled craft.

1903 *Daily Chron.* 7 Jan. 3/2 The Bow inkstand and craft-bowl. 1928 *Britain's Industrial Future* III. xiv. § 3. 155 The Craft Unions, which in general are the oldest, aim at combining men who pursue the same skilled trade, whatever industry may employ them. 1928 *Daily Express* 24 Feb. 5/2 Another institution..where games and craftwork are an important part of convalescent treatment.

Craggedness. (Later U.S. example.)

1805–9 J. J. Henry *Camp. agst. Quebec* (1812) 181 A bleak and dreary coast and country, whose craggedness inspired disagreeable sensations.

Cra·ggly, *a.* ? *U.S.* = Craggy *a.* 2.

1886 *Harper's Mag.* Nov. 868/2 These overhanging ancient orchards, lichened and craggly..do they not speak to us?

Cram, *v.* Add: 1. c. To plaster the interstices between the logs of a house. *U.S.*

1781 *Cal. Virginia St. Papers* I. 561 [He has received no assistance from the latter except in] cramming between the loggs. 1837 *Southern Lit. Messenger* III. 217 A plain building of sawed logs, *crammed*, as we say in Virginia, with mud.

Cram-jam, *adv.* [Emphatic combination of stems of Cram *v.* and Jam *v.*] Chock- or cram-(full). So **Cram-jam** *v. trans.*

1880 *Punch* 25 Sept. 142/1 The house was cram-jammed from ceiling to floor by an audience that showed itself decidedly appreciative and strictly critical. 1905 *East Coast Visitor* 17 Aug. 7/3 I've seen these flats cram-jammed with fowl of all sorts. 1909 *Daily Chron.* 8 Mar. 3/2 That garden was simply cram-jam full of them.

Cramp, *v.* Add: 4. c. *trans.* and *intr.* To deflect or turn to one side. *U.S.*

1883 'Mark Twain' *Life Mississippi* x. 99 Cramp her up to the bar! What are you standing up through the middle of the river for? 1924 W. M. Raine *Troubled Waters* iii, She tried to cramp to the left.

Crampet. Add: 4. A wall-hook.

1901 Waterhouse *Conduit Wiring* 24 The first straight run or runs may be fixed up in position by means of saddles, clips or crampets, as the case may require. 1909 W. S. Ibbetson *Electric Wiring* x. 183 The conduit may be fixed to walls by means of saddles, crampets, or clips.

Cranberry. 3. Add: *cranberry bog, field, marsh, meadow, pie, sauce, vine*; **cranberry gatherer, rake** *U.S.*, an implement used in gathering cranberries.

1833 *Ind. Q. Mag. Hist.* XV. 251 A visit to a *cranberry bog..where..I got my feet wet. 1885 *Outing* (U.S.) VII. 178/2 Our pitcher-plant..grows abundantly in a cranberry bog. 1893 B. Torrey *Footpath-Way* 200, I came to a barbed-wire fence which bounded the *cranberry field. 1895 *Funk's Standard Dict.*, *Cranberry-gatherer. 1845 Mrs. Kirkland *Western Clearings* 127 A *cranberry-marsh about half an hour from the village. 1685 *Rec. Providence*, R. I. IV. 227 His meaddow, called *cranberry Meadow, betwixt the said Meaddow & ye Rockey hill. 1863 'Gail Hamilton' *Gala-Days* 49 [You] go..mounting..to the moderate sublimity of a cranberry-meadow. 1893 B. Torrey *Footpath-Way* 197, I walked down the bay shore..meaning to go into a large cranberry meadow. 1854 Mary J. Holmes *Tempest & Sunshine* iv. 54 He started on his mission laden with..a big *cranberry pie. 1869 Mrs. Stowe *Oldtown Folks* xxvii. 340 Cranberry pies, huckleberry pies. 1849 *Cultivator* VII. 52, I have used a wooden machine, made like a *cranberry rake,..to gather my clover-seed this season. 1767 J. Adams *Diary* 8 Apr., Tufts..determined to go over and bring [them]..to dine upon wild goose and *cranberry sauce. 1854 Maria S. Cummins *Lamplighter* xix, She doesn't know anything about nursing, let her go back to her cranberry sauce and squash pie. 1839 *Trans. Mich. Agric. Soc.* (1855) VI. 264 Most of the swamps and marshes are covered with a luxuriant growth of sedge, tamarack, and *cranberry vines. 1893 B. Torrey *Footpath-Way* 201 Long rows of newly planted cranberry vines.

Cranberrying, *gerund.* Gathering cranberries.

1881 Sally P. McLean *Cape Cod Folks* xvi. 275 She hires a room, and Beck she's saved a little money cranberryin'.

Crane, *sb.*[1] 3. b. (Earlier example.)

1780 E. Parkman *Diary* 292 Mr. Beeton has made a Crane for our West Room Chimney.

Cranial, *a.* Add: *Cranial index*, the ratio of the width of the skull to its length (see quot.).

1908 A. Wilson *Education, Personality & Crime* xv. 125 The Cranial Index is found by multiplying the width of the skull by 100, and dividing by the length.

Craniate (krēⁱ·niět), *a.* and *sb. Zool.* [ad. mod.L. *crāniātus*: see Craniata.] A. *adj.* Having a skull or cranium. B. *sb.* A member of the *Craniata.*

1880 A. S. Packard *Zool.* (ed. 2) 401 The Vertebrates are divided into the skulless or *acraniate*..and the skulled or *craniate* (*Craniota*). 1900 G. C. Bourne *Compar. Anat. Anim.* I. 24 The craniate vertebrates. 1909 E. S. Goodrich *Cyclostomes & Fishes* 1 The great gap which separates the lowest known Craniate from *Amphioxus.*

Crank, *sb.*[1] 6. Add: *crank-arm, -joint*; **crank-case**, the case or covering in which the crank-shaft of a motor engine is enclosed; **crank-chamber** (see quot. 1906); **crank-pit**, a pit in which a crank revolves.

1889 Hasluck *Model Engin. Handybk.* (1900) 14 The bed-plate is..cut away to allow the *crank-arm and cross-head to pass. 1911 *Encycl. Brit.* XVII. 1005/1 In a turning piece a perpendicular let fall from its connected point upon its axis of rotation is the arm or crank-arm. 1904 *Motor Boat* 29 Sept. 228/1 Lamp oil is a rather imprudent thing to carry aboard, as some unwise friend may mistake it for engine lubricant and put a charge or two into the *crank-case. 1920 *Cornhill Mag.* Sept. 311 For forgetting to put any oil in the crank-case, he was stopped fourteen days' pay. 1904 *Motor Boat* 22 Sept. 215/2 Each cylinder has a bore of 90 mm..; both are cast together..and are mounted on a cast iron *crank chamber. 1906 *Motors* (Badm. Libr., ed. 4) 139 The crank chamber, or base chamber, as it is usually termed, forms the base of the cylinders. Its use for lubricating purposes is very important. 1922 *Times* 20 June 6/5 The cylinders are cast in one with the crank-chamber, a practice forgivable in a low-priced chassis. 1839 *Knickerbocker Mag.* XIII. 346 He..commenced..oiling the piston-rod and *crank-joints. 1893 *Daily News* 17 Oct. 3/5 The body of the deceased was found in the *crank pit.

Crank, *sb.*[2] 1. Delete † *Obs.* and add quot.:

1909 Margaret B. Saunders *Litany Lane* I. v, A glimpse ..of grey west tower half hidden by high buildings, then re-appearing by some quaint crank of street or turning.

Crank, *v.*[1] Add:

8. To move or operate (a motor engine) by a crank. Also *intr.* to turn a crank, as in starting a motor engine. Also with *up.*

1908 *Smart Set* June 91 The chauffeur..jumped out, and began to crank her up. 1909 Forrest R. Jones *Gas Engine* 181 Small motors are 'cranked' or otherwise turned by hand. *Ibid.* 183 The cranking should be done immediately after the gas is turned on. *Ibid.*, Then crank up to a fair speed and close the switch. *Ibid.* 184 Until the motor has been cranked up to high speed. 1920 V. W. Pagé *Automobile Starting*, etc. (ed. 6) 424 If the starting motor rotates but does not crank the engine. *Ibid.* 453 And still the starting motor makes no effort to crank the car. 1924 W. M. Raine *Troubled Waters* vi. 59 Silently she watched him crank the car and drive away. 1929 J. B. Priestley *Good Companions* 194 The car refused to start again. She cranked away until she was breathless and aching.

transf. *a* 1910 'O. Henry' *Rolling Stones* 231 Mike, the proprietor, who was cranking the cash register, heard.

Crankism. *U.S.* (Earlier example.)

1882 *Congress. Rec.* 13 Feb. 1166/2 Such mathematics..is contaminated with congenital infirmity... It is crankism applied to figures.

Crap-, comb. form of *Craps, as in *crap-game, -house, -shooter, -shooting, -table.*

1903 *N. Y. Even. Post* 23 Sept., There may be a few small poker and *crap games, but the big gambling houses have shut up shop. *a* 1906 'O. Henry' *Trimmed Lamp* etc. 243 A cigar store near the Bowery that was running a crap game in the back room. 1916 Donald Thompson *In Russia* i. (1918) 3 A crap game was started. 1888 *Missouri Republ.* Feb. (Farmer) When arrested he was in the negro *crap-house kept by Alex. Wells. 1905 *N. Y. Even. Post* 22 Aug. 6 The action of two Brooklyn plain-clothes men in rounding up a dozen boy '*crap-shooters'. 1926 J. Black *You Can't Win* iv. 27, I soon came to know the poker players, crap shooters and dice sharks. 1890 *Ann Arbor R.* Feb. 27 Young boys congregating there for the purpose of *crap-shooting. 1902 T. M. Young *Amer. Cotton Industry* 103 At the *crap-table he [*sc.* the negro] will often lose or win at a sitting a sum equal to the profits of his labour for a whole year.

Crape, *sb.* Add: 3. b. **crape ring.** *Astr.* (see quot.); **crape-tree** *U.S.* = *crape-myrtle.*

1902 *Encycl. Brit.* XXV. 733/2 Saturn's rings...It is now well established that the dusky or *crape ring, which is on the inside of the brighter one, is really in the nature of an inner border of the bright ring, the one shading off imperceptibly into the other. 1920 C. Harris *Eve's Husb.* 113 We were sitting upon a bench near a flowering pink *crape tree.

Crape, *v.*[1] (Earlier U.S. examples.)

1774 P. V. Fithian *Jrnl.* (1900) 184 Her Hair..was crap'd up, with two Rolls at each Side. *Ibid.* 224 Her head tho' was powdered white as snow, & crap'd in the newest taste. 1787 Lucinda Orr *Jrnl. Young Lady Va.* (1871) 19, I am this moment going to crape and dress. *Ibid.* 23, I am just up, and am going to seat myself for Sibby to crape my hair.

Craps. *U.S.* [Of obscure origin, but cf. *crabs*, Crab *sb.*[1] 9.] A game of chance played with dice. *To shoot craps*: to play at this game. Also *Comb.* (see *Crap-).

1843 J. H. Green *Expos. Gambling* 88 The Game of Craps..is a game lately introduced into New Orleans, and is fully equal to faro in its..ruinous effects. 1853 Mayne Reid *Rifle Rangers* ii. 22 So I stepped into a shanty whar they wur a-playin craps. 1859 Matsell *Rogue's Lexicon* 111 Craps or props, a game peculiar to Boston. 1888 *St. Louis Globe Democrat* (Farmer) A party of colored deck hands were playing craps. 1902 T. M. Young *Amer. Cotton Industry* 103 The besetting weakness of the negro is gambling, and his favourite game is 'craps'. 1903 *N. Y. Sun* 12 Nov. 1 Two young toughs came along and started to shoot craps. 1922 Mulford *Black Buttes* ii. 20, I never saw a redhead yet that could shoot craps worth a damn.

b. (Also *crap.*) A losing throw or 'shoot' of 2, 3, or 12 in the game of craps.

1911 Webster s.v. *Craps*, The caster..loses if it [*sc.* his throw] is 2, 3, or 12 (called a crap). 1916 D. Thompson *In Russia* i. (1918) 3 A crap game was started. Just when you would reach for the money, after seeing '7' or '11' on the dice, the boat would give another roll and 'craps' would appear.

Crapulosity (kræpiŭlǫ·sĭti). [f. L. *crāpulōs-us* Crapulous *a.* + -ity.] Inclination to drunkenness.

1887 Browning *Fust & his Friends* 108 Pride seized me at last as Concupiscence first, Crapulosity ever: true Fiends, every one.

Crash, *sb.*[1] Add:

4. *Hunting.* The outcry made by hounds when they find the game. Also *fig.*

1781 P. Beckford *Thoughts on Hunting* xiii. 167 Where are all your sorrows,..one halloo has dispelled them all.—What a crash they make! 1837 Apperley ('Nimrod') *Chace, Turf, & Road* (1843) 41 There is no crash now, and not much music... At the pace these hounds are going there is no time for babbling. 1919 Masefield *Reynard* 85 But the whimpering rose to a crying crash By the hollow ruin of Tineton Ash.

5. *Theatr.* a. (See quot. 1891.) b. A basket filled with fragments of glass or pottery, used to imitate the sound of the breaking of windows, etc.

1891 Farmer *Slang*, *Crash*, the machine used to suggest the roar of thunder; a noise of desperate (and unseen) conflict; an effect of 'alarums, excursions' generally. 1921 R. M. Heath *Art of Production* 70 'Glass crash', ready off L. up stage.

6. *Aviation, Motoring*, etc. The act, or an instance, of crashing. (See *Crash *v.* 6 a.) Also *attrib.*, as **crash helmet**, a helmet worn as a protection in case of crashing.

1918 McCudden *5 Yrs. R.F.C.* 167 It is the ambition of every youthful pilot to down a Hun in our lines—and then land a crash alongside. *Ibid.* 185 About the end of May I had my first crash, on a Bristol Scout that I was delivering to J— G—. 1923 *Motor Cycling* 26 Sept. 659/2 Lowe's retirement was due to a crash caused by a burst front tyre. 1923 *Motor Cycle* 20 Sept. Advts. p. xlvii, 5,000 New Crash Helmets, Tutz patent, ex-R.A.F. 1929 *Star* 21 Aug. 8/2 Air Crash that caused 7 deaths.

7. **crash-dive**, a sudden dive made by a submarine when surprised or in imminent danger. Also **crash-dive** *v. trans.*

1922 E. K. Chatterton *Q-Ships* viii. 97 The U-boat would then make a crash-dive towards the bottom. 1928 C. F. S. Gamble *North Sea Air Station* xii. 177 As soon as those aboard the submarine saw the seaplane, they 'crash-dived' the boat.

Crash, *sb.*[2] Add:

2. The name of a tint in textile fabrics.

1927 *Daily Express* 2 Apr. 6 In shades of Peach, Bracken, Sunburn, Caramel, Gold, Crash, White. 1927 *Daily Mail* 12 July 1 Colours:..Silver, Blush, Crash, etc.

Crash, *v.* Add:

2. Delete *rare.* Now freq. with adv. Also *fig.*

1886 'Maxwell Gray' *Silence of Dean Maitland* III. iv, He longed for the..high stone roof to crash in and hide him from that terrible gaze. 1893 Mary E. Mann *In Summer Shade* xxviii, Bob..crashed over and fell in his blood at his murderer's feet. 1903 R. Langbridge *Flame & Flood* v, She was prepared for some new development which must crash in on her ignorance. 1924 D. H. Lawrence *England, my England* 172 Seats had crashed over.

6. a. *intr.* Of an aeroplane or its pilot: To fall or come down violently with the machine out of control, by which the machine is damaged or destroyed. Also of a motor car or its occupant: To suffer damage which puts the car out of action. Also *fig.* to suffer a sudden breakdown in business, etc.

1915 *War Illustrated* 6 Nov. 288/2 Cpl. Bennett disabled the German machine, which crashed to earth. 1918 McCudden *5 Yrs. R.F.C.* 122 One of our machines had crashed about a mile away and..both occupants were dead. *Ibid.* 164 The Hun went down and crashed. 1919 P. Bewsher *Green Balls* 231 He's getting very low! My God! Did you hear that! He's crashed! 1923 *Motor Cycling* 26 Sept. 657/2 The first casualty was..one of the favourites, who crashed on Bray Hill, his machine catching fire. 1927 F. E. Baily *Golden Vanity* xv, Secretaryships to magnates are so precarious. Moreover, if French crashed, who would give his ex-secretary a job? 1928 C. F. S. Gamble *North Sea Air Station* Introd. 26 The onomatopoeic word 'crash', used in the literature of aviation, was coined by Captain J. D. B. Fulton of the Royal Field Artillery and Royal Flying Corps.

b. *trans.* To land (an aeroplane) in such a manner that it is injured or destroyed by the act of landing.

1915 Rosher *In R.N.A.S.* (1916) 69 Our aerodrome here is a beastly small one. I have had several narrow shaves already of running into things, and feel sure that before long I shall 'crash' something. 1919 A. E. Illingworth *Fly Papers* 26 'If you want a walking stick', I said, 'crash a machine yourself—don't come pinching mine'. 1928 C. F. S. Gamble *North Sea Air Station* i. 44 This machine was crashed as a result of a forced landing. *Ibid.* ix. 136 The last-named officer crashed his machine on landing (owing to the bad condition of the ground).

c. To disable (an enemy aeroplane) so that it is wrecked on hitting the ground. Also *fig.*

1919 *Athenæum* 18 July 632/1 Men in the R.F.C. in France always swore it [*sc.* the Hotel Cecil, H.Q. of Air Ministry] was staffed with villains who were betraying and 'crashing' the fighters.

Crasher (kræ·ʃəɹ). [f. Crash *v.* + -er[1].]

1. Something that crashes or makes a crash; a loud harsh blow or percussion. Also *fig.*

1887 T. Darlington *Folk-speech S. Cheshire*, *Crasher*, a lie. 1922 A. S. M. Hutchinson *This Freedom* II. iv, Flick, rat-tat! What a crasher! You can feel it echo! 1928 Eden Phillpotts in *Sunday Dispatch* 16 Sept. 2 He told the fatal tale to me...It was..of course a crasher for Archibald.

2. = *gate-crasher.

1924 *Daily Express* 13 Nov. 3/4 'Crasher'—a man who comes in without an invitation. 1928 *Ibid.* 12 July 8/6 The procedure of these 'crashers' is to wait until a function is well started and then to stroll into the hotel [etc.]. 1928 *Sunday Dispatch* 15 July 1 The dance 'crasher' has a most insidious rival in the dance 'cadger', declares a prominent hostess.

Crasized (krēⁱ·saizd), *a.* [f. Crasis + -ize + -ed.] Subjected to grammatical crasis.

1914 A. Plummer *St. Mark* 371 The crasized form is found in the best MSS.

Crassier (krasye). [Fr.] A dump or rubbish-hill.

1916 *Times Hist. War* VI. 372 Opposite Grenay and west of Loos were two large slag heaps, known as the Double Crassier, bristling with mitrailleuses. 1920 *Chambers's Jrnl.* 275/1 Its piles of timber and extensive *crassiers* (pit-banks or dumps).

Cratægin (krātī·dʒin). [f. mod.L. *Cratægus* hawthorn + -in[1].] A bitter principle contained in the bark of hawthorn twigs.

1895 *Naturalist* 23 The bark of the branches [of the hawthorn] has a bitter principle, cratægin, and also amygdalin.

Crate, *v.* [f. the sb.] *trans.* To pack in a crate or framework. Hence **Cra·ted** *ppl. a.*, **Cra·ting** *vbl. sb.*

1872 Eggleston *Hoosier Schoolm.* xi. 65 The boys thought 'twas funny to crate me. 1897 *Outing* (U.S.) XXX. 366/1 Crated and swathed in white clothes, it appeared like a mummy. 1900 Kipling in *Daily Express* 20 June 4/5 Neatly-piled boxes of rivets and a mass of crated ironwork. 1901 Holland *Mousmé* 265 The heavier articles, a man came and crated for me.

Crater, *sb.* 4. Add: Also, the cavity formed by the explosion of a shell. Also *attrib.*

1855 E. B. Hamley *Story Campaign Sebastopol* xxvii. 282 A magazine..had been blown up by a shell—..no serious damage was done by this explosion, which left..a vast crater like a quarry. 1914 *Scotsman* 26 Dec. 8 Seamed with dugouts, burrows, trenches,..and pitted with craters. 1919 P. Bewsher *Green Balls* 200, I can see dotted around the fields the great craters of the shell-holes. 1919 G. K. Rose *2/4th Oxf. & Bucks Lt. Infty.* ii. 24 The Somme 'craterfield'. 1921 Bewsher *51st Div.* 117 A belt of marshy country, just east of the mine crater. 1926 *Encycl. Brit.* Suppl. I. 228/2 A 6-in. howitzer mine shell..produces a cylindrical crater about four yards across and 10 ft. deep. *Ibid.* 239 Each tank was given some saphead, crater post, or communication trench to deal with.

Crater, *v.* [f. the sb.] a. *intr.* To form a crater or hollow. b. *trans.* To obstruct or destroy (a road or *terrain*) by craters formed by mines or mine shells. Also **Cra·tered** *ppl. a.*

1884 *Cassell's Fam. Mag.* 576/1 This arrangement is found to give a better light than the solid rod, which is apt to 'crater' or become hollow in its burning end. Compound rods..do not crater in this way. 1921 *Times Lit. Suppl.* 8 Sept. 570/4 The Second [German Army] could not get beyond Albert on account of difficulties in the cratered area. 1922 *Glasgow Herald* 22 Mar. 10 A number of roads had been cratered and a certain number of bridges blown up.

Cravat, *sb.* Add: 1. c. A scarf or necklet of lace, fur, etc., worn by women and girls.

1903 *Westm. Gaz.* 26 Nov. 4/2 Things..of the lacy kind.. little collar-cravats, &c. 1904 *Daily Chron.* 19 Mar. 8/2 Talk no longer of stoles, boas, and ruffles, but of cravats, for by that name the necklets sold for early spring wear prefer to be known. 1905 *Westm. Gaz.* 11 Nov. 13/2 The cravat effect of the ermine on the shoulders is charming. 1909 *Ibid.* 2 Jan. 2/3, I worked at cravat-making, and helped my sister with her four children.

e. *Surg.* (See quot. 1901.)

[1884 W. Pye *Surgical Handicraft* II. viii. 78 The first and most obvious use of this [triangular or scarf] bandage is to simply tie it round..with a reef knot, it having been previously folded up into a cravat.] 1901 Dorland *Med. Dict.* (ed. 2), *Cravat*, a form of bandage made by folding a triangular piece of cloth from its apex towards the base.

Crave, *sb.* Add: b. *Scots Law.* A demand or claim addressed to the court. (Cf. Crave *v.* 1 c.) Also **Cra·ving** *vbl. sb.* in the same sense.

1913 *Act 2 & 3 Geo. V*, c. 28 Sched. ii. (23) The sheriff may, at any time after the expiry of the inducie, upon a written craving being endorsed on the initial writ, decern in terms of the crave of the initial writ.

Crawfish, *v. U.S.* (Earlier examples.)

1848 *Congress. Globe* Feb. 277/3 No sooner did they see the old British Lion rising up.., than they crawfished back to 49°. 1850 L. H. Garrard *Wah-To-Yah* i. (1927) 18 Others slowly 'crawfished', hiding, by their singular way of crouching.

Cra·wfishing, *vbl. sb.* and *ppl. a.* Fishing for crawfish. Also *fig.*

1883 Keighley *Who are you* 102 Where the sturdy crawfishing children sat. 1903 *Daily Chron.* 8 June 9/2 It is only natural that by crawfishing for a good reference this steward neglects the men who actually do the hard work.

Crawk, *v.* [Imitative.] *intr.* To utter a hoarse sound, squawk: also *trans.* with *out.* Also as *sb.*

1845 *Round Preacher* 94 Not many hours 'ud pass afore they'd crawk out for the loaves and fishes. 1889 Rose T. Cooke *Steadfast* xxvi. 287 A cooped barnyard fowl, that crawks, and cheeps. 1928 D. H. Lawrence *Rainbow* iv. 108 There was a sharp crawk of expostulation as one of the hens shifted over. 1930 *Aberdeen Press & Jrnl.* 26 Sept. 6/3 The eagle retired, crawking out his discomfiture.

Crawl, *sb.*[1] Add: b. A walk at a leisurely pace. In *beer-crawl, gin-crawl, pub-crawl*, a slow progress from one drinking place to another. *slang.*

1902 *Daily Chron.* 3 Dec. 5/2 The cockney 'beer crawl'. 1905 *Ibid.* 28 Mar. 4/6 Glasgow's most fashionable Sunday parade, the 'crawl' on Great Western-road. 1927 *Blackw. Mag.* Sept. 336/2 During our evening gin crawls in the various camps.

c. A high-speed swimming stroke, in which the swimmer, lying face-downwards, usually with the face submerged, makes alternate overhand arm-strokes assisted by the quick movement of the legs. In full *crawl-stroke.*

1903 A. Sinclair & W. Henry *Swimming* (ed. 4) 89 A young swimmer named R. Cavill, who revolutionised all ideas about speed swimming for short distances by introducing a further modification of this style [*sc.* the 'Trudgen'], which was at once termed the 'crawl' stroke. 1912 F. Sachs *Complete Swimmer* 144 The double over-arm and crawl racers. 1926 *Westm. Gaz.* 10 Sept., To the school children across the Atlantic the 'crawl' is as natural as the ancient 'breast' stroke to the average British child.

d. *Crawl-out*: a back-out. *U.S.*

1903 A. H. Lewis *The Boss* 184 That's a crawl-out,..an' it aint worthy of you.

Crawl, *sb.*[2] 2. (Earlier examples.)

1682 T. A. *Carolina* 28 If near their Market or Harbor they bring them [*sc.* turtles] in Sloops alive, and afterwards keep them in Crauls. 1740 *New Hist. Jamaica* (ed. 2) 183 None shall hunt any Gang of Dogs within Four Miles of any Crawl or Settlement.

Crawler. Add:

1. c. One who swims the crawl-stroke.

1912 F. Sachs *Complete Swimmer* 149 The majority of crawlers will complete one length of a bath—usually about 30 yards—without breathing at all.

4. A domesticated animal of slow movements. *Austral.*

1890 'R. Boldrewood' *Col. Reformer* xviii, The herd.. consisted almost wholly of the well-bred station 'crawlers', as the stockmen term them from their peaceable and orderly habits.

5. Chiefly *pl.* An infant's overall garment in which it can crawl without spoiling its ordinary clothes.

1923 *Daily Mail* 11 Jan. 4 Children's Crawlers. 1923 *Weekly Dispatch* 18 Feb. 15 A new style of crawler has just been designed. 1926 *Brit. Weekly* 30 Dec. 360/3 A tiny boy in crawlers.

6. Applied to a kind of tractor moving on an endless chain.

1922 *Encycl. Brit.* XXXII. 739/1 The crawler type..can pass over marshy land where the wheeled tractor would be mired. 1926 *Ibid.* Suppl. III. 796/1 The crawler tractor had one or two continuous-chain tracks on which it ran and which it carried with it.

Crawling, *vbl. sb.* Add: b. **crawling-board** (see quots.).

1901 *Daily Chron.* 25 Nov. 7/3 A crawling-board used on a roof in connection with a ladder. 1902 *Law Rep.* I.K.B.D. 494 A crawling board, which was a contrivance ordinarily used in the repair of roofs, and consisted of a wooden plank about 18 to 20 feet long and 10 inches wide, across which were nailed transverse pieces of wood.

Crawlsome (krǭ·lsəm), *a.* [f. Crawl *v.* + -some.] Addicted to mean, worm-like behaviour. Hence **Craw·lsomeness.**

1900 H. Lawson *Over Sliprails* 73 We'd be sure to.. reckon that it was done out of nastiness or crawlsomeness, and feel a contempt for him accordingly. 1904 *Delta* (N. Queensl.) *Advocate* in *Westm. Gaz.* 21 Mar. 4/2 In the whole course of their crawlsome, insanitary lives.

Cray [2]. *Australian.* = Crayfish 3 b.

1916 C. J. Dennis *Ginger Mick* 46 We'll 'ave a cray fer supper when I comes a-marchin' 'ome.

Cray·fish, *v.* [f. Crayfish *sb.*] *intr.* To move like a crayfish. Cf. Crawfish *v.*

1900 H. Lawson *Over Sliprails* 63 The steamer was just crayfishing away from a mud island, where she had tied up for more wool.

Cray·fishing, *vbl. sb.* [f. Crayfish *sb.* 3.] The catching of crayfish.

1835 J. H. Ingraham *South-West* I. xvi. 174 Others were engaged in the delicate amusement of cray-fishing.

Crazia (kra·tsia). Pl. **crazie** (-ie). [It., ad. G. *kreuzer* Kreutzer.] A copper coin of Tuscany, the twelfth part of a lira.

1787 Beckford *Lett. Italy* (1805) I. 259 Four crazie only, somewhat less than three pence English. 1897 *Daily News* 5 July 3/6 Tuscany [postage stamps] 9 crazie on white, unused, 7*l.*

Crazy, *a.* Add:

4. c. Extremely eager. *colloq.*

1779 [see 4 in Dict.]. 1839 C. Clark *John Noakes* lxxxii, But so crazy all for Tiptree wor, They coodn't thussins stay. 1859 in *Chicago Tribune* 11 Oct. (1929) VIII. 1, I am crazy to have a carpet like Mr. Laflins. 1883 J. Hay *Bread-winners* xi. 175, I see you are crazy to go and talk to Miss Dallas. 1895 Susan Hale *Lett.* 294 They were crazy that I should talk about the celebrated people I have known. 1926 J. Black *You Can't Win* iii. 19 Well, if you're so crazy about a job, I'll make one for you.

5. Used (after *crazy-quilt*) to denote a garden walk or pavement of irregular pieces of flat stone or tile between which rock plants are often grown.

1923 *Daily Mail* 13 Jan. 11 Stone walks, either crazy or rectangular. *Ibid.* 19 Feb. 6 Visitors will pass by old red brick and crazy paths to a sunk lawn. 1925 A. S. M. Hutchinson *One Increasing Purpose* III. xvi, Under the blue tile..of the crazy-paving just by the rain-water butt. 1927 H. C. Bailey *Mr. Fortune, Please* 173 Along the house was a terrace with crazy pavement in which saxifrage grew. *Ibid.* 223 Mrs. Pemberton's garden was a pleasant place of crazy paving and rock plants.

Creakily (krī·kili), *adv.* [f. Creaky *a.* + -ly[2].] In a creaky manner, with a creaky sound.

1909 *Daily Chron.* 27 Aug. 7/6 One treading softly..the other loudly, creakily, and importantly. 1920 *Blackw. Mag.* Oct. 525/1 A steamer creakily blowing off regular jets of steam.

Creaking, *vbl. sb.* a. Delete † *Obs.* and add example:

1923 *Chambers's Jrnl.* Oct. 638/1 The 'creaking' of the partridges still hung in the stagnant air.

Cream, *sb.*[2] Add:

2. f. The collection of globules of rubber which rise to the surface of the latex in the manufacture of india-rubber.

1903 *Seeligmann's Indiarubber* 57 The hydrocarbide elements solidify on the surface into a sort of thick cream. 1914 H. Brown *Rubber* 71 The latex is diluted with water and is allowed to stand until the 'cream', consisting of the rubber globules, rises to the surface... The cream is afterwards converted into solid rubber by pressure [etc.].

7. Also (as in *cream cake*) used to designate many other confections cooked with cream, or filled with whipped cream or Devonshire cream, as *cream bun, scone, slice*, etc.

1869 E. Eggleston *Mr. Blake's Walking-Stick* i. 15 [He] rolled his soft lips about, as though he had a cream tart in his mouth. 1889 *Kansas Times & Star* 5 Oct., What they [*sc.* school boys] dote on most in pastry is cream puffs. 1891 *Encycl. Pract. Cookery* (ed. T. F. Garrett) I. 469/2 Cream Scones...will take from ten to twelve minutes to cook. 1894 Cream bun [sold in London]. 1897 *Hearth & Home* 2 Dec. 171/2 Devonshire Cream Buns. 1899 *Cassell's Dict. Cook.* 160 Cream Biscuits..Cream Fritters. *Ibid.* 161 Cream Pancakes ..Cream Pudding. *Ibid.* 162 Cream Sauce..Cream Toasts. 1906 *Mrs. Beeton's Househ. Management* 906 Cream Buns. 1915 May Byron *Cake Bk.* 71–2 Cream Scones.

Cream, *v.* Add: 2. c. Of the latex of india-rubber: To form a collection of globules of rubber on the surface. Hence **Creamed** *ppl. a.*

1903 *Seeligmann's Indiarubber* 56 Coagulation by creaming after doubling the volume of the latex with water. 1914 H. Brown *Rubber* 69 This behaviour, which is termed 'creaming',..is only shown by certain latices... If the creamed globules are separated from the liquid..they coalesce to form a mass of rubber. *Ibid.* 71 Castilloa latex ..creams very readily.

7. To prepare (fish, chicken, etc.) in a cream sauce.

1906, 1908 [see *Creamed *ppl. a.* 2].

8. To work (butter and sugar, or yolk of eggs and sugar) into a creamy consistency.

1889 R. Wells *Pastry Cook & Confect. Guide* 30 Then start and cream the butter and sugar together. 1891 *Encycl. Pract. Cookery* (ed. T. F. Garrett) I. 839/2 Cream ½ lb. of butter, add ½ lb. of caster sugar. 1906 *Mrs. Beeton's Househ. Management* 914. *Ibid.* 916 Cream the butter and sugar together until thick and white. 1915 May Byron *Cake Bk.* 132 Cream eight ounces of butter with eight ounces of sugar. *Ibid.* 139 Cream four ounces of castor sugar with six yolks.

9. To treat (the skin) with a cosmetic cream.

1927 *Daily Express* 14 Oct. 3/6 To have their ankles massaged, creamed, and drilled into the approved slender lines of grace and beauty.

Creamed, *ppl. a.* 2. Add: Of chicken, fish, etc.: Cooked with cream, prepared in a cream sauce.

1906 *Mrs. Beeton's Househ. Management* 1517 Creamed Lobster..Creamed Peas. 1908 *Practitioner* Sept. 369 Later on creamed chicken or fish may be given.

3. Of butter: Beaten to a cream. Cf. *Cream *v.* 8.

1891 *Encycl. Pract. Cookery* (ed. T. F. Garrett) I. 216/2 Creamed butter..is best adapted for making cakes and some kinds of pastry. 1906 *Mrs. Beeton's Househ. Management* 1116 Creamed butter for sandwiches.

4. Having a creamy surface. Cf. *Cream *v.* 9.

1925 *Blackw. Mag.* Nov. 583/1 Her neck and the sweep of a cheek were smooth and creamed as a fresh-peeled almond.

Creamer. Add: c. A cream-jug. *U.S.*

1877 Mrs. E. S. Ward *Story of Avis* 237 That rose-curlew on the creamer is like a singing leaf, I think. 1893 'O. Thanet' *Stories Western Town* 215 But she remembered the silver service, the coffee-pot,..the creamer,..the sugar-bowl.

Creamery. Add: 1. (Earlier example.)

1872 *Rep. Vermont Board Agric.* I. 164 Mr. Bliss spoke of the creameries in New York.

b. (Earlier and later examples.)

a 1877 *N. Y. Bulletin* (Bartlett) In the general features of the butter market there is no change. The fine creameries are considered well sold at 23 cts.;..Western creamery, 22 cts. 1909 *Public Ledger* (Philad.) 24 June 12/4 Butter..desirable grades of both solid-packed creamery and prints.

c. **creamery butter**, butter made at a creamery, as distinguished from that made at a private dairy; so **creamery print** (Print *sb.* 5).

1894 *Field* 9 June 846/2 The average price realised for Irish *creamery butter was 88s. f.o.r. at this creamery. 1901 *Daily News* 7 Jan. 8/7 Two standards, one for the creamery butter and one for the more heavily salted butter known as Irish. 1909 *Public Ledger* (Philad.) 24 June 12/4 Pennsylvania and other nearby *creamery prints.

Creamily (krī·mili), *adv.* [f. Creamy *a.* + -ly[2].] With a creamy tint or surface.

1906 Frances Campbell *Dearlove* 24 Peaches like mother-o'-pearl creamily yellow.

Crease, *v.*[2] 3. Add: Also *transf.* (*U.S.*)

1913 Mulford *Coming of Cassidy* vii. 119 The drawing bar-tender,..dazed from shock of a ball that 'creased' his head. *Ibid.* x. 162 They creased you!

Creasing, *vbl. sb.*[2] Add:

1. b. (See *Crease *v.*[2] 3.) *U.S.*

1853 [Paxton] *Stray Yankee in Texas* 38 The 'creasing' of a horse is a feat which..would electrify a northern jockey.

Create, *v.* Add:

1. d. To design (a costume): see *Creation 5 c.

1930 *Daily Tel.* 7 Apr. 7/7 A brown mixture tweed suit.. created by Schiaparelli.

5. *intr.* To make a fuss, grumble, 'go on' *about* (something). *slang.*

1919 *Athenæum* 8 Aug. 729/1 'Creating' is presumably an abbreviation of 'creating (or making) a fuss'.

Creation. Add: 2. b. The formation or floatation of a business company.

1898 *Westm. Gaz.* 15 Mar. 6/1 An Australian Brewery Creation. *Ibid.* 6/3 Engineering creations are becoming quite plentiful. This week end will witness the flotation of the old-established business of Jesse Ellis and Co.

3. b. At Cambridge University before 16 Oct. 1926, the ceremony on Commencement Day in which the professors in the various faculties (or other officials for some degrees) recited the names of those who had been admitted doctors (doctors designate) during the past year and the senior proctor the names of those who had been admitted masters (inceptors).

1860 *Univ. Cambr., Method Proceed. Arts* 26 The Inceptors in every year become complete Masters of Arts by creation on the commencement day. 1902 *Student's Handbk. Cambridge* 341 The day appointed for the..process known as 'creation' in the case of Masters and Doctors in the various faculties.

4. b. Used in various phrases with *all* (see quots.), or as an exclamation; also *to beat* or *lick creation*, to surpass everything. *U.S. colloq.*

1834 S. Smith *Sel. Lett. Downing* 14 But when in all creation any of 'em will be finished I guess it would puzzle a Philadelphy lawyer to tell. 1839 *Yale Lit. Mag.* IV. 363 (Th.) He pulls like all creation, as the woman remarked when the horse ran away with her. 1843 Haliburton *Attaché* II. ix. 159 'Creation, man,' said Mr. Slick, 'I have done it..and you didn't know it.' *Ibid.* xii. 230 Creation! how he looked. 1853 *Knickerbocker Mag.* Sept. 122 (Th.) 'Heavenly marcies!' sez she, 'if that don't beat creation!' 1862 'E. Kirke' *Among Pines* xiii. 237 Go to Wilmington and telegraph all creation. 1888 *Detroit Free Press* Aug. (Farmer) Beats all creation how I mistook. 1891 Farmer *Slang* s.v. *Creation*, *To beat* or *lick creation* (American), to overpower; excel; surpass; to be incomparable.

5. b. *spec.* The first representation on the stage of a dramatic character or rôle; a dramatic character 'made' by a particular artist. (Cf. Create *v.* 2 c and F. *création.*)

1872 *Gentl. Mag.* Feb. 195 One of Mr. Irving's latest successes has been the 'creation' of Jingle in the version of 'Pickwick'. 1881 *Punch* 17 Dec. 288/1 The character of Maximilian..was doubtless written expressly for Robson, and, therefore, as one of that actor's 'creations' carries with it a Robsonian tradition.

c. A costume, etc. designed by an expert *modiste.* Also applied to other kinds of 'confection'.

1878 *Cassell's Fam. Mag.* IV. 107/2 The 'Empress' is another of this season's creations. 1884 *Pharmaceutical Jrnl.* 22 Nov. 407/1 A fresh, clear healthful complexion.. comforts the mind and eye far more than all the pearl-white and rose-pink 'creations'. 1887 Kipling *Plain Tales fr. Hills, Three and—an Extra* (1889) 12 It was what *The Queen* calls 'a creation'. 1898 *Daily News* 17 Sept. 6/2 A recent 'creation'—to use the curious technical word—consists of dark blue repp with heliotrope velvet let in. 1921 *13th Ann. Drapery* etc. *Exhib.* Advt., Our creations are bought throughout the world, where the demand exists for Furs which are correct. 1930 Jane Dashwood *Three Daughters* xvi, Judy, radiant in a tiara and a creation of Rosalie's.

Creativity (krīăti·vĭti). [f. Creative + -ity.] Creative power or faculty; ability to create.

1875 A. W. Ward *Engl. Dram. Lit.* I. 506 The spontaneous flow of his [*sc.* Shakspere's] poetic creativity. 1926 A. N. Whitehead *Relig. in Making* iii. 90 The creativity whereby the actual world has its character of temporal passage to novelty. *Ibid.* 152 Unlimited possibility and abstract creativity can procure nothing.

Creator. Add: 2. b. One who 'creates' a dramatic character or rôle. (Cf. *Creation 5 b.)

1872 *Gentl. Mag.* June 715 Her representation had always this want of dramatic propriety for those who had witnessed the original creator of the part.

c. One who 'creates' or designs a costume, etc. (see *Create *v.* 1 d, *Creation 5 c).

1901 *Westm. Gaz.* 23 May 3/1 Everything seemed so absolutely simple, and yet so absolutely impossible to any other creator.

Creature. See also *Critter.

Credentialled (krĭde·nʃăld), *ppl. a.* Furnished with credentials.

1891 *Sat. Rev.* 10 Jan. 47 A person himself qualified and credentialled by almost every possible kind of passage through the Academic mill. 1928 *Sunday Dispatch* 5 Aug. 8 The credentialled spiritualist in a semi-scientific Bloomsbury 'college'.

Credenza (krĕde·ntsă). [It.] A sideboard. (Cf. Credence *sb.* 7.)

1880 Shorthouse *John Inglesant* xxviii, Below and beside these were credenzas and cabinets upon which luxury and art had lavished every costly device and material.

Credit, *sb.* Add:

13. d. A kind of 'distinction' awarded in some examinations to examinees obtaining more than a certain percentage of the maximum marks in a subject. *colloq.* (Officially styled *pass-with-credit.*)

1917 *Regul. Oxf. & Camb. Schools Exam. Board* 49 Candidates who attain a sufficiently high standard in one or more of the subjects comprised in the several Divisions will be awarded a pass-with-credit in each of those subjects.

e. An entry in the record of a pupil or student certifying that he or she has qualified in some course of study. *U.S.*

1904 E. G. Dexter *Hist. Educ. U.S.* 288 On the basis of 'credits', one credit representing a subject pursued daily.. for one year in the secondary schools, forty-five credits is the usual requirement.

14. **credit-draper**, a 'travelling' draper who delivers goods on credit; **credit insurance**, insurance against bad debts; **credit letter**, a letter of credit (see 10 b); **credit man**, a clerk who has charge of the credit accounts in a business.

1897 *Westm. Gaz.* 24 Apr. 2/3 [In] 'Lads' Love'..Nathan Murdoch, a *Credit Draper. 1903 *Daily Chron.* 17 Oct. 7/7 A case of considerable importance to travelling and credit drapers was decided at the Thames Police Court yesterday. 1925 *Daily Tel.* 13 May 4/4 A good deal of attention has been drawn during the past year to what is known as *credit insurance. 1929 *Encycl. Brit.* VI. 655/1 If it is worth a trader's while to accept a risk then a credit insurance company will generally undertake a proportion unless the transaction is obviously a gamble. 1903 A. Adams *Log Cowboy* ii. 22 Your *credit letter is good anywhere you need supplies. 1915 *Lit. Digest* (N. Y.) 21 Aug. 377/3 Big order comes in from Jones & Co. Everybody pleased—except that office kill-joy, the *credit man.

Creditable, *a.* Add:

3. Capable of being ascribed *to.*

1904 *Rep. Librarian Congress* 32 Many documents creditable to that period can be judged to be so and assigned to their proper group only by internal evidence.

Creditor. Add:

5. *attrib.*, as *creditor-account, -nation.*

1899 *Westm. Gaz.* 8 Sept. 7/3 *Creditor-account balances. 1897 *Daily News* 30 Nov. 4/6 This country, the great *creditor nation of the world. 1906 *Westm. Gaz.* 27 Mar. 9/1 The creditor nations of Europe, as well as the debtor nations of South America. 1919 J. L. Garvin *Econ. Foundations of Peace* 445 America's new position as a great creditor-nation.

Creed, *sb.*² *Telegraphy.* The designation of an automatic tape-printing machine invented by F. G. *Creed.* Usually *attrib.*, as *Creed printer, system, translator.*

1916 T. E. Herbert *Telegr.* (ed. 3) 363 The Creed receiving perforator. *Ibid.* 368 The Bille Receiver, like the Creed, reproduces perforated Wheatstone tape. *Ibid.* 375 The Creed Translator. 1923 H. H. Harrison *Print. Telegr. Systems* 208 The Creed recorder. *Ibid.* 261 The Creed was the first of this class [*sc.* translators]. *Ibid.* 266 The 1920 design of Creed printer. 1928 A. E. Stone *Text Bk. Telegr.* 284 The Creed System. *Ibid.* 286 The Creed Printer.

Creek, *sb.*¹ **8.** Add: *creek-bed, -side* (earlier examples), *-timber* (U.S.); **creek-gum,** the Australian gum-tree, *Eucalyptus rostrata.*

1903 S. E. White *Forest* xiv. 196 If we..followed a *creek-bed..we should have made our discovery. 1898 Morris *Austral Eng.* 178 *Creek Gum. 1930 Palmer *Men are Human* x. 89 The sun, visible through a gap in the creek-gums, hung fixed in the sky. 1649 *Maryland Hist. Mag.* VIII. 59 We..went along the said *creeke side to the Head thereof. 1751 C. Gist *Jrnls.* 63 Set out down the said Creek Side N 3 M. 1864 B. Taylor *H. Thurston* ii. 30 The great elms by the creek-side had not yet shed all of their tawny leaves. 1836 Edward *Hist. Texas* 36 We find..[the] prairie ..relieved by *creek timbers and solitary groves.

Creek, *sb.*³ [tr. Algonkin *maskoki* creeks.] A North American Indian of the Muskhogean family. The tribe is now settled in Oklahoma.

1741 *Coll. S. Carol. Hist. Soc.* IV. 12 The Creek Indians ..sensible of the Danger approaching, acquainted our Traders..with it. *Ibid.* 20 He had also sent Commissions into the Creek Nation. 1761 *Pennsylvania Gaz.* 1 Oct. 2/3 The French Officers at Albama invited the Creek headman to a talk at that fort. 1775 Adair *Amer. Ind.* 2 A large body of the English Indian traders, on their way to the Choktah country, were escorted by a body of Creek and Choktah warriors. 1789 W. Bartram *Creek & Cherokee Indians* in *Trans. Amer. Ethnol. Soc.* (1853) III. i. 11 The Cricks, or, as they call themselves, Muscoges, or Muscogulges, are a very powerful confederacy. 1792 — (*title*) Travels through North and South Carolina,..the extensive territories of the Muscogulges or Creek confederacy, and the country of the Chactaws. 1828 *Encycl. Metrop.* (1845) XIX. 54/2 The Lower Creek Indians. 1837 *Penny Cycl.* VIII. 146/1 Creek Indians were, at the beginning of the present century, one of the most powerful native tribes within the limits of the United States of America. 1921 *Hist. Amer. Lit.* I. ii. i. 209 Gaily dressed Creeks, quite oriental in appearance.

Creek-bottom. *U.S.* [Creek *sb.*¹ 2 b.] Level ground beside a stream or brook.

1831 Peck *Guide for Emigrants* ii. 91 (*heading*) River and Creek Bottoms. 1857 Olmsted *Journ. Texas* (1861) 81 The soil of the creek-bottoms bears good cotton. 1858 *Texas Alm.* 78 The timber..is chiefly confined to the river and creek bottoms. 1874 Eggleston *Circuit Rider* iv. 45, I will open that crick bottom, and then I shall make some money.

Creeklet. Add: **2.** A small stream, rivulet. (See Creek *sb.*¹ 2 b.) *Colonial.*

1884 Bracken *Lays of Maori* 91 One small creeklet, day by day, murmurs.

Creep, *sb.* Add:

7. *Geol.* (Cf. 3.) A gradual movement of disintegrated rock due to atmospheric changes, water, etc.; the slow displacement of strata or the earth's crust by expansion or contraction, or under compressive strain; more explicitly *continental, crust, tangential creep.*

1903 T. M. Reade *Evol. Earth Structure* ii. 45 The tangential creep and ridging up. *Ibid.* ix. 134 The horizontal expansion..will produce, by small increments and minor alternations, a creep, ending in an anticlinal fold. 1904 tr. *Suess' Face of Earth* I. 115 Those cases of overthrusting which are distinguished from faults under the name of *Wechsel* or *Schlächten* in Germany, and known in England as *creeps.* 1906 Chamberlin & Salisbury *Geol.* III. 312 Continental creep along the steep slope between the continental platforms and the oceanic basins.

8. Of a bar of steel, etc.: A very slow increase in length under excessive stress. Cf. *Creep *v.* 8.

1924 F. C. Lea in *Proc. Inst. Mech. Engin.* II. 1066 At stresses slightly above this the creep was continuous and the bar broke. *Ibid.* 1072 It will thus stand a higher stress without creep. 1928 *Daily Express* 29 June 6 Investigations are being made into the 'creep' in metals.

9. The slip of the belt on the pulley drum, or wheel over which it runs.

1909 W. C. Unwin *Machine Design* I. 448 Creep of belt.

10. A creeping motion between the rim of a wheel and a rubber tyre. Cf. *Creep *v.* 11.

1908 *Westm. Gaz.* 5 Mar. 4/3 The rims of the R. W. wheel allow no creep with a properly inflated tyre.

Creep, *v.* Add:

4. e. Of salts in solution: To rise in crystals upon the sides of the containing vessel.

1900 *Nature* 4 Oct. 562/1 Dr. Tronton gave a short account of his experiments on the creeping of liquids, and on the surface tensions of mixtures. He has found that the tendency of certain liquids to creep up the sides of their containing vessels is due to such liquids being mixtures. 1901 W. R. Cooper *Prim. Batteries* 195 When evaporation of a salt takes place in a glass vessel, crystals form on the vessel near the surface of the solution; and..the crystals grow upwards and finally grow over the top of the vessel. This 'creeping', as it is termed, is avoided in Leclanché cells by dipping the tops of the glass pots into ozokerite or paraffin wax. 1911 T. Mather *Ayrton's Pract. Electr.* 194 Their compactness, portability, freedom from all creeping of the salts.

8. Also, to increase very gradually in length under excessive stress.

1899 J. A. Ewing *Strength Mater.* 24 When a load exceeding the elastic limit is applied the strain which occurs at once is followed by a continued 'creeping' or supplementary deformation. 1911 — in *Encycl. Brit.* XXV. 1014/1 The elastic limit is the point..at which a tendency to creep is first seen. 1924 F. C. Lea in *Proc. Inst. Mech. Eng.* II. 1053 The problem is to find the safe stress at which the material will not change form or creep. *Ibid.* 1072 At 11.40 a.m. on the 11th the specimen had crept 0·2 millimetre, but at 11.40 a.m. on the 14th the creeping had ceased.

10. Of soil, etc.: To be gradually moved or dislocated.

1843 J. Phillips in *Rep. Brit. Assoc.* (1844) 61 This seemed to be the result of a 'creeping' movement of the particles of rock along the planes of cleavage. 1855 — *Man. Geol.* 85 Thus the mica and chlorite which generally meet the surfaces of lamination, appear to have been shouldered about, without being fused, twisted in their structural planes, and subject to that curious minute folding which is often observed as one of the effects of cleavage structure in delicate and pliable shells in slates, for which the term 'creep' was used by the author in 1843.

11. Of a rubber tyre. (Cf. *Creep *sb.* 10.)

1903 *Motoring Ann.* 300 It is claimed for the Collier tyre that it cannot possibly creep. 1908 *Westm. Gaz.* 25 Feb. 4/2, I understand that they have a great tendency to creep.

12. Of a belt or rope: To slip or slide backwards on the pulley. (Cf. *Creep *sb.* 9.)

1922 F. V. Hetzel *Belt Conveyors* 124 A poorly made belt ..will creep more and cause more wear than a good belt.

Creepage (krīˑpėdʒ). [f. Creep *v.* + -age.] Gradual movement.

1903 *Electr. World & Engin.* 7 Nov. 777 (Cent. D. Suppl. s.v. *Oil-thrower*) Special oil throwers are provided to prevent the creepage of oil along the shaft.

Creeper. Add: **2. c.** (Earlier U.S. example.)

1849 D. J. Browne *Amer. Poultry Yd.* (1855) 71 Creepers, so called from the shortness of their legs..are rather to be considered as accidental deformities collected from unhealthy families of Bantams.

11. b. creeper bridge, rope, a bridge or rope of twisted creepers stretched across a tropical river; **creeper chain** *Mining*, an endless chain fitted with grips or hooks for traction of mine-cars, etc.

1892 H. W. Hughes *Coal-mining* 383 No better appliance has been introduced for minimising the cost of conveying tubs about the heapstead than that known as the 'finger' or 'creeper' chain...It consists of an endless chain travelling under the tubs, provided at intervals with vertical projecting pieces of iron fastened to the links. 1894 *Westm. Gaz.* 16 Jan. 5/3 A creeper rope tied from bank to bank. 1909 *Ibid.* 30 Dec. 5/4 We finally managed to get another creeper bridge between the island and the opposite bank, and hauled the women and children to a place of safety.

12. A pupil in the tea-planting trade in Ceylon.

1893 *Field* 8 Apr. 510/3 'Creepers', as they are called, are constantly coming out to learn tea. 1894 *Standard* 2 Jan. 5 A 'creeper', it seems, is the technical term for a pupil whose parents pay a high premium to have him taught the art and mystery of tea-planting in Ceylon. 1921 Ld. F. Hamilton *Here, There & Everywhere* ii. 48 [In Ceylon] Planters are divided locally into three categories: the managers,..the assistants,..and the premium-pupils, known as 'creepers'.

13. *Cricket.* A ball which keeps low after pitching.

1927 *Daily Tel.* 14 June 6/1 A 'creeper' from Larwood got rid of Twining.

Hence **Creeˑpered** *ppl. a.*, having (Virginia) creeper growing on the walls; **Creeˑperless** *a.*, destitute of this ornament.

1894 *Pall Mall Gaz.* 20 July 3/3 Down in the hollow is a glimpse of the creepered farmhouse. 1904 H. G. Wells *Food of Gods* I. ii. § 1 The little house was creeperless. 1906 Galsworthy *Man of Property* I. vii, The creepered trellis round the garden. 1921 — *To Let* III. ix, The moonlight.. fell..on the windows of the creepered house.

Creepie. 2. *U.S.* (Example.)

1871 Schele de Vere *Americanisms* (1872) 380 A tailless fowl is in Pennsylvania called a *bunty*, and a small speckled kind a creepy (S. S. Haldeman).

Creeping, *ppl. a.* Add: **2. a.** Applied to a flaw or crack in steel.

1902 *Daily Chron.* 1 May 6/3 From an examination of the broken parts a 'creeping' flaw was found in the cross-section. 1914 H. Brearly *Case-hardening Steel* 110 Such cracks, generally spoken of as 'creeping cracks', are not often found in brittle material.

b. *Creeping Jesus*, a person who slinks about or hides himself from fear of being ill-treated. *slang.*

c 1818 Blake *Everlasting Gospel* Wks. (1927) 137 If he [*sc.* Christ] had been Antichrist, Creeping Jesus, He'd have done any thing to please us. 1827 — *Lett.* Ibid. 1138 God keep you and me from the divinity of yes and no too—the yea, nay, creeping Jesus. 1871 Pulman *Rustic Sketches* (ed. 3) 88 Creeping-jesus, applied to a person who seeks to hide himself in pursuit of sport or otherwise. 'Jack crawled ääder the weeld ducks lik' a creeping-jesus'.

c. *Creeping barrage* (Mil.): see *Barrage and add quot.

1919 G. K. Rose *2/4th Oxf. & Bucks Lt. Infty.* 129 Our methods of attack..consisted, broadly speaking, in the advance of lines of Infantry behind a creeping barrage.

d. *Creeping paralysis*: locomotor ataxia. Also *fig.*

1913 Dorland *Med. Dict.* (ed. 7) s.v. *Paralysis.* 1926 W. Deeping *Sorrell & Son* I. iii. 11 He remembered that he had won his M.C. by 'doing something' as a protest against the creeping paralysis of intense fear.

Creepy-crawly, *a.* Add: Also *transf.* and *fig.* Sneaking, servile; (of feelings, etc.) full of eerie or uncanny suggestion. Also as *sb. pl.* A creepy-crawly feeling.

1891 Lucas Malet *Wages of Sin* VII. iii, I'm ever so hungry, and there's cold creepy-crawlies running up my legs. 1902 *Daily Chron.* 5 Dec. 4/5 The creepy-crawly atmosphere of 'Wuthering Heights'. 1907 *Ibid.* 1 Apr. 4/4 His way is mostly the creepy-crawly way...There's nothing heroic, or splendid, or even dignified, about his methods.

Crème (krẽm, krɛˑm). Also **crême.** [Fr., = Cream *sb.*²]

1. A name for various syrupy liqueurs, as *crème de menthe* (peppermint), *crème de vanille, crème de noyau.* (Cf. Cream *sb.*² 2 e.)

1892 *Encycl. Pract. Cookery* (ed. T. F. Garrett) I. 477/1 *Crêmes*, a French term applied to certain cordials and liqueurs, to indicate the cream-like smoothness of these manufactures. 1899 *Cassell's Dict. Cookery* 382/2 Noyau, or Crême de Noyau, is a sweet cordial flavoured with bitter almonds. 1903 *Daily Mail* 11 Sept. 3/3 Crême de menthe, with its strong peppermint flavour, is the one almost exclusively favoured by ladies.

2. Meat, fish, or vegetables, baked in white sauce and covered with bread-crumbs.

[1901 C. H. Senn *New Cent. Cookery Bk.* 307 Petites Crêmes de Veau à l' Ecarlate.]

3. Phr. *Crème de la crème*, the élite, the very pick of society.

1860 *Once a Week* 28 July 119/2 The elders—the *crème de la crème*, or those initiated into the highest mysteries of the sect. 1867 S. W. Baker *Nile Tribut.* xvii. 451 The society in this district was not *crême de la crême.* 1898 Farjeon *Miriam Rozella* xi, Need I say that he and Lady Laverock move in the best society, and are *crême de la crême?*

Cremnophobia (kremnofōu·biă). *Path.* [mod. L., f. Gr. κρημνός overhanging cliff: see -phobia.] Morbid dread of precipices or steep places.

1903 Dorland *Med. Dict.* (ed. 3).

Creodonta (kriodǫ·ntă), *sb. pl.* [mod.L., f. Gr. κρέας flesh + ὀδοντ-, ὀδούς tooth.] A group of extinct carnivorous mammals, whose remains are found in the Eocene and Miocene. Anglicized **Creodont** (krīˑodǫnt), *sb.* and *a.*

1883 W. H. Flower in *Encycl. Brit.* XV. 442/1 The suborder *Creodonta.* 1891 Flower & Lydekker *Mammals* 607 The more typical Creodonts appear..to be..closely related to the true Carnivora. 1903 H. Johnston *Brit. Mammals* 115 *note*, No Creodont..has ever been discovered which possessed more than three true molars. *Ibid.* 188 The Creodont Carnivores.

Creolism. Delete *Obs.* and add quot.

1893 *Athenæum* 7 Oct. 484/1 Though he had been born in Misiones (Paraguay), yet, as the son of a lieutenant-governor of a department and removed to Spain at an early age, he did not suffer from the disabilities of creolism.

Creolized (krīˑǝlaizd), *ppl.a.* [-ed¹.] Naturalized in the West Indies.

1880 Cable *Grandissimes* iii. 20 The most thoroughly Creolized Américain.

Creosotal (krīosōuˑtăl). [f. Creosote *sb.* + -al.] A mixture of phenol carbonates prepared from creosote, used as an internal antiseptic.

1899 *Nature* 15 June 154/2 The treatment of phthisis by guiacol carbonate and creosotal. 1910 *Encycl. Brit.* VII. 410/1 In phthisis creosote is now superseded by both its carbonate (creosotal)..and by guiacol itself. 1928 Kingzett *Chem. Encycl.* (ed. 4), *Creosote Carbonate* (also known under the commercial name of 'creosotal').

Creosote, *sb.* **2.** Add: **creosote-plant** (earlier U.S. example).

1854 J. R. Bartlett *Personal Narr.* I. iv. 94 Rosin wood, or creosote plant, a most disgusting, strong-smelling shrub.

Crêpe, *sb.* Add examples of more recent fabrics.

1907 *Daily Chron.* 15 July 8/4 The crêpe de soie..is of the plainer kind, without a printed border. 1923 *Weekly Dispatch* 11 Feb. 15 This dinner gown of amber crepe Romain. 1923 *Daily Mail* 14 Feb. 6 A very pretty gown of blue crêpe romaine. *Ibid.* 19 Apr. 8 The bride's gown was of white crêpe perle. 1925 *Good Housekeeping* Apr. 142/3 The crêpe twist [of acetate silk]. 1928 *Sunday Express* 8 July 3 Crepe malika, a lovely material,..is one of the few innovations which are finding favour with the most important dress artists.

2. In full *crêpe rubber*: Indiarubber rolled into thin sheets with a corrugated surface.

1907 *Brit. Trade Jrnl.* 1 Sept. in W. H. Johnson *Para Rubber* (1909) 117 After the crêpe rubber has left the vacuum drier. *Ibid.* 118 The first packing of the crêpe in the box. 1909 W. H. Johnson *Para Rubber* (ed. 2) 114 The manufacture of crêpe rubber..consists in passing the freshly coagulated rubber through a washing machine. 1914 H. Brown *Rubber* 75 The corrugated sheet known as crêpe... The crêpe rubber, after drying, is sometimes converted into blocks by submitting it to pressure in steel moulds.

3. *Comb.*: **crêpe paper,** a thin crinkled paper resembling crêpe.

1915 *Chemists' Windows* 27 Crêpe paper or plain stiff materials have enough 'body' to remain in pleat.

Crêpeline (krēˑpalīn). Also **crepoline.** [Fr., dim. of *crêpe* Crêpe.] A light thin material of silk or silk and wool used for women's dresses.

1882 Caulfeild & Saward *Dict. Needlework* 93/2 *Crêpeline, Crêpon*, or *Crape Cloth*, a dress material, having a silken surface, much resembling crape, but considerably thicker. 1898 *Daily News* 10 Dec. 6/3 Another novelty is crêpoline cloth,..as soft as cashmere. 1909 *Westm. Gaz.* 9 Oct. 15/1 Crêpolines, silk combined with wool.

Crépinette (krēpineˑt). [Fr., dim. of *crépine*: see Crepine 2.] Minced meat with sauce or farce, wrapped in pieces of pork caul.

1907 Escoffier *Mod. Cookery* 462 Shape the *crépinettes* thus formed rectangularly. 1911 *Francatelli's Mod. Cook* 331 Crepinettes of Partridge à la d'Estaing. 1926 *Mrs. Marshall's Cookery Bk.* 142 Brush over the crépinettes with a little warm thin glaze.

Crêping (krēˑpiŋ), *vbl. sb.*

1. The crimping or frizzing of hair.

1889 *Daily News* 30 Dec. 6/6 The mistake of too tightly crimping—or, to use the new word, crêping—the hair.

2. The production of crêpe rubber.

1909 W. H. Johnson *Para Rubber* (ed. 2) 123 A large size pair of breaking-up and crêping machines.

Crepis (krīˑpis). [L. *crēpis*, a. Gr. κρηπίς base, foundation, the plant ox-tongue.]

1. *Bot.* A plant of the cichoraceous genus so named, the cultivated species of which have pink, white, light-purple, or orange flowers.

1822 Loudon *Encycl. Gardening* (1824) Gen. Index, Crepis, ..of easy culture. 1904 R. J. Farrer *Garden Asia* 246 Twinkling gold of crepis. 1919 — *Engl. Rock-Garden* I. 243 No Crepis is worthy of admission to the rock-garden..except the following: *C. incisa..; C. rubra..;* and *C. lagoseris.*

2. *Biol.* A sponge-spicule forming the central axis of a desma.

1909 E. A. Minchin *Sponges* 134 Each desma is formed typically by secondary deposits of silica upon a true spicule termed the *crepis* or foundation.

Cresceˑndo, *v.* [f. the sb.] *intr.* To increase gradually in loudness or intensity.

1900 *Westm. Gaz.* 2 July 2/1 A faint whir crescendoes rapidly into the shrill whoop of a steam-siren. 1901 *Ibid.* 12 Nov. 2/1 The trolly-cars, with their booming note which crescendoes up the scale with increasing speed and diminuendoes with the slackening of it. 1903 R. Langbridge *Flame & Flood* xvi, A bubbling torrent of vituperation that crescendoed as she leapt in air..and decrescendoed, as.. she turned away. 1927 *Daily Express* 24 Oct. 10/3 'The season'..starts in November, crescendoes to its height in January and February, to die away in April.

Crescent, *sb.* **6.** Add:

More fully, *crescent bun, roll.* (Cf. *Croissant.)

1899 *Daily News* 23 Sept. 3/1 Crescent rolls and hot milk.

Crescent, *a.* Add:

2. b. *The Crescent City*, New Orleans. Hence *Crescent citizen*, a native of New Orleans. *U.S.*

Crescent City of the Northwest, Galena in Illinois (De Vere *Amer.* 663).

1835 J. H. Ingraham *South-West* I. 91, I have termed New Orleans the Crescent city,..from its being built around the segment of a circle formed by a graceful curve of the river. 1851 A. O. Hall *Manhattaner in N. Orleans* 64 Your true-blooded Crescent citizen. 1854 Mayne Reid *Hunters' Feast* i. 7 Most of them were the annual birds of passage from New Orleans,..sojourning here till the cold frosty winds of November should drive that intruder [*sc.* yellow fever] from the 'crescent city'. 1890 *Congress. Rec.* 27 May 5349/1 That majestic inland sea, whose importance..gives to the 'Crescent City' the second position in the list of export cities of the western hemisphere. 1909 *Springfield Weekly Republ.* 11 Mar. 1 He never was in New Orleans, and..the president was in the Crescent City about a month ago.

Crescograph (kreˑskǒgraf). [Badly f. L. *cresc-ĕre* to grow + -o- + -graph.] An instrument invented by Sir Jagadis Chunder Bose for recording the rate of growth in plants.

1917 J. C. Bose in *Proc. R. Soc.* B. (1919) XC. 364 The High Magnification Crescograph. 1918–19 — *Life Movements in Plants* I–II. 157 High Magnification Crescograph. *Ibid.* 169 Magnetic Crescograph. *Ibid.* 255 Balanced Crescograph.

Cress (kres), *v.* [Cf. *cress*, var. Crease *v.*²] *trans.* To raise a rib on (an edge tool). Hence **Creˑsser,** an operative who does this. So **Cressed** *ppl. a.*, (of a metal tube) reduced slightly in diameter at the end.

1921 *Dict. Occup. Terms* (1927) § 254.

Creˑstedness. [f. Crested *a.*] The property of having a crest.

1849 D. J. Browne *Amer. Poultry Yd.* (1855) 57 The hens, too, vary in their degree of crestedness, some not having above half a dozen feathers in their head dress.

Crestless, *a.* Add:

2. *gen.* Without a tuft, top, ridge, or the like.

1908 A. S. M. Hutchinson *Once Aboard the Lugger* I. ii. 33 It welled, rose deeply;..crestless, flinging no intoxicating spume. 1908 *Daily Chron.* 31 Aug. 7/2 Great shiny blue crestless jays flitted over the scrub.

Cretaceous, *a.* Add: **B.** *sb.* (with *the*). *Geol.* The Cretaceous system or period.

1906 Chamberlin & Salisbury *Geol.* III. 160 In the Black Hills, the Cretaceous has in some places a thickness of no more than 1000 feet. *Ibid.* 162 The Appalachian mountains, ..which had been reduced to a peneplain by the close of the Cretaceous. 1910 *Encycl. Brit.* VII. 415/1 There is a very general unconformity and break between the Lower and Upper Cretaceous. *Ibid.*, With the opening of the Cretaceous in Europe there commenced a period of marine transgression.

Cretacic (krītæˑsik), *a.* and *sb. Geol.* = Cretaceous *a.* and *sb.

1887 *Amer. Naturalist* XXI. 449 Total thickness of the Cretacic of the West, about four thousand nine hundred feet.

Cretan (krīˑtăn), *a.* and *sb.* [ad. L. *Crētānus.* The forms used in the various translations of the Bible are, in Acts ii. 11 *Cretes* (Geneva and A.V.), in Titus i. 12 *Cretayns* (Tindale and Coverdale), *Cretyans* (Cranmer), *Cretians* (Geneva and A.V.); Rheims and Douay have *Cretensians*, and R.V. *Cretans* in both places.] **A.** *adj.* Of or belonging to the island of Crete in the Mediterranean. **B.** *sb.* A native of Crete.

Cretan bull, the bull beloved by Pasiphae. *Cretan carrot*, the plant *Athamanta cretensis*, used in medicine. *Cretan hemp*, bastard hemp.

1596 Shaks. *Tam. Shrew* I. i. 175 When with his knees he kist the Cretan strond. 1654 Ogilby *Virgil, Bucolicks* v. 24 *note*, That excellent Cretan Archer. *c* 1790 *Encycl. Brit.* (1797) V. 532/2 In order to distinguish the true Cretans from strangers, they were named *Eteocretes.* 1819 Shelley *Peter Bell 3rd* III. xiii, Lunches and snacks so aldermanic..Where reigns a Cretan-tongued panic. 1820 — *Œd. Tyr.* II. ii. 3 What though Cretans old called thee City-crested Cybele? 1821 Campbell (*title*) Song of Hybrias the Cretan. 1841 De Quincey *Homer & Homeridæ* Wks. 1863 V. 325 A Cretan mountaineer. *Ibid.* 327 Identifying Homer himself as in some measure a Cretan by his habits of life. 1874 Hardy *Far fr. Mad. Crowd* xxv, He was perfectly truthful toward men, but to woman lied like a Cretan. 1915 *Edin. Rev.* Jan. 127 Compare the Cretan and Dionysiac Oreibasiai or Mountain-Rites.

Cretin. Add: Also *transf.* (see quots.).

1922 R. C. Punnett *Mendelism* 79 One of the best-pedigreed of all sports is the 'cretin' sweet-pea, a monstrous form so called from its fancied resemblance to a gaping mouth with a protruding tongue. *Ibid.* 124 Again there is a peculiar monstrous form of flower known as the cretin.. which is recessive to the normal flower.

Cretinoid (krīˑtinoid), *a.* [See -oid.] Resembling a cretin or cretinism.

1873 Sir W. Gull in *Trans. Clin. Soc.* (1874) VII. 180 (*title*) On a Cretinoid State supervening in Adult Life in Women. 1886 *Buck's Handbk. Med. Sci.* II. 20 Myxœdema..Cretinoid disease.

Creusot (krözo). A gun made by the Schneider Company at Le Creusot, Saône-et-Loire, France.

1899 *Daily News* 11 Dec. 7/7 Putting one big Creusot and one Howitzer out of action. 1901 'Linesman' *Words Eyewitness* (1902) 99 A 96-pounder Creusot gun...The Creusot and the pom-pom.

Crevasse, *sb.* **2.** *U.S.* Add earlier example. Also *fig.*

1812 Brackenridge *Views Louisiana* (1814) 179 The terrors excited by a *crevasse* or breaking of the levee. 1879 G. W. Cable *Old Creole Days* (1905) 104 The Anglo-American flood that was presently to burst in a crevasse of immigration upon the delta.

Crèvecœur (krẹvkör). [Fr., = break-heart.] A variety (usually black) of the domestic fowl of French origin, resembling the houdan in body, but characterized by a comb consisting of two large coral-red horns. Also abbrev. **Crève** (crève).

1855 *Poultry Chron.* III. 285 The Crèvecœur fowls. *Ibid.* 286 The Crèvecœurs exhibited at Baker Street. 1872–4 L. Wright *Bk. Poultry* 415 The Crève is the bulkiest in appearance of all the French races. 1883 *Daily News* 3 Oct. 2/2 The pretty Houdans and Crèvecœurs. 1904 S. W. Thomas in *L. Wright's Bk. Poultry* (ed. Ludlow) 452/1 The spiral crest is gone, and so is the Crève comb. *Ibid.* 456/1 The very finest Crèves even now attain greater size than the largest Houdans.

Crevette (kraveˑt). [Fr., = shrimp.] A deep shade of pink, shrimp-pink.

1884 *Cassell's Fam. Mag.* May 371/1 Blues, greens.. salmon-pink, and the deeper crevette, or shrimp-pink. 1890 *Daily News* 5 July 3/4 Costumes of the colours known as crevette and eau-de-Nil.

Crevicing (kreˑvisiŋ), *vbl. sb.* (See quots. and Crevice *sb.* 1 b.) Also *attrib.*

1876 Joaquin Miller *First Families* xv. 127 A lot of picks and pans, and tom irons, and crevicing spoons, that lay up against the wall. 1886 Anderson *Prospector's Handbook* 117 Crevicing—Collecting gold in the crevices of rock. 1888 C. D. Ferguson *Exp. Forty-niner* ix. 129 It was all crevicing, that is, working the crevices in the rocks.

Criant (krəiˑănt, ‖kriaṅ), *a.* [a. F. *criant* crying, loud, pr. pple. of *crier* to Cry.] 'Loud', garish.

1876 'Ouida' *Winter City* i, A *criant* bit of furniture hurt her as the grating of a false quantity hurts a scholar. 1884 *Tablet* 805/1 (Stanf.) There is nothing garish or *criant* in either of these canvases.

Criard (krəiˑăɹd, ‖kriar). [Fr.] = prec.

1924 *Blackw. Mag.* June 774/1 Man and label were equally *criard.* *Ibid.* Aug. 237/1 The palace furniture was equally *criard.*

Crib, *sb.* Add:

10. b. The enclosure for trapped fish in a pound-net. *U.S.*

1873 *Rep. U.S. Fish Commission* I. 264 The pound-nets.. have several parts, termed the 'leader', the 'heart', the 'pot', 'bowl', or 'crib', and the 'tunnel'. 1884 Knight *Dict. Mech.* Suppl., *Crib* (Fishing), the bowl or pound of a Pound Net.

14. *U.S.* (Earlier example.)

1776 C. Carroll *Jrnl.* (1845) 47 The smaller rafts are called *cribs.*

20. crib-bite *v.*, to have the practice or habit of crib-biting; **crib-breakwater** *U.S.*, a breakwater made of cribwork; **crib-bridge,** a bridge whose piers are formed of cribs (see Crib *sb.* 13); **crib-cracker** *slang*, a burglar (see Crib *sb.* 3 b); **crib-dam** *U.S.*, a dam formed of cribs; **crib-muzzle,** a muzzle worn by a horse to prevent crib-biting.

1844 H. Stephens *Bk. Farm* II. 229 He continued to *crib-bite or wind-suck in spite of it. 1879 *Rep. Chief of Engineers, U.S. Army* II. 1588 (Knight) *Crib breakwater. 1899 *Westm. Gaz.* 8 Dec. 2/1 What military engineers call a '*crib' bridge. 1879 *Punch* 3 May 201/1 A bludgeon as big As a *crib-cracker's nobby persuader. 1883 G. R. Sims *How the Poor Live* ii, His talents as a 'cribcracker' and his adventures as a pickpocket. 1906 *Daily Chron.* 5 Dec. 6/6 The house is adequately protected against burglars and is proof against the amateur crib-cracker. 1852 *Punch* 9 Oct. 161/1 He..From cly-faking to *crib-cracking turned. 1877 *Rep. Chief of Ordnance, U.S.A.* 354 (Knight) *Crib dam. 1884 Knight *Dict. Mech.* Suppl., *Crib Muzzle* (Manége), a muzzle used to correct the equine habit of cribbing.

Crib, *v.* Add:

2. c. To place (Indian corn) in a crib. *U.S.*

1745 Macsparran *Diary* 41 Harry finished cribbing ye corn. 1779 *Narrag. Hist. Reg.* I. 95 Cribbed our corn. 1831 Peck *Guide for Emigrants* II. 151 The value of the crop, then, before it is cribbed, is one hundred and twenty-five dollars. 1874 Eggleston *Circuit Rider* i. 17 Now, boys, crib your corn.

Cribellum (kribeˑlǒm). *Zool.* [L. *cribellum*, dim. of *cribrum* sieve.] An additional spinning organ, having numerous fine pores, situated in front of the spinnerets in certain spiders. Also **Criˑbellated** *a.*, having a cribellum.

1888 Rolleston & Jackson *Forms Anim. Life* 524 *note*, In a few Spiders a chitinoid plate, the cribellum, lies in front of the spinnerets. 1926 T. H. Savory *Brit. Spiders* 97 The British cribellated spiders.

Cribo (krəiˑbo, kriˑbo). [Native name.] A large West Indian snake, *Spilotes corais.*

1871 Kingsley *At Last* ii, This snake..has no power against another West Indian snake, almost equally common, namely, the Cribo. 1918 W. H. Hudson *Far Away* xii. 176 The Cribo of Martinique..kills and swallows the deadly fer-de-lance.

Crichton (krəiˑtən). The surname of James *Crichton* of Clunie (1560–85?), a Scottish prodigy of intellectual and knightly accomplishments; qualified by *admirable*, it is used allusively for any man who excels in all kinds of studies and pursuits. Hence *Admirable Crichtonism*; also *Crichtoˑnian* adj.

The epithet which became traditional was first applied in Johnstone's *Heroes Scoti* (1603) 41 Iacobus Critonius Clunius, Musarum pariter ac Martis alumnus, omnibus in studiis, ipsis etiam Italis admirabilis. In English it appeared first in Urquhart's *Jewel* (1652) 112 The admirable Crichtoun..did ..present himself to epilogate this his almost extemporanean Comedie.

1812 T. Amyot *Life of Windham* I. 139 [Windham] was the admirable Crichton of his age and country. *a* 1845 Barham *Ingol. Leg.* Ser. III. *Brothers of Birchington*, Like a small boy at Eton, Who's not quite a Crichton. 1889 *Blackw. Mag.* CXLVI. 707/1 The..endless resource and Admirable Crichtonism of Robert Hazel. 1890 *Punch* 11 Jan. 15/2 *Algy*...You lucky dog, you possess all the accomplishments I lack! *Jim*...Oh, nonsense! Why, you're making me out a regular *Crichton!* 1900 *Academy* 3 Feb. 99/2 Matthew, the self-taught, listening intelligently to a German song while he is swimming, is a little too Crichtonian.

Cricket, *sb.*² Add:

1. b. Used allusively for: Fair play, honourable dealings with opponents and rivals. *To play cricket*: to act fairly, to play the game. *Not cricket*: not playing the game; not fair, straight, honourable, or sporting.

1900 *Westm. Gaz.* 5 June 2/2 We should be very much surprised if the Duke really thought that to dissolve would be 'cricket'. *Ibid.* 31 July 1/3 We believe that the feeling is very widespread that it would not be 'cricket' to get back to power again as the result of an appeal to the country. 1911 W. De Morgan *Likely Story* 313 It is scarcely fair play to make a merit of patience—isn't cricket, as folk say nowadays. 1922 *Daily Mail* 14 Nov. 10, I appeal to the Conservatives to do what is patriotic and honourable and to play 'cricket'. 1930 Van Dine *Scarab Murder* 20 It didn't seem cricket to leave the poor devil there.

Crickle (kriˑk'l), *v.* [Echoic.] *intr.* To make a sharp, thin sound; to make a succession of sharp sounds. Hence **Criˑckle** *sb.*

1883 Stallybrass tr. *Grimm's Teut. Myth.* III. 929 You hear him [*sc.* the wild hunter] bluster in the air, so that it 'crickles and crackles'. 1926 *U. F. Ch. Mission Rec.* Aug. 361/1 There ran a crickle of wind in the thatch.

Crickle-crackle. Delete †*Obs.* and add:

1914 W. J. Locke *Fortunate Youth* xiii, I like to feel that He's in the wind or in the crickle-crackle of the earth.

Cri de cœur (kridkör). [Fr., = 'cry of heart'.] An utterance of distress or anguish.

1930 *John o' London's Weekly* 15 Mar. 919 From first to last it is a *cri de cœur.* 1930 *Punch* 23 Apr. 450 Until I read the *cri de cœur* from Soviet Russia..I had not realized how difficult it must be in a Communistic country..to advertise.

Crime, *sb.* **4.** Add: **crime sheet,** in the army, a list in which the names of offenders and their offences are entered.

1915 D. O. Barnett *Lett.* 41 Spent the morning filling up 'crime sheets' with all their offences. 1917 Empey *From Fire Step* 150 The Sergeant-Major keeps what is known as the Crime Sheet. When a man commits an offence, he is 'Crimed'—that is, his name, number, and offence is entered on the Crime Sheet.

Crime, *v.* Delete *rare* and add: Now in army use.

1917 [see prec.]. 1929 C. E. Montague in *Mercury Story Bk.* 178 You know, Sergeant, the sort of a squadroon it is where a man's never crimed.

Crimean (krəimīˑăn), *a.* [f. *Crimea*, name of a peninsula lying between the Sea of Azov and the Black Sea, the chief seat of a war (1854–6)

between Russia and Turkey (with its allies).] *Crimean shirt*, a shirt worn by colonials in the Australian bush.

1895 'R. Boldrewood' *Crooked Stick* iii. 80 A young man, whose Crimean shirt and absence of necktie denoted..the presumed abandon of bush life. 1927 Bennett *Christison* x. 110 Christison gave Mickey a Crimean shirt.

Crimes (krəimz), *int.* Later modification of Crimine.

1874 *Slang Dict.* s.v. *Crikey.* 1891 Farmer *Slang*, Crimini, Criminey, or Crimes. 1929 Raymond *Family that was* II. ii, Crimes! I'm moving in the Upper Ten, I think.

Criminaloid (kriˑminăloid). [f. Criminal *sb.* + -oid.] A man with a tendency towards crime; a first offender as opposed to a habitual criminal.

1895 Lombroso *Female Offender* 308 A middle type between criminaloids and born criminals. 1909 *Westm. Gaz.* 5 Jan. 2/1 The common incarceration of offenders manufactures the criminal out of the juvenile, the criminaloid and the single offender.

Crimmer: see *Krimmer.

Crimp, *sb.*³ Add: **1. b.** A fold or crease. Also *collect. U.S.*

1874 *Rep. Vermont Board Agric.* II. 410 Fineness of fiber can be judged by its appearance to the eye, by its feeling when touched and by its fineness of crimp. *Ibid.* 411 Style of wool is judged by its crimp; the number of crimps to an inch of very fine wool is from twenty-seven to twenty-nine. 1922 Sandburg *Slabs Sunburnt West* 10 If these bother respectable people with the right crimp in their napkins..forgive us.

c. *To put a crimp in* or *into*: to do something to thwart or block. *U.S. slang.*

1896 G. Ade *Artie* xii. 106 They'll put a crimp in him if things come their way. 1911 H. S. Harrison *Queed* xxv. 321 They never forgive a man who puts a crimp into the party. 1918 *Nation* (N.Y.) 7 Feb. 166/1 All plans passed through their hands, and they took particular pleasure in putting a crimp into the Fire God. *fig.* 1919 H. L. Wilson *Ma Pettengill* viii. 256 It put a crimp into his sunny nature—all this armed pursuit of him.

Crimp, *a.* Add: **3. b.** (See quot.)

1904 *Technol. & Sci. Dict.* (ed. Goodchild & Tweney), *Crimp Cloth*, a form of cotton weaving in which longitudinal sections of the cloth are uniformly crimped or crinkled purposely.

Crimper¹. **2. c.** (Earlier example.)

1877 Eliz. S. Phelps *Story of Avis* ii. 31, I think I could have patented a crimper that would make a simpler system of punctuation in your finger than this.

Crimping, *vbl. sb.*¹ **3.** Add: *Crimping board.*

1837 W. Jenkins *Ohio Gaz.* 158 A last factory, producing 14,000 lasts, 200 boot trees, and 200 crimping boards per annum.

Crimple, *sb.* Substitute Now *dial.* and *U.S.* for *Obs.* and add:

1862 C. C. Robinson *Dial. Leeds* 278 Where the breadth of muslin was narrow the 'crimple' was made by means of a penknife and the thumb. 1881 McLean *Cape Cod Folks* vi. 131 Teacher,..how shiny those crimples in your hair look, with that streak of sun lighting on 'em!

Crimpy (kriˑmpi), *a.* [f. Crimp *a.* or *v.*¹ + -y¹.] Having a crimped appearance, frizzy.

1888 [see Crimp *sb.*³ 1 in Dict.]. 1894 *Daily News* 24 July 5/7 The special petroleum wash dried more quickly..and left the hair more crimpy.

Crimsony (kriˑmzəni), *a.* [f. Crimson *a.* + -y¹.] Somewhat crimson, resembling crimson.

1844 *Florist's Jrnl.* (1846) V. 17 The crimsony scarlet. 1905 Holman Hunt *Pre-Raph.* II. 70 With a crimsony lustre. 1909 Margaret B. Saunders *Litany Lane* I. vi, The dim crimsony browns, the curious blue-greens.

Crin (krin, ‖kræṅ). [Fr., = horsehair.] A fabric made from horsehair alone or combined with vegetable fibre. *Crin végétal*, a substitute for horsehair made from the fibre of the European and North African fan-palm, *Chamærops humilis.*

[1858 Simmonds *Dict. Trade, Crin*, the French name for horsehair.] 1875 *Encycl. Brit.* I. 565/1 The most important fibre is the *crin vegetal*, or vegetable horse hair, produced from the dwarf palm (*Chamærops humilis*), with which a vast portion of the uncultivated parts of the country [*sc.* Algeria] is covered. 1900 *Daily News* 9 June 6/6 The crin or horsehair (sometimes called crinoline) hat is poetic enough. 1900 *Traveller* 4 Aug. 112/2 A big floppy crin hat, trimmed with..black lace. 1909 *Westm. Gaz.* 3 June 8/3 There is a large hat of black crin. 1923 *Daily Mail* 9 Feb. 11 A similar shape of blue crin straw and satin ribbon.

Crinkled, *ppl. a.* Add: **crinkled (tissue) paper,** paper crinkled lengthwise, made in various colours, used for making paper flowers and for decorative purposes.

1895 *Army & Navy Co-op. Soc. Price List* 526 Crinkled tissue paper. For making Fancy Lamp Shades. 1921 *Dict. Occup. Terms* (1927) § 559 Crinkled paper machine operator.

Criˑnkle-root. *U.S.* The two-leaved pepperwort, *Dentaria diphylla.*

1889 *Century Dict.* 1899 Van Dyke *Fisherman's Luck* iv. 74 Crinkle-root is spicy, but you must partake of it delicately, or it will bite your tongue.

Crinkliness (kriˑŋklinės). [f. Crinkly *a.* + -ness.] Crinkly condition.

1927 R. A. Freeman *Certain Dr. Thorndyke* II. xv, Mr. Wamploe's advice produced on Polton's countenance a smile of most extraordinary crinkliness.

Crinkly, *a.* Add: **b.** Characterized by a succession of crinkling sounds.

1827 J. Wilson *Noctes Ambr.* Wks. 1855 I. 330 Does my voice come from my heart in a crinkly cough, as if the lungs were rotten? 1911 Hugh Walpole *Mr. Perrin* iii, The white, crinkly sound of the silk of her dress against the table.

Crio-. Add: **Criˑophore,** a statue or other representation of a figure carrying a ram. So **Crioˑphorous** *a.*

1921 G. A. F. Knight *Nile & Jordan* xiii. 160 Criophorous sphinxes lined the avenues of Thebes and other cities.

Criollo (kriǫˑlo). [a. Sp. *criollo* native to the locality: see Creole.] A variety of cacao-bean.

1908 H. H. Smith *Cacao Planting* 39 Strong growing forastero or calabicillo, bearing the finest criollo beans. *Ibid.*, Good buds from pure criollo stocks. 1929 *Encycl. Brit.* V. 947/1 The finest type of bean, the criollo, is grown in Venezuela, Ceylon, Java, Samoa, Madagascar and Nicaragua; but in Ceylon, and other places, criollo is being replaced by forastero. *Ibid.* XXIII. 52/1 There are two grades of Venezuelan cacao—the *criollo* or native, and the *trinitario*, or Trinidad.

Cripes (krəips), *int.* Vulgar perversion of Christ in the exclamation *(By) cripes!* (Cf. *Crimes.)

1910 Davis *From Selection to City* xii. 107 'By cripes!' he gasped, 'I've lost th' cheques'. 1920 *Blackw. Mag.* June 775/2 I'd have put him through ut, be cripes. 1924 Galsworthy *White Monkey* I. iii, 'Cripes! Ain't he took bad!' 1929 *Sunday Dispatch* 13 Jan. 2/4 You've sold me a pup! But, by cripes, I'll..let you have it back. 1930 Priestley *Angel Pavement* iv. 177 That's what it was—oh, cripes!—awful hole!

Cripple, *sb.* Add: **3.** *U.S.* (Earlier and later examples.)

1675 *New Jersey Arch.* (1880) I. 115 The great Swamp or Cripple which backs the said two Necks of land. 1678 *New Castle Court Rec.* 305, 800 acres Called the mussel Cripple. 1679 *Ibid.* 286 A small slipe of ground stretching..along the Kripple towards the fence of the Towne Dyche. 1720 *Pennsylvania Col. Rec.* (1852) III. 111 Through the Swamp and Cripple..to Little Hollanders Creek. 1832 J. F. Watson *Tales Olden Times* 57 Through that cripple browsed the deer.

5. cripple-timber, a short timber used in positions where one of the ordinary size would be too long.

1874 Knight *Dict. Mech.*, *Cripple-timber*, studding or scantling used in narrow situations, where they are necessarily shorter than their fellows, as the cripple-studding from the rafters to the floor-joists in attics finished with a collar-beam ceiling. A jack-timber.

6. A cattle disease. *dial.* and *Austral.*

1897 *Penrith Obs.* 7 Dec. (E.D.D.) Ass t'coo doctor what ails a coo when it'll eat a body's kytle, er owt else but gerse—that's cripple. 1929 *Times* 1 July 15/6 Lack of minerals in pastures causes innumerable diseases, such as..'cripples' ..in Australia.

Cripplingly (kriˑpliŋli), *adv.* [f. Crippling *ppl. a.* + -ly².] So as to cripple or disable.

1899 *Daily News* 18 Feb. 6/3 The new skirts are very long, cripplingly so. 1927 *Daily Express* 4 Nov. 3/4 Be teetotal! From the point of view of human society the case is unanswerable. The damage, the cost, the contamination are cripplingly unbearable.

Crisp, *sb.*¹ Delete †*Obs.* and add:

6. A banknote or banknotes. *slang.*

a 1889 *Modern Society* (Barrère & Leland), He..cashed a cheque for £100 and handed over the crisp.

7. An overdone piece of anything fried or roasted. Usually in phr. *to a crisp.*

1872 'Mark Twain' *Sketches* 215 Not just frizzled up a bit, but literally roasted to a crisp! 1899 Morrow *Bohem. Paris* 44 It was sometime before Haidon could realize that he was not burned to a crisp. 1911 H. S. Harrison *Queed* xxi. 258, I became absorbed in a book I was reading, and Jim came back to find the bacon a crisp.

8. *pl.* Fried and dried slivers of potato (done up in a packet).

1929 *Star* 21 Aug. 13/3 Potato Crisp Factory.

Crisp, *v.* Add:

1. b. To fold (cloth) which has just been woven.

1892 in *Eng. Dial. Dict.* 1927 *Daily Tel.* 21 June 8 The cloth may be crisped (folded lengthwise), rolled or lapped.

Crispi-, comb. form of L. *crispus* Crisp *a.*, as in **Crispifloˑral** *a.*, having curled flowers; **Crispifoˑlious** *a.*, having curled leaves. (B. D. Jackson 1900.)

Criss (kris). [Variant form of w. midl. dial. *cress*, = Crease *sb.*² (sense 3).] The curved top of the stand on which tiles are made.

1881 *Instr. Census Clerks* (1885) 87 Brick, Tile-Maker, Burner, Dealer. Criss Maker. 1921 *Dict. Occup. Terms* (1927) § 474 *Criss maker* (tile making); a carpenter who makes criss.

Criss-cross, *sb.* Add:

2. b. A network of intersecting lines.

1881 C. De Kay *Vision of Nimrod* vii. (Cent. Dict.) The country gleaming With silvery crisscross of canals. 1901 *Daily Express* 28 Aug. 4/6 A great boulevard..hemmed in all round by the criss-cross of narrower streets. 1928 A. Bennett *Vanguard* xxxii. 214 A criss-cross of streets dotted with a thousand towers.

c. *fig.* The state of being at cross-purposes.

1907 *Daily Chron.* 23 Feb. 3/1 The practice of one manufacturing country assisting another with the sinews of war was described by Mr. Zangwill as 'a topsy turvy criss-cross, and Gilbertian'. 1909 *Westm. Gaz.* 20 Sept. 2/3 The absurd criss-cross of the authorities who look after us at play-time.

Crista (kriˑstă). [L., = crest.] A ridge or crest; *spec.* in various anatomical and zoological senses.

1849–50 Weale *Dict. Terms*, *Crista*, a crest; the apex or highest part of a shrine. 1889 *Jrnl. Morph.* III. 300 The crista, a cord-like ridge running the full length of the dorsal surface of the capsule.

Cristobalite (kristobæˑləit). [f. the name of Cerro San *Cristobal*, near Pachuca, Mexico: see -ite¹.] An oxide of silica, SiO_2, occurring in small octahedral crystals.

1888 *Min. Mag.* VIII. 36 A New Mineral. Cristobalite... An analysis..gave 91 per cent. of silica and 6 per cent. of oxide of iron and alumina. 1920 *Brit. Museum Return* 144 Artificial minerals (cristobalite, fayalite, rhodonite, apatite, spinel..) from furnace slags. 1925 J. Joly *Surface-Hist. Earth* iii. 64 Quartz..undergoes an allotropic modification ..at atmospheric pressure. It changes into cristobalite—which is a low-density form of quartz.

Critter, freq. U.S. dial. var. of Creature, q.v. sense 2 b.

1815 D. Humphreys *Yankee in Eng.* 41 Cooking for the crew, and taking care of the dum critturs. 1834 S. Smith *Sel. Lett. Downing* 86 Bears and wolves and such kind of critters. 1852 *Trans. Mich. Agric. Soc.* III. 332 It is a hard matter to make the critters I speak of ever weigh 200 lbs. 1886 *Harper's Mag.* Sept. 582/2 First they wrote home that it was beautiful—climate and critters and everything. 1923 'B. M. Bower' *Parowan Bonanza* vi. 65 She..can sling a pack or rope a critter better than lots of men that draw wages for doing it.

Croak, *v.* Add:

5. b. *trans.* To kill. *dial.* and *U.S. slang.*

1877 F. Ross, etc. *Gloss. Holderness*, *Crooak*,..N. and E., to kill. 1910 E. A. Walcott *Open Door* vii. 83 'I never done it!' he gasped. 'I never hurt nobody. Who's been croaked?' 1923 L. J. Vance *Baroque* xxvii. 173 If that ever got out, sister'd be croaked, and Angelo would get his simultaneous. 1930 *Punch* 26 Feb. 236 It was fairly clear that he had been croaked.

Croat (krōuˑæt). [ad. mod.L. (pl.) *Croatæ* (F. *Croate*, G. *Kroat*), ad. Serbo-Croatian *Hrvat*, formerly pronounced (*χrwát*). Cf. Cravat (from a later variety of pronunciation).] A native of the former Austrian province of Croatia, now forming part of Yugoslavia; one of a race descended from the tribe which occupied that country in the seventh century. **b.** A soldier of a former French cavalry regiment. *Hist.*

1704 *Milit. Dict.* (ed. 2), *Croat*, properly the People of Croatia: but in France there is a Regiment of Horse so call'd...These Croats are commanded upon all desperate Service. 1749 Fielding *Tom Jones* VI. ii, Brother, you are absolutely a perfect Croat; but as those have their Use in the Army of the Empress Queen, so you likewise have some Good in you. *c* 1790 *Encycl. Brit.* V. 555/2 The Croats derive their origin from the Sclavi. 1862 *Chambers's Encycl.* III. 324/2 The Croatians are warlike, but the name Croats is employed to designate light-cavalry regiments in the imperial army, in which Magyars and others are mingled with true Croatians. 1920 H. Fisher *Studies Hist. & Pol.* 207 Croat and Slovene newspapers. 1920 *Edin. Rev.* July 46 Two new divisions formed under ex-Austrian officers, mostly of Croat nationality.

Croatian (kroǭˑʃiăn), *a.* and *sb.* [f. mod.L. *Croatia*, f. *Croatæ*: see prec. and -ian.] **A.** *adj.* Of or belonging to the Croats. **B.** *sb.* **1.** A Croat. **2.** The language of the Croats, belonging to the Balto-Slavic group.

1555 Eden *Decades* (Arb.) 290 The Bohemians, Croatians, and Sclauons. 1837 *Penny Cycl.* VIII. 161/2 The Damascene plum furnishes the favourite drink of the Croatians. *Ibid.*, The Croatian language is a dialect of the Sclavonian. 1885 *Encycl. Brit.* XVIII. 785/1 There are two main branches of Slavonic. The so-called Southern or South-Eastern branch embraces Russian, Ruthenian (in Galicia), Bulgarian, Servian, Croatian, and Slovenian. 1921 *Glasgow Herald* 8 Jan. 6 Their intrigues with the Croatian separatists.

Croc². Colloq. abbreviation of Crocodile.

1921 *Blackw. Mag.* Jan. 102/1 The 'croc' is the one African animal regarding which nobody has any idea of sportsmanship. 1925 *Ibid.* Sept. 419/1 With loud yells to scare away any crocs that might be lurking round.

Croc-chien (krǫʃyæṅ). [Colonial F., f. *croc* fang + *chien* dog.] A West Indian name for any climbing plant of the genus *Desmoncus*, so called from the hooked spines attached to all parts of their leaf-stalks.

1871 Kingsley *At Last* iii, The prickly climbing palm, the Croc-chien, or Hook-dog. *Ibid.*, As the Spanish soldiers ran from the English, one of them was caught in the innumerable hooks of the Croc-chien.

Crochet, *sb.* **2.** Add: *crochet-hook, -pin.*

1849 *Family Friend* I. 78/2 The Penelope Crochet Hook is invented by Mrs. Warren. 1860 *Ladies' Companion* 37 A coarse Crochet Hook. 1881 *Instr. Census Clerks* (1885) 44 Crochet Hook Maker. 1909 *Daily Chron.* 8 Dec. 9/2 By putting the crochet-pin into the upper half of the stitch.

Crocheting (krōuˑʃiˌiŋ), *vbl. sb.* [f. Crochet *v.* + -ing¹.] The making of crochet-work; crochet-work. Also *attrib.*

1883, 1891 [see Crochet *v.*]. 1901 *Daily Chron.* 17 Sept. 7/1 She..at once took up her crocheting. 1921 *Dict. Occup. Terms* (1927) § 375 A crocheting machine to make lace.

Crock, *sb.*³ **3.** Add: Now only, a broken-down or physically debilitated person. *colloq.*

1889 *Illustr. Bits* 13 July (Farmer) I say..you are getting a bit of a crock—failing fast, I should say. 1930 Rose Macaulay *Potterism* IV. iii. 149 Shall we be a race of clever crocks, or..be robust imbeciles?

Crock, *v.*² Add: **c.** To impart colour or dye to other articles, to stain: said also of the colour.

1855 *Knickerbocker Mag.* XLV. 566 A pair of green gloves ..had 'crocked off' very generously to whatever was in contact with them. 1885 A. Watt *Leather Manuf.* 322 The clear colours do not 'crock' so easily, and the little that does come off is hardly noticeable.

Crock, *v.*⁴ [f. Crock *sb.*³ 2, *3.] *intr.* To collapse, give way, break down. Also *trans.*, to cause to collapse. Often with *up.* Hence **Crocked** *ppl. a.*, hurt, damaged, disabled.

1893 *Idler* Mar. 221 An oarsman who is likely to 'crock up'. 1896 *Westm. Gaz.* 12 Dec. 2/1 Smith has crocked his knee. 1900 *Ibid.* 17 Dec. 8/2 The northern player, who is less likely to get 'crocked' than the Richmond man. 1906 *Daily Chron.* 26 Sept. 7/5 He had his knee crocked last season. 1926 *Spectator* 12 June 983/1 Dressing is accomplished quickly considering my crocked-up hand. 1928 *Observer* 19 Feb. 28/6 Slogging home against the present stream would safeguard a crew against crocking later on.

Crocky (krǫˑki), *a.*² [f. Crock *sb.*³ + -y¹.] That is a crock; broken-down, physically enfeebled.

1906 *Westm. Gaz.* 18 Sept. 10/1 Among the parts of a crocky engine. 1907 Conan Doyle *Through Magic Door* 109 The crockiest of spectators had a better chance of life than the magnificent young athlete. 1920 Rose Macaulay *Potterism* IV. iii. 149 Crocky imbeciles.

Crocodile. Add: **1. c.** = *crocodile skin.*

1908 *Daily Chron.* 15 Aug. 3/2 A large crocodile letter-case. 1908 *Westm. Gaz.* 19 Nov. 4/2 All the upholstering is in crocodile.

d. A mechanical appliance with a notched or serrated edge suggestive of the upper jaw of a crocodile: (*a*) used with a builders' crane as a means of attaching the chain (see quot. 1901); (*b*) = *crocodile squeezer.*

1869 (in MS. Note-book). 1884 W. H. Greenwood *Steel & Iron* (ed. 2) 302 The bloom, when finished at the crocodile. 1901 M. Beazeley *Let. to Editor*, The crocodile is used to bring the point of suspension over the centre of gravity of any mass that has to be lifted..when..the lewis-hole cannot be sunk at the centre of gravity.

4. b. Applied to any long procession of moving objects close together.

1928 *Manchester Guardian Weekly* 17 Aug. 136/2 Those roads which, unlike the Brighton and Eastbourne roads, do not carry an endless and snorting crocodile of cars. 1930 Pertwee *Pursuit* I. xi. 55 Transport would pile up before and behind you in a ceaselessly cursing crocodile.

5. *crocodile-like* adj.; **crocodile-bird,** the Egyptian black-headed plover, *Pluvianus ægyptius*, so called from its habit of eating the insect parasites of the crocodile, probably the trochilos of ancient writers; **crocodile shears,** shears used in cutting into lengths and removing the faulty ends of steel or iron bars; **crocodile squeezer,** a machine with a pivoted upper jaw, used in the process of removing impurities from metals by the application of pressure.

1868 A. C. Smith *Attractions Nile* II. 255 *Charadrius spinosus*..in all probability the true '*crocodile bird' or *trochilus* of Herodotus. 1621 in Foster *Engl. Factories Ind.* (1906) 347 These viprous, dessemblinge, and *crockadillike curs. 1897 Anne Page *Afternoon Ride* x, A large iguana, almost crocodile-like in its proportion. 1884 W. H. Greenwood *Steel & Iron* 347 Puddled bars are..sheared hot either by *crocodile or guillotine shears. *Ibid.* 301 The single alligator or *crocodile squeezer has two broad flat jaws. *Ibid.* 302 The crocodile squeezer makes about 60 strokes per minute.

Crocus. 5. Add: *crocus-bed.*

1891 M. O'Rell *Frenchm. Amer.* 60 A..crocus-bed effect.

Crœsus (krīˑsǒs). The Latin form of the name of a king of Lydia (Gr. Κροῖσος) in the sixth century B.C., who was famous for his riches, used allusively in phr., as *Crœsus' wealth, as rich as Crœsus*, and hence typically for: A very rich man.

1650 Trapp *Comm. Prov.* xxx. 8, I shall not envie the richest Crœsus or Crassus upon earth. 1754 H. Walpole *Lett.* (1857) II. 389 A contest between two young Crœsus's, Lord Thanet and Sir James Lowther. 1883 Miss Braddon *Golden Calf* xii, Ida, left alone amidst all the fascinations of the chief shop in a smart county town, and feeling herself a Crœsus.

Crofterize (krǫˑftəraiz), *v.* [f. Crofter¹ + -ize.] *trans.* To convert into a croft-tenancy. So **Crofterizaˑtion.**

1907 *Times* 7 Oct. 9/4 Nor do the Scottish Lowlands.. desire the crofterization of the Lowland counties. 1908 *Ibid.* 11 Mar. 11/5 Amendments which shall not interfere with the crofterizing of the Scottish Lowlands.

Croisette. Delete †*Obs.* and add:

1906 *Daily Chron.* 11 Oct. 3/2 To pay to the Administration, in the form of a tax, a certain number of croisettes—brass rods in the form of a St. Andrew's cross. 1920 A. Stratton *Engl. Interior* 72 French doorways of the Louis XIV. period, with surrounding architraves broken at the top with *croisettes* and surmounted by a frieze.

Croissant (krwasaṅ). [a. F. *croissant*, properly pres. pple. of *croître* (:–L. *crescĕre*) to increase.] = *Crescent *sb.* 6.

1899 Morrow *Bohem. Paris* 139 The odor of hot rolls and croissants. 1928 Rose Macaulay *Keeping up Appearances* i. § 2 Foaming coffee and milk, the crusty roll, the little tender croissant.

Crokerism (krōuˑkəriz'm). [f. the surname *Croker* + -ism.]

1. The political principles of John Wilson Croker (1780–1857).

1851 Carlyle *New Lett.* (1904) II. 114, I was reading in the *Quarterly Review*:—very beggarly Crokerism, all of copperas and gall and human baseness. 1927 *Observer* 9 Oct. 16/4 When Randolph Churchill set out to revive his party, what did he do? He swept away Crokerism.

2. In U.S. politics, the political following and influence of Richard Croker (born 1843), who made himself master (*c* 1888) of the Tammany organization and subsequently attained to great power in the government of the state of New York. Hence **Croˑkerist,** an adherent of Crokerism; also *attrib.*

1897 *Daily News* 4 Nov. 3/4 Evidence..that Crokerism had brought New York to almost the lowest possible point. 1900 *Westm. Gaz.* 27 Oct. 6/2 Mr. Roosevelt..urged.. the killing of Crokerism in the State. 1901 *Daily Chron.* 3 Oct. 5/7 The supporters of Crokerism and corruption..are opposed by the advocates of good government with freedom from bosses. *Ibid.* 1 Nov. 6/3 He will..vote the whole Fusionist 'ticket' or the whole Crokerist 'ticket' as it is offered to him.

Cro-Magnon (kromæˑnyoṅ). [The name of a cave in Dordogne, France, where prehistoric remains were discovered in 1868.] A prehistoric European race of mesolithic or neolithic age, characterized by very large and long heads, low foreheads, very broad face, deep-set eyes, and tall stature.

1868 in Lartet & Christy *Reliq. Aquit.* (1875) 99 The Cro-Magnon race. 1874 *Leisure Hour* 31 Oct. 697 Outline of Cro-Magnon skull as seen in front. 1881 Jas. Geikie *Preh. Eur.* 23 The second race is called by the same anthropologist [*sc.* M. de Quatrefages] the 'Cro-Magnon race'. 1882 *Amer. Antiquarian* Apr.–July 242 Cromagnon skulls in Bavaria. 1900 Ripley *Races Eur.* 173 The Cro-Magnon head. 1912 R. Munro *Palæolithic Man* 200 All the skeletons of the Cro-Magnon type found in the Grimaldi caves. 1927 Haldane & Huxley *Anim. Biol.* xiii. 331 Cromagnon man.

Crombec (krǫˑmbek). [Used in this form by Le Vaillant *Histoire naturelle des oiseaux d'Espagne* 1802; f. Du. *krom* crooked + *bek* Beak *sb.*] A book-name for the South African warbler, *Sylvietta rufescens.*

[1875–84 Layard *Birds S. Afr.* 303 Sylvietta rufescens... The 'Stomp-stertje' of the Dutch colonists, and the 'Crombec' of Le Vaillant.] 1901 Stark & Sclater *Birds S. Afr.* II. 117 Sylviella [*sic*] pallida. The Zambesi Crombec. 1908 Haagner & Ivy *Sk. S. Afr. Bird Life* 80.

Cronk (krǫŋk), *a. Austral. colloq.*, orig. *Racing slang.* [Origin unknown.] Of a horse: Unfit to run in a race, or dishonestly run as though unfit; said also of the race. Hence *gen.* Unsound, liable to collapse; also, obtained by fraud.

1891 Nat. Gould *Double Event* xvii, He'd never ride another 'cronk' race, he vowed. 1892 *Sydney Bulletin* 12 Nov. (Funk) 'Cronk' financial institutions. 1893 *Herald* (Melbourne) 4 July 2/7 (Morris) The word 'cronk', Mr. Finlayson explained, meant 'not honestly come by'. 1900 H. Lawson *On Track* 39 'It's always the way!'..'I knew the beggar would turn up!..And the only cronk log we've had, too!' *Ibid.* 157 Generosity isn't understood nowadays, and what the people don't understand is either 'mad' or 'cronk'.

Crook, *sb.* **13.** For *U.S. colloq.* read *orig. U.S.* and add: Now esp. a professional criminal or an associate of criminals, one who is recognized as belonging to the criminal classes.

1886, 1891 [in Dict.]. 1891 *The Sun* (N.Y.) 19 June 6/4 (Funk) The slang word 'crook' now bids fair to be recognized in the statutes and consequently to be adopted as good English in the courts of law. A bill regulating admissions to the prison at Marquette excludes, among other classes of individuals specified, those known to be 'crooks' in police parlance. 1896 *Westm. Gaz.* 17 July 2/1 A crook what kep a little crib Dad went to when things was too lively. 1903 *Daily Chron.* 3 Nov. 5/4 All the saloon-keepers, and gamblers, and crooks, and confidence men, in fact all the predatory elements of society are..working for a Tammany victory. 1909 *Ibid.* 19 June 3/2 The people here..are clever and rather interesting scamps. Were they on a slightly lower social level they would be called 'crooks'.

B. *adj.* Crooked, dishonest.

1929 Martindale *Risen Sun* 173 When sport goes crook, what can remain wholesome?

Hence **Crooˑkdom,** the realm of crooks.

1921 *Glasgow Herald* 23 Apr. 4 The brilliant amateur investigator, whose uncanny intuition and superman brain have paralysed the ranks of 'crookdom'. 1929 *Daily Express* 7 Jan. 9 Story of a careless young athlete's adventures in crookdom.

Crook, *v.*¹ Add: **1. d.** *To crook the little finger* or *the elbow*: to drink (esp. with implication of excess). *slang*, orig. *U.S.*

1836 *Philad. Publ. Ledger* 2 Aug. (Th.) William Martin was fined for, as he quaintly expressed it, crooking his little finger too often. 1859 Bartlett *Dict. Amer.* (ed. 2) s.v., To crook one's elbow or one's little finger, is to tipple. 1884 Besant & Rice *With Harp & Crown* xix, The secretary.. might have done great things in literature but for his unfortunate crook of the elbow. As he only crooks it at night, it does not matter to the hospital.

Crooked, *a.* Add:

1. b. *Crooked stick*: see Stick *sb.*¹ 12.

3. b. (Now in general use.)

1898 *Daily News* 27 Aug. 6/6 Telling him that he rather thought he had bought 'a crooked lot'. 1902 *Daily Chron.* 26 Aug. 6/6 In the event of his being found..to be dealing in 'crooked' things, or refusing to give information as to where he got his stuff.

5. *crooked-necked* (spec. applied to a variety of squash: cf. Crook-neck).

1796–1801 Fessenden *Orig. Poems* (1806) 134 Like a nice crook'd neck'd squash on the ground. 1841 *Lowell Offering* I. 79 (Th.) Over the fire-place was our crooked necked squashes.

Crookes (kruks). The name of Sir William *Crookes* (1832–1919), English scientist, used attrib. or in the genitive to designate phenomena observed and apparatus invented by him. **Crookes** or **Crookes's (dark) space,** the dark space between the negative glow and the cathode of a vacuum tube, observed when the pressure is very low; also called *cathode dark space, cathodic dark space.* **Crookes** or **Crookes's layer,** (*a*) the layer of vapour underlying any mass or liquid in the spheroidal state, insulating it from the surface on which it rests; (*b*) = *Crookes (dark) space.* **Crookes's radiometer**: see Radiometer 2. **Crookes rays,** = *cathode rays.* **Crookes's tube,** a vacuum tube in which the rarefaction is carried to a high degree, so that electric discharges produce phosphorescent glows in the form of layers and strata. **Crookes** or **Crookes's vacuum,** an extremely high vacuum in which molecular atoms have free play.

1884 A. Daniell *Princ. Physics* 325 Let us now suppose that the particles recoiling from the heated surface do not meet other molecules, but impinge on the walls of the vessel. A layer of particles in such a condition is called a Crookes' layer. 1885 *Encycl. Brit.* XIX. 249/1 In Crookes's radiometer the free path is very long. 1891 *Cent. Dict.* s.v. *Vacuum-tube*, A Crookes's tube..used by Mr. William Crookes in his investigation of what he has called radiant matter. 1892 G. F. Barker *Physics* 329 The layer of vapor which has to support the drop is called a Crookes layer. 1893 J. J. Thomson *Recent Res. Electr. & Magn.* 108 Next to this [*sc.* the negative electrode] there is a comparatively dark region..called sometimes 'Crookes' space' and sometimes the 'first dark space'. 1902 *Encycl. Brit.* XXVIII. 47/2 The Crookes dark space. 1906 *Amer. Jrnl. Sci.* Ser. IV. XXII. 312 The extremely tenuous condition of the residual elementary gas or gases in a Crookes tube. 1910 *N. Hawkins' Electr. Dict.*, *Crookes' Effect*, the radiant effect produced in a vacuum glass tube in which the exhaustion has been carried to a high degree, when electricity is discharged through it between suitable electrodes.

Hence **Crookesian** (kruˑksiăn) *a.*, pertaining to Crookes or to instruments invented by him.

1899 *Science Siftings* XVI. 117/2 The Crookesian scale-pan. *Ibid.*, Crookesian radiometer.

Crookesite (kruˑksəit). *Min.* [f. *Crookes + -ite¹.] Selenide of copper, thallium, and silver.

1877 Dana *Text-bk. Min.* 213 Crookesite...Formerly regarded as selenide of copper or berzelianite.

Crook-neck. *U.S.* (Earlier example.)

1844 Whittier *Pumpkin* 15 Fields..Where crook-necks are coiling and yellow fruit shines.

Crooˑk-necked, *a.* (Cf. Crook-neck and *Crooked *a.* 5.)

1818 *Massachusetts Spy* 11 Nov. (Th.) Upwards of ten tons of the best crook-necked winter Squashes.

Crop, *sb.* Add: **14.** (Earlier and additional American examples.)

1653 *Plymouth* (Mass.) *Rec.* 2 The mark of his cattle is a cropp on the left eare. 1709 *Portsmouth* (N.H.) *Rec.* 262 A crope and sli[t]. 1841 *Ibid.* 386 The ear mark..is a crop of the right ear. 1869 *Overland Monthly* III. 126 He asked me if I had seen a red mulley cow, with a crop and an underbit in the right and a marked crop in the left.

22. crop-bound *a.*, (of birds) unable to pass food through the crop; **crop-end,** a piece of metal cut off a bar of rolled iron or steel to remove imperfections and to reduce the bar to standard length; **crop-head,** a crop-end cut from that end of a bar of iron or steel which is at the top during the process of cooling and where most of the imperfections occur; **crop hogshead** *U.S.* (see quot.); **crop movement** (see Movement 8); **crop-over,** in the West Indies, the end of the sugar-cane harvest on a plantation, and the accompanying celebrations; **crop-writer** *U.S.*, an authority on crops.

1854 *Poultry Chron.* I. 136 '*Crop-bound' fowls. 1897 *Daily News* 29 Dec. 7/2 The bird..had become crop-bound, and in order to remove the obstruction an incision five inches long was made in the crop. 1880 *Encycl. Brit.* XIII. 332/1 Cuttings, '*crop ends,' and 'scrap' of various kinds, often not very largely inferior in value to the bar iron. 1884 W. H. Greenwood *Steel & Iron* (ed. 2) 347 Cutting off the rough or crop-ends of puddled, finished, or other bars. 1903 *Sci. Amer. Suppl.* 21 Feb. 22687 (Cent. D. Suppl.) The rough ends—'*crop heads'—are cut off and are placed..in a car for shipment to any part of the works. 1784 J. Smyth *Tour U.S.* II. 138 The weight of each hogshead must be nine hundred and fifty pounds neat, exclusive of the cask, for less a note will not be given under the name of a *Crop hogshead. 1909 *Westm. Gaz.* 14 June 12/1 The *crop movement began very early last year, and the farmers were paid for their wheat and other products promptly. 1894 Robson *Story of our Jamaica Mission* 35 The grinding routine of slavery was relieved at '*crop-over' and Christmas times. 1897 *Yearbk. U.S. Dept. Agric.* 67 (Cent. D. Suppl.) Educated and practically trained meteorologists, *crop writers, printers, and messengers are on duty.

Crop, *v.* Add: **6.** Also *absol.*

1879 Tourgee *Fool's Err.* xviii. 91 They didn't require me to leave, only to stop selling horses to niggers and letting them crop on shares.

b. *trans.* To grow or rear as a crop.

1921 *Discovery* Feb. 48/1 The pest..remains in existence until potatoes are again cropped in the field.

Cropper². **1.** Add: *spec.* a shearing machine in iron and steel work; also, the workman who operates it.

1884 Knight *Dict. Mech.* Suppl., *Cropper*, a powerful hand machine for shearing off bolts or rod iron. 1921 *Dict. Occup. Terms* (1927) § 279 *Cropper* (iron and steel rolling); forge cropper, mill cropper and shearer; a shearer or a hot sawyer who cuts off badly shaped ends of finished bars of iron or steel after rolling.

Cropper[4]. Add: Also *cropper boy, work.*
1881 *Instr. Census Clerks* (1885) 40 Letter-Press Printing: ..Cropper Hand. 1888 JACOBI *Printers' Vocab.* 28 *Cropper*, a short term for the 'cropper' small printing platen machine. 1896 *Daily News* 30 Oct. 10/6 Compositor (young). Jobbing and cropper. 1901 *Daily Chron.* 3 Dec. 9/7 Printers.—Young man seeks Situation in machine room; good reference for Cropper work. 1903 *Ibid.* 4 Mar. 9/7 Printers.—Cropper boy wanted. 1921 *Dict. Occup. Terms* (1927) § 529 *Machine minder*, platen; cropper hand; has charge of platen machine.

Cro·ppie. *U.S.* [Of obscure origin.] (See quot. 1889.)
1889 FARMER *Americanisms*, *Croppie*, a local name for a species of green bass found in Lake Minnetonka. 1892 *Gentlewoman's Bk. Sports* I. 73 We caught bass, croppie, sun perch and pickerel. 1895 *Outing* (U.S.) XXVI. 62/1 Seeing schools of sunfish, perch, rockbass, and croppies.

Cropping, *vbl. sb.* Add: **4.** *Comb.*, as **cropping shears** = **crocodile shears*.
1873 *Spons' Dict. Engin.* VI. 2122 Two pairs of cropping shears at 55 revolutions a minute. 1884 W. H. GREENWOOD *Steel & Iron* (ed. 2) 348 The crocodile, cropping, or alligator shears.

Croquis (kroki). [Fr.] A rough draught; a sketch, study.
1888 *Athenæum* 7 Jan. 23/2 The volume will be illustrated with etchings and *croquis*. a 1895 LOCKER in T. H. Ward *Engl. Poets* (1918) V. 525 He sent her this copy containing His comical little *croquis*.

Cross, *a.* **1. d.** Add: Also *cross-swell, -tide.*
1867 SMYTH *Sailor's Word-bk.*, *Cross-swell*, this is similar to a cross-sea, except that it undulates without breaking violently. *Ibid.*, *Cross-tide*, the varying directions of the flow amongst shoals that are under water. 1891 KIPLING *Light that Failed* (1900) 265 A boisterous little cross-swell swung the steamer disrespectfully by the nose. 1903 — *Five Nations, Cruisers* viii, 'Twixt wrench of cross-surges or plunge of head-gale. 1903 *Q. Rev.* Apr. 486 Like vortices upon a surface of water swept by violent cross-tides.

Cross, *v.* Add: **5.** Also (one limb) *over* another.
1881 MRS. RIDDELL *Senior Partner* ii. I. 29 She crossed her soft white hands one over the other. 1886 'MAXWELL GRAY' *Silence of Dean Maitland* II. i, Staring at the sky, with one leg crossed over the other. 1902 'SETON MERRIMAN' *Vultures* xxv, The captain..crossed one leg over the other.
7. Also *absol.*
1924 ROSE MACAULAY *Orphan Island* xiv. § 2. 176 Miss Smith had the sloping, flowing hand of the ladies of her period, and often crossed and recrossed.
b. (Earlier U.S. examples.)
1786 WASHINGTON *Diaries* III. 30 This day finished crossing the ground in the Neck designed for Oats. *Ibid.* 172 In the Neck began to cross the Plowing in the homestead.. in order to sow oats.
8. Also *transf.*
1904 LILLIE T. MEADE *Love Triumphant* IV. ii, An ugly sneer crossed his lips.

Cross-. Add:
5. *cross current* (fig. uses).
1891 MEREDITH *One of our Conq.* xxv, It was a happy cross-current recollection. 1899 MORLEY in *Westm. Gaz.* 18 Jan. 5/1 There have been cross-currents, and it was impossible either inside the House of Commons or elsewhere that Sir William Harcourt could speak with the authority of a united party. 1899 *Westm. Gaz.* 26 Jan. 2/2 Cross-current politics.
6. b. *cross-pollenate*. **d.** *cross-petition.*
1904 *Westm. Gaz.* 7 Dec. 7/2 The husband denied various acts described as cruelty by the wife, and *cross-petitioned for judicial separation. 1923 *Daily Mail* 28 Feb. 5 Her husband..cross-petitions for the dissolution of his marriage. 1920 *Chambers's Jrnl.* 238/1 Budding and *cross-pollenating.
9. *cross-banter, -correspondence, -inquiry, -suit, -summons.*
1928 *Daily Express* 11 Sept. 5/5 The greetings and *cross banter had the ring of complete enjoyment. 1911 W. F. BARRETT *Psychical Research* xv. 228 The new and noteworthy feature is what the investigators of the phenomena have called *cross-correspondence. 1895 *Daily News* 10 June 5/4 A *cross-inquiry officer. 1923 *Daily Mail* 28 Feb. 5 In this case there are *cross-suits. One, by the wife.., her husband..cross-petitions for the dissolution of his marriage. 1927 *Daily Express* 17 Aug. 7, I hope that I shall live to see the day when motorists will be able to take out *cross-summonses against careless pedestrians.
B. cross-border *a.*, that forms a border across; also **cross-bordered** *a.*; **cross-boy** *Austral.*, a dishonest man, a crook; **cross-break**, a break across a lode of ore or strata of rocks; **cross cause** *Law*, a cause in which each of the litigants has a suit against the other; **cross-colouring** *Geol.*, colour-markings in strata caused by the introduction of extraneous matter by the action of water; **cross-fault** *Geol.*, a fault which crosses the strike of the displaced strata; **cross-ferry** = FERRY *sb.*[1] 2, 3; **cross-flute**, a transverse flute (see FLUTE *sb.*[1] 1); **cross-hair**, a fine strand of spider's web stretched across the focal plane of a telescope or microscope, usually forming a cross with another similar strand; **cross-mouth chisel**, a cylindrical boring chisel with a diametrical blade; also *cross-mouthed chisel*; **cross-nibbed** *a.*, having the points of the nib crossed; **cross-rail**, a horizontal rail of a door or other framework; **cross-reel** *v.*, to wind (yarn) on a reel with a reciprocating movement; so *cross-reeling*; **cross-rib**, (*a*) *Arch.* (see quots.); (*b*) in a side of beef, a sternal rib running crosswise to the body; **cross-saddle**, a saddle on which the rider sits astride; also as *adv.*, on a cross-saddle, astride; **cross-seizing** *Naut.*, a seizing in which a number of turns of rope cross an equal number in the opposite direction; **cross-shed** (see quot. 1874); **cross-shot** (*b*) *Lawn Tennis*, a shot placed in the court diametrically opposed to the player; **cross-sleeper**, a sleeper laid transversely across a tramway or railway track as a support for the rails; **cross-surge, -swell**: see *CROSS *a.* 1 d; **cross-talk**, (*a*) see quots. 1910, 1922; (*b*) altercation, back-chat; so **cross-talker**; **cross-tide**: see *CROSS *a.* 1 d; **cross tube** (see quot. 1888); **cross-volley** (cf. *cross-shot* above); **cross-warp weave, cross-weaving**, weaving in which the warp-threads are crossed in regular order; **cross-wind** *v. trans.*, to wind yarn on a reel in such a way that the strands of one layer cross those of the previous layer at an acute angle; so **cross-wind** *sb.*
1894 T. W. FOX *Mech. Weaving* 156 If a *cross-border machine is employed, a considerable saving in cards results in the manufacture of handkerchiefs..with a border all round. *Ibid.*, Certain classes of fabrics, such as *cross-bordered, swivel, and compound. 1890 'R. BOLDREWOOD' *Miner's Right* xv, He believed all the '*cross boys' of all the colonies were congregated here. 1909 *Westm. Gaz.* 30 Mar. 11/4 Low values caused by *cross-breaks. 1768 BLACKSTONE *Comm.* III. xxvii. 451 When there are *cross causes, on a cross bill filed by the defendant against the plaintiff in the original cause, they are generally contrived to be brought on together, that the same hearing and the same decree may serve for both of them. 1902 *Science* 31 May 869 (Cent. D. Suppl.) *Cross-colouring. 1900 *Geogr. Jrnl.* (R.G.S.) XVI. 461 Both longitudinal and *cross-faults..in the Eastern Alps. 1900 *Westm. Gaz.* 2 May 10/1 Nine *cross-ferries, two of which carry vehicular traffic. 1903 *Daily Chron.* 20 Feb. 6/7 Vehicular cross-ferry traffic was suspended. 1876 STAINER & BARRETT *Dict. Mus. Terms* 172/2 *Cross-flutes were known to the Greeks by the name plagiaulos (πλαγίαυλος), and to the Romans as *tibia obliqua*. 1902 *Westm. Gaz.* 2 July 2/3 How this the flute, and that the cross-flute wrought. 1884 KNIGHT *Dict. Mech.* Suppl. 322/1 A telescope fitted with a *cross hair. 1922 MCCONKEY *End of Age* 50 The cross-hairs of God's telescope of prophecy are centered upon it. 1874 KNIGHT *Dict. Mech.*, **Cross-mouth Chisel*, a boring-chisel of a cylindrical form with a diametrical blade. 1896 *Daily News* 26 Sept. 3/5 *Crossmouthed chisels of hardest tool steel. 1913 E. F. BENSON *Thorley Weir* iv, A splash of grey, as if the brush had spluttered like a *cross-nibbed pen. 1880 *Spons' Encycl. Industr. Arts* II. 739 In the interior of the frame-work, is fitted a conical grid, having its apex downwards, and resting on a *cross-rail at a short distance from the bottom. 1894 T. W. FOX *Mech. Weaving* 153 A hole is drilled in the cross rail near each end of the upper griffe frame. 1902 *How to Make Useful Things* 13/2 The bottom cross-rail is..3½ in. less in length than the width of the end of the fowl-house. 1890 NASMITH *Mod. Cotton Spinning Mach.* xiii. 267 The hanks being reeled, they are, if *cross reeled, dyed or bleached, and, if in leas, bundled. 1852–61 *Archit. Publ. Soc. Dict.* I. 167/1 **Cross rib* (Fr. *arc doubleau*), a rib from one pier or pillar across to its respond, square with the vault to which the rib belongs. ..Willis calls it the transverse rib, and it is often called the arch rib. 1902 R. STURGIS *Dict. Archit.* III. 289 The wall ribs (*formerets*) and cross ribs (*arcs doubleaux*) were.. pointed. 1897 W. E. NORRIS *Clarissa Furiosa* xxxiii, That his daughter..would..ride to hounds in a *cross-saddle. 1897 *Westm. Gaz.* 22 Dec. 4/2 The cross-saddle position assumed by women on 'bikes'. 1905 *Daily Chron.* 1 Aug. 3/3 One of our Royal Princesses is to be taught to ride cross-saddle. 1883 *Man. Seamanship for Boys* 109 A *Cross Seizing is used when the rigging is turned in with the end up. 1874 KNIGHT *Dict. Mech.*, **Cross-shed*, the upper shed of a gauze-loom. 1894 T. W. FOX *Mech. Weaving* 225 *O* shows the lifting for an open shed, and *c* that for a cross shed. 1895 H. W. W. WILBERFORCE *Lawn Tennis* xii. 43 It may be a difficult *cross-shot. 1902 *Westm. Gaz.* 1 July 4/3 His cross-shots to the left-hand corner swift and sure. 1841 *Penny Cycl.* XIX. 255/1 The use of *cross-sleepers..needs little remark. 1888 *Encycl. Brit.* XXIII. 506/2 The rail was spiked through to a longitudinal timber laid on cross sleepers. 1910 *N. Hawkins' Electr. Dict.*, **Cross Talk*, conversation over one telephone circuit overheard in the telephone of another circuit, when their wires run side by side. This fault is due almost entirely to electrostatic induction. 1917 'IAN HAY' *Carrying on* i. 18 Each bus is in charge of the identical pair of cross-talk comedians who controlled its destinies in more peaceful days. 1922 *Glazebrook's Dict. Applied Physics* II. 859/1 Cross-talk is interference between adjacent telephone circuits due to the transmission of speech energy from one circuit to another. 1923 *Daily Mail* 23 Jan. 5 The 'cross-talk' sketch 'The Haunted House'. 1930 *Times Lit. Suppl.* 27 Mar. 276/3 Some of the crosstalk of the American shop-girls is entertaining. 1907 *Daily Chron.* 1 May 6/4 Those pioneer *cross-talkers, the Christy Minstrels. 1884 KNIGHT *Dict. Mech.* Suppl., *Cross tube boiler. 1888 *Lockwood's Dict. Mech. Engin.*, *Cross Tubes*, the heating tubes in a steam boiler—usually applied to boilers of the vertical type. 1905 *Daily Chron.* 20 Mar. 3/3 The American *cross-volleys which may bring the English players a little nearer the net in doubles. 1843 *Penny Cycl.* XXVII. 179/1 **Cross Weaving*.—This term may be conveniently applied to those varieties of woven fabric in which the warp-threads..cross over or twist around one another, thus forming a plexus or interlacing independent of that produced by the weft. 1874 KNIGHT *Dict. Mech.*, *Cross-weaving Loom*, a loom for weaving with a crossed warp. 1892 NASMITH *Students' Cotton Spinning* 360 *Cross winding is resorted to when the hank is to be dyed. 1927 T. WOODHOUSE *Artif. Silk* 91 A cross-wind or V-shaped wind.

Cross-bar, *sb.* Add: **1. c.** (See quot.)
1884 KNIGHT *Dict. Mech.* Suppl., *Cross-bar* (Fire-arms), the small bar in a break-joint breech-loader, which, when the barrels are falling, presses out the extractor.

Cro·ss-ba:rring, *vbl. sb.* [f. CROSS-BAR *v.* + -ING[1].] A cross-bar, a transverse bar. Also *collect.*
1884 J. H. GURNEY *Diurnal Birds Prey* 116 The tail is grey, with some remains of brown cross-barring.

Cro·ss-connect, *v. Electr.* [CROSS- 4 c.] *trans.* To interchange the connections of (electric wires). Also in *ppl. a.* and *vbl. sb.* Hence **Cro·ss-conne:ction**, the arrangement of wires in this way. **Cro·ss-conne:ctor**, the device used to effect this.
1875 KNIGHT *Dict. Mech.* 2512/2 To cross-connect wires is to interchange them, so that a current from one wire is shifted to another at one station and then back again at a farther station, to work around a faulty station. 1884 P. HIGGS *Magn. & Dyn.-Electr. Mach.* 261 The segments of the collector are internally cross connected. 1893 SLOANE *Electr. Dict.* 157 *Cross-Connecting Board*, a special switch board used in telephone exchanges and central telegraph offices. Its function is, by plugs and wires, to connect the line wires with any desired section of the main switchboard. *Ibid.* 158 *Cross Connection*, a method of disposing of the effects of induction from neighboring circuits by alternately crossing the two wires of a metallic telephone circuit, so that for equal intervals they lie to right and left, or one above and one below. 1894 W. P. MAYCOCK *Electric Lighting* II. vii. (ed. 2) 205 The cross-connectors consisting of copper rings with two lugs. 1910 *N. Hawkins' Electr. Dict.*, *Cross Connected Dynamo*, a dynamo having the coils of its armature connected to corresponding bars of the commutator.

Cro·ss-cou:nter. *Boxing.* [f. CROSS- 10 + COUNTER *sb.*[5] 3.] A blow at the head delivered across an opponent's lead-off with the other hand.
1889 MICHELL *Boxing* (Badm. Libr.) 166 The answer to this cross-counter is to deliver the right at the face of the counterer.

Cross-country, *a.* Add:
1891 *Harper's Mag.* Aug. 364/2 Some cross-countrymen [*sc.* horsemen] brush such things aside as trivial.

Cro·ss-cut, *sb.* Add:
2. b. A cut sawn across a log.
1861 *Congress. Globe* 2 Mar. 1354/2 In the west..we sometimes do what we call 'sawing a cross cut'. It always requires two to perform the operation well.

Cross-cut, *a.* **1.** (Earlier examples.)
1645 *Early Connect. Probate Rec.* I. 31 My sonne..shall have..my long cross cut saw. 1677 *New Castle Court Rec.* 138 The Plaintiff hath attached..two or three Chests and a crascut saw. 1686 *Narrag. Hist. Reg.* III. 105, 1 crosscut saw..1 hand saw. 1735 *New-York Gaz.* 1 Sept., Hand saws, Tennet Saws, Cross-cut-Saws. 1754 *Boston News-Letter* 23 May, Imported from London..the best..cross-cut saws. 1760 WASHINGTON *Diaries* I. 122 They spent 25 minutes more in getting the cross cut saw, standing to consider what to do. 1768 *Massachusetts Gaz.* 25 Aug. (Th.) The lightning was attracted by a cross-cut saw lying against the chimney.
2. (Earlier example.)
1827 *Maryland Hist. Mag.* XVII. 246 They will prefer proceeding to Philadelphia by the cross-cut canal.

Cro·ss-cu:tting, *vbl. sb.* [f. CROSS-CUT *v.* + -ING[1].] The action of cutting across.
1805 R. W. DICKSON *Pract. Agric.* I. 345 Repeated cross-cuttings with the plough and harrowings. 1896 *Daily News* 16 Dec. 8/4 He had done 326 feet of cross-cutting still in ore.

Cro·ss-dye, *v. trans.* To dye a cotton and wool fabric in which the cotton warp has been dyed before weaving. Hence **Cro·ss-dye** *sb.*, a colour used in cross-dyeing; **Cro·ss-dyeing** *vbl. sb.*
1885 HUMMEL *Dyeing Textile Fabrics* 466 The cotton warp may be dyed black, brown, dark blue, drab, &c., before weaving, in which case only the woollen or worsted weft is dyed subsequently. The finished goods are then said to be 'cross-dyed'.

Crossect (krǫse·kt), *v.* [f. CROSS + L. *secare*, *sectum* to cut.] *trans.* To divide transversely.
1860 TROLLOPE *Castle Richmond* xxxiii, These had since been bisected and crossected, and intersected. 1927 *Glasgow Herald* 1 Sept. 8 The Exchequer crossects our income.

Cross-head, *sb.* Add:
1. b. Any beam across the top of a piece of mechanism.
1844 H. STEPHENS *Bk. Farm* I. 417 The draught shackle.. is held in its place upon the cross-head..by the draught-bolt. *Ibid.* II. 134 The handle..terminates in a crosshead. 1884 *Science* III. 314 Two side-screws, carrying the top crosshead. 1884 KNIGHT *Dict. Mech.* Suppl., *Cross Head*, a cruciform-shaped four-handled bar, at the upper end of a drill-rod or earth-auger. 1888 *Encycl. Brit.* XXIII. 151/1 Thus avoiding torsion of the polar axis at the expense of greatly increased length of the cross-head. 1901 S. MERWIN & WEBSTER *Calumet K* xvi. 322 Another endless series of cups was carrying the wheat aloft. It went over the cross-head and down a spout.
3. *Mining.* A heading running across a vein.
1877 RAYMOND *Statist. Mines & Mining* 197 At the point of connection the eastern limit of the south vein is defined by a cross-head.., and to the east of this cross-head no trace of the fissure has as yet been found.
4. cross-head brasses *pl.*, the brass bearings of the cross-head of a steam or other engine; **cross-head pin**, the pin by which the connecting-rod is attached to the piston-rod.
1895 *Daily News* 26 July 3/1 No. 80 torpedo boat..broke down owing to a defect in the *crosshead brasses. 1887 D. A. LOW *Machine Draw.* (1892) 51 The *cross-head pin need not be drawn separately, and the isometric projection of the bush at (*b*) may be omitted. 1889 HASLUCK *Model Engin. Handybk.* (1900) 91 The hole in cross-head must be broached out till the cross-head pin will nearly fit it.

Cro·ss-hea:ding. *Mining.* A transverse heading (see quots.).
1900 *Coal & Metal Miners' Pocketbook* (ed. 6) 582 *Cross-*

Heading, a passage driven for ventilation from the airway to the gang-way, or from one breast through the pillar to the adjoining working. *Cross-Heading*, or *Cross-Gateway*, a road kept through goaf and cutting off the gateways at right angles or diagonally. 1904 *Technol. & Sci. Dict.* (ed. Goodchild & Tweney), *Cross Heading* (Mining), a drift or passage from one level to another for ventilating purposes.

Crossing, *vbl. sb.* **11.** Add: **crossing-gate**, a gate at a level crossing which is closed to road traffic when a train is due; **crossing-place** (earlier examples of U.S. use).
1929 *Star* 21 Aug. 7/2 The railway crosses the road in several places without *crossing-gates. 1763 WASHINGTON *Diaries* I. 193 A common causay through at the *crossing place would most certainly lay all that Arm dry. 1832 R. COX *Adv. Columbia River* xxiv. 249 The river at the crossing-place was between three and four hundred yards wide. 1847 C. LANMAN *Summer in Wilderness* xiv. 86 There was a crossing place on the Mississippi, where a good marksman might take one almost any time.

Cross-lining. Add: **b.** The action of fishing with a cross-line, cross-fishing.
1897 *19th Cent.* Aug. 199 Cross-lining for trout has lately been prohibited. 1900 *Daily News* 16 Aug. 3/2 A large landowner, who has..succeeded in stopping cross-lining on Lough Corrib. 1907 *Westm. Gaz.* 13 Dec. 4/2 A daring spirit suggested the project of cross-lining.

Cross-lots, *adv. phr. U.S.* (See CROSS *prep.* and LOT *sb.* 6 a.) Also *attrib.*
1851 S. JUDD *Margaret* I. xiv. (ed. 2) 88 They come..by numerous foot paths cross-lots [*ed.* 1845, xiv. 103 across the lots] and through the woods. 1873 'MARK TWAIN' & WARNER *Gilded Age* xxi. (1883) 154 The cross-lots path she traversed to the Seminary.

Cross-over. Add **2. b.** Anything so arranged that one part crosses over another; *spec.*, the front of a dress or wrap so arranged.
1909 *Westm. Gaz.* 2 Jan. 11/1 An evening dress in satin Rajah, with the bodice arranged in a cross-over.
3. Delete *U.S.*: Also of a tramway.
1895 *Daily News* 15 Oct. 3/2 At the starting point are four crossovers to suit any arrangement of traffic. 1901 *Westm. Gaz.* 29 Nov. 10/2 The castings necessary for the cross-overs on electric tramways. 1928 *Daily Express* 22 Nov. 11/1 The cross-overs available were at Beckenham Junction and Penge.
4. The crossing over of the current from one side of a river to the other.
1902 *Encycl. Brit.* XXVII. 533/1 Just below the Pass of Lillo there is a cross-over in the current.
5. *Biol.* (See quots.)
1919 R. C. PUNNETT *Mendelism* (ed. 5) 144 It is upon the proportion of 'crossover' gametes as compared with 'non-crossover' gametes that the distances between the factors along the chromosomes have been determined. 1920 L. DONCASTER *Introd. Cytology* 224 The American investigators call these exceptional combinations cross-overs, since in the combinations of *Ab* and *aB*, *A* and *a* are regarded as having crossed over from their normal combinations and to have exchanged places.
6. *attrib.* or as *adj.* That crosses over; characterized by having a part that crosses over another.
1893 M. GRAY *Last Sentence* III. ii, White pinafore, cross-over shawl, and velvet hat. 1905 *Westm. Gaz.* 8 July 13/2 The cross-over bodice. 1906 *Ibid.* 15 Feb. 4/1 A cross-over ring set with a large brilliant and a cabochon emerald.
b. *Cross-over block, road* (see quots.).
1893 SLOANE *Electr. Dict.* 158 **Cross-over Block*, a piece of porcelain or other material shaped to receive two wires which are to cross each other. 1888 *Lockwood's Dict. Mech. Engin.*, **Cross-over Road*, a short diagonal line of rails on permanent way, provided with a pair of points or switches at each end, and connecting two parallel lines of rails together. 1893 *Athenæum* 8 July 68/1 'Crossings' imply something more than merely the gaps left in the rails for a cross-over road. 1896 *Daily News* 18 Dec. 8/2 He let the goods train on to the up main line, but did not pull over the cross-over road points for the goods train to go across to the down line.

Cross-point, *sb.* Add:
3. *Math.* A point at which there is a crossing.
1877 CAYLEY *Math. Papers* (1896) X. 318 When the curve described by *P* passes through *V*, the curves described by the two points *P′* will unite together at this point (*W′*) as a node; viz. they will form a figure of eight, the crossing being at the cross-point (*W′*), which corresponds to the branch-point *V*.
4. *pl.* The points of a railway cross-over.
1896 *Westm. Gaz.* 13 July 2/2 When the train has to pass over cross-points.

Cro·ss-point, *v. Naut.* [f. the sb.] *trans.* To point (a rope) by plaiting the nettles crosswise. Hence **Cro·ss-pointing** *vbl. sb.*, the action of pointing a rope in this manner; rope so pointed.
1883 *Man. Seamanship for Boys* 185 *Q.* How do you cross-point a rope? *A.* Man-ropes are sometimes made of cross-pointing.

Cro·ss-re:ference, *v.* [f. the sb.] *trans.* To provide with a cross-reference; to refer to by a cross-reference. Hence **Cro·ss-re:ferencing** *vbl. sb.*
1909 in *Cent. Dict.* Suppl. 1914 *Cath. Encycl.* XVI. 88 Where several forms of the same name occur, all the references are grouped under one spelling to which the other forms are duly cross-referenced. 1922 *Daily Mail* 7 Dec. 10 It saves the unnecessary labour of cross-referencing.

Cross-road. Add:
2. b. *fig.* A point at which two or more courses of action diverge; a critical turning-point.
1852 *Hogg's Instructor* VIII. 90/1 He had met with four cross-roads, and he knew not which to follow. 1898 *Nat. Rev.* Aug. 908 To place him at the cross roads of starvation and revolt. 1915 *War Illustrated* 6 Mar. 54 Britons at cross-roads of Honour, Glory and Death. 1924 E. Y. MULLINS (*title*) Christianity at the Cross Roads.
3. *attrib.* Also *cross-roads.*
1868 *Putnam's Mag.* June 715/1 Now and then an enterprising specimen of the breed set up a 'cross-roads grocery'. 1884 'C. E. CRADDOCK' *Tenn. Mts.* I. 21, I dunno whether ye holped ter rob the cross-roads store or no. 1905 *Forum* Apr. 485 To place an obstacle in the way of the cross-roads politicians.

Cross-section, *sb.* (Earlier examples.)
1835 A. GRAY *Lett.* (1893) 52 A cross-section shows the same structure as the rattan. 1870 *Spons' Dict. Engin.* II. 389 A front elevation and cross-section of a boiler. 1874 *Ibid.* VIII. 2924 The converting department, shown in ground plan by Fig. 6996, and in cross-section by Fig. 6998. 1878 J. H. BEADLE *Western Wilds* x. 143 Five men were twenty days felling it, the object being to have it sawed into cross-sections to be shipped eastward to Europe.

Cro·ss-se:ction, *v.* [f. the sb.] *trans.* To make a cross-section of; to cut into cross-sections.
1890 D'OYLE *Notches* 52 They were going down to 'cross-section' the old railway survey which ran through our valley. 1897 *Outing* (U.S.) XXX. 126/2 Much of the ground is.. conveniently bounded and cross-sectioned by roads. 1908 *Westm. Gaz.* 22 Aug. 14/1 The eye would then cross-section its words, reading the lateral parts in indirect vision.

Cro·ss-se:ctional, *a.* [f. CROSS-SECTION *sb.* + -AL.] Of or pertaining to a cross-section.
1874 *Spons' Dict. Engin.* VIII. 2931 The difference in cross-sectional area between the two ends of the ram is the area acted upon by the water to lift it. 1896 tr. *H. Du Bois' Magnetic Circuit* 60, *S* is the cross-sectional area of the bar-magnet. 1916 H. BARBER *Aeroplane Speaks* 94 The cross-sectional dimensions must be correct. 1924 W. E. GIBBS *Clouds & Smokes* 137 The cross-sectional area is many times that of the fume.

Cross-stone. (Later U.S. example.)
1867 *Amer. Naturalist* July 264 A boulder..containing large crystals of staurotite, or cross-stone.

Cro·ss-tie. [CROSS- 4.] A transverse connecting piece (of timber, etc.).
1849 *Rep. U.S. Comm. Patents* (1850) 158 The arrangement of cross ties and stays in the interior part of the hub. 1858 SIMMONDS *Dict. Trade*, *Cross-tie*, a railway sleeper; a connecting band in building. 1868 *Rep. to Govt. U.S. Munitions of War* 129 These cross-ties are formed with a curve in their centre part to clear the lower portion of the breech of the gun. 1886 *Encycl. Brit.* XX. 244/1 The longitudinals are connected and kept to gauge by transoms or cross-ties at intervals. 1890 *Harper's Mag.* May 888/1 Across this ditch two old 'cross-ties' made a bridge to the railway. 1901 S. MERWIN & WEBSTER *Calumet K* ii. 22 Did you ever try to shove five hundred foot coils over a mile of crossties? 1908 *Daily Chron.* 14 Nov. 8/6 A few variations in frame design..taking the form of auxiliary cross-ties and supplementary diagonals.

Cross Timber(s). *U.S.* (See quot. 1859.)
1835 W. IRVING *Tour Prairies* xviii. 102 That scattered belt of forest land..commonly called the 'Cross Timber'. 1838 C. NEWELL *Hist. Rev. Texas* 166 Near the 'cross timbers' there is a saline atmosphere. 1859 BARTLETT *Dict. Amer.*, *Cross Timbers*, a belt of forest or woodland, from five to thirty miles in width, which extends from the Arkansas River in a southwesterly direction to the Brazos, a distance of four hundred miles. 1887 *Amer. Naturalist* XXI. 448 The formation is seen between the east and west Cross-Timbers of Texas, and the thickness is not given.

Cro·ss tongue. [CROSS- 4 a.] A cross-grained tongue of wood used to give extra strength to a joint in woodwork. Hence **Cro·ss-tongue** *v.*, to provide with a cross tongue.
1876 *Encycl. Brit.* IV. 489/2 Surfaces..formed of inch or inch and quarter boards joined with glue, and a cross or feather tongue ploughed into each joint. 1901 *J. Black's Carp. & Build.*, *Home Handicrafts* 86 In the back and sides the grain of the wood runs vertically, the back being necessarily cross-tongued in two places. 1904 *Technol. & Sci. Dict.* (ed. Goodchild & Tweney), *Cross Tongue*, a thin slip of wood with the grain at right angles to its length.

Cro·ss-town, *a.* and *adv. U.S.* [CROSS- 4.]
A. *adj.* Lying, leading, or going across a town.
1894 *Congress. Rec.* 28 May 5413/1, I do not believe that on the L street, or, as it is called, this cross-town road, it is possible for a cable or electric motor to be successfully used. 1900 G. BONNER *Hard Pan* i. 10 Then he hastened his steps, and a few blocks farther on boarded a cross-town car. 1902 *Ann. Amer. Acad. Pol. & Soc. Sci.* XX. 307 The payment of two fares..to go a short distance on cross-town lines. 1906 'O. HENRY' *Four Million* xv. (1916) 152 A cross-town street in the older central part of the city.
B. *adv.* Across the town.
1906 'O. HENRY' *Four Million* xvi. (1916) 165 The crowd in the gutter scattered, and the fine hansom dashed away 'cross-town.

Cross-walk. (See CROSS- 4 a.)
1808 *Boston Selectmen* 21 Dec., To have two cross walks laid of flat stones. 1904 *N. Y. Even. Post* 16 May 7 The Government service answers very well as a cross-walk in getting over a trying period in a young man's life.

Crosswise. Add: **B.** *adj.* Cross, placed across; transverse.
1903 *Westm. Gaz.* 10 Sept. 4/2 Its crosswise pelerine. 1927 *Observer* 4 Dec. 16/4 The cross-wise streets..are growing more and more canyon-like. *Ibid.*, The crosswise thrust of traffic at every block.

Crossword, cro·ss-word. [CROSS- 4 c.] In full *crossword puzzle*: a puzzle in which a pattern of chequered paper has to be filled in from numbered clues with words which are thus formed horizontally and vertically and/or diagonally.
1924 (*title*) The Cross Word Puzzle Book. 1925 *Punch* 1 July 724 The allure of Epstein and Oxford trouserings has been for the few; the Cross-word Puzzle captivated the general. 1927 *Observer* 3 Apr. 7 Particularly that spot known to crossword solvers as the acnestis. 1928 GALSWORTHY *Swan Song* II. iv. 141 Religion used to be red-hot politics, then it became caste feeling, and now it's a crossword puzzle.

Crotal, variant of CROTTLE, used *attrib.* or *adj.*: = of the colour of lichen, golden-brown.
1904 S. GWYNN *Fishing Holidays* Pref., For salmon I have done best with a sort of fiery brown or 'crotal' colour. 1905 *Westm. Gaz.* 15 Sept. 7/2 The brown *crotal* tint of the seaweed. 1907 *Ibid.* 26 Dec. 2/3 When Autumn wears her crotal gown.

Crotalism (krōu·tăliz'm). *U.S.* [f. mod.L. *Crotalaria* + -ISM.] A disease of horses in the Missouri region of the United States, caused by eating the plant *Crotalaria sagittalis* (rattleweed or rattlebox).
1900 *Yearbk. U.S. Dept. Agric.* 308 The diseases resulting from plant poisoning known as *locoism* and *crotalism*, which prevail in some parts of the West and Northwest.

Crotch. Add: **6.** *U.S.* (Earlier examples.)
1725 *Lancaster Rec.* 240 We marched to ye crotch of ye River. 1780 E. PARKMAN *Diary* 204 Mr. Andrews and Mr. Gale..have got to ye crotch of ye Road.
8. crotch-bound *a.*, lacking flexibility at the crotch of the body.
1893 *Outing* (U.S.) XXII. 154/2 Green never ran, but wobbled..he was slightly crotch-bound, and had in consequence a 'rigging stride'.
9. *Billiards.* In the three-ball cannon game a small space, usually four and a half inches square, at each corner of the table.
1889 *Cent. Dict.* 1890 CHAMPLIN & BOSTWICK *Y. F. Cyc. Games* 82 (Funk) In match games,..when the centers of both object-balls are within a crotch, the player is not allowed to make more than three caroms unless he force one of the balls out of the crotch.

Crotch (krǫtʃ), *v. U.S.* [f. the sb.] *trans.* To notch (a log) on opposite sides to provide a grip for the hooks in hauling.
1905 *Terms Forestry & Logging* 34.

Crotchet, *sb.*[1] **13.** Add: **crotchet letter**, one having a hook-shaped hair-line.
1887 *Script Letters for Perforating & Sewing*, Crotchet letters b v f r w.

Croup, *sb.*[2] **3.** Add: **croup-kettle**, an apparatus consisting of a kettle and lamp used for providing a continuous stream of vapour for inhalation or to keep the air humid.
1884 KNIGHT *Dict. Mech.* Suppl., *Croup Kettle*, a small kettle and alcohol lamp for quickly raising a steam for inhalation in cases of croup.

Croustade (krusta·d). [F., f. *crouste*, older form of *croûte* CRUST.] A crisp piece of bread, fried or baked and scooped out into a mould, to receive a filling of meat or other savoury; also, a hollowed shape of rice or pastry for the same purpose.
1845 BREGION & MILLER *Pract. Cook* 41 *Croustades*, fried crusts of bread. 1846 SOYER *Cookery* 160 Prepare the croustades as above, and make a good purée of fowl. 1865 'OUIDA' *Strathmore* xi, Congregate at luncheon, and take *croustades* and conversation together! 1892 *Encycl. Pract. Cookery* (ed. T. F. Garrett) I. 481/1 The Croustade may be made of Bread or Paste of any kind. *Ibid.*, Line a dozen small Croustade-moulds with the rolled-out paste.

Crout, *sb.* Add: Also *Comb.*
1886 *Congress. Rec.* App. 117/1 A crout-eating, pretzel-stuffing, beer-swilling Dutchman.

Croûte (krūt). [Fr., = CRUST.] A crust of bread, toasted or fried, served as a foundation for certain dishes.
[1846 SOYER *Cookery* 473 Croute aux Truffes.] 1907 ESCOFFIER *Mod. Cookery* 782 Set these croûtes in a crown on a round dish, and garnish their midst with a rocky pyramid of plombière ice.

Croûton (krū·toṅ). [F., f. *croûte* CRUST.] A small piece of toasted or fried bread used in soups and to garnish stewed dishes and minces. Also, any small piece used for garnishing.
1816 J. SIMPSON *Cookery* 33 (Stanford) Garnish with either paste or crouton. 1846 SOYER *Cookery* 60 Put some croutons in the tureen, with twenty very small *quenelles de volaille*. 1892 *Encycl. Pract. Cookery* (ed. T. F. Garrett) I. 481/2 Croûtons of aspic jelly are made in almost any shape... Croûtons for garnishing or soup. 1907 ESCOFFIER *Mod. Cookery* 535 Border the dish with neatly-cut *croûtons* of pale jelly. 1921 *Contemp. Rev.* Sept. 374 A purée or cream soup with crackers or croûtons.

Crow, *sb.*[1] Add: **3.** *To eat crow* (examples).
1885 C. L. NORTON *Polit. Americanisms* in *Mag. Amer. Hist.* XIII. 199 'To eat crow' means to recant, or to humiliate oneself. 1904 *Newark Advertiser* 12 July 4 There appears to be one disappointed man who can't eat his crow without making faces over it.
11. crow-bait, *spec.* an old or worn-out horse; **crow-blackbird** (examples); **crow-fig**, the berry of the nux vomica tree; **crow-flight**, a direct course, a straight line; **crow-pheasant**, an East Indian bird, *Centropus rufipennis*; **crow-pick** *v.*, to inspect coal and to free it from stones and rubbish; **crow-picker**, an inspector of coal.
1887 TOURGEE *Button's Inn* 149 What right have you to drive a glandered *crow-bait? 1898 H. S. CANFIELD *Maid of Frontier* 109 That old crow-bait of his would have starved to death. a 1906 'O. HENRY' *Trimmed Lamp* etc. 73, I think I like your horses best. I haven't seen a crowbait since I've been in town. 1920 HUNTER *Trail Drivers of Texas* 98 At this I..rounded up my 'crow bait' and pulled out for home. 1870 *Game Laws Mass.* in *Fur, Fin & Feather* (1872) 72 Any undomesticated birds..except birds of prey, *crow blackbirds [etc.]. 1872 *Rep. Vermont Board Agric.* 333 The most common of all the Blackbirds is that called Crow Blackbirds. 1830 *Oxford Jrnl.* 30 Oct. 3 He struck her; which exasperated the poor woman so much as to induce her to poison herself with *crow-fig. 1858 *Morning Chron.* 16 Sept. 8 (Cassell) It is thought that he has been poisoned with crow-fig, the berry of the nux vomica. 1895 BLOXAM *Chem.* (ed. 8) 760 Nux-vomica, or crow-fig, contains about 1 per cent. of strychnine. 1885 *Science* 7 Aug. 108/2 We clambered over the hills and spurs in the usual '*crow-flight of the Karens. 1876 P. ROBINSON *In my Indian Garden* 7 The *crow pheasant stalks past with his chestnut wings drooping by his side. 1883 E. H. AITKEN *Tribes on my Frontier* 155 That ungainly object the *coucal*, crow-pheasant, jungle-crow, or whatever else you like to call the miscellaneous thing. 1920 *Glasgow Herald* 13 May 6 To *crow-pick each hutch as it passes the steelyard. 1921 *Dict. Occup. Terms* (1927) § 047 **Crow picker*; inspects shale in mine before it is loaded, to see that only clean shale is loaded. 1922 *Glasgow Herald* 12 July 10 Frae crawpickers that craw us O' hauf oor hardwon rakes;..Deliver us, O Lord!

Crow (krōu), *v.*[2] *S. Afr.* [S. African Du., a. Nama *cho·rá* to dig for water.] *trans.* and *intr.* To dig with a pointed stick.
1853 GALTON *Trop. S. Africa* iii. (1889) 48 This method of digging is called in Dutch patois 'crowing' the ground, thus, 'crow-water', means water that you have to crow for, and not an open well, or spring. 1878 WOOD *Uncivilized Races* I. 313 The Damara wife..crows her own ground nuts. 1896 BRYDEN *Tales S. Afr.* 47 With this last implement she can the more easily crow up their dinner.

Crow·-bar. orig. *U.S.* (Earlier examples.)
1797 *Baltimore Town Rec.* 106 The Commissioners planted a Stone upon Part of an Iron Crow Bar drove into the Earth. c 1805 *Deb. Congress* 1806–7 (1852) 1136 Salt is found in form of a solid rock, and may be dug out with the crow-bar. 1816 PICKERING *Vocab.* 74 *Crow-bar*, an iron crow, or simply, a crow. (Used in New England.)

Crowd, *sb.*[3] Add: **2. c.** (Earlier U.S. examples.)
1840 *Congress. Globe* Apr., App. 376/2, I became satisfied that Democracy had but few charms for that crowd. 1847 C. LANMAN *Summer in Wilderness* v. 37 All who could, made their escape and the leader of this crowd was Black Hawk himself.
d. *May* (*might, would*) *pass in a crowd*: does not fall so far short of the standard as to be noticed, is not conspicuously below the average. *colloq.*
4. *crowd psychology, suggestion*, etc. (cf. *MASS *sb.*[2]).
1924 W. B. SELBIE *Psych. Relig.* 157 The whole thing comes from crowd suggestion. *Ibid.* 204 The whole subject [*sc.* conversion] is an interesting branch of the study of crowd psychology.

Crowd, *v.*[1] Add:
2. b. Also with *through*.
1852 E. BENNETT *Mike Fink* i. 13/2 But crowd her through, my hearty, for I'm in a hurry.
c. To hurry. (*intr.* and *trans.*) *U.S. colloq.*
1838 *Knickerbocker Mag.* XII. 506 Well, children, don't *crowd* the old man so; give him time. 1840 *Ibid.* XVI. 258 Simon Schultz crowds me so, that I have no comfort of my life. a 1861 T. WINTHROP *John Brent* v. 53, I might perhaps make it a new story; but I crowd on now to the proper spot where this drama is to be enacted. *Ibid.* xix. 209 He crowded on, more desperately, as a lover rides for love. 1876 *Rep. Vermont Board Agric.* III. 627 He is for ever crowding and rushing, so as to get some particular piece of work done by such a time. 1903 A. ADAMS *Log Cowboy* vi. 80, I didn't crowd matters.
3. Also, to push *back, down* (also *fig.*).
1830 *Mass. Spy* 14 July (Thornton) He was carting timber, and stepped upon the cart tongue to crowd some sticks back with his feet. 1874 *Rep. Vermont Board Agric.* II. 732 You are crowding him down to a gold basis. *Ibid.* 764 The excavation was..stopped upon a clean pebbly bottom, into which an iron bar could be crowded down its length. 1880 CABLE *Grandissimes* xl. 318 He crowded his hat fiercely down over his curls and plunged out.
5. b. *intr.* Of a train: To have its rear coaches thrust forward against those in front.
1907 *Westm. Gaz.* 16 Oct. 7/3 Although in rapid sequence every pair of wheels in the train is braked, the tendency is for the train to 'crowd', as railwaymen say.
7. c. Also *U.S. colloq.* in various contexts.
1851 J. J. HOOPER *Widow Rugby's Husb.* 128 Dad drat my upper leather ef any man shall crowd my feeling's that way. 1868 *Congress. Globe* 19 Feb. 1263/3 [Such an argument as] this is 'crowding the mourners'. 1872 'MARK TWAIN' *Sketches* 322 You ought to respect their little prejudices..and put up with their little foibles, until they get to crowding you too much. 1897 — *Following Equator* xlvii. 441 They crowded him so that he had to give himself up. 1904 W. H. SMITH *Promoters* xix. 282, I don't want to crowd the mourners at your end of the line. 1911 A. M. SIMONS *Social Forces Amer. Hist.* 50 Holland was crowding Spain for first place in the commercial world.
e. *U.S.* (Example.)
1853 BRIGHAM YOUNG *Jrnl. of Discourses* 5 Dec. (1854) I. 340/1 [I have never] distressed a man for what he owes me, or crowded any person in the least.
8. Also with *off, up.*
1881 *Amer. Naturalist* XV. 31 The yellow catkins were actually crowding off the leaves. 1901 S. MERWIN & WEBSTER *Calumet K* vi. 108 It takes a pretty lively man to crowd me off the end of a wire. 1910 *Springfield Weekly Republ.* 6 Jan. 1 The price of cotton is being crowded up higher than conditions of supply and demand warrant.

Crowded, *ppl. a.* Add:
1. b. *fig.* Full of events or experience of life.
1816 SCOTT *Old Mort.* xxxiv. *motto*, One crowded hour of glorious life Is worth an age without a name.

Crowdedness. Add mod. examples of various senses.
1895 SCHLICH *Man. Forestry* III. 181 As long as the degree of crowdedness is not too great. 1928 MARY WEBB *House in Dormer Forest* I. vi. 69 The phrase pleased him because of its crowdedness. 1930 SIR O. LODGE in *Aberdeen Press & Jrnl.* 9 Sept. 6/2 The great crowdedness of space.

Crow·dy, *a.* [f. CROWD *v.*[1]] Somewhat crowded.
1827 J. F. COOPER *Prairie* i. (1879) 10 There is country left, it is true,..but to my taste, it is getting crowdy.

Crowfoot, *sb.* Add: **2. f.** A grass, *Dactyloctenium ægyptiacum*, common in the southern States; also, the plant *Eleusine indica*: more definitely *crowfoot-grass*. (Cf. *CROW'S FOOT 6.) *U.S.*

Crowfoot (krōu·fut), *v. Naut.* [f. the sb.] *trans.* To fasten with small cords and a block (see CROWFOOT *sb.*).
1883 *Man. Seamanship for Boys* 44 Reef points..are crow-footed in the middle.

Crow-hop, *sb. U.S.* [CROW *sb.*[1] 1.] A hopping movement like that of a crow. Also **Crow-hop** *v. intr.*, to hop like a crow.
1903 *Wide World Mag.* Apr. 548 The ways they try to throw their riders may be classed under three heads. The first is known as the crow-hop. 1907 S. E. WHITE *Arizona Nights* I. xiv. 207 Sometimes we crow-hopped solemnly around and around the prostrate Schwartz.

Crown, *sb.* Add:
6. d. *Crown and anchor*, a gambling game (see quot.).
1927 W. E. COLLINSON *Contemp. Eng.* 32 Crown and Anchor is played by means of dice marked with crowns, anchors, hearts, etc. and a board similarly marked.
19. b. *Naut.* The arching or camber of a ship's deck or deck-beams.
1894 W. H. WHITE *Man. Naval Arch.* (ed. 3) 61 The provisions of the Act of 1854 may be briefly summarized. Spaces 'solely occupied by and necessary for the proper working of the boilers and machinery' are measured. These spaces include the internal volume of the ship, below the deck forming the 'crown' of the engine and boiler-rooms.
c. The arched surface of a bowling-green. (Cf. **crown green*.)
1897 *Encycl. Sport* (1911) I. 332/1 In Lancashire each green has a 'crown' varying in rise and slope.
31. b. Short for CROWN-GLASS.
1854 *Tomlinson's Cycl. Useful Arts* I. 761/1 Regarding glass as a chemical,..the various kinds have been distributed in the following manner: 2..English crown,..3..foreign crown. 1902 *Encycl. Brit.* XXV. 41/2 The experiments of the eminent Jena glass-makers with phosphate crowns and borate flints. *Ibid.*, A triple combination of ordinary crown and flint with a boro-silicate flint.
c. The boring end of a diamond or similar drill.
1883 *Encycl. Brit.* XVI. 444/1 The working part of the drill consists of the so-called crown, which is a short piece of tube made of cast steel, at one end of which a number of black diamonds are fastened into small cavities.
d. A term used to designate the fineness of wire used in carding operations.
1884 MCLAREN *Spinning* (ed. 2) 211 The crown..is the number of wires in 1 inch along it.
35. crown-arch, an arched plate supporting the crown-sheet of a locomotive; **crown-bar**, a bar serving the same purpose as a crown-arch (Knight); **crown-bark**, Peruvian bark obtained from *Cinchona officinalis*; **crown-berry**, the Cape cranberry, *Dovyalis rhamnoides*; **crown borer**, a drill having a cutter equipped with diamonds or steel teeth for boring purposes; **crown-bud**, the flower-bud of a chrysanthemum shoot that forms after the plant 'breaks' or branches (*first crown bud*) or, if this is removed, the bud that forms on the secondary shoot (*second crown bud*); **Crown Derby**, trade name of the Derby porcelain during a period of its manufacture (see *DERBY 6), bearing a crown as an additional distinguishing mark; **crown green**, a bowling green which is higher at the middle than at the sides; **crown lens**, the convex lens of an achromatic lens, made of crown-glass; **crown tuber**, a tuber of which the lower part is root and the upper part stem or crown, as in beetroot and carrot.
a 1884 *Railroad Gazette* XXII. 356 (Knight) *Crown arch. 1880 C. R. MARKHAM *Peruv. Bark* 233 The *crown barks of Loxa. 1907 SIM *Forests & For. Flora Col. Cape Gd. Hope* 132 '*Crownberry' is in use at East London, and may have originated in the crown-like calyx of *D*[*ovyalis*] *rhamnoides*. 1902 *Encycl. Brit.* XXXI. 643/1 Attempts are being made to substitute a rotary '*crown' borer for the percussion drill in sinking wells for petroleum. 1900 *Book of Gardening* (ed. W. D. Drury) 140 These growths form buds (termed *crown buds)..These buds..are taken out, and another shoot is made, which produces a 'terminal', or second crown, bud. 1906 *Daily Chron.* 17 Nov. 9/5 When growing for an individual flower of the largest size, a crown bud is generally selected. 1883 *Daily News* 18 Dec. 3/7 The dessert service of *Crown Derby china which is to be presented to Mr. Gladstone. 1906 ELIN. GLYN *Visits Eliz.* 85 When he saw the best Crown Derby smashed on the floor. 1902 *Encycl. Brit.* XXVI. 327/2 There are two kinds of green—one the *crown, and the other the level. 1928 *Observer* 15 Apr. 29/5 What are known as Crown greens. 1834 P. BARLOW in *Phil. Trans.* CXXIV. 202 The *crown lens must be made concave and the flint lens convex. 1845 T. DICK *Pract. Astron.* iv. § 5. (1857) 89/2 The predominating refraction of the crown lens disposed the achromatic rays to meet at a distant focus. 1900 L. H. BAILEY *Cycl. Amer. Hort.* 404/1 **Crown-tuber*, a tuber of which the top is stem and the lower part root, as the radish.

Crown, *v.*[1] Add:
5. b. To furnish (a road) with a crown.
1907 S. E. WHITE *Arizona Nights* I. xvi. 232 They ploughed her [*sc.* a road], and crowned her, and scraped her.
6. c. *Dentistry.* To put an artificial crown on (a tooth).
1904 *Dental Surgeon* 3 Dec. 80/2 Crowning Live Teeth. 1907 *Westm. Gaz.* 23 Oct. 9/1 The teeth were crowned.
d. *intr.* To rise in the centre.
1900 *Circular Twin-Wheel Cycle Co.* 5 Practice in steering and turning on roads that crown.

Crowner[1]. **2.** *U.S.* (Earlier and later examples.)
1815 *Massachusetts Spy* 31 May (Th. 146) This is the crowner, the cap-sheaf. 1922 ALICE BROWN *Old Crow* xxvii. 320 Isn't that a joke, Rookie? Charlotte would say it's the crowner.

Crow's foot. 4. (Earlier U.S. examples.)
1830 O. W. HOLMES *Myst. Visitor* 6, What if the creature should arise,..And swallow down a sophomore, Coat, crow's-foot, cap, and all! 1835 *Class Poem Harvard* 18 in B. H. Hall *College Words* (1851) 88 The corded crow's-feet, and the collar square.
b. A mark or symbol resembling a bird's foot.
1871 *Scribner's Monthly* II. 502 [A chart] adorned at this point by the crowfeet that call for a chain of mountains.
6. = *CROWFOOT *sb.* 2 f.
1849 *Rep. U.S. Comm. Patents, Agric.* (1850) 156 'Crow's foot'..grows with great vigor, though an annual grass.

Croy (kroi). *Sc.* [Inferred from early Sc. *croys*, pl. of *cro* wattled enclosure for catching fish: cf. CREW[2], CROO, CRUIVE.] A structure in a river designed to hold back the water and restrict it to a certain channel.
1825 *Jamieson's Dict.* Suppl. 1874 KNIGHT *Dict. Mech.*, *Croy*, a mound or structure projecting into a stream, to break the force of the water on a particular part and prevent encroachments. 1908 *Baily's Mag.* May 380 Croys may be convenient for casting from. 1909 W. L. CALDERWOOD *Salmon Rivers Scot.* 70 At Edradynate the system of croy-building has been carefully developed by Mr. H. W. Johnston, so that in one large pool alone..there are eleven croys.

Croydon. Add: **2.** Trade name for a heavy calico; also a kind of cotton sheeting.
1910 *Encycl. Brit.* VII. 277/2 (*Cotton*), *Croydon*, which seems to be an arbitrary trade name, is a heavy, bleached, plain calico, usually stiff and glossy in finish.

Croze, *v.*[1] (Earlier U.S. example.)
1849 *Rep. U.S. Comm. Patents* (1850) 386, I also claim the apparatus for chamfering and howelling and crozing.

Crozier (krōu·ziəɹ). [f. CROZE *v.*[2] + -IER.] One who opens and refolds hat-bodies in the making of felt hats.
1921 *Dict. Occup. Terms* (1927) § 429.

Crucifixion. Add: **2. c.** (See quot.) So **Crucify** *v.*
1917 EMPEY *From Fire Step* 149 The famous Field Punishment No. 1. Tommy has nicknamed it 'crucifixion'. It means that a man is spread-eagled on a limber wheel two hours a day for twenty-one days. During this time he only gets water, bully beef, and biscuits for his chow. You get 'crucified' for repeated minor offences.

Cruciform, *a.* Add: of a girder (see quot.).
1928 V. W. PAGE *Mod. Aircraft* 67 *Cruciform girder*, the structure, consisting of vertical and horizontal transverse girders, which is fitted at the stern of a rigid airship for the purpose of supporting the inboard ends of the sternposts of the fins or the rudderposts.

Crude, *a.* Add:
1. b. *Crude fibre*, the cellulose residue obtained in the chemical analysis of vegetable matter.
1895 CROSS & BEVAN *Cellulose* 165 'Crude Fibre'.—'Rohfaser'. 1901 — *Researches on Cellulose* 16 The product of this treatment, viz. 'crude fibre', is a mixture, containing furfuroids and lignone compounds. 1910 *Encycl. Brit.* V. 606/2 In the analysis of fodder plants,..the residue obtained after successive acid and alkaline hydrolysis is the 'crude fibre' of the agricultural chemist.
c. *Crude oil*, natural mineral oil.
1896 B. REDWOOD *Petroleum* I. 215 The crude oil of Upper Burma. *Ibid.*, The solid hydrocarbons present in crude petroleum. 1911 *Encycl. Brit.* XXI. 317/2 Paraffins are found in all crude oils.
11. As *sb.* **a.** Crude oil (see *1 c).
1916 T. J. HOOVER *Concentrating Ores by Flotation* (ed. 3) 123 Russian crude. 1921 J. E. POGUE *Econ. Petroleum* 79 The details of a complete refinery differ according to the type of crude employed. *Ibid.* 82 Asphaltic crudes, such as those of the Gold Coast. 1922 D. T. DAY *Petrol. Industry* II. 12 A high-priced, stock-producing crude.
b. *pl.* Crude or unconcentrated ore. *Austral.*

Cruise, *v.* Add:
2. To prospect for timber. (Cf. *CRUISER 3.) *U.S.*
1895 *Outing* (U.S.) XXVII. 218/2, I found he was off 'cruising' (i.e. hunting up good timber tracts).

Cruiser. Add:
1. b. A yacht constructed or adapted for cruising, as distinguished from a 'racer'.
1879 in E. Bonnaffé *Dict. Angl.* 1888 *Encycl. Brit.* XXIV. 724/2 As to the number of yachts now afloat, cruisers as well as racers, the British yacht fleet..now numbers..3000 yachts.
c. A large police-car. *U.S.*
1929 *Saturday Evening Post* 7 Dec. 68/2 The cruisers are high-powered seven-passenger touring cars manned by a crew of four.
2. *transf.* One who tours or travels about on land.

1927 *Observer* 25 Sept. 24 With the coming of autumn motor wanderers begin to plan their foreign tours...It is certainly an excellent axiom that the perfect motor cruiser is happiest when he makes no plans at all.
3. A prospector. *U.S.*
1893 *Scribner's Mag.* June 695/1 My first day's experience as a 'Cruiser' or 'Landlooker'. 1909 S. E. WHITE *Rules of Game* V. viii, Even if a cruiser in the old days happened to look down on this, he wouldn't realize how good it was.
b. A long-legged boot. *U.S.*
1902 S. E. WHITE *Blazed Trail* xvii. 125 Dressed in broad hats, flannel shirts, coarse trousers tucked in high-laced 'cruisers'. 1903 — *Forest* x. 129 He brought to light.. 'cruisers' of varying degree of height.
4. *Boxing.* Short for *cruiser-weight* (see *5).
1928 *Daily Tel.* 28 Feb. 16 Poor heavy-weights. Gallant 'cruisers'.
5. *attrib.* and *Comb.*, as *cruiser squadron*; *cruiser-built* adj.; **cruiser-weight** *Boxing*, 'light-heavy' weight, not exceeding 12 stone 6 lb. (between middle and heavy).
1902 *Westm. Gaz.* 7 May 5/1 *Cruiser-built merchantmen. 1901 *Ibid.* 30 July 6/2 *Cruiser squadrons. 1922 *Daily Mail* 11 Nov. 11 Jack Bloomfield, the *cruiser-weight champion. 1923 *Ibid.* 10 Jan. 9 He will go for the cruiser-weight trophy.

Cruller. *U.S.* (Earlier example.)
1808 PIKE *Sources Mississ.* (1810) II. App. 11 A dish of tea.., boiled meat and crullers.

Crumb, *sb.* Add:
1. c. In artificial silk manufacture (see quots.).
1927 M. H. AVRAM *Rayon Industry* 259 Following the steeping operation the blocks of alkali-cellulose are shredded. In this operation, which is usually carried out in a machine called a shredder or disintegrator, the cellulose is reduced to very finely divided particles called crumbs. 1929 T. WOODHOUSE *Artif. Silk* (ed. 2) 104 The action of the internal parts of the kneader breaks up the [alkali-cellulose] sheets effectively into small particles similar to small breadcrumbs, and hence these particles are called 'crumbs'.

Crumen (krū·men). *Zool.* [ad. L. *crumēna* purse.] The suborbital gland in deer and antelopes, secreting a waxy substance.
1875 W. H. FLOWER in *Proc. Zool. Soc.* 160 There was no suborbital gland or crumen [in a musk-deer]. 1883 — in *Encycl. Brit.* XV. 348/2 The suborbital gland or 'crumen' of Antelopes and Deer.

Crump, *sb.*[4] Add:
2. The sound of a heavy shell or bomb exploding; hence, the shell itself. *Crump-hole*, a hole or crater made by a shell. *Soldiers' slang.*
1914 *Times* 10 Dec. 6/1 The heavy shell..ending in a loud 'crump' as it bursts on the ground. 1915 D. O. BARNETT *Lett.* 180 Suddenly a yellow cloud leaped up three times as high as the tower itself..and after a bit there was the deuce of a crump. *Ibid.* 220, I got buried by a six-inch crump. 1915 BOYD CABLE *Between Lines* 254 There was some fancy driving past them crump holes in the road. 1916 BEAN *Lett. from France* (1917) 75 We can hear the *crump, crump, crump* of heavy explosives almost incessantly. 1917 P. GIBBS *Battles of Somme* 171 The enemy was 'lathering' the field of observation with every kind of 'crump' and shell.

Crump, *v.*[2] Add:
4. To bombard with heavy shells. *Soldiers' slang.*
1915 BOYD CABLE *Between Lines* 254 We could hear the blighters crumpin' away back down the road behind us. 1916 *Blackw. Mag.* Jan. 125/1 You may imagine with what methodical solemnity the Bosche 'crumps' the interior of that constricted area. 1920 J. C. F. FULLER *Tanks in Gt. War* 54 The ground had..become severely 'crumped' in places.

Crumpet. Add:
4. *slang.* **a.** A trivial term of endearment.
1900 G. SWIFT *Somerley* 40 You're Ophelia, Scrubby; but don't you go winking at the johnnies in the stalls, you giddy little crumpet!
b. The head. *Balmy* or *barmy on the crumpet*: wrong in the head, 'cracked': see *BALMY *a.* 7. Also *off one's crumpet.*
1891 [see *BALMY *a.* 7]. 1902 *Strand Mag.* Mar. 298 He placed his hand against his forehead. 'Barmy on the crumpet', he observed. 1909 H. G. WELLS *Tono-Bungay* III. iii. 276, I heard my aunt admit that one of the Stuart Durgan ladies did look a bit 'balmy on the crumpet'.

Crumple, *sb.* Add:
2. *fig.* The act of giving way or collapsing. (Cf. *CRUMPLE *v.* 5 c.)
1909 H. G. WELLS *Ann Veronica* vii. 240 The other's a crumple-up—just surrender. Funk! I'll see it out.

Crumple, *v.* Add: **5. c.** (with *up*). To give way, collapse (under hostile pressure or attack).
1898 *Westm. Gaz.* 17 May 2/2 It may be well that the Spanish defeat should not be too immediately overwhelming. It may help to keep Spain stable internally if she does not 'crumple up' at once.
7. *fig.* To deprive of strength and energy.
1892 KIPLING *Barrack-room Ballads, Yng. Brit. Soldier* iv, For the sickness gets in as the liquor dies out, An' it crumples the young British soldier.

Crumply, *a.* Add: **b.** Having crumpled horns.
1885 'C. E. CRADDOCK' *Prophet Gt. Smoky Mtn.* iii. 59 Dorinda, hunting for the vagrant 'crumply cow', paused sometimes. *Ibid.* 70.

Crunchable (krʊ·nʃăb'l), *a.* [f. CRUNCH *v.* + -ABLE.] Capable of being crunched or crushed.
1906 WELLS *In Days of Comet* I. iv. § 3 The coal-cellar.. opened, and diffused small crunchable particles about the uneven brick floor.

Crunchingly (krʊ·nʃiŋli), *adv.* [f. CRUNCHING *ppl. a.* + -LY[2].] In a crunching manner; with a crunching action or sound.
1843 A. J. SYMINGTON *Harebell Chimes* (1849) 24 While there crisp'd 'neath her feet The snow crunchingly. 1927 *Chambers's Jrnl.* 79/1 Carwardine stepped out on to the shingle, with no particular caution as to noise—quite crunchingly, in fact.

Crunchy (krʊ·nʃi), *a. colloq.* [f. CRUNCH *v.* or *sb.* + -Y[1].] Characterized by crunching; fit for crunching or for being crunched. Hence **Cru·nchiness**, quality of being 'crunchy'.
1892 W. BESANT in *Pictorial World* 6 Feb. 434/2 Showing molars of a whiteness and crunchiness both beautiful and awful. 1928 *Daily Express* 14 June 4 The ripe-corn flavour and delightful 'crunchiness'..make it unusually tempting. 1929 *Ibid.* 3 Jan. 5 The crispest and crunchiest of nuts from Brazil.

Crunkle (krʊ·ŋk'l), *v.*[3] [Echoic.] *intr.* To make a harsh dry sound, as by grinding the jaws. Hence **Cru·nkling** *vbl. sb.*
1882 FLOYER *Unexpl. Baluch.* 362 The 'crunkling' noise of so many feeding together. 1900 *Westm. Gaz.* 5 Sept. 2/3 The crabs..crunkled loud and long.

Cruse. b. Add: Also *widow's cruse.*

Crush, *sb.* Add:
2. d. *To have* or *get a crush on*: to be enamoured of, take a strong fancy to. orig. *U.S. slang.*
1914 GERTR. ATHERTON *Perch of Devil* I. 31 Some of the younger married women..get a crush on some other woman's husband. *Ibid.* 186 To be jealous you've got to have a fearful crush. 1917 WILL IRWIN *Reporter at Armag.* 349 'She has a crush on our military chauffeur', said the doctor. 1928 *Punch* 2 May 484/1 Gervase and Pontefract had had a quiet sort of masculine crush on Joyce for some time.
e. Hence, a person whom one is 'gone on'.
1929 JELLIFFE & WHITE *Dis. Nervous Syst.* (ed. 5) 335 They tend to be aggressive, domineering and often play the man role with their schoolmates, or 'crushes'.
4. c. A number of persons; a 'crowd'. orig. *U.S. colloq.*
1924 A. J. SMALL *Frozen Gold* i. 40 Any one of that crush would do murder for no more than that 500 dollars reward.
d. A body of troops; a unit of a regiment. *Soldiers' slang.*
1916 BOYD CABLE *Action Front* 151 You want to ask something about someone in the old crush [*sc.* regiment]. 1927 *Observer* 12 June 10/3 The best recruiter is the man who is pleased with his 'crush'.
e. A funnel-shaped fenced passage along which cattle are driven one by one for branding. *Austral.*
1872 C. H. EDEN *My Wife & I in Queensland* iii. 69 A crush, which is an elongated funnel, becoming so narrow at the end that a beast is wedged in and unable to move. 1889 MRS. CAMPBELL PRAED *Romance of Station* ii, The 'crush', or branding lane. *Ibid.* iv, Those animals which were drafted through the crush into the mob destined for sale. 1895 *Chambers's Jrnl.* 702/2 A crush—that is, long lines of parallel fences just wide enough for one horse to pass at a time—was erected; they were driven into this long lane.
6. b. *spec.* in *Geol.* with reference to compression, thrust, or shattering of rock: as *crush-breccia, -conglomerate, -line, -material, -movement, -plane, -zone.*
1893 GEIKIE *Text-bk. Geol.* (ed. 3) 703 Dykes of 50 or 60 yards in breadth are reduced, where one of these crush-lines crosses them obliquely, to a thickness of no more than four feet. 1903 M. M. OGILVIE-GORDON in *Trans. Edin. Geol. Soc.* VIII. 30 The previous investigators of Fassa Valley failed to recognise the presence of the innumerable crush-planes with extremely low hade. 1903 *Nature* 12 Feb. 359/1 This passage-zone had been the great crush-zone of the district. 1904 *Ibid.* 16 June 166/1 The post-Bala crush-movements. 1930 PEACH & HORNE *Geol. Scotl.* 62 The belt of sheared rocks and flinty crush-material.

Crush, *v.* **3. b.** Add: Also, *to crush one's way.*
1893 F. F. MOORE *I Forbid Banns* xlvii, He came into the room just now and crushed his way up to her at once.

Crusher. 2. Add: A crushing blow.
1888 F. W. J. HENNING *Recoll. Prize Ring* 18 Caunt now got closer for a try, but missed an intended crusher.

Cru:socrea·tinin. *Physiol. Chem.* Also -ine. [app. incorrectly f. Gr. χρυσός gold.] A leucomaine of the creatinin group, obtained from muscular tissue.
1910 *Practitioner* June 829 Leucomaines in fresh muscular tissue:—Xantho-creatinin...Cruso-creatinin.

Crusoe (krū·so). One who is shipwrecked on a desert island, like the hero of Defoe's romance. Also *attrib.* and *Comb.*, as *Crusoe life*, *-like* adj. and adv. Hence **Cru·soeing**, living like Crusoe.
1888 STEVENSON *Lantern-Bearers* i. in *Across the Plains* (1892) 210 And then you might go Crusoeing, a word that covers all extempore eating in the open air. 1907 *Daily Chron.* 3 July 5/5 There he had built himself a habitation, Crusoe-like, out of brushwood. 1908 *Ibid.* 16 July 1/5 Blades of penknives were fashioned into needles, hair-combs were made from bush thorns, and altogether the men led a regular Crusoe life. 1926 *Chambers's Jrnl.* 104/1 No other island ..has accommodated more Crusoes during the last three centuries than Chatham Island. *Ibid.*, There is another and fell aspect of Crusoeing, however—an aspect which most fiction-writers carefully ignore.

Crust, *sb.* Add: **5. c.** *U.S.* (Earlier example.)
1809 A. HENRY *Travels* 146 The crust upon the snow cutting his legs..to the very bone.
7. b. Impudence, effrontery. *slang.*
1924 P. G. WODEHOUSE *Inimitable Jeeves* xiv, The blighter had the cold, cynical crust to look me in the eyeball without a blink. 1927 — *Small Bach.* xviii. 243 When a woman has the crust to disparage the morals of one of the finest young fellows who ever came out of the golden West.
13. b. *spec.* in *Geol.* (see 4 b), as *crust-block, -fold, -fracture, -lag, -movement, -strain, -stress, -torsion.*
1897 *Geogr. Jrnl.* June 669 There are two primary and permanent kinds of crust-movements. 1900 *Ibid.* Jan. 48 The great Rocky Mountain-Andes fold,..the longest and most continuous crust-fold of the present day. 1900 M. M. OGILVIE-GORDON *Ibid.* Oct. 457 That phenomena of crust-torsion were induced by any combination of crust-pressures. *Ibid.*, The original cause of crust-strains. *Ibid.* 460 Old crust-forms and crust-fractures, especially such as allow occasional intrusion and outlet of volcanic material, are determining factors in the distribution of the subsequent deposits. *Ibid.* 461 Gigantic crust-creep of overthrust masses. 1903 in *Trans. Edin. Geol. Soc.* VIII. 177 The form of the sill-complex was capable of being re-moulded periodically in harmony with the localised crust-stresses. 1907 *19th Cent.* Aug. 220 The remarkable crust-movements exhibited over a wide area. 1926 *Chambers's Jrnl.* 598/2, I would..hazard also the suggestion that crust-lag may be a potent factor, in conjunction with shrinkage of the earth's crust, in the causation of earth-tremors and earthquakes. 1929 *Encycl. Brit.* II. 980/2 According to current views of the mechanics of mountain-folding, a crust-block of old and hard rocks is always present, which receives the pressure of the thrust causing the folding.

Crusta (krʊ·stă). The L. original of CRUST, used in some scientific senses and combinations; as **a.** *Zool.* The hard integument or shell of crustaceans and some molluscs and insects (= CRUST *sb.* 6); **b.** *Bot.* The crustaceous thallus of some lichens; **c.** *Anat.* The lower part of the *crus cerebri*; **d.** *Path.* A scab or eschar (= CRUST *sb.* 3); **e.** *Crusta fibrosa*, *c. petrosa*, the cement of a tooth (CEMENT *sb.* 4); **f.** *Crusta phlogistica*, the buffy coat of the blood when coagulated; **g.** *Crusta lactea*, an eruptive disease of infants at the breast, milk-scab, milk-blotch.
1806 *Med. Jrnl.* XV. 33 Crusta Lactea..sometimes proves a very severe..disease; in some families attacking every child at the age of a few weeks. 1866 *Treas. Bot.*, *Crusta*, the upper surface of lichens. 1876 T. BRYANT *Pract. Surg.* (ed. 2) I. 537 The crusta petrosa is formed on the gradually elongating root through the agency of the dental sac or capsule which surrounds the forming tooth crown. 1929 *Encycl. Brit.* IV. 12/2 The superficial part (crusta) of each crus..consists of motory and sensory nerve fibres. *Ibid.* XXI. 874/1 Surrounding the dentine where it is not covered by enamel is the 'cement' or 'crusta petrosa', a thin layer of bone.
h. *Antiq.* A thin plate of embossed metal, etc., inlaid on a vessel, wall, or other object.
1842 BRANDE *Dict. Sci.*, etc., *Crustæ*, in Gem Sculpture, a gem engraved for inlaying on a vase or other object. 1910 *Encycl. Brit.* XIV. 627/2 The *proscenium* of the Odeum was lined with *crustae*, or 'marble-veneering', under one inch thick. 1911 *Ibid.* XXIII. 484/1 The *crustae*, or plaques decorated in repoussé, which were mounted on smooth silver cups. *Ibid.*, Cups adorned with golden *crustae*.

Crustacean, *a.* Add:
2. Of the wings of an aeroplane.
1928 *Daily Tel.* 10 Apr. 4 'Crustacean' wings, in which the metal lifting surface itself takes the stresses.

Crustal, *a.* Add: esp. of the crust of the earth or moon.
1883 A. WINCHELL *World-Life* 402 (Cent. Dict.) The addition of crustal layers upon the exterior [of the moon]. 1898 *Jrnl. Sch. Geog.* (U.S.) Oct. 286 Long ago the crustal rocks were crowded together in a great system of wrinkles. 1924 SKERL tr. *Wegener's Orig. Cont. & Oceans* 14 An explanation of mountain building must take into account immense tangential crustal movements.

Crusting, *vbl. sb.* **2.** *U.S.* (Earlier example.)
1839 C. F. HOFFMAN *Wild Scenes* I. xviii. 92 'Crusting' is the term applied to taking large game amid the deep snows of winter, when the crust of ice which forms upon the surface after a slight rain is enough to support the weight of a man, but gives way at once to the hoofs of a moose or a deer.

Crustless (krʊ·stlės), *a.* [See -LESS.] Made without a crust.
1927 *Daily Tel.* 6 Dec. 2 English crustless cheese.

Cry, *sb.* **14.** Add: See also quot. 1873.
1873 J. H. BEADLE *Undevel. West* ii. 57 The coach drags heavily, the wheels often causing a disagreeable 'cry' in the sand and soda.
19. *To follow in the cry*: to be in the following crowd of undistinguished or unimportant people.
1928 *Manchester Guardian Weekly* 27 July 72/1 Timmis is not always a mere follower in the cry. *Ibid.* 31 Aug. 172/2 In 'the provinces' we can hardly muster a coterie; we are content to follow in the cry, to be merged to be an insignificant part of the great world.

Cry, *v.* **18. b.** *fig.* (U.S. example.)
1849 D. J. BROWNE *Amer. Poultry Yd.* (1855) 74 A cross between the Cochin-China, and some other large eastern fowl, which, at present, has nearly or quite 'cried back'.

Cryable (krəi·ăb'l), *a.* [f. CRY *v.* + -ABLE.] That may be cried or wept over.
1897 *Daily News* 22 Mar. 9/4 Tragedy means a cryable play. 1908 S. E. WHITE *Riverman* xxi. 188 What laughable and cryable mistakes she made only those who have encountered a like situation could realize.

Cry-baby. (Earlier U.S. examples.)
1851 ALICE CARY *Clovernook* 274 You had better be still, cry-baby. 1854 MARY J. HOLMES *Tempest & Sunshine* xiii. 180, I wouldn't be such a cry-baby, anyway.
Hence **Cry-baby** *v. intr.*
1902 WISTER *Virginian* vii. 85, I am not crybabying to the judge.

Cryoconite, mod. form of KRYOKONITE. See also quot. 1924.
1922 C. S. WRIGHT & R. E. PRIESTLEY *Glaciology* 111

Cryoconite holes which have at one time definitely contained water. 1924 *Nature* 22 Mar. 418/1 The authors adopt the term 'cryoconite' for wind-blown sand in the ice. 1925 Odell in E. F. Norton *Fight for Everest, 1924* 311 The so-called 'cryoconite holes' or 'dust wells'.

Cryogenic (kraiodʒe·nik), *a.* [f. Cryogen + -ic.] Of or pertaining to cryogens or to the production of low temperatures.

1902 Dewar in *Encycl. Brit.* XXX. 287 Within recent years several special cryogenic laboratories have been established.

Cryohydric (kraiohai·drik), *a.* [f. Cryohydr-ate + -ic.] Of or pertaining to a cryohydrate. *Cryohydric point* or *temperature*, the freezing-point of a cryohydrate.

1902 *Encycl. Brit.* XXVIII. 569/1 This can only occur at the cryohydric temperature. 1903 *Amer. Chem. Jrnl.* Mar. 205 Such a system can exist only at its cryohydric temperature, and the composition of the solution is fixed. 1910 *Encycl. Brit.* XI. 371/2 The solution must necessarily become saturated with respect to both ice and salt, and this can only occur at the cryohydric temperature. 1929 *Ibid.* XXII. 111/2 Cryohydric Points.

Cryoscopic, Cryoscopy, modern ff. Kryoscopic, Kryoscopy.

1900 *Rep. Brit. Assoc.* 167 The cryoscopic behaviour of substances possessing constitutions similar to that of the solvent. 1903 *Nature* 15 Jan. 263/1 The methods of exact cryoscopy. 1908 *Practitioner* Sept. 435 In differential diagnosis, he regards cryoscopic examination as of great importance. 1909 *Ibid.* Nov. 664 Kümmel is satisfied in such cases with the cryoscopy of the blood. 1910 *Ibid.* Mar. 305 Cryoscopy of the separated urines. 1927 E. W. H. Groves *Synops. Surg.* (ed. 8) 568 The freezing-point is known as the cryoscopic index.

Cryptæsthesia (kriptɪspī·ziă). *Psychics.* Also -esthesia (-espī·ziă). [f. Gr. κρυπτός (see Crypto-) + αἴσθησις perception + -ia¹.] Supernormal knowledge, whether telepathic or clairvoyant.

1923 tr. *C. Richet's 30 Yrs. Psych. Research* II. ii. 64 Nearly the whole of subjective metapsychics can be reduced to a single phenomenon which the magnetizers of a past age called 'lucidity' or 'clairvoyance'..; which is now called telepathy.. I propose to name it cryptesthesia. 1926 *Spectator* 9 Oct. 601/2 The dowser..is a person endowed with a subconscious supernormal cryptesthesia.

Cryptic, *a.* Add: **3.** *Zool.* Serving for concealment, as markings or coloration.

1890 Poulton *Colours of Animals* xvii. 338 Cryptic colours. Protective and Aggressive Resemblances.

Crypto-. 1. Add: **Cryptomne·sia** [after *amnesia*] (see quots.). Hence **Cryptomne·sic** *a.*

1903 Myers *Hum. Pers.* I. p. xvi, *Cryptomnesia*, submerged or subliminal memory of events forgotten by the supraliminal self. *Ibid.* II. 136 'Cryptomnesia' (as Professor Flournoy calls submerged memory). *Ibid.* 140 This cryptomnesic automatism. 1916 tr. *Jung's Coll. Papers Anal. Psychol.* 91 The rudimentary glossolalia of our case has not any title to be a classical instance of cryptomnesia. *Ibid.*, The cryptomnesic image arrives at consciousness through the senses.

Cryptogenetic (kriptodʒĕne·tik), *a. Path.* [f. Crypto- + -genetic.] Of a disease: Of obscure or unknown origin. Also (in the same sense) **Cryptogenic** (-dʒe·nik), **Cryptogenous** (-ǫ·dʒĕnəs) *adjs.* [see *-genic, *-genous].

1908 R. Park *Mod. Surg.* I. 87 Cryptogenetic or spontaneous septicemia is a term applied to those cases in which the port of entry of the germs is no longer visible—*e.g.*, a hypodermic puncture—or cannot be positively determined. 1908 *Practitioner* Feb. 249–50 Cryptogenic pernicious anaemia...So-called 'cryptogenic' sepsis, or pyaemia.

Cryptomeria (kriptomī·riă). [mod.L. (Don), f. Gr. κρυπτός (see Crypto-) + μέρος part. So named because the seeds are hidden or enclosed by scales.] An evergreen coniferous tree (*C. japonica*) allied to the cypresses, a native of North China and Japan, and now extensively cultivated in England; the Japanese Cedar.

1852 R. Fortune *Journ. Tea Countries China* xviii. 304 The beautiful *Cryptomeria*, or Japan cedar. 1863 Alcock *Capit. Tycoon* I. iv. 103 A long avenue of cryptomerias and pines. 1886 *Athenæum* 17 July 72/1 The valleys..are filled with..acacias, cedars, cryptomerias, and chestnuts. 1895 'Clive Holland' *Japanese Wife* vii, The grove of giant camellias, camphor-wood trees, and cryptomerias. 1904 Sladen *Playing the Game* xii, An avenue of tall cryptomerias.

Cryptozoic (kriptozōu·ik), *a.* [f. Gr. κρυπτός (see Crypto-) + ζωή life + -ic.]

1. *Biol.* Defining a class of fauna composed of animals living a concealed or hidden life (see quots.); also, belonging to this class.

1895 A. Dendy *Presid. Addr. Section D Austral. Assoc. Adv. Sci.* 1 The Cryptozoic Fauna of Australasia...I use the word 'Cryptozoic' for want of a better. 1898 Parker & Haswell *Zool.* (1910) II. 637 Cryptozoic forms, which live under stones, logs of wood, &c., such as Land-Planarians, Peripatus, Centipedes, and Woodlice. 1911 *Encycl. Brit.* XXI. 707/1 The majority of marine Planarians are nocturnal or cryptozoic, hiding away during the period of low tide to avoid desiccation of their soft sticky bodies and coming out at night or during high tide to feed.

2. *Geol.* Designating limestones whose organic origin cannot be recognized by the naked eye.

1911 *Encycl. Brit.* XXII. 266/2.

Crystal, *sb.* Add: **4. c.** *fig.* (*a*) Applied to a statement regarded as a crystallization; (*b*) a prophecy derived from crystal-gazing.

1902 *Westm. Gaz.* 6 Nov. 2/3 The Cleveland by-election will always be memorable if only for the fact that the crystal has had a new form given to it. 1914 *Concise Oxf. Dict.* Addenda, *Crystal* colloq., view of the future thus obtained [*i.e.* by crystal-gazing], prophetic utterance.

12. *Wireless.* A piece of mineral (natural or artificial) used, in contact with a metal or another piece of mineral, to 'rectify' an oscillatory current, i.e. to allow it to pass through in one direction only. This device is called a *crystal detector* or *rectifier*. *Crystal receiver, set*, a receiving set in which the detector is a crystal.

1913 *Year-Bk. Wireless Telegr.* 419 Crystal Detector, a form of oscillation detector depending on the fact that certain crystals (*e.g.*, carborundum) allow current to pass through them more readily in one direction than in the other. 1918 W. H. Eccles *Wireless Telegr. & Teleph.* (ed. 2) 512 Thermoelectric Detector, Crystal Rectifier. 1923 J. A. Fleming *Wireless Telegr. & Teleph.* 20 The most generally used crystal is now galena (sulphide of lead). 1923 Hawkhead & Dowsett *Wireless Telegr.* 129 A good commercial crystal detector..should rectify with very small changes in potential. *Ibid.* 223 Crystal Receiver. 1924 E. T. Larner (*title*) Crystal Sets. 1925 B. E. Jones (*title*) Loud-speaker Crystal Sets. 1926 J. A. Fleming *Electr. Educator* I. 379/2 This detector consists of two crystals, zincite and chalcopyrites, in contact. 1928 W. James in *Morning Post* 26 Jan. 13/4 A crystal detector cannot amplify; a valve can and does.

B. 2. c. crystal-gazing, -vision, concentration of one's gaze on a ball of rock-crystal in order to obtain a telepathic or hallucinatory picture; similarly **crystal-gazer**; cf. *crystal-seer, -seeing* in Dict.

1889 *Proc. Soc. Psych. Research* V. 486 Recent Experiments in Crystal-vision. *Ibid.* 501 Crystal-seers. *Ibid.* 502 Examples of crystal-seeing. *Ibid.* 507 Crystal-gazing. 1898 A. Lang *Making of Religion* v. 90 Crystal Visions, Savage and Civilised. *Ibid.* 95 The crystal-gazer. 1919 M. K. Bradby *Psycho-analysis* 5 We read of automatic writing and painting of visions seen by crystal-gazers and clairvoyants. 1920 Rose Macaulay *Potterism* III. i. 108, Thought-readers, crystal-gazers, mediums and planchette-writers.

Crystalline, *sb.* Add:

6. A light soft dress-material.

1903 *Daily Chron.* 25 July 8/4 Crystalline differs very little from mousseline de soie, for it is a thin fabric with a silky sheen upon it, and a very charming one for afternoon summer frocks. 1923 *Daily Mail* 8 May 14 Soft crepe finish crystalline.

Csardas (tʃā·rdāʃ). Also *erron.* **czardas.** [Magyar.] A Hungarian national dance.

1883 'Ouida' *Wanda* vi, They ended their dances with the Hungarian czardas. 1886 W. J. Tucker *E. Europe* 217 The bewildering postures and maddening antics of the Csárdás. 1888 E. Gerard *Land Beyond the Forest* II. 245 Whenever the csardas comes to an end there is a violent clapping of hands to make the music resume.

Cuadrilla (kwadri·lya). [Sp.: see Quadrille *sb.*²] The troupe or following of a matador.

1893 Chapman & Buck *Wild Spain* v. 67 The *Espada*, or Matador, receives on the day from £120 to £200, including the services of his cuadrilla or troupe, which consists of two picadors, three banderilleros, and a cachetero. 1898 *Daily News* 11 Aug. 7/1 The crowd, blaming the bull, instead of the toreador and his cuadrilla, insisted on that animal being killed.

Cub, *sb.*¹ Add: **2. c.** A junior member of the organization known as 'Boy Scouts' (see Scout *sb.*³ 2 c). In full *wolf-cub*.

1922 A. Povser (*title*) The Cub Song Book. 1923 *Daily Mail* 11 June 16 Boy Scouts and Cubs furnished a guard of honour. 1927 *Ibid.* 12 July 10/4 A Hastings Rover Cubmaster. 1927 *Daily Tel.* 21 June 3/2 A child who had fallen into a mill stream..was rescued by a local cubmistress.

3. b. *spec.* An apprentice or beginner. *U.S.*

1883 'Mark Twain' *Life Mississippi* xii. 115 The pilot not on watch takes his 'cub' or steersman..and goes out in the yawl. *Ibid.* 117 Nothing delights a cub so much as an opportunity to go out sounding.

5. cub-bear; (sense *2 c) *cub-master, -mistress*; (sense *3 b) *cub-engineer, -pilot, -reporter.*

1834 H. Brackenridge *Recoll.* vii. 79 Some would rather pass for cub bears than be disappointed in their endeavours to attract attention. 1883 'Mark Twain' *Life Mississippi* iv. 45 They..learned to disappear when the ruthless 'cub'-engineer approached. *Ibid.* v. 47, I want to be a cub-pilot. 1908 A. Ruhl *Other Americans* ii. 9 The mere gringo feels like a cub reporter at the office of a campaign committee.

Cuban (kiū·băn), *a.* and *sb.* [See -an.] **A.** *adj.* Of or pertaining to Cuba. **B.** *sb.* A native or inhabitant of Cuba.

Cuban heel, a high, comparatively straight heel (in shoes).

1850 (*title*) Cuba and the Cubans; comprising a History of the Island. 1877 *Encycl. Brit.* VI. 679/1 Great sympathy had long been shown for the Cubans by the people of the United States. *Ibid.*, The yearly campaigns up to the present time have shown that in the eastern interior the Cuban patriots are practically invincible. 1878 *Chambers's Encycl.* III 349/1 The Cuban sugar-trade. *Ibid.* 350/1 'Cuba for the Cubans', is the watchword of the creoles. 1885 R. L. & F. Stevenson *The Dynamiter* 144 Story of the Fair Cuban. 1909 *Public Ledger* (Philad.) 24 June 5 Turned-sole Oxfords..Cuban heels. 1926 *Contemp. Rev.* Aug. 180 Among the mass of the Cuban peasants, the Cuban politician ..strikes a responsive chord.

Cubanize (kiū·bănaiz), *v.* [See -ize.] *trans.* To claim a right of protection or partial control over (a weaker but independent state), as the United States are alleged to have done with regard to Cuba. Hence **Cu:baniza·tion.**

1922 *Q. Rev.* July 151 The various Yankee associations whose ultimate aim is the attraction of Mexico within the political orbit of the United States, and its 'Cubanisation' by treaty. 1924 *Countries of the World* xv. 1525/1 Among Cuba's other claims to fame may be placed the fact that its political status has originated a new verb—to Cubanise... It is a quasi-protectorate of America and the word was invented to express this relation.

Cubbed (kɒbd), *ppl. a. poet.* [f. Cub *sb.*¹ + -ed ².] Possessed of cubs.

1889 Tennyson *Demeter & Perseph.* 54, I envied human wives, and nested birds, Yea, the cubb'd lioness.

Cubby. 1. (Earlier U.S. example.)

1868 *Congress. Globe* 2 June 2762/3 [Many of the national banks] keep a little cubby of an office, loan no money,..and yet draw interest on their circulation.

Cube (kū·bē), *sb.*² A South American plant the root of which contains a principle known as rotenone, used as an insecticide.

1930 *Sci. Amer.* Nov. 391 The cube plant now grows in a part of South America where the climate is similar to that of the Malay States.

Cubically, *adv.* Add: In the form of a cube or cubes.

1855 J. R. Leifchild *Cornwall* 61 Rocks rising cubically.

Cubicle. Add:

2. *Electr. Engineering.* A chamber or compartment to hold a switch-gear apparatus.

1911 J. F. C. Snell *Power House Design* 347 The oil-break switches are contained within glazed brick cubicles. *Ibid.* 349 The operating gallery and cubicle gallery in the Bahia Blanca power house. 1927 *Daily Tel.* 14 Mar. 4 Switch-gear cells and cubicles constructed of moulded stone.

Cubism (kiū·biz'm). [ad. F. *cubisme*, f. *cube* Cube *sb.*] A phase of post-impressionistic art in which the representation or design is based on the cube and other geometrical figures, and which lays emphasis upon volume as the important feature of objects. Hence **Cu·bist** [F. *cubiste*], an artist who adopts this style; also *attrib.* and as *adj.* Also **Cubi·stic** *a.*, **Cubi·stically** *adv.*

'The word "Cubism"..dates from 1908 and was pronounced for the first time, according to M. Léonce Rosenberg, by a member of the Hanging Committee of the Salon des Indépendants. As a canvas by Georges Braque was being carried by, this person exclaimed, "*Encore des Cubes! assez de cubisme!*" A journalist seized on the *mot* and spread it abroad, and the painter concerned, together with his associates, accepted the nickname and confessed themselves Cubists' (Rutter *Evol. Mod. Art* 80).

1911 *Illustr. Lond. News* 21 Oct. 648/1 Paris is perturbed by the Cubism and the Cubists of the Salon d'Automne. 1911 *Lit. Digest* (N.Y.) 18 Nov. 914/1 The cubists take the blocks of the pavement as their medium for interpreting the external world. 1913 tr. *Gleizes & Metzinger's Cubism* 16 To understand Cézanne is to foresee Cubism. 1915 A. J. Eddy *Cubists & Post-Impress.* 72 Cubism is simply a systematic use of planes. 1915 W. H. Wright *Mod. Painting* 187 Those whose criterion is prettiness are naturally attracted to Whistlerian and Cubistic modes. 1917 W. J. Locke *Red Planet* x. 113 All their talk was of Hauptmann and Sudermann..and in art—Heaven save the mark—the Cubist school. 1920 R. Fry *Vision & Design* 186 It is interesting to consider his Cubist period, since Marchand's reaction to Cubism is typical of his nature. 1921 P. M. Turner *Apprec. Painting* 193 There are a number of perfectly sincere painters who, being cubist by conviction, will probably continue to practise its principles. 1924 Galsworthy *White Monkey* II. ii. 133 [Painter to model] 'No, I shouldn't be treating you cubistically'. 1928 — *Swan Song* III. xiii. 317, I remember the first shows in London of those post-impressionists and early Cubist chaps.

transf. 1915 A. J. Eddy *Cubists & Post-Impress.* 64 A form of dramatic representation that is essentially Cubist, Futurist, and Orphist in its expression. 1926 W. J. Locke *Old Bridge* II. vi, The..German tourist and his cubistically attired wife. 1927 S. Vines *Movements* 3 Mr. Blunden is a case in point, this critic claiming him for the Georgians, while that one will allege that cubistic symptoms have characterised, if not marred, his later work. 1927 *Observer* 6 Mar. 21/3 A few [ladies' coats] display cubistic ideas, amusing to study in detail.

Cubitus (kiū·bitǒs). *Ent.* [L.: see Cubit.] (See quot.)

1826 Kirby & Sp. *Entomol.* III. 369 *Cubitus*, the fourth and elongated joint [in the first pair of legs in Hexapods], answering to the Tibia in the legs.

Cuckle-, Cuckold-bur, U.S. varr. Cockle-bur.

1821 T. Nuttall *Trav. Arkansa* ii. 58 The cornfields, at this season of the year, are so over-run with cuckold-burrs (*Xanthium Strumarium*)..as to prove extremely troublesome to woollen clothes.

Cuckoo, *sb.* Add:

3. b. A person, individual. *slang.*

1924 Galsworthy *White Monkey* I. ix. 77 'Don't worry, we'll dig up the just-right cuckoos, somehow'. 'A Chinese Minister would be perfect', mused Fleur.

9. cuckoo-fish *U.S.* (mod. example); **cuckoo fowl** (see quot.).

a 1884 J. C. Brevoort in Goode *Nat. Hist. Aquat. Anim.* (1884) 257 When freshly taken from the water they grunt quite loudly, whence their popular name of Grunter, or *Cuckoo-fish. 1849 D. J. Browne *Amer. Poultry Yd.* (1855) 55 *Cuckoo Fowl, of the Norfolk Farmyards, England, Barn-Door Fowl, of the English and Anglo-Americans.

Cuckoo (ku·kū), *a. U.S. slang.* [f. the sb.] Crazy, out of one's wits.

1923 P. G. Wodehouse *Inimit. Jeeves* xvii. 241 He pottered about the room for a bit, babbling at intervals. The boy seemed cuckoo. 1928 *Collier's* 29 Dec. 28/1 When everything..failed to reduce Jack's bulk, I was nearly cuckoo with rage and fear.

Cucumber. 4. Add: **cucumber-beetle, -bug, flea beetle** *U.S.* (see quots.); **cucumber-wood** *U.S.*, the wood of the cucumber-tree.

1861 *Trans. Ill. Agric. Soc.* (1865) V. 435 The various remedies adopted to check the ravages of the *cucumber beetle, would be appropriate. *Ibid.* 432 This insect..comes so near in its colors and markings to the *Diabolica vittata*, or '*cucumber-bug', that care must be taken to prevent mistake. 1877 *Rep. Vermont Board Agric.* IV. 154 The *Cucumber Flea Beetle,..a little black beetle..sometimes attacks the raspberry. 1904 'O. Henry' *Cabbages & Kings* x. 161 Johnny Atwood..prated feebly of cool water to be had in the *cucumber-wood pumps of Dalesburg.

Cucumber-tree. *U.S.* (See Cucumber 4.)

1781–2 Jefferson *Notes on Virginia* (1787) 38 Cucumber-tree. Magnolia acuminata. 1784 J. Filson *Kentucke* 23 The cucumber-tree is small and soft, with remarkable leaves, [and] bears a fruit much resembling that from which it is named. 1797 Morse *Amer. Gazetteer* s.v. *Territory*, The more useful trees are..elm, cucumber tree, lynn tree. 1832 D. J. Browne *Sylva Amer.* 205 The cucumber tree sometimes exceeds 80 feet in height. 1834 *Southern Lit. Messenger* I. 98 The customary variety of oak, ash maple and hickory presents itself, mingled with the cucumber tree (*Magnolia Acuminata*). 1895 'C. E. Craddock' *Myst. Witch-Face Mt.* iii. 56 Near at hand, a cucumbertree with its great, broad green leaves and its deep red cones..gave the only touch of color.

Cud, *sb.* **4.** Add: **cud-chewer,** a ruminant animal.

1927 Haldane & Huxley *Anim. Biol.* iv. 112 In cud-chewers like the cow and sheep.

Cuddleable (kɒ·d'lăb'l), *a. colloq.* [See -able.] = Cuddlesome.

1928 E. Wallace *Again the Three Just Men* 32 The Lord has given you kissable lips and a cuddleable body. 1928 *Daily Express* 18 May 11/1, I do not want a brainless doll, but I would like a jolly, lovable, cuddleable woman.

Cuddlesome, *a.* Delete *nonce-wd.* and add quots.:

1893 *Ardrossan & Saltcoats Herald* 1 Sept. 3 The crowd of cuddlesome darlings in nice frocks. 1923 *Daily Mail* 27 Feb. 7 A rattlesnake has produced a family of thirty babies. There is nothing of cuddlesome, infant softness about these tenfold triplets.

Cuddly, *a.* Delete *nonce-wd.* and add to def.: Such as invites cuddling; = Cuddlesome.

1915 Galsworthy *Freelands* xxxvi, She laid her face beside his on the pillow...It made everything seem cuddly and warm. 1923 *Daily Mail* 16 Mar. 14 Cuddly toys appeal to babies. 1924 D. H. Lawrence *England* 55 He put his arm round her and drew her a little nearer to him, in a very warm and cuddly manner. 1927 P. G. Wodehouse *Small Bach.* i. § 1. 6 'Are you trying to convey the idea that she is short and stout?' 'Oh, no, sir, not stout. Just nice and plump. What I should describe as cuddly.'

Cuddy². **1.** *Naut.* (Earlier Amer. examples.)

1641 Winthrop *Hist. New Eng.* 34 He threw himself in at the door of the cuddy. 1652 *Plymouth Col. Rec.* III. 16 The surges being violent, bee was beaten of the fore cuddey of the said boate into the water, and soe ended his life.

Cue, *sb.*¹ **2. b.** (Later U.S. example.)

1831 P. Wingate in B. Peirce *Hist. Harvard Univ.* (1833) 219 We were allowed at dinner a cue of beer, which was a half-pint.

Cuff, *sb.*¹ **4.** Add: *cuff-links.*

1915 'Bartimeus' *Tall Ship* iv. 75 This liberal display of fine linen and flashing cuff-links.

Cuffee, cuffy (kɒ·fi). *U.S.* [A personal name formerly common among negroes.] **a.** A negro; also used as a generic name. **b.** *transf.* A black bear.

1824 J. Doddridge *Notes* 21 When the bear approached him, he sprang out and halloed at him; but cuffee..jumped at him with mouth wide open. 1837 *Southern Lit. Messenger* III. 86 The song ceased, and the cuffee advanced in silence. 1844 'Jon. Slick' *High Life N. Y.* I. 74 Jest as I was a thinking this, the cuffy come into the room. 1862 'Artemus Ward' *His Bk.* (1865) 61 Praps I'm bearin down too hard upon Cuffy.

Cuffer². *dial.* or *slang.* [f. s.w. dial. *cuff* vb., to talk over, discuss, relate + -er¹.] A yarn or story.

1887 Farrell *How He Died* 65 You made me start to pitch you this most interesting cuffer. 1898 P. H. Emerson *Marsh Leaves* 188 He'll spin up a rare cuffa along with old Jenks. 1899 F. T. Bullen *Idylls Sea*, etc. xxv. 219 The time-honoured 'cuffer' or yarn was going its soothing round. 1923 *Blackw. Mag.* May 661/1 There's plenty of cuffers, as they're called, about mermaids, phantom ships, dripping corpses, and such like.

Cuirass, *sb.* Add: **4. c.** In full *cuirasse band*, a band made of linen pressed in layers to protect a cycle tyre.

1906 *Daily Chron.* 28 Nov. 9/2 The winter and tropical tyre..consists of a smooth vulcanised cover, with cuirasse band put on top by hand. 1907 *Ibid.* 12 Oct. 9/4 The Paris cuirasse band...Unlike the Sphinx, the cuirasse becomes an integral part of the tyre, being attached inside the cover.

Culching, cultching (kɒ·ltʃiŋ), *vbl. sb.* [f. Culch, cultch.] The practice of strewing an oyster-bed with culch. Also *attrib.*

1894 *Westm. Gaz.* 3 Apr. 5/3 A Burnham cultching boat. 1904 *Nature* 17 Mar. 466/1 The process known as 'culching', that is, scattering the floor of the bed with rock, loose coral, and so on, to afford the necessary anchorage for the byssus of the young oyster.

Culicicide (kiū·lisisaid). Also **culicide** (kiū·lisaid). [f. L. *culex, culicis* gnat: see -cide I.] An insecticide to destroy gnats and mosquitoes.

1901 L. O. Howard *Mosquitoes* 197 The non-spreading qualities of corn-oil, however, as well as its price, remove it from the list of good culicides. 1901 *Practitioner* Mar. 263 By fumigating the rooms occasionally with some such culicicide as the dried flowers of the chrysanthemum.

Culicifuge (kiū·lisifiūdʒ). [f. L. *culex, culicis* gnat + -fuge.] (See quot.)

1901 Dorland *Med. Dict.* (ed. 2), *Culicifuge*, a preparation intended to prevent the attacks of gnats and mosquitoes.

Culicine (kiū·lisəin), *a.* and *sb. Ent.* [ad. mod.L. *Culicina* (pl.), f. *culex, culicis* gnat: see -ine¹.] **A.** *adj.* Belonging to the sub-family *Culicina* or gnats. **B.** *sb.* A member of this sub-family.

1921 G. H. Carpenter *Insect Transf.* 198 Less abundant in these countries than the Culicine gnats are the Anophelines. 1923 H. M. Lefroy *Entom.* 419 The Anophelines hang parallel to the surface..but the Culicines hang at an angle. 1929 R. Matheson *Mosquitoes N. Amer.* 36 The species of Culicine mosquitoes have widely varying larval habits.

Cull, *sb.*³ Add: **2.** Also *fig.*

1919 H. L. Wilson *Ma Pettengill* viii. 253 It made him feel like a social cull or an outcast, or something.

3. a. *U.S.* (Earlier example.) Also *cull lumber*.

1865–6 *Trans. Ill. Agric. Soc.* VI. 647 Culls are a quality manufactured from winding, worm-eaten, shaky or dry-rot timber, badly manufactured, or less than sixteen (16) inches in length. 1897 Moore *How to Build* ii. 23 The 'cull' lumber should be put in the closets, storerooms, and upper or attic rooms.

Cull, *v.*¹ Add: **4.** To pick out (calves) according to their quality. Also *absol. Australian.*

1927 Bennett *Christison* xii. 125 Christison used to cull on clearly defined lines. At first coarse calves were culled.

Culler. Add:

1. b. *spec.* as the name of a town official.

1663 *Boston* (Mass.) *Town Rec.* VII. 15 Francis Hudshon and Ralph Sammies are made choice of by the Selectmen for to be Cullers of fishe. *Ibid.* 20 Cullour of staves, Edward Belcher. 1684 *Cambridge* (Mass.) *Rec.* 272 Culler of bricks for the Town. 1696 *Manchester* (Mass.) *Rec.* 70 Att ye same towne meettinge John Bishope was chosen culler of staves and other goods. 1697 *Ibid.* 76 Clark of the market and culler of fish and staves. 1781 *Baltimore Town Rec.* 43 Jacob Dawson appointed Garbler, Culler of Staves.

c. *local.* (See quot.)

1906 *Vict. Co. Hist., Cornwall* I. 521/2 Many comparatively rough blocks [of slate-rock] are refused by the contract men, and these are passed on to men and boys called cullers, who are paid a fixed price, and make as much out of them as they can.

Culmen. 1. Delete †*Obs.* Still in use, esp. in fig. applications.

1928 C. T. Onions in *Times* 19 Apr. 10/7 The Oxford English Dictionary is the culmen [of a series of lexicons].

Culminate, *v.* **4.** Delete *rare* and add modern instances.

1896 Earl of Rosebery in *Westm. Gaz.* 12 Sept. 5/1 This brings to a head and culminates all the nameless massacres in Asia Minor. 1904 *Omaha Bee* 25 Sept., A romance extending over several years was culminated. 1927 *Daily Express* 25 Apr. 1/5 They decided that an immediate ceremony would culminate their childhood romance.

Culmination. Add: **3.** [Cf. It. *colmare.*] The raising of land by the deposition of silt.

1838 F. Macerone *Mem.* II. 62 The process of culmination is particularly successful if practised high up a river much liable to winter floods.

Cult, *sb.* Add: **2. b.** Now freq. used *attrib.* by writers on the archæology of primitive cults.

1901 A. J. Evans *Mycen. Tree & Pillar Cult* 25 Aniconic Cult Images. *Ibid.* 77 Cult Scenes relating to a Warrior God and his Consort. 1903 *Folk-Lore* Sept. 264 The image of the patron deity, usually a simple copy of the cult statue. *Ibid.* 269 Inscriptions found at various cult-centres. 1906 D. G. Hogarth in *Proc. Brit. Acad.* 1905–6 375 Small objects dedicated in that temple, among which are several cult-figurines of the Goddess. 1928 Peake & Fleure *Steppe & Sown* 104 Already in Early Minoan times the double axe had become, not only a symbol of authority, but a cult object.

Cultching: see *Culching.

Cultellus (kɒlte·lǒs). Pl. **cultelli** (-ai). *Ent.* [L., dim. of *culter* knife.] Each of the lancet-like mandibles of many blood-sucking Diptera.

1899 D. Sharp *Insects* II. 443 Cultelli (mandibles of other anatomists).

Cultic (kɒ·ltik), *a.* [f. Cult *sb.* + -ic, perh. after G. *kultisch.*] Of or pertaining to a religious cult.

1898 Peritz in *Jrnl. Bibl. Lit.* XVII. 117 Whether as divinity, devotee, or cultic official, woman shares cultic duties with man. 1925 G. B. Gray *Sacrifice in O.T.* 193 Though of course women reckoned their descent from Levi, they did not exercise the special cultic Levitical service. 1925 J. E. McFadyen in A. S. Peake *People & Bk.* 216 Gunkel maintains that, though they [*sc.* the psalms] originated in poetry composed for the cult, most of them no longer presuppose any cultic action.

Cultivated, *ppl. a.* **2.** Add: Of the voice or utterance, indicating refinement in its user.

1908 *Westm. Gaz.* 2 Jan. 8/1 The prisoner is a well set-up and well-dressed man with a cultivated voice.

Cultivation. Add: **2.** Also *attrib.*, as *cultivation field, zone*; **cultivation paddock,** the part of an Australian station used for the raising of crops. (Foreign and Colonial.)

1853 C. St. Julian & Silvester *Prod. N.S.W.* 170 (Morris) Few stations of any magnitude are without their 'cultivation paddocks'. 1893 F. Adams *New Egypt* 94 An open space in the desert, beyond the cultivation fields. 1896 *Daily News* 2 Jan. 5/6, I hope to establish cultivation zones in the province of Havana. 1902 *Westm. Gaz.* 13 Dec. 2/1 Posy..went over the fence into the cultivation paddock.

c. Short for *cultivation paddock* (see above).

1910 Davis *Our Selection* xvi. 151 The kangaroo started across the cultivation, heading for the grass-paddock.

Cultual (kɒ·ltiuăl), *a.* [ad. F. *cultuel*, f. L. *cultus* Cultus.] Of or pertaining to a cult or organized religious worship.

1906 *Westm. Gaz.* 17 Dec. 2/3 Catholic Cultual Associations. 1912 Von Hügel *Eternal Life* 163 There is nothing necessarily superstitious in..Cultual Acts.

Cultural (kɒ·ltiŭrăl), *sb.* [f. Cultural *a.* 2.] A factor in human culture.

1904 *Nation* (N.Y.) 8 Dec. 466/1 There has been..an interaction between all human culturals, namely, between industry, knowledge, art, conduct, and religion.

Cultural, *a.* Add:

3. Relating to civilization, esp. that of a particular country at a particular period.

1875 Whitney *Life Lang.* 172 All these widely-sundered tribes of men, found at the dawn of history in every variety of cultural condition. 1884 *Science* IV. 21/2 In its cultural development, China stands wholly for itself. 1898 *Daily News* 30 Aug. 5/1 The gigantic cultural problems awaiting solution in the Russian Empire. 1909 *Westm. Gaz.* 22 Apr. 5/2 The Professor [Doerpsfeld] says the excavations reveal several distinct cultural deposits. 1909 A. H. Keane *Centr. & S. Amer.* (ed. 2) I. 48 The southern extremity of the cultural zone.

4. *Bacteriology.* Relating to culture-media or to the character of the micro-organisms grown upon them.

1900 *Jrnl. Exper. Med.* V. 259 The bacillus recovered by us from our several autopsies always showed the same cultural characters.

Culturally, *adv.* Add:

2. *Bacteriology.* With reference to culture-media or their development.

1893 *Daily Tel.* 29 Sept. 4/6 A fatal case..is officially described as 'culturally indistinguishable from true cholera'. 1906 *Practitioner* Nov. 635 Culturally, it possesses no features by means of which it may be readily distinguished from other diplo- or streptococci. 1908 *Ibid.* Jan. 68 Ruppell found that there was a striking resemblance between the non-virulent strains of meningococci and ordinary gonococci, morphologically, culturally, and as regards their immunising power against virulent meningococci.

Culture, *sb.* Add: **3. c.** *culture plate*; **culture medium,** a substance, solid or liquid, in which bacteria or other micro-organisms are cultivated.

1899 G. Newman *Bacteria* i. 27 The sunlight acts prejudicially upon the *culture medium. 1906 J. B. Burke *Orig. Life* 97 If cyanogen is a half-living thing..it is only natural to try if it would form growths in culture media. 1907 *Westm. Gaz.* 9 Oct. 12/1 The feet of the fly..are so formed as to make effective carriers of germs, and as an illustration of what a single fly can do in this way he showed a photograph of a *culture plate upon which a captured fly had been allowed to walk.

5. b. *spec.* The civilization of a people (esp. at a certain stage of its development or history).

1871 E. B. Tylor (*title*) Primitive Culture. 1903 C. Lumholtz *Unknown Mexico* I. 117 A thrifty people whose stage of culture was that of the Pueblo Indians of to-day.

c. *attrib.* and *Comb.*, as *culture-condition, -instincts*; *culture-loving* ppl. adj. Also *spec.* in *Anthropology*, as *culture-hero, -heroine, -legend, -myth, -province, -stock, -zone.*

1897 Mary Kingsley *W. Africa* 28 The present *culture-condition of West Africa. *Ibid.* Pref. p. ix, Your superior *culture-instincts may militate against your enjoying West Africa. 1905 *Daily Chron.* 15 June 3/1 The *culture-loving Catholic Gael. 1909 *Westm. Gaz.* 2 Jan. 11/2 A modernised, constitutional, culture-loving Turkish State.

1907 A. C. Haddon in *Anthropol. Ess.* 183 The death dances were introduced into the Western Islands by two *culture heroes from New Guinea. 1901 *Contemp. Rev.* Mar. 455 The ancient '*culture-heroine'. 1903 *Daily Chron.* 11 June 3/1 The hero-tales and *culture-legends of the prehistoric period of the Hebrews. 1902 *Encycl. Brit.* XXV. 373/2 *Culture provinces. 1908 *Daily Chron.* 5 Mar. 3/2 Human *culture-zones.

Culture, *v.* Add: **2.** *Bacteriology.* To grow (a micro-organism) upon a culture medium.

1908 *Practitioner* Sept. 463 The ovary and tube (unopened) were despatched..with a request to see what organism could be cultured, and to make a vaccine.

Culturization (kɒ·ltiŭrəizē¹·ʃən, -tʃər-). [f. Culture *sb.*: see -ize, -ization.] The process of making (a people or country) cultured.

1918 *Hist. Amer. Lit.* I. II. v. 273 All his translations.. are a witness to Bryant's knowledge of foreign tongues and literatures, to his part in the culturization of America.

Cultus. Add: **3.** *attrib.*, as *cultus-type*; **cultus-image, -statue,** an image or statue set up in connexion with the cultus of a deity.

1906 D. G. Hogarth in *Proc. Brit. Acad.* 1905–6 376 A well-known type of cultus-image..a traditional cultus-type ..of Phrygian or Cappadocian origin.

Cumberland. Used to designate the fashion of cutting up a pig's carcase in which the ham is cut away and cured separately.

1905 W. H. Simmonds *Practical Grocer* III. 103 It pays to sell the ham separately and convert the rest of the side into 'Cumberland cut' bacon or 'Irish rolls'.

Cumbrian (kɒ·mbriăn), *a.* (and *sb.*). [f. med.L. *Cumbria*, f. W. *Cymry*:—prehist. W. **kombrogī*, pl. of **kombrogos* lit. fellow-countryman (W. *bro*:—**mrog-* region).]

1. Belonging to the ancient British kingdom of Cumbria, which included Cumberland. As *sb.*, a native of this kingdom.

2. Belonging to Cumberland, or its system of rocks; also, more widely, belonging to the Lake District and its fells; *sb.* a native of Cumberland.

1778 T. West *Guide Lakes Cumb.*, etc. (1789) 6 The travelled visitor of the Cumbrian lakes. 1833–4 J. Phillips *Geol.* in *Encycl. Metrop.* (1845) VI. 584/2 The analogous arches of limestone, which begird the primary district of the Cumbrian lakes. 1837 *Penny Cycl.* VIII. 223/2 The Cumbrians have been undeservedly said to be litigious. *Ibid.*, Cumbrian peasantry have various festive meetings, called the *kirn*, or harvest-home, sheep-shearing, merry nights, and upshots. 1882 *Encycl. Brit.* XIV. 40/1 Kentigern,..the restorer of Christianity among the Cumbrians. 1901 A. G. Bradley *Lake District* 4 The simple dalesman,..canny Cumbrian as he is. 1902 W. G. Collingwood *Lake Counties* 38 There have been many Cumbrian poets, most of them, like Wordsworth at Grasmere, cottage folk. Haskett Smith *Ibid.* 259 Leaving out Langdale, which runs down into Westmorland, there are five purely Cumbrian dales.

Cumulet (kiū·miŭlĕt). A high-flying variety of fancy pigeon.

1876 *Bazaar, Exchange & Mart* 12 Jan. 74/3 Pair splendid white eyed cumulets. 1910 A. H. Osman *Pigeon Bk.* 131.

Cumulo-. Add: **cumulo-nimbus** (see quots.).

1887 *Leisure Hour* 570/2 Similar cumulus and cumulo-nimbus forms range in latitude from London to near Cape Horn. 1928 D. Brunt *Meteorol.* iii, Cumulo-nimbus is the thunder-cloud. It frequently takes the form of towers or anvils.

Cunarder. (Earlier U.S. examples.)

1869 C. L. Brace *New West* i. 23 Take the matter of coal alone..burned at the rate it is on a Cunarder. 1873 'Mark Twain' & C. D. Warner *Gilded Age* lv. 494 He pointed out where the Cunarders lay when in port.

Cup, *sb.* Add: **4.** Also, a depression in the skin forming a rudimentary eye in certain low-grade animals. Also *eye-cup* or *cup-eye*.

1927 *Glasgow Herald* 9 July 4 In some of the sea-worms ..we start with diagrammatically simple 'cup-eyes',..and gradually pass to very elaborate 'cup-eyes'. *Ibid.*, A minute optic skin-cup. 1929 *Encycl. Brit.* XX. 628/2 Eye-spots are found in Medusae, starfishes, and some Annelid worms. ..The first step..is the sinking of the eye-spot into a pit-like depression, thus forming an eye-cup (optic cup). *Ibid.*, The cells situated at the back of the cup.

5. (Earlier and later U.S. examples.) Cf. *cup-and-ring* in *13 d.

1819 W. Faux *Memorable Days Amer.* (1823) 284 He would have bought [land] from Mr. Birkbeck, but could get only a 'cup', that is, a swamp. 1886 *Outing* (U.S.) Nov. 107/1 He [*sc.* the grizzly] had passed the end of the butte, and descended into a shallow cup in the plain.

13. c. Additional combinations and quots.

1894 *Daily News* 26 Feb. 5/1 Those mighty cup-fighters, the Blackburn Rovers. 1895 *Ibid.* 21 Feb. 5/5 The Wednesday men are noted cup-tie fighters. 1901 *Westm. Gaz.* 22 Apr. 7/3 A typical 'cup-fighting' team. 1902 *Encycl. Brit.* XXIX. 329/2 The expression 'a cup horse' is understood to imply an animal capable of distinguishing himself over a long distance at even weights against the best opponents. 1905 *Daily Chron.* 14 Apr. 8/1 A special brand of play known as 'the Cup-tie game'. *Ibid.* 25 Dec. 3/4 Old Internationals and Cup-final players. 1910 *Westm. Gaz.* 14 Mar. 14/2 The cup-holders were defeated in their first match.

d. cup-and-ring, designation of a type of marks found cut in megalithic monuments, consisting of a circular depression surrounded by concentric rings; **cup-cake,** orig. *U.S.*, a cake baked from ingredients measured by the cupful, or baked in small cups; **cup-custard** (U.S. examples); **cup-fungus,** any discomycetous fungus having a cup-shaped ascoma; cf. *cup-mushroom*; **cup-head,** a hemispherical head to a bolt; hence **cup-headed** *a.*; **cup-mark, -marking,** a shallow cup-like depression found cut in rocks or stone monuments (see 5); also **cup-marked** *a.*; **cup-mouthpiece** (see quot.); **cup-plant** *U.S.* (examples); **cup-sculpture** = **cup-marking*; **cup-shrimp** (see quot.); **cup-stone,** a stone or rock surface inscribed with cup-marks.

1867 J. Y. Simpson *Arch. Sculpt.* 2 *Cup and ring cuttings. 1875 C. Maclagan *Hill Forts*, etc. Index, Cup and Ring Sculpturings. *Ibid.* 41 On one monolith..are some 'cup and ring markings'. 1900 *Daily News* 11 Oct. 6/1 A rude dial at West Kirby looks like an example of 'cup and ring stones'. 1919 *Proc. Soc. Antiq. Scot.* LIII. 23 The cup-and ring-marked stone which was found near this spot. 1886 *Harper's Mag.* Dec. 134/2 Cousin Carry with her eternal *cup-cake. 1890 Mary E. Wilkins *Humble Romance*, etc. *Unwilling Guest* 271 Mis' Steele made some cup-cake to-day...She put a cup of butter and two whole cups of sugar in it. 1911 E. Ferber *Dawn O'Hara* viii. 109 There were little round cup cakes made of almond paste that melts in the mouth. 1924 *Mrs. Beeton's Cake-making* 24 Cup Cakes, Plain (American Recipe.) Take 3 level cupfuls of flour, 1 cupful of sugar, ½ cupful of butter, 1 cupful of milk...Bake in shallow tins or small cups. 1862 'G. Hamilton' *Country Living & Thinking* 72 We had *cup-custards at the close of our breakfast that morning. 1866 Mrs. Whitney *L. Goldthwaite* x, Cup-custards, even, disappeared,—cups and all. 1910 *Encycl. Brit.* XI. 341/2 Owing to the shape of the fruit-body many of these forms are known as *cup-fungi, the cup or apothecium often attaining a large size. 1929 *Ibid.* (ed. 12) III. 827/2 The *cup-head or coach-bolt. 1884 *Proc. Soc. Antiq. Scot.* XVIII. 110 Edge of Rock with *Cup-marks. 1919 *Ibid.* LIII. 22 The fracture on one side cuts across a cup-mark. 1867 *Ibid.* (1870) VII. 270 A Kist, with a *cup-marked Cover. 1875 C. Maclagan *Hill Forts*, etc. 45 The cup-marked stone figured on Plate XI. 1898 *Geogr. Jrnl.* XI. 681 Inscribed and cup-marked stones. 1867 J. Y. Simpson *Arch. Sculpt.* 7 In the centres of the remaining six series of circles there are no *cup-markings. 1877 W. Greenwell *Brit. Barrows* 341 A square piece of the same stone..which has a circular pit or cup-marking on each face. 1911 *Encycl. Brit.* XVIII. 947/1 **Cup-Mouthpieces.*—Brass wind instruments are played by means of cup or funnel-shaped mouthpieces, generally made of silver... The shallower the cup the more suitable it is for producing the higher harmonics. 1846–50 A. Wood *Class-bk. Bot.* 336 *Silphium perfoliatum.* *Cup-plant. 1870 *Amer. Naturalist* IV. 580 Another species of the same genus, called the cup plant (*Silphium perfoliatum*)..is common in the moist ravines. 1911 Calman *Life of Crustacea* 245 A smaller species..(*Leander squilla*), and another very similar species..*L. adspersus*,..are said to be sold on some parts of the English coast as '*Cup Shrimps'.

Cup, *v.* Add:

3. b. To lodge or contain as in a cup.

1889 Bret Harte *Cressy* ii, Her chin cupped in the hollow of her hand. 1907 *Daily Chron.* 17 Oct. 8/5 Dene, cupped by the hills that guarded every outlet.

c. *Golf.* To lodge (the ball) in a 'cup' or depression of the ground. (See Cup *sb.* 5.)

1896 W. Park *Golf* 95 A cupped ball gives room for playing one of the finest strokes in golf. 1905 H. Vardon *Compl. Golfer* 81 When the ball is really badly cupped. 1909 *Westm. Gaz.* 11 May 12/2 The cleek is only for use when the ball lies cupped.

5. *trans.* To make concave or cup-shaped, form into a cup.

1909 Mrs. Stratton-Porter *Girl of Limberlost* xv. 299 'Are you afraid she is going?' Elnora asked. 'If you are, cup your other hand over her for shelter.' 1911 *Encycl. Brit.* XXVII. 39/2 Power presses for working sheet-metal articles include those for cutting out the blanks, termed cutting-out or blanking presses, and those for cupping or drawing the flat blank into shape. *Ibid.*, The cupping of the blank being effected by the downward motion of the plunger.

Cupid. Add: **1.** *Cupid's bow*, a popular name for lips curved like the double-curved bow of Cupid. *Cupid's darts* (see quot. 1910).

1875 Sir T. Seaton *Fret-Cutting* 139 It gives the lip that shape called *Cupid's Bow. 1904 B'ness von Hutten *Pam* IV. viii, He's a sweetly pretty youth..with a cupid's-bow mouth. 1929 J. L. Hodson *Grey Dawn* I. i, Big brown eyes, cupid's bow mouth and broad forehead. 1910 *Encycl. Brit.* XII. 272/1 This form of the mineral [göthite] has long been known as onegite, and the crystals enclosing it are cut for ornamental purposes under the name of '*Cupid's darts' (*flèches d'amour*).

4. A variety of dwarf sweet pea.

1903 *Daily Chron.* 16 July 7/4 A collection of 'Cupids' —a dwarf variety—in pots.

5. (With small initial.) A kind of small jam tart; a love-well. Also *cupid-cake.* ? *U.S.*

Cupola, *sb.* **1.** Add: Sometimes *spec.* the dome of the building in which the French Academy meets (*la coupole de l'Institut*).

1900 *Westm. Gaz.* 21 June 1/3 It is only by a majority of one that M. Hervieu is called 'under the cupola'. 1920 *Edin. Rev.* Oct. 276 These guardians of the Cupola. *Ibid.* 279 On the 20th of March 1919, M. René Boylesve.. was received under the Cupola by the poet, M. Henri de Regnier.

2. *cupola-furnace* (U.S. examples).

1837 W. Jenkins *Ohio Gazetteer* 55 In a circle of five miles, ..there are 11 stores, a cupola furnaces, two oil mills. 1849 Chamberlain *Indiana Gazetteer* 319 It contains two large blast furnaces, two cupola furnaces, one forge.

Cupolated (kiū·pǒlē¹ted), *a.* Delete † *Obs. rare*⁻¹ and add quot.:

1924 *Contemp. Rev.* Jan. 78 Their carbuncled, cupolated tops.

Cupper². *Oxford University slang.* [f. Cup *sb.* + *-er ⁶.] A series of intercollegiate matches played in competition for a cup.

1903 *Oxf. Mag.* 11 Feb. 214/1 Hockey.—...We are drawn against Magdalen in the second round of the 'Cupper'. 1928 *Observer* 18 Mar. 13/4 The final of 'the rugger cupper'.

Cuppy, *a.* **b.** (*Golf.*) Add: *Cuppy lie*, the position of a ball when it lies in a 'cup' or shallow depression. Said also of the ball.

1886 H. Hutchinson *Hints Game Golf* 32 If it [*sc.* the ball] lie 'cuppy', a jerking stroke will be necessary. 1901 W. J. Travis *Pract. Golf* (1903) 46 It is better to..play each shot the same way—except in the case of a very cuppy lie. 1922 P. G. Wodehouse *Clicking of Cuthbert* 88 Mortimer.. found his ball in a nasty cuppy lie.

Cupram (kiū·prăm). *Chem.* [f. L. *cupr(um* copper + Am)monia.] Ammoniacal copper carbonate, used as a fungicide. 1911 Webster.

Cuprammo·nia. Also *erron.* cupra-ammonia. = next.

1927 M. H. Avram *Rayon Industry* 497 The cupra-ammonia cellulose process.

Cuprammonium (kiūprămōu·niǒm). Also *erron.* **cupra-ammonium.** [f. L. *cuprum* copper + Ammonium.] A solution of copper oxide in ammonia, which has the property of dissolving cellulose. Chiefly as the designation of a method of making artificial silk.

1921 T. Woodhouse tr. *Foltzer's Artif. Silk* 29 Despeissis Artificial Silk (Cuprammonium Process). *Ibid.* 36 Cuprammonium Solution..is a solution of copper oxide in ammonia. It is a blue liquid known to chemists as Schweitzer's reagent. 1925 *Good Housekeeping* Apr. 142/2 Cuprammonium silk. 1927 Avram *Rayon Industry* 192 The cupra-ammonium solution of cellulose. *Ibid.* 497 Cupra-ammonium Rayon.

Cuprea (kiū·priă). [L., fem. of *cupreus* Cupreous *a.*] *Cuprea bark*, the coppery-red bark of the S. American tree *Remijia pedunculata* (and other species), one of the sources of quinine.

1884 *Pharmaceutical Jrnl. & Trans.* 23 Aug. 141/1 The china cuprea, which we now know to be derived from *Remijia pedunculata*. *Ibid.*, The alkaloid of cuprea bark. 1886 *Encycl. Brit.* XX. 186/2 A few years ago it was discovered that a bark imported from..Colombia under the name of cuprea bark and derived from *Remijia pedunculata*, *Triana*, and other species, contained quinine.

Cupreine, -in (kiū·prī,in). *Chem.* [f. *Cuprea + -ine⁵, -in¹.] A cinchona alkaloid contained in cuprea bark.

1886 *Encycl. Brit.* XX. 185/1 Homoquinine has been shown..to be decomposed on treatment with caustic soda into quinine and a new alkaloid, cupreine.

Cupro-. Add: **Cu:pro-ni·ckel,** an alloy of copper and nickel used as a sheathing for army-rifle bullets.

1905 *Kynoch Jrnl.* Jan.–Mar. 18 The bullet is sheathed with a cupro-nickel envelope. 1922 *Encycl. Brit.* XXX. 135/2 This jacket is made from cupro-nickel which..contains from 80% to 85% copper and from 15% to 20% nickel.

Cuproid. Add:

2. A trade name for a preparation of cuprous oxide used in artificial-silk manufacture.

1921 T. Woodhouse tr. *Foltzer's Artif. Silk* 123 Instead of metallic copper, this firm used cuprous oxide, Cu_2O, and the special preparation which they obtained is termed 'cuproid'. The product appears as a commercial article in the form of pulverized cuprous oxide.

Curate. Add:

2. b. *The curate's egg*: taken as a type of something of mixed character (good and bad).

Originating in a story of a meek curate who, having been given a stale egg by his episcopal host, stated that 'parts of it' were 'excellent' (*Punch* 9 Nov. 1895, p. 222).

1905 *Minister's Gazette of Fashion* Aug. 141/1 The past spring and summer season has seen much fluctuation. Like the curate's egg, it has been excellent in parts.

5. *jocular.* A small extra poker, meant for use, not ornament.

1891 *N. & Q.* 7th Ser. XII. 206/2 A 'curate' is a small auxiliary poker with a steel point, intended for use, in contradistinction to the elaborate fire brasses, which are only kept for show.

6. In Ireland, a spirit-grocer's assistant.

1909 M. Hayden & Hartog in *Fortn. Rev.* Apr. 781 'Curate'..is the assistant to a 'spirit grocer', such as most grocers are in Ireland. 1914 Jas. Joyce *Dubliners, Grace* (1926) 169 These two gentlemen and one of the curates carried him up the stairs and laid him down again on the floor of the bar.

Curating (kiūǝ·rĕtiŋ), *vbl. sb.* [-ing¹.] Acting as curate; performing the duties of a curate.

1831 W. Cobbett *Two-penny Trash* Jan. 159 Non-residence, or stipendiary curating. 1907 H. Begbie *Vigil* II. 23, I am to commence vicar. No curating. *Ibid.* v. 68 You have begun curating for me already.

Curative. II. (U.S. example.)

1857 D. E. E. Braman *Inform. Texas* i. 15, I place great confidence in the frequent outward use of cold water, as a preventive and curative.

Curb, *sb.* Add: **12. b.** The body of curbstone brokers. *U.S.*

1903 *Nation* (N.Y.) 4 June 446 The Stock Exchange and the 'curb'..gave..plain evidence what their opinion was.

15. curb-market, -price, -stocks *U.S.* (cf. Curb-stone b).

1914 *N. Y. Herald* 17 Nov. 6/4 Prices again strong in curb market. 1915 *World's Work* (N.Y.) Oct. 641 Unlisted (Curb) Stocks. 1930 *San Antonio* (Texas) *Light* 31 Jan., Closing Curb Prices.

Curb, *v.*² **3.** (Earlier U.S. example.)

1836 J. Hall *Statist. West* vii. 101 In the west..wells are curbed with hollow logs.

Curbed, *ppl. a.*² Add:

3. Of a horse: Affected with a curb (Curb *sb.* 4).

1861 *Trans. Ill. Agric. Soc.* IV. 375 A narrow-quartered, splinted, curbed mare.

Curbing, *vbl. sb.*² **2.** (Earlier U.S. example.)

1838 J. Hall *Notes Western States* viii. 106 After removing the rich soil, a stratum of hard clay presents itself, then gravel, and then another layer of clay, all of which are so compact as to require no curbing.

Curb-stone. b. *U.S.* (Earlier example.) Also **curbstone operator.**

1848 W. Armstrong *Stocks* 7 This class comprehends..all those petty operators and non-descripts, who have neither a local habitation or scarcely, a name, that are dignified by the title of curb-stone brokers. 1861 *Knickerbocker Mag.* June LVII. 635 All sorts of brokers, from the leading houses down to the curbstone 'operator'. 1868 R. B. Kimball *Undercurrents* 321 It is rather a habit with the Curb-stone operator when he gets severely winged, to go into the cigar business.

Curdy, *a.* **3.** Add mod. quots.

1859 Lever *Davenport Dunn* xxxvi, His curdiest salmon declined, his wonderful 'south-down' sent away scarcely tasted. 1892 Hutchinson *Fairway Island* i, We'll eat this [salmon] that had the tide-lice on him. He'll be fine and curdy.

Cure, *sb.*¹ Add: **9.** Still in use in the cod-fishery. Also, a catch of fish so treated.

1883 Shea *Newfoundland Fisheries* 7 (Fish. Exhib. Publ.) The cure of the fish requires much care and judgment. ..The best cure is effected when the weather is variable. 1902 *Encycl. Brit.* XXXI. 143 The fish caught round the Newfoundland coast are generally of good quality, but the Labrador cure..is often very inferior.

11. After F. *cure*, G. *kur, cur* (see Kurbaal): A period of residence at a health-resort, under medical regimen, in order to restore or benefit one's health. Also *comb.*, as *cure-guest* (= G. *kurgast*), *-seeker.*

1898 *Daily News* 22 July 5/1 One of the speakers was an old cure servant. 1905 *Westm. Gaz.* 11 Sept. 10/2 The number of cure-guests registered [at Carlsbad]. 1906 *Ibid.* 27 Aug. 8/1 Cure-seekers at Homburg. 1908 T. P. O'Connor *Campbell-Bannerman* 123 He rarely took the cure [at Marienbad]. *Ibid.*, The severe waters which the other cure-guests were taking.

12. The vulcanization of indiarubber. Also applied, with defining word (*hard, soft cure*), as a designation of different brands. (See also quot. 1923.)

1907 H. L. Terry *India-rubber* 32 Fine Para rubber.. varies slightly in its properties and price according as it is 'Up-river hard cure' or 'Island soft cure'. 1908 H. A. Wickham *Parà Rubber* 24 Extraction and cure of the rubber *latex*. *Ibid.* 29 The antiseptic smoke-cure. 1909 *Westm. Gaz.* 9 Nov. 12/1 Fine Hard Cure Para Rubber. 1922 H. E. Simmons *Rubber Manuf.* 48/2 This variation in rate of cure or vulcanizing capacity. *Ibid.* 98/1 There are two general methods of vulcanization, namely, what is known as the 'cold cure' and the 'hot cure vulcanization'. 1923 B. D. W. Luff *Chem. Rubber* 19 In works practice, and indeed in technical literature, the term 'cure' is frequently employed instead of 'vulcanisation'. While this has the merit of brevity, it is unfortunately used also to denote the 'smoking' of wild or cultivated rubber in the course of its preparation. *Ibid.* 136 Hydrochloric acid gives a rubber having a slower rate of cure. *Ibid.* 137 The effect of alum in retarding the cure of the rubber.

Cure, *v.*¹ Add: **5. b.** *absol.* or *intr.* To effect a cure; often in *kill or cure* (see Kill *v.* 7 e).

1593 Shaks. *2 Hen. VI*, v. i. 99 Whose Smile and Frowne, like to Achilles Speare Is able with the change, to kill and cure. 1764–1875 [see Kill *v.* 7 e]. 1787 Cowper *Stanzas Bill Mortality* 27 No med'cine, though it often cure, Can always balk the tomb. 1908 *Smart Set* Sept. 82/1 Buttermilk is good for it...Warranted to cure in thirty days or money refunded.

7. (Earlier Amer. example.)

1633 *Virginia Statutes* (1823) I. 205 That [tobacco] which shall be cured that present yeare.

c. *spec.* To dry (hay, etc.) properly for keeping. Also *intr.*, to undergo this process.

1750 W. Ellis *Mod. Husbandman* V. ii. 11 (E.D.S.) The cutting, curing, and inning of barley-crops. 1787 Washington *Diaries* II. 256 Carried the Pease and the Vines which appeared to be cured into one end of the Tob[acc]o House. 1837 Colman *Rep. Agric. Mass.* (1838) 38 [They] have this year cut and cured 75 tons of hay. 1840 J. Buel *Farmer's Comp.* 218 The advantage of curing clover in the cock is this, that when cured by being spread, the leaves and blossoms are dry long before the stems are cured, or sufficiently dry. 1873 J. H. Beadle *Undevel. West* xxxv. 749 The grass, dead ripe, stands cured to a bright yellow.

intr. 1873 J. H. Beadle *Undevel. West* ii. 58 It then cures upon the grounds, and stands through the year looking very much like bunches of broom-sedge. 1887 [see Cure *v.*¹ 7 b in Dict.]. 1888 *Harper's Mag.* Mar. 567/1 Judging by the grass (which cures into the most nutritious feed as it stands) there had been no lack of rain during the summer.

9. *intr.* To reside for some time at a health-resort, following a regimen for the benefit of one's health. See *Cure *sb.*¹ 11.

1902 *Westm. Gaz.* 22 Aug. 2/1 Those who have come up to 'cure' at Davos. 1905 *Ibid.* 9 June 10/1 They 'cured' together on the balcony, and rowed together on the lake.

10. *trans.* To vulcanize (indiarubber).

1880 *Encycl. Brit.* XII. 841/2 The calendered sheets are generally cured between folds of wet cloth. 1902 C. O. Weber *Chem. India Rubber* 299 'Dry heat cured' waterproof fabrics. *Ibid.*, 'Cold cured' cloth. 1907 H. L. Terry *India-rubber* 79 Goods cured by Dry Heat..are less likely to be damaged by copper than those which are cold cured. 1908 H. A. Wickham *Parà Rubber* 29 The standard rubber known in commerce as 'fine Parà' is smoke-cured. *Ibid.* 32 The weight of the cured rubber should approximate very nearly that of the *latex* used. 1922 H. E. Simmons *Rubber Manuf.* 48/2 They cured all their samples at a temperature of 140 C.

b. *intr.* To become vulcanized, undergo vulcanization.

1922 H. E. Simmons *Rubber Manuf.* 48/2 A rubber which cures an hour and forty-five minutes more quickly than plain or smoked sheets. *Ibid.* 49/1 A rapid curing rubber. 1923 B. D. W. Luff *Chem. Rubber* 136 Sulphuric acid gives a slow-curing rubber if used in slight excess.

Curelessness (kiūǝ·ɹlesnĕs). The quality or condition of being cureless.

1891 Kipling & Balestier *Naulahka* xiii, Her heart torn with the curelessness of it all.

Curetonian (kiuǝtōu·niăn), *a.* and *sb.* Designation of the Syriac version of the Gospels discovered by the Rev. William *Cureton*, and edited by him from the MS. in 1858.

1861 Scrivener *Introd. Crit. N. T.* 236 The Curetonian Syriac. *Ibid.* 237 *note*, Such cases..are common to the Curetonian with the Peshito. 1904 F. C. Burkitt (*title*) Evangelion Da-Mepharreshe: The Curetonian Version of the Four Gospels. *Ibid.* II. 17 *note*, Where the photograph clearly agreed with the Curetonian against the Peshitta.

Curettage (kiure·tāʒ). *Surg.* [Fr.: see Curette and -age.] The application of the curette; scraping or cleaning by means of a curette.

1897 W. Anderson *Surg. Treat. Lupus* 8 Various supplementary measures have been added to the curettage. 1908 *Practitioner* Feb. 180 No more than a curettage of the growth was attempted.

Curettement (kiure·tmĕnt). *Surg.* [See prec. and -ment.] = *Curettage.

1908 *Practitioner* Dec. 787 The right ovary had been removed elsewhere five years ago, at which time currettement had also been done.

Curf (kǝ̄ɹf). *local.* Also **carf, kerf.** [var. f. Carf, Kerf.] One of the strata of the Portland beds of stone.

1839 *Civil Eng. & Arch. Jrnl.* II. 375/2 A middle or curf bed occurs only in the southernmost of the quarries. 1893 *Spons' Mechanics' Own Bk.* (ed. 4) 564 Then..the Bastard-Roach, Kerf, or Curf is reached.

Curia. Add:

4. *Hist.* **a.** Each of four electoral bodies in the Austrian constitution of 1861. **b.** Each of three bodies, representing respectively the nobles, knights, and towns, into which the members of the estates of Bohemia were divided in 1446.

1907 *Westm. Gaz.* 28 May 2/1 How false was the idea given by the old Curia Parliament of what were the feelings and the aspirations of the people of Austria. 1908 *Ibid.* 16 Jan. 2/1 He wished to see Bohemia divided into curias —Germans being governed by a German, and Czechs by a Czech curia. 1910 *Encycl. Brit.* III. 26/1 (Austria). *Ibid.* IV. 126/2 (Bohemia).

Curiara (kūriā·ra). The native name in Venezuela and Colombia for a dug-out canoe.

1910 H. J. Mozans *Up the Orinoco* 174 *note*, The curiara is smaller than the bongo or falca. 1910 M. B. & C. W. Beebe *Our Search* 12 A network of narrow channels.. allowed us to explore the far interior in our shallow curiara or dug-out. 1927 *Chambers's Jrnl.* 290/1 Their curiaras are very strong and carefully made.

Curie (kiūǝ·ri, ‖küri). [Named in honour of M. Pierre & Mme Marie *Curie*, who discovered radium.] A standard unit of radium emanation, being the quantity in equilibrium with one gram of radium. Also **Cu·riegram.**

1913 E. Rutherford *Radioactive Subst.* 479 At the Radiology Congress in Brussels in 1910, it was decided to call this equilibrium quantity a 'curie', in honour of M. and Mme Curie...It is convenient to use the term millicurie as a smaller unit. 1929 *Encycl. Brit.* VI. 875/2 *Curiegram*,.. the quantity of radium emanation in equilibrium with one gram of radium. This unit is subdivided into the millicuriegram and the microcuriegram.

Curing, *vbl. sb.* **3.** *curing-room* (examples).

1833 B. Silliman *Man. Sugar Cane* 46 The line of the floor..deviates only six inches in the curing rooms. 1878 *Rep. Vermont Board Agric.* 79 In connection with..the manufacturing room was the curing room.

Curious, *a.* **16** and **17.** Add: Used in booksellers' catalogues as a euphemistic description of erotic or pornographic works.

1925 Aldous Huxley *Those Barren Leaves, Mrs. Aldwinkle* v. (1927) 55 The publications of the Purity League figure invariably under the heading 'Curious' in the booksellers' catalogues.

-curist (kiūǝ·rist). As the second element of compounds such as *mind-curist, sure-curist* (= one who dabbles in mind-cure, etc.).

1889 *Cent. Dict.* 1907 *Practitioner* Apr. 580 Whether the engineer calls himself Christian Scientist, or Mind Curist, or Hypnotist, matters nothing.

Curl, *sb.* **3.** Add: Phr. *in curl, out of curl*: said of hair which is kept curled, or which has gone straight. Also fig. *to go out of curl*: to lose one's activity and 'vim', to become limp.

1924 Galsworthy *White Monkey* I. ix, 'If you got pneumonia', he said, 'I should go clean out of curl.'

Curl, *v.*¹ Add: **9.** *Cricket.* **a.** *intr.* Of the ball: To turn in after pitching; also, to turn in its flight before pitching. **b.** *trans.* Of the bowler: To cause (the ball) to curve in the air.

1888 *Cricket* (Badm.) ii. 54 Apart from breaking or curling, the ball may shoot or bump. 1900 Warner *Cr. in Many Climes* 83 He makes the ball curl in the air. 1904 *Westm. Gaz.* 21 May 3/1 When he first came to England,..he had that 'curl-in-the-air ball' to a very marked degree. *Ibid.*, Trott shone as a baseball player, and it is to this that he owed his power of curling a ball.

Curled, *ppl. a.* Add: **3. c.** Of wood: Having a wavy or curly grain. Chiefly in *curled maple*.

1813 H. Muhlenberg *Catal. Plants* 84 (*Alnus undulata* or *crispata*) Waved alder or curled alder. 1832 D. J. Browne *Sylva Amer.* 107 It sometimes happens that in very old trees, the grain instead of following a perpendicular direction, is undulated, and this variety is termed Curled Maple. 1851 C. Cist *Cincinnati* 249 There are no finer ornamental woods in the world for furniture, than those of American growth, the black walnut, cherry and curled maple. 1855 *Trans. Mich. Agric. Soc.* VI. 528 Much of this [maple] timber is curled and some bird's-eyed.

Curlicue. (Earlier U.S. examples.)

1844 'Jon. Slick' *High Life N. Y.* II. 54, I writ out my name..and handed it over, curlecues and all. *Ibid.* 155 We made a curlecue round both the ships.

Cu·rlicue, *v. U.S.* [f. the sb.] *trans.* and *intr.* To bend elaborately or fantastically.

1844 'Jon. Slick' *High Life N. Y.* I. 11 A kind of picket fence made out of iron, all *curlicued* over on the sides. *Ibid.* 66 Then her arms went curlecueing over her head.

Curl-leaf. [Curl *sb.* or *v.*] = Curl *sb.* 4.

1886 *Harper's Mag.* July 283/1 Foreign varieties and their hybrids are sometimes afflicted with the curl leaf.

Curly, *a.* **3.** Add: *curly maple* (see *Curled 3 c).

1909 Mrs. Stratton-Porter *Girl of Limberlost* xi. 218 In an expressed crate was a fine curly-maple dressing table.

Curly-wurly (kǝ̄·ɹli,wǝ̄·ɹli), *a. dial.* and *colloq.* [See Curlie-wurlie *sb.* in Dict.] Twisting and curling.

1853 Cadenhead *Bon-accord* 187 (E.D.D.) Wi' a' their curly-wurly stanes. 1907 N. Munro *Daft Days* xix, The dusting of the stair-rauls and the parlour beltings—the curly-wurly places, as she called them.

Curragh (kɒ·răχ, kɒ·rā). *Ireland* and *Isle of Man.* [Ir. *corrach* marsh, Manx *curragh* moor, bog, fen.] Marshy waste ground; *spec.* the proper name of the level stretch of open ground in Co. Kildare, famous for its race-course and military camp.

1664 in *Lex Scripta Isle of Man* (1819) 144 Digg and take away Timber in and out of the Curraughes on the North Side. 1894 Hall Caine *Manxman* vi. i, The bog-bane to the rushy curragh, say I, Nancy. 1908 — in *M. A. P.* XX. 362 A widower living alone in some little mud cottage on the curragh.

Currajong, var. Kurrajong.

Currant. 4. Add: **currant-borer, -worm** (U.S. examples).

1867 *Amer. Naturalist* June 223 The *currant-borer moth (*Trochilium tipuliforme*) darts about the leaves on hot sunny days. 1886 *Harper's Mag.* Aug. 447/2 There are three species of the currant-borer. 1867 *Amer. Naturalist* June 222 The *Abraxas? ribearia* of Fitch, the well-known *Currant-worm, defoliates whole rows of currant bushes. 1886 *Harper's Mag.* Aug. 447 The natural history of the currant worm and moth.

Currant jelly. A preserve made of the strained juice of boiled currants heated and mixed with sugar in a preserving-pan. Also in fig. context. Also *attrib.*, as *currant-jelly dog*, a harrier.

1747 Mrs. Glasse *Cookery* 145 To make Curran Jelly. Strip the Currants from the Stalks, put them in a Stone Jar [etc.]. 1761 W. Gelleroy *Lond. Cook* 303 To make Currant Jelly. 1831 *Athenæum* 31 Dec. 852/1 Swallowing the bitter powder of instruction by enclosing it in the currant jelly of amusement. 1851 *Illustr. Lond. News* 11 Jan. 27/3 Those agents of woodcraft, called, in flippant parlance, 'currant-jelly dogs'. [1923 H. Cox *Dogs and I* xvii. 145 Those which are contemptuously termed 'Red Currant Jelly Dogs'..are composed either of Beagle Harriers or..dwarf Foxhounds.]

Cu·rranty, *a.* [See -y¹.] Full of currants.

1876 Miss Braddon *J. Haggard's Dau.* ix, Certain rock-cakes, seedy and curranty.

Currency. Add: **4. c.** Formerly a name for native-born Australians, as distinguished from *sterling*, or English-born. (See 4 b and the quots. there marked *fig.*) Also *attrib.* and *adj.*

1827 P. Cunningham *N. S. Wales* xxi. II. 53 Our Currency lads and lasses are a fine interesting race. 1828 *Ibid.* (ed. 3) 48 The Currencies grow up tall and slender, like the Americans. 1894 W. C. Dawe (*title*) The Confessions of a Currency Girl. 1899 *Macm. Mag.* June 127/1 The boys when questioned would say: 'I'm not English; I'm Currency'.

6. currency note, paper money used as currency, esp. the £1 and 10*s.* notes issued by the Treasury for circulation as legal tender during the war of 1914–18; a Treasury-note.

1893 Kipling *Many Invent., In the Rukh*, The currency notes accumulated in the drawer. 1915 *Proclamation* in *Jrnl. Instit. Bankers* Mar. 113 Payment for the order at its face value in coins or currency notes. 1920 *Discovery* May 145/1 Our over-issues of currency notes. 1922 *Encycl. Brit.* XXXI. 969/2 The 1914 Act..allowed an issue of £1 and 10*s.* currency notes by the Treasury.

Current, *sb.* **8.** Add: **a. current meter,** also, see quot. 1868. **b.** Various obvious combs.

1862 *Catal. Internat. Exhib.* II. XIII. 13 As these instruments have no break pieces or current reversers they cannot get out of order. 1866 R. M. Ferguson *Electr.* (1870) 185 A contrivance for this purpose is called a rheotome or current-break. 1868 Haskoll *Land & Marine Survey.* (1886) 209 The current meter is useful also to ascertain the velocity of under currents. 1884 Higgs *Magn. & Dyn.-Electr. Mach.* 207 The current closers and interrupters. *Ibid.* 272 The current-energised rotating helix. 1888 Bottone *Electr. Instr. Making* (1894) 192 The current reverser for the Wheatstone single needle telegraph. 1927 *Daily Tel.* 31 Jan. 5 The plate current-grid volts.

Current, *a.* **3.** Add: *current account*, an account kept by a customer at a bank to meet his current expenses.

1875 H. Fisher *Opening* etc. *Spec. Bank Accts.* 1 The opening, working, and closing of certain classes of Current and Deposit Accounts. 1883 J. Hutchison *Pract. Banking* II. 112 A number of the accounts in the Deposit Ledgers might with propriety be transferred to the Current Account Ledgers. 1899 *Westm. Gaz.* 1 Sept. 6/3 It is the depositor, rather than the current-account customer, who is victimised by this custom.

Curse, *sb.* Add: **3. b.** = Cuss *sb.* 2.

1791 R. Tyler *Contrast* III. i. (1887) 55 There was a poor, good-natured, curse of a husband, and a sad rantipole of a wife. 1853 B. Young in *Jrnl. Discourses* I. 83 We have known Gladden Bishop for more than twenty years, and know him to be a poor, dirty curse. *Ibid.* 169 Why don't you do it, you poor miserable curses?

c. An angler's name for a very small gnat or midge.

1889 F. M. Halford *Dry-Fly Fishing* vi. 116 'Curses', or black midges or gnats. 1899 *19th Cent.* Jan. 122 The monstrously minute 'curse'.

5. curse-word = *cuss-word* (Cuss *sb.* 3).

1897 R. M. Stuart *Simpkinsville* vii. 225 The popular after-dinner 'curse word story' of the cloth would never have been tolerated in Simpkinsville.

Cursus. Add: **d.** The regular varying cadences which mark the end of sentences and phrases, esp. in Greek and Latin prose.

1904 H. A. Wilson in *Jrnl. Theol. Stud.* V. 387 Prof. E. Norden has traced the use of the 'cursus' in Classical writers, Greek as well as Latin. 1910 *Encycl. Brit.* VIII. 304/1 The *cursus* or prose rhythm of the pontifical chancery

of the 11th and 12th centuries. 1910 A. C. Clark (*title*) The Cursus in Mediaeval and Vulgar Latin.

Curtain, *sb.*[1] Add:

3. b. *Mil.* (In full *curtain of fire, curtain fire.*) A concentration of rapid and continuous artillery or machine-gun fire on a designated line or area, to prevent the advance or retreat of enemy troops, or to clear the way for the combatant's advance. Also, a concentration of fire to block the progress of aeroplanes.

1916 Boyd Cable *Action Front* 114 Shells began to batter at their parapet, and to prepare a curtain of fire along their front. 1920 D. A. Macalister *Field Gunnery* (ed. 4) 157 During an attack..the batteries, acting in concert, establish the 'curtain of fire' or 'barrage'. 1922 *Encycl. Brit.* XXX. 98/2 The idea also was evolved of barrage fire, a curtain of bursting shell to be put up in the path of the raiders.

c. A contrivance consisting of wooden slats which can be rolled up: a number of these are used to form a dam or weir. Also *attrib.*, *curtain-dam, -valve, -weir.*

1913 B. F. Thomas & Watt *Improvem. Rivers* (ed. 2) II. 616 Curtain Dams... The Cameré curtain..consists of narrow horizontal strips of wood hinged together, and capable of being rolled up by an endless chain. *Ibid.* 640 The space between the two rows [of shutters] was then filled with water by opening curtain-valves. 1927 E. Weymann *Dams* 586 The curtains are suspended from hooks on the face of the frames. 1929 *Encycl. Brit.* XXIII. 483/1 The curtain weir... In it wooden curtains that can be rolled up from the bottom were substituted for the needles in the Poirée weir.

8. curtain-call, a call for an actor to appear after the fall of the curtain (see 2); **curtain-fall,** the fall of the curtain at the end of an act or scene; the situation or tableau when the curtain falls; also *fig.*

a 1909 'O. Henry' *Roads of Destiny* xxi. 353 Uncle Sam has nine *curtain-calls holding Miss Panama by the hand. 1909 *Westm. Gaz.* 17 Apr. 1/3 Thirty 'curtain calls' rewarding play and players. 1920 P. G. Wodehouse *Damsel in Distress* xii. 144 He felt a wave of stage-fright such as he had only once experienced before in his life—on the occasion when he had been young enough to take a curtain-call on a first-night. 1904 *Westm. Gaz.* 30 Mar. 4/2 The sad *curtain-fall of universal commonplace. 1907 *Ibid.* 10 June 3/1 Pride..forbids him to propose until close on the final curtain-fall. 1909 *Daily Chron.* 26 Jan. 5/6 'A Merry Christmas!' he shouts light-heartedly at curtain-fall.

Curtate, *a.* Add:

2. *Economics* and *Statistics.* Shortened or limited according to some formula or rule.

1927 Bowley & Stamp *Nat. Income 1924* 21 When the averages of these curtate groups are taken, that for women is often higher than for men. 1927 B. C. Hoskins *Insur. Lexicon* 134 If payments cease with the last payment preceding the death, the annuity is said to be 'non-apportionable', or 'without proportion', or 'curtate'. 1929 *Encycl. Brit.* VIII. 973/1 This expression..is technically known as the curtate expectation of life. No allowance is included in the formula for that portion of life-time lived by each individual in the year of his death.

Curvature. Add: **1. c.** *Curvature of space* (or *space-time*), in the theory of relativity, a generalization of the notion of curvature applied to space of four (or of *n*) dimensions.

1920 A. S. Eddington *Space Time & Gravit.* x. 158 We thus get the idea that space-time may have an essential curvature on a great scale independent of the small hummocks due to recognised matter. 1923 — *Math. Th. Relativity* v. 149 Curvature of space and time. 1927 — *Stars & Atoms* 83 Mass produces a curvature of space.

Curve, *sb.* Add:

B. 5. *Physics, Statistics,* etc. A line drawn from point to point so as to represent diagrammatically a continuous variation of quantity.

1884 *Pharmaceut. Jrnl. & Trans.* 26 July 77/2 The object of these curves was to show clearly some of the most important factors in the growth of crops. 1899 temperature curve [see Temperature 10]. 1909 Karl Pearson *Problem Pract. Eugenics* 11 The curve for all possibly reproductive wives is amply verified by the curve for young wives. 1910 W. E. Dalby in *Rep. Brit. Assoc.* (1911) 695 The curves of mileage, passengers carried, and goods carried increase regularly with the increase of capital.

C. curve-billed (epithet of a N. American thrush); **curve-plotting,** the graphic representation of a curve in a plan or diagram by means of points marked on coordinates.

1881 *Amer. Naturalist* XV. 217 The *curve-billed thrush (*H[arporhynchus] curvirostris*). 1905 Ashe & Keiley *Electr. Railways* 6 *Curve plotting is accomplished by means of a series of perpendicular and parallel lines.. termed coördinates.

Curved, *ppl. a.* Add: *Curved fire,* gun-fire with an angle of elevation or departure exceeding that of direct fire.

The angle is variously estimated: see quots.

1883 G. Mackinlay *Text Bk. Gunnery* 161 Indirect or curved fire. Fire from guns, with reduced charges, and from howitzers and mortars, at all angles of elevation not exceeding 15°. 1902 *Text Bk. Gunnery* II. iv. 214 When the curvature of the trajectory becomes considerable, as in High Angle and Curved Fire. 1907 O. M. Lissak *Ordn. & Gunnery* 358 Direct Fire is with high velocities, and angles of elevation not exceeding 20 degrees. Curved Fire is with low velocities, and angles of elevation not exceeding 30 degrees. 1917 W. H. Tschappat *Ord. & Gunnery* 426 For convenience of discussion curved fire will be considered as firings with elevations between 15° and 40° and high-angle fire as firings with elevations above 40°. 1920 D. A. Macalister *Field Gunnery* 19 *Curved Fire.*—Where the angle of elevation is not above 30°.

Curvometer (kəɪvǫ·mĭtəɪ). [f. Curve *sb.* + -meter.] An instrument for measuring the length of a curve. 1902 *Encycl. Brit.* XXX. 578/1.

Curvulate (kə·ɪviŭlĕɪt), *a.* [f. L. *curvus* Curve *a.*, with dim. termination as in *lingulate, virgulate.*] Slightly curved. 1889 *Cent. Dict.*

Curvy (kə·ɪvi), *a.* [-y [1].] Having a curve or curves; full of curves, marked with curves.

1902 *Westm. Gaz.* 23 Oct. 3/2 The collar and the quaint curvy applications on the skirt should be of guipure lace.

Cusec. Abbreviation, used by engineers, of '*cu*bic foot per *sec*ond'.

1913 B. F. Thomas & Watt *Improvem. Rivers* (ed. 2) I. 46 The abbreviation 'second-feet' which is frequently used in America instead of 'cubic feet per second', has the equivalent of 'cusecks' among the Anglo-Indian engineers. 1915 Housden *Is Venus Inhabited?* 37 We should need a continuous flow of 20,000,000 cusecs. 1922 *Q. Rev.* Jan. 79 Taking the high flood discharge at Baghdad as 250,000 cusecs (i.e. cubic feet of water per second), then the escapage amounts to 242,000 cusecs.

Cush (kuʃ), colloq. shortening of *cushion* in sense 3 c. Also as verb.

1905 *Westm. Gaz.* 21 Oct. 4/1 It is like watching a game of billiards with wooden cushes and beechwood balls.

Cush *v.*, var. *cosh* (see *Cosh *sb.*[3]). Hence **Cu·sher.**

1923 Packard *Four Stragglers* I. ii, 'A bit of a "cushing" expedition, was it?'..'Just the usual bash on the head with a neddy.' *Ibid.* II. iv, That was the method of the 'cusher'.

Cushag (ku·ʃəg). *dial.* Also -og. [Manx *cuishag vooar* lit. big stalk.] The common ragwort, *Senecio Jacobæa.*

1887 Hall Caine *Deemster* xxiv, There's gold on the cushags yet. 1894 — *Manxman* II. xxii, Philip plucked the cushag. 1900 *Westm. Gaz.* 1 Oct. 2/3 The term 'weeds' is defined as including thistles, cushags, and common docks.

Cush-cush. [Native name.] A species of yam, *Colocasia esculenta,* used as a food in the West Indies.

1871 Kingsley *At Last* ii. (1892) 26 Great roots of yam and cush-cush. *Ibid.* 37 Wild cush-cush roots.

Cushion, *sb.* Add:

3. c. Also of a bagatelle board.

1837 D. Walker *Games & Sports* 89 There are likewise two small cushions placed against the sides.

e. A small dam or body of water to catch the water falling from a weir.

1927 W. G. Bligh *Irrig. Wks.* (ed. 3) 109 The system of providing water cushions to canal falls by lowering the floor below the bed of the channel down stream.

f. A sweetmeat in the shape of a cushion.

1921 Louisa Thorpe *Bonbons & Simple Sugar Sweets* 49 Satin Cushions... With a pair of scissors cut the mixture into small cushions and leave them until quite firm.

Cushioned, *ppl. a.* Add:

1. e. *fig.* Of the voice: Soft and smooth, velvety.

1909 *Daily Chron.* 20 Jan. 5/6 Complaining for two hours against fate in that cushioned voice of hers. 1920 Galsworthy *In Chancery* II. xiii, There was comfort in her cushioned voice.

Cu·shioning, *ppl. a.* [f. Cushion *v.* + -ing [2].] Forming a cushion.

1887 Tourgee *Button's Inn* 304 The soft..snow..may have formed a cushioning mass saving him from instant death.

Cushiony, *a.* Add: *fig.* = *Cushy *a.*

1908 *Daily Chron.* 25 Feb. 4/4 A lot of them have rare cushiony jobs.

Cushy (ku·ʃi), *a. slang.* Also **cushey.** [Anglo-Ind., f. Hind. *khush* pleasant.] Of a post, job, etc.: Easy, comfortable, 'soft'. Of a wound: Not dangerous or serious.

1915 D. O. Barnett *Letters* 44 The billets here are very good..and we have rooms to ourselves... It's all very cushey and nice. 1916 *Blackw. Mag.* Jan. 91/2 I've got a cushy wound. 1916 *Daily Mail* 1 Nov., He's got a cushy job. 1917 Gibbs *Battles of Somme* 146 All our men who have had the luck to get a 'cushie wound'. 1928 E. Waugh *Decl. & F.* I. iii, I was sent to Ireland on a pretty cushy job connected with postal service. 1929 A. Waugh *Three Score & Ten* 214 For two months,..thank Heaven, we'll be in a cushy section.

Cuss, *sb. U.S.* **2.** (Earlier example.)

1775 *Narrag. Hist. Reg.* III. 263 A man that..was noted for a damn cuss.

Cuss, *v. U.S.* Add: (Earlier and later examples.)

1835 R. M. Bird *Hawks of Hawk-hollow* II. xx. 244, I hit the 'oss on the 'ead, and cuss the bit of his master! 1873 Aldrich *Marj. Daw* etc. (1885) 217 A vicious drop of rain.. fell upon the wick of our tallow candle, making it 'cuss', as Ned Strong described it. 1897 'Mark Twain' *Following Equator* vi, See him weep, hear him cuss between the lines!

b. With *out.* (See quot. 1881.)

1881 *N.Y. Times* 18 Dec. in *N. & Q.* 6th Ser. V. 65/1 *Cuss out,* to subdue by overwhelming severity of tongue. 'He cussed that fellow out', *i.e.* he annihilated him verbally. 1901 S. E. White *Westerners* xvi. 134 Clearly he could not 'cuss out' the delinquents as they deserved.

Cussed, *a.* orig. *U.S.* (Earlier examples.)

1840 *Knickerbocker Mag.* XVI. 323 Blast the 'cussed old imp!' 1841 *Ibid.* XVII. 154, I had a twelve-pounder out of the water, when my cussed line broke.

Cussedly, *adv.* (Earlier U.S. example.)

1846 Corcoran *Pickings* 10, I never keeps low company, and you is so cussedly vulgar.

Custard. 2. b. Add: **custard pie; custard-powder,** a preparation in powder form for making custard by mixing it with milk; **custard tree,** the tree bearing the custard-apple.

1869 Mrs. Stowe *Oldtown Folks* xxvii. 340 *Custard pies, apple pies. 1861 H. Beasley *Druggist's Gen. Receipt Bk.* 278 *Custard Powder [recipe]. 1808 T. Ashe *Trav.* x. 85 [Custard Island abounds] with the papaw, which is vulgarly known by the name of the *Custard tree.

Custard-apple. Add: Also *attrib.*

1819 E. Evans *Pedestrious Tour* 284 The papaw resembles the locust, or custard apple tree.

Custom, *sb.* **6.** Add: **custom-made** *a. U.S.*, made to order or to measure; similarly **custom garment, -shop, -tailor, -work.**

1905 *Washington Star* 24 Nov. 5 Advt., Double or Single-Breasted Sacks, as perfect-fitting as the finest *custom garments. 1888 *Chicago Inter-Ocean* (Farmer) Mr. Bond abominated *custom-made clothing... He put comfort before style, and independence before tailors' plates. 1899 W. D. Howells *Ragged Lady* 65 That's a custom made slipper, and the price..was seven dollars. 1851 C. Cist *Cincinnati* 176 Two thirds of these at least, are made here, wholesale or at *custom shops. 1903 *N.Y. Times* 26 Sept. 6 Advt., *Custom tailors charge for suits like these $35. 1851 C. Cist *Cincinnati* 175 Fine and coarse work for foreign markets, and *custom work for home consumption. *Ibid.* 176 Custom-work boot and shoemakers.

Customer, *sb.* Add: **5. b.** A fox that affords good sport in the field. Also, a player or athlete who offers to take on or compete with a champion.

1843–54 R. S. Surtees *Handley Cross* xxxiv. (1901) I. 271 A light-coloured fox beat him so often as to acquire the name of the 'old customer'. 1896 *Westm. Gaz.* 5 Dec. 4/2 A. R. Downer is the latest 'customer' for Bredin. He last night telegraphed..expressing his willingness to run the new professional 350 yards for £50 a side. 1898 *Ibid.* 17 Nov. 9/1 At a second attempt Scraptoft Gorse produced the right sort of customer. 1898 J. A. Gibbs *Cotswold Village* xiv. (1912) 329 An old dog fox, the hero of many a good run in recent years from these coverts (an 'old customer' in fact). 1899 *Westm. Gaz.* 15 Feb. 9/2 Almost immediately a fox went away, and he proved to be a real customer.

Cut, *sb.*[2] Add:

12. b. Intentional absence from or deliberate omission to attend (a service, etc.).

1920 W. T. Grenfell *Labrador Doctor* ii. 16 Attendance at chapel was compulsory, and no 'cuts' were allowed.

23. b. *To have* or *take a cut*: to make a slight meal with a slice of meat. *U.S.*

1770 Washington *Diaries* I. 383 Had a cold cut at Mrs. Campbell's. 1773 *Ibid.* II. 102 [They] calld here, but would not stay dinner, taking a Cut before it. 1816 U. Brown *Jrnl.* in *Maryland Hist. Mag.* XI. 230 At last comes to an Orniary [= Ordinary], fed and took a cut.

c. A number of cattle cut out from the herd. *U.S.*

1888 Roosevelt in *Century Mag.* Apr. 860/2 As the animals of a brand are cut out they are received and held apart by some rider detailed for the purpose, who is said to be 'holding the cut'. 1907 S. E. White *Arizona Nights* I. vi. 112 The round-up Captain appointed two men to hold the cow-and-calf cut, and two more to hold the steer cut.

27. Also, a portion of a field cut, or intended for cutting, at one time. *U.S.*

1765 Washington *Diaries* I. 216 Finished sowing Wheat at the Mill—viz 19 Bushls in ye large cut within the Post and Rail fence and 6 B. in ye small cut. 1770 *Ibid.* 399 Morris at Doeg Run began to sow his third Cut of Wheat. 1855 *Florida Plant. Rec.* 132 The Cotton in the lower most cut of prelow will avrige knee high, the next two cutes will not avrige quit wast high.

Cut, *v.* Add:

8. c. *To cut fine*: to allow only the minimum or a very small margin of profit, etc. on.

1896 *Daily News* 24 July 8/6 The making of clothes was, he added, 'cut very fine'.

9. d. *To cut and cover*: to plough so that the furrow-slice is turned over on an unploughed strip. *U.S.*

1840 [see *'61 below]. 1861 *Trans. Ill. Agric. Soc.* IV. 111 Mr. Mills is not in favor of any implement that 'cuts and covers'. Col. Harris..says that cutting and covering is practiced by some of the Scioto farmers.

13. b. Also of land, to yield as a crop.

1754 *Essex Inst. Hist. Coll.* XLIII. 90 The Pasturing good..and cuts enough to keep all the stock. 1840 J. Buel *Farmer's Comp.* 211 One acre of good grass will cut three tons of hay, or keep a cow... Four acres of lean, poor grass will cut little more..than three tons of hay. 1872 *Rep. Vermont Board Agric.* 351 It would cut only hay enough to winter four cattle. 1921 R. D. Paine *Comr. Rolling Ocean* x. 169, I quit the sea for a spell to run my own place—she cuts thirty ton o' hay.

14. c. *transf.* = 56 d. *U.S.*

1903 A. Adams *Log Cowboy* ii. 13 Flood had the first pick, and cut twelve bays and browns.

15. *To cut across* (fig.).

1927 Carr-Saunders & Jones *Soc. Struct. Eng. & Wales* 83 But these other associations cut across industrial, occupational, and income classifications.

16. b. esp. *U.S.* with *trail.* Also *ellipt.*

1899 T. Hall *Tales* 19 One of his men dashes breathlessly in..with the exciting report that he has cut the raiders' trail. 1903 A. Adams *Log Cowboy* vii. 90 If you have no authority to cut this trail then you don't cut this herd. *Ibid.*, They were merely cutting (trail cutting) in the interest of the immediate locality.

19. b. (Earlier examples.) *To cut round*: to make a display. *U.S.*

1834 D. Crockett *Life* 63, I saw a little woman streaking it along through the woods like all wrath, and so I cut on too. *Ibid.* 65, I took my eldest brother..and cut out to her father's house to get her. 1848–52 Mrs. Whitcher *Widow Bedott P.* (1856) 91 They say she cut round and hollered and laffed and tried to be wonderful interestin'. *a* 1859 *N.Y. Spirit of Times* (Bartlett) Instead of sticking to me as she

used to do, she got to cuttin' round with all the young fellows, just as if she cared nothin' about me no more. 1879 F. R. Stockton *Rudder Grange* viii. 86 [The dog] was only cuttin' round because he was so glad to get loose.

c. To get up *behind* a vehicle. *U.S.*

1860 O. W. Holmes *Prof. Breakf.-t.* viii. 171 Here is a boy that loves to..chalk doorsteps, 'cut behind' anything on wheels or runners [etc.].

21. Also, to lower the prices in (a trade list).

1930 *Publishers' Circular* 5 July 5/3 Many publishers have told us they are cutting their lists.

33. d. To cease to support politically. *U.S.*

1904 *N.Y. Even. Post* 6 Sept. 2 Information..that Mr. Bell, the Republican nominee for governor, was being cut by the farmers of Chittenden County because of his policy.

41. *To cut loose.* **c.** To begin to act freely; to start off; to commence an attack; to let oneself go. *U.S.*

1900 G. Ade *More Fables in Slang* (1902) 182 She would approach the Piano timidly and sort of Trifle with it for a while, and say they would have to make Allowances, and then she would Cut Loose and worry the whole Block. 1901 S. E. White *Westerners* xviii. 157 You just ought to see him when he cuts loose. 1920 W. M. Raine *B. O'Connor* 244 It was York shot Reilly, after Cork had cut loose at him. 1918 E. M. Roberts *Flying Fighter* 66 My lorry had been seen, however. As I was taking it round a corner the Huns cut loose and caused me to go down that road as fast as the motor would take me. 1921 R. D. Paine *Comr. Rolling Ocean* xi. 196 He just now cut loose with 'Goodness gracious..I should call this the deuce of a mess'.

49. *To cut didoes* (Dido [2]), *dirt* (Dirt *sb.* 6 d), *eyes, (no) ice, the painter* (Painter [2] 2 b), *a splurge, a swath* (Swath [1] 3 c), *to waste* (Waste *sb.* 10 d): see the sbs. For *cut one's loss(es), cut prices,* see *Loss *sb.*[1] 4, *Price *sb.*

52. Cut back. c. *Bread-making.* (See quot.)

1907 J. Kirkland *Mod. Baker* I. 99 When it has been lying altogether ten hours, it [*sc.* dough] should be cut in pieces and turned from one end of the trough to the other, and well kneaded. The kneading operation should be repeated in another hour's time; but dough need not be cut back, only well kneaded, and four sides folded up. Machine-made dough ought not to require cutting back at all.

d. *intr.* In a cinema play or scenario: To return to a previous scene by repeating a picture of that scene. (See *Cut-back *sb.* 2.) Also *trans.* (with the play as obj.). Also *cut* simply.

1913 E. W. Sargent *Techn. Photoplay* (ed. 2) 91 The same device may be used to get rid of a dinner scene... We cut-back to some other action. 1916 *Ibid.* (ed. 3) 184 If you can not use a crowd perhaps you can cut to some single person who overlooks the crime and later tells the story. *Ibid.* 191 Another effective use is cutting from a person unknowingly approaching destruction to the person who seeks to bring about the catastrophe. *Ibid.* 193 It is well to remember..that not all plays may be cut back.

54. Cut in. c. In recent use also, to drive a motor-vehicle between two others which are passing each other in opposite directions, instead of keeping behind the one until the other has passed. Also *transf.*

1922 *Encycl. Brit.* XXXII. 1027/2 Two-way radio-telephony enabling two communicators..to 'cut in' or interrupt each other. 1925 *Don'ts for Motorists* 55 Cutting in is another evil practice. *Ibid.* 100 How to avoid accidents. ..Don't 'cut in'. 1926 *Weekly Disp.* 5 Sept. 1/1 He is supposed to have been reported for cutting in at the second and eleventh tees.

d. In recent use also *spec.*, (*a*) to employ a telephone so as to listen to conversation between other parties; (*b*) to supersede a partner during a dance.

1904 W. H. Smith *Promoters* xxv. 348 That telephone is 'cut in' and I have a number of friends..who are listening through it. 1921 R. D. Paine *Comr. Rolling Ocean* viii. 135 Excuse me, but may I cut in? Miss Crozier wants to see you right away. 1928 *Daily Express* 14 Dec. 19 The American practice known as 'cutting-in'..consists..of any man who wishes to dance tapping the shoulder of another man who is already dancing and abducting his partner.

55. Cut off. h. Also, in recent use *spec.* to deprive of communication by telegraph or telephone; to stop (one) from talking.

1891 E. S. Ellis *Check No. 2134* v. 38 The company can't afford to be cut off this way. 1926 J. Black *You Can't Win* vi. 68 She might git worked up about your troubles and ask a lot of dam' fool questions. Cut her off.

56. Cut out. a. Freq. *fig.* in recent use: To stop doing or using (something); to leave off, do without, omit, drop: esp. in imper. phr. *cut it out.*

a 1910 'O. Henry' *Sixes & Sevens* xviii. 209 To be frank with you, Whatsup, I've cut out the dope. 1914 Gertr. Atherton *Perch of Devil* I. 137 If it were more the primal instinct..so much the worse, the more reason to 'cut it out'. 1921 R. D. Paine *Comr. Rolling Ocean* vi. 110 Will you cut out the booze while you are ashore in Jamaica? 1924 W. M. Raine *Troubled Waters* viii. 85 We'd better cut out threats. They lead to trouble. 1928 F. N. Hart *Bellamy Trial* iii. 96, I thought she'd make him cut it out.

d. (Earlier U.S. examples.)

1869 *Overland Monthly* III. 126 Another rides in, selects a stray brand and 'cuts it out', by chasing it out with his horse. 1874 J. H. McCoy *Hist. Sk. Cattle Trade* 79 Whilst from six to ten cow boys hold the herd together the ranchman with one or two assistants separate such as are suitable. This process is termed 'cutting out'.

q. To finish shearing. *Austral.*

1890 *Melbourne Argus* 20 Sept. 13/6 When the stations 'cut out', as the term for finishing is.

r. *trans.* To disconnect (an electric circuit, etc.). Also *intr.* of the motor.

1920 *Chambers's Jrnl.* May 350/1 By means of a switch near the keyboard the organist can cut the motor in and out as desired. 1922 *Ibid.* Aug. 556/2 The dynamo is cut out automatically. 1917 *Blackw. Mag.* May 804/1 We continued in a westerly direction, with one cylinder still cutting out. 1924 A. W. Judge *Mod. Motor Cars* III. 75 Which causes the hammer to vibrate and to cut-out the battery circuit. 1926 H. H. U. Cross *Electric Lighting* etc. (ed. 4) 264 When the gears are fully enmeshed, the electro-magnet is..cut out by a disconnecting switch. 1928 *Motor Manual* (ed. 27) 110 When the dynamo speed falls below a certain minimum the device cuts out or opens the charging circuit. 1930 *Daily Express* 16 Aug. 5/5 When aero engines were much more liable to cut out and force one down in isolated places.

58. Cut under. (Earlier U.S. example.)

1859 Bartlett *Dict. Amer.* (ed. 2), *To Cut under,* to undersell in price. New York.

59. Cut up. o. *trans.* To 'kick' up (a disturbance). *U.S.*

a 1848 *Knickerbocker Mag.* (Bartlett) A wild bull of the prairies was cutting up shines at no great distance, tearing up the sod with hoofs and horns. 1902 McFaul *Ike Glidden* ii. 11 It was not Ike that cut up the mischief this time.

p. To conduct or manage (a contest) fraudulently. *Sporting slang.*

1923 *Daily Mail* 16 Jan. 7 Georges Carpentier, M. Descamps, his manager, and M. Hellers, the manager of the coloured boxer Siki, have been acquitted by the French Boxing Federation of having arranged and 'cut up' the fight in which Siki was declared victor. 1923 *Weekly Disp.* 13 May 7, I read in newspapers now that more than half the races under National Hunt rules are cut up, and that jockeys and trainers are out to rob the public.

61. Cut-and-cover. Also *Agric.* (see *9 d). *U.S.*

1840 J. Buel *Farmer's Comp.* 113 The cut-and-cover practice is still worse as it leaves..two thirds of the soil, undisturbed by the plough. 187. *Rep. Vermont Board Agric.* IV. 93 The old Dutch wooden plow..[was] used among the stumps and roots of the newish lands, with the plowman's ideal of cut and cover.

Cut, *ppl. a.* Add:

2. b. Of money (see *Cut-money.). *U.S.*

1844 in C. Cist *Cincinnati Misc.* 5 The early settlers coined cut money, that is to say the dollar was cut into four equal parts. *Ibid.* 6 As late as 1806..the business house in Philadelphia in which I was apprentice, received over one hundred pounds of cut silver.

3. b. *Cut bank,* a bank formed by a river cutting into it. *U.S.*

1836 S. Cummings *Western Pilot* 68 You pass close by this cut bank of the bar. 1884 'Mark Twain' *Huck. Finn* xv. 127 In about a minute I come a-booming down on a cut bank with..big trees on it..That cut bank was an island.

6. *U.S.* freq. in recent use in *cut rates.*

18.. *Boston Jrnl.* (Farmer) The plain people who enjoy a spectacular, musical, and dramatic season at cut rates. 1904 F. Lynde *Grafters* xiii. 163 If the cut rates should be withdrawn and the railroad activities cease. 1907 *N.Y. Even. Post* (semi-weekly ed.) 14 Feb. 6 The evangelist was referred to as a man who 'stole members from other churches by offering cut rates to heaven'.

12. b. *cut-glass, -leaf, -paper, -steel.*

1875 Mrs. Stowe *We & Neighbors* xxxii. 303, I arranged it in my high *cut-glass dish and covered it with foamy billow of whites of eggs. 1923 E. F. Wyatt *Invis. Gods* I. ii. 16 *Cut-leaf birch flickered their light foliage in summer. 1891 Kipling *Light that Failed* (1900) 9 The boy who..had decorated Amomma's horns with *cut-paper ham-frills. 1896 *Westm. Gaz.* 10 Dec. 3/2 A *cut-steel buckle.

d. *cut-chopping, -drive, -lob.*

1907 P. A. Vaile *Mod. Lawn Tennis* 87 A cut lob should drop straighter than a lifted one. 1908 *Westm. Gaz.* 27 June 11/2 The latter's cut-drives and crisp volleying proved more than usually effective. 1927 *Daily Express* 11 June 13/5 The 'cut-chopping' by Miss Ryan was fierce and fast in the first set.

Cut-away, *a.* (*sb.*). Add: **c.** [f. Cut *v.* 51.] *adj.* 'Having a cutting action; as, a cutaway harrow' (Webster 1911). *sb.* 'That part of a machine which cuts away; as, the cutaway of a harrow' (Funk 1928).

Cu·t-back, *sb.* [f. Cut *v.* 52.]

1. *Gardening.* A plant which has been pruned by cutting off shoots close back to the main stem.

1897 *Garden* 21 Aug. 141 The 'cutbacks' [*sc.* young vines] planted in March. 1920 *19th Cent.* July 173 Too often they [*sc.* roseries] consist of little more than serried rows of 'cut-backs'.

2. *Cinematography.* A scene which is a return to a previous action in the play.

1913 E. W. Sargent *Techn. Photoplay* (ed. 2) 90 Originally the cut-back was used to close up a gap in the action, to obviate the actual showing of a crime [etc.]. 1916 *Ibid.* (ed. 3) 360 *Cut-back*—One or more returns to a previous action, either to avoid the showing of prohibited action, to raise the effect through contrast or to quicken the action. 1927 *Sunday Times* 27 Feb. 6/4 In the last ten minutes a 'cut-back' occurs, and the quarrel and killing are reconstructed. *Ibid.* 15 May 10/5 The discovery of the 'close-up' and the 'cut-back' has always been accredited to Griffith.

Cute, *a.* **2.** *U.S.* (Earlier and later examples.)

1834 C. A. Davis *Major Downing's Lett.* 214 I'm goin' to show you about as cute a thing as you've seen in mary a day. 1849 N. P. Willis *Rural Lett.* xviii. 155 'Purty 'cute tool' says my neighbor. 1857 D. H. Strother *Virginia Illustr.* ii. 166 'What cute little socks!' said the woman. 1879 F. R. Stockton *Rudder Grange* vi. 61 [The flat] was so cute, so complete. 1881 A. A. Hayes *New Colorado* vii. 97 The way that Smart Aleck hollered when we swung round some of them 'cute' curves. 1900 *Daily News* 15 Nov. 6/5 A small and compact wooden house, what the Americans would call 'cute'. 1908 *Daily Chron.* 21 Apr. 3/3 American visitors who are used to wide rectangular streets are delightfully bewildered when I take them through sinuous byeways and tortuous alleys. They proclaim it 'just too cute and lovely'.

Cuteness. (Later U.S. examples.)

1845 *Knickerbocker Mag.* Aug. (Bartlett) He had a pair of bright, twinkling eyes, that gave an air of extreme cuteness to his physiognomy. 1872 H. M. Stanley *How I found Livingstone* xii. 464 Very fine people and singularly remarkable for commercial ''cuteness' and sagacity. 1903 *Booklovers' Mag.* Dec. Advt., The illustration gives but a faint idea of the beauty and cuteness of the calendar itself.

Cutey, cutie (kiū·ti). *U.S. slang.* [f. Cute *a.*] A clever or smart girl.

1921 R. D. Paine *Comr. Rolling Ocean* viii. 130 Her friends thought she was a cutey for turning the trick. 1927 J. Barbican *Confess. Rum-Runner* xiv. 149 He goes about with a high-stepping cutie who's ace-high on the face and figure. 1930 *Punch* 12 Mar. 284/2 Only two flappers ('cuties', Percival whispered to me).

Cuthbert [2]. A name given during the war of 1914–18 to a man who secured a post in a Government Office or the Civil Service expressly to evade military service.

1917 *Evening News* 25 Jan. (in a cartoon by 'Poy').

Cut-in, *sb.* [See Cut *v.* 54.]

1. The act of striking in, entering *for* (a race), etc.

1898 *Westm. Gaz.* 21 June 9/2 Herminius himself, with all his weight, is likely to have a cut in for the same race.

2. *Cinematography.* A sub-title or 'leader' thrown on the screen during a scene, and thus 'cutting into' the action. Also called *cut-in leader.*

1916 E. W. Sargent *Techn. Photoplay* (ed. 3) 164 If the leader is placed directly in a scene, generally as the spoken words of some character, it is termed a cut-in leader, and is written 'cut-in'... It is termed a cut in because the joining girl takes a pair of scissors and cuts the scene to permit its insertion. 1921 Lescarboura *Cinema Handbk.* 21 *Cut-In*—Anything inserted in a scene which breaks its continuity.

3. A device for starting a motor engine by completing the electric circuit.

1924 A. W. Judge *Mod. Motor Cars* III. 74 A more common form of cut-in is that depending upon electro-magnetic action. *Ibid.* 76 There are many other forms of electrical, thermostatic, and mechanical 'cut-out' and 'cut-in' devices for the battery-dynamo and battery-ignition circuits. 1929 *Motor Electr. Manual* (ed. 4) 119 A cut-out (which is also a cut-in) is an essential control device between the dynamo and the battery.

Cutlass, *sb.* **2. cutlass-fish** (example).

1884 Goode *Nat. Hist. Aquatic Anim.* 335 The name 'Cutlass-fish', which is current for the same species [*sc. Trichiurus lepturus*] in the British West Indies.

Cut-line. *Cut-line drawing* (see quot. 1912).

1912 M. Drake *Engl. Glass-painting* 183 Once a panel.. has been made up, the panes composing it should be laid in their places on a sheet of paper and their outlines traced by a pencil run round their edges. This sheet of paper will serve the glazier as a 'cut-line' drawing when the panels are handed to him for re-leading. 1923 — *Doom Window* xxv. 290 Cartoons began to be completed, and Reinecke and Sophie now made the cut-line drawings.

Cu·t-money. *U.S.* [*Cut *ppl. a.* 2 b.] (See quots.)

1822 J. Woods *Engl. Prairie* 230 We found change at these towns very scarce; what there was, was mostly cut-money; that is, when change is wanted they often cut dollars, half-dollars, and quarter-dollars, into smaller pieces with an ax or chisel. 1824 W. N. Blane *Excursion* 257, I was obliged to cut a silver dollar, into quarters, and even into eights; a practice so common in the Western States, that the cut-money as it was called, was the only change that could be had in Missouri.

Cut nail. *U.S.* (See Cut *ppl. a.* 3, quot. 1874.)

1795 J. Scott *U.S. Gazetteer* 1288/2, 3 nail manufactories for cut nails. 1809 *Deb. Congress* 13 Aug. 2250 The manufacture of cut nails was born in our country. 1835 *Southern Lit. Messenger* I. 260 In the city..there are..two manufactories for cut nails. 1860 Holmes *Prof. Breakf.-t.* v. 152 The cut nails of machine-divinity may be driven in, but they won't clinch.

attrib. 1817 S. R. Brown *Western Gaz.* 316 Also, more mercantile stores,..one cut nail factory. 1878 *Congress. Rec.* 28 Jan. 612/1 An improvement nearly as important.. as was the cut-nail machine in malling nails.

Cut-off, *sb.* Add: **2.** *U.S.* (Earlier examples.) Now used in other countries. Also, a lateral canal dug across a bend in a river or formed by the flood action of the river itself (also *attrib.*).

1773 *Acts Gen. Assembly Georgia* (1881) 300 To make any such cut off as shall be thought necessary from River to River. *Ibid.*, In such Cuts off and Clearing. 1817 S. R. Brown *Western Gaz.* 222 It is about four miles across the several branches of the Pascagola..intersected by bayous and cut-offs. 1821 T. Nuttall *Trav. Arkansa* vi. 98 The latter proceeds from the bayou,..the bayou or cut-off continuing to the southwest. 1913 B. F. Thomas & Watt *Improvem. Rivers* (ed. 2) I. 27 When a bend has become almost a complete curve, the river breaks through the intervening neck of land and forms a cut-off. *Ibid.* II. 337 The entire river was dammed at or near the upper part of a sharp bend, and a cut-off or lateral canal was dug across the bend from the pool thus formed. *Ibid.* 367 Cut-off walls resting on the river-bed.

b. *U.S.* (Earlier and later examples.)

1807 Pike *Sources Mississ.* (1810) 64 Observed Mr. Grant's trackes going through it; found his mark of a cut off, (agreed on between us) took it, and proceeded very well. 1818 *Boston Weekly Messenger* 23 July (Th.) They pointed [it] out to him as being a nigh cut-off to the high road. 1857 W. Chandless *Visit Salt Lake* I. 107 Two more days, over a 'cut off', little travelled, brought us within a few miles of the mountains. 1908 *Westm. Gaz.* 31 Dec. 3/1 The Great Western's Ashendon to Aynho 'cut-off', which will provide that company with a new route to Birmingham, nineteen miles shorter than its existing one. 1924 W. M. Raine

Troubled Waters iii. 29 Evidently she was taking the cut-off back to the ranch, unaware that the bridge had been washed out by the freshet.

3. e. In a magazine rifle, a device which prevents the feeding of cartridges from the magazine into the chamber, and enables the rifle to be used as a single-loader.

1890 [see 3 c in Dict.]. 1898 *Daily News* 9 May 3/1 Magazine Cut-off. 1904 *Westm. Gaz.* 9 Dec 7/2 As the Navy considered that a cut-off was necessary this..is fitted to all naval rifles. 1919 Boyd Cable *Old Contemptibles* ix. 141 In a twinkling every man..had his rifle muzzle over the parapet, and his fingers busy with magazine and cut-off.

f. An automatic safety device for shutting off light, esp. the light of a cinema-projector.

1906 *Daily Chron.* 28 June 2/7 Automatic cut-off devices. 1923 C. N. Bennett *Kinematography* 46 Immediately before the condenser..is a safety device called the hand light cut-off. *Ibid.* 47 There is a second cut-off fitted to all professional projectors... It is the automatic light cut-off. 1923 F. A. Talbot *Moving Pictures* ix. 119 The 'cut-off', an automatic safety shutter, mounted between the lamp and the film, which falls to intercept the light when the machine is at rest.

Cut-out, *sb.* Add: Also, in motor-vehicles an appliance that gives a free opening to the exhaust gases.

1905 *Motor Cycle* 2 Jan. 6 An exhaust cut-out. 1906 *Daily Chron.* 17 July 3/3 Nothing is easier than to have a 'cut-out' in the exhaust pipe, worked by a wire from the steering column, and so produce this noise and eliminate the back pressure whenever you wish. 1907 *Public Opinion* 17 May 628/2 The attention of the Committee of the Royal Automobile Club has been called to the increase in the use of sirens and exhaust cut-outs by certain motorists. 1908 *Westm. Gaz.* 5 May 4/3, I opened the cut-out, and applied the exhaust whistle.

2. a. The space formed by a piece or section being cut out (as of a floor).

1850 A. O. Hall *Manhattaner New Orleans* 30 Above the bar and post-office (the former..looked down upon through a wide cut-out in the floor) are the..reading-rooms of the merchants.

b. A railway or canal cutting.

1898 *Engineering Mag.* XVI. 116/1 The dredge by which the cut-outs were excavated and embankments constructed.

c. A figure cut out (or designed for cutting out) of paper, cloth, cardboard, or wood; also, appliqué.

Such figures are used for photographing as part of a cinematographic scene.

1905 Calkins & Holden *Art of Mod. Advertising* 10 The grocer must be supplied with attractive counter slips, 'hangers', window-cards, 'cut-outs', posters and other forms of lithographed matter. 1920 E. G. Lutz *Animated Cartoons* 84 This model, specifically spoken of as a 'cut-out', is pushed over the background under the camera and photographed. 1927 — *Motion-Pict. Cameraman* 169 A series of cut-outs for a continued action. 1927 *Daily Express* 27 Sept. 5/2 Cut-outs are all the rage—cut-outs in wood and in cardboard painted. 1927 *Ladies' Home Jrnl.* Dec. 68/3 It would be easy enough to adapt for the purpose the various animal cut-outs and illustrations. 1927 *Home Notes* 17 Dec., Embroidered Appliqué and Making Directions Supplied with Each Cut-Out.

d. A portion excised from a play, cinema film, etc.

1918 *America* (N.Y.) 20 July 352/1 A list of the cut-outs is marked on the permit so that an inspector visiting the theatre can see whether those parts are omitted.

3. An act of cutting out cattle from the herd. *U.S.*

1907 Mulford *Bar-20* xi. 120 In this contest Hopalong Cassidy led his nearest rival, Red Connors,..by twenty cut-outs. 1920 — *J. Nelson* xxiii. 254 Sam saw no use of collecting infants only to have them turned loose at the cut-out.

b. A place where cut-out animals are collected.

1920 Hunter *Trail Drivers of Texas* 98 Our camp was the catch and cut-out for all the other horses.

c. The finish of shearing, end of shearing-time. *Austral.*

1900 H. Lawson *Over Sliprails* 33 It was within a couple of days of cut-out, so I told Mitchell—who was shearing—that I'd camp up the Billabong and wait for him.

Cut-out, *a.* [See Cut *v.* 56 j and Cut *ppl. a.* 11.] Formed by cutting out a piece of paper, cloth, cardboard, etc., or of the piece cut out. Cf. *Cut-out *sb.* 2 c.

1799 [see Cut *ppl. a.* 11 in Dict.]. 1898 *Westm. Gaz.* 4 June 7/2 The slate-coloured cut-out frames, on which the prints are mounted. 1927 E. G. Lutz *Motion-Pict. Cameraman* 162 Cut-out figures photographed in sequence. 1929 *Publishers' Circular* 22 June 73 Attractive cut-out figures, in full colours.

Cut-over, *a.* and *sb. U.S.* [See Cut *v.* 57 b and Cut *ppl. a.* 11.]

A. *adj.* Cleared of timber by cutting.

1899 *Westm. Gaz.* 6 Jan. 10/2 At least 90 per cent. of the cut-over lands [on the Pacific coast] are of absolutely no value for agricultural purposes. 1911 H. Quick *Yellowstone N.* xii. 338 The solitary guest which is the only thing that brings the haunch to the spit in the Minnesota cut-over forest.

B. *sb.* An area on which the timber has been cut.

1922 Titus *Timber* vi. 60 If we had known we could have gone north..into the hardwood cutover and made a go of it.

Cut-rate. *attrib. U.S.* (See *Cut *ppl. a.* 6.)

1904 *Daily Chron.* 15 June 7/3 During the first eleven days of June one out of every eighty of the cut-rate arrivals was ordered back to Europe. *a* 1909 'O. Henry' *Roads of Destiny* xv. 237 A clerk in the Cut-rate Drug Store.

Cut sheet. India-rubber cut into sheets from a pressed block.

1907 H. L. Terry *India-rubber* xii. 161 Cut sheet rubber. *Ibid.* 162 A good deal of English cut sheet goes to Paris. 1920 *Seeligmann's Indiarubber* (ed. 2) 146 The great use of blocked rubber consists in the manufacture of cut sheet and English sheet. 1923 B. D. W. Luff *Chem. Rubber* 17 This 'cut sheet', as it was and still is called, was adapted to many purposes, surgical appliances, tubing and overshoes being made at an early date.

Cut-stone. *attrib.* (See Cut *ppl. a.* 3.)

1836 *Knickerbocker Mag.* VIII. 193 A depth of eight feet and width of ninety feet, with cut-stone locks. 1882 *Econ. Geol. Illinois* II. 57 All the principal limestone formations in this county afford good building stone..and some of them afford a superior article, suitable for cut-stone work.

Cutter, *sb.*[1] Add:

1. b. *cutter-out,* also *spec.* in *U.S.*, one who separates cattle from a herd.

1910 Mulford *Hopalong Cassidy* iii. 28 Each of the cutters-out rode after some calf. 1920 — *J. Nelson* xxv. 259 There was only one pair of ropers..and only three cutters-out.

c. *Cutter-in,* a motorist who cuts in between two vehicles going in opposite directions (see *Cut *v.* 54 c).

1928 *Daily Express* 5 June 9/1 The cutters-in, and the speed-at-any-price merchants who spoil travelling. *Ibid.* 26 June 10/2 The cutter-in and the speeder-up..are the causes of..accidents.

8. cutter-dredge, a river-dredge fitted with knives; **cutter-wheel** (earlier U.S. example).

1849 *Rep. Comm. Patents* (1850) 231 We are aware that planing machines have been made with cutters on the face of the cutter wheel. 1913 B. F. Thomas & Watt *Improvem. Rivers* (ed. 2) I. 100 The cutter dredge,..in which the material is loosened by a series of knives shaped so that they will not clog, fastened to a shaft and revolving close to the end of the suction pipe.

Cutter, *sb.*[2] **3.** *U.S.* (Earlier and later examples.)

1804 Fessenden *Terrible Tractoration* 80 Then condescend to be my crony And guide my wild Parnassian pony, Till our aerial cutter runs, Athwart a wilderness of suns! 1811 *Massachusetts Spy* 1 May (Th.) The horse and cutter advertised in your paper has been found... The post bags which were in the cutter, [etc.]. 1912 Canfield *Squirrel Cage* I. ix. 88 Women used to sleigh-ride in a little cutter just big enough for one and a half.

Cut-throat. Add:

5. b. In full *cut-throat trout*: a trout, *Salmo clarkii,* of the lakes and rivers of N.W. America; the typical form has a red mark under the jaw.

6. Also *fig.* and *transf.*

1848 W. Armstrong *Stocks* 31 [Harlem rail road stock] is generally considered to be most essentially a 'cut-throat stock'. 1903 *Westm. Gaz.* 17 Jan. 3/1 The wide valley of the Po, where, in nine months of the year, the cut-throat *tramontana* is a frequent visitant.

b. *Cut-throat euchre*: three-handed euchre, in which one player plays against the other two. Also applied to dummy bridge.

1904 Eleanor A. Tennant *A B C of Bridge* 100 Cut-Throat Bridge. Though the above is the simplest way of playing three-handed Bridge, Cut-throat has great attractions for some people. 1907 *Hoyle's Games* 131 Three-Handed Bridge, Cut-Throat, or Dummy Bridge. *Ibid.* 223 Euchre...Cut-Throat, or Three-Hand. 1928 F. Tennyson Jesse *Many Latitudes,* etc. 167 We played cut-throat and had a rather dejected evening.

Cutting, *vbl. sb.* Add:

3. b. A quantity that may be cut.

1902 S. E. White *Blazed Trail* xxvii. 191 'Its a fine country,' went on Thorpe so everyone could hear, 'with a great cutting of white pine.'

9. *Cutting-in*: (*a*) the action of starting a motor engine by some device which closes the circuit.

1924 A. W. Judge *Mod. Motor Cars* III. 74 When the dynamo speed is low, the spring holds the contacts apart, but as soon as the 'cutting-in' speed is attained [etc.]. 1928 *Motor Manual* (ed. 27) 110 A dynamo has what is termed a definite 'cutting-in' speed, which means that at, say, 400 revolutions per minute, it begins to generate effective current, which, by the action of a device known as the cut-out, connects the dynamo to the battery and charges it.

(*b*) See *Cut *v.* 54 c.

1930 *Times* 26 Mar. 11/3 [He] said one of the most serious offences was 'cutting in', and the motorist who was passed in this way would be the only witness against the offending driver.

d. *Cutting-out* = sense 1 c.

1877 R. E. Strahorn *Hand-bk. Wyoming* 35 Our artist has given a very fair representation of the 'cutting out' scene. 1884 W. Shepherd *Prairie Exper.* 34 This cutting-out goes on all the day long. 1890 'R. Boldrewood' *Squatter's Dream* ii. 13 He's the best cutting-out horse. 1910 W. M. Raine *B. O'Connor* 75 I'm running this cutting-out expedition. 1920 Mulford *J. Nelson* xxv. 255 Selecting from their best cutting-out animals, saddles were hastily changed, [etc.].

10. *cutting-cylinder, -edge, -plate.* Also quots. for *cutting-bed, -knife, -room.*

1881 Carpenter *Microscope* (ed. 6) v. 229 The circular *cutting-bed, instead of being fixed on the upper end of the cylinder, is made to screw upon it. 1909 *Daily Chron.* 11 June 7/5 Each colour is rolled out in long sheets, and passes through separate rollers upon which what is known as a '*cutting cylinder' is rotating continuously, one to each colour. 1929 *Encycl. Brit.* XIV. 166/2 In this process the scratched material is rolled into a continuous sheet, and led..under a revolving 'cutting cylinder'. 1825 Loudon *Encycl. Agric.* § 501 It resembles a large..shovel, strongly prepared with iron on the *cutting edge. 1831 *Mech. Mag.* 23 July 334 The cutting-edges must be parallel to each other. 1909 A. Berget *Conquest of Air* II. v. 212 Angle of cutting edge, 7 degrees. 1927 Carr-Saunders & Jones *Soc. Struct. Eng. & Wales* 207 No one supposes that it is possible to put a sharp cutting-edge on a leaden blade. 1925 F. Walton *Linoleum* 48 An octagonal cylinder, arranged with a number of *cutting knives. 1876 Preece & Sivewright *Telegraphy* 195 The *cutting-plate itself is in the form of a screw, and thus acts both as a drill and cutting-plate. 1902 *Daily Chron.* 25 Oct. 7/6 At the rear is a *cutting-room, where meat is cut up.

Cuttoe. (Earlier Amer. examples.)

1771 *Boston Even. Post* 4 Mar., Advt. (Th.) [Public vendue of] Pen-knives, Razors, Cuttoes, Jack Knives, &c. 1772 *Massachusetts Spy* 9 Apr. (Th.) Thimbles, Cuttoe knives, &c.

Cutty, *a.* Add:

5. Capable of cutting, sharp.

1903 Kipling in *Windsor Mag.* Sept. 364/1 We'll draw fine, freehand, tribal patterns on their backs with the cutty edges of mussel-shells.

Cut-under, *sb.* Add:

2. Cutting of prices.

1851 C. Cist *Cincinnati* 313 The next effect will be a general reduction on the margin of profit in commercial operations—a system of cut-under will be pursued.

Cut-up, *sb.* Add:

1. b. A person who 'cuts up' or capers. *U.S. slang.*

a 1906 'O. Henry' *Trimmed Lamp* etc. 226 Kappelman, the painter, was the cut-up..he got up from his chair and waltzed down the room with a waiter. 1912 R. W. Chambers *Common Law* v. 157 Jests emanating from the boarding-house cut-up—a blonde young man with rah-rah hair and a brier pipe. 1921 R. D. Paine *Comr. Rolling Ocean* viii. 129 As a college cut-up he was the star comedian of the campus.

c. *fig.* A damaging criticism or review.

1928 Galsworthy *Silver Spoon* II. vi, He says there's a snorting cut-up of it [*sc.* a new publication] in 'The Protagonist'.

Cuvage (küvāʒ). [Fr., f. *cuve* Cuve.] The vatting of wine; the time allowed for this.

1893 P. E. Muskett *Art Living in Australia* 215 The 'cuvage' is the length of time the contents are left in the fermenting-vat.

Cuvierian (kiuvi,iə·riăn), *a.* [f. *Cuvier* (see below) + -ian.] Of, pertaining to, or named after the French naturalist Georges Cuvier (1769–1832); characteristic of his methods or system of classification.

Cuvierian ducts, two short transverse venous ducts in the vertebrate fetus which return the blood from the cardinal sinuses to the heart. *Cuvierian organs* (see quot. 1910).

1856 *Chambers's Jrnl.* 27 Sept. 207/2 A Cuvierian examination of the various articles. 1905 H. S. Pratt *Vertebr. Zoöl.* 52 Joining each end of the transverse sinus venosus is a large and conspicuous duct or sinus called the Cuvierian duct. 1910 Parker & Haswell *Zool.* I. 428 In the Holothurians..the 'Cuvierian organs' are simple filiform glandular tubes,..connected with the cloaca.

Cyanamide (under Cyan- 2). Add: Also, a compound of this with an alkaline earth metal; *spec.* = calcium cyanamide ($CaCN_2$), used as a fertilizer and as a source of other nitrogen compounds.

Cyanamide process, the production of calcium cyanamide by the reaction between calcium carbide (CaC_2) and nitrogen at a high temperature.

1914 J. Knox *Fixation Atmosph. Nitrogen* 88 The metallic cyanamides are derivatives of cyanamide, H_2CN_2. 1922 Partington & Parker *Nitrogen Industry* 188 The second important method of nitrogen fixation—viz., the cyanamide process. 1926 J. F. Crowley in *Waeser's Atmosph. Nitr. Industry* p. xiv, Cyanamide has been found to be a useful fertiliser for particular soils.

Cyanicide (səiæ·nisəid). *Metallurgy.* [f. Cyan- 2 + -cide 1.] A substance (esp. salts of copper and iron) which consumes cyanides.

1895 M. Eissler *Cyanide Process* 33 To remove such soluble salts or 'cyanicides' as may be present. 1896 T. K. Rose *Metall. Gold* (ed. 2) xvi. 348 These substances..act as 'cyanicides', destroying large quantities of the solvent by direct or indirect oxidising effects. 1904 Julian & Smart *Cyaniding* xxviii. 202 The principal cyanicide remaining in the Rand concentrates is the basic ferric sulphate.

Cyanide. Add: *Cyanide process.* **a.** A method of extracting gold and silver from ores by treatment with a dilute solution of potassium cyanide.

1895 M. Eissler (*title*) The Cyanide Process for the Extraction of Gold.

b. The fixation of atmospheric nitrogen by chemical reaction at high temperatures so as to form alkali cyanides or other cyanogen derivatives.

1926 *Waeser's Atmosph. Nitr. Industry* 486 The Cyanide Processes.

Cyanide gauze: an antiseptic gauze impregnated with a cyanide, used in dressing wounds.

1895 *Arnold & Sons' Catal. Surg. Instr.* 726 Double Zinc-Cyanide Gauze. 1913 A. Bennett *Regent* ii. § 4 He did nothing but cover up the place with a bit of cyanide gauze. 1925 R. W. G. Hingston in E. F. Norton *Fight for Everest, 1924* 350.

Cy·anide, *v. Metallurgy. trans.* To treat with a cyanide; to subject to the cyanide process (in metallurgy). Hence **Cy·anider, Cy·aniding** *vbl. sb.*, **Cy:anida·tion.**

1894 *N. Brit. Daily Mail* 30 July 5 Cyaniding syndicates. 1895 M. Eissler *Cyanide Process* 39 The cost of cyaniding was as follows. 1896 *N. Amer. Rev.* Apr. 479 The development of certain wet processes, cyanidation..has supplemented the work. 1896 *Daily News* 10 Dec. 2/7, 2,666 tons cyanided, producing 352 ozs. 1900 J. Park *Cyanide Process* vi. 73 Dry-crushing with cyanidation will soon be entirely displaced by wet-crushing with cyanide. *Ibid.* 75 Roasting previous to Cyaniding. *Ibid.* App. 124 The many worries which the use of cyanide entails on even the successful cyanider. 1915 T. K. Rose *Metall. Gold* (ed. 6) xiii. 281 The roasting of gold ores as a preliminary to chlorination or cyanidation.

Cyanize (səi·ănəiz), *v. Chem.* [f. Cyan- 2 + -ize.] *trans.* To fix (atmospheric nitrogen) in the form of cyanides; to convert into cyanides. Hence **Cy·anized** *ppl. a.*, **Cy·anizing** *vbl. sb.*, **Cy:aniza·tion.**

1926 *Waeser's Atmosph. Nitr. Industry* 499 In order to determine whether pure nitrogen is necessary for cyanisation. *Ibid.* 501 The cyanising apparatus. *Ibid.*, The cyanised briquettes contained 19 per cent. of sodium cyanide. *Ibid.* 507 Mond cyanises briquettes of barium carbonate and charcoal in a ring furnace.

Cycladic (siklæ·dik), *a.* [f. L. *Cyclades* pl., a. Gr. Κυκλάδες (νῆσοι islands) + -ic.] Of or pertaining to the Cyclades, a group of islands in the Aegean, lying in a circle round Delos; *spec.* designating, or pertaining to, the prehistoric civilization of these islands.

1920 *Discovery* June 178/2 'Cycladic'..is sometimes substituted for 'Minoan' when one speaks exclusively of the island sites outside of Crete. 1921 *Brit. Museum Return* 60 Large beaked jug of later Cycladic style.. From Melos or Thera. 1927 Peake & Fleure *Priests & Kings* 113 These [sub-periods] have been named in the same way, ranging from Early Cycladic I to Late Cycladic III.

Cyclamen. Add: **c.** The shade of colour characteristic of the red cyclamen flower.

1923 *Daily Mail* 29 Jan. 1 In shades of Powder Blue.. Cyclamen,..Flamingo, Pink. 1926 *Spectator* 24 Apr. 750/2 Sleeveless cardigan, in various shades of cyclamen, rose marie and saxe.

Cycle, *sb.* Add: **10. c.** *Physics.* A recurring series of operations, as in internal combustion motors, in which heat is imparted to or taken away from a working substance, which consequently produces mechanical work, and is finally brought back to its original state. **d.** *Electr.* A full period, or complete positive and negative wave, of an alternating current. (The number of cycles per second is the measure of frequency.)

1929 A. F. Collins *Aviation* 148 An airplane engine.. works on what is called the four-stroke cycle principle... In an airplane engine there is only one explosion, or power stroke, for every four strokes of the piston... After the power stroke is completed three more strokes must take place before there is another explosion stroke and, hence, another power stroke. Then the series of strokes, or cycle, as it is called, begins all over again, and this is what is meant by a four-stroke cycle engine.

12. cycle-car, a light motor-driven vehicle with three (rarely four) wheels.

1914 *Morning Post* 9 Feb. 5 A Cyclecar Paperchase.

Cyclery (səi·kləri). *U.S.* [f. Cycle *sb.* 11.] A bicycle shop.

1897 *Trans. Mississippian* (Council Bluffs) Apr. 20 Advt., Council Bluffs Cyclery. 1899 J. F. Fraser *Round World on Wheel* xxxvii. 484 There is a cyclery—that's an American word—where machines are hired out at a shilling an hour.

Cyclette (səikle·t). [Fr.: see -ette.] A small (motor) bicycle.

1898 *Daily News* 15 Nov. 7/6 The one-mile motor cyclette race. 1923 *Daily Mail* 28 Feb. 6 The Paris-Nice Trial. How the motor cyclettes fared under strenuous conditions.

Cyclic (si·klik), *sb.* [See Cyclic *a.* 2, 5.]

1. Short for *cyclic poem* or *cyclic poet.*

2. *Math.* Short for *cyclic curve.*

Cyclic, *a.* Add:

7. *Org. Chem.* Of, pertaining to, or characterized by the 'closed chain' formation; opposed to *aliphatic.* See also *Alicyclic, *Carbocyclic, *Heterocyclic, *Isocyclic.

1913 *Bloxam's Chem.* (ed. 10) 544 The cyclic or closed-chain series. 1923 T. H. Pope *Molinari's Org. Chem.* 616 Cyclic compounds.

Cyclically (səi·klikăli), *adv.* [f. Cyclical + -ly [2].] In a cyclic or cyclical way; in cycles.

1895 *Athenæum* 1 June 710/1 Mr. Burstall commenced the reading of a paper 'On the Measurement of a Cyclically Varying Temperature'.

Cyclo-. Add: **Cyclobra·nchian,** a mollusc of the sub-order *Cyclobranchia.* **Cyclohe·xane** *Chem.* = hexamethylene or naphthene, C_6H_{12}, occurring in petroleum. **Cyclople·gia** *Path.* [Gr. πληγή stroke], paralysis of the ciliary muscle. Hence **Cyclople·gic** *a.*, producing cycloplegia; *sb.* a cycloplegic agent. **Cyclostro·phic** *a. Meteorol.*, denoting that component of the deflective force of a wind which is due to the curvature of its path. **Cyclothy·mia** *Path.* [Gr. θυμός mind, temper], cyclic insanity. Hence **Cyclothy·miac, -thy·mic** *adjs.* and *sbs.* (a person) affected with this.

1837 *Penny Cycl.* VIII. 248/2 *Cyclobranchians. 1839 *Ibid.* XIII. 485/1 With regard to the marine species [of Limacineans], which Cuvier has approximated to these, M. de Blainville observes that they constitute his genus *Peronia* in his order of Cyclobranchians. 1925 A. W. Judge *Automob. Engines* 10 A mixture of 20 parts benzole and 80 parts *cyclohexane will enable an engine to be run at 200 lb. per sq. in. compression pressure. 1919 W. B. Faraday *Gloss. Aeronaut. Terms* 31 The portion of the [pressure] gradient which is balanced by the flow on account of the earth's spin is called the geostrophic component, and the remaining portion, which is balanced by the curvature of the air's path, is called the *cyclostrophic component. 1921 tr. *A. Adler's Neurot. Constit.* 187 Dementia præcox, paranoia and *cyclothymia. 1929 tr. *A. Adler's Probl. Neurosis* 27 A cyclothymia beginning late in life. 1926 W. McDougall *Outl. Abnormal Psych.* 353 Most of us..are liable to mild alternations of this kind, moods of 'excitement' and of depression... When the liability to such alternations is well marked, the personality is said to be of the *cyclo-thymic type. *Ibid.* 356 *note,* Cyclo-thymics, in whom periods of energetic euphoria alternate with despondent impotence.

Cyclone. 2. Add: **cyclone cellar** *U.S.*, a cellar intended to give shelter during a cyclone; also *fig.*

1904 G. H. Lorimer *Old Gorgon Graham* 125 This was one of those holy moments..when an outsider wants to pull his tongue back into its cyclone cellar. 1910 *N.Y. Even. Post* (semi-weekly ed.) 7 Feb. 3 An iron cyclone cellar is a novelty.

Cyclonish (səi·klǭniʃ), *a.* Somewhat cyclonic (*fig.*).

1893 *Nation* (N.Y.) 15 July 32/2 She is altogether of the 'breezy', indeed cyclonish, western type—a good tempered girl with no end of go.

Cyclopean, *a.* Add:

1. b. *Zool.* Designating one form of the eyes of trilobites (see quot.). Also **Cyclopic** (-ǫ·pik) *a.*

1906 Sollas tr. *Suess' Face of Earth* II. 213 In the case of *Aeglina armata*..the enlargement of the eyes is so far advanced that they meet from side to side in the middle, and Barrande calls this the *cyclopean* form. 1924 *Ibid.* V. Index, Cyclopic form of Trilobite eyes.

Cy·clostyle, *v. trans.* To print (copies) by cyclostyle.

1897 *Westm. Gaz.* 3 July 2/3 Note the gradual rise from the cyclostyled circular to the printed appeal. 1928 *Daily Express* 5 Mar. 2/3 No candidate can be directly boosted by name in any matter printed, typed, or cyclostyled.

Cylinder, *sb.* **9. b.** Add: *cylinder card* (see 5), *gun* (see 5), *machine, saw, seal* (see 4 a), *stove.*

1812 *Deb. Congress* 12 June (1853) 2188 In the year 1762 *cylinder cards were first made use of by Mr. Peel. 1892 Greener *Breech-loader* 141 An old or true *cylinder gun will not..put three pellets into a pigeon thirty yards distant. 1907 *Cambr. Mod. Hist. Prosp.* 90 The *cylinder machine has immensely increased the speed at which it is possible to print well. 1851 C. Cist *Cincinnati* 181 They are..fed to a *cylinder saw, which cuts them into staves of the proper thickness and curve. 1892 W. M. F. Petrie *Ten Years' Digging in Egypt* (1893) 198 *Cylinder seals. 1922 *Guide Babylonian & Assyrian Antiq.* (Brit. Mus.) (ed. 3) 82 Cylinder seal..of Syrian type. 1927 Peake & Fleure *Priests & Kings* 64 Some of the Egyptians used mace-heads and cylinder-seals almost exactly similar to those found somewhat later in Mesopotamia. 1898 E. N. Westcott *David Harum* 162 The proximity of wet boots and garments to the big *cylinder stove.

Cylindered (si·lindəɹd), *ppl. a.* [See -ed [2].] Having a cylinder or cylinders (of a specified number or type).

1899 *Daily News* 14 Sept. 7/5 The engine..is one of Mr. Drummond's latest type of four-wheel-coupled inside cylindered express locomotives. 1908 *Westm. Gaz.* 14 May 4/2 As a hill-climber the Argyll, with its 120 by 140 cylindered engine, has great claims.

Cylindra·ceo-. Used in *Zool.* as combining form of Cylindraceous.

1822 J. Parkinson *Outl. Oryctol.* 195 A straight cylindraceo-tubular operculated shell. 1887 W. Phillips *Brit. Discomycetes* 161 Asci cylindraceo-clavate.

Cylindrite (sili·ndrəit). *Min.* Also **kyl-.** [ad. G. *kylindrit,* f. Gr. κύλινδρος Cylinder; see -ite [1].] A compound of sulphur, lead, antimony, and tin. So named from the shape of the crystals.

1896 Chester *Dict. Min.*, Kylindrite.

Cymba (si·mbă). *Zool.* [L., = boat.] A boat-shaped sponge-spicule.

1887 Sollas in *Encycl. Brit.* XXII. 417/2 This..C-shaped spicule..may be termed a *cymba.*

Cymblin(g, cymling. *U.S.* Varr. Simlin.

1781–2 Jefferson *Notes on Virginia* (1787) 40 Cymlings. *Cucurbita verrucosa.* 1796–1806 B. Hawkins *Lett.* 211 They made beans, ground peas, cymblins. 1829–32 J. P. Kennedy *Swallow B.* IV. vi. 100 Little garden-patches..where cymblings..flourished. 1885 'C. E. Craddock' *Prophet Gt. Smoky Mtn.* ix. 160 Ef ever thar war a empty cymblin' its yer head.

Cymometer (səimǫ·mĭtəɹ). *Electr.* [See Cyma and -meter.] An instrument for measuring wave length, frequency, etc.

1918 W. H. Eccles *Wireless Telegr. & Teleph.* (ed. 2) Glossary, *Cymometer,* a kind of wave-meter (*q.v.*). 1926 S. O. Pearson *Dict. Wireless Terms, Cymometer* (Fleming's), a wave-meter in which both the inductance and the capacity are varied simultaneously by the operation of one handle.

Cymoscope (səi·mǫskǫup). *Electr.* [See Cyma and -scope.] A wave-detecting device used in wireless telegraphy.

1906 J. A. Fleming *Princ. Electric Wave Telegraphy* vi. 353.

Cymotrichous (səimǫ·trikəs), *a. Anthrop.* [f. Gr. κῦμα wave (see Cyma) + θρίξ, τριχός hair.] Having wavy hair. **Cymo·trichy,** wavy-hairedness.

1909 A. C. Haddon *Races of Man* Gloss., *Cymotrichi*:.. cymotrichous. 1924 *Ibid.* 5 *Cymotrichy,* or smooth, wavy and curly hair. *Ibid.* 6 Some cymotrichous peoples have very hairy bodies.

Cypress [1]. **4.** Add: *cypress brake, plank, shingle*; **cypress gall** *U.S.* (see quot. 1837); **cypress-knee** *U.S.* (earlier examples); **cypress pine** *Austral.*, a tree of the genus *Callitris*; **cypress vine,** the quamoclit.

1868 *Putnam's Mag.* May 592/1 One would not..be surprised..to hear a[n]..iguanodon crashing..through yon *cypress-brake. 1819 E. Dana *Geogr. Sketches* 173 The *cypress galls, (so called), the poorest species of land, have, below their surface, veins of a remarkably fine clay. 1837 J. L. Williams *Territory of Florida* 89 Pine barren swamps ..when covered with small coast cypress trees and knees, are usually, but improperly, termed cypress galls. 1784 J. F. D. Smyth *Tour U.S.* II. 235 *Cypress knees, closely intermixed with a matted body of strong fibrous roots. 1791 W. Bartram *Trav. Carolina* 91 From these roots grow woody cones, called cypress knees, four, five, and six feet high. 1817 S. R. Brown *Western Gaz.* 145 A number of conical excrescences rising from its base to the height of eight or ten feet, called cypress knees. 1836 *Southern Lit. Messenger* II. 288 His tail..mounted suddenly upwards like a cypress knee. 1875 E. King *Southern St. N. Amer.* 383 The gleaming water out of which rise thousands of 'cypress-knees'. 1847 Leichhardt *Jrnl.* i. 13 It was covered with *cypress-pine, and an Acacia. 1885 *Spons' Mechanics' Own Bk.* 131 Cypress pine (*Callitris columellaris*) is a plentiful tree in Queensland. 1725 *Maryland Hist. Mag.* VII. 279 The new Covering the shed of the Vestry house with feather edged *Cyprus Plank. 1724 *Ibid.* VI. 1 [The house] was well shingled with good *cypress shingles. 1785 Washington *Diaries* II. 411 Bought 28,430 good Cyprus shingles. 1828 *Deb. Congress* 2 Apr. 2112, 60,000 Cypress Shingles. 1857 A. Gray *First Less. Bot.* (1866) 101 The corolla of the Phlox..and of the *Cypress-Vine are of this sort. 1868 *Rep. U.S. Comm. Agric.* (1869) 205 Cypress vine, (*Quamoclit vulgaris*).

Cypress-swamp. *U.S.* [Cypress [1] 2.] A swamp having a growth of cypress.

1736 Wesley *Jrnl.* 22 Dec., In an hour or two we came to a cypress-swamp. 1737 *Ibid.* 2 Dec., Cypress-swamps are mostly large ponds, in and round which cypresses grow. 1766 J. Bartram *Jrnl.* (1769) 11 A cypress-swamp, at the upper end of which oaks and palmettos join the river. 1817 S. R. Brown *Western Gaz.* 11 Canebrakes along the river; and sometimes cypress swamps. 1868 *Putnam's Mag.* May 594/2 Stretching..in the rear of these great sugar-estates are the immense cypress-swamps of Louisiana. 1886 *Outing* (U.S.) VIII. 59/2 In the lonely fastnesses of a cypress swamp with only the alligator for company.

Cyprianic (sipriæ·nik), *a.* [ad. mod.L. *Cyprianicus,* f. *Cyprianus.*] Of, pertaining to, or characteristic of St. Cyprian (Thascius Cæcilius Cyprianus), bishop of Carthage, martyred 258 A.D.

1695 J. Sage (*title*) The Principles of the Cyprianic Age. 1696 G. Rule (*title*) The Cyprianick Bishop examined and found not to be a Diocesan. *a* 1861 W. Cunningham *Hist. Theology* Wks. 1863 I. 164 The Cyprianic bishop was very different from the modern one. 1916 J. Rendel Harris *Testimonies* I. viii. 77 We have an almost contemporary witness for the Cyprianic text. *Ibid.* xiv. 127 Justin starts with the first chapter of the Cyprianic Christology. 1920 *Christian World* 19 Aug. 8/4 We need for the recovery of Christian unity a man of Cyprianic grasp, though not of Cyprian's opinions.

Cyprid (səi·prid). *Zool.* An entomostracous crustacean of the family *Cyprididae* (see Cypris).

1913 H. M. Cadell *Story of Forth* i. 8 Other shale seams are almost entirely composed of minute entomostraca or cyprids.

Cypriote (si·priǫt), **Cypriot** (si·priǫt), *a.* and *sb.* [ad. Gr. Κυπριώτης, f. Κύπρος Cyprus. The earlier name is Cyprian.] **a.** *adj.* Belonging to Cyprus. **b.** *sb.* A native or inhabitant of Cyprus; the dialect (ancient or modern) of Cyprus.

1750 *Universal Mag.* July 4/1 For a while he triumphed over the Tyrians, Sidonians, and Cypriots. 1797 R. Heron *Collect. Voy. & Trav.* 198 St. Spiridion, the Cypriot. 1837 *Penny Cycl.* VIII. 261/2 Almost every house has a garden, of which the Cypriotes are very fond. 1878 *Murray's Handbk. Trav. Turkey in Asia* (ed. 4) 179/1 The Inscriptions found..in Cyprus are in three languages: 1. Cypriote. *Ibid.* 182/1 Androcles..was present in the Cypriote fleet which supported Alexander. 1920 J. A. Robertson *Hidden Rom. N.T.* I. 20 The wealthy Cypriote Mnason, who entertained Paul. 1920 Buckle *Disraeli* VI. 300 The occupation of Cyprus ensured the fair treatment of the Cypriot Greeks. 1920 *Q. Rev.* July 38 This Cypriote School, with its grand Græco-Oriental seriousness, had many ramifications, one of which, the Palyrene..lasted down to the third century A.D. 1927 *Times* (weekly ed.) 25 Aug. 208/3 The Cypriots in Egypt.

Cypripedium (sipripī·diə̆m). [See Cypripedin.] An orchid of the genus so named.

1884 M. T. Masters in *Encycl. Brit.* XVII. 816/2 In place of the six stamens we commonly find but one (two in *Cypripedium*). 1902 *Westm. Gaz.* 31 Dec. 10/1 Cypripedium orchids. 1904 Farrer *Garden Asia* 250 On the shelving banks of grass in open places [grows] the cypripedium.

Cyrillian (siri·liăn), *a.* and *sb.* Relating to Saint Cyril, bishop of Alexandria (376–444 A.D.) or his doctrine; a follower of Cyril.

1917 Bartlet & Carlyle *Christianity in Hist.* v. v. 602 The Apollinarian or Cyrillian Christology.

Cyst-. Add: **Cyste·ctomy** [Gr. ἐκτομή], surgical removal of a cyst.

1910 *Practitioner* Mar. 377 The performance of cystectomy.

Cysticotomy (sistikǫ·tŏmi). *Surg.* [f. mod.Gr. κυστικός Cystic (duct) + -tomy.] Incision into the cystic duct.

1901 Dorland *Med. Dict.* 1908 *Practitioner* Dec. 826 A stone was extracted after the incision of the cystic duct (Cysticotomy).

Cystitic (sisti·tik), *a.* Affected with cystitis.

1910 *Practitioner* July 44 Distended cystitic bladder gave way.

Cysto-. Add: **Cysto·scopy** [Gr. σκοπιά look-out, watch], examination of the bladder with the cystoscope. **Cysto·stomy** [Gr. στόμα mouth], the formation of an opening into the bladder by incision.

1908 *Practitioner* Sept. 434 *Cystoscopy is of great use in determining the character of the fluid issuing from each ureter. 1909 *Ibid.* Nov. 664 Cystoscopy and ureteral catheterization are necessary. 1910 *Ibid.* Mar. 377 As a general

rule the operation of cholecystectomy shows a higher mortality than cholecystostomy, but in Rimann's statistics the reverse is the case (cystectomy 3·4 per cent. and *cystostomy 14·3 per cent.).

Cytase (sai·teis). *Biol. Chem.* [f. Gr. κύτος, taken as = cell (see -CYTE), with ending after *diastase*.] An enzyme found in grass-seeds which has the property of decomposing cell-walls; = *COMPLEMENT *sb.* 5 i. Hence **Cytasic** (saitæ·zik) *a.*

1895 W. Jago *Bread-making* 123 The enzyme, which thus dissolves the parenchymatous cell-walls of the endosperm, has received the name Cytase. Cytase is secreted by the embryo during germination. 1899 J. R. Green *Soluble Ferments* (1901) vii. 90 The existence of cytase has not been known for many years, our acquaintance with it dating back only to 1886, when it was discovered by De Bary. *Ibid.* xxi. 304 *Bacillus mesentericus vulgatus* has been shown to be possessed of diastasic, inverting, cytasic, and peptonising power. 1901–5, 1903 [see *COMPLEMENT *sb.* 5 i].

Cyto-. Add: **Cy·tochrome** (see quots.); **Cy·todiagno·sis**, diagnosis by examining the cell-contents of effusions into the serous cavities of the body (Dorland 1903). **Cytolo·gic, Cytolo·gical** *adjs.*, pertaining to cytology. Hence **Cytolo·gically** *adv.* **Cyto·logist**, one who studies cytology. **Cyto·lysis**, the dissolution of cells. Hence **Cytoly·tic** *a.* **Cy·tomorpho·sis**, the series of changes undergone by cells. **Cy·tophil** *a.*, having affinity for cell-substance. **Cytoto·xic** *a.*, pertaining to cytotoxin. **Cytoto·xin**, a substance developed in the blood serum, having a toxic effect on cells. **Cyto·trophy** (see quot.). **Cy·tozyme** (see quot.).

1901 Dorland *Med. Dict.* (ed. 2), *Cytochrome, a nerve-cell having an ill-developed cell-body, in which the stained nucleus appears to be completely surrounded, and does not exceed in size the nucleus of a leukocyte. 1925 *Glasgow Herald* 1 Aug. 4 A recently discovered..pigment called cytochrome. 1927 A. V. Hill *Living Machinery* iv. 130 Cytochrome contains an atom of iron attached to a fairly complicated chemical substance. 1908 *Practitioner* Oct. 621 The method of *cytodiagnosis..usually gives satisfactory results, especially in the case of pleural exudates. 1898 *Academy* 11 June 761/2 On the *Cytological Features of Fertilisation. 1908 *Practitioner* Aug. 306 A cytological examination of the blood. 1908 W. E. C. Dickson (*title*) The Bone-marrow: a Cytological Study. 1908 *Practitioner* Apr. 525 The infected region..should be bacteriologically and *cytologically examined. 1919 Osler in *Proc. Class. Assoc.* 28 In the action and interaction of physical forces the *cytologist hopes to find the key to the secret of life itself. 1923 H. G. Wells *Men like Gods* II. ii, This Cedar was a cytologist, and he was in charge of the arrangements for this improvised sanatorium. 1907 *Brit. Med. Jrnl.* 20 Apr. 923/1 There seems to be some toxic condition produced which overcomes natural resistance, resulting in *cytolysis. 1904 *Keene's Bath Journal* 28 May 5/5 The '*cytolytic' milk of a cow has been tried.... The word 'cytolytic' has not yet found its way into biological dictionaries. 1910 *Practitioner* Feb. 199 The virulence of the cocci was evidenced..by the cytolytic findings. 1908 C. S. Minot (*title*) The Problem of Age, Growth, and Death; a Study of *Cytomorphosis. 1902 Vaughan & Novy *Cellular Toxins* (ed. 4) 182 In the first place,..the body cells must possess toxophil side chains... In the second place, a given substance, in order to be toxic, must possess certain *cytophil side chains. Both the toxophil groups of the cell, and the cytophil groups of the toxin may be designated as haptophorous bodies. 1907 *Practitioner* Aug. 191 The result of *cytotoxic activity. 1915 *Ibid.* Jan. 171 (*title*) Pituitary Insufficiency And A Pituitary Antiserum or *Cytotoxin. 1901 G. N. Calkins *Protozoa* 217 The phenomena of *cytotrophy, or the mutual attraction of two or more cells. 1927 Haldane & Huxley *Anim. Biol.* viii. 166 A waxy substance called *cytozyme produced by the breaking-up of cells.

Czechize (tʃe·kaiz), *v.* [f. CZECH + -IZE.] *trans.* To make Czech in character, language, etc. So **Czechiza·tion.**

1920 *Glasgow Herald* 21 Sept. 8 If Magyarisation was bad, Czechisation is little better. 1927 *Contemp. Rev.* Feb. 173 Efforts to 'Czechise' place-names and to impose the Czech language.

Czechoslovak (tʃekoslōu·væk), *sb.* and *a.* A native of the new state called Czechoslovakia, which includes Bohemia, Moravia, and the northern Slavs of the extinct Austrian Empire. As *adj.*, belonging to this state. Also **Cze:choslova·kian** *a.* and *sb.*

1917 Namier (*title*) The Czecho-Slovaks. An oppressed nationality. 1920 Pokorný & Selver (*title*) The Czecho-slovak Republic, its economical, industrial and cultural resources. 1929 (*title*) An Anthology of Czechoslovak literature, selected and translated..by P. Selver.

Czigany (tsigā·ni), *sb.* and *a.* = TZIGANE.

1922 *Blackw. Mag.* June 717/1 The *Czigány* folk-songs are part of the people's life.

D

D. Add: **2.** *D-shaped* (examples); also *D-front*, *D link*; *D-fronted* adj.

1883 Gresley *Gloss. Coal-m.* 72 *D Link*, a flat iron bar attached to chains, and suspended from a hemp rope to a windlass at surface. It is a loop in which one man is lowered and raised in an engine-pit. 1890 W. J. Gordon *Foundry* 135 A closed crucible with a D-shaped opening in one of its sides. 1895 *Westm. Gaz.* 22 Nov. 5/3 D-shaped and oval tubes. 1908 *Ibid.* 16 Nov. 4/2 A D-front limousine. *Ibid.* 19 Nov. 5/2 A 'D'-fronted landaulette.

III. 3. D. = Dame, as D.B.E., Dame Commander of the British Empire (established 1917); = Deputy, as D.A.A.G., Deputy Assistant Adjutant General; D.A.G., Deputy Adjutant General; D.A.Q.M.G., Deputy Assistant Quarter Master General; = diameter; = Dictionary, as D.N.B., Dictionary of National Biography; = distinguished, as D.C.M., Distinguished Conduct Medal (established 1862); D.F.C., D.F.M., Distinguished Flying Cross, Medal (established 1918); D.S.C., D.S.M., D.S.O., Distinguished Service Cross (established 1914), Medal (1914), Order (1886); D.M.O. = Director of Military Operations. D.O.M. = L. *Deo Optimo Maximo*, to God best and greatest; D.Z.A. (see quot.). D.S. (*dal segno* from the sign); d.d.d., D.D.D. (*dat, dicat, dedicat* gives, devotes, and dedicates); d.d., D.D. (*dono dedit* gave as a gift). See also *DORA, *D.T.

1899 *Westm. Gaz.* 8 Nov. 2/1 Calling into consultation.. the D.A.A.G. for Topography. 1901 'M. Gray' *Four-Leaved Clover* i, He's got a D.S.O. You 've got to deserve a D.S.O., mind you, before you get it. 1903 Gosse in *Life & Lett.* (1931) 287 To see if anything has been overlooked by the *D.N.B.* 1910 *N. Hawkins's Electr. Dict.*, D, abbreviation for diameter, in electrical calculations. 1914 *Daily Express* 10 Nov. 6/3 Our fellows were extraordinarily brave, and I think several of them should get the D.C.M. 1918 E. A. Mackintosh *War, the Liberator* 100 If you want a D.S.O. Or a small M.C. or so Don't go crawling rashly out When there's nobody about. 1919 G. K. Rose *2/4th Oxf. & Bucks Lt. Infty.* 151 Next morning Private Hatt, who for his exploit gained the D.C.M., crawled into our lines. 1922 *Blackw. Mag.* Mar. 356 Plymouth sent a 'D.Z.A.' *Note*, International Code—'Allow me to congratulate you'. 1930 *N. & Q.* 4 Oct. 245/2 There was a good sprinkling of D.S.O.'s and O.B.E.'s. *Ibid.* 11 Oct. 257/2 Corrigendum for the D.N.B.

b. D and P., D.W.: see quots.

1909 *Practitioner* Feb. 262 D.W. stood for distilled water. 1924 *Brit. Jrnl. Photographic Alm.* 333 The appliances used in a..D and P (developing and printing) establishment.

Dabber. Add: **1. d.** (See quot.)

1921 *Dict. Occup. Terms* (1927) § 139 *Dabber-up*; dabs clay round furnace doors to make air-tight and keep in heat.

Dabbler. Add: **3.** (See quot.) Hence **Dabbling** *sb.*

1881 *Cassell's Family Mag.* VII. 85/2 Two dabblers of different sizes should be procured..for laying the background smooth and even [in painting on china]. *Ibid.* 87/1 Wash over the..ground-work..with light sweeps of the brush, ..then take the dabbler and..dab rapidly and evenly. *Ibid.*, It will..draw off the colour if the dabbling is persisted in.

Dabchick. Add:

2. A small yacht of five tons or under.

1895 *Daily News* 3 Sept. 7/3 An amateur yacht race..in which several one-raters and dabchicks started. 1896 *Ibid.* 4 June 2/6 The dabchicks sailed the second match of the week yesterday round the short course at Leigh.

Dabitis (dæ·bitis). *Logic.* [L., = you will give.] The mnemonic term for that indirect mood of the first figure of syllogisms in which the major premiss is universal and affirmative, and the minor premiss and conclusion are particular and affirmative.

Dacha (dæ·kă). Also 8 **dacca, dacka,** 9 **dakka, dakha, daka, dagga.** [Hottentot (Khoi-Khoin) *dachab*.] A South African name for *Cannabis indica*, Indian hemp, used by the natives as a narcotic. Also applied to other plants, as Red Dacha, *Leonotis leonurus*. Also *attrib.*

1785 G. Forster tr. *Sparrman's Voy.* I. 145 *Bucku* (*diosma*) and wild *dacka* (*phlomis leonurus*) which are known both by the colonists and the Hottentots to be as efficacious as they are common. 1835 Moodie *Ten Yrs. S. Afr.* I. 41 Many of these people [*sc.* Hottentots] have ..a pernicious habit of smoking a plant called 'dacha'. ..The 'dacha rookers' are held in great contempt by the tobacco smokers of their nation. 1852 Godlonton *Kaffir War* 306 (Pettman) His dacha sack at the saddle-bow. 1894 C. H. W. Donaldson *With Wilson in Matabeleland* vii. 140 It is exceedingly entertaining to watch these boys 'dakha-smoking'. 1912 *East London Dispatch* 28 June 9 (Pettman) The red dagga or 'Mfincafincane' of the Kaffirs. 1921 *Blackw. Mag.* Jan. 110/2 They are..much addicted to smoking a drug which is known as 'daka'.

Dacian (dēi·ʃiăn), *a.* (*sb.*) [f. *Dacia* + -AN.] Of or belonging to, a native of, Dacia, a country of south-eastern Europe, which became a Roman province.

1818 Byron *Ch. Har.* IV. cxli, *There* were his young barbarians all at play, *There* was their Dacian mother—he, their sire, Butcher'd to make a Roman holiday. 1837 *Penny Cycl.* VIII. 281/2 Domitian celebrated his pretended exploits against the Dacians by assuming the title Dacicus. 1877 *Encycl. Brit.* VI. 758/2 He advanced to the Dacian capital. *Ibid.*, The Dacians come forward as one of the most powerful enemies of Rome.

Dacryo-, combining form of Gr. δάκρυον tear, as in **Da:cryocysti·tis**, inflammation of the tear-sac.

1848 Dunglison *Med. Lex.* (ed. 7). 1908 *Practitioner* Feb. 288 Acute and chronic dachryocystitis [*sic*] are usually associated with epiphora.

Dacryon (dæ·kripn). *Anat.* [mod.L., a. Gr. δάκρυον tear.] The point of juncture of the lachrymal, frontal, and upper maxillary bones; the lachrymal point.

1878 Bartley tr. *Topinard's Anthropol.* 235.

Dactylate (dæ·ktilēit), *a. Anat.* [f. DACTYL (or its source) + -ATE^{2}.] Having finger-like processes, digitate.

1890 Billings *Nat. Med. Dict.*

Dactylically (dækti·likăli), *adv. Prosody.* [f. DACTYLIC *a.*: see -LY^{2}.] With a dactylic rhythm.

1891 Stevenson *Vailima Lett.* (1895) 85 'Ulufanua the isle of the sea,' read that verse dactylically and you get the beat.

Dactylo-. Add: In terms relating to the taking of finger-prints: **Da·ctylogram** [Gr. γράμμα letter], a finger-print. **Dactylo·scopy**, the examination of finger-prints; hence **Da:ctylosco·pic** *a.*

1908 *Boston Transcript* 10 Oct., An interesting illustration of the practical value of the science of dactyloscopy. 1910 *Let. to J. A. H. Murray* 5 Mar., The dactyloscopic records of the Boston Police Department. 1913 Dorland *Med. Dict.* (ed. 7), *Dactylogram*, a finger-print taken for purposes of identification. 1921 *Discovery* Oct. 257/1 You would not find two dactylograms alike, says Galton,..if you were to examine a series of 64,000,000. *Ibid.* 259/1 [Poroscopy] is infinitely more fruitful in results than the one known by the name of dactyloscopy. *Ibid.* 259/2 In all cases of dactyloscopic analysis.

Dad (deformation of *God*). Add: *U.S.* esp. with verbs and pa. pples.

1834 Carruthers *Kentuckian in N.Y.* I. 216 I'll be dad shamed if it ain't all cowardice. 1845 [W. T. Thompson] *Chron. Pineville* 67 (Th.) Dadfetch me if [etc.]. *Ibid.* 74 I'll be dadfetcht if [etc.]. 1884 'C. E. Craddock' *Tenn. Mts.* I. 45 Dad-burn that..idle poultry. *Ibid.* III. 141 That dad-burned scoundrel. 1901 Harben *Westerfelt* xiv. 195 'Don't act so dadratted foolish,' he said. *Ibid.* xxii. 300 Yes, dad burn it; you know she loves you. 1911 R. D. Saunders *Col. Todhunter* vi. 84 I'll be dadblamed if I know what's goin to come of it all some day! 1927 *Hollis St. Theatre Progr.* (U.S.) 19 Sept., But who'd think where buildings are tall Business could be so dadburned bum?

Dada^{2} (da·da). [Fr.; title of a review which appeared at Zurich first in 1916, founded by Tzara (a Roumanian), Arp (an Alsatian German), and Huelzenbeck (a German).] Applied to a short-lived movement among writers of French poetry, whose chief tenet was that the sound of what is written is alone of importance. Hence **Da·daism**, the theory or practice of these writers. So **Da·daist, Dadai·stical** *a.*

1920 *Athenæum* 13 Aug. 221/2 The movement 'Dada'.. has its headquarters in Paris, and its principal promoters are Francis Picabia and Tristan Tzara, neither of whom is of French nationality. *Ibid.*, Mr. Dent defines Dadaism as being a 'whole-heartedly æsthetic movement', in contradistinction to 'papaism' and 'nanaism'. *Ibid.* 222/2 [Guillaum Apollinaire's] most advanced, most nearly dadaistical poetry. 1920 *Times Lit. Suppl.* 2 Sept. 569/3 M. Mille still believes in *bon sens*, clarity and humour as valuable assets in art, a belief which has got him into serious trouble with the Dadaistes. 1920 *Glasgow Herald* 27 Nov. 6 It is when we try to give our vague raptures a coherent form that the troublesome part of our task begins. This the Dada decadent tries to escape. 1921 *Cornhill Mag.* Dec. 700 The riff-raff of the studios whom it would have been a politeness even to call 'Dadaists'.

Daddler (dæ·dləɹ). *slang.* Also **dadler.** A farthing.

1907 *Daily Chron.* 26 July 4/7 An East-end carman..assures us that a farthing is a dadler. 1908 *Ibid.* 5 Feb. 4/7 He could not recognise the daddler—which is a farthing, or the stiver or the 'yennyp' that indicates the penny.

Daddy. Add:

2. Various slang uses (see quots.).

1859 *Slang Dict.*, *Daddy*, the stage manager.—*Theatr.* 1860 [*adds*] The person who gives away the bride at weddings. 1865 *Daddy*; at mock raffles, lotteries, &c., the Daddy is an accomplice, most commonly the getter up of the swindle, and in all cases the person that has been previously arranged to win the prize. 1874 *Daddy*, the old man in charge—generally an aged pauper—at casual wards. 1886 *Graphic* 10 Apr. 399/2 The manager himself is sometimes known as the 'gorger', and 'daddy' is the stage-manager.

Dafadar, variant form of DUFFADAR.

1849 Eastwick *Dry Leaves* 69 A Dafadár of Captain Christie's corps. 1921 *Glasgow Herald* 25 Mar. 7 A force of one dafadar and ten sowars of mounted police.

Daffingly (dæ·fiŋli), *adv.* [f. *daffing*, pres. pple. of DAFF *v.*^{1} + -LY^{2}.] Sportively.

1901 D. S. Meldrum *Conquest of Charlotte* III. xix, 'Ah! he's married: that's crucial,' I said, daffingly. 1907 J. H. McCarthy *Needles & Pins* xx, 'I should have taken a great fancy to you,' he answered daffingly, 'if I had been a free man when we met.'

Daffle (dæ·f'l), *v. dial.* or *colloq.* [f. DAFF *v.*^{1} + -LE.] *intr.* To become silly, daft, or wandering; to act stupidly or inanely.

1796 Marshall *Rur. Econ. Yorks.* Gloss. (E.D.S.) s.v., 'He daffles', he wanders, or falters in his speech or conversation. 1853 R. S. Surtees *Sponge's Sp. Tour* xxxvi, If your old man is done daffling with your draft, I should like to have the pick of it.

Daffy (dæ·fi), *sb.*^{1} [The name of Thomas *Daffy*, an English clergyman of the seventeenth century.] Orig. in *Daffy's elixir*, a medicine given to infants, 'tinctura sennæ composita' (Dunglison), to which gin was commonly added; hence, a slang name for gin itself.

1776 *Hibernian Jrnl.* 8–10 Apr., Daffy's Elixir, Just imported. 1821 *The Fancy* I. 304 (Farmer) While carrying on his new vocation as publican, Jack did not deny himself the use of drops of daffy. 1828 *Sporting Mag.* XXI. 435 His predilection for daffey of late years grew upon him. 1838 Dickens *O. Twist* ii, [A little gin] to put into the blessed infants' Daffy. 1857 Trollope *Barchester T.* xxiii, Not got a coral—how can you expect that he should cut his teeth? Have you got Daffy's Elixir? 1861 Mayhew *Lond. Labour* IV. 430 When I goes in where they are a havin' their daffies—that's drops o' gin, sir. 1871 *London Figaro* 15 April (Farmer) [If the baby] should bawl persistently..he would..thoroughly dose it with daffy. 1882 *Punch* 29 Apr. 193/2 A good many of them..had been partaking freely of *daffy*.

Daffy (dæ·fi), *sb.*^{2} *colloq.* (orig. *dial.*) Abbreviated f. DAFFODILLY. So **Da·ffying** *sb.* (see quot.).

1871 *Leisure Hour* 25 Mar. 184/1 Another of our rustic treats..was going to gather daffodils.... In Herefordshire this little festival was called Daffying. 1878 *Cumbld. Gloss.*, *Daffy-doon-dilly*, *Daffy*, the daffodil. 1925 *Sunday at Home* June 536/2 Little winds just rose on purpose to stir the daffies. 1928 *Daily Express* 28 Mar. 3/3 Despite the fact that this has been a bad season for 'daffies' owing to a recent spell of frost in Cornwall.

Daffy (dæ·fi), *a. dial.* or *slang.* [f. DAFF *sb.*, *v.*^{1}; cf. *DAFFLE *v.*] = DAFT *a.* 3.

1884 *Upton-on-Severn Gloss.*, *Daffy*, simple, soft. 1896 G. Ade *Artie* iii. 24 She'd make anybody daffy. 1902 *Munsey's Mag.* XXII. 491/2, I want to know what this new affair is. If I'm daffy, there's the reason. 1908 Mulford *Orphan* xiv. 180 Old man Gordon was daffy on education, which is a good thing to be daffy over. 1921 R. D. Paine *Comr. Rolling Ocean* xv. 258 England was daffy over spy stories during the war. 1922 *19th Cent.* Feb. 270 Guess the poor old devil's gone daffy.

Dag (dæg), *sb.*^{5} *dial.* or *slang.* [prob. altered from DARG (one's) task.] A feat of skill; chiefly *pl.* esp. in *doing dags* (see quots.).

1879 *N. & Q.* 5th Ser. XII. 128/1 'I'll do you (or your) dags.'—An expression used by children of young, and sometimes of older, growth, meaning, 'I'll do something that you cannot do.' 1886 Elworthy *W. Som. Word-bk.* s.v., To 'set a dag' is to perform some feat in such a way as to challenge imitation.... There's a dag for you—do it if you can. 1886 *Fun* (Farmer) He was very fond of what, in schoolboy days, we used to call doing dags. 1898 *Daily News* 4 Oct. 6/3 What does your entertainment principally consist of?..Doing 'dags' to make the people laugh. 1902 *Windsor Mag.* June 114/1 Wearing it in your hat shows that you don't funk me. It's doing my dags to touch you.

Dagga, variant of *DACHA.

Dagger, *sb.* Add:

6. c. = DOG-SHORE.

1838 *Civil Eng. & Arch. Jrnl.* I. 384/2 At 11 o'clock the dagger was knocked down, and the beautiful vessel..glided majestically into the river. 1896 *Strand Mag.* XII. 325 Being simultaneously released .. these weights instantly fall, and .. bring down the daggers, thus removing all obstacle to the passage of the ship down the ways.

Daggett (dæ·gėt). Also **degote, degut(t.** [ad. Russ. деготь *degotĭ*.] A dark tar obtained by the distillation of the bark of the European white birch, and used in the preparation of Russia leather, and as a local application for diseases of the skin.

1861 *Chambers's Encycl.* II. 104/1 [The birch] yields also the B[irch] Tar, or *Degutt*. [1875 *Encycl. Brit.* III. 698/1 An empyreumatic oil, called *diogott* in Russia.] 1890 Billings *Nat. Med. Dict.*, *Daggett*, birch-tar. 1901 Dorland *Med. Dict.* (ed. 2), *Degote*,..tarry oil of white birch.

Dagher (dæ·gəɹ), *sb.* Also **dargha, dagga.** [Kaffir *u-Daka* mud, clay, mortar (cf. *im-Daka* dark, dirty, muddy).] A kind of mortar used in

South Africa, composed of mud, cow-dung, and blood mixed together. Hence as *vb.*, to smear with dagher.

1880 H. M. Prichard *Friends & Foes* 282 Kafir women.. smear the walls and floor with 'dargha'. 1893 Blennerhassett & Sleeman *Adv. Mashon.* 32 We had heard..that 'daghering' and 'smearing' would be essential parts of our duties. 1899 W. H. Brown *On S. Afr. Frontier* 63 The houses were built of 'dagga' (mud), brick, and corrugated iron. 1905 *Blackw. Mag.* Mar. 389/1 The room was floored with dagga—anthill earth brought to a high stage of hardness and mahogany-like polish by frequent dressings of bullock's blood and kraal manure.

Dago. Add: (Earlier examples.)

1832 Ames *Two Years in Navy* (1833) I. 145 These *Degos* [of Minorca], as they are pleasantly called by our people, were always a great pest. 1858 *Knickerbocker Mag.* Jan. 7 And so, Bill, you served as a ingineer with these ere blamed Dagos, you say.

2. Spanish or Italian (language).

1901 H. McHugh *John Henry* 32 She said she was svelte. I guess that's Dago for a shine.

3. *attrib.*, as **dago red**, Italian red wine.

1906 A. Walcott *Open Door* xii. 146 You know I'm.. pleased when the meal can be washed down only with ..'dago red'.

Daguerrean (dăge·rĭăn), *a.* Also **Daguerryan, -ian, Daguerreian.** [See DAGUERREOTYPE.] Pertaining to Daguerre or the daguerreotype; photographic.

1844 *Yale Lit. Mag.* IX. 381 His imitative bump is certainly 'large'—so large, in fact, that it becomes almost Daguerryan in its workings, in that its productions only want an appearance of life and health to counterfeit the original. 1851 C. Cist *Cincinnati* 161 Daguerrean rooms. 1878 Abney *Photogr.* ix. 63 The method of developing the Daguerrean image. *Ibid.* xxxiii. 264 Both of these eminent physicists employed the Daguerrean process with the greatest success in these researches. 1889 *Anthony's Photogr. Bull.* II. 5 A full fledged daguerrean artist.

Dah (da). [Burmese. See also *DAO, *DHA.] A short sword with a heavy back, used also as a knife, especially in Burma; also *attrib.*

1831 Jas. Bell *Syst. Geog.* IV. 588 A short sword called *dah*, having a blade of about a foot and a half in length. 1839 H. Malcom *Trav. S.-E. Asia* I. II. iii. 247 Their chief tool, and one used for all manner of purposes, from the felling of a tree to the paring of a cucumber, is the dah. The handle is like that of a cleaver, and the blade like a drawing-knife. 1858 C. T. W. *Six Months Brit. Burmah* xiii. 104 The Burman has few agricultural implements... A cart, plough, dah (or sword-knife), and sickle are about all he requires. 1881 Kipling *Departm. Ditties*, *What Happened* ix, Amid the jungle-grass..grinned and jabbered Little Boh Hla-oo and cleared the dah-blade from the scabbard. 1908 Sir H. Jones in *Life* (1924) 207 [He] was finished promptly by the native and his *dah*. 1923 *Blackw. Mag.* Sept. 304/2 Thrust into his coloured sash were two silver-mounted dahs.

Dahil, var. *DAYAL.

Dahlgren (dā·lgren). Now *Hist.* In full *Dahlgren gun*: A cast-iron smoothbore gun invented by J. A. Dahlgren in 1856.

1862 *Chambers's Encycl.* III. 394 Dahlgren guns, made to fire shells or hollow shot, have been introduced to a considerable extent in the United States navy. 1867 H. Latham *Black & White* 86 Each [gunboat] was armed with two 15-inch Dahlgrens. 1876 Voyle & Stevenson *Milit. Dict.* (ed. 3) s.v., The Dahlgren 11-inch was once a formidable gun on the seas.

Dahllite (dā·hləit). *Min.* [Named *dahllit* (1888) after T. and J. *Dahll*: see -ITE^{1}.] Phosphate and carbonate of calcium found as a yellowish crust on apatite.

1892 *Dana's Min.* (ed. 6) 866 Phosphates or Arsenates with Carbonates, Sulphates, Borates... Dahllite $2Ca_3P_2O_8 . CaCO_3 . \frac{1}{2}H_2O$.

Dahoman (dăhōu·măn), *a.* (*sb.*) Also **Dahomean, Dahomeyan.** [f. the name of the country *Dahomey* or the tribal name *Dahomeh*.] Of or pertaining to, a native of, the West African state of Dahomey.

1837 *Penny Cycl.* VIII. 285/2 The captains of these forts.. were now prisoners in the Dahoman camp. *Ibid.*, The Dahomans..made their appearance on the coast. 1851 Forbes (*title*) Dahomey and the Dahomans. 1877 *Encycl. Brit.* VI. 766/2 The Dahomans have at several times penetrated along the beach towards the east as far as Badagry. 1883 Moloney *W. Afr. Fisheries* 50 It has been for some time conveniently contrary to the Dahomean fetish to cross water.

Dail Eireann (dǭl ē·rən). [Ir., = assembly of Ireland.] The Sinn Fein Parliament in Ireland. Also abbreviated **Dail.**

1919 *Times* 21 Jan. 9/4 A committee had been nominated 'to select Irish technical terms for the work of "An Dail Eireann,"' the Gaelic appellation of the new Irish Parliament. *Ibid.* 22 Jan. 9/4 The first word in English was spoken when the Dail had been in session for about three-quarters of an hour. 1921 *Punch* CLX. 254/3 The Government should enter into unconditional negotiations with Dail Eirann. 1923 *Contemp. Rev.* Sept. 332 Parliament has been sitting continuously ever since the last Dail elections.

Dailiness. Delete *rare*, and add quots.:

1898 A. Bennett *Man from North* xix, The drab dailiness of her existence in Carteret Street. 1899 *Academy* 14 Oct. 432/1 That which Mrs. Meynell has well called the 'dailiness' of life. 1906 *Daily Chron.* 22 May 6/6 All necessary implication of dailiness has long disappeared from the word 'journal'. 1906 E. V. Lucas *Wand. in Lond.* i. 9 Perhaps a touch of grime is not unnecessary. Perhaps houses can be too clean for the truest human dailiness.

Daily, *a.* Add:

1. b. *Daily girl*, etc. Also as *sb.* short for this.

1921 *Dict. Occup. Terms* (1927) § 900 *Daily servant, daily girl*..: a non-resident general servant. *Mod.* I can't get anybody to live in. I have to be content with a daily.

B. *sb.* (orig. *U.S.*)

1833 Paulding *Westward Ho* I. xxi. 190 'Make out an estimate of the cost of establishing a paper.' 'A daily, sir?' 'Ay, a daily, if you wish.' 1840 *Knickerbocker Mag.* XVI. 382 Mr. Morse..was reading his 'daily'. 1851 C. Cist *Cincinnati* 74 These are all dailies, tri-weeklies, and weekly reissues of dailies.

Dairy, *sb.* Add:

2. b. Dairy produce. *U.S.*

1882 *Narragansett Hist. Reg.* I. 226 Farmers used to sell their dairy in the Boston market.

4. *dairy cow, produce*; **dairy butter**, butter made at a private dairy; **dairy herd**, a herd of milch-cows.

c1830 *Glouc. Farm Rep.* 17 in *Libr. Usef. Knowl.*, *Husb.* III, The twenty heifer-calves are bred to keep up the stock of dairy-cows. 1844 H. Stephens *Bk. Farm* III. 835 Cows being kept for the express purpose of yielding dairy produce. *Ibid.* 1387 Cattle..—food given to dairy cows. 1881 Sheldon *Dairy Farming* 5/2 Whilst a cow is kept in the dairy herd. 1927 Peake & Fleure *Peasants & Potters* 43 A small and docile dairy-herd. 1928 *Daily Express* 3 Feb. 5/2 Instruction is given in the management of small dairy herds.

Dais. Add:

2. c. *Freemasonry.* (See quots.)

1879 A. G. Mackey *Encycl. Freemasonry* 201/1 The dais is the elevated portion of the eastern part of the Lodge room, which is occupied by Past Masters and the dignitaries of the Order. 1925 Sir A. Hardinge *Life H. H. M. Herbert* I. 223 The crippling decisions of the Grand Master and the 'Dais' or board. *Ibid.*, The 'Dais' was consternated at the audacity of so young a brother.

Daisy, *sb.* Add:

1. c. Slang phr. *Under the daisies*: dead. *To turn one's toes to the daisies*: to die.

1842 Barham *Ingol. Leg.* Ser. II. *Babes in the Wood* iv, Be kind to those dear little folks When our toes are turned up to the daisies. 1866 G. Macdonald *Ann. Q. Neighb.* xi. I. 356, I shall very soon hide [my name] under some daisies. 1928 S. Vines *Humours Unreconciled* xxi. 268, I think she's drinking herself under the daisies, so to speak.

6. b. *U.S. slang.* (See sense 5.) Also as *adv.*

1887 F. Francis Jr. *Saddle & Mocassin* x. 189 Well, if he can kick anything out of a Government mule, he's a daisy burro. 1892 *Harper's Mag.* Feb. 438/1 A passenger informed on him for having his coat unbuttoned. Daisy passenger, wasn't it? 1902 S. E. White *Blazed Trail* xxxvii. 252 She's my daisy Sunday best-day girl. 1905 Rex Beach *Pardners* v. (1912) 130 The noose sailed up and settled over him fine and daisy.

7. **daisy fleabane** *U.S.*, **daisy-tree** (see quots.).

1856 A. Gray *Man. Bot.* (1860) 198 *Erigeron annuum*, *Daisy Fleabane. Sweet Scabious. *Ibid.* 199 *E. strigosum*, Daisy Fleabane. 1872 *Rep. Vermont Board Agric.* I. 279 *Erigeron annuum* and *E. strigosum*, Daisy Fleabanes, acrid plants, mingle their coarse stalks quite too freely with the hay from newly seeded land. 1898 Morris *Austral Engl.*, *Daisy Tree*, two Tasmanian trees, *Astur stellulatus*, ..and *A. glandulosus*.

Dajaksch (dā·yakʃ). The arrow-poison of Borneo.

1864 P. M. Braidwood in *Edin. Med. Jrnl.* X. 123 The Physiological Actions of Dajaksch, an Arrow Poison, used in Borneo. 1890 Billings *Nat. Med. Dict.*

Daka, dakha: see *DACHA.

Dakhma (dā·kmă). Also **dokhma, dokhmeh.** [Pers.] = Tower of Silence (see SILENCE *sb.* 2 c).

1865 *Chambers's Encycl.* VII. 300 Their dead are not buried, but exposed on an iron grating in the Dokhma, or Tower of Silence, to the fowls of the air. 1912 H. G. Rawlinson *Bactria* iii. 40 Alexander promptly ordered the *dakhmas*, or Towers of Silence, to be closed.

Dakin (dēi·kin). The name of H. D. *Dakin*, of the Herter Laboratory, New York, designating a solution of sodium hypochlorite used as an antiseptic.

1920 Martindale & Westcott *Extra Pharmacop.* (ed. 17) I. 56 Dakin's (Stronger) Hypochlorite Solution. 1927 T. Sollman *Man. Pharmacol.* (ed. 3) 165 The addition of Dakin's solution to blood prevents clotting. 1928 Edmunds & Gunn *Cushny's Textbk. Pharmacol.* (ed. 9) 160 Dakin's solution is prepared by adding chlorinated lime to a solution of sodium carbonate.

Dakka, variant of *DACHA.

Dale^{3}. **1.** Add: also *attrib.*, as *dale hose*.

1889 Welch *Text Bk. Naval Archit.* xi. 129 A flexible hose, known as a dale hose, is led from the delivery nozzle of the pump to the pipe in the deck plate communicating with the compartment to be flooded.

Dalle^{2}. **2.** *U.S.* (Earlier examples.)

1839 J. K. Townsend *Narr. Journ. Rocky Mts.* xv. 358 Here Mr. M'Leod and myself debarked, and the men ran the dall. 1844 Lee & Frost *Oregon* xviii. 198 The next object to be noticed is the Small Dalls two miles further up. 1846 De Smet *Oregon Missions* (1847) 231 The distance from the cascades to the dalles is about forty-five miles. *Ibid.* 232 The third day we arrived at the great dalles.

Dalo (dā·lo). [Fiji.] = TARO.

1879 *Encycl. Brit.* IX. 156/2 The taro or dalo..is grown in ditches, by streams, or on irrigated ground.

Dalripa (dæ·lripă). [a. Norw. *dalrjupa*. Cf. RIPA^{1}, RYPE.] The Norwegian ptarmigan.

1889 *Cent. Dict.* 1896 *Blackw. Mag.* July 92/2 The willow-grouse or dalryper is treated in very similar fashion.

Dalton (dǭ·ltən). The name of the high school (at *Dalton*, Mass., U.S.A.) in which the educational method devised by Miss Helen Parkhurst was first adopted, which consists essentially in dividing up the year's work into monthly 'assignments' which the pupils contract to carry through (with certain preliminary aids) on their own responsibility and with their own discipline. Hence **Da·ltonize** *v. trans.*, to manage or arrange on this educational method; **Da:ltoniza·tion**; **Da·ltonism**, the method itself.

1922 Helen Parkhurst *Educ. on Dalton Plan* ii. 15 The Dalton Laboratory Plan provides that means by diverting his energy to the pursuit and organization of his own studies in his own way. *Ibid.* iv. 40 Demonstrating the superiority of the Dalton Plan from the point of view of economy. 1924 A. J. Lynch *Individual Work & Dalton Plan* 34 The teaching of arithmetic under the Dalton Plan. *Ibid.* 47 Convinced Daltonians recognise at once that assignments are the heart and centre of the plan. *Ibid.* 124 He could find no fault with any other Dalton teacher. 1927 Aldous Huxley *Proper Studies* 117 The first step in the Daltonization of a school consists in the abolition of class rooms and the substitution of specialist rooms. *Ibid.* 125 In a well-run Daltonized school the problem of discipline solves itself. *Ibid.* 133 These ancient seats of learning [*sc.* Oxford and Cambridge] were Daltonized long before Daltonism was invented.

Dam, *sb.*^{1} Add: **4. d.** A reservoir or tank, as of loam and brick construction, in which metal is collected for heavy castings.

1901 Bolland in Webster *Dict.*

e. A soft rubber guard to protect a tooth from saliva while it is being prepared for filling. *U.S.*

1872 L. P. Meredith *Teeth* (1878) 117 By the use of the rubber-dam inconvenience and unsuccessful operations may be avoided. 1875 *Dental Cosmos* XVII. 514 The next step is the application of the 'rubber dam' to the four teeth.

Dam (dām), *sb.*^{5} Also **daum, dawm.** [Hind. *dām*.] An East Indian copper coin of the value of one fortieth of a rupee.

1781 Fr. Balfour *Forms of Herkern* 39 The sum of twenty one lacks of dams. 1801 R. Patton *Asiat. Mon.* 182 A crore of dams. 1871 E. Balfour *Cycl. India* (ed. 2) II. 10. 1884 *Encycl. Brit.* XVII. 343/1 The gold coinage and the silver rupee are seldom seen [in Nepal], the ordinary currency consisting of the copper dāms and paisā, and the mōhar or half rupee.

Damage, *sb.* **5.** Add: Common in recent use.

1875 Holland *Sevenoaks* xxii. 303 What's the damage for the sort o' thing ye're drivin' at this morning? 1888 A. C. Gunter *Mr. Potter of Texas* xi, 'What's the damage?' 'Damage?' echoes Lubbins, not understanding this Americanism. 'Yes, how much do I owe?'

Damaged, *ppl. a.* Add: **b.** *Damaged goods*: merchandise that has become deteriorated in quality by exposure to the elements, unsaleability, etc. Also *fig.* of persons.

1816 J. Scott *Visit to Paris in 1814* 211 Damaged goods of every description, were brought out for the Cossack market. 1840–1 S. Warren *Ten Thousand a Year* i, Didn't I feel like damaged goods, just then! 1872 *Porcupine* Aug. 330/3 Everything seemed to be done in some shops to steal money and pass off damaged goods. 1911 tr. Brieux (*title*) Damaged Goods [tr. of *Les Avariés*].

Damascene. B. 2. Add: *attrib.* and *Comb.*

1880 G. C. M. Birdwood *Industr. Art India* I. 141 A vast establishment of..damascene workers, chiefly for ornamenting arms. 1882 Caulfeild & Saward *Dict. Needlework* 139/1 Damascene Lace.... The difference between it and Modern Point lace..consists in the introduction into Damascene of real Honiton sprigs, and the absence of any needle-worked Fillings.

Damassé. Add: **B.** *adj.* Woven like damask.

1882 Caulfeild & Saward *Dict. Needlework*, *Damassé*, a French term applied to all cloths manufactured after the manner of damask, in every kind of material. 1896 *Godey's Mag.* Apr. 443/2 White damassé mohair.

Dambo (dæ·mbo). *Central Africa.* Also **damba.** [Mang'unja *dambo* treeless grass-covered plain, open glade in the bush.] A grassy clearing.

1907 *Macm. Mag.* Jan. 194 Large open patches, or *dambos*, covered with fresh green grass and well-watered. 1916 *Cornhill Mag.* Mar. 385 Crossing those 'dambos' in the fierce heat of the day. 1927 *Observer* 20 Nov. 21 Northern Rhodesia, which consists mainly of orchard bush interspersed with dambas.

Dame. 1. Delete †*Obs.*, and add: The title given to Benedictine nuns who have made their solemn profession (cf. DAN, DOM); also, any fully professed nun.

c1425 *Hampole's Psalter* Metr. Pref. 24 At a worthy recluse prayer cald dame merget Kyrkby. 1590 in *Cath. Rec. Soc. Publ.* V. 192 Dame Isabel Whitehead an ancient religious woman. a1700 *Ibid.* IX. 335 She leaving the world went over to the English Benedictine Dames of our Blessed Lady of Consolation. *Ibid.* 339 The Rd Dames, Dame Magdalena, D. Augustina, D. Maria, and D. Clementia. 1795 in B. Ward *Dawn Cath. Revival* (1909) II. xxiii. 82 The three houses of English Dames at Paris. 1867 Drane *Chr. Schools* II. iv. 179 Dame Mabel Wafre, abbess of Godstow. 1906 P. Nolan (*title*) The Irish Dames of Ypres.

7. d. The title of lady members of the Order of the British Empire; also *Dame Commander*, *Dame Grand Cross*.

1917 *Times* 2 June 6/1 The New Order of the British Empire... Degrees of classification for women,..(1) Dame Grand Cross, (2) Dame Commander, (3) Dame Companion. 1930 *Ibid.* 1 Jan. 14 Made a Dame of the Order of the British Empire for her services to aviation.

Dame de compagnie (dam də koṅpan'i). Also, semi-anglicized *damdecompany*. [Fr.; lit. 'lady of company'.] A paid female companion.

1784 in *H. Walpole's Lett.* (1858) VIII. 518 *note*, The duchess brought with her, as a *dame de compagnie*, a Frenchwoman. 1832 *Edin. Rev.* July 481 The female professor,

late *dame de compagnie* to La Fayette. 1848 Thackeray *Van. Fair* xxxii, Marry a drawing-master's daughter, indeed!—marry a *dame de compagnie*—for she was no better, Briggs. 1885 'L. Malet' *Col. Enderby's Wife* II. iii, A nice, gentle, little person in grey, who put in an appearance at dinner—*dame de compagnie*, I suppose. 1897 *Sat. Rev.* 5 June 641 'Mees' became a 'damdecompany' to an old Contessa.

Damenisation (dāmĕnəizēi·ʃən). *Mus. Hist.* [f. the syllables *da me ni* + -IZATION.] The use of the syllables *da, me, ni, po, tu, la, be* in solmization for the notes of the scale, advocated by Graun (died 1759).

1889 Rockstro in *Grove's Dict. Mus.* III. 551/2.

Damewort (dēi·mwɒɹt). [f. DAME + WORT.] A book name for the garden rocket, *Hesperis matronalis*; = DAME'S-VIOLET.

1796 Withering *Brit. Plants* (ed. 3) III. 587 *Hesperis inodora*..Scentless Damewort.

Damfool (dæmfū·l). *colloq.* Also (*jocular*) **damphool, -phule.** [f. *DAMN *a.* + FOOL *sb.* 4.] A damned fool; *transf.* a foolish thing or affair. Also *attrib.* or as *adj.*, foolish, stupid. Hence **Damfoo·lishness.**

1886 'F. Anstey' *Fallen Idol* xi. 216 When I open the note I see in Greek characters, and forgif me that I rebeat such words to you at all, but I see written there—'Do not a damfool be!' 1900 Kipling in *Daily Express* 20 June 4/5 'Fighting heroically' in some damfool trap he's walked into with his eyes open! 1908 G. H. Lorimer *J. Spurlock* iv. 66 The grasshopper is n't the only damphool in the good old summer-time. *Ibid.* xii. 328 It's all damfoolishness. a1909 in J. R. Ware *Passing Engl.* 103 Now, Hennery, I am going to break you of this damfoolishness, or I will break your neck. 1911 H. S. Harrison *Queed* vii. 84 Something loose in his belfry, as ye might have surmised from thim damfool taxdrools. 1913 W. J. Locke *Stella Maris* ii, It's perhaps the only tremendous thing in my damfool of a life.

Damianist (dēi·miănist). [f. the name *Damian* + -IST.] A follower of Damian, patriarch of Alexandria in the 6th century, who denied the separate godhead of the three persons of the Trinity. Also **Da·mianite.**

1727–38 Chambers *Cycl.*, *Damianists*, a branch of the antient Acephalous Severites. 1894 *National Obs.* 29 Dec., Damianist.

Damine (dēi·min, -əin), *a. Zool.* [f. L. *dama* deer + -INE^{1}.] Belonging to or characteristic of the fallow deer, *Cervus dama*.

1891 Flower & Lydekker *Mamm.* 323 Damine group of existing Deer.

Dammar. Add: In full **dammar pine, dammar tree**, any tree yielding dammar resin.

a1815 W. Roxburgh *Flora Indica* 436 In the Bednore country, it is called the Dammar tree by the English, and blossoms during the hot season. 1829 Loudon *Encycl. Plants* (1836) 802 *Agathis* Salisb. Dammar Pine. 1846 Lindley *Veg. Kingd.* 229 Liquid storax is thought to be yielded by the Dammar Pine. 1880 C. R. Markham *Peruv. Bark* 347 The *Canarum strictum*, or black dammer tree.

Dammed, *ppl. a.* Add later quots. with *up*:

1899 *Westm. Gaz.* 17 May 8/1 In a dammed-up glacial valley. 1904 Gallichan *Fishing Spain* 115, I made a few casts with the fly over a dammed-up pool.

Dammit (dæ·mit), for *damn it*, used in comparative phrases.

1908 E. Wallace *Angel Esquire* xii, 'Outside as quick as dammit!' he cried.

Damn (dæm), *a.* and *adv.* Also **damn', dam'.** Clipped f. DAMNED *ppl. a.* (See also *DAMFOOL.)

1775 *Narrag. Hist. Reg.* III. 263 A man that..was noted for a damn cuss. 1776 *Ibid.* I. 304 You damn old Tory Raskel. 1787 *Mirror* 164 Don't beef and butter go off damn soberly? 1882 in T. M. Healy *Lett. & Leaders* (1928) I. 150 T. P. quoted my answer as 'I'm damn glad'. 1897 Flandrau *Harvard Episodes* 4 You've gone through the whole damn thing yourself. *Ibid.* 218 'But he isn't bad, really bad.' 'No, certainly not; merely a damn fool.' 1901 Merwin & Webster *Calumet K* iv. 62 My only order was, 'Clear the road—and be damn quick about it'. 1903 Kipling *Five Nations* 199 I've known a lot o' people ride a dam' sight worse than Piet. 1918 W. J. Locke *Rough Road* xviii, It's all dam funny! 1928 D. L. Sayers *Bellona Club* iii, If you understand that..you understand a damn' sight more than I do. 1928 E. Wallace *Again the Three Just Men* 209 It's none of your dam' business.

Damned, *ppl. a.* Add: **4.** In the Southern U.S., a common epithet added to *Yankee*.

1812 *Niles' Weekly Reg.* III. 45/1 Take the middle of the road or I'll hew you down, you d——d Yankee rascal. 1818 Fearon *Sk. Amer.* 210 His friend..said that there was 'nothing in America but d—d Yankies and rogues, and that it was not fit for a dog to live in'. 1833 H. Barnard in *Maryland Hist. Mag.* XIII. 361 It is only surpassed by their hatred of the d—d Yankees. 1837 *Knickerbocker Mag.* X. 381 As they [*sc.* inhabitants of Gulf-states] come to the North to be educated, they herd with the Carolinians at our colleges and schools; continually quarreling among themselves, and slandering each other, they only agree to hate the 'd—d yankees'.

c. Substantival use of superlative in phr. *One's damnedest*: the worst one can do; the utmost evil or harm possible; also *ironically* = one's very best.

1830 [see DAMNED 4]. 1845 J. J. Hooper *Adv. Simon Suggs* xii. 144, I..tried my d—dst, but it wouldn't grind no way. 1891 H. Herman *His Angel* 176 Now do your damnedest at your peril. 1928 S. Vines *Humours Unreconciled* xviii. 237 She..had done her 'damnedest' to please him.

Damnonian (dæmnōu·niăn), *a.* [f. med.L. *Damnonii* sb. pl.: see -IAN.] Of or pertaining to the Damnonii, ancient inhabitants of Devon and Cornwall.

1849 Kingsley *Prose Idylls, North Devon, Clovelly* (1873) 279 Far and wide over the Damnonian moors. 1876 *Encycl. Brit.* V. 302/1 The Damnonian kingdom of Devon and Cornwall.

Damnum (dæ·mnǝm). [L., = hurt, harm, damage.] A legal wrong: see quot. 1862.

1828 *Congress. Debates* IV. I. 424 (Stanf.) It is a loss which gives no legal title to indemnity; it is a *damnum*, but a *damnum*, as the law has it, *absque injuria*. 1862 J. W. Smith *Man. Com. Law* 264 Damnum is such a damage, whether pecuniary or perceptible, or not, as is capable, in legal contemplation, of being estimated by a jury.

Dampen, *v.* **3.** (Earlier and later U.S. examples.)

1827 J. F. Cooper *Red Rover* I. xv. 246 It is seldom that ..he is dampened with salt water. 1902 C. C. Munn *Rockhaven* i. 9 We took a handful o' matches, an' dampenin' 'em, rubbed the ends round the eyes..o' the critter. 1906 H. D. Pittman *Belle of Blue Grass C.* xxi. 302 The heavy dews.. fell upon her, dampening her hair.

Dampener. Add: Also *fig.*

1920 *Glasgow Herald* 5 Nov. 11 Socialism has received a decided dampener.

Damper. Add: **1. c.** An operative who damps the materials used in various manufactures.

1921 *Dict. Occup. Terms* (1927) § 429 *Damper* (boots); wetter; soaks leather bends in clean soft water. *Ibid.*, *Damper-down* (boots); smooths bottom of sole of a boot or shoe with a pad of clean, white flannel, damped with special solution.

2. c. In an organ: A thumping-board (see THUMPING *vbl. sb.* b).

4. b. *Electr.* (See quot.)

1906 A. Russell *Altern. Curr.* II. 191 In order to prevent phase swinging, Hutin and Leblanc provided the field magnets with 'amortisseurs', or 'dampers', which tend to prevent any relative change between the positions of the magnetic field due to the armature and the field due to the field magnets.

Damping, *vbl. sb.* Add: Also *damping-off*, the decay of seedlings or cuttings due to excessive damp; *damping-out* (DAMP *v.* 1 d); **damping-coil**, in a galvanometer or dynamometer, a coil used to check vibrations of the needle, etc.; **damping roll, roller**, a roller or cylinder used for damping in certain processes.

1906 A. Russell *Altern. Curr.* II. 192 The ordinary field magnet coils must act to a certain extent like *damping coils. 1919 F. O. Bower *Bot. Living Plant* 413 When Mustard and Cress are sown thickly, and kept too warm and damp, the seedlings are liable to the disease of '*damping-off', the plants quickly rotting with an unpleasant smell. 1912 *Q. Rev.* July 242 The *damping-out of oscillations cannot be expected to be as rapid. 1904 *Technol. & Sci. Dict.* (ed. Goodchild & Tweney), **Damping Rolls*, metal cylinders of small diameter used for damping paper.

Damster (dæ·mstəɹ). *U.S.* [f. DAM *sb.*^{1} 1 + -STER.] The superintendent of a logging dam.

a1861 T. Winthrop *Life in Open Air* (1863) 18 The damster..received us with hearty hospitality. *Ibid.* 24 Hardly less important is the Damster.

Danaid. Add: **b.** A butterfly of the family *Danaidæ*.

1892 W. L. Distant *Naturalist in Transvaal* 65 The female Hypolimnas being present with the Danaids.

Danain (dæ·neɪin). *Chem.* [f. mod.L. *Danais* (generic name) + -IN^{1}.] A glucoside, $C_{14}H_{14}O_5$, contained in the root of *Danais fragrans*. Also **Danaidin** (dænēi·idin): see quot.

1886 *Jrnl. Chem. Soc.* L. 173 This substance, to which the author gives the name *danain*, has the composition $C_{14}H_{14}O_5$, and splits up into half its own weight of glucose, and a resinous amorphous compound, *danaidin*, which probably has the composition $C_{22}H_{20}O_6$.

Danaine (dæ·neɪin), *a.* (*sb.*) *Ent.* [ad. mod.L. *Danainæ*, f. generic name *DANAIS: see -INE^{1}.] Of or belonging to, a member of, the subfamily *Danainæ* of butterflies.

1901 E. B. Poulton *The. of Mimicry Afr. Butterfl.* 2 All of them possess a dark tip to the fore wing crossed by a white bar, as in the Danaine butterfly. *Ibid.*, The abundant black-and-white Danaines. 1913 *Oxf. Univ. Gaz.* 4 June 951/2 The rare Danaine butterfly *Amauris ansorgei*.

Danais (dæ·neɪis). [mod.L., a. Gr. Δαναΐς.] A butterfly belonging to the genus so named.

1878 P. Robinson *In my Indian Garden* 101 The coppery Danais flitted at ease about the shrubs. 1892 W. L. Distant *Naturalist in Transvaal* 65 Birds may..make an experimental dash at a *Danais*.

Dance, *sb.* Add:

6. d. Also *transf.*

1883 *19th Cent.* Sept. 537 He calls this policy 'the policy of salutary agitation', which I irreverently translate: 'the St. Vitus' dance policy'. 1897 *Syd. Soc. Lex.*, *St. Vitus' dance of the voice*, a name for Stammering.

7. *dance-frock*; **dance-cellar** *U.S.*, a dancing-saloon beneath the ground level; **dance-hall, -house** *U.S.* (earlier examples).

1855 *Knickerbocker Mag.* XLV. 363 This is the *dance-cellar of notorious Jim Poole! 1904 *Westm. Gaz.* 18 Feb. 4/2 An accordion-pleated lace net is one of the prettiest *dance-frocks I have seen for some time. 1858 *Mass. Acts & Resolves* 125 Any person who shall offer to view..any..show, concert, or *dance-hall exhibition of any description shall be punished by a fine. 1855 *Knickerbocker Mag.* XLV. 364 The tattered curtain of a *dance-house. 1868 *Rep. U.S. Comm. Agric.* (1869) 176 All their [*sc.* Esquimaux] houses and casinos, or dance-houses, are built from it [*sc.* spruce]. 1876 Mrs. Stowe *We & Neighbors* xli. 375 He told me that he was in the constant habit of passing through the dance-houses, and talking with people who kept them.

Dance, *v.* Add:

8. To rejoice over by dancing round (a captured scalp) in the manner formerly practised by North American Indians.

1841 Catlin *N. Amer. Indians* I. 31 After having been formally 'danced', as the saying is, (i.e. after it [*sc.* a scalp] has been stuck up upon a pole,..and the warriors have danced around it for two or three weeks at intervals). 1846 Sage *Scenes Rocky Mts.* (1859) 126 Rarely did we return empty-handed from the foeman's land—without..scalps to dance.

Danchi (dɒ·ntʃi). Also **dhanicha, dhuncheo, dhun-chi, dunchee.** [Bengali.] A tropical shrub, *Sesbania aculeata*; also, the bast fibre obtained therefrom.

a1815 Roxburgh *Flora Indica* 571 Cultivation of the Dhunchi plant. 1866 *Treas. Bot.* s.v. *Sesbania*, *S. aculeata*, the Danchi of India, is an erect slightly branched annual. 1887 Moloney *Forestry W. Afr.* 312 'Dhunchee' or 'Danchi'..Cultivated about Calcutta during the rains.

Dancing, *vbl. sb.* **b.** Add: *dancing-class, -list, -party, -teacher*; **dancing-partner** (see quot.).

1870 Mrs. Stephens *Married in Haste* xxxi. 172 Constance had never felt..pleasure in departing for her *dancing classes. 1871 Mrs. Stowe *Pink & White Tyranny* xxi. 263 Her *dancing-list seemed in a fair way to be soon filled up for the evening. 1921 *Dict. Occup. Terms* (1927) § 899 **Dancing partner*..., an expert dancer engaged by proprietor or manager of dancing hall or by individual dancer, to act as partner when required and to teach ball-room dancing. 1889 *Kansas Times & Star* 13 Dec., The *dancing party given by Mrs. Kirk Armour and her sister, Mrs. Ed Smith, at the Casino last night was the most brilliant social event of the early winter. 1880 Cable *Grandissimes* xliii. 336, I could be..a *dancing-teacher.

Dandelion. 3. Add: **dandelion coffee** *U.S.*, a preparation from dried dandelion roots; **dandelion greens** *U.S. dial.*, fresh dandelion leaves used as a green food or herb.

1886 *Harper's Mag.* Sept. 578/2 If you'd asked pleasanter, I should just as soon told you that we use *dandelion coffee. 1887 Mary E. Wilkins *Humble Romance* 234 There were ..two old women—one..searching for *dandelion greens among the short young grass. 1889 Rose T. Cooke *Steadfast* xvii. 190 Dandelion greens is better 'n a doctor.

Dander, *sb.*^{3} (U.S. examples.)

a1800 *Spirit of Farmer's Museum* (1801) 278 An infant child..had ever since its birth, been grievously afflicted with a certain disorder in the head, called by the learned, 'the dander, or dandriff'. 1860 Holland *Miss Gilbert's Career* viii. 131 A young man that..keeps the dander all off his coat collar..always makes a good husband. 1875— *Sevenoaks* v. 65 I've took more nor three quarts o' dander out iv 'is hide.

Dander, *sb.*^{4} *U.S.* (Earlier examples.)

1834 C. A. Davis *Lett. J. Downing* 34 He was as wrathy as thunder—and when he gets his dander up, it's no joke, I tell you. 1834 D. Crockett *Life* 89 So sullen is the Indian, when his dander is up, that he would sooner die than make a noise.

Dandie Dinmont (dændi di·nmənt). Also shortened to **Dandie.** [Name of a character in Sir Walter Scott's novel *Guy Mannering* (q.v. ch. xxii, 'Dandy Dinmont's Pepper and Mustard terriers', and Note C).] A breed of terriers from the Scottish borders, having short legs, long body, and rough coat. Also *attrib.*

1848 *Sporting Life* 8 Jan. 246/1 The dog celebrated by Sir Walter Scott as the Pepper and Mustard, or Dandie Dinmont breed. 1859 'Stonehenge' *Shot-gun* 77 The Dandie Dinmont..is an excellent rabbit dog. 1862 J. Brown *Our Dogs* 29 From this dog descended Davidson (the original Dandie Dinmont) of Hyndlee's breed. 1875 Mrs. Stowe *We & Neighbors* i. 7 A rough coated Dandie Dinmont terrier. 1894 R. B. Lee *Mod. Dogs (Terriers)* 287 He has never known one of his Dandies show the 'white feather'. 1925 *Chambers's Jrnl.* 772/1 The two so-called Dandies.

Dandy, *sb.*^{1} Add: **2.** (U.S. examples of *a dandy*.) Also, in colloq. phr. *For dandy*, for effect.

1822 *Pennsylv. Intelligencer* 3 Dec. (Th.) The reader will suppose this was a dandy of a thing, since it was on writing paper. 1887 *Harper's Mag.* June 160/1 'Death loves a shining mark', and she hit a dandy when she turned loose on Jim. 1897 Susan Hale *Lett.* 319 Mrs. B. was a dandy, she didn't fuss nor worry. 1897 Mary Kingsley *W. Africa* 387, I go to bed early, thankfully observing that the gay mosquito curtain is entirely 'for dandy'—decorative and not defensive. 1919 H. L. Wilson *Ma Pettengill* iv. 111 It was just one punch, though a dandy.

7. b. *attrib.* and *Comb.*

1881 *Instr. Census Clerks* (1885) 42 Dandy Roll and Dandy Roll Mould Maker. 1895 *Daily News* 19 June 9/3 Dandy rolls,..all kinds of machinery apparatus and fittings used in the trade of a paper-maker's engineer and dandy roll maker. 1921 *Dict. Occup. Terms* (1927) § 363 *Rover, dandy*; *dandy minder*..; minds dandy roving frame, which further attenuates and twists slubbing from gill roving frame.

B. *adj.* **2.** Fine, splendid, first-rate. *U.S. colloq.*

1794 *Massachusetts Spy* 27 Aug. (Th.) My uncle Cuthbert blew out a prodigious puff of my dandy tobacco. 1898 P. L. Ford *Hon. Peter Stirling* 163 'If I was as big as him', said one, 'I'd fire all the peelers'. 'Wouldn't that be dandy?' cried another. 1902 Harben *Abner Daniel* 243, I know the place like a book,..an' it's a dandy investment. 1908 Mulford *Orphan* vi. 73, I got yore smokin', Orphant!..Here she is, right side up and fine and dandy!

1909 S. E. White *Rules of Game* I. i, 'How's Mrs. Orde..?' he inquired. 'Mrs. Orde is fine and dandy.'

b. As *adv.* Finely, splendidly. *U.S.*

1908 S. E. White *Riverman* xli. 323 'She's holding strong and dandy', said Orde.., examining critically the clumps of piles.

Dandydom (dæ·ndidəm). [f. Dandy *sb.*1 + -dom.] The condition of a dandy; the world of dandies.

c 1850 in *Daily Chron.* (1902) 4 Nov. 3/2 It 'flustered the realms of dandydom'. 1885 *Society in London* 155 A glorified dragoon who has reached the apotheosis of old dandydom. 1899 *Strand Mag.* Mar. 273/2 He was..reduced to a state of dilapidated dandy-dom.

Dandyishly (dæ·ndiˌiʃli), *adv.* [f. Dandyish + -ly 2.] Like a dandy, in the manner of a dandy.

1868 *Good Words* 1 Nov. 699 Dandyishly dressed in spotless white linen.

Dandyize, *v.* (See after Dandy *sb.*1) Add: *trans.* To dandify.

1846 in Worcester. 1855 in Ogilvie Suppl.

Dane gun. A gun used in the Guinea Coast area of West Africa.

1900 *Daily News* 25 Sept. 8/3 In the village were found 300 Dane guns, 40 rifles, three Martini-Henry carbines. 1901 *Daily Chron.* 31 Aug. 3/4 Three Ashantis, armed with their long dane guns. 1920 *Blackw. Mag.* Mar. 384/2 Every man or boy who could wield a spear or hold a dane gun.

Daneq (dā·nek). Also danic. [Arab. دانق *dāneq.*] An Arabian weight, one sixth of a dirhem; also, a small silver coin of this weight.

1884 J. Payne *Tales from Arabic* I. 277, I will pay thee a dirhem, when I enter the city; or take of me four danics now.

Dang, *sb. slang.* [f. Dang *v.*] A damn, cuss.

1906 Somerville & Ross *Irish Yesterdays* 113 He wouldn't give a dang for them.

Danger, *sb.* C. Add: *danger area, -point, -spot, -zone*; **danger angle,** (*a*) *Naut.* the angle enclosed by lines drawn from two known points to a point marking the limit of safe approach to a danger to navigation, so that a ship by steering a course keeping the two known points at a larger or smaller angle will avoid the danger; (*b*) *Gunnery* (see quot. 1918); **danger building,** at Woolwich Arsenal, a building in which are carried on the most dangerous operations in making ammunitions; **danger line,** a line, real or imaginary, representing the division between safety and danger.

1902 *Encycl. Brit.* XXXI. 109/2 To avoid an unnecessarily wide détour in rounding points and shoals, extensive use is now made of both horizontal and vertical *danger angles...The vertical danger angle enables similar results to be attained by measuring the vertical angle subtended by a known height. 1918 E. S. Farrow *Dict. Mil. Terms, Danger Angle,* the angle which the tangent to the trajectory at the point of splash makes with the plane containing the point of splash and parallel to the horizontal plane through the muzzle of the piece in the firing position. 1929 *Star* 21 Aug. 12/4 The gas leak..which made a portion of New Bridge-street a '*danger area'. 1899 *Daily News* 8 June 3/4 The *Danger Buildings, East Laboratory, Woolwich Arsenal. 1903 *Westm. Gaz.* 22 June 7/3 Timekeeper in the danger building. 1890 *Congress. Rec.* 5 June 5654/2, I believe the good sense of our law-makers will still hold us inside the *danger line of peril. 1902 *Monthly Weather Rev.* 3/1 The December floods of the Tennessee..continued considerably above the danger lines for the first few days. 1873 *Cassell's Mag.* (N.S.) VIII. 70/1 In the excursion season, stock and servants are alike taxed to the *danger point. 1897 *Daily News* 22 Apr. 6/3 The Macedonian difficulty, which is the real danger-point. 1910 *Westm. Gaz.* 6 Apr. 2/3 The axle is the danger-point in all heavy vehicles which are run at high speeds. 1905 *Ibid.* 4 Oct. 3/2 The *danger-spot in our new Treaty with Japan..is the provision for 'insuring the independence and integrity of the Chinese Empire'. 1928 Oppenheim in *Strand Mag.* July 17 Their danger spot was turning into the Brompton Road here without exciting suspicion. 1907 *Westm. Gaz.* 5 Feb. 7/3 An alarming fire broke out in the City *danger-zone soon after six o'clock last night. 1925 E. F. Norton *Fight for Everest, 1924* 58 Anywhere beyond the Base Camp may be considered as the 'danger zone'. 1927 *Observer* 5 June 19/2 The chief new feature [of contract bridge] introduced in America has been what is known as the 'Vulnerable' or 'Danger Zone'. A side is said to be 'vulnerable' when it has won its first game.

Dangered, *ppl. a.* Add mod. poetic examples.

1819 Keats *Otho* I. i. Poems (1889) 423 This danger'd neck is saved. 1915 *Oxford Mag.* 21 May 317/1 High Powers that love this dangered folk.

Dangersome, *a.* (Earlier U.S. examples.)

1890 *Odd Leaves* 172 (Th.), I knew it war a dangersome place for a well man to go in, much less a one-leg cripple. 1851 J. J. Hooper *Widow Rugby's Husb.* 50 It was dangersome for me to stay on the deck.

Dangle, *sb.* Delete *rare* and add quots. for sense: An object that dangles.

1909 *Cent. Dict.* Suppl., *Dangle-money*, an early Chinese bronze coinage, so called from its resemblance to and former use as dangles of a musical instrument. 1909 Margaret B. Saunders *Litany Lane* I. ix, A pair of long jet earrings representing funeral urns with cloths over them had replaced the usual golden dangles. 1911 Webster s.v., A dangle of curls.

Danian (dē^i·niăn), *a. Geol.* [f. L. *Dania* Denmark, f. *Danus* Dane: see -an.] Epithet of the uppermost division of the cretaceous system in France and Belgium.

1882 Geikie *Text-bk. Geol.* 803 The uppermost division, or Danian, of the Continental chalk appears to be absent in England, unless its lower portions are represented by some of the uppermost beds of the Norwich Chalk. 1893 tr. *E. Kayser's Comp. Geol.* 314 In the North of France the succession of the Upper Cretaceous rocks closely resembles that of England; but still higher zones are represented, and these are united under the term Danian. 1925 *Countries of the World* xxx. 3072/1 A beautiful stone resembling marble is secured from phosphatic beds of Danian Age.

Daniel (dæ·nyəl). The name of the biblical character (see Dan. i–vi) used typically for: An exemplary judge, a person of infallible judgement. Also *attrib.* and *Comb.*

1596 Shaks. *Merch. V.* iv. i. 223 A Daniel come to judgement, yea a Daniel. *Ibid.* 333 A second Daniel, a Daniel Jew. 1898 *Westm. Gaz.* 9 Nov. 2/3 His Daniel-like appeal to the writings on the wall.

Daniell (dæ·niĕl). [The name of John Frederic *Daniell*, English physicist (1790–1845), inventor of Daniell's hygrometer constant battery, etc. (see below).] **a.** A unit of electricity equal to 1·124 volts. **b.** Short for *Daniell cell.*

1871 *Engl. Mechanic* 430/2 The improved Daniell devised by me. 1878 G. Chrystal in *Encycl. Brit.* VIII. 93/2 The sawdust Daniell, invented by Sir Wm. Thomson (1858), is very convenient when portability is desired. 1884 Higgs *Magn. & Dyn.-electr. Mach.* 222 In this battery the value of the electromotive force, *e*, of each element is 2 (that of a Daniell being 1).

c. Used attrib. or in genitive to designate the various inventions of Daniell or their modifications.

1842 G. Francis *Dict. Arts*, etc., Daniell's Constant Galvanic Battery. 1872 Atkinson tr. *Ganot's Physics* 639 The current produced by a Daniell's battery is constant for some hours. 1873 F. Jenkin *Electr. & Magn.* xi. § 9 In the galvanic cell known as Daniell's cell, the electrodes are copper and zinc. 1878 *Encycl. Brit.* VIII. 114/2 A Daniell's cell consists, in its usual form, of a copper vessel containing a saturated solution of blue vitriol or sulphate of copper, in which is placed a porous cylinder containing dilute sulphuric acid. 1884 Higgs *Magn. & Dyn.-electr. Mach.* 233 If the instrument were always graduated with a Daniell cell. 1902 *Encycl. Brit.* XXVI. 735/1 In cells of the Daniell type.

Danish, *a.* Add: *Danish balance*: a form of balance consisting of a graduated beam with a weight at one end and a movable fulcrum which indicates by its position the weight of any object attached to the other end of the beam.

1837 Hebert *Engin. & Mech. Encycl.* I. 128.

Danite (dæ·nait). [f. *Dan*, the name of one of the sons of Jacob and of the tribe of Israel founded by him + -ite 1.] A member of an alleged secret order of Mormons supposed to have arisen in the early days of that sect to act as spies and suppressors of disaffection.

1857 *Congress. Globe* 24 Feb. App. 289/3 They suppose that there is a secret society existing there, called Danites, Shanpips, or Destroying Angels. *a* 1861 T. Winthrop *John Brent* xxix. 306 He might too have an undiscriminating senile terror of any letter going to America, lest it should set Danites upon his track. 1882 Waite *Adv. Far West* 252 The Danites are expected to act as spies upon the federal officers and other gentiles; to watch the feelings and spirits of the saints, and to report the first indications of disaffection. 1883 *Encycl. Brit.* XVI. 826/2 To counteract the efforts of his enemies, a secret society was organized in Smith's favour in October 1838, called the Danites, with the avowed purpose of supporting Smith at all hazards. 1905 *Daily Chron.* 22 June 3/1 The duties of the Danites, or 'avenging angels'.

Danization (dænizē^i·ʃən). [f. Dane: see -ization.] The act of making anything Danish, or making it conform to Danish fashion.

1918 C. G. Robertson *Bismarck* iv. 157 To Holstein incorporation with Denmark meant de-Germanisation and Danisation.

Dano- (dē^i·no), used as comb. form of *Danus* Dane, Danish, = 'Danish and', as *Dano-Irish*.

1880 *Encycl. Brit.* XIII. 252/2 The many feuds between the Irish clans in which the Dano-Irish shared. *Ibid.*, During the independence of the Dano-Irish kingdom of Dublin.

Dansant (daṅsaṅ), fem. **dansante** (daṅsaṅt), *a.* (*sb.*) [Fr., pr. pple. of *danser* to Dance.] Accompanied by dancing, as in *thé dansant* (erron. *-ante*), an afternoon entertainment at which there is dancing and tea is served; *soirée dansante*, an evening party with dancing.

1841 *Punch* 28 Aug. 83/2 The elegant *soirées dansantes*, nightly held at the 'Frog and Fiddle'. 1845 *Ibid.* 26 July 52/1 Among the fashionable parties of the season we have observed the frequent announcement of a *Thé Dansante*, or a dancing tea. 1849 Thackeray *Pendennis* vii, What did Lady Snapperton do..at her *déjeuné dansant* after the Bohemian ball? 1854 — *Newcomes* xiv, Mrs. Toddle Tompkyns's *soirée dansante* in Belgrave Square. 1858 *Punch* 29 May 214/1 Two medical students..got up an impromptu *Thé Dansante*. 1872 E. Braddon *Life in India* v. 151 The projection of balls and parties *dansantes*.

b. *sb.* = *thé dansant*.

1921 *Glasgow Herald* 17 Nov. 5 It must not be confused with the tea frock that owes its origin to the *dansant*.

Danter (da·ntəɹ). *local.* A female superintendent of a silk-throwing department.

1867 Simmonds *Dict. Trade* Suppl., *Danter*, a person engaged in silk-throwing operations. 1877 E. Leigh *Cheshire Gloss.* 1881 *Instr. Census Clerks* (1885) 67. 1921 *Dict. Occup. Terms* (1927) § 355.

Dantonist (dæ·ntŏnist). [f. the name of *Danton* + -ist.] A follower of Georges Jacques Danton (1759–94), one of the leaders in the French revolution. So **Dantonesque** *a.*, resembling the style of Danton; **Danto·nian** *a.*, of or pertaining to Danton (*Dicts.*).

1879 *Encycl. Brit.* IX. 606/2 Two parties..the *Exagérés*, or Hebertists..and the Modérés, the Dantonists. 1899 A. H. Beesly *Danton* 316 The indictment against the Dantonists. 1901 *Daily Chron.* 31 Dec. 3/1 He who had corrected the proofs of the Dantonist appeal for mercy. 1924 *Contemp. Rev.* Apr. 420 He can cut a knot with a phrase of Dantonesque audacity. 1928 *Sunday Express* 10 June 10/5 Camille Desmoulins was one of..the Dantonists.

Dan(t)zig (dæ·nzig, -tsig). Name of a city near the mouth of the Vistula and of the district containing that city, used *attrib.* chiefly to designate kinds of timber grown in that district, as *Dantzig deal, fir, oak.* **Dantzig beer,** a black syrupy beer made at Dantzig. **Dantzig spruce,** beer made by adding a decoction of the buds or cones of spruce.

1855 Ogilvie Suppl., Black-beer, or Dantzic. 1862 *Chambers's Encycl.* IV. 334/2 It [*sc.* the Norway spruce fir] is the ..Danzig Deal of the market. 1871 S. T. Aveling *Carpentry & Joinery* 9 The weight of a cubic foot of English oak generally considered seasoned is about 50 lb...Of Dantzic oak about 48. 1879 *Encycl. Brit.* IX. 223/2 The well-known 'Danzig-spruce' is prepared by adding a decoction of the buds or cones to the wort or saccharine liquor before fermentation. 1889 Welch *Text-Bk. Naval Archit.* 111 The wood employed [for decks] is generally Dantzic fir.

Danubian (dāniū·biăn), *a.* [f. med.L. *Danubius, Danuvius,* Gr. Δανούβιος: see -ian.] Of or pertaining to, bordering on, the river Danube.

Danubian corn, Indian corn grown in south-eastern Europe for chicken food. *Danubian reed*, the giant reed *Arundo donax*, cultivated in Australia.

1854 *Punch* 6 May 191/1 The aggression of Russia upon the Danubian Principalities. 1864 *Chambers's Encycl.* VI. 511/2 Moldavia and Walachia,..forming the so-called Danubian Principalities. 1875 *Encycl. Brit.* II. 700/1 The Danubian provinces. 1878 Gladstone *Sp. Berlin Treaty* 27 The union of the Danubian Principalities. 1911 Webster, Danubian reed. 1927 Peake & Fleure *Priests & Kings* 138 Their civilization, which in many respects resembled that of Thessaly, is known as Danubian.

Dao (dā·o). Also dhao; *Dah, *Dha. [Native name.] = *Dah.

1876 Voyle & Stevenson *Milit. Dict.* (ed. 3), *Dhao*, a Burman tool or weapon (half chopper, half sword) used in clearing jungle and in cutting down trees. 1884 *Encycl. Brit.* XVII. 163/2 The only implements of tillage being the *dáo* or hill knife, and a *koddli* or hoe. 1923 *Blackw. Mag.* May 569/2 They..are armed with..spear and *dao*.

Dapicho (dæ·pitʃo). Also dapico. [Cf. Guarani *tapicha.*] A South American name for the caoutchouc obtained from various species of *Hevea*.

1864 Watts *Dict. Chem.* II. 305 *Dapicho* or *Zapis*,..the dirty-white spongy caoutchouc which exudes from the roots of *Siphonia elastica*. 1880 *Encycl. Brit.* XII. 837/1 Rubber is obtained..in Venezuela from *Hevea brasiliensis*, there called dápi or dápiche.

Dapping (dæ·piŋ), *vbl. sb.* [f. Dap *v.* + -ing 1.] Fishing by a method in which the bait is allowed to dip or bob lightly on the water. So **Da·pper,** one who daps. **Dap** *sb.*, the bait used in dapping.

1799, 1867 [see s.v. Dap *v.*]. 1908 *Westm. Gaz.* 13 June 11/3 Heavy trout being captured with the natural insect on 'dapping' tackle. 1920 *Glasgow Herald* 17 July 4 A position from which he can lower his 'dap' on to the water without drawing the fishes' attention. *Ibid.*, The floating imitation of the dry-fly fisher or the dapper's living lure. 1928 *Daily Express* 28 July 4/6 The patient 'dapper', who thrusts his rod between the branches of over-hanging foliage and dangles a blue-bottle temptingly at the extremity of a 3x cast.

Dapple, *sb.* 2. (Later U.S. examples.)

1868 Lowell *Lett.* (1894) I. 404, I should like to lie under a tree for a year with no other industry than to watch the dapples of sunlight on the grass. 1878 B. F. Taylor *Between Gates* 262 The green turf..invited you to sit down on the dapple of a shadow every few minutes.

Dapple-grey. b. *absol.* (Modern U.S. example.)

1858 Teresa Viele *Following the Drum* 35 The term 'Vermont horses' was soon after our arrival most potently realized in the possession of a pair of dapple greys.

Dard (dārd), *sb.* and *a.* Of or pertaining to, a member of, any of various Turko-Iranian tribes of Dardistan, in northwest India.

1879 *Encycl. Brit.* (ed. 9) X. 598/1 The Dards are described as decidedly Aryan in features. 1902 *Ibid.* (ed. 10) XXVIII. 729/2 Eleven different languages, which have all been usually classed together under the name Dard. 1920 *Blackw. Mag.* May 620/1 The 'Indians' to whom Herodotus refers are none other than the Dards. *Ibid.*, In Ladakh to this day we find pure Dard settlements.

Dare, *sb.*1 1. (Earlier modern U.S. example.)

1876 'Mark Twain' *Tom Sawyer* i. 8, I dare you to knock it off and anybody that 'll take a dare will suck eggs.

2. (Modern U.S. example.)

a 1904 H. R. Martin *Tillie* 13, I would love to play in the evening if I had the dare.

Dare, *v.*1 B. 5. (Later U.S. example.)

1886 *Harper's Mag.* Dec. 105/2 Jabe Pennell begun to hunt him an' dare him.

Dariole. Add:

2. A savoury of various kinds, esp. one of which the main ingredients are flour, butter, milk, and eggs, baked or steamed in a *dariole mould*. b. A dariole mould.

1846 Soyer *Cookery* 507 Darioles. Line (very thinly) a dozen small dariole moulds with paste. 1892 *Encycl. Pract. Cookery* (ed. T. F. Garrett) I. 575/1. 1893 *Mrs. Beeton's Cookery Book* § 768 Oyster darioles. 1895 *Army & Navy Co-op. Soc. Price List* 15 Sept. 308 Dariols, Plain. Do. Fluted. 1901 *Daily Chron.* 23 Nov. 8/4 Line some dariole moulds thinly with tomato aspic...Set a dariole on each slice of tomato. 1903 *Ibid.* 21 Mar. 8/5 Darioles à la Maraschino. 1930 *Daily Mail* 6 June 15/3 Dariole of salmon is made with flaked cooked salmon, set in a mould with aspic jelly, sliced hard-boiled eggs, and shrimps.

Dark, *sb.* 1. *Dark of the moon* (later U.S. examples).

1871 Eggleston *Hoosier Schoolm.* x. 87 But it must be rendered in the dark of the moon. 1889 Farmer *Americanisms* 193 *Dark Moon* or *Dark of the Moon*, the period between the moon's change from 'full' to 'new'. Also provincial in England.

Dark, *a.* Add: 3. d. Of blood or race.

1895 Paston *Study in Prej.* ii, There is dark blood in us ..; our great grandmother was a beautiful half caste.

13. c. **dark and bloody ground** *U.S.*, the state of Kentucky; **dark-arches,** a British noctuid moth of the genus *Xylophasia* (see *Arch *sb.* 7); **dark-line** *a.*, of or pertaining to the dark lines in a spectrum due to the selective absorption of light of certain wave-lengths; **dark space,** one or other of two non-luminous regions (the *Cathode or *Crookes or *first dark space* and the *Faraday or *second dark space*) in a vacuum tube traversed by an electric discharge; also *dark discharge*.

[1777 *Cal. Virginia St. Papers* I. 283 When the said Henderson & Co., proposed purchasing the lands below the Kentucky, the Dragging Canoe told them it was the bloody Ground, and would be dark, and difficult to settle it.] 1832 Paulding *Westward Ho!* I. i. 8 This smiling, fruitful region ..still retains..the ominous, melancholy appellation of 'The *Dark and Bloody Ground'. 1835 C. F. Hoffman *Winter West* II. 138 We crossed the stream near 'Bryant's Station', one of the most celebrated spots in the annals of 'The Dark and Bloody Ground'. 1888 *St. Louis Daily Globe Democrat* (Farmer) The McCoy and Hatfield feud shows that Kentucky will not willingly surrender its designation of the dark and bloody ground. 1832 J. Rennie *Butterfl. & Moths* 65 The *Dark Arches..appears the end of June and beginning of July. 1878 *Encycl. Brit.* VIII. 64/1 The *dark spaces that sometimes appear in the spark in gas at the atmospheric pressure...When the discharge takes place in highly rarefied gas, a dark space of this kind almost always separates the positive from the negative light...Pending further investigation, Faraday called it the *dark discharge. 1928 W. M. Smart *Sun, Stars & Universe* vi. 83 Certain groups of lines which are known to belong to the arc spectra of the elements concerned..together with their *dark-line counterparts in the solar spectrum. 1881 S. P. Thompson *Elem. Less. Electr. & Magn.* II. iv. (1899) 307 The kathode exhibits a beautiful bluish or violet glow, separated from the conductor by a narrow *dark space. 1902 *Encycl. Brit.* XXVIII. 47/2 Next after the negative glow comes a second comparatively non-luminous space,..called by some writers the 'second negative dark space', and by others the 'Faraday dark space'.

Darkfall (dā·ɹkfǫl). [f. Dark *sb.* + Fall *sb.*1] The coming on of dark; dusk, nightfall.

1897 'O. Rhoscomyl' *White Rose Arno* 292, I can have fifteen of them here by darkfall.

Da·rkling, *sb.*2 [subst. use of Darkling *a.*] = Dark *sb.* 1, 1 b.

1903 *Westm. Gaz.* 13 Jan. 2/3 At darkling of the moon. 1909 H. G. Wells *Tono-Bungay* iv. i. 343 She carried some rugs for me through the shrubbery in the darkling.

Darling, *a.* Add: c. Sweetly pretty or charming, 'sweet'. *affected.*

1854 *Punch* Mar. 116 Isn't it the darlingest, sweetest, prettiest, little dear darling darling! Oh! did you ever!! 1906 *Ibid.* 21 Mar. 215/1 You have a darling little note-book ..to match your frock. 1908 Beatrice Harraden *Interplay* 373 It is perfectly darling of you to have chosen Hughie.

Darling2. The name of a river in Australia used *attrib.* in the names of certain plants growing in its neighbourhood; also **Darling shower,** a local name for a dust-storm.

1898 Morris *Austral Engl.*, *Darling Shower*, a local name in the interior of Australia, and especially on the River Darling, for a dust storm, caused by cyclonic winds. 1899 *Westm. Gaz.* 20 Feb. 10/1 The Riverina breeds a particularly distressful variety of dust-storm known as 'Darling showers'.

Darmoor, darmur (dā·ɹmuəɹ). A coarse cotton fabric, such as is sometimes used in America for salt-sacks.

1866 S. W. Baker *Albert N'yanza* II. vi. 242 Ibrahim.. bought me a piece of coarse cotton cloth of Arab manufacture (darmoor) for clothes for myself.

Darn, *sb.*2 *U.S.* [Cf. next.] *By darn*, used as a form of asseveration. Also *not to care a darn*.

1840 C. F. Hoffman *Greyslaer* II. iv. 206 But, by darn, the capting's cleared out without speaking to one..but ourselves. 1854 Mary J. Holmes *Tempest & Sunshine* xxiv. 330, I don't care a darn how many Miss Betsy's I git. 1890 Marah E. Ryan *Told in Hills* 92, I don't care a darn about the sheep just now.

Darn, *adv.* and *a. U.S.* [Possibly identical with *darn*, var. of Dern *a.* See G. P. Krapp *Engl. Lang. in Amer.* I. 118–126.]

A. *adv.* Extremely, intensely.

1789 Webster *Diss. Engl. Lang.* 385 The word (*dern*) is in common use in New England and pronounced *darn*. It has not, however, the sense it had formerly; it is now used as an adverb to qualify an adjective, as *darn sweet*; denoting a great degree of the quality. 1797 D. Mackintosh *Rational Ess. Engl. Gram.* 82 We say, dea'rn or da'rn, heark'en, heart', hearth'. 1869 Barnum *Struggles & Triumphs* (1871) 146 Darn glad to see you, by hokey; I came down here to have lots of fun. 1892 *Century Mag.* June 264 It was a darn good churn too.

B. *adj.* 'Blessed', 'confounded'. Also *absol.*

1840 C. F. Hoffman *Greyslaer* III. iv. 141 'Jim, you've done the darn thing agin us to-night, and no mistake' said one. 1899 Susan Hale *Lett.* 348 You know they are all here improving their minds, learning some darn thing or other. *c* 1904 H. R. Martin *Tillie* 40 To fill out blanks answerin' to a lot of darn-fool questions 'bout one thing and 'nother. 1924 A. J. Small *Frozen Gold* iii. 87 I'm doing my darnest to drive you out of Cedar Falls.

Darn, *v.*1 Add: c. *transf.* To mend (a hole in a wall, road, etc.) by filling-in.

1801 W. Beattie *Fruits of Time Parings* (1873) 24 (E.D.D.) He staps wi' strae ilk navus bore, And ilka crevice darns. 1850 'H. Hieover' *Pract. Horsemanship* 146 There is a mode of keeping our present roads in order, that I have heard termed 'darning' them; i.e. if a part is seen somewhat lower than the surface, the unbroken pieces of granite are got up to it, and there left to be crushed by the wheels of carriages.

2. To ornament or embroider with the darning stitch.

1882 [see s.v. *Darning *vbl. sb.* 3]. 1900 L. F. Day *Art in Needlework* 108 The flower stalk is defined by darning the first row in a darker colour. *Ibid.*, The background is darned diaper fashion.

Darn, *v.*2 (= 'confound'. Earlier U.S. examples.)

1809 A. B. Lindsley *Love & Friendship* 8 Darn my skin 'f you wouldn't dewe it. 1825 Paulding *J. Bull in Amer.* iii. 36 If I don't have him before the justice, darn my soul. 1830 [H. H. Porter] *Betrothed of Wyoming* x. 135 His ideas took another turn and he exclaimed 'Darn them, what do I care for them!'

Darnation, darnationed. (Examples.)

1839 *Lex. Observer & Rep.* 10 Apr., Sal. don't be so darnation skitterish. 1840 *Daily Pennant* (St. Louis) 9 May (Thornton, s.v. *Chip*) It wouldn't take so much..to make it a darnation sight riz-er. 1878 Mrs. Stowe *Poganuc People* iii. 33 If I didn't hold on to him he'd have us all to the darnation in five minutes.

Darned, *ppl. a.*1 Add: 2. Formed, made, or ornamented with the darning-stitch.

1882 Caulfeild & Saward *Dict. Needlework* 145/2 The Darned Embroidery most practised in Europe has been chiefly worked upon cotton. 1909 *Westm. Gaz.* 27 Feb. 15/2 The theatre or afternoon dress is of darned filet over satin or cashmere. *Ibid.* 7 Aug. 15/1 Darned net, such as was worn about 1830, or even earlier, looks very well.

Darned, *pa. pple., ppl. a.*2, and *adv.* (Early U.S. examples.)

(*a*) 1808 J. N. Barker *Tears & Smiles* 18 I'll be darned, sir, if I think this is the way. *c* 1815 Paulding *Bucktails* II. ii. (1847) 33 I'll be darned but I guess I've lost my way.

(*b*) *c* 1815 Paulding *Bucktails* III. i. (1847) 43 Serving a man don't make him my master, by a darn'd sight. 1834 C. A. Davis *Lett. J. Downing* 41 'What'..'do you want another report?' 'Not by a darn'd sight', says he. 1890 Marah E. Ryan *Told in Hills* 123 She..was 'the darndest, cutest, little customer he ever saw'. 1904 W. H. Smith *Promoters* xviii. 269 Darndest fellow to take things up that way.

absol. 1916 H. L. Wilson *Somewhere in Red Gap* ii. 71 How little we think when we had ought to be thinking our darndest!

(*c*) 1806 L. Beach *Jonathan Post Free* 23 Drove down old Squire Herdy's cattle—darn'd ugly creatures to drive. 1822 Woodworth *Deed of Gift* 45, I have taken a liking to you, 'cause you are so darn'd pretty. 1888 *Harper's Mag.* July 323/2 In Colorado the man who tells the first story has a darned poor show.

Darner. Add: 2. b. A darning-machine.

1876 J. S. Ingram *Centenn. Exposition* x. 346 The Complete Darner. *Ibid.* 347 The top..could be removed for the insertion of a ball of darning-cotton into the swell of the 'darner'.

c. A darning-ball or similar device.

1909 *Daily Chron.* 25 May 9/1 Even the embroiderer who does not use a hoop will find it more convenient in working stockings to do the embroidery over a darner.

Darning, *vbl. sb.* Add: 1. c. Embroidering with the darning-stitch; also = darning-stitch.

1882 Caulfeild & Saward *Dict. Needlework* 148/1 The embroidery is done in Satin stitch or in plain Darning.

3. *darning-cotton* (see *Darner 2 b); **darning-egg** = *darning-ball*; **darning-machine,** a machine for darning hose or clothes (Knight *Dict. Mech.* Suppl. 1884); **darning-needle** (see also Devil *sb.* 25 b); **darning-stitch,** (*b*) a straight stitch used in embroidery to make a regular open-work pattern.

1925 Ellen Glasgow *Barren Ground* III. ii. 410 Dorinda ..slipped her *darning-egg into one of Nathan's socks. 1882 Caulfeild & Saward *Dict. Needlework* 148/2 Fillings for the centre of any designs that are not worked in Satin or *Darning stitch. *Ibid.* 149/1 Darn the thick lines up and down in Point de Reprise or plain Darning stitch.

Daroo-tree. The Egyptian sycamore, *Ficus Sycomorus*.

1814 H. Salt *Voy. Abyssinia* 229 Here we encamped, close to two daro trees.

Dart, *sb.* Add:

1. d. A light pointed missile thrown at a target in the indoor game called *darts*.

1901 *Stationer, Printer*, etc. 1 June 322 Ring Boards. Dart Boards. Parlour Cricket. 1916 H. G. Wells *Mr. Britling* I. v. § 11 Dart-throwing and ring-throwing stalls. 1924 B. Gilbert *Bly Market* 18 Coconut Saloons. Shooting Galleries. Dart-Saloons. *Ibid.* 419 Darts, darts, darts, penny a dart. Over 50 wins the prize...No skill needed. 1929 *B'ham Post* 12 Jan., A peculiar thing I noticed was that two darts, such as they use in public-houses, were near the body.

6. c. The name of a type of aeroplane, used for attacking warships.

1925 Fraser & Gibbons *Soldier & Sailor Words & Phrases, Darts*, a device used in the earlier part of the War for attacking troops from an aeroplane...Also, the name of a type of small, very fast aeroplane, intended for attacking warships by diving down at high speed and dropping a torpedo when at close range and just clear of the water. 1928 *Times* 23 Mar. 19/2 We saw three of her [*sc.* The Eagle, aircraft-carrier's] 'Dart' machines appear as specks in the blue, to dive and to attack the Furious with torpedoes.

7. b. (One's) fancy or favourite. *Austral.*

1895 in Morris *Austral Engl.* (1898) 115 'Fresh strawberries eh!—that's my dart', says the bushman when he sees the fruit lunch in Collins-street.

Darter. 5. (Earlier U.S. example.)

1881 *Amer. Naturalist* XV. 147 The author gives the results of a large series of examinations of the stomachs of darters, perches, bass, and sunfishes.

Dartmoor (dā·ɹtmūəɹ, -mōəɹ). A district in Devonshire, from which the convict prison near Princetown is named, and which produces special breeds of ponies and sheep (named from it).

1831 Youatt *Horse* iv. 59 The Dartmoor pony is larger than the Exmoor, and, if possible, uglier. 1837 — *Sheep* vii. 252 The South Downs never succeeded well on the heath-clad hills of the Dartmoor sheep. 1902 *Encycl. Brit.* XXV. 189/2 Native ponies include those variously known as English, New Forest, Exmoor, Dartmoor. *Ibid.* 194/2 The Dartmoor is a hornless, longwool, white-fleeced sheep. 1906 *Westm. Gaz.* 24 Sept. 8/1 An intelligent Dartmoor, that would follow its master like a dog.

Dartwood. [Dart *sb.*] A small West Indian rubiaceous tree, *Chomelia fasciculata*, used for darts.

1909 *Cent. Dict.* Suppl.

Darwinian, *a.* Add:

3. **Darwinian curvature,** curvature convex on the side to which the stimulus is applied, induced in the tip of a root by mechanical irritation; **Darwinian tubercle,** a projection sometimes present on the edge of the human external ear believed by some scientists to be a relic of the pointed ear of quadrupeds; also called *Darwin's point, process, tip, tubercle*.

1885 *Encycl. Brit.* XIX. 60/2 It has been shown that the mere presence of the drop of shellac is sufficient to induce the Darwinian curvature, and microscopical examination has proved that the part touched by the shellac had died away. 1890 Billings *Med. Dict.*, *Darwinian tubercle*.., eminence on edge of helix of external ear, believed to correspond with end of pointed ear of apes, and therefore considered a vestige.

Dash, *sb.*1 Add:

7. c. Sometimes implying the use of strong language; hence as a mild substitute for *devil*.

1898 A. Nicholas *Idyl of Wabash* 64 A dreadful thought which if put in print would have contained a dash. 1903 Lord R. Gower *Rec. & Remin.* 312 Who the Dash is this person, and what the Dash does he here?

f. One of the two signals (the other being the dot) which in various combinations make up the Morse alphabet. Also *dash-and-dot*, more usually *dot-and-dash*, q.v. s.v. Dot *sb.*1 8.

1859 Shaffner *Telegr. Man.* 469 Whether the dots, spaces, and dashes be long or short, they should be uniform. 1873 F. Jenkin *Electr. & Magn.* xxii. § 4 Morse signals are sent by a simple key...A short depression or mere tap sends the short elementary signal technically called a *dot*; a longer depression sends the second elementary signal technically called a *dash*. 1883 Ogilvie Suppl., *Dash-and-dot*, consisting of dashes and dots; as, the dash-and-dot alphabet.

12. (Later U.S. example.)

1911 J. C. Lincoln *Cap'n Warren's Wards* ii. 15 He says the buggy dash is pretty well scratched up.

b. Now esp. in motor vehicles.

1906 *Daily Chron.* 14 Nov. 9/3 The coil and commutator, being fixed on the dash, are always in front of the driver. 1907 *Westm. Gaz.* 18 Nov. 7/2 The 35-h.p. open side-entrance phaeton..is particularly attractive with its aluminium dash. 1919 *Autocar Handbk.* (ed. 9) 253 A second lamp placed somewhere on the dash. 1929 *Daily Express* 10 Jan. 3/1 The car is fitted with electrical devices with lights on the dashfront to keep the driver informed when anything goes wrong with the lubrication or the ignition.

Dash, *v.*1 Add: 16. b. **dash-piston, -plate** (see quots.); **dash-pot,** esp. in an arc-lamp.

1888 *Lockwood's Dict. Mech. Engin.*, *Dash Piston, the piston sliding in the dash pot of a Corliss engine, whose release by a spring closes the steam or exhaust valves, and whose concussion is deadened by the springs or buffers enclosed in the dash pot. *Ibid.*, *Dash Plates or *Division Plates*, plates sometimes fixed in a marine boiler in line with, and over, the tubes, in order to prevent the crown plates of the fire-box from being exposed to the action of the flame when the ship heels over heavily. 1878 in *J. Dredge's Electr. Illum.* (1885) II. App. p. lxiv, The arm of the lever may be at right angles to the carbon, one end being weighted and the other attached to the core of a solenoid; the core may have a *dash-pot action. 1879 *Ibid.* p. lxxxvii, The lamp is adjusted so that the magnets shall carry a definite load, and to insure a steady motion a dash-pot, having the cylinder movable and the plunger fixed, is employed. 1902 *Encycl. Brit.* XXVIII. 86/1 The arc-lamp mechanism is provided with a dash-pot, or contrivance in which a piston moving nearly air-tight in a cylinder prevents sudden jerks in the motion of the mechanism.

Dash-board. 1. Add: Also in motor vehicles, the partition between the engine and front seat (cf. *Dash *sb.*1 12 b).

1904 A. B. F. Young *Compl. Motorist* iv. 114 A cooling apparatus has now been fitted behind the bonnet and in front of the dashboard. 1925 Warwick Deeping *Sorrell & Son* v. § 1 Sorrell remained by the car. He liked the colour of it, and the compact brightness of the dash-board.

Dashed, *ppl. a.* 3. Also *advb.*, deucedly, confoundedly.

1893 W. S. Gilbert *Utopia* II, How utterly dashed absurd.

Dasheen (dæʃī·n). Also dashen. [ad. F. *de Chine* of China.] An araceous tropical food-plant, having a farinaceous root that may be cooked like the potato; the Trinidad potato.

1913 W. H. Page in *Life* (1922) I. 128 I'm going to grow dasheens.

Dasher. 2. (Earlier U.S. examples.)

1846 *Rep. U.S. Comm. Patents* (1847) 233 What I claim as my invention..is the combination of the vertical dasher with the oscillating dashers. 1848 in Drake *Pion. Life Kentucky* v. 93 The latter stages of the process [*sc.* of churning], when the butter rises on the dasher.

Dassie vanger (dæ·si væ·ŋgəɹ). *S. Afr.* [= Du. *dasje* Dassy + *vanger* catcher.] The black eagle, *Helotarsus ecaudatus*.

1889 Bryden *Kloof & Karroo* 273 A great black mountain eagle. We know him at once for a berghaan (cock of the mountain), or dassie-vanger (coney-eater). 1893 Newton *Dict. Birds* 132.

Dastoor, -ur, -i: see Dustoor, -y.

1909 Maud Diver *Candles in Wind* i, Is the *subbardusti* gentleman up there a toll-gate keeper that we should offer him *dasturi*? *Ibid.* viii, It was *dastur*; and there was no more to be said. 1926 *Blackw. Mag.* June 756/1 It was his custom—*dastur*—respected by his people and the British Resident.

Dasylirion (dæsili·riǫn). [mod.L., f. Gr. δασύς thick + λείριον lily.] A Mexican plant of the liliaceous genus of this name, having ornamental foliage, cultivated as a greenhouse evergreen plant.

1880 *Encycl. Brit.* XII. 262/1 The Dasylirions have stout woody stems and large heads of narrow leaves.

Dasypeltis (dæsipe·ltis). [mod.L., f. Gr. δασύς thick + πέλτη small shield.] A small harmless egg-eating snake of the genus of this name found in central and south Africa. Hence **Dasype·ltid, -oid** *adjs.* and *sbs.*

1887 *Encycl. Brit.* XXII. 194/2 A very peculiar genus of snakes, Dasypeltis, represented by three species only, is the type of a separate family. 1927 Haldane & Huxley *Anim. Biol.* xi. 223 The egg-eating snake, Dasypeltis.

Datal, *a.* Delete *rare* and add: b. Containing or including the date (as of a charter).

1837 T. D. Hardy *Rot. Chart.* Pref. 31 The Datal clause in Anglo-Saxon charters generally..precedes the names of the witnesses. *Ibid.* 34 William the Conqueror..also commemorated historical occurrences in his datal clauses. 1858 *Topographer & Genealogist* III. 120 Same seal and datal clause.

Datcha (dæ·tʃă). Pl. **datche.** [Russ.] A Russian country-house.

1896 *Edin. Rev.* Jan. 83 Russian officials run down to their *datchas*, or country houses. 1905 *Westm. Gaz.* 18 Aug. 8/1 Everyone who can leaves the town during the hot weather —the rich for their estates and the rank and file for *datcha* life in the country round. 1905 *Daily Chron.* 9 Sept. 4/5, I was privileged to visit one of these datche and to dine with the family.

Date, *sb.*1 4. Add: **date-fish** *U.S.*, a date-shell or piddock.

1838 *Knickerbocker Mag.* XI. 446 Each separate raisin therein embedded, bearing much resemblance to the date-fish in his rock. 1884 Goode *Nat. Hist. Aquatic Anim.* 707 Some cousins (*Zirphæa crispata, Platydon cancellatus*, etc.) are esteemed delicacies on the coast of California under the name of 'Date-fish'.

Date, *sb.*2 Add: 2. c. An engagement or appointment at a particular time; esp. in *to have* (*got*), *to make a date. U.S. colloq.*

1896 G. Ade *Artie* vii. 65, I s'pose the other boy's fillin all my dates? 1902 J. M. Forman *Journey's End* iii. 42, I must be going on. I've a date to keep. 1906 'O. Henry' *Four Million* 176, I made a date for dinner this evening. 1913 J. L. Vance *Baroque* xv. 93, 'll give you a ring, and make a date. 1928 M. Baring *Comfortless Mem.* iii, Mr. Donne can't come; he's got a date.

7. *To date*: to the present time or moment. Cf. Up to date (1868–).

8. **date-box,** an apparatus for indicating the date; usually a box containing rollers which can be turned by handles at the side, so as to show through openings in the front the letters and figures denoting the month and day; **date-cancel** *v.*, to cancel by a written or stamped date; **date-stamp,** a stamp with adjustable types, used in recording the date of posting or delivery of a letter or parcel, receipting a bill, receiving a book, and the like.

1929–30 *Unemployment Book* 2 *Date-cancel stamps immediately. 1909 *Daily Chron.* 2 July 5/3 Mr. Buxton has undertaken that the *date-stamps shall not in future bear the name of the firms.

Date, *v.* Add: 2. Also *colloq.* in *pass.* To have its date fixed by some circumstance. Hence *intr.* To bear evidence of its or one's date or period, to betray its or one's date by the style or manner.

1895 *Westm. Gaz.* 13 Mar. 5/1 Every portion of a picture was 'dated' from every other portion of it. 1901 *Daily Chron.* 17 May 6/6 In the four or five years it has been laid aside it [*sc.* a play] has not 'dated' in the slightest degree. 1915 H. G. Wells *Research Magnificent* Prelude 9 He had found the word 'Bushido' written with a particularly flourishing capital letter, and twice repeated. 'This was inevitable', said White...'And it dates..Yes—this was early'. 1925 *Sat. Rev.* 7 Nov. 1 Younger men say with contemptuous brevity that his views 'date'. 1927 *N. & Q.* CLIII. 269 This kind of gibe is at the time..immensely diverting; but it does not sustain itself well in cold print.. for it is the misfortune of flippancy to 'date'. 1927 *Mus. Assoc. Proc.* 1926–7 47 A recent revival showed that the work had 'dated' a little, as the phrase goes. 1928 Galsworthy *Swan Song* III. xvi. 341, 'I respected old Forsyte' he said to his son..' He dated, and he couldn't express himself, but there was no humbug about him.'

Dateless, *a.* Add: 1. b. Free from engagements or appointments. *U.S.*

1923 *N. Y. Tribune* 25 Apr., The young men at Northwestern University have agreed to join the young women of that institution in observing three dateless nights each week.

Dato (dā·to). Also datoo, datto, datoh. [Malay داتق *dātoq* grandfather, title of respect or distinction.] A landowner or chief in the Philippine Islands, Sulu, and other Malayan countries.

1867 Smyth *Sailor's Word-bk.*, *Datoo*,..a Malay term of rank, and four of whom form the council of the sultan of the Malayu Islands. 1897 *Geogr. Jrnl.* (R.G.S.) Jan. 36 The Galas district is nominally under the charge of the Dato. [1902 *Encycl. Brit.* XXIX. 754 [Sultan Abubakar's] principal adviser, the Dâto' Mêntri.] 1925 *Chambers's Jrnl.* 46/1 The Malay point of view was well expressed by a certain *Datoh*, or landowner of good birth.

Daub, *sb.* 5. Add: *daub-boy, -grinder, -mixer* (Dict. Occup. Terms, 1921).

Daughter. Add:

1. b. The female offspring of an animal or plant.

1887 W. S. Blunt *Land War in Ireland* (1912) 218 The Sheykh..showed us a filly he had, the daughter of one of Ali Sherif's horses.

c. Used in pl. in the names of various women's societies, as *Daughters of the American Revolution* (1890), *of the Confederacy* (1894), etc. Also *sing.*, a member of one or other of these societies. *U.S.*

1911 R. D. Saunders *Col. Todhunter* i. 4 Working the Daughters of the Confederacy as a political proposition. *Ibid.* 7 Mrs. Todhunter, an ardent Daughter had gone early in the day.

7. *daughter-land, -nation.*

1901 *National Rev.* Nov. 347 The conduct of these daughter nations during our South African struggle. 1903 *Westm. Gaz.* 3 June 9/3 Everyone was too busy talking about their grand Imperial theories, and the duties of the mother-country, to bother about the dull little domestic facts that are worrying the daughter-land. 1905 *Spectator* 11 Feb. 205/1 The great self-governing daughter-nations.

b. *Biol.*, etc. Applied to things having the relation of offspring of the first generation, or resulting from a primary division or segmentation.

1876 *Trans. Clinical Soc.* IX. 137, I cut down upon the tumour so as freely to expose it, and then punctured it, when a quantity of clear water escaped, and with it two or three small daughter cysts. 1901 Dorland *Med. Dict.* (ed. 2) s.v. *Cyst, Daughter cyst*, a small cyst developed from the wall of a larger one. 1924 J. A. Thomson *Science Old & New* xliv. 257 A non-cellular organism multiplies by division, budding and spore-forming, and its daughter-units separate off.

Daulian (dǭ·liăn), *a.* [f. mod.L. *Daulias* used as the generic name of the nightingale (*D. luscinia*), a. Gr. Δαυλιάς lit. woman of Daulis, Procne, who was changed into a nightingale.] *Daulian bird*, an affected appellation of the nightingale.

1894 *Daily News* 22 Jan. 5/1 That tiny modest tome [*sc.* Keats's Poems of 1817], a brown Daulian bird in brown paper. 1904 *Westm. Gaz.* 9 June 12/1 Until three years ago the existence of the Daulian birds in Devonshire was strenuously denied. 1909 *Ibid.* 12 May 5/1 Londoners who want to hear the Daulian birds with complete certainty must now journey to Kew or Chingford.

Dauncy (dǭ·nsi), *a. U.S.* (and *dial.*). [var. of Donsy *a.*] Sickly; delicate, not robust.

1846 E. W. Farnham *Life in Prairie Land* iv. (1855) 39, I shall give her enough to eat and wear, and I dont calculate she'll be very dauncy if she gets that. 1874 Eggleston *Circuit Rider* vi. 61 You look powerful dauncy, said the old man. 1880 *Antrim & Down Gloss.* 31 *Donsy, Dauncey*, sick, sick-looking. 1892 Marah E. Ryan *Pagan of Alleghanies* v. 82 He ain't one o' yer skim-milk, dauncy ones. His is stout as a young bull.

Davidic (dēⁱvi·dik), *a.* [f. personal name *David* + -ic.] Of or pertaining to David as king of Israel, or as the reputed author of the Psalms. Also **Davi·dical** *a.*

1827 Coleridge *Table-t.* 10 Mar., I apprehend many of the Psalms to be Davidical only, not David's own compositions. 1865 *Chambers's Encycl.* VII. 819/1 The first [book]..contains the Davidic Jehovistic psalms. 1877 *Encycl. Brit.* VI. 841/2 We cannot well stop short of the admission that the Psalter must contain Davidic psalms. 1883 *Ibid.* XVI. 54/1 Amos foretold the redintegration of the Davidic kingdom. 1918 E. Grubb *Relig. Experience* 186 The glories of the ancient Davidic monarchy.

Daviesite (dē^i·vizait). *Min.* [f. the name of Thomas *Davies*, mineralogist (1837–91), of the British Museum: see -ite 1.] A colourless oxychloride of lead occurring in prismatic crystals.

1889 *Min. Mag.* May 171 Crystals of..an Oxychloride of Lead (Daviesite), from Mina Beatriz, Sierra Gorda, Atacama, South America.

Daw (dǭ), *a.* [Of obscure origin; Ir., Gael. *dath* 'colour' has been suggested.] Of a pale primrose colour, as the eyes of certain game fowl.

1856 Roscoe in Tegetmeier *Poultry Bk.* 100 Black-breasted reds..have a fine long head; daw eyes. 1856 Tegetmeier *Ibid.*, The required 'daw eye'..is that which resembles the gray eye of a jackdaw. 1872 L. Wright *Bk. Poultry* 277 There never was a Malay with red eyes; they are invariably pearl, yellow, or daw. 1913 W. Bateson *Mendel's Princ. Heredity* 110 Malay fowls are peculiar in having a pale, yellowish white iris—the 'daw-eye' of fanciers.

Dawk, *sb.*2 b. Add: *dawk-* or *dâk-bag, boat*; **dawk-** or **dâk-wallah,** a letter-carrier.

1828 *Asiatic Costumes* 40 The dauk-wala is dispatched from the post-office every day with his bundle of letters. 1872 E. Braddon *Life in India* vii. 260 The arrival at any village of the *dâk-walla* (letter-carrier) with a letter is an event to be remembered and talked of. 1923 *Blackw. Mag.* Nov. 678/2 My old *dâk-wallah*..had scented the battle from afar. 1926 *Ibid.* Nov. 587/1 An 'Urgent' dak bag arrived from the Agency with a letter from Baird. 1928 *Ibid.* Jan. 5/2 The correspondence came to an abrupt stop. Great soggy chunks of silence filled the incoming dâk-bag.

Dawn, *sb.* Add: 1. b. An opalescent colour resembling that seen in the sky at dawn.

1894 *Daily News* 11 Apr. 3/1 Palest pink and blue shot silk, called by the poetic name of 'Dawn', because it suggests the union of those colours in the early morning sky. 1927 *Daily Express* 21 Mar. 2 Colours include cedar, green, silver, new blue, dawn or bois de rose.

Daxie (dæ·ksi) Colloquial pet-form of Dachshund.

1899 *Daily News* 28 Oct. 7/5 They (like Daxies again) delight in playing tricks. 1900 *Ibid.* 22 Dec. 6/3 Coercion distinctly disagreeing with daxies!

Day, *sb.* Add: 6. (The astronomical day is now reckoned from midnight to midnight.)

d. *Thirty days, sixty days*: a month, two months. *Canada* and *U.S.*

e. *Of a day*: lit. lasting only a day, ephemeral; transitory, fleeting, fugitive.

1746 Wesley *Serm.* I. Pref. § 5, I am a creature of a day, passing through life as an arrow through the air. 1746 Hervey *Medit. & Contempl.* (1789) 39 Phantoms of a Day. 1834 *The Rival Sisters* 14 Man—the insect of a day. 1865 M. Arnold *Ess. Crit.* Ser. I. Pref., Apparitions of a day.

7. c. Used without a preposition. *U.S.*

1905 *N. Y. Even. Post* 20 May 4 Day before yesterday the President was again in a state of terrific determination. *Ibid.* 26 Sept. 6 Day after election people will want to know [etc.].

8. d. That period of the day allotted by usage or law for work; as, *an eight-hour day.* (See *Eight hours, *Working-day.)

1850 *Working Man's Friend & Fam. Instr.* 14 Dec. 300/1 Being at the rate of 4s. 2d. per day of ten hours. 1870 *Chambers's Jrnl.* 10 Sept. 586/2 In government workshops, ..by special act of Congress, eight hours has been constituted a legal day's work. 1880 C. Marvin *Our Public Offices* (ed. 2) 121 [They] worked hard the whole of the seven hours of their official day. 1884 J. E. T. Rogers *Six Cent. Work & Wages* xii. 327 It is plain that the day was one of eight hours. 1889 R. Tangye *One and All* vii. 116 In 1871 a great agitation sprung [*sic*] up amongst the operative engineers at Newcastle-on-Tyne in favour of a nine hours' day. 1893 *Engl. Illustr. Mag.* 293/1 Mr. Morley has from the first taken a clearly defined position on the question of the length of the labour day.

9. c. *The Day* (esp. as translation of G. *Der Tag*): the appointed day.

1914 O. Seaman in *Punch* 9 Dec. 470/1 [German Crown Prince loq.] Thank Father's God that I can say My constant aim was Peace; I simply lived to see the Day (*Den Tag*) when wars would cease.

19. **Day in (and) day out,** every day for an indefinite number of successive days, continuously. **Day off,** a day away from work. **Day out,** a day away from home or one's lodgings; *spec.* a servant's free day; also *fig.*

1828 Carr *Craven Gloss.* s.v., 'Day in and day out', all the day long. 1848 *Punch* 4 Nov. 182/2 The Servant-Girl's Idea of Life;—one long day out with 'the journeyman'. 1869 *Ibid.* 20 Mar. 111/2 Having made this a holiday with a view to having a 'day out', my landlady had not had notice to call me at any particular hour. 1890 *Peel City Guardian* 4 Jan. 5/5 It was Fayle's day out, and he made the most of the chances offered. 1893 *Engl. Illustr. Mag.* 488/2 The bus-driver spends his 'day off' in driving on a pal's bus, on the box-seat by his pal's side. 1904 Kipling in *Windsor Mag.* Dec. 10/1 Whatever 's done, let us remember that 'e's given us a day off. 1908 A. E. T. Watson *Turf* 17 It may not have been the animal's 'day out', it may do better later on. 1927 *Public Opinion* Jan. 56/3 The British Broadcasting Company will have to offer, day in and day out, a service. *Ibid.* Feb. 109/2 Work—day in day out—and not much money.

20. b. *To make a day of it*: see Make *v.*1 18 c. *To call it a day*: to consider that one has done a day's work. *Between two days* U.S.: overnight.

1860 Holland *Miss Gilbert's Career* xv. 277 We are going to make a day of it. 1876 J. H. Beadle *Western Wilds* xxvi. 406 Some ne'er-do-well who had defrauded the State and other creditors by departing between two days. 1902 McFaul *The Glidden* ii. 12 Hadn't been't he left town 'tween two days he'd be good way on the road to the pen'tentiary now. 1926 J. Black *You Can't Win* iv. 27 At six you come on and stay till ten and call it a day.

23. *day-fall* (poet.); *day-old* adj. (also *sb.* = day-old chick).

1897 F. Thompson *Ode to Setting Sun* Poems 112 Who set Upon her brow the *day-fall's carcanet? 1925 *Chambers's Jrnl.* 68/2 Shelley, although he had turned Quaker, would still have 'dabbled his fingers in the day-fall, and littered the floor of heaven with his broken fancies'. 1907 *Daily Chron.* 8 July 4/4 Many poultry-keepers dispose of several thousand *day-old chicks every season. 1928 *Daily Tel.* 11 May 19/4 Day-olds from reliable pedigree strains cost only 21s. a dozen.

24. **day boy, day girl,** a boy, girl employed as a domestic servant by the day; **day-car, -coach** *U.S.*, an ordinary passenger carriage as distinguished from a sleeper; **day editor,** the editor in charge of a newspaper during the day; **day-feeder,** an animal that feeds in the day-time; **day-nurse,** a nurse who is employed for day work; one who has charge of a day nursery; **day nursery,** (*a*) a nursery where children are cared for during the day while their mothers are at work; (*b*) a nursery used by children during the day (as distinguished from *night nursery*).

1904 *Westm. Gaz.* 26 Sept. 6/3 (Accident in Tennessee) *Day-car and day-car were telescoped, buckled, and thrown over. 1887 C. B. George *40 Yrs. on Rail* xi. 226 A passenger on his way to the dining-car came out of the *day coach into the ladies' end of my car. 1924 W. M. Raine *Troubled Waters* vii. 68 I'm going forward to the day coach. 1873 W. Mathews *Getting on in World* xiv. 218 Mr. Brooks..acting as leading editor [of the *New York Express*], reporter, *day editor, night editor, and even type-setter. 1877 *Harper's Mag.* Dec. 53/2 The day editor in charge. *a* 1889 W. H. Flower (Cent. Dict.), *Day-feeder. 1871 *Food Jrnl.* 2 Jan. 679 Mothers sending their little ones to the care of professional *day nurses while they are at work. 1850 *Household Words* II. 110/1 These institutions were to be *Day-Nurseries for the children of the poor. 1884 *Harper's Mag.* Apr. 782/2 A 'Day Nursery and Temporary Home for Children', charging two cents a day to busy mothers. 1886 *Pop. Sci. Monthly* XXVIII. 686 (Cent. D.) The day-nurseries which benevolence has established for the care of these little ones. 1896 *Mr. Gladstone: In the Evening of his Days* 70 (Illustration) The Day Nursery at Hawarden Castle. 1908 Stacpoole *Patsy* ii, They were in the day nursery, which was also the schoolroom.

Dayabeah, variant of Dahabeeyah.

1905 E. F. Benson *Image in Sand* i, A couple of dayabeahs moored to the bank were a blaze of Syrian awnings.

Dayak, var. *Dyak.

Dayal (dā·yăl). *Anglo-Ind.* Also dahil, dhyal. = Dial-bird (q. v. for etymology).

1855 *Orr's Circle Sci., Org. Nat.* III. 307 The Dayal.. which..is called the Magpie Robin by the English residents in Ceylon. 1893 Newton *Dict. Birds* 133 Dayal, or more correctly it would seem, Dhyal (corrupted into Dial-bird), the Hindostani name commonly adopted by Anglo-Indians.

Dayan (dayā·n). Pl. **dayanim.** [Heb.] A judge.

1880 *Encycl. Brit.* XIII. 687/1 Each congregation requires the services of a dayan or religious chief. 1892 Zangwill *Childr. Ghetto* I. 4 The Dayanim, those cadis of the East End, administered justice. 1902 *Daily Chron.* 3 Jan. 5/1 The Rev. B. Spiers, the Dayan of the Beth Hamedrash of London. 1928 *Daily Tel.* 3 Jan. 10/4 Dayan Dr. Feldmann.

Day-break. Add: Phr. *To make day-break*: to announce the dawn of day.

1872 *Routledge's Ev. Boy's Ann.* Dec. 5 When the flag-ship 'made day-break' with one of her guns.

Daye (dāi). Also 8 **dy,** 9 **daee, dhye, [dyah], dai.** [f. Hind. *dāi*, Pers. *dāyah*.] In N. India and Persia, a nurse; a wet-nurse; a midwife.

1782 *India Gaz.* 12 Oct. (Y., Suppl.) Dy (Wet-nurse) 10 Rs. 1810 T. Williamson *East India Vade-Mecum* I. 341 The *Dhye* is more generally an attendant upon native ladies. [1883 C. J. Wills *In Land of Lion & Sun* xxix. 326 The 'dyah', or wet-nurse, is looked on as a second mother.] 1920 *Outward Bound* Oct. 82/1 The doctor and her least dangerous *dai* (nurse) clambered into the waiting barouche. 1927 *Other Lands* Apr. 89/2 The indigenous dais are.. absolutely ignorant.

Day labour. Add later quots.

1839 De la Beche *Rep. Geol. Cornwall*, etc. xv. 569 Though in some mines day-labour is also used under ground. *a* 1861 T. Winthrop *John Brent* i. (1862) 11 In a few months more, I should have spent my last dollar and have gone to day labor, perhaps among the Pikes. 1898 W. St. Clair Baddeley *Cotteswold Shrine* 76 At the same hour ended his day-labours. 1911 *Rep. Labour & Soc. Cond. Germany* III. vi–vii. 207 Half the labour is piece and the other half is day labour.

Daylight. Add: 4. (Later U.S. examples.)

1852 E. Bennet *Mike Fink* i. 14/1 We'll catch the fever and ager,..and that'll shake the daylights out o' us. 1883 Nye *Baled Hay* 79 The driver bangs the mule, that is ostensibly pulling his daylights out. 1921 R. D. Paine *Comr. Rolling Ocean* ii. 22 Putting seven of 'em in irons after they shot the daylights out of me left us mighty short-handed.

6. **daylight-loading** *a.*, (of a film-spool, cartridge, etc.) adapted for loading by daylight without the use of a dark-room; **daylight-saving,** a method of securing a longer period of daylight at the end of the day by making use of a fictitious time (see Summer time 2), viz. by putting the clock forward (e.g. an hour).

1902 *Photographic Catal.*, Rollable *daylight loading Films. 1908 *Hansard's Parl. Deb.* Ser. iv. CLXXXIV. 155 *Daylight Saving Bill...Mr. R. Pearce...in moving the Second Reading said that the object of the Bill was to promote the earlier use of daylight in the summer. 1916 *Ibid.* Ser. v. LXXXII. 321 The advocates of daylight saving are adept in securing the consent of one body of opinion on the ground that some other body has adopted it with enthusiasm. 1924 *Punch* 24 Sept. 338 Two more.. weeks of daylight-saving.

Hence **Day·lighter,** one of a body of men who sought to enforce the decrees of the Land League in Ireland by violence during the daytime; **Day·lighting** *vbl. sb.*

1886 *St. James's Gaz.* 25 Nov. 11/2 Seeing the '*Daylighters' she ran into the room where she knew the gun to be and closed the door. 1894 *Daily Tel.* 2 Apr., A case of '*daylighting' instead of moonlighting has been reported to the local police.

Day·-lighted, *a.* [f. Daylight.] Light; *fig.* open, unconcealed.

1887 Mary E. Wilkins *Humble Romance* 124 Everything, down to his love-making was prompt, and earnest, and day-lighted with John Elliot. 1889 *Cent. Dict.*, *Daylighted*, light, open. [With quot. from R. L. Stevenson, in which the correct reading is *daylit.*]

Daytimes (dē^i·taimz), *adv. U.S.* [f. Daytime + advb. -s.] In the daytime, during the day.

1854 Maria S. Cummins *Lamplighter* xvii, Willie was very busy daytimes, but was always with them in the evening.

Dazzle, *sb.* Add:

3. The use of splashes of various colours on sea-going vessels so as to make the constructional parts unrecognizable. Hence **Dazzle** *v. trans.*, to camouflage in this way. Also *Comb.* in *dazzle-painted, -painting* (in quot. 1920 transf.).

1917 *Admiralty Order* 2 July (MS.), The 'Dazzle' painting of a ship with large patches of strong colour in a carefully thought-out pattern and colour scheme. 1919 *Times* 29 May 8/1 'Dazzle', to use the term employed by the camouflage department of the Admiralty. *Ibid.* 5 June 10/2 A 'dazzle' painted ship is on the whole more visible against sky and sea than the usual grey vessel, and this was its chief disadvantage. Furthermore, 'dazzle' painting was designed for short range, at which it is impossible to conceal a vessel against its background. 1919 N. Wilkinson *Ibid.* 9 June 6/4 Dazzle painting was never intended for use on 'ships of the line', but only for merchantmen..and war vessels working with them. 1919 *War Slang* in *Athenæum* 11 July 583/2 The other service [*sc.* the Navy] invented 'dazzle'. 1920 *Blackw. Mag.* Oct. 94/2 A geological 'dazzle-painting' in ochre and red, brown, purple, and buff. 1920 *Glasgow Herald* 12 Mar. 7 A number of lantern slides were shown of ships 'dazzled' during the war. 1922 *Ibid.* 28 Apr. 9 A 'tramp' steamer, 'dazzle' painted. 1928 C. F. S. Gamble *North Sea Air Station* xxii. 400 It was decided that all flying-boats should have their hulls 'dazzle-painted'.

Dea, Deac, abbrev. of Deacon 1 c, d. (*U.S.*)

1821 *Massachusetts Spy* 28 Feb. (Th.) Deac Josiah Bridge. *Ibid.* 4 Apr., Dea. Ebenezer Read. 1852 *Yale Lit. Mag.* XVII. 345 (Th.) In the goodly village of Q. Dea. Pip lived. 1907 *Springfield Weekly Republ.* 17 Jan. 11 Dea Wilson was among the foremost of the town's citizens.

Deacon, *sb.* Add:

1. f. The cleric who acts as principal assistant at a solemn celebration of the Eucharist; the 'gospeller'. (Cf. sense 5 and Subdeacon 2.)

1440 in Peacock *Engl. Ch. Furnit.* (1866) 181 One whole vestiment for Priest Deacon and Subdeacon. 1483 Caxton *Gold. Leg.* 133b/1 A preest a deken & a subdeken all reuested goyng to thaulter as for to saye masse. *c* 1618 Moryson *Itin.* IV. (1903) 439 When the pope..sings Masse himselfe, with one Cardinall seruing him as Deacon, and another as subdeacon. 1701 in *Cath. Rec. Soc. Publ.* VII. 101 His Deacon, Subdiacon & Acolythe were his 3 sons, brothers to yᵉ Nonne. 1851 Pugin *Chancel Screens* 26 The Epistle and Gospel were sung by the deacon and sub-deacon, from marble desks.

6. **deacon-seat** *U.S.* (earlier example).

1851 J. S. Springer *Forest Life* 71 Directly over the foot-pole..and in front of the fire, is the deacon-seat. This seat constitutes our sofa or settee.

7. 'A hunter's name for the young of the elk or wapiti' (*Cent. Dict.* Suppl. 1909).

8. 'The skin of a very young or aborted calf. It must weigh less than 8 pounds' (Webster 1911). *U.S.* [After Deacon *v.* 2 b.]

1889 *Cent. Dict.*

Deacon2. The name of H. *Deacon*, the inventor, used attrib. or in the possessive to denote his process for the making of chlorine gas from hydrochloric acid by the use of a catalyst.

1876 *Encycl. Brit.* V. 491/1 The production of chlorine by Deacon's process. 1921 *Dict. Occup. Terms* (1927) § 143 Deacon plant man, deacon process man.

Deacon, *v.* Add: 2. b. (Earlier example.)

1838 H. Colman *Rep. Agric. Mass.* (1839) 53 In this case some calves were raised; but most of them were killed at four days old. Throughout the county of Berkshire this mode of dealing with the calves is termed 'deaconing' them.

3. To make or ordain deacon. (Cf. Priest *v.* 2.)

1889 *Cent. Dict.*

Deactivation (dīˌæktivē^i·ʃən). [f. De- + *Activation.] Loss of radioactivity.

1904 *Sci. Amer. Suppl.* 20 Feb. 23523 (Cent. D. Suppl.) He finds that the law of deactivation is still the same throughout this range of temperature.

Dead, *a.* Add:

A. 2. c. Of pain: Dull and continuous, as opposed to sharp and sudden pain.

1863–76 Curling *Dis. Rectum* (ed. 4) 25 He complained of suffering from a dead, aching pain. 1894 Helen H. Gardener *Unoff. Patriot* 348 She only sat and stared, and was conscious of the dull dead pain.

d. (*a*) *proleptically*, who is 'as good as dead', certain to die or to be killed, past recovery; (*b*) in hyperbolical phrases expressing extreme exhaustion, fatigue, or indisposition.

[1598 Shaks. *Merry Wives* IV. ii. 44 Why then you are vtterly sham'd, & hee's but a dead man.] 1813 Annabella Milbanke *Diary* (MS.) At home dead. 1894 *Pall Mall Mag.* Feb. 583 I'm nearly dead from being boxed up in the house all day. 1906 *Daily Chron.* 9 Aug. 8/5 He could not tell her bluntly..that Wilson was practically a dead man.

12. c. *Electr.* Of a circuit or conductor: Carrying or transmitting no current. Similarly of a wire, etc.

1903 A. H. Beavan *Tube, Train*, etc. xi. 134 The studs are 'alive' while the car is over them, and 'dead' as soon as it has passed. 1906 *Westm. Gaz.* 13 July 5/2 There was another stoppage..caused by a 'dead' car.

13. b. esp. in *dead white*, where there is now often mixture of sense 31 (cf. C. *2 b).

1863 Mrs. H. Wood *Verner's Pride* xiv, The dead white of the roses was not more utterly colourless than Sibylla's face.

16. b. Of a horse: Not intended to win, fraudulently run in such a way that it cannot win: chiefly in *dead one, dead 'un.* (Cf. *Corpse 2 f.) *slang.*

1864 *Baily's Mag.* June 121 A horse which has been regarded occasionally as a dead one has proved lively enough to beat the winner of the Two Thousand. 1868 *Lond. Rev.* 11 July 38/2 (Farmer) The stable and owners might safely lay against what was technically a dead 'un from the first. 1880 H. Smart *Social Sinners* v, Lord, what 'dead 'uns' he did back, to be sure! 1922 *N. & Q.* 12th Ser. XI. 206/2 *Dead meat.* Horses which are not out to win are so described.

18. b. Of a house: Uninhabited.

1879 J. W. Horsley *Jottings from Jail* (1887) 17 Me and the screwsman went to Gravesend, and I found a dead 'un (uninhabited house), and we both went and turned it over. 1896 A. Morrison *Child Jago* 231 On the look out for a dead 'un. 1922 *Daily Mail* 8 Aug. 2/2 We thought it was a 'dead' house, but we walked into a girl's room and she squealed.

c. *Mil.* Out of range. (Cf. *dead angle* in D. 2.)

1899 *Westm. Gaz.* 9 Dec. 5/3 Besides the great advantage which we shall reap from the smashing power of these howitzers against field defences, we shall also find them most valuable to search out hollow or hidden ground 'dead' to other fire. 1900 *Daily News* 5 May 3/2 A high and rather steep hill, surrounded by a good deal of 'dead' ground. 1919 *Proc. Soc. Antiq. Scot.* LIII. 38 There is not a single piece of 'dead' ground in the whole fortress.

20. Of a locality, etc.: That has lost its former prosperity or glory.

1875 Annie Wood (*title*) The Dead Cities of the Zuyder Zee; a Voyage to the Picturesque Side of Holland, from the French of Henry Havard. 1905 Rivela & Pernull (*title*) The Dead Cities of Sicily. 1909 *Daily Chron.* 13 Apr. 4/5 My memory lingered with the people in the 'dead cities' [of Holland] who had spent their Easter with old-world simplicity.

d. *Typog.* That has been used or is no longer required, as copy after composition, or type ready for distribution or discarded.

1874 Knight *Dict. Mech.* I. 679 *Dead-letter, Print.*: Type which has been used for printing, and is ready for distribution. Dead-matter. 1898 J. Southward *Mod. Printing* I. xxiv. 154 The 'dead' letter..would, if of uniform face, constitute in itself a strong fount.

e. Of a cinema set: Out of use.

1929 Edington *Studio Murder Myst.* i, The skeletons of 'dead' sets clothed in flowing veils of gray.

21. (Illustrations of use in various games.) Also *dead-ball* attrib. Cf. *Dead wood.

1875 *Encycl. Brit.* III. 407/1 (Baseball) A ball which hits the bat without being struck at, or the person of the striker or umpire, is a dead ball and out of play. 1876 *Ibid.* IV. 180/2 A 'dead bowl' is one knocked off the green, or against one lying in the ditch, or an illegally played bowl, and must at once be removed from the green. 1889 *Laws of Cricket* (1890) 6, 33. A batsman being out from any cause the ball shall be 'Dead'. 1900 *Ibid.* 4, 33a. If the ball, whether struck with the bat or not, lodges in a batsman's clothing, the ball shall become 'Dead'. 1902 *Encycl. Brit.* XXVIII. 426/2 So the game [*sc.* Rugby football] proceeds until the ball is once more 'dead'—that is, brought to a standstill. 1905 *Westm. Gaz.* 30 Nov. 8/3 [Rugby football] The necessity of lengthening the playing area to admit of the extensions behind the goals to the 'dead-ball' line.

b. *Golf.* Of the ball: Placed so near the hole that it can be holed with certainty at the next stroke.

1881 R. Forgan *Golfer's Handbk.* iii. 30 If you can possibly win a 'half' [i.e. halve a hole] by running your ball 'dead' at the side of the hole,..then the cautious game is to be preferred. 1891 H. G. Hutchinson *Golf* (ed. 6) 83 Missing a four-inch put which your partner has left you..and receiving the cheery consolation, 'Never mind, partner, never mind—another time I'll try to lay you dead'. 1909 P. A. Vaile *Mod. Golf* v. 73 A man may lie 'dead' off a run up, but I am referring now to the well-lofted shot that falls 'plump' within an easy put of the hole and scarcely moves.

c. Lacking resiliency, having no spring.

1895 H. W. W. Wilberforce *Lawn Tennis* ix. 29 This form of game..arose from the very wet and dead state of the courts. 1909 P. A. Vaile *Mod. Golf* viii. 120 You will do well, should you have to choose [a driver] for yourself, to exercise moderation. Avoid too much spring. Don't have a 'dead' one. 1930 *Morning Post* 16 July 16/2 So well did Squires and Peach perform on the dead pitch that the Kent total of 317 was passed without the loss of another wicket.

22. c. Of molten metal: Thick and sluggish, either from insufficient melting, or from having stood too long in a ladle. Cf. *Deadmelt *v.*

1884 W. H. Greenwood *Steel & Iron* xviii. (ed. 2) 425 Extreme 'dead-melting' produces a metal that runs dull and dead.

29. *Dead load*, a load whose weight is constant and invariable.

1888 *Lockwood's Dict. Mech. Engin.* 1891 *Scribner's Mag.* X. 7 The greater engine-power will add to the dead load, thus still further diminishing the vessel's capability for carrying.

Supplement, p. 3873; Corrigenda, p. 4092; Spurious words, p. 4093; Books quoted, p. 4094

31. Hence *dead-earnest* in attrib. use.
1883 'Mark Twain' *Life Mississippi* xviii. 223 Ritchie's good-natured badgering was pretty nearly as aggravating as Brown's dead-earnest nagging.

d. (Later U.S. example.)
1920 Mulford *J. Nelson* xii. 131 Striking into a dead run as he approached the rocky hump in the trail.

e. Absolutely certain or safe.
1876 Joaquin Miller *Unwritten Hist.* xv. 227 It 's your pot, Prince, take it down. You hold the papers, called us on a dead hand, you did, but this was no bluff of mine. 1882 Waite *Adv. Far West* 264 'No' said he, 'I shall not go into anything new unless it is a "*dead thing*", in fact', said he 'it must be *very dead*.'

32. a. *Dead and alive*: see Dead-alive. Also *Dead and buried, done (for, with)*; *dead-and-gone* (attrib.).
1863 *All Year Round* IX. 473/1 The grave of Carthage, and other dead and buried cities of the Carthaginians. 1892 J. L. Kipling *Beast & Man in India* i. (ed. 2) 7 Buddhism has been dead and done with in India proper for centuries. 1897 Stuart Erskine *Lord Dullborough* v, We ..saw some six-months'-old playbills, announcing some dead-and-gone performance. 1909 *Westm. Gaz.* 10 Mar. 11/2 It is urged that the intellect of the Poll-man is starved and himself broken on the wheel of a dead-and-done system.

e. *To be dead on*: cf. Death 16.
1891 Scrivener *Fields & Cities* 22 These boys always were 'dead' on a rat, no matter what its size.

f. *To be dead nuts on*: see Nut *sb.*[1] 6.

B. 6. (Examples of *dead-meat*.) *Dead-pulled wool* = dead wool (Webster 1911).
1897 *Westm. Gaz.* 18 May 2/3 One hideous monster was seen in the Park last week, puffing and rocking along and looking as much out of place as a dead-meat van in a Jubilee procession. 1908 *Ibid.* 22 July 4/3 If we are soon to get cheap beef and mutton it must be by developing the dead-meat trade.

7. *On the dead*: in dead earnest, honestly. *U.S. slang.*
1902 H. L. Wilson *Spenders* xxix. 340 Say, on the dead, Uncle Peter, I wish you'd come. 1903 A. H. Lewis *The Boss* 184 But, on the dead! I'd like to learn how you.. reconcile yourselves to things.

C. 2. esp. *dead certain, level*; *Dead-broke, *Dead-sure.
1845 *Cultivator* II. 92 As I ..come out upon the high prairie with the wind 'dead ahead'. *a* 1861 T. Winthrop *Canoe & Saddle* 280 Prairie-land lies dead level for leagues. 1883 'Mark Twain' *Life Mississippi* xxxix. 414 We'll cotton-seed his salad for him..that's a dead-certain thing. 1904 W. H. Smith *Promoters* v. 92 For a dead easy mark in a business way, commend me to a preacher. 1908 G. H. Lorimer *J. Spurlock* i. 19 It was like having one of those mushy girls dead gone on you. 1923 'B. M. Bower' *Parowan Bonanza* i. 15 'You're dead right, old girl', Bill agreed.

b. in *dead white*, pure white; flat or lustreless white (cf. A. *13 b).
1796 Kirwan *Elem. Min.* (ed. 2) I. 327 Its colour white, two opposite faces silvery white, two others dead white or yellowish. 1825 J. Nicholson *Oper. Mech.* 640 If it is to be finished flat, or, as the painters style it, dead white, grey, fawn, &c. 1857 G. A. Lawrence *Guy Liv.* xxx, The straight, beautifully-turned ankle, cased in dead-white silk. 1920 Rose Macaulay *Potterism* II. i. 67 Jane, in a square-cut, high-waisted, dead white frock. 1924 D. H. Lawrence *England, my England* 110 She turned white—dead white.

D. 2. dead-bird (see quot. 1898); **dead block** (see quot.); **dead-box**, a vehicle used for conveying dead bodies out of a mine; **dead-burnt** *a.*, so strongly heated in the burning as to lose the power of absorbing water; **dead-drop** (see quot.); **dead duck** *U.S. slang*, a person who has failed financially; a person or thing that has become nearly worthless; **dead earth** *Electr.* = **dead ground*; **dead-end** *Electr.* (see quot. 1925); also *fig.* (cf. *Blind alley); hence as *vb.*, to bring to a dead end; **dead finish**, (*a*) *Austral.*, any of several Australian trees or shrubs, esp. *Albizzia basaltica* or *Acacia farnesiana*, also the thicket formed by such trees; (*b*) *Austral. colloq.*, the 'limit' or extreme point (with regard to excellence, endurance, etc.); **dead-fold**, a sheep pen; similarly *dead pen* (dial.); **dead furrow**, a furrow between two ridges; **dead ground** *Electr.*, perfect connexion with the earth; **dead horse** (see Horse *sb.* 18); **dead-house** (earlier example); **dead leaf** *Aviation*, an aeroplane whose movement is like that of a falling dead leaf; as *adj.* resembling a dead leaf, of the colour of a dead leaf; **dead loads** *U.S.*, great quantities; **dead marine** (see Marine *sb.* 4 d); **dead metal**, metal left unburnished; **dead wagon** *U.S.*, a vehicle for conveying the dead.
1892 Stevenson & Osbourne *Wrecker* xxii Can't you give us a '*dead bird' for a good trade-room? 1898 Morris *Austral English*, *Dead-bird*, in Australia, a recent slang term, meaning 'a certainty'. The metaphor is from pigeon-shooting, where the bird being let loose in front of a good shot is as good as dead. 1884 Knight *Dict. Mech.* Suppl., **Dead Blocks*.., blocks projecting from the end of a freight car to receive the concussion when the buffer springs are compressed. 1897 *Daily News* 12 May 5/7 He arrived at the pit's mouth in the *dead-box, having fainted whilst below. 1903 *Nature* 19 Nov. 64/2 Under favourable conditions gypsum actually breaks up at 63°·5, and forms insoluble anhydrite found in nature and identical with *dead-burnt gypsum. 1904 *Technol. & Sci. Dict.* (ed. Goodchild & Tweney), *Dead burnt*, a term applied to lime which has become vitrified by fusion of calcium silicate in the limekiln. 1928 *Daily Express* 13 July 4 Do simple fancy dives first, such as sitting dives, arm balances, and *dead-drops. The last-named is performed like a 'header', but with arms extended above the head, then fall into the water rigid, without springing or making any other movement. 1888 *N. Y. Clipper* (Farmer) Long Branch is said to be a *dead duck. 1882 R. M. Ballantyne *Battery & Boiler* x. (1883) 102 We have found *dead earth. 1910 *Hawkins' Electr. Dict.* 109/1 *Dead earth*, in telegraphy, a fault in the line involving a complete grounding or connection with the earth; a total earth. 1914 *Work* 26 Sept. 490/2 When cables are earthed intentionally the connection is complete, or a 'dead earth'. There are also 'partial earths' when a cable..leaks. 1925 P. J. Risdon *Crystal Receivers & Circuits* 10 The unused portion of the coil, although not directly in the circuit, is joined on to it, and produces an effect known as *dead-end loss. 1928 *Observer* 15 Jan. 5 He deplores the fate of boys who get into dead-end employments. 1928 *Daily Tel.* 24 July 12/1 Young men..who are either working into a dead end or engaged in an industry that has a restricted future. 1921 *Blackw. Mag.* Nov. 641/2 Engineers..are not dead-ended so easily. 1881 A. C. Grant *Bush Life* xiv, 'He's the *dead finish—go right through a man', rejoins Sam, rather sulkily. 1885 Finch-Hatton *Advance Australia* xvii. 272 On the western slopes, rose-wood, myall, dead-finish, plum-tree..all woods with a fine grain suitable for cabinet-making and fancy work. 1889 J. H. Maiden *Useful Native Plants* 355 *Acacia farnesiana*...Sometimes called by the absurd name of 'Dead Finish'. This name given to some species of *Acacia* and *Albizzia*, is on account of the trees or shrubs shooting thickly from the bottom, and forming an impenetrable barrier to the traveller, who is thus brought to a 'dead finish' (stop). 1902 J. H. M. Abbott *Tommy Cornstalk* 64 There are few colloquialisms more expressive of wearisome disgust, dissatisfaction and discontent than is 'Dead Finish'. It is almost synonymous with 'the Last Straw'. 1907 *Daily Chron.* 18 Mar. 4/4 There is a corporation which grows roses to compete with Nature's 'dead finish' trees. 1897 L. Robinson *Wild Traits* vi. 168 A sudden change of diet from the frugal fare on the hill-turf and in the '*dead-fold' to that of lush cereals [etc.]. 1906 G. A. B. Dewar *Faery Year* 32 The dead-fold is formed of wattle hurdles bound about with swathes of straw. 1873 *Trans. Dep. Agric. Illinois* X. 94 The land between the rows should be plowed toward the trees, so as to have the '*dead furrow' in the center, to allow the water to pass off freely. 1910 *Hawkins' Electr. Dict.* 109/1 **Dead ground*, the same as dead earth. 1805-9 J. Henry *Camp. agst. Quebec* 134 Many carioles.. passed our dwelling loaded with the dead ..to a place, emphatically called the '*dead-house'. 1896 *Daily News* 17 Oct. 6/5 A woollen skirt of a *dead-leaf shade. 1904 *Daily Chron.* 24 Oct. 8/1 A smart gown of dead-leaf brown. 1918 E. S. Farrow *Dict. Mil. Terms*, *Dead Leaf*, in aviation, the term applied to an aircraft when its movement resembles that of a falling dead leaf. 1873 'Mark Twain' & Warner *Gilded Age* xxvii. 247 There's *dead loads of peat down there somewhere. 1874 Knight *Dict. Mech.*, **Dead-metal*, metal, such as gold or silver, left with dead or lustreless..surface. 1894 *Outing* (U.S.) XXIV. 7/1 *Dead wagons, hospital ambulances and sanitary corps vehicles were the most prominent objects in the streets.

Dead beat, *sb.*[2] *U.S. slang.* (Earlier quot.)
1875 'P. V. Nasby' *Eastern Fruit* vii. 48 True, he was besieged by 'dead beats',..but..they got very little the better of him.

b. (See quot.)
1877 Bartlett *Dict. Amer.* (ed. 4), *Dead-beat*, a mixture of ginger-soda and whiskey, taken by hard drinkers after a night's carousal.

Dead-bea·ten, *ppl. a.* (See Dead-beat *ppl. a.*)
1875 Holland *Sevenoaks* i. 3 One by one—sick, disabled, discouraged, dead-beaten—they drifted into the poor-house.

Dead-beatism. *U.S. slang.* [f. Dead-beat *sb.*[2]] Worthlessness.
1882 *Congress. Rec.* 25 Jan. 615/1 [Are we] going to put a premium on judicial trumpery and dead-beatism?

Dead-beatness. [f. Dead-beat *a.*] Utter exhaustion.
1907 M. C. Harris *Tents of Wickedness* III. v. 299 The light came streaming in at the window that in the dead-beatness of last night everyone had forgotten to close.

Dead-broke, *ppl. a.* (1851–): see *Broke *ppl. a.* 3.

Deaden, *v.* Add: **4. e.** To make impervious to sound; = Deafen *v.* 3.
1926 Connington *Death at Swaythling Court* vii. 121 The kitchen is next the workshop and the walls are very badly deadened, so I could hear voices talking next door.

Deadener. Add: **b.** *Logging.* (See quot.) *U.S.*
1905 *Terms Forestry & Logging* 34 *Deadener*, a heavy log or timber, with spikes set in the butt end, so fastened in a log slide that the logs passing under it come in contact with the spikes and have their speed retarded.

Dead-eye. Add: **c.** (See quot.)
1874 Knight *Dict. Mech.*, *Dead-eye*, the eye-bolt or staple on the gunwale of a canal-boat to which the towing-line is bent.

Deadfall. Add: **1.** (Earlier U.S. examples.)
1829 *Massachusetts Spy* 8 July (Th.) In the act of getting in, the log or dead-fall fell upon his back and held him fast. 1843 Carlton *New Purchase* I. 2 We.., were setting dead-falls and snares.

b. *attrib.* with *trap.*
1902 S. E. White *Blazed Trail* xvii. 128 He had bound together..several of the oddly shaped pine timbers to form a species of dead-fall trap.

2. c. *U.S.* (Examples.)
1903 A. Adams *Log Cowboy* xvi. 251 'There's a deadfall down here on the river'; says he, 'that robs a man coming and going'. 1910 J. Hart *Vigilante Girl* iv. 52 Let's shake this deadfall. Come along, we'll go over to the Arcade.

Deadhead, *sb.* Add: **3.** *U.S.* (Earlier example. Also *attrib.* and *transf.*)
1848 Bartlett *Dict. Amer.* App. s.v., Persons who drink at a bar, ride in an omnibus, or railroad car, travel in steam-boats, or visit the theatre without charge, are called *dead heads.* 1863 *Rep. Maine Board Agric.* 15 The milch cow which barely pays the expense of keeping and care is a 'dead head' yielding no profit. 1887 C. B. George *40 Yrs. on Rail* ii. 32 Once in a while the conductor found it desirable to eject some would-be dead-head passenger while between stations. 1892 *Congress. Rec.* 31 May, App. 385/1 The free-delivery service is burdened by the collection and delivery of thousands of dead-head matter under the 'penalty-postage system'.

b. Used predicatively without article.
1873 'Mark Twain' & Warner *Gilded Age* xxx. 275 Senators and Representatives..always traveled 'dead-head' both ways. 1888 *Portland Transcript* 14 Mar. (Farmer) [Those letters] which had to do with the stage business and went dead-head.

c. A non-combatant accompanying a fighting-force.
1867 J. N. Edwards *Shelby*, etc. xxi. 396 Accompanied by at least five hundred 'dead-heads', loafers, and amateur cavalry gentlemen.

4. In full *dead head log*, a sunken or submerged log. *U.S.*
1902 S. E. White *Blazed Trail* lv. 380 He was enabled to catch the slanting end of a 'dead head' log whose lower end was jammed in the crib. 1905 *Terms Forestry & Logging* 34. 1907 *Black Cat* June 17 Numerous 'dead-heads' bobbed in the current like otters swimming with the stream.

5. as. adj. Headlong.
1906 'O. Henry' *Four Million* 115, I made a dead-head scramble for the doors.

Dead-head, *v.* Add: *transf.* of logs: To jam.
1922 Titus *Timber* viii. 79 Your hardwood will begin dead-heading in a hurry. *Ibid.* x. 89 If the raft goes to pieces and that one log dead-heads.

Deadheadism. *U.S.* (Earlier example.)
1857 *N. Y. Tribune* (Bartlett), I had never experienced the blessed privilege of deadheadism.

Dead-heat, *sb.* Add: *fig.* A state or position of exact equality.

Dead-heat, *v. intr.* Add: Const. *with.*
1902 *Daily Chron.* 21 May 3/5 Hitherto the London and North-Western have deliberately 'dawdled' over the thirty miles after Crewe, so as to only 'dead-heat' with their competitors. 1922 *Daily Mail* 22 Nov. 7 Chuck-a-Penny distinguished himself..by dead-heating with Eton and dividing the spoils.

Deading, *vbl. sb.* Delete †*Obs.* and add:
2. Something which deadens.
1874 Knight *Dict. Mech.*, *Deading*,..the clothing or jacket around a steam boiler or cylinder to prevent radiation of heat.
3. Work not directly productive; = Dead-work 2.
1883 Gresley *Gloss. Coal-m.* 1921 *Dict. Occup. Terms* (1927) § 042 *Deading man, deadwork man*; excavates with pick and shovels into tubs other material than coal where necessary.

Dead letter. Add:
3. *Typog.* See *Dead *a.* 20 d.

Dea·dlighted, *a.* [f. Dead-light + -ed[2].] Provided with a dead-light.
1926 F. W. Crofts *Inspector French & Cheyne Mystery* iii, He..tried to break through the door, the bulkheads and the deadlighted porthole.

Dead-line. Add: **2. b.** *gen.* A line beyond which it is not permitted or possible to go.
1917 F. S. Henry *Printing for School & Shop* xi. 183 If the chase is one that just fits the bed of the press, make certain that the type does not come outside of the dead line on the press. 1929 *Publishers' Weekly* 27 July 349 Deadline for *Poetry's* $250 prize poem contest is September 1.

Deadlock, *v.* Add: *intr.* To come to a deadlock.
1903 *N. Y. Even. Post* 25 Nov. 6 The Legislature would have deadlocked over the vote had not Gov. Odell come to his rescue.

Deadly, *a.* Add: **8. b.** Characterized by dead accuracy. So *deadliness.*
1905 *Daily Chron.* 24 Aug. 6/4 A lack of deadliness in approaching. 1909 P. A. Vaile *Modern Golf* v. 95 The peculiarity of the stymie stroke, played parallel with the ground, is its deadly direction.

Dead man. Add: **4. b.** *Logging.* (See quot.) *U.S.*
1905 *Terms Forestry* etc. 34 *Deadman*, a fallen tree on the shore, or a timber to which the hawser of a boom is attached.

Dead man's handle. In electric trains, the controlling handle which must be kept pressed down for the current to pass, so that the current is automatically cut off and the train brought to a standstill should the driver release his grasp through illness or accident.
1911 Webster. 1924 *Westm. Gaz.* 2 Dec., The Dead Man's handle..is a safety device for pulling up Underground trains.

Dead-melt (de·dmelt), *v. trans.* To keep (metal) at a melting heat until it becomes perfectly fluid. Hence **Dead-melting** *vbl. sb.*
1880 *Encycl. Brit.* XIII. 341/2 If cast immediately it is found that a much larger quantity of gas separates during solidification, rendering the steel porous, than is evolved if the metal is dead-melted, *i.e.*, allowed to remain melted for an extra half hour or more. *Ibid.*, The 'dead melting' effect of the extra time allowed in fusing steel for the molten metal to stand in the furnace after fusion is brought about is due [etc.]. 1884 W. H. Greenwood *Steel & Iron* (ed. 2) 425 Too long exposure to the heat, or extreme 'dead-melting', produces a metal that runs dull and dead. 1919 *Nature* CIII. 169/1 There is a particular equilibrium at which no chemical reaction takes place. The heat is then what is called 'dead-melted'.

Dead-sure, *a.* [Dead *adv.* 2.] Absolutely sure or certain.
1589 [see Dead *adv.* 2]. 1873 J. H. Beadle *Undevel. West* i. 34 One thought a seavoyage a dead sure thing. 1891 *Harper's Mag.* Dec. 54/1 Some large opportunity is dead sure to present itself to me if I wait. 1897 *Scribner's Mag.* Sept. 297/2, I was dead frozen sure that I had a sure tip on a wheat deal. 1906 *Springfield Weekly Republ.* 12 July 3 His scouts..report that Moran [a candidate for governor] has a dead-sure thing.

Dead weight. Add: **4.** *attrib.*
1894 *Westm. Gaz.* 7 May 3/1 Dead-weight expenses have almost reached the irreducible minimum. 1903 *Ibid.* 28 Jan. 9/3 Her dead-weight carrying capacity 18,400 tons. 1905 *Daily Chron.* 16 May 4/4 There is dead-weight debt, and there is remunerative debt. 1927 T. Woodhouse *Artificial Silk* 16 A dead-weight safety valve.

Dead wood. Add: **1.** Also *attrib.*
1814 J. Taylor *Arator* 183 They [*sc.* hogs] are the cause of dead wood fences which render..labour unproductive.

b. *fig.* (Earlier and later examples.)
1857 *San Francisco Call* 7 Jan. (Th.) Let such men but have a sure thing, or, as Californians say, the deadwood, and they will bet their last farthing. 1888 H. Clews *28 Yrs. Wall Street* 349 Most of the members of the Legislature thought they had got the 'deadwood' on the Commodore.

c. *fig.* Inactive members of a business house.
1903 *McClure's Mag.* July 326 No dead wood is taken into the concern unless it is through the supposed necessities of family or business relations.

3. *fig.* Useless material. Also *attrib.*
1887 *Sci. Amer.* 1 Oct. 209/1 The commissioner [of patents] has made some effort..to cut the deadwood out of the examining and clerical forces left him as a legacy by his predecessor. 1928 *Daily Express* 11 Aug. 9/5 These papers do not receive any advertising support from us unless they make a price which we consider is adequate when you cut out their dead-wood circulation. 1929 *Daily Tel.* 15 Jan. 6/3 Amalgamations of what have hitherto been competing concerns are being formed, the specific objects being to cut out any dead-wood which may be handicapping the smooth working of the machine, to promote efficiency by the pooling of brains and experience.

4. Used *attrib.* as an intensive.
1876 'Mark Twain' *Tom Sawyer* xxxv. (1885) 306 No! Oh, good licks, are you in real dead-wood earnest, Tom?

Deady, *a.* [f. Dead *a.* + -y[1].] Suggestive of death, deathlike.
1921 *Chambers's Jrnl.* 846/2 There was something in the atmosphere of the house that was used-up and deady.

Deaf, *a.* **7.** Add: **deaf-ear**, (*c*) the ear-lobe of the domestic fowl.
1854 *Poultry Chron.* I. 225 The cock..should have large wattles, and a clear white deaf-ear. 1855 *Ibid.* III. 92 Is the white deaf ear more important than a clear flight? *Ibid.* 443 The importance of white deaf-ears seems however to have been overlooked by some of the competitors.

Deal, *sb.*[2] Add:
4. b. (Now in gen. English use, and often applied to international as well as to inter-party agreements.)
1928 *Manchester Guardian Weekly* 10 Aug. 102/2 We are ..dependent on Parisian sources for information about our latest deal with the French. *Ibid.* 104/1 [He] tries to explain the attitude of British Liberalism towards the naval deal.

c. *A fair deal*: equitable treatment (in a bargain, settlement, etc.). *A square deal*: see *Square *a.* 8 b.
1928 *Daily Chron.* 9 Aug. 6/2 The men have had a fair deal.

Deal, *sb.*[3] **2.** Add: *Native deal*, the wood of the Australian pine, *Nageia elata.*
1889 J. H. Maiden *Useful Native Plants* 589 *Podocarpus elata*,..Native Deal, Pencil Cedar [etc.].

Dealer. Add:
5. A jobber on the Stock Exchange.
1837 *Penny Mag.* VI. 186/2 Dealers in bills purchase them either to get a commission, or in return for goods exported. 1870 *Gentl. Mag.* New Ser. V. 484 The dealers were almost unable to sell stock of any kind. 1890 *Cassell's Sat. Jrnl.* June 724/3 A jobber was engaged in 'banging' the market... Another dealer saw through the trick. 1902 *Encycl. Brit.* XXV. 23/2 Much of the work of the Stock Exchange account is carried out by a department of that institution corresponding to the bankers' clearing house. Its function is to bring into direct communication the ultimate buyer and the ultimate seller as represented by their respective brokers, thus eliminating, for the purposes of the settlement, the middleman known as the 'dealer' or 'jobber'. 1907 *Westm. Gaz.* 25 Mar. 9/3 Those dozens of other dealers are on the look-out for orders from brokers whose clientèle lies amongst the great body of the public.

Dealing, *vbl. sb.* Add: *attrib.*, *dealing-book* (Stock Exch.).
1899 *Westm. Gaz.* 19 July 8/2 Dealing-books that have been innocent for weeks of more than two or three bargains a day have been filling rapidly. 1907 *Ibid.* 25 Mar. 9/3 There..is one man very much absorbed in his dealing-book.

Deaner (dī·nəɹ). *slang.* [Immediate origin uncertain, but prob. ultimately identical with Denier, Denarius.] A shilling.
1846 R. L. Snowden *Mag. Assistant* 342 Shilling, Deaner, also twelver. 1864 *Times* 12 Oct. 11/6 One woman said, 'Where's the "deaner"'. 1904 *Daily Chron.* 27 Dec. 4/4 I've played it [*sc.* a cornet] six hour for a deaner and a haddock-bone disguised in batter as a bit o' cold, fried fish. 1922 *Contemp. Rev.* Sept. 367 A shilling..is frequently a 'deener' [in cockney speech].

Deanstonize (dīnstənaiz), *v.* [f. place-name *Deanston*, in the west of Perthshire + -ize.] *intr.* To follow the system of subsoil-ploughing practised by James Smith at his farm at Deanston; *trans.* to treat (land) in this way.
[1846 *Farmer's Mag.* Ser. II. XIV. 195/2 The engineering works designed and executed at the Deanston establishment. 1850 *Ibid.* XXII. 67/2 Whether the Deanston system [of drainage] of 30 inches, or the more recent, and now more fashionable, one of 48 inches is the best.] 1898 *Dict. Nat. Biog.* LIII. 58/2 The word 'Deanstonising' passed into common use to signify deep ploughing and thorough draining.

Dearborn. *U.S.* (Earlier examples.)
1820 *Massachusetts Spy* 15 Mar. (Th.), I don't live extravagantly—I keep a little Dearborn waggon. 1825 Weems *Letters* III. 358 It might be well to set Jesse out with a coarse little dearborn cart. 1825 J. M. Cobbett *Lett. fr. France* 216 The farmers and tradesmen use a little wagon, precisely that which in America is called the *Dearborn.*

Death. Add: **12. d.** *To do* (a thing) *to death*: to overdo it; *esp.* to repeat too often or *ad nauseam.*
a 1889 in Barrère & Leland *Dict. Slang* s.v. *Done to death*, Caricature of Academy pictures done to death in comic journals with utmost regularity for many past years. 1909 W. S. Sparrow *Hints on House Furnishing* II. iii. 134 Diapered patterns for wall-papers and carpets..were 'done to death'.

13. b. *To go one's death*: to do one's utmost. *U.S. colloq.*
1833 Crockett *Sketches* 74 My little boys at home will go their death to support my election. *Ibid.* 173 You think they don't go their death upon a jig, but they do. 1835 Longstreet *Georgia Scenes* (1840) 199 I'll go my death upon you at the shooting match. 1878 *Scribner's Mag.* XV. 400/1 The consulship at Rio Janeiro is vacant, and being worth $6,000, he is moved to 'go his death on Rio'.

16. Orig. *U.S.*
1842 *Spirit of Times* (Philad.) 10 Mar. (Th.) We need not say that this medicine is death on colds.

17. *As sure as death.*
1766 Goldsm. *Vicar Wakef.* xix, As sure as death there is our master and mistress come home. 1831 Miss Ferrier *Destiny* xlviii, Oh, as sure as death, then, that's just owning that you are going to be married.

19. death-angle, a corner of a military position where serious losses have taken place; **death camash, quamash**, a plant of the western U.S., the bulb of which is poisonous to cattle; **death-cloth**, the head-covering of the Jews worn for prayer; **death-cup**, the poisonous fungus *Amanita phalloides*; **death-fetch** *U.S.* (cf. Fetch *sb.*[1] 2); **death-roll**, a list of names of those who have been killed in an accident or battle.
1889 R. Johnson *War Secession* xxiii. 383 (Funk) The fighting around the '*death-angle', as the soldiers called it, was kept up till past midnight. 1884 Miller *Plant-n.*, *Zygadenus venenosus*, '*Death Quamash', Hog's Potato. 1905 Dorothea Gerard *Improb. Idyl* 255 The white stripes of the '*death-cloth' in which he had been saying his prayers. 1904 *Westm. Gaz.* 6 Oct. 10/1 The '*death-cup' is very abundant in woods in this country. 1891 *Harper's Mag.* Oct. 815/1 Any unusual occurrence fell under the suspicion of being a *death-fetch. 1873 *Porcupine* XIV. 725/2 Two other actresses also appear on this week's *death-roll. 1878 *Sunday at Home* 28 Sept. 624/2 Our death-roll..contains ..so many names that we must dismiss each with the briefest mention. 1906 *Westm. Gaz.* 17 Oct. 10/1 The terrible disaster at Seaham in 1880, when the death-roll approximated to nearly 200.

Death-bed. *attrib.* Add: often (with derogatory implication) in *death-bed confession, repentance* (also *transf.* = a belated change of conduct or policy).
1691–8 Death-bed repentance [in Dict.]. 1888 A. C. Gunter *Mr. Potter of Texas* vi, Curse him and his death-bed confession!

Death-place (de·þplə's). [f. Death + Place *sb.*] The place where a person dies.
1830 Moore *Byron's Life & Lett.* II. 778 His lost friend's melancholy deathplace, Missolonghi. 1901 *Spectator* 28 Sept. 430/1 Why..is the deathplace of Constantius given as Mopsucrenam? 1906 *Daily Chron.* 19 Dec. 4/5 Brocket Hall, Herts, ..the death-place of two Premiers, Lord Melbourne and Lord Palmerston. 1908 *Westm. Gaz.* 16 Nov. 9/2 Violating the precedents which prescribe the death-place of the rulers of China.

Death-song. [Death *sb.* 18 a. Cf. G. *todesgesang*, earlier † *todtengesang.*] A song sung immediately before death, or to commemorate the dead. In U.S. *spec.* with reference to Indian customs.
a 1780 [see Death *sb.* 18 a]. 1818 Eastburn *Yamoyden* (1834) I. 295 And thus his death-song wildly woke. 1843 *American Pioneer* II. 225 Four of the missionaries..were then led into the camp of the Delawares, where the death-song was sung over them. 1876 Joaquin Miller *Unwritten Hist.* ii. 39 They will not revisit their own camp..until it is first visited by their priest or medicine man, who chaunts the death-song.

Deathward. Add: **B.** *adj.* Tending towards death.
1854 'Grace Greenwood' *Haps & Mishaps* 43 O immortal stones,..mocking..the mournful mortality, the deathward throbbing, of the brows ye encircle! 1882 Swinburne *Tristram of L.*, etc. *8 Yrs. Old* iii, Sounds of dying and dawning years, Now quickened on his deathward way. 1899 *Daily News* 17 Oct. 8/3 A pleasant-looking, neatly-dressed woman on the deathward side of fifty.

Deb (deb). Colloq. U.S. abbreviation of Débutante. Also **De·bby.**
1926 *Ladies' Home Jrnl.* July 26 One of my deb cousins makes a transcendent cocktail. 1927 *Sunday Express* 10 July 10 It appears that her comments on society have roused the ire of the great army of debutantes...How the angry 'debs' propose to deal with their victim..I cannot imagine. 1928 *Sunday Dispatch* 9 Dec. 11/2 The impossibility of parents doing any of the old kind of chaperonage in the hours kept by the present day (or night) 'debbies' during their present season.

Debadge (dībæ·dʒ), *v.* [f. De- II. 2 a + Badge *sb.*] *trans.* To deprive of the badge which in the war of 1914–18 exempted a man from military service.
1916 *Daily Mail* 23 Sept. 5/7 All single men under, say, twenty one, to be immediately debadged. *Ibid.* 1 Nov. 5/5 This practice of capturing debadged men has been brought prominently before the Man-Power Board.

Debag (dībæ·g), *v.* *University slang.* [f. De- II. 2 a + Bag *sb.* 16.] *trans.* To remove the 'bags' from.
1914 C. Mackenzie *Sinister St.* III. vi, At Oxford..we should be out of sympathy with him, even up to the point of debagging him. *Ibid.* vii, 'We ought to debag him', he cried. Appleby was thereupon debagged; but as..he continued to walk about trouserless and dispense hospitality without any apparent loss of dignity, the debagging had to be written down a failure. 1927 *Daily Express* 5 Oct. 3/3 If the Gun Room wishes to pay a tribute to one whom it loves, it de-bags the adored after dinner; if the Gun Room wishes to hurt the feelings of one it hates, it de-bags the hated one after dinner.

Debating, *vbl. sb.* **b.** Add: **debating club** = *debating society*; **debating point**, a point which, though not essential to the matter in hand, furnishes a useful or interesting subject for debate.
1840 *Knickerbocker Mag.* XVI. 262 We instituted a *debating club, in which I soon became prominent and popular. 1843 *American Pioneer* II. 204 In the absence of other means of improvement, debating clubs were formed in some neighborhoods. 1928 *Daily Tel.* 9 Oct. 6 'I do plead for the liberties of the people of England more than any of you do.' It was not a bad *debating point, if such things had then been of any avail.

Debel, *v.* Delete †*Obs.* and add:
1886 R. F. Burton *Arab. Nts.* (1903) 11 Doing battle for the weak and debelling the strong [after Virgil's *debellare superbos*]. 1897 H. N. Howard *Footsteps Proserpine* 12 Many mourned by man, by fate debelled.

Debitable (de·bităb'l), *a.* [f. Debit *v.* + -able.] That can be debited.
1895 *19th Cent.* Oct. 650 Salaries and establishments out of, but debitable to, India. 1899 *Westm. Gaz.* 12 Oct. 5/3 The monthly maintenance is estimated at £11,000 sterling, all of which is debitable to England.

Debouchure. (Earlier U.S. example.)
1832 *Louisville Directory* 110 The deposites of alluvial earth at the lower extremity of the Canal, or debouchure, could not be removed.

Débridement (debridmaṅ). *Surg.* [Fr., f. *débrider* to unbridle.] The operation of removing constriction by the incision of tissue.
1854 Mayne *Expos. Lex.*

Debris. Add:
2. *attrib.* and *Comb.*: **debris-cone**, a cone formed by the accumulation of volcanic ejecta and debris.
1890 Dana *Char. Volcanoes* 113 The cone was found to be literally a debris-cone, not a lava-cone or cinder-cone in any part. *Ibid.* 171 Between 1880 and 1882 another debris cone began in the basin of Halema'uma'u. 1895 — *Man. Geol.* (ed. 4) 285 The basin contained a debris-cone made of the fallen blocks, and not at all of ejected material.

Debt, *sb.* **5.** Add: *debt-collecting, -collector, -reduction*; **debt-raiser**, one who undertakes to raise money to pay off a debt; **debt-slave**, one who is in slavery for the redemption of debt; so **death-slavery.**
1897 *Westm. Gaz.* 13 Apr. 2/1 But not by any means must it be supposed that the work of the County Courts is confined to *debt-collecting. *Ibid.*, The small debt-collecting work which now largely occupies them. *a* 1852 in G. B. Hill *Talks about Autographs* (1896) 3 F.-M. the Duke of Wellington begs to inform Mr. Snip that he is neither the Marquis of Douro's steward nor Mr. Snip's *debt collector. 1881 *Instr. Census Clerks* (1885) 121. 1899 *Westm. Gaz.* 19 May 3/1 Lord Salisbury may be an admirable political '*debt raiser'. 1905 *Daily Chron.* 1 Feb. 6/1 We have handed over £93,376 more towards *debt reduction. 1895 Mrs. Grindrod *Siam* 40 People still sell themselves and their families to a wealthy chief, who will pay off their debts contracted through thriftlessness or gambling. These *debt slaves give service for a specified term. 1895 Swettenham *Malay Sketches* 229 The revolting practice of *debt-slavery.

Debunk (dībʌ·ŋk), *v.* *U.S.* [f. De- II. 2 + *Bunk *sb.*[4]] *trans.* To remove the 'nonsense' or false sentiment from; hence, to remove (a person) from his 'pedestal' or 'pinnacle'.
1927 *Daily Express* 18 Apr. 4/2 The 'New York Evening Post' advertises that it has employed as its chief reporter for the trial Mr. W. E. Woodward, author of the novel 'Bunk'. He is also the author of a recent life of Washington, 'debunking' the national idol by removing the aura of false sentimentality from his name. 1927 *Brit. Weekly* 29 Dec. 327/2 The somewhat ruthless process which in America is called 'debunking'—that is, pricking pretentious bubbles [etc.]. 1930 *Times Lit. Suppl.* 6 Mar. 174 The present fashion for 'debunking' great men. *Ibid.* 13 Mar. 217 He is not indeed a 'debunker', but he is as far from being a blind hero-worshipper. *Ibid.* 8 May 378 The aim of 'debunking' a reputation that has been swollen by the uncritical eulogies of contemporaries.

Debus (dībʌ·s), *v.* *Army slang.* [f. De- II. 2 + Bus *sb.*] *intr.* To alight from motor transport.
1915 *Times* 12 Mar. 10/1 The words 'embuss' and 'debuss' have been consecrated in Staff orders. Many is the battalion which has received orders to 'embuss' at dusk at X, and 'debuss' at Z. 1917 *Ibid.* 28 Sept. 9/5 This Division had already had a very hard time...From the moment of 'de-busing' its life was made very difficult for it. 1927 *Observer* 13 Nov. 17/5 One of the officers..announced.. that the infantry were 'de-busing'.

Débutante. Add: *attrib.*
1900 Elin. Glyn *Visits Eliz.* (1906) 102 By far the prettiest débutante frock. 1904 *Daily Chron.* 14 June 4/4 Lord Northampton's postponed ball for his débutante daughter. 1907 *Ibid.* 16 July 4/5 One of the débutante beauties of this season.

Decahydrate (dekăhəi·drĕt). *Chem.* [f. Deca- + Hydrate.] A compound containing ten molecules of water. So **Decahy·drated** *a.*
1880 Lunge *Sulphuric Acid* II. 6 The solubility of the decahydrated salt in water rises from 0° to 34° C. with the temperature. 1902 *Science* 24 Jan. 146 (Cent. D. Suppl.) The equilibrium conditions were determined by the solid salt being in the form of the decahydrate.

Decapod, *sb.* Add: **2.** A heavy-freight ten-wheeled locomotive originating in the United States.
1902 Prout & Soule in *Encycl. Brit.* XXXII. 150/2 'Ten-coupled' type [of engine], with a leading axle. This originated in America, where it is known as the 'Decapod'. 1903 *Westm. Gaz.* 25 Feb. 5/2 'Decapod'! New Hustling Locomotive for G.E.R. 1906 *Daily Mail* 17 Dec. 5/7 Messrs. Robert Stephenson and Co. of Darlington have just completed three..huge 'decapod' locomotives.

Decapsulate (dikæ·psiŭlĕ't), *v.* *Surg.* [f. De- II. 2 a + Capsule *sb.* + -ate[3].] *trans.* To remove the capsule of. Hence **Decapsula·tion**, the removal of the capsule.
1907 *Practitioner* Oct. 471 The decapsulation of the normal healthy kidney. *Ibid.* Dec. 778 The renal artery of a cat, whose corresponding kidney had been decapsulated and fixed two months previously.

Decarbonization. Add: **b.** Removal of carbon deposit from an internal combustion engine.
1912 *Motor Manual* (ed. 14) 232 Certain preparations in liquid form are sold for which it is claimed that, when injected in the cylinders, decarbonization and thorough cleansing is effected.

Decarbonize, *v.* Add: **b.** To remove carbon deposit from (an internal combustion engine). Also *absol.*
1925 *Morris Owner's Manual* 70 Materials required—for decarbonizing only—are the standard tool kit and a bottle of gold size. *Ibid.*, The head has to be lifted to decarbonize. *Ibid.* 71 When decarbonizing the Morris engine.

Decarbonizer (dīkā·ɹbŏnəizəɹ). [f. Decarbonize *v.* + -er[1].] One who or that which decarbonizes; *spec.* see quot. 1921.
1911 Webster. 1921 *Dict. Occup. Terms* (1927) § 449 *Decarboniser* (sugar refining); attends a number of steam-heated cylinders..in which animal charcoal is decarbonised after revivification in char kiln.

Decastich. Add mod. example.
1891 S. R. Driver *Introd. Lit. O. T.* (1892) 376 A short poem on the value of industry to the farmer consisting of a decastich.

Decasualize (dikæ·ziuăləiz), *v.* [f. De- + Casual *a.* + -ize.] *trans.* To remove the casual element from (labour). Hence **Deca·sualiza·tion**, the abolition of casual labour.
1892 T. H. Nunn in *Toynbee Record* V. 30 A permanent decasualization of labour at the Docks. 1893 *Rep. Agencies & Methods Unemployed* 12 (Parl. Papers LXXXII) In other cases, such as that of the 'decasualisation' of the docks, the displaced 'unemployed' may, to a large extent, be an inefficient 'residuum'. 1907 *Toynbee Hall Ann. Rep.* 1906–7 34 In its demand for nationalisation before means are taken to decasualise labour. 1910 *Fabian News* XXI. 16/2 Taxi-driver desires to decasualize his profession by acquiring regular clientèle. 1928 *Daily Tel.* 15 May 12/4 Bermondsey contains a large number of casual riverside labourers, whose decasualisation has been the steady aim of the Port authorities.

Decathlon (dekæ·þlŏn). [f. Gr. δέκα ten + ἆθλον contest.] In the modern Olympic games, a composite contest consisting of ten specific events.
1920 *Glasgow Herald* 23 Aug. 10 In the stadium proper most of the morning was given up to a succession of Decathlon events, including hurdles, throwing the discus, and pole jump. 1924 *Ibid.* 12 July 9 The preliminaries of the 100 metres decathlon. 1928 *Daily Tel.* 6 Nov. 19/4 The Springboks' Decathlon champion..broke down.

Decatize (de·kătəiz), *v.* [f. F. *décatir* to deprive of lustre.] *trans.* To subject (woollen cloth) to the action of steam in order to give it a permanent lustre.
1909 *Cent. D.* Suppl. 1921 *Dict. Occup. Terms* (1927) § 384 Decatising machine minder.

Decaudation (dīkǫdē^i·ʃən). [f. Decaudate: see -tion.] Removal of the tail or 'tails'.
1897 *19th Cent.* May 805 Decaudation with mutilation is seen in *bike* for *bicycle*. 1927 *Daily Tel.* 9 Aug. 8/5 The decaudation and blanching and unstiffening of the waiter are another phase of the transformation which has abolished the frock-coat and the silk hat and women's hair.

Deceased, *ppl. a.* **1.** Add: *transf.* Of a deceased person.
1906 *Times* 29 Aug. 11/2 London and North-Western stock was noticeably plentiful for delivery, and was said to have been sold heavily during the account on behalf of a deceased estate.

Decelerate (dīse·lĕrĕ't), *v.* [f. De- + L. *celer* swift + -ate[3], after *accelerate.*] *trans.* To diminish the speed of; to cause to go slower. Also *absol.* or *intr.*
1899 *Times* 30 Sept. 3/5 The 7.45 a.m. ex Exeter..is decelerated nine minutes. 1902 *Westm. Gaz.* 22 Oct. 2/1 Two years ago this timing was decelerated by 5 min. 1916 (Dec.) *Railway Notice*, The Passenger Train Service will be considerably curtailed and decelerated. 1924 *Public Opinion* 26 Apr. 399/3 Pushing the third button decelerates the whole system. 1928 *Evening Standard* 18 Mar., There would be a catastrophe if you decelerated too suddenly.

Deceleration (dīselĕrē^i·ʃən). [f. prec.: see -tion.] The action or process of decelerating a railway train, etc.
1897 *Daily News* 20 July 5/2 As far as the Great Northern and Caledonian Companies are concerned, 'deceleration' has been the order of the day in making the summer arrangements. 1900 *Ibid.* 24 Mar. 5/6 These alterations and 'decelerations' affect only Chatham trains. 1922 *Field* 18 Feb., Our travel was one of smooth acceleration and deceleration. 1926 *Bulletin* 1 Dec. 5/6 Drive cautiously and avoid sudden acceleration or deceleration.

Decelerator (dīse·lĕrĕ'təɹ). [f. *Decelerate *v.* + -or.] An apparatus for reducing the speed of an engine.
1907 *Westm. Gaz.* 18 Nov. 6/3 The decelerator which automatically throttles the engine whenever the clutch is disengaged.

December. Add: *attrib.* **December moth** (see quot.).
1832 J. Rennie *Butterfl. & M.* 38 The December Moth (*Pœcilocampa Populi*, Stephens) appears in December.

Decent, *a.* Add: **5. b.** Kind, not severe, accommodating. *colloq.* (orig. *schoolboy's*?).
1910 Harker *Master & Maid* xvii. (1923) 232 Fellows had told him how cut up old Nick was when that chap died in his house, and Bruiser was a jolly sight decenter than old Nick. *Ibid.* xx. 277 He was a very decent chap, quite a man of the world. 1928 W. Deeping *Old Pybus* ix. § 3 The pater has been rather decent.

Decentralist (dīse·ntrălist). [f. Decentralize: see -ist.] One who believes in a policy of decentralization.
1920 *Glasgow Herald* 18 Mar. 9 The struggle between the Centralists and the Decentralists or Regionalists in the matter of administration. 1921 *Q. Rev.* Apr. 398 The Centralists and Decentralists are about equal in numbers.

Decentralization. Add: Also *attrib.*
1898 *Daily News* 8 Sept. 5/1 The recommendations of Lord Lansdowne's decentralisation Committee. 1906 *Daily Chron.* 23 Jan. 5/2 The decentralisation schemes introduced by the late Government. 1908 *Ibid.* 12 May 6/4 With these larger and wider reforms the Decentralisation Commission has nothing to do. 1909 *Westm. Gaz.* 1 Mar. 2/2 The report of the Indian Decentralisation Commission.

Decentralizer (dīse·ntrăləizəɹ). [f. Decentralize *v.*] = *Decentralist.
1898 Bodley *France* I. 36 The venerable savant, himself a decentralizer.

Decerebrate (dīse·rĭbrĕt), *a.* [f. De- + Cerebrum: see -ate[2].] Deprived of the cerebrum, having the brain removed. Also **Decerebra·tion**, the removal of the brain.
1901 Dorland *Med. Dict.* (ed. 2), *Decerebration*, the removal of the brain in performing craniotomy. 1902 *Encycl. Brit.* XXXI. 744/1 The decerebrate monkey exhibits 'cataleptoid' reflexes. Father Kircher's *experimentum mirabile* with the fowl and the chalk line succeeds best with the decerebrate hen. 1915 Sir W. Osler in H. Cushing *Life* (1925) II. 484 It [*sc.* shell shock] is a sort of psychical decerebration... I suppose it is the shock and strain. 1927 Haldane & Huxley *Anim. Biol.* vi. 139 A 'decerebrate' animal, i.e. one in which the cerebral hemispheres have been removed, though unconscious, can to some extent adjust its standing posture. 1929 *Psyche* Jan. 8 As regards the hundred fundamental qualifiers (adjectives) any but a decerebrate preparation should be able to elicit the relationship of contradictory or contrary for exactly half the list.

Decian (dī·ʃiăn), *a.* [f. *Decius* + -an.] Of or pertaining to the Roman emperor Decius or his reign (A.D. 249–251), and esp. the persecution of Christians which took place under him.
1847 C. Maitland *Ch. in Catacombs* iv. 104 The Decian persecution at Carthage. 1869 T. W. Allies *Formation Christendom* II. xii. 323 At the eve of the great Decian persecution in 249. 1877 *Encycl. Brit.* VI. 746/2 The *lapsi*, or those who had fallen away through fear during the beat of the Decian persecution.

Decibar (de·sibāɹ). *Meteorol.* One tenth of a bar.
1914 [see *Bar *sb.*[6]].

Deciduoma (dīsidiu,ōu·mă). *Path.* Pl. **-ata.** [mod.L., f. Decidua + *-oma.] A tumour probably caused by portions of the decidua remaining after abortion. *Deciduoma malignum*, a malignant and cancerous deciduoma.
1890 Billings *Med. Dict.* 1907 F. J. McCann *Cancer of the Womb* xi. 119 The deciduoma malignum consists as a rule of a small primary growth. *Ibid.* 122 Deciduoma may occur at any age during the child-bearing period. 1908 *Practitioner* Mar. 413.

Decim[2] (de·sim). Abbreviation of Decimetre.
1898 *Rev. Brit. Pharm.* 53 When volumetric analysis was a matter of 'decims'. 1899 *Phil. Mag.* Ser. v. XLVIII. Fig. 1 Decim: the first Metret.

Decinormal (desin̄ǫ·ɹmăl), *a.* [f. Deci- + Normal *a.*] Having one tenth of a normal or usual strength, *spec.* denoting a chemical solution in which one litre contains one tenth of the gram-molecule or gram-equivalent of the dissolved substance.
1863 F. Sutton *Syst. Handbk. Volumetric Anal.* 19 The decinormal solutions may be made either by weighing 1/10 atom of test direct and diluting to 1000, or by diluting 100 parts of normal solution to 1000. 1898 *Rev. Brit. Pharm.* 32 Deci-normal silver nitrate.

Decivilize, *v.* (Earlier U.S. example.)
1831 Mrs. Holley *Lett. Texas* (1833) 43 It sometimes happens that a white man from the States, who has become somewhat *decivilized* (to coin a word), is substituted.

Deck, *sb.*[1] Add:
3. b. By extension, any kind of floor or platform; esp. the platform or roadway of a deck-bridge (see III below).
1883 *Specif. Alnwick & Cornhill Rlwy.* 45 The girders are connected by a wrought-iron deck. 1910 A. Williams *Engineering Wonders of World* III. 282 The old suspension truss, which could then be removed piece by piece to make room for the upper deck.

c. *Aviation.* A main aeroplane surface, esp. of a biplane or multiplane.
1910 A. Williams *Engin. Wonders of World* III. 7/2 The biplane, with two 'decks' set one above the other.

4. b. The floor of a tramcar or omnibus. *Top* or *upper deck*, the upper floor or compartment of a double-decked vehicle. Cf. *Double-deck.
1903 [implied in *Double-decked *a.*]. 1906 *Daily Chron.* 11 Sept. 7/1 The cars..have no upper deck, and carry only thirty-six passengers, as compared with accommodation for sixty-six in and on the double-deck pattern. 1921 *Dict. Occup. Terms* (1927) § 474 Top decks of double-decked tramcars.

c. The floor of a pier, landing-stage, or jetty; *spec.* a lower part used for the embarking and disembarking of passengers. (Cf. *Decking 2.)
1872 *Porcupine* XIV. 314/2 The decks of the three stages being swept pretty clear, by the devastating fire of the enemy. 1876 *Ibid.* XVIII. 330/1 Its deck is fairly rotting away.

III. *deck-cabin, -car, -cricket, -dandy, -feed pump, hoisting engine, -passage, -passenger* (U.S. examples), *-planking, plating, -scrubber, -tent, -trumpet*; **deck-boy**, a boy employed on the deck of a vessel; **deck-bridge** (*b*) (example); **deck-feather** (see quot.); **deck-framing** (see Framing *vbl. sb.* 4); **deck-hand** (earlier U.S. examples); **deck-lander**, an aeroplane designed so as to be able to land on a ship's deck; **deck-light, -load** (U.S. examples); **deck-pot**, a pot used on whaling vessels to receive the scraps; **deck-stringer** *Shipbuilding*, a stringer (see Stringer 5 b) supporting the deck-beams.
1900 *Westm. Gaz.* 22 Mar. 5/2 Prisoner said he was *deck-boy on board the *Carisbrook Castle.* 1908 *Ibid.* 28 Aug. 12/1 The owner..sent his son, the deck-boy, down to the engineer. 1874 Knight *Dict. Mech.*, **Deck-bridge*, one in which the track occupies the upper stringer, as distinguished from one in which the track..rests on the lower stringer. 1902 *Westm. Gaz.* 28 July 2/1 He..writes pictured postcards at the *deck-cabin table. 1891 *Scribner's Mag.* X. 278 *Deck cricket, quoits, and cock-fighting enliven the forenoons. 1879 *Encycl. Brit.* IX. 7/1 *Deck feathers, the two centre tail-feathers. 1874 Knight *Dict. Mech.*, **Deck-feed Pump* (Nautical), a hand-pump used for washing decks, feeding the boiler, etc. 1894 *Outing* (U.S.) XXIV. 396/1 Everything else, including the *deck-framing and deck is of the same kind of material as those used in a regular battleship. 1844 *Knickerbocker Mag.* XXIII. 88 On board of one of the steam-boats on the Mississippi, I encountered a *deck-hand, who went by the name of Barney. 1846 Sol. Smith *Theatr. Apprenticeship* 146 The fees were paid, the deck-hand gathered his bundle, and we walked down to the landing. 1853 J. G. Baldwin *Flush Times Alabama* 96 Could not interest procure service as a deck-hand on a steam-boat? 1928 *Daily Tel.* 18 Sept. 11/4 It [*sc.* the autogiro] should be able to act as a *deck-lander on almost any ship. 1849 N. Kingsley *Diary* 7 Mate arrived today, Mr. Webb, put in *deck lights and scuttle to house on deck. 1757 *Essex Inst. Hist. Coll.* XLVI. 273 They hove overboard the *Deck load of Lumber. 1837 *Gaz. Illinois* App. III. 324 A **deck* passage..:—The deck for such passengers is usually in the midships. 1883 'Mark Twain' *Life Mississippi* vi. 79 He only traveled deck passage because it was cooler! 1835 J. H. Ingraham *South-West* I. ix. 106 Their former owners with well-lined purses return home as *deck passengers on board steamboats. 1872 Eggleston *End of World* xxviii. 187 He passed through to the place where the steerage or deck passengers are. 1889 Welch *Naval Archit.* ix. 110 *Deck Plating and Planking. 1904 *Sci. Amer. Suppl.* 5 Mar. 23551 The oil flows freely..into the pots, while the refuse.. is thrown into another receptacle, called the 'deck-pot. 1920 *Blackw. Mag.* Apr. 509/2 He..belaboured them methodically with a *deck-scrubber. 1874 *deck stringer [see Stringer 5 b]. 1874 Thearle *Naval Archit.* 102 The deck-stringer plate. 1838 J. F. Cooper *Eve Effingham* I. ii. 52 A capital watch..and a *deck-trumpet, in solid silver.

Deck (dek), *sb.*[2] *Anglo-Indian.* Also **dekh.** [Hind. *dekha* sight, *dekhnā* to see, look at. Cf. *Dekko.] A look, peep.
1853 W. Arnold *Oakfield* .iv. 85 Some officer, stopping, as he passed by,..'just to have a dekh at the steamer'. 1886 Yule & Burnell *Hobson-Jobson*, Deck.

Deck, *v.* Add: **6.** In lumbering: To pile *up* (logs) on a skidway. *U.S.*
1901 *Munsey's Mag.* XXV. 392/1 Other men pile—technically, 'deck'—them [*sc.* logs] exactly as in the woods. 1905 *Terms Forestry & Logging* 35 Deck up.

Deck-chair. A folding cane-panelled chair, usually with adjustable leg rest, used primarily on the deck of a ship as seating accommodation for passengers. Also popularly applied to a hammock chair.
1886 [see Deck *sb.* III]. 1888 W. S. Caine *Trip round World* i. 3 Ladies are grouped about in pleasant corners in easy deck-chairs. 1903 'Guy Thorne' *When it was Dark* (1905) 369 Spence sank into a deck-chair. 1904 *Daily Chron.* 6 Oct. 8/1 At eleven o'clock soup and crackers..are served and little deck-chair groups are formed. 1926 *Spectator* 11 Sept. 372/2 To spend one's leisure lying on a deck-chair.

Decker[1]. Add:
2. One who rolls logs on a skidway. *U.S.*
1902 S. E. White *Blazed Trail* viii. 57 He decided to advance Bob Stratton to the post, that 'decker' having had more or less experience the year before. 1905 *Terms Forestry & Logging* 35.

Deckie (de·ki). [f. Deck *sb.*[1] + -ie.] A decker, a deck-hand.
1913 *Q. Rev.* Apr. 435 This 'deckie'..has usually no more knowledge of seamanship than a ploughboy. 1927 *Scots Observer* 8 Jan. 2/3 One of the 'deckies' said he would manage the job.

Decking, *vbl. sb.* Add:
2. Also in extended uses (see *Deck *sb.*[1] 3 b, 4 c).
1883 *Specif. Alnwick & Cornhill Rlwy.* 45 The superstructure consists of two wrought-iron plate girders..connected together by cross-bracing and by a decking of curved strips. 1897 *Daily News* 3 May 2/1 Piles, beams, and decking. 1898 *Ibid.* 4 Oct. 3/2 A huge decking..is being constructed in the river. *Ibid.* 12 Dec. 3/3 It was some time before the decking of the pier collapsed. 1900 *Westm. Gaz.* 29 Dec. 5/2 Some of the decking of St. Leonards pier was wrenched away by the waves. 1905 *Daily Chron.* 9 Jan. 5/2 A quantity of decking [of the pier] was torn up on the land side.

3. In lumbering: The action of piling logs on a skidway. Also attrib. *decking-chain. U.S.*
1901 *Munsey's Mag.* XXV. 392/1 A decking chain more than three hundred feet long is required to roll the logs to their places. 1902 S. E. White *Blazed Trail* xi. 83 A shout of surprise or horror would have stopped the horse pulling on the decking chain.

Deckled (de·k'ld), *a.* [f. Deckle + -ed.] Formed by a deckle; deckle-edged.
1906 C. G. McCrie *Contemp. Portraits of Reformers* (dust-jacket) Vellum gilt, gilt top, deckled edges.

Declaration. Add:
6. *ellipt.* = Declaration of Independence.
1837 *Knickerbocker Mag.* X. 444 He was a distinguished man;..read 'the Declaration' on every Fourth-of-July.

8. b. In the game of bridge, the naming of the trump suit or the declaring of 'no trumps' by any of the players.
1905 in W. Dalton '*Saturday' Bridge* (1910) 12 [Rules] 48. If the dealer does not wish to exercise his option [of declaring], he may pass it to his partner.., and his partner must thereupon make the necessary declaration...49. If the dealer's partner make the trump declaration without receiving permission from the dealer, the eldest hand may demand: I. That the declaration so made shall stand. II. That there shall be a new deal. 1910 *Ibid.* 38 The declaration at Bridge affords an opportunity for the exercise of certain qualities which were never called into use in the game of Whist. *Ibid.* 39 The most expensive declaration..being No Trumps, when the value of each trick is twelve points.

Decla·re, *sb.* [f. Declare *v.* 11.] An act of declaring in the game of poker.
1887 S. Cumberland *Queen's Highway* 279, I raised Browne's last declare to the extent of the limit.

Declare, *v.* Add: **5. e.** *Cricket.* To close an innings before the usual ten wickets have fallen. orig. 'to *declare* the innings at an end'.
[1889 *Laws of Cricket* 54 On the last day of a match, and in a one-day match at any time, the in-side may declare their innings at an end.] 1897 *Encycl. Sport* I. 245/2 *Declare*, to close an innings. 1901 *Daily News* 5 June 4/4 Warwickshire made 532 for four wickets, and then declared.

9. b. *Racing.* To announce the withdrawal of (a horse) from a race for which it has been entered; said also of a horse.
1847 *Weekly Times* 9 Oct., Stakes of 10 sovs each, 5 f[orfeit], and only 3 if declared. 1897 *Westm. Gaz.* 5 Feb. 9/2 Two Grand National winners have just declared.

11. b. In the game of bridge, to make or name the trump suit, or to announce the intention to play 'no trumps'.
1905 in W. Dalton '*Saturday' Bridge* (1910) 12–13 [Rules] 47. The dealer..has the option of declaring which suit shall be trumps...55. The player who has declared the trump shall have the first right [of doubling].

c. 'In billiards, to name or designate the particulars as to the balls, the pocket, etc. of (a shot about to be played)' (Webster 1911).

Declarer. Add:
3. b. In the game of bridge, one who declares (*Declare *v.* 11 b). So **Decla·ring** *ppl. a.*
1905 in W. Dalton '*Saturday' Bridge* (1910) 13 [Rule] 57. The declarer of the trump shall have the right to say whether or not the double shall stand. 1910 *Ibid.* 242 A declaration of 'Two Hearts' offers a free double to the opponents when the declaring side is 16 up, or more. 1921 *Sat. Westm. Gaz.* 1 Oct. 17/1 In playing a no-trump hand, declarer is recommended to bear in mind the calls.

Déclassé (deklase), *sb.* and *a.* fem. **-ée.** [Fr., pa. pple. of *déclasser* Declass *v.*] Reduced or degraded from one's social class, that has lost caste. Often *absol.* with *the* or in *pl.*
1887 *Fortn. Rev.* Aug. 227 It is only the *déclassé*, the ne'er-do-well, or the really unfortunate, who has nothing to call his own. 1905 *Spectator* 28 Jan. 144/2 Pamela.. quits the company of artists and actresses, *declassés* and *divorcées.* 1921 *Glasgow Herald* 3 Aug., The attempt by a body of declassés to form the policy of the entire working-class of this country. 1921 *Times Lit. Suppl.* 29 Sept. 626/2 A girl of any family may, by force of circumstances, become *déclassée.*
So **Déclassement** (deklasmaṅ).
1891 *Jrnl. Roy. Statist. Soc.* June 383 The primary school ..is rapidly leading to a general *déclassement.*

Declination. 11. Add: **declination axis**, that axis of an equatorial telescope which is at right angles to the polar axis, and to which is attached at one end the telescope and at the other the declination circle, so called because when the position of the telescope is changed by turning the declination axis there is an alteration in the declination of the object viewed; **declination circle**, (*b*) the graduated circle which marks the declinations of the heavenly bodies; **declination compass**, a compass which measures the magnetic declination; **declination magnet**, a magnet used in determining the magnetic declination and the magnetic axis.
1835 *Mech. Mag.* XXIV. 210/2 On these rollers turns the *declination axis. 1888 *Encycl. Brit.* XXIII. 146/2 The equatorial in its simplest form consists of an axis parallel to the earth's axis, called the 'polar axis'; a second axis, at right angles to this, called the 'declination axis'; and a telescope fixed at right angles to the latter. 1891 *Anthony's Photogr. Bull.* IV. 368 The Lick telescope is simply a magnified equatorial..with a polar axis in bearings and a declination axis at right angles to it. 1905 *Westm. Gaz.* 17 Apr. 1/3 A large equatorial with a 26-in. photographic refractor at one end of the declination axis and a 30-in. reflector at the other. 1835 *Mech. Mag.* XXIV. 211 Y is the *declination circle, fixed on the declination axis. 1888 D. Gill in *Encycl. Brit.* XXIII. 149/1 The declination circle is attached to the farther end of the declination axis. 1862 *Chambers's Encycl.* III. 461/1 The ordinary compass which must be used by making allowance for declination, is a *declination compass. 1883 *Encycl. Brit.* XV. 238/1 The first step is to remove the torsion as far as possible from the suspension fibre by hanging to it a brass plummet E of the same weight as the *declination magnet. After this weight has come to rest, it is replaced by the declination magnet. 1899 *Daily News* 3 Mar. 5/2 They have placed out here a declination magnet, a dip instrument for the inclination of the needle, and a deflexion instrument.

Decline, *sb.* Add: **1. f.** That stage of a disease at which the symptoms begin to abate.
1848 Dunglison *Med. Lex.* (ed. 7).

Decline, *v.* Add: **13. d.** *Chess.* To refuse to take a piece or pawn offered.
1873 G. H. D. Gossip *Chess-Player's Man.* 705 The Queen's Gambit accepted and declined. 1899 E. E. Cunnington *How to Play Chess* 48 P-QKt4, offering the sacrifice of a P. to get an attack. Black need not take it (he may retreat the B to Kt3), in which case the Opening is called the Evans declined.

Decli·vitously, *adv.* [f. Declivitous + -ly[2].] In a steep manner; down a steep slope.
1930 Locke *Tombarel* vii. 215 The path lands you declivitously into the Place Georges Clemenceau.

Declutch (dīklʌ·tʃ), *v.* [f. De- + *Clutch *sb.*[1] 6 a.] *intr.* To disengage the clutch of a motor vehicle.
1905 *Daily Chron.* 21 Mar. 7/4 Without once using a brake, changing his gear, declutching or slipping the clutch. 1906 *Westm. Gaz.* 16 July 5/1 The driver of the 'bus declutched at the top of the hill. 1925 *Morris Owner's Manual* 10 The expert driver will have recourse to double declutching.

Decode (dīkōu·d), *v.* [f. De- I. 6 + Code *sb.*[1]] *trans.* To decipher or translate (a coded message); to interpret (a communication written in a code) by means of the key. Also *absol.* and *fig.*
1896 *N. Brit. Daily Mail* 28 Aug. 5 The message was decoded. 1897 *Westm. Gaz.* 26 Jan. 2/1 If it seems desirable, I shall decode and publish at my own time. *Ibid.* 18 May 7/1 The decoded cables. 1897 *Times* 30 June 9 The cipher telegrams in which they and Mr. Rhodes are concerned, and which have now been decoded. 1899 *Daily Chron.* 13 May 4/3 There was at first a little doubt as to the decoding. The cipher was a new one and they had not mastered it. 1904 *Daily News* 26 Oct. 7/2 The process of coding and decoding is a long one.

Decohere (dīkohī·ɹ), *v.* *Electr.* [f. De- + Cohere.] **a.** *trans.* To restore (a coherer) to its normal condition of sensitiveness. Also *absol.*, and *intr.* for *pass.*
1902 *How to make Useful Things* 5/1 The purpose of the tapper is to decohere the filings after they are affected by the etheric waves. *Ibid.* 6/1 The tapper keeps busily at work decohering in response to the continuously closing circuit caused by the waves.
Hence **Decohe·rence, Decohe·sion; Decohe·rer**, a device for bringing a coherer back to its normal condition.
1899 Marconi in *Jrnl. Inst. Electr. Engin.* XXVIII. 275 This coherer forms part of a circuit..which circuit works a trembler or decoherer and a recording instrument. 1902 *Science* 21 Mar. 466 (Cent. D. Suppl.) After a short description of the single contact coherer used by him and an explanation of the so-called decohesion, he calculated how near the metallic surfaces must be brought together. 1903 *Science Abstracts* VI. Section B. 128 The self-induction of the telephone may have been sufficient to cause the decoherence. 1913 *Work* 4 Oct. 7/2 The decoherer circuit.

Decoke (dīkōu·k), *v.* [f. De- II. 2 + Coke *sb.*] = *Decarbonize.
1928 *Daily Express* 19 May 13/2 My advice to all motorists who are puzzled about..the 'knocking' which invariably accompanies carbonisation, is that they should lose not an hour in getting the engine 'decoked'. *Ibid.* 31 May 3/7 Good car, but wants decoking.

Décollement (dekolmaṅ). *Med.* [Fr., f. *décoller*, f. De- + *coller* to glue.] Separation of tissue from surrounding parts.
[1848 Dunglison *Med. Lex.* (ed. 7), *Décollement*, the state of an organ that is separated from the surrounding parts, owing to destruction of the cellular membrane which united them. The skin is *décollé*, i.e. separated from the subjacent parts.] 1908 *Practitioner* Sept. 455 (from French) The third danger zone is behind in the neighbourhood of the portal vein and vena cava. Injury to these vessels may be avoided by practising 'decollement' of the duodenum. ..The stage of decollement being completed, ablation may be proceeded with.

Décolletage (dekoltāʒ). (Also **decoltage.**) [Fr.: see Décolleté.]
1. The low-cut neck of a bodice.
1894 *Season* X. 34/2 Into the breast pleats are placed fan-shaped gores..loosely smocked into the decoltage. 1896 *Westm. Gaz.* 14 Mar. 3/2 The sleeves and upper bodice are in creamy white chiffon, and the dark line round the décolletage of black jet. 1902 *Queen* 10 May 816/2 A soft fold of pink silk at the decolletage.

2. Exposure of the neck and shoulders by the low cut of the bodice. Also *fig.*
1894 *Sat. Rev.* LXXVIII. 596 Such art as that of John Oliver Hobbes, so typically feminine in its discreet décolletage, is not truth but effect. 1921 *Public Opinion* 8 July 37/3 A bold *decolletage* of shoulders still young and white. 1924 *Blackw. Mag.* Nov. 678/1 *Skeletta's* ever-increasing décolletage had a sort of embarrassed fascination for us.

Décolletée (dekolte). (Now disused?) [fem. pa. pple. of *décolleter*: see Decolleté.] The low cut neck of a bodice.
1907 *Daily Chron.* 2 July 10/5 Mohair braid round the décolletée and armpits in bretelles and as bands on the skirt. 1908 *Ibid.* 24 Aug. 7/5 Décolletée and sleeves are in Malines.

Decolo(u)rize, *v.* Add: **b.** *intr.* To lose colour, to become colourless.
1908 *Practitioner* Feb. 205 Characteristics of the gonococcus...Its characteristic half-moon shape, and the fact that it decolourises with Gram's method.
Hence **Deco·lo(u)rized** *ppl. a.*
1879 *St. George's Hosp. Rep.* IX. 509 Decolorised blood-clot. 1890 W. J. Gordon *Foundry* 177 Decolourized indigo.

Decomposing, *ppl. a.* Add: **decomposing furnace**, 'a chemical furnace, used in the soda industry in decomposing chloride of sodium with sulphuric acid' (Knight); **decomposing man** (see quot. 1921).
1876 *Sci. Amer. Suppl.* 305 (Knight 1884) *Decomposing furnace. 1881 *Instr. Census Clerks* (1885) 60 Alkali Manufacture...*Decomposing Man. 1921 *Dict. Occup. Terms* (1927) § 143 *Deacon plant man,..decomposing man*; a process man who makes chlorine gas by acidising hydrochloric acid gas.

Decompress (dīkǫmpre·s), *v.* [f. De- + Compress *v.*] *trans.* To relieve the air pressure on (one who has been working in compressed air) in an air-lock before returning to the outside air. Also *absol.* Hence **Decompre·ssing** *vbl. sb.*; **Decompre·ssion**, the process of relieving pressure, the restoration to the pressure of the outside air; *Surg.* the removal of a flap of the skull to relieve intercranial pressure; so **Decompre·ssive** *a.*
1906 *Westm. Gaz.* 27 Jan. 10/1 The men who controlled the airlocks, and were subjected to compression and decompression every few minutes, were in no case affected. 1910 H. Cushing in *Mod. Med.* (ed. Osler & McCrae) VII. 457 Tumor-Palliation (Decompressive Operations). *Ibid.* 458 When it is desirable to end a fruitless exploration of the hemisphere with a palliative decompression, the osteoplastic flap may be removed *in toto.* *Ibid.*, We have had over 70 subtemporal decompressions for tumor. 1911 *Engineer* 10 Mar. 243/1 To decompress slowly but continuously. 1925 *Literary Digest* 27 June 24/1 When they have finished their labors, it is necessary that they be 'decomprest', that is, slowly restored to normal air conditions. *Ibid.*, The two air-locks..are used in putting the compress-air workers gradually under pressure and for decompressing them after they have finished work. *Ibid.*, To reduce most materially the period of 'decompression' of divers.

Decompressor (dīkǫmpre·sǫɹ). [f. *Decompress *v.* + -or.] An apparatus for reducing compression in a motor engine.
1923 *Daily Mail* 7 June 12 An ingenious decompressor to lower the engine compression..for easy starting.

Decongestive (dīkǫndʒe·stiv), *a.* and *sb.* *Path.* [f. De- II. 1 + Congestive *a.*] **a.** *adj.* That relieves congestion. **b.** *sb.* A decongestive agent. So **Deconge·stion.**
1903 *Med. Record* 1 Aug. 167 (Cent. D. Suppl.) Treatment ..by electricity..has a decongestive local action. 1908 *Practitioner* Oct. 569 Heat relieves the pain, not by the old-fashioned theory of 'de-congestion', but by causing hyperæmia.

Decontrol (dīkǫntrōu·l), *sb.* [De-.] The removal of control, *spec.* the removal of government control. Hence **Decontro·l** *v.*
1919 G. H. Roberts in *Times* 14 Feb. 3/1, I am told that every one wants to get rid of Government control...The moment I can see those conditions safeguarded in respect of any commodity, decontrol will come. *Ibid.* 3/2, I do not propose to risk decontrolling any commodity while there is the slightest possibility of decontrol resulting in higher prices. 1923 *Daily Mail* 27 Jan. 8 Rent decontrol. 1923 Ramsay MacDonald in *Parl. Debates* CLX. 21 To decontrol a certain block of middle-class tenants..will do more harm than good. Look at what happens the moment decontrol comes. Either the rent goes up, or what is more likely the house will be sold.

Décor (dekǭr). [Fr., a. L. *decor* Decor(e).] The scenery and furnishings of a theatre stage; also, the lay-out or method of display of an exhibition, entertainment, etc.
1927 *Observer* 5 June 11/2 Despite the producer's hortatory notes, the ingenuity of the décor, and some very clever acting. 1927 *Daily Tel.* 16 Aug. 12/5 The new décor of 'The Mikado'. 1927 *Observer* 24 July 18/3 Olympia last week marked a revolution in exhibition *décor.* 1931 *Times Lit. Suppl.* 29 Jan. 76/2 This author..seems to lavish all his art ..on fitting to them [*sc.* his characters]..a telling *décor.*

Decorate, *v.* Add: **2. c.** *spec.* To deck (a town) with flags and bunting.
1852 *Illustr. Lond. News* 26 June 504/2 The *façade* of the market was tastefully decorated with tri-coloured banners. 1872 *Porcupine* 29 June 201/2 The whole display was organized and paid for by a committee of tradesmen in the streets which were decorated. 1882 *Standard* 28 Apr. 6 Has the town been beflagged and decorated?

Decoration. Add: 2. b. *pl.* Flags, wreaths, etc., put up at festival times or on occasions of public rejoicing.

1887 *Jubilee Celebr. Cambr.* 16 The townspeople..putting out their decorations earlier than they probably otherwise would have done.

4. The composition placed in the head of a rocket which makes the display when the case explodes.

1873–4 W. H. Browne *Art of Pyrotechny* 23 The rocket is now ready for its cap or pot which is to contain the stars or other decorations that are to be used. 1888—*Firework Making* 74 The first decorations that I shall notice are rocket stars.

Decortication. Add: *spec.* in surgical use.

1909 *Practitioner* Nov. 661 Where the surgeon finds during the course of a nephrectomy that the decortication of the sac is very difficult.

Decoudun (dĕkū·dən). [Named after Jules *Decoudun*.] A calender ironing machine of French invention, first made in England in 1876.

1889 *Laundry Management* p. xxi, The Decoudun Ironer. ..The decoudun varies in size and construction with each maker. A simple form consists of a polished metal bed (concave) and a heavy roller, fitted in a strong cast-iron frame. 1905 *Daily Chron.* 23 Feb. 9/2 Wanted to purchase, Decoudon Ironer, a Cudlipp Perfect preferred. *Ibid.* 31 Oct. 9/5 Laundry.—Wanted really good calender hands, for calender and Decoudun. 1911 *Encycl. Brit.* XVI. 282/1. 1921 *Dict. Occup. Terms* (1927) § 918 Decoudun hand.

Decoy, *sb.*[2] 6. Add: **decoy keeper,** a decoy-man; **decoy ship,** one used to decoy enemy vessels.

1881 *Instr. Census Clerks* (1885) 39 Decoy Man, *Decoy Keeper. 1921 *Dict. Occup. Terms* (1927) § 910 Decoy keeper, decoy man. 1915 *War Illustrated* III. 262/2 *Decoy ships flying a neutral flag. 1923 Churchill *World Crisis, 1915* 290 Our two principal devices for destroying the German submarines were the Bircham Indicator Nets and the Decoy Ships, afterwards called the Q-boats. 1925 Fraser & Gibbons *Soldier & Sailor Words, Decoy Ships*, a name for certain vessels (also known as 'Mystery Ships' and 'Q-Ships'), introduced in 1915.

Decoyment (dĭkoi·mĕnt). [f. Decoy *v.*: see -ment.] The action or fact of decoying.

1841 H. S. Foote *Texas & Texans* I. 59 Abominable treachery [was] practiced for the decoyment of the confiding Montezuma into captivity.

Decretorial (dekrĭtōᵊ·riăl), *a.* Transfer †*Obs.* to 1 and add to 2:

1909 Geo. Tyrrell *Christianity at Cross Roads* 179 He understood this destination as more than moral or decretorial, as an inherent potentiality of His spirit. 1921 *Glasgow Herald* 18 Apr. 7 The argument..which that gentleman plainly considers decretorial.

Decretum (dĭkrī·tŏm). [L.] A decree; sometimes short for *Decretum Gratiani*.

1600 W. Watson *Decacordon* (1602) 163 The *decretum* of the order obserued in all elections. 1817 *Parl. Debates* 939 (Stanford) The *decretum* of the Irish synod was promulgated in Dublin. 1888 *Encycl. Brit.* XXIV. 639/1 The Decretum specially inculcated subjection of the wife to the husband.

Dedes (dī·des). [Javanese.] A perfume obtained from the rasse.

1817 Raffles *Java* I. 50 Musk, called dedes, is procured from the rasé. 1843 *Penny Cycl.* XXVI. 406/2 This is the *Rasse* of the Javanese, who term the odoriferous secretion *dedes* or *jibet*.

Dedifferentiate (dīdifĕre·nʃiˌeɪt), *v. Biol.* [f. De- + Differentiate.] *intr.* Of an organ: To lose its special form or function. Hence **Dedifferentiated** *ppl. a.*; **Dedifferentiation**, the loss of form or function, simplification of structure.

1921 J. S. Huxley in *Discovery* Feb. 28/2 Such a process, which we may style dedifferentiation followed by redifferentiation, is clear evidence of the possibility of reversing development. 1926 *Glasgow Herald* 18 Sept. 4 A good example of the dedifferentiated inert state of suspended animation is the 'brown body' of some of the moss-animals. 1927 Haldane & Huxley *Anim. Biol.* ix. 179 Eventually they will lose almost all signs of their previous differentiated structure... They have lost differentiation—in other words, have undergone dedifferentiation. *Ibid.* 180 When the tadpole metamorphoses into the frog, some of its tissues start to dedifferentiate.

Dedolomitization (dīdǫlŏmitaizē·ʃən). *Min.* [f. De- + Dolomitize *v.* + -ation.] The changing of dolomite into rock of another kind. So **Dedo·lomitize** *v.* (Cent. D. Suppl. 1909).

1907 J. J. H. Teall in Geikie *Geol. Struct. N.-W. Highl. Scot.* 461 In extreme cases no dolomite is left; in others there is only partial dedolomitisation. 1930 Peach & Horne *Geol. Scotl.* 113 Another method of dedolomitization should be added to those enumerated by Teall.

Deductible, *a.* Delete *rare* and add quots. (also **Dedu·ctable**):

1894 *Westm. Gaz.* 14 Aug. 2/1 Now tax is deductable either at the rate actually in force at the date of payment. 1913 *Standard* 3 Apr. 11/4 A dividend entrusted to an agent for payment on a date before April 6 is chargeable with the duty in force for the year 1912–13, and the duty is deductible notwithstanding that payment in individual cases may not happen to be claimed until after that date. 1918 *Nation* (N.Y.) 7 Feb. 169/1 Advances against future payments to the insured..deductible at the maturity of the policy. 1925 *Glasgow Herald* 30 Jan. 9 The time within which..discount was deductable under the contract.

Dee, *v.* Add: b. = Damned.

1889 Kipling *From Sea to Sea* ii. Wks. 1900 I. 256 Dee fool. It's different in Upper Burma.

De-emanate (dīˌe·mănēɪt), *v.* [f. De- + Emanate.] *trans.* To deprive (a radioactive substance) of the power of sending out radioactive emanations. Hence **De-emana·tion.**

1904 E. Rutherford *Radio-activity* 216 Thus de-emanation does not permanently destroy the power of thorium of giving out an emanation. *Ibid.*, The de-emanated thoria was dissolved. 1913 Dorland *Med. Dict.* (ed. 7), *Deëmanate*, to deprive of the property of giving off radioactive emanations.

Deemstership (dī·mstəʃip). [f. Deemster + -ship.] The office of Deemster in the Isle of Man.

1894 Hall Caine *Manxman* III. iii, Let the Deemstership go to perdition. 1902 *Daily Chron.* 28 Mar. 5/2 When he retired from his deemstership of the Isle of Man in 1897.

Deep, *sb.* Add: 3. d. *Cricket.* The deep field (see *Deep *a.* IV. c).

1906 Beldam & Fry *Gt. Bowlers & Fielders* 438 A fine example of the throw in from 'the deep'. 1924 Selincourt *Cricket Match* iv. (1928) 89 One catch in the deep which he had held in a school cricket match..was still vividly remembered.

Deep, *a.* Add: 1. b. Also of a theatrical set scene.

1918 H. Croy *How Motion Pictures are Made* 90 Audiences ..demanded real rooms, with the result that 'deep' sets replaced the painted representations.

c. *In deep water* (fig. phr.; cf. Psalm lxix. 2, 14): in trouble, difficulty, or distress; in distressful (esp. impecunious) circumstances.

1867 Trollope *Chron. Barset* xxxiv, Once he had been very nearly in deep water because Mrs. Proudie had taken it in dudgeon that a certain young rector, who had been left a widower, had a very pretty governess for his children. [1886 Stevenson *Kidnapped* xxiii. 275 I thought it seemed deep water for Alan to be riding, who had no better battle-horse than a green purse and a matter of five pounds. Cf. quot. 1926 s.v. Deepish *a.*]

d. *To go (in) off the deep end*, etc.: to let oneself go, give way to emotion or passion.

1921 *Times Lit. Suppl.* 22 Dec. 853/3 Saint-Saens rarely, if ever, takes any risks; he never, to use the slang of the moment, 'went in off the deep end'. 1922 Joad *Highbrows* vi. 186 She passed her life metaphorically at the end of a diving-board, ready at the slightest provocation to go in at the deep end. 1923 *Weekly Dispatch* 21 Jan. 5 Mr. Nicholas Hannen..plays the second fiddling husband admirably, except when, once or twice, he goes off the deep end a trifle too explosively. 1924 Galsworthy *White Monkey* II. iv, Would it not be more in the mode, really dramatic—if one 'went over the deep end', as they said, just once? 1930 *Punch* 12 Mar. 300/1 There are fathers who, when their sons get the sack..go off the deep end.

2. b. Also in trivial use, *so many deep* = having so many engagements or obligations.

1921 *Discovery* Sept. 242/2 He proposed to her, and she accepted him—if he would wait his turn; she was four deep already!

3. c. *spec.* Far below the surface of the ground: said of mining operations. *Deep lead* (see Lead *sb.*[2] 6).

1839 *Penny Cycl.* XV. 239/2 Even in very deep shafts, when complete, daylight may be seen from the bottom. 1899 *Daily News* 3 May 3/5 Deep-level mines and deep-level mining. 1902 *Daily Chron.* 2 Dec. 6/5 Mr. Chapman maintained that it was possible so to ventilate even a deep-level tube railway that passengers 'would not notice any difference between the atmosphere in the tunnels and the atmosphere on the street level'. 1906 *Ibid.* 21 Mar. 6/6 Some of his 'deep-sinking' projects were at first considered symptoms of insanity. 1921 *Dict. Occup. Terms* (1927) § 581 *Deep sinking labourer*; navvy or miner engaged in sinking deep holes or shafts.

IV. a. *deep-well.*

1874 Knight *Dict. Mech.*, *Deep-well Pump*, a pump specifically adapted for oil and brine wells which are bored of small diameters and to great depths. 1906 *Daily Chron.* 5 Sept. 3/3 To allow these deep-well waters..to run heedlessly to waste, is a policy of which a later generation of Australians may have bitter cause for complaint.

b. *deep-bosomed* (Gr. βαθύκολπος), *-faced*, *-rutted* adjs.

1848 Buckley *Iliad* 346 Trojan (dames) and *deep-bosomed Dardanians. 1876 Pater *Greek Studies* (1895) 81 The deep-bosomed daughters of the Ocean. 1905 R. Garnett *Shakespeare* 56 Not all deep-bosomed earth's wide fruitfulness. 1909 *Westm. Gaz.* 14 Aug. 2/3 The brown-faced, deep-bosomed peasant women. 1908 *Westm. Gaz.* 23 Dec. 4/1 A number of golfers playing with *deep-faced, round-headed drivers. 1836 T. Hook *G. Gurney* I. iii. 217 At the corner of the *deep-rutted lane. 1899 *Daily News* 19 Oct. 6/1 Transports stopped in the deep-rutted roads. 1906 *Daily Chron.* 10 Mar. 4/4 There is a sort of road, steep, winding, deep-rutted down to the stream.

c. **deep-draught** *a.*, of a vessel that draws or displaces deep water; **deep field** *Cricket*, that part of the field which is near the boundary, esp. behind the bowler; also, a fieldsman or his position there; **deep-milking,** the production of a good yield of milk; so *deep-milker*; **deep-rooter,** something which takes deep root; **deep-sinker** *Austral.*, (*a*) a drinking-glass of the largest size, so called from a fanciful resemblance to a deep mine shaft; (*b*) the drink served in such a glass; **deep tank,** a tank for water ballast, formed by cutting off a part of a ship's hold.

1908 *Westm. Gaz.* 30 Oct. 11/4 None of our inward water-borne traffic enters the Port in *deep-draft vessels. 1900 *Ibid.* 22 June 3/1 There is scarcely a bowler nowadays who does not station at least one man in the *deep-field. *Ibid.* 3/2 Our first two batsmen..succeeded in getting the ball between his deep fields. 1881 Sheldon *Dairy Farming* 5/2 It is important that she should be a '*deep milker' *Ibid.* 36/2 Deep milking..is a question of breeding and training. 1833 *Ridgemont Farm Rep.* 148 in *Libr. Usef. Knowl., Husb.* III, The large, heavy, slow-fattening but *deep-milking cows of this country. 1923 *Discovery* Sept. 244/2 The deep-milking propensity of some cows may be transmitted through the bull to the next generation of female calves. 1898 *Westm. Gaz.* 19 Mar. 2/1 Her first cousin..is a *deep-rooter, and must be looked after betimes. 1927 *Smallholder* 26 Mar. 105/2 The main-crop, deep-rooters should be sown at the end of May. 1897 *Argus* 15 Jan. 6/5 (Morris) A tumbler—whether medium, small, or *deepsinker.

Deep, *adv.* Add: 3. *deep digging, ploughing.*

1844 H. Stephens *Bk. Farm* I. 641 On the broad principle that deep ploughing ought to be the rule.

Deeping. Add: 2. The making of deep theatrical set scenes. Cf. *Deep *a.* 1 b.

1918 H. Croy *How Motion Pictures are Made* 90 As the number of producing companies began to increase rivalry resulted and everywhere was there 'deeping'.

Deepish (dī·piʃ), *a.* [f. Deep *a.* + -ish [1].] Somewhat or rather deep.

1879 Miss Bird *Lady's Life Rocky Mountains* 197 We crossed a deepish stream on the ice. 1920 *Blackw. Mag.* July 86/2 It's only a deepish scratch. 1925 A. S. M. Hutchinson *One Increasing Purpose* I. xx. 128 Rather, rather deepish things. 1926 *Spectator* 6 Mar. 408/2 The Government was now in deepish water.

Deep-water. [Deep *a.* 1.] Used *attrib.* or as *adj.* Having, relating or pertaining to deep water.

1795 [see Deep *a.* IV. a]. 1874 J. W. Long *Wild-Fowl Shooting* 15, I shall..separate them into two distinct classes which I shall term respectively the *deep-water* and the *shoal-water* varieties [of wildfowl]. 1880 *Harper's Mag.* Aug. 341/2 He sat down..to the business of hand-lining for deep-water fish. 1890 [see Deep *a.* IV. a]. 1897 *Westm. Gaz.* 19 Oct. 8/1 The new scheme will embrace a new deep-water dock. 1909 *Daily Chron.* 8 Sept. 7/3 It is a natural deep-water harbour.

Deep-waterman (dī·pˌwǭ·tərmæ̆n). [f. *deep water* + Man *sb.*[1]] A sea-going vessel as opposed to a coaster.

1906 *Daily Chron.* 21 Mar. 6/4 Owners, not of 'deep-watermen' only, but of coasting craft as well. 1909 *Ibid.* 13 Aug. 3/1 What of the hundreds of fine deep-water men that still fly the Red Ensign? 1925 Rex Clements *Gipsy of Horn* 57 This..constitutes the time-honoured decoration of a deep-waterman.

Deer. Add: 4. (U.S.) *deer-gun, -hunt, -hunter, -leather, -trace.*

1834 *Southern Lit. Messenger* I. 157 Double barrelled guns, *deer guns, ducking guns. 1843 Carlton *New Purchase* I. xxi. 195 We had a *deer hunt..somewhat remarkable in itself. 1828 A. Sherburne *Mem.* ii. (1831) 51 Nor were we any ways equal to those *deer hunters in travelling this wilderness. 1751 *Narrag. Hist. Reg.* I. 216 Feloniously taking ..in *deer leather, and money to the value of one thousand and eighty pounds. 1897 J. L. Allen *Choir Invis.* ii. (1918) 13 Beyond which he struck a narrow *deer-trace, and followed that.

b. **deer-ball,** an underground fungus of the genus *Elaphomyces*; **deer-bleat** *U.S.*, an instrument serving to imitate the bleating of a deer; **deer-drive** (earlier U.S. example); **deer-fly** *U.S.*, a fly infesting the Virginian deer; **deer foot** *U.S.* (see quot.); **deer-grasshopper,** a locustid insect of Malay, of the genus *Mecopoda*, characterized by its ability to take long leaps; **deer-horn,** (*a*) the material of a deer's horn; (*b*) *U.S.*, a large rough mussel of the Mississippi, *Trigonia* or *Unio verrucosa*, the shell of which is used for making buttons; **deer-meat** *U.S.* (example); **deer paddock,** a paddock in which deer are kept; **deer-stand,** a station for the shooters at a deer-drive; **deer-yard** *U.S.* (earlier example).

[1640 Parkinson *Theat. Bot.* 1320 *Tubera cervina.* The *Deares underground balles or Mushromes are another sort of these Tuberaes.] 1854 Mayne *Expos. Lex.*, Deer-Ball. 1866 *Treas. Bot.*, *Deer balls*, a synonym of Hart's Truffles, Lycoperdon Nuts, and *Elaphomyces*. 1853 Marcy & McClellan *Explor. Red River* vi. 50 The idea occurred to me of attempting to call them with a *deer-bleat, which one of the Delawares had made for me. 1835 *Southern Lit. Messenger* I. 614 Almost every morning a company started, with hounds and horns, on a '*deer drive'. 1903 S. E. White *Forest* ix. 105 The question of flies..in its wide embracement of mosquitoes, sand-flies, *deer flies, black-flies and midges. 1905 *Terms Forestry & Logging* 35 *Deer foot*, a V-shaped iron catch on the side of a logging car in which the binding chain is fastened. 1900 *Proc. Zool. Soc.* 854 The enormous leaps of..the 'Belalang Rusa' or *Deer Grasshopper. 1843 Carlton *New Purchase* I. xvii. 122 A powder horn, and its loader of *deer-horn. 1880 *Encycl. Brit.* XII. 167/2 Deer-horn is almost exclusively used for handles by cutlers and walking-stick and umbrella makers. 1897 *Daily News* 1 Feb. 6/2 A saddle, probably Burgundian workmanship of 1400, composed of polished deer-horn plates. 1846 Sage *Scenes Rocky Mts.* (1859) 149 *Deer-meat at this season of the year is very poor eating. 1786 Washington *Diaries* III. 27 Returned to the erection of my *Deer paddock, which the bad weather had impeded. 1835 J. H. Ingraham *South-West* II. 137 After a farther ride of a mile..we arrived at the '*deer-stand'. 1849 C. Lanman *Alleghany Mts.* viii. 58, I discovered a large spot of bare earth, which I took to be a *deer-yard.

Deerberry. (Earlier U.S. example.)

1838 *Southern Lit. Messenger* IV. 25 We..admired..the rich crimson deer-berry, which was very abundant.

Deerlet. Add to def.: *spec.* the chevrotain.

1883 *Cassell's Nat. Hist.* II. 336 In the Water Deerlet of West Africa the external toes are smaller, whilst..each metacarpal..is independent of its neighbour, the Javan Deerlet differing in having the third and fourth fused into a 'cannon' bone. 1924 *Glasgow Herald* 8 Nov. 4 While camels chew the cud they resemble the old-fashioned chevrotains or deerlets in having only three chambers in their 'stomach' instead of the usual four.

Deer-lick. *U.S.* (Earlier examples.)

1778 *Maryland Jrnl.* 2 June (Th.), I never saw a Deer-lick. Hunters have told me that Deer frequent those places for the mud. 1819 Faux *Memorable Days Amer.* (1823) 234, I saw a deer-lick, at which I dismounted and took a lick. 1840 in *Trans. Mich. Agric. Soc.* (1855) VI. 289 Several saline springs and deer-licks were examined in the valley and vicinity of Maskego river.

Deer-mouse. *U.S.* (Earlier examples.)

1841 Catlin *N. Amer. Ind.* I. 194 A small 'deer mouse', of which little and very destructive animals their lodges contained many. 1865 S. Tenney *Man. Zool.* 73 The White-footed, or Deer Mouse..of Labrador and Virginia..is three to four inches long to the tail. 1876 J. Burroughs *Winter Sunshine* iii. 72 He is known to the farmer as the 'deer mouse'.

Deer-stalker. 1. (Earlier U.S. example.)

1849 Pritts *Mirror of Border Life* 686 In one of the loneliest of these glens..well known to the deer-stalker, there flourished a few years since a weeping-willow.

Deevey (dī·vi), *a. colloq.* Also **devey, devy, deevie.** [Affected alteration of *Divvy *a.*] Delightful, sweet, charming.

1900 Elin. Glyn *Visits Eliz.* (1906) 4 Miss La Touche happened to be next me, so she spoke to me, and said my hat was 'too devey for words'. 1904 Benson *Challoners* xi, 'Martin,' she cried, 'you are too deevey!' 1905 *Punch* 8 Mar. 178/1 Do look at this sweet little monkey on the organ! Isn't he deevie! 1906 *Ibid.* 13 June 422/2, I had the most *devy* doll you can imagine. 1909 Vachell *Paladin* i, The affair..was so appropriate, so obviously fashioned in heaven, so 'deevy'—a word coined in those days, and now regrettably become obsolete. 1930 Sackville-West *Edwardians* i, 17 Tommy, you're going, aren't you? How too deevy!

Hence **Dee·vily** *adv.*

1905 E. F. Benson *Image in Sand* vii, How too deliciously eerie! How deevily mysterious!

Defalcation. 5. (Earlier U.S. example.)

1831 *Deb. Congress* 9 May 911 The defalcations of post-masters.

Defalcator. (Earlier U.S. example.)

1806 Fessenden *Democr. Unv.* II. 84 Public defalcators.

Defatted (dīfæ·tĕd), *a.* [f. De- + Fat *sb.*[2] + -ed.] Destitute of fat or fats.

1923 Dreyer in *Times* 15 June 11/6 If the bacillus is 'defatted'..it no longer retains the acid stain. *Ibid.*, Dr. A. C. Inman..began..to treat cases of human tuberculosis with the 'defatted' antigen. 1924 *Glasgow Herald* 15 Feb. 6 These 'defatted' vaccines.

Default, *sb.* Add:

3. *attrib.* and *Comb.*: Dealing or connected with a default, as *default authority, interest, price.*

1897 *Westm. Gaz.* 29 July 5/3 If a client borrowed £100, say, and paid off £90, 'default interest' at the rate of one halfpenny per shilling per week...was at once charged on the £10 in arrear. 1908 *Daily Chron.* 13 May 7/7 While the county council is the default authority in case of the failure of the district council in sanitation, the Local Government Board is the default authority in case of the district council's failure to do what is needed in housing. 1909 *Westm. Gaz.* 9 Nov. 8/2 The Army authorities saying that if plaintiffs would not take the cattle the beasts would subsequently be issued at default prices.

Defaulted (dīfǭ·ltĕd), *ppl. a.* Transfer †*Obs.* to 1 and add:

2. Not paid by reason of default.

1897 *Westm. Gaz.* 26 May 5/1 Nearly all the bonds issued of late by the Greek Government in respect of defaulted interest having found their way to London.

Defaulter. c. (Earlier U.S. example.)

1806 Webster, *Defaulter*, one who fails in payment, a debtor.

Defeatism (dĭfī·tiz'm). [ad. F. *défaitisme*, f. *défaite* Defeat *sb.*: see -ism.] Conduct tending to bring about acceptance of defeat, esp. by action on civilian opinion.

1918 *Observer* 9 June. 1922 *Daily Mail* 13 Nov. 10 At an order from the leaders, the Labour Press has broken into a campaign of defeatism, lamenting that organised capital is still too strong to admit of any possible chance of the levy becoming law this time. 1926 C. L. Graves *Hubert Parry* II. 79 He was as far removed from foolish optimism as from 'defeatism'. 1928 Galsworthy *Swan Song* 124 To acknowledge the limitations of human nature was a sort of defeatism. 1930 H. Redwood *God in Slums* 128 Religion must throw off its defeatism.

So **Defeatist** (dĭfī·tist) [F. *défaitiste*], one who advocates defeatism; also *attrib.* or as *adj.*

1918 *Times* 19 June 6/4 The Independent Nationalist Press ..has applied the label 'defeatist' to those Nationalists who voted for a moderate policy at the Irish Convention. 1920 *19th Cent.* Mar. 556 The shop-stewards, too, in the great factories in Berlin and other towns were disloyal and 'defeatist'. 1921 'N. Angell' *Fruits of Victory* vii. 207 The repression of pacifist and defeatist propaganda during the War. 1921 *19th Cent.* Jan. 151 Throughout the Great War, as in the Japanese War, he was a defeatist. 1922 Sir B. Thomson *Queer People* xxiv. 282 The second Russian Revolution turned the heads of the Pacifists and Defeatists in England.

Defeminize (dīfe·minəiz), *v.* [f. De- + L. *femina* woman + -ize.] *trans.* To deprive of feminity; to unwoman. Hence **Defeminiza·tion.**

1900 *Amer. Jrnl. Psychol.* July 546 The most defeminized of these specimens, who are so prone to diminutives suggesting endearment. 1905 *Daily Chron.* 25 May 3/6 He thought this was 'monstrous and de-feminised'. 1907 *Ibid.* 9 Mar. 4/6 The so-called Feminism tends in reality to the 'defeminisation' of women. 1907 *Standard* 23 Mar., There was no need for women's suffrage, which would defeminise women.

Defence, *sb.* 5. Add: Also, a defending force.

1916 Boyd Cable *Action Front* 27 The defence, demoralised by that tornado of explosion, was pushed a good fifty yards further back.

Defendant, *a.* 2. Delete ? *Obs.* and add:

1896 *Daily News* 24 Nov. 5/7 Detailing my instructions to the defendant surgeon. 1907 *Westm. Gaz.* 6 Dec. 9/1 The defendant directors. 1927 *Pocket Oxf. Dict.* s.v., The defendant company.

Defender. Add:

1. e. *Sport.* The holder of a championship, cup, etc., who defends the title (opp. to *challenger*).

Defensor. Add:

4. *Eccl.* An officer in charge of the temporal affairs of a church.

[1875 Smith & Cheetham *Dict. Chr. Antiq.* I. 33/2 In Rome..the *Defensores* became by the time of Gregory the Great a regular order of officers.] 1905 Dudden *Greg. Gt.* I. 327 A certain defensor of the Milanese Church, named Valentinus.

Deferred, *ppl. a.* Add: (Earlier U.S. examples of modern special uses.)

1792 A. Hamilton *Wks.* (1885) II. 330 The 1st of January, 1802, when the deferred debt will become redeemable. 1796 *Deb. Congress* (1849) 792 A sum..will then become due and payable on the deferred stock. *Ibid.* 793 Additional revenue..will..discharge..the accruing annuity arising from the Deferred Debt.

b. *Deferred payment*, payment by instalments. *Deferred rate*, cheaper rate charged for a telegram, cable, etc. which may be delayed in transit; so *Deferred telegram*, one not for immediate delivery.

1884 Walker *Pol. Econ.* III. iii. 115 The Standard of Deferred Payments, usually called the Standard of Value. 1896 *Chambers's Jrnl.* 26 Sept. 610/1 It is this system of 'deferred payment', as it may be called, that enables the speculator to deal in shares although he may not possess any appreciable capital. 1898 Morris *Austral Eng.*, *Deferred payment*, a legal phrase. 'Land on deferred payment'; 'Deferred payment settler'; 'Pastoral deferred payment'. These expressions in New Zealand have reference to the mode of statutory alienation of Crown lands. 1907 *Westm. Gaz.* 18 June 4/2 The introduction of the deferred-payment system in connexion with the automobile business. 1908 *Ibid.* 3 Apr. 10/1 All deferred rate telegrams are posted instead of being wired. 1929 *Times* 2 Feb. 8/3 The cost of 'Urgent' telegram to be 1s., and 'Deferred' 6d., for 15 words.

Deficient, *sb.* Add: 4. = Defective *sb.* 2 b.

1906 F. Thoresby in *Westm. Rev.* Jan. 39 There are the deficients, *i.e.*, those who from, or before birth, or by reason of their rearing, or both, never have..a fair start. 1927 Carr-Saunders & Jones *Soc. Struct. Eng. & Wales* 213 [Authorities] vary notoriously...Some are active, while others close their eyes to the existence of deficients within their areas.

Define, *v.* 2. b. Add: (Examples of active use.) In more recent use also *refl.*

1859 Geo. Eliot *Lifted Veil* ii, I..saw the light floating vanities of the girl defining themselves into the systematic coquetry, the scheming selfishness, of the woman. 1888 Mrs. H. Ward *R. Elsmere* xv, The slender figure suddenly defined itself against the road. *Ibid.* xxxii, The difficulties began to define themselves more sharply. *Ibid.* xliii, The half-coherent enigmatical sentences..began gradually to define themselves. 1908 *Smart Set* Sept. 6 The great crystal stars barely defined the mountain and the tall, slender shafts..of the royal palm.

Deflate, *v.* Add:

1. b. *intr.* for *pass.* Of an inflated object: To be emptied of the inflating gas.

1902 *Daily Chron.* 2 Sept. 4/5 Mr. Spencer turning aside from the deflating balloon.

2. To reduce (an inflated currency). Also *absol.* to pursue a policy of deflation. b. *intr.* for *pass.* To be reduced by deflation.

1919 R. G. Hawtrey *Currency & Credit* 352 Every country will seek to keep pace with its neighbours. If one does not deflate its currency as quickly as the others the exchanges will turn against it. 1922 *Glasgow Herald* 7 Aug. 8 All of these costs..would require to deflate to pre-war standard to enable the sixpenny loaf to reappear. 1923 R. McKenna in *Daily Mail* 27 Jan. 3 If at this stage we made no further effort to deflate, trade would soon recover. 1926 *Westm. Gaz.* 30 July, To 'deflate' the franc from 240 or 200..to a level of only 25 to the £ is beyond the realms of practicability.

Hence **Defla·ted** *ppl. a.*

1894 *Sat. Rev.* 8 Dec. 618/1 There are narrow edges to the rims on which a deflated tyre would rest.

Deflation. Add:

2. *Geol.* The removal of solid particles by the wind, leaving the rocks exposed to the weather.

1898 J. Geikie *Earth Sculpture* 20 The transporting action of the wind, or 'deflation' as it is termed, goes on without ceasing. 1910 Lake & Rastall *Text-bk. Geol.* 73 Erosion by wind divides itself naturally into two parts—removal by material or *deflation*, which of course comes under the heading of transport, and actual corrosion or wearing away of the rocks by the dynamical effect of moving sand.

3. The action or process of deflating currency.

1919 R. G. Hawtrey in *Rep. Brit. Assoc.* (1920) 252 To restore a depreciated unit to its normal gold value requires a measure of deflation. Deflation, which is a reversal of the process of inflation, must mean a decrease in the aggregate of money incomes. 1920 *Glasgow Herald* 11 May 10 The process of deflation likely to result from the new rights of the Federal Reserve system to discount on a graded scale. 1923 *Guernsey Star* 25 Jan., The primary ground on which a policy of gradual deflation is recommended is that it raises the exchange value of the pound sterling in relation to the dollar and hastens our return to the gold standard.

Deflationary (dĭflē·ʃənări), *a.* [f. *Deflation 3 + -ary [1].] Of or pertaining to deflation.

1920 *Glasgow Herald* 21 Aug. 7 The transition from an inflationary to a deflationary period in prices. 1929 *New Statesman* 1 June 231 The falling price level of recent years has been in large part the result of a world-wide deflationary movement which has inevitably reacted on credit and unemployment.

Deflationist (dĭflē·ʃənist). [f. *Deflation 3 + -ist.] One who advocates a policy of deflation. Also *attrib.* or as *adj.*

1921 *Glasgow Herald* 10 Feb. 4 If the deflationists have their way, the pound will be raised again to the value of 20s. 1922 *Edin. Rev.* July 194 The decision to get back to gold would divide the country into inflationists and deflationists. 1928 *Observer* 19 Feb. 18/2 The policy of the Seiyukai is positive and inflationist, while that of the Minseito is negative and deflationist.

Deflator (dĭflē·tər). [f. Deflate *v.* + -or.] A thing which deflates.

1896 *Westm. Gaz.* 2 Nov. 9/1 Some person..had strewn the road with a number of 'boot protectors', perhaps the most deadly deflator that could be constructed.

Deflectable (dĭfle·ktăb'l), *a.* [f. Deflect *v.* + -able.] Capable of being deflected.

1895 *Funk's Standard Dict.* 1925 *Contemp. Rev.* July 89 Woman..being less deflectable and in her nature more impressionable [than man].

Deflocculation (dīflǫkiŭlē·ʃən). [f. De- + Flocculation.] Separation into floccules.

1904 *Nature* 7 July 238/2 The removal of the finest particles from the surface soil is attributed to deflocculation induced by the use of sodium nitrate.

Defluvium (dĭflū·viə̆m). [L.] A falling off, especially of the hair, also the bark of a tree, from disease.

[1848 Dunglison *Med. Lex.* (ed. 7).] 1906 *Practitioner* Nov. 692 All loss of hair is abnormal, and the popular belief in a physiological defluvium is false.

Deforestation, Deforesting *vbl. sb.* (Earlier U.S. examples.)

1874 *Rep. Vermont Board Agric.* II. 501 But now, because of these early clearings and succeeding deforestations, the lowlands have become drier and warmer. *Ibid.*, There are many compensations accompanying the deforesting of the country.

Deformation. Add: 3. b. *Bot.* Any malformation or abnormal growth.

1862 *Once a Week* VII. 135/2 The calyx, when this deformation is about to take place, has not ceased to exercise its vital power of development. 1866 *Treas. Bot.*, *Deformation*, an alteration in the usual form of an organ by accident or otherwise. 1900 B. D. Jackson *Gloss. Bot. Terms, Deformation*, a malformation or alteration from the normal sense.

c. *Geol.* The process by which a stratum, mass or rock, or portion of the earth's crust undergoes change of form, usually by compression. (Cf. next.)

1882 Geikie *Text-bk. Geol.* 312 Evidences of actual deformation within the mass of rock. 1905 Chamberlin & Salisbury *Geol.* I. 547 It is theoretically possible that deformation of the sub-crust may result from the internal transfer of heat without regard to external loss.

Deformational (dīfǫɹmē·ʃənăl), *a.* [f. Deformation + -al.] Of or pertaining to deformation.

1903 *Nature* 12 Feb. 359/1 Several deformational movements had affected this district.

Defreeze (dīfrī·z), *v.* [f. De- + Freeze *v.*] *trans.* = next.

1901 *Westm. Gaz.* 22 July 10/2 A new process of 'defreezing' is now being tried. 1922 *Evening News* 20 Dec. 4/3 When these birds, only lightly frozen for the voyage, are 'defrozen'—the trade term.

Defrost (dīfrǫ·st), *v.* [f. De- + Frost *v.*] *trans.* To unfreeze (frozen meat or other provisions).

1895 *Daily News* 29 May 8/4 It was believed that Queensland defrosted beef could be brought into formidable competition with American chilled. 1895 *Austral. Pastoralist Rev.* 15 Aug. p. viii, The difficulties hitherto attaching to the defrosting of Beef and Mutton. 1908 *Daily Chron.* 22 Oct. 8/5 The Judge: What did you provide Trinity College with? Witness: A lot of defrosted mutton, sir. 1924 *Glasgow Herald* 19 Aug. 7 The electrical defrosting process experiments which were recently undertaken in Melbourne.

Defterdar (deftərdā·r). Also 6–7 **teftadar,** 8 **tefterdar,** 9 **daftardar, dufterdar.** [Hind. *daftardār*, f. *daftar* Dufter + *-dār* holder.] A Turkish officer of finance, *esp.* the accountant general of a province; also formerly, the Turkish minister of finance.

1599 Hakluyt *Voy.* II. I. 292 Vnder him be three subtreasurers called *Teftadars*. 1601 W. Biddulph in T. Lavender *Trav. Four Englishm.* (1612) 75 *Defterdare*, that is, treasurer of Aleppo. 1615 Sandys *Trav.* III. 211 Tendring to the *Teftadar* or Treasurer the reuenew of that Sanziackry. 1796 Morse *Amer. Geog.* II. 463 The first minister of finances is called Defterdar. 1836 Lane *Mod. Egypt.* I. 154 The Defturda'r, having caused the Na'zir to be brought before him, asked him [etc.]. 1902 *Encycl. Brit.* XXXIII. 508/1 A complete budget of receipts and expenditure is drawn up by its *defterdar*.

Defy (dĭfai·), *sb.*[2] *U.S.* [app. a new formation on Defy *v.*] A challenge, defiance.

1897 *Harper's Mag.* Jan. 231 He sent out the last defy to the enemy in 1800. 1910 in *W. James' Mem. & Studies* (1911) 396 Roaring my fierce defy.

Degenerate (dĭdʒe·nĕrĕt), *sb.* [subst. use of the adj.] One who has lost, or has become deficient in, the qualities proper to the race or kind; a degenerate specimen; *esp.* a person of debased or perverted physical or mental constitution.

1890 Havelock Ellis *Criminal* iii. (1910) 51 Näcke.. found the skulls of women..abnormal, and among degenerates generally..the stigmata of degeneracy are more common in women. 1895 tr. *Nordau's Degeneration* I. iii. 18 In the mental development of degenerates, we meet with the same irregularity that we have observed in their physical growth...That which nearly all degenerates lack is the sense of morality and of right and wrong. 1919 M. K. Bradby *Psycho-analysis* 17 The fact..is compatible with his being a genius or a degenerate, a scoundrel or a valuable citizen.

Degenerate, *v.* 5. Delete †*Obs.* and add:

1870 Curteis *Bampton Lect.* (ed. 3) p. xxviii, The nation is being degraded by drink and degenerated by impurity. 1893 J. Pulsford *Loyalty to Christ* II. 131 The one seeking to regenerate, and the other to degenerate yet more and more the soul's nature. 1921 MacNeill *Celtic Irel.* 17 Acquired habits..can degenerate and recreate a nation.

Degote: see *Daggett.

Degradation [1]. Add: 7. *Organic Chem.* The systematic reduction of the molecule of a compound into others of less complex structure.

1904 *Nature* 24 Mar. 504/1 A method of preparation of aldehydes and the systematic degradation of acids.

Degrade, *v.* 8. Add: Also occas. at Oxford University (now disused). Now at Cambridge, to take a specified examination when one is above the standing prescribed for it.

1906 *Oxf. Univ. Gaz.* 29 May 654/2 John O. Aglionby.. was granted permission to degrade till Trinity Term, 1907, and to offer Modern History.

b. See quot. 1883; now at Oxford University, to supplicate for a lower degree than that for which one originally entered.

1883 *Cassell's Encycl. Dict.*, *Degrade*,..to take a lower degree than one is entitled to;..to descend from a higher to a lower class. 1921 (Nov. 4) *Oxford Univ. Registry Acc. Bks.* (MS.), Wing, J. L...Degrading to B.Litt. £1.

Degrain (dĭgrē·n). [f. De- + Grain *sb.*[1]] Used *attrib.* designating leather from which the grain has been removed. Hence **Degrai·ned** *a.*

1925 *Civil Service Supply Assoc. Ltd. Catal.* 133 Men's Glove Department...Degrain Mocha finish. 1928 *Daily Express* 1 Nov. 8/1 Degrained Glove...Made from supple Degrain skins.

Degras (dəgra·, de·grās). [F. *dégras*, f. *dégraisser* to remove grease from, with assimilation to *gras* fat.] A fat or grease obtained by the treatment of hides with fish-oil and potash as a commercial article or as a by-product in the manufacture of leather, especially chamois leather; also, wool-grease. See also quot. 1904.

1882 *Encycl. Brit.* XIV. 390/2 This uncombined oil is washed out with a warm potash solution, and the fat so recovered, known as *degras*, forms a valuable material for the dressing of common leather by curriers. 1898 C. Salter tr. *Andés' Anim. Fats* 204 Dégras, Tanner's Grease, Leather Grease...The substance indicated by the above names was originally a waste product obtained in the preparation of chamois (shamoy) leather. *Ibid.*, In composition, dégras is nothing more or less than emulsified fat, *i.e.*, a fat existing in an extremely fine state of division in a suitable liquid, so that it forms a mass of buttery or salve-like consistency. 1904 *Technol. & Sci. Dict.* (ed. Goodchild & Tweney) s.v., Artificial Degras is made by adding tallow to cod oil (and sometimes red oil and wool grease), and incorporating with a neutral soap.

b. *Comb.*: **degras-former,** a brown, resinous constituent of tanners' degras, the presence of which promotes the emulsification of the fish-oils used in currying and tanning.

Degree, *sb.* Add:

1. c. *Degree-cut* in gem-cutting: = Trap-cut.

6. e. *Third degree* (U.S.): see *Third *a.*

7. In legal use.

1880 *Encycl. Brit.* XIII. 87/2 Each inn confers this status or degree [*sc.* of barrister] on its own members only. 1885 *Law Jrnl.* 13 June 364/1 That his Royal Highness..be called to the degree of the Utter Bar.

14. A percentage of the basic element or pure material of a substance; as, a soda of ninety degrees.

15. *Comb.*, as *degree-day, -fee*; *degree-conferring, -granting* adjs.

1903 *Westm. Gaz.* 21 July 2/2 The *degree-conferring Universities of the United Kingdom. 1906 *Daily Chron.* 27 July 6/7 To make the Nottingham University College a degree-conferring University. 1900 G. Swift *Somerley* 164 When the dance and *degree-day were over. 1897 *Daily News* 23 Apr. 7/4 Many of the *Degree-Fees have..been raised. 1895 *Westm. Gaz.* 27 July 5/3 It..had never been adequately encouraged by *degree-granting Universities. 1896 *Daily News* 20 Feb. 5/4 The larger degree-granting institutions.

Degression (dĭgre·ʃən). Transfer †*Obs.* to 1 and add: 2. The decrease in the rate of taxation in a degressive scale.

1896 Palgrave *Dict. Pol. Econ.* II. 244/1 Graduated taxation therefore technically includes progression, degression, and regression. 1906 *Westm. Gaz.* 9 June 2/1 The income-tax so long planned in France..is English both in its taxation by schedules and in its exemptions of the less wealthy payers, though it effects the last-named result by a more complete scheme of 'degression' than is in operation here. *Ibid.* 31 July 5/3 If any change was made in the direction of degression by which everybody would first be taxed at the higher rate and then have to apply for abatements.

Degressive (dĭgre·siv), *a.* [f. L. *degress-*, ppl. stem of *dēgredī* to descend.] In taxation, of or pertaining to schemes in which the rate decreases successively on sums below a certain limit. Hence **Degre·ssively** (Webster 1911).

1911 S. J. Chapman *Outl. Pol. Econ.* xxxii. 379 *Degressive taxation* means that large incomes are taxed at a higher rate than smaller incomes, but not in a degree which involves as great a proportional sacrifice for the former as for the latter.

Dégringolade (degrængolad). [Fr., f. *dégringoler* to descend rapidly.] A rapid descent; deterioration, decadence; change from bad to worse.

1883 *Sat. Rev.* 24 Nov. 648/1 The *dégringolade* of Tokka and the catastrophe of Obeid. 1906 W. De Morgan *Joseph Vance* xxxv. 346 This last is a short chapter, but is a record of a steady *dégringolade*. 1909 *Westm. Gaz.* 29 May 5/3 We..share her distress in the ensuing dégringolade. 1926 *Spectator* 29 May 900/1 This *dégringolade*, this falling back into an undrained, unfenced, unploughed, unweeded prairie. 1926 *Nation* 24 July 460/1 The franc has this week looked the penny in the face, and has acquired a momentum in decline which suggests that a *dégringolade* is close at hand, unless prompt and effective measures are really taken.

Dehæmatize (dīhī·mătəiz), *v.* Also **dehematize.** [f. De- + Gr. αἱματ-, αἷμα blood + -ize.] *trans.* To deprive of blood.

1903 *Med. Record* 7 Mar. 362 (Cent. D. Suppl.). 1913 Dorland *Med. Dict.* (ed. 7).

Dehæmoglobinize (dīhīmoglōu·binəiz), *v.* Also **dehemo-.** [f. De- + Hæmoglobin + -ize.] *trans.* To remove hæmoglobin from (the red blood-corpuscles).

1903 *Jrnl. Trop. Med.* 2 Nov. 337/2 A very large thick, slowly-dried, unfixed blood film, dehæmoglobinised and stained by immersion in a weak watery solution of an aniline dye.

Dehair (dīhēᵊ·ɹ), *v.* [f. De- + Hair *sb.*] *trans.* To remove the hair from (a skin), to unhair. Hence **Dehai·rer.**

a 1909 *Mod. Amer. Tanning* 37 (Cent. D. Suppl.). 1921 *Dict. Occup. Terms* (1927) § 338 *Unhairer* (tannery); *dehairer*; (i) a beam man who spreads hides or skins on wooden beam; scrapes hair, by hand, with two-handled knife; (ii) passes hides or skins from lime pits, between unhairing machine, removing hairs.

Dehalogenize (dīhæ·lodʒĕnəiz), *v.* [f. De- + Halogen + -ize.] *trans.* To deprive of one or more of the halogens.

1883 *Jrnl. Soc. Chem. Industry* 29 Apr. 171/1 Dehalogenising Benzotrichloride.

De haut en bas (də o taṅ ba). [Fr., lit. 'from high to low'.] With an air of conscious superiority or condescension. Also *attrib.* and *Comb.*

1697 Vanbrugh *Relapse* I. ii, If you treat him *de haut en bas*. 1778 H. Walpole *Let. to W. Mason* 4 July, The Congress has ratified the treaty with France, and intend to treat the Commissioners *de haut en bas*. 1868 *Good Words* 1 Aug. 516/1 A de-haut-en-bas-like drawling gait. 1886 *Athenæum* 12 June 773/2 Whose utterances, moreover, though treated somewhat *de haut en bas*, are among the most sensible of all. 1910 *Westm. Gaz.* 12 Jan. 12/1 The cable companies.. took up a very de haut en bas attitude.

Deho·rn, *v.* [De- II. 2.]

1. *trans.* To deprive (an animal) of horns. Also *absol.* and *fig.* Hence **Deho·rn** *sb.*, a dehorned animal (Western U.S.) (Funk, 1895); **Deho·rner.**

1888 *Missouri Republ.* 15 Feb. (Farmer) Dehorning is performed when the calf is young, and the tips of the horns movable. 1888 Dehorn, Dehorner [see De- II. 2]. 1889 Farmer *Americanisms* 197/1 The preferred age at which to dehorn is in the second year of the animal's life. 1914 *Boston Even. Transcript* 6 June 2/1 Four years ago they dehorned the speaker.

2. (See quot.)

1905 *Terms Forestry & Logging* 35 *Dehorn*, to saw off the ends of logs bearing the owner's mark and put on a new mark (Kentucky).

Dehydracetic (dīhəidrăsī·tik), *a. Chem.* [f. De- + Hydr(o- + Acetic.] Designating or pertaining to an acid ($C_8H_8O_4$), obtained by heating aceto-acetic ester.

1872 Watts *Dict. Chem.* VI. 543.

Dehydrogenated (dīhəi·drǫdʒĕnēᵊtĕd), *ppl. a. Chem.* [f. Dehydrogenate *v.* + -ed [1].] Deprived of its hydrogen.

1909 *Chambers's Jrnl.* Oct. 686/1 A direct conversion of the gas into alcohols and dehydrogenated alcohols.

Dehydrogenation (dīhəidrǫdʒĕnē·ʃən). *Chem.* [f. Dehydrogenate: see -ation.] = Dehydrogenization.

1866 Odling *Anim. Chem.* 129 The oxidation or dehydrogenation of uric acid.

Deiamba (diˌæ·mbă). Also **diamba.** [Native name.] Congo tobacco.

1851 R. O. Clarke in *Hooker's Kew Jrnl.* III. 9 (*title*) Short notice of the African Plant Diamba, commonly called Congo Tobacco. 1861 Bentley *Man. Bot.* 637 Indian hemp is also used for smoking. The plant is also known under the name of *Diamba* in Western Africa. 1864 Watts *Dict. Chem.* II. 309 Deiamba.

Deificatory (dĭ·ifikētəri), *a.* Delete †*Obs.* and add:

1902 A. M. Fairbairn *Philos. Chr. Relig.* II. II. ii. 474 He is not conceived as the subject of a deificatory process.

Deiters (dəi·tərz, ‖dai·tərs). The name of Otto Friedrich Carl *Deiters*, German anatomist (1834–63), applied to certain cells and processes recognized by him.

1890 Billings *Med. Dict.* 1902 *Encycl. Brit.* XXXI. 742/2 Certain cerebellar cells send processes down to the cell-group in the bulb known as the nucleus of Deiters, which latter projects fibres down the spinal cord.

Déjeuner. Add: b. Short for *déjeuner-service.*

1875 E. Meteyard *Wedgwood Handbk.* 395 A déjeuner consists of a tray, one or more cups and saucers, occasionally a teapot, a cream jug, and a slop basin.

c. *attrib.*

1851 *Illustr. Catal. Gt. Exhib.* III. 726/1 Communion and déjeûne services. *Ibid.* 748/2 Papier maché 'standish', 'déjeûner tray', and bottle-stand. 1865 'Ouida' *Strathmore* xii, In the breakfast-room every déjeûner delicacy was waiting. 1875 J. Grant *One of Six Hundr.* x, A *déjeûner* service of splendid Wedgwood ware. 1899 *Westm. Gaz.* 5 July 1/3 Messrs. Christie sold yesterday the déjeuner-service of Napoleon I.

Dekabrist (de·kăbrist). Also **Deca-.** [f. Russ. *Dekabrĭ* December + -ist.] One who took part in a military conspiracy which broke out in St. Petersburg on December 26th, 1825, on the accession of the Emperor Nicholas to the throne.

1882 Ogilvie (Annandale). 1885 *Encycl. Brit.* XIX. 649/1 The unfortunate conspiracy of the Dekabrists. 1920 *19th Cent.* Sept. 420 *Russian Women* gives a description of the wives of the Dekabrists, aristocrats but our first revolutionists. 1925 *Glasgow Herald* 5 Mar. 4 Prince Wolkonsky, as became a descendant of a Dekabrist, was a Liberal.

Dekko (de·ko). *Army slang.* [f. Hind. *dekho*, imperative of *dekhnā* to look: cf. *Deck *sb.*[2]] A look. Also as vb.

1894 *Daily News* 8 Sept. 6/3, I had a 'dekho' round every 'house' in the place, but couldn't see you. 1917 A. G. Empey *From the Fire Step* 232 '*Dekko*', to look; a look at something. 1920 M. A. Mügge *War Diary of Square Peg* 219 Dekko.—Look! 1927 E. Thompson *These Men thy Friends* 63 'You haven't had a proper *dekko*, padre' he protested.

Delafossite (delăfǫ·səit). *Min.* [a. F. *delafossite* (1873), f. the name of G. *Delafosse*: see -ite [1].] An oxide of iron and copper, perhaps a mixture, cleavable into thin opaque lamellæ.

1880 Dana *Min.* (ed. 5) App. II. 16. 1914 *Brit. Mus. Return* 225.

Delanouite (delæ·nuəit). *Min.* [a. F. *delanouite* (1856), f. the name of J. *Delanoue*: see -ite [1].] A kind of clay of a rose-red colour.

1868 Dana *Min.* 459.

Délassement (delasmaṅ). [Fr., f. *délasser*, f. *dé-* De- + *las* weary.] Relaxation.

1854 Thackeray *Newcomes* xxii, Clive (who had taken a trip to Paris with his father, as a *délassement* after the fatigues incident on his great work)..declared the thing was rubbish. 1860 Russell *Diary India* I. 56 We had the *délassements* of many meals, and music, and whist, and songs at night. 1906 W. De Morgan *Joseph Vance* xxiv. 232 Illusion—hallucination—*délassement* of the senses—that sort of thing.

Delay, *sb.* Add: 3. *attrib.* (Cf. next.)

1879 *Man. Artill. Exerc.* II. 51 Delay Action for base of Battering Shell. 1900 *Daily News* 11 Apr. 5/6 Delay-action projectiles. 1918 in C. F. S. Gamble *N. Sea Air Station* xv. 280, 100-lb. bombs with 2½ seconds delay fuses.

Delayed, *ppl. a.*[1] Add: **delayed-action fuse,** a fuse which delays the action of the shell until it has penetrated the object struck.

1892 *Chambers's Jrnl.* 560/1 A delayed-action fuse. 1909 *Westm. Gaz.* 2 Jan. 13/3 The thickest armour-plate can now be pierced by projectiles fitted with a delayed-action fuse.

Dele. Add: Also as *sb.*, an instance of the use of the sign so called.

1727–51 Chambers *Cycl.* s.v. *Correction*, There are different characters used to express different corrections, *v. gr.* D or ₰ *dele* for anything to be effaced, or left out. 1821 Dibdin *Bibliogr., etc. Tour* I. 129, I could discover...that..he wished me to..leave him to his *deles* and *stets*!

Hence **Dele** (dī·lī), *v.* = Delete *v.* 2.

1705 S. Sewall *Diary* 24 Dec. (1879) II. 150, I deled the Title, *In Obitum Crucis*. 1765 *N. Carolina Col. Rec.* (1890) VII. 81 To the *deleing* the Clause..we..agree. 1869 R. Morris *Spenser's Wks.* App. i. (1893) 689/2 The comma after ape should be deled.

Dele·ctify, *v.* [f. L. *dēlect-* (see Delect *v.* and -fy).] *trans.* To delight.

1834 W. G. Simms *Guy Rivers* 78 So spake another of the company, who, having been much delectified with the trial, had been particularly solicitous in his cries for order.

Delegate, *sb.* 3. *U.S.* a. (Earlier examples.)

1774 *Jrnl. Contin. Congress* I. 15 [To] be appointed..as delegates, on the part of this province, to attend and assist in the General Congress of delegates from the other Colonies. 1777 *Act Confed. Art.* 5 Delegates shall be annually appointed in such manner as the legislature of each state shall direct, to meet in Congress [etc.].

Delegation. 3. b. *U.S.* (Earlier examples.)

1775 *Jrnl. Contin. Congress* II. 16 We, the subscribers, do..signify our assent to, and approbation of, the above Delegation. 1787 Jefferson *Writ.* (1894) IV. 441 The members of the Pennsylvania delegation..came in.

Delicate, *a.* Add:

8. b. Also colloq. phr. *in a delicate condition* or *state of health*: pregnant.

1850 Dickens *Dav. Copp.* xxvii, Mrs. Micawber being in a delicate state of health, was overcome by it. 1910 Sanger *Seventy Years a Showman* (1927) 184, I was the more concerned as Mrs. Sanger was in a delicate condition.

c. Characterized by the fastidious use of slight quantities.

1908 *Animal Managem.* (War Office) 127 Occasionally a timid, delicate feeder will be met.

Delicatessen (de:likăte·sən). orig. *U.S.* [G. *delikatessen*, Du. *delicatessen*, ad. F. *délicatesse* (see Delicatesse).] Delicacies or relishes for the table; esp. *attrib.*, in *delicatessen shop, store.* b. *ellipt.* A delicatessen shop.

1889 *Kansas Times & Star* 7 Nov., Burglars broke into Blake's delicatessen store..and..made an awful mess of the juicy stuff, canned and bottled. 1896 *Voice* (N.Y.) 25 June 6/3 A delicatessen store on upper Third avenue. 1896 G. H. Putnam *Books & their Makers* I. 249 A dealer in *delicatessen*. 1904 'Alan Dale' *Wanted: A Cook* 28 To-night, Anna has provided us what she calls a delicatessen dinner. 1904 *N.Y. Even. Post* 30 June 14 Advt., Our Modern Delicatessen Department on the fifth floor is prepared to furnish estimates for picnic luncheons. 1905 *Ibid.* 13 Nov. 7 Next week's opening of Mr. Conried's operatic delicatessen store on Broadway. 1908 *Daily Chron.* 8 Jan. 8/3 The German delicatessen shops which are now becoming such a feature in London life. 1930 *Daily Tel.* 8 Apr. 9/6 The New York women,..in their skyscraper niches, where everything can be done by electricity, with the delicatessen and.. prepared food as a stand-by.

Delictal (dĭli·ktăl), *a.* [f. Delict + -al.] Of, pertaining to, or of the nature of a delict.

1913 H. Goudy in *Ess. Legal Hist. Congr. Hist. Stud.* 208 Where..a delictal action was not strictly penal..it transmitted both actively and passively.

Delight, *sb.* Add:

4. In the name of the sweetmeat called *Turkish delight* (see Turkish *a.* 2 b), formerly *Lumps of Delight* (tr. Turkish *rāhat luqūm*) (whence mod. Gr. λουκοῦμι), altered from Arab. *rāhatu 'l halqūm* ease for the throat, by association with *luqmat*, pl. *luqam* piece, and apprehended as meaning 'pieces of delight'.

1870 [see Turkish *a.* 1]. 1875 Miss Alcott *Eight Cousins* v, Phebe..crunched the 'Lump of Delight' tucked into her mouth. 1894 *Daily News* 4 June 7/7 The Turkish, or rather Greek, sweetmeat known as Rahat Loukoums, or 'Lumps of Delight'.

Delight, *v.* 1. *absol.* Add quots.:

1904 'Lillie T. Meade' *Love Triumphant* v, I mean to go to London..to meet my equals. I shall dazzle, I shall delight. 1908 Gertrude Atherton *Gorgeous Isle* iii, There had been much to delight and awe.

Delilah (dĭləi·lă). Also 6–8 **Dalilah.** The name of the woman who betrayed Samson to the Philistines (see Judges xvi), used allusively to mean a temptress or treacherous love.

1594 J. King *On Jonas* xlvi. (1597) 630 You who esteeme.. to be the dearlings of the pleasure of Egypt, and be set vpon the knees of the Delilah of this world. 1614 T. Adams *Fatal Banket* i. Wks. (1629) 169 If Dalilah inuite Sampson, ware his lockes; she will spoile the Nazarite of his hayres; there are many Dalilahs in these dayes. 1678 Butler *Hud.* III. ii. 1115 [Ye] Transform'd all Wives to Dalilahs, Whose Husbands were not for the Cause. 1768 H. Brooke *Fool of Qual.* xiii. III. 30, I have no foreign Dalilahs, no secret amours. 1879 J. C. Shairp *Robert Burns* vi. 141 Other Delilahs on a smaller scale Burns met with during his Dumfries sojourn. 1893 F. Adams *New Egypt* 63 This is about as far as the French Delilah dare at present go in the public incitements of her young Egyptian Samson.

Delineative, *a.* (Earlier U.S. example.)

1841 H. S. Foote *Texas & Texans* I. 40 Others were perspicuously delineative of current events.

Delineator. Add: 3. (See quots.)

1874 Knight *Dict. Mech.*, *Delineator* 1. (*Tailoring.*) A pattern formed by rule; being expansible in the directions where the sizes vary, as indicated by the varying lengths obtained by measurement. 2. (*Surveying.*) A perambulator, or geodetical instrument on wheels, with registering devices for recording distances between points [etc.].

Delint (dĭli·nt), *v.* [f. De- + Lint [1].] *trans.* To remove the fibre from (cotton or similar seeds). Hence **Deli·nter.** So **Deli·nt** *sb.* (see quot. 1904).

1902 *Westm. Gaz.* 2 Jan. 7/2 A new process for delinting and hulling the cotton seed. 1904 L. L. Lamborn *Cotton-seed Products* 34 Linters, or delint, as the short fiber is also called, find extensive application in the arts. *Ibid.* 50 The delinter is similar in construction to the gin for seed cotton. 1921 *Dict. Occup. Terms* (1927) § 159 *Delinter*;..attends and feeds machine which removes short fibres adhering to cotton seeds, after long fibres have been detached in ginning process.

Deliver, *v.*[1] Add: 8. d. Colloq. phr. *To deliver the goods*: see *Goods *sb. pl.*

9. e. *intr.* Of a road: To discharge traffic.

1895 *Daily News* 1 Oct. 3/1 The Committee thinking it desirable that the new thoroughfare shall deliver directly into and on a level with the Strand.

Delivery. Add:

9. *attrib.* and *Comb.*: *delivery cart, -roller, -tube, -van, wagon*; **delivery box, order** (see quots.); **delivery pipe,** a pipe through which liquids are ejected, *spec.* from a pump; also, a service-pipe; **delivery-valve,** a discharge valve.

1888 *Lockwood's Dict. Mech. Engin.*, *Delivery Box, the upper or delivery chamber of a series of two or three throw pumps, into which the liquid is lifted by the pistons and from which it is delivered. 1859 Measom *Illustr. Guide Lanc. & Carlisle Railw.* 115 Advt., Tradesmen's *Delivery Carts and Vans. 1882 R. Bithell *Counting-house Dict.* (1893), *Delivery Order*, a..document, entitling..the legal holder thereof, to the delivery of any goods..of the value of forty shillings, or upwards, lying in any dock, port, wharf, or warehouse. 1924 *Times Trade & Engin. Suppl.* 29 Nov. 245/1 Ownership in goods can be transferred by mere endorsement of a bill of lading or a delivery order...A delivery order, or formal request, signed by the owner of goods, that they be delivered to the firm or person named, or to 'bearer', must be lodged with the bill of lading or freight release. 1888 *Lockwood's Dict. Mech. Engin.*, *Delivery Pipes*, the series of pipes through which the liquids drawn up by pumping machinery are ejected. 1889 Hasluck *Model Engin. Handybk.* (1900) 111 To connect the delivery-pipe union. 1895 *Daily News* 14 Sept. 5/1 It was noticed that this water had the power to dissolve the lead of the delivery pipes. 1874 Knight *Dict. Mech.*, *Delivery-roller*, that roller in a carding, paper, or calendering, or other machine, which conducts the object finally from the operative portions of the apparatus. 1879 Noad & Preece *Electricity* 221 The *delivery tube conducts the gases into a graduated receiver. 1874 Knight *Dict. Mech.*, *Delivery-valve*, that valve through which the discharge of a pumped fluid occurs, as the upper valve of the air-pump in the condensing steam-engine, through which water is lifted into the hot-well. 1906 *Westm. Gaz.* 22 Feb. 11/1 For the purpose of manufacturing in England motor-cars, motor-omnibuses, and *delivery-vans. 1907 *Ibid.* 21 Nov. 4/3 Delivered free by express motor delivery-van. 1889 *Kansas Times & Star* 14 Dec., The sign painted on one side of the *delivery wagon going to the various schools with supplies.

Della Robbia (de·lă rɒ·biă). [Proper name of a family of Italian painters and sculptors of the fifteenth century.]

1. Used attrib. to designate the enamelled terra-cotta ware made by Luca Della Robbia and his successors. b. Any similar ware.

1787 Beckford *Lett. fr. Italy* (1805) I. 307 Some curious specimens in Terra della Robbia. 1878 *Lloyd's Weekly* 19 May 5/4 (Stanford) A mural tablet in Della Robbia ware. 1886 *Encycl. Brit.* XX. 589/2 Though Luca was not the inventor of the process [*sc.* the production of terra-cotta reliefs covered with enamel], yet his genius so improved and extended its application that it is not unnaturally known now as Della Robbia ware.

2. *Printing.* The name of a kind of type.

1917 F. S. Henry *Printing for School & Shop* vi. 79 Mr. Bullen further subdivides roman letters into two groups—*Display Types* and what he calls *Publicity Types*. The second includes Cheltenham, Della Robbia, Pabst Oldstyle, and Bewick Roman.

Delomorphic (dīlǫmǭ·ɹfik), *a. Anat.* [f. Gr. δῆλος visible + μορφή form + -ic.] Having a definite form, *spec.* denoting certain cells of the gastric glands of the stomach. Also **Delomo·rphous** *a.*

1890 Billings *Med. Dict.*, *Delomorphous cells*, large parietal cells of secretory portion of peptic glands. 1891 W. D. Halliburton *Chem. Physiol. & Path.* 633 Cells of a different nature called parietal cells (Heidenhain), delomorphic cells (Rollett), or oxyntic cells (Langley).

Deloul (delū·l). Also **delool, delul.** [Arab. ذلول *delūl* lit. obedient.] A dromedary.

1853 Layard *Discov. Nineveh & Babylon* xi. 236 *note*, I use the word 'dromedary' for a swift riding camel, the *Deloul* of the Arabs, and *Hejin* of the Turks. 1855 R. F. Burton *El-Medinah* xx. II. 225 Bedouins bestriding naked-backed 'Deluls'. 1875 *Encycl. Brit.* II. 242/1 The 'hejeen', or dromedary, sometimes also called 'delool', or 'facile'.

Delouse (dīlau·z), *v.* [f. De- + Louse *sb.*] *trans.* To clear of lice. Hence **Delou·sing** *vbl. sb.* and *ppl. a.*

1919 *Library Assoc. Rec.* Sept. 6 The inhabitants of each barrack went in turn to the delousing station on the other side of the island, where the delousing process took three days. 1921 *Glasgow Herald* 9 July 7 The fact that there were no adequate means of delousing these men. 1929 A. Forbes *Hist. Army Ordn. Serv.* III. ii. 46 Disinfectors for de-lousing clothing.

Delphine (de·lfin). Also **-in.** [ad. L. Delphinium.] A deep blue like that of the indigo-blue delphinium.

1909 *Cent. Dict.* Suppl. s.v. *Blue*, *Delphin blue*, a mordant coal-tar color of the oxazin type. 1923 *Daily Mail* 28 May 1 Shades: Lemon,..Champagne, Delphine.

Delphinium. Add: b. = prec.

1923 *Daily Mail* 23 Apr. 6 Exclusive colourings, including..Delphinium, Saxe. 1927 *Observer* 9 Oct. 21 Nut Brown, Cocoa, Delphinium.

Delta. Add:

3. b. *Electr.* In a three-phase alternator, the triangular figure formed by the connecting of the three wires of the transmitting circuit to the junction of the three coils; chiefly used *attrib.*, as **delta connexion,** a method of connecting the coils to the wires of the transmitting circuit in this manner.

1902 *Encycl. Brit.* XXVII. 582/2 Any three-phase winding may be changed over from the star to the delta connection. *Ibid.* 592/1 If the three coils are closed upon themselves in a mesh or *delta* fashion.

4. **delta-connexion** (see above); **delta-plain, -plateau,** a sand plain; **delta rays** or *δ-rays*, rays of low penetrative power emitted by radium, polonium, uranium, and perhaps by other radio-active substances.

1902 *Delta connection [see above]. 1892 R. D. Salisbury *Geol. Surv. New Jersey* 101 (Cent. D. Suppl. s.v. *Delta-plain). 1903 *Amer. Geol.* Sept. 163 For such topographic forms professor Davis long since proposed the name of delta-plain or delta-plateau, instead of sand-plain.

Deluginous (deliū·ginəs), *a.* [Fantastically f. Deluge after *ferruginous, salsuginous.*] Like a deluge.

1835 Darley *Nepenthe* II. 60 He..enthralls Earth in deluginous ocean. 1923 *Glasgow Herald* 15 Nov. 8 The deluginous flooding of its markets. 1924 *Ibid.* 15 Apr. 8 When the Great War broke deluginous over the world.

Delusion. Add: 3. b. A fixed penchant *for* (something). *U.S.*

1901–2 *Rep. Kansas State Board Agric.* 52 (Cent. D. Suppl. s.v. *Dished*) There was a time when swine-breeders had a delusion for 'dished faces' and heavy jowls.

De luxe (də lüks). [Fr., lit. 'of luxury'.] Luxurious, sumptuous; of a superior kind.

1819 edition de luxe [see Luxe 2]. 1865 'Ouida' *Strathmore* viii, I wonder governments don't tax good talk; it's quite a luxury, and they might add *de luxe*. 1885 edition de luxe [see Luxe 2]. 1890 trains de luxe [see Luxe 2]. 1908 *Westm. Gaz.* 6 June 5/1 We are conscious of something de luxe, but not oppressed by the sense of it.

Delvauxite (delvǭ·ksəit). *Min.* [ad. G. *delvauxit* (1845), f. the name of Professor *Delvaux* de Teuffe: see -ite [1].] A variety of dufrenite. Also **Delvau·xene** [F. *delvauxine* (1838)].

1864 Church in *Chemical News* 24 Sept. 145/1 The formula 2 Fe₂O₃.PO₅ + 24 HO is assigned to delvauxite. 1868 Dana *Min.* 584 Church also demonstrates that the delvauxite of Liege is only a wet dufrenite. *Ibid.*, The delvauxene is from Besnau, near Visé, in Belgium.

Delve, *v.* 9 (Earlier U.S. example.)

1838 Caroline Gilman *Recoll. Southern Matron* xxix. 204 The poor mother..delving at her needle.

Demagnetized (dīmæ·gnĕtəizd), *ppl. a.* [f. Demagnetize + -ed [1].] Deprived of magnetic quality.

1876 Preece & Sivewright *Telegr.* 246 A demagnetised needle.

Demagogue, *v.* Delete *nonce-wd.* and add modern U.S. examples.

1850 *Congress. Globe* 24 July App. 946 In Ohio, the master-spirits of the party, while demagoging upon the stump, have promised the people [etc.]. 1867 *Ibid.* 16 Mar. 146/1 There was a great temptation presented to members of the Republican party now to demagogue. 1876 *Congress. Rec.* 1 July 4338/1, I have not been one of those..trying to cut down a few dollars for the purpose of demagoguing before the county.

2. *trans.* To deal with (a matter) after the fashion of a demagogue.

1897 *Congress. Rec.* 20 Feb. 2041/2 Here is a plain, common-sense question, not to be demagogued in any way.

Demantoid (dĭmæ·ntoid). [f. Sw., Du. *demant* diamond + -oid.] A green variety of garnet having a brilliant lustre.

1892 E. S. Dana *J. D. Dana's Min.* 442 Demantoid is a grass-green to emerald-green variety [of garnet] with brilliant luster. 1895 Anderson *Prospector's Handbk.* (ed. 6) 96 Garnet...Demantoid, green. 1897 *Edin. Rev.* Oct. 346 The demantoid or Bobrovka garnet. 1920 *Brit. Museum Return* 144 Demantoid with fibrous enclosures.

Demarcator (dī·mɑːkeɪtər). [f. Demarcate + -or.] One who marks out boundaries.

1898 *Daily News* 25 Feb. 6/3 English demarcators and French got on together excellently well. 1900 *Ibid.* 22 Dec. 7/2 The demarcators failed to agree, and there is now a tremendous question between the two countries as to the lines drawn on the map by their respective experts.

Demargarinated (dīmā·ɹgărinēᵊtĕd), *a.* [f. De- + Margarin + -ate [3] + -ed [1].] Of an oil, having the stearin or solid part removed.

1920 W. Clayton *Margarine* 10 A deposit of 'stearin' ensues.., and if this is removed a 'winter' oil is obtained... Such winter oils are also said to be 'demargarinated'.

Démenti (demaṅti). [Fr., f. *démentir* to give the lie.] In modern use applied esp. to an official contradiction of a published statement.

1598–1883 [see Dementie]. 1918 *The Crime* II. v. 228 The semi-official organ seeks to defend the reports of Pourtalès against the English *démentis*. 1921 *Contemp. Rev.* Jan. 103 My information contradicts the dementis published by the *Deutsche Tageszeitung*.

Demerara (demĕrē·ră, demĕrā·ră). The name of a region of British Guiana, used to designate a kind of raw cane-sugar, originally and chiefly brought from Demerara, the crystals of which have a yellowish-brown colour.

1848 *Sugar Question* II. 72 With a long price of 42s. for Demerara sugar, and more labour, the estates could go on. 1880 *Encycl. Brit.* XI. 251/1 The 'Demerara crystals' are very popular for their purity and saccharine strength. 1895 *Young Woman* Dec. 98/2 Sprinkle them with a little Demerara sugar to form a crisp brown coating. 1901 *Brit. Med. Jrnl.* 4 May 1119/2 The West India Committee have caused several grocers to be prosecuted..for selling yellow crystals as Demerara sugar.

Demerit, *v.* Add:

2. b. To lower in status by cancelling of merit.

1895 *Century Mag.* Oct. 843/2 He stands a fair chance of being demerited and punished until his hope of release before he is of age is almost extinguished.

Demersal (dĭmɜ̄·rsăl), *a.* [f. L. *demersus*, pa. pple. of *dēmergĕre* to submerge: see -al.] Of the eggs of fishes: Sinking to the bottom of the sea, deposited at or near the bottom. Of fishes: Living near the bottom.

1889 *Nature* 13 June 159/2 The herring with its demersal eggs, fixed firmly to the bottom. 1911 *Ann. Rept. Sea Fish.* 1909 p. vi. in *Parlt. Papers* XXIV, Demersal fish landed from each 'Area' of the North Sea. 1915 A. Meek in *Rep. Dove Mar. Lab. Cullercoats* 14 The region where the demersal fry are mainly congregated. 1925 *Public Opinion* 16 Oct. 376/1 This increase was most marked in the bottom living or demersal fish.

Supplement, p. 3873; Corrigenda, p. 4092; Spurious words, p. 4093; Books quoted, p. 4094

Demersion. Add: **2.** Organic matter lying at the bottom of the sea.

[1919 *Nature* 31 July 438/2 There remains the 'Demerson', that extremely plenteous floating organic matter..derived from the..planktonic forms which 'rain down'..from the upper waters to the depths below.] 1923 [see *Benthos].

Demidoffite (demidǫ·fəit). *Min.* [a. Sw. *demidovit* (1856), f. the name of the Prince de *Demidov.*] A variety of chrysocolla.

1868 Dana *Min.* 403 Demidoffite occurs at Tagilsk, Urals, in mammillated crusts of a sky-blue color.

Demi-mondaine (dəmi,mondēn). [Fr.; f. Demi-monde.] A woman of the demi-monde.

1894 *Nation* (N.Y.) 12 July 29/1 The conclusion is irresistible that he has been fooled into believing *demi-mondaines* women of good society. 1898 W. J. Locke *Idols* xxi. 211 Her manner was that of the insolently luxurious demi-mondaine.

Demiourgos (dīmiau·ɹgǫs). A strict transcription of Gr. δημιουργός (see s.v. Demiurge).

1923 J. P. Nunn *Education, Data & First Princ.* 192 The 'pure' geologist still presses for the kind of understanding of the earth's structure that we might ascribe to the demiourgos who made it. 1924 W. B. Selbie *Psychol. Relig.* 56 The familiar conception of the demiourgos in gnostic philosophy.

Demi-reputable (demi,re·piŭtăb'l), *a.* [f. Demi- + Reputable: see Demi-rep.] Of doubtful reputation. Also **De:mi-reputa·tion.**

1897 W. J. Locke *Derelicts* xvii. 224 That fashionable demi-reputable world which had drawn him to his precipice. 1909 Marg. B. Saunders *Litany Lane* x, People with doubtful histories, women of demi-reputation.

Demi-semi. Add recent examples.

1901 *Contemp. Rev.* Mar. 358 England..no longer..employed the demi-semi-educated to educate the voters. 1906 *Daily Chron.* 1 May 3/1 Among the demi-semi-educated a laugh can always be raised by sitting down upon a silk hat! 1908 *Ibid.* 13 May 7/7 In the demi-semi-rural districts on the outskirts of towns.

Demiss. 1. Delete †*Obs.* or *arch.* and add:

1837 Manning in Leslie *Life* (1921) 269, I wrote a very soft, demiss rejoinder. 1888 Doughty *Arabia Deserta* I. 253 Not timid as the demiss Damascene Christians. 1903 Bryce *Studies in Contemp. Biog.* 53 By appearing too demiss or too unenterprising in foreign affairs.

Demit (dīmi·t), *sb.* *U.S. Freemasonry.* Also **dimit.** [f. Demit *v.*2] Written permission to leave a lodge, granted to a mason.

1856 R. Morris in A. G. Mackey *Encycl. Freemasonry* (1879) 221/2 A 'demit', technically considered, is the act of withdrawing, and applies to the Lodge and not to the individual. 1879 *Ibid.* 220/1 The granting of 'a dimit' does not necessarily lead to the conclusion that the Mason who received it has left the Lodge. He has only been permitted to do so. *Ibid.* 221/2 'A demit' is..an Americanism of very recent usage.

Demnition (demni·ʃən). Chiefly *U.S.* Euphemistic pronunciation of Damnation 3 b.

1838 [see *Bow-wow 2 e]. 1840 Poe *Business Man* Wks. IV. 168 A democratic rabble is *so* obtrusive, and so full of demnition mischievous little boys. 1888 *San Francisco Weekly Exam.* 22 Mar. (Farmer) It was demnition hot.

Demo, U.S. abbreviation of Democrat 2.

1796–1801 Fessenden *Orig. Poems* 57 In vain each demo spouts and billows. 1806 — *Democr. Unveiled* I. 117 Nothing did demos any good But syllogisms made of wood.

Demob (dīmǫ·b), *v.* Colloq. abbreviation of Demobilize.

1920 *Glasgow Herald* 2 June 11 Some young soldiers..who had been recently demobbed. 1921 *Ibid.* 5 Feb. 7 The unemployed demobbed men. 1922 W. J. Locke *Tale of Triona* v. 56 The impecunious demobbed. 1926 *Spectator* 26 June 1075/1 He was 'demobbed' in 1902.

Democrat. 3. *U.S.* (Earlier example.)

1873 *Trans. Dep. Agric. Illinois* X. 65 Landing at the depot about midnight, they were conveyed in a 'Democrat' at break-neck speed to the Railroad House.

Démodé (demōu·de, ‖demode), *a.* [Fr., = Demoded.] Out of fashion.

1896 *Westm. Gaz.* 7 Mar. 3/2 A chance of reincarnation for some demodé white satin bodice. 1900 *Daily News* 16 Oct. 6/6 There is fashion in art, as in everything else, and the démodé painter soon passes into an obscurity which he does not deserve. 1928 *Observer* 26 Feb. 15/5 Ibsen, demodé as he is, seems to have the quality of the mountain that does not move. 1930 *Time & Tide* 4 Apr. 451 This does not mean that Mr. Birrell's mind is *demodé*.

Demogra·phical, *a.* = Demographic. Also **Demogra·phically** *adv.*

1902 *Daily Chron.* 7 Nov. 4/2 The application of what we might almost call demographical method to departmental studies of the French Revolution. 1904 *Biometrika* Jan. 100 Buénos-Ayres is a town which is altering demographically in two very sensible ways.

Demoiselle. Add:

2. c. A fish of the genus *Pomacentrus.*

1884 Goode *Nat. Hist. Aquatic Anim.* 275 The Demoiselle and the Cichlid Families. 1926 Beebe *Arcturus Adv.* xii. 315 Out from this very coral rock in its path there would shoot a diminutive demoiselle, fins erect in righteous wrath.

d. The tiger-shark, *Galeocerdo tigrinus.*

a 1889 Playfair (Cent. Dict.).

Demon. Add:

2. e. Applied to a being of superhuman or 'diabolical' energy, skill, etc. (cf. 3 a *spec.*).

1876 *Coursing Calendar* 21 A demon of a hare got up for Rose and Bar Girl. *Ibid.* 315 It was hard lines indeed for Mr. Watson to meet with such a demon of a hare for the decider. 1899 *Westm. Gaz.* 6 Feb. 3/1 He is a demon of accuracy.

3. demon star, Algol [Arab. ال غول the demon: see Ghoul], the β star of Perseus.

1895 *Funk's Standard Dict.* 1909 *Daily Chron.* 1 Sept. 7/3 Algol, the Demon Star.

Demonomaniac (dīmōno,mēi·niæk). [f. Demonomania: see -ac.] One who believes himself to be possessed by a devil.

1891 tr. *C. Lombroso's Man of Genius* III. i. 173 For the demonomaniacs of a hundred years ago..are now substituted the modern paranoiacs. 1920 Chesterton *New Jerus.* ix. 177, I do not say that psychologists admit the discovery of demoniacs; and if they did they would doubtless call them something else, such as demonomaniacs.

Demonstration. Add:

8. *attrib.*, chiefly in sense 5.

1883 [see sense 5 in Dict.]. 1899 *Westm. Gaz.* 16 June 4/1 The demonstration farm of the Northumberland County Council at Cockle Park. 1902 Lanteri *Modelling* Introd. 1 The notes of which I made use for my demonstration-classes at the Royal College of Art. 1902 *Rep. Brit. Forestry* 9 in *Parlt. Papers* XX. 1215 That two areas for practical demonstration be acquired...We suggest that the Alice Holt Woods in Hampshire be made available as soon as possible to serve as a Demonstration Area. 1907 *Westm. Gaz.* 22 May 12/2 The Board of Education recognises gardening as a school subject...To each school is allotted a demonstration plot, which is used by the teacher for object-lessons. 1908 J. J. Findlay (*title*) The Demonstration Schools Record. 1909 *Westm. Gaz.* 26 Jan. 4/1 To..give demonstration flights.

Demoralize, *v.* Add: **2. b.** *intr.* for *pass.* To lose moral strength or character.

1903 R. Langbridge *Flame & Flood* xxi. She had demoralised beneath the unwise admiration of her mereness which she received from Maurice.

Demoralizingly (dīmǫ·rălaiziŋli), *adv.* [f. Demoralizing *ppl. a.* + -ly 2.] In a demoralizing manner; to a demoralizing degree.

1926 W. J. Locke *Old Bridge* iv. xii, It seemed..so demoralizingly vicious to drink a friend's cocktails or whisky behind closed doors.

Demosthenian, *a.* (Earlier U.S. example.)

1834 *Deb. Congress* 10 Mar. 843 This Demosthenian pouring-out of the shreds and patches of old Grecian orations.

Demote (dīmōu·t), *v.* orig. *U.S.* [f. De- + (Pro)mote.] *trans.* To reduce to a lower rank or class. Hence **Demo·tion.**

1895 *Funk's Standard Dict.* 1900 *Daily News* 26 May 6/7 When absentees returned to school, the masters were unwilling to 'demote' them. 1901 *Smithsonian Rep.* (1902) 75 Promotion and demotion, i.e., advancement in 'age' (rank) by common consent in recognition of prowess, etc., with correlative reduction in 'age' as the penalty for cowardice. 1919 *Daily Mail* 7 Oct. 5/4 Major-General Biddle..is shortly to be 'demoted' to brigadier. 1929 R. A. Fisher *Genet. The. Nat. Selection* 226 The agencies controlling promotion or demotion.

Demoticist (dīmǫ·tisist). [f. Demotic 1 + -ist.] A student of demotic script. Also **Demo·tist.**

1902 *Encycl. Brit.* XXVII. 726/2 Though demotic has not yet received serious attention at Berlin, the influence of that great school has made itself felt amongst demotists, especially in Switzerland, Germany, America, and England. 1911 *Year's Work Class. Stud.* 188 The use made in the syntax of the writings of the modern demoticists..is..quite fresh and very interesting.

Den, *v.*1 **2.** *To den up.* U.S. colloq. (Earlier example.)

1843 *American Pioneer* II. 171 In that climate [*sc.* of Canada] the bears usually den up in the winter, and lie in something of a torpid state.

Denatant (dīnēi·tănt), *a.* [f. De- + Natant.] Of migrating fishes: Swimming with the current. Hence **Denata·tion,** the migration of fishes in the direction of the current.

1915 [see *Contranatant]. 1920 *Rep. Dove Mar. Lab. Cullercoats* 38 A consideration of our herring shoals from the standpoint of denatation.

Denationalism (dīnæ·ʃənăliz'm). [f. Denationalize: see -ism.] The loss or deprivation of national character. Also **Dena·tionalist,** one who would deprive a people of its national identity.

1916 Stanford & Forsyth *Hist. Music* (1925) 305 The nationalists and the denationalists. 1923 *Glasgow Herald* 29 Mar. 9 International control of the Rhineland and the Saar meant denationalism of the people.

Denaturalizer (dīnæ·tiŭrălaizəɹ, -tʃəɹ-). [f. Denaturalize + -er 1.] One who or that which denaturalizes.

1832 *Crisis* 19 May 31/3 Man..the great denaturalizer of other animals, has exerted his deforming powers most remarkably..upon himself. 1905 *Westm. Gaz.* 28 Mar. 4/2 That ideal 'de-naturaliser' which would..solve the whole problem.

Denaturant (dīnēi·tiŭrănt, -tʃəɹ-). Also -ent. [f. Denature *v.* + -ant 1.] A substance added to alcohol and other commodities as a denaturing agent. (Cf. Denature *v.* 2.)

1905 *Westm. Gaz.* 4 Apr. 5/2 Alcohol similar in purity to methylated spirits before the denaturent is added. 1906 *Daily Chron.* 15 Sept. 3/4 The problem of a cheap, available and efficient denaturant. 1920 *Auto* 4 Mar. 248/2 A real denaturant, which will leave the fuel effective for its purpose, but destroy its qualities as a substitute for drinkable spirit. 1922 *Chambers's Jrnl.* 624/2 Alcohol of 95 per cent. purity was used without denaturents.

Denaturate (dīnēi·tiŭreit, -tʃəɹ-), *v.* [f. De- + Nature + -ate 3.] = Denature *v.*

1895 Lunge *Sulphuric Acid* (ed. 2) II. 14 Decomposing the salt for saltcake..is avoided by 'denaturating' the salt under official supervision. 1904 *Daily Chron.* 4 Aug. 3/5 A proper denaturating medium is not known.

Denaturize (dīnēi·tiŭraiz, -tʃəɹ-), *v.* [f. De- + Nature + -ize.] = Denature *v.* 2. Hence **Denaturiza·tion,** denaturation.

1898 *Trans. Amer. Inst. Electr. Engin.* 139 (Cent. D. Suppl.). 1905 *Westm. Gaz.* 26 Jan. 2/2 The general idea is that if the alcohol be denaturised..it should be subject to no impost.

Dendrite. Add: **3.** *Anat.* Each of the short branching filamentous outgrowths of a nerve-cell.

1900 W. S. Hall *Physiology* 535 The dendrites, or protoplasmic processes, resemble more closely in appearance the cell-body itself than does the axon. 1902 *Encycl. Brit.* XXV. 394/2 In the simplest cases the dendrites carry the sensory impulse to the nerve-cell. 1927 Haldane & Huxley *Anim. Biol.* i. 40 Shorter branched outgrowths (dendrites).

Dendron (de·ndrǫn). *Anat.* [a. Gr. δένδρον tree.] = *Dendrite 3.

1901 Dorland *Med. Dict.* (ed. 2).

Dener (dī·nəɹ). *slang.* A shilling. Cf. *Deaner.

1907 *Daily Chron.* 26 July 4/7 In Ireland the 'denarius' lingers in the name for a shilling—a dener. 1908 *Ibid.* 5 Feb. 4/7 Here we come to classic reminiscences of the denarius! It is a 'bob', and 'owt deners' is a florin.

Dengue. (Earlier U.S. examples.)

1828 *Charleston Courier* 15 July, The Dengue. This..epidemic exists at this time in our city. *Ibid.* 9 Aug. 1830 *Amer. Beacon* (Norfolk, Va.) 9 Nov. 2/2 A rheumatic fever, pronounced by the physicians to be the celebrated Dengue of 1818, made its appearance.

Denia (dī·niă). The name of a Mediterranean seaport of Spain in the province of Alicante used attrib. to denote the products grown in that neighbourhood, as *Denia grape, Denia orange*; also ellipt. for these.

1845 Dodd *Brit. Manuf.* V. 102 The 'Lexias' produce a dry wine, the 'Denias' a sweet wine. 1904 *Westm. Gaz.* 12 Aug. 10/1 Quantities of new Denia grapes flood the market.

Denidation (dīnidēi·ʃən). *Path.* [f. De- + L. *nidus* nest: see -ation.] The removal of the nidus for a fertilized ovum.

1874 J. H. Aveling in *Obstetr. Jrnl.* July 212 Nidation has been likened to gestation. Denidation may be compared with parturition.

Denier 3. Add: **4.** A unit of weight, equal to about 8½ troy grains, by which silk yarn is weighed and its fineness estimated. Hence **Denie·r** *v. trans.*, to ascertain the fineness (of silk yarns) in deniers; **Denie·rer.**

1839 Ure *Dict. Arts* 1105 The first of these raw silks will have a *titre* of 20 to 24 deniers. 1858 Simmonds *Dict. Trade, Denier*,..in Italy, a small weight equal to about a grain, by which silk is weighed. 1887 *Colonial & Indian Exhib., Rep. Col. Sect.* 341 The general sizes [of silk] seem to be 16 to 20 deniers, but it will range from about 10 to 24 deniers, single thread. 1921 *Dict. Occup. Terms* (1927) § 149 *Tester, silk*; *denierer, examiner*; samples, weighs and tests artificial silk for quality when spun. 1927 T. Woodhouse *Artificial Silk* 78 Finally the hanks are weighed..to ascertain the denier count. 1928 (Jan. 11) *British Celanese, Ltd.* (To shareholders) Artificial silk yarns in all the forms and grades which correspond to any deniers existing and offered in the trade...Finest single filament denier thread, being approximately 0·5 to 2 denier.

Denkli (de·ŋkli). *Indian.* [Hind. (Hindi) *ḍhenklī.*] A contrivance used in India for raising water for purposes of irrigation.

1902 *Encycl. Brit.* XXIX. 592/1 In India this is known as the *denkli* or *paecottah*; in Egypt it is called the *shadúf*.

Denmark (de·nmāɹk). The name of one of the Scandinavian countries, used attrib., as in *Denmark satin.*

1858 Simmonds *Dict. Trade.* 1882 Caulfeild & Saward *Dict. Needlework, Denmark Satin*, a kind of worsted stuff employed for the making of women's shoes, measuring 27 inches in width.

Denounce, *v.* Add: **6. b.** *absol.* or *intr.*

1837 E. G. G. Howard *Old Commodore* iii, He first petitioned, then remonstrated, and, foolish boy! at last denounced. 1888 Mrs. H. Ward *Robert Elsmere* xl, I went to confront, to denounce you!..I went to denounce..and the Lord refused it to me.

Dent, *ppl. a.* **3.** *U.S.* Add: Also *ellipt.* Also, see quot. 1909.

1853 *Trans. Mich. Agric. Soc.* V. 125 The land..was planted..with the 'Indian Yellow Dent'. 1873 *Trans. Dep. Agric. Illinois* X. 77 The Dent Corns—White and Yellow Dent, Large White, and Yellow Dent. 1909 W. Bateson *Mendel's Princ. Heredity* 264 According as the seeds [of maize] are opaque or semi-transparent, the varieties are distinguished as 'Dent' or 'Flint'.

Dental, *a.* Add: **1. c.** Engaged in dentistry or dental work, as **dental mechanic,** an operative who makes artificial dentures; **dental moulder,** one who moulds artificial teeth for dentures; **dental surgeon,** a dentist.

1921 *Act* 11 & 12 *Geo. V* c. 21 § 3 (1) The occupation of a *dental mechanic. 1921 *Dict. Occup. Terms* (1927) § 118 *Dental moulder.

3. Provided or fitted with toothed projections.

1849 *Rep. U.S. Comm. Patents* (1850) 312 The application of a dental faced crushing side to a hopper.

Dentaria (dentē·riă). *Bot.* [mod.L., fem. sing. of L. *dentarius* pertaining to the teeth, so called from the toothed roots of the plant.] A plant of the cruciferous genus so named, toothwort.

1886 M. Arnold *Lett.* (1895) II. 327 The dentarias too are beautiful.

Dented, *ppl. a.* Add:

3. b. Of Indian corn (see Dent *ppl. a.* 3). *U.S.*

1855 *Trans. Mich. Agric. Soc.* VI. 151 My mode of harvesting is, to cut up the corn as soon as it is generally dented, or glazed.

Dentelle. 3. Add: *dentelle border, tooling* in bookbinding.

1890 *Catal. Exhib. Bk.-bindings Grolier Club* 11 Dentelle *Border.* A tooled pointed border with finely dotted or Gascon ornaments in imitation of lace. *Ibid.* 21 [Book] Blue morocco; doublé with blue morocco, large dentelle tooling.

Dentex (de·nteks). [L.] An acanthopterygious fish of the genus of that name, common in the waters of the Levant.

1880 Günther *Fishes* 389 Dentex—..Marine fishes rather locally distributed in the Mediterranean. 1925 *Countries of World* IV. 2673/1 The dentex and barracada pike.

Denudant (dīniū·dănt). [f. Denude *v.* + -ant 1.] That which denudes; *spec.* in *Geol.*, an agent or agency which removes disintegrated matter and lays bare the underlying rock or formation.

1894 J. Geikie *Gt. Ice Age* (ed. 3) 259 Its [*sc.* the boulder-clay's] chief denudant has evidently been running water.

Department, *sb.* Add:

5. department store, orig. *U.S.*, a large shop dealing in a variety of articles.

1896 *Congress. Rec.* 7 Apr. 3661/2 [He] seems to think that a department store is the great curse of the country and the devilfish which ought to be killed. 1903 *Forum* Oct. 223 A certain department store in Chicago contains in its equipment no fewer than 53 elevators. 1911 R. W. Chambers *Common Law* ii. 45 One of those bread-and-butter objects that the department shops call a 'Miss'. 1928 *Daily Mail* 25 July 4/3 One big department store, where Japanese paper fans are priced from 3¾d. to 3s. 6d. each, is selling 1,000 a day.

Departmental, *a.* Add: **3.** Consisting of or comprising several departments.

1924 *Times Trade & Engin. Suppl.* 29 Nov. 235/2 The departmental stores and the larger retail shops throughout the Western States. 1928 Alonza James *Commerce* i. 53 Departmental stores contain under one roof many departments. It is possible to purchase groceries, boots and shoes, furniture, clothing, toilet requisites, as well as listen to the latest jazz music from the orchestra.

Departme·ntalist. An adherent or advocate of departmentalism.

1928 *Manch. Guardian Weekly* 31 Aug. 175/1 It will not be possible for departmentalists and lawyers of backward countries to be any longer unconscious of their own imperfections.

Depatriation (dīpætriēi·ʃən). [f. Depatriate: see -tion.] The removal from one's or its country.

1918 *Oxf. Mag.* 21 June 342/2 To rescue works of art of the first importance from the swift-flowing tide of depatriation.

Dependability (dīpendăbi·lĭti). [f. Dependable: see -ility.] The quality of being dependable, reliability.

1901 F. T. Bullen *Sack of Shakings* 264 Next to the Trades in dependability..are the west winds of the regions north and south of the Tropics. 1922 *Daily Mail* 7 Nov. 8 Renowned for entire Dependability. 1928 *Daily Express* 21 Apr. 10/3 That essential solidity and dependability that every wise woman seeks in her life mate.

Depersonalization (dīpɜ̄ːɹsənălaizēi·ʃən). [f. Depersonalize + -ation.] The action of depersonalizing or fact of being depersonalized.

1907 Illingworth *Doctr. Trin.* x. 191 Madness, prison, suicide may be the end, and all equally symbolise the destruction of proper personality, or, to use a modern term, the depersonalisation, to which transgression leads. 1912 F. von Hügel *Eternal Life* 69 A certain depersonalization of his conception of this same Christ. 1929 *Times* 14 Aug. 6/3 That progress means the 'de-personalization' of the individual.

Deplane (dīplēi·n), *v.*2 [f. De- + *Plane *sb.*3] *intr.* To descend from an aeroplane.

1923 *Blackw. Mag.* July 11/2 Dudley left me, saying..that he was to 'deplane' [*sc.* by parachute] now. 1929 *Morn. Post* 28 Oct., Two new words, 'enplane' and 'deplane'.

Depo, U.S. var. of Depot.

1819 E. Evans *Pedestrious Tour* 180 The Hudson..the great maritime depo of the state.

Deport, *v.* Add: **5. b.** In Indian use, = *Detain *v.* 1. So **Deporta·tion** = *Detention 7.

1909 Visct. Morley *Indian Speeches* 144 Great uneasiness is growing in the House of Commons as to the matter of deportation. You know what deportation means. It means that nine Indian gentlemen on December 13 last were arrested and are now detained. *Ibid.* 149 If he is one of these nine deported men, he is not put into contact with criminal persons. 1910 V. Chirol *Indian Unrest* vii. 99 The deportation struck just at that type of agitator whose influence is most pernicious because it is most subtle. 1914 Mrs. Besant *India & the Empire* 123 Harmless men like my friend Lajpat Rai, who is here, are deported or imprisoned without trial.

Deportable (dīpōə·ɹtăb'l), *a.* [f. Deport *v.* + -able.] Punishable by deportation.

1891 Stevenson *Vailima Lett.* (1895) 100 This intervention would have been a deportable offence.

Deportee (dīpoɹtī·). [f. Deport *v.* + -ee 1.] One who is or has been deported; *spec.* in Indian use, = *Détenu.

1895 *Westm. Gaz.* 13 Dec. 5/1 One party of fifteen deportees from Constantinople having been massacred. 1909 Morley *Recoll.* (1917) II. 309 The failure to tell the deportee what he is arrested for. 1910 V. Chirol *Indian Unrest* vii. 99 The grounds on which Government announced the release of these deportees last winter were even more unhappily chosen than the moment for the announcement. 1914 *Morn. Post* 3 Feb. 9/4 To intercept the Umgeni and give the deportees an opportunity of returning to their homes.

Deposit, *sb.* **6.** Add: *deposit account* (earlier U.S. example); (sense 3) *bed, gold, mines.*

1851 C. Cist *Cincinnati* 89 Their average *deposit account during that period was about eight hundred thousand dollars. 1849 C. Lanman *Alleghany Mts.* i. 11 Heretofore the gold ore of Lumpkin county has been obtained from what is called the *deposit beds. *Ibid.* 17 The *deposit gold is extracted from the gravel by means of a simple machine called a rocker. 1833 H. Barnard in *Maryland Hist. Mag.* XIII. 346, I..hired a horse for 50 cents to go down to see the *deposite mines, which are spread over the whole country.

Depot. 7. Add: **depot-wagon** *U.S.*, 'formerly a square-box wagon with a detachable top; now a rockaway with a trap-door at the rear end which can be converted into a baggage-rack' (*Cent. Dict. Suppl.*).

1908 *Daily Chron.* 29 Sept. 7/1 Resisting a little as he drew her out, down the stairs, and aided her to enter the depot-wagon.

Hence **Depot** *v. trans.*, to place in a depot.

1921 H. G. Ponting *Gt. White South* 274 When near the summit, Captain Scott told off four more of the party to depôt their surplus and return.

Deprecating (de·prĭkēitiŋ), *ppl. a.* [f. Deprecate *v.* + -ing 2.] That deprecates or expresses disapproval or disavowal; deprecatory.

1871 L. W. M. Lockhart *Fair to See* xviii, A bright, but withal deprecating, smile on her lovely face. 1919 Wodehouse *Damsel in Distress* xi, Albert waved a deprecating hand. 1925 Mrs. Belloc Lowndes *Some Men & Women* 199 With a queer, half-deprecating, half-humorous look on his handsome face.

Depreciating, *ppl. a.* (Earlier U.S. example.)

1777 J. Adams *Wks.* (1854) IX. 463 There is so much injustice in carrying on a war with depreciating currency that we can hardly pray with confidence for success.

Depressent. Variant of Depressant *sb.*, a depressing influence.

1894 Stevenson & Osbourne *Ebb-Tide* i. v. 87 So strong a tonic to the merely weak, and so deadly a depressent to the merely cowardly.

Depressingness (dīpre·siŋnės). [f. Depressing *ppl. a.* + -ness.] The quality of being depressing.

1923 *Glasgow Herald* 9 June 7, I wonder if he finds 'pervading depressingness' in these verses. 1927 *Chambers's Jrnl.* 3/2 More likely to stop a fellow from getting back to the mark, by its wretched 'depressingness'.

Depressor. Add: **4.** *Electr.* A device in the return circuit for keeping the potential in that circuit the same as that of the earth.

1909 *Cent. Dict.* Suppl. s.v., A depressor or crusher is essentially of the same nature as a booster, but is applied to the regulation of the return circuit instead of the insulated circuit.

Deprint (dī·print), *sb.* [f. De- + Print *sb.*] An offprint. Hence **Depri·nt** *v.* (*Cent. Dict.* Suppl.).

1885 Skeat in *Academy* 22 Aug. 121/3 Various terms, such as 'deprint', 'exprint', &c., have been proposed to denote a separately printed copy of a pamphlet. 1895 (*title*) Modern Language Notes: Deprints of Articles by George C. Keidel, Ph.D...Baltimore, Md. 1895.

Depth. IV. Add: **depth bomb, charge,** a bomb capable of exploding under water.

1918 E. S. Farrow *Dict. Mil. Terms* s.v., Submarines..are pursued and destroyed by dropping *depth bombs from the observing aircraft or warship. 1917 *War Illustrated* 18 Dec. 361 Telegraph to seamen..who prepare to drop *Depth Charges to destroy U-boat. 1920 *Blackw. Mag.* Mar. 315/2 The depth-charge thrower, which later came into common use..was as yet far from perfection. 1928 C. F. S. Gamble *N. Sea Air Station* Introd. 14 Lieutenant Williamson..described how depth-charges (he said 'bombs exploding so feet under the surface of the water') might possibly be used to destroy submarines.

Depula (de·piŭlă). *Embryol.* [mod.L., irreg. dim. of Gr. δέπας goblet.] The stage in the development of a fertilized egg-cell which succeeds the blastula and precedes the gastrula.

1892 E. Ray Lankester tr. *Haeckel's Hist. Creat.* (ed. 4) II. 159 Depula. (Hooded larva.) Hood-shaped larva with body-cavity (Blastocœl) and primary intestine (Progaster) ('Gastrula invaginata').

Deputize. 2. Add illustration of wider use.

1900 *Westm. Gaz.* 27 Sept. 5/2 Sir Samuel Scott being absent in South Africa, has cabled the neighbouring Tory candidate, Mr. Boulnois, to deputise for him. 1904 *Daily Chron.* 15 Sept. 3/6 He was called upon at various times to deputise for other high officials. 1906 *Sat. Rev.* 30 June 807 With the exception of Mr. Stead and Mr. T. P. O'Connor, the representatives of the press were deputising in the absence of their chiefs. 1915 *Observer* 31 Jan. 9/6 Mrs. Levison..deputising for Lady Jellicoe, read to the company a letter.

Deracialize (dīrēi·ʃălaiz), *v.* [f. De- + Racial + -ize.] *trans.* To remove racial characteristics or features from. So **Deracializa·tion.**

1899 Patten *Devel. Engl. Thought* 365 Religious leaders, no longer deracialized by education, are dissatisfied with foreign platitudes and commonplaces. 1907 *Westm. Gaz.* 21 Feb. 2/2 The good service they have rendered by deracialising (so to speak) the elections. 1931 Sir A. Keith *Ethnos* 27 Where Huxley went wrong was in believing that when Europeans belonging to separate racial stocks..were planted together..they became, if I may coin a term, deracialized. *Ibid.* 90, I am convinced that deracialisation is possible.

Déraciné (derasine), *a.* (*sb.*) [Fr.: see Deracinate.] 'Uprooted' from one's (national or social) environment. Also *sb.*

1921 *19th Cent.* May 770 The unseen Jew *déraciné* provides munitions of argument for the revolutionary group. 1926 J. Buchan *Dancing Floor* i. vi, She rides well, but her manners are atrocious. Lord, how I dislike these *déracinés*!

Derate (dīrēi·t), *v.* [f. De- + Rate *sb.*1] *trans.* and *intr.* To diminish the burden of rates (upon). Hence **Dera·ting** *vbl. sb.* and *ppl. a.*

1928 Churchill in *Hansard's Parl. Deb.* Ser. v. CCXVI. 849 Twelve months will be required after that Bill is passed, to enable the new valuation to be made for the purposes of de-rating. *Ibid.* 869 The cost of the complete de-rating of agriculture is about £4,750,000. 1928 *Daily Express* 22 June 2/4 [He] asked the Government to expedite their derating scheme, which is expected to be worth £3,000,000 a year to the coal industry. 1928 *Daily Tel.* 17 July 11/4 [He] proposed to derate hospitals supported by voluntary subscriptions.

Deratization (dīrætəizēi·ʃən). [f. De- + Rat *sb.*1 + -ization.] The getting rid of rats.

1914 *Standard* 13 Oct. in *N. & Q.* 11th Ser. X. 386 The Board of Trade communication gives a translation of the circular, in the course of which it more than once uses the curious word 'deratization', meaning, apparently, the clearing away of rats. 1921 *Glasgow Herald* 28 May 5 A discussion on 'Deratisation of Ships at British Ports'. 1929 *Ministry of Health*, Stat. Rules & Orders No. 832 The Public Health (Deratisation of Ships) Regulations.

Derby. Add:

1. d. Applied to any kind of important contest.

1909 *Daily Chron.* 17 June 5/6 The twenty-ninth Medway Barge Sailing Match, known locally as 'the barge Derby'. 1914 *Daily Express* 3 Oct. 3/1 A local Derby [*sc.* football match] between Liverpool and Everton.

2. b. A kind of sporting-boot having no stiffening and a very low heel.

1901 *Daily News* 23 Feb. 6/4 The Prince Consort is represented..as wearing low-heeled, square-toed 'Derbies', with buckles on them. 1904 *Westm. Gaz.* 15 Apr. 10/2 Russia calf Derbys for shooting-boots.

5. *Derby scheme*: in the war of 1914–18 a recruiting scheme initiated in October 1915 by Lord Derby. Also *Derby recruit* and simply *Derby*, a soldier recruited under this scheme.

1915 *Times* 4 Dec. 9/6 Last week of the Derby Scheme. *Ibid.* 20 Dec. 9/2 Men who have been attested and classified under the Derby scheme. 1917 P. Gibbs *Battles of Somme* 177 Old English regiments with new men in them, including some of the 'Derby recruits'. 1918 McCudden *Five Yrs. R.F.C.* 198 It was at that time [Feb. & Mar. 1917] that the 'Derby' scheme was operating. 1925 E. Fraser & Gibbons *Soldier & Sailor Words* s.v., Men of the 'Groups' of 'Derbies', awaiting their turn to be called up,..wore armlets lettered 'G.R.' (General Reserve).

6. Denoting a variety of porcelain made at Derby, *esp.* a soft-paste porcelain made from about 1750, Crown Derby being a variety made from 1784, and Derby Crown being a modern imitation of old Crown Derby ware.

1875 Tiffin (*title*) A Chronograph of the Bow, Chelsea and Derby Porcelain Manufactories. 1885 *Encycl. Brit.* XIX. 641/2 The Derby under-glaze blue was remarkably fine.

7. *Derby* or *Derbyshire cheese*, a hard, pressed cheese made from partly skimmed milk, produced chiefly in the Derbyshire district.

1905 W. H. Simmonds *Pract. Grocer* III. 79 The true 'Derbyshire' cheese..is a small cylindrical or flat and thin cheese of pale colour, and generally of rich, buttery quality. 'Derby Goudas' are a variety shaped like the Dutch Gouda. 1902 *Encycl. Brit.* XXVII. 355/2 Derby cheese in its best forms is much like Leicester, being 'clean' in flavour and mellow.

Hence **De·rbyed** *a.*, wearing a Derby hat (*U.S.*).

1905 Howells in *Harper's Mag.* Mar. 560 One of the few cylindered or derbyed heads in the swarming processions of Piccadilly.

Deregister (dīre·dʒistəɹ), *v.* [f. De- + Register *sb.*1] *trans.* To remove from a register. Hence **De-registra·tion.**

1924 *Glasgow Herald* 19 Nov. 11 Disobedience would almost certainly have caused de-registration of the union under the Arbitration Act. 1925 *Ibid.* 23 Jan. 10 Mr Justice Powers indicated plainly that he would deregister the union if he did not receive a pledge that the men would obey the award. 1927 *Observer* 4 Dec. 17/5 As the Federation, by a triple refusal, in March, May, and October, to obey the award, is in flagrant contempt of court, it should, it is held, be promptly deregistered.

Derisive. Add: **b.** That causes derision, ridiculous.

1896 *Westm. Gaz.* 25 Feb. 2/1 In thirteen years he has brought a paper costing money to keep it going and with a derisive circulation to the front rank of the world's journalism. 1923 *Daily Mail* 15 May 8 Germany has provided only a derisive amount to make good that cruel injury.

Derisory, *a.* Add: **b.** = prec.

1923 *Westm. Gaz.* 19 Mar., In comparison with what it was hoped to do the result is derisory. 1923 *Daily Mail* 5 June 8 Of the total German payments for reparations France has received in cash or kind the derisory amount of £14,500,000, and England the equally preposterous amount of £5,700,000.

Derivation 1. Add:

1. d. Borrowing, in an organ: see *Borrow *v.*1 2 b. So **Deri·ved** *ppl. a.* = *Borrowed *ppl. a.* 2 b.

1905 T. Casson *Pedal Organ* 22 It is true that they often call the borrowing by another name, such as 'transmission', 'derivation' and even 'duplication', but that is not straightforward.

Derivative, *a.* Add:

4. *Geol.* **a.** Of fossils: Occurring in rocks other than those to which they are native. **b.** Of rocks: Formed from materials derived from older rocks.

1871 Lyell *Student's Elem. Geol.* Index, Derivative shells of the Red Crag. 1894 J. Geikie *Gt. Ice Age* (ed. 3) 371 The shells which they occasionally contain are probably, in most cases, derivative—they do not occupy the positions in which the molluscs themselves lived. 1904 *Technol. & Sci. Dict.* (ed. Goodchild & Tweney) s.v., Conglomerates, sandstones, shales, and clays are good examples of derivative rocks.

Derive, *v.* **11.** Add: In recent journalism extensively used, prob. as a gallicism.

1895 tr. *Paul Bourget's Outre-mer* ii. 36 How all literature derives from him [*sc.* Shakespeare] in every English-speaking country. 1899 *Daily News* 28 Nov. 6/5 As a draughtsman he derives from Charles Keene. 1901 *Ibid.* 22 Jan. 5/4 The theory of the mediæval empire derives immediately from Rome. 1907 *Daily Chron.* 18 Oct. 4/6 Thackeray derived straight from Goldsmith. 1908 *Ibid.* 16 Sept. 3/3 In the beginning the American portrait painters..derived from England as England had derived from Flanders and Italy.

Derived. Add: **d.** *Derived fossils* (Geol.), fossils occurring in formations other than those to which they are native. Cf. *Derivative *a.* 4.

1904 *Technol. & Sci. Dict.* (ed. Goodchild & Tweney), *Derived Fossils*...Such fossils need to be distinguished from those which actually lived during the period when their matrix was laid down.

Derivometer (derivǫ·mĭtəɹ). Delete † *Obs.* and add quot.:

1928 *Times* 15 Aug. 13/6 The afterpart of the cabin..contained the derivometer for measuring the airship's deviation from the straight course.

Dermale (dəɹmē·lĭ). [mod.L., neut. sing. of *dermalis Dermal.] Each of the spicules of a sponge which support the dermal membrane.

1898 Sedgwick *Text-bk. Zool.* I. 91 Dermalia are spicules in relation with the bounding membrane of the sponge.

Dermato-. Add: **De:rmatocly·sis** (see quot.) **De:rmatosco·pic** *a.*, having the faculty of perceiving variations of light by means of the skin alone. (Many other terms are given in medical dicts.)

1908 *Practitioner* Apr. 436 *Dermatoclysis, or the subcutaneous injection of large quantities of water or normal saline solution. 1898 *Geogr. Jrnl.* (R. G. S.) XII. 452 *Actinia, Medusæ, Velelia, Spongiaria*, etc., when subjected to light of greater or less intensity, give evidence of sensations to which the name of '*dermatoscopic' is given.

Dermo-. Add: **De·rmochrome,** a coloured illustration of the skin. **Dermographia, Dermo·graphism,** an irritable condition of the skin in which lines drawn on it leave a reddish elevated mark.

1903 *Lancet* 9 May 1308/2 Portfolio of Dermochromes. By Professor Jacobi of Freiburg in Breisgau. 1908 *Practitioner* Feb. 252 From these individuals we get a history of attacks of urticaria, whilst they may even show dermographism.

Dermoid. Add: **B.** *sb.* A dermoid cyst.

1897 *Allbutt's Syst. Med.* III. 686 The intraperitoneal dermoids may be very numerous. 1908 *Practitioner* Apr. 469 A dermoid often produces an indentation of the bone.

Dermotrich (dɜ̄·ɹmətrik). Also in L. form **-trichium.** [f. Dermo- + Gr. τριχ-, θρίξ hair.] A mesoblastic dermal fin-ray of fishes.

1904 *Q. Jrnl. Microsc. Sci.* (N.S.) XLVII. 512 In all the fins of the true Pisces there are present dermal rays of mesoblastic origin, the dermotrichia. 1909 *Cent. Dict.* Suppl., Dermotrich.

Dern, *sb.* var. of Darn (= damn). *U.S.* (Earlier examples.)

1874 Eggleston *Circuit Rider* (1895) 120, I tole him as how I didn't keer three continental derns fer his whole band. 1876 'Mark Twain' *Tom Sawyer* vi. 56, I wouldn't give a dern for spunk-water.

Dern, U.S. var. of *Darn *a.*

1876 'Mark Twain' *Tom Sawyer* ix. 84 I'd druther [rather] they was devils a dern sight. 1883 — *Life Mississippi* xviii. 219 'Where was you born?' 'In Florida, Missouri.' 'Dern sight better stayed there!' 1919 T. K. Holmes *Man fr. Tall Timber* xviii. 220 The dern fool! Thirty thousand against thirty millions!

Dern, U.S. var. of Darn *v.* (= damn).

1883 'Mark Twain' *Life Mississippi* xviii. 226 'Dod dern' was the nearest he ventured to the luxury of swearing. 1890 H. C. Bunner *Short Sixes* (1891) 100 'Dern you', said the keeper to Dr. Tibbitt.

Derned, U.S. var. of Darned *a.* (= damned).

1873 J. H. Beadle *Undevel. West* xxi. 403 [He] was rich afo' the war; derned poor now. 1898 H. S. Canfield *Maid of Frontier* i. 6 The derned rangers will have to make the same ride.

Dernier. Add: **c.** *The* (or *le*) *dernier cri* [lit. the last cry]: the very latest fashion. Also in predicative use.

1896 *Westm. Gaz.* 10 Dec. 3/2 At a moment when cut-steel is *le dernier cri*. 1906 *Ibid.* 13 June 6/7 There was a time when the lisp was, so to speak, the 'dernier cri'. 1928 *Daily Express* 16 June 5/5 That is why they wear hats and gowns that they are told are le dernier cri. *Ibid.* 9 Nov. 5/4 Any old necklace can be made modern and 'dernier cri'.

Derricking (de·rikiŋ), *vbl. sb.* and *ppl. a.* [f. Derrick *sb.* + -ing 1, 2.] **a.** *vbl. sb.* The action of operating the jib of a derrick-crane. **b.** *ppl. a.* Operating as a derrick.

1888 *Lockwood's Dict. Mech. Engin.* s.v. *Derrick*, Portable cranes..are provided with movable jibs, whose mechanism for derricking is made in various types.

Derrid (de·rid). [f. mod.L. *Derris*: see below.] A tarry substance obtained from the bark of the root of *Derris* (or *Deguelia*) *elliptica*, used by the people of the Malay archipelago as a fish poison.

1891 *Jrnl. Soc. Chem. Industry* X. 268.

Derringer. *U.S.* (Earlier example.)

1854 J. R. Bartlett *Personal Narr. Explor. Texas* I. iii. 48 My carriage driver carried a pair of Deringer pistols.

Derry (de·ri). *Austral.* [?jocular adaptation of *derry* in the refrain *derry down.*] = Down *sb.*3 5.

1896 *Argus* 19 Mar. 5/9 (Morris) Have you any particular 'derry' upon this Wendouree?

Dertrum (dɜ̄·ɹtrǒm). *Zool.* Also **dertron.** [mod.L., ad. Gr. δέρτρον beak.] The extremity of the upper bill of a bird when in any way distinguished from the rest of the beak.

1893–6 Newton *Dict. Birds.*

Derzie, -y, variants of *Durzee.

Desai (de·sai). *Anglo-Indian.* Also 7 **desie,** 9 **desaye, dessai.** [Marathi *desāī.*] A native Indian revenue official, or petty chief.

1698 Fryer *Acc. E. India & P.* 120 The Desie or Farmer, who squeezes the Countryman, as much as the Governor does the Citizen. 1800 Wellington *Suppl. Desp.* (1858) II. 116 He has sent 300 horse to seize the dessays of the villages which you mention. 1835 Jas. Bird tr. *Order in Mirat-i-Ahmadi* 408 (Y.) The Desayes..made a complaint at Court. 1883 *Pioneer Mail* 24 Jan. (Y.) The Desai of Sawantwari has arrived at Delhi on a visit. 1885 G. S. Forbes *Wild Life in Canara* 20 They were also instructed to rendezvous..under their Dessaies at any point which might be threatened.

Desaxé (dezakse), *a.* Also -axe. [Fr., f. *dés-* Dis- + *axe* axis.] Out of line with the axis of the cylinder; off-set.

1906 *Daily Chron.* 14 Nov. 9/3 The setting of the crank-shaft desaxes, or out of line with the cylinders. 1908 *Westm. Gaz.* 4 June 4/2 An uncommon feature of the Metallurgique engine is the setting of the crank-shaft *desaxés*—that is to say, the centre of the crank is set slightly out of line with the centre of the cylinder. *Ibid.* 17 Nov. 5/2 The off-set crank-shaft, or *désaxes*, as it is more familiarly termed. 1912 *Motor Manual* (ed. 14) iii. 66 Principle of Offset Cylinder, or Desaxe Crankshaft Setting.

Descended, *ppl. a.* Add:

2. That has descended, fallen, or dropped.

1903 W. M. Eccles (*title*), Imperfectly descended testis.

Descent. Add:

1. g. The descent of Christ into hell.

1882 Westcott *Hist. Faith* vi. (1883) 76 The eternal meaning of Christ's Descent, Resurrection, Ascension, Session in heaven, as set forth in our Creed. 1894 Swete *Apostles' Creed* v. 56 The doctrine of the Descent had found a place in three synodical declarations. *Ibid.* 57 Cyril..assigns great importance to the Descent, making it one of his ten primary *credenda*.

Description. 3. b. (Recent U.S. example.)

1902 S. E. White *Blazed Trail* xvii. 127 Entering the sections..in his note-book; taking in only the 'descriptions' containing the best pine.

Descriptive. Add:

2. *Descriptive geometry* (= F. *géométrie descriptive*, Monge 1794–5): that branch of geometry in which the relations of lines and figures are studied in their projections on two planes.

1880 *Encycl. Brit.* XI. 359/2 The department of descriptive geometry. 1885 C. Leudesdorf tr. *Cremona's Projective Geom.* 50 Projective Geometry..dealing with projective properties..is chiefly concerned with descriptive properties of figures.

Desensitize (dīse·nsitaiz), *v.* [f. De- + Sensitive + -ize, after *sensitize.*] *trans.* To reduce the sensitiveness of. Also *intr.* Hence **Dese·nsitizer,** a preparation which desensitizes; **Dese·nsitizing** *ppl. a.* and *vbl. sb.*

1904 *Brit. & Col. Printer* 10 Mar. 15/2 Don't leave the plate too long out of the bath or it will desensitise. 1921 *Glasgow Herald* 9 Mar. 7 A single bottle contains enough solution for the desensitising of hundreds of small plates. *Ibid.* 6 Apr. 7 The discovery of phenosafranin as a desensitiser. *Ibid.* 11 May 7 The desensitising properties of pheno-safranine. 1922 *Brit. Jrnl. Photogr. Alm.* 368 The desensitising action. *Ibid.* 369 The transparent backing..acts as a powerful desensitiser.

Desert, *sb.*2 **5.** Add: *desert-brown, -grey*; *desert-frequenting, -haunting, -worn* adjs.; **desert-lemon** *Austral.*, a rutaceous tree, *Atalantia glauca*, bearing a small acid fruit; **desert oak** (see Oak 3 b); **desert polish,** the polish imparted to rocks or other hard surfaces by the friction of the wind-blown sand of the desert; **desert varnish,** a film of iron oxide or quartz on rocks polished by wind-blown sand.

1923 *Daily Mail* 5 Mar. 13 Nigger, Regal Blue, Grey, *Desert Brown. 1905 *Westm. Gaz.* 28 Aug. 10/2 This species (*Varanus griseus*) is a large, *desert-frequenting lizard. 1906 *Ibid.* 1 Oct. 4/3 The kiang [*sc.* wild ass] is a desert-frequenting species. 1901 *Ibid.* 2 Jan. 2/1 Two stalwart sportsmen with..their *desert-grey hounds gliding near them. 1894 R. B. Sharpe *Handbk. Birds Gt. Brit.* I. 122 From its pale coloration this Pipit might be considered a *desert-haunting bird. 1889 J. H. Maiden *Useful Native Plants* 8 *Atalantia glauca*,..'Native Kumquat', '*Desert Lemon'. 1896 W. B. Spencer *Rep. Horne Sci. Exped.* i. 49 The region of the '*Desert Oak' (*Casuarina Decaisneana*). 1903 Geikie *Text-bk. Geol.* (ed. 4) 436 On the sandy plains of Wyoming, Utah,..surfaces even of such hard materials as chalcedony are etched into furrows and wrinkles, acquiring at the same time a peculiar and characteristic glaze ('*desert-polish'). 1904 Van Hise *Treat. Metamorphism* in *U.S. Geol. Surv.* Monograph 47. 547 In arid regions the hardened film has frequently been smoothed by the wind-blown sand, so as to present a polished surface. Such polished hardened films are known as '*desert varnish'. 1890 'R. Boldrewood' *Col. Reformer* ix, Sun-burned and *desert-worn passengers.

Desertion. Add:

1. b. A person who deserts.

1898 H. G. Wells *War of Worlds* i. xvii, The Midland Railway Company had replaced the desertions of the first day's panic.

Desexualize (dīse·ksiŭălaiz), *v.* [f. De- + Sexual + -ize.] *trans.* To deprive of sex or sexual characters, to deprive of the distinctive qualities of a sex.

1894 *Idler* Sept. 195 The most highly cultured, mentally most richly endowed women I have known—not *desexualised.* 1919 Bradby *Psycho-analysis* (1920) 50 They regard all human energy as sexual, or 'libido', though Jung holds that it may become de-sexualised by turning from a sexual aim to non-sexual surrogate. 1926 *Spectator* 19 June 1038/2 The self-flatterer who, because of a misdirected sense of sin desexualizes the human form that he may pride himself on his idealization of it.

b. To castrate.

1913 Dorland *Med. Dict.* (ed. 7).

Deshmukh (dē·ʃmuk). *Indian.* Also **desmook, désmúkh.** [Marathi *deçmukh.*] A hereditary revenue officer in India.

1801 R. Patton *Asiat. Mon.* 210 The *desmooks*, or official zemindars, who had preceded him in the subordinate financial management of the country. 1841 Elphinstone *Hist. India* II. 461 They were left in charge of the nearest désmúkh, or other revenue officer.

Designate, *a.* Add: *spec.* in the University of Cambridge.

1878 *Cambr. Univ. Cal.* 5 There are three days of general admission to the title of Bachelor Designate of Arts in every year. 1892 *Ordinances of Cambr. Univ.* 152 At the creation of Doctors of Law in every year, the names be arranged in order of seniority according to the seniority of the Doctors Designate as Masters of Law. 1925 *Cambr. Univ. Cal.* 85 Bachelors in Arts, Law, Medicine, Surgery, and Music remain 'Bachelors designate' until the 31st of December.

Desirable, *sb.* Add: **2.** One who is desirable.

1664 H. More *Antid. Idolatry* viii. 93 The highest of all desirables, that is, God himself. 1853 R. S. Surtees *Sponge's Sp. Tour* xvi, Certainly all parties concurred in placing him high on the list of 'desirables'. 1904 *Daily Chron.* 21 Sept. 8/5 Nor did the individual who spoke proudly of 'moving in a circle'—of 'desirables'—realise the vulgarity of the expression. 1905 *Westm. Gaz.* 21 June 8/2 The real undesirables..would have to be kept back and looked after until they became 'desirables'. 1908 *Ibid.* 26 June 2/1 Could not the undesirables be got rid of, and the desirables multiplied?

Desk, *sb.* **5.** Add: **desk-room** *U.S.*, space for a desk rented in a business office.

1868 A. B. Kimball *Undercuts* 9, I occupied an office—no, I had 'desk-room' in a basement office. 1870 Medbery *Men & Myst. Wall Street* 117 Many of the operators, as well as the smaller brokers,..have simply desk-room.

Desmoncus (desmǫ·ŋkǒs). *Bot.* [mod.L., f. Gr. δεσμός bond + ὄγκος hook.] A climbing plant of the genus of palms of this name, common in tropical America.

1899 Rodway *Guiana Wilds* 14 His head grazed by the formidable hooks which hung from the horrid desmoncus.

Desolatingly (de·sŏlĕitiŋli), *adv.* [f. Desolating *ppl. a.* + -ly 2.] In a manner that desolates or saddens.

1901 'L. Malet' *Counsel of Perfection* xiv, These desolatingly encouraging persons. 1909 H. G. Wells *Tono-Bungay* i. iii. 81 A drab-coloured passage..not only narrow and dirty but desolatingly empty.

Despecialize (dīspe·ʃălaiz), *v.* [f. De- + Special + -ize.] *trans.* To eliminate as a specialist or specialized vocation. **b.** *intr.* To pass from a specialized to a general condition. Hence **Despecializa·tion.**

1896 F. L. D. Herbertson tr. *P. de Rousiers' Lab. Quest. Britain* ii. iii. 190 Service is a very *despecialised* trade, at any rate in ordinary families, where a man-servant is an unknown luxury. *Ibid.* iii. i. 253 The increasing despecialisation of the worker. 1898 *Edin. Rev.* Apr. 281 The whole tendency of the age of machinery has been to..de-specialise the average workman. 1903 Patten *Heredity & Soc. Progr.* 61 Emotion is the same force expressed as feeling, and in conscious beings is the index of the despecialization and regeneration acting within them. *Ibid.*, The despecialized part is not restored, but a new specialization begins in the part affected by the emotion.

Desperate, *a.* Add: **4. c.** Desperately in love.

1835 *Knickerbocker Mag.* V. 301 They were, it was plain to see, quite desperate with each other.

Despisement (dīspəi·zmĕnt). Delete †*Obs.* and add:

1886 C. A. Briggs *Messianic Proph.* 398 Her days of oppression and despisement are over. 1887 *Critic* 27 May (Farmer) An uncomfortable sensation of over-familiarity bordering on despisement.

Des(s)atine, more freq. forms of Dessiatine.

1814 Dessatine [in Dict.]. 1898 B. Redwood *Rep. on Schibaieff's Petrol. Refinery* 6 Two other plots, about four dessatines in area. 1901 *Daily Chron.* 29 Aug. 5/1 The Tsar is said..to own in private property, mostly in the Baltic Provinces, a million desatines of land.

Dessert. Add: Also 9 *U.S.* **desert.**

1. b. *U.S.* (Earlier example.)

1833 H. Barnard in *Maryland Hist. Mag.* XIII. 379 The desert was pudding—cherry pie—and strawberries, cream and sugar.

Dessous (desū·). [Fr., = below, underneath.]

1. Underwear.

1901 'Clive Holland' *Mousmé* 285 Mousmé had adopted the dainty *dessous* of Western woman. 1902 Elin. Glyn *Refl. Ambrosine* 237 The tiniest pink satin slippers peeped out of billows of exquisite *dessous.*

2. Phr. *Dessous des cartes*: the underside of the cards as they lie face downwards when dealt; *fig.* a secret aim or object, explanation, etc. kept in reserve.

1756 Ld. Chesterfield *Let. to Dayrolles* 26 Nov., Misc. Wks. 1777 II. 435 There must be some *dessous des cartes*, some invisible wheels within wheels, which..I cannot guess at. 1820 Mrs. Opie *Tales* IV. 271 Sir Walter and Arthur laughed at this *dessous des cartes.* 1885 'L. Malet' *Col. Enderby's Wife* iv. iii, Just a little something behind, an explanation, you know, a *dessous-des-cartes.*

Destool (dīstū·l), *v.* [f. De- + Stool *sb.*] *trans.* To remove (a chief) from his 'stool'. Hence **Destoo·lment.**

1929 Rattray *Ashanti Law & Const.* 82 Failure to accept such guidance and advice was a legitimate cause for destoolment. *Ibid.* 83 The person of a Chief was..invested with sanctity, just so long as he sat upon the Stool of his dead ancestors. This is the reason why there was a reaction the moment a Chief was destooled.

Destroyer. Add: **b.** Short for *torpedo-boat destroyer*, q.v. s.v. Torpedo boat b.

Destroyer was the proper name of an American torpedo-boat in 1882 (see *Leisure Hour*, 1882, 637/2, quoting *Brooklyn Eagle*). An earlier name for the torpedo-boat destroyer was *torpedo(-boat) catcher* (see *Catcher 3).

1893 torpedo-boat-destroyer [see Torpedo boat b]. 1899 torpedo-destroyer [see Torpedo *sb.* 4]. 1893 *Revue gén. des Sciences* IV. 458 (Bonnaffé) Le *Destroyer* était amarré à 30m, 48 d'un bassin. 1894 *Daily News* 11 June 6/5 This type of boiler..is being put into most of the 'destroyers' which are being built for the Government. 1895 *Ibid.* 27 July 3/1 The Rocket, another destroyer, ..will not be ready for sea until Wednesday next. 1897 *Pop. Sci. Monthly* Nov. 139 It is becoming difficult to obtain the requisite area in screws of 'destroyers' without either resorting to an abnormal width of blade or to a large diameter. 1898 Kipling *Fleet in Being* ii. 23 Would she—and a fast cruiser can do this—try to rush her by night, destroyer-fashion? 1899 *Daily News* 25 July 6/6 She is the gunboat in charge of one of our destroyer divisions. 1927 *Daily Tel.* 28 June 12/1 Large cruisers, destroyer-leaders, and submarines. 1929 W. J. Locke *Jorico* 124 He strode up and down with the air of the Commander of a Destroyer going into his first action.

Destroying, *ppl. a.* Add: *Destroying angel*, = *Danite.

1857 [see *Danite]. 1872 'Mark Twain' *Roughing it* xii. (1882) 71 Half an hour..later we changed horses, and took supper with a Mormon 'Destroying Angel'.

Destructional (dīstrʊ·kʃənăl), *a.* [f. Destruction + -al.] Of or pertaining to destruction; formed by destructive agencies, *spec.* by denudation.

1904 *Amer. Jrnl. Sci.* Jan. 38 The steep cliff is clearly in both cases a destructional surface from which material has fallen away.

Destructivity (dīstrʊkti·vĭti). [f. Destructive *a.* + -ity.] Destructiveness. Also **Destru·ctivism.**

1902 *Encycl. Brit.* XXVII. 609/1 With the result that seismic destructivity can be accurately expressed in mechanical units. 1927 *Weekly Times* 19 May 562/1 It [*sc.* Marxism] demolishes the foundation of an individualistic society. On the continent this is now called destructivism.

Detached, *ppl. a.* Add: **b.** Of persons, their conduct, etc.: Characterized by detachment (see Detachment 4 b, and next).

1924 Anne D. Sedgwick *Little French Girl* ii. xi, She might be detached, and even callous; but she was not brazen. *Ibid.* iv. i, Someone quite, quite detached and devoted must fall in love with her.

Detachment. 4. b. Add: More widely, freedom or aloofness from ordinary occupations, concerns, attachments, or the like.

1888 H. James in *Harper's Mag.* Feb. 342/2 Her detachment, her air of having no fatuous illusions, and not being blinded by prejudice, seemed to me at times to amount to an affectation. 1915 R. Brooke in *Coll. Poems* (1918) Mem. 147 One just hasn't, though, the time and detachment to write, I find. 1924 Anne D. Sedgwick *Little French Girl* ii. xi, 'C'était un bien méchant homme', Madame Vervier remarked in a tone of surpassing detachment. 1926 Churchill in W. R. Inge *Lay Thoughts of a Dean* 166 That sense of detachment and impartiality, that power of comprehending the other man's point of view.

Detail (dītē·l), *v.*2 [f. De- II. 2 + Tail *sb.*1] *trans.* To deprive of its tail.

1837 Marryat *Snarleyyow* xxxvi. The dog had been detailed. 1900 G. Swift *Somerley* 148 His de-tailed coat looked like a ragged Eton jacket.

Detailed, *ppl. a.* Add:

2. *Mil.* Appointed to a particular duty; seconded.

1874 *Rep. Vermont Board Agric.* II. 617 We have in connection with the college, a detailed United States army officer, but what he is to do I do not know.

Detain, *v.* **1.** Add: *spec.* in Indian use, to place (a political offender) in confinement. Cf. *Detention 1 and *Détenu.

1918 *Rep. Comm. Rev. Conspiracies* 86 in *Parlt. Papers* VIII, Such men are the leaders and organizers of the movement. They are now detained or their arrest is intended under Regulation III of 1818.

Detainure. (Later U.S. example.)

1816 U. Brown *Jrnl.* in *Maryland Hist. Mag.* XI. 363 The Expence of my Detainure in Cumberland on the Above Account with my 2 Horses.

Detartarizer (dītā·ɹtăraizəɹ). [f. De- + Tartar *sb.*1 + -ize + -er 1.] An apparatus for purifying or softening water. 1911 Webster.

Detective, *a.* and *sb.* Add: **A.** *adj.* *Detective camera*, a hand camera adapted for taking instantaneous photographs.

1881 *Brit. Jrnl. Photogr.* 28 Jan. 44/2 A form of the detective camera, in which the finding arrangement and the stock of slides are omitted, is in progress. 1882 *Year-Bk. Photogr.* 27 Among novel apparatus we may mention..Mr. Bolas' so-called 'Detective Camera'. 1888 *Brit. Jrnl. Photography* 18 May 305 The subject of detective cameras is capable of considerable subdivision.

B. *sb.* attrib. *detective force, -inspector.*

1888 A. C. Gunter *Mr. Potter of Texas* xx, Sergeant Brackett, of the British detective force. 1898 *Westm. Gaz.* 27 Nov. 7/2 Detective-inspector Egan said that he arrested the prisoner upon the charge.

Detectivism (dīte·ktiviz'm). [f. Detective + -ism.] The activities of a detective, detective work.

1894 *Academy* 23 June 514/2 An incredible piece of detectivism. 1896 *Athenæum* 15 Aug. 225 Literary detectivism of a high order. 1905 *Book-Lover* 10/2 A sea story with a little detectivism and plenty of humour in it.

Detector. Add: **3. f.** A high-frequency rectifier used in wireless telegraphy.

1895 S. P. Thompson *Elem. Less. Electr. & Magn.* ii. xiv. (1899) 557 Using such a detector,..Lodge has shown how these electric waves can pass hundreds of feet through walls. 1898 *Science Siftings* 11 June 117/2 A Hertz-wave 'detector' resistance included in the circuit. 1902 *Encycl. Brit.* XXXIII. 232/2 The coherer, or detector, is inserted between the earth and the outer end of this last wire. 1924 *Wireless Weekly* 8 Oct. 744/2 Seven valves (all 'peanuts'), used successively as first detector, oscillator valve, three stages of intermediate frequency, second detector valve, and one stage of transformer-coupled note-magnification. 1928 *Morning Post* 6 Feb. 3/4 The nature of the circuit connected to the detector helps to determine the amplification.

4. In full *bank-note detector*: A published list of current bank-notes, formerly in use as a guide to their real value. *U.S.*

1893 *Congress. Rec.* 25 Aug. 936/2 We had throughout Indiana, Illinois, and Ohio what is known as blue-dog and yellow-pup, where every man had to carry a detector with him.

Detent (dīte·nt), *sb.*2 Delete †*Obs.* and add: The holding back or inhibition.

1907 W. James *Mem. & Studies* (1911) 256 They are forces of detent in situations in which no other force produces equivalent effects, and each is a force of detent only in a specific group of men. 1929 R. Bridges *Test. Beauty* iv. 150 A pinprick or a momentary whiff or hairbreadth motion freeth the detent of force.

Détente (detãnt). [Fr., = loosening, relaxation.] The easing of strained relations, esp. in a political situation.

1908 *Times* 17 Aug. 5/4 A change in the European situation..had..set in...The characteristic feature of this transformation may be called a *détente*. 1921 Von Hügel in L. S. Hunter *John Hunter* 213 The profound impression of a comforting *détente* made upon my mind by my first contact with his spirit. 1928 *Daily Tel.* 29 May 9/5 To bring about an early détente in Turco-Persian relations.

Detention. Add:

1. *spec.* in Indian use, of the confinement of a political offender. Cf. *Détenu.

1909 Visct. Morley *Indian Speeches* 146 There is no fixed limit of time of detention. 1920 *Statem. Moral & Mat. Progr. India* 26 in *Parlt. Papers* XXXIV. 744 The continued detention of dangerous characters already under control or in confinement.

5. *attrib.*: **detention barrack** *Mil.*, a recent name for a military prison; **detention camp,** in the war of 1914–18 a camp in which aliens and others were kept under restraint; **detention money,** a sum of money held back until certain conditions are fulfilled.

1906 *Act 6 Edw. VII* c. 2 § 6. 5 A soldier sentenced to imprisonment..may be confined in a *detention barrack. 1898 *Westm. Gaz.* 12 July 7/3 The Union rate of wages, overtime, and *detention money are paid. 1902 *Daily Chron.* 27 Nov. 4/7 The cable contract detention money payable when the cables had proved satisfactory.

Détenu. Add: Also *spec.* A political prisoner in India.

1918 (*title*) Report of Sir N. Chandavarka and Mr. Justice Beachcroft on Detenus and Internees in Bengal. 1920 Sir H. V. Lovett *Hist. Indian Nat. Movem.* vii. 196 The Committee recommended the release of six only of all the above enumerated *détenus.*

Determa (dītɜ̄·ɹmă). Also 8 **tetermer.** [Native name.] A native wood of Guiana.

1769 [Bancroft] *Nat. Hist. Guiana* 80 The Tetermer Tree grows to near fifty feet in height. 1851 *Illustr. Catal. Gt. Exhib.* iv. i. 984/2 Determa, transverse and vertical sections, from River Demerara. 1858 Simmonds *Dict. Trade, Determa*, a native wood of Guiana, which is used for masts, booms, and planking for colonial craft.

Determinant, *sb.* Add:

4. *Biol.* In Weismann's theory of heredity, a secondary unit of germ-plasm supposed to determine the character of a cell or group of cells (hence called a *determinate*) in the organism.

1893 tr. *Weismann's Germ-Plasm* i. 57, I shall designate the cells or groups of cells which are independently variable from the germ onwards as the 'hereditary parts' or 'determinates', and the particles of the germ-plasm corresponding to and determining them, as the 'determining parts' or 'determinants'. *Ibid.* 59 A determinant is always a group of biophors. 1905 *Westm. Gaz.* 30 Mar. 2/1 Selection acts on the determinants and produces the variations once so plausibly attributed to the Lamarckian principle of acquired characters. 1920 *Cambr. Bulletin* Feb. 16 Germ-cell Determinants.

Determinantal (dītɜ̄ɹminæ·ntăl), *a.* Add: Consisting of or expressed in determinants.

1867 C. L. Dodgson *Elem. Treat. Determinants* 12 The determinantal coefficient of any Element of a square Block is the Determinant of its complemental Minor.

Determinate, *ppl. a.* Add: **C.** *sb.* *Biol.* (See prec.)

1893 tr. *Weismann's Germ-Plasm* i. i. 58 Similar hereditary parts or determinates may be observed in butterflies, in which the colours on the wings often form very complicated lines and spots of slight extent but of great constancy.

Determine, *v.* Add:

14. c. *absol.* or *intr.* To give a (certain) direction.

1863 O. M. Mitchell *Astron. Bible* 157 A time finally comes when a preponderance determines in favor of the attraction of one sun above all others.

Determiner 1. Add: **1. d.** *Biol.* = *Determinant *sb.* 4.

1909 W. Bateson *Mendel's Princ. Heredity* 79 Hitherto we have spoken of the determiner for such a colour as grey in rabbits and mice as 'dominant' over the colours lower in the scale, as black or chocolate...We shall then speak of the determiner for grey as epistatic to that for black. 1922 R. C. Punnett *Mendelism* (ed. 6) 113 A female determiner incapable of carrying sex-limited factors.

Detin (dīti·n), *v.* [f. De- II. 2 + Tin *sb.*] *trans.* To remove the tin from (scrap tin plate).

1909 *Cent. Dict.* Suppl. 1923 *Glasgow Herald* 15 Aug. 7 The major portion of the old tins was disposed of after being detinned and pressed into billets. 1929 *Times* 21 Sept. 7/4 Scrap metal..suitable for detinning.

Detonate, *v.* Add: **1. d.** Of an internal combustion engine: To make a clinking or hammering noise, owing to some defect in the machinery. Cf. *Knock *v.*

1928 *Daily Tel.* 16 Oct. 17 Why the motor engine 'pinks', 'knocks', or, as it is technically termed, 'detonates'.

Detonation. Add:

1. b. A hammering noise occurring in the machinery of an internal combustion engine, in motor engines caused chiefly by faulty ignition or carburation and worn or loose bearings. Cf. *Knock *sb.*

1912 *Motor Manual* (ed. 14) vi. 201 With super-compression of the charge instead of a gradual expansion of the ignited gases a 'detonation' occurs.

Detort, *v.* Transfer †*Obs.* to 1 and 2 and add:

3. *Biol.* *intr.* To become straight (cf. *Detortion 3).

1930 G. R. de Beer *Embryol. & Evol.* vii. 54 There is no possibility whatsoever of mistaking these detorting forms for the 'torting' forms for which we search in vain.

Detortion, -sion. Add:

3. *Biol.* The straightening or straight condition of an organism whose ancestors were twisted.

1902 *Encycl. Brit.* XXX. 796/2 Not an absence of torsion, but an actual detorsion of the visceral commissure. 1913 Dorland *Med. Dict.* (ed. 7), *Detorsion*, the correction of a curvature or deformity. 1930 G. R. de Beer *Embryol. & Evol.* vii. 54 That intermediate stages are not *a priori* impossible is proved by the fact that intermediate stages in detorsion in later Gastropods are not wanting.

Detour, *v.* Add: **b.** *trans.* To send by a detour.

1905 *N. Y. Even. Post* 18 Sept., The Missouri Pacific is detouring its St. Louis-Kansas City trains over the Burlington Railway via Chillicothe.

Detoxicate (dītǫ·ksikeit), *v.* Delete *nonce-wd.* and add:

1906 *Practitioner* Nov. 590 Focalisation of the infection in the liver, with disturbance of its detoxicating mechanism. 1927 *Observer* 7 Aug. 2 It detoxicates the blood and keeps it clean and free-running.

Hence **Detoxica·tion,** the action of depriving of poisonous qualities; also **Detoxifica·tion. Deto·xicator,** that which detoxicates.

1906 *Practitioner* Nov. 586 A reducer and detoxicator of toxic substances. *Ibid.* 593 The detoxication of the poisons found in the blood. 1906 Dorland *Med. Dict.* (ed. 4), *Detoxification*, reduction of the toxic properties of poisons. 1913 *Ibid.* (ed. 7), Detoxication.

Detractation (dītræktēi·ʃən). Delete †*Obs.* and add:

1888 H. S. Salt *Shelley* 141 Against Shelley he never uttered a word of detractation.

Detrainment (dītrēi·nmĕnt). [f. Detrain *v.*2 + -ment.] The action of detraining.

1899 *Westm. Gaz.* 9 Dec. 6/1 Three trains of mounted troops have been detrained at Arundel,..being covered in their detrainment by the New Zealand Mounted Infantry. 1916 Ld. E. Hamilton *First 7 Div.* (1917) 156 On October 11th the detrainment of the 2nd A.C. was completed. 1928 *Observer* 18 Mar. 13/1 All detrainments of the assault divisions were made well back on a wide front.

Detribalize (dītrai·bǎləiz), *v.* [f. DE- + TRIBAL + -IZE.] *trans.* To render (a person) no longer a member of a tribe; to destroy the tribal habits of.
1920 *Contemp. Rev.* Sept. 397 Numbers of natives who, through living in close contact with the settlers have become quite detribalised. 1927 *Public Opinion* 272/1 White men have detribalised him. 1927 *Other Lands* Jan. 59/1 Two types, the tribal native and the detribalized native.

Detrimental, *a.* Add: **b.** *Detrimental surface* (of an aeroplane): see quot.
1916 BARBER *Aeroplane Speaks* 58 Active Drift, which is the drift produced by the lifting surfaces. Passive Drift, which is the drift produced by all the rest of the aeroplane—the struts, wires, fuselage, under-carriage, etc., all of which is known as 'detrimental surface'.

Deuce[1]. **2.** Add: **deuce-game** (see quot. 1897); **deuce-set,** a set in which each side is level, having won five or more games.
1886 *Cassell's Fam. Mag.* Oct. 704/2 It also scores back to deuce points and deuce games. 1897 *Encycl. Sport* I. 621/2 *Deuce-game*, the game won, which makes the score in games level when each side has won more than five. 1908 *Westm. Gaz.* 16 Nov. 14/1 Losing the first game after a deuce set.

Deurbanize (dīˌǝ·ɹbǎnəiz), *v.* [f. DE- + URBAN *a.* + -IZE.] *trans.* To deprive (a district) of its urban character. Also *fig.*
1924 *Public Opinion* 15 Feb. 154/3 Its work is to deurbanise the minds of British rulers. 1927 *Observer* 29 May 7 Can we de-urbanise England? Or will all our efforts to empty the towns merely result in urbanising the countryside?

Deuteranopia (diūtěrǎnōu·piǎ). *Path.* [mod. L., f. DEUTERO- + mod.L. *anopia* blindness (f. Gr. privative ἀν- + ὤψ eye).] Green-blindness. Also **Deu·teranope,** one who is affected with deuteranopia.
1901 *J. M. Baldwin's Dict. Philos. & Psychol.* I. 274 *Deuteranopia*, ..the name proposed by v. Kries for what was formerly called green-blindness. 1902 *Ibid.* II. 787 The wave-length which corresponds to the colourless sensation, *W*, is different for the two sorts of colour-defectives, proteranopes and deuteranopes.

Deutero-. Add: **Deu·terocone,** the inner and anterior cusp of an upper premolar of mammals. **Deu:teroco·nid,** the corresponding cusp of a lower premolar. **Deu·terograph,** a duplicate written or printed passage. **Deutero·merite,** a deutomerite. **Deu·terotheme,** a stem used as the second element of a compound word. **Deutero·tokous** *a.*, of or pertaining to deuterotoky. **Deutero·toky,** that form of parthenogenesis in which the virgin female produces offspring of both sexes. **Deu:teroto·xin,** any one of the second of four groups of diphtheria toxins.
1896 *Proc. Zool. Soc.* 5 May 563 The antero-external cusp ..develops first, the antero-internal or *deuterocone second. 1894 R. B. GIRDLESTONE (*title*) *Deuterographs. Duplicate Passages in the Old Testament. 1896 FARRAR in *Expositor* Jan. 36 We can explain..the repeated occurrence in the same book of deuterographs. 1888 ROLLESTON & JACKSON *Anim. Life* 858 *note*, The proto- and *deutero-merite. 1914 *N. & Q.* 11th Ser. X. 142/1 Mr. Searle has accidentally omitted *hād* from his list of *deuterothemes of O.E. personal names on p. xvii of his 'Onomasticon'. 1895 F. G. SINCLAIR in *Cambridge Nat. Hist.* V. 141 It is a curious fact that the result of parthenogenesis in some species is the production of only one sex, which in some Insects is female, in others male; the phenomenon in the former case is called by Taschenberg Thelyotoky, in the latter case Arrhenotoky; *Deuterotoky being applied to the cases in which two sexes are produced. 1901 DORLAND *Med. Dict.* (ed. 2). **Deuterotoxin*, any one of the second of the four groups of diphtheria-toxins. 1904 *Brit. Med. Jrnl.* 10 Sept. 567 We have three different toxins with different toxicity and different avidities to the antitoxin, viz. the prototoxin, the deuterotoxin, and the tritotoxin.

Deuterocanonicity (diūtěroˌkænǝni·sĭti). [f. mod.L. *deuterocanonicus* + -ITY.] The condition or quality of being deuterocanonical.
1909 J. RENDEL HARRIS *Odes & Ps. Solomon* (1911) 4 We may perhaps describe their [*sc.* the Psalms'] position as the penumbra of uncanonicity, or, rather of deuterocanonicity.

Deuterogamy. Add: **b.** *Bot.* A form of nuclear fusion in certain cryptogams, subsequent to and superposed on the sexual act.
1898 P. GROOM in *Trans. Bot. Soc. Edinb.* 8 Dec. 140 Bearing in mind the analogy to the sexual act, we may describe these nuclear unions as being cases of deuterogamy.

Devalorize (dīvæ·lǒrəiz), *v.* [f. DE- + VALOR + -IZE: see VALORIZATION.] *trans.* To lower the value of. Hence **Devaloriza·tion.**
1925 *Glasgow Herald* 1 Apr. 8 To face honestly the question of devalorising the franc. 1928 *Observer* 15 July 12/2 So that he and they may equally share the devalorisation.

Devaluate (dīvæ·liuˌeɪt), *v.* [f. DE- + VALUE *sb.* + -ATE[3].] *trans.* To reduce or annul the value of; to deprive of value.
1898 W. J. LOCKE *Idols* xiii. 128 He is relying on his speech to-morrow to devaluate the evidence. 1924 *Glasgow Herald* 1 Mar. 8 The country has gone a great length in the direction of devaluating the vote by conferring it on men whose politics are as immature as themselves.

Devaluation (dīvæliuˌeɪ·ʃǝn). [f. prec. or next: see -ATION.] The process of devaluating or fact of being devaluated.
1914 *Engl. Hist. Rev.* Jan. 140 The devaluation of the ancient Merovingian pence. 1921 *Glasgow Herald* 10 Dec. 8 Devaluation has an important bearing on Lord Inchcape's criticism of teachers' salaries. 1922 *Ibid.* 12 May 9 The probable further devaluation of the mark.

Devalue (dīvæ·liū), *v.* [f. DE- II. 2 + VALUE *sb.*] *trans.* = *DEVALUATE.
1918 *Guardian* 24 Oct. 847/3 The chemist has succeeded in devaluing the ruby. 1925 *Glasgow Herald* 29 Apr. 10 To return to the gold standard on the basis of a devalued sovereign.

Devastatingly (de·vǎstĕˌtiŋli), *adv.* [f. DEVASTATING *ppl. a.* + -LY[2].] In a devastating manner: often used trivially.
1905 *Daily Chron.* 28 Sept. 4/6 The devastatingly tidy housemaid. 1927 *Observer* 15 May 8 A man in whom a natural violence of lust and temper is restrained by the unnaturally strict taboos of his childhood's environment, but breaks loose all the more devastatingly when his inhibitions are removed by drink. *Ibid.* 21 Aug. 5 The devastatingly betraying sentences of Theodore Parker. 1928 *Daily Tel.* 15 May 8 His conversation..is positive, narrow-minded, egregiously self-satisfied, impregnably commercial, but it is devastatingly entertaining.

Develop, *v.* Add:
3. d. *Chess.* Phrases. *To develop one's game*: to pursue a certain plan, carry out intended tactics. *To develop a piece*: to bring that piece towards or into a position where it is of service.
1847 STAUNTON *Chess-Player's Handbk.* 22 In chess, this is attempted by the first player putting a Pawn en prise of the enemy early in the game, by which he is enabled more rapidly and effectually to develope his superior Pieces. *Ibid.* 147 Leaving him the option of exchanging Knights or of protecting his K.P., either of which would afford you an opportunity of developing your game. 1864 *Chess Player's Mag.* 52 Black, it seems, had no other chance of developing his game than to give up Rook for Knight at this point. *Ibid.* 80 Black's game is now fully developed; their Bishops are strongly posted, and..their game, we think, was preferable.
e. To show the details of (a piece of work) in a drawing (cf. *DEVELOPMENT 7 d).
1888 [see *DEVELOPMENT 7 d].
5. d. To reveal, bring to light. *U.S.*
1889 *Kansas Times & Star* 8 May, A census of Kansas City's saloons develops the startling fact that there are about 1,000. *Ibid.* 16 July, A search for the pioneer bicyclist hereabouts developed Dr. Henderson, who proudly rode a wheel on our streets in 1880. 1900 *Publishers' Circular* 15 Dec. 617/2 The inquiry did not develop any new facts.
e. To come to light, become known. *U.S.*
1903 *N. Y. Even. Post* 17 Sept., A new feature of the shooting developed to-day, when it was discovered that [etc.]. 1927 *N. Y. Times* 29 Sept. 1/6 It developed that Beach had been pressed for money.
7. c. (with cross-influence of sense 9 b). To exhibit the symptoms of (a disease or ailment). *colloq.*
Mod. I'm sorry to be away from work, but I have developed a bad cold.

Developable, *a.* Add: **c.** *Photogr.* Capable of being developed (see DEVELOP 5 b).
1878 ABNEY *Photogr.* (1881) 30 An exposure in the camera to produce a developable image would have to be very prolonged. 1892 *Photogr. Ann.* II. 85 New Theory of the Developable Image. 1907 *Westm. Gaz.* 26 Oct. 13/2 They take only a short time to produce a developable condition in the emulsion.

Developed, *ppl. a.* (see under DEVELOP *v.*). Add: *Chess.* (See *DEVELOP *v.* 3 d.)
1898 *Westm. Gaz.* 26 Feb. 3/3 Unnecessarily moving a developed piece.

Developer. Add: **c.** *Photogr.* An operative who develops photographs.
1899 *Daily News* 28 Apr. 5/2 We had two men on the train—our regular developer and his assistant. 1921 *Dict. Occup. Terms* (1927) § 527.
d. An apparatus for developing a person's muscles.
1900 SANDOW *Strength* 41 The great value of the Developer lies in the fact that it serves to render the muscles pliable. *Ibid.*, Exercise with the rubber Developer affords a welcome change from work with the dumb-bells. 1907 *Westm. Gaz.* 17 Jan. 4/2 With regard to the use of grip dumb-bells and the developer, they are not intended for the abnormal development of any one muscle.

Developing, *vbl. sb.* (see under DEVELOP *v.*). Add: *developing-cup, -machine*; **developing (out) paper** *Photogr.*, paper on which the image remains invisible during printing and is afterwards developed.
1878 ABNEY *Treat. Photogr.* xvi. 118 The solution should be flowed back into the *developing cup. 1884 T. C. HEPWORTH *Photogr. Amat.* 149 Wavy markings on a developed plate may generally be traced to dirty dishes or developing-cups. 1921 *Dict. Occup. Terms* (1927) § 398 *Developing machine minder (textile printing). 1890 *Anthony's Photogr. Bull.* III. 166 Any one who has ever manipulated *developing paper. 1918 *Photo-Miniature* XV. Mar. (Gloss.), Developing Out Papers (D.O.P.).

Development. Add:
1. b. In mod. use: A fact or circumstance emerging or coming to light. (Cf. *DEVELOP *v.* 5 e.)
1928 *Publishers' Weekly* (N.Y.) 24 Nov. 2191 The October '27 issue of *The Outlook* was devoted almost entirely to confessions and developments proving Vanzetti's innocence.
3. d. The developing of the potentialities of an estate, property, site, etc. by laying it out, building, mining, or the like: freq. attrib., esp. in *development work.*
1885 [in Dict. sense 11]. 1897 *Daily News* 4 Jan. 2/1 During the year an unusual amount of development work was done on the producing mines. 1898 *Westm. Gaz.* 21 Apr. 4/3 Advance moneys for development purposes. 1900 *Daily News* 11 June 2/1 Development operations have been carried out upon the Le Roi, No. 2 Property. 1909 *Westm. Gaz.* 11 Feb. 11/4 About 5,000 ft. of development work has been done on the claims.
7. d. The working out of details in a technical drawing.
1888 *Lockwood's Dict. Mech. Engin.*, *Development*.—(1) A drawing is said to be developed when certain working details are drawn in full. Thus a propeller blade is developed when the various transverse sections are shown;..a plate or templet is developed when it is so marked out that if cut to the developed lines and then bent, it will form the envelope of some definite geometrical figure. 1904 *Technol. & Sci. Dict.* (ed. Goodchild & Tweney).
10. b. *Chess.* The disposition of the forces for attack or defence at an early stage of a game.
1864 *Chess Player's Mag.* 195 The difficulty of meeting the many new developments of the attack, especially those resulting from 9 Q.Kt. to B.3rd, has led to a reaction in favour of the move Q.Kt. to R. 4th. 1865 *Ibid.* 48 In order to fix a Pawn at his Q. fifth, and so obstruct the development of Black's cavalry. 1889 FREEBOROUGH & RANKINE *Chess Openings* (1893) 13 There are two styles of development; the attacking and the defensive. In the one the pieces are spread about to secure the greatest possible command of the board. In the other they are kept together mutually supporting or defending each other. *Ibid.* 14 When you cannot see your way to an attacking move, play a development move.
11. development rock, rock of inferior value removed during the development of a gold-mine. See also *3 d.
1900 *Daily News* 17 Oct. 2/4 The mill during the past two months has been hampered by the necessity of crushing low grade development rock, removed in order to render rock of average value available. *Ibid.*, Crushed 1,021 tons development rock.

Deverbative (dīvɜ̄·ɹbǎtiv). *Gram.* [f. DE- + VERB, after *denominative.*] A word formed on or derived from a verb.
1913 J. M. JONES *Welsh Gram.* 381 Other Aryan stem-forms, mostly deverbatives and denominatives.

Deviable (dī·viǎb'l), *a.* [f. L. *dēviāre* (see DEVIATE) + -ABLE.] That can be caused to deviate; capable of being deflected. Hence **Deviabi·lity** (*Cent. Dict.* Suppl. 1909).
1913 J. COX *Beyond the Atom* iii. 50 The α rays [from radio-active substances] bear a positive [electric] charge... Though deviable by magnetic and electric fields, the amount of deviation is minute compared with that of kathode rays or β rays.

Deviation. Add: **3. d.** *spec.* (*a*) *Deviation of the complements*, in *Biol. Chem.*, the prevention of the complements from acting upon the receptors. (*b*) *Embryol.* Divergence in the development of an animal from the ontogenetic stages of its ancestor.
1906 *Practitioner* Dec. 748 Another and much more important and serious cause of failure comes about by means of the phenomenon described by Neisser and Wechsburg, and known as the 'deviation of the complements'. 1930 G. R. DE BEER *Embryol. & Evol.* xv. 102 The appearance of characters in the early stages of development is caenogenesis, and these characters which loom so largely in neoteny and deviation are flies in the Haeckelian ointment of recapitulation.

Devil, *sb.* Add:
8. Various other contrivances (see quots.).
1874 KNIGHT *Dict. Mech.*, *Devil*, a machine for making wood screws. 1890 W. J. GORDON *Foundry* 72 A herculean metallic disk, grimly named the 'devil', armed with steel cutters on its circumference that takes off a pound of shavings at every revolution. 1901 *Farm, Field & Fireside* 13 Dec. 362/2 Large surfaces are dealt with by burning, an instrument called a 'devil' being generally employed by painters for 'burning off' doors, panels, etc. 1904 *Technol. & Sci. Dict.* (ed. Goodchild & Tweney), *Devil* (Foundry), a small portable grate containing a charcoal fire, used for drying the internal surfaces of a mould. (Plumb.) A plumber's firepot; used for heating solder, etc.
9. b. *Devils on horseback* = angels on horseback (see *ANGEL 9).
1909 *Cent. Dict.* Suppl.
11. Also, a dust-storm in South Africa.
1897 BADEN-POWELL *Matabele Camp.* 284 A 'Devil' with its roaring pillar of dust and leaves, comes tearing by. 1900 *Daily News* 3 Apr. 3/1 The 'dust devils' that sweep across the blustering plain. 1901 *Westm. Gaz.* 16 Mar. 3/1 The 'devil' in South Africa will pick up boots and tins of sardines, even bottles of whisky and saddle bags.
17. *Devil take the hindmost*: see HINDMOST *a.* 1 b.
23. c. *devil-driven* adj.
1926 'LUCAS MALET' *Dogs of Want* v. § 3 Lonely and devil-driven. 1926 M. LEINSTER *Dew on Leaf* II. i, Jack is lonely, wretched, devil-driven.
24. devil-crab, the velvet crab, *Portunus puber*; **devil dance** (cf. *devil dancer*); **devil-devil,** in Australian folk-lore (see quot.); **devil-grass** (U.S. example); **devil-on-the-coals** *Austral.*, a small damper hastily baked in hot ashes; **devil-wood** (U.S. examples).
1871 DARWIN *Desc. Man* II. ix. 269 When a *Devil-crab (Portunus puber) was seen..fighting with a *Carcinus mænas*, the latter was soon thrown on its back. 1899 GRANT ALLEN in *Strand Mag.* June 655/2 Prickly devil-crabs. 1930 G. E. O. KNIGHT *Intim. Glimpses Myster. Tibet* 29 The *Devil Dances of Tibet..represent either some historical, legendary, or mythological event. 1900 H. LAWSON *Over Sliprails* 108 Black Jimmie shifted away from the hut [of the dead woman] ..for the '*devil-devil' sat down there. 1872 *Rep. Vermont*

Board Agric. 289 *Triticum repens.* Its various English names, Couch... Witch and *Devil Grass, attest how widespread it is becoming. 1862 POLEHAMPTON *Kangaroo Land* 77 Instead of damper we occasionally made what is colonially known as '*devils on the coals'. 1832 D. J. BROWNE *Sylva Amer.* 225 The wood..when perfectly dry—is excessively hard and very difficult to cut and split—hence is derived the name of *Devil Wood. 1844 LEE & FROST *Ten Yrs. Oregon* vii. 81 A species of maple called green-maple, or 'devil-wood', remarkable for its toughness.
25. b. devil's darning-needle *U.S.* (earlier examples).
1809 W. IRVING *Knickerb.* VI. iv. (1825) 245 They..bore as a standard three Devil's-darning-needles, *volant*, in a flame coloured field. 1830 PAULDING *Chron. Gotham* 14 Gnats, flies, and devil's darning-needles.

Devil, *v.* Add: **1. d.** To treat harshly.
1823 W. FAUX *Mem. Days* 216 Go..tell our great Father, the President, how we are deviled and cheated.
2. b. *fig.* To ply with questions or chaff; to 'grill'; to trouble, annoy. *U.S.*
1891 *Harper's Mag.* June 78/2, I be powerful sorry I kem a-devilin' ye hyar this time o' night fur nuthin'. 1896 *Congress. Rec.* 21 Dec. 384/2 All the members of..the 'hog combine' were on their feet, deviling him and asking him questions. 1906 B'NESS VON HUTTEN *What became of Pam* II. xiii, Don't devil me, Pam; I haven't slept for a week, trying to think. 1910 W. M. RAINE *B. O'Connor* 229 Go in and devil him. 1924 MULFORD *Rustlers' Valley* xiii. 151 The cook was stirring about the kitchen when they dismounted at his door and devilled him for hot coffee.

Devil-may-care. Add: Also used subst.
1857 G. W. THORNBURY *Songs of Cavaliers* 120, I and some seventy devil-may-cares Rode to Bristol. 1928 *Manchester Guardian Weekly* 21 Sept. 230/3 An air of devil-may-care.

Devil's bit. 3. *U.S.* (Examples.)
1815 D. DRAKE *Cincinnati* ii. 87 [List of plants used in medicine] Devilsbit. 1836 D. B. EDWARD *Hist. Texas* ii. 43 Let us look at some of the roots and plants below, such as the devils bit, the blood-root. 1871 SCHELE DE VERE *Americanisms* (1872) 406 A medicinal plant (Aletris farinosa), which, under the name of Devil's Bit is highly esteemed in the West for its virtues.

Devil's-guts. Add: **c.** The Australian plant *Cassytha filiformis.*
1889 J. H. MAIDEN *Useful Native Plants* 14 This and other species of *Cassytha* are called 'Dodder-laurel'. The emphatic name of 'Devil's guts' is largely used. It frequently connects bushes and trees by cords, and becomes a nuisance to the traveller.

Deviltry. (Earlier U.S. example.)
1788 *Massachusetts Spy* 28 Aug. (Th.) His shoes were made of the leather of hypocrisy, tanned with the bark of presumption and curried in the shop of deviltry.

Devirilize (dīvi·riləiz), *v.* [f. DE- + VIRILE + -IZE.] *trans.* **a.** To deprive of virility, to devitalize. **b.** To deprive of manly qualities. Hence **Devirilizaˑtion.**
1901 *Amer. Jrnl. Psychol.* XII. 277 The devirilized effects of transcendental and idealistic habits of thought. 1920 W. J. LOCKE *House of Baltazar* v, These new women are out for the devirilisation of man.

Devolution. Add:
9. b. In Irish politics, with reference to a scheme proposed as a substitute for Home Rule.
1898 J. REDMOND in *Parl. Deb.* Ser. IV. LIII. 379 It is perfectly evident..that Liberal popular opinion in England is in the direction..of the diminution of the magnitude of the Home Rule question, from 1886 and 1893, down to some scheme of devolution and federalism. 1907 A. S. T. GRIFFITH BOSCAWEN *14 Yrs. Parl.* 323 In the middle of the summer holidays [1905] the country had been startled by the promulgation by Lord Dunraven and his friends of a plan of 'devolution' of Irish Government, which was neither Unionism nor Home Rule, but a sort of half-way house, in which Irishmen of all persuasions were to live in happiness for ever after. 1907 *Daily Chron.* 9 May 4/6 The vehement language in which some of the Orange Members spoke of resistance to Mr. Birrell's Irish Council scheme might.. almost justify fears of another 'Devolution War'.

Devolutionary (dīvǒliū·ʃǝnǎri), *a.* [f. DEVOLUTION + -ARY[2].] Of or pertaining to, characterized by devolution.
1896 *Daily News* 1 June 8/3 The symptoms of a coming devolutionary change. 1920 *Glasgow Herald* 17 Apr. 6 He has arresting ideas of the Clyde Valley as a devolutionary unit.

Devolutionist (dīvǒliū·ʃǝnist). [f. DEVOLUTION + -IST.] One who believes in or advocates the principles of (political) devolution.
1905 *Westm. Gaz.* 20 Feb. 1/2 Sir West Ridgeway, now a Devolutionist. 1920 *Glasgow Herald* 17 Apr. 6 Everyone is a convinced devolutionist to-day.

Devon (de·vǝn). Name of a county in the south-west of England, designating (*a*) a breed of cattle noted for the quality of their milk, (*b*) a breed of sheep.
1837 YOUATT *Cattle* (L.U.K.) iii. 15 The skin of the Devon, notwithstanding his curly hair, is exceedingly mellow and elastic. 1837 *Penny Cycl.* VIII. 454/1 The North Devon oxen are famed for their docility... A cow bred from a North Devon by a Yorkshire bull... The milk of the pure Devon cow. *Ibid.* 454/2 South Devon nott, brown face and legs, long wool, pure. 1844 H. STEPHENS *Bk. Farm* II. 172 The Devons may perhaps be classed among the Galloways and Angus. 1851 *Ibid.* (ed. 2) II. 144/1 Lord Farnham's Devon ox, slaughtered in Dublin in 1828. 1881 SHELDON *Dairy Farming* 33/2 The North Devons..may be regarded as the true Devons.
b. *Angling.* Name of an artificial fly.
1924 *Blackw. Mag.* Apr. 492/1, I..fished out across the stream with a heavy Devon.

Devonshire (de·vǝnʃǝɹ). = prec.; used attrib. to designate various articles manufactured, produced, or animals reared in Devonshire, or characteristic of Devonshire; as *Devonshire cider, Devonshire sheep*; **Devonshire cream,** a thick rich clotted cream; **Devonshire slipper** (see quot. 1921).
1825 LOUDON *Encycl. Agric.* 991 *Devonshire cream*, is a term applied in the county of that name, sometimes to sour curd, and sometimes to sour cream. 1837 YOUATT *Sheep* vii. 253 The Devonshire notts, or polled sheep used, forty or fifty years ago, to be at least middle-woolled, if not short-woolled sheep. 1845 DODD *Brit. Manuf.* V. 176 Straw-plait... There are several descriptions of plait made in England—such as.. the 'Devonshire'. 1865 E. BURRITT *Walk to Land's End* viii. 269 That most delectable of luxuries, Devonshire or clotted cream. 1881 *Instr. Census Clerks* (1885) 57 Devonshire Slipper Maker. 1907 GOSSE *Father & Son* (1916) 129 A coating of that rich Western whitewash which looks like Devonshire cream. 1921 *Dict. Occup. Terms* (1927) § 344 *Devonshire slipper maker*; a brown saddler who makes the fitting known as a slipper for one type of lady's side saddle.

Devulcanize (dīvʌ·lkǎnəiz), *v.* [f. DE- + VULCANIZE.] *trans.* To restore (vulcanized india-rubber, etc.) to its former condition.
1899 *Engl. Mechanic* 19 May 316 Any one who can devulcanise indiarubber 'so as to make it soluble in benzine' will assuredly take out a patent for the process.

Dew, *sb.* Add: **5. e.** *dew-damp* adj.
1899 A. R. COWAN *Hist. Kiss* 86 The grass, still dew-damp in the glade. 1906 T. S. MOORE *Poems* 29 She..ordered the dew-damp hair.

Dewalee (dīwā·lī). Also 7 dually, 9 divali, diwali, dewallee. [Hind. *dīwālī*, ad. Skr. *dīpāvalī* (*dīpālī*) row of lights, f. *dīpa* light, lamp.] A Hindu festival with illuminations held on the day of the new moon in the month Aśvina or Kārttika.
1698 FRYER *Acc. E. India & P.* 110 The first New Moon in October, is the Banyans Dually. 1820 T. COATS in *Trans. Lit. Soc. Bombay* (1823) III. 211 The Dewallee, Deepaullee, or Time of Lights, takes place twenty days after the Dussera, and lasts three days. 1849 E. B. EASTWICK *Dry Leaves* 84 The Dīwālī happening to fall on this day, the whole river was bright with lamps. 1883 MONIER WILLIAMS *Religious Thought & Life in India* 432 The Dīvālī is celebrated with splendid effect at Benares.

Dewater (dīwǭ·tǝɹ), *v.* [f. DE- + WATER *sb.*] *trans.* To remove the water from.
1923 *Glasgow Herald* 10 Oct. 10 There is now more hope of getting through 'dewatered' roadways. 1929 *Times* 10 May 22/3 The Lagan Navigation Company shall..dewater such portion of the canal [*sc.* the Ulster Canal].

Dew-bow (diū·bōu). [f. DEW *sb.*, after *rainbow*.] A halo resembling a rainbow, occurring on a dew-covered surface.
1909 *Cent. Dict.* Suppl. 1920 *Conquest* May 346/1 That curious phenomenon known as the dew bow. *Ibid.* 346/2 The..author may have seen a dew bow effect at his feet.

Dewdrop. Add: **b.** A glass bead resembling a drop of dew.
1880 *Harper's Mag.* June 31/1 'Grass-work' consists in the fastening of small glass beads or 'dew-drops' to the artificial blades.

Dewindtite (dīwi·ntəit). *Min.* [Named after Jean *De Windt*, Belgian geologist: see -ITE[1].] (See quot.)
1922 *Mineral Mag.* XIX. 339 Dewindtite... Hydrated phosphate of uranium and lead..occurring as a canary-yellow powder at Kasolo, Katanga [in the Belgian Congo].

Dewmink. *U.S.* (See quot.)
1781 S. PETERS *Hist. Connecticut* (1829) 193 Larks, humilitys, whipperwills, dewminks. *Ibid.*, The dewmink, so named from its articulating those syllables, is black and white, and of the size of an English robin.

Dew-pond (diū·pǫnd). [DEW *sb.*] A shallow pond, usually of artificial construction, fed by the condensation of water from the atmosphere, occurring on downs where there is no adequate water-supply from springs or surface-drainage.
See A. J. and G. Hubbard *Neolithic Dew-ponds & Cattle-ways* (ed. 2) 1907, and E. A. Martin 'Some Considerations concerning Dew-ponds' in *Trans. South-Eastern Union of Scientific Soc.*, 1908, pp. 66 ff.
1877 H. P. SLADE (*title*) Short practical treatise on dew ponds. 1879 *Athenæum* 14 June 757/1 The Wiltshire farmers, having learned the value of 'cloud ponds' or 'dew ponds', have formed them at much expense on the tops of the hills. 1902 CORNISH *Naturalist Thames* 128 The dew-ponds..have kept their water, while the deeper ponds in the valleys have often failed. 1903 KIPLING *Five Nations, Sussex* vi, Only the dewpond on the height Unfed, that never fails. 1905 A. J. & G. HUBBARD *Neolithic Dew-ponds* 2 The gang of dew-pond makers commence operations by hollowing out the earth for a space far in excess of the apparent requirements of the proposed pond. They then thickly cover the whole of the hollow with a coating of dry straw. The straw ..is covered by a layer of well-chosen, finely puddled clay, and the upper surface of the clay is then closely strewn with stones.

Dexter[2] (de·kstǝɹ). [Said to have originated from the name of a Mr. *Dexter*, who is credited with having established the breed.] A breed of small hardy Irish cattle originating from the Kerry breed. Also called *Dexter Kerry.*
1880 *Encycl. Brit.* XIII. 225/2 The variety known as the 'Dexter', a cross between the 'Kerry' and some unknown breed, is shorter and plumper than the pure 'Kerry'. 1899 *Daily News* 20 June 9/5 The best dexter animal in the show. *Ibid.* 21 June 9/1 The dainty Jersey or pigmy Dexter and Kerry. 1902 *Encycl. Brit.* XXV. 192/2 The Dexter breed... Until recently it was called the Dexter Kerry.

Dextral. Add:
1. c. That uses the right hand in preference to the left, right-handed: see DEXTRALITY 2.
1871 *Lancet* I. 49 On Dextral Pre-eminence by William Ogle M.D. 1904 *Westm. Gaz.* 6 Aug. 11/3 As if fate had chosen to make it a dextral child.

Dha (dā). Also dhar. [Burmese.] = *DAH, *DAO.
1859 J. W. PALMER *New & Old* 421 (Cent. Dict.) The Burmese dropped their lances and dhars. 1920 *Blackw. Mag.* June 834/2 The two men were allowed to come on after they had deposited their guns and *dhas*.
b. A Burmese measure of length.
1821 P. KELLY *Univ. Cambist* (ed. 2) I. 115 The Dha, or Bamboo, consists of 7 royal Cubits; 1000 Dhas make 1 Dain, or Birman League. 1888 *Encycl. Brit.* XXIV. 490/1 Burmah.—..dha 154 inches.

Dhall, var. of DAL.
1923 *Nature* CXI. 626/2 The addition of oatmeal and dhall to the British ration.

Dhaman (dā·mǎn). *Indian.* [Hindi (Skr. *dharmana*).]
1. a. The grass *Pennisetum cenchroides*, used for fattening cattle. **b.** The dhamnoo, *Grewia elastica.*
1887 MOLONEY *Forestry W. Afr.* 248 Dhaman of Punjab.
2. The rat-snake.
1878 P. ROBINSON *In my Indian Garden* 92 A pair of gorgeous dhaman snakes. 1927 *Chambers's Jrnl.* 493/2 The dhaman, though not poisonous, turns a somersault and hits you with its tail. *Ibid.* 495/1 The local natives all think that the dhaman or 'rat snake', is the female of the cobra.

Dhamnoo (dæ·mnū). *Indian.* [Hind.] An East Indian tiliaceous tree, *Grewia elastica*, or the timber therefrom.
1846 LOUDON *Veget. Kingd.* 372 The wood of Grewia elastica, called Dhamnoo, affords timber highly valued for its strength and elasticity.

Dhan (dān). *Indian.* [Hind. *dhān*, a. Bengali *dhāna* rice, grain, *dhānā* fried barley, rice, etc. (Skr. *dhāna*).] Rice in the husk.
a 1815 ROXBURGH *Flora Indica* (1832) II. 201 Dhan the Bengalee name of the plant, and the unhusked rice, and Chaul the clean rice. 1858 SIMMONDS *Dict. Trade, Dhan*, a vernacular name in parts of Hindustan for rice. 1908 *Animal Managem.* (W.O.) 299 In Burma, unhusked rice (*dhan*), and in Madras, koolthi, is issued instead of gram or barley.

Dhandh (dænd). *Indian.* Also dhand. A lake or swamp of the territorial division of Sind in India.
1887 *Encycl. Brit.* XXII. 91/1 In the cold season the lakes or *dhandhs* are covered with wild geese, *kulang*, ducks, teal, curlew, and snipe. 1926 *Blackw. Mag.* Dec. 807/1 Any swamp or overflow water or tank or jhil in Sind is a dhand. 1928 *Ibid.* Mar. 389/1 In that year the dhand extended more than a hundred miles north and south, and ten to thirty miles east and west. *Ibid.* 389/2 Several canals took off from the dhand.

Dhani (dɒ·ni). Also dhunny. A kind of palm, the leaves of which are often used for making thatch in the tropics.
1926 *Chambers's Jrnl.* 85/2 Bamboo matting, jungle-wood boards, and dhunny thatch make ready prey for flames. 1926 *Blackw. Mag.* June 731/2 She arrived soon after seven at the steamer anchorage, beyond the flat islands of dhani palm and mangrove swamp. *Ibid.* Dec. 718/1 Huts..squalid and filthy and stinking, but for the most part newly roofed with dhani thatch against the rains. *Ibid.* 732/2 There was a sampan with a hooped covering of dhani leaves.

Dharma (dā·ɹmǎ). *Indian.* Also dharm, dhurm. [Skr., = decree, custom.] Right behaviour, virtue, righteousness; in Buddhism, the law.
1862 MAX MÜLLER *Chips* (1867) I. ix. 196 The second and third baskets [*sc.* canonical books of the Buddhists] are sometimes comprehended under the general name of *Dharma*, or law. 1876 *Encycl. Brit.* IV. 429/2 The customs of the law (Dharma) are good both for this world and the world that is to come. *Ibid.* V. 190/2 Before the caste assembly the Dhurm, or caste custom, is sometimes appealed to. 1926 *Other Lands* Apr. 84/2 The missionary is the most dreadful enemy you have to meet, the greatest enemy of dharma and Hindu national life in the present age.

Dharmsala (dā·ɹmsālā). *Indian.* Also dharma sala, dhurmsalla, durhmsallah, dhormsal. [Hind. (Skr. *dharmsālā*, f. *dharma* custom, decree, *sālā* house).] A building devoted to religious or charitable purposes, *esp.* a rest-house for travellers.
a 1805 WELLINGTON *Disp.* (Stanford). 1826 HOCKLEY *Pandurang Hari* I. 255, I then proceeded to the *durhm sallah*, or place where travellers put up, and where I had left the two females. 1838 *Penny Cycl.* XII. 233/2 A *Dharma Sala*, one or more sheds or buildings for the accommodation of the mendicants or travellers who are constantly visiting the math. 1920 *Chambers's Jrnl.* 434/1 Even the precincts of the regimental mosque and *dharmsala* (Sikh temple) were examined. 1922 *Blackw. Mag.* Oct. 550/2 At the door of the *dhormsal* I was met by some of the priests.

Dhobi. Add: **dhobie('s) itch,** ring-worm affecting the arm-pit and crotch in hot moist climates.
1890 BILLINGS *Med. Dict.*, *Dhobie's itch*, Tinea circinata tropica of scrotum, thighs, and perineum; so called in India. 1910 *Practitioner* Jan. 16 The name 'Dhobie itch' is used to denote several kinds of troublesome eczema generally first appearing on the covered hairy regions of the body.

Dhoon (dūn). *Indian.* Also dhun, doon, dun. [Hind. *dūn*, a. Hindi *dūna* valley.] Any of the flat valleys lying parallel to the base of the Himālayas dividing the sub-Himalayan hills into two ranges, *spec.* the valley of Dehra.
1814 *Asiatic Jrnl.* (1816) II. 151 *Mewoici* in the far-famed Dhoon, the *Tempe* of Asia. 1877 *H. M. Elliot's Hist. India*

VII. 106 Khalilu-lla Khán..having reached the Dún. 1879 MEDLICOTT & BLANFORD *Geol. India* 521 A repetition of low ridges and intervening dúns. 1922 *19th Cent.* Jan. 46 In the lower valleys and hollows, or *dhuns*.

Dhoona (dū·nǎ). [Skr. *dhūna.*] A resin obtained from the Indian tree *Shorea robusta.*
1846 LOUDON *Veget. Kingd.* 394 The dhoona or dammer pitch, generally used in India for marine purposes, and as incense. 1924 *Public Opinion* 20 June 582/1 The odour of dhoop (incense) and dhoona greeted our breath.

Dhoop (dūp). *Indian.* [Hindi, Bengali *dhūpa* incense, resin, gum.] An Indian plant, *Vateria indica*, also the pitch obtained therefrom.
1851 *Illustr. Catal. Gt. Exhib.* IV. I. 877/1 Piney resin of dhoop tree..from Canara... Different sorts of dhoop, a perfume, from Nepal, Bhotan. 1924 [see *DHOONA].

Dhudheen, var. of DUDEEN.
1867 P. KENNEDY *Banks Boro* xxiv, Their hands went into their pockets more than once in search of the treacherously-consoling *dhudheen*. 1905 *Daily Chron.* 7 July 5/7 Removing his clay dhudheen from his lips.

Dhuine-wassel, var. of DUNIWASSAL.
1905 *Daily Chron.* 7 July 5/7 Scottish Dhuine wassels with aggressive feathers in front of their Tam o' Shanter caps. 1920 *Blackw. Mag.* Apr. 517/1 Kilted Hebridean dhuine-wassels.

Dhunchee: see *DANCHI.

Diabeah, variant of DAHABEEYAH.
1864 J. A. GRANT *Walk across Africa* 366 Baker led us to his 'diabeah', or Nile pleasure-boat.

Diablotin. Add: **b.** In the West Indies, a rare bird of the petrel family, *Œstrelata hæsitata.* **c.** A name in Trinidad for the guacharo.
1823 LATHAM *Gen. Hist. Birds* VII. 366 They [*sc.* Trinidad Goatsuckers] were served up without the heads or feet, under the name of Dumpy Ducks, or Diablotins. 1880 *Encycl. Brit.* XI. 227/1. 1891 *Ibis* Ser. VI. III. 131 The Capped Petrel or Diablotin (*Œstrelata hæsitata*) formerly bred on the tops of the mountains of Dominica. 1924 *Glasgow Herald* 28 Oct. 3 The diablotin bird, one of the petrel family, now believed to be extinct.

Diabolo (dəiæ·bǒlo). [It., = devil.] The game of the devil-on-two-sticks revived under this name. Also, the wooden top with which the game is played. Hence **Dia·bolist,** a player of the game.
The game consists in balancing and spinning a double-headed top on a string (which is supported on two sticks), throwing it into the air, and catching it again.
1907 *Fry's Mag.* Mar. 582 The Devil Game: Diabolo. *Ibid.* 586/2 It is not difficult to learn to spin the diabolo. *Ibid.* 587/2 The diabolo game can be played by sides of almost any number. 1907 *Westm. Gaz.* 25 Sept. 12/1 The inventor of the modern Diabolo is M. Gustave Phillipart, a French engineer, well known in the automobile world. 1922 JOAD *Highbrows* iv. 135 They invent some quaint form of amusement like diabolo or roller-skating.

Diacetic (dəiˌǎsī·tik), *a.* *Chem.* [f. DI-[2] + ACETIC.] *Diacetic acid*, an acid found in the urine in certain abnormal conditions, esp. when diabetes is present. Hence **Diacetonu·ria, Diacetu·ria,** the presence of diacetic acid in the urine.
1890 BILLINGS *Med. Dict.*, *Diaceturia*,..excretion of acetic acid in urine. 1906 DORLAND *Med. Dict.* (ed. 4) s.v. *Acid*, Diacetic acid. 1908 *Practitioner* Feb. 197 Urine did not contain acetone nor diacetic acid.

Diact (dəi·ækt). *Zool.* Shortened form of next.
1887 tr. *F. E. Schulze* in *Challenger Rep., Zool.* XXI. 36 The two rays of a diact belong either to the same or to different axes. *Ibid.*, A..typical diact structure.

Diactine (dəiˌæ·ktin), *a.* and *sb.* *Zool.* [f. DI-[2] + *ACTINE.] **A.** *adj.* Of a sponge spicule of the monaxon type: Having two rays, pointed at both ends. **B.** *sb.* A straight or curved spicule with two rays. Also **Dia·ctinal** *a.*
1888 SOLLAS in *Challenger Rep.* XXV. p. liii, Diactine (*diactina*).—A monaxon in which growth proceeds in both directions along the axis.

Dial, *sb.*[1] Add: **8. b. dial (tele)phone,** an automatic telephone (cf. next).
1931 *Punch* 27 May 564/2, I like the dial telephone. Bless its funny little dial! *Ibid.*, One can do such a lot with the dial phone without getting into a hot exchange of snappy come-backs.

Dial, *v.* Add:
4. To indicate on or with a dial (a number to be called up on an automatic telephone). Also *absol.* to make a call on an automatic telephone.
1922 *Glasgow Herald* 9 Aug. 9 Subscribers will communicate with each other by 'dialing' the required number and obtaining immediate connection without the intervention of an operator. 1927 *Daily Express* 28 Oct. 3/1 The ringing tone tells you, after you have dialled the number you want, that the automatic system is ringing the other subscriber's bell. 1928 *Daily Tel.* 28 Feb. 15 She goes to the 'central supply conveyor', at which, by dialing on an indicating switchboard, she lets the store know her requirements. 1930 *Punch* 21 May 579/1, I keep meeting people who are quite worn out with dialling all day.

Dialling. 4. Add: **dialling tone,** the sound produced by a telephone where automatic exchanges are in operation, showing that the line is in order and that the user can proceed to dial.
1927 *Daily Express* 28 Oct. 3/1 The dialling tone is heard as soon as you place the receiver to your ear—if your line is in order.

Diamanté (dǐǎmā·nte). [Fr., f. *diamant* DIAMOND.] Material to which a sparkling effect is given by the use of powdered glass or crystal or of (paste) brilliants. Also *attrib.*
1904 *Daily Chron.* 3 May 6/4 The duchess was in black with diamanté wings in her hair. 1909 *Ibid.* 20 Mar. 4/6 A long stole-like panel of crystal and diamanté embroidery. *Ibid.* 18 Aug. 4/5 Garnitures of pale blue silk embroidery and diamanté. 1923 *Weekly Dispatch* 29 Apr. 15 The gown being draped Greek fashion and trimmed with bands of diamanté.

Diameter. Add: *Tactical diameter*, the perpendicular distance between a ship's original line of advance, and her position when she has turned 180° from that line, under the given angle of helm. *Final diameter*, the diameter of the practically circular path which a ship traverses if after turning through 180° the helm is still kept over.
1882 W. H. WHITE *Man. Naval Archit.* (ed. 2) 631.

Diamond, *sb.* Add:
1. d. *pl.* Shares in a diamond-mine.
1905 *Daily Report* 22 Mar. 1/2 Lace Diamonds have been bought from Johannesburg. 1907 *Daily Chron.* 28 Oct. 1/7 In Mines diamonds declined. 1909 *Westm. Gaz.* 31 Aug. 8/3 Diamonds hard. Diamond shares maintained their strength.
5. d. *U.S.* (Earlier example.)
1888 *Outing* (U.S.) May 120/2 Joe Start has retired from the diamond and keeps a saloon.
e. In a safety bicycle, the lozenge-shaped frame of steel tubing. More fully *diamond frame.* (Now disused.)
1897 *Outing* (U.S.) XXIX. 488/2 Those had canvas luggage-cases in the diamond of their wheels. 1898 *Cycling* 26 Valises which fit into the 'diamond' of the frame. 1917 *Cycling Man.* 2 Diamond frame, with horizontal top tube.
12. diamond hitch *U.S.* (examples); **Diamond State** *U.S.*, the state of Delaware.
1888 ROOSEVELT in *Century Mag.* June 202 An expert packer, versed in the mysteries of the '*diamond hitch', the only arrangement of the ropes that will insure a load staying in its place. 1904 ELIZ. ROBINS *Magnetic North* I. 223 You see him..throwing the diamond hitch as he goes from camp to camp for gold and freedom. 1918 MULFORD *Man fr. Bar-20* x. 101 The diamond hitch which held the bulging tarpaulin in place. 1869 *Congress. Globe* 20 Dec. 262/2 Pass this bill, and you strike down the sovereignty of the States,..and my own little '*Diamond State' is crushed.

Diamorphine (dəiǎmǭ·ɹfīn). *Chem.* [f. DIA-[2] + MORPHINE.] A drug usually called heroin (an acetyl derivative of morphine).
1914 *Chemist & Druggist* LXXXV. 819/2 The name 'diamorphine' cannot be regarded as satisfactory. 1916 P. W. SQUIRE *Comp. Brit. Pharmacopœia* 551 Diamorphine Hydrochloride..is described officially as the hydrochloride of an alkaloid obtainable by the action of acetic anhydride on morphine. 1920 *Act* 10 & 11 *Geo. V* c. 46 § 8 The drugs to which..this Act applies are morphine, cocaine, ecgonine and diamorphine (commonly known as heroin).

Diana. Add: **1. e.** *transf.*
1784 COWPER *Task* IV. 517 Nymphs were Dianas then, and swains had hearts That felt their virtues. 1897 *Westm. Gaz.* 25 Oct. 2/1 Some of these fair Dianas are clad in divided skirts.

Diapasonal (dəiˌǎpē·zǝnǎl), *a.* [f. DIAPASON *sb.* + -AL.] Of or pertaining to the diapason or melody. Also **Diapaso·nic** *a.*
1928 *Daily Tel.* 31 Jan. 8 There was no 'diapasonal excess', which a distinguished Mus. Doc. has declared to be the abuse of modern organ-playing. 1928 *Observer* 8 Apr. 9/4 The trills, roulades, cascades, and diapasonic fertility of 'Zampa'.

Diaphanous, *a.* Add: Also *fig.*
1927 G. MURRAY *Class. Tradition* 104 Poems..which attain an indescribable and as it were diaphanous beauty by almost nothing but their rhythm.

Dia-phototropic (dəi·ǎfōtotrǫ·pik), *a.* *Biol.* [f. DIA-[1] + PHOTOTROPIC.] Indifferent to the action of light. Hence **Dia-photo·tropism.**
1929 J. C. BOSE *Growth & Tropic Movem. Plants* xiii. 133 Dia-phototropism and Negative Phototropism. *Ibid.* 134 Three stages of phototropic action may be distinguished.

Diaphragm, *sb.* **4. a.** Add examples of the use of the diaphragm in a camera.
1878 ABNEY *Treat. Photogr.* xxix. 205 In the doublet lens the position of the diaphragm is important. 1892 *Photogr. Ann.* II. 38 The diaphragm case. *Ibid.* 39 A flare spot is ..really the reflection of the diaphragm aperture. 1918 *Photo-Miniature* XV. Mar. (Glossary), *Diaphragm Shutter*, one working approximately in the position of the diaphragm in the doublet lens. Constructed of leaves or blades which open and then close the aperture in the exposure shutter.

Diapsid (dəiˌæ·psid), *a.* [f. DI-[2] + Gr. ἀψίς, ἀψιδ- arch.] Having two temporal arches, like the reptiles of the sub-class *Diapsida.* So **Dia·psidan** *a.*

Diarchal (dəiˌā·ɹkǎl), *a.* Also diarchial, dyarchal, -ial. [f. DIARCHY + -AL.] Of or pertaining to a diarchy (see below).
1921 *Glasgow Herald* 11 Mar. 10 Among the Ministers recently elected under the new 'Dyarchal' system was an Indian who had been previously convicted on charges of conspiracy. 1921 *Evening Standard* 20 May 4/3 Mr...Sastri ..took a prominent part in the dyarchal reforms in India. 1924 *Observer* 3 Aug. 5/1 In Bengal, the Diarchal plan is in suspense. 1927 *Ibid.* 27 Mar. 11/2 The diarchial system had to be suspended. *Ibid.* 13 Nov. 18/2 The dyarchial system [in India].

Diarchic (dəiˌā·ɹkik), *a.* Also dyarchic. [f. DIARCHY: see -IC.] = prec. So **Dia·rchical** *a.*
1920 *Edin. Rev.* Oct. 386 The diarchic character of the Swiss Government. 1921 *Spectator* 5 Feb. 161/2 The preposterous dyarchical constitution forced upon India by Mr. Montagu. 1926 *Contemp. Rev.* Feb. 240 He broke every rule of the diarchic principle. *Ibid.* Mar. 274 The dyarchic executives.

Diarchy. Add: Revived, chiefly in the form **dyarchy,** to describe the system of provincial governments in India established by the Government of India Act of 1919 (9 & 10 Geo. V).
1917 L. CURTIS *Papers Princ. Dyarchy* (1920) 105 Self-government in any large country thus involves the operation of two authorities with separate mainsprings side by side. The word 'dyarchy'..has been coined to denote this principle and for convenience I shall use it. 1919 LD. CHELMSFORD in *Blue Bk. E. India Const. Reform* Cd. 123. 55 in *Parl. Papers* XXXVII, The only method by which this can be attained is one which involves the division of the functions of government between two different sets of authorities, a method which has been compendiously styled 'dyarchy'. 1920 SIR H. V. LOVETT *Hist. Indian Nat. Movem.* 163, etc. 1921 *Glasgow Herald* 4 June 6 To exempt Burma from the operation of this system, which is known as Dyarchy.

Diasporic (dəiˌǎspǫ·rik), *a.* [f. DIASPORA: see -IC.] Of or pertaining to the Dispersion.
1895 *Expositor* Aug. 139 The Diasporic Jewish Christians who were 'intermediate' between the strict Jewish Christian and the free Gentile Christian.

Diathermal, *a.* Delete †*Obs.* and add:
1923 *Blackw. Mag.* Nov. 584/2 The Diplomatic Body's process of diathermal hibernation.

Diathermic, *a.* Add: **2.** Of or pertaining to diathermy. Also **Diathe·rmically** *adv.*, by means of a diathermic current.
1910 *Brit. Med. Jrnl.* 12 Nov. 1547/2 During diathermic operations the blood vessels and lymph channels are securely sealed. 1929 MARTINDALE *Risen Sun* 100 They were sure I liked heat, and pumped an incredible amount, diathermically, into me each day.

Diathermy (dəi·ǎþǝɹmi). [f. Gr. διά through + θερμός heat + -Y[3].] Application of electric currents of low tension and high amperage to produce heat in those parts of the body that lie below the surface.
1910 *Archives Roentgen Ray* June 19 Diathermy is but one phase of d'Arsonvalisation, which, besides the production of heat, has other physiological effects dependent on the tension, length, form and frequency of the waves. 1910 *Brit. Med. Jrnl.* 12 Nov. 1547/2 Diathermy, or thermo-penetration, describes the heating of diseased tissue by electrical currents of high frequency. 1911 *Ibid.* 14 Oct. 900/1 The now familiar diathermy apparatus. 1929 *Times* 19 Apr. 16/3 Dr. F. D. Howitt visited Craigwell House and again applied the diathermy treatment to the King. 1929 MORRIN in *Irish Jrnl. Med. Sci.* Apr. 183 Such coagulation of cancerous growths is carried out with a very powerful diathermy apparatus.

Diatonism (dəiˌæ·tǒniz'm). *Mus.* [f. DIATONIC: see -ISM.] Diatonic system.
1927 *Music & Lett.* July 325 An insipid diatonic scheme which lacks the primitive freshness of Beethoven's diatonism. 1928 G. COOKE *Theory of Music* 19 Recent attacks upon conventional and arbitrary Diatonism.

Diaxon (dəiˌæ·ksǫn). *Med.* Also -one. [f. DI-[2] + *AXON.] A nerve-cell having two axons.
1901 DORLAND *Med. Dict.* (ed. 2).

Dibatag (di·bǎtæg). [Native name.] A variety of antelope, *Ammodorcas clarkei*, found in Somaliland, having recurved horns ringed at the base.
1902 *Encycl. Brit.* XXV. 454/1. 1904 *Nature* 8 Sept. 458 The dibatag, or Clarke's gazelle.

Diblastic (dəiblæ·stik), *a.* [f. DI-[2] + Gr. βλαστός germ: see BLASTULA.] Having a twofold origin; composed of two germ-layers.
1901 G. N. CALKIN *Protozoa* 26 Colonies [of Protozoa] do not form a distinct tissue of cells as in the blastula stage of Metazoa, while a still stronger point is that they never form a diblastic embryo.

Dibs[2] (dibz). [Arab. دبس *debs* = Heb. דבש *debash* honey, wine syrup.] A thick sweet syrup made from grape-juice in Eastern countries; also, a similar syrup made from dates.
1841 E. ROBINSON *Bibl. Res. Palestine* II. 442 The finest grapes are dried as raisins; and the rest being trodden and pressed, the juice is boiled down to a syrup, which under the name of *Dibs* is much used by all classes wherever vineyards are found. 1864 TWEEDIE *Lakes & Rivers of Bible* 62 He will fetch fresh-baked bread, and a supply of dibs—a kind of honey made from grapes.

Dichoptic (dəikǫ·ptik), *a.* *Zool.* [f. DICHO- + OPTIC *a.*] Of certain insects: Having the eyes widely separated.
1899 D. SHARP in *Camb. Nat. Hist.* VI. 440 When the eyes of the two sides meet in a co-adapted line of union the Insect is said to be 'holoptic', and when the eyes are well separated 'dichoptic'.

Dickensian, *a.* Add: **b.** *sb.* An admirer of Dickens or his works.
1905 (*title*) The Dickensian, a Magazine for Dickens Lovers and Monthly Record of the Dickens Fellowship.

Dicker, *sb.*[2] *U.S.* Add: **2.** Articles or commodities as a medium of exchange or payment.
1880 *Harper's Mag.* May 907/1 An old watch and shotgun..that he had taken as 'dicker' on accounts.

Dicker, *v.* **Dickering,** *vbl. sb.* *U.S.* (Earlier examples.)
1802 *Port Folio* II. 268 *note* (Th.) Dickering signifies all that *honest* conversation, preliminary to the sale of a horse, where the parties very laudably strive in a sort of gladiatorial combat of lying, cheating, and overreaching. 1834 C. A. DAVIS *Lett. J. Downing* 47 'Here', say I, 'Squire Biddle, I have a small trifle I should like to dicker with you'.

Dicky, dickey, *sb.* Add: **1.** (Earlier U.S. examples.)
1836 *Knickerbocker Mag.* VIII. 203 Jack Marlinspike,

who had been first dickey of an Indiaman. 1839 *Ibid.* XIII. 40 To hear our second dickey (an old man) talk about the nor'west coast.
9. c. An extra seat at the back of a two-seater motor car which can be closed down when not in use.
1912 *Motor Manual* iv. 139 On most two-seaters a light, detachable, rear single or dickey seat can be arranged for if specially desired. 1926 W. DEEPING *Sorrell & Son* v, I'll take it round to a garage for you, sir. Luggage in the dicky?
d. In other extended uses.
1907 *Macm. Mag.* Feb. 314, I..went to the leadsman's dicky, or little projecting platform, on the starboard side. *a* 1922 T. BURT *Autobiog.* (1924) 94 The hauling-engine, called the 'dickey', was at the surface.

Dicot, Dicotyl. Abbreviations of DICOTYLEDON.
1877 SIR J. D. HOOKER in *Life* (1918) II. xxxix. 236, 1. Monocots. 2. Dicots. *a.* Angiosp. *b.* Gymnosp. 1877 LE CONTE *Elem. Geol.* (1879) 354 Types..of the Monocotyls on the one hand, and the Dicotyls on the other. 1890 *Athenæum* 22 Nov. 702/1 Thus placing the monocots and dicots on a lower level than the cycads. 1903 *Amer. Jrnl. Sci.* Dec. 416 The main development of the early Dicotyls and other plants constituting the best horizon markers took place in the late Jurassic. 1907 SIR J. D. HOOKER in *Life* (1918) II. xxix. 22 You ask why 'in the British Flora of Mr. Bentham and myself I begin Dicots with Ranunculaceae'!

Dictamnus (diktæ·mnǒs). [L.: see DITTANY.] A plant of the genus of this name, esp. of the cultivated species *Fraxinella.*
1922 *Glasgow Herald* 5 Aug. 6 The dictamnus is easily raised from seeds.

Dictaphone (di·ktǎfōun). [irreg. f. DICTATE + *-phone* as in GRAMOPHONE.] A proprietary name for a machine which records and subsequently reproduces for transcription words spoken into it.
1907 *Daily Chron.* 3 July 3/5 The 'dictaphone', an adaptation of the phonograph. 1920 *Chambers's Jrnl.* 264/2 A familiar object in many business and editorial offices is the dictaphone, an instrument which records on wax cylinders letters or articles spoken into it. 1920 *Glasgow Herald* 22 May 5 Typing for half an hour an aggregate of 3991 words from dictaphone records. 1926 J. J. CONNINGTON *Death at Swaythling Court* xvi, You know he's an expert on gramophones and dictaphones and all that kind of truck. ..He got a dictaphone record of a telephone message from Hubbard to his clerk.

Dictionary. 3. Add:
1911 H. BRADLEY in *F. J. Furnivall* ii. 8 In April 1900, when I gave my annual report on my dictionary work to the Philological Society. 1929 CATH. I. DODD *Apples & Quinces* IV. ii. 146 When Amanda grew tired of teaching she got work on a big Dictionary in Oxford... It was over the Dictionary work that Amanda made the acquaintance of Mr. Jasper Stafford. *Ibid.* v. ii. 156 Amanda went back to Oxford and Dictionary-making.

Dictograph (di·ktǒgrɑf). [irreg. f. L. *dictum* thing said, word + -GRAPH.] A proprietary name for a machine capable of recording in one room sounds or conversation made in another, having a sound-magnifying device as a substitute for the mouthpiece of the telephone.
1907 *Times* 26 June 12/4 Mr. [K. M.] Turner of New York ..had the honour of exhibiting the Dictograph before the King and Queen. 1912 *Times* (weekly ed.) 23 Feb., Indianapolis advices..say that a 'dictograph' which was concealed in the office soon after John McNamara's arrest enabled Government stenographers in the room below to take the daily conversations. 1926 *Spectator* 20 Mar. 520/1 Among inventions for great captains of industry, I looked with awe upon the Dictograph Telephone.

Dictyonal (di·ktiǝnǎl), *a.* *Zool.* [f. mod.L. *Dictyonina*, f. Gr. δίκτυον net.] Pertaining to, or characteristic of, the *Dictyonina*, a suborder of sponges of the order *Hexactinellida*, in which the parenchymal spicules coalesce in a firm and regular skeleton. Hence **Dictyonale** (di·ktiǝnǝl), one of the spicules which become fused to form the skeleton of a dictyonal sponge.
1887 tr. *F. E. Schulze* in *Challenger Rep., Zool.* XXI. 265 Hexactinellida in which the principal hexacts are already at an early stage united into a connected and compact (dictyonal) framework.

Dictyonine (di·ktiǝnəin), *a.* *Zool.* [ad. mod.L. *Dictyonina*: see prec.] = prec. Also **Dictyoni·nal** *a.*
1887 tr. *F. E. Schulze* in *Challenger Rep., Zool.* XXI. 489 As a Lyssacine every Dictyonal form must still begin its development, though this stage may only perhaps last for a very short time. And thus there was at any stage the possibility of the Dictyoninal form becoming again reduced to a Lyssacine. *Ibid.* 496 Even in the Silurian period both Lyssacine and Dictyonine forms appear to be present.

Dictyoxylon (diktiǫ·ksilǫn). [mod.L., f. Gr. δίκτυον net + ξύλον wood.] One of a genus of palæozoic fossils occurring in the coal-measures of Europe, and represented by stems exhibiting radiating wedges of wood.
1896 *Naturalist* Jan. 28 The Dictyoxylons of the Coal Measures.

Diddle, *sb.* Add: **4.** A slight and rapid movement in dancing.
1835 LONGSTREET *Georgia Scenes* 12 Rhoda Nobles swam through the reel like a cork on wavy waters, giving two or three pretty little perch-bite diddles as she rose from a coupee.

Diddums (di·dǝmz). [= *did 'em*, i.e. Did they (tease you, etc.)?, with addition of plural *s*.] An expression of commiseration addressed to children, and jocularly to adults. Hence **Diddum** *v. trans.*, to say 'diddums' to.
c 1880 [remembered by a correspondent]. 1901 E. F. BENSON *Dodo* vii, It bored her to say 'Didums' for an indefinite period, and she did not believe it amused the baby. 1926 *Spectator* 1 May 795/1 On being 'diddumed' when sleeping..it [*sc.* a cat] opened its eyes crossly. 1928 *Internat. Jrnl. Psycho-Analysis* IX. 17 Where an hysteric will spend endless time consciously rejecting, say, an obscene word, the obsessional will spend the same time in an agony of confusion over a simple nursery phrase, e.g. 'Diddums' or 'Ducky'. 1928 ROSE MACAULAY *Keeping Up Appearances* viii, Sometimes they inquire..as to the past life in general of the object of their solicitude, as 'Was he?' or 'Diddums?'

Dido[2]. *U.S.* (Earlier examples.)
1831 L. OSBORN *Life of Jeremy Levis* II. VI. x. 315 Then cutting a few more didos (if I may apply so vulgar a phrase to a man of the Doctor's refinement), he would add [etc.]. 1835 D. P. THOMPSON *Adv. Timothy Peacock* 170 Must all the world know all the didos we cut up in the lodge-room?

Die, *sb.*[2] (Earlier U.S. examples.)
1825 J. NEAL *Bro. Jonathan* I. 398 (Th.), I wonder [the dog] didn't go mad; or make a die of it. 1848 *Stray Subj.* 195 (Th.) I'm afraid I'm going to make a die of it. I'm going to create a vacancy.

Die, *v.*[1] **3.** Add: *To die in one's boots* or *shoes, with one's boots on*: to die a violent death, *spec.* to be hanged; also *U.S.*, to die in harness (see *BOOT *sb.*[3] 1 c).
1694, 1837 [see SHOE *sb.* 2 d]. 1712 [in Dict.]. 1873, etc. [see *BOOT *sb.*[3] 1 c]. 1886 B. HARTE *Snowbound* 109 *note*, 'To die with one's boots on'. A synonym for death by violence, popular among South-western desperadoes, and the subject of superstitious dread.

Die-hard. Add:
B. 2. Applied to (*a*) those who were prepared to 'die in the last ditch' in their resistance to the Home Rule Bill of 1912; (*b*) those members of the Conservative party who followed the leadership of the Marquess of Salisbury in 1922. Hence applied to any one who is extremely conservative on a political or other issue. Also *attrib.*
1912 *Tatler* 9 Oct. 32a, One of the 'Die-hards'. Lord Willoughby de Broke speaking recently at Ballyroney against Home Rule for Ireland. 1922 *Times* 18 Oct. 14/2 Diehards demand freedom. Lord Salisbury on Coalition. 1922 *Daily Mail* 25 Oct. 10 Mr. Chamberlain said: Politics have many vicissitudes. A few days ago I was orthodox; to-day I am a 'Die-hard'. *Ibid.* 3 Nov. 13 Die hard, the section of Conservatives led by Lord Salisbury who were hostile to Mr. Lloyd George's Premiership and Home Rule. 1923 E. A. ROSS *Russian Soviet Republ.* 395 The die-hard Tories. 1927 A. T. HAGG *Labour Community Song Bk.* 6 The Tory Die-hards in their clubs They sing this plaintive song. 1930 *Daily Tel.* 15 May 14/3, I always feel at home ..where I can hear a Liberal thought expressed. The only place where I do not feel at home is where there is die-hard thought or left-wing Socialist thought.
3. A variety of Scottish terrier.
1900 *Westm. Gaz.* 9 July 3/1 To anyone in doubt as to a suitable dog to take up as household guard or companion the Scottish terrier, often called the 'Die-hard', or Aberdeen terrier, and the Dandie Dinmont, immortalised by Sir Walter Scott, are strongly recommended. 1921 *Melbourne Argus* 13 Sept. 5 The name 'Die-Hards' has been given to the well-known black or brindle Scottish terrier.
Hence **Die-hardism** (dəi·hāɹdiz'm), the principles, tenets, or spirit of a die-hard.
1922 *Glasgow Herald* 8 Mar. 8 If the atmosphere of co-operation can be created, 'die-hardism' will be painlessly asphyxiated. 1923 *Ibid.* 28 July 8 There is a core of 'die-hardism' in all sincerely held convictions, and its language does not consist only of 'outworn shibboleths'. 1926 *Spectator* 17 Apr. 695/2 Those half-dead persons whom one may see..sitting in their clubs, reading the newspapers, are partly responsible, with their die-hardisms and inhibitions, for keeping up a spirit of pessimism in Young England. 1926 *Manch. Guardian Weekly* Sept. 181/1 Mr. Churchill has reversed his former die-hardism and struck out boldly.

Diener, var. *DENER.
1930 PALMER *Men are Human* xxix. 273 I'd like a diener for every quart of whisky the old boy's sunk in his day.

Diesel (dī·zǝl). Name of Dr. Rudolf *Diesel* of Munich, the inventor, used attrib. to designate a type of oil-engine, in which air alone is drawn into the cylinder, this air being so highly compressed that the heat generated ignites the oil when it enters the combustion space. Also *Comb.*
1894 B. DONKIN *Text-bk. Gas, Oil, & Air Engines* Index 413 Diesel engine. 1894 — *Rational Heat Motor* 53 The three vertical cylinders of the Diesel motor. 1905 H. ALLEN *Gas & Oil Eng.* (1907) 267 Test of a 500 B.H.P. Diesel Oil Engine. 1916 *Motor Ship & Motor Boat* 30 Nov. 379, 1200 h.p. Diesel-engined Auxiliaries. 1929 *Oil Engine Power Plant Handbk.* (ed. J. Kuttner) 79 The Buckeye Vertical Diesel Engine is of the solid injection, four cycle type, securing its ignition from the heat of compression.

Diet, *sb.*[1] **7.** Add: **diet-sheet,** a paper showing the daily diet of the inmates of an institution.
1902 J. H. M. ABBOTT *Tommy Cornstalk* 182 We all lay in, or upon, our beds with our board-mounted diet-sheets in our hands. 1904 *Windsor Mag.* Jan. 274/1 The Steward.. composes the hospital diet-sheet. 1920 *Chambers's Jrnl.* 825/1 In the diet-sheet of this prison appeared on two days a week 'turtle-soup'.

Dietheroscope (dəiˌīþe·rǒskōup). [f. Gr. δι- two + αἰθήρ ETHER + -O- + -SCOPE.] An instrument invented by M. G. Luvini of Tunis for measuring the variations in atmospheric refraction, usually consisting of a telescope having additional lenses or mirrors which bring two images of any object into the field of vision.
1878 *Haydn's Dict. Dates* (ed. 16), *Dietheroscope*, an apparatus for geodesy and teaching optics, constructed by G. Luvini, of Tunis, and announced, April, 1876. 1889 *Times* 21 Mar. 3/3 There are also Luvini's dietheroscope for observing the changes of atmospheric refraction optically.

Dietitian (dəiˌěti·ʃǎn). orig. *U.S.* Delete *rare* and add (also **dietician**):
1905 *Springfield Weekly Republ.* 29 Dec. 16 The dietitian's work consists in ordering food and preparing the dietary for the patients. 1906 *Daily Chron.* 14 Aug. 5/3 An ex-graduate of Harvard, and an experienced dietician. 1928 *Daily Express* 2 Aug. 2/3 An outline of each day's menu is supplied to the steward's department by the dieticians on board.

Dietl (dī·t'l). Name of Joseph *Dietl*, an Austrian physician (1804–1878) in *Dietl's crisis*, 'sudden severe attacks of nephralgic or gastric trouble, chills, fever, nausea, and vomiting, and general collapse' (Dorland).
1907 *Practitioner* Dec. 750 In such cases [of movable kidney] as present symptoms, the severity of these may present every gradation from a dull aching pain in the back to the acutest paroxysms of renal pain. To the latter the name of Dietl's crisis is commonly applied. 1908 *Ibid.* June 784 A Dietl's crisis in intermittent hydroneph[r]osis.

Diff., colloq. abbrev. of DIFFERENCE *sb.*
1910 O. JOHNSON *Varmint* iv. 58 'What's the diff?' said the Tennessee Shad, yawning. 1919 *Punch* 28 May 427/1 But Lallie couldn't see the diff between a man and a novelist.

Different, *a.* Add:
1. c. *slang.* Out of the ordinary, special, *recherché.*
1912 CANFIELD *Squirrel Cage* iii, What a perfectly lovely couch. . Why, it is so beautifully *different*! *Ibid.* xviii, To avoid being 'queer' and 'different' one had to play a good hand [at Bridge]. 1930 *Publishers' Weekly* 8 Feb. 709/1 They are always striving to write a piece of copy that will be 'different', that 'will hit the reader right between the eyes'. *Ibid.* 15 Mar. 1554/1 A 'different' book ad appeared in the Sunday, March the 9th, New York *Herald Tribune.* 1930 *Publishers' Circular* 22 Mar. 376 Will war books never cease? Perhaps not; but at least some may be different. 1930 *Punch* 26 Mar. (Cigarette advt.), —— are *different.* 1930 *Week-end Rev.* 7 June 467 Ireland this year! For a 'different' holiday, with all the charms of foreign travel and none of the disadvantages.

Differential. Add:
A. *adj.* **4. b.** *esp.* Applied to mechanism devised for imparting differing velocities, e.g. to the two halves of the driving axle of a car (so that the wheels revolve at different rates when turning a corner).
1902 A. C. HARMSWORTH *Motors & Motor-Driving* x. 213 The differential gear acts on the principle of the action of the pair-horse whippletree and equalising bar. 1903 *Sci. Amer.* 7 Feb. 91/2 Single-chain-drives are more popular than ever, although..it looked as if the double outside chain drive to both rear wheels from a differential counter-shaft would supplant this form. 1904 A. B. F. YOUNG *Compl. Motorist* iii. 62 A separate shaft, parallel with the rear axle, called the differential shaft, driven by bevel gearing from the secondary shaft in the gear case. 1908 *Westm. Gaz.* 16 Jan. 4/2 In conformity with the latest ideas in live-axle construction, the differential case is assembled horizontally. 1925 *Morris Owner's Man.* 26 If any adjustments to the differential bearings are required. *Ibid.*, This adjusting sleeve is easily accessible through an opening on the upper side of the differential carrier.
5. Operating differently on different kinds of material.
1900 *Geogr. Jrnl.* (R.G.S.) XV. 652 The facts collected pointed to the conclusion that this type of valley was due to differential preglacial decay.
B. *sb.* **4.** A differential gear, *spec.* of a motor vehicle.
1902 *Daily Chron.* 30 June 6/2 When he broke the differential of his 70 h.-p. Panhard car 50 kilometres from the finish. 1905 *Westm. Gaz.* 17 Feb. 8/2 A motor-boat requires no differential. 1925 *Morris Owner's Man.* 26 The bearings take the load and thrust of the differential.
5. (See quot.)
1884 KNIGHT *Dict. Mech.* Suppl., *Differential* (Electricity), a coil of electrified wire having such relation to another electrified coil or to an armature (or needle) common to both as to produce polar action contrary to that produced by such other coil. (Electric Lamps), a conductor of high relative resistance—used with electric lamps in series,—which operates in the twofold capacity of shunting surplus current to the next lamp, and of shortening the arc of its own lamp, so as to maintain equal action in all lamps of the series.

Differentiate (difěre·nʃiˌeɪt), *sb.* [f. the vb.] A variety of a rock, differentiated by its constituents.
a 1925 DALY in J. Joly *Surface-Hist. Earth* i. 32 The 'obvious and long recognized hypothesis that augite andesite is a differentiate from basalt'.

Differentiatingly (difěre·nʃiˌeɪtiŋli), *adv.* [see -LY[2].] So as to differentiate.
1879 J. MORISON in *Expositor* IX. 106 He immediately adds differentiatingly a servant of Jesus Christ.

Differentiator (difěre·nʃiˌeɪtǝɹ). [f. DIFFERENTIATE *v.* + -OR.] One who or that which differentiates; *spec.* in *Math.* an instrument for calculating or indicating differential coefficients; in *Biol.* a modified or specialized part, organ, etc.
1894 *Times* 11 Aug. 11/1 It was..advisable to have a 'differentiator'..and this was difficult to construct, because any irregularities in a curve were magnified in its differential coefficients. 1924 J. HUXLEY in *Discovery* June 77/1 Some influence had spread from it [*sc.* the grafted dorsal lip]

 Supplement, p. 3873; Corrigenda, p. 4092; Spurious words, p. 4093; Books quoted, p. 4094

which made the tissues of the host build themselves up in the special and orderly way of differentiation. It was a differentiator.

Difficult, *a.* **2.** a. Delete *arch.* and add recent examples (after F. *difficile*). Cf. DIFFICILE 3.
1904 *Westm. Gaz.* 20 Jan. 3/2 Lady Verona refers to her husband as 'rather difficult'. 1929 *Times* 2 Feb. 10/1 A letter from a 'difficult' customer.

Difformed (dif*ǫ*·ɹmd). Delete †*Obs.* and add: *Bot.* Of unusual form or shape.
1887 W. PHILLIPS *Brit. Discomycetes* 35 Club difformed, compressed, obtuse, distinct. *Ibid.* 174 These burst out through the bark in little heaps, much crowded and difformed.

Difformity. 1. For †*Obs.* read *Obs.* exc. *poet.*
1929 R. BRIDGES *Test. Beauty* IV. 1191 Exuberant difformity of disorder'd growth.

Dig, *sb.*[1] Add: **5.** *U.S.* (Earlier example.)
1837 *Harvardiana* III. 283 in B. H. Hall *College Words* (1856) 158 [He] yet is no elaborate dig, Nor for rank systems cares a fig.
6. *pl.* Lodgings (cf. DIGGING 5). *colloq.*
1893 *Stage* 11 May 16/2 'Being in the know' regarding the best 'digs' can only be attained by experience. 1905 *Varsity* 16 Nov. 79/1 An invitation from a friend in digs. 1908 A. S. M. HUTCHINSON *Once Aboard the Lugger* I. 27, I have heard that one can work far better by living near the hospital in digs. 1922 MRS. A. SIDGWICK *Victorian* xxv. 190 He had achieved the entry of the studios through a cousin with whom he had shared digs.

Dig, *v.* Add: **1.** Also *transf.*, to make incisions with action resembling digging.
1930 W. A. THORPE in *Connoisseur* Oct. 226/2 To produce relief motives the operator has to 'dig' with his wheel at a steep angle to the surface.
d. To have 'diggings', lodge. *colloq.*
1914 C. MACKENZIE *Sinister St.* II. xi, Soon it would come to the point of declaring outright that he did not want to dig with him. 1920 W. T. GRENFELL *Labrador Dr.* iv. 64 Two or three classmates would 'dig' together.
11. Dig in. d. *intr.* or *refl.* To excavate a trench or trenches and dug-outs in order to withstand an attack or consolidate a position. Also *fig.*, to establish oneself in a position.
1917 EMPEY *From Fire Step* 145 The machine-gunners went over with the fourth wave to consolidate the captured line, or 'dig in', as Tommy calls it. 1918 E. S. FARROW *Dict. Mil. Terms*, 'Digging in' is frequently replaced by the expression Consolidate Captured Line. 1919 J. B. MORTON *Barber of Putney* xvi. 263 Word came back that they [*sc.* a platoon] were to go to a certain point and dig in. 1922 *Daily Mail* 21 Nov. 8 The most alarming of Sir Percival Phillips's disclosures is that our 'limpets' in Mesopotamia are digging themselves vigorously in.
13. Dig out. *fig.* To obtain, get hold of, or get out by search or effort.
1864 [in Dict.]. 1877 *Gentl. Mag.* CCXL. 596 This last-named prince..had hidden himself in a cupboard in the midst of a roll of carpet, and was with difficulty dug out to be girt with the sword of Othman. 1887 *Harper's Mag.* May 884/2, I don't believe it is worth while to dig out the glasses. 1929 P. WILLIAMS *Jacob's Ladder* xix. 269 It was Carolyn who..dug out two old volumes of eighteenth century pictures lying forgotten in a cupboard. 1930 *Daily Express* 30 July 3/7 England..may need more batsmen of the type who have to be dug out.
14. Dig up. d. To obtain; to search out. Also *absol.* *U.S. slang.*
1895 *Century Mag.* Sept. 674/1, I heard he was tryin' to dig up a trade with a man who's got a mine over in the Slocan country. 1909 'O. HENRY' *Options* (1916) 47 So Ogden digs up a deck of cards and we play casino. 1910 W. M. RAINE *B. O'Connor* 21 Dig up, Mr. Pullman, Go way down into your jeans.

Digby (di·gbi). [Name of a seaport of Nova Scotia.] A herring caught and cured at Digby. In full *Digby chicken* or *chick* (see CHICK *sb.*[1] 4).
1889 G. HEAD *Forest Scenes Wilds N. Amer.* 40 A small species of herring...They are extremely delicate, and are salted in great quantities every year. They have gained the nick-name of Digby chickens. 1862 *Chambers's Encycl.* III. 557/2 A variety of small herrings or pilchards, which are smoked and dried for export; they have a high flavour, and are known in trade as Digbies.

Digester. Add: **4. d.** An apparatus used in the preparation of artificial silk from wood.
1927 T. WOODHOUSE *Artificial Silk* 19 The chips are then blown up to the top of the wood-boiling house into large silos, from which the digesters are filled.

Digger. Add: **2. e.** An Australian or New Zealander, *spec.* in the war of 1914–18. *colloq.*
1919 *War Slang* in *Athenæum* 8 Aug. 727/2 [The soldier] gave nicknames to the Overseas troops, as 'Aussies', 'Diggers', or 'Dincums' for Australians. 1925 FRASER & GIBBONS *Soldier & Sailor Words*, *Digger*, an Australian; also a New Zealander. The name originated for Australians in the old gold-mining days. 1929 MARTINDALE *Risen Sun* 14 Where my experience of the Diggers really began was a little club in the Turl, to which hospital cases came.
6. digger's delight *Austral.*, a species of speedwell, *Veronica perfoliata*, so called from the supposition that it grows only on auriferous soil.
1878 W. R. GUILFOYLE *1st Bk. Bot.* 64 (Morris) Digger's Delight...A pretty, blue-flowering shrub with smooth stem-clasping leaves. 1888 D. MACDONALD *Gum Boughs* 147 Such native flowers as the wild violet, the shepherd's purse, or the blue-flowered 'digger's delight'.

Digging, *vbl. sb.* **4.** (Earlier U.S. examples.)
1814 BRACKENRIDGE *Views Louisiana* 148 The mode of working the mines is exceedingly simple. The word *diggings*, by which they are known, very well designates the appearance of these places. *Ibid.* 151. 1823 S. H. LONG *Exped. Rocky Mts.* I. 93 Near his house are the diggings so often mentioned in this region as objects of curiosity.

Diggy (di·gi), *a.* *colloq.* [f. DIG *sb.*[1] 4 b + -Y [1].] Inclined to give sly digs.
1904 *Daily Chron.* 26 Mar. 3/3 General Frey is very 'diggy' against what we should have thought he would have found to be equally fine representatives of our Indian Army—the Sikhs. 1906 *Ibid.* 23 Jan. 3/1 Our official German critics..are always very 'diggy' towards Buller.

Digitorium (didʒitō·riəm). [f. DIGIT *sb.* + -ORIUM.] A small portable keyboard used for exercising and strengthening the fingers in piano-playing; a dumb piano.
1876 STAINER & BARRETT *Dict. Mus. Terms.* 1921 *Times* 15 Jan. 1/3 Wanted, Digitorium.—State size and price.

Digonal (di·gŏnăl), *a.* *Cryst.* [f. DI-[2] + Gr. γωνία angle + -AL.] Denoting an axis of binary symmetry, *spec.* one of the six axes of an isometric crystal at right angles to the dodecahedral faces.
1890 G. H. WILLIAMS *Elem. Crystallogr.* (ed. 2) iii. 47 *note*, One [set of axes] is the set of intersection-lines between the principal and secondary planes of symmetry...[They] are normal to the faces of the rhombic dodecahedron and are called the digonal. 1898 *Nature* 27 Jan. 309 Only digonal, trigonal, and hexagonal axes [of symmetry] are possible with crystals.

Dihedral, *a.* Add:
1. *Dihedral angle*, (also) the angle formed by any two meeting or intersecting planes or plane faces, *spec.* the angle formed by the wing pairs of an aeroplane. *Dihedral board*, an instrument used in measuring and correcting the dihedral angle of the wings of an aeroplane.
1909 *Westm. Gaz.* 11 Mar. 4/1 The problem of automatic transverse stability is solved by giving the aeroplanes a dihedral angle or keels. 1916 C. C. TURNER *Aircraft of To-day* viii. (1917) 140 Inherent stability is secured..by a dihedral setting of the wings, i.e. sloping up to right and left from the body. 1916 H. BARBER *Aeroplane Speaks* ii. 74 It is a necessary condition [of stability] that the neutral lift lines of the two surfaces, when projected to meet each other, make a dihedral angle. *Ibid.* iii. 108 Another method of securing the dihedral angle, and also the angle of incidence, is by means of the dihedral board.
B. *sb.* A dihedral angle.
1916 H. BARBER *Aeroplane Speaks* ii. 80 It is sometimes advanced that the lateral dihedral increases the 'spill' of air from the wing-tips and that this adversely affects the lift-drift ratio.

Dihybrid (dəihai·brid). *Biol.* [f. DI-[2] + HYBRID.] A hybrid descended from parents differing in two characters. Also *attrib.* Hence **Dihy·bridism.**
1910 R. C. PUNNETT *Mendelism* (ed. 2) 34 Where the original parents differ in two pairs of characters, the case is termed one of dihybridism. *Ibid.* 62 In the dihybrid cases ..the two pairs of characters behave quite independently, in so far as the process of segregation was concerned.

Diionic (dəi,əi,ǫ·nik), *a.* [f. DI-[2] + ION + -IC.] Producing two ions by electrolytic dissociation.
1904 *Physical Rev.* XIX. 370 The conductivity and transference values of neutral diionic salts.

Dik-dik (di·kdik). Also **dikdik, dig(-)dig.** [Native name in Abyssinia (?).] Any of several small African antelopes.
1895 *19th Cent.* Sept. 489 Besides lion and rhinoceros there were..Gerenook, Dik-Dik (*Nanotragus Saltii*),..and many kinds of birds. 1906 *Daily Chron.* 23 Mar. 3/3 The dainty little Somali dik-dik. 1912 *The State* July 30 (Pettman) Later on I shot a dik-dik, a pretty little buck but little bigger than a hare. 1920 *Blackw. Mag.* May 660/1 There is nothing to be seen of wild life save occasional tracks of dik-dik.

Dike (dəik), *sb.*[2] and *v.*[2] *U.S. slang* or *colloq.* [Of obscure origin.] (See quots.)
1871 SCHELE DE VERE *Americanisms* 597 *Dike*, denoting a man in full dress, or merely the dress, is a peculiar American cant term as yet unexplained. To be *out on a dike* is said of persons, mainly young men, who are dressed more carefully than usual, in order to pay visits or to attend a party. 1902 CLAPIN *Dict. Amer.* 159 *Dike*, to attire oneself faultlessly for social purposes. *Diked out*, to be dressed up, with connotation of being in one's best clothes. 1923 WATTS *Luther Nichols* 62 All right for you..comin' round here all diked out like Sunday.

Dikelet (dəi·klet). [f. DIKE *sb.* + -LET.] A small or low dike.
1901 S. E. WHITE *Westerners* xix. 175 She was accustomed to perch on a neighbouring dikelet, near a claim.

Dikh (dik). *Anglo-Ind.* Also **dik(k.** [Hind.] Trouble, worry, vexation.
1873 W. HERLEY *Lay Med. Darjeeling* (Y.) And if his locks are white as snow, 'Tis more from dikh than age! 1923 KIPLING *Land & Sea Tales* 243 There has been great *dikh* in this case? *Ibid.* 246 There has been great *dikh-dari* [i.e. trouble-giving].

Dikkop (di·kǫp). *S. Afr.* Also **dikop, dicoop.** [Afrikaans; f. Du. *dik* thick + *kop* head.] The stone curlew. Also *fig.* (= thickhead).
1858 DRAYSON *Sporting Scenes* 17 One or two of the bustard tribe are also found here, and are called the *diccop*, *coran*, and *pouw*. 1873 tr. *J. Verne's Meridiana* xvi. 148 The hunters shot..some '*dikkops*', whose flesh is very delicate eating. 1891 LD. R. CHURCHILL in *Daily Graphic* 17 Aug. 5 Eleven snipe, one dikkop, one wild turkey, one blue crane. 1903 GLANVILLE *Diamond Seekers* 116 They're playing dik-kop...The dik-kop drops his wing and shams hurt to lead you off. 1913 PETTMAN *Africanderisms*, *Dikkop*, a term of reproach meaning numskull, blockhead.
b. A form of blue tongue (see *BLUE TONGUE 1).
1877 BAINE *Gold Regions S. E. Africa* 75 One of whose horses was standing apart suffering from the 'dikop' form of horse sickness.

Dilapidated, *ppl. a.* Add: *Comb.*
1926 M. LEINSTER *Dew on Leaf* viii. § i, The doctor knocked at a faded green door of a dilapidated-looking house.

Dilex, variant of *dillesk*, DULSE.
1883 J. B. BLOOMFIELD in N. Okoshi *Fisheries Japan* 27 (Fish. Exhib. Publ.) A kind of seaweed called dilex, which they found upon the rocks.

Dill, *sb.*[1] **3.** Add: *dill-pickle* (U.S.).
1916 H. L. WILSON *Somewhere in Red Gap* v. 217 A big dill pickle, two deviled eggs, and a half of one of these Camelbert [*sic*] cheeses.

Dilly (di·li), *a.* *colloq.* The first syllable of *delightful* (dĭləi·tfŭl) + -Y [6].
1909 *Punch* 26 May 362/1, I sent out the ordinary cards ..with 'Dancing' in one corner of the card, but in the *other* corner was 'Bare feet'. Wasn't it a dilly idea? 1922 JOAD *Highbrows* iii. 103 Have you heard that new waltz, 'Luscious Love'? It's simply dilly.

Dilly-dally, *sb.* Delete † *Obs.* and add: Also, a dilly-dallying person.
1929 VACHELL *Virgin* ix. 155 I'm serving on our Green Committee. I'm making the dilly-dallies sit up and howl.

Dilo (dī·lo). The Fijian name for the domba, *Calophyllum Inophyllum*. Also *attrib.*, as *dilo oil, tree.*
1874 *Treas. Bot.* Suppl. 1879 *Encycl. Brit.* IX. 156/2 The dilo.., the oil from its seeds being much used in the [Fiji] islands.., in the treatment of rheumatism. 1894 B. THOMSON *S. Sea Yarns* 184 His arm was thick and knotted as yon dilo-tree.

Dilutee (dəiliutī·). [Badly f. DILUTE *v.* + -EE [1].] An unskilled worker who takes a place hitherto occupied by a skilled worker.
1918 *Times* 8 Feb., That 'dilutees' under 32 and fit for general service should be taken first. 1921 *Glasgow Herald* 7 Mar. 12 The 50,000 dilutees whom the Government were particularly anxious to force upon the building trade. 1923 G. D. H. COLE *Trade Un. & Munit.* 135 Before any skilled men were taken for the army, all 'dilutees' of military age and fitness should first be removed.

Dilution. Add: **4.** The substitution of unskilled for skilled workers.
1919 *Daily Mail Year Bk.* 111/1 True, the dilution of labour includes the employment of a large contingent of unskilled men besides women. 1921 *Ibid.* 60/2 Dilution by taking in unskilled and partially skilled men, and particularly ex-Service men. 1923 J. D. HACKETT *Labor Terms* in *Management Engin.* May, *Dilution*, the practice of placing unskilled workers in positions hitherto occupied by skilled workers.

Dime, *sb.* **2.** Add: *The dimes*, money. *U.S.*
1854 MARY J. HOLMES *Tempest & Sunshine* viii. 114 'No matter about her temper—has she got the dimes?' said Raymond.
b. *dime novel* (earlier example).
1865 A. H. STEPHENS *Diary* (1910) 424 A little primer-looking sort of a child's book. It was a dime novel.

Dimension, *sb.* **5.** Add: **dimension lines,** straight lines usually having an arrow at each end, indicating the parts or lines to which the figured dimensions refer in a technical drawing.
1887 D. A. LOW *Machine Draw.* 5 Dimension lines and centre lines are best put in of different colour. 1902 P. MARSHALL *Metal Tools* 18 The marking of dimension lines on metal surfaces is generally done with a steel scriber.

Dimension, *v.* Add: **2.** *trans.* To mark the dimensions on (a working drawing, diagram, or sketch). Chiefly in *pa. pple.*
1885 *Marine Engineer* 1 Apr. 27/1 Twenty-five large plates of fully dimensioned drawings. 1887 D. A. LOW *Machine Draw.* 5 Many a good drawing has its appearance spoiled through being slovenly dimensioned. 1892 *Ibid.* 99 Rough dimensioned sketches. 1904 *Westm. Gaz.* 28 July 2/1 All parts being carefully illustrated by dimensioned drawings. 1907 *Install. News* Oct. 1/2 Diagrams are more valuable when dimensioned.

Dimeric (dəime·rik), *a.* [f. DIMER(OUS + -IC.] **a.** *Zool.* Bilateral, having a right and left side. **b.** *Bot.* = DIMEROUS b.
1897 L. H. BAILEY in *Ann. Rep. Smithsonian Inst.* 455 A comparison of bilateral or dimeric animals with rotate or polymeric animals. 1900 B. D. JACKSON *Gloss. Bot. Terms.*

Dimery (dəi·mĕri). *Bot.* [f. DIMEROUS + -Y [3].] The condition of being dimerous.
1902 *Encycl. Brit.* XXV. 433/2 The pentamery and dimery of Dicotyledones.

Dimidiately (dimi·diĕtli), *adv.* [f. DIMIDIATE *a.* + -LY [2].] In a dimidiate manner.
1857 T. MOORE *Handbk. Brit. Ferns* (ed. 3) 168 Dimidiately sub-quadrate. 1887 W. PHILLIPS *Brit. Discomycetes* 51 Cup subsessile, externally pruinose, dimidiately elongated, or obliquely contorted.

Dimini (dimī·ni). Also **Dh-.** [Gr. Διμήνι.] The name of a locality of north-eastern Greece used to designate a kind of pottery ornamented with spirals, found there by excavation.
1912 WACE & THOMPSON *Prehist. Thess.* 16 Painted pottery, Dhimini ware. 1925 V. G. CHILDE *Dawn Eur. Civiliz.* 69 The invaders [of Eastern Thessaly]..introduced a new pottery, Dimini ware, rather coarser than the older fabric.

Diminished, *ppl. a.* **1.** Add: *Diminished return* (cf. *DIMINISHING *ppl. a.* 1 b).
1870 *McCulloch's Princ. Pol. Econ.* 199 The greatest possible amount of capital and labour may be employed in

fashioning raw produce and adapting it to our use, and in transporting it from where it is produced to where it is consumed, without a diminished return.

Diminishing, *vbl. sb.* Add: **3.** *attrib.* **diminishing glass,** an instrument which causes objects to appear smaller than they appear to the naked eye; **diminishing rod,** that part of the mechanism of a cotton-roving machine which gives the bobbins of roving their conical ends.
1896 *Daily News* 28 May 2/2 Diminishing and magnifying glasses such as are used by artists. 1890 NASMITH *Cotton Spinning* x. 168 The slide in its reciprocal vertical movement causes, by means of the 'diminishing rod' or 'hangar bar', the upper cradle to oscillate in its centre.

Diminishing, *ppl. a.* **1. b.** Add: esp. in *law of diminishing returns*: the observed fact that the expenditure of labour or capital beyond a certain point does not produce a proportionately corresponding return.
1884 F. A. WALKER *Pol. Econ.* II. 23 The great comprehensive principle to which we give the name, 'the law of diminishing returns in agriculture'. 1892 *Peel City Guardian* X. 8/1 With a diminishing money return has naturally come a luke-warmness towards the crop. 1892 A. MARSHALL *Elem. Econ. Industry* iii. (1898) 115.

Diminuendo (diminiuęˑndo), *v.* [f. the sb.] *intr.* To grow less, to become fainter.
1901 *Westm. Gaz.* 12 Nov. 2/1 Their booming note crescendoes up the scale with increasing speed and diminuendoes with the slackening of it. 1905 *Daily Chron.* 27 Oct. 6/4 The wail of Niobe diminuendoes in the receding distance.

Dimit, variant of *DEMIT.

Dimmer, *sb.* Add: *spec.* a device for reducing the brilliance of a light. Also *fig.*
1909 *Century Dict.* Suppl., *Dimmer*, in *elect.*, an adjustable reactive coil used for reducing the amount of light of incandescent lamps. 1913 *Work* 14 June 212/1 The resistance of the dimmer coils. 1916 H. L. WILSON *Somewhere in Red Gap* ix. 378 It was a suit that the automobile law in some states would have compelled him to put dimmers on. 1926 H. T. WILKINS *Marvels Mod. Mechanics* 236 Levers on these dials operate the 'dimmers'.

Dimmer, *v.* (Earlier example.)
1873 LELAND *Egypt. Sketch-bk.* 22 He..looked over the top-rail at the beautiful Monte Christo, which was dimmering in the distance.

Dimoric (dəimǫ·rik), *a.* *Pros.* [f. DI-[2] + MORA[1] 3 + -IC.] Containing two *moræ*; having the length of two short syllables.
1901 [see TRIMORIC].

Dimorphobiotic (dəimǭɹfo,bəiǫ·tik), *a.* [f. DI-[2] + Gr. μορφή form + βίωσις way of life + -IC.] Exhibiting alternation of generations; having a parasitic and a non-parasitic stage in the complete life history.
1901 *Jrnl. Exper. Med.* VI. 79 [Grassi] advanced..the hypothesis..that *Anguillula intestinalis* was a dimorphobiotic parasite like *Ascaris nigrovenosa*.

Dimplingly (di·mpliŋli), *adv.* [f. DIMPLING *ppl. a.* + -LY [2].] With a dimpling face.
1907 M. C. HARRIS *Tents of Wickedness* II. iv. 166 She said very daintily and dimplingly [etc.].

Dinar[2] (dinā·ɹ). [Serb, etc. *dinar*, ad. L. DENARIUS.] The monetary unit of Jugoslavia.
1924 M. M. STOJADINOVIC *Financial Pos. Kingd. Serb, Croates & Slovenes* 9 For the period April 1st 1924 to April 1st 1925 it is estimated that the amount of cash payments for already concluded agreements should amount to 200 million dinars. 1926 *Jugo-Slavia 1927–8* 3 The changes in the economic conditions of this country, which were the consequences of the stabilisation of the dinar. 1927 *Economic Jugoslavia* 34 The National Bank..has paid up capital to the amount of 30 million dinars.

Dinarian (dinẹ̄·riăn), *a.* *Geol.* [f. *Dinara*, a mountain in Dalmatia + -IAN.] Denoting a division of the Triassic rocks between the Tirolian and the Scythian series.
1903 GEIKIE *Text-bk. Geol.* (ed. 4) 1108 The Scythian and Dinarian stages are developed in the coast province of Eastern Siberia.., where Brahmanian and Anisian cephalopods have been discovered.

Dinaric (dinæ·rik), *a.* [f. *Dinara*, a mountain in Dalmatia + -IC.] Denoting a mountain range which extends in a south-easterly direction along the eastern side of the Adriatic, and a race of people inhabiting the coast of the northern Adriatic, characterized by tall stature, a very short head, dark wavy hair, and straight or aquiline nose.
1833 *Penny Cycl.* I. 387/1 The Dinaric Alps. 1862 *Chambers's Encycl.* III. 572/1 Dinaric Alps, that branch of the Alpine system which connects the Julian Alps with the western ranges of the Balkan. 1900 DENIKER *Races of Man* 333 Dark, brachycephalic, tall race, called Adriatic or Dinaric, because its purest representatives are met with along the coast of the Northern Adriatic and especially in Bosnia, Dalmatia, and Croatia. 1924 *T. P.'s & Cassell's Weekly* 13 Sept. 658/2 The pyramid-headed man from the Dinaric lands. 1928 C. DAWSON *Age of Gods* xvi. 370 There is..no evidence for the occurrence of the Dinaric type in the neolithic period.

Dinas (di·năs). [f. *Dinas* Rock, in the Vale of Neath, Wales.] Used *attrib.* in **Dinas brick,** fire-brick made from **Dinas clay,** a kind of rock consisting almost entirely of silica.
1875 URE *Dict. Arts* (ed. 7) I. 532 Stone Bricks.—These are manufactured at Neath, in Glamorganshire...They are usually known as the 'Dinas bricks'. 1879 *Encycl. Brit.* IX. 844/1 Dinas clay, which is really nearly pure silica. 1880 *Ibid.* XIII. 294/2 Dinas brick, which perfectly resists the ordinary steel melting temperatures of coke-fired furnaces.

Dine, *v.* **1. b.** Add: *To dine in*: to dine at home or at one's place of residence.
1888 MRS. H. WARD *Robt. Elsmere* I. v, The college cook ..mounted to his room..to inquire whether he would 'dine in'.

Dingaan('s) apricot. A Natal name for the Kei-apple, the acid fruit of *Aberia Caffra*.
1853 E. ARMITAGE in *Jas. Chapman's Trav.* (1868) II. 449 The Kei apple, or Dingan's apricot, invaluable for forming thorny fences and yielding a pleasant fruit. 1891 R. RUSSELL *Natal* 31 The Dingaan apricot, or Kaw apple.

Ding-a-ling. [Echoic.] = DING *sb.*[2]
1894 ELIZ. L. BANKS *Campaigns Curios.* 77, I was awakened by the ding-a-ling of the front-door bell.

Dingar (di·ŋgăɹ). A large wild bee of East India, *Apis dorsata*.
1899 D. SHARP in *Cambr. Nat. Hist.* VI. 70 The fondness of bears for the honey of the 'Dingar', as this species [*sc.* *Apis dorsata*] is called, is well known.

Dingbat. *U.S. slang.* [f. DING *v.*[1] + BAT *sb.*[2]] (See quot. 1889.)
1864 G. A. SALA in *Daily Tel.* 19 Oct., Little John, erst a hog-driver..and recently in trouble for manufacturing bogus 'dingbats'. *Ibid.* 1 Nov., I paid for my Kissingen in five-cent 'dingbat' or 'spondulick'—two of the many names given to the fractional currency. 1889 FARMER *Americanisms*, *Ding-bat*, this word seems to be applied to anything that can be thrown with force or dashed violently at another object. 1926 J. BLACK *You Can't Win* vi. 65 If you was some kind of a rank dingbat you wouldn't have been invited down here.

Ding-dong, *sb.* Add: **1. b.** *fig.*
1928 *Manch. Guardian Weekly* 19 Oct. 301/1 Accustomed to cut a good figure in the ding-dong of public argument.

Dinge (dindʒ), *sb.*[2] [f. DINGE *v.*[2], or back-formation from DINGY *a.*] Dinginess.
1846 ELIZ. D. BANCROFT *Lett. from Eng.* (1904) 12, I cannot get accustomed to the London dinge. 1854 THACKERAY *Newcomes* xxxv, A noble dinge, a venerable mouldy splendour. 1860 — *Roundabout Papers, De Juventute* (1863) 117 The dinge and wrinkles of their wretched old cotton stockings. 1916 GALSWORTHY *Apple Tree* § 8 His mood threw a dinge even over the children.

Dinger (di·ŋəɹ). *dial.* and *U.S.* [f. DING *v.*[1] 3.] Something superlative.
1892 *Leeds Merc. Suppl.* in *Eng. Dial. Dict.* s.v. 1904 *Daily Capital* (Topeka) 1 June 4 The alfalfa crop this year is going to be a 'dinger'.

Dingled (di·ŋg'ld), *a.* [f. DINGLE *sb.* + -ED [2].] Having dingles.
a 1912 COLVIN *Mem.* (1921) 134 An enchanting fir-belted, green and dingled oval glade.

Dingus (di·ŋŏs). *S. Afr.* Also **dinges.** [f. Du. *ding* thing.] (See quot. 1913.)
1898 FOSSICKER *Kloof Yarns* in *The Empire* 27 Aug. (Pettman) 'Where d'ye find the animile?' 'Animal, Mr. Pike?' 'The dingus—the gentleman who lumbers round in space.' 1913 PETTMAN *Africanderisms*, *Dinges*, thing, almost universal in its application, things animate and inanimate in Dutch-speaking districts are all of them *dinges* if the speaker fails to recall their names. 1928 *Blackw. Mag.* Jan. 30/1 Even an oiler, sent in an emergency to start such a homely inadequate dingus, can do no more.

Dingy, *a.* Add:
2. b. Also, 'drab', dull.
1920 H. G. WELLS *Outline of Hist.* 201 Narrow and dingy-spirited specialists.
c. As an epithet in the vernacular name of certain butterflies.
1832 J. RENNIE *Butterfl. & Moths* 20 The Dingy Skipper ..appears about the end of May and middle of July. *Ibid.* 69 The Dingy (*M[amestra] furva*). *Ibid.* 142 The Dingy Wave..appears in June. 1876 *Encycl. Brit.* IV. 596 Plate XXIX, *Hesperia tages* (Dingy Skipper).

Dining, *vbl. sb.*
2. *dining-hall* (U.S. examples); **dining-coat** *U.S.*, a dinner jacket.
1907 LADY GROVE *Social Fetich* 152 'Tuxedo', 'dining coats', or 'dinner jackets'. 1831 PECK *Guide for Emigrants* 247 A boarding-house, including a *dining hall,.. two kitchens, a pantry [etc.]. 1870 'FANNY FERN' *Ginger-Snaps* 237 Mrs. Fire-Fly..swept into the dining hall in a train about six yards long.

Dinka (di·ŋkă). [ad. native name *Jeng*, pl. *Jangé*.] An individual of a powerful and numerous group of Nilotic negroes. **b.** The language spoken by this group.
1875 *Encycl. Brit.* II. 118/2 The Dinka may supply examples of forming the plural by internal change, *ran*, 'man'; *ror*, 'men'. 1884 *Ibid.* XVII. 317/1 *note* 1, The same expression 'jet black' is applied by Schweinfurth to the Upper-Nilotic Shilluks, Nuers, and Dinkas. 1900 E. S. GROGAN in *Daily News* 27 Feb. 5/7 Four days before reaching Bahr el Jaraf I was attacked by Dinkas. 1926 *Blackw. Mag.* Oct. 561/2 Wol explained in the Dinka dialect the reason and object of my sudden visit. *Ibid.* 562/1 The native Dinka never hurries unless he is being hunted.

Dinkel (di·ŋkəl). [G.] A variety of wheat, *Triticum monococcum*.
1866 *Treas. Bot.* 1928 V. G. CHILDE *Most Anc. East* ii. 43 The uncultivated form of another variety of wheat, *Triticum monococcum* or dinkel, grows in the Balkans [etc.].

Dinkum (di·ŋkŏm), *sb.* and *a.* *Austral.*, *dial.*, and *slang.* Also **dincum.** [Origin unknown.]
A. *sb.* **1.** Work.
1888 'R. BOLDREWOOD' *Robbery under Arms* v, It took us an hour's hard dinkum to get near the peak. 1891 ADDY *Suppl. Sheffield Gloss.* 18, 'I can stand plenty o' dincum.' This word is used by colliers at Eckington.
2. An Australian (see B).
1919 [see *DIGGER 2 e].
B. *adj.* Honest, genuine, real. Phr. (Australian) *dinkum oil*, the honest truth. Cf. '*Fair dinkum!* fair play' (E.D.D.).
1916 *Anzac Bk.* 22/2 'Ere's some er the dinkum coc'nut ice the tart useter make. 1916 C. J. DENNIS *Ginger Mick* 87 That's the dinkum oil frum Ginger Mick. 1921 *Spectator* 5 Feb. 169/1 This, as we Australians say, is 'dinkum'. 1924 *Public Opinion* 7 Mar. 230/2 The answer must be dead honest, as a friend of mine used to say 'Cross my heart straight dinkum'. 1925 FRASER & GIBBONS *Soldier & Sailor Words*, *Dinkum oil*, a colloquial phrase meaning 'Correct Information'. 1925 *Spectator* 21 Nov. 930/1 Every 'dinkum Bushman'. 1930 GROOM *Merry Christmas* iii. 21 I'll strike a dinkum business deal with you—fair and square.

Dinky (di·ŋki), *a.* (*sb.*). orig. *dial.* and *U.S.* *colloq.* Also **dinkie, -ey.** [f. DINK *a.* or *v.*]
1. Neat, trim, dainty.
1858 M. PORTEOUS *Souter Johnny* 29 Ye'll observe yon dinkie pile In your ain cauf-lan'. 1893 *Columbus* (Ohio) *Dispatch* 8 Apr., The British Artillerymen wore little dinky caps with a yellow band. 1896 G. ADE *Artie* xvii. 154 I'll come hot-footin' in here with my knee-pants and a dinky coat. 1904 'O. HENRY' *Cabbages & Kings* x. 169 A train of cars was waitin' for us on a dinky little railroad. 1905 E. PHILLPOTTS *Secret Woman* I. i. 16 You're all angel yourself—all, to the dinky dimple there at the corner of your li'l mouth. 1909 S. E. WHITE *Rules of Game* III. xxiv, What's those dinkey little reports..amount to, anyhow? 1915 *Punch* 20 Jan. 49, I shall have a couple of the dinkiest little wounded subs to show you. 1917 'CONTACT' *Airman's Outings* 224 Winkle, the dinky Persian with a penchant for high life, has presented the family with five kittens. 1929 DESMOND COKE *Monkey Tree* xvi, Miss Des Vaux asserted her superiority by saying that it was a 'dinky notion'.
2. Tiny. *s.w. dial.*
1880 *W. Cornwall Gloss.* 1880 MRS. PARR *Adam & Eve* xxviii, You must leave me a dinkey little corner to squeeze into by.
B. *sb.* Applied to small contrivances; *spec.* an apparatus of smaller size than the usual standard, e.g. a donkey-engine for doing work which requires small horse-power; a pair of wheels on an axle used to carry the weight of a beam or pole in erecting structures or wire lines; a small locomotive used for shunting, etc.
1905 *Terms Forestry & Logging*, *Dinkey*, a small logging locomotive. 1909 *Cent. Dict.* Suppl. 1911 WEBSTER.

Dinner, *sb.* **2.** Add: *dinner-alarm, -gong*; **dinner-bucket** *U.S.* = *dinner-pail*; **dinner-call,** a formal call upon one's host after a dinner party; **dinner-card,** a card bearing a name and indicating a person's place at a dinner-table; **dinner-dance,** a dinner followed by dancing; **dinner-horn** *U.S.*, a horn used to announce dinner on a farm; **dinner jacket,** a dress-coat without tails worn in the evening as a less formal alternative to the swallow-tailed coat; **dinner-pail** *U.S.*, a pail in which a workman carries his dinner with him; **dinner-pot,** a large pot in which dinner is cooked; **dinner speech,** an after-dinner speech; so *dinner-speaking*; **dinner-tin** = *dinner-pail.
1851 C. CIST *Cincinnati* 172 Bells of all sizes, from a *dinner alarm to the largest class of church bells. 1901 *Scribner's Mag.* XXIX. 404/2 Billy put on his coat, took his *dinner-bucket. 1897 HOWELLS *Landlord at Lion's Head* 84 He never paid his *dinner-call. 1907 M. C. HARRIS *Tents of Wickedness* I. iii. 35 His *dinner-card lay on the side of the cloth next her, and she..glanced at it. 'Mr. Paul Fairfax'—so that was his name. 1901 *Lady's Realm* X. 613/1 From one *dinner-dance to the next. 1910 *Westm. Gaz.* 15 Apr. 5/2 A dinner-dance—quite a small affair. 1838 *Knickerbocker Mag.* XII. 227 How startling is the sound of the *dinner-gong! 1900 *Westm. Gaz.* 7 June 2/1 The vultures had gathered as usual at the sound of their dinner-gong. 1838 CAROLINE GILMAN *Recoll.* vi. 51 The business was scarcely settled, when the *dinner-horn sounded. 1849 *Congress. Globe* 10 Jan. App. 80/2 The dinner horn will be heard across broad fields, and will be answered by the keen appetites attendant upon honest labor. 1856 *Trans. Mich. Agric. Soc.* VI. 55 [Exhibited] 6 farm dinner horns. 1867 'T. LACKLAND' *Homespun* III. 290 From that time until the dinner-horn sounds, no tented field..ever furnished a busier..spectacle. 1894 *To-day* 17 Mar. 182/1, I see that the so-called '*dinner-jacket' is getting to be the regular wear at the theatres. 1900 H. HARLAND *Cardinal's Snuff-box* iv, A youngish, presentable-looking creature, in a dinner-jacket. 1924 GALSWORTHY *White Monkey* I. iv, Full fig, or dinner jacket? 1904 *N. Y. Even. Post* 19 Feb. 3 Thousands of men with their *dinner-pails on their way to work. 1904 *Philad. Publ. Ledger* 26 Aug. 8 Four years ago the 'full dinner-pail' was the battle cry of the national campaign. 1855 M. M. THOMPSON *Doesticks* xxxv. 319 A hole in a board which was painted in admirable imitation of a *dinner pot. 1871 MRS. STOWE *Sam Lawson* 119 A gret iron pot as big as your granny's dinner-pot with an iron bale to it. 1910 *Westm. Gaz.* 11 Apr. 8/3 Mr. W. W. Jacobs..said..*Dinner-speaking was a gift which was never put into his stocking. 1890 *Harper's Mag.* Apr. 799/2 The modern *dinner speech is a happy blending of sparkling banter, [etc.].

Dinoflagellate (dəinoflæ·dʒĕlĕt), *a.* (*sb.*) *Zool.* [ad. mod.L. *Dinoflagellata.*] Of, pertaining to, or characteristic of the *Dinoflagellata*, an order of flagellate infusorians, having two flagella. Also as *sb.*, one of the *Dinoflagellata*.
1901 G. N. CALKINS *Protozoa* 260 The dinoflagellate *Ceratium hirundinella*.

Diocletian (dəiǒklī·ʃăn). Name of the Roman Emperor C. Aurelius Valerius Diocletianus, used *attrib.* (as if an adj. in -IAN, like *DECIAN) to denote the persecution of the Christians which took place in his reign (303 A.D.).
[1837 *Penny Cycl.* VIII. 504/1 This was the last persecution under the Roman empire, and it has been called by the name of Diocletian.] 1846 C. MAITLAND *Church in Catacombs* iv. 94 Towards the time of the Diocletian persecution. 1878 J. HUTCHESON *Church its Life & Work*, The Diocletian persecution.

Diode, *a.* Add: **2.** *Wireless Telegr.* Designating a two-electrode valve.
1921 W. H. ECCLES *Contin. Wave Wireless Telegr.* I. 257 A bulb with two electrodes, namely, anode and cathode, is called a diode tube. *Ibid.* 306 This example shows plainly that two constants are required to define the chief properties of a diode. 1926 R. W. HUTCHINSON *Wireless* viii. 139.

Dionine (dəi·ǒnin). [app. f. DI-[2] + arbitrary element *-on-* + -INE[5].] A proprietary name for ethyl morphine hydrochlorate, used as a local anæsthetic.
1901 DORLAND *Med. Dict.* (ed. 2), Dionin. 1907 *Practitioner* Aug. 250 A solution of dionine, 1 per cent.

Dioptre, var. of DIOPTER 5.
1907 *Practitioner* June 820 Patient was myopic to 2·0 dioptres. 1910 *Ibid.* July 69 A sudden increase of several dioptres in the degree of optic neuritis present.

Dioscuric (dəiǒskiū·rik), *a.* [f. Gr. Διόσκουροι, f. Διός, gen. of Ζεύς Zeus + κοῦροι, κόροι boy, son + -IC.] Of, pertaining to, or resembling the legend of the twins Castor and Pollux. Also **Dioscu·rian** *a.* Hence **Dioscurism** (dəiǫ·skiŭriz'm).
1903 J. RENDEL HARRIS *Dioscuri* 42 Let us..examine a third case of twin saints in the Christian calendar, and test it..for Dioscurism. *Ibid.* 47 We naturally enquire..whether there are any Dioscuric features about them. *Ibid.* 61 The popular religion was deeply tinctured with Dioscurism.

Diose (dəi·ōus). *Chem.* [f. DI-[2] + -OSE[2].] = *BIOSE.
1904 *Jrnl. Phys. Chem.* VIII. 509 Dioses, trioses, tetroses.

Diosphenol (dəiǫsfī·nǫl). *Chem.* [f. DIOS(MIN + PHENOL.] A camphor obtained from the oil of *Barosma betulina*.
1888 *Jrnl. Chem. Soc.* LIV. 1205 Acetyldiosphenol is obtained by mixing diosphenol with anhydrous sodium acetate and excess of acetic anhydride, and heating at 145° in a closed tube.

Dip, *sb.* Add: **1. g.** A receptacle from which a prize may be obtained by dipping. *Lucky dip* = LUCKY-BAG 1.
1915 'BARTIMEUS' *Tall Ship* vii. (1916) 129 Pennies..to be extracted at great personal risk from an electric dip. 1927 W. E. COLLINSON *Contemp. Engl.* 20 Here one could for a small sum put one's hand into the..lucky dive (dip) and draw out a prize.
5. b. *Mining.* Short for *dip-head* (see 11 in Dict.).
1877 *Encycl. Brit.* VI. 69/1 The drawing roads for the coal may be of three different kinds,—(1) levels driven at right angles to the dip,..(2) rise ways, known as jinny roads, jig-brows, or up-brows,..(3) dip or down-brows, requiring engine power. 1883 GRESLEY *Gloss. Coal-M.*, *Dip*.., a heading or other underground way driven to the deep...It is usual to drive a pair of dips about 10 yards apart every 180 yards or so.
6. b. (See quot.)
1874 KNIGHT *Dict. Mech.*, *Dip*,..The slight downward inclination of the arms of an axle...(Fortification.) *a.* The superior slope of a parapet. *b.* The inclination of the sole of an embrasure.
8. b. A grade of turpentine. (See quot. 1884, and cf. *DIPPING *vbl. sb.* 2 b.)
1863 'E. KIRKE' *Life in Dixie's Land* 226 [The Abolitionists have] long, lean, tommerhawk faces, as white as vargin dip. 1884 C. S. SARGENT *Rep. Forests N. Amer.* 517 The following grades of turpentine are recognised in the trade: 'Virgin dip'..the product the first year the trees are worked; 'Yellow-dip'—the product of the second and succeeding years. 1896 *Pop. Sci. Monthly* Feb. 473 The *dip* or crude turpentine is emptied.
9. b. *pl.* Dough-boys. *Austral. colloq.*
1859 BUNCE *Trav. with Leichhardt* 161 Dr. Leichhardt gave the party a quantity of dough-boys, or, as we called them, dips. *Ibid.* 171 Dr. Leichhardt ordered the cook to mix up a lot of flour, and treated us all to a feed of dips.
11. dip-compass = *dipping-compass; **dip equator,** a line drawn through places where there is no magnetic dip; **dip-regulator** (see quot.); **dip-roller,** a form of roller used in printing-works for taking up ink; **dip-slope,** the surface-slope of ground when parallel to the dip of the strata over which it lies; **dip-stick gauge** (see quot.).
1897 *Strand Mag.* Mar. 344/2 Its [*sc.* the Pole's] variable position was approximately determined by Sir James Clark Ross by help of the *dip compass. 1883 *Encycl. Brit.* XVI. 164/2 The line of no dip is called the magnetic or *dip equator. 1884 KNIGHT *Dict. Mech.* Suppl., **Dip Regulator*, a device used in gas works for regulating the seal of the dip-pipes in the hydraulic main, and for drawing off the heavy tar from the bottom of the main without disturbing the seal. 1874 *Ibid.*, **Dip-roller* (Printing), a roller to dip ink from the fountain. 1900 *Geogr. Jrnl.* (R. G. S.) XV. 220 Its [*sc.* the Arun's] course was determined by the original *dip-slope of the Wealden dome. 1902 H. J. MACKINDER *Britain & Brit. Seas* ix. (1907) 121 The original consequent drainage of the dip-slope. 1925 ODELL in E. F. Norton *Fight for Everest, 1924* 295 This is vividly shown in Somervell's wonderful photograph taken from 28,000 feet, where one is looking down the dip slope of the series. 1927 *Observer* 4 Dec. 11/4 The near side of the engine [*sc.* of a new Ford motor vehicle] carries the self-starter and the oil-filler and *dip-stick gauge only, and has almost a European appearance.
b. In various attrib. uses of sense 5.
1839 URE *Dict. Arts* 964 Where the coal-measures are horizontal, and the faults run at a greater angle than 45° to the line of bearing, they are termed dip and rise faults. *Ibid.* 968 The true dip-line of the plane which leads to the outcrop. *Ibid.* 974 On the dip side of the gallery. *Ibid.* 992 The subterraneous fire broke forth with two heavy discharges from the dip-pit. *Ibid.* 994 In the dip-mine a double tram-road is laid. 1877 *Encycl. Brit.* VI. 63/2 Galleries driven at right angles to these [*sc.* the dip head level and lodgment level] are known as 'dip' or 'rise headings', according to their position above or below the pit bottom. 1879 *Ibid.* X. 297/1 A quarry is usually worked to the dip of a rock, hence the strike-joints form clean-cut faces in front of the workmen as they advance. These are known as 'backs,' and the dip-joints which traverse them as 'cutters'. *Ibid.* 303/1 Dip-faults will often be observed to deviate considerably from the normal direction of dip. 1882 GEIKIE *Text-bk. Geol.* 502 In general they [*sc.* joints of stratified rocks] have two dominant trends, one coincident, on the whole, with the direction in which the strata are inclined from the horizon, and the other running transversely at a right angle or nearly so. The former set is known as dip-joints, because they run with the dip or inclination of the rocks. 1883 GRESLEY *Gloss. Coal-M.*, *Dip Split*, a current of intake air directed into or down a dip or deep district of a mine. 1887 P. MCNEILL *Blawearie* 24 The firm..had turned their whole force of men into the dip-workings, in order to exhaust the coal bordering on the march.

Dip, *v.* **5.** *To dip snuff* (U.S.). Add: Also *absol.*
1853 *Putnam's Mag.* Feb. I. 142 (Th.) This horrible practice, called in Lower Virginia and North Carolina dipping, is of respectable standing. 1857 T. B. GUNN *N. Y. Boarding Houses* 221 (Th.) She was suspected of a mysterious habit denominated in Southern parlance 'dipping',—in other words of chewing snuff. 1864 J. T. TROWBRIDGE *Cudjo's Cave* xxxiv. 332 For this excellent woman snuffed, 'dipped' and smoked. 1865 S. ANDREWS *South since War* (1866) 181 The native North-Carolinian..'chaws' and she 'dips'. *Ibid.* 182 Women of most classes 'dip'.

Dipeptide (dəipe·ptəid). *Chem.* Also **-id.** [f. DI-[2] + PEPT(IC + -IDE.] Any of several substances formed by the union of two amino-acids in the process of digestion.
1903 *Jrnl. Chem. Soc.* LXXXIV. I. 694 Derivatives of Dipeptides and their Behaviour towards Pancreas Ferments. 1906 *Ibid.* XC. I. 326 Formation of a Dipeptide by Hydrolysis of Silk Fibroin.

Diphase (dəi·fēɪz). = DIPHASIC.
1910 *Hawkins' Electr. Dict.* 118/1 *Diphase*, a term sometimes used for two phase.

Diphtheroid, *a.* Add: **B.** *sb.* A pseudo-diphtheria bacillus.
1908 *Practitioner* Jan. 138 The true diphtheria bacillus, and not one of these diphtheroids.

Diphthongism (di·fþǫŋiz'm). [f. DIPHTHONG *sb.* + -ISM.] The development of diphthongs.
1892 HAKE *Mem. Eighty Yrs.* 204 The laws of diphthongism and accent.

Diphyletic (dəifile·tik), *a.* [f. DI-[2] + Gr. φυλή, after *phyletic*.] Having two lines of descent, derived from two distinct sets of ancestors; also, of or pertaining to a classification of groups of animals in accordance with the view that they have a diphyletic origin; hence **Diphyle·tically** *adv.*
1902 *Nature* 25 Sept. 526 The 'Myriapoda', if a natural group, are diphyletic. 1903 *Amer. Nat.* Jan. 74 The diphyletic origin of the birds as represented by the Ratitæ and Carinatæ. 1912 G. E. SMITH in *Rep. Brit. Assoc. Adv. Sci.* 578 Yet others claim a diphyletic origin for Man from the Apes.

Diplacusis (diplăkiū·sis). *Path.* [mod.L., f. DIPLO- + Gr. ἄκουσις hearing.] Double hearing, the hearing of two notes when only one is produced, due to the hearing of a different tone in each ear, or to the arousing of two tonal sensations in the same ear.
1890 BILLINGS *Med. Dict.* 1895 E. B. TITCHENER tr. *Külpe's Outl. Psychol.* 299 The abnormality (*diplacusis*) may be restricted to a single ear.

Diplanar (dəiplē·năɹ), *a.* [f. DI-[2] + PLANAR.] Of or pertaining to two planes.
a 1865 SIR W. R. HAMILTON *Elem. Quarternions* (1866) 113 Any two quarternions (or quotients), which have different planes (intersecting therefore in a right line through the origin), may be said, by contrast, to be Diplanar.

Dipleurogenesis (dəi:plū·rodʒe·nĕsis). [f. DI-[2] + Gr. πλευρά side + γένεσις GENESIS.] Bilateral symmetry, the two-sided form assumed by the higher members of the animal kingdom; also, evolution through the acquisition of bilateral symmetry.
1896 L. H. BAILEY *Survival of Unlike* i. 17 We may, therefore, contrast these two great lines of ascent which, with so many vicissitudes, have come up through the ages, as Dipleurogenesis and Centrogenesis.

Dipleurula (dəiplū·riŭlă). [mod.L., dim. of DIPLEURA.] A supposed bilaterally symmetrical ancestor of the echinoderms.
1902 *Encycl. Brit.* XXVII. 620/1 We reach the conception that this supposed bilateral ancestor (or *Dipleurula*) may have become fixed.

Diplo-. Add: **Di:plobacilˑlus,** a form of bacillus in which the cells occur in pairs. **Diploco·ccal, Diplococˑcic** *adjs.*, of, pertaining to, or produced by diplococci. **Diploco·ccoid** *a.*, resembling diplococci. **Diploge·nesis,** (*b*) the supposed change of germ plasm produced by changes due to environment, bringing about inheritance of acquired characteristics. **Diplogra·phic** *a.* = *diplographical*. **Di:plomye·lia,** 'longitudinal fissure of spinal cord, giving an appearance of duplication' (Billings, 1890).
1899 *Jrnl. Exper. Med.* (1900) V. 213 The occurrence of acid-resisting diplococci or *diplo-bacilli. 1908 *Practitioner* Feb. 203 The diplobacillus of Morax-Axenfeld. 1903 *Med. Record* 27 June 1047 (Cent. D. Suppl.) *Diplococcal. 1908 *Lancet* 15 Feb. 484/1 A diplococcal infection of the spinal sac. *a* 1909 *Buck's Handbk. Med. Sci.* IV. 398 (Cent. D. Suppl.) *Diplococcic. 1910 *Practitioner* Apr. 489 The characteristic *diplococcoid arrangement of the germs. 1896 *Nat. Sci.* Nov. 288 Cope's theory of *Diplogenesis. 1823 J. ELMES *Mem. & Life C. Wren* 23 In 1647..he had a patent granted him for seventeen years, for a *diplographic instrument for writing with two pens.

Diplodocus (diplǫ·dǒkǒs). [mod.L., f. Gr. διπλόος double + δοκός a beam.] An individual of the extinct genus of gigantic herbivorous dinosaurs of the order Sauropoda, of which remains have been found in the Upper Jurassic of Colorado and Wyoming. Also *allusively*.
1890 *Guide Exhib. Galleries Departm. Palæontol. Brit. Mus.* II. 9 The *Diplodocus*, an animal intermediate in size between *Atlantosaurus* and *Morosaurus*. 1905 *Daily Chron.* 13 May 6/6 The diplodocus which lived and died about 4,000 centuries ago. 1905 *Westm. Gaz.* 6 July 2/1 Divo Pietro Aretino, the heroic literary blackguard, the diplodocus of the reptile press. 1927 HALDANE & HUXLEY *Anim. Biol.* xi. 242 Diplodocus (herbivorous, gigantic, and semi-aquatic). 1928 G. B. SHAW *Intell. Woman's Guide Socialism* xlii. (1929) 162 Adam Smith's eighteen men are as extinct as the diplodocus.

Diploid. Add: **B.** *adj.* *Biol.* Of a somatic cell: Having double the number of chromosomes characteristic of germ cells.
1927 HALDANE & HUXLEY *Anim. Biol.* ii. 60 The 2*n* or diploid number of chromosomes..found in the body-cells being reduced to *n*.

Diplomatize, *v.* Add: **1.** (Later U.S. example.)
1834 *Knickerbocker Mag.* IV. 120 Ladies were invited..to prepare themselves for future honors..by becoming Latinized, Graecised, mathematicized, and at length diplomatized.
3. Delete *rare*; later examples.
1898 *Daily News* 6 Aug. 7/3 Italian unity is owing in great part to the work of the people with Garibaldi, and Cavour did nothing but diplomatize the movement. 1906 *Daily Chron.* 24 Dec. 4/6 Count Nicholas Ignatieff who may be said to have 'diplomatised' the Russo-Turkish War of 1877.

Dipode (dəi·pǒud), *a.* and *sb.* [ad. Gr. διποδ-, δίπους having two feet.] **A.** *adj.* Biped. **B.** *sb.* A lizard with rudimentary pectoral limbs, so that it appears to have only two feet.
1889 *Cent. Dict.*

Dipolar, *a.* Add: **dipolar bath** (see quot.).
1906 *Practitioner* Dec. 773 The di-polar bath, in which both electrodes are in the bath with the patient.

Dipped, *ppl. a.* Add: **1. c.** *transf.* Extended or carried below a surface or level.
1925 J. PENDEREL-BRODHURST & LAYTON *Gloss. Eng. Furniture*, *Dropped or Dipped Seat*, the seat of a chair having a concave upper surface between the two side rails. 1929 *Evening News* 18 Nov. 10 A wonderfully flared skirt dipped at sides.

Dippel's oil. [f. the name of the discoverer J. C. *Dippel* (1672–1734), German alchemist.] Bone oil. In full *Dippel's animal oil*.
1840 *Penny Cycl.* XVI. 415/1. 1904 *Technol. & Sci. Dict.* (ed. Goodchild & Tweney).

Dipper. Add: **5.** (Earlier U.S. example.)
1783 E. PARKMAN *Diary* 298 Tin tunnel.., two tin dippers.
b. *U.S.* (Earlier example.)
1842 *Lowell* (Mass.) *Offering* II. 234, 236 (Th.), You all know the Dipper? Yes, it is in the Great Bear. The Little Dipper is in Ursa Minor.
c. In full *dipper dredge*, an American dredging boat or machine (see quots.).
1877 *Encycl. Brit.* VII. 465/1 The dipper dredge consists of a barge, with a derrick-crane reaching over the stern, suspending a large wrought-iron bucket which brings up the dredged material. 1879 *Scribner's Monthly* Nov. 55/1 The channel has also been assisted somewhat in its development, by an Osgood dipper dredge. 1884 KNIGHT *Dict. Mech.* Suppl., *Dipper*, a form of dredging machine which has a large ladle on the end of a spar.
7. b. As the name of various mechanical devices or instruments.
1925 *Morris Owner's Man.* 28 In the bottom case are fitted the troughs for feeding oil to the connecting-rod big ends through the oil dippers which are fitted to same. 1928 *Daily Express* 28 Sept. 9 It should be made compulsory for all motorists to have dippers affixed to their headlights.

Dipping, *vbl. sb.* Add: **2. b.** A grade of turpentine. (Cf. *DIP *sb.* 8 b.) *U.S.*
1832 D. J. BROWNE *Sylva Amer.* 232 The turpentine thus procured is the best, and is called pure dipping.
3. *dipping-machine, -tank, -trough, -vat*; **dipping-compass,** an instrument for measuring the inclination of the magnetic needle, an inclinometer; **dipping-wheel** *U.S.*, a wheel consisting of revolving buckets or nets set in a river for catching fish.
1886 C. SCOTT *Sheep-farming* 145 The material best adapted for making the tub of a *dipping machine is concrete... On a sheep farm the *dipping-trough should be always the landlord's property, and a fixture. 1903 *Daily Chron.* 10 Feb. 6/4 The molten spelter, with which the *dipping tanks were filled ready for the day's work. 1884 KNIGHT *Dict. Mech.* Suppl., **Dipping Vat*, the trough containing fine glazing slip in which biscuit ware is dipped to be covered with the material which, baked on, forms glaze. *Ibid.*, **Dipping Wheel*, a contrivance used in Southern rivers to meet local demand for fish. It is set in the stream so as to be turned by the current, and has a number of dip-nets which raise the fish and tumble them out at the axis in the manner of the scoop-wheel.

Dippy (di·pi), *a.* *slang.* [Origin obscure; ? f. DIP *v.*] Mad, insane, crazy.
1922 J. A. DUNN *Man Trap* xii. 167, I got lost there... Damned fool. No water! Too much sun! Went dippy and threw away everything. 1928 E. WAUGH *Decl. & F.* III. iii, Old Prendy went to see a chap What said he'd seen a ghost; Well, he was dippy, and he'd got A mallett and a saw. 1930 PRIESTLEY *Angel Pavement* vii. 353 The daughter she talks about seems to be completely dippy.

Diprionid (dəiprəi·ǒnid), *a.* = DIPRIONIDIAN *a.*
1888 ROLLESTON & JACKSON *Anim. Life* 769 Specimens of diprionid Graptolites.

Dipylon (di·pilǫn), *a.* and *sb.* *Gr. Archæol.* Also **Dipylum.** Pl. **dipyla** (di·pilă). [L., a. Gr. δίπυλον, neut. of δίπυλος double-gated, f. δι- two + πύλη gate.] **A.** *sb.* A double gateway in which the two gates are placed side by side, *esp.* a gateway in Athens on the northwest side of the city. **B.** *adj.* Denoting or pertaining to the Dipylon of Athens; *spec.* designating a style of Greek pottery belonging to the Geometric period found during excavations near this gate, or a similar Bœotian ware of the same period and of similar style.
1835 *Penny Cycl.* III. 10/1 The direction of the wall from the Ilissus along the south and west sides of the city to the Dipylum is quite clear. 1896 *Daily News* 12 June 5/1 Through the modifications of the Dipylon period..the fashions of Greek ladies were always changing. 1902 *Encycl. Brit.* XXV. 572/2 We engrave an excerpt from a Dipylon vase. *Ibid.* 759/1 The discovery of the Dipylon Gate, the principal entrance of ancient Athens. 1911 PETRIE *Revolutions of Civilisation* iii. 59 The rise of a new art began to dawn in the dipylon vases.

Direct, *a.* Add:
2. c. Also applied to gunnery fire with an elevation not exceeding 15°.
1879 *Man. Artill. Exerc.* I. v. 24 Direct fire at masonry is either for demolition or for breaching.
6. d. *Direct action*, (*b*) the exertion of pressure on the community by industrial workers through any action which is directly effective, such as strikes, sabotage, or demonstrations, in order to force political measures on the Government, as distinguished from action through parliamentary representatives. Hence *direct-actionist*.
1912 J. R. MACDONALD *Syndicalism* iv. 24 The Programme of Direct Action. 1919 *Times* 28 June 14/3 He had been a direct actionist for 35 years. 1920 S. & B. WEBB *Trade Unionism* 672 The vast majority of Trade Unionists object to Direct Action..for objects other than those connected with the economic function of the Direct Actionists...Trade Unionists..are not prepared to disapprove of Direct Action as a reprisal for Direct Action taken by other persons or groups. 1920 *Edin. Rev.* Oct. 361 The root idea of direct action dates back in this country to Chartist days. In practice, direct action almost invariably implies either a sectional strike by a particular group or groups of labour, or a general strike by all groups of labour combined. 1926 *Morn. Post* 7 Oct. 11/5 They really think the failure of this industrial action will cause a swing round from the direct actionists to the politicians.
f. Of or pertaining to the work and expenses actually incurred during production as distinct from subsidiary work and overhead charges, i.e. to prime or initial costs or charges; also, applied to labour employed for the construction of works directly (without the intervention of a contractor).
1895 A. FIELDHOUSE *Student's Adv. Book-keeping* (1910) 215 The more immediate or direct cost of production. 1898 S. S. DAWSON *Accountant's Compend.* 71/1 The prime cost ..is the original or direct cost of same. 1903 *Encycl. Accounting* II. 263 These 'expenses' or charges are broadly divisible into 'direct' and 'indirect'. 1922 J. D. HACKETT in *Management Engineering* Feb., Absence, such as is being considered here, applies mainly to direct or 'productive' labor and not to indirect or 'non-productive' employees. 1923 *Ibid.* May, *Direct Labor*, work done exclusively in the making of a product, in contradistinction to subsidiary work also necessary for production. 1925 RYALL *Primer of Costing* 49 Direct labour may therefore be defined as—'Labour applied to a works order which can be measured and directly charged to that order or product'. 1930 *Daily Mail* 1 Aug. 7/7 The Office of Works is about to substitute direct labour for the present system of work done by contract.
g. Of a dye: Not requiring a mordant, substantive.
1902 *Encycl. Brit.* XXVII. 558/1 Direct Colours.—The characteristic feature of the dyestuffs belonging to this class is that they dye cotton 'direct'. *Ibid.* 558/2 Wool and silk are dyed with the Direct Colours in the same manner as cotton. 1904 *Technol. & Sci. Dict.* (ed. Goodchild & Tweney) s.v. *Dye*, The Direct Cotton Colours or Substantive Dyes, also known as the Benzidine Colours.
h. Designating a process by which iron or steel is obtained direct from the ore without passing through the stage of cast iron.
1875 *Ure's Dict. Arts* (ed. 7) II. 941 Chenot's sponge may be obtained by an 'internal' or 'direct' method, in which the ore is reduced..by a hot current of carbonic-oxide gas. 1880 *Encycl. Brit.* XIII. 291/1 The 'direct' methods of Clay, Chenot, Yates, Blair, Snelus, Du Puy, Siemens, and others. 1884 W. H. GREENWOOD *Steel & Iron* xi. 212 The direct processes necessitate the use of purer and richer ores and fuels than the indirect processes.
i. direct-connected *a.* = next (*a*); **direct-coupled** *a.*, (*a*) coupled without intermediate transmission device; (*b*) *Wireless Telegr.*, of an antenna or aerial, 'connected electrically with one point of a closed oscillation circuit in syntony with it and earthed' (Webster 1911); **direct coupler** (see quot.); **direct current** *Electr.*, a current flowing in one direction only, as distinguished from an alternating current; also *attrib.*; **direct (extra or) induced current,** 'a momentary current of the same direction as the inducing current, produced by the stopping or removing the latter; also, a similar current produced by the removal of a magnet' (W. 1911); **direct spark,** designating a form of magneto-ignition in an internal combustion engine.
1901 *Feilden's Mag.* IV. 441/2 A *direct-coupled electrically-driven fan. 1910 G. W. PIERCE *Wireless Telegr.* 96 Direct coupled transmitting and receiving circuits. 1916 *Standard. Rules Amer. Inst. Electr. Engin.* 97 **Direct Coupler*, a coupler which magnetically joins two circuits having a common conductive portion. 1893 D. C. JACKSON *Electro-Magn.* I. 92 A current constant in direction, but not necessarily so in value, is often called a *Direct Current. 1893 *Jrnl. Soc. Arts* XLI. 623/2 The general merits of alternate-current, as against those of the direct-current systems. 1906 A. RUSSELL *Altern. Curr.* II. 2 One advantage that direct current machines have over alternators is that they are self-exciting. 1915 HAWKHEAD & DOWSETT *Techn. Instr. Wireless Telegr.* 83 A direct current may be passed through a known resistance and the amount of heat generated may be measured. 1916 *Standard. Rules Amer. Inst. Electr. Engin.* 21 A Direct-Current Compensator or Balancer comprises two or more similar direct-current machines.. directly coupled to each other. 1863 E. ATKINSON tr. *Ganot's Elem. Treat. Physics* 670 When the circuit is opened the induced current formed is in the same direction as the principal current, and hence it is called the *direct extra-current. 1866 *Ibid.* (ed. 2) 702 A *direct induced current, that is, one in the same direction as the principal one. This is known as the extra current. 1908 *Westm. Gaz.* 16 Nov. 5/2 The adoption of the high-tension *direct-spark magneto ignition.

Dire·ctedness. [f. DIRECTED *ppl. a.* + -NESS.] The quality of being directed.
1922 J. Y. SIMPSON *Man & Attainm. Immort.* xii. 267 The specificity of action, the directedness, the working out of what looks like purpose.

Directee (direktī·). [f. DIRECT *v.* + -EE.] One who is directed or is under direction.
1928 G. B. SHAW *Intell. Woman's Guide Socialism* lxx. (1929) 337 By paying the director more than the directee it creates a difference of class between them.

Direction. 11. Add: **direction-finder** *Wireless Telegr.* (see quot. 1919); so *direction-finding*.
1913 *Year-Bk. Wireless Telegr. & Teleph.* 307 Direction-finding from ship-board. *Ibid.* 316 The uses of the direction-finder. 1919 R. STANLEY *Wireless Telegr.* I. 387 An instrument for use on board ships, called the 'Wireless Direction Finder'. *Ibid.* II. 270 A direction-finding aerial system. 1919 H. WARD *Techn. Terms Wireless Telegr.* 39 *Direction Finder*, two Bellini-Tosi aerials at right angles, each of which has in middle of lower side a coil which acts inductively upon another coil in detector circuit, which is capable of being swung until parallel with either aerial coil. 1920 *Discovery* May 131/2 The Marconi direction-finder not only receives wireless signals; it also indicates the direction of the sending station. 1921 L. B. TURNER *Wireless Telegr.* 178 Direction-finding stations on land..are usually grouped in pairs at the ends of a suitable base line, so that the intersection of the two orientations determined gives the position of the source of signal, e.g. a ship or an aeroplane. *Ibid.* 180 Observations with a direction-finding receiver. 1928 C. F. S. GAMBLE *N. Sea Air Station* xviii. 313 Submarines..whose presence had been detected largely by direction-finding wireless telegraphic stations.

Directional, *a.* Add: **4.** Of or pertaining to the direction or guidance of affairs.
1921 *Glasgow Herald* 5 Mar. 6 The responsibility of so improving his directional control of the conditions of working. 1922 *Ibid.* 21 Mar. 7 Their doctrine of one directional authority. 1928 *Daily Express* 26 Sept. 1 All directional and organisation expenses.
5. *Wireless Telegraphy.* Concerned with the record of directions indicated by signals received from a vessel, etc. Also *sb.*, a directional signal.
1914 R. STANLEY *Wireless Telegr.* 179 To illustrate the effect of directional aerials at the sender and at the receiver. 1922 *Encycl. Brit.* XXX. 45/1 There are two methods by which 'directional wireless' (as it is termed) can be employed. 1930 *Aberdeen Press & Jrnl.* 26 June 7/1 An occasional directional message from the Cape Race wireless station was the only guidance they could pick up.

Directive, *sb.* Delete †*Obs.* and add: *spec.* a general instruction how to proceed or act.
1911 *Encycl. Brit.* XX. 720/1 The ecclesiastical régime ..arrogated to itself the right of interfering by means of 'Directives' with the political life of nations. 1914 tr. *F. von Bernhardi's How Germany makes War* x. 206 He had to make the best of politely advising, of obligingly leaving it to the direction of the directives, and of similar makeshifts.

Directivity (direkti·vĭti, dəi-). [f. DIRECTIVE + -ITY.] The quality or state of being directed by a vital force or power as distinguished from the physical forces, *spec.* as a theory of evolution.
1903 *Daily Chron.* Apr., That directivity which could not be explained without the power of the Deity behind it. 1907 *Hibbert Jrnl.* Oct. 150 Sheep, oxen, horses, and even geese may be feeding in the same grass-land. In each case the molecular compounds of the grass are identical, but they find themselves ultimately disposed in very different arrangements in the different animals. This can only be possible under the influence of directivity, but 'directing' differently in each creature.

Directoire (dire·ktwāɹ), *a.* and *sb.* [Fr.; see DIRECTORY *sb.* 6.] **A.** *adj.* Of or pertaining to, or in imitation of, a style of dress prevalent at the time of the French Directory, characterized by its extravagance of design and its imitation of Greek and Roman costume. **B.** *sb.* A hat of this style.
1878 *Cassell's Family Mag.* 756 The Directoire..very nearly obscures the face. 1888 *Weldon's Illustr. Dress-maker* Dec., The Empire and Directoire styles are steadily increasing in popularity. 1896 *Godey's Mag.* Feb. 214/2 An immense *directoire* bow of ribbon or chiffon. 1904 *Daily Chron.* 18 June 8/2 Such hats, with their picturesque brims, are known as Directoires. 1908 *Westm. Gaz.* 22 Apr. 4/3 Her hat is Directoire-shape. 1908 *Daily Chron.* 16 June 4/5 Worth has made a feature of Directoire gowns for Ascot. 1924 *Drapery Catal.*, Ladies Summer-weight Stockinette Directoire Knickers.

Diremption. Add: **c.** *Bot.* An abnormal separation or displacement of leaves.
1869 MASTERS *Veget. Teratol.* 87 The term 'diremption' has sometimes been applied to cases where leaves are thus apparently dragged out of position. 1900 B. D. JACKSON *Gloss. Bot. Terms*, *Diremption*, the occasional separation or displacement of leaves.

Dirge, *v.* Add: **b.** To sing as a dirge.
1895 *Punch* 5 Oct. 162/2 They might all dirge in chorus the old duet of 'Again we come to thee, Savoy'.
c. *intr.* To utter a dirge.
1907 MULFORD *Bar-20* xxi. 206 Shortly afterward the mournful cry of a whip-poor-will dirged out on the early morning air. 1921 *Chambers's Jrnl.* 211/2 The dead tops of the Gwynfrwyn trees were swaying and dirging dismally.

Dirgee, var. of *DURZEE, tailor.

Dirigibility (di:ridʒibi·lĭti). [f. DIRIGIBLE *a.*: see -ILITY.] The quality of being dirigible.
1902 *Westm. Gaz.* 25 Mar. 9/2 Proving the dirigibility of the aerostat. 1903 *Ibid.* 16 Nov. 7/3 Wireless dirigibility experiments. 1908 *B'ham Inst. Mag.* Jan. 254 The problem of..perfect dirigibility of dynamic flying machines.

Dirigible, *a.* Add: **B.** *sb.* A dirigible balloon or airship.
1907 *Daily Chron.* 26 July 5/6 He had been up in a captive balloon, but never before in a dirigible. 1910 *Daily Mail* 6 June 8/1 Night-flying dirigibles. 1927 *Glasgow Herald* 28 Apr. 15 A new dictionary of air terms has been compiled...So far as England is concerned, the word 'dirigible' will disappear and only 'airship' remain.

Dirk, *sb.* **2.** *dirk-knife* (U.S. example).
1843 CARLTON *New Purchase* I. xx. 189 Tom [was] talking and laughing away like a fellow whittling poplar with a dirk knife!

Dirned, U.S. var. of DURNED *adv.*
1873 J. H. BEADLE *Undevel. West* xx. 369 Him and two other Cherokees..scared some Eastern fellers dirned near to death.

Dirt, *sb.* **6. c.** *To eat dirt*: also (*U.S.*), to make a humiliating confession or retractation.
1891 FARMER *Slang* s.v. *Dirt*, *To eat dirt*,..to retract. 1902 CLAPIN *Dict. Amer.*, *Eat dirt*, to retract, to be penitent, the Yankee equiv. of 'to eat one's words'.
7. d. dirt-line, a layer of dirt and debris accumulated on the surface of a glacier and imprisoned by the seasonal layer of snow; **dirt track,** a course (*a*) made of cinders and brickdust for motor-cycle racing; (*b*) composed of soil, esp. as distinguished from turf, for flat-racing.
1894 J. GEIKIE *Gt. Ice Age* (ed. 3) 30 *note*, The beds of snow..being usually marked off by a '*dirt-line' or crust formed of a mixture of dust, small grit, and occasional remains of insects. 1902 *Encycl. Brit.* XXIX. 335/2 Practically all flat racing in the United States is held on '*dirt-tracks', *i.e.*, courses with soil specially prepared for racing, instead of turf courses. 1924 MASEFIELD *Sard Harker* I. 63 The road was not macadam but dirt-track, with soft going, after the first mile. 1928 *Daily Tel.* 20 Mar. 14/2 Motor-cycle racing on 'dirt tracks', a form of sport very popular in Australia. 1928 *Times* 2 July 6/7 Dirt Track Racing.

Dirt, *v.* Add: **2.** To cover with earth. *U.S.*
1903 A. ADAMS *Log Cowboy* xiv. 221 It now only remained to sod over and dirt the bridge thoroughly.

Dirt-eater. Add: *spec.* one of a class of 'poor whites' in some parts of the southern United States (see quot. 1895).
1840 C. F. HOFFMAN *Greyslaer* III. xii. 223 Even Bettys, little fastidious as he was, recoiled from the fare which these 'Dirt Eaters', as the Indians called them, placed before him. 1845 J. J. HOOPER *Adv. Simon Suggs* vii. (1848) 88 'What do you aim to bury your dead Injuns Cap'en?' sarcastically enquired the little dirt-eater. 1866 *Ret. Agric. Soc. Maine* 46 It rests with you..whether you will take rank with the poor whites, the dirt-eaters of the South, or with the best classes of the north. 1895 *Funk's Stand. Dict.*, *Dirt-eater*, one of a non-slaveholding class in the slave states of the Union: so called by the supporters of slavery.

Di·rt-road. *U.S.* [DIRT *sb.* 3.] An unmade road, having merely the natural surface.
1852 MRS. STOWE *Uncle Tom's C.* vii. 62 Der's two roads to de river—de dirt road and de pike. *Ibid.*, Haley.. thought that it lay in favour of the dirt road aforesaid. 1884 'C. E. CRADDOCK' *Tenn. Mts.* 39 From the summit of the mountain could be seen for many a mile the dirt-road in the valley. 1897 *Outing* (U.S.) XXIX. 385/2, I found myself on a level and reasonably smooth dirt-road. 1906 J. MCGEORGE in *Engineering Mag.* June 382 Our dirt roads are simply a

heap of soil scraped up into a ridge by the farmer's scrapers. 1917 MATHEWSON *Sec. Base Sloan* vi. 75 A few scattered houses indicated the dirt road in that direction.

Di·rt-roofed, *a. U.S.* [DIRT *sb.* 3.] Having an earthen roof.
1873 J. H. BEADLE *Undevel. West* xxxiv. 734 To his joy he came upon a dirt-roofed log-house. 1899 T. HALL *Tales* 273 Slowly..the sole representative of the law in Skull Gulch ambled into his dirt-roofed log cabin.

Di·rt-washer, -washing. (See DIRT *sb.* 3 c.)
1869 S. BOWLES *Our New West* ix. 179 The dirt-washers swept eagerly over the rich surface deposits. *Ibid.*, The old and simple dirt washing for gold was resumed.

Dirty, *a.* Add: **2. b.** Also *absol.* in phrase *To do the dirty*: to play a dirty trick.
1914 *Daily Express* 13 Nov. 514 The Germans have been 'doing the dirty' on us by donning khaki and kilts to approach our trenches. 1915 D. O. BARNETT *Lett.* 157, I hope our friends the 133rd will..do the dirty on their Prussian friends. 1929 PRIESTLEY *Good Comp.* III. v. 607 Anyhow they did the dirty on yer. 1930 MOTTRAM *Europa's Beast* xii. 282 If you've been doing the dirty on my friends.
6. Also *dirty-looking* adj.
1818 W. TUCKER *Family Dyer & Scourer* i. (ed. 2) 7 A kind of dirty looking green.

Dirzie, variant of *DURZEE.

Dis (dis), *v. Printer's slang.* Colloq. abbreviation of DISTRIBUTE *v.* 5. Hence **Dis** *sb.*, type ready for distribution.
1889 BARRÈRE & LELAND *Dict. Slang*, *Diss* (printers), abbreviation for distribution, *i.e.*, printed off type—to be returned to its respective cases, and re-composed. 1899 SOUTHWARD *Mod. Printing* II. 168 It is not necessary for an operator to read the matter to be 'dis'd'. *Ibid.* 169 The type being ordinary 'dis', and in no way assorted. 1903 'No. 7' *25 Yrs. in 17 Prisons* x. 96 There was 'pie' to the left of us, 'pie' to the right of us..and what had only taken a week to 'set up' took nearly a month to 'dis'. *Ibid.* xii. 115 For the first week or two I was put upon 'dissing'.

Disablement. Add: **3.** *attrib.*
1898 *Westm. Gaz.* 23 June 9/1 A crushing liability for death and disablement claims. 1898 *Daily News* 25 June 6/6 The first 26 weeks' disablement pay. 1920 *Act 10 Geo. V* c. 10 § 2 The rate of disablement benefit.

Disaccharide (daisæ·kărəid, -id). *Chem.* Also -id. [DI-[2] 2 c.] = *BIOSE.
1895 [see *BIOSE]. 1905 E. F. ARMSTRONG in *Proc. R. Soc.* B. LXXVI. 592 The enzymes which are capable of inducing the hydrolysis of disaccharides or bioses.

Disaffiliation (di·săfiliē·ʃən). [f. DISAFFILIATE *v.*: see -TION.] The action of disaffiliating.
1927 *Glasgow Herald* 9 Mar. 11 The ground upon which disaffiliation is urged. 1927 *Observer* 10 July 14/6 The announcement of the disaffiliation of the Union of Post Office Workers. 1927 *Glasgow Herald* 3 Oct. 13 The disaffiliation of societies which have not carried out the decisions of the conference debarring Communists from membership.

Disagreeable, *a.* **3. b.** (Earlier U.S. example.)
1836 *Knickerbocker Mag.* VIII. 151 Had I not become accustomed to such dangers, I should have felt very disagreeable.

Disamenity (disăme·nĭti, -ī·nĭti). [f. DIS- 9 + AMENITY.] *pl.* The disadvantages or drawbacks of a place or time.
1924 *Glasgow Herald* 19 Apr. 4 The disamenities of warm countries in the summer time. *Ibid.* 29 Nov. 4 The disamenities attendant on the growth of civilisation.

Disappear, *v.* Add: **1.** Also with advb. expressions introduced by preps.
1837 E. HOWARD *Old Commodore* I. iv. 111 Richard Stubbs..disappeared down the Jacob's ladder. 1842 LEVER *Jack Hinton* lii, A mounted party..entering one of the gates of the city, disappeared from our sight. 1881 MRS. RIDDELL *Senior Partner* viii. Like a man in a dream, young McCullagh..disappeared from outward view. *Ibid.* xxii, The boy disappeared into the retirement of the back room. 1888 MRS. H. WARD *R. Elsmere* v, Almost every year he disappeared to France. *Ibid.* x, Rose caught a gray dress disappearing up the little stairs.
3. *trans.* To cause to disappear.
1897 *Chem. News* 19 Mar. 143 We progressively disappear the faces of the dodecahedron.

Disappoint, *v.* **2.** Add: Also *absol.*, to cause disappointment.
1842 LEVER *Jack Hinton* ix, The Duke has disappointed so often, that he is sure to go now. 1881 MRS. RIDDELL *Senior Partner* xxxii, I shall look out for you at Waterloo at a quarter to five, and trust you will not disappoint. 1927 *Daily Tel.* 3 May 16 Innuendo [a racehorse] has disappointed in the past when fancied.

Disarmingly (disā·ɹmiŋli), *adv.* [f. DISARMING *ppl. a.* + -LY [2].] In a disarming manner; so as to disarm opponents.
1905 *Daily Chron.* 11 Mar. 7/2 Hascombe smiled disarmingly. 1920 *Blackw. Mag.* Dec. 714/2 A name..which she..disarmingly admitted there was small prospect of her ever otherwise being able to change. 1928 *Daily Tel.* 21 Aug. 8/5 He is a business man himself, speaking in terms which are disarmingly straightforward.

Disassemble (disăse·mb'l), *v.* Delete *Obs.* and add: **b.** To take to pieces, to take apart. (The opposite of *ASSEMBLE *v.*[1] 2 b.)
1922 *Short Stories* Feb. 41/2 This generating plant was partly disassembled. 1930 *Sci. Amer.* Nov. 389 The entire 50-foot line can be assembled or disassembled in six minutes.

Disassociation. Add: **b.** = *DISSOCIATION 3.
1906 M. PRINCE (*title*) The Disassociation of a Personality.

Disazo- (disæ·zo). *Chem.* [f. Gr. δίς twice + AZO-.] A combining form used in organic chemistry to denote the presence in the molecule of a compound of two azo groups. Also used *attrib.* as *disazo*.
1891 ROSCOE & SCHORLEMMER *Treat. Chem.* III. III. 353 Disazobenzene..is obtained from the corresponding amidodisazobenzene by diazotizing and boiling with alcohol. 1913 BLOXAM & LEWIS *Chem.* (ed. 10) 719 Disazo-dyestuffs..contain the ·N:N· group twice, and are of three kinds. 1930 HACKH *Chem. Dict.* 250/1 *Disazo compound*, a compound containing two azo groups of the type R.N:N.R.–N:N.R. Many dyes belong to this group.

Disboscation. (Modern U.S. example.)
1874 *Rep. Vermont Board Agric.* II. 477 Does the disboscation of forests predispose to a diminution in the pluvious character of a region?

Disbursal (disbə̄·ɹsăl). [f. DISBURSE *v.* + -AL.] The act of disbursing, disbursement.
1589 in *Rep. Hist. MSS. Comm., Var. Coll.* (1904) III. 49 Divers disbursalles..as for some bookes. 1895 GRACE M. KIMBALL in *Manch. Guardian* 30 Sept. 6/8 Accommodation ..upstairs for the disbursal and reception of goods. 1898 in *Westm. Gaz.* 9 Mar. 2/3 All moneys received shall be duly acknowledged, and their disbursal shall be controlled by the Mansion House committee.

Disc [3]. Abbreviation of DISCONNECTED.
1916 BOYD CABLE *Action Front* 275 The wire was pronounced disconnected, or 'disc', as the signaller called it.

Discard, *sb.* Add:
1. c. *gen.* The fact of being discarded; dismissal. Also, the act of dismissing or abandoning.
1787 DALRYMPLE *Jrnl. Young Lady Virg.* (1871) 29 Nancy had an admirer lately..He got his discard yesterday. 1906 *Daily Chron.* 29 Sept. 5/4 'The Chief's' sudden discard of South Africa and adoption of Protection under the name of Tariff Reform.
2. b. *fig.* and *gen.*
1905 *Smart Set* Oct. 14/1 I'm much obliged to the lady; but she goes to the discard, too. 1927 H. E. FOSDICK *Pilgr. Palestine* 260 One surely does not mean to sweep into the discard as spiritually futile the elaborate symbolism of Eastern worship.

Discarnate, *a.* Transfer †*Obs. rare* to sense 1 and add:
2. Divested of the flesh or the body, disembodied.
1895 *Westm. Gaz.* 5 Nov. 2/3 Any *à priori* belief in a discarnate existence of one's personality. 1901 J. H. HYSLOP in *Proc. Soc. Psychical Research* XVI. 216 We ought to expect *a priori* that a discarnate memory should be defective in its communications from a transcendental world. 1903 MYERS *Hum. Pers.* II. 274 We cannot simply admit the existence of discarnate spirits as inert or subsidiary phenomena. 1920 *Public Opinion* 9 July 34/3 It is rash to claim that a given phenomenon..must..be due to discarnate influences. 1922 E. PHILLPOTTS *Grey Room* iv. 106 This death-dealing ghost, or discarnate but conscious being.
So **Discarna·tion**, disembodiment.
1901 *Contemp. Rev.* Aug. 221 The discarnation of personality in death.

Discerptor (disə̄·ɹptəɹ). [f. L. *discerpt-*, ppl. stem of *discerpĕre*: see -OR.] One who disjoins.
1904 *Nature* 17 Mar. 464/2 The first discerptor [of the genus *Cimex*] was Fabricius.

Discharge, *v.* **1. c.** Delete † and add:
1899 *Daily News* 12 June 3/4 Kennerley was not aware that the firearm was loaded, and it discharged in his face.

Dischargeable, *a.* Delete *rare* and add:
1897 *Daily News* 20 July 5/6 The notes are dischargeable on August 1st, 1900.

Dischargee (dis,tʃaɹdʒī·). [f. DISCHARGE *v.* + -EE.] A person who is discharged.
1894 *Scottish Rev.* July 58 Government finds place for its deserving dischargees in its public service.

Disciple, *sb.* **3.** Add: The name was suggested by Alex. Campbell of Lexington, Kentucky, in 1832.
1835 J. MARTIN *Gaz. Virginia* 76 The precise distinction between the regular Baptist and the Reformers, called the disciples of Christ, not being in all cases drawn.

Disco-. Add: **Di·scoplasm, Di·scotriæne** (see quots.).
1900 tr. *Ehrlich & Lazarus's Histol. Blood* 51 The *discoplasm loses its power of retaining the hæmoglobin, and gives it up to the blood plasma in ever increasing quantity. 1913 DORLAND *Med. Dict.* (ed. 7), *Discoplasm*, the structural part of a red blood-corpuscle. 1888 SOLLAS in *Challenger Rep.* XXV. p. lvii, Varieties of the Triæne..**Discotriæne*..The cladome is a disc in which separate cladi are not distinguishable; and the axial rods representing them extend but a short distance from the cladal origin. *Ibid.*, The discotriæne combines in itself the characters of the desma and the ordinary spicule.

Discohere (diskohī·ɹ), *v.* [f. DIS- 6 + COHERE *v.*] Early synonym of *DECOHERE.
1899 *Standard* 8 May, The current causes a small hammer to strike the coherer and to cause the filings to discohere, so that the circuit may be completed and broken at will.

Discommodious (diskǫmōu·diəs), *a.* Delete †*Obs.* and add examples of modern pedantic use:
1897 N. MUNRO in *Blackw. Mag.* Nov. 593/2 [A fashion] discommodious for warm weather. 1928 *Ibid.* Feb. 160/2 Confound and blister that blasted German and all his damned discommodious works.

Disconcert, *v.* **2.** Add: Also *absol.*
1908 *Smart Set* Sept. 47 She was conscious of a baffling reserve, a poise that disconcerted.

Disconcertingly (diskǫnsə̄·ɹtiŋli), *adv.* [f. DISCONCERTING *ppl. a.* + -LY [2].] In a disconcerting manner.
1898 *Westm. Gaz.* 5 Apr. 2/2 The Japs have found it disconcertingly expensive. 1900 H. G. WELLS *Love & Mr. Lewisham* xi, He regarded Lewisham critically and disconcertingly over gilt glasses. 1906 GALSWORTHY *Man of Property* I. i, He had sherry-coloured eyes, disconcertingly inattentive at times.

Disconformable, *a.* Delete †*Obs.* and add:
1925 in E. F. Norton *Fight for Everest, 1924* 295 The true nature of this important junction it is difficult to tell, but it has the appearance of being a disconformable one.

Disconne·cting, *vbl. sb.* [f. DISCONNECT *v.* + -ING [1].] The action of separating. Also *attrib.*, as **disconnecting engine** (see quot.).
1888 *Lockwood's Dict. Mech. Engin.*, *Disconnecting Engine*, a double engine, usually of the compound type, in which the cylinders can either be used in combination, or each separately from the other.

Discrimination. Add: **1. c.** (See quot.)
1923 J. D. HACKETT *Labor Terms* in *Management Engineering* May, *Discrimination*, the act of employing non-union workers to the exclusion of union workers.
5. *attrib.* and *Comb.*: **discrimination reaction** *Psychol.*, a reaction in which the movement of response is delayed until the mind of the subject has identified the stimulus; **discrimination time** *Psychol.*, the total duration of the time of such reaction, or the time necessary for the identification of the stimuli.
1898 E. B. TITCHENER *Prim. Psychol.* 260 In the *discrimination reaction, he [*sc.* the subject] moves when he has apperceived some one of two or more familiar stimuli. 1894 tr. *W. Wundt's Hum. & Anim. Psychol.* 279 By subtracting the previously determined simple time from this longer time we get a *discrimination-time.

Disease, *sb.* **1.** (Revived in recent use with the spelling *dis-ease*.)
1909 *Daily Chron.* 17 May 3/1 Perhaps he..kept dark the apprehensions of his artist soul, communicated his ease not his dis-ease. 1922 A. S. M. HUTCHINSON *This Freedom* II. x. 166 They were in a curious dis-ease whose occasion was not to be defined. 1925 — *One Increasing Purpose* III. xiv, She had a curious dis-ease in meeting socially doctors whom also she met professionally.

Diseuse (dī·zȫz). [Fr., fem. = talker.] A female artiste who specializes in monologue. Also less freq. masc. **Diseur.**
1896 *Cosmopolitan* XX. 444 She is only a concert-hall singer (or diseuse, to use a newly-coined and specific title). 1903 *Daily Chron.* 20 June 8/2 Mme. Anna Thibaud, the celebrated *diseuse*. 1927 M. BARING *Tinker's Leave* xxv, Bielor played songs, and Zurova, a well known *diseuse* sang.

Disfellowship, *v. U.S.* (Earlier example.)
1831 *Troy* (N.Y.) *Watchman* 3 Sept. (Th.) They were disfellowshipped by the association.

Disfiguringly (disfi·giŭriŋli, -fi·gəɹ-), *adv.* [f. DISFIGURING *ppl. a.* + -LY [2].] In a disfiguring manner; so as to disfigure.
1911 MRS. H. WARD *Case of R. Meynell* i, Certain lines on the forehead..showed themselves disfiguringly. 1923 BARING-GOULD *Early Remin.* ii. 23 Telegraph stations planted..most disfiguringly, on the summit of church towers.

Disgorger. Add: Also *spec.* in the manufacture of effervescing wine, one who temporarily removes the cork from a bottle of wine after secondary fermentation in order to allow the yeasty sediment to be blown out by the escaping gas.
1900 SADTLER *Hand-bk. Industr. Org. Chem.* (ed. 3) 207 With the sediment thus on the cork it goes into the hands of a workman called a 'disgorger', who, holding the bottle still neck downward, proceeds to liberate the cork by slipping off the agrafe, and when the cork is three-fourth parts out he quickly inverts the bottle.

Dish, *sb.* Add: **5.** Also, more commonly, the condition of wheels having such concavity; the amount of such concavity.
1810 [in Dict.]. 1837 W. B. ADAMS *Carriages* 98 Some wheels ..get more dish than others. 1844 H. STEPHENS *Bk. Farm* III. 1154 The third or front wheel may be found without dish. 1888 *Encycl. Brit.* XI. 311/1 The dish is considerable, amounting to 2 inches in the 5-foot wheel. 1891 *Fur, Fin & Feather* Mar. 167 The left hind wheel of his wagon is out of dish.
10. dish-cross, -rim, Sheffield plate appliances for keeping dishes warm at table; **dish face,** the face of a dog when the nose is higher at the tip than at the stop (cf. *dish-faced*); **dish-keel** (see KEEL *sb.*[1] 1 b).
1908 B. WYLLIE *Sheffield Plate* 75 '*Dish-crosses' or 'spiders'..served two purposes: either to keep a hot dish from marking the polished tables..or to support a spirit-lamp which kept the contents of the dish above hot. 1908 H. N. VEITCH *Sheffield Plate* 136 These dish-crosses..are suitable for both round and oval dishes. 1893 *Kennel Gaz.* Aug. 214 Jess III is spoilt by her *dish face. 1874 THEARLE *Naval Archit.* 72 The hollow or *dish keel is a variety of the flat keel system. 1774 in B. Wyllie *Sheffield Plate* (1908) 71 *Dish-rims. 1908 B. WYLLIE *Ibid.* pl. lxxi, Revolving Dish Stand for round or oval dish. Possibly this is what was meant by a 'dish-rim'.

Dish-cloth. Add: **2. Dishcloth gourd,** the gourd or the plant of any of the species of *Luffa* of which the spongy inner portion of the fruit may be used as a cloth. 1911 WEBSTER.

Dished, *ppl. a.* Add: **d.** Of the face of an animal: Concave in profile (cf. **dish-face*).
1878 *Trans. Ill. Dept. Agric.* XIV. 210 The head was short and fine, with a dished face and rather thin jowls. 1908 *Animal Managem.* 21 The face..'stag-faced' or 'dished'.

Dishouse, *v.* **1.** Add: also, to deprive of a habitation. Chiefly in **Dishou·sed** *ppl. a.* (also *absol.*), **Dishou·sing** *vbl. sb.*
1900 *Daily News* 4 Jan. 3/1 The evil of dishousing

altogether would be substituted for the evil of living in places unfit for habitation. 1900 *Ibid.* 8 Jan. 7/1 Such considerations as the fate of the dishoused. 1901 *Westm. Gaz.* 5 Sept. 2/3 To secure sites for the dishoused. 1902 *Ibid.* 13 Dec. 5/1 The dishousing of the inhabitants of the slums. 1921 *Contemp. Rev.* Oct. 451 Large closing orders are out of the question because of the dishousing they would occasion.

Dish-rag (di·ʃræg). *U.S.* [DISH *sb.* 10.] **a.** A dish-cloth. **b.** *transf.* The dishcloth gourd.
1873 'MARK TWAIN' & WARNER *Gilded Age* vii. 81 We used to have a calf that et apples and just chawed up dish-rags like nothing. 1904 *N.Y. Tribune* 22 May, A novel enterprise, that of raising dishrags, is being exploited by a number of Southern California horticulturists. These curious vegetables assume the form and appearance of cucumbers, and hang on the vines until their green coats become brown and dry like parchment.

Dish-washer. 2. (U.S. example.)
1889 *Kansas Times & Star* 9 July, The patent new dish washer washes a bushel of dishes in a few minutes.

Di·sh-wa·tery, *a.* [See -Y [1].] Resembling dish-water. Also *fig.*
1910 W. JAMES *Mem. & Studies* xi. (1911) 284 Mawkish and dishwatery. 1928 *Sunday Express* 8 Jan. 9/4 Then came the soup. Great greasy tins of a dish-watery liquid.

Disinhibition (disinhibi·ʃən). [f. DIS- 9 + INHIBITION.] (See quot.)
1927 PAVLOV tr. *G. V. Anrep's Conditioned Reflexes* iv. 67 We are now afforded some justification for regarding disinhibition, as we did a short while ago, as being the 'inhibition of an inhibition'.

Disi·ntegratively, *adv.* [f. DISINTEGRATIVE + -LY [2].] In a disintegrative manner, in a way that causes disintegration.
1874 SIMON *Rep. Med. Dept. P.C.* 30 July 6 A force.. acting disintegratively upon organic matter.

Disinterest, *sb.*
2. Delete †*Obs.* and add:
1896 *Sat. Rev.* Suppl. Christmas 4/2 We here see Morris working, with entire disinterest, at his work, and caring above all things for fine workmanship. 1905 *Globe* 19 Sept., The American Press..reproached Japan with her want of disinterest.
3. (Add examples and cf. next.)
1900 *Pilot* 1 Sept. 283/1 The general reader may, without confessing to a heart of stone, feel a certain disinterest in weather and Mrs. Bouveries, however nice and however ill. 1904 *Sat. Rev.* 9 Jan. 34 The whole election was a model of quiet disinterest.

Disinterested, *a.* **1.** Delete † ? *Obs.* and add:
1928 in C. F. S. Gamble *N. Sea Air Station* xiii. 222 Being disinterested with the rest of the proceedings, I opened the file and began to read the theory of Wave Transmission. 1928 *Daily Express* 21 June 11/4 She is listless and disinterested. 1928 *Sunday Dispatch* 8 July 15/2 The English public is disinterested in its theatre.

Disk. Add: **2. d.** A phonograph or gramophone record. Also, see quot. 1929 [2].
1888 *Leisure Hour* 209/1 A disc about eleven inches in diameter can, it is said, contain four minutes' talk. 1907 *Sound Wave & Talking Mach. Record* Dec. 60/2 The world today always associates Edison's phonograph with a cylinder apparatus, but the first phonograph we look at in this patent is a disc (he called it a disk) machine. 1919 A. SEYMOUR *Good-bye-ee!* 37 A gramaphone record with the picture of a foxterrier on the disc. 1929 *Sunday Dispatch* 20 Jan. 16 A fine disc by his orchestra. 1929 *Photoplay* Apr. (Dict. Talkie Terms), *Disc*, the wax record, like a phonograph record, on which sound is recorded.
8. c. *disk-cutter, -fan*; also in the names of American agricultural machines, as *disk-cultivator, -drill, -harrow* (example), *-plough*; **e.** also instrumental and similative, as *disk-adjusting, -capped, -like* adjs.; **disk-anvil** (see quot.); **disk-crank,** a crank composed of a disk or a pair of disks and a crank-pin; **disk electrode** (see quot. 1884 [1]); **disk pile,** an iron pile, having a disk or flange as a foot, used for foundations in sand; **disk-winding** *Electr.*, an armature winding in which the convolutions are flat.
1898 *Cycling* 54 *Disc-adjusting bearings. 1884 KNIGHT *Dict. Mech.* Suppl., **Disk Anvil*, a strengthening plate or reinforce placed inside the bead of a cartridge to support the impact of the striking pin which explodes the fulminate. 1928 *Daily Express* 17 Aug. 2/7 The system of milk distribution by means of *disc-capped bottles. 1888 *Lockwood's Dict. Mech. Engin.*, **Disc Crank*, or *Crank Disc*, or *Crank Plate*, a crank of circular outline in which the metal is so disposed that the varying motion of the connecting-rod is suitably balanced. 1835 URE *Philos. Manuf.* 198 A toothed pinion..gives each *disc-cutter a quick rotatory motion on its centre. 1884 KNIGHT *Dict. Mech.* Suppl., *Disk Cutter*, an instrument for cutting circles of thin glass for covers of microscopic objects on slides. 1907 L. H. BAILEY *Cycl. Amer. Agric.* I. 207 The *disc drill is also used very extensively in many sections of the country. 1884 KNIGHT *Dict. Mech.* Suppl., **Disk Electrode*,..an electrode for telegraphic instruments in which the connection is secured by the contact of the peripheries of two disks. 1884 P. HIGGS *Magn. & Dyn.-electr. Mach.* 104 A kind of voltaic battery in which only one metal was employed, the disk-electrodes of which were rendered active by polarisation. 1903 *Westm. Gaz.* 9 Dec. 8/2 The air..is drawn out by a *disc-fan. 1907 L. H. BAILEY *Cycl. Amer. Agric.* I. 385 The revolving *disc harrow or plow, with its concave discs moving obliquely through the soil. 1893 TUCKEY *Amphioxus* 137 A *disc-like thickening of the hypoblast. 1902 *Westm. Gaz.* 3 Sept. 10/2 Disc-like expansions of the fingers and toes. 1895 *Ibid.* 19 Dec. 8/2 The structure is..to be supported on *disc piles sunk to a depth of 30 ft. in the sand. 1881 *U.S. Patent* 15 Mar. 9603 *Disk plow. 1907 [see *disk harrow* above]. 1902 *Encycl. Brit.* XXVII. 577/2 The fourth or *disc winding was in principle employed in many of the earliest machines.

Di·sking, *vbl. sb.* [f. DISK *sb.* 2.] Cultivation with a disk-plough. *Disking machine* (see quot.).
1884 KNIGHT *Dict. Mech.* Suppl., *Disking Machine*,..a steam-cultivating implement to be drawn by an engine over sod or plowed sod. 1917 *Ninth Crop Bulletin* (Wash., D.C.) 5 Apr. 4/2 Disking and plowing has commenced.

Disloyalist. (Earlier U.S. examples.)
1863 *Boston Sunday Her.* 24 May 1/3. 1870 *Congress. Globe* 7 July 5310/3 The county of Monroe [in Missouri] was the place where disloyalists fleeing from other counties took shelter all the time.

Dismayingly (dismē·iŋli), *adv.* Delete †*Obs.* and add:
1918 M. & J. FINDLATER *Penny Monypenny* III. iv. 300 It was now dismayingly hot. 1926 *Chambers's Jrnl.* 337/2 She would have found it dismayingly difficult to conduct the most juvenile class.

Dismiss, *v.* Add: **3. c.** To free from (an office) by a formal discharge. *U.S.*
1907 *Springfield Weekly Republ.* 7 Mar. 14 Rev. T. Claire Luce..who recently resigned on account of ill-health, was Monday formally dismissed by a council representing the neighbouring churches.
10. c. To discharge or acquit (an accused person).
1904 *N.Y. Times* 30 Apr. 9 Judge McCann of the Police Court had received requests from women all over the city asking that Mrs. Wiggs be dismissed.

Dismoded (dismōu·dĕd), *a.* Anglicization of *DÉMODÉ.
1898 *Blackw. Mag.* Nov. 693/2 A tune dismoded, common. 1907 *Ibid.* Sept. 428 His ambition was the ambition now wholly dismoded, to make scholars and gentlemen. 1917 *Daily Mail* 25 Aug. 2/4 The works of Frith, Leighton, and other dismoded veterans. 1922 *Blackw. Mag.* June 806/1 The men of genius who are its peculiar glory seem dismoded to the anarchs who write in hopeless competition with them.

Dismountable (dismau·ntăb'l), *a.* [f. DISMOUNT *v.* + -ABLE.] Capable of being dismounted. Of a gun or cannon: Capable of being removed from its carriage for transport.
1711 *Fingall MSS.* in *10th Rep. Hist. MSS. Comm.* App. v. 168 The garrison had a battery..which..was not dismountable, by reason of its lowness. 1900 *Engineering Mag.* XIX. 789/2 A gun made dismountable, that it may be easily carried by men or animals. 1903 *Westm. Gaz.* 17 Nov. 9/1 The gun is provided with..dismountable shields.

Disorderly, *a.* Add: **B.** *sb.* A disorderly person.
1852 MUNDY *Antipodes* (1857) 200 A brace of disorderlies in handcuffs. 1855 *Illustr. Lond. News* 21 July 74/1 One of the drunk and disorderlies. 1905 *Daily Chron.* 9 Oct. 5/3 The Pope was obliged to threaten the disorderlies with expulsion from the Vatican.

Disordination (disǫɹdinē·ʃən). (Modern examples.)
1896 *Pop. Sci. Monthly* Feb. 521, I would propose the term *disordination*, the etymological opposite of coordination. 1897 *Educ. Rev.* XIII. 52 The phenomena of hypnotic disordination or disruption of consciousness.

Disowner (disōu·nəɹ). [f. DISOWN *v.*] One who disowns.
1895 J. SMITH *Perm. Mess. Exodus* ix. 126 The disowners of God.

Dispatch, *sb.* **12.** Add: *dispatch-carrier*; **dispatch-boat** (earlier example); **dispatch money** (see quot. 1923); **dispatch note,** a memorandum required to be made in addition to the customs declaration for foreign parcel post; **dispatch rider,** one who rides on horseback or bicycle to carry dispatches; so **dispatch riding; dispatch-vessel** = *dispatch-boat*.
1807 *Deb. Congress* (1852) 614, I received by a *despatch boat an invitation to dine. 1905 *Daily Chron.* 1 Aug. 3/1 A *dispatch-carrier for the Foreign Office. 1878 *Law Jrnl. Rep.* Q.B. XLVII. 513/1 If the Court shall be of opinion that..*despatch-money..is to be paid per working day of twelve hours. 1923 *D. Maclachlan's Merchant Shipping* (ed. 6) 428 Despatch money is a term which designates a payment which the Shipowner agrees to make for time saved out of the lay-days. 1892 *Post Office Guide* Oct. 383 Parcels for Foreign Countries must..be accompanied by a *Despatch Note. 1899 *Daily News* 18 Oct. 7/2 A report brought from the north by *dispatch riders, via Vryburg. 1907 *Daily Chron.* 10 Jan. 9/5 An interesting *dispatch-riding test from Newcastle and London to Manchester. 1809 *Deb. Congress* 21 Feb. 432 There may be time for the *despatch vessel to go to France and return.

Dispatching (dispæ·tʃiŋ), *vbl. sb.* Add: also Comb. **dispatching-sheet** (see quot.).
1918 H. CROY *How Motion Pictures are Made* 254 On shipment of the film the photographer makes out a title and a despatching-sheet which shows the light conditions.

Dispenser. Add: **3. b.** An attendant who serves out aerated water at a soda-fountain.
1925 *Daily Tel.* 13 May 20 Soda water dispenser required, to supervise six fountains.

Dispensing, *vbl. sb.* **b.** Add: **dispensing-counter,** a counter at which medical prescriptions are made up.
1898 *Rev. Brit. Pharm.* 14 The syrup of glucose generally used at the dispensing-counter.

Dispeo·plement. [f. DISPEOPLE *v.*] The process of dispeopling, depopulation.
1841 H. S. FOOTE *Texas & Texans* I. 14 To mark its dreadful course with the dispeoplement of her infant towns and villages.

Dispermy (dəi·spə̄ɹmi). *Biol.* [f. DI-[2] + Gr. σπέρμα seed + -Y [3].] The entrance of two spermatozoa into a single egg. Hence **Dispe·rmic** *a.*
1896 E. B. WILSON *The Cell* 335 Dispermy. 1905 *Rep. Brit. Assoc.* 432 Dispermic eggs.

Disperse (dispə̄·ɹs). *Chem.* The verb-stem used *attrib.* in **disperse phase, system** (see quots. 1927); also **dispersed phase.** So **Dispersion, Dispersoid** (see quots. 1915, 1919, 1924, 1927).
1915 WASHBURN *Princ. Phys. Chem.* 361 If we imagine any phase within a given system to be gradually broken up into smaller and smaller particles, then as the size of these particles gradually decreases the surface of contact between this phase and its neighbors will correspondingly increase and the effects of forces of the nature of surface tension.. will gradually become more apparent, and these surface forces will eventually begin to be an important factor in determining the fugacities of the molecular species composing the system. Whenever this situation exists to an appreciable extent..we have what is called a disperse system or a dispersoid. *Ibid.*, The degree of dispersion of a dispersed phase is usually defined as the ratio of its surface to its volume. 1919 E. HENDRICK *Chem. Everyday Life* 74 Soap is a colloid, and when we get a little of it in a great deal of water we have it in dispersion. 1923 W. CLAYTON *Theory Emulsions* 1 That liquid which is broken up into globules is termed the dispersed phase. 1924 A. FINDLAY *Phys. Chem.* 173 A colloidal sol..consists of finely divided particles (the dispersed phase) distributed throughout a dispersion medium. 1927 CROCKER & MATTHEWS *Th. & Exper. Phys. Chem.* 273 *Dispersator*, a protective colloid used to stabilise colloidal solutions made mechanically, e.g., in the Plauson mill. *Disperse phase*, the discontinuous constituent of a colloidal solution corresponding to the solute in true solution. *Disperse system*, any colloidal solution. A two-phase system with greatly developed surfaces. *Ibid.* 274 *Dispersion medium*, the continuous phase in a colloidal solution, corresponding to the solvent in true solution.

Dispersedness. (Modern U.S. example.)
1897 *Atlantic Monthly* LXXX. 544 It..gives added cohesion to a great institution whose topographical dispersedness is surpassed only by its enormous enrollment.

Dispiral (dəispəiə·răl), *a. Bot.* [f. DI-[2] + SPIRAL *sb.*] = *DISPIROUS *a.*
1899 W. H. PEARSON *Hepaticæ Brit. Isles* I. 15 Elaters in almost all cases dispiral, rarely monospiral or 3–4 spiral.

Dispireme (dəispəi·rīm). *Cytology.* Also -em. [f. DI-[2] + Gr. σπείρημα spire, coil.] (See quot. 1896.)
1890 SIR W. TURNER *Cell Theory* 31 In the..dispirem stage, the chromatin threads thicken and shorten. 1896 E. B. WILSON *The Cell* 336 *Dispireme*..., that stage of mitosis in which each daughter-nucleus has given rise to a spireme.

Dispirous (dəispəi·rəs), *a. Bot.* [f. DI-[2] + Gr. σπεῖρα coil, spiral + -OUS.] Of the elaters of the *Hepaticæ*: Having double spirals.
1900 B. D. JACKSON *Gloss. Bot. Terms.*

Displacement. Add: **3. d.** *Bot.* Abnormality in the position or form of a leaf or organ.
1869 MASTERS *Veget. Teratol.* 89 Instances of displacement of leaves arising from suppression.
4. *attrib.* and *Comb.*, as *displacement apparatus* (see 3 c), *cylinder, lubricator*.
1874 GARROD & BAXTER *Mat. Med.* (1880) 277 Place the bark in a *displacement apparatus and percolate with the diluted hydrochloric acid. 1888 *Lockwood's Dict. Mech. Engin.*, **Displacement Cylinder*, an auxiliary cylinder belonging to some gas engines, by which the constituents of the charge are forced into the working or power cylinder. **Displacement Lubricator*, a lubricator which acts by the difference in the sp. gr. of oil and of water. An impermeator is one form of displacement lubricator.

Display, *sb.* **5.** Add: **display hand,** (*a*) one who sets up display-type; (*b*) a pyrotechnist employed chiefly to assist in firework displays.
1896 *Daily News* 1 Dec. 12/7 Compositor.—First-class Jobbing and Display Hand seeks situation. 1921 *Dict. Occup. Terms* (1927) § 148 *Display hand*..; *pyrotechnist*; assists at firework display, lighting fuses [etc.].

Disposedly, *adv.* Add: In mod. instances echoing the 'high and disposedly' of quot. 1610 in Dict., used = with lofty dignity.
1904 FARRER *Garden Asia* 187 Go-betweens conduct the negotiations, high and disposedly as Queen Elizabeth. 1907 J. H. MCCARTHY *Needles & Pins* viii, The company.. marched up the aisle very disposedly. 1924 P. G. WODEHOUSE *Leave it to Psmith* ix. § 5. 195 Through the belt of rhododendrons..a portly form..made itself visible, moving high and disposedly in the direction of the back premises.

Dispossessed, *ppl. a.* Add: Also *absol.* with *the*.
1901 *Macm. Mag.* Apr. 411/2 Throughout Ireland, on the whole, Protestants are the possessors, Catholics the dispossessed. 1909 *Englishwoman* Apr. 305 Woman rebelled because she belonged to the classes of the dispossessed.

Disquieten (diskwəi·ĕt'n), *v.* [f. DIS- 6 + QUIETEN *v.*] = DISQUIET *v.*
1921 *Glasgow Herald* 9 Mar. 10 Her condition is disquietening. *Ibid.* 23 Sept. 7 In view of disquietening reports as to their activities in the Near East. 1928 L. ROSSITER *Sex Age* viii, She turned, bewildered and disquietened, from the sickening turmoil.

Disquietingly (diskwəi·ĕtiŋli), *adv.* [f. DISQUIETING *ppl. a.* + -LY [2].] In a disquieting manner.
1922 *Public Opinion* 23 June 580/1 A tendency to change strangely and disquietingly. 1918 *Britain's Industr. Future* (*Lib. Ind. Inq.*) IV. xxvii. 398 In some industrial centres there is a disquietingly high percentage of registered unskilled workers between the ages of eighteen and twenty-five.

Disraelian (dizrē·liăn), *a.* [f. name of Benjamin *Disraeli*, first Earl of Beaconsfield (1804–1881), prominent Tory politician and prime minister.] Pertaining to or characteristic of Disraeli or his opinions, measures, or writings.

1901 *N. Amer. Rev.* Feb. 252 The great Disraelian Myth, which has changed the most un-English of all our Prime Ministers into an almost sacramental Symbol of Patriotism. 1927 *Observer* 11 Dec. 15/2 A devout Disraelian Tory. 1927 H. MILES tr. *A. Maurois' Disraeli* 296 Even abroad the altogether Disraelian boldness of this *coup* was extolled.

Disrelate (disrĭlē·t), *v.* [See DISRELATED *ppl. a.*] *trans.* To sever the connexion between, cause to have no connexion with.
1654 J. OWEN *Doctr. Saints Persev.* xv. 353 True Believers who only are the members of Christ disrelate themselves to him. 1895 *Westm. Gaz.* 25 Nov. 2/3 Something analogous to a sense of prudery has caused the author slightly to disrelate the two contestants for Lois.

Disremember, *v.* (Earlier and recent U.S. examples.)
1815 in *Doc. Hist. Amer. Industr. Soc.* (1910) IV. 25. I belonged to the Society about fifteen months; as to the constitution I disremember, the rules I recollect. 1928 BYRNE *Destiny Bay* viii. 382 Either in Ohio or Illinois, I disremember which.

Disrobing, *vbl. sb.*: (see after DISROBE *v.*). Add quots. illustrating recent currency.
1903 MCNEILL *Egregious Engl.* 58 The bare business of robing and disrobing takes up pretty well half her waking day. 1912 L. A. HARKER *Mr. Wyckerly's Wards* x, Neither of them cared a whit for Jane-Anne and her disrobings.

Disrupture, *sb.* (Earlier Amer. example.)
1782 JEFFERSON *Notes Virginia* (1787) 27 The evident marks of their disrupture and avulsion from their beds by the most powerful agents of nature corroborate the impression.

Dissava (disā·vă). Also 7 dissauva, 8 dissuava, dissave. [Sinhalese *disāwa*.] A governor of a district of Ceylon.
1681 R. KNOX *Hist. Rel. Ceylon* 35 He gives order to his *Dissava's* or Governors of the Countreys to..choose out Boyes. *Ibid.* 50 Next under the Adigars, are the *Dissauva's*. 1720 DE FOE *Captain Singleton* 294 The King of the Country..sent down a *Dissuava*, or General, with an Army. 1803 R. PERCIVAL *Ceylon* 258 The Dissauvas, as long as they hold their office, are allowed by the king a certain portion of land for their services. 1859 J. E. TENNENT *Ceylon* II. 91 The dissave of Oovah..placed himself at the head of the insurgents.

Dissection. 7. Add: Applied to wounds, etc. contracted by dissectors.
1884 T. BRYANT *Pract. Surg.* (ed. 4) I. ii. 122 Dissection wounds.

Dissector. Add: **b.** A dissecting instrument.
a 1860 ALB. SMITH *Med. Student* (1861) 6 He perpetually carries a Dublin dissector under his arm. 1910 *Practitioner* July 118 If the appendix..is concealed under massive granulations, careful search with swab, blunt dissector and the occasional use of scissors will rarely fail to bring it into view.

Dissociated (disōu·ʃiēted), *ppl. a.* (See under DISSOCIATE *v.*) Add: *Psychol.* Characterized by the disjunction of associated mental connexions or the disaggregation of consciousness. *Dissociated personality*, a pathological state of the mind in which two or more distinct personalities exist in the same person. (Rarely used as active verb.)
1911 I. H. CORIAT *Abnormal Psychology* 7 When an experience or complex has become dissociated, it tends to act automatically, and cannot be controlled by the will. 1912 B. HART *Psychol. Insanity* iv. 47 That the continuous stream of her thought had been interrupted by the sudden appearance of a 'dissociated system of ideas'. 1918 C. S. MYERS *Present-day Applic. Psychol.* 35 Irène had undergone a severe shock owing to the death of her mother. ..Shortly after, Irène began to develope a dissociated personality. 1919 BRADBY *Psycho-Anal.* 68 If we cannot readily recall such principles at will for a critical overhauling then we are in danger of becoming 'dissociated', of doing the thing and not knowing why we do it. *Ibid.* 70 It links up proverbial knowledge of human nature with the phenomena of 'dissociated personality'. 1922 *Encycl. Brit.* XXXII. 200/1 As a little girl of three, 'Doris Fischer' was thrown down violently by her drunken father, and so sustained a psychic fracture, which 'dissociated' her into 'Margaret' and 'Real Doris'. 1924 W. B. SELBIE *Psychol. Relig.* 291 It is not necessary to presuppose a secondary personality or a dissociated consciousness.

Dissociation. Add: **3.** *Psychol.* The process or result of breaking up associations of ideas.
1890 W. JAMES *Princ. Psychol.* I. 506 What is associated now with one thing and now with another tends to become dissociated from either...One might call this the law of dissociation by varying concomitants. 1890 J. M. BALDWIN *Handbk. Psychol.* (ed. 2) 218 The part played by dissociation is evident. If there were no such breaking up of representations, imagination would be simply memory.
b. The disintegration of consciousness, the state in which a person suffers from dissociated personality.
1897 E. PARISH *Halluc. & Illus.* 71 If we..seek for some quality common to all the various states in which hallucinations occur, we shall find that their most striking characteristic is the dissociation of consciousness. 1908 W. MCDOUGALL in *Brain* July 257 That cerebral dissociation of some degree is at least one of the essential features of the hypnotic state can..hardly be doubted. 1922 *Encycl. Brit.* XXXII. 200/1 Other cases of dissociation (e.g. the 'Watseka Wonder').

Dissoconch (di·sokǫŋk)., *Zool.* [f. Gr. δισσός double + CONCH.] The shell of a mollusc in the veliger stage; also, the shell of an adult bivalve.
1888 JACKSON in *Proc. Boston Soc. Nat. Hist.* XXIII. 543 In the oyster..this [*sc.* the earlier] shell is not single, but double-valved, and, therefore, deserves a distinct name, as it precedes the dissoconch or true shell.

Dissogony (disǫ·gŏni). *Biol.* [f. Gr. δισσός double + γόνος offspring.] A form of reproduction among the *Ctenophora*, in which there are two periods of sexual maturity in the same individual, one in the larval and another in the adult form. Hence **Disso·gonous** *a.*
1896 LYDEKKER *Roy. Nat. Hist.* VI. 477 In at least one species (*Eucharis multicornis*) sexually mature larvæ, or larvæ which are capable of reproduction as such, also occur; these, when completely developed, become once more capable of reproduction as adults;—a method of multiplication which has been called dissogony.

Dissolve, *v.* Add: **7. b.** In cinematography, to cause (a picture) to become faint or fade away (*into* another); similarly *intr.* (cf. 13); also in **Disso·lving** *ppl. a.* Hence **Disso·lve** *sb.*, the act or process of dissolving a picture; a dissolving scene in a cinema film; a piece of apparatus with the aid of which this is produced. **Disso·lver,** an apparatus for dissolving a picture; also *attrib.*
1912 F. H. RICHARDSON *Motion Picture Handbk.* (ed. 2) 375 The lamps of a dissolver should each one be connected just as though the other one did not exist. *Ibid.* 377 To construct a home-made dissolver shutter. *Ibid.* 378 A dissolving effect with one lens is an impossibility. *Ibid.*, Your dissolver lens must be matched. 1915 *Ibid.* (ed. 3) 604 The upper dissolver lamp must be supplied with amperage equal to the projection machine arc. *Ibid.* 606 Dissolving moving picture. *Ibid.*, Many operators who run two machines dissolve one reel into the next. 1918 HOMER CROY *How Motion Pictures are Made* vii. 176 The second means of accomplishing a fade picture is by means of the dissolving shutter...The dissolving shutter is a mechanical device which, while the shutter is revolving, is closed by a blade slowly passing over the opening until it is entirely closed. *Ibid.* 178 The so-called 'dissolve', by which the figures of the scene gradually disappear while those of a succeeding scene slowly take their place. 1923 F. A. TALBOT *Moving Pictures* xx. 274 The conventional type of studio camera..is equipped with what is known as the mechanical automatic 'dissolve'.

Dissuader (see under DISSUADE *v.*). Add: Also, a thing which dissuades.
1883 M. ARNOLD *Lett.* (1895) II. 216, I relied on a dissuader from you.

Distearin (dəistī·ărin). *Chem.* [f. DI-[2] + STEARIN.] That form of stearin derived from glycerin by the replacement of two of the three OH groups by stearyl groups.
1873 RALFE *Phys. Chem.* 48 Stearic acid forms with glycerin 3 compounds, Monostearin, Distearin, and Tristearin. 1879 [see MONOSTEARIN].

Distemperer. Delete *rare* and add:
1881 *Instr. Census Clerks* (1885) 52 Colourer. Decorator. Distemperer. 1901 *Daily Chron.* 10 Sept. 9/7 Painter, Distemperer.—Good brush hand wants Work.

Distensile (diste·nsəil, -il), *a.* Delete †*Obs.* *rare*, add quots., and extend def.: Also, capable of distending or causing distention.
1879 *St. George's Hosp. Rep.* IX. 337 Over the whole of this tumour could be felt well-marked distensile pulsation. 1902 *Encycl. Brit.* XXXI. 360/2 As a result of these fibrous changes there is interference with the blood current, since the vessels become unyielding yet frangible, instead of distensile and elastic, tubes. 1907 *Practitioner* Nov. 621 This distensile force would have been amply sufficient to cause dilatation of the ventricular cavity. 1910 *Ibid.* Apr. 482 Forcible inflation under pressure may also be done by compressing the india-rubber tube between the distensile bulb and the proximal glass tube.

Distinguished, *ppl. a.* **4.** Add: *Distinguished Service Order* (abbrev. D.S.O.), an order of distinction for British naval, military, and air force commissioned officers, instituted 9 Nov. 1886. *Distinguished Conduct Medal* (abbrev. D.C.M.), a distinction, instituted in 1862, awarded to warrant officers, non-commissioned officers, and men for distinguished conduct in the field. Also *Distinguished Service Cross* (D.S.C.), *Flying Cross* (D.F.C.), *Service Medal* (D.S.M.), *Flying Medal* (D.F.M.): see quots.
1862 in *Royal Warrants*, etc. (1864) 289 No retrospective action will be given to the warrant in question, so far as 'distinguished conduct' medals without annuity or gratuity are concerned. 1914 *Times* 19 Oct. 3/5 His Majesty has been pleased to approve of the establishment of a medal, to be called the Distinguished Service Medal, to be awarded to chief petty officers, petty officers, men, and boys of all branches of the Royal Navy, to non-commissioned officers and men of the Royal Marines, and to all other persons holding corresponding positions in his Majesty's Service afloat, for distinguished conduct in war in cases where the award of the Conspicuous Gallantry Medal would not be applicable. His Majesty has further approved of the award of the Conspicuous Service Cross (to be designated in future the Distinguished Service Cross) to all officers below the rank of Lieutenant-Commander in addition to the officers previously eligible for this Decoration. 1918 *Ibid.* 3 June 7/5 'The Distinguished Flying Cross', to be awarded to officers and warrant officers for acts of gallantry when flying in active operations against the enemy...'The Distinguished Flying Medal', to be awarded to non-commissioned officers and men for acts of courage or devotion to duty when flying, although not in active operations against the enemy.

Distinguo (disti·ŋgwo). [L., = I distinguish.] A distinction in thought or reasoning.
1920 *Contemp. Rev.* Mar. 364 When one hears that put in so unqualified a way, certain *distinguos* at once present themselves to the mind.

Distortion. Add: **4.** The uneven frequency response of electrical apparatus, usually causing bad reproduction. Hence **Disto·rtionless** *a.*
1914 ROLFE-MARTIN *Wireless Telegr.* 117 It is found that, owing chiefly to dielectric losses in the condenser, the distortion has a still greater weakening effect on radiating power. 1921 *Jrnl. Inst. Electr. Engineers* Apr. 397/2 For satisfactory transmission of speech the circuit should also be practically 'distortionless'. 1925 *Chambers's Jrnl.* 220/1 The invention of a new distortionless [telegraph] cable. 1928 *Morning Post* 16 Feb. 13/4 Too much grid bias causes distortion by reducing the high tension current.

Distraction. Add: **1. f.** *Surg.* The action of drawing apart normally opposed surfaces.
1901 DORLAND *Med. Dict.* (ed. 2).

Distress, *sb.* **5.** Add: (sense 2 c) *distress call, light, message, signal, signalling*; **distress committee,** a committee set up to help people in distressed circumstances; **distress work,** work provided for people in distress.
1913 *Year-Bk. Wireless Telegr. & Teleph.* 319 Accumulators, enabling the ship to issue *distress calls. 1905 *Daily Chron.* 21 Sept. 1/7 The establishment of *distress committees. 1885 *Encycl. Brit.* XVIII. 818/1 Inextinguishable *distress-lights. 1921 *Discovery* Apr. 92/2 A *distress message is preceded by a signal consisting of three dots, three dashes, and three dots sent as one sign, and repeated at short intervals. This is usually alluded to as the S.O.S. signal. 1873 *Porcupine* 6 Sept. 361/1 It is necessary for all craft to carry a gun for use in making *distress signals. 1913 *Year-Bk. Wireless Telegr. & Teleph.* 318 *Distress Signalling. 1905 *Daily Chron.* 13 Nov. 4/4 The *distress work is not provided except in emergencies.

Distressed. Add: **c.** Upon which a distress is levied.
1896 *Westm. Gaz.* 24 June 3/1 The Government had never said they could discriminate between land distressed and land not distressed.

Distributary, *a.* and *sb.* Add: **A.** *adj.* **2.** *spec.* in *distributary canal, channel, river*.
1926 *Spectator* 24 Apr. 736/2 To excavate additional distributary canals and flood channels.
B. *sb.* **2.** A river branch which flows away from the main stream without returning to it, as in a delta.
1863 J. FERGUSSON in *Q. Jrnl. Geol. Soc.* XIX. 328 One consequence of any such alteration in the course of the main stream is, that the initial or terminal oscillation of any tributary or distributary is continually altering its position. 1881 *Times* 16 Aug. 3/6 [A river's] breaking up into distributaries as it approaches the sea. 1891–2 *13th Ann. Rep. U.S. Geol. Surv.* (1893) III. 171 The canal skirts the slopes of the foothills to the north on a changing grade, the object of which is to diminish its discharge as the various distributaries are diverted from it.

Distributing, *vbl. sb.* **b.** Add: **distributing box** *Electr.*, a box containing apparatus for the distribution of an electric current; **distributing-table** *Printing*, an inking-table.
1913 V. B. LEWES *Oil Fuel* 109 The wires for each lamp.. should be carried to the lamp from a *distributing-box placed outside the pump-room or companion. 1890 W. J. GORDON *Foundry* 190 His new perfecting machine was fitted with the *distributing-table and 'end motion' of the composition inking-rollers.

Distributism (distri·biutiz'm). [Short for **Distri·butivism,** f. DISTRIBUTIVE *a.* + -ISM.] The theory of the 'distributive state' (Hilaire Belloc), in which the possession of personal property is to be assured to all. Hence **Distri·but(iv)ist.**
1915 E. BARKER *Pol. Tht. in Engl.* viii. 223 Mr. Belloc's Distributivism. 1926 *G. K.'s Weekly* 18 Sept. 13/1 In Switzerland distributism is not confined to economics..and distributists who [etc.]. 1927 *Ibid.* 17 Sept. 605 Nor do we decide how far machinery may be used in the Distributist State. 1927 *Church Times* 22 July 105/2 With the extreme revolutionaries of the Clyde, and with Guild Socialists and distributists represented by Sir Henry Slesser, Mr. Lloyd George and his capitalist friends can have nothing in common.

Distributive, *a.* Add:
2. b. *Distributive fault*, a fault in which the displacement is distributed among several parallel planes at short distances from one another instead of being confined to a single plane.
1905 CHAMBERLIN & SALISBURY *Geol.* I. 494 Sometimes the faulting is distributed among a series of parallel planes,.. thus giving rise to a distributive fault.

Distributor. b. Add: *Electr.* An apparatus for distributing an electric current. 1911 WEBSTER.

District, *sb.* Add: **3. b.** attrib. *General district fund, rate* (see quot.).
1902 *Encycl. Brit.* XXX. 318/2 As a general rule, all the expenses of carrying into execution the Public Health Acts in an urban district fall upon a fund which is called the general district fund, and that fund is provided by means of a rate called the general district rate.
d. *U.S.* (Earlier example.)
1792 *Mass. Acts & Resolves* (1895) 185 The first district shall consist of the Counties of Suffolk Essex & Middlesex & shall be entitled to choose four representatives.
f. A territorial division of the Methodist communions comprising a number of circuits.
1839 [see CIRCUIT *sb.* 6]. 1885 [see sense 6 in Dict.].
g. Short for *Metropolitan District Railway*; also *pl.* shares in this railway.
1898 *Westm. Gaz.* 29 Nov. 8/1 We cannot find any sufficient reason for the recent rise in Districts. 1902 *Ibid.* 29 May 7/3 To travel on the District from Ealing to the Mansion House and back, third-class, will in the future cost 8d. 1909 *Ibid.* 16 July 10/3 Districts were also good in tone at 17½.

6. district attorney *U.S.* (example); also as *v.*; **district court** (earlier example); **district curves,** in terrestrial magnetism, curves obtained by joining the successive points where isogonals, isoclinals, etc., intersect the lines of latitude; **district judge** (earlier example); **district lines** = **district curves*; **district messenger,** one employed by the District Messenger Service (see quot.); **district nurse,** a nurse who serves a rural district; so *district nursing*; **district school** (later U.S. examples); **district system** *U.S.*, a system of electing members to the House of Representatives by electing one member for each district of a State (see sense 3 d in Dict.).
1856 S. MORDECAI *Virginia* vii. (1860) 101 The office of *district attorney in the United States Court of Virginia. 1873 'MARK TWAIN' & WARNER *Gilded Age* liv. 493 The district attorney..opened the case for the state. 1922 ALICE BROWN *Old Crow* vi. 67 You're district-attorneying it a trifle too much to interest me...This isn't a third degree. 1791 WASHINGTON *Diaries* IV. 186 The *District Court is held in it [*sc.* Salisbury]. 1800 WEEMS *Lett.* II. 150, I can't think of the Dumfries District Court with patience. 1902 *Encycl. Brit.* XXX. 461/1 [Rücker and Thorpe] found where isogonals, isoclinals, &c., cut the lines of latitude. The curves obtained by joining these successive points of intersection on a map are called *district lines or curves. 1789 *U.S. Stat. Large* I. 73 And it be further enacted That there be a court called a District Court..to consist of one judge.. called a *District Judge [etc.]. 1911 *Chambers's Jrnl.* I. 208/1 The *District Messenger Service was founded in London in 1890 for the purpose of introducing..the electric call-box system. 1902 *Encycl. Brit.* XXXI. 298/1 *District nursing, which is the highest and most exacting branch of the profession...A *district nurse should be able to do everything for the patient. 1854 MARY J. HOLMES *Tempest & Sunshine* viii. 111 He handed him five hundred dollars, telling him..to send her for two years to the *district school. 1874 *Rep. Vermont Board Agric.* II. 609 Until I was twenty-five, laboring on the farm in summer and teaching district school in winter. 1902 *Encycl. Brit.* XXXIII. 581/2 The House of Representatives is composed of members elected by popular vote...Each State is at liberty under the Constitution to adopt either the 'general ticket' system, *i.e.*, the plan of electing all its members by one vote over the whole State, or to elect them in one-membered districts (the '*district system').

District, *v.* Add: Orig. and chiefly *U.S.*
1792 *Mass. Acts & Resolves* (1895) 184 Resolve for districting the commonwealth, for the purpose of choosing federal representatives. 1806 WEBSTER, *District*, v.t. to divide into circuits or parts.

Disturb, *v.* Add:
1. d. *refl.* To put oneself out by moving, etc. (e.g. in order to oblige a person).
1831 T. L. PEACOCK *Crotchet Castle* iii, The stranger was rising up, when Mr. Crotchet begged him not to disturb himself. 1888 MRS. H. WARD *Robt. Elsmere* xiii, 'Can I find anything for you?' he said springing up. She hesitated a moment, then..she said..: 'Pray don't disturb yourself. I know exactly where to find it.'

Disunionist. (Earlier U.S. example.)
1831 *Deb. Congress* 15 June 3572 Those who denounce them ..are branded as disunionists and nullifiers.
So **Disunionism.** (Earlier U.S. reference.)
1855 *Boston Post* 24 Aug. 2/1.

Ditch, *sb.*[1] Add:
1. c. Calcutta, so called in allusion to the Mahratta Ditch (see MAHRATTA 3). *slang.*
1886 YULE & BURNELL *Anglo-Ind. Gloss.*, *Ditch*; and *Ditcher*, disparaging sobriquets for Calcutta and its European citizens.
d. The ground (formerly a trench) immediately surrounding a bowling green.
1861 *Chambers's Encycl.* II. 289/1 If a bowl..strikes the jack, and then rolls into the ditch, it reckons as if on the green. 1886 *Rules of Bowling* 16 When the jack is run into the ditch by a bowl in the regular course of the game. 1902 *Encycl. Brit.* XXVI. 328/1 There is no excuse for short play on the part of the first players; their bowls would be far better in the ditch.

Ditch, *v.*[1] Add:
8. *intr.* To take to a ditch, take refuge in a ditch.
1876 *Coursing Calendar* 73 Scotch Broth passed his opponent, but puss ditching, the course ended.

Ditcher. Add: **2.** (Earlier U.S. example.)
1846 *Rep.* (U.S.) *Comm. Patents* (1847) 236 Having thus fully described my improved ditcher what I claim therein as new..is [etc.].
4. A bowl which runs or is driven off the green.
1886 *Rules of Bowling* 17.
5. A resident in Calcutta (cf. *DITCH *sb.*[1] 1 c). *slang.*
1886 [see *DITCH *sb.*[1] 1 c]. 1909 *Westm. Gaz.* 17 June 8/1 The existence of the unfortunate ditchers left to themselves in the off season. 1923 *United Free Ch. Miss. Rec.* June 248/1 Residents in Calcutta are sometimes referred to in prints of origin other than Bengal as 'Ditchers'.

Ditching, *vbl. sb.* **c.** *ditching-machine* (earlier U.S. examples).
1838 H. W. ELLSWORTH *Valley Upper Wabash* iv. 35 The recent improvements in ditching machines. 1846 *Rep.* (U.S.) *Comm. Patents* (1847) 306 What I claim therein as new..is the combination of the two ditching machines. 1854 J. R. BARTLETT *Personal Narr.* II. xxii. 18 In one place I saw a ditching machine in operation.

Dite, *sb.*[2] Also dit. Phr. *Not to care a dit(e)*: not to care at all.
1907 *Westm. Gaz.* 7 Sept. 23/1 'Don't care a dite', Sylvia said despondently. 1920 *Blackw. Mag.* Oct. 488/2, 'I suppose your major won't mind that?' 'Not a tuppenny dit.'

Dithematic (dəiþimæ·tik), *a.* [f. DI-[2] + THEMATIC.] Of a word: Containing two significant themes or stems. Also as *sb.*
1916 WEEKLEY *Surnames* 26 These Teutonic names were originally all dithematic [*sic*]. 1922 — in *N. & Q.* 12th Ser. XI. 52/2 Some old Teutonic dithematic.

Dither, *sb.* Add: **b.** A state of tremulous excitement or apprehension; chiefly in phr. *all of a dither*.
1819 'PAUL BOBBIN' (J. Butterworth) *Sequel to Lanc. Dial.* 6 (E.D.D.) I'm aw on o' dither, if th' wynt bo sturs a twig. 1899 WATTS-DUNTON *Aylwin* xii. 331 The sight o' both on us..might make the poor body all of a dither if she was very ill. 1929 PRIESTLEY *Good Comp.* III. ii. 500 They'll rehearse all right...When it comes to the night, all of a dither. 1931 E. SACKVILLE-WEST *Simpson* III. xvii, She quickly pulled herself together, feeling that such a state of dither would not, if she showed it, illustrate her name.

Dithyrambically (diþiræ·mbikăli), *adv.* [f. DITHYRAMBIC: see -ICALLY.] In or as in dithyrambs; with dithyrambic or 'lyrical' expression.
1891 SYMONDS in *Biog.* (1895) II. 332 Tell me if you would like me to write what I think about their excellence—not dithyrambically, as here, but soberly as art requires. 1905 *Spectator* 11 Mar. 371/1 M. Santos-Dumont writes interestingly, if dithyrambically, of the future of the airship.

Ditto, *v.* Add: **b.** To say or do 'ditto'.
1894 HELEN GARDENER *Unofficial Patriot* 299 They are sulking in their tents and we are dittoing in ours. 1901 *Westm. Gaz.* 22 Mar. 2/1 No, Mr. Balfour knew nothing of Lord Lansdowne's communication. 'Nor I,' dittoed Lord Cranborne.

Di·ttograph, *v.* [f. the sb.] *pass.* To be repeated by dittography.
1897 *Expositor* June 409, X. 22 c is certainly 'dittographed' from v. 22 a. 1906 DRIVER *Jeremiah* 349 The ה at the end is simply dittographed from the following word.

Divali, diwali, var. ff. *DEWALEE.

Dive, *sb.* Add: **1. b.** *Aviation.* A precipitate descent. (Cf. **nose-dive*.)
1914 ROSHER *In R.N.A.S.* (1916) 13 When in the air, he bawls in your ear, 'Now when you push your hand forward, you go down, see!' (and he pushes your hand forward and you make a sudden dive).
3. dive-keeper *U.S.* (examples).
1890 *Nation* (N.Y.) 8 May 367/1 Gamblers, dive-keepers, and rumsellers. 1909 S. E. WHITE *Rules of Game* I. xvi, One of the saloon keepers at Twin Falls...This dive-keeper.. had offered transportation.
b. In wider use, a more or less concealed building or place affording a sanctuary or hiding-place.
1892 STEVENSON & OSBOURNE *Wrecker* viii, I visited Chinese and Mexican gambling-hells, German secret societies, sailors' boarding-houses, and 'dives' of every complexion of the disreputable and dangerous. 1897 *Daily News* 17 Apr. 3/1 From highway into byway they go; now up into tottering garret, then down into dim dive. 1910 *Westm. Gaz.* 25 Jan. 4/1 This dingy 'dive' can boast of many glorious memories.

Dive, *v.* Add: **1. c.** *Aviation.* To descend or fall precipitously with increasing momentum.
1908 H. G. WELLS *War in the Air* iv. § 5 He could feel the airship diving down, down, down. 1914 ROSHER *In R.N.A.S.* (1916) 37, I switched on and off, and dived down through the opening to 1,000 feet. 1916 H. BARBER *Aeroplane Speaks* 136 *Dive*, to descend so steeply as to produce a speed greater than the normal flying speed.

Diver. 2. Add: In Natal, the cormorant.
1906 *Natal Mercury Pictorial* 703 (Pettman) I notice a number of those ugly, useless, and predaceous birds known as divers in the Bay.

Diversion. Add:
6. *attrib.* and *Comb.*: **diversion-cut,** a channel made to divert impure water past a reservoir; **diversion weir,** a weir erected to divert water from a river to the head of an irrigating canal.
1874 KNIGHT *Dict. Mech.*, **Diversion-cut*, a channel to divert past a reservoir a stream of impure or turbid water which would otherwise flow into the reservoir. A by-wash. 1891–2 H. M. WILSON in *13th Ann. Rep. U.S. Geol. Surv.* (1893) III. 231 One of the latest..*diversion weirs constructed in this country is that built at the head of the Turlock and Modesto canals.

Diversity. Add:
4. *attrib.* **diversity factor** *Electr.* (see quots.).
1905 *Fabian Tract* 1106 When we speak of a good diversity factor we mean that the generating station is so happily situated that it meets a regular and constant maximum demand for diverse purposes...A continuous 'diversity factor' makes a good 'load factor'. 1916 *Standardization Rules Amer. Instit. Electr. Engin.* 17 *Diversity Factor*, the ratio of the sum of the maximum power demands of the subdivisions of any system or parts of a system to the maximum demand of the whole system or of the part of the system under consideration, measured at the point of supply.

Diverter. Add: **b.** *Electr.* (See quots.)
1909 *Cent. Dict.* Suppl. s.v. *Diverter*, *Electrical diverter*, a form of combined lightning guard and fuse for telephonic and other electrical apparatus. 1910 *N. Hawkins' Electr. Dict.*, *Diverter*, in electric traction, a name given to a certain type of motor starting-coil, probably because some of the applied voltage is diverted from the motor in forcing the current through the coil against its resistance.

Divesian (dəivī·siăn), *a. Geol.* [f. *Dives*, a river in France.] Denoting a division of the Jurassic system in the vicinity of Dives and other parts of France.
1903 GEIKIE *Text-bk. Geol.* (ed. 4) II. 1150 Upper Callovian (Divesian).

Divide, *sb.* **2.** Add: *The Great Divide*, the watershed of the Rocky Mountains; *fig.* a dividing or boundary line; *spec.* the boundary between life and death.
1879 MISS BIRD *Lady's Life Rocky Mts.* v. 65 The Snowy Range, the backbone or 'divide' of the continent. 1887 HOWORTH *Mammoth & Flood* 256 This catastrophe..is the great Divide when history really begins. 1907 MULFORD *Bar-20* xxiii. 226 Snip! goes his bill an' th' snake slides over th' Divide. 1908 — *Orphan* xi. 139 If he was killed, he would have company across the Great Divide. 1909 *Daily Chron.* 16 Sept. 1/2 He was good to Ruth, and she, too, loved him. But between them still was 'the great divide'. She could not forget that he had bought her for a string of nuggets. 1930 *Times Lit. Suppl.* 24 July 601/1 In view of the extent of the chronological divide.

Divide, *v.* **8.** Add: Also with *up*.
1914 E. CANNAN *Wealth* v. 82 Even the pasture was divided up with the small exceptions which we see in the 'commons' of the present day.

Divided, *ppl. a.* Add: **1. d.** *Divided axle*: see quot. *Divided skirt*: see SKIRT *sb.* 1.
1874 KNIGHT *Dict. Mech.*, *Divided Axle*, one bisected at its mid-length.

Di·videndless, *a.* [See -LESS.] Without dividends.
1899 *Westm. Gaz.* 26 Jan. 8/1 If the Hyderabad-Deccan Company were in its infancy instead of having laboured on through thirteen years of a dividendless career. *Ibid.* 2 Mar. 8/1 The dividendless stock of the District Railway. 1920 *Glasgow Herald* 4 Sept. 10 It may be noted that shareholders again go dividendless.

Divident, *a.* **A. 1.** Add: esp. in *divident fence, line* (cf. next).
1644 *Col. Rec. Conn.* I. 105 There shall be a liberty for ether party of 12 inches from the divident lyne. 1697 *Conn. Hist. Soc. Coll.* XIV. 462 To maintain the Divident fence between the said Longs home lott and this parcell of land. 1703 *Col. Rec. Conn.* IV. 445 This Court doth allow of the divident line agreed upon by the inhabitants of Plainfield to be the dividing line of their township.

Dividing, *ppl. a.* Add: Earlier examples of *dividing line*; also *dividing bounds, fence*.
1640 *Conn. Hist. Soc. Coll.* XIV. 106 Which field abutteth ..on the deviding lyne betwene the South & North Side. *Ibid.* 257 To make and mayntaine the halfe of the div(i)deing fence. 1680 *Col. Rec. Conn.* III. 69 They agreed that the dividing bounds should be at Ashowat to Wongushock. 1751 C. GIST *Jrnls.* 65 The dividing Line between Carolina and Virginia. 1760 WASHINGTON *Diaries* I. 133 Also run round the fields in the lower pasture according as the dividing fence is to go.

Diving, *vbl. sb.* **b.** Add: **diving-board,** a board projecting some distance over the water, from which a swimmer dives.
1893 SINCLAIR & HENRY *Swimming* (Badm. Libr.) iv. 108 A spring diving-board is generally used for running headers.

Division, *sb.* Add:
1. e. *Biol.* In cytogenesis, the separation of the protoplasm of the mother-cell into two or more daughter-cells. In zoology, the breaking up of an organism into two or more parts which develop into new individuals of the typical form of the organism, as distinguished from reproduction from a bud.
1880 *Encycl. Brit.* XII. 13/1 Four types of Cytogenesis may be distinguished: (1) Rejuvenescence; (2) Conjugation; (3) Free-cell formation; and (4) Division. 1901 T. H. MORGAN *Regeneration* 149 The breaking up of lumbriculus or of a planarian into pieces that form new individuals is a typical example of division.
10. c. Also *pl.* The parade of a ship's company according to its divisions.
1915 'BARTIMEUS' *A Tall Ship* iii. (*A Captain's Forenoon*) 54 Nine o'clock, sir; all ready for divisions. *Ibid.* 55 A moment later the bugle overhead blazed forth 'Divisions'.
e. In the Civil Service, the technical designation of the several grades of clerks.
1876 *Order in Council* 12 Feb. in *Guide Employm. Civil Service* (1886) 17 A Lower Division of the Civil Service shall be constituted. It shall consist of men clerks and of boy clerks, engaged to serve in any department of the State to which they may, from time to time, be appointed or transferred. *Ibid.* 19 Promotion from the Lower to the Higher Division of the Service shall not be made without a special certificate from the Civil Service Commissioners. 1892 S. SAVILL *Civil Service Coach* 2 The salaries of Clerks in the Second Division..shall commence at 70*l.* per annum. 1898 *Guide Employm. Civil Service* 15 Second Division Clerkships...The Second Division forms at present the rank and file of the permanent Civil Service.
f. Any of the three grades of imprisonment to which certain misdemeanants may be sentenced (see quots.).
1865 *Act 28 & 29 Vict.* c. 126 § 67 In every Prison to which this Act applies Prisoners convicted of Misdemeanor, and not sentenced to Hard Labour, shall be divided into at least Two Divisions, One of which shall be called the First Division; and whenever any Person convicted of Misdemeanor is sentenced to Imprisonment without Hard Labour it shall be lawful for the Court..to order..that such person shall be treated as a Misdemeanant of the First Division, and a Misdemeanant of the First Division shall not be deemed to be a Criminal Prisoner within the Meaning of this Act. 1898 *Act 61 & 62 Vict.* c. 41 § 6 Prisoners..not sentenced to penal servitude or hard labour, shall be divided into three divisions. ..Where a person is..sentenced to imprisonment without hard labour, the court may..direct that he be treated as an offender of the first division or as an offender of the second division. If no direction is given by the court, the offender shall, subject to the provisions of this section, be treated as an offender of the third division.

Supplement, p. 3873; Corrigenda, p. 4092; Spurious words, p. 4093; Books quoted, p. 4094

g. A section of a railway line. Also *attrib.* U.S.
1887 C. B. George *40 Years on Rail* xii. 254 My plan.. is to have a book to be called the division book kept by each company. 1891 C. Roberts *Adrift Amer.* 71 Every line in the United States is divided into divisions of various lengths.. Each division is under the supervision of a man who is called a division road master. *Ibid.* 96 Wallace was a division terminus. 1892 Gunter *Miss Dividends* 10 This citizen soldier..had been one of the division engineers of the Union Pacific Railway.

Divisional, *a.* 2. Add: *Divisional Court*: see Division 10.
1928 *Daily Mail* 3 Aug. 10/6 In recent years the trend of decisions is very different and reached its culminating point in the Divisional Court this year.

Divisionism (divi·ʒəniz'm). [f. Division + -ism.] The practice of painting with pure colours, and of achieving the effect of mixed colours by the juxtaposition of contrasting colours instead of by mixing the desired shade on the palette. Hence **Divi·sionist**, a painter who follows this practice; also *attrib.* or as *adj.*
1901 L. Villari *Giovanni Segantini* 53 His 'divisionist' drawings. *Ibid.* 73 In this replica he began to apply the system of divisionism. 1920 *Times Lit. Suppl.* 18 Nov. 745/4 Cézanne, with his insistence upon the volumes of objects, rebelled against the disintegration of form which was the logical consequence of divisionism. 1921 *Edin. Rev.* Apr. 311 The Futurists accepted the Divisionism and complementarism of the Neo-Impressionists. 1926 Rutter *Evol. Mod. Art* 41 A Divisionist painter desiring a grey..places on his canvas little touches, say, of pure violet in juxtaposition to little touches of a yellowish green.

Divot, *sb.* Add: *Golf.* A piece of turf cut out with a club by a player in making a stroke.
1891 H. G. Hutchinson *Golf* 9 With an iron club an unskilful player is much more likely to cut fids of turf—*golfice*, 'divots'—out of the green.

Divulse, *v.* (Modern U.S. example.)
1897 *Trans. Amer. Pediatric Soc.* IX. 55 Dr. Lesser..performed tracheotomy, and divulsed the stricture through the wound.

Divvers (di·vəɹz). *Oxford University slang.* [f. first syllable of Divinity + *-er⁶ + -s (representing the pl. *moderations*).] Divinity moderations, the first public examination in Holy Scripture.
1905 *Varsity* 30 Nov. 109/3 Those who are in for 'Divvers' should make sure of knowing all about St. Stephen's Speech. 1913 *Isis* 8 Feb. 184/2 Honour Mods. and Divvers behind him and Groups before.

Divvy, *sb.* and *v.* (Earlier U.S. examples.)
1881 A. A. Hayes *New Colorado* xi. 156 The two men, unsuspicious of danger were 'divvying up' the spoils in the middle of the road. 1883 J. Hay *Bread-winners* x. 150 'You surely do not intend—' 'To strike Saul for a divvy?'

Divvy (di·vi), *a. slang.* [f. first syllable of Divine (A. 5 b) + -y¹; cf. *Deevey.] 'Divine', 'heavenly.'
1903 *Daily Chron.* 1 Aug. 8/1, I heard one of them say that 'the dimpy was divvy, and this, when translated, meant that a certain dinner party was divine.

Dix (dis). [Fr.] The lowest trump in bezique and other games; also, in pinocle, a certain score of ten points, or the trump entitling the player to it.
1908 R. F. Foster *Pinochle* 5 In two-hand, any player holding the dix may exchange it for the trump card immediately after winning a trick.

Dix-huitième (dizwityɛm), *a.* [Fr., = eighteenth.] Of or belonging to the eighteenth century.
1920 *Times Lit. Suppl.* 26 June 538/1 In a charming and characteristically dix-huitième manner.

Dixie¹ (di·ksi). Also [dechsie], dixey, dixy. [Hind. *degchi, -cha*, a. Hindi *degachī, -chā*, Panjabi *dekachī, degāchī, -chā*, a. Pers. *degcha*, dim. of *deg*, *dig* iron pot, kettle, cauldron.] An iron kettle or pot, used by soldiers for making tea or stew.
[1879 Mrs. A. E. James *Ind. Househ. Managem.* 40 Six dechsies and covers. *Ibid.* 45 A few *dechsies* (copper pots).] 1900 *Westm. Gaz.* 23 Mar. 8/1 On halting at Klip Drift we immediately got down our dixies [*sic*] and made tea for all. 1900 *Daily News* 10 July 3/2 The 'billy' is what Tommy calls a 'dixie'. 1901 *Westm. Gaz.* 26 June 8/1 With much difficulty water was procured from a spruit over a mile away, and the 'dixey' boiled. 1916 H. G. Wells *Mr. Britling* II. iv. § 14 They shelled us again next day and our tea dixy was hit. 1916 *Anzac Bk.* 41/1 Tea made in the stew dixie, and tasting more of dixie and stew than of tea.

Dixie² (di·ksi). U.S. [Of doubtful origin. Suggested explanations are cited by Bartlett (ed. 4), Farmer *Americanisms*, and in the *Century Dict.* (Cycl. of Names).]
1. The southern United States; the South. Also *Dixie('s) Land.*
1861 G. P. Putnam (*title*) Before and After the Battle; a day and night in 'Dixie'. 1863 *Ret. Agric. Soc. Maine* (1864) 19 Sheep step in to furnish..what every one must acknowledge to be a very excellent substitute for 'Dixie's product' [i.e. cotton]. 1864 W. Pittenger *Daring & Suffering* 35 That coat..I wore all through Dixie. 1866 C. H. Smith *Bill Arp* 139 I'm a good Union reb, and my battle cry is Dixie and the Union. 1879 Tourgee *Fool's Err.* v. 21, I am considering the idea of removing my household gods to Dixie. 1901 W. Pittenger *Gt. Locom. Chase* 101 Now I will succeed, or leave my bones in Dixie. 1903 *N.Y. Times* 20 Dec. 5 Nearly 400 exiles from Dixie Land gathered at the annual dinner of the Southern Society.
b. The music or words of the song of 'Dixie'.
1904 *Minneapolis Times* 23 June 8 The orchestra in a Georgia theatre quieted a panic-stricken crowd by playing 'Dixie'. 1921 H. S. Harrison *Queed* xxi. 261 From far away floated the strains of 'Dixie', crashed out by forty bands.
2. (See quots.)
1873 J. H. Beadle *Undevel. West* xxx. 660 'Dixie wine' as the Mormons call it, is rather strong and pungent. *Ibid.* 661 All that part of Mormondom south of the rim of the Great Basin is called Dixie, and extends some distance into Arizona.

Dizoic (dəizōᵘ·ik), *a. Zool.* [f. Gr. δι- Di-² + ζῷον animal + -ic.] Producing two young; applied to a spore producing two sporozoites.
1901 Calkins *Protozoa* 153. 1903 [see Monozoic 2].

Dizygotic (dəizəigǫ·tik), *a. Biol.* [f. Di-² + Zygote + -ic.] Formed by the development of two distinct zygotes.
1930 *Nature* 15 Nov. 766 Dizygotic twins are..on the whole inferior to their brothers and sisters in the physical measurements, but this is certainly not the case with monozygotic twins.

Dizzy, *a.* Add: 3. b. (U.S. examples.)
1878 J. H. Beadle *Western Wilds* xxxv, Dance houses and saloons multiplied and 'dizzy doves' gave an air of abandon to the streets. 1888 *Texas Siftings* 29 Sept. (Farmer) Professional beauties or maidens, commonly called dizzy blondes. 1889 *Kansas Times & Star* 4 Nov., Many of the local clergy last night warned the church members ..against a 'Dizzy Blonde' company coming to one of the theaters soon.
c. Startling, astonishing. *slang.*
1896 G. Ade *Artie* xvii. 158 They was out there in them dizzy togs cuttin' up and down the track. 1897 *Daily News* 10 Aug. 5/2 Four straw hats with 'dizzy bands'. 1921 R. D. Paine *Comr. Rolling Ocean* v. 84 When she limped into Brest a week overdue, the admiral called it a dizzy miracle.

Dizzyite (di·zi,əit). [f. *Dizzy*, nickname of Benjamin Disraeli (see, e.g., *Punch* 3 Apr. 1852) + -ite.¹] A follower or admirer of Disraeli (cf. *Disraelian).
1903 Meynell *Disraeli* I. 61 Dizzyites..must marvel that one who received this close confidence could afterwards be jaunty at the expense of the dead woman whom Disraeli 'so truly loved'. *Ibid.* II. 483 If Disraeli bore his traducers no grudge, it would be superfluous indeed for true Dizzyites to bear them any.

Djati (dʒā·ti). Also d'jatti. [Malay *jātī*.] The teak tree.
1908 *Westm. Gaz.* 9 June 5/3 Java teak, known as d'jatti.

Djebba, djibba(h), variants of Jibbah.
1896 *Daily News* 23 Oct. 2/1 They had turned their tattered djebbas inside out. 1904 *Daily Chron.* 27 July 8/2 The djibbah is produced in full, warm reds, purples, blues, and orange hues. 1909 H. G. Wells *Ann Veronica* vii, A purple djibbah with a richly embroidered yoke. 1927 *Spectator* 17 Dec. 1081/1 The books..are sold by ladies in djibbas.

Do, *sb.*¹ Add:
2. b. *esp.* An entertainment or show (see quots. in Dict.); hence (orig. *jocular*), a military or naval engagement, raid, or other 'show'.
1915 Cable *Between Lines* 110 We are about the first Terrier lot to be in a heavy 'do' in the forward trenches.
4. An injunction to do (something specified). Only when coupled with *don't*: see Don't.
1902 'Stancliffe' (*title*) Golf Do's and Don'ts. 1920 G. C. Bailey *Complete Airman* 190 Between this and the next lesson the pupil should be encouraged to think well over the 'dos' and 'don'ts' of his trip.

Do, *v.* Add: A. 2. c. γ. (American examples of *don't* = does not.)
1670 *Rhode Isl. Hist. Soc.* X. 102 Evidence of..River being more than 11 miles long, but how much more dont say. 1774 P. V. Fithian *Jrnl.* (1900) 202 A Sunday in Virginia dont seem to wear the same Dress as our Sundays to the Northward. 1782 *Essex Inst. Hist. Coll.* I. 13/2 It dont all discorage me in the least. 1813 Paulding *John Bull & Br. Jon.* ii. 9 The old saying that a man don't know when he is well off. 1835 R. M. Bird *Hawks of Hawk-hollow* I. xi. 143, I wonder she don't sing; for a speaking voice, she has the richest *soprano*. 1862 O. W. Norton *Army Lett.* 120 It don't take ten thousand acres here to support one family.
3. d. *dial.* and U.S. done.
1847 in D. Drake *Pioneer Life Kentucky* iii. 63 The weavil..'done' great injury to that grain. 1849 N. Kingsley *Diary* 56 Anna done the fair thing last night. 1850 *Ibid.* 117 [We] worked in the old place and done middling well. 1873 'Mark Twain' & Warner *Gilded Age* xxxiii. 307, I think it done him good. 1924 W. M. Raine *Troubled Waters* xxi. 226 The little boss done right not to take that Cheyenne bid for the doggies.
B. 6. f. *It isn't done*: it is forbidden by custom, opinion, or propriety; it is bad form. *colloq.*
1879 E. Gosse in Charteris *Life & Lett.* (1931) 126 We haven't the originality to think of dying. It's never done here, in our set. 1911 R. W. Chambers *Common Law* i, 'You know', he said, 'models are not supposed to come here unless sent for. It isn't done in this building.' 1926 Ethel M. Dell *Black Knight* I. viii, 'Oh, but you couldn't—you couldn't—live there by yourself!' protested Joyce. 'It isn't done, Ermine. It wouldn't be fitting.' 1928 *Observer* 29 Jan. 22/1 Undergraduates regard the conduct of the night of December 13 as the sort of thing that 'isn't done'.
11. a. With person as obj. = to operate on, attend to.
1901 *Daily Chron.* 16 Oct. 5/2 The [vaccinated] man who ..has been 'done in the leg'. *Mod.* I will do you next, sir (= I will cut your hair, shave you, etc. next).
e. Phr. *Done to the wide* or *the world*: absolutely done for, defeated, etc. *colloq.*
1922 *Daily Mail* 6 Dec. 11 He came again after appearing 'done to the world' more than once. 1925 Fraser & Gibbons *Soldier & Sailor Words*, *Done to the wide*, utterly beaten.
f. Also *to do in the eye.*
1891 Dixon *Dict. Idiomatic Phrases* s.v., The jockey did your friend in the eye over that horse. 1908 *Punch* 20 May 367/1 Done in the eye again. What on earth do you expect?
m. To provide food, etc. for (a person); to treat or entertain (*well*). *To do oneself well*: to make liberal provision for one's creature comforts. *slang.*
1897 (Apr. 23) *Correspondent*, They do you well at the White Lion. 1897 *Punch* 23 Oct. 185/1 The nightmare of an artist who does himself not wisely but far too well, at an unnecessary supper. 1902 *Daily Chron.* 16 Aug. 3/4 For ten francs a day one is done well there. 1902 *Westm. Gaz.* 25 Aug. 2 His Majesty has been to Westminster Abbey, and the Crystal Palace,..and Madame Tussaud's—really we think that on the whole we have done him very well. *Ibid.* 22 Oct. 3/3 The man who had done himself fairly well on everyday cooking. 1928 *Daily Express* 7 Sept. 1/1 They do you well, with plenty of eggs, cream, [etc.].
15. b. Also, to make shift to live *on* (a limited income).
1924 Rose Macaulay *Orphan Island* xviii. 237 'Is that a good living wage?' he asked her; and she answered that they could just do on it, no more, with what she herself earned.
16. Hence *do or die* as adj. phr., expressing determination to be deterred by no danger or difficulty.
1902 *Westm. Gaz.* 1 Mar. 4/1 She dips the first pen into the ink with a do-or-die expression. 1907 *Daily Chron.* 26 Sept. 4/6 The dominant motive with all was hatred of the foreign yoke, and the 'do-or-die' determination to shake it off. 1907 *National Church* 15 Oct. 273/1, I confess that I do not agree with the stalwarts...And I certainly am not impressed with their 'do or die' earnestness.
20. b. Hence *trans.* To do for, suffice, satisfy (a person). *colloq.*
1846 *Congress. Globe* 20 July 1118, I have just enough [money] to do me to the end of the session. 1880 *Congress. Rec.* 22 Jan. 491/1, I should like to have ten minutes, but it will do me just as well in the morning. 1926 W. Deeping *Sorrell & Son* xiii, 'What's it to be, Do? An orange cocktail?' 'Yes, that will do me.' 1928 Galsworthy *Swan Song* I. iv. 25 Leicester Square would do me all right.
31. b. In illiterate, esp. negro, speech, used with pa. pples., esp. *done gone*; sometimes with inf. as *done make*. U.S.
1836 *N. Y. Spirit of Times* (1846) 22 (Th.) He had done gone three hours ago. *Ibid.* 94 I'd done got the licker, and I was satisfied. 1845 [W. T. Thompson] *Chron. Pineville* 107 (Bartlett) The horse and cart is done gone, and everything in it. 1854 Mary J. Holmes *Tempest & Sunshine* ii. 24 I've done let my best horse and nigger go off with a man from the free States. 1873 J. H. Beadle *Undevel. West* xix. 356 People have done forgot they had any Injun blood in 'em. 1887 G. W. Cable in *Century Mag.* Nov. 96/1 'You done had supper?' she asked. 1897 R. M. Stuart *Simphkinsville* 23, I see my pipe has done gone out while I've been talkin'.
34. c. *Nothing doing*: *lit.* nothing being done, or transacted; no business on foot; hence (*slang* or *colloq.*) an announcement of refusal of a request or offer, failure in an attempt, etc.
1858 *Leisure Hour* 25 Mar. 186/2 There's nothing doing now. 1870 *Porcupine* 26 Mar. 503/3 A friend of mine hailed an outfitter the other day, 'How is business?' 'Nothing doing.'
1910 *N. Y. Evening Post* 13 Dec. 7 Spottford offered the porter a dime. The negro waved it aside and said: 'Nothing doing; my price is a quarter at least'. 1915 'Ian Hay' *First Hundred Thou.* xx. 302 'Na pooh!'..also means, 'Not likely!' or 'Nothing doing!' 1921 R. D. Paine *Comr. Rolling Ocean* i. 5 I'm all through. Nothing doing. 1928 *Boston Even. Transcript* 30 Mar. 15/7, I looked in the dictionaries. 'Nothing doing!' 1930 Maugham *Gent. in Parlour* x. 46 Then my girl asked me to marry her...I told her there was nothing doing.
45. **Do down.** b. To overcome, master, get the better of, bring to grief. *colloq.*
1911 H. Walpole *Mr. Perrin & Mr. Traill* viii. 154 He saw nothing but a spiteful and malignant world trying, as he phrased it, to 'do him down'. 1923 *Daily Mail* 12 Mar. 6 Sir Arthur Griffith-Boscawen..said they had been done down by what had been rightly called an act of treachery. 1924 D. H. Lawrence *England, my England* 228 Poor Fanny! She was such a lady, and so straight and magnificent. And yet everything seemed to do her down. 1928 *Daily Express* 2 July 7 Mr. Cairns, the magistrate: You want all the brains you possess to deal with two women of that relationship. Your wife, plus your mother-in-law, can do you down sober, much less [*sic*] drunk.
45. **Do in.** b. To bring disaster upon, do a great injury to, ruin; often, to murder, kill. *slang.*
1905 *Daily Chron.* 22 May 6/3, I heard people tell her to do me an injury, throw glasses at me, and 'do me in'. 1906 *Ibid.* 11 Dec. 4/4 It seems funny that the first blooming order I got in Enfield I should be done in. 1912 Shaw *Pygmalion* III, Liza (darkly) My aunt died of influenza: so they said. *Mrs Eynsford Hill* (clicks her tongue sympathetically)!!! *Liza* (in the same tragic tone) But it's my belief they done the old woman in. 1917 I. A. R. Wylie *Duchess in Pursuit* 60 'Dear Sir John' (the Duchess had scrawled)—'I am not murdered—"done in" I think is the local expression.' 1918 W. J. Locke *Rough Road* vi, If you engage a second-rate man..who isn't used to this make of car, he'll do it in for you pretty quick. 1919 J. B. Morton *Barber of Putney* xiv. 235 'Yes', said Graves. 'That's what did my nerves in. Still sleep bad.' *a* 1928 Cadbury in C. F. S. Gamble *N. Sea Air Station* xii. 194 As an awful sea got up about noon we knew he must be done in unless he was picked up. 1928 Galsworthy *Swan Song* I. ix. 66 That house had 'done in' her father.
47. **Do off.** c. To deck up. U.S.
1839 Mrs. Kirkland *New Home* xxxiv. 227, I..reconnoitred the company who were 'done off' (indigenous,) 'in first-rate style', for this important occasion.
d. To partition off. U.S.
1874 *Rep. Vermont Board Agric.* II. 514, I have also one small room done off for storing butter in the fall.

50. **Do over.** b. = *make over* (Make *v.* 92 d). U.S.
1908 *Smart Set* Sept. 84/1 If only somebody would 'do over' Browning into English.
52. **Do up.** f. To get the better of; to settle in some way. U.S.
1901 S. Merwin & H. K. Webster *Calumet K* vi. 111 Max did him up good last night, when he was blowing off about bringing the delegate around. 1902 Eliz. L. Banks *Newspaper Girl* 11 Instead of being allowed to 'do her up', I was instructed to give her a 'good send-off'. 1904 W. H. Smith *Promoters* ii. 54 The thing to do is to do up your competitor. 1906 'O. Henry' *Four Million* 121, I have many times told you those Dagoes would do you up.

Dobber. U.S. (Additional example.)
1836 *Knickerbocker Mag.* VII. 14 His tangent now is the lithsome bamboo, his sine the buoyant dobber, that taketh the gauge of bite or nibble.

Dobe, 'dobe (dōᵘ·bi). U.S. Colloq. shortenings of Adobe.
1883 Nye *Baled Hay* 135 The dobe pig pens..are not true to nature. 1897 *Outing* (U.S.) XXIX. 582/1 The afternoon monsoon..howls..as if it would tear the stubborn little 'dobe shanties off the earth. 1904 'O. Henry' *Cabbages & Kings* iv. 73 Grass huts, 'dobes, five or six two-story houses. *Ibid.* vi. 104 A 'dobe house in a dirty side street.

Dobermann (dōᵘ·bəɹmæn). [Name of *Dobermann*, a German of Thuringia. See also *Pinscher.] In full *Dobermann pinscher*: A kind of German hound with smooth coat and docked tail.
1925 G. W. Little *Dog Bk.* (facing p. 274) One of the greatest Dobermann Pinschers ever imported to America. 1928 *Sunday Express* 24 June 11 A German named Dobermann, of Aplolba, Thuringia..spent his life experimenting with different breeds, and at last, in the middle of the last century, he produced specimens of the 'Dobermann Pincher'—and died before disclosing his secret.

Dobie, doby, varr. of *Dobe. Also *attrib.* and *Comb.* U.S.
1857 W. Chandless *Visit Salt Lake* II. i. 146 Sun-baked bricks, called 'dobies', a corruption of the word 'adobe', are the sole building material. *Ibid.* v. 214 The dobie-maker, the mason, the shingle-layer. *Ibid.* vii. 249 He'll only have to pay the dobie-layer. 1878 J. H. Beadle *Western Wilds* xxii. 348 He told of digging ditches, building fences and making dobies. *Ibid.* xxx. 660 The neat white *dobie* houses. 1885 *Outing* (U.S.) VII. 52/1 Half sand and the other half 'doby'-mud. 1891 C. Roberts *Adrift Amer.* 86 These bricks..although they are spelt 'adobes', I always heard ..spoken of as 'dobies'.
b. (See quot.)
1857 W. Chandless *Visit Salt Lake* II. i. 146 The fifty dollar California pieces..were called 'dobies', because octagonal.

Dobra (dō·brā). [Pg.] A former Portuguese gold coin worth about £3 12*s.*
1920 Alan Graham *Follow Little Pict.* xxv, The chest was packed to the brim with gold—guineas from England, louis from France, doubloons from Spain, dobras from Portugal.

Doc (dǫk), U.S. colloq. abbrev. of Doctor.
1854 R. Glisan *Jrnl. Army Life* 24 Nov. (1874) 149 Don't you think, Doc., ague makes a fellow powerful weak? 1887 F. Francis Jr. *Saddle & Mocassin* viii. 146 Anyhow, Doc Gilpen the Marshal jumped him [= took him to task]. 1904 G. H. Lorimer *Old Gorgon Graham* 173 Doc was cribbing those powerful Sunday evening discourses from a volume of Beecher's sermons. 1920 Mulford *J. Nelson* vi. 60 I'd like to shake hands with th' coyote that lugged th' Doc off to fix that laig.

Docete (dōᵘ·sīt). [Anglicized form.] A member or follower of the Docetæ; a Docetist.
1894 Illingworth *Pers. Hum. & Div.* i. 11 Had Christ been..a mere appearance as with the Docetes.

Dock, *sb.*³ Add:
4. *In dry dock* (fig.): out of employment. *colloq.*
1929 Vachell *Virgin* iii. 55 June found herself in dry dock, and likely to remain there.
b. *In dock*: in hospital. *War slang.*
1919 *Athenæum* 11 July 582/2 'Dock', hospital, is..probably from 'in dock'. *Ibid.* 22 Aug. 791/2 While 'in dock' (*i.e.* in hospital) one lay upon 'biscuits'.
6. b. *Theatr.* Accommodation for scenery that has to be removed quickly from the stage.
1898 E. O. Sachs *Mod. Opera Houses* III. Suppl. I. 24 At each side of the stage the counterweight boxes practically form enclosing walls with a number of openings leading to a series of 'scene' docks on each side. The arrangement of these side docks..is essentially of French origin, and they afford a very ready means for the disposal of scenery which has to be quickly removed from the stage. *Ibid.* 34 There is a dock for each sequence of 'traps', so that the 'wings' belonging to each 'entrance' can always be kept in the dock opposite it.
7. **dock-glass**, a large wine-glass for wine-tasting; **dock-head** (earlier American examples).
1911 *Concise Oxf. Dict.*, *Dock-glass. 1922 'Langa Langa' (H. B. Hermon-Hodge) *Up against it in Nigeria* x. 180 A dock-glass of rum..soon transformed me from a quasi-corpse into an exhilarated and hungry man. 1657 *Boston Town Rec.* II. 142 To sett up a building att the west end of the house..by the *dock head. 1692 S. Sewall *Diary* I. 354 By the Dock-head Mr. Willard struck in. 1736 *Boston Town Rec.* XII. 139 The Watch House at the Dock-head.

Dock, *sb.*⁴ *attrib.* Add: **dock brief**, a brief handed direct to a barrister in court, who has been selected by a poor prisoner, standing in the dock, to defend him. (Cf. Docker ³.)
1909 *Daily Chron.* 30 Apr. 6/7 The 'dock brief'..is the only exception to the rule that briefs must come through a solicitor. 1928 *Daily Tel.* 10 Jan. 9 Barristers who are not anxious to accept dock briefs are entitled to leave the court on hearing a prisoner ask for one.

Dock, *v.*¹ Add:
2. b. To deprive (a person) of part of his pay as a fine. *colloq.* (orig. *dial.*).
1822 *Cobbett's Weekly Reg.* 13 Apr. 81 Hence arose numerous schemes for *docking* you in this quarter. 1891 *Rutland Gloss.* s.v., Mr. A— has docked his men as last Saturday, I suppose. 1891 *Harper's Mag.* Nov. 888/2 Each man was 'docked', or charged, seventy-five cents a month for medical services. 1901 S. Merwin & H. K. Webster *Calumet K* vii. 128 Every man that drops anything into the bins gets docked an hour's pay. *Ibid.*, I guess we won't take the trouble to dock you.

Dockage¹. (Earlier Amer. example.)
1669 *Boston Town Rec.* VII. 151 The..peece of land with all..accomodations and benefitts with wharfige, dockage, moreage [etc.].

Dockland (dǫ·klænd). A newspaper name for the poor districts about the London docks.
1904 *Daily Chron.* 21 Sept. 6/2 Clarkson-street School..is situated in the heart of Dockland. 1922 *Weekly Dispatch* 19 Nov. 8 For him there is glamour even in the mean streets of dockland. 1922 *Daily Mail* 12 Dec. 7 The Dockland Mission, formerly known as the Malvern Mission, in Canning Town. 1929 *Times* 7 Feb. 9/4 His work there won the whole-hearted love and devotion of Dockland.

Docksman (dǫ·ksmæn). [f. *docks* (see Dock *sb.*³ 5) + Man *sb.*¹] A man employed at a dock or docks; *spec.* see quot. 1921.
1921 *Dict. Occup. Terms* (1927) § 745 *Docksman*, one of a team of men who open and shut dock gates by means of capstan. 1929 *Daily News* 25 July 5/6 The former Cardiff docksman.

Dockyard. Add: **dockyardman**, a man permanently employed in a Government dockyard.
1837 Dickens *Pickw.* ii, Soldiers, sailors,..and dockyard men. 1906 *Outlook* 20 Nov. 495/2 Dockyardmen who are in danger of losing that *otium cum dignitate* which they have regarded as their perquisite. 1908 *Daily Chron.* 5 Oct. 5/4 The men of the salvage corps who have worked at raising the Gladiator for the last six months, and the bluejackets and dockyardmen who have assisted. 1909 *Pall Mall Gaz.* 12 Apr. 3/2 Naval men, or dockyardmen, which practically amounts to the same thing, raised Torpedo-boat No. 99 after she was sunk off Berry Head.

Docmac (dǫ·kmæk). [Ar. *doqmāq* mallet.] A large edible catfish, *Bagrus docmac*, common in the Nile.
1887 Günther in *Encycl. Brit.* XXII. 68/1 The 'Bayad' (*B[agrus] bayad*) and 'Docmac' (*B. docmac*)..grow to a length of 5 feet, and are eaten.

Doctor, *sb.* Add:
6. Also, a wizard or medicine-man in a savage tribe.
1858 *Compendium of Kaffir Laws & Customs* 123 Doctors are not entitled to fees, except a cure is performed, or the patient relieved.
b. In the West Indies, S. Africa, and W. Australia, a cool sea-breeze which usually prevails during part of the day in summer. *colloq.*
1740 [in Dict.]. 1856 Fleming *Southern Africa* iv. 62 The South-easter, from blowing all pestilent vapours and effluvia out to sea..has obtained the local epithet of '*the Doctor*'.
c. One who mends or repairs; as a chair doctor. *colloq.*
11. *Naut.* (Earlier U.S. examples.)
1821 *Massachusetts Spy* 1 Aug. (Th.) The cook, at sea, is generally called doctor. 1835 J. H. Ingraham *South-West* I. vi. 69 All [the crew] neatly dressed in white trousers and shirts, even to the sable 'Doctor' and his 'sub'.
b. A name for a certain class of shipping broker (see quot.). *colloq.*
1899 *Daily News* 2 Mar. 9/1 The owner, nervous about a vessel, wants a further insurance, and the 'doctor' procures it for him...The 'doctor' is a broker who deals particularly with the overdue vessels.
13. Also, **doctor's gum**, the West Indian tree *Rhus Metopium*; also, see quot. 1887.
1858 [see Hog gum]. 1887 Moloney *Forestry W. Afr.* 279 Hog or Doctor's gum, Gamboge tree (*Symphonia globulifera*).

Doctorand (dǫ·ktŏrænd). Also in L. form doctora·ndus (pl. -i). [G., ad. med.L.] A candidate for a doctor's degree.
1912 R. S. Rait *Life Med. Univ.* ii. 32 When our young English Doctorand received the permission of his Rector to proceed to his degree. 1921 *Edin. Rev.* Jan. 72 Increasing numbers of *doctorandi* sought admission to his laboratory.

Dod- (Dod *sb.*¹), used as an intensive with verbs and pa. pples. U.S. *vulgar.* See also *Dodgast *v.*, *Dod-rot *v.*
18.. *Southern Sketches* (Bartlett 1859) I'll be dod fetched if I meant any harm. 1908 Mulford *Orphan* xiii. 164 'Dod-blasted postage stamp of a pelt', he grumbled.

Dodderer (dǫ·dərəɹ). [f. Dodder *v.* + -er¹.] One who dodders; one infirm in body or mind; a feeble or inept person.
1917 W. J. Locke *Red Planet* xi. 131 Do you think I'm a blind dodderer? 1926 *Public Opinion* 23 Apr. 420/1, I am constantly meeting ponderous dodderers who are sure civilisation is in rapid decay. 1930 A. P. Herbert in *Punch* 14 May 551, I see now that I have been a difficult old dodderer upon this subject.

Doddering, *ppl. a.* (see under Dodder *v.*). Add: Now freq. Mentally feeble or inept; futile, footling. Hence **Do·dderingness.**
1908 *Fabian News* XIX. 82/2 Mr. Justin McCarthy, in his rather doddering introduction, explicitly warns us against Mr. Sheehy-Skeffington's portraiture of Davitt as an anti-clerical politician. 1915 Wodehouse *Something Fresh* iii, The amiable dodderingness which marked every branch of his life. 1926 *Brit. Weekly* 23 Sept. 529/3 Your puir, toom, dodderin', fushionless kirk.

Doddery (dǫ·dəri), *a.* [f. Dodder *v.* + -y¹.] Apt to tremble or totter, from age or infirmity; shaky.
1919 Buchan *Mr. Standfast* xvii, When he got on his feet he was as doddery as an old man. 1921 *Chambers's Jrnl.* May 325/1 The old man..seemed to have become very doddery as he descended from the buggy.

Dodecapropheton (dōᵘ:dĕkăprŏfī·tǫn). [Gr. δωδεκαπρόφητον (Epiphanius).] The book of the twelve minor prophets.
1897 T. K. Cheyne in *Expositor* Jan. 41 The earlier commentators on the Dodecapropheton.

Dodecyl (dōᵘ·dĭsil). *Chem.* [f. Dodeca- + -yl.] The univalent radical $C_{12}H_{25}$, of which dodecane is the hydride. Hence **Dodecylene** (dōᵘde·silīn), each of several isomeric liquid hydrocarbons, $C_{12}H_{24}$, of the ethylene series.
1889 Muir & Morley *Watts' Dict. Chem.* II. 413/2 Dodecyl alcohol $C_{12}H_{25}OH$. *Ibid.*, Dodecylene...Got by distilling the potash-soap derived from herring oil.

Dodgast, *v.* U.S. *vulgar.* [f. *Dod- + *gast*, prob. for Blast *v.* 10. Cf. *Dod-rot *v.*] In imprecatory and expletive use: To 'confound', 'curse'. Chiefly in **Do·dgasted** *ppl. a.*
1888 *Detroit Free Press* (Farmer) It's a dodgasted funny thing,..but it's a fact. 1908 Mulford *Orphan* ix. 103 What can we do when our cayuses are so dod-gasted tired? 1909 *N. Y. Observer* 2 Sept. 319/2 Well, dodgast you, get in the stern there. 1914 W. J. Locke *Fort. Youth* xxi, It's a pity, sonny—a dodgasted pity!

Dodge, *sb.*¹ Add: 2. b. *On the dodge*: engaged in crooked or dishonest proceedings.
a 1910 'O. Henry' *Sixes & Sevens* v. 67, I don't think I ought to close without giving some deductions from my experience of eight years 'on the dodge'. It doesn't pay to rob trains.

Dodge, *v.* Add: 13. *To dodge Pompey* (see quot.). *Austral. slang.*
1930 Billis & Kenyon *Pastures New* iii. 46 Browne detailed the laws passed, not to encourage the overlander, but rather to counteract his habit of stealing grass—'dodging Pompey', as it was known.

Dodger. Add: 2. U.S. (Earlier examples.)
1831 Peck *Guide for Emigrants* II. 152 Dodgers are masses [of corn meal] like small loaves of bread, prepared in a similar manner [i.e. with water or milk], and baked in the spider or skillet. 1832 Mrs. F. Trollope *Dom. Mann. Amer.* I. 83 Hoe cake, johnny cake, waffle cake, and dodger cake.
5. A screen on the bridge of a steamer to afford protection from spray, etc.
1898 C. Hyne *Capt. Kettle* x. 260 Under shelter of the dodgers on the upper bridge. *Ibid.* 262 Kettle hung on behind the canvas dodgers at the weather end of the bridge.
6. A game.
1928 *Daily Tel.* 30 Oct. 7/2 The dodger,..Throw and sit, and King of the Castle.

Dodgy, *a.* Add: Also of things.
1898 Shaw *Mrs. Warren's Prof.* I. i, Take care of your fingers: theyre rather dodgy things, those chairs.

Dodrat, var. of *Dod-rotted *ppl. a.*
1897 *Outing* (U.S.) XXX. 273/2 This is the dodrattest place I ever struck.

Dod-rot, *v.* U.S. *vulgar.* [f. *Dod- + Rot *v.*] = *Dodgast *v.* Hence **Do·d-rotted** *ppl. a.*
1842 *American Pioneer* I. 347 'Dod rot'em', said the old hunter, 'I would not let them have a bushel'. 1885 'C. E. Craddock' *Prophet Gt. Smoky Mtn.* vi. 121 'Dod-rot that critter', exclaimed the sheriff, angrily. 1887 *Century Mag.* (Farmer) 'You ketch us with yer dodrotted foolin'', says he. 1911 R. D. Saunders *Col. Todhunter* vii. 100 That dod-rotted old lady is a-movin' Heaven and earth to make a match.

Dœgling (dö·gliŋ). [Native name in the Faröe Islands.] The beaked whale, which yields *dœgling oil*. Hence **Dœglic** (dö·glik) *a.*, in *dœglic acid*, obtained by saponification of dœgling oil.
1890 Roscoe & Schorlemmer *Treat. Chem.* III. II. 483 Dœglic Acid, $C_{19}H_{36}O_2$. The glyceride of this acid forms, according to Scharling, the principal part of the dœgling train oil.

Dog, *sb.* Add:
15. n. *To put on dog*: to assume pretentious airs. *colloq.*
1915 Kipling *Fringes of Fleet* (1916) 36 Ah! That's the king of the Trawlers. Isn't he carrying dog too! Give him room! 1924 W. J. Locke *Coming of Amos* xii, I don't want to put on dog, but the Lord didn't give me physical strength for nothing. 1926 — *Old Bridge* II. v, Young Blake puts on dog and condescends to take the order.
17. a. in ref. to greyhound racing, as *dog-race, -racer, -racing, -track.*
1864 *Chambers's Jrnl.* 502/2 Betting more than you can afford upon a dog-race. 1865 *Ibid.* 657/2 They are also fond of dog-racing. 1875 *Ibid.* 254/1 Excluded from enjoying the pleasures of bull-baiting, the Lancashire rough falls back on dog-racing or some similar sport which admits of betting. *Ibid.*, Manchester..being the headquarters of the rabbit-courser;..and the colliery districts generally, of the dog-racer. 1928 *Observer* 25 Mar. 16/6 The Ministry of Health has decided that Wimbledon must put up with a dog-track, however much the Council and inhabitants may resent it. 1928 *Manchester Guardian Weekly* 10 Aug. 113/4 The Dog-racing bill.
18. a. **dog-musher** U.S., one who uses a dog-team

for sledging; **dog-sled** (earlier example); **dog-team**, a team of dogs used for drawing a sled; **dog-town** (earlier example).
1907 Jack London *White Fang* 215 *Dog-mushers' cries were heard..They saw, up the trail, two men running with sled and dogs. 1823 S. H. Long *Exped. Rocky Mtns.* I. 186 By..preparing their saddles and *dog-sleds. 1865 *Rep. U.S. Comm. Agric.* (1869) 174 The warm sun at noon melts the snow a little forming a hard crust. Over this the dog-sleds can go anywhere. 1928 *Publishers' Weekly* 16 June 2461 The author worked as a *dog-team freighter in Alaska during the gold-rush. 1854 J. R. Bartlett *Personal Narr.* I. iv. 70 The vast domains of this community, or '*dog-town', as they are usually called.
b. **dog's age** U.S., a long time; **dog's body** (see also quots. below); **dog's chance**, the poorest chance; cf. *dog-chance* in 18 a in Dict.
1836 *Knickerbocker Mag.* VII. 17 That blamed line gale has kept me in bilboes such a *dog's age. 1916 H. L. Wilson *Somewhere in Red Gap* v. 175 Booming pained surmises through the house as to what fearful state it would get to be in if she didn't fight it to a clean finish once in a dog's age. 1919 T. K. Holmes *Man fr. Tall Timber* v. 55, I don't get a letter once in a dog's age from any of them. 1924 Rex Clements *Gipsy of Horn* 38 Sea-biscuits soaked into a pulp with water and sugar, are known as '*dogs-body'. 1928 *Daily Express* 3 Apr. 13/2 A midshipman is known..in the service as a 'snottie'...If he is a junior midshipman he is also a 'dog's body'. I defy anyone to be accurate and sentimental about a snottie who is a dog's body. 1902 *Captain* VII. 542/1 They all felt that Adderman's wouldn't have a *dog's chance when Ardenwood College had got fairly going.
c. **dog salmon**, a salmon of the species *Oncorhynchus keta* and *O. gorbuscha* of the Pacific coast; **dog-winkle**, the marine gastropod *Purpura lapillus*.
1881 *Amer. Naturalist* XV. 178 The males of all the species in the fall are usually known as *dog salmon, or fall salmon. 1901 *Westm. Gaz.* 16 Dec. 3/1 The Tyrian purple of the ancients can be obtained from the common *dog-winkle (*purpura lapillus*).

Dog-brier. (Later U.S. example.)
1840 C. F. Hoffman *Greyslaer* II. xi. 42 A spot where some huge rocks, covered only with dog-briers let down the light..into the forest.

Dog-collar. 2. Add: *spec.* used as a derogatory term for the clerical collar.
1868 *Good Words* 1 July 445/1 He wore the dress, clerical 'dog-collar' included, in which Roman Catholic priests usually take their walks abroad. 1931 *Tablet* 21 Feb. 234/2 Jewish Rabbis..as well as Free Church pastors, are often seen wearing what the profane call 'dog-collars'.
b. *attrib.*
1903 *Daily Chron.* 17 Oct. 8/4 The latest ornaments for the throat are of the dog-collar pattern. 1904 *Ibid.* 3 Nov. 5/6 Diamond dog-collar necklet.

Dogeate (dōᵘ·dʒe̦ɪt). [f. Doge + -ate¹.] = Dogate.
1923 *J. Buchan's Nations of To-Day, Italy* 5 In the Dogeate of Pietro Orseolo.

Dog-fennel. (U.S. example.)
1873 E. Eggleston *Myst. Metrop.* 12 A country road where the dog-fennel blooms almost undisturbed by comers and goers.

Dog-fight. Add:
2. *transf.* A general shindy or mêlée.
1917 Kipling *Diversity of Creatures* (1917) 208 The pitiless Whips were even then at the telephones to head 'em up to another dog-fight. 1919 A. E. Illingworth *Fly Papers* 79 The battle develops into a 'dog-fight', small groups of machines engaging each other in a fight to the death. 1927 F. E. Baily *Golden Vanity* xiv, No dividend, reserve fund wiped out, and a dog-fight at the annual general meeting. 1928 C. F. S. Gamble *N. Sea Air Station* xxii. 400 It was decided that all flying-boats should have their hulls 'dazzle-painted'..so that a pilot could, in a 'dog-fight', know at a glance who was in a particular machine.

Dogged, *a.* 3. Add vulgar phrase: *It's dogged as does it*: persistency and tenacity win in the end.
1867 Trollope *Last Chronicle of Barset* lxi, There ain't nowt a man can't bear if he'll only be dogged...It's dogged as does it. 1896 *Daily News* 27 June 8/1 All his own writing seems to have been done in about three hours a day. 'It's dogged as does it,' he has been wont to explain.

Doggery. 4. U.S. (Earlier examples.)
1835 D. P. Thompson *Timothy Peacock* 140 (Th.) A sort of Dutch doggery, or sailor's hotel, situated near the wharf. 1843 R. Carlton *New Purchase* xxii. 212 He has agents to treat at his expense at every doggery. 1853 J. G. Baldwin *Flush Times Alabama* 65 An altercation had arisen at the grocery (fashionably called doggery).

Dogging, *vbl. sb.* (see under Dog *v.*). Add: Grouse-shooting over dogs, as distinguished from 'driving'. Also *attrib.*
1894 [see *dogging vbl. sb.*, s.v. Dog *v.*]. 1904 *Westm. Gaz.* 19 Aug. 4/2 On the 'dogging' moors..the actual shooting will begin as soon as it becomes legal. 1905 *Kynoch Jrnl.* Jan.–Mar. 41 Very soon after dogging operations were commenced on August 12th. 1907 *Westm. Gaz.* 16 Aug. 4/2 If he wants to spread his shooting out over many days..he can do this on the 'dogging' method. 1908 *Ibid.* 14 Aug. 5/2 When the shooting-time came for 'the dogging men'. 1928 *Daily Tel.* 26 June 13/5 The shooting extends to 16,000 acres and is an excellent dogging moor.

Doggo (dǫ·go), *adv. slang.* [Of obscure origin: prob. f. Dog *sb.*] *To lie doggo*: to lie quiet, to remain hid. Also occas. with other verbs.
1893 Kipling *Many Invent.*, *Love-o'-women* 259, I wud lie most powerful doggo whin I heard a shot. 1916 Rosher *In R.N.A.S.* 141 In the meanwhile lie doggo and do come down this week-end. 1918 Vachell *Some Happenings* iv, You'll play doggo and keep out of sight. 1924 *Blackw. Mag.* Sept. 352/2, I stayed doggo in the scrub. 1924 A. J. Small *Frozen Gold* i. 36 That Indian is lying doggo. 1924 Rose Macaulay *Orphan Island* iii. 39 Islands..are chancey little devils. They lie doggo, saying nothing, just below the horizon, while you steam by.

Doggy, doggie, *sb.* Add: 3. An officer who assists an admiral in his duties. *Naval slang.*
1921 *Blackw. Mag.* July 50/2 Is the Admiral going to have a doggie?

Doggy, *a.* Add: 4. Of Latin: Debased, corrupt. (See Dog *sb.* 17 e.) *colloq.*
1898 *Daily News* 3 Jan. 6/3 He spoke Latin! patristic Latin of the doggyest order.

Dog-house. (Later U.S. examples.)
1879 F. R. Stockton *Rudder Grange* vii. 77, I had no dog-house as yet. 1898 Susan Hale *Lett.* 338 Behind the dog-house there is a warren of..four small animals.

Dogie, dogy (dōᵘ·gi). U.S. [Of obscure origin.] A motherless calf on a cattle range.
1903 A. Adams *Log Cowboy* vii. 86 Before you could say Jack Robinson our dogies..were running in half a dozen different directions. 1911 H. Quick *Yellowstone N.* v. 126 To them as think strange of ten thousand steers, even dogies, bein' bought by a busted boomer. 1920 Hunter *Trail Drivers of Texas* 151 It took us just exactly three months and twenty days to drive a herd of southern 'dogies' from Red River.
attrib. 1911 H. Quick *Yellowstone N.* v. 124 The Old Man ..was a one-lunger when this dogie enterprise started. 1920 Hunter *Trail Drivers of Texas* 130 A dogie calf that had got into the herd several days before.

Dog-leg, *a.* Add: b. *Dog-leg hole*, in *Golf.*
1907 *Daily Chron.* 17 Aug. 7/2 There are two or three very fine specimens of the dog-leg kind of hole. 1909 *Westm. Gaz.* 30 Apr. 4/2 There is the occasional variety of the 'dog-leg' hole, where the player has to go round an angle.
2. Applied to an inferior quality of tobacco. U.S.
1863 'E. Kirke' *My Southern Friends* iii. 48 The other [apartment] was densely crowded with logwood, 'dog-leg', ..and cistern water. 1868 *Congress. Globe* 18 Mar., App. 287/1 Watching the neighbors pitch horseshoes for dog-leg tobacco. 1891 Marah E. Ryan *Pagan of Alleghanies* ii. 25 Then the black-and-tan man treated himself to a fresh chew of 'dog-leg'.

Dog-legged, *a.* Add: b. Of a fence (see Dog-leg *a.*). *Austral.*
1900 H. Lawson *Over Sliprails* 95 A spidery dog-legged fence.

Dogoned, var. of Dog-goned *a.*
1868 *All Year Round* 19 Sept. 353/2 He looks the dogondest cuss ever since Jim Ford left. 1872 E. Eggleston *End of World* xxiii. 158 Clark township don't want none of 'em, I'll be dog-oned if it do.

Dog's-ear, *sb.* 2. U.S. (Earlier example.)
1840 R. H. Dana *Bef. Mast* iv, The first [man] on the yard goes to the weather earing, the second to the lee, and the next two to the 'dog's ears'.

Dog-wolf. Add: 2. = Wolf-dog 2.
1907 Sodenkamp in *Kennel Encycl.* I. 159 At a dog show at Spa, in 1882, several 'Dog-wolves' were exhibited, and the animals so termed in the catalogue.

Dog-wood. Add: 3. b. = *dog-wood bark* (see 4).
1843 R. Carlton *New Purchase* xxxiv. 16 Give them their dog-wood and cherry-bitters every morning into the bargain!

Doing, *vbl. sb.* Add: 1. c. A scolding, dressing-down. *colloq.*
1880 *Antrim & Down Gloss.*, *Doing off*, a scolding. 1923 Lady Astor in *Parlt. Deb.* CLXVI. 1782 The hon. Member for Dundee has given me a tremendous doing.
4. *pl.* Materials for a specified adjunct of a dish or meal (in quot. 1856 *fig.*); also, a made or fancy dish. U.S. *local.*
1838 E. Flagg *Far West* II. 72 'Well, stranger, what'll ye take: wheat-bread and chicken fixens, or corn-bread and common doins?' by the latter..being signified bacon. 1843 R. Carlton *New Purchase* II. xl. 58 A snug breakfast of chicken fixins, eggs, ham-doins, and corn slapjacks. 1856 *Knickerbocker Mag.* Apr. XLVII. 406 (Th.) Pretty girl there in the black fixings, and white arrangements, with blue doings. 1859 *Ibid.* LIII. 317 Tell Sal to..have some flour-doins and chicken-fixins for the stranger. *Ibid.* 318 Instead of 'store-tea' they had only saxifrax tea-doins, without milk. 1881 J. C. Harris *Uncle Remus* i. 18 Sposen' you drap roun' termorrer an' take dinner wid me. We ain't got no great doin's at our house, but I speck de old 'oman..kin sorter scramble roun' 'en git up sump'n. 1908 *Dialect Notes* III. iv. 306 *Doing(s)*,..prepared dishes, especially fancy dishes.
b. (orig. *War slang.*) Applied to any concomitant, adjunct, or 'etcetera', or anything that happens to be 'about' or to be wanted.
1919 *War Slang* in *Athenæum* 25 July 664/2 'Doings', practically anything: 'Pass the doings.' 1925 Fraser & Gibbons *Soldier & Sailor Words*, *Doings, the*, a word with every kind of meaning and application. E.g., In quarters, 'Pass the doings', might mean bread, salt, a pack of cards, or anything at hand. 'Ill have a drop of the doings' (i.e., whatever drink there is going). 'Here comes Jerry with the doings' (i.e. an enemy aeroplane sighted). 1927 W. E. Collinson *Contemp. Engl.* 101 Doings for gravy, salt, sugar, pepper, milk or anything wanted at a particular time for a particular purpose.

Dole, *sb.*¹ 6. Add: *The dole*: the popular name for the various kinds of weekly payments made from national or local funds to the unemployed since the war of 1914–18. Phr. (*to be* or *go*) *on the dole*: to be in receipt of such unemployment relief.
1919 *Daily Mail* 11 June 8/4 You won't draw your out-of-work dole of 29s. this week. 1923 L. Allen Harker *Master & Maid* (new ed.) xx. 265 If only I'd danced an Irish jig I believe I could have got the whole of them to increase the dole. 1925 *Westm. Gaz.* 26 Mar., 3,000 Aliens on the Dole. 1926 *Good Housekeeping* July 188/2 Profiteers, dole-drawers and music-hall artists—in fact, the only people who have any money to-day. 1928 *Britain's Industrial Future* (*Lib. Ind. Inq.*) 277 To speak of Unemployment Benefit as 'the dole' is to misrepresent the facts.

Dolichocephal (dǫlikose·fəl). [ad. mod.L. Dolichocephali *pl.*] A dolichocephalic person. Also *adj.*
1876 tr. *O. Peschel's Races of Man* 55 If the index [of breadth] sinks below 74, we speak of 'dolichocephal', narrow or long skulls. 1901 G. Sergi *Mediterranean Race* I. 12 The present populations of southern Germany are in great part brachycephals, among whom mesocephals are rare and dolichocephals quite isolated. 1912 A. C. Haddon *Wand. Peoples* 16 The tall, fair, blue-eyed dolichocephals of north Europe.

Dolichomorphic (dǫlikomǭ·ɹfik), *a. Ethnol.* [f. Gr. δολιχός long + μορφή form + -ic.] Having disproportionately long bodily members, as the head and neck.
1930 R. L. Sutton *Long Trek* 162 In bodily conformation, the typical Mbulu is dolichomorphic. The head is considerably longer than it is wide, the neck is long, the chest is phthisical.

Doll (dǫl), *v.*² *colloq.* [f. Doll *sb.*¹ 2.] *trans.* To dress *up* finely; to deck *up*. Also *intr.* (for *refl.*).
1906 *Even. Standard* 31 Aug. 3/3 The time fellows spent in dolling up before taking a wheel. 1916 H. L. Wilson *Somewhere in Red Gap* ix. 378 Jeff said he'd also doll up in his dress suit and get shaved. 1917 Mathewson *Sec. Base Sloan* xix. 261 He was..all dolled up in fancy togs. 1921 *Public Opinion* 9 Sept. 252/1 Keturah dolled herself up a little but not too much. 1927 M. Eiker *Over the Boat-Side* 269 She had been exquisitely costumed. If she ever did run into Reverdy, she hoped it would be some time when she was dolled. 1928 Galsworthy *Swan Song* II. xiii. 216 He supposed his fellow-guests were 'dolling up' (as young Michael would put it) for this ball.

Dollar. Add: 3. b. The value of a dollar; an amount answering to this. U.S.
1851 C. Cist *Cincinnati* 231 Geo. S. Stearns..makes yearly eight thousand dollars of printing inks.
6. *dollar-bill, -note* (earlier examples); **dollar store** U.S., a shop in which each article is priced at a dollar.
1831 *Deb. Congress* 22 Feb., App. p. cxxxix, Taking the issues of one, two, and three dollar notes, in the Eastern States as a guide. *a* 1861 T. Winthrop *Canoe & Saddle* (1862) 21 Have we not all been educated..by handling the dollar-bills of civilization? 1887 *Harper's Mag.* July 245/2 Those houses are built, for the most part, by wealthy Hebrews, brokers or dollar-store men.
b. with reference to the pursuit and worship of 'the almighty dollar' (see quot. 1837 in 3).
1892 Stevenson & Osbourne *Wrecker* ix, Of all forms of the dollar-hunt, this wrecking had by far the most address to my imagination. 1897 *Outing* (U.S.) XXX. 373/1 Our striving, dollar-chasing people. 1900 *Daily News* 25 Sept. 4/6 The dollar-hunting Americans. 1901 *Westm. Gaz.* 5 July 2/1 The father is regarded as the dollar-grinding machine. 1902 *Ibid.* 9 May 9/1 What if the American Dollar-Kings hold the keys to the railway depots of the great Western Continent? 1906 *Fabian News* XVI. 7/1 It is not life but the dollar-hustle which is copious, vehement and bold for this hundred-million nation. 1906 *Westm. Gaz.* 17 Dec. 2/1 Washington society escapes the dollar-mark with entire success. 1920 *Blackw. Mag.* Aug. 139/1 Manhattan Dollardom trooped into the Ritz-Carlton carrying flasks.

Do·ll-ba·by. U.S. [Doll *sb.*¹ 2.] A doll. Also *attrib.*
1807 Jefferson *Let. Writ.* (1898) IX. 83 The dresses of the annual doll-babies from Paris. 1853 J. G. Baldwin *Flush Times Alabama* 42 She never had more than a thimbleful of brains in her doll-baby head. 1887 Mrs. Smedes *Mem. Southern Planter* vii. (1880) 57 Let us light the candles and play with your doll-babies. 1897 R. M. Stuart *Simpkinsville* 59 Same ez if a doll-baby was to commence to talk by machinery.

Do·ll's house. Also dolls' house, U.S. doll house. [Doll *sb.*¹ 2.] A miniature toy house made for dolls; hence, applied to a diminutive dwelling-house.
1852 Dickens *Bleak House* vi, A habitable doll's house. 1882 H. F. Lord *Nora* p. v, To a public unused to Ibsen's surprises, *A Doll's House* [Norw. *Et Dukkehjem*] is a misleading title. 1904 *Daily Chron.* 2 July 8/1 The little stone houses..and their diminutive doll's-house windows. 1924 (*title*) The Book of the Queen's Dolls' House. 1926 W. Deeping *Sorrell & Son* xxiv, Christopher spent a week-end with Thomas Roland in his doll's house at Chelsea. 1928 F. N. Hart *Bellamy Trial* ii. 44 He'd made Polly a wonderful doll house.

Dolly, *sb.*¹ Add: 4. h. A platform with a roller used as a truck. U.S.
1901 S. Merwin & H. K. Webster *Calumet K* vi. 104 Other gangs were carrying them [*sc.* planks] away and piling them on 'dollies' to be pulled along the plank runways to the hoist. *Ibid.* xiii. 246 And every stick that leaves the runway has got to go on a dolly.
5. **dolly-bag**, a small bag or purse carried by women.
1927 Mottram *Spanish Farm Trilogy* 595 She carried the day's takings clasped to her breast, in a solid little leather dolly-bag.

Dolly, *a.* Add: b. *Games.* Designating a simple or 'soft' catch, shot, etc.
1895 in *Eng. Dial. Dict.* s.v. 1904 *Daily Chron.* 17 Aug. 7/3 Wells received a 'dolly' catch and bowl off the splice. 1909 *Westm. Gaz.* 2 Mar. 12/2 Till then he had played a grand game, and had saved many clever shots, only in the end to be beaten by a 'dolly one'.

Do·lomite, *v.* [f. the sb.] = Dolomitize *v.*
1913 V. B. Lewes *Oil Fuel* 32 The carbon dioxide dissolved in the brine under enormous pressure would slowly become absorbed in actions upon the mineral matter present, such as forming carbonates and soluble bicarbonates of magnesia, thus dolomiting the calcareous deposits.

Doloroso (dǫlŏrōᵘ·so), *a. Mus.* [It.: see Dolorous *a.*] As a direction to the performer: Plaintive, pathetic.
1876 Stainer & Barrett *Dict. Mus. Terms.*

Dolphin. Add: 6. f. (See quot.) U.S.
1905 *Terms Forestry & Logging* 35 *Dolphin*, a cluster of piles to which a boom is secured.

Dom³ (dōᵘm). Also dome. [Hind. *Ḍōm*, f. Sanskr. *Ḍōma, Ḍōmba.*] A member of a Dravidian menial caste, of Bengal, Behar, and the North-Western Provinces.
1828 H. H. Wilson in *Asiatic Researches* XVIII. 47 Nābhāji..was by birth a *Dom*, a caste whose employ is making baskets and various sort of wicker work. 1869 *H. M. Elliot's Races N.W. Prov.* I. 84 Ramgarh and Sahankot, on the Rohini, are also Dom forts. *Ibid.* 85 The Magahya Doms of Champāran are a race of professional thieves. 1872 Sherring *Hindu Tribes* 400 The Dom is generally considered by Hindus to be the type and representative of all uncleanness. 1891 H. H. Risley *Ethnogr. Gloss.* I. 243 When a man has been ejected from his own caste for living with a Dom woman.

Dome, *sb.* Add:
4. c. The head. U.S. *slang.*
1918 C. Sandburg *Cornhuskers* 60 Your bony head..Those grappling hooks..The dome and the wings of you. 1921 R. D. Paine *Comr. Rolling Ocean* ix. 160 He got tired of trying to shove the book stuff into ivory domes like yours.
6. **dome fastener**, a kind of spring fastener for a glove; **dome-headed** *a.*, having a large, well-rounded head.
1910 *Daily Chron.* 14 Mar. 6/4 Ladies' Kid Gloves..with 2 or 3 dome fasteners. 1910 H. G. Wells *Mr. Polly* vii. 153 A certain high-browed gentleman living at Highbury... This dome-headed monster of intellect alleges [etc.].

Domestic, *a.* and *sb.* Add: A. *adj.* 2. *Domestic economy, science*; **domestic workshop**, a workshop in a private dwelling-house.
1778 [see Economy 2]. 1797 F. M. Eden (*title*) The State of the Poor, or an History of the Labouring Classes in England,..in which are particularly considered, Their Domestic Economy, with respect to Diet, Dress, Fuel, and Habitation. 1878 *Act* 41 *Vict.* c. 16 *margin*, Period of employment.. for children and young persons in domestic workshop. 1915 'Bartimeus' *A Tall Ship* ii. 37 Cooking and laundry, and hygiene—domestic science it's called.
3. (Recent examples.)
1898 *Daily News* 12 May 6/7 London..began buying later, and this, combined with heavy domestic buying, sent prices upward rapidly. 1903 *Churchman* (U.S.) 14 Nov. 608 The domestic postage on this copy of the Churchman is 2 cents. The foreign postage is 3 cents.
b. (Recent example.)
1907 J. L. Howe *Inorg. Chem.* 213 The ammonia process ..for many years furnished the only domestic soda, the larger part of that used being imported.
B. *sb.* 4. b. *sing.* A specific article of home manufacture.
1894 Mary J. Jaques *Texan Ranch Life* 113 The large spinning wheel, with which Mrs. B...made by hand the 'domestic' (calico) for her household. 1905 F. Hopkinson Smith *At Close Range* 74 Sam..tilted his domestic at a higher angle, and went out to view the harbor. *Ibid.* 85 This done, he drew out a domestic from the upper pocket, bit off the end, slid a match along the well-worn seam and blew a ring out to sea.

Domett. Add: In more recent use domette.
1901 *Daily Chron.* 23 Nov. 8/3 Close-grained cloth coats, lined with fur, or with satin, or sandwiched with domette between it and the cloth. 1910 *Practitioner* Mar. 367 A many-tailed bandage of domette.

Dominance. Add:
2. *Biol.* The character of being dominant in cross-bred descent. See *Dominant *a.* 6.
1902 W. Bateson *Mendel's Princ. Hered.* 119 The Facts in regard to Dominance of Characters in Peas. *Ibid.*, The dominance of the smooth form over the wrinkled. 1916 J. Wilson *Man. Mendelism* 24 If the pairs in which the parents differ are clearly defined at the hybrid generation as regards dominance and recessiveness. 1925 T. H. Morgan *Evol. & Genetics* 151 The Dominance of the Wild Type Genes.

Dominant, *a.* and *sb.* Add: 6. *Biol.* Applied by Mendel to a marked parental character which is transmitted to a cross-bred descendant.
See Mendel in *Abhandlungen des naturforsch. Vereines in Brünn* IV. 1865.
1900 W. Bateson in *Jrnl. Royal Hort. Soc.* XXV. 58 In the case of each pair of characters there is thus one which in the first cross prevails to the exclusion of the other. This prevailing character Mendel calls the dominant character, the other being the recessive character. 1925 C. C. Hurst *Exper. in Genetics* 246 In each pair, when crossed, Mendel found the first-named character dominant over the other. 1925 T. H. Morgan *Evol. & Genetics* 151 The genes that arise by mutation have been found to be largely recessive to the genes already present in the original type which are said, therefore, to be dominant to the new genes.
7. *Forestry.* Overtopping other trees; said esp. of those trees in a forest which have their crowns free to light on all sides.
1893 J. Nisbet *Sel. Trees Woodland Crops* 21 Four classes of stems become distinguishable, viz., (1) predominating, (2) dominant, (3) dominated, and (4) suppressed. 1908 A. M. F. Caccia *Gloss. Techn. Terms Ind. Forestry*, *Dominant*, a tree which has raised its crown above the level of the surrounding trees. 1930 *Indian Forestry Rec.* XV. 1. 2 Dominant Trees, including all trees which form the uppermost leaf canopy and have their leading shoots free.
B. *sb.* 3. *Biol.* A marked parental character which is transmitted to cross-bred descendants; an organism exhibiting such character.
1900 W. Bateson in *Jrnl. Royal Hort. Soc.* XXV. 58 In this generation the numerical proportion of dominants to recessives is..as three to one. 1905 Punnett *Mendelism* 10 There are dominants which breed to the dominant character, and are therefore pure. 1913 *Oxf. Univ. Gaz.* 4 June 948/2 *Hypolimnas..dubius*, Beauv., proved to be a Mendelian dominant, and *H. anthedon*, Boisd., recessive. 1920 Pringle-Pattison *Idea of God* 80 *note*, Reinke's 'dominants'..seem to resemble Driesch's entelechies or psychoids.

Dominie, domine. Add:
3. **dominie-apple** U.S., a large variety of apple.
1867 J. A. Warder *Amer. Pomology* 430 Domine..Fruit large, flat, regular. 1876 J. Burroughs *Winter Sunshine* vii. 158 If they were the dominie apples..he certainly would [hasten his sermon].

Dominion. Add: 2. b. Applied individually in sing. or generally in pl. to countries outside England or Great Britain under the sovereignty or suzerainty of the English crown; †formerly, to the principality of Wales; *the Old* or *Ancient Dominion*, Virginia, U.S.A.
1606 *First Charter Virginia* in H. W. Preston *Amer. Hist.* (1886) 9 The said several Colonies and Plantations,.. they being of any Realms, or Dominions under our Obedience. 1623–4 *Act* 21 *Jas. I* c. 3 Within this Realm, or the Dominion of Wales. 1682 *Acts of Assembly Virginia* (1727) I. 142 His Majesty's Subjects, being in this his Majesty's Dominion of Virginia. 1684 *Ibid.* 146 Inhabitants of this his Majesty's Colony and Dominion of Virginia. 1700 *Act* 11 & 12 *Will. III* c. 12 § 1 Commanders in Chief of Plantations and Colonies within his Majesty's Dominions beyond the Seas. *Ibid.* c. 19 § 7 Any Prisons..belonging to any County of this Realm, or the Dominion of Wales. 1808 *Deb. Congress* 7 Apr. (1852) 2024 In 1798, everything went on merrily—no dissentients, except one or two States, the Old Dominion and her eldest daughter. 1824 H. C. Knight ('A. Singleton') *Lett. fr. South & West* 69 (Thornton) The chief sickness in this ancient dominion, is in the autumn. 1828 *Richmond Whig* 16 Feb. 2/3 (ibid.) His idea of the Ancient Dominion is very much confined to that part of the State which lies below and near to the tide water. 1850 Foote in *Congressional Globe* 28 Jan. 237/2 [Richmond] that famous metropolis of the Ancient Dominion.
(*b*) Designating the larger self-governing British colonies. The title was given *spec.* to Canada in 1867 (1 July) and to New Zealand in 1907 (28 Sept.).
1867 *Act* 30 & 31 *Vict.* c. 3 § 3 The Provinces of Canada, Nova Scotia, and New Brunswick shall form and be One Dominion under the Name of Canada. 1901 *Proclamation Edw. VII* 4 Nov. 2 The following addition shall be made to the Style and Titles at present appertaining to the Imperial Crown of the United Kingdom and its Dependencies; that is to say, in the Latin tongue, after the word 'Britanniarum', these words 'et terrarum transmarinarum quæ in ditione sunt Britannicâ'; and in the English tongue, after the words 'of the United Kingdom of Great Britain and Ireland', these words, 'and of the British Dominions beyond the Seas'. 1901 *Act* 1 *Edw. VII* c. 15 An Act to enable His most gracious Majesty to make an Addition to the Royal Style and Titles in recognition of His Majesty's dominions beyond the seas. 1907 *Times* 1 Mar. 10/2 They had found themselves in complete agreement with the Premiers and Ministers of Defence of the King's Dominions across the seas. *Ibid.* 22 Apr. 14/2 The Prime Ministers of the self-governing Dominions. 1910 Clough (*title*) History of the British Dominions beyond the Seas (1558–1910). 1912 A. B. Keith *Respons. Govt. in Domin.* III. 1313 Since the Colonial Conference of 1907 Dominion is a technical term for the self-governing Colonies. 1930 *Daily Tel.* 27 May 10, I look forward to the day when Indian liberty will be enlarged in order that she will take her place as a fully self-governing Dominion in the Dominions of the Empire.

Domino. Add:
3. d. Hence *subst.* (see quot. 1874). *It is domino with*: it is all up with, there is no hope for. *slang.*
1874 *Slang Dict.* s.v., A domino means either a blow, or the last of a series of things, whether pleasant or otherwise. 1898 *Daily News* 10 Feb. 7/3 The young delinquent sullenly declared that James struck him first, whereupon he 'gave him domino for himself'. 1927 *Chambers's Jrnl.* 45/1, I thought it was domino with me and my little schemes.
e. *To make (the) domino*: to go out at the game of dominoes; also *fig.* to anticipate the end.
1890 'Berkeley' *Dominoes & Solitaire* 11 Sometimes each hand constitutes a game in itself; and when this is so, the player who makes 'domino' wins. 1892 C. Santley *Student & Singer* (ed. 3) 24 At the rehearsal of Rossini's 'Stabat Mater', in my eagerness, I did not notice the bar's rest before the 'Amen', and performed a solo, which called forth some witty remark from Benedict about the future career of the singer who made the 'domino', and some merriment at my expense from the orchestra.
g. pl. *The dominoes*: the keys of a piano. *Box of dominoes*: a piano. *slang.*
1889 Barrère & Leland *Dict. Slang*, *Domino thumper* (theatrical), a pianist. 1891 Farmer *Slang*, *Dominoes*..2. (colloquial). The keys of a piano.
h. A design or picture printed on paper from a wood-block and coloured. Hence *domino-paper*, an early kind of wall-paper decorated with these designs. [F. *domino, papier dominoté.*]
1924 N. McClelland *Hist. Wall-papers* 20 The industry which gave the *Dominotiers* their name was the making of 'domino papers', which consisted principally of marbleized papers and again of others with little figures and grotesques, crudely printed from wood-blocks and coloured by hand. These 'dominos' were made in Rouen and in other cities.. of France. 1926 Sugden & Edmondson *Hist. Engl. Wall-paper* 27 In France, 'domino' papers are regarded as the real forbears of paper-hangings. *Ibid.* 28 'Domino' papers were usually small—16½ in. by 12½ in.—and all the earliest were 'marbled'.

Don, *sb.*¹ 1. c. Add: **Don Juane·sque** *a.*, **Don Quixote** (examples).
1898 W. Graham *Last Links* 33 Byron's manner was tinged with a vein of *Don-Juanesque recklessness. 1926 W. J. Locke *Old Bridge* III. ix, Where her father was a Don Juanesque clerk in a factory. 1900 Conan Doyle *Gt. Boer War* x. 167 His long thin figure, his gaunt *Don-Quixote face. 1902 *Pall Mall Gaz.* 4 Jan. 6/3 The Woman's Suffrage Society has again made its voice heard in the land...This Don Quixote of a society has made an assault upon the most solid of windmills.
6. (Example of the shortened form.)
1897 *Daily News* 16 Mar. 8/3 Two detectives..saw the prisoners playing Don.

Donah. *slang.* See Dona 2.

Donate (dōᵘ·ne̦ɪt), **donat** (dōᵘ·næt), *sb.* [ad. med.L. *dōnātus, -a*, pa. pple. of *dōnāre* to give.] One who is aggregated to a religious order and imparts to it his worldly goods, without becoming a member.
1902 Bedford & Holbeche *Order Hosp. St. John Jerus.* 207 In addition to Members there should be Honorary Associates and Donats—..the Donats being persons who, from an appreciation of the works of the Order, had contributed to its funds. 1911 *Encycl. Brit.* XXIV. 13/1 Affiliated brethren (*confratres*) and 'donats' (*donati*, i. e. regular subscribers..to the order in return for its privileges). 1925 C. S. Durrant *Flem. Mystics & Engl. Martyrs* 45 Here [at Diepenveen] he saw about a hundred veiled nuns with no small number of lay sisters, donates, and servants.

Donate, *v.* 1. Example of U.S. use.
1928 S. Vines *Humours Unreconciled* xxi. 270 Godly millionaires..'donating' motors and villas at climatic stations to their missionaries abroad.

Donation. 4. Add: **donation act** U.S. (see quot.); **donation party** (earlier examples).
1894 *Congress. Rec.* 17 July 7572/2 Certain lands disposed of under the act of Congress approved Sept. 27, 1850, and the acts amendatory and supplemented thereto,..commonly known as the '*donation act'. 1845 S. Judd *Margaret* II. v. 290 One day there was a *donation party at our house. 1846–52 Mrs. Whitcher *Widow Bedott P.* xxiii. 249 They agreed to give him four hundred dollars a year and a donation party every winter.

Donatism, Donatist, Donative, Donatory. The pronunciation of the first syllable is now generally (dōᵘ).

Donkey. Add:
3. b. **donkey-drop** *colloq.*, a slow, high, dropping ball; **donkey-jacket**, a thick jacket worn by workmen as a protection against wet, mud, etc.; **donkey's breakfast** *Sailors' slang* (see quot.); **donkey's ears** (or **years**) *jocular slang* [arising from such an expression as *years and years—and donkey's years*, with punning allusion to the frequent pronunciation of *ears* as *years*], a very long time; **donkey-sled** U.S. (see quot.); **donkey-work**, hard unattractive work.
1890 Lyttelton *Cricket* 69 Slow round-hand bowling,.. known by the contumelious designation of '*donkey-drops'. 1906 *P.T.O.* I. 21/2 There are worse 'donkey-drops' than those he sends down. 1927 *Daily Tel.* 14 June 9/1 He is content to play 'donkey drops' back into court, awaiting the right ball to hit. 1929 *Morning Post* 4 Oct., Members of the City Corporation wanted to know at yesterday's meeting at the Guildhall what a *donkey jacket is... Mr. Gower explained that the jacket was one with leather shoulders and back. 1901 W. C. Russell *Ship's Adv.* iii, Explaining..that the term '*donkey's breakfast* signified the bundle of straw which sailors who are reckless of their money ashore carry on board ship with them as a bed. 1916 E. V. Lucas *Vermilion Box* lxxvii. 86 Now for my first bath for what the men call '*Donkey's ears', meaning years and years. 1927 H. Walpole *Great Trad.* xvi, I was at the wedding, you know,..'aving worked for Miss Janet and her sister donkey's years. 1928 S. Vines *Humours Unreconciled* ix. 121 He hasn't talked emotionally to me for donkey's years. 1929 Vachell *Virgin* xii. 190 Winkie was famous for his luncheons, but never, not for donkey's years, had he asked young girls to help to eat them. 1905 *Terms Forestry & Logging* 35 '*Donkey sled*, the heavy sled-like frame upon which a donkey engine is fastened. 1920 *Nat. Rev.* Apr. 145 Most of the '*donkey-work of this preposterous League has fallen on British shoulders. 1928 *Sunday Dispatch* 8 July 20/5 It would never do for a player to bat and not take his share of the donkey-work afterwards!

Donnée (done). [Fr., fem. pa. pple. of *donner* to give.] The subject, theme, or motif of a story, play, etc.
1878 H. James *Fr. Poets & Novelists* 136 The *donnée* of 'Le Père Goriot' is typical. 1879 — *Hawthorne* v. 123 The subject, the *donnée*, as the French say, of the story, does not quite fill it out. 1925 *Glasgow Herald* 29 Aug. 4 In the same tale données from classical myth are also to be encountered.

Donnishly (dǫ·nišli), *adv.* [-ly².] In a donnish manner.
1924 Rose Macaulay *Orphan Island* vii. 76 Mr. Thinkwell signed to him, donnishly, with his hand, to stop talking.

Donnybrook (dǫ·nibruk). [The name of *Donnybrook*, Dublin, Ireland, a town once famous

for its annual fair.] A scene of uproar, disorder, and free fighting; a riotous and uproarious meeting.
1900 *Daily Tel.* 19 Feb. (Ware *Passing Eng.*) The Destroyers' Donnybrook. 1909 *Westm. Gaz.* 13 Dec. 8/2 The Irish election campaign has opened with real 'Donnybrooks'.

Donsie, donsy, *a.* **2.** Add: also, poor, low; low-spirited. *U.S.* (Cf. *DAUNCY *a.*)
1805 *Lancaster* (Pa.) *Jrnl.* 2 Oct. (Th.) Citizen Lafferty must have a 'doncy' opinion of the cause, when he is afraid to bet even. 1853 *Yale Lit. Mag.* XVII. 223 (Th.) [She brought some letters] to my room, to keep me from feeling 'donsy'.

Doo-da, doodah (dū·da). *slang.* [From the refrain *doo-da(h)* of the plantation song 'Camptown Races'.] Phr. *all of a doodah*: in a state of excitement, 'all on wires'.
1915 ROSHER *In R.N.A.S.* (1916) 97, I had lunch with the R—s and five daughters (swish, I was all of a doo-da!). 1928 S. VINES *Humours Unreconciled* xiii. 165 It was the evenings, clearly, that made her 'all of a religious doodah'. 1929 PRIESTLEY *Good Comp.* II. iii. 307, I don't care if a man's been fifty years in the business, there's the same old thrill comes back. Opening night—all of a doodah!

Doodle, *sb.* Add: **2.** A doodle-bug. *U.S.*
1887 *Harper's Mag.* July 276/1 She wondered how the nice, fat little round 'doodles' were getting on in their tin can under the house; she never had had such a fine box of bait.
3. doodle-bug *U.S.*, a tiger-beetle, or the larva of this, used as bait.
1876 'MARK TWAIN' *Tom Sawyer* viii. 76 Doodle-bug, doodle-bug, tell me what I want to know! 1877 BARTLETT *Dict. Amer.* (ed. 4), *Doodle bugs*, a kind of beetles which live in holes in the ground. By calling *doodle* several times near their holes, it is said the bugs will come out. Louisiana. 1903 S. E. WHITE *Forest* vii. 81, I never hesitate to offer them [*sc.* trout] any kind of a doodle-bug they may fancy. *fig.* 1918 MULFORD *Man fr. Bar-20* xviii. 193 'You're a fine pair of doodle-bugs'...'Don't you know an opportunity when you see one?'

Doodle-doo. Playful shortening of COCK-A-DOODLE-DOO.
1904 BARRIE *Peter Pan* v. (1928) 133 HOOK (*slowly*). Cecco, go back and fetch me out that doodle-doo. 1907 D. O'CONNOR *Peter Pan Picture Bk.* 53 He was silenced by a shrill and piercing cock's-crow from the cabin. 'Someone must bring me out that doodledoo', roared the Captain.

Doonga (dū·ngā). *India.* Also **dunga.** [Hind. *dūnga.*] A flat-bottomed dug-out with a square sail.
1905 *Westm. Gaz.* 3 Jan. 2/1 A line of stretchers was winding in and out past the dungas—all laden. 1922 *Chambers's Jrnl.* 759/2 There is the house-boat, the *doonga*—a species of long canoe, with a sloping rush roof.., in which you live. 1925 *Ibid.* 77/1 At Srinagar Durrant hired a large doonga-houseboat.

Door. 8. Add: **door-casing, -facing, -trim** *U.S.* = DOOR-CASE; **door-knob,** a door-handle; **door-prairie** *U.S.* (see quot.); **door-stone** (later example); **door-window,** a window reaching to the floor and opening like a door.
1887 MARY E. WILKINS *Humble Romance* 2 He lounged smilingly against the *door-casing, jingling his scales, and waiting for the woman. 1845 W. G. SIMMS *Wigwam & Cabin* Ser. I. 99, I had been hewing out some *door-facings for a new corn-crib and fodder-house. 1877 *Congress. Rec.* 26 Nov. 705/1 This man.., was sitting up in the door with his feet on the door facing. 1846 *Rep. Comm. Patents* (1847) 63 Several improvements have been patented for improvements in *door-knobs. 1837 *Southern Lit. Messenger* III. 737 The '*door prairies' which..take their name from the fact that they communicate with one another by an opening like a door. 1872 *Rep. Vermont Board Agric.* I. 62 The old apple trees..showered their luscious bounties, ruddy and golden, about the *door-stones of our old homesteads. 1905 *N. Y. Even. Post* 30 Dec. 12 Advt., The corridors, floors, stairways, *doortrims and walls are of marble. 1897 *Outing* (U.S.) XXX. 462/1 Above, outside the hotel, could be seen long *door-windows. 1899 *Daily News* 23 May 5/7 Instead of an ordinary window, I have substituted large French folding doors...My bedroom is also upon the same principle, and the door windows are ever open. 1907 *Westm. Gaz.* 31 Aug. 2/3 He bounded out through the wide-open French window...Vincent slammed the door-window behind him as he jumped.

Doorman (dōə·rmæ̆n).
1. = DOORSMAN.
1904 *Daily Chron.* 26 July 6/4 A publican whose doorman ejected a customer. 1905 *Westm. Gaz.* 27 June 9/1 Employment as porter, odd-man, lift-man, or door-man. 1927 *Blackw. Mag.* Nov. 701/1 At this moment entered the discreet white-clad doorman.
2. A farrier's assistant.
1896 *Daily Chron.* 25 Aug. 9/5 Farrier—Young man wants Job as doorman and jobbing. 1897 *Daily News* 10 May 11/5 The present scale of pay is 5s. a day for doormen and 6s. for firemen. 1901 *N. & Q.* 9th Ser. VIII. 184/2 [advt. in provincial newspaper] Wanted, doorman, able to nail well.

Door-mat. Add: *fig.* applied to a person upon whom people 'wipe their boots'.
1930 G. SAINTSBURY in *Observer* 20 Apr. 5/5 She is not such a nullity and 'doormat' as Miss Byron.

Door-step. Add: *attrib.* = belonging to, or carried on at, the front-door of private houses; door-to-door.
1906 *Daily Chron.* 4 Jan. 4/1 Dr. Cooper's fight is in every respect a 'doorstep' affair. 1908 *Ibid.* 20 Feb. 3/5 All the prisoners concerned in the 'doorstep' campaign. 1909 *Westm. Gaz.* 25 Oct. 9/2 We still want doorstep workers.

Door-yard. *U.S.* (Earlier example.)
1841 J. F. COOPER *Deerslayer* ii, Old Tom calls this sort of a wharf his door-yard.

Doosuti (dūsū·ti). [Hind. دوسوتا *dosūtā* (*do* two, *sūt* thread).] A kind of Indian linen.
1908 *Animal Managem.* (War Office) 306 For cold bandages use thin doosuti or linen.

Dooted, var. of DOTED (sense 2).

Dop, *sb.*[3] *S. Africa.* [S. Afr. Du.]
1. A drinking-cup; a basin.
1920 *Chambers's Jrnl.* Aug. 482/1 The vessel, or 'dop', is then lifted off and the full effect of the operation [*sc.* cutting men's hair] is disclosed.
2. Cape brandy, made from grape-skins. In full *dop brandy.*
1894 C. H. W. DONALDSON *With Wilson in Matabeleland* xi. 251 'Dop' (the usual name for Cape Brandy). 1895 SCULLY *Kafir Stories* 18 Jim..got his daily number of tots of poisonous 'dop' brandy. 1896 *Johannesburg Weekly Times* 8 Aug. 8 Several samples of whiskies, Cape dop, and Cape brandy were examined. 1897 BADEN-POWELL *Matabele-land Camp.* 347 We just had sufficient 'dop' (Dutch brandy) to give everybody a tot in which to drink her health. 1901 *Westm. Gaz.* 11 May 5/1 A bottle of 'Dop'—or Cape gin. 1910 'R. DEHAN' (Clo. Graves) *Dop Doctor* xiii. 98 'Dop', being the native name for the cheapest and most villainous of Cape brandies, has come to signify alcoholic drinks in general. 1921 *Chambers's Jrnl.* 647/1 The Cape 'dop' bottle brought oblivion to his tortured mind.

Dope, *sb.* Add: **1. b.** A varnish applied to the cloth surface of aeroplane parts, in order to increase strength and to keep them taut and air-tight. Also, a liquid preparation applied to air-ship covering, to increase gas-tightness.
1912 *Aeroplane* 19 Dec. 607 Cellon...The Fabric Dope used by the leading British and Continental Aeroplane and Hydro-aeroplane Builders. 1916 H. BARBER *Aeroplane Speaks* 142 *Strut, Dope*, a strut within a surface, so placed as to prevent the tension of the doped fabric from distorting the framework. 1917 *Times* 1 June 9/5 The King and Queen ..went on through..the seaplane department, and the 'dope' room. 1918 in *Aeroplane Handbk.* (ed. A. J. Swinton 1920) 144 The Germans at the beginning of the war used acetate dope and covered it with transparent oil varnish.
c. Applied more widely to any kind of material applied to a surface or used in an operation.
1915 E. POOLE *Harbor* 60 Joe's father vaccinated about a score of children that week. The 'dope' he used was mailed to him by a drug firm. 1923 F. A. TALBOT *Moving Pictures* 57 This is the substance forming the base or thin strip of film serving as the support for the sensitised emulsion, and which is called 'dope'. 1924 WEBSTER Addenda, *Dope*...5. *Photogr.* A varnish used to facilitate retouching, block out portions of a negative, etc. 1928 *Sunday Dispatch* 8 July 9/5 'Dope finish' [is a slang expression] for face paint and powder.
3. 'Opium, especially the thick treacle-like preparation used in opium-smoking' (*Cent. Dict.* Suppl. 1909); hence applied to stupefying drugs and narcotics in general, or to alcoholic drink. Also *attrib.*, esp. in **dope fiend,** a drug addict. orig. *U.S.*
1889 *Kansas Times & Star* 8 Oct., The oldest of the trio, an Irishman from County Cork, was very hilarious... The 'dope' made him 20 years younger and very pugnacious. 1895 J. L. FORD *Lit. Shop* ix. (1896) 130 Opium-joints,—those mysterious dens in which..the fumes of the burning 'dope' cloy the senses. 1896 G. ADE *Artie* viii. 71, I would advise you to stop smokin that double X brand of dope. 1896 F. J. MASTERS in *Chautauquan* Oct. 60/1 In San Francisco, large confiscations of 'dope' are made nearly every week. 1896 *N. Y. Sun* Dec., 'A dope fiend'..a victim of the opium habit. 1915 R. H. DAVIS *With the Allies* 158 With the desperation of a dope fiend clutching his last pill of cocaine. 1922 *Public Opinion* 5 May 420/3 The cabarets in Constantinople are a meeting place for all the world's dope purveyors.
b. 'A person under the influence of, or addicted to the use of, some dope' (*Cent. Dict.* 1909).
4. *spec.* **a.** A medical preparation administered to a race-horse for the purpose of faking his condition.
1900 *Westm. Gaz.* 30 Oct. 7/3 It is administered in capsules, given in a gelatine of varying thickness according to the required time when the 'dope' is desired to take effect. 1913 *Badm. Mag.* Jan. 88 A dope proper may be administered [to a horse] as a powder laid on the tongue, as a drink—usually given in old ale—or by the hypodermic syringe.
b. A mixture of petrol, alcohol, etc., sometimes used as a fuel for racing cars.
5. Information concerning the performances, condition, etc. of a racehorse which may give assistance in judging of his possibilities (cf. *dope-book, -sheet* in *6); hence, (*a*) information designed to gloss over or disguise facts, (*b*) information or statement of particulars in general, esp. for journalistic use. Phr. *to hand (out) the dope*: to supply the necessary information. orig. *U.S.*
1901 H. McHUGH *John Henry* 77 I've known Tommy for a long time, so he feels free to read his dope to me. 1904 W. H. SMITH *Promoters* iii. 72 Unless you cover your dope with a sort of angel-of-light coating that would fool Gabriel himself, you'll never get there. 1905 REX BEACH *Pardners* i. (1912) 26 He handed me the dope: 'In re Olive Troop Morrow *vs.* Justus Morroe'. 1909 S. E. WHITE *Rules of Game* II. iii, Gosh! I get sick of handing out dope to these yaps. 1917 EMPEY *From Fire Step* 103, I was to send the dope to Cassell and he would transmit it to the Battery Commander as officially coming through the observation post. 1919 *Detective Story Mag.* XXVIII. I. 13, I suggested it to a detective, but he laughed at me and said the article was nothing but '*dope*'. 1920 *Public Opinion* 9 July 43/3 Your patent dialectic dope By gulps we take with zest. 1921 R. D. PAINE *Comr. Rolling Ocean* iii. 41, I thought you were asleep on your feet. The wrong dope. 1921 *19th Cent.* May 748 He does not quite believe that the Bolshevik leaders themselves believe in their doctrines. He strongly suspects that on their part it is mainly 'dope'. 1922 H. L. FOSTER *Adv. Trop. Tramp* x. 140 Run up to Bolivia and get the dope on this affair.
b. *gen.* Something designed to deceive or bamboozle; a fraudulent design or action; a piece of deception or humbug; also, a person employed in a fraudulent transaction.
1915 FROEST & DILNOT *Crime Club* vi, I want you to find out who's marketing the dope. *Ibid.* xii, 'I reckon it [*sc.* a pistol] is liable to go off,' agreed the other grimly. 'Especially if you try to put any of the funny dope over on me.' *Ibid.*, 'Don't pull any of that dope on me', said Coyne sharply. 1925 N. VENNER *Imperfect Impostor* ii, It's his idea. I am just the humble dope; the clay pigeon.
6. *attrib.*: **dope-book** *U.S. slang*, 'a miscellaneous collection of racing information' (*Cent. Dict.* 1909); **dope fiend** (see *3); **dope-sheet,** 'a list of race-horses, giving the record of their performances in previous races' (*Cent. Dict.* 1909).

Dope, *v. slang.* orig. *U.S.* [f. DOPE *sb.*]
1. *trans.* To administer dope to (a person, a horse); to stupefy with a drug; to drug.
1889 BARRÈRE & LELAND *Dict. Slang* s.v., Doping is the stupifying men with tobacco prepared in a peculiar way. Nine out of ten saloons in the slums employ doping as a means to increase their illicit revenue. *American Newspaper.* 1891 FARMER *Slang*, *Dope v.* (American), to drug with tobacco. Also *Doping* = the practice. 1900 *Westm. Gaz.* 23 Oct. 8/2 They urge a liberal investment on the American horse, and confidentially impart the information that the animal is 'doped'. 1902 H. L. WILSON *Spenders* xxxv. 429 That guy that doped me, he wa'n't satisfied with my good thirty-dollar wad. 1915 C. S. JONES *Hohenzollern* 169 The King (who, if we are to believe his fair companion, used to be liberally doped) would awake from a trance at a *séance* to find his *inamorata* in his arms. 1919 H. L. WILSON *Ma Pettengill* ii. 62 To say nothing of doping him with asperin and quinine and camphor and menthol and hot tea and soothing words. 1919 GERTRUDE PAGE *Veldt Trail* xix. 200 'They must have kept him [*sc.* a horse] pretty short of food'..'Or doped him', suggested Birkdale. 1922 *Blackw. Mag.* May 632/2 He ladled into his nose sufficient snuff to have doped an ordinary man.
fig. 1908 G. H. LORIMER *J. Spurlock* iii. 41, I was so doped with my siren song that I steered straight for the rocks. 1928 SHAW *Intell. Woman's Guide Socialism* l. (1929) 218 Boycotting the Churches as mere contrivances for doping the workers into submission to Capitalism.
2. To treat with an adulterant, etc.; to 'doctor'.
1898 *Let.* in *Congress. Rec.* App. 223/1 They will run their flutter mills and mixers, and dope the flour to suit themselves. 1913 *Sunday Times* (Trenton, N. J.) 2 Mar. 1 Alternative offered to the water drinkers of Trenton: Typhoid if the water isn't 'doped' with hypochlorite of lime; an itch if it is.
3. To apply 'dope' to (the outer fabric of an aeroplane or air-ship).
1917 *Times* 1 June 9/5 Some hundreds of girls were engaged in 'doping' the fabric which covers the planes, rudders and ailerons. 1922 *Encycl. Brit.* XXX. 59/1 [Airship.] Cotton..appears to have some advantages owing to its great uniformity of contraction when doped. 1928 C. F. S. GAMBLE *N. Sea Air Station* Introd. 10 The envelope was 'doped' with aluminium paint on its top side and with yellow pigment on the lower portions.
4. *To dope out.* **a.** To make out; to find out, discover; to get the truth about.
1906 'O. HENRY' *Four Million, Green Door* 181 All the same, I believe it was the hand of Fate that doped out the way for me to find her. 1913 BIGGERS *Seven Keys to Baldpate* ii. 31 Ther's something I haven't quite doped out. That is—who's trespassing, me or you? 1915 R. H. DAVIS *With the Allies* 10 We would study the morning papers and ..from them try to dope out the winners. 1918 CAROLYN WELLS *Vicky Van* xv. 180, I dope out all this has to be so. 1919 P. G. WODEHOUSE *Damsel in Distress* ii. 30 Nature had it all doped out for me to be the Belle of Hicks Corners. 1922 *Short Stories* Feb. 102/2 'How'd you dope it out, Kid?' asked one. 'Tell us how you could do such good detective work.' 1926 J. BLACK *You Can't Win* xxiii. 367, I had all the criminal lawyers in San Francisco doped out like race horses by this time.
b. To work out; to get hold of.
1906 'O. HENRY' *Four Million* xviii. (1916) 191 He's doped out a fifty-dollar bill, anyway. 1919 *Detective Story Mag.* XXVIII. I. 6 He might have doped out a corking yarn about how the Phantom..made everybody believe that the explosion killed him. 1922 *Short Stories* Feb. 175/2, I didn't have time to dope out any plot till I got back to Denver.
Hence **Doped** *ppl. a.*; **Do·ping** *vbl. sb.* and *ppl. a.* Also **Do·per,** one who dopes; one who administers, or takes, drugs.
1900 *Daily News* 14 Nov. 8/4 'Doping' meant the administration to a horse of certain medical preparations, with the object of either stimulating or retarding the animal's progress in a race. 1903 *Westm. Gaz.* 15 Sept. 5/2 The Jockey Club propose to pass a rule forbidding doping in any shape or form. 1903 *N. Y. Sun* 23 Nov. 12 A 'doped' cigar was given to him in a pool and billiard room, and it had pretty near the same effect on him as knockout drops. 1913 *Daily Mail* 11 Mar. 7/5 'Doped' Athletes...It is well known..that the Russian skaters take such stimulants [as strychnine]. 1913 *Badm. Mag.* Jan. 89 A doped animal will run till it is done, mad drunk with the drug. *Ibid.*, A regular doper always tries his horses at home. 1913 *Aeroplane* 13 Mar. 303/1 The shiny surface of well 'doped' wings. 1914 *Racing Calendar* 23 July, I was unable to obtain evidence of the presence of a doping agent. 1921 *Blackw. Mag.* Apr. 535/2 She rejoined the remainder of the passengers.., having in her hands a

doped handkerchief. 1922 *Ibid.* Jan. 124/1 He might publish in his doped and venal press the felicitations that were showered upon him. 1923 P. G. WODEHOUSE *Inimitable Jeeves* xiv, To tell me we ought to cook Harold's food ourselves to prevent doping. 1926 *Chambers's Jrnl.* 515/1 So the old reprobate's dopings had told at long last.

Dopey: see *DOPY *a.*

Doppelganger (dǫ·pəlgæ:ŋəɪ). Also **dopple-.** [Properly *doppelgänger* (-geŋəɪ), f. *doppel* double + *gänger* goer, agent-n. of *gehen* to go.] = DOUBLE-GANGER I.
1895 *Denham Tracts* (Folklore Soc. 1895) II. 79 Hell-hounds, dopple-gangers, boggleboes. 1907 N. MUNRO *Daft Days* xxviii, Miss Macintosh is surely your doppelganger.

Doppler (dǫ·plaɪ). The name of Christian *Doppler* (Austrian mathematician and physicist, died 1853), designating a principle defined by him (see quot. 1888).
1888 C. A. YOUNG *Gen. Astron.* 202 Not infrequently it happens that certain lines of the spectrum are crooked and broken in connection with sun spots...Such phenomena are caused, according to Doppler's principle, by the swift motion of matter towards or from the observer. *Note*, Doppler's principle is this: that when we are approaching, or approached by, a body which is emitting regular vibrations, then the number of waves received by us in a second is increased, and their wave-length correspondingly diminished. 1909 *Westm. Gaz.* 9 Dec. 2/1 The Doppler or Doppler-Fizeau principle..first applied to the velocity of stars in the line of sight by Sir William Huggins. 1926 H. MACPHERSON *Mod. Astron.* 34 The application of Doppler's principle to the measurement of the rotation and atmospheric motions of the Sun. *Ibid.* 119 The Doppler principle was first applied to the study of stellar motions as far back as 1868.

Dopy (dōu·pi), *a. slang.* Also **dopey.** [f. *DOPE *sb.* 3.]
1. Heavy or stupefied, as with a drug.
1896 *N. Y. Sun* Dec., A man who acts as if under the influence of the poppy drug is said to be dopy. 1900 G. ADE *More Fables in Slang* (1902) 179 A Young Man with Hair who played the 'Cello. He was so wrapped up in his Art that he acted Dopey most of the time. 1919 BRANDER MATTHEWS *Ess. English* (1921) 112, I began to hear men assert that they felt *dopy*, *i.e.* sluggish, as though they had taken an opiate. 1924 A. J. SMALL *Frozen Gold* iii. 97 Henderson was still a bit dopey [after a blow on the head].
2. Of the nature of or containing dope or a narcotic.
1925 E. WALLACE *Melody of Death* xii. 212 'Will you have a cigar?..You need not be scared of them'...' There is nothing dopey or wrong with these.'

Dor, *sb.*[1] **4. dor-bug** *U.S.* (earlier example).
1837 *Southern Lit. Messenger* III. 590 An enormous doorbug [*sic*] or hedge-chafer..bounced..into the room.

Dor, dorm, school slang shortenings of DORMITORY.
1920 *Blackw. Mag.* Oct. 479/1 No fag may, *proprio motu*, enter Lower, still less Middle or Upper fifth 'dors'. 1927 ANNE MACDONALD *Dorty Speaking* iii, I found Midge in the dorm when I went up to change for tea.

Dora (dōə·rā). A jocular personification of the '*D*efence *o*f the *R*ealm *A*ct', the name being an acrostic of the initials of the title, and at the same time forming a familiar feminine proper name. The Act was first passed in August, 1914, and provided the Government with wide powers during war.
1918 'IAN HAY' *Last Million* vi. 68 We are up against official secrets again. A lady called Dora: you will become well acquainted with her. 1921 *Punch* CLX. 293/2 To judge by his description, Dora's daughter [Emergency Powers Act of 1920] will not be a whit less drastic in her action than the old lady herself. 1929 GUEDALLA *Missing Muse* 194 These imbecile restrictions, which are the last legacy of 'Dora' to her grateful heirs.

Dorcas[1]. Add: **Dorcas Society** (earlier U.S. example); also short for 'Dorcas society' or 'meeting'. Hence **Do·rcasing,** working for a 'Dorcas'.
1833 *Knickerbocker Mag.* I. 157 A message from a Dorcas society. 1894 BARING-GOULD *Queen of Love* xx. II. 40 Aunt Beulah will not be home for an hour. She is Dorcasing. 1900 UPWARD *Eben. Lobb* 39 Getting ready for a Dorcas that came to our house once a quarter to have tea and work for the heathen.

Dorcas[2] (dǭ·ɪkăs). [mod.L., a. Gr. δορκάς deer, gazelle.] A genus of antelopes, including the common gazelle.
1836 OGILBY (Cent. Dict.). 1893 LYDEKKER *Horns & Hoofs* 180 The last of the Asiatic gazelles in which the females are horned is the Dorcas gazelle.

Dori, variant of DORY *sb.*[2]
1903 *Month* Aug. 146 The little flat-bottomed doris, holding two or three men, drift away. 1927 *Observer* 4 Dec. 21/2 The moutier's day begins at two in the morning, when he goes out from the smack, with one other man, in a small boat called a 'doris'.

Dormitory, *sb.* Add: **1. b.** In universities and colleges: A building in which students reside; a hall of residence; a hostel. *U.S.*
1892 *Univ. of Chicago Quart. Cal.* 9 Students are advised to make their residence in the dormitories. 1903 CLARK HOWARD in *N. Y. Even. Post* 7 Oct. 7 There are four regular domitories or halls for women at Oxford. 1906 *Athens Female College* 7 The dormitories will accomodate about 100. 1913 J. K. LORD *Hist. Dartmouth Coll.* 487 In 1899 the old home..was converted into a small dormitory for twenty men.
c. *jocular.* A suburb of a large town, regarded as merely a sleeping place for those who work in the town during the day.
1923 *Westm. Gaz.* 6 Feb., The steady expansion of London's working centres and the ever-increasing sprawl of its surrounding dormitories. 1930 *Times* 12 May 9/5 Moreover, it is said, West Fulham is but a London dormitory—a place where voters sleep, and have their interests elsewhere.

Dormy, *a.* Add: **dormy house,** a hostel, generally run in connexion with a golf club, in which members may be accommodated for the night. (With jocular reference to *dormitory*.)

Dornick[2]. *U.S.* Also **donnick, don(n)ock, darnick.** [Cf. Ir. *dornog* handful, small stone.] A pebble, stone, or small boulder.
1840 *Daily Pennant* (St. Louis) June 18 (Thornton) That ar man he tooks up a dornick, and made a heap of cavortins. 1869 'MARK TWAIN' *Innoc. Abr.* xxxv, Darnick from the tomb of Abelard and Heloise. 1878 J. H. BEADLE *Western Wilds* 185 (Thornton) He gathered a dornick, and was just drawin' back to send the strange dog where there's no fleas.

Doronicum (dǫrǫ·nikǒm). [mod.L., a.mod. Gr. δορονίκον, ad. Arab. *doronakh.*] A plant of the asteraceous genus so named, esp. any of the species used for herbaceous borders.
1892 S. R. HOLE *Bk. about Garden* 27 That group of iris (germanica) and doronicum reminds us of the cohorts of the Assyrians, 'all gleaming with purple and gold'. 1921 G. JEKYLL *Colour Schemes for Flower Garden* 27 Tulip Chrysolora of fuller yellow, yellow Wallflowers, the tall Doronicum, and..several patches of yellow Crown Imperial.

Do·rothy bag. [f. female proper name *Dorothy*.] A woman's open-topped hand-bag slung by loops from the wrist.
1909 *Westm. Gaz.* 23 Aug. 9/1 A 'Dorothy' bag, containing a quantity of jewellery. 1923 *Daily Mail* 15 Jan. 15 An effective Dorothy bag for evenings.

Dorothy Perkins (dǫ·rəþi pǭ·ɪkinz). Also simply **Dorothy.** [Personal name.] A popular variety of climbing rose which bears clusters of double pink flowers.
1904 T. W. SANDERS *Roses & their Cultivation* 36 Free-growing roses like Dundee Rambler, Thalia,..Dorothy Perkins. 1908 J. H. PEMBERTON *Roses* 314 Dorothy Perkins (Wich.) Jackson & Perkins, 1901.—Shell pink, white centre. —Very vigorous pillar. 1912 H. H. THOMAS *Complete Gard.* 110 Liberties may be taken with the Dorothy Perkins class of rose that would lead to disappointment with other kinds. 1913 — *Rose Bk.* 13 *Dorothy Perkins.*—The most popular of all wichuraiana roses, bearing large clusters of big, double, rich pink blossoms. 1915 *Star* 5 Aug. 2/6 Suburban gardens round London are aflame with blooming 'Dorothys'.

Dorp. Delete †*Obs.* Still in use in reference to Dutch S. Africa.
1902 *Daily Chron.* 23 Apr. 7/3 The most remote 'dorp' has not been too far placed beyond the reach of the fertilising stream. 1902 J. H. M. ABBOTT *Tommy Cornstalk* 13 The dorp represented the Bush township. 1920 *Contemp. Rev.* Feb. 197 In the *dorps* and the *backveld*, society, business, religion, and politics are closely interwoven.

Dorsi-. Add: **Dorsico·rnu,** the dorsal cornu of the spinal cord (Dorland, 1903). Hence **Dorsico·rnual** *a.* **Do·rsiflex** *v. trans.*, to bend towards the dorsum. **Dorsifle·xion,** flexion or bending towards the dorsum or dorsal surface. **Dorsi-ve·ntral** *a.*, **-ventra·lity** = DORSO-*ventral*, *-ventrality*.
1890 *Buck's Handbk. Med. Sci.* VIII. 528 The myelic cornua are strictly dorsal and ventral,..permitting the adjectives *dorsicornual and ventricornual. 1908 *Practitioner* Oct. 561 The ankles can be *dorsiflexed, until the dorsum of the feet touches the shin. 1895 OLIVER tr. *Kerner's Nat. Hist. Plants* II. 697 The oophyte is a lobed band-like thallus with marked *dorsi-ventrality.

Dorsum. 2. Delete *nonce-use* and add recent example.
1905 W. G. HOLMES *Justinian & Theod.* I. 27 The moat.. follows the trend of the ground as it rises on either side from the beach to the dorsum of the peninsula.

Dory, *sb.*[2] Add: In *Comb.*, as *dory-becket*, *-fishing*, *-mate*, *-roding*; *dory-modelled*, *-shaped* adjs.
1897 KIPLING *Capt. Cour.* 154 Fiddling helplessly with a *dory-becket. *Ibid.* 163 Men had met one another before, *dory-fishing in the fog. *Ibid.* 178 It's yours and welcome, Harve, because we're *dory-mates. 1919 *Hist. Amer. Lit.* II. II. x. 9 The reader asks resentfully what they are doing in this *dory-modelled *galère*, painted green below with a border of blue. 1897 KIPLING *Capt. Cour.* 52 A tiny anchor ..and some seventy fathoms of thin brown *dory-roding. 1897 *Outing* (U.S.) XXX. 386/2 The boat..is *dory-shaped, nine feet long.

Dos-à-dos (dozado), *adv. phr., sb.* [Fr.] **A.** *adv. phr.* Back to back. **B.** *sb.* A seat, carriage, or the like, so constructed that the occupants sit back to back.
1837 J. F. COOPER *Europe* I. 43 Some one kindly told him that they no longer danced *dos-à-dos*. 1859 *Habits of Good Society* xiv. 349 A liberal supply of ottomans, *dos-à-dos*, and sofas. 1882 DE WINDT *Equator* 119 The street cab of Batavia is a 'dos-à-dos' literally so called, as the passenger sits with his back to the driver's, thus forming a mutual support.

Dosage. Add: **1. b.** In electrotherapeutics and radiotherapeutics: The intensity of current, X-rays, or the like, applied in a particular case.
1893 A. S. ECCLES *Sciatica* 56 Care must be taken not to exceed the dosage either in strength or duration. 1912 BYTHELL & BARCLAY *X-ray Diagnosis & Treatment* 121 It is necessary to be extremely cautious until some idea is obtained as to the amount of dosage the skin will stand. 1918 R. KNOX *Radiography & Radio-therap.* (ed. 2) II. 424 The various systems of measuring the X-ray dosage. *Ibid.* 511 The most difficult question in radium treatment is that of dosage. 1928 *New Statesman* 28 July 510/1 The most careful and experienced practitioner may sometimes cause an X-ray burn after dosage which he has used..without injury on hosts of occasions.

Dose, *sb.* Add: **1. b.** The application of a given quantity of electricity, X-rays, or the like.
1912 BYTHELL & BARCLAY *X-ray Diagnosis & Treatment* 117 Heavy doses may occasionally produce a strong skin reaction. 1918 R. KNOX *Radiography & Radio-therap.* (ed. 2) II. 424 An erythema dose is one which causes slight erythema to appear within fifteen to twenty-one days. *Ibid.* 428 If the total dose is to be administered in several sittings. *Ibid.* 514 Exposures, with large quantities of radium in well-filtered doses, may be given up to twenty-four hours.

Dosology, Dosometer: see DOSIOLOGY, DOSIMETER in Dict.

Dossy (dǫ·si), *a. slang.* [Cf. Sc. *doss* neat, spruce, *dossie* small, neat, well-dressed person.] Stylish, smart. Hence **Do·ssily** *adv.*
1889 GILBERT *Brigands* in *Standard* 9 Nov. 3 (E.D.D.) We are dossy and neat From head to our feet. 1900 *Daily News* 31 July 8/2 What with the ladies' bonnets and blokes' dossy hats. 1903 'MARJORIBANKS' *Fluff-hunters* 42 A dossy Sloane Street milliner. *Ibid.* 95 A dossily dressed girl.

Dot, *sb.*[1] Add: **4. b.** *To a dot*: exactly, precisely. *U.S.*
1854 MARY J. HOLMES *Tempest & Sunshine* xv. 215 That was one of Tempest's capers to a dot. 1866 *Congress. Globe* 18 June 3235/3 He understands it to a dot. 1881 *Ibid.* 20 Apr. 356/1 That is the question. That is it to a dot. 1887 TOURGEE *Button's Inn* 189 'That'll suit me to a dot'.
c. *To put dots on*: to bore, weary. *slang.*
1919 *War Slang* in *Athenæum* 8 Aug. 727/2 If a man is boring or tiresome he is said to 'put dots on one'.
5. e. *Morse telegraphy.* (See *DASH *sb.*[1] 7 f.)

Dot, *v.*[1] Add: **6.** *trans. To dot off*: to tick off (in counting on the fingers).
1904 LILLIE T. MEADE *Love Triumphant* I. ii, She recounted a little list of famous women,..dotting them off on her slender fingers.
7. To hit, strike; to give (a person) a black eye. Phr. *to dot* (a person) *one. slang.*
1896 JACOBS *Many Cargoes* 239 Put your dooks up...I'm going to dot you! 1911 A. NEIL LYONS *Clara* xxi. 237 Some of us might dot you one.
8. *intr.* To limp (*off*).
1924 *Chambers's Jrnl.* 124/2 The ungrateful little brute ..dotted off, wagging his skinny tail.

Dotard. A. *sb.* Add: **3.** (See quot.)
1884 GOODE *Nat. Hist. Aquatic Anim.* 58 The Harbor Seal, *Phoca vitulina.* The young are there [*sc.* in Newfoundland] also called 'Rangers', and when two or three years old..receive the name of 'Dotards'.

Dote, *sb.*[1] Add: **4.** Decay in wood. (Cf. DOTE *v.*[1] 4.) *U.S.*
1874 KNIGHT *Dict. Mech.* 564/1 *Clear-stuff*, boards free from knots, wane, wind-shakes, ring-hearts, dote, sap. 1905 *Terms Forestry & Logging* 35 *Dote*, the general term used by lumbermen to denote decay or rot in timber.

Dotted, *ppl. a.*[1] Add: Of engraving: Executed by dots instead of lines; stippled. = F. (*manière*) *pointillée.*
1897 R. E. GRAVES in *Dict. Nat. Biog.* L. 58/2 He [*sc.* Ryland] adopted the 'chalk' or dotted manner of engraving. 1908 A. M. HIND *Hist. Engraving* (1911) 290 We have already noted dotted work in plates of Giulio Campagnola.

Dotter, *sb.* Add: **2.** A device in which a pencil dots an oscillating target fixed to a gun when fired without ammunition, used in training gunners to take aim.
1903 *Daily Chron.* 25 June 4/5 Neither Captain Percy Scott nor his dotter were on view. 1906 *Ibid.* 5 June 2/3 Admiral Percy Scott's dotter and aiming apparatus.

Doty, *a. dial.* Add: Also **doaty.** Hence **Do·tiness.**
1885 *Spons' Mechanics' Own Bk.* 167 'Doatiness': a speckled stain found in beech, American oak, and others.

Double, *sb.* Add: **3. i.** esp. in phr. *at the double.* Also *fig.*
1865 *Chambers's Jrnl.* 213/1 Intellect not only marches, but marches at the 'double'. *Ibid.* 470/1 Ellsworth detailed twenty men.., and went at 'the double' down Pennsylvania Avenue. 1883 *Army Regulations* II. x. 242 A certain number of movements are to be performed at each drill at 'the double'.
n. Further instances (e.g. = double bedroom, double event, double snipe, two 'tots' of whisky, two centuries scored by a batsman in one match).
1891 NAT. GOULD *Double Event* xxvi, Messrs Isaacs and Moses..were always ready to lay the double. *Ibid.*, If he loses the Derby we may go for a recovery in the cup. But ..Ike is confident he will win the double. 1902 *London Mag.* June 438/2 The men who play both cricket and football well..the best 'first-class doubles' who were at Oxford or Cambridge. 1920 *Field* 2 Oct. 488/2 There were several 'doubles' (a fish on each of the two hooks used on the line) of red gurnet and bream. 1920 G. BURRARD *Notes on Sporting Rifles* 33 A hammerless ejector double rifle is the best and quickest to reload...Next come hammerless non-ejectors, and then hammer rifles, but a double is a *sine qua non.* 1921 *Spectator* 19 Mar. 357/1 A few snipe rose. We got four of them, two being 'doubles'. 1922 J. SYRETT *Alf, Old Chum* 99 'You've 'ad a lot of doubles to-night, Mr. Powell', Flo remarked...'Don't want to go 'ome screwed again to-night, does yer?' 1929 *Star* 21 Aug. 17/1 When he reached his second hundred of the match, for no batsman before has twice done the 'double' in Test Matches. 1931 *Times* 16 Mar. 2/7 Large doubles [*sc.* bedrooms] now available.

o. = *double feast* (see *DOUBLE *a.* 6).
*c*1690 in *The Month* (1882) Jan. 122 And his feast kept as a duble annualy upon yᵉ 2nd of Octobre. 1759 CHALLONER *Let.* 4 May in E. H. Burton *Life* (1909) II. xxiii. 7 He.. will come over to receive his consecration here: and therefore I should be obliged to you if you would obtain for him ..a license to have this performed on any *double*. 1762 *Evening Office of Church* (ed. 2) 303 The Transfiguration of our Lord Jesus Christ. A greater double. 1850, 1885 [in Dict., sense 3 n].
p. Double-screened coal.
1931 *Times* 16 Mar. 19/7 Lanarkshire [coal]..trebles.. doubles..singles.

Double, *a.* Add:
A. 5. *To live* (or *lead*) *a double life*: to sustain two different characters in life, one virtuous and respectable, the other immoral or blameworthy. Often of a married man who keeps a mistress.
1892 ZANGWILL *Childr. Ghetto* viii. (1893) 83 Esther led a double life, just as she spoke two tongues. 1907 MR. JUSTICE GRANTHAM in *Times* 19 Dec. 9/4 The woman must have been murdered by a man who was leading a double life. ..The prisoner had been leading a double life. 1924 E. WALLACE *Sinister Man* xxxv, She had never imagined that this gawk of a girl..could lead what was tantamount to a double life.
6. *Double blank*: a domino with both halves of its face blank. *Double chin*: a chin with a fold of flesh under it (cf. *double-chinned*, quot. 1387 in DOUBLE *a.* C. 1). *Double coal*: a superior kind of coal (the application varying locally). *Double consciousness*: a hypnotic condition in which the patient seems to lead two lives, oblivious in either state of his experiences in the other. *Double crown*: a size of printing-paper (20 × 30 in.). *Double elephant*: see ELEPHANT 10. *Double fault*: two consecutive faults at tennis. *Double feast* [eccl. L. *festum duplex*]: a feast on which the antiphons are recited in full before and after the psalms and canticles. *Double figures*: a total or score, esp. of runs at cricket, higher than nine and less than one hundred. *Double foolscap*: a size of paper (writing 16½ × 26½ in., printing 17 × 27 in.). *Double-nelson* (see quot. 1889). *Double pneumonia*: pneumonia affecting both lungs. *Double room*: a *DOUBLE BED room. *Double salt*: a compound salt composed of two salts in chemical combination. *Double shuffle*: see SHUFFLE *sb.* 5. *Double vision*: diplopia.
1868 SALA *Notes & Sk. Paris Exhib.* iv. 34 The houses.. gave to the outskirts of Paris an odd affinity to a city built of dominoes set on end. The double-sixes and double-fours, with here and there a *double-blank in the shape of a dead-wall. 1927 P. G. WODEHOUSE *Small Bachelor* i. § 4. 20 It has been well said of Sigsbee H. Waddington that, if men were dominoes, he would be the double-blank. 1832 *double chin [see CHIN *sb.* 1]. 1803 JOS. PLYMLEY *Agric. Shropsh.* 54 Coal, called the *double-coal. 1839 URE *Dict. Arts* 962 A section of the Quarrelton coal..showing the overlapped coal and the double coal. 1879–81 MISS JACKSON *Shropsh. Word-bk.*, *Double-coal*, a good coal for manufacturing purposes, much used. 1920 W. GIBSON *Coal Gt. Britain* 207 The Seven Feet Coal..is the chief coal, but below it the Double and Bench coals are workable. 1891 *Spectator* 20 June, Cases of *double-consciousness,—that is, cases in which the patient appears to have at one time one set of memories dating from one date, and at another time another set of memories dating from another date. 1897 *Westm. Gaz.* 22 Dec. 9/1 Billposting..at One Penny per *Double-crown Sheet per Week. 1921 A. W. MYERS *Twenty Yrs. Lawn Tennis* 128 A universal 'Oh!' echoed round the arena when Wilding served a *double fault. *Ibid.* 156 He served half a dozen double faults and two foot-faults. *a* 1225 *Ancr. R.* 70 Euerich urdeie of be yer holdeð silence, bute ȝif hit beo *duble feste. 1440 in Peacock *Eng. Ch. Furniture* (1866) 182 For great doble feastes and principall feastes. 1486 *Rec. St. Mary at Hill* (1905) 13 Euery Sonday & euery double feest, pryncipall feest, & solempne feest. 1514 *Ibid.* 19 Vppon high and doble ffestes. 1534 tr. *Lyndewode's Const. Angliæ* 25 b, The feast of saint George the martyr shal be kept doble, after the maner of the more doble feaste. 1614 SPELMAN *Orig. Four Terms* Eng. Wks. II. (1727) 92 The Feast..of St. Peter and Paul on the 29th of June was a double Feast. 1884 *Boy's Own Paper* Summer No. 26 Watch the ball, keep your temper, and don't be afraid; For that is the way *double figures are made. 1894 *Times* 25 May 11/3 Mr. Mitchell for once in a way failed to reach double figures. 1889 W. ARMSTRONG *Wrestling* (Badm.) 233 Probably the most dangerous move in Lancashire and Cornwall and Devon wrestling..is what is called the '*Double Nelson'...To get behind an opponent, place both arms under his, and clasp your hands round the back of his neck and thus bend his head forward till his breast-bone almost gives way. 1903 J. J. MILLER *Scottish Sports* 127 So Ingram slipped on a double-Nelson, pinned him down for the requisite 30 seconds, and then politely assisted him to rise. 1892 OSLER *Princ. Med.* 525 *Double pneumonia presents no peculiarities other than the greater danger connected with it. 1929 *Encycl. Brit.* XVIII. 100/2 Usually pneumonia affects one lower lobe but it may extend to the whole lung or even to parts of both lungs (double pneumonia). 1926 FANNIE KILBOURNE *Dot & Will, Vacation* (1929) 193, I would change to a single room in the hotel which was a little cheaper than the *double one..we had. 1931 *Times* 1 June 10/3 A large double room and private bathroom. 1849 D. CAMPBELL *Inorg. Chem.* 176 These *double salts are known as manganese alums. 1889 G. A. BERRY *Dis. Eye* 504 The *diplopia* or *double vision to which the condition gives rise. 1922 *Encycl. Brit.* XXX. 975/1 Paralysis of the muscles of the eye, producing diplopia or double vision.
C. 1. *double-bottomed*, *-tracked*, *-triggered* (examples); **double-threaded** *a.* (of a screw; also *transf.*).
1833 B. SILLIMAN *Man. Sugar Cane* 60 His apparatus is composed of a *double bottomed copper boiler, covered by a dome. 1909 *Westm. Gaz.* 18 Mar. 4/1 The propeller is.. made up of two portions of a *double-threaded screw. 1910 *Daily Chron.* 28 Jan. 6/3 'A Will in a Well' is a double-threaded mystery story. 1887 C. B. GEORGE *40 Yrs. on Rail* v. 91 Accidents are reduced to a minimum, owing to good management and to the *double-tracked roads. 1839 Z. LEONARD *Adv.* (1904) 70 In a hurry, the one that was accustomed to the single trigger, caught up the *double triggered gun.
2. *double-motor, -spiral, -standard*; **double-beat sluice** (see quot.); **double-gate table,** a gate-table with two hinged movable legs to support leaves.
1931 F. M. DU-PLAT-TAYLOR *Reclam. Land fr. Sea* 72 *Double-beat or compensated cylindrical sluices. 1908 *Daily Report* 5 Sept. 8/2 A 3 ft. 6 in. oak *double-gate table. 1910 *Chambers's Jrnl.* 24 Dec. 55/2 A *double-motor aeroplane. 1928 PEAKE & FLEURE *Steppe & Sown* 96 *Double-spiral ornaments made of copper wire. 1867 J. LAING *Theory of Business* iv. (1868) 59 The *double-standard system is found to cause one of the two metals involved to be treated as bullion.
3. *double-board* vb.; **double-fault** *v. intr.* (Tennis), to serve two consecutive faults; hence **double-faulter; double-iron** *v. trans.*, to shackle with irons on both legs (cf. *double-ironed* in 4 in Dict.); **double-shuffle** *v. intr.*, to perform a double shuffle.
1874 *Rep. Vermont Board Agric.* II. 512 My plan was to *double board and cleat the main body of the barn, having a basement or cellar under the whole barn. 1921 A. W. MYERS *Twenty Yrs. Lawn Tennis* 136 Dixon *double-faulted in the eleventh game and lost it. *Ibid.* 78 The brilliant server and smasher became a *double-faulter and a snatcher at lobs. 1922 TILDEN *It's All in the Game* 118 Vincey took the first point on Dave's net but double-faulted away the next. 1927 *Daily Express* 6 June 1 Tilden.. double faulted. 1897 P. WARUNG *Tales Old Régime* 42 Here, guard! *double-iron this man. 1909 MARG. B. SAUNDERS *Litany Lane* I. i, Toeing, tipping, *double-shuffling, hopping.
4. double-opposed *a.*, of an engine, having two or more pairs of cylinders on opposite sides of the common crank-shaft; **double-screened** *a.* (see quot. 1921).
1908 *Westm. Gaz.* 20 Nov. 4/3 A 9-h.p. runabout fitted with a *double-opposed air-cooled engine. 1909 *Ibid.* 23 Mar. 4/2 A..double-opposed horizontal four-cylinder engine. *Ibid.* 1 Apr. 4/2 The double-opposed horizontal engine, which is made with two, four, and six cylinders. 1905 *Daily Chron.* 4 May, *Double-screened Nuts. 1921 C. E. EVANS *Hints Coal Buyers* 56 Double Screened coal, indicates coal that has been screened at the Colliery, and screened also over two open screens in the spout at the Dock Tip, that is to say, 'Double Screened' at time of shipment.

Double, *v.* **1. e.** Add: Also *absol.*
1918 H. CROY *How Motion Pictures are Made* v. 124 A young man, doubling for a leading lady in a bit of hazardous fire jumping.

Doublé (duble), *a.* [Fr., = lined.] Of a book binding: Made with a *doublure.*
1890 *Catal. Exhib. Bk.-bindings Grolier Club* 11 When the inside of the cover is lined with leather it is termed *doublé*. *Ibid.* 27 Garnet morocco, with ornament in mosaic and gold; doublé, blue morocco, with border of foliage and flowers.

Double-barrelled, *a.* **2.** (Earlier U.S. example.)
1777 *Maryland Jrnl.* 9 Sept. (Th.) The event of this double-barreled scheme has been, that the colonel and his party are defeated.

Double bed. A bed to accommodate two persons. Also *attrib.* So **Double-bedded** *a.*, having a double bed or two single beds.
1866 MRS. WHITNEY *L. Goldthwaite* iii, Ours is a double-bedded room. 1925 G. BURRARD *Big Game Hunting* 280 A good warm rug or blanket, preferably double-bed size. 1931 *Times* 16 Mar. 22/1 Large double bed room.

Dou·ble-bi·tter. [f. DOUBLE- C. 2 + BIT *sb.*[1] + -ER[1].] A double-bitted axe.
1904 ELIZ. ROBINS *Magnetic North* I. 247 Then the Colonel would give a little start, turn about, lift his double-bitter and swing it in frontier fashion.

Double-cross, *sb. slang.* [f. DOUBLE *a.* + CROSS *sb.* 29.] An act of treachery to both parties (orig. in gaming or sport), esp. by pretended collusion with each; more widely, betrayal of the other party in a (dishonest) transaction.
1874 *Slang Dict.*, *Double cross*, a cross in which a man who has engaged to lose breaks his engagement, and 'goes straight' at the last moment. 1887 *Referee* 21 Aug. 1/3 (Farmer) A double cross was brought off. Teemer promised to sell the match, and finished by selling those who calculated on his losing. 1896 G. ADE *Artie* ix. 79 Every time I see him over at the city hall he's whisperin' to one o' them red-necked boys and fixin' it to give somebody the double-cross. 1905 REX BEACH *Pardners* ii. (1912) 53 Now, he allus found himself planning how to hand Mr. Lo the double cross and avoid complications. 1910 W. M. RAINE *B. O'Connor* 214 'Think you're getting the double-cross?' asked Leroy. 1920 A. E. W. MASON *Summons* xii, There was always a certain amount of money for the man who would work the double cross.
Hence **Double-cross** *v. trans.*, to give or hand (a person) the double-cross; loosely, to cheat; also *absol.*; **-crosser; -crossing** *vbl. sb.* and *ppl. a.*
1904 'O. HENRY' *Cabbages & Kings* x. 161 'Twas thus I was double-crossed by the Tropics through a family failin' of goin' out of the way to hunt disturbances. 1910 W. M. RAINE *B. O'Connor* 240 Nothing like being on the spot to prevent double-crossing. 1915 P. G. WODEHOUSE *Something Fresh* i, A wealthy uncle who subsequently double-crossed them by leaving his money to charities. 1926 J. BLACK *You Can't Win* iv. 42 This song is a favorite among negroes when in great trouble, such as..being double-crossed by a friend. 1927 *Observer* 10 July 17/5 This was apparently part of a deep-laid plot, for the Nationalists now consider they have been double-crossed. 1928 *Hearst's International* Aug. 156/3 Are you going to be a dirty thief and a double-crosser? 1928 *Collier's* 18 Aug. 6/4 'You're a double-crossing rat,' I said.

Double-deck. [See DOUBLE *a.* C. 2 and DECK *sb.*] Used *attrib.* in designations of structures having two platforms, floors, or planes one above the other. So **Double-decked** *a.* [DOUBLE *a.* C. 1].
1867–8 *Trans. Ill. Agric. Soc.* VII. 460 Sheep arrive here from the west in single decked cars, but leave in double decked ones. 1903 A. H. BEAVAN *Tube, Train, Tram, & Car* xv. 212 Electric omnibuses..double-decked. 1906 [see *DECK *sb.*[1] 4 b]. 1910 A. WILLIAMS *Engin. Wonders World* II. 49/2 The makers claim that..it [*sc.* the Scherzer Rolling Lift Bridge] could be made double-decked. *Ibid.* 267/1 The double-deck floor accommodates four elevated railway tracks. 1917 C. C. TURNER *Aircraft of To-day* ii. 34 The 'double-deck' type of rectangular planes.

Double-decker. Add: **b.** orig. *U.S.* (Examples.)
1878 *Design & Work* IV. 324/3 [Quoting U.S. newspaper] The car is a double-decker. 1887 *Harper's Mag.* Sept. 557/2 The street-cars are double-deckers, with seats upon the roof as well as within. 1895 *Popular Sci. Monthly* Apr. 757 The 'double decker' or two-story cars.
c. In various technical uses: A loaf baked with a smaller upper portion; a woman's dress consisting of two skirts or flounces, one above the other; a miner's cage made in two stories; a double-decked aeroplane.
1902 *Fortn. Rev.* June 1008 The English 'double-decker' is a fearful and wonderful production that errs on the side of heaviness. 1902 *Westm. Gaz.* 30 Oct. 3/1 The double-decker costume sketched has each of its flounces bordered with..grey and white squirrel. 1902 *Daily Chron.* 12 Nov. 8/6 A number of workmen were being brought up out of the mine..in the double decker cage. 1917 C. C. TURNER *Aircraft of To-day* viii. 137 Chanute made 700 glides in his 'double-decker' without an accident.

Double dummy: see DUMMY *sb.* 2.

Double Dutch: see DUTCH B. *sb.* 2 b.

Double-eagle. *U.S.* [f. DOUBLE *a.* + EAGLE *sb.* 5.] A gold coin of the value of twenty dollars.
1859 BARTLETT *Dict. Amer.* (ed. 2) 185 There are also double eagles of twenty dollars. 1872 E. EGGLESTON *End of World* xxvi. 179 He..piled the double-eagles like a fortification in front of him. 1886 *Harper's Mag.* Dec. 36 Then the spokesman took a golden double-eagle from his belt. 1902 S. E. WHITE *Blazed Trail* viii. 61 His wages were twenty-five dollars a month, which his van bill would reduce to the double eagle.

Double-e·dgedness. The quality or condition of being double-edged.
1901 JASTROW *Fact & Fable in Psychol.* 165 With peculiar obliviousness to the double-edgedness of his remark, he writes [etc.]. 1908 *Dublin Rev.* Oct. 281 He did not realize the double-edgedness of epigram when delivered in the wrong time and place, to the wrong person.

Double event. [EVENT *sb.* 2 e.] orig. in *Racing*, applied to the winning by a horse, competitor, or team, of two races or matches at the same meeting or in the same season; hence *gen.* applied to two occurrences, acts, or performances of any kind. Also *attrib.*
1863 *Illustr. London News* 566/3 They are not anxious to back anything for the 'double event'. 1872 *Gentl. Mag.* Dec. 696 He then 'backed himself for the double event' and went in for 'second schools', the last bar to a B.A. taking up mathematics. 1885 EARL OF SUFFOLK, etc. *Racing* (Badm. Libr.) xiv. (1889) 268 The double-event betting. 1888 *Peel City Guardian* VI. 2/3, I was not codding, dear old boss, when I gave you the tip...Double event this time. ..Jack the Ripper. 1891 NAT GOULD (*title*) The Double Event. 1898 *Cycling* 62 Most of the special burning oils are satisfactory, provided that 'double-event' oils are eschewed. 1899 *Chambers's Jrnl.* 25 Nov. 823/1 The reasons for a display of disgust at a 'double event' [*sc.* the birth of twins]. 1915 KIPLING *Fringes of Fleet* 30 It was a simple calculation of comparative speeds and positions, and when it was worked out she decided to try for the double event.

Dou·ble-head, *v. U.S.* [Cf. DOUBLE-HEADER b.] *intr.* Of a train: To run with two engines.
1904 *Delineator* Sept. 374 A heavy freight train had double-headed up the mountain, and at the summit the leading engine had been cut off to run down ahead of the train.

Double-headed, *a.* Add: Of a train: Running with two engines. Of an electric locomotive (see quot. 1905).
1902 *Daily Chron.* 21 May 3/5 So heavy a train..doubtless ..will always be 'double-headed'. 1905 *Ibid.* 12 Jan. 8/5 The locomotive is double-headed, and controllable at either end, so that no turning is necessary.

Double-header. Add: **c.** In baseball and lacrosse, the playing of two games in succession on the same day by the same opposing teams. *U.S. & Canada.* **d.** *Logging.* (See quot.) *U.S.*
1905 *Terms Forestry & Logging* 35 *Double header*, a place from which it is possible to haul a full load of logs to the landing, and where partial loads are topped out or finished to the full hauling capacity of teams.

Doublet. Add: **2. d.** A story told twice over (as in the book of Genesis), or a saying in the Synoptic Gospels occurring in two different con-

texts, and hence regarded as derived from distinct sources.
1906 F. C. BURKITT *Gospel Hist.* 14 One of the really striking features about the narrative in Genesis..is the number of Doublets, *i.e.* stories told twice over. *Ibid.* 163 At the first glance they are real doublets; *i.e.* different accounts of the same event drawn from different sources.

Double-team, *v. U.S.* [f. DOUBLE *v.* 1 + TEAM *sb.* 3.] *intr.* To bring double force to bear *on* one.
1860 *Congress. Globe* 12 Jan. 424/2 In respect to the Senator's allusion to 'double-teaming' upon him..I do not exactly agree with my friend from Mississippi. 1865 MRS. CHESNUT *Diary fr. Dixie* (1905) 346 Grant had double-teamed on Lee. 1904 T. WATSON *Bethany* (1920) 197 On the next day we double-teamed on one section of his army.
b. With *it*: To act in combination.
1884 'MARK TWAIN' *Huck. Finn* xix. 183 'Old man' said the young one, 'I reckon we might double-team it together'.

Doubleton (dʌ·b'ltən). *Card-playing.* [f. DOUBLE *a.*, after *singleton.*] In whist and bridge: Two cards only of one suit, in a player's hand.
1906 *Westm. Gaz.* 11 Aug. 14/1 B's ten of hearts is nearly sure to be a lead from the best of three—it cannot be a singleton...Similarly, if it is a doubleton [etc.]. 1922 *Evening News* 10 Apr. 8/6 Do not lead from a doubleton (a suit of two cards only) about which you have no information. 1927 *Observer* 20 Mar. 25 When he holds a singleton or weak doubleton of a suit.

Double-tongue, *v. intr. Music.* To apply the tongue with a quick vibratory action to the teeth and hard palate alternately in producing staccato or rapidly repeated notes on the flute or cornet.
1876 STAINER & BARRETT *Dict. Mus. Terms.* 1880 [see TONGUING *vbl. sb.*]. 1898 *Daily News* 25 Feb. 6/6 A flute solo, in which florid passages and difficult double-tongueing were executed with the timbre of a Barrett or a Radcliff.

Doubletree (dʌ·b'ltrī). *U.S.* [f. DOUBLE *a.* + TREE *sb.*, after U.S. *single-tree* = SWINGLETREE.] The cross-piece to which the swingletree of a carriage, plough, etc. is attached.
1847–64 WEBSTER (citing *Haldeman*) s.v. *Single-tree*, A single-tree is fixed upon each end of another cross-piece, called the double-tree, when two horses draw abreast. 1874 KNIGHT *Dict. Mech.*

Double wall. In full *double wall knot*: see WALL-KNOT. Hence **Double-wall** *v.*
1801 J. J. MOORE *Brit. Mariner's Vocab.* M 2, Double wall Knot. 1808 D. LEVER *Yng. Sea Officer's Sheet Anchor* 5 To Double Wall this Knot...The knot will appear..having a double wall, and single crown. 1834 *Tough Yarns* (1858) 31 Occasionally he would turn 'em end-for-end, and begin with the prayer first, knotting it with a double-walled damme, ..crowned with an Amen. 1841 R. H. DANA *Seaman's Man.* vii. 37 Make the single wall slack, and crown it... Thus made, it has a double wall. *Ibid.* 38 It may be double walled by next passing the strands under the walling on the left of them.

Doubt, *sb.*[1] **1. b.** Add phr. *To give* (an accused person) *the benefit of the doubt*: to give a verdict of Not Guilty where the evidence is conflicting; to assume his innocence rather than guilt. Hence in wider use, to incline to the more favourable or kindly decision, estimate, or the like.
1860 T. INMAN *On Myalgia* 104 We should more frequently give our patients the 'benefit of our doubts', and abstain from attempting to cure an inflammation [etc.]. 1892 [in Dict.].

Douche, *sb. Comb.* Add: *douche-can, -glass.*
1908 *Practitioner* Oct. 579 At first I used an ordinary enamelled tin douche-can. *Ibid.*, It is an advantage..to be able to watch the limb which is being congested, and so I now use a cylindrical douche-glass.

Dough, *sb.* Add: **2. b.** Money. *U.S. slang.*
1851 *Yale Tomahawk* Feb. (Th.) He thinks he will pick his way out of the Society's embarrassments, provided he can get sufficient dough. 1896 G. ADE *Artie* ii. 12, I pulled in the dough and picked up the cards. 1903 *N. Y. Even. Post* 31 Oct. 4 Its attitude is simply that of a millionaire buyer of votes. 'We've got the dough' is the cry of the conspirators in the 14th Street. 1919 *War Slang* in *Athenæum* 22 Aug. 791/2 'Dough' denotes money, but more especially the weekly pay.
attrib. 1904 *N. Y. Even. Post* 7 Nov. 3 This is Tammany's regular annual 'dough day'—that is, the day on which the district leaders come to Tammany Hall for election day funds. 1906 *Ibid.* 24 Oct. 4 In the country, election day without some sort of 'dough-bag' is an unheard-of thing. No 'dough-bag' means no votes.
5. *dough-bait, -cake* (examples); *dough-like* adj.; **dough-head** (example).
1904 *Westm. Gaz.* 19 Nov. 3/1 On the bank..men and boys..are fishing with quill-floats and *dough-bait, the least artistic form of sport. 1844 LEE & FROST *Oregon* xxii. 290 Becoming quite hungry we got out some flour, and baked some *dough cakes. *a* 1861 T. WINTHROP *John Brent* v. 53 Sternly common viaticum of pork, dough-cakes, and coffee. 1854 MARY J. HOLMES *Tempest & Sunshine* xv. 222 He inwardly accused them all of being '*doughheads'.. 1928 A. B. CALLOW *Food & Health* 25 The 'indigestibility' of very new bread is due to its *dough-like consistency.

Dough-boy. Add: **2.** An infantry soldier. *U.S. colloq.*
In allusion to the 'large globular brass buttons of the infantry uniform' in the American civil war.
1867 MRS. CUSTER *Tenting on Plains* xvii. 532 She was so accustomed to fast riding with our cavalry, she does not know how to treat a dough-boy. 1904 *N. Y. Times* 13 June 6 A disgusting practice which reduced a bold cavalier to the level of a 'doughboy' at once. 1920 BOK *Americanization of Ed. Bok* (1921) 410 He found himself in one of the numerous little towns where our doughboys were billeted.

Dough-face. 1. Substitute: A mask made of dough. Also *transf.*
1809 *Deb. Congress* 23 Feb. (1853) 1509 It is something like dressing ourselves up in a dough-face and winding-sheet to frighten others. 1820 *Massachusetts Spy* 22 Mar. (Th.) They saw their dough faces in the glass and were frightened. 1883 E. EGGLESTON *Hoosier School-Boy* xviii. 120 Two boys from the neighborhood, who had joined the party, agreed to furnish dough-faces for them all.
2. (Earlier example.)
1833 H. BARNARD in *Maryland Hist. Mag.* XIII. 272 What a set of 'dough faces' have we got here to be frightened into a repeal of their Tariff.

Douglas's pouch. *Anat.* [Name of James *Douglas*, English physician (1675–1742).] A sac of the peritoneum which dips down below the posterior surface of the uterus. Also *Douglas's cul-de-sac, space.* Hence **Douglasitis** (dʌglăsəi·tis), inflammation of Douglas's pouch (Dorland 1903).
1890 BILLINGS *Med. Dict.*, Douglas's cul-de-sac...D.'s pouch. 1899 *Jrnl. Anat. & Physiol.* XXXIII. 368 Freund, on Douglas' cul-de-sac. 1907 *Practitioner* Apr. 472 A boggy, ill-defined, and very tender swelling present in Douglas's pouch. *Ibid.* Nov. 678 Ulcer stitched, Douglas's space opened, and drainage tube inserted.

Doukhobors (dū·kobǭɪz), *sb. pl.* Also **Dukh-.** [ad. Russ. *Dukhobórets*, pl. *-bortsy*, spirit-wrestler or -denier.] A Russian fanatical sect who migrated in large numbers to Canada because they refused military service.
1897 [see SPIRIT *sb.* 23 c]. 1899 *Westm. Gaz.* 24 Apr. 3/2 Some of the Russian Doukhobors who have been expelled for refusing to participate in war. 1899 *Daily News* 30 May 5/2 Several settlements of the persecuted sect of the Doukobohrs [*sic*] are established there [*sc.* in Canada]. 1921 R. M. JONES *Later Periods of Quakerism* II. xx. 836 The persecution of the Doukhobors in Trans-Caucasia.

Douma, variant of *DUMA.

Dourine (dū·rīn). [F. *dourin.*] A contagious disease of horses transmitted by copulation and caused by the parasite *Trypanosoma equiperdum.*
1903 M. H. HAYES *Vet. Notes* (ed. 6) 510 Dourine is a specific disease which at first appears as an inflammation of the surface of the genital organs, and which causes grave alterations in the nervous system of the attacked animal. *Ibid.* 511 Mares are more liable to acute dourine than stallions.

Douro (dū·ro). [Fr., a. Sp. *duro.*] A Spanish coin of the value of five francs.
1905 *Daily Chron.* 21 June 5/4 That the Moorish Government should pay 9,000 douros by way of compensation. 1905 *Westm. Gaz.* 12 Sept. 2/1 No, my daughter, a douro, that is sufficient. Another sou would be excessive. 1908 *Ibid.* 21 July 5/1 The new law provides that all these Seville douros shall be confiscated. 1925 *Chambers's Jrnl.* June 383/2 He proposes forty douros as a fair price...A douro is equal to five francs.

Douroucouli (dūrukū·li). Also **douroucoli, durukuli, doura-, dorocouli.** The native name for monkeys of the S. American genus *Nyctipithecus*; a night-ape.
1891 FLOWER & LYDEKKER *Mammals* 714 The Douroucoulis. 1894 H. A. FORBES *Primates* I. 166 The Douroucolis. 1897 *Q. Rev.* Oct. 434 The *Douracoulis* or Night Apes are truly nocturnal animals...The group ranges from Costa Rica and Nicaragua to the south of Paraguay. 1902 F. E. BEDDARD *Mammalia* 560 The Douroucouli Monkeys.

Douser. Add: *Cinema.* (See quot.)
1921 LESCARBOURA *Cinema Handbk.* 21 *Douser*, the manually operated door in the projecting machine, which intercepts the light before it reaches the film.

Dove, *sb.* Add: **1. d.** = *dove-colour* (5 b).
1895 *Bow Bells* 29 Mar. 322/1 Sortie-de-bals..are almost always in neutral tints—dove, gray, or fawn. 1903 *Daily Chron.* 21 Nov. 8/4 Aubergine accords with dove charmingly.
5. b. dove-marble, marble of a dove-colour; **dove-party** *U.S.* (see quot.).
1872 *Rep. Vermont Board Agric.* 675 The first mills at Swanton were wholly employed in the manufacture of grave-stones from the *dove-marble. 1886 *Harper's Mag.* Dec. 159/2 The '*dove parties' composed of the wives of cabinet officers and foreign ministers..were exceedingly lively and popular.

Dover's powder. *Pharmacy.* A preparation of opium and ipecacuanha (*pulvis Doveri*) prescribed by Dr. Thomas *Dover* (1660–1742) as an anodyne diaphoretic.
1854 MAYNE *Expos. Lex.* 1887 *Buck's Handbk. Med. Sci.* V. 325/1 Dover's Powder..: Powdered Opium 10 parts, Ipecac. 10 parts, Sugar of Milk 80 parts.

Dowd, *sb.*[1] Add examples of recent currency, which appears to be due to a new back-formation from DOWDY *a.*
1899 *Westm. Gaz.* 30 Oct. 3/2 She's a dowd to-day. 1904 *Ibid.* 23 June 4/2 Only a duchess may dare to be a dowd just now.

Dowel, *sb.* **3. dowel-pin** (U.S. example).
1901 S. MERWIN & H. K. WEBSTER *Calumet K* i. 6 Then he hammered the timber down on the iron dowel pins.

Dower, *sb.*[2] **4.** Add: **dower-chest,** an ornamental chest or coffer made to hold a bride's marriage-outfit (cf. *CASSONE); **dower-land** (earlier U.S. example).
1922 *Daily Tel.* 12 June 20/1 Antique walnut cabinets, *dower chest. 1925 N. VENNER *Imperfect Impostor* iv, There was an old oak dower chest, curiously carved. 1927 *Daily Tel.* 14 June 3/1 A fine old carved dower chest of the Henry VIII. period. 1769 WASHINGTON *Diaries* I. 325 Rid over my *dower Land in York. [*Note*, Land belonging to Mrs. Washington's estate.]

Dowitcher (dau·itʃəɪ). [? ad. G. *Deutscher* (doi·tʃəɪ) German.] An American long-billed snipe of the genus *Macrorhamphus.*
1872 COUES *Key N. Amer. Birds* 252 Brown-back. Dowitcher. 1888 LEES & CLUTTERBUCK *B.C. 1887* xvii. (1892) 182 The long-billed dowitchers are very much like large snipe, of a pale cinnamon colour.

Down, *sb.*[3] Add: **2. b.** An act of throwing down, as in wrestling. In American football: see quot. 1897.
1840 W. G. SIMMS *Border Beagles* 134 He downed him: a fair stupid down. 1893 W. K. POST *Harvard Stories* 22 After three downs Spofford dropped back. *Ibid.* 24 On the fourth down, the ball would be Harvard's. 1897 *Encycl. Sport* I. 425/1 *A down.*—The term used to indicate the number of attempts made to advance the ball. Each side has three tries in which to advance the ball five yards. The end of each try, *i.e.* when the ball is held by the opposing side, is a down. As soon as the five yards have been gained it is first down again. 1927 *Observer* 11 Dec. 16/3 After the kick-off the side that has the ball must gain ten yards in a maximum of four 'downs'. Otherwise it loses the ball.
5. Chiefly in phr. *to have a down on*: to dislike, regard unfavourably, be ill-disposed towards.
1878 in R. Brough Smyth *Aborig. Queensland* I. 129 Blacks never like a quarrel to be of long standing:..nothing would make a man more miserable than to think that some of his tribe had a 'down' on him. 1904 *Daily Chron.* 8 Dec. 8/1 Why this 'down' on an always useful, sometimes dainty, garment? 1928 S. VINES *Humours Unreconciled* xiii. 179 Somebody'd got a down on him.

Down, *a.* Add:
1. d. Of payment: see DOWN *adv.* 12.
1930 *San Antonio* (Texas) *Light* 31 Jan. 14/6 Small down payment, balance like rent.

Down, *adv.* Add:
14. b. (So many points, etc.) behind one's opponent in a game; opposed to *up*.
1894 *Times* 16 June 16/1 [He] lost the [golf] match by four down, and two to play. 1897 *Encycl. Sport* I. 472/2 A player is said to be down when his opponent has won one or more holes [more] than he has. 1907 H. H. HILTON *Golfing Remin.* 103 At the fourteenth hole he was one down.
15. Later examples, in the phrase *down to date* (after UP TO DATE).
1897 'MARK TWAIN' *Following the Equator* xxv. 244 He was down to date with them, too. 1901 *Daily Chron.* 1 Nov. 5/2 An author of the most down-to-date ballads of the barrack-room. 1930 *Morning Post* 4 Mar. 7/5 The most down-to-date dictionaries.
25. c. *Down charge*: the order given to a setter or pointer in training to drop when the game rises and the shot is fired.
1833 *New Sporting Mag.* V. 259/1 Some sportsmen..make him down charge when the bird is missed. *Ibid.* 260/1 Call out directly, 'Down charge!' 1859 STONEHENGE *Shot-gun & Sporting Rifle* II. i. 129 He puts up the birds, calling out 'Down charge' at the same moment in a loud voice. 1882 W. N. HUTCHINSON *Dog Breaking* ii. § 27. 16 You may, whilst he is lying down (in order to teach him the 'down charge'), go through the motions of loading. 1886 LD. WALSINGHAM, etc. *Shooting* (Badm. Libr.) I. 324 His obedience to 'down charging' being frequently enforced. *Ibid.* 334 Provided the dog is fairly cured of chasing, taught to 'down-charge', find, return, and keep at heel.
VII. Down along: in, or to, the West Country. Also *attrib.*, and *sb.* (= the West Country). *dial.*
1871 KINGSLEY *At Last* i, Their faces lighted up at the old pass-word of 'Down-Along'; for whosoever knows Down-Along, and the speech thereof, is at once a friend and a brother. 1899 *Westm. Gaz.* 12 Jan. 3/3 The people of the 'down-along' country are slow in putting thoughts into words. 1905 E. PHILLPOTTS *Secret Woman* III. xiii, Henceforth I shall come down-along once a year to visit you. 1907 *Westm. Gaz.* 18 Dec. 4/2 In his 'Devonshire Characters' ..there is a true tang of 'Down-along' in every page. 1929 F. C. BOWEN *Sea Slang* 40 *Down Along.* Sailing coastways down Channel.

Down, *prep.* Add: **1. c.** *Down cellar*: in the cellar or basement. *U.S.*
1855 M. THOMPSON *Doesticks* x. 84 A patent medicine palace, with a..conservatory down cellar. 1870 'FANNY FERN' *Ginger-Snaps* 142 When we place a young plant down cellar and shut out light and sunshine. 1871 MRS. STOWE *Sam Lawson* 7 Ef ye should be down cellar, and the candle should go out, now? 1877 MRS. E. S. WARD *Story of Avis* 141, I wonder if it wouldn't help you out to go down cellar and stir the ice-cream.
2. d. *Down the course*: said of a horse which is not among the leading competitors in a race.
1920 A. E. W. MASON *The Summons* xx. 202 All our horses were down the course...They weren't running in their form at all. 1923 *Daily Mail* 11 Jan. 9 Certain horses which ran second or third in the great 'chase at Aintree were 'down the course' this week at Birmingham. *Ibid.* 5 Mar. 9 What about the big and powerful stables..whose horses are down the course one day and up the next, according to the betting?

Down, *v.*[2] Add: **1.** *To down tools*: to refuse to go on working, to go on strike. Hence *down-tools* is used attrib. to designate such action.
1898 *Westm. Gaz.* 7 Apr. 6/3 The men..have ruined their position by..suddenly downing tools. 1913 *Daily Express* 4 Mar. 1/5 The 'down-tools' movement seems to have arisen spontaneously out of the engineers' dissatisfaction at not securing the twopence an hour increase when they asked for it. 1919 *Brit. Manuf.* Nov. 39/2 The recent 'down-tools' policy of the workers. 1923 *Daily Mail* 3 Mar. 13 Yesterday some hundreds of men who did not receive their notice.. to 'down tools' on the previous day left their work.

b. *fig.* To overthrow, to get the better of.
1898 H. S. Canfield *Maid of Frontier* 43 We will have trouble in finishing the gang after Harriott is downed. 1900 *Westm. Gaz.* 26 July 1/2 He sees a chance of 'downing' his political opponents. 1904 F. Lynde *Grafters* xviii. 233 'A determination to make my brag good.' 'To down the ring, you mean?' 'Yes; to down the ring.' 1926 W. Deeping *Sorrell & Son* I. i. § 5 The thing is not to love your neighbour, but to be able to make it unsafe for him to try and down you.

c. To drink down.
1922 Mulford *Tex* x. 145 Silently he poured out a drink and downed it mechanically.

2. b. To die down. *U.S.*
1924 W. M. Raine *Troubled Waters* xvii. 180 The rumour would not down that one of the prisoners had turned State's evidence.

Down and out. orig. *U.S.* [Down *adv.* 5, Out *adv.* 19 c.] Completely without resources or means of livelihood; 'on one's beam ends'; absolutely 'done'. Also *absol.* ('the down and out') and as *sb.*
1889 *Kansas Times & Star* 28 Nov., The brewers, saloon-keepers and sports will meet..to provide a turkey feast for the 'down and outs' in their line. *a* 1906 'O. Henry' *Trimmed Lamp* etc. 186 I'm down and out; but I'm no traitor to a man that's been my friend. 1917 Jeffery Farnol *Definite Object* vi. 49, I don't want 'em to think I'm floatin' around with a down-an'-out from Battyville. 1921 H. Walpole *Young Enchanted* III. vi, Everybody over forty is tired and down and out, and everybody under thirty has swelled head. 1922 G. M. Trevelyan *Brit. Hist. 19th Cent.* xxiii. 375 France was down and out. 1923 H. L. Foster *Beachcomber in Orient* x. 215 Nowhere in my travels had I ever found a city so full of the down-and-out as was Singapore at that particular moment. 1924 W. B. Selbie *Psych. Relig.* 87 The down-and-outs converted there. 1928 H. Walpole *Wintersmoon* III. v, Next to Wildherne was a down-and-out with holes in his boots. 1928 Galsworthy *Swan Song* III. vi. 259 'You've never been down and out, I imagine, Mr. Forsyte?' 'No', answered Soames.

Hence **Down-and-out** *v. trans.*, to do for, destroy. **Down-and-outer,** one who is 'down and out'. **Down-and-outness.**
1909 *Springfield Weekly Republ.* 4 Mar. 2 Compliments from political enemies follow the most distinguished down-and-outer of his day into the seclusion of private life. 1914 Gertrude Atherton *Perch of Devil* II. 298 You don't..put it over without running the risk of being shot by some sort of down-and-outer. 1916 Boyd Cable *Action Front* 186 That machine-gun upstairs is a certain invitation to sudden death and the German gunners to down and out us. 1922 H. L. Foster *Adv. Trop. Tramp* ii. 20 The down-and-outers of whom my old sea-captain had spoken. 1926 *Blackw. Mag.* Aug. 235/2 In the process of investigating the reason for their down-and-outness, he considered that the applicant had been a knave.

Down-draught. Add: **3.** The drawing or displacing of water by an object as it sinks.
1899 Bullen *Way Navy* 24 The down-draught of the anchor had sucked him after it almost to the bottom.

Down-easter (see Down *adv.* 28). (Additional example.) Also applied to a ship.
1835 [see *Dumbfish]. 1925 Rex Clements *Gipsy of Horn* 84 If this ship was a 'down-easter' she'd be flauntin' a main-royal. 1929 F. C. Bowen *Sea Slang* 40 *Down Easter.* Originally a native of the State of Maine, which turned out some magnificent men, or a sailing ship built there.

Dow·n-fold. *Geol.* A synclinal fold or depression. So **Dow·n-folded** *a.*, (of strata) dipping on each side towards a common axis.
1902 Mackinder *Britain & Brit. Seas* vi. 71 To the very top it consists of down-folded beds. *Ibid.* 80 The valleys are floored with strips of carboniferous limestone still preserved in the Old Red downfolds. Geographical valley and geological downfold here coincide with a precision that is rare. 1920 *Glasgow Herald* 15 Oct. 7 The oil did not come from the arches or anticlines, but from the downfolds, (synclines).

Down grade. (Earlier U.S. examples.) Also as *adv.*
1876 Joaquin Miller *Unwritten Hist.* vi. 96 He [*sc.* the stage-driver] said:—'boys, I am on the down grade, and can't reach the brake!' and sank down and died. And so it is that 'the down grade,' an expression born of the death of the old stage-driver, has a meaning with us now. 1878 B. F. Taylor *Between Gates* 13 The down grade has begun. Let the engines take breath. 1902 S. Merwin & H. K. Webster *Calumet K* xi. 199 They'd all strike like a freight train rolling down grade.

Downily, *adv.* Add: **2.** Artfully, cunningly.
1929 C. E. Montague *Disenchantment* v. § ii. 72 He could soothe the couch of a wounded sergeant by telling him ..how downily the old colonel..had timed his enteric inoculation.

Downing Street. A short street running out of Whitehall towards St. James's Park and containing the Foreign Office and the official residence (No. 10) of the prime minister: hence used as a synonym for the Government of the day.
1849 Thackeray *Pendennis* xxxi, Look! here comes the Foreign Express galloping in. They will be able to give news to Downing Street to-morrow. 1858 *Leisure Hour* 18 Nov. 728/1 The decrees and counsels of Downing Street will be heard simultaneously in Pekin or Canton. 1920 K. Jones *Fleet St. & Downing St.* 330 Thus would Fleet Street and Downing Street at last understand one another. 1920 [H. Begbie] *Mirrors of Downing St.* 7 The private opposition he [*sc.* Lloyd George] encountered in Downing Street.

Down lead. *Wireless Telegraphy.* [Down *adv.* 38.] (See quot. 1919.)
1913 *Work* 23 Aug. 413/2 The aerial..should be at least 100 ft. to 150 ft.. including down leads. 1919 H. Ward *Techn. Terms Wireless Telegr.*, *Down lead*, wire connecting elevated portion of aerial to the instruments.

Down-looking, *a.* (Earlier U.S. examples.)
1788 *Maryland Jrnl.* 9 May (Th.) Lindsey, a down-looking fellow, had on a new flaxen shirt. 1800 *Aurora* (Philad.) 23 July, A number of sneaking down-looking fellows, who occasionally assembled in a group.

Downsman (dau·nzmǝ̆n). [Down *sb.*[1] 2.] A native or inhabitant of the (Sussex) Downs.
1906 *Academy* 20 Jan. 63/1 The Downsman in the city May not his home forget. 1921 S. Leslie *Manning* 44 Morning after morning in the grey mist the shepherds and downsmen could hear the bell of their vigilant pastor. 1927 *Observer* 5 June 6/3 [He] founded the Society of Sussex Downsmen.

Downsome (dau·nsǝ̆m), *a. colloq.* or *dial.* [See Down *adv.* 18, Down *a.* 3.] Inclined to be down or dispirited.
1888 F. R. Stockton *The Dusantes* iii, When you left us at 'Frisco we felt pretty downsome. 1894 Blackmore *Perlycross* viii. 61 Then I just looked in at the *Bush*, because my heart was downsome.

Down South, *adv.* *U.S.* [Down *adv.* 2, 4.] In or into the States south of Mason and Dixon's line.
1862 'E. Kirke' *Among Pines* i. 12 Old Abe he's gwine to come down Souf. *Ibid.* iii. 60 Away down South in Dixie. 1884 'Mark Twain' *Huck. Finn* xxxiii, There was plenty other farmer-preachers like that,.. down South.

Dow·nstrea·m, *adv.* (*a.*). [Down *prep.* 3.] Down the stream, in the direction of the current, towards the mouth of a river. Also (*to the*) *downstream of.*
1864 [see Down *prep.* 3]. 1869 Blackmore *Lorna D.* vii, Even an otter might float downstream. 1900 *Westm. Gaz.* 10 July 2/2 He found the sudd of the flood..still in the White Nile, downstream of Lake No...Dr. Schweinfurth.. found the 'sudd' to the downstream of Lake No, as before. 1929 Belloc *Joan of Arc* iii. 62 The French forces lay downstream.

b. as *adj.*
1842 *American Pioneer* I. 70 Steam-boats seem almost to say, we will do your up-stream business for nothing, if you will give us your down-stream business. 1890 Morris *News from Nowhere* ii. (1913) 8 Even the up-stream bridges..are scarcely daintier, and the down-stream ones are scarcely more dignified and stately.

Down-town, *a.* and *sb.* *U.S.* [See Down *prep.* 2 b and 3.]

A. *adj.* Situated in the lower, or more central, part of the town.
1870 J. K. Medbery *Men & Myst. Wall Street* 67 On these securities therefore the down-town banks make call loans. 1876 Ingram *Centen. Expos.* v. 155 Foreign orders.. were obtainable the same as at the down-town office. 1891 *Congress. Rec.* 28 Jan. 1906/1 The second ward of the city of New York..is what is called a down-town ward, a business ward. 1906 'O. Henry' *Four Million* ix. (1916) 101 To-morrow he would go into the roaring downtown district and find work. 1911 H. S. Harrison *Queed* ii. 17 He would spend all his time in his room, apparently having no down-town occupation.

B. *sb.* The lower or business part of a town.
1851 H. Melville *Whale* i, Its extreme down-town is the Battery. 1905 *N.Y. Even. Post* 4 Mar. 5 One of the diversions of downtown yesterday was watching the sure movements of a steeplejack.

Down under, *adv.* [Down *adv.* 4.] At the antipodes; in Australia, New Zealand, etc. Also *attrib.* and *sb.* (after a prep.).
1908 *Daily Chron.* 31 Oct. 4/6 The Bishop of London.. does not take a very active interest in the 'down under' section of his see. 1909 *Westm. Gaz.* 11 Jan. 12/1 The same could happen 'down under' if New Zealand..were bracketted with New South Wales and Queensland. 1916 *Anzac Bk.* 145/2 Macaulay's prophecy concerning the man from 'down under' sitting on the ruins of London Bridge. 1922 *Daily Mail* 9 Dec. 11 The steeplechaser Kinlark, a gift to the Prince from 'down under'. 1928 *Daily Express* 17 Feb. 4 Mr. Collins, the captain of the last visiting Australian team, was a stipendiary steward 'down under'.

Down wind: see Wind *sb.*[1] 18 a.

Downy, *a.*[2] Add: **3. b.** *Downy hickory.*
1846 J. W. Abert in Emory *Military Reconn.* 387 Here we noticed the white hickory, or downy hickory.

c. Downy woodpecker *U.S.* (see quot.).
1872 *Rep. Vermont Board Agric.* 321 The Downy Woodpecker (*Picus pubescens*, Linn.) a black and white bird, usually not over six inches long.

Doxographer (dǫksǫ·grăfǝɹ). [f. mod.L. *doxographus* (Diels 1879), f. Gr. δόξα opinion + -γραφος writer: see -er[1].] A writer who collects and records the opinions or *placita* of the Greek philosophers. Hence **Doxogra·phical** *a.*, of or pertaining to the doxographers; **Doxo·graphy,** a collection of philosophical opinions.
1892 J. Burnet *Early Greek Philos.* 371 By the term *doxographers* we understand all those writers who relate the opinions of the Greek philosophers. *Ibid.* 374 The doxography [of the *Lucullus*] has come through the hands of Kleitomachus. *Ibid.* 375 Short doxographical summaries are to be found in Eusebios [etc.]. 1908 J. Adam *Relig. Teachers of Greece* xiii. 267 We have doxographical testimony to show that Diogenes pronounced the soul to be imperishable. *Ibid.* 268 The doxographers sometimes ascribe to him [*sc.* Democritus] the doctrine of a single world-soul or Deity identical..with the aggregate of fiery atoms in the world. 1919 *Jrnl. Hellen. Stud.* 180 The Greek doxographers know of no astronomer before Thales.

Doxologize, *v.* **a.** Add: More *gen.* To give glory to God.
1919 R. Harris *Orig. Doctr. Trinity* 9 It must be remembered that the Church doxologised before it defined.

Doxology. Add: **c.** *gen.* An utterance or ascription of praise and thanksgiving.
1906 *Sat. Rev.* 3 Feb. 131 It may be only here and there that cheers have been given in dissenting places of worship for the Liberal candidate, and triumphant doxologies sung for his return.

Doyenne (dwaye·n). [orig. F. *doyenné*, in full *poire de doyenné*, lit. 'deanery pear'.] A variety of pear. More fully *Doyenne pear.*
1781 Miller *Gard. Dict.* s.v. *Pyrus* 35 Le Doyenné, *i.e.* The Deans Pear. 1822 Loudon *Encycl. Gardening* (1824) § 4437 Doyenné. *Synonym.* Dean's pear. 1860 Hogg *Fruit Manual* 181 Fruit small, roundish-obovate, or Doyenné-shaped. 1867–8 *Trans. Ill. Agric. Soc.* VII. 506 We know that the Bartlett and the White Doyenne have no two things exactly in common. 1872 *Rep. Vermont Board Agric.* 109 A yearly crop of the finest Doyenne pears, in size, colour and quality, of any I have ever seen.

Dozy, *a.*[1] **2.** *U.S.* (Earlier and later examples.)
1871 Schele de Vere *Americanisms* (1872) 464 *Dozy* and *dozed* are said in Pennsylvania of timber beginning to decay and unfit for use, while the decay is yet hardly perceptible, but the timber already brittle. (S. S. Haldeman.) 1928 D. H. Lawrence *Kangaroo* viii. 166 Refined young men.. writing with a guarded kind of friendliness..as dozy as ripe pears in their..heaviness.

Drab, *sb.*[2] and *a.* Add:

B. *adj.* **c.** In comb. with other names of colours.
1894 R. B. Sharpe *Handbk. Birds Gt. Brit.* (1896) I. 12 Sides of neck and under surface of body drab-grey. 1905 *Westm. Gaz.* 15 May 10/2 The rather soft fur of the under-parts is drab-brown.

C. *sb.* **1. b.** *fig.* A dull or lifeless appearance or character.
1903 *Daily Chron.* 31 Dec. 5/1 Despite the fact that so many of his works wore a drab, still those who knew him best recognised that the drab was the colour of his experience. 1909 *Westm. Gaz.* 4 Feb. 1/3 It is the one sustained note of colour in the dreary drab of Irish life.

Draba (drē·bă). *Bot.* [mod.L., ad. Gr. δράβη a kind of cress.] A plant of the genus of cruciferous herbs so named, found in temperate and arctic regions, cultivated as a hardy annual, biennial, and perennial alpine plant.
1777 W. Curtis *Flora Lond.* I. Plate 49, Vernal Draba or Whitlow Grass. 1895 Vines *Students' Text-bk. Bot.* 603 Latiseptal silicula of Draba.

Drabble, *sb.* Add: **3.** A wet mass. *U.S.*
1893 'O. Thanet' *Stories Western Town* 3 There was a drabble of dead leaves on the sidewalk.

Drabble, *v.* **2.** Add examples of wider use.
1903 Kipling *Five Nations, Cruisers* vii, Across the sad valleys all drabbled with rain. 1923 *Chambers's Jrnl.* 89/2 Thews who..drabbled graybeards in their blood.

Drabi (dræ·bi). [See quot. 1920.] A muleteer.
1920 *Chambers's Jrnl.* 296/2 (Indian frontier) The lot of the muleteer (or *drabi*, as he is generally called, this being the native rendering of the English word 'driver.') is never a very easy one. 1920 *Blackw. Mag.* Nov. 569/2 (Mahsud-land) Mule drabis. 1927 E. Thompson *These Men thy Friends* 125 A fool of a *drabi*, who had left his mules and stumbled off, seeking India that lay to the east.

Drably (dræ·bli), *adv.* (see under Drab *sb.*[2] and *a.*). Add: Also *fig.* Without brightness or colour, dully, uninterestingly.
1905 *Westm. Gaz.* 19 Sept. 10/1 Few guess that the dahlia ..has had a drably unromantic origin. 1918 *Cornhill Mag.* June 616 The desirability of expressing thoughts fully and truly in words..is too drably presented to the child. 1927 *Sunday Express* 1 May 9 Their novels look drably old-fashioned.

Dracocephalum (drēkǫse·fălǝ̆m). *Bot.* [mod.L., f. Gr. δράκων dragon + κεφαλή head.] A labiate plant of the genus so named, found in temperate Europe and Asia, a few species of which are cultivated as hardy perennial herbs.
1904 Farrer *Garden Asia* 237 The pallid gleam of a dracocephalum.

Draconiform (drăkǫ·nifǫ̆ɹm), *a.* [f. L. *dracon-, draco* Dragon: see -form.] Resembling a dragon in shape.
1888 Dunlop *Prose Fiction* I. 450 The accessory emblem of a draconiform monster.

Draft, *sb.* Add: **2. c.** A member of a selected military detachment.
1914–16 E. A. Mackintosh *War, the Liberator* (1918) 23, I know the drafts are good men I know they're doing well. 1916 Boyd Cable *Action Front* 110 I've seen one-half the battalion wiped out in one engagement and built up with drafts.

d. = *draft ewe* (see 7).
1844 H. Stephens *Bk. Farm* III. 1107 Drafts are ready for sale in September. 1886 C. Scott *Sheep-farming* 107 Ewes and gimmers at 34/4½, being 3/– a head more than the drafts.

Draft, *v.* **1.** Add: Also *transf.*
1927 *Observer* 4 Dec. 20/7 Mr. Smith will be nominated. Mr. Coolidge will be 'drafted' by acclaim of the Convention. The Republicans will win.

Drafter. Add: **3.** A draught-horse.
Cf. 1876 *Whitby Gloss.*, *Draughters*, waggon-horses. 1906 *Springfield Republ.* 7 Feb. 2 Advt., A nice lot of well-broken useful horses, consisting of all classes from the nice, pleasant driver to the large, strong, rugged drafter.

Drag, *sb.* Add: **3. e.** The slow-moving portion of a cattle-herd which is being driven. Hence *drag-driver. U.S.*
1888 T. Roosevelt in *Century Mag.* Apr. 862/1 The rest [of the men] are in the rear to act as 'drag-drivers', and hurry up the phalanx of reluctant weaklings. 1920 Hunter *Trail Drivers of Texas* 44, I went up the trail twice, and drove the drag both times. *Ibid.* 151 All the men were in front of the cattle except myself, the drag driver, and the cook. *Ibid.* 172 We left the drags together in another herd. 1924 W. M. Raine *Troubled Waters* x. 101 I'm plumb fed up with the dust of the drag driver.

f. Feminine attire worn by a man when impersonating a woman; also, a party attended by men wearing feminine attire. *slang.*
1870 *Reynold's Newsp.* 29 May (Farmer) We shall come in drag. 1870 *London Figaro* 23 June (Farmer) Not quite so low..as going about in drag. 1887 *Referee* 24 July (Ware), I don't like to see low coms. in drag parts. 1927 *Sunday Express* 13 Feb. 5/5 A drag is a rowdy party attended by abnormal men dressed in scanty feminine garments, singing jazz songs in high falsetto voices.

g. Influence, 'pull'. *U.S. slang.*
1896 G. Ade *Artie* xii. 105 He knows I've got a drag in the precinct. *Ibid.* xvii. 160 If you've got any drag with him.

9. *drag-rope* (U.S. example); **drag-line,** (*a*) *Geol.*, each of a series of striæ which form a fringe on the lee-side of older striæ; (*b*) *Aeronautics*, a guide rope; **drag-mill** = Arrastre; **drag-saw** (U.S. example); **drag-seine** *U.S.*, a haul-ashore seine (*Cent. Dict.* 1890 s.v. *seine*[1]); hence **drag-seining** *vbl. sb.*
1886 T. C. Chamberlin in *7th Ann. Rep. U.S. Geol. Surv.* (1888) 201 It clearly shows the older set by the *drag-lines on their lee sides. 1922 *Glasgow Herald* 28 Sept. 7 Drag-line excavators. 1884 Knight *Mech. Dict.* Suppl., **Drag Mill*, another name for the arrastra. 1856 E. E. Hale *If, Yes, & Perhaps* (1868) 147 The sled is fitted with two *drag-ropes, at which the men haul. 1867 *Rep. Iowa Agric. Soc.* (1868) 220 *Drag-saw, for cutting logs into fire-wood. 1888 Goode *Amer. Fishes* 179 The method chiefly practiced by the colonists of New England was that of *drag-seining.

Drag, *v.* Add:

6. b. *Stock Exchange.* To be sluggish or inactive.
1906 *Daily Chron.* 19 Sept. 1/7 Stock markets were heavy. Consols dragged.

13. (From Drag *sb.* 6 a.) To follow the line of scent of (an animal); to trail.
1772 Washington *Diaries* II. 133 Went out after Breakfast with the Dogs, dragd a fox an hour or two, but never found [it]. 1786 *Ibid.* III. 12 Never got a fox afoot, tho I dragged one to Mr. Robt. Alexander's Pocoson.

Dragée. Add: In recent use not restricted to sweetmeats serving as a vehicle for drugs; often, a chocolate drop.

Dra·ggle-tai·ledness. [-ness.] Draggle-tailed condition or character.
1889 E. F. Knight '*Falcon*' *on the Baltic* iv. 62 The outrageously bad taste and gaudy draggletailedness of English girls of the same degree. 1904 *Westm. Gaz.* 2 Nov. 1/3 The terrible draggletailedness of some of the women.

Dragon[1]. Add:

10. c. A very powerful armoured tractor.
1926 *Glasgow Herald* 8 Apr. 11 The tanks, dragons, light and heavy guns, cookers, etc. 1927 *Sunday Express* 1 May 7 Just as these 'tankettes' will largely supersede the infantry, so will the 'dragons' supersede horse-teams for bringing up the guns.

Drag-out: see *Knock-down.

Drail (drēl), *v.*[2] *U.S.* [f. Drail *sb.*] *intr.* To fish with a drail.
1873 *Rep. U.S. Fish. Comm.* I. xiv. 248 The usual method of taking them [*sc.* bluefish] with the line is by drailing or trolling. 1888 Goode *Amer. Fishes* 180 It is not known when the custom of drailing for mackerel was first introduced.

Drain, *sb.* Add: **1. c.** (Later U.S. examples.)
1816 U. Brown *Jrnl.* in *Maryland Hist. Mag.* XI. 49 What the people here call a Drain; I would call it a Gully, 20 or 25 feet deep. 1823 J. Fowler *Jrnl.* 144 Crossing over and down a small dream about two miles wide..we went up a small Branch. 1836 W. Irving *Astoria* III. 76 About noon, the travellers reached the 'drains' and brooks that formed the head-waters of the river.

Drainage. 4. Add: *drainage-canal, -line, -outfall*; **drainage-basin,** the area of land drained by a river and its tributaries; **drainage cycle,** the initiation, development, and maturity of drainage of any given region to the time of interruption introduced by new conditions; **drainage-level,** a tunnel in an underground working for collecting the water from upper levels so that it can be pumped out.
1885 Geikie *Text-bk. Geol.* (ed. 2) 352 The proportion of mineral matter in river-water varies with the season...Its amount and composition depend upon the nature of the rocks forming the *drainage-basin. 1900 *Westm. Gaz.* 20 Sept. 8/1 The opening of the *drainage canal has given Chicago an excellent supply of pure water. 1903 W. G. Tight *U.S. Geol. Surv. Professional Paper* No. 13. 76 The deformations of the basin during the development of this old *drainage cycle. 1882 Geikie *Text-bk. Geol.* 922 The permanence of *drainage-lines is one of the most remarkable features in the geological history of the continents. 1911 F. O. Bower *Plant-Life on Land* 16 Conspicuously near to the *drainage-outfalls.

Draining, *vbl. sb.* **4.** Add: **draining-board,** a grooved and sloping board on which utensils are put to drain after they have been washed; so *draining-table.*
1906 *Westm. Gaz.* 30 Apr. 4/2 Few sculleries are equipped with a *draining-board. 1895 *Army & Navy Co-op. Soc. Price List* 15 Sept. 230 Plate Rack and Folding *Draining Table Combined.

Drainless, *a.* Add: **2.** Unprovided with drains.
1902 Sir H. Rumbold *Recoll. Diplomatist* I. 38 They were badly lighted and worse paved, drainless and malodorous.

Drake[2]. **2.** Add:
drake-fly, also, a may-fly, used in angling.
1833 T. Hook *Parson's Dau.* I. v, A dab at killing trout; drake-fly, wasp-fly, or stone-fly, all one to him. 1928 H. Williamson *Tarka the Otter* 58 The summer drake-flies.. hatched from their cases on the water and danced over the shadowed surface.

b. Prefixed to the names of birds of the duck kind to denote the male of the species.
1907 in *Zoologist* (1908) Apr. 124 A drake Shoveler seen on the river at Eaton.

Dramatism (dræ·mătiz'm). Add:

2. Dramatic quality.
1880 Mrs. J. H. Ewing in Horatia K. F. Ewing *J. H. Ewing* (1896) 222 Her writing is glorious—Imagination limited—Dramatism—nil! 1901 'Linesman' *Words Eye-witness* (1902) 165 The infamous stage management of the thing rather aided than detracted from its unspeakable dramatism.

Dra·m-shop. Chiefly *U.S.* [Dram *sb.*[1] 3 b.] A shop or bar where spirituous liquor is sold in drams or small quantities.
1761 J. Adams *Wks.* (1850) II. 122 Taverns and dram-shops are therefore placed in every corner of the town. 1775 in J. S. Loving *Boston Orators* (1852) 673 The commanding officer will accordingly..put a stop to Dram Shops. 1799 *Aurora* (Philad.) 27 Mar. (Th.) Does he or Brother Eyerley mean to keep a dram-shop? 1824 P. Horry *Life F. Marion* vi. (1833) 47 If there was a devil's house (a dram shop) hard by. 1839 [see Dram *sb.*[1] 6]. 1849 Parkman *Oregon Trail* 445 We passed..Boone's grocery and old Vogle's dram-shop. 1875 Holland *Sevenoaks* i. 2 A row of stores and dram-shops and butchers' establishments.

Drapery, *sb.* **6.** Add: **drapery drudge,** man, an artist employed by another artist to paint the drapery in a composition.
1861 Drapery drudge [in Dict.]. 1894 H. Gamlin *G. Romney* 90 Unlike Reynolds and Gainsborough, he employed no drapery men.

Draping (drē·piŋ), *ppl. a.* Hanging in graceful or 'artistic' folds.
1898 *Daily News* 7 May 8/4 A stiff collar on which are drawn folds of some softly draping stuff. 1903 Langbridge *Flame & Flood* xx, Vases with the draping honeysuckle.

Draught, *sb.* Add: **24.** Phrase. *To feel the draught* (fig.): see *Feel *v.* 6 b.

48. c. draught arm, a handle used in drawing liquid from a beer-machine or soda-water fountain; **draught-excluder,** an apparatus for excluding draughts (see quot. 1895); **draught-proof** *a.*, fitted so as to be proof against draughts; **draught-screen,** a screen for keeping off draughts; **draught-scroll,** a scroll for regulating the draught of the roving on a spinning-mule; **draught-table,** a table on which the game of draughts is played.
1901 *Westm. Gaz.* 11 Nov. 11/1 Before entering into any arrangements with the vendors of the various taps or *draught arms at present being offered. 1895 *Army & Navy Co-op. Soc. Price List* 15 Sept. 187 Patent *Draught Excluder. This simple invention consists of a roller covered with plushette, which revolves between two brass brackets when the door is opened or closed. 1909 *Lady's Realm* July 271/2 A most effectual draught excluder. 1908 *Westm. Gaz.* 17 Nov. 4/2 When closed it is entirely *draught-proof. 1929 *Evening News* 18 Nov. 5/1 It seats a pilot and two passengers in an enclosed draught-proof cabin. 1922 F. Niven *Justice of the Peace* x, Behind the *draught-screen was the sound of soap-lather and water. 1894 C. Vickerman *Woollen Spinning* 233 The form of the *draft-scroll has to be varied in diameter at different points to suit the twine at different portions of the draft. 1756 Payne *Draughts*, The *Draught-Table must be placed with an upper White Corner towards the Right Hand.

Draughting, *vbl. sb.* Add: **draughting-table,** one used in drawing designs, plans, etc.
1901 S. Merwin & H. K. Webster *Calumet K* xiii. 247 Bannon was sitting in the office chair with his feet on the draughting-table.

Dravidian (drăvi·diăn), *a.* and *sb.* [f. Skr. *drāviḍa* pertaining to *Draviḍa*, name of a province of southern India. (See Tamil etym.)] **A.** *adj.* Of or pertaining to Dravida or its inhabitants or their language. **B.** *sb.* **a.** A member of the race inhabiting southern India and parts of Ceylon. **b.** Any of the group of languages spoken by the Dravidians. Hence **Dravi·dianism.**
1856 R. Caldwell *Gram. Dravidian Lang.* 503 The Coorgs, whose Drâvidianism cannot be questioned. *Ibid.* 527 The builders of the cairns had settled in India earlier than the Drâvidians. 1871 E. Balfour *Cycl. India* (ed. 2) II. India 39/2 That geographical distribution of the Kol and Dravidian languages. *Ibid.* 42/1 The uncivilized Dravidian speaking tribes are genuine Dravidians who have in a great measure escaped the culture which the more exposed tribes have received. 1884 D. Aubrey *Lett. fr. Bombay* 149 Every scheme appears to have been tried to draw the Hindoo, the Iranian, the Jain, the Dravidian to Christ. 1920 H. G. Wells *Outl. Hist.* 78/1 Dravidian in South India. *Ibid.* 79/1 The Himalayas etc. divided off the Dravidians from the Mongolians, the canoe was the chief link between Dravidian and Southern Mongol. 1924 A. Huxley *Little Mexican & Other Stories* 58 Two expatriated Hindus and a couple of swarthy meridional Frenchmen, who might pass at a pinch as the Aryan compatriots of these dark Dravidians. 1928 C. Dawson *Age of the Gods* iv. 82 The Dravidian was pictured as a mere jungle-dwelling savage. *Ibid.* 83 The modern Dravidian-speaking Brahui.

Dravidic (drăvi·dik), *a.* [f. *Draviḍa*: see prec. and -ic.] = prec. adj.
1888 *Amer. Antiquarian* X. 59 They first entered India, became mingled with the Dravidic race, and afterward were driven out.

Draw, *sb.* Add:

1. c. Short for *draw-poker* (see Draw- a). *U.S. colloq.*
1876 Joaquin Miller *Unwritten Hist.* x. 157 The man ..took a quiet game of 'draw' with the boys at the Howlin' Wilderness, and won at once the title of Judge. 1891 *Scribner's Mag.* X. 278 A small game of draw shortens the dying hours.

2. b. The act of drawing a revolver in order to shoot. *U.S.*
1857 T. H. Gladstone *Kansas* v. 54 With my hand upon the pistols..he didn't stand out long. But I felt pretty bad..till I got the draw on him. 1903 C. T. Brady *Bishop* i. 9 He had the reputation..of being the quickest man on the draw..in the Territory. 1908 Mulford *Orphan* iii. 37 And they would have gotten it, too, only I beat them on the draw.

7. *U.S.* (Earlier examples.)
1786 *Maryland Jrnl.* 3 Nov. (Th.) A draw is placed over the deepest water, for permitting vessels to pass and repass. 1789 Morse *Amer. Geog.* 181 The draw..is designed to require the strength of two men only in raising it. *a* 1817 T. Dwight *Trav. New Eng.* etc. (1821) I. 403 The draw [of Haverhill bridge] is thirty feet in length, and is easily raised by means of a lever. 1832 *U.S. Stat.* c. ccxxvi. (1856) IV. 582 Provided, That the said bridge be so constructed as to have a draw therein suitable for the safe passage of vessels of the largest dimensions.

b. A drawer. *U.S.*
1748 *N. H. Probate Rec.* III. 565, I give..my chist of draws to my dafter Lidea. 1764 *Boston Even. Post* 30 Jan. (Th.) A Chest of Draws. 1775 *Essex Inst. Hist. Coll.* XIII. 188 You know I can take a Draw at a time and lay them in the same manner into Dr Gardners. 1829 in W. L. Mackenzie *Lives Butler & Hoyt* (1845) 50 That celebrated receptacle of Chancery papers..the draw or bushel-basket ..of his venerable predecessor. 1862 Lowell *Biglow P.* Ser. II. vi. 1 Once git a smell o' musk into a draw, An' it clings hold.

Draw-. Add: **draw-cord** = *draw-string*; **draw-frame** = *drawing-frame* (see Drawing *vbl. sb.* 6 a); **draw-horse** (U.S. example); **draw-shave** (*b*), a surgical instrument resembling a drawing-knife for removing thin slices of tissue from the interior of a cavity (Dorland 1913); **draw-string** (earlier U.S. examples); **draw-tub** *U.S.* (see quot.).
1840 W. G. Simms *Border Beagles* 376 [I] have nothing to do but tie a few threads and lay a *draw-cord through the end-loops of the net. 1901 T. Thornley *Holmes' Cotton Spinning* 191 *Drawframes. 1913 W. S. Taggart *Cotton Spinning* (ed. 5) II. 4 A complete draw-frame. 1845 S. Judd *Margaret* I. xvii. 160 Near Hash stands the *draw-horse on which he smooths and squares his shingles. 1845 Mrs. Kirkland *Western Clearings* (1846) 127 It was Miss Celestina Pye, and she certainly had no *draw-strings in her lips just then. 1872 Eggleston *End of World* xiii. 89 She pulled out the folds of the chintz curtains, hanging on its draw-string half-way up the window. 1874 *Rep. Vermont Board Agric.* II. 719 The 'sap-gatherer' or '*draw-tub', as it is called, is a hogshead containing from one hundred to one hundred and fifty gallons.

Drawback, *sb.* Add:

2. b. *Bookselling.* A rebate of the paper tax given under certain conditions to the King's printers and the Oxford and Cambridge University presses. *Hist.*
1796 (*title*) The Poems of Ossian...Printed for A. Strahan and T. Cadell: And sold by T. Cadell Jun. and W. Davies. ..MDCCXCVI (Drawback). 1797 (*title*) An Historical Essay on the Ambition and Conquests of France...London Printed for J. Debrett...1797. (Drawback.)

Draw-bar. 2. orig. *U.S.* (Examples.)
1670 *Groton Rec.* (1880) 36 A gat or a sufficient pair of draw barrs to [be] Kept and maintained at the end [of] Natha[niel] Lawrences field. 1671 *Portsmouth* (R.I.) *Rec.* 159 He letting in a paire of Draw barrs at each end the sayd Lane. 1811 *Massachusetts Spy* 3 Apr. (Th.) There were a pair of draw bars about twelve or fifteen yards from [his] door. 1836 *Southern Lit. Messenger* II. 162 On every side I was met by gates, drawbars, and gaps. 1888 Macon *Uncle Gabe Tucker* 23 Some people gwine to git lef' de wus sort when dey jump de eberlasting draw-bars.

Draw-boy. Add:

2. An article exposed for sale in a shop window at a very low price to attract customers. *slang.*
1865 *Slang Dict.*, *Draw-boy*, a cunning device used by puffing tradesmen.

Drawer[1]. Add: **7. b.** *Printing.* = Tympan 4.
1896 De Vinne *Moxon's Mech. Exerc., Printing* 410 The pasting down of the vellum on the inner side of the tympan (now known as the drawer).

8. *drawer-off* (in various trades: see Dict. Occup. Terms, 1921).
1908 *Westm. Gaz.* 9 Oct. 3/1 'Drawers-off' in saw-mills.

Drawing, *vbl. sb.* Add: **1. b.** *U.S.* (Earlier examples.)
1846–52 Mrs. Whitcher *Widow Bedott P.* v. 53 She went to borrer sonethin or other—a loaf o' bread or a drawin' o' tea. 1855 Haliburton *Nat. & Hum. Nat.* II. 350 'I believe', she said, 'I have a drawing of tea left,' and taking from the shelf a small mahogany caddy, emptied it of its contents.

6. drawing-string (earlier U.S. example).
1829–32 J. P. Kennedy *Swallow-B.* II. xviii. 225 Faces shortened as if with drawing-strings.

Drawing-knife. (Earlier Amer. examples.)
1645 *Early Connect. Probate Rec.* I. 21 A gunn,..on[e] auger, one draweing knife. 1650 *Essex Inst. Hist. Coll.* XLIII. 71 Three axes, too wedges & a drawing knife.

Drawing-room[1]. Add:

3. b. Used allusively to qualify a version of a story, etc. fitted by its observance of the proprieties for the society of the drawing-room.
1877 *Porcupine* 20 Jan. 676/3 It was desirable to modify the language a little, and the drawing-room version ran thus. 1909 Balfour in *Daily Chron.* 23 Sept. 1/3 The Prime Minister's Birmingham version of the Budget struck me.. as having been intended for what I may call drawing-room use. 1915 Rosher *In R.N.A.S.* (1916) 82 What do you think of this story, the latest from the trenches? It's not quite a drawing-room one!

Hence **Draw·ing-roomy** *a.*, characteristic of the drawing-room, as being over-refined, insipid, etc.
1906 *Daily Chron.* 18 May 9/3 Miss Evelyn Millard's Desdemona was a disappointment. She was terribly drawing-roomy. 1907 *Ibid.* 18 June 6/4 The sentiment was sometimes rather drawing-roomy.

Drawl, *v.* **3.** Add: Often with quoted words as obj.
1842 Lever *Jack Hinton* xxx, 'Them chaps always recover', drawled out the doctor in a dolorous cadence. 1878 Stevenson *New Arab. Nts.* II. 66 'Ye — es', drawled Northmour.

Drawn, *ppl. a.* Add: **1. b.** *Drawn-in*, (of a rug or mat) made of small cuttings of material drawn through a canvas foundation.
1901 *Harper's Mag.* CII. 661/2 Her mother had only drawn-in rugs, which Ellen had watched her make.

Dray, *sb.*[1] Add: **1. b.** A sled used in dragging logs in the woods. Also *attrib.* and *Comb. U.S.*
1902 S. E. White *Blazed Trail* vii. 49 When are you going to dray-haul that Norway [pine] across Pine Lake? *Ibid.* 52 A number of pines had been felled out on the ice, cut in logs, and left in expectation of thick ice enough to bear the travoy 'dray'. 1905 *Terms Forestry & Logging* 36 *Dray*, a single sled used in dragging logs. One end of the log rests upon the sled.

4. dray-road (see quot. 1905).
1905 *Terms Forestry & Logging* 36 *Dray road*, a narrow road, cut wide enough to allow the passage of a team and dray. 1907 *Westm. Gaz.* 14 Dec. 14/1 For four hot and weary days I had tramped along lonely and disused dray-roads and bridle-paths that led from a little mining township in the northern part of New South Wales to the coast.

Dray, *v.* Add: Also *to dray in.* *U.S.*
1905 *Terms Forestry & Logging* 36 *Dray in, to*, to drag logs from the place where they are cut directly to the skid-way or landing.

Hence **Dray·ing** *vbl. sb.* Also *attrib.*
1906 'O. Henry' *Four Million* 248 A single gentleman connected with the draying business. 1906 — *Rolling Stones* (1915) 13 You can get me a bunch of draying contracts.

Dreadnought, *sb.* Add: **2.** The name of the first British battleship (launched on 18 Feb. 1906) of a powerful type superior in armament to all its predecessors; hence, the name of a class of battleships having their main armament entirely of big guns of one calibre. (Now disused.)
1906 *Outlook* 20 Oct. 495/2 The Atlantic Fleet will consist of three *Dreadnoughts* and five of the *Canopus* class. 1908 *Westm. Gaz.* 14 Aug. 2/2 The mysterious *Dreadnoughts* which are being built in this country for the Brazilian Government. 1909 *Daily Chron.* 23 Mar. 1/1 Our Dreadnought strength and our strength in pre-Dreadnought ships, in comparison with those of Germany. 1909 *Westm. Gaz.* 13 Apr. 9/1 Three and a half years is still practically the time I count on for 'Dreadnought'-building. 1914 *Daily Express* 26 Nov. 2/4, 7 Dreadnought Zeppelins: Airships built for the Invasion of Britain. 1915 *Ibid.* 23 Jan. 1/5 Vessels of the Dreadnought era.

Dream, *sb.*[2]. Add: **4. g. dream-book,** a book containing interpretations of dreams; **dream-child,** a child seen in a dream.
1803 Weems *Lett.* II. 272 To that list you may add..Some *dream books, dreaming Dictionaries and above all, some Pilg. Progress. 1854 *Poultry Chron.* I. 514 The gift of a Napoleon's Dream Book necessarily contracts the intellect. 1909 Jane Barlow *Irish Ways* 17 There are fair-sized country towns, whose shops might be thoroughly ransacked without bringing to light any literary wares of more account than a dream-book. 1913 P. Colum *Castle Conquer* x, I bought ear-rings and brooches, dream-books and fortune-books, buckles and combs. 1822 Lamb *Elia*, *Dream-Children; A Reverie. 1903 *Westm. Gaz.* 28 Mar. 2/1 He's only my Dream-child. Some women have to be content all their life with Dream-children.

Drea·mlessness. [-ness.] Dreamless condition.
1905 E. F. Benson *Image in the Sand* xiii, Something that had mingled with sleep, but was previous to her deep dreamlessness.

Dredge, *sb.*[1] **b.** Add: *dredge-catch, -chock.*
1891 *Scribner's Mag.* X. 473 At the sides of the vessels there are long iron-rollers, 'dredge-catches' and 'dredge-chocks'.

Dredge, *sb.*[2] **4.** Add: *dredge-fork*; **dredge corn** (see quot.).
1917 *Statutory Rules & Orders* 2 in *Parl. Papers* XXVI. 402 For the purposes of this Order, '*Dredge Corn' shall mean a mixture of cereals, whether or not grown together, containing more than one cereal as a main constituent. 1891 *Scribner's Mag.* X. 469, I began to see a great glass case ..containing..a *dredge-fork: an oyster knife.

Dredging, *vbl. sb.* **c.** Add: *dredging-bucket, -steamer.*
1860 Abbott *South & North* 65 A few dredging-steamers were also slumbering upon the mud. 1872 *Porcupine* 29 June 198/3 Set the dredging-buckets to work, and scooped it all away.

Dreelite (drī·lǝit). *Min.* Also **dreeite.** [a. F. *dréelite*, named by Dufrenoy (1835) after E. de *Drée*: see -lite and -ite[1] 2 b.] Sulphate of barium and calcium in small pearly-white crystals.
1836 *Amer. Jrnl. Sci.* XXX. 380 Dreelite, a new Mineral Species. 1896 Chester *Dict. Min.*, Dreeite, Dreelite.

Dreibund (drai·bunt). [G., f. *drei* three: see *Bund.] The triple alliance formed in 1882 between Germany, Austria, and Italy.
1914 *Scotsman* 1 Oct. 6/6 Vienna journals triumphantly dwelt on the solidarity of the Dreibund.

Dreikanter (drai·kantǝɹ). [G., = three-cornered things, f. *drei* three + *kant* corner.] Angular and prismoidal pebbles the faces of which have been cut by wind-blown sand.
1903 *Nature* 10 Dec. 143/1 A collection of wind-worn pebbles of quartz and quartzite from an old raised beach near Waverley, North Island, New Zealand,..was exhibited by the president. They have been cut by the sand driven by the wind into the characteristic *Dreikanter.* 1920 *Brit. Museum Return* 137 Three dreikanten [*sic*] from the Bunter Sandstone of Nottingham.

Dresden (dre·zdǝn). Name of a town in Saxony, used attrib. or absol. to designate a variety of white porcelain made at Meissen near Dresden, and characterized by elaborate decoration and figure pieces in delicate colourings. Hence (often attrib.) used to designate anything of a delicate or feeble prettiness.
1752 [see China *sb.*[1] 3 b]. 1753 Hanway *Trav.* II. 226 Fourteen apartments filled with China and Dresden porcelain. 1756 [see Porcelain 1]. 1885 *Encycl. Brit.* XIX. 640/1 Perhaps the chief specialty of Dresden porcelain consists in its statuettes and group of figures, the best of which were made between 1731 and 1756 under the superintendence of a sculptor named Kändler. *Ibid.*, The increase of prices given for old Dresden. 1905 W. Holman Hunt *Pre-Raph.* I. 49 Etty was cramped by a taste for Dresden-china prettiness. 1908 *Daily Chron.* 28 Aug. 1/1 His own Dresden-china doll of a wife.

Dress, *sb.* Add:

4. a. *dress-case*; **dress-basket,** a travelling case for a woman's dresses; **dress-length,** a piece of material sufficient to make a dress; **dress-reform,** a movement to make dress more practical; so *dress-reformer*; **dress-shield,** a piece of waterproof material fastened under the arms of a woman's bodice to protect it from perspiration; a dress-preserver.
1895 *Army & Navy Co-op. Soc. Price List* 15 Sept. 1358 *Dress Basket, fitted inside with 1 Tray and Webbing Straps. 1899 T. M. Ellis *Three Cat's-Eye Rings* 25 Her trunk and her dress-basket were already loaded in. 1905 *Daily Chron.* 24 Apr. 6/2 We..'kiss again with tears' across the dress-basket. 1897 *Westm. Gaz.* 9 Dec. 3/2 The travelling '*dress-case' that combines dressing-bag and trunk. 1899 *Westm. Gaz.* 3 Aug. 3/2 These..low broad dress-cases, that, if necessary, can go under a railway carriage seat. 1889 *Young Ladies' Jrnl.* 1 Jan. 21/1 Advt., A full *dress-length of beautiful cloth. 1907 *Daily Chron.* 16 May 5/7 The wife of a native chief who was given a dress length by Lord Kitchener. 1889 *Kansas Times & Star* 16 Mar., Anna Jenness Miller's *dress reform disciples now number about 400 here. *Ibid.* 7 Mar., Mrs. Jenness Miller, *dress reformer, is back in New York from her Western lecture tour. 1905 *Daily News* 26 Sept. 5/1 Sewn on the inside of the bodice were two rubber *dress-shields.

b. *dress-boots* (example), *hat, -parade* (earlier example); **dress-carriage,** a carriage reserved for state or semi-state occasions; **dress rehearsal** [short for *full-dress rehearsal*; also †*dressed rehearsal* (see Dressed, quot. 1793)], a rehearsal of a drama in costume, esp. the final rehearsal before the first public performance; also *fig.*
1851 C. Cist *Cincinnati* 178 He employs from 75 to 125 hands, all upon fine work of men's *dress boots..and fine shoes. 1897 *Daily News* 8 Feb. 5/4 Many of these are what one might call semi-state carriages, but are known as *Dress Carriages. 1902 *Westm. Gaz.* 7 Aug. 10/1 His Majesty has.. intimated a wish that dress carriages might come in vogue again for evening Court functions...In the early days of.. Queen Victoria dress carriages were always used by those commanded to attend the Court. 1787 Dalrymple *Jrnl. Young Lady Virg.* (1871) 19, I shall wear my Great-Coat and *dress Hat. 1862 O. W. Norton *Army Lett.* 105 By the time I get back it will be time for *dress parade. 1865 Mrs. Stowe *House & Home P.* 75 You gave him a bad *dress-rehearsal. 1874 *Porcupine* 24 Oct. 469/1 A dress rehearsal of 'The Black Prince' at St. James's Theatre. 1897 *Encycl. Sport* I. 563/2 After several undress and dress rehearsals the master may venture to ask a field to meet him. 1917 *Strand Mag.* Dec. 538 If you'll have one dress rehearsal, I'll promise to leave you in peace for the duration of the war. 1925 A. J. Toynbee *Surv. Internat. Affairs 1920–23* 46 It [*sc.* the Reparation Question] served as a 'dress rehearsal' for the First Session of the Assembly of the League of Nations.

Dress, *v.* Add: **11. c.** *trans.* To weigh (a specified amount) on removal of the skin and offal.
1873 *Rep. Vermont Board Agric.* II. 186 These steers.. were sold in market..dressed 1,570 pounds, amounting to $231,58. 1895 [see Dress *v.* 13].

13. j. *Type-founding.* To finish (types or lines of type) after casting, by grooving and smoothing them and adjusting their height and alignment.
1683 Moxon *Mech. Exerc., Printing* xxi. ¶ 2 This pair of Dressing-sticks will serve to Dress Brevier, Long-Primmer, and Pica. 1839 W. Nichol in T. C. Hansard *Print. & Type-founding* 231 The letters are then set up in a long stick, and again dressed. 1888 J. Southward in *Encycl. Brit.* XXIII. 699/2 The types are then dressed and the picker takes them in hand.

Dresser[1]. Add:

1. b. A dressing- or toilet-table. *U.S.*
1906 'O. Henry' *Four Million, Unfinished Story* 180 Dulcie took a last look at the pictures on the dresser..and skipped into bed.

Dresser[2]. Add: **1. b.** *Type-founding.* An operative who finishes types or lines of type after casting or who controls a type-dressing machine.
1846 Dodd *Brit. Manufactures* VI. 45 The long frame, filled with a single line of type, is removed to the dresser. 1888 J. Southward in *Encycl. Brit.* XXIII. 699/2 The dresser..slips them into a long stick..and..cuts with a plane a groove in the bottom.

Dressing, *vbl. sb.* Add:

3. Also with *down* (see Dress *v.* 9).
1876 *Coursing Cal.* 223 Blucher was much faster in the stretches than Folly, who got a genuine dressing down. 1893 W. K. Post *Harvard Stories* 70 The poor man got such a dressing down that Randolph presented him with full forgiveness. 1911 H. S. Harrison *Queed* xiii. 146 She must doff all gloves and give the little Doctor the dressing-down of his life. 1925 E. F. Norton *Fight for Everest, 1924* 21 The following morning, when they were coming up for a second dressing I thought I would add a little dressing down on my own account.

4. c. (Later U.S. examples.)
1833 B. Silliman *Man. Sugar Cane* 20 The most speedy remedy for such soils consists in..the addition of a dressing of ashes. 1882 *Rep. Maine Board Agric.* XXVI. 50 The farmer finds he can plant but little corn, because he has but little dressing.

5. a. dressing-sack (example). **b. dressing forceps** (see quot. 1884); **dressing-house,** a house for dressing ore.
1816 Hutchison *Pract. Obs. Surg.* (1826) 180 By dilating the meatus urinarius with a common pair of *dressing forceps. 1879 *St. George's Hosp. Rep.* IX. 772 Passing a pair of dressing-forceps through the joint to the lowest part of its outer aspect. 1884 Knight *Dict. Mech.* Suppl., *Dressing Forceps*, an instrument used in applying and removing dressings. 1872 *Rep. Vermont Board Agric.* 628 The same track takes it [*sc.* the ore] to the *dressing house at the foot of the hill. 1883 J. Hay *Bread-winners* x. 153 She was in the summer afternoon condition which the ladies call '*dressing sack'.

e. *Printing* (see Dress *v.* 3 b) *dressing-bench, -block, -hook.* **f.** *Type-founding* (see *Dress *v.* 13 j) *dressing machine, plane, stick.*
1683 Moxon *Mech. Exerc., Printing* xix. ¶ 7 The *Dressing-Bench. *Ibid.* ix. ¶ 3 The *Dressing-Block..is to run over the Face of the Form, and..to be gently knock't upon.., that such Letters as may chance to stand up higher than the rest may be pressed down. *Ibid.* xx. ¶ 2 The *Dressing-Hook. 1888 J. Southward in *Encycl. Brit.* XXIII. 699/2 A machine, which produces types that do not require rubbing or dressing...The casting machine and the *dressing machine are...mounted on a common frame...The letters pass through a channel one by one into the dressing machine. 1695 in H. Hart *Century of Typography* (1900) 55 Utensils for Printing. 4 *Dressing Planes. 3 Dressing Blocks. 1683 *Dressing-stick [see *Dress *v.* 13 j].

Dressing-case. (Later U.S. examples.)
1838 J. F. Cooper *Home as Found* xxvi. (1873) 443 The dressing-case was complicated and large, having several compartments. 1858 Teresa Viele *Following the Drum* 96, I sat on a dressing-case in the sand, patiently watching the operation. 1891 Eggleston in *Century Mag.* Feb. 542 The satin cravat is against the looking-glass on the dressing-case.

Driblet, *sb.* Add:

4. *Driblet-cone*, a cone produced by the successive ejections of small quantities of lava.
1895 Dana *Man. Geol.* (ed. 4) 271 Driblets pile up the fantastic driblet-cone, which has no crater but simply a hole for the projection of lava in small liquid masses, drops, driblets, or worm-like streamlets.

Driedness (drai·dnės). [f. Dried *ppl. a.* + -ness.] Dried condition. Also *dried-up-ness.*
1907 Galsworthy *Country House* III. ii. 231 The strange yellow driedness of his face. 1923 *United Free Ch. Miss. Rec.* June 248/1 Dried-up-ness is of the essence of the thing.

Drift, *sb.* Add:

2. e. *Aeronautics.* The horizontal component of the reaction produced by the detrimental and lifting surfaces of an aeroplane in flight: cf. *Lift *sb.*[2] 5 e.
1896 H. S. Maxim in *Aeronautical Ann.* 50 (Cent. D. Suppl.). 1909 *Westm. Gaz.* 25 Feb. 4/1 One of the most ardent experimenters..who adopted the daring plan of jumping off a hill 45 ft. high with the object of ascertaining the proportion between lift and drift. 1916 Barber *Aeroplane Speaks* 2 Drift,..sometimes, though rather erroneously, called Head Resistance. 1920 *19th Cent.* July 145 The object of camber is to obtain the maximum lift, and to reduce the drift.

f. *Astron.* Either of two streams of stars of which the universe is supposed to consist. Also *drift curve.*
1907 H. H. Turner in *Westm. Gaz.* 26 Mar. 8/2 Do we belong to one of these drifts more than the other? The disparity in velocity rather suggests that we do. 1928 W. M. Smart *Sun, Stars & Universe* x. 172 The feature of the curve is that the great majority of the stars appear to be moving in or near the direction of the solar antapex and comparatively few in or near the opposite direction; expressing it somewhat differently, we say that the general tendency of the proper motions is in the direction of the antapex. Such a distribution of proper motions is called a drift. *Ibid.* 174 If the stars with which we are dealing were moving about in space with quite haphazard motions, we should obtain,..from the observed proper motions of stars within a restricted part of the sky a single drift curve...We have seen that if we envisage the sky as a whole, the prominent drifts in the different parts of the sky are directed towards a definite point on the celestial sphere.

9. b. Also *fig.*
1897 *Daily News* 3 May 4/1 They are not beggars..; they are merely human drift—men who live on 'nuffin'.

10. b. drift-peat, a deposit of peat in or associated with a glacial drift.
1894 Geikie *Gt. Ice Age* (ed. 3) 308 The drift-peat and timber that underlie the Carse-deposits of the 45 to 50-ft. level.

19. c. drift angle *Naval Arch.*, angle of leeway (see Lee-way); **drift oyster,** an Australian oyster, *Ostrea subtrigona*, supposed to be subject to drift; **drift-weed** (*a*), also *fig.*
1882 W. H. White *Man. Naval Archit.* (ed. 2) 621 The angle between this tangent and the keel-line, or '*drift-angle' (*angle de dérive*). 1906 E. L. Attwood *War-Ships* (ed. 2) 237 At the point P, where OP is drawn perpendicular to the centre line of the ship, there is no drift angle, as the tangent to the circle through P is the centre line of the ship. 1883 E. P. Ramsay *Food Fishes N.S. Wales* 43 (Fish. Exhib. Publ.) The so-called *Drift Oyster of the Sydney Oystermen. 1906 Somerville & Ross *Irish Yesterdays* 223 She belonged to the *drift-weed of the household. 1909 *Daily Chron.* 14 June 9/2 These dreadful drift-weeds of the great city.

Drift, *v.* Add:

1. c. Also with *in.* (Cf. *Blow *v.* 12 d.) orig. *U.S.*
1884 Marg. Deland *Old Chester Tales* (1899) 43 Peter, with a pretty girl on his arm, drifted in out of the windy and rainy darkness. 1921 R. D. Paine *Comr. Rolling Ocean* viii. 141, I drifted in for a minute to listen to a nigger with a bully voice.

2. b. To allow or cause (a fishing-net) to be borne by the current. Also *absol.* *U.S.*
1850 N. Kingsley *Diary* 118 [We] drifted the seine across the river and floated down with the current. *Ibid.* 119 They drifted once more and made up the number of 51 salmon.

c. To drive (cattle or horses). Also with *in.* *U.S.*
1903 A. Adams *Log Cowboy* iv. 51 The Rebel and Blades were following, to drift in what cattle we had held on our left. *Ibid.* vi. 85 We were drifting them back towards the trail. 1920 Hunter *Trail Drivers of Texas* 50 [They said] they would drift the horses along with two outfits instead of four.

d. *Fly-fishing.* To allow (the fly) to float down stream.
1907 *Westm. Gaz.* 29 Nov. 3/1 By casting or 'drifting' the dry-fly on a long line down stream to the fish.

7. *Mining.* (Earlier U.S. examples.)
1849 *President's Message Congress* II. 505 After drifting on that vein some 30 feet, all signs of copper disappeared. *Ibid.*, He..is now drifting in on a vein on a level with the surface.

Drifter. Add: **d.** A wind causing snow to drift.
1924 A. J. Small *Frozen Gold* ii. 49 A confused..blur of whining blizzards, roaring drifters, flat calm cold-snaps.

e. An object which is allowed to float freely in the sea to determine ocean-currents.
1900 *Geogr. Jrnl.* (R.G.S.) XV. 275 On the voyage from Iceland to Jan Mayen in 1896 twenty drifters were thrown overboard.

f. A man following an aimless, irresolute, or vagrant way of life.
1908 *Daily Chron.* 28 Sept. 4/7 The drifter drifts to California, and brings up there because..he can drift no further. 1922 *Short Stories* Feb. 25/1 The trampers ain't all hoboes, some of 'em being just drifters. 1926 Deeping *Sorrell & Son* xxviii. 275 For months he had had a sense of drifting, and his character was not that of a drifter.

Drifting, *vbl. sb.* Add:

2. *spec.* in *Mining* (see Drift *v.* 7). Also *attrib.*
1882 *U.S. Rep. Precious Metals* 70 This mine has been worked by the drifting method. *Ibid.* 640 The workings in the drifting ground.

Drift-wood. Add: esp. wood carried down by a river. *U.S.*
1785 Washington *Diaries* II. 396 It would probably be frequently choaked with drift wood, Ice, and other rubbish. *Ibid.* IV. 79 The river there is..full of small islands occasioned by drift wood lodging on the rocks. 1821 J. Fowler *Jrnl.* 26 The men waided over and geathered drift wood for the night. 1848 J. F. Cooper *Oak Openings* I. iii. 47 The drift-wood choked the channel. 1850 H. C. Watson *Camp-fires Revol.* 67 That exposed our boats to being all the time tangled in the drift-wood and bushes. 1884 'Mark Twain' *Huck. Finn* vii. 44 The river was coming up pretty fast, and lots of drift-wood going by on the rise.

Drill, *sb.*[2] **7. b.** Add: *drill-hall*; **drill-book,** a manual of instruction in military drill; **drill-order** (see *Order *sb.*).
1846 *United Services Mag.* II. 235 The French *drill-book. 1900 *Daily News* 15 May 3/3 The Queensland Mounted Infantry contingent seem to have engrafted sufficient drill-book into their common-sense methods. 1906 W. Wood *Enemy in our Midst* vii. 73 On a certain assumption which was that an enemy would work according to drill-book and rule-of-thumb. 1878 *Chambers's Encycl.* III. 671/1 *Drill-halls, in which drill can be carried on comfortably in any kind of weather, are now common. 1891 *Scribner's Mag.* X. 565 Entertainments are also given in the drill hall every Friday evening.

Drill, *sb.*[3] Also *attrib.*, as *drill baboon, monkey.*
1905 *Daily Chron.* 29 Apr. 7/1 The finest *drill baboon ever seen in confinement is in the Bellevue Gardens. 1898 *Westm. Gaz.* 15 Feb. 11/3 The *drill monkey, the most costly and rare of its kind in the gardens.

Driller[2]. Add:

1. c. A ship used for carrying out drilling operations.
1896 *Westm. Gaz.* 31 Dec. 5/2 The driller *Delta*, which was engaged in operations for the widening of the approaches to Devonport Harbour.

Drilling, *vbl. sb.*[2] **3.** Add: *drilling-machine* (earlier example); **drilling-plant** = Rig *sb.*[6] 3.
1847 *Rep. U.S. Comm. Patents* (1848) 73 Letters patent have been granted for a *drilling machine. 1913 V. B. Lewes *Oil Fuel* 63 The form of *drilling plant or 'rig', as it is generally called.

Drink, *sb.* Add: **6.** *U.S.* (Earlier examples.)
1832 Paulding *Westward Ho!* I. 121 Sing dumb, or I'll throw you into the drink. 1840 *Knickerbocker Mag.* XVI. 43 Down by the drink The wolves howled so loudly he slept not a wink. 1849 N. P. Willis *Rural Lett.* viii. 79 My catechiser lives above me on the drink (his name for the river).

8. c. *drink-sodden* adj.
1897 *Westm. Gaz.* 13 Jan. 2/1 Many a heart that has long been too drink-sodden for any human passion. 1904 H. G. Wells *Food of Gods* III. iii. 240 The drink-sodden wretchedness of the painted women at the corner. 1908 *Daily Chron.* 10 Nov. 4/7 If they presented themselves in a drink sodden condition.

Drink, *v.*[1] **12. e.** Add: Also in other analogous uses.
1746 Francis tr. *Hor., Sat.* I. iii. 24 He drank the Night away Till rising Dawn. 1836 Dickens *Sk. Boz, New Year*, The musicians exhibit unequivocal symptoms of having drunk the new year in.

Drinkery. (Earlier U.S. examples.)
1840 J. P. Kennedy *Quodlibet* 222 The Sergeant took a small frame house next door to Sim Traver's Refectory,— or rather as Sim called it, his Drinkery. 1845 T. J. Green *Texian Exped.* xix. 368 We wended our way up town, and called into the first open 'drinkery'.

Drinking, *vbl. sb.* **4.** Add: *drinking-place, -saloon* (examples), *-shop*; **drinking-nut** (see quot.).
1909 *Chambers's Jrnl.* Apr. 256/1, I met a stalwart native ..with..a dozen '*drinking-nuts' (young cocoa-nuts), the ice-creams of the Pacific. 1870 'Fanny Fern' *Ginger-Snaps* 91 The man who..takes that child to bar-rooms and *drinking places. 1875 Mrs. Stowe *We & Neighbors* xli. 378 After this we went out..to go through the..drinking places. 1864 B. Taylor *H. Thurston* xvii. 221 He halted before the red light of a *drinking-saloon. 1875 Mrs. Stowe *We & Neighbors* xli. 377 Finally we alighted before a plain house in a street full of drinking-saloons. 1891 Kipling *Light that Failed* xv, When Dick entered the *drinking-shop which was one source of her gains.

Drip, *sb.* **8.** Add: **drip coffee-pot,** a percolating coffee-pot; **drip-feed,** used attrib. to designate a method of lubrication by which the oil percolates in drops; **drip-point, -tip** *Bot.* (see quot. 1897).
1897 *Outing* (U.S.) XXIX. 574/1 He..produced a jar of coffee and the *drip coffee-pot. 1907 *Westm. Gaz.* 18 Nov. 6/3 The neat four-sight *drip-feed lubricator. *Ibid.* 27 Dec. 4/2 No adjustment of the drip-feed points is necessary, as the pumps send a continuous stream of oil to the various parts. 1916 *Motor Cyclists' A.B.C.* 115 Lubrication (Automatic Drip Feed). 1900 B. D. Jackson *Gloss. Bot. Terms*, *Drip-point, Drip-tip. 1897 Willis *Flowering Plants* I. 154 The *drip-tip..or acuminate leaf-apex.

Dripped (dript), *ppl. a.* [f. Drip *v.*] That has been allowed to drip or percolate.
1909 'O. Henry' *Options* (1916) 30 But if you're ever in the Middle West just mention my name and you'll get foot-warmers and dripped coffee.

Dripper. Add:

2. A pen in which sheep are put after they have been dipped, having a floor sloping towards the bath, so that the dip which falls off the sheep flows back into the bath.
1886 C. Scott *Sheep-farming* 145 The dripper of a bath consists of a couple of pens capable of holding from thirty to forty sheep, set upon a water-tight floor.

Drive, *sb.* Add:

1. spec. of cattle or logs (cf. sense 3). *U.S.*
1873 J. H. Beadle *Undevel. West* xxxiii. 718 Each company comes down on a 'drive', hunting such logs as have lodged along the way. 1890 *Harper's Mag.* July 240/1 They [*sc.* cowboys] have little to do when not on the drive or in branding time. 1902 S. E. White *Blazed Trail* ii. 7 Customarily a jobber is paid a certain proportion of the agreed price..so much when the 'drive' down the waters of the river is finished. 1920 Hunter *Trail Drivers of Texas* 53 A cheap rate..had been perfected for..the..cowboys returning home after the drives.

c. (Earlier examples.) Also of a hound in coursing.
1833 Crockett *Sketches & Eccentr.* 196 We were soon on foot, moving merrily forward to a small hurricane which had been agreed upon for a drive. 1843 *American Pioneer* II. 55 There were four drives, or large hunts, organized during the winter. 1876 *Coursing Calendar* 5 Dovedale got up first, through puss bearing to her side; Thunder then took a good drive and turned.

g. An organized effort to collect money for a special purpose; an organized campaign. *U.S.*
1890 *Ann Arbor R.* 1 Mar., Advt., Ladies, we are going to give you a Benefit and it will be the drive of the season. 1928 *Washington Star* 9 Dec., The drive for $100,000 to buy a site for the Lutheran College will get under way tomorrow night at a dinner in the Lee House. 1928 *Britain's Industrial Future* (*Lib. Ind. Inq.*) III. xix. 258 The Board of National Investment should devise means for facilitating the continuous, direct sale of National bonds of low denomination, through the Banks and the Post offices. The remarkable American 'drive' for the sale of Liberty Bonds during the War affords a model which is capable of adaptation. 1930 *Publishers' Weekly* 15 Feb. 858/2 In this 'Plant Your Home' drive [*sc.* campaign for the outdoor living-room].

h. *Whist drive*: see Whist *sb.*[3] b.

2. b. (Examples.)
1835 J. H. Ingraham *South-West* II. 132 We..proceeded to the 'drive'..as the hunting station is technically termed. *Ibid.* 137 An extensive 'drive' or forest frequented by deer.

6. A driving-gear.
1901 S. Merwin & H. K. Webster *Calumet K* xiv. 263 He's putting in three drives entirely different from the way they are in the plans. 1902 *Harmsworth's Motors* 191 A very smooth and silent drive without the spreading or bursting action of the bevels. 1912 *Motor Man.* (ed. 14) 74 Three speeds and a reverse are provided, with direct drive on top speed.

Drive, *v.* Add: **8.** Also in *Golf.*
1801 Strutt *Sports & Past.* II. iii. 81 The game consists in driving the ball into certain holes made in the ground. 1856 'Stonehenge' (J. H. Walsh) *Brit. Rural Sports* III. I. ii. 503/2 The score depends upon the number of strokes required by each party to drive their ball from hole to hole. 1862 *Chambers's Encycl.* IV. 823/2 Crack-players will drive a ball above 200 yards. 1892 R. Barclay *Batch of Golfing Papers* 42 He drives with the 'Bulger', as so many of the best players do nowadays.

17. c. With *under*: To suppress.
1920 Rose Macaulay *Potterism* v. 180, I hadn't known, until that moment, because I had driven it under, how large a part of my brain believed that Gideon had perhaps done this thing.

Drive-. drive-wheel (U.S. example).
1887 George *Forty Years on Rail* ii. 28 'The drive-wheels will slip', was their crushing argument.

Driven, *ppl. a.* Add: **3.** Of a stake, tube, nail, etc.: Forced into a solid material. *Driven well*, a tube-well.
1875 Knight *Dict. Mech.* s.v. *Well-tube*, The driven-well, invented..1862.

Driver. Add: **1. b.** A horse for driving, as distinguished from a hunter, roadster, etc. *U.S.*
1876 *Rep. Vermont Board Agric.* III. 168 Stylish, enduring roadsters, trotters and gentlemen's drivers, standing from fifteen to fifteen and one-half hands high. 1902 McFaul *Ike Glidden* viii. 61 That is a pretty good driver you've got here. *Ibid.* 66 All prosperous people there keep a 'driver' and a 'trader'.

2. c. (Later U.S. example.)
1887 *Century Mag.* Nov. 110/1 A 'driver' is the foreman of a gang of laborers. On some plantations the title of foreman is coming into use, the negroes objecting to the old word.

f. An overseer, bailiff. *Ireland.*
1847 Tuke *Visit to Connaught* (1848) 20 The landlord's 'driver' was pursuing his calling, seizing almost every little patch of oats or potatoes. 1848 *Ibid.* 63 The younger Mr. Walshe with two drivers, had come and pulled down the roofs of their houses.

g. Short for *driver-ant.*
1897 Mary Kingsley *W. Africa* 626 Bad language, such as I am accustomed to when a lord of creation gets drivers on him.

Driveway. (Earlier U.S. examples.)
1838 H. Colman *Rep. Agric. Mass.* (1839) 80 The building should be so placed that the barn floor could be laid upon the beams, and the drive-way be into the end directly under the roof. 1870 *Congress. Globe* 2 Feb. 966/3, I doubt as to the policy of allowing this railroad to go along exactly in the track of where we propose to have a public drive-way.

Driving, *vbl. sb.* Add:

1. b. *Bee-culture.* The removal of bees to a new hive in artificial swarming.
1875 *Encycl. Brit.* III. 502/1 Considering, first, straw skeps, the common hive of the country, the operation to be pursued is known as 'driving'.

3. c. Pertaining to the driving of game, as *driving-moor.*
1896 *Westm. Gaz.* 12 Dec. 7/2 The Scottish driving moors, of which the best are situated in Inverness-shire.

Driving, *ppl. a.* **1.** Add: **driving force, power,** the force or power by which an engine or vehicle is driven, motor force or power; often *fig.*
1856 [in Dict.]. 1874 Knight *Dict. Mech.* I. 948/2 The great weight of this wheel is..to carry the machine over the one half of its period in which the driving-power is absent. 1905 *Sketch* 26 July 38/1 The driving power [*sc.* of a dirigible balloon] is supplied by two 50 horse-power Bucket motors. 1909 F. Harris *The Man Shakespeare* 369, I always think of him as a ship over-engined; when the driving-power is working at full speed it shakes the ship to pieces. 1924 G. Frankau *Gerald Cranston's Lady* i. § 2 Other qualities than decision shewed in Gerald Cranston's countenance. From it..there radiated a force; a driving power; a poised and dominant individualism that bespoke the born leader. 1927 M. Pupin *New Reformation* 214 A cosmic stream of solar energy from which everything that lives and breathes on this terrestrial globe derives its driving-force, just as the mill on the mountain side derives its driving-power from the mountain stream.

Drizzle, *v.* Add:

4. *intr.* To pick the gold thread out of tassels or embroideries into which it was woven; so *drizzler, drizzling* (also *attrib.*).
1896 *Godey's Mag.* Feb. 177/2 Drizzling—which was nothing more or less than picking the gold thread out of old gold tassels, braid [etc.]. *Ibid.* 178/1 One of the Countess's principal grievances against the Prince seems to have been that he was a confirmed drizzler; she says Leopold would sit by her hour after hour diligently and indefatigably drizzling...

The tall Prince..bending over his elegant drizzling-box of tortoise-shell.

Drome (drōᵘm). Short for *AERODROME.
1915 ROSHER *In R.N.A.S.* (1916) 41, I crashed into the atmosphere first thing this morning and flipped around for 55 minutes. By then I was as cold as —, so pitched in the 'drome. 1919 'BERTA RUCK' *Disturbing Charm* xiii, I've been carting some young lunatic, who's lost his 'bus or something, back to his 'drome.

Dromomania (drǫmǒmē¹·niă). [f. Gr. δρόμος running: see -MANIA.] A mania for roaming.
1901 DORLAND *Med. Dict.* 1906 W. JAMES *Mem. & Studies* (1911) 248 Hitherto such freaks of impulse have received Greek names (as bulimia, dromomania, etc.).

Dromotropic (drǫmǒtrǫ·pik), *a.* *Bot.* and *Physiol.* [f. Gr. δρόμος race + τροπικός (see TROPIC *a.* 4).] (See quots.) Hence **Dromo·tropism.**
1900 B. D. JACKSON *Gloss. Bot. Terms* (Additions), *Dromotropism*, the irritability of climbing plants which results in the spiral growth (Macmillan); adj. *dromotropic.* 1902 *Encycl. Brit.* XXXI. 733/2 The centrifugal cardiac nerves influence the frequency, the force of contraction, and the conductivity of the excitatory wave (chrono-, ino-, and dromo-tropism of Engelmann). 1913 DORLAND *Med. Dict.* (ed. 7), *Dromotropic*, affecting the course or conductivity, as of a nerve-fiber. *Dromotropism*, interference with the conductivity of a muscle.

Drool, *sb.* *U.S.* [Cf. DROOL *v.*] Drivelled matter; also *fig.* drivel, nonsense.
1867–9 *Trans. Ill. Agric. Soc.* VII. 179 The drooled matter is filled with air bubbles, and may be described as a 'frothy' drool. 1911 H. S. HARRISON *Queed* xxv. 314 Say, Doc, I been readin' them reformatory drools of yours. 1928 *Daily Express* 6 Aug. 11 That sentimental drool.

Drool, *v.* Add: *fig.* to talk drivel or nonsense. Hence **Droo·ling** *vbl. sb.*
1921 R. D. PAINE *Comr. Rolling Ocean* vii. 118 You might think you were somebody, to hear you drool. 1923 P. G. WODEHOUSE *Inimit. Jeeves* xii. 130, I never know, when I'm telling a story, whether to cut the thing down to plain facts or whether to drool on and shove in a lot of atmosphere. 1924 LLOYD GEORGE in *Glasgow Herald* 22 Nov. 10 The peppery leaders of the 'Morning Post', the dull-witted leaders of 'The Times', and the droolings of the 'Observer'.

Drop, *sb.* Add: **12. d.** = DROP-KICK.
1845 *Rules Footb. Rugby School* § 7 Kick out must not be from more than..twenty five yards, if a punt, drop, or knock on.

14. (Earlier examples.)
1869 A. K. MCCLURE *Rocky Mts.* xxiv. 233 So expert is he with his faithful pistol, that the most scientific of rogues have repeatedly attempted in vain to get 'the drop' on him. 1876 JOAQUIN MILLER *First Families* xii. 105 It was strange that Sandy did not pull.., at all events he had the 'drop', and could afford to wait..and see what he [*sc.* the Parson] would do.

17. b. *Thieves' slang.* A receiver of stolen goods; a fence.
1915 *Times* 19 Mar. 5/5 The Magistrate.—I thought that they called these men 'fences'. Mr. Pearce.—Perhaps the fashion has changed. One usually associates a 'drop' with a more serious offence.

Drop, *v.* Add: **6.** Also with *through.*
1865 *Punch* 13 May 189/2 The debate 'dropped through' at a quarter to six.

9. b. To come casually *to* knowledge of something. *colloq.*
1901 MARAH E. RYAN *Montana* viii. 118 As I slipped out through the back door before your visitors left, I dropped to the fact that you had some damage done to that left arm.

13. c. To plant (corn) by letting fall on prepared ground. *U.S.*
1854 T. D. PRICE *MS. Diary* 22 May, Afternoon dropped corn. 1909 MRS. STRATTON-PORTER *Girl of Limberlost* xi. 218, I earned it myself, dropping corn, sticking onions, and pulling weeds.

d. To form by dropping from a shot-tower into a water-cistern.
1892 GREENER *Breech-Loader* 165 Lead shot is of two kinds: that which is moulded, as large buckshot, and that which is 'dropped', as the ordinary small shot.

e. *To drop a brick*: see *BRICK *sb.*[1] 5 c.

30. Drop out. *intr.* To disappear from one's or its place in a series or order; to fall out of a plan or arrangement.

Drop-. Add: 'arranged so as to drop or let down', as *drop-end, -frame, -shelf, -window*; *drop-in, drop-over* in *attrib.* use; **drop-cake,** a small cake made by letting batter drop from a spoon into hot fat, or on a greased pan to be baked in an oven; **drop-cannon** *Billiards*, a variety of cannon; **drop-forge** *v.*, to forge by means of a drop-press; also in *vbl. sb.* (*concr.*) and *ppl. a.*; **drop-frame,** (see above) also, a bicycle frame having the top bar lowered or depressed; so *drop-framed* adj.; **drop-jaw,** the canine disease of paralytic rabies; **drop-lamp** *U.S.* (example); **drop-light,** (*b*) a suspended electric lamp; **drop-line,** also, a hand-line used in fishing; **drop-out** *Rugby Football*, a drop-kick made from within the player's twenty-five-yard line; **drop-pattern** (see quot.); **drop scone** (see SCONE 1); **drop-shot** = *drop-stroke*; **drop-stitch,** openwork in stocking-web; **drop-stroke** *Lawn Tennis*, a stroke which causes the ball to drop abruptly after clearing the net; so **drop-volley**; **drop-title,** a title which is set comparatively low on the first page; **drop-worm,** the larva of any of various moths, which drop from trees by a thread of silk.
1879 MRS. WHITNEY *Just How* 83 May also be baked as cookies, in muffin rings; or *drop-cakes, in your small drop-cake rings. 1904 *J. P. Mannock's Billiards Expounded* 336 The plain '*drop cannon' which is employed to gather the balls between the two top pockets. 1909 *Westm. Gaz.* 2 Feb. 12/3 He unexpectedly missed a rather wide drop-cannon from hand. 1928 *Daily Mail* 31 July 1/2 Settee has *drop end. 1897 *Westm. Gaz.* 7 Jan. 7/2 Cleeks and irons made of *drop-forged steel. 1897 *Outing* (U.S.) XXX. 278/2 The hammers that are pounding out the drop-forgings. 1909 *Westm. Gaz.* 13 July 5/1 A nickel chrome steel drop forging. 1909 *Engineer* CVII. 277 Drop forgings are cheaper and more accurate than hand forgings. 1898 *Westm. Gaz.* 18 Nov. 9/1 In Professor Lilly's triangulated frame will be found an attempt by a skilled engineer to overcome the '*drop'-frame difficulty. 1906 *Bazaar, Exch. & Mart Suppl.* 12 Oct. 1481/2 Gentleman's cycle, 23 in. drop frame. 1928 *Daily Tel.* 16 Oct. 7 Another feature demanded by lady drivers is a drop-frame for the divisional window between the front and rear seats. 1898 *Cycling* 91 The *drop-framed safety. 1921 *Spectator* 16 Apr. 485/2 Above this French window is a *drop-in fanlight. 1900 *Yearbk. U.S. Dept. Agric.* 233 (Cent. D. Suppl.) The dumb form of rabies is very common, and many persons know it as '*drop jaw' who have no idea of its true nature. 1891 *Century Mag.* Apr. 940 A long discussion..was held..between the young people sitting by the *drop-lamp. 1904 KATH. C. THURSTON *John Chilcote* viii, The *drop-light from the ceiling being directly above his head. 1847 C. LANMAN *Summer in Wilderness* xxvi. 158, I..with a *drop-line have taken, in twenty minutes, more trout than I could eat in a fortnight. 1897 *Encycl. Sport* I. 430/2 *Drop-out is a drop-kick from within 25 yards of the kicker's goal line...If the ball pitch in touch the opposite side may have it dropped out again. 1905 *Westm. Gaz.* 12 Dec. 9/2 From the drop-out Cambridge began an attack. 1897 STEPHENSON & SUDDARDS *Textbk. Orn. Design Woven Fabrics* iv. 49 This placing or 'dropping' of one diamond below another..gives the essence of the *drop pattern. 1916 A. S. NEILL *Dominie Dismissed* ix. 118 Margaret..invited me to sample some *drop-scones she had been making. 1905 *Daily Chron.* 16 Feb. 8/5 A *drop-shelf, with chains attached to one of the panels. 1908 *Captain* Aug. 453/1 They never practice its [*sc.* the lob's] antithesis, the *drop-shot. 1927 *Observer* 20 Mar. 27/3 Mixing up deep drives and clever drop-shots. 1905 *Smart Set* Oct. 9/2 Kind o' openwork, like a lady's *drop-stitch sock. 1923 *Daily Mail* 29 June 1 French Lisle Thread Stockings..Drop-stitch design. 1897 WILBERFORCE *Lawn Tennis* xi. 39 The cross-*drop stroke is considerably easier to make backhand from the backhand court. 1897 *Encycl. Sport* I. 621/2 *Drop-stroke*, a stroke by which the ball is made to drop dead, just clearing the net. 1893 WISE & SMART *Bibliography of Ruskin* I. 189 There is no title-page, the '*drop-title' on page 1 reading 'Memorandum of Association of the Guild of St. George'. 1907 *Westm. Gaz.* 9 Nov. 12/3 The *drop-volley..was one of her favourite strokes. 1927 *Daily Express* 4 May 13/7 She would leap forward and summarily cut short the rally with a deft drop-volley. 1901 *Daily News* 3 Jan. 6/4 A door with window, and on either side of the latter a *drop window. 1926 *Glasgow Herald* 26 June 9 The drop-windows permit of ready means of ventilation on warm days. 1862 T. W. HARRIS *Insects Injur. Veget.* 415 In Philadelphia and the vicinity, cases of a similar kind [*sc.* an *Oiketicus*] are very common on many of the trees,..which are often very much injured by the insects inhabiting them. These are there popularly called *drop-worms and basket-worms.

Droplet. Add: *Droplet infection*, infection conveyed by fine droplets of mucus sprayed into the air when a person opens his mouth to speak, cough, etc.
1904 *Westm. Gaz.* 20 Sept. 7/2 In the act of loud speaking, fine droplets of mucus are sprayed from the mouth into the air...It has been shown that by reading aloud for half an hour B[acillus] prodigiosus may be disseminated from the mouth to a distance of 24 ft. in front. 1929 *Times* 12 June 16/4 The prevalence and mode of spread of minor epidemics in residential schools, especially those believed to be spread by 'droplet infection'.

Dropper. Add: **4.** (Later U.S. example.)
1881 MCLEAN *Cape Cod Folks* iii. 54 There was a marked and cheerful variety in the nature of the droppers-in at the Ark.

5. e. *Hort.* A young bulb of certain bulbous plants, *esp.* a small bulb developed at the apex of a downward shoot growing from the base of the parent bulb.
1900 B. D. JACKSON *Gloss. Bot. Terms*, *Dropper*, the young bulb of a tulip, not of flowering size. 1907 *Annals of Botany* XX. 429 The 'Droppers' of *Tulipa* and *Erythronium.* 1929 A. D. HALL *Bk. Tulip* 22 Occasionally also it will be noticed..that a stolon has started away from the base of the old bulb, turned downward and formed a bulb at the extremity...These bulbs are called 'droppers' and differ in no respect from other offsets.

Dropping, *vbl. sb.* Add: **5. b.** *pl.* The waste material cast off from a machine in certain processes of textile manufacture.
1902 HANNAN *Textile Fibres of Commerce* 115 The primary impurities from each of the two processes of opening and scutching are known as the droppings.

Drosera (drǫ·sĕră). [mod.L., f. Gr. δροσερός dewy.] A plant of the genus so named, the sundew; also applied to the drug prepared from the roots and leaves of this plant, which is used as a remedy in bronchial diseases.
1846 LINDLEY *Veget. Kingd.* 433 The common Droseras are rather acid. 1880 *Encycl. Brit.* XIII. 135/1 Insects seem to be attracted by the leaves of *Drosera.* 1909 *Rami-Syrup* 3 Tincture of drosera. 1928 MARTINDALE & WESTCOTT *Extra Pharm.* (ed. 19) 854 Drosera not found specific.

Droseraceous (drǫsĕrē¹·ʃəs), *a.* *Bot.* [f. *DROSERA + -ACEOUS.] Of or belonging to the *Droseraceæ*, the sundew family of insect-eating plants.

Droserin (drǫ·sĕrin). [f. *DROSERA: see -IN [1].] An antiseptic and digestive ferment derived from *Drosera* and other insectivorous plants.
1880 *Encycl. Brit.* XIII. 139/2 Droserin seems to be present in the secretion of all those insectivorous plants which possess the power of digestion.

Drosophyllum (drōᵘsǒfi·lǒm). *Bot.* [mod.L., f. Gr. δρόσος dew + φύλλον leaf.] A plant of the genus of droseraceous plants so called, which consists of a single species, *Drosophyllum lusitanicum*, found in Portugal and Morocco.
1880 *Encycl. Brit.* XIII. 134/1 *Drosophyllum* occurs only in Portugal and Morocco. 1901 *Daily News* 5 Jan. 9/1 The lecturer..told how the drosophyllum went in for a sticky exudation that acted not as a deterrent, but as an actual death-trap. 1909 *Daily Chron.* 18 Feb. 7/5 Portuguese farmers use the fly-catching drosophyllum instead of mechanical flytraps to clear their houses of insects.

Drot, U.S. variant of DRAT *v.*
1834 W. GUY SIMMS *Guy Rivers* II. 100 Drot the man..who hasn't the courage to get in a passion. 1845 J. J. HOOPER *Adv. Simon Suggs* ii. 20 Drot it! what do boys have daddies for, any how?

Drought. Add: **2.** *Absolute drought*, a period of fourteen or more consecutive days without rain. *Partial drought*, a period of twenty-eight or more consecutive days with a very small average rainfall per day.
1880 *British Rainfall* 112, (1) 'Absolute Droughts,' or all periods of 14 or more consecutive days absolutely without rain; and (2) 'Partial Droughts,' or all periods of 28 days or upwards in which the total fall was less than a quarter of an inch. 1899 *Daily News* 12 June 7/2 With all the dry weather we had last year there was not one case of an absolute drought in London.

5. *drought-resisting* adj.
1916 *Nature* XCVII. 333/2 Special drought-resisting wheats. 1927 KENDREW *Climates of Continents* 54 Drought-resisting bushes.

Dro·ve wo̱rk. [See DROVE *v.*[3] and *sb.* 4.] The dressing of masonry with a drove or broad chisel, as distinguished from broached and striped work.
1883 *Specif. Alnwick & Cornhill Rlwy.* 5 The face-work is ..to be..dressed in the manner that is technically called 'Drove Work'.

Drown, *v.* **1.** Delete (Now *unusual*) and add quots.:
1895 A. SYMONS *Poems* (1907) I. 119, I sicken with a wild desire, I drown in sweetness. 1924 ANNE D. SEDGWICK *Little French Girl* I. viii. 70 She had the sensation of drowning yet of keeping calm while she drowned. 1928 *Manchester Guardian Weekly* 31 Aug. 152/1 Public opinion is like the crowd that watches a man drown while convinced that something ought to be done.

5. c. *Tobacco culture.* *pass.* To be injured by long-continued rain followed by hot sunshine.
1897 *Yearbk. U.S. Dept. Agric.* 33 (Cent. D. Suppl.) This tobacco was cut after being drowned or scalded.

Drowse, *v.* Add:
2. b. Also with *away, off.*
1885 W. W. STORY *Fiammetta* (1886) 39 He..now and then drowsed away into a half sleep. 1908 *Smart Set* Sept. 101/2, I must have drowsed off.

Drudge, *sb.* Add:
1. b. *drudge-horse* (later U.S. example).
1849 N. KINGSLEY *Diary* 72 Mr. Potter is at work at harnesses for drudge horses.

2. The performance of drudgery.
1892 STEVENSON & OSBOURNE *Wrecker* xv, With every day it took harder driving to keep them to the daily drudge.

Drudgy (drʊ·dʒi), *a.* [f. DRUDGE *sb.* + -Y [1].] Having the character of a drudge.
1863 'GAIL HAMILTON' *Gala-Days* 288 If a woman lets herself become shabby, drudgy, and commonplace as a wife.

Drug, *sb.*[1] Add:
1. b. *spec.* Now often applied without qualification to narcotics and opiates; esp. in *attrib.* use, as *drug-addict, -evil, -fiend* (*FIEND 4 e), *-habit*, etc.
1902 *Daily Chron.* 7 Nov. 5/6 Two remedies to the drug-evil were suggested by the Bishop of Kensington. 1905 *Ibid.* 2 May 5/7 The drug-taking Chilcote. 1906 RIDER HAGGARD *Benita* xix, It was as though the power of the drug-induced oblivion..had reasserted itself. 1906 BENSON *House of Defence* i, The raptures of these drug-effects. 1907 *Public Opinion* 17 May 622/1 The cure of a drug-logged man by a Christian Scientist. 1922 E. F. MURPHY *Black Candle* iii. 31 The drug habit affects all classes of society in Canada. 1928 F. B. YOUNG *My Brother Jonathan* 271 Wheeler..whose yellow skin suggested..the coloration of a drug-addict. 1929 J. COURNOS tr. *Stories Soviet Russia* 78, I had thought you were a drug-fiend. 1931 H. WALPOLE *Above the Dark Circus* II. ix, She was a hopeless drug addict.

3. *drug-shop* (U.S. example); **drug clerk** *U.S.*, an attendant in a drug-store; **drug-disease,** (*a*) a morbid state caused by the excessive use of a drug; (*b*) in homœopathic medicine, the symptoms noted after the administration of any drug for experimental purposes; **drug-rash,** a rash caused by the taking of a drug.
a 1910 'O. HENRY' *Rolling Stones* 128 The *drug clerk looks sharply at the white face half concealed by the high-turned overcoat collar. 1902 *Encycl. Brit.* XXIX. 312/2 The manifestations of drug action thus produced are carefully recorded, and this record of '*drug-diseases', after being verified by repetition on many 'provers', constitutes the distinguishing feature of the homœopathic materia medica. 1908 *Practitioner* Sept. 466 They act like tonics and prevent the development of *drug-rashes. 1836 *Knickerbocker Mag.* VIII. 74 A *drug-shop..where you can obtain soda powders.

Drug, *v.*[2] Add: **3.** *intr.* To take or be in the habit of taking drugs; *esp.* to indulge in narcotics.
1895 *Funk's Standard Dict.*

Dru·g-store. *U.S.* [DRUG *sb.*[1]] A druggist's shop, also dealing extensively or mainly in other articles, as toilet requisites, stationery, magazines and newspapers, light refreshments, etc.
1845 J. J. HOOPER *Adv. Simon Suggs* v. 52 The windows of the great drug store cast forth their blaze of varied lights. 1857 D. BRAMAN *Inform. Texas* ii. 24 There are twelve stores here, among which are two drug stores and a book store. 1873 ALDRICH *Marj. Daw* etc. 7 The bone was very skilfully set by the surgeon who chanced to be in the drug-store where Flemming was brought after his fall. 1897 R. M. STUART *Simpkinsville* 94 They rise from their comfortable chairs tilted back against the weather-boarded fronts of their respective drug-stores. 1903 *N.Y. Even. Post* 24 Sept. 8 It hardly pays to keep the [soda] fountains going in the drugstores. 1908 *Westm. Gaz.* 18 Aug. 3/1, I took them to a chemist's or I beg pardon: a drug-store.

Drum, *sb.*[1] Add: **1. d.** Now esp. *To beat* or *thump the big drum*: to make loud or clamorous advertisement, protest, or the like.
1907 *Q. Rev.* Apr. 393 It was left to the Navy League to thump the big drum. [1930 *Church Times* 4 July 3 Even the Bishop of London hesitates when the Protestant drum is loudly beaten.]

6. g. The cartridge-holding receptacle of a machine-gun; also, the contents of one of these.
1888 [in Dict.]. 1890 W. J. GORDON *Foundry* 29 To the breech is fixed a drum with 104 bullets. 1916 BOYD CABLE *Action Front* 198 Can you fill the cartridges into these drums while I shoot? 1928 *Daily Tel.* 24 Apr. 12/6, I gave him a drum and he went down underneath me.

9. d. A bundle. *To hump one's drum*: see HUMP *v.* 2. *Austral.*
1866 W. STAMER *Recoll. Life Adventure* I. 304 Our ci-devant millionaire..'humping his drum', [would] start off for the diggings to seek more gold. 1872 C. H. EDEN *My Wife & I in Queensland* i. 17 They all chaffed us about our swags, or donkeys, or drums, as a bundle of things wrapped in a blanket is indifferently called. 1886 F. COWAN *Australia* 31 (Morris) The Swagman: bed and board upon his back—or, having humped his drum and set out on the wallaby.

13. drum fire (see quot.); **drum-fishing,** fishing for drum-fish; **drum winding,** an armature winding in which the wire is wound on the cylinder's surface from end to end; so **drum wound** *a.*
1918 E. S. FARROW *Dict. Mil. Terms*, *Drum Fire*, a common name given to the artillery barrage or curtain of fire. Continuous bombardment, like the rolling of drums. 1855 *Knickerbocker Mag.* XLVI. 499 So highly enjoyed is *drum-fishing among our bail-fishers. 1902 *Encycl. Brit.* XXVII. 582/1 The development of the modern *drum winding from the shuttle-wound Siemens armature. 1893 W. P. MAYCOCK *Electric Lighting* II. vii. 196 The armature is *drum wound. 1904 R. M. WALMSLEY *Electricity in Service of Man* ii. i. 756 A method of arranging the connections of drum-wound armatures..consists in winding and insulating the coils separately before placing them on the core.

14. *drum-and-fife, drum-and-trumpet* (see HISTORY *sb.* 2).
1874 [see HISTORY *sb.* 2]. 1899 *Westm. Gaz.* 14 Dec. 3/2 They are both drum-and-fife supporters of their particular views. 1928 *Daily Tel.* 14 Aug. 5/3 We have had enough of drum-and-trumpet history.

Drum, *v.* Add: **5.** To solicit orders; to canvass. *U.S.*
1839 C. F. BRIGGS *Harry Franco* I. xiii. 90 Augustus..had drummed in Arkansas, and collected in the lithograph cities of the west. 1882 *Congress. Rec.* 315/1 The merchants ..have many thousands..drumming for business in every town. 1901 *Chambers's Jrnl.* Dec. 827/1, I was 'drumming' for one of the two great houses which divided the wool and the hides of the Argentine.

Drumhead. **5.** Add:
1899 *Westm. Gaz.* 22 Dec. 10/1 What he calls 'drum-head letters,' written by soldiers at the front before and after battle. 1908 *Daily Chron.* 25 May 7/7 A drum-head service held in the camp of the Essex Imperial Yeomanry.

Drumin (drʊ·min). *Chem.* Also -ine, drummine. [f. the specific name of the plant: see -INE [5].] A crystalline alkaloid obtained from *Euphorbia drummundi*, said to have anæsthetic properties.
1886 *Australian Med. Gaz.* Oct.

Drunk, *ppl. a.* and *sb.*[2] Add:
1. *Drunk and disorderly*: the official form of a charge in police court procedure. *Drunk and incapable*: see INCAPABLE *a.* 5.
1874 H. C. GREENWOOD *Magisterial & Police Guide* 610 *margin*, Offences. Drunk and disorderly persons. 1893 T. MARRIOTT *Constable's Duty* 76 Offence Defined...Every person who..is found to be drunk and disorderly.

B. *sb.* **1.** (Earlier U.S. example.)
1839 C. F. BRIGGS *Harry Franco* II. vii. 78, I have kept money enough to have a good drunk.

Drused (drūzd), *a.* [DRUSE [1].] = DRUSY *a.*
1895 STORY-MASKELYNE *Crystallogr.* 172 Forms..which exhibit ridged or 'drused' surfaces.

Dry, *sb.* Add: **5.** (from DRY *a.* 11 a) A prohibitionist. orig. *U.S.*
1918 *Literary Digest* (N.Y.) 17 Aug. 39 The 'drys' lose the State by only a bare majority. 1922 *Ibid.* 16 Dec. 12 The 'drys' broadly base their satisfaction on the fact that no previously 'dry' State reversed itself in the election. 1930 *Daily Express* 6 Nov. 2/1 An active 'Dry'.

Dry, *a.* Add: **11. a.** (Later example.)
1916 *Literary Digest* (N.Y.) 1 Jan. 4/2 About as much 'dry' territory 'going wet' as there was of 'wet' territory 'going dry'. 1922 [see *DRY *sb.* 5].

C. 2. a. *dry-feed* vb.; **dry-clean** *v. trans.*, to clean (clothes and other textiles) without using water; so *dry-cleaner, dry-cleaning* vbl. sb. and ppl. adj.; **dry-dyeing** *vbl. sb.*, dyeing with dyes soluble in spirit.
1818 W. TUCKER *Family Dyer & Scourer* (ed. 2) i. 20 For *dry cleaning Clothes of any Colour. 1897 *Chambers's Jrnl.* 25 Sept. 620/2 A firm of so-called 'dry-cleaners' of wearing apparel. 1899 *Westm. Gaz.* 9 Mar. 3/1 A dry cleaning cloth ball. *Ibid.* 20 Apr. 3/3 The present extraordinary perfection of dry-cleaning. *Ibid.*, A good gown, dry-cleaned, is a much better thing than an inferior new one. Of course I do not pretend that all dry-cleaners are equally good. *Ibid.* 12 Oct. 3/2 How well they may dry-clean at home by the use of benzoline. 1908 *Daily Report* 27 Aug. 6/4 The conditions under which women and girls work in dry-cleaning establishments, where benzine is largely used. 1911 R. W. CHAMBERS *Common Law* viii. 232 Her gown needs dry-cleaning. 1904 *Westm. Gaz.* 8 Sept. 4/2 *Dry-dyeing is simply dyeing with aniline dyes soluble in spirit. 1907 *Daily Chron.* 8 July 4/4 New systems of *dry-feeding young and adult stock.

3. dry-blower *Austral.*, a term of opprobrium (cf. BLOWER [1] 5); **dry-blowing** *Austral.* (see quot.); **dry camp** *U.S.*, a camp or halt where there is no water; **dry diggings,** (*a*) in S. Africa, diamond diggings at which the diamondiferous material is disintegrated by exposure to the atmosphere; (*b*) *U.S.* diggings on high land or a hill-side away from a river; **dry-dike** = *dry-stone dike* (see DIKE *sb.* 6 b); so *dry-diked* adj., *dry-diker*; **dry farmer** *U.S.* (see next); **dry farming** *U.S.*, farming without a good supply of water; **dry norther** *U.S.*, a north wind not accompanied by rain; **dry spell,** a period of at least fifteen consecutive days to none of which is credited as much as ·04 inch of rain; **dry stone** *a.* (earlier U.S. example); **dry-wall** *v.*, to furnish with a dry wall; to build a dry wall; **dry-walling,** walling without mortar; so **dry-waller**; **dry-wash** *U.S.*, the dry bed of an intermittent stream.
1895 *Queenslander* 7 Dec. 1069 Every other man you meet in Coolgardie..is either a lord, a colonel, a captain, a doctor, an expert, an agent, a sharebroker, or a sharper; all the rest are dudes, drunkards, and *dryblowers, professional liars, and loafers. 1894 *Argus* 28 Mar. 5/5 (Morris) When water is not available, as unfortunately is the case at Coolgardie, '*dry blowing' is resorted to. This is done by placing the pounded stuff [*sc.* alluvial ore] in one dish, and pouring it slowly at a certain height into the other. If there is any wind blowing it will carry away the powdered stuff; if there is no wind the breath will have to be used. 1873 J. H. BEADLE *Undevel. West* xxviii. 615 We..find a pool with water enough for our horses, and to fill our jugs, as we must make a '*dry camp' to-night. 1887 *Outing* (U.S.) X. 4/2 We halted on an open place at the edge of a cañon and went into dry camp. 1920 HUNTER *Trail Drivers of Texas* 312 The round up boss..called for two or three men..to make what is called a 'dry camp'. 1851 in *19th Cent.* (1889) June 970 The cradles were at work washing the earth brought from his claims upon the *dry diggings. 1873 F. BOYLE *To the Cape for Diamonds* 123 Four 'dry diggings':—New Rush..Old De Beers, Dutoitspan, and Bultfontein. 1889 K. MUNROE *Golden Days* x. 111 The dry diggings were those of hill-sides, or in gulches containing no steady supply of water. 1899 LACY *Pictures of Travel* 173 The 'dry diggings' are thirty miles to the south-east of Pniel. They are so called because the gems are not found in river-wash, but in dry tufa, which has apparently never been in contact with water. 1910 J. HART *Vigilante Girl* xxiv. 326 It had been a 'dry diggings', and the skeleton line of a long flume ran thread-like along the mountains. 1920 HUNTER *Trail Drivers of Texas* 43 This being Dry Diggings, meaning no gold to be found,..we all scattered. 1907 *Macm. Mag.* Jan. 196 The platform..was some fifty feet above the valley, and the stones on its face, which was almost perpendicular, appeared to be irregularly *dry-dyked. 1905 *Spectator* 11 Feb. 211/1 In the Boer War the '*dry dikers' of a certain East Yorkshire regiment used to be asked to volunteer to build 'sangars'. 1912 WASON *Friar Tuck* iii. 36 Next came the *dry farmer. 1919 H. L. WILSON *Ma Pettengill* v. 155 The forlorn shack of a dry-farmer. 1908 *Sci. Amer.* 22 Aug. 120 '*Dry farming' consists in so preparing the soil in semi-arid regions that it will catch what little annual rainfall there is, and store it within reach of the roots of the plants to be grown. 1871–3 *Texas Almanac* 97 The people here in Texas divide these winter storms into 'wet northers' and '*dry northers'. 1927 *Observer* 15 May 22 A..*dry plate clutch. 1887 *Dry spell [see SPELL *sb.*[3] 5 b]. 1919 *British Rainfall* 27 A Dry Spell is a period of fifteen or more consecutive days no one of which is a 'Wet Day'. 1770 WASHINGTON *Diaries* I. 380 The Mason's went to laying Stone in the walls of the water Pit (*dry stone). 1886 ELWORTHY *W. Somerset Word-bk.*, *Dry-waller...*Dry-walling. 1921 G. JEKYLL *Colour Schemes for Flower Garden* 67 It is a plant for dry banks, tops of rock-work and dry-walling. *Ibid.* 86 An earth bank four and a half feet high, *dry-walled on both sides. 1922 *Daily Mail* 10 Nov. 8/5 A dry-waller has to be born, not made. So old William told me when I found him dry-walling. 1928 PEAKE & FLEURE *Steppe & Sown* 116 A certain amount of dry walling was used. 1926 MULFORD *Cassidy's Protégé* ix. 110 A bridge spanned a *dry-wash, dry most of the year.

Dry, *v.* Add: **2. c.** *To dry straight*: to come right in the end. *colloq.*
1897 W. J. LOCKE *Derelicts* xxii, I shall miss you terribly —at first—but it will all dry straight, Yvonne.

5. Dry up. d. (Earlier U.S. examples.)
1855 F. S. MARRYAT *Mts. & Molehills* xiv. 257 One of the miners told him..that 'if he didn't "dry up" he'd chuck him out of the stage'. 1862 'GAIL HAMILTON' *Country Living & Th.* 94 Men can talk 'slang'. 'Dry up' is nowhere forbidden in the Decalogue.

Dryas (drəi·æs). [L.: see DRYAD etym.] A tufted rosaceous plant of the genus so named, found in arctic and alpine regions.
1829 LOUDON *Encycl. Plants* 454. 1927 *Glasgow Herald* 26 Mar., A thin carpet of Arctic-Alpine vegetation such as a white-flowered dryas and dwarf-willows.

Dry-dock, *v.* Add: Also *fig.*
1882 *Li-quor Christmas Annual* II. 83/2 They had the ability and tact to live by fraud without being overhauled by Justice and dry-docked.

Dry goods. (Additional U.S. examples.)
1806 WEEMS *Lett.* II. 334 If you can make by the Dry Good commerce 2, or 3000$ per an...I really think you ought to embrace the offer. 1815 *Ibid.* III. 126, I may get the decks clear for..some dry goods. 1860 S. MORDECAI *Virginia* iv. 58 The first specimen in Richmond of the Broadway style of dry goods palaces. 1902 O. WISTER *Virginian* iv. 43 The new day and its doings began around me in the store, chiefly at the grocery counter. Dry-goods were not in great request. 1904 TOM WATSON *Bethany* (1920) 6 Bethany had a dry-goods store.

Dryness. Add: **4.** The condition of being 'dry' or without alcohol. *U.S.*
1920 *Contemp. Rev.* July 79 'Dryness' in America is enormously increasing the consumption [of sugar] there. 1927 *Observer* 24 July 9/2 President Coolidge will..run as a staunch champion of 'dryness'.

Dry·salted, *ppl. a.* Salted and dried, as distinguished from pickled.
1885 [see DRY *a.* C. 2]. 1930 *Times* 22 Mar. 18/6 Pork (drysalted clear bellies).

Dso. Add: Also **Dzo.**
1897 *Geog. Jrnl.* (R.G.S.) July 36 The male *dso* is used for ploughing. 1927 *Glasgow Herald* 3 May 6 These Dzos gave excellent milk, and were fertile 'inter se'.

D.T. (dī·tī·). Also **D.T.'s** (dī·tī·z). The initials of DELIRIUM TREMENS used as a word.
1858 'MEGATHYM SPLENE' *Almæ Matres* 33 The disease called D.T. (heaven forbid I should write it in full). 1865 *Soiled Dove* xxvii, I wish to God I could get D.T., and then I should go mad and cut my throat. 1880 G. R. SIMS *Ballads of Babylon, Beauty & Beast* iv, A titled churl Who had just got round from a bad *d.t.* 1907 *Daily Chron.* 30 Aug. 7/3 'D.T.'s' without drunkenness. 1910 DAVIS *From Selection to City* ix. 82 He started to shake as if he had the d.t.'s.

Dual, *a.* (*sb.*) Add: **A.** *adj.* **3.** In technical use; esp. *dual control* (of an aeroplane); hence *attrib.* and *dual-controlled* adj.
1909 *Westm. Gaz.* 22 July 8/3 Some system of what is known as dual ignition for the modern high-class..motor-car. 1911 A. G. CLARK *Motor Car Engin.* I. 173 Diagram of Wiring for Dual System. *Ibid.* 175 Bosch Dual Magneto. *Ibid.* 177 Bosch Dual Wiring. 1912 *Motor Manual* (ed. 14) 51 Bosch dual-ignition system. 1912 J. ARMSTRONG *Motor* 156 A well-designed type of dual disc-clutch. 1914 *Scotsman* 8 Oct. 9/1 The number of 'dual-purpose' boats, equipped to burn both coal and oil, includes 38 battleships, 17 battle-cruisers, and 21 light cruisers. 1914 *Aeroplane* 15 July 60/2 Even if the 'Herring Pond' is crossed previously by a single or dual control machine. *Ibid.* 12 Aug. 164/2 The Beatty School, with its dual control Wright biplanes. 1917 A. G. CLARK *Motor Car Engin.* II. 73 Having in view the high efficiency of the modern magneto, it may be accepted that the dual ignition will only be fitted on the more expensive and high-powered cars to facilitate starting up. 1917 C. C. TURNER *Aircraft of To-day* vii. 114 The dual-engine aeroplane. *Ibid.* xi. 184 A common method of tuition is on machines with dual control. 1928 *Times* 13 Aug. 18/7 A Shorthorn is, and always has been, a dual-purpose animal. 1930 *Aberdeen Press & Jrnl.* 18 Mar. 7 A Grebe dual-control aeroplane. 1930 *Daily Tel.* 24 July 10/4 The machine was dual-controlled.

B. *sb.* **3.** In chess problems, a choice in White's continuations. Hence **Dual** *v.* in *pass.*, to admit of a dual solution.
1875 *City London Chess Mag.* 116 The Black Pawn on the K R file is here omitted as superfluous, and the above-mentioned duals entirely eliminated. 1903 *Daily Chron.* 11 July 8/7 Your problem is dualled by 22 17. 1906 A. C. WHITE *Tours de Force* p. xxxiii, If White is allowed a choice of continuations, such a choice is called a dual, or multiple, continuation. There are two kinds of duals: Absolute duals ..and minor duals.

Duar (dū·ɑɹ). Also douar. [Arab., f. Semitic root meaning 'round'.] An Arabian village.
1899 *Daily News* 6 Nov. 7/2 At the duar of Charifin a man stole a donkey. 1900 A. E. W. MASON *Miranda of the Balcony* x, He [*sc.* the Arab] belonged to a douar, a tent village, you understand. 1908 *Westm. Gaz.* 16 Apr. 5/2 The duar or village of the Kaid of the Ouled Buziri.

Dub (dʊb), *sb.*[5] *Criminals' slang.* [Cf. DUB *v.*[3]] A key, especially one used for picking locks. Hence **Du·bsman** (or abbrev. **Dubs**), a turnkey, gaoler.
a 1700 B. E. *Dict. Cant. Crew*, *Dub*, c. a Pick-lock-key. 1789 G. PARKER *Life's Painter* 139 A bunch of young dubs by her side. 1821 D. HAGGART *Life* (ed. 2) 31 We seized him, took the dubs, bound, and gagged him. 1839 AINSWORTH *Jack Sheppard* II. xii, Oh! give me a chisel, a knife, or a file, And the dubsmen shall find that I'll do it in style! 1887 HENLEY *Villon's Good Night* (Farmer) You coppers' narks, and dubs, What pinched me when upon the snam. 1923 *Chambers's Jrnl.* 716/1, I pulled the dub of the outer jigger from his sack.

Dub, *sb.*[6] *U.S. slang.* [Perh. related to DUB *v.*[1] 11, DUBBED *ppl. a.* 4.] A poor hand at anything.
1896 G. ADE *Artie* i. 4 What kills me off is how all these dubs make their star winnins. 1902 H. L. WILSON *Spenders* xxx. 353 People can talk all they want to about your bein' just a dub—I won't believe 'em. 1905 *Smart Set* Oct. 18/1 I've made up my mind that I ain't goin' to keep on bein' a common dub all my life. 1911 H. QUICK *Yellowstone N.* 43, I was coming on pretty well for a dub. 1916 BOYD CABLE *Action Front* 8 The Schmidt customer crowd didn't need to know a thing about me being here unless he was dub enough to tell 'em. 1921 R. D. PAINE *Comr. Rolling Ocean* vi. 99 He..says the officers are dubs and most of the boys muckers.

Dub, *v.*[4] *slang.* [Origin obscure.] *intr.* *To dub up*: to pay up.
1840 *Comic Almanack* 36 'Come, dub up!' roars a third; and I don't mind telling you..that I..took out the sovereign and gave it. 1845 *Punch* Oct. 147/1 He has been compelled to 'dub up' out of his own pocket. 1852 MUNDY *Antipodes* (1857) 36 The juniors are compelled to *dub up.*

Dub, *v.*[5] *U.S. slang.* [Cf. *DUB *sb.*[6]] *intr.* To go or act aimlessly or ineffectively.
1896 G. ADE *Artie* xvi. 146 I'd been readin' them con story-books about pickin' flowers and goin' fishin' and dubbin' around the woods out in the country.

Dubber[1]. Add: **2.** An implement for trimming hides. *U.S.*
1850 L. H. GARRARD *Wah-to-Yah* iv. (1927) 61 Bringing.. buffalo skins down to the required thinness, by means of the dubber.

Dubbin: see DUBBING *vbl. sb.* 4. Hence **Du·bbined** *a.*, treated with dubbin.
1825 JAMIESON, *Dubbin*, the liquor used by curriers for softening leather, composed of tallow and oil. 1855 J. DAVIES *Races of Lancashire* in *Trans. Philol. Soc.* 230 *Dubbin*, a kind of paste used by shoemakers. 1896 J. K. SNOWDEN *Web of Old Weaver* vii. 77, I was seeking a pot of dubbin on the top shelf of her cupboard. 1899 M. CORBETT *Bottled Holidays* 147 An omnibus odorous of freely-dubbined boots. 1928 *Daily Express* 11 Oct. 3/3 Wearing enormous dubbined boots.

Dubby (dʊ·bi), *a.* *colloq.* and *dial.* [f. DUB *v.*[1] + -Y [1].] Blunt; short, dumpy.
1865 JENNINGS *Obs. Dial. w. Eng.* 35 *Dub, dubbed, dubby*, ..blunt; not pointed; squat. 1872 F. W. ROBINSON *Wrayford's Ward* III. 208 A nose that young ladies, I believe, call 'dubby'. 1904 ELLEN T. FOWLER & FELKIN *Kate of Kate Hall* xxiii, A dubby piece of blacklead that couldn't write two consecutive words.

Dublin (dʊ·blin). The name of the capital of the Irish Free State, formerly of Ireland; as in **Dublin prawn,** the small lobster *Nephrops norvegicus.*
1915 E. R. LANKESTER *Diversions of Naturalist* 100 Another lobster of our markets is the little one known as the 'Dublin prawn', which is common enough on the Scotch and Norwegian coasts, as well as that of Ireland.

Dubs[1] (dʊbz). *The Dubs*, the nickname given to the men of the Royal Dublin Fusiliers.
1899 *Daily News* 20 Nov. 4/5 One of the 'Dubs' shot through the left leg and both arms. 1900 *Ibid.* 29 Mar. 3/4 It is as good as a tonic to get into conversation with the 'Dubs'.

Dubs[2] (dʊbz). *local.* [Short for *doubles.*] (See quots.)
1823 E. MOOR *Suffolk Words* s.v., A player knocking two out of the ring cries 'dubs!' to authorize his claim to both. 1882 MARY H. FOOTE *Led-Horse Claim* iv. 62 'What is it the boys say when they play marbles?'..'Fend dubs!' Hilgard suggested. 1896 *Dialect Notes* (Amer. Dial. Soc.) I. 220 In Missouri..dubs means, not doublets, but that the player has blundered, and by crying 'dubs' is entitled to play again.

Dubster (dʊ·bstəɹ). *U.S. slang.* = *DUB *sb.*[6]
1904 *N.Y. Tribune* 1 May, They seize upon the latest clever dubster and cry him up as a wizard of wit and wisdom.

Duchesse (dʊ·tʃes, ‖ düʃe·s). [Fr., = duchess.]
1. *Duchesse satin, satin duchesse*, a very soft kind of satin.
1878 *Cassell's Family Mag.* IV. 365/1 Duchesse satin is the widest, and at the same time far the best. 1884 *Pall Mall Gaz.* 9 Aug. 9/1 A long train of cream duchesse satin. 1894 *Times* 19 Sept. 10/4 Charged..with stealing a large quantity of silk and satin duchesse. 1895 *Army & Navy Co-op. Soc. Price List* 15 Sept. 1095/2 Coloured Satins. Duchesse.

2. *Duchesse lace*, a variety of Brussels pillow-lace, worked with fine thread in large sprays.
1882 CAULFEILD & SAWARD *Dict. Needlework* 166/2 Duchesse Lace is worked with a finer and different thread to that of Honiton. 1902 *Encycl. Brit.* XXX. 110/2 'Duchesse' and Bruges lace are the chief pillow-made laces.

3. (See quot.)
1878 *Cassell's Family Mag.* IV. 168/2 For balls..there are the Duchesse and Marquise sleeves. The Duchesse covers two-thirds of the arm, and is finished off with frills..and lace.

4. *Duchesse dressing chest, table*, a dressing-table with a swing-glass. *Duchesse toilet cover, set*, a cover for a dressing-table, or a set of covers consisting usually of one long runner, one smaller, and two very small mats.
1895 *Army & Navy Co-op. Soc. Price List* 15 Sept. 1102/2 Duchesse Toilet Covers. 1906 *Lady's World* Nov. 156/1 Very dainty Duchesse toilet sets can be made by placing some of these floral squares on a foundation of coloured silk. 1922 *Daily Tel.* 12 June 20/1 Burr walnut duchesse tables and washstands. 1930 *Ibid.* 5 Apr. 21/7 Duchesse dressing chests.

Duck, *sb.*[1] Add: **1. e.** *ellipt.* Duck-shot.
1687 S. SEWALL *Letter Bk.* 64 Six tone of shott, of which three ton Goose, two tone Duck, one pigeon. 1775 *Jrnls. Cont. Congress* III. 426 Procure a quantity of duck and powder. 1845 W. G. SIMMS *Wigwam & Cabin* 334 Draw the loads, Scip, and put in some of the high duck.

3. b. Often *a duck of a...*; and applied to things as well as persons.
1841 *Punch* 18 Sept. 112/1 If our remarks were made with an affectionate eye to the young ladies of the satin-album-loving school, we should assuredly style this 'a duck of a picture'. 1841 W. L. REDE *Sixteen String Jack* I. ii, Oh, isn't he a duck of a fellow! 1891 FARMER *Slang* s.v., A duck of a bonnet.

4. Also, a fellow, 'customer'. *U.S. slang.*
1889 K. MUNROE *Golden Days* xxiv. 261 He was the duck that stole Paddy's horse. 1903 A. ADAMS *Log Cowboy* ix. 125, I can't quite make out this other duck, but I reckon he's some big auger. 1904 W. H. SMITH *Promoters* v. 100 As you said, Goldsby, Slosher's a slick duck.

9. b. *transf.*
1929 W. J. LOCKE *Jorico* 226 She was something of a lame duck of a craft.

10. b. *Sydney duck* (Australian), a convict.
1873 JOAQUIN MILLER *Unwritten Hist.* viii. (1876) 120 There are some hard names given on the Pacific; but when you call a man a 'Sydney duck' it is well understood that you mean blood.

11. a. *duck-hunt.*
1847 C. LANMAN *Summer in Wilderness* xxviii. 196, I.. started on a duck hunt down the river Raisin.

12. duck-disease *colloq.*, shortness of leg; also *ducks' disease*; **duck shot** (U.S. example); **duck-shover** *Austral.*, a cabman who does not wait his turn in the rank, but touts for passengers; so *duck-shoving*; **duck walk,** a duckboard track (see *DUCKBOARD).
1925 E. FRASER & GIBBONS *Soldier & Sailor Words*, *'Ducks' disease*, short legged. 1928 S. VINES *Humours Unreconciled* viii. 103 Mr. Sheepshanks..soon got his host expanding a theory of the 'duck-disease', as he facetiously called the shortness of leg from which the Japanese were suffering. 1851 R. GLISAN *Jrnl. Army Life* vi. (1874) 57, I had a fine opportunity to plunge a whole charge of *duck shot into his side. 1898 MORRIS *Austral Eng.*, *Duck-shover. 1908 *Westm. Gaz.* 18 Jan. 3/2 A swanker and a duck-shover. 1870 *N. & Q.* 4th Ser. VI. 111 '*Duck-shoving'..is the term used by our Melbourne cabmen to express the unprofessional trick of breaking the rank, in order to push past the cabman on the stand for the purpose of picking up a stray passenger or so. 1896 *Otago Daily Times* 25 Jan. 3/6 (Morris) 'Duck shoving', a process of getting passengers which operated unfairly against the cabmen who stayed on the licensed stand and obeyed the by-law. 1917 *War Illustrated* 28 Apr. 239/2 The '*duck-walk' is laid for easy crossing of difficult surfaces.

Duck, *v.* Add: **2. b.** To back out, withdraw; to make off, abscond. orig. *U.S. slang.*
1896 G. ADE *Artie* ii. 9, I think I'll have to duck on that present. 1910 W. M. RAINE *B. O'Connor* 249 Coming through the cañon Del Oro in the night, he ducked; I reckon he's in Mexico now. 1911 H. S. HARRISON *Queed* xxi. 270 It's about over. And now I must pay for my fun—duck back to the office. 1915 H. L. WILSON *Ruggles of Red Gap* ii. (1917) 26, I duck out every morning before she's up. 1919 P. G. WODEHOUSE *Damsel in Distress* xvi, He saw me, too, and what do you think he did? Ducked down a side-street, if you please.

c. *trans.* To get away from, to avoid, dodge (a person or thing). *U.S.*
1896 G. ADE *Artie* vi. 55 And purty soon he duck's 'em and comes over an' touches me for two cases. 1926 J. BLACK *You Can't Win* vii. 80 We'll get a passenger train out of Cheyenne, kid, if we can duck Jeff Carr. 1928 *Daily Tel.* 6 Nov. 13/3 (American Election) Both sides, he says, have 'ducked' the problems of Labour and foreign policy.

6. *trans.* and *intr.* In the game of Bridge (see quots.).
1905 R. F. FOSTER *Complete Bridge* 263 Ducking..is refusing to part with the command of your own suit, and is usually resorted to in situations in which no finesse is possible. *Ibid.* 264 The dealer sees that it is impossible to catch the K, Q, 10 of spades, so he ducks the suit by leading a small card. *Ibid.* 266 As there is no card in dummy's hand but the club ace that will bring the suit into play, that card must be kept as a re-entry until the third round, and the first two rounds of the suit must be ducked. *Ibid.* 312 *Ducking.*—Refusing to win tricks when able to do so. 1928 *Daily Express* 27 Aug. 4 You can frequently make the most of a suit by deliberately losing the first trick. This method of play, called 'ducking', is founded not only on the law of average probabilities but also on the expectation that the cards are normally distributed.

Duckboard (dʊ·kbōᵊɹd). [f. DUCK *sb.*[1] + BOARD *sb.*] Usually *pl.* In the war of 1914–18, a slatted timber path laid down on wet or muddy ground in the trenches or in camps; also in wider use. Also *attrib.* Hence **Du·ck-boarded** *a.*, furnished with duckboards.
1917 *War Illustrated* 17 Mar. 109 Walking wounded are helped along the duck-boards that flank the light railways. *Ibid.* 14 July 467 They..flung duck-board bridges over the Douve river. 1919 G. K. ROSE *2/4th Oxf. & Bucks Lt. Infty.* 31 For four miles the path lay along a single duck-board track, capsized or slanting in many places. *Ibid.* 72 The day was spent in..rebuilding dug-outs or laying fresh duckboards (wooden slats to walk on in the trenches). *Ibid.* 73 A duck-boarded communication trench. 1925 E. FRASER & GIBBONS *Soldier & Sailor Words*, *Duckboard glide*, a common term for after-dark movements along the trenches, when secrecy and quietness was essential... *Duckboard harrier*, a despatch 'runner' or messenger, whose duty took him along the duckboards in the trenches. 1926 *Glasgow Herald* 9 Jan. 9 Certain underground stations are feeling the effects of the flood, particularly that of Mirabeau, where duckboards have been laid upon the platform.

Ducker[1]. Add: **3.** A duck-hunter.
1903 *N.Y. Sun* 8 Nov., The professional ducker goes about his work in an entirely different manner. Killing ducks with these men is a business.

Ducking[3]. (Later U.S. examples.)
1904 *N.Y. Times* 10 May 4 Advt., Splendid selection of duckings from which to make them [*sc.* awnings]. 1920 HUNTER *Trail Drivers of Texas* 177 The silver..was placed in duckin' sacks.

Ducky (dʊ·ki), *a.* *colloq.* [f. DUCK *sb.*[1] + -Y [1].] In affected or juvenile speech an emotional epithet of commendation: see *DUCK *sb.*[1] 3 b.
1897 *Westm. Gaz.* 5 Apr. 10/1 She remembers making his first dress with its 'ducky buttons'. 1905 M. BARNES-GRUNDY *Vacil. Hazel* 111 The duckiest, little bronze beetle, ..mounted in gold. 1905 *Punch* 8 Mar. 178/1 Only see how prettily he's scratching his ducky little ear. 1927 *Ibid.* 14 Sept. 285/1 You can wear one of those ducky little lace caps.

Duct. Add:
5. Also, a conduit for an electric cable.
1901 *Westm. Gaz.* 11 Apr. 7/2 The work of laying the cable ducts has practically finished.

7. In *attrib.* use = affecting the epithelium of the mammary glands, as *duct-cancer, -cyst, -papilloma.*
1864 *T. Holmes' Syst. Surg.* IV. 680 Duct-cysts. Perfectly closed cysts..but having an opening communicating with a duct. 1889 *Lancet* 21 Dec. 1278/1 In duct cancer of the breast he had not observed eczematous appearances. 1910 *Practitioner* Apr. 469 When a duct-papilloma obstructs one of the large ducts near the nipple.

Dud, *sb.* Add: **4.** A counterfeit thing, as a bad coin, a dishonoured cheque; in the war of 1914–18 applied *spec.* to an explosive shell that failed to explode; hence (cf., however, sense 3 in Dict.) applied contemptuously to any useless or inefficient person or thing. (Cf. next.)
1897 *Daily News* 14 Jan. 2/2 He admitted that he knew that he ought not to have sold the piracies, and that such works were known as 'Duds'. 1908 *Westm. Gaz.* 28 Jan. 4/1 Gambling with 'Duds'..A 'dud' car is a worthless contraption, which..has arrived at a stage when it would be dear at any price. 1908 *Captain* Apr. 23/2 We want talent, not duds. 1915 *Blackw. Mag.* Feb. 141 Our weary hearts rejoice When Silent Susan sends us down a dud! 1915 BOYD CABLE *Between Lines* 254 One of these [shells] was a dud an' didn't burst. 1915 ROSHER *In R.N.A.S.* (1916) 97, I..spent the whole of the afternoon trying to get my beastly engine to go. It's an awful dud. 1920 *Punch* 1 Sept. 168/1 He..has..been irritated by his school-boy son derisively addressing him as an 'old dud'. 1923 S. BALDWIN in *Public Opinion* 30 Nov. 531/1 All the torpedoes they carry are duds. 1927 R. THORNDIKE *Slype* xi, And then you wants to know the reason of their putting a dud in charge of a public building. 1928 GALSWORTHY *Swan Song* III. xvi. 345 It's when you don't understand that you feel such a dud.

Dud, *a.* [app. adj. use of DUD 3, *4.] Counterfeit; failing to answer to its description or to perform its function; worn out; useless; unsatisfactory.
1903 *Daily Chron.* 29 July 9/4, I..got him to give me half a crown for a dud ring. 1904 *Ibid.* 13 May 6/3 Wanted comedy and dramatic sketches. Something with life and go in it. No Dud stuff required. 1915 ROSHER *In R.N.A.S.* (1916) 130 As luck would have it, the weather was dud. 1917 *Blackw. Mag.* May 803/2 It was soon afterwards that our engine went dud. 1917 'CONTACT' *Airman's Outings* 267 They wanted a plan of some new defences on which the Hun had been busy during the spell of dud weather. 1918 W. J. LOCKE *Rough Road* xviii, 'It's a dud sort of a place, Durdlebury,' said he. 'Dud?' He laughed. 'It never goes off.' 1920 *Punch* 20 Oct. 309/1 Give me some dud messages. 1929 *Star* 21 Aug. 14/4 Hitherto, he has met with rotten luck in Africa. Seemed to strike one dud patch after another.

Due, *a.* Add: **9. d.** advb. in *Due to*: = owing to (OWING *ppl. a.* 3 b). Frequent in *U.S.* use.

10. b. On the point of (doing something). With inf. *U.S. colloq.*
1921 R. D. PAINE *Comr. Rolling Ocean* ii. 22 These.. relatives of his had never taken the trouble to find out whether he amounted to anything or not...Well they were about due to find out.

11. due-bill *U.S.* (earlier examples).
1800 in C. Cist *Cincinnati* (1841) 173 A number of due bills. 1841 J. F. COOPER *Deerslayer* vii, Though there's them about that would look upon you more as a due-bill for the bounty than a human mortal.

Duff, *sb.*[1] (Earlier U.S. example.)
1838 *Knickerbocker Mag.* XI. 446 And oh! that 'duff'.. that plum duff!..of a Sunday!

Duff, *v.*[2] *Golf.* [Back-formation f. DUFFER *sb.*[2]] *trans.* To perform (a shot) badly, by hitting the ground first behind the ball and thus driving the ball only a short distance. Also *fig.* to make a mess of, muff.
1897 *Encycl. Sport* I. 469/1 The verb 'to duff' does not mean..to play as a 'duffer' or hopelessly bad player, but simply to hit the ground first, behind the ball, so that the ball is struck with the upper edge of the face, and sent only a short way into the air. *Ibid.* 469/2 Duffing is very frequently caused by the player having his ball too near his right foot. 1906 *Westm. Gaz.* 8 Sept. 3/1 At the first duffed shot. 1909 *Ibid.* 30 Apr. 12/2 Mayo duffed his approach. 1924 *Glasgow Herald* 15 June 11 He made one solitary slip when he duffed his putt on Wee Bogle.

Duffer, *sb.*[2] Add: **1. b.** *Duffer's fortnight*, a fortnight of the angling season during which trout are supposed to be caught easily.
1927 *Observer* 19 June 27/4 That period of imbecility the so-called 'duffer's fortnight'. 1928 *Daily Express* 28 May 4/5 This annual festival of the Mayfly inaugurates the 'Duffers' Fortnight'.

Dufterdar, variant of *DEFTERDAR.

Dug-out, *sb.* Add:
2. (Earlier U.S. examples.) Also *attrib.*
1855 in J. A. Thomson *80 Yrs'. Remin.* (1904) I. 171, I live in a dug-out tent [at Balaklava], which is pretty warm, with a capital fire-place made out of potato tins! 1860 BRIGHAM YOUNG *Jrnl. Discourses* VIII. 293/1 When you have built splendid habitations, be as willing to leave them as you would to leave a dug-out. 1873 J. H. BEADLE *Undevel. West* xxxi. 685 The unhappy traveler, if compelled to seek shelter in winter, will find it in a Swedish 'dug-out'.

b. *spec.* applied to the roofed shelters used in trench warfare. Also *attrib.*
1904 *Westm. Gaz.* 7 Dec. 7/1 The following telegram from General Sakharoff..has been received at St. Petersburg:.. Our troops, thanks to their dug-outs, warm clothing, and plentiful food, do not suffer from the cold. 1914 D. O. BARNETT *Lett.* (1915) 19 A dug-out in the reserve trenches. 1914–16 E. A. MACKINTOSH *War the Liberator* (1918) 23 And I shall see no more The gallant friendly faces Framed in my dug-out door. 1919 G. K. ROSE *2/4th Oxf. & Bucks Lt. Infty.* 26 Desire Trench..was a shallow disconnected trough upholstered in mud and possessing four or five unfinished dug-out shafts. *Ibid.* 63 A bombed dug-out is the last word in 'unhealthiness'.

3. A channel made by digging. *U.S.*
1854 BARTLETT *Pers. Narr. Explor. Texas*, etc. II. xlv. 535 A little further we came to a 'dug out'—that is, a passage cut or dug across a bar.

4. A superannuated officer in temporary service. Also *transf.* applied to any person of out-of-date appearance or ideas. orig. *Army slang.*
1912 *Blackw. Mag.* June 805/2 From his turn-out, he was probably a prehistoric 'dug-out', a 'was-bird' of 'weird' early Victorian ideas. 1916 H. G. WELLS *Mr. Britling* II. ii. 232 A new untried man—usually a dug-out in an advanced state of decay—is stuck into the job. 1918 W. J. LOCKE *Rough Road* vii. 75 The Colonel was immensely proud of them and sang their praises to any fellow dug-out who would listen to him. 1920 *Q. Rev.* July 139 Retired officers and civilians, the much sneered at 'Dug-outs'..saved the situation.

Du·g-up, *a.* [See DIG *v.* 14.] Exhumed; unearthed.
1897 *Daily News* 23 Jan. 5/5 When the loud laughter which greeted this dug-up relic had died away. 1900 *Westm. Gaz.* 20 Jan. 4/2 The facts which this 'dug-up' material discloses are all to Thackeray's credit. 1921 GALSWORTHY *To Let* I. xii, Thought her father had some 'ripping' pictures and some rather 'dug-up'.

Du·g-way. *U.S.* [DUG *ppl. a.*] A road made by digging.
1718 *Lancaster Rec.* 183 Neer where the path now goes, to witt the parth [*sic*] called the dugway. 1819 E. DANA *Geogr. Sketches* 43 The spacious dug ways by the side of, and around the adjoining hills, gave them the facility of speedily gaining their fort. 1870 J. H. BEADLE *Life in Utah* 219 Descending to the valley by a dangerous 'dug-way', we forded Green River. 1873 — *Undevel. West* viii. 148 A narrow 'dug-way'..cut by cross ravines.

Duk-duk (du·kduk). [Native name.] A (member of a) secret society among the natives of Neu Pommern, Bismark Archipelago, which executes justice on the rest of the tribe and practises sorcery and mysterious rites.
1883 W. POWELL *Wand. Wild Country* 61 The Duk-duk ..may be spoken of as the administration of law, being judge, policeman, and hangman all in one. 1884 *Encycl. Brit.* XVII. 372/2 Justice is executed, and tabus, feasts, taxes, &c., arranged, by a mysterious disguised figure, the 'duk-duk'. 1896 tr. *Ratzel's Hist. Mankind* I. 133 The weak chiefs of Melanesia, in order not to be quite powerless, apply the mystic Duk-Duk system to their own purposes. 1908 *Athenæum* 11 Apr. 444/2 The Dukduk of Melanesia. 1929 ELIZ. A. WEBER (*title*) The Duk-Duks. Primitive and Historic Types of Citizenship.

Duke, *sb.* Add:
3. d. *The Duke's*: short for (*a*) the Duke of Cambridge's Own (Middlesex Regiment); (*b*) the Duke of Wellington's (West Riding Regiment).
1900 *Westm. Gaz.* 20 July 5/1 The force that was engaged ..was composed of the Duke of Cambridge's Own and the Irish and Belfast Yeomanry. The Dukes were 125 strong. 1925 E. FRASER & GIBBONS *Soldier & Sailor Words* s.v. *Nicknames*, *Duke's, The*, the Duke of Wellington's (West Riding Regiment).

Dukie (diū·ki). [-IE, -Y [6].] *The Dukies*, familiar name of the boys (soldiers' sons and orphans) of the Duke of York's Royal Military School. Also *sing.*
1906 *Daily Chron.* 27 Aug. 4/4 A big detachment of 'the Dukies'. 1908 *Ibid.* 23 Jan. 6/3 Enough to fire the imagination of the very dullest 'Dukie' in the school. 1927 *Daily Tel.* 28 June 7 The 'Dukies'..were given a farewell at the station.

Dulce, *sb.* **2.** *U.S.* (Earlier examples.)
1844 G. W. KENDALL *Santa Fé Exped.* II. i. 31 Among the higher order of Mexicans the dinner finishes with fruits, dulces or sweetmeats. 1858 TERESA VIELE *Following the Drum* 186 Then came the dessert, dulcies of candied cactus and melons.

Dulcin (dʊ·lsin). *Chem.* [f. L. *dulcis* + -IN [1].] A very sweet crystalline substance, paraphenetol carbamide, used as a sugar substitute in diabetes.
1895 *Buck's Handbk. Med. Sci.* Suppl. 844 Dulcin. $C_6H_4.OC_2H_5.NH_2.NH.CO$. 1912 *Jrnl. Chem. Soc.* CII. II. 104 Detection and Identification of 'Saccharin' and 'Dulcin' in Beverages, Foods, Drugs, Cosmetics, etc.

Dulcitone (dʊ·lsitoᵘn). [f. L. *dulcis* sweet + TONE *sb.*] (See quot. 1927.)
1909 *Chambers's Jrnl.* Mar. 206/2 The dulcitone is a musical instrument on the lines of the pianoforte. 1923 R. NOBLE *Shakespeare's Use of Song* 17 The dulcitone, which is portable and is capable of being performed upon by an actor or actress of moderate musical accomplishment. 1927 *Grove's Dict. Mus.* (ed. 3), *Dulcitone*, a keyboard instrument somewhat similar in effect to the Celesta, in which graduated steel tuning-forks are struck by hammers. The compass is usually five octaves from bass A.

Dull, *a.* Add:
7. c. Defining a grade of tobacco leaf.
1849 *Rep. U.S. Comm. Patents, Agric.* (1850) 322 There ought, if the quality of the crop will permit, to be four sorts of tobacco, 'Yellow', 'Bright', 'Dull', and 'Second'.

8. b. dull emitter valve *Wireless* (see quot. 1924).
1923 *Exper. Wireless* Nov. 97 The development of the dull emitter has been a more closely-guarded secret than any other manufacturing process connected with radio engineering. 1924 *Harmsworth's Wireless Encycl.* II. 761/1 A dull emitter valve is a valve used in wireless work that has been specially designed and made to operate on a minimum voltage for the heating of the filament.

Dulosis (diulōᵘ·sis). *Ent.* [mod.L., a. Gr. δούλωσις, f. δουλοῦν to enslave, f. δοῦλος slave.] The practice of enslaving colonies or individuals of colonies of other ants, exhibited by certain genera of ants. Hence **Dulo·tic** *a.*, slave-holding.
1904 *Biol. Bulletin* May 257 Dahl is mistaken in supposing that L[eptogenys] bismarckensis is a dulotic ant. 1908 *Westm. Gaz.* 21 Jan. 2/1 The custom of 'dulosis'..exists in its pure and unadulterated form in two—the *Formica sanguinea* and the *Polyergus rufescens.* 1925 A. D. IMMS *Textbk. Entom.* 571 From temporary social parasitism the next step is exhibited by dulosis or slavery. 1928 W. M. WHEELER *Social Insects* 289 Yet another Myrmicine genus, Harpagoxenus..must be included among the dulotic, or slave-making ants.

Duma (dū·mă). Also (in Fr. form) douma. [Russ. дума *duma.*] In Russia, an elective municipal council. *The Duma*, the elective legislative council of state, Gosoudarstvennaia Duma, established in 1905 by a ukase of Czar Nicholas II and abolished in 1917. Hence **Du·maist,** a member of a duma or the Duma.
1886 *Encycl. Brit.* XXI. 70/2 Since 1870 the municipalities have had institutions like those of the zemstvos...The executive is in the hands of an elective mayor and an *uprava* which consists of several members elected by the *duma.* 1905 *Daily Chron.* 16 Feb. 5/1 The Douma will consist of delegates of the district councils, each sending five. 1905 *Times* 19 Aug. 7/2 The *Duma* is established for the preliminary study and discussion of legislative propositions which, according to the fundamental laws, will be submitted to the supreme autocratic authority by the Council of the Empire. 1905 *Outlook* 12 Aug. 892 (Cent. Dict. Suppl.) [The plan] was received with derision by the zemstvoists and dumaists at their Congress in July. 1906 *Daily Chron.* 2 Aug. 1/7 M. Herzenstein, a wealthy Dumaist,..has been shot dead..in Finland.

Dumb, *a.* Add: **7. b.** Foolish, stupid. (Chiefly of persons.) *U.S. colloq.*
Possibly after G. *dumm* or Du. *dom.*
1823 J. F. COOPER *Pilot* II. iii. 39 'They're a dumb race', said the cockswain,..'now, there was our sargeant, who ought to know something' [etc.]. 1825 — *L. Lincoln* ix. (1859) 133 Do you think the Boston people so dumb as not to know the law? 1846–52 MRS. WHITCHER *Widow Bedott P.* xxix. 369 How could you be so dumb, Peggy? 1892 *Harper's Mag.* Feb. 441/1 My, but men are dumb. A woman would have caught on long ago. *c* 1904 H. R. MARTIN *Tillie* 14 And he used to be dummer yet than what he is now. *Ibid.* 58, I got religion a plenty, but I don't hold to no sich dumm thoughts!

8. *Dumb ague* (earlier U.S. example). Also *dumb fever.*
1832 [R. BAIRD] *Valley Mississippi* viii. (1834) 85 These maladies are intermitting and remitting billious fevers—.. which have received the names of 'ague', 'dumb fever' and 'chill and fever'. 1837 *Knickerbocker Mag.* X. 414 To this cause [*sc.* violent exertion] he attributed the 'dumb ague', that laid him up when the first snow commenced.

B. 3. A dumbfish. *U.S.*
1825 J. F. COOPER *L. Lincoln* xiv. (1859) 199 A real dumb is not to be despised, especially when served up in a wrapper, and between two coarser fish, to preserve the steam.

4. [Short for *DUMBHEAD] A foolish or stupid person. *U.S. colloq.*
1928 *Daily Express* 4 Dec. 10/3 A 'dumb' is a stupid person, and if he's dumb enough he'll probably drive you 'cuckoo' or crazy.

C. b. dumb-play = DUMB SHOW 2.
1920 *Chambers's Jrnl.* 374/1 A violent dumb-play of smoothing the hair and arranging the coats of pyjamas. 1921 *Glasgow Herald* 10 Feb. 6 Certain M.P.'s did take the part of actors and were duly taken and their dumb-play shown on the screen.

Dumb-bell, *sb.* Add: **2. b.** (After *DUMB *a.* 7 b.) A stupid person, a blockhead. *U.S. slang.*

Dumbfish. *U.S. local.* [Of doubtful origin; also called *dumbed fish* in 18th c. (1762–). Cf. the later DUNFISH.] Codfish cured by the process of dunning (see DUN *v.*[1] 1 b).
1762 *Boston Even. Post* 11 Jan. Advt. (Th.) Choice Dumb Fish and Connecticut Pork. 1772–6 J. ANDREWS *Lett.* 337 Finally determined to admit Dumb fish and rice to be brought up as articles of provision. 1792 [see DUMB *a.* 8]. 1809 W. IRVING *Knickerb.* III. vi. (1820) 198 They have been called *dumb-fish* ever since. 1835 PAULDING *John Bull & Br. Jon.* xix. 80 These Down Easters are excellent good boatmen, as well as great takers of..a certain fish called dumbfish.

Du·mbhead. *U.S. slang.* [f. *DUMB *a.* 7 b + HEAD *sb.*, after G. *dummkopf*, Du. *domkop.*] A blockhead.
1921 MULFORD *Bar-20 Three* xi. 125 Have I got to do *all* the thinking for this crowd of dumbheads?

Dumb-iron (dʊ·məiəɹn). [See DUMB *a.* 8.] A carriage-spring composed of two half-elliptic springs joined at the ends. In the chassis of a motor car, each of the pair of curved forward ends of the frame-side members to which one end of each front spring is fixed.
1907 *Westm. Gaz.* 19 Dec. 4/2 The distinctive frame is of pressed steel, slightly narrowed from the dashboard, tapered, and turned down in front so as to form its own dumb-irons, thus making the connexion for the forward ends of the springs. 1920 *London Mag.* June 334/1 The sharp dumb-irons dug into the bank, and the car reared itself on end. 1928 *Daily Tel.* 16 Oct. 17 Saukey's tool box..which fills the usual blank space between the dumb irons, curved to follow the line of the dumb iron.

Dumb-waiter. **2.** *U.S.* (Examples.)
1856 COZZENS *Sparrowgr. Papers* vi. 68 We have put a dumb waiter in our house. 1876 J. S. INGRAM *Centennial Exposition* iii. 69 The general kitchen whence the food is distributed throughout the upper stories by means of dumb waiters. 1890 *Harper's Mag.* Apr. 744/1 She clutched the door of the dumb-waiter, which stood ajar.

Dum casta (dʊm kæ·stă). *Law.* [Short for *dum sola et casta vixerit* as long as she shall live alone and chaste.] A clause in a deed of separation in which it is provided that the husband's allowance to the wife shall be conditional upon her continuing to lead a chaste life.
1905 *Law Jrnl. Rep., Prob.* LXXIV. 3/1 The main subject to be regarded is the temptation to which the wife may be exposed; and in this respect it appears a material precaution that the limitation *dum casta* should be inserted. 1906 *Westm. Gaz.* 29 Mar. 7/2 The question..was whether it was a condition of the allowance of £100 that a *dum casta* or chastity clause should be inserted.

Dumdum (dʊ·mdʊm). [f. *Dum Dum*, name of a town and military station near Calcutta, the seat of the arsenal for the Indian army.] In full *dumdum bullet*: A metal-cased bullet with a soft core uncovered at the point, which expands on impact, first produced at the Dum Dum arsenal. (The name was first used of the Mark IV. Lee-Metford bullet.) Hence **Du·mdum** *v. trans.*, to convert into a dumdum bullet.
1897 *Westm. Gaz.* 14 Dec. 7/3 The piper hero, Findlater, was wounded in the ankle with a Dum Dum bullet. 1898 *Ibid.* 25 Mar. 3/1 That the War Office authorities are not responsible directly for Dum-dumming the Lee-Metford bullets. 1898 *Times* 28 June 13/6 The Dum Dum bullet, now..superseded. 1899 *Westm. Gaz.* 25 Nov. 6/1 Any man can 'Dum-Dum' his own cartridges in a very few minutes by merely filing the nickel envelope off the nose of the bullet. 1906 *Ibid.* 27 Mar. 9/2 It is impossible that the Kaiser can know or approve of the adoption of the dum-dum.

Dumminess. Add:
2. A condition of defective intelligence in the horse, following acute inflammation of the brain (see *DUMMY *sb.* 3 b). *U.S.*
1903 *U.S. Dept. Agric., Rep. Diseases Horse* 11 In dumminess, or immobility, the hanging position of the head and the stupid expression are rather characteristic.

Dummy, *sb.* Add:
2. b. *Bridge.* In full *dummy hand*: The hand of the dealer's partner; in auction bridge, the partner's hand of the player who makes the first call in the accepted declaration; also, the holder of this hand after his or her cards are laid down.
1894 'BOAZ' *Bridge* 5 After the first player has played a card, the dealer plays his partner's hand, which, like Dummy, is placed face upwards on the table. 1901 R. F. FOSTER *Bridge* 17 After laying down his cards..the dummy takes no further part in the play, and is not allowed to make any remarks or suggestions. 1901 W. DALTON *Bridge Abridged* 23 With very bad cards in your own hand, there is a slightly increased possibility of an exceptional hand in your Dummy. *Ibid.*, After the first card is led the Dummy hand is exposed. 1905 in W. Dalton '*Saturday*' *Bridge* (1906) 14 The duty of playing the cards from that hand, which is called Dummy, ..shall devolve upon the dealer. 1906 *Ibid.* 21 The player who cuts the lowest card deals first, and has the Dummy, throughout the first rubber. 1910 *Ibid.* (ed. 9) 230 (Auction bridge) Z leads to the first trick, and A's hand is exposed on the table, and A becomes the dummy for that deal.

3. b. A horse whose senses are dulled, after acute inflammation of the brain. *U.S.*
1901 *Jrnl. Exper. Med.* VI. 66 The duration of the disease varies from a few hours to a week, the average being perhaps 72 hours. Horses which recover are said to become 'dummies'—animals with a permanent cerebral lesion and defective intelligence.

5. Also *dummy engine* (see quot. 1864 in Dict.).
1889 *Kansas Times & Star* 10 Oct., Mike Ross sued the East Fifth Street railway for damages, a dummy engine causing a runaway, seriously injuring his horse.

e. *In dummy* = 'in dummy form' (see quot. 1893 in Dict., sense 5).
1898 A. J. BALFOUR in *Parl. Deb.* Ser. IV. LIX. 768 The Report has been presented in dummy, and is now being proceeded with.

f. In full *dummy teat*: An indiarubber teat put into a baby's mouth to soothe it.
1903 *Science Siftings* 22 Aug. 269/1, I never saw the child but it had a dummy in its mouth. 1906 *Chemist & Druggist* LXIX. 648/2 There has been little progress in the shape of the 'dummy teat'. 1921 *Sunday at Home* Feb. 257/2 She smiled and crowed and dropped her dummy.

g. *Dentistry.* (See quot.)
1902 *Encycl. Brit.* XXVII. 418/2 When artificial crowns are supported not by natural tooth-roots but by soldering them to abutments, they are termed dummies.

h. Rugby Football. *To give* or *sell the dummy*: to feign to pass the ball so as to deceive one's opponent.
1907 'OLD INTERNATIONAL' *Rugby Guide* 27 Feinting, 'giving a dummy', or pretending to pass is a useful adjunct

to the numerous other qualifications of a good centre. *a* 1924 J. E. Raphael *Mod. Rugby Football* (1918) 125 A little judicious 'dummy' giving might be very effective in securing an opening. 1920 *Times* 8 Nov. 6/3 R. C. Pickles 'sold the dummy' really cleverly to score again for Gloucestershire.

7. dummy-head, applied to torpedoes which are provided with a thin copper head and filled with water for target practice; so **dummy-headed** *a.*

1906 *Daily Chron.* 8 Sept. 5/3 A large proportion of the dummy-headed torpedoes struck her hull. 1923 *Daily Mail* 22 June 5 The 'planes released six dummy-head aerial torpedoes.

Dump, *sb.*4 Add: **1. b.** The practice of dumping goods (see *Dump *v.*1 2 c); also, the goods dumped.

1884 *Congress. Rec.* 1 May 3663/1 It is this dump that we want to stop; it is protection against this dump that the protective system seeks to accomplish. 1908 *Westm. Gaz.* 8 Apr. 9/2 The present 'dump', which has assumed such amazing proportions in the eyes of the alarmists.

c. A collection of provisions, ammunition of war, apparatus, or general equipment forming a depôt; hence, a place used for a depôt of this kind; more widely, any material or articles deposited for use later, or the place of such deposit.

1915 *Daily Mail* 30 Dec. 4/6 The Dump! Just a pile of old clothes, battered helmets, decrepit boots, kit bags, shirts, socks, boots—all the little personal properties of soldiers. 1916 Buchan *Battle of Somme* 55 That same day we..took a 'dump' of German stores. 1918 E. M. Roberts *Flying Fighter* 61 One night about six o'clock I received orders to report at an engineers' dump known as Hyde Park Corner. 1922 *Blackw. Mag.* June 767/2 She had gone home to collect dumps. 1925 in E. F. Norton *Fight for Everest, 1924* 353 A dump for stores..would seem to be essential half-way between Camps II and III. *Ibid.* 361 To provide dumps of reserve cylinders on the mountain. *Ibid.* 643 To make a dump of some ropes and pegs at the foot of the ice slopes.

4. *dump-boat, -car, -cart, -heap, -hook, -ore, -wagon.*

1889 *Kansas Times & Star* 18 Nov., The big city *dump-boat that sank to the river bed at the foot of Grand avenue has been refloated. 1924 Haskin *Amer. Govt.* (revised ed.) 425 The trains of *dump cars used in carrying away this vast amount of earth. 1890 *Harper's Mag.* Sept. 557/1 Presently Adoniram clattered out of the yard in his two-wheeled *dump cart. 1903 *Daily Chron.* 2 Mar. 6/1 There is not a mile of public road fit to run a dump-cart over. 1881 A. A. Hayes *New Colorado* vii. 106 The hills having been quite stripped of trees and covered with gray '*dump-heaps'. 1905 *Terms Forestry & Logging* 36 **Dump hook*, a levered chain grab hook attached to the evener to which a team is hitched in loading logs. A movement of the lever releases the hook from the logging chain without stopping the team. 1877 Raymond *Mines & Mining* 308 Those months in which custom-ore and *dump-ore were run. 1874 — *6th Rep. Mines* 405 The ore is brought from the mine to a *dump-pile. 1884 [in Dict.]. 1868 *Rep. U.S. Commissioner Agric.* (1869) 357 Wheelbarrows, carts, or *dump-wagons will be necessary.

Dump, *v.*1 Add: **2. c.** To import, or throw on the market, in large quantities and at low prices; *spec.* to offer for sale (surplus goods), esp. abroad, at less than the ordinary trade prices. Also *absol.* Often in *ppl. adjs.* and *vbl. sb.*

1884 *Congress. Rec.* 1 May 3663/1 The surplus dumped from foreign pauper markets is the great bane of our industries. 1903 *Westm. Gaz.* 8 Sept. 2/2 Those who base their case on (*a*) decreasing exports, and (*b*) the dumped state of iron and steel. 1903 *Daily Chron.* 25 Sept. 3/7 'Dumping' is in our eyes a great sin. 1903 Earl of Rosebery in *Westm. Gaz.* 26 Nov. 2/2 Canada..has in the last two years dumped down in Great Britain nearly as much iron as all the dumping countries put together. 1904 Grafton *Treasury* Oct. 8/1 The..capitalists desire this, as it..enables them to dump their surplus production on foreign countries. 1908 *Westm. Gaz.* 30 Mar. 10/2 As for the dumping scare,..there is nothing in it. *Ibid.* 4 May 2/2 You appear to think that he dumps for the sake of dumping. 1916 *Economist* 4 Mar. 458/1 We hear of large stocks of cheap manufactures that will be dumped upon us. 1928 *Britain's Industr. Future* (*Lib. Ind. Inq.*) i. v. 50 They showed that the practice of dumping demoralises the world-market to the ultimate disadvantage of all concerned.

d. To make a dump of; to deposit in or as in a dump (see *Dump *sb.*4 1 c).

1919 A. P. Herbert *Secret Battle* viii. 154 We call them the Old Duds, and we believed that..they were dumped upon us by way of penalty. *Ibid.* 165 Philpott..accused him hotly of dumping the rations carelessly anywhere. 1919 G. K. Rose *2/4th Oxf. & Bucks Lt. Infty.* 35 A pile of logs dumped in the wrong place. 1925 E. F. Norton *Fight for Everest, 1924* 52 There to prepare the camp and dump tents and stores for it. *Ibid.* 77 Odell and Lhakpa Tsering should collect the dumped stores. *Ibid.* 137, I dumped the oxygen apparatus and immediately went off along the probable route Mallory and Irvine had taken.

Dump (dɒmp), *v.*3 [Cf. *dump* (dial.) to blunt.] *trans.* To shorten (the toe) by rasping the front wall of a horse's hoof. Hence **Du·mping** *vbl. sb.*

1908 *Animal Management* (War Office) 226 'Stumping up' or 'dumping' the toe...Dumping is very occasionally necessary with flat feet in order to get the nails high enough up the wall to give a secure hold.

Dumper. Add: **c.** One who, or a country or community which, dumps goods (*Dump *v.*1 2 c).

1903 *Daily Chron.* 24 Oct. 5/2 They would not have supported the fiscal policy of Mr. Chamberlain, for they were 'dumpers', who sold shoes to the poor below cost-price. *Ibid.* 21 Nov. 6/3 How long do you think that the dumpers will be content with only dumping unfinished goods? 1919 *Economist* 11 Oct. 568/2 Germany as a 'Dumper'.

Dumpoked (dɒ·mpōukt), *a.* *Anglo-Ind.* [ad. Hind. *dampukht*, f. Pers. *dem* breath, hot + *pukhte* cooked.] Applied to a baked dish of meat boned and stuffed. Hence **Du·mpoke**, a baked dish of this kind, especially a boned and stuffed chicken or duck.

1696 Ovington *Voy. Suratt* 397 A dumpoked Fowl. 1698 Fryer *Acc. E. India & P.* 93 These Eat highly of all Flesh Dumpoked, which is Baked with Spice in Butter. *Ibid.* 404 Baked Meat they call Dumpoke which is dressed with sweet Herbs and Butter, with whose Gravy they swallow Rice dry Boiled. 1879 Mrs. A. E. James *Ind. Househ. Managem.* 89 *Dumpoke* is a boned chicken, its form preserved, only all the bones extracted; it is stuffed with a rice forcemeat, and you cut it through in slices.

Dumpty, *sb.* Add: = next, c.

1923 *Sunday at Home* Apr. 385/1 The girl..was sitting on an enormous dumpty close to her father's big chair.

Dumpy, *sb.* Add: **c.** A low stuffed seat or cushion; a humpty.

d. A short umbrella.

1927 *Glasgow Herald* 11 Mar. 10 The dumpy reduced its dimensions severely, while now and then an umbrella-stick has been carried by men.

Dun, *a.* Add: **1. b.** Of a horse: Of a light yellow or sand colour.

1841 Barham *Ingol. Leg.* Ser. ii. *Smuggler's Leap* (1905) 318 Smuggler Bill, he looks behind, And he sees a Dun horse come swift as the wind, And his nostrils smoke and his eyes they blaze Like a couple of lamps on a yellow post-chaise!

Dun, *v.*1 **1. b.** *U.S.* (Earlier example.)

1818 *Massachusetts Spy* 23 Dec., When cod-fish is dunned, it ought not to be boiled at all.

Dundreary (dɒndrīə·ri). [Name of Lord *Dundreary*, a character in T. Taylor's comedy *Our American Cousin* (produced in New York in 1858).] In allusive attrib. uses, esp. *Dundreary whiskers*, long side whiskers worn without a beard. Also *absol.* in *pl.*

1862 *Englishwoman's Dom. Mag.* Aug. 183 Bodger..came to understand (in a Dundreary manner) a little more about Bradshaw. 1864 *Chambers's Jrnl.* 17 Sept. 595/2 It was only a summer scarf, of the sort that is called Dundreary. 1867 'Pips' *Lyrics & Lays* 141 Full proud is he, I ween, Of his Dundreary whiskers. 1882 'F. Anstey' *Vice Versa* xvii, Bushy black whiskers, more like the antiquated 'Dundreary' type than modern fashion permits. 1894 C. G. Harper *Revolted Woman* ii. 39 This fashion was the 'Piccadilly-weeper' variety of adornment, known at this day—chiefly owing to Sothern's impersonation of a contemporary lisping fop—as the 'Dundreary'. 1906 Galsworthy *Man of Property* i. i, His cheeks, thinned by two parallel folds, and a long clean-shaven upper lip, were framed within Dundreary whiskers. 1929 C. H. Smith *Bridge of Life* ii. 38 The older men wore beards, Dundrearys or side whiskers; the middle-aged, mustaches.

Dunducketty, dunduckity (dɒndɒ·kĕti, -iti), *a.* [app. f. Dun *a.* + Duck *sb.*1] In phr. *dunducketty mud-colour*: of a dull, drab colour.

1818 Lady Morgan *Autobiog.* (1859) 29 She..makes parties for us of all sorts of colours—pink, blue, gray, and a colour I have supplied her with (not from the rainbow), dunducketty mud colour. [1847 Halliwell, *Dunduckitymur*, an indescribable colour, but rather dull. *Suffolk.*] 1897 Mary Kingsley *W. Africa* 420 It is better than all white, or dunduckety mud-colour paint.

Dunfish. *U.S. local.* (Earlier examples.)

1818 *Massachusetts Spy* 23 Dec., Dun-fish. When cod-fish is dunned, it ought not to be boiled at all. 1819 J. Hopkinson *Let. to D. Webster* 19 Apr., I have heard you Boston folks brag that the codfish we get are not the thing; but you have a certain animal called a 'Dun fish' much superior. 1841 Whittier *St. John* 26 They had loaded his shallop With dun-fish and ball.

Dunker1. (Earlier example.)

1751 G. Croghan *Jrnl.* 61 A Dunkar from the Colony of Virginia..requested Liberty of the Six Nation Chiefs to make [a settlement] on the River Yogh-yo-gaine.

Dunlop (dɒ·nlɒp). The name of a parish in Ayrshire, Scotland, designating an unskimmed-milk cheese originally made there.

1834 Youatt *Cattle* (L.U.K.) 137 The Dunlop sweet-milk cheese has a peculiarly mild and rich taste. 1878 *Chambers's Encycl.* II. 786 Dunlop Cheese..is now manufactured in the dairy districts of Scotland generally. 1905 W. H. Simmonds *Pract. Grocer* III. 79 The Dunlop is a rather rich cheese, similar in general quality to Derbyshire or Gouda, but larger in size.

Dunnage, *sb.* ¶. (Earlier U.S. example.)

1834 *Knickerbocker Mag.* III. 81 The crew were disposed in various groups about the deck..; some with their clothes-bags beside them, turning it to account in overhauling their dunnage.

Dunnage, *v.* (Earlier U.S. example.)

1849 in G. A. Thompson *Handbk. Pacific & Cal.* 17 See also that the bottom of the canoe is properly 'dunnaged', that is, laid with long strips of wood to keep your luggage or bed from getting wet.

Dunno (dɒno, dŭnōu·), also **dunna(w)**, etc., colloq. ff. *don't know.*

1842 G. P. R. Pulman *Sketches, Equestrianship* 34 There I vlounder'd like a zow, An' ramm'l'd out I dun-no how. 1848 Lowell *Biglow Papers* Ser. i. vii, I dunno as it's ushle to print Poscrips. 1867 P. Kennedy *Banks Boro* xxiii, Now indeed I *dunna* what to do. 1888 Burnett *Stable Boy* ii, I dun naw wat ta du!

Dunt, *sb.*1 Add: **1. d.** (See quot. 1924.)

1924 *Jrnl. Roy. Aeronautical Soc.* Mar. 198 Special temperature conditions are brought about by vertical currents of air. The vertical currents usually consist of a hot stream of air rising or a cold stream falling. In flying into such a current the airship will experience a 'dunt'. The 'dunt' received will depend on two actions—one the dynamic action of the current, and the other the sudden change in lift due to change in temperature. 1928 E. F. Spanner *Gentlemen Prefer Aeroplanes* vi. 43 Moderate clouds—unavoidable temperature 'dunts'—and so on. *Ibid.* x. 71 When the vessel meets 'temperature "dunts"' and other atmospheric irregularities.

Duodenectomy (diū:odĕne·ktŏmi). *Surg.* [f. Duodenum + Gr. ἐκτομή cutting out.] Partial or total excision of the duodenum.

1908 *Practitioner* Sept. 454 Codivilla is the only surgeon, who, operating on the pancreas, has performed a duodenectomy.

Duodeno- (diū̆odī·no), comb. form of Duodenum, = relating to the duodenum and another part denoted by the following element, as *duodeno-jejunal* adj., pertaining to the duodenum and the jejunum.

1886 *Buck's Handbk. Med. Sci.* II. 537 Duodeno-cholecystostomy. 1887 *Ibid.* V. 606 The little pocket which lies behind this (duodeno-jejunal recess). 1901 Dorland *Med. Dict.* (ed. 2), *Duodenocholecystostomy*.., the operation of forming a communication between the gall-bladder and the duodenum. 1906 *Practitioner* Dec. 761 The duodeno-jejunal junction. 1907 *Ibid.* Nov. 680 A large hernia into the duodeno-jejunal pouch. 1908 *Ibid.* Nov. 712 The duodeno-pyloric constriction.

Duplet (diū·plėt). Delete † *Obs.* and add:

1922 F. W. Aston *Isotopes* 96 The atoms may be coupled together by one or more 'duplets' held in common by the complete sheaths of the atoms.

Duplex, *a.* Add:

1. c. Designating the type of human eyes that has a layer of pigment over the iris, which causes the iris to be black, brown, or green.

1911 A. D. Darbishire *Breeding & Mendelian Discov.* 276 Duplex eyes are those which have a layer of brown pigment in front of the iris. 1925 C. C. Hurst *Exper. Genetics* 273 The eyes in which two kinds of pigments are present; the one, yellow-brown in colour, deposited on the outer or anterior surface of the iris; the other, blue-black in colour, deposited on the inner or posterior surface of the iris. Such eyes I propose to call *duplex*. *Ibid.*, To the duplex type belong the various shades of eyes with both anterior and posterior pigments.

Duplex querela (diū·pleks kwĕrī·lă). [Law Latin, lit. twofold complaint.] (See quot. 1763.)

1763 Burn *Eccl. Law* I. 113 When the bishop doth without good cause refuse..to admit and institute a clerk to the church to which he is presented, the clerk may have his remedy..by the way of a duplex querela; that is to say, if a bishop doth refuse, then before the archbishop in his court of appeals; if an archbishop doth refuse, then before the delegates. And if the bishop doth admit the clerk, and then doth refuse to institute him; the clerk..being refused or unjustly delayed, and complaining to the judge of appeals thereof; the judge is wont to write to the bishop in form of law, and this writing they call a duplex querela. This duplex querela is to contain a monition to the bishop, or to his vicar general..that within a certain time..he admit the party complaining; and also a citation, whereby the bishop may be cited to appear..to shew cause why..the right of institution is not devolved to the superior judge. 1768 Blackstone *Comm.* III. xvi. 247. 1931 S. Royle Shore in *Church Times* 20 Feb. 223/1 The Clerk might have commenced proceedings by *Duplex querela* in the Arches Court, but for weighty reasons this was turned down.

Dupondius (diupɒ·ndiŭs). *Roman Antiq.* [L.] A bronze or brass coin of the value of two asses.

1601 Holland *Pliny* xxxiii. iii. II. 462 Like as the weight in brasse of two pound, they named Dipondius [*sic*]. 1853 Humphreys *Coin Collector's Man.* II. 378 The second bronze, which was called the dupondius, or double as, was ..exactly half the sestertius. 1921 *Brit. Museum Return* 81 A dupondius of Nero.

Dupuytren (düpüi·tren). The name of Baron Guillaume *Dupuytren* (1777–1835), French surgeon, used in the genitive to designate certain conditions observed or appliances invented by him. **Dupuytren's contraction,** a contracted condition of the fingers and palm due to inflammatory hyperplasia of their tissues; **Dupuytren's fracture,** fracture of the fibula just above the malleolus; **Dupuytren's paste** (see quot. 1886); **Dupuytren's splint,** a splint to prevent eversion in Pott's fracture.

1879 in *Brit. Med. Jrnl.* (1880) 19 June 919/1 Dupuytren's Fracture of the Fibula. 1883 *T. Holmes & Hulke's Syst. Surg.* I. 1093 Dupuytren's splint is often used, and is good when properly applied. 1886 *Buck's Handbk. Med. Sci.* II. 7 Dupuytren's paste was made of from six to ten parts by weight of arsenic, and one hundred of calomel. *Ibid.* III. 159 Dupuytren's Finger-contraction.—This deformity is dependent chiefly upon chronic disease and contraction of the palmar aponeurosis. 1887 *Ibid.* V. 197 Dupuytren's Method. A method of amputating at the shoulder-joint. 1898 *Treves' Syst. Surg.* I. 870 Dupuytren's splint..a 'long splint' in miniature, should be padded with increasing thickness from the knee down to the ankle. 1908 *Practitioner* Feb. 279 Treatment of Dupuytren's contraction by thiosinamine.

Duralumin (diuræ·liumin), **Duraluminium** (diuræliumi·niŏm). [Trade name, f. L. *dūrus* hard + Alumin(ium).] A light aluminium alloy, comparable in strength and hardness to soft steel, used esp. in the manufacture of aircraft.

1910 *Blackw. Mag.* July 4 In the Barrow [air] ship another aluminium alloy called duralumin is employed. 1917 A. G. Clark *Motor Car Engin.* II. 53 A metal which has recently come into prominence on account of remarkable properties that it possesses is duralumin, which is manufactured by Vickers, Limited...This material combines lightness with great strength, has an excellent elongation, and

may be forged. 1920 T. G. Andrews & Benson *Aeroplane Design* 15 Duralumin is composed of aluminium, copper manganese, and magnesium. 1921 *Glasgow Herald* 8 July 8 The aerohydrotor parts will be made chiefly of duraluminium wire stayed. 1925 E. F. Norton *Fight for Everest, 1924* 131 The duralumin carriers. 1928 C. F. S. Gamble *N. Sea Air Station* Introd. 10 This hull was twelve-sided, the framework being built of the alloy duralumin.

Durance. **3.** (Later U.S. attrib. example.)

1744 Jas. MacSparran *Diary* 18 Oct. (1899) 21 My wife put her red Durance Petticoat in the Frame and Betty and she is at work thereon.

Duranta (diuræ·ntă). Also **durantia.** [mod. L., f. name of C. *Durante* (d. 1590), an Italian herbalist.] A shrub of the verbenaceous genus so named, found in tropical America.

1829 Loudon *Encycl. Plants* 522. 1927 *Chambers's Jrnl.* 278/3 A twig of Durantia on which were some yellow berries.

Duration. Add:

3. *Army slang.* The term of service for which the soldiers who joined the British army in 1914 were recruited, from the term of enlistment 'for four years or the duration of the war'. *For the duration*: until the end of the war; hence, for an unconscionably long time.

1916 *Punch* 12 July 51 'I've got a lot of contracts to finish.' 'How long will they take?' 'Oh, about three years—or the duration of the War.' 1925 Fraser & Gibbons *Soldier & Sailor Words, Duration, for the*, a phrase often used colloquially to express weariness and impatience...Men, for instance, whose relief was long overdue might be heard complaining 'Are we going to stop here for the duration?' 1930 *Times Lit. Suppl.* 17 Apr., Nothing so prosaic as 'doing one's bit' would have kept an Italian heart up 'for the duration'.

Durative (diūə·rătiv), *a.* (*sb.*). [f. Dure *v.* + -ative.] Continuing; not completed; *Gram.* applied to a form which marks action as going on. Also as *sb.* Hence **Durati·vity.**

1889 W. R. Morfill *Russ. Gram.* 40 Durative verbs on taking a prefix become perfective. 1904 J. H. Moulton in *Expositor* Nov. 360 In οἱ ἀπολλύμενοι, strongly durative though the verb is, we see its perfectivity in the fact that the goal is ideally reached. *Ibid.* 361 'Ἀγωνίζεσθαι is only used in the durative present, but καταγωνίσασθαι..is a good perfective. 1906 *Ibid.* Dec. 441 Other futural presents..have no lack of durativity about them. 1912 Wright *Compar. Gram. Gk. Lang.* § 424 (2) An action is said to be cursive, durative or imperfective when it denotes continuous action without any reference to its beginning or end, as in English *I am striking* compared with *I strike*.

Durchmusterung (duɹχ³mu·stəruŋ). *Astr.* [G., f. *durch* thoroughly + *musterung* muster.] The name given to certain extensive catalogues of stars containing their magnitudes and approximate positions. The oldest of these, from which the name was adopted into general use, was Argelander's Durchmusterung of the Northern Heavens.

1892 Proctor & Ranyard *Astron.* 724 According to Littrow's analysis of Argelander's magnitudes, there are in the region included in the *Durchmusterung* survey 1,001 stars between the 5th and 6th magnitudes. 1902 Newcomb *Stars* 46.

Duress, *v.* (Modern U.S. example.)

1870 *Congress. Globe* 5 July 5197/3, I never heard of a man who was duressed into an office to hold and exercise the functions of it during a period of four years by duress.

Durham (dɒ·rəm). Name of a county in the north of England, designating a breed of shorthorn cattle originating there, now generally called shorthorns.

1834 Youatt *Cattle* (L.U.K.) 229 The circumstance which brought the improved short-horns into most extensive notice was the production of the 'Durham Ox'. 1875 *Encycl. Brit.* I. 303/1 These [*sc.* long-horned cattle], however,..have now been entirely superseded by the shorthorn or Durham breed. 1902 *Ibid.* XXV. 190/2 The Shorthorn..is still termed the Durham breed in most parts of the world except the land of its birth.

Durn, U.S. variant of *Darn, *Dern.

1888 *Portland Transcript* (Farmer), I'll bet I could make as good-lookin' a burst as any o' these,—an' mebbe a durn sight better. 1898 H. S. Canfield *Maid of Frontier* 176 It was as much as a man's life was worth to say 'durn' out loud. 1902 Harben *Abner Daniel* 198, I axed 'em what they tuck me fer—did I look like a durn fool?

Durwan (dūɹwā·n). *Anglo-Ind.* Also 8 **derwan, dirwan, door-van,** 9 **darwan.** [Hind. (a. Pers.) *darwān.*] A porter or door-keeper.

1773 E. Ives *Voy. to India* 50 Derwan. These are properly porters, who sit at the gate to receive messages, &c. 1781 *Bengal Gaz.* 14 Apr. (Yule) A Door-van is well known to be the alarm of the House. 1784 in W. S. Seton-Karr *Sel. fr. Calcutta Gaz.* (1864) I. 12 A most extraordinary and horrid murder was committed upon the Dirwan of Thomas Martin, Esq. 1874 *Calcutta Rev.* LIX. 207 In the entrance passage..is a raised floor with one or two open cells in which the *darwāns* (or door keepers) sit, lie and sleep. 1926 *Blackw. Mag.* June 726/2 His durwan..refused to awaken a sleeping man.

Durzee (dɒ̄·ɹzi). *Anglo-Ind.* Also **derzie, -y, dirge, dirzie, dir(d)jee, dirgee, durjee, dhurzie, dhirzie.** [Hind. (a. Pers.) *darzī*, *darjī* (Pers. *darz* sewing, hem).] A native tailor.

1812 Maria Graham *Jrnl. Resid. India* 30 (Yule) The dirdjees, or taylors, in Bombay, are Hindoos of respectable caste. *a* 1847 Mrs. Sherwood *Life* (1854) 300 Dirges, and Dobes. 1879 Mrs. A. E. James *Ind. Househ. Managem.* 41 The things for minor furnishings..you can, with the aid of the native *durzees* (tailors), soon make up into coverings, curtains, and blinds. 1884 D. Aubrey *Lett. fr. Bombay* 204 Their parents have no wish to make 'dirzees' or tailors of them. 1894 Mrs. Dyan *Man's Keeping* i, Manufacturing, with the incompetent aid of her durzee, a gown for the ball. 1907 Mrs. B. M. Croker *Company's Servant* xix, The Bazaar's chief 'Dirzee' was engaged in overhauling his cricketing flannels. 1920 Harker *Montagu Wycherly* ii. xiii. 117 He asked for the very Dhirzee who sat working on the verandah. 1922 *Blackw. Mag.* Feb. 183/2 The regimental dhurzee.

Dusky, *a.* Add: **1.** (U.S. example.)

1855 *Knickerbocker Mag.* XLVI. 222 In the marshes the black or dusky duck, willet, black-headed gull, and dapper-rail or mud-hen rear their young.

5. As *sb.* Dusky colour.

1886 Newton in *Encycl. Brit.* XXI. 846/1 Beneath it [*sc.* the shrike] is nearly white or..barred with dusky.

Dust, *sb.*1 Add: **6.** (Later U.S. example.)

1873 Joaquin Miller *Unwritten Hist.* iii. (1876) 56 'Why don't you pay me, and be off?' '..Haven't got the dust. Can't liquidate.'

8. b. *dust-laying, -raising*; *dust-proof* adj.

1899 *Westm. Gaz.* 18 July 2/1 Water-carts sprayed the road with grateful *dust-laying streams. 1902 *Ibid.* 11 Sept. 7/3 Oil is the latest dust-laying agent. 1882 *Leisure Hour* 414/2 The fittings are massive and *dust-proof. 1898 J. Southward *Mod. Printing* I. iv. 26 One of the most useful recent innovations is to make the racks 'dust-proof'. 1903 Beatrice Harraden *Kath. Frensham* 272 A long, straggling, *dust-raising line of about 50 conveyances. 1908 *Westm. Gaz.* 22 Dec. 4/2 On the mere off-chance of minimising in an infinitesimal degree their dust-raising propensities.

e. dust-blister, a blister in a rubber tyre caused by the entry of dust into a cut; **dust-cover,** bookseller's name for the paper cover or jacket in which a new book is usually issued and which often contains an illustration to the work or information about it or its author, designed to attract buyers; **dust-flow,** a stream or land-slide of volcanic ashes saturated with water; **dust-jacket** = **dust-cover*; **dust-pan** (earlier U.S. example); **dust-sheet,** a sheet for covering furniture or the like to keep off dust; **dust-up,** disturbance, uproar; a brisk bout in rowing, boxing, etc. (cf. 5 b); **dust-veil,** a veil worn to keep off the dust; **dust-wind,** a wind bringing dust-storms; **dust-wrapper** = **dust-cover*.

1898 *Cycling* 67 *Dust blisters occur from the entry of dust into a neglected cut. 1921 *Sat. Westm. Gaz.* 17 Sept. 14/1 The *dust-cover..suggests that the book will be of service not only in schools but also as 'an entertainment for home-reading'. 1913 *Times Lit. Suppl.* 22 Feb. 126/1 The lurid dust cover. 1925 Aldous Huxley *Those Barren Leaves*, Concl. i. (1927) 346 'This thoughtful young writer..' would be quoted from the reviewers on the dust-cover of her next book. 1904 E. O. Harvey in *Science* 1 July 24 (Cent. D. Suppl.) Clouds of steam rising from the crater, accompanied from time to time by *dust-flows. 1928 *S. J. Looker's Book-lover's Catal.* Jan. 5 The Life and Letters of Emily Dickinson ..in *dust jacket. 1928 *Observer* 24 June 8 The book is sent out by Constable's in a particularly attractive dust-jacket. 1841 A. Bache *Fire-Screen* 68 She brought in a *dust-pan and brush. 1904 *B'ham Inst. Mag.* Nov. 43 A splendid house ..wholly superseding the clothes-horse and *dust-sheet structure. 1907 *Westm. Gaz.* 17 Aug. 4/3 The big town-house was depressing in its shroud of dust-sheets. 1897 *Daily News* 6 Mar. 7/3 They turned at the Lasher, and after a *dust-up for about a minute in Iffley Reach did a nice piece of paddling back to the raft. 1897 Hinde *Congo Arabs* 152 An American nigger said..they ain't had such a dust-up in this hole since creation. 1928 *Sunday Express* 3 June 20/1 Maxie Rosenbloom..and George West have had some rare 'dust-ups'. 1901 *Geog. Jrnl.* (R.G.S.) XVIII. 91 Observations, outline and relief of the region,..temperature in the interior, *dust-winds, temperatures of wells and springs [etc.].

Dust, *v.*1 **10.** (Earlier U.S. example.)

1873 Joaquin Miller *Unwritten Hist.* xxxii. (1876) 407 Some chipmenks dusted down the road and across the track.

Dust-brand. (Earlier U.S. example.)

1849 *Rep. U.S. Comm. Patents, Agric.* (1850) 393 The sooty powder on the flowering parts of corn-plants, called smut, chimney-sweepers, and dust-brand, is formed of the spores of another uredo.

Duster. Add:

5. *Naval.* An ensign. *The red duster*, the red ensign flown in the Mercantile Marine. *slang.*

1904 *Eastern Morn. News* 27 June, A regatta..of the duster boats for the championship of the Humber. 1918 *Punch* 27 Mar. 206/1 She's dipped her dingy duster in the spray of all the seas.

Dustering (dɒ·stəriŋ). [f. Duster + -ing 1.] Material such as is used for dusters.

1910 H. G. Wells *Mr. Polly* ii. 33 He was now hanging long strips of grey silesia and chilly-coloured linen dustering.

Dusty, *a.* Add:

1. b. Of wine: Containing sediment.

1886 J. Noble *Handbk. Cape Gd. Hope* 275 Notwithstanding the large amount of alcohol which they [*sc.* Cape wines] contain, they are not clear and always somewhat 'dusty'.

5. dusty miller, also (*c*) a species of moth. *U.S.*

1909 Gene Stratton-Porter *Girl of Limberlost* xii. 243 Small insects of night gathered, and at last a little dusty miller, but nothing came of any size.

Dutch, *sb.*2 *slang.* [Abbreviation of Duchess.] A costermonger's wife; often *old Dutch.*

a 1889 Mitchell *Jimmy Johnson's Holiday* (Barrère & Leland) He made a vow he'd never row With his old Dutch again. 1889 Barrère & Leland *Dict. Slang* s.v., (Popular), a *Dutch*, a wife. 1893 A. Chevalier *My Old Dutch*, There ain't a lady livin' in the land As I'd 'swop' for my dear old Dutch! 1901 R. C. Lehmann *Anni Fugaces* 128, I detected a coster..with some one to act as his Dutch.

Dutch, *a.* Add:

3. b. Dutch doll, a jointed wooden doll; **Dutch garden** (see quots. 1872, 1899); so **Dutch gardening; Dutch pink,** a yellow lake pigment; also *slang*, blood; **Dutch roll,** a roll in skating, executed by gliding with the feet parallel and pressing on the alternate edges of each foot.

1797 Lady Anne Barnard in *South Africa* (ed. W. H. Wilkins, 1901) 57 What they [*sc.* Dutch ladies] want most is shoulders and manners. I know now what is meant by a '*Dutch doll'. 1824 Scott *Redgauntlet* Let. iii, All thy motions, like those of a great Dutch doll, depending on the pressure of certain springs. 1926 W. Deeping *Sorrell & Son* vii, Her head was as neat as the head of a Dutch doll. *a* 1772 T. Whately in A. F. Sieveking *Praise of Gardens* (1899) 197 To get too, as far as can be, the advantage of natural prospects, the artificial mounts of the flat *Dutch gardens should here be introduced. 1872 Shee *My Garden* 584 The chief peculiarities of a Dutch garden may be said to consist in its being seen at one glance;..in the utmost symmetry being observed in all its parts..; in its trees being clipped sometimes into curious shapes and figures..; in its having long serpentine or straight walks..; [etc.]. 1899 S. R. Hole *Our Gardens* 277, I asked an old gardener whether he could tell me anything about Dutch Gardens, and he made answer, 'They be bits o' beds with edgings o' box, and gravel walks, and four sloping banks forming a square outside, and they be pratty toys for children, and very snug for varmint'. 1902 Triggs *Formal Gardens* plate 58 Holland House, Kensington. The Dutch Garden. 1896 *Dutch gardening [see Dutch *a.* 5]. 1853 'C. Bede' *Verdant Green* ii. iv, That'll take the bark from your nozzle, and distil the *Dutch pink for you, won't it? 1858 Simmonds *Dict. Trade, Dutch-pink*, a painter's yellow colour, obtained from *Reseda luteola*. 1881 Jas. Bell *Anal. Foods* i. 22 The leaves were slightly coloured with Dutch pink to impart a bloom. 1893 *Durham Univ. Jrnl.* X. 103 Others have in spite of honourable endeavour been obliged to content themselves with mediocre achievement and *Dutch roll.

4. *Dutch lunch, party, supper, treat*, one at which each person contributes his or her own share. *U.S.*

1895 *Funk's Stand. Dict., Dutch treat* (Slang, U.S.), an entertainment in which each pays for himself. 1904 *Columbus Post-Dispatch* 21 Aug., Dancing was enjoyed by all as was the Dutch lunch which was partaken of at intervals during the evening. 1904 *Dallas Morning News* 10 Sept. 6 Depriving themselves of money they need to buy plug-cut and Dutch suppers with. 1927 *Observer* 8 May 13/3 Dutch parties are rather more elaborate, in that while the hostess provides the dance floor, music, table, service, and cutlery, her friends bring along the drinks and the viands, raiding their family cellars and larders.

B. 3. a. Latterly *U.S.*

1845 in C. Cist *Cincinnati Misc.* 198 Shall we infer from the above that the Indians and Germans have one common origin? If so, the Dutch are the real natives.

c. *To beat the Dutch* (modern U.S. example).

1906 Mary E. Wilkins-Freeman *By Light of Soul* 277 'Well, you women do beat the Dutch', said her brother.

Dutchman. Add: **1.** (Later U.S. examples.)

1807 *Balance* (Hudson, N.Y.) 10 Mar. 75, I think they call him German, though he is not a Dutchman. 1841 W. G. Simms *Scout* xxi. (1882) 234 The dull, drowsy, beef-eyed Dutchmen..the Hessian boobies. 1872 Eggleston *Hoosier Schoolm.* vii. 74 The robbery at 'the Dutchman's' (as the only German in the whole region was called).

b. The name given in the Far East to any man of northern Europe; also used by British sailors in this sense or to include any foreign sailorman.

1892 Stevenson & Osbourne *Wrecker* (ed. 2) 194 *note*, In sea-lingo (Pacific) *Dutchman* includes all Teutons and folk from the basin of the Baltic; *Scattermouch*, all Latins and Levantines. 1907 *Daily Chron.* 21 Dec. 6/6 'Only fifty years ago', he remarked, 'we gave the generic name of Dutchman to all the representatives of Western civilisation in the Far East'. 1925 Fraser & Gibbons *Soldier & Sailor Words, Dutchman*, the British seafarers' name for sailormen in general, natives of Northern Europe: Dutchmen proper, Danes, Swedes, Russians, Germans. Finns are excepted. 1928 *Daily Express* 20 July 2/7 British sailors refer to foreigners employed on vessels as 'Dutchmen'.

4. Also in other applications. (See quots.) *U.S.*

1905 *Terms Forestry & Logging* 36 *Dutchman*, a short stick placed transversely between the outer logs of a load to divert the load toward the middle and so keep any logs from falling off. 1909 *Cent. Dict.* Suppl., *Dutchman*, a layer of suet fastened with skewers into a roast of lean beef or mutton.

Dutchy (dɒ·tʃi), *sb.* [f. Dutch + -y 6.] A familiar or contemptuous name for a Dutchman or German.

1864 J. T. Trowbridge *Cudjo's Cave* iv. 39 See here, Dutchy! ye haint been foolin us, have ye? 1890 H. C. Bunner *Short Sixes* (1891) 83 'Say, Dutchy!' he roared. The German stood aghast. 1901 *Daily Chron.* 12 Aug. 6/1 The captain of the ship insulted him by saying, 'Here's another Dutchy who wants to be an American'.

Duty. **7.** Add: **duty-man** = *duty-sergeant*; **duty-paid** *a.*, on which duty is paid; **duty-pay,** a bonus paid for work done outside the ordinary routine-work.

1906 *Westm. Gaz.* 15 Sept. 4/1 Prepared to join the suggested training battalion for a further period of six months, as non-commissioned officers and '*Duty-men'. 1930 Snowden *Sp. in Ho. Comm.* 15 July, The extent to which *duty-paid stocks of lace are being re-exported with the intention of re-importing them duty free. 1880 C. Marvin *Public Offices* (ed. 2) 67 Most of these extras..had something handsome attached to them in the way of gratification money or '*duty-pay'.

Duvetyn (diū·vėtīn, dɒ·vtin). Also **-tine, -tyne.** [f. F. *duvet* down.] The trade name of a

soft material of worsted and silk with a fine downy nap, used for women's coats and dresses.

1913 *Trade Marks Jrnl.* 10 Sept. 1434 Duvetyn..Silk Piece Goods. 1921 *Glasgow Herald* 19 Feb. 5 The upper part, which had a high calyx collar buttoned at the left side, was of dark duvetine. 1922 *Tatler* 18 Oct. Advts. p. w, This Hat can also be copied in Duvetyn, in all shades, at 2½ Gns. *Ibid.* 130/2 A new fabric known by the name of crocodile duvetyn. 1923 G. G. Denny *Fabrics & how to know them* 41 The so-called silk duvetyn usually has a fine mercerized cotton warp and spun silk filling. 1924 *Scribner's Mag.* Aug. 200/2 She was wearing a new dark blue duvetyne suit.

Duxeen (dɒ·ksīn). [Patented by the *Dux* Chemical Solutions Co., Bromley-by-Bow, London. See *-een 1.] A paper used as a book covering, made in imitation of bookbinders' cloth.

1920 *Trade Marks Jrnl.* 24 Nov. 2215. 1921 *Caxton Mag.* XXIII. 127. 1927 *Longmans' Class. Catal. Educ. Works* 11.

Dvornik (dvǭ·ɹnik). [Russ. двóрникъ, f. дворъ court, house.] A house-porter.

1903 *Westm. Gaz.* 17 Jan. 10/1 The duties of the dvorniks, a sort of assistant police. 1923 *Blackw. Mag.* Feb. 203/2 The 'dvornik' had been with the family for years.

Dwarf, *sb.* Add:

2. b. The name (G. *zwerg*) given by Dr. Hertzsprung in 1905 to the red stars belonging to the class of smaller stars of greater density as distinguished from the larger diffuse stars or 'giants'.

1921 *Discovery* Sept. 236/1 After this stage is reached and the star attains a certain density, it falls off rapidly in temperature, and becomes a cooling dwarf.

Dwarfism (dwǭ·ɹfiz'm). [f. Dwarf *sb.* + -ism.] The condition or character of being a dwarf or undersized.

1919 *Nature* 3 Nov. 304/1 One of these forms of dwarfism is known to medical men as achondroplasia, because the growth of cartilage is particularly affected.

Dwelling, *vbl. sb.* **4.** Add: *dwelling-room* (local U.S.).

1837 *Knickerbocker Mag.* X. 432 The coffin was placed in the centre of the largest apartment, in country phrase, the 'dwelling-room'.

Dwerg (dwǭɹg). Pseudo-archaic form of Dwarf *sb.*, simulating OE. *dweorg*.

1892 Kipling *Lett. Trav.* (1920) 76 A puff of the warm night wind among the flares set the whole line off again in a crazy dance of dwergs. 1896 — *Seven Seas, Neolithic Age* ii, And the troll and gnome and dwerg, and the Gods of Cliff and Berg Were about me and beneath me and above.

Dwindling, *sb.* Add: *U.S. local.* (See quot.)

1911 *Essex Inst. Hist. Coll.* XLVII. 14 The small creeks into which the marsh lots slope are called 'dwindlings'.

Dyad. **3.** Add: **dyad axis** *Cryst.*, an axis of binary symmetry. 1909 *Cent. Dict.* Suppl.

Dyadic, *sb.* Add: **2.** *Math.* **a.** A sum of dyads. **b.** 'The science of reckoning with a system of numerals in which the ratio of values of successive places is two' (Cent. Dict. 1889).

1884 [see Prefactor].

Dyak (dəi·æk). Also **Daya(c)k, Dayakker.** [Native name.] A member of one of the aboriginal tribes of Borneo in the Malay archipelago; the language of this tribe.

1836 *Penny Cycl.* V. 189/2 The mines are only wrought by the Dayacks. 1876 *Encycl. Brit.* IV. 58/1 The Dyaks, Dayaks, or Dayakkers are..broken into numerous tribes. 1880 *Ibid.* V. 818/1 Among the other languages which have been reduced to writing and grammatically analysed are the Balinese..the Dayak, and the Macassarese. 1893 A. Russan & Boyle *Orchid Seekers* xii. 134 Squatting on their 'tail-mats' to the Collector's right hand..were the Dyaks; on the left lay the Malays. *Ibid.* xiii. 151 On every side rose cries of terror in Malay and Dyak. 1927 *Weekly Times* 29 Sept. 434/2 Dyaks of Borneo.

Dyarchal, etc.: see *Diarchal, etc.

Dye, *v.* **1. c.** (For *dyed in the wool* in fig. use, see Wool *sb.*2 1 g.)

2. b. Delete † before *into* and add:

1891 Clo. Graves *Field of Tares* 62, I saw a lovely flush rise in her cheeks and dye her sweet white throat into crimson.

Dying, *vbl. sb.* **1. b.** Add: *Dying-back*: see Die *v.*1 14.

1921 *Times Lit. Suppl.* 8 Sept. 574/3 Its silviculture [*sc.* of Sal] is very difficult, more especially the question of the dying-back of its seedlings.

Dynamic *a.* and *sb.* Add: **A. 8.** *Dynamic equator* (see quot.).

1883 *Encycl. Brit.* XVI. 165/1 The line connecting all the points where the magnetic intensity is least is called the dynamic equator.

Dynamite, *sb.* Add: **1. b.** *transf.* In the name of a plant used as a fish poison in New Guinea.

1928 F. E. Williams *Orokaiva Magic* 211 The vine *Anisi* (which belongs to the genus *Derris*), known as 'New Guinea Dynamite' because it is used for killing or stunning fish.

Dynamite, *v.* Add: Also *fig.*

1903 *Westm. Gaz.* 30 July 3/1 Mr. Chamberlain..tried to dynamite discussion by declaring that the rejection of the Bill would mean the infringement of treaty obligation.

Dynamo. Add: **b.** Also *fig.*

1904 Dowden *Browning* 327 Any stream of moral electricity worked from a dynamo of the will.

Dynamophone (dəinæ·mofōun, di-). [f. Dynamo- + *-phone* of *telephone*.] A form of dynamometer in which the twist of a revolving shaft is measured by means of mounted telephones.

1902 *Science* 29 Aug. 339 (Cent. Dict. Suppl.).

Dynamotor (dəi·nămōutǫɹ). [f. Dyna- + Motor.] A combined electrical motor and generator with one field magnet and two armatures, or with one armature upon which are two windings, one which receives current as a motor and the other which generates current as a dynamo.

1908 *Westm. Gaz.* 30 Mar. 5/2 For starting purposes supplementary power is obtained by means of an electric machine, best described as a dynamotor. 1910 *Hawkins' Electr. Dict.* 133/2 Another form of dynamotor is called the continuous alternating transformer.

Dys-. Add: **Dy·schronous** *a.*, not agreeing as to time, separate as to time. **Dyspho·tic** *a.* *Phytogeography*, badly lighted, having little light; also, occurring or growing where there is little light, as at certain depths of water.

1902 *Science* 4 July 5 (Cent. D. Suppl.) [Consciousness] can make synchronous impressions *dyschronous in their effects, and dyschronous impressions synchronous. 1903 tr. *A. F. W. Schimper's Plant Geog.* 811 The flora of the *dysphotic region [in fresh-water lakes] is composed almost exclusively of microphytes, Diatomaceae in particular.

Dysgenic (disdʒe·nik), *a.* [f. Dys- + *-genic.] Exerting a detrimental effect on the race, *spec.* opposed to *eugenic*.

1915 W. R. Inge *Outspoken Ess.* (1921) 41 Its [*sc.* frequent war's] dysgenic effect, by eliminating the strongest and healthiest of the population, while leaving the weaklings at home to be the fathers of the next generation. 1922 *Edin. Rev.* July 46 Encouraging the dysgenic art of fortune-hunting. 1926 *Spectator* 1 May 804/2 Conceptive control has been an almost entirely harmful or dysgenic factor. 1928 G. B. Shaw *Intell. Woman's Guide Socialism* xxxviii. 150 Division of society into classes, with the resultant dysgenic restrictions on marriage.

Dytiscus (dəiti·skŏs, di-). [mod.L.: see Dytiscid.] A beetle of the genus of water-beetles so named. Also *attrib.*

1902 Cornish *Naturalist Thames* 26 The great carnivorous water-beetle, the dytiscus..will rise by night from the surface of the Thames. *Ibid.*, A dytiscus beetle.

E

E. III. Add: E.D.D. = English Dialect Dictionary. E.D.S. = English Dialect Society. E.E.T.S. = Early English Text Society. E.H.P. = (*a*) effective horse power; (*b*) electrical horse power. E.I. = East India. E.I.C. = East India(n) Company. E.M.F., e.m.f. = electromotive force. E.P.D. = excess profits duty.

1884 *Nature* 16 Oct. 595/1 In a circuit of uniform temperature, if metallic, the sum of the E.M.F. is zero by the second law of thermodynamics. 1891 Schick *Lydgate's Temple of Glas* Introd. p. xii, Dr. Erdmann's forthcoming edition of the *Story of Thebes*, for the E.E.T.S. 1898 J. J. M. Innes *Sir H. Lawrence* 103 The E.I. Board. 1905 E. B. Titchener *Exper. Psych.* II. 120 The practical unit of E.M.F...is the volt. 1905 N. H. Schneider *Study Electr.* 76 The e.m.f. is raised. 1919 J. A. Fleming *Thermionic Valve* vii. 225 The same plate battery may be used to provide E.M.F. in the plate circuits of all the valves. 1920 *Conquest* June 360/1 An average of about £50 [in cost] per E.H.P. at power house must be allowed. 1921 *Times* 4 Feb. 11/4 The End of E.P.D.

Each, *a.* **1. d.** Add: *Each way*: a racing term denoting that a horse has been backed for a win and a place. Also *attrib.*

1869 *Cassell's Mag.* IV. 170/2 One pound on Blue Gown each way. 1897 E. H. Cooper *Mr. Blake* vi, I'll just go and put a little bit on Highborn for this race..; only fifty pounds or so each way. 1925 G. Frankau *Masterson* xvi, Cynthia had decided to 'risk a couple of Bradburys each way'. 1929 *Star* 21 Aug. 16/2, I should think he may be a good each-way bet. 1930 *Daily Mail* 17 June 14/2 Sun Glory..has a useful each-way chance.

Eagle, *sb.* Add: **1.** Also in U.S. allusive use.

1861–2 *Trans. Ill. Agric. Soc.* (1865) V. 203 The clang of mighty forges, fashioning out the sinews of war, to guard the eagle of liberty. 1904 *N. Y. Even. Post* 14 Sept. 1 Mr. Fassett was toying with those dear but haggard phrases.. and generally making the eagle scream.

c. (Later example.)

1849 *Congress. Globe* 16 Feb., App. 114 This gentleman thought proper to denominate me the 'Eagle from Harper's Ferry'.

d. *Golf.* A score of two under bogey or par.

1922 C. Leitch *Golf* xii. 202 Barnes..holed his putt for a 3, so securing what is known in American golfing parlance as an 'eagle'. 1926 P. G. Wodehouse *Heart of a Goof* iv. 135 When he had got that 'eagle' on the third, he had looked bored. 1927 *Observer* 3 Apr. 29/1 [He] let loose a whole flock of 'birdies' and 'eagles' with which he captured the remainder of the holes. 1928 *Daily Express* 9 July 17/7 He accomplished an 'eagle' two for the 351 yards.

2. d. *U.S. Mil.* A device worn on the shoulder, indicating the rank of a colonel.

1865 Boudrye *Fifth N.Y. Cavalry* 184 Col. Hull..was killed. He was a gallant young officer, who had but recently borne the eagle.

e. = *eagle button* (see *10).

1812 *Niles' Weekly Reg.* II. 131/1 Cockades and eagles.. have been bought or made.

5. (Earlier U.S. examples.)

1786 in *Amer. Museum* (1789) II. 182 There shall be two gold coins; one..to be stamped with the impression of the American eagle, and to be called an eagle. 1789 *Gazette of U.S.* (N.Y.) 14 July (Th.) The Eagle containing 10 dollars of 50d. is worth 2 guineas, and rather more. 1809 Fessenden *Pills Poetical* 16 Were eagles, in embargo times, As plentiful as cents and dimes. 1816 *Niles' Weekly Reg.* IX. 370/2 The president tendered several eagles in gold to cover the costs. 1854 Mary J. Holmes *Tempest & Sunshine* xiii. 84 At the same time managing to slip an eagle into the hands of the honest clerk.

10. eagle button, a button bearing the device of an eagle.

1897 J. L. Allen *Choir Invis.* ii. (1918) 11 As he joined them, three other young men—Federalists—sauntered past, wearing black cockades, with an eagle button on the left side.

Eagle-hawk. Add:

2. An Australian bird of prey, *Aquila audax*.

1827 in Bischoff *Van Diemen's Land* (1832) 177 The eagle-hawk pouncing upon them for his prey. 1848 J. Gould *Birds of Australia* I. pl. 1 *Aquila Fucosa*..Wedge-tailed Eagle...Eagle Hawk, Colonists of New South Wales. 1886 Kendall *Poems* 159 The fierce-featured eagle-hawk flies—afraid as a dove is afraid. 1911 C. E. W. Bean *'Dreadnought' of Darling* xii. 105 A big black eagle-hawk.

Ear, *sb.*1 Add:

1. c. *To give one's ears* (earlier U.S. example). *To have one's ear(s) to the ground*: fig. to be on the alert regarding the trend of public opinion.

1796–1801 Fessenden *Orig. Poems* (1806) 128 Jove tells his peers He'd give his ears For such an hour as this is. 1920 *Nat. Rev.* Apr. 142 On the eve of a Presidential Election campaign, when practical politicians have their ears to the ground.

h. *To get* (a person) *up on his ears*: to make him indignant. So *to be on one's ear*. *To get up* or *go off on one's ear*: to rouse or bestir oneself. *U.S.*

1871 *Galveston News* 4 May (De Vere) They..said that I was lightning, when I got up on my ear. 1881 A. A. Hayes *New Colorado* v. 77 Wouldn't that just get some of his high-toned relations up on their ear? 1882 Howells *Mod. Instance* xxix. II. 144, 'I can cut your acquaintance fast enough,..if you're really on your ear!' 'I'm on my ear', said Ricker. 1889 Farmer *Americanisms* s.v., *To get up* or *go off on one's ear*, to bestir oneself; to rouse oneself to a great effort. 1907 M. C. Harris *Tents of Wickedness* iii. iv. 255, I only hope Paul Fairfax won't read it and get on his ear!

3. d. *To believe one's ears*: to credit what one hears. (Chiefly with negative expressed or implied.)

1886 H. Conway *Living or Dead* viii, He..blamed my partner, who could scarcely believe his ears.

15. a. *ear-hook, -scoop, -spoon, -spud.*

1929 *Encycl. Brit.* XIV. 202/2 The aortic tourniquet, the wire needle, the *ear hook, the sinus forceps. 1921 *Chambers's Jrnl.* 719/2 Some peculiarly shaped *ear-scoops. 1928 V. G. Childe *Most Anc. East* viii. 189 Tweezers..were combined with prickers and earscoops in regular reticules. *c* 1325 *Gloss. W. de Bibbesworth* in Wright *Voc.* 146 Cakenole *gloss* *herespon. 1878 *Sunday at Home* 6 July 424/2, I made several purchases, such as..ear spoons. 1921 *Chambers's Jrnl.* 763/2 Toilet implements as toothpick, tweezers, ear-spoon. 1928 *Daily Express* 16 June 3/7 Soak the entire external canal of the ear in warm olive oil... Repeat this process for a week. At the end of that period it will be found possible to remove the wax with a small ear-spoon. 1927 D. McKenzie *Dis. Throat, Nose, Ear* (ed. 2) 462 Removal of foreign body from the External Auditory Meatus by *Ear-spuds.

16. ear-bob *dial.* or *slang* (additional U.S. examples); **ear-bone,** a bone of the ear; **ear chair,** an armchair or easy chair having side pieces fixed near the top of the back; **ear-flap,** also, a flap of material covering the ear; hence **ear-flapped** *a.*; **ear-fly,** a gad-fly belonging to the genus *Chrysops*, esp. *C. vittatus*, which attacks the ears of horses; **ear-hoop** *U.S.*, an ear-ring; **ear-lappet,** also *U.S.* = **ear-tab*; **ear-lid,** delete † and add quots.; **ear-lock** (later examples); **ear-muff** *U.S.*, a protection for the ears in cold weather; **ear-phone,** (*a*) a device applied to the ears for listening in to wireless broadcasting; (*b*) a device to aid defective hearing; **ear-piece,** an apparatus or a part of one designed to be fitted to the ear, as of a telephone or a wireless receiver; **ear-plug,** (*a*) an ornament worn in the lobe of the ear; (*b*) a wad of cotton-wool, wax, or other substance placed in the ear to prevent an inrush of cold air or water; **ear-roll,** in a leather helmet, a roll of leather behind the ear; **ear-tab** *U.S.*, a tab, esp. one affixed to either side of a fur cap, to protect the ear in cold weather (= sense 13); **ear-tone,** a tone due to the constitution of the ear itself and not to the surrounding air waves.

1846 McKenney *Memoirs* I. vi. 121 Finger-rings..and *ear-bobs. 1863 Louisa M. Alcott *Hospital Sk.* 35 (Cent.) A pair o' ear-bobs. 1681 Grew *Musæum* i. v. i. 82 Part of the *Ear-Bone of a Whale. 1901 *Jrnl. R. Microsc. Soc.* 138 Ear-bones of Opossum. 1915 Shipley & MacBride *Zool.* (ed. 3) 644 The evolution of the ear-bones in Mammalia. 1930 *Times* 25 Mar. 31/7 'Derbyshire' and Grandfather '*Ear' Chairs. 1925 E. F. Norton *Fight for Everest, 1924* 51 *Ear-flapped caps. 1917 Sanderson & Peairs *School Entom.* 136 The Horse-flies. *Tabanidæ*...Some are called *Ear-flies, some Gad-flies. 1808 *Massachusetts Spy* 18 May (Th.) A large assortment of *Earhoops, of different sizes. 1845 S. Judd *Margaret* i. x. 64 Many wore ear-hoops of pinchbeck, large as a dollar. 1864 B. Taylor *H. Thurston* vi. 79 Woodbury recognised, projecting between *ear-lappets of fur, the curiously-planted nose..which belonged to the Rev. Mr. Waldo. 1871 Huxley *Anat. Vert.* 250 The tympanic membranes [of the crocodile] are exposed, but a cutaneous valve, or *earlid, lies above each, and can be shut down over it. 1930 *Times* 3 July 10/5 Nature..has not provided against assaults upon the hearing, and we have no 'ear-lid' by which we can shut out noise. 1854 J. R. Bartlett *Pers. Narr.* II. xxx. 230 Their *ear-locks either hang loose, or are braided in several strands. 1867 Lowell *Fitz Adam's Story* 431 His ear-locks gray, striped with a foxy brown, Were braided up to hide a desert crown. 1889 *Kansas Times & Star* 30 Nov., A young chap got off a train from the South today...Said they wore no flannels, gloves or *earmuffs down at Shreveport. 1893 *Funk's Stand. Dict., Ear-muff*, one of a pair of adjustable cloth coverings for the ear, usually secured in place by a spring, and worn as a protection against cold. 1904 'O. Henry' *Cabbages & Kings* x. 168 'Twas a fine Chinchilla overcoat, Arctic overshoes, fur cap and ear-muffs, with elegant fleece-lined gloves and woolen muffler. 1924 *Glasgow Herald* 24 Dec. 6 With a slight effort of the imagination we can forget *earphones and valves. 1927 *Radio Times* 22 Apr. 145/1 One might even suppose that you had never in your life put on a pair of earphones or listened to a loud speaker. 1928 J. F. Barnhill *Nose, Throat & Ear* 583 Ear phones..are the most serviceable present means of aiding impaired hearing. *a* 1843 *ear-pieces [in Dict.]. 1853 Markham *Skoda's Auscult.* 29 The ear-piece may be convex, concave, or plane, provided the disk forming it be truly perpendicular. completely. 1904 F. Lynde *Grafters* xxvii. 332 The train-master dropped the ear-piece of the telephone. 1909 *Practitioner* Dec. 862 The ear-pieces should fit closely and accurately into the external auditory meatus. 1910 *Hawkins' Electr. Dict.* 134/1 *Ear Piece*, that portion of a telephone receiver designed to rest against the ear of the listener. 1916 Boyd Cable *Action Front* 185 The earpiece receiver strapped tightly over one ear. 1928 Galsworthy *Swan Song* i. iv. 29 Soames..took up the earpieces of the wireless. 1904 *Nature* 9 June 138/1 Numerous copper ornaments.. such as pendants and *ear-plugs. 1904 *Daily Chron.* 5 Sept. 8/3 We should like..to see the use of ear-plugs spread, for many cases of ear trouble are brought into activity by the inrush of water during diving or swimming. 1909 *Westm. Gaz.* 23 Sept. 12/3 One of the regulations was that competitors had to wear *ear-rolls to facilitate their hearing when other riders wished to overtake them. 1922–3 *Halford Cycle Co. Ltd.* 110 Helmets. Leather, with Ear Rolls. 1855 *Knickerbocker Mag.* Feb. 199 In stable-yards, old-looking black boys, in cat-skin caps, with *ear-tabs to them. 1909 *N. Y. Even. Post* 28 Jan. (Th.) With the first really cold weather of the winter, there appeared on Broadway the vendors of ear-tabs. 1901 E. B. Titchener *Exper. Psychol.* I. 40 The first difference-tone..is an *ear-tone and not an air-tone.

Ear, *sb.*2 Add: **b.** *Ear of corn*, a head of Indian corn. Also *ellipt.* *U.S.*

1622 Mourt *Relat. Plant. Plymouth* 21 We..found a fine new Basket full of very faire corne of this yeare, with some 36. goodly eares of corne. 1697 S. Sewall *Diary* I. 462 He was Carting Ears of Corn from the uper Barn. 1831 Peck *Guide for Emigrants* ii. 156 The ears [of Virginia corn] are usually five or six feet, and often more from the ground. 1852 D. G. Mitchell *Dream Life* 199 Broad rustling leaves, and ears half glowing with crowded corn. 1880 Webster Suppl. s.v. *Head*, In the U.S., *ear* is used of Indian corn alone.

c. *Ear-corn*, Indian corn, maize; esp. corn on the cob. *U.S.*

1872 Eggleston *End of World* xx. 140 Put a bushel of ear-corn in the great wash-boiler.

Ear, *v.*2 Add: **b.** Of Indian corn. *U.S.*

1888 *Vermont Agric. Rep.* X. 48, I plant..with the hills far enough so that the stalks will fully ear. 1896 *Ibid.* XV. 71 Usually it [*sc.* the Red Cob] does not ear.

Ear, *v.*4 [f. Ear *sb.*1 8.] *trans.* To fit with ears.

1851 C. Cist *Cincinnati* 181 [The staves] are then..eared and handled.

Earlet. Add: **2. d.** = Tragus, esp. when largely developed as in some bats.

1837 *Penny Cycl.* VII. 25/2 The ears are large, insulated and lateral, with an internal earlet. 1845 *Encycl. Metrop.* XXV. 1072/1 Ears large, the tragus or earlet always existing. 1904 *Speaker* 24 Dec. 315/2 The earlet, a curious development of the tragus in insectivorous bats.

Early, *a.* Add:

7. Special collocations: as, **early-closer,** one whose place of business is closed one afternoon in the week; **early closing,** orig. designating a movement for the reduction of the daily hours of labour in wholesale and retail trades; now, the system by which business premises are closed for the day at the end of the morning on a particular day of the week; also, the closing of public houses earlier at night; also *attrib.* or *adj.*; **early door,** a door at a theatre which is opened at a specified time before the ordinary door at an enhanced price; also *attrib.*; **early Victorian** *a.*, belonging to or characteristic of the early years of Queen Victoria's reign, its literature, fashions, etc.; also as *sb.*; often derogatory.

1906 *Daily Chron.* 28 July 7/6 Thus giving *early-closers and Saturday-afternooners a chance. 1847 *Howitt's Jrnl.* 248/2 The *early closing movement. 1849 *Hogg's Instructor* III. 24/2 The Metropolitan Early Closing Society. 1851 *Household Words* 1 Nov. 126/2 That early-closing movement which has fastened the portals of all those magnificent palaces of linen-drapery. 1852 *Illustr. London News* 17 Jan. 50/3 Early-closing Movement in the Iron Trade. 1856 *Ibid.* 27 Dec. 652/4 Early Closing Hosiery Establishment. 1881 *Household Words* 12 Nov. 53/2 That Saturday 'early closing' ..must be a vast boon to shop-people. 1888 *Boy's Own Paper* Christmas Number 34/1 Wednesday was our early-closing day. 1902 *Encycl. Brit.* XXXII. 685/2 Scottish Early Closing of Public-houses Act. 1901 *Daily Chron.* 6 June 7/2 London playgoers are familiar with the iniquitous '*early-door' system, under which grasping managers trade on the fears of their nervous patrons. 1883 *Engl. Illustr. Mag.* Nov. 89/2 The late Georgian or *early Victorian age. 1896 'H. S. Merriman' in *Lady's Realm* Dec. 129/1, I was a youth—in the mahogany age—early Victorian, you know. 1896 F. Harrison (*title*) Early Victorian Literature. 1906 *Fortn. Rev.* Nov. 880 We invite the humour of the gods if we look down on the early Victorians. 1908 *Westm. Gaz.* 31 Oct. 15/3 The bonnets..were positively early-Victorian in size, and quite early-Victorian in the dainty pale silk frillings which framed most becomingly the face and the hair.

b. In collocations used *attrib.*

1897 Mary Kingsley *W. Africa* 65 The pottery has a very early-man look about it. 1900 *Westm. Gaz.* 9 Jan. 2/1 The shock of that early-dawn disaster. 1906 *Daily Chron.* 2 June 9/1 The abolition of early-season events for two-year-olds.

Earmark. 1909 *Westm. Gas.* 23 Apr. 8/2 Much of the early-morning work is performed entirely alone.

Ear-minded, *a. Psychol.* [f. EAR *sb.*1 + MINDED *a.*] Having a marked tendency to carry on mental operations most readily by auditory images; thinking in sounds.

Hence **Ear-mindedness**.

Ear-ringed, *a.* [f. EAR-RING + -ED *2.*] Wearing ear-rings.

Earth, *sb.*1 Add: **4.** *To run to earth*: to chase (the quarry) to its earth; *fig.* to capture or find (something sought for) after a long search. Similarly *to go to earth*, said of the quarry, *etc.*

b. *Electr.* (Substantive *def.* and *quot.*). Connexion of a wire conductor with the earth, either accidental with the result of leading a current to dangerous difference of potential or intentional (as for the purpose of providing a return path for a telegraph current, etc.).

9. *c.* (Quots. illustrating wider use, chiefly in interrogative and negative contexts.)

B. II. earth almond *U.S.* (see CHUFA); earth glacier, a glacier of land-waste and snow occurring in the spring; earth-life, terrestrial existence; Earth-Mother (*tr.* Ger. *erdmutter*), in mythology and folklore, a spirit or being taken as a symbol of the earth; also = MOTHER EARTH 1; earth-pig, *transl.* Du. *aardvarken* or AARD-VARK; earth-portrait *Electr.*, an earthed return circuit, as distinguished from a metallic return; also *attrib.*; earth-shrinkage *Geol.*, the reduction of the earth's diameter and volume by contraction; earth-squirrel = GROUND-SQUIRREL 1 *b*; earth-tilting (see quot.); earth-wire *Electr.*, wire carried from a conductor into the earth, esp.

to prevent contact from the leakage of current from one wire into another; hence earth-wire *v.*, -wired *ppl. a.*, -wiring *vbl. sb.*

Ease, *v.* Add: **I.** Also *U.S.* with *up*.

4. *c.* (*U.S.* example.)

5. To move, lift, or shift *down* gradually or gently, *or* into a person's pocket.

7. To relax or cease one's efforts, *pres.* in rowing; also with *up*. To ease of = to stop rowing (Cf. sense 4 *c*).

Easterliness (*i*stəlines), *sb.* [f. EASTERLY *a.* + -NESS] Easterly quality or condition.

Easterly, *a.*2 Add: **2. b.** *sb.* An easterly wind.

10. Ease off. **b.** Freq. *in easy money*. orig. *U.S.*

Eastern, *a.* Add: **1. b.** Situated in, of pertaining to the, (north-) eastern parts of the United States.

Easternism (*i*stə̄ni'm). [f. EASTERN + -ISM.] Eastern characteristics, practices, etc.; tendency to make Eastern in character.

Easternmost, *a.* (Earlier *U.S.* example.)

East-side. *U.S.* [f. EAST D. 1 *b* + SIDE *sb.*] That section of New York City which lies on the east side of Manhattan (to the east of Fifth Avenue). Also *attrib.* Hence **East-sider**, one who lives on the East-side.

Eastward. Add: **A.** *b. Comb.* east-wardness.

Eastwardly, *a.* Add: b. also, facing the east.

East wind. Add: **b.** In the game of mah jong the name given to the player who, by drawing a disk or by a throw of the dice, is entitled to choice of seats.

Easy, *a.* Add: **B.** (Recent U.S. examples.)

9. *Stand easy*: an order in military use allowing a greater freedom of posture than 'stand at ease'.

16. Eat off. **b.** To clear off (a crop) by feeding it with cattle: said also of the cattle. Also *absol.*

17. Eat out. In phrases with *heart*.

18. Eat up. *fig.* To traverse (a distance, ground) rapidly.

Eater. Add: A fruit that eats well, or is intended to be eaten uncooked (cf. COOKER 2).

Eatery (*i*təri). *U.S.* [f. EAT *v.* + -ERY *2 b.*] An eating-house.

Eating, *vbl. sb.* Add: **1. c.** Also *pl.* = Food.

Eau. Add: *l. Messenger* VII. 286/2 Good eatings there, light-bread, fried bacon and eggs, waffles, butter-cakes—coffee and buttermilk.

Eaves. **3.** Add: *eave(s)-run*, *-shoot*, *-spout*, *-trough* (designating various forms of gutter or spout to catch the drip from eaves).

2. *On the eaves* (*U.S.*).

Ebb, *v.* Add: **2. b.** *To be on the ebb*.

Ebbed, *ppl. a.* Add: Also with *down*.

Ebon, *sb.* Add: A negro. *U.S.*

Ebonize, *v.* Add: **2.** *intr.* To take an ebony colour.

Ebullioscopic (*i*bŭ′liŏskŏ′pik), *a.* [f. EBULLIOSCOPE + -IC] Of or pertaining to the ebullioscope or ebullioscopy.

Ebullioscopy (*i*bŭ′liŏ′skŏpi). Of or pertaining to the ebullioscope.

Ecactine (ek,æ′ktə̆in). *Zool.* [f. Gr. ἐκ out of, from + δκτίς, δκ- ray.] The distal ray of a sponge-spicule; cf. *ENACTINE.

Ecardinate (ek,a′di‐nāt), *a.* [f. mod.L. *Ecardines* (f. ε- without + *cardo* hinge) + -ATE 2.] *Zool.* Of, belonging to, or characteristic of the *Ecardines* (hingeless mollusc).

Ecbole (e′kbōle). *Chem.* Also -in. [f. Gr. ἐκβολή, f. ἐκβάλλειν to throw out, expel.] A bitter alkaloid found in ergot, ergotinine.

Ecbolin, variant of *EKKA.

Eccedroma (eksε′drōmə). *Path.* [mod. f. Gr. ἐκ out + σ- journey: cf. ~OMA.] A tumour growing from a cartilage.

Eccles (e′k′lz). [Name of a town in Lancashire.] *Eccles cake*, a kind of fancy cake resembling a Banbury cake, but usually round.

Ecdemic (ekdε′mik), *a.* [f. Gr. ἐκδημικός, f. ἐκδημεῖν to be out, after ENDEMIC *a.*] Occurring away from the place where it is endemic.

Ecdemite (e′kdəmə̆it). *Min.* (Named (1877) *ekdemi*, f. Gr. ἐκδημεῖν unusual: see -ITE.] Chloro-arsenite of lead, found in small, yellow masses, foliated or granular.

Ecgonine (e′kgŏnin). *Chem.* [f. Gr. ἔξγονος (f. out of, out + γόνος born) + -INE 2.] A base obtained by the decomposition of cocaine.

Echinus. Add: **8.** Also in *Bridge*, a signal to the leader indicating how many cards his partner holds of the suit led (plain-suit echo), or that the third player can trump in on a suit in the third round (peter-echo).

Écorché (ekɔrše). *Painting and Sculpture.* [F., pa. pple. of *écorcher* to flay.] A subject so treated as to expose the muscular system.

Éco-. Also **Ectobla′stic** *a.*, of or belonging to an ectoblast. **Ectocho′ndral** *a. Anat.*, having external calcification.

Écossaise. 2. (See quot.)

Éda′m, **Eder**, variants of *EKKA, *EKKER.

Éclair (eklē′r). [F., lit. lightning.] A small pastry made of flour, butter, and eggs, coated with chocolate icing, etc., filled with whipped cream or custard.

Édam (ē′dəm). [Du., f. place-name *Edam* near Amsterdam.]

Édenite (ē′dīnə̆it). *Min.* [Named (1839) *edenite*, f. *Edenville* near New York: see -ITE.] An aluminous variety of hornblende.

Edestin (ĭde·stin). *Chem.* [f. Gr. ἐδεστός eatable + -IN[1].] A vegetable globulin occurring in wheat, rye, etc.
1896 *Jrnl. Chem. Soc.* LXX. I. 400 The proteid which is soluble in saline solutions the author shows to be edestin, or vegetable vitellin.

Edge, *sb.* Add:
2. d. Of temper (cf. *EDGY *a.* 4).
1916 BOYD CABLE *Action Front* 224 The company commanders found him with rather a sharp edge to his temper.
e. *To have an edge on* (a person): to have a grudge against, or an advantage over. *U.S.*
1896 *Daily News* 18 Mar. 7/5, I expect that when I am gone, especially from your own people, who always had an edge on me, and for no reason. 1929 *Publishers' Weekly* 14 Sept. 1060 Here we have the edge on our rivals, not only because of our superior location, but also because we are reputedly reckless about reducing prices.
4. b. *To be on edge*: to be excited or irritable (cf. *2 d).
1900 *Daily News* 4 Oct. 6/1 For me there was to be no sleep far into that night, for my nerves were upon edge. 1908 R. W. CHAMBERS *Firing Line* v. 56 I'm all on edge over this landscape scheme.
6. b. See also RAZOR *sb.* 1 b.
7. c. *Edge of regression* (see REGRESSION 3 b).
12. a. **edge-laid** adj.; **b.** *edge-milling, nailing*; **edge grindstone, key, -metal, plane, -rolled** *a.* (see quots.); **edge-runner,** an apparatus for grinding ores by means of a heavy disk which runs on its edge in a circular mortar; **edge-setter, -zone** (see quots.).
1884 KNIGHT *Dict. Mech.* Suppl., **Edge grindstone*, one the peripheral edge of which is the portion utilized; as distinguished from surface grindstone. **Edge key*, a tool used in boot-making for rubbing and burnishing the edges of soles. The disks are made of patterns: plain, convex, scotch edge, fluted, etc. **Edge laid belt*, one made by cutting up the hides into strips of the width of the intended thickness of the belt, and setting them on edge. 1839 URE *Dict. Arts* 961 The coal-seams thus upheaved [*sc.* at a high angle], are called *edge-metals by the miners. 1883 GRESLEY *Gloss. Coal-m.* 1883 *Encycl. Brit.* XV. 156/2 Profiling or *edge-milling machines are a still more recent application of the milling-tool system. 1876 *Ibid.* IV. 493/1 For side or *edge nailing..clasp-nails..are used. 1874 KNIGHT *Dict. Mech.*, **Edge-plane.* 1. (Wood-working.) A plane for edging boards, having a fence, and a face with the required shape; flat, hollow, or round. 2. (Shoe-making.) A plane for shaving the edges of boot and shoe soles. 1880 ZAEHNSDORF *Art Bookbinding* 170 *Edge-rolled, when the edges of the boards are rolled, either in blind or in gold. 1883 H. G. HARRIS *Plate Glass* 146 The pieces of limestone are further crushed under a pair of '*edge-runners'. 1883 *Encycl. Brit.* XVI. 463/2 Edge-runners (Chilian mills). 1891 *Engineer* 9 Jan. 36 Edge runner grinding mill. 1884 KNIGHT *Dict. Mech.* Suppl., **Edge setter*, a small lathe for burnishing the edges of boot soles. In the Tayman edge setter the shoe is carried on a jack and the burnisher held in the hand. 1902 *Encycl. Brit.* XXV. 459/2 A fold of soft tissue extending to a greater or less distance over the theca, and containing ..a cavity continuous over the lip of the calicle with the cœlenteron. This fold of tissue is known as the *edge-zone. 1904 *Ann. & Mag. Nat. Hist.* XIII. 22 The epitheca is that part of the skeleton secreted by the edge-zone.

Edge, *v.*[1] Add: **7.** *Cricket.* To deflect (the ball) with the edge of the bat.
1906 *Daily Chron.* 28 July 7/4 Seeing his first ball edged by Rhodes over the slips. 1927 *Observer* 7 Aug. 18/2 Being inclined to edge the ball.

Edger. Add:
4. An operative in various crafts (see quots.).
1909 *Daily Chron.* 26 June 8/5 Optician's Edger wanted. 1921 *Dict. Occup. Terms* (1927) § 105 *Edger*, a fettler who smoothes edges and joints of clay ware articles with a knife, leather or sponge before firing. *Ibid.* § 429 *Black edger* (gloves)..stains, with a blackened pad, as received from machinist, the white edge left on black kid gloves.
5. *Cricket.* A ball that is deflected with the edge of the bat.
1905 *Daily Chron.* 16 Aug. 5/6 Aided by an extraordinary quantity of luck in respect of edgers and extras, the Australians succeeded in getting within 67 of the English total. 1906 *Ibid.* 28 July 7/5 Tunnicliffe, who repeated that edger and then mis-hit one just short of Goatly at mid-on.

Edgily (e·dʒili), *adv.* [f. EDGY *a.* + -LY[2].] In an edgy manner; irritably, testily.
1837 MANNING in Leslie *Life* (1921) 269 He answered rather edgily and defensively. 1922 'M. ARLEN' *Piracy* III. ix. § 3 'You are making a butt of me, Virginia', he complained edgily.

Edging, *vbl. sb.* Add: **3. c.** *Photogr.* A narrow strip of albumen, gelatin, or india-rubber along the edge of a collodion dry plate.
1885 ABNEY *Photogr. with Emulsions* (ed. 3) 247 The plate is given an edging by placing the moistened end of the spill beneath the thumb of the right hand, and drawing it round the edge of the plate. By this means a 'safe edge' is given to it.
6. *attrib.* in various senses.
1884 KNIGHT *Dict. Mech.* Suppl., **Edging and dividing bench*, a circular saw of special adaption for sawing blocks into voussoir shapes, used in one form..of car-wheels. 1880 *G. Turner's Catal. Tool Wks. Sheffield* 24 Common Grass Plot *Edging Knives. 1874 KNIGHT *Dict. Mech.*, **Edging machine*, a machine for edging boards to a given pattern. An edger. 1841 MRS. J. W. LOUDON *Ladies' Comp. Flower Garden* 117/2 *Gentiana acaulis* is frequently used as an *edging plant. 1907 *Macmillan's Mag.* 825 Lepidoptera seek out this sunny retreat and suck the edging plants.

Edgy, *a.* Add:
4. Having one's nerves on edge; irritable; testy.
1837 [see *EDGILY]. 1864 WEBSTER. 1914 KIPLING *Dog Hervey, Divers. Char.* (1917) 149 'I say', he began hurriedly, 'do you mind if I come in here for a little? I'm a bit edgy.' 1915 J. BUCHAN *39 Steps* i. 33 Then I could see that he began to get edgy again. He listened for little noises. 1924 *Chambers's Jrnl.* 555/1 The horses were very nervous and edgy for the rest of the day. 1929 S. AUMONIER *Ups & Downs* 514 That its mood was tense and 'edgy' was evident from the way in which the members spoke and behaved.

Edh (eð), name of the Anglo-Saxon letter, or the phonetic symbol, ð ('crossed d').
1875 *Encycl. Brit.* I. 612/2 In order to express the corresponding sonant (heard in '*that*', and confusedly denoted by the same compound *th*) a stroke was drawn across the simple d (đ), and the new letter was called *edh*.

Edifier (e·difaiəɹ). Delete *rare* and add quots.
1832 CARLYLE *Ess.*, *Boswell's Johnson* (1872) IV. 117 The true Spiritual Edifier and Soul's-Father of all England. 1909 *Westm. Gaz.* 22 Jan. 3/1 The real edifiers. 1921 *Glasgow Herald* 19 Feb. 6 The professional edifiers of British youth.

Edisonite (e·disənait). *Min.* [f. name of Thomas Alva *Edison*, American inventor (1847–1931) + -ITE[1].] Titanic acid occurring in golden-brown orthorhombic crystals.
1888 *Amer. Jrnl. Sci.* Ser. III. XXXVI. 274, I therefore propose for it the name *Edisonite*, after Mr. Thomas Alva Edison. 1889 *Jrnl. Chem. Soc.* LVI. 354 Edisonite, a fourth form of Titanic Anhydride.

Edition de luxe: see LUXE 2.

Editio princeps (ĭdi·ʃio pri·nseps). Pl. **editiones principes** (ĭdiʃiō·nīz pri·nsipīz). [mod.L.] The first printed edition of a book.
1802 T. F. DIBDIN *Introd. Knowl. Rare & Val. Ed.* 4 This editio princeps contains but nine comedies. 1815 J. SCOTT *Visit to Paris* (ed. 2) 237 The room of the *Editiones principes*, contains every thing to gratify the taste of the bibliographer. 1875 *Encycl. Brit.* III. 656/2 Azzoguidi's *editio princeps* of Ovid. 1885 LIGHTFOOT *Apostolic Fathers* I. 113 A misprint of the editio princeps.

Editor. Add: **3. b.** A person in charge of a particular section of a newspaper, e.g. of the financial news (*city editor*: see *CITY 9).
c. The literary manager of a publishing house. *U.S.*
1930 *Publishers' Weekly* 5 Apr. 2096 Far more attention might well be given the West's peculiar needs by Eastern editors.
d. *attrib.* (appos.), as *editor-manager, -proprietor, -publisher.*
1899 *Westm. Gaz.* 20 May 1/3 Editor-manager of the *Oxford Chronicle*. 1906 *Ibid.* 20 Sept. 10/2 The editor-proprietor of the 'Studio'. 1907 *Ibid.* 8 Nov. 12/1 The staff, from the editor-publisher downward.

Editorial, *a.* Add: **b.** *spec.* Written by the editor of a newspaper, as distinct from news items.
1802 *Deb. Congress* 25 Feb. (1851) 796 The editorial part of the paper..was supposed to come from the pen of Mr. Hobby. 1816 *Niles' Weekly Register* X. Index, Editorial articles. 1877 *Harper's Mag.* Dec. 109/1 [He] thoroughly worked an idea into an editorial leader.
B. *sb.* (Earlier U.S. examples.)
1844 *Knickerbocker Mag.* XXIII. 114 A drawer containing ..unfinished letters, half-written editorials, incidents of travel. 1850 D. WEBSTER *Private Corr.* (1856) II. 365 The editorial in the Courier..is exactly in the right spirit.

Edmonsonite (e·dmənsənait). *Min.* [f. name of George *Edmonson* (1798–1863), headmaster of Queenwood College, Hampshire + -ITE[1].] An alloy of iron and nickel found in meteorites.
1882 W. FLIGHT in *Phil. Trans.* CLXXIII. 888 Edmonsonite..occurring in the Cranbourne meteorite.

Edriophtha·lmate, *a.* [See EDRIOPHTHALMIAN.] Of or pertaining to the *Edriophthalma*. Also **Edriophtha·lmatous, -mic** *adjs.*
1904 *Ann. & Mag. Nat. Hist.* Feb. 154 In the Edriophthalmate orders no similar arrangement is known.

Educand (ediŭkæ·nd). [ad. L. *ēducandus*, gerundive of *ēdūcāre* to EDUCATE.] One who is to be educated.
a 1909 PETTY (Cent. D. Suppl.) We wish therefore that the educands be taught to observe. 1917 J. ADAMS *Student's Guide* 6 We have a case where the teacher is all educator, and the pupil all educand. 1927 — *Errors in School* 44 Preparing the educand to take his place in the world.

Educatable (e·diŭkeităb'l), *a.* [f. EDUCATE *v.* + -ABLE.] = EDUCABLE. Hence **E:ducatabi·lity.**
1868 ALCOTT *Tablets* 105 (Cent. D.) Not letters but life chiefly educate if we are educatable. 1894 C. C. STOPES *Brit. Freewomen* 153 A constantly expanding view of the educatability even of ordinary girls. 1926 *Glasgow Herald* 21 July 10 Some fishes are 'more intelligent', or, as Dr. Longley puts it, 'have a greater degree of educatability' than others.

Eduction. 5. Add: **eduction-port,** an exhaust port.
1874 KNIGHT *Dict. Mech.* 774/1.

Edwardian, *a.* Add:
3. Belonging to or characteristic of the reign of Edward VII. Also **Edwa·rdine.**
1908 *Westm. Gaz.* 28 Sept. 2/2 That the Edwardian age is more placidly disposed towards such a threat [*viz.* 'your beer will cost you more'] than the times of the King's great-grandfather, George III. 1910 *Tablet* 14 May Suppl. 792/2 One event of the Edwardine reign afforded to the Catholics of this country satisfactions that were all their own, the union of the King of Spain and the Princess Ena. 1926 *Chambers's Jrnl.* 462/1 He sleeked his Edwardian moustache. 1927 M. SADLEIR *Trollope* 3 To the critical eye of Edwardian and Georgian enlightenment the mid-Victorians have appeared smug and hypocritical and selfish. 1930 *B'ham Post* 24 Apr. 15/2 Most Edwardian little girls enjoyed a foretaste of the permanent wave—but without the permanence—suffering the infliction of tightly-twisted 'curl rags' at night.
B. *sb.* **1.** An alumnus of a school of King Edward VI's foundation, of St. Edward's School, Oxford, or of King Edward VII School, Sheffield.
1873 *S. Edward's Sch. Chron.* Apr. 15/2 Then with a kick S. Edward's chief raises the ball on high; And above their adversaries' heads the Edwardians see it fly. 1875 *Ibid.* July 154/2 The captain of the Old Edwardians. 1919 GILSON in *Serv. Rec. K. Edw. Sch., B'ham* (1920) Introd., [His] unrivalled knowledge and memory of Old Edwardians.
2. A person belonging to the period of Edward VII.
1920 *Times Lit. Suppl.* 23 Sept. 617/2 Beguiled to sleep towards the end of last century..and suddenly awoken in a world of earnest Edwardians. 1929 S. AUMONIER *Ups & Downs* 147 He was an Edwardian of Edwardians..surprisingly gracious, tactful and charming.

Eel. **6.** Add: **eel-back** *U.S.* (see quot.); **eel-cat,** a channel catfish, *Ictalurus anguilla* or *I. punctatus*; **eel-pot** (earlier example); **eel-schuit,** an eel-boat.
1884 GOODE *Nat. Hist. Aquatic Anim.* 183 The Smooth Flounder,..*Pleuronectes glaber*,..may be distinguished from the former [*sc.* the Flat Fish] by its smooth skin, which has given to the species, in some localities, the name '*Eel-back'. 1898 JORDAN & EVERMANN *Fishes N. & Middle Amer.* 2789 The *eel cat rarely attains a greater weight than 5 pounds. 1648 T. SHEPARD *Clear Sunshine* (1833) 59 All winter they sell Brooms, Staves, *Elepots, Baskets. 1905 M. A. WYLLIE *London to the Nore* iv. 42 Gaily painted and varnished Dutch *eel-schuits.

Ee·l-grass. A plant with long narrow leaves: (*a*) the aquatic herb *Vallisneria spiralis*; (*b*) the common sea-wrack *Zostera marina*. U.S.
1806 *Baltimore Even. Post* 19 Feb. 3/3 (Th.) A young man at Sullivan [Maine] saw a Fox go down to some eel-grass, and roll himself up in it. 1837 COLMAN *Rep. Agric. Mass.* (1838) 58 The eel-grass is of little value except as litter. 1864 [in Dict. s.v. EEL]. 1867 *Amer. Naturalist* May I. 164 Go to the nearest brook, gather..a root of the Eel grass, [etc.]. 1880 BESSEY *Botany* 473 Order Hydrocharideæ.—This contains the Eel Grass, *Vallisneria spiralis*. 1888 GOODE *Amer. Fishes* 65 Jungles of eel-grass and meadows of lily pads. 1893 B. TORREY *Footpath-Way* 39 The beach was strewn with sea-weeds and eel-grass.

Eeling (ī·liŋ), *gerund* and *vbl. sb.* [f. EEL *sb.*] Fishing for eels.
1780 *Narrag. Hist. Reg.* I. 104 Made an eel spear. Went eeling. *Ibid.*, Went an eeling. 1843 *Knickerbocker Mag.* XXII. 426 No clammin', no eelin', and no pastur to feed your cows onto. 1895 *Outing* (U.S.) XXVI. 406/2 When he couldn't go eeling.

Eel-pout. Add: **1. c.** The mutton-fish, *Zoarces anguillaris*. *U.S.* 1889 *Century Dict.*

Eel-skin. Add: **b.** *U.S.* = PASTER 2, STICKER[1] 5.
1877 BARTLETT *Dict. Amer.* (ed. 4), *Eel-skin*, a thin, narrow slip of paper, with the name of a candidate on one side, and coated with mucilage on the other, so as to be quickly and secretly placed over the name of an opponent, on a printed ballot.

Ee·l-worm. A nematode worm resembling an eel, injurious to plants. (Cf. EEL 3.)
1890 E. A. ORMEROD *Injurious Insects* (ed. 2) 52 These eel worms (*Tylenchus devastatrix*) are too small to be observed without the help of a magnifier. 1897 *Yearbk. U.S. Dept. Agric.* 568 What appeared to be eel worms, or nematodes, were observed in potato stalks, causing the foliage to turn yellow. 1901 *Dundee Advertiser* 15 Jan. 4/3 'Tulip-root', a disease [of oats] caused by a minute eel-worm.

-een (īn), *suffix*[1], ultimately derived from L. *-īnus*, *-īna* adj. suffix, through F. *-in, -ine*, as in †*damaskeen* (1551), *canteen* (1737), *tureen* (1706), *bombazeen* (18th–19th century variant of *bombasine*). *Bombazeen* apparently furnished the model for *velveteen* (1795, *velvatean* 1776), on which followed *sateen* (an alteration of *satin*).

-een (īn), *suffix*[2], ad. Ir. dim. suffix *-ín*, as in *buckeen* (1793), *colleen* (1828), *dudeen* (1841), *girleen* (1836), *jackeen* (1840), *poteen* (1812), *spalpeen* (1780), *squireen* (1809).

E'enamost (ī·nămoust), *adv.* *English* and *U.S. dial.* Also α. e'en a most, a'most; β. enymost, eeny(-)most, enermost. [f. *e'en* EVEN *adv.* + *a'most* ALMOST *adv.*] Even almost; nearly.
α. 1736 PEGGE *Kenticisms* (E.D.S.), *E'en a'most*, almost. 1839 *Havana* (N.Y.) *Republ.* 21 Aug. (Th.) [The whale's head] was e'en a most off. 1843 HALIBURTON *Attaché* I. xiv. 253 The repudiation of debts..has lowered us down e'en a'most to the bottom of the shaft. 1891 H. FREDERIC *Copperhead* etc. (1894) 208 'I could e'en a'most 'a' thought it was Alvy talkin'', was what he said.
β. 1833 C. A. DAVIS *Major Downing* 168 It was made so long ago he has enymost forgot it. 1840 *Crockett Almanac* 2 The sun will be enermost hid. 1845 S. JUDD *Margaret* I. xiv. 113 He..has got the whole Bible eeny most by heart. 1870 MRS. STOWE *Oldtown Fireside Stories* (1871) 189 Then he'd jaw and scold so that she was eenymost beat out.

-eer, *suffix*[1]. Add:
The spelling *-eer*, replacing the older *-ier*, became frequent in the early 17th century. *Mountaineer* and *Waistcoateer* (a prostitute) afford early instances, and are also exceptional examples of the use of this suffix. A few formations denote inanimate objects, as *gazetteer* (1704), *muffineer* (1806–7).

In the latter part of the 17th century gerundial and (to a less extent) participial formations on agent-nouns in *-eer* appeared, and increased in the course of the following century, as *auctioneering* (1733), *buccaneering* (1703), *electioneering* (1790), *engineering* (1720), *parliamenteering* (1711), *privateering* (1664), *volunteering* (1691). These, being formed directly on the sbs. in *-eer*, do not necessarily imply the existence of a corresponding infinitive or finite verbal form, though an early example actually appears in *mutineered* (1682). Some of these formations, e.g. *parliamenteering*, were in commoner use than the original sb.; occasionally, as in *revolutioneering*, no sb. exists, *-eering* itself being used as a suffix.

-eer, *suffix*[2], representing Du. *-eren*, ad. F. infinitive ending *-er*; as in *domineer* (Shakspere), ad. Du. †*domineren*, ad. F. *dominer* to DOMINATE; *commandeer* (1881), ad. Cape Du. *commanderen*, ad. F. *commander* to COMMAND.

Effect, *sb.* Add:
1. d. Any of various phenomena of physical science, e.g. those connected with electric currents, usually named after the first discoverer or describer of the appearance.
1881 S. P. THOMPSON *Elem. Less. Electr. & Magn.* 343 This phenomenon of heating (or cooling) by a current, where it crosses the junction of two dissimilar metals (known as the 'Peltier effect', to distinguish it from the ordinary heating of a circuit where it offers a resistance to the current, which is sometimes called the 'Joule effect'). *Ibid.* 346 This effect, known as the Thomson effect from its discoverer Sir W. Thomson, is opposite in iron to what it is in copper or zinc. 1894 *Ibid.* 563 Kerr's Effect. Dr. Kerr showed in 1877 that a ray of polarized light is also rotated when reflected at the surface of a magnet or electromagnet. 1904 R. M. WALMSLEY *Electr. Serv. of Man* v. 295 The Faraday Effect. 1913 P. PHILLIPS *Sci. of Light* 82 The Zeeman Effect..is perhaps the most important magnetic effect. 1927 A. S. EDDINGTON *Stars & Atoms* 52 The Einstein effect is proportional to the mass divided by the radius of the star. *Ibid.* 75 Owing to the Doppler effect a moving atom absorbs a rather different wave-length from a stationary atom. 1929 *Nature* 31 Aug. 354 Cooling a neon tube in liquid air, to reduce the thermal broadening of the lines by the Doppler effect.
e. In various technical uses: see quots.
1902 *Encycl. Brit.* XXIX. 180/1 With a factor of effect 0·7, the net muzzle energy is 0·7 × 4 × 92·4881 = 259 foot-tons. 1904 *Technol. & Sci. Dict.* (ed. Goodchild & Tweney), *Effects*.., the separate vacuum units of a multiple effect evaporator. *Ibid.* s.v. *Evaporators*, Multiple evaporators are generally operated under a vacuum, and may be either single, double, or triple Effects.
f. Psychology. *Law of effect*: see quots.
1922 R. S. WOODWORTH *Psychol.* 392 The law of effect, stated as objectively as possible, is simply that the successful or unsuccessful outcome or effect of a reaction determines whether it shall become firmly linked with the stimulus, or detached from the stimulus and thus eliminated. 1929 *Encycl. Brit.* XVIII. 683/1 The so-called 'Law of Effect', ..which refers..more particularly to the acquisition of skill, and to the formation of habit.
3. b. Also of music.
1870 *Porcupine* 19 Mar. 492/3 The other perfectly unique 'Spohr effects' produced during the performance of this cantata.

Effectism. Delete *nonce-wd.* and add:
1889 *Harper's Mag.* Nov. 964/1 The vice which has been very graphically called *effectism*, or the itch of awaking at all cost in the reader vivid and violent emotions. *Ibid.* 965/1 The result of *effectism* when allowed full play.
Hence **Effectist** (efe·ktist), one who aims at effect. Also **Effe·ctivism.**
1889 *Harper's Mag.* Nov. 965/2 The *effectists* who delight genteel people at all the theatres. 1892 *Ibid.* Nov. 960/1 No desire for startling effectivism ever disturbed the calm serenity of his style.

Effector (efe·ktəɹ). **1.** As a variant of EFFECTER, q.v. in Dict.
2. *Biol.* In attrib. use or as adj., or sb., applied to an organ which shows the specific effect of a nervous reaction.
1906 C. S. SHERRINGTON *Integrative Action Nerv. System* i. 7 An *effector* organ, e.g., gland cells or muscle cells. *Ibid.* ix. 309 The conductor mediating between receptor and effector. *Ibid.*, At the deep, i.e. effector, end the branching of the conductive stem places it in touch not with one effective cell but with many. 1920 T. P. NUNN *Education: its Data & First Princ.* 166 Connector-axons which make their way to effector-neurones entirely outside the cord. 1927 SHUMWAY *Vert. Embryol.* 186 The sense organs (receptors) from the nerves (transmittors) by which stimuli are passed on to the muscles or glands (effectors). 1927 RANSON *Anat. Nerv. System* 18 A sensitive mechanism for receiving stimuli and conducting them to the appropriate organs of response. These organs..are known as effectors.

Efferve·scingly, *adv.* [f. EFFERVESCING *ppl. a.* + -LY[2].] In an effervescing manner, sparklingly.
1898 *Westm. Gaz.* 15 June 3/1 He speaks briskly and effervescingly.

Efficiency. Add: **3.** The ratio of useful work performed to the total energy expended.
Radiant or *luminous efficiency*, the ratio of the light-giving radiation of a source of light to the total radiation.
1879 G. B. PRESCOTT *Speaking Telephone* xiv. 465 The true comparative measure of the efficiency of dynamo-electric machines. 1887 *Encycl. Brit.* XXII. 496/1 The efficiency of furnace and boiler is the ratio which the amount of heat taken up by the water bears to the whole potential energy of the fuel. In good boilers this efficiency is about 0·7. 1902 *Ibid.* XXXIII. 418/1 The ratio between the power given out by a transformer and the power taken up by it is called its efficiency, and is best represented by a curve, of which the ordinate is the efficiency expressed as a percentage, and the corresponding abscissæ represent the fractions of the full load as decimal fractions. 1929 *Ibid.* (ed. 14) VIII. 290/1 The 'efficiency' of a lamp is measured in lumens per watt.

Effigurate (efi·giŭrĕt), *ppl. a.* *Bot.* [f. EF- (= *ec-, ex-*) + FIGURATE.] Having a definite form; also, fully developed in its subordinate parts.
1872 W. A. LEIGHTON *Lichen-Flora* (ed. 2) p. xxiv, *Effigurate*, having a distinct form or fringe. 1886 HOLMES & GRAY *Brit. Fungi, Lichens* 6 When its [*sc.* of the thallus] circumference is radiate or stellate, it is effigurate.

Effigy. Add: **3.** **effigy-mound,** an earth mound in the shape of an animal.
1886 *Amer. Jrnl. Archæol.* II. 66 Bancroft..places Pidgeon and Lapham on an equal footing, as the original discoverers of the 'effigy mounds'. 1929 *Encycl. Brit.* (ed. 14) XV. 928/2 In Wisconsin the most interesting mounds are the effigy mounds—earthen forms of mammals, birds and reptiles. *Ibid.*, The purpose of these effigy mounds is probably totemic.

Effleurage (eflöräʒ), *sb.* *Massage.* [F., f. *effleurer* to skim.] A centripetal stroking movement made with the flat or the heel of the hand. So **Effleurage** *v. intr.*, to massage a part or a limb with this movement.
1886 MURRELL *Massage* iii. 10. 1890 KELLGREN *Man. Treatment* 9 The effleurage may be very superficial or deep. 1894 A. C. HALE *Massage* 133 Separate the fingers and effleurage thoroughly over and round the malleoli.

Effort, *sb.* Add:
2. b. Often used somewhat trivially or jocularly for any kind of achievement or result of activity.
1871 L. W. M. LOCKHART *Fair to See* xxiii, His first attempt [*sc.* the letter itself] ran thus..and he tried again... This effort was also torn up in despair. 1924 ANNE D. SEDGWICK *Little French Girl* I. vii. 59 The Venus is an effort of Ruth's.
c. *Mech.* (See quots. 1842, 1875.)
1842 FRANCIS *Dict. Arts*, *Effort*, the force with which a body in motion tends to produce an effect, whether the effect be really produced or impeded. 1875 RANKINE *Mech. Text-Bk.* (ed. 2) 205 A direct force is..distinguished, according as it acts with or against the motion of the point..by the name of effort, or of resistance, as the case may be. 1883 *Encycl. Brit.* XV. 764/2 If the component along the direction of motion acts with the motion, it is called an effort.

Effortful (e·fŏ́ɹtfŭl), *a.* [f. EFFORT *sb.* + -FUL.] Exhibiting, full of, or requiring effort.
1900 *Academy* 1 June 473/1 At its most effortful it is strained and excited—a painfully obvious striving beyond the poet's power. 1926 SIR O. LODGE in *Brit. Weekly* 4 Nov. 120/4 A life of value is always a strenuous and effortful life. 1927 C. C. MARTINDALE *Christ is King* ii. 34 It is usually more effortful to do right than to do wrong. 1927 *Manchester Guardian Weekly* Sept. 169/2 The effortful conscious striving towards an æsthetic and philosophical ideal.

E·ffortlessness. [f. EFFORTLESS *a.* + -NESS.] The character or quality of being effortless.
1889 W. BOYD CARPENTER *Perm. Elem. Relig.* vii. 253 He passed from the effortless stage, through the stage of pain and effort, and on again to the stage of effortlessness. 1904 *Daily Chron.* 18 Apr. 3/2 And, in spite of its effortlessness, how splendid in technique. 1923 *Public Opinion* 28 Dec. 643/2 He gave an impression of effortlessness in the calm ease of his manner. 1928 *Observer* 8 Jan. 21/4 That effortlessness and comparative noiselessness of the engine.

Effusion. **1. d.** Add: *effusion-aperture, -plug.*
1901 M. W. TRAVERS *Exper. Study Gases* 281 The effusion-plug, or partition containing the effusion-aperture, was placed at or near the lower extremity of the glass tube.

Effusive, *a.* Add: **1. b.** *Geol.* Of an igneous rock: Poured out on the earth's surface in a state of fusion and afterwards solidified; so *effusive period*, the period in which effusive rocks were formed. Also *sb.*, an effusive rock.
1895 A. HARKER *Petrol.* 128 The two periods of consolidation were styled by Rosenbusch the 'intratelluric' and the 'effusive'. 1897 G. P. MERRILL *Treat. Rocks* 60 To divide the eruptive rocks into two general groups: first, the intrusive or plutonic rocks; and second, the effusive or volcanic rocks. 1903 *Amer. Jrnl. Sci.* XVI. 121 An origin contemporaneous with that of the Rossland effusives. 1903 A. GEIKIE *Text-Bk. Geol.* (ed. 4) 197 The effusive or volcanic rocks (Erguss-gesteine). 1905 JAS. GEIKIE *Struct. & Field Geol.* 206 Effusive rocks..are of two types, crystalline and fragmental. 1915 LINDGREN *Igneous Geol. Cordilleras* 273 Basalt is probably the most widely spread of the Tertiary effusives.

Egalitarian (ĭgælitē·riăn), *a.* Delete *nonce-wd.* and add quots. Also *sb.*, one who asserts the equality of mankind.
1894 *Daily News* 21 July 5/2 The Scot..is, of course, the most 'egalitarian' of mankind. 1898 J. E. C. BODLEY *France* I. 162 In warlike but egalitarian France. 1909 BELLOC *Marie Antoinette* 377 The violent egalitarian mood which had now for a year and more driven the military fury of the Republic. 1920 *19th Cent.* July 10 A variant of the superman as noxious as the mediocrity or the egalitarian.

Egbo (e·gbo). [Alege *egbo*; cf. Efik *ekpe*, Bulom *ugbo, igbo*.] A native secret society at one time existing as a political bond between the various towns in Old Calabar.
1876 *Encycl. Brit.* IV. 649/2 The only political bond of union between the various towns is the Egbo. 1920 *Chambers's Jrnl.* 799/2 The Old Calabar custom of 'Egbo'..The penalty of death was incurred by any unauthorised person looking at an 'Egbo' runner as he passed through the town.

Egeria (ĭdʒĭə·riă).
1. In *Roman Mythology*, the name of a prophetic nymph, supposed to be the instructress of Numa Pompilius, and regarded as the giver of life; *transf.* a tutelary divinity.
1621 BURTON *Anat. Mel.* (1624) To Rdr. b, My Mistris Melancholy, my Ægeria, or my *malus Genius*. 1818 LADY MORGAN *Fl. Macarthy* (1819) III. ii. 82 Why may not I have my Egeria or my dæmon, as well as another? 1826 DISRAELI *Viv. Grey* III. vi, It is in these moments, that Nature becomes our Egeria. 1890 *Athenæum* 24 May 670/2 With the help and counsel of Beatrice, who turns his Egeria, he wins fame in law and politics.
2. *Astron.* One of the small planets or asteroids between the orbits of Mars and Jupiter discovered by De Gasparis, 2 Nov., 1850.
1865 BRANDE & COX *Dict. Sci. Lit. & Art* I. 754/2.

Egg, *sb.* Add:
3. b. In full *egg coal*: see quots. *U.S.*
1885 *Encycl. Brit.* XVIII. 501/2 (Pennsylvania) The market sizes being designated egg, stove, chestnut, pea, and buckwheat. 1900 *Coal & Metal Miners' Pocketbk.* (ed. 6) 434 Egg passes over 2" mesh, and through 2½" mesh. *Ibid.* 585 Egg coal, anthracite coal that will pass through a 2½" square mesh and over a 2" square mesh.
c. An egg-shaped tea-infuser.
1894 MRS. DYAN *Man's Keeping* xvi, She watched him pour the water into the teapot on to the silver egg full of the fragrant leaves.
d. *Cricket.* = DUCK'S EGG b.
1898 RANJITSINHJI *With Stoddart's Team in Australia* x. 195 Gregory..was yorked first ball... Iredale also secured an 'egg'.
e. An aerial bomb. *slang.*
1917 *War Illustrated* 13 Jan. 524/2 That seaplane..having some explosive 'eggs' to drop. 1918 E. M. ROBERTS *Flying Fighter* 335 *Eggs*, bombs weighing twenty pounds and upward filled with high explosives and 'laid' in Hunland.
4. *A bad egg* (earlier U.S. example). *Good egg* (slang): (*a*) an excellent person or object; (*b*) an exclamation of enthusiastic approbation.
1853 *Capt. Priest* 319 (Th.) In the language of his class, the Perfect Bird generally turns out to be 'a bad egg'. 1914 C. MACKENZIE *Sinister St.* III. x, It doesn't look a hundred quid to a tanner on his blue. Bad luck. He's a very good egg. *Ibid.* xii, Oxford was divided into Bad Men and Good Eggs. 1915 D. O. BARNETT *Lett.* 56 We are going to do this regularly, and I think it is a very good egg. 1915 WODEHOUSE *Something Fresh* x. § 3 'She isn't going to sue me for breach?' 'She never had any intention of doing so.' The Hon. Frederick sank back on the pillows. 'Good egg!' he said with fervour. 1922 — *Clicking of Cuthbert* x. 256 'Well?' we said, anxiously. 'I like it,' said the editor. 'Good egg!' we murmured. 1929 S. AUMONIER *Ups & Downs* 418 Hullo, Pan! Good egg!
c. *Old egg*: a familiar form of address = old chap, old fellow, old sport.
1919 *Punch* 5 Mar. 190/2 Cheerio, old egg. 1927 A. ARMSTRONG *Patrick Engaged* ix. § 3 'You'd be arrested.. and spoil the whole show', replied Patrick tersely. 'Sorry, old egg, sorry!'
6. *egg-coloration, -mass, -stage.*
1912 J. A. THOMSON *Biol. Seasons* II. 177 A stereotyped kind of *egg-coloration. 1889 MARY E. BAMFORD *Up & Down the Brooks* 45 The bright-yellow *egg-mass. 1921 *Brit. Museum Return* 119 An exceedingly fine egg-mass of *Natica sp.* from Scotia Bay, South Orkneys. 1883 F. DAY *Indian Fish* 26 (Fish. Exhib. Publ.) They have their enemies in the *egg stage..and during their maturity.
b. *egg-gatherer, -hunting.*
1855 *Knickerbocker Mag.* XLVI. 223 Upon the approach of the egg-gatherers, with little or no dissenting clamor, they rise up in one vast, dangling-legged body. *Ibid.*, As egg-hunting is viewed by our country people as a species of 'picnicking', lovers and their mistresses..are the principal actors in these excursions.
c. *egg-ended, -eyed, -faced, -headed* adjs.
1859 RANKINE *Steam Engine* § 63 The ends of '*egg-ended' cylindrical boilers. 1875 *Plain Needlework* 10 Abel Morrell's '*egg-eyed' needles. 1921 *Glasgow Herald* 26 Sept. 6 He will find the *egg-faced man there. 1920 W. DEEPING *Second Youth* iv, A little *egg-headed pedant.
7. **egg albumin,** the principle found in the white of egg; **egg-and-spoon race,** a foot race during which the competitors are required to carry an egg in a spoon with which it has been picked up; see also quot. 1894; **egg-apparatus** *Bot.*, the group of three cells at the micropylar end of the embryo-sac in seed plants, only one of which is fertile; **egg-assorter** (see quot.); **egg-barrel,** a barrel-like egg; **egg-bread** *U.S.*, bread made of the meal of Indian corn, eggs, etc.; **egg-burster** = **egg-tooth*; **egg-capsule,** a natural envelope containing eggs; **egg-chain,** a chain of the egg-cases of certain fishes; **egg-cleavage,** the process of division that occurs in a fertilized egg-cell; **egg-cosy,** a cover to keep a boiled egg warm (see COSY B. 2); **egg-eater,** a South African name for a snake of the genus *Dasypeltis*; **egg-end,** an egg-shaped cap of a cylindrical boiler; **egg-fruit,** the fruit of the egg-plant; **egg-guide** *Ent.*, a movable flap at the external opening of an oviduct to guide the eggs as they are laid; **egg powder,** an artificially prepared substitute for eggs in cookery; **egg-purse** = **egg-capsule*; **egg-raft, -rope, -string,** a connected series of eggs laid by various insects; **egg-stand,** a stand or frame for holding a set of egg-

cups; **egg-tooth,** a small, hard, white protuberance developed in the embryo bird and reptile which is used to crack the egg and is cast off after hatching; **egg-tube,** an oviduct, esp. of an insect; **egg-webb** = **egg-raft*; **egg-whip,** an egg-whisk.
1871 *Jrnl. Chem. Soc.* XXIV. 572 Some properties of *Egg Albumin. 1919 J. B. COHEN *Class-Bk. Chem.* II. 94 Of the albumins, egg- and serum-albumin are the most important. 1894 *Daily News* 8 Sept. 5/3 The gentlemen had a turn in the *egg-and-spoon race, in which the competitors had to punt with one hand and balance an egg on a spoon with the other. 1902 *Encycl. Brit.* XXV. 434/2 Of the three energids of the *egg-apparatus, one alone is normally functional as the egg. 1874 KNIGHT *Dict. Mech.*, **Egg-assorter*, a device by which eggs are assorted according to quality; being so placed that a strong light is brought upon them. 1889 MARY E. BAMFORD *Up & Down the Brooks* 132 The *egg-barrels of the Harlequin Cabbage-bug. 1854 MARY J. HOLMES *Tempest & Sunshine* viii. 118 *Egg-bread which Southern cooks know so well how to make. 1862 *Southern Hist. Soc. Papers* XII. 26 (Th.) The table was spread with rich egg-bread, fried ham, and pure coffee. 1911 R. D. SAUNDERS *Col. Todhunter* ii. 29 The Missouri supper of fried chicken, egg-bread, butterbeans and corn on the ear. 1920 *Brit. Museum Return* 121 The *Egg-burster of Encephalous Fly-larvæ. 1883 *Encycl. Brit.* XVI. 653/2 When *egg-capsules are formed they are often of large size, have tough walls, and in each capsule are several eggs floating in a viscid fluid. 1921 *Brit. Museum Return* 119 A string of egg-capsules containing young examples of *Buscyon perversum*. 1870 *Amer. Naturalist* III. 286 These *egg-chains are sometimes two feet in length. 1899 J. A. THOMSON *Science of Life* 123 The primary processes of *egg-cleavage, and the establishment of the germinal layers. 1894 EDITH Œ. SOMERVILLE & ROSS *Real Charlotte* xxxv. (1918) 255 The *egg-cosy that his wife had crocheted for him. 1906 *Westm. Gaz.* 3 Nov. 6/2 The sale of pin-cushions, d'oyleys, and knitted egg-cosies was unprecedented. 1909 *Lady's World* Dec. 284 The egg cosy made in the form of a cock's head and comb. 1887 *Encycl. Brit.* XXII. 194/2 A..genus of snakes, *Dasypeltis*...In Cape Colony these snakes are well known under the name of 'eyer-vreter', i.e. '*egg-eaters'. 1911 *East London Dispatch* 1 Sept. 7 (Pettman) The Egg-eater lives almost entirely on eggs, which it eats in a curious fashion. 1892 *Daily News* 23 May 6/1 A soup cauldron holding about 140 gallons was improvised from the '*egg end' of a steam boiler. 1887 *Harper's Mag.* Jan. 310/1 A dozen well-grown plants will supply a large family with *egg-fruit. 1898 A. S. PACKARD *Text-bk. Entom.* 183 In the Acrydiidæ the external opening of the oviduct is bounded on the ventral side by a movable, triangular, acute flap, the *egg-guide. 1862 *Englishwoman's Dom. Mag.* Sept. 230/2 With the mysteries of making *egg-powder we are quite unacquainted. 1864 *Chemist & Druggist* 193 It seems that certain cooks..are in the habit of buying and using egg powders. 1921 *Chambers's Jrnl.* 375/2 The cockroach..is very careful in the selection of a suitable site to place her *egg-purse. *Ibid.*, Each egg-purse [*sc.* of a cockroach] contains sixteen eggs, arranged in two rows, with the ends from which the larvæ will emerge pointing towards the top. 1927 *Observer* 18 Sept. 8 The *egg-raft is laid by the many species of that group of mosquitoes, the *Culicinæ*, represented by our common gnat. 1891 *Nature* 10 Sept. 457 Each *egg-rope is moored to the bank by a thread. 1848 H. R. FORSTER *Stowe Catal.* 60, 2 *egg-stands; and 4 cups. 1909 BENNETT *Old Wives' Tale* II. i. § 3 The resplendent egg-stand holding twelve silver-gilt egg-cups and twelve chased spoons to match. 1888 ROLLESTON & JACKSON *Anim. Life* 222 In *Nephelis* and *Clepsine*..'*egg-strings', produced by the continuous division of a cell, lie free in the capsular cavity. 1893 NEWTON *Dict. Birds* 36 The '*egg-tooth'..is developed in the embryos of all birds as a small whitish protuberance or conglomeration of salts of calcareous matter, deposited in the middle layers of the epidermis of the tip of the upper bill. 1826 KIRBY & SP. *Entomol.* IV. xlii. 148 The ovaries, or *egg-tubes as they are sometimes called. 1895 D. SHARP in *Camb. Nat. Hist.* V. 137 The number of egg-tubes varies greatly in different Insects. 1889 MARY E. BAMFORD *Up & Down the Brooks* 45 These *egg-webs are clear above the water. 1910 *Daily Chron.* 23 Apr. 7/5 Beat with an *egg whip until smooth and glossy.

Egg-cup (e·gkʊp). A cup-shaped vessel to hold an egg. Hence **E·ggcupful** (usually *egg-cupful*), as much as will fill an egg-cup.
1837 DICKENS *Pickw.* xvi, There's nothin' so refreshin' as sleep, sir, as the servant-girl said afore she drank the egg-cupful of laudanum. 1848 H. R. FORSTER *Stowe Catal.* 117, 6 egg-cups. 1870 [in Dict., EGG *sb.* 6 a]. 1871 *The City-Road Mag.* I. 263 We drank all but boiling coffee at half a piastre an egg-cupful. 1905 H. G. WELLS *Kipps* I. v. 88 An egg-cupful of brandy.

Egger, *sb.*[2] (Earlier U.S. examples.)
1834 AUDUBON *Ornith. Biog.* II. 370 Turtles..deposit their eggs in the burning sand, and clouds of sea-fowl arrive every spring for the same purpose. These are followed by persons called 'Eggers'. 1849 D. J. BROWNE *Amer. Poultry Yd.* (1855) 310 A class of persons called 'eggers', who follow.. the avocation of procuring the eggs of wild birds.

Egger (e·gəɹ), *sb.*[4] [prob. f. EGG *v.*[2] + -ER[1].] One who dresses white leather; a tawer.
1921 *Dict. Occup. Terms* (1927) § 338 *Tawer*; egger and washer; treats skins with alum, by hand, to produce soft, white leather for gloves, etc.

Eggery (e·gəri). [f. EGG *sb.* + -ERY.] A collection of eggs; an establishment for producing eggs.
1846 WORCESTER, *Eggery*, a nest of eggs. 1910 *Daily Chron.* 21 Mar. 4/7 A Western Canadian paper declares that next to the discovery of a gold-mine the most profitable investment is the 'importation of a batch of well-disposed hens and the establishment of an up-to-date eggery'.

Egging, *vbl. sb.*[2] Add: **2.** The laying or production of eggs, as in *egging season, time.*
1905 *Westm. Gaz.* 4 May 4/1 Among the risks which attend the breeding of game birds, frost at the 'egging' time is not the least serious. 1909 *Ibid.* 14 May 5/1 This is the 'egging' season, and outlying nests of pheasants and partridges may be disturbed.

Eggless (e·glės), *a.* [f. EGG *sb.* + -LESS.] Without eggs.
1904 H. G. WELLS *Food of Gods* I. iv. 92 The two surviving hens..spent their remaining years in eggless celebrity. 1909 *Daily Chron.* 2 Feb. 4/7 The recipe for an eggless omelette. 1915 *Even. News* 20 Jan. 7 Eggless and Less Egg Cookery.

Eggy, *a.* **a.** Add: *spec.*, as in quot.
1901 *Farm, Field & Fireside* 13 Dec. 357/3 If it has laid eggs, or is within a short time of laying, it is also detected. These birds are called 'eggy'.

Eglestonite (e·g'lztənait). *Min.* [f. name of Thomas *Egleston*, an American mining engineer (1832–1900) + -ITE[1].] A native oxychloride of mercury, occurring in brownish isometric crystals.
1903 *Amer. Jrnl. Sci.* Ser. IV. XVI. 258 The eglestonite crystals are usually easily recognized. 1912 *Brit. Museum Return* 196 Eglestonite and calomel from Palo Alto, California.

Églomisé (eglomize), *a.* and *sb.* [Fr., f. name of *Glomy*, a Parisian picture-framer of the 18th cent. So It. *agglomizzato*, G. *eglomisiert*.] Applied to glass painted on the back, and used by Glomy for frames.
1897 A. HARTSHORNE *Old Eng. Glasses* 343 To the last quarter of the eighteenth century belong also those florid painted panels—'églomisés'—inserted in the bottoms. 1912 *Catal. Wks. Art J. E. Taylor sold at Christie's* Lot 85 A portable altar of églomisé and silver-gilt. The base is further enriched with two églomisé plaques.

Egocentric (egose·ntrik), *a.* [f. EGO + CENTRE *sb.*, after *geocentric, heliocentric*.] Centred in the ego; in vague or popular use, self-centred, egoistic.
1897–8 *19th Ann. Rep. Bur. Amer. Ethnol.* 831 An earlier ethnocentric system born of the primeval egocentric cosmos of inchoate thinking. 1901 *Baldwin's Dict. Philos. & Psychol.* II. 194/2 For the ego-centric point of view is substituted the homocentric. 1919 *The Spirit* iii. 97 The instincts, the radical fault in most of which is their selfish and egocentric character. 1926 *19th Cent.* July 83 The girl of to-day absorbs a freedom-loving and egocentric conception of life.
Hence **E:gocentri·city,** the state or quality of being egocentric; self-centredness.
1903 *Amer. Jrnl. Psychol.* July–Oct. 100 Ziehen limits the hysterical constitution to emotional instability, egocentricity, craving for attention. 1918 E. JONES *Psycho-analysis* (ed. 2) 632 Its ruthless and absolute egocentricity. 1928 *Brit. Weekly* 22 Mar. 593/1 In this book the first personal pronoun occurs with a frequent and monotonous egocentricity.

Egomania. Delete *humorous* and add quots.:
1895 tr. *M. Nordau's Degeneration* 241. 1895 *Times* 21 Nov. 11/2 He panders either to the morbid egomania of the sitter or to the snobbism of his readers. 1901 *Academy* 18 May 427 There is not much reasoning with nerves and temperament; and as for 'egomania', was she not shut up with a mirror all her life? 1924 W. B. SELBIE *Psych. Relig.* 140 Instances abound of religious individualism degenerating into egoism and producing even egomania.

Egomaniac (egomē·niæk). [f. prec. after *monomaniac*, etc.] One who suffers from egomania.
1890 *Daily News* 8 July 6/1 To the end she is an egomaniac, and her religion is but another expression of the sensuousness that is the active principle of her being. 1895 *Westm. Gaz.* 25 Feb. 2/1 The Ego-maniac—the degenerate who is too feeble of will to control his thoughts by a regard to the welfare of society. 1914 *Daily Express* 17 Nov. 4 The crazy egomaniac who has deluged Europe with blood. 1915 C. S. JONES *Story of Hohenzollern* 199 So ruthless and imperious as to become that most dangerous of lunatics—a confirmed egomaniac! 1920 *Glasgow Herald* 20 Nov. 5 Pretensions that had grown to egomaniac heights. 1921 GALSWORTHY *To Let* II. ii, I know those enthusiastic egomaniac gentry.

Eguttulate (igʊ·tiŭlĕt), *a.* *Bot.* [f. E-[3] + GUTTULATE.] Without spots.
1887 W. PHILLIPS *Brit. Discomycetes* 29 Sporidia lanceolate, hyaline, eguttulate.

Egyptian, *a.* and *sb.* Add: **A. 2.** **Egyptian lily,** the white arum, or trumpet lily, *Richardia æthiopica*; = CALLA 2; **Egyptian millet,** (*a*) *Penicellaria spicata*, (*b*) *Pennisetum typhoideum*; **Egyptian onion** (see quot.); **Egyptian pea,** the chick pea, *Cicer arietinum*; **Egyptian privet,** henna.
1845–50 MRS. LINCOLN *Lect. Bot.* 191 The elegant exotic, Calla ethiopica, or *Egyptian lily. 1883 *Encycl. Brit.* XVI. 321/1 Bajree, sometimes also called *Egyptian Millet, a Guinea corn. 1880 *Ibid.* XII. 285/1 The Tree Onion or *Egyptian Onion..produces small bulbs instead of flowers. *Ibid.* XI. 36/2 Gram, or Chick-pea, called also *Egyptian Pea, or Bengal Gram. 1825 LOUDON *Encycl. Agric.* § 1057 The henné or *Egyptian privet. 1877 *Encycl. Brit.* VII. 710/2 *Lawsonia alba*, or Egyptian privet, which is said to be a flower of Paradise. 1880 *Ibid.* XI. 654/1 [Henna] is called Egyptian privet.
6. **Egyptian binding, pound, wheel, wind** (see quots.).
1727–38 CHAMBERS *Cycl.* s.v. *Bookbinding*, The manner of binding Books in Volumes, i.e. of gluing the leaves together, to roll them on round pieces, or cylinders of wood..we call *Egyptian-binding. 1902 *Encycl. Brit.* XXVII. 695/2 The authorized expenditure for administrative purposes was originally fixed at £E. 5,237,000. *Note*, The *Egyptian pound = £1 0s. 6d. 1793 [EARL DUNDONALD] *Descr. Estate of Culross* 9 Sir George Bruce erected machinery, consisting of the *Egyptian wheel, commonly called chain and bucket, to drain the Coal to the dip of the old workings. 1867 LADY HERBERT *Cradle L.* vii. 196 A well of water worked by a thoroughly Egyptian wheel. 1880 *Encycl. Brit.* XII. 435/1 The Egyptian Wheel or Noria. 1902 *Ibid.* XXXII. 187/2 In the Gulf of Suez the westerly, or '*Egyptian', wind occurs frequently during winter.
B. *sb.* **4.** The Hamitic language of Egypt.
1646 J. GREGORY *Notes & Obs.* (1650) To Rdr., This Booke of ours..may be read in..Coptick or Ægyptian. 1842 *Visitor or Monthly Instructor* 409/1 It ain't Greek at all: except, perhaps a few words. What ain't Greek is Egyptian; and what ain't Egyptian is Greek. 1857 S. BIRCH in J. G. Wilkinson *Egyptians* 182 Enlightened rulers prided themselves in speaking foreign tongues..Cleopatra spoke seven, Egyptian among the number. 1875 WHITNEY *Life Lang.* 254 In this [*sc.* 'Hamitic'] family, the Egyptian occupies the same commanding position as the Chinese. 1877 *Encycl. Brit.* VII. 721/2 The inscribed and written character of Egyptian was the hieroglyphic.
5. a. A mother-of-pearl shell from Egypt. **b.** An Egyptian cigarette.
1885 *Encycl. Brit.* XVIII. 447/2 The Arabs still obtain from this district [*sc.* Jiddah and Koseir] a quantity of mother-of-pearl shells, which are shipped from Alexandria, and come into the market as 'Egyptians'. 1892 *Whitehall Rev.* 22 Oct. 8/1 She could tell Russians from Egyptians, and sometimes took a mild Havannah with her B and S in the smoking-room. 1905 *Westm. Gaz.* 28 Oct. 10/2 A box of Egyptians.

Egypticity (īdʒipti·siti). [f. *Egypt* + -ICITY.] The character or quality of being Egyptian (see quot. 1895).
1888 *Expositor* Sept. 219 The Pentateuch—Egypticity and Authenticity. 1895 W. H. TURTON *Truth of Christianity* x. 147 The Egypticity of the narrative. By this is meant that the part of the Pentateuch in which reference is made to Egyptian customs, seasons, and names appears to be written with correct details throughout. 1921 G. A. F. KNIGHT *Nile & Jordan* xxviii. 384 The reference..is thoroughly Egyptian, and testifies to the 'Egypticity' of the book.

Egyptizing (ī·dʒiptaiziŋ), *ppl. a.* [f. *Egypt* + -IZE + -ING[2].] Becoming Egyptian in character; adopting Egyptian characteristics.
1847 J. LEITCH tr. *C. O. Müller's Anc. Art* § 240 The Egyptising image of the god of Heliopolis. 1923 *Weekly Westm. Gaz.* 24 Mar. 16/2 The art of two great and widely different empires knew its Egyptising phases.

Egypto-, repr. stem of Gr. Αἰγυπτος Egypt, in comb. (= Egyptian and ...) as *Egypto-Abyssinian, -Arab, -Arabic, -Caucasian, -Syrian, -Turk.*
1831 *Athenæum* 3 Dec. 787/3 All..were obviously of Arabian or Egypto-Caucasian extraction. 1874 P. B. RANDOLPH *Seership* 73 Nor do I see any reason why the white women of Western Europe..should not be..as..successful..as their Arabian and Egypto-Syriac sisters. 1879 *Chambers's Jrnl.* 174/2 The Egypto-Syrian forces. 1884 *Illustr. Lond. News* 9 Feb. 130/1 Peace had been completely restored on the Egypto-Abyssinian frontier. 1893 F. ADAMS *New Egypt* 16 Even these fanatical Egypto-Turks,..even these degraded Egypto-Arabs. 1911 WEBSTER s.v. *Saracenic*, The square or polygonal minarets in diminishing stories of the Arabic or Egypto-Arabic style.

Eh, *int.* Add:
3. Used interrogatively, as a request for the repetition or explanation of something that has just been said: = What do you say? *colloq.* or *vulgar.*
1837 T. BACON *Impressions in Hindostan* II. 149 Eh? What's that, Sackville? a 1845 HOOD *Hood's Own* Ser. II. (1860) 26 'The mail bags are on board—and it's more than my post is worth to put back'. 'Eh? What? How?' exclaimed the Oddity. 1869 *Chambers's Jrnl.* 595/2 'Eh?' said the old clerk, at last detecting my intrusion. I repeated my business. 1903 C. MARRIOTT *House on Sands* xvi, 'Ass!' muttered Lanyon, with a diabolical grin. 'Jelly-belly!' 'Eh?' said Sir Peter, blankly. 'Your health', replied Lanyon, gravely, raising his glass. 1905 H. G. WELLS *Kipps* III. i. 321 'I'm going to build a house, Ann.' 'Eh?' said Ann suddenly, as if awake. 'Build a house.'

Eidetic (əide·tik), *a.* *Psychol.* [ad. G. *eidetisch*, ad. Gr. εἰδητικός, f. εἶδος form.] Applied to an image which revives an optical impression with hallucinatory clearness. So *eidetic ability*, etc. Also *sb. pl.* (tr. G. *eidetik*): see quot. 1930. Hence **Eide·tically** *adv.*, by an eidetic image.
1924 G. W. ALLPORT in *Brit. Jrnl. Psych.* Oct. 100 The true eidetic image, in distinction to the visual memory-image, revives the earlier optical impression when the eyes are closed, in a dark room, and sometimes when the eyes are normally open, with hallucinatory clearness. *Ibid.* 101 Children with less eidetic ability frequently need to be instructed regarding the nature of the phenomenon. *Ibid.* 120 Eidetic imagery is a common possession of children. 1925 C. FOX *Educat. Psychol.* 81 The inability to discriminate between hallucinations and normal mental imagery and the mental confusion thereby entailed is responsible for a psychological abortion called the 'eidetic image'. 1929 *Encycl. Brit.* VIII. 112/1 An object may be eidetically seen either immediately after it has been removed from sight or after a considerable period of time..has elapsed. 1930 O. OESER tr. *Jaensch's Eidetic Imagery* 1 Eidetics—the theory of eidetic or perceptual images.

Eifel (əi·fəl), the name of a plateau in Western Germany used *attrib.* to designate a subdivision of Middle Devonian in the region so named, and the rocks. Hence **Eifelian** (əifī·liăn) *a.*
1879 *Encycl. Brit.* X. 341/2 Stringocephalus group, consisting of the great Eifel limestone with underlying crinoidal beds. [1882 A. GEIKIE *Text-Bk. Geol.* 702 Eifélien, Shales (Schistes de Couvin). 1894 *Geol. Mag.* Oct. 474 The Eifélien and the *Stringocephalus* beds of the Middle Devonian.] 1895 DANA *Man. Geol.* (ed. 4) 626 The Lower, Middle, and Upper divisions are named (1) the Rhénan, (2) the Eifelian, and (3) the Famennian. 1912 JUKES-BROWNE *Strat. Geol.* (ed. 2) 217 Middle Devonian. This also comprises two divisions, the Eifelian and the Givetian.

Eight, *a.* and *sb.* Add: **B. 2. b.** Also *the* (..) *eight*, the eight-oar crew of any society chosen to represent it in races.

1871 [in Dict.] 1892 *Pall Mall Gaz.* 22 Mar. 3/1 The 'Varsity eight has departed for Putney. 1896 *Daily News* 20 Jan. 5/1 After leaving..Oxford, where he rowed in the eight, he took a curacy at Fulham. 1926 BUCHAN in *Mod. Short Stories, Far Islands* 196 In his first year he rowed seven in the Eight.
4. A shoe of the eighth size.
1913 GERTRUDE PAGE *Where Strange Roads* ix. (ed. 14) 79 My wife takes large eight's in shoes.
5. slang phr. *One over the eight*: intoxicated.
C. *eight-manned, -oared, -rowed, -spoked, -wheeled* adjs.; *eight-bore, -ounce, eight-and-sixpenny*; *eight-bearer, -company, -dog*; *eight-pointer, -wheeler, -yarder*; **eight-box system,** a system of voting in South Carolina; **eight-coupled** *a.*, having eight coupled wheels; **eight-day clock** (earlier examples); **eight-foil** *Her.* (see quot.).
1906 B'NESS VON HUTTEN *What became of Pam* I. ii, The new hat, an *eight-and-sixpenny confection from the Tottenham Court Road. 1908 *Westm. Gaz.* 17 Dec. 7/2 An *eight-bearer yellow chair. 1874 J. W. LONG *Wild-Fowl Shooting* 23 For flight-shooting, an *8-bore [gun] is as large as is advantageous, and a 10 is sufficiently small. 1902 *Encycl. Brit.* XXXII. 732/2 In order to restrict the ignorant negro vote,..the General Assembly in 1882 instituted an electoral system which enforces an educational qualification by requiring the voter (who is secluded) to select his ticket himself and deposit it in the appropriate box. The system has become known as the '*Eight-Box' system, and has been imitated in other states. 1900 *Daily News* 26 June 3/5 An *eight-company battalion. 1900 *Locomotives & Railways* Jan. 10/2 Twenty *8-coupled compound goods. 1902 *Encycl. Brit.* XXXII. 150/2 'Eight-coupled' total-adhesion type; now found on a good many English railways. 1903 *Westm. Gaz.* 3 Oct. 7/3 One of the standard eight-coupled goods engines. 1904 C. S. LAKE *Locomotive* 60 Goods engines with eight-coupled wheels. 1750 *Boston News-Letter* 11 Jan., A beautiful *8 Day Clock. 1784 in Wallace Nutting *Clock Bk.* (1924) No. 33 Common eight-day repeating Clocks. 1876 *Coursing Calendar* 56 An *eight-dog stake was added to the card in the evening. 1847 *Gloss. Terms Brit. Her.*, *Huitfoil*, **Eight-foil*, or *Double quatrefoil*, an eight leaved flower used as a mark of cadency for the ninth son. 1897 *Daily News* 3 Feb. 6/4 A woman riding one among seven men on an *eight-manned wheel. 1893 W. K. POST *Harvard Stories* 305 Now began that most pathetic spectacle, the finish of a beaten *eight-oared crew. 1886 *Outing* (U.S.) VIII. 161/1 On one side an *eight-ounce rod, a thread of silk [etc.]. 1909 *Daily Chron.* 28 Sept. 4/5 A good *eight-pointer, weighing over 15 stone. 1837 *Rep. Agric. Mass.* 24 The Pickwacket corn, an early *eight-rowed variety. 1849 *Rep. Comm. Patents, Agric.* (1850) 101 Maize. The eight-rowed and twelve-rowed varieties are mostly used. 1868 *Rep. U.S. Comm. Agric.* (1869) 431 A small variety of eight-rowed corn. 1884 P. HIGGS *Magn. & Dyn.-electr. Mach.* 33 The armature consists of an *eight-spoked wheel. 1906 *Daily Chron.* 1 Mar. 7/2 *Eight-wheeled first and third-class carriages. 1904 *Westm. Gaz.* 28 Dec. 3/1 A special mail train consisting of twelve *eight-wheelers. 1930 *Morning Post* 17 June 14/7 He holed an *eight-yarder for a 2 at the sixth.

Eighteen, *a.* (*sb.*) Add: **2. b.** *pl.* A sheet of eighteen pages; a book in 18mo.
1683 MOXON *Mech. Exerc., Printing* II. 55 When a Twelves, Eighteens, etc. is wrought. 1795 *Hull Advertiser* 19 Dec. 4/3 A purposely manufactured wove paper, in Octodecimo or Eighteens. 1808 STOWER *Printers' Gram.* 199 A plan for imposing a half sheet of eighteens. 1839 T. C. HANSARD *Print. & Type-Founding* 168 Works done in sixteens, eighteens, twenty-fours, or thirty-twos.
3. *eighteen-hole* (golf-course); *eighteen-tonner.*
1907 *Westm. Gaz.* 21 Sept. 9/1 The opening of Matlock's new *eighteen-holes golf course. 1888 B. MOORE (*title*) To Gibraltar and Back in an *Eighteen-Tonner.
b. As in *eighteen-twenties*, the years between 1819 and 1830.
1906 *Daily Chron.* 16 Oct. 4/4 A collection of poems by Frances Ridley Havergal, belonging to the eighteen-seventies. 1909 *Westm. Gaz.* 24 Mar. 2/1 She has abundance of 'sensibility', as that word was understood in the eighteen-twenties. 1924 GALSWORTHY *White Monkey* II. ix, The Hotch-potch Club went back to the eighteen-sixties. 1929 SUSAN ERTZ *Galaxy* x, The eighteen-nineties came, with their revival of interest in literature and painting. 1929 (*title*) The Eighteen-seventies: essays by Fellows of the Royal Society of Literature. Ed. H. G. Granville-Barker. 1930 (*title*) The Eighteen-Eighties. Ed. W. De la Mare.

Eight hours. Usually *attrib.*, as in *eight hours'* (*hour*) *day*, a working-day of eight hours, esp. regarded as the maximum for industrial workers.
1867 in S. WEBB *Trade Unionism* (1920) 309 Such a measure of legislative restriction as shall secure a uniform Eight Hours Bill in factories, exclusive of meal-times. 1869 C. L. BRACE *New West* v. 60 The effort to gain a larger share of the profits of capital by means of an Eight-Hour Law. *Ibid.* 61 From all we can hear, the eight hour movement will soon fall to the ground. 1891 S. WEBB & H. COX (*title*) The Eight Hours Day. 1895 J. BURNS in *Encycl. Brit.* (1902) XXXII. 668/1 Higher wages and eight hours for Government workmen—all these things were in the direction of helping the unemployed. 1899 *Daily News* 6 Mar. 7/1 It should never be forgotten that Alfred was the inventor of the eight hour day. 1902 *Encycl. Brit.* XXXII. 668/1 English public opinion was sceptical when the Trades Union Congresses declared themselves powerless to establish an eight hours' working day without the help of the State. 1910 J. F. FRASER *Australia* 202 The eight hours' day is operative throughout the Commonwealth.

Eightsome (ē·tsəm), *a.* Add: [See -SOME[2].] Also *sb.* = an eightsome reel.
1875 W. ALEXANDER *Ain Folk* 246 They..caper through the 'eightsome' figure with louder 'hooch-hoochs!' than before. 1905 *Westm. Gaz.* 15 Sept. 7/2 A host of charming young Highland girls, with the tartans and badges of their clans, danced the eightsomes and the Reel of Tulloch. 1926 *Glasgow Herald* 7 June 8 The dancing of Scottish reels, foursomes, eightsomes, and sometimes even a sixteensome.

Eight-square, *a.* (Recent U.S. example.)
1907 S. E. WHITE *Arizona Nights* I. i. 4 He..carried across his saddle a heavy 'eight square' rifle.

Eighty, *a.* (*sb.*) Add: **2. c.** A half of a quarter section of land, comprising eighty acres. *U.S.*
1845 MRS. KIRKLAND *Western Clearings* 2 Section-corners and quarter-stakes, eighties and forties, and fractions, are plain enough when one is habituated to them. 1872 *Amer. Naturalist* VI. 77 The whole surface of the plains is sere and brown save some 'eighties' or larger tracts that are fenced. 1913 MRS. STRATTON-PORTER *Laddie* xi. (1917) 204 Then I hurried..across the west eighty to the woods.
3. *eighty-ton* (gun).
1874 *Porcupine* 18 Apr. 37/1 The construction of an 80-ton gun at Woolwich is stated to be decided upon. 1880 E. MAITLAND in *Encycl. Brit.* XI. 292/2 In the 80-ton gun powder cubes of 1½ in. edge are used. 1888 A. C. GUNTER *Mr. Potter of Texas* iii, That was the first eighty-ton gun fired in war.

Eiko (əi·kōu). Short for *EIKONOGEN.
1890 *Anthony's Photogr. Bull.* III. 20 Eiko has not yet.. shown all it can do. 1892 *Photogr. Ann.* II. 45 Eiko stock solution.

Eikonogen (əikɒ·nŏdʒen). *Chem.* [Discovered by M. Andresen, of Berlin; f. Gr. εἰκονο-, εἰκών image, ICON + -GEN.] A developing agent used in photography (see quot. 1889). Also *attrib.*
1889 *Jrnl. Soc. Chem. Ind.* 31 Dec. 958 This acid was the first amidosulphonic acid of naphthol ever obtained, and it is the sodium salt of the said acid which has recently been introduced as a photographic developer under the name of 'Eikonogen'. 1890 *Anthony's Photogr. Bull.* III. 25 Eikonogen for lantern slides is cheaper and easier than any other developer. 1892 *Photogr. Ann.* II. p. vii, Eikonogen Cartridges only require the addition of water when it is ready for use. *Ibid.* 96 The addition of a very few drops of J. Emerson Reynold's tetrathiocarbamide-ammonium bromide to the eikonogen developer.

Einkorn (əi·nkɒ̄n). [G., f. *ein* one + *korn* seed.] An inferior variety of wheat, *Triticum monococcum.*
1924 J. A. THOMSON *Science Old & New* xliii. 250 Inferior cultivated wheats like Emmer, Spelt, and Einkorn. 1928 PEAKE & FLEURE *Steppe & Sown* 54 It is believed that their predecessors [in Eastern Thessaly], like the early peasants in the Danube basin, had cultivated einkorn.

Einsteinian (əinʃtainiăn), *a.* [f. the name of Albert *Einstein* + -IAN.] Pertaining to or characteristic of Einstein or his theories.
1925 JOAD *Mind & Matter* 46 In an Einsteinian universe the velocity of light is the greatest velocity possible. 1928 *Observer* 25 Mar. 9/4 Einsteinian physics.

Eirenical, variant of IRENICAL.
1890 GASQUET & BISHOP *Edw. VI & Bk. Com. Prayer* 28 The choice of Quignon's work for a model had an aspect almost eirenical. 1891 *Tablet* 3 Jan. 11 The whole Pastoral ..is decidedly eirenical.

Eisegesis (əisĭdʒī·sis). [f. Gr. εἰς in, into + *-egesis* of EXEGESIS.] The interpretation of a word or passage (of the Scriptures) by reading into it one's own ideas. Hence **Eisege·tical** *a.*
1878 SCHAFF *Through Bible Lands* I. v. 53 The eisegetical manner of those allegorical and typological exegetes who make the Scriptures responsible for their own pious thoughts and fancies. 1892 *Evangelist* (N.Y.) 3 Mar. 4/4 (Funk) Dr. Elliot..held firmly to the doctrine that exegesis, and 'eisegesis', is the province of the student of the Scriptures.

Eisteddfodic (esteðvɒ·dik), *a.* [f. EISTEDDFOD + -IC.] Of or belonging to the Eisteddfod.
1877 RHYS *Lect. Welsh Philol.* vi. 314 *Ofydd*..is defined to be an Eisteddfodic graduate who is neither bard nor druid, and translated into ovate. 1894 *Daily News* 31 May 5/4 One of the Eisteddfodic conductors. 1923 SIR H. JONES *Old Mem.* i. 29, I pass over the Eistedfodic prizes we won.

Eis wool. [G. *eis* ice.] (See quot. 1882.)
1882 CAULFEILD & SAWARD *Dict. Needlework*, *Eis wool* (sometimes written 'Ice Wool'), a very fine glossy description of worsted wool, made of two-thread thickness, and employed double for making shawls. 1891 *Queen* 17 Oct. 639/3 Twelve balls of eis wool are required.

-eity, termination of nouns of quality or condition corresp. to adjs. in -EOUS, on the model of L. *idoneus* IDONEOUS, late L. *idoneitās* IDONEITY (1617), scholastic L. *homogeneus* HOMOGENEOUS, *homogeneitās* HOMOGENEITY (1625). Among other early examples are *spontaneity* (1651), *subterraneity* (1686), *consentaneity* (1798). Two exceptional mod.L. formations *ecceitās* (f. *ecce* lo, behold), *velleitās* (f. *velle* to will) gave ECCEITY (1549), VELLEITY (1618).

Ejecta (ĭdʒe·ktă), *sb. pl.* [neut. pl. of pa. pple. of L. *eicĕre*, f. *e-* out, forth + *iacĕre* to cast.]
1. The matter ejected from a volcano.
a 1889 *Amer. Meteor. Jrnl.* III. 109 (Cent. D.) Dust and other ejecta played but a secondary part in the production of the phenomena. 1890 *Nature* 16 Oct. 601/2 It may be thought that any volcanic ejecta would speedily melt the snow upon which they fell. 1902 *Daily Chron.* 11 Sept. 6/2 On the afternoon of the 3rd the ejecta was of the colour of sulphur.
2. *Path.* That which is ejected in vomiting.
1908 *Practitioner* Oct. 601 Frequent vomiting,..the ejecta being often blood-stained and sometimes faecal.

Ejector. Add: **2.** *ejector rifle.*
1920 G. BURRARD *Notes on Sporting Rifles* 68 Spare fore sights, extractors in the case of ejector-rifles.

Ekka (e·kă). *Anglo-Ind.* Also **ecca, ecka.** [Hind. *ekka* (Skr. *eka* one).] A small one-horsed vehicle used in India.
1811 F. B. SOLVYNS *Les Hindous* III, Ekka..perhaps the simplest carriage that can be imagined, being nothing more than a chair covered with red cloth, and fixed upon an axle-tree between two small wheels. The Ekka is drawn by one horse. 1886 KIPLING *Departm. Ditties* (1888) 21 The Waler jumped an *ekka* just above the City Drain. 1892 *Pall Mall Gaz.* 21 Dec. 3/2, I am going to take an ecka. 1895 MRS. CROKER *Village Tales* (1896) 148 His wife had real silver tyres to the wheels of her ekka! 1922 *19th Cent.* Oct. 592 The bullock carts, the loaded camels, the eccas, the elephants, of typical India.
attrib. 1890 KIPLING *Plain Tales, Thrown away* 23 The *ekka*-pony..had gone home. 1899 *Westm. Gaz.* 25 Oct. 3/1 Ekka bells.

Ekker (e·kəɹ). *University* or *school slang.* [See *-ER[6].] = EXERCISE *sb.* 7.
1891 SARA J. DUNCAN *Amer. Girl in London* 254 Walking for what in the vulgar tongue might be called exercise, but here [*sc.* in Oxford] was 'ekker'. 1901 *Winchester Coll. Notions* 40 Most houses have Ekker Rolls, the amount of compulsory exercise varying from four to six hours a week.

Ekphore, etc.: see *ECPHORE, etc.

El (el). *U.S.* [Short for ELEVATED *ppl. a.*] An elevated railway. (Cf. *L.)
a 1906 'O. HENRY' *Trimmed Lamp* etc. 121 Behold Ikey as he ambles up the street beneath the roaring 'El' between the rows of reeking sweatshops.

Elaborate, *v.* Add:
3. *intr.* To become elaborate.
1876 H. SPENCER *Princ. Sociol.* I. § 103 This custom elaborates as social development goes through its earlier stages. 1903 LANGBRIDGE *Flame & Flood* xx, These [*sc.* preparations] she discovered had augmented and elaborated to a considerable extent.

Elabrate (ĭlæ·brĕt), *a.* *Ent.* [f. E-[3] + LABRUM + -ATE[2].] Without a distinct labrum or upper lip.
1826 KIRBY & SP. *Entomol.* xlvi. IV. 308 Elabrate (*Elabratum*). When an imperfect mouth has Mandibulæ, Maxillæ, Labium, and Maxillary Palpi, or what perform their office, but no Labrum.

Elaioplast (ĭlai·ŏplæst). *Cytology.* Also **elæo-.** [f. Gr. ἔλαιον oil + -PLAST.] A globular body consisting of granular protoplasm and drops of oil.
1902 *Encycl. Brit.* XXVII. 334/1 In the Hepaticæ, oil-bodies are found which may have some relation to elaioplasts. *Ibid.*, The eye-spot which is found in motile cells of the Algæ, *Protococcus, Englena*, etc., may also have something in common with the elaioplast.

Elamite (ī·lămait). [-ITE[1].] An inhabitant or native of Elam. Also *attrib.*
1526 TINDALE *Acts* ii. 9 Parthians, Medes and Elamyts, and the inhabiters of Mesopotamia. 1880 *Encycl. Brit.* XI. 135/1 It [*sc.* Nestorian Christianity] was successfully preached to the Bactrians, the Huns, the Persians, the Indians, the Persarmenians, the Medes, the Elamites. 1928 C. DAWSON *Age Gods* iv. 83 The ancient Elamite tongue.

Elaphure (e·lăfiuəɹ). [ad. mod.L. *elaphurus*, f. ἔλαφος stag + οὐρά tail.] A species of deer, *Elaphurus davidianus*, of northern China. So **E:laphurine** *a.*
1872 *Trans. Zool. Soc.* VII. 336 The Elaphure is..very distinct in the form of its horns from every other described species of the genus [*Cervus*]. 1891 FLOWER & LYDEKKER *Mammals* 321 The Elaphurine group is represented..by *Cervus davidianus*.

Elapoid (e·lăpoid), *a.* [f. mod.L. ELAPS + -OID.] Of, belonging to, or resembling the *Elapidæ*.
1895 *Athenæum* 14 Dec. 838/2 *Boulengerina stormsi*, an elapoid snake from Lake Tanganyika.

Elasmobranchian (ĭlæzmobræ·ŋkiăn), *a.* and *sb.* *Zool.* = ELASMOBRANCH. 1889 *Cent. Dict.*

Elasmosaurus (ĭlæzmosǭ·rŭs). *Palæont.* Also anglicized **-saur.** [mod.L., f. Gr. ἐλασμός metal plate + σαῦρος lizard.] An extinct marine reptile.
1879 *Encycl. Brit.* X. 359/2 One of the most extraordinary of these reptilian forms was the *Elasmosaurus*—a huge snake-like form 40 feet long, with slim arrow-shaped head on a swan-like neck rising 20 feet out of the water. 1924 J. A. THOMSON in *Glasgow Herald* 5 July 4 One of them, Elasmosaurus, seems to have been 45 feet in length, half consisting of neck.

Elasmothere (ĭlæ·zmoþiəɹ). *Palæont.* [ad. mod.L. *elasmothērium* (also used), f. Gr. ἐλασμός metal plate + θηρίον beast.] A large extinct rhinoceros the remains of which are found in the Pleistocene.
1927 PEAKE & FLEURE *Hunters & Artists* 32 Another grass-eating rhinoceros from Siberia, usually known as the Elasmothere.

Elastance (ĭlæ·stăns). *Electr.* [irreg. f. ELASTIC + -ANCE.] The capacity of a dielectric for opposing an electric charge or displacement.
1890 W. P. MAYCOCK *Pract. Electr. Notes* (ed. 2) 48 Elastance is the reciprocal (or reverse) of Permittance; the comparative elastance of a dielectric is called its elastivity. For instance, a dielectric of great permittance has little elastance and *vice versâ*. 1890 *Electrician* 14 Nov. 41 The use of the words decalescence, reluctancy, reluctivity, elastance, elastivity, permittivity, might be well deferred till they are more generally adopted. 1893 HEAVISIDE *Electromagn. Theory* I. ii. § 31. 29 The formal relation of reluctance to reluctivity with magnetic force and induction, is the same as that..of elastance to elastivity with electric force and displacement.

Elastic, *a.* and *sb.* Add:
A. *adj.* **4.** (partly attrib. use of the sb.) Applied to fabrics (or articles made of them) containing threads or thin strips of rubber usually covered by a woven material. *Elastic sides*: pieces of such fabric

forming the sides or insertions in the sides of a boot; also *attrib.*, as *elastic side boots*, and ellipt. = boots of such a make. Hence *elastic-sided* adj.
1851 *Illustr. Catal. Gt. Exhib.* III. III. 525/1 Elastic side, dress, and other boots. *Ibid.* 579/2 Corset, made to fasten in the front with patent spring clasp, and gauze elastic sides. ..Boots and shoes, with elastic sides, made by sewing pieces of India-rubber to the upper leather and then to the sole. 1856 [in Dict.]. 1858 SIMMONDS *Dict. Trade*, *Elastic-bands*, belts, braces, gaiters, &c., made with threads of caoutchouc, either naked or covered. 1874 KNIGHT *Dict. Mech.*, *Elastic-fabric loom*, one having mechanical devices for stretching the rubber threads or shirrs, and holding them at a positive tension while the fabric is woven. 1880 *Encycl. Brit.* XII. 842/1 The threads used in making elastic webbing are usually cut from spread sheets. 1899 SOMERVILLE & ROSS *Irish R.M.* 295 Narrow feet in elastic-sided cloth boots. 1902 MRS. BARNES-GRUNDY *Thames Camp* 30 A man with a soft felt hat and elastic-sided boots. 1905 — *Vocill. Hazel* 292 An elastic-sided-booted woman.

B. *sb.* (Earlier example.)
1847 in H. Howe *Hist. Collect. Ohio* 48 With the *elastics* supplied by the ladies, for a halter..the young dog passed from the shores of time.

Elastivity (ilæsti·viti). *Electr.* [irreg. f. ELASTIC + -IVITY.] The property of a dielectric by virtue of which the flow of current between points having difference of potential is restrained.
1890, 1893 [see *ELASTANCE]. 1890 W. P. MAYCOCK *Pract. Electr. Notes* (ed. 2) 48 The comparative elastance of a dielectric is called its elastivity.

Elatement (ilē¹·tmĕnt). Delete † *Obs.* and add quots.
1894 *Leisure Hour* Jan. 146/2 Impossible to describe the child's elatement. 1922 MRS. A. SIDGWICK *Victorian* xv. 117 A note of elatement in his voice.

Elative, *a.* Add: **c.** *Gram.* Having an absolute superlative force. Also *sb.*, an absolute superlative.
1906 J. H. MOULTON *Gram. N.T. Grk.* I. 78 In the NT the obsolescence of the superlative, except in the elative sense is most marked. *Ibid.*, Mt. 11[20] may show the elative—'those very numerous mighty works'. *Ibid.* 97 The repetition of an adjective produces an elative. 1915 A. H. MᶜNEILE *St. Matt.* 59/2 'Ἐλάχιστος..may be elative, 'very small'.

Elbow, *sb.* Add:
1. b. Delete † *Obs.* and add quot.
1908 *Animal Managem.* (War Office) 330 For the horse, a small sausage-shaped pillow, long enough to surround the pastern..will be found to prevent the elbow touching the ground when lying down. *Ibid.* [see *elbow-brushing* in '5].

4. g. *To lift one's* (or *the*) *elbow*: to drink immoderately. Similarly, *to crook the elbow*: see *CROOK *v.*[1]
1916 W. J. LOCKE *Wonderful Year* xiv. 205 It was he.. who..when, *pauvre garçon*, he lifted his elbow too often himself, gave her the taste for alcohol. 1928 *Daily Express* 7 Mar. 15/4 Many a young man who has been lifting his elbow too frequently in Dublin is packed off to Melleray for a cure.

5. elbow-brushing (see quot.); **elbow-pipe**, a pipe having a bend resembling an elbow; **elbow-sleeve**, a sleeve reaching only to the elbow.
1908 *Animal Managem.* (War Office) 330 *Elbow brushing in the camel is a serious condition resulting from the friction of the elbow pad against the side in animals which are tied in at the elbow and whose toes are turned out. 1861 SIR W. FAIRBAIRN *Iron* 166 An *elbow-pipe..establishes a communication..between the blast-pipe and the tuyere. 1883 *Specif. Alnwick & Cornhill Rlwy.* 22 Proper elbow pipes and connections to be made with existing drains. 1899 *Daily News* 24 June 4/6 Some of the smart people compromise by adopting *elbow sleeves with very long gloves rucked up the whole length of the fore-arm. *Ibid.* 22 July 4/3 Elbow sleeves have come in with the heat.

Elbow-chair. (Earlier and later U.S. examples.)
1696 S. SEWALL *Diary* I. 438, I reach'd the elbow chair to him and with my Arms crowded him into it. 1835 *Knickerbocker Mag.* V. 221 Rising from his elbow-chair. 1852 D. G. MITCHELL *Dream Life* 183 The old elbow chair is in its place.

Elder, *a.* and *sb.*[3] Add:
A. *adj.* **1. c.** *Elder statesman*, in Japan, a member of a body of retired statesmen and nobles who act as confidential advisers of the emperor.
1921 [see *GENRO]. 1923 *19th Cent.* Jan. 138 The exclusive powers of the *genro*, or elder statesmen, are passing with the men themselves.

B. *sb.* **4. b.** An order of priests in the Catholic Apostolic Church.
1828 E. IRVING *Doctr. Incarn.* Ep. Ded., Writ. 1865 V. 7 These Sermons on the Incarnation..you received with all acceptation; and the Elders whom God hath set over you made choice of them to stand first in these volumes. 1876 *Encycl. Brit.* V. 238/1 Four-and-twenty priests, divided into the four ministries of 'elders, prophets, evangelists, and pastors'...The understanding is that each elder, with his co-presbyters and deacons, shall have charge of 500 adult communicants in his district.

c. In New England, a minister of any denomination.
1874 B. F. TAYLOR *World on Wheels*, etc. I. xix. 140 Take a young fellow from Hamilton or Rochester..and call him Elder, as his country brethren and sisters always will. *Ibid.* 141 Elders Card and Cook. 1921 R. M. JONES *Later Periods Quakerism* I. iv. 120 *note*, Even now in the rural districts of New England a minister of any denomination is called 'Elder'.

Eldonian (eldō^u·niăn), *a.* [f. the name of John Scott, Earl of *Eldon* + -IAN.] Belonging to or characteristic of Lord Eldon, regarded as typical of 'diehard' toryism. Also **Eldonine** (e·ldənəin) *a.*
1876 W. CORY *Lett. & Jrnls.* (1897) 419 A fusion of Benthamic legislation with Eldonine evolution. 1898 *Daily News* 8 July 4/7 His Toryism is Eldonian and antediluvian. 1900 *Ibid.* 31 Dec. 4/7 The century, considered from a political point of view, may be divided into the Eldonian, the Peelite, the Palmerstonian, and the Gladstonian eras. 1926 *London Merc.* May 104 An Eldonian Tory still describes a type peculiar to the English temperament, and never, perhaps for that reason, personally unpopular.

Election. Add: (Also *U.S.* 'lection.)
7. b. The choosing between two rights by a person who derives one of them under an instrument in which a clear intention appears that he should not enjoy both.
1891 G. SERRELL *Equitable Doctrine Election* 6 Election is often said to rest on an implied condition.

8. election bun, cake *U.S.*, varieties of fancy bread; **election-commissioner**, one of a body of men appointed to inquire into corrupt practices during an election or (*U.S.*) to take charge of an election; **election court**, a court for the election of magistrates or officers; **election district** *U.S.*, a district created for the purposes of elections; **election petition**, a petition brought against a member of parliament for illegal practices during his election campaign; **election sermon** *U.S.*, one delivered on the occasion of an election.
1859 O. W. HOLMES *Prof. Breakf.-t.* ii. 52 [He] recollects he had a glazed *'lection bun, and sat eating it, and looking down on the Common. 1869 MRS. STOWE *Oldtown Folks* v. 48 Aunt Nancy Prime, famous for making *election-cake and ginger pop. 1878 *Harper's Mag.* LVII. 581/1 Polly.. nursed him up with a mug of flip and a lot o' lection cake. 1889 ROSE T. COOKE *Steadfast* vi. 73 Nobody in Trumbull could make..such shortcakes, 'lection cake, or pound cake. 1902 *Encycl. Brit.* XXVI. 369/1 A prosecution for any of the above offences cannot be instituted more than a year after the offence was committed, unless an inquiry by *Election Commissioners takes place. *a* 1656 BRADFORD *Plymouth Plant.* II. (1856) 189 At ye spring of ye year, about ye time of their *Election Court, Oldam came againe amongst them. 1685 S. SEWALL *Diary* I. 12 They would have had them made a report..next Tuesday, but agreed to be next Election Court. 1799 in *Ann. 7th Congress* 2 Sess. 1411 In every *election district in the country. 1835 *Southern Lit. Messenger* I. 218 One or two..get a resolution passed for a general caucus of the whole party, in the town, or election district. 1839 *Act* 2 & 3 *Vict.* c. 38 (*title*) An Act to amend the Jurisdiction for the Trial of *Election Petitions. 1840 *Penny Cycl.* XVII. 278/2 In 1741, Sir Robert Walpole..was ..driven from office by a vote upon the Chippenham election petition. 1868 *Act* 31 & 32 *Vict.* c. 125 § 11 The Trial of every Election Petition shall be conducted before a Puisne Judge of One of Her Majesty's Superior Courts of Common Law. 1885 *Encycl. Brit.* XVIII. 705/1 By the Act of 1879 the trial of an election petition is conducted before two judges instead of one, as before. 1644 *Rec. Massachusetts Bay* (1853) II. 71 The printer shall have leave to print the *election sermon, wth Mʳ Mathers consent. 1685 S. SEWALL *Diary* I. 92 This day his Election Sermon came out.

Electioneer (ĭlekʃəniə·ɹ), *sb.* [f. ELECTION + -EER, after *auctioneer*, etc.] = ELECTIONEERER.
1895 *Pall Mall Gaz.* 26 July 8/1 In the Yorkshire Constituencies. The Champion Electioneer. 1905 *Jrnl. Educ.* Apr. 272/2 To secure that the professorship shall not necessarily go to the most successful electioneer. 1928 *Daily Express* 11 Oct. 11/1 The Liberal electioneers at once denounced it as a 'Tory trick'.

Electioneer, *v.* (Later U.S. examples.)
1817 in Fearon *Sketches* (1818) 146 One who intrigued and bargained for the office, and openly electioneered for himself. 1836 CROCKETT *Exploits & Adv. Texas* (1837) 11 For this reason he came out openly to electioneer against me. 1843 CARLTON *New Purchase* xviii. 139 Numbers go to see their neighbours, or to hear the news, and not a few to electioneer.

Electioneering, *vbl. sb.* (Earlier example.)
1774 W. GORDON *Hist. Amer. Rev.* (1788) I. 252 Caucusing ..answers much to what we style parliamenteering or electioneering.

Elective, *a.* and *sb.* Add: **A.** *adj.* **3. b.** Of college or high-school studies: Subject to the student's choice; optional. So *elective system. U.S.*
1847 in *Ann. Rep. Harvard Coll.* 1883–4 14 The elective system is now given up in this department. 1868 C. W. DILKE *Greater Brit.* I. vii. 89 The system of elective studies pursued at Michigan [University] is one to which we are year by year tending in the English universities. 1880 *Harper's Mag.* July 254/1 In the German Universities the studies are all elective and optional; in the colleges of the United States compulsory. 1890 J. G. FITCH *Notes Amer. Schools* 59 In the high schools and universities the practice of prescribing 'elective' subjects is very common.

B. *sb.* **2.** A subject of study specially selected by the student in a college or university; an optional subject or course of study. *U.S.*
1876 J. D. WHITNEY in *Life* (1909) 330, I shall have an elective this winter in economical geology. 1895 *Cal. Univ. Nebraska* 212 The elective in the History of Sculpture and Painting will be given at three o'clock. 1901 *Westm. Gaz.* 30 May 12/1 At Yale, where the study of this language had been neglected for many years, more than a hundred students have chosen it as one of their 'electives'. 1902 CORBIN *American at Oxford* 167 The idea of grouping electives is the fundamental difference between English and American education. 1926 *Amer. Oxonian* July 100 Oxford is a school for specialists. There are no minors, no electives, nothing but majors.

Electoral, *a.* Add: **1. b.** *Electoral college* (see quot. 1889). *U.S.*
1812 *Steele Papers* II. 687 The sense of each district may then be pretty generally represented in the Electoral College. *a* 1850 CALHOUN *Wks.* I. 175 In case the electoral college fails to choose a Vice-President, the power devolves on the Senate to make the selection. 1889 *Century Dict.*, *Electoral college*, a name informally given to the electors of a single State, when met to vote for President and Vice-President of the United States, and sometimes to the whole body of electors. 1903 R. L. ASHLEY *Amer. Govt.* 274 The work of the Electoral College.

4. *Electoral Act*, an act determining the method of parliamentary election.
1875 *Encycl. Brit.* III. 290/2 The Constitution Act of 1856 and the Electoral Act of 1858. *Ibid.*, The Electoral Act of 1865 (29 Vic. c. 279). 1906 *Westm. Gaz.* 7 Feb. 2/2 The precedent of the Commonwealth Electoral Act.

Electric, *a.* and *sb.* Add: **A.** *adj.* **2, 2 b.** Additional examples and quots.: also, **electric chair** *U.S.*, a chair in which persons condemned to death are electrocuted; **electric chorea** (see quot.); **electric hare**, an artificial hare made to run by electricity, used in coursing; **electric storm** *Meteorol.*, a violent disturbance of the electrical condition of the atmosphere, often causing interference with telegraphic communication; **electric torch**, (*a*) a gas-lighter operated by electricity (Knight *Dict. Mech.* 1874); (*b*) a contrivance consisting essentially of an electric lamp enclosed in a portable case containing a battery.
1891 A. E. KENNEDY in *Elect. in Daily Life, Househ.* 239 The first application of electricity to household purposes was presented by the *electric bell early in the [19th] century. 1889 *Peel City Guardian* 8 June 6/2 The preparations, which are to consist of taking a seat in an *electric chair. 1903 *N. Y. Even. Post* 28 Oct. 12 Two men were sentenced to die in the electric chair. 1890 BILLINGS *Med. Dict.*, **Electric chorea*, a peculiar disease of northern Italy, characterized by sudden, shock-like muscular contractions, with progressive atrophy and paralysis. 1927 *Punch* 27 July 85/3 A greyhound race at the White City had to be re-run last week because the *electric hare ran too fast. 1902 *Encycl. Brit.* XXX. 449/1 A transverse difference of *electric potential (Hall effect). 1882 *Proc. R. Inst. Gt. Brit.* X. 69 Siemens' Lichterfelde *Electric Railway, now running at Berlin. 1902 *Encycl. Brit.* XXVI. 228/1 An overhead electric railway runs from the Zoologischer Garten to the Schlesisches Thor. 1919 E. HENDRICK *Chem. Everyday Life* 99 *Electric steel is the latest method whereby the steel is heated, and the required ingredients added in an electric furnace. 1906 *Springfield Weekly Republ.* 14 June 16 A severe *electric storm, accompanied by a high wind, swept over Springfield. 1859 SHAFFNER *Telegr. Man.* 142 Soemmering's *Electric Telegraph of 1809. 1868 *Act* 31 & 32 *Vict.* c. 110 An Act to enable Her Majesty's Postmaster General to acquire, work, and maintain Electric Telegraphs. 1902 *Windsor Mag.* June, Advt. p. xxv/2 The 'Ever-Ready' Portable *Electric Torch. 1916 BOYD CABLE *Action Front* 3 The list of damages discovered by the glare of an electric torch. 1888 *Encycl. Brit.* XXIII. 495/2 Another method of effecting *electric traction is to carry a store of energy on the car or on a special locomotive. *Ibid.* 495/1 An *electric tramway 6 miles long connecting Portrush and Bushmills, in the north of Ireland. 1871 *Leisure Hour* 18 Nov. 720/2 The *electric wave, produced by a few pieces of copper and zinc. 1895 S. P. THOMPSON *Electr. & Magn.* II. xiv. § 516 In the case of true electric waves, portions of the energy of the current..are thrown off. 1902 *Encycl. Brit.* XXVIII. 55/2 Electric waves must be passing through the dielectric surrounding a condenser in the act of discharging.

B. *sb.* **3.** Short for (*a*) *electric lamp, light*, (*b*) *electric motor car, railway, tramcar*, etc.
1886 *Harper's Mag.* July 314/1 The light of common day ..is preferable to any manner of..alabaster lamps, or even the latest improvement in electrics. 1890 *Boston* (Mass.) *Jrnl.* 3 Mar. 1/7 Do the electrics travel too fast for the public safety? 1892 SUSAN HALE *Lett.* 269 There are cables, and electrics, but these haven't entirely driven out the horse. 1896 *Peterson Mag.* Jan. 65/2 [They] would no more enter an 'electric' than they would give up wearing mitts all day. 1897 KIPLING *Capt. Cour.* 215 Harvey..was asleep before his father could shade the electrics. 1898 — *Fleet in Being* vi. A triple row of white and purple electrics. 1905 ELIN. GLYN *Viciss. Evangeline* 166 In the twinkle of an eye we were rolling in the electric to Willis's. 1909 *Westm. Gaz.* 2 Sept. 9/1 Underground electrics. 1922 MARG. B. HOUSTON *Witch-man* ix. 99 Mrs. Morse..climbed breathlessly back into the electric. 1924 SUSAN GLASPELL *Fidelity* iv. 33 She told him..that Mrs. Blair had come for Mrs. Franklin in her 'electric' and they had gone to a tea. 1926 E. WALLACE *Clue of Twisted Candle* xiii, He felt for the switch of the electric.

Electric eel. (Also **electrical eel.**) [tr. mod. L. *gymnotus electricus*.] = GYMNOTUS.
1775 *Phil. Trans.* LXV. I. 102 An Account of the *Gymnotus Electricus*, or Electrical Eel. [1775 A. GARDEN *Ibid.* 107 The person to whom these animals belong, calls them Electrical Fish.] 1794 *Medical Extracts* II. xii. 121 *note*, Vandelott makes two species of the electric eel, the black and reddish. 1802, 1836 [see ELECTRICAL 2]. 1838 *Penny Cycl.* XI. 510/2 The electric-eel is said to communicate shocks so violent that men and even horses are overpowered by them.

Electric ray. = TORPEDO *sb.* I.
1862 COUCH *Brit. Fishes* I. 119. 1880 *Encycl. Brit.* XII. 649/2 The electric rays (*Torpedinidæ*). 1880–4 DAY *Fishes Gt. Brit. & Irel.* II. 331.

Electricute (ĭle·ktrikiūt), a proposed substitute for *ELECTROCUTE *v.*: see quot. So **Ele·ctricuter, Electricu·tioner, Electricu·tion** (in Dicts.).
1893 F. A. MARCH in *The Chautauquan* Apr. 21 (Funk) A Latin word for execute, to go with electric, or a Greek word to go with electro is wanted. The Latin word execute makes electri-execute, which would contract into electricute.

Electrifiable (ele·ktrifəi,ăb'l), *a.* [f. ELECTRIFY + -ABLE.] Capable of being electrified.
1828–32 WEBSTER.

Electrification. Add:
1. b. The action or process of electrifying a railway system or the like.
Earlier attempts to provide a term for this were *electrolisation* and *electrilisation*, with a verb *electralise* (sic) = *ELECTRIFY *v.* 1 b.
[1900 *Westm. Gaz.* 15 Feb. 4/1 The electrolisation of the inner circle, with its twenty-six stations. *Ibid.* 15 Aug. 3/1 The complete electrolisation of London tramways. 1901 J. BURNS in *Standard* 4 Mar., If Londoners had only done in 1895 what they did on Saturday, three-fourths of the tramways would have been electralised. 1901 *Westm. Gaz.* 28 Aug. 4/3 Americanised companies which go in for the 'standard' system of electrilisation.]
1901 *Westm. Gaz.* 2 Jan. 8/3 The character of the coal consumed..has altered the position for the worse...The one possible remedy is electrification. *Ibid.* 6 June, District Railway Electrification. 1904 *Daily Chron.* 26 Aug. 7/4 Electrification Perils. Risk Entailed by the Transformation of the 'Underground'. 1921 *Dict. Occup. Terms* (1927) § 561 Electrification ganger.

3. *fig.* The condition or state of being electrified or excited. (Cf. ELECTRIFY *v.* 2.)
1878 FR. A. KEMBLE *Rec. Girlhood* I. iv. 113 The tragedy was ended, and I had electrified the audience, my companions, and, still more, myself; and so, to avert any ill effects from this general electrification, Mrs. Rowden thought it wise and well to say to me [etc.]. 1892 *Leisure Hour* Aug. 657/1 Her electrification by Mr. Belport's proposal.

Electrify, *v.* Add: **1. b.** To introduce electric power into (a system of railways, etc.).
1900 *Westm. Gaz.* 17 Oct. 9/3 It is not very astonishing that the directors of the District Railway should be in no violent hurry to start upon the electrifying of their line.

Electro-. Add:
Ele:ctro-ana·lysis *Chem.*, electrolytic analysis; so **Ele:ctro-analy·tical** *a.* **Ele:ctro-bra·sser** (see quot.). **Ele·ctrobus**, an omnibus propelled by electricity; also *attrib.* **Ele:ctro-ca·rdiogram** *Path.*, a tracing giving a record of the electric currents produced in the body by the heart-beats of a patient. **Ele:ctro-ca·rdiograph**, the apparatus used in registering electro-cardiograms; hence **Ele:ctro-cardiogra·phic** *a.*, **Ele:ctro-cardio·graphy. Ele:ctro-che·mically** *adv.*, in accordance with the laws of electro-chemistry. **Ele:ctro-che·mist**, one who practises electro-chemistry. **Electro-chronograph** (earlier U.S. example). **Ele:ctro-co·ntact**, applied to a submarine mine which is exploded by means of electricity. **Ele:ctro-co·pper** *v.*, to coat with copper by electrolysis. **Ele:ctro-cu·lture**, the use of electricity in the growing of crops. **Ele:ctro-fa·rmer**, one who uses electricity for the cultivation of farm-produce; so **Ele:ctro-fa·rming. Ele:ctro-kinema·tics**, the theory of the distribution of currents in conductors. **Electro-motograph**: see MOTOGRAPH. **Ele:ctro-o·ptical** *a.*, of or pertaining to electro-optics. **Ele:ctro-pneuma·tic** *a.*, pertaining to a combination of electrical and pneumatic power; so **Ele:ctro-pneuma·tics. Ele:ctro-sy·nthesis**, chemical synthesis effected by electricity. **Ele:ctro-therapeu·tical** *a.*, of or pertaining to electro-therapeutics. **Ele:ctro-the·rapist, -therapeu·tist**, one who practises electro-therapy. **Ele:ctro-the·rmal, -the·rmic** *adjs.*, relating to heat derived from electricity. **Ele:ctro-tra·ctor**, a tractor driven by electricity. **Ele:ctro-tro·pic** *a.*, of, pertaining to, or exhibiting electrotropism. **Electro·tropism** = *ELECTROPISM. **Ele:ctro-va·lency**, a state of atomic linkage due to the 'sharing' of electrons; so **Ele:ctro-va·lent** *a.*
1903 *Elect. World & Engin.* 28 Mar. 530 (Cent. Suppl.) The differences observed in the *electro-analysis of mercury from a potassium cyanide solution are due to an attack of the platinum disc serving as cathode and to the solubility of platinum in potassium cyanide. *Ibid.* 21 Nov. 853 *Electro-analytical methods. 1921 *Dict. Occup. Terms* (1927) § 278 **Electro-brasser*..effects electrolytic deposition of brass on better types of finished screws. 1906 *Westm. Gaz.* 20 Apr. 11/1 The London *Electrobus Company. *Ibid.* 4 Dec. 6/3 About January..the first of the electrobuses will be placed in regular running. 1904 *Sci. Amer.* 5 Mar. 197/3 The human *electrocardiogram discovered by A. D. Waller. 1927 A. V. HILL *Living Machinery* iii. 117 The second record is a normal 'electro-cardiogram' accompanied by a 'phonocardiogram'. 1913 *Q. Jrnl. Med.* July 442 The Two Installations, Electro-phonograph and *electro-cardiograph, are arranged side by side. 1927 A. V. HILL *Living Machinery* iii. Pl. xii, String galvanometer ('electrocardiograph') as used for recording currents produced by the human heart. 1916 MACCULLUM *Pathol.* 477 *Electrocardiographic tracings, which give a clear idea of the movements of the heart. 1913 DORLAND *Med. Dict.* (ed. 7), *Electrocardiography. *a* 1889 *Sci. Amer. Suppl.* 8814 (Cent. D.) The *electro-chemically equivalent amount of copper sulphate. 1885 *Jrnl. Franklin Inst.* Feb. 81 The man skilled in its science [*sc.* electro-metallurgy] and art may appropriately be styled an *electro-chemist. 1851 C. CIST *Cincinnati* 302 The invention of the *electro-chronograph by Professor Locke of our city. 1888 *Encycl. Brit.* XXIII. 449/2 This is done..in *electro-contact mines by a circuit closer in the mine. 1898 *Westm. Gaz.* 28 May 2/1 The electro-contact mine is fired by an electric cable leading from the shore. 1873 SPON *Workshop Rec.* Ser. I. 212/2 Steel, iron, zinc, lead, and tin which have been previously *electro-coppered. 1902 WEBSTER Suppl., *Electro-culture. 1917 *Electrical Rev.* 6 July 21/1 Though only just beginning to attract public attention, •lectro-culture is by no means a new idea. 1920 *Electrician* 27 Aug. 223/2 Experiments were made as to the effect of applying electro-culture to three varieties of potato. 1926 *Electro-Farming* Mar. 294/2 Outside his cheery comfy house, The *electro-farmer stands. 1921 R. B. MATTHEWS in *Jrnl. Inst. Electr. Engin.* (1922) LX. 725/1 This use of the term '*electro-farming' must be interpreted in its broadest sense, i.e. whether the electrical medium provides merely mechanical methods..or whether the methods are exclusively electrical. 1885 *Encycl. Brit.* XIX. 3/1 *Electrokinematics. 1899 *Daily News* 1 July 4/5 This Westinghouse *electro-pneumatic signalling plant. 1902 *Encycl. Brit.* XXXII. 147/2 In the electro-pneumatic system a full-size semaphore is used. 1898 LORENZ tr. Löb (*title*) Electrolysis and *Electrosynthesis of Organic Compounds. 1908 *Practitioner* Oct. 609 The other sections, namely, Dermatological, *Electro-therapeutical, Epidemiological. 1909 *Ibid.* Dec. 870 The electro-therapeutical Department, West London Hospital. 1899 *Westm. Gaz.* 19 July 10/1 Oculists, and *electro-therapeutists. 1928 *Sunday Dispatch* 23 Dec. 5/6 Even Grosvenor-street having a dressmaker and an electro-therapeutist. 1928 *Daily Express* 16 May 7 An *electro-therapist. 1883 SIR W. THOMSON *Pop. Lect.* (1889) I. 134 Joule's *electro-thermal method. 1902 *Encycl. Brit.* XXVIII. 123/2 In 1885 the brothers Cowles patented a process for the electrothermal reduction of oxidized ores. 1899 *Engineering Mag.* June 495/1 *Electrothermic methods have been in use for a number of years in connection with the production of aluminium, sodium, potassium, etc. 1926 *Electro-Farming* Mar. 309 The Essentials of *Electro-Tractor Design. 1927 N. V. SIDGWICK *Electr. The. Valency* 84 Covalencies, unlike *electrovalencies, are directed forces. *Ibid.* 83 The electronic structure which we assign to an atom in a molecule depends on whether we regard its attachments to other atoms as *electrovalent or covalent.

Electrocute (ĭle·ktrŏkiūt), *v.* [f. ELECTRO-, after EXECUTE *v.*] *trans.* To put to death by means of a powerful electric current.
1889 *Voice* (N.Y.) 1 Aug., Kemmler, the murderer sentenced to be 'electrocuted'. 1890 *Boston* (Mass.) *Jrnl.* 3 May 5/6 The important thing to consider is that the State has a large number of murderers which it can neither hang nor 'electrocute'—as the new phrase hath it. 1890 *Congress. Rec.* 8375/1 That the gentleman..should be 'electrocuted' by the Kemmler process recently adopted in the state of New York. 1924 A. HUXLEY *Limbo* 84 It was as though he were about to be electrocuted.

b. *transf.* To kill in any way by electricity.
1909 *Yorkshire Post* 4 Aug. 4/5 [A boy] who was electrocuted on the Mersey Railway last Saturday. 1913 *Daily Mail* 13 Jan. 3/2 The horse..was struck by the wire and instantly electrocuted.

Electrocution (ĭlektrŏkiū·ʃən). [f. prec.: see -TION.] Execution by electricity.
1890 *Even. News* 6 May 4/1 The Supreme Court of the United States has refused to grant a writ of habeas corpus in the case of the wife murderer under sentence of electrocution. 1890 *Columbus* (Ohio) *Dispatch* 4 Aug., Buffalo parties invited to witness the Kemmler electrocution. 1902 *Encycl. Brit.* XXVI. 379/1 Sentence of death is executed by hanging by the neck except in New York and Ohio, where it is carried out by 'electrocution', or by passing through the body of the convict a current of electricity of sufficient intensity to cause death and until death is caused.

Electrode. Add: Also *attrib.*
1902 *Encycl. Brit.* XXVIII. 123/2 Ordinarily carbon is used as the electrode material. 1907 *Trans. Faraday Soc.* July 70 Electrode Potentials in Liquid Ammonia.
Hence **Ele·ctrodeless** *a.*, destitute of electrodes.
1893 *Athenæum* 13 May 609/2 Mr. E. C. Rimington read a paper 'On Luminous Discharges in Electrodeless Vacuum Tubes'. 1899 *Daily News* 29 June 6/5 The electrode-less or ring discharge in various gases.

Electromobile (ĭle·ktrŏmō^u·bil). (Disused.) [f. ELECTRO- after *automobile*.] A motor vehicle driven by electricity. Also *attrib.*
1899 *Automotor* Nov., Accumulators for Electromobiles. 1900 G. ILES *Flame, Electr. & Camera* 148 An electromobile cab. 1906 (*title*) Steam Car and Electromobile Review. 1907 *Daily Chron.* 12 Nov. 7/4 The new electromobile garage, the largest in the world.

Electromotivity (ĭle:ktro,moti·viti). [f. ELECTROMOTIVE + -ITY.] Electromotive power.
1900 *Phil. Trans.* Ser. B. CXCIII. 128 The original positive current of a freshly excised eyeball has two factors: electromotivity of the cut end of the optic nerve and electromotivity of the disturbed retina.

Electron[2] (ĭle·ktrǫn). *Physics.* [f. ELECTR(IC + *-on* in *anion, cation, ion*.] The smallest supposed component of matter, associated with (or consisting of) an invariable charge of negative electricity.
1891 *Trans. Roy. Dublin Soc.* Ser. II. IV. 583 A charge of this amount is associated in the chemical atom with each bond... These charges, which it will be convenient to call *electrons*, cannot be removed from the atom; but they become disguised when atoms chemically unite. 1902 *Fortn. Rev.* June 1023 Larmor's hypothesis of electrons, which supposes a kind of an electric atom, a charge not associated with ordinary matter. 1902 *Nature* 18 Sept. 488 The conception ..that the ultimate atoms of matter involve positive and negative electrons. 1927 A. S. EDDINGTON *Stars & Atoms* 16 The electron is the lightest thing known, weighing no more than 1/1,840 of the lightest atom.

b. *attrib.*: **electron theory** = *electronic theory* (see next).
1903 CROOKES in *Science* 26 June 1001 (Cent. D. Suppl.) The electron theory fits and luminously explains Ampere's idea that magnetism is due to a rotating current of electricity round each atom of iron. 1921 *Discovery* Sept. 226/2 The corresponding electron velocities are so small that it is difficult to measure them. *Ibid.*, We must recognise that wave radiation and electron radiation are in a sense mutually convertible.

Electronic (ĭlektrǫ·nik), *a.* *Physics.* [f. *ELECTRON[2] + -IC.] Of or pertaining to an electron or electrons.
Electronic theory, the theory that the chemical atom consists of electrons having orbital or vibratory motions under the influence of the forces acting between them.
1902 J. A. FLEMING (*title*) Electronic Theory of Electricity. 1905 AGNES M. CLERKE *Mod. Cosmogonies* x. 175 An electronic theory of gravitation. 1906 J. B. BURKE *Orig. Life* xi. 191 Three states of electronic aggregation. 1922 J. MILLS *Within the Atom* xi. 147 Whenever electronic impacts give rise to radiation, the energy associated therewith is always proportional to the frequency. *Ibid.* xii. 159 Only in a highly evacuated tube would there be the possibility of large electronic orbits. 1927 N. V. SIDGWICK (*title*) The Electronic Theory of Valency.

Electrophone (ĭle·ktrŏfō^un), *sb.* [f. ELECTRO- + -PHONE.] An instrument for transmitting sounds by means of electric currents. Also *attrib.* Hence **Ele·ctrophone** *v.*, to transmit (a speech, etc.) by this instrument. **Electropho·nic** *a.*, of or pertaining to an electrophone. **Electropho·nically** *adv.*
1868 *Chambers's Encycl.* X. 510/2 The electrophone may be adapted to the telephone. 1897 *Daily News* 6 Dec. 8/7 An 'electrophonic conversazione'. 1898 *Westm. Gaz.* 22 July 5/1 People who could hear Melba, Jean de Reszke, and the rest through the electrophone. 1900 *Ibid.* 13 Feb. 10/2 An electrophonically-heard sermon. 1904 *Ibid.* 20 Jan. 8/2 The rapidity with which the words spoken by Mr. Chamberlain in the Guildhall were electrophoned to Langham-place. 1921 *Glasgow Herald* 30 Mar. 9 By means of wireless and an electrophone device British troops on the Rhine are to be entertained at bi-weekly concerts. 1922 *Ibid.* 22 Dec. 9 The Radio Association anticipates a popularity for wireless telephony far exceeding that of the electrophone.

Electropism (ĭle·ktrŏpiz'm). *Bot.* [f. ELECTRO- + Gr. -τροπος turning + -ISM.] Curvature of growth in plants due to slight electric currents.
1898 tr. *Strasburger's Bot.* 263 The existence of electropism in plants shows clearly that an irritability may be present, from which no direct benefit is ordinarily derived. 1900 B. D. JACKSON *Gloss. Bot. Terms* 85/1 *Electropism*, the electric impulse which governs certain plant-functions.

Electrotechnic (ĭlektrote·knik). [f. ELECTRO- + TECHNIC.] *pl.* The technics of electricity. Hence **Ele:ctro-tech·nical** *a.*; **Ele:ctro-techni·cian**, one who is versed in electrotechnics.
1886 S. P. THOMPSON (*title*) Dynamo-Electric Machinery, a Manual for Students of Electrotechnics. 1896 *Daily News* 1 Dec. 5/5 A commercial as well as an electro-technical success. 1902 *Encycl. Brit.* XXXII. p. xxxii, In close touch with the Engineering Laboratory should be a Laboratory for Electro-Technical Industries. 1927 *Daily Express* 21 Dec. 11/7 Engineers who are to take charge of large machines, locomotive drivers and electro-technicians, where instant and accurate response to any change in conditions is essential, are tested by another machine.

Elegant, *a.* **8.** (Earlier U.S. examples.)
1772 *Mass. Spy* June 11 (Thornton) In the evening they exhibited some elegant fireworks from the balcony. 1817 M. BIRKBECK *Journ. Amer.* 152 You hear of an *elegant* mill, an *elegant* orchard, an *elegant* tanyard, &c...The word implies eligibility or usefulness in America, but has nothing to do with taste. 1822 J. WOODS *Engl. Prairie Illinois* 203 This negro said, some very *elegant* potatoes grew on this land last year. 1837 PECK *Gaz. Illinois* I. 38 Mr. Brigham has an elegant farm on one of these mounds.

Element, *sb.* Add:
14. c. The bottom class in some English Roman Catholic schools or colleges.
1908 *Stonyhurst Mag.* in *Tablet* 25 Apr. 646/2 We are informed that any boy from Rhetoric down to Elements may join the class.

Element, *v.* **2.** (Recent U.S. example.)
1905 GREENSLET *J. R. Lowell* 2 When we endeavor to add to our portrait of his personality some analysis of the things that elemented it.

Elemental, *a.* Add: **B.** *sb.* An entity or a force which is regarded by occultists as capable of producing physical manifestations.
1877 H. P. BLAVATSKY *Isis* Pref. p. xxx, These elementals are the principal agents of disembodied but never visible spirits. 1894 H. NISBET *Bush Girl's Rom.* 235 So that we may not be horrified or shy aside at the sight of the strange beings and elementals that surround us. 1923 RIDER HAGGARD in *Westm. Gaz.* 7 Apr., Did they suppose that God Almighty would permit a Pharaoh..thousands of years after his own death..to loose what spiritualists called an Elemental?

Elementalism (elĭme·ntăliz'm). Delete *nonce-wd.* and substitute:
1. A method or theory which divinizes the elemental powers of nature.
1863 [in Dict.]. 1882 OGILVIE Suppl., *Elementalism*, the theory which identifies the divinities of the ancients with the elemental powers. *Gladstone.*
2. A system based upon elemental forces or characters.
1921 *Glasgow Herald* 8 Jan. 4 An incompetent charlatan, performing in public under the guise of 'sublime elementalism' his worthless exercises. 1921 *Times Lit. Suppl.* 17 Feb. 106/4 To reduce two women, one the embodiment of inherited fastidiousness, the other touched with intellectual greatness, to a common level of elementalism.

Elemic (ĕle·mik), *a.* *Chem.* [f. ELEMI + -IC.] Epithet of a crystalline acid existing in elemi.
1878 *Jrnl. Chem. Soc.* XXXIV. 440 The solution of elemic acid is lævogyrate, deviating the ray 3·5°...Its formula is $C_{35}H_{56}O_4$ or $(C_5H_8)_7O_4$, thus showing elemic acid to be allied to bryoïdin, amyrin, and other derivatives of terpene, C_5H_8.

Eleonorite (e:lĭŏnō^u·rəit). *Min.* [Named (1880) *eleonorit*, f. *Eleonore* the name of a mine in the Dünsberg near Giessen.] = BERAUNITE.

1881 *Jrnl. Chem. Soc.* XL. 525. 1883 *Encycl. Brit.* XVI. 405/2.

Elephant. Add:
1. d. *To see the elephant* (U.S. slang): to see life, the world, or the sights (as of a large city); to get experience of life, to gain knowledge by experience. Also *to show* or *get a look at the elephant*.
[1840 A. B. LONGSTREET *Georgia Scenes* 10 (Thornton) That's sufficient, as Tom Haynes said when he saw the elephant.] 1844 G. W. KENDALL *Santa Fé Exped.* I. 108 There is a cant expression, 'I've seen the elephant' in very common use in Texas. 1846 W. T. PORTER *Quarter Race Kentucky* 87 (Th.), I axed him if he'd ever seen the elephant. 1849 N. KINGSLEY *Diary* 86, [I] went up town and saw the Elephant, and it almost baffles description. [1850 T. T. JOHNSON *Sights in Gold Region* 324 (Thornton) If you think we have not shown you enough of the elephant..please to mount him and take a view for yourself.] 1857 *Quinland* II. xviii. II. 126 The 'Fox and Crow' is one of the famous sights in New York. It is never missed by the countryman or the foreigner, who is searching after the 'elephant'. 1878 J. H. BEADLE *Western Wilds* iii. 45 My friend Will Wylie, who had seen the elephant in its entirety, from trunk to tail. 1906 'O. HENRY' *Four Million* 87 He makes his rounds every evening, while you and I see the elephant once a week.

e. As the emblem of the Republican party. *U.S.*
1904 *Chicago Tribune* 20 June 6 The selection..will.. handicap the republican elephant in the coming race.

f. In full *elephant-colour*: A fashion shade simulating the grey colour of the elephant. Cf. *elephant-grey* below.
1875 *All Year Round* 278/1 So admirably is elephant-colour copied. 1894 *Queen* 6 Oct. 574/1 The shade of cloth used..being known as 'Elephant'. 1923 *Daily Mail* 7 June 6 In Almond Green,..Mole, Elephant, Honey.

10. b. *Army slang.* (See quot. 1925.)
1917 EMPEY *From Fire Step* 152 One gun..had the exact range of our 'elephant' dug-out entrance. 1919 *War Terms* in *Athenæum* 15 Aug. 759/1 Elephant, corrugated iron shelter. Baby elephant, small corrugated iron shelter. 1919 G. K. ROSE *2/4th Oxf. & Bucks Lt. Infty.* 10 Battalion Headquarters..were comfortable enough with many 'elephant' dug-outs and half a farm-house for a mess. 1925 FRASER & GIBBONS *Soldier & Sailor Words*, *Elephant (and Baby Elephant) Dug-Out*: A dug-out made with semi-circular linings of heavy corrugated iron. The two names refer to the two sizes issued.

11 and **11 b. elephant grass**, a cat-tail, *Typha elephantina*, of which the leaves are used for baskets, etc., and the pollen (in India) for flour; **elephant-grey** = *1 f; **elephant-rain** (see quot.); **elephant's foot** (earlier example).
a 1815 ROXBURGH *Flora Indica* (1832) III. 566 *Elephant grass...Elephants are fond of it. 1895 MRS. CROKER *Village Tales* (1896) 15 We marched two and two,..glancing askance at every bush, at every big tuft of elephant grass. 1906 *Westm. Gaz.* 28 Dec. 2/1 Long grass in Uganda, 'elephant grass', grows from fifteen feet to twenty feet high. 1896 *Daily News* 12 Sept. 6/2 '*Elephant' grey is another favourite. 1906 *Westm. Gaz.* 7 Apr. 18/2 A tailor suit of elephant-grey facecloth. 1921 G. JEKYLL *Colour Schemes Flower Garden* 2 The trunks of the Spanish Chestnuts are elephant-grey. 1895 KIPLING *2nd Jungle Bk.* 215 A light spring rain—*elephant-rain they call it—drove across the Jungle. 1845–50 MRS. LINCOLN *Lect. Bot.* 186 The *elephant's-foot (*Elephantopus*), a low, hairy-leaved plant, with purple, ligulate florets.

Elevate, *v.* Add: **6. b.** *absol.*
1886 'M. GRAY' *Silence Dean Maitland* III. vi, It was the kind of sorrow that purifies and elevates.

Elevated, *ppl. a.* **1.** Add: Also (U.S.) *elevated railroad, railway* (examples), *road*; so *elevated train*. Also *ellipt.* as *sb.* = elevated railway, etc.
1874 KNIGHT *Dict. Mech.*, Elevated Railway. 1880 *Harper's Mag.* Sept. 563 The buzzing which vibrates in the air comes from an elevated railway. 1882 *Leisure Hour* 413/2 The variegated lamps of the frequent trains on the 'Elevated', like aerial fire-serpents, pervaded the city. 1884 *Encycl. Brit.* XVII. 465/2 After a long period of clamorous discontent, the remedy was applied in 1878 by the construction of what is known as the Elevated Railroad. 1886 *Ibid.* XX. 240/2 The New York Elevated Railroad. 1890 *Century Mag.* Nov. 45 In those days there were no elevated roads. 1901 *Scribner's Mag.* XXIX. 454/1 In the street the Ninth Avenue Elevated train roared by... The cobble-stones on Sixth Avenue were shining under the Elevated. 1904 *Booklover's Mag.* Sept. 354, I could almost fancy I was on an elevated train bound for Harlem. 1906 'O. HENRY' *Four Million* 8 Standing under a gas-light and looking over the elevated road at the moon.

Elevator. **3. a.** (Earlier examples.)
1787 in *Rep. U.S. Comm. Patents* (1849) I. 574 One of which [machines], denominated by the said Oliver Evans an elevator, is calculated by its own motion to hoist the wheat or grain from the lower floor..to the upper loft of such mill. 1795 I. WELD *Trav. N. Amer.* I. 35 The elevators are inclosed in square wooden tubes.

d. (Earlier examples and attrib. uses.)
1872 MARIETTA HOLLEY *Betsy Bobbet* (1891) 295 She spoke up and says she, 'Here is the elevater, be carried up'. 1879 F. R. STOCKTON *Rudder Grange* i. 4 You had to go up to them in an elevator. 1890 *Congress. Rec.* 8123/2 On this list there are firemen, watchmen, elevator men. 1902 *Encycl. Brit.* XXVIII. 129/1 A..plunger, which..carries the elevator-cage on its upper end. *Ibid.* 130/2 The walls..of the elevator shaft. 1904 F. LYNDE *Grafters* xxiv. 300 When the door of the elevator-cage clacked again, Kent was waiting.

4. *Aeronautics.* **a.** An elevating screw. **b.** A rudder device for lifting or steering an aircraft vertically.
1871 *English Mechanic* 27 Jan. 448/2 The side elevators would not only raise but poise the car. 1916 H. BARBER *Aeroplane Speaks* (1918) 138.

Eleven, *a.* and *sb.* Add:
A. *adj.* **2. c.** *Eleven o'clock* (U.S. and dial.), *eleven hours* (Sc.), a refreshment or slight repast taken at eleven o'clock.
1808 JAMIESON, *Eleven-hours*, a luncheon; so called from the time that labourers or children get their meridian. 1845 S. JUDD *Margaret* II. i. 214 Men and boys were seen going to the tavern for their eleven o'clock. 1888– in *Eng. Dial. Dict.* s. v.

C. elevenpenny, comb. form of *eleven pence*, as in **elevenpenny bit** *U.S.*, a coin of the value of twelve and a half cents; = LEVY *sb.*[3]
1826 *New-Harmony Gaz.* 3 May 256/2 (Th.) There were many poor people that would have made the shirts for three elevenpenny bits apiece. 1842 *Congress. Globe* 9 July, App. 699 (Th.) The bones of the biggest statesman.., ground into dust, would not be worth an elevenpenny bit. 1891 KIPLING *Light that Failed* ix, The one-and-elevenpenny umbrella.

Elevener (ĭle·v'nəɹ). Add: One who takes a drink at 11 a.m. *U.S.*
1807 JANSON *Stranger in Amer.* 299, I know of no custom more destructive than that which is practised by slingers and eleveners.

Eleventh, *a.* and *sb.* Add: **A. 1.** Also *eleventh-hour* used attrib. or as adj.
1897 FLANDRAU *Harvard Episodes* 230 So, in response to John's eleventh-hour prayers, he did what he could. 1904 *Daily Chron.* 24 Oct. 5/4 An eleventh-hour alteration in the arrangements for the return of Queen Alexandra from Copenhagen.

4. Delete † *Obs.* and add quot.:
1880 C. H. H. PARRY in Grove *Dict. Mus.* I. 437 The chord of the dominant eleventh, when complete..is hardly likely to be found unabridged. *Ibid.* 438 [Some] theorists ..repudiate the chords of the eleventh and thirteenth.

Elfin, *a.* and *sb.* Add:
B. *sb.* **4. elfin-tree**, a dwarfed alpine tree; **elfin-wood**, a wood composed of such trees.
1903 tr. *A. F. W. Schimper's Plant-Geogr.* 704 We contrast alpine grassland, alpine shrubland, and alpine desert with those of the lowlands, and retain for alpine forest merely the title elfin-wood. *Note*, 'Elfin-wood' and 'elfin-tree' are the terms introduced here as the equivalents of 'Krummholz'. *Ibid.* 705 Elfin-tree..is characterized by a short, gnarled, often oblique or horizontal stem, and long serpentine branches, which are bent in all directions.

Elia (ī·liă). The pseudonym adopted by Charles Lamb. Hence **Eliaism** (ī·liăiz'm), a characteristic Elian essay. **E·lian** *a.*, pertaining to or characteristic of the *Essays of Elia* or their author, Charles Lamb; *sb.* an admirer of 'Elia'.
1854 PATMORE *Friends & Acq.* I. 99 Lamb, in his exquisite Eliaism, 'Blakesmoor in H—shire'. 1903 in *Dobell's Catal.* June 31/2 It is a comfort to think that there are so many good and true Elians in the world. 1905 *Athenæum* 3 June 681/1 Many of the new letters are of no literary account; perhaps a score have the true Elian *cachet*. 1913 *Times Lit. Suppl.* 23 Aug. 555/2 Mr. Tillyard renounces all claims to satisfying 'every Elian'. 1929 *Daily Express* 3 Jan. 8/5 The Elian Chinaman's device for roasting pork.

Elidible (ĭlai·dĭb'l), *a.* [f. ELIDE *v.* + -IBLE.] That may be elided.
1878 G. CONWAY *Versification* 67 Theoretically, there is no interval between the elidible vowels of separate phrases.

Eligibleness (e·lidʒĭb'lnės). [f. ELIGIBLE *a.* + -NESS.] Eligibility.
1828–32 WEBSTER. 1877 G. P. FISHER *Begin. Christ.* 49 The right of suffrage, and eligibleness to office.

Eliminant. Add: **B. 2.** *Med.* An agent which eliminates deleterious matter from the system.
1887 MOLONEY *Forestry W. Afr.* 417 Recommended as an eliminant in malignant cholera. 1907 *Practitioner* Oct. 557 Stoeltzner states that the intestinal mucosa acts both as absorbent and eliminant of lime-salts.

Eliminating (ĭli·mine¹tiŋ), *ppl. a.* [f. ELIMINATE *v.* + -ING[2].] That eliminates.
1888 *Pall Mall Gaz.* 13 Sept. 4/1 The eliminating influence of the battle-field. 1909 *Westm. Gaz.* 9 June 14/3 To face the ordeal of the eliminating competition.

Eliminator. Add: **b.** Any apparatus which eliminates a battery (high or low tension or grid bias) by enabling a wireless to be worked from any electricity supply.
1928 *Morn. Post* 9 July, The rectifier intended for inclusion in high tension battery eliminators.

Elinvar (e·linvāɹ). (See quot. 1923.)
1923 *Glazebrook's Dict. Applied Physics* V. 320/1 Elinvar (short for *elasticity invariable*) is an alloy of iron and nickel, with a considerable admixture of other metals or metalloids, possessing an invariable modulus of elasticity (Young's modulus). 1928 J. E. HASWELL *Horol.* 263 Dr. Guillaume's researches have been continued, however, and in 1913 he invented an alloy of nickel-steel with a percentage of chromium, which he has named 'Elinvar' (derived from 'Elasticity invariable'). 1929 *Daily Tel.* 8 Jan. 8/6 Dr. Charles Édouard Guillaume..is the inventor of three metallic alloys of great importance, invar, elinvar, and platinite.

Elizabethanism (ĭlizăbī·þăniz'm). [See -ISM.] Manner or style, or a particular feature of these, characteristic of the reign of Queen Elizabeth of England (1558–1603).
1895 S. BAKER in *Life* (1919) II. xxxiii. 207 He who would write a translation like those of the Elizabethans must above all things avoid Elizabethanisms. 1897 *Daily News* 10 May 9/1 Complaint is heard of his 'affected Elizabethanisms'. 1909 CHESTERTON in D. Figgis *Vis. Life* Introd. p. vii, The latest Elizabethanism has differed not only from the actual Elizabethan work, but from other revivals of it.

Elizabethine (ĭlizăbī·þəin), *a.* and *sb.* [f. the name of *Elizabeth* of Hungary (1207–31) + -INE[1].] **a.** *adj.* Of or belonging to the order of St. Elizabeth. **b.** *sb.* A nun of this order.
1909 *Catholic Times* 12 Mar., She discovered the relics of St. Elizabeth in the Elizabethine convent in Vienna. *Ibid.*, The convent of the Elizabethines in the same city.

Elk[1]. Add:
1. b. (U.S. examples of collect. sing.)
1807 GASS *Jrnl.* 38 The men..killed two elk, four deer and one porcupine. 1837 W. IRVING *Capt. Bonneville* (1895) II. 132 After a time they came in sight of a gang of elk. 1850 N. KINGSLEY *Diary* 109 Saw two elk among the tulas. 1890 H. P. WELLS *City Boys in Woods* 108 (*Plate*) A group of elk.

2. b. In Anglo-Indian use, the SAMBUR.
1884 W. RICE *Indian Game* 95 Sâmbar deer, beautiful animals one sometimes hears miscalled the elk. 1890 BAKER *Wild Beasts* (1891) 414 Sâmbar deer, miscalled elk in Ceylon.

4. elk-hound, a dog of Scandinavian origin specially adapted for hunting the elk, having a thick and weather-resisting coat of a grey colour with black tips, and a thick tail curled over the back; **elk-wood** (U.S. examples).
1878 *Kennel Club Stud Bk.* 213 Norwegian *Elbehound [*sic*]. 1889 *Kennel Gaz.*, Swedish Elk Hound. 1895 *Kennel Club Cal.* (1896) XXIII. 436 Foreign Dogs...Norse (Elk-hound). 1907 R. LEIGHTON *New Bk. Dog* 491 Prominent among these varieties [of Norwegian Bear-hounds] is the Elk-hound, which may be termed the Scandinavian Pointer, for, as well as for elk and bear-hunting, it is used as a gun-dog for blackcock. 1908 *Kennel Encycl.* II. 588 The true Elk or Bear hound is distinctly by nature a hunting dog, hailing originally from Swedish Lapland or Jemtland...The dogs are designated by their owners 'Svenske Hunder'. 1814 F. PURSH *Flora Amer. Sept.* I. 381 *Elk-wood. *Magnolia tripetala.* 1834 *Southern Lit. Messenger* I. 97 The underwood is mostly streaked maple or elkwood (the *Acer Striatum* of Michaux). 1880 *Harper's Mag.* July 182/2 Vines and elk-wood cover both sides (of the rock).

Ell[2]. Read: *U.S.* = L 2 a.
1875 HOLLAND *Sevenoaks* xii. 157 Can't we put on an ell when we want it? 1876 'MARK TWAIN' *Tom Sawyer* ix. 81 A single minute later he was..creeping along the roof of the 'ell' on all fours. 1904 TOM WATSON *Bethany* (1920) 9 So it came to pass that two handsome rooms were built in the front of the west end of the old house, forming an 'ell' thereto.
attrib. 1892 HOWELLS *Mercy* 367 Matt could see a light in the ell-chamber.

Ellagitannic (elădʒitæ·nik), *a.* *Chem.* Also **ellago-**. [f. ELLAGIC + TANNIC.] *Ellagitannic acid*, an acid resembling ellagic acid, derived from the tannin of divi-divi and myrobalanes.
1891 *Jrnl. Chem. Soc.* LX. II. 918 This new ellagotannic acid, $C_{14}H_{10}O_{10}$, has already been obtained in an impure form by Löwe, from the fruit of myrobalan and divi-divi.
Also **Ellagitannin** (elădʒitæ·nin).
1895 *Naturalist* 25 Ellagotannin $C_{14}H_{10}O_{10}$, which is the most highly oxidised of vegetable astringents. 1898 *Proc. Chem. Soc.* 104 The presence of ellagic acid has also been detected, and thus besides gallotannin, ellagitannin is also present.

Elm, *sb.* Add: **2. Dutch elm**, *Ulmus suberosa*.
1731 MILLER *Gard. Dict.* dd/3 The Dutch Elm affords the worst Timber. 1882 *Garden* 11 Nov. 419/3 A form of Wych Elm entitled to specific rank is the Dutch Elm.

5. elm beetle, Elm City (also *City of Elms*) *U.S.* (see quots.); **elm butterfly**, a butterfly whose larva feeds on the leaves of the elm, as the comma-butterfly (*Grapta comma-album*).
1876 *Field & Forest* II. 12 One [insect] found destroying the foliage of the elm, pronounced..to be *Galeruca calmariensis*, the *elm beetle. 1872 PACKARD *Study Insects* Index 692/1 *Elm butterfly. 1843 *Yale Lit. Mag.* VIII. 328 Some inconsiderate hard-hearted beauty, that was supposed to reside somewhere in the '*City of Elms'. 1871 SCHELE DE VERE *Americanisms* (1872) 664 New Haven in Connecticut, is known throughout the United States as *Elm City, from the number and magnificent size of the elm-trees that adorn the public squares and most of the principal streets.

Elohim. Add: **c.** *attrib.* = ELOHIMIC *a.*
1875 *Encycl. Brit.* III. 637/1 It is still possible to reconstruct at least the Elohim document. 1886 *Ibid.* XX. 30/1 The Elohim psalms..have undergone a common editorial treatment distinguishing them from the rest of the Psalter.

Elohism (elō^u·hiz'm). [f. ELOHIM + -ISM.] The worship of Elohim.
1888 *Edin. Rev.* Apr. 502 It was the task of the great prophets..to bring Israel back to the primitive Elohism of the patriarchs.

Eloquent, *a.* Add:
4. *fig.* Clearly expressive *of*.
1873 PROCTOR *Exp. Heaven* 123 To the Almighty every atom in infinite space is eloquent of the universe itself. *a* 1882 ROSSETTI *House of Life* iv, Close-kissed and eloquent of still replies. 1885 A. FORBES *Souvenirs of some Continents* 208 His whole attitude eloquent of discouragement.

Elsewhence (e·lshwens), *adv.* Delete †*Obs. rare*[−1] and add quots.
1864 W. SMITH *Smaller Lat. Dict.* (1879), *Aliundē*, *adv.* (ali·unde) lit. else-whence. 1892 *Pall Mall Gaz.* 9 Dec. 1/2 He has learnt..not only the lesson of reticence from his Chief, but a certain lesson in vivacity to boot elsewhence.

Elul (ī·lvl). The name of one of the Jewish months, being the twelfth of the civil and sixth of the ecclesiastical year.
1535 COVERDALE *Neh.* vi. 15 The wall was fynished on the fyue & twentyeth daye of the moneth Elul. 1611 *Bible* 1 Macc. xiv. 27 The eighteenth day of the moneth Elul, in the hundred threescore and twelft yeere. 1753 CHAMBERS *Cycl.* Suppl. 1886 *Encycl. Brit.* XXI. 126/2 What we do know from a calendar of the intercalary month Elul II. is that in that month the 7th, 14th, 19th, 21st, and 28th days had a peculiar character. 1907 *Daily Chron.* 10 Aug. 4/6 With the advent of the Jewish month of Ellul, of which to-morrow is the first day, a religious revival annually takes place in Jewry.

Elutriator (ĭliū·trie¹təɹ). [f. ELUTRIATE *v.* + -OR.] An apparatus for elutriating.
1922 *Nature* CIX. 497/1 Prof. Lowry then showed 'A New Elutriator for Rapid Use', especially adapted for use in factories.

Elytro-, comb. form of Gr. ἔλυτρον sheath, used = VAGINA in various medical terms (Billings *Med. Dict.*, etc.).

Email (emā·l). [Fr., = enamel.] Used *attrib.* in **email-ink**, coloured ink used on glass, porcelain, etc. **Email ombrant** *Pottery*, a process in which the impressions of the design appear as shadows (see quots.).
1874 KNIGHT *Dict. Mech.*, *Email-ombrant*, a process which consists in flooding colored but transparent glasses over designs stamped in the body of earthenware or porcelain. 1880 C. A. JANVIER *Pract. Keramics* 95 In these the pattern is..exactly the opposite of the *emaux ombrants*. 1884 KNIGHT *Dict. Mech.* Suppl., *Email ink*...Colored inks —black, white, red, blue—used with a quill on glass, porcelain, ivory, marble, bone, mother of pearl, or metal.

Emanant (e·mănănt), *sb.* *Math.* [ad. pres. pple. of L. *ēmānāre* to EMANATE.] The result of operating upon a quantic with the operator $(x'd/dx + y'd/dy + \ldots)$.
1853 J. J. SYLVESTER *Math. Papers* (1904) I. 582 When the order of the emanant is the same as the degree of the function (supposed to be rational and integral) from which the emanant proceeds, the form of the original function is reproduced in the final emanant. 1860 CAYLEY *Math. Papers* (1891) IV. 604 The coefficients of the successive terms λ^m, $\lambda^{m-1}\mu$, etc. are said to be the emanants of the quantic $(*)(x, y)^m$.

Emanation. Add:
1. d. *Math.* The process of finding successive emanants.
1853 J. J. SYLVESTER *Math. Papers* (1904) I. 582 The process of emanation is one of incessant occurrence in the theory of invariants. 1856 CAYLEY *Math. Papers* (1889) II. 321 The facients $(X, Y, \ldots)$ may be termed the facients of emanation, or simply the new facients.

5. *Chem.* The heaviest of the inert gases, an element (no. 86) produced by radioactive disintegration.
1904 E. RUTHERFORD *Radio-Activity* 226 Red-hot magnesium would not retain an emanation consisting of radio-active hydrogen, or red-hot zinc-dust, an emanation consisting of radio-active carbon dioxide. *Ibid.*, Since the matter which produces the phenomena of excited radio-activity is derived from the emanation of thorium and of radium, the name *emanation X* will be given to it. 1927 N. V. SIDGWICK *Electronic The. Valency* 7 Radium in Group II becomes emanation in Group 0.

Emanatist. Delete *rare* and add *attrib.*
1866 LIDDON *Bampton Lect.* vii. (1867) 646 These Emanatist doctrines. *Ibid.* 647 The Nicene Fathers..were able.. to vindicate for the word its Catholic sense, unaffected by any Emanatist gloss.

Emancipation. Add: **2. a.** (U.S. example.) *Emancipation Day*, the day, Jan. 1, 1863, when by President Lincoln's *Emancipation Proclamation* the slaves in the Southern States were declared to be free.
1834 *Southern Lit. Messenger* I. 88 The abolitionists find fault with colonization because, say they, its aim is to postpone or prevent emancipation. 1861 O. W. NORTON *Army Lett.* 29, I am fully satisfied..that it [*sc.* the war] cannot be ended without the emancipation proclamation. 1865 *Nation* I. 163 (Cent. Dict.) Was the Emancipation Proclamation legally operative and efficient the moment it was uttered? 1905 *Hartford Courant* 3 Jan. 10 The 42nd anniversary of Emancipation Day was celebrated last evening by the colored people of this city.

Emanometer (emănǫ·mĭtəɹ). [irreg. f. EMANATE *v.* + -METER.] An instrument which furnishes a diagnosis of a disease by testing the emanations of a patient. Also *attrib.*
1923 *Westm. Gaz.* 2 Mar., Boyd's Emanometer. 1924 *Glasgow Herald* 23 Jan. 8 The emanometer, which..was invented by a San Franciscan doctor and improved by Dr. Boyd, of Glasgow. 1925 HORDER *Comm. conc. Electr. React.* 43 Report on Emanometer tests conducted with Dr. W. G. Boyd at Glasgow, June, 1924.

Embanker (ĕmbæ·ŋkəɹ). [f. EMBANK *v.* + -ER[1].] One who makes an embankment.
1851 WIGGINS *Embanking* 80 The embanker may..always test the time it will take to freshen and to admit the growth of clover by experiments on the soil from different spots. 1896 *Contemp. Rev.* Aug. 203 Barrowers,..embankers,..and bricklayers.

Embargo, *sb.* Add: **embargo act, law** *U.S.*, a statute, e.g. that of 1807–8, 1812, and 1813, forbidding the clearing of foreign merchant vessels from any port except by the special permission of the President.
1809 *Repertory* (Boston) Jan. 27 (Thornton) The Embargo laws were called *O grab me* laws. 1883 *Encycl. Brit.* XV. 301/2 Everything prospered until the Embargo Act of 1808, cutting off commerce and the coast trade, struck Maine in a vital point.

Embarkation. **1.** *attrib.* Add quots.
1899 *Westm. Gaz.* 9 Nov. 10/2 As the ship was about to sail, investigations were made, and..the embarkation officer went aboard to see the supply. 1904 *Daily Chron.* 6 Sept. 6/7 The embarkation staff at the port.

Embarras, *sb.* **2.** *U.S.* (Earlier examples.)
1814 H. M. BRACKENRIDGE *Views Louisiana* 203 At the distance of every mile or two,..there are *embarras*, or rafts, formed by the collection of trees closely matted, and extending from twenty to thirty yards. *Ibid.* 208 Passed an *embarras*, N.E. side, the most difficult since we started.

Emblaze (ĕmblē¹·z), *sb.* [Cf. EMBLAZE *v.*[2]] = EMBLAZONRY I b.
1892 *Harper's Mag.* LXXXIV. 194 Dragons and monsters, crescents, stars and all the arrogant emblaze of heraldry.

Emblema (emblī·mă). [L.: see EMBLEM *sb.*] An ornament in relief, either carved or mounted, on jewellery, vases, etc.
1842 *W. Smith's Dict. Grk. & Rom. Antiq.* 1880 C. T. NEWTON *Art & Archæol.* 265 Embossed and cut out in outline, like the *emblemata* of later Greek art. 1885 *Encycl. Brit.* XIX. 181/1 A seated figure of Athene—an 'emblema' soldered on, in very high relief.

Embolic, *a.* Add:
2. *Embryology.* Characterized by emboly; invaginate.
1883 E. R. LANKESTER in *Encycl. Brit.* XVI. 653/1 The embolic Paludina. 1884–5 SEDGWICK & HEATHCOTE tr. *Claus' Zool.* 114 The two-layered gastrula is, as a rule, developed from the blastosphere by invagination (embolic invagination). 1888 ROLLESTON & JACKSON *Anim. Life* p. xxvi, The latter [*sc.* larger cells of the blastosphere] undergo invagination or *emboly*, that is to say they sink inwards, obliterating more or less completely the blastocoele. The result is an invaginate, or embolic Gastrula.

Embolism. Add:
3. b. *Path.* An obstruction in a blood-vessel. (Cf. sense 3 and EMBOLUS 2.)
1902 *Encycl. Brit.* XXXI. 565/2 The small vessels are sometimes blocked by masses of organisms only, producing minute embolisms.

4. In the Eucharistic canon of Eastern liturgies = EMBO-LISMUS 2.
1881 WESTCOTT & HORT *Greek Test.* App. 9 The embolism, or expanded last double petition. 1883 *Encycl. Brit.* XVI. 509/1 The 'canon'..(except in the Nestorian liturgy) concludes with the Lord's Prayer and 'embolism'. 1904 *Rock's Ch. Fathers* II. xi. IV. 105 The Lord's Prayer was said as at the end of the Canon, with its bidding before it and its embolism after it.

Embolium (embǫ·liŏm). *Ent.* [mod.L., a. Gr. ἐμβόλιον insertion, f. ἐν in + βολ-, var. of root of βάλλειν to throw.] The marginal part of the corium in some heteropterous insects.
1889 *Cent. Dict.* 1895 COMSTOCK *Insects* 125 Classification of the Heteroptera...In certain other cases, a narrow piece on the costal margin of the corium is separated by a suture; this is the *embolium*. 1899 G. H. CARPENTER *Insects* 187 The *corium*..in most families reaches to the costa, but in one is separated from that edge by a narrow *embolium*.

Embracive (ĕmbrē¹·siv), *a.* [f. EMBRACE *v.* + -IVE.] **1.** *nonce-use.* (See Dict.)
2. Embracing or tending to embrace all. Hence **Embra·cively** *adv.*
1897 *Academy* 18 Sept., Fiction Suppl. 70/1 'George Du Maurier in three volumes' would be a fair embracive title. 1899 *Westm. Gaz.* 22 Apr. 7/2 General Sir W. Olpherts, V.C., in replying for 'The Army' embracively spoke of the American Army. 1902 *Academy* 16 Aug. 178/1 The 'characteristics of the time' and the 'natural lineaments of contemporary people' may have found no embracive novelist. 1920 *Edin. Rev.* Oct. 357 Important deities have been omitted from this brief catalogue, which is much more representative than embracive. 1930 *Punch* 18 June 683 Perhaps he is too embracive, for it is doubtful if Mr. William Nicholson should be grouped with purely comic artists.

Embrithite (e·mbriþəit). *Min.* [a. G. *embrithit*, f. Gr. ἐμβριθής heavy + -ITE[1].] A variety of boulangerite.
1854 DANA *Syst. Min.* (ed. 4) II. 81. 1883 *Encycl. Brit.* XVI. 395/1 Plumbostib or Embrethite, from Nerchinsk.

Embri·ttle, *v.* [f. EM- + BRITTLE *a.*] *trans.* To render brittle.
1902 *Encycl. Brit.* XXIX. 574/2 Sudden cooling hardens and embrittles steel and cast iron. 1903 H. M. HOWE *Iron, Steel*, etc. 257 The coarsening and embrittling of low-carbon steel.

Embroidery. Add: **6.** *attrib.* and *Comb.*
1880 L. HIGGIN *Handbk. Embroidery* i. 1 'Embroidery needles' for ordinary crewel handwork. 1882 CAULFEILD & SAWARD *Dict. Needlework* 197/1 Embroidery needles..for canvas work..are short, thick, and blunt, and the eye is wide and long. *Ibid.*, Embroidery paste is used for two purposes in needlework: one to make two materials adhere together, the other to strengthen and stiffen Embroidery at the back. 1899 *Daily News* 28 June 8/4 A gigantic embroidery-like cloth of gold. 1909 *Englishwoman* Apr. 232 The lace-making and embroidery industry.

Embryo-, combining form of Gr. ἔμβρυον EMBRYON, as in **E:mbryoca·rdia**, an affection of the heart in which its action resembles that of the fœtal heart. **E:mbryopla·stic** *a.*, pertaining to or participating in the formation of the embryo (Billings *Med. Dict.* 1890). **E·mbryoscope**, an instrument for examining embryos; so **E:mbryosco·pic** *a.* **E:mbryospa·stic** *a.*, applied to instruments designed to bring away a child from the uterus without injury. **E:mbryoto·mic** *a.*, pertaining to or used in embryotomy.
1908 OSLER & MᶜCRAE *Syst. Med.* IV. 275 Tachycardia with *embryocardia exhibits phenomena which correspond to a prolonged series of extrasystole. 1908 *Practitioner* Feb. 291 With gradual heart weakness and signs of dilatation, the long pause is greatly shortened, the sounds approach each other in tone, and have a fœtal character (embryocardia). 1909 ALLBUTT & ROLLESTON *Syst. Med.* VI. 499 The name 'embryocardia'..is pedantic if it means merely a very rapid heart; misleading if it means that the heart has undergone some reversion to a fetal state. 1889 GEDDES & THOMSON *Evol. Sex* 103 The minute area of formative protoplasm [that] the observers of to-day look down upon through their *embryoscopes. 1828 *Lancet* 5 Apr. 4/2 A case requiring the use of *embryospastic instruments. *Ibid.*, Instruments..designed to bring away the child by reducing its bulk, and those again which are intended to abstract the fœtus without injury..the latter may be called the embryospastic instruments, the former the *embryotomic.

Embryogenical (e:mbriodʒe·nikăl), *a.* [See -ICAL.] = EMBRYOGENIC.
1895 *Pop. Sci. Monthly* July 395 Degeneration in general results from embryogenical troubles.

Embryoma (embriō^u·mă). Pl. **-mata.** *Path.* [f. EMBRYO + *-OMA.] A tumour composed of fœtal tissues.
1903 J. H. TEACHER in *Jrnl. Obstet. & Gynæcol.* July 54 Either at once (congenital tumours) or after an interval (mixed tumours of later life) this developes into an imperfect organism—a teratoma or embryoma. 1906 *Practitioner* Nov. 664 V. Bonney..derives teratomata and embryomata, ..not originating in pregnancy, from cell seclusions formed normally, or abnormally, during embryonic life.

Embryonically (embriǫ·nikăli), *adv.* [f. EMBRYONIC *a.*: see -ICALLY.] In (the) embryo.
1883 M. FOSTER & F. M. BALFOUR *Embryol.* (ed. 2) 255 The atrophy of the dorsal section of the embryonically large canal of the spinal cord. 1899 E. GRIFFITH-JONES *Ascent through Christ* 377 In prophecy He was as it were embryonically incarnated.

Embryoniferous (embriŏni·fĕrəs), *a.* *Bot.* [f. EMBRYO + -(I)FEROUS.] Producing or bearing an embryo.
1819 LINDLEY tr. *Richard's Observ. Fruits & Seeds* 29 An examination of the embryoniferous cavity. 1834 R. BROWN *Misc. Bot. Wks.* (1866) I. 570 The remains of the embryoniferous areolæ, from four to six in number, were still visible.

Embus (embv·s), *v.* [f. EM-1 a + BUS *sb.*, after *embark*.] **a.** *intr.* To mount a bus or transport vehicle. **b.** *trans.* To transport by 'bus'.
1915 [see *DEBUS]. 1927 *Daily Tel.* 13 Sept. 10/3 Using the mechanised transport thus released for embussing the headquarters. 1929 D. RORIE *Medico's Luck* vii. 141 On the 24th July we left Clairmarais for Lederzeele, and 'embussed'..for the XVIII Corps.

Embusqué (anbüske). [subst. use of pa. pple. of F. *embusquer* to ambush.] One who escaped war service by working in a government office or the like; a 'Cuthbert'.
1920 *Blackw. Mag.* May 586/2 These particular *embusqués*, who made Egypt a byword during the War. 1926 *Spectator* 7 Aug. 207/2 The best scenes are those between the poor *embusqué* and his wife.

Emerge, *v.* **4.** Add: Also said of the production of a type by such a process as evolution.
1912 G. E. SMITH in *Rep. Brit. Assoc.* 582 When the true mammal emerged.

Emergence. **2.** Add: Also said of the result of an evolutionary process: cf. prec.
1912 G. E. SMITH in *Rep. Brit. Assoc.* 577 The gradual emergence of human traits from the uncouth simian features of our ancestors. 1912 GEDDES & THOMSON *Evolution* 102 It is undeniably difficult to discover the factors in his emergence and ascent.

Emergency. Add:
4. c. *Cricket*, etc. An emergency man, a substitute.
1862 in W. G. Grace *Cricketing Remin.* i. (1899) 12 With this ball (presented by M.C.C. to E. M. Grace), he got every wicket in 2nd innings, in the match played at Canterbury, August 14, 15, 1862, Gentlemen of Kent v. M.C.C. for whom he played as an emergency, and in which, going in first, he scored 192 not out.

5. Now esp. in general adj. sense 'used, issued, called upon, or arising in an emergency'.
1896 *Daily Chron.* 15 Aug. 11/6 She had been asked by the medical officer to take charge of the emergency brandy. 1898 *Daily News* 13 May 5/2 The emergency ration is never served out for more than five days consecutively. 1900 *Jrnl. Soc. Arts* 21 Sept. 802/2 The fitting of emergency brakes. 1902 *Young Engineer* I. 47/2 Doors are provided both for regular use and as emergency exits. 1903 *Westm. Gaz.* 11 Sept. 8/1 Directly the current between the Bank Station and the stations as far as the British Museum was cut off, an emergency current was turned on. 1904 *Baltimore American* 13 June 6 The emergency offices of the Baltimore American. 1904 F. F. MOORE *Original Woman* xxiv, He was a man who always had at hand an emergency exit opening outward by which he could escape from any situation that was getting too hot for him. 1915 *Lit. Digest* (N.Y.) 21 Aug. 348/1 All of the [beaver-]ponds are equipped with 'emergency exits' in the form of holes in the bank. 1920 *Act* 10 *Geo. V* c. 5 (*title*) An Act to continue temporarily certain emergency enactments. 1921 *Dict. Occup. Terms* (1927) § 729 *Emergency man*..a tramway conductor..who is held in readiness to replace anyone of depot cashier's assistants who may be on leave or sick. 1925 A. S. M. HUTCHINSON *One Increasing Purpose* I. xx, 'Have you a girl on your staff called Glade?' 'Not on my staff...Miss Glade is one of my emergency-calls. I get her when I want her, if she is available.' 1926 W. DEEPING *Sorrell & Son* xxx, He asked you to do an emergency job for him in the theatre. 1929 *Star* 21 Aug. 12/1 Glamorgan's emergency bowlers.

6. *Bot.* = EMERGENCE 4.
1876 *Encycl. Brit.* IV. 90/2 When the cells of hairs are hardened by thickening of the cell-wall..they are called Prickles...By some these are not considered as hairs, but are termed emergencies.

Supplement, p. 3873; Corrigenda, p. 4092; Spurious words, p. 4093; Books quoted, p. 4094

Emergent. B. *sb.* 1. Add: In wider use: Something that emerges.

1920 *Challenge* 15 Oct. 337/2 The growing estrangement [between England and Ireland] which is the mildest emergent from the tragedy. 1928 Joad *Future of Life* vi. 105 The mind is an 'emergent' upon the combination of two constituents—namely the body and what Professor Broad calls the 'psychic factor'.

Emeritus, *a.* (Earlier U.S. example.)

1794 *U.S. Register* (Philad.) 119 Emeritus professor of divinity.

Emersonian (emərsōᵘ·niăn), *a.* and *sb.* [f. the name of the American author Ralph Waldo *Emerson* (1803–1882) + -IAN.]

A. *adj.* Of, pertaining to, or characteristic of Emerson or his writings. B. *sb.* An admirer or follower of Emerson. Hence **Emerso·nianism.**

1851 *Family Friend* July 120/2 (*title*) Emersonian Treasures. 1870 *Gentl. Mag.* July 160 He 'planted himself', in Emersonian language, 'upon his instincts'. 1883 *Century Mag.* XXVII. 930 It is hard to reconcile Arnold's criticism of Emerson's poetry with what many of us feel to be its beauty and value. It is irritating to Emersonians to be compelled to admit that his strain lacks any essential quality. 1884 J. Hawthorne in *N. Amer. Rev.* Aug. 166 To be Emersonian is to be American. 1888 *Athenæum* 24 Mar. 372/2 In later life he [*sc.* A. B. Alcott] went about the American cities as a peripatetic philosopher, displaying in 'conversations' the Emersonian jewels and Transcendental wares. 1928 *Hist. Amer. Lit.* I. 352 The volatile and heady liquid known as Emersonianism.

Emery, *sb.* Add: 1. b. A case containing emery: cf. *emery bag* (below).

1900 Mary E. Wilkins *Love of Parson Lord* 47 Her scissors, her emery, her thread were on the ground. *Ibid.* 49 An emery of painted velvet in an ivory case.

3. *emery grinding, shaping*; **emery bag** (see quot. 1895); **emery-cake,** a compound of emery and beeswax; **emery planer,** a planer having an emery wheel as a cutter instead of a blade.

1895 *Funk's Stand. Dict.*, *Emery bag, a small bag or case filled with emery; used for keeping needles bright and clean. 1905 *Daily Chron.* 6 Apr. 4/7 A minority of Englishwomen who chafed against their educational inequalities, who loathed their emery-bag destiny. 1853 Ure *Dict. Arts* (ed. 4) I. 644 *Emery-cake consists of emery mixed with a little beeswax. 1884 Knight *Dict. Mech.* Suppl., *Emery Grinding Machine. 1902 *Encycl. Brit.* XXVIII. 154/1 Emery grinding operations may be divided into four classes. 1883 *Ibid.* XV. 157/1 Emery wheels are now mounted for use in a great many different ways,—either on slide-rests as turning tools, in *emery planers and *emery shaping machines.

Emigrant, *sb.* Add: Freq. *attrib.* in sense 'of, pertaining to, or used by emigrants', as *emigrant camp, car, company, road, ship, trail, vessel.*

1842 *Amer. Almanac* (Boston) 321 The emigrant ship called the Governor Fenner..comes in collision with the Nottingham Steamer. 1845 Fremont *Exped.* 107 The usual emigrant road to the mountains. *Ibid.* 133 The edge of the wood..was dotted with the white covers of emigrant wagons. *Ibid.* 179, I had determined to leave the emigrant trail. 1846 Sage *Scenes Rocky Mts.* (1859) 30 Here, most of the..emigrant companies remain encamped for several weeks. 1849 Parkman *Oregon Trail* 105 The white tents and wagons of an emigrant camp. 1852 *Mass. Acts & Res.* 314 The consequence is, that emigrant vessels discharge at New York. 1858 *Penn. Rail Road Annual Rep.* 14 The rolling stock ..consisted..of 31 Emigrant Cars. 1883 Nye *Baled Hay* 56 The tourists..got them onto the emigrant train.

Emilian (ĭmi·liăn), *a.* and *sb.* Also 9 **Æmilian.** [f. *Emilia* + -AN.] Of or pertaining to Emilia, a department of Northern Italy; a native or inhabitant of Emilia; the dialect of Italian spoken there.

1660 E. Warcupp *Italy* i. 82 At Piacenza begins the Emilian Way. 1776 Gibbon *Decl. & F.* xiv. (1782) I. 505 From Milan to Rome, the Æmilian and Flaminian highways offered an easy march of about four hundred miles. 1878 *Encycl. Brit.* VIII. 701/1 The dialects..of Upper Italy, including Genoese, Piedmontese, Venetian, Æmilian, and Lombard. 1880 *Ibid.* XIII. 435/1 The side of the Apennines, where the great Emilian Way..preserves an unbroken straight line from Rimini to Piacenza. *Ibid.* 493/1 Characteristic of the Piedmontese, the Lombard, and the Emilian is the continual elision of the unaccented final vowels. *Ibid.*, Gallo-Italian and more specially Emilian characteristics. 1893 G. A. Greene *Ital. Lyrists* Introd. p. xxx, The Tuscans, Emilians, and Romans must be classed together. 1904 E. G. Gardner *Dukes & Poets in Ferrara* 10 Transfigured in the glow of an Emilian sunset.

Emission. 3. (Earlier Amer. example.)

1729 Franklin *Paper Currency* Wks. 1905 II. 141, I appeal to those immediately concerned..whether Land has not risen very much since the first Emission of what Paper Currency we now have.

Emissivity (ĭmisi·vĭti). [f. Emissive + -ity.] Emissive or radiating power of heat or light; *spec.* in *Physics* (see quot. 1902).

1880 *Encycl. Brit.* XI. 577/2 We define thermal emissivity as the quantity of heat per unit of time. *Ibid.*, The first thoroughly trustworthy experiments giving emissivities in absolute measure. 1884 Tait *Light* 248 We now define the emissivity of a body at a given temperature, for a particular radiation, as the ratio of its emission of that radiation to the emission of the same radiation by a black body at the same temperature. 1891 *Proc. Royal Soc.* L. 166 The Thermal Emissivity of Thin Wires in Air. 1902 *Encycl. Brit.* XXVII. 189/2 Fourier defined another constant expressing the rate of loss of heat at a bounding surface per degree of difference of temperature between the surface of the body and its surroundings. This he called External Conductivity, but the term Emissivity is more convenient.

Emit, *v.* 6. (Earlier Amer. examples relating to currency.)

1716 *Jrnls Ho. Repr. Mass.* I. 160 An Act for the making and Emitting the Sum of One Hundred Thousand Pounds in Bills of Credit on this Province. 1775 *Jrnls. Cont. Congress* III. 390 Report the number and denomination of the bills to be emitted.

Emma, used in telephone communications and in the oral transliteration of code messages for *m*, as in *emma gee*, for *m.g.* = machine gun; *ack emma*, for *a.m.* = ante meridiem; *pip emma*, for *p.m.* = post meridiem; *toc emma*, for *t. m.* = trench mortar.

1919 *War Slang* in *Athenæum* 18 July 632/2 'Emma Gee', 'Tock Emma', and a host of others. 1920 *Blackw. Mag.* Oct. 468/1 They can bet on tools being downed by three pip emma signal time.

Emmenagogue, *a.* Delete † *Obs.* and add:

1861 Bentley *Man. Bot.* 625 *Petiveria alliacea* is reputed sudorific and emmenagogue. 1874 Garrod & Baxter *Mat. Med.* 232 Myrrh..is supposed to possess antispasmodic and emmenagogue properties. 1887 Moloney *Forestry W. Afr.* 328 All parts of this plant are said to be emmenagogue.

Emmenthaler (e·mɑntālər). [Name of locality in Switzerland.] A variety of pressed cheese resembling gruyère.

1902 *Encycl. Brit.* XXVII. 355/2 Of the varieties of cheese made in Switzerland, the best known is the Emmenthaler.

Emmer (e·mər). [Upper G. *emmer* (OHG., MHG. *amer*).] A species of wheat. Also *attrib.*

1921 G. A. F. Knight *Nile & Jordan* iii. 32 One of the names of the primitive 'emmer-corn' in Babylonia was *bututtu*, which is akin to the Egyptian *bôti*. 1924 J. A. Thomson *Science Old & New* xliii. 250 According to Aaronsohn, there is strong evidence for regarding the Hermon wheat as the ancestor of Emmer. 1928 V. G. Childe *Most Anc. East* ii. 43 The wild ancestor of emmer wheat (*Triticum dicoccum* with fourteen chromosomes) is alleged to grow native in Western Persia and Mesopotamia, in Syria and Palestine.

Emotionable (ĭmōᵘ·ʃənăb'l), *a.* [f. Emotion + -able.] = Emotional 2.

1889 *Univ. Rev.* III. 46 The secret of his supremacy over an emotionable nation. 1893 H. W. Lucy in *Daily News* 6 May 5/5 Mr. Asquith, not ordinarily an emotionable man.

Emotionlessness (ĭmōᵘ·ʃənlĕsnĕs). [f. Emotionless + -ness.] The character or condition of being emotionless.

1921 T. R. Glover *Jesus in Exper. of Men* xiii. 219 One of their ideals was 'Emotionlessness'. 1926 *Chambers's Jrnl.* 357/1 The whole face had a suggestion of emotionlessness acquired by habit.

Empathy (e·mpăþi). *Psychol.* [Rendering (after Gr. ἐμπάθεια) of G. *einfühlung* (Lipps), f. *ein* in + *fühlung* feeling.] The power of entering into the experience of or understanding objects or emotions outside ourselves.

1912 *Academy* 17 Aug. 209/2 [Lipps] propounded the theory that the appreciation of a work of art depended upon the capacity of the spectator to project his personality into the object of contemplation. One had to 'feel oneself into it'...This mental process he called by the name of *Einfühlung*, or, as it has been translated, *Empathy*. 1913 J. M. Baldwin *Hist. Psychol.* II. 126 *note*, 'Æsthetic semblance' is the equivalent of 'empathy'. 1928 'Rebecca West' *Strange Necessity* 102 The active power of empathy which makes the creative artist, or the passive power of empathy which makes the appreciator of art. 1928 *Observer* 29 July 5 Joyce, like Proust, is the possessor of a violent empathy.

Empennage (empe·nĕdʒ). [Fr., f. *empenner* to feather (an arrow).] An arrangement of stabilizing planes at the stern of an aeroplane or airship; also, the tail-surfaces or tail-plane.

1909 A. Berget *Conquest of Air* II. i. 132 The empennage will comprise a surface placed well to the rear of the sustaining surface..to which it will be joined. 1911 *Aero* Nov. 232/1 The construction of the empennage or fixed 'nonlifting' tail plane. 1912 S. L. Walkden *Aeroplanes in Gusts* xii. 95 This..only defines the path AH more obstinately than before, unless the empennage is made with considerable spread in the fore-and-aft direction. 1926 *Chambers's Jrnl.* 580/1 In every aeroplane the tail unit or 'empennage' comprises the rudder,..the elevators,..and the fin.

Emperor. Add: 4. b. *ellipt.* for *emperor fish, emperor penguin.*

1927 *Times* (weekly ed.) 3 Feb. 115/3 The King penguins.. are, next to the Emperors, the largest of the family. 1929 S. E. Napier in *Times* 2 Aug. 14/1 'Emperors', beautiful fish of about 30 lb., and of a rich red colour all over.

6. **emperor fish,** a brilliant-coloured chætodont food fish; **emperor goose,** a goose of Alaska, *Philacte canagica*, having handsomely variegated plumage; **emperor penguin,** the largest of the penguin family, *Aptenodytes imperator.*

1896 Lydekker *Royal Nat. Hist.* V. 344 The splendidly-coloured *emperor-fish (*H*[*olacanthus*] *imperator*)..ranges from the east coast of Africa to the Indian and Malayan seas. 1872 Coues *Key N. Amer. Birds* 283 Painted Goose. *Emperor Goose. Wavy bluish-gray, with lavender or lilac tinting. 1885 *Encycl. Brit.* XVIII. 492 '*Emperor' and 'King' Penguins. 1895 Lydekker *Royal Nat. Hist.* IV. 546 The king-penguin..and the still larger emperor-penguin. 1905 R. F. Scott *Voy. 'Discov.'* I. 148 A small colony of Emperor penguins in process of moulting exhibited the most dishevelled appearance.

Emphasizer (e·mfăsəizər). [f. Emphasize *v.* + -er [1].] One who or that which emphasizes.

1887 *Outing* (U.S.) X. 111/1 By way of an emphasizer, striking the table a blow with his fist. 1922 H. W. Fowler in *S.P.E. Tract No. XI* 20 We have come to such a pass with this emphasizer [*sc. literally*] that [etc.].

E·mphasizing, *vbl. sb.* [f. Emphasize *v.* + -ing [1].] The action of the verb.

1888 Mrs. H. Ward *Robt. Elsmere* I. vi, The emphasising rather than the surrender of self.

Emphatic. 1. Add: Also *sb. pl.* Emphatic words or phrases.

1873 Gilbert *More 'Bab' Ballads, Lost Mr. Blake* iii, I have known him to indulge in profane, ungentlemanly emphatics. 1905 *Daily Chron.* 23 Oct. 3/4 His emphatics, his luxuriant indulgence in the use of the 'and'.

Empiecement (empī·smĕnt). [ad. F. *empiècement*, f. *em-* = *en-* + *pièce* Piece *sb.* + -ment.] A piece of ornamental material inserted in a garment as a trimming.

1899 *Daily News* 26 Jan. 6/3 The cape matched the dress, and its empiecement and storm collar were covered with steel embroidery. 1902 *Westm. Gaz.* 17 Apr. 3/1 The skirt of this costume has the popular empiecement about the waist. 1927 *Observer* 13 Mar. 25 Empiecements in artistic and other geometrical designs are inserted on some, bars of a contrasting material on others.

Empire, *sb.* Add:

5. b. *The Empire*: (*b*) Great Britain with its colonies and dependencies; the British Empire. (Cf. *British Empire*: see *British *a.* 2 b.)

1772 R. Cumberland Advt. to *Fashionable Lover* p. vi, Wherever..I have made any attempts at novelty, I have found myself obliged to dive into the lower class of men, or betake myself to the out-skirts of the empire. 1776 Adam Smith *W. N.* v. iii. II. 586 Countries which contribute neither revenue nor military force towards the support of the empire. 1847 in J. C. Byrne *Twelve Years Wand. Brit. Colonies* (1848) II. iii. 86 This gentleman asked whether the colony was to remain the sink-hole of the empire. 1862 *Englishwoman's Dom. Mag.* Jan. 136 'The Hope of the Empire'—the Prince of Wales. 1900 J. Chamberlain in *Daily News* 25 Oct. 4/4 Was it too much to say that in this last twelve months the Empire had been born anew? 1902 Earl of Meath in *Times* 18 July 8/2 Their fellow-subjects in other portions of the Empire. 1904 *Daily Chron.* 15 Nov. 6/7 Lord Rosebery, in his capacity of principal guest at a dinner of the Oxford Colonial Club last night, replied to the toast of the 'Empire'. 1917 R. Muir *Char. Brit. Empire* 13 The British Navy has made the growth of the Empire possible.

(*c*) the rule of Napoleon Bonaparte as Emperor of the French, 1804–14, or the period of this.

1830 W. Hazlitt *Life Nap. Buonaparte* III. 114 If the reign of terror excited their fears and horror, the establishment of the Empire under Buonaparte seemed even a greater affront and encroachment on their pride and privileges. 1902 J. H. Rose *Life Napoleon I* I. 470 At Metz the troops and populace fretted against the Empire and its pretentious pomp. 1904 R. M. Johnston *Napoleon* viii. 111 In 1805 began the first of the three great cycles of the wars of the Empire. 1924 R. B. Mowat *Diplom. Napoleon* xiii. 132 Bonaparte had ushered in the Empire by proclaiming his contempt for the law of nations.

8. *empire-builder, -building, -grown* adj., *-maker, -making*; **Empire City** *U.S.* (examples); **Empire Day,** May 24, the birthday of Queen Victoria, usually observed as a (school) holiday in the British Empire, and instituted as a memorial of the assistance given by the colonies to the mother country in the South African war of 1899–1902; **Empire Marketing Board,** a body set up to superintend and promote the development of the market in Great Britain for the produce of the dominions; **Empire State** *U.S.* (examples); **empire-waisted** *a.*, having a waist of a type fashionable under the French Empire.

1894 *Westm. Gaz.* 30 June 6/1 A reference to Mr. Cecil Rhodes's work as *empire-builder. 1909 Visct. Morley in *Westm. Gaz.* 10 June 7/1 As if Shakespeare and Burns and Bunyan and Swift and all the rest of that superb gallery were not the greatest of British Empire-builders. 1898 *Daily News* 12 Aug. 6/1 His exploits in the *Empire-building line. 1854 Mary J. Holmes *Tempest & Sunshine* xvi. 104 When you return, I shall probably be looking on the dust, smoke, and chimneys of the *Empire City. 1857 W. Chandless *Visit Salt Lake* II. v. 222 The mint julep, that in the Crescent City you may enjoy for ten cents, costs you twelve and half in the Empire city. 1904 *N. Y. Tribune* 24 Oct. 5 Thursday's formal opening of the subway will mark a distinct red letter day even in the mighty rubric of the Empire City. 1902 *Times* 18 July 8/1 Lord Meath..wrote suggesting that May 24..should be observed as an official holiday under the title of '*Empire Day'. 1905 Earl of Meath *Addr. Exeter Hall 24th May* 11 The 'Empire Day' movement desires to promote amongst the rising generation a deeper sense of patriotic and of civic duty. 1901 *Empire Rev.* I. 370 A concession in support of *Empire-grown wine. 1903 *Daily Chron.* 5 Dec. 4/4 Whether we had 'Empire-grown' cotton, or depended chiefly on American supplies. 1903 *Westm. Gaz.* 1 June 12/3 Gazing out across the silent waters at the granite hills that have seen the passage of how many *empire-makers. 1894 *Daily News* 29 Jan. 5/2 Mr. Rhodes is an *Empire-making man. 1927 *Daily Tel.* 5 Mar. 8/7 The *Empire Marketing Board for the development of the market for Dominion produce in Great Britain. 1835 *Knickerbocker Mag.* V. 51 Show him the public works of the *Empire State, as well as those of Pennsylvania. 1841 J. Q. Adams in *Congress. Globe* Sept. App. 433 If there is an 'Empire State' in this Union, it is Delaware..[but] if my forty friends from New York choose to call it the Empire State, I will not quarrel with them. 1860 *Leisure Hour* 29 Nov. 765/2 Illinois, the 'Empire State' of the mighty West. 1862 *Trans. Ill. Agric. Soc.* (1865) V. 693 Ours is now the Empire State of the West. 1889 Farmer *Americanisms* s.v., The term *Empire State of the South* has been applied to Georgia. 1903 *N. Y. Even. Post*, The saloon men of Tennessee have not, perhaps, the literary finish..of their brethren in the Empire State. *a* 1910

'O. Henry' *Sixes & Sevens* xiii. 146 High-collared, baggy, *empire-waisted, ample-skirted.

b. Applied to styles of furniture, etc. characteristic of the period of the French Empire (see *5 b (*c*)).

1879 *Encycl. Brit.* IX. 849/2 The 'empire' style, a stiff, affected classicalism, prevailed in France during the reign of Napoleon. 1889 R. Brook *Elem. Style Furnit.* 29 As in all other French styles, 'Empire' was closely imitated in this country. *Ibid.*, It is impossible to have a better authority on 'Empire' Furniture, than the book of designs published in Paris, by the architects, Percier and Fontaine, in 1809. 1901 E. Singleton *Furnit. of our Forefathers* II. 573 Empire sofa owned by Mrs. William Young, Baltimore, Md. 1904 H. E. Binstead *Furnit. Styles* x. 116 It is never difficult to determine what is Empire. 1905 A. Hayden *Chats on Old Furnit.* 208 The wood used for..Empire cabinets is rich mahogany.

Emplace, *v.* Delete *rare*, and add quots. in spec. sense of providing an emplacement for guns.

1900 *Daily News* 22 Jan. 3/2 This morning the Boers emplaced a five-pounder at the brick fields, and proceeded to drop shells into the market square. 1904 *Daily Chron.* 28 May 5/4 A series of batteries, strongly emplaced, crowded the crest of the hill. 1915 J. Buchan *Hist. War* V. 26 They had an ordinary range of four to five miles, and this allowed them to be emplaced well to the rear out of any danger from the enemy.

Emplane (emplēᵗ·n), *v.* [f. Em- 1 a + *Plane *sb.*[3]] *trans.* and *intr.* To take or go on board an aeroplane.

1923 *Westm. Gaz.* 2 July 3/2 Two Vickers-Victoria machines arrived, and emplaned the distressed garrison. 1930 *Air* July 292 The Prime Minister and Miss Ishbel MacDonald emplaning for a week-end in Edinburgh.

Empleomania (emplīōmēᵗ·niă). [Sp., f. *empleo* employ + Mania.] A mania for holding public office.

1878 Lowell in *Century Mag.* (1898) Nov. 144/1 The *empleomania*, which is the dry-rot of Spain. 1920 *Glasgow Herald* 23 Oct. 12 The evil which has sapped the vigour of so many nations—'empleomania'—has made its insidious way into British administrative departments. 1922 *Ibid.* 4 Jan. 4 This creed, adoption of which begets the insanity of empleomania..has had a stranglehold upon the whole Ibero-American Continent.

Employ, *sb.* Add: 4. An owner or body of owners of a ship. *U.S. Naut.*

1840 R. H. Dana *Bef. Mast* xxxi. 291 *note*, So high was the reputation of 'the employ' [*sc.* the owners of the ship] among men and officers.

Employability (èmploi,ăbi·lĭti). [f. Employable + -ity.] The character or quality of being employable.

1926 A. M. Carr-Saunders *Eugenics* vii. 157 Categories (a) and (b) of employability account for 89·4 per cent. of the men and 88·2 per cent. of the women. 1927 *Daily Tel.* 28 June 7/2 The scheme..is for the purpose of so improving the general employability of young unskilled men.

Employee. Delete *rare* exc. *U.S.* and add pronunciation (èmploi·ī) and quots.:

1891 *Pall Mall Gaz.* 23 Oct. 2/1 To arrange a forty-eight hour week for the few binders, while retaining the fifty-four hours for the bulk of the employees. 1906 *Daily Chron.* 9 May 5/5 'I don't like this affectation of "employee"', observed Judge Addison, in the Southwark County Court. 'I prefer English words.' 1909 *Ibid.* 15 Dec. 1/3 The employee shares in the company are 50,000 of £1 each. 1928 *Britain's Industr. Future* (*Lib. Ind. Inq.*) III. Argt. 141 The stimulation of employee-ownership under schemes of profit-sharing and investment by employees.

¶ In U.S. now often written **employe, employ.**

1923 Childs & Cornell *Office Administr.* 258 The training of a new employe. 1930 *Herald-Examiner* 30 June, The 3,400 employes of the Elgin National Watch Company went on a vacation Friday. 1930 *Chicago Daily News* 25 Aug., The first annual picnic of employes of The Daily News and their families.

Empressé (aṅpre·se), *a.* [Fr., pa. pple. of *empresser*, f. *em-* = *en-* + *presser* to Press.] Eager, zealous.

1837 J. F. Cooper *Recoll. Eur.* II. 42 Exceedingly *empressés* in their manner towards the Great Unknown. 1877 L. W. M. Lockhart *Mine is Thine* xvii. (1879) 160 (Stanford) Be low, be depressed, but, at the right moment, *empressé* and earnest. 1906 W. De Morgan *Joseph Vance* xxxiii. 325 'Was he very *empressé* in his manner?' I asked. 'Spooney, do you mean?'

Empting, *vbl. sb.* (Examples.)

1839 Mrs. Kirkland *New Home* xviii. 120 Mrs. Doubleday..keeps her husband's house..in unexceptionable trim. Her *emptin's* are the envy of the neighbourhood. [For 1884 read 1848.] 1889 Rose T. Cooke *Steadfast* vi. 74 Everybody wanted some of her 'empt'ins' to set their own. 1902 Clapin *Dict. Amer.* 173 *To run emptins*, to show signs of not holding out well, as for instance a speech or an enterprise of any kind.

Empty, *a.* and *sb.* B. *sb.* Add: An empty cab or taxi; an empty house or premises.

a 1859 L. Hunt in *Personal Traits Brit. Authors* (1885) 241, I found him [*sc.* a cabman] returning from Hammersmith, and he said as an empty he would take me for half-fare. 1905 *Westm. Gaz.* 23 Aug. 8/2 Property owners throughout the various suburbs of London are making loud complaint of the steady increase in the proportion of 'empties'.

Empyema. The more frequent pronunciation is now (empəi,ī·mă).

Emulant (e·miŭlănt). [a. L. *æmulant-, æmulans*, pr. pple. of *æmulārī* to rival.] One who emulates; a rival.

1878 *Scribner's Monthly* XV. 212/1, I..could not avoid furtive glances, every now and then, at the emulants.

Emulsifier (ĭmʌ·lsifəi,əɹ). *Chem.* [f. Emulsify + -er [1].] An agent which effects the emulsification of a fixed oil.

1888 *Chemist & Druggist* XXXII. 28/2 An Emulsifier Wanted. 1902 C. J. S. Thompson *Pract. Dispensing* 28 When making an emulsion the oil to be emulsified should be added to the emulsifier. 1928 *Manchester Guardian Weekly* 26 Oct. 323/4 Milk..is being produced in increasing quantities from an 'emulsifier'.

Emulsion. Add: 4. *Photog.* A mixture consisting of a silver compound held in suspension in collodion or gelatin, used in coating plates, films, etc. Also *attrib.*

1877 *English Mechanic* 23 Nov. 261/2 Emulsions..consisting of collodion and silver, ready for pouring upon plates. 1878 Abney *Treat. Photogr.* 115 All the different varieties of the emulsion processes. *Ibid.* 153 If a glass plate has to be coated with the emulsion, the same directions as those given for coating emulsion plates should be followed. 1908 *Westm. Gaz.* 18 Jan. 14/2 The emulsion side of the film or plate. *Ibid.* 25 July 14/2 This positive can be made on a silver emulsion plate. 1921 *Dict. Occup. Terms* (1927) § 148.

Emulsoid (ĭmʌ·lsoid). *Chem.* [f. Emuls(ion + -oid.] A colloid capable of redissolving after desiccation at ordinary temperatures.

1918 Webster Addenda. 1925 J. Alexander *Colloid Chem.* 27 The reversible colloids are therefore called *emulsoids* and the irreversible colloids *suspensoids.*

En (en). The name of the letter N. In *Printing*, the half square, formerly of the type n, used as a unit for measuring the amount of printed matter in a line, page, etc. Also *attrib.* (Cf. Em.)

1785 in Stower *Printer's Gram.* xvii. (1808) 419 The ems and ens at the beginnings and ends of the lines not to be reckoned in the width. 1793 *Ibid.* 419 That em and en quadrats..be included. 1888 *Pall Mall Gaz.* 10 Sept. 11/2 The 'justifier'..spaces out the lines with great regularity and in so short a time that 20,000 ens per hour is about the average output. 1891 *Printers' Register* 7 Dec., 49,000 American ems, equal to 98,000 English ens. 1921 *Glasgow Herald* 22 Feb. 10 The first scale paid to linotype operators was 3d. per thousand 'ens'.

En (aṅ). [Fr. prep., = in; as (a).] **En attendant,** in the meantime. **En avant,** forward. **En axe** (see quot.). **En barbette**: see Barbette. **En clair,** in ordinary language (not in cipher). **En cœur,** in dressmaking, heart-shaped, V-shaped. **En coquille** (see quot. 1882). **En déshabillé,** in undress; also *fig.* (see Dishabille). **En évidence,** in evidence, in the forefront, conspicuous(ly). **En famille,** in or with the family, as one of the family, at home. **En fête,** in festival array, keeping holiday. **En garçon,** as a bachelor. **En grand seigneur,** like a lord. **En grande tenue,** in full dress. **En l'air,** 'in the air'; (of troops) unsupported. **En noir,** on the black side. **En pantoufles,** lit. 'in slippers', hence, in a free and easy atmosphere. **En pension,** as a boarder. **En permanence,** permanently. **En plein air,** in the open air. **En prince,** like a prince, in a princely manner. **En prise** *Chess*, in a position to be taken. **En rapport,** in harmony or sympathy (*with*). **En règle,** in due form. **En retraite,** in retirement, on half pay. **En revanche,** in return, as a quid pro quo. **En route**: see Route *sb.* 5. **En suite**: see Suite 5. **En ventre sa mère,** in the womb, unborn. **En ville,** away from home. Also En bloc, En tout cas.

1743 H. Walpole *Lett.* (1857) I. 276, I hope in time to have poems upon him...**En attendant*, I have sent you some pamphlets to amuse your solitude. 1800 Maria Edgeworth *Belinda* xii, *En attendant* here are your two hundred guineas. 1816 J. Simpson *Visit to Flanders, 1815* (ed. 4) 122 The man who, when the lives of others were concerned, could only cry, '*en avant, en avant'. 1823 Byron in Moore *Lett. & Jrnls.* (1875) 935 But never mind—*en avant!* live while you can. 1852 tr. *Bourrienne's Mem. N. Bonaparte* xiv. 176 (Stanford) 'Very well', said the chief consul, '*en avant*—let us proceed'. 1901 R. Sturgis *Dict. Archit.* 178/2 A monument is said to be **en axe* with a street when the centre line of the street passes through the centre of the monument. Two rooms are said to be *en axe*, or an opposite window or door, or two opposite doors, are said to be *en axe* when the axis of the room, pavilion, wing, or whole building passes through them, or even when they are centred upon one another with deliberate care to bring them exactly opposite. 1897 *en clair [in use at the Foreign Office]. 1928 *Daily Tel.* 17 July 10/7 Making 'en clair' wireless signals. 1874 *Echo* Dec. (Stanford) Opened **en cœur* or square. 1882 Caulfeild & Saward *Dict. Needlework.* 1878 *Cassell's Family Mag.* Apr. 295/1 The skirt is..bordered with a flounce *en coquille. 1882 Caulfeild & Saward *Dict. Needlework, En Coquille*, the French term to denote 'shell-shaped'. The ribbon or lace is laid like a succession of scallop-shells, one above or over the other, in groups of threes. 1698 Lister *Journ. Paris* (1699) 35 A young Gentleman in a Fur Cap *en dishabille. 1808 *Edin. Rev.* Oct. 133 A powerful mind *en deshabille*, and free from the fetters of study. 1877 Reade *Woman Hater* vii. (Stanford) Let me catch her *en déshabillé*, with her porter on one side, and her lover on the other. 1818 Lady Morgan *Fl. Macarthy* II. i. 6 Mr. Crawley now placed himself *en evidence at his window. 1886 S. Buxton *Handbk. Pol. Quest. Day* (ed. 7) 153 The anxiety of members to keep themselves *en évidence*. 1729 Swift *Poems, Libel on Dr. Delany* 3 Deluded mortals, whom the great Choose for companions *tête-à-tête*; Who at their dinners, '**en famille*, Get leave to sit where'er you will. 1787 Beckford *Italy* (1834) II. 55 We passed the day quite *en famille* at Belem with a whole legion of Marialvas. 1843 Thackeray *Men's Wives* Misc. 1857 IV. 86 It was vary kaind of you to come upon us *en famille*, and accept a dinner *sans cérémonie*. 1915 P. Jones *War Lett.* (1918) 140 Flemish is almost always used by the people *en famille*. 1865 'Ouida' *Strathmore* xxxii, Paris was **en fête*. 1888 *Lancashire Even. Post* 3 Feb. 2/4 Haslingden Liberalism..is to be *en fête* this evening on the occasion of its annual soirée. 1811 Miss L. M. Hawkins *C'tess & Gertr.* (ed. 2) I. 248 (Stanford) He soon settled himself again, **en garçon*, in chambers. 1866 Mrs. H. Wood *Elster's Folly* xvii, He was living quite *en garçon*, with only one man. 1929 S. McKenna *Happy Ending* II. i, Mark Tollesbury will be in London *en garçon*. 1831 Disraeli *Yng. Duke* IV. i, [It] prevented him from receiving his friends **en grand seigneur* in his hereditary castle. 1834 Greville *Leaves fr. Diary* (1883) 41 A farce at which all the Court **en grande tenue* was obliged to attend. 1872 W. Chaffers *Keramic Gallery* I. 59 A lady in the costume of Louis XIV., *en grande tenue*. 1927 *Blackw. Mag.* June 749/2 He found the Rissaldar-major *en grande tenue* just back from a wedding. 1808 Wellington *Disp.* (1838) IV. 130 Its retreat to the sea should be considered in some degree **en l'air*. 1891 'L. Malet' *Wages of Sin* v. i, I wait on circumstances. My plans are rather distractingly *en l'air* every way just at present. 1918 Farrow *Milit. Dict.* 204 *En l'air*. ..Said of troops when too far from the main body, either to render assistance or to receive support. 1905 Mrs. H. Ward *Marr. W. Ashe* II. xi. 197 She must know that everything she does is seen there **en noir*. 1930 *Time & Tide* 2 May, His secretary..had a little work up his sleeve, all ready to be printed and published on the morrow of France's burial, in which he was to be exposed '*en pantoufles'. 1818 **en pension* [see Pension *sb.* 6 c]. 1889 *Athenæum* 14 Sept. 351/1 The persistence with which Mrs. Markenfeld..remains *en pension* in a gloomy house with such abominable company. 1848 Thackeray *Van. Fair* liii, There were dirty trays, and wine-coolers *en permanence. 1872 E. Braddon *Life in India* v. 178 His Lares and Penates are erected *en permanence*. 1888 E. Drummond in *Practitioner* Oct. 258 Typhus..is..very uncommon amongst the class of people..who are well fed and well housed, and live largely a life **en plein air*. *a* 1700 Evelyn *Diary* 16 Jan. 1678–9, A French merchant, who had his house furnish'd **en Prince*. 1885 'L. Malet' *Col. Enderby's Wife* II. iv, I was assured that you would be treated *en prince*. 1821 *Kaleidoscope* 13 Mar. 294/2 [He] had the privilege of taking such of the pieces..as might be **en prise*. 1902 *Encycl. Brit.* XXVIII. 758/2 B moves anywhere not *en prise*. 1857 Lady Morgan *Mem.* (1862) I. 23 An Irish audience was always **en rapport* with the stage. 1837 C. MacFarlane *Banditti & Robbers* 39 (Stanford) Many of these Calabrians were banditti..and afterwards became robbers **en règle*. 1880 L. Fagan *Panizzi* I. 42 Panizzi's passport being perfectly *en règle*. 1849 Thackeray *Pendennis* i, Specimens of the costume of a military man **en retraite*. 1860 W. H. Russell *Diary in India* I. 57, I receive as a reward for my services..a post, with which I am well satisfied. I live in it for years. I use all my energies in it, and for me there is no future except *en retraite*. 1841 C'tess Blessington *Idler in France* I. 308 She offers him, **en revanche*, a cane, buttons, or a pin—in short, some present. 1883 L. Oliphant *Altiora Peto* vii. 125 She gave a comical look at that lady's waist and elbows, which was evidently *en revanche* for the well-bred stare to which she had been subjected. 1891 *Law Times* XC. 461/2 Beyond all question, for many purposes, a child **en ventre sa mère* is considered as being alive. 1860 *Once a Week* 11 Feb. 152/1 (Stanford) She was so huffy that I told Blot I would dine **en ville* for a short time. 1884 F. Boyle *Borderland* 336 The horrid cookshops which send dinners *en ville*.

-en, *suffix* [6], the ending of the past participle of many strong verbs, as *broken, spoken, sunken*. OE. *-en*, corresp. to OFris. *-en*, OS. *-an*, (M)Du. *-en*, OHG. *-an* (MHG., G. *-en*), ON. *-enn, -inn* (Sw. *-en*), Goth. *-ans*:—prim. Germ. *-enaz, -anaz* (Indo-Eur. *-ĕnos, -ŏnos*), of which some languages generalized one and some the other, a third type *-iniz* (Indo-Eur. *-enis*) being represented by mutated forms in OE., e.g. *cymen* (:—**kuminí-*), pa. pple. of *cuman* to Come, beside *cumen* (:—**kumena-*).

Enable, *v.* 5. Delete † *Obs.* and add quots.

1892 *Daily News* 2 Feb. 3/3 It will also enable the inclusion of others. 1902 A. Nutt *Leg. Holy Grail* 27 This has been held by some scholars to enable the dating of the romance.

Enabling, *ppl. a.* Add: *Enabling act*, a legislative enactment enabling or empowering a person or corporation to take certain action.

1873 J. H. Beadle *Undevel. West* xix. 364 Let Congress pass an enabling act for that Territory. 1919 *Public Gen. Acts* Index 609 Enabling Bill, The. See Church of England Assembly (Powers) Act (c. 76).

Enamel, *sb.* Add:

1. e. *U.S.* (See quot.)

1832 *Deb. Congress* 13 Nov. App. 31 The last layer [of the road] which will make up the nine inches, and will constitute its enamel, or wearing surface.

5. **enamel prism,** each of the microscopic rods of which the enamel of the teeth is composed.

1877 *Encycl. Brit.* VII. 234/1 The enamel is composed of microscopic rods,—the enamel fibres, or enamel prisms.

Enamel, *v.* Add: 2. e. To paint with enamel paint (cf. Aspinall). Also *absol.*

1889 *Pall Mall Gaz.* 17 Oct. 1/3 The craze for enamelled furniture and enamelled nick-nacks gets worse and worse. Everybody enamels. Bachelors enamel their own furniture and rooms.

Enantioblastic (enæ̆nti,oblæ·stik), *a.* *Bot.* [f. Gr. ἐναντίος opposite + βλαστός (-blast) + -ic.] Having the radicle turned away from the micropyle. Also **Enantiobla·stous** *a.* (B. D. Jackson).

1878 Henfrey *Elem. Bot.* (ed. 3) 157 The radicle generally points to the hilum (homoblastic), rarely away from it (enantioblastic). 1887 Bentley *Man. Bot.* (ed. 5) 347 We

have already observed, that the radicle as a general character is turned towards the micropyle...Some apparent exceptions to these relative positions occur..when the radicle is described as enantioblastic.

Enantiomorph (enæ·nti,omǫɹf). [ad. G. *enantiomorph* (Naumann), f. Gr. ἐναντίος opposite + μορφή form.] A form which is related to another as an object is related to its image in a mirror; a mirror image. Also *adj.* = **Enantiomo·rphic, -mo·rphous** *adjs.*; whence **-mo·rphously** *adv.* So **Enantiomo·rphism, Ena·ntiomorphy,** the condition or property of being enantiomorphous, esp. in *Cryst.*

1885 A. Crum Brown in *Encycl. Brit.* XIX. 312/1 Two figures or two portions of matter are said to be enantiomorph to each other when these forms are not superposable, i.e., the one will not fit into a mould which fits the other, but the one is identical in form with the mirror image of the other. *Ibid.*, As an example of enantiomorphism we may take our two hands, which will not fit the same mould or glove, but the one of which resembles in figure the mirror image of the other. *Ibid.* 313/2 The crystallographic theory of enantiomorph crystals. *Ibid.* 314/1 We now know a considerable number of cases where..both enantiomorphs have been discovered, and many where only one has as yet been found. 1895 Story-Maskelyne *Crystallogr.* vi. § 150. 169 The configuration of the one tetartohedron will then correspond to that of the other as seen in a mirror. In a word, the two tetarto-symmetrical forms are enantiomorphous. 1895 *Bloxam's Chem.* (ed. 8) 600 The sodium-ammonium racemate..has the same crystalline form as the tartrate, but whilst all the crystals of this salt are exactly alike, those of the racemate differ from each other in the position of a certain unsymmetrical face; this is on the right hand in the one kind and on the left hand in the other (*enantiomorphous*). 1898 *Nature* 8 Sept. 454/1 Enantiomorphism is possible only in the case of asymmetric solid figures. *Ibid.* 454/2 The special one-sided asymmetry of the base will modify its mode of combination with the two enantiomorphous acids. *Ibid.* 455/1 Asymmetric agents can only display selective action in dealing with enantiomorphs. 1898 *Jrnl. Chem. Soc.* LXXIII. 608 The question of the proportion in which enantiomorphously related crystals are deposited. 1900 Larmor *Æther & Matter* 209 Enantiomorphy [of a molecule] reverses the signs of all its electrons and perverts their relative position. 1902 H. A. Miers *Min.* 50 Two supplementary forms which are similar but not identical are said to be 'enantiomorphous'; all forms which have neither a centre nor a plane of symmetry are enantiomorphous to another form. 1929 *Times* 2 Feb. 8/3 The whole is a perfect enantiomorph (mirror image) of the coast of Holland and the Zuyder Zee.

Enantiotropic (enæ̆ntĭ,otrǫ·pik), *a.* *Physical Chem.* [f. Gr. ἐναντίος opposite + -τροπος turning + -ic.] That can be transformed in opposite directions. Hence **Enantio·tropy.**

1900 *Jrnl. Chem. Soc.* LXXVIII. II. 83 Enantiotropy of Tin. 1903 H. C. Jones *Princ. Inorg. Chem.* 172 Substances which like sulphur exist in two phases of the same state of aggregation, and the two phases can be reciprocally transformed into one another by changing the temperature, are known as enantiotropic. 1904 A. Findlay *Phase Rule* 42.

En bloc (aṅ blok), *adv. phr.* [Fr.] In a block, as a whole. Also *attrib.*

1877 L. W. M. Lockhart *Mine is Thine* xii. (1879) 115 (Stanford) You judge all your old friends, *en bloc*, simply from your own point of view. 1888 *Contemp. Rev.* Jan. 81 We are bound to take Nature *en bloc*, with all her laws and all her cruelties, as well as her beneficences. 1900 *Westm. Gaz.* 11 July 2/2 We agree, *prima facie*, that there is every kind of objection to *en bloc* disfranchisements. 1905 *Spectator, Lit. Suppl.* 28 Jan. 111/1 He was all but ready to..accept the tenets of the elder Church *en bloc*. 1908 *Westm. Gaz.* 17 Nov. 5/3 This machine is the new 1909 model, the en bloc engine, four-speed gear-box, and thermo-syphon cooling denoting the only departure from standard practice. 1914 C. W. Dyson Perrins *Italian Bk.-illustr.* p. v, To rescue them.. from the perils of the auction by persuading the owner to sell them to me *en bloc*. 1930 G. R. de Beer *Embryol. & Evol.* i. 10 It is not the 'stage' which is shifted *en bloc*, but certain characters which may be peculiar to that stage.

Encallow (enkæ·lōᵘ), *sb. local.* = Callow *sb.* 3. Hence **Encallow** *v.*

1836 *Penny Cycl.* V. 408/1 The encallow, as it is technically called, or the top-soil. 1850 E. Dobson *Bricks & Tiles* 21 The first operation [in digging clay] is to remove the mould and top soil...In London the vegetable mould is called the encallow, and the operation of removing it, encallowing. 1884 C. T. Davis *Manuf. Bricks* 103.

Encasement. Add: 2. The act of encasing; the condition of being encased; *spec.* in *Bee-keeping.* Also *concr.* (see quot. 1875).

1825 *New Monthly Mag.* XVI. 598 This incasement of our feet in icy boxes was very annoying. 1875 J. Hunter *Manual Bee-keeping* (1884) 15 In the case of a strange Queen's appearance in the hive..the stranger is seized by the Workers, who gather round her and form a closely packed ball..technically called 'an encasement'. 1888 F. R. Cheshire *Bees* II. 431 During examination..an encasement of the queen in her own hive is commenced.

Encashable (enkæ·ʃăb'l), *a.* [f. Encash *v.* + -able.] Capable of being cashed.

1927 *Daily Tel.* 7 Mar. 2 This loan bears ½ per cent. more interest than the Savings Bonds, but whereas the latter are encashable at any time without loss of capital, the price receivable for the Conversion Loan would depend on the market value when sold.

Encephalo- (ense·fălo), comb. form of Gr. ἐγκέφαλος brain, as in **Ence·phalolith,** a concretion in the brain (Billings). **Encephalo·logy,** a description of the brain; the science of the brain. **Ence·phalomala·cia,** softening of the brain. **Ence·phalomeni·ngocele,** protrusion through a fissure in the skull of brain-substance with the attached membranes.

1824 (*title*) *Encephalology, or a very brief Sketch of Drs Hirnschadel's Ologies of the Cranion and Phren perfected by the Rationals. 1877 tr. *von Ziemssen's Cycl. Pract. Med.* XII. 181 Certain observers have firmly maintained the opinion that the so-called *encephalomalacia is always an inflammatory process. 1912 Adami & McCrae *Pathol.* 487 The result of such embolism is encephalomalacia. 1905 *T. H. Green's Pathol.* (ed. 10) 11 They [*sc.* pouches in the cranium] may contain brain-substance (*encephalocele*), or brain-substance and fluid (**encephalo-meningocele*).

Encharm (entʃā·ɹm), *v.* Delete † *Obs.* and add quots.

c 1854 Carlyle in W. Holman Hunt *Pre-Raph.* (1905) I. 358 Christ..encharming the simple by His love and loveliness. 1890 Mrs. Hungerford *Life's Remorse* I. xv. 200 Such a knowledge of horseflesh as should encharm the soul of any Irishmen.

Enchondrosis (enkǫndrōᵘ·sis). [f. Enchondroma + -osis.] An enchondroma arising from cartilage.

1873 T. H. Green *Introd. Pathol.* (ed. 2) 137 The enchondromata must for the most part be regarded as innocent growths. Those homologous forms which originate from cartilage, and have been called 'enchondroses', differ in all respects from the heterologous. 1908 *Practitioner* Dec. 763 On the inner aspect of the second toe there is an enchondrosis.

Enchylema (enkilī·mă). *Biol.* [mod.L.: see En-[2] and Chyle.] The fluid part of protoplasm.

1886 *Science* VIII. 125/1 This basal substance, enchylema, is probably more or less nearly fluid during life. 1888 Rolleston & Jackson *Anim. Life* p. xxi, Protoplasm.. appears sometimes to be structureless, but as a rule it is more or less vesicular, consisting of a denser substance (mitome) enclosing droplets of a more fluid character (enchylema, paramitome). 1902 *Encycl. Brit.* XXXII. 41/2 A framework distinct from granules and enchylema.

Encirclement (ensə̄·ɹk'lmĕnt). [f. Encircle *v.* + -ment.] The act or fact of encircling.

1920 H. G. Wells *Outl. Hist.* 456/2 Their [*sc.* the French] government set about the encirclement of the colonies and their subjugation in a terrifyingly systematic manner. 1927 *Observer* 24 July 14/2 A ring of Verey lights..that exaggerated..the encirclement and nearly completed it.

Enclosed, *ppl. a.* Add: *spec.* of communities of religious who are secluded from relations with the outside world.

1905 *Athenæum* 30 Sept. 431/1 Catherine de' Ricci belonged to an enclosed community of Dominican Tertiaries.

Enclosure. 4. b. (Early U.S. example.)

1776 *Jrnls. Cont. Congress* IV. 107 Two letters from General Schuyler..with an account of his expedition to Tryon county, with 9 enclosures.

Encoffined (enkǫ·find), *ppl. a.* [f. Encoffin *v.* + -ed [1].] Enclosed in a coffin.

1907 tr. *K. Werder's Hamlet's Myst.* 49 The secret of the encoffined and unprovable crime. 1908 *Daily Chron.* 17 Aug. 5/6 An encoffined body.

Encoignure (aṅkonʸūr). [Fr., f. *en-* in + *coin* corner.] A piece of furniture, esp. of ornamental design, made with an angle to fit into a corner.

1848 H. R. Forster *Stowe Catal.* 22 A pair of very handsome encoigneures, of rich buhl on tortoiseshell.

Encomienda (enkōᵘmie·ndă). [Sp., = commission, charge, sb. corresp. to the vb. *encomendar* to commit, charge; cf. med.L. phr. *in commendam* (see Commendam).] (See quot. 1885.)

1818 *Amer. State Papers* For. Rel. (1834) IV. 325 (Stanford) All these regulations were found ineffectual to secure the Indians against the rapacity of the encomenderos, and encomiendas were abolished. 1877 *Encycl. Brit.* VI. 174/1 That system of *repartimientos* or *encomiendas* which was afterwards to work such cruel mischief among the conquered. 1885 *Ibid.* XVIII. 677/2 'Encomiendas', or grants of estates on which the inhabitants were bound to pay tribute and give personal service to the grantee.

Encompass, *v.* Add:

6. Used for Compass *v.*[1] 2.

a 1889 P. Robinson *Under the Sun* 201 (Cent. Dict.) Whatever the method employed for encompassing his death. 1889 Mrs. H. Lovett Cameron *Lost Wife* iv, What earthly reason could Captain Thistleby have for encompassing my destruction?

Encoop (enkū·p), *v. poet.* [f. En-[1] + Coop *sb.*[1]] *trans.* To coop up.

1867 J. B. Rose tr. *Virgil's Æneid* 267 Again besieged, again encooped in hold. 1906 T. Hardy *Dynasts* II. I. viii. 172 Her fleet at any minute can encoop Yours in the Baltic.

Encore, *v.* Add: Also *absol.* or *intr.* To call out 'encore'; to ask for an encore of a song, etc.

1888 *Cassell's Encycl. Dict.*

Encroach (ènkrōᵘ·tʃ), *sb.* Delete †*Obs. rare* and add quots.

1920 *Conquest* Nov. 39/3 Rocks are affected by micro-fungi, and may crumble as a result of their encroach into crevices and their subsequent action. 1924 *Chambers's Jrnl.* Nov. 714/1 From a line square of posts, bordering on the marshes, and on the mud-flats' farthest encroach, the one safe track leads shoreward.

Encrustation, var. of Incrustation.

1923 *Daily Mail* 24 Jan. 6 The heavy encrustation of swollen buds on every twig. 1923 H. G. Wells *Outl. Hist.* 206/1 There was no effective prohibition of superstitious practices..and supplementary worships. At an early stage [of Buddhism] a process of encrustation began.

Encyclopædian, *sb.* 1. Delete *Obs. rare*[−1].

1902 H. White in *Outing* (U.S.) June Advts., What I needed first was the encyclopædian's ideal of what an encyclopædia ought to be.

Encyclopædically (ènsəiklopī·dikăli), *adv.* [f. Encyclopædic: see -ically.] In an encyclopædic manner; comprehensively.

1856 Rossetti *Lett. to Allingham* (1897) 160, I found his knowledge of early Italian art beyond that of any one I ever met,—*encyclopædically* beyond that of Ruskin himself.

Encyst, *v.* Add: Also *absol.* or *intr.*

1896 tr. *Boas' Zool.* 86 A great many forms..have the power of encysting.

End, *sb.* Add:

2. b. An outlying part of a village or small country town, usually preceded by a descriptive name.

1906 *Bungalow* Dec. 8/2 It is the typical 'end' so beloved of the novelist, the disreputable quarter which the parsimonious squire neglects.

3. e. *Archery.* (*a*) The place at which a mark is set up. (*b*) The number of arrows shot from one end of a range.

1801 T. Roberts *Engl. Bowman* 288 End.—The place where a mark is fixed. 1836 in Hargrave *Archery* (1845) 89 Any member who shall draw an arrow before the *end* has been determined by the Judges, shall forfeit his right to count for such arrow. 1879 M. & W. Thompson *Archery* 52 (Cent. Dict.) By the rules of the York Round three arrows to each archer constitute an end. 1887 *H. A. Ford's Archery* 289 On July 5, 1877, he made 3 golds in one end at 100 yards.

f. One stationed at the extremity of a line of players; a wing. *U.S.*

1899 A. H. Quinn *Pennsylv. Stories* 22 The ends and the backs came together as though drawn by a magnet and the pyramid toppled and fell.

g. *Coalmining.* Phr. *On the end*: see quots.

1867 W. W. Smyth *Coal* 140 A far better proportion of round coal will be obtained by working on the end, *i.e.*, in the direction of such cleat. 1892 H. W. Hughes *Coal-m.* 158 If the face is parallel to the cleat, the coal is said to be 'on the end'.

5. d. A share or portion; a part or side. *U.S.*

1926 J. Black *You Can't Win* ix. 105 Didn't him and Smiler bring it [= $200] up here for my end of that chippy gambling house's bankroll? 1928 *Publishers' Weekly* 30 June 2598 To talk to such a person about the editorial end of a publishing business means little or nothing.

6. e. (See quot.)

1885 *Spons' Mechanics' Own Bk.* 169 'Ends' are pieces of plank, deal, or batten less than 8 ft. long.

7. c. in attrib. uses of phrases, as *end-account, end-August, -September*; *end-of-December, end-of-term* (also *end-of-termy* adj.).

1902 *Westm. Gaz.* 12 June 7/2 The end-of-December account. 1903 *Ibid.* 21 Aug. 9/1 The final details of the end-August settlement. 1905 *Ibid.* 22 Sept. 9/1 Business in Kaffirs for the End-September settlement. 1909 *Ibid.* 9 Dec. 10/1 The end-of-the-year requirements are likely to be satisfied. 1911 H. Walpole *Mr. Perrin* iii. 42 The end-of-termy feelings. 1923 *Manchester Guardian Weekly* 10 Aug. 106/1 Smith Minor has been cruelly flogged by an avaricious head master who had discovered that his end-of-term rose-bowl was only electro plate instead of the solid silver which he had stipulated in his letter to the lad's parents. 1928 *Daily Chron.* 9 Aug. 8/6 The falling off in the average shown in latest developments, accentuated by end-account sales.

17. b. Also *right* or *straight on end*: (*a*) consecutively, uninterruptedly; (*b*) immediately.

[1778 strait on end: see Straight *adv.* 2 c.] 1837 T. Hook *Jack Brag* i, The fox going away right on-end across a heavy country. 1867 Smyth *Sailor's Word-bk.*, *Right on end*, in a continuous line; as the masts should be. 1883 Baring-Gould *John Herring* xi. I. 154, I be going to die right on end, I be.

19. d. *End-to-end*: applied to the (motoring) course extending from one end of Britain to the other, i.e. from John o' Groats to Land's End.

1908 *Daily Report* 20 July 9/1 The start for the end-to-end run. 1909 *Daily Chron.* 14 Aug. 6/5 The first attempt ever made to drive a sidecar and passenger over the End-to-End course.

20. a. *End on.* Recent instances of attrib. use.

1888 *Encycl. Brit.* XXIV. 366/1 Several ships have been built for the 'end-on attack'. 1894 *Pall Mall Gaz.* 23 Oct. 2/1 Ships built mainly for end-on fire. 1898 Kipling in *Morn. Post* 10 Nov. 5/1, I meant my shot for an end-on shot. 1910 *Install. News* IV. 59/1 In a Tungsten lamp only 50% of the light is directed below the horizontal and the end-on candle power.

(*b*) 'Working a seam of coal, &c., at right angles to the cleat, or natural planes of cleavage' (Gresley, 1883).

b. *End up.* Also attrib. (*end-up*) of the nose: Snub, turned-up.

1850 H. C. Watson *Camp-Fires Revol.* 311 The broad face; the short, end-up nose; the light and red hair.

c. Phr. *All ends up*: out-and-out, 'anyhow'.

1921 A. W. Myers *Twenty Yrs. Lawn Tennis* 19 Barrett beat him 'all ends up' in an early round.

22. f. *To keep one's end up* (also *to keep* or *hold up one's end*): to sustain one's part or bear one's share fully in an undertaking or performance.

1878 Mrs. Stowe *Poganuc People* vi. 63 Nobody can say she hain't been a good yoke-fellow; she's kept up her end. 1887 Tourgee *Button's Inn* 131 She'd be worn out..trying to keep up her end [of the work]. 1892 Stevenson & Osbourne *Wrecker* 21 Do you think..that a man who can paint a thousand-dollar picture has not grit enough to keep his end up in the stock market? 1899 *Westm. Gaz.* 24 Nov. 5/1 Colonel Baden-Powell and his gallant garrison will have to keep their end up unassisted. 1903 'O. Henry' *Rolling Stones* (1915) 88 The Diamond Cross'll hold its end up with a man who'll look after its interests. 1928 *Observer* 18 Mar. 15/3 Not a single woman who appears..in this play is able to keep her end up after the cosmic announcer informs the inhabitants of the world that the world is about to end.

25. *Comb.*, with sense 'placed at the end', 'coming at the end'; as *end-artery, -body, -bud, -bulb, -situation, -spurt, -stop, -wood*; **end game** *Chess, attrib.* uses; **end-gate** *U.S.*, the movable board at the rear of a wagon, = Tail-board; **end-hole** (see quot.); **end-measure,** a measure of length defined by the distance between points in the surfaces of the ends of a bar; **end-papers** *pl.*, the blank leaves placed at the beginning and end of a book; **end-piece,** a piece forming the end of a box, etc.; in watchmaking, the support for the end of a pivot; **end-product** *Chem.*, the substance finally produced; **end table** *U.S.*, a table with a flat side suitable for placing at the end of a couch or settee; **end-value** *Math.* (see quot.).

1883 J. Coats *Pathol.* 35 There are parts of the body in which the arteries are distributed to a perfectly definite piece of tissue, and have no anastomotic connections. In the case of such arteries, to which Cohnheim gives the name of *End Arteries, the results of obstruction are very serious. 1875 *Encycl. Brit.* I. 861/2 Nerve fibres at their peripheral extremities terminate in connection with peculiar structures, named *end-bodies, terminal bodies. *Ibid.*, The peripheral end-bodies in the skin. 1903 Dorland *Med. Dict.* (ed. 3), *End-body*, that one of the two elements of the serum of an immunized animal which serves actually to kill the bacteria. The other element, the Between-body or Immune-body, simply fastens the end-body to the bacteria. The end-body is also called the complement and addiment. 1900 J. S. Kingsley *Vert. Zool.* 68 Allied to the sense organs of the lateral line are structures known as *end buds. 1887 *Buck's Handbk. Med. Sci.* V. 150/2 In the clitoris these *end-bulbs (genital end-bulbs)..are round, elongated, or oval. 1898 *H. Morris's Hum. Anat.* (ed. 2) 1076 The spheroidal end-bulbs of Krause, found in the conjunctiva and mucous membrane. 1897 *Westm. Gaz.* 15 Feb. 4/1 A fine *end-game player. 1899 *Ibid.* 1 June 6/3 Skill in end-game play. 1905 *Emporia* (Kan.) *Gaz.* 3 Mar., Henry kept right on lamming the *end-gate of the band wagon of reform with a poker. 1911 H. Quick *Yellowstone N.* vi. 165 Two boys..tied to the feed-rack by Allen's hired man and spanked with the end-gate of his wagon. 1877 *Encycl. Brit.* VI. 576/1 (*Cribbage*) The go, *end hole, or last card is scored by the player who approaches most nearly to thirty-one. 1902 *Nature* 7 Aug. 350/1 The verification in 1890–7 of standard *end-measures (mètres à bouts). 1818 *Art Bk.-binding* 31 Common marble paper pasted between the first and second leaf of the *end-papers. 1846 Dodd *Brit. Manuf.* VI. 94 The end-papers are..glued to the boards. 1901 *Athenæum* 4 May, The end-papers were a little spotted, but the general condition was splendid. 1839 *Penny Cycl.* XIII. 118/1 The *end-pieces, when real diamonds are used, are what are called rose-diamonds, and are procured from Holland, where they are cut. 1878 Abney *Treat. Photogr.* 216 A movable end-piece through which the plate passes into the holder. 1881 [in Dict.]. 1907 B. C. A. Windle *Sci. Facts* 10 The element thorium appears to be constantly engaged in generating from itself another solid element which again decays, its *end-product being so far unknown. 1908 *Practitioner* Mar. 390 Such simple end-products of proteid digestion, as leucin and tyrosin. 1911 *Encycl. Brit.* XXII. 800 After the radioactive transformations have come to an end, each of the elements uranium and thorium and actinium should give rise to an end or final product. 1851 C. Cist *Cincinnati* 206 Circular, center, card, and *end tables. 1902 *Encycl. Brit.* XXVIII. 549/2 The numbers *a* and *b* which limit the interval are usually called the 'lower and upper limits'. We shall call them the 'nearer and further *end-values'.

End, *v.*[1] Add: 2. Also with *off, up.*

1884 G. Allen *Philistia* III. 250 Capital sentence to end off one's speech with. 1926 *Ladies' Home Jrnl.* Aug. 109 Those things you use to divide off words and end up sentences with.

III. 8. *trans.* To furnish with an end of a particular kind, for protection or ornament.

1889 *Cent. Dict.* s.v., To end a cane with an iron ferrule.

9. To put *up* on end; to up-end.

1889 *Cent. Dict.*, *End*..to set on end; set upright. 1890 *Century Mag.* Aug. 617/1 We ended-up an old plank.. against the twelve-foot brick wall.

¶ *To end or mend*: see *to mend or end* (Mend *v.* 12 c).

1671 S. Collins *Pres. State Russia* 9 It is a strange chastisement to kill, seeing the design hereof was never intended to end people, but to mend them. 1820 Scott *Monast.* xix, My fate calls me elsewhere, to scenes where I shall end it or mend it. [1823 Byron *Juan* x. xlii, This is the way physicians mend or end us.]

Endamasked (endæ·măskt), *ppl. a.* [f. Endamask *v.* + -ed [1].] Coloured with or as with damask.

1856 *Titan Mag.* Nov. 403 The down-bent eyes, the cheek's endamask'd glow.

Endarch (e·ndaɹk), *a.* *Bot.* [f. Gr. ἔνδον End(o- + ἀρχή beginning, origin.] Having a single protoxylem, or several protoxylems surrounding a central parenchyma.

1900 B. D. Jackson *Gloss. Bot. Terms.* 1902 Tansley in *Encycl. Brit.* XXV. 413/1.

Endeavourer (ènde·vərəɹ). Delete †*Obs.* and add: b. Also *spec.* (in full, *Christian Endeavourer*). A member of the Christian Endeavour Society, a religious association which originated in the United States in 1881.

1897 *Helping Words* Nov. 247 'There are some directions in the Bible that you can't follow.'..'That is a remarkable admission for an Endeavourer to make.' 1900 H. Lawson *On Track* 136 At one end of the table a Christian Endeavourer endeavouring.

Endellionite (ende·liŏnəit). *Min.* [f. *Endellion*, Cornwall + -ite [1].] A variety of bournonite.

1854 Dana *Min.* (ed. 4) II. 80.

Endemism (e·ndĕmiz'm). [f. Endemic + -ism.] The character or quality of being endemic.

1886 *Encycl. Brit.* XX. 126/1 In their fauna also the Pyrenees present some striking instances of endemism. 1931 *Nature* 7 Mar. 338 The endemism is tremendous, and the fauna has the aspect of great antiquity.

Endite (e·ndəit), *sb.*[2] *Zool.* [f. Gr. ἔνδον within + -ite [1].] An appendage on the inner side of the limbs of a branchiopod crustacean.

1888 Rolleston & Jackson *Anim. Life* 532 The Phyllopod type of appendage,..with its branchia and external respiratory plate, and its series of internal lobes or endites. 1902 E. R. Lankester in *Encycl. Brit.* XXV. 695/2 The limb of the lowest Crustacea, such as Apus, consists of a corm or axis which may be jointed, and gives rise to outgrowths.. on its inner and outer margins (endites and exites). *Ibid.*, It is by the specialization of two 'endites' that the endopodite and exopodite of higher Crustacea are formed. *Ibid.* 696/1 The conversion of the Arthropod's limb into a jaw..is effected by the development of an endite near its base into a hard.. gnathobase.

Endlichite (e·ndlikəit). *Min.* [ad. G. *endlichit*, named after F. M. *Endlich*, director of the Lake Valley mines, New Mexico.] An arsenio-vanadate of lead.

1885 Genth in *Amer. Phil. Soc.* XXII. 367 Endlichite, or Vanadium-Mimetite, a new species...The name has been suggested by Mr. N. H. Muhlenberg. 1886 *Jrnl. Chem. Soc.* L. 26 Lead Arsenio-vanadate—Endlichite. 1887 *Ibid.* LII. I. 347 The crystals..corresponding exactly with the description given by F. A. Genth and G. vom Rath of the species named by them endlichite.

E·nd-man. Also **end man.** [f. End *sb.* + Man *sb.*[1]]

1. A man at an end of a line or row; *U.S.* the man at either extremity of the semicircle of performers in a negro minstrel entertainment, a corner-man.

1869 E. P. Hingston in *A. Ward's Lect.* Pref. Note 40 All 'end-men' of the burnt-cork profession have used Artemus Ward as a mine. 1886 *Harper's Mag.* Nov. 837/1 Binns..sang..appearing to Roxy as he sang as delightful a personage as an end man. 1889 *Century Dict.* s.v., In the early days of negro minstrelsy each troupe had two end-men...The larger troupes have since had two, and sometimes four, of each class of end-men. 1909 De Leon *Belles, Beaux & Brains of 60's* 356 Emmett was the star of Birch and Backus, as endman.

2. One who holds advanced views; an extremist.

1884 *Science* 8 Aug. 113/1 A very long series of resolutions, expressing the sentiments of a few end men on most of the open questions in the broad sphere of modern life, were approved.

Endo-. Add: **E·ndobio·tic** *a.* *Bot.* (see quot.). **E·ndoblast** *Biol.*, the inner substance of the endoderm. **Endoca·nnibalism** [G. *endocannibalismus*, Steinmetz, 1896], the practice of eating parents and relatives. **E·ndocervici·tis** *Path.*, inflammation of the membrane of the cervix uteri. **E·ndochone** *Zool.*, the innermost structure of a chone. **Endo·chylous** *a.* *Bot.*, situated inside the chlorenchyma. **Endocli·nal** *a.* *Geol.*, of the nature of an **E·ndocline,** a fan-fold of anticlinal type. **E·ndocorpu·scular** *a.* *Path.*, within a corpuscle. **Endodro·mic, Endodynamomo·rphic** *adjs.* (see quots.). **Endoga·stric** *a.* *Path.*, situated within the abdomen. **Endoglo·bular** *a.* *Path.*, occurring within a globule. **E·ndognath** *Zool.*, the inner branch of the oral appendage of a crustacean. **E·ndogoni·dium** *Bot.*, a gonidium formed within a receptacle. **Endogo·nium** *Bot.* (see quot. 1866). **E·ndometri·tis** *Path.*, inflammation of the endometrium. **Endome·trium** *Anat.*, the membrane lining the uterus. **E·ndomyocardi·tis** *Path.*, inflammation of the lining and muscular substance of the heart. **E·ndopericardi·tis** *Path.*, inflammation of the endocardium and pericardium simultaneously. **Endophlœ·um** *Bot.*, the liber of bark. **Endophy·tic** *a.* (*a*) *Bot.*, of, pertaining to, or of the nature of an endophyte; (*b*) *Ent.*, penetrating or living within plants, etc. (also **Endo·phytous** *a.*). **E·ndopod** = Endopodite. **E·ndopodi·tic** *a.*, of or pertaining to the endopodite. **Endopsy·chic** *a.*, that is within the soul. **Endosi·phon,** the internal tube of cephalopods; hence **Endosi·phonal, -nate** *adjs.* **E·ndosome,** the innermost part of a sponge. **Endo·steal** *a.*, situated or occurring in the interior of a bone. **Endo·stracum,** the inner layer of the shell of a crustacean. **Endothe·cium** *Bot.*, the inner layer of the ripe anther. **Endotho·rax** *Anat.*, the internal processes of the thorax or cephalothorax of arthropods. **Endoto·xin,** a toxic substance set free during the process of bacteriolysis which fails to induce the production of an antitoxin by the animal body. **E·ndotra·cheal** *a.*, within the trachea.

1900 B. D. Jackson *Gloss. Bot. Terms*, **Endobiotic*, living within as a parasite. 1900 Deniker *Races of Man* 148 *Endocannibalism is but the remains of a natural state of primitive man. 1879 *St. George's Hosp. Rep.* IX. 443 One case [of retroversion of uterus] was accompanied by severe *endocervicitis. 1888 Rolleston & Jackson *Anim. Life* 795 The funnels or chonae are divided by a constriction into an outer part, the ectochone, long and cylindrical, and an inner part, the *endochone, short and more or less hemispherical. 1903 Groom & Balfour *Schimper's Plant-Geogr.* 11 This aqueous tissue is..within the chlorenchyma (*endochylous), as in Cactaceæ. 1901 *Rep. Brit. Assoc. Adv. Sci.* 625 The Silurian tableland, its endless overfolds, its *endoclinal and exoclinal structures. 1901 *Practitioner* Mar. 276 The new generation of *endo-corpuscular parasites. 1901 A. B. Basset *Elem. Cubic & Quartic Curves* 14 All curves of an even degree, except conics, may consist of two or more perigraphic portions which may lie entirely within or entirely without one another. In the former case the curves will be called *endodromic, and in the latter exodromic. 1930 *Nature* 19 July 89 *Endodynamomorphic soils are those in which external factors have not yet exerted their full influence and which are therefore immature. 1888 Rolleston & Jackson *Anim. Life* 795 The *endogastric septa of Haeckel. 1902 *Encycl. Brit.* XXX. 795/2 Ultimately the coil becomes ventral or endogastric. 1901 *Practitioner* Mar. 303 The progressive development of the *endoglobular parasites. 1899 *Proc. Zool. Soc.* 705 The middle lobe of the *endognath (the proximal division of the *lacinia externa* in Boas's nomenclature). 1881 Carpenter *Microsc.* (ed. 6) § 311 These **endogonidia*..being set free by the dissolution of the wall of the parent-cell soon enlarge. 1866 *Treas. Bot.*, **Endogonium*, the contents of the nucule of a *Chara*. 1918 R. Knox *Radiog. & Radio-Therap.* II. (1923) 523 Chronic *endometritis. 1907 *Practitioner* Dec. 792 The *endometrium was normal. 1912 Adami & McCrae *Pathol.* 647 The histological appearances of the endometrium in certain stages of the menstrual cycle. 1908 *Practitioner* Mar. 319 An acute *endo-myocarditis of the infundibulum. 1907 *Ibid.* June 734 Structural disease of the tricuspid orifice of inflammatory origin.. is presumably evidence of an intense and widespread *endopericarditis. 1861 Bentley *Man. Bot.* 85 Liber or Inner Bark, or *Endophlœum. 1898 tr. *Strasburger's Bot.* 308 Some species also are *endophytic and inhabit cavities in other plants. 1902 *Encycl. Brit.* XXV. 439/1 There is a reciprocal symbiosis between the Angiosperm and the fungus which is endophytic, only rarely ectophytic. 1902 *Ibid.* XXVIII. 563/2 Endophytic parasites. *a* 1889 C. V. Riley (Cent. Dict.) The larvæ of the castnians are.. *endophytous, boring the stems and roots of orchids and other plants. 1893 T. R. R. Stebbing *Crustacea* 36 The main branch or principal flagellum is the true *endopod. 1880 Huxley *Crayfish* 218 The inner or *endopoditic division of the antenna. 1922 Joan Riviere tr. *Freud's Introd. Lect. Psycho-anal.* 240 The *why* of the symptom, its tendency, is..always an *endo-psychic process. 1927 C. Mackenzie *Vestal Fire* I. i, A *frisson* that no endopsychic censor is capable of providing. 1883 Hyatt in *Proc. Boston Soc. Nat. Hist.* 261 The '*endosiphon', here spoken of for the first time by that name, is the internal tube long known in Actinoceras, and lately demonstrated in Piloceras. *Ibid.* 273 The *endosiphonal tube is narrow and regular. 1883 — *Proc. Amer. Assoc. Adv. Sci.* XXXII. 328 The *endosiphonate..types [of cephalopods]. 1887 Sollas in *Encycl. Brit.* XXII. 415 A reticulation of ectosome on the one side and of endoderm and mesoderm, i.e., *endosome, on the other. 1885 *Endosteal [see *Ectosteal]. 1880 Huxley *Crayfish* iv. 194 This zone [*sc.* the ectostracum] may be distinguished from the *endostracum which makes up the rest of the exoskeleton. 1832 Lindley *Introd. Bot.* 128 The lining of the anther has received particular illustration from M. Purkinje, who calls it *endothecium. 1878 Bell tr. *Gegenbaur's Comp. Anat.* 249 These processes ..are found chiefly in the head and thorax in many orders of the Insecta..where they form a complicated structure known as the '*endothorax'. 1906 A. C. Abbott *Bacteriol.* (ed. 7) 568 We now regard the toxic action of these bacteria to be due to the formation of *endotoxins or intracellular toxins. 1907 *Jrnl. Amer. Med. Assoc.* 923 The serum injected into the patient has brought about a local disintegration of the gonococci and a liberation of endotoxins. 1910 *Practitioner* June 861 *Endotracheal stenosis, due to syphilis.

Endocrine (e·ndokrəin), *a.* and *sb.* *Anat.* Also -crin. [f. Gr. ἔνδον Endo- + κρίνειν to separate. Cf. F. *glandes endocrines* (Gottignies, 1912), Sp. *glándulas endocrinas* (R. Mollá, 1912), It. *ghiandole endocrine* (G. Ghedini, 1913), *endocrinico* (ibid.).] Denoting a gland having an internal secretion which is poured into blood or lymph; a ductless gland, as the thyroid, pituitary, and adrenal glands. As *adj.* also = endocrinal.

Dorland's *Med. Dict.*, 1913, has *endocrin* with the erroneous def. 'The internal secretion of a gland'.

1913 Sir E. Schäfer *Introd. Study Endocrine Glands* (1914) 5 Organs..passing such material into the blood or lymph are termed internally secreting or endocrine organs. 1914 *Lancet* 12 Sept. 714/1 The organs of internal secretion, or endocrine glands. 1921 Lichty in *Amer. Jrnl. Med. Sci.* CLIX. 800 Thyroid and other endocrin disturbances. 1923 Blumgarten in *N. Y. Med. Jrnl.* CXV. 393 The diagnostic and therapeutic rôle of the endocrines. 1924 R. Muir *Pathol.* 721 Several of the endocrine glands exert ..a co-ordinated action on the metabolism of carbohydrates. 1925 Laird *Our Minds & Their Bodies* 52 Secretions from the endocrines. 1925 W. J. H. Sprott tr. *Kretschmer's Physique & Char.* 84 Whether the thyroid plays here a rôle as primary cause of an endocrine nature..one cannot say for certain. 1927 Haldane & Huxley *Anim. Biol.* ix. 190 The endocrine system or sum total of the ductless glands.

Hence **E·ndocrinal, Endocrinic** (-kri·nik), **Endocrinous** *adjs.*, pertaining to, of the nature of, or relating to endocrine organs; **Endocrino·logy,** the physiology of the endocrines; whence **Endocrino·logist.**

1913 Dorland *Med. Dict.*, Endocrinology. 1914 *Brit. Med. Jrnl.* 14 Feb. 369/1 Deficiency of endocrinic glandular secretion. 1914 *Lancet* 4 Apr. 952/2 Influence of the Endocrinous Glands upon Uterine Hæmorrhage. 1919 *Nature* CIV. 208/1 'Endocrinology', or physiology of the internally secreting glands. 1923 *Glasgow Herald* 10 Nov. 4 Variations in the endocrinal or regulatory system. 1930 *Times Lit. Suppl.* 25 Dec. 1103/1 For the endocrinologist

there are three papers dealing respectively with the chemical properties of the oxytocic principle of the pituitary gland, with oestrin and with a comb-growth-promoting substance obtained from testes and urine.

Endoderm. Add: **2. c.** *attrib.*
1885 M. Foster in *Encycl. Brit.* XIX. 14/2 The endoderm cells..are almost wholly taken up in the chemical work of digesting and assimilating the food received into the cavity, the lining of which they form. 1902 *Ibid.* XXXI. 794/2 Just as in Anthozoa and Ctenophora the reproductive function and the function of excretion are largely the work of the endoderm cells.

Endogamy. Add: **2.** *Bot.* The fusion or coalescence of two or more female gametes.
1900 B. D. Jackson *Gloss. Bot. Terms.*

Endogenesis (endodʒe·nĕsis). *Biol.* [mod.L., f. Gr. ἔνδον within + γένεσις origin, production.] The production of or the giving rise to structures from within. 1909 *Cent. Dict.* Suppl.

Endogenetic (e:ndodʒĭne·tik), *a.* [f. as prec.: see -genetic.] **a.** *Path.* Developed internally. **b.** *Biol.* Produced from within. **c.** *Geol.* Formed from solutions.
a 1889 Dunglison *Med. Dict.* (1893), Endogenetic. 1902 *Encycl. Brit.* XXV. 439/2 The inflorescence may be endogenetic, the ovule may consist of nucellus alone, and frequently there is no ovule. 1904 *Amer. Geol.* Apr. 229 Endogenetic rocks may also be called nonclastic, since they are never composed of fragments of older rocks, as are the clastic rocks.

Endogenous, *a.* Add:
d. *Geol.* Formed within a mass of rock, or within the earth's surface; *spec.* applied to intrusive rock changed by contact with surrounding rocks.
1859 Page *Handbk. Geol. Terms, Endogenites,* fossil stems and fragments exhibiting the endogenous structure are so termed. 1878 T. S. Hunt *Chem. & Geol. Ess.* xi. 196 The endogenous character of this granite is well shown by its banded structure. 1890 [see *Exogenous].

Endopterygotic, -ous (e:ndopterigǫ·tik, -igōᵘ·təs), *adjs. Ent.* [f. mod.L. *Endopterygota,* f. Gr. ἔνδον within + πτερυγωτός winged.] Belonging to the division *Endopterygota* of insects, which develops its wings inside the body. So **Endopte·rygote** *a.* = prec.; also as *sb.,* a member of the *Endopterygota*; **Endopterygo·tism,** the condition of being endopterygotous.
1898 *Proc. Intern. Zool. Congr.* 248 (Cassell's Suppl.) The great majority of existing insects are endopterygotic. 1902 *Encycl. Brit.* XXIX. 502/2 Some of the Palæozoic insects, though we infer them to have been exopterygotous, were really endopterygotous. 1902 [see *Anapterygotism].

Endorse, *v.* Add:
1. e. To make an entry of an offence on the back of (a licence, e.g. of a publican or motorist).
1902 *Parl. Deb.* CI. 1436 The justices will not exercise the power given them of endorsing licenses, the effect of which, on the third endorsement, would be to deprive a man of the value of his license.
2. c. To declare one's approval of, 'crack up' (a person or thing). So **Endo·rsement.** *U.S.*
1914 *Concise Oxf. Dict., Endorse* (vulgar in advertisements), declare one's belief in. 1914 H. G. Wells *Englishm. looks at World* 61 *note,* Larkinism comes to endorse me since this was written. 1925 *Publishers' Weekly* 26 Dec. 2013/1, I am told..that even the endorsing of articles by prominent stage-folk is now not so eagerly sought after by astute manufacturers. 1926 *Ibid.* 20 Feb. 563 The New York Times, The New York Post,..and many others endorsed the book so highly that we are now setting it up ourselves. *Ibid.* 18 Sept. 960 From the standpoint of the man or woman who endorses college and college education.

Endoscopic (endoskǫ·pik), *a.* [f. Gr. ἔνδον Endo- + -σκοπος viewing + -ic.]
1. (See s.v. Endo- in Dict.)
2. *Math.* Characterized by the treatment of coefficients 'with reference to their internal constitution as composed of roots or other elements' (Sylvester). Hence **Endosco·pically** *adv.*
1853 Sylvester *Math. Papers* (1904) I. 431 In the second section I proceed to express the residues and syzygetic multipliers in terms of the roots and factors of the given functions; the method becoming as it may be said endoscopic instead of being exoscopic, as in the first section. 1893 *Correspondent,* An algebraic form may be viewed endoscopically or exoscopically.

Endosmo·tically, *adv.* [f. Endosmotic *a.*: see -ically.] In an endosmotic manner.
1881 Semper *Anim. Life* 184 They [*sc.* desert-snails] may ..be capable of absorbing a larger amount of water endosmotically through the skin than the snails living in our damp climates. 1884 tr. *Claus' Zool.* 307 The nutritive fluid passes endosmotically into the body parenchyma.

Endothelioma (e:ndoþīliōᵘ·mă). *Path.* [f. Endothelium + *-oma.] A malignant growth developed from endothelium. Hence **Endothelio·matous** *a.*
1880 tr. *von Ziemssen's Cycl. Pract. Med.* IX. 344 Under the name of primary melanotic endothelioma of the liver, Block recently described a case of diffuse or infiltrated pigment cancer. 1886 *Buck's Handbk. Med. Sci.* II. 812/1 *Endothelioma* (psammoma) of the optic nerve consists of alveolar connective tissue, in which cells lie embedded in more or less concentric layers. 1888 J. F. Payne *Gen. Pathol.* 302 Endothelioma is a name sometimes given to this [*sc.* psammoma] and other growths originating in, and composed of, endothelium. 1894 D. J. Hamilton *Pathol.* II. 738 Cylindromatous endotheliomata are found in various parts of the brain or projecting into the brain from the membranes. 1906 *Practitioner* Nov. 666 The endotheliomatous areas consisted of tubules, columns or sheets of cells.

Endothermic (endoþə·ımik), *a. Chem.* [f. Endo- + Thermic *a.*] Characterized by, or attended with, the absorption of heat. So **Endothe·rmous** *a.*
1884 M. M. P. Muir *Princ. Chem.* 254 To found a system of classification on the difference between exothermic and endothermic changes. 1890 *Bloxam's Chem.* (ed. 7) 141 When C is burnt into CO_2 by $2N_2O$, it evolves 40,400 more units of heat than when burnt in O_2, showing that, contrary to the usual law, heat is evolved in the decomposition of the N_2O, amounting to 20,200 units per molecule. Such a compound is said to be endothermic. 1898 *Nature* 18 Aug. 375 The true chemical equivalent of light energy can only be measured by means of an endothermic irreversible reaction. 1902 *Encycl. Brit.* XXV. 37/1 Such endothermic bodies are nearly always found to show considerable violence in their decomposition.

Endowment. Add:
5. *attrib.* and *Comb.*: (sense 2) **endowment assurance, insurance,** a form of life insurance providing for the payment of an endowment or fixed sum to the insured person at a specified date, or (usually) to his representatives on his death, should that take place before the specified date of payment; **endowment (insurance) policy,** a policy which provides for payment according to the above method.
1880 *Encycl. Brit.* XIII. 168/2 Endowment-Assurances. 1898 *Westm. Gaz.* 5 Feb. 6/3 The Equity and Law seems to be the only office to which the public should take their endowment assurance business. 1898 *Daily News* 26 Feb. 8/1 The favourite system of insurance is the endowment plan, is it not?

Endurably (endiūᵊ·răbli), *adv.* [f. Endurable *a.* + -ly [2].] In an endurable manner; so as to be endured. In recent Dicts.

Endurance. Add:
1. c. Of inanimate things: The power of holding out; the capacity (e.g. of steel) of withstanding strain.
1890 *Daily News* 13 Nov. 5/7 Her speed was 18 knots an hour. Her coal endurance is given as 475 tons stowage, and with that stowed she could have steamed 7,000 miles.

Endways, *adv.* **2. b.** (Later U.S. example.)
1871 'Mark Twain' *Screamers* 31 He was all ready for the dog too, and knocked him endways with a rock when he came to tear him.

Enemy, *sb.* and *a.* Add: **A. III.** *Comb.*: instrumental, as *enemy-controlled, -occupied* adjs.
1918 *Act* 8 & 9 *Geo. V* c. 31 § 8 Any property belonging to a company which is an enemy-controlled corporation. 1920 J. M. Keynes *Econ. Conseq. Peace* 108 To maintain the civilian French population in the enemy-occupied districts.
B. 2. Delete '*rare* in modern use' and add quots.:
1891 Meredith *One of our Conq.* xxxiv, The young..have either emotion or imagination to fold them defensively from an enemy world. 1902 *Westm. Gaz.* 5 Aug. 6/3 Stock requisitioned during the late war from private enemy owners. 1909 *Ibid.* 5 Apr. 1/3 The destination..is presumed to exist if the goods are consigned to enemy authorities, or to a contractor established in the enemy country who..supplies articles of this kind to the enemy. *Ibid.* 2/1 If goods consigned to any trader supplying an enemy population could be seized. 1915 J. H. Morgan tr. *German War Bk.* 113 Usages of war in regard to enemy territory and its inhabitants. 1915 *N.Y. Tribune* 30 Mar. 8/3 British naval officers in their reports have also referred to 'enemy' ships and fleets.

Eneolithic, var. Æneolithic.
1911 J. L. Myres *Dawn Hist.* x. 224 The result was a long chalcolithic (or as the Italians say, eneolithic) phase, in which good cheap stone and bad expensive bronze were in use concurrently. 1913 *Engl. Hist. Rev.* Jan. 134 In the neolithic and eneolithic ages.

Energid (enə·rdʒid). *Biol.* [a. G. *energid* (Sachs in *Flora* 1892 and 1895), f. *energie* Energy: see -id [2].] The nucleus of a cell together with its active cytoplasm regarded as a vital unit.
1897 *Nat. Science* Dec. 393 We may introduce that change from the word cell to that of energid (Sachs). *Ibid.,* The distinguishing characteristic of an energid is the living element (protoplasm and nucleus), whilst that of a cell is the membrane. 1900 I. B. Balfour tr. *Goebel's Organ. Plants* I. 24 A polyergic plant is either an energid-colony or *coenobium* (cellular or non-cellular) in which a division of labour between the several energids has not yet appeared and each energid is capable of living for itself; or the energids exhibit a division of labour and although in union with one another are therein different from one another—they form an energid-dominion. 1902 *Encycl. Brit.* XXV. 434/2 Of the three energids of the egg-apparatus, one alone is normally functional as the egg.

Energism (e·nəɹdʒiz'm). *Ethics.* [ad. G. and mod.L. *energismus,* f. late L. *energīa* Energy: see -ism.] The theory that the supreme good does not lie in pleasure but in a contented activity of mind. Hence **Energi·stic** *a.*
1899 Thilly tr. *Paulsen's Syst. Ethics* i. 223 The energistic view..holds: The will does not aim at pleasure, but at an objective content of life, or, since life consists solely of action, at definite concrete activities. I regard the latter conception as the correct one. My view may, therefore, be characterized as teleological energism. 1913 *Hastings' Encycl. Relig.* VI. 511/1 'Energism' is Paulsen's title for his revived Greek position. In this third use of the term it [*sc.* happiness] includes, rather than excludes, perfection as an end.

Energize, *v.* Add: **1. b.** (In modern technical use.)
1886 P. Benjamin *Age of Electricity* 80 An electro-magnet is energized or de-energized..by simply establishing or stopping the current in the coil. 1909 *Westm. Gaz.* 12 Jan. 4/3 The Blaisdell energised solid tyre.
2. (Examples illustrating more recent usage.)
1895 *Contemp. Rev.* Jan. 16 That Law would revive and energise the moment our backs were turned. 1908 *Westm. Gaz.* 11 Dec. 2/1 The stray Tories who chanced to go with the Liberal tide in 1906, and who now energise on the Liberal benches. 1920 *Pilgrim* Oct. 105 The act of speaking makes words..the actual vehicle and expression of a concrete personality here and now locally energising in them. 1922 J. Y. Simpson *Man & Attainm. Immortality* i. 8 Theology ..must in some degree be a knowledge of the world as an expression of God, and of Him as energising in and through it.

Energy. Add: **7.** *attrib.* and *Comb.*: as *energy-carrying, -change, consumption, -producing.*
1905 *Westm. Gaz.* 28 Apr. 2/1 The *energy-carrying power of a beam of light. 1884 M. M. P. Muir *Princ. Chem.* 453 The *energy-changes attending the formation of various compounds. 1909 *Install. News* III. 109/1 The *energy consumption should not be below 500 watts. 1909 *Daily Chron.* 8 July 6/4 An *energy-producing food.

Enfantillage (aṅfaṅtiyāʒ). [Fr., f. *s'enfantiller* (f. *enfant* child): see -age.] A childish action or prank.
1914 E. Sidgwick *Duke Jones* 384 The talk distracted itself again owing to Charles' enfantillages.

Enfant terrible (aṅfaṅ teribl). [Fr., = terrible child.] A child who embarrasses his elders by untimely remarks; *transf.* a person who compromises his associates or his party by unconventional or ill-considered action.
1851 *Fraser's Mag.* Mar. 322/1 He..seemed to tell all these stories just as an *enfant terrible* might, without fully understanding them. 1854 Thackeray *Newcomes* xxi, Miss Ethel..never mentioned this part of her talk with Mrs. Mason. But the *enfant terrible,* young Alfred, did: announcing to all the company at dessert, that Ethel was in love with Clive. 1885 'L. Malet' *Col. Enderby's Wife* III. v, That *enfant terrible* of Mrs. Farrell's is not coming back, I trust.

Enfe·vered, *ppl. a.* [f. Enfever *v.* + -ed [1].] Fever-stricken.
1893 *Pall Mall Mag.* I. 887 His enfevered brain. 1901 *Daily Chron.* 2 July 3/1 Whilst the last chill comes To that enfevered clay and makes it pure.

Enfleurage (aṅflörāʒ). [Fr.] The process of extracting perfumes from flowers by means of fats such as lard and olive oil: Inflowering.
1855 Piesse *Art of Perfumery* 15 Absorption, or Enfleurage. 1880 *Encycl. Brit.* XIII. 595/2 The aroma is extracted by the process known as 'enfleurage', *i.e.,* absorption by a fatty body, such as purified lard or olive oil. 1884 *Ibid.* XVII. 748/1.

Enfold, *v.* Add: **4. b.** *Surg.* To enclose (an ulcer) in a fold of the organ (e.g. the stomach) by stitching together the walls on either side. So **Enfo·lding** *vbl. sb.,* the operation.
1903 *Lancet* 29 Aug. 592/1, I decided to infold the entire ulcerated area without opening the stomach. *Ibid.,* Simple infolding of the ulcer should prove efficient.

Enforceability (enfōᵊ:ısăbi·lĭti). [f. Enforceable + -ity.] The character or quality of being enforceable.
1925 *Glasgow Herald* 9 Sept. 10 The danger of 'a Legislature which has grown accustomed to pass any number of laws without concern for their consequences or their enforceability'. 1928 *Britain's Industr. Future* (*Lib. Ind. Inq.*) III. xvii. 212 The possibility of obtaining legal enforceability for their decisions.

Engage, *v.* **5. b.** (Earlier Amer. examples.)
1760 Washington *Diaries* I. 109 Accompanied Mrs. Bassett to Alexandria and engaged a Keg of Butter of Mr. Kirkpatrick, being quite out of that article. 1770 *Maryland Hist. Mag.* XII. 358 Pray write to Coolidge and send an Express to him to Engage the Corn and to send it up as soon as possible.

Engagement. 2. d. Add: *engagement-ring.*
1875 Mrs. Stowe *We & Neighbors* xxxix. 372 Angie wore on her finger an engagement-ring. 1900 Elin. Glyn *Visits Eliz.* (1906) 73 He seemed to have forgotten that it was arranged for him to give Victorine the engagement ring that evening and say a few appropriate words to her.

Engagingness. Delete † *Obs.* and add quots.
1727 Bailey vol. II, *Insinuatingness,*..insinuating Nature, Engagingness. 1906 G. Saintsbury *Caroline Poets* II. 371 A certain quality of engagingness which it has.

Engelmann (e·ŋgəlmăn). The name of Dr. G. *Engelmann* of St. Louis, an American botanist, used *attrib.* or in the genitive to designate a spruce (*Picea engelmanni*) growing in British Columbia and the Rocky Mountains.
1902 *Encycl. Brit.* XXVI. 391/1.

Engine, *sb.* Add:
5. c. (Delete †*Obs.*) Still used for appliances used in the illicit catching of salmon.
1861 *Act* 24 & 25 *Vict.* c. 109 § 11 No fixed Engine of any Description shall be placed or used for catching Salmon in any inland or tidal Waters. 1873 *Salmon Fishery Act* 270 The nets were illegal fixed engines. 1923 *Act* 13 & 14 *Geo. V* c. 16 § 11.
11. *engine-hose.*
1838 *Knickerbocker Mag.* XII. 373 A small engine-hose.. coiled up like a huge snake on the deck.

Engineer, *sb.* Add: **5. b.** (Later U.S. example.) Also *humorously,* a team-driver. *U.S.* In recent use applied to one who controls any kind of engine and is responsible for the running of the machinery.

1878 J. H. Beadle *Western Wilds* iii. 53, I took a position as engineer of a six-mule team. 1903 *N. Y. Times* 1 Oct. 1 The engineer tried to stop his train before it struck the party. 1921 *Dict. Occup. Terms* (1927) §§ 353, 458, 950, etc.

Engineer, *v.* **2. b.** (Earlier U.S. examples.) Also, to manœuvre, 'shepherd'.
1864 Sala in *Daily Tel.* 7 July, The lobbying or engineering a bill through the Legislature. 1865 S. S. Cox *Eight Yrs. Congress* 99 When he undertakes to engineer a resolution through this House for the expulsion of a brother member. 1889 *Sat. Rev.* 16 Mar. 299/2 The jealousies and interests of workmen against employers are engineered remorselessly by professional wirepullers. 1890 *Fortn. Rev.* May 716 To 'engineer' a party..throughout a holiday expedition in a foreign country is an arduous..undertaking.

Engineering, *vbl. sb.* **2.** Add: *engineering shop, yard.*
1919 *Brit. Manufacturer* Nov. 24/1 Engineering shops. *Ibid.* 24/2 Engineering yards.

Englacial (englēi·ʃiăl), *a.* [f. En- [1] + Glacial.] Embedded in or passing over the surface of a glacier. So **Engla·cially** *adv.*
1891 R. D. Salisbury *Geol. Surv. New Jersey* 87 (Cent. D. Suppl.) On one of the Alaskan glaciers..an englacial stream appears at the surface of the ice,..pursues a superglacial course for a short distance, and plunges again beneath an ice arch and pursues for an undetermined distance an englacial course. 1905 Chamberlin & Salisbury *Geol.* I. 268 A surface load..buried by snow and ice..is englacial. 1925 Odell in E. F. Norton *Fight for Everest, 1924* 315 The medial moraine from the north-east shoulder of Everest, carried englacially.

England. 2. Add: *Old England*: the 'old country' (as distinguished from *New England*).
1638 *Essex Inst. Hist. Coll.* IV. 184/1 George Ropes is to have 20 acres of Land to be laid out for him at his retorne from old England. 1680 *New Castle Court Rec.* 397, I bequeath itt to my brother & sister in ould England. *a* 1700 Evelyn *Diary* 26 May 1671, The condition of New England..as to their regard to Old England.

English, *sb.* **2.** Delete † *Obs.* and add later quots. Also, the English word or equivalent (*for*).
1824 *Oriental Herald* I. 90 Whose patience is equal to the reading of the 'Bahar Damash' in Dr. Scott's English? 1864 Alford (*title*) The Queen's English. 1890 T. Hardy *Three Notable Stories, Melancholy Hussar* ii. 170 Phyllis used to say that his English, though not good, was quite intelligible to her. 1926 Kearton *Naturalist's Pilgr.* vii. 74 'What are they mining for..Herr Sonbergh?' 'Ah', he exclaimed, 'I know quite well, but I cannot remember the English for it.' 1930 *N. & Q.* 11 Oct. 270/1 Throughout the English is apt, for spaces, to be careless and dull.
7. *Billiards.* = Side *sb.*[1] 14 d. *U.S.*

Englishism. Add:
2. An English idiom or form of speech.
1895 *Funk's Stand. Dict.* 1923 *Blackw. Mag.* Aug. 203/2 We..did the best we might with blunt Englishisms.

Englishize (i·ŋgliʃəiz), *v.* [f. English *a.* + -ize.] *trans.* To make English.
1858 *Brownson's Q. Rev.* Apr. 190, I want the Church Americanized no more than I want her..Englishized or Gallicized. 1921 *Blackw. Mag.* Sept. 281/1 F...had been accustomed to meet the Englishised Indian in the privacy of his board-room in London. 1928 *Sunday Dispatch* 22 July 22/3 The Englishised sport from the other side of the Atlantic.

Englishman. Add: **2.** An English ship.
1823 J. F. Cooper *Pilot* xxxiii, Griffith saw his own ship borne away from the Englishman. 1885 W. C. Russell *Strange Voy.* iv, She was not an Englishman, though I really forget the nationality of the colour she flew at the peak.

Englobe, *v.* Add: **2.** *Biol.* To absorb within a blood-globule, amœba, or the like. So **Englo·bed** *ppl. a.*; **Englo·bement,** the process or state of being englobed or absorbed.
1902 *Encycl. Brit.* XXXI. 536/2 Red blood corpuscles are often englobed by this amœba. 1902 *Jrnl. Exper. Med.* VI. 155 The bodies of englobed parasites. *Ibid.,* The englobement of parasites in the liver is more active at certain periods of the cycle.

Engram (e·ngræm). *Psychol.* [f. Gr. ἐν En- + γράμμα letter.] A permanent change in the nucleus of a cell, due to stimulus, which is transferred to the germ-cells and thus becomes heritable. So **Engraphy** (e·ngrăfi), the action of exciting an organism in such a way that a permanent change or engram results. So **Engra·phic** *a.,* of or pertaining to engraphy; **Engra·phically** *adv.*
1914 L. Simon tr. *R. Semon's Mneme* (1921) 24 When an organism has been temporarily stimulated and has passed, after the cessation of the stimulus, into the condition of 'secondary indifference', it can be shown that such organism..has been permanently affected. This I call the engraphic action of a stimulus, because a permanent record has been written or engraved on the irritable substance. I use the word engram to denote this permanent change wrought by a stimulus. *Ibid.,* The sum of such engrams in an organism may be called its 'engram-store'. *Ibid.* 32 Neither can such influences act engraphically. *Ibid.* 274 The engram-association is a result of engraphy and becomes manifest on ecphory. 1923 B. Duffy tr. *R. Semon's Mnemic Psych.* 325 It is only through ecphory that we first get to know the existence of engraphy, and there can be no ecphory unless preceded by engraphy. 1925 C. Fox *Educat. Psychol.* 10 When a child simultaneously sees his nurse and receives food, both the optical stimulus and the taste stimuli produce their engraphic effects and the engrams are permanently associated. 1927 Joad *Mind & its Workings* 40 What I am aware of when I appear to remember something is not the past occurrence which, as I say, I remember, but a present state or modification of my body. This present state or modification is called an engram.

Enhance, *v.* **4. b.** Add: In modern use, (of property, etc.) to increase in value or price.
1889 *Century Dict.* s.v., A debt enhances rapidly by compound interest. 1892 *Pall Mall Gaz.* 15 Nov. 3/2 Until the property enhanced sufficiently to sell. 1904 *N. Y. Even. Post* 31 Mar. 2 With stationary or diminishing incomes, their living expenses are constantly enhancing.

Enhanced, *ppl. a.* Add: **b.** *Spectroscopy.* Applied to the lines of a metallic spectrum which are strengthened, or which only appear, under the action of the spark.
1903 Lockyer & Baxandall in *Phil. Trans.* Ser. A. CCI. 211 The majority of the lines are due to metallic vapours, the enhanced lines and the arc lines being of about equal prominence. 1907 Sir N. Lockyer *Spectroscopic Comp. Metals* 24 The enhanced lines of titanium are..considerably weaker in the stellar spectrum than in the sun. 1922 *Encycl. Brit.* XXX. 298/2 The 'enhanced lines' of strontium 4077 and 4215 are relatively strong in stars of high luminosity and weak in those of low luminosity.

Enhancive (enhɑ·nsiv), *a.* Also *U.S.* enhansive. [f. Enhance *v.* + -ive.] That tends to enhance or intensify; *spec.* designating a sentence of which the second part is more forcible than the first, or the second part itself.
1853 Edwards & Taylor tr. *Kühner's Grk. Gram.* 499 A copulative coördinate sentence is either annexive or enhansive. 1889 *Blackw. Mag.* Nov. 708 What so..enhancive of the glow of the bright firelight..as that delightful ball of warm dark-grey fur coiled up upon the hearth? 1904 A. B. Davidson *Theol. O. T.* 99 *Elohim*—a plural not numerical, but simply enhancive of the idea of *might.*

Enhat (enhæ·t), *v.* [f. En- 1 b + Hat *sb.*] *trans.* To invest with a cardinal's hat.
1925 *Times Lit. Suppl.* 26 Nov. 795/1 The rings ceremonially presented to Cardinals when enhatted. 1925 *Times* 18 Dec. 13/2 Five Cardinals Enhatted.

Enhypostasia (enhəipostēi·ziă). *Theol.* [mod. L., f. Gr. ἐνυπόστατος really existent.] **a.** Substantial or personal existence. **b.** Personality existing not independently but in union with another personality; often describing the human nature of Christ as related to His divine nature as God the Son. So **Enhyposta·tic** *a.*
1877 Schaff in Smith & Wace *Dict. Chr. Biog.* I. 495/1 The Anhypostasia, Impersonality, or, to speak more accurately, the Enhypostasia, of the human nature of Christ. 1917 H. M. Relton *Study Christol.* 226 The doctrine of the Enhypostasia..secures that the self-consciousness of the God-Man is a single-consciousness which is not purely human, nor merely human, but truly human.

Enlarge, *v.* Add: **2. d.** *Photog.* To make a picture larger than (the original negative). Also *absol.*
1871 *English Mechanic* 24 Feb. 549/3 Cheap Enlarging Camera. *Ibid.* 5 May 166/2 [A] condenser..for enlarging with a ½ plate lens. 1878 Abney *Treat. Photogr.* Index, Enlarged photographs. 1903 A. Watkins *Watkins Man.* 43 Daylight Enlarging. *Ibid.* 44 In commencing..to calculate enlarging exposures. *Ibid.,* The indicated exposure will be right for a decidedly dense negative without taking into account the increase for the enlarging factor. *Ibid.* 47 Most photographers want to enlarge from a negative of settled size to one size of paper.

Enlargedness. (Later U.S. example.)
1805 D. McClure *Diary* (1899) 105 Desire to be thankful for that freedom and enlargedness, with which I am sometimes favored.

Enlargement. Add:
1. c. *Photog.* The process of enlarging a picture; a negative or print made of a larger size than the original.
1871 *English Mechanic* 17 Mar. 621/2 The inner body of large camera for enlargement. 1878 Abney *Treat. Photogr.* xxix. 209 It can also be shown that an enlargement from a small negative is better than a picture of the same size taken direct as regards sharpness of detail. 1884 — *Instr. Photogr.* (ed. 6) 188 Enlarged negatives can be produced either by making an enlarged transparency, or by enlarging the negative from it in the camera. In all cases of enlargement the camera must be employed. 1903 A. Watkins *Watkins Man.* 47 The five separate influences which decide an enlargement exposure.

Enlist, *v.* **3.** (Earlier Amer. example.)
1716 *Jrnls. Ho. Repr. Mass.* I. 149 If the interested can find so many that will Inlist themselves for that Service.

Enlisting, *vbl. sb.* (Earlier Amer. examples of *attrib.* use).
1757 in *Lett. to Washington* II. 125 The Treasurer this Day sends..Money to pay the Volunteers & Draughts their enlisting Money. 1775 *Rec. New Hampshire Comm. Safety* 27 Sent him..Six blank enlisting orders.

Enneastyle (e·niăstəil), *a. Arch.* [f. Gr. ἐννέα nine + στῦλος column.] Having nine columns or pillars.
1875 *Encycl. Brit.* II. 410/2 An enneastyle arrangement.

Enochian (inōᵘ·kiăn), *a.* [f. *Enoch* + -ian.] Of, belonging to, or characteristic of Enoch the patriarch (see Gen. v. 24), or the apocryphal Book of Enoch. Also **Eno·chic** *a.*
1902 *Encycl. Brit.* XXV. 496/1 Slavonic Book of Enoch... This new fragment of the Enochic literature has only recently come to light. 1919 S. C. Carpenter *Christianity acc. Luke* iv. 41 [Our Lord's] actual use of the Enochian conception [of the Messiah]. 1920 J. Rendel Harris *Testimonies* II. x. 84 Peter's use of the Enochic writings makes in the direction of a close relation between his citations from them and his citations from Isaiah.

Enol (ī·nǫl). *Chem.* [app. for *henol, f. Gr. ἑν-, stem of εἷς one + -ol.] One of the several compounds containing the unsaturated alcoholic group, .CH: C(OH). Hence **Eno·lic** *a.,* of or pertaining to an enol.
1894 *Jrnl. Chem. Soc.* LXVI. II. 433 Compounds containing the group: C:C(OH) are said to be 'enolic'. *Ibid.* 434 No evidence supporting the existence of the tautomeric enolic form sometimes attributed to malonic acid was obtained. 1902 *Encycl. Brit.* XXVI. 725/1 In some cases compounds are obtained from it [*sc.* ethylic aceto-acetate] which are clearly of an enolic form..*i.e.,* a form which is both an ethenoid and an *ol* or alcohol.

Enophthalmus, -mos (enǫfþæ·lmŏs, -ǫs). *Path.* [mod.L., f. Gr. ἐν in + ὀφθαλμός eye.] Abnormal retraction of the eyeball into the orbit.
1892 Gradle in *Hare's Syst. Pract. Therap.* 1075 The.. receding of the eyeball into the orbit, enophthalmos, is apparently produced by any condition of emaciation or extreme anæmia. 1907 *Practitioner* Nov. 734 The intermittent exophthalmos occurs when the head is depressed, such as occurs in stooping, whereas enophthalmos follows when the head is in the erect position.

Enough, *a., sb.,* and *adv.* Add: **A.** *adj.* **1.** Also *U.S. dial.* in phr. *enough sight better,* etc. Cf. Sight *sb.*[1] 2 b.
1845 S. Judd *Margaret* I. xiv. 110 Their music is enough sight better than ours. 1856 Alice Cary *Married* 63 Granmam likes Hal, in fact, enough sight the best. 1887 Mary E. Wilkins *Humble Romance* 160 If it's got to be done by anybody I'd enough sight rather 'twoud be done by the town. 1891 — *New Eng. Nun* 407 They'd keep dusted 'nough sight cleaner. 1911 J. C. Lincoln *Cap'n Warren's Wards* xvi. 251 It was enough sight damper amongst the seats than in those cloth waves.
B. *adv.* **3.** With comparatives: Amply, sufficiently. *U.S. dial.*
1846–52 Mrs. Whitcher *Widow Bedott P.* xvi. 163 Its enough ginteeler 'n them flambergasted blue and yaller things. 1897 R. M. Stuart *Simpkinsville* 18 You'd see one thet was enough pinker an sweeter 'n the rest to make you climb for it.

Enregister, *v.* For '*rare* in mod. use' substitute 'Revived in recent use as a gallicism', and add quots.:
1896 *McClure's Mag.* VI. 479/2 The works of men too numerous to be enregistered here. 1918 *Times Lit. Supp.* 21 Mar. 137/2 The three hundred thousand enregistered by the barrister Chenaux. 1928 *New Statesman* 27 Oct. 81 The young spiders..are obeying what is nowadays a racially enregistered tropism to climb.

Enregistration (e:nredʒistrēi·ʃən). [f. Enregister *v.*: see -ation.] The registering, on the brain, of previous actions, so that performance becomes automatic or instinctive.
1922 J. Y. Simpson *Man & Attainm. Immortality* xi. 241 Increased cerebral development involves in some way a wider and more complex range of enregistration and combination of action and reaction, and so, through the presence of alternatives, of choice. 1927 *Glasgow Herald* 24 Mar. 4 Experiments with rats that quickly master a labyrinth of the Hampton Court maze type point to an enregistration of tactile and muscular sensations. 1930 J. A. Thomson in *John O' London's Weekly* 8 Mar. 878/3 Enregistration of the past is characteristic of life.

Enrolled, *ppl. a.* (Earlier U.S. examples.)
1789 *Ann. Congress* I. 6 July 49 The House had appointed a Committee..for the purpose of examining an enrolled bill imposing duties on tonnage. 1835 *Indiana Ho. Repr. Jrnl.* 145 The joint committee on enrolled bills have this day compared the following engrossed bills of the Senate with the enrolled bills, and find the same correctly enrolled.

Enrolling, *ppl. a.* [f. Enrol *v.* + -ing [2].] That enters on a roll or list.
1838 *Indiana Ho. Repr. Jrnl.* 6 The House proceeded to the election of Enrolling Clerks. *Ibid.* 143 The duties of Enrolling Secretary of the Senate.

Ensellure (ense·liuə, ‖aṅsęlür). *Anthrop.* [Fr. f. *en-* + *selle* saddle + *-ure.*] (See quot.)
1900 Deniker *Races of Man* 93 Ensellure—that is to say, the strongly marked curve of the dorso-lumbo-sacral region —is especially marked among Spanish women. *Ibid.,* Ensellure is also more marked among Negroes than among Whites.

Ensemble, *sb.* Add: **1. b.** A woman's suit or complete dress (e.g. for afternoon or evening wear).
1927 *Weekly Dispatch* 6 Nov. 16 A simple ensemble..in shades of brown. *Ibid.,* The afternoon ensemble is by no means dead. 1930 *Daily Express* 8 Sept. 5/5 White rabbit, brocade, velvet..add considerable chic to the evening ensemble.
3. *Mus.* The united performance of all voices or all instruments in a piece of concerted music, or of a chorus and orchestra; also, the manner in which this is done.
1844 *Musical Examiner* 28 Sept. 809 It was really possible for five principal vocalists to achieve a perfect *ensemble.* 1880 *Grove's Dict. Music* II. 659/2 A feeling of carelessness which the conductor must be quick to detect lest the *ensemble* be marred thereby. 1915 Fuller-Maitland in *Musical Quarterly* I. 83 We must put up with *ensemble* when we want to talk of that part of music, which is produced by the co-operation of several performers. *Ibid.,* Much care is required to secure a good ensemble in a vocal piece. 1927 *Observer* 27 Nov. 14/4 The ensemble between pianoforte and violoncello was good. 1929 *Encycl. Brit.* VIII. 616/2 The 'ensemble numbers' of an opera (trio, quartet and so forth). By extension the term is applied to the process of combining in this manner and to the skill with which it is accomplished. Thus in this sense it may be said that the ensemble of a choir or of a quartet was poor.
4. *Math.* A collection or combination of systems.
1902 J. W. Gibbs *Statist. Mech.* 116 A microcanonical ensemble of systems. *Ibid.* 169 The time-ensemble, or ensemble of phases through which a single system passes in the course of time. *Ibid.* 190 A grand ensemble is therefore composed of a multitude of petit ensembles.

Ensete (ensī·ti). [Native name.] The Abyssinian banana, *Musa Ensete.*
1864 J. A. Grant *Walk Across Africa* p. xv.

Ensiform, *a.* Add: *sb.* = *ensiform cartilage.*
1907 *Practitioner* Oct. 467 Even when it travels directly downwards, in the same line as the pulmonary murmur, it [*sc.* an aortic murmur] travels much further, and is usually clearly audible at the ensiform.

Ensign, *sb.* **9.** Add: **ensign-fly,** a parasitic hymenopterous insect of the family *Evaniidæ.*
1894 Comstock *Man. Insects* 628 We have named these insects Ensign-flies, because they carry the abdomen aloft like a flag. 1897 — *Insect Life* 86.

Ensilation (ensilēi·ʃən). [f. Ensilate *v.*: see -tion.] The preserving of green fodder in a pit.
1885 *Nature* 22 Oct. 606/1 The life of the plant under the restricting conditions of ensilation.

Ensnarl, *v.*[1] Delete †*Obs.* and add quots.
1890 P. Brooks *New Starts in Life* xiv. 239 Shall life be one great deep stream of joy, ever and anon darkening and ensnarling itself in suffering, but always unsnarling and brightening itself again? 1894 W. R. Thayer *Poems New & Old* 19 The soul of Halid is ensnarled in a secret and pardonless crime. 1924 *Public Opinion* 1 Aug. 104/2 Exhibiting an amazing capacity to get at the ensnarled kinks of the mind and soul.

En-Soph (en sōᵘf). Also -sof. [Late Heb. אין סוף *ēn sōf* no end.] In Cabbalistic doctrine, the absolute infinite and incomprehensible God. Hence **Enso·phic** *a.*
1693 Ensophick [in Dict.]. 1865 C. D. Ginsburg *Kabbalah* 64 No one has seen the *En Soph* at any time. 1873 Leland *Egypt. Sketch-Bk.* 202 The supermundane and ensophic universe. 1902 *Jewish Encycl.* III. 468/1 An expression of the will of the En-Sof is not necessary in the act of emanation.

Enstool (enstū·l), *v.* [f. En- [1] + Stool *sb.* 1 e.] *trans.* To place (a chief) on his 'stool'.
1895 *Times* 16 Nov. 5/4 The King of Kokofu..is one of the three chiefs who, by ancient custom, perform the ceremony of 'enstooling' the King of Kumassi as King paramount [of the Ashanti Confederation]. 1895 *Daily News* 25 Nov. 3/5 The enstooling of Prempeh on March 26, 1886. 1925 *Public Opinion* 11 Oct. 396/1 Should a Chief be enstooled.

Ensuant (ĕnsiū·ănt), *a.* Delete † *Obs.* and add: **2.** Following or consequent *on.*
1897 *Daily News* 21 Oct. 7/7 His condition, ensuant on a paralytic stroke, left little room for hope. 1900 *Ibid.* 2 July 5/6 The stoppage of trade ensuant on the war.

En suite: see Suite.

Enswamped, *ppl. a.* (Later U.S. example.)
1821 T. Nuttall *Trav. Arkansa* vi. 108, I was now obliged more deeply to wade through the enswamped forests,..which surround the habitable prairie lands.

Entad (e·ntæd), *adv. Anat.* and *Zool.* [f. Gr. ἐντός within + *-ad.] On or towards the inner side or interior; in or into a position nearer to the centre.
1882 Wilder & Gage *Anat. Technol.* 27 The dura (mater) may be described as *ectad* of the brain, but *entad* of the cranium.

Ental (e·ntăl), *a. Anat.* and *Zool.* [f. Gr. ἐντός within + -al.] Inner; internal.
1882 Wilder & Gage *Anat. Technol.* 27 The need of other terms than those in use was so generally and so strongly felt among the students in the Anatomical Laboratory of Cornell University that the suggestion to employ *ental* and *ectal* was welcomed. 1889 *Buck's Handbk. Med. Sci.* VIII. 111 The ental surface of the pia.

Entanglement. Add:
3. *Mil.* An extensive barrier arranged so as to impede an enemy's movements; an abatis formed of trees and branches, or an obstruction formed of stakes and barbed wire.
1834–47 J. S. Macaulay *Field Fortif.* (1851) 89 The boughs of the brushwood..interlacing with one another, will thus form a very good obstacle, called an entanglement. 1876 Voyle & Stevenson *Milit. Dict.* (ed. 3) s.v., A good entanglement can be made with stakes and wire. 1899 *Westm. Gaz.* 17 Nov. 2/1 Where a wood enters into the scheme of defence, an abattis—in this case called an 'entanglement'—forms naturally one of the best resources of the defenders. 1916 Boyd Cable *Action Front* 47 Slowly and cautiously, with the officer leading, they began to wend their way out under their own entanglement. 1917 [see Wire *sb.* 1 e].

Entente (aṅtaṅ·t). [Fr.] An understanding; most freq. used as a shortening of *Entente cordiale. **b.** A group of states or powers connected by an entente cordiale.
1877 L. W. M. Lockhart *Mine is Thine* xxxv. (Stanf.) Esmé held out her hand, which he took; and thus the friendly entente was sealed! 1883 Lady Bloomfield *Remin.* II. 47 Just at the moment that the King was proclaiming the happy *entente* with Austria. 1884 *Fortn. Rev.* XLII. 1 We have been constantly urged to maintain the policy of *entente cordiale* with France. 1907 *Times* 20 Apr. 8/2 But was there not an *entente* which must be the great ideal of every Briton—the *entente cordiale,* the *entente commerciale* between Great and Greater Britain? 1907 *Westm. Gaz.* 16 Aug. 2/2 The reforms introduced in the Macedonian vilayets by the *entente* Powers. 1908 *Daily Chron.* 14 Aug. 1/5 Why, asked Mr. Lloyd George, cannot we have an agreement with Germany, seeing that Great Britain has already concluded ententes with France, Russia, and the United States? 1920 *Glasgow Herald* 5 Aug. 7 The young Austrian republic, whose existence would be endangered unless the Entente intervened. 1923 *Westm. Gaz.* 23 Jan., The Little Entente (Roumania, Czecho-Slovakia, and Jugo-Slavia).
Hence **Ente·ntist,** one who favours an entente.
[1915 *Times* 30 Aug. 5/6 Oh! you stupid Quadruple Ententists!] 1924 *Glasgow Herald* 24 Jan. 7 Carlotti, the Italian Ambassador at Petersburg and an Ententist.

Entente cordiale (aṅtaṅt kordyal). [Fr.] A friendly understanding, esp. one between two or more political powers or states; with special reference to the understanding arrived at between England and France in 1904, and between these two countries and Russia in 1908 (cf. prec.). Also *attrib.*
1844 T. Raikes *Jrnl.* (1857) IV. 400 Still less had he [*sc.* the Emperor of Russia] the slightest wish or intention to derange or counteract this *entente cordiale* between England and France, which has been blazoned over Europe. 1845 Ford *Hand-bk. Spain* I. 227 But all this breeds bad blood and mars, on the Spaniards' part, the *entente cordiale.* 1847 H. Greville *Diary* (1883) Ser. I. 189 If Guizot remains in office Normanby must be recalled, as the only chance of a renewal of the *entente cordiale.* 1870 Lowell *Among my Bks., Lessing* 320 Something that would break the *entente cordiale* of placid mutual assurance. 1904 *Spectator* 31 Dec. 1070/1 The Cologne Gazette last week discounted M. Jaurès's reply to Count von Bülow, and warned its readers that the *entente cordiale* with England was aimed against Germany. 1908 *Times* 11 Mar. 11/6 The agreements which constitute the *entente cordiale* with France.

Ententophil, -phile (aṅtaṅ·tofil), *a.* and *sb.* [f. *Entente + -(o)phil, -phile.] (One who is) friendly to a particular *entente.*
1920 *Glasgow Herald* 9 May 9 (Greece) A Government formed with the least possible delay should declare itself ententophile. *Ibid.* 15 June 7 Signor Meda is the most Ententophile, or the least Germanophile, personality of the 'Popular Party'. *Ibid.* 14 Oct. 6 M. Take Jonescu,..the staunchest Ententophile in Eastern Europe. 1920 *19th Cent.* Nov. 793 Seven of their ships..by an act of Ententophil.. took refuge in Italian ports.

Entepicondyle (entepikǫ·ndil). *Anat.* [f. Gr. ἐντός within + Epicondyle.] The process just above the inner condyle of the humerus. So **Entepico·ndylar** *a.*
1893 *Athenæum* 18 Nov. 701/2 An entepicondylar (ulnar) foramen in the humerus. 1897 Parker & Haswell *Zool.* II. 496.

Enter, *v.* Add:
20. d. To get (land) recorded in a land-office in one's name as the intending occupier. *U.S.*
1835 in H. Howe *Hist. Coll. Ohio* 387 Much land was entered in the county, and many settlements made. 1843 R. Carlton *New Purchase* xiv. 100 Out there, a settlement usually takes its name from the person that first 'enters the land', i.e. buys a tract at the land office. *a* 1856 P. Cartwright *Autob.* xviii. (1858) 236 He..had some three hundred dollars hoarded up to enter land. *Ibid.* 239 Money was very scarce, and what little there was, was generally kept close to enter lands when our Congress should order sales. 1871 Schele de Vere *Americanisms* (1872) 173 All other lands can be obtained by entering them. 1884 H. Butterworth *Zigzag Journ. Western States* 217 'What does it usually cost to make a farm on government land?'.. 'It costs fourteen dollars to enter one hundred and sixty acres of land.'
22. c. To put down or cause to be put down upon the record. Also with *up.*
1896 A. Pulling *Law Rep., Five Years' Digest* 679 The defendant failed to appear, and judgment was entered. 1920 *Act* 10 & 11 *Geo. V* c. 67 § 41 (3) Judgments obtained or entered up in the Supreme Courts of Northern Ireland. 1930 *Daily Express* 6 Nov. 7/2 No judgment was entered.

Enteric, *a.* Add: **B.** *sb.* Enteric fever.
1900 *Westm. Gaz.* 31 Jan. 5/2 The preventive inoculation for enteric. 1926 W. R. Inge *Lay Thoughts* 99 Two of the worst scourges, enteric and tetanus.

Entering, *vbl. sb.* **3.** Add: **entering edge** *Aeronautics,* that edge of a surface which is the front edge in flight; called also *leading edge.*
1908 Sir H. Maxim *Artif. & Nat. Flight* 100 Our planes must have a certain length of entering edge—that is, the length of the front edge must bear a certain relation to the load lifted.

Entero-. Add: **Entera·lgia** *Path.,* pain in the intestines, colic. **Entere·ctomy** *Surg.,* removal of a portion of the intestine. **Entero-anastomo·sis** *Surg.,* the joining of two portions of an intestine so as to make a continuous tube. **Enterochlo·rophyl** *Chem.,* a form of chlorophyl present in some animals. **E·nterocœle** *Biol.,* the body-cavity or cœloma; hence **Enterocœ·lic** *a.* **Enterocoli·tis** *Path.,* inflammation of the small intestine and colon. **Enterody·nia** *Path.,* = *enteralgia. **Entero-entero·stomy** *Surg.,* an operation for forming a permanent opening between two non-continuous portions of the intestine. **Enteroki·nase** *Chem.,* a kinase found in the intestinal mucous membrane. **Enterone·phric** *a. Zool.,* designating a nephridial system in which the septal nephridia open into the intestine. **Enteropto·sis** *Path.,* prolapse of the intestines. **Entero·rrhaphy** *Surg.,* the sewing up of a wound in the intestines. **E·nterospasm** *Path.,* spasmodic contraction of the intestine. **Entero·stomy** *Surg.,* the operation for making a permanent opening into the intestine. **E·nterotome,** an instrument for opening the intestinal canal.
1848 Dunglison *Med. Lex.,* *Enteralgia. 1886 *Buck's Handbk. Med. Sci.* II. 231/2 Enteralgia is a term sometimes applied to colic, but more often to a neuralgia of the intestines without spasm. 1897 *Trans. Amer. Pediatric Soc.* IX. 119 These cases are common in the practice of every physician and are commonly diagnosed as 'gastralgia' or 'enteralgia'. 1877 tr. *von Ziemssen's Cycl. Pract. Med.* VII. 662 In case ..the volvulus cannot be withdrawn,..it has been recommended to excise it completely (*enterectomy), and then.. to insert the upper end through an opening into the cæcum (Hacken), and to ligate the other: *entero-anastomosis. 1908 *Practitioner* Mar. 368 To..wait for an improvement in the patient's condition to perform an enterectomy. *Ibid.* Sept. 459 Entero-anastomosis without resection. 1883 C. A. MacMunn in *Proc. Royal Soc.* XXXV. 133 It..can be detected in the bile of specimens of *Helix* after a six months' fast; for this colouring-matter, since it is found in the appendages of the enteron, the name *enterochlorophyll is proposed. 1888 Rolleston & Jackson *Anim. Life* 117 The secretion of the liver is acid, and has been found to have a diastatic and a peptic action in *H. pomatia.* It contains enterochlorophyl in *Helix pomatia.* 1884 tr. *Claus' Zool.* 116 The body cavity..may be developed secondarily as a split in the mesoderm (cœlom), or as outgrowths from the rudiment of the rudimentary canal (archenteron), in which case it is known as an *enterocœle body cavity. 1888 *Nature* 2 Feb. 334/2 The 'Schlauchförmiger Kanal'..being *enterocœlic in origin. 1888 Rolleston & Jackson *Anim. Life* 592 The anterior enterocœlic pouch. 1857 Dunglison *Med. Lex.,* *Enterocolitis. 1886 *Buck's Handbk. Med. Sci.* II. 435/1 In entero-colitis the inflammation is mostly confined to the lower end of the ileum. 1848 Dunglison *Med. Lex.,* *Enterodynia. 1874 Garrod & Baxter *Mat. Med.* 450 Painful affections of the stomach and duodenum, as in gastrodynia, enterodynia. 1903 *Med. Record* 28 Feb. 352 (Cent. D. Suppl.) *Entero-enterostomy. 1908 *Brit. Med. Jrnl.* 18 Jan. 140/2 Entero-enterostomy, or the Y-shaped junction, avoided. 1902 *Jrnl. Chem. Soc.* LXXXII. II. 680 Snake venom..contains a substance (enzyme) which has the properties of Pawlow's *enterokinase. 1908 *Practitioner* Sept. 447 Succus entericus, which contains the activating enterokinase. 1919 K. N. Bahl in *Q. Jrnl. Microsc. Sci.* LXIV. I. 101 The elaborate '*enteronephric' type of the nephridial system in Pheretima. 1902 *Encycl. Brit.* XXXI. 550/2 Displacements downwards of the stomach and transverse colon, along with a movable right kidney and associated with dyspepsia and neurasthenia, form the malady termed by Glénard *enteroptosis. 1907 *Practitioner* Dec. 771 Patients with very lax abdominal walls and marked enteroptosis. 1889 *Buck's Handbk. Med. Sci.* VIII. 299/1 The immediate restoration of the continuity of the gut by circular *enterorrhaphy. 1901 Dorland *Med. Dict.,* *Enterospasm. 1908 *Practitioner* Aug. 219 A localised enterospasm. 1889 *Buck's Handbk. Med. Sci.* VIII. 328/2 In cases in which strangulation was the marked feature..*enterostomy could ..do nothing to relieve. 1848 Dunglison *Med. Lex.,* *Enterotome. 1882 Wilder & Gage *Anat. Technol.* 70 The enterotome supplied in post-mortem cases is a pair of long scissors, one blade of which is enlarged and rounded, and projects beyond the other so as to precede it in opening an intestine.

Enteron (e·ntĕrǫn). *Anat.* Pl. **entera.** [mod. L., a. Gr. ἔντερον an intestine.] The alimentary canal or gut.
1878 Bell tr. *Gegenbaur's Comp. Anat.* 165 Separate glands are almost always absent from the mid-gut of the Vermes, but the epithelium is generally found to be different from the epithelia of the other divisions of the enteron. 1880 *Encycl. Brit.* XII. 548/1 By the formation of a mouth to the sac, the enteron acquires the functions of a digestive retort. 1927 Haldane & Huxley *Anim. Biol.* xii. 268 The mouth leads into a cavity called the coelenteron, because it fulfils the functions both of the coelom and of the enteron or gut of higher forms.

Entertainee (entəɹtēinī·). *rare.* [f. Entertain *v.* + -ee.] One who is entertained.
1839 J. F. Cooper *Home as Found* v. (1878) 84 Miss Ring was inviting, with her eyes, a number six to join the circle, her ambition being dissatisfied with five entertainees.

Entertainment. Add: **13.** *Comb.,* **entertainment tax,** a tax which became operative on August 1, 1918, levied on attendance at public entertainments.
1922 *Punch* 25 Oct. 385 Admission to the Carlton Club for the meeting of Unionist M.P.'s last Thursday was free. No entertainment tax.

Enthuse, *v. U.S.* **a.** (Earlier example.)
1859 *Congress. Globe* 16 Feb. 1058/3 They are what they call in the country 'enthused'—run mad on the subject [of Cuba].

Entire, *a.* Add:
5. d. *Her.* Of a bearing, e.g. a cross: Attached to the sides of the shield.
1825 W. Berry *Encycl. Her.* I. Bb 2/1 *Entire,* or *Throughout,* sometimes called *fixed* and *firm,* being attached to the sides of the shield, as a *cross pattée entire.* 1873 Aveling *Boutell's Her.* 43 Crosses are sometimes borne entire, that is, they cover the whole field.
e. *Skating.* Of a movement: Beginning and ending at the centre.
1882 Monier-Williams *Figure Skating* (1883) 29 The term 'Entire' signifies a Cross Roll at the centre, either forward or backward, as indicated by the call. *Ibid.* 30 The word 'Entire' is declared to mean a forward cross roll at the centre as well as a back cross roll.

Entitative, *a.* Add examples of more recent currency:
1890 *Tablet* 29 Nov. 860 The vexed question as to the entitative simplicity or not of the living principles of mere plants and brute animals. 1907 *Dublin Rev.* July 188 St. Thomas, with all the Scholastics, maintained the absolute entitative distinction of God from creatures. 1909 M. H. Dziewicki *Wyclif's De Ente* 243 *marg.,* The commission of sin as an entitative act.

Entitle, *v.* **4.** Add: Also *absol.*
1897 *Daily News* 19 Jan. 5/4 A post that does not entitle to a seat in the Lords.

Ento-. Add: **Entobra·nchiate** *a. Zool.,* having concealed or internal gills. **Entoch·ondral** *a. Anat.,* situated or occurring within the substance of a cartilage. **Entoco·don** [Gr. κώδων bell] (see quot.). **E·ntocœle** *Zool.,* that portion of the gut-cavity of certain polyps which lies between a pair of mesenteries (see quots.); so **Entocœ·lic** *a.* **Entode·rmal, -mic** *adjs.,* of or pertaining to the endoderm. **Entomere** *Embryol.,* each of the more granular cells produced by segmentation of the primitive ovum. **Entopla·stral** *a.,* pertaining to the entoplastron. **Entopla·stron** (see quot.). **Entoscle·rite** *Ent.,* an internal sclerite. **Entose·ptum,** in corals, a septum developed interiorly. **Entosole·nian** *a.* [Gr. σωλήν channel, gutter], having an internal neck. **Entoste·rnite** *Anat.,* an internal fibro-cartilaginous plate giving support to a series of muscles in various arthropods. **Entoste·rnum** *Ent.,* an internal process or system of processes of the sternum of an arthropod. **Entotri·ceps,** the inner head of the triceps muscle of the arm. **Ento·trophous** *a.,* having the characteristics of the *Entotrophi,* a suborder of insects whose jaws seem sunk in the head.
1888 Rolleston & Jackson *Anim. Life* 560 In the *Cidaridæ* or *Entobranchiate *Desmosticha.* 1889 A. Macalister *Hum. Anat.* 38 The mesoblastic tissue..is replaced by bone in either of two ways, which are called respectively ectochondral and *entochondral ossification. 1888 Rolleston & Jackson *Anim. Life* 747 The bell and velum are formed.. from an *entocodon or ectodermic thickening. 1885 G. H. Fowler in *Q. Jrnl. Microsc. Sci.* XXV. 578 To those chambers which lie between a 'pair' of mesenteries the term *entocœle is applied. 1887 G. C. Bourne *ibid.* Aug. 34 The intermesenterial chambers or entocœles of the pairs to which they belong project far deeper into the calyx than the remaining chambers in Seriatopora. 1902 *Trans. Linnean Soc.* Oct. 304 The appearance of a new mesenterial pair is followed very closely by the outgrowth of a tentacle from its entocœle. 1888 *Q. Jrnl. Microsc. Sci.* XXVIII. 5 The tentacles are probably *entocœlic only. 1902 *Trans. Linnean Soc.* Oct. 304 The tentacles are outgrowths of both the entocœlic and exocœlic mesenterial chambers. 1884 tr. *Claus' Zool.* 100 The *entodermal lining of the gastro-vascular canals. 1886 *Buck's Handbk. Med. Sci.* III. 172/1 The division of the margin of the ectodermal disk into two parts, one resting directly on the *entodermic yoke. 1890 Billings *Med. Dict.,* *Entomere. 1896 Lydekker *Roy. Nat. Hist.* V. 77 Owing to the absence of the unpaired *entoplastral bone. 1871 Huxley *Anat. Vert.* 202 The *entoplastron and the two *epiplastra* correspond with the median and lateral thoracic plates of the Labyrinthodont *Amphibia.* 1902 *Proc. Zool. Soc.* 17 June 174 From the middle of its area arises a stout, hooked *entosclerite, which projects backwards into the cavity of the prosoma. 1885 G. H. Fowler in *Q. Jrnl. Microsc. Sci.* XXV. 578 The septa lying in these two classes of chambers are similarly called exosepta and *entosepta. 1903 *Ann. & Mag. Nat. Hist.* Feb. 147 The union of the entoseptum within each pair of the second cycle mesenteries with the adjoining exosepta. 1897 *Smithsonian Rep.* (Nat. Mus.) (1899) 306 *Lagena Globosa*..aperture leading into a short internal neck (*entosolenian). 1888 Rolleston & Jackson *Anim. Life* 526 An *entosternite or chitinoid fibrocellular plate. 1902 *Nature* 25 Sept. 529 The entosternite of Mygale. 1902 *Encycl. Brit.* XXV. 527/2 The affinity between Limulus and the Arachnids, indicated by the presence of a free suspended *entosternum or plastron or entosternite in both. 1882 Wilder & Gage *Anat. Technol.* 263 The origin of the middle division of the *entotriceps. *Ibid.* 266 The cephalic division of the entotriceps. 1895 *Cambr. Nat. Hist.* V. 174 The family Japygidae is..*entotrophous.

En tout cas (aṅ tu ka). [Fr., = in any case or emergency.] A parasol which also serves the purpose of an umbrella.
1876 *Echo* 30 Aug. (Stanford). 1889 *Chambers's Jrnl.* 28 Dec. 827/1 The parasol and the popular *en tout cas.* 1915 Galsworthy *Little Man* etc. 39 Maud comes running, ..dragging a bull-dog..by the crutch end of her en-tout-cas. 1928 *Daily Express* 17 July 5/2 The useful en-tout-cas that will withstand a summer shower.

Entrain, *v.*[1] Add: **2.** *spec.* Of a fluid: To carry (particles) along by its flow; *spec.* of steam which carries along particles of water through a pipe or particles of sugar from an evaporating pan during the manufacture of sugar. Hence **Entrai·ner,** 'a device for saturating a current of gas or steam with liquid, usually a hollow or pocket for collecting a liquid in such a way that it will be picked up by a passing current of gas or steam' (*Cent. Dict.* Suppl.); **Entrai·nment** [1], the action of a fluid in carrying particles along.
1892 *Mod. Lang. Notes* Nov. 393 *Entrain, entrainement*— evidently from Fr. *entrainer.* The action of carrying over particles of syrup or sugar by the steam exhausted from vacuum-pans in boiling sugar. 1902 *Sci. Amer. Suppl.* 27 Dec. 22558 (Cent. D. Suppl.).

Entrain, *v.*[2] Add:
2. *intr.* To go on board a train.
1890 *Daily News* 8 Apr. 3/3 The troops should be back.. in sufficient time to..entrain for London. 1899 *Ibid.* 21 Nov. 5/4 The debarkation and entraining of the troops as they arrive here is being carried out rapidly...The troops entrain at the docks. 1914 R. Brooke *Coll. Poems* (1918) Mem. p. cxxx, We..entrained in the last train left.

Entrainment [2] (entrēi·nmĕnt). [f. Entrain *v.*[2] + -ment.] The act or fact of entering a train.
1891 *Pall Mall Gaz.* 8 July 2/2 The early hour of entrainment is..still maintained.

Entrance, *sb.* **2. d.** (Later U.S. example.)
1886 C. D. Warner *Their Pilgr.* xi. (1888) 253 Paying their entrance, and passing through the turnstile..they stood in the Congress Spring Park.
6. *Naut.* (Later U.S. example.)
1886 *Outing* (U.S.) IX. 125/1 The Pocahontas was a failure. She had a fine entrance, but was too heavy in her counters for fast sailing.

Entredeux (aṅtrədȫ). *Dressmaking.* [Fr., lit. = between two.] An insertion of lace, linen, or other material.
1850 *Harper's Mag.* I. 432 (Stanford) Embroidered *entredeux.* 1902 *Daily Chron.* 1 Feb. 8/3 A milk-white gown, most delightfully arranged about the waist in corselet form by means of lace entredeux. 1904 *Ibid.* 3 May 8/5 A way of using medallions and entredeux of stitched linen on gowns of fine cloth. 1928 *Observer* 12 Feb. 23 Such felts are.. simple compared to many another which is complicated by endredeux of straw.

Entrée. Add: **2.** Also *attrib.*
1846 Soyer *Gastron. Regenerator* 713 New pagodatique entrée dish. 1901 *Connoisseur* Dec. 275/2 A nice pair of Sheffield plate entrée dishes.

Entrenching, *vbl. sb.* (Earlier U.S. examples of *entrenching tools.*)
1775 *Rec. New Hampshire Comm. Safety* 9 [He] went.. to Medford, with Blanketing, Entrenching Tools, etc. 1776 J. Thacher *Military Jrnl.* 46 Then follow the carts with the entrenching tools.

Entre nous (aṅtrənu). [Fr.] Between ourselves.
1818 Byron *Don Juan* I. lxxxiv, I only say suppose it— *inter nos,* (This should be *entre nous,* for Julia thought In French, but then the rhyme would go for nought). 1824 Laetitia M. Hawkins *Annaline* I. 272, I suspect, entre nous, that the man acted under the directions of his master.

Entrepreneur. Add: **c.** *gen.* A manager.
1852 Carlyle in Froude *Life* (1884) II. 107 A public set of rooms—*Kursaal* they call such things,..all supported by gambling, all built by one French gambling *entrepreneur.* 1871 J. C. Young *Mem. C. M. Young* I. vi. 208 The great violinist [Paganini] has shut himself up in close confinement since his arrival in this country, and refused to receive any one but his *entrepreneur* and his dentist.
d. *Pol. Econ.* One who undertakes an enterprise; *esp.* a contractor (whether an individual or a corporation) acting as intermediary between capital and labour.
1885 F. A. Walker *Pol. Econ.* 167 The employer, or entrepreneur, receiving profits. *Ibid.* 365 The state as capitalist is at no small disadvantage; as entrepreneur, that disadvantage is vastly aggravated. 1889 R. T. Ely *Introd. Pol. Econ.* (1891) 170 We have..been obliged to resort to the French language for a word to designate the person who organizes and directs the productive factors, and we call such a one an *entrepreneur.* 1922 F. Lavington *Trade Cycle* iii. 19 In modern times the entrepreneur assumes many forms. He may be a private business man, a partnership, a joint stock company, a co-operative society, a municipality or similar body. 1930 J. M. Keynes *Treat. Money* I. 159 Entrepreneurs will sometimes begin to act before the price-changes which are the justification of their action have actually occurred.

Entry. Add: **1.** Also, the beginning of his part by a performer in a canon or similar musical composition; also *attrib.* in *entry sign.*
1879 *Grove's Dict. Mus.* I. 390/2 Those who can stand the enormous strain which is implied in the recollection of every *nuance* and the exact entry of every instrument in a long and complicated work. 1897 J. S. Shedlock tr. *H. Riemann's Dict. Mus.* 220/1 Entry Signs are the marks in a canon (of which only one part is written out) for the entry of the imitating parts...The sign which a conductor gives to a player or singer to come in after a long pause is also called an Entry Sign.
8. *Card of entry,* in card games, a card the playing of which secures the lead for the player.
1884 'Cavendish' *Whist* (ed. 14) 135 In case his only card of entry in that suit should be an honour. 1910 W. Dalton *'Saturday' Bridge* ii. (ed. 9) 53 When you hold six or more cards of a black suit, thoroughly established, and one other card of entry, No Trumps should always be declared at the score of love.
4. c. The initial training of young hounds (cf. Enter *v.* 18 b); now, more commonly *collect.,* young hounds who are being entered. Also *transf.,* the younger generation.
1845 Youatt *Dog* (1858) 127 There must always be a little flesh in hand for the sick, for bitches with their whelps, and for the entry of young hounds. 1856 'Stonehenge' *Brit. Sports* iv. 124/2 Remembering that your chance of good sport through this season and the next depends more upon your young entry than upon the old draft-hounds. *Ibid.* 125/1 In order to have an opportunity of rating the young ones for speaking to 'riot', while under the fresh recollections of the encouragement which they have received in their entry to their own particular game. 1881 *Encycl. Brit.* XII. 315/2 The young entry are sure to run riot. 1897 *Encycl. Sport* I. 543/2 It is better to keep steadily on, confining hounds as much as possible to covert, or the entry will forget what they have learned. 1899 Somerville & Ross *Irish R.M.* vi. 130 Dr. Jerome Hickey was having a stirring time with the young entry and the rabbit-holes. 1924 J. Buchan *Three Hostages* vii, Thank God that we have a man like him among the young entry.
6. (For *Obs.* read Now *U.S.*)
1907 *Springfield Weekly Republ.* 24 Oct. 1 An act of the Legislature which became operative with the entry of the month.
10. *entry-card, -list, -money* (earlier U.S. examples), *-way*; **entryman** *U.S.,* one who enters upon a homestead with the intention of settling.
1908 *Westm. Gaz.* 13 Aug. 4/1 It was only with the greatest difficulty that the R.A.C. managed to get anything like a representative *entry list. 1886 *N. Amer. Rev.* Jan. 59 The *entryman, under the timber culture act, is not compelled to plant any trees until the third year from date of entry, when if he likes he may file a relinquishment of his claim, and the land is again open for entry. 1803 *Steele Papers* I. 417 The *Entry-Money you mentioned is paid. 1804 *Ibid.* II. 791 The entry money for each coalt shall be [a specified number of] dollars. 1854 Mary J. Holmes *Tempest & Sunshine* iii. 44 There was no *entry way to the building. 1889 Rose T. Cooke *Steadfast* xxii. 236 His study door opened from the left hand of the little entry-way into which they stepped from without.

Enucleate (ĭniū·kli₁ėt), *a. Biol.,* etc. [ad. L. *enucleatus,* pa. pple. of *enucleare* to Enucleate.] Without a nucleus.
1889 *Cent. Dict.* 1910 F. Keeble *Plant-Anim.* iv. 113 The enucleate green cell may be connected by fine processes with another green cell still possessed of nuclear substance. 1921 L. W. Sharp *Cytol.* 69 Klebs found that enucleate cells of *Spirogyra* may continue for some time to form starch.

Enu·cleated, *ppl. a.* [f. Enucleate *v.* + -ed [1].] Having the kernel extracted. Also *fig.*
1885 Sir R. F. Burton *Arab. Nts.* VII. 14 *note,* Arab 'Ajwah', enucleated dates pressed together into a solid mass. 1900 *Daily News* 17 May 6/3 The most enucleated invalid might stand the intellectual strain of the 'Southern Cross' and the 'Northern Lights'.

Enunciator. b. (Earlier U.S. example.)
1846 *Rep. U.S. Comm. Patents* (1847) 101 Letters patent have also been granted for an improved enunciator, for use in hotels, &c.

Enuresis (eniurī·sis). *Path.* [mod.L., f. Gr. ἐνουρεῖν to urinate in.] Incontinence of urine.
1800 tr. *Cullen's Nosology* 173. 1822–7 Good *Study Med.* (1829) V. 509 Paruria incontinens...This is the enuresis of most of the nosologists. 1907 *Practitioner* Apr. 542 For a year past he had had terrors practically every night, and often..enuresis. 1909 *Lancet* 1 May 1245/2 He had frequently known nocturnal enuresis to persist after very thorough removal of adenoids and tonsils.

Envelope, *sb.* Add: **6.** *attrib.* and *Comb.,* as *envelope cementer, cutter, flap, folder.*
1891 Kipling *Light that Failed* (1900) 191 A letter with a black M. on the envelope flap. 1901 *Daily Chron.* 16 Apr. 8/6 Envelope Cutter. 1904 *Ibid.* 12 Jan. 10/6 Envelope Cementer wanted...Envelope Folder wanted.

Environmental, *a.* Add illustrations of more recent currency. Hence **Environme·ntally** *adv.,* with reference to or by means of (one's or the) environment.
1884 *Mind* July 338 Environmentally-initiated Sensations are classified according to the nature of the agent by which they are aroused. 1891 *Blackw. Mag.* CL. 853/1 Some general environmental cause appears to be necessary for the explanation of the facts. 1918 *Times Lit. Suppl.* 2 May 205/1 A cell may environmentally acquire a new property and keep it. 1920 A. S. Pringle-Pattison *Idea of God* 75 Terms like stimulus, response, behaviour, all imply the notion of selection, the power of adaptation to environmental change. 1928 *Daily Tel.* 21 Aug. 13/1 If you cannot indict a nation, neither can you fully describe a nation, environmentally or spiritually.

Envision (envi·ʒən), *v.* [f. En- [1] + Vision *sb.*] *trans.* To see as in a vision.
1921 L. Strachey *Q. Vict.* viii. 221 His blackest hypochondria had never envisioned quite so miserable a Catastrophe. 1925 *Chambers's Jrnl.* Dec. 800/1 Namitie..resigned himself apparently to envisioning her in the arms of his perfidious cousin. 1927 *Observer* 15 May 6 Karel Capek has..envisioned a world in which atomic energy, having been harnessed, first provides mankind with a new religion and then sets all the world at war.

Enwheel, *v.* For †*Obs.* read *Obs.* exc. in echoes of Shakespeare's use.
1897 F. Thompson *New Poems, Assumpta Maria* 42 The Presence-hall where Angels Do enwheel their placèd King. 1912 L. A. Harker *Mr. Wycherly's Wards* ix, Enwheel'd around with love on every hand.

Enzyme (e·nzəim). *Chem.* Also *U.S.* enzym. [ad. G. *enzym* (Kühne, 1876), f. mod.Gr. ἔνζυμος leavened, f. Gr. ἐν in + ζύμη leaven.] An unorganized ferment; see Ferment *sb.* 1.
1881 W. Roberts in *Proc. Royal Soc.* XXXII. 146, I would suggest the desirability of adopting this term [G. *enzym*] into English, with a slight change of orthography, as 'enzymes', and also of coining from this root the cognate words which are requisite for clear and concise description. The action of an enzyme may be designated *enzymosis,* and the nature of the action may be spoken of as *enzymic.* 1890 A. S. Lea in *Jrnl. Physiol.* XI. 254 The word 'zymolysis' might be conveniently used to denote..the changes produced by the enzymes or unorganised ferments. 1898 J. R. Green in *Ann. Bot.* XII. 491 The alcoholic fermentation of sugar is effected by the activity of an enzyme or soluble ferment. 1927 Haldane & Huxley *Anim. Biol.* iv. 106 Each digestive enzyme is a definite substance with the property of bringing about, or enormously speeding up, a particular chemical reaction.
Hence **Enzy·mic** *a.*
1881 [see above]. 1899 J. R. Green *Soluble Ferments* i. (1901) 12 Additional instances of enzymic powers. 1905 J. L. Baker *Brewing Industry* 99 The unorganised ferments were termed 'enzymes' and their action spoken of as 'enzymic action'.

Eolienne (iᵢəlie·n). Also æ-. [ad. F. *éolienne,* fem. of *éolien,* f. Gr. αἰόλος quick-moving, glittering, sheeny + *-ien* = -ian.] A fine dress fabric of silk and wool. Also *attrib.*
1902 *Westm. Gaz.* 27 Feb. 3/2 Crêpes de Chine and Éoliennes and taffetas. 1909 *Ibid.* 28 June 5/3 Éolienne skirts trimmed with lace. 1918 *Home Chat* 4 May 106 A

Supplement, p. 3873; Corrigenda, p. 4092; Spurious words, p. 4093; Books quoted, p. 4094

tunic..of..fine coating serge, or wool Eolienne. 1930 *Glasgow Herald* 17 Apr. 4 A navy blue aeolienne frock.

Eolith (ī·olip). *Archæol.* [f. Eo- + Lith, after *neolith*. Cf. F. *éolithe*.] The name given to certain flints which have been found in Tertiary deposits in England, France, and elsewhere, which have been claimed to be the earliest traces of human handiwork, but whose origin is much disputed.

1896 A. H. Keane *Ethnol.* 74 Other modern savages, who are quite incapable of fashioning any of these British *eoliths*, as they have been called. 1907 T. R. Holmes *Anc. Brit.* 26 Flints of divers shapes..which have been termed 'eoliths', or stone implements of a dawning age. 1921 R. A. S. Macalister *Text-bk. European Archæol.* I. 148 Certain flint flakes to which the name 'Eoliths' has been given.

Eolithic (īoli·pik), *a.* *Archæol.* [f. Eo- + Lithic, after *neolithic*, *palæolithic*. Cf. F. *éolithique* (G. de Mortillet).] Pertaining to the earliest age of man that is represented by the use of worked flint implements.

1888 T. Wilson in *Rep. Smithsonian Inst.* (1890) 604 The first or Eolithic period belongs entirely to the tertiary geologic epoch. 1892 J. A. Brown in *Jrnl. Anthropol. Inst.* XXII. 94, I venture to suggest the following four divisions of the Stone age..1. Eolithic; Roughly hewn pebbles and nodules..found on the plateaux of the chalk. 1920 *Keane's Man Past & Pr.* 10 The tools exhibit deliberate flaking, and mark the transition between eolithic and palaeolithic work.

Eosinophil (īosi·nǝfil), *a.* and *sb.* *Phys.* Also -phile. [f. Eosin + -o- + -phil, -phile. In F. *éosinophile*.] **a.** *adj.* Having an affinity for eosin, staining readily with eosin. **b.** *sb.* A cell or histologic element readily stained by eosin. Hence **Eosinophi·lic, Eosino·philous** *adjs.* (= a above). **Eosinophi·lia**, a condition of the blood marked by the formation and accumulation of an excess of eosinophil cells.

1899 J. R. Green *Soluble Ferments* xxii. 382 An eosinophilous substance diffused out of the nucleus into the cytoplasmic zone. 1905 *Medical Annual* 140 Of 158 non-infected persons 91·1 per cent had under 5 per cent of eosinophiles. *Ibid.*, The eosinophilia may persist some time after the disappearance of ova. 1907 Adami *Inflammation* (ed. 3) 82 During the height of the infection the eosinophils were found in the blood-vessels, actively migrating into the peritoneal cavity. 1907 *Practitioner* Sept. 455 The Eosinophil Cells. *Ibid.* 246 The distribution of the eosinophilic leucocytes in a fatal case of Hodgkin's disease. 1910 Armit *Ehrlich & Lazarus' Anæmia* 97 The Eosinophile Cells..are recognised by a coarse, shotty granulation, which shows considerable avidity for the acid dyes. *Ibid.* 167 The Post-infective Form of Eosinophilia...There may even be a distinct eosinophilic leucocytosis. 1912 Adami & McCrae *Pathol.* 99 All verminous parasites set up eosinophilia, an increase in the number of eosinophile leukocytes in the circulating blood. *Ibid.* 128 The leukocytes that take part [in inflammation] are the polynuclear..cells, the lymphocytes, and the eosinophiles.

Epacme (epæ·kmi). *Biol.* [f. Gr. ἐπί upon + ἀκμή Acme.] The period preceding the acme of development in the ancestral history of organisms.

1887 Hyatt in *Proc. Boston Soc. Nat. Hist.* XXIII. 405 Haeckel used also the term Anaplastology for the physiological relations of the stages of progressive growth and those of the epacme of groups.

Epacris (epæ·kris). [mod.L.] A plant of the genus of shrubs so named (see Epacrid).

1841 *Florist's Jrnl.* (1846) II. 137 A 'New Subscriber'.. wishes to know the reason his Epacrises are losing their foliage. 1884 'R. Boldrewood' *Melb. Mem.* xi. 77 Special species of Epacris grew there. 1885 Hayter *Carboona* 7 Of our tribe she is the flower, Lily, epacris and orchid.

Epagomenal, Epagomenous (epægǫ·mĕnăl, -ǝs), *adjs.* = Epagomenic, intercalary.

1906 *Expositor* Apr. 342 The five epagomenous days of the year. 1928 C. Dawson *Age of Gods* vii. 151 The Egyptian solar calendar with its 12 months of 30 days and 5 epagomenal days, which is so marked an improvement on the Babylonian lunar year.

Epana-. Add: **Epanaleptic** (-le·ptik) *a.* [Gr. ἐπαναληπτικός], characterized by epanalepsis or repetition of a word or phrase. **Epana·phoral** *a.*, characterized by epanaphora.

1927 F. J. E. Raby *Hist. Chr. Latin Poetry* iii. 96 Luxorius..shows a vicious taste for the cento and for *epanaleptic verses. 1906 *Athenæum* 10 Mar. 303/2 Under cover of all this *epanaphoral fury..Mr. Campbell has in more than one instance shifted his ground.

Eparchæan (epaɹkī·ăn), *a.* *Geol.* Also -ean, -ian. [f. Ep- (= after in time or sequence) + Archæan.] Resting upon or following the Archæan. Algonkian.

1896 J. W. Judd *Student's Lyell* 437/2 These strata the American geologists propose to call Algonkian, and as alternative names they have proposed 'Eparchian' (lying on the Archæan), 'Agnotozoic'.., and 'Proterozoic'.

Eparterial (epaɹtīǝ·riăl), *a.* *Anat.* [See Ep-.] Situated above the pulmonary artery (see quots.).

1902 D. J. Cunningham *Anat.* 939 On the right side..the first bronchial branch is placed above the pulmonary artery, and in consequence it is termed the eparterial bronchus; all the others lie below the artery, and are termed hyparterial bronchi. 1921 A. Keith *Hum. Embryol.* (ed. 4) 349 The bronchus of the upper right lobe..commonly lies above its artery—that is to say, it is eparterial. The other bronchi are hyparterial.

Epedaphic (epĕdæ·fik), *a.* *Phytogeogr.* [f. Gr. ἐπί upon (see Epi-, Ep-) + ἔδαφος ground, soil + -ic. Cf. *Edaphic.] Pertaining to or dependent on atmospheric conditions.

1902 I. B. Balfour in *Encycl. Brit.* XXV. 430/1 The varying climatic or environmental conditions to which Angiosperms may be exposed in their wide distribution, including those of the soil, edaphic, those of the atmosphere, epedaphic, and those of water, aquatic.

Épée (*epe*). [Fr., = sword.] The sharp-pointed sword used in duelling and (blunted) in fencing. Hence **Épé(e)ist**, an épée fencer.

1889 W. H. Pollock, etc. *Fencing* 112 The fencer who has never handled the practice *épée* may at first find some difficulty when he exchanges the foil for it. 1910 *Encycl. Brit.* IX. 668/1 English *épéists* have also been coming to the front. *Ibid.* 668/2 Épée fencing can be, and often is, conducted indoors. 1910 *Westm. Gaz.* 11 Apr. 14/1 Mr. Seligman is a very fine épéeist. 1922 Laking *Eur. Armour* V. 59 The Court or 'small' sword, the use and rules of which are practically identical with those of the modern *épée*.

Epeiric (epǝi·rik), *a.* *Geol.* [f. Gr. ἤπειρος mainland, continent + -ic.] Of or pertaining to continents or their formation.

1925 J. Joly *Surface-Hist. Earth* iii. App. 65 We are justified in ascribing the epeiric seas, attending the coming of a revolution, to the density-changes arising from the change of state of a basaltic substratum.

Epeirid (epǝi·rid). *Zool.* [ad. mod.L. *Epeiridæ* (see below), ? f. ἐπί on + εἴρειν to string together.] Any member of the family *Epeiridæ* of spiders (which includes all the web-spinners). Also *attrib.* or *adj.*

1881 O. Pickard-Cambridge *Spiders of Dorset* II. 587 The studding of the lines of their snares, by some Epeirids, with viscid globules intended to entrap their prey. *Ibid.*, The cross-lines of Epeirid snares. 1902 *Trans. S. Afr. Philos. Soc.* XI. p. xlvi, The garden..was tenanted by numerous Epeirid spiders (*Argyope australis*). 1909 A. E. Shipley *Arachnida* 408 Perhaps our commonest Epeirid, *Meta segmentata*.

Epeirogenic (epǝiǝrodʒe·nik), *a.* *Geol.* [f. Gr. ἤπειρος mainland, continent + *-genic.] Of or pertaining to the formation of continents. Also **Epeirogene·tic** *a.* [-genetic], in the same sense. **Epeiroge·nesis, Epeiro·geny** [-genesis, -geny], the formation of continents; the deformation of the earth's crust by which continents and ocean basins are produced.

1890 G. K. Gilbert *Lake Bonneville* viii. 340, I shall take the liberty to apply to the broader movements the adjective *epeirogenic*...The process of mountain formation is *orogeny*, the process of continent formation is *epeirogeny*, and the two collectively are diastrophism. 1894 J. W. Spencer in *Geol. Mag.* 449 The gentle but varying amount of epeirogenic deformation. 1898 J. E. Marr *Princ. Stratigr. Geol.* 32 Those wide-spread, fairly uniform movements which are spoken of as epeirogenic or continent-forming. 1903 A. Geikie *Geol.* (ed. 4) II. 1428/1 Epeirogeny or continent-making. 1925 J. Joly *Surface-Hist. Earth* x. 162 The relations which exist between epeirogenic movements and glacial phenomena. *Ibid.* 189 Orogenesis and epeirogenesis ..are forms of diastrophism.

Epenchyma (epe·ŋkimă). *Bot.* [mod.L., f. Gr. ἐπί (see Epi-) + ἔγχυμα infusion, after Parenchyma.] A term used by Nägeli for the cambium and the tissue (fibro-vascular) which arises from it: contrasted with Protenchyma.

1875 Bennett & Dyer tr. *Sachs's Bot.* 103.

Ependyma. Add: Also **ependyme**. Hence **Epe·ndymal** *a.*, pertaining to the ependyma. **Ependymi·tis**, inflammation of the ependyma (Dorland 1901).

1897 Parker & Haswell *Zool.* II. 94 A purely non-nervous epithelial layer (ependyme). 1902 D. J. Cunningham *Anat.* 419 The ependymal cells. *Ibid.* 436 The ependymal layer. 1910 *Practitioner* July 65 Definite signs of post-basic meningitis or ependymitis about the fourth ventricle were found.

Epe·nthesized, *ppl. a.* [See -ize.] Of a letter or sound: Inserted by or resulting from Epenthesis.

1880 A. S. Wilkins & England *Curtius' Grk. Vb.* 216 The epenthesised ι.

Ephebeum (efībī·ǝ̆m). *Antiq.* [L., a. Gr. ἐφηβεῖον, f. ἔφηβος Ephebe.] A court in the palæstra for the young men to exercise themselves.

1697 Potter *Antiq. Greece* I. viii. 40 (Plate). 1851–2 *Archit. Publ. Soc.*, *Detached Ess.*, *Baths* 3/1 The ephebæum (or young men's hexedra). 1901 R. Sturgis *Dict. Archit.*, *Ephebeion*; *-eum*. In Greek archæology, a place for the youths (*epheboi*) to exercise; hence, in Greco-Roman archæology, any place for gymnastic exercises, as in connection with Roman thermæ.

Ephedrin (e·fĕdrin). *Med.* Also -ine. [See -in [1].] (See quot. 1892.)

1892 *Jrnl. Chem. Soc.* LXII. II. 893 Ephedrine from *Ephedra monostachia*...The alkaloid thus obtained, ephedrine, is not the only one which has received this name. Nagai, of Tokio, extracted an alkaloid from *Ephedra vulgaris* var. *helvetica*, to which he gave this name. 1929 Morrin in *Irish Jrnl. Med. Sci.* Apr. 184 In cases where the blood-pressure falls very low, ephedrin will control the fall.

Ephelcystic (efelsi·stik), *a.* *Gram.* Also -kustic (-kiū·stik). [Gr. ἐφελκυστικός attracted, suffixed.] In Greek grammar, designation of the letter ν (νῦ ἐφελκυστικόν) added for euphony to a word ending in a vowel when the following word begins with a vowel.

1870 E. C. Brewer *Dict. Phr. & Fable* 603/2 *N*, added to Greek words ending in a short vowel.., and 'l' added to French words beginning with a vowel, when they follow a word ending with a vowel (as *si l'on* for *si on*), is called N or L, 'ephelcystic'.

Ephelis (efī·lis). *Med.* Pl. ephelides (efī·lidez). [a. Gr. ἔφηλις (or ἐφηλίς), in pl. rough spots on the face, or perh. freckles.] A freckle.

1908 *Practitioner* Aug. 348 Some dermatologists include freckles, lentigo, or ephelides under the heading of sexual pigmentation.

Ephorate. Add: = Ephoralty in both senses.

1841 [in Dict.]. 1897 *Daily News* 26 Apr. 8/6 The two native bodies, the Athenian Ephorate and the Society of Antiquities. 1923 W. W. Tarn in *Hellenistic Age* 134 Then, having captured the ephorate, they were able to prevent him [*sc.* Agis] carrying out both his proposals together. *Ibid.* 135 He [*sc.* Cleomenes] also abolished the ephorate.

Ephyra (e·firă), **Ephyrula** (efi·riŭlă). *Zool.* [Gr. Ἐφύρα, Ionic -η, L. *Ephyre*, name of a Nereid and of an Oceanid. *Ephyrula* is a diminutive.] An embryo jellyfish, after separation from the scyphistoma.

1897 Parker & Haswell *Zool.* I. 161 The saucer-like bodies separate from one another, and each, turning upside down, begins to swim about as a small jelly-fish called an *Ephyrula*. ..The umbrella of the ephyrula is divided into eight long bifid arms. 1916 H. S. Pratt *Invertebr. Anim.* 125 Each disc is called an ephyra..and is a young medusa or jellyfish, which on becoming free grows in time to be a sexual animal. 1923 R. Lulham *Zool.* (ed. 2) 41 Scyphistoma undergoing fission. Several Ephyrae have already floated off.

Epialid: see *Hepialid.

Epibenthos (epibe·nþǫs). [f. Epi- + *Benthos.] The whole body of organisms living on the sea-floor of the continental shelf or littoral zone. Hence **Epibe·nthic** *a.*

1902 *Encycl. Brit.* XXXIII. 933 The fauna of this zone.. may be distinguished as the *epibenthos*. *Ibid.*, The epibenthic fauna.

Epiblastic (epiblæ·stik), *a.* *Biol.* Belonging to the Epiblast.

1887 A. C. Haddon *Study Embryol.* 36 The blastoderm of a newly-laid egg..consists of a definite epiblastic layer and an inferior irregular mass of rounded cells. 1893 A. M. Marshall *Vert. Embryol.* 371 The small epiblastic villi of the lower pole of the vesicle. 1921 A. Keith *Hum. Embryol.* (ed. 4) 12 An epiblastic or ectodermal set [of cells].

Epiboly (epi·bǝli). *Embryol.* Also **epibole** (-ǝ̄lī). [Gr. ἐπιβολή a throwing or laying on.] The inclusion of one set of segmenting cells within another by reason of the more rapid division of the latter. Hence **Epibolic** (epibǫ·lik) *a.*

1887 A. C. Haddon *Study Embryol.* 33 The gastrula in the Frog is thus formed partly by invagination (*embolé*), partly by overgrowth (*epibolé*). 1897 Parker & Haswell *Zool.* I. 205 The stage has been produced, not by a process of invagination or tucking-in, but by one of epiboly or overgrowth. *Ibid.* 257 The process by which the germinal layers have become formed is..a process of epibolic gastrulation. 1914 E. W. MacBride *Embryol.* I. 171 The formation of a cap of small ectoderm cells resting on larger endoderm cells and gradually investing the latter by the process termed epibole.

Epibranchial (epibræ·ŋkiăl), *a.* *Zool.* [See Epi-.] Of or belonging to the segment next below the pharyngobranchial in a branchial arch. As *sb.*, this segment.

1846 Owen *Comp. Anat. Vertebr.* 116 The fourth arch consists of the cerato-branchial, the epi-branchial, and the pharyngo-branchial pieces. 1875 Huxley & Martin *Elem. Biol.* (1877) 119. 1892 C. S. Minot *Hum. Embryol.* 651 A chain of epibranchial organs. 1893 A. M. Milnes *Vert. Embryol.* 40 Along the mid-dorsal line of the pharynx is a deep epibranchial groove.., lined by a single layer of long columnar ciliated cells. 1921 A. Keith *Hum. Embryol.* (ed. 4) 243 At the upper end of each cleft depression there develop remarkable sense-organs, known as the epibranchial placodes. 1929 W. Garstang in *Q. Jrnl. Microsc. Sci.* LXXII. 152 Epibranchial flaps eventually grow downward over the gill-slits of both sides to form the belated atrium.

Epicacuana, illiterate var. Ipecacuanha.

Epicanthus (epikæ·nþǝ̆s). *Anat.* [f. Epi- + Canthus. Cf. Gr. ἐπικανθίς = Encanthis.] A fold of skin which sometimes covers the inner canthus, esp. in Mongols. Hence **Epica·nthic** *a.*

1901 Dorland *Med. Dict.* (ed. 2), Epicanthus. 1913 A. Keith *Hum. Embryol.* (ed. 3) 196 The curious epicanthic fold..is represented in all races during foetal life. *Ibid.* 197 Epicanthic or Mongolian fold.

Epicardium (epikā·ɹdiǝ̆m). Pl. -ia. [f. Epi-, after Pericardium.]

1. *Anat.* The innermost layer of the pericardium, closely investing the heart.

1902 D. J. Cunningham *Anat.* 747 The epicardium, or visceral portion of the pericardium.

2. *Zool.* In certain ascidians, each of two hollow outgrowths from the pharynx, connected with the process of budding.

1893 A. H. L. Newstead in *Q. Jrnl. Microsc. Sci.* XXXV. 125 The perivisceral cavity of Ciona corresponds to the epicardium of Clavellina. 1914 E. W. MacBride *Embryol.* I. 626 The conjoined inner walls of the epicardia form a kind of visceral peritoneum, enwrapping heart, pericardium, and intestine. 1929 W. Garstang in *Q. Jrnl. Microsc. Sci.* LXXII. 158 Pharynx produced behind the endostyle into a pair of diverticula ('epicardia').

Hence **Epica·rdiac, Epica·rdial** *adjs.*

1893 A. H. L. Newstead in *Q. Jrnl. Microsc. Sci.* XXXV. 123 Two tubes are first formed as outgrowths of

the pharynx [in Clavellina], called by van Beneden and Julin [1887] the 'epicardiac tubes'. 1908 *Practitioner* Nov. 638 In the first group of cases there is simple adhesion between the peri- and epi-cardial layers. 1911 *Encycl. Brit.* XXVII. 390/1 There are..two main types of budding [in compound Ascidians]...There is first the 'stolonial' or 'epicardiac' type. 1914 E. W. MacBride *Embryol.* I. 626 The epicardial tubes or epicardia.

Epicaridan (epikæ·ridăn), *a.* and *sb.* *Zool.* [f. mod.L. *Epicarides* (f. Gr. ἐπί upon + καρίς shrimp) + -an.] Of or belonging to (a member of) the genus *Epicarides* containing isopods parasitic on shrimps.

1931 B. W. Tucker in *Q. Jrnl. Microsc. Sci.* LXXIV. 1 On the effects of an Epicaridan Parasite, Gyge branchialis, on Upogebia littoralis.

Epiclesis (epiklī·sis). *Liturgiology.* Also **epiklesis**. [Gr. ἐπίκλησις, f. ἐπικαλεῖν to call upon, invoke.] In Eastern liturgies, a part of the prayer of consecration in which the presence of the Holy Spirit is invoked to bless the gifts on the altar and the worshippers.

[1838 W. Palmer *Orig. Liturg.* II. 134 The immediate or proper prayer of consecration..may be divided into two particulars: first, the prayer itself, or ἐπίκλησις, in the language of the primitive church; and, secondly, the commemoration of our Lord's deeds and words at the last supper.] 1878 *Encycl. Brit.* VIII. 653/2 In Quæstio 107 it is laid down that immediately on the pronunciation of the *Epiclesis*, transubstantiation takes place. 1925 *Contemp. Rev.* Oct. 426 Many Anglo-Catholics desire the introduction of the *Epiklesis*, or Invocation of the Holy Spirit, at the time of the consecration of the elements.

E·picontine·ntal, *a.* *Geol.* [See Epi-.] (See quot.)

1905 Chamberlin & Salisbury *Geol.* I. 11 Those shallow portions of the sea which lie upon the continental shelf, and those portions which extend into the interior of the continent with like shallow-depths, such as the Baltic Sea and the Hudson Bay, may be called epicontinental seas, for they really lie *upon* the continent, or at least upon the continental platform.

Epicormic (epikǭ·ɹmik), *a.* *Forestry.* [f. Epi- + Corm [2] + -ic.] Of a shoot or branch: Growing from a dormant bud which has been suddenly exposed to the light and air.

1909 P. T. Maw *Pract. Forestry* 149 With some trees, especially Oak and Chestnut, an unduly thick canopy will often cause..the flushing of latent buds along the stem, and epicormic branches will be thrown out. 1921 R. C. Hawley *Silviculture* 135 The isolated position of the standards with full light from all sides..often results in the formation of epicormic branches on trees which have not an adequate crown development.

Epicrisis (epi·krisis). [Gr. ἐπίκρισις determination, judgement, f. ἐπικρίνειν to decide, determine.] A Massoretic appendix to each book of the Old Testament, stating the number of letters, verses, and chapters, and quoting the middle sentence of the whole book.

1878 *Encycl. Brit.* VIII. 832/1 That the Massoretes themselves recognized no real separation [between the books of Ezra and Nehemiah] is shown by their epicrisis on Nehemiah.

Epicritic (epikri·tik), *a.* *Psychol.* [f. Gr. ἐπικριτικός adjudicatory (cf. prec.).] The epithet chosen by Head to designate the finer and more recently evolved sensations of touch: distinguished from *protopathic*.

1905 H. Head, etc. in *Brain* XXVIII. 107 To this form of sensibility we propose to give the name 'epicritic', since it is peculiarly associated with the localisation and discrimination of cutaneous stimuli. 1920 W. H. R. Rivers *Instinct & Unconscious* iv. 23 Epicritic sensibility may be only a greater perfection of protopathic sensibility. 1920 *Discovery* Nov. 340/1 From a physiological aspect, the distinction of protopathic from epicritic sensibility is, so far, devoid of neurological basis.

Epicyclic, *a.* Add examples of recent application to the gear of motor vehicles. Also *sb.*

1906 *Daily Chron.* 9 June 3/5 Another kind of gear, known as the epicyclic, its principle resembling that of the differential. 1907 *Westm. Gaz.* 13 Nov. 9/1 Three-speed epicyclic gear. 1910 *Ibid.* 1 Feb. 4/2 Many of the old epicyclics failed solely for the reason that their designers were too niggardly with the wearing surfaces.

Epicyte (e·pisǝit). *Biol.* [f. Epi- + -cyte.] The investing membrane of a cell.

1903 E. Ray Lankester *Zool.* I. II. 179 The cuticle or epicyte [in Gregarines] is a membrane secreted by the ectoplasm, usually of some thickness.

Epidendrum (epide·ndrǝ̆m). Also -dendron. [mod.L., f. Gr. ἐπί upon + δένδρον tree. Cf. Epidendral, -ic.] An epiphytic orchid of the genus so named, native to S. America and the W. Indies.

1829 Loudon *Encycl. Plants* 760. 1842 *Florist's Jrnl.* (1846) III. 212 A fine orchidaceous plant, with the habit of an Epidendron. 1890 W. Watson *Orchids* 237 The list of useful garden Epidendrums is a fairly long one. 1910 C. H. Curtis *Orchids* 100 All Epidendrums are evergreen.

Epidermolysis (epidǝɹmǫ·lisis). *Path.* [f. Gr. ἐπιδερμίς Epidermis + -o- + λύσις a loosening or releasing.] A loosened state of the epidermis.

1901 Dorland *Med. Dict.* 1909 W. Bateson *Mendel's Princ. Hered.* 220 In epidermolysis transmission through unaffected persons occurred in some of the strains. 1922 R. C. Punnett *Mendelism* 202 Epidermolysis bullosa, a disease in which the skin rises up into numerous bursting blisters.

Epidiascope (epidǝi·ăskǫup). [f. Epi- + Dia-[1] + -scope.] A magic lantern made to project images of both opaque and transparent objects. Hence **Epidiasco·pic** *a.*

1903 *Nature* 19 Feb. 376/1 The epidiascope, a new optical lantern,..is primarily intended for the projection on the screen of opaque bodies, such as insects, coins, fossils, diagrams, &c., in their natural colours. It is equally serviceable for projection of transparent objects. 1907 *Practitioner* Dec. 860 An epidiascopic demonstration. 1927 *Brit. Jrnl. Photogr. Alm.* 345 The Ica Hand Epidiascope.

Epidosite (epi·dǝsǝit). *Min.* [f. Gr. ἐπίδοσις a free or additional giving, f. ἐπιδιδόναι (see Epidote) + -ite [1].] (See quots.)

1866 Lawrence tr. *Cotta's Rocks* 355 Epidosite, or pistacite rock.—Epidote usually combined with some quartz. 1868 Dana *Syst. Min.* (ed. 5) 284 [Epidote] sometimes forms with quartz an epidote rock, called epidosyte. 1880 — *Man. Geol.* (ed. 3) 75 Epidosyte.—Pale green to pistachio-green. Consists of epidote mixed with quartz. 1893 A. Geikie *Geol.* (ed. 3) 183 Epidosite.

Epidotized (e·pidǝtǝizd), *ppl. a.* [f. Epidote + -ize + -ed.] Altered metamorphically into epidote. So **E:pidotiza·tion**.

1888 Teall *Brit. Petrography* 150 The epidotisation of the felspar is an alteration process. 1930 Peach & Horne *Geol. Scotl.* 79 Beds with abundant pebbles of epidote and epidotized felspar.

Epidural (epidiū·răl), *a.* *Anat.* [f. Epi- + Dura (mater) + -al.] Situated upon or outside the dura mater.

1895 *Buck's Handbk. Med. Sci.* Suppl. 608/2 There are two layers of dura [in the spine], an ectal (periosteal) and an ental (myelic), the interval between them constitutes an epidural space. 1902 D. J. Cunningham *Anat.* 558 The spinal dura mater..is separated from the walls of the spinal canal by an interval, the epidural space, which is occupied by soft fat and a plexus of thin-walled veins.

Epifocal (epifōu·kăl), *a.* *Geol.* [See Epi- 1.] Situated above the focus of an earthquake.

1902 J. Milne in *Encycl. Brit.* XXVII. 608/1 Causes which should produce magnetic effects within an epifocal district. 1910 — *Ibid.* VIII. 817/2 (*Earthquake*) That part of the surface of the earth which is vertically above the centre is called the *epicentre*; or, if of considerable area, the epicentral or epifocal tract.

Epigamic (epigæ·mik), *a.* *Zool.* [f. Gr. ἐπί upon + γάμος marriage + -ic. Cf. Gr. ἐπίγαμος marriageable.] Relating to the mating of animals and the characteristics of colour, etc., which serve to attract the opposite sex during courtship.

1890 Poulton *Colours of Animals* xvii. 338 Epigamic Colours. Colours displayed in courtship. 1926 H. Mack in *Contemp. Rev.* Sept. 369 This fact..if it were ascertained for a large number of species, would help to illuminate the subject of epigamic colours.

Epigeal, *a.* Add: **b.** Of cotyledons: Borne above ground after germination.

1861 Bentley *Man. Bot.* 773 They burst through the coats, and rise out of the ground in the form of green leaves.., in which case they are epigeal. 1884 Henfrey *Elem. Bot.* (ed. 4) 652 The seed-leaves..are pushed up above ground, and become epigeal. 1913 H. Bateson *Mendel's Princ. Heredity* 36 In *Phaseolus* hypogeal cotyledons are dominant to epi-geal.

Epigenesis. Add to etymology: The word is used by W. Harvey, *Exercitationes* 1651, p. 148, and in the English *Anatomical Exercitations* 1653, p. 272. It is explained to mean 'partium superexorientium additamentum', 'the additament of parts budding one out of another'.

Epigenetic, *a.* Add:

2. *Geol. & Phys. Geog.* 'A term applied to those rivers whose courses have been determined by the slope of a once overlying series of strata, now removed by erosion so as to disclose rock-structures of another arrangement; superposed; inherited' (*Cent. Dict.* Suppl. 1909).

Epigeous, *a.* Add: = *Epigeal b.

1844 Lindley *Elem. Bot.* Gloss.

Epigon (e·pigǫn). More recent form of Epigone [1].

1890 J. H. Stirling *Gifford Lect.* xii. 231 Any true follower of Hume, any genuine aufgeklärt *epigon* of his. 1890 W. Cory *Lett. & Jrnls.* (1897) 553 Anglo-Catholics, a second crop, the Epigons, started vestments. 1926 *Contemp. Rev.* July 22/1 The epigons of the fighters for freedom.

Epigonic (epigǫ·nik), *a.* *Zool.* [f. Gr. ἐπίγονος (see Epigone [1]) + -ic.] Descended from common parents. So **Epigony** (epi·gŏni) [Gr. ἐπιγονή offspring, descendants + -y [4]], breeding or descent from common parents.

1904 Poulton *Ess. Evol.* (1908) 61 Breeding from common parents or from a common parthenogenetic or self-fertilizing parent may be spoken of as Epigony or the production of Epigonic evidence.

Epigyne (e·pidʒǝin). *Zool.* [ad. mod.L. *epigynum*, f. Gr. ἐπί Epi- + γυνή woman, female. Cf. Epigynous *a.*] The ovipositor, or the external genital plate, in spiders or arachnids. Also in mod.L. form **Epigynum** (epidʒǝi·nǝ̆m).

1875 Cambridge in *Encycl. Brit.* II. 273/1 These have a common exterior orifice (vulva)..and connected with this opening there is frequently an epigyne, or ovipositor. 1892 *Trans. Linnean Soc.* Ser. II. Zool. V. 297 The epigynum or external genital plate..entirely closes the genital aperture. 1900 *Proc. Zool. Soc.* 387 The under surface of the body is whitish except the small yellow-brown epigyne. 1916 H. S. Pratt *Invertebr. Anim.* 415 Between them [*sc.* the lung spiracles] is the genital pore which, in the female, is covered by a plate..called the epigynum.

Epileptically (epile·ptikăli), *adv.* [-ly [2].] As if affected with epilepsy.

1913 Kipling *Diversity of Creatures* (1917) 211 The House sang at the tops and at the bottoms of their voices,..epileptically beating with their swelled feet.

Epimedium (epimī·diǝ̆m). *Bot.* [mod.L., f. L. *epimēdion*, Gr. ἐπιμήδιον.] Any plant of the genus of hardy perennials so named.

1898 tr. *Strasburger's Text-bk. Bot.* 516 Species of *Mahonia* and *Epimedium* are cultivated as garden plants. 1900 W. D. Drury *Bk. Gard.* 293 Epimediums are useful plants for shady positions. 1901 *Cassell's Dict. Gard.* 321/2 The Epimediums will thrive well in shady places, and even under trees.

Epimerite (epi·mĕrǝit). *Zool.* [f. Gr. ἐπί Epi- + μέρος part + -ite [1].] (See quots.)

1885 E. Ray Lankester in *Encycl. Brit.* XIX. 854/1 There is frequently if not always present, either in early growth or more persistently, an anterior proboscis-like appendage (the epimerite) growing from the protomerite. The epimerite serves to attach the parasite to its host, and may for that purpose carry hooklets. 1921 Parker & Haswell *Zool.* (ed. 3) I. 85 Sometimes the protomerite is produced in front into a process ending in a rounded enlargement, the epimerite, which may be provided with radiating spine-like projections.

Epinephrin (epine·frin). *Chem.* Also -ine. [f. Gr. ἐπί upon + νεφρός kidney + -in [1].] An early name for *Adrenalin.

1899 *Jrnl. Chem. Soc.* LXXVI. I. 395 Epinephrine, the active material of suprarenal capsules. 1908 *Practitioner* Mar. 422 The active principle from the medulla of the suprarenal capsule is now generally known as adrenalin, though other terms have been applied, such as suprarenin, epinephrin.

Epineural, *a.* Add:

2. *Zool.* Lying over and parallel to a nerve. Said of various processes in echinoderms, etc.

1906 E. W. MacBride *Echinodermata* 515 In Echinoids the ambulacral groove has become converted into a canal called the 'epineural canal'. 1914 — *Embryol.* I. 254 The epineural sinus [in arthropods]..derives its name from the circumstance that it lies above the rudiments of the ganglia of the ventral nerve cord. *Ibid.* 495 Epineural flaps. *Ibid.*, The epineural roof which covers in each radial nerve cord of the adult. *Ibid.* 514 The epineural ridges. *Ibid.*, These epineural canals meet in a central epineural space, roofed over by a membrane termed the epineural veil.

Epipalæolithic (e:pipæli,ǫli·þik), *a.* *Archæol.* [Epi- 1.] Belonging to the period next after the palæolithic.

1924 W. J. Sollas *Anc. Hunters* (ed. 3) 602 *note*, We use the term Azilian in general to denote an age or stage which Dr. Obermaier designates 'Epipalæolithic' and others less appropriately 'Mesolithic'. 1928 V. G. Childe *Most Anc. East* ii. 33 Others [*sc.* rock-paintings] belong to the immediately succeeding epipalæolithic period.

Epipharynx (epifæ·riŋks). *Zool.* [Epi- 1.] (See quots.)

1826 Kirby & Sp. *Entomol.* III. xxxiii. 359. 1872 Packard *Insects* 29 The roof of the mouth is formed by the *labrum* and the *epipharynx*.., a small fleshy tubercle concealed beneath the labrum. 1897 Parker & Haswell *Zool.* (ed. 3) I. 592 A projection of the roof of the mouth cavity (*epipharynx*) is present in some Insects. 1909 A. E. Shipley *Arachnida* 459.

Epiphenomenal (e:pifīnǫ·minăl), *a.* [f. Epiphenomenon + -al.] Of the nature of an epiphenomenon; relating to epiphenomena.

1899 J. Ward *Naturalism & Agnosticism* II. 100 From the standpoint of naturalism a world described in such terms is epiphenomenal. 1924 *Glasgow Herald* 29 Aug. 10 He maintained that mind was not epiphenomenal. 1929 C. S. Myers *Psychol. Conceptions* 22 The old view expressed by Spencer..was that consciousness has arisen as an 'epiphenomenal' product of living matter whence physiological processes became too complex to work automatically.

Epipheno·menalism. [f. prec. + -ism.] The theory that consciousness is an epiphenomenon, i.e. a secondary result and by-product of the material brain and nerve-system. So **Epipheno·menalist**, one who holds this theory; also *adj.*

1899 J. Ward *Naturalism & Agnosticism* II. 34 Doctrine of conscious automatism or psychical epiphenominalism examined. 1903 A. E. Taylor *Elem. Metaphysics* 317 The epiphenomenalist theory is largely adopted by the workers in the physical sciences. 1915 G. F. Stout *Man. Psychol.* (ed. 3) 98 Perhaps the word which best characterises the general position is epiphenomenalism. Consciousness is regarded as a superfluous apparition or phenomenon which unaccountably crops up at a certain stage in the course of material processes. 1922 W. R. Inge *Outspoken Ess.* Ser. II. 6 Not only does epiphenomenalism (as Plotinus said long ago) 'make soul an affection, or disease, of matter'.

Epiphenomenon. Add:

b. *spec.* in *Psychol.* Applied to consciousness regarded as a by-product of the material activities of the brain and nerve-system.

1899 J. Ward *Naturalism & Agnosticism* II. 37 The newly coined phrase *epiphenomenon* (or, as the Germans say, *Begleiterscheinung*). 1902 — in *Encycl. Brit.* XXXII. 57/1 No 'mental chemistry'..can generate objective reality from feelings or sense-impressions as psycho-physically defined. *Note*, Nothing shows this more plainly than the newly-coined term *epiphenomenon* now applied in this connexion. 1913 J. M. Baldwin *Hist. Psychol.* II. 60 The charge of materialism..is frankly accepted..by those, such as Maudsley, who accept the 'epiphenomenon' theory of consciousness; to them consciousness is merely a by-product, a spark thrown off by the engine, the brain.

Epiphloem (epiflōu·em). *Bot.* Also -phlœum. [f. Gr. ἐπί upon, Epi- + φλόος = φλοιός bark: see Phloem.] The outermost bark.

1848 Lindley *Introd. Bot.* I. (ed. 4) 193. 1866 *Treas. Bot.* 1109/2 *Suber*.., cork. The epiphlœum of bark, when it acquires an elastic soft texture, and is preternaturally enlarged. 1900 B. D. Jackson *Gloss. Bot. Terms*, Epiphloem.

Epiphysial, *a.* *Anat.* Also in the form epiphyseal.

1889 *Buck's Handbk. Med. Sci.* VIII. 336/2 Diffuse Epiphyseal Osteitis. 1908 *Practitioner* Oct. 531 The slightest tap on the point of either of these fingers gave her intense pain, referred to a spot corresponding with the epiphyseal line.

Epiphysis. Add:

3. The pineal gland. In full *epiphysis cerebri*.

1887 A. C. Haddon *Study Embryol.* 199 Vertebral epiphyses are peculiar to Mammals. 1889 *Buck's Handbk. Med. Sci.* VIII. 175/1 The *epiphysis* (pineal gland) is not regarded as an important neural ingredient of the brain.

4. In sea-urchins, a calcareous piece attached to each half of an alveolus of a sea-urchin.

1906 *Cambr. Nat. Hist.* I. 526 [Echinus] Each tooth is firmly fixed by a pair of ossicles.—Their upper ends are connected by a pair of ossicles called 'epiphyses'. These two epiphyses meet in an arch above.

Epiphysitis (epifisǝi·tis). *Path.* [-itis.] Inflammation of an epiphysis (sense 1) or of the cartilage which separates it from the main bone.

1889 *Buck's Handbk. Med. Sci.* VIII. 346/1 The most common disease of the hip-joint is tubercular epiphysitis, occurring in the growing bone of children. 1908 *Practitioner* Apr. 507 The left elbow was swollen, and the condition was thought to be an epiphysitis.

Epiplankton (epiplæ·ŋktǫn). *Zool.* [Epi- 1.] That portion of the plankton occurring from the surface of the sea to a depth of about one hundred fathoms. Hence **E:piplankto·nic** *a.*

1911 *Encycl. Brit.* XXI. 721/2 (*Plankton*) The fauna to which light and warmth are more or less necessary..may be termed the *epiplankton*. 1923 W. A. Herdman *Founders Oceanogr.* 231 Epi-, Meso- and Bathy-plankton.

Epiplasm (e·piplæz'm). *Biol.* [f. Epi- + Plasm.] Protoplasm remaining over after the formation of spores. Hence **Epipla·smic** *a.*

1906 M. Hartog in *Cambr. Nat. Hist.* I. 96 (*Sporozoa*) Some of the cytoplasm of the original cells remains over unused, as 'epiplasm', and ultimately degenerates.

Epipod (e·pipǫd). *Zool.* Shortened form of Epipodite.

1893 T. R. R. Stebbing *Crustacea* 41 Huxley supposes that this valve may represent the epipod. 1911 — in *Encycl. Brit.* XVII. 457/1 In the maxillipeds and the trunk-legs it is common to find..a seven-jointed stem, the endopod, from which may spring two branches, the epipod from the first joint, the exopod from the second.

Epipteric (epipte·rik), *a.* *Anat.* [f. Gr. ἐπί upon + πτερόν wing + -ic.] *Epipteric bone* or *ossicle*, a small Wormian bone sometimes found between the parietal and the great wing of the sphenoid. Also *sb.* = epipteric bone.

1902 D. J. Cunningham *Anat.* 127 They [*sc.* Wormian bones] occur commonly about the pterion, and in this situation are called epipteric bones (Flower). 1904 A. Keith *Hum. Embryol.* 199 The fontanelle ossifications form Wormian bones. They occur most frequently at the posterior angles of the parietal (Lambda and Asterion), but they are also common at the Pterion (epipteric Wormian) and rare at the Bregma.

Epipterygoid (epipte·rigoid), *a.* *Anat.* [Epi- 1.] Situated above the pterygoid; the designation of a bone in the skull of certain lizards (see quot.). Also *sb.* = this bone.

1897 Parker & Haswell *Zool.* II. 297 Extending nearly vertically downwards from the pro-otic to the pterygoid is a slender rod of bone, the epi-pterygoid.

Epipubic (epipiū·bik), *a.* *Anat.* [See next.] Situated on the pubis; of the nature of an epipubis.

1897 Parker & Haswell *Zool.* II. 162 [Elasmo-branchii] In some cases a median epipubic process projects forwards from the pelvic arch. *Ibid.* 489 [Marsupials, Echidna] With the anterior border of the pubes are articulated a pair of large epi-pubic or 'marsupial' bones.

Epipubis (epipiū·bis). *Anat.* [Epi- 1.] A cartilage or bone in front of the pubis in marsupials.

1897 Parker & Haswell *Zool.* II. 282 Attached to the anterior border of the pubic region there occurs in many Urodela and in Xenopus, a rod of cartilage, forked in front, the *epipubis*. 1904 A. Keith *Hum. Embryol.* Index 393.

Epirrhema (epirī·mă). *Antiq.* [ad. Gr. ἐπίρρημα, f. ἐπί upon, after + ῥῆμα word, saying.] In the Attic Old Comedy, a speech addressed by the Coryphæus to the audience after the Parabasis. Hence **Epirrhema·tic** *a.*

1835 W. R. Hamilton tr. *Süvern's Ess. Birds Aristoph.* 96 The second epirrhematic parabasis. 1887 *Amer. Jrnl. Philol.* VIII. 183 His [*sc.* Zielinski's] theory of the original 'epirrhematic' composition of a comedy as compared with the 'epeisodic' of a tragedy.

Episcopalia (episkǭpā·liă), *sb. pl.* [neut. pl. of late L. *episcopālis* Episcopal.] Episcopal belongings, e.g. vestments, buildings.

1903 *Daily Chron.* 23 Jan., To St. Joseph's College at Mill-hill testator left his episcopal vestments and other episcopalia. 1924 Bent *Med. Papacy* 13 Symmachus was a busy builder, and in his erection of *episcopalia* over against the vestibule of St. Peter's may be seen the first beginnings of the Vatican.

Episcotister (episkǫti·stǝɹ). [f. Gr. ἐπισκοτίζειν to throw a shadow or darkness over, f. ἐπί upon + σκότος darkness: see -ist and -er [1].] An apparatus for admitting light into a darkened room by means of adjustable discs.

1905 Titchener *Exper. Psychol.* II. 80 The episcotister is placed as close as possible to the screen. 1909 C. S. Myers *Text-bk. Exp. Psychol.* 362.

Episematic (episimæ·tik), *a.* *Biol.* [f. Epi- + Sematic.] Designating natural colours, markings, etc. which serve to assist animals of the same species to recognize each other. (Opposed to *Aposematic.)

1890 Poulton *Colours of Animals* xvii. 337 Recognition Markings..assist an individual of the same species, and are termed Episematic. *a* 1908 — *Ess. Evol.* 357 Episematic Colours are the logical antithesis of Aposematic, their object being to assist in keeping friends together instead of keeping enemies at a distance.

Episperm (e·pispǝɹm). *Bot.* [f. Gr. ἐπί upon + σπέρμα seed: see Epi- and Sperm *sb.*] The exterior covering of a seed. Hence **E·pispermic** *a.*

1819 Lindley tr. *Richard's Observ. Fruits & Seeds* 17 The covering or integument peculiar to the seed being the most exterior of its constituent parts, I give it the name of Episperm. *Ibid.* 32 If..the entire kernel..is immediately covered over by the episperm, it is called epispermic. 1861 Bentley *Man. Bot.* 337 The terms most frequently used, are *testa* or *episperm* for the outer coat.

Epispore. Add:

2. *Zool.* in Sporozoa (see quot.).

1903 E. Ray Lankester *Zool.* I. II. 189 The spore-envelope or sporocyst [in Gregarines] consists of two layers, an outer clear and delicate epispore, and an inner refringent and tough endospore.

Epistasis (epi·stăsis). [Gr. ἐπίστασις a stopping, stoppage, f. ἐφιστάναι to stop, check.]

1. *Med.* The checking of any discharge, as of blood, menses, or lochia (Dorland *Med. Dict.* 1901).

2. A scum, or pellicle, as on the surface of urine (Dorland 1901).

3. *Zool.* A condition of arrested development in the early evolutionary period of a group of organisms. 1903 in *Cent. Dict.* Suppl.

4. *Biol.* In Mendelian inheritance, the expression of one character to the exclusion of another not of the same allelomorphic pair. (Cf. *Epistatic *a.*)

Epistasy (epi·stăsi). *Biol.* [ad. Gr. ἐπιστασία, parallel form to ἐπίστασις: see prec.] = *Epistasis 4.

1929 *Encycl. Brit.* XI. 489/2.

Epistatic (epistæ·tik), *a.* *Biol.* [f. Gr. ἐπιστατικός, adj. corresponding to ἐπίστασις *Epistasis.] Of a Mendelian character or factor: Able to exclude, or prevent the development of, another character (though not allelomorphic). Const. *to*, *on*, *over*. (Opposed to *hypostatic*.)

1909 W. Bateson *Mendel's Princ. Heredity* (1913) 41 (*Primula*). The magenta shades have a factor epistatic to crimson and pink. Blue is hypostatic to all the red shades. *Ibid.* 98 The pale ivory is due to a factor epistatic on the bright yellow. 1910 L. Doncaster *Heredity* 75 The presence of a higher member of the series obscures or prevents the development of the lower. This is expressed by saying that grey is 'epistatic' over black and chocolate, and black over chocolate.

Epistemolo·gically, *adv.* [-ly [2].] In an epistemological manner; with reference or in regard to epistemology.

1906 *Westm. Gaz.* 9 June 3/2 Epistemologically..Von Hartmann is a transcendental realist who ably defends his views. 1919 Pringle-Pattison in *Mind* Jan. 4 There is nothing which I believe to be epistemologically more unsound than this identification of the knower's knowledge or experience with the reality of the object he knows.

Epistemologist (e:pistimǫ·lŏdʒist). [-ist.] One who is versed in epistemology.

1902 *Encycl. Brit.* XXXII. 55/2 It is only epistemologists, and notably Kant, who so describe individual experience. 1925 J. E. Turner *Theory Direct Realism* 34 This systematic connection is ignored by Stout, as also by epistemologists in general.

Epistlar (epi·stlăɹ), *a.* [irreg. f. Epistle *sb.* + -ar, after Epistolar.] Designating the epistle or south side of the altar.

1883 Dixon *Hist. Ch. Eng.* III. 193 Standing at the Epistlar wing of the altar.

Epistom(e. Add: The Latin form *epistoma* is also used. Also applied to similar parts in arachnids, molluscs, etc.

1880 Huxley *Crayfish* 155 In front of the mouth, the sternal region which appertains, in part, to the antennæ, and, in part, to the mandibles, is obvious as a broad plate..termed the *epistoma*. 1897 Parker & Haswell *Zool.* I. 328 (Molluscs), A small lobe—the epistome..—overhangs the mouth and lies between it and the anus. *Ibid.* 499 The head exhibits no segmentation: its sternal region is formed largely by a shield-shaped plate, the *epistoma*, nearly vertical in position. 1909 *Cambr. Nat. Hist.* IV. 291 In *Pterygotus* there is a well-developed epistome..between the mouth and the front margin of the carapace.

Epithalamus (epiþæ·lămǝ̆s). *Anat.* [f. Epi- 1 + Thalamus (sense 1).] (See quots.)

1902 D. J. Cunningham *Anat.* 501 The epithalamus, which comprises the pineal body and the habenular region. 1921 A. Keith *Hum. Embryol.* (ed. 4) 103 In the upper region will be differentiated the optic thalamus, the epithalamus (the pineal body with its ganglia and commissures) and the metathalamus or geniculate bodies.

Epithallus (epiþæ·lǝ̆s). *Bot.* [f. Epi- 1 + Thallus.] (See quot.)

1911 *Encycl. Brit.* XVI. 579/1 The term *epithallus* is sometimes applied to the superficial dense portion of the cortical layer.

So **Epithalline** (epiþæ·lǝin) *a.*, situated or growing upon the thallus.

Epithecium (epiþī·ʃiǝ̆m). *Bot.* [mod.L., f. Epi- 1 + Thecium.] The surface of the fruiting disc in certain lichens and fungi.

1911 *Encycl. Brit.* XVI. 581/2 The apices [of the paraphyses] are usually cemented together into a definite layer, the *epithecium*.

Epitheliomatous (e:pipīliōu·mătǝs), *a.* *Path.* [-ous.] Pertaining to, of the nature of, epithelioma.

1881 *Trans. Obstetr. Soc. Lond.* XXII. 7 The disease was an ordinary epitheliomatous cervix. 1908 *Practitioner* Sept. 355 A squamous-celled epitheliomatous ulcer.

Epitheted, *ppl. a.* Add: **c.** Designated by an epithet too coarse or violent to repeat. *jocular.*

1896 *Punch* 21 Nov. 241/2 Mr. Jones's compliments, Sir, and *when the epitheted substantive* is this noise going to stop? 1905 *Daily Chron.* 1 July 4/4 No London fire engine has such precedence as the 'Varsity boat. If you make it 'easy all' with your epitheted clumsiness in a boat—it is ten-and-sixpence.

Epitoke (e·pitǫuk). *Zool.* [ad. Gr. ἐπίτοκος fruitful, bearing offspring, f. ἐπί Epi- 1 + τόκος a bringing forth, birth.] The posterior sexual part of the body of certain annelids. Hence **Epi·tokous** *a.*

1911 J. A. Thomson *Biol. Seasons* III. 261 In some of our British shore-worms..a remarkable change occurs in the body at the breeding season. So striking is the transformation in some instances, that the breeding ('epitokous') phase has been mistaken for a distinct species. 1916 H. S. Pratt *Invertebr. Anim.* 283 In many (Polychæta) the anterior part of the body is sexless and is called the atoke, while the hinder part is sexual and is called the epitoke.

Epitoxoid (epitǫ·ksoid). [Epi- 1.] A toxoid which has less affinity than the toxin for the corresponding antitoxin.

1903 [see Toxoid].

Epitrichium (epitri·kiǝ̆m). *Anat.* [mod.L., f. Gr. ἐπί upon + τρίχιον, dim. of θρίξ hair.] A thin membrane which overlies the epidermis and hair during fœtal life, usually disappearing before birth. Hence **Epitri·chial** *a.*

1887 A. C. Haddon *Study Embryol.* 100 The epidermis of Amphioxus permanently remains as a single layer. In all other embryo Vertebrates, the epiblast, from being single, becomes double layered, owing to the primitive epiblast giving rise to a layer of flattened epithelial cells, the epitrichial layer. 1902 D. J. Cunningham *Anat.* 734 A thin membrane, termed the epitrichium. 1913 A. Keith *Hum. Embryol.* (ed. 3) 451 The epitrichium,..so named because the hairs are developed beneath it, and when they grow out in the sixth month this surface layer of flat epithelium is shed.

Epoch. 7. Add: **epoch-marking** *a.*, journalistic alteration of *epoch-making*.

1895 *Westm. Gaz.* 15 Jan. 2/2. 1919 J. L. Garvin *Econ. Found. Peace* 272 Consent by the United States to administer Constantinople and the Straits, Armenia and Palestine, would be an epoch-marking step in itself. 1923 *Daily Mail* 16 Jan. 7 This epoch-marking experiment.

Éponge (epoṅʒ). [Fr., = sponge.] Some sort of dress-fabric.

1928 *Daily Express* 11 July 5/5 For a bathing-coat try to find flowery éponge or any other bright fabric.

Eponychium (eponi·kiǝ̆m). *Anat.* [mod.L., f. Gr. ἐπί upon + ὄνυξ nail.]

1. The horny embryonic structure whence the nail is developed.

2. The nail-skin; a film of epidermis which covers the body of the nail for a limited distance.

1892 C. S. Minot *Hum. Embryol.* 555 The epitrichial layer over the area has received the special name of *eponychium* from Unna. 1902 D. J. Cunningham *Anat.* 734 The part [of the epitrichium] which persists over the root of the nail is termed the eponychium, and covers the proximal part of the lunula.

Epoophoron (epoǫ·fǒrǫn). *Anat.* [mod.L., f. Ep- + *oophoron* ovary (f. Gr. ᾠόν egg + -φορος bearing, bearer).] = Parovarium.

1883 M. Foster & F. M. Balfour *Elem. Embryol.* (ed. 2) 224 The sexual part becomes in the cock the after-testes or coni vasculosi...In the hen it forms part of the epoophoron of Waldeyer, and is composed of well-developed tubes with yellow pigment. 1887 *Buck's Handbk. Med. Sci.* V. 520/2 The parovarium (Syn., paroöphoron, epoöphoron, corpus pampiniforme (Wrisberg), organ of Rosenmüller) in the human female, is a structure having a vertical diameter of 15 to 25 mm. 1904 A. Keith *Hum. Embryol.* (ed. 2) 125.

Epsilon (epsǝi·lǫ̆n). [Gr. ἒ ψιλόν, lit. 'bare e', i.e. 'e and nothing else' = short e written ε and not αι.] The fifth letter of the Greek alphabet (Ε, ε); *Astron.* denoting the fifth star in a constellation.

c 1400 Maundev. (1839) iii. 20. 1842 *Penny Cycl.* XXII. 448/2 ε (4) and ε (5) Lyræ. 1930 A. J. Quirke *Forged, Anon. & Suspect Documents* 77 Affectation of letter-forms of unconventional type...A typical example is the use of the Greek 'epsilon' for small *e*. *Ibid.* 100 Examination of small 'e'..If Greek 'epsilon' form is used, [etc.]. 1931 *Times Lit. Suppl.* 1 Jan. 10/3 The epsilon-shaped E [i.e. ε].

Equalita·rianism. [-ism.] Belief in the natural equality of mankind.

1920 H. G. Wells *Outl. Hist.* 512/2 The dominant liberal ideas were freedom and a certain vague equalitarianism. 1921 *Q. Rev.* July 140 In fifth-century Athens, where equalitarianism ran to such a ridiculous extreme that gradually all civil offices were distributed among the citizens by lot. 1922 G. M. Trevelyan *Brit. Hist. 19th Cent.* v. 84 *note*, Equalitarianism on board ship is proverbially dangerous.

Equalization. Add: *Board of equalization*, in certain state and county governments of the U.S., a board of commissioners appointed to make uniform the valuations set by local assessors.

1889 *Century Dict.* 1904 *Los Angeles Express* 11 Aug. 4 Phoenix, Ariz. Members of the territorial board of equalization are in session here.

Equalize, *v.* Add: **8.** *intr.* To become equal.

1906 *Amer. Naturalist* June 427 The temperature in the outer and inner layers had equalized to a large extent.

Equate (ī·kwet), *a.* *Ent.* [ad. L. *æquatus*, pa. pple. of *æquare* to make level or smooth.] Comparatively smooth.

1826 Kirby & Sp. *Entomol.* IV. 269 *Equate*, without larger partial elevations or depressions.

Equation. Add:

7. equation box = *equational box* (see next); equation table, a table showing the time a clock should indicate when the sun is on the meridian.

1895 *Funk's Standard Dict.* s.v. *Equational*, *Equation box. 1731 *Explan. Equation of Time* (title-p.), The *Equation Table for Adjusting Watches and Clocks to the Motion of the Sun. 1850 Denison *Clock & Watch-m.* 19 This [sundial]..with the equation-table will give the means of correcting a clock on any fine day.

Equational, *a.* Add:

2. *Mech.* Of gearing, etc.: Equalizing, adjusting. *Equational box* (see quot.).

1874 Knight *Dict. Mech.*, *Equational box*,..a differential gearing used in the bobbin and fly machine for the adjustment of different degrees of twist, for different yarns.

3. *Biol.* Designating mitotic cell-division in which the different elements of the chromatin are divided equally between the daughter nuclei.

1920 W. E. Agar *Cytol.* 50 Now in a meiosis with tetrad formation of the Copepod type it follows that if both the joints represent division planes, one division must be longitudinal (or *equational*, since the resulting daughter chromosomes receive similar sets of chromatin elements), and the other division must be transverse (or *reductional*, since each resulting daughter chromosome receives only one half of the set of chromatin elements).

Equator. Add:

3. b. *Rainfall equator* (see quot.). *Thermal equator*, the line which passes through places of greatest heat on the earth's surface.

1927 Kendrew *Climates Cont.* 45 In the south of Kamerun at about lat. 3° N. we find the rainfall 'Equator'..where rain falls throughout the year, with two well-marked maxima at the equinoxes.

d. *Aeronautics.* 'The line along which the plane of the maximum horizontal section cuts the envelope of an aerostat' (W. B. Faraday *Gloss. Aeronaut. Terms* 1919).

1784 P. H. Maty *New Review* July 61, 64 men who kept the machine in by ropes fixed to its equator. 1815 J. Smith *Panorama Sci. & Art* (1826) II. 151 From this equator proceeded ropes, by which was suspended a car in the form of a boat, a few feet below the balloon. 1838 M. Mason *Aeronautica* 268 An opening, however, of about four feet in length which appeared above the equator of the balloon, soon brought it down again. 1900 *Westm. Gaz.* 1 May 2/1 A balloon loses but little of its lifting power if a rent is made below the equator.

e. *Biol.* Of an egg (see quots.).

1913 J. W. Jenkinson *Vertebr. Embryol.* 95 The structure and symmetry of the egg, its axis, poles, and equator. *a* 1915 — *Lect. Exper. Embryol.* 7 The equator of the egg is the plane passing through the centre at right angles to the axis.

Equatorial, *a.* Add:

1. c. Pertaining to the equator of a balloon (cf. prec. 3 d).

1838 M. Mason *Aeronautica* 30 In shape it [*sc.* a balloon] somewhat resembles a pear; its upright or polar diameter exceeding the transverse or equatorial by about one-sixth.

3. *Biol.* (Cf. prec. 3 e.)

Equatorial plate, in mitosis, the group of chromosomes when arranged in the equatorial plane of the spindle.

1887 A. C. Haddon *Study Embryol.* 19 At the stage when the chromatin is equatorially situated (the 'equatorial plate', which is the equivalent of the wreath and aster stage), the achromatin forms a well-marked spindle-shaped bundle of fibres. 1902 E. B. Wilson *Cell* (ed. 2) 68 The chromosomes group themselves in a plane passing through the equator of the spindle, and thus form what is known as the equatorial plate. 1909 J. W. Jenkinson *Exper. Embryol.* 22 Segmenting ova...1. The radial type. Here the first division is meridional, the second meridional and at right angles to the first, the third equatorial—or more often latitudinal—and at right angles to both the preceding. 1913 — *Vertebr. Embryol.* 40 The plane at right angles to the axis and including the centre of the egg is equatorial.

Equi-. Add: **Equice·llular** *a.* *Biol.*, made up of similar cells. **Equimole·cular** *a.*, having an equal number of molecules. **Equira·tional** *a.* *Math.*, characterized by equal ratio.

1890 E. Ray Lankester in *Encycl. Brit.* XXIV. 810/2 The unicellular or *equicellular Protozoa. 1922 F. W. Aston *Isotopes* 19 Solutions of two different compounds of lead in *equimolecular proportions. 1873 J. Pryde *Pract. Math.* 287 *Equirational progression.

Equid (e·kwid). [ad. mod.L. *equidae*, f. *equus* horse.] A member of the family *Equidae*, which embraces horses, asses, and zebras.

1928 V. G. Childe *Most Anc. East* ii. 25 The zebra, and perhaps another equid.

Equilibrator (īkwi·librētǫɹ). [f. Equilibrate *v.* + -or.] A device for maintaining or restoring equilibrium, as in a flying-machine, or between the primary and secondary currents in a phototelegraphic apparatus.

1908 *Westm. Gaz.* 18 Aug. 4/2 All flying-machines..are liable to be brought more or less suddenly to earth by a wrong movement given to the equilibrator. 1909 *Ibid.* 11 Mar. 4/2 The pilot..might..by skilful manipulation of the equilibrator, succeed in recovering his equilibrium.

Equinely (ī·kwǝinli), *adv.* [f. Equine *a.* + -ly [2].] In an equine manner; like a horse.

1899 *Pearson's Mag.* Apr. 395/1 At the end of this course a man is supposed to be entirely at home on his horse, and with it to do everything that is humanly and equinely possible. *a* 1906 'O. Henry' *Trimmed Lamp* etc. 86 The chestnut approving his new rider, danced and pranced, reviling equinely the subdued bays.

Equinity. (Later U.S. example.)

1898 H. S. Canfield *Maid of Frontier* i. 5 The enormous load of Texas saddle, gun, blanket,..crushed them into mere semblances of equinity.

Equipotential, *a.* Add:

3. *Biol.* Of a germ or embryo: Having equal potentialities. Hence **E:quipotentia·lity**.

1908 H. Driesch *Sci. & Philos. Organism* I. 83 Though ectoderm and endoderm have their potencies equally distributed amongst their respective cells, they possess different potencies compared one with the other. And the same relation is found to hold for all cases of what we may call elementary organs: they are 'equipotential', as we may say, in themselves, but of different potencies compared with each other. 1909 J. W. Jenkinson *Exper. Embryol.* 282 This conception, of the absolute equipotentiality of the parts, as we have already had occasion to remark, is erroneous. 1920 L. Doncaster *Introd. Cytol.* 118 It is maintained by Driesch and others that eggs of this type are equipotential systems, that is to say, they are not differentiated before fertilisation into regions of different potentiality, and any part of the egg is capable of giving rise to any part of the embryo.

Equity. Add: **5. c.** (See quot. 1928.) orig. *U.S.*

1904 E. S. Meade in *Pol. Sci. Q.* Mar. 50 Its preferred stock is quoted at..prices which indicate a general conviction that the equity in the company is worth little. 1926 *Times* 30 Apr. 15/6 Your wife in a fur coat or a smart 'ensemble,' in which she has a 20 per cent. equity. 1928 *New Statesman* 28 July, Finance Suppl. p. vi, Out of the combined issued capital of £16,629,000 the public put up 93 per cent. of the cash required, but received only 21·8 per cent. of the equity—that is the balance of profits remaining after the fixed dividends have been paid on the Preferred capital. 1930 *Times* 11 Feb., Financial Rev. p. iii/2 It was widely imagined that more money was to be made in high pressure equities than in anæmic mortgages.

attrib. 1930 *Daily Express* 8 Sept. 10/2 Purchasers of equity securities of the speculative type.

Equivalve (ī·kwivælv), *a.* (*sb.*) *Zool.* [See Equi-.] Having both valves alike in shape and size. As *sb.*, a bivalve mollusc with both valves alike. Also **Equiva·lvular** *a.*

1897 Parker & Haswell *Zool.* I. 650 [Pelecypoda] As a general rule the right and left valves are alike, or nearly so, the shell being therefore equivalve.

Equivolu·minal, *a.* *Physics.* [See Equi-.] Having an equal unchanging volume (see quot.).

1899 Ld. Kelvin in *Phil. Mag.* XLVII. 480 On the Application of Force within a Limited Space, required to produce Spherical Solitary Waves, or Trains of Periodic Waves, of both Species, Equivoluminal and Irrotational, in an Elastic Solid. *Note*, By 'equivoluminal' I mean every part of the solid keeping its volume unchanged during the motion.

Er (5ɹ). Used to express the inarticulate sound or murmur made by a hesitant speaker. Also as *vb.*

1862 *St. James's Mag.* Mar. 481 Oh!—er—Well I think it was a—er—little fête at—at—Dear me—where was it? 1878 *Porcupine* XX. 681/2 Those ladies and gentlemen.. who have had the advantage of—er—being—er—confined in Newgate prison. 1904 Whitechurch *Canon in Residence* (1906) 4 Mr. Smith said, 'Er, can I have a bed?' 1912 Wright-Henderson *Annabel* i. 9, I think, Mr. Buckle, if you would slightly modulate—er—that is—. *Ibid.* viii. 122 Have you decided yet what—er—. 1924 Rose Macaulay *Orphan Island* xxi, Grandmamma's—er—adultery (if you will pardon the crude word). 1931 *Time & Tide* 12 Sept. 1057 He ahs and ers, and hums and hawes his way through an incredibly fatuous pronouncement.

-er, *suffix* [6]. Introduced from Rugby School into Oxford University slang, orig. at University College, in Michaelmas Term, 1875; used to make jocular formations on sbs., by clipping or curtailing them and adding *-er* to the remaining part, which is sometimes itself distorted. Among the earliest instances are *Footer [3] (= football), Rugger [2] (1893), Socker (1891); Togger (1897), Tosher [3] (1889); *Brekker, *Divvers, *Ekker.

Other familiar examples are *Bedder, *bed-sitter* = bed-sittingroom, *collekkers* = collections (see Collection 8), *Cupper [2], and (formerly) *rudders* = rudiments (of divinity), *stragger* = stranger. Examples of proper names are *Adders* = Addison's Walk, *Bodder* = Bodleian, *Jaggers* = Jesus (College), *Quaggers* = The Queen's College. (Cf. Madan *Oxford outside the Guidebooks* xxv.)

1899 *Daily Tel.* 14 Aug. in Ware *Passing Engl.* 175 The triumph of this jargon was reached when some one christened the Martyrs' Memorial the 'Martyrs' Memugger'. 1903 D. F. T. Coke *Sandford of Merton* ii. 10 *note*, 'Wagger-pagger-bagger' for the receptacle of torn-up letters and the like. 1904 *Daily Chron.* 25 Mar. 4/7 Mr. Gladstone was 'the Gladder'. An undergraduate left his 'bedder' in the morning to eat his 'brekker' in his 'sitter'; later he attended a 'lecker', and in the afternoon he might run with the 'Toggers' (torpid races) or take some other form of 'ecker'. 1912 *Tatler* 23 Oct., Suppl. 40 The 'Pragger-Wagger', it should be explained, is the new name given to the Prince of Wales. 1914 D. O. Barnett *Lett.* (1915) 13 The P-Wagger came to see us yesterday. I met him coming off parade, and threw a hairy salute.

Era. Add: **4. c.** *Era of good feeling(s*, in U.S. Hist., a period during the presidency of Monroe (1817–24), when there was virtually only one political party. Also *transf.*

1817 *Columbian Centinel* 12 July (Th.) (*heading*) Era of Good Feelings. 1851 H. A. Garland *Life J. Randolph* II. 78 During the 'era of good feelings', and the undisturbed repose of Mr. Monroe's administration, [these ideas] had been widely disseminated. 1904 *N. Y. Herald* 22 Sept. 4 The nomination was made unanimously, and the era of good feeling continued throughout the naming of the rest of the ticket.

6. **era-making** *a.* = epoch-making.

1894 tr. *von Weizsäcker's Apostolic Age* I. 188 The era-making significance of the treaty. 1929 R. A. Cram *Cath. Ch. & Art* iv. 53 The great monastic sovereignty..that had grown out of the first and era-making beginnings at the hands of St. Benedict.

Ercles (5·ɹklīz), Bottom's pronunciation of 'Hercules'; 'Ercles vein' is a stock quotation. (See *Mids. N.* I. ii. 31, 42.)

1901 *Standard* 9 Apr. 4/7 Mr. J. B. Glacier, in his opening speech, was in the Ercles vein, and dwelt on perils overcome and triumphs gained.

Erector. Add: **1. b.** As a spec. designation of an engineer who works at the assembling of engines and other iron and steel structures.

1892 *Daily Chron.* 28 Apr. 9/2 Engineer, Fitter, or Erector. 1905 *Westm. Gaz.* 18 Dec. 7/1 Charles Grove, a foreman erector of steel work.

c. A machine used in erecting iron and steel structures.

1895 *Daily News* 31 Oct. 6/5 These 'erectors' are two hydraulic appliances for lifting up and fixing in position the ponderous segments of the iron ring constituting the exterior of the tunnel. 1909 *Daily Chron.* 19 May 3/4 The tunnel shield, complete, with hydraulic erector.

Eremurus (erīmiū·rǝ̆s). *Bot.* [mod.L., f. Gr. ἐρῆμος solitary + οὐρά tail.] A hardy herbaceous perennial plant of the liliaceous genus of plants so named, the cultivated species of which bear spikes of yellow, white, lilac, or brown flowers.

1829 Loudon *Encycl. Plants* 278. 1900 W. D. Drury *Bk. Gard.* 325 Eremuri are noble plants. 1901 *Cassell's Dict. Gard.* I. 323/1 A good but not too heavy soil suits the Eremuruses.

Erewhonian (erīwōu·niăn), *a.* and *sb.* [f. *Erewhon*, title of a book (partial reversal of *Nowhere*) by Samuel Butler, published 1872 and describing a form of utopia: see -ian.] Of, belonging to, or characteristic of the book *Erewhon*, the utopia described in it, or the principles inculcated. **b.** *sb.* An inhabitant of Erewhon.

1897 *Daily News* 16 June 5/2 The Erewhonian plan of counting disease as a crime. 1900 *Ibid.* 10 Dec. 9/6 The Erewhonian Professors, Hanky and Panky. 1921 *Edin. Rev.* July 28 The exhortation which persuaded Samuel Butler's Erewhonians to destroy all their machines. *Ibid.* 36 The Erewhonian policy of breaking up the machines is manifestly impossible in this country. 1927 *Observer* 25 Sept. 16/6 The Erewhonian paradox of imprisoning the invalid is not wholly a barren one.

Ergastulum (ǝɹgæ·stiŭlǝ̆m). *Rom. Antiq.* Pl. -ula (-iŭlă). [L., after Gr. ἐργαστήριον workshop, with altered suffix.] A private prison or house of correction for slaves.

1885 R. S. Storrs *Div. Orig. Christianity* v. 159 As workers on farms, they..slept at night in the cells of the ergastula, under-ground. 1891 Farrar *Darkn. & Dawn* xxxi, The ergastulum is half-subterranean. Its windows are narrow, and high above our heads.

Ergates (5·ɹgătīz). *Ent.* [Gr. ἐργάτης workman.] The worker ant.

1910 W. M. Wheeler *Ants* 97 The worker (ergates) is characterized by the complete absence of wings.

Hence **Ergata·ndromorph** [Gr. ἀνήρ, ἀνδρός man, -μορφος -form], an ant that combines worker and male characters. **E·rgatane:r** (Iǝɹ) [Gr. ἀνήρ man], a male ant resembling a worker. **E·rgatogy·ne** [Gr. γυνή woman], a worker-like ant with female characters. **Ergatoid, E:rgatomo·rphic** *adjs.*, worker-like. **E:rgatote·lic** *a.* (see quot.).

1910 W. M. Wheeler *Ants* 94 The ergatanēr, ergatomorphic, or ergatoid male resembles the worker in having no wings and in the structure of the antennæ. *Ibid.* 96 The ergatogyne, ergatomorphic, or ergatoid female, is a worker-like form, with ocelli, large eyes, and a thorax more or less like that of the female, but without wings. *Ibid.* 99 The ergatandromorph..is an anomaly similar to the [gynandromorph] but having worker instead of female characters combined with those of the male. *Ibid.* 120 In these [*sc.* honeybees] only the secondary instincts are manifested in the queen, while the worker retains the primary series in full vigor and thus more clearly represents the ancestral female of the species. This type may therefore be called ergatotelic. 1915 Donisthorpe *Brit. Ants* 114 Wasmann records a mixed ergatandromorph with only the colour of the head like that of the worker. 1927 *Glasgow Herald* 16 July 4 The ergatoids can reproduce ergatoids, besides workers and soldiers.

Ergo, *sb.* 1. (Later U.S. example.)
1867 Lowell *Fitz Adam's Story* 31 His fancy's thrall, he drew all ergos thence, And thought himself the type of common sense.

Ergogram (ɜ·ɪgǒgræm). [f. Gr. ἔργον work + -GRAM.] A record made by an ergograph.
1904 G. S. Hall *Adolescence* I. 150 Endurance as measured by ergograms. 1918 C. S. Myers *Psychol.* 8 After sufficient rest, complete recovery occurs, so that a second ergogram equal to the first is obtainable.

Ergograph (ɜ·ɪgǒgrɑf). [ad. It. *ergografo* (A. Mosso), f. Gr. ἔργον work: see -GRAPH.] An instrument which measures and records work done by the muscles. Hence **Ergogra·phic** *a.*, **Ergo·graphy.**
1892 *Sat. Rev.* 9 Apr. 430/2 The action of the brain on the muscles, as demonstrated by experiments made with the ergograph. 1897 E. W. Scripture *New Psychol.* 230 The ergograph..consists of a rest in which the arm is fixed so that the middle finger can be moved alone without involving any of the others. 1898 *Daily News* 25 Nov. 6/3 His ergographic curves, and his abdominal respiratory curves, are duly recorded. 1909 C. S. Myers *Text-bk. Exper. Psychol.* 184 Ergography.—The work performed by an active muscle ..may be best determined by means of graphic records. *Ibid.* 186 An ergographic record. *Ibid.* 383 The ergograph ..is especially adapted for the study of simple movements in which very few muscles are involved.

Ergophobia (ɜɪgǒfōu·biă). *jocular.* [f. Gr. ἔργον work + -PHOBIA.] Fear of work.
1905 W. D. Spanton in *Brit. Med. Jrnl.* 11 Feb. 300/2 He has discovered that it often pays better to idle and loaf about than to work, and the consequence is that a new disease has been engendered, which I have termed 'ergophobia'. 1905 *Daily Chron.* 26 May 5/7 Ergophobia.. means a hatred or terror of work...It is a new disease which a medical paper has recently called attention to. 1921 A. D. Godley in *19th Cent.* Dec. 986 Ergophobia—a recognised if not a notifiable disease.

Ergostat (ɜ·ɪgǒstæt). *Med.* [f. Gr. ἔργον work + στατός adj., standing.] (See quots.)
1890 Billings *Med. Dict.*, *Ergostat*.., an apparatus for regulating and measuring the amount of muscular effort put forth during a given time, as in prescribed exercise. 1901 Dorland *Med. Dict.*, *Ergostat*, a machine to be worked for muscular exercise, for the cure of obesity, etc.

Ergosterol (ɜɪgǫ·stĕrǫl). *Chem.* Earlier **ergosterin.** [f. Ergot + *-sterol* as in Cholesterol: see -OL.] An inert alcohol derived from ergot.
1889 *Jrnl. Chem. Soc.* LVI. 408 Ergosterin..is completely dissolved by sulphuric acid without discoloration. 1906 *Ibid.* XC. II. 202 As obtained by Bömer's method..from the fat of rye, ergosterol contains a small amount of a product which forms small, white flocks melting at 60–61° and is non-saponifiable, but the nature of which is unknown. 1927 *Nature* 24 Sept. 440/2 Irradiated ergosterol possesses extraordinarily potent anti-rachitic activity. 1928 A. B. Callow *Food & Health* 51 Ergosterol..was present in minute quantities in what was formerly thought to be pure cholesterol.. When ergosterol is irradiated it acquires the property of preventing or curing rickets, that is to say, it becomes vitamin D.

Eria. Add: Also (anglicized) **eri**: The silkworm that produces this silk. Also *eria moth, worm.*
1839 Ure *Dict. Arts* II. 1104 The *Arrindy*, or *Eria* worm, and moth, is reared over a great part of Hindustan. 1866 *Chambers's Encycl.* VIII. 724/1 The 'Eria', or 'Arrindy' silkworm, native of India. 1887 *Encycl. Brit.* XXII. 60/2 The eria or arrindi moth of Bengal and Assam, *Attacus ricini*, which feeds on the castor-oil plant. 1923 *Nature* CXI. 411/2 It appears that all the recognised diseases are prevalent, and those of the mulberry, muga, and eri worms are the same.

Erigeron (ĕri·dʒərǫn). Delete *Obs.* and add: b. A hardy herbaceous perennial plant belonging to the modern genus of that name, bearing daisy-like flowers.
1829 Loudon *Encycl. Plants* 704. 1900 W. D. Drury *Bk. Gard.* 270 Erigerons are summer-flowering composites with beautiful star-shaped flowers. 1901 *Cassell's Dict. Gard.* I. 325/2 Snails and slugs are frequently very destructive to Erigerons in late autumn.

Erinaceous, *a.* See also Herinacious.

Erineum (ĕri·nĭŭm). *Bot.* [mod.L., f. Gr. ἐρίνεος woolly, f. ἔριον wool.] A pathological growth of the epidermis of plants caused by certain mites.
Formerly supposed to be caused by a fungus to which *Erineum* was given as the generic name.
1916 H. S. Pratt *Invertebr. Anim.* 438 A fuzzy spot or erineum is a dense mass of twisted hairs, among which the mites live.

Erinoid (e·rinoid). Proprietary name (perhaps f. *Erin* Ireland) of a semi-plastic material manufactured from casein by Erinoid Ltd., Lightpill, Stroud, Gloucestershire, and serving as a substitute for horn, amber, ebony, etc.
1915 *Chemist & Druggist* LXXXVI. 646 'Erinoid'..is put to a great number of uses, many of them connected with druggists' sundries. 1930 *Daily Express* 30 July 2/1 [A] fountain pen..in either green erinoid with rolled gold bands or plain black.

Ernestine (ɜ·mĕstəin), *a.* *Hist.* [f. *Ernest*, proper name = G. *Ernst.*] Designating the elder or electoral line of the house of Frederick of Saxony, originating from his son Ernest (1441–86).
1841 *Penny Cycl.* XX. 493/2 Albert and Ernest, who were the founders of the Albertine and Ernestine lines. 1866 *Chambers's Encycl.* VIII. 515/2 The Ernestine, which was also the elder or electoral line. 1904 *Westm. Gaz.* 23 Nov. 2/3 The Ernestine line of the House of Saxony to which the late Prince Consort belonged. 1911 *Encycl. Brit.* XXIV. 270/1 This deed transferred the electoral title..from the Ernestine to the Albertine branch of the house.

Erogenous (erǫ·dʒĭnəs), *a.* Variant of Erogenic.
Both words are incorrectly formed.
1915 C. R. Payne tr. *O. Pfister's Psychol. Method* 155 Those places which are important for the gaining of sexual pleasure, we call erogenous zones. 1925 C. Fox *Educat. Psychol.* 237 Any portion of the skin or mucous membrane which yields a feeling of pleasure when stimulated is described as an erogenous zone.

Eros (ī·rǫs, e·rǫuz). Pl. **Erotes** (erōu·tez); **Eroses** (ī·rǫsĕz, e·rǫuzĕz). [L. *Erōs*, a. Gr. ἔρως.]
1. Love, the god of love, or a representation of him: = Cupid.
1775 J. Bryant *Mythol.* I. 510 Under this characteristic they represented an heavenly personage, and joined her with Eros, or divine Love. 1817 Byron *Manfred* II. ii. 93 He who from out their fountain dwellings raised Eros and Anteros. 1864 Tennyson *Islet* 11 A bevy of Eroses apple-cheek'd. 1877 Patmore (*title*) The Unknown Eros and other Odes. 1888 A. H. Smith *Catal. Engr. Gems Brit. Mus.* 127 Silenus..threatening to flog Eros, who is held up by two other Erotes. 1896 Farnell *Cults Gk. States* II. 625 The only ancient centres of Eros-worship were Thespiae and Parion. 1904 Budge *3rd & 4th Egypt. Rooms Brit. Mus.* 229 Erotes, or Cupids, holding grapes and thyrsus with wreath. 1924 tr. *Freud's Coll. Papers* II. 261 This masochism would be a witness and a survival of that phase of development in which the amalgamation, so important for life afterwards, of death-instinct and Eros took place. 1928 *Times* 14 Dec. 10/4 Mr. John Murray's suggested new site for the Shaftesbury memorial..would be an excellent one but for the fact that 'Eros' would then be lost to view from the principal approach roads to Piccadilly-circus.
2. *Astr.* An asteroid discovered by Witt at Berlin in 1898. It comes at times nearer the earth than any heavenly body except the moon.
1926 H. Macpherson *Mod. Astron.* 92 Eros..comes at perihelion within the orbit of the Earth, from which it is then distant but thirteen million miles.

Erotica (ĕrǫ·tikă). [a. Gr. ἐρωτικά, neut. pl. of ἐρωτικός amatory, f. ἐρωτ-, ἔρως love.] Matters of love; often in booksellers' catalogues as a heading for items of erotic literature.
1854 (*title*) Erotica. The Elegies of Propertius. 1913 H. Jackson *Eighteen Nineties* v. 122 The romance..in its unexpurgated form, suggests deep knowledge of that literature generally classed under *facetiæ* and *erotica* by the booksellers.

Erotogenic (ĕrōutodʒe·nik), *a.* [f. Gr. ἐρωτο-, ἔρως love + -GENIC.] = Erogenic *a.*
1922 Joan Riviere tr. *Freud's Introd. Lect. Psycho-analysis* 264 The gratification obtained can only relate to the region of the mouth and lips; we therefore call these areas of the body *erotogenic zones*. 1924 tr. *Freud's Coll. Papers* II. 39 A certain degree of directly sexual pleasure is produced by the stimulation of various cutaneous areas (erotogenic zones).

Erotoma·niac. [f. Erotomania: see Maniac.] A victim of erotomania. Also *attrib.* or *adj.*
1858 Bucknill & Tuke *Man. Psychol. Med.* 212 The erotomaniac is..the sport of the imagination. 1895 J. A. Noble in *Contemp. Rev.* Apr. 494 The impudences..of the erotomaniacs. *Ibid.* 496 Erotomaniac literature. 1895 *Ch. Times* 5 Apr. 398/1 This kind of erotomaniac fiction. 1921 *Spectator* 16 Apr. 497/1 Outside an asylum for erotomaniacs, the world is not governed by perpetual storms of unrestrainable animal passion.

Erraticism (eræ·tisiz'm). [See -ISM.] Erratic tendencies.
1907 *Daily Chron.* 18 Jan. 9/6 Pronounced Erraticism [in golf-play]. 1920 *19th Cent.* July 6 In various ways his erraticism threatened actual danger to the allied cause. 1928 T. C. Chamberlin *Two Solar Families* Introd. p. xxi, Their courses were all-wayward. And yet their erraticisms are accompanied with spectacular brilliancy.

Ersatz (ɜ·zæts, ‖e·rzats). [G., = compensation, replacement.] A substitute or imitation (usually, an inferior article instead of the real thing). Also *attrib.* or *adj.*
1919 *War Terms* in *Athenæum* 1 Aug. 695/1 Another word not seldom met with is 'ersatz'. It is the German 'substitute'. 1927 *Daily Express* 30 Sept. 1/1 It will merely be an imitation Parliament, an 'Ersatz' Parliament, designed to fulfil the immediate needs of the Dictatorship. 1930 *Observer* 9 Mar. 12 The coffee..will be..tempered with a judicious mixture of 'ersatz'.

Erstwhile, *adv.* Add: Also *adj.* = former. (Cf. *whilom*.)
1901 L. Housman *Two Widows of Chadsey* in *Odd Pairs* (1925) i, Her erstwhile rival. 1903 McNeill *Egregious English* 31 The erstwhile portly mother of daughters. 1909 *Westm. Gaz.* 21 Aug. 13/1 A tottering pleasure-resort, whose erstwhile patrons look more longingly every year at the pretty and easily reached villages of Normandy and Brittany.

Eructated, *ppl. a.* [f. Eructate *v.* + -ED[1].] Vomited.
1869 C. L. Brace *New West* i. 13 The reeling state-rooms, smelling of oil, bilgewater and eructated dinner.

Erven, pl. of Erf[2], *South African*, garden plot.
1902 *Westm. Gaz.* 14 Apr. 10/1 The erven (acres) in question were granted to these Reservists by the Government. 1905 *Tarka Herald* 4 Feb., For the purpose of leading storm water..to their erven.

-ery, *suffix.* Add:
2. b. In recent U.S. use, after *bakery* (= baker's shop or works), this suffix has gained considerable currency in denoting 'a place where an indicated article or service may be purchased or procured', as *beanery, bootery, boozery, breadery, cakery, carwashery, drillery, eatery, hashery, lunchery, mendery, toggery.*

Eryngium (ĭri·ndʒiŭm). [mod.L., f. L. *eryngion*: see Eryngo.] A hardy perennial plant of the umbelliferous genus of plants so named, bearing blue or white flowers.
1900 W. D. Drury *Bk. Gard.* 270 Eryngiums are handsome plants with..large branching heads of Thistle-like flowers. 1901 *Cassell's Dict. Gard.* I. 327/2 These Eryngiums may be transplanted safely when young.

Erythræmia (eriþrī·miă). *Path.* [mod.L. (W. Türk), f. Gr. ἐρυθρός red + αἷμα blood.] A disease characterized by a persistent increase of the red blood-corpuscles.
1908 Osler in *Lancet* 18 Jan. 143. 1908 *Practitioner* Apr. 461. 1912 *Osler's Princ. Med.* (ed. 8) 757.

Erythrism (e·riþriz'm). [f. Gr. ἐρυθρός red + -ISM.]
1. Redness of the hair and beard (Dorland 1901); abnormal or excessive redness (in the plumage of birds or hair of mammals).
1930 E. W. Hendy *Wild Exmoor* 297 Erythrism, or excess of red colouration, may be produced..by feeding birds upon red pepper.
2. A red variety (of some recognized species). (Cf. Melanism 1 b.)
1893 *Athenæum* 28 Jan. 124/3 Mr. Hose thought that this species might possibly be only an erythrism of *S[emnopithecus] chrysomelas*. 1908 J. H. Gurney in *Zoologist* Apr. 136 A good example of the same erythrism was that by Mr. McLean in the autumn of 1906.
Hence **Erythri·smal, Erythri·stic** *adjs.*, exhibiting erythrism.
1923 *Glasgow Herald* 17 Mar. 6 The variety, technically called 'erythristic', occurs among ferrets as well as among polecats.

Erythritol (eri·þritǫl). *Chem.* [f. Erythrite + -OL.] A tetrahydric alcohol obtained chiefly from lichens and algæ.
1900 *Jrnl. Chem. Soc.* LXXVIII. I. 579 The algæ *Trentepohlia Jolithus*..when extracted with ether, yields erythritol. 1923 Bernthsen *Org. Chem.* viii. 210 Erythritol (Butane-tetrol) occurs in the free state in *Protococcus vulgaris*.

Erythro-. Add: **Ery·throblast,** a rudimentary red blood-corpuscle; hence **Erythrobla·stic** *a.* **Ery·throcyte,** a red blood-corpuscle; hence **Erythrocy·tic** *a.* **Ery·throcythæ·mia** = *Erythræmia. **Erythropla·stid** = *erythrocyte.*
1890 Billings *Med. Dict.*, *Erythroblasts. 1898 *Allbutt's Syst. Med.* V. 651 None of the leucocytes of the blood becomes transformed into red corpuscles, these being formed from special cells—'erythroblasts'—in the bone-marrow. 1908 Osler & McCrae *Syst. Med.* IV. 600 A considerable number of the immature cells of the adult marrow, including many of the erythroblasts, possess a considerable degree of affinity for basic coloring matters. 1908 *Practitioner* Feb. 239 The *erythroblastic tissues of the marrow. 1908 Osler & McCrae *Syst. Med.* IV. 679 The disease is due to a primary hyperplasia of the erythroblastic bone-marrow. 1898 *Allbutt's Syst. Med.* V. 413 The red corpuscles or *erythrocytes. 1908 Osler & McCrae *Syst. Med.* IV. 600 We speak of the..blue-stained erythrocyte as polychromatophilic. 1905 Osler *Princ. Med.* (ed. 6) 748 An increase in the number of the red blood-corpuscles—*erythrocythæmia. 1908 *Practitioner* Feb. 234 According to the degree in which the parent cell has developed along the leucocytic or *erythrocytic route. 1878 S. W. Mitchell in *Amer. Jrnl. Med. Sci.* July 17 *note*, The foot and hand disorder I am about to describe may be conveniently labelled *Erythromelalgia. 1921 A. Keith *Hum. Embryol.* (ed. 4) 336 At every period of life the red blood corpuscles (*erythroplastids) arise from erythroblasts.

Erythrol (e·riþrǫl). *Chem.* [f. Gr. ἐρυθρός red + -OL.]
1. An earlier name for *Erythritol.
1901 Dorland *Med. Dict.* (ed. 2).
2. (See quot. 1908.)
1901 Dorland *Med. Dict.* (ed. 2). 1908 *Practitioner* Feb. 279 For butyric fermentation, is used erythrol, a red powder insoluble in water, which is a double iodide of bismuth and cinchonidine. 1910 *Ibid.* Feb. 277 Erythrol tetranitrate is said to have less effect than liquor trinitrini.

Erythronium (eriþrōu·niŭm). [mod.L., ad. Gr. ἐρυθρόνιον, a plant of the satyrion kind.] A plant of the liliaceous genus of plants so named, bearing cyclamen-like flowers.
1900 W. D. Drury *Bk. Gard.* 326 Erythroniums range between 6 in. and 9 in. in height. 1901 *Cassell's Dict. Gard.* I. 329/1 Erythroniums should be as short a time out of the soil as possible.

Erythrosin (eri·þrǫsin). *Chem.* [irreg. f. Gr. ἐρυθρός red + -IN[1].] A red colouring matter obtained from fluorescein by the action of iodine, used in photography and as a histological stain.
1891 *Jrnl. Camera Club* V. 123–7. 1892 *Photogr. Ann.* II. 72 Plates sensitised with erythrosin and erythrosin silver. 1908 *Jrnl. Chem. Soc.* XCIV. I. 669 When silver nitrate is added to an excess of a dilute solution of erythrosin, a much more intensely coloured colloidal solution of the silver salt of erythrosin is obtained.

Esactine (es,æ·ktəin). *Zool.* [f. Gr. ἐς, εἰς into, to + ἀκτίς, -ῖν- ray.] The proximal ray of a sponge-spicule: cf. *Ecactine.
1888 [see *Ecactine, Tylroclad].

Esau (ī·sǫ). Name of the elder of the twin sons of the patriarch Isaac, who sold his birthright to his brother Jacob for 'a mess of pottage' (Gen. xxv. 25 ff.), used symbolically for: One who prefers present advantage to permanent rights or interests.
1662 Brooks *Crown & Glory of Christ.* 82 He that is a Cato without, and a Nero within; a Jacob without, and an Esau within..is ripened for the worst of torments. 1828 *Congress. Debates* IV. I. 1226 (Stanford) He would again call the attention of..the political Esaus of our tribe to the predicament in which they stand. 1845 Browning *Flight of Duchess* xvii, Smooth Jacob still robs homely Esau. 1849 Kingsley *North Devon* Misc. (1859) II. 240 Esau is a dumb soul, especially here in England; but he has as deep a heart in him as Jacob. 1859 Thackeray *Virgin.* lxxxiv, I turned from Esau, and I clung to Jacob. And now I have my reward, I have my reward! 1889 Stevenson *Master of Ballantrae* (1911) 118 'Ah! Jacob', says the Master. 'So here is Esau.'

Escalator (e·skălēⁱtəɹ). orig. *U.S.* [Formed from stem of Escalade after *elevator*.] A moving staircase made on the endless chain principle, so that the steps ascend or descend continuously, for carrying passengers up or down.
1904 *Daily Chron.* 21 Nov. 5/5 [New York] There are to be four elevator shafts, besides stairways and 'escalators'. *a* 1906 'O. Henry' *Trimmed Lamp* etc. 132 You will perceive that the Bee-Hive was not a fashionable department store, with escalators and pompadours. 1910 *Daily News* 2 July 10 In the course of the hearing counsel referred to a proposed moving staircase as an 'escalator'. 1923 *Spectator* 29 Sept. 411/2 Three escalators will serve the Bakerloo Tube.

Escape, *sb.*[1] Add:
4. c. An outlet for a liquid; *esp.* a sluice or gate for the outlet of surplus water in a canal. Also *attrib.*, as *escape-drain, -head, water.*
1891 *Daily News* 31 Oct. 6/4 The Koshesha Escape, or Barrage...The escape is constructed to discharge 2,000 million cubic metres in twenty days in good Nile years. 1893 *Pall Mall Gaz.* 30 Jan. 3/1 The revolution of these caps whips the skim-milk through a broad escape. 1907 W. G. Bligh *Irrig. Wks.* x. 274 In places on a canal where an Escape or a Branch takes off, a regulating bridge across both works is generally necessary. *Ibid.* 280 An Escape Head should, if practicable, be combined with a fall. 1911 W. Willcocks *Irrig. Mesopot.* 27 Every canal system needs its escapes. 1913 Willcocks & Craig *Egypt. Irrig.* II. 465 The escape waters of the canals and larger water-courses should be allowed to enter the escape-drain by means of regulators at the tails of the canals.

Escapee. (Earlier U.S. example.)
1865 Whitman *Specimen Days* (1892) 62 Some three or four hundred more escapees from the confederate army came up on the boat.

Escapement. Add:
3. In a pianoforte (see quot.).
1896 A. J. Hipkins *Pianoforte* Gloss., *Escapement*, a space that is left between the hammer at its full rise and the strings, necessary for the strings to vibrate and to prevent jarring.

Escargot (ɛskargo). *Cookery.* [Fr.] An edible snail.
1892 *Encycl. Pract. Cookery* (ed. T. F. Garrett). 1926 *Glasgow Herald* 26 Mar. 10 I've savoured an escargot.

-escence, *suffix*, forming sbs. corresponding to adjs. in -ESCENT, as *effervescence, iridescence.*

Eschatocol (e·skătokǫl). [G. *eschatokoll* (It. *escatocollo*, F. *eschatocole*), f. Gr. ἔσχατος last + κόλλα glue. Cf. πρωτόκολλον Protocol. Martial (II. vi. 3) has ἐσχατοκόλλιον end of a papyrus roll.] The concluding section of a charter, containing the attestation, date, etc.; a concluding clause or formula.
1897 F. W. Maitland *Domesday Bk.* 247 Such words as a charter has about 'consent'..may occur in the eschatocol, the clause which deals with the execution and attestation of the instrument. 1904 E. Barker in *Engl. Hist. Rev.* Jan. 152 In regard to the dating we find originally a separation, the year going into the protocol, the month and regnal year into the eschatocol. But by the middle of the twelfth century the whole date is put into the eschatocol.

Eschatolo·gically, *adv.* [f. Eschatological *a.* + -LY[2].] In relation to eschatology.
1922 A. E. Garvie *Beloved Disciple* ix. 199 Whether we interpret these functions spiritually or eschatologically.

Eschato·logize (-dʒəiz), *v.* [See -IZE.] *trans.* To give an eschatological character to.
1919 S. C. Carpenter *Christianity acc. S. Luke* vii. 101 The first Evangelist has 'eschatologized' an originally non-eschatological saying.

Eschea·tment. [f. Escheat *v.* + -MENT.] Forfeiture or lapsing by escheat.
1869 Blackmore *Lorna Doone* xxiv, On pain of a heavy fine or escheatment. 1919 E. MacNeill *Phases Irish Hist.* (1920) 312 The new grants were not preceded..by..any escheatment or invalidation of the existing contract.

Escort, *v.* Add: c. To 'keep company' or 'walk out' with (a woman). *U.S.*
1890 *Harper's Mag.* Oct. 716/2 A whisper also went the rounds that Dick Jones was escorting Miss Turner.

Escortage (eskǭ·ɹtĕdʒ). *U.S.* [f. Escort *v.* + -AGE.] The action of escorting.
1898 P. L. Ford *Hon. Peter Stirling* 153 She likes my company and finds my escortage very convenient. 1911 H. S. Harrison *Queed* xiii. 146 At nine, as it chanced, she was to go out under the escortage of Charles Gardiner West.

Escudo (eskū·do). [Sp., Pg.:—L. *scūtum* shield. Cf. Scudo, Écu.] A Spanish and Portuguese silver coin of the value of a crown. Also applied to other coins, gold or silver, in American countries.
1915 Ethel C. Hargrove *Progressive Portugal* 262 In 1913, the Portuguese Authorities altered the denomination of the coinage from milreis and reis to escudos and centavos. 1920 *Chambers's Jrnl.* 404/2 The escudo, which normally.. is of the value of nearly four shillings and sixpence. 1925 *Glasgow Herald* 14 Aug. 6 The paper, escudos nominally equivalent to a French franc.

Escutcheon. Add: 3. g. = *milk-escutcheon* (Milk *sb.* 10).
1881 Sheldon *Dairy Farming* 6/2 This reversed hair is the so-called 'escutcheon'. 1912 F. T. Barton *Cattle, Sheep & Pigs* 18 The escutcheon may extend over the whole of the hind quarters and the udder.

-ese. Add: On the model of derivatives from authors' names were formed Journalese (1882), Newspaperese (1889).
1898 F. Harrison in *19th Cent.* June 941 As Mat Arnold said to me..'Flee Carlylese as the very devil!' Yes! flee Carlylese, Ruskinese, Meredithese, and every other *ese*. 1899 *Golf Illustr.* 14 July 134 American 'golfese'. 1906 *Daily Chron.* 2 Aug. 3/2 Deplorable guide-bookese.

Eskimo (e·skimǫu). Also **Esquimaux** (8 **-eaux, Eskima**). Pl. **-oes, -os** (ǭuz), **-aux** (ǭu). [ad. Da. *Eskimo* (Sw. *Eskimå*), ad. F. *Esquimaux* pl., corrupt ad. an Amer. Indian word (cf. Abnaki *Eskimantsic*, Ojibway *Ashkimeq*) meaning 'eaters of raw flesh' (cf. Cree *aski* raw, *mow* he eats).]
1. A member of a N. American race inhabiting the Arctic coast from Greenland to Alaska. (Their own name for themselves is *Innuit*.) Used as sing. and pl. Also *attrib.*, as *Eskimo dog.*
1744 Dobbs *Hudson Bay* 49 The East Main...Here the Nodway or Eskimaux Indians live. *Ibid.* 203 A vocabulary of English and Eskima words. 1791 J. Long (*title*) Voyages and Travels of an Indian Interpreter...To which is added.. a List of Words in the Iroquois, Mohegan, Shawanee, and Esquimeaux Tongues. 1792 G. Cartwright *Labrador* 7 The Esquimaux from Ice and snow now free, In Shallops and in Whale-boats go to Sea. 1845 Youatt *Dog* 55 The Esquimaux Dog is a beast of burden and of draught. *Ibid.* 56 The Esquimaux Indian goes in pursuit of the seal. 1850 Latham *Nat. Hist. Var. Man* 289 The difficulties presented by the Eskimo language. *Ibid.* 290 The Eskimo is essentially a Mongol in physiognomy. 1870 *Amer. Naturalist* III. 83 Esquimaux Curlew (*Numenius borealis*) breeds near Fort Benton. 1875 H. Rink (*title*) Tales and Traditions of the Eskimo. *Ibid.* p. viii, Words..peculiar to Eskimo life.
2. The language of this people. Also applied to a jargon used in intercourse between Eskimos and whites and consisting mainly of Eskimo words.
1850 Latham *Nat. Hist. Var. Man* 290 From the grammar of Fabricius, the Eskimo was soon known to be a language of long compound words. 1916 E. W. Hawkes *Labrador Eskimo* 6 Lieut. Lucas, who had acquired a knowledge of Eskimo. 1929 *Encycl. Brit.* VIII. 709/1.
3. (See quots.). Also *attrib.*
1922 *Glasgow Herald* 11 Oct. 8 Chocolate eggs filled with ice-cream and known as 'Eskimos'. 1928 Turnbow & Raffetto *Ice Cream* 57 Chocolate-coated ice cream bars were introduced in 1921 as 'Eskimo Pies'.

Esotericism (esote·risiz'm). Add quot. So **Esote·ricist,** one who holds esoteric doctrines. Also **Eso·terist** (Funk's *Stand. Dict.*).
1885 Mrs. H. Ward *Amiel's Jrnl.* II. 315 Yes, but still a certain esotericism [*orig.* ésotérisme] is inevitable, since critical, scientific, and philosophical culture is only attainable by a minority. 1891 *Review of Rev.* 15 June 522/2 She [*sc.* Madame Blavatsky] made all her 'esotericists', as she called them, send her their photographs. 1892 *Ch. Times* 1 Apr. 337/1 Further on the esotericist is identified with the Rationalist.

Espada (espā·da). Also erron. **espardo.** [Sp., = It. *spada*, Fr. *épée* sword.] = Matador 1.
1902 *Encycl. Brit.* XXVI. 460/1 Two *matadors* or *espardos* are engaged in each day's fight. 1923 Ld. Curzon *Tales Trav.* 215 Just as the *espada* lunged with the sword..the bull..was upon him. 1926 *Blackw. Mag.* Sept. 290/2 Bull-fighting requires great courage in the bull-fighters from the espada to the mozo.

Espadrille (espadri·l). Also **-illo.** [Fr., a. Prov. *espardillo*, f. *espart* Esparto.] A canvas shoe with soles of twisted rope, worn in the Pyrenees.
1892 *Daily News* 16 June 5/4 'Espadrilles', or shoes with woven rope soles, are likely to come into favour with running men. 1907 Baring-Gould *Pyrenees* 123 Mauléon..has become the centre of manufacture of the espadrillos. 1923 *Blackw. Mag.* Aug. 162/1, I crept through the thickets in my rope-soled espadrilles.

Esperanto (espĕræ·nto). [Orig. the pen-name (Dr. *Esperanto* = Dr. Hoping-one) used by the inventor on the title-page of his book *Langue internationale; préface et manuel complet*, 1887.] An artificial language invented for universal use by Dr. Ludovik Lazarus Zamenhof, a Polish physician. Its vocabulary consists of roots common to the chief European languages, with endings normalized.
1898 R. H. Geoghegan (*title*) The International Language 'Esperanto'. 1903 *Daily Chron.* 13 Jan. 5/2 Esperanto is, in fact, a vocal international shorthand. 1922 C. R. Buxton *In a Russian Village* xvi. 70 Petrov..called himself by the Esperanto name, 'Pecnego'.
Hence **Espera·ntic** *a.*, resembling Esperanto. **Espera·ntist,** one who is versed in Esperanto; also *attrib.*
1905 *Westm. Gaz.* 4 May 10/2 The Congress of Esperantists. 1909 M. L. Jones *Advantages of Esperanto* 2 To my Esperantist friends of The Yorkshire Federation. 1909 'Ian Hay' *Man's Man* vii, He first of all abused them with all the resources of an almost Esperantic vocabulary. 1922 C. R. Buxton *In a Russian Village* xvi. 70 He was a fluent Esperantist.

Essayi·stic, *a.* [f. Essay *sb.* + -ISTIC.] In the style of a literary essay.
1895 *Thinker* VIII. 404 The young pastor thinks himself obliged by the weight of custom to press much that is humanistic and essayistic into the ministrations of the truth.

Ess bouquet (e·sbukeⁱ·). [Short for *essence de bouquet*.] The trade name of a perfume.
1855 Piesse *Art of Perfumery* 118 Ess Bouquet...A mere contraction of 'essence' of bouquet. 1892 *Askinson's Perfumes* 175 The title Ess. Bouquet is an abbreviation of the full name given above [*i.e.* Essence des Bouquets]. 1905 *Westm. Gaz.* 8 Aug. 10/1 Queen Alexandra..has recently abandoned her favourite Ess Bouquet to some extent and taken to Sweet Pea. 1920 *Deite's Soap-making* (ed. 2) 222 'Ess-Bouquet' Soap.

Esse. Add: 2. b. Used in recent times in the sense of 'essential being or nature', esp. in contrast with *bene esse.*
1899 H. P. Hughes in *Daily News* 21 Oct. 7/1 So long as your clergy believe that Episcopacy is essential not only to the bene esse, but to the esse of the Church. 1920 *The Life of Faith* 23 June 619/2 The great missionary meeting on the Saturday morning..is not the *esse* of the movement. 1929 I. M. Clark *Ch. Discip. in Scot.* 208 Some form of law will be necessary to regulate her [*sc.* the Church's] life and protect that distinctive character which is her *esse*.

Essence, *sb.* Add: 8. *Of the essence of* (orig. legal): indispensable to. (Cf. F. *de l'essence de*.)
1873 *Act* 36 & 37 *Vict.* c. 66 § 25 (7) Stipulations..as to time or otherwise, which would not before the passing of this Act have been deemed to be or to have become of the essence of such contracts in a Court of Equity. 1931 *Morn. Post* 21 Aug. 8/2 While time is of the essence of the contract to retrieve the situation, discussion still proceeds.
11. **essence-peddler** *U.S.*, a skunk.
1850 *Knickerbocker Mag.* Apr. 361 It is a vulgar mistake that the porcupine has the faculty of darting his quills to a distance, as the essence-peddler has of scattering his aromatic wares. 1862 Lowell *Biglow P.* Ser. II. iii. 292 With means about 'em (Like essence-peddlers) thet 'll make folks long to be without 'em. 1890 Mrs. Custer *Following Guidon* xiv. 200 As soon as that essence-peddler saw fit to move on, the major-general commanding would issue his order to march.

Essentialize (ĕse·nʃăləiz), *v.* Delete † and add: In recent use: To raise to essential character, express the essential form of.
1913 *Westm. Gaz.* 22 Feb. 5/1 Its difficulties and restrictions, instead of essentialising his thought, have frustrated it. 1922 *Times Lit. Suppl.* 5 Jan. 10/1 A poet [*sc.* Dante] in whom the manifold passions and cultural movements of his time were essentialized and ennobled into the highest poetical utterance. 1923 *Glasgow Herald* 19 Apr. 4 The essentialising flame of Rembrandt's genius. 1930 Nan Shepherd *Weatherhouse* x. 181 Garry went drunk to bed, but not with whiskey. Again he had seen life essentialised.

Essenwood (e·sənwud). [Partial transl. of S. Afr. Du. *eschenhout*, f. Du. *esch* ash + *hout* wood.] (*a*) The South African ash, *Ekebergia capensis*; (*b*) Cape mahogany, *Trichilia emetica.*
1910 J. Buchan *Prester John* vi, We took a path up the Berg among groves of stinkwood and essenwood.

Essive (e·siv). [ad. Finn. *essiivi*, f. L. Esse, with termination ad. L. *-īvus*.] The designation of one of the fifteen cases of the Finnish noun, expressing a continuous state of being, existence in a specified state or capacity.
1890 C. N. E. Eliot *Finnish Gram.* 22 The essive.. expresses a state of being regarded as continuous. *Ibid.* 23 The suffix *-na*, called here essive. 1905 Jespersen *Hist. Engl. Lang.* 5 Essive, indicating the state in which anybody or anything is.

Establishable, *a.* Delete † *Obs.* and add:
1918 *Hist. Amer. Lit.* II. III. i. 259 The facts of his biography which are well established or establishable.

Estamin. Add: Also spelled **estamene**, as the name of a woollen cloth for dresses.
1862 *Catal. Internat. Exhib., Brit.* II. No. 4019. 1897 *Daily News* 8 Apr. 8/5 Estamene serges with their diagonal ribs or plain woolly surface.

Estampage (ĕstæ·mpĕdʒ, ‖estanpāʒ). *Archæol.* [Fr., f. *estamper* to stamp.] A squeeze or impression on paper of an inscription.
1887 *Academy* 24 Dec. 427/3, I made complete estampages.. of the Asoka inscription at Kālsi. 1888 J. Burgess *Epigraphia Indica* I. 1 Methods of taking direct inked impressions from stone, also, have been devised; and *estampages* can thus be taken, having the advantages of presenting a direct reading of the inscription on the inked face and a mould from it on the back, so that the slightest scratch on the stone is retained on a carefully-taken impression. 1903 Wickremasinghe *Epigraphia Zeylanica* I. p. iii, From these estampages..it was arranged that I should edit the texts for publication. As to the scrupulous care taken in the preparation of ink-estampages there need not be the slightest doubt.

Estate, *sb.* Add:
14. *attrib.* and *Comb.*: **estate agent,** one who acts as steward or manager of a landed estate; one who conducts business in the sale of houses and land; hence **estate agency**; **estate duty,** a graduated charge levied by the State on real or personal property at the death of the owner.
1912 *Estate Agents, Archit. & Surveyors* 5 The *Estate Agency profession. 1880 *Harper's Mag.* Sept. 565 '*Estate agent?' he next asked. 1884 *The 'Estate Agent'* 3 House and Estate Agents. 1886 S. W. Mitchell *R. Blake* xx. (1895) 188 It seems to her natural that an unknown Yankee estate-agent should wish to marry a woman of assured social place. 1894 *Act* 57 & 58 *Vict.* c. 30 § 1 There shall be levied..upon the principal value..of all property real or personal..which passes on the death of such person a duty called '*estate duty' at the graduated rates hereinafter mentioned. 1896 *Act* 59 & 60 *Vict.* c. 28 § 16 The estate duty payable in respect of any annuity.

Estatification (ĕstæ̆tifikēⁱ·ʃən). [f. Estate *sb.* + -FICATION.] The integration of separate property interests into a common estate. So **Esta·tify** *v. trans.* [-FY], **Esta·tified** *ppl. a.*
1921 H. C. Dowdall in *Law Q. Rev.* XXXVII. 167 It would solve many difficulties of legal theory..if in some circumstances thought were directed more to the estatification of interests and less to the incorporation of persons. 1926 *Ibid.* XLII. 466 When you and I..each invest £100 in the G.W.R...we estatify our interests in our £100 in the estate of the G.W.R., in which we then have an interest; and when I incorporate my private business..I estatify my business in a separate estate distinct from the rest of my property. 1930 — *Estatification* 36 A group of estatified interests governed by the company.

Esteemed, *a.* Add: Much in vogue as a complimentary epithet in commercial correspondence.
1903 *Daily Chron.* 25 Feb. 7/2 Sir, yours of even date to hand. If you can make it convenient, we should be glad if you could come on Wednesday morning to try on your esteemed favour.

Ester (e·stəɹ). *Chem.* [Invented by the German chemist L. Gmelin.] A compound ether derived from an oxygenated acid.
[1852 Watts tr. *Gmelin's Hand-bk. Chem.* VII. 190 *Ethers du troisième genre.* I formerly distinguished these compounds by the name of Naphthas produced by oxygen-acids (*Naphthen durch Sauers[t]offsäuren erzeugt*); but I now propose for them the term *Ester*.] *Ibid.* 215 Compound Ethers formed by Oxygen-acids (Ester). 1889 Muir & Morley *Watts' Dict. Chem.* II. 466 A compound ether (or ester) is a hydrogen salt in which the typical hydrogen has been displaced by an alkyl. 1899 E. F. Smith tr. *V. von Richter's Org. Chem.* 139 Just as salts result from the union of metallic hydroxides with acids, so esters are formed by the combination of alcohols with acids. 1906 *Practitioner* Nov. 593 The rapidly fermentable fruit and malt sugars, esters, and higher alcohols.
attrib. 1907 *Jrnl. Chem. Soc.* XCII. I. 383 Ester-Acids of Sulphur-substituted Carbonic Acids with Aliphatic Hydroxy-Acids. 1921 *Jrnl. Soc. Dyers & Colourists* XXXVII. 268/1 Acetyl silk, the new ester-silk.
Hence **E·sterify** *v.* [-FY], to convert, or be converted, into an ester. **E:sterifica·tion,** the process of forming an ester; the conversion of an acid into its ester. Also **E·sterize** *v.*, **E:steriza·tion.**
1898 *Nature* 6 Jan. 239/1 The authors have made experiments on the esterification of many cinnamic acids. 1902 *Rep. Brit. Assoc.* (1903) 586 The rate of esterification of methyl hydrogen succinate. 1907 *Practitioner* June 864 Arhovin..is a product of diphenylamin and the esterified thymol-benzoic acid. 1920 Cross & Bevan *Paper-Making* 27 Esterifying reagents.

Esth (esþ), *a.* and *sb.* [G. *Esth, Ehst.*] = next.
1868 S. Baring-Gould in *Fraser's Mag.* LXXVIII. 535/1 The Esths..speak a language closely allied to the Finnish. *Ibid.* 536/1 The poem was published in Esth, with a translation into German. *Ibid.* 542/2 Turja is the Esth name for Norway. 1910 *Encycl. Brit.* IX. 798/1 The Esths, Ehsts or Esthonians.

Esthonian (esþōu·niăn), *a.* and *sb.* Also **Estonian.** [f. mod.L. *Est(h)onia* (f. *Esth, after *Saxonia*, etc.) + -AN.]
A. *adj.* Of or belonging to Esthonia (native name Eesti), now an independent Baltic republic, stretching along the south coast of the Gulf of Finland. B. *sb.* A native of Esthonia. Also, the native language (akin to Finnish).
1795 *Varieties of Literature* I. 23 Esthonian poetry. *Ibid.*, The Esthonians..have an extremely soft, delicate, and tender articulation. 1842 [Lady Eastlake] *Resid. Shores Baltic* II. xvi. 62 Nothing can exceed the hospitality of the Estonians. 1863 R. G. Latham *Nationalities of Europe* I. 129 *Ma*, in Estonian, means *land*. *Ibid.* 132 The Estonian instrument is the harp. 1874 A. H. Sayce *Princ. Compar. Philol.* 322 *note*, *Wanna Issi* in Esthonian means 'the old father'. 1895 W. F. Kirby *Hero of Esthonia* I. p. xvi, The Finns, the Esthonians, and the Lapps..speak very similar languages. 1925 O. Rutter *New Baltic States* xi. 199 Estonian folklore owes something to the Finnish.

Estrada (estrā·da). [Pg.:—L. *strāta* (see Street).] In the Brazilian rubber trade, a winding path or road connecting a series of trees. Also in Fr. form **Estrade.**
1906 *Westm. Gaz.* 12 July 9/3 The estradas (or roads) which are being worked produce at least 250 kilos of rubber per harvest. 1913 R. H. Lock *Rubber* 20 [Brazil] To each seringueiro or collector are assigned from 100 to 150 trees, which are connected by a winding path, or *estrade*, cut through the undergrowth...Beginning at sunrise the seringueiro makes two rounds of his estrade. 1921 *Glasgow Herald* 3 May 10 From one estrada in six months about one ton of rubber may be obtained.

Estray, *a.* (Later U.S. examples.)
1876 *Rep. Vermont Board Agric.* III. 426 Many..of these new varieties of grain are *not* new...They are old varieties estray..from remote quarters..of the globe. 1889 *Harper's Mag.* June 138/2 A farmer living near a middle Georgia town, one day found an estray cow in his pasture.

Estufa. *U.S.* (Earlier examples.)
1844 J. J. Webb *Memoirs* 32 The old men who..directed the ceremonious worship of the Indians in the Estufa. 1845 J. Gregg *Commerce of Prairies* I. 271, I have myself descended into the famous *estufas* or subterranean vaults.

Etærio (ētĭ·rio). *Bot.* = Hetærio.
1844 Lindley *Elem. Bot.* Gloss., *Etaerio, Etairium* (adj. *Etairionar*). Such an aggregate fruit as that of the Ranunculus or Strawberry. 1861 Bentley *Man. Bot.* 316 When the achænia borne by a single flower are so numerous that they form more than a single whorl or series, they constitute collectively an *etærio*. 1896 *Henslow's Wild Flowers* 102 The cluster of drupels is called an etaerio.

Etager, -ier, U.S. ff. Étagère.
1851 C. Cist *Cincinnati* 204 Fancy dressing bureaus.. corner etagers with closets. 1859 in *Chicago Tribune* 11 Oct. (1929) VIII. 1, I am crazy to have..an etagier like Mrs. Neef's.

Étalage (etalāʒ). [Fr., f. *étaler* to display.] Display.
1900 *Daily News* 4 Sept. 4/3 A constant étalage of jewellery. 1925 *Blackw. Mag.* Oct. 493/2 The *étalage* in the window betrayed a small grocer's shop.

Eta palm. Variant of Ita-palm.
1866 G. W. Bennett *Illustr. Hist. Brit. Guiana* 228 The Eta Palm (*Mauritia flexuosa*) is a beautiful tree and is adored by the Indians for the numerous uses to which it can be applied.

Eta patch. *Aeronautics.* See quots.
1918 W. E. Dommett *Dict. Aircraft* 25 *Goosefoot*, a method of attaching the rigging on the envelope, often called an 'Eta Patch'. 1919 W. B. Faraday *Gloss. Aeronaut. Terms* 57 *Eta Patch*, a means of attaching rigging to the envelope consisting of a large fan-shaped patch made up of several thicknesses of fabric and reinforced with webbing bands and terminating in a metal ring. [1921 L. F. Plugge *Gloss. Aeronaut. Terms* 87 Vient du nom du dirigeable anglais 'Eta' où cette pièce fut utilisé pour la première fois.]

Étatisme (etatizm). [Fr., f. *état* State + *-isme* -ISM.] Extreme development of the power of the State over the individual citizen.
1923 *Contemp. Rev.* Aug. 195 What one might almost call the fetishism of the State, an extreme form of *étatisme*. 1926 *Spectator* 2 July 6/2 That hideous thing which later the French called *Étatisme* produced a social and political atmosphere in which a free man could hardly breathe. *Ibid.* 24 July 122/2 It must not be thought that we should like to see the British spirit of individual liberty subjected to any such trial of extreme *étatisme*.

Et cetera. 2. a. *attrib.* Add quots.:
1898 *Daily News* 15 July 6/2 Colonial affairs..formed a sort of etcetera department of the War Office. 1900 *Ibid.* 23 May 6/3 The nickname, Etcetera Department, sometimes given to the English Home Office.

Eternality (ītəɹnæ·liti). Delete † *Obs.* and add:
1926 A. N. Whitehead *Science & Mod. World* 121 Every scheme for the analysis of nature has to face these two facts, change and endurance. There is yet a third fact to be placed by it, *eternality*, I will call it.

Eternally, *adv.* 2. b. (Later U.S. example.)
1850 W. R. Ryan *Upper & Lower California* I. 310 If you'll sell it me..I'll be etarnally obliged to you.

Etherical (iþe·rikăl), *a.* Delete † *Obs.* and add quot. (which refers to Ether 5).
1920 *Conquest* May 317/2 The plant..responds to different rays of the vast etherical spectrum, from the extreme ultra-violet to the longest wireless electrical waves.

Etherism. Add: 2. Addiction to taking ether; cf. next, 2.
1888 N. Kerr *Inebriety* 108 Etherism is the antipodes of opiumism.

Etherist (ī·þĕrist). [-IST.]
1. One who administers ether to a patient.
1884 Sir H. Thompson *Tumours of Bladder* 25 If the etherist permits the patient any power of resisting with the abdominal muscles, the effort is hopeless.
2. One who is addicted to taking ether as a stimulant or intoxicant.
1888 N. Kerr *Inebriety* 109 At first he took chloral and opium, then he devoted himself to ether, and has been an etherist for some years.

Etheromania (īþĕromēⁱ·niă). *Path.* [f. Ether (Gr. αἰθήρ, αἰθέρος) + -MANIA.] A morbid addiction to the consumption of ether as a stimulant or intoxicant. So **E:theroma·niac,** an ether addict.
1889 N. Kerr *Inebriety* (ed. 2) 122 Etheromania has been a contributory cause of insanity in cases treated at asylums in the North of Ireland. 1894 *Ibid.* (ed. 3) 138 A gentleman aged 35 had been an etheromaniac for three years. 1909 *Westm. Gaz.* 13 Feb. 14/3 Etheromania is largely on the increase in South-west Russia.

Ethicality (eþikæ·liti). [-ITY.] Right doing according to customary standards, as opposed to the morality of the individual conscience.
1889 J. H. Stirling *Philos. & Theol.* (1890) 90 What immediately presented itself to him [*sc.* Socrates] was, as we may term it, the ethicality of the past, which, shaken in the present, promised but poorly for the future. So it was, in his hands, that ethicality became morality.

Ethicism (e·þisiz'm). [-ISM.] Devotion to ethics or ethical ideals; tendency to moralize.
1895 W. D. Howells in *Harper's Mag.* Nov. 867/2 Their art..was marred by the intense ethicism that pervaded the New England mind for two hundred years. 1900 F. Harrison in *Daily News* 12 Nov. 7/4 A scientific theory of social duty,..ethicism founded on a solid and comprehensive science of man. 1908 *Mod. Philol.* V. 623 This means that he ..rejected ethicism, declamation, narration, and description.

Ethicist. Add quots. (Sometimes = one who supports morality or ethics in opposition to religion.)
1891 *Monist* I. 556 A scientific ethicist has to proceed like any other naturalist. 1905 *Daily Chron.* 29 Nov. 3/3 Able to make their understanding 'issue in act,' as the Oxford ethicists used to say. 1907 H. Begbie *Vigil* xix. 307 He would play the part of ethicist and point people to the highest example of human perfection. 1908 *Lit. Guide* 1 Aug. 121/1 A Rationalist or an Ethicist can seldom get credit for what he does, however good his intentions.

Ethico-. Add: **E:thico-so·cial.**
1905 *Spectator* Lit. Suppl. 28 Jan. 119/1 Modern ethico-social guides, such as Stevenson, Whitman, and Maeterlinck. 1920 *Red Triangle* May 352/2 Every Church is trying to overcome every danger which is trying to destroy its ethico-social being. 1924 W. B. Selbie *Psychol. Relig.* 102 The social element in these early forms of ritual..points to a tribal consciousness which has in it at least the beginnings of an ethico-social outlook.

Ethiopian, *a.* and *sb.* Add: A. 1. c. *Ethiopian sour gourd* = Baobab.
1640– [see *sour gourd*, Sour *a.* 10].

Ethiopianism (īþiōu·piăniz'm). [-ISM.] A movement or propaganda in favour of 'Africa for the Africans'.
1906 *Daily Chron.* 13 Feb. 5/4 The rising in Natal is now officially declared..to be the result of the teaching of Ethiopianism, namely 'South Africa for the Black races'. 1910 J. Buchan *Prester John* vii. 131 It is what they call 'Ethiopianism', and American negroes are the chief apostles.

Ethnic, *a.* and *sb.* B. *sb.* Add:
2. *Greek Antiq.* An epithet denoting nationality, derived from or corresponding to the name of a people or city [= ἐθνικόν (Steph. Byz.)]. Also gen.
1828 Cramer *Anc. Greece* III. Index, The Greek ethnic of each town or place has been subjoined where there was authority for it. 1902 D. G. Hogarth *Nearer East* 194 Where the 'Arab' (to use the ethnic widely) lives under conditions similar to the Greek, he resembles him. 1921 C. T. Seltman *Temple Coins Olymp.* 103 The dies..upon which the full ethnic ΓΑΛΕΙΩΝ appears. 1921 *Brit. Mus. Return* 79 The ethnics of Damastium and Pelagia.

Ethology. Add:
4. *Zool.* The branch of Natural History which deals with an animal's actions and habits, its reaction to its environment. [Gr. ἦθος nature or disposition (of animals); in pl., customs, haunts.]
1897 Parker & Haswell *Zool.* I. 9 The whole question of the relation of the organism to its environment gives us a final and most important branch of Natural History which has been called Ethology or Bionomics. 1910 W. M. Wheeler *Ants* 124 Their ethology, that is, their functional aspect (physiology and psychology).

Etiquettical (etike·tikăl), *a.* [-ICAL.] Pertaining to etiquette.
1838 Miss Pardoe *River & Desert* II. 33 Death..has resumed its etiquettical observances. 1887 Mrs. Custer *Tenting on Plains* (1893) 42 But it was too much for his etiquettical instincts. 1900 G. Swift *Somerley* 107 We shouted directions at one another, and, in the interest of the moment, forgot the 'Miss' and 'Mr.' and other etiquettical matters.

Eton (ī·t'n). The name of a college, the largest of the ancient public schools, founded by Henry VI on the Thames opposite Windsor. a. *Eton blue*, a light blue adopted as the school colour.
1883 J. Brinsley-Richards *7 Yrs. at Eton* 306 A birch tied with Eton blue ribbon and rosettes. 1899 T. M. Ellis *Three Cat's-Eye Rings* 93 Looking at her wonderingly from his wide Eton-blue eyes. 1899 *Captain* II. 14/2 A very gorgeous equipage, with much Eton blue about it. 1908 *Daily Chron.* 4 Apr. 4/6 Philips..rushed off to a neighbouring haberdasher's, and demanded a piece of Eton blue ribbon or silk.
b. *Eton collar*: a broad stiff white collar worn outside the jacket by Eton boys (and many others); also, a similar collar as part of a woman's costume.
1887 *Army & Navy Co-op. Soc. Price List* 1095 Boys' Collars and Cuffs. The Eton. 1895 *Ibid.* 1160 Boys' front with Eton collar. 1925 *Queen* 22 Apr. 11 Its prim Eton collar, its daintiness of finish with its jabot and cuffs of pleated lawn.
c. *Eton crop*, a fashion of cutting women's hair close to the head all over. Hence *Eton-cropped* ppl. adj.
1926 E. Wallace *Square Emerald* 9 The masculinity of the powerful face was emphasized by the grey hair cut close in an Eton crop. 1927 A. Monkhouse *Alfred the Great* 248 Maud was a trim, competent schoolgirl, long-legged, Eton-cropped. 1930 *Punch* 29 Jan. 126/1 A young thing whose essential plainness is emphasised rather than concealed by an Eton crop.
d. *Eton jacket*: a short black broadcloth jacket, with an open front and broad lapels, pointed at the back and cut square at the hips, worn by boys at Eton (and elsewhere); also, a garment of similar cut worn by women. Hence *Eton-jacketed* ppl. adj. *Eton suit*: a boys' suit consisting of Eton jacket with trousers and waistcoat; also, a women's suit of skirt and front with similarly cut jacket. Often simply *Eton* and in pl.
1881 *Punch* 15 Oct. 170/3 The coat having no tails, could serve as an Eton jacket to a growing youth. 1882 'F. Anstey' *Vice Versâ* ii, Two small boys..in Eton jackets and broad white collars. 1892 *Queen* 28 May 888 'With a stout heart', published in 1874,..delighted an Eton-jacketed public. 1894 *Million* V. 377/2 Among the ladies riding was Lady —, in an Eton suit and blue sailor hat. 1925 *Blackw. Mag.* July 80/2 The Eton jacket (or 'tum-coat') was reserved for Sundays.
1899 *Westm. Gaz.* 6 Jan. 3/2 The natty little Eton that in the South so often replaces the coat in the *costume tailleur*. 1900 *Daily News* 8 Sept. 6/3 Two-thirds of the smart dresses are now made with an Eton or bolero over a more or less ornamental front. 1900 *Captain* III. 405/2 The spectacle of Jim in Fourth Form Etons would have been too entrancing a sight.

Étrenne (etrɛn). [Fr., older *estreine*:—L. *strena.*] A New Year's gift.
1834 K. H. Digby *Mores Cath.* v. vii. 234 The faithful were forbidden to give etrennes. 1880 Disraeli in Buckle *Life* (1920) VI. 505 Osborne has sent me, as an *étrenne* a most beautiful book. 1883 *Sat. Rev.* 24 Mar. 377/1 Mme. de Witt's magnificent volume belongs to the class of *étrennes*.

Etruscology (itrɒskǫ·lŏdʒi). [f. L. *Etruscus* Etruscan + -LOGY.] The study of Etruscan history and antiquities.
1928 *Observer* 15 Apr. 12 There is also [at Perugia] a yearly course on Etruscology. *Ibid.* 17 June 12 Some recent admirably illustrated volumes [in German] on Etruscology. 1928 *Times* 7 June 12/3 The International Congress recently held at Florence demonstrated the great interest taken in the science of Etruscology.
Hence **Etrusco·logist,** one versed in Etruscology.
1894 *Athenæum* 24 Mar. 385/1 The chief interest and expectation of Tuscan archæologists and of all Etruscologists in Italy are turned to..Vetulonia.

Eucaine (yū·keⁱ,əin, -ēⁱ,in, yukēⁱ·n). *Pharm.* Also -in. [f. Eu-, after Cocaine.] A name for two compounds (eucaine A and B) used as local anæsthetics.
1896 *Chemist & Druggist* XLVIII. 597 Eucaine is employed like cocaine as a hypodermic solution of the hydrochloride. 1897 *Jrnl. Chem. Soc.* LXXII. I. 499 Eucaine,..whose chloride is used in commerce as a substitute for cocaine. 1907 *Practitioner* Apr. 473 Under eucaine, combined with a very little general anaesthetic, the abdomen was quickly opened.

Eucalypt. Delete *rare* and add:
1877 F. von Müller *Botanic Teachings* 7 (Morris s.v. *Gum*) The vernacular name of gum-trees for the eucalypts. 1880 Nutt *Palace Ind.* 11 Stems of the soaring Eucalypts that rise Four hundred friendly feet to glad blue skies. 1887 Moloney *Forestry W. Afr.* 228 A collection of fresh seeds of such Eucalypts as deserved trial. 1892 *Pall Mall Gaz.* 4 Oct. 2/3 The beautiful timber—the red and Huon pines, as well as the more utilitarian eucalypts (hard wood). 1893 D. C. Murray *Time's Revenges* vii, A forest of eucalypt closed in the band. 1898 *Queensland Year Bk.* 96 Great eucalypts spread their huge arms overhead.

Eucalyptian (yūkăli·ptiăn), *a.* (*sb.*) [See -IAN.] Belonging to the genus *Eucalyptus*. Also *sb.*, a tree of this genus; = prec. Also **Eucaly·ptic** *a.*
1870 Gordon *Bush Ballads* Ded. 8 The gnarl'd knotted trunks Eucalyptian. 1873 J. B. Stephens *Black Gin*, etc. 6 This eucalyptic cloisterdom. 1901 *Harper's Mag.* CII. 708/1 The huge, white-armed eucalyptians overhead.

Eucalyptus. Add: Popularly used as short for *eucalyptus oil*, an antiseptic and disinfectant.
1885 *Buck's Handbk. Med. Sci.* I. 262/2 Odor and expense serve to tell against eucalyptus preparations. 1888 *Brit. Med. Jrnl.* 21 Apr. 849 Eucalyptus acts chiefly on nerve centres. 1895 *Lancet* 3 Aug. 268 The soap is pleasantly medicated with 'sanitas' and eucalyptus. 1898 *Ibid.* 12 Nov. 1304/2, I made a mask of cotton-wool and soaked it with eucalyptus and olive oil.

Euchre, *sb.* Add: Also **euker.**
1. (U.S. examples.) Also *attrib.*
1841 *Southern Lit. Messenger* VII. 54/2 A month ere I embarked I lost at euker. 1850 L. H. Gerard *Wah-To-Yah* xix. (1927) 220, I thought of..the 'poker' an' 'euker' I'd played to rendevoo an' Fort William. *Ibid.* xx. 243 Jim Beckwith..found himself..at Greenhorn settlement, 'raking' the 'plews' from the less fortunate euchre and poker players.
2. (Earlier U.S. example.)
1876 B. Harte *G. Conroy* vi. ii, And where am I now? Echo answers 'where?' and passes for a euchre!

Euchre, *v.* Add: 2. *intr.* To play euchre.
1841 *Southern Lit. Messenger* VII. 54/2 Go down and drink your strong compounded potion, and euker in a warmer atmosphere.

Eucone (yū·koun), *a.* *Ent.* [f. Eu- + Cone *sb.*] Of the eyes of certain insects: Having a well-developed or true cone.
1885 S. J. Hickson in *Q. Jrnl. Microsc. Sci.* XXV. 230 The crystalline cone of the 'eucone eyes'. 1888 Rolleston & Jackson *Anim. Life* 502 The vitreous cells..are reduced to feeble remnants inclosing a solid crystalline cone composed of 2–5 parts, the eucone eyes of other Insecta...In pseudocone and eucone eyes the seven cells are grouped round a central axis.

Eucy·clic, *a.* *Bot.* [Eu-.] Cyclic with alternate isomerous whorls.
1878 Henfrey *Elem. Bot.* (ed. 3) 91 A flower thus presenting all the whorls is called complete or eucyclic.

Eugenically (yudʒe·nikăli), *adv.* [f. Eugenic: see -ICALLY.] In regard to eugenics; from a eugenic point of view.
1912 *Q. Rev.* July 65 The propagation of the eugenically fit. 1922 *Edin. Rev.* July 46 It is eugenically bad, making early marriage impossible, or encouraging the dysgenic art of fortune-hunting. 1928 *Daily Express* 1 June 10/4 Wondering why he has not gone in for the great adventure. ..Is he eugenically unfit?

Eugenist (yū·dʒĭnist). [See Eugenic and -IST.] A student or advocate of eugenics.
1909 Saleeby *Parenthood* p. ix, Some years ago I ventured to coin the word eugenist, which is now the accepted term. 1921 W. R. Inge *Lay Thoughts* (1926) 247 Prudent eugenists are in no hurry to advocate legislation.
attrib. 1921 W. McDougall *Nat. Welfare* p. vii, This great gap in the eugenist argument. 1928 *Daily Express* 16 Jan. 8/7 Candidates for marriage..may be faced..with a searching Eugenist standard of physical fitness.

Eugeogenous (yūdʒi,ǫ·dʒĭnəs), *a.* [f. F. *eugéogène* (Thurmann 1849): see Eu- and -*GENOUS.] Of rock: That readily decomposes into good soil, as distinguished from *dysgeogenous.*
1863 J. G. Baker *North Yorkshire* 152 They are due south of the hills of the eugeogenous range and based upon their slope.

Euglenoid (yuglī·noid), *a.* (*sb.*) *Zool.* [f. mod.L. *Euglēna* (see def.: f. Eu- + Gr. γλήνη pupil of the eye) + -OID.] Resembling, akin to, or like that of, the *Euglena*, a genus of *Flagellata*. Also *sb.*, a member of the family *Euglenaceæ.*
1885 E. R. Lankester in *Encycl. Brit.* XIX. 852/2 The movements now become neither vibratile nor amœboid but definitely restrained, and are best described as 'euglenoid'. *Ibid.* 857/1 Euglenoidea...Fam. 6. Astasina. Colourless, metabolic, or stiff Euglenoids. 1888 Rolleston & Jackson *Anim. Life* 843 Chromatophores..are numerous, small, round, or oval in Euglenoids. 1906 *Cambr. Nat. Hist.* I. 124 *Euglena*..shows a peculiar wriggling motion, waves of transverse constriction passing along the body from end to end...Such motions are termed 'euglenoid'.

Eulachon, -an, variants of Oolakan.
1866 J. K. Lord *Naturalist in Vancouver Isl.* I. 88 A fish ..called by the natives *Eulachon* or Candle-fish. 1888 Goode *Amer. Fishes* 476 They [*sc.* trout] are taken in Frazer River at the time of the eulachon run, but they probably then ascend the river to feed upon the eulachon, and not for spawning purposes. 1889 *Century Dict.* s.v. *Candle-fish*, The fish is..used..for the manufacture of eulachon-oil, proposed as a substitute for cod-liver oil in medicine.

Eumerism (yū·mĕriz'm). *Biol.* [f. Gr. εὖ well (see Eu-) + μερισμός division into parts (see Merism).] The aggregation of like parts in a regular series in the formation of an organism. So **Eumeri·stic** *a.*, having the character of such an aggregation. **Eumerogenesis** (yū·mĕro,dʒe·nĕsis), the formation of an organism by successive production of like parts in a regular series; hence **Eu:merogene·tic** *a.*, marked by or resulting from eumerogenesis. **Eu·meromo:rph,** an organic form resulting from eumerogenesis; hence **Eu:meromo·rphic** *a.*, having the character of such a form. (Opposed to Dysmerism, Dysmeristic, etc.)
1881 E. R. Lankester in *Encycl. Brit.* XII. 554/2 An original unit like those which constitute the composite organism has freely budded, and repeated its own structure in the well-marked units which remain conjoined to form an arborescent or linear aggregate. This is 'eumerogenesis', and such aggregates may be termed eumeristic. *Ibid.* 555/1 Thus, using the terms eumeromorph and dysmeromorph, we have—(1) synthesized eumeromorph simulates normal dysmeromorph; (2) analysized dysmeromorph simulates normal eumeromorph.

Eunomian (yunōu·miăn), *sb.* (*a.*) *Ch. Hist.* [See -AN.] A follower of Eunomius, bishop of Cyzicus in the 4th century A.D., who developed the Arian heresy into the extreme form of anomœanism. Also as *adj.* Hence **Euno·mianism.**
c 1449 Pecock *Repr.* v. iii. 499 The sect of Acyanys and of Ennomynyarys [*sic*]. 1574 R. Bristow *Motives Cath. Faith* To Rdr. ¶iiij, Ye Aetians, the Eunomians, the Macedonians. 1607 T. Rogers *39 Art.* i. (1633) 6 The Eunomeans, and Tretheites. 1788 Gibbon *Decl. & F.* xli. IV. 205 Theodosius had been educated in the Eunomian heresy. 1880 E. Venables in *W. Smith's Dict. Chr. Biog.* II. 288 Eunomianism, as a cold, logical system, wanted the elements of vitality. 1893 W. M. Ramsay *Church in Empire* xviii. 448 Did the Eunomian differ from the Catholic only in point of doctrine?

Eunuchoid (yū·nŭkoid), *a.* (*sb.*) [See -OID.] Resembling, or characteristic of, a eunuch. Also as *sb.* Hence **Eu·nuchoidism.**
1906 *Rep. Brit. Assoc.* 703 (heading) Observations made on an 'Eunuchoid' Subject in the Cambridge Anatomy School. 1925 W. J. H. Sprott tr. *Kretschmer's Physique & Char.* 26 A growth in length which indicates eunuchoidism. *Ibid.* 73 Disposition of fat according to the eunuchoid plan. *Ibid.* 86 Schizophrenes and eunuchoids. 1928 *Cowdry's Spec. Cytology* 1231 Eunuchoid conditions.

Euonymin (yuǫ·nimin). *Pharm.* Also -ine. [Discovered by G. Romm. See -IN[1], -INE[5].] A bitter principle derived from *Euonymus atropurpureus.*
1878 *Dispensatory of U.S.* (ed. 14) 402. 1886 *Jrnl. Chem. Soc.* L. 72 The bark of *Euonymus europæus* contains no euonymin. 1898 *Rev. Brit. Pharm.* 19 There is neither footnote nor synonym to say it is Euonymin. 1910 *Practitioner* June 833 A hepatic stimulant, such as podophyllin, euonymin, rhubarb.

Eupad (yū·pæd). *Pharm.* [f. the initials of *E*dinburgh *U*niversity *P*athological *D*epartment (where the mixture was invented) with jocular reference to Eu- and Pad *sb.*[3], quasi 'good pad'.] A mixture of bleaching powder and powdered boric acid, used as an antiseptic dry dressing. It evolves hypochlorous acid.
1915 *Brit. Med. Jrnl.* II. 129/1. 1920 Martindale & Westcott *Extra Pharmacopœia* (ed. 17) I. 55.

Euphemizer (yū·fĭməizəɹ). [f. Euphemize *v.* + -ER[1].] One who speaks euphemistically.
1890 C. Martyn *Wendell Phillips* 186 He was the one outspoken man in a nation of euphemizers.

Euphonion, an early form of Euphonium.
1862 *Catal. Internat. Exhib., Brit.* II. No. 3377, An Euphonion or solo bass in B flat.

Euphratean (yufrē·tĭăn), *a.* [f. *Euphrates* + -AN.] Bordering on the river Euphrates.
1902 D. G. Hogarth *Nearer East* 220 Trade between east and west has deserted the painful Euphratean routes. *Ibid.* 222 The route taken by the Persian *haj*, after visiting the Euphratean shrines.

Euquinine (yū·kwinīn). *Pharm.* [See Eu-.] A white crystalline tasteless powder derived from quinine, for which it is sometimes used as a substitute.
1898 *Jrnl. Chem. Soc.* LXXIV. I. 282 Euquinine (quinine ethylic carbonate, $C_{20}H_{23}N_2O\text{-}O\text{-}COOEt$), is obtained by the action of ethylic chlorocarbonate on quinine. 1901 *Practitioner* Mar. 269 Euquinine—a derivative of quinine—is at present on its trial.

Eurafrican (yuəræ·frikăn), *a.* and *sb.* [f. *Europe* + *Africa* + -AN.]
1. *Anthrop.* Designation of a dark-skinned race which inhabited regions on both sides of the Mediterranean.
1899 A. H. Keane *Man: Past & Present* 444 The right of citizenship is to be withdrawn from such time-honoured names as 'Hamitic', 'Semitic'..in favour of 'Mediterranean', 'Eurafrican', and other upstarts. 1910 J. L. Myres in *Encycl. Brit.* XIV. 217/1 Whether this type is more conveniently designated by the word *Iberian*, or by some other name ('Eur-african', 'Mediterranean', &c.). 1928 V. G. Childe *Most Anc. East* ii. 39 The so-called Eurafrican, Mediterranean, or Brown race.
2. Designation of the 'Coloured People' of S. Africa, descendants of Hottentots and other natives with white admixture.
1927 W. M. Macmillan *Cape Colour Question* 283 All recent restrictive legislation, designed for the 'segregation' of the Natives, classes the 'Eurafricans' with the Europeans. 1927 *Times* (weekly ed.) 24 Nov. 586/1 The coloured or Eurafrican workers.

Eurasian, *a.* and *sb.* A. *adj.* 1. Add: Applied to a movement in Russia, since the revolution, which regards Russia in Europe and Asia as a distinct civilization. Also as *sb.* Hence **Eura·sianism.**
1923 Mirsky in *Contemp. Rev.* Aug. 197 Such are the Eurasians. They have, of course, nothing to do with those of the name in India...The pith of the Eurasian doctrine is that Russia is not part of Europe, nor of Asia either, but a world of itself...Eurasianism is a quite recent growth.

Eurhythmic, *a.* Add: B. *sb. pl.* A system of rhythmical bodily movements, *esp.* dancing exercises, with musical accompaniment, freq. used with an educational object. Hence **Eurhy·thmic(al** *adjs.*, **Eurythmi·cian, Eurhy·thmist.**
1915 A. S. Neill *Dominie's Log* v. (1918) 57, I recently read an illustrated article by (or on?) Jacques Dalcroze, the inventor of the method, and the founder of the Eurhythmics School near Dresden. 1920 *Challenge* 21 May 44/3 In the Eurythmics of M. Jacques Dalcroze..the dancer expresses by improvized postures the emotions aroused by music. 1921 H. F. Rubinstein tr. *Jaques-Dalcroze's Rhythm, Music & Educ.* 195 The art of the Eurhythmist is self-sufficient. *Ibid.* 196 Eurhythmic exercises enable the individual to feel and express music corporally. *Ibid.* 206 Eurhythmicians watching exercises performed by fellow-students. 1923 *Daily Mail* 17 Mar. 10 An eurhythmical display under the command of M. Jaques-Dalcroze. 1924 J. J. Findlay in V. Davis *Modern Teaching* (1928) 101 The eurythmist does not neglect or despise the body; he accepts the counsel of the trainer, but he leads his pupils to fix their attention on rhythmic values. 1925 C. Fox *Educat. Psychol.* 84 Dancing and eurhythmics in school.

Europasian (yūərop,ēⁱ·ʃăn), *a.* and *sb.* [f. *Europe* + *Asia* + -AN.] = *Eurasian.
1928 (*title*) Russia in Resurrection..By an English Europasian. *Ibid.* 177 The Europasian Movement. 1930 *Times Lit. Suppl.* 4 Sept. 703/1 'Europasian' sympathizers. 1931 *Ibid.* 8 Jan. 18/3 Russia is again turning to the East (a theory ..in which the..'Europasians' find cause for rejoicing).

European, *a.* 1. Add:
European plan (U.S.), the method or practice at a hotel of charging for lodging and service without inclusion of meals. Contrasted with *American plan.*
1847 *Tom Pepper* I. 201 Her establishment was conducted on the 'European plan', and silver forks and finger-glasses were things of course. 1889 *Harper's Mag.* Aug. 484/3 Is this hotel on the European plan?

Europe·anly, *adv. rare.* [-LY[2].] In a European way or style.
1902 S. Lane-Poole *Story of Cairo* i. 27 Mean and uneven offices and tenements, neither Europeanly regular nor Orientally picturesque.

Eurygnathism (yūəri·gnăþiz'm). [See -ISM.] Eurygnathous character.
1890 H. Ellis *Criminal* iii. 52 Microcephaly of the frontal region,..eurigmatism [*sic*; ed. 3 (1901) so eurignathism]. 1911 *Encycl. Brit.* XXII. 424/2 Eurygnathism..is the lateral projection of jaw bones so characteristic of the Mongolic races.

Euryscope (yūə·riskoup). *Photog.* [f. Gr. εὐρύς broad + -SCOPE.] A kind of wide-angle lens.
1890 W. E. Woodbury *Encycl. Photogr.* 277. 1892 *Photogr. Ann.* II. p. v, The Rapidity of this series is equal to that of the Rapid Euryscopes. 1902 *Encycl. Brit.* XXXI. 694/2 Voigtländer's 'Euryscopes'..are..still largely in use.

Eusol (yū·sǫl). *Pharm.* [f. initial letters of *E*dinburgh *U*niversity *sol*ution: cf. *Eupad.] A solution of free hypochlorous acid, prepared from bleaching powder, used as an antiseptic and bactericide.
1915 *Brit. Med. Jrnl.* II. 129/1. 1920 Martindale & Westcott *Extra Pharmacopœia* (ed. 17) I. 52 Eusol has been most extensively used to wounds.

Eustatic (yustæ·tik), *a.* *Geol.* and *Physiogr.* [ad. G. *eustatisch*; see Eu- and Static *a.*] Of a land area: Not subject to depression or elevation; thoroughly established.
1906 tr. *E. Suess' Face of Earth* II. 538.

Euthysymmetrical, a. Cryst.

Euxanthic, a.

Euxanthone.

Evacuation.

Evangeliar (ēvanǵẽliar). Also **Evangeliary** (-iäri) and in l. form.

Even, a.

Even, v.

Evening, sb.

Evener.

Eventualize (vē'ntiuəlăiz), v.

Even, adv.

Ever, adv.

Everglade. U.S.

Everlasting.

Evertor (īvŏ'ətŏɹ). Anat.

Every, a.

Everydayness.

Everyman (e'vriman).

Everywhere, adv.

Evolute (e'vŏliut), v. intr.

Evolutionally (e·vŏliū'ʃŏnali), adv.

Evolve, v.

Ennise (ī'nəiz). v.

or hear the like?

Exarch (e'ksäk), sb. Bot.

Exarchate (e'ksäkeit, eksä'ʀkeit).

Ex-, prefix.

Exarch, sb.

Excavate, v.

Excavator.

Exceed, v.

Excelsin (ekse'lsin). Chem.

Exceptor (ekse'ptŏɹ). Delete †Obs. and add.

Excess, sb.

Exchange, sb.

Excise, sb.

Exciter.

Excise, v.

Exclusive, a. and sb.

Exempt, ppl. a. and sb.

Exemption.

Exercise, sb.

Exhibit, v.

Exhibition.

In London.

Exes (e'ksiz). sb. pl.

Excelsior (ekse'lsiŏɹ).

Excursion, sb.

Excuse, sb.

Ex gratia (eks grē'ʃiă).

Exhaust, sb.

Executive, a. and sb.

Exemplification.

Excelsior.

Exhibitionism (eksibi'ʃaniz'm). [f. Exhibition + -ism.]

Exhibitionist. Delete rare and add.

Exhorter, sb.

Ex hypothesi (eks həipŏ'ʈhĕsi), [mod.L.]

Exilarch (e'gzilăk). Jewish Hist.

Exit, sb.

Exite (e'ksit), Gram.

Exlex (e'ksleks), a.

Ex-libris. Delete rare and add.

Ex-libristic, a.

Exmeridian (eksmerī'diăn), a.

Exmoor (e'ksmuɹ, -mɔɹ).

particular breeds of ponies and sheep which it produces.

Exocrine (e'ksŏkrəin), a.

Ex officio.

Exogenous, a.

the continent, so far as through marine waters, may be said to have been endogenous.

Exonian (egzōu'niăn). [f. L. Exonia Exeter: see -IAN.]

Exotherm (e'ksŏþŏɹm). Chem.

Exothermous, a.

Exotospore (e'ksŏtŏspɔɹ). Zool.

Expanding, ppl. a.

Expansion, sb.

Expansional (ekspæ'nʃŏnăl), a.

Expansionism (ekspæ'nʃŏniz'm). Add quots.

Expansionist. Add quots.

Explain, v.

Expansional, a.

Expectant, ppl. a.

Expenditor (ekspe'nditŏɹ).

Romney Marsh.

Experience, sb.

Experience, v.

Exotherm, Chem.

Experient, a. and sb.

Experiment, sb.

Experiment, v.

Experimentee. Delete rare and add.

Expertise (ekspŏɹtī'z).

Expert, sb.

Expertism (e'kspŏɹtiz'm). Delete nonce-wd.

Explain, v.

Explicand (ekspliĭkæ'nd).

Explicit, adv.

Explosive, a. and sb.

Explanatively, adv.

Explicable, a.

Explicit, a.

Exemplification.

Explanatory.

Explicand.

Explore, v.

Exploring, ppl. a.

Explosibility (eksplŏuzibi'liti).

Explosion.

Explosive, a. and sb.

Exponentially, adv.

Exponentiation.

Expose (ekspŏu'z), sb.

Expository, a.

Expositorially, adv.

Expostulatory.

Exposure.

Exposure, v.

Express, sb.

Express, sb.

C. sb.1 3. U.S. (Earlier examples.)
1839 Knickerbocker Mag. XIII. 24 Means for defraying the expenses of express-men. 1844 D. Lee & Frost Ten Yrs. Oregon xix. 224 The Hudson Bay Company's Express..is a communication by which despatches are sent annually from Vancouver to Canada. 1848 Congress. Globe 23 June 870/1 The present arrangement was diverting [public money] into the pockets of private expresses. 1859 R. H. Dana Bef. Mast, Twenty-four Yrs. After (1869) 380 The dock..and the streets..were densely crowded with express-wagons and hand-carts to take luggage.

c. **express agent**, the agent of an express company; **express car**, a railway carriage for conveying packages, etc., sent by express.
1867–8 Trans. Ill. Agric. Soc. VII. 522 They can be handled as roughly, almost, as these *express agents handle boxes. 1873 Trans. Dep. Agric. Ill. X. 247 That is, for the railroads to take charge of all the goods that consignor does not desire to be delivered by the express agents. 1891 E. S. Ellis Check No. 2134 i. 5 On the first run made by Arthur Helmuth, in place of the regular express agent and baggage master. 1910 J. Hart Vigilante Girl xxvii. 376 This was the room of the man who filled the manifold offices of station-master, ticket-agent, express-agent. 1871 Schele de Vere Americanisms (1872) 357 Next to the locomotive comes another feature peculiar to American trains—the *express-car. 1879 F. R. Stockton Rudder Grange vii. 76 My package was wheeled to the express-car.

Express, v.1 U.S. (See after Express sb.1; earlier and later examples.)
1716 Jrnls. Ho. Repr. Mass. I. 81 Isaac Winslow Esq., brought down..several letters that had been expressed to his Honour the Lieut. Governour from the Eastward. 1892 Stevenson & Osbourne Wrecker x, Did he express his baggage, ma'am? asked Pinkerton. 1903 N. Y. Even. Post 22 Sept. 2 The trunks were expressed to Sullivan County, where the honeymoon was to be.

b. To send by express delivery (see Express a. 4 d).
1899 Brit. Postal Guide Jan. 18 A Letter may be posted in any Letter Box, from which it will be collected by a Postman and be expressed on reaching the proper office. 1930 Daily Express 6 Nov. 1/1, I telephoned to my mother to express my passport to me at Croydon.

Hence **Expre·ssed** ppl. a.2 U.S., sent by express.
1909 Gene Stratton-Porter Girl of Limberlost xi. 218 In an expressed crate was a fine curly-maple dressing table.

Expressionable (ėkspre·ʃənăb'l), a. [f. Expression + -able.] Capable of showing expression.
1892 Blackw. Mag. CLI. 43/2 Mozart..discovered the soul-reaching and expressionable capacity of instrumental music. 1908 Bram Stoker in Daily Chron. 15 Jan. 8/4 The mouth is an orator's mouth; clear cut, expressionable.

Expressionism (ėkspre·ʃəniz'm). [f. Expression + -ism.] The methods, style, or attitude of expressionists, esp. in artistic technique.
1923 MacGowan & Jones Continental Stagecraft iii. 27 A Symbolism that is far on the way towards Expressionism. Ibid. 31 Expressionism..is a violent storm of emotion beating up from the unconscious mind. 1924 A Dukes Youngest Drama 136 Realism and expressionism represent attitudes of mind and not uses of theatrical machinery. 1924 Anne D. Sedgwick Little French Girl II. iv. 132 Giles..felt that he could not adequately defend his theories, which rested upon an objection to the use of the body as a means of primitive expressionism. 1925 H. Carter New Spirit European Theatre 220 Expressionism is simply expression taking the form of a new technique for the purpose of giving the most intense effect..to the species of drama that expressed pre-war and war time insurrectionary tendencies. 1926 Rutter Evol. Mod. Art 112 The Expressionism of the Russo-Polish artist Wassily Kandinsky.

Expressionist. Add modern examples; now esp. in reference to artistic technique (see prec.).
1921 Galsworthy To Let I. i, They were all Expressionists now, he had heard, on the Continent. 1924 New Statesman 2 Aug. 494/2 Elmer Rice's play, The Adding Machine..has two or three expressionist scenes, but is for the most part not in the expressionist manner. 1927 Sunday Times 13 Feb. 6/3, I suggest that an expressionist setting would suit it down to the water's edge. 1927 Observer 11 Sept. 6 A cocaine romance written by one of the most gifted of those men who joined the band of expressionists early in the movement.

Expressionistic (ėkspreʃəni·stik), a. [f. Expressionist + -ic.] Of, pertaining to, or produced by expressionists; characterized by expressionism.
1921 Galsworthy To Let III. x, She had begun to exchange her Empire for her Expressionistic furniture. 1924 Glasgow Herald 17 July 4 An example of the expressionistic type of drama. 1927 Ibid. 6 Oct. 6 Careless, expressionistic young men. 1928 Observer 29 Jan. 15/4 His expressionistic ingenuity achieved many stimulating effects.

Expropriating (ekspróu·pri,ēɪtiŋ), ppl. a. [see -ing 2] Dispossessing, depriving of property.
1908 H. G. Wells First & Last Things 104 A class conflict between the expropriated Many and the expropriating Few. 1910 Daily Chron. 24 Mar. 4/3 The expropriating authority is in justice bound to appropriate such land for all time.

Expulsatory (ekspʊ·lsătəri), a. [f. L. expulsat-, -are (see Expulse v.) + -ory 2.] Of or pertaining to expulsion.
1910 Practitioner Mar. 406 When its [sc. the uterus'] muscular fabric is engaged in expulsatory efforts..pain of extreme intensity is endured.

Expulsion. Add: Also attrib., as expulsion order.
1905 Act 5 Edw. VII c. 13 § 3 The Secretary of State may ..make an order (in this Act referred to as an expulsion order) requiring an alien to leave the United Kingdom within a time fixed by the order, and thereafter to remain out of the United Kingdom.

Expunct (ekspʊ·ŋkt), v. Delete †Obs. and add:
1847 Madden Layamons Brut I. 127 Written at first eldade, and the a subsequently expuncted. Ibid. III. 460 The ancient scribes, who often in such cases expunct the superfluous letter. 1868 Skeat Havelok 21 note, The MS. has 'ig', but the g is expuncted. 1908 — in N. & Q. 10th Ser. IX. 116/1 The scribe first of all copied 'Ætheredes' as 'Atheredys',..and after that he..divided it as 'At beredys', and then, by expuncting h, produced 'At eredys'.

Exsiccator. Add: Also, a drying agent.
1892 Photogr. Ann. II. 78 Exsiccators and Drying Agents.

Exstulpate (e·kstʊlpēɪt), v. Zool. [f. ppl. stem of mod.L. *exstulpāre, representing G. ausstülpen to turn inside out.] trans. To extrude, push out, as an eversible papilla, or other process. Hence **Exstulpa·tion.**
1899 Cambr. Nat. Hist. VI. 256 The larva..possesses several finger-like pouches that can be exstulpated at the end of the body. Ibid. 363 There is a gland in the osmeterium, and as a result a strong odour is emitted when the exstulpation occurs.

Extend, v. 1. b. Add: esp. pass. and refl. of a horse: To exert itself to the full; to go 'all out'; so, of a runner, oarsman, etc.; hence gen. to put forth all one's efforts.
1856 'Stonehenge' Brit. Sports 332/1 The horse is made to extend himself. 1886 [in Dict.]. 1915 P. G. Wodehouse Something Fresh v, The Blandings chef had extended himself in honour of the house-party, and had produced a succession of dishes which, in happier days, Mr. Peters would have devoured eagerly. 1921 Baily's Mag. Jan. 3/2 The flying Pharmacie, who has not only won all the eight races in which she has taken part, but has never been really extended for a single stride. 1923 P. G. Wodehouse Inimitable Jeeves xiii, He delivered an address of twenty-six minutes by Claude's stop-watch. At a village wedding, mark you! What'll he do when he really extends himself! 1931 Morn. Post 25 Feb. 16/3 Corpus held their place at the Head of the River without being extended.

Extended, ppl. a. Add: 2. c. In Insurance (see quots.).
1911 Webster, Extended insurance, insurance for the full face of a policy on which payments are stopped, granted for an additional period in consideration of retaining part or all of the cash surrender value of the policy. 1925 Act 15 & 16 Geo. V c. 69 § 4 A further period thereafter ending on such date as the Minister may by order prescribe, not being a date later than the first day of the insurance year commencing next after the end of the aforesaid deficiency period (the aggregate of which two periods is in this section referred to as 'the extended period'). 1928 Britain's Industrial Future (Lib. Ind. Inq.) IV. xx. 278 Claimants to 'extended' benefit.

Extender. Add:
1. b. Painting. A substance used to let down strong colours.
1920 F. H. Jennison Manuf. Lake Pigments (ed. 2) 53 There is a considerable difference between the base of a lake, and the filler or extender that is used in the paint trade to let down strong colours.
4. University Extender, a University Extension lecturer (see Extension 9 g).
1893 National Observer 11 Nov. 652/1 The University Extender is a familiar type. 1894 19th Cent. XXXVI. 207 The University Extender exults in the hapless ones who attend his ministrations.

Extension. Add: 9. a. spec. in a camera, the distance by which the front part carrying the lens can be drawn away from the back part carrying the screen.
1893 Jrnl. Soc. Arts XLI. 3 Mar. 381/1 With this form of lens system there can be only one definite extension of camera..in which the entire system is aplanatic. 1928 Photo-Miniature XV. Mar. (Gloss.).
b. Also (orig. U.S.), an addition to (esp. the rear of) a house or other building, usually not so high as the main building; an annex.
1867 [see extension-room in 10]. 1889 Century Mag. Mar. 781/1 They were making beds together in the extension. 1889 Century Dict. s.v., A dining-room extension. 1903 Ruth Hall Pine Grove House 12 The tin roof blew off the extension one windy night.
10. c. extension bag, table, top; **extension lens**, a lens that may be used in a combination to increase its focal length (see quot.).
1904 Delineator Oct. 547 With the genial season arrived every kind of drummer. They came with *extension bags filled with samples. 1908 Nature 17 July 280/1 The replacement of the back component by a lens of greater focal length, increasing the focal length of the objective by about 50 per cent. we referred to some time ago, the alternative back lens being known as an '*extension lens'. 1851 C. Cist Cincinnati 202 One of the remarkable articles..is an *extension table. 1864 [in Dict.]. 1876 J. S. Ingram Centen. Expos. xi. 382 From Crete, Illinois, we saw some very handsome extension-tables, the extra leaves of which were packed away in grooves in the legs when not in use. 1893 Kate D. Wiggin Polly Oliver v. 53 The dining-room just holds, by a squeeze, the extension-table and four chairs. 1887 Tourgee Button's Inn 92 A comfortable *extension top might be raised at will to protect the driver from sun or storm.

Extensionally (ėkste·nʃənăli), adv. [see -ly 2.] By way of extension.
1903 Nature 3 Sept. 411 A class may be defined either extensionally, by an enumeration of its terms, or intensionally, by the concept which denotes its terms.

Extensionless (ėkste·nʃənlės), a. [-less.] Without extension.
1929 A. N. Whitehead Enq. Princ. Nat. Knowledge 112 An extensionless moment of time.

Extensive, a. Add: 3. d. Econ. Applied to methods of cultivation in which a relatively small crop is obtained from a large area at the minimum of attention and expense: opposed to Intensive a. 5.
1832 [see Intensive a. 5].

Extensometer (ekstensǫ·mɪtəɪ). Also -ometer. [f. L. extensus, pa. pple. of extendere + Extend + -ometer.] An instrument for measuring the alteration of form of a bar of metal under the influence of temperature or stress.
1887 Proc. Physical Soc. VIII. 183 Screw-Micrometer Extensometer. 1902 Encycl. Brit. XXXIII. 10/1 Extensometers, or apparatus for observing the small deformation which a test-piece in tension or compression undergoes before its limit of elasticity is reached.

Extent, sb. Add:
7. Campanology. See quot. 1904.
1904 Bulwer Gloss. Techn. Terms Bells 14 Extent.— (a) The full number of distinct 'changes', of which a 'method' admits, is the 'extent' of the 'method'. (b) The full number of times a bell, or some definite combination of bells, can occupy a given position, without repetition of any one of the 'changes' containing such bell, or bells, in that position. 1928 Daily Tel. 27 Nov. 10/7 Three 'extents' (i.e. 720 changes each) upon the six large bells to three different methods, 2,160 changes in all.

Exterior, a. and sb. B. sb. Add: 1. b. An outdoor scene; a cinema picture made out of doors.
1918 Croy How Motion Pictures are Made 74 The few pictures that had been made were made outdoors, in the open—'exteriors', as they are called.

Exteriorist (ėkstīə·rĭrist). [f. Exterior a. + -ist.] One who judges by outward appearances.
1912 G. Tyrrell in Autobiogr. I. 183, I was also largely an exteriorist, and did not realise..how compatible outward carelessness is with inward earnestness.

Externalist. Add: b. One who believes in the external origin of certain forms of skin disease.
1902 Encycl. Brit. XXXI. 568/1 The German school, most of its leaders being pupils of the great Hebra, tend to look to external irritants as the cause of the great majority of diseases, and they are often described as 'externalists'.

Extero-ceptive (e·kstĕrǫse·ptiv), a. Physiol. [irreg. f. L. exterus exterior + -ceptive of Receptive.] (See quots.) Also **E·xtero-ceptor.**
1906 C. S. Sherrington Integr. Action Nerv. Syst. 130 There exist..two primary distributions of the receptor organs, each a field in certain respects fundamentally different from the other. The surface field lies freely open to the numberless vicissitudes of the environment...This field, extero-ceptive as it may be called, is rich in the number and variety of receptors which adaptation has evolved in it. Ibid., The reaction of the animal to stimulation of one of its extero-ceptors excites certain tissues, and the activity thus produced in these latter tissues excites in them the receptors, which are proprio-ceptors. 1927 Haldane & Huxley Anim. Biol. i. 24; v. 123.

Extinction. Add: 5. Petrography. (See quots.) So **Extinguished** a.
1882 Geikie Text-bk. Geol. 189 In searching for the crystallographic system to which a mineral in a microscopic slide should be referred, attention is given to the directions in which the mineral appears dark, in other words, to the directions of its extinction, between crossed Nicols. It is extinguished when two of its axes of elasticity for vibrations of light coincide with the principal sections of the two prisms. 1912 tr. Weinschenk's Petrogr. Meth. 67 Maximum brightness is obtained when the vibration directions of the crystal are at 45° to those of the nicols. It diminishes upon further rotation and passes gradually over into complete darkness when these directions are respectively parallel. This latter position is also called the position of extinction, and the vibration directions in the crystal, the extinction directions. Ibid. 71 Extinction is of especial importance in the investigation of cleavage pieces. Ibid. 70 Extinction Curve for Diopside. Ibid., In triclinic minerals the determination of the extinction angles is of value only when the orientation of the section upon which they are observed is accurately known. 1921 A. Holmes Petrogr. Meth. 126 When a transparent mineral fragment is rotated between crossed nicols various phenomena may be observed according to the nature of the mineral and the orientation of the fragment. If the object remains dark, and is therefore isotropic, the total extinction indicates an amorphous or cubic (isometric) mineral in an unstrained condition, or a basal section of a uniaxial mineral (tetragonal, hexagonal, or trigonal). Ibid., Except by rare coincidence in all sections of triclinic crystals, the extinction is neither straight nor symmetrical, but is symmetrically inclined to the edge, cleavage, or twin-direction which gives the crystallographic orientation. The angle between any such direction and the nearest extinction is the extinction-angle.

Extinguisher. 3. Add: extinguisher-shaped adj.; **extinguisher moss**, a moss whose peristome closes inwards when touched by water.
1821 S. F. Gray Nat. Arr. Brit. Plants I. Encalypta...*Extinguisher-moss. 1876 Encycl. Brit. IV. 161/2 [illegible] Barham Ingol. Leg., Hand of Glory 23 A shocking bad hat, *Extinguisher-shaped. 1903 Ld. R. Gower Rec. & Reminisc. 16 The towers with their extinguisher-shaped roofs. 1909 A. Morrison Green Ginger, Absent Three 27 The wide fireplace and its blazing embers, stuck with black extinguisher-shaped beer-warmers.

Extra, a., adv., and sb. Add: A. adj. e. Cricket. Extra cover (point), a fieldsman whose position is between cover-point and mid-off, but more distant than either from the batsman's wicket; also, his position in the field.
1897 Ranjitsinhji Jubilee Bk. Cricket ii. 50 There is no need to treat extra-cover separately. The position is a cross between cover and mid-off, and its duties are a mixture of the duties required in those two places. 1897 Encycl. Sport I. 217 Extra cover point. Ibid., For slow and medium paced

bowling, a man at long on and extra cover is almost necessary. 1911 Warner Bk. Cricket 74, I prefer to see him at cover or extra-cover.

C. sb. In sense: 'an additional issue of a newspaper' (earlier U.S. examples).
1849 Willis Rural Lett. xix. 168 As to other and more general 'Boziana' are they not written in the Dailies and glorified in the 'Extras?' 1870 Scribner's Monthly I. 115 Newsboys..forsook the 'extra'. 1883 'Mark Twain' Life Mississippi xx. 237 At Napoleon, Arkansas, the same evening, we got an extra, issued by a Memphis paper, which gave some particulars.

b. U.S. (See quot. 1838.)
1836 Knickerbocker Mag. VIII. 348 The plunge of the wheels of the 'extra', as they sank..in the rugged road. 1838 J. F. Cooper Home as Found ii. 35 Mr. Howel informed him that an extra in America meant a supernumerary coach, to carry any excess of the ordinary number of passengers. 1849 Willis Rural Lett. 203 We felt ourselves compensated for paying nearly double price for our 'extra', by the remarkable alacrity with which the coach came to the door after the bargain was concluded. 1860 Holland Miss Gilbert's Career xx. 366 The coach and Cheek were detained as 'an extra' to take over the bridal party.

c. A spell of extra sentinel duty. U.S. Mil. slang.
1889 Farmer Americanisms, Extra (American cadet), an extra is a punishment imposed on Saturday and Sunday, when general leave is granted to all except those who are thus doomed to do extra sentinel duty.

d. An extra item in a program, as a dance.
1900 Elin. Glyn Visits Eliz. (1906) 105 When we got to the ball-room an extra was on.

Extra-. 1. Add: **Extrabra·nchial** Anat., outside of the branchial arches; also as sb., an extra-branchial cartilage. **Extra-ma·rginal**, outside the field of consciousness. **Extra-me·ntal**, beyond the mind, independent of mental apprehension. **E:xtramorai·nic**, of glacial origin though occurring in regions beyond the outermost terminal moraine. **Extra-o·vate**, exterior to the egg; also as sb., a part of the ovum extruded through a rupture in the membrane.

Also in many other combinations of obvious meaning (see quots.).
1877 W. K. Parker & Bettany Morphol. Skull 39 Four *extrabranchial cartilages..,parallel to the ceratobranchials. Ibid., The fifth branchial arch has no gill-pouch behind it, no rays, and no extrabranchial. Ibid. 343 The extra-branchials of the Dogfish are..superficial cartilages related to the branchial arches. 1888 G. H. Fowler in Q. Jrnl. Microsc. Sci. (N.S.) XXVIII. 16 The pseudo-costæ occurring at the lip of the calicle of this species of Lophohelia which are produced by *extra-calicular calicoblasts. 1896 Phil. Trans. Ser. B. CLXXXVII. 147 Mussa is a genus which produces intracalycinal and *extracalycinal buds almost with equal facility. 1890 Billings Med. Dict., *Extra-ciliary fibres, those derived from outer surface of dentate nucleus of cerebellum (corpus ciliare), and joining the tractus semicircularis. 1901 Science 1 Feb. 184 (Cent. D. Suppl.) *Extraconscious. 1914 tr. Maeterlinck's Unknown Guest iii. 120 In all these extraconscious matters [i.e. above the unconscious cerebration]. 1913 Dorland Med. Dict. (ed. 7), *Extracorporeal, outside of the body: said of the stages of a parasite passed elsewhere than in the host. 1901 Practitioner Mar. 274 Laveran formerly regarded these forms of the parasite as *extra-corpuscular. 1925 Cushing Life Osler I. 491 Lest one lose track of Osler in his daily rounds in the hospital wards during the recital of all these *extracurricular matters. 1789 Sir W. Scott in J. Haggard Rep. Consist. Cases (1822) I. 34 Supposing the jury..had been of opinion it was extra-parochial,—that the place may be so, and not *extra-diocesan, is not to be denied. 1897 Westm. Gaz. 14 July 1/3 The island [sc. Lundy] is extra-diocesan and extra-parochial. 1907 Practitioner Nov. 731 The causes of exophthalmos..tumours of the optic nerve, which are either intra-dural or *extra-dural. 1919 S. Paget Sir V. Horsley viii. 127 The removal of part of a large extra-dural tumour. 1913 Dorland Med. Dict., *Extra-embryonic, not a part of the embryo proper: applied to that portion of the embryo outside of the umbilical stalk. 1902 Encycl. Brit. XXXI. 419/1 In the Permo-Carboniferous series..In certain cases the structure was further complicated by the appearance of *extrafascicular zones exterior to the whole stelar system. 1902 W. James Varieties Relig. Exper. 233 Feelings which are *extra-marginal and outside of the primary consciousness altogether. a 1909 Buck's Handbk. Med. Sci. III. 260 (Cent. D. Suppl.) Infra-conscious or extra-marginal psychical activities. 1880 Winchell Preadamites (ed. 2) 271, I maintain that the derivative theory implies the perpetual exertion of *extra-material power which is tantamount to creation. 1886 McCosh Psychol., Cognitive Powers i. 27 All knowledge obtained through the senses is discerned as *extra-mental, that is, as out of and beyond the perceiving mind. 1903 C. A. Strong Why the Mind has a Body 214 Extra-mental realities. 1903 Geikie Text-bk. Geol. (ed. 4) 1339 Deposit of the *extramorainic high-terrace schotter. 1902 Encycl. Brit. XXV. 433/2 These nectaries, often termed nuptial, to distinguish them from similar ones which occur upon parts of the plant away from the flower (*extranuptial). 1893 J. Loeb Biol. Lect. 52 (Cent. D. Suppl.) It often happens that the *extra-ovate receives its nucleus later. 1907 Practitioner Apr. 481 Old cases, in which there is no fear of severe haemorrhage, may be treated *extra-peritoneally. 1918 Osmond Myst. Poets Engl. Ch. viii. 286 There are many today to whom mysticism, to be genuine must be *extra-phenomenal. 1901 Dorland Med. Dict. (ed. 2), *Extrapolar, situated or occurring outside, or not between, the poles, as of a battery. 1875 Encycl. Brit. III. 710/2 The tongue-shaped and fenestrate *extra-stapedial.

Extract, sb. 2. c. Add: Also in fuller form extract wool.
1888 Encycl. Brit. XXIV. 661/1 Extract wool is that which is recovered from rags of various cloths in which cotton and wool are variously woven together.

Extracted (ėkstræ·ktėd), ppl. a. [f. Extract v. + -ed 1.] Derived, drawn out, in senses of the vb.; spec. in Biol., produced by Mendelian methods.
1694 W. Salmon Bate's Dispens. (1713) 198/1 An extracted and digested Tincture of Mars. 1905 A. B. Darbishire in Biometrika Jan. 25 (Cent. D. Suppl.) By pairing such hybrids with extracted albinos we should, in the Mendelian view, produce equal numbers of albinos and dark-eyed hybrids.
b. Extracted honey: honey separated from the uncrushed comb by centrifugal force or by gravity; so extracted comb.
1881 T. W. Cowan Brit. Bee-Keeper's Guide Bk. 88 Pure extracted honey will usually granulate if kept at a low temperature. 1897 Bartrum & McClelland Bees in Bar-Frame Hive 11 Extract at a distance..from the hives, in a room into which the bees cannot penetrate; return extracted comb at night. 1905 Hasluck Beehives & Bee Keepers' Appliances 116 A number of hives are worked for extracted honey.

Extractor. 3. Add: an instrument for extracting honey from the combs.
1886 F. G. Jenyns Bk. about Bees 150 When the bee-keeper wishes to obtain the greatest possible quantity of honey he ..uses to a great extent the machine called an extractor.

Extrality (ekstræ·lĭti). Syncopated form of *Extraterritoriality.
1926 Spectator 9 Jan. 38/1 The connecting link between the Anti-British campaign and the question of abolishing extrality is the Russian policy. 1927 Glasgow Herald 5 Mar. 11 Such questions as 'extral[i]ty' and 'concessions' were not strange words in Japanese ears. 1929 New York Times 6 Sept. 24/3 That China has suffered grievously as a result of 'extrality' (as it is now commonly called).

Extramurally (ekstrămiū·răli), adv. In an extramural way.
1927 Observer 5 June 7/2 The University College of the South-West is the youngest of our University institutions; but during the short period of its career it has developed considerably both intra- and extra-murally.

Extraneous, a. Add:
2. d. Mus. (See quots.)
1876 Stainer & Barrett Dict. Mus. Terms, Extraneous modulation, a modulation in an extreme or unrelated key. Ibid. s.v. Modulation, When a remote key is reached by relative keys, the modulation is by some said to be extraneous.

Extrapolate (ekstræ·pǫlēɪt, e·kstrăpǫlēɪt), v. [f. Extra + -polate of Interpolate v.] trans. To obtain by extrapolation; also absol., to practise extrapolation. Also transf.
1831 Gladstone Let. in Chas. Wordsworth Ann. Early Life (1891) 91 They inserted the letter.., but extrapolated or metabolised a part where I had mentioned Canning. 1874 Jevons Princ. Sci. II. 120 If we wish to assign by reasoning results lying beyond the limits of experiment, we may be said, using an expression of Sir George Airy, to extrapolate.

Extrapolation. Add more recent examples illustrating wider and extended uses.
1903 Agnes M. Clerke Probl. Astrophysics 67 The range allowed to perilous processes of extrapolation can be restricted. 1916 Sir O. Lodge in Hibbert Jrnl. Oct. 151 Does dominance of that kind give to that splendid science.. the right to make a gigantic extrapolation and sprawl over all the rest of the universe? 1922 J. Y. Simpson Man & Attainm. Immortality i. 16 By extrapolation of the curve of our knowledge we can reconstruct within the range of conceivability, if not of probability, the course of process. 1924 Skerl tr. Wegener's Orig. Continents & Oceans 135 By the use of linear extrapolation at a depth of 100 km. in the continental block, a temperature of 2500° C. is reached, a figure far above the melting-point of igneous rocks. 1929 R. A. Fisher Genet. Thé. Nat. Selection 219 From a series of comparable census investigations some such extrapolation should be feasible.

Extra-special, a. [See Extra B. a. note.] Applied to the latest editions of certain London evening newspapers; also sb. any of such editions. Now often colloq. = exceptionally good or fine.
1897 Pearson's Mag. Aug. 221/2 The St. James' Gazette, in an extra special edition, announced [etc.]. 1897 Truth, Christmas Number 25 Dec. 13/2 Strange forms came out upon her,..And offered 'Hextry-speshuls'. 1901 Punch 31 July 86/1 The magazines, the newspapers, the extra-specials of the twentieth century. 1902 Captain VII. 8/1 I'm playing owl.., for one or two extra-special reasons. Mod. He wore a very extra-special buttonhole for the occasion. Is there anything extra-special for tea?

Extra-spective (ekstrăspe·ktiv), a. [f. L. extra outside + -spective of introspective.] Not introspective, regarding external objects rather than one's own thoughts and feelings. Cf. *Extrospective.
1926 Public Opinion 6 Aug. 132/2 He is of the introspective rather than the extra-spective order.

Extraterritoriality. (Extended later to denote the right of jurisdiction of a country over all its nationals abroad.) Cf. *Extrality.
1869 Daily News 8 Jan., In Rome, at one time, this extra-territoriality was made to extend to the inhabitants of the quarter in which the residence of an Ambassador was situated. 1901 Westm. Gaz. 28 Jan. 1/2 To do in China what we have just done in Japan and are anxious that others should do in Egypt—abolish the principle of extra-territoriality, and submit ourselves one and all..to the laws and institutions of China. 1928 G. W. Keeton (title) The Development of Extraterritoriality in China. 1931 T. F. Millard (title) The End of Extraterritoriality in China.

Extravagation (ekstrævăgēɪ·ʃən). Delete †Obs. and add quots.
1849 A. D. Fillan Stories of Rebellions 39 To check all froward desire of extravagation on the part of Major Drummond. 1899 C. K. Paul Mem. 304 M. Renan never could understand how it was people were so little tolerant of his own extravagations.

Extraversion. Transfer † Obs. rare to sense already in Dict., and add:
2. Psychol. The fact of having the thoughts and activities exclusively directed to things outside the self: opp. to *Introversion. (Cf. quot. 1692 in Dict.) So **E·xtravert** sb. [cf. *introvert], one characterized by extraversion (also attrib.); **E·xtraverted** ppl. a. (cf. Extravert v.), said of such a person, or of his activities, etc.
1916 tr. Jung's Coll. Papers Anal. Psychol. 288, I propose to use the terms 'Extraversion' and 'Introversion' to describe these two opposite directions of the libido. Ibid. 289 I will call 'regressive extraversion' the phenomenon which Freud calls 'transference' (Übertragung), by which the hysteric projects into the objective world the illusions, or subjective values of his feelings. Ibid., We say that he is extraverted when he gives his fundamental interest to the outer or objective world, and attributes an all-important and essential value to it. Ibid. 348 The extraverted type sends his libido to a certain extent externally. Ibid. 349 An extravert can hardly conceive the necessity which compels the Introvert to conquer the world by means of a system. 1924 Alice G. Ikin in Brit. Jrnl. Med. Psychol. IV. 304 In 'altroversion' psychic energy is not consistently directed inwards or outwards as in introversion or extraversion, but can flow freely either way. Ibid. 214, I have suggested the use of the term altroversion for the socialisation of either the introverted or extraverted types..with balance between the self and the environment. Ibid., The personality which thus combines introvert and extravert reactions..could be called an 'altrovert'..[as that] resulting from a one-sided synthesis of interest and libido, with over emphasis on ego and object respectively, is called an introvert or an extravert. 1926 Geraldine Coster Psycho-Analysis for Normal People 38 The extravert goes out to people and things, enjoys contacts and shrinking from solitude and meditation.

Extremal (ėkstrī·măl). Math. [f. Extreme + -al.] In the calculus of variations, a curve the integral along an arc of which may be a maximum or a minimum; a stationary curve.
1901 Ann. Mathematics Ser. II. II. 112 The Notion of a Field about the Extremal C. Ibid., Secondly, we shall assume that a one-parameter family of extremals, y = φ (x, γ) exists.

Extremist. Add: One who holds extreme views or advocates extreme measures, esp. as a member of a party; also adj. So **Extre·mism.** **Extremistic** (ekstrĭmi·stik) a., of or pertaining to extremists or extremism.
1907 Daily Chron. 28 Aug. 5/2 Bepin Pal, the Extremist leader. 1920 Sir H. V. Lovett Hist. Ind. Nationalist Movem. 69 The reception committee was broken up by a gang of Extremists. Ibid. 240 This doctrine is the direct result of Extremism. 1921 Telegr. Inform. Mopla Reb. (Parl. Papers XXVI.) 50 Certain Extremist Muhammadan agitators..have been..working up the people of the Khilafat. 1921 19th Cent. July 148 The Fascismo was born in the provinces, where the extremistic menace was strongest.

Extro-spective (ekstrǫspe·ktiv), a. [f. Extro- + -spective of introspective.] = *Extra-spective.
1925 J. E. Turner Theory Direct Realism v. 51 It [sc. the inherence of existence] is offered as an accurate description of consciousness, confirmed both by psychological introspection, intro- and extro-spective, and the logical exclusion of any alternative.

Extroversion. Add:
3. Psychol. = *Extraversion 2.
1920 Challenge 21 May 44/3 [In eurhythmics] the gestures represent an extroversion or objectivisation of the libido.

Extrovert (e·kstrovɜ̄ɪt), sb. Psychol. [Perverted f. *Extravert after *Introvert (cf. Extro-).] = *Extravert; also attrib. So **E·xtroverted** ppl. a. = *Extraverted.
1918 Phyllis Blanchard in Amer. Jrnl. Psychol. Apr. 165 Jung's hypothesis of the two psychological types, the introvert and extrovert,—the thinking type and the feeling type. 1920 Times Lit. Suppl. 1 Apr. 205/4 The external always throws him [sc. George Herbert] back into himself, and then his thoughts turn outwards for confirmation... He is, in the language of modern psychology, both introvert and extrovert, yet never an egotist. 1920 Challenge 21 May 44/2 An extrovert soldier faced with the problem of escape from war conditions. 1923 Westm. Gaz. 21 Mar., Any one of us will display either the introverted or the extroverted attitude. 1925 C. Fox Educat. Psychol. 254 The first is called the extroverted type, because in the main he goes outside himself to the object. 1926 W. McDougall Outl. Abnormal Psych. 440 The characteristic neurosis of the extrovert is hysteria, while that of the introvert is neurasthenia or psychasthenia. 1930 Music & Lett. XI. i. 45 One might suspect the temperamental incompatibility to exist only between romantic composers and an extroverted nation.

Extrude, v. Add: 1. d. To shape (metal) by forcing it through dies. Hence **Extru·ded** ppl. a.
1913 Lockwood's Dict. Mech. Engin. (ed. 4), Extruded Metal.

Exudate, sb. Delete rare—1 and add quots.
1906 Dorland Med. Dict., Exudate, a substance thrown out by exudation; any adventitious substance deposited in or on a tissue by a vital process or a disease. 1907 Gordon Abel's Labor. Handbk. Bacteriol. 164 Pus and various pathological exudates.

Exumbrella (eksʊmbre·lă). Zool. [mod.L., f. L. ex out + Umbrella 7 b.] The aboral or outer surface of the umbrella of a jelly-fish. Hence

Exumbre·llar a., of or pertaining to the exumbrella.
1886 A. W. Greely Arctic Service II. 400 The genus Nauphanta is a characteristic one, and is remarkable in the peculiar sculpturing of the exumbrella, the division of the umbrella on the exumbral side into a central and coronal or peripheral zone. 1888 Rolleston & Jackson Anim. Life 745 The mesoglaea of the aboral aspect of the bell is much thickened to form the umbrella s. exumbrella. Ibid. 783 note, If the Ephyra be regarded from the dorsal, i.e. exumbrellar aspect. Ibid. 784 The sense-bodies are usually protected by a dorsal, i.e. exumbrellar covering-piece or hood. 1897 T. J. Parker & Haswell Text-bk. Zool. I. 124 The convex outer surface of the bell or umbrella..by which the zooid was originally attached to the blastostyle is distinguished as the ex-umbrella, the concave inner surface as the sub-umbrella. 1907 Gentl. Mag. July 97/2 The tentacles ..imbedded in ridges of jelly of the exumbrella.

Ex-voto. Add: Also attrib.
1823 R. Bakewell Trav. Tarentaise I. 354 Ex voto inscriptions.

Eye, sb.1 Add: 3. b. To keep one's eye skinned or peeled: see the pples. Eyes and no eyes: used to express the difference between an observant and an unobservant person; so, said of or to a person who fails to observe; hence used as the title of a book or series of books dealing with the observation of natural objects.
1795 Aikin & Barbauld Evenings at Home (1805) IV. 95 Eyes, and No Eyes; or, The Art of Seeing. 1865 Miss Yonge Clever Woman Fam. iii, 'There is a wonderful charm in a circumscribed view, because one is obliged to look well into it all.' 'Yes; eyes and no eyes apply there,' said Rachel. 1867 (title) Eyes and no eyes. A magazine of meteorology and natural history. 1901 Cassell's 'Eyes and No Eyes' series.
f. Applied in local names to a prominent natural object, such as a hill or island.
1837 Penny Cycl. IX. 165/2 Ireland's Eye, a rocky picturesque island of thirty acres. 1891 Dixon Dict. Idiomatic Eng. Phrases s.v. Eye, The eye of the Baltic—Gothland, or Gottland, an island in the Baltic. 1904 Daily Chron. 14 Sept. 5/1 A low rugged hill, nicknamed 'Kuropatkin's eye'.
5. To cut eyes or one's eye: to cast a glance. U.S.
1827 L. Dow Jrnl. (1850) 177/2 Went to New York, took steamboat to New Brunswick thence stage No. 7, strangers crosses words and cut eyes. 1837 Southern Lit. Messenger III. 233 'Why, we thought about here' said be 'that you were cutting your eye at Miss Gatty'. 1885 'C. E. Craddock' Prophet Gt. Smoky Mtn. xv. 288 Ter see him cut his blazin' eye aroun' at ye, ye'd low ez he'd never hearn o' grace.
(b) The glad eye: a movement of the eyes designed to attract a person of the opposite sex.
1911 Punch 22 Nov. 382/2 The lover, the elderly philanderer, the girl with the glad eye. 1913 'Ian Hay' Happy-go-lucky ii, Miss Welwyn..from the safe harbourage of her mother's arms, was endeavouring to administer to him what is technically known, I believe, as The Glad Eye. 1922 Daily Mail 13 Dec. 11 This is tantamount to cutting the owner of a bad horse on one side of the street and giving him the glad eye on the other. 1923 W. L. George Hail, Columbia! iv. 119, I have never seen an American girl give to a man in the street what the English call the 'glad eye'.
c. To turn a blind eye: to refuse to take any notice of a situation, state of affairs, etc. A single eye: see Single a. 14 b.
1925 Odell in E. F. Norton Fight for Everest, 1924 290 The Tibetans appear to turn a blind eye to the wholesale slaughter involved in the collection..of over 10,000 specimens by our ardent Natural Historian. 1925 E. F. Norton Ibid. 127 Not detracting by its impression from the vision of such as can behold with more than single eye.
7. A straight eye (see Straight a. 7).
12. c. Also applied to the dark spot in hens' eggs.
1895 Pearson's Weekly 18 May 712 The yolk of one average-sized hen's egg (from which the 'eye' has been removed).
d. An eye-like spot in the wings of insects; an ocellus. (Cf. *Eyelet sb. 3.)
1876 Encycl. Brit. IV. 595/2 The Peacock Butterfly.. conspicuous from the 'eyes' on the upper surface of its wings. Ibid. 596/2 Tropæa luna,..with wings of a lemon colour, each with a 'transparent eye'.
14. Also Eyes of the ship, and (simply) eyes.
1890 W. C. Russell Ocean Trag. II. xix. 134 Sleeping as he did, right in the 'eyes', he got the very full of the motion. 1908 Westm. Gaz. 29 Apr. 4/1 There was also a man in the look-out—at what was called the eyes of the ship.
16. b. The bright red spot observed through the mica or glass-covered sight hole of a blast furnace.
1884 W. H. Greenwood Steel & Iron vii. 126 A small slide containing a glass or mica plate, through which the state of the furnace may be observed; the bright spot thus seen is known as the 'eye of the furnace'. 1888 Lockwood's Dict. Mech. Engin. s.v., The eye of a furnace is that spot or area embraced or commanded by the sight holes.
c. The centre of a target; = Bull's-eye 7.
1874 Knight Dict. Mech.
d. Mining. A mass of ore left in the mine to be worked when other ore is becoming scarce or inaccessible. Hence fig., the most profitable part of a possession or enterprise; a 'plum'; a tit-bit left to the last.
1839 De la Beche Rep. Geol. Cornw., etc. 561 The ores thus left in various places are often termed the eyes of the mine; and when it may be necessary, in abandoning the mine,..to remove them, it is termed, picking out the eyes of the mine. 1905 Westm. Gaz. 9 Mar. 9/2 We do not want anybody to come in and 'pick the eyes' out of our districts —to take away the profitable load and leave the unprofitable one.
27. a. eye-colour, -trouble; (Cosmetics) eye-black, -pencil; (sense 21 b) eye-block. b. eye-training.
1927 Sunday Express 20 Mar. 1 The police found little besides some lipstick and *eyeblack. 1928 Daily Express 14 June 10/5 A vow of total abstinence from mouth-paint and eye-black. Ibid. 29 Nov. 1/5 Miss Negri sets a new fashion among cinema actresses. Her cheeks are not enamelled, her eyes are free from belladonna and 'eye black', her lips are naturally red. 1884 Knight Dict. Mech. Suppl., *Eye Block, a tackle block with an eye or loop above, for shackle or lashing. 1912 R. C. Punnett Mendelism 204 It was natural that *eye-colour should be early selected as a subject of investigation. 1925 C. Fox Educat. Psychol. 26 The physical characters were such things as stature, length of arm, cephalic index, eye-colour, etc. 1902 Westm. Gaz. 20 Nov. 6/3 Sticks of grease-paint, *eye-pencils, lip salve. 1907 Daily Chron. 24 Sept. 4/4 The effect of free *eye-training in the development of mental powers. 1896 Westm. Gaz. 24 Sept. 1/3 Mr. Gladstone's *eye-trouble.
28. **eye-area**, in decorative art a device consisting of the eye and eyelashes, and sometimes the cheek-fold; **eye-bath**, a cup-shaped vessel designed to fit the orbit of the eye, used to apply a lotion to the eye; **eye-box** Tanning, a box in a leach in which the height of the liquor can be seen; **eye-cap** U.S., the eye-bone; **eye-case** Ent., in a pupa, the part that covers the eye; **eye douche**, an apparatus for douching the surface of the eye; **eye fly**, a minute fly which in summer-time in the East is troublesome to the eyes of men and beasts; **eye-frame**, the frame of an eye-glass or spectacle-lens; **eye-ground**, the fundus of the eye; **eye-minded** a. Psychol., tending to a frequent use of visual imagery; thinking in terms of the printed or written word rather than of the spoken word; having a mental constitution chiefly or exclusively visual, so that thoughts and memories take the form of visual images; so **eye-mindedness**, the condition of being eye-minded; **eye-opener** (a) U.S. (earlier examples); (d) a person who reveals facts to others; **eye-panel**, a conventional representation of an eye taking the shape of a panel; **eye-plate**, a chitinous sclerite in which the eyes of Acarina are placed; **eye-ring**, a circular space within which the eye of the user of an optical instrument must be placed in order to obtain the full field of view; **eye-strain**, weariness or strained condition of the eyes resulting from excessive or improper use of the eyes, or uncorrected defects of vision; so eye-straining sb. and adj.; **eye-veil**, a veil which reaches down as far as the eyes; **eye-ward**, a ward for eye patients in a hospital; **eye wire**, wire forming the metal frames of spectacles; **eye-worker**, one whose work needs special use of the eyes.
1895 Haddon Evol. Art 36 The six rays are but a symmetrical coalescence of two pairs of *eye-areas. Note, I have adopted the term 'eye-area' to denote the eye device which includes the eye, the eye-lashes, and often the cheek-fold of that side. 1830 J. & S. Maw's Catal., *Eye Baths. 1848 H. R. Forster Stowe Catal. No. 629. 137 An eye-bath. 1857 Trans. Mich. Agric. Soc. VIII. 170 The orbits of the eye, the *eyecap or bone, not too projecting, that is may not form a fatal hindrance in lambing. 1826 Kirby & Sp. Entomol. xxxi. III. 250 Just below the base of the antennæ-case you may discern the *eye-cases (Ophthalmo-theca). 1855 Family Economist III. 83 *Eye-douche. 1884 [see Dict. s.v. Eye 27]. 1815 Kirby & Sp. Entomol. iv. (1818) I. 131 A very minute black fly..which, because it flies in swarms into the eyes, is very troublesome, and..is called there [sc. in India] the *eye-fly. 1881 Instr. Census Clerks (1885) 47 Optician...*Eye Frame Maker. 1900 Jrnl. Exper. Med. 25 Oct. 196 The *eye grounds..were normal. 1910 Practitioner July 97 Mental and moral deterioration in the one.., normal eye-grounds and active pupils in the other. 1901 E. B. Titchener Exper. Psychol. I. i. 196 The purely *eye-minded man would recognise persons, things and places by their look, and would recall events as a panorama of views. 1818 Fearon Sk. Amer. 252 At table there is neither conversation nor yet drinking; the latter is effected by individuals taking their solitary '*eye openers', 'toddy', and 'phlegm dispersers'. 1846 Corcoran Pickings 75 A 'pig and whistle' is the only reg'lar eye opener. a 1861 Winthrop John Brent xxii, Others, who, fuddled last night, are limp in their lazy beds, till soda-water lends them its fizzle. Eye-openers these of moderate calibre. 1928 Manchester Guardian Weekly 31 Aug. 174/4 He felt his mission to be that of an agitator, of an eye-opener, of a merciless yet undogmatic critic. 1895 Haddon Evol. Art 23 The eye has become enormously enlarged, and constitutes what I propose to term an *eye-panel. 1903 Ann. & Mag. Nat. Hist. Nov. 505 The comparative structure of the hard chitinous parts of the body, especially of the *eye-plates, mouth-organs, and palps. 1902 tr. P. Drude's Theory of Optics 77 The exit-pupil is often called the *eye-ring, and its centre is called the position of the eye. 1874 S. Weir Mitchell in Med. & Surg. Reporter (Philad.) XXXI. 67 (heading) Headaches.. from *eye strain. 1898 G. M. Gould Biogr. Clinics (1905) III. 497 Eyestrain was ruled out by careful tests. 1909 Practitioner Dec. 779 Of all the causes of eyestrain the most frequent is the presence of an error of refraction. 1871 English Mechanic 380/3 *Eye-straining. 1923 Kipling Land & Sea Tales 185 Cold, nose-running, eye-straining work. 1928 Daily Express 4 June 5/3 The *eye-veil fashion..is good for the races. 1879 St. George's Hosp. Rep. IX. 465 The average stay of a patient in the *eye-wards.. was 25·84 days. 1881 Instr. Census Clerks (1885) 96 *Eye Wire Maker. 1898 G. M. Gould Biogr. Clinics (1905) III. 500 A seamstress or..any hard-pushed *eye-worker.

Eye, v. Add: 7. intr. Of eggs: To form eyes. (See Eye sb.1 12 c.)
1904 Daily Chron. 25 Mar. 8/3 The eggs take from six weeks to three months to 'eye', as it is called.

Eyebrow. 1. Add: To raise an eyebrow: to show surprise.
1918 Strachey Emin. Victorians (1929) 26 The most steady-going churchman hardly raises an eyebrow at it now.

Eyeglassy (əi·glɑsi), a. colloq. [f. Eye-glass sb. + -y 1.] Pertaining to or characteristic of one who wears an eye-glass; allusively, haughtily superior or contemptuous.
1871 Meredith Harry Richmond xxi, The interior of the Casino seemed more hostile. I remarked it to him. 'A trifle more eyeglassy' he murmured. 1906 Cassell's Mag. Apr. 553/1 Mr. Rodder only laughed—the pleasant laugh that wasn't eye-glassy.

Eyelet, sb. 3. Add: spec. on a butterfly's wing; an ocellus.
1832 J. Rennie Butterfl. & M. 23 The Eyed Hawk. Wings..; second pair rosy at the base, the tips much paler, with a large blue eyelet near the posterior angle. 1832 T. Brown Bk. Butterfl. & M. (1834) I. 120 The wings are angular,..with large compound eyelets, reddish in the centre.

Eyer. Add: b. A maker of eyes in needles.
1881 Instr. Census Clerks (1885) 45 Needle Maker...Eyer.

Eye-wash (əi·wɒʃ). [f. Eye sb.1 + Wash sb. 3.]
1. Lotion for the eye.
1866 [see Eye sb.1 28].
2. Something that is intended to interfere with clear vision; something said or done in order to give the impression that all is as it should be; humbug, blarney. slang.
1884, 1889 [see Eye sb.1 28]. 1913 Aeroplane 20 Mar. 327/2 Well as this may do as 'eye wash', it is not the real thing. 1916 Bean Lett. from France (1917) 197 The ignorance which ..flies to the conclusion that everything written and spoken about the horrors of this war is humbug, and what the Army calls 'eyewash'. 1919 'Ian Hay' Last Million ii, The greater the fuss a regiment made about its appearance—'eye-wash', we called it—the better its work in the field. 1919 War Slang in Athenæum 8 Aug. 728/1 Anything complimentary is termed 'eyewash'. 1920 Blackw. Mag. July 91/2 Kemp went ashore to pay a polite visit to the local Sheikh, as 'eye-wash' against our real activities.

Eyra (əi·ră). [mod.L., a. native name.] A wild cat of S. America, Felis eyra, of a uniform reddish colour, with a long slender body and short legs.
1873 Proc. Zool. Soc. 2 A specimen of the Eyra Cat..with other animals, all stated to have been brought from Maranham, Brazil.

Eyrie. Now the commonest spelling of Aerie.
1861 [see Aerie].

F

F. Add: III. 3. F.A. = Football Association. F.A.F. = Fresh Air Fund. F.A.Q. (f.a.q.) or S. (s.) = free alongside quay or ship. F.D. = Fidei Defensor, Defender of the Faith. F.G. = fine grain. F.G.A. = free of general average. F.I.T. = free in truck. F.M. = field-magnet. F.O. = Foreign Office. F.O.B. (f.o.b.) or R. (r.) = free on board or rail. F.O.T. = free on truck. F.S. (f.s.) = foot-second (see *Foot sb. 35).
1871 English Mechanic 17 Mar. 615/3 Medium rifle powder ..is still used..under the name of 'powder shell F.G.' (fine grain). 1880 C. Marvyn Our Public Offices (ed. 2) 203 Everything at the F.O. revolves round the Library. 1880 Encycl. Brit. XI. 304/2 It is considered that with field guns the velocity of the projectile at the moment of bursting should not fall below 800 f.s. Ibid. 326/2 Formerly at Waltham Abbey both musket (F.G.) and cannon powder (L.G.) were granulated in the same machine at the same time. 1888 Lockwood's Dict. Mech. Engin., F.A.S., free alongside ship. Engages to deliver goods on the wharf without extra charge. Ibid., F.I.T., free in truck. Engages to load goods in railway trucks without extra charge. Ibid., F.O.R., Free on rail. Signifies the placing of goods on the railway without extra charge. F.O.T., free on truck. The same as F.I.T. 1890 Economist 22 Feb. Suppl. 12/1 Bleach opened firm in January at £7 16s per ton for hard wood, f.o.b., and £7 5s per ton for soft wood f.o.r. 1892 in W. Pickford Assoc. Football (1905) I. 112 The meetings of the F.A. are carried out under rules of procedure. 1894 W. P. Maycock Electr. Lighting & Power Distrib. (ed. 2) II. viii. § 134 The F. Ms. of an alternator must be separately excited. 1894 Field 9 June 846/2 The average price realized for Irish creamery butter was 88s f.o.r. at this creamery. 1902 Encycl. Brit. XXIX. 171/1 Velocities ranging from 100 to 2800 feet per second (f/s). 1905 Kynoch Jrnl. July-Sept. 156 Accuracy does not demand a muzzle velocity higher than 2,300 f.s. 1907 Westm. Gaz. 22 July 3/2 Known as the F.A.F.—three letters that have grown as familiar as P.P.C. or F.O.B. or any other of the abbreviations of social or commercial life. ..Without distinction of creed or race, the F.A.F. takes away the children of the slums from the festering alleys.. of London. 1928 Daily Mail 25 July 19/3 Oats: Plate f.a.q. afloat 27s. 3d. 1930 Morning Post 18 Nov. 15/4 The first round proper of the F.A. Cup.
b. F.F. or F.F.V. (A member or descendant of one of the) first families of Virginia. U.S.
1847 Knickerbocker Mag. June XXIX. 495 (Th.) F.F.V. A Virginia scion insisted that [these letters] were an abbreviation he had seen used in the navy to represent 'First Family in Virginia'. 1850 Odd Leaves 178 (Th.) [He was] the first of his race to acknowledge that he was not an F.F. 1853 F. W. Thomas J. Randolph etc. 286, I came from one of the first families in Virginia, one of the F.F.V.'s. 1861 Lowell Biglow P. Ser. II. i. 217 She's an F.F...an' prouder'n the Gran' Turk. 1862 O. W. Norton Army Lett. 115 The home ..gave much evidence that the owner is..in name and pretention an F.F.V. 1873 J. H. Beadle Undevel. West xxxiii. 710 The F.F.V's wonder how the farmer can get through the winters in New York. 1905 Springfield Weekly Republ. 5 May 2 He was by every line of descent an F.F.V.
c. Photogr. F. = Focal length. Used in combination with numbers to indicate the ratio between the focal length of the lens and the diameter of the stop.
1892 C. H. Bothamley Ilford Man. Photog. v. 34 For example, f/8 and f/16 mean that the diameter of the stop is, in the first case, one-eighth, and, in the second case, one-sixteenth of the focal length of the lens. 1903 A. Watkins The Watkins Man. (ed. 2) 42 Instead of having to work out afresh the value of the diaphragm, it is much more convenient to regard the lengthening of the camera as a separate influence which I have named the F factor. Ibid. 43 The F factor to allow for the lengthened focus of the lens, and S the value of the subject. Ibid. 45 The F figure (distance of image to lens in terms of focus of lens) is always the same as the degree of enlargement plus 1. 1928 Photo-Miniature XV. Mar. (Gloss.), F (f/·) Numbers —denote the 'speed' of a lens. About the most rapid lens is f/3 to f/4·5...The f/ number is the number of times the diameter of the stop will divide into the focal length of the lens. 1919 Brit. Jrnl. Photogr. Alm. 238 In almost all lenses the diameter of the stop which really determines the F. No. is a little greater than the real diameter owing to the converging action of the front lens.

Faam, variant of *Faham.

Fabianine (fəᵘ·biănin). Chem. [f. Fabiana, a genus of South African shrubs + -ine 5.] A colouring matter contained in the flowers of Fabiana imbricata. Also **Fa·bianol**, the odoriferous constituent of the volatile oil contained in the dried twigs of Fabiana imbricata.
1899 Jrnl. Chem. Soc. LXXVI. i. 448 The aqueous extract contained chrysatropic acid, choline, fabianaglucotannoid and—after boiling with 1 per cent. sulphuric acid—fabianol.

Fabianism (fəᵘ·biăniz'm). [f. Fabian a. + -ism.] The principles of the Fabian Society. Hence **Fa·bianist.**
1900 G. B. Shaw (title) Fabianism and the Empire. 1918 H. Dalton in E. Marsh R. Brooke 26 During our years at Cambridge, Fabianism was at its high tide. 1924 Blackw. Mag. Sept. 393/1 Fabianism touched her during her last year at school.

Fabric, v. Delete †Obs. and add quots.
1921 Public Opinion 14 Oct. 375/1 All these were dreamed and fabricked out for immediate material benefit. 1926 W. A. White Woodrow Wilson 352 This high dream of peace, that he fabricked upon the anvil of a three years' debate.

Fabrica (fa·brika). [Sp.] A factory.
1902 Encycl. Brit. XXVI. 146/1 Every town and village full of 'fabricas', with their tall chimneys. 1924 Chambers's Jrnl. Oct. 649/2 The silk factories are not so popular with the young women of the district as the ordinary fabrica.

Fabrication. 1. Delete 'Now rare' and add:
1930 (July 15) U.S. Advt., The fabrication of the books themselves was intrusted to craftsmen who are masters of the art of printing and binding.
concr. 1674 Moxon Tutor to Astron. & Geog. (ed. 3) App. 201 A Sphear is complicated of Lath-like Circles to represent each Orb, and is not an intire Orb as a Globe is, so that you may see the several Fabrications that are made within it. 1893 Whitby Gaz. 8 Dec. 2/7, I thought all our masts, funnel, and the whole fabrication, boats and all, would surely go.

Fabricator. Add: 3. Archæol. A flint implement, probably used in the making of arrows.
1872 J. Evans Anc. Stone Implem. 367 A characteristic specimen of the tool to which I have provisionally assigned the name of 'flaking-tool' or fabricator. 1877 W. Greenwell Brit. Barrows 35 Those [sc. articles found in barrows] of flint, include hatchets; scrapers;..fabricators or flaking tools. 1907 T. R. Holmes Anc. Brit. 75.

Face, sb. Add: 2. To open one's face: to open the mouth, to speak. U.S. slang.
1896 G. Ade Artie iii. 26 If you open your face to this lady again tonight, I'll separate you from your breath.
4. A slap in the face: a rebuff, an insult.
1861 [see Slap sb.1 2 a].
e. Lacrosse. The action of facing (see *Face v. 4 c), corresponding to the bully in hockey. Also face-off.
1900 Daily News 29 Mar. 7/5 Kent opened proceedings with a goal by Jones immediately after the 'face'. 1900 J. C. Isard in Football, Hockey, & Lacrosse 178 When the game is opening, with the face-off at the centre.
7. b. To run one's face (earlier example). Also to travel on or upon one's face. U.S.
1845 J. J. Hooper Adv. Simon Suggs v. 63 It was, therefore, time to 'run his face'. 1856 Knickerbocker Mag. Nov. XLVIII. 504 [I] must travel on my face after this, when I want to go through the College. 1859 Yale Lit. Mag. XXV. 60 (Th.) If you have not a ready tongue, and cannot travel upon your face, you had better [etc.].
10. b. To save one's face: see Save v. 8 f; also to save face. To lose face [tr. Chinese tiu lien]: to be humiliated, lose one's credit, good name, or reputation; similarly, loss of face.
1876 R. Hart Land of Sinim (1901) 225 Arrangements by which China has lost face. 1916 'Jack London' Lost Face (1918) 27 He had lost face before all his people. 1928 Galsworthy Swan Song i. 5 They've got to save face. Saving face is the strongest motive in the world. 1929 Times 3 Aug. 11/3 Each wishes to concede only what can be conceded without loss of 'face'.
12. a. Also Golf, the slope or cliff of a bunker.
1881 Forgan Golfer's Handbk. 33 Face,..the sandy slope of a bunker. 1891 H. G. Hutchinson Golf (ed. 6) 33 In the typical niblick shot the ball lies in a heel-mark or other cup in the sand, with the face of the bunker in front. 1897 Encycl. Sport I. 466/1 Shall I play it backwards, or sideways on to the grass, or try to get it over the face of the bunker nearer the hole? 1910 B. Darwin Golf Courses Brit. Isles 105 We may be just short with our second..and we shall be battering the bunker's unyielding face till our card is shattered and wrecked.
13. c. On the face of it (fig.): on a merely superficial view, obviously, plainly, prima facie.
1882 Knowledge II. 70 The whole theory was absurd on the face of it. 1926 J. J. Connington Nordenholt's Million vi, It certainly seemed on the face of it to be a very useless accomplishment.
15. b. The striking surface of a golf-club, cricket-bat, hockey-stick, or tennis-racket; the inside of the net of a lacrosse-stick.
1881 Forgan Golfer's Handbk. 8 The head [of a full-sized Driver] weighs 7 oz. or 8 oz., and is distinguished from those of the 'Spoon' family by its 'face' being straight and almost perpendicular. 1887 Grace Cricket 49 It is much better to hold the face of the bat towards the umpire—nothing is gained by showing him the edge. 1891 H. G. Hutchinson Golf (ed. 6) 15 The maker's name gives you a fine guide to the centre of the face, which is the intended point of impact. 1897 Encycl. Sport I. 469/1 (Golf) The lofted face enables the player to start the ball straight. Ibid. 606/2 (Lacrosse) The leading string is then joined to the face of the gut by means of other pieces of gut, and the crosse is complete. Ibid. 613/2 (Lawn tennis) Avoid lop-sided or small-faced rackets, and see that the grain in the frame runs equally round the face. 1900 H. F. P. Battersby in Football, Hockey, & Lacrosse 85 Sticks are made up with the grain running, broadly speaking, in one of two ways: either parallel to the plane of the face, or at right angles to it. 1909 P. A. Vaile Mod. Golf i. 13 It is a mistake in the driver or brassy to have the face too shallow.
26. (sense 1) face-bleach, -hair, -massage, -paint, -powder, -screen, -towel, -wash; face-high adj.
1907 Daily News 3 Sept. 2/7 A *face-bleach for removing all discolorations from the skin. 1927 Peake & Fleure Peasants & Potters 122 Scanty *face-hair save for a chin tuft in the male. 1905 Westm. Gaz. 15 June 7/1 The sea went, *face-high, just within reach of Gregory. 1896 K. M. Caffyn Quaker Grandmother 259 She..would have her usual *face massage done then. 1900 Daily News 3 May 7/4 Departments for manicure, pedicure, and face-massage. 1925 Illustr. Lond. News 23 Jan. 120/1 Egyptian women used..malachite, as the ingredient of a *face-paint. 1858 Illustr. News of World 17 Apr. 175/4 Saunders's Face Powder..beautifies the complexion. 1879 Chemist & Druggist XXI. 481/1, 60 grammes of..Face Powder, a mixture of talc with a small proportion of white magnesia, coloured faintly red with cochineal. 1920 Punch 15 Sept. 219/1 A lady with a Russian name, no back to her gown and green face-powder. 1890 W. J. Gordon Foundry 159 The men around in *face-screens and leg-guards. 1925 R. A. Knox Viaduct Murder vi. 59 The *face-towel was distinctly mentioned in the washing-list. 1926 Agatha Christie Murder of R. Ackroyd x. 127 He wouldn't even buy new face towels, though I told him the old ones were in holes. 1907 Daily News 3 Sept. 2/7 A *face-wash for improving the complexion. 1911 E. Ferber Dawn O'Hara iii. 34 A motherly hug..enveloped me in an atmosphere of liquid face-wash, strong perfumery and fried lard.
27. **face-ache** (earlier U.S. example); **face-brick** U.S., a special brick used for facing buildings, etc.; a facing-brick; also, face-work of brick; **face-cloth**, (b) a woollen cloth with a smooth surface; (c) a cloth for washing the face; **face decoration**, decoration (of pottery) with a face or faces; so face-decorated adj.; **face-glass**, the glass window of a diver's helmet; **face harden** v. trans., to harden the surface of (metal) by case-hardening, chill casting, or other process; also fig.; **face-lifting**, a method of improving facial beauty by an operation in which the skin is tightened and the wrinkles smoothed out; **face-line**, (a) the alignment of the face of a structure, etc.; (b) pl. the lines or wrinkles of the face; **faceman**, a miner who works at the face; **face-piece** = *face-glass; **face-plate**, (c) a plate protecting some piece of machinery; **face-symbol** Cryst., the symbol designating the face or plane of a crystal; **face-urn**, an urn decorated with a face or faces; **face-work**, the exterior of masonry, the material forming the outside of a wall or the like.
1854 Mary J. Holmes Tempest & Sunshine ii. 40 It was more of a *face-ache. than the genuine toothache. 1878 Congress. Rec. 25 Jan. 548/1 In consequence of the limit placed upon the cost of the building, it was found necessary to adopt *face-brick. 1901 R. Sturgis Dict. Archit. s.v. Brick, Face Brick, one of a superior quality used for the face of a wall. 1909 Century Dict. Suppl. s.v. Face-work, In a brick wall, the face work may be of what are called face-brick, and laid in thinner points. 1898 Westm. Gaz. 29 Sept. 3/2 Dark plaid skirts and *face-cloth coats. 1928 Daily Express 27 Dec. 5/2 Smooth face cloth and fox. 1921 Chemist & Druggist CXII. 663/1 A novelty in the way of face cloths. 1928 Peake & Fleure Steppe & Sown 91 The curious pottery with *face decorations reminds us of the *face-decorated handles of pots from Cemetery A at Kish in Mesopotamia. 1896 Strand Mag. XII. 356/1 It is useless to butt the *face-glass or wildly knock your head against the inside of the helmet. 1874 Porcupine 21 Feb. 742/3 They were seen to join in the revelry and devilry as drunken as the most *face-hardened of their companions. 1896 Westm. Gaz. 28 Feb. 6/3 All thick armour is face-hardened on the Harvey principle. 1922 F. Courtenay Physical Beauty 57 The 'face-raising' or '*face-lifting' process which does away with wrinkles, mouth and eyelines and sagging cheeks, by literally 'lifting' off part of the old face and replacing it. 1928 Sunday Dispatch 16 Dec. 9/4 A youthful appearance is considered an advantage, and face-lifting is a common thing among men. 1883 *Face line [see 26 in Dict.]. 1906 Daily Chron. 13 July 3/3 They are the real Rembrandt. There is a deep furrow in the brow; the face-lines are bitten as by acid. 1909 Westm. Gaz. 6 Mar. 16/1 The work of erecting the new intermediate ribs between the old bridge and the new face-line is now in progress on all the spans. 1921 Glasgow Herald 21 Apr. 5 The effect of the new offer on the wages of '*facemen'. 1908 Westm. Gaz. 21 Sept. 5/3 A big round-topped helmet which contains a small glass *face-piece through which the wearer can see. 1884 Knight Dict. Mech. Suppl., *Face-plate, a covering plate for an object to receive wear or shock. 1880 Athenæum 17 Jan. 86/3 How to convert the *face-symbols of Naumann into those of Miller. 1927 Peake & Fleure Priests & Kings 147 The *face-urns..do not seem to belong to the invading people who founded HissarlikII. 1838 Civil Engin. & Arch. Jrnl. I. 330/1 What is called Flemish bond consists in the disposition of the bricks on the outside, or *face-work. 1909 Daily Chron. 5 Aug. 1/3 The face-work of the old parapet having been re-erected.

Supplement, p. 3873; Corrigenda, p. 4092; Spurious words, p. 4093; Books quoted, p. 4094

Face, *v.* Add:
3. *To face out of countenance*: to confront and disconcert (cf. COUNTENANCE *sb.* 6 b). *To face up*: *intr.* to show a bold face; with *to*, to confront, oppose (a person, etc.).
1854 *Punch* 27 May 222/1 Is he to be faced out of countenance by a young whipper-snapper? 1924 D. H. LAWRENCE *England, my England* 109 She faced up at the truck where the two men stood up in the wind. 1925 MRS. BELLOC LOWNDES *Some Men & Women, Gun Room* 161 She was a woman who always faced up to the realities of life. 1926 *Hutchinson's Best Story Mag.* Nov. 21 Margery faced her up. 'What I have I hold', she answered.
4. *To face the music*: see MUSIC *sb.* 11.
c. *Lacrosse.* To place (the ball) between the crosses of two players of opposing sides, for instance, as a preliminary to the commencement of the game.
1867 *Laws of La Crosse* 6 Should the ball lodge in any spot inaccessible to the 'crosse' it may be taken out by the hand and immediately placed on the 'crosse', but should an opponent be checking and cry 'face', it must be faced for. 1882 *Rules of Lacrosse* 15 Should the ball lodge in any place inaccessible to the crosse, it may be taken out by the hand; and the party picking it up must 'face' with his nearest opponent. 1897 E. T. SACHS *Lacrosse* 117. 1910 [see *FACING *vbl. sb.* 2 b].
5. b. esp. *pass.* To be confronted *with*.
1920 *Challenge* 21 May 44/2 An extrovert soldier faced with the problem of escape from war conditions.
8. e. With *off*. To turn aside (*spec.* the current of a stream).
1887 RUSKIN *Præterita* II. 394 A little logwork to face off the stream at its angles.
14. Also with *up*.
1883 *Specif. Alnwick & Cornhill Rlwy.* 10 All bolt-holes to have bosses cast on them, which are to be faced up. 1889 HASLUCK *Model Engin. Handybk.* (1900) 113 If all the flange joints are faced up absolutely true.

Faced, *ppl. a.*[2] **1.** Add: Of a golf-club, tennis-racket, etc. (see *FACE *sb.* 15 b), as *long-faced, short-faced* adjs.
1893 H. G. HUTCHINSON *Golfing* 21 These short-faced clubs. 1897 *Encycl. Sport* I. 467/2 A straight-faced club. *Ibid.* 613/2 [see *FACE *sb.* 15 b]. 1909 P. A. VAILE *Mod. Golf* viii. 120 Don't choose a big-headed club, and avoid a long-faced one.

Fach (fāχ). [G., compartment, partition, division.] A line of work or business; a department of activity; (one's) métier.
1920 SANTAYANA *Char. & Opin. U.S.* v. 143 Very professional in tone and conscious of his *Fach*. 1923 *Contemp. Rev.* June 757 The Eldorado of story-tellers whose *Fach* is the portrayal of luxurious vice.

Facial, *a.* Add: **4. b.** = *face-massage. U.S.*
1914 GERTRUDE ATHERTON *Perch of Devil* I. 84 I've got fourteen heads to dress..and most of them want a facial, too.

Facies. Add:
1. b. *Path.* The appearance or expression of the face.
1907 *Practitioner* Apr. 520, I can only recall one facies which at all suggested the condition of *bien-être* associated with the acquired disease. 1908 *Ibid.* Feb. 292 The facies gray. 1909 *Ibid.* Feb. 205 The disorder produces such a change in the personal appearance and mental activity of the patient that its 'facies' is pathognomonic.
2. b. *spec.* in *Geol.* (see quots.).
1849 [in Dict. sense 2]. 1882 GEIKIE *Text-bk. Geol.* 615 Every well-marked formation is characterized..by a general assemblage or *facies* of organic forms. 1895 H. S. WILLIAMS *Geol. Biol.* 69 The term *facies* is used in a particular sense in geology to apply to the particular composition or condition of a formation in a given region. 1910 LAKE & RASTALL *Text-bk. Geol.* 285 When a geological series or system is in one district composed chiefly of limestone and in another of clays and shales, it is usual to speak of these different types of deposit as different 'facies'. 1924 tr. *A. Wegener's Orig. Continents & Oceans* 46 These alkaline rocks are very striking in the absolutely similar development of the plutonic, dyke, and volcanic facies.

Facile princeps (fæ·sili pri·nseps). [L.] Easily first, the acknowledged leader or chief.
1834 GREVILLE *Mem.* (1874) III. xxii. 64 In the prime of life,..*facile princeps* in the House of Commons. 1858 A. TROLLOPE *Three Clerks* I. ii. 33 He..soon became *facile princeps* in the list of habitual idlers. 1861 *Two Cosmos* I. vi, The *facile princeps* of the Whig Attorneys. 1879 SIR G. G. SCOTT *Lect. Mediæval Archit.* II. 253 [St. Sophia's] is *facile princeps* among structures on the pendentive domical principle. 1887 MARQUIS OF SALISBURY in *Times* 20 Dec. 7/3 In that [*sc.* political tergiversation] he is *facile princeps*, and has left all competitors behind.

Facing, *vbl. sb.* Add: **2. b.** *Lacrosse.* (Cf. *FACE *v.* 4 c.)
1910 *Westm. Gaz.* 22 Apr. 14/3 Facing is no longer to be regarded as a penalty.

Facio- (fē·ʃio), used as combining form (see -o-) of L. *facies* face, as in **facioplegic** *a.*, pertaining to paralysis of the face; etc. (see quots.).
1901 DORLAND *Med. Dict.* (ed. 2), *Faciobrachial*, pertaining to the face and arm. *Faciocervical*, affecting the face and neck. *Faciolingual*, pertaining to the face and tongue. *Facioscapulohumeral*, pertaining to the face, scapula, and arm. 1910 OSLER & MCCRAE *Syst. Med.* VII. 124 The facio-scapulo-humeral type [of progressive muscular dystrophy]. 1922 *F. W. Price's Textbk. Pract. Med.* 1577 When the wasting begins in the face (facio-scapulo-humeral type). 1922 A. A. STEVENS *Pract. Med.* 916 In a few instances recurrent facial paralysis seems to have been an accompaniment of migraine (facioplegic migraine).

Façon de parler (fasoṅdparle). [Fr.] A way or manner of speaking; a mere phrase or formula.
1806 *Edin. Rev.* Jan. 494 Philostratus..introduces the high priest of Serapis saying, (in the time of Vitellius) 'and who can alter the sacred institutions of Egypt?' Was this a mere *façon de parler*? 1813 WELLINGTON *Disp.* (1838) X. 161, I hope that this mode of considering an omission which can easily be rectified, is only a *façon de parler*. 1886 H. G. HUTCHINSON *Hints Golf* 56 A mere golfing *façon de parler*. 1907 W. DE MORGAN *Alice-for-Short* xlii. 439 Which was palpably a lie, taken literally; but was a *façon-de-parler* that passed muster, taken leniently.

Fact, *sb.* Add:
8. *Comb.*, as (sense 6) *fact-crammed* adj.
1894 *Westm. Gaz.* 4 Apr. 3/1 It was a clever fact-crammed speech. 1907 *Daily Chron.* 16 Jan. 3/2 A fact-crammed encyclopædia.

Factional, *a.* Add: Also *sb.* A member of a faction.
1904 *N. Y. Even. Post* 5 July 5 At his left sat the Harrison factionals of Chicago.

Factionalism (fæ·kʃənăliz'm). [f. FACTIONAL *a.* + -ISM.] A condition characterized by faction; tendency to factional differences; the factional spirit.
1905 *Springfield Weekly Republ.* 31 Mar. 2 Factionalism within the republican party in Wisconsin. 1922 *Glasgow Herald* 21 Feb. 8 Italy..suffers in her political life from the ineradicable vice of factionalism. 1926 *Contemp. Rev.* Nov. 594 The provinces would be less subject to civil factionalism if the incentive to obtain control of Peking were absent.

Factionally (fæ·kʃənăli), *adv.* [f. FACTIONAL *a.* + -LY[2].] By means of faction.
1893 *Columbus Dispatch* 16 Sept., It will be their purpose to not factionally prolong the session.

Factionism (fæ·kʃəniz'm). [See -ISM.] The factionist spirit or tendency; = *FACTIONALISM.
1930 *New Statesman* 18 Jan. 458/2.

Factor, *sb.* Add: **7. b.** *Biol.* In Mendelian theory, any of the physiological units which are held to cause the development in the offspring of certain characters present in the parent.
1907 PUNNETT *Mendelism* (ed. 2) 24 Every zygotic cell, being formed by the fusion of two gametes, is a double structure, and contains two factors belonging to any given pair of characters. *Note*, By this term [*sc.* factor] it is convenient to denote the physical basis for the unit character which exists in the gamete. Tallness in the pea is a unit character, and is transmitted from one generation to another by the 'tall' factor in the gamete. 1910 DONCASTER *Heredity* 56 If the factor tallness is present it makes itself visible, and therefore the short peas in F_2 should contain no tall factor. *Ibid.* 136 In Mendelian inheritance, the hereditary determinant of a particular character is spoken of as the factor for that character. 1921 *Conquest* Sept. 491/3 Mendel..introduced the idea of germinal factors, which are to heredity what the atoms of Dalton were to chemistry. 1927 HALDANE & HUXLEY *Anim. Biol.* ii. 62 These units are called factors of heredity, or sometimes still more shortly the *genes*. 1930 G. R. DE BEER *Embryol. & Evol.* ii. 14 The internal and transmitted factors are by themselves unable to 'produce' an animal at all.
8. *Factor of safety*: the ratio between the load which a structure or material is capable of supporting and the load which it is required to support, between the stress which causes it to break and the stress that it is required to stand; also, between the elastic limit of the structure and the usual load.
1858 [see SAFETY 6]. 1866 RANKINE *Usef. Rules* 205 Factors of safety for perfect materials and workmanship,..Dead Load 2. Live Load 4. 1876 *Encycl. Brit.* IV. 296/2 In designing a girder the load which it will have to carry is multiplied by a number called the factor of safety, varying from 3 to 6. 1877 W. H. WHITE *Man. Naval Archit.* 377 Supposing a factor of safety of 8 to be taken instead of 10, the safe working load..for timber subject to compressive strains would be about three-eighths of a ton per square inch. 1910 *N. Hawkins' Electr. Dict.*, *Factor of safety*. 1. A term expressive of a determined limit to which materials or machines shall be subjected; the safety limit. 2. In wiring, the ratio between the breaking stress of a wire and the maximum tension to which it is subjected in overhead suspension.

Factorially (fæktō·riăli), *adv.* *Biol.* [f. FACTORIAL *a.*[1] + -LY[2].] By reference to factors.
1913 W. BATESON *Mendel's Princ. Heredity* 84 In all the cases yet studied the genetic properties of the pied types can be represented factorially by regarding the pattern or distribution of the colour as due to a distinct factor or to its absence.

Factorization (fæktŏrəizē·ʃən). *Math.* [f. FACTORIZE *v.* + -ATION.] The resolution into factors.
1886 G. CHRYSTAL *Text-bk. Algebra* I. 112 Every known identity resulting from the distribution of a product of such factors, when read backwards gives a factorisation. 1888 C. SMITH *Algebra* 60 The factorisation of x^3-8 is for many purposes complete in the form $(x-2)(x^2+2x+4)$.

Factory. 6. Add: *factory butter* (U.S.), *-girl* (earlier U.S. example), *system*; *factory-made* pple. (and sb.); **factory cloth** = *factory-cotton*.
1888 *Vermont Agric. Rep.* X. 14 *Factory butter secures an average higher price than its patrons could secure it if they made it at home. 1872 MARIETTA HOLLEY *My Opin.* (1891) 205 Merrymac calico and *factory cloth. 1833 S. BRECK *Recoll.* (1877) App. 275 *Factory-girls were introduced. 1904 *Daily Chron.* 23 Aug. 5/4 The over-decorated *factory-made furniture of Michigan and Ohio. *Ibid.* 28 Dec. 4/5 Cheapest line of factory-mades. 1905 *Ibid.* 13 June 7/2 Practically all shoes are factory-made in the United States. 1847 *Knickerbocker Mag.* XXX. 512 Such shallow observers betray an entire ignorance of the *factory system.

Factualness (fæ·ktiuălnės). [f. FACTUAL + -NESS.] The state of being factual.
1906 C. A. BRIGGS & VON HÜGEL *Papal Comm. & Pentat.* 29 The massive factualness, the serried, interdependent ranks of fact upon fact. 1925 *Public Opinion* 14 Aug. 153/3 Even the compassionate pity they arouse does not lift the weight of their seriousness and factualness from the reader's breast.

Faculty. 5. Delete †*Obs.* and add:
1889 *Cent. Dict.*, *Faculty*...6. In the law of divorce (commonly in the plural), the pecuniary ability of the husband, in view of both his property and his capacity to earn money, with reference to which the amount of the wife's alimony is fixed. 1894 [see 12 below].
9. b. The whole teaching staff of a college or university. *U.S.*
1829 *Western Monthly Rev.* III. 111 Exposition of the System of Instruction and Discipline pursued in the University of Vermont. By the Faculty. 1843 *Yale Lit. Mag.* IX. 66 That was all I could ever get from him on the subject—'that the Faculty were funny fellows, very—had sent him off for laughing'. 1846 *Knickerbocker Mag.* XXVIII. 9 This body [of trustees]..is composed of men..who are not obliged to consult the Faculty of the college in regard to proposed changes. 1893 W. K. POST *Harvard Stories* 79 There are many classes and individuals..as firmly established..as the Faculty.
12. (sense *9 b) *faculty business, list, meeting*; **faculty psychology**, a term for those systems of psychology in which certain mental faculties were held to be the forces and powers accountable for the phenomena of mind; so *faculty psychologist*; **faculty tax** (example of survival in U.S.); **faculty theory**, the theory of taxation according to which every man should help to bear public burdens according to his ability.
1877 MRS. E. S. WARD *Story of Avis* 74 Some pressing *Faculty business took him..to Professor Dobell's house. 1911 H. S. HARRISON *Queed* xviii. 218 The president sat up late going over his *faculty list. *Ibid.*, There was one man on the staff that West objected to from the first *faculty meeting. 1886 *Encycl. Brit.* XX. 41/1 To free us from the mythology and verbiage of the '*faculty-psychologists'. 1909 *Cent. Dict.* Suppl. s.v. *Psychology*, C. von Wolff (1679–1754) is regarded as the typical faculty-psychologist. 1897 tr. *W. Wundt's Outl. Psychol.* 11 The *faculty-psychology considered these class-concepts as psychical forces or faculties, and referred psychical processes to their alternating or united activity. 1911 E. R. A. SELIGMAN *Income Tax* 398 The only other state in which the *faculty tax lasted during the nineteenth century is South Carolina. 1894 — *Progress. Taxation* (1908) 205 The *faculty theory of taxation is very old. That a man should contribute to the public burdens in proportion to his ability or faculty is a principle which dates back to the middle ages...For a long time..the best practical test of faculty was supposed to be general property. 1896 C. C. PLEHN *Introd. Public Finance* ii. ii. 84 Each citizen should contribute as he is able. They claim that it is easier to measure ability than it is to measure benefit. This theory is called the faculty theory, the term 'faculty' having been found in this sense in early tax laws.

Facundity (fǎkv·nditi). Delete †*Obs.* and add:
1921 *Times Lit. Suppl.* 17 Feb. 110/4 Two love sequences ..have a fine poetic facundity, but that is all.

Faddishly (fæ·diʃli), *adv.* [f. FADDISH + -LY[2].] In a faddish or finical manner.
1928 *Collier's* 10 Nov. 35/2 The sufferer generally eats poorly and faddishly.

Fade (fēⁱd), *sb.*[1] Transfer † *Obs.* and add:
2. *Cinematography.* The action or an act of 'fading' (see *FADE *v.*[1] 7); also freq. *fade-in* or *fade-out*, the gradual brightening up or blacking out of a picture. Also *attrib.*
1918 CROY *How Motion Pictures are Made* 175–6 It was in such experiments that the principle of fade was discovered, by means of which a scene could be made gradually to grow plainer until the full details were before the audience. This in photographic parlance came to be known as the fade-in. *Ibid.*, Slowly the details of the picture are faded in until not only the girl's features are plain, but also the surrounding setting. The reverse of this—the gradual elimination of the scene—came to be known as fade-out. *Ibid.*, The second means of accomplishing a fade picture is by means of the dissolving shutter. *Ibid.*, The diaphragm fade is open to the objection that with an iris that never closes completely it is impossible to make a complete fade. 1919 *Amat. Photographer & Photography* 592/2 After two hundred feet of any picture they could find their way blindfolded..to the fade-out of the lovers. 1922 MACBEAN *Kinemat. Studio Technique* 71 The number of turns in which a 'mix' or 'fade' should be accomplished. 1923 *Strand Mag.* Oct. 350 As I glance around me at this extremely good luxury, and see through it, like a fade-out at the movies, that abhorrent little bedroom in the purlieus of Bloomsbury. 1930 *Times* 26 Mar. 17/4 We may expect the 'close-ups' and 'fade-outs' of happy lovers to be accompanied by the scent of..roses.
b. *transf.* *Fade-out*: Disappearance; death. Cf. the earlier *FADE-AWAY.
1924 A. J. SMALL *Frozen Gold* i. 39 It isn't natural for a whole tribe of stick-at-nothings to be able to do a fade-out like that. 1930 *London Mercury* Feb. 324 Personally I don't want a sticky fade-out yet.

Fade, *v.*[1] Add:
6. b. Of sound: To die away (cf. *FADING *vbl. sb.* c).
1879 G. B. PRESCOTT *Sp. Telephone* ix. 287 The voice increased or faded out in proportion as the telephone was directed towards or receded from the pole of the dipping needle. 1924 *Wireless Ann.* 21 Without a word of warning, the signal 'fades' to nothing.
c. Now often with *away, out*: To disappear from the scene, obliterate oneself.
1924 A. J. SMALL *Frozen Gold* i. 39 When that gang fades out of one camp, I hear all about it inside twenty-four hours. 1929 PRIESTLEY *Good Comp.* I. ii. 63 'My wife', Mr. Rathbury muttered, fading out.
7. *Cinematography. trans.* To cause (a picture,

etc.) to pass gradually *in* or *out*, i.e. to appear or disappear on the screen.
1918 CROY *How Motion Pictures are Made* 177 The fourth method of fading a picture is by means of a chemical process. *Ibid.*, This shutter device for fading out a picture may be operated automatically or by hand. 1922 MACBEAN *Kinemat. Studio Technique* 82 On occasions..it is necessary ..to fade or mix titles into a scene to which they relate.
b. *transf.* of wireless transmission.
1927 *Observer* 11 Sept. 21 Why can't we have the crowd noises faded in? If it is properly handled it won't interfere with the man who is reading the race. *Ibid.* 30 Oct. 26 It was faded out in the middle of Mr. Chesterton's speech.
Hence **Fa·der**, an apparatus for controlling the volume of sound in a talking-picture.
1931 B. BROWN *Talking Pictures* 102 The fader and volume control.

Fa·de-away. *U.S.* [FADE *v.*[1] 6.] An act of disappearance.
1911 H. S. HARRISON *Queed* v. 56 She had only pretended to die in order to make a fade-away with the gate receipts. 1912 C. MATHEWSON *Pitching in a Pinch* i. 11 Many persons have asked me why I do not use my 'fade-away' oftener when it is so effective.

Faded, *ppl. a.* Add: Also *faded-out*.
1874 *Rep. Vermont Board Agric.* II. 600 They are about shedding their coats, with large patches of unshed, faded-out hair upon either side.

Fading, *vbl. sb.* Add: **b.** *Cinematography.* (See *FADE *v.*[1] 7.) Also *ppl. a.*
1918 CROY *How Motion Pictures are Made* 176 Fading in or out is accomplished by four different methods. 1922 MACBEAN *Kinemat. Studio Technique* 65 The operations of 'fading in' and 'fading out'..are..effected with the diaphragm. *Ibid.* 78 'Mixing' from a 'Fading-in' Title. *Ibid.* 82 The film is then wound back to the beginning of the 'fading' with the lens closed.
c. The periodic variation in intensity of wireless signals, due to in- and out-phase effects.
1923 *Wireless Rev.* 23 June 128/2 Manchester and Newcastle both appear to be suffering very badly from fading. 1924 *Ibid.* 20 Feb. 355/1 Fading is always confined to distant signals (not necessarily weak signals). 1927 *Glasgow Herald* 1 Jan. 9 A site where interference and what is technically known as 'fading' would be reduced to a minimum. 1930 *Morning Post* 18 Aug., The difficulty lies more in the reception of the medium wave stations. These are subject to variations in strength, owing to fading.

Faenza (fa,e·nza). Name of a city in the province of Ravenna, Italy, used *attrib.* to designate the pottery made there in the sixteenth century.
1885 *Encycl. Brit.* XIX. 627/2 Faenza plate (tondino), with border in deep ultramarine blues, and central coat of arms in rich orange and red. 1904 *Technol. & Sci. Dict.* (ed. Goodchild & Tweney), *Faenza Ware*, a distinctive term given to a fine sort of pottery originally made at Faenza near Bologna, in Italy.

Færoese: see *FAROESE.

Fag (fæg), *sb.*[4] *slang.* [Abbreviation of FAG-END. (Cf. FAG *sb.*[2] 2.)] The fag-end of a cigar or cigarette; hence applied to cheap brands of cigarettes.
1888 *Sat. Rev.* 30 June 786/2 They..burn their throats with the abominable 'fag', with its acrid paper and vile tobacco. 1893 *Pick-me-up* 14 Oct. 45/2 Stimulants he calls 'booze' and a cigarette a 'fag'. 1898 *Engl. Dial. Dict.* s.v., Here [*sc.* at Redruth] we are often asked by youngsters to 'chuck' them 'a fag'—and whole cheap cigarettes are also often called fags. 1908 *Ch. Times* 7 Feb. 173/1 He gathered into a leather pouch the remains of his cigarettes, and left the room. 'What does he do with all those fags?' asked Conway. 1928 GALSWORTHY *Swan Song* iv. 24 Cinemas, fags, and football matches—there would be no real revolution while they were on hand.

Fagaceous (fǎgē·ʃəs), *a.* [f. mod.L. *Fagaceæ* (typical genus *Fagus* 'beech'): see -ACEOUS.] Belonging to or characteristic of the family *Fagaceæ*; pertaining to or resembling the beech.
1902 WEBSTER Suppl.

Faggot, *sb.* **10.** Add: **faggot-iron**, iron, in the form of bars or masses, made from welding together a faggot or pile of iron bars; **faggot-stitch**, needlework in which two pieces of material are joined together by stitching resembling the fagoting of drawn-thread work; so *faggot-stitching*.
1903 *Daily Chron.* 13 June 8/4 A lace and canvas epaulette pelerine, the seams of which are separated by faggot-stitch. 1928 *Sunday Express* 3 June 8 The frills, which were not more than half an inch wide, were set in with faggot stitching.

Faggot, *v.* Add:
1. d. *Embroidery.* To ornament (needlework) by FAGGOTING; also, to join (two pieces of material) by faggot-stitch.
1900 MARY E. WILKINS *Parson Lord* 117 She has hemstitched and fagoted everything. 1904 *Daily Chron.* 3 May 5/4 They are joined with an insertion, or are faggoted together to make kimonas for morning wear.

Faggoted (fæ·gŏtėd), *ppl. a.* [f. FAGGOT *sb.* or *v.* + -ED.] Made into faggots. *Faggoted iron* (see quots.). Also *attrib.*
1848 W. TEMPLETON *Locomotive Steam-Engine* (ed. 2) 29 The best wrought iron, fagoted and welded together, generally termed fagoted iron. 1874 KNIGHT *Dict. Mech.*, Fagoted Iron Furnace.

Fagin (fē·gin). The name of a character in Dickens's 'Oliver Twist', a Jew who trained children to be thieves and pickpockets; allusively used for a thief or trainer of thieves.
1847 *Punch* 2 Oct. 125 The Fagin of France after condemnation. (*Slightly altered from* 'Oliver Twist'.) 1905 *Daily Chron.* 14 Apr. 6/6 Thieves' kitchen kept by two modern Fagins...This school of crime bore outwardly the innocent semblance of a greengrocery and ice-cream shop... The two Fagins who conducted it were..both Italians. [1907 *Ibid.* 17 May 3/4 The Fagin-like person who has hitherto been King of the Nile.]

Fagine (fē·dʒin). *Chem.* Also -in. [f. L. *fagus* beech + -INE[5].] An alkaloid obtained from the nuts of the common beech *Fagus sylvatica*.
1838 R. D. THOMSON in *Brit. Annual* 337 Fagin. 1846 LOUDON *Veget. Kingd.* 291 The husks of the common Beech-tree yield a narcotic extractive, called Fagine. 1860 *Chambers's Encycl.* I. 804/2 A volatile, narcotic, poisonous principle, called Fagine, is..found in it [*sc.* beechmast].

Fagmaster (fæ·gmɑstəɹ). [f. FAG *sb.*[1] 2 + MASTER *sb.*[1]] A boy who has a junior boy as his fag, a fagger.
1876 ALBEMARLE *50 Yrs. of My Life* I. 293 One day I had to take a pair of my fagmaster's shoes to 'Cobbler Foots' to be mended. 1895 *Q. Rev.* Oct. 283 Probably he would have been..cobbed by his fagmaster as an incorrigible toast-burner. 1920 *Blackw. Mag.* Oct. 483/2 One small boy, Harker minor,..was told by his fagmaster that he would be licked for 'fighting' as soon as he was well.

Faham (fā·ăm, fā·ăm). *Bot.* Also **faam**. [So Fr.] An orchid, *Angræcum fragrans*, from Bourbon and Mauritius, used as a substitute for China tea, and medicinally; also, the leaves so used.
1858 SIMMONDS *Dict. Trade*, Faham-tea. 1861 [see *BOURBON 3 d]. 1862 *Chambers's Encycl.* IV. 211/2 Faam, or Faham..much prized in the East for the delightful fragrance of its leaves.

Fail, *v.* Add:
12. e. With negative and const. *to* with inf., of a thing, circumstance, situation, influence: Not to have the effect of, not to result in doing something.
1920 *Engl. Hist. Rev.* Jan. 143 Turenne..was a protestant, a circumstance which could not fail to prejudice Louis.
14. c. *trans.* To fail to pass (an examination). *colloq.*
1909 H. G. WELLS *Tono-Bungay* III. ii. 244 He failed some dreadful examination and had to go into the militia. *Mod.* She failed even School Certif.

Fain (fēⁱn), *v.*[2] Chiefly *school slang*, orig. *dial.* = FEN *v.*[2] Used in the expression *fains* or *fain(s) I, fain it, fainits*: see quots.
1870 *N. & Q.* 4th Ser. VI. 415/2 'Fains', or 'Fain it'—A term demanding a 'truce' during the progress of any game, which is always granted by the opposing party. *Ibid.* 517/1 A boy who had 'killed' another at marbles, that is hit his marble, would call out 'Fain it', meaning 'You mustn't shoot at me in return'; or if a boy was going to shoot, and some inequality of surface was in his way, which he would have cleared away, his antagonist would prevent him by calling out 'Fain clears'. *Ibid.* 517/2 If a prefect wants anything fetched for him and does not say by whom, those who wish to get off going say 'Fain I'. 1889 BARRÈRE & LELAND *Dict. Slang*, *Faints*, in vogue among schoolboys to express a wish temporarily to withdraw from participation in the particular sport or game being played. 1891 FARMER *Slang*, Fains! Fainits! Fain it!

Fainéantism (fēne,ăntiz'm). [f. FAINÉANT + -ISM.] = FAINEANTISE.
1873 *Bookseller* 2 July 549/1 He had little tolerance for anything like fainéantism, or shirking in those about him. 1898 *Star* 3 Jan. 1/7 Old Russia, with its fainéantism, its childish superstition, its base and effeminate pleasures.

Faint, *a.* Add:
7. b. Of food: Not fresh, tainted. *local.*
1902 *Westm. Gaz.* 25 Oct. 2/3 This meat hadn't been trimmed. I admit it was 'faint'.

Fair, *sb.*[1] **2.** *fair-ground* (earlier examples).
1741 LADY POMFRET *Lett.* (1805) III. 247 The fair-ground; which is a square enclosure, with..shops of all sorts on each hand. 1857 *Trans. Ill. Agric. Soc.* 25 Choose a spot of ground ..south of this city for fair grounds. 1862 O. W. NORTON *Army Lett.* 106 It looks like the road near a county fair ground.

Fair, *a.* and *sb.*[2] Add: **A.** *adj.* **1. b.** Also in comparative.
1878 J. H. BEADLE *Western Wilds* xxix. 451 The fairer section of our party are startled at the crowds of men in the streets.
d. Also *arch.*
1820 SCOTT *Abbot* xi, 'So much for your lineage, fair sir', replied his companion.
10. *Fair wages* (attrib.).
1894 S. WEBB *Hist. Trade Unionism* 386 A hundred and fifty local authorities have now (1894) adopted some kind of 'Fair Wages' resolution. 1902 *Encycl. Brit.* XXXII. 692/1 The extent to which a 'fair wages clause', in some form or another, has been inserted in public contracts. 1907 *Westm. Gaz.* 3 Sept. 7/1 The committee appointed to consider the fair-wages resolution.
d. *spec.* in games.
1867 *Routledge's Handbk. Football* 41 Knocking on and throwing forward are disallowed: in case of this rule being broken a catch from such a knock or throw shall be equivalent to a fair catch. *Ibid.* 47 A Fair Catch is a catch from a kick, or a knock on from the hand but not from the arm of the opposite side, or a throw on, when the catcher makes a mark with his heel provided no one else on his side touch the ball. 1896 R. G. KNOWLES & MORTON *Baseball* 23 If the ball falls exactly on the foul line, it is a fair hit, unless it rolls into foul territory.
e. *Fair game*: see GAME *sb.* 10 b.
11. c. Unquestionable, absolute, complete, thorough. *dial.*, *Austral.*, or *slang.*
1872 E. J. IRVING *Fireside Lays* 232 The sichts an' the soun's that we witnessed, Amaist made me greet for fair shame. 1889–98 Fair cop [see *COP *sb.*[2] 1]. 1916 *Anzac Bk.* 31/2 'Ee's a fair cow, 'e is.
B. *sb.*[2] **1. c.** *For fair*: completely, altogether. *U.S. slang.*
1903 *N. Y. Times* 5 Dec. 5, 'I seem to be putting my foot in it for fair', said the green marine. 1916 H. L. WILSON *Somewhere in Red Gap* viii. 352 Pete must of [= have] been crazy for fair about that time.

Fair, *v.* Add: **1. b.** Also *dial.* and *U.S.* with *off* or *up.*
a 1859 *Western Tales* (Bartlett) He..moved to the North, and whenever he see a fog risin', took to his bed, and kept it till it fair'd off. *a* 1859 *N. Y. Spirit of Times* (ibid.) There's going to be a nasty fog to-night,..call me if it fairs up. 1859 W. WHITE *Northumb. & Border* 448 The squall lasted for nearly two hours. When it 'faired up', the son said [etc.]. 1899 T. D. PRICE *MS. Diary* 28 Apr., Rain in morning but faired up and good day. 1903 A. ADAMS *Log Cowboy* viii. 110 The weather in the meantime had faired off.
3. Also of an aeroplane (cf. *FAIRING *vbl. sb.*[2]).
1922 *Encycl. Brit.* XXX. 21/1 To reduce resistance, exposed parts may be 'faired'.

Fair-haired, *a.* Add: **c.** *fig.* Darling, favourite. (Cf. WHITE *a.* 9, WHITE BOY.)
1916 J. W. GERARD *Face to Face with Kaiserism* vii. (1918) 76 The [German] Government published a certificate in the *Official Gazette* to the effect that I was their fair-haired boy, etc.—very nice of them.

Fairily (fē·rili), *adv.* [f. FAIRY *a.* + -LY[2].] In a fairy-like manner.
1864 TENNYSON *Islet* 18 Fairily-delicate palaces shine.

Fairing (fē·riŋ), *vbl. sb.*[2] [f. *FAIR *v.* 3 + -ING[1].] The action or result of making the lines of a vessel suitable for its easy passage through water or air; the line or curvature so made, or the structure added for this purpose.
1867 SMYTH *Sailor's Word-bk.*, *Fairing*, sheering a ship in construction. Also, the draught of a ship. 1916 H. BARBER *Aeroplane Speaks* 137 *Fairing*, usually made of thin sheet aluminium, wood, or a light construction of wood and fabric; and bent round detrimental surface in order to give it a 'fair' or 'stream-like' shape. 1927 *Daily Tel.* 6 Sept. 11/3 The fairing of the wings into the fuselage. *attrib.* 1930 *Daily Express* 23 May 11/5 The fairing piece at the extreme end of the tail, which performs no actual function in the operation of the airship, was slightly damaged.
b. (See quot.)
1922 *Encycl. Brit.* XXX. 21/1 In other countries cable has continued to be used, frequently duplicated, the cables lying one behind the other with a wood 'fairing' between them.

Fair Isle (fē·rəil). Name of one of the Shetland islands used attrib. to designate woollen articles knitted in certain designs characteristic of the island.
1851 *Illustr. Catal. Gt. Exhib.* III. III. 585/2 Fair Isle socks, gloves, vest piece, comforter, and cap. 1913 *Queen* 25 Oct. Advts. p. i/3 Allover Fair Isle Jumpers. *Ibid.*, Fair Isle Knitting Yarn, in 2-ply yellow, green, blue and red. 1924 *Tourist* Winter Sports No. 20 Shetland wool with Fair Isle border. 1925 *Queen* 8 Apr. 19 Attired in her Fair Isle jersey.

Fairly and squarely, *adv.* (see under FAIR AND SQUARE). (Earlier U.S. example.)
1862 *Congress. Globe* 27 Mar. 1402/2, I..doubt..the ability of these guns to remain in their position if..struck fairly and squarely by shot from the enemy.

Fair-top boot. *U.S.* [FAIR *a.* 1 f.] A boot topped with light-coloured leather.
1799 in C. Cist *Cincinnati* (1841) 159 As an illustration of fashions..fair-top boots. 1826 *Rhode Isl. American* Let. 2 Mar. (Th.) His usual dress in the Senate is a blue coat,.. drab small-clothes, and fair-top boots. 1853 J. G. BALDWIN *Flush Times Alabama* 22 He dressed in the old-fashioned fair-top boots and shorts. 1860 S. MORDECAI *Virginia* iii. 48 His tall and burly form arrayed in fair-top boots [etc.].

Fairway. Add:
b. *Golf.* That part of a golf-course between a tee and putting-green which consists of short grass.
1910 B. DARWIN *Golf Courses Brit. Isles* 18 Hillocks have risen as if by magic in the middle of the fairway. 1912 *Golf. From the Times* i. 12 The flanking bunkers, set on the edges of the fairway, are as often as not wholly outside the range of practical politics as far as his tee shot is concerned. 1923 *Daily Mail* 18 Jan. 9 The maintenance staff..are busy on the fairways and teeing grounds.
c. *Lawn tennis.* The middle of a court.
1927 A. W. MYERS in *Daily Tel.* 30 Aug. 10/5 The court ..was soft and yielding near the base-lines, even if true enough in the fairway.

Fairy, *sb.* and *a.* Add: **A.** *sb.* **6.** Euphemism for: A catamite. *slang.*
1925 F. LONSDALE *Spring Cleaning* II, *Mona.* I say, what's the fairy's name? *Richard.* Happily for the moment I have forgotten it. 1929 R. HUGHES *High Wind in Jamaica* iv, 'Who are they?' Emily asked the Captain...'Who are who?' he murmured absently...'Oh, those? Fairies.' 'Hey! Yey! Yey!' cried the mate.
C. 2. fairy bells, a kind of musical instrument; **fairy cycle**, a small cycle for young children; **fairy lights**, (*a*) a kind of night light; (*b*) small coloured lights used in illuminations out of doors and often hung among trees; (*c*) perversion of 'Verey light'.
1895 *Army & Navy Co-op. Soc. Price List* 15 Sept. 1664 *Fairy Bells. 1927 *Times* 6 July 13 A girl of six..riding her *fairycycle. 1928 *Daily Express* 2 June 7/3 The boy was pushing his fairy cycle near his home when a collision occurred between two motor-cars, one of which killed him. 1871 *Engl. Mechanic* 24 Nov. 244/2 A long crescent of *fairy-lights, glimmering on the coast-line. 1886 *Colon. & Ind. Exhib. Official Catal.* 166 Advt., New Patent 'Fairy'

Lamps and 'Fairy' Lights. 1891 *Strand Mag.* Aug. Advt. i 'Fairy' Light. With Double Wicks. 1895 *Army & Navy Co-op. Soc. Price List* 15 Sept. 20 Night Lights...Fairy Lights, to burn in the 'Fairy Lamps'. 1927 W. E. COLLINSON *Contemp. Eng.* 98 Fairy lights (Verey lights to send up the S.O.S. or distress signals).

Fairyology (fē·riǫ·lŏdʒi). [f. FAIRY + -OLOGY.] The study of fairies. Hence **Fairyo·logist**, one who studies fairies.
1859 *Denham Tracts* (*title*) A few Fragments of Fairyology. 1908 *Daily Chron.* 11 Dec. 4/4 Mr. Dion Clayton Calthrop, the 'fairyologist' of all others—to quote Mr. Tree's quaint phrase.

Fairy-tale (fē·ri,tēⁱl). [f. FAIRY + TALE *sb.*; rendering F. *conte de fées*.] **a.** A tale about fairies. Also *gen.*, fairy legend, faerie. **b.** An unreal or incredible story. **c.** A falsehood. Also *attrib.* Hence **Fai·ry-tale-ish** *a.*
1750 (*title*) A new Collection of Fairy Tales. 1797 J. MOSER (*title*) Moral Tales; consisting of the Reconciliation,..a Fairy Tale, in the modern style. Clementia and Malitia; a Fairy Tale, in the ancient style. 1864 TENNYSON *Aylmer's Field* 89 He..Had..told her fairy-tales, Show'd her the fairy footings on the grass. 1887 RUSKIN *Præterita* II. 244 [Shakespeare's] Henry V. is only a king of fairy tale. 1900 *Daily Tel.* 4 July (Ware) Mr. Kruger, for the information of his sympathisers in America, has told a Chicago journalist one of his pretty little fairy tales, the only truth in which is that some burghers are again taking up arms. 1914 *Scotsman* 16 Sept. 6/4 The Russians have neither 'landed in nor passed Great Britain on their way to France or Belgium', nor are they now on French or Belgian soil. The whole story has been a gigantic fairy tale. 1920 O. DOUGLAS *Penny Plain* ix, It would be very nice and fairy-tale-ish!

Fait accompli (fɛtakoṅpli). [Fr.] An accomplished fact.
1845 R. FORD *Handbk. Spain* I. 337 This is now a *fait accompli*. 1872 E. BRADDON *Life in India* v. 179 After the overland route was a *fait accompli*, the rules of the services ..restricted the servants of the East India Company from enjoying much of their leave westward of the Cape of Good Hope. 1895 *Bow Bells* 16 Aug. 177/2 It will be very interesting to see..whether various other suggestions..will also become fait accompli. 1905 MRS. H. WARD *Marriage of W. Ashe* II. viii. 139 Elizabeth knew that his appearance in the conversation invariably meant a *fait accompli* of some sort.

Faith, *sb.* **14.** Add: *faith-state.*
1896 J. H. LEUBA in *Amer. Jrnl. Psychol.* Apr. 315 That state of confidence, trust,..which we have found, more or less tersely expressed, in every conversion considered is the Faith-state. 1902 W. JAMES *Var. Relig. Exper.* 505. 1924 W. B. SELBIE *Psych. Relig.* 158 To induce what psychologists call the faith state may be a very great and wonderful thing if the object of faith is worthy, i.e. God or Christ.

Faithist (fē·þist). [f. FAITH *sb.* + -IST.] A member of a sect whose religion is based on revelations contained in the 'Kosmon Bible' or 'Oahspe' and on angelic communications. Also *attrib.*
1907 *Westm. Gaz.* 25 June 10/1 The Faithist Community, which has established a modest footing in Balham, and whose comprehensive gospel ranges from the creation of man to the 'glory and labours of the gods and goddesses of the Etherian Heavens'. 1921 *Glasgow Herald* 21 Sept. 10 Mr. F. T. A. Davies, founder of the Faithist movement in England. 1928 *Sunday Dispatch* 29 July 9/5 The Faithists originated in America. There are only two or three hundred in Great Britain—most of them in London and the Home Counties.

Fake, *v.*[2] Add: **1.** Also *absol.*
1908 *Smart Set* Sept. 39, I knew that..it had no curative power and I didn't want to be caught faking.
b. *spec.* To conceal the defects of (an animal) by colouring hair or feathers.
1874 [see Dict., sense 1]. 1895 STABLES *Our Friend the Dog* vii. 73 *Faking*—Dyeing, staining, clipping, or otherwise interfering with the dog's coat or appearance, to hide defects and deceive the judge or public.
c. To fit *up* as a makeshift.
1929 ABU NADAAR in *Mercury Story Bk.* 95 He managed to fake up some sort of a hand-crusher for the quartz.

Fakir. Add: **1. b.** *erron.* for FAKER *U.S.*, pronounced (fē·kəɹ).
1902 A. D. MCFAUL *Ike Glidden* xvii. 127 Each day brought its new characters, fakirs, peddlers, schemers and promoters. 1903 *N. Y. Even. Post* 31 Oct. 5 One may see at almost any of the downtown corners a street fakir selling shoestrings.

Falasha (fală·ʃă). [Abyssinian *falasha* exile, immigrant.] One of a group of people in Abyssinia holding the Jewish faith. Also as *collect. sing.*
1790 J. BRUCE *Trav.* I. 404 The Falasha..are a people of Abyssinia, having a particular language of their own;.. they are now, and ever were, Jews. 1869 S. P. GOODHART tr. J. M. Flad (*title*) The Falashas (Jews) of Abyssinia. 1875 *Encycl. Brit.* I. 63/2 A race of Jews, known by the name of Falashas, inhabit the district of Samen. 1908 *Daily Chron.* 6 Mar. 3/5 Proposed School for the 'Falashas' of Abyssinia.

Fall, *sb.*[1] Add: **14. d.** In full *fall-notch*: A notch made on that side of a tree indicating the direction in which the tree is intended to fall.
1893 G. D. LESLIE *Lett. to Marco* xxxviii. 253 Then what they called the fall was made; this was a larger and deeper notch on the side the tree was intended to fall...By the proper placement of the fall-notch, the tree was eventually brought down due west. When the fall had been carefully cut with the axe, a long, narrow saw was worked through the stem.
23. c. Also, a flap overhanging a bookshelf.
1897 F. J. BURGOYNE *Library Construction* 50 Falls should be of some cheaper material than leather.
29. fall-block, either of the two lower blocks of a boat's falls; **fall-leaf** *U.S.*, a table-leaf which can be let down; also *attrib.*; **fall-line**, an imaginary line drawn through a number of rivers where they make a sudden descent, as at the edge of a plateau; *spec.* such a line in the eastern United States marking the western limit of the Atlantic coastal plain; **fall-notch** = *14 d; **fall-piece** *U.S.*, the flap of a pair of breeches; **fall-pipe**, (*a*) the sloping inlet pipe of a water-ram; (*b*) the pipe conveying rain-water from a roof, etc. to the ground; **fall tube**, (*a*) a tube in a mercury air pump through which the mercury falls carrying with it the air from the vessel in which it is desired to make a vacuum; (*b*) the supply pipe of a water motor.
1874 KNIGHT *Dict. Mech.* s.v. *Davit*, When the boat is lowered the hooks of the *fall-blocks are cast off simultaneously. 1883 *Man. Seamanship for Boys* 136 Fall Blocks, for Top-Tackle Pendants. 1853 B. F. TAYLOR *Jan. & June* (1871) 204 It was the old table with the *fall leaves. 1882 WAITE *Adv. Far West* 189 [A] fall-leaf table. 1902 LD. AVEBURY *Scenery of Eng.* 481 A similar line along the junction of the uplands with the sea-plain is known in the United States as the '*fall line'. 1883 *fall-notch [see *14 d]. 1837 *Knickerbocker Mag.* IX. 157 The pantaloons..with a perpendicular opening in front, which I should think must be much more convenient than the old-fashioned *fall-pieces. 1888 *Lockwood's Dict. Mech. Engin.*, **Fall Pipe*, a drive pipe. 1929 *Daily Tel.* 22 Jan. 12/4 When cornered he slid down a fallpipe. 1894 *Westm. Gaz.* 1 May 7/2 The *fall tube is about two metres in diameter. 1904 *Technol. & Sci. Dict.* (ed. Goodchild & Tweney) s.v. *Air Pumps*, Mercury is poured into a large funnel (A), and flows through the tubes AB and BC into the 'pump head' D, from which it falls down the 'fall tube' DE, whose length is greater than the height of the barometer.

Fall, *v.* Add:
19. d. Also of the batsman: To be out.
1882 PARDON *Australians in Eng.* 147 Grace fell to a catch at long-on. 1888 R. H. LYTTELTON *Cricket* (Badm. Libr.) 344 Ridley again fell to Patterson, with the total at 16.
e. *To fall over one another* or *each other* (fig. phr.): to 'scramble' for the first place, engage in rough-and-tumble rivalry.
1904 W. H. SMITH *Promoters* viii. 144 Capitalists are getting ready to fall over each other in availing themselves of the opportunity of utilizing the situation.
26. d. Of tobacco leaves: To lose freshness after cutting.
1849 *Rep. U.S. Comm. Patents, Agric.* (1850) 320 Let it [*sc.* tobacco] lay on the ground for a short time to 'fall' or wilt.
e. *Leather-manufacture.* Of a skin: To become soft and pliable.
1885 H. R. PROCTER *Text-bk. Tanning* xxi. 226 The bate must be used tepid, and not too strong. The skins 'fall' (lose their plumpness) in it rapidly, and become extremely soft and fine to the touch.
32. b. (Modern quot. for northern usage.)
1892 H. R. MILL *Realm of Nature* i. 3 They alone fall to be considered here.
38. Also const. *upon.*
1906 E. PHILLPOTTS *Portreeve* III. iv, The rest of the party fell upon a few moments of silence after they had got out of earshot. *Ibid.* xiv, She marked how he fell once more upon a fitful gloom.
59*. Fall for —. To be captivated or carried away by; to yield to the attractions of; (in a bad sense) to be taken in by. orig. *U.S. slang.*
1911 L. J. VANCE *Cynthia* 179 There's only one sensible thing...And I think I can see you falling for it. 1916 H. L. WILSON *Somewhere in Red Gap* v. 186 Even Mis' Judge Ballard fell for it, though hers were made of severe black with a long coat. 1919 — *Ma Pettengill* x. 292 Herman fell for it all—all this old stuff. 1924 ROSE MACAULAY *Orphan Island* xix. § 1. 250 European critics, for ever falling for new things, would fall most certainly for this. 1926 GALSWORTHY *Silver Spoon* II. viii, 'Francis Wilmot? Oh! he's "fallen for" Marjorie Ferrar'. 1926 *Publishers' Weekly* 30 Jan. 327 Can't you picture the susceptible swain falling for books of love stories? 1927 *Sunday Express* 4 Sept. 5, I have got a play here by some Frenchman about how you live with a guy who has got a wife. The guy falls for you until his wife trips him. Then there's a bed-room scene. 1929 FARJEON *Underground* xxi, I held out my pocket-case, and said I'd found it on the floor of the hotel. 'Is it yours?' I asked. To my surprise, he fell for it beautifully.
60. Fall from —. c. Delete † and add:
1872 C. E. MAURICE *Stephen Langton* iv. 254 The followers of Louis were falling from him.
84. Fall down. f. To 'come to grief'; to collapse, fail. Often with *on*. *slang.* orig. *U.S.*
1873 J. H. BEADLE *Undevel. West* xxxii. 704 We'll reach Sioux City by 5 o'clock if we don't fall down...But we did 'fall down' just at noon, running hard aground. 1899 J. L. WILLIAMS *Stolen Story* etc. 223 It amazed him every time a new reporter..fell down on a story. 1913 F. H. BURNETT *T. Tembarom* ii, I'll put up a mighty hard fight before I fall down. *Ibid.* iii, Vouldn't have fell down on that order for twenty-five dollars. 1928 *Publishers' Weekly* 26 May 2175 We know of many cases where we fell down on buying books written by authors that had had successful books before. 1928 *Daily Tel.* 14 Aug. 10/4 If we fall down on the job of absorbing these 10,000 men of good stock and stamina.

Fall-away, *sb.* Add: **2.** A falling off.
1878 B. F. TAYLOR *Between Gates* 232 On midsummer the Yo Semite is less of a fall than a fall-away.

Fall-back, *a.* *U.S.* Of a chaise, etc.: Having a back which can be let down.
1767 *Boston Gaz.* 12 Oct. (Th.) A Fall-back Chaise for sale. 1768 *Essex Inst. Hist. Coll.* XI. 38 He also has five fall-back chaises, one fall-back curricle. 1832 *Coll. New H. Hist. Soc.* III. 37 He was the proprietor of a fall back chaise.

Fall-down, *sb.* *U.S.* [FALL *v.* 84.] **a.** A device forming part of a trap. **b.** A downfall; a reverse.
1853 F. W. THOMAS *J. Randolph* 106 There stood the trap with the fall-down about ten feet from us. 1889 *Kansas Times & Star* 13 Dec., There was prosperity in about every line of business here, except the undertakers' and for the latter's fall down, much thanks.

Fallen, *ppl. a.* **4.** *absol.* with *the*: Add: Those who have died in battle.
1914 W. D. NEWTON *War* xi. 119 The corpses of the fallen were trodden and ground beneath stumbling heedless soles. 1917 L. BINYON (*title*) For the Fallen and other poems. 1919 *Times* 12 Nov. 16/5 The majority of the citizens willingly consented to pay a tribute to the memory of the fallen.

Fallenness (fǭ·l'n,nės). [f. FALLEN *ppl. a.* + -NESS.] The state of being fallen; *esp.* degenerateness consequent upon the Fall.
1871 W. GRAHAM *Lect. Ephesians* 364 It teaches the fallenness of our whole nature. 1913 W. H. MOBERLY in *Foundations* 283 What is important is not an historical Fall, but the fact of 'fallenness'. 1923 *Expos. Times* July 439/2 It fails to express the fallenness of man's original animalism and degradation.

Faller. Add: **2.** Also *U.S.*
1905 *Terms Forestry & Logging* 37 *Faller*, one who fells trees.
5. b. A kind of stamp (see quots.).
1884 KNIGHT *Dict. Mech.* Suppl., *Faller*, a vertical stamp in a fulling, milling, or stamping machine; usually lifted by cams and allowed to drop vertically and endwise. *Ibid.*, *Faller Machine*, a machine with vertical stamps or fallers, used in milling goods.

Falling, *vbl. sb.* **7.** Add: *attrib.* (= felling) in *falling axe, rope, wedge.*
1875 G. C. DAVIES *Rambles School Field-Club* viii. 67 A 'falling rope'..that men attach to the top of a tree when they wish to cut it down. 1905 *Terms Forestry & Logging* 37 *Falling ax*, an ax with a long helve and a long, narrow bit, designed especially for felling trees. *Falling wedge*, a wedge used to throw a tree in the desired direction, by driving it into the saw kerf.

Falling, *ppl. a.* Add:
2. *Falling diphthong*: see DIPHTHONG *sb.* note.
5. Applied to weather in which rain, snow, or hail falls or may be expected. *dial.* and *U.S.*
1733 FRANKLIN *Poor Richard's Almanac* 6 Windy and falling weather. 1760 WASHINGTON *Diaries* I. 112 The morning..promised much rain or other falling weather. 1780 in *Coll. New H. Hist. Soc.* IX. 176 Cloudy but no falling weather. 1838 CAROLINE GILMAN *Recoll. Southern Matron* xxv. 172 It looks like falling weather, and my old drab will come in well to-day. 1859 BARTLETT *Dict. Amer.* (ed. 2) s.v. *Weather*, 'We are going to have falling weather', means that we are going to have rain, snow or hail. 1884– in dial. glossaries (Gloucester, Hereford, Warwick, Worcester). 1919 H. L. WILSON *Ma Pettengill* v. 165 Will you look at that mess of clouds? I bet it's falling weather over in Surprise Valley.

False, *a.* Add:
2. d. or by any restrictive action or influence.
1768 BLACKSTONE *Comm.* III. viii. 127 To constitute the injury of false imprisonment there are two points requisite: 1. The detention of the person; and, 2. The unlawfulness of such detention. 1880 T. E. HOLLAND *Jurispr.* 111 A man has a right to go where he pleases, so long as he does not interfere with the rights of others, and anyone who prevents him from so doing, whether by constraint actually applied, or by such show of authority or force as has an effect on the will equivalent to actual constraint, is said in English law to be guilty of 'false imprisonment'.
6. b. *False starter*: see quot.
1923 J. D. HACKETT *Labor Terms* in *Management Engineering* May, *False Starter*, one who has been selected, tested, and approved by the employment department but who fails to start work.
8. b. Law. *False issue*: an issue introduced by counsel in order to conceal the real issue. *False pretences*: misrepresentations made to convey a false impression. Also *false representation.*
1757 *Act* 30 *Geo. II* c. 24 § 1 All persons who knowingly and designedly, by false pretence or pretences, shall obtain ..money, goods, wares or merchandizes, with intent to.. defraud any person..of the same. 1831 [J. BANIM] *Smuggler* (1833) I. xi. 139 Made prisoners in it, upon false pretences. 1836 *Mag. Dom. Econ.* I. 92 Indictable for obtaining money under false pretences. 1858 False representation [see REPRESENTATION 4]. 1861 *Act* 24 & 25 *Vict.* c 96 § 88 It shall be sufficient in any Indictment for obtaining or attempting to obtain any such Property by false Pretences to allege that the Party accused did the Act with Intent to defraud, without alleging an Intent to defraud any particular Person. 1903 *Westm. Gaz.* 12 June 10/1 Mr. Robson: Then your lordship does not specify any false issues that you say I raised? His Lordship: The false issue you raised was whether or not the uncle was justified in going to the detective to find out the wife's residence instead of going to the father, and there were hours in the Divorce Court occupied upon that point. 1907 *Daily Chron.* 28 Aug., When charged he pleaded guilty to three charges of obtaining goods on false pretences.
13. d. Also in more general sense.
1902 *Encycl. Brit.* XXXII. 605/1 Where pheasants exist in any number, a 'false covert' of spruce and fir loppings should be made at the point to which it is desirable to force the birds.
i. Photog. *False image*: an extra image made on the plate at the same time as the image proper by a defective lens.

1892 *Photogr. Ann.* II. 39 Another troublesome fault is what is called a ghost, or false image. 1918 *Photo-Miniature* XV. Mar. (Gloss.), *False Image*, an extra image, usually unsharp and often inverted, which a defective (doublet) lens will give on the plate at the same time as the image proper.
14. c. *False alarm*: an alarm without foundation, given either purposely to deceive or under misapprehension of danger. Now often *transf.* or *gen.*
1594 [see ALARM *sb.* 8]. 1802 C. JAMES *Milit. Dict.* s.v. *Alarm*, False-Alarms, are stratagems of war, frequently made use of to harrass an enemy, by keeping them perpetually under arms. 1834 tr. *Jacquemont's Journ. India* I. 214 My pistols and watch were almost in his way; but, disturbed ..by some noise or false alarm, he had not time to choose. 1847 ANNE BRONTË *Agnes Grey* xvii, There was 'no need to be in such agitation about the matter—it might prove a false alarm after all'. 1873 *Gentleman's Mag.* X. 587 The false alarm..was made the occasion of a discussion.., which ended in the Lord Mayor advising his civic brethren to wait and see. 1900 *Daily News* 7 Dec. 3/2 Any day the giving of a false alarm might cause the deaths of persons endangered by fire, and whom the Brigade did not reach in time.
15. In various technical uses: see quots.
1854 *Poultry Chron.* I. 488 On inspecting the windpipe from the root of the tongue, I found congestion and swelling of the glottis and rima glottidis, but no false membrane such as I should have found in a child. 1873 T. H. GREEN *Introd. Pathol.* (ed. 2) 265 In croup the exuded materials coagulate principally upon the surface of the membrane, where, together with the newly-formed cellular elements, they form the false membrane. 1879 *St. George's Hosp. Rep.* IX. 702 Sore-throats without anything that can fairly be called false membrane. 1880 *Encycl. Brit.* XII. 180/2 Immediately within the opening of the nostril [of a horse], the respiratory canal sends off on its upper and outer side a diverticulum or blind pouch (called 'false nostril') of a conical form. 1882 CAULFEILD & SAWARD *Dict. Needlew.*, *False hem*, this is applied to a fold-over at the extreme edge of any portion of dress or other article..which has the appearance of a hem..but is not one. 1883 *Man. Seamanship for Boys* 97 Cardinal Points...False Points. So called because they borrow their names from the two points between which they come. 1883 *Encycl. Brit.* XV. 235/2 Such a point is called a false north pole, and we see that the existence of two true north poles necessitates the existence of a false north pole. 1886 *Ibid.* XXI. 404/2 These portions go on growing in a direction at an angle with the previous one, but still in contact, and thus produce the 'false-branching' to which the *Cladothrix* owes its name. 1888 *Lockwood's Dict. Mech. Engin.* s.v. *False Water*, When steam is generated very rapidly in a boiler, the immediate effect is a rapid rising of the water level in the gauge cocks, due to the increase in volume caused by admixture of steam. This sudden increase is termed false water. 1902 *Encycl. Brit.* XXXIII. 99/2 *False Station*.—When the theodolite cannot for any reason be placed over the centre of a station, if the distance be measured, and the theodolite reading of it be noted, the observed angles may be reduced to what they would be at the centre of the station. False stations have frequently to be made in practice.
e. *False grain*: a fresh crop of small sugar crystals formed during the process of sugar manufacture when syrup is introduced into the crystallizing pans in order to increase the size of the formed crystals.
1900 SADTLER *Hand-bk. Industr. Org. Chem.* (ed. 3) 132 The process of admitting successive portions of fresh syrup after the 'grain' has once formed is used in the development of large crystals. It must be used with judgment though, or the new syrup starts a new set of minute crystals, making what is called 'false grain'.
16. c. *False dawn, morning, sunrise* [tr. Arab. *ṣubḥ kāḏib*]: a transient light which precedes the true dawn by about an hour, a phenomenon common in the East.
1832 MORIER *Zohrab* i, Do tell me..whether that be the dawn or the false dawn? 1868 E. FITZGERALD *Omar* (ed. 2) ii, Before the phantom of False morning died. 1879 E. ARNOLD *Lt. Asia* v. 54 Then slept he..But rose e'er the False-Dawn. 1928 *Daily Express* 23 Aug. 8/3 A flickering false-sunrise.
17. *False core*: see quots.
1843 HOLTZAPFFEL *Turning* I. 338 *note*, The term false-core is employed by the brass founder to express the same thing as the drawback of the iron founder. The former calls every loose piece of the mould not intended for holes, a false core. 1874 KNIGHT *Dict. Mech.*, *False-core*, a part of a pattern which is used in the undercut part of a mold, and is not withdrawn with the main part of the pattern, but removed by a lateral draft subsequently. 1907 A. MCWILLIAM & LONGMUIR *Foundry Practice* 95 In light work these removable parts of a mould are termed 'false cores', and in heavy work 'drawbacks'.

False-card, *v. intr.* To play a false card (see FALSE *a.* 2 g).
1589 WARNER *Alb. Eng.* VI. xxx. 132 Nay, be it that he should espie false carding, what of it? 1902 ELWELL *Bridge* 82 The dealer false-cards so that the adversaries will not know that he holds the queen. 1923 *Daily Mail* 23 June 6 A simple case of false-carding is where declarer holding ace, king of a suit led by an opponent takes the first trick with the ace in order to convey the idea that he does not possess the king...Many players false-card without rhyme or reason.

Falutin, *sb.* and *a.* = HIGHFALUTIN.
1921 T. R. GLOVER *Pilgrim* 118 He does not use of the Church the splendid language of Paul, still less the falutin of some second century Christians. 1928 *Observer* 12 Feb. 17/5 The Swarajists..would have..sought to flout Parliament with falutin phrases.

Falx. Add: **2.** *Ent.* Each of the pair of prehensile claws of the proboscis of a spider.
1875 *Encycl. Brit.* II. 272/1 These organs are often called mandibles, but more generally..*falces*. 1885 H. O. FORBES *Nat. Wand. East. Archipelago* III. vi. 216 With the rapidest motion..it [*sc.* a spider] flashed its falces into my flesh.

Famennian (fāme·niăn), *a.* *Geol.* Also -ien. [ad. F. *famennien*, f. *Famenne*, a district of western Luxemburg.] Epithet of the uppermost division of the Devonian rocks in Belgium and northern France, consisting of the Condrusian psammites above and the Famenne shales below.
1888 PRESTWICH *Geol.* II. 581 Famennian system. 1893 GEIKIE *Text-bk. Geol.* (ed. 3) 787 In Brittany also, Devonian strata are found, including representatives of the Famennian groups with Cypridinas and Goniatites. 1894 J. D. DANA *Man. Geol.* (ed. 4) 627 In the Eifel, the three divisions, the Rhénan, Eifelian and Famennian are well developed. 1909 SOLLAS tr. *Suess' Face of Earth* IV. 61 Five species of Avicula (Leptodesma) which the Chemung stage possesses in common with the Famennian of Belgium.

Familial (fămi·liăl), *a.* [ad. F. *familial*, f. L. *familia* family + -AL.] **a.** *Med.* Occurring in members of a family, characteristic of a family.
1903 *Amer. Jrnl. Psychol.* July–Oct. 100 The chronic constitutional type, said to be to a large extent familial. 1910 *Practitioner* June 809 It is a familial defect rather than an acquired disease. 1925 H. CUSHING *Osler* I. 432 Instances in which the disease [*sc.* Angina Pectoris] has shown hereditary or familial tendencies.
b. Of, pertaining to, or characteristic of a family.
1907 SALEEBY in *Daily Chron.* 6 June 4/4 The parental or familial attitude towards education. 1919 CONRAD *Arrow of Gold* IV. ii. 163 A remote ideal which yet may belong to his familial tradition. 1929 JOSEPHSON *Zola* plate facing 492 A Familial Scene in the Garden of Zola's English Retreat.

Familistère (famili̇̄stɛ̄r). [Fr.] = FAMILISTERY.
1880 *Encycl. Brit.* XI. 265/2 A palatial *familistère* with accommodation for 400 families. *a* 1889 *Sci. Amer. Suppl.* 8761 (Cent. D.) In 1859 Godin put up a large building called the *familistère*, for the accommodation of 300 families, adding a theater, school-house, etc. 1899 *Daily News* 15 Sept. 3/2 The famillistère [*sic*] founded by M. Goudin at Guise.

Famille (famiy). [Fr., = family.] Phr. *famille de robe*: a lawyer's family. (See ROBE *sb.* 4 b.)
1857 J. W. CROKER *Ess. Fr. Rev.* iv. 161 Pierre Louis Rœderer, born about 1756 of a respectable *famille de robe*. 1881 MISS THACKERAY *Mme. de Sévigné* ii. 10 A..gentle heiress belonging to a respectable *famille de robe*.
b. *Famille rose*: Chinese enamelled porcelain of which the predominant colour is red. *Famille verte*: enamel ware of which the predominant colour is green.
1898 GULLAND *Chinese Porcelain* 174 Famille Verte. So called from the decoration being chiefly in green enamel. *Ibid.* 192 Famille Rose. So named from a rose tint in greater or lesser quantity being employed in the decoration. 1903 *Daily Chron.* 7 July 2/7 A large famille-rose cistern. 1904 E. DILLON *Porcelain* 106 We may probably associate with the beginning of this reign [*viz.* Kien-lung (1735–1795)]..the first use of the *rouge d'or* which has given its name to a well-known class of porcelain—the *famille rose*.

Family. Add: **6. b.** (In botany 'family' is now used, as in zoology, for a division of an order, and has therefore superseded the term 'natural order'; e.g. order *Rosales*, family *Rosaceæ*.)
11. family allowance, an allowance paid to workers in proportion to the size of their families; **family portrait**, a portrait of a member of a family in whose possession it remains as an heirloom or a relic; **family-room** *U.S.*, = *living-room*.
1928 *Britain's Industr. Future* (*Lib. Ind. Inq.*) III. Argt. 139 The minimum wage should be fixed for each industry..; the introduction of *Family Allowances may be found desirable by industries to which they are suited. 1928 *Manchester Guardian Weekly* 6 Jan. 5/2 A living wage laid down by the State, to pay which industry must be reorganised by State action, family allowances, [etc.]. 1931 *N. & Q.* 20 June 447/2 Is not the fifteenth century too early for *family portraits? 1884 HOWELLS *S. Lapham* xix. 356 Indicating the *family-room, he added, 'She's in there'. *Ibid.* xxv. 461 He heard talking in the family room.

Fan, *sb.*[1] Add: **5. d.** *Geol.* See quots. and *CONE *sb.*[1] 1 d. Also *attrib.* in *fan-delta, -terrace.*
1864 HAAST *Rep. Form. Canterbury Plains* 19 The term 'delta' in geology is confined to the alluvial deposits of a river at its mouth, falling either into the sea or into a lake; but thinking that giving such a name to the alluvial accumulations of the rivers in this island, showing some peculiarities, would impart an erroneous impression, Dr. Hector and myself, in drawing up a synopsis of the geological formations of New Zealand, have adopted for the formation of those subaerial accumulations the expression 'Fan', for those of regular water-courses; and of 'Half-cone', for those of intermittent mountain torrents, and we shall for the future use these two expressions. 1873 F. DREW in *Q. Jrnl. Geol. Soc.* XXIX. 446 At the mouth of each of these [gorges] are alluvial fans, which project out into the flat of the river-alluvium. *Ibid.* 447 The fan is properly a flat cone, having its apex at the mouth of the ravine. *Ibid.* 448 The only difference of form between an alluvial fan..and the fan talus sketched in fig. 2 is in the degree of slope. *Ibid.* 455 The course of events was, that after the formation of that fan the main river lowered its bed, cutting through its own alluvium; this caused the fan-stream to cut through its fan. 1883 H. MILLER in *Proc. R. Phys. Soc.* VII. 290 Fan Terraces, or Lateral Delta Terraces. 1890 GILBERT in *U.S. Geol. Survey Monograph* I. 81 *footnote*, The 'alluvial fan' of Drew is the 'alluvial cone' of American Geologists, and there would be some reason for preferring 'fan' to 'cone' if it were necessary to employ a single term only. It is convenient to use them as synonyms, employing 'cone' when the angle of slope is high and 'fan' when it is low. 1902 in LD. AVEBURY *Scenery of Eng.* 482 The vale of Neath contains a series of such cones or 'fans' of gravel. 1930 *Nature* CV. 322/2 The wind-worn grains of magnetite brought northward from the great fan-deltas of the Adour system.
e. That portion of the side-bars of a saddle which projects behind.
1908 *Animal Managem.* (War Office) 169 The projecting portion of the side bars behind is known as the 'fan'. *Ibid.* 179 The part of the pannel corresponding to the 'burr' or 'fans' stitched across to keep the hair from re-entering.
6. f. In a motor car, an apparatus for sending a current of cold air through the radiators. Also *attrib.*
1900 *Motor-Car World* May 178/2 The motor..is cooled by means of a fan driven from the periphery of the fly-wheel. 1909 *Westm. Gaz.* 27 Apr. 4/1 The cylinders had kept so cool by the fan-blower that I could almost keep my hand on the combustion head. 1912 *Motor Manual* (ed. 14) iii. 64 An alternative method which avoids the use of a separate fan, is provided by fan-vaned arms in the fly-wheel. 1925 *Morris Owner's Man.* 14 The Fan Belt Adjustment.
10. a. *fan-blower* (earlier U.S. example).
1846 *Rep. U.S. Comm. Patents* (1847) 84 The fan blowers now used in steamboats for blowing the fires in the furnaces are generally made from two to three feet in diameter.
e. In various *attrib.* uses relating to the ventilation of a mine by means of a fan.
1883 GRESLEY *Gloss. Coal-mining* 101 *Fan Drift*, a short tunnel leading from a short distance from the top of the upcast shaft to the fan chamber or casing in which the fan runs, along which the whole of the return air is drawn by the fan... *Fan-shaft*. 1. A shallow pit-shaft sunk beneath a fan connecting it with the fan drift. 2. The upcast shaft where a fan is in use. 1908 *Westm. Gaz.* 9 Mar. 7/4 The fan-drift connecting the present downcast pit with the existing fan has at last been completed. 1921 *Dict. Occup. Terms* (1927) § 047 *Fan boy, fan man*,..turns handle of small ventilating fan to ventilate heading not served by main air current. 1927 *Daily Tel.* 7 June 12/5 The dismissal of three fanmen who refused to do certain work.
11. fan consonant, a consonant pronounced with the edges of the tongue more extended than is usual in making analogous sounds, as in the Arabic 'emphatic' consonants; **fan-delta**, see *5 d; **fan draught**, a system of supplying air in boiler furnaces by means of mechanically driven fans; **fan-head** *U.S.*, the hooded merganser of N. America, *Merganser cucullatus*, the male of which has a fan-shaped crest.
1902 SWEET *Primer Phonetics* (ed. 2) 36 *Fan (spread) consonants..are modifications of point and blade consonants. [1908 — *Sounds Engl.* 45, *tl, dl* occur in Irish English as substitutes for þ, ð respectively; in them the fan modification is supplemented by a slight raising of the back of the tongue.] 1894 W. H. WHITE *Man. Naval Archit.* (ed. 3) 563 *Fan draught is also of great value under unfavourable conditions, such as hot weather, calms, or following winds, giving a command of steam not possible with funnel draught. 1897 *Outing* (U.S.) XXX. 58/1 The hooded merganser, generally termed '*fan-head' owing to its beautiful crest, is a fish duck.

Fan, *sb.*[2] (abbrev. of FANATIC). Delete †*Obs.* and add: Re-formed in mod.Engl. (orig. *U.S.*) to denote: A keen and regular spectator of a (professional) sport, in early use esp. of baseball; hence, a keen follower of a specified hobby or amusement, and *gen.* an enthusiast for a particular person or thing.
1889 *Kansas Times & Star* 26 Mar., Kansas City baseball fans are glad they're through with Dave Rowe as a ball club manager. 1896 G. ADE *Artie* xvii. 158 I'm goin' to be the worst fan in the whole bunch. 1901 *Dialect Notes* II. 139 *Fan*, a base ball enthusiast; common among reporters. 1914 *Daily Express* 3 Oct. 3 First League football 'fans' in London can have a joyous time to-day. 1915 *Film Flashes* 13 Nov. 1 It is quite usual for a picture 'fan' to come out of one theatre and immediately cross the road to another. 1920 W. T. GRENFELL *Labrador Dr.* iv. 56 Among my acquaintances there were not a few theatre fans. 1921 A. W. MYERS *Twenty Yrs. Lawn Tennis* 142 This was sheer spectacular tennis, dear to the hearts of the American 'fans'. 1928 S. VINES *Humours Unreconciled* xiii. 168 What about..your League of Nations and disarmament fans? 1928 B. NICHOLS *Star-spangled Manner* xxi. 247, I felt..that she might have been a little less obviously solicitous of the radio fans.

Fan, *v.* Add:
1. b. (Later U.S. examples.)
1879 TOURGEE *Fool's Err.* xxxvii. 261 Whoever got 'fanned out'—it was always our own folk that did it. 1908 A. RUHL *Other Americans* x. 151 One dreams of..a Broadway policeman marching down upon them leisurely with a night-stick and fanning them away.
2. b. Also, to move smartly; to clear *out. U.S. slang.*
1902 O. WISTER *Virginian* xv. 168 This hyeh train?.. Why, it's been fanning it a right smart little while. 1905 REX BEACH *Pardners* v. (1912) 120 He saw I was drunk, and fanned out, me shootin' at him with every jump.
3. Also, to stir (water) in this way; hence *intr.* or *absol.*
1886 *Outing* (U.S.) VIII. 161/1 The trout..is balancing himself on the hard sandy bottom, his fins slowly fanning the water. 1898 *Daily News* 15 June 4/7 It is commonly in steady weather that you see the trout with their heads a quarter of an inch beneath the surface, and with their tails fanning expectantly.
b. Also in mod. *U.S. slang.*
1907 MULFORD *Bar-20* viii. 86 Then I wants a drink an' he goes an' fans a knife at me. 1916 H. L. WILSON *Some-*

where in Red Gap iii. 85 Ketch me not ready to fan the old forty-four!

6. c. *intr.* To spread out in the shape of a fan; to assume a fan-like shape.

1926 *Hutchinson's Best Story Mag.* Nov. 59/1 His black tangle of beard, fanning over his knees ruffled in the wind.

d. *trans.* To cover (an area) by fanning (*FANNING *vbl. sb.* 5 b). *U.S.*

1901 H. W. WILSON *With the Flag to Pretoria* II. 472 It was our..task to 'fan' this [*sc.* a wooded valley], as an American officer would say, by scattering a ceaseless shower of bullets throughout its length.

7. (Later U.S. examples.)

1916 TITUS *I conquered* vi. 84 His quirt fell...He fanned his pony again, and the beast grunted in his struggles for increased speed in the climbing. 1918 MULFORD *Man fr. Bar-20* ix. 100 Cussed if I wouldn't 'a' give six pesos, U.S. to 'a' seen that cougar a-fannin' you!

Fanar, Fanariot(e), variants of PHANAR, PHANARIOT.

1819 T. HOPE *Anastasius* (1820) I. 41 He..plunged headlong into all the intrigues of the Fanar. *Ibid.* 70 The persons of the Fanariote grandees were of a piece with their habitations. *Ibid.* 77, I had had my share of the second-hand insolence, which the Fanariotes take very quietly from the Turks. 1838 *Penny Cycl.* X. 194/2 A crowd of Fanariotes always followed the new Hospodars. *Ibid.*, The bankers of the Fanar. 1856 *Mem. F. Perthes* I. 411 The cruel exactions of the Greek princes, and insatiable Fanariots. 1878 DISRAELI in Buckle *Life* (1920) VI. 320 A perfect Greek of the Fanar. 1886 *Encycl. Brit.* XX. 20/1 The Fanar quarter of Constantinople.

Fanciable (fæ·nsiăb'l), *a.* [f. FANCY *v.* + -ABLE.] **a.** That may be fancied or imagined. **b.** To which a fancy may be taken.

1930 W. HOLTBY in *Time & Tide* 14 Feb. 213 The less fanciable evidences of his physical ailments. *Mod.* It looks very fanciable.

Fancy, *sb.* and *a.* Add: **A.** *sb.* **14.** Often = **fancy cake* (below).

1891 *Confectioners' Union* 15 Oct., Advts. p. iii, Fondant, Jellies, Gelatine goods,..and other Fancies. *Ibid.* 15 Nov. 633/2 The room where Christmas fancies are being packed by a small army of girls. 1894 SKUSE *Complete Confect.* 110 There are a great number of fancies made from grain sugars, sold about Christmas time.

B. 2. fancy-girl *slang* = *fancy-woman*.

1930 A. P. HERBERT *Water Gipsies* xxii, Let's hear the rest now—out with it! You been his fancy-girl?

C. *adj.* **1.** *fancy cake*, etc. See also next.

1893 HÉRISSE *Pastry Making* 8 Fondant Icing..for icing fancy pastry-cakes. *Ibid.* 97 Fancy Ornamental Meringues. (Meringues décorées). 1912 *Ibid.* 20 Dip in the fancy cakes or pastry with the point of a penknife or fork.

c. Also as *sb.*, short for *fancy pelargonium*, etc.

1904 BROTHERSTON *Bk. Carnation* 17 'Fancies' include a large variety of flowers with markings and colours of the most diverse kinds. 1905 *Westm. Gaz.* 8 Sept. 12/2 Two fancies were certificated.

3. e. *Fancy religion*. (See quot.)

1925 E. FRASER & GIBBONS *Soldier & Sailor Words, Fancy religion*, a very old Service colloquial term in both Navy and Army for a creed or denomination not Church of England, Roman Catholic, or Presbyterian, before the War the three authorized creeds.

Fancy bread. [FANCY *sb.* and *a.* C. 1.] Bread not of the ordinary texture, size, and weight of the standard 'household' and 'cottage' loaves.

1801 *Times* 9 Mar., Germans, who make what they call French or fancy bread, particularly to please the appetites of foreigners. 1841 *Guide to Trade, Baker* 65 Fancy Bread, Ginger-bread, Buns, Rolls, Muffins and Crumpets, etc. 1853 *Fraser's Mag.* June XLVII. 680/2 A large assortment of fancy breads. 1894 *Daily Tel.* 5 Dec. 5/3 He brought witnesses to show that the article was 'fancy'—that is to say it was baked by itself. 1904 *Westm. Gaz.* 23 Aug. 4/1 Fancy bread is for the future to be defined as that which is 'made up into separate rolls, twists, or other shapes, each of which is less than one pound in weight'. 1908 *J. Kirkland's Mod. Baker* II. 165 The greatest diversity of opinion prevails amongst bakers as to what is fancy bread. The rough interpretation of the term as recognized by the Bread Laws is: Bread that cannot readily be mistaken for plain bread. The distinguishing mark in this case is some difference in shape or in glaze; but the baker in a technical sense gives the term fancy bread a much wider meaning, and makes it include all sorts which involve more labour in manufacture, or entail greater cost for materials.

Fancy work. Add: Also *fig.*

1907 W. P. KER *Eliz. Voyagers* Coll. Ess. 1925 I. 3 The importance and the novelty of their matter seem to prevent any excessive rhetoric; they cannot afford the time for fancy work. 1929 *Daily Express* 7 Nov. 19/1 They cut out all fancy work and went straight ahead for goal.

Fandangle. (Earlier U.S. example.)

1835 *Southern Lit. Messenger* I. 361 What is the use of all these fandangles of lace?

Fanda·ngle, *v.* *U.S.* [f. the sb.] *intr.* To philander, flirt, 'carry on'.

1901 *Munsey's Mag.* XXVI. 583/1 A nice pirate,..to be going on talking and fandangling with pretty girls.

Fandango. 1. Add: Also *fig.*

1894 PHIL ROBINSON in *Monthly Packet* Feb. 152 The hippopotamus does not indulge in these fandangoes. 1928 E. BLUNDEN *Undertones of War* xix. 197 The usual free-verse fandango of brick mounds and water-holes.

Fandom. *U.S.* [f. *FAN *sb.*[2] + -DOM.] The world of enthusiasts for some sport or amusement.

1928 *Publishers' Weekly* 30 June, Ty Cobb, the idol of baseball fandom.

Fanfare, *sb.* Add:

c. A style of bookbinding or book-ornamentation in which the design is characterized by its intricacy and by the absence of a regular or geometrical pattern.

1895 ZAEHNSDORF *Sh. Hist. Bookbinding* 22 A development of the 'fanfare' sprays of foliage. *Ibid.*, The graceful ornamentation known as 'fanfare' is attributed to the Eves. ..The name of 'fanfare' was given to this style of work in the last century, when Charles Nodier had a volume entitled 'Les Fanfare et Courvées Abbadesques' bound for him by Thouvenir.

Fanfoot (fæ·nfut). *Pl.* **fanfoots** or **fanfeet.** [f. FAN *sb.*[1] + FOOT.] **a.** A species of gecko having fan-shaped toes. **b.** A collectors' name for a moth of the genus *Polypogon*.

1832 J. RENNIE *Butterfl. & Moths* 146 Polypogon..The Common Fan-foot..The Clay Fan-foot. 1863 *W. Smith's Dict. Bible* II. s.v. *Lizard*, The Fan-Foot Lizard (*Ptyodactylus Gecko*).

Fang, *sb.* Add: **IV. 9.** *attrib.* and *Comb.*: **fang-bolt,** a bolt having a spiked nut or washer, used for attaching iron to wood; **fang-hole,** the cavity in the jaw into which a tooth fits.

1881 J. W. BARRY *Railway Appliances* 73 *Fang-bolts consist of bolts long enough to pass through the sleepers, with a screw cut on the lower end to fit a wide flat nut, having on it fangs or short spikes. 1883 *Lockwood's Dict. Mech. Engin.*, *Fang Bolt*, a bolt in which the nut is a triangular plate with teeth for biting into timber, the bolt being tightened by revolving the head and shank. 1908 *Animal Managem.* (War Office) 36 As the tooth [of a horse] grows up, the *fang-hole becomes filled in with tooth substance of a lighter colour than the remainder.

Fango (fæ·ŋgo). *Med.* [It., = F. *fange*.] A kind of mud obtained from the thermal springs of Battaglia in Italy, used in the treatment of gout, rheumatism, and other ailments.

1904 E. RUTHERFORD *Radio-Activity* 363 'Fango'—a fine mud obtained from hot springs in Battaglia, Northern Italy. 1905 *Jrnl. Balneology* Jan. 5 The annual visits of several patients to Italy for the sole purpose of taking a course of fango-packs. 1906 *Christian World* 22 Mar., I have just returned from a trial of 'Fango' at the Royal Hotel and Baths, Matlock Bath.

Fanned (fænd), *ppl. a.* [f. FAN *v.* + -ED[1].] That has been freed from chaff by means of a fan; winnowed.

1845 F. DOUGLASS *Life* (1846) 66 Hughes was clearing the fanned wheat from before the fan.

Fanning, *vbl. sb.* Add: **5. b.** (See quots.) *U.S.*

1898 *Science Siftings* XV. 79/1 The destructive area of the gun can..be greatly increased by moving it gently from side to side while it is being fired...This process is known as fanning. 1907 MULFORD *Bar-20* i. 11 'Fanning' is the name of a certain style of gun play and was universal among the bad men of the West.

Fanny[2] (fæ·ni). *Navy slang.* [? The female name.] A can to hold drink.

1904 *Daily Chron.* 11 Aug. 3/2 Many total abstainers drawing their grog and leaving it in the 'fanny' for the benefit of the mess. 1925 E. FRASER & GIBBONS *Soldier & Sailor Words*, *Fanny*, a name for the receptacle holding the bluejackets' 'tot' of rum. 1926 *Blackw. Mag.* Dec. 823/2 On board a British man-of-war the same..vessel is called a 'fanny'...Tea made in a billy or fanny is the best to be had.

Fanny[3]. The word formed by the initials of *First Aid Nursing Yeomanry* accommodated to the form of the name *Fanny*.

1918 E. S. FARROW *Dict. Mil. Terms.*

Fanny Adams (fæ·ni æ·dəmz). *Navy slang.* [The name of a young woman who was murdered *c* 1810 and whose body was cut into pieces and thrown into the river at Alton in Hampshire.] Tinned meat.

1889 BARRÈRE & LELAND *Dict. Slang*, *Fanny Adams* (naval), tinned mutton. 1927 *Blackw. Mag.* Feb. 259/2 'Fanny Adams' (or preserved mutton) brought from the ship.

Fantasia. 1. Add: Also of literary compositions.

1896 'J. O. HOBBES' (*title*) The Herb-Moon. A Fantasia. 1919 G. B. SHAW *Heartbreak House* p. xlix, Heartbreak House: a Fantasia in the Russian manner on English themes. 1922 D. H. LAWRENCE (*title*) Fantasia of the Unconscious.

Fantasist (fæ·ntăsist). [f. FANTASY + -IST.] One who 'weaves' fantasies.

1923 *Glasgow Herald* 10 May 6 Wilde, a chartered fantasist. 1928 *Observer* 1 Jan. 5/2 The Fantasists or Special Geniuses! *Ibid.* 2 Sept. 5 There is, I believe, no agreement among statisticians as to the number of H. G. Wells's. There are the sociologist and the fantasist and the novelist and the prophet.

Fantee (fæ·ntī). Also **Fanti, Fante.** A negro of a tribe closely related to the Ashantees, inhabiting the Gold Coast. Also, the language of this tribe.

1819 BOWDICH *Mission to Ashantee* 344, I have heard about half a dozen words in the Fantee, which might be said to be not unlike the same nouns in the Welsh language. *Ibid.* 345 The Fantee word *umpa* (*true, indeed*). [1868 D. L. CARR & F. P. BROWN (*title*) Mfantsi Grammar.] 1875 *Encycl. Brit.* II. 681/1 The separation of Fantees and Ashantees is ascribed to a famine which drove the former south, and led them to live on *fan*, or herbs, while the latter subsisted on *san*, or Indian corn, etc. (whence the names Fantees and Santees). 1879 *Ibid.* X. 756/1 Fante dialects are spoken, not only in Fanti proper, but in Afutu or the country round Cape Coast. *Ibid.*, A Fanti..can converse without much difficulty with a native of Aquapem or Ashantee. *Ibid.*, The Aquapem, which is based on the Akem but has imbibed Fanti influences.

b. Phr. *To go fantee*: to join the natives or a district and conform to their habits.

1886 KIPLING *Departm. Ditties, Giffen's Debt* (1888) 81 *Imprimis* he was 'broke'. Thereafter left His regiment and,..having lost the balance of his friends, 'Went Fantee'—joined the people of the land. 1888 — *Plain Tales fr. Hills, Miss Youghal's Sais*, He was perpetually 'going Fantee' among natives. 1930 CHESTERTON *Four Felons* 190 He was a white man, or whitish man, who had gone fantee, and wore nothing but a pair of spectacles.

Fantod, variant of FANTAD.

1885 'MARK TWAIN' *Huck. Finn* xvii, These was all nice pictures,..but I didn't somehow seem to take to them, because..they always give me the fan-tods. 1910 *Sat. Westm. Gaz.* 1 Jan. 6/1 Sundays inside of a house gives you the fan-tods. 1920 GALSWORTHY *In Chancery* I. v, You mustn't get into a fantod, it 'll never do.

Far, *adv.* Add: **2.** *Far and wide*: see WIDE *adv.* 1 b.

8. a. *far-going, -travelled* adjs.

1852 J. A. ROEBUCK *Hist. Whig Min.* II. 32 *note*, This view was exceedingly offensive to the *far-going reformers. 1889 GRETTON *Memory's Harkback* 135 A far-going Whig. 1896 *Daily News* 7 Dec. 7/6 A too far-going concession to democracy. 1867 H. LATHAM *Black & White* 25 A *far-travelled well-read agreeable host. 1905 *Westm. Gaz.* 9 Sept. 2/3 Far-travelled tourists.

Faraday (fæ·rădeɪ). The name of Michael *Faraday* (1791–1867), English electrician and chemist, used attrib. or in the genitive to designate certain phenomena observed, apparatus invented, and principles enunciated by him.

Faraday or **Faraday's (dark) space,** in a vacuum tube traversed by an electric discharge the dark space observed between the positive column and the negative glow when the pressure is low; also called the *second dark space*. **Faraday's disk,** a metallic disk capable of producing an electric current by revolving on a metallic axis in a magnetic field. **Faraday effect** (see quot. 1900). **Faraday's electric bag,** an instrument invented by Faraday to prove that a charge of static electricity is distributed on the outside surfaces of bodies. **Faraday's laws,** the principles of electrolytic phenomena enunciated by Faraday. **Faraday** or **Faraday's tubes** (see quot. 1904).

1881 *Jrnl. Chem. Soc.* XXXIX. 286 The more experimental methods were refined, the more completely were the exactness and generality of Faraday's law confirmed. 1889 LODGE *Mod. Views Electr.* (1892) 308 The only substance in which the Faraday effect is large, is iron. 1893 J. J. THOMSON *Electr. & Magn.* 3 The Faraday tubes either form closed circuits or else begin and end on atoms. *Ibid.* 111 Next after the negative glow comes a second comparatively non-luminous space..called..the 'Faraday space'. 1900 W. WATSON *Text-bk. Physics* 862 The Faraday Effect.—In 1845 Faraday discovered that when a beam of plane polarised light is passed through a magnetic field in the direction of the lines of force, the plane of polarisation of the light is rotated owing to its passage through the field. *Ibid.* 889 Faraday tubes. 1902 *Jrnl. Chem. Soc.* LXXXII. II. 300 Faraday's law, so far as the weight of substance deposited by a given amount of electricity is concerned, may be regarded as an absolutely exact law of nature. 1902 *Encycl. Brit.* XXVIII. 48/2 In the unstriated discharge the temperature is constant in the positive column, diminishes in the Faraday dark space. 1904 *Technol. & Sci. Dict.* (ed. Goodchild & Tweney), *Faraday tubes*, the part of a dielectric enclosed within a tubular surface formed by a number of lines of force drawn infinitely close together from the boundaries of an area on which there is a unit charge of electricity.

Faradimeter (færădi·mɪtəɪ). [f. FARAD + -(I)METER.] An instrument for determining in farads the electrostatic capacity of a condenser. Also **Farado·meter, Fa·rad-me·ter.**

1902 S. SLOAN in *Lancet* 22 Mar. 830/1 The Faradimeter, an instrument for measuring currents from induction coils for therapeutic use.

Far-away, *a.* etc. Add:

A. *adj.* **2. b.** Of a voice: Sounding faint as if from a distance.

1897 MARY KINGSLEY *W. Africa* 216 A quaint, falsetto, far-away sort of voice. 1900 H. LAWSON *On Track* 83 Then be commenced to speak—..to talk in that strange, absent, far-away tone that awes one. 1926 *Glasgow Herald* 30 Sept. 5, I heard his voice sounding in a far-away and curious tone.

C. *sb.* **2.** Part of a cinema film taken at a distance, as distinguished from a 'close-up'.

1926 BASIL MAINE *Receive It So* 29 Seeing that for nine-tenths of the house these things appeared as 'far-aways', the whole point of them was lost.

Farce (fāɪs), *sb.*[1] Delete †*Obs.* and add:

1904 *Daily Chron.* 4 May 10/5 The hollow should be filled with a rich veal farce.

Farce, *v.*[1] Add: **7.** See FARSE *v.*

1857 [see FARSE]. 1894 *Athenæum* 28 July 128/2 A peculiar feature in the recitation is the 'farcings' of each psalm, *i.e.*, the introduction of sentences, generally giving some application of the psalm to Christ. 1895 *Liturgy of Holy Apostles Adai & Mari* 1 There is no farcing at feasts, but a Hallelujah is said. 1899 *Westm. Gaz.* 6 Apr. 1/3 A libretto with a touch of poetry in it, an intelligible story and humorous, hardly farced. 1907 J. M. MANLY in *Mod. Philol.* IV. 585 None of these gradual variations caused legend or farced epistle to become anything other than legend and farced epistle.

Farcicalize (fā·ɪsikălaiz), *v.* [f. FARCICAL *a.*[1] + -IZE.] *trans.* To make farcical, to make into a farce. Hence **Fa:rcicaliza·tion.**

1928 *Sunday Express* 8 Apr. 4 'The Flag Lieutenant', Further Adventures of,..Over-farcicalised. *Ibid.* 16 Dec. 4 Farcicalisation of the cave man theme.

Fardel, *sb.*[1] Add:

1. b. The omasum, or third stomach, of ruminants. Also *fardel-bag*.

1862 *Chambers's Encycl.* IV. 245/1 Fardel-bound, a disease of cattle and sheep, consists of impaction of the fardel bag.

1908 *Animal Managem.* (War Office) 16 The..'manyplies' or 'fardel' (omasum).

4. fardel-bound *a.*, costive, denoting a condition in cattle and sheep in which food is retained in the folds of the omasum.

1825 LOUDON *Encycl. Agric.* 976 Costiveness also brings on a colic in them, called clue bound, fardel bound, etc. 1844 H. STEPHENS *Bk. Farm* II. 255 The fardlebound of cattle and sheep is nothing more than a modification of the disease in horses called stomach-staggers, which is caused by an enormous distention of the stomach. 1862 [see *1 b].

Fare, *sb.*[1] **5. b.** (Earlier and later examples of U.S. sense.)

1792 BELKNAP *Hist. New Hampsh.* III. 214 The fish of the summer and fall fares is divided into two sorts. 1828 A. SHERBURNE *Mem.* x. (1831) 217 The old gentleman had just arrived from the ocean with a fare of fish. 1875 HOLLAND *Sevenoaks* xi. 139 The whalers had returned with scantier fares year after year. 1886 *Harper's Mag.* Dec. 105/1 He come by with his fare o' fish, an' hove to to see what I was gittin. 1904 *N. Y. Even. Post* 18 June, The prices brought by the 'fares', which are..cargoes of fresh or salted fish.

Far East. [FAR *a.* 1 a, EAST *sb.*] The extreme eastern regions of the Old World, esp. India, China, and Japan.

1894 G. N. CURZON *Problems of Far East* i. 7 No introduction is needed in presenting the Far East to an English audience. 1898 *Westm. Gaz.* 1 Jan. 2/3 The Emperor's Far-East policy. 1906 *Q. Rev.* Jan. 287 The main interest of Great Britain in the Far East. 1911 *Ibid.* July 245 The great conflict which for many months bathed the Far East in blood weakened Russia in Europe.

So **Far-Eastern** *a.*, of or belonging to the Far East.

1888 *Peel City Guardian* 14 July 7/4 One firm has the monopoly of this Far-Eastern *pari mutuel*. 1900 *Black & White Budget* 25 Aug. 649/1 The Far Eastern question is a new one to American diplomacy.

Fare-you-well. *U.S. colloq.* [f. phr. *fare you well*, FARE *v.*[1] 9.] *To a fare-you-well*: to the last point; to the utmost degree; completely.

1910 W. M. RAINE *B. O'Connor* 77 The little cuss has got me bluffed to a fare-you-well. 1911 R. D. SAUNDERS *Col. Todhunter* i. 3 The fight's begun, and we've got to rally around old Bill Strickland to a fare-you-well. 1924 W. M. RAINE *Troubled Waters* x. 101 'Who is boss of the round-up this year?'..'Rowan is, and believe me he worked us to a fare-you-well. He's some driver, Mac is.'

Far-flung, *a.* [FAR *adv.* 8 a.] 'Flung', 'cast', or extended far or to a great distance.

1896 KIPLING *Seven Seas, Native-Born* ix, To the far-flung fenceless prairie. 1897 — *Recessional* i, Lord of our far-flung battle-line. 1902 *Daily Chron.* 31 Jan. 3/5 The tangled, far-flung story of the once semi-Royal house of Douglas. 1925 B. N. ODELL in E. F. Norton *Fight for Everest, 1924* 292 A far-flung head tributary of the Dzakar Chu. 1927 H. E. FOSDICK *Pilgr. Palestine* 23 This far-flung vista of the land he loved.

Farinaceous, *a.* Add:

5. Characterized by flour. *Farinaceous city, colony*, playful names for Adelaide and southern Australia, from the large export of wheat.

1873 A. TROLLOPE *Australia & N. Z.* II. 184 [Adelaide] has also been nicknamed the Farinaceous City. 1902 *Daily Chron.* 7 May 7/1 Before emigrating to the 'farinaceous colony'.

Farkleberry. *U.S.* = SPARKLEBERRY.

1845–50 MRS. LINCOLN *Lect. Bot.* App. 181/2. 1856 A. GRAY *Man. Bot.* 248 *Vaccinium arboreum*, the Farkleberry, a tall species of this section, with evergreen leaves, probably extends northward into Virginia.

Farm, *sb.*[2] Add:

5. b. With qualification, extended to tracts of water devoted to the breeding or rearing of some animals, as *fish-farm, oyster-farm, terrapin-farm*, etc. (see these words).

1866 *Chambers's Jrnl.* 22 Sept. 601/1, I saw no farm of mussels.

9. and **9 b.** *farm-building, -labour, -land* (earlier U.S. examples); **farm-hand** (U.S. examples); **farm-market** *U.S.*, a market for books among the farming or agricultural population.

1660 *Early Conn. Prob. Rec.* 51 Six Mile Island..with *farme buildings..upon it. 1843 *Cultivator* X. 85 In unpropitious weather for out door employment your *farm hands can go to threshing out grain. 1878 WHITMAN *Specimen Days* (1892) 108 He was about the best specimen of a young country farm-hand I ever knew. 1868 *Rep. U.S. Comm. Agric.* (1869) 322 When *farm labor is too valuable to be used in hunting very small game and fishing. 1638 *Watertown* (Mass.) *Rec.* 4 The *Farmland at the further end shalbe for a Common. 1645 [see QUARTERLAND]. 1695 *Plymouth* (Mass.) *Rec.* 93 A Raing run and settled between Samuell Riders land..and James Clarkes farm land. 1859 [in Dict.]. 1930 *Publishers' Weekly* 12 July 175 In many states the bulk of the population, if towns of under 5,000 population are included, is predominantly rural. It is known as the *farm market.

Farmer. *Naut. slang.* (See quot.)

1886 R. BROWN *Spunyarn & Spindrift* vi. 89 I'm a farmer to-night, and means to have a quiet and peaceful night's rest. *Note*, A sailor calls himself a farmer when he has neither wheel nor look-out during a night.

Far niente (fār nie·nte). [It.; = to do nothing.] Idleness. (Usually DOLCE FAR NIENTE.)

1819 T. HOPE *Anastasius* (1820) II. vii. 124, I determined ..to indulge in the supreme pleasure of the Italians—the *far niente*. 1894 'MAX O'RELL' *John Bull & Co.* 271 Allow him to pass his life in the softest of *far nientes*.

Faroese (fɛ̄ᵊro,ī·z, færo,ī·z), *a.* and *sb.* Also **Faröese, Færoese, Feroese.** [f. *Faröe* + -ESE, after Sw. *Färöarna*, Da. *Færøerne* = Icel. *Færeyskr*, f. *Færeyjar*, f. *fær* sheep + *ey* island.] **A.** *adj.* Of or pertaining to the Faröe Islands, their inhabitants, or the language spoken by them. **B.** *sb.* **a.** A native or inhabitant of the Faröe Islands. **b.** The language of the Faröe Islands, which is a variety of Norse.

1851 *Illustr. Catal. Gt. Exhib.* III. III. 552/1 Faroese and Danish St. Luke. 1855 GREIG *Cruise Yacht Maria* 15 Immediately after we anchored, a Feroese gentleman came on board. *Ibid.* 25 The Feroese are very long-lived. 1898 RUSSELL-JEAFFRESON *Faröe Isl.* 15 The religion of the Faröese..is Lutheran. *Ibid.* 99 The child cried out in Faröese, 'Nüg me up'. *Ibid.* 103, I collected..as many of the old Faröese proverbs as I came across. 1908 W. G. COLLINGWOOD *Scandin. Brit.* 259 The 'Norn' is shown to be fairly pure Norse, with a very slight sprinkling of Danish, Færoese, Frisian and English words. *Ibid.* 260 Phonetic changes like those in Icelandic and Færoese.

Far-off, *a.* Add: **1. d.** Of a look: Dreamy, far-away.

1870 MORRIS *Earthly Par.* (1896) III. 463 Scarce happy 'neath his far-off moody gaze. 1876 *Mr. Gray & his Neighbours* II. 41 Alice Gray was very pale, and with that far-off look in her eyes, which those who are to die young have more than others.

Faroish (fɛ̄ᵊro,iʃ, fæ·ro,iʃ), *a.* [f. *Faroe* + -ISH[1].] = *FAROESE *a.* Also **Farish** (fɛ̄ᵊ·riʃ, fæ·riʃ) *a.*

a 1889 CHILD *Ballads* I. 315 (Cent. Dict.) The Swedish.. Danish, and Faroish ballads. 1898 *Blackw. Mag.* Aug. 245 A collection of Farish ballads. 1905 ANNANDALE *Faroes* 14 It is only some fifty or sixty years since Farish began to be written. *Ibid.* 131 A Farish cottage is generally clean, an Icelandic farmhouse is almost as often airless, filthy, and verminous.

Farrash, var. FERASH.

1873 H. BLOCHMANN tr. *Ain I Akbari* I. 47 Besides, there are employed a thousand Farrāshes, natives of I'rān, Tūrān, and Hindustan. 1894 SAFAR NAMEH *Persian Pict.* 162 It belonged to the Shah's *farrash*. 1921 *Blackw. Mag.* June 707/2 My farrash entered with a telegram.

Far-reaching (stress variable), *a.* [f. FAR *adv.* 8 + REACHING *ppl. a.*] That reaches far; extensive (*lit.* and *fig.*); exerting an influence or producing an effect which extends far in space or time.

1824 NEWMAN *Poems, To H. E. N.* xii, The dusky heath far-reaching. 1860 RUSKIN *Unto this Last* ii. (1896) 59 That which seems to be wealth may in verity be only the gilded index of far-reaching ruin. 1874 H. SIDGWICK *Meth. Ethics* 245 A fundamental conflict of ideas, which appears more profound and far-reaching in its consequences the more we examine it. 1894 *Pop. Sci. Monthly* XLIV. 572 Geology formed a subject of far-reaching importance. 1900 *Daily News* 1 Mar. 2/1 A number of far-reaching caves.

Hence **Far-rea·chingly** *adv.*, **Far-rea·chingness.**

c 1850 BAGEHOT *To R. C. Ch.* iii. Wks. 1915 I. 12 With head of power and thoughts of light, As Britain seas, far-reachingly. 1893 *Harper's Mag.* May 821 The most far-reachingly beneficial expression of this fostering policy. 1901 S. BUTLER in *Mem.* (1919) I. 264, I was oppressed and scared by the far-reachingness and daring of what I had done.

Farrow, *sb.* **5.** (Earlier U.S. example.)

1836 D. B. EDWARD *Hist. Texas* v. 79 They have more.. milk than they know how to dispose of, except they are well stocked with farrow sows.

Farther, *a.* Add: **3. b.** *Farther East* = *FAR EAST.

1876 *Fraser's Mag.* Jan. 1/2 There came another thunder-clap tending once more to direct men's eyes from the near to the farther East. 1902 MAHAN *Retrospect & Prospect* 160 It is..the principal sea route between Europe and the Farther East.

Far West. *U.S.* [FAR *a.* 1 a, WEST *sb.*] The more remote area lying to the west of the earlier settlements in the United States. Originally applied to what is now the *Middle West*.

1830 *Deb. Congress* 8 May 920/2 Sir, I am from the West, although not from the 'far, far West'. 1832 *Ibid.* Feb. 290 Some of the descendants of illustrious families have gone to the far West. 1835 *Southern Lit. Messenger* I. 615, I do not believe that the prairies of the 'far West' can exhibit more luxuriant fields of corn. 1839 Z. LEONARD *Adv.* (1904) 187 The idea of being within hearing of the end of the Far West inspired the heart of every member of our company with a patriotic feeling. 1843 CARLTON *New Purchase* I. 2 In a part of what was, at the time of this journey, the Far West. 1867 *Rep. Iowa Agric. Soc.* (1868) 437 The few settlers we have are mostly poor people who have sought homes in the far west. 1881 A. A. HAYES *New Colorado* vii. 108 Surely this is at variance with the traditions of the Far West.

Hence **Far-Wester,** a white settler in, or inhabitant of, the 'Far West'; **Far-Western** *a.*, of or belonging to the Far West.

1843 CARLTON *New Purchase* I. 112 True honest-hearted far westers unadulterated by foreign or domestic scum. 1844 [see FAR *adv.* 8 c]. 1845 *Knickerbocker Mag.* XXVI. 283 There is a county in one of our far-western states which numbers just four whigs. 1874 B. F. TAYLOR *World on Wheels*, etc. I. vi. 50 Such touches of border-life give a Far Western train a character of its own. 1887 C. B. GEORGE *40 Yrs. on Rail* xi. 234 The hearty 'Wall stranger', with which a Far Wester greets his neighbor on the train, immediately does away with reserve.

Fasci (fa·ʃi), *sb. pl.* [It., pl. of *fascio* bundle, burden, assemblage, group:—pop.L. *fascium* for L. *fascis* bundle: see FASCES.] Groups of men organized politically, such as those (*fasci dei lavoratori*) in Sicily *c* 1895, and those of the Fascisti (e.g. the *fascio interventista* of 1915).

1902 *Encycl. Brit.* XXIX. 649/1 To produce in Sicily a discontent of which Socialist agitators took advantage to organize the workmen of the towns and the peasants of the country into groups known as *fasci*. 1921 *Public Opinion* 20 May 464/3 The first Fasci (composed of ex-soldiers) began to show signs of resistance and opposition to the Communists. 1922 *Q. Rev.* Jan. 144 A considerable proportion of the poet's legionaries in Fiume was drawn from the Fasci in different Italian towns.

Fascia. Add: *attrib.* in *fascia-board* (see FACIA).

1926 W. DEEPING *Sorrell & Son* i. § 2 Painted in white letters on a black fascia-board 'John Verity—Dealer in Antiques'.

Fascinatedly (fæsine·tĕdli), *adv.* [f. FASCINATED *ppl. a.* + -LY[2].] In a fascinated manner.

1894 MRS. DYAN *Man's Keeping* (1899) 83 The lady stared fascinatedly on.

Fascinator. Add: **c.** A head covering worn by women and made of a soft material. (Now disused.)

1900 *Athenæum* 1 Sept. 285/1 A fascinator being a knitted kerchief or hood which women put round their heads. 1908 *Scribner's Mag.* Feb. 177 A scant worsted 'enchanter' or 'fascinator', I think she called it, thrown over her head and shoulders. 1909 *Daily Chron.* 8 Dec. 9/4 A lovely shawl of eider, Shetland, or any fine wool..can be utilised as a fascinator, or shoulder wrap.

Fascine, *sb.* **3.** Add: *fascine-net*.

1872 *Game Laws Penn.* in *Fur, Fin & Feather* 115 Such contrivances..as are commonly known as fish-baskets, brush or facinenets.

Fasciola (fāsəi·ŏlă). *Anat.* [L., small bundle.] The dentate convolution of the brain, the *fascia cinerea* or *dentata*.

1882 WILDER & GAGE *Anat. Technol.* 478 Fasciola...The somewhat thickened margin of cinerea along the fimbria. In man the ventral portion has commonly been called *fascia dentata*; in the cat, however, there is no denticulation, and the name fascia is certainly misleading; hence the senior author proposed to employ *fasciola* for the whole.

Fasciole (fæ·sioᵘl). [f. mod.L. *fasciola*.] **1.** *Ent.* A narrow band of colour, a small fascia. **2.** *Zool.* One of the bands of minute tubercles, bearing modified spines, in spatangoid sea-urchins. Hence **Fa·sciolet,** = 1 above.

1826 KIRBY & SP. *Entomol.* IV. xlvi. 302 *Fasciolet*, a short fascia. 1850 E. FORBES *Brit. Organic Rem.* III. plate x. 2 A fasciole of tertiary spines. 1888 ROLLESTON & JACKSON *Anim. Life* 558 Clavulæ, found only in *Spatangidæ*, are minute spines..attached to minute tubercles which form regular bands known as *fascioles* or *semitæ*.

Fascism (fæ·ʃiz'm, fæ·siz'm). Also in It. form **Fascismo** (faʃi·zmo). [ad. It. *fascismo*, f. *fascio* bundle, group: see *FASCI and -ISM.] The principles and organization of the Fascists.

1923 *Q. Rev.* Jan. 148 A section of the Press..now veered completely round to the cause of Fascism. The Fascist terror increased in intensity. 1923 *Contemp. Rev.* Nov. 557 Fascism in Germany will never be more than one of several factors. 1925 *Weekly Westm. Gaz.* 10 Jan. 320/2 The outrages which have been associated with Fascism have gradually alienated much of the support which it won two years ago. 1921 *19th Cent.* July 148 The Fascismo was born in the provinces, where the extremistic menace was stronger. 1923 *Contemp. Rev.* Jan. 44 We do not want Fascismo in this country.

Fascist (fæ·ʃist, fæ·sist). Also in Italian form **Fascista** (faʃi·sta). *Pl.* **Fascisti** (faʃi·sti). [ad. It. *Fascista*, formed as prec.: see -IST.] One of a body of Italian nationalists, which was organized in March 1919 to oppose Bolshevism in Italy, and, as the *partito nazionale fascista*, under the leadership of Signor Mussolini assumed control of the Italian government in October 1922; *transf.* applied to similar organizations in other countries. Also *attrib.*

1921 *Times* 1 Jan. 9/6 The *Fascisti* are certainly paying back..the Socialists in matters of violence. 1921 *Glasgow Herald* 30 Mar. 9 A party of Fascisti from Perugia visiting Città di Castello burned the Labour Bureau. 1921 *Public Opinion* 20 May 464/1 For the moment the Fascisti are acting as a sort of Government bodyguard for the elections and Fascist candidates find a place..on the Government lists. 1922 *Daily Mail* 17 Nov. 7 Signor Mussolini, the Fascist leader, to-day made his first speech in the Chamber. 1923 *Ibid.* 26 Feb. 7 The gala ball organised by the London branch of the Fascisti party in aid of the fund for the Fascista Home in London. 1929 WALPOLE *Hans Frost* ii. 146 At Venice..a Fascist official at the railway station had been abominably vulgar.

Hence **Fa:scistiza·tion,** the action or process of making Fascist.

1925 *Glasgow Herald* 20 May 10 The complete 'fascistisation' of Italy. 1927 *Observer* 27 Nov. 12 The salient pronouncements of the Grand Council were the following:— 1. Direct control by the State of the schools where 'Fascistisation' has proceeded apace, but not as yet thoroughly enough to meet the case. 1928 *Ibid.* 26 Aug. 6/5 It is but a step further along that road which, ultimately, leads to the total 'Fascistization of the country'.

Fashion, *sb.* **14.** Add: **fashion-book,** a book describing and illustrating new fashions in dress.

1878 *Harper's Mag.* Apr. 764/2 The pictures were merely an improved reproduction of the men and women of the fashion-books.

Fassanian (fæsē·niăn), *a.* *Geol.* [f. *Fassa*, a district in Tyrol, from which the Fassa valley takes its name.] Denoting a group of strata forming the lower group in the Tirolian series in the Mediterranean triassic province.

1903 GEIKIE *Text-bk. Geol.* (ed. 4) 1106.

Fast, *a.* Add: **1. h.** (See quot.)

1913 DORLAND *Med. Dict.* (ed. 7), *Fast*, resistant to destruction or to staining: said of bacteria.

8. c. Also of scales: Indicating more than the actual weight.

1908 *N. Y. Even. Post* (semi-weekly ed.) 7 May 5 Such people lose heavily if the scales on which their purchases are weighed daily are fast only half an ounce.

11. fast-footed *a.* *Cricket*, denoting the action or method of keeping the right foot firm in batting; **fast-goer** (earlier U.S. example).

1897 *Encycl. Sport* I. 228/2 The '*fast-footed' style of hitting. 1907 *Westm. Gaz.* 21 Aug. 7/1 To play right over it in attempting a fast-footed drive. 1868 H. WOODRUFF *Trotting Horse* xxx. 253 She was..introduced to the very best society of *fast-goers on the Bloomingdale..road.

Fast, *v.*[2] Add: **3. b.** To cause to fast or be without food.

1854 *Poultry Chron.* I. 15 Before they are killed, they should be fasted at least fourteen hours.

Fasten, *v.* Add:

7. c. *intr.* To become fixed or fastened together.

1829 SCOTT *Old Mort.* Note x, The iron hasps [of the window]..fastened in the inside. 1850 SMEDLEY *F. Fairlegh* iv, The macintosh..fastening round the neck with a hook and eye. 1924 ANNE D. SEDGWICK *Little French Girl* II. viii, A dark silk dress..fastening at the breast with a great old clasp of wrought gold.

8. Also with *up*.

1908 J. S. FLETCHER *Paradise Crt.* v. ii, Was he..to be fastened up there like a rat in a trap for—how long?

b. *intr.* To close with fastenings.

1862 G. MACDONALD *D. Elginbrod* II. xxiv, He could find no fastening upon it [*sc.* a door]. 'No doubt', thought he, 'it does fasten, in some secret way or other'.

12. d. Also with *to*.

1881 MRS. RIDDELL *Senior Partner* xxxv, One of the nephews..insisted on fastening himself to Mr. Snow.

e. = FIX *v.* 6 c.

1881 MRS. RIDDELL *Senior Partner* xvi, Fastening her kinsman with a cold steely eye.

Fat, *a.* and *sb.*[2] Add:

A. *adj.* **2. e.** Of larger size than is usual, large in comparison with others of the same species.

1877 *Encycl. Brit.* VII. 368/2 The Fat Dormouse (*Myoxus glis*) is larger than the British species. 1877 A. B. HORTON in Moloney *Forestry W. Afr.* (1887) 38 Nuts well supplied with flesh, or what is technically called 'fat nuts'.

f. *Fat herring*: = MATIE.

1863 [see MATIE]. 1879 *Encycl. Brit.* IX. 259/2 'Maties', or fat fish, in which the milt or roe is quite undeveloped. 1883 WALLEM *Fish Supply Norway* 15 (Fish. Exhib. Publ.) The Norwegian fat herring is considered to be the very best herring in the world.

3. c. Of a spark.

1902 A. C. HARMSWORTH *Motors & Motor-driving* viii. 162 The magneto machine itself seems, and is, inexhaustible... It also gives a fine 'fat' spark, which adds to the efficiency of the explosion.

5. Of quicklime: Nearly pure, and therefore slaking easily.

1904 *Technol. & Sci. Dict.* (ed. Goodchild & Tweney), *Fat Lime*, a nearly pure lime (calcined white chalk).

10. c. *A fat lot*: a large amount, a great deal: always *ironical* and implying 'very little, hardly any'.

1899 C. J. CUTCLIFFE HYNE *Further Adv. Capt. Kettle* i, Shows what a fat lot of influence this Etat du Congo has got. 1913 'IAN HAY' *Right Stuff* vi, Rot! Fat lot you know about it, Dilly. 1916 CLOUSTON *Two's Two* ix. 69 'And a fat lot of good they'll be!' scoffed Archibald.

14. fat acid = SEBACIC *acid*; **fat colour,** stale mixed paint which has become greasy owing to exposure; **fat crab** *U.S.*, a crab ready to shed its shell; **fat edge,** a superfluous rim of paint left on the edge of a surface; **fat-headedness,** stupidity; **fat-tail,** a fat-tailed sheep.

1904 *Technol. & Sci. Dict.* (ed. Goodchild & Tweney) s.v., *Fat colour is sometimes used for painting rough work, being thinned down with turpentine or benzene before use. *Ibid.*, A professional painter guards against *fat edges. 1891 KIPLING *Light that Failed* viii, The *fat-headedness of deliberately trying to do work that will live. 1915 WODEHOUSE *Something Fresh* iii, If you want any further proof of your young man's fat-headedness, mark that. 1888 *Castle Line Guide to S. A.* 55 (Pettman) The *fat-tails held their own for many years.

B. *sb.*[2] **1. b.** *pl.* or *collect. sing.* (*attrib.*) Fat cattle or sheep. *Austral.*

1886 C. SCOTT *Sheep-farming* 137 Sheep intended for the fat market. 1894 A. ROBERTSON *Nuggets* 132 What say ye to him goin' to Melbourne to see the flock o' fats sold at the Flemington Yards? 1910 DAVIS *From Selection to City* xiii. 112 We had to hold them together on the camp while the fats were cut out.

2. c. Also *Mining*. (See quot.) *U.S.*

1883 J. H. BEADLE *Western Wilds* xxxv. 584 Here and there..are sometimes found little accretions of pure silver which miners speak of as 'the fat of the vein'.

6. a. *fat-formation, -former, -mass.* **b.** *fat-forming, -splitting* adjs.

1909 *Daily Chron.* 8 July 6/4 *Fat-formation in the body ..is not to be regarded as a mere accretion or addition of the fat we consume to the tissues of the frame. 1886 C. SCOTT *Sheep-farming* 41 A ton of good linseed cake contains of *fat-formers 1308 lbs.; of flesh-formers, 582 lbs. 1893 F. F. MOORE *I Forbid Banns* xxxiv, She knew the flesh-formers from the fat-formers, and partook of both. 1847 *Rep. U.S. Comm. Patents* (1848) 116 With respect to the *fat-forming principle..the proportions of the different parts of the grain stand thus. 1872 HUMPHRY *Myol.* 5 In addition to the four *fat-masses disposed with the longitudinal series of vessels are four deep fat-masses lying beneath the four lateral muscles. 1890 BILLINGS *Med. Dict.*, **Fat-splitting ferment*, steapsin. 1907 *Practitioner* Aug. 320 The steapsin, or fat-splitting ferment of the pancreatic juice.

c. fat-body, in arthropods, amphibians, and insects, a mass consisting of connective tissue and globules of fat, forming a reserve store of nutritious matter; **fat-cake** *Austral.* (see quots.); **fat-fish,** the blue-fish; **fat liquor,** a mixture of soap and oil used in leather manufacture for softening hides; also as *vb.*; **fat-tree,** one of a class of trees of temperate zones, including chiefly the soft-wooded trees such as the birch, lime, and conifers, which, at the beginning of winter, convert the starch of the bark and wood into fat, and reconvert it into starch in the spring.

1901 *Cambr. Nat. Hist.* VIII. 52 All Amphibia possess *Fat-bodies. They consist of richly vascularised lymphatic tissue, the meshes of which are filled with lymph-cells, globules of fat and oil. *Ibid.*, There is in some Anura..a mysterious organ, intercalated between the fat-body and the testis or ovary. 1927 HALDANE & HUXLEY *Anim. Biol.* iv. 113 In the frog fat is stored in special fat-bodies. 1865 W. HOWITT *Discov. in Australia* II. 15 *Fat-cakes, made of flour, and fried in their pan, a bush dainty. 1898 MORRIS *Austral Eng.*, *Fat-cake*, a ridiculous name sometimes applied to *Eucalyptus leucoxylon*. 1905 *East London Dispatch* 7 Aug. (Pettman) When opened the stomach usually contains large lobes of fat—hence the name *fat-fish. 1904 *Technol. & Sci. Dict.* (ed. Goodchild & Tweney), **Fat Liquor*, an emulsified solution of soap and oil in warm water, used for softening mineral tanned leather... First used by Ed. Kent on Dongola leather. 1903 FLEMMING *Pract. Tanning* 22 The leather is then ready to be stained or colored, fat-liquored, put out on the grain and treated in the finishing operations. *Ibid.* 127 The leather treated with it [*sc.* palmetto] takes even cooling and carries the fat-liquor well. 1903 tr. *A. F. W. Schimper's Plant-Geog.* 437 In the group of *fat-trees, which are chiefly soft-wooded species, such as conifers, birches, and lime-trees, all the starch in the cortex and wood is converted into fat.

Fat, *v.* Add: **3. d.** *trans.* In the manufacture of leather, to smear over with a fat liquor.

1903 FLEMMING *Pract. Tanning* 166 The leather is now treated as usual, and fatted or oiled.

Fate, *sb.* **5.** Add: **fate-line** *Palmistry*, a line in the palm of the hand supposed to indicate a person's fate in worldly affairs.

1896 SPARK *Sci. Palmistry* 252 Islands...On the Fate line—fate, handicapped by relatives, or lover. 1898 *Daily News* 23 Nov. 2/4, I told you I was born mad, with my fate-line upside down. 1898 *Cheiro's Guide to the Hand* 110 The happiest mark of marriage on the Line of Fate is when the Influence Line lies close to the Fate Line.

Fatha, variant of *FATIHAH.

Father, *sb.* Add: **1. f.** Also *father-in-church*.

1871 MRS. H. WOOD *Dene Hollow* vi, 'I shall want you to stand father-in-church to this young lady', said Geoffrey to the clerk.

4. *Like a father*: in a paternal, authoritative, or severe manner.

1830 PAULDING *Chron. Gotham* 64 If she wont listen to reason, I will talk to her like a father.

8. b. *Father Christmas*: the personification of Christmas as a benevolent old man with a flowing white beard, wearing a red sleeved gown and hood trimmed with white fur, and carrying a sack of Christmas presents. *Father Time*: see TIME *sb.* 25.

a 1800 in Brand *Pop. Antiq.* (1813) I. 373 Lordings, in these realms of pleasure Father Christmas yearly dwells. 1860 *Christmas Tree* 189 'Tis now, when once more from his lair Old Father Christmas issues forth. *Ibid.* 190 Hail, Father Christmas! Come, and bring Thine ancient merriment and glee. 1864 *Chambers's Bk. of Days* II. 740/2 Old Father Christmas, bearing, as emblematic devices, the holly bough, wassail-bowl, etc. 1919 *Punch* 24 Dec. 538 Uncle James (who after hours of making up rather fancies himself as Father Christmas).

9. c. (U.S. examples of *Father of waters*, etc.; in later use *spec.* the Mississippi.)

1813 *Niles' Weekly Reg.* V. Suppl. 176/2 The Mississippi is the Nile of America. The aborigines who resided on its banks, called it Mechaseba, or Father of waters. 1818 FEARON *Sk. Amer.* 257 The facilities of export afforded by those 'fathers of waters', the Ohio, Mississippi, and Missouri. 1834 H. BRACKENRIDGE *Recoll.* xix. 237 About noon we..came in sight of the 'father of rivers'. 1836 J. HALL *Statist. West* iii. 46 The traveler is struck with the magnitude..of the stream which has been so appropriately called, the Father of waters. 1857 *Trans. Mich. Agric. Soc.* VIII. 193, I was..more than a hundred miles on the sunset side of the father of floods. 1878 B. F. TAYLOR *Between Gates* 23 Fox river, Rock river, Mississippi, the old Father of them all.

12. father-right [G. *vaterrecht*], the supremacy of the father in a family in which descent follows the male line; **father-rule,** the rule of the father of a family as distinguished from the rule of the male relatives of the mother where descent follows the female line; patriarchy.

1907 *Folk-Lore* June 245 The passage from motherright to *fatherright. *a* 1909 tr. *L. Gumplowicz's Outl. Sociol.* 53 (Cent. D. Suppl.) Father-right. *Ibid.* 112 *Father-rule.

Fatherhood. Add:

1. e. The position of being the 'father' or oldest member of a society, esp. of the House of Commons.

1899 *Daily News* 24 Apr. 7/3 The House decided informally that the Fatherhood rested with whoever had been longest in the House. 1907 *Westm. Gaz.* 23 May 2/3 The 'Fatherhood' of Sir Henry Campbell-Bannerman.

Fathering, *vbl. sb.* Delete †*Obs.* and add:

1894 G. EGERTON *Discords* 60 The want-wit inconsistency that forgives the man that begat the brat and treats with pitiless scorn the helpless result of his fathering. 1894 *Athenæum* 24 Feb. 238/3 The fathering of bairns. 1894 DU MAURIER *Trilby* III. VII. 19 Taffy..was equal to any burden or responsibility all this instinctive young fathering might involve. 1903 *Daily Chron.* 16 Oct. 3/4 There was too much fathering. The settlers were fathered by their priests, fathered by their King. 1920 H. G. WELLS *Outl. Hist.* 122 The divine fathering and birth of Amenophis III.

Fa·therlandless, *a.* Used as tr. G. *vaterlandlos*: Unpatriotic.

1898 *Daily News* 11 July 3/4 A Conservative Deputy at Dirschau lately called five Liberal electors who voted for the Polish candidate 'Vaterlandlose gesellen' (unpatriotic 'Fatherlandless' fellows). 1915 T. F. A. SMITH *Soul of Germany* 274 Every Socialist, in my opinion, means an enemy to Empire and Fatherland. They are the Fatherlandless enemies of the divine order of things.

Fathership. Add: **b.** = *FATHERHOOD 1 e.

1899 *Westm. Gaz.* 28 Dec. 3/3 The 'Fathership' falls upon Lord Templemore. 1901 *Ibid.* 22 Apr. 1/1 The successor of the late Mr. Villiers in the 'fathership' of the House of Commons. 1910 *Ibid.* 16 Feb. 2/3 Mr. Balfour..lost his chance of the 'Fathership' by a like accident.

Fathom, *sb.* **6.** Add: **fathom-fish** *U.S.*, fish that are tied together in series and sold by the fathom.

1849 A. ROSS *Adv. Oregon River* vi. (1904) 109 To prepare them [*sc.* the ulichans] for a distant market, they are laid side by side, head and tail alternately, and then a thread run through both extremities links them together, in which state they are dried, smoked, and sold by the fathom, hence they have obtained the name of fathom-fish.

Fatigability (fætigăbi·lĭti). Also **fatiguability** (fătī·g-). [f. FATIGABLE: see -ILITY.] Susceptibility to fatigue.

1913 DORLAND *Med. Dict.* (ed. 7), *Fatigability*, easily susceptible to fatigue. 1919 J. A. HADFIELD in *The Spirit* III. 79 A man's fatiguability is tested by tying a weight to his finger [etc.].

Fatigue, *sb.* Add:

1. c. Physics. *Fatigue of elasticity, elastic fatigue*, etc.: see quots.

1892 G. F. BARKER *Physics* 143 A curious phenomenon called the 'fatigue of elasticity' has been observed in solids which shows very clearly the effect of molecular friction. When a wire is vibrated torsionally, there is always a displacement of the zero-point to one side or the other, according to the direction of the original torsion; this disturbance requiring hours or even days for its disappearance. If the wire be kept vibrating, however, the molecular friction is greatly increased. 1899 *Nature* 6 July 239/2 Experiments on an iron wire..showed distinct fatigue of elasticity. 1922 *Glazebrook's Dict. Applied Physics* II. 505/1 Photoelectric Fatigue.—The photoelectric activity of a metal surface which has been freshly polished diminishes as the time that has elapsed since the metal was polished is increased. This is known as the 'fatigue' of the Hallwachs effect.

d. *Physiol.* A condition of cells or organs caused by excessive activity and characterized by loss of power due to the formation of waste products.

1900 W. P. LOMBARD in *W. H. Howell's Text-bk. Physiol.* (ed. 2) II. 70 The fatigue which results from functional activity has, therefore, a twofold cause, the decrease in energy-holding compounds available for work and the accumulation of poisonous waste matters.

3. b. *pl.* (Earlier U.S. example.)

1836 HILDRETH *Dragoon Campaigns Rocky Mts.* I. vii. 51 We have not yet received our uniforms..but even in our 'fatigues', we make an imposing appearance when mounted.

4. *fatigue duty, party, uniform* (earlier U.S. examples); also *fatigue duty man, fatigue frock, trousers*; **fatigue-fever,** a high temperature consequent upon excessive muscular exertion and due to an accumulation of poisonous products in the system; **fatigue products, stuff,** the accumulation of products in the body caused by oxidation of tissue after fatigue.

1856 R. GLISAN *Jrnl. Army Life* xxiv. (1874) 336 The present custom of employing soldiers while in the garrison, on almost continuous hard *fatigue duty. 1867 J. N. EDWARDS *Shelby* xx. 354 Shelby gathered up his *fatigue dutymen and opposed front to front. 1898 *Cycling* 27 Riding too far or too fast leads to '*fatigue fever'. 1813 *Niles' Weekly Reg.* III. 295/2 *Fatigue frocks. 1847 in H. Howe *Hist. Collect. Ohio* 490 It was at night..and they [*sc.* the soldiers] were dressed in fatigue frocks. 1794 *American Pioneer* (1842) I. 351 This morning the *fatigue party ordered yesterday began to fortify and strengthen the fort. 1909 *Westm. Gaz.* 8 June 9/2 To eliminate from the muscles what pathologists know as '*fatigue products'. 1901 DORLAND *Med. Dict.* (ed. 2), **Fatigue-stuff*, toxic material due to tissue-degeneration after excessive fatigue. 1813 *Niles' Weekly Reg.* III. 295/2 *Fatigue trowsers. 1836 J. HILDRETH *Dragoon Campaigns Rocky Mts.* I. iii. 28 Attired in what I afterwards learned to be the *fatigue uniform.

Fatigued, *ppl. a.* Add: **c.** Worn, shabby.

1894 *Daily News* 22 Jan. 5/1 Preferring a fatigued brown calf binding to a new suit of leather for 'Tom Jones'. 1897 *Ibid.* 20 Nov. 8/3 The renovation of a dress that has seen some wear, and consequently has that fatigued appearance.

d. *Physics*. (See *FATIGUE *sb.* 1 c.)

1892 G. F. BARKER *Physics* 144 If an electrically vibrated tuning-fork be kept in motion for a long time, its elasticity appears to become fatigued. 1899 *Nature* 6 July 239/2 There is no apparent reason why too large an initial oscillation should be given always to the fatigued wire and to the unfatigued wire.

Fatihah (fā·tiha). Also **fatha, fattah.** [Arab. *fātiḥa, fātḥa* opening, f. *fataḥa* to open.] The short first sura of the Koran, used by Mohammedans as a prayer.

1863 *Chambers's Encycl.* V. 818/1 Immediately after the introductory fattah or exordium, follows the longest chapter. 1883 E. ARNOLD *Pearls of Faith* xlv, 'Gabriel! why stay'st thou me?'..'Since at this hour the Fâtihah should be read'. 1916 J. RENDEL HARRIS *Testimonies* I. v. 41 He begins his discourse with an imitation of the Fatha, or opening chapter of the Koran.

Fatimite (fæ·timəit), *a.* and *sb.* Also **Fat(h)emite, Fathimite, Fatimid(e.** [f. Arab. *Fatimah* + -ITE[1].] **A.** *adj.* Descended from Fatima, the daughter of Mohammed by his first wife, Khadija. **B.** *sb.* A descendant of Fatima and her husband, Ali; a member of the Arabian dynasty which ruled in parts of northern Africa from A.D. 908–1171, and during some of that period in Egypt and Syria.

1727–38 CHAMBERS *Cycl.*, Fathimites, or Fathemites. *c* 1789 *Encycl. Brit.* (1797) III. 4/2. *c* 1791 *Ibid.* VII. 177/1 Fathemites, Fatemites, or Fathimites. 1838 *Penny Cycl.* X. 207/1 Obeidallah, the first Fatimide caliph. 1883 *Encycl. Brit.* XVI. 587/1 With the reign of Moktadir is connected one of the greatest events in the history of the Caliphate, the foundation of the Fâtimite dynasty. 1897 *Daily News* 8 Apr. 8/1 In 1072 the Holy City was possessed by the Fatimite Caliph of Egypt. 1902 *Daily Chron.* 20 June 4/2 The Fatimid Caliphate.

Fatling, *sb.* Add: Also *transf.* of a person.

a 1861 WINTHROP *John Brent* vii. 72 'Well, boys!' said the unpleasant fatling, approaching again.

Fatness. 1. c. (Later U.S. examples.)

1814 J. TAYLOR *Arator* 172 This [*sc.* using bottom lands for tillage and grazing] is owing to the extreme fatness of the soil. 1849 E. BRYANT *California* ii. 23, I never saw a soil indicative of a higher degree of fatness.

Fattah, variant of *FATIHAH.

Fatty, *a.* Add:

1. c. Of quicklime: = *FAT *a.* 5.

6. *Fatty series*: a group of carbon compounds derived from methane and having a chain-like structure. *Fatty-tailed sheep*: = fat-tailed sheep (see FAT *a.* 13).

1864 J. A. GRANT *Walk Across Africa* 31 'Doomba' or fatty-tailed variety. 1897 REMSEN *Org. Chem.* 147 The acids with which it [*sc.* glycerin] is in combination are mostly members of the fatty acid series. 1913 DORLAND *Med. Dict.* (ed. 7), *Fatty series*, the open-chain series.

B. *sb.* A fat person: esp. as a nickname.

1822 R. RICHARDSON *Trav. Medit.* II. xix. 266 Well-built fatties, with double mouldings in the neck and chin. 1891 FARMER *Slang*, *Fatty*, a jocular epithet for a fat man; a comic endearment for a fat woman. 1913 E. F. BENSON *Thorley Weir* ix. 317 He proposed to her twice, the old fatty.

Faucalize (fǭ·kăləiz), *v.* [f. FAUCAL + -IZE.] *trans.* To add a faucal element to (a sound).

1919 SIR H. H. JOHNSTON *Comp. Stud. Bantu & Semi-B. Lang.* I. 36 The faucalizing of *w*. 1920 MISS A. WERNER in *Man* XX. 14 How do you faucalise *w*?

Fault, *sb.* Add:

1. c. Delete †*Obs.* and add quots. Also without *for* (after F. *faute de*).

1867 EMERSON *Terminus* 21 And, fault of novel germs, Mature the unfallen fruit. 1874 SWINBURNE *Bothwell* II. xiv. (1882) 195 Though it be evil made for fault of time.

9. A flaw or dislocation in ice.

1860 [in Dict.]. 1925 N. E. ODELL in E. F. Norton *Fight for Everest, 1924* 314 That the ice above the Trough was undergoing severe stress was apparent not only from its foliation, but also from the faults—'flaws' or 'tear-faults'—that had been extensively developed in this area.

11. (sense 9), as *fault-bundle, -fissure, -plane*; **fault-block,** a mass of displaced rock between two faults; **fault-scarp,** the upthrow side of a fault remaining as a line of cliffs; **fault vein,** a vein of mineral filling a fault; **fault-vent,** a volcanic vent occurring at a fault.

1897 W. B. SCOTT *Introd. Geol.* 248 If two parallel dislocations hade toward each other, they form a trough fault and include a wedge-shaped *fault block. 1925 N. E. ODELL in E. F. Norton *Fight for Everest, 1924* 292 At one point in the gorge a fault block had been turned through 90°. 1900 *Geogr. Jrnl.* (R.G.S.) XVI. 464 Varied arrangements in *fault-bundles and fault-polygons. 1855 J. R. LEIFCHILD *Cornwall Mines* 87 In some instances..the *fault-fissures are open. 1903 GEIKIE *Text-bk. Geol.* (ed. 4) 372 Another remarkable instance of the..fault-fissure type was furnished by the great Japanese earthquake of 28th October 1891. 1900 *Geogr. Jrnl.* (R.G.S.) XVI. 466 Inclined *fault-planes with downthrow towards one trough. 1897 W. B. SCOTT *Introd. Geol.* 248 It is comparatively seldom that the upthrow side of a fault is left standing as a line of cliffs; when such is the case, the cliffs form a *fault scarp. 1905 CHAMBERLIN & SALISBURY *Geol.* I. 490 The cliff above the edge of the downthrow side is a fault-scarp. 1903 *Nature* 3 Sept. 413/2 During the geological periods when the *fault-vent continued intermittently active.

Fault, *v.* **9.** Add: Also *intr.*

1905 CHAMBERLIN & SALISBURY *Geol.* I. 496 Faulting is probably one of the common causes of earthquakes. 1927 *Daily Express* 5 July 11/4 A geological inexactitude which appears to have faulted or slipped from peaceful churchyard surroundings to a boisterous life in the ocean waves.

Faultage (fǭ·ltédʒ). [f. FAULT *sb.* 9 + -AGE.] Faults considered collectively, faulting.

1899 *Geogr. Jrnl.* (R.G.S.) XIII. 272 Well-marked lines of faultage going down to the bases of the mountains.

Faunally (fǭ·năli), *adv.* [f. FAUNAL *a.*[2] + -LY[2].] As regards the fauna of a district or epoch.

1872 *Amer. Naturalist* VI. 342 These two regions are as diverse faunally as they are in physical features. 1887 *Ibid.* XXI. 447 This formation..displays a number of divisions, which differ both lithologically and faunally.

Faunule (fǭ·niul). [ad. mod.L. *faunula*, dim. of FAUNA.] A subdivision of a fauna; *esp.* a local group of fossils representative of a fauna.

1928 C. L. FENTON & M. A. FENTON in *Amer. Midland Natural.* Jan. II. I. 21 A zonule is the stratum or strata which contain a faunule.

Faute de mieux (fot də myö). [Fr.] For want of better.

1766 CHESTERF. *Lett.* (1774) II. 501 The seals..were offered first to Lord Egmont, then to Lord Hardwicke; but, after their going a begging for some time, the Duke of — begged them, and has them *faute de mieux*. 1828 LYTTON *Pelham* xxxii, At seven o'clock, up came a *cotelette pannée—faute de mieux*, I swallowed the composition. 1865 'OUIDA' *Strathmore* ii, Still they were better than nothing, and were peppered *faute de mieux* that day.

Fauteuil. Add:

b. The seat of a member of the French Academy; hence, membership of the Academy.

1883 *Standard* 23 Aug. 5/2 (Stanford) The number of Academic *fauteuils* would be fixed. 1910 *Glasgow Herald* 28 Apr. 9 The creation..of the class of Senior Academicians, whose fauteuils automatically became vacant.

c. A seat in a theatre, an omnibus, etc. designed to resemble an armchair. Popularly pronounced (fōᵘ·til).

1901 *Playgoer* 15 Oct. 38/1 Fine *fauteuils* for sixpence.. or stage box seats for ninepence. 1902 MACHRAY *Night Side of London* vii. (1906) 124 You abandon your fauteuil, get out of the smoke-laden..atmosphere, and pass out into the street. 1925 A. P. HERBERT *Laughing Ann* 37 Oh, I likes a bit of enjoyment on a Friday, I like to sit in the fautles an' be grand. 1931 *Morning Post* 20 Aug. 8/3 With their covered-in tops, resilient springs, and voluptuous *fauteuils*, the latest omnibuses have become so attractive that one often feels..disinclined to get off.

Faveolus (fāvī·ŏlŏs). *Pl.* **-i.** [mod.L., dim. of *favus* honeycomb.] A small depression, like a cell of a honeycomb.

1882 *Encycl. Brit.* XIV. 562/1 The apothecia of several calcicole lichens..have the power..of forming minute faveoli in the rocks.

Faverolle (fæ·vəɹǫl, fævərǫᵘ·l). [f. place name *Faverolles*.] One of a breed of domestic fowls originated in France by crossing light Brahmas or Dorkings with Houdans.

1902 L. WRIGHT *New Bk. Poultry* (1905) 457/1 Faverolles have for some time been common in the northern part of France, where they are regarded as simply useful fowls. *Ibid.* 457/2 The colour of the Salmon Faverolles cock is quite different from that of the hen.

Favositoid (fævǫsəi·toid), *a.* [f. FAVOSITES + -OID.] Pertaining to, or resembling, the genus *Favosites*.

1904 *Amer. Jrnl. Sci.* Ser. IV. XVIII. 136 The septa of a favositoid coral.

Favour, *sb.* Add: **3. d.** *Ombre* and *Quadrille*. (See quots.)

1902 LD. ALDENHAM *Ombre* 46 Favor..consists..in a preference given to one suit—usually Diamonds (*Oros*). *Ibid.*, One of his antagonists, having a good hand in Diamonds, outbids him, and demands *Favor*, intending to play the Simple game.

Favourable, *a.* Add:

5. b. Of a patient's condition, progress, etc.: Satisfactory; favouring recovery.

1903 *Westm. Gaz.* 8 July 7/1 Seeing that his condition was so favourable.

Favoured, *ppl. a.*[1] Add quots. illustrating the *attrib.* use of 'the most favoured nation'.

1902 *Encycl. Brit.* XXVII. 164/1 By extending to a third nation privileges granted to particular countries, the most favoured nation article began to be framed. 1909 *Westm. Gaz.* 17 Aug. 2/1 Having secured a most-favoured-nation clause in her commercial treaty with China in 1896. 1928 *Manch. Guardian Weekly* 26 Oct. 328/2 In the agreement will be two main clauses dealing with most-favoured-nation treatment.

Favourite, *sb.* and *a.* **B.** *adj.*:

2. *Ombre* and *Quadrille*. *Favourite suit*, the suit which has preference over the others. Also simply *favourite*.

1763 LADY SARAH LENNOX *Lett.* (1901) I. 132 Mr. Bunbury and I won a vole in favourite in the last deal of all some time ago. 1820 HOYLE *Games* (1835) 281 The favourite suit is determined, either by drawing a card, or otherwise fixing upon a suit at the commencement of the party; and during the whole game, each player, asking leave in that suit, has a preference before others who have a good hand in a different suit.

Favrile (favrī·l). Formed as a trade name by L. C. Tiffany, the inventor of the glass, in 1894, from FABRILE *a.*, to denote a kind of glass characterized by rich colouring, iridescence, and enamelling.

1902 *Encycl. Brit.* XXIX. 8/1 The so-called 'Favrile' glass of Messrs. Tiffany of New York owes its effect entirely to surface colour and lustre.

Fawnish (fǭ·niʃ), *a.* [f. FAWN *sb.*[1] 3 + -ISH[1].] Somewhat fawn, resembling fawn in colour.

1895 *Daily News* 31 May 2/1 The rest of the dress being a negation in fawnish cream colour. 1909 MARG. B. SAUNDERS *Litany Lane* I. i, Looming out of the fawnish mist shone the great golden glory of the world.

Fay, *v.*[1] **2. b.** *U.S.* (Earlier and later examples.)

1847 D. P. THOMPSON *Locke Amsden* 138 (Th.), I have no notion of spoiling sense to make it fay in with book rules. 1906 P. LOWELL *Mars & its Canals* 347 The explanation of the canals as threads of vegetation fays in with the one which has been found to meet the requirements of the blue-green areas.

Faze, *v.* *U.S.* (Earlier examples.)

1843 CARLTON *New Purchase* I. xix. 174 This didn't *faze* me, only I steps back for my old camlit cloak. 1859 *Harper's Weekly* 16 July (Th.) Such a stomach that even a dram of nitric acid would not faze it.

Feather, *sb.* Add:

11. b. Also on other animals.

1884 G. STABLES *Our Friend the Dog* vii. (1895) 74 *Feather*—The long hair on chest, legs, and tail, &c., of some breeds. The hair generally. 1897 *Outing* (U.S.) XXX. 413/1 The coat [of the Russian wolfhound] is long...forming a liberal 'feather' upon the legs, chest, belly and hind-quarters. 1914 *N. Z. Farmer* Apr., Although the General Trend of the hair [*sc.* on the part between the hock and the vulva of a cow] is in an ascending direction there are variations on certain points where changes in the direction of the growth makes the hair stand up on ridges, sometimes forming figures. These variations are called feathers. There are in all seven feathers. 1 The Oval feather. 2 The Buttock feather. 3 The Babine feather. 4 The Vulvous feather. 5 The Bastard feather. 6 The Thigh feather. 7 The Dart feather.

c. The foamy crest of a wave.

1838 *Civil Eng. & Arch. Jrnl.* I. 272/1 The feather only of each wave would be seen. 1896 *Daily News* 10 July 3/6 White feathers from their bows.

18. a. *feather-boa*.

1895 *Army & Navy Co-op. Soc. Price List* 15 Sept. 1041 Black and Coloured Feather Boas. 1902 *Queen* 15 Feb. Advt. 2nd sheet, Lace Berthes and Feather Boas.

19. feather ball, a golf-ball stuffed with feathers (cf. *FEATHERY *a.* 4); **feather-curler,** one employed in curling feathers; so *feather-curling*.

1893 H. G. HUTCHINSON *Golfing* 4 Before the days of gutta-percha. Men played with '*feather balls'—that is, balls of leather stuffed..tightly with feathers. 1881 *Instr. Census Clerks* (1885) 79 *Feather..Curler. 1895 *Daily News* 4 Apr. 5/6 Earning fifteenpence a day as a feather-curler.

Feather, *v.* Add: **11. b.** To fix (paddle-floats) so as to offer the least resistance while descending into, or ascending out of, the water. (Cf. FEATHERING *ppl. a.* b.)

1847 *Rep. U.S. Comm. Patents* (1848) 71 Another for improvements in the mode of feathering the floats of paddle wheels.

Feather-duster. **1.** (See FEATHER *sb.* 19 in Dict.) **2.** An American Indian. *U.S. slang.*

1907 MULFORD *Bar-20* ix. 103, I had a little argument with some feather dusters. 1908 — *Orphan* iv. 40 Show me the feather-dusters in war paint.

Feather-edge, *sb.* Add: attrib. *feather-edge steps* (see quot.).

1876 *Encycl. Brit.* IV. 473/1 It is usual to make the steps of somewhat a triangular shape, so as to present a continued soffit. In this case they are called arris, or feather-edge steps.

b. A wire edge. (See quot.)

1901 *J. Black's Carp. & Build., Home Handicr.* 32 Sometimes, by over-grinding,..a 'feather-edge' is produced. This is a little film of steel projecting from the true edge.

2. *fig.* An over-fine edge. *U.S.*

1891 *Harper's Mag.* July 210/1 Let the pony have a little fun...This takes the feather-edge off him. 1903 A. H. LEWIS *Boss* 59 An'..not to put a feather-edge on it, I thought I'd run you over, an' see if they'd been fixin' you.

Feather-edge, *v.* (Earlier Amer. example.)

1648 *Dedham* (Mass.) *Rec.* 157 A schoole house to be built...the stayers [to be] made, the sides boarded feather-edged & rabbited.

Feathering, *vbl. sb.* **1.** Add: Of a paddle-wheel: see *FEATHER *v.* 11 b.

1849 *Rep. U.S. Comm. Patents* (1850) 447 Many applications have been made based upon alleged novelties in the feathering of the vertical float paddle wheel.

Feather-weight. Add: **4.** *attrib.*

1905 *Daily Chron.* 28 June 3/2 A 'feather-weight' laid paper of a durable kind is employed. 1908 *Ibid.* 3 Aug. 6/6 Green's mount was a featherweight Raleigh.

Feathery, *a.* Add:

4. Of golf-balls: Stuffed with feathers. Also as *sb.*

1891 R. FORGAN *Golfer's Handbk.* 34 The so-called 'feathery' variety of golf balls exclusively held the field. These 'featheries' were made of leather, stuffed with feathers.

Feature, *sb.* **4. c.** Add: in recent Comb. = forming a special feature in a magazine, newspaper, etc.

1928 *Publishers' Weekly* 16 June 2440 When a single Sunday newspaper sometimes has three or four feature stories about authors.

Feature, *v.* Add: **4.** To exhibit as a 'feature'; to make a special feature or display of, make a special attraction of. orig. *U.S.*

1888 *St. Louis Globe Democrat* 29 Apr. (Farmer) The biggest thing I saw at the wedding was a lot of glassware and block tin knives and forks, which were featured in one of the rooms. 1889 FARMER *Americanisms*, *Featured, to be*, to be displayed; to be set out to the best advantage, literally to be made a feature. 1906 *Westm. Gaz.* 24 Sept. 9/3 The way in which Miss Clifford had been 'featured' and 'billed' in preference to herself. 1907 *Times* (weekly ed.) 28 June 402 Every day for weeks past it has 'featured' articles..on the Japanese question. 1928 *Publishers' Weekly* 12 May 1932 You will know then why so many booksellers feature Macaulay books. *Ibid.* 9 June 2352 All three [books] will be featured in a lavish and spectacular joint display. 1928 G. B. SHAW *Intell. Woman's Guide Socialism* (1929) 444 The Government posters 'feature' precisely the same epithets. 1929 *Times* 1 Aug., The Louvre, Oxford-circus, are featuring coats and skirts and top coats for Scotland in new designs.

b. *spec.* To exhibit as a prominent feature in a dramatic piece, esp. on 'the films'; to 'star'.

1897 *Metropolitan Mag.* (N.Y.) Nov. 383/2 A company that includes in addition to the 'featured' members, [etc.]. 1923 *Westm. Gaz.* 22 Jan., Balzac's 'The Eternal Flame', featuring Miss Norma Talmadge. 1927 *Daily Chron.* 29 Mar. 6 She said she had been 'featured' in 22 or 23 different pieces in America. 1928 *Manchester Guardian Weekly* 7 Dec., Suppl. p. ix/1 A young man in trouble and not a handsome middle-aged gentleman featuring himself through five acts.

Feaze, *v.* *U.S.* Var. FAZE *v.* (Cf. FEEZE *v.* 2.)

1906 *Springfield Weekly Republ.* 27 Dec. 1 The gentlemen at the head of the Standard oil trust will not be feazed or troubled a bit by these revelations. 1907 MULFORD *Bar-20* ix. 96 I've bit on so many of them rumours that they don't feaze me no more. 1916 'B. M. BOWER' *Phantom Herd* ix. 143 That..rather feazed the Happy Family for a few minutes.

Febricule (fe·brikiul). Anglicised form of FEBRICULA.

1887 R. L. STEVENSON *Merry Men* (ed. 2) 228 A febricule when I digest.

Febronian, *a.* Add: Also *sb.*, a follower of Febronius.

1884 ADDIS & ARNOLD *Cath. Dict.* 346/2 The Pope's power was to be reduced to that which Febronians supposed him to have exercised in the first three centuries. 1895 W. WARD in *19th Cent.* Nov. 797 Protestants of the sixteenth and seventeenth centuries were succeeded by Febronians and Jansenists in the eighteenth.

Fechner (fe·χᵊnəɹ). The name of Gustav Theodor *Fechner* (1801–87), the founder of German experimental psychology, used in the genitive to designate laws, formulæ, etc. of his invention.

1876 *Mind* I. 455 It is thus quite possible to give a physical interpretation to Fechner's law without implying anything 'inconceivable'. 1887 LADD *Physiol. Psychol.* (1890) 365 The significant addition which Fechner has made to Weber's law consists in the assumption that all just observable differences are equally great. It is therefore also called 'Fechner's law'. 1892 tr. *Ziehen's Physiol. Psychol.* 54 The logarithmic formula of Fechner's Law. *Ibid.* 55 The undoubted advantage of being able to explain or account for Fechner's Formula entirely in accordance with the spirit of the natural sciences. 1897 SCRIPTURE *New Psychol.* 441 Upon such considerations as these, Bernoulli developed formulas equivalent to the differential and logarithmic ones we have spoken of when considering Fechner's law. 1909 MYERS *Exper. Psychol.* 86 When a white sector upon a black ground is very slowly turned on the colour wheel, a series of black bands in the form of radii may be observed on that part of the white surface which first stimulates the eye... With somewhat more rapid rotation, especially under bright illumination, various colours, called Fechner's colours, may be visible on the white surface.

Fechnerian (feχᵊnīᵊ·riăn), *a.* Relating to G. T. *Fechner* (see prec.). So **Fe·chnerism** (in recent Dicts.).

1909 *Westm. Gaz.* 15 May 4/2 These Fechnerian ideas.

Fecula: see FÆCULA.

Feculent, *a.* Add: Also *sb.* A starch, a starchy substance or food.

1908 *Practitioner* Feb. 280 Feculents and sugar must be limited in the diet.

Feculose (fe·kiŭlōᵘs). *Chem.* [f. FÆCULA + -OSE[2].] (See quot. 1928.)

1920 CROSS & BEVAN *Paper-Making* 309 'Feculose'. is being employed in increasing quantities as a substitute for gelatine. 1928 KINGZETT *Chem. Encycl.* (ed. 4) 272 *Feculose* is an acetylated starchy product used by treating dry starch with glacial acetic acid at 120° C., using, if desired, small additions of mineral acids or formic acid as accelerators.

Fecund, Fecundity. Distinguished from *fertile, fertility* (see quots.).

1866 J. M. DUNCAN *Fecundity*, etc. 3 By fertility or productiveness I mean the amount of births as distinguished from the capability to bear... By fecundity I mean the demonstrated capability to bear children; it implies the conditions necessary for conception in the women of whom its variations are predicated... In short, fertility implies fecundity, and also introduces the idea of number of progeny; while fecundity simply indicates the quality without any superadded notion of quantity. 1904 *Brit. Med. Jrnl.* 23 Apr. 769 A difference is drawn between fecundity and fertility. Thus women of Irish birth in Australia are less fecund than women born either in New South Wales or in Scotland, but they are more fertile. In other words fewer Irish women have children, but to those who are fecund more children are born.

Fed, *sb.* *U.S.* (Earlier examples.)

1788 *Maryland Jrnl.* 3 June (Th.) The famous Dr. Spring asked a lady on which side she was, fed. or antifed. *a* 1800 *Spirit of Farmers' Mus.* (1801) 56 There Feds shall cease to charge the Antis, With making Frenchmen rule brave yankees.

Fed, *pa. pple.* Slang phr. *to be fed up*: to be surfeited or disgusted (*with*), bored to death, or tired to breaking-point. Also with emphasizing expressions, as *fed to the* (*back*) *teeth*; occas. without *up*.

[1882 F. ARNOLD *Three Cornered Essays* (1886) 4 Fed up to the eyelids, it is no care to him that there are other people all otherwise than so well off.] 1900 *Westm. Gaz.* 13 Nov. 2/3 It may be quite true that, to use an expression often heard in South Africa just now, the men are 'fed up' with the war. 1906 *Daily Chron.* 22 Mar. 9/5, I am about 'fed-up' over this motor-car. 1914 *Even. News* 19 Sept. 4/1 We have also seen hundreds of German prisoners, mostly looking 'fed up'. 1916 BOYD CABLE *Action Front* 32 'I'm just about fed up with him', said Gunner Donovan bitterly. 1922 A. S. M. HUTCHINSON *This Freedom* IV. iv. 293 Oh, those sickening scarves and things, they were eternally knitting, that wasn't war work. It was fun at first. They were fed to death with doing them now. 1924 A. J. SMALL *Frozen Gold* iii. 78 He had the air of a man who was utterly and finally fed-up with the eternal effort of keeping the upper hand of the worst. 1928 WODEHOUSE in *Strand Mag.* July 4 Her aspect was that of a girl who is fed to the teeth. 1930 MACKAIL *How Amusing* 342 It made me feel pretty fed with the old boy.

Fedai (fe·dāi). Pl. **fedai, fedais.** [Pers. فداي courageous, valiant, volunteer.] = ASSASSIN 1.

1875 *Encycl. Brit.* II. 723/1 When the sheikh required the services of any of them, the selected *fedais* were intoxicated with *hashish*. 1909 *Westm. Gaz.* 15 Feb. 2/1 Thousands of them became 'fedai', men ready to sacrifice themselves for the common good. 1921 *Glasgow Herald* 13 Sept. 7 Seventeen Fedai, otherwise reckless desperadoes, are stated to have been specially brought to Constantinople for the purpose of committing murders.

Federal, *a.* and *sb.* Add: **A.** *adj.* **3. c.** *Federal City*, Washington, as the capital of the United States.

1847 *Knickerbocker Mag.* XXIX. 536 She..last winter travelled with her uncle as far as the Federal City.

B. *sb.* (Earlier example.)

1867 J. N. EDWARDS *Shelby*, etc. iii. 52 The dead were buried by the Federals, and the wounded cared for in the hospitals.

Federator (fe·dĕrēᵗəɹ). [f. FEDERATE *v.* + -OR.] One who or that which makes a federation; one who takes part in a federation.

1879 JAS. MARTINEAU *Ess.* (1891) IV. 271 It's [*sc.* religion's] power..as a federator of nations..is freely admitted. 1901 *Wide World Mag.* VI. 472/2 Professor Bickerton himself paying on the same scale as any other Federator.

Fedora (fĕdōᵊ·rā). [f. *Fédora*, title of a drama by V. Sardou.] A low soft felt hat with a curled brim and the crown creased lengthways, worn by both men and women.

1916 LEACOCK *Moonbeams* ii. 23 There was no use in my having bought a sage-green fedora in Broadway. 1927 L. BROMFIELD *Possession* ix. 46 He took off..his brown fedora hat. *Ibid.* xvii. 100 In place of a warm skating cap he wore a Fedora hat pulled over his ears. 1930 E. V. KNOX in *Punch* 26 Feb. 236 He carried a cheap black fedora in his hand.

Fee, *sb.*[4] Variant of FAY *sb.*[3]

1839 [in Dict.]. 1864 *Jrnl. R. Agric. Soc.* XXV. II. 371 The earth overlying the marl, technically called 'fee' or 'rid'. *Ibid.*, The fee was in the first instance carefully removed from the upper surface of the marl.

Feeble, *a.* **9.** *feeble-minded* (add quot. for technical definition).

1908 *Rep. Comm. Care & Control Feeble-Minded* VIII. 324 'Feeble-minded', *i.e.*, persons who may be capable of earning a living under favourable circumstances, but are incapable from mental defect existing from birth or from an early age: (*a*) of competing on equal terms with their normal fellows; or (*b*) of managing themselves and their affairs with ordinary prudence.

Feebling (fī·bliŋ). [f. FEEBLE *a.*: see -LING[1].] A weakling, a feeble person.

1891 H. A. BEERS *Init. Studies* vii. (1896) 216 [Henry James] has exhibited types of the American girl, the American business-man, the æsthetic feebling from Boston. 1896 *Westm. Gaz.* 13 June 2/1 To shriek with horror at them, the sign of a feebling. 1914 BARING-GOULD *Ch. Revival* 151 The Church was supplied with feeblings as candidates for Orders.

Feed, *sb.* Add: **3. c.** Also, food, fare (for human beings). *U.S. colloq.*

1818 FEARON *Sk. Amer.* 194, I guess whiskey is all the feed we have on sale. 1835 *Knickerbocker Mag.* V. 304 A John Smith lives next door, to whom half my choice rounds and sirloins, selected personally in the market,—for I love good feed,—are sent without distinction. 1867 SUSAN HALE *Lett.* (1919) 27 The cook is French and feed delicious. 1888 NYE *Baled Hay* 31 He will..absorb a given amount of feed.

5. d. *Theatrical slang.* = FEEDER 11.

1929 PRIESTLEY *Good Companions* II. i, Joe over there..is as good a feed as you could wish for. *Ibid.*, You couldn't want a better dancer... The only thing is, he won't feed. I never struck a worse feed.

6. a. *U.S.* (sense 3 and 3 b) *feed-bin, -lot, -stable, -station, -stuff, -yard*; (sense 5) *feed-bar*; *feed-cock, -hole* (earlier examples). **b.** (sense 3) *feed-chopper.*

1876 J. S. INGRAM *Centennial Expos.* ix. 298 The radiating arms..act against the *feed-bar. 1898 MARG. DELAND *Old Chester Tales* 250 The open space between the stalls and the *feed-bins should be the stage. 1916 H. L. WILSON *Somewhere in Red Gap* vii. 304 Rex II [beagle] didn't get in till next day and looked like he'd come through a *feed chopper. 1833 B. SILLIMAN *Man. Sugar Cane* 56 It is drawn up into the vacuum pans..by the *feed cocks. 1874 J. W. LONG *Amer. Wild-Fowl Shooting* 37 A quick loading flask, i.e., one having a large *feed-hole to the charger, should also be used. 1911 H. QUICK *Yellowstone N.* vi. 165 Two boys..had met in Allen's *feed-lot to fight a duel. 1902 O. WISTER *Virginian* ii. 13, I took its dimensions, twenty-nine buildings in all,—..one *feed stable, and..others. 1910 W. M. RAINE *B. O'Connor* 106 Jay Hardman's place, a tumble-down *feed-station on the edge of town. *a* 1909 'O. HENRY' *Roads of Destiny* ix. 157 There was a *feedstuff famine in Mexico. 1911 H. QUICK *Yellowstone N.* iv. 109 One, two, three farmsteads we passed, with its white house hidden in trees, low hog-houses, its *feed yards.

7. feed-back (circuit) *Wireless* (see quot. 1923); **feed-block** (see quot. 1902); **feed check,** a valve placed between the feed-pipe and the boiler, to prevent return of feed-water; **feed collector** (see quot.); **feed-door** (earlier U.S. examples); **feed-floor** *U.S.*, a floor off which cattle, etc., can eat food; **feed gear,** the mechanism of feed-motion; **feed-mouth** = *feed-door*; **feed-room** *U.S.*, a dining-room; **feed-strip,** a cartridge belt for a machine gun; **feed-table,** a table indicating the food values of fodders; **feed-tank,** also, a tank to hold liquid fuel; **feed-trough,** also *U.S.* a trough in which food for animals is placed; **feed-tub,** the supply vessel of an evaporator; **feed-wire** = FEEDER 10.

1923 *Harmsworth's Wireless Encycl.* 913/1 The term *feed back* is applied to any radio-telegraph circuit in which one part of the circuit is coupled to another part in order to transfer some part of the energy in the one circuit to the other circuit. 1930 *Morning Post* 14 July 3 If the receiver is well designed, so that low-frequency feed-back is negligible, a filter circuit is not needed. 1895 LUKIN *Maxim Machine Gun* 11 What keeps the extractor at its highest until the cartridge is drawn from the *feed block? *Ibid.* 21 When loading for rapid fire, the crank handle is turned over to buffer spring twice and the belt is pulled through the feed block. 1902 *Encycl. Brit.* XXX. 401/2 The feed-block through which the belt of cartridges is fed to the gun. 1928 C. F. S. GAMBLE *N. Sea Air Station* xvi. 295 A left-hand feed-block, which was instantly interchangeable with the right-hand feed-block. 1895 *Daily News* 17 Dec. 3/5 To repair *feed check valve. 1908 *Westm. Gaz.* 25 Apr. 2/3 Off they went into the stokehole, where the Third put two of them to mind the feed-checks. 1902 *Encycl. Brit.* XXVI. 264/1 A horizontal cross-tube of square section, called a *feed collector, which extends the whole width of the [marine water-tube] boiler. 1872 *Rep. Vermont Board Agric.* I. 635 The ore..is landed at the *feed door of the furnace. 1877 RAYMOND *Statist. Mines & Mining* 269, 10 ft. 6 ins. from tuyeres to feed-door. 1867 *Rep. Iowa Agric. Soc.* (1868) 104 Put them [*sc.* hogs] in small yards with a good plank *feed-floor. 1892 *Lockwood's Dict. Mech. Engin.* (ed. 2), **Feed Gear*, the mechanism, usually automatic, by which the extent of the operations of cutting tools used in machines is governed. 1895 *Daily News* 27 July 3/1 The torpedo boat destroyer Ferret, which broke down..owing to the defective working of her automatic feed gear. 1833 B. SILLIMAN *Man. Sugar Cane* 34 An opening into the furnace, called the *feed-mouth, for the supply of fuel and the regulation of the fire, is left. 1887 TOURGEE *Button's Inn* 142 A great towel ..hung inside the *feed-room door. 1902 *Encycl. Brit.* XXX. 404/2 The breech-block..driving a cartridge in front of it out of the *feed-strip. 1886 C. SCOTT *Sheep-farming* 33 He can only examine the *feed tables..and guess at the quality of his own fodders. 1886 *Marine Engineer* 1 Feb. 283 Storage-tanks..being connected by pipes to the small *feed-tanks situated above the boiler. 1845 A. WILEY in *Indiana Mag. Hist.* XXIII. 212 To come with their wagons, and grain, and hay, and *feed troughs and watering buckets. 1854 BARTLETT *Pers. Narr. Explor. Texas* etc. II. 12 All [the wagons] had to be provided with feed-troughs. 1867 *Rep. Iowa Agric. Soc.* (1868) 148 Our market is in the feed-troughs. 1878 *Rep. Vermont Board Agric.* 109 The *feed tub will be high enough for the sap to run from that to the evaporator. 1909 *Westm. Gaz.* 16 Apr. 8/1 Killed.. while testing some electric *feed wires.

Feed, *v.* Add:

6. c. Also, *trans.* and *intr.*, to supply another character with cues. (Cf. FEEDER 11.)

1929 PRIESTLEY *Good Companions* II. i, You couldn't want a better dancer... The only thing is, he won't feed. *Ibid.*, The chap that feeds has to ask the comedian questions. 1930 MACKAIL *How Amusing* 66 I've had laughs I've earned, and laughs the other fellow's earned by my feeding him.

g. *Football.* To give a pass to.

1889 BARRÈRE & LELAND *Dict. Slang* s.v., To *feed*, to support. 1897 *Encycl. Sport* I. 417/2 The way in which he can aid his side in attacking is by passing to, or, as it is called, feeding his forwards.

8. b. (Earlier and later examples. Also with *out.*) Also, to supply (food) *to* persons. *U.S.*

1818 in *Trans. Ill. State Hist. Soc.* 1910, 158 They either have to feed out their corn or their cattle get very poor. 1852 *Trans. Mich. Agric. Soc.* III. 145, I feed almost every thing, hay, oats, straw, [etc.]. 1867 *Rep. Iowa Agric. Soc.* (1868) 148 Corn is husked and cribbed and fed out to stock. 1904 *Grand Rapids Even. Press* 2 June 3 The professor.. fed snake sandwiches to his college class at a party. 1911 R. W. CHAMBERS *Common Law* viii. 237 Rita..fed them bits of cassava and crumbs of cake.

Feed-box (fī·dbǫks). [f. FEED *sb.* + BOX *sb.*[2]] **a.** A box for containing fodder. **b.** A box containing the feeding apparatus of a machine.

1867 *Rep. Iowa Agric. Soc.* (1868) 118 The plan of allowing the colt..to eat all the corn it can from feed boxes..is a mistaken idea. 1872 *Rep. Vermont Board Agric.* I. 149 Put all into a water-tight feed box. 1886 C. SCOTT *Sheep-farming* 80 A number of small feed boxes, suitable for feeding the ewes in the pens. 1890 D'OYLE *Notches* 128 Then he looked to the wants of his horse, and putting a feed into the 'feed-box' of hers too, went back to the house. 1895 KIPLING in *Pall Mall Gaz.* 26 June 2/3 As if he had his nose in a feed-box and was looking for something nice. 1902 *Encycl. Brit.* XXX. 404/1 The platform on the top of the feed-box [of a machine gun] through which the teeth of the smaller feed-wheel project.

Feeder. Add:

7. d. = *feeder-line.*

1858 SIMMONDS *Dict. Trade*, *Feeder*...a branch railway, running into the main-trunk line. 1902 *Encycl. Brit.* XXIX. 443/1 All the leading trunk lines, with their principal feeders.

12. *attrib.* **feeder line, feeder railway,** branch lines linking up outlying districts with the main lines of communication; **feeder main,** a main supplying electricity to branch-wires.

1895 *Westm. Gaz.* 6 June 6/2 The policy of building what are known as *feeder lines is one that is much advocated by politicians who take an active interest in the future of India. 1903 EARL OF CROMER in *Daily Chron.* 30 Jan. 5/5, I want feeder lines to Kassala. 1893 *Jrnl. Soc. Arts* 5 May 622/2 A pair of omnibus bars,..from which all the *feeder mains run off to the various circuits of the distribution. 1895 *Westm. Gaz.* 6 June 6/2 The question of *feeder railways, whether on a standard or meter gauge, had also attracted some attention.

Feeding, *vbl. sb.* Add:

1. (Examples of modern techn. senses.)

1897 *Encycl. Sport* I. 404/2 Many aver that..Alan Rotherham was the first to reduce the art of feeding to a science. 1929 PRIESTLEY *Good Companions* II. i, This feeding I'm talking about..is a name in the profession for working up to gags.

4. *feeding-ground* (other U.S. examples), *-hole, -land* (earlier U.S. example), *-room, -trough.*

1647 *Essex Inst. Hist. Coll.* V. 223/1 Wee have granted to him 200 acres of *feeding grounde. 1874 J. W. LONG *Amer. Wild-Fowl Shooting* 161 The ducks will be seen..coming to the feeding-grounds. 1868 JOYNSON *Metals* 71 In this country the *feeding hole of the furnace is generally closed. 1901 *Feilden's Mag.* IV. 436/1 With a steeper inclination.. to a 'feeding-hole' for the admission of refuse from the platform above. 1669 *Watertown* (Mass.) *Rec.* 99 If any such sheep be taken vpon comon *feeding land. 1910 *Blackw. Mag.* Mar. 614/1, I was wet, miserable, and tired, so I passed into the common *feeding-room. 1825 J. NICHOLSON *Operat. Mechanic* 403 The flax is fed or supplied in handsfull on the *feeding-trough. 1867 'T. LACKLAND' *Homespun* II. 170 It will pay you well to feed your beast..in the feeding-trough under the shed.

b. feeding bag, a nose-bag for a horse (cf. *feed-bag*, FEED *sb.* 6 a).

1812 *Niles' Weekly Register* II. 131/1 The purveyor of public supplies advertises for..3000 nose or feeding bags.

Feel, *v.* Add: **1. d.** Also, to search *out*, to ascertain, by feeling or testing.

1835 LONGSTREET *Georgia Scenes* 242 These [chills] I had to bear for the space of a minute or two before I could *feel out* my hat. 1928 *Publishers' Weekly* 9 June 2376, I cannot stress enough..the necessity of feeling out the possibilities of a book before giving a large order.

5. c. *To feel out* (see quot.).

1925 E. FRASER & GIBBONS *Soldier & Sailor Words*, *Feel out*, of Artillery ranging until a desired target or objective is attained.

6. b. Slang phr. *To feel the draught*: to be seriously incommoded.

1925 *Westm. Gaz.* 27 Apr., When the wind changed it might be the Conservative Party which would be feeling the draught.

d. Also *to feel one's feet.*

1889 *Farmer's Mag.* Dec. 217 Trees put in now cannot be expected to succeed as well as those that are already beginning to 'feel their feet'.

Feeler. Add: **5.** A device which moves a control lever in the weaving of artificial silk.

1927 T. WOODHOUSE *Artif. Silk* 131 When the weft is nearly exhausted in the shuttle, an electric circuit is completed; this causes a single feeler under the circular magazine to move a control lever which ensures that the next change of weft will place in the shuttle a bobbin with the same kind of weft as that just finished.

Feeling, *vbl. sb.* Add: **11.** *attrib.* and *Comb.*: (sense 9), esp. after G. compounds of *gefühl*, e.g. *gefühlston* (Wundt).

1899 G. F. STOUT *Man. Psychol.* 60 Besides having cognisance of an object, we are usually, if not always, pleased or displeased, satisfied or dissatisfied with it, and sometimes partially the one and partially the other. This feeling-attitude pre-supposes the existence of cognition. *Ibid.* 62 Feeling-tone is a generic word for pleasure and pain. *Ibid.* 63 In the complex emotion of anger there is included a specific feeling-attitude distinct from being pleased or the reverse. 1900 *Amer. Jrnl. Psychol.* Apr. 307 The manner in which delusions are formed is the *feeling-tone* of pleasantness and unpleasantness. 1901 E. B. TITCHENER *Exper. Psychol.* I. I. ii. 54 Likeness may mean 'likeness of *feeling-effect*'. 1919 M. K. BRADBY *Psycho-analysis* 58 Certain unconscious factors..give the complex its peculiar feeling-tone. *Ibid.* 150 A woman who heard the first maroon announcing the Armistice on November 11th, 1918, responded with an instantaneous feeling-thought. 1920 PRINGLE-PATTISON *Idea of God* 120 The feeling-tone of the secondary qualities and their intimate connexion with the higher emotional life. 1920 T. P. NUNN *Educ., Data & Princ.* (1923) 125 Feeling-spread is almost wholly biological imitation. *Ibid.* 134 Pugnacity is an example of the instincts in which the feeling-element is a definite emotion.

Feelingness (fī·liŋnĕs). [f. FEELING *ppl. a.* + -NESS.] Emotional quality or character.

1870 G. MEREDITH *Lett.* (1912) I. 216 The feelingness of your letter to Mickleham was much felt there. 1901 MRS. F. H. BURNETT *Making of Marchioness* II. vi, 'I do *love* him so', she whispered hysterically. 'I do so *love* him, and I shall so *miss* him!' with the italicised feelingness of old.

Féerie (fē·ĕri). Also **féery, feërie.** [F. *féerie*, f. *fée* fairy; see FAIRY *sb.*] A spectacular theatrical production involving the representation of fairy scenes and characters.

1878 *Lloyd's Weekly* 19 May 7/2 (Stanford) A magnificent *féery*, in which five Nubian lions are announced as about to make their *début*. 1886 *Athenæum* 24 July 116/3 M. Victorien Sardou is at work on a *féerie*, or rather a piece for children, intended for the Port-Saint-Martin. 1895 *Daily News* 5 Feb. 5/4 It is not strictly an opera, but is described as a dramatic feërie, entitled 'The Royal Infants'.

Feeze, *sb.* **2.** *U.S.* (Earlier example and reference.)

1825 J. NEAL *Bro. Jonathan* II. 315 By snum; but you're a precious fellow!—in a feeze, I dare say, at receiving a decent letter from your sweetheart. 1843 HALIBURTON *Sam Slick in Eng.* ii. (= quot. *a* 1863).

Fei (fē·i). [Tahitian vernacular name of the plant and fruit.] In Polynesia and New Caledonia, a species of plantain or wild banana, *Musa fehi.*

1888 *Encycl. Brit.* XXIII. 24/1 The wild plantain (*fei*). 1894 STEVENSON & OSBOURNE *Ebb-Tide* I. ii, Five Kanakas ..were squatted round a basin of fried feis.

Feinne (fīn). Also **Fein.** [Gaelic.] = *FIAN(N.

1782 T. F. HILL in *Gentl. Mag.* LII. 570/2 The songs relating to the Feinne, and their Chieftain, Fion-mac-Coul. *Ibid.* 571/1 The whole host of the Feinne, or Fingalians. 1872 J. F. CAMPBELL *Leabhar na Feinne* 33 Fionn and the Feinne were the successors of Cumhal and Cuchullin. 1891 *Youthful Exploits of Fionn* 96 A company of the old Feinne. 1891 A. MACDOUGALL *Folk & Hero Tales* 35 The Fein looked at each other.

Feint. In commercial use, the usual spelling of FAINT *a.* 5 c.

1874 *Stationers' Hand-bk.* 72 Feint only, the term for a book having merely feint blue lines across the page from left to right. 1895 *Army & Navy Co-op. Soc. Price List* 15 Sept. 525 Foolscap Paper—Ruled with Money Columns and Feint Lines.

Feis (feʃ, fæʃ). Pl. **feiseanna.** Also **fes(s.** [a. Ir. *feis, fess* meeting, assembly.]

1. An assembly of kings, chiefs, etc., being a kind of early Celtic parliament.

1792 *Encycl. Brit.* IX. 313/1 Ollam Fodla..erected a grand seminary of learning, and instituted the *Fes*, or triennial convention of provincial kings, priests, and poets, at Feamor or Tarah in Meath. 1880 *Ibid.* XIII. 250/2 He summoned a convention (*feis* or *fess*)..to assemble at Druimceta. 1898 HERON *Celtic Ch.* 19. 1905 *Daily Chron.* 15 June 3/1 The whole scheme of [old Irish] national life turned on central feiseanna—social, legislative, and literary functions.

2. An Irish festival which provided competitions in singing, dancing, acting, music, and handicrafts, resembling the Welsh Eisteddfod.

1896 *Daily News* 2 Oct. 5/2 The 'Feis' extending over four days. 1896 *Westm. Gaz.* 3 Oct. 8/1 The *Feis* is announced to take place next May. 1910 *Daily Chron.* 3 Jan. 3/4 In her incidental reference to latter-day Feiseanna. 1916 *N. & Q.* 12th Ser. II. 71 The feis portions of local shows.

Feist, variant of FIST *sb.*[2]

Feldsher (fe·ldʃəɹ). Also **feldschar, feldscher.** [ad. Little Russ. *felcher*, Russ. *fel'dsherŭ*, ad. G. *feldscher* field surgeon.] An army surgeon. In Russia, a surgeon's assistant, a hospital orderly.

1877 D. M. WALLACE *Russia* I. v. 104 There is not exactly a doctor, but there is a Feldsher in the village. 1916 H. WALPOLE *Dark Forest* I. iv, Like an old feldschar in my village who hates our village Pope. 1925 *Contemp. Rev.* June 752 In Russia the place of doctor or nurse is often filled by a 'feldscher' or half-trained doctor only.

Félibre (fēlibr). [F. *félibre*, a. mod. Prov. *felibre* doctor of the law.] A word used by F. Mistral (1830–1914) to designate a member of the brotherhood which was founded by J. Roumanille for the maintenance and purification of Provençal as a literary language, and also for the promotion of the artistic interests of the South of France.

1902 *Encycl. Brit.* XXXII. 44/1 Greatest of them all, the true and acknowledged forerunner of the *félibres*, Jacques Jasmin (1798–1864), the hairdresser of Agen. *Ibid.* 45/1 The *félibres* are in no sense of the word the direct successors of the troubadours. 1904 *Westm. Gaz.* 27 May 12/2 The Félibres, who have just been celebrating their jubilee.

Hence **Féli·brian** *a.*, relating to the Félibres, or to the Provençal literature produced by them; **Féli·brism** (fēˡ·libriz'm), the movement instituted by the Félibres; the principles underlying that movement.

1908 *Daily Chron.* 16 Jan. 4/4 He plunged into the centre of things Félibrian. 1911 *Daily News* 11 Mar. 6/4 The literary output of Félibrism has been mainly poetic.

Félibrige (fēlibriʒ). [F. *Félibrige*, ad. Prov. *Felibrige*, f. *felibre*: see prec.] The name of the society formed by the Félibres.

1902 *Encycl. Brit.* XXXII. 44/2 The most widely read of the *Félibrige* publications is the *Armana Prouvençau*, which.. contains much of the best work of the school. 1907 *Daily Chron.* 14 Nov. 3/3 Two other pioneers of the 'Félibrige' movement, Roumanille and Mathieu.

Fell (fel). Name of John *Fell* (1625–86), dean of Christ Church and bishop of Oxford, designating the founts of type and matrices procured by him for the Oxford University Press, the use of which has been revived in recent years.

1900 H. HART *Cent. Oxf. Typography* p. ix, All doubts and conjectures as to where most of the Fell types were purchased may..now be regarded as disposed of. 1922 UPDIKE *Printing Types* II. 199 Caslon and Fell revivals.

Fellah, representing an affected pronunciation of FELLOW *sb.*

1912 A. C. DOYLE *Lost World* vi. 84 Young fellah my lad.

Feller[1]. Add: **4.** A sewer in various trades.

1894 *N. Brit. Daily Mail* 5 Sept. 4 The wages of the fellers, whether on day work or on piece work, ranged from 1s 6d to 2s 6d. 1921 *Dict. Occup. Terms* (1927) § 404 *Finisher*, tailor's finisher; feller; sews by hand, sleeve linings, vest arm holes. *Ibid.* § 411 *Feller*, sews seams of gloves with a particular kind of felling stitch on treadle machine.

Feller[2] (fe·ləɹ). Vulgar or affected (cf. *FELLAH) form of FELLOW *sb.* 9. Also in jocular phr. *young feller-me-* (or *my-*) *lad*, orig. used vocatively with an implication of disapproval or reproof; hence as compound sb. designating young men of a frivolous or irresponsible character.

1880 *Punch* 20 Nov. 234 Why, there was an Actor, by Jingo! and a scientific chap, and an artist feller. 1897 KIPLING *Capt. Cour.* 17 You've nigh slep' the clock around, young feller. 1909 P. G. WODEHOUSE *The Swoop!* vi. 86 Not so much of your eight hundred and seventy-five, young feller me lad. 1913 MRS. HARKER *Ffolliots of Redmarley* xxiv. (1919) 321, I beheld Miss Bax seemingly in difficulties with two young feller-me-lads, who evidently had no intention of going on. 1925 B. TRAVERS *Mischief* v, Now, listen, young feller-me-lad. It's about that place at Richmond. [1926, 1929: see *FELLOW *sb.* 9.]

Fellmonger. Add: In modern use restricted to an operative who works skins.

1845 DODD *Brit. Manuf.* V. 195 There are in Bermondsey several manufacturers called fellmongers, whose business it is to bring sheep-skins into a certain state of preparation before the leather-dresser commences his operations thereon. 1921 *Dict. Occup. Terms* (1927) § 338 *Fellmonger*, general term for any person employed in fellmongery trade, e.g. washing sheep skins, painting pelt side of skins with chemicals to facilitate subsequent pulling [etc.].

Hence **Fe·llmongered** *a.*, **Fe·llmongering** *vbl. sb.*

1895 *Austral. Pastoralist Rev.* 15 Aug. 284 The very large quantity of fellmongered wool sold in Sydney. 1897 *Daily News* 7 Oct. 2/2 Fellmongering and leather dressing premises.

Fellow, *sb.* Add: **7.** Now extended to women holders of such positions.

1899 *Westm. Gaz.* 24 Nov. 10/1 A lady 'research' Fellow already exists in Wales. 1921 *Oxf. Univ. Cal.*, Somerville College... Lady Carlisle Fellow. 1923 *Ibid.*, Somerville College..Official Fellow—Research Fellows.

9. *Young fellow-me-* (or *my-*) *lad*: see *FELLER[2].

1926 SPANNER *Navigators* 36 This young fellow-me-lad seems to have spent ten minutes or so diving in and out among the wreckage. 1929 W. DEEPING *Roper's Row* iv. § 1 There were young fellow-my-lads who began to take notice.

Fellowly (fe·loᵘli), *a.* and *adv.* Delete † *Obs.* and add quots. illustrating revival in poet. and rhet. use.

1883 G. MEREDITH *Woods of Westermain* iv, Love it [*sc.* the light] so you could accost Fellowly a livid ghost. 1898 T. HARDY *Wessex Poems, The Temporary the All* i, Change and chancefulness in my flowering youthtime, Set me sun by sun near to one unchosen; Wrought us fellowly, and despite divergence, Friends interblent us. 1903 *Travel* May 3 The fellowly enfolding of the night. 1928 W. J. JAPP *Wayfarings* viii. 93 The revealings of a spirit fellowly and accordant with his own.

Felting, *vbl. sb.* Add: **1. b.** Of the hair (see quot. 1848).

1848 DUNGLISON *Med. Lex.* (ed. 7), *Felting*,..a term applied to the hair when inextricably interlaced, as occurs occasionally in women from inattention. 1864 W. T. FOX *Skin Dis.* 75 Canities, Felting.

Female, *a.* Add: **10. b.** *Female close* = *feminine close* (see FEMININE *a.* 6 b, quot. 1844).

1928 E. BLOM *Limitations of Music* 85 Mendelssohn uses female closes to excess.

Femaleness (fī·meˡlnĕs). Delete *nonce-wd.* and add: **2.** *Biol.* The quality of being female.

1894 H. DRUMMOND *Ascent of Man* vii. 315 That this division into maleness and femaleness should run between almost every two of every plant and every animal in existence, must have implications of a quite exceptional kind. *Ibid.* 323 What exactly maleness is, and what femaleness, has been one of the problems of the world. 1902 *Encycl. Brit.* XXXII. 210/1 That maleness and femaleness may be regarded as expressing metabolic alternatives open to the germ-cell in its development. 1930 G. R. DE BEER *Embryol. & Evol.* iii. 22 The various organs and parts of the body do not all switch over from maleness to femaleness together.

Femic (fe·mik), *a.* *Min.* [f. *fe, m*, initial letters of *ferro-magnetian* (see *FERRO- 1) + -IC.] (See quots.)

1909 *Cent. Dict.* Suppl. s.v. *Rock*, The second group contains all other pyrogenetic minerals which are free from alumina... This group is called *femic* (mnemonic of *ferromagnesian*, the predominant character of the group). 1912 J. W. GREGORY *Making of Earth* iv. 64 These minerals belong to the series which, owing to their poverty in silica, are known as basic minerals; some of the most important contain ferrum (iron) and magnesium as their chief constituents, and are therefore called femic, a word formed from the letters Fe and Mg, the chemical symbols for those metals.

Feminal (fe·minăl), *a.* Transfer † *Obs.* to sense in Dict. and add: **2.** = FEMININE *a.* 4.

1907 *Ladies' Field* 10 Aug. 357/1 Combine the perfection of physical strength with the highest type of feminal beauty. 1922 C'TESS BARCYNSKA *Webs* xxv. 207 In her emotional tumult, sheerly feminal, she believed every word she said.

Feminine, *sb.* **1. b.** Add: *The eternal feminine* as a literal rendering of G. *das ewige weibliches* (Goethe).

1892 [in Dict.]. 1898 *Daily News* 5 Sept. 6/2 The Eternal Feminine played a larger part in Oxford social life in the earlier part of the eighteenth century than she has since done. 1912 W. J. LOCKE *Aristide Pujol* ix, His quest being little Jean and not the eternal feminine.

Feminism. Delete *rare* and add:

2. [After F. *féminisme.*] The opinions and principles of the advocates of the extended recognition of the achievements and claims of women; advocacy of women's rights. (Cf. WOMANISM.)

1895 *Athenæum* 27 Apr. 533/2 Her intellectual evolution and her coquettings with the doctrines of 'feminism' are traced with real humour. 1897 *Daily News* 6 Sept. 8/6 You alluded, Mr. Goldwin Smith, somewhat disparagingly, to that phase of feminism which is so curious a feature of the present day. 1908 *Daily Chron.* 7 May 4/7 In Germany feminism is openly Socialistic.

Feminist (fe·minist). [ad. F. *féministe*, f. L. *fēmina* woman: see -IST.] An advocate of feminism. Often *attrib.* Also **Fe·mininist.**

1894 *Daily News* 12 Oct. 5/5 What our Paris Correspondent describes as a 'Feminist' group is being formed in the French Chamber of Deputies. 1895 *Critic* 2 Feb. 90/2 The writer depicts Ford as the deepest 'femininist' in the Shakespearian constellation. 1898 *Daily Chron.* 15 Oct. 5/1 The lady Parliamentary reporter is the latest development of the feminist movement in New Zealand. 1904 *Athenæum* 26 Nov. 730/2 There have been feminists who claimed George Eliot as the rival of Thackeray. 1920 W. J. LOCKE *House of Baltazar* v. 56 We're out of this feminist hurly-burly. 1930 *Manchester Guardian* 15 Sept. 7/7 Feminists are rare birds in Russia.

Hence **Feminì·stic** *a.*

1908 *Westm. Gaz.* 11 Sept. 6/3 Some thinkers in Hungary anticipate feministic developments even in Turkey. 1912 *Englishwoman* Mar. 261 This society is only feministic in so far as it strives to give women better opportunities.

Femino- (fe·minoᵘ), used as combining form (see -O-) of L. *fēmina* woman, = female. **Femino-nu·cleus** *Embryology*, the female pronucleus.

1884 [see MASCULO-].

Femoro- (fe·mŏro), used as combining form (see -O-) of FEMUR = pertaining to the femur and (another part); also = femoral.

1848 DUNGLISON *Med. Lex.* (ed. 7), *Femoro-tibial*, belonging to the femur and tibia. 1872 HUMPHRY *Myol.* 22 This femoro-fibular muscle appears to represent the short or femoral origin of the biceps. 1901 DORLAND *Med. Dict.*, *Femorocele*, femoral hernia.

Fence, *sb.* Add: **5. c.** *On the fence* (earlier U.S. examples). *On the other side of the fence* (U.S. example). *To mend* (or *look after*) *one's fences*, of a member of Congress, to renew contact with the electors.

1828 *Richmond Whig* 13 Aug. 1/5 (Th.) There are certain Administration Editors, Editors for a long time on the fence, who occasionally undertake..to sit as censors upon their fatigued and dusty brethren. 1834 [R. BAIRD] *Valley Mississippi* xviii. 360 The demons of discord are on the fence, ready to pounce down upon the unsuspecting public, on either side. 1888 *Texas Siftings* 7 July (Farmer) Journals on the other side of the fence will represent him to be a weak, feeble old man. 1888 *Congress. Rec.* 16 Aug. 7646/1 [They] are at home seeking renomination or looking after their fences. 1889 BARRÈRE & LELAND *Dict. Slang*, *Mend fences, to* (American), to mend or repair fences for a man is to attend to his interests. 1906 H. L. WEST in *Forum* Apr. 444 An early adjournment of the session is deemed essential in order that the members may go home to mend their fences, as the saying is.

10. b. *fence-post* (earlier U.S. example).

1853 B. F. TAYLOR *Jan. & June* (1871) 13 Life..laid away in 'Patent Burial Cases' and fastened to rails and fence-posts.

11. fence-arbour, a piece in a combination lock which connects the spindle and the tumblers; **fence corner** *U.S.*, (*a*) one of the four corners of a fenced enclosure; (*b*) one of the many angles made by a zig-zag rail fence; also *attrib.*; **fence-man** *U.S.*, one who practises 'sitting on the fence', who avoids taking a side in an issue; **fence-rail** *U.S.*, a long, rough rail for fencing, split from a small log; **fe·nce-rider** *U.S.* (see quot. 1920); **fence-riding** *U.S.*, 'sitting on the fence'; avoidance of committing oneself to one or other of two contrary policies; **fence-row** *U.S.*, a fence with the row of shrubs and other vegetation which frequently grows up under its protection.

1902 *Encycl. Brit.* XXXII. 360/1 A balanced *fence arbour. 1829–32 J. P. KENNEDY *Swallow B.* I. xiv. 153 He slowly went to the *fence corner, and untied his horse. 1845 J. J. HOOPER *Adv. Simon Suggs* i. 14 Simon and Bill were in a fence corner very earnestly engaged at 'seven up'. 1855 *Knickerbocker Mag.* XLV. 197 Posting himself at night in a fence-corner, he saw her at one end of a hollow log. 1874 E. EGGLESTON *Circuit Rider* xxviii. 272 Patty climbed upon a fence-corner. 1886 *Harper's Mag.* Oct. 808/2, I was a couple o' fence corners from 'em. 1901 S. E. WHITE *Claim Jumpers* iv. 64 It was..not as large as a good-sized rat, quite smaller than our own fence-corner chipmunks of the East. 1829 *Lett. 'Columbus'* (Boston) 19 *Fence-man. 1848 *N. Y. Herald* 14 Oct. (Bartlett 1859) All the fence-men, all the doubters, all the seekers after majorities, will now bustle up. 1889 FARMER *Americanisms* s.v. *Fence*, The possessors of highly developed bumps of caution are called *fence men*; they run with the hare and hunt with the hounds, an operation which receives the equally descriptive name of *fence-riding*. 1802 ELLICOTT *Jrnl.* 3 It was then placed on a *fence-rail which was covered with frost. 1814 J. TAYLOR *Arator* 177 Small common fence rails.. will last with less labour..than any I have ever tried. 1829–32 J. P. KENNEDY *Swallow B.* I. xxiii. 239 The mill-pond..wasted away, like a chestnut fence-rail under the united attacks of sun and wind. 1853 J. G. BALDWIN *Flush Times Alabama* 110 Buck Jones..seized a fence rail, grasped it in both hands, and..hurled the same. 1872 E. EGGLESTON *End of World* xxxviii. 238 I've knowed boys who'd throw a rock at a fence-rail and hit a stump. 1909 R. A. WASON *Happy Hawkins* 207, I met the foreman o' the E.Z. outfit ridin' into town to see if he couldn't pick up a *fence-rider. 1920 HUNTER *Trail Drivers of Texas* 298 The fence rider, also called the 'line rider', is employed to ride fences and repair them. *a* 1859 *N. Y. Mirror* (Bartlett) The dividing line..admits of no *fence-riding; the candidate must be on one side or the other. 1868 *Congress. Globe* 17 July (De Vere) This question is one of clear right and wrong, and there can be no fence-riding, when the rights of four millions of men are at stake. 1889 [see '*fence-man*]. 1842 *American Pioneer* I. 43, I was alone, clearing out a *fence row, about a quarter of a mile from the house. 1855 *Trans. Mich. Agric. Soc.* VI. 144 The fence rows were free from weeds and bushes. 1858 J. A. WARDER *Hedges & Evergreens* II. 229 Many kinds of trees..are to be taken from their natural position in open woods, fields or fence rows. 1901 N. L. BRITTON *Man. Flora N. United States* 952 Along fence-rows in partial shade.

Fence, *v.* **6.** Add: Also *transf.*, to ride on either side of. *U.S.*

1910 W. M. RAINE *B. O'Connor* 215 Alice Mackenzie might have searched the west..and not found..two such riders..as fenced her that day.

Fence-viewer. *U.S.* (See FENCE *sb.* 11.)

1676 *Connecticut Public Rec.* II. 276 Lnt Joseph Orton is by this Court appoynted..to administer oathes to fence viewers. 1686 in Temple & Sheldon *Hist. Northfield, Mass.* (1875) 102 The fence about the Great Meadow shall be made up.. according to the judgment of the fence-viewers. 1706 *Rec. Muddy River & Brookline, Mass.* (1875) 92 Voted that John Winchester jun'r & Edward Devotion should serve as Fence viewers. 1736 in Temple & Sheldon *Hist. Northfield, Mass.* (1875) 16 Fence viewers were chosen, who were ordered to lay out ye fence and proportion it to each proprietor. 1771 H. PELHAM in *Copley-Pelham Lett.* (1914) 125 She will apply to the Fence viewers to have the Fences made upp. 1843 CARLTON *New Purchase* xxii. 209 From Governor down to a deputy constable's deputy and fence-viewer's clerk's first assistant. 1858 J. A. WARDER *Hedges & Evergreens* I. x. 162 Fence-viewers [are] to assign the portions to each occupant when they cannot agree. 1886 [in Dict.]. *fig.* 1880 *Scribner's Monthly* Feb. XIX. 504 You are likely to start from its shelter a hare..or you may catch glimpses of a brown wood wren. .. These are the fence viewers of the wood lot.

Fencing, *vbl. sb.* **7.** Add: (sense 1) *fencing-room*; (sense 3) *fencing-stuff* (U.S.).

1897 *Outing* (U.S.) XXX. 200/1 The contest was held March 20th in the *fencing-room of the New York Athletic Club. 1645 *Springfield* (Mass.) *Rec.* I. 183 Every man cut his *fencinge stuff upon his owne grounde. 1680 *Braintree* (Mass.) *Rec.* 19 That no person..shall fall cutt or carry away any wood, timber [or] fencing stuff. 1893 B. TORREY *Footpath-Way* 72 No wonder such fields do not pay for fencing-stuff.

Fendered (fe·ndəɹd), *ppl. a.* [f. FENDER *sb.* + -ED[2].] Provided with a fender or fenders.

1795 R. DODD *Rep. Improv. Hartlepool* 8 This pier..well fendered, piled, &c. 1927 *Blackw. Mag.* Sept. 363/2 The tug thrust her fendered nose against the timbers.

Fenestrated, *ppl. a.* Add:

4. Of a surgical instrument: Having openings or loops at the grasping end.

1881 *Trans. Obstetr. Soc. Lond.* XXII. 46 These forceps, fenestrated longitudinally. 1884 KNIGHT *Dict. Mech.* Suppl., *Fenestrated Instruments* (surgical), said of instruments such as some forceps, scoops, enucleators, etc., the grasping ends of which have openings, or loops which engage and partially embrace the object. 1854 W. PYE *Surg. Handicraft* 23 The patterns of a few of these forceps are given here. On the whole, the most satisfactory is the 'fenestrated'.

Feng-shui (fœ ŋʃūi). Also 8 **fong-choui,** 9 **fung-shui.** [Chinese, f. *feng* wind + *shui* water.] In Chinese mythology, a system of spirit influences, good and evil, which inhabit the natural features of landscapes; hence, a kind of geomancy for dealing with these influences in determining sites for houses and graves.

c 1789 *Encycl. Brit.* (1797) IV. 679/2 The greater part of the Chinese are of opinion that all the happiness and misfortunes of life depend upon the *fong-choui*. 1883 *Ibid.* XV. 204/1 The *feng-shui*, or 'wind-and-water' magic, is a system the practitioners of which regulate the building of houses and tombs by their local aspects. 1906 W. DE MORGAN *Joseph Vance* xxvii. 252, I think what the Chinese call the Feng-Shui of the sofa-back had a good deal to answer for.

Ferme·ntal, *a.* Delete † *Obs.* and add quots.:

1753 CHAMBERS *Cycl. Suppl.* s.v. *Zymology*, The fermental principles of acid and sulphur connatural to that oil [*sc.* oil of vitriol]. 1922 *Glasgow Herald* 21 Aug. 7 Sugar or any other kind of fermental food.

Fermentum (fəɹme·ntŏm). [med.L. use of L. *fermentum* yeast, FERMENT *sb.*] In the mediæval church, a portion of a consecrated wafer reserved and brought to a priest about to say Mass, as a token of Christian communion.

1884 ADDIS & ARNOLD *Cath. Dict.* s.v. *Reservation*, A supposed decretal of Pope Innocent to Decentius proves that the Bishop of Rome sent the *fermentum* or consecrated host 'per titulos'—*i.e.* to the chief churches of the city. 1902 *Encycl. Brit.* XXXII. 220/2.

Fermorite (fɜ̄·ımŏrəit). *Min.* [f. name of L. L. *Fermor*, of the Geological Survey of India + -ITE[1].] An arsenate and phosphate of lime and strontia found in the manganese deposits of India.

1910 G. T. PRIOR & SMITH in *Nature* LXXXIII. 513.

Feroese, var. *FAROESE.

Ferozone (fe·rozōᵘn). Also **ferro-.** [Proprietary name, app. arbitrarily formed.] A precipitating substance, consisting chiefly of iron protosulphate, for treating sewage.

1888 *Patent Specif.* No. 11663. 1889–90 *Proc. Assoc. Munic. & County Engin.* XVI. 38 The 'ferrozone' or magnetic ferrous carbon. 1898 [see POLARITE].

Ferra (fe·rā). [Local It.] The fresh-water herring, *Coregonus fera.*

1807 [see POLLAN]. 1879 *Encycl. Brit.* X. 152/1 The Lake of Geneva is not so rich in fish as many of the smaller lakes of Switzerland... The 'fera' (*Coregonus fera*) is economically the most important species. 1925 *Glasgow Herald* 5 Aug. 8 The 'ferra' of Lake Geneva.

Ferranti (ferænti), name of S. Z. *Ferranti*, used attrib. to designate certain electrical devices invented by him, and a phenomenon first observed in connexion with the Ferranti cables in London. See quots.

1892 SLOANE *Electr. Dict.* (1898), *Ferranti Effect*, an effect as yet not definitely explained, observed in the mains of the Deptford, Eng., alternating current plant. It is observed that the potential difference between the members of a pair of mains rises or increases with the distance the place of trial is from the station. 1902 *Encycl. Brit.* XXX. 596/2 The Ferranti continuous-current ampere-hour meter. *Ibid.* XXXIII. 424/2 The Ferranti rectifier is much employed for rectifying alternating current for arc lighting purposes. 1910 *N. Hawkins' Electr. Dict.*, *Ferranti Cable*, a type of electrical conductor designed to carry high tension currents, consisting of concentric tubes of copper separated by an insulation of paper saturated with black mineral wax.

Ferrazite (fe·răzəit). *Min.* [f. name of Jorge Belmiro de Aranjo *Ferraz*, of the Geological Survey of Brazil + -ITE[1].] A hydrated phosphate of lead and barium.

1919 *Amer. Jrnl. Sci.* Ser. IV. XLVIII. 353. 1921 *British Museum Return* 157 Ferrazite, a 'fava' from the Brazilian diamond-washings (a new species named after the donor) by Dr. J. B. de Aranjo Ferraz.

Ferris (fe·ris), name of an American engineer, G. W. G. *Ferris*, used attrib. to designate an amusement device, the *Ferris wheel*, invented and first erected by him for the World's Columbian Exposition in Chicago in 1893 (see quot. 1897).

1893 *Sci. Amer.* 9 Sept. 169/1 The World's Columbian Exposition—A view from the Ferris wheel. 1897 R. JOHNSON *World's Columb. Expos.* I. 77 The feature at the Exposition that corresponded in its character with the Eiffel Tower at the Paris Exposition of 1889 was the Ferris Wheel —an enormous wheel two hundred and fifty feet in diameter, projected into the air, hung upon supports of steel framework by an axle thirty-two inches in diameter, forty-five feet long, and weighing fifty-six tons... On the periphery of the wheel were hung thirty-six passenger cars, each with a seating capacity of forty to sixty persons. 1927 *Blackw. Mag.* Sept. 358/2 Two ferris wheels squeaked like pigs in agony.

Ferrite. Add:

3. *Metallurgy.* Pure metallic iron as separated out from iron carbides in the cooling of steel.

1890 H. M. HOWE *Metall. Steel* I. 164. 1900 *Engineering Mag.* XIX. 752/1 Iron in its pure state consists of crystalline ferrite granules. *Ibid.* 753/1 The changes caused by heat in the form and size of the ferrite granules depend..upon the condition of the metal when heating begins. 1902 *Encycl. Brit.* XXIX. 572/1 Slowly cooled steels in general consist essentially of a mixture of ferrite and cementite.

Ferro-. Add: **1.** Various other names of minerals.

1891 *Jrnl. Chem. Soc.* LX. II. 992 *Ferro-goslarite, a New Variety of Zinc Sulphate. 1877 DANA *Text-bk. Min.* 338 Columbite. Niobite. *Ferroilmenite. 1902 MIERS *Min.* 471 Biotite (*Ferro-magnesian Mica). 1889 *Amer. Jrnl. Sci.* Ser. III. XXXVIII. 244 *Ferronatrite..occurs in stellate groups of a pale, whitish green color, forming nearly spherical nodules; it is in general similar to pale wavellite in appearance. 1902 MIERS *Min.* 547 Ferronatrite, $Na_3Fe^{III}(SO_4)_3.3H_2O$. 1903 *Jrnl. Chem. Soc.* LXXXIV. II. 556 *Ferropallidite.—This name was given to a white, granular mineral which occurs with römerite at Alcapa rossa, Calama, Chili.

b. *Metallurgy.* In names of alloys with the meaning of 'iron and', as *ferro-aluminium.* Also **Ferro-alloy,** an alloy of iron and some other metal.

1905 *Electr. Rev.* 31 Mar. 517/2 The production of special steels and *ferro-alloys. 1908 *Jrnl. Chem. Soc.* XCIII. II. 1496 The production of ferro-alloys from a mixture of the oxides with ferric oxide is a comparatively simple matter. 1928 KINGZETT *Chem. Encycl.* (ed. 4) 395 Ferro-alloys are used in the steel industry to remove oxygen and nitrogen from molten steel, or to introduce into the steel a small proportion of the metal. 1890 *Jrnl. Chem. Soc.* LVIII. II. 1471 *Ferro-aluminium is composed of iron, aluminium, manganese, silicon, and carbon, and resembles ferro-tungsten in appearance. 1910 *Ibid.* XCVIII. II. 508 The Behaviour of Goldschmidt's *Ferroboron and Manganese-boron on Heating in Chlorine and Hydrogen Sulphide. 1920 *Ironmonger* 18 Dec. 97/1 The other steel-making alloys dealt with include chromium alloys,..ferro-titanium, ferro-uranium, ferro-boron. 1878 *Jrnl. Chem. Soc.* XXXIV. 772 The discovery of chrome-steel and *ferrochrome by Berthier in 1821. 1894 *Ibid.* LXVI. II. 452 *Ferrochromium..contains crystals, the hardness of which = 6, whilst that of the magma = 4·2. 1902 *Ibid.* LXXXII. II. 533 Volumetric Estimation of Molybdenum in Molybdenum Steel and *Ferro-Molybdenum. 1885 *Ibid.* XLVIII. I. 462 Malleable *ferronickel and ferrocobalt. 1882 *Ibid.* XLII. 118 *Ferro-silicon. 1908 *Westm. Gaz.* 22 Dec. 2/3 Anything more dangerous to carry than casks of ferro-silicon cannot well be imagined... Ferro-silicon is used in the manufacture of steel, and there is a Board of Trade order on the subject of its conveyance. 1893 *Jrnl. Chem. Soc.* LXIV. II. 97 *Ferrotitanium can only be dissolved by fusion with sodium hydrogen sulphate and treatment with cold water. 1911 *Ibid.* C. II. 157 The Analysis of *Ferro-Uranium. 1904 *Ibid.* LXXXVI. II. 824 *Ferrovanadium, containing 33 per cent. of vanadium, is made by igniting in the electric furnace the precipitate obtained by mixing sodium vanadate, iron sulphate, and sodium carbonate in the requisite proportions.

2. b. In names of various substances containing iron, or consisting of iron and something else, as *ferro-glidin, -plasma* (see Dorland's *Med. Dict.*).

1902 *Encycl. Brit.* XXXI. 724/2 Ferro-proteids, proteids combined with an iron-containing molecule. The best-known of these is the colouring matter of the blood, hæmoglobin, which consists of about 96 per cent. of a globulin linked with about 4 per cent. of hæmatin.

3. *Photog.* **Ferro-ga·llic** *a.*, designating a process by which specially sensitized paper is developed by immersion in a solution of gallic acid; *ferro-gallic paper*, printing paper which has been sensitized with a special solution for development by the ferro-gallic process. So *ferro-gallic sensitizer.* **Fe·rro-print** (see quot.).

1902 *Encycl. Brit.* XXXI. 703/2 For architects and engineers, cyanotype and *ferro-gallic papers are prepared in rolls of considerable width for the direct reproduction of tracings and drawings, as blue or black prints by these methods. 1918 *Photo-Miniature* XV. Mar. (Gloss.), *Ferro-Gallic Process*, for copying plans giving black lines on white ground. 1919 *Brit. Jrnl. Photo. Alm.* 253 Ferro-gallic, or black-line paper. *Ibid.* Index, Ferro-gallic sensitiser. 1914 *Literary Year-bk.* 494 *Ferro-print*, Ferro-gallic and ferro-prussiate. Prints made from salts of iron sensitizers, principally used for plans and copying tracings in blue or black lines.

Ferro-concrete (fe·roᵘ,kǫ·nkrīt). [FERRO-.] Concrete reinforced by having embedded in it iron or steel bars, netting, or the like: see *CONCRETE *sb.* 3. Also as adj., composed or constructed of ferro-concrete.

1900 *Patent Specif.* No. 8831. 1902 GALBRAITH in *Trans. Soc. Engineers* 6 Oct. 177 Ferro-concrete..is the combination of iron, or more strictly speaking, steel and concrete. *Ibid.*, The Hennebique System of Ferro-concrete Construction. 1904 C. F. MARSH *Reinforced Concrete* 1 The combination of iron and concrete as a material for building.. called armoured concrete, ferro-concrete, concrete-steel, and reinforced concrete. 1905 *Daily Chron.* 10 June 4/4 Ferro-concrete houses. 1908 *Westm. Gaz.* 13 Aug. 8/1 A promenade deck with ferro-concrete floor. 1914 *Scotsman* 12 Oct. 8/7 The tall white ferro-concrete telegraph posts lining many of the main roads. 1927 *N. & Q.* 9 July 35 In a building of ferro-concrete any fire of contents was isolated.

Hence **Fe·rro-concre·tor.**

1921 *Dict. Occup. Terms* (1927) § 579 *Ferro-concretor* tips, pours, or shovels wet concrete,..brought to his machine mixed, into wooden casings or moulds.

Ferrozone: see *FEROZONE.

Ferry, *sb.*[1] Add:

3. c. Used allusively with reference to Charon's ferry (see CHARON). *To take the ferry*: to die.

1895 MEREDITH *Amaz. Marr.* xxviii, The Lethean ferry-boatload. 1928 GALSWORTHY *Swan Song* III. vi. 266 What are you going to do with your pictures when you take the ferry? Leave them to the nation?

d. Used jocularly to describe the passage between England and New York, Australia, or New Zealand.

1902 C. HYNE *Mr. Horrocks Purser* 57 They see funny things on the Atlantic ferry which rich young men get mixed up in. 1907 *Daily Chron.* 11 June 10/4 Nearly all the Australian States are now offering assisted passages to selected immigrants... Why should not the Imperial Government take a hand in this, and in certain cases contribute the other £6, and thus realise the 'free ferry'? 1930 C. E. LEE (*title*) The Blue Riband: The Romance of the Atlantic Ferry.

5. b. ferry-house (earlier U.S. examples).

1791 W. BARTRAM *Trav. Carolina* etc. 470 The ferry-house being on the opposite shore I hoisted my travelling blanket on a pole for a signal. 1821 T. DWIGHT *Trav. New Eng.* II. 444 We found nothing in the ferry-house.

Fess, 'fess, *v.* *U.S.* Aphetic for CONFESS *v.*

1840 *Knickerbocker Mag.* XVI. 112 It would be a sad thing to die here all alone in the woods with a lie in your mouth; so 'fess clean. 1930 *Randolph Enterprise* (W.Va.) 20 Nov. 1/1 The joke is on him and he may as well 'Fess up' to it.

Fest (fest). *U.S.* [a. G. *fest.*] A festival or special occasion.

1889 *Kansas Times & Star* 24 June, Bob Ricketts won the gold medal at the shooting fest of the Kansas City Gun Club Saturday.

Festival, *a.* and *sb.* **B.** *sb.* Add:

1. b. Also applied to recurrent celebrations such as the annual series of performances held in honour of Shakespeare at Stratford-on-Avon. Also *attrib.*

1864 *Chambers's Jrnl.* Shaks. Tercentenary No. 2/1 At the present moment, when a grand Tercentenary Festival of the birth of Shakspeare is about to be celebrated at his native place. 1909 *Englishwoman* Apr. 298, I am convinced that there is enough appreciation of Wagner in England to build a modest festival theatre. 1926 *Publishers' Weekly* 1 May 1474/2 The annual Shakespeare festival at Stratford-on-Avon. 1930 *Times Lit. Suppl.* 3 July 551/3 A festival production of *The Pretenders.*

Festschrift (fe·st,ʃrift). Pl. **-en, -s.** [G., lit. 'festival-writing'.] A collection of writings in book form presented to a scholar or savant on the occasion of his attaining to a certain age or period in his career.

1901 *Engl. Misc. Furnivall* 491 An English Miscellany or 'Festschrift' in Dr. Furnivall's honour. 1931 *Periodical* June 100 Dr. Cowley..contributed to the Sir Arthur Evans and the Reginald Lane Poole *festschrifts*. 1931 *Times Lit. Suppl.* 1 Oct. 757/3 Lectures, collected papers and *Festschriften.*

Fetch, *sb.*[1] Add: **1. c.** *A far* or *long fetch*: a long distance to travel.

1903 JACK LONDON *People of Abyss* xi. 138 The day was half gone, and it was a far fetch to Stepney. 1919 SIR W. N. SHAW *Man. Meteorol.* IV. 50 The heavy cloud in winds from the North which have a long 'fetch' over the North Sea.

Fetch, *v.* Add: **4.** (U.S. example.)

1860 HOLLAND *Miss Gilbert's Career* xxvii. 470, I thought you'd fetched me once, but somehow it didn't stick.

9. b. *To fetch the farm*: see FARM *sb.*[2] 8.

a 1889 *Evening News* (Barrère & Leland), The dodges which would take place to 'fetch the farm'. 1900 *Pall Mall Mag.* Oct. 203 To 'fetch the farm' was, and still is, the current slang equivalent for getting round the doctor.

18*. Fetch through. *intr.* To win through.

1912 R. F. SCOTT *Last Exped.* (1913) I. 593 Though we constantly talk of fetching through, I don't think any one of us believes it in his heart.

19. Fetch up. i. (Earlier and later examples. Also *trans.*)

18.. J. C. NEAL *Dolly Jones* (Bartlett s.v. *Bust*), I was soon fotch'd up in the victualling line—and I busted for the benefit of my creditors. 1848 BARTLETT *Dict. Amer.*, *To Fetch up*, to stop suddenly... We often hear the phrase 'He fetched up all standing' that is, he made a sudden halt. It is a nautical vulgarism. 1857 *Quinland* I. 27 His little, tough, jet-black, Canadian horses, fairly wallowed in the snow, as he drove in a large circle round the house, and 'fetched up' at the front door. 1879 WHITMAN *Specimen Days* (1892) 139, I made quite a western journey, fetching up at Denver, Colorado. 1890 *Buckskin Mose* ii. 25 Waukegan was designated as the place where he might probably fetch up. 1898 E. N. WESTCOTT *David Harum* 175, I..walked alongside the el'phant..till they fetched up inside the tent. 1906 *Springfield Weekly Republ.* 11 Oct. 1 If he tries often enough he may fetch up in Congress.

j. To bring up, rear, or train children. *U.S.*

1848 W. E. BURTON *Waggeries* 88 (Th.) 'Where was you raised, old fellow?' 'Raised?' 'Yes, raised,—fotched up.' 1869 MRS. STOWE *Oldtown Folks* xx. 237, I was fetchin' on her up to work for her livin' as I was fetched up. 1870 *Putnam's Mag.* Nov. (De Vere) How you were the child of a missionary, and from your cradle had been fetched up for the work.

Fetcher. Add: **1. c.** Something which 'fetches' or attracts. (Cf. FETCH *v.* 4.) *U.S.*

1909 R. A. WASON *Happy Hawkins* 83 But this business was sure a fetcher to me. *Ibid.* 146 Well, that was a fetcher.

Fe·tch-up, *sb.* [f. vbl. phr. *fetch up*, FETCH *v.* 19 i.] A coming to a stand-still; stopping.

1866 MRS. WHITNEY *L. Goldthwaite* x, It isn't the fall that hurts,—it's the fetch-up.

Fêting (fēˡ·tiŋ), *vbl. sb.* The action of FÊTE *v.*

1895 *Westm. Gaz.* 11 Sept. 1/3 It would be absurd to expect as much *fêting* and feeding among the Liberal as among the Conservative rank and file.

Fetish, *sb.* **4. a.** Add: *fetish-bird, phœnix.*

1895 *Blackw. Mag.* Aug. 229/2 From the ashes of one fetich phoenix arose another equally strong. 1925 R. M. OGDEN tr. *Koffka's Growth of Mind* 347 If a white man shoots an invulnerable fetish-bird, this does not destroy the bird's invulnerability in their eyes.

Fetticus (fe·tikŏs). *U.S.* Also **vetticost.** = CORN-SALAD.

1848 BARTLETT *Dict. Amer.*

Feudist. Add: **3.** A person who has a feud with another. *U.S.*

1901 *Munsey's Mag.* XXV. 614/1 To speak of his feud to a feudist is a serious breach of the mountain etiquette. *a* 1909 'O. HENRY' *Roads of Destiny* viii. 130 The punchers from that ranch were more relentless and vengeful than Kentucky feudists. 1922 *Daily Mail* 13 Dec. 9 Neighbours, formerly the best of friends, are now virtually feudists. 1927 A. NEVINS *Emergence Mod. America* 252 A gang of horse thieves and outlaws; moonshiners, hunters and feudists.

Feuing (fiū·iŋ), *vbl. sb.* *Sc.* The action of FEU *v.*

1893 DK. ARGYLL *Unseen Found. Soc.* xvii. 536 No exclusive or preferential right of leasing, or of purchasing, or of feuing, had ever been conceded to local bodies. 1909 *Westm. Gaz.* 7 Aug. 2/1 The Scottish feuing method.

Fever, *sb.*[1] **1. c.** Add: Also *fever and ague* U.S., intermittent fever.

1676 S. SEWALL *Diary* I. 22 Told..of the death of Goodman Titcomb..after about a fortnight sickness of the Fever and Ague. 1828 A. SHERBURNE *Mem.* xi. (1831) 243, I was violently attacked with that distressing disease, the fever and ague. 1846 *Knickerbocker Mag.* XXVII. 55 Fever-and-ague riots among the ditches and green ponds. 1874 R. GLISAN *Jrnl. Army Life* xxxi. 444 They would be prostrated with the various forms of malarious fever—such as fever and ague.

Feyness (fēˡ·nĕs). [f. FEY *a.* + -NESS.] Fragile delicacy.

1926 *Spectator* 9 Oct. 568/1 That queer, elusive 'feyness'.. of Miss Fay Compton. 1930 *Time & Tide* 24 May 677 That ethereal physique and effect of feyness which has helped her to so many of her successes.

Fian(n (fīn). [Irish.] A member of the ancient Irish militia, one of the soldiers of Fionn mac Cumhail; = FENIAN *sb.* 1. Also *attrib.*

1787 M. YOUNG (*title*) Ancient Gælic Poems respecting the Race of the Fians, collected in the Highlands of Scotland in the years 1784–1786. 1879 [see FENIAN A. 1]. 1891 J. G. CAMPBELL *Fians* p. xii, The Fian heroes are to this day prominent in proverbs and riddles. 1910 D. A. MACKENZIE *Elves & Heroes*, The Ossianic or Fian Cycle.

Fiat, *sb.* **3.** Add: Also *fiat dollar*; **flat town** *U.S.* (see quot.).

1879 *Congress. Rec.* 17 May 1438/1 You now have the 'fiat dollar'..redeemable in pulp. 1879 *Harper's Mag.* Dec. 30/1 Atlanta is a 'fiat' town, and was put where she is by act of Legislature.

Fiat, *v.* Add: **b.** To declare by a 'fiat'.

1879 *Congress. Rec.* 17 May 1438/1 You can 'fiat' eighty-five cents to be worth a hundred cents.

Fiatism (fai·ătiz'm). *U.S.* [f. FIAT *sb.* + -ISM.] The principle or practice of making money legal tender by a 'fiat' of the government. Hence **Fi·atist,** one who believes in or advocates fiatism.

1896 *N. Amer. Rev.* CLXIII. 698 The protective theory as applied to our tax laws, and the theory of fiatism as applied to our currency issues, have introduced..the elements of legislative control to such an extent that [etc.]. *Ibid.* 701 Those..who..repudiated the doctrines of the fiatist, the Populist and the Socialist. 1904 J. G. CANNON in *N. Y. Times* 23 June 2 When the first battle was fought against greenback or fiat money, whatever they were on the Atlantic Coast, they were fiatists in the West.

Fiat lux (fai·æt lʊks). [L., = let there be light.] Used allusively with reference to Gen. i. 3.

a 1680 CHARNOCK *Disc. Knowl. God* Wks. 1684 II. 405 The new Creation as well as the old begins with a *Fiat lux*. 1905 *Daily Chron.* 21 Apr. 3/1 The death-knell of tyranny in these islands, a *fiat-lux* in the history of the Western hemisphere.

Fibre, *sb.* **8.** Add: **fibre-faced** *a.*, (*a*) having a facing or coat of fibre; (*b*) *U.S.*, (paper) having a surface composed of visible fibres; **fibre needle,** a gramophone needle made of fibre; **fibre-plant,** any plant which produces a fibre of commercial value; **fibre-stitch** (see quot.).

1884 KNIGHT *Dict. Mech.* Suppl., **Fiber-faced Paper*, a means of security against the restoration of the surface of check or draft-paper after it has been tampered with. It consists in imbedding in the pulp..a layer of fibers, the outer ends of which are then raised in the form of a nap [etc.]. 1922 *Times* 20 June 8/5 At right angles to this disc is a fibre-faced wheel which is mounted on a castellated shaft, along which it can be slid by means of the 'gear' lever. 1922 S. A. MAYCOCK *Handbk. Gramophone* v. 32 My own experiences with *fibre needles. 1929 P. WILSON & G. W. WEBB *Mod. Gramophones* 153 A fibre needle, in a sound-box specially made for it. 1887 MOLONEY *Forestry W. Afr.* 277 'Buaze' *fibre plant of the Zambesi (*Securidaca longipedunculata*). 1882 CAULFEILD & SAWARD *Dict. Needlework*, **Fibre Stitch*, a stitch used in Honiton and other Pillow Laces to make open leaves, with a fibre running down their centres.

Fibrilia (faibri·liă). [mod.L.] A fine vegetable fibre used as a substitute for cotton in the manufacture of fabrics.

1861 *Illustr. Lond. News* 18 May 476/2 Fibrilia is a generic term given in the United States to fibres obtained from a large number of plants. *Ibid.*, A paper..was read at a recent meeting of the French Academy when tissue made from fibrilia were shown.

Fibrin. 2. Add: **fibrin-ferment,** = THROMBIN; **fibrin-globulin,** a globulin contained in fibrinogen (Dorland, 1913); **fibrin-hyaloidin** (see quot.).

1876 *Jrnl. Chem. Soc.* I. 945 The author [*sc.* Alex Schmidt] proceeds to show..that *fibrin-ferment is not a body pre-existing in the blood, which was originally in the red blood corpuscles, and only after its exit from the body passed over into the plasma. 1897 *Daily News* 9 Jan. 7/7 The symptoms of poisoning by fibrin ferment. 1898, 1900 fibrin ferment [see THROMBIN]. 1920 *Jrnl. Chem. Soc.* CXVIII. I. 688 *Fibrin-hyaloidin obtained from fibrin, $C_{29}H_{54}O_{24}N_2$, is different from those [*sc.* hyaloidins] already discussed.

Fibrinate (fai·brineˡt), *v.* [f. FIBRIN + -ATE[3].] *trans.* To add fibrin to (the blood).

1871 A. MEADOWS *Man. Midwifery* (ed. 2) 357 Either we may defibrinate the blood, or we may add something to prevent or retard coagulation... The fibrinating method is on the whole, perhaps, not quite so satisfactory. 1910 *Practitioner* Jan. 54 The haematocele contains red fibrinated blood-clot.

Fibring (fai·briŋ), *vbl. sb.* [f. FIBRE *v.*] The action of the verb FIBRE; also, an instance of this.

1893 TUCKEY *Amphioxus* 146 The transverse fibring..of the notochord plates.

Fibrinoid (fai·brinoid). *Path.* [f. FIBRIN + -OID.] (See quots.)

1910 *Practitioner* Jan. 43 The muscle so invaded stains feebly, and the presence of these cells in them has brought about a fibrinoid or necrotic change. 1913 DORLAND *Med. Dict.* (ed. 7), *Fibrinoid*, the substance formed in the process of caseation of tissues: so called because it resembles canalized fibrin.

Fibrinose (fai·brinoᵘs). [f. FIBRIN + -OSE[2].] An albumose derived from fibrin.

1909 *Cent. D.* Suppl. 1913 DORLAND *Med. Dict.* (ed. 7).

Fibrinosis (faibrinōᵘ·sis). *Path.* [mod.L., f. FIBRIN + -OSIS.] A condition marked by excess of fibrin in the blood.

1901 DORLAND *Med. Dict.*

Fibrinuria (faibriniūᵊ·riă). *Path.* [f. FIBRIN + -URIA.] Passage of fibrin in the urine.

1890 BILLINGS *Med. Dict.* 1896 *Brit. Med. Jrnl.* 29 Aug. 531/2 Docent Dr. Klein writes an interesting article on fibrinuria... The disease is very rare.

Fibro-. Add: **Fi·bro-adeno·ma,** a glandular tumour containing fibrous tissue. **Fi·bro-ca·seose** (Dorland 1903), **-ous** *adjs.*, both fibrous and caseous. **Fi·bro-cicatri·cial** *a.*, consisting of fibrous tissue and scar. **Fi·bro-cyst,** a fibrous tumour which has undergone cystic degeneration. **Fi·bro-endothelio·ma,** an endothelioma containing fibrous tissue. **Fi·bro-lipo·ma**, a lipoma containing fibrous tissue; hence **Fi·bro-lipo·matous** *a.* **Fi·bro-papillo·ma**, a papilloma containing fibrous tissue.

1892 *Brit. Med. Jrnl.* 23 Apr. 862/2 A large *fibro-adenoma removed from the left breast of a girl. 1908 *Practitioner* Feb. 182 What was apparently a fibro-adenoma of the prostate was enucleated. *Ibid.* Mar. 423 A *fibro-caseous lesion due to tuberculosis. *Ibid.* Jan. 44 The *fibro-cicatricial bands. 1881 *Trans. Obstetr. Soc.* XXII. 129 A *fibro-cyst of the uterus. 1908 *Practitioner* Jan. 16 A slow-growing, non-vascular *fibro-endothelioma. 1889 *Brit. Med. Jrnl.* 11 May 1062/1 *Fibro-lipoma of Labia Majora. *Ibid.*, A *fibro-lipomatous growth. 1884 Thompson *Tumours of Bladder* 66 The bleeding is more continuous and free than in '*fibro-papilloma'.

Fibroid, *a.* Add: **b.** Designating diseases characterized by the formation or inflammation of connective tissue.

1874 Fagge in *Pathological Trans.* XXV. 64 A series of cases of fibroid disease of the heart. *Ibid.* 67 Towards the apex of the left ventricle..there was advanced fibroid growth. 1891 Taylor *Pract. Med.* (ed. 2) 424 Fibroid Phthisis.—This form may supervene upon chronic pleurisy and chronic pneumonia. 1918 *Act* 8 & 9 *Geo. V* c. 14 *title*, The disease known as fibroid phthisis or silicosis of the lungs.

Fibrolysin (fəibrǫ·lisin). [f. Fibro- + Lysin.] A soluble combination of sodium salicylate and thiosinamin used, as an injection, to break up fibrous tissue.

1906 *Practitioner* Dec. 828. 1910 *Ibid.* Apr. 470, I am not aware that fibrolysin has been tried in mastitis.

Fibrose (fəi·brōus), *v.* *Med.* [f. Fibrose *a.*] *intr.* To form fibrous tissue. Hence **Fi·brosed** *ppl. a.*; **Fi·brosing** *vbl. sb.* and *ppl. a.*

1879 *St. George's Hosp. Rep.* IX. 133 Lungs (some fibrosing or caseous). *Ibid.* 156 Indolent fibrosing tubercle at the apices of the lungs. 1897 *Brit. Med. Jrnl.* 11 Dec. 1728/1 The lower lobe of each lung was completely fibrosed. 1909 *Practitioner* Feb. 210 On examination of the fibroid, it is found shrunken and fibrosed throughout.

Fibrosis (fəibrōu·sis). *Path.* [mod.L., f. L. *fibra* Fibre: see -osis.] The development in an organ of fibrous tissue; fibroid degeneration.

1873 *Brit. Med. Jrnl.* I. 4 Arterio-capillary fibrosis. 1886 *Buck's Handbk. Med. Sci.* II. 174/2 Cirrhosis. Synonyms.—Sclerosis,..Chronic Fibrosis. 1893 *Brit. Med. Jrnl.* 2 Dec. 1214/2 Ordinary fibrosis of the kidney. 1906 *Practitioner* Dec. 730 The fibrosis steadily invades the lung parenchyma.

Hence **Fibro·tic** *a.*, of, pertaining to, or characterized by fibrosis.

1893 *Brit. Med. Jrnl.* 2 Dec. 1214/2 The difficult problems presented by fibrotic kidneys. 1906 *Practitioner* Dec. 730 Chronic inflammations of the bronchi, the pleura, or the lungs, which, having failed to resolve, become fibrotic. 1910 *Ibid.* June 781 Between 45 and 50 the liability to fibrotic metritis, endometritis, and mucous polypi diminishes.

Fibrositis (fəibrosəi·tis). *Path.* [f. Fibrose + -itis.] Inflammatory hyperplasia of the white fibrous tissue.

1910 *Lancet* 12 Mar. 713/2 Muscular rheumatism.—This affection is always a fibrositis. *Ibid.*, Muscular fibrositis of the shoulder.

Fibrous, *a.* **1. b.** Add: *Fibrous grass*, a Tasmanian grass, *Stipa semibarbata*, the stem of which splits into fibre when the seed is ripe.

1862 W. Archer *Prod. Tasmania* 41 (Morris).

Fice (fəis). *U.S.* Variant of Fise 2.

1845 J. J. Hooper *Adv. Simon Suggs* vii. 88 I'll bury you, you little whifflin fice. 1854 R. Glisan *Jrnl. Army Life* xi. (1874) 138 Its resemblance is between that of a small fice and grey squirrel. 1860 *Richmond Enquirer* 10 July 1/5 (Th.) John Bell may indeed be a very 'little dog'—yea, a most excellent fice. 1874 E. Eggleston *Circuit Rider* ix. 89 Dogs set up a vociferous barking, ranging in key all the way from the contemptible treble of an ill-natured 'fice' to the deep baying of a bull dog.

attrib. 1843 *Missouri Reporter* (St. Louis) 29 June (Th.) Did you ever see a pack composed of five or six little fice dogs, barking furiously?

Ficelle. Add: **1.** Also *ficelle-coloured* adj.

1900 *Westm. Gaz.* 5 Feb. 2/1 Hat of ficelle-coloured straw. 1927 *Observer* 12 June 11/4 Ficelle coloured lace.

2. A device, trick, artifice.

1920 in H. G. Wells *Outline Hist.* 125 *note*, True, raids on women were a real cause of war, but they were also a very favourite *ficelle* of fiction.

Fichued (fi·ʃūd), *a.* [f. Fichu + -ed [2].] Draped or covered with a fichu.

1928 Galsworthy *Swan Song* II. xiii. 219 Over her fichued shoulder.

Fiction. 6. Add: *fiction-monger* (earlier U.S. example).

1835 J. P. Kennedy *Horse-Shoe Robinson* ii. 32 If any one, hereafter, should tell your story, he will be accounted a fiction-monger.

Fictioneer (fikʃəniə·ɹ). [f. Fiction + -eer.] A writer or inventor of fiction (senses 3 and 4). Hence **Fictionee·ring** *vbl. sb.* and *ppl. a.*

1923 D. A. Wilson *Carlyle till Marr.* III. xvi. 213 Carlyle had as little patience as Irving with sentimental fictioneering. *Ibid.* xxvii. 246 Fictioneering biographers. *Ibid.* IV. iii. 265 A fictioneer would say the story has no plot. 1927 *Scots Observer* 30 July 1/3 He does his job of fictioneering gaily.

Fictioner (fi·kʃənəɹ). [f. Fiction + -er [1].] A writer of fiction; a novelist.

1916 L. P. Jacks *Philos. in Trouble* 116 Divine Fictionism..Actor Camelius will address the Divine Fictioners today in the Temple of Light. 1924 G. Overton *Cargoes for Crusoes* 215 There are present in this novel the two requisites of Mr. Lucas's art as a fictioner.

Fid, *sb.* Add:

5. b. A heap; *pl.* 'heaps', 'crowds'. Also as an exclamation = Great!

1899 Kipling *Stalky & Co.* (1900) 17 Fids! Fids! Oh, Fids! I gloat! Hear me gloat! 1920 *Blackw. Mag.* Oct. 473/1 Look at the dirty blighters on that hill there! Fids of 'em! 1926 *Ibid.* Mar. 353/2 Little fids of snow.

8. fid-hook (see quot. 1905).

1851 J. S. Springer *Forest Life* 108 (Th.) He examines above all the 'fid-hook' and the 'dog-hook', the former that it does not work out, the latter that it loose not its grappling hold upon the tree. 1905 *Terms in Forestry & Logging* 37 *Fid hook*, a slender, flat hook used to keep another hook from slipping on a chain.

Fid, *v.* Add: Also with *out*, and in *ppl. a.* and *vbl. sb.*

1883 *Man. Seamanship for Boys* 30 Holes in the heel of topmasts, for the top tackle pendants to reef through for housing, striking, or fidding. *Ibid.* 220 The cringle is.. fidded out. 1901 W. C. Russell *Ship's Adventure* 342 A full-rigged ship must have fidded topmast and fidded topgallant-mast.

-fid (fid), terminal element representing L. *-fidus* cleft, divided, related to *findere* to cleave, as in *bifid*, *palmatifid*, *pinnatifid*, *trifid*, which are ad. L. *bifidus*, mod.L. *palmātifidus*, etc.

Fidate (fəi·deit), *v.* *Chess.* [f. med.L. *fīdāt-*, ppl. stem of *fīdāre*.] *trans.* To give (a piece) immunity from capture. So **Fida·tion**.

1910 H. J. R. Murray in *Brit. Chess Mag.* 230 This left the white pieces unprotected on QR 7 and QKt 7 and in typical mediaeval fashion they were fidated, i.e. made immune from capture. *Ibid.*, The necessity of preserving the original solution..made the Rook's fidation a restricted one: the King could not take it, but the Knight could still do so. 1913 — *Hist. Chess* 570 In one problem, men are fidated (*atreguado*) and their capture is prohibited. *Ibid.* 679, BS 13 prevents this by fidating Bd 4 from the King and renders the fidation of the P unnecessary.

Fiddle, *sb.* Add:

1. b. *As fine as a fiddle* U.S., = as fit as a fiddle. *To hang up one's fiddle* (early U.S. examples). *To play third fiddle*: to be the third party.

1811 *Massachusetts Spy* 20 Mar. 4/1 But pleasures are brittle as glass, Although as a fiddle they're fine. 1815 Humphreys *Yankey in Eng.* 37, I am as fine as a fiddle. 1837 J. K. Paulding *St. Nicholas* (1836) 78 Pleasure sleighs, which, at that period it was the fashion among farmers to have as fine as fiddles. 1836 Dunlap *Mem. Water Drinker* II. 6 He does not hang his fiddle up behind the street-door when he comes home. 1870 Mrs. Stowe *Oldtown Fireside Stories* (1871) 185 Wal, you see, from the time that Bill Elderkin come and took the academy, I could see plain enough that it was time for me to hang up my fiddle. 1889 'Edna Lyall' *Derrick Vaughan* ii, I took care to drop behind, having no taste for the third-fiddle business.

3. d. *Ceramics.* A rack in which pieces of ware are placed to drain after having been dipped in liquid glaze.

1825 J. Nicholson *Oper. Mech.* 473 Hollow pieces and blue-printed ware, are placed on hair sieves, or on four pieces of sheet iron, from two to three feet long, called a *fiddle*.

4. f. A swindle. *U.S.*

1874 *Slang Dict.*, *Fiddle*...In America, a swindle or an imposture.

8. fiddle-back, (*b*) an Australian scarabæid beetle, *Schizorrhina australasiæ* (Morris); (*c*) *colloq.* a chasuble having a fiddle-shaped back; **fiddle-boat** (see quot.); **fiddle-drill,** a drill rotated by a string and bow, a bow-drill.

1890 W. J. Gordon *Foundry* 120 The *fiddle-boat being two boats, or rather two sections of a boat, rigged catamaran fashion and having the wheel in the middle. 1888 *Lockwood's Dict. Mech. Engin.*, *Bow Drill*, a *fiddle drill.

Fideism (fəi·dī,iz'm). [f. L. *fides* faith + -ism.] A mode of thought according to which knowledge depends upon a fundamental act of faith. Hence **Fi·deist, Fidei·stic** *a.*

1885 [see Traditionalism]. 1895 *Dublin Rev.* Apr. 313 *note*, As to Fideism, see Dr. Hettinger's interesting classification of its four stages, as corresponding to the four stages of Rationalism, in his 'Fundamental Theologie', 1879, vol. ii. pp. 348–9. 1908 *The Programme of Modernism* 142 *note*, Such scepticism destroys the certitude of the fact of revelation and ends in blind fideism. 1909 *Cath. Encycl.* VI. 68/2 Fideism owes its origin to distrust in human reason, and the logical sequence of such an attitude is scepticism. *Ibid.*, For some fideists, human reason cannot of itself reach certitude in regard to any truth whatever. *Ibid.*, It is also a fideistic attitude which is the occasion of agnosticism..and other modern forms of anti-intellectualism. 1912 F. von Hügel *Eternal Life* II. xii. 344 Rome is finely free from all Fideism or Pietism.

Fie, *int.* Add: **3. b.** as sb. *fie-for-shames* U.S., trousers.

1847 *Knickerbocker Mag.* XXIX. 386 Following the general practice I usually, in pulling off my 'fie-for-shames', hung them up to the ceiling of the state-room opposite the door.

Fiedlerite (fī·dlərəit). *Min.* [Named *fiedlerit*, 1887, after Baron von Fiedler, mine director of Laurium, Greece: see -ite [1].] A chloride or oxychloride of lead.

1899 *Jrnl. Chem. Soc.* LXXVI. II. 433 The new mineral, paralaurionite, may at a cursory glance be easily mistaken for laurionite or fiedlerite.

Field, *sb.* Add:

19. b. In designations of crops grown solely for feeding to cattle, and covering a large area, as *field-hay*; **field-pea,** *Pisum arvense*.

1895 C. J. Cornish *Wild England of To-day* 242 '*Field-hay', as the produce of the rye-grass, sainfoin, clover, and trefoil is called, is a new feature in the country. 1858 *Field pea [see Pea [1] 2 b]. 1892 Fream *Elem. Agric.* (ed. 2) 240 The field-pea, of which there are several sorts, distinguished by bearing a blue blossom, should be sown as early as possible in the spring.

21. field-dinner *U.S.*, a picnic dinner; **field driver** (earlier examples); **field editor** *U.S.* (see quot.); **field events,** certain athletic events (see quot. 1912), as distinguished from events on the running track; **field-grey** [tr. G. *feldgrau*], the regulation colour of the uniform of a German infantryman; **field hand** (earlier examples); **field labourer** = *field hand* (*b*); **field-man,** (*c*) a surveyor; **field-negro** *U.S.*, a negro field hand; **field-notes** (earlier examples); **field-regulator, -rheostat** (see quots.); **field spaniel,** a variety of spaniel closely allied to the cocker; **field-trash** (see quot.).

1857 E. Stone *Life Howland* xii. 282 A *field dinner and Rhode Island clam bake..was announced. 1695 *Manchester* (Mass.) *Rec.* 65 Genkin Williams and Samuell Lee wear chosen Howards or *field Drivers. 1736 *Boston Town Rec.* XII. 153 Voted, That Mr. Nathanael Tuttle be Haward or Field-driver. 1923 H. M. Swetlans *Industrial Publishing* 54 On a paper covering a wide territory there may be an assistant editor (sometimes called *field editor) stationed at each important center. 1901 *Westm. Gaz.* 30 Mar. 8/2 In the five '*field' events there was one more surprise. 1912 E. H. Ryle *Athletics* 19 'Field events' (*i.e.*, long-, high- and pole-jumping, weight-putting, hammer- and discus-throwing, and hurdling). 1929 Bretherton (*title*) Khaki or *Field-Grey? 1929 E. Sutton tr. *Zweig's Case of Sergeant Grischa* II. ii, They came in their threadbare field grey. 1835 J. H. Ingraham *South-West* II. 254 The third and lowest class consists of those slaves who are termed '*field-hands'. 1845 F. Douglass *Life* (1846) 58, I was now for the first time in my life a field hand. 1860 Abbott *South & North* 279 A little handful of slaveholders may be exempted from paying wages to..their *field-laborers. 1903 *Sci. Amer. Suppl.* 31 Jan. 22,647 (Cent. Suppl.) The *fieldmen of the Geological Survey have been the pioneer surveyors of the natural features of the vast regions which constitute half the continent. 1812 [Paulding] *Beauties Bro. Bull-us* 52 The democrats of the South despise the democrats of the North as much as they do their *field-negroes. 1818 Fearon *Sk. Amer.* 239 The price of good field negroes is now about eight hundred dollars. 1845 W. G. Simms *Wigwam & Cabin* Ser. II. 204 Mr. Carrington and myself had begun to take interest in the issue thus tacitly made up between the field negro and his visiter. 1806 in *Ann. 9th Congress* 2 Sess. 1002 He was retained as a necessary assistant to the principal surveyor in copying *field notes. 1841 C. Cist *Cincinnati* 152 From these field-notes, the plats, or maps..are prepared. 1849 *President's Message Congress* II. 572 United States geological survey of public lands in Michigan—Field notes. 1919 W. H. Marchant *Wireless Telegr.* (ed. 2) 297 *Field Regulator. A variable resistance forming part of the field circuit of a motor or a dynamo. 1923 *Harmsworth's Wireless Encycl.* 918/2 A field regulator is a device for varying the strength of the field magnets in a dynamo or electric motor. *Ibid.* 919/1 From the wireless point of view, the chief use of field regulators is to provide a convenient means for regulating the charging-rate of a dynamo used to recharge accumulators. 1910 *Hawkins' Electr. Dict.*, *Field Rheostat*, an adjustable resistance used to vary the strength of the magnetic field of a shunt wound dynamo or motor. 1867 J. H. Walsh *Dogs Brit. Isl.* 36 Field Spaniels...The heavy, large-eared, well-feathered, short-legged '*field-spaniels', have been known for years as 'springers'. 1897 *Encycl. Sport* I. 319/2 There are four varieties of field spaniels,..the Clumber, the Sussex, the Black, and the any-other-colour. 1793 B. Edwards *Hist. Brit. Colonies W. I.* II. 221 Refuse, or *field-trash, (i.e.) the decayed leaves and stems of the canes; so called in contradistinction to cane-trash.

Field (fīld). Name of Edward *Field* (of Messrs. Merryweather & Sons) used attrib. to designate a form of engine boiler tube invented by him.

1887 *Encycl. Brit.* XXII. 498/1 Tubes of this kind (called Field tubes) are used..where it is necessary to get up steam with the least possible delay. 1895 *Model Steam Engine* 53 The steam cylinders and pumps are horizontal and fixed on a rigid wrought iron frame, the boiler being at the hind end. They are on the 'Field' system.

Field, *v.* Add:

5. c. *fig.* To 'catch', 'pick up'.

1902 *Daily Chron.* 2 Sept. 3/1, I would get an agile and hard-skinned man to field the novels as they come. 1908 *Ibid.* 20 Apr. 4/6 From Good Friday to the following Tuesday, if you stay in London, you have to field splashes of paint and skirt ladders. 1909 *Ibid.* 18 Nov. 4/6 The Correctors of the Press are demanding the proper consideration of men who field the mistakes of careless writers.

6. *Football.* To put into the field.

1922 *Daily Mail* 1 Dec. 11 The F.A. played four professionals in the defence, but fielded an amateur forward line. *Ibid.* 6 Dec. 12 North Midlands hope to field a powerful fifteen in to-day's match v. Warwickshire. 1927 *Morn. Post* 24 Oct. 13/3 The Oxford side fielded against the United Services was a more workmanlike lot.

Field-land. Transfer †*Obs.* to **a** and **b** and add: **c.** Land suitable for cultivation. *U.S.*

1851 A. O. Hall *Manhattaner* 129, I have seen a million dollars worth of property..plantations; field lands; sugar-houses.

Fiend. Add: **4. e.** With qualifying word or phr.: One who is much devoted to or skilled in some subject; one who is addicted to some practice or habit, esp. one of an injurious character, as *dope fiend*, *opium fiend*. orig. *U.S. slang*.

1889 Farmer *Americanisms* s.v., The free lunch fiend..is one who makes a meal off what is really provided as a snack. He pays for a drink, but shamefacedly manages in this way to get something more than his money's worth. 1896 dope fiend [see *Dope *sb.* 3]. 1911 Webster s.v., An opium fiend. ..He is a fiend in mathematics; a botany fiend. 1925 H. G. Wells *Christina Alberta's Father* vi. § 8 There you see.. artists' models and drug-fiends. 1926 Dearden *Understanding Ourselves* I. xiv. 151 We can no more resist our daydreaming than the morphia-fiend his drug. 1929 Graves *Good-Bye to All That* xxviii. 377 He had been upset that morning by a letter from an autograph-fiend.

Fie·ndish, *a.* Add: Also as *adv.*, excessively, horribly.

1891 Susan Hale *Lett.* (1919) 258 As all the Continent is fiendish cold, we did wisely.

Fierce, *a.* Add:

1. c. (See quot.)

1912 *Motor Manual* 166 Complaints are occasionally made of what is called a 'fierce' clutch. In other words, the clutch will not slide or slip in, but permits the engine to take hold suddenly, and almost takes the starting control from the driver's hands.

d. *fig.* Characterized by wild or brutal conduct, manners, etc.

1923 *R. S. Frampton's Catal.*, Old Fierce Novel.—Paul Periwinkle, or the Pressgang.

5. c. Outrageous. *U.S. slang*.

a 1906 'O. Henry' *Trimmed Lamp* etc. 6 How can you wear a waist like that, Lou?..It shows fierce taste. *Ibid.* 210 But it's fierce, now, how cynical I am, ain't it?

7. Also, violently. *U.S. slang*.

1927 H. Rose in *Atlantic Monthly* Mar. 338, I broke a finger on my right hand. It ached fierce.

Fiery, *a.* Add: **4. d.** *Cricket.* Causing the ball to fly up after pitching. (Cf. *Fire *sb.* 15.)

1882 Pardon *Austral. in Eng.* 181 The wicket was fiery and the outfielding rough. 1893 *Baily's Mag.* Oct. 255/1 Fiery wickets are not at all desirable, since they introduce an element of danger into the game which is customarily absent.

7. d. fiery thorn *U.S.* (see quot.).

1858 J. A. Warder *Hedges & Evergreens* II. 276 Fiery Thorn is an evergreen with dark foliage and bright-red berries.

Fiesta (fie·stā). [Sp., feast.] In Spanish America, a religious festival; also, any festivity or holiday.

1885 *U.S. Cons. Rep.* No. 59. 257 (Cent. D.) On holidays or *fiestas*. 1923 *Blackw. Mag.* Nov. 697/1 The failure of the great June *fiestas* owing to continued rains. 1925 *Chambers's Jrnl.* 123/1 Except for an occasional 'Fiesta', they have to supply their own brand of entertainment.

Fife, *sb.* Add: **1. c.** *Fife and drum*: taken as typical instruments of martial music; often *attrib.* in lit. sense, and fig. = martial, militant (cf. *drum-and-fife*, *Drum *sb.* [1] 14).

Song, Here they come, Fife and drum.

1900 *Westm. Gaz.* 14 Feb. 3/2 The 'Captains Courageous' of the House were by no means unanimous in his favour. The Under-Secretary for War had not many fife-and-drum supporters in their ranks. 1923 B. Whitlock *J. Hardin & Son* I. v. 69 In the line there was a fife and drum corps.

Fifer [2] (fəi·fəɹ). [f. *Fife* + -er [1].] A native or inhabitant of Fife, a county of Scotland.

1891 Farmer *Slang*. 1897 R. Wallace in *Daily News* 23 Nov. 3/6 He knew that the outside and envious critic was in the habit of telling Fifers that they worked the idea of a kingdom of Fife for a good deal more than it was worth. 1901 *Daily Chron.* 14 Oct. 5/2 The London 'Fifers' do not forget in exile the engaging qualities of their native county. 1908 *Westm. Gaz.* 12 May 7/2 We Scots outside 'the Kingdom' know it takes 'a long spoon to sup wi' a Fifer'. 1927 *Glasgow Herald* 14 May 9 The average Fifer..has more of Gaelic blood in him than the average Lewisman.

Fifth, *a.* and *sb.* Add: **C.** *Comb.* **fifth nerve,** either of the fifth pair of cranial nerves (see Trifacial, Trigeminal).

1836–9 *Todd's Cycl. Anat.* II. 270 The fifth nerve is attached to the surface of the brain on either side of the pons Varolii, at a distance of three-fourths of an inch from its middle line. 1875 *Encycl. Brit.* I. 881/2 The Trifacial or fifth is the largest cranial nerve. 1890 Billings *Med. Dict.*, *Trifacial neuralgia*, neuralgia in the distribution of the fifth nerve. 1931 *Daily Tel.* 19 Jan. 11/3 The Archbishop is suffering from severe fifth nerve neuralgia.

b. In Quaker use: *fifth day* (i.e. of the week); similarly *fifth month*, May.

1799 E. Fry in S. Corder *Life* (1853) 63 Fifth Month, 1st. 1821 *Ibid.* 318 My beloved daughter, Rachel, was married last Fifth-day, the 23rd, at Runcton. 1868 G. G. Channing *Early Recoll. Newport, R.I.* 231, I went frequently to hear him at the fifth-day [*sc.* Thursday] meetings.

Fifty, *a.* and *sb.* **C.** *Comb.* Add: **fifty-six** *dial.* and *U.S.*, a fifty-six pound weight.

a 1800 *Sp. Farmers' Museum* (1801) 176 He had no notion of hanging a fifty-six to his chin, for the sake of lengthening his face to the taste of a wilful audience. 1886 *W. Somerset Word-bk.*, *Vifty-zix*,..a weight of 56 lbs.—the usual name for a half-hundredweight stone.

Fifty-fifty, *adv.* and *a.* *colloq.* (orig. *U.S.*). [f. Fifty *sb.* 1.] **A.** *adv.* On a basis of fifty per cent. (or one half) each; half-and-half, equally. **B.** *adj.* Equal, shared equally; half-and-half.

1913 Wodehouse *Little Nugget* vi. 121 Say, Sam, don't be a hawg. Let's go fifty-fifty in dis deal. *Ibid.* xii. 209 Would a fifty-fifty offer tempt you? *Ibid.* xiv. 248 'Fifteen per cent. is our offer', he said. 'And to think it was once fifty-fifty!' 1926 H. L. Wilson *Somewhere in Red Gap* vi. 263 And she glared at Cousin Egbert with rage and distrust splitting fifty-fifty in her fevered eyes. 1921 R. D. Paine *Comr. Rolling Ocean* i. 9, I intend to divide the worries with you fifty-fifty. 1924 *Daily Mail* 28 Nov. 10/5 [He] did not take a fifty-fifty chance that the bedroom door he would enter by was the right one. It was pointed out to him the day before. 1929 Farjeon *Underground* ii, Perhaps half the impetus of rising was supplied by the shock he had just received. Shock and heroism may have been fifty-fifty. 1929 *Nebraska Alumnus* June 167 Child raising is a fifty-fifty job for the parents.

Figaro (fi·gārǫ). *slang*. [The name of the hero in *Le Barbier de Séville*, and *Le Mariage de Figaro* of Beaumarchais (1732–99).] A barber.

1865–74 *Slang Dict.*, *Figaro*, a barber; from *Le Nozze di Figaro* [of Mozart]. 1886 *Globe* 18 Mar. 3/2 (Farmer) There is wailing and weeping among a certain section of the army, the Figaros, which has been despoiled at one fell swoop [*viz.* by an order of French War Minister permitting soldiers to wear their beards]. 1922 *Contemp. Rev.* Mar. 334 [He] one day asked his Figaro who he thought was the richest man in the town.

Fight, *sb.* Add:

2. d. *Fight-off*, a contest to decide a tie in a fencing match.

1930 *Morning Post* 14 July 15 In the fight-off, Armstrong worried at his enemy's arm with an incessant attack.

Fight, *v.* Add: **2. a.** Of an animal: To struggle for freedom or mastery. Also *trans.* To strive with (a horse, etc.) for mastery. *U.S.*

1850 'H. Hieover' *Pract. Horsemanship* 179 If you find he at all fights against you..stand now on no ceremony with him. 1875 [in Dict.]. 1908 Mulford *Orphan* i. 13 He mounted and fought the animal for a few minutes, just as he always had to fight it. 1920 Hunter *Trail Drivers of Texas* 231, I 'fought' cattle for nine years almost night and day.

4. b. *To fight fire.* (Cf. *Fire *sb.* B. 2.)

1865 *Chambers's Jrnl.* 29 July 470/1 They took away from the local firemen their apparatus, and proceeded in their own way to 'fight fire'.

Fighting, *vbl. sb.* **3. b.** Add:

fighting chance, an opportunity of succeeding by great effort; **fighting drunk, -tight** *adjs.*, *colloq.*, drunk to a state of quarrelsomeness; **fighting-fit** *a.*, fit to fight; hence *fighting-fitness*; **fighting-top** *Naut.*, a circular platform placed on an elevation on the mast of a warship, on which guns and armed men can be placed.

1889 *Kansas Times & Star* 20 Feb., With a somewhat divided party, but having a *fighting chance of success. 1894 *Outing* (U.S.) XXIV. 295/1 The captain decided to..land the sailor so as to give him a fighting chance for his life in the hospital. 1894 *Congress. Rec.* 1 Feb. 1786/1 He can not be beaten out of hand. He will have a fighting chance. 1908 *Daily Chron.* 17 Nov. 4/7 Those who are acting like hooligans or who are '*fighting' drunk. 1909 *Westm. Gaz.* 1 Oct. 3/3 Jim's Sarah she come 'ome fighting drunk the other night. 1894 A. Morrison *Mean Streets* 131 Neddy Milton was not quite *fighting-fit. 1894 H. Drummond *Ascent of Man* 267 Fitness in the stormy days of the world's animal youth was necessarily *fighting-fitness. *a* 1889 *Chicago Tribune* (Barrère & Leland), A quarter of a dollar would buy enough sour mash to make an ordinary man *fighting tight. 1896 *Naval Annual* (ed. T. A. Brassey) I. 32 The foremast has two *fighting-tops...The mainmast has only one fighting-top. 1915 *Nature* XCVI. 182/1 On board our battleships a range-finder of this kind is placed in one of the fighting-tops on the masts.

Fighting, *ppl. a.* Add:

1. c. In colloquial designations of various regiments, qualifying the regimental number, in allusion to specific episodes in their history.

Fighting Fifteenth, the 15th Hussars; **Fighting Fifth,** the Northumberland Fusiliers; **Fighting Fortieth,** the Prince of Wales' Volunteers; **Fighting Ninth,** the Norfolk Regiment.

1871 *Chambers's Jrnl.* 23 Dec. 802/2 The 'Fighting Fifth'..was distinguished by its men wearing a white plume in the cap. 1888 *Nicknames in the Army* 32, 15th (King's) Hussars...The 'Fighting Fifteenth'. 1890 *Standard* 25 Apr. 3/4 (Farmer) The Northumberland Fusiliers, better known as the Fighting Fifth. 1891 Farmer *Slang*, *Fighting Fifth*.. Other nicknames were The Shiners..The Old Bold Fifth ..and Lord Wellington's Body Guard.

d. *Mining.* (See quots.)

1860 *Engl. & For. Mining Gloss.* (ed. 2) 72 *Fighting* applies to the ventilation when reversed, as the upcast becoming the downcast, and *vice versâ*. 1883 Gresley *Gloss. Coal-m.* 105 When the weight or pressure of the ventilating current of air in a mine becomes equal or nearly so in both the downcast and upcast shafts, and no appreciable movement is caused in the air,..the pit is said to be fighting.

Figure, *sb.* Add: **19. c.** (Earlier and later examples.) Also *figure four trap*.

1837 J. C. Neal *Charcoal Sk.* I. 38 The most beautiful notions are all lost for want of a trap; an intellectual Figgery Four. 1847 H. Howe *Hist. Collect. Ohio* 275 The [wolf] trap was set by a figure four, with any kind of meat except that of wolf's. 1853 Lowell *Our Own* Digression D 114 So bait your moral figure-of-fours to catch the Orson public. 1862 *Trans. Ill. Agric. Soc.* (1865) V. 734 Boys..capture them by means of a 'figure four' trap. 1919 H. L. Wilson *Ma Pettengill* viii. 243 Lew Wee..made a figure-four trap, and put something for bait on the pointed stick and set the trap.

20. b. *Big figure*, in phrases *to do things on the big figure*, *to go* (or *come*) *the big figure*: see *Big B. *To go the whole figure* U.S.: to go the whole way; to act in a thoroughgoing fashion.

1838 [Asa Green] *Glance at New York* (Bartlett 1859), A foo-foo, or an outsider, is a chap that can't come the big figure. 1839 *Havana* (N.Y.) *Republ.* 21 Aug. 369 (Th.), I was determined to go the hull figure, and see all. 1840 J. P. Kennedy *Quodlibet* xii. (1872) 180, I can tell you that he goes the whole figure against rotation in this individual.. case. 1855 Haliburton *Nat. & Hum. Nat.* xii. II. 142 Sally was death on lace, and old Aunt Thankful goes the whole figure for furs. 1864 J. T. Trowbridge *Cudjo's Cave* iii. 37 The time may come when we will have to..go the whole figure with the free north, or drift with the cotton states. 1914 H. James *Ivory Tower* Notes 309 The..momentous season or scene,..in which she goes the whole figure.

22. b. *pl.* The name of the first form in certain Jesuit schools and colleges, divided into High (or †Great) and Low (or †Little) Figures: corresponding to the Rudiments or Accidence of other places.

1629 Wadsworth *Pilgr.* iii. 12, I was promoted to the first forme called the Figures. 1713 in B. Ward *Hist. St. Edmund's Coll.* (1893) 58 What we call the Accidence they call Figures, which they divide into two years, one for the lower, the second for the higher. 1716 M. Davies *Athen. Brit.* III. 2 Their Humanity-Schools..are subdivided, and call'd Little Figures..then great Figures or Rudiments. 1736 in E. H. Burton *Life Bp. Challoner* (1909) I. ii. 17, I have at this very day..39 in Figures only. 1893 B. Ward *Hist. St. Edmund's Coll.* iv. 58 *note*, The two classes of 'Figures' were changed very shortly after this [1713] into three classes of 'Rudiments', and this term has survived at St. Edmund's to the present day. At Ushaw the older title of 'Figures' is now in use. 1913 *Ushaw Mag.* Dec. 170 The Rev. William Lamb, who for a year had taught High Figures as a professor. *Ibid.* 278 The most interesting game of the year was that between Grammar and High Figures.

Figure, *v.* Add:

12. b. (*trans.*, also with *down*) To reckon, calculate. Also with obj. clause. *U.S.*

1865 *Congress. Globe* 9 Feb. 671/3, I have not figured the number of square miles that there will be. 1891 *Fur, Fin & Feather* Mar. 170 By this time Sagebrush and I had got the whole thing figured down pretty fine in our own minds. 1901 *Chambers's Jrnl.* Sept. 633/1 Only this morning I was figuring that the work should bring us enough to put all straight and sow next year again. 1913 *N. Y. Even. Post* 8 Sept. 1/6 Yale men figure that the bones have lain where found from 5,000 to 20,000 years.

(*b*) *To figure on* or *upon* (fig.): to think over, consider; to count on, anticipate, expect. *U.S.*

1837 *Congress. Globe* App. 247/1, I..cannot understand the Secretary's report. I figured upon its data until I threw down my slate in despair. 1877 Bartlett *Dict. Amer.* (ed. 4) s.v., 'Figure on that' means to consider it; to think it over. Western. 1904 Gene Stratton-Porter *Freckles* 241 In figuring on their not coming that day he failed to reckon with the enthusiasm of the Bird Woman. 1905 *Smart Set* Oct. 17/1 But I'm figurin' on gettin' hold of some more land. 1906 *N. Y. Even. Post* 13 Oct. 5 He is not figuring on any extensive defection on their part. 1907 *Smart Set* Feb. 96, I hadn't figured on that. 1909 *N. Y. Even. Post* 7 Jan. (Th.) We always figure on supplying more lenses in July and August than in all the rest of the year.

(*c*) To make estimates or lay plans *for*. *U.S.*

a 1889 *Burlington Free Press* (Farmer) The next evening we came to a drove of small pigs and began to figure for one.

15. Figure out. c. Also, more widely, to estimate or calculate; hence, to work out, make out. Chiefly *U.S.*

1833 C. A. Davis *Lett. J. Downing* (1834) 41 As I said before, I'm stump'd about that Bank of U.S.; and I want you to help me figure it out. 1888 'R. Boldrewood' *Robbery under Arms* xlvii, We took a couple of days figuring it out at the Hollow. Starlight had a map, and we plotted it out, and marked all the stages which could be safely made. 1902 G. H. Lorimer *Lett. Self-made Merchant* i. 5 You can't have to be very bright to figure out which one started the demand. 1903 *N. Y. Sun* 1 Nov. 5 The telegraph lines began to have trouble, and for a while the experts couldn't figure out what was the matter. 1905 *Smart Set* Oct. 17/2 'I'll figure it out after a while', he said. 'It ain't exactly worryin' me sick yet.' 1910 W. M. Raine *B. O'Connor* 12 Now, this is how I figured it out.

Fijian, Feejeean (fīdʒī·ăn), *a.* and *sb.* (Also **Feegeean.**) [f. *Fiji*, native name of the principal island of the Fiji archipelago + -an.] **A.** *adj.* Of or pertaining to Fiji or the Fiji islands or people. **B.** *sb.* A native or inhabitant of Fiji or the Fiji islands; the Fiji language.

1838 J. Williams *Miss. Enterpr. S. Sea Isl.* p. xviii, Cruel Rite of the Fijians. 1846 in *Wesleyan-Meth. Mag.* (1847) Apr. 221/1 Thus is laid the foundation of another Feejeean war. 1860 Mrs. Smythe *10 Months in Fiji Isl.* (1864) 112 He wrote a letter to him, which Mr. Waterhouse read aloud, in Fijian. 1861 *Ibid.* 206 A narrow patch of ground supplies the wants of a Fijian household. 1865 Lubbock *Prehist. Times* 356 The fortified towns of the Feegeeans had an earthern rampart. 1875 Jevons *Money* 25 Among our interesting fellow-subjects, the Fijians, whale's teeth served in the place of cowries. 1877 *Encycl. Brit.* VI. 798/2 The Fijians jump half round from side to side with their arms akimbo. 1879 *Ibid.* IX. 157/1 The Fijian character was till lately proverbial for every savage abomination. 1885 Codrington *Melanes. Lang.* 4 It is desirable to use the term Polynesia strictly to indicate the region of the East Pacific to the West of which Melanesia begins with the Fijian group. 1885 *Encycl. Brit.* XIX. 423/2 In Fijian the word *luve* means either a son or a daughter. 1921 W. Deane *Fijian Soc.* 208 It is at feast-time that the Fijian earns for himself the reputation of being a good eater.

Fijo (fī·χo). [Sp. *fijo* fixed, settled.] A standing regiment.

1902 *Encycl. Brit.* XXVI. 643/2 The disciplinary corps of military convicts styled *Fijo de Ceuta*. 1928 *Blackw. Mag.* May 642/2 The 'fijo' or permanent regiment of Palermo was small.

Fike, var. of Fyke *U.S.*, bag-net.

1871 *Game Laws N. Y.* in *Fur, Fin & Feather* (1872) 28 It shall not be lawful for any person to take eels in fikes or pots.

Fikey (fəi·ki). *S. Afr.* [ad. Du. *vaatje*, dim. of *vaat* Vat.] (See quot. 1913.)

1891 E. Glanville *Fossicker* xix, One of the three rose up,..took a final pull at the water 'fikey', and stretched himself on the bare ground. 1913 Pettman *Africanderisms*, *Fikey*.., a small keg for water, generally forming part of the furniture of a transport wagon.

Fikiness (fəi·kinės). Chiefly *Sc.* Also **feikieness, fykiness.** [f. Fikie *a.* + -ness.] Restlessness, agitation; the action of taking much trouble.

1889 Barrie *Window in Thrums* xiv, Her feikieness ended in his surrender. 1892 N. Dickson *Auld Sc. Min.* 128 I'm sure ye ken as weel as me that love's just an unco fykiness o' the mind.

Filament. Add: **2. b.** *Astr.* A narrow thread-like streamer of the sun's corona.

a 1869 J. Nasmyth in Duncan *Midnight Sky* 224 The filaments in question are seen..at the edges of the luminous surface. 1871 *English Mechanic* 24 Nov. 243/1 The chromosphere is surmounted by filaments like brilliant hairs. 1902 *Encycl. Brit.* XXVII. 630/2 The drawings in the volume quoted show its polar rays, wings, interlacing filaments, and rifts as they are now known to be, as well as the forms and details of the prominences.

5. *attrib.*, as *filament battery*, *current*.

1919 *Radio Rev.* Oct. 47 The filament battery is used to supply the anode circuit voltage, as well as for lighting the filament. 1921 W. H. Eccles *Contin. Wave Wireless Telegr.* I. 266 The filament current and the length of the filament which could be used directly on a 10-volt battery at a temperature of 2,300° K. 1923 *Harmsworth's Wireless Encycl.* 922/1 *Filament battery*, expression used to describe all types of batteries used for energizing the filament of a valve employed in receiving from another wireless apparatus.

Filaria (filē·riă). [mod.L., f. L. *filum* thread.] A member of the genus *Filaria* of threadworms. Also *attrib.*

1883 P. Manson *Filaria Sanguinis Hominis* 51 Filarial periodicity is an adaptation of the habits of the filaria to those of the mosquito. 1886 C. Scott *Sheep-farming* 94 This second growth of grass, from the droppings of previous stock on the same land, often harbours the germs of various diseases, and particularly those of filaria and tapeworm. 1897 Mary Kingsley *W. Africa* 686, I have seen the eyes of natives simply swarming with these filariæ. 1897 *Daily News* 8 Feb. 6/2 From its decaying body the filaria larvæ escape into the water. 1901 L. O. Howard *Mosquitoes* 141 The Filaria embryos..lose their hyaline envelope. 1932 *Nature* CIX. 379/1 The filarias and their allies, which live in the connective tissues.

Filariasis (filērĭə·sis). *Path.* [f. mod.L. *Filaria + -asis.] A disease caused by the presence of filariæ in the blood and lymph vessels. Also **Filario·sis** (see quot. 1888).

1888 *Brit. Med. Jrnl.* 29 Sept. 728/2 The term 'filariosis' [Dr. Lancereaux] applies to the entire group of pathological conditions resulting from infection of the organism by the *filaria sanguinis hominis*. 1895 *Ibid.* 20 July 160/1 Dr. Austin Flint..advocates the use of methylene blue in chyluria and filariasis. 1907 *Philippine Jrnl. Sci.* II. 1 The rarity of filariasis in the Philippines.

Filasse (fila·s). [Fr., = tow. Cf. *Fillis.] Vegetable fibre prepared for manufacture.

1858 Simmonds *Dict. Trade*. 1895 *Daily News* 3 Dec. 2/3 Ramie, whose fibre produces a substance called filasse, similar to flax.

File, *sb.* [2] Add:

7. d. An individual soldier.

1903 *Med. Record* 7 Feb. 227 (Cent. D. Suppl.) The poor file who has to carry it, as well as his gun and various other accoutrements. 1916 Boyd Cable *Action Front* 105 'Dusty Miller', the next file on his left,..spoke to him.

11. (sense 4) *file copy*, *cover*; *file-closer* (earlier U.S. example); **file mark,** 'the note indorsed by a clerk or recording officer upon a document filed, usually consisting of the word *filed* and the date of filing' (Cent. Dict.).

1836 J. Hildreth *Dragoon Campaigns Rocky Mts.* I. vi. 48 Next in order of inspection came the adjutant, and, commencing at the right of the line, 'told off' the battalion by equal troops, the subalterns taking their stations in the rank of *file-closers. 1899 *Daily News* 23 Jan. 4/7 Prudent swains might find a *file copy extremely useful in general emergencies. 1909 *Daily Chron.* 2 Sept. 4/7 The file copy of 'The Daily Chronicle' of the same date. 1930 D. L. Sayers *Strong Poison* vi, I don't think you could get a first edition in London for love or money. We have nothing here but our own file copies. 1925 in E. F. Norton *Fight for Everest, 1924* 349 A few *file covers are useful to keep the correspondence on various subjects separate.

File (fi·lė), *sb.* [3] Also **fileadh, filidh.** [Gaelic *file*, *fileadh*, *filidh* bard, poet.] The name given in Irish to one of the orders of Druids.

1876 *Encycl. Brit.* V. 303/1 The *Fili* truly represents the *Ouáteis*, or vates, who formed one of the orders of Druids, mentioned by Strabo. 1880 *Ibid.* XIII. 250/2 The *filid*, whom we shall conventionally call bards..were part of the transformed Druidic order...An ollam fili, the highest grade of the order, was entitled to a large retinue of pupils. 1898 Heron *Celtic Ch.* 30 Entrance into the ranks of the Ollamhs and the Fileadh (or poets).

File, *v.* [3] **4. c.** *U.S.* Add: Also with *on*.

1871 E. Eggleston in *Scribner's Monthly* II. 254 The half-breed who had 'filed on' the claim alongside Lindsley's.

Filet (fi·lėt). Also **fillet.** [a. F. *filet* thread.] A kind of net or lace having a square mesh. Also *attrib.*, as *filet lace*, *net*, *veiling*.

[1882 Caulfeild & Saward *Dict. Needlew.* 233/1 Guipure d'Art.—In this lace, also known as Filet Brodé and Filet Guipure, we have the modern revival of the Opus Filatorium.] 1904 *Technol. & Sci. Dict.* (ed. Goodchild & Tweney), *Fillet ground*.., a net with absolutely square holes, similar to canvas, but more defined and 'lacey' in appearance. Made upon all descriptions of lace machinery. 1907 *Westm. Gaz.* 9 Mar. 13/2 The lace might be of cream silk filet. 1907 *Daily Chron.* 25 June 8/3 The new filet designs. 1908 *Westm. Gaz.* 8 Aug. 13/2 The square spotted filet veiling. *Ibid.* 28 Dec. 5/1 A brown filet net trimmed with small rosettes of velvet. 1909 *Daily Chron.* 6 July 4/4 She's got on a sort of filet-lace. I thought they went out with the Georges. 1931 *Evening Standard* 29 Jan. 5/3 Fadeless artificial silk filet net.

Filibuster, *sb.* Add: **4.** An act of obstruction in a legislative assembly. *U.S.*

1915 *Morn. Post* 13 Feb. 8/3 It has been decided..to suspend the filibuster in order to attend to important appropriations. 1917 *Daily Chron.* 5 Mar. 1/7 The bill..was talked to death. Its last hours were spent in a filibuster against Senator Lafollette. 1923 E. F. Wyatt *Invis. Gods* III. iii. 121 There was a three hours' filibuster against the civil service clause.

Filibuster, *v.* **2.** (Earlier examples.)

1863 *Congress. Globe* 29 Jan. 607/3 He was not engaged.. in voting with the filibustering gentlemen. *Ibid.* 20 Feb. 1134/1 His friends filibustered all night in this hall.

Filibusterism. *U.S.* (Earlier example.)

1854 *California Pioneer* Jan. (Bartlett) Every foot of Mexican soil is now under the dominion, language, laws, usages, and liturgy of fillibusterism.

Filicic (fili·sik), *a.* *Chem.* [f. L. *filic-*, *filix* fern + -ic.] Pertaining to or derived from ferns. *Filicic acid*, the dibutyric ether of phoroglucin, obtained from the rhizome of the common male fern. Hence **Fi·licin, Filici·nic** *a.* (see quots.).

1886 *Buck's Handbk. Med. Sci.* III. 65/1 The most characteristic ingredient of Male Fern is filicic acid. 1889 *Jrnl. Chem. Soc.* LVI. 54 Filicic acid..has the composition $C_{14}H_{16}O_5$. 1892 *Ibid.* LXII. I. 380 Experiments show that the poisonous properties of fern extract are due to an amorphous substance which is the true filicic acid. The acid is readily converted into its lactone, by simply boiling its ethereal solution. The lactone is named filicin. 1898 *Ibid.* LXXIV. I. 41 By heating filicin (filicic acid)..phenol, phloroglucinol, and a new acid, filicinic acid, $C_{11}H_{14}O_4$, were obtained.

Filing, *vbl. sb.* [3] Add: **c.** *attrib.*, as *filing cabinet*, *case*.

1911 H. S. Harrison *Queed* xxv. 329 West went to a *filing cabinet in the corner of the room. 1930 *Daily Express* 6 Nov. 3/2 There are scores of new type-writers..and filing cabinets, telephone instruments and..telephone boxes for the use of the ninety delegates and their staffs. 1911 H. Quick *Yellowstone N.* ii. 32, I was over at the *filing-cases.

Filio-pietistic (fi·li,opəi,ėti·stik), *a.* [f. L. *filius* son + Pietistic.] Marked by excess of filial piety. (*contemptuous.*)

1893 C. F. Adams *Massachusetts* 49 The historians of the Massachusetts filio-pietistic school. 1897 *Q. Rev.* Apr. 532 The 'filio-pietistic' school [of American historians]. 1902 *Daily Chron.* 19 June 4/1 The 'filio-pietistic' spirit of the New England writers in American history.

Filipinize (fi·lipinəiz), *v.* [f. *Filipino + -ize.] *trans.* To make Philippine in character. Hence **Filipiniza·tion.**

1923 *Glasgow Herald* 28 Apr. 8 The administrative services have been almost completely Filipinised. 1924 *Life & Work* Feb. 30/1 A Dual Government for eight years marked by a sweeping Filipinisation of the services. *Ibid.* 31/1 A Reserve Fund of 41 million dollars was handed over by the Americans to the Filipinised Government.

Filipino (filipī·no). [Sp., f. (*las Islas*) *Filipinas* the Philippine islands.] A native of the Philippine islands, especially one of Spanish or mixed blood. Also **Filipina** (-ī·nā) fem.

1898 *Daily News* 16 Dec. 4/6 Though there may be no guarantee of American citizenship for the Filippinos, the islands will become a part of the Union. 1902 *Encycl. Brit.* XXXI. 668/2 Filipinos had for generations been ordained in the priesthood. *a* 1909 'O. Henry' *Roads of Destiny* xxi. 352 A Southerner is as good as a Filipino any day.

attrib. 1902 *Encycl. Brit.* XXXI. 668/2 Ever ready to join issue against any Filipino movement. 1918 Farrow *Dict. Mil. Terms*, *Filipino ration*, the ration for use of Filipino scouts, consisting of 70 per cent of fresh beef or canned meat, 20 per cent of bacon, and 10 per cent of fish.

Fill, *sb.* [1] Add: **2. b.** (Earlier examples.)

1850 *Congress. Globe* Apr., App. 531/1 It was like..making deep cuts and large fills with a view to construct a railroad. 1873 J. H. Beadle *Undevel. West* xxiv. 507 There is not.. a difficult 'cut' or 'fill' for over two hundred miles.

c. In Poker: A hand in which every card helps to complete the set, as a flush, or 'run'; a full hand, or 'full house'.

1887 Stuart Cumberland *Queen's Highway* 276 If I drew for a 'fill' I 'filled', it is true, only to find that some one at the table had drawn a 'full hand' of a higher denomination.

Fill, *sb.* [2] **1.** (Later U.S. examples.) Now *dial.*: see Eng. Dial. Dict.

1845 D. Webster *Priv. Corr.* (1856) II. 202 He could not follow them any more than a dray-horse can jump out of the fills. 1849 D. Nason *Jrnl.* 34 They..set their feet upon the fills, and jog off.

Fill, *v.* Add:

1. f. In Poker: To complete (a 'full house', flush, straight, etc.) by drawing the necessary cards; also, to improve (one's hand) by drawing complementary cards: *intr.* or *absol.*, to make a flush, etc.; also, (of the flush, etc.) to become complete.

1882 *Poker* 31 Scott drew to 'fill a straight and a flush both'. 1885 [in Dict., sense 1 c]. 1887 Stuart Cumberland *Queen's Highway* 279 By-and-by I found myself with three kings in my hand, and hoping to 'fill' I took two cards. Chance favoured me, and I 'filled'. 1889 R. Guerndale *Poker Bk.* 25 To fill your hand, to improve it by the draw. 1895 'Templar' *Poker Manual* 43 Sometimes the ante-man or the straddler will come in, if there has been no raise, on three to a straight or flush, drawing two cards. Such hands rarely fill. 1901 D. Curtis *Sci. Draw Poker* 56 If the three cards held be the Queen, Jack and nine it is evident that either the ten and eight, or the King and ten, would fill. *Ibid.* 78 Theoretically, the Flush should be filled oftener than the Straight. *Ibid.* 79 If B then fills he is getting 11 to 1. 1913 A. B. Loucher *Poker* 13 The next process is that of drawing to fill the hands.

3. c. *intr.* Of the eyes: To fill with tears.

1871 *Two Little Bruces* ix, 'I'm..tired..', said Clemmie, with filling eyes. 1905 *Westm. Gaz.* 14 Jan. 2/3 The blue-grey eyes filled as the girl got quietly into bed.

d. Of a horse's legs: To become œdematous. Also *pass.*

1907 *The Horse* (ed. J. W. Axe) VI. 364 Œdema..frequently occurs in the legs of horses, when they are said to 'fill'. *Ibid.* VIII. 380 Some, which are commonly spoken of as 'filled' legs, are generally the outcome of slight temporary disturbance of the general system.

7. c. *To fill the bill*: see *Bill *sb.* [3] 8 c.

12. a. (Later U.S. example.)

1836 *Congress. Globe* Jan., App. 50/2 From age to age, they [*sc.* the negroes] have filled this saying ['Cursed be Canaan'].

c. (Earlier and later examples.)

1860 *Richmond Enquirer* 2 Nov. 1/7 The Executive of the State is making the most strenuous efforts to fill the orders for arms that come to him from all parts of the State. 1926 D. L. Colvin *Prohibition in U.S.* 171 During the campaign he filled one hundred and twenty-five speaking engagements.

14. b. To put or throw *into* (a receptacle) by way of filling it.

1884 *Encycl. Brit.* XVII. 742 Measured quantities..of [oil-seed] meal are filled into woollen bags. 1906 *Springfield Weekly Republ.* 12 Jan. 13 The New Englander curses gold mining. Billions of good, hard New England cash have been filled into those little black holes.

15. Fill in. d. *To fill in the time*: to occupy oneself during a period of inaction.

1905 W. Bodie *Bodie Bk.* 135 It is simply to fill in the time while I am deciding how to act.

Filled, *ppl. a.* **1.** (Add example, = stuffed.)

1843 Carlton *New Purchase* viii. 51 Why should we trespass on patience with the account of..steaks, filled chickens, plum puddings, and the curious dish of what-nots?

Filler [1]. Add: **1.** (In mining.)

1883 Gresley *Gloss. Coal-m.*, *Filler*, one who fills at a working place or in a stall. 1921 *Dict. Occup. Terms* (1927) § 042 *Filler*.., shovels coal into trams or tubs or upon conveyor at coal face. 1928 *Observer* 12 Feb. 21/4 The full effect of the reduction will be felt only by the hewers, fillers, and a few others.

c. A filling machine or apparatus.

1895 *Army & Navy Co-op. Soc. Price List* 15 Sept. 252/2 Boiler Fillers, galvanized, 2 gall. *Ibid.* 309 Oil Fillers, 1 pint. 1901 *Daily Chron.* 10 Sept. 9/1 Mineral Waters.—Experienced respectable young man, accustomed Riley's filler.

2. (Earlier U.S. example.) Also in *Forestry* (see quot. 1916) and in various technical uses applied to objects, compositions, etc. employed to fill gaps or to bring something to a required solidity, etc.

1874 *Congress. Rec.* 10 Jan. 558/1 They will not give beyond so much for a certain class of fillers and a certain class of wrapper. 1895 *Street Railway Jrnl.* Apr. 252 'Filler' wire strand, consisting of 19 wires of the same size with the small wires inserted so as to make the outer wires of the strand tangent to the circumscribed circle. 1904 Sabin *Paint & Varnish* (1917) 406 The very best filler that can ever be put on wood is a good varnish. 1904 *Technol. & Sci. Dict.* (ed. Goodchild & Tweney), *Filling up*, the process of bringing a surface to a level before painting or between the application of the coats..A good filler for a plastered surface is made by mixing fine plaster of Paris, whiting, and warm size. 1904 *Electr. Rev.* 11 Sept. 450 (Cent. D. Suppl.) The floor framing consists of six sills, the four centre ones being six-inch 'I' beams with wood fillers extending the entire length of car. 1916 J. W. Toumey *Seeding & Planting* 70 When the original cost of the seeding or planting can be materially reduced by the use of so-called fillers, i.e. inexpensive species which serve to occupy a portion of the area, but which are removed in the early thinnings.

Filler [3] (filē·ɹ). [Magyar *fillér*.] A Hungarian coin, the hundredth part of a krona.

1904 *Statesman's Year-Bk.* 416 Nickel:—The twenty-heller (20-fillér) piece. 1927 *Observer* 9 Oct. 11/3 Buyers of the fifty-filler 'Trianon' brooch. 1928 *Ibid.* 15 Apr. 12 Nádosy earned four *filler* a day.

Filleting, *vbl. sb.* Add: **3.** *Spinning.* = Fillet *sb.* [1] 3.

1884 W. S. B. McLaren *Spinning* 81 Leather filleting with very strong teeth set in it.

Filling, *vbl. sb.* **3.** (Earlier U.S. example.) Also, in cigar-making: see quots.

1812 *Niles' Weekly Reg.* II. 9/1 Much of it [*sc.* wool]..may be wrought into..worsted chain or warp for woollen weft or fillings. 1864 *Congress. Globe* 3 June 2706/3 Cigars are made of Connecticut grown wrappers and the best qualities filled with Cuba filling. 1898 *Westm. Gaz.* 15 Dec. 2/1 'Fillins! What may they be?' 'Why, they're the inside of noo cigars, of course.' 1902 *Chambers's Jrnl.* May 302/2 Each leaf will give on an average two 'wrappers' or outside covers for cigars and when used for such the remainder of the leaf is used for 'filling'.

4. filling-engine (see quot.); **filling-station,** a depot for the supply of petrol, oil, etc., to motorists; a petrol station.

1874 Knight *Mech. Dict.*, *Filling-engine..., a machine in which waste and floss silk from the..silk-machinery is disentangled, and the fibers laid parallel. 1928 J. N. Hall *Mid-Pacific* viii. § 4. 173, I should not be surprised to learn that there is now a *filling-station or a moving-picture theater on the very spot where this scene took place. 1929 *Chicago Tribune* 22 Jan. 6/1 They robbed four gasoline filling stations. 1929 R. R. Moton *What the Negro Thinks* 213 In that same city a Negro cannot get gas at a filling station patronized by whites.

Fillis (fi·lis). Also **phillis.** [Variant of *Filasse.] A kind of loosely-twisted string, made of hemp (*hemp fillis*) or of jute (*jute fillis*), used by horticulturists as a tying material.

1900 *Oxford rope-dealer's price-list*, Fillis, Hemp, and Jute.

Film, *sb.* Add:

3. b. *Photog.* Now *esp.* such a coating or layer of gelatin or collodion mounted on a flexible sheet of celluloid, and made either in the form of a roll containing several exposures, or into a pack (see *film pack* in *7 b).

1890 [in Dict.]. 1902 *Encycl. Brit.* XXXI. 687/2 Instead of glass plates, flexible films of celluloid and other materials are available in single sheets like plates, or in rolls enclosed in opaque paper. 1903 Watkins *Watkins Man.* 50 The great convenience of daylight changing with rollable films. 1918 *Photo-Miniature* XV. Mar. (Gloss.) s.v., Roll film, flat or cut film. 1919 *Brit. Jrnl. Phot. Almanac* 244 Autographic film..is one by which the title of the subject can be impressed on each section of the film by the action of light.

c. A celluloid roll of film used in the production of cinema pictures.

1897 C. M. Hepworth *Anim. Photogr.* 60 In a short time commercial cinematographic films will be as good in their way as the best lantern slides on the market. *Ibid.* 99 Cinematograph films are usually manipulated in the dark-room. 1901 *Brit. Jrnl. Photogr.* 738/1 No attempt has yet been made to make a national collection of cinematograph films. 1907 C. Urban *Cinematograph* 22 Every piece of exposed film that does not reach the depository is effectively destroyed. 1910 *Punch* 15 June 433/1 Messrs. Pathé, who have conceived the idea of showing the news of the week on films at the cinematograph theatres. 1911 *Ibid.* 20 Dec. 464/3 The Latest Films...Mr. J. W. H. T. Douglas making two runs. (Film 1,800 yards long). 1928 *Daily Express* 12 Apr. 8/6 A length of film, comprising a number of small photographs, is placed in the transmitter.

d. A cinematographic representation of a story, drama, episode, event, etc.; a cinema performance; *pl.* the cinema, the pictures, the movies. (See also *7 c.)

1911 *Times* 22 Sept. 6/2 The great majority of heroic and patriotic films shown here make United States sailors and roughriders the heroes. 1912 *Field* 14 Sept. 548/2 A cinema film of myself boxing a round or two. 1913 *Punch* 14 May 388/2 When half-a-dozen persons in the same film write letters they all do it in the same hand-writing. 1923 F. A. Talbot *Moving Pictures* 72 The films emanating from the European studios. 1927 *Times* 23 Dec. 11/4 The American film *The King of Kings*.

7. b. In sense 3 b, as *film base*, *-camera*, *-carrier*, *-holder*, *-punch*, *roll*, *side*; **film pack,** an assemblage of cut films fitted in a case or holder.

1889 *Anthony's Photogr. Bull.* II. 361 The film side of the plate. 1890 *Ibid.* III. 22 Where a film roll is used, one is tempted to make a great many utterly useless pictures. *Ibid.* 312 We have to use 'film carriers' which up to date have been complicated, unsafe. 1900 *Westm. Gaz.* 10 May 9/2 Nine hand-cameras out of every ten are film-cameras. 1903 *Brit. Jrnl. Photogr.* 19 June 490/2 The Film Pack consists of a light tight sheath made of black press board, with an opening in one side corresponding in size to the exposure, into which are folded thirteen strips of black, chemically pure paper..; each of twelve of these..has fastened to the inner side a sheet of film. 1918 *Photo-Miniature* XV. Mar. (Gloss.), *Film Pack*, a cardboard or metal holder containing, usually, 12 cut films so placed in it that, by pulling in succession projecting paper tabs, the films are brought into position for exposure in the camera and then carried in turn to the back of the pack...A magazine film-holder. 1923 F. A. Talbot *Moving Pictures* 62 It was necessary to discover.. a new film-base. Cellulose could not be avoided as the basic constituent. *Ibid.* 88 The film-punch for indicating exposure changes upon the edge of the film in a camera.

c. In sense *3 d, as *film actress*, *fan* (see *Fan *sb.*[2]), *-hero*, *-producer*, *-super*, *trade*, etc.; **film-goer,** a frequenter of the cinema; **film-star,** a star actor for the cinema.

1914 *Even. News* 8 Oct. 2/1 It is 'up to' the American film trade to see that the evidence of the camera gets a fair reception. 1918 H. Croy *How Motion Pictures are Made* vi. 134 The director..gives him what might be called his film cues. 1920 *Q. Rev.* July 182 The only kind of ending the film-producers can think of for this or any other type of drama. 1921 *Punch* 12 Jan. 21/1 Two leading film actresses have made runaway marriages. 1923 *Weekly Dispatch* 28 Jan. 1 She had become absolutely 'film-struck'. 1923 *Chambers's Jrnl.* Mar. 180/1 A number of very beautiful women have earned untold riches as 'film-stars'. 1924 Galsworthy *White Monkey* II. ii, The lurid professions—film super, or mannequin. 1925 W. Deeping *Sorrell & Son* xv. § 1 He hated crowds, he—the crowd's film-hero. 1927 *Sunday Express* 26 June 4 Every film-goer likes to feel that he is up-to-date in cinema affairs. 1928 *Observer* 15 Apr. 5/4 Filmcraft is little understood.

Hence **Fi·lmdom** [-dom], the realm of cinematographic production and producers; the cinema world.

1927 *Sunday Express* 12 June 18/3 One of filmdom's finest mansions is Pickfair. 1928 *Weekly Dispatch* 15 Apr. 9/1 His remarkably liberal outlook on filmdom.

Film, *v.* Add: **3.** *trans.* **a.** To photograph (moving objects) for use in a mutoscope.

1899 *Westm. Gaz.* 21 Sept. 4/1 Professors of medicine are 'filming' their patients' muscles.

b. To photograph for use in a cinema; to exhibit as a cinematographic production; to put on 'the films' or 'the screen'.

1915 A. S. Neill *Dominie's Log* viii, I have seen *Hamlet* filmed. 1915 *Even. News* 18 Feb. 6 The Monkey's Paw...The Most Thrilling Mystery-Drama Ever Filmed. 1915 Irwin *Men, Women & War* 15 We filmed a Belgian troop of cavalry going into action. 1918 H. Croy *How Motion Pictures are Made* 110 The filming of this is put last to give the carpenters time to complete it. 1920 *Q. Rev.* July 183 Hallo, here's a big success, let's film it! 1920 *Glasgow Herald* 11 Sept. 7 Churchmen are invited to write thrilling Biblical scenarios to be filmed for exhibition at afternoon services.

4. *intr.* To be (well or ill) suited for film-acting or for reproduction on the films.

1928 *Observer* 26 Feb. 20/2 [He] 'films' very well indeed. 1928 *Sunday Dispatch* 22 July 4/2 He had had a film test, at the conclusion of which he was told that he filmed remarkably well.

Filmable (fi·lmăb'l), *a.* [f. *Film *v.* + -able.] Capable of being filmed or adapted to the cinema.

1921 *Glasgow Herald* 25 Mar. 7 Full of 'filmable' incident. 1926 *Spectator* 17 July 88/2 A reason, incidentally, why Dickens is not really filmable. 1928 *Daily Tel.* 25 Sept. 12/5 To find fresh filmable 'material'.

Filmic (fi·lmik), *a.* [f. *Film *sb.* 3 d + -ic.] Of or pertaining to the films.

1930 *Time & Tide* 23 Aug. 1080 They do seem to have an eye for the filmic possibilities of subjects. 1930 *Times Lit. Suppl.* 18 Sept. 728/2 Debating the merits of various types of 'filmic' art.

Filter, *sb.* Add:

3. b. *Photog.* A screen to cut out rays which interfere with correct colour-rendering; = *colour-filter* (see *Colour *sb.* 18).

1900 [see *Colour *sb.* 18]. 1912 *E. J. Wall's Dict. Photogr.* (ed. 9) 335 Most makers of orthochromatic..plates also supply filters specially adapted for use with their plates.

c. A device used in telephony and wireless reception for the elimination or attenuation of alternating currents of undesired frequencies or undue prominence.

1920 *Radio Rev.* July 505 By a combination of the two types of filter [*sc.* infra- and ultra-] only currents between the two frequency limits are transmitted. *Ibid.*, When using a number of such filters thermionic valve amplifiers may be connected between successive filters to prevent reaction of the output circuit on to the input circuit. 1923 *Exper. Wireless* Dec. 149/1 An electric filter is an apparatus which enables us to separate into its various parts an electric current made up of a combination of different frequencies. 1923 *Harmsworth's Wireless Encycl.* 933 A filter is generally employed with high-frequency amplifiers for preventing signals from other stations than the one sought being amplified.

5. filter cell (see quot.); **filter circuit** = 3 c above; **filter-condenser,** a condenser forming part of a wave trap or filter circuit; **filter-paper** (examples); **filter-passer,** a filter-passing bacillus; **filter-passing** *a.*, (of a virus or bacterium) so small as not to be arrested by the finest filter.

1928 Kingzett *Chem. Encycl.* 278 **Filter cell*, a proprietary infusorial earth used as a filtering and decolorizing agent. 1920 *Radio Rev.* July 505 A number of special *filter circuits designed with the object of allowing certain frequencies to pass and cutting out others. 1924 *Exper. Wireless* July 614/2 Systems of multiple amplifiers and filter circuits..for the purpose of suppressing unduly prominent frequencies. 1923 *Harmsworth's Wireless Encycl.* 934/1 The *filter condenser is varied until the interfering sound is eliminated. 1929 R. L. Duncan & Drew *Radio Telegr.* 507 Filter condensers are of the fixed type and employ either a mica or paper dielectric. 1849 D. Campbell *Inorg. Chem.* 18 A few grains of recently-heated spongy platinum, in a small piece of *filter paper. 1892 *Photogr. Ann.* II. 109 Dried on pure filter paper. 1919 *Nature* CIV. 210/2 The infective agents of the common exanthemata..are at some period of their life-history so small as to be included amongst the '*filter-passers'. 1930 *Morning Post* 24 Nov. 3 'Ultra-microscopic' or '*filter passing' virus.

Filter, *v.* Add: **1. d.** In *Telephony* and *Wireless* (see *Filter *sb.* 3 c).

1924 *Discovery* Mar. 72/1 It is an extremely instructive experience to listen, first to an unfiltered, and then to a filtered transmission [of wireless telephony]. *Ibid.*, The filtering out of atmospherics has already been carried to a high level of success..at Ongar.

Filterable (fi·ltərăb'l), *a.* Also **filtrable.** [f. Filter *v.* + -able.] Able to pass through the pores of a fine porcelain filter.

1913 Dorland *Med. Dict.* (ed. 7), Filtrable. 1922 *Glasgow Herald* 21 Feb. 10 A number of animal diseases besides foot-and-mouth disease are caused by filterable viruses. 1928 *Daily Tel.* 10 July 9/4 Dr. Gye's theory of the causation of cancer by a filtrable virus.

Filtering, *vbl. sb.* **2.** Add: **filtering-bed,** a filter-bed; **filtering-cloth,** material for filtering.

1908 *Westm. Gaz.* 24 Jan. 5/4 The filtering-beds of the New River works at Hornsey. 1909 *Ibid.* 23 Feb. 2/1 Filtering-cloths.

Filthy, *a.* **6.** quasi-*adv.* (Later U.S. example.)

1843 *Knickerbocker Mag.* XXI. 122 His trousers [were] 'filthy dirty' and pulled up above the tops of his boots.

Fin, *sb.* Add:

3. d. A fin-like appendage to a ship's bottom; a fin-keel; also, a centreboard.

1885 *Marine Engineer* 1 Apr. 8/1 But it is possible to fit fins, flappers, or shutters.., to the run of a ship so as to be flush with the plates. 1893 *Outing* (U.S.) XXII. 147/1 The fin is of Tobin bronze, one-quarter inch think, six feet long on upper edge. 1897 *Ibid.* XXX. 468/1 Their hulls..are enormously strong, so as to restrain the heavy weight of the fin.

e. In aircraft (see quots.).

1836 *Mag. Dom. Econ.* I. 92 There is no fulcrum upon which any oar, paddle, fin, wing or any thing else, can possibly act. 1852 *Illustr. London News* XX. 468/1 By means of the handles at the outer sides, the apparatus contained in the case can be turned round at pleasure, and the position of the fins altered, thus enabling the operator to steer the balloon. 1910 C. C. Turner *Aerial Navigation of Today* iv. 54 Leppig's Balloon, 1812. It was to be driven by a fin propeller, worked by hand. 1916 Barber *Aeroplane Speaks* 137 *Fin*, additional keel-surface, usually mounted at the rear of an aeroplane. 1920 *Discovery* Mar. 78/1 An elliptically-shaped gas-bag provided with a conical-shaped tail filled with air, to which a rudder and stabilising fins are attached.

Fin, *v.* Add: **4.** *To fin it* or *fin its way*: to swim, as a fish.

a 1861 T. Winthrop *Canoe & Saddle* (1862) 134 In midsummer salmon fin it along the reaches of Whulge. 1894 *Outing* (U.S.) XXIV. 140/1 For this [stump] the rascal [trout] steers, as fast as he can fin his way.

Finalism (fəi·năliz'm). See Dict. s.v. Final *a.* and *sb.* Add:

1909 Sorley *Interpr. Evol.* 24 'The organization of nature', says Kant, 'has in it nothing analogous to any causality we know'. It is not mechanism; nor, again, is it finalism. 1920 Pringle-Pattison *Idea of God* 370 He develops his own account of 'creative' evolution in contrast with the two rival theories of mechanism and finalism.

Finalist (see after Final). Add:

2. Any of the competitors that are left in for the final contest (see Final *sb.* 2 c).

1898 *Bury Times* 2 Nov. 2/3 Two of the finalists,.. just before the race started, publicly appealed to the Baths Committee to withdraw the objectionable clause. 1902 *Westm. Gaz.* 1 July 4/3 The finalists in the Gentlemen's Doubles Championships. 1906 *Daily Chron.* 25 May 1/7 The finalists in the Amateur Golf Championship.

Finance, *sb.* [1] **8.** Add: **finance bill** (see quot.).

1901 Courtney *Working Const. U. K.* 24 What used to be called the Customs and Inland Revenue Bill, received in 1894 the name of the Finance Bill.

Find, *v.* Add: **18.** Also simply *found* = all found. *U.S.*

1853 B. F. Taylor *Jan. & June* (1871) 273 A story..he wouldn't have whispered for twelve dollars a month 'and found'. 1923 'B. M. Bower' *Parowan Bonanza* iv. 48, I got him cheap for yuh. Three dollars and found.

19. d. In Harrow School phraseology (see quot. 1905). Also as *sb.* (see quot. 1899).

1899 *Captain* I. 471/1 A 'find' consists of a number of Sixth Form boys, who are privileged to have their breakfast and tea together in one of their own rooms. 1905 Vachell *The Hill* x. 218 You will find together. Of course Scaife can find with you, if you wish. *Footnote.* 'Finding' is the privilege, accorded to the Sixth Form, of having breakfast and tea served in their own rooms instead of in Hall. *Ibid.* xi. 244 They no longer shared No. 7..but they still 'found' together.

20. Find out. e. *absol.* or *intr.* To make a discovery; to discover a fact, the truth, etc.; also with prep. *about*.

1862 G. Macdonald *D. Elginbrod* II. ii, 'I don't like the pigs—I don't know where they are.' 'Well, we must find out.' 1881 Mrs. Riddell *Senior Partner* xxxi, 'Who might that one be?' 'I am thinking ye'll have to find out for yourself.' 1893 Mary E. Mann *Summer Shade* xix, 'He has found out about Mrs. Le Grice's bill,' said Lally to herself. 1894 Beatrice Harraden *Varying Moods, Umbrella Mender*, Perhaps death brings peace. I shall soon find out about that. 1913 Gallichan *Like Stars that Fall* xi, Supposing your husband found out? There might be a devil of a row. 1927 May Sinclair *Anthony Waring* xviii, Tony determined to find out. Aunt or no aunt, he would go to her.

Fine, *a.* Add: **7. f.** In colloq. expressions such as *to cut fine*, *to run fine*, with advb. force: With a very slight margin of time or space.

1890, 1892 [see Run *v.* 36 d]. 1899 *Chambers's Jrnl.* 30 Sept. 694/1 If by..chance I was cutting it fine. 1908 *Pearson's Weekly* 5 Mar. 606/2 Running it fine.

g. *Cricket.* Less square with the wickets and nearer the line of flight of the ball.

1895 *Sunlight Year Bk. Sports* 13 The batsman is in a better position for cutting late or 'fine'.

B. *sb.* *pl.* **e.** In various technical senses.

1880 J. Dunbar *Pract. Papermaker* 14 Fines consist of fine white cottons [*sc.* rags]. 1904 *Westm. Gaz.* 28 July 3/2 Breaking up much waste rock into fines. 1908 *Ibid.* 22 Oct. 13/1 All fines [= fine ores] are discharged into the tank over the head of the funnel with great force.

D. *Comb.* **3. fine-axe** *v. trans.*, to face (stone) to a smooth surface by tapping with a mason's axe; **fine-etcher** (see quot. 1921).

1886 H. C. Seddon *Builder's Wk.* 82 *Fine axed is a more careful description of single axed work. 1895 *Daily News* 18 June 6/4 All kinds of Scotch granites, polished and fine-axed. 1921 *Dict. Occup. Terms* (1927) § 526 **Fine etcher*.., an experienced etcher capable of undertaking all etching processes except line etching.

Fine champagne (fīn ʃampan'). [Fr., = eau-de-vie *fine* de la *Champagne* 'fine brandy of Champagne' (of the district of Angoumois and Saintonge).] Old liqueur brandy. Also abbreviated *fine* in fine (de la) maison, old brandy 'of the house'.

1868 Sala Notes & Sk. Paris Exhib. 167 We shall require sixty bottles of cognac, *fine champagne*. 1875 Vizetelly Wines of World 19 The Enrageat,..Folle Blanche, or crazy vine, which prevails so extensively in the Deux-Charentes, and from whose fruit *fine champagne* cognac is distilled. 1928 A. E. W. Mason Prisoner in Opal xxiii, So! Some coffee and some *fine de la maison*? 1928 Observer 11 Mar. 12/2 The wine waiter has had the habit of insidiously proposing a 'fine maison' to the customer who wants an old brandy.

Fine-cut, *a.* and *sb.* [Fine *adv.*]

A. *adj.* Finely cut. (See Fine *a.* D. 3.) *U.S.*

1878 Congress. Rec. 5 June 4164/2 Gentlemen of fortune..can very well afford..to chew their fine-cut tobacco.

B. *sb.* A kind of fine-cut tobacco. *U.S.*

1854 H. H. Riley Puddleford 100 (Th.) He chewed a paper of fine-cut every day. 1864 Congress. Globe 3 June 2707/3 On tobacco, cavendish, plug, twist, fine cut, and manufactured of all descriptions. *a* 1909 'O. Henry' Roads of Destiny xxi. 355 Haven't got a chew of fine-cut on you, have you?

Fine gentleman. Add: Also *attrib.* or as *adj.* Hence **Fine-ge·ntlemanism, Fine-ge·ntlemanship.**

1866 Athenæum 24 Nov. 676/2 The evanescent air of fine gentlemanism. 1874 L. Carr Judith Gwynne xvii, That boredom is one of the necessary traits of fine gentlemanism. 1883 Contemp. Rev. June 899 The spirit of fine gentlemanship. 1928 Smart Set Sept. 49/1 Your fine-gentleman airs sit ridiculously on you.

Fine hair, *sb.* [Fine *a.* 7.] (See quot. 1901.)

1897 C. T. Davis Manuf. Leather (ed. 2) 109 Besides the hair proper, the animal hide is covered with a short down, similar to what is found on the arms and legs of the human body. This down is known to the tanners as fine-hair. 1901 Addyman tr. Villon's Leather Industry 359 *Fine hair*, long, fine but coarser than wool, as the rabbit.

Hence **Fine-hair** *v. trans.*, to remove the fine hair or down from (a skin).

1897 C. T. Davis Manuf. Leather (ed. 2) 158 The best time for fine-hairing is after the drenching, as the grain of the skins is then cleaner and the fine hairs more easily seen. 1903 H. R. Procter Leather Manuf. 180 After bating, the hides are usually 'worked' ('scudded', 'fine-haired') on the beam, to remove dirt and grease.

Fine-hand, *a.* [Fine *a.* 7 d.] Written in a fine or delicate hand. Also *fig.*

1845 Caroline M. Kirkland Western Clearings 154, I want a fine-hand copy. 1846 Knickerbocker Mag. XXVII. 279 How many recollections of early school-days,..of coarse and fine-hand pens. 1878 B. F. Taylor Between Gates 228 From this rock the horse-trail climbs to the right for Nevada Fall and a fine-hand affair, a foot-trail, trends up to the left of Vernal Fall.

Finely, *adv.* 8. Add: *finely-axed*, fine-axed (*Fine *a.* D. 3).

1902 Daily Chron. 13 Oct. 7/1 The pedestal is of finely-axed Kemnay granite.

Finery[1]. Add: 4. *Comb.*: **finery-ironer, -machinist** (see quots.).

1895 Westm. Gaz. 16 Apr. 3/2 Of the ironers: four made incomplete weeks; one worked 72,..and one (the finery ironer) 75½. 1908 Daily Chron. 12 June 9/6 Laundry.—Wanted finery ironers. 1921 Dict. Occup. Terms (1927) § 918 *Finery machinist*, general term for any person ironing delicate articles by machine in a laundry.

Fine-tooth, *a.* [Fine *a.* 7 d. Cf. *fine-toothed* (Fine *a.* D. 3).] Of a comb: Having fine and closely-set teeth. Also in fig. phrases.

1839 H. Malcom Trav. South-Eastern Asia I. ii. 37 *note*, Friends who wish to make little presents to the Karen Christians, might send fine-tooth combs. 1849 Rep. U.S. Comm. Patents (1850) 267 Improvement in making Ivory fine-tooth Combs. 1878 B. F. Taylor Between Gates 246 As slender in the distance as a fine-tooth comb. 1891 Century Mag. Feb. 595 I'll go through this town like a fine-tooth comb but what I'll find him. 1911 H. S. Harrison Queed xxi. 266 You could scrape this town with a fine-tooth comb without finding anybody of his age that wasn't in the war.

Finetop. *U.S.* [Fine *a.* 7.] *Finetop grass*, the meadow and pasture grass also known as *herds-grass*, etc.

1856 Rep. Mass. Board Agric. I. 26 Redtop, Finetop, Burden's Grass, Dew Grass, Herds Grass of Pennsylvania and Southern States.

Finger, *sb.* Add:

5. a. Also, a quarter of an inch.

1901 J. Black's Carp. & Build., Home Handicrafts 35 The laths should be laid a 'finger', that is, a ¼in. apart.

c. *U.S.* (Earlier and later examples.)

1886 Harper's Mag. Oct. 678/1 Even 'two fingers', said the artist, standing at the bar, had little effect in allaying the impression of terror out there. 1907 Daily Chron. 13 June 4/4 The man who sells his vote for three fingers of whisky or a glass of beer.

8. *esp.* A banana.

1894 [in Dict.]. 1895 Daily News 26 Aug. 5/2 This..is a shorter and stouter plant than the tropical banana, and often bears from 150 to 250 'fingers' in a bunch.

15. **finger-ache,** used symbolically for a slight or negligible pain; **finger-bar** (earlier U.S. examples); **finger-beam** *U.S.*, = *finger-bar*; **finger-berry,** in Queensland, the native loquat, *Rhodomyrtus macrocarpa*; **finger-board,** (*a*) *U.S.*, = Finger-post; (*b*) a gradient post; **finger-grass** (U.S. example); **finger-hold,** something by which the fingers can hold; also *transf.*; **finger-impression, -mark,** now always **finger-print,** with specific reference to the recording by the police of impressions taken from the finger-tips of criminals and suspects; also *attrib.*; hence **finger-print** *v. trans.*, to take the finger-prints of; **finger-spin,** spin imparted to a cricket ball by the fingers, as an element in bowling; also *attrib.*; **finger-work,** (*a*) work executed with the fingers; (*b*) the play of, or manipulation by, the fingers.

1872 Tennyson Gareth & Lynette 86 And thee..Who never knewest finger-ache, nor pang Of wrench'd or broken limb. 1865–6 Trans. Ill. Agric. Soc. VI. 52 Patent Cold Rolled Reaper and Mower *Finger Bars. 1867–9 Ibid. VII. 312 The greatest objections to a joint in the finger-bar of a mower. 1852 Trans. Mich. Agric. Soc. III. 158 Lapping the *finger beam above or below. 1902 Encycl. Brit. XXXII. 109/1 The '*Finger Berry' or 'Native Loquat' (*Rhodomyrtus macrocarpa*) makes a good jam. 1845 in D. Drake Pioneer Life Kentucky ix. 235 At their..forks there were no *finger boards, and not many living fingers to point out the true way. 1883 F. S. Williams Our Iron Roads iv. 95 Gradients..vary considerably as we may see by the finger-boards placed on the lines for the guidance of the engine-driver. 1856 Rep. Mass. Board Agric. I. 85 The stems of the *finger grass are from one to two feet high. 1909 Daily Chron. 21 Aug. 7/4 Wherever it [*sc.* samphire] can get *finger-hold in the rough face of the cliff, it shows in abundance. 1923 A. Train His Children's Children xviii. 219 The relief of him who, having plunged part way down the face of a precipice, has caught a finger-hold in a crevice. 1923 H. L. Wilson Oh, Doctor! xii. 135 'Yes', assented Seaver; 'one of these movie actors that can bite nails in two and throw a horse over a fence and climb up the side of a church with only a finger hold.' 1903 Westm. Gaz. 16 Nov. 5/1 Witness told him that his *finger-impression had been found on a pane of glass on the roof of the building. 1906 Daily Chron. 24 Oct. 1/7 Two men who are so much alike that they can be distinguished only by their finger impressions. 1891 Galton in Proc. Roy. Soc. 28 May 540 Methods of indexing *Finger-Marks. 1891 — in 19th Cent. Aug. 304 *Finger-prints have been proposed over and over again before now as a means of identification. 1903 Daily Chron. 9 Feb. 8/7 The finger-print system of identification. 1905 Westm. Gaz. 7 Feb. 8/2 The finger-print expert from Scotland Yard. 1905 Daily Chron. 4 Apr. 5/6 Three pairs of well-worn gloves ..were used by the thieves to prevent any finger-print clues being left. 1921 Discovery Oct. 259/1 The finger-print archives of the Lyons Police Laboratory. 1905 Daily Chron. 13 Sept. 7/4 A prisoner..seldom objects to being *finger-printed. 1923 Glasgow Herald 2 Nov. 6 Demanding that every new-born child be finger-printed when registered. 1905 Westm. Gaz. 1 July 2/3 Bowlers with plenty of *finger-spin are most likely to take wickets on the mat. 1906 Ibid. 8 May 2/1 Finger-spin bowlers like Schwarz, Faulkner, and Vogler. 1927 Observer 17 Apr. 17/4 [He] only needs more power of finger-spin to be a match-winning bowler. 1849 *finger-work [in Dict., sense 14]. 1906 Practitioner Dec. 826 The great drawback of this treatment is that it..must be minutely carried out, demanding..a great deal of finger-work. 1906 Westm. Gaz. 10 Aug. 3/1 There was never before so clear an exposition of balance, of swing, and of finger-work in bowling. 1927 Observer 29 May 14/5 [His] first recital showed promise...Mozart does not suit his style: it needs better finger-work and not so much arm and body and pedal.

Finger, *v.* Add: 3. Also with *over*.

1853 Kingsley Hypatia xix, Her..splendid jewels, which she had been fingering over as a child might its toys. Ibid. xxvi, She fitted the two pieces together again and again, fingering them over.

6. b. *intr.* To be manipulated with the fingers.

1927 W. W. Bishop Pract. Handbk. Mod. Libr. Catal. 33 The tests of a card are the cleanness and speed with which it 'fingers' in consultation, and the fastness of its color.

Fingerpoll (fi·ŋgəɹpǫl). *S. Africa.* [ad. Afrikaansch *vingerpol*, f. *vinger* finger + *pol* shrub.] A plant, *Euphorbia caput-medusæ*, characterized by a bunch of finger-like growths, and providing a nourishing food for cattle.

1889 Baydon Kloof & Karroo 258 Spent and foundered oxen,..when fed with fingerpoll, regained vitality. 1890 Annie Martin Home Life on Ostrich Farm 58 Another of our many eccentric-looking plants, the *finger-poll*.

Fi·nger-tip. The tip of a finger; *Archæol.* used *attrib.* to designate ornamentation made with the tips of the fingers. Phr. *to the finger-tips* = through one's whole body, 'from top to toe', throughout; *at one's finger-tips* (see Finger *sb.* 3 e).

1842, 1883 [see Finger *sb.* 14]. 1886 Kipling Departmental Ditties 45, I redden to my finger-tips. 1905 Strand Mag. June 702/1 He has at his finger-tips every stroke in the game. 1907 Daily Chron. 21 Jan. 3/5 Alive with science to the finger tips. 1928 Crawford & Keiller Wessex from the Air 10 If it was constructed, as he concludes, by the finger-tip people. Ibid. 200 The fragment of a typical finger-tip urn. 1929 F. Hackett Henry the Eighth viii. 417 He was a magnate to his finger-tips. 1929 Childe Danube in Prehist. 364 Biconical or open urns with finger-tip ornament.

Fingo (fi·ŋgo). Also **fengu.** [f. Kaffir *ama-fengu* destitute people in search of work, f. *fenguza* to seek service.] The designation of certain races formerly occupying the country west and north-east of Durban, Natal, and now of the remnants of these (see quot. 1902).

1836 Grahamstown Jrnl. 109 (Pettman) The Fingoes residing on the missionary station, displayed..considerable firmness and courage. 1850 Appleyard Kafir Lang. 41 *note*, The term *Amafengu* is a conventional national epithet, first applied to the *Fingoes* by the Kafirs, but now in general use amongst themselves. 1883 Encycl. Brit. XVI. 517/1 The South African races, Hottentots and Kaffres, Fingoes and Bechuanas, Basutos and Zulus. 1902 Ibid. XXX. 3/1 The formerly degraded but now respected and civilised Fingos or Fengus, who give their name to the district of Fingoland, and also form the bulk of the population in the Idutywa Reserve.

Finickiness (fi·nikinės). Also **finn-.** [f. Finicky *a.* + -ness.] The quality or condition of being finicky; exceedingly affected or over-fastidious character.

1833 Nyren Yng. Cricketer's Tutor (1902) 114 It was thought a piece of finnikiness by those simple and homely yeomen. 1920 Glasgow Herald 23 Dec. 4 Sensitive to the point of finnickiness.

Finicky, *a.* (Earlier U.S. examples.)

1839 Poe Devil in Belfry Wks. 1865 II. 388 He was really the most finnicky little personage that had ever been seen in Vondervotteimittiss. 1857–8 Trans. Ill. Agric. Soc. (1859) III. 473 We desire to be neither coarse or finicky. 1873 E. Eggleston Myst. Metrop. xxxv. 303 You a'n't so finicky 'bout vittles as you was.

Finify, *v.* (Later U.S. and dial. examples.)

1847 Robb Squatter Life 73 (Bartlett) If this new judge is the slicked up, finefied sort on a character they pictur' him, I don't want to see him. 1891 'C. E. Craddock' in Harper's Mag. Jan. 222/1 They [*sc.* the wimmin] air obleiged ter set out a table all tricked up an' finified off. 1895 Rye E. Anglian Gloss., *Finify*, to be over-nice in doing anything.

Finish, *sb.* Add: 6. *finish fight* U.S., a fight to a finish.

1909 R. A. Wason Happy Hawkins 143 The' ain't nothin' ever satisfies a civilized human except a finish fight.

Finish, *v.* Add: 5. Also with *up*.

1878 Harper's Mag. Nov. 892/2 Shall we finish up and have done with it, with a song at the end? 1902 Machray Night Side London i. 21 Others vanish into the night..finishing up..at some night-club, or in some other den.

d. Of a competitor in a sporting contest: To come to the end of a course or race (in a certain condition or 'place').

1881 [in Dict., sense 5]. 1894 G. Moore Esther Waters ii, He told me..to bring the colt along and finish up close by where he would be standing. 1929 Star 21 Aug. 16/2 Every horse he has backed has finished out of the first three.

Finishment. (Modern U.S. examples.)

1872 E. Eggleston End of World viii. 59 This 'rithmetic preacher can't make a finishment of this sublunary speer by addition. 1873 Leland Egypt. Sketch-Bk. 103, I should say, in finishment of this chapter, that one leaves the dervish performance with mixed emotions.

Finitize (fəi·nəitəiz), *v.* [f. Finite *a.* + -ize.] *trans.* To make finite.

1917 Pringle-Pattison Idea of God xvi. 321 Professor Howison..seems to use the idea of self-consciousness entirely as a principle of separation and exclusion, which finitizes even what he calls 'the Supreme Instance', the 'absolutely perfect mind, or God'. 1930 Monument to St. Augustine 257 In his account of Kant, Hegel reproaches him with a shallow finitizing, whereas Spinoza represents for him an impracticable infinitizing.

Finity. Add more recent example; also semi-*concr.*, an instance of finiteness.

1899 H. Wright Depopulation 57 There seemed no finity to the vista of country the eye followed. 1903 Beatrice Harraden Kath. Frensham ii. x. 199 Infinities which one ..could see were finities blending with each other imperceptibly.

Fink[1] (fiŋk). *S. Africa.* [a. Du. *fink* finch.] Any of various birds of the family *Ploceidæ*.

1896 Clairmonte Africander 2 A flock of long-tailed mousebirds, called *finks*, would dash past to settle in a *rooihout* tree. 1897 Anne Page Afternoon Ride 62 The Kafir fink swaying on the grass.

Fink[2]. *U.S.* 'One who engages as a strike-breaker but is inexperienced in the work to be done' (Funk's Standard Dict. 1928).

Finlander (fi·nlændəɹ). [f. *Finland* + -er[1].] An inhabitant or native of Finland.

1727 P. Kinck in Phil. Trans. XXXV. 357 A Letter to James Theobald, Esq., giving an Account of the Norwegian Finns, or Finlanders. 1808 in Monteith's Narr. Conq. Finland (1854) 53 The Finlander regiments entering the service of His Imperial Majesty shall not be employed against Sweden..during the present war. 1838 Penny Cycl. X. 274/1 The Laplander is of the same extraction as the Finlander, and calls himself a 'Samelada or Same'. 1854 [see Finn]. 1920 Contemp. Rev. Dec. 792 Finnish-speaking Finlanders.

Finney (fi·ni). Local name of finnan haddock. Also **finnie haddie.**

1851 Mayhew Lond. Labour I. 77/1 Smoked or dried haddocks (often called 'finnie haddies'). 1906 Daily Chron. 10 May 1/4 Finneys, kippers, bloaters, 2s. 6d. per box...Fish Docks, Grimsby.

Finno- (fi·no), used as comb. form of Finn or Finnic to designate race combinations and language groups of Finns or Finnish with other elements.

1879 J. S. Keltie in Encycl. Brit. IX. 219/1 The term Finns has a wider application than Finland, being, with its adjective Finnic or Finno-Ugric or Ugro-Finnic, the collective name of the westernmost branch of the great Uralo-Altaic family. 1885 Whitney Ibid. XVIII. 779/2 The nearer relation of the Samoyed is with the Finno-Hungarian. 1888 Keane Ibid. XXIV. 1/1 The Ural-Altaic, Finno-Tatar, or 'Turanian' languages. 1896 — Ethnol. 200 We have in Europe..mixed Finno-Slavs, Slavo-Teutons, Kelto-Teutons, but no Finno-Slav, Slavo-Teutonic or Kelto-Teutonic tongues.

Fin(n)sko, finnesko (fi·nsko). [Norw. *finnsko*, f. *Finn* Finn + *sko* shoe.] In Norway, a boot made of birch-tanned reindeer skin with the hair left on.

1890 tr. Nansen's 1st Crossing Greenland I. 47 The two Lapps had two pair of 'finnesko' each. 1911 R. F. Scott Last Exped. (1923) iv. 103 We have..served out two pairs of finnesko (fur boots) to each traveller. 1928 Daily Tel. 27 Nov. 10/6 Leather boots to replace the finsko which the men were wearing.

Finos (fi·nos), *sb. pl.* [Sp., pl. of *fino* Fine *a.*] Wool of the second grade from the merino sheep.

1887 Bonwick Rom. Wool Trade 56 In 1798 he [*sc.* Sir Joseph Banks] divided the wool into the three classes, after the Spanish method, of *terceros*, the coarsest, *finas* [sic], the middle sort, and *raffinos*, the choicest.

Finsen (fi·nsən). The name of Niels R. *Finsen* (1860–1904), Danish physician, used *attrib.* to designate a certain treatment of skin diseases by actinic rays and apparatus used in applying it.

1902 Brit. Med. Jrnl. 31 May 1324/2 A small ulcerating surface, which resisted treatment by Finsen's light. Ibid. 25 Oct. 1319/2 The pathological changes in the skin produced by the rays from a Finsen lamp. 1903 Ibid. 3 Jan. 24/1 The Finsen treatment in lupus vulgaris. 1907 Practitioner Nov. 721 The Finsen-light treatment of lupus. 1911 Allbutt's Syst. Med. IX. 480 Intra-nasal lupus can be rarely reached with Finsen's apparatus. 1913 Dorland Med. Dict. (ed. 7), *Finsen light*, light consisting principally of the violet and ultra-violet ray.

Fip. *U.S.* (Earlier examples.)

1822 Philad. Freeman's Jrnl. 5 Sept. (Th.) A dispute now commenced between two persons respecting some cents and a 'fip'..: one asserting that there were two 'fips', and the other that there was but one. 1833 Ind. Q. Mag. Hist. XV. 244 He would not let us pass through the fense without a 'fip', that is 4½ cents. 1838 Knickerbocker Mag. XI. 244 A man can always go to an inn with a 'fip' in his pocket, and find a welcome, when he could find one no where else. 1845 S. Judd Margaret ii. vii. 313, I havn't hardly a hair left to my hide, or a pewter fip in my pocket.

Fipenny. Add: **fipenny bit, piece** *U.S.* = Fip.

1836 Southern Lit. Messenger II. 455/1 We give the amount of six such volumes then for forty cents—or one of them for very little more than a fi'penny bit. 1840 W. G. Simms Border Beagles (1855) 252 [The boy had] the tempting reward of a fip-penny piece before him. 1843 Carlton New Purchase xxvii. 253 To lay out even a fippenny-bit must have become a matter for very solemn reflection.

Fir. 4. Add: **fir balsam,** the silver fir of Canada, *Abies balsamea*; **fir sawfly,** *Lophyrus abietis*, especially harmful to the fir tree.

1810 Michaux Arbres I. 18 Sylvir fir,..*Fir balsam,..[or] Balsam of Gilead tree. 1862 T. W. Harris Insects Injur. Veget. (ed. 3) 520 The pine and *fir saw-flies, described by Kollar.

Fire, *sb.* Add:

A. 3. g. *To play with fire*: to trifle with dangerous matters, esp. at the risk of moral disaster.

1887 J. Grant (*title*) Playing With Fire. 1888 Kipling Plain Tales fr. Hills, His Wedded Wife (1890) 150 There is no sort of use in playing with fire, even for fun. 1907 Daily Chron. 9 Oct. 4/6, I should like to sound a note of warning, for, as one who plays with fire, he can only expect to get burnt. 1925 A. S. M. Hutchinson One Increasing Purpose iii. xvi, Looking back upon herself in those fire-playing days. 1928 Galsworthy Swan Song v. 33 If—on second thoughts, she wanted to play with fire.

5. e. *A brand from* or *out of the fire*: see Brand *sb.* 3 b. *To save out of the fire*: to preserve as a remnant from a disaster or catastrophe. *To pull* or *snatch out of the fire* [after Jude 23]: to rescue from destruction or ruin.

1855 Trollope Warden xix, To be sure Puddingdale is only four hundred, but that would be saving something out of the fire. 1924 Lambton Men & Horses 120 Well, I pulled that race out of the fire. 1927 Daily Tel. 11 Oct. 5/6 The winner pulling the match out of the fire after being down 2 sets to 1. 1928 Observer 10 June 27/4 The best snatcher of a match out of the fire that we ever had.

f. *To pull the chestnuts out of the fire*: used (with reference to the fable of the monkey using the cat's paw to extract roasting chestnuts from the fire) of the employment of another to undertake the dangerous part of an enterprise. (See *N. & Q.* 6th Ser., 1883, VII. 286, VIII. 34.)

[1586 G. Whitney Emblems 58 The ape, did reache for Chestnuttes in the fire,..he with a whelpe did close, And thruste his foote, into the Embers quick, And made him, pull the Chestnuttes out perforce.] 1657 [see Cat's paw 2]. [1754 Richardson Grandison III. 358 He makes her fight his battles for him; and become herself the cat's paw to help him to the ready-roasted chestnuts.] 1855 Kingsley Westward Ho! ix, I am..ready to make a cat's paw of him or any man, if there be a chestnut in the fire. 1886 [see Union-ist A. 1. c]. 1930 Snaith Unforeseen ii. xxi, He was the guy who pulled the financial chestnuts out of the fire.

15. *Cricket.* Tendency (of a ball) to fly up erratically or (of the ground) to cause the ball to fly up.

1888 A. G. Steel in Cricket (Badm. Libr.) iii. 161 A good long run..gets way and 'fire' on to the ball. 1897 Ranjitsinhji Jubilee Bk. Cricket 70 Coming from a high elevation, a ball..has more fire or 'devil' in it. Ibid. 80 There is something to be done with the ball when..the wicket has fire in it.

B. 1. g. *fire-call, -chief.*

1897 Daily News 30 Nov. 5/1 Our *fire-call system in London. 1906 Westm. Gaz. 26 Apr. 7/1 Within a very few minutes of the fire-call being rung. 1889 Kansas Times & Star 21 Sept., Our gallant *fire chief was elected first vice-president.

2. (sense 5) *fire-fighter, -fighting.*

1903 Westm. Gaz. 16 June 4/3 The 'invention' and arrangement of the display..is the work of a practical *fire-fighter of great experience..who has been for a long time the chief officer of the Hampton Fire Brigade. 1904 Forum Oct. 274 The most modern equipment should be at the command of the fire fighters. 1906 Daily Chron. 20 Apr. 7/1 The efforts of five thousand fire fighters are useless, because there is no longer any water with which to attack the flames. 1918 Nation (N.Y.) 7 Feb. 168/1 Automobile fire-engines.. manned by a sufficient force of trained fire-fighters. 1897 L. J. Gage in Open Court xi. 213 The *fire-fighting force is divided into 109 companies. 1897 Westm. Gaz. 22 Nov. 9/1 Chemical engines, water-towers, and other time-saving and fire-fighting apparatus. 1903 Daily Chron. 5 May 7/1 The present week is an interesting one in the history of fire-fighting. 1918 Nation (N.Y.) 7 Feb. 168/1 The completeness of the fire-fighting equipment..constituted a most reassuring factor of safety.

5. **fire-back** (earlier U.S. example); **fire-bag** *U.S.*, (*a*) a bag for carrying shot; (*b*) see 1 c of Comb. in Dict.; (*c*) a bag containing implements such as are used by Indians for making a fire; **fire-barrier** (see quot.); **fire-bed** *attrib.*, suitable for grate or furnace bottoms; **fire-blight,** chiefly *U.S.*, a form of blight affecting plants or trees, producing a scorched appearance of the leaves; **fire-board, -chamber** (earlier U.S. examples); **fire command** *Mil.*, a number of guns or batteries under one officer, the smallest unit of fire control; **fire-company** (examples); **fire-control** *Mil.* and *Naval*, the regulation or control of the fire of each gun of a battery; also, the central station from which the commanding officer can exercise such control; also *attrib.*; **fire-crack,** a crack formed by heat, *spec.* in metal when it is being reheated or annealed; **fire-cracker** *U.S.*, = Cracker 6; also *colloq.*, a revolver; **fire-crome** = Fire-hook (*a*); **fire-cure** *v. trans.*, to cure (tobacco or leather) by means of fire; hence **fire-curing** *vbl. sb.*; **fire-discipline** *Mil.*, the training of men to fire exactly as directed by the commander, so that the work of a unit is co-ordinated; **fire-dog** (earlier U.S. example); **fire dropper,** a man who removes the fire from the fire-box of a locomotive at the end of a journey; **fire-fight** *Mil.*, the struggle to establish fire superiority over the enemy; **fire-gang,** a gang of incendiaries; **fire-guard,** (*b*) *U.S.* a member of a fire-brigade; (*c*) a strip of burned grass preventing the spreading of fire; **fire-guard** *v.*, to surround (land) with a fire-guard (*c*); **fire-hat** *U.S.*, a hat for a fireman; **fire-lighting** = *fire-hunting* (see *Fire-hunt); **fire-line** = **fire-guard* (*c*); **fire-painting,** unusual effects of colouring and glazing produced by a special kind of firing; so **fire-painted** *a.*; **fire position** *Mil.*, a position from which fire is opened by an attacking force during an advance; **fire-range** = Range *sb.* 12; **fire-ranger,** a Canadian official who keeps watch against the occurrence of forest fires; **fire-risk,** (*a*) the risk of loss by fire; (*b*) the obligation of a fire-insurance company to make good loss by fire; (*c*) property insured against fire; **fire-room** (earlier example); (*b*) a furnace-room of a building or stokehold of a ship; **fire-shooting** = *fire-hunting* (see *Fire-hunt); **fire-step** = **firing-step*; **fire-stick,** (*c*) an implement used for stirring up a fire; **fire-stop,** (*a*) = *fire-bridge* (see Dict.); (*b*) a device designed to stop the spread of fire, *spec.* incombustible material placed in open parts of a structure; so **fire-stop** *v.*; **fire-trace** = **fire-guard* (*c*); **fire-trench** *Mil.*, a deep and narrow trench from which firing takes place; **fire-walk,** the ceremony of walking barefoot over hot stones, performed as a religious rite by the Fijians and others, and formerly as an ordeal in European countries; so **fire-walker, -walking.**

1846 Rep. U.S. Comm. Patents (1847) 249 The *fire-backs of fireplaces have been made separate. 1769 Massachusetts Gaz. 2 Feb. (Th.) Some silk 'lately found in a *fire-bag'. 1844 Bp. of Montreal Jrnl. (1845) 103 The powder-horn and the fire-bag, in which the shot is carried loose, are slung upon belts crossing each other upon the breast. 1892 Harper's Mag. Mar. 497/1 The Sioux..each carried a fire-bag, a quiver, and a brightly painted shield. 1918 Farrow Dict. Mil. Terms, **Fire Barrier*, a protection against poisonous gases. The burning of dry material giving a line of high and hot flames and little smoke may, under favorable circumstances, lift the wave of gas when it arrives at the trench. 1851 C. Cist Cincinnati 213 One thousand tons *fire-bed and sheet-iron. 1750 *fire-blight [see Dict.]. 1849 Rep. U.S. Comm. Patents, Agric. (1850) 271 Pears suffer much from fire-blight especially on very rich ground. 1857–8 Trans. Ill. Agric. Soc. (1859) III. 346 The fire blight ..has..done much injury to the orchards of this state. 1867–8 Ibid. VII. 503 There are several distinct diseases, all grouped together under the general name of 'Fire Blight'. 1867 Amer. Naturalist Apr. I. 110 Cylindrical bark borers, which are little round black weevil-like Beetles, often causing 'fire-blight' in pears, etc., are now flying about fruit trees to lay their eggs. 1838 J. H. Ingraham Burton II. xii. 194 There was..a flower-vase containing a daisy upon the shining red hearth before a flaunting paper *fireboard. 1845 Knickerbocker Mag. XXV. 446, I went out of the bed-room into the 'sitting-room' where was a black mantel-piece and fire-board, almost as high as the ceiling. 1846 Rep. U.S. Comm. Patents (1847) 211, I also claim the air passage below the *fire chamber. 1918 E. S. Farrow Dict. Mil. Terms, **Fire Command*, in coast artillery, two or more battery commands, the additional fire control stations and accessories, and the personnel assigned to the fire command. 1817 S. R. Brown Western Gaz. 344 A *Fire Company; a public library. 1835 Southern Lit. Messenger I. 259 The remaining expenses are on account of the public markets, fire companies, salaries of officers, [etc.]. 1841 C. Cist Cincinnati 47 They have power to establish..fire companies. 1849 Chamberlain Indiana Gazetteer 373 There are in the town..two fire companies and engines. 1880 Harper's Mag. July 208/2 Several of the members belonged to the volunteer fire-companies, then in the height of their glory. 1886 J. H. A. Macdonald Common Sense on Parade 118 What is wanted is the conviction in the mind of every instructor..that his men should never leave a parade without having gained something in fire discipline,—that is, that *fire control drill be one of the main points in view as a necessary part of the work to be performed on every occasion when men are being drilled, [etc.]. 1907 Westm. Gaz. 3 May 7/1 Stand on the deck amidships, look up at the vast tripod which supports the fire-control. *a* 1928 in C. F. S. Gamble N. Sea Air Station xv. 241, I had a very pleasant minute or so wondering which I was going to hit—the wireless masts or the monitor's fire-control top. 1862 Catal. Internat. Exhib. II. x. 12 Cliff's patent enamelled clay retort is.. adapted for the use of gas works, by its..freedom from *fire-cracks. 1898 Engineering Mag. XVI. 147/2 The Influence of Bismuth on Brass, and its Relation to Fire-Cracks. 1849 in Harper's Mag. (1878) Jan. 274 The signal for starting was the exploding of *fire-crackers by the hundred boxes. 1852 Mrs. Stowe Uncle Tom's C. xxiii, The boy is..a perfect fire-cracker when excited. 1857 Quinland I. 120 Here is everything you want,..fire-crackers, powder, shot. 1894 Outing (U.S.) XXIV. 106/1 You drop that little firecracker or I'll send you after your father! 1901 S. E. White Westerners xx. 182 Peter was barking like a bunch of fire crackers. 1902 G. H. Lorimer Lett. Self-made Merchant vi. 76 It isn't possible to make so much noise with a fire-cracker as with a cannon. 1846 *fire croom [see Crome]. 1899 Athenæum 2 Sept. 329/2 The head of a great fire-hook or fire-crome was noted. 1847 Rep. U.S. Comm. Patents (1848) 170 The following experiment..shows that *fire-curing is not necessary. 1899 Atlantic Monthly LXXXIII. 758/2 The pliant sandals of fire-cured skin. *a* 1909 U.S. Dept. Agric. Rep. 65. 34 (Cent. Suppl.) Tobaccos that have been fire-cured, as the plug tobaccos. 1886 *fire discipline [see **fire-control*]. 1897 Cavalry Tactics xvii. 121 Fire discipline must be strictly enforced, both to ensure accurate shooting at the indicated object and to control the ammunition expenditure. 1905 Daily Chron. 25 May 5/4 The whole Aldershot infantry force..swept forward regardless of everything, including the rules of fire-discipline. 1792 Massachusetts Spy 1 Mar. 3/1 [He] caught a *fire-dog, which he threw with such force that he knocked down one of the ruffians. 1898 L'pool Weekly Courier 9 Apr. 2/7 He was a *fire dropper—drawing the fires from locomotives. 1899 Westm. Gaz. 23 Nov. 2/1 The excitement of a *fire-fight at short ranges. 1898 Ibid. 18 Jan. 2/3 There have been plenty of *fire-gangs in the past, the last of any note being broken up in 1891. 1851 C. Cist Cincinnati 168 There are besides, two hook and ladder companies, and one company of *fire guards. 1874 J. C. McCoy Hist. Sk. 217 An impassable barrier would be created between the unburned grass within the encircled tract, and that upon the outside of the 'fire-guard'. Ibid., A large adjacent tract of land..will be '*fire-guarded', in order to secure a winter range from the ravages of prairie fires. 1851 C. Cist Cincinnati 213 George E. Minister..makes..*fire hats. 1849 C. Lanman Lett. Allegheny Mts. vi. 48 In killing wild animals he pursues but two methods, called '*fire-lighting' and 'still-hunting'. 1905 Terms Forestry & Logging 10 **Fire line*, a strip kept clear of inflammable material as a protection against the spread of forest fire. 1927 W. H. Todd Tiger, Tiger! 108, I walked down a jungle ride, or fire line. 1909 E. A. Barber Pottery & Porcelain U.S. (ed. 3) 494 By this process *Fire-Painted ware may be produced successfully in all colors and lustres. Ibid., The *Fire Painting will again be restored in all its prismatic brilliancy. 1905 Westm. Gaz. 15 May 4/1 Cavalry could do next to nothing, and artillery could seldom find really effective *fire-positions. Ibid. 13 June 3/1 The most favourable spot for your individual fire-position. 1899 Westm. Gaz. 19 May 2/1 The kitchen, with its..huge *fire-range. 1928 Daily Express 29 Aug. 2/5 The British Columbia *fire ranger, whose look-out station is on Mount Cartier, 9,000 feet above sea level. 1907 Install. News June 4/2 The *fire risk aspect of any particular installation. Ibid. Mar. 7/1 The Gunpowder Manufactory at Minden, where Simplex Screwed Conduits have been used because of the fire risk. 1741 N.H. Probate Rec. III. 8 Also they are to find one convenient *fire-room and wood sufficient to maintain one Fire. 1836 Southern Lit. Messenger II. 734 Passing the fire-room, where they were just firing up, I stopped. 1880 Harper's Mag. Oct. 793 Yet even on the *Seawanhaka* it appears that the fire-room..was unprotected. 1903 A. H. Lewis The Boss i. 8 As for a bed, if it should be summer time, what should be finer than the docks? Or if winter, than the fire-rooms of the tugs? 1904 S. E. White Blazed Trail Stories iv. 70 Factory owners ..raised up their voices in bitterness over flooded fire-rooms. 1876 Habberton Jericho Road x. 95 He had done '*fire-shooting' near springs elsewhere. 1916 War Illustrated 23 Dec. 449/1 Bill got upon the *fire-step, placed his rifle against the wall, [etc.]. 1896 J. C. Harris Sister Jane 100 Sister Jane, armed with a '*fire-stick (a heavy piece of metal weighing four or five pounds)..was..making an effort to get to the door. 1900 Ann. Rep. Smithsonian Inst. (Nat. Mus.) 180 In the same plate are included a pair of wooden fire sticks or tongs [of the Tulare Indians]. 1911 Webster, *Fire-stop. 1926 Mulford Cassidy's Protégé iv. 41 The farms he had dreamed of were now no more than memories, their boundary furrows and firestops rank with triumphant bunchgrass. 1895 W. R. Fisher Forest Protection IV. 547 Wherever forests are surrounded by inflammable undergrowth such as heather, grass, etc., *fire-traces of sufficient breadth should be made along their boundaries, and internal fire-traces are also required for all extensive inflammable forest areas...Before burning fire-traces, the soil-covering is usually cut on guide-lines on either side of the trace. 1905 Terms Forestry & Logging 10. 1909 Strand Mag. Apr. 365/2 He dived down into the *fire-trenches. 1916 Boyd Cable Action Front 103 The deep ditch with a narrow platform along its front that was the forward fire trench. 1926 Infantry Training I. 8 Traverse, a buttress of earth, etc. provided between two adjacent portions of a fire or communication trench. 1898 Westm. Gaz. 26 July 3/2 The Fijian *fire-walk. 1900 Proc. Soc. Psychical Res. Feb. 11 Colonel Haggard saw the fire-

walk done in Tokio, on April 9th, 1899. 1898 Westm. Gaz. 28 June 4/3 The *fire-walkers then approached..and..walked leisurely across and around the oven. 1899 Daily News 25 Jan. 4/6 There was a *fire-walking ceremony at Benares the other day. 1904 Athenæum 13 Feb. 216/1 An interesting lecture on 'The Fijians and their Fire-Walking'.

b. **fire-grass** (*b*) *U.S.*, a kind of grass which springs up on burnt land (cf. *fire-weed*); **fire-leaves** (earlier example); **fire-lily,** a name given to certain plants bearing brilliant flowers.

1821 T. Dwight Trav. New Eng. (1823) IV. 50 Immediately after the fires a species of grass springs up, sometimes called *fire grass. 1796–1806 B. Hawkins Lett. 46 There is a plant in bloom called by the whites wolfs tongue or *fire leaves. 1871 Mrs. Stowe Sam Lawson 170 A tall straight *fire-lily, black, spotted in its centre..rose like a jet of flame. 1878 — Poganuc P. xix. 211 There, under the burning August sun, the ground shot up those ardent flower-flames well called fire-lilies.

c. **fire-beetle** (see quot.); **fire-brat,** a thysanurous insect found in bakehouses; **fire-bug** *U.S.*, the glow-worm; **fire-finch,** a name given to several weaver birds from the red plumage of the male in the breeding season.

1862 T. W. Harris Insects Injur. Veget. (ed. 3) 55 *Elater* (*Pyrophorus*) *noctilucus*, the night-shining Elater, is the celebrated *cucuio* or *fire-beetle of the West Indies. 1895 Cambr. Nat. Hist. V. 186 The bakers call these Insects [*sc.* *Thermobia furnorum*] *fire-brats, apparently considering them to be food of heat. 1797 Mass. Spy 30 Aug. (Thornton) These may be more properly stiled 'Fire Bugs'; they are differently formed from common Bugs. *a* 1872 J. M. Bailey Folks in Danbury 40 (ibid.) [The lamp] don't give more light than a fire-bug. 1897 Daily News 6 Feb. 8/3 Australian *firefinches.

Fire, *v.*[1] Add: 2. e. To set fire to (forest land) in order to produce pasturage-land.

1908 Westm. Gaz. 15 Apr. 10/1 Complaints..that we do not fire enough of the forest..where there is pasturage.

11. b. (Earlier examples.) Also *trans.*

1836 Southern Lit. Messenger II. 734 Passing the fire-room, where they were just firing up, I stopped. 1840 Knickerbocker Mag. XVI. 227 Come, gentlemen, 'fire up, fire up!' as the steam-boat engineer says. 1855 R. Glisan Jrnl. Army Life xiv. (1874) 190 He neglected to fire up properly and take in fuel at the proper time. 1857 E. Stone Life Howland xii. 267 The time required to 'fire up', and set the engine again in motion, delayed the arrival. *trans.* 1865–6 Trans. Ill. Agric. Soc. VI. 320 It can be attached..in less time than is required to fire up a steam fire engine. 1867 Rep. Iowa Agric. Soc. (1868) 168 Rye.—No market but one distillery, it has not been fired up for six months. 1903 N. Y. Even. Post 13 Oct. 1 Then the two statesmen fired up their cigars.

15. d. *Photog.* To release (the shutter). Also intr. in *To fire off at*, to take a snapshot of (see Shoot *v.* 22 f).

1892 Photogr. Ann. II. 51 What is the object of firing off at a street view..with the shutter set at 1/50 second when 1/25 would be fast enough? Ibid. 349 The shutter release..appears to lift the mirror and fire the shutter much more efficiently.

Fireable (fəi·ərăb'l), *a.* Delete †*Obs.* and add quot.

1900 Times (weekly ed.) 3 Aug. Suppl. p. iii/4 American coal, in consequence of being very firable, is not screened out.

b. Of a fire-arm: Capable of being discharged.

1898 Westm. Gaz. 26 May 4/2 The *Don Juan de Austria* had only two fireable guns.

Fired, *ppl. a.* Add:

6. Of the case of a cartridge: Used, having had the cartridge discharged.

1892 Greener Breech-loader 65 Such processes as cocking the locks and taking out the fired cases. 1902 Encycl. Brit. XXX. 402/2 The extractor holds a cartridge and a fired case ready to be pushed into the empty breech and ejector-tube respectively...The lock is withdrawn taking with it the fresh cartridge from the belt and the now fired case.

Fire-eater. 2. b. *U.S.* (Earlier examples.)

1852 Fisher in Life & Corr. Quitman (1860) II. xvii. 178 Men of the two extremes, Free-soilers and Fire-eaters, hasten into parties. 1858 Congress. Globe Mar., App. 290/2, I tell you, southern men, I am ready to strike hands with fire-eaters and exterminate the race.

Fire-fang, *v.* (Later U.S. example.)

1896 Vermont Agric. Rep. XV. 72 There is danger if ensilage contains more than 25 per cent of dry matter that it will fire-fang in the silo.

Fi·re-hunt, *sb.* *U.S.* [Fire *sb.* B. 3 b.] A hunt by night in which lights are used to reveal or attract the game.

1788 Mary Dewees Jrnl. (MS.) 172 Had Several Gentlemen to dine on board the Arke expecting a fire hunt of some deer. 1831 Peck Guide Emigrants ii. 48 Mr. Flint [see *Fire-hunting 1826] gives the following animated description of what is called the 'Fire hunt'. 1852 [see Fire *sb.* B. 3 b].

Hence **Fi·re-hunt** *v. trans.*, to hunt (animals) with lights; also *intr.*, to carry out a fire-hunt; **Fi·re-hunter; Fi·re-hunting** *vbl. sb.*

1775 A. Burnaby Trav. N. Amer. 88 An act of parliament ..prohibits..that very destructive practice, taken from the Indians, of fire-hunting. 1824 [see Fire *sb.* B. 3 b]. 1826 T. Flint Recoll. Ten Yrs. Mississippi 339 The most interesting hunts [in Louisiana] are practised at night, and are called fire-huntings. 1843 Carlton New Purchase 164 We feel tempted to give Uncle Tommy's 'morakalus' escape in fire-hunting! 1845 Knickerbocker Mag. XXV. 214 As to deer, fire-hunting, still-hunting, or up in the fork of a tree by night..it is all one to Harry. 1868 Amer. Naturalist Oct. II. 472 [When deer hide by day and feed by night] fire-hunting may take the place of still hunting. 1875 E. King Southern States N. Amer. 417 The sportsman..may 'fire-hunt' the deer in the forests. 1876 Habberton Jericho Road x. 96 He puzzled his brain to know who the men might be. Fire-hunters? Ibid. x. 97 Two, or three men at most, were as many as ever composed a fire-hunting party. 1885 [see Fire *sb.* B. 3 b].

Fire-water. 2. orig. *U.S.* (Earlier example.)

1817 J. Bradbury Trav. Amer. 156 He informed me that they called the whiskey fire water.

Fire-work. Add: 2. b. Necessaries for making a fire. *U.S.*

1847 H. Howe Hist. Collect. Ohio 188 The necessary appendages of his journey would be an axe, a pocket compass, fire works, and blanket and bells.

Firing, *vbl. sb.* 8. Add: **firing-glass,** a table-glass with an unusually thick base; **firing-step** *Mil.*, a board or ledge in a trench, upon which soldiers stand when firing.

1905 Bate Engl. Table Glass 72 '*Firing' glasses..having a thick and massive base with which to knock on the table when applause was to be given. 1923 Weekly Disp. 30 Sept. 7/4 Short Jacobite firing-glasses. 1916 Boyd Cable Action Front 254 He..leaped on the *firing step, and hurled himself over after him.

Firm, *a.* and *adv.* C. *Comb.* 1. b. Add: **firm-footed** = *fast-footed* (*Fast *a.* 11).

1907 Westm. Gaz. 20 Aug. 3/2 A hitter of the firm-footed school. 1928 Daily Tel. 15 May 10/1 He attempts, firm-footed, to drive the ball which is pitched a couple of feet wide of the off-stump.

Firm, *v.* Add: 7. b. *To firm up*: to become firm, to stiffen; esp. of stocks and shares. Hence **Firming-up** *vbl. sb.*

1899 Daily News 30 Oct. 2/6 A gradual firming-up of prices. 1907 Daily Chron. 9 Dec. 1/7 One or two Argentine Rails firmed up. 1929 Daily Express 7 Nov. 2/7 Then all firmed up on trade and Cuban buying.

First, *a.* (*sb.*) and *adv.* Add: A. *adj.* I. 2. b. (Later U.S. examples of special use.)

1922 Titus Timber xxii. 201 Humphrey was going down state the first of the week to hunt an investor. 1926 Publishers' Weekly 16 Jan. 147 When the first of the year had passed.

4. Also in phr. *of the first order* [F. *du premier ordre*]. (*To put*) *first things first*: a catch phr. used to denote a policy of giving the first place to the most important things.

1794 [see Order *sb.* 4]. 1895 R. L. Douglas in Bookman Oct. 33/1 A diplomatist of the first order. 1920 W. Riley Yorkshire Suburb 136 The dear lady was..incapable..of putting first things first. [1926 A. Bennett Lord Raingo xix, Just like her! She would put last things first.] 1931 News Chron. 28 Apr. 3/3 'First things first' must be the guiding principle.

II. 7. g. A first edition; a first-class railway carriage or compartment; the first known or discovered example or specimen of a thing.

1922 M. Sadleir Excurs. Vict. Bibliogr. 6, I have contrived..to keep myself fairly supplied with 'reading firsts'. 1924 G. McLeish's Catal. 13 Essential to the collection of 'modern firsts'. 1925 B. Travers Mischief iv, The train arrived and Eleanor..was easily spotted, being alone in the firsts. 1932 F. Buck & E. Anthony Bring 'em back Alive 215 There is no bigger thrill in the game than bringing back rare 'firsts' [i.e. an animal that has not been seen alive before in the country to which it is brought].

B. *adv.* 1. f. *First off*: at the first blush, at the first go-off, in the first place, to begin with. *U.S.*

1891 'L. Malet' Wages of Sin v. i, What anger is not righteous first off in the estimate of the enraged one? 1897 Howells Landlord at Lion's Head 445 First off, you know, I thought I'd sell to the other feller. 1910 W. M. Raine B. O'Connor 39 Four's right. First off Neil, then the fellow I took to be the Wolf. 1915 Nation (N.Y.) 10 June 646/1 Men of science..no longer admit first off what simple good sense shows to us.

C. *Comb.* 2. **first aid** (examples); also *attrib.* and *fig.*; **first-fleeter** *Austral. slang* (see quots.); **first-footer,** one who goes first-footing; **first offender** (see Offender *note*); **first pointed** *Arch.*, = Early English (see Early *a.* 4 b); **first polar** *Math.* (see quot.); **first-spear,** in pig-sticking, the first thrust which draws blood; also, the man who makes it.

1882 P. Shepherd (*title*) *First Aid to the Injured. 1892 Medical Annual 602 Dressing (First Aid). 1907 Chambers's Jrnl. 26 Oct. 768/1 A first-aid chemical fire-extinguisher. 1926 W. Deeping Sorrell & Son i. § 2 The porter applied first aid to their piece of luggage. 1848 Haygarth Bush Life Australia viii. 93 A man who, by his own account, is of so long standing in the neighbourhood as to have been what is called in the colony a '*first fleeter'. 1850 Dickens Househ. Words I. 418/2 He was a 'first fleeter', that is, came over with Governor Phillips in the first fleet. 1897 Daily News 25 Sept. 2/6 Scottish '*first-footers' in the fifteenth century awoke the night echoes with a mild and 'soughing' Tra-la-la. 1926 Glasgow Herald 30 Dec. 6 The red herring which your Dundee 'first-footer' carries with him as a lucky emblem. 1869 Temple Bar XXV. 541 We ought to temper justice with mercy in dealing with all *first offenders. 1875 Encycl. Brit. II. 427/1 The *First Pointed, Lancet, or Early English style to which the transitional work thus led up. 1886 F. G. Lee Edw. VI. i. 58 A first-pointed chapel and charnel-house. 1877 Encycl. Brit. VI. 720/2 The points of contact are found as the intersections of the curve $u = 0$ by a curve depending on the position of the arbitrary point, and called the '*first polar' of this point; the order of the first polar is $= m - 1$, and the number of intersections is thus $= m(m - 1)$. 1898 Encycl. Sport II. 92 The object of the run is to kill the pig, and not entirely for getting the honour of '*first spear'. Ibid., First spear...Transferred frequently to the man who makes it. 1920 Blackw. Mag. Jan. 112/2 Much of the supreme joy in pig-sticking lies in the successful struggle for first-spear and in outgeneraling and outriding one's friends. Ibid., A first-spear which merely pricks the pig in the buttock, is a matter for shame.

b. In attrib. uses of syntactical collocations, as *first-edition copy*, *first-magnitude star*; see also First-class B., First-fruit 4, First-rate A. 2.

a 1860 Alb. Smith Med. Student (1861) 61 First-session pupils receive turkeys and fresh-looking loins of pork from their friends in the country. 1892 Greener Breech-loader 174 Loaded with first quality powder. 1897 Daily News 1 June 3/2 To establish themselves once more in their former first line positions. 1904 Westm. Gaz. 28 May 2/3 First-category Cossacks of the Chitinsk, Argunsk, and Veckhni Udinsk regiments. 1905 Ibid. 14 Mar. 12/1 Any privileges which go with a first-cabin ticket. Ibid. 9 June 10/1 A first edition copy of 'Richard III'. Ibid. 13 Nov. 12/1 The only first-magnitude star in the track of the moon. 1906 Daily Chron. 21 July 1/7 The third best first-wicket stand on record. 1906 Westm. Gaz. 24 Aug. 4/2 The nests which are marked and inspected by way of tests are always first-brood nests. 1912 L. J. Vance Destroying Angel xvi, A lighthouse—probably a first-order light—with its characteristic flash, not duplicated anywhere along this section of the Atlantic coast. 1921 A. R. Lord Princ. Politics vi. 156 This crude, first-sight democratic theory.

First class. b. *ellipt.* Add: = first-class accommodation or fare.

1852 H. W. Dulcken tr. Ida L. Pfeiffer's Visit Holy Land i. 23 The first-class to Constantinople costs 120 florins.

First-cla·sser. *colloq.* [f. First class + -er[1].] A person or thing of the first class.

1925 Glasgow Herald 28 Mar. 9 These [matches] are exclusively 'first-classers'. 1927 Daily Tel. 7 June 3/1 The first-classers are a mere..drop in the cricket ocean.

First-day. (Additional U.S. examples.)

1811 R. Sutcliff Trav. N. Amer. xiii. (1815) 257, I attended Merion meeting, it being 1st day. 1842 American Pioneer I. 166 The fifty-first anniversary of the First Day, or Sunday School Society, was held at 146 Chesnut Street.

First-handedness (fɜ̄ɹsthæ·ndėdnės). [f. First hand + -ed + -ness.] The quality or condition of being first-hand or of an original character.

1905 Daily Chron. 3 May 8/5 It may breed distrust as to the first-handedness of some brilliant toilettes whose origin we could never account for. 1926 M. Baring Daphne Adeane x, That first-handedness; that habit..of taking nothing for granted.

Firstness (fɜ̄·ɹstnės). Delete †*Obs. rare* and add:

c 1380 Wyclif Sel. Wks. I. 172 Oo firstnesse of love shulde we have to us silf, and to oure fadir and oure modir. 1895 Mrs. W. K. Clifford Flash of Summer vii, Daffodils ..—the bell-like single ones; and their tender firstness appealed to her. 1924 Glasgow Herald 4 Sept. 4 A first novel, ..with a freshness and spontaneity not always synonymous with 'first-ness' in novel-writing. 1927 Blackw. Mag. June 828/2 An odd kind of distinction should halo the person who is the very first to see something or to do something which hitherto humanity has not seen or done...The value of these 'firstnesses' is by no means equal.

Fiscalism (fi·skăliz'm). [f. Fiscal + -ism.] Fiscal principles or policy, esp. in relation to the questions of free trade and protection.

1892 tr. Schäffle's Imposs. Soc. Democr. 193 The old-fashioned fiscalism. 1902 Daily Chron. 15 July 8/7 Two out of every three members spoken to declared that they will fight regardless of fiscalism for the House of Representatives having effective control of the purse. 1906 Ibid. 27 Mar. 6/7 Seeing that they are Free Traders, and most of us are Protectionists, their talking fiscalism would not be very helpful.

Fiscality. Add: Also, fiscal policy; *pl.* fiscal matters.

1904 W. D. Gainsford What is the Fiscal Question? 7 Such is Cobden Club Fiscality. 1904 Westm. Gaz. 13 Jan. 9/1 The rascalities of the Education Act would be set aside by the fiscalities of the food-tax. 1904 Fabian News XIV. 4/1 Fiscalities occupy much space. 1905 Daily Chron. 14 Dec. 4/6 One eye on Fiscalities and the other on Mr. John Burns's costume.

Fisetin (fisi·tin, fi·sĭtin). *Chem.* [f. G. *fisett-*(*holz*) young fustic + -in[1].] A yellow crystalline colouring matter obtained from fustet.

1873 Jrnl. Chem. Soc. XXVI. 72 Fisetin, the colouring matter of Fiset wood, was regarded by Bolley as identical with quercetin. The author gives to it the formula $C_{15}H_{10}O_6$. 1886 Ibid. L. 894 Fisetin occurs in fustet.

Fish, *sb.*[1] Add: 1. f. Applied to the turtle.

1898 Westm. Gaz. 9 Nov. 3/1 The sea round about the West Indies is the happiest hunting-ground for green turtle. The fish (the dealers describe them as fish) are usually taken in the manner described. 1908 Daily Chron. 6 Nov. 7/3 The 'fish', as they are called in the trade, are probably as tenacious of life as any animal.

6. b. *fish-bait, -craft* (U.S. example), *-line, -spear* (later U.S. example).

1870 'Fanny Fern' Ginger-Snaps 275 Won't the laundress rub the skin off her knuckles when she tries to get the *fish-bait off your ruffled skirt. 1866 Game Laws Conn. in Fur, Fin & Feather (1872) 34 Shall forfeit the value of the seine and *fish-craft used for said purpose. 1864 J. T. Trowbridge Cudjo's Cave xliii. 451 Arms and head hung down, causing him to resemble..a frog hooked on for bait at the end of a *fish-line. 1837 R. M. Bird Nick of Woods II. xi. 144 Upon this pillar..were laid or suspended sundry Indian utensils of the kitchen and the field,..wooden bowls..*fish spears [etc.].

c. *fish-ball* (earlier U.S. examples), *-chowder* (example), *-stock.*

1854 Shillaber Mrs. Partington 100 The breakfast was waiting for him, the *fishballs were getting cold. 1873 Aldrich Marj. Daw, etc. 90 She averted her head in making up the fish-balls. 1891 Scribner's Mag. X. 106 We had our dinner at noon..of *fish chowder and potatoes. 1787 J. Farley Lond. Art of Cookery (ed. 4) 166 Take what quantity may be wanted of *fish-stock. 1883 Annie Thomas Mod. Housewife 51 The receipt for a fish-stock which is as strengthening and succulent as can well be desired.

d. *fish-breeder* (earlier U.S. example); *fish-breeding* (U.S. example).

1868 Rep. U.S. Comm. Agric. (1869) 323 The efforts of *fish breeders will be called into requisition to restore the salmon to those waters. Ibid. 320 The information concerning *fish-breeding experiments..was quite full and satisfactory.

7. **fish-basket,** (*a*) a basket used for carrying fish (see 6 b); (*b*) *U.S.*, a creel for catching fish; **fish-bed** (U.S. example); **fish-blooded** *a.*, cold-blooded; **fish-brant** *U.S.*, a snow-goose; **fish-commissioner,** an officer appointed to superintend fisheries; **fish-cow** = Cow-fish 1; **fish-crow** (earlier examples); **fish-eye, fish's eye,** a variety of moonstone; **fish-farming** (U.S. example); **fish-feast, festival** *U.S.*, a festival held by American Indians at the beginning of the salmon season; **fish-flake** (earlier U.S. examples); **fish-fry** *U.S.*, a picnic where fish is fried and eaten; **fish geranium,** an evergreen shrub (*Pelargonium inquinans*); **fish guano** (earlier U.S. example); **fish-hatcher,** one who rears fish from spawn; so **fish-hatchery,** a place for the rearing of fish by artificial means; **fish-hatching** *vbl. sb.*; **fish-horn,** a tin horn used on fishing-boats or by sellers of fish; **fish ladder** (earlier U.S. example); **fish-leaves,** the pondweed *Potamogeton natans*, the flat leaves of which were formerly supposed to give shelter to fish; **fish-manure** (U.S. example); **fish-marten** (see quot.); **fish moth** = *Fish-tail *moth*; **fish-oil** (earlier U.S. example); **fish-poison,** a name given to various plants which have an intoxicating effect upon fish, causing them to float helplessly on the surface of the water; **fish pole** *U.S.*, a pole used as a fishing-rod; **fish-scrap** (U.S. example); **fish-story** (earlier U.S. examples); **fish-ward** = *fish-warden*; **fish-way** (earlier U.S. examples).

1844 S. S. Haldeman in Schele de Vere Americanisms (1872) 351 Various species are abundantly caught..in *fish-baskets, made of lath-work, with diverging walls of stone. 1867 Game Laws Penn. in Fur, Fin & Feather (1872) 100 It shall not be lawful to take, catch, or kill..any fish, by means of any fish-basket. 1868 Rep. U.S. Comm. Agric. (1869) 75 Bones of marine animals are so abundant as to have induced Professor L. Agassiz, twenty years ago, to call it the '*fish bed' of the Charleston Basin. 1898 Westm. Gaz. 14 Jan. 3/1 Not that the historian is *fish-blooded and without predisposition. 1923 Daily Mail 27 Feb. 8 The Ministerial policy of fish-blooded neutrality. 1874 J. W. Long Amer. Wild-Fowl Shooting 243 The snow-geese are all called *fish-brant. 1866 Game Laws Vt. in Fur, Fin & Feather (1872) 63 The Governor is hereby authorized..to appoint two persons, to be styled *fish commissioners. 1860 Mayne Reid Odd People 359 The *manatee*, or '*fish-cow'. 1834 Audubon Ornith. Biog. II. 268 The *Fish-Crow *Corvus ossifragus*, Wils[on]. 1870 Amer. Naturalist III. 287 The Fish-crows..are running over the wet sands. 1882 E. W. Streeter Prec. Stones (ed. 3) 96 The '*Fish's Eye' becomes red by transmitted light, undergoing the same changes as a bead of Schmetze paste. 1868 Rep. U.S. Comm. Agric. (1869) 330 Area for *fish-farming. 1837 W. Irving Capt. Bonneville (1895) II. 163 It was now the season of the annual *fish-feast, with which the Indians in these parts celebrate the first appearance of the salmon in this river [*sc.* the Columbia]. 1845 De Smet Oregon Missions (1847) 119, I arrived among the Arcs-a-plats in time to witness the grand *fish festival, which is yearly celebrated. 1767 Boston Gaz. 26 Jan., Advt. (Th.) Several Fish Houses, and *Fish Flakes now fit for Curing Fish. 1819 Massachusetts Spy 19 May 4/3 While attending the fish flakes at Windmill Point. 1853 J. G. Baldwin Flush Times Alabama 80 In the science of getting up and in getting through a..*fish fry, the Virginian..was first. 1895 Century Mag. Oct. 830/1 Fish-fries and picnics are arranged that you may spend or gamble away your money with a free hand. 1898 H. S. Canfield Maid of Frontier 168 The young clerks and lawyers..concocted a 'fish-fry'. *a* 1909 'O. Henry' Roads of Destiny ix. 153 A little party of peaceable rustics assembled for a fish fry. 1862 Trans. Ill. Agric. Soc. (1865) V. 581, I remarked to her, on viewing some *fish geraniums..how much their scent was like that emitted from the scales of a fresh fish. 1870 Rep. Mass. Board Agric. I. 196 '*Fish guano'..consists of the dry residuum of the fish-oil factories on the New England coast. 1868 Rep. U.S. Comm. Agric. (1869) 336 The result was successful beyond the expectation of the amateur *fish-hatchers. 1885 *fish hatcheries [see Hatchery]. 1897 Congress. Rec. 8 Jan. 602/2 A bill granting to the state of Washington certain lands..for the purpose of a fish hatchery. 1868 Rep. U.S. Comm. Agric. (1869) 319 The Chinese..have practised *fish-hatching successfully for centuries. 1883 Goode Fish. Indust. U.S.A. 59 This being needed for fish-hatching purposes, another larger steamer..has just been built. 1856 Cozzens Sparrowgr. Papers iii. 38 Mrs. Sparrowgrass asked me who that was 'blowing a *fish-horn'. 1860 Holland Miss Gilbert's Career xix. 351 The instrument leaping out into various angular flourishes, as if a fish-horn had got above its business and were ambitious of the reputation of a key-bugle. 1870 Game Laws Cal. in Fur, Fin & Feather (1872) 137 [He] may superintend..the construction of fish-ways and *fish-ladders. 1868 Rep. Mass. Board Agric. i. 105 *Fish manures, the product of the oil-fisheries on our coast..sell at about forty-five dollars per ton. 1904 P. Fountain Great North-West x. 104 The tree-fox, or tree-cat, of the trappers. This is *Mustela pennanti*, often called the *fish-marten. 1859 Mann Natal 171 (Pettman) It is one of nature's beneficent compensations that the *fish moth is devoid of wings. 1803 Ann. 7th Congress 2 Sess. 349 It appears that Great Britain..has secured effectually the carrying..of our *fish-oil, tobacco, pot and pearl ashes. 1846 Lindley Veget. Kingd. 384 Serjania triternata is also employed as a *fish poison. 1866 Treas. Bot., Fish-poison, *Lepidium Piscidium*. Jamaica, *Piscidia Erythrina*. 1884 Miller Dict. Plant-n. 1834 Visit to Texas ix. 88 We touched [a flame] to a few of the tall canes, at this season as dry as *fish poles. 1841 J. F. Cooper Deerslayer xiv. 99 Deerslayer..played with the end of a fish-pole in the water. 1881 N. Y. Times in Goode Amer. Fishes (1888) 112 These smacks are engaged..for the oil-rendering and *fish-scrap works on Barren Island. 1819 St. Louis Enquirer 8 Dec. (Th.) A *fish story!..In consequence of the shoals of white-fish which occupied and choaked the channel between Bois Blanc Island and Amberstburgh, the steamboat could not pass. 1823 Missouri Intelligencer 28 Jan. (Th.) That's 'a fish story', but mine's a true one. *c* 1843 O. Russel Jrnl. (1921) 129, I have frequently seen those 'fish stories' published with the original very much enlarged. 1870 Game Laws N. H. in Fur, Fin & Feather (1872) 166 All nets..may be seized by any *fish ward. 1866 Game Laws Vt. ibid. 63 To direct..the construction of *fishways. 1867 Amer. Naturalist I. 165 Mr. Theodore Lyman..exhibited models of fish-ways.

Fish, *v.*[1] Add:

4. b. To use as a bait in fishing.

1922 Times Lit. Suppl. 27 Apr. 273/3 Fishing the floating fly with a very fine cast. 1927 Observer 24 July 26/3 Mackerel skin, on a single hook, cast and fished like a fly.

9. *intr.* Of water: To provide (good or bad) sport for anglers.

1898 Daily News 4 Oct. 9/3 The Arun continues to fish badly. 1904 Daily Chron. 13 Jan. 5/2 It is a loch that fishes best in the early part of the year. 1910 Westm. Gaz. 26 Feb. 16/4 The Avon was fishing well for roach.

Fisher. 6. b. Add: *fisher-wife*.

1868 Miss Braddon Dead-Sea Fruit xxxix, The rough fishermen and brawny fisherwives. 1887 Ruskin Præterita II. vi. 200 A fisher-wife doll from Calais. 1895 Month Sept. 52 All the fisher-wives we dressed alike in short petticoats of blue stuff.

Fisher[2] (fi·ʃəɹ). *colloq.* [f. the name of Sir Warren *Fisher*, Permanent Secretary to the Treasury from 1919.] Temporary name for a currency note (esp. of £1). Cf. *Bradbury.

1922 Daily Mail 18 Dec. 7 A 'Bradbury' or a 'Fisher' are terms that have practically passed into the language. 1923 Motor Cycling 14 Nov. 35/2 The Bench mulcted him of a couple of Fishers and warned him as to his future behaviour.

Fish-gig. (Later U.S. example.)

1866 Atlantic Monthly Mar. 278/2 They were prevented from ascending by what appears to have been an ordinary fish gig.

Fish-hook. 3. Add: **fish-hook cactus** *U.S.*, a cactus with hooked spines.

1875 Amer. Naturalist IX. 20 *Mammillaria phelosperma* Engel., or 'the fish-hook cactus', is found as a rarity in rocky clefts, at this season adorned with its bright red fruit. 1907 S. E. White Arizona Nights i. xiii. 196 Denton ran across some fishhook cactus, which we cut up and chewed.

Fishiness. Add: 2. *fig.* 'Shadiness', questionableness. *colloq.*

1919 Wodehouse Damsel in Distress xiv, The extreme fishiness of Albert's sudden production of a cousin from America.

Fishing, *vbl. sb.*[1] Add: 5. a. *fishing-gear* (earlier example); *fishing-light, -party, -spear, -station.* (All *U.S.*)

1839 Knickerbocker Mag. XIII. 406 To throw by my *fishing gear, and sit upon rocks. 1845 Caroline M. Kirkland Western Clearings 120 Nobody broke his windows or pulled the shingles off his roof to make *fishing-lights or quail-traps. 1838 Caroline Gilman Recoll. Southern Matron xxvi. 176 *Fishing parties, and the chase soon occupied his leisure moments. 1849 Parkman Oregon Trail 35 She sat down and entertained us..with anecdotes of fishing-parties. 1840 C. F. Hoffman Greyslaer i. xi. 122 The torches..enable them..to approach sufficiently near to destroy him with their *fishing spears. 1841 J. F. Cooper Deerslayer ii. 12 Fishing-spears, rods, nets. 1836 Southern Lit. Messenger II. 747 He..under pretence of making inquiries at a small *fishing station, sailed down the river alone. 1845 Frémont Exped. 186 A favorite fishing station among the Indians.

b. **fishing-plummet** (see quot.); **fishing-pole,** a pole used as a fishing-rod; **fishing warden** = *fish-warden.* (All *U.S.*)

1872 Amer. Naturalist VI. 225 Girdled, globular or oval pebbles, which have been designated '*fishing-plummets', are very abundant. 1873 Aldrich Marj. Daw, etc. 75 He rigged himself up a *fishing-pole. 1870 Game Laws N.H. in Fur, Fin & Feather (1872) 167 Any town..may..choose one or more *fishing wardens.

Fishing, *ppl. a.* 1. Add: *Fishing eagle*, a fish-eagle. *Fishing hawk*, a fish-hawk.

1688 Fishing hauk [in Dict.]. 1781–2 Jefferson Notes Virginia (1787) 72 *Accipiter piscatorius*..Fishing hawk. 1835 R. M. Bird Hawks of Hawk-hollow i. vi. 85 They are no true fishing-hawks, after all. Ibid. vii. 94 The Solitude..[was] broken by..the plaintive scream of the fishing eagles.

Fishling. (Earlier U.S. example.)

a 1861 T. Winthrop Life in open Air (1863) 33 Only petty fishlings, weighing ounces.

Fish-tail. Add: c. **Fish-tail moth** *South Africa* = Silver-fish 2.

1891 Monteiro Delagoa Bay 129 Some people call them fish-tail moths—why 'moths' it would be difficult to discover.

Fishy, *a.* 6. (Earlier U.S. example.)

1840 J. P. Kennedy Quodlibet 75 Jesse being..a little amphibious in his politics, or, in Mr. Fog's expressive language, *rather fishy*.

Fission (fi·ʃən), *v.* [f. Fission *sb.*] *intr.* To undergo fission.

1929 Sir Jas. Jeans Universe Around Us 226 The development of the hypothetical chaos has now been traced through five generations of astronomical bodies, chaos—nebulae—stars—binary systems—sub-systems, to which a sixth generation must be added if the stars of the sub-system happen to fission further.

Fist, *sb.*[1] 1. c. *To make a* (*good*, etc.) *fist of*, *at* something. (Earlier U.S., dial., and other examples.)

1833 A. Greene Dod. Duckworth ii. 8 You hadn't ought to tax any thing..seeing you've made such a fist of it. 1838 Caroline Gilman Recoll. Southern Matron v. 46 He reckoned he should make a better fist at farming than edicating. 1841 W. G. Simms Kinsmen II. 24 (Th.) You made a poor fist of this business. 1869 A. C. Gibson Folk-sp. Cumb. 177 Thoo *hes* mead a fist on't. 1876 Hardy Ethelberta xlvi, 'Tis a poor fist I can make at hearing anything. 1894 (Amer.) Dial. Notes (1896) I. 330 'To make a bad fist of it': to make mistakes or do work incorrectly. 1920 Galsworthy In Chancery iii, He made a poor fist of sleeping.

4. **fist-fight** (later U.S. example).

1873 J. H. Beadle Undevel. West iv. 88 Dances, drunks and fist-fights met with a sudden interruption.

Fist, *sb.*[2] 3. *U.S.* (Earlier and later examples. Cf. *Fice.)

1850 L. H. Garrard Wah-To-Yah iv. (1927) 60 In our lodge were three huge curs and four cross feists. 1872 E. Eggleston End of World xliv. 287 It reminded me of a little fice-t dog I had when I was a leetle codger.

Fit, *sb.*[2] 3. d. (Earlier U.S. examples.)

1844 G. W. Kendall Santa Fé Exped. (De Vere) The man ran after the thievish Indian, and the corporal cried out to him to give him fits if he caught him. *a* 1848 Dow Jr. Patent Serm. I. 54 (Th.) Either flax out your opponent, or give nature special fits in the undertaking. 1851 Knickerbocker Mag. Jan. XXXVII. 102 He's given the Mexicans, to their pain, Such charming fits—and will again.

Fit, *a.* 5. b. quasi-*adv.* (Later U.S. example.)

1856 Knickerbocker Mag. Oct. XLVIII. 433 Then she laughs fit to kill.

Fit, *v.*[1] 8. *fig.* Add: Freq. *refl.* of persons, and const. *to, into*.

1919 Bradby Psycho-anal. 52 His consequent difficulty in fitting himself in to life. Ibid. 247 He cannot fit himself in happily to his surroundings.

Fitch (fitʃ), *sb.*[3] Also **fetch.** [Origin unknown.] In basket-making, a kind of plait in which two canes or osiers are twisted together in the same direction so as to enclose a crossing weft at each half-turn. Also = *fitch-rod*, one of the canes so used. Hence **Fitch** *v.*

1910 T. Okey in Encycl. Brit. III. 482/2 The 'fitch'.. employed for skeleton work such as cages and waste-paper baskets. 1912 Rep. Cambr. Anthropol. Exped. Torres Straits IV. 64.

Fi·t-out. See Fit *sb.*[4] 4 and add U.S. example.

1844 G. W. Kendall Santa Fé Exped. II. xix. 363 A cruel bit,..which causes the horse to curve his neck, champ, and froth..at the mouth, completes the fit-out of the Mexican gentleman.

Fitter, *sb.*[1] Add: 2. (Examples.)

1851 C. Cist Cincinnati Advt., Brass and iron founders; fitters of wrought iron welded pipe, for steam, gas, etc. 1905 Terms Forestry & Logging 37 *Fitter*, 1. one who notches the tree for felling and after it is felled marks the log lengths into which it is to be cut; 2. one who cuts limbs from felled trees and rings and slits the bark preparatory to peeling tanbark.

b. *Tailoring* and *Dressmaking*. One who is engaged to supervise the cutting out and making of garments, or the alteration of ready-made garments to suit customers' requirements.

1858, 1885 [in Dict., sense 2]. 1896 Daily News 10 Dec. 7/2 She will find that the fitter who receives her presides..at the table where her orders are being carried out. 1906 Daily Chron. 17 July 5/2 She sent the defendants notice that unless they sent a fitter up to make the dress right on the Monday it would be of no use to her. 1921 Dict. Occup. Terms (1927) § 405 *Fitter, dressmaker's fitter*, in charge of workrooms in large establishment..; fits garments requiring alterations and takes customers' measurements for length of skirt, etc.

Fitting, *vbl. sb.* Add: 1. b. The action or an act of fitting on a garment in tailoring and dressmaking.

1930 London Mercury Feb. 320 They had had to cancel two fittings and three dress shows.

Fit-up (fi·tʌp). *slang.* [f. verbal phr. *to fit up* (see Fit *v.*[1] 11 d).] A stage or other theatrical accessory that can be fitted up for the occasion. Hence (in full *fit-up company*), a travelling theatrical company which carries makeshift scenery and properties that can be fitted up for the occasion.

1883 Referee 22 July (Ware) The 'fit-up' towns..are the towns which do not possess a theatre [etc.]. 1885 J. K. Jerome On the Stage v, He had been a member of a fit-up company that travelled with a complete Shaksperian *répertoire* and four set scenes. Ibid. xvii, However, I never did join a booth. ..The nearest I approached to anything of the kind was this fit-up. 1898 Westm. Gaz. 5 Mar. 4/3 We venture to guess that there will be many a fit-up dressing-room on the enormous stage of Old Drury on this memorable day. 1899 Daily News 18 July 3/6 St. George's-hall..is a much more suitable place for operatic representations than the 'fit-up' in the Royal Academy concert room. 1901 Westm. Gaz. 4 Nov. 10/1 His early, struggling, happy days with his father when they took the road with a little fit-up show. 'Fit-up, indeed!' he used to say with a laugh; 'why, our whole fit-up went into a couple of brown-paper parcels!' 1902 B'ham. Inst. Mag. Oct. 38 The difficulties of 'stage fit-ups' and

(Dictionary text in multiple columns — Oxford English Dictionary Supplement. Entries include:)

FIVE. ... **Five Nations.** ... **Five-figure** ... **Fivepenny.** ... **Fivesome.** ... **Five-square.** ...

Fix. ... **Fixate.** ... **Fixer.** ... **Fixing.** ... **Fixation.** ... **Fixature.** ... **Fixity.** ... **Fixture.** ... **Fix-up.** ... **Fixz.** ...

Fizgig. ... **Fizzer.** ... **Fizzle.** ... **Fizz.** ... **Fizzy.** ...

Flackey, s. ... **Flag**, sb. ... **Flagellate.** ... **Flagellation.** ... **Flagged.** ... **Flagstone.** ... **Flail.** ... **Flamingant.** ... **Flaith.** ...

Flame, sb. ... **Flambé.** ... **Flamenco.** ... **Flaming.** ... **Flammule.** ... **Flan.** ... **Flanch.** ...

Flanching, vbl. sb. ... **Flanders.** ... **Flange.** ... **Flangeless.** ... **Flank**, v. ... **Flanker**, sb. ... **Flanky.** ... **Flannel.** ... **Flannelled**, ppl. a. ... **Flap.** ... **Flapping.** ... **Flappy.** ... **Flare.** ... **Flapper.** ... **Flapjack.** ... **Flary.** ... **Flaser.** ...

Flasher. ... **Flasqued.** ... **Flat**, a., adv. ... **Flash.** ... **Flat-boat.** ... **Flat-cap.** ... **Flat-foot.** ... **Flat-footed.** ... **Flat-head.** ...

Supplement, p. 3873; Corrigenda, p. 4092; Spurious words, p. 4093; Books quoted, p. 4094.

B. *attrib.* **flat-head adder** = sense 3; **flat-head Indian** = sense 1 (hence **flat-head horse**).
1847 De Smet *Oregon Missions* 33 Father De Smet..was sent on a visit..to the Flathead Indians. *a* 1861 T. Winthrop *John Brent* vii. 68 The little villain's mount was a red roan, a Flat-head horse. 1875 *Amer. Naturalist* IX. 10, I have known the Flat-head Adder or Blowing Viper, *Heterodon platyrhinos*, to eat the heads of the common eel. 1879 *Encycl. Brit.* VIII. 837/1 In a legend of the Flathead Indians.

Hence **Fla·t-head** *v. trans.*, to flatten the head of.
a 1861 T. Winthrop *Canoe & Saddle* (1862) 204 One infant ..was being flat-headed.

Flatness. Add: **3. b.** *Flatness of field* (see quots. and *flat field* s.v. *Flat *a.* 15).
1878 Abney *Photogr.* 206 On the distance of the diaphragm from the lens is dependent the amount of distortion, as is also the size of the picture which the lens is capable of defining; whilst at the same time the flatness of the field is also in a great measure due to a large distance being maintained between them. 1884 *Encycl. Brit.* XVII. 805/2 To get tolerable definition and flatness of field a stop must be added. 1919 *Brit. Jrnl. Photogr. Alm.* 238 Flatness of field means the property of giving equal definition in all parts of the plate when photographing a flat subject with the lens pointed squarely to it.

Flat-out. *U.S.* [f. verbal phr. *to flat out* (see Flat *v.*[2] 4 b).] A failure, a fiasco.
1886 *Century Mag.* Mar. 727/1, I didn't know it was goin' to be s'ch a perfect flat-out.

Flatstone (flæ·tstoun). [f. Flat *a.* + Stone *sb.*] **1** and **2.** (See Dict. s.v. Flat *a.* 15.)
3. A horizontal grave-stone.
1855 *Parl. Papers* XLI. 1. 52 Flatstone, not exceeding 6 ft. 6 in. by 3 ft. *Ibid.* 53 Memorial, consisting of a flat stone over such grave, in remembrance of one person .. £1 10s.

Flatted (flæ·tėd), *a.*[2] *Sc.* [f. Flat *sb.*[2] + -ed[2].] Divided into or constructed as flats.
1913 *Chamb. Etym. Dict.* Suppl., *Concierge*, .. a door-keeper, esp. in a flatted house. 1921 *Glasgow Herald* 28 Jan. 10 English visitors..are sometimes astonished at our flatted houses.

Flatten, *v.* Add:
2. b. *intr.* Aviation. *To flatten out*: to bring an aeroplane into a position parallel with the ground. Also, of the aeroplane: to assume such a position.
1913 *Aeroplane* 17 Apr. 453/1 Apparently he tried to flatten out too quickly. 1914 Rosher *In R.N.A.S.* (1916) 37, I just managed to flatten out and straighten up a little as I hit the ground sideways. 1917 C. C. Turner *Aircraft of To-Day* vii. 116 When the sea is calm the pilot often finds it anything but easy to see when to flatten out to 'land'.
4. *fig.* Also with *down.*
1924 *History* Oct. 209 The general average flattened down to a moderate thirteen shillings.

Flatter, *sb.*[2] Add: **3.** In diving, striking the water with the body in a flat or horizontal position.

Flatter (flæ·təɹ), *sb.*[4] [f. Flat *sb.*[3] 4 b + -er[1].] One who couples and uncouples trucks at a flat in a coal-mine.
1894 *Times* 11 Oct. 4/6 After two years or so..the trapper is advanced to the rank of a flatter. His occupation then consists in coupling or uncoupling the trucks or wagons. 1921 *Dict. Occup. Terms* (1927) § 043 *Flat keeper*, flat coupler-on; flatman, flatter; couples full and uncouples empty tubs at 'flat' or working face terminus of haulage system.

Flatter, *v.*[1] Add:
9. b. To show to the best advantage, make effective, emphasize the good points of.
1904 *Westm. Gaz.* 11 Feb. 4/2 A dark blue velvet will flatter diamonds remarkably. *Ibid.* 27 Aug. 2/3 The wickets at Nottingham..flatter batsmen enormously. 1909 *Ibid.* 27 Feb. 15 1 A good white shoe worn with a white dress flatters the foot immensely.

Flattering, *ppl. a.* Add:
3. b. *Flattering unction*: see Unction 5 b.

Flatwoods (flæ·twudz). *U.S.* [f. Flat *a.* + Wood *sb.*[1]] Low-lying timber land; applied especially to types of well-wooded land in Ohio, Alabama, and Florida.
1887 'C. E. Craddock' *Keedon Bluffs* 169 The cattle..had been ..driven home to the farms in the 'flat-woods'. 1908 R. W. Chambers *Firing Line* ix, Where have you been for a week? In the flat-woods. *Ibid.* x, Those lemon-tinted butterflies which haunt the Florida flat-woods.

Flaunching: see *Flanching *vbl. sb.*

Flavenol (flæ·vėnǫl). *Chem.* [f. *Flavone + -*en* + -ol.] A colourless crystalline derivative of quinolin.
1883 *Jrnl. Chem. Soc.* XLIV. 600 Acetylflavenol is obtained by boiling flavenol with an excess of acetic anhydride for an hour.

Flavin. Add:
2. (In form *flavine.*) A yellow crystalline base, $C_{13}H_{12}N_2O$, used as an antiseptic.
1917 *Jrnl. Chem. Soc.* CXII. 1. 241 This substance, 'flavine,' kills *Staphylococcus aureus* at 1:20,000 in water containing 0.7% peptone. 1922 *Encycl. Brit.* XXX. 155/1 Flavine differed from all the other antiseptics in that it acted more powerfully in the presence of blood serum than it did in water.

Flavinduline (flevi·ndiuləin). *Chem.* [f. Flavo- + Induline.] A coal-tar dye producing a light yellow.
1899 *Jrnl. Chem. Soc.* LXXVI. 1. 239 Flavinduline..as a type of the azonium bases, readily reacts with methylene compounds, yielding characteristic colorations.

Flavol (flǣ·vǫl, flæ-). *Chem.* [f. L. *flavus* yellow + -ol.] A yellow crystalline compound, $C_{14}H_8(OH)_2$, a derivative of anthracene.
1883 *Jrnl. Chem. Soc.* XLIV. 74 Flavol, $C_{14}H_8(OH)_2$, is formed when the fusion with potash is continued until the mass becomes intensely black, and gives off a tarry odour.

Flavoline (flǣ·volin). *Chem.* [f. *Flavol + -ine[5].] A crystalline compound, $C_{16}H_{13}N$, prepared synthetically from quinoline.
1882 *Jrnl. Chem. Soc.* XLII. 1067 On distillation with zinc-dust, the phenol is converted into a new base, flavoline, $C_{16}H_{13}N$, which distils above 360° as a yellowish oil.

Flavone (flǣ·voun). *Chem.* [f. Flavo- + -one.] A colourless synthetic crystalline substance, the parent-substance of a number of yellow vegetable dyes; also, any of the derivatives of this substance.
1897 *Jrnl. Chem. Soc.* LXXII. 1. 425 Flavone, $C_{15}H_{10}O_2$, is formed by the condensation of ketocumaran with benzaldehyde, and separates in almost colourless crystals melting at 108°. 1921 *Ibid.* CXX 1. 682 The bromides of *o*-acetoxyphenyl styryl ketones yield flavones..according to the substituents in the benzene nucleus.

Flavonol (flǣ·vǫnǫl). *Chem.* [f. *Flavone + -ol.] A yellow crystalline compound from which several vegetable dyes are obtained.
1898 *Jrnl. Chem. Soc.* LXXIV. 1. 327 Morin differs from quercetin and other flavonol derivatives in colour.

Flavour, *v.* Add:
1. b. To have the flavour *of*, to savour.
1887 Marie Corelli *Thelma* 1. xii, A strange sickening sense of unrest that flavoured of despair. 1897 *Westm. Gaz.* 4 Mar. 3/3 Though they flavour more of antiquity and the early Victorian era than of novelty.

Flawy, *a.* **2.** (Earlier U.S. example.)
1807 P. Gass *Jrnl.* 78 The wind became flawy and the sailing bad.

Flax, *sb.* Add:
7. e. Referring to the colour of the flower of the flax, as *flax-blue, flax-flower blue.*
1899 *Daily News* 20 May 8/6 Flax-flower blue, a lovely shade that seems to reflect the summer sky itself. 1900 *Ibid.* 21 July 6/5 Flax-blue Irish linen.

Flax, *v.* **2. a.** *U.S.* (Earlier and later examples with *out.*)
a 1848 Dow Jr. *Patent Serm.* I. 54 (Th.) Either flax out your opponent, or give nature special fits in the undertaking. 1903 (*Amer.*) *Dialect Notes* II. 351 *Flax out*, v. phr. to wear out, be weary. 'I'm all flaxed out.'

Flax-seed. **2.** *U.S.* (Earlier example.)
1862 *Trans. Ill. Agric. Soc.* (1865) V. 485 A wheat stubble, full of Hessian flies in the 'flax seed' or pupa state.

Flea, *sb.* **6.** Add: **flea-bag,** also, a soldier's sleeping-bag; **flea-bug** *U.S.* = *flea-beetle.*
1915 Rosher *In R.N.A.S.* (1916) 41, I am going to invest in a Jaeger *flea bag. 1930 Pertwee *Pursuit* 1. xi. 58 He snaked his feet into his flea bag. 1877 *Rep. Vermont Board Agric.* IV. 158 It is very lively in its movements, and is sometimes called *flea-bug.

Flea-bit, *a.* (Later U.S. example.)
1830 O. W. Holmes *Poems, Daily Trials* 15 The small-voiced pug-dog welcomes in the sun, And flea-bit mongrels ..give answer all.

Pleasome (flī·sŏm), *a. jocular* (in association with *gleesome*). [f. Flea *sb.* + -some[1].] Full of fleas.
1853 J. Payn *Poems* 79 (*On our Dog Jock*) A gleesome fleasome affectionate beast. 1884 Kipling *Other Verses* 53 Gentle *Bandar*, an inscrutable Decree, Makes thee a gleesome fleasome Thou, and me a wretched Me. 1924 *Blackw. Mag.* Feb. 220/1 The still fleasome but now gleesome puppy.

Flèche. Add: **2. b.** In decorative art, a representation of a spire in carving or metal-work.
1862 *Catal. Spec. Exhib. Wks. Art S. Kens. Mus.* 60 Châsse..in the shape of a church, surmounted in the centre of the roof with a 'flèche' or spire.
3. *Fencing.* (See quots.)
1928 *Daily Tel.* 17 July 17/7 With the épée Walter met his most dangerous opponent..in the first round, and beat him with a rapid flèche attack on the body. 1930 *Morning Post* 14 July 15 In the concluding series Armstrong's pace embarrassed Mowlam into an ill-timed flèche.
4. One of the twenty-four points on a backgammon board.
1867 *Bohn's Hand-bk. Games* 381 Backgammon is played ..upon a quadrangular..board, on which are figured 24 points or *flèches*, of two colours, placed alternately...The points or flèches are numbered from 1 to 12 of each colour [*sc.* in a diagram]. 1897 R. F. Foster *Complete Hoyle* 617.

Fléchette (fleʃe·t). [Fr., dim. of *flèche* arrow.] A missile resembling a dart, dropped from aircraft.
1915 F. A. Talbot *Aeroplanes & Dirigibles* 141 Another missile which has been introduced by the French airmen.. is the steel arrow, or 'fléchette' as it is called. 1915 Grahame-White & Harper *Aircraft Gt. War* 247 The first use of 'flechettes' in the war was at the beginning of September.

Fleck (flek), *v.*[3] U.S., var. of Flick *v.*[2]
1887 Tourgee *Button's Inn* 124 'You handle that as if there were eggs in it', laughed the other, flecking the whip. 1888 'C. E. Craddock' *Broomsedge Cove* xxiii. 424 He experimented with some delicate flecking touches of the bow. 1918 C. Sandburg *Cornhuskers* 50 He lived flecking lint off coat lapels.

Fled, *ppl. a.* Add:
2. Of pottery: Liable to crack at a late stage of manufacture by a too rapid change of temperature during or after a firing. *Fled ware*, ware cracked after the bisque firing.
1904 *Technol. & Sci. Dict.* (ed. Goodchild & Tweney).

Fleece, *sb.* **6.** Add: *fleece-roller* (Austral.).
1890 'R. Boldrewood' *Col. Reformer* xii, Sheepwashers, shearers,..fleece-rollers.

Fleet, *sb.*[1] Add:
1. *Fleet in being*: a phrase first used by the Earl of Torrington after the engagement off Beachy Head in 1690 to describe a fleet, which, though inferior to that of the enemy, is able to hamper his movements.
[1690 Earl Torrington *Sp. to Ho. Comm.* (1710) 29 Most Men were in fear that the French wou'd invade; but I was always of another Opinion,..for I always said, that whilst we had a Fleet in being, they wou'd not dare to make an Attempt.] 1898 Kipling (*title*) A Fleet in Being. 1899 A. T. Mahan *War with Spain* (1900) 76 It is indeed as a threat to communications that the fleet in being is chiefly formidable. 1902 *Encycl. Brit.* XXXII. 501/1 Of late years controversy has raged round this phrase, 'a fleet in being' and the strategic principle which it expresses.
2. Revived in the sense of: A number of vehicles or aircraft forming a definite group or 'unit'.
1889 *Kansas Times & Star* 7 May, A fleet of hacks was cruising around to take them to their..homes. 1905 *Daily Chron.* 11 Sept. 5/6 At five o'clock, when the motor fleet drew up. 1908 air-fleet [see *Air *sb.* B. II b]. 1911 *Chambers's Jrnl.* 767/1 The vast sum of money..expended on..a single Dreadnought might better be devoted to creating a whole fleet of dirigibles and aeroplanes. 1914–15 W. J. Locke *Jaffery* iii, Barbara has gone away with the Daimler,..and as I don't keep a fleet of cars, I had to choose between this and the donkey-cart. 1924 F. J. Haskin *Amer. Govt.* (revised ed.) 433 Large fleets of trucks and automobiles.
4. *fleet-action, engineer, -men.*
1901 J. Blake *How Sailors Fight* iv. 91 As the first phase of a *fleet action the captains of the various warships meet together on the admiral's flagship. 1910 *Daily Chron.* 17 Mar. 3/5 The fleet action of the future will..develop into an aggregation of duels between opposing battle units. 1901 J. Blake *How Sailors Fight* ii. 44 A *fleet engineer is always on duty in South Wales, and it is his business to recommend to the Government the coal they shall include in their contracts. 1904 *Daily Chron.* 1 Feb. 3/3 It will encourage straight shooting among the *fleetmen. 1905 *Ibid.* 19 July 5/6 The magic personality of British fleetmen. 1909 *London Mag.* Aug. 605/2 To cheer the fleetmen as they march through the streets.

Fleet, *sb.*[2] **2. b.** Add: **Fleet Street,** a street in London devoted largely to the production and publication of periodical journals; hence *allusively*, the newspapers generally, the journalistic press, journalism.
1904 Sir J. R. Robinson *50 Yrs. Fleet St.* 236 The passion for letter-writing to newspapers is recognised in Fleet Street as a distinct form of mental aberration. 1905 H. Leach *Fleet St.* 87 A faculty for quick and perfect condensation is one of the most valuable possessions of the Fleet Street man. *Ibid.* 143 Fleet Street has its particular specialists for several of the courts of law. *Ibid.* 189 Their [*sc.* editors'] differences show how impossible it is for Fleet Street to tell what the morrow will bring forth for it. 1920 [see *Downing Street]. 1927 *Scots Observer* 12 Mar. 11/3 Shabbiness and flyblowness represent a Fleet Street tradition that has been broken.

Fleetful (flī·tful). [f. Fleet *sb.*[1] + -ful 2.] As many as would make a fleet; *transf.* a large number.
1899 *Westm. Gaz.* 21 Feb. 2/2 The public would have paid for a fleetful of ships. 1908 Dinneen tr. *Keating's Hist. Irel.* II. 165 The king gave him a fleetful, that is, two thousand two hundred, and they put out to sea. 1923 S. Gwynn *Hist. Irel.* v. 45 The 'fleetfuls' of foreign students who came to attend surprisingly advanced teaching.

Flem (flem). An abbreviation of Fleming[1].
1909 *Daily Chron.* 20 Aug. 3/3 Rubens..This exuberant, robust, vivacious Flem. 1925 *Contemp. Rev.* Mar. 312 The Flems outnumber the Walloons in Belgium.

Flemingin (flemi·ndʒin). *Chem.* [f. *Flemingia* + -in[1].] An orange-red crystalline powder, $C_{12}H_{12}O_3$, obtained from *Moghania congesta* (*Flemingia congesta* of Roxburgh), used in dyeing.
1898 *Jrnl. Chem. Soc.* LXXIII. 661 Flemingin..under the microscope, is seen to consist of star-shaped groups of small prismatic needles.

Flesh, *sb.* Add: **12. b.** *flesh-forming* adj.
1873–4 *Rep. Vermont Board Agric.* II. 232 These roots contain about one third as much flesh-forming matter as does our best hay.
13. flesh-split, that part of a split hide or skin which is nearest the flesh.
1897 C. T. Davis *Manuf. Leather* (ed. 2) 429 Flesh splits are splits which are finished on the flesh side. The usual weight of the flesh splits is from 1½ to 3½ pounds. 1904 *Technol. & Sci. Dict.* (ed. Goodchild & Tweney) s. v. *Bag Hides*, The lower or Flesh Split is used for insoles and stiffeners in boots.

Flesh, *v.*
4. b. Delete †*Obs* and add quots.
1909 H. G. Wells *Tono-Bungay* II. i. 103 We've fleshed ourselves a bit, eh? *a* 1911 *Century Mag.* (Webster) A rangy bay that ought to be fleshed for six months.
c. *intr.* for *pass.* To acquire flesh, become (more) fleshy.
1872 Susan Coolidge *What Katy did* xii, I seem to have fleshed up since then.

Fleshing, *vbl. sb.* **7. fleshing-knife** (earlier U.S. example).
1812 *Niles' Weekly Reg.* I. 25 Jan. 390/1 The subscriber.. at short notice can furnish tanner's fleshing knives.

Fleshmonger. Add: **3.** A slave-dealer.
1845 F. Douglass *Life* (1846) 4 Cruel as the deed may strike any one to be, for a man to sell his own children to human flesh-mongers, it is often the dictate of humanity for him to do so.

Fletcherian (fletʃīə·riăn), *a.* [f. the name of John *Fletcher* (1579–1625), English dramatist + -ian.] Of, pertaining to, or characteristic of Fletcher.
1907 *Westm. Gaz.* 3 Apr. 4/1 It is curious..that FitzGerald should have made his translations of Calderon so strongly Fletcherian in style. 1921 *Spectator* 19 Feb. 236/2 We all know how this new flower flourished and ramped in the Fletcherian garden and was taken up by the poet's dramatic imitators.

Fletcherism (fle·tʃəriz'm). [f. the name of Horace *Fletcher* (1849–1919), American author + -ism.] The practice of thorough mastication advocated by Fletcher. So **Fle·tcherite,** a follower of Fletcher; **Fle·tcherize** *v. trans.*, to masticate thoroughly. Also *fig.*
1904 *Daily Chron.* 31 Oct. 4/7 The Fletcherites preach the gospel of chewing. 1905 *Ibid.* 30 May 4/4 'Fletcherising' means much monetary economy. 1907 *Practitioner* June 852 The Fletcherites, who, so far from not giving two bites to a cherry, insist on thirty-two to a mashed potato. 1909 H. James in Orcutt *Quest Perf. Bk.* (1926) 88 It is impossible save in a long talk to make you understand how the blessed Fletcherism..lulled me, charmed me, beguiled me. 1910 'O. Henry' *Strictly Business* xvii. 203 Annette Fletcherized large numbers of romantic novels. 1922 P. G. Wodehouse *Adventures of Sally* ii. 41 The raffish mongrel was apparently endeavouring to fletcherize a complete stranger of the Sealyham family.

Fleur. Add:
2. b. In names of artificial silk materials, as *fleur de chine, fleur de soie* (also *fleursoie*).
1927 *Daily Express* 5 Apr. 3 It is practically impossible to tell the newest material 'fleur de Chine' from crêpe de Chine. 1928 *Times* 9 May 10/4 A draped gown of parchment fleur de soie, trimmed with old lace. 1928 *Daily Express* 23 July 5/2 Fleursoie, a soft firm material rather like triple georgette.

Fleuss (flois). The name of H. A. *Fleuss*, used *attrib.* to designate apparatus designed by him.
1882 *Rep. Inspectors of Mines for 1881* 463 Fleuss' breathing apparatus and lamp. 1883 *Encycl. Brit.* XVI. 467/1 Persons equipped with the Fleuss breathing apparatus can now enter mines after explosions. 1902 *Ibid.* XXXII. 190/1 The small Fleuss machine will produce about 1½ lb of ice in one operation of 20 minutes. 1904 *Technol. & Sci. Dict.* (ed. Goodchild & Tweney) s. v. *Air Pumps*, A great improvement in mechanical pumps has been made of recent years in what is called the Fleuss Pump. 1906 *Ibid.* s.v. *Tyres*, The Fleuss Tyre possesses no inner tube, but the edges of the cover overlap and fit together closely enough to retain the air. 1909 *Westm. Gaz.* 22 Feb. 8/1 'The Fleuss', he added, 'is the prototype of all apparatus using compressed oxygen and caustic soda, and it has already proved its value in mine rescue-work.'

Flew[2] (flū). [Probably a variant of Flue *sb.*[2]] 'A layer or fold of cloth as it comes from the loom' (*Cent. Dict.* Suppl. 1909). So **Flew·ing,** 'the process of examining cloth for blemishes in weaving by folding it upon the front of the loom as it is unrolled from the cloth-beam' (ibid.).
1895 R. Marsden *Cotton Weaving* 479 The first method [of cloth-looking] may be said to be that of 'flewing' it, which is probably the oldest form, and a survival from the days of handloom weaving. When the weaver has completed a piece of cloth, it is 'pulled out' from the cloth beam of the loom, being folded in 'flews' or layers upon the slay cap of the loom.

Flex (fleks), *sb.*[1] [Abbreviation of *Flexible *sb.*] Flexible insulated wire used in electric lighting. Also *attrib.*
1907 *Install. News* July 10/2 A flat piece of vulcanite.. provided with three holes, the bottom two being used to take the flex. 1922 *Daily Mail* 18 Dec. 1 Electric Iron, Complete with Flex cord and Adaptor. 1927 *Glasgow Herald* 6 Sept. 6 Found dead on his bed with wireless earphones on his head and a piece of flex, connecting with the crystal set, in his mouth.

Flex (fleks), *sb.*[2] *Math.* [f. L. *flexus*, f. *flectere* to bend.] A point of inflexion (see Inflexion 3).
1866 Cayley *Coll. Math. Papers* (1892) V. 521 The stationary inenut, or cusp, considered as..a particular case of the double inenut, is a spinode; to render this notation symmetrical, we require certain new terms, say link, as the correlative to node, and flex as the correlative to cusp... The ordinary singularities of a plane curve would thus be the node, the cusp, the link, and the flex.

Flexible, *a.* Add:
1. b. In modern mechanical and electrical usage (see quots.). Also as *sb.* = *Flex *sb.*[1]
1859 Rankine *Steam Eng.* (1861) 126 Flexible Tube and Diaphragm Valves. 1874 Knight *Dict. Mech.* s.v., Thirion's flexible coupling is used for conveying power from one shaft to another when they are not in line. 1888 *Lockwood's Dict. Mech. Engin., Flexible Crank Shaft*, a crank shaft in which the strains due to the rigidity of an unyielding mass compelled to revolve under conditions of strain due to the want of alignment of its bearings, are reduced and minimised by the introduction of flexible joints in its length...*Flexible Hose*, piping made either of india-rubber or leather. 1907 *Install. News* May 11/1 Conductors (excepting flexibles) may be enclosed in steel conduits. 1909 *Ibid.* II. 186/1 Flexible cord surface wiring. 1918 E. S. Farrow *Dict. Mil. Terms, Flexible*, a term applied to a dirigible balloon in which a flexible gas container is held in shape only by the pressure of gas within and to which the load is hung. This characterizes the whole non-rigid system of airships.

Flexing (fle·ksiŋ), *vbl. sb.* [f. Flex *v.* + -ing[1].] The action of the verb Flex.
1902 *Westm. Gaz.* 9 May 10/1 Those earth movements which have resulted in the flexing and fracturing of strata. 1920 *Blackw. Mag.* July 71/1 Never a tremor of wing except just the flexing and twisting of the tips for balance.

Flexure. Add:
8. *attrib.* and *Comb.*: (sense 7) **flexure-fault,** a fault in strata where flexure has occurred.
1895 Dana *Man. Geol.* (ed. 4) 109 Not unfrequently a flexure changes, in one direction or the other, into a fault...Many examples of such flexure-faults have been described..from the plateaus of Colorado.

Fli·bbertigi·bbet, *v.* [f. Flibbertigibbet *sb.*] *intr.* To play the flibbertigibbet; to gad about frivolously.
1921 Galsworthy *To Let* 1. i, His daughter *would* flibberty-gibbet all over the place like most young women since the War.

Flick, *sb.*[1] Add: **1. d.** *Cricket.* A quick turn of the batsman's or bowler's wrist in playing or delivering the ball; also, a turn of the ball.
1897 Ranjitsinhji *Jubilee Bk. Cricket* 73 There is a certain amount of 'flick' from the fingers, but this is quite different from the twist of the slow bowler. *Ibid.* 84 Spin imparted by wrist 'flick'. 1903 Jephson in *Cricket* (ed. H. G. Hutchinson) 91 The varying 'flicks' or 'whips' of the wrist. *Ibid.* 112 Two or three long loose strides, two at a trot, and an arm swinging round like a flail, a good length, great pace, and on any wicket at times a considerable flick back from the off.
e. *pl.* The films, the pictures; *sing.* a moving picture, a cinema performance. *slang.*
1926 E. Wallace *Square Emerald* xv, We'll occupy the afternoon with a 'flick.' I love the movies—especially the romantic ones. 1931 *Repertory* (Oxford) 18 Apr. 9/1 Hand in hand with the Muse of the Theatre departs the appropriate feminine deity who presides over the 'flicks'.

Flick, *v.*[2] Add:
2. c. *Cricket.* (*a*) Of the bowler: To deliver (a ball) with a flicking movement of the wrist. Also *intr.* said of the ball so delivered.
1903 Jephson in *Cricket* (ed. H. G. Hutchinson) 110 Bowling with a long bouncing run, he can make the ball flick higher and faster from the pitch than any other bowler. *Ibid.* 116 He 'flicks' the ball as we have all seen many a wrathful billiard-player do when returning the white from a most unexpected pocket. 1920 E. R. Wilson in *Cricket* (Badm.) 102 He [*sc.* Simpson-Hayward, the underhand bowler] 'flicked' the cricket ball as if it were a billiard ball.
(*b*) Of the batsman: To play (the ball) with a slight turn of the wrist.
1897 *Encycl. Sport* I. 223/2 The two wrists moving the bat with a sort of 'flicking' movement, impossible to describe. 1903 Warner in *Cricket* (ed. H. G. Hutchinson) 62 Short and straight balls, if they do not get up to any height, may be flicked round on the on side by a quick turn of the wrist. 1904 *Daily Chron.* 8 July 7/2 His success lies in the flicking of the straight, good-length ball to leg. 1927 Noble *Those 'Ashes'* 176 Gregory..was all at sea to Larwood, whom he flicked three times dangerously through the slips.
4. *fig.* To 'touch up'.
1923 *Challenge* 2 Feb. 390/1 The parody that follows.. flicks the whole super-sensitive school of novelists very neatly.

Flicker, *sb.*[3] Add:
2. b. A rapidly fluctuating or intermittent light; also, the sensation caused by such a light.
1893 O. N. Rood in *Amer. Jrnl. Sci.* Sept. 173 For the determination then of the reflecting power, for example of a vermilion disc, it was only necessary to select from the series a gray disc which when combined with it in equal parts gave no perceptible flicker. 1902 *Encycl. Brit.* XXX. 238/2 When in the comparison of lights of different colour the flicker vanishes, the sensation of colour is greatly diminished. 1913 F. A. Talbot *Moving Pictures* 7 The regularity of this recurring damping wave, described as 'flicker', set up severe eye-strain.
3. *attrib.* **flicker method,** the use of flicker photometry; **flicker photometer,** an instrument for measuring the relative intensities of light from two different sources by measuring the flicker or observing the absence of flicker when the field of view is illuminated alternately by the two sources of light; so **flicker photometry.**
1902 *Amer. Jrnl. Psychol.* XIII. 139 The brightnesses of these colors were determined by Rood's '*Flicker-method.' *Ibid.* 145 Shades of gray paper were selected by the 'Flicker Method', differing as little as possible from the brightness of the colors used. 1910 *N. Hawkins' Electr. Dict.*, **Flicker Photometer*, a type of photometer in which rotating mirrors of diffusing screens are employed in order to give rapidly alternating impressions from both lamps. 1912 H. Bohle *Electr. Photom.* 46 Experience shows that a Flicker photometer gives more consistent results than any other type when comparing lights of different colours. 1902 *Encycl. Brit.* XXX. 238/1 *Flicker photometry.

Flicker, *v.* Add: **7. b.** To cause to move in a fitful and unsteady manner; to indicate by a flicker.
1903 R. Langbridge *Flame & Flood* viii, He watched her eye-lashes flicker dismissal. *Ibid.* xxii, There was yet a partial inhumanity which licked its lips..which..burned as fiercely on the side of justice as injustice,..flickering an equal encouragement to '*I can't* go!' and—'I must!' 1907 *Munsey's Mag.* Dec. 303/1 [They] entered the castle..; the torches flickering weird shadows as they walked between them.

Flickerless (fli·kəɹlės), *a.* [f. Flicker *sb.*[3] + -less.] Without flickers, producing no flicker.
1922 M. J. Wrigley *The Film* 117 Mr. Martin Harper.. has the credit to his name of producing the 'Extralite' flickerless shutter.

Flicky (fli·ki), *a.*[2] [f. Flick *sb.*[1] + -y[1].] Of or pertaining to a flick, jerky.
1897 Ranjitsinhji *Jubilee Bk. Cricket* 127 There is something distinctly jerky and flicky in this projection of the elbow and straightening of the arm.

Flight, *sb.*[1] Add:
1. f. The action or art of travelling through the air in a flying machine; now restricted to travel in such machines as are capable of effective control (and so distinguished from a voyage in a balloon).
1784 *Universal Mag.* Sept. 358 We again took our flight [in a balloon], and ascended to near 1200 feet. 1835 *Nautical Mag.* Oct. 613 It is related that the aërial ship took her first flight in a waggon. 1852 *Household Words* IV. 98/2 Exertions he had undergone in preparing for the flight. 1879 *Encycl. Brit.* IX. 308/1 It is not necessary to enter upon a history of artificial flight. 1904 *Pall Mall Mag.* Jan. 19/2 Nor is it an easy task to calculate an air-ship's speed. On these flights up and down the Mediterranean coast, [etc.]. 1909 *Daily Chron.* 19 Mar. 4/5 Lilienthal..shares with Pilcher.. and Le Bris, the honour of being the pioneer of modern experiments in gliding flight. 1926 H. Barber *Aeroplane Speaks* 1 The Elementary Principles of Flight.
g. An instance of this; a voyage in a flying machine.
1909 *Aero* 25 May 14/1 Mr. J. T. C. Moore-Brabazon has made several short flights with the *Bird of Passage* at Shellness. 1912 *Aeroplane* 26 Dec. 637/2 Their Yuletide present takes the form of a ticket for a passenger flight at Hendon. 1928 *Times* 22 Mar., [The King of Afghanistan's] first flight in any civil aircraft, and his only flight since he visited Europe.
h. A Royal Air Force unit consisting of about five or six machines.
1914 Rosher *In R. N. A. S.* (1916) 25 We shall not get our squadron together until the end of January...We may, however, go over in pieces, a flight at a time. 1915 *War Illustrated* 27 Nov. 345 This branch of the Army is organized in what are called wings, divided into squadrons, and subdivided into flights. 1917 *Blackw. Mag.* July 121/1 Twelve officers flew to France with the flight to which I belonged.
6. d. *Cricket.* The control of the trajectory and pace of the ball in its flight before pitching. (Cf. *Flight *v.* 7.)
1903 Jephson in *Cricket* (ed. H. G. Hutchinson) 88 He.. possesses a wonderful command of length,..a considerable variation of flight. *Ibid.* 106 He was..one of the most difficult of medium-paced bowlers, for the flight was so deceptive. 1911 P. F. Warner *Bk. Cricket* 74 Every slow left-hander should cultivate 'flight'.
13. d. (Earlier U.S. example.)
1813 *Niles' Weekly Register* V. Add. A. 6/2 It was extended with flights to draw the meal towards the Hopper.
14. b. In titles of officers of various ranks in the Royal Air Force.
1926 H. Barber *Aeroplane Speaks* 27 The Flight-Sergeant is awaiting the Pilot's orders. 1917 *Blackw. Mag.* Mar. 380/2 'Good-night, you chaps,' said one of the flight-commanders. *Ibid.* May 800/1 The good work of my pilot had brought him a flight commandership. 1928 C. F. S. Gamble *North Sea Air Station* iv. 75 Flight Commander (relative rank of Lieutenant, R.N.). Flight Lieutenant (relative rank of Lieutenant, R.N.). Flight Sub-Lieutenant (relative rank of Sub-Lieutenant, R.N.).

Flight, *v.* Add: **7.** *Cricket.* To vary the trajectory and pace of (the ball) in its flight before pitching.
1927 Noble *Those 'Ashes'* 24 Lockton..flighted and turned the ball well. 1931 *Daily Mail* 7 May 13/3 Slow bowling is useless unless the ball is pitched up to the batsman, or, rather, is made to appear to pitch up to him. That is what is commonly called flighting, persuading a batsman to play forward when he should play back.

Flim-flam, *v.* *U.S.* (Later examples.)
1903 O. Kildare *My Mamie Rose* 72 'Flim-flamming'... Doubling a bill in a number of them and counting each end of it as one separate bill. 1904 Eliz. Robins *Magnetic North* ii. 144 But I didn't know *you'd* get flim-flammed out o' your boots. 1911 H. Quick *Yellowstone N.* xi. 290 Financial ingenuity has found a way to flim flam the devil himself.

Hence **Flim-flammer** *U.S.* (Later example.)
1903 *N. Y. Sun* 20 Nov. 8 They are about as fine a bunch of grafters and flim-flammers as have been got together in some time.

Flimmer, *v.* (Later U.S. examples of extended use.)
1918 C. Sandburg *Cornhuskers* 17 Canada thistle blue and flimmering larkspur blue. *Ibid.* 114 The shafts across her bed are flimmering.

Flinch, *sb.* [f. Flinch *v.*[1]] Flinching.
1829–32 J. P. Kennedy *Swallow B.* I. xx. 205 Thar's no flinch in me, you may depend upon it. 1922 A. S. M. Hutchinson *This Freedom* II. ii. 91 But she came back bravely from her flinch.

Flinders[2] (fli·ndəɹz). The name of Captain Matthew *Flinders* (1774–1814), English navigator and explorer, used attrib. in **Flinders bar(s),** a soft iron bar or bundle of rods, placed vertically near a ship's compass to correct deviation due to magnetic induction and to lessen the heeling-error.
1902 *Encycl. Brit.* XXVII. 181/2 A method of correcting deviation by means of a bar of vertical iron so placed as to correct the deviation nearly in all latitudes. This bar, now known as a 'Flinders bar,' is still in general use. 1924 Rex Clements *Gipsy of Horn* (1925) 217 The binnacle was useless..for the Flinders-bars had gone with the sky-light.

Flindosa (flindōu·ză). *Austral.* [Corruption of *Flindersia*, a genus of trees, f. the name of Captain Matthew *Flinders*: see prec.] The rasp-pod or Australian beech, *Flindersia australis.* So **Flindo·sy.**
1898 Morris *Austral Eng.*

Flinkite (fli·ŋkəit). *Min.* [ad. G. *flinkit* (1889), f. the name of Gustav *Flink*, Swedish mineralogist.] A basic arsenate of manganese, occurring in greenish-brown crystals in Sweden.
1892 Dana *Syst. Min.* (ed. 6) 802 Flinkite...Occurs with caryopilite and sarkinite at the Harstig mine near Pajsberg, Sweden.

Flint, *sb.* Add: **8. c.** ellipt. for *flint-corn* (see *10).
1857 *Trans. Ill. Agric. Soc.* III. 63, I plant the white flint. It is rather on the gourd seed order. 1883 *Encycl. Brit.* XV. 100/2 The 'Flint' varieties are most common east of Lake Erie and north of Maryland. 1913 W. Bateson *Mendel's Princ. Heredity* 264 Analogous observations have been made in regard to Maize, especially by Lock. According as the seeds are opaque or semi-transparent, the varieties are distinguished as 'Dent' or 'Flint'.
9. b. *flint-chipper.* **c.** *flint-headed* adj. (earlier U.S. example).
1872 *Amer. Naturalist* VI. 208 Unfinished specimens suggest that variety was continually aimed at by the '*flint chipper'. 1843 Carlton *New Purchase* I. 2 Shadows of branching antlers and *flint-headed arrows caused many a darkness in his path.
10. flint-corn, the name of certain varieties of maize having very hard grains; **flint-gun** (earlier U.S. example).
1705 Beverley *Hist. Virginia* (1722) 126 The one [grain] looks as smooth, and as full as the early ripe Corn, and this they call **Flint-Corn.* 1837 Colman *Rep. Agric. Mass.* (1838) 20 The best kinds of flint corn weigh 60 lbs. to the bushel. 1872 E. Eggleston *End of World* viii. 60 The relative merits of 'gourd-seed' and 'flint' corn. 1894 *Vermont Agric. Rep.* XIV. 47 Where the whole corn is put in..say of the Flint corn, is there not a good deal of waste by imperfect digestion? 1837 W. Irving *Capt. Bonneville* (1895) II. 133 Their *flint guns were at fault, and missed fire.

Flinty, *a.* Add: **2. b.** *spec.* applied to varieties of maize (cf. *flint-corn*, *Flint *sb.* 10).
1818 J. Taylor *Arator* 227 The small flinty forward kind [of corn] producing from 2 to 6 ears on a stalk, inspired the most hope. 1876 *Trans. Ill. Dep. Agric.* XIII. 301 The French raised almost entirely the hard, flinty corn, from which hominy was manufactured.
4. flinty-slate (see quot.).
1879 A. Geikie in *Encycl. Brit.* X. 238/1 Flinty-slate (Lydian-stone, Hornstone) is a siliceous shale or mudstone.. breaking with a conchoidal or splintery fracture.

Flip, *sb.*[1] Add: **2.** In *U.S.* = custard.
3. flip-iron *U.S.* = *flip-dog.*
1869 Mrs. Stowe *Oldtown Folks* xxxvii. 480 Draw the flip-iron from the fire and stir the foaming bowl.

Flip, *sb.*[2] Add:
2. b. *Gunnery.* The springing of the barrel of a gun at the moment of discharge.
1903 *Kynoch Jrnl.* June–July 101/2 The flip, or springing of the barrel may entirely counteract the increase in jump. 1904 *Ibid.* Jan.–Mar. 63 The flip was evidently not entirely vertical since the direction varied as well as the elevation. 1905 *Ibid.* April–June 80 There is the probability that the 'jump' or 'flip' of the rifles will not be quite the same. 1925 G. Burrard *Notes on Sporting Rifles* (ed. 2) 75 They do not take into account the effect of jump or flip. This varies in every individual rifle and barrel.
4. A flight in an aircraft; a trip in an aeroplane. *colloq.* or *slang.*
1914 Rosher *In R.N.A.S.* (1916) 28 It was much too foggy for my trip to Hartlepool yesterday afternoon, but I went for a short flip around. 1920 *Blackw. Mag.* Feb. 167/2 The *Morse* arrived, untouched, on 4th March, after a two months' 'flip'. 1929 *Daily Express* 7 Nov. 2/1, I went to Croydon and went up again for a short 'flip'.

Flip, *v.* Add:
8. To fly in an aircraft. *colloq.* or *slang.*
1915 Rosher *In R.N.A.S.* (1916) 41, I crashed into the atmosphere first thing this morning and flipped around for 55 minutes.

Flip-flap, *sb.* Add:
3. d. In a place of amusement or the amusement section of an exhibition, etc., a machine with long moving arms to which passengers are raised on platforms (see quot. 1908).
1908 *Daily Chron.* 3 Apr. 7/2 The..huge steel arms [are] 150 ft. in length, much like the main shaft of a crane, greatly magnified...These arms will be slowly raised until their extremities cross in the air, 150 ft. above the level, and then each will complete the semi-circle. Suspended from..the band of each steel arm will be a car containing passengers... The flip-flap is built on the cantilever principle with heavy counter weights. 1922 Mrs. A. Sidgwick *Victorian* xxii, He is going to have millions of Japanese lanterns and a Flip-Flap and an open air café like at Earl's Court.

Flip-flop, *sb.* Add: **c.** A somersault. Cf. Flip-flap B. *sb.* 3 a. *U.S.*
1902 G. H. Lorimer *Lett. Self-made Merchant* xvii. 245 And when a fellow's turning flip-flops up among the clouds, he's naturally going to have the farmers gaping at him. 1929 *Liberty* 30 Nov. 43/1 Turning hand-springs and flip-flops all over the sawdust covered floor.
d. As advb.
1904 H. G. Wells *Food of Gods* II. i. 145 She..passed, flip-flop, within three yards of them.

Hence **Flip-flopping,** a flip-flop sound.
1897 *Outing* (U.S.) XXX. 176/1, I could hear a vigorous flip-flopping going on beyond the weeds, and I knew the captive was a trout.

Flitch, *sb.*[1] Add:
3. c. In full *flitch-plate*, a strengthening plate added to a beam, girder, or any woodwork.
1888 *Lockwood's Dict. Mech. Engin., Flitch*, a plate of metal or of wood bolted to an otherwise weak and unstayed beam or structure in order to strengthen and support it. *Flitch Plate*, a broad thin plate or rolled bar used in building up flitch beams or plated work. 1912 *Motor Man.* (ed. 14) iii. 89 To build the frame up of stout section ash and bolt on steel 'flitch' plates to the sides.

Flivver (fli·vəɹ), *sb.* orig. *U.S. slang.* [Of obscure origin.]
1. A person or thing that has a damaging or deleterious influence; 'a failure, fizzle, bungle' (Webster, Add. 1918).
1915 H. L. Wilson *Ruggles of Red Gap* xiii. (1917) 230 That Jackson lad has offered me about ten thousand of them vegetable cigarettes, but I'll have to throw him down. He's the human flivver. Put him in a car of dressed beef and he'd freeze it between here and Spokane.
2. A cheap motor car or aeroplane. Also, 'a destroyer of 750 tons or less' (*Funk's Stand. Dict.* 1928).
1920 *Glasgow Herald* 21 July 9 May be I will disguise the Shamrock as a 'flivver' (as the Ford car is known here). 1921 R. D. Paine *Comr. Rolling Ocean* i. 4 It was a shabby, weary-looking flivver that rolled its bones over the sun-baked ruts. 1924 W. M. Raine *Troubled Waters* vi. 58 Rowan McCoy drove his new car—it was a flivver, though they did not call it that in those days. 1926 *Ladies' Home Jrnl.* Apr. 39 Won't it be amusing when we can..step into our little up-shooting flivvers at the back door? 1927 *Punch* 2 Feb. 135/1 He has successfully fought the villain Trust; his workmen all own 'flivvers'; there has never been a strike.

Hence **Fli·vver** *v.*, to travel in a flivver; also to fail, to come short of success.
1913 L. J. Vance *Destroying Angel* vi. 74 If the production flivvers, I'll need that thirty cents. 1927 *Bulletin* 11 Apr. 14/1, I was finding the desert a bit flat when you flivvered in.

Float, *sb.* Add: **6. b.** A 'wave' or crowd. *U.S.*
1873 J. H. Beadle *Undevel. West* xviii. 329 Their mode of life engenders a love of gaming, and following close upon them..is a 'float' of gamblers, strikers, [etc.].
8. e. A structure fitted to the alighting gear of a flying-machine to enable it to float on water.
1897 *Strand Mag.* June 717/1 The conical vessel in front is an empty float, whose use is to keep the whole from sinking if it should fall in the water. 1909 *Flight* 30 Jan. 63/1 Delagrange..has ordered a set of special floats for his aeroplane. 1913 *Aeroplane* 17 Apr. 453 Labouret..'stalled' the machine, fell over sideways, and smashed..the right float. *Ibid.* 455 The concertina floats on this machine are evidently a great success. 1928 C. F. S. Gamble *North Sea Air Station* Introd. 13 Experiments with various types of floats and flotation bags for aeroplanes.
9. a. Also, a device which floats on and regulates the motor spirit in the carburettor of a petrol motor.
1901 *Motor-Car World* Mar. 42/1 The Float. 1902 A. C. Harmsworth *Motors & Motor-Driving* vii. 112 F is a float with wire attached to indicate the height of the petrol. 1912 *Motor Man.* (ed. 14) 10 When the float sinks it opens a small valve and allows the petrol to flow in till a certain level is reached. The float then rises and closes the valve.
22. *U.S.* (Later example.)
1841 J. Buchanan *Wks.* (1908) IV. 345 We have wisely determined to put down forever the practice of granting what are called 'floats'.
24. float-anchor = *floating anchor*; **float-carburettor,** a carburettor in which the feed is regulated by a float; **float-chamber,** the chamber containing a float (sense *9 a); **float-feed,** a device for controlling the feed of a liquid by means of a float; also *attrib.*; **float-gold** (earlier U.S. example); **float-ironed** *a.*, ironed by means of a float roll calender; so **float-ironing; float needle,** the indicator of a float (sense *9 a); **float-road** *U.S.* (see quot.); **float-rock** = *float-mineral*; **float roll calender, machine,** an ironing machine constructed with springs and resilient padding to the rollers, so that articles with buttons, etc. may be passed through without damage; **float-seaplane,** a seaplane equipped with floats.
1897 *Outing* (U.S.) XXX. 259/1 Securing the *Otter* by means of a '*float-anchor'. 1901 *Motor-Car World* Mar. 42/1 Should petrol run over at the jet when the pressure is on, give the spindle in the centre of the *float-chamber a few turns with a screwdriver to grind in the needle valve. When the engine is not running keep the spring on the *float needle. 1902 A. C. Harmsworth *Motors & Motor-Driving* vii. 115 The method of supplying petrol to the carburetter is on the same principle..., *float feed. 1907 *Westm. Gaz.* 28 Nov. 4/1 The carburetter is of the float-feed type. *Ibid.* 5 Dec. 4/2 Carburetter..of the usual float-feed spray type. 1873 Joaquin Miller *Unwritten Hist.* xvi. (1876) 231 They had found only a few bars with *float gold. 1927 *Daily Tel.* 11 May 17/5 Laundry for sale...Good-class family and *float-ironed services. 1905 *Terms Forestry & Logging* 37 **Float road*, a channel cleared in a swamp and used to float cypress logs from the woods to the boom at the river or mill. 1902 H. L. Wilson *Spenders* i. 15 He was talking about some likely *float-rock he'd picked up over that way last summer. 1926 *Laundry Jrnl.* 23 Oct. Suppl. p. iii, *Float-Roll with Hamilton Padding and full vacuum attachment. 1928 C. F. S. Gamble *North Sea Air Station* xiii. 212 The flying-boat is not so fast, nor has it the same ceiling, as *float-seaplanes.

Float, *v.* Add:
5. d. To be deflected *from* its position.
1896 *McClure's Mag.* VI. 490/2 In technical language, the core had 'floated' an eighth of an inch from its position.
9. *U.S.* (Additional examples.)
1875 Holland *Sevenoaks* x. 134 They floated for deer at night. 1885 *Outing* (U.S.) Oct. VII. 80/2 'Kill any deer over there?' 'No,' said Carl, 'we floated two nights, but it was terrible foggy'.
11. d. To clear *out* by floating. *U.S.*
1873–4 *Rep. Vermont Board Agric.* II. 226 The washing in brine is done to float out imperfect kernels.

Floatation. Add: **1. b.** The separation of the particles of finely pulverized ore by utilizing their relative capacity for floating on a given liquid.
1908 *Westm. Gaz.* 1 Aug. 15/1, 11,775 tons of dump tailings were treated by the flotation process. 1927 *Daily Express* 15 July 10/1 The original ore is readily amenable to treatment by flotation.
3. *attrib.* (sense 1) **floatation bag** = *Float *sb.* 8 e.
1928 [see *Float *sb.* 8 e].

Floater. Add: **1. a.** *spec.* (*a*) A golf-ball capable of floating in water.
1897 *Westm. Gaz.* 30 Mar. 9/2 There are bournes from which no ball, not e'en a floater, returns. 1921 *Punch* CLX. 134/1 The only theme to-day discussed Is 'Shall we standardise the Floater?' 1927 *Daily Express* 29 Sept. 9 Many leading American professionals ask that the 'floater' be adopted as the official standard ball.
(*b*) A piece of float-ore.
1921 *Chambers's Jrnl.* 508/1 The molybdenite-seeker next proceeds to work in earnest by breaking all the loose 'floaters' or detached boulders, and collecting all the flakes that are set free in bags. 1928 *Sunday Dispatch* 25 Nov. 3/5 The chance discovery..of a large 'floater,' or piece of gold-bearing quartz.
(*c*) A cask, buoy, or bottle containing a message, thrown into the sea and left to float.
1898 *Geog. Jrnl.* (R.G.S.) XII. 527 Several 'floaters', or receptacles for messages, had been thrown overboard before reaching the neighbourhood of Cape Farewell.
(*d*) A dead body found floating in water. *U.S. slang.*
1897 [in letter from Washington University, St. Louis]. 1898 *Westm. Gaz.* 28 July 8/1 Bodies found in the water, which are known at the [New York] Morgue as 'floaters'.
2. e. A tanning vat.
1897 C. T. Davis *Manuf. Leather* (ed. 2) 403 The skins are handled daily..for a month in 'floaters' in liquor of about 20 degrees.
3. b. *Insurance.* A policy in general terms. (Cf. *Floating *ppl. a.* 5 b.)
1900 *Policy-holder* 6 June 441/2 The Norwich Union is largely interested..by specific amounts and by floaters... Messrs. John McNairn and Co. had a £20,000 floater from the North British.
4. *U.S.* **a.** (Further examples.)
1847 *Knickerbocker Mag.* XXIX. 329 Early the next morning the 'floaters' were marched in single file with votes in hand, to the ballot box. 1905 D. G. Phillips *Plum Tree* 14 Those 'floaters' had to keep the ballot in full view.
b. (Earlier examples.)
1873 J. H. Beadle *Undevel. West* xxiii. 455 There are clerks, agents..and perhaps fifty 'floaters', making up the American population. 1878 — *Western Wilds* iii. 45 A man ..failed, lost hope, and sank into a 'floater'.
5. A mistake, 'bloomer'. *slang.*
1925 A. Huxley *Those Barren Leaves* I. i, What she called in her jovial undergraduatish moments, a 'floater'. 1929 P. G. Wodehouse in *Legion Bk.* 110 It's just when our intentions are best that we always make the most poisonous floaters.

Floating, *ppl. a.* Add: **1.** (Additional examples.)
1838 *Southern Lit. Messenger* IV. 26/1 The noise of steam, and the dissonant voices of the crowd subside, and give place to the regular thump of the floating hotel [*sc.* a steamer]. 1843 *Knickerbocker Mag.* XXII. 85 The Knickerbocker-Steamer, that floating palace of the Hudson. 1912 *Chambers's Jrnl.* 184/2 A floating factory means an old steamer of three to four thousand tons, a size which has annually been increased...By using the larger size of steamers the owners are able to fit them with plant not only for trying out the blubber..but also with plant for turning the carcasses into oil and guano.
3. b. (See quot.)
1888 *Lockwood's Dict. Mech. Engin.* s. v., When the lever of a weigh-bridge or of a testing machine is in equal balance it is said to be floating.
5. b. Of an insurance policy: Variable as to certain details, as a policy of marine insurance which covers a certain class of goods or all goods shipped between specified ports, or a policy which insures goods of a certain class the specific articles of which are liable to change.
1839 *Southern Lit. Messenger* V. 7/1 The packets, by their 'floating policies of insurance' offer another inducement to shippers. 1902 *Encycl. Brit.* XXIX. 527/2 As it frequently happens that merchants desire to have all their shipments covered, by whatever vessel they may come, they require insurance in general terms; such a policy is termed a *floating* policy.
6. floating axle, a live axle in which the revolving part turns the wheels while the weight of the vehicle is carried on the ends of a fixed axle housing; **floating battery** (*a*) (later example); (*b*) *Electr.* (see quot. 1910); **floating mill** *U.S.*, a mill so constructed as to float in a river and be worked by the current; also *attrib.*; **floating vote, voter** *U.S.* (see Floater 4 a).

1907 *Westm. Gaz.* 26 Nov. 4/3 The famous '*floating' back axle. 1866 E. A. Pollard *Southern Hist. War* I. 60 The *floating battery dismounted two of the parapet guns [of Fort Sumter]. 1878 *Encycl. Brit.* VIII. 72/2 De la Rive's floating battery. 1910 *N. Hawkins' Electr. Dict., Floating Battery*, a storage battery employed in a parallel system to discharge into or be charged by the system as required. 1817 S. R. Brown *Western Gaz.* 52 It has a post office, and a *floating mill anchored abreast of the town. 1888 *Lockwood's Dict. Mech. Engin., Floating Mill Wheel*, a water wheel, having its bearings in a boat moored in the stream of a rapidly flowing river, which turns the wheel and performs work for which it is suitable. 1847 *Knickerbocker Mag.* XXIX. 328 Such constitute what in common parlance is called the '*floating vote'. 1905 D. G. Phillips *Plum Tree* 14 Those stiff-armed men were the '*floating voters' of that ward of Pulaski.
b. In the names of certain grasses (see quots.). *U.S.*
1856 *Rep. Mass. Board Agric.* I. 22 Floating Foxtail, (*Alopecurus geniculatus*). *Ibid.* 50 The Floating Meadow Grass, or Common Manna Grass.

Floating-out. [f. vbl. phrase *to float out* (see Float *v.* 11).] The action of floating a ship out of dock. Also *attrib.*
1896 *Daily News* 18 Sept. 6/7 The floating-out of dock of the battleship Illustrious at Chatham Dockyard. 1899 *Ibid.* 29 June 5/5 Her floating-out weight was 1,500 tons.

Flobert (flōu·bəɹt, ‖flobɛr). The name of a French armourer, used attrib. in *Flobert cartridge, rifle.*
1904 *Kynoch Jrnl.* Jan.–Mar. 33 The Flobert cartridge is notable as being an evolution of the percussion cap.

Flocculus. Add: **3.** *Astr.* **a.** Applied to the wisps of luminosity in a nebula.
1826 Sir J. Herschel in *Mem. Astron. Soc.* II. 491 The flocculi [in the nebula of Orion], instead of being generally round, are drawn out into little wisps.
b. A name given by Hale to cloudy wisps or masses covering the sun's surface, revealed when the sun is photographed with the spectroheliograph.
1904 G. E. Hale & Ellerman in *Astrophys. Jrnl.* XIX. 42 It has now seemed best..to suggest the name *flocculus* to distinguish a mass of vapor from the facula which may or may not lie below it. *Ibid.*, The term 'flocculi' is applied indiscriminately to all bright or dark clouds of vapor photographed in projection on the Sun's disk, without distinction of level. 1915 G. E. Hale *Ten Yrs. Wk. Mount. Observ.* 20 The spectroheliograph..discloses extensive clouds of calcium, hydrogen, iron, and other vapors, which..are recorded (as flocculi). *Ibid.* 21 At the lower level of the calcium flocculi the period of rotation at the sun's equator is 24.8 days.

Flogging, *vbl. sb.* Add:
2. d. *Army slang.* (See quot.)
1919 *War Terms* in *Athenæum* 1 Aug. 695/2 'Flogging,' the illegal disposal of Army goods. [Cf. 1925 E. Fraser & Gibbons *Soldier & Sailor Words, Flog*, to: to sell something not the vendor's own to dispose of.]

Flood, *sb.* **8.** Add: **flood-light,** artificial light projected in quantity from different directions so that dark shadows are completely eliminated; also, a light forming part of a system for illuminating ground in this way; also *attrib.*; hence **flood-light** *v. trans.*, to illuminate with flood-light; **flood-lighting,** the action of illuminating with flood-lights; also, flood-lights collectively; also *attrib.*; so **flood-lit** *a.*; **flood-plain** (earlier example); **flood-way,** (*a*) a piece of flooded road or path; (*b*) a channel constructed for the purpose of taking the flood-waters of a river; **flood-wood** (earlier U.S. example).
1925 A. E. Newton *Greatest Bk. in World* 82 From either side of the proscenium arch two *flood-lights played upon the actors. 1925 *Cady & Dates' Illum. Engin.* 410 The light may be projected from flood-light projectors. 1928 *Daily Tel.* 29 May 10/5 From thirty flood-light projectors the Royal Pavilion was bathed in amber, red, and green. 1930 *Aberdeen Press & Jrnl.* 29 Mar. 7/1 It would be useless to turn a 'flood-light' on to any article which cannot stand this searching test. 1923 Luckiesh *Light & Color* 256 Tall or isolated buildings are particularly attractive when *flood-lighted. 1928 C. F. S. Gamble *North Sea Air Station* ix. 131 By flood-lighting the sky with flares placed on the tops of balloons. 1917 *Electr. News* 26, 48 A Resumé of *Flood-lighting. 1923 J. W. T. Walsh *Lighting & Photom.* 188 The illumination of open spaces..may often be carried out satisfactorily by a floodlighting equipment. 1927 Mary Borden *Flamingo* II. ii, It was, of course, most beautiful at night against the dark, when Peter's flood-lighting streamed over it to make it translucent as ice. 1928 *Daily Express* 6 Aug. 15/1 Its walls, brilliantly *flood-lit,..are made almost entirely of sheets of glass. 1873 J. H. Beadle *Undevel. West* xxx. 656 West of the 'Buckskin' was a singular *flood plain some six miles wide. 1889 Gretton *Memory's Harkback* 108 Near Tewkesbury and Upton there was a nasty bit of *flood-way. 1928 *Manchester Guardian Weekly* 31 Aug. 178/3 The construction of a 'floodway' leaving the main stream [of the Mississippi] at Bird Point, near Cairo. 1821 *Massachusetts Spy* 6 Feb. (Th.) There are two short carrying places in this distance, occasioned by *flood-wood.

Flood, *v.* Add: **3. b.** To drive *out* by floods.
1910 *Westm. Gaz.* 21 June 8/3 The flooded-out attendants.
4. d. To become flooded.
1908 *Daily Report* 24 Aug. 9/1 A carburettor which persistently floods is not uncommon. 1912 *Motor Man.* 13 A persistent tendency to flood..due to a punctured float.

Floor, *sb.*[1] Add: **1.** Phr. *To wipe the floor with*: see Wipe *v.* 9 e.
7. b. *The floor* (Cricket colloq.): the ground. So *to put a catch on the floor* (Cricket colloq.): to fail to hold it.
1903 *Strand Mag.* XXV. 624/2 A large majority of them [*sc.* catches] were 'put on the floor'.
14. *floor-space.*
1876 J. S. Ingram *Centennial Expos.* v. 150 It occupied about one-seventh of the entire floor-space in that structure. 1896 M. Beaumont *Joan Seaton* 113 The floor-space was so great, that there was no crowding.
15. floor-leader *U.S.*, a leader in debate, esp. in legislative assemblies; **floor-manager** *U.S.*, a 'master of ceremonies' at a dance; **floor-timber,** (*b*) *U.S.* timber for flooring; **floor-walker** *U.S.* (earlier example).
1899 *Congress. Rec.* 11 Feb. 1764/2 Congress has witnessed very few more successful 'floor leaders. 1906 *Springfield* (Mass.) *Weekly Republ.* 8 Feb. 11 Representative Payne.. is titular republican floor leader in the House. 1887 *Harper's Mag.* May 967/1 Jerry, as one of the *floor-managers, was gorgeous. 1902 Harben *Abner Daniel* 47 The floor-managers piloted the dancers down-stairs. 1851 C. Cist *Cincinnati* 325 'Floor timbers..are here furnished. 1876 F. R. Stockton in *Scribner's Monthly* Feb. 599/2, I next went into a store a few doors further up Broadway. When I entered I approached the *floor-walker.

Floorer. Add:
1. b. In the game of skittles, a throw with the first of three balls which floors all the pins.
1883 *Cassell's Bk. Sports* 128 The only play that will secure a floorer is to throw the ball with a good round-handed swing, imparting to the ball what in billiards would be called a 'side', and so that the edge of the ball alights on the right-handed shoulder of the front pin. 1928 *Daily Express* 31 Mar. 3/4 A scroll on which are inscribed the names of members who have scored floorers. 1930 A. P. Herbert *Water Gipsies* xxi, A stranger to the game could not have told how it happened, but in less than a second the frame was clear—not one pin standing—a 'floorer'.

Flooring, *vbl. sb.* **5.** *flooring-board* (earlier U.S. example), *-machine.*
1851 C. Cist *Cincinnati* 237 Every other building article, panel doors, blinds,..*flooring-boards and plank, [etc.]. 1847 H. Howe *Hist. Collect. Ohio* 372 There are now in operation within the corporate limits..2 *flooring machines.

Floose (flūs). Also **falus, faloos, floos, flus(e).** [See Fluce *sb.*] A small coin of north Africa, Arabia, India, and other neighbouring countries.
1625 in Foster *Engl. Factories India* (1909) III. 71 There money goeth by the caffala, of which 9½ maketh a doller and 60 fluse to a caffala. 1858 Simmonds *Dict. Trade, Floose*, the tenth part of a danim, a petty money of Bussorah and other parts of Arabia. 1906 *Daily Chron.* 2 May 7/6 To-day a well-dressed man, who sees a European passing in the street, extends his hand, and mutters something about 'flus'. 1907 *Daily Mail* 18 Jan. 6/4 Often have I bestowed upon him a *floos* for bread.

Flop, *sb.* Add: **4. b.** A turn-round; a sudden change of policy or party. *U.S.*
1904 *Springfield* (Mass.) *Weekly Republ.* 7 Oct. 2 That a flop by the most militant of the unionists is under contemplation has been denied. 1911 H. S. Harrison *Queed* xviii. 230 So ran the editorial, which was offensively headed 'West's Fatal Flop'.
c. A failure, collapse, or decline. Also, a book or play which is a failure.
1893 Farmer *Slang, Flop.* 2...A sudden fall or 'flop' down. 3...A collapse or breakdown. 1899 *Westm. Gaz.* 28 Jan. 6/2 There has been a flop in Trunks, but Canadas have been good. 1927 *Sunday Express* 15 May 5/7 Nearly all the American turns prove a flop. Yet they think they can command the earth. 1930 *Publishers' Weekly* 18 Oct. 1851 These authors every once in a while write a flop.
d. A 'flabby' or 'soft' person. *slang.*
1909 H. G. Wells *Tono-Bungay* II. iv. 171 All the little, soft feminine hands, the nervous ugly males, the hands of the flops, and the hands of the snatchers! 1923 *Glasgow Herald* 12 Dec. 10 If that little flop..believes he can play fast and loose with the moral consciousness of this nation. 1930 R. Fraser *Rose Anstey* xii. 301 You funny little man...You're simply a flop.
5. *flop-eared* (earlier U.S. example); **flop-house,** a doss-house.
1845 J. J. Hooper *Adv. Simon Suggs* ii. 28 You..gnatty, *flop-eared varmint! 1927 *Scots Observer* 26 Mar. 20/3 The lowest of the derelicts spent the night..in a '*flophouse' (which is worse than the lowest 'model'). 1930 *Harper's Mag.* July 133 The Welfare Council of New York had to charter an old barge..as an overflow flop house.

Flop, *adv.* and *int.* Add: Also *fig.*
1930 *Daily Express* 6 Sept. 4/2 Every one adopts a 'wait and see' policy, and business goes 'flop'.

Flop, *v.* Add: **2. b.** Also without *over*; and *trans.* to cause to change sides; to bring over. *U.S.*
1904 *Omaha Bee* 3 Sept. 6 A number of New York newspapers have flopped to the support of Parker. 1904 *Springfield* (Mass.) *Weekly Republ.* 16 Dec. 8 Mr. Roche flopped the Boston Pilot to the support of the republican candidate.
c. To 'go flop', collapse. *slang.*
1919 P. G. Wodehouse *Damsel in Distress* viii, The summertime number [in a theatre] flopped on the second night. 1928 *Observer* 15 July 15/1 If..the play 'flops' after a run of..three or four nights.

Flopper (flǫ·pəɹ). *U.S.* [f. Flop *v.* 2 b.] One who deserts to the opposite side, esp. in politics.
1904 *Louisville Courier Jrnl.* 17 Aug. 4 There are always floppers. The mere circumstance that somebody deserts his party and goes over to the other proves nothing. 1905 *N.Y. Even. Post* 28 Dec. 1 Assemblyman Rogers is a flopper because he withdrew from the speakership race and re-entered it.

Floppy, *a.* Add: Also *fig.*
1905 Sladen *Playing the Game* ix, She's such a young heifer—she's at the floppy sentimental age.

Florencite (flǫ·rĕnsəit). *Min.* [f. name of W. *Florence* + -ite[1].] A hydrated phosphate of alumina and cerium earths.
1899 *Min. Mag.* (1900) XII. 244 Florencite was first discovered as a rare constituent of the cinnabar-bearing sands of Tripuhy, near Ouro Preto, Minas Geraes, Brazil. *Ibid.* 247 The chemical composition of florencite is..very similar to that of hamlinite.

Florida. Add: **Florida moss** = Long-beard 2, *Tillandsia usneoides.*
1888 G. Trumbull *Bird Names* 75 A large bunch of 'Florida moss'. 1924 *Contemp. Rev.* Jan. 95 Giant trees hung with florida moss.
b. A variety of orange grown largely in Florida.
1892 Susan Hale *Lett.* (1919) 270 Oranges are delicious... I think they must be Floridas. 1896 *Daily News* 24 Dec. 3/2 The difficulty with 'Floridas' is the cost of the transit, owing to the very great tenderness of their skins.

Floridean (flǫri·diăn), *a.* [f. mod.L. *Florideæ* (f. L. *floridus* Florid) + -an.] Of or pertaining to the *Florideæ.*
1902 *Encycl. Brit.* XXV. 272/1 The colourless granules of *Florideæ*..have been called floridean-starch.

Floridian (flǫri·diăn), *a.* and *sb.* [f. Florida + -ian.] **A.** *adj.* Of, pertaining to, or associated with Florida; *Geol.*, of or pertaining to a group of strata of the Pliocene series extending through the Atlantic states of North America, or to the corresponding geologic age. **B.** *sb.* **a.** An inhabitant of Florida. **b.** *Geol.* The Floridian group of strata.
1870 *Amer. Naturalist* III. 400 It is called Grape Fruit by the Floridians. *Ibid.* 401 A species grows in Mexico, but whether identical with the Floridian we do not know. 1888 *Amer. Anthrop.* I. 342 Along the coast from Labrador to the Floridian peninsula. 1895 Dana *Man. Geol.* (ed. 4) 884 Marine Tertiary of the Atlantic and Gulf Borders. 3. Pliocene period. Floridian Epoch. 1903 Geikie *Text-bk. Geol.* (ed. 4) II. 1298 The Floridian series, in which have been recognised—(*a*) a lower group (Caloosahatchie, Waccamaw), and (*b*) an upper group, variously termed De Soto and Croatan.

Floristic (flǫri·stik), *a.* and *sb.* [f. Flora: see -istic.] **A.** *adj.* Of or pertaining to the study of plants with reference to their distribution. **B.** *sb. pl.* That branch of phytogeography which deals with the distribution and abundance of plants. So **Flori·stically** *adv.*
1909 *Warming's Œcol. Plants* 1 Floristic plant-geography is concerned with—1. The compilation of a 'Flora', that is, a list of species growing within a larger or smaller area... 2. The division of the earth's surface into natural floristic tracts..according to their affinities...3. The sub-division of the larger natural floristic tracts—floristic kingdoms—into smaller natural tracts. *Ibid.* 145 Grassy surfaces lining a railway differ floristically according to the aspect. 1918 L. Huxley *Life Sir J. D. Hooker* II. 414 This great floristic work was fitly rounded off by his completion of the 'Ceylon Flora'. 1928 V. G. Childe *Most Anc. East* iii. 50 To find a floristic and faunistic environment comparable to that encountered by the most ancient Egyptians one must travel far upstream into the monsoon zone.

Florule (flǭ·riŭl). Anglicized form of Flo-rula.
1894–5 *16th Ann. Rep. U.S. Geol. Surv.* 1. 535 In view of the fact that in both countries [*sc.* Portugal and America] a number of distinct horizons showing the progressive change in the flora throughout that period have yielded fossil plants in such a way that, if the Portuguese beds were as fully developed as are the American ones, each of these florules might also be compared, the subject becomes rather fascinating.

Flossy, *a.* Add: Also *fig.* Saucy, impertinent, 'fresh'. *U.S. slang.*
1900 G. Ade *More Fables in Slang* (1902) 136 He'd show you if you could get Flossy with a Lady, even though she Works. 1903 A. H. Lewis *Boss* 122 He's as flossy a proposition as ever came down the pike. 1922 Titus *Timber* i. 14 Do you list that with your references? Your luck with these flossy young petticoats?

Flots (flǫts, ‖flo), *sb. pl.* [Fr., pl. of *flot* wave.] Trimmings of lace or loops of ribbon arranged in overlapping rows.
1882 Caulfeild & Saward *Dict. Needlework, Flots*, a French term, used to signify successive loops of ribbon or lace arranged to lie over-lapping one another in rows, so as to resemble the flow of small waves...What is called a Flôt-bow is made after the same style. 1902 *Daily Chron.* 12 Apr. 8/3 The long flots of frills.

Flouncy (flau·nsi), *a.* Also -ey. [f. Flounce *sb.*[2] + -y[1].] Having flounces, flounced.
1900 *Westm. Gaz.* 20 Sept. 3/2 A deep-kilted flouncy chiffon. 1906 *Daily Chron.* 31 Aug. 5/7 Floppy hats and skirts, all 'fluffy' and 'flouncy', have come into vogue again. 1909 H. G. Wells *Tono-Bungay* I. i. 15 Shiny and flouncey clothing. 1927 *Sunday at Home* June 525/2 Flouncy petticoats..are giving way in Spain to modern styles.

Flounder, *sb.*[1] Add: **2. c.** A drowned corpse. *slang.*
1889 Barrère & Leland *Dict. Slang.*

Flour, *sb.* **3.** *flour-dredger* (U.S. example), *loaf, man, -shoot.*
1867 'T. Lackland' *Homespun* i. 125 Spoons, and knives, and rolling-pins, and '*flour-dredgers. 1868 A. Sherburne *Mem.* ii. (1831) 53 He withdrew and sent us in some '*flour loaves. 1848 *Knickerbocker Mag.* XXXI. 221 The butcher's bill, the coal man's bill, the '*flour man's bill, the house rent, were all quickly settled. 1880 T. Hardy *Trumpet-Major* xxxii, The miller entered the mill as if he were simply staying up to grind. But he continually left the *flour-shoot to go outside and walk round.

| FLOUR. | 381 | FLUKE. | FLUKED. | 382 | FLUX. |

FLOUR.

4. flour-worm, the larva of any one of the flour-beetles or flour-moths.

FLOURING. Add: **1. a.** and *trans.*

FLOW, *v.* **3.** *Add:*

FLOW, *sb.* **14.** *(f. 1. Geol.)* A gradual increase or deformation of rocks.

8. flow-blue, a blue colour applied to pottery or porcelain which diffuses readily through the glaze; **flow-glaze,** coloured glaze applied to the top of a vessel and allowed to run down the sides of the irregular strata; **flow-ometer,** an instrument for measuring rate of flow (of gas, liquid fuel, etc.); **flow-pipe,** the pipe by which hot water leaves the boiler in a system of heating; **flow-structure** *Geol.,* the structure in igneous rock produced by the flow of the molten mass before solidifying.

3. a. Also, of animals.

8. *(Earlier U.S. example.)*

FLOWAGE. *Add:* (Earlier example.)

b. *Geol.* and *Mech.* Gradual internal alteration in structure of a viscous solid by intermolecular movement.

FLOWED, *ppl. a. U.S.* **1.** *Flow b.* + -ED.] Flooded.

FLOWER, *sb.* **Add: 3.** *No flowers:* an intimation that floral tributes are not desired at a funeral; hence, no sign of mourning or regret.

13. a. *flour-sweet oil.*

13. b. *flour-sweet* (U.S. example).

(many further subentries)

FLOWER, *v.* **1. b.** *Add:* Also with *into.*

FLOWERY, *a.* *Add:* **1. c.** *Flowery Empire, Kingdom, Land,* or *Nation* [transl. Chinese *hwa kwo*]: China. *Flowery Land* also = Florida.

FLUAVIL. *Chem.* [ad. F. *fluavile* (Payen, *Comptes Rendus,* 1852, XXXV. 188).]

FLUE *see* FLU *sb.*

FLUFFILY, *adv.* [f. FLUFFY *a.* + -LY.] In a fluffy manner or condition, like fluff.

FLUFFMENT *(fleˈ°fmĕnt),* *dial.* and *U.S.* [f. FLUFF *sb.*[1] or *v.*[1] + -MENT.] Something of a light or loose texture *(dial.* and *U.S.).*

FLUFFY, *a.* *Add:* **1. c.** *fig.,* often with reference to personal character or intellect.

FLUFFLY, *sb.* *Add:* **b.** Also *examples of extended uses.*

FLY, *sb.*[1] *Add:*

FLY, *v.*[2] *Add:* Later examples.

FLYER. *Add:* **1. b.** An aviator.

FLYING, *vbl. sb.* *Add:* **1. b.** The action of guiding or piloting aircraft, or of travelling in aircraft.

FLYING-BOAT, *sb.* A boat which can fly or is able to rise from and settle on the water.

FOLD.

ETCHER *Gainsborough* 88 The fold of the fields and the grouping of trees. 1930 *Morning Post* 17 June 20/5 Delight-house in a fold of the Downs.

h. *Geol.* The folding or curvature of strata.

1863 DANA *Man. Geol.* 104 One fold or flexure in the rocks may succeed to another, or they may form interrupted series. 1879 *Encycl. Brit.* X. 300/1 The prevalent strike of a region determined by the direction of the axes of the great folds into which the rocks have been thrown. 1885 LYELL *Elem. Geol.* (ed. 4) 61 Stratified rocks have their strata usually bent into parallel folds forming anticlinal and synclinal curves. 1894 DANA *Man. Geol.* (ed. 4) 104 Fan-shaped folds are common on a small scale in schists, and occasionally they may occur on a scale of mountain magnitude. The facts at Mont Blanc in the Alps are explained on the idea of such a fold.

7. *attrib.* **fold-mountain** (see quot. 1908).

1908 J. W. GREGORY *Geog.* 34 Fold-mountains arise from the crumpling of bands of the earth's crust by lateral pressure. Such fold-mountains resemble the wrinkles formed when a table-cloth is pushed across a table. 1925 J. JOLY *Surface-Hist. Earth* i. 24 The great Eastern Eurasian Chains of fold-mountains.

Fold, *v.*[1] Add: **1. e.** Now esp. with *up*.

1914 *Daily Mail* 21 Feb. 10/1 One of the little seats that folded up when they were not required.

6. In mod. use freq. with *together*.

1771 H. MACKENZIE *Man Feel.* 223 He folded his hands together. 1853 KINGSLEY *Hypatia* x, Her hands folded together before her. 1894 BEATRICE HARRADEN *Varying Moods* 60 She folded her hands together on the buckle of her waist-belt.

8. Also const. certain advs. and prepositions.

1906 K. TRASK *Night & Morn.* 34 Take me, Leonidas, to thy strong arms—..fold me from the whole wide world. 1915 H. MACKAY *London, One Nov.* 46 The mystery of things the twilights fold away.

Folder, *sb.* Add: **h.** A folding case for loose papers.

1922 *Brit. Stationer* 11 Dec. 66 Folders for name and number system. 1930 A. PALMER *Company Secretarial Practice* 182 To file the copies in a folder.

Folding, *vbl. sb.*[1] **3.** Add:

1848 H. W. HAYGARTH *Bush Life in Australia* v. 48 As soon as the fleece is taken off, it is laid upon the 'folding-table',..and after being shaken..it is folded up neatly.

Foliary (fōu·liări), *a.* [ad. mod.L. *foliaris*, f. L. *folium* leaf.] = FOLIAR *a.*

1898 *Nature* 15 Dec. 147/1 The foliary organs are found separately in the shales and ironstone nodules.

Folie (foli). [Fr.; see FOLLY.] Madness, insanity, mania. Chiefly in various pathological terms (see quots.).

1803 *Edin. Rev.* II. 163 The maniac appears perfectly composed, makes the best and most correct answers to the questions put to him; but, if set at liberty, immediately becomes furious. This kind of derangement..is what is vulgarly called *folie raisonnante*. 1848 DUNGLISON *Med. Lex.* (ed. 7), *Folie*, insanity—*f. des Ivrognes*, delirium tremens. 1880 *Encycl. Brit.* XIII. 109/2 To this condition foreign authorities have applied the term *folie circulaire*...After intervals of comparative sanity, the patient manifests symptoms which run their course through the prodromal, the acute, and the demented stages, on again to recovery. 1890 BILLINGS *Med. Dict.*, *Folie raisonnante*, constitutional emotional insanity of Krafft-Ebing. 1913 DORLAND *Med. Dict.* (ed. 7), *Folie à deux*, communicated insanity. 1914 W. J. LOCKE *Jaffery* viii, This is absurd. It's megalomania —*la folie des grandeurs*.

Folk. Add:

3. c. *Folk of peace* [mistransl. of Gael. *daoine sidhe*, lit. people of the fairy hill or of the fairies (cf. Ir. *bean sidhe* BANSHEE), by confusion with *sithe*, gen. of *sith* peace]: fairy folk, fairies. *Sc.*

1875 *Encycl. Brit.* II. 203/2 The Highlanders call them the folk of peace. 1893 R. L. STEVENSON *Catriona* i. i, I am nameless, like the Folk of Peace.

4. c. People who are eminently respectable. *U.S.*

1839 CAROLINE M. KIRKLAND *New Home* v, It's a rattle-snake; the Indians call them massisangas [*i.e.* massasaugas] and so *folks* calls 'em so too. 1844 CATH. M. SEDGWICK *Tales* 200 There was considerable earthenware and silver teaspoons, and it was evident they had lived like folks. 1867 LOWELL *Fitz-Adam's Story* 544 'Why, where in thunder were his horns and tail?' 'They're only worn by some old-fashioned pokes; They mostly aim at looking just like folks.'

6. folk-dance, a dance of popular origin; the music for such a dance; also **folk-dance** *v.*; **folk-dancing** *vbl. sb.*; **folk-laws,** customary laws of the people and especially the *Leges Barbarorum*, the laws of the Germanic peoples; **folk-music,** music of popular origin; hence **folk-musician**; so **folk-tune**; **folk-play,** a play written for acting by the people of a town; **folk-psychology** [tr. G. *völkerpsychologie*] = ETHNOPSYCHOLOGY; **folk-singer,** a singer of folk-songs; so **folk-singing.**

1909 ELIZ. BURCHENAL (*title*) *Folk-dances and singing games. 1912 C. J. SHARP *Folk Dancing in Schools* 4 The three main types of folk-dance found in England are:—(1) The Morris Dance. (2) The Sword Dance. (3) The Country Dance. 1927 *Observer* 2 Oct. 19/4 He defied anyone who *folk-danced to be unhappy. 1908 *Amer. Physical Educ. Rev.* Oct. 375 The place of *folk dancing. 1927 *Observer* 2 Oct. 19/4 If there was more singing of the old songs and more folk-dancing. 1884 *folk-law [see Dict. 5 b]. 1898 E. JENKS *Law & Politics Middle Ages* ii. 32 While France and Germany have their feudal laws..England is still in the twilight of the folk-laws. 1907 C. J. SHARP *Engl. Folk Song* Introd. p. ix, It is impossible to say how far the *folk-music that has survived in a county like Somerset is..truly representative of English folk-song as a whole. *Ibid.* 34 The *folk-musician..is under no such temptation [*sc.* to make music for the sake of making it]. 1889 *Cent. Dict.*, *Folk-psychology. 1924 R. M. OGDEN tr. *Koffka's Growth of Mind*

49 Comparing child-psychology with folk-psychology. 1907 C. J. SHARP *Engl. Folk Song* Introd. p. viii, Only those, perhaps, who have been brought into close contact with the old *folk-singers of to-day, can fully realize how intimately *folk-singing and folk-dancing have..been bound up with the social life of the English village. 1927 *Observer* 12 June 13/2 Altogether more than fifty folk-singers and craft workers hailing from all parts of French Canada were gathered together. 1931 *Times Lit. Suppl.* 30 Apr. 344/4 The free rhythm and florid ornament..characteristic of Greek *folk-singing. 1907 C. J. SHARP *Engl. Folk Song* Introd. p. x, The *folk-tune presents many problems of absorbing interest to the musical theorist. 1914 — *Folk Singing in Schools* 5 The folk-tunes which have recently been collected from the English peasantry.

Folk-song (fōu·k,sǫŋ). Earlier folk's song. [f. FOLK + SONG *sb.*, after G. *volkslied.*] A song originating from 'the people'; also *collect. sing.*

1847 *Howitt's Jrnl.* 17 Apr. 212/1 The Three Little Roses. A German Folk's song. Translated by Mary Howitt. 1870 Folk-Song [see FOLK 5 b]. 1871 *Cornhill Mag.* Nov. 573 In a large collection of folk-songs from all the chief Dravidian languages, not one may be called immoral, not one cheerful. 1875 *Encycl. Brit.* III. 283/1 It was not till the publication of Allan Ramsay's *Evergreen* and *Tea Table Miscellany*, and of Bishop Percy's *Reliques*, that a serious effort was made to recover Scotch and English folk-songs from the recitation of the old people who still knew them by heart. 1880 'MARK TWAIN' *Tramp Abr.* xvi, Germany is rich in folk-songs,..but 'The Lorelei' is the people's favourite. 1883 *Grove's Dict. Mus.* III. 584/2 In some countries of Europe the development of the Song can be followed from the primitive form of folk-song to the highest type of artistic composition. 1887 *Contemp. Rev.* Mar. 338 The idyllic bond between shepherd and sheep has formed the subject of many quaintly graceful Roumanian folk-songs. 1907 C. J. SHARP (*title*) English Folk Song.

Folksy (fōu·ksi), *a.* *U.S.* [f. *folks*, pl. of FOLK + -Y [1].] Sociable.

1871 SCHELE DE VERE *Americanisms* (1872) 474 Even an adjective, folksy, has been made, which is used in Virginia and the South. 1886 *Harper's Mag.* Dec. 107/2 She's dreadful folksy for a girl that's had to live alone on a far island. 1890 *Ibid.* Dec. 138/2 I'd kind o' thought 'twould be folksy an'..cheerful. 1891 ROSE T. COOKE *Huckleberries* 331 I'm real folksy; grasshoppers ain't no neighbours to me.

Follow, *sb.* Add:

1. b. A supplementary portion in a restaurant.

1910 A. A. MILNE *The Day's Play* 213 At most restaurants you can get a second help of anything for half-price, and that is technically called a 'follow'.

3. Follow-on. *attrib.*

1897 *Badminton Mag.* Apr. 441 The original 'follow-on' limit was 100. 1899 GRACE *Cricket. Remin.* 229 The compulsory follow-on innings.

4. Follow-through. *Golf*, etc. The action or an act of following through (see *FOLLOW *v.* 20*).

1897 *Encycl. Sport* I. 465/1 Both force and direction are imparted by what is technically known as the 'follow through'. 1904 *Daily Chron.* 28 Apr. 3/2 It is..worthy of note that after the ball has departed, when the follow-through is nearly completed, Vardon's gaze is still fixed on the spot whence it has flown. 1905 *Westm. Gaz.* 10 Nov. 4/2 If he had hit it with the straight-forward, follow-through stroke. 1920 D. J. KNIGHT in *Cricket* (Badm. Libr.) 27 Another great factor of the batsman's art is what is known as the follow through. 1924 F. G. LOWE *Lawn Tennis* 46 The wrist brings the striking face square with the ball, and after impact gradually turns the striking face over until at the finish of the 'follow through' it almost faces the ground. 1931 *Times Lit. Suppl.* 17 Sept. 699/3 The upward swing of a bait-rod (that gentle easy follow-through).

b. Applied to an organization which attends to the after-care of patients.

1926 *Socialist Rev.* Jan. 308 He should be familiar with what is meant by 'follow-through Departments', for the condition of a patient five years after he leaves is a good test of the Hospital's efficiency.

5. Follow-up. The continuation of an action, investigation, circularizing, etc.

1923 J. D. HACKETT *Labor Terms* in *Management Engineering* May, *Follow-Up*, methods used by the personnel department to maintain friendly relations with employees. 1929 *Saturday Even. Post* (N.Y.) 14 Dec. 13/2 It's the follow-up of that injunction gag.

Follow, *v.* Add:

1. Also with advs., e.g. *about*, *in*, *out*.

1749 GOADBY *Apol. Life Bampfylde Moore Carew* (1768) 48 Parson Bryant followed him out. 1860 W. COLLINS *Woman in White* xi, I opened the door for her in silence, and followed her out. 1866 MRS. MIRIAM C. HARRIS *Christine* xxx, Richard followed his brother slowly out into the path. 1877 A. SEWELL *Black Beauty* xlviii, I used to come to him in the field and follow him about. 1910 E. MARIA ALBANESI *Love of Anne Lambart* 59 He follows me about like a dog.

2. c. To provide (a thing) *with* a sequel (cf. *21 c) or a successor.

1671 HEAD & KIRKMAN *Engl. Rogue* IV. (1680) 128 At the first blow, I thought he had cut me in two, following that with three or four more. 1901 *Daily Chron.* 14 Dec. 8/2 He had arranged to follow 'Iris' with..'My Lady Virtue'. 1907 *Smart Set* Jan. 72 Her efforts to follow 'Anchored' with other stories.

3. c. To attend (the body of a deceased person) to the grave. Also *absol.* To attend a person's funeral. *colloq.*

1819 C. WOLFE in *Rem.* (1827) 155 Last night I helped to lay poor M— in his coffin, and followed him this morning to his grave. 1820 *Kaleidoscope* New Ser. I. 142/3 His brothers ..agreed to follow the body to the grave. 1831 [J. BANIM] *Smuggler* (1856) I. xi. 111 They renewed their cries for 'Hood! to follow in the funeral!' 1857 *Chambers's Jrnl.* 5 Dec. 354/2 You are likely to be following another party as your own dear departed to his or her long home. 1897 HALL

CAINE *Christian* I. viii, Gimme a black cloth on the corfin, my dear, and mind yer tell 'im to foller. 1902 *Westm. Gaz.* 18 Dec. 12/2 In Norfolk it is customary to speak of attending a funeral as 'following' the remains.

15. b. Const. *on.*

1888 MRS. H. WARD *Robt. Elsmere* I. iii, That state which so often follows on the long confinement of illness. 1903 LANGBRIDGE *Flame & Flood* ii, A rich-souled organ poured out its absolution; following on the voice of the violin.

20*. Follow through. *intr. Golf*, etc. To continue the stroke, after the ball has been struck, to the full extent of the swing. (Cf. *FOLLOW *sb.* 4.)

[1895 HUTCHINSON *Golf* iv. (ed. 5) 87 The difficulty..of getting the club to follow easily through after the ball.] 1897 *Encycl. Sport* I. 464/1 The player should have the habit, so important in this 'following through', of regarding the ball merely as a point *through* which the club head is to pass in the course of its circuit. *Ibid.* 469/2 It [*sc.* slicing] can only be cured by earnest endeavours to 'follow through'. 1909 P. A. VAILE *Mod. Golf* xiv. 197 The timing of the stroke, so that the head of the driver..runs into the line of flight of the ball, hits it truly, and then follows through in a true vertical plane.

21. Follow up. c. = sense *2 c.

1795 T. PAINE *Age of Reason* II. 66 Matthew..follows up this part of the story of the guard..with a second part. 1905 W. BODIE *Bodie Bk.* 173, I must explain these two statements, and then follow them up by a third.

22. *Comb.*: **follow-me-lads** *sb. pl.* [cf. F. *suivez-moi-jeune-homme*]: curls or ribbons hanging loosely over the shoulder; also *sing.*, *U.S. colloq.*, an attractive furbelow in a woman's costume.

1872 *Spectator* (Farmer), 'Follow-me-lads' are not in themselves very pretty, though, like any other fashion, they become the Princess. 1874 *Slang Dict.*, *Follow-me-lads*, curls hanging over a lady's shoulder. 1902 J. B. GREENOUGH & KITTREDGE *Words Eng. Speech* 190 Kiss-me-quick, hug-me-tight, follow-me-lads,—names for articles of female attire. 1928 KATH. H. BROWN *The Father* i, Miss Evelina Amberley, in all her frills and laces and follow-me-lads, as scalloped and frilled and fluted as her name. *Ibid.* ix, The knife sawed through Aunt Euphemia's follow-me-lad, slashed out a thick chunk of somber plush.

Following, *ppl. a.* Add:

6. In various technical usages.

1839 URE *Dict. Arts* 979 When a coal has a following or roof stone, which regularly separates with the coal. 1883 GRESLEY *Gloss. Coal-m.*, *Following dirt*, loose shale, etc., in a thin bed forming the roof of a coal seam. *Ibid.*, *Following-up bank*, a breadth of about 6 yards of coal taken off on either side of a leading bank. 1888 *Lockwood's Dict. Mech. Engin.*, *Following edge*, that edge of the blade of a screw propeller which leaves the water behind it, as distinguished from the leading edge. *Following joints.* The rings of which cylindrical boilers are built, being lap jointed, fit one within the other. Instead, therefore, of being parallel cylinders, they are necessarily frustra of cones, and as the joints all lap in one direction, they are termed following joints. *Following steady*, a steady which is attached to the back of the side rest of a lathe, and which embraces the work behind or after the tool and follows it along with the rest.

Fomorian (fǫmōᵊ·riăn). [f. Ir. *fomor* pirate (f. *fo* under + *muir* sea) = Gael. *famhair* + -IAN.] A sea-rover; a name given in Irish legend to the early invaders of Ireland.

1876 *Encycl. Brit.* V. 300/2 That the Fomorian and *Tuatha Dé Danaan* contests are mythological there can be no doubt. 1898 JAS. HERON *Celtic Church* 5 Partholonians, Nemedians, and Fomorians, or sea-rovers, are..the first.. to take possession [of Ireland].

Fons et origo (fǫnz et ǭrai·go). [L.] The source and origin (*of*).

[1809, etc. examples of *fons et origo mali*: see Stanford's Dict. Anglicised Words.] 1897 *Westm. Gaz.* 12 Nov. 2/2 If we may reserve our opinion on the one point which was the *fons et origo* of Liberal Forwardism—the Eastern Question. 1927 A. H. MCNEILE *Introd. N. T.* 285 Papias, the *fons et origo* of many problems. 1930 *Times Lit. Suppl.* 20 Nov. 955/3 The *fons et origo* of the downfall of the West.

Food, *sb.* Add: **2. b.** *transf.*, as in *skin food*.

1908 *Queen* 30 May 932/1 The introducer of the Russian skin food Valaze is Dr. Lyruski. 1912 *Ibid.* 30 Nov. 1006/1 It is a skin food in the truest sense and really works wonders with the skin.

7. *food faddist*, *-fish* (earlier example), *product*, *tax*, *ticket*.

1910 *Daily Chron.* 14 Apr. 4/2 The '*food faddists' or 'food reformers'. 1927 W. E. COLLINSON *Contemp. Engl.* 38 Some of the food-faddists went beyond the vegetarian stage and became fruitarians. 1865 J. G. BERTRAM (*title*) The harvest of the sea. A contribution to the natural and economic history of the British *food fishes. 1875 *Congress. Rec.* 26 Feb. 1804/1 A good many States have already established a system for the introduction of food-fishes. 1897 *Daily News* 6 Mar. 6/4 The Select Committee on *food products adulteration. 1906 *Daily Chron.* 5 June 5/4 To enable Government inspectors to supervise, from hoof to can, the preparation of meat food-products. 1913 *Punch* 22 Jan. 67 *Food taxes. 1907 *Westm. Gaz.* 12 Oct. 13/1 The *food-ticket is invaluable, when money might prove a danger. 1909 *Ibid.* 30 Jan. 2/2, I felt also bound to refuse the gift of a food-ticket until their cases had been investigated.

b. *food-taxer*, *-taxing*.

1903 *Westm. Gaz.* 19 Aug. 5/1 Mr. Arnold-Forster a *food-taxer. 1906 *Daily Chron.* 13 Feb. 4/2 There was something for the Food-taxers also, for..the matter of food-taxes is 'not a question of principle'. 1905 *Ibid.* 25 Mar. 7/4 This *food-taxing policy.

8. food-card, a card used in the rationing of food to indicate the amount of food allowed to a person for a specified period of time; **food-controller,** an official having control of food supplies; **food-values,** in dietetics, the relative nourishing

power assigned to foods; **food vase, vessel,** names given to a form of pot which succeeded the beaker in the round barrows of Great Britain; **food-vessel men,** the people of a Middle Bronze Age.

1918 *Times* 6 Feb. 8/2 *Food cards taken out for children educated at boarding schools. 1923 E. A. ROSS *Russian Soviet Republ.* 113 Bread- and food-cards of four different colors were issued to four class divisions of the population. *Ibid.* 114 In the spring of 1920 there were only eight thousand adults in Petrograd who had not taken out food-cards, i.e. had not gone to work. 1916 *Act 6 & 7 Geo. V* c. 68 § 3 For the purpose of economising and maintaining the food supply of the country during the present war, it shall be lawful for His Majesty to appoint a Minister of Food under the title of *Food Controller. 1907 *Chambers's Jrnl.* 29 June 495 The York Health and Housing Reform Association has published a table of *food-values. 1909 *Ibid.* Jan. 6/2 The average Chinese and Japanese diet is rather richer in food-values than the average American. 1915 *Lit. Digest* (N.Y.) 4 Sept. 479/2 Advt., A nourishing and appetizing first course like..Tomato Soup..contributes rich food-value. 1871 *Archaeologia* XLIII. 385 One of the four *food-vases.. is ornamented with fine punctures at the bottom. *Ibid.* 378 *Food vessels are rare in the barrows of Wiltshire and the South of England. *Ibid.* 383 Food vessels, almost alone of British *fictilia*, are in rare cases furnished with covers. 1872 J. EVANS *Anc. Stone Implem.* 200 A smaller hammer-head.. was found with a small 'food vessel' accompanying an interment near Doune.

Foo-foo (fū·fū). Also fou-fou. [Ashanti (Twi) *fufū*. Cf. Cuban Sp. *fufú*.] A kind of dough made out of plantains.

1851 *Illustr. Catal. Gt. Exhib.* IV. I. 977/2 This mass [of plantain boiled whole], beaten in a mortar, constitutes the *foo-foo* of the negroes [of British Guiana]. 1858 SIMMONDS *Dict. Trade*, *Foo-foo*, a negro name for dough made from plantains; the fruit being boiled and then pounded in a mortar. 1899 RODWAY *Guiana Wilds* 54 There were fou-fou soup, pepper-pot, barbecued meat, and piles of oranges. 1924 *Glasgow Herald* 8 Nov. 5 The women pounded their 'fou-fou' in the courtyard of the [Ashanti] village.

Fool, *sb.*[1] and *a.* Add: **6. fool-water** (see quot.).

1837 *Knickerbocker Mag.* X. 413 The disturber..by the Indians appropriately named 'fire-water', and more emphatically '*fool-water', was happily beyond their reach.

B. *adj.* Freq. in U.S.

1805 L. DOW *Jrnl.* Wks. 1806 II. I. 76, I showed the contrast of a gentleman and a fool deist. 1842 *Congress. Globe* 25 Jan. App. 153 (Th.) All the fool Federal fandangoes that disgraced the country. 1854 MARY J. HOLMES *Tempest & Sunshine* ii. 25 Tempest..can hardly wait till I'm dead before she spends my money on fool fixins. 1862 SUSAN HALE *Lett.* (1919) 13 Everybody talking such fool nonsense as sometimes almost to prevent digestion. 1897 *Congress. Rec.* 21 Jan. 1018/2 If you had availed yourselves of the information you would not have given the fool votes you did. 1902 HARBEN *Abner Daniel* 2 Oh, Alan, don't you see he's goin' to ruin us with his fool notions? 1912 R. A. WASON *Friar Tuck* xxiii. 165 It was the foolest lookin' group I was ever part of. 1914 GERTR. ATHERTON *Perch of Devil* I. 111 Men are..as selfish as..fool women have.. made them. 1924 W. M. RAINE *Troubled Waters* xxiii. 245 You've heard that fool story about Norma and Mac.

Fooler (fū·lǝɹ). [f. FOOL *v.* 3 + -ER[1].] A person or thing that 'fools' one.

1909 R. A. WASON *Happy Hawkins* 316 They finally located a mine that looked good-natured an' generous; but it was a fooler.

Fool-proof (fū·lprūf), *a.* orig. *U.S.* [f. FOOL *sb.*[1] + PROOF *a.* 1 b.] Proof against even the incompetence of a fool; simple and straightforward so as to respond to the most inexperienced or careless handling; safeguarded against every sort of accident. Hence **Foo·l-proofness,** the quality of being fool-proof.

1902 A. C. HARMSWORTH *Motors & Motor-driving* 309 The car..is comparatively 'fool-proof'. 1904 *Westm. Gaz.* 24 Oct. 2/2 The car is so 'simple' that my daughters drive it—'fool-proof' the Americans call it. 1906 *Ibid.* 24 Apr. 10/2 Not even a coffin-shaped bottle is 'fool-proof', however. 1908 H. H. SMITH *Cacao Planting* 34 Such a pump is said to be practically fool-proof, and capable of being understood and operated by a native labourer of the lowest degree of intelligence. 1911 GRAHAME-WHITE & HARPER *Aeroplane* 318 It is a difficult task to construct a flying machine which shall be 'fool-proof'. 1924 W. R. INGE *Lay Thoughts* (1926) 220 Everywhere we find the same demand to make life easy, safe, and fool proof. 1928 GALSWORTHY *Swan Song* III. ii. 231 A base of operations with a fool-proof title was essential.

Foolscapped (fū·lzkæpt), *pa. pple.* and *ppl. a.* [f. FOOL'S-CAP + -ED[2].] Furnished with a fool's-cap.

1909 NOYES in *Westm. Gaz.* 26 Aug. 1/3 Poor fool's-capped scholars. 1918 *Hist. Amer. Lit.* I. 265 He was never laurelled like Byron, never foolscapped like Keats by critics or public.

Foot, *sb.* Add: **7.** Also *by the* or *per foot run*: by the linear foot (see RUN *ppl. a.* 12).

1847 SMEATON *Builder's Man.* 183 Plasterer's work is in part measured by the yard and foot square, and in part by the foot run. 1887 *Daily News* 6 July 7/4 The Cheap Wood Company are selling 2 by 4 at ½d. per foot run.

d. As a measure of coal gas: The amount of gas contained in one cubic foot of space.

1838 *Penny Cycl.* XI. 88/2 A sufficient quantity of gas was turned on to give a light equal to that of a mould candle; the consumption in this case was a foot and a half per hour. 1862 *Chambers's Encycl.* IV. 640/1, 1000 cubic feet will last as long as 20 candles. 1879 *Encycl. Brit.* X. 96/1 These holders are each capable of storing 2 million cubic feet of gas. *Ibid.* 99/2 A burner passing 7 feet of gas per hour.

22. b. In *Archery* (see quot.).

1923 *Daily Mail* 18 July 3 Several of the Woodmen..

made what are known as 'thumbs'..and 'foots', the arrow in this case lying against one leg of the target.

29. b. *To get the foot of.* (Earlier U.S. example.)

1829–32 J. P. KENNEDY *Swallow B.* I. 248 She got the foot of them [*sc.* dogs] so far, that she found she could get back to her nest.

30. d. *To have* or *set one's foot on the neck of*: (fig.) to hold completely in subjection: see NECK *sb.*[1] 3 a.

32. On foot. d. Of cattle-flesh: Alive, before being slaughtered for food.

1846 M'KENNEY *Memoirs* I. ix. 217, I told him that I knew that beef could be purchased in Missouri and Illinois, on foot, at from one dollar to one dollar and fifty cents per hundred pounds.

34. e. esp. in names of speed and control appliances on vehicles, as *foot-accelerator*, *-brake*, *-braking*, *-clutch*, *-starter*; also *foot-acted*, *-operated* adjs.

1888 *Lockwood's Dict. Mech. Engin.*, Foot Brake. 1905 *Westm. Gaz.* 17 Oct. 4/2 Many motorists who find the working of a foot-clutch trying. 1908 *Ibid.* 16 Jan. 4/2 A foot accelerator is also fitted. *Ibid.* 30 Jan. 4/1 A large foot-operated contracting brake. 1908 *Daily Chron.* 21 Nov. 9/4 The three-speed gear in association with a foot-acted brake. 1925 *Morris Owner's Man.* 11 Both foot and hand brakes operate on drums fitted to the back wheels.

35. foot-drop *Path.*, a permanently extended position of the foot, due to paralysis of the flexor muscles; **foot-piece,** (*b*) the wooden support for the foot in a wood clog skate; **foot-plate,** (*b*) *Anat.* (see quot. 1901); (*c*) each of the metal mounts which support the foot in a metal skate; **foot-rule,** also *fig.*; **foot-second,** (*a*) a unit of velocity, being the speed necessary to traverse one foot per second; (*b*) = *CUSEC; **foot-stock,** (*a*) = **foot-plate* c; **foot-ton,** a unit of energy, being the amount necessary to raise one ton through the height of one foot; **foot-work,** (*d*) in other games, agility, sureness and accurate placing of the feet.

1920 *Glasgow Herald* 8 July 4 Conditions affecting the feet..e.g. *foot-drop, corns and contracted toes, clawfoot. 1856 'STONEHENGE' *Brit. Sports* 522/1 The *foot-piece is generally a solid block of hard wood, flat above and shaped to the boot, and rounded below with a longitudinal groove to receive the iron. 1898 *Encycl. Sport* II. 361/2 The *foot plates, or mounts, one for the sole and one for the heel, are best made of light metal. 1901 DORLAND *Med. Dict.* (ed. 2), *Foot-plate*, the plate that forms the base of the stapes. 1910 *Practitioner* Feb. 237 In a typical specimen the stapes will be seen to be fixed to the oval window by bone either along the margin of the foot-plate or by bony processes passing from the limbs of the ossicle. 1903 *Westm. Gaz.* 16 June 2/2 The advantage of having a *foot-rule, so to speak, by which to test agreements for purchase. 1904 *Daily Chron.* 12 May 3/2 Mr. Richard Bagot's work may not always satisfy the critical foot-rule. 1908 *Westm. Gaz.* 9 June 1/2 It was Mr. Chamberlain who had pointed to exports as a foot-rule with which he wanted us to measure up our trade as a whole. 1901 'LINKSMAN' *Words Eyewitness* (1902) 147 A velocity of 2500 '*foot-seconds'. 1905 *Kynoch Jrnl.* July–Sept. 156 In the Government back-pressure gun, a muzzle velocity of 2,400 feet sec. is practicable. 1892 *Gentlewoman's Bk. Sports* I. 131 My own skates have metal *footstocks. 1888 *Lockwood's Dict. Mech. Engin.*, **Foot Ton*, a unit used in calculation, signifying one ton lifted one foot high. *Ibid.* s.v. *Unit*, The great primary mechanical units used by engineers are the Joule, or unit of heat; the foot pound or ton; the inch pound, or inch ton, and the H.P. 1902 *Encycl. Brit.* XXIX. 176/2 The energy in foot-tons..of a shot weighing *w* lb. 1908 *Daily Chron.* 25 June 3/3 (Tennis) It is *foot-work that wins. 1921 A. W. MYERS *Twenty Yrs. Lawn Tennis* 167 So well controlled was her footwork.

b. With adv.: **foot-up** *Rugby football*, in scrummaging, the lifting of either foot by any member of the front row of forwards on either side before the ball is fairly put in the scrummage. Also *attrib.*

1921 E. H. D. SEWELL *Rugby Football* 361 Inadvertent offside, foot-up,..are..absolutely unavoidable at times. 1927 WAKEFIELD & MARSHALL *Rugger* 183 The forwards.. merely leant up against one another while the front row tried trick hooking and foot-up tactics. *Ibid.* 185 He must be careful..not to be penalised..for foot-up.

Foot, *v.* Add:

2. Also of a ship: To move or sail with speed. Also with *it*. (In windward sailing, denoting speed as distinguished from pointing.)

1899 *Daily News* 4 Oct. 3/1 Shamrock, under clever handling, and footing splendidly, again took the lead. 1901 *Daily Chron.* 27 Sept. 5/7 His boat seemed to be footing it better. 1905 *Ibid.* 19 May 5/5 The latter boat was closely pursued by Hamburg, which was footing splendidly.

9. c. (Earlier U.S. example.)

1844 *Lowell* (Mass.) *Offering* IV. 76 I'll drink with him, even if I have to foot the bill.

Footage (fu·tedʒ). [f. FOOT *sb.* + -AGE.]

1. *Mining.* A piece-work system of paying miners by the running foot of work; the amount paid; also, the amount mined.

1902 WEBSTER Suppl. 1909 *Westm. Gaz.* 9 Dec. 10/4 The output was 15,800 tons, or 2·15 tons per head, and the development footage 3,700. 1923 *Glasgow Herald* 31 May 16 The fathoms broken in the stopes were 234,960 against 192,784, the development footage 104,447 against 87,159, the tons milled 3,786,666 as compared with 3,447,736. 1927 *Sunday Times* 23 Jan. 5 The Development Footage sampled totalled 5,530 feet.

2. The length in linear feet of cinematographic film used in photographing a scene, play, etc. Also *attrib.*

1916 'B. M. BOWER' *Phantom Herd* ii. 22 He visualized a stampede and the probable amount of footage it would

require. 1918 H. CROY *How Motion Pictures are Made* v. 128 Directors..craftily working to keep the production expense as low as possible, do not altogether forget the footage possibilities of an exterior love-scene. *Ibid.* vi. 150 The amounts are added up and a footage rate determined. 1927 *Daily Express* 5 Dec. 13 The total amount of film 'footage' devoted to him.

Foot-bridge. [FOOT *sb.*] A bridge for foot-passengers only.

1375 *Creation* 1139 in Horstm. *Altengl. Leg.* (1878) 138 Ouer a diche þat tre þe3 deden leye..For to ben a fot brigge. 1506 [see FOOT *sb.* 35]. 1645 *New Haven Col. Rec.* I. 210 A foote bridge formerly made over the Mill River into the Necke. 1710 *Boston Town Rec.* II. 117 Mr. John Oliver and others..have of Late Layd Timber or plank as a foot bridg over the slip. 1807 [see FOOT *sb.* 35]. 1863 MRS. WHITNEY *F. Gartney's Girlh.* xxvii, A pretty little foot-bridge crossed it. 1888 'C. E. CRADDOCK' *Broomsedge Cove* iii. 49 The foot-bredge over the ruver air nigh under water by this time.

Foot-coal. [FOOT *sb.* 18.] An underlying stratum of coal.

1712 [see FOOT *sb.* 35]. 1840 *Knickerbocker Mag.* XV. 105 About a foot from the bottom of every vein, there is a layer of earth..This divides it into 'foot-coal' and 'upper coal'. 1879 MISS JACKSON *Shropsh. Word-bk.* 91.

Footer, *sb.*[1] Add: **6.** (See quot.)

1927 T. WOODHOUSE *Artificial Silk* 95 In the manufacture of stockings..two machines are used...One of these machines, termed the 'legger', knits the upper and longer part of the stocking, whereas the other machine, termed the 'footer', knits the remainder of the stocking.

Footer (fu·tǝɹ), *sb.*[3] orig. *University slang.* [f. FOOTBALL: see *-ER[6].] Football. Also *attrib.*

1896 *Westm. Gaz.* 12 Dec. 1/3 Who'd have thought of finding the old smug at a footer match? 1899 E. PHILLPOTTS *Human Boy* 235 He had changed in the dormitory for 'footer'. 1906 *Varsity* 29 Nov. 147/3 Two enthusiasts in 'footer' clothes. 1911 H. WALPOLE *Mr. Perrin* v. 83 There's a most ripping footer match this afternoon, sir. 1912 HUGH WALPOLE *Prelude to Adventure* v, Every time I put on my footer boots. 1925 G. WARWICK DEEPING *Sorrell & Son* xvi, To perform on the footer field with a lot of young louts.

Foot-evil. *U.S.* [FOOT *sb.* 1.] A disease affecting the feet of cattle.

1845 FRÉMONT *Exped.* 259 Many animals are destroyed.. by a disease called the foot evil. 1867–8 *Trans. Ill. Agric. Soc.* VII. 144 The disease known to stock-growers as foot evil or foules, to which our native cattle are occasionally liable.

Foot-fault (fu·tfǫlt). *Lawn Tennis.* [f. FOOT *sb.* + FAULT *sb.*] A fault or infringement of the rules made by overstepping the base-line while serving. Hence **Foo·t-fault** *v. intr.*, to make a foot-fault; *trans.*, to record a foot-fault against (a player). **Foo·t-faulter, Foo·t-faulting** *vbl. sb.*

1902 *Westm. Gaz.* 6 Oct. 4/3 The ex-champion was annoyed at being several times pulled up for 'foot-faulting'. *Ibid.* 23 Oct. 6/2 The New Lawn Tennis Laws. The Foot-Fault Difficulty Abolished...The feet of more than one 'crack' had to be carefully watched by relentless linesmen to detect the slightest inclination to foot-fault. 1909 *Ibid.* 9 Feb. 12/2 The ruling..that players who..lift the left foot before throwing up the ball, or while doing it, and then do the same with the right foot before the ball leaves the racket, are foot-faulters. 1921 A. W. MYERS *Twenty Yrs. Lawn Tennis* 114 Larned..was the foot-fault judge in the Davis Cup doubles...When he foot-faulted,..he signalled to the umpire with his hand and the man in the chair called the foot-fault. 1922 TILDEN *It's All in the Game* 35 In his anxiety he foot-faulted and his first serve was wasted. 1927 *Daily Express* 6 June 1 Tilden was foot-faulted by a special umpire in the fifth game of the third set.

Foot-folk (fu·tfōuk). Delete †*Obs.* and add: In mod. use a new formation, prob. partly after G. *fussvolk*, as in quot. 1859 in Dict.

1876 MORRIS *Æneids* VII. 793 A cloud of foot-folk follow him. 1903 *Daily Chron.* 11 Dec. 3/4 The British footfolk at close grips are the very devil. 1905 *Ibid.* 24 June 4/6 The Scottish army consisted almost exclusively of foot-folk.

Foo·t-gear. [FOOT *sb.* 1.] Boots, shoes, or similar covering for the feet.

1837 [see FOOT *sb.* 34 a]. 1869 TOURGEE *Toinette* ix. (1881) 101 The heavy brogans and a part of the gray stockings which formed her foot-gear. 1872 *Congress. Globe* 7 May 3917/1 Then, except the matter of gloves and mittens, it is foot-gear only that is made of kip-skins? 1891 *Scribner's Mag.* X. 279 The proper foot-gear is the canvas shoe with rubber sole. 1904 S. E. WHITE *Silent Places* viii. 81 A man's standing..can be accurately gauged by the magnificence of his foot-gear.

Footguards. For 'Now ... Guards' read: The Footguards now comprise the Grenadier Guards, the Coldstream Guards, the Scots Guards, the Irish Guards, and the Welsh Guards.

Foot-hill (fu·thil). orig. *U.S.* [FOOT *sb.* 18.] A hill forming a lower eminence at the foot of a mountain or mountain-range.

1859 G. A. JACKSON *MS. Diary* 9 Camped at some springs in the foothills. 1870 W. GLADDEN in *Scribner's Monthly* I. 153 The road leading to it passes over and among a series of conical foot-hills that rest against the base of the mountains. 1873 J. H. BEADLE *Undevel. West* xv. 253 In California, everything under two thousand feet high is called a hill; if it leads up to a mountain, a foothill. 1879 [see FOOT *sb.* 35]. 1882 *Rep. Prec. Metals U.S.* 262 The mineral belt is in the western foot-hills of the Verde range of mountains. 1916 J. B. THOBURN *Hist. Oklahoma* II. 4 The Black Mesa is in reality one of the foot-hills of the Rocky mountains.

Footing, *vbl. sb.* Add:

1. d. The stamping of hop-flowers into large canvas bags for preservation.

1876 *Encycl. Brit.* IV. 273/1 'Footing', that is, letting the empty bag drop through a hole in the floor, and having the hops stamped down by one man, whilst two others filled.

Footler (fū·tlǝɹ). [f. FOOTLE *v.* + -ER[1].] One who footles.

1923 *Daily Mail* 22 June 7 Urbane persiflage directed against 'footlers', bores, and busybodies. 1923 UNA L. SILBERRAD *Lett. Jean Armiter* ix. 191 The rest are just footlers who'd piffle and gas.

Footlights. Add: *Across the footlights*: see *ACROSS B. 2 b.

Footling (fū·tliŋ), *ppl. a.* [f. FOOTLE *v.* + -ING[2].] That footles or trifles; 'drivelling', 'blithering'; hence of things.

1896 [in Dict. s.v. FOOTLE *v.*]. 1905 G. B. SHAW in *Daily Chron.* 15 Mar. 6/3 They are paraphrases of great works, made by footling people. 1907 *Daily Chron.* 2 Apr. 4/4 That dreary room..with its footling little lace window curtains. 1923 A. BENNETT *Things that have interested me* Ser. II. 20 A perfectly footling popular play which fails to be popular. 1930 THURSTON *Man in Black Hat* x. 181, I had heard it before from fatuous idealists and footling divines.

Foo·t-log. *U.S.* [FOOT *sb.* 1.] A log used as a foot-bridge.

1863 T. D. PRICE *MS. Diary* 24 Jan., Helped put foot-log over run by my water-gate. 1869 *Overland Monthly* III. 9 Balancing over the deepest on round foot-logs, where one is moderately certain to slip off at critical places. 1873 J. H. BEADLE *Undevel. West* xxii. 446 An important bridge has been washed away, leaving only a foot-log, on which the passengers cross. 1881 TOURGEE *Zouri's Christmas* vi, Then they crossed the foot-log together.

Foo·t-loose, *a.* *U.S.* [Cf. FOOT *sb.* 35.] Free to act as one pleases; not hampered by any ties.

1873 J. H. BEADLE *Undevel. West* xxxi. 669 All my friends who were 'footloose' had the 'Arizona fever'. 1904 F. LYNDE *Grafters* xxvii. 347 If the mine should happen to explode..it'll be a comfort to have a foot-loose friend or two on the outside to pick up the pieces of us. 1910 W. M. RAINE *B. O'Connor* 52 We went in together for all the kinds of spreeing that young fellows who are footloose are likely to do. 1924 — *Troubled Waters* x. 104 Oh, she's nice enough, when she isn't a little divvle. The trouble is she isn't foot-loose.

Footsek, variant of *VOETSAK.

Foot-slog (fu·tslǫg), *v.* [f. FOOT *sb.* + SLOG *v.* 2.] *intr.* To go on foot; to tramp, march. Also with *it*. Hence **Foo·t-slog** *sb.*, a tramp, march; **Foo·t-slogger,** a foot-soldier, infantryman, pedestrian.

1894 C. H. W. DONALDSON *With Wilson in Matabeleland* ix. 198 Some of the Johannesburg 'Foot-Sloggers'..were doing damage in the village. 1906 *Macm. Mag.* Apr. 472 Must get in and foot-slog it, that's all. 1916 'PETER' *Trench Yarns* iv. 34 I'm not a Shop gunner, y' know. I'm only a miserable footslogger! 1925 B. TRAVERS *Mischief* viii, Another long foot-slog..in squelching shoes. 1927 *Chambers's Jrnl.* June 392/1, I..had to foot-slog until I could find a British Consul to borrow from. 1928 *Sunday Express* 28 Oct. 14/3 A long, long way to Berlin, especially for the poor bally foot-sloggers who did the fighting and the dying.

Footstep. 6. Add: *attrib.*: **footstep bearing** = sense 5 d.

1887 D. A. LOW *Machine Draw.* 110 Plan and sectional elevation of a footstep bearing for an upright shaft. 1888 *Lockwood's Dict. Mech. Engin.* 147 Footstep bearings are.. made adjustable by placing the bearing in the centre of a ring casting.

Footstool. 1. c. *U.S.* (Earlier and later examples.)

1821 T. DWIGHT *Trav. New Eng.* (1823) III. 231 We felt a total superiority to all the humble beings who were creeping on the footstool beneath us. 1859 *Congress. Globe* 18 Feb. 1122/1, I would give that power [of declaring war] to no President—none that has ever stood upon this footstool. 1906 *N.Y. Globe* 20 Feb. 8 This New York of ours, regarded by many the wickedest city on the footstool.

Footwear (fu·twe°ɹ). orig. *U.S.* [f. FOOT *sb.* 1 + WEAR *sb.* 3.] Clothing for the feet; boots, shoes, etc.

1881 [see FOOT *sb.* 34 a]. 1922 *Daily Mail* 1 Nov. 8 Women and girls, with their short skirts, neat footwear, and other prevailing fashions.

Foozled (fū·z'ld), *ppl. a.* [f. FOOZLE *v.* + -ED[1].] Bungled; esp. of a stroke in *Golf*.

1899 *Westm. Gaz.* 25 Aug. 3/1 Foozled drives or missed approaches. 1909 *Ibid.* 22 Jan. 5/2 A round freely interspersed with foozled tee shots.

So **Foo·zling** *vbl. sb.*, bungling.

1927 J. ADAMS *Errors in School* 187 In his playing the pupil finds no lack of errors, mistakes, foozlings, call them what you will.

For, *prep.* Add:

8. Also, in preparation for or anticipation of (the stated time of a meeting, etc.).

1900 *Athenæum* 5 May 545/1 The Annual Dinner of the Society will take place on Wednesday, May 16..at 7, for 7.30 P.M. 1929 E. WALLACE *Iron Grip* viii, You can please yourself about accepting..No. 109 Grosvenor Place, and the hour is 7.30 for 8.

13. e. *To be for it* (fǫ·rit): (orig. *Mil. slang*) to have one's name on the crime sheet, i.e. to be marked down for punishment or trouble; hence, to be in for trouble.

1915 'IAN HAY' *First Hundred Thou.* xvi. 214 No more trial trips; no more chaperoning! This time, we decided, we were 'for it'. 1915 *War Illustr.* 21 Aug. 22/1 Then it is that he realises so acutely that if anything happens to his pilot he is 'for it', as the current flying phrase has it. 1917 P. MACGILL *Brown Brethren* iv. 68 If Captain Thorley finds 'im missin' he'll be for it. 1919 *War Slang* in *Athenæum*

25 July 664/1 'You're for it', *i.e.*, for the 'orderly room'. *Ibid.* 1 Aug. 695/1 'On the peg,' to be charged with a 'crime'. 'You'll be for it,' the sergeant's threat of 'the peg'. 1926 *Punch* 28 Apr. 466/1 Major Atlee..declared that if the discipline of a unit broke down it was the officer in charge who should be 'for it'. 1928 GALSWORTHY *Swan Song* II. vi. 152 We've come to ask you to lead a forlorn hope. Don't smile! You're 'for it' as they say in this Bonzoid age.

Forage, *sb.* **4.** *forage-bag*, *-hat* (U.S.); **forage-cap** (earlier U.S. example); **forage-master** (later U.S. example).

1812 *Niles' Weekly Register* II. 131/1 The purveyor of public supplies advertises for..3000 *forage bags. 1837 *Southern Lit. Messenger* III. 82 He advanced, and gracefully bowing, took off his *forage cap. 1889 *Century Mag.* Apr. 901/2 Five troopers, sitting loosely in their saddles.. *forage-hats set well over their eyes [etc.]. 1861 *U.S. Army Regul.* 149 No wagon-master or *forage-master shall be interested..in any wagon or other means of transport employed by the United States.

Foramen. Add: Also with defining name, as *foramen of Magendie*, *of Monro*, *of Winslow*.

1848 DUNGLISON *Med. Lex.* (ed. 7). 1907 *Practitioner* Aug. 267 A hernia into the foramen of Winslow was discovered. 1910 *Ibid.* July 48 The two lateral ventricles communicate with each other and with the third ventricle by means of the foramina of Monro. *Ibid.* 50 The orifice in the ependyma roofing the fourth ventricle, which is called the foramen of Magendie.

Forbesite (fǫ·ɹbzait). *Min.* [ad. G. *forbesit*, f. the name of David *Forbes*, who first analysed it: see -ITE[1].] (See quot.)

1868 DANA *Min.* (ed. 5) 560 Hydrous Bibasic Arseniate of Nickel and Cobalt. Under this name D. Forbes describes ..a mineral occurring in the desert of Atacama in veins in a decomposed dioryte...Kenngott names it Forbesite.

Force, *sb.*[1] Add: **4. d.** *U.S.* (See quots.)

1834 W. G. SIMMS *Guy Rivers* II. 97 The force of the traveller—for such is the term by which the number of his slaves are understood—was small. 1845 — *Wigwam & Cabin* Ser. I. 178 The crop..had been so great as to be beyond the ability, to gather in and harvest, of the 'force' by which it was made. 1859 BARTLETT *Dict. Amer.* (ed. 2), *Force*, in the South, the slaves of a planter able to work in the field. 1871 SCHELE DE VERE *Americanisms* (1872) 475 *Force* is a common name for a gang of laborers, whether they are Irishmen at work on a railway, or negroes employed on a plantation.

15. b. *Tennis.* (See quots.) Also *attrib.*

1890 J. M. HEATHCOTE *Tennis* (Badm. Libr.) 50 The Force is the usual resource of a player who must try to win at very 'close chase', or who returns a ball which comes 'fair-off' from the end-wall. *Ibid.* 124 *Force*, a stroke played, either direct or boasted, for the dedans with some strength. 1927 *Daily Tel.* 26 Apr. 17/1 Some admirable tennis was seen, with good returns, short chases, and accurate forces.

Force, *v.*[1] Add: **8. b.** *Tennis.* To use the force stroke (see prec. 15 b).

1890 J. M. HEATHCOTE *Tennis* (Badm. Libr.) 52 It is impossible to force as severely, difficult to force as accurately, with a back-hand as with a fore-hand stroke.

9. *To force* (a person) *on*, *upon* (something). Delete † and add:

1856 DE QUINCEY *Confess.* 238 Nervous irritation forced me ..upon frightful excesses; but terror from anomalous symptoms sooner or later forced me back. *Ibid.* 269 The..riotous prodigality of life naturally forces the mind more powerfully upon the antagonist thought of death. 1903 LANGBRIDGE *Flame & Flood* xxiv, Her lack of money had forced her back upon the most respectable costume which she had.

12. Also *absol.*

1854 *Poultry Chron.* I. 624/2 If you wish to *force*, you have nothing more to do than give the male bird an extra good feed in the afternoon. [1902 *Encycl. Brit.* XXXI. 878/1 The following is the 'mash' ration on a successful American Egg-farm, and represents a high forcing diet.]

Fo·rce-bill. *U.S.* [FORCE *sb.*[1] 5.] A bill authorizing the use of military force to prevent civil disorder.

1833 *Deb. Congress* 27 Feb. 1818 He was pledged to meet this force bill fairly and openly, and he should do it. 1872 *Congress. Globe* 2 Apr. 2110/1 He proposed in the tariff bill to hold out the olive branch of peace to South Carolina, and in the force bill to hold out the sword. 1893 *Congress. Rec.* 28 Feb. 2300/1 The so called 'force bill' has been consigned to its political grave. 1910 *Atlantic Monthly* Sept. 292 There is in the American nation a fixed hostility to the employment of troops at polling-places. It is a fact that every administration which has ever passed a force bill has lost the House of Representatives at the next election.

Forced, *ppl. a.* Add:

7. In ventilation, etc., artificially produced, as in *forced air*, *draught*, *feed*, *induction* (usually attrib.).

1885 *Marine Engineer* VII. 39/1 On the Application of Moderate Forced Draught to the Furnaces of Small Steam Vessels. 1887 *Encycl. Brit.* XXII. 496/2 Where forced draught has been substituted for chimney draught. 1898 *Westm. Gaz.* 18 May 2/3 In our service we are satisfied with a forced draught trial of four hours as a rule. 1901 *Feilden's Mag.* IV. 441/2 The forced-air draught fans... Forced-air draught is preferable to steam blast. 1907 *Westm. Gaz.* 19 Nov. 4/2 Forced feed lubrication. 1909 *Ibid.* 12 Aug. 4/2 Designing an engine on the forced-induction principle.

Force majeure (fors maʒȫr). [Fr., = superior strength.] Irresistible force or overwhelming power, such as an act of God, etc.

1858 SIMMONDS *Dict. Trade*, *Force-majeure*, a French commercial term for unavoidable accidents in the transport of goods, from superior force, the act of God, &c. 1883 *Academy* 8 Sept. 158/1 Tyranny, upheld by law, will generally be 'tempered' by outrage, so long as a *force majeure* prevents its being met in any other way. 1886 *Macm. Mag.* Sept. 342/1 They [*sc.* politicians] will not combine except under *force majeure*. 1902 *Encycl. Brit.*

XXV. 112/1 The expression 'act of God'..is not synonymous with *force majeure*; but it includes every loss by *force majeure* in which human agency, by act or negligence, has had no part. 1907 W. DE MORGAN *Alice-for-Short* i, Hindered from..determined effort by a *force-majeure* trying to the temper but heroically endured. 1916 'PETER' *Trench Yarns* v. 51 *Force majeure* being on George's side, the transaction was accomplished to the accompaniment of awful threats as to George's lurid future.

Forceps. 3. Add: **forceps-tail,** an American species of scorpion-fly.

1867 *Amer. Naturalist* I. 279 The Forceps-tail, or Panorpa, *P. rufescens*..is found in bushy fields and shrubbery.

Forcer[2]. Add: **1. b.** One who produces forced crops.

1789 J. ABERCROMBIE (*title*) The Complete Kitchen Gardener and Hot-bed Forcer. 1902 *Westm. Gaz.* 4 Apr. 8/2 There are forcers who have a dozen large hothouses devoted solely to Easter lilies. 1905 *Ibid.* 21 Feb. 12/1 A 'forcer' in Kent gets a living from strawberry-forcing on less than half an acre of land.

Forcherite (fǫ·ɹʃǝrait). *Min.* [ad. G. *forcherit*, f. the name of V. *Forcher*, the discoverer: see -ITE[1].] A variety of opal found in Styria.

1892 DANA *Min.* (ed. 6) 195 Forcherite..an orange-yellow opal, colored by orpiment...It is from Knittenfeld, in Upper Styria.

Forcing, *vbl. sb.* **3. a.** Add: **forcing-jet,** a jet of exhaust steam used in making a forced draught (*Cent. Dict.* Suppl. 1909).

Forcing-pump. = FORCE-PUMP 2.

1838 *Civil Engin. & Arch. Jrnl.* I. 322/1 A substitute for the Forcing-pump in supplying Steam Boilers.

Forcive (fǫ·ɹsiv), *sb.* *Physics.* [f. FORCE *sb.*[1] + -IVE.] A system of forces.

1890 LD. KELVIN *Math. & Phys. Papers* III. 457 *note*, Forcive is a word which has been introduced by my brother, Prof. James Thomson, to denote quite generally any system of forces such as, for example, a force or a number of forces acting on a rigid body, or on any system of particles, or any distribution of bodily or surface force on an elastic or fluid body. *Ibid.*, An example of a circuital forcive is, the triangle of forces or the polygon of forces, in elementary statics, by which I mean forces numerically equal to the sides of the triangle or polygon and applied in the lines of the sides, not as sometimes meant, forces applied in parallel lines through one point. 1899 — in *Phil. Mag.* XLVII. 480 The forcive which must be applied to the boundary.

Ford (fōᵊɹd), *sb.*[2] The name of Henry *Ford* (1863–), an American manufacturer of motor vehicles, used to designate these, esp. as typical of cheap makes of car.

1914 *Scotsman* 14 Oct. 12/1 Ford Chassis £105. 1918 *Automobile Engineer* Mar. 85/2 The minimum-priced car, represented by the Ford. 1920 *Blackw. Mag.* Jan. 105/2 It is the sort of road that even a Ford would hesitate to tackle. 1925 A. P. HERBERT *Laughing Ann* 48 Like the starting of a Ford.

Ford, *v.* Add: **1. b.** (Modern U.S. example.)

1903 A. ADAMS *Log Cowboy* vii. 88 You can hardly imagine what a difference there is in fording this herd, between a cool cloudy day and a clear hot one.

Fording, *vbl. sb.* (Earlier U.S. example.)

1815–16 *Niles' Weekly Reg.* IX. Suppl. 165/1 The dams are to be made with fording places.

Fore-. 5. Add:

fore-caddie, a caddie who goes in advance of the players to watch where the balls fall; **fore-car,** an obsolete form of motor-cycle having the passenger's seat in front; **fore-hock,** the hock of the fore-leg of pork or bacon; **fore-intestine** (see quot.); **fore-kidney** = PRONEPHROS; **fore-milk,** (*a*) the first milk drawn from the cow at each milking; (*b*) the colostrum (Dorland, 1901); **fore-stone,** also, the front cross-piece of a blast-furnace; **fore-truck,** a truck attached to a locomotive engine, a bogie-truck.

1890 A. LANG in H. G. Hutchinson *Golf* (Badm. Libr.) 17 In the time of..James II (then Duke of York), we hear of the '*fore-cadie' who ran in front, to mark the ball down. 1904 *Motor Cycle* 11 Apr. 348/1 One of the most highly developed *forecars we have yet seen. 1908 *Westm. Gaz.* 21 May 4/3 My machine was a three-wheeler, known in those days as a forecar. 1923 R. E. DAVIES *Pigs & Bacon Curing* 29 The side may be made into smaller cuts by either of the following divisions:—First: *fore hock, thick streaky, thin streaky, flank, gammon, corner, long loin, back and ribs, and collar. 1898 A. S. PACKARD *Text-bk. Entom.* 299 The *fore-intestine (stomodœum of the embryo). 1892 J. A. THOMSON *Outl. Zool.* 404 The pronephros or *fore-kidney persists. 1904 *Daily Chron.* 15 July 3/7 Thousands of bacteria have been found in the '*fore' milk, whereas the 'middle' milk was..germ-free. 1908 *Stratford-on-Avon Herald* 24 July 7/1 The rejection of foremilk and the discontinuance of wet milking. 1839 URE *Dict. Arts* 756 The front of the furnace is open for about 12 inches from the lower part of the front cross-piece called *fore-stone. 1891 KIPLING *Light that Failed* xv, Let me come into the bogie truck of the train. There is a *fore-truck, isn't there?

Fore-and-after. Add: **a.** (Later U.S. example.)

1891 *Scribner's Mag.* X. 781 The big 'fore-and-after' now showing a torch-light, rushed at almost ten-knot speed across the bows of the propeller.

c. A kind of dance.

1841 *Southern Lit. Messenger* VII. 767/2 The fiddler would be sawing away for life and death, and two or three couple in the floor—men and women—dancing fore and afters. *Ibid.* 768/2, I was one of six sailors and women in a regular fore and after.

Fore-bay. **b.** (Earlier U.S. example.)

1844 in C. Cist *Cincinnati Misc.* 38 His only chance of escape was to cross the forebay of the mill, where if the stretch would have proven too great for his horse to leap, he must lose him and cross on the timbers.

Fore-carriage. Add: **c.** The front seat of a fore-car (see *FORE- 5).

1904 A. B. F. YOUNG *Complete Motorist* 170 The motor-bicycle..with its fore-carriage or trailer.

Foreclosure. *attrib.* Add: *foreclosure action.*

1905 *Westm. Gaz.* 15 May 2/1 [The] suggestion of a foreclosure without a foreclosure action. 1929 *Encycl. Brit.* IX. 494/2 A foreclosure action is brought by the mortgagee against the mortgagor in the chancery division of the High Court in England.

Foreconscious (fōᵊ·ɹkǫ·nʃǝs), *a.* *Psychol.* [f. FORE- + CONSCIOUS *a.*] Belonging to that portion of the mental field the memory traces of which may be more or less readily recalled. Also *absol.*

1915 C. R. PAYNE tr. *Pfister's Psych. Method* 47 Freud distinguishes foreconscious ideas which lack only the conscious investment of energy, from the real unconscious, but attributes to this distinction more practical than theoretical value. 1920 T. P. NUNN *Educ. Data & 1st Princ.* (1923) 49 The complex may be on the 'fore-conscious' level—that is the ideas belonging to its activity, though forgotten, may be capable of being recalled. 1921 *Sat. Westm. Gaz.* 1 Oct. 16/2 The fore-conscious or marginal region of the mind.

Forehand, *a.* and *sb.* Add:

A. *adj.* **5.** *Lawn Tennis.* **a.** Said of a stroke made by holding the racket with the palm of the hand turned forwards, a stroke on the right-hand side. **b.** Applied to the right-hand court or right-hand corner or side of a court.

1889 H. W. W. WILBERFORCE *Lawn Tennis* 21 When about to make a forehand stroke, the feet should be apart. *Ibid.* 36 Supposing it [*sc.* the return] comes to the player's forehand, he may..return it in the direction it came but at an acuter angle. *Ibid.* 37 From the forehand court the return will be either—(*a*) Down the line..(*b*) Across the court. 1890 C. P. HEATHCOTE *Tennis*, etc. (Badm. Libr.) 212 The moment it is seen that the ball will come to the fore-hand, the left foot should be brought across and in front of the right. 1921 A. W. MYERS *Twenty Years Lawn Tennis* 9 He attacked the Australian's backhand corner (the forehand corner of a right-handed player) very adroitly. 1929 *Morn. Post* 13 July 16/2 The Forehand Grip.

B. *sb.* **3.** (See quot. 1908.)

1764 *Museum Rusticum* II. 165 [Mares that are] small limbed, with a moderate-sized head, and a good forehand. 1908 *Animal Managem.* (War Office) 20 The 'forehand' [of a horse] includes head, neck and fore limb.

4. Lawn Tennis. *On the forehand*: forehanded.

1908 H. S. MAHONY in A. W. Myers *Complete Lawn Tennis Player* 246 Of their ground-play, especially on the forehand, there is nothing to be said but praise. 1924 G. W. HILLYARD *Forty Years Lawn Tennis* 69 He..never did acquire the right method of hitting the ball on the forehand.

C. *adv.* *Lawn Tennis.* (See quot.)

1925 S. LENGLEN *Lawn Tennis* 24 The ball is cut forehand when it is struck below the centre of its circumference and across from right to left.

Forehanded, *a.* Add: **3.** *Lawn Tennis.* Played forehand. Also *advb.*

1889 H. W. W. WILBERFORCE *Lawn Tennis* 29 It is much more difficult to volley a high lob backhanded than forehanded. 1890 C. P. HEATHCOTE *Tennis*, etc. (Badm. Libr.) 218 The over-hand twist, given fast or slow and fore-handed as well as back-handed. 1908 A. W. MYERS *Complete Lawn Tennis Player* 129 Lawford attempted to take them forehanded. 1922 A. E. CRAWLEY *Lawn Tennis Do's & Don'ts* 27 The receiver is in doubt whether to play it forehanded or backhanded.

Foreha·ndedness. *U.S.* [f. FOREHANDED *a.* 2.] The quality of being 'forehanded'.

1840 DANA *Bef. Mast* (1854) 272 Regular habits, forehandedness (if I may use the word) in worldly affairs. 1898 MAHAN *Ld. Nelson* II. 277 The incident shows at once the forehandedness of Nelson. 1905 *Springfield Weekly Republ.* 8 Dec. 1 The attempt..to persuade people to do their Christmas shopping early appears to be making headway. Such forehandedness is in the interest of the buyers.

Forehander (fōᵊ·ɹhæ:ndǝɹ). *Lawn Tennis.* [f. FOREHAND + -ER[1].] A forehand stroke.

1922 A. E. CRAWLEY *Lawn Tennis Do's & Don'ts* 25 If you hold [the racket] across your chest, you may be too late for a forehander.

Foreign, *a.* Add: **2. d.** Of a railway: Belonging to another company, as *foreign car*, *line*.

1897 *Rep. Cambrian Railway*, Foreign Lines.

8. *Foreign legion*: see LEGION 1 b.

14. Further examples of combs. of the type of *foreign-owned* (= owned by a foreigner, of foreign ownership).

1898 *Westm. Gaz.* 16 June 1/3 A foreign-controlled department of public works. 1898 *Daily News* 5 Nov. 6/3 The commander of the foreign drilled troops. 1905 *Daily Chron.* 22 Nov. 6/3 Our corn is part home-grown and part foreign-grown. 1906 *Ibid.* 13 Aug. 4/7 The foreign-trained fitters and machinists.

Foreigner. Add:

1. c. *pl.* Foreign stocks and shares.

1898 *Westm. Gaz.* 14 Feb. 9/1 Foreigners are quiet. 1904 *Ibid.* 10 May 11/1 The Account Changes in Foreigners.

Fo·relady. *U.S.* = FOREWOMAN b.

1889 FARMER *Americanisms*, *Forelady*, a forewoman. 1904 *N. Y. Even. Post* 6 Oct. 3 Advt., Help Wanted. Designer and Forelady for long-established waist factory near Chicago. *a* 1906 'O. HENRY' *Trimmed Lamp* etc. 12 Two of the most 'refined' women in the store—a forelady and a cashier—had a few 'swell gentlemen friends'. 1906

U. SINCLAIR *Jungle* x. 125 Miss Henderson, the forelady in her department. 1909 *Public Ledger* (Philadelphia) 24 June 14/1 Umbrella forelady, to take charge of finishers in large umbrella factory.

Foresite (forǝ·zait). *Min.* [ad. G. *foresit*, f. name of G. F. *Foresi* of Porto Ferrajo, Elba: see -ITE[1].] A hydrous silicate of aluminum and calcium.

1875 DANA *Min.* App. II. 1877 — *Text-bk. Min.* 325 Foresite.—Resembles stilbite in form. 1914 *Brit. Mus. Return* 226 Granite with a crystallined cavity containing pollucite, tourmaline, foresite, etc., from Elba.

Forest, *sb.* Add: **4. a.** *forest fire.*

1880 *Harper's Mag.* July 317/2 A large portion of Southern New Jersey was laid waste by forest fires. 1896 *Vermont Agric. Rep.* XV. 82 She has directed him to..determine.. the extent and cause of forest fires.

d. *forest-born* (modern examples).

1837 *Southern Lit. Messenger* III. 238 The walls..once resounded with the accents of the forest-born Demosthenes. 1841 FOOTE *Texas & Texans* I. 120 It was in fact perfectly natural..that 'forest-born' orators [should have come forward] to rouse..the spirit of resistance.

Forestian (fǫre·stiăn), *a.* *Geol.* [f. FOREST + -IAN.] (See quots.)

1895 *Jrnl. Geol.* III. 241. 1903 GEIKIE *Text-bk. Geol.* (ed. 4) 1313 Professor James Geikie..has come to the conclusion that there were really in Europe six glacial intervals embraced within what is called the Glacial Period...These he arranges and names as in the subjoined table:—..Upper Forestian or 5th Interglacial Epoch, shown by a buried forest, with a fauna and flora indicative of a temperate and dry climate...Lower Forestian or 4th Interglacial Epoch, embracing the great fresh-water lake of the Baltic Area (*Ancylus*-beds), the lower forests under peat bogs, and the *Littorina*-clays of Scandinavia in part. 1926 *Glasgow Herald* 20 Jan. 13 Dealing with the Scotland of that remote time, Dr. Ritchie..showed that Early Man reached Scotland before the Upper Forestian epoch.

Fore-stick. *U.S.* (Earlier examples.)

1793 *Massachusetts Spy* 7 Mar. (Th.) He found his companion lying in a large body of live coals, her head on the backlog and knees on the forestick. *a* 1800 *Sp. Farmer's Museum* (1801) 167, I kicked over my forestick, and saw by this man's uneasy countenance that he must be no more nor less than a Jacobin. 1825 J. NEAL *Bro. Jonathan* I. 33 [She was] watching the current of sparks that rushed up the chimney whenever the 'back log' moved or the 'fore-stick' parted in the fire. 1845 S. JUDD *Margaret* I. xvii. 158 A great fire, composed of a huge green back log, a large green forestick. 1860 HOLLAND *Miss Gilbert's Career* xxiv. 429 The doctor and Aunt Catherine were sitting before the deep wood-fire..the doctor trying to read a newspaper and punching the forestick.

Foreteach, *v.* Delete *Obs.* and add:

1876 MORRIS *Æneids* x. 843 The father's soul foretaught of ill, afar their wail he knew. 1909 WASHBOURNE tr. *Sermons of St. Bernard* 152 They are foretaught by the Holy Spirit.

Forete·llable, *a.* [f. FORETELL *v.* + -ABLE.] Capable of being foretold.

1912 F. VON HÜGEL *Eternal Life* 212 The very range and slowness of such an immense, assumedly necessary, foretellable evolution. 1927 H. G. WELLS in *Sunday Express* 20 Feb. 12/3 A foretellable disaster.

Foretop. 3. (Later U.S. examples, of sheep.)

1866 *Ret. Agric. Soc. Maine* 149 They all had the large foretop on the forehead. 1874 *Rep. Vermont Board Agric.* II. 416 When young they should have good foretop, and the skin a light pink.

Forfar (fǫ·ɹfaɹ). The name of the county town of Forfarshire, Scotland, used attrib. to designate a kind of linen cloth which is chiefly made there.

1902 A. REID *Royal Burgh Forfar* 384 Forfar linen grew more famous in the mart than its brogues had ever been.

Forge, *sb.* **6. b.** Add: **forge-scale** = *hammer-scale* (HAMMER *sb.*[1] 7).

1883 *Specif. Alnwick & Cornhill Rlwy.* 9 To substitute a portion of forge scales or cinders.

Forget, *sb.*, variant of FORGETT.

1886 [see *FOURCHETTE 1 d]. 1921 *Dict. Occup. Terms* (1927) § 429 Side pieces for fingers of glove (called fourchettes or forgets).

Forget, *v.* Add: **1.** Used *colloq.* in admonitory phrases. orig. *U.S.*

1888 *Detroit Free Press* 6 Oct. (Farmer *Amer.*) You don't want to fool with those Quakers any, and don't you forget it. 1908 ELIZA C. HALL *Aunt Jane of Kentucky* ii. (1909) 32 He was the Rev. Lemuel Page, and don't you forgit it.

3. Also, *to forget about*: Not to recall the facts concerning; not to remember to take action in the matter of. *colloq.*

1897 NAT. GOULD *Seeing him through* xix, He had forgotten about that, it was such a long time ago. *a* 1915 R. BROOKE in *Collected Poems* (1918) Mem. p. xxv, I often wonder whether I haven't written several of them myself under a pseudonym, and forgotten about it.

Forget-me-not. 4. Add: *forget-me-not ring.* Also *ellipt.* for this.

1863 MRS. WHITNEY *F. Gartney's Girlh.* xx, There was the forget-me-not ring lying in her box of ornaments. *Ibid.* xxiv, You must wear this, now, and keep the forget-me-not for a guard.

Forging, *vbl. sb.*[2] [f. FORGE *v.*[3] + -ING[1].] = CLICKING *vbl. sb.* b.

1843 YOUATT *Horse* 393 A singular species of over-reaching, termed forging or clicking. 1892 in Funk's *Standard Dict.*, In *forging*, a horse merely hits one of his forward shoes with his hind shoes, making a disagreeable noise, but does not cut or injure his feet as in over-reaching.

Forgivableness (fǫɹgi·văb'lnės). [f. FORGIVABLE *a.* + -NESS.] The quality of being forgivable. So **Forgivably** (fǫɹgi·văbli) *adv.*

1898 A. B. BRUCE in *Expositor* Aug. 105 When general unbelief prevails in the forgivableness of transgression, it is a truth worth proclaiming. 1926 *Spectator* 29 May 917/2 The quality which distinguishes his great prototype Pepys, we mean the quality of forgivableness. 1927 *Sunday Times* 13 Mar. 6/4 [The part] was quite ludicrously, if forgivably, presented by a substitute.

Forgottenness (fǫɹgǫ·t'nnės). [f. FORGOTTEN + -NESS.] The state of being forgotten; oblivion.

1924 *Brit. Weekly* 4 Sept. 483/4 Archbishop Leighton's writings are apt to be relegated to forgottenness to-day. 1924 L. M. WATT *Prayers Public Worship* 159 Awake them from the lethargy of forgottenness.

Fork, *sb.* Add:

10. d. The part of a bicycle frame in which the (front or back) wheel revolves; also *attrib.*, as *fork-blade*, *-crown*, *-end*, *-head*.

1871 *Engl. Mechanic* XIII. 144 Can any reader give me a description of socket and fork of 'Ariel' bicycle? 1880 *Scott. Football Ann.* Advt., The Howe Bicycle, all the latest improvements, hollow oval fork, &c. 1898 *Echo* 19 Nov. 2/5 The 'Mohawk' people have improved their fork crowns. 1898 *Cycling* 48 The fork ends. 1902 *Captain* VII. 83/1 The fork head of the Raleigh. 1908 *Daily Chron.* 7 Nov. 7/1 In a fog it is better to carry one's lamp on the fork-blade than high up.

e. The forked prop which supports the mantle in an incandescent gas burner.

1913 *Work* 14 June 219/3 Clay forks for incandescent mantles.

12. c. (Earlier Amer. examples.)

1692 in *Maryland Hist. Mag.* I. 11 [It is therin described as] Being in the forks of Gunpowder River by the side of the said River. *c* 1700 *Rec. Providence* (R.I.) XI. 183 Two trees in the forke of the brooke.

g. *Chess.* A simultaneous attack on two pieces, esp. by a knight.

1656 BEALE *Royall Game of Chesse Play* vii, Forke is, that when you see two of the enemies Noble-men standing in the same ranke, and but one house betwixt them, advance a pawne, guarded with an other, unto the middle house before them both, and you may commonly take one of them. 1688 R. HOLME *Armoury* (Roxb. Club 1905) 66/2 A Fork or dilemma, is a way of takeing a chesse man, by runing vp a pawn to the rank next two great men of the aduerse part standing in one rank with a house betweene them, where if one be saued, the other wilbe taken. 1761 HOYLE *Ess. Chess* A 4, Take care of a Fork or a Check by Discovery, or a Stale mat. 1764 LAMBE *Hist. Chess* 98 A Fork is, when an adverse Pawn must take one of your Pieces, by standing upon a Square of the next Line, between two of them. 1889 R. F. GREEN *Chess* (1894) 17 The annexed diagram shows an example of a frequent and fatal fork. The White Knight, it will be observed, attacks both the Black King and Queen.

Fork, *v.* Add: **1. c.** *Chess. trans.* To attack (two pieces) simultaneously with the same piece.

1745 HOYLE *Piquet & Chess* 61 Take care that no guarded Pawn of your Adversary's fork two of your Pieces. 1891 FREEBOROUGH *Chess Endings* 116 The Queen may be forked by a diverging check, with the Kt, preceded by B-Kt 7 ch. 1891 SWINTON *Chess for Beginners* 73 Sometimes a Pawn can play a shrewd trick by 'forking' two pieces. 1899 CUNNINGTON *Mod. Chess Primer* 20 There is nothing, in chess, more dangerous than to allow one of your opponent's men to.. 'fork' two of your men by one move.

5. (Earlier examples with *over*.) Also *to fork up*.

(*a*) 1839 *Observer & Reporter* May 18 The gambler should fork over his illgotten gains. 1849 D. NASON *Jrnl.* 113 As he was the biggest man I had to fork over $1·25. 1866 GREGG *Life in Army* xv. 132 Every person..forks over his picayune. (*b*) 1839 *Observer & Reporter* Nov. 23 Well then, fork up, and be quick. 1843 *Punch* V. 86/2 'Oblige me with that hod,' and 'Have the kindness to hand me that gimlet,' are phrases which might be well substituted for a request to 'chuck' or 'fork up' 'this here' and 'that 'ere'. 1857 *Quinland* III. iii. II. 167 The plethoric dog of a New Jersey Jew has got the 'tin', and will fork up as soon as the matter is fixed. 1871 *Scribner's Monthly* I. 601 So the governor forked this up, though it's my selection entirely.

10. To bestride or mount (a horse). *U.S.*

1903 A. ADAMS *Log Cowboy* xix. 295 So fork that swimming horse of yours and wet your big toe again in the North Platte. 1920 HUNTER *Trail Drivers of Texas* 245 Throw your rope and whatever it falls on, fork him.

Forked, *ppl. a.* **8.** Add: **forked-tail.**

1849 *Rep. U.S. Comm. Patents* (1850) 621 Only two other birds he knew perform such a feat, the forked-tail hawk and the swift or chimney swallow.

Fork-lightning. = *forked lightning*, FORKED *ppl. a.* 1.

1862 'G. HAMILTON' *Country Living & Thinking* 210 They [*sc.* the birds]..moved by a sudden impulse, hopping along again in a fork-lightning kind of way.

Forlornity (fǫɹlǫ·rnĭti). [f. FORLORN *a.* + -ITY.] Forlornness.

1904 B'NESS VON HUTTEN *Pam* III. ii, 'Oh!' she added, breaking into rueful laughter at the sight of his fat forlornity. 1922 *Contemp. Rev.* Oct. 489 In their rusty forlornity.

Form, *sb.* Add: **5. d.** *Librarianship.* (See quot. 1913.) Chiefly *attrib.*, as *form-catalogue*, *-class*, *-entry*, *-list*.

1876 C. A. CUTTER *Rules Dict. Catal.* Contents, Form-catalogue. *Ibid.* 14 *Form-entry*, registry under the name of the kind of literature to which the book belongs. *Ibid.* 49 In the catalogues of libraries consisting chiefly of English books, if it is thought most convenient to make form-entries under the headings Poetry, Drama, Fiction, it may be done. *Ibid.*, There is no reason but want of room why only collections should be entered under form-headings. *Ibid.*, In the case of English fiction a form-list is of such constant use that nearly all libraries have separate fiction catalogues. 1913 QUINN *Library Catal.* 30 Form-Catalogue is one in which the entries are arranged according to the forms of literature and the languages in which the books are written,

either alphabetically or according to the relations of the forms to one another.

11. *A matter of form*: a point of formal procedure; orig. a legal phrase; hence *colloq.* = a merely formal affair; a point of ordinary routine.

1787 [in Dict.]. 1824 H. J. STEPHEN *Princ. Pleading* ii. § 1. 254 As the party has no option in accepting the issue, when well tendered, and as the similiter may in that case be added for him, the acceptance of the issue when well tendered, may be considered as a mere matter of *form*.

22. (sense 6 b) *form-room*; **form-class, -factor** (see quots.); **form-genus**, a form or phase of the life-cycle of a microfungus, etc. which has been regarded as a distinct genus; so **form-species**; **form-letter**, a circular with blanks for the insertion of relevant particulars.

1905 *Terms Forestry & Logging* 12 *Form class, all trees in a stand so similar in form that the same form factor is applicable in determining their actual volume. 1895 SIR W. SCHLICH *Man. Forestry* III. 36 Under '*form factor' is understood the proportion which exists between the volume of a tree and that of a regularly-shaped body which has the same base and height as the tree. 1886 *Encycl. Brit.* XXI. 401/2 When vigorously growing and dividing, the Schizomycetes as a rule present certain definite forms, which are at any rate so constant under constant conditions that they can be figured and described with such accuracy and certainty that good observers have regarded them as fixed species, or at least as '*form-species' or '*form-genera'. 1900 B. D. JACKSON *Gloss. Bot. Terms* 174/2 The form-genus *Oidium*. 1922 SINCLAIR LEWIS *Babbitt* iii. § 3 The fortnightly *form-letter, to be mimeographed and sent out to a thousand 'prospects'. 1897 BLEACKLEY *Short Innings* xv, The bell..signified that all the boys should be in their *form rooms. 1899 KIPLING *Stalky* 105 Why aren't you down watchin' cricket?..You mustn't frowst in a form-room. 1907 MISS C. L. THOMSON *Teaching Engl.* 11 The form-room library, under the control of the form mistress.

Form, *v.*[1] Add: **1. g.** *Electr. trans.* To prepare (plates for a storage battery) by coating one with red lead and the other with litharge by means of a direct charging current. Also *intr.* for *pass.*

1893 SLOANE *Electr. Dict.* 72 Two lead plates..are 'formed', by exposure to an electrolyzing current of electricity in one direction, while they are immersed in dilute sulphuric acid. 1902 *Encycl. Brit.* XXV. 26/2 They required too much time to 'form'. *Ibid.* 28/2 The positive plates..are formed (that is, covered with peroxide) by charging them, and leaving them on open circuit (repose) alternately. 1926 R. W. HUTCHINSON *Wireless* 51 The current is first passed through the electrolyte in the direction *A* to *K*, with the result that *A* is peroxidised; it is then reversed, in which step the oxygen at *K* forms PbO_2 there, while the hydrogen at *A* reduces the existing PbO_2 to porous spongy lead. This operation is several times repeated, with the final result that the last anode (positive plate) has a thick coating of dark brown lead peroxide, while the last kathode (negative plate) is coated mainly with metallic lead of a greyish colour in a porous spongy condition, readily acted on by the SO_4 during discharge. The process is known as 'forming' the plates.

8. c. esp. in the orders *Form fours!* and *Form two deep!*

1889 *Infantry Drill* 152 The companies that will form the side faces will form fours in the required direction. *Ibid.* 154 On the words Form Two-Deep, the original rear-rank men will take one pace to the rear. 1915 'IAN HAY' *First Hundred Thous.* i, 'Squoad—'Shun! Move to the right in fours. Forrm—*fourrrs*!'..'On the command "form fours", odd numbers will stand fast.'..'Forrm—two *deep*!'

Form- (fǭɹm), a combining form of FORMIC, used to designate various chemical and proprietary preparations, as *formal, formamidine, formanilid, formeston*, etc.

1901 *Jrnl. Chem. Soc.* LXXX. i. 254 The limiting proportion of *formal or acetal produced is decreased by the presence of water. 1901 DORLAND *Med. Dict.*, *Formal*, methylal or methylene dimethylate..; a clear, fragrant liquid. It is anesthetic and hypnotic. 1901 *Ibid.*, **Form-albumin*, a formaldehyd and casein compound; a yellowish powder, used as a wound-antiseptic. 1863 *Jrnl. Chem. Soc.* XVI. 74 In a partial vacuum, which reduces the boiling point to 140°, *formamide may be distilled without the slightest decomposition. 1867 BLOXAM *Chem.* 549 Oxamide is the representative of a large class of bodies, known as the *amides*, which may be defined as substances capable of being converted, by the assimilation of the elements of two equivalents of water, into the ammonia-salts from which they are derived. Some other..members of this class are here enumerated, together with the corresponding ammonia-salts —Formamide, .. $NH_2.C_2HO_2$ — Formiate of ammonia. 1869, 1890 [see Dict.]. 1881 *Jrnl. Chem. Soc.* XLI. 266 The solid..obtained by the action of the substance, 2 HCN + 3 HCl, upon alcohol is..*formamidine. 1889 MUIR & MORLEY *Watts's Dict. Chem.* II. 563/1 *Formamidine*,..formed from the compound $(HCN)_{2}$ 3HCl by decomposing it with alcohol at 100°; the products being formic ether and formamidine. 1929 *Encycl. Brit.* I. 810/2 *Formamidine*, is only known in the form of its salts, the crystalline hydrochloride being obtained by the action of ammonia on the hydrochloride of formimido-ethyl ether. 1852 W. GREGORY *Handbk. Org. Chem.* 377 *Formanilide, the analogous compound to which, formamide, is not known. 1901 DORLAND *Med. Dict.*, *Formanilid*, a substance, $HCO.NH.C_6H_5$, resembling acetanilid: an anodyne, antipyretic, and local anesthetic. 1908 *Practitioner* Feb. 280 Combination [of pure eston] with formic acid produced a more energetic substance. This has been called '*Formeston,' the acetic acid of one of the valencies of the alumina hydrate being replaced by formic acid. 1925 T. L. STEDMAN *Med. Dict.*, *Formeston*, aluminum aceto-formate, a dusting powder similar to eston and subeston.

Formaldehyde (fǭɹmæ·ldǐhəid). *Chem.* [f. FORMIC *a.* 1 + ALDEHYDE.] A colourless gas, formic aldehyde, largely used in aqueous solution as a disinfectant and as a preservative in synthetic resins and varnishes. Also *attrib.*

1873 *Jrnl. Chem. Soc.* XXVI. 885 Formaldehyde and Diphenyl yield a hydrocarbon which separates from chloroform in small crystals. 1897 *Westm. Gaz.* 9 June 10/1 Dr. Billings says that he has a perfect disinfectant in the gas formaldehyde. 1903 *Brit. & Col. Printer* 19 Nov. 6/4 The glutinous material in the fabric is rendered insoluble by the formaldehyde treatment. 1920 *Chambers's Jrnl.* 477/1 A most powerful germ-destroyer—formaldehyde. 1929 *Encycl. Brit.* XIX. 212/1 Formaldehyde-phenolic resins.

Formalin (fǭɹmălin). Also -ine. [f. *FORMAL(DEHYDE + -IN[1].] An aqueous solution of formaldehyde, used as a disinfectant. Also *attrib.* Hence **Fo·rmalinize** *v. trans.*, to treat with formalin.

1893 *Specif. Pitt's Patent* 5 Apr. No. 7038 The new antiseptic material, herein called formalin,..contains 40% of pure formaldehyde combined with 60% of water. 1895 *Analyst* July 167 The addition of formalin to milk may be deemed admissible. 1901 *Westm. Gaz.* 25 July 5/3 The formalin treatment of consumption. 1907 *Practitioner* Apr. 570 The use of formalinised gut is advised. 1908 *Ibid.* Jan. 47 A simple and convenient method [of sterilisation] is treatment by formalin vapour.

Formant (fǭɹmănt). *Phonetics.* [ad. G. *formant* (L. Hermann), ad. L. *formant-, -ans*, pres. pple. of *formāre* to FORM.] The characteristic pitch of a vowel-sound.

1901 *Nature* 26 Dec. 187/2 A vowel, according to him [*sc.* Hermann], is a special acoustic phenomenon, depending on the intermittent production of a special partial, or 'formant' or 'characteristique'. The pitch of the 'formant' may vary a little without altering the character of the vowel. 1930 *Times Lit. Suppl.* 3 July 545/1 Later investigators have developed a theory of the vowel as a *formant*, which, though occupying a definite region of pitch, nevertheless manages somehow to affect the whole sound-complex.

Forma pauperis (fǭɹme̞ pǭ·pĕris). [L.] = *in forma pauperis* (s.v. ‖ IN 4). Also †*under forma pauperis*.

1607 MIDDLETON, etc. *Widow* II. i, I scorn to get thee under *forma pauperis*. 1633 T. ADAMS *Exp. 2 Peter* ii. 6. 621 Doe they not sue for their inheritance in heaven, *Forma pauperis*; refusing to give the least scrap of their superfluitie for eternall life? 1907 *Daily Chron.* 4 Mar. 3/5 In the Divorce Court..fees to the lawyers are supposed to be paid even in formâ pauperis causes.

Formation. Add:

1. b. *Electr.* The action or process of 'forming' accumulator plates.

1895 S. P. THOMPSON *Electr. & Magn.* 519 During the subsequent process of 'formation' the hardened paste is reduced on one plate..and peroxidized on the other. 1926 R. W. HUTCHINSON *Wireless* 51 To obviate the tedious 'formation' of the Planté plates, Faure coated the plates, prior to charging, with a paste of red lead (Pb_3O_4) and sulphuric acid.

5. b. *Bot.* An assemblage of plants of a similar character or environment.

1900 B. D. JACKSON *Gloss. Bot. Terms.* 1904 *Science* 18 Mar. 467 (Cent. Dict. Suppl.) The persistent misuse by many ecologists of the word '*formation*', when referring to plant societies or associations.

Formative, *sb.* Add: *gen.* A formative agent.

1907 GALSWORTHY *Country House* I. iv, That essential formative of character, east wind.

Formatore (fǭɹmatō·re). [It., agent-n. f. *formare* to form.] A modeller in wax or plaster.

1862 *Catal. Internat. Exhib., Brit.* II. No. 5451 Formatore to the Science and Art Department, the Trustees of the British Museum, and the Royal Academy of Arts. 1899 *Proc. Zool. Soc.* 776 Assistant formatore in the Museum.

Formed, *ppl. a.* Add:

1. b. *Electr.* (see *FORM *v.*[1] 1 g).

1904 *Technol. & Sci. Dict.* (ed. Goodchild & Tweney) 3/2 In the original cells used by Planté the coating of oxides of lead was formed by immersing ordinary leaden plates in a dilute acid, passing the current, then discharging, and repeating this process a number of times. Cells made in this way are sometimes termed 'Formed cells'. 1926 R. W. HUTCHINSON *Wireless* 51 The nascent oxygen at *A* will convert the $PbSO_4$.. there into PbO_2, while the nascent hydrogen at *K* will reduce the products there to the metallic state; thus the electrodes are again in their 'formed' condition, viz. lead peroxide (PbO_2) at *A*, lead (Pb) at *K*.

Former, *sb.*[1] Add:

1. b. *Electr.* One who attends to the 'forming' of accumulator plates.

1921 *Dict. Occup. Terms* (1927) § 302 Storage battery former.

4. *attrib.* and *Comb.*, as **former-wound** *a.*, of an armature coil, wound on a former before being mounted.

1902 *Encycl. Brit.* XXVII. 583/2 The former-wound coils have the advantage that they are perfectly symmetrical and interchangeable. 1906 A. RUSSELL *Altern. Curr.* II. 328 The winding of the stator of a polyphase motor is simple. It may be made up of rectangular former-wound coils, that is, coils which are wound into shape on a rectangular wooden block before being fixed on the stator.

-former. [f. FORM *sb.* 6 b + -ER[1].] In schools, a member of a specified class or form, as *sixth-former*.

1927 J. ELDER *Thomasina Toddy* xi, Sixth and Fifth formers who were in the Elevens. *Ibid.* xii, They gained on the Sixth-formers' boat. 1928 *Daily Express* 31 Aug. 15/2 One of them inquired of a small fourth-former whether he had seen any suspicious characters about.

Former, *a.* Add: **1. e.** Used to designate a former holder of an office; = English *ex-*. *U.S.*

1905 *N. Y. Herald* 5 Feb. 47 Former President Cleveland is among the arrivals of the week at the Lakewood Hotel. 1919 H. L. MENCKEN *Amer. Lang.* 118 Such clumsy quasi-titles as ex-United States Senator,..and former Chief of the Fire Department.

Forming, *vbl. sb.* Add: **b.** *Electr.* = *FORMATION 1 b. Also *attrib.*

1902 *Encycl. Brit.* XXV. 26/2 Faure..greatly shortened the time required for 'forming' by giving the plates a preliminary coating of red lead. 1921 *Dict. Occup. Terms* (1927) § 302 s.v. *Former*, A forming tank, a lead-lined wooden container filled with sulphuric acid. 1923 *Harmsworth's Wireless Encycl.* II. 956/1 The process of 'forming' in accumulators consists of converting the paste in the grids of the plate into an active mass containing lead peroxide in the case of the brown positive plate, and grey porous metallic lead in the negative plate.

Formo-[2] (fǭɹmo), used as combining form of *FORMALDEHYDE, designating various formaldehyde preparations.

1874 *Jrnl. Chem. Soc.* XXVIII. 755 Formoguanamine..exhibits a slight alkaline reaction. 1896 *Ibid.* LXX. i. 628 Marcourt's 'Formopyrine'... The substance obtained by Marcourt..on allowing antipyrine and formaldehyde to remain together in solution, is identical with methylenediantipyrine.

Formol (fǭ·ɹmǫl). *Pharm.* [f. *FORM(ALDEHYDE + -OL.] = *FORMALIN.

1894 *Brit. Med. Jrnl.* 22 Dec. 1429/2 Formol was introduced by Professor Leber; it was supplied under two names —formol or formaline. 1907 *Practitioner* Oct. 571 When 240 grammes..of crystals of permanganate of potash were placed in an ordinary three-gallon pail, and..17 fluid ounces of formol, poured on to them, sufficient gas was evolved to disinfect 1,600 cubic feet of space.

Formosan (fǭɹmō·săn), *a.* and *sb.* [f. *Formosa*, orig. fem. (sc. *insula* island) of L. *formōsus* beautiful; orig. the Portuguese name for the island Taiwan: see -AN.]

A. *adj.* Of or pertaining to the island of Formosa or its inhabitants. **B.** *sb.* A native of Formosa; the native language of the Formosans, one of the Malayo-Polynesian group of languages.

1704 PSALMANAZAR *Descr. Formosa* 122 The Formosan Alphabet. 1731 R. MILLAR *Hist. Propag. Christ.* II. viii. 318 Mr. Robert Junius..translated certain psalms into the Formosan language. 1879 *Encycl. Brit.* IX. 416/2 The Formosan fauna has been but partially ascertained. 1898 W. A. PICKERING *Pioneering in Formosa* 33 The climate of the Formosan capital is exceedingly fine..except for an occasional 'north-easter'. 1902 *Encycl. Brit.* XXIX. 685/1 Upon the Chinese Government properly devolved the duty of punishing its subjects, the Formosans.

Formose (fǭ·ɹmōᵘs), *sb.* *Chem.* [ad. G. *formos* (Lörs), f. *FORM(ALDEHYDE: see -OSE[2].] A mixture of sugars obtained by the action of milk of lime on formaldehyde.

1886 *Jrnl. Chem. Soc.* L. 610 Formose, $C_6H_{12}O_6$, is obtained by shaking a 3·5 to 4 per cent. solution of formaldehyde with an excess of milk of lime.

Formularism (fǭ·ɹmiŭlăriz'm). [f. FORMULARY + -ISM.] Rigid adherence to or dependence on formularies. So **Fo·rmularist.**

1896 T. HARDY *Jude the Obscure* II. i. 95 The well-known three, the enthusiast, the poet, and the formularist. 1927 *Observer* 30 Oct. 7 The cut-and-dried formularism of the Socialist theory.

Formulate, *v.* Add examples of more extended use.

1893 A. CONAN DOYLE *Mem. Sherlock Holmes* 12, I listened..to the dialogue of the two detectives. Gregory was formulating his theory. 1906 PHILLPOTTS *Portreeve* I. x, She..stood for the moment powerless to formulate a clear pathway through this thicket of ideas. 1907 *Smart Set* Mar. 134 He resolved to send her some volumes of Ruskin and to formulate a graduated course of reading. 1910 ALBANESI *For Love of Anne Lambart* 91 Anne began to put into movement the scheme that had formulated itself in her mind. 1924 ANNE D. SEDGWICK *Little French Girl* I. vii. 69 It was strange to her, as she spoke to feel how deeply she knew all this about Giles, though she had never before formulated it to herself.

Hence **Fo·rmulator.**

1919 K. PEARSON in C. Goring *Eng. Convict* (1919) Introd. 12 The use by the formulator of a thoroughly unscientific method does not justify us in rejecting his hypothesis.

Forra(r)der: see *FORWARDER.

Forsythia (fǭɹsəi·þiă). [mod.L., f. the name of William *Forsyth* (1737–1804), English botanist: see -IA[1].] Any plant of the ornamental oleaceous genus of spring-flowering shrubs so named, which are cultivated for their bright-yellow bell-shaped flowers.

1814 O. O. RICH *Amer. Plants* 57. 1905 *Daily Chron.* 2 Aug. 3/1 Daffodils in the grass under drooping Forsythia. 1927 E. H. M. COX *Evol. Garden* xiii. 250 The Forsythias with bright yellow flowers. 1931 *Morn. Post* 25 Feb. 6/3 R—'s forsythias and cherries towered up 12 feet.

Fort, *v.* (Later U.S. examples.)

1834 CROCKETT *Narr. Life* vii. 52 The fort was built right in the middle of a large old field, and in it the people had been forted so long and so quietly, that they didn't apprehend any danger at all. 1838 *Southern Lit. Messenger* IV. 295 The settlers were sometimes forted. 1851 W. DE HASS *Hist. Western Virginia* 315 Of those forted at Grave creek, was a William McIntosh, wife and child.

absol. 1853 B. YOUNG *Jrnl. Discourses* I. 165 Suppose we should say to all the wards in this city, the time has come to fort up. 1878 J. H. BEADLE *Western Wilds* xii. 186 They lit on the Yorker and his friends and druv 'em back into Miller's Store, when they forted and held their own.

Fortescue (fǭ·ɹtĕskiū). *Austral.* [perh. alteration of the pop. name *forty skewer* after the proper name *Fortescue.*] A scorpænoid fish, *Pentaroge marmorata.*

1874 HILL in Tenison-Woods *Fish N. S. W.* (1882) 49 The scorpion or Fortescue..bear that name no doubt in memory of the pain they have hitherto inflicted; and for its number and array of prickles it enjoys in this country the *alias* 'Forty skewer' or 'Fortescue'. 1882 *Ibid.* 49 The 'Fortescue'..is a common fish in Port Jackson, with a very long dagger-shaped preorbital spine. 1896 F. G. AFLALO *Nat. Hist. Australia* 228 Fortescue (*Pentaroge*)..is a terrible pest, lurking among the *débris* in the nets and all but invisible.

Fortified, *ppl. a.* Add: **b.** Denoting animals that have been immunized against diseases.

1904 *Daily Chron.* 4 July 7/6 Serum taken from 'fortified' beasts.

c. (See quot.)

1913 DORLAND *Med. Dict.* (ed. 7), *Fortified milk*, milk made more nutritious by the addition of cream or white of egg.

Fortissimo, *adv.* Add: **B.** *sb.* A very loud passage or point; *fig.* a high pitch of excitement.

1928 *Observer* 5 Feb. 12/5 The hard and sudden fortissimos. 1928 *Daily Express* 17 Mar. 9/7 As this jazz harmony reached its fortissimo. 1931 E. SACKVILLE-WEST *Simpson* III. xiii, Flinging a fortissimo of emotion—whether of anger or of delight—with sudden and deafening violence on to everything which twitched the robe of his soul.

Fortress, *sb.* **2. b.** Add: *fortress-castle, -city, -palace.*

1906 *Westm. Gaz.* 16 Aug. 2/3 No Imperial *fortress-castle is strong enough to Germanise the vast plains where peer and peasant alike are still passionately Polish. 1909 *Ibid.* 22 Feb. 1/3 The buried *fortress-city of Jericho. 1905 *Ibid.* 11 Sept. 3/1 The gloomy *fortress-palaces.

Fortune, *sb.* **9.** Add: *fortune-favoured* adj.; *fortune-seeker.*

1898 *Daily News* 6 Oct. 6/7 The more *fortune-favoured individuals. 1915 W. J. LOCKE *Jaffery* i, He had put poor old Jaffery and fortune-favoured me in the shade. 1906 *Daily Chron.* 5 May 4/7 A vast throng of *fortune-seekers.

Forty, *a.* and *sb.* Add: **A.** *adj.* **e.** *The forty hours* (also qualifying *devotion*, etc.; It. *le quarant'ore*): in the R. C. Church, the continuous exposition of the Host for forty hours, used as an occasion of special devotion or intercession.

1756–9 BUTLER *Lives Saints* (1845) XI. 118 The saint..ordered the forty hours' prayer for his recovery. 1839 K. H. DIGBY *Mores Cath.* IX. iii. (1847) III. 41/2 The devotion of the forty hours prayer instituted by a poor Capuchin friar, Joseph of Milan. 1869 *Life Mother Margaret Hallahan* vii. 189 During the Octave of Corpus Christi this year the Devotion of the Forty Hours was for the first time celebrated in St. Catherine's Convent. 1922 *Cath. Encycl.* Suppl. 29/1 The Forty Hours' Adoration.

B. *sb.* **5.** One fourth of a quarter section of land, comprising forty acres. *U.S.*

1845 CAROLINE M. KIRKLAND *Western Clearings* 2 Eighties and forties..are plain enough when one is habituated to them. 1873 E. EGGLESTON *Myst. Metrop.* i. 19 It was just so many quarter sections, 'eighties', and 'forties' to be bought low. 1902 S. E. WHITE *Blazed Trail* i. 13 The men who were to fell the trees, Radway distributed along one boundary of a 'forty'. 1913 GENE STRATTON-PORTER *Laddie* xiv. (1917) 276, I had thought we would commence on the east forty when planning the work [of ploughing].

6. A period of forty minutes' play.

1913 *Field* 25 Oct. 904/2 Light forwards are bound to be worn down in two 'forties' by heavier.

7. A sharper. *Australian slang.*

1927 M. M. BENNETT *Christison* xxii. 194 Their numbers swelled with rowdies and 'forties'—gambling sharpers who travelled from shed to shed making five pounds by cheating for every five shillings they earned.

C. 1. *forty-acre* (see *B. 5); **forty-footer**, a forty-foot yacht; **forty-rod** *U.S.* (earlier examples).

1887 C. B. GEORGE *Forty Yrs. on Rail* xi. 227, 'I live just over there', pointing to his house across a *forty-acre lot. 1902 *Essex Inst. Hist. Coll.* XXXVIII. 256 The schooner-yacht 'Excelsior' was one of the earliest of the '*forty-footers'. *c* 1871 'MARK TWAIN' *Sketches* Wks. 1900 XIX. 77 Trading for *forty-rod whisky..has played the everlasting mischief. 1873 J. H. BEADLE *Undevel. West* xiii, The standard drink is whisky—'stone fence', 'forty-rod', and 'tarantula-juice'.

2. forty-eight, (*b*) *pl.* a sheet of a book folded into forty-eight leaves; (*c*) the forty-eight preludes and fugues of J. S. Bach; **forty-eightmo**, the size of a book in forty-eights.

1808 STOWER *Printers' Gram.* 192 A Half Sheet of Forty-eights, with Two Signatures. 1839 T. C. HANSARD *Print. & Type-Founding* 168 Forty-eights to be paid 2s. per sheet extra. 1872 H. C. BANISTER *Music* III. xxxvi. (1889) 206 Bach's Fugue in C♯ Minor, No. 4 of the 48. 1888 JACOBI *Printers' Vocab.*, *Forty-eightmo*, a sheet of paper folded into forty-eight leaves. 1902 *Westm. Gaz.* 29 Dec. 1/3 Those famous fugues and preludes known to all musicians as the 'Forty-Eight'.

b. forty-niner *U.S.* (earlier examples).

1873 J. H. BEADLE *Undevel. West* xv. 268 The 'voyage of Jason and the Argonauts' is no doubt a poetic account of the '49-ers' of Greece. 1878 B. F. TAYLOR *Between Gates* 96 There is an association of Forty-niners.

Forty-five. Add: **c.** A revolver of ·45 calibre. *U.S.*

1898 H. S. CANFIELD *Maid of Frontier* i. 7 He uz [= was] wearin' a shiny nickel plated forty-five. *a* 1909 'O. HENRY' *Roads of Destiny* xviii. 296 He could handle the trigger of a forty five with skill. 1926 J. BLACK *You Can't Win* iii. 21 He owned the latest pattern of repeating rifle and a couple of 'forty-fives'.

Forward, *a.* and *sb.* Add: **A.** *adj.* **4.** Also of delivery.

1930 M. CLARK *Home Trade* 107 'Forward delivery' [means] that the goods will be delivered..at a future date.

C. *sb.* **4.** Also in various other games.

1895 J. M. BROWN *Polo* 78 The two 'forwards', No. 1 and No. 2, should work together, and, if possible, be exactly the same class of player. 1897 *Encycl. Sport* I. 517/2 All the forwards should make a point of taking passes with their sticks. 1929 *Encycl. Brit.* III. 182/2 The duty of the forwards [in basket-ball] is primarily to make goals.

Forwardal (fǭɹwǭ·ɹdăl). [f. FORWARD *v.* + -AL.] = FORWARDING.

1911 *Supt. Govt. Printing India* Form No. 283 Books. The book..is available, price Rs. — inclusive of forwardal charges.

Forwarder (fǭ·ɹwəɹdəɹ), *a.* and *adv.* [compar. of FORWARD *a.* and *adv.*] Further forward. Often in jocular colloq. use in the (orig. dial. or vulgar) form **forra(r)der** (fǭ·rədəɹ), in the phr. (*to get*) *no* or *any forra(r)der*.

1796 MME. D'ARBLAY *Camilla* x. vii, She ventured to bend forwarder, to take a view of the side wings. 1796–7 JANE AUSTEN *Pride & Prej.* III. xiii, Kitty is forwarder than either of us. 1811–13 — *Mansf. Park* I. xviii, Without his being much the forwarder. 1862 SPENCER *First Princ.* (1867) 33 And so on in an infinite series, leaving us at last no forwarder than at first. 1898 *Daily Tel.* 15 Dec. (Ware) Whether the Liberal Forwards will get any 'forrader' over the light claret [etc.].

Forwarding, *vbl. sb.* **3.** Add: *forwarding agency, establishment, house.*

1837 W. JENKINS *Ohio Gaz.* 126 It has..ten heavy forwarding houses, connected with lake and canal transportation. 1847 H. HOWE *Hist. Coll. Ohio* 43 The harbor of Ashtabula..has several forwarding establishments. *Ibid.* 331 Toledo..has..9 forwarding and commission houses. 1897 *Outing* (U.S.) XXX. 197/2 The tourist should look after his own mount..and he should not send it by an independent forwarding agency.

Forwardly, *adv.* **3.** Delete *U.S.* and add:

1907 *Practitioner* Nov. 643 A forwardly displaced kidney.

Fossa. Add: Also with qualifying phrase.

1907 *Practitioner* Aug. 268 The pouch in which this hernia took place was formed by the inconstant fossa of Waldeyer. *Ibid.* 269 The inferior mesenteric vein, which is the guide to the fossa of Landzert.

Fossa, foussa (fǫ·să, fū·să). [Malagasy.] A civet-like animal of Madagascar, *Fossa daubentoni*, or *Cryptoprocta ferox.*

1883 *Encycl. Brit.* XV. 435/2, 436/1. 1887 CHISHOLM tr. *Vogt & Specht's Nat. Hist. Anim.* I. 184 The Fossa of the Malagasies or in scientific nomenclature Cryptoprocta ferox.

Fosse. Add: **2. b.** In full *fosse-road*, = *FOSSE-WAY.

1882 *Encycl. Brit.* XIV. 424/2 The Fosse road from Lincolnshire..passes by Leicester to Watling Street; the *Via Devana*..joins the Fosse at Leicester on its way to Chester.

Fosse-way (fǫ·swē̆). *Hist.* (Usually with cap.) Also **foss-way.** [f. FOSSE 2 + WAY *sb.*[1]] Any of the great Roman roads in Britain, so called from the ditch or fosse on each side.

1610 HOLLAND *Camden's Brit.* I. 562 Thus much of the Feldon, or champion part, which, that ancient Fosse-way (a thing that would not bee overpassed) cutteth overthwart. *c* 1790 *Encycl. Brit.* (1797) V. 26/1 The fosse-way, which comes from Scotland, passes through this county and town to Totness in Devonshire. 1838 *Penny Cycl.* X. 381/1 From Aquæ Solis the Foss-way continued its course in a pretty direct line to Ischalis (Ilchester), of which town it forms the principal street. 1876 *Encycl. Brit.* V. 792/2 The junction of the Fosse-way with the Ermin and Icknield streets.

Fossildom (fǫ·sĭldəm). [f. FOSSIL *sb.* + -DOM.] The condition or character of being a fossil or a lifeless piece of antiquity.

1898 *Daily News* 3 Dec. 5/7 Spurious vulgar fossildom secretly urges members to oppose this non-party measure. 1905 J. RICKABY *Development* 48 Protestantism, even Anglican Protestantism, is essentially fossildom.

Fossor. Add: **2.** A burrowing hymenopter, as the digger-wasp.

1899 *Cambr. Nat. Hist.* VI. 95 The apterous condition of the females of the Mutillides and Thynnides is very anomalous in the Fossors.

Foster-mother. Add: **2.** An apparatus for rearing chickens hatched in an incubator.

1911 J. W. HURST *Successful Incub.* 78 A cheap form of ordinary lamp should never be used, as is sometimes attempted..by makers of home-made brooders and foster-mothers. 1914 *Poultry* 2 Jan. 1042 When my Chicks are in your Foster-Mothers I can rest comfortably at night, and so can the Chicks.

Foucault (fu·ko). The name of J. B. L. *Foucault* (1819–1868), French physicist, used attrib. and in the genitive to designate experiments or discoveries made, or apparatus designed, by him; as *Foucault current*; *Foucault's gyroscope, pendulum experiment, prism*, etc.

1863 ATKINSON tr. *Ganot's Physics* 632 Foucault's experiment.—This consists in projecting on a screen the image of the charcoal points produced in the camera obscura at the moment at which the electric light is formed. 1879 *Encycl. Brit.* X. 197/2 Foucault's pendulum experiment. 1883 ATKINSON tr. *Ganot's Physics* (ed. 11) 869 The currents..produced in solid conductors and which are converted into heat, are often spoken of as Foucault currents. 1883 GLAZEBROOK *Phys. Optics* 338 Foucault's prism is constructed in a similar manner [as a Nicol's prism], only the Canada balsam is done away with. 1887 MENDENHALL *Cent. of Electr.* 189 Foucault's first automatic regulator. 1892 G. F. BARKER *Physics* 835 Foucault's interrupter..consists of an arm supported on a vertical spring, carrying an armature at one end and a vertical platinum contact-point at the other. 1902 *Encycl. Brit.* XXIX. 195/1 Foucault's gyroscope. 1906 A. RUSSELL *Altern. Curr.* II. 326 Foucault's disc. 1929 *Encycl. Brit.* IX. 551/1 Eddy or 'Foucault currents' induced in a copper disc moving in a strong magnetic field.

Fougade (fugā·d). Delete † and add quot.

1904 *Daily Chron.* 4 June 5/5 The explosion of a number of mines and fougades.

Foul, *a.*, etc. Add: **A.** *adj.* **1. b.** *Foul brood* (earlier U.S. examples). Hence **Foul-broody** *a.*, infected with foul brood.

1868 *Rep. U.S. Comm. Agric.* (1869) 278 The foul-brood fungus, which I have named *Cryptococcus alvearis*, belongs to the smallest of the fungoid forms. 1868 *Amer. Naturalist* June II. 196 An insect..producing the well-known disease called 'foul-brood', which is analogous to the typhus fever of man. 1875 J. HUNTER *Man. Bee-keeping* 193 Twenty stocks..were foul-broody, and I lost them all.

13. b. Revolting, disgusting. *slang.*

1930 A. P. HERBERT *Water Gipsies* xxi, 'Hullo, Gordon! My dear, it's a *foul* night. Arctic!' She shivered charmingly. 1930 *Punch* 20 Aug. 200/1 'How foul!' I said... 'How dare the creature long to meet me!'

C. *adv.* **6. foul-hooked** *a.*, hooked anywhere on the body except in the mouth.

1898 *Westm. Gaz.* 6 Oct. 4/2 Without doubt this fish was foul-hooked, though it was surely a heavy one. 1908 *Ibid.* 11 Sept. 4/1 A large salmon has been foul-hooked by, and has broken away from, anglers roach-fishing in the Trent at Wilford.

Found, *ppl. a.* Add: **3.** *absol.* in *pl.* Advertisements of found articles, usually in phr. *losts and founds.*

1913 G. B. DIBBLEE *Newspaper* 126 The most important groups of classified advertising are as follows: financial, theatrical, public notices, losts and founds, educational.

Foundation. Add: **7.** Also *attrib.*

1882 [in Dict.]. 1907 *Westm. Gaz.* 9 Mar. 13/2 Such a coat is..mounted on a foundation silk.

8. b. Also applied to persons, etc. belonging to or associated with the foundation of a society or institution.

1900 *Westm. Gaz.* 28 June 1/1 The Royal herd and flock at Sandringham were established in 1863, when the foundation animals were selected from some of the best stocks in England. 1928 *Daily Mail* 31 July 8/5 The subscription will be 5s. a year for foundation members.

Fountain. Add: **2. b.** A metal vessel containing aerated water for drinking; a box containing ice and a coil through which aerated water is drawn (= **soda-fountain*). *U.S.*

1873 J. H. BEADLE *Undevel. West* xxxi. 675 A drink equal to the best soda from fountains. 1874 KNIGHT *Dict. Mech.*

Fountaining (fau·ntĕniŋ), *ppl. a.* [f. FOUNTAIN + -ING[2].] = FOUNTING *ppl. a.*

1883 G. MEREDITH *Day of Dau. of Hades* x, A chariot, cleaving the storm, Clove the fountaining lake with a plough. 1923 *Glasgow Herald* 5 Sept. 8 When the sun plays on the foam the impression of innumerable fountaining pearls is conveyed. *Ibid.* 11 Dec. 6 The pale fountaining gold of the clumps of tall windlestraws.

Fountain pen. [f. FOUNTAIN 4 + PEN *sb.*[2]] A pen containing a reservoir of ink (see quot. 1738).

1710 M. HENRY *Expos. Bible, Zechariah* iv. 2 Without any further Care they [*sc.* lamps] received Oil as fast as they wasted it, (as in those which we call Fountain Inkhorns, or Fountain Pens). 1738 CHAMBERS *Cycl.*, *Fountain Pen* is a sort of pen, contrived to contain a great quantity of ink, and let it flow by gentle degrees; so as to supply the writer a long time, without a necessity of taking fresh ink. 1758 E. STONE tr. *Bion's Constr. Math. Instruments* (ed. 2) 85 Of the Fountain-Pen... When the afore-mentioned Pen is to be used, the Cover must be taken off, and the Pen a little shaken, in order to make the Ink run freely. 1789 MISS BURNEY *Diary*, etc. 18 Aug. (1842) 51, I took my fountain pen, and wrote my rough journal. 1833 *Mechanics' Mag.* XIX. 319/1 The introduction of this paper will go far to supersede the use of fountain-pens of all kinds. 1885 *Encycl. Brit.* XVIII. 484/1.

Four, *a.* and *sb.* Add:

B. *sb.* **1. b.** The figure (4) denoting this number.

2. f. *pl.* A light meal taken in the fields at four o'clock in the afternoon. *local.*

1823 MOOR *Suffolk Words* 27. 1849 RAYNBIRD *Agric. Suffolk* 296 The names 'fources' and 'elevens', given to these short periods of rest and refreshment, show when taken. 1887 E. S. SUFFLING *Land of Broads* (ed. 2) 266 At 4 p.m., when they have their 'fourses'. 1895 C. J. CORNISH *Wild Eng. of To-day* 243 The workmen rest for their 'elevenses' and 'fourses'.

C. *Comb.* **1. a.** *four-cylinder, -day, -mile.*

1902 *Westm. Gaz.* 8 Sept. 7/3 Quadruple expansion *four-cylinder engines of 4,000 horse-power. 1903 *Daily Chron.* 24 Mar. 5/2 The new De Glehn four-cylinder compound express locomotive. 1902 *Ibid.* 1 Sept. 5/2 The half-yearly *four-day closing of the British Museum reading room. 1909 *Westm. Gaz.* 3 Sept. 12/1 Thus making the first four-day westward voyage. 1897 HINDE *Fall of Congo Arabs* 115 The whole crowd jumped into the river, here about a hundred yards wide, with a *four-mile current. 1903 KIPLING *Five Nations* 90 From the Four-mile Radius roughly to the plains of Hindustan.

2. four-ball *a.*, defining a foursome at golf in which four balls are used, the best ball on each side counting at each hole; **four-baller**, a golfer playing in a four-ball match; **four-cycle** = *FOUR STROKE 2; **four-figure** *a.*, consisting of 'four figures', i.e. a thousand pounds or over; **four-place** *a.*, said of mathematical tables worked out to four places of decimals (four-figure tables); **four-seater**, a car with seating accommodation for four people, also *attrib.*; **four-spot**, a card marked with four spots; **four-walled** *a.*, having or inclosed within four walls; **four-walls**, the walls of a room or a house; hence, *allusively*, in reference to confinement within the limits of a (small) building.

1904 *Westm. Gaz.* 25 Mar. 4/1 The players in a *four-ball match. 1909 *Ibid.* 8 Mar. 12/2 Four-ball foursomes. 1927 *Observer* 31 July 15/5 A selfish '*four-baller,' intent solely on his own pleasure, has blocked the way. 1909 *Westm. Gaz.* 25 Mar. 4/1 It is open to question if a two-cycle engine will ever be produced which will show the same economy of fuel as the *four-cycle. 1924 *Times, Trade & Engin. Suppl.* 29 Nov. 250/3 Four-cycle double-acting engines. 1877 *Porcupine* 17 Feb. 741/1 The same modest *four-figure price. 1886 *Encycl. Brit.* XXIII. 13/1 A *four-place table. 1927 CAREY & GRACE (*title*) Four-Place Mathematical Tables with Forced Decimals. 1909 *Westm. Gaz.* 16 Nov. 4/2 The famous 15-h.p. *four-seater touring-car. 1922 *Times* 20 June 8/5 The increased convenience and comfort of a four-seater. 1920 MULFORD *J. Nelson* x. 100 I'm layin' down as fine a pair of *four-spots as I've ever held. 1905 *Daily Chron.* 18 Aug. 3/7 A *four-walled prison life. 1908 WALLACE *Children Chapel* 7 The four-walled coach-court of the public inn. [1834 tr. *Jacquemont's Journ. India* I. 156, I was much more comfortable under it..than within *four naked walls.] 1849 N. P. WILLIS *Rural Lett.* 17 Between five in the morning and 'flower-shut' I feel as if four walls and a ceiling would stop my breath. 1922 E. PERCY (*title*) If Four Walls Told. 1930 M. C. C. HARRISON & H. A. CARTWRIGHT (*title*) Within Four Walls.

Fourchette. Add:

1. d. *Glove-making.* The forked piece between two adjacent fingers of a glove; a forgett. Also *Comb.*, as *fourchette-cutter, -puncher.*

1862 *Catal. Internat. Exhib., Brit.* II. No. 4942 The Children's [gloves] have an improved fourchette. 1881 *Instr. Census Clerks* (1885) 76 Thumb and Fourchette Cutter and Puncher. 1886 *Chambers's Jrnl.* 226/2 He cut pieces for the thumbs and fourchettes or sides of the fingers—usually pronounced 'forgets'.

e. The disposition of troops in furcated lines.

1866 R. L. DABNEY *Life T. J. Jackson* 532 These [*sc.* lines] formed a vast, obtuse *fourchette*, presenting its concavity toward the enemy.

2. *Card games.* (See quots.)

1885 R. A. PROCTOR *Whist* 241 King and Knave make the *fourchette* to the Queen led; Queen and ten make the *fourchette* to the Knave; and so on. 1898 'CAVENDISH' *Whist* 102 When you have the *fourchette* it is almost always right to cover. 1906 'CUT-CAVENDISH' *Complete Bridge Player* 131 A fourchette is the combination of cards in one hand immediately above and below the card led, such as knave, nine, sitting over the ten. It applies to the cards of the second player over the leader, and to the cards of the third player over the second. 1907 *Westm. Gaz.* 18 May 14/1 In the unusual case of holding a hand that is full of fourchettes, the middle heart is the correct opening.

Fourcroea: see *FURCRÆA.

Fourdrinier (fuədri·nie). *Fourdrinier machine*, a paper-making machine invented by C. and S. Fourdrinier, printers of the early part of the 19th century. Also *Fourdrinier cloth*, the special wire cloth used for draining the pulp in the machine; *Fourdrinier loom*, the machine in which the wire cloth is made.

1874 *Art of Paper-Making* 164 They certainly well deserve to be immortalised in the name of the present Fourdrinier. *Ibid.* 182 It is this shaking movement, though it is very trifling (about ½ inch), which makes the Fourdrinier paper superior to that made on a cylinder-machine. 1874 KNIGHT *Dict. Mech.*, *Fourdrinier-machine*, a paper-making machine, the first to make a continuous web.

Fourer (fǭ·rəɹ). *Cricket.* [f. FOUR + -ER[1].] A hit from which four runs are scored.

1875 *Field* 8 May 458/1 Boys made a 'fourer'. 1901 R. H. LYTTELTON *Out-door Games* 14 The public only applaud him [*sc.* the batsman] when he hits a fourer. 1927 *Observer* 29 May 28/5 At the other end I'll make old Brown bowl full half-volleys wide of the off-stump and have an outer ring of three to save the fourers.

Four flush, *sb.* *U.S.* [FLUSH *sb.*[3] 1.] In poker, a flush containing only four (instead of five) cards; a bob-tail flush. Hence *attrib.*, lacking in genuineness.

1887 J. W. KELLER *Draw Poker* 35 If in opening a pot a player finds in his hand a pair and a four flush, or four straight, he may break his pair. 1904 *N. Y. Even. Post* 20 Feb. 10 Mayor Harrison's assertion that the Sunday closing law is a 'four-flush' law..one that was meant to deceive and not meant for actual enforcement.

Hence **Fou·r-flusher**, a pretender, humbug.

1910 *Outlook* 25 June 376 Many doubted his intention, and one newspaper called him a 'four-flusher'. 1916 'B. M. BOWER' *Phantom Herd* ii. 30 Some of the four-flushers..kept eyeing that bluff. 1920 A. B. BAXTER *Parts Men Play* xxi. § 1 Vot you mean, you great big fourflusher? 1921 R. D. PAINE *Comr. Rolling Ocean* vi. 106, I could have sized up this Maddigan four-flusher if he had merely walked across the campus in my freshman year. 1924 W. M. RAINE *Troubled Waters* ii. 22 You're a fine bunch of four-flushers.

Four-flush, *v.* *U.S.* [f. the sb.] *intr.* To act in a 'bluffing' fashion.

1920 I. OSTRANDER *How Many Cards?* 245 I've an idea that Waverly is four-flushing financially..and is in on a percentage of Cutler's games.

Fou·r-footer. [f. FOUR *a.* + FOOT *sb.* + -ER[1].] A creature having four feet, a quadruped.

1920 GALSWORTHY *In Chancery* II. x, 'Strange life a dog's,' said Jolyon suddenly: 'the only four-footer with rudiments of altruism, and a sense of God!'

Four hundred. *U.S.* [FOUR *a.* 3.] (See quot. 1895.)

1889 *Century Mag.* Apr. 857/2 Her sayings and doings were as much a part of tea and dinner table gossip as they would be if she lived today and belonged to the 'four hundred'. 1895 *Sun* (N. Y.) 1 Feb., The term Four Hundred has no actual meaning. It is a general phrase which stands for an exclusive association of people who represent the very best Society in this city. 1906 MARY E. WILKINS FREEMAN *Light of the Soul* 93 People in Edgham aped society, they even talked about the 'four hundred'.

Four-in-hand. Add: **1. b.** A kind of necktie of the variety designed to be tied in a loose knot with hanging ends.

1892 four-in-hand tie [see 3]. 1902 SUSAN HALE *Lett.* (1919) 374 The young men in Tuxedos, four-in-hands, panamas. *a* 1909 'O. HENRY' *Roads of Destiny* x. 166 While trying to figure out Jimmy's method of tying his four-in-hand he cordially gave information. 1909 *Public Ledger* (Philadelphia) 24 June 5/1 Knitted and French Four-in-hands, made of fiber and short lengths of silk. 1919 T. K. HOLMES *Man fr. Tall Timber* xix. 224 She had fashioned..a crimson four-in-hand to be tied at the low, rolling collar of her blouse.

Fournier (fū·rnie). The name of P. S. *Fournier* (1712–68), French engraver and type-founder, used to designate a style of type originated by him.

1902 DE VINNE *Plain Printing Types* 146 *note*, Attempts have been made to return to the Fournier point by making it in accord with the new measures. *Ibid.* 155 *note*, In the Fournier system 1000 points made 35 centimetres. 1930 H. CARTER *Fournier on Typefounding* p. xxxv, The traditional 'Fournier point', long used in Belgium, was ·013728 English inch.

Fourré (fū·re, ‖ fure). [F. *fourré*, pa. pple. of *fourrer* to dip, thrust.] A kind of cream mixture in which nuts, fruit, etc. are dipped to make fondants; the sweetmeat itself.

1921 *Dict. Occup. Terms* (1927) § 435 *Dipper, fourré*,..heats fourré mixture (cream) in a steam-heated pan..; throws in almonds or other sweet centres and picks them out, covered with fourré, with a spoon.

Fourreau (fu·ro). [F. *fourreau* sheath, scabbard.] An under-slip. (Cf. SLIP *sb.*[3] 4 c.)

1921 *Glasgow Herald* 22 Jan. 4 A fourreau of black charmeuse, with which..is worn a simple over-dress of crepe de chine. 1927 *Observer* 10 Apr. 22 The whole dress is also slit from throat to hem, permitting a glimpse of a contrasting fourreau.

Four-spot. *U.S.* [FOUR *a.* C. 2.] A playing card having four symbols or 'pips'.

1878 B. F. TAYLOR *Between Gates* 193 We are a four-spot of dirty spades.

Four stroke. [FOUR *a.*, STROKE *sb.*[1]]

1. A stroke in billiards by which four points are scored.

1868 J. ROBERTS *Billiards* (1869) 225 A four stroke may be made by pocketing the white and spot-white balls, or by making a cannon and pocketing an opponent's ball.

2. *attrib.* In internal combustion engines, designating a cycle of operations which consists of four strokes, intake, compression, combustion, and exhaust, as *four-stroke cycle, engine.*

1906 *Motor Boat* 12 July 14/1 A four-stroke engine. 1912 *Motor Manual* 4 The Four-stroke 'Cycle' of Operations. 1929 *Encycl. Brit.* XV. 881/2 Practically all automobile engines operate on what is called the four stroke cycle.

Fourth, *a.* and *sb.* Add: **A.** *adj.* **2. b.** *Fourth of July* (earlier examples. Hence *Fourth-of-Julyism.* Also later examples of *Fourth*).

(*a*) 1807 WEEMS *Letters* II. 369 From these reflections..we may collect some good fourth-of-July ideas. 1809 W. IRVING *Knickerb.* VI. viii. (1825) 280 The dinner went off much the same as do our..fourth of July banquets. 1834 *Southern Lit. Messenger* I. 156, I do not know that the celebration of a Fourth of July in a country village has ever been thought worthy of appearing in print. 1874 B. F. TAYLOR *World on Wheels*, etc. II. i. 183 A Fourth-of-Julyism has somehow become an object of contempt.

(*b*) 1830 S. BRECK in *Recoll.* (1877) 91 On the Fourth, being a national holiday, there was a great parade on the Common. 1854 W. G. SIMMS *Southward Ho!* xiii. 253 Ordinarily admirable, our dinner on the glorious Fourth was worthy of the occasion. 1872 E. EGGLESTON *End of World* xi. 76 No more electin' presidents,..no more Fourths,..no more nothin. *a* 1909 'O. HENRY' *Roads of Destiny* xiii. 206 It reminds me of a Fourth I helped to celebrate down in Salvador.

B. *sb.* **6.** A player who comes in to make a party of four in a game.

1902 ELIN. GLYN *Refl. Ambrosine* 159 The men played Bridge. Augustus made one of the fourths.

C. *Comb.* **fourth arm** (see *ARM *sb.*[2] 9); **fourth dimension**, a supposed or assumed dimension, additional to length, breadth, and thickness (see DIMENSION 3 *note*); hence **fourth-dimensional** *a.*, of or relating to the fourth dimension, *fig.* superhuman, extraordinary; hence **fourth-dimensionalism**; **fourth (cranial) nerve**, the trochlear nerve; **fourth party** *Engl. Hist.*, a group of politicians (1880–85) led by Lord Randolph Churchill, forming a party independent of the three existing political parties; **fourth-proof** *a.* *U.S.*, highly refined; of a high grade or quality; **fourth ventricle**, a rhomboidal cavity situated between the medulla oblongata and the pons Varolii in front and the cerebellum behind.

1904 C. H. HINTON in *Harper's Mag.* July 232/2 If it became necessary to assume the existence of five atoms at equal distances from one another in a molecule, there would be evidence of a *fourth dimension. 1908 *Westm. Gaz.* 28 July 2/1 A forcible proof of superhuman or *fourth-dimensional power. 1909 SIR O. LODGE *Survival of Man* (1916) 123 In some unknown or fourth-dimensional manner. 1921 *Quest* Oct. 55 These few crude remarks on *fourth-dimensionalism and the time-enigma are ventured solely as the tentative opinions of a layman. 1875 *Encycl. Brit.* I. 881/1 The *Trochlearis* or *fourth, the smallest cranial nerve. 1890 BILLINGS *Med. Dict.*, *Trochlear nerve*,..fourth cranial nerve, the motor nerve for the superior oblique muscle of the eye. 1880 SIR H. WOLFF in W. S. Churchill *Ld. R. Churchill* (1906) I. 160 My dear Randolph,—After you left yesterday I received two very handsome tributes to the *Fourth Party. 1897 J. MCCARTHY *Hist. Own Times from 1880 to Jubilee* 27 Now came Lord Randolph with his new group, having its distinct individual purpose, and it claimed to be recognised as the Fourth party. 1828 A. SHERBURNE *Mem.* i. (1831) 24 My share was..from thirty to forty gallons of *fourth proof Jamaica rum. 1835 J. F. COOPER *Monikins* vi. (1860) 92 Those parts..being indicated by touches of red, nearly as bright as Fourth-proof brandy. *a* 1861 T. WINTHROP *John Brent* ix. 91 I'd seen 'em gettin' up the sham kind [of miracle],..and I knowed the fourth-proof article. 1877 *Encycl. Brit.* VII. 147/2 The floor of the *fourth ventricle in the brain.

Fowling, *vbl. sb.* **2.** *attrib.* Add: *fowling-gun* (U.S.).

1847 *Knickerbocker Mag.* XXX. 239 Reader, in your younger days you have, no doubt, left your fowling gun slyly hid in a fence corner.

Fox, *sb.* Add: **16. fox-walk** = *FOX-TROT *sb.* 1.

1879 TOURGEE *Fool's Err.* xxxvi. 248 Pressing on now in the swinging fox-walk, which he took whenever the character of the road, or the mood of his rider demanded.

b. fox-snake, -squirrel (examples).

1857 *Trans. Ill. Agric. Soc.* II. 658 They are also found in the stomachs of the milk-snake,..and of the large *fox-snake (Scotophis vulpinus). 1688 CLAYTON *Virginia* 5 in *Phil. Trans.* XVIII. 123 The first is the great *Fox Squirrel, much larger than the English, and gray. 1791, 1844 [see Fox *sb.* 16 b]. 1851 R. GLISAN *Jrnl. Army Life* (1874) 89 Animals most common to this country that are good for food are..fox squirrel [etc.].

c. fox-grass, (*b*) *U.S.* a salt-marsh grass of New England.

1837 COLMAN *Rep. Agric. Mass.* (1838) 18 The next grass is the Red grass or Fox grass, a very fine reedy grass, abundant and excellent.

Fox, *v.* **2. c.** Delete † and add quots.

1835 LONGSTREET *Georgia Scenes* 63 Has he foxed you? 1906 E. PHILLPOTTS *Portreeve* I. xv, Don't fox yourself to think that. That's mad. *Ibid.* II. xviii, Love makes a man cunning... I foxed you fifty times. 1928 *Collier's* 29 Dec. 28/3 Fay's hard to fox.

e. To disguise or make confused. *U.S.*

1876 JOAQUIN MILLER *Unwritten Hist.* xv. 210 Klamat kept an eye constantly on his rifle when not foxing the trail and eyeing the pursuers.

Foxaline (fǫ·ksălin). [Fanciful formation on FOX *sb.*] Imitation fox-fur.

1907 *Ladies' Field* 12 Jan. Advt., White Foxaline long Stole. 1923 *Daily Mail* 16 Apr. 4 White Foxaline Tie. 1927 *Daily Express* 13 Sept. 5/2 Grey Chinese cat (sometimes called foxaline). 1930 *Daily Tel.* 9 Apr. 9/6 Grey and Fawn Foxaline.

Fo·x-coloured, *a.* (See FOX *sb.* 16.)

1641, 1879 [see FOX *sb.* 16]. 1808 T. ASHE *Trav. Amer.* xvii. 159 Between ninety and an hundred American birds have been described..as follows: fox coloured thrush. 1845 S. JUDD *Margaret* II. i. 226 A thin stream of water emerging from a long line of fox-coloured cotton thistle. 1867 *Amer. Naturalist* Mar. I. 54 Ornithological Calendar for March 20th to 31st...Fox-colored Sparrows arrive.

Fox-fire. (Additional U.S. examples.)

1829–32 J. P. KENNEDY *Swallow B.* I. xxviii. 311 The fox-fire—as the country people call it—glowed hideously from the cold and matted bosom of the marsh. 1872 E. EGGLESTON *End of World* xxxii. 210 The 'fox-fire', rotting logs glowing with a faint luminosity, startled her several times. 1886 *Harper's Mag.* Dec. 97/2 The night hunter..waits in the darkness to observe his 'fox-fire' obscured ere he pulls the trigger. 1920 HUNTER *Trail Drivers of Texas* 149 There is where you could see phosphorescence (fox fire) on our horses' ears.

Fo·x-grape. (See FOX *sb.* 16 c.)

1648 B. PLANTAGENET *New Albion* iv. 24 There are four sorts of Grapes,..the second the great foxe and thick Grape, after five moneths reaped being boyled and salted, and well fined, it is a strong red Xeres. 1657, 1683, 1849 [see FOX *sb.* 16 c]. 1705 R. BEVERLY *Virginia* (1722) 116 A second Kind..grow upon small Vines and in small Bunches; but are..of a rank Taste when ripe, resembling the smell of a Fox, from whence they are called Fox-Grapes. 1815 D. DRAKE *Cincinnati* ii. 83 The..fox grape and mountain-chestnut oak are still scarcer [than flowering locust]. 1836 MARY A. HOLLEY *Texas* v. 87 Almost every variety of grape is native in Texas, from the large fox-grape down to what is called the chicken-grape. 1886 S. W. MITCHELL *R. Blake* xxvi. (1895) 297 About them on the stunted cedars the fox grapes hung thick.

Fox-trot, *sb.* **1.** (See FOX *sb.* 16 and add earlier quot.)

1887 *Outing* (U.S.) May X. 118/1 'Come Peggy, old boy', said Jim, as he led off at a fox trot.

2. A modern dance, of American origin, characterized originally by two measures of slow movement followed by two measures of rapid movement.

The origin of the name has been attributed by some to a dancing-master named *Fox.*

1917 LEACOCK *Frenzied Fiction* v. (1919) 70 The others were dancing the fox-trot to the victrola on the piazza. 1919 D'EGVILLE *How & what to dance* (1922) 55 The Fox-Trot is a dance of many steps, and to the casual observer every-

body seems to have different ones. 1920 E. SCOTT *All about Latest Dances* 68 The true basis of the American Fox-Trot is an alternation of four slow and four or eight quick movements, depending on the step chosen. 1923 — *A.B.C. of Dancing* 84 The foxtrot is not a dance in the sense that the waltz and polka are dances because it has no distinctive rhythm and no characteristic step or figure.

Hence **Fo·x-trot** *v. intr.*, to dance a fox-trot; **Fo·x-trotter**, one who fox-trots, **Fo·x-trotting** *vbl. sb.*

1919 *Punch* 26 Feb. 166/2 I've fox-trotted in Stranraer, Irish-jigged in Mullingar. 1920 E. SCOTT *All about Latest Dances* 72 Some fox-trotters spin round at intervals on the soles of their feet. 1921 R. D. PAINE *Comr. Rolling Ocean* v. 75 A dozen couples..fox-trotted in a clear space of the forward deck. 1928 F. N. HART *Bellamy Trial* i. 18 He seems to have spent most of his time perfecting his golf game and his fox-trotting abilities.

Foyer. Add:

1. b. *Path.* The focus or centre of infection.

1902 *Encycl. Brit.* XXVII. 51/1 Each nation is pledged to notify the others of the existence within its own borders of a 'foyer' of cholera.

Frabjous (fræ·bdʒəs), *a.* A nonsense-word invented by 'Lewis Carroll' (C. L. Dodgson), app. intended to suggest 'fair' and 'joyous'; used vaguely by others, e.g. = 'egregious'. Hence **Fra·bjously** *adv.*

1872 'L. CARROLL' *Through Looking-Glass* i. 24 O frabjous day! Callooh! Callay! 1899 KIPLING *Stalky* 144 Oh, you frabjous asses! *Ibid.* 244 You're a dirty little schoolboy. Besides bein' frabjously immoral.

Fraction, *sb.* Add:

6. *Chem.* One of the parts into which a substance is separated by fractionation.

1904 F. SODDY *Radio-Activity* 18 If the active barium chloride was fractionally crystallised, the activity tended to concentrate in the least soluble fraction. 1905 GARROD & HELE in *Jrnl. Physiol.* XXXIII. 198 The destruction of the aromatic fractions of proteids. 1913 A. R. WARNES *Coal Tar Distill.* 52 When it is not desired to recover the anthracene, the heavy creosote and anthracene oil fractions are sometimes not separated, but worked as one fraction.

7. A portion of a section of land. *U.S.*

1815 D. DRAKE *Cincinnati* vi. 202 The principal wall or embankment, encloses an entire block of lots and some fractions. 1837 PECK *Gaz. Illinois* I. 77 Fractions are parts of quarter sections intersected by streams or confined claims. 1847 in H. Howe *Hist. Coll. Ohio* 206 Matthias Denman..had purchased the fraction of land on the bank of the Ohio, and the entire section adjoining it on the north. 1901 S. E. WHITE *Westerners* xviii. 156 Thar is a lode..over on the J. G. fraction that's shore th' purtiest bit of quartz lead you ever see.

Fractional, *a.* Add: *Fractional currency* (example). *Fractional note*, a note in fractional currency. *Fractional section* = *FRACTION *sb.* 7.

1831 PECK *Guide Emigrants* III. 294 The town is laid out of fractional sections thirteen and fourteen. 1863 *Stat. at Large U.S.A.* (1864) XII. 711 In lieu of postage and revenue stamps for fractional currency, and of fractional notes, commonly called postage currency,..the Secretary of the Treasury may issue fractional notes of like amounts in such form as he may deem expedient. 1878 *Congress. Rec.* 29 Jan. 638/2 [Silver] is not like our fractional notes, a promise to pay. It is payment. *Ibid.* 4 Feb. 727/2 The fractional currency had become so ragged and so dirty that people were willing to surrender it for almost anything.

b. *Chem.* Of, pertaining to, or resulting from fractionation. *Fractional distillation*: see DISTILLATION 3.

1887 A. M. BROWN *Anim. Alkaloids* 24 The bodies which crystallize are afterwards separated the one from the other by fractional precipitation.

Hence **Fractionally** *adv.* Add: *Chem.* So as to separate into fractions.

1888 *Nature* 8 Nov. 39/2 The chloride was next fractionally distilled. 1904 F. SODDY *Radio-Activity* 17 If the active barium chloride was fractionally crystallised. 1921 LEWKOWITSCH & WARBURTON *Oils, Fats & Waxes* (ed. 6) I. 672 The glycerides of the lower fatty acids can be fractionally distilled in a complete vacuum without undergoing decomposition.

Fracto- (fræ·kto), used as comb. form of L. *fractus* broken, in terms of meteorology (see quots.).

1917 MCADIE *Princ. Aërography* 115 The true cumulus..is often torn by strong winds,..('fracto-cumulus'). *Ibid.*, If the mass of nimbus is torn up into small patches..they may be called 'fracto-nimbus', the 'scud' of the sailors. 1926 — *Man & Weather* 68 The word *fracto*..is now in general use to designate a cloud form in which the mass is broken into small divisions.

Fracturable (fræ·ktiŭrăb'l, -tʃərăb'l), *a.* [f. FRACTURE *v.* + -ABLE.] That can be fractured.

1897 *Kodak News* May 6 Nor should there be anything easily fracturable. 1911 H. S. HARRISON *Queed* xxxi, He might fracture all of the decalogue that was refinedly fracturable.

Fracture, *sb.* **6.** Add: **fracture-box**, a combination of splints used to encase a broken limb. Also *Geol.* (of fracture in the earth's crust) *fracture-line, -system.*

1879 *St. George's Hosp. Rep.* IX. 685 The dislocation was easily reduced under ether..and the limb was put up in a fracture-box. 1922 *Encycl. Brit.* XXXI. 214/2 Rectilinear and regularly intersecting fracture-systems. 1925 J. JOLY *Surface-Hist. Earth* viii. 140 The long rift valley of South Australia, mainly meridional in direction, as well as meridionally-directed fracture-lines along the eastern side of that continent.

Fracture, *v.* Add: **3.** *Phonology.* (*trans.*) To subject to fracture. Hence **Fractured** *ppl. a.* = *BROKEN *ppl. a.* 1 c.

1888 ELLIS *E. E. Pron.* v. 496 The peculiar manner of fracturing the vowels in the A-, A', Æ, E-, EA', O' words by prefixing an accented (ee) or (*ii*) and reducing the vowel itself to indistinct (ɐ).

Frænulum. Add: Also **frenulum** (frē·niŭlə̆m).

2. *Ent.* A bristle or group of bristles attached to the base of the hind wing in many Lepidoptera, and interlocking with a process on the front wing, thus uniting the two wings of a side in flight.

1892 G. F. HAMPSON *Fauna Brit. India, Moths* I. 6 The fore and hind wings of the majority of families of moths are united by a 'frenulum' arising from the base of the costa of the hind wing and fitting into a 'retinaculum' on the fore wing. 1898 A. S. PACKARD *Entomol.* 122 In many Lepidoptera they [*sc.* the wings] are loosely connected by the loop and frenulum. 1899 D. SHARP *Insects* II. 316 The bristle is called the 'frenulum', the structure that retains it a 'retinaculum'.

Fragarol (frǣ·gărǫl). *Chem.* [? f. mod.L. *Fragaria* the strawberry genus + -OL.] The butyl ether of β-naphthol, used for making a synthetic perfume.

1923 E. J. PARRY *Durvelle's Perfumes* 75 The substance known under the name fragarol, with its slightly fruity odour, is the corresponding butyl ether. 1925 BUNBURY & DAVIDSON *Coal Tar Products* 158 The only derivatives of β-naphthol which are employed in making up synthetic perfumes are the methyl, ethyl, and butyl ethers, known as Nerolin (or Yara-Yara), Nerolin II (or Bromelia), and Fragarol respectively.

Fragment (frægme̞nt), *v.* [f. the sb.] *trans.* To break or separate into fragments.

1901 H. MCINTOSH *Is Christ Infallible?* (1902) 76 They vainly dream that they can fragment and vivisect the Spirit's embodiment and environment of Christ's teaching. 1919 OSLER in *Proc. Class. Assoc.* 27 Specialism..has fragmented the specialities themselves in a way that makes the outlook hazardous.

Frail, *sb.*[3] *slang.* [Subst. use of FRAIL *a.*] A woman.

1931 ERIC LINKLATER *Juan in America* II. xvi. 177 Without bullets whistling through the air to frighten him and threaten widowhood for the ravished frail.

Frail, *v.* *U.S. dial.* [prob. f. dial. *frail* flail.] *trans.* To beat, thrash. Hence **Frai·ling** *vbl. sb.*

1851 *Arkansas Doctor* 82 (Th.) The old man plainly told her..be would frail her worse than a dog would a pole-cat. *Ibid.* 123 (Th.) He..did not like the thought of getting a frailing for it. 1890 J. C. HARRIS in *Century Mag.* Dec. 287/1 He uped an' frailed me out, an' got the gal to boot. 1896 *Peterson Mag.* Jan. 89/2 A frailing with a dead branch left him [*sc.* a mule] unmoved. 1901 W. CHURCHILL *Crisis* I. xii. 97 Reckon I'd frail 'em good ef he catched hold of me with his black hands.

Fraise (frē̆z, ‖ frę̄z), *sb.*[4] [Fr., = strawberry.]

1. *Her.* A conventional strawberry-flower used as a bearing.

1896 J. WOODWARD *Her.* I. 341 A charge resembling the cinquefoil is the Fraise, or strawberry flower, which in Scottish armory is recognised as a distinct bearing:..as in..the arms of Fraser: Azure, three fraises argent.

2. The colour of crushed strawberries.

1923 *Daily Mail* 19 Feb. 1 Also in plain colours..Lemon, Fraize [*sic*], Coral, and Ivory.

Fraising, *vbl. sb.* [f. FRAISE *v.*] A palisade.

1821 T. DWIGHT *Trav. New Eng.* (1823) II. 178 He fastened, with the skewer, the corner of his blanket round a picket of the fraising.

Frame, *sb.* Add:

4. d. Geom. *Frame of reference*: a set of coordinates by means of which the movements of a body or group of bodies are described.

1929 *Encycl. Brit.* I. 870/1 A co-ordinate is always measured with respect to a fixed origin or base or frame of reference of some sort... We often need to change the frame of reference in the middle of a piece of work.

10. (Recent U.S. example.)

1904 HARBEN *Georgians* 299 Half a dozen expert workmen were putting up the frame of a two-storied building on massive pine sills.

b. (U.S. examples.) Also = FRAME-HOUSE 2.

1732 *Boston Town Rec.* XII. 40 Henry Gibbs has very lately Incroched on the Towns Land on Dock Square by Erecting Frames thereon. 1841 C. CIST *Cincinnati* 41 Of these last [buildings] 200 were brick and 121 frames. 1873 J. H. BEADLE *Undevel. West* xxi. 405 The log houses here are superior in style to those in most new countries... There are few frames.

c. *ellipt.* as adj. (= FRAMED) or sb. (= FRAMEWORK). *U.S.*

1816 U. BROWN *Jrnl.* in *Maryland Hist. Mag.* X. 268 The 3rd House is Log and frame with Double Porches. 1836 J. HALL *Statist. West* iv. 66 The dwelling houses are usually large edifices of brick or frame. 1872 'MARK TWAIN' *Roughing it* xiii. (1882) 74 Block after block of trim dwellings, built of 'frame' and sunburnt brick. 1897 J. L. ALLEN *Choir Invis.* ii. (1918) 9 Rude dwellings of logs now giving way to others of frame and of brick. 1924 MULFORD *Rustlers' Valley* iv. 38 The street was a busy one in front of a line of lighted buildings, frame, one-story shacks all.

11. e. The rigid part of a bicycle. Hence *frame-bag* (a bag for carrying articles, fixed within the frame).

1871 *Engl. Mechanic* 10 Feb. 491/3 The great ease in riding..the makers attribute to the form of the frame. 1897 *Westm. Gaz.* 14 Aug. 7/2 In the frame bag was a package containing blocks of writing paper. 1898 *Cycling* 8 Lacking the elaborate plant of the great firms—especially that for frame building—they are apt to fit their frames together untruly.

f. The skeleton of a motor vehicle or aeroplane, supporting the machinery and body; see also quot. 1918. Also *attrib.*

1900 W. W. BEAUMONT *Motor Vehicles* I. 232 The frame is built up of tubes, and is carried on double-leaf springs on the front axle, which carries stud axles at its ends with forwardly projecting steering arms. 1906 *Ibid.* II. 221 The frame is of the wood and steel flitch build like the Panhard; and the engine is carried on a suspended subsidiary underframe. 1902 *Motors & Motor-Driving* II. x, A frame which has some diagonal stays or parts which act as diagonals is very desirable, though few car frames are so made. 1909 *Flight* 20 Feb. 103 *Frame*, in French, the term 'chassis' is sometimes used, but more often the word 'fuselage' on account of the bodies of most monoplanes being spindle-shaped. *Ibid.*, *Half-Elliptic Frames*, a frame of the fusiform type which has been curtailed at the middle. 1918 W. E. DOMMETT *Dict. Aircraft*, *Frame*, extensions to the car of a non-Rigid Airship which distribute the weight more evenly over the envelope; the keel of a Semi-Rigid Airship; the hull of a Rigid Airship. 1921 *Chambers's Jrnl.* 341/1 The rattle and jolt of the little frame-car and the noise of the motor made conversation..inaudible. 1929 *Encycl. Brit.* XV. 893/2 The type of frame which has become practically standard consists of two longitudinal beams..with cross members spanning between them at intervals... The frame with the mechanical parts of the car assembled upon it is called the chassis.

g. In Pool, the triangular form used in setting up the balls; also, the balls as set up, or the round of play required to pocket them all; similarly in Skittles and Tenpins; also, one of the several innings forming a game.

1890 C. C. MOORE *Games of Pool* 79 These balls are placed in the form of a triangle upon the table, as in Pyramids, a wooden frame or 'triangle' being employed to save trouble and insure correctness. 1897 R. F. FOSTER *Compl. Hoyle* 608 (Tenpins) Each player rolls ten frames or innings. 1910 *Hints on Skittles, Offic. Rules* 23 The Frame shall be 4-ft. 6-in. square, the Plate circular, 3-in. in diameter, and 22½-in. from centre to centre. *Ibid.* 24 The ball is not dead until it is motionless on, or off the frame. 1929 *Encycl. Brit.* III. 978/1 The teams roll one frame (2 balls) on one alley, and for the next frame alternate and use the other alley. 1930 A. P. HERBERT *Water Gipsies* xxi, There were thirty competitors for the Cup, and each of them played seven frames.

12. b. *Cinematography.* One of the series of small pictures on a film (see quot. 1913).

1913 E. W. SARGENT *Photoplay* (1916) 362 *Frame.* A single photograph in the roll of film. A picture one inch wide by three-fourths of an inch high. There are sixteen of these frames to the foot. 1918 H. CROY *How Motion Pictures are Made* 32 The light revealed the postures of the dancer as she appeared on the 'frames' in front of the viewing aperture. 1927 E. G. LUTZ *Motion-Picture Cameraman* 16 One frame or section of film.

13. d. An open box of slats in which bees build and which can be removed from the hive. Also *attrib.*

1673 *Phil. Trans.* VIII. 6097 The Frame for the Bees to fasten their Work upon. 1875 J. HUNTER *Man. Bee-keeping* 137 Select a frame of comb. 1881 *Gardening Illustr.* III. 123 Remove the top, and four or five of the frames, so as to let the bees drop in the hive. *Ibid.*, The bees will run up into the frame hive. 1904 *Daily Chron.* 17 Sept. 8/5 The new, clean, and manageable frame-hive.

15. (sense 10) *frame barn, building* (earlier U.S. examples), *dwelling, shop, tenement*; *frame-built* adj.; **frame aerial** *Wireless Telegr.*, an aerial composed of a rectangle or loop of wire, adapted for directional reception.

1921 *Wireless World* 10 Dec. 562/2, I can receive the Dutch Concert..on a..*frame aerial. 1924 *Wireless Weekly* 8 Oct. 745/1 A good range of receivers, including reflex sets using small frame aerials. 1831 PECK *Guide Emigrants* 182 He may put up a *frame barn. 1827 DRAKE & MANSFIELD *Cincinnati* iv. 36 A *frame building..is at present used by the Society as a Synagogue. 1841 C. CIST *Cincinnati* 19 Two frame buildings were also added during the same time. 1797 F. BAILY *Jrnl. Tour N. Amer. 1796–7* (1856) 228 Cincinnati may contain about three or four hundred houses, mostly *frame-built. 1829–32 J. P. KENNEDY *Swallow B.* I. xix. 192 Half a dozen *frame dwellings..were scattered over the landscape. 1796 *Aurora* (Philad.) 15 Apr. (Th.) That certain one-story *Frame Shop in front, and Two Story Frame Messuage [etc.]. 1799 *Ibid.* 13 Aug. (Th.) *Frame tenement at Auction. 1836 CROCKETT *Exploits & Adv. Texas* (1837) 65 He made fast an immense cable to the frame tenement where the theft had been perpetrated.

Frame, *v.* Add: **7. b.** *To be framed up*: to be suitable *for*. *U.S. colloq.*

1909 S. E. WHITE *Rules of Game* II. i. 110 Fresno..is a nice, well-built city... But it is not framed up for tourists.

8. e. *To frame up*: to prearrange (an event) surreptitiously and with sinister intent; to plan in secret; to fake the result of (a contest, etc.). orig. *U.S. slang.*

1910 E. A. WALCOTT *Open Door* vii. 86 'An' then he frames up dis job on me', said Jimmy bitterly. 1913 MULFORD *Coming of Cassidy* vii. 119 As long as this deal was framed up, we'll say it was this mornin'. 1919 *Detective Story Mag.* 25 Nov. XXVIII. 5 If you give me the signal I'll frame up something. 1921 R. D. PAINE *Comr. Rolling Ocean* vii. 121 All I need is a little work with your catcher, to frame up signals and so on.

11. To concoct a false charge or accusation against; to devise a scheme or plot with regard to; to make the victim of a 'frame-up'.

1922 TITUS *Timber* xxvi. 234 So they were after Bryant were they? They were framing him? 1926 MULFORD *Cassidy's Protégé* iv. 40 He had seen honest men framed,

 Supplement, p. 3873; Corrigenda, p. 4092; Spurious words, p. 4093; Books quoted, p. 4094

and guilty men let off for political reasons. 1926 J. Black *You Can't Win* xxii. 347 The police..knew I was trying to frame myself out; they began framing me in. 1927 *Observer* 6 Nov. 21 Her heart has been given to Tom Mix, who, in consequence, is 'framed'. 1931 *Daily Tel.* 19 Jan. 11/6 They're for ever after me all the time, trying to frame me.

Framed, *ppl. a.* Add: *spec.* in U.S. of houses. (Cf. Frame *sb.* 15.)

1639 [in Dict.]. 1784 *Maryland Jrnl.* 11 May, Advt. (Th.) A large framed House almost as good as new. 1823 E. James *Long's Exped. Rocky Mts.* I. 82 This town..contained..several framed dwellings of two stories. 1834 *Southern Lit. Messenger* I. 29 The links of graduation between the rude cottage and what they styled the 'framed house'. 1837 Peck *Gaz. Illinois* II. 133 The rough..cabin is giving place to comfortable framed or brick tenements.

Frame-house. 2. *U.S.* (Earlier examples.)

1796 *Aurora* (Philad.) 28 Nov. (Th.) To be Sold, An Elegant Three Story Frame House. 1797 F. Baily *Jrnl. Tour N. Amer.* (1856) 219 He begins then to think of erecting himself a frame-house. 1818 Paulding *J. Bull & Br. Jon.* i. 6 Building himself a fine frame house, [Jonathan] began to be quite snug and comfortable.

Frame-up. orig. *U.S. slang.* [See *Frame *v.* 8 e.] Anything that has been prearranged or concocted, esp. with a sinister intent; a conspiracy or plot, e.g. for the purpose of incriminating a person on false evidence.

1907 Rex Beach *Barrier* vii. (1908) 100 You go about it queer...Your frame-up may work double. 1913 Mulford *Coming of Cassidy* vii. 116 The crookedness would not come more than once in a deal if the frame-up was 'single-odd'. 1919 *New Appeal* (Girard, Kans.) 11 Jan. 1/5 They were the victims of a frameup inspired by class hatred. 1924 *Westm. Gaz.* 12 Feb., The Government, he said, were guilty of manufacturing a plot which never existed. He claimed that the plot was from beginning to end a 'frame-up'. 1927 Agatha Christie *Big Four* iv, Some one put those little glass figures amongst my traps. It was a frame-up.

Franchisal (frɒ·ntʃizăl, -tʃəiz-), *a.* [f. Franchise + -al.] Of or belonging to the franchise.

1897 Maitland *Domesday Bk.* 80 With feudal justice therefore we contrast 'franchisal' justice.

Franchise, *sb.* Add:

2. c. *Marine Insurance.* A percentage below which the underwriter incurs no responsibility.

The term was borrowed from French practice, but the English application differs from the French; cf. 1857 M. Hopkins *Handbk. Average* 140 In some foreign policies the warranty has a rather different signification. It not only requires that the damage should amount to a certain proportion of the value of the goods insured, but it gives to the assured, in case of Average, only that portion of the loss which exceeds the agreed limit, which is there called the *franchise*, or *affranchisement*.

1895 W. Gow *Marine Insur.* 192 It has been arranged that all claims falling short of a certain amount or percentage should not attach to the policy covering the goods. This amount or percentage is termed the *franchise*. *Ibid.* 195 Nowadays in England when the franchise is once reached, the whole amount of average including the franchise is paid by the underwriter. 1929 V. Dover *Marine Insur.* (ed. 3) 240 Once the franchise is reached the policy pays in full. *Ibid.* 330 Unless a franchise of 5 *per cent.* is attained.

Franchised, *ppl. a.* Add: **4.** Of a company: Possessing special powers or rights conferred on the ground of public utility. *U.S.*

1908 *Munsey's Mag.* Nov. 165/2 His attitude toward the franchised and privileged monopolies of Washington.

Franco-. Add: *Franco-Canadian.*

1845 *Knickerbocker Mag.* XXV. 59 The ever-noisy sailors, with their strange Franco-Canadian *patois*, 'made the air vocal with sweet sounds'.

Francomania (fræŋkomē·niă). [See -mania.] A craze or excessive liking for France and for things French. Hence **Francoma·niac.**

1899 *Daily News* 8 May 8/2 From 1750 to the Revolution, Anglo-mania in France was fostered by Franco-mania in England. 1908 *Daily Chron.* 4 Mar. 6/6 That Francomaniac, Frederick the Great.

Francophobia (fræŋkofōᵘ·biă). [See -phobia.] Dread or dislike of France or the French, tending to become an obsession.

1900 *Fortn. Rev.* May 722 To deny Frenchmen the quality of courage in the face of danger is really to push Francophobia beyond the bounds of common sense. 1928 *Manch. Guardian Weekly* 10 Aug. 104/1 In his indignation M. Jacques Bainville, of the 'Liberté', brings a direct charge of Francophobia.

Frankenstein (fræ·ŋkənstəin). The title-character in a romance by Mrs. Shelley (1818), who constructed a human monster and endowed it with life. Commonly misused allusively as a typical name for a monster who is a terror to his originator and ends by destroying him.

1838 Gladstone in *Murray's Handbk. Sicily* (1864) p. xlvi, They [*sc.* mules] really seem like Frankensteins of the animal creation. 1889 S. Webb in *Fabian Ess.* 38 The landlord and the capitalist are both finding that the steam-engine is a Frankenstein which they had better not have raised. 1907 *Sat. Rev.* 6 Apr. 414/1 Is Great Britain creating for herself something of a Frankenstein monster on the Nile?

Franker. Add: Also, an instrument for franking postal matter.

1925 *Glasgow Herald* 5 Jan. 8 There are addressers, duplicators,..postal frankers and cheque writers.

Frankfurt (fræ·ŋkfəɹt), **Frankfurter** (fræ·ŋkfəɹtəɹ). *U.S.* [G. *Frankfurter wurst* Frankfurt sausage. Cf. Frankfort.] A highly-seasoned German sausage.

1902 G. H. Lorimer *Lett. Self-made Merchant* x. 127 Only last week the head of our sausage department started to put out a tin-tag brand of frankfurts. 1908 — *J. Spurlock* vii. 147, I told the Major that he had undoubtedly got hold of the hottest dog in the frankfurter can.

Frankincense. 2 and 3. (Earlier U.S. examples.)

1803 A. B. Lambert *Descr. Genus Pinus* 23 Frankincense Pine. Plains consisting of dry sand, and sea coasts, in N.A., are abundantly stocked with this species of pine. 1858 J. A. Warder *Hedges & Evergreens* 249 *Pinus taeda*, the Frankincense or Loblolly, is a lofty American tree.

Franklin[2] (fræ·ŋklin). *U.S.* [f. the name of Benjamin *Franklin* (1706–1790).]

1. A lightning-conductor.

1817 J. Palmer *Jrnl. Trav. U.S.* (1818) 104 in *N. & Q.* 11th Ser. III. 487 Franklins, or conductors, are a certain safe-guard, and generally used. *a* 1862 S. Breck *Recoll.* ii. (1877) 71 Our professor of natural philosophy was desirous to erect on the old lofty tower..a lightning-rod, very properly called at that time a 'Franklin'.

2. *Franklin stove*, a form of stove for heating a room, devised by Franklin.

1841 *Congress. Globe* Aug., App. 452/3 The booby..was told that the Franklin stove would save half the wood. 1846 *Rep. U.S. Comm. Patents* (1847) 361 A design for an ornamental Franklin stove. 1881 Howells *Mod. Instance* xii. 154 The landlord had kindled a fire on the hearth of the Franklin stove in his parlor. 1895 J. L. Ford *Lit. Shop* i. (1896) 2 From where I lie I can see a Franklin stove, a pair of brass andirons.

b. *ellipt.* = Franklin stove.

1817 J. Palmer *Jrnl. Trav. U.S.* (1818) 14, 15 in *N. & Q.* 11th Ser. III. 486 In the best room some have an iron fire-place called a Franklin; these look very neat, and will much sooner heat a room than the open fire-place. 1867 Lowell *Fitz Adam's Story* 288 And bushed asparagus in fading green Added its shiver to the franklin clean. 1879 B. F. Taylor *Summer-Savory* x. 95 Within the wide door was the bar-room, with a great hospitable Franklin and chuckle-headed andirons with slender crooked necks.

Frantic, *a.* Add: **2. b.** *colloq.* In exaggerated use = 'Terrific', 'awful'. So **Fra·ntically** *adv.*

1908 *Punch* 26 Feb. 152/2 I'm working simply most awfully hard for Ireland just now. I've bought a ghastly heap of poplin..and a frantic lot of Limerick lace. *Mod.* I'm in a frantic hurry. He is frantically busy.

Frappé, *a.* Add: Also as *sb.*, an iced drink or mixture. *U.S.*

1922 *Glasgow Herald* 13 May 6 Besides untold recipes for cobblers, coolers, highballs, frappés, daisies, sangarees.

Frasnian (fræ·sniăn), *a.* and *sb.* *Geol.* Also -ien. [ad. F. *frasnien*, f. *Frasne* in Belgium.] **A.** *adj.* Belonging to the lower of the two groups of strata of the Upper Devonian in western Europe. **B.** *sb.* This group of strata.

1882 A. Geikie *Geol.* 701 In the Belgian and Eifelian tracts they have been subdivided as under:..Famennien..Frasnien. 1894 *Geol. Mag.* Oct. 474 The Frasnien series in the North of France and Belgium.

Frat (fræt). *U.S. College slang.* Abbreviated form of *Fraternity 7. Also *attrib.*, as *frat-house*, *-man*.

1899 A. H. Quinn *Pennsylv. Stories* 186 But any Frat would have wanted Harington. 1909 *Daily Chron.* 9 Feb. 4/4 The Frat-man is one of a group of about fifteen students. ..Frat-houses may be expensive or cheap. 1926 *Ladies' Home Jrnl.* Nov. 12 It's a frat house.

Fraternal, *a.* Add: *Fraternal order*, a brotherhood or friendly society. *U.S.*

1889 *Kansas Times & Star* 7 June, The Iron Hall, a western fraternal order, is in session here this week. 1905 B. G. Phillips *Plum Tree* 267 Local machine leaders of Scarborough's party, with corruptible labor and fraternal order leaders.

b. *sb.* A friendly meeting of ministers of religion of a town or district.

Fraternity. Add: **7.** A literary or social association of the alumni of a college or university; a 'Greek-Letter' Society. *U.S.*

Each society is named by the initials of two or three Greek words, as the 'Phi Beta Kappa' of William and Mary College, Va.

1777 in F. W. Shepardson *Phi Beta Kappa* (1915) 9 [At the January meeting of 1777..a mode of initiation was reported.] 'I, A.B. do swear..to prove true, just, and deeply attached to this our growing fraternity.' 1844 in A. P. Jacobs *Psi Upsilon Epitome* (1884) 180 Catalogue of the Psi Upsilon Fraternity. 1879 in *Alpha Delta Phi* (1882) xxxi, An act to incorporate the Executive Council of the Alpha Delta Phi Fraternity and to provide for the organization of New Chapters. 1883 W. R. Baird (*title*) American College Fraternities. 1901 H. D. Sheldon *Student Life* 224 In general, the fraternities dominate the smaller colleges,..although an occasional revolt on the part of the non-fraternity men sometimes occurs. 1902 J. Corbin *American at Oxf.* 54 In Balliol there are three debating clubs, and they are of course in some sense rivals. Like the fraternities in an American college, they look over the freshmen each year pretty closely.

attrib. 1899 A. H. Quinn *Pennsylv. Stories* 59 He could not help seeing that the Fraternity men were in general the best dressed. 1902 J. Corbin *American at Oxf.* 269 The fraternity houses so widely diffused in America offer almost a counterpart of the halls of the golden age of the mediæval university. 1909 S. E. White *Rules of Game* I. xi. 61, 'I see you're a College man', said he, indicating Bob's fraternity pin. 1927 *Saturday Even. Post* 24 Dec. 19/3 There was heartbreaking rivalry among us to secure fraternity pins from the boys who possessed them.

8. Used by Galton for: The brothers (and sisters) of a family collectively.

1889 F. Galton *Nat. Inheritance* 234 *note*, A Fraternity consists of the brothers of a family, and of the sisters after the qualities of the latter have been transmuted to their Male Equivalents.

Fraud, *sb.* **6.** Add: **fraud order** *U.S.*, an official order prohibiting the delivery of letters to a firm or individual suspected of making illegal use of the postal service.

1906 *Macm. Mag.* Apr. 469 In the United States, the Post Office can get a 'fraud-order' against an advertiser, by virtue of which authorities have power to open letters addressed to him and return money to the senders.

Fraunhofer (frau·nhōᵘfəɹ). The name of Joseph von *Fraunhofer* (1787–1826), a Bavarian optician, used, chiefly in *Fraunhofer's lines*, to specify the lines of the spectrum, esp. the dark lines of the solar spectrum.

1863 Atkinson *Ganot's Physics* (1866) 421. 1879 *Encycl. Brit.* IX. 728/1.

Frawn. Add: Also fraughan, fraun.

1869 P. Kennedy *Evenings on Duffrey* xix. 208 They might ..gather..fraughans in the woods. 1892 Jane Barlow *Bogland Studies* 69 Wee frauns. 1906 *Temple Bar* June 553 They trod the heather and fraughan beneath them. 1914 'G. A. Birmingham' *Lost Tribes* xi, Under their shelter fraughan bushes nestled, their black fruit already ripening.

Frazzle, *sb.* Add examples (chiefly U.S.) of phr. *to a frazzle* in fig. expressions denoting complete exhaustion or extinction.

1865 Gordon in Church *Ulysses Grant* (1897) 318 Tell General Lee, I have fought my corps to a frazzle. 1872 *Congress. Globe* 30 May, App. 578/2 They..got great big long brushes..and they whipped them all into frassels. There are welts on me now. 1881 J. C. Harris *Uncle Remus* xi, Brer Fox dun know Brer Rabbit uv ole, en he know dat sorter game done wo' ter a frazzle. 1882 *Southern Hist. Soc. Papers* X. 504 (Th.) All these causes combined dwindled the Army of Northern Virginia away to a mere frazzle, as General Gordon expressed it. 1905 *Washington Star* 24 Nov. 22 The Becham machine whipped Blackburn to a frazzle, giving him the first real defeat he had ever experienced. 1908 *Westm. Gaz.* 3 Nov. 7/3 Mr. Roosevelt, when asked for his opinion on the result, said, 'We have got them beaten to a "frazzle".' 1921 Mulford *Bar-20 Three* viii. 101 I'm aiming to ride him [*sc.* his horse] to a frazzle.

Frazzle, *v.* Now *slang* or *colloq.* (Earlier U.S. example.) Also *intr.* and in ppl. adj. (*frazzled-out*).

1872 *Congress. Globe* 30 May, App. 577/3 The ends of the switches were all frazzled. 1896 J. C. Harris *Sister Jane* 344 He's the genuine article, guaranteed not to rip in the seams or frazzle at the sleeves. 1912 J. H. Moore *Ethics & Educ.* 34 Many a frazzled-out member of society owes his failure in life to no greater misdemeanour than the mere failure to make connection with his calling. 1913 J. London *Son of Sun* viii. 285 Loose ends of rope stood out stiffly horizontal, and, when a whipping gave, the loose end frazzled and blew away.

Freak, *sb.*[1] **5.** Add: Also quasi-*adj.* to denote something abnormal or capriciously irregular.

1898 *Daily News* 17 Mar. 6/5 'The yellow kid', a personification of 'freak' or sensational journalism. 1907 *Westm. Gaz.* 26 Sept. 7/2 The boats which have been built for this race of recent years are freak boats pure and simple. 1907 *Daily Chron.* 5 Oct. 4/4 Conditions in America seem particularly favourable to the propagation of freak religions. 1908 *Westm. Gaz.* 7 Mar. 8/1 The production of freak fruits, such as white blackberries..and seedless oranges.

Free, *a.* Add: **10. b.** *Free fight* (orig. U.S.). (Earlier example.)

1855 *Knickerbocker Mag.* XLV. 130 The fight is free!—There is naught to pay.

11. b. Of the movements of molecules, atoms, ions: Unrestricted by other molecules, etc. *Free path*: the distance which a molecule, atom, or ion traverses without encountering another and without colliding with the sides of the containing vessel.

1881 Sir W. Thomson in *Proc. Royal Inst.* IX. 520 Observation and measurement of the free path of an individual atom. 1883 *Encycl. Brit.* XVI. 616/2 The distance traversed by the type molecule..from one encounter to another..is called its free path. 1902 *Ibid.* XXVIII. 31/1 The free path of the ion.

20. b. Also *free to admit*.

1921 Mulford *Bar-20 Three* xiv. 179 An' I'm free to admit that I'm cussed glad to be settin' here.

D. 2. free association *Psychol.*, in an experiment based on the association of ideas, an association freely made by the person undergoing the test without suggestion or control on the part of the experimenter; **free food**, food imported free of tax or duty; also *attrib.*; **free-fooder**, a politician who opposes taxes on food; **free (public) house** (see sense 31, quot. 1858); **free list**, a list of things on which, or persons from whom, payment is not required; hence **free list** *v.*; **free lover** (earlier U.S. example); **free lunch** *U.S.*, a lunch given gratis by saloon-keepers to attract customers; also *attrib.*; hence **free-luncher**; **free pass**, authority to travel on a railway, etc., or to enter a place of entertainment without payment; **free path** (see sense *11 b); **free place**, education in a secondary school awarded free to a scholar from an elementary school; also *attrib.*; **free union** [F. *union libre*], cohabitation of a couple without marriage; **free verse** = *Vers libre; hence **free-verser**, **-versifier**.

1905 E. B. Titchener *Exper. Psychol.* II. i. 192 We show him a word; he is to react when the word has suggested

something, no matter what. The word *sea* may arouse the idea of land or water or ships or some particular sea or some particular incident at sea,—anything it likes. Associations of this sort are termed, technically, *free* associations. 1903 *Westm. Gaz.* 17 June 7/2 The *free food Unionists. 1903 *National Rev.* Aug. 893 Though calling themselves *Free Fooders, they are not in favour of Free Food. 1905 *Spectator* 7 Jan. 13/2 Such a supposition..is surely strange as coming from convinced Free-fooders. 1927 W. E. Collinson *Contemp. Engl.* 80 Tied houses and *free houses. 1930 *Daily Express* 16 Aug. 10/2 To bring about in large regional areas the compulsory merging of brewery companies, including 'free' houses. 1833 *Deb. Congress* 20 Feb. 1749 The gentleman moved to strike the article of cotton out from the *free list of imports. 1845 *Ann. U.S. Treas. Rep.* 6 An adequate revenue will still be produced, and permit the addition to the free list of salt and guano. 1855 M. Thompson *Doesticks* xxvi. 229 The Bowery Theatre..where they announce a grand 'benefit' five nights in the week, for the purpose of cutting off the free list. 1856 [see Free *a.* 32]. 1870 Medbery *Men & Myst. Wall St.* 20 The securities.. are divided into two classes, known respectively as the Regular and the Free List. 1909 *Daily Chron.* 13 Apr. 5/2 Cocoa was *free listed on the ground that..it was a common necessity of life. 1858 *Baltimore Sun* 28 June (Bartlett) Abolitionists, spiritualists, and *free lovers. 1889 *Kansas Times & Star* 25 June, Two..Saloon keepers here were notified by the police department to discontinue the *free lunches at their places. 1908 G. H. Lorimer *J. Spurlock* v. 87, I had mapped out the most complete little free-lunch route in New York City. *a* 1909 'O. Henry' *Roads of Destiny* iv. 58 [His] memories of the old hotel are limited to his having been kicked out from its free-lunch counter in 1873. 1898 *Daily News* 15 July 6/6, I felt flattered myself, a mere *free-luncher, when I saw the great Joseph, with the income of a prince, thus deigning to superintend my viands. 1857 *Trans. Ill. Agric. Soc.* II. 2 The railroad company sent *free passes over their whole line. 1894 [see Free *a.* 32]. 1907 *Parl. Debates* 15 May 1054 These *free places..would be for Public Elementary School children who would not be asked to compete with children outside but who would only be asked to pass a qualifying examination. 1909 *Daily Chron.* 28 July 5/5 The distinction between fee-paying and free-place scholars. 1920 *Rep. Departm. Committee on Scholarships & Free Places* 2 To qualify as a 'free place' pupil the child must have attended a Public Elementary School for a certain period previously. *Ibid.* 35 The existing provision of free places in secondary schools appears to us inadequate. 1926 *Rep. Educ. of Adolescent* 133 The Free Place Examination is conducted in writing. 1931 *Times Lit. Suppl.* 1 Oct. 742/4 Marriage, companionate marriage, *free unions, are considered intimately. 1908 Noyes *W. Morris* 119 The so-called '*free-verse' experiments, with abrupt and meaningless jerks or bumps. 1926 W. R. Inge *Lay Thoughts* 31 A cubist or a free-verse writer. 1926 *Glasgow Herald* 1 Feb. 8 Those among the *free-versers who are not purely imbecile are disgruntled, sarcastic, and gloomy.

Free-board. 2. Add: *transf.* and *fig.*

1898 Kipling *Day's Work* 268 (*Bread upon the Waters*), I saw Mrs. McPhee swell and swell under her *garance*-coloured gown. There is no small free-board to Janet McPhee, nor is *garance* any subdued tint. 1925 J. Joly *Surface-Hist. Earth* iii. 54 The change of buoyancy of the magma which must arise if the substratum changes from the solid to the liquid state...How will this change affect the 'freeboard' of the continents? When we melt basalt in the laboratory we easily float granite in the fluid rock. It floats with a good free-board, and appears to preserve its buoyancy indefinitely.

Free Church. Add: **3.** (With small initials.) A church in which the seats are free. *U.S.*

1835 J. Martin *Gaz. Virginia* 126 It contains several dwelling houses—one free church—one common school. 1835 A. A. Phelps in *Life W. L. Garrison* (1885) II. 63 He has since been requested to preach the sermon to the Free Church in Hartford. 1860 *Massachusetts Acts & Resolves* c. 181 An act to incorporate the trustees of the free church of Saint Mary, for sailors.

Freedom. **10.** *Degree of freedom.* Add: **b.** *Phys. Chem.* The number of factors in a system, which can be varied independently without altering the number of phases.

1904 A. Findlay *Phase Rule* ii. 15 We shall therefore define the number of degrees of freedom of a system as the number of the variable factors, temperature, pressure, and concentration of the components, which must be arbitrarily fixed in order that the condition of the system may be perfectly defined. 1924 H. S. Taylor *Phys. Chem.* II. 1169 Every independent positional coordinate thus implies a possibility of motion or a 'degree of freedom'. Thus, our point molecule has three degrees of freedom.

15. *freedom-loving* (earlier examples).

1841 Foote *Texas & Texans* I. 102 The descendants of.. freedom-loving ancestors in Texas nobly resolved to imperil their lives. 1866 Gregg *Life in Army* xxviii. 244 Thousands of freedom-loving Germans have spoken deeply in condemnation of this monster iniquity.

Free-for-all, *a.* and *sb.* *U.S.* [Free *a.* 10 b.] **a.** *adj.* Open to all. **b.** *sb.* A fight, etc. in which any one may take part.

1881 [see Free *a.* 10 b]. 1902 S. E. White *Blazed Trail* xxvii. 175 In a free-for-all knock-down-and-drag out, kicking, gouging, and biting are all legitimate. 1918 Mulford *Man fr. Bar-20* vi. 56 From the noise it appeared to be turning into a free-for-all. 1923 L. J. Vance *Baroque* xiv. 85 The girl quietly lifted the lower sash, letting in..cacophony of a domestic free-for-all in one of the neighboring flats. 1931 *Amer. Speech* VII. Oct. 49 [Lumberjacks'] 'free-for-all' when the 'shanty men' join the 'bull pen boys' around the box stove.

Free-growing, *a.* [Free *adv.*] Growing freely.

1824 Loudon *Encycl. Gard.* (ed. 2) 396 The species of stocks for fruit-trees are divided into what are called free-growing and dwarfing stocks. 1868 *Rep. U.S. Comm. Agric.* (1869) 198 Neither is it [*sc.* the silver maple] liable to produce suckers, an objectionable tendency peculiar to some free-growing trees. 1902 *Daily Chron.* 1 Apr. 2/1 The free-growing heralds of spring (*sc.* daffodils).

Freeha·ndedness. [f. Freehanded *a.*] Openhandedness, liberality.

1888 Lowell *Lit. & Pol. Addresses* (1914) 214 The power of the political boss is built up..by his freehandedness in distributing the property of other people.

Free lance. 2. Add: *attrib.* (in quot. 1927 = working for oneself and not for an employer).

1901 *Westm. Gaz.* 7 Mar. 9/1 Someone who calls himself a free-lance journalist. 1927 Carr-Saunders & Jones *Soc. Struct. Eng. & Wales* 62 Free-lance professional men, doctors and barristers for instance. *Ibid.* 75 When members of a free-lance profession take salaried positions.

Hence **Free-lance** *v. intr.*, to act as a free lance; **Free-lancing** *vbl. sb.* and *ppl. a.*

1904 *Westm. Gaz.* 6 May 2/3 Lord Londonderry..has done a bit of free-lancing himself in his non-Ministerial days. 1907 *Ibid.* 27 Mar. 4/2 Some free-lancing Parliamentary iconoclast. 1909 *Daily Chron.* 7 Apr. 4/7 If the clergy were allowed to free-lance in each other's parishes. 1915 W. J. Locke *Jaffery* i, He had a terrible time for a dozen years or so, taking pupils, acting, free-lancing in journalism.

Free State. 2. *U.S.* (Earlier examples.)

1820 *Deb. Congress* 9 Feb. 1209 Population in the free States we know increases with greater rapidity than in the slaveholding States. 1837 *Southern Lit. Messenger* III. 644 The various police trials of negro offenders in the different cities of the free states. 1845 F. Douglass *Life* (1846) 107, I have been..asked how I felt when I found myself in a Free State.

Free trade. 2. (Earlier U.S. example.)

1812 *Niles' Weekly Reg.* III. 61/2 The Essex may be known by a flag bearing the motto—Free Trade and Sailors Rights.

Free-trader. Add: **1. c.** A trader not in the service of a company. *U.S.*

1837 W. Irving *Capt. Bonneville* (1895) I. 66 Waylaying and dogging the caravans of the free traders, and murdering the solitary trapper. 1846 Sage *Scenes Rocky Mts.* (1859) 213 We..halted with a camp of free traders and hunters. 1871 Eggleston *Duffels* iv. (1893) 108 [He was] bent on spending the rest of his life as a 'freetrader' in British America. 1902 S. E. White *Conjuror's House* iv. 39 Brooding on his imprisonment the Free Trader forgot his surroundings.

3. (Earlier U.S. example.)

1832 *Deb. Congress* 6 June 3305 He admits a fact which the free traders have always found it difficult to explain, that goods do not usually rise under an increase of duties.

Free wheel, free-wheel. [Free *a.* 14.] The rear wheel of a bicycle arranged so that it can rotate freely while the pedals remain stationary; also *attrib.* Hence **Free-wheel** *v. intr.*, to ride with a free wheel; **free-wheel gear**, a non-rigid steering gear of a motor vehicle, as distinguished from locked gear; **Free-wheeled** *a.*, having a free wheel; **Free-wheeler**, a free-wheel bicycle.

1899 *Westm. Gaz.* 17 Nov. 7/1 The free-wheel device..is.. *the* novelty of the show. 1900 *Isle of Man Exam.* 3 Nov. 7 The recent free wheel contests. 1900 *Captain* III. 80/2 All these free wheeled machines made a clicking noise. 1901 *Westm. Gaz.* 18 Sept. 8/1 Injuries sustained while riding a free-wheel machine down Knockholt Hill. 1902 A. C. Harmsworth *Motors & Motor-Driving* x. 217 Free-wheel steering gear. 1903 *Motor Cycle* 31 Mar. 10/2 There is nothing incongruous in the sight of a club of bicyclists—some of them propelling their bicycles by muscular power at all times, except when free-wheeling downhill. 1905 *Mosquito* Aug. 4 They thoroughly enjoyed the ride coming back and free-wheeled the whole way. 1908 E. M. Sneyd-Kynnersley *H.M.I.* viii. 78 It was the first year of 'free-wheelers'. 1909 'R. Andom' *On Tour with Troddles* 185 We had a magnificent run for miles without putting an ounce of pressure on the pedals. Most of the time we free-wheeled.

Free-will. **3. b.** Add:

1823 *Baptist Mag.* IV. 32 Some who usually assembled with those denominated Free-will Baptists. 1847 H. Howe *Hist. Coll. Ohio* 348 The village contains 1 Free Will Baptist, 1 Methodist and 1 Universalist church.

Freeze, *v.* Add: **4. d.** *To freeze out*: to die out through freezing.

1872 *Trans. Dep. Agric. Illinois* 73 They [*sc.* strawberry plants] dry out and freeze out worse in a loose and well aerated sand. 1873 *Rep. Vermont Board Agric.* 128 Alsike luxuriates in damp soils, and will not freeze out as red clover.

e. To become stiff or motionless. *U.S.*

1908 S. E. White *Riverman* iii. 27 But Orde..had frozen in an attitude of attentive listening. 1912 Mulford & Clay *Buck Peters* iii. 49 Dave froze in his position. 'Meanin'?' he asked, coldly. 1916 H. Titus *I conquered* ix. 109 Of a sudden the horse froze, stopped his breathing.

7. b. *U.S.* (Earlier examples.)

1867 'Mark Twain' *Amer. Drolleries* 62 They would let that man go on and pay assessments.., and then they would close in on him and freeze him out. 1869 C. L. Brace *New West* v. 69 They can..lay assessments to bring a stock down to the lowest point, thus 'freezing out' the unhappy stockholders. 1882 *N.Y. Times* 2 Feb. (Th.) John A. Walsh became the contractor on the route after the original contractor had been 'frozen out'.

Free·ze-out. *U.S.* [Freeze *v.* 7.]

1. A variety of the game of poker in which the players, as fast as they lose their capital, drop out, all the stakes going to the last player left in. In full *freeze-out poker*.

1877 *Harper's Monthly* Oct. 799 (Bartlett) They doant do nuthin' but drink whiskey and play frease aout poker. 1887 F. Francis Jr. *Saddle & Mocassin* 61 The boys was having a little game of 'freeze out' last night. 1889 Farmer *Americanisms* s.v., In *freeze out* poker..no player, when his money is exhausted, can borrow, or continue in the game on credit under any circumstances. 1907 Tarkington *His own People* iv. 61 I'll put it up against that tin automobile of yours, divide chips even and play you freeze-out for it.

2. An act of 'freezing' or forcing out.

1883 J. Hay *Bread-Winners* x. 151 They organized a freeze-out against him. 1904 F. Lynde *Grafters* xiv. 190 By that time enough of the stock will have changed hands.. and the freeze-out will be a fact accomplished.

Freezer. Add: **4.** In *Chasing*, a punch for producing a frosted groundwork. (Cf. Frieze *v.*[2] 3.) Also **Freezing tool.**

1887 L. L. Haslope *Repoussé Work* 23 A small punch, called a freezing tool, which produces a small star. 1898 T. B. Wigley *Goldsm. & Jeweller* 79 Punches of various shapes, called chasing tools...Freezer. Mat. Dead Mat. Hair Mat.

Freeze-up. [f. phr. *freeze up*.] The condition of being stopped by frost; a frozen condition (of a water tank, motor cylinder jacket, etc.).

1879 [see Freeze *sb.*[1]]. 1904 J. Lynch *3 Yrs. Klondike* 129 A couple of steam-engines had been..brought to Dawson last October just before the freeze-up. 1912 *Motor Manual* (ed. 14) 177 If the motor-house is continually heated..there will be no risk of a freeze-up.

Freezing, *ppl. a.* 1. Add: quasi-*adv.* in adj. phr. *freezing cold* (cf. *boiling hot*).

1907 *Smart Set* Mar. 96 They transferred from the first stifling car to the second one, freezing cold.

Freezy, *a.* Add: freezing cold.

1902 O. Wister *Virginian* xxiii, Thought it looked pretty freezy out where yu' war riding.

Freight, *sb.* Add: **4.** *U.S.* (Later examples.)

1887 C. B. George *Forty Yrs. on Rail* v. 83 A freight had made an effort to run from Winnetka to Evanston. 1899 Tarkington *Gentl. Indiana* x. 166 It began to be generally believed that they had escaped by the one-o'clock freight. 1922 Titus *Timber* xx. 183 The morning freight came down. 1922 Marg. B. Houston *Witch-man* i. 14 There were four trains a day in Innessburg, not counting the freights.

5. (U.S.) *freight agent*, *car* (earlier and later examples), *conductor*, *depot*, *house*, *room*, *-train* (earlier and later examples), *wagon*, *yard*.

1843 *Rep. Western R.R.* 17 *Freight-agent. 1875 *N. Amer. Rev.* CXX. 403 He has been promoted to the office of freight-agent. 1841 *Ann. Rep. Boston & Worc. R. R.*, *Freight-car. 1887 M. Roberts *Western Avernus* 238 He ..was standing up between the freight-cars, with his feet on the coupling. 1905 *Springfield Weekly Republ.* 7 July 12 The boy attempted to climb on to one of the freight cars. 1872 E. B. Tuttle *Boy's Bk. Indians* (1882) 75 Two *freight conductors brought in their trains. 1904 Harben *Georgians* 1 The long, brick *freight depot. 1906 *Springfield Weekly Republ.* 4 Oct. 7 What the English call a 'railway goods station', and what we call a freight depot. 1880 *Harper's Mag.* Mar. 580/1 The only *freight-house of the line at Boston could hold but two freight-cars. 1889 *Kansas Times & Star* 16 Mar., The Rock Island railway will build two big freight houses. 1918 *Essex Inst. Hist. Coll.* LIV. 218 They should be run as one road, thus doing away with the expensive separate staffs, repair shops, freight houses, etc. 1899 Tarkington *Gentl. Indiana* xix. 354 The doors of the *freight-room were thrown open. 1845 *Ann. Rep. Boston & Worc. R. R.*, *Freight-train. 1887 M. Roberts *Western Avernus* 35 We found there was a freight train leaving this town at one o'clock. 1906 *Harper's Mag.* July 309 The wind brought the noise of a freight-train. 1855 Barnum *Life* 69 My father..ran a *freight wagon to Norwalk. 1889 K. Munroe *Golden Days* ix. 91 Holstead and Thurston soon had their modest outfit..on board an Oregon freight wagon. 1910 J. Hart *Vigilante Girl* viii. 122 Behind these were.. waiting stage coaches, and behind them freight wagons. 1899 Tarkington *Gentl. Indiana* xii. 201 One of my sergeants found him in the *freight-yards about four-o'clock. 1903 *N.Y. Times* 24 Sept. 5 Two youths..were seen prowling about the freight yards.

Freight, *v.* **2.** Add: Also *absol.*

1878 J. H. Beadle *Western Wilds* iii. 46 He was freighting thence to Montana, the owner of mules and wagons worth five thousand dollars. 1920 Hunter *Trail Drivers Texas* 163 My father sold them several yoke of old oxen which he had freighted to Mexico with.

Freighter. **2.** Also, one who owns or conducts a freight wagon or train of wagons.

1874 B. F. Taylor *World on Wheels* I. v. 43 You meet now and then a 'freighter', as the ox-expressmen of plain and prairie are called. 1876 *Fur, Fin & Feather* Sept. 162 Freighters pass through it regularly. 1881 *Amer. Naturalist* XV. 30 Freighters..always replace the broken spokes or felly with one made from green Mesquit. 1891 *Fur, Fin & Feather* Mar. 184 There [they] hire what they call a freighter's wagon and a driver that can cook. 1907 S. E. White *Arizona Nights* I. xvi. 229 It happened to be..a freighter without the fear of God in his soul.

3. (Earlier U.S. examples.)

1839 *Southern Lit. Messenger* V. 5/2 The Great Britain is now sailing as a mere freighter, and larger vessels are sailing as packets. 1859 R. H. Dana *Bef. Mast, Twenty Yrs. After* (1869) 381 Capacious freighters and passenger-carriers to all parts of the great bay.

b. A freight-wagon. *U.S.*

1885 *Century Mag.* Nov. 65/1 Heavily loaded freighters were lurching in. 1921 Mulford *Bar-20 Three* xiii. 147 Pete Jarvis was proud of his new sixteen-foot freighter. 1929 *Randolph Enterprise* (W. Va.) 14 Nov. 1/3 The Conestoga Wagon, known as the freighter, hauled travelers too.

French, *v.* Add: **6.** *intr.* To take French leave. *U.S. slang.*

1907 *N.Y. Times* 14 Sept. 18 The midshipman recently recommended for dismissal from the Naval Academy for 'frenching' from his ship during the late summer cruise.

7. Of tobacco, cotton, or other plants: To become diseased and distorted. (Cf. Frenchman 4.)

1852 *Florida Plantation Rec.* 67 My Corn Crop Looks better than it did Last year; this time it have Frenched a

Little, I see, in Places. 1888 *Congress. Rec.* 17 May 4069 Then [the cotton-plant] begins to blight, then comes frenching and the shedding of squares and formes.

Frencher. (Earlier U.S. example.)

1827 J. F. Cooper *Prairie* xxv. (1879) 328 And so it was atween the Frenchers of the Canadas and the red-coated English.

Frenchie, variant form of Frenchy *sb.*

1916 Boyd Cable *Action Front* 89 Now I wonder who it is. A Frenchie by his tunic sleeve.

Frenchman. Add:

5. A knife used in pointing brickwork.

1885 *Spons' Mechanics' Own Bk.* 591 This Frenchman is simply an old dinner-knife ground to a point, the tip of which is turned down square to form a hook.

6. The red-legged partridge, *Caccabis rufa*.

1893 *Baily's Mag.* Oct. 258/1 The red leg, the very much-abused 'Frenchman' of the English fields.

Frenulum: see *Frænulum.

Frequency. Add: **4. b.** *Electr.* The number of complete cycles per second of an alternating current. Also in comb., as *frequency-changer*, *-converter*, *-indicator*, *-meter*, *-raiser*, *-teller*.

1891 *English Mechanic* 24 July 469/2 Fairly good results have been obtained by a frequency as low as 15,000 to 20,000 per second, and a potential of about 20,000 volts. 1893 *Jrnl. Soc. Arts* 11 Aug. 842/2 We speak of the frequency of the current meaning the number of complete cycles in a second. 1904 R. M. Walmsley *Electr. in Service of Man* I. xiv. I. 514 To a current which..would show + and − loops following one another with the same frequency as the loops of E.M.F. 1926 G. G. Blake *Radio Telegr. & Teleph.* 234 The main object of the foregoing frequency raisers has been to obtain an increase of frequency from comparatively low frequency alternators. 1928 G. E. Sterling *Radio Manual* 22 If the alternating current has a very high frequency. *Ibid.* 32 Frequency Meters. *Ibid.* 152 The Frequency Changer.

c. *Statistics.* The ratio of the number of actual to the number of possible occurrences of an event, within a given interval of time. Also *attrib.*, as *frequency-curve*, *-distribution*, *-polygon* (see quots.).

1897 K. Pearson *Chances of Death* I. 14 However unable we may be to predict the result of a single trial, the frequencies of many trials distribute themselves around the mode in a perfectly orderly manner. *Ibid.* 16 This curve is the so-called frequency curve. *Ibid.* 272 The frequency distribution. *Ibid.* 273 If the tops of these lines be joined we obtain a frequency polygon. 1906 W. P. Elderton *Frequency-curves* ii. 5 If statistics are arranged so as to show the number of times, or frequency with which, an event happens in a particular way, then the arrangement is a frequency distribution...It is necessary to have a name for the formula used to describe such distributions, and the term frequency-curve has been adopted for the purpose...The drawings of distributions, such as those in the diagram, are called frequency polygons or histograms. 1911 G. U. Yule *Theory of Statistics* vi. 76 The manner in which the observations are distributed over the successive equal intervals of the scale is spoken of as the frequency-distribution of the variable. *Ibid.* 87 Such an ideal limit to the frequency-polygon or histogram is termed a frequency-curve.

Fresh, *a.*[1], *adv.*, and *sb.*[1] Add:

A. *adj.* **6.** *fresh air* used in attrib. phrases, as *fresh-air fiend* or *maniac*, etc.

1901 'R. Andom' *Troddles* xiv. 166 He didn't want to go down there spreading the impression that we were a waif-and-stray party or the protégés of a Fresh Air Fund. 1908 *Daily Chron.* 6 July 4/4 The fresh-air cure has been..very much boomed of late years...One result of this has been the evolution of what I may term the fresh-air maniac. 1909 *Sat. Westm. Gaz.* 16 Oct. 6/2 An out-of-door, fresh-air cry. 1927 W. E. Collinson *Contemp. Engl.* 39 Before the war we had our fresh air fiends...and the hatless brigade.

10. c. Of a cow: Yielding a renewed or greatly increased supply of milk; coming into milk. *U.S.*

1884 *Vermont Agric. Rep.* VIII. 29 The cows will go dry for a time during the hot weather in summer and be fresh in fall. 1896 *Ibid.* XV. 67 This [inoculating of cream] may be done by using a 'starter' made from cream of the skim-milk of a fresh cow.

B. *adv.* **2. fresh-find** *v. trans.*, to find (a deer) after the scent has been lost.

1780 in C. P. Collyns *Chase Wild Red Deer* (1862) 193 He was fresh found lying in a rush-bed. 1799 *Ibid.* 209 Here they fresh found him. 1855 in J. Fortescue *Stag-hunting* (1887) 189 Still persevered in hopes of fresh finding him in Haddon. *Ibid.* 190 We had fresh found our deer. 1899 *Westm. Gaz.* 18 Aug. 3/1 A clever huntsman..usually succeeds in fresh-finding his deer.

C. *sb.*[1] **5.** A freshman. *U.S.* (college slang).

1837 *Knickerbocker Mag.* IX. 250 The president's *fresh* came in, and handed me a suspension-bill, and left me, with a mock bow.

Fresh, *a.*[2] orig. *U.S.* [A use of prec., perhaps influenced by G. *frech* saucy, impudent.] Forward, impertinent, free in behaviour.

1848 Bartlett *Dict. Amer.* App., *Fresh*, forward; as 'don't make yourself too fresh here'; that is to say, not quite so much at home. 1887 F. Francis Jr. *Saddle & Mocassin* 136 What's the matter, then? Has Piggy been too 'fresh'? 1902 H. L. Wilson *Spenders* xxiii. 270 And when she goes out and says that isn't right they tell her she's too fresh. 1904 'Alan Dale' *Wanted: A Cook* 199, I smiled, and was about to speak, when she rose, and in a loud voice, cried: 'Say, you're too fresh! Where d'ye think ye are?' 1908 G. H. Lorimer *J. Spurlock* ii. 26 That [remark] was pretty fresh, and my only excuse for doing it was that I couldn't think of anything fresher. 1928 S. Vines *Humours Unreconciled* iii. 41 A woman who does that sort of thing has no business to turn one down as soon as one gets a little bit fresh.

Hence **Fre·shness**, forwardness, impertinence.

1901 *Munsey's Mag.* XXIV. 791/1 He had once heartily 'larruped' a new hand who had exhibited an unpleasing 'freshness' when speaking of her. 1928 J. C. Lincoln *Silas Bradford's Boy* 13 The captain's dignity was slightly ruffled by what he considered freshness on the part of his nephew.

Fresh, *v.* **1.** Delete †*Obs.*, and add U.S. and recent examples. Also with *up*.

1835 J. P. Kennedy *Horse Shoe Robinson* I. 66 Put a sprinkling of salt in a bucket o' water,..it sort of freshes the cretur up like. 1897 Kipling *Capt. Cour.* 260 The fresh air will fresh Mrs. Cheyne up. 1910 *Westm. Gaz.* 16 Apr. 16/2 The rains have freshed the trout streams.

Freshen, *v.* Add: **1. d.** To become fresh (see *Fresh *a.*[1] 10 c). *U.S.*

1931 *Randolph Enterprise* (W. Va.) 9 Apr. 2/2, I have for sale 2 year old Jersey heifers to freshen in April and two Jersey cows,..one of them fresh now.

3. *Naut.* *To freshen the nip* (earlier examples; also *fig.*: cf. Nip *sb.*[2] b).

1827 J. F. Cooper *Red Rover* iii. (1881) 51 Profiting by the occasion 'to freshen his nip', as he quaintly called swallowing a pint of rum and water, he continued his narrative. 1841 *Southern Lit. Messenger* VII. 764/1 After going into the saloon (grog-shop) to 'freshen the nip'—as they professionally called taking a glass of brandy and water—they led me into the upper tier of boxes. 1859 [see Nip *sb.*[1] 1 c].

Freshman. **2.** Add: Applied also to female students (in their first year). *U.S.*

1897–8 *Vassar Coll. Catal.* 90 Freshman Class. Adair, Barbara. Affeld, Antoinette [etc.].

b. freshman-class *U.S.* (earlier examples).

1805 D. McClure *Diary* (1899) 8, I..was examined & admitted into the Freshman Class at Yale College. 1832 *Collect. New Hampsh. Hist. Soc.* III. 9 He was..in 1751.. admitted a member of the freshman class in Harvard University at the age of twelve years. 1842 *Knickerbocker Mag.* XIX. 433 From time immemorial a playful animosity has existed between the freshman and sophomore classes.

Freshwater, *a.* Add: **1. b.** *U.S.* (See quot. 1925.)

1881 *Harper's Mag.* Jan. 224/1 'There is enough to send him through college.'..'In a fresh-water college?'..'Why not, for a fresh-water boy? He will always live in the West.' 1903 C. T. Brady *Bishop* xii. 230 He had just entered the preparatory class of a little Eastern Fresh-water college. 1925 Krapp *English Lang.* I. 135 One speaks also..of regions further inland with the qualifying adjective freshwater, as in *freshwater towns* or *freshwater colleges*, the adjective carrying with it some implication of rusticity and provincialism.

Freshwoman. Delete † and add mod. examples.

1871 *Scribner's Monthly* II. 347 To bring them where they can enter as Freshmen, or Freshwomen. 1885 *Academy* 21 Nov. 347 (Girton Dram. Soc.) A fresh-woman—if that is the girl-equivalent of fresh-man—is to play the second lady.

Fret, *v.*[1] **9.** Add: Often const. *about*, *after*, *at*, *over*, *upon*.

1788 B. Franklin *Autobiog.* (1909) 79 Fretting about the money Collins had got from me. 1837 E. G. G. Howard *Old Comm.* III. 69 Timothy began to fret upon it. 1854 W. Collins *Hide & Seek* I. vii. 247 Don't forget the letter, sir, for I shan't fret so much after her, when once I've got that! 1865 Mrs. Miriam C. Harris *Christine* xi, She went through life..fretting at her lot. 1899 A. Skeel & W. H. Brearley *King Washington* 224 In vain the captain fretted over the delay.

10. (Example of modern technical use.)

1897 W. J. Sykes *Princ. & Pract. Brewing* 481 Often the secondary fermentation becomes unduly excited; the beer is then said to 'fret' or 'kick up'.

Fretty, *a.*[2] Add: **c.** Of beer: Characterized by fretting or secondary fermentation (see Fret *v.*[1] 10, Fretting *vbl. sb.*[1] 2).

1897 W. J. Sykes *Brewing* 382 Beers produced from such contaminated waters show a great tendency, especially marked in hot weather, to become 'fretty', go turbid, turn sour.

Freudian (froi·diăn), *a.* [See -ian.] Of or pertaining to Dr. Sigmund *Freud*, the psycho-analyst of Vienna (born 1856), or his teaching. Also *sb.*, a follower or adherent of Freud. Hence **Freu·dianism, Freu·dism**, the teaching or system of Freud; a characteristic specimen of this.

1910 *Amer. Jrnl. Psychol.* Apr. 289, I recently dreamt that I was travelling to Italy on my way to the next Freudian Congress (which is to be held in March). 1915 E. B. Holt *Freudian Wish* Pref. p. vi, The idea has gone abroad that the term 'Freudian' is somehow synonymous with 'sexual'. 1919 *Athenæum* 23 May 360/2 Curative treatment based on Freudian theories. 1919 B. Low *Psycho-Analysis* 10 The Freudian theory and technique, and these alone, constitute Psycho-Analysis. 1921 *19th Cent.* Mar. 475 The out-and-out Freudian..held the stage. *Ibid.* 477 The attitude of the new school towards Freudism. 1922 Woodworth *Psychol.* xix. 505 The Freudian would shake his head at our interpretation of the lightning dream. 1923 *Times Lit. Suppl.* 12 Apr. 245/2 Once or twice he strains us with a Freudianism. 1924 E. & C. Paul tr. *Wittels' Sigmund Freud* 225 Able thinkers who have no intimate connexion with Freudianism. 1924 C. Hamilton *Prisoners of Hope* 149 Lady George.. began singing 'Not for Joe, oh no, no', which, for some Freudian reason, had come into her mind out of the rag-bag of her childhood.

Friction, *sb.* **5.** Add: **friction-ball** (earlier U.S. example); **friction-drive**, a transmission of power by means of friction-gear.

1813 *Niles' Weekly Register* IV. 111/2 The wheels of both boats and carriages are provided with double ratchets reversed, or *friction cups and balls. 1907 *Motor Boat* 19 Sept. 190/2 The cargo-winch should have a *friction drive and a good brake for lowering. 1927 T. Woodhouse *Artif. Silk* 54 By these means, and a suitable combined belt, wheel, and friction drive, the trough can be tilted, when desired.

Frictionally, *adv.* Add: By means or by way of friction.

1927 T. Woodhouse *Artif. Silk* 90 These vertical discs impart motion frictionally to horizontal discs.

Friedreich (frī·draiχ). Name of N. *Friedreich* (1825–82), German physician, used in the genitive in designations of hereditary locomotor ataxia.

1887 *Buck's Handbk. Med. Sci.* V. 198/1 Friedreich's Disease. Hereditary locomotor ataxia—the family form of locomotor ataxia. 1907 *Practitioner* Apr. 484 Friedreich's Disease. 1910 Osler & McCrae *Syst. Med.* VII. 131 Friedreich's ataxia.

Friesian, var. of Frisian *a.* and *sb.*, as the name of a breed of cattle.

1923 R. Wallace *Farm Live Stock* (ed. 5) 222 The general type of the Friesian is that of a large dairy animal. *Ibid.* Index, Friesian (or Fresian) British cattle. 1926 J. A. S. Watson, etc. *Cattle-Breeder's Handbk.* 46 It is many years since certain shrewd dairy-farmers in England and Scotland imported Friesian cattle from their native home. *Ibid.* 48 For crossing purposes..the British Friesian is supreme.

Frie·zing, *vbl. sb.*[2] [f. Frieze *sb.*[2] or *v.*[2]] Frieze-work. Also *attrib.*

1769, *c* 1850 [see Frieze *v.*[2] 2]. 1899 *Westm. Gaz.* 17 May 5/2 The large amount of window space will contrast pleasingly with the plain friezing above. 1911 Webster, *Friezing machine*, a machine for making edge moldings on wood-work.

Friezy, *a.* Add: **2.** Resembling frieze.

1890 J. H. Pearce *Esther Pentreath* I. iii, Covering him over with Tom's friezy coat. 1892 *Northumbld. Gloss.* s.v., A friezy coat is made of a kind of rough home-spun yarn. 1901 *Westm. Gaz.* 25 July 3/1 The Highwayman coat,.. formed of a friezy tweed or homespun.

Frighten, *v.* **b.** Add: with *off* (adv. and prep.).

1861 Geo. Eliot *Silas M.* xiv. 261 If you can't bring your mind to frighten her off touching things, you must..keep 'em out of her way. 1904 Lillie T. Meade *Love Tri.* IV. x, I frightened those fellows off, didn't I, Beaufort?

Frighteningly (frəi·t'niŋli), *adv.* [f. Frightening *ppl. a.* + -ly[2].] In a manner that frightens.

c 1854 [see Dict. s.v. Frighten *v.*]. 1906 W. J. Locke *Beloved Vagabond* xi, The backward vista down the years is too frighteningly long. 1921 Galsworthy *To Let* I. ii, She was frighteningly self-willed. 1922 A. S. M. Hutchinson *This Freedom* IV. i. 251 Her mother had scalded her hand and had cried out to her, frighteningly.

Frightfully, *adv.* **2 b.** Add: Not now restricted to unfavourable reference, but merely = 'awfully', greatly, very. *colloq.* or *slang*.

1875 *Punch* 24 July 31/1 Everything is..'How deliciously frightful!' 'How frightfully charming!' 1928 Galsworthy *Swan Song* I. v. 39 With more jaw, and deeper set eyes, but frightfully like Jon! *Ibid.* III. vii. 308, I don't know that I approve of it frightfully.

Frightfulness. Add: Used during the war of 1914–18 to render G. *schrecklichkeit*, implying a deliberate policy of terrorizing the enemy (esp. non-combatants) as a military resource.

1915 D. O. Barnett *Lett.* 115 We are having a quiet time to-day, without any frightfulness for a change. 1915 P. Gibbs *Soul of War* 155 It was only when special orders for 'frightfulness' had been issued,..that the rank and file of the enemy's army committed its brutalities. 1924 J. S. C. Bridge *Hist. France* II. 119 Attributing to the French the deliberate pursuit of a policy of 'frightfulness'.

Frigo (frī·go). *Soldiers' slang.* [Fr., short for *viande frigorifiée*.] Chilled or frozen meat.

1919 *Athenæum* 11 July 582/2 With the entry of America into the war came a mob of Yankeeisms—'frigo,' frozen meat; 'kookenette,' a cooker.

Frill, *sb.*[1] Add:

1. c. esp. in pigeons (see quots. 1860, 1879); hence, a pigeon having a frill (cf. *frill-back* in 5).

1860 B. P. Brent *Pigeon Bk.* 53 The eye..is of a pearl or gravel colour..very different from the Turbit's,..and the frill is rarely so long. 1879 L. Wright *Practical Pigeon Keeper* xiv. 165 The fourth and last property is frill. *Ibid.*, If the frill, or group of re-curved feathers on the breast is to extend [etc.]. 1890 *Daily News* 8 Jan. 2/4 Oriental frills, imported 20 years ago from Turkey and Smyrna.

d. orig. *U.S.* and *Austral.* (Earlier and later examples.)

1870 *Sacramento paper* (De Vere) I can't bear his talk, it's all frills. 1871 Schele de Vere *Americanisms* (1872) 603 *Frills*, denotes, in California and the West generally, any assumption of style. 1885 'Mark Twain' *Huck. Finn* v, You've put on considerable many frills since I been away. *Ibid.*, He cussed me for putting on frills, and trying to be better than him. 1891 E. Kinglake *Australian* 157 Do not put on what the Americans call 'frill'. 1892 Kipling *Barrack-room Ball.*, *Oonts* 12 It's the commissariat camel puttin' on 'is bloomin' frills! 1900 G. Bonner *Hard Pan* vi. 194 She suffered from none of that rancor which the boarder who is suspected of 'putting on frills' is liable to arouse. 1928 Galsworthy *Swan Song* iii. 23 The first book was born too still for anything. A sort of 'African Farm,' without the spiritual frills—if you remember it.

e. *fig.* A thing or feature which is merely ornamental; an embellishment. Usually in a derogatory sense.

1893 Farmer *Slang*, *Frills*, swagger; conceit; also accomplishments (as music, languages, etc.); and culture; *cf.*, Man with no frills. 1904 *N.Y. Tribune* 13 Oct. 6 The Board of Education should be encouraged in its tendency to lop off a few 'frills' from the curriculum and add the time saved to the substantial parts of the course. 1909 *Westm. Gaz.* 4 Aug. 4/1 A full-fledged Parliament.., a Speaker, a Mace, and all the frills and furbelows still considered essential to Parliamentary Government. 1926 'Q' *On the Art of Writing* vii. 133 The editor of a mining paper in Denver, U.S.A., boldly the other day laid down this law, that niceties of language were mere 'frills'. 1919 Mrs. L. F. Cody *Buffalo Bill* 21 There were no frills about Will Cody's story as he told it to me.

Frilling, *vbl. sb.* Add: **1. b.** *fig.*

1899 C. J. Cutcliffe Hyne *Further Adv. Capt. Kettle* vi, Great masses of foliage growing to the crown of the splintered heights, with a surf frilling. 1903 *Westm. Gaz.* 2 Mar. 8/2 A mid-day meal of stewed steak and frillings.

Frilly, *a.* (under Frill *sb.*[1]). Add: Full of frills; resembling frills. Also *fig.* **b.** *sb. pl.* Frilled undergarments. *colloq.* Hence **Fri·lliness**, frilly character; also *fig.*

1890 Mrs. Eliz. Custer *Following the Guidon* xiv. 202 Our ..era-glasses looked just a little 'frilly' in such a place, but they were really useful. 1899 *Westm. Gaz.* 21 Sept. 3/2 Fluffy, frilly wraps. 1900 *Ibid.* 10 July 3/1 Capelines..more or less frilly and floppy. 1902 *Ibid.* 20 Nov. 3/1 The effect was delightfully rippling and frilly. 1904 B'ness von Hutten *Pam* I. iii, Pamela in a frilly nightgown. 1911 H. S. Harrison *Queed* vi. 75, I am a clerk,..and office girl. My official title of course, is a little more frilly. 1922 *Glasgow Herald* 22 Mar. 10 [He] insisted upon the need for a thorough elementary education..even if less attention were paid to the 'frilly' subjects than at present.

1900 Elin. Glyn *Visits Eliz.* 16 Lady Doraine and that horrid Smith creature made a place for me in the empty hammock between them, and, as I knew my 'frillies' were all right, I hammocked too. 1927 *Daily Express* 27 June 13/4 There are bargains to be found from fur coats to 'frillies'.

1909 *Westm. Gaz.* 3 July 15/1 Once more everything is tending towards paniers, frilliness, flounces, and full skirts. 1927 *Daily Express* 27 Apr. 3/2 There was, surely, more feminity, more coy frilliness..about the evening dresses than last year. *Ibid.* 23 Sept. 3/3 The food was nourishing and English—..none of your Frenchified frillinesses.

Fringe, *sb.* Add:

2. b. Also in wider use: An outer edge or margin of any kind, material or immaterial; an outer limit of a country, area, or population. Also *attrib.* = existing on the edge or margin of an area or region.

1898 Q. Victoria in *Daily News* 20 Dec. 5/4 All these people ask is to be allowed to do their daily task in peace.. and to have a little fringe of play. 1902 D. G. Hogarth *Nearer East* 162 The density of this Fringe population depends on fertility. *Ibid.* 181 It is necessary to detach the Arabs, who are found in the Arabian and Mesopotamian Fringe, from the central Semitic group. *Ibid.* 185 The outer desert ring has up to now proved effective to separate this loose unity from the Fringe populations. *Ibid.* 221 This system of railways..will serve to neutralise the immemorial tendency of this Fringe to display upon a superficial area.. a *congeries* of human groups bitterly antagonistic in tradition and hope. 1926 J. Geddie (*title*) The Fringes of Edinburgh.

c. Also *Grecian fringe*.

1878 *Cassell's Fam. Mag.* IV. 175/2 None of that affected 'Grecian fringe' with which modern 'girls of the period' strive to hide what little forehead they possess.

3. fringe-net, a net intended to confine a fringe of hair (2 c); hence **fringe-netted** *ppl. a.*; **fringe-variation** *Chess* (see quot. 1907).

1899 *Westm. Gaz.* 10 June 2/1 She was now engrossed with a refractory *fringe-net. 1909 Marg. B. Saunders *Litany Lane* I. vi, Her round face, tightened up in a stiff frame of fringe-nets. *Ibid.* x. Provincial mayoress..with *fringe-netted hair. 1898 *Brit. Chess Mag.* 472 It would not be very difficult to find quite a goodly collection of two-movers in which every specimen contained the weakness of a '*fringe' variation. 1907 Blackburne *Terms & Themes of Chess Problems* 54 A variation which does not spring naturally from the position, but had been tacked on by the employment of men which have otherwise no effect upon the solution is known as a 'Fringe Variation'.

Fringe, *v.* Add:

4. *intr.* (with adv.) To spread like a fringe *away*, *out*, *over*, etc.

1883 'Mark Twain' *Life Mississippi* ix. 112 Do you see where the line fringes out at the upper end and begins to fade away? 1899 C. P. Allen *What is Liberalism?* viii. 43 Its limits fringe away from it like a huge penumbra. 1901 *Westm. Gaz.* 15 Aug. 2/1 Exmoor..is for the most part in the west of Somerset, but it fringes over into the north-eastern part of Devon.

Fringing, *vbl. sb.* Add: The appearance of a rim or border of false colour on the outline of an object photographed.

1921 *Conquest* Oct. 511/2 The moment motion of any rapidity occurs the objectionable defect of 'fringing' makes itself apparent.

Frisesomorum (frəi:sesŏmōᵊ·rŏm). *Logic.* The mnemonic term for that indirect mood of the first figure of syllogisms in which the major premise is particular and affirmative, the minor universal and negative, and the conclusion particular and negative. Also called **Frisesmo.**

1849 Mansel *Aldrich* 65 *note*, The five indirect moods of the first figure were called Baralip, Celantes, Dabitis, Fapesmo, Frisesmo. 1884 J. N. Keynes *Formal Logic* 199 Similarly, *Fapesmo* and *Frisesomorum* (the *Fesapo* and *Fresison* of Figure 4) have no corresponding direct moods.

Frisk, *v.* **4. a.** Add: To run the hand rapidly over (a person or his clothing), in search for a concealed weapon, smuggled goods, etc. *U.S. slang.*

1920 I. Ostrander *How Many Cards?* 65 When you frisk this man Hill at Headquarters, if you find a pair of gloves on him keep them aside till I get there. 1929 C. E. Merriam *Chicago* 289 To take the police away from the task of frisking hip pockets and inspecting refrigerators. 1930 E. V. Knox in *Punch* 26 Feb. 236 His arm was twisted during the course of the interview, and his person was frisked on the chance of finding a gun.

Frisure. Delete †*Obs.* and add recent example.

1927 *Daily Express* 4 Oct. 9/6 Other resolutions declared that bobbed and shingled heads should have a higher frisure than formerly.

Fritz (frits). German nickname for *Friedrich* (= Frederick). Hence in *War-slang* used for: A German, *esp.* a German soldier (as typical of the German army); also, a German shell, aeroplane, submarine, etc.

1915 D. O. Barnett *Lett.* 174 By that time, of course, Fritz had made himself scarce. 1916 *Daily Mail* 1 Nov. 4/4 An effective bombardment of the enemy's lines or a successful trench raid [is] described by Tommy as 'strafing the Fritzes'. 1919 G. K. Rose *2/4th Oxf. & Bucks Lt. Infty.* 54 At night it seemed probable that a patrol of a few brave men could crawl right up to the German wire and listen, or by setting foot in them enquire whether 'Fritz' was at home in his trenches or no. 1919 J. B. Morton *Barber of Putney* xiv. 228 Anyone'd think you was the first bloke that ever done a Fritz in.

Frizziness (fri·zinės). [f. Frizzy *a.* + -ness.] Frizzy style or character.

1906 W. J. Locke *Beloved Vagabond* iii. 36, I criticised her straight Teutonic fringe and fanfarouaded on the captivating frizziness of Janna's hair. 1912 L. A. Harker *Mr. Wycherly's Wards* xvii, Your type is severe and classical; 'frizziness' would be quite dreadful and incongruous.

Frock, *sb.* Add:

5. c. *transf.* A *député* or politician.

[1917 Sir H. Wilson *Diary* (1927) I. 342 It makes it all the more necessary to put off the next meeting of the Frock Coats till after that date.] 1919 *Ibid.* II. 177, I think the Frocks have gone mad. They sit and talk all day. 1921 Sir W. Orpen *Onlooker in France* xiv. 100 A little mass of black frock-coated figures—'frocks' as we called them. 1926 *Blackw. Mag.* Oct. 455/2 These deputies were not as the 'frocks' of 1914–18, remarkable only for their ignorance of matters military. 1928 *Observer* 26 Aug. 5 Contemptible as a soldier, Lord George was impossible as a 'frock'.

6. frock dress, a form of court dress (see quot. 1875).

1875 *Dress worn by Gentlemen at Court* 3 Frock Dress is worn at Dinners and Evening Parties, where uniform is not worn, and consists of Dress Coat lappelled, Waistcoat, Breeches or Pantaloons, with white Cravat. 1903 *Westm. Gaz.* 17 Nov. 1/1 'Windsor Uniform—Frock dress' is the order for evening attire at Court this week.

Frog[1]. Add: **7.** *frog-spear.*

1891 *Fur, Fin & Feather* Mar. 196 If the tourist likes frogs' legs..a frog spear is handy but not necessary.

8. frog-eye, a disease of tobacco which produces white spots on the leaves (Cent. D., Suppl. 1909); so **frog-eyed** *ppl. a.* (Webster *Suppl.* 1902); **frog-face**, a face like that of a frog; *Path.*, a deformity of the nose and eyes caused by a polypus in the nose; **frog-farm** *U.S.*, a place where frogs are bred for market; so **frog-farming** *vbl. sb.*; **frog-hop**, a jerky leap like that of a frog.

1873 George Eliot *Middlemarch* xxxiv, A little round head with bulging eyes—a sort of *frog-face. 1884 M. Mackenzie *Dis. Throat & Nose* II. 385 The most marked symptoms [of enchondromata of the nose] an obstruction of the nasal passages, and deformity in advanced cases amounting to 'frog-face'. 1901 *Westm. Gaz.* 2 Aug. 10/1 There are extensive *frog farms in Indiana and Illinois. 1927 *Blackw. Mag.* Sept. 292/2 The bear fled in ungainly *frog-hops, whining pitifully.

b. frog-lily *U.S.*, the American yellow water-lily, *Nymphaea advena*.

1889 *Harper's Mag.* May 860/2 From its filthy habits it [*sc.* the yellow nuphar] has been called, with some justice, the frog-lily.

Frog[2]. **b.** Add: **frog-band**, a band running from above the wall below the coronary band to join the frog; **frog-pad** = Cushion *sb.* 4 b.

1831 Youatt *Horse* Contents p. vi, The Anatomy of the Foot...The coronary ligament; the coronary ring; the *frog-band. 1908 *Animal Managem.* (W.O.) 219. *Ibid.* 217 A firm, soft cushion, sometimes called the '*frog pad' or 'cushion of the heels'.

Frog[4]. (Earlier U.S. example.)

1846 *Rep. U.S. Comm. Patents* (1847) 95 Frogs are used having guards or grinders on their outsides, and double inclined planes up and down, by which the wheels are guided to the right track.

Froggish, *a.* (Earlier U.S. example.)

a 1861 T. Winthrop *John Brent* xxii. 240 Thanks La Grenouille, rover of the wilderness, for thy froggish instinct.

Froglet (frɒ·glėt). [See -let.] A small or young frog.

1907 W. De Morgan *Alice-for-Short* xxi, Just one chirp of a nightingale or trill of a flute from a froglet. 1929 J. Huxley *Ess. Pop. Sci.* xvii. 196 The brusque transformation of tadpole into froglet.

Fro·g-pond. Chiefly *U.S.* [Frog[1] 1.] A pond frequented by frogs.

1635 *Essex Inst. Hist. Coll.* IV. 92/1 Half of the playne ground betwixt that and the frog pond. 1748 *N. H. Probate Rec.* III. 625, I give unto my son Ebenezer the one half of my woodland...Excepting three acres of sd woodland lying at the west of a frog pond. 1799 *Aurora* (Philad.) 28 May (Th.) The hero who performed such wonders at the Kensington (Philad.) frog-pond. 1838 Caroline Gilman *Recoll.* xxxv. 254, I involuntarily paused at the frog-pond, for there seemed a kind of society in their voices. 1863 'Gail Hamilton' *Gala-Days* 33 It [*sc.* Boston] has..a Frog-pond. 1882 *Congress. Rec.* 18 Jan. 497/1 [The language] is sufficiently precise to cut off headwaters and frog-ponds..and it applies to main rivers exclusively. 1891 'L. Malet' *Wages of Sin* v. iii, The daily routine of frog-pond existence would become deadly dull if King Stork should abdicate.

Hence **Fro·gpondian**, a Bostonian.

1880 *Harper's Mag.* Oct. 78/1 Poe retorted that the poem was good enough for Frogpondians.

Frolicky, *a.* (See Frolic *sb.*; modern U.S. example.)

1883 Nye *Baled Hay* 88 They was just frolicky and gay because they felt good.

From, *prep.* **15. a.** Add: (*to get*) *from under*: (to extricate oneself or escape) from a difficulty or a 'tight place'. *U.S.*

1916 *Lit. Digest* (N.Y.) 8 Jan. 88/2 Ed. Gwinner and C. B. Comstock, the Pittsburg members of the Federal clan, were the next to 'get from under'.

Front, *sb.* (and *a.*). Add:

7. e. *spec.* with *the*: The promenade of a seaside resort, often with adjoining gardens.

1904 *Ward, Lock & Co.'s Guide Isle of Man* 44 The Queen's Promenade..is the part of the Front most favoured by visitors with a taste for quiet. 1920 *Glasgow Herald* 17 July 7 For them the 'front', palpitating with cheerful humanity, is Elysium.

9. e. The front part of a woman's garment.

1889 *Daily News* 23 July 7/2 The travelling mantle.. buttons the whole way down the front, and is provided with over-fronts which fall straight from the shoulders...These fronts are lined with yellow and pink..surah. 1891 *Ibid.* 25 June 6/2 A rather similar dress..has the front in gold-coloured silk muslin held with clasps of yellow topaz. 1895 *Army & Navy Co-op. Soc. Price List* 15 Sept. 1036 Cape in Amazon Cloth, solid Fur Collar and trimmed down Fronts.

10. a. *To get in front of oneself*: to hurry, 'hustle'. *U.S. slang.*

1907 *Daily Chron.* 21 Oct. 6/4 There is a common American phrase, which expresses better than anything else the curious effect of this policy of 'hustle' upon the national temperament. They say that a man gets 'in front of himself'.

11. = *front-pipe* (see *14).

1879 *Organ Voicing* 12 Zinc is frequently used for basses and 'fronts'.

b. *Front of*, in front of. *U.S.*

1843 Carlton *New Purchase* xv. 110 Front of the fire-place was the parlour. 1871 Mrs. Stowe *Sam Lawson* 45 Wall, she was a standin' front o' this.

c. As a command: To the front, forward.

1907 *N.Y. Even. Post* (semi-weekly ed.) 13 May 6 The register clerk [at a Shanghai hotel] assigns you to a room, and instead of 'Front!' he shouts 'Boy!'

13. In various more or less technical uses.

1897 *Encycl. Sport* I. 267/2 It ruins the tyres, and, if applied to the front wheel, puts a great strain on the front forks. *Ibid.* 493/1 It often happens in heavy shooting that the recoil of the second barrel causes the front trigger to cut the first joint of the fore-finger. 1902 *Captain* VII. 474 Crabb front rim brake. 1907 *Daily Chron.* 11 Nov. 7/4 The front axle being..used for both steering and driving alike. 1908 *Westm. Gaz.* 18 Jan. 7/2 Front pressure over the area of a railway carriage must be from 25lb. to 35lb. per sq. foot before the stability of the train is imperilled. 1908 *Daily Chron.* 3 July 6/4 This front-cover picture. 1925 *Morris Man.* 68 When the front axle is off the ground, the pedal should be depressed.

b. *Phonetics.* Applied to sounds in the formation of which the fore-part of the tongue touches or is raised towards the front of the hard palate.

1867 A. M. Bell *Vis. Speech* 52 Front. The Front of the Tongue contracting the oral passage between it and the roof of the mouth. *Ibid.*, Front-Mixed. The Front and the Point of the Tongue both raised. *Ibid.* 58 The 'Front-divided' Consonant has its side apertures within the palatal arch. 1888 H. Sweet *Engl. Sounds* 2 Front vowels are rounded by the lips only.

14. front-action *a.* (see quots.); **front-bencher**, an occupant of a front bench (q.v. in Dict.); **front brake** = **front-wheel brake*; **front brick**, brick for the front of a building; **front door** (earlier U.S. example); **front-driven** *a.*, designating a motor car in which the power is transmitted to the front wheels; **front flight** = first flight (see Flight *sb.*[1] 8 d); also *attrib.*; **front foot**, a linear foot along the front of a plot of ground (cf. *foot front* in 11); **front line** = Front *sb.* 5; also *attrib.*; **front matter** *U.S. Typogr.*, all matter in a book that precedes the text (such as title-page, preface, table of contents, etc.); **front name** *U.S.* (earlier example); **front office** *Thieves' slang*, police headquarters; **front page**, the front outside page of a newspaper; often *attrib.* to indicate an important or striking piece of news; **front-piece** *Theatrical*, a small play acted in front of the curtain (cf. Front *sb.* 7 f); **front-pipe**, each of the row of pipes which form the front of an organ, often gilded or otherwise decorated; **front rank**, the first or foremost rank; also *attrib.*; **front-ranker**, a person (ship, etc.) of the highest class or of leading position; **front trench** *Mil.*, the trench nearest the enemy; **front wheel**, the foremost or either of the foremost wheels upon which a vehicle runs; also *attrib.*, as *front-wheel brake*.

1881 Greener *Gun* 209 Back-action locks..tend to weaken the stock at the grip more than *front-action locks. 1907 *Ibid.* (ed. 8) 144 If the mainspring [of the lock]..is placed before the tumbler, it is 'front action' or 'bar'. 1907 *Westm. Gaz.* 31 Aug. 1/3 Each Unionist *Front-Bencher will have to do a double or treble turn. 1919 G. B. Shaw *Heartbreak House* (1927) p. ix, Where were our front benchers to nest if not here? 1925 *Morris Man.* 68 From the points near the ends of the front number plate to the

*front brake assemblies. 1865 *Trans. Ill. Agric. Soc.* VI. 39 Best Brick Machine for making fine *Front Brick. 1749 *N. H. Probate Rec.* III. 754 We set off to the Heirs of Eleanor Shackford,..the Privilege of the *Front Door Entrys below and above stairs. 1907 *Daily Chron.* 11 Nov. 7/4 The *front-driven vehicle is much less liable to sideslip than when the front wheels are merely pushed forward from the rear. 1899 *Westm. Gaz.* 1 Dec. 4/2 The field gradually tailed off and only the *front-flight men were able to keep on terms. 1902 *Daily Chron.* 5 Dec. 3/4 A department of the chase upon which front-flight men of the shires may be inclined to look down. 1873 E. Eggleston *Myst. Metrop.* 12 Corner lots were once sold for a hundred dollars the *front foot. 1889 *Kansas Times & Star* 30 Mar., John Taylor bought the southwest corner..about $1,700 a front foot. 1915 'Ian Hay' *First Hundred Thou.* xviii. 248 That sudden disturbance in the *front-line trench. *Ibid.* 251 Our front-line parapet. 1919 Boyd Cable *Old Contemptibles* xv. 243 If the front line there was pushed back. 1919 G. K. Rose *2/4th Oxf. & Bucks Lt. Infty.* 36 My company supplied parties to carry wire and stakes up to the front line. 1919 'R. Andom' *Traddles in Trenches* xi, We'll soon be up in the front line now. 1931 *Times Lit. Suppl.* 12 Feb. 116/4 From a vast mass of published diaries..by officers and men whose duties brought them constantly into the front line, Professor Cru, himself a front-line soldier, has studied the fundamental nature of war. 1909 *Cent. Dict.* Suppl., *Front matter. 1930 *Publishers' Weekly* 4 Oct. 1660/2 We have cast-off your manuscript and estimate it will make 8 pages of front-matter and 248 pages of text. 1877 Bartlett *Dict. Amer.* (ed. 4), **Front name*, Christian name. 'The familiar manner in which the telegraph handles my front name', i.e. in calling him Ben. 1901 J. Flynt in *McClure's Mag.* Apr. 571/2 The *Front Office itself could not tell for a certainty the number of first-class thieves who are on the streets at this moment. 1930 *Publishers' Weekly* 31 May 2732/1 Realizing that such announcements would have *front-page value. a 1889 *Evening News* (Barrère & Leland) At the Gaiety..a farce, 'Lot 49', by Mr. Fisher, as a *front piece to 'Frankenstein'. 1907 *Daily Chron.* 9 Nov. 4/4 Thirty-four full-length plays and seven front-pieces. 1855 E. J. Hopkins *Organ* 73 Tin does not soon become tarnished; hence its peculiar appropriateness for ungilded '*front pipes'. 1905 T. Elliston *Organs & Tuning* 393 The front pipes to be of stout V.M. zinc silvered with aluminium leaf. 1899 *Westm. Gaz.* 10 Mar. 4/3 Mr. Fox, another *front-rank costumier. 1905 *Ibid.* 25 Mar. 15/1 The eagerness which was displayed by some '*front-rankers' to get a 'line' of the Ceylon Pearl Syndicate's underwriting. 1914 in E. C. Barnes *Alfred Yarrow* (1923) xxvii. 260 The *Firedrake* and *Lurcher* were looked upon as two front-rankers. 1928 *Manchester Guardian Weekly* 7 Dec., Suppl. p. vi/1 It is a long time since a year's verse list was led by so many front rankers. 1916 Boyd Cable *Action Front* 143 The stretcher-bearers carried their burden into the *front trench. 1878 *Design & Work* IV. 218/1, 52 in. Wolverhampton..with lamp and pouch, *front wheel brake. 1900 *Captain* III. 463/2 Gamage's Holborn Front Wheel Rim Brake. 1902 A. C. Harmsworth *Motors & Motor-Driving* x. 218 The automobilist should frequently jack up the front of his car so that the front wheels are free of the ground. 1904 *Technol. & Sci. Dict.* (ed. Goodchild & Tweney) 147/2 The front wheel brake usually carries two blocks on a horseshoe-shaped clip. 1908 *Westm. Gaz.* 3 Nov. 4/1 The Allen-Liversidge system of front-wheel braking.

Front, *v.*[1] Add: **11.** *Phonetics.* To pronounce with the tongue in a front position, i.e. touching or raised towards the hard palate; to palatalize. Hence **Fronted** *ppl. a.*, **Fronting** *vbl. sb.*

1888 H. Sweet *Engl. Sounds* 36 The fronting is carried out most fully with the point nasals and stops. *Ibid.*, These fronted consonants again in their turn influence a preceding sound. *Ibid.* 37 [This sound] fronts the preceding ʃ. 1907 H. C. Wyld *Hist. Study Mother Tongue* viii. 160 A natural inference is that..*e* being a front vowel, fronted the preceding consonant. 1929 *Encycl. Brit.* I. 1/2 These [changes] are due to fronting..or to rounding.

Frontal, *a.* Add:

2. c. Of or pertaining to the façade of a building; *spec.* in *Gr. Art*, pertaining to front or full-face view of a sculptured object (cf. next).

1895 *Funk's Standard Dict.* s.v., The frontal effect of a fine building. 1905 P. Gardner *Gramm. Gr. Art* v. 57 One finds figures stooping, or kneeling, or in a variety of other attitudes; but the frontal law still holds.

Frontality (frɒntæ·lĭti). [f. Frontal *a.* + -ity, after Da. *frontalitet* (Julius Lange): so G. *frontalität*, F. *frontalité*.] A principle in sculpture, according to which the figure is carved or moulded as viewed from the full front.

In the strictest style, the figure is divided by an imaginary plane into two symmetrical halves, with no bending to either side.

1905 P. Gardner *Gramm. Gr. Art* v. 56 Lange has expounded in detail his theory of frontality in early art. 1910 E. A. Gardner *Six Greek Sculptors* 34 The bold modelling of the figure, and the skill with which the twist of the body is rendered, make it worthy of notice in its departure from the rigid 'frontality' of early art. 1920 *Q. Rev.* July 39 A new decorative style of portraiture, of which the leading characteristic was a return to the frontal view of primitive Greek art. That is to say, 'frontality' became, as in the archaic periods, the basic principle of composition.

Frontally (frɒ·ntăli), *adv.* [f. Frontal *a.* + -ly[2].] By a frontal attack.

1900 *Westm. Gaz.* 2 Feb. 7/1 Thus Buller, in order to relieve Ladysmith, must frontally force a tremendous position held by 10,000 or 12,000 of the best riflemen in the world.

Frontier, *sb.* and *a.* Add: **A.** *sb.* **4. b.** *U.S.* (Earlier examples.)

1803 *Steele Papers* I. 374, I dislike the Country as a frontier. 1838 *Southern Lit. Messenger* IV. 294 In this situation he..passed his days upon the frontier. 1842 *Amer. Pioneer* I. 226 Of all the men I ever knew he was the best qualified to live on a frontier where there were savages..to contend with. 1848 J. F. Cooper *Oak Open.* I. iv. 59 Gershom had seen more of the peculiar life of the frontiers than his companion. 1856 R. Glisan *Jrnl. Army Life* (1874) 327 An equal number of sharp-shooters enlisted from the whites on the frontier.

B. *adj.* **1.** 'Frequent in *U.S.* (sense 4 b) from 17th cent.'

b. *Frontier Colt*, a Colt revolver for frontier use; also *ellipt.* *U.S.*

1918 Mulford *Man fr. Bar-20* v. 50 He..did not care to call attention to his wooden-handled, flare-butt Frontiers. *Ibid.* viii. 78 A plain Frontier Colt peeked coyly from his hip.

Fro·ntierless, *a.* [See -less.] Having no frontier or dividing line.

1925 *The Inner Life* ix. 165 The English layman as he comes to receive the Holy Communion in his parish Church, finds himself caught up into a Fellowship which is frontierless.

Frontiersman. Add: *Legion of Frontiersmen*, an organization intended to enrol for irregular service men with colonial or frontier experience.

1905 *Times* 11 Apr. 8/1 A corporation to be called the 'Legion of Frontiersmen'. 1906 *Daily Chron.* 21 May 7/1 Mr. Roger Pocock, founder and hon. secretary of the Legion of Frontiersmen. 1930 *Times* 8 Nov. 8/7 A movement has been set on foot for the formation of a Maritime Command of the Legion of Frontiersmen.

Fronto-. Add: *fronto-central*, *-ethmoidal* adjs.

1908 *Practitioner* Jan. 19 The *fronto-central and parietal regions. *Ibid.* June 795 The..*fronto-ethmoidal cells.

Front yard. *U.S.* [Front *sb.* (*a.*) 13.] A piece of ground or garden in front of a house.

1835 J. H. Ingraham *South-West* II. 114 Southerners, with the exception of the cultivation of a few plants in a front yard, pay little regard to horticulture. 1838 — *Burton* II. vii. 106 Meeting Caroline in one of the avenues of the front yard, he delivered his message. 1861–2 *Trans. Ill. Agric. Soc.* (1865) V. 198 The front yard is well laid out, and filled with fruit, ornamental trees, shrubs and plants. 1897 'Mark Twain' *Following Equator* xxix. 282 There cannot be another town in the world that has no..weed-grown front-yards of the poor. 1908 *Westm. Gaz.* 29 May 1/3 'The front-yard', as my old farming friend in the train informed me, was mostly grass. 1916 H. L. Wilson *Somewhere in Red Gap* ii. 69 The Piedmont Queen dahlia bulbs I'd ordered for the front yard.

Frost, *sb.* Add: **4. b.** A detrimental influence.

1911 R. D. Saunders *Col. Todhunter* viii. 112 They're the ones that's puttin' a frost on the Strickland campaign fund.

c. *jocular.* One who disappoints expectations; one who tries to humbug or mislead; a 'fraud'.

1916 Boyd Cable *Action Front* 123 'You old frost!' he said gaily, 'there's no need to keep it up any longer now.'

7. c. **frost-grape** *U.S.* (earlier examples).

1845–50 Mrs. Lincoln *Lect. Bot.* App. 186/1 *Vitis vulpina*, frost-grape. 1849 *Rep. U.S. Comm. Patents Agric.* (1850) 443 Besides the common 'frost-grape' of the East, we have some excellent native varieties.

Frost-bite, *sb.* Add: Also, the effect of frost on a plant.

1862 *Trans. Ill. Agric. Soc.* (1865) V. 570 The bitter, smoky taste..arises wholly from frost-bite.

Froth, *sb.* **4.** Add: **froth-blower** *jocular*, a beer-drinker: adopted as the title of a certain charitable organization.

1905 *Daily Chron.* 25 Mar. 6/4 The quaintly-named 'Froth Blowers'..are a little group of twenty-four working men. 1927 *Times* 25 June 9/7 A company limited by guarantee under the title of 'Ye Ancient Order of Froth-Blowers, Limited', has been registered to take over all or part of the property and liabilities of the incorporated Ancient Order of Froth-Blowers. 1927 *Punch* 9 Feb. 146/2 England might have remained part of the Scandinavian empire, with a fixed Nordic physiognomy and a population of blue-eyed froth-blowers. 1928 *Times* 8 Feb. 5/3 In 1924 Mr. Herbert Temple ..desired to benefit certain charities. He invented the name 'Ancient Order of Frothblowers'. 1928 'Sapper' *Female of Species* xvii, Now then, boys, once again—and all together —Froth Blowers for ever.

Frothy, *a.* **3.** Add: Used to describe very light, tenuous dress-material. Hence **Fro·thiness.**

1901 *Westm. Gaz.* 10 Jan. 3/2 In evening frocks and tea-gowns there is still a very marked liking for frilled frothy edges. 1930 *Times* 13 Mar. 11/6 The outstanding feature is the frothiness of the dresses made from perishable materials with their innumerable frills, flounces, and furbelows.

Frotton (frotoǹ). [Fr., f. *frotter* to rub. The termination *-on* denotes a tool or implement.] In early block-printing, a dabber or burnisher used to press the damp sheet upon the inked block.

1893 E. G. Duff *Early Printed Bks.* 17 It consists of three sheets of paper, each of which contains an impression from a block...They are printed by means of the frotton in light-coloured ink. 1911 Hessels in *Encycl. Brit.* XXVII. 511/2 Then a sheet of damp paper was laid upon it [*sc.* the block], and the back of the paper was carefully rubbed with some kind of dabber or burnisher, usually called a *frotton*, till an impression from the ridges of the carved block had been transferred to the paper.

Frou-frou, *v.* [f. Frou-frou *sb.*] *intr.* To move about with a rustle of draperies. Only in *frou-frouing*.

1905 *Truth* 18 May 1289/2 Frou-frouing femininities. 1909 Marg. B. Saunders *Litany Lane* II. xvii, She found herself floating and frou-frouing up Majorson's monastic stairs.

Frowst (fraust), *sb. colloq.* Also **froust.** [Back-formation from Frowsty *a.*]

1. At Harrow School: see quots.

1880 [W. G. Baillie] *Hugh Russell at Harrow* 12 Can't you let a fellow take his frowst the very second morning? [Glossary: *Frowst*, extra time in bed on Sundays, saints' days and whole holidays.] 1905 Vachell *The Hill* v. 113 *note*, Lying in bed in the morning when there is no First School is a 'frowst'. By a subtle law of association, an armchair is also a 'frowst'. 1920 Galsworthy *Captures* (1923) 60 Ruding..looked right down on me in my old 'froust', as we called arm-chairs.

2. The close and fusty air of a room which is over-warm or over-crowded and without adequate ventilation.

1907 'J. Halsham' *Lonewood Corner* 130 For the manufacture of froust trust the elementary schools! 1921 *Blackw. Mag.* Apr. 453/1 Poor Colin..had to listen in candle-lit frowst [in a dug-out] to the banalities talked by the Brigadier. 1929 D. Coke *Monkey Tree* vii, He liked the cheap room and its genial frowst.

Frowst, *v.* Substitute for def.: To take pleasure in staying in a warm, close, 'fuggy' atmosphere. Hence **Fro·wster.**

1929 'A. Berkeley' *Wychford Poisoning Case* xxiii. 280 'Hallo, you frowsters!' cried Sheila, bursting without warning into the room.

Frowstiness (frau·stinės). [f. Frowsty *a.* + -ness.] Frowsty quality; fustiness, stuffiness.

1923 *Daily Mail* 21 June 10 To clear his lungs of their over-night 'frowstiness'. 1926 W. J. Locke *Old Bridge* III. ix, The old frowstiness of dirt had given place to the fragrance of cleanliness.

Frowzled (frau·z'ld), *ppl. a.* *U.S.* Rumpled, tousled, dishevelled, frowzy (*Cent. Dict.* Suppl. 1909). Also **Frowzly** (frau·zli), *a.* (in quot. *frowsly*), in similar sense.

1901 *Harper's Mag.* CII. 665/1 Look at the poor thing's hair! Only see how frowsly it is.

Frozen, *ppl. a.* Add:

1. b. *The frozen limit* (colloq.): the hard and fast limit; the *ne plus ultra* of what is objectionable or unendurable. See *Limit *sb.* 2 h.

1917 W. H. L. Watson *Adv. Despatch Rider* x. 216, I don't mind their machine-guns, but their Minnenwerfer are the frozen limit! 1920 H. C. McNeile ('Sapper') *Bull-Dog Drummond* i. § 1 Only his eyes redeemed his face from being what is known in the vernacular as the Frozen Limit.

c. *Billiards.* Used to designate a ball at rest in close contact with another ball or a cushion.

1904 J. P. Mannock *Billiards* II. 275 When the object is frozen to the side cushion. *Ibid.* 287 Here we have the red ball 'frozen' or 'tight up' against an end cushion. *Ibid.* 293 A ball 'frozen' on a cushion.

d. Of credits, assets, etc.: Impossible to liquidate or realize at maturity or other given time. (Opposed to Liquid *a.* 6.)

1922 *Daily Mail* 16 Dec. 9 Germany has an immense quantity of 'frozen credits' locked up in this country. 1923 *Ibid.* 9 Jan. 7 A large part of British assets..were temporarily 'frozen'. 1929 *Encycl. Brit.* IX. 876/2 *Frozen credit*, credit (generally bank-loans) which has been extended but which the creditors find it impossible or highly inexpedient to collect at maturity or at any given time...In such a case the bank will often renew or extend the loan, and this credit is said to be *frozen*, a term signifying the opposite of 'liquid' as applied to credit, capital or assets. 1930 *Times* 24 Mar. 23/5 The opportunity to accomplish this liquidation of over $10,000,000 of frozen assets.

e. Of a journal and its bearing: Immovable by reason of expansion consequent upon imperfect lubrication. 1895 *Funk's Standard Dict.*

Fruit, *sb.* Add: **2. e.** *Old* (*tin of*) *fruit*: a term of familiar address. (Cf. *old bean*.) *slang.*

1923 *Daily Mail* 8 Feb. 6 Was she simply bursting to address him Gaily as her 'dear old tin of fruit'? 1928 *Ibid.* 25 July 10/6 Then their politeness. No slapping a friend on the back with a 'What cheer, old fruit?'

5. Applied to the boll of the cotton-plant. *U.S.*

1854 *Florida Plant. Rec.* 89 Still they [= there] is a good deal of grown and half grown fruit on the cotton.

8. a. *fruit farm*, *-juice*, *lot*, *pulp*, *year*. **b.** *fruit-farmer*, *-grower* (earlier example), *-growing* sb. and ppl. adj. (earlier example), *-raising*.

1872 *Trans. Dep. Agric. Illinois* 65 The first consideration in the establishment of a *fruit farm is accessibility to market. *Ibid.* 66 The *fruit farmer can raise cheap pork in his apple and peach orchards. 1854 *Trans. Ill. Agric. Soc.* I. 70 The fruit and *fruit growers of seven states were represented. *Ibid.* 135 *Fruit growing..has not increased any faster than the growing of other agricultural produce. 1872 *Trans. Dep. Agric. Illinois* 66 A soil adapted to the growth of forest trees is..the best for fruit growing. 1849 *Rep. U.S. Comm. Patents Agric.* (1850) 106 This perhaps is the best *fruit-growing district of the State. 1880 *Jrnl. Chem. Soc.* XXXVIII. 354 Behaviour of *Fruit-Juices of Different Ages with Reagents. 1912 *Chambers's Jrnl.* Mar. 173/2 It is very beautiful up behind the *fruit-lot among the rocks and the pine-trees. 1887 *Colon. & Indian Exhib., Rep. Col. Sect.* 131 Importing a large quantity of fresh fruit, and what is called '*fruit-pulp' from Tasmania. 1887 Moloney *Forestry W. Afr.* 339 The fruit-pulp is eaten and also prepared into a pleasant beverage. 1906 *Westm. Gaz.* 28 Aug. 6/1 To avail themselves of any cheap and defective fruit-pulp for the making of jam. 1854 *Trans. Ill. Agric. Soc.* I. 500 The fact that *fruit raising here is attended by drawbacks. 1891 C. D. Warner in *Harper's Mag.* Jan. 168/2 California has much to learn about fruit-raising and fruit-curing. 1811 R. Sutcliff *Trav. N. Amer.* ii. (1815) 45 This was likely to be a very abundant *fruit year.

9. fruit-cake (earlier U.S. example); **fruit cocktail**, a preparation of fruit used as an appetizer or refreshment; **fruit-cup**, a drink made from fruit; **fruit-gatherer**, an implement for gathering fruit from tall trees; **fruit-jelly**, a fruit-flavoured table-jelly; **fruit-moth** = *codling-moth* (Codling[2] 4); **fruit-netting**, nets or network containing

fruit; **fruit salad**, fruits, usually uncooked, cut up and mixed in a bowl with sugar, cream, etc.; **fruit steamer**, a steam vessel engaged in carrying fruit; **fruit (tree) bark beetle**, *Scolytus rugulosus*, which burrows beneath the bark of fruit-trees.

1915 *Let. to Editor from Royal Bot. Gardens, Kew*, One of the commonest insects that mine under the bark of trees, including the pear, is Scolytus rugulosus, the *fruit bark beetle. 1848 E. Bryant *What I saw in California* xi. 162 The prejudice against the grasshopper '*fruit-cake' was strong at first, but it soon wore off. 1928 *Saturday Even. Post* 12 May 107/1 Mr. Montgomery had taken a morsel of *fruit cocktail. 1931 *N. & Q.* 4 Apr. 241/2 Where *fruit-cup, ices and wonderful cakes were served. 1846 *Rep. U.S. Comm. Patents* (1847) 19 A *fruit-gatherer, of very ingenious and simple construction, has been patented. 1910 *Daily Chron.* 10 Feb. 1/5 A fruit-gatherer attached to a pole and armed with cutting teeth. 1875 *Encycl. Brit.* I. 172/1 Jams, marmalades, and *fruit jellies. 1862 T. W. Harris *Insects injur. Veget.* (ed. 3) 484 *Carpocapsa Pomonella*, the codling-moth, or *fruit-moth of the apple. 1846 *Knickerbocker Mag.* XXVIII. 67 The *fruit-netting over the stern amply filled with the products of that luscious land. 1892–4 *Encycl. Cookery* (ed. T. F. Garrett) 657/1 *Fruit Salad. 1887 Susan Hale *Lett.* (1919) 181 My idea is to come home in one of those *fruit-steamers from Gibraltar. 1921 R. D. Paine *Comr. Rolling Ocean* vii. 111 Nothing ever happened excepting the arrival of the fruit steamers which took on thousands of bunches of bananas. 1898 E. A. Ormerod *Orchard & Bush Fruit Insects* 197 *Fruit-tree Bark Beetle.

Fruitarian. Add: also as *adj.*

1902 H. Begbie *Sir John Sparrow* x. 150 The form of eating which I practise..is not vegetarian, but fruitarian. 1903 *Sci. Amer.* 10 Oct. 255/2 Fruits contain little protein, and nuts are relied on in the fruitarian plan of eating to balance the ration.

Hence **Fruita·rianism**, the principles or practice of fruitarians.

1902 H. Begbie *Sir John Sparrow* xiv. 221 We flee from before the face of vegetarianism, fruitarianism, theosophy, and religious manias. 1908 *Practitioner* Mar. 401 Vegetarianism, fruitarianism, and even zomotherapy may suit a few. 1930 E. T. Thurston *Man in Black Hat* viii. 149 The medical profession at the moment approves of fruitarianism.

Fruity, *a.* Add: **3.** *colloq.* Full of rich or strong quality; highly interesting, attractive, or suggestive. Cf. *spicy*, *juicy*.

1900 Tighe Hopkins *Silent Gate* ii. 45 When pulled up short, his language was of the Dials, fruity. 1915 T. Burke *Nights in Town* 337 A popular murder, fruity, cleverly done, and with a sex interest. 1921 Wodehouse *Indiscr. Archie* 299 It's here now. The dickens of a fruity picture. 1925 *Weekly Westminster* 19 Sept. 522/3 Mr. John Garside's Young Launcelot is more intelligent, even if it is like the work of a fruity comedian without his fruitiness. 1928 S. Vines *Humours Unreconciled* xv. 201 An unusually 'fruity' political scandal connected with bribery.

Frumpiness (frɒ·mpinės). [f. Frumpy *a.* + -ness.] The quality or condition of a frump.

1912 C. N. & A. M. Williamson *Heather Moon* I. v. 59 Aline tried to think that she was the weirdest frump in the world...The thing was to hurry her away in all her frumpiness. 1924 *Sunday at Home* Feb. 258/1, I am going to take you up and save you from frumpiness and spinsterhood.

Frumpishly (frɒ·mpiʃli), *adv.* [-ly[2].] In a frumpish manner; like a frump or dowdy.

1927 *Daily Tel.* 23 Aug. 8/5 The middle-aged matron refuses definitely to take a back seat. She does not feel a frump. Why, then, should she dress frumpishly?

Fry, *v.*[1] Add: **1.** With *up*: To 'hot up' (cold viands) in a frying-pan.

1899 G. B. Burgin *Bread of Tears* I. v, 'What are you cooking there, Fenella? It smells good.' 'Frying up the cold fowl,' said Fenella.

c. *To fry the fat out of*: to subject to extortion. *To fry out fat*: to obtain money by pressure. *U.S. slang.*

1890 *Congress. Rec.* 10 July 7088/1 That process which in the U.S. is called the 'frying of fat' out of people. *Ibid.* 16 July 7790/1, I did not suppose there had been any authority of law for 'frying the fat' out of the manufacturers in the last presidential campaign. 1904 *Nation* (N.Y.) 28 Apr. 321 His main qualification is admitted to be that of a good collector of funds. No one could, in the historic phrase, fry out more fat.

Frying, *vbl. sb.* **2.** Add: **frying-basket**, a vessel for frying fish, etc., made of metal basket-work.

1888 *Mrs. Beeton's Bk. Househ. Man.* xi. 369 Iron saucepans or stewpans, frying-pans and frying-baskets. 1928 *Daily Mail* 9 Aug. 3/5 Use a frying basket,..let the fish fry a nice golden brown.

Fuchsia. Add: **d.** A red colour like that of the fuchsia flower, fuchsia-red.

1923 *Daily Mail* 5 Mar. 13 Colours: Peach, Apple, Apricot, Mauve, Fuchsia, Periwinkle. 1930 *Times* 29 Nov. 16 A colour scheme of fuchsia and gold predominates.

Fuchsinophil, -phile (fuksi·nǒfil, -fəil), *a.* and *sb.* *Phys.* [f. Fuchsine + -phil, -phile.] **A.** *adj.* Readily stained by fuchsine. **B.** *sb.* A cell or other element readily stained by fuchsine. Also **Fuchsino·philous** *a.* = A. (Dorland 1901).

1911 W. K. Hunter *Rec. Adv. Hæmatol.* 31 Azurophile and fuchsinophile granules are absent from the myeloblast. 1913 Gruner *Biol. Blood-Cells* 206 There are no azur or fuchsinophile granules.

Fudge, *int.* and *sb.* **B.** *sb.* Add:

4. A patch of print, esp. a piece of late news, inserted in a newspaper page; also, a machine or cylinder for printing such patches. Also *attrib.*, as *fudge-space*; **fudge-box** (see quot. 1929).

1899 *Daily News* 23 Sept. 5/1 The blank space left for 'fudge' while the evening paper is being printed off is caused by the presence of the empty fudge-box. 1902 *Daily Mail* 27 June 7/5 After the paper has passed through the big cylinders that print the entire sheets, it goes past the small cylinder which prints the contents of the 'fudge box' in the vacant space. 1910 E. Wallace *Nine Bears* vi. 45 'Issued at 4.10', he said, glancing at the 'fudge' space, where the result of a race had been printed. 1929 *Encycl. Brit.* XVIII. 508/1 This late news is printed into the blank spaces by a contrivance called a 'fudge box' which is circular in form and into which are secured linotype slugs. The 'fudge' is fastened on to an auxiliary cylinder equipped with inking mechanism.

5. A soft-grained sweetmeat prepared by boiling together milk, sugar, butter, and chocolate or maple sugar. orig. *U.S.*

1897 *Confectioner's Price List*, Chocolate fudge. 1902 *Queen* 3 May 763/1 The greatest 'stunt' among college students is to make *Fudge*. *Ibid.*, Nut Fudges...Fruit Fudge. 1905 *Buffalo Express* 16 Jan. 2 The overturning of an alcohol lamp over which some girls were cooking fudge.

Fuel, *sb.* Add: **1.** Also applied by extension to the fireclay and asbestos which the flames of a gas fire or stove make incandescent.

3. b. fuel food, food which maintains steady heat in the body; **fuel oil**, oil used as fuel in an engine or furnace; **fuel-value**, the value of a combustible article as fuel; also in reference to the amount of heat-energy imparted to the body by a given article of food.

1905 *Daily Chron.* 14 July 4/4 At the present period of year there is comparatively little demand for *fuel-food. 1893 *Power* Mar. 6 A contract..for the supply of all *fuel oil required during 1893. 1886 *Lett. fr. Donegal* (ed. Col. Maurice) 36 Bog once 'cut out' does not grow again, and the *fuel-value is permanently lost to the land. 1928 A. B. Callow *Food & Health* 18 Water cannot be burnt in the body, and therefore has no fuel-value.

Fuelling (fiū·eliŋ), *vbl. sb.* [f. Fuel *v.* + -ing[1].] The action of laying in, or furnishing with, fuel; supply or storage of fuel. Also *attrib.*

1921 *19th Cent.* June 1063 At each port, facilities for fuelling and for receiving the various supplies which a fleet requires must..be forthcoming. *Ibid.* 1068 There are numerous minor ports available as temporary fuelling bases. 1927 *Glasgow Herald* 14 July 11 The broad Imperial development of the science of fuelling.

Fug (fɒg), *sb. colloq.*, orig. *dial.* and *school slang.* [? Related to Fogo. Cf. *Fuggy *a.*] A thick, close, stuffy atmosphere, esp. that of a room overcrowded and with little or no ventilation.

1888 [E. F. Benson] *Sketches fr. Marlborough* i. 16 Seating himself in the most comfortable chair, as a consolation for the prevailing fug. 1915 'Bartimeus' *A Tall Ship* iv. 78 We get up quite a good fug in our casemate at night. *Ibid.* ix. 171 'Pouf!' he exclaimed. 'What a fug!' And elevated his nose with a sniff. 1923 Silberrad *Lett. Jean Armiter* x. 214 Can you smell the cold damp fug of those wet Sunday afternoons..? 1925 *Chambers's Jrnl.* 556/1 The 'fug' that could be got up inside these huts was sheer bliss to many a trench-weary soldier during the war. 1927 G. W. Deeping *Kitty* xvii, It [*sc.* a sickroom] smelt like a greenhouse, full of soft fug.

Hence **Fug** *v. intr.*, to stay in, and enjoy, a stuffy atmosphere. Also with *up*.

1889 Barrère & Leland *Dict. Slang*, *Fug, to* (Shrewsbury), to stay in a close, stuffy room. 1920 W. T. Grenfell *Labrador Dr.* ii. 35 Others were 'fugging' in the house or had gone to bed. 1921 A. S. M. Hutchinson *If Winter Comes* ii. v. 122, I like it a jolly sight better than fugging up in those carriages with all that gassing crowd.

Fugato, *adv.* Add examples of *sb.* and *attrib.* use.

1876 Stainer & Barrett *Dict. Mus. Terms*, *Fugato*, in the fugue style; a composition containing fugal imitation, but which is not in strict fugue form. 1891 E. Prout *Fugue* § 358 Passages of imitation, provided that all the voices take part in them, will very often be also fugato passages. *Ibid.* § 359 The freedom allowed in fugato. 1903 *Travel* May 28 A fugato entry for the lower strings. 1906 *Grove's Dict. Mus.* II. 118/1 Beethoven was particularly fond of the fugato.

Fuggle (fɒ·g'l). Also **Fuggle's.** A variety of hops.

1898 *Westm. Gaz.* 5 Sept. 7/3 All good sound hops suitable for copper use, such as the fuggle. 1902 *Times* 5 Sept. 2/5 Bramblings that are picked are small..but fuggles have developed most. 1908 *Westm. Gaz.* 25 Sept. 9/2 The growers of 'Fuggles' and other comparatively hardy kinds. 1910 *Encycl. Brit.* XIII. 679/2 The variety known as Fuggle's, a heavy-cropping though slightly coarse hop, has been much planted in the Weald of Kent.

Fuggy (fɒ·gi), *a. colloq.*, orig. *dial.* and *school slang.* [f. *Fug *sb.* + -y[1]; or Fug may be a back-formation from this. Cf. Fog *sb.*[2] and Foggy *a.*] Of the air in a room: Close, stuffy, and smelly, from want of ventilation. Of persons: Addicted to living in such an atmosphere.

1888 [E. F. Benson] *Sketches fr. Marlborough* i. 15 How beastly fuggy this place is. *Ibid.* vi. 58 He was rude enough to say that I was a fuggy beast. 1889 Barrère & Leland *Dict. Slang*, *Fuggy* (Shrewsbury), stuffy. 1900 *Globe* 12 Jan. 3/1 They missed the warm, and it must be owned often 'fuggy' heat of their old cabins. 1921 *Chambers's Jrnl.* 189/1 In the fuggy comfort of the engineers' mess. 1923 Silberrad *Lett. Jean Armiter* iv. § 3. 102 He came up to the window and I opened it—the artists are rather a fuggy lot indoors.

Fughetta (fuge·tă). *Mus.* [It., dim. of *fuga* Fugue. Cf. G. *fughette*.] A short, condensed fugue. Also *attrib.*

1876 Stainer & Barrett *Dict. Mus.* 1891 E. Prout *Fugue* § 351 In the form most frequently met with, a fughetta is an abridged fugue. *Ibid.* § 356 Another variety of the fughetta form. 1898 *Westm. Gaz.* 19 Dec. 10/2 The Finale, ..with..its fughetta based..on the first subject of the first movement.

Fugue, *sb.* Add:

2. *Psychopathol.* The impulsive flight or wandering of a neurotic from his accustomed haunts followed by his appearing in some distant place, with or without memory of what has happened in the interval. [So used by French writers on the subject.]

1925 E. & C. Paul tr. *P. Janet's Psychol. Healing* 595 The subject cannot tell us about the incidents of the fugue, or explain why he ran away. 1925 J. Laird *Our Minds & Their Bodies* iv. 86 There is a palpable difference between man's behaviour in somnambulism, or in a fugue, or in masked epilepsy, and ordinary human conduct. 1925 C. Burt *Young Delinquent* 439 Amnesic Fugues.

Fuhrt-sack, variant of *Voetsak.

Fulcrum. Add: **2. c.** The stem or median part of the incus of the mastax of certain rotifers.

1886 C. T. Hudson *Rotifera* I. 118 The trophi consist mainly of two ribbed rami, attached to a long narrow plate (the fulcrum). 1896 M. Hartog *Rotifera* in *Cambr. Nat. Hist.* II. 210 In the ventral wall of the gizzard of most Ploima is a median piece, the *fulcrum*, from which run forwards and upwards two pieces, the *rami*, which are hinged on the fulcrum. The Y-shaped structure formed of these three pieces is called the *incus* (anvil).

d. In trilobites (see quot.).

1909 H. Woods *Trilobites* in *Cambr. Nat. Hist.* VI. 234 At some distance from the axis the pleurae are bent downwards and backwards. The point where this bend occurs is called the 'fulcrum'; it divides the pleura into an internal and an external part.

e. *Ent.* A chitinous portion of the pharynx.

1910 C. G. Hewitt *House Fly* 12 The Fulcrum.—This chitinous portion of the pharynx..lies on the lower part of the head and in the rostrum. 1925 A. D. Imms *Entomol.* 597 Situated within this region is a complex framework of chitin known as the *fulcrum*, which forms a kind of case enclosing the pharynx, and is present in almost all Diptera.

Fulcrumed (fɒ·lkrǒmd), *pa. pple.* [See -ed.] Supported *on* (some object) as fulcrum.

1927 T. Woodhouse *Artif. Silk* 41 The upper ends of the two vertical rods *N* are attached to the two ends of the lever *O* fulcrumed on the shaft *P*.

Fulfil, *v.* Add: **5.** *refl.* Of a person: To work out one's destiny; to develop one's gifts and character to the full. (A development of Tennyson's use: see Dict.)

1920 Rose Macaulay *Potterism* III. i. § 8. 117 In what place, under what conditions, would Oliver Hobart now fulfil himself, now carry on the work so faithfully begun on earth? *Ibid.* vi. v. § 8. 259 Jane would, no doubt, fulfil herself in the course of time, make an adequate figure in the world she loved.

b. *absol.*

1539 *Bible* (Great) Matt. v. 17, I am not come to destroye, but to fulfyll. 1862 G. Macdonald *D. Elginbrod* I. v, Hugh promised and fulfilled.

Fulgorid (fɒ·lgǒrid), *sb.* and *a.* *Ent.* [ad. mod.L. *Fulgoridæ*, f. the generic name *Fulgora*, a. L. *Fulgora* goddess of lightning, f. *fulgur* lightning: see -id[3].] **A.** *sb.* An insect of the homopterous family *Fulgoridæ* which includes the lantern-flies. **B.** *adj.* Belonging to this family.

1899 D. Sharp *Insects* II. 576 The wax of Fulgorids is used by the Chinese for candles. 1913 *Zoologist* Ser. IV. XVII. 281 Some notes on a Luminous South African Fulgorid Insect (Rhinortha Guttata). *Ibid.* 289 With approach of cold weather all signs of the Fulgorid parasites disappeared.

Fulgurante (fülgürānt). [Fr., fem. of *fulgurant*: see Fulgurant.] A glistening dress-material.

1922 *Daily Mail* 21 Nov. 8 A gown of lovely silver grey fulgurante. *Ibid.* 24 Nov. 6 The wedding dress is a beautiful silver grey fulgurante gown. 1923 *Ibid.* 19 Jan. 8 A lovely débutante's frock of ivory fulgurante.

Fuliguline (fiuli·giŭləin), *a.* *Zool.* [f. mod.L. *Fuligula* (f. L. *fūlīgo* soot) + -ine[1].] Of or belonging to the sub-family *Fuligulinæ* or sea-ducks, of which *Fuligula* is the typical genus.

1862 H. G. Adams *Wild Flowers, Birds*, etc. 273 The *Fuligulinæ*, or Fuliguline birds. 1893 [see *Anatine].

Full, *sb.*[4] *Kent.* [Probably a use of Full *sb.*[3]] A ridge of shingle or sand pushed or cast up by the tide. Hence **Full** *v.*[4] *trans.*, to form such a ridge on (the beach).

1864 *Proc. Instit. Civil Engin.* XXIII. 187 The sandy foreshore..has a small shingle 'full' at the top. *Ibid.* 195 The spit..is formed of parallel 'fulls' of beach. 1864 F. Drew *Geol. Country betw. Folkestone & Rye* 16 The beach is gradually 'fulled', that is pebbles are heaped up in front of the breaker, generally forming a small ridge. 1902 W. H. Wheeler *Sea-Coast* 36 In calm weather the face of the bank becomes heaped up, assuming what is termed a 'full', or ridge and hollow, parallel to the coast. 1902 Ld. Avebury *Scenery of Eng.* 163 It [*sc.* North Weir Point] consists of a series of curved concentric ridges or 'fulls'..forming a projecting cape or 'Ness'. 1907 *1st Rep. Royal Comm. Coast Erosion* App. 144/2 The successive fulls of Dunge Beach.

Full, *a.*, etc. Add:

A. *adj.* **11.** *Full and by*: also *fig.*

1930 *New Statesman* 5 July 412/1 And, take it full and bye, it is one of the very few things to be honoured in our nature.

12. a. *full-size*, *-tank*, *-term*, *-voice*.

1888 Hasluck *Model Engin. Handybk.* (1900) 41 The Figs. are reduced from *full-size drawings. 1927 W. H. Todd *Tiger, Tiger!* 25 The water..had already reached to within a foot or so of the designed *full-tank level. 1907 Maloney tr. P. Budin (*title*) The Nursling: the Feeding and Hygiene of Premature and *Full-term Infants. 1927 V. McNabb *Cath. Ch. & Philos.* iii. 119 The *full-voice assertion of the rights of reason to reason.

d. full-choke, a gun with the maximum amount of choke-boring; **full-hand** *Poker* = *Full house 2; **full load** *Aeronautics*, the dead load plus the useful load (Webster *Addenda* 1924); **full pitch** *advb. phr.*, without the ball having first touched the ground; so **full-pitched** *a.*; **full score** *Mus.*, a score in which the parts for all voices and instruments are given on separate staves.

1881 Greener *Gun* 387 A *full choke is constricted to the extent of 30 to 40,000ths of an inch. 1892 — *Breech-loader* 134 The 16-bore full-choke, with barrels 30 inches in length. 1895 *Outing* (U.S.) XXVII. 65/1, I have ruined too many fine birds with the full-choke to want to use it any more. 1895 H. G. Hutchinson *P. Steele* i. 29 One or two [balls] went over the wicket altogether, and were taken, *full pitch, by the wicket-keeper. *Ibid.*, He..sent..ball after ball *full-pitched. 1876 Stainer & Barrett *Dict. Mus. Terms*, *Full score.

C. *adv.* **5. b. full-fashioned**, of a garment (esp. a stocking) shaped to the full proportions of the body; also *transf.*

1883 [in Dict.]. 1927 T. Woodhouse *Artif. Silk* 92 Originally, the spring beard needles were used in full-fashioned (flat) machines. *Ibid.* 95 Needles have to be taken out of action when it is desired to decrease the width of any part of the full-fashioned fabric...This possibility of effecting various changes in the width according to the amount of material required for various parts of the human body, gave rise to the term 'full-fashioned'.

Full, *v.*[2] **1. b.** Of the moon (earlier and later U.S. examples). Also said of the tide.

1794 Eliz. Drinker *Jrnl.* (1889) 237 The moon fulled this morning about 8 or 10 o'clock. 1809 Fessenden *Pills Poetical* 7 She [*sc.* the moon] fills moreover, when she fulls, Their plainest bills so full of bulls. 1878 B. F. Taylor *Between Gates* 40 It is as if a poor little aster should full like the moon and be a dahlia. 1912 L. J. Vance *Destroying Angel* xix, He should be able to catch the tide just as it was nearing high water. Allowing it to swing him north-west until it fulled, he ought to be a third of the way across by the time it slackened.

Full-blood, *a.* (Earlier U.S. examples, of animals.)

1812 *Niles' Weekly Register* II. 408/1 His full blood merino ram lamb. 1837 Colman *Rep. Agric. Mass.* (1838) 53, I have had some of the full-blood and some of the mixed breed. 1849 *Rep. U.S. Comm. Patents Agric.* (1850) 88 Sheep.. ranging in quality from half to full-blood merino.

B. *sb.* A full-blooded person or animal.

1846 Sage *Scenes Rocky Mts.* (1859) 214 They [*sc.* half-breed children] were more beautiful..than the same number of full-bloods,—either of whites or Indians. 1864 *Rt. Agric. Soc. Maine* 9 Those [sheep] exhibited were mostly Spanish Merinos..most full bloods. 1873 J. H. Beadle *Undevel. West* xix. 358 One may travel for days in the Territory, and never see a full-blood. 1888 *Vermont Agric. Rep.* X. 38, I breed Jerseys; have no full-bloods but high grades.

Full-blooded, *a.* (Earlier U.S. examples.)

1786 *Maryland Jrnl.* 31 Mar. (Th.) A number of full-blooded Colts and Fillies. 1801 *Steele Papers* I. 218 The present Secy. altho' a full blooded Yankee, as we call him in these parts, knows the importance of this place. 1810 *Massachusetts Spy* 25 Apr. 3/1 Forty-five full-blooded Merino Sheep. 1812 *Niles' Weekly Register* II. 408/1 His full blooded merino ram lamb.

Fullerphone (fu·lərfōun). [f. name of Major A. C. *Fuller* + *-phone* in *telephone*.] A telegraphic instrument used in war-signalling.

1920 *Glasgow Herald* 2 Mar. 7 The claim of Major A. C. Fuller in respect of the 'Fullerphone'. 1922 *Encycl. Brit.* XXXII. 491/2 The fullerphone is a telegraph instrument, the essential point of which is the changing at the receiving end of a steady current into an intermittent current of audible frequency, while at the same time the current in the line remains steady. 1928 E. Blunden *Undertones of War* xxvi. 253 The mechanism of the 'fullerphone' or 'power buzzer'.

Full-face. [See Full *a.* 8, quots. 1702, 1876, 1895.]

1. *attrib. phr.* = Full-faced *a.* 2.

1909 *Daily Chron.* 4 Mar. 1/3 The Halcyon was struck a heavy full face blow on the port quarter.

2. *Printing.* A full-faced type.

1892 [see Face *sb.* 22]. 1903 *J. J. Little Bk. Types*, etc. (N.Y.) 409 Bold Face.—A fullface letter similar to the roman, containing both hair lines and heavy strokes.

Full-faced, *a.* Add: **3.** Of type: Bold-faced.

1824 J. Johnson *Typogr.* II. i. 10 Being cast in all the various sizes, both Full-faced and Open.

Full house.

1. An assembly or audience which fills the building in which a performance is given or a meeting is held. Also, a session of a legislative or deliberative body, in which all or most of the members are present in their usual capacity (*Funk's Standard Dict.* 1895).

[Cf. 1662–3 s.v. House *sb.*[1] 4 g, and 1710 s.v. Full *a.* 1.] 1828 *Ohio* 22 Mar. 164/1 A party of itinerant Maromeros (or rope dancers) held their exhibition in the large walled yard .., to about eight hundred people; which was considered as a very 'full house'.

2. *Poker.* A hand containing three of a kind and a pair (next in value below four of a kind). Also *fig.*

1887 *Puck* (U.S.A.) 7 Sept. 21/2 Noah drew to pairs and got a full house [in the ark]. 1908 Mulford *Orphan* xxi. 267 You two make a pair of aces what can beat any full-house ever got together. 1922 — *Tex* iii. 33 Tex wondered what the crowd would say if he should lean over and pull a royal flush out of Williams' ear, or a full-house from the nephew's nose. 1929 Eric Linklater *Poet's Pub* xxv. 274 He had filled the kitty roof-high, bluffed the four-ace-players, scared the full-house-holders.

Full-ri·gger. [See Rigger[1] 4.] A full-rigged vessel. Also *fig.*

1899 Cutcliffe Hyne *Further Adv. Captain Kettle* vii, Image nodded towards the deserted vessel. 'Fine full-rigger, hasn't she been?' 1907 *Daily Chron.* 27 Dec. 3/2 A well-found full-rigger of 600 tons. 1908 *Ibid.* 17 Dec. 3/3 Instead of being the fine fullrigger that it might have been, it is, comparatively, only a topsail schooner.

Full time. The complete tale of hours normally allotted to daily or weekly work or school-attendance. Chiefly *attrib.* (hyphened) and advb.

1898 *Daily News* 13 Dec. 5/7 The half-time system..does irretrievable hurt to the full-time scholars as well. 1912 *Rep. Labour & Social Conditions in Germany* III. vi.–vii. 89 Full-time employment. *Ibid.* 97 Full time is worked all the year round. *Ibid.* 104 All the factories we visited were running full time. 1921 *Act 11 & 12 Geo. V* c. 51. § 77 (2) Any young person..shown..to be under suitable and efficient full-time instruction. a 1926 in Fowler *Dict. Mod. Engl. Usage* 737/2 That motherhood is a full-time job all worth-while mothers will readily admit. 1927 Bowley & Stamp *Nat. Income 1924* 31 The general average increase in weekly full-time wages.

Fulminate, *v.* Add:

10. *Path.* Of a disease: To develop suddenly and severely. (Cf. *Fulminating *ppl. a.* 3.)

1910 *Practitioner* June 744 A gland presumably tuberculous...Sooner or later such a gland almost always fulminates, that is to say, rapidly bursts its capsule and allows the broken-down contents to invade the surrounding lymphoid tissues.

Fulminating, *ppl. a.* Add: **1.** (Earlier U.S. example of *fulminating powder*.)

1804 Fessenden *Terrible Tractoration* 142 Sound Discord's jarring tocsin louder, Than Howard's fulminating powder.

3. *Path.* Of a disease: Coming on suddenly with intense severity; foudroyant; = Fulminant *a.* 2.

1901 Dorland *Med. Dict.* (ed. 2). 1908 K. W. Goadby in *Brit. Med. Jrnl.* 22 Aug. 477/1 Two cases of fulminating pyorrhœa alveolaris specifica. 1910 *Practitioner* Feb. 204 Fulminating cases of infection with virulent organisms.

Fulvo-, used as combining form of Fulvous, meaning 'having a reddish-yellow hue', as *fulvo-aeneous*, *-hyaline*, *-rufous* adjs.

1887 W. Phillips *Brit. Discomycetes* 256 Exterior fulvo-rufous.

Fumagine (fiū·mădʒin, -in). *Bot.* [Fr., f. Fumago.] A sooty mould on plants, caused by the parasitic fungus *Fumago*.

1913 D. Grant tr. *E. Bourcart's Insecticides* etc. 393 (Gloss.) Fumagine is the term applied to the black coating which appears on certain plants infested by plant lice or cochineals (scale insects). This coating is formed by the black mycelium of a fungus which lives solely on the saccharine liquid, the honey-dew, which the insects project on the leaves.

Fumaroid (fiū·măroid), *a.* *Chem.* [f. Fumaric + -oid.] Of the character of or resembling that of fumaric acid.

1895 *Bloxam's Chem.* (ed. 8) 595 Many cases of stereoisomerism are believed to be explicable by formulæ resembling those given above, so that the expressions *maleinoid* and *fumaroid* structure are used.

Fumarolic (fiūmărǫ·lik), *a.* [f. Fumarole + -ic.] Of or belonging to a fumarole, formed by a fumarole.

1903 *Science* 3 Apr. 543 The placing of various ore deposits of many well-known districts in such classes as fumarolic, solfataric, pneumatolytic, etc...seemed to the speaker to be premature.

Fumaryl (fiū·măril). *Chem.* [f. Fumaric + -yl.] The bivalent radical, $C_2H_2(CO)_2$, of fumaric acid.

1864 Watts *Dict. Chem.* II. 747 Chloride of Fumaryl. 1890 *Bloxam's Chem.* (ed. 7) 565 Fumaryl dichloride.

Fumatorium (fiūmătō·riǒm). [mod.L.: see Fumatory *sb.*] An air-tight compartment in which vapour is generated to destroy germs or insects on plants. 1902 Webster Suppl.

Fumble, *v.* Add:

6. Forming combs., as *fumble-fisted*, *-footed* adjs.

1847 Halliwell, *Fumble-fisted*, very awkward in handling things. *Suffolk.* 1877 A. Sewell *Black Beauty* xxxi. 149, I don't know what is the matter with this horse, he goes very fumble-footed. 1926 A. Brent Smith *Studies & Caprices* 150 Music which even the most fumble-fisted can play with pleasure.

Fume, *sb.* **8.** Add:

fume-chamber, **-closet**, **-cupboard**, **-pipe**, ventilation contrivances for getting rid of noxious gases generated in laboratory work.

1905 *Strand Mag.* Apr. 422/1 It is..fitted up with.. 'muffles'..fume chambers, [etc.]. 1913 *Oxf. Univ. Gaz.* 4 June 943/2 [Apparatus of the pharmacological laboratory] fume chamber. 1921 A. E. Munby *Laboratories* 34 Fume hoods on the benches are sometimes provided in the form of a metal or wood tube or boxing with a small hood 9 or 10 ins. square attached to a ventilating trunk in the bench. *Ibid.* 35 Fume cupboards or draught closets..consist of a wood-framed glazed case in which the experiment is performed, with some special means of ventilation. *Ibid.* 44 Fume Pipe for Benches or Lecture Table.

Fume, *v.* Add: **6. b.** quasi-*trans.* with a sentence or words as obj.: To utter irritatedly. Also with *away*: To pass or spend (time) fuming.

1897 W. W. Jacobs *Skipper's Wooing* xii, Glover fumed the afternoon away. 1907 *Munsey's Mag.* Dec. 392/1 'What are you doing—guying us?' fumed Bailey. 1908 *Smart Set* Sept. 76/2 'Good Gad, Titcomb,' fumed Parmalee,..'it's a chamber of horrors.'

Fumed, *ppl. a.* (at end of Fume *v.*). Add: *fumed oak*, oak which has been darkened by exposure to ammonia vapour. (Cf. Fumé *a.* b and Fumigated *ppl. a.*)

1902 *Idler* Nov. 255 Bookcase in Fumed Oak. 1910 *Encycl. Brit.* XI. 301/1 'Fumigated' or 'fumed' oak. 1915 T. Burke *Nights in Town* 110 There is one of those ubiquitous fumed-oak bookcases.

Fumerole, variant of Fumarole.

Fun, *sb.* Add: **2. b.** *Like fun* (earlier U.S. example).

1833 C. A. Davis *Lett. J. Downing* (1834) 24 And began to laugh like fun.

c. Exacting or difficult duty; dangerous and exciting goings-on. *Soldiers' slang.*

1897 *Daily News* 13 Sept. 7/1 From the soldier's point of view, indeed, as expounded by themselves, the engineer officers who are engaged in carrying out some of the Sirdar's plans get much more than their fair share of 'the fun'. 1898 *Westm. Gaz.* 28 Oct. 3/1 It is possible that there may be rare fun by-and-by on the Nile.

3. fun fair, a fair (or that part of a fair) which is devoted to amusements and side-shows; **fun-maker**, a jester.

1925 A. Huxley *Those Barren Leaves*, *F. Chelifer* iii. (1927) 106, I cannot claim to bring every attraction of the *Fun Fair into your place of labour—only the switchback, the water-shoot and the mountain railway. 1904 *Daily Chron.* 12 Nov. 5/6 Mr. James Welch to be Prominent *Fun-maker at Drury Lane. 1906 R. L. Ramsay *Skelton's Magnyf.* (E.E.T.S.) p. xcvii, The two fun-makers of the morality are the brothers Fancy and Folly.

Function, *v.* **1.** Add more recent examples of the meanings derived immediately from F. *fonctionner*.

1897 Grant Allen *Evol. Idea of God* iii. 46 We..know.. consciousness ceases altogether at death, when the brain no longer functions. 1898 J. A. Hobson *Ruskin* 166 It is a condition of the effective functioning of capital, as the latter is of the effective functioning of labour. 1904 *Daily Chron.* 19 Aug. 3/2 The marvellous mechanism and functioning of the universe. 1907 *Ibid.* 31 Aug. 4/7 This joy does not 'function,' as the French so charmingly say, over the present sample of autumnal weather in a month that should strictly be August. 1918 *Times* 18 Apr. 8/3 The agencies of obstruction and party intrigue which will immediately begin to function in every section of the political arena. 1924 Galsworthy *White Monkey* I. viii, There are rules of the game which must be observed, if society is to function at all.

Functional, *a.* Add:

1. b. Relating to the system which specializes and divides the functions of managers, workers, or employés in a business, factory, etc. *U.S.*

1903 F. W. Taylor *Shop Management* § 234 'Functional management' consists in so dividing the work of management that each man from the assistant superintendent down shall have as few functions as possible to perform. *Ibid.* § 240 The four functional bosses who are a part of the planning department. *Ibid.* § 245 Functional Foremanship. 1911 — *Princ. Sci. Management* 65 It is necessary, therefore, to provide teachers (called functional foremen) to see that the workmen both understand and carry out these written instructions. Under functional management, the old-fashioned single foreman is superseded by eight different men, each one of whom has his own special duties. 1930 M. Clark *Home Trade* 198 Foremen are of the type termed 'functional'.

Fu·nctionalism. [f. Functional *a.* + -ism.] Regard for the function and purpose of a building as regulating its shape and style.

1930 *Observer* 29 June 20 Sugar-cube architecture, or to be impressively abstract 'Functionalism'. *Ibid.* 5 Oct. 19 This is what is called the architecture of functionalism. The architectural form arises purely out of the purpose of the building.

Functionalize, *v.* Add: *U.S.* In the theory of business management: To distribute or assign (work) with due regard to the special function of the individual worker. Hence **Fu·nctionaliza·tion**, the system governing such assignment of work.

1923 R. H. Lansburgh *Industr. Management* 55 Functionalization has brought with it basic changes in the structure of industrial organizations. *Ibid.* 60 These functionalized foremen. *Ibid.* 63 Functionalized departments working through one foreman. 1925 W. H. Leffingwell *Office Management* 108 As business grows ever larger and becomes increasingly functionalized and specialized. *Ibid.* 118 The functionalization of all industrial departments.

Fundamentalism (fɒndăme·ntăliz'm). [f. Fundamental *a.* + -ism.] A religious movement which became active among various Protestant bodies in the United States after the war of 1914–18, based on strict adherence to traditional orthodox tenets (e.g. the literal inerrancy of Scripture) held to be fundamental to the Christian faith; opposed to *liberalism* and *modernism*.

1923 *Daily Mail* 24 May 8 Mr. William Jennings Bryan ..has been exerting the full force of his great eloquence in

a campaign on behalf of what is termed 'Fundamentalism'. 1925 K. Lake *Relig. Yesterday & To-morrow* 63 There has been in America some surprise at the sudden rise of Fundamentalism in the last five years. 1927 *Observer* 5 June 5/3 Fundamentalism and the Klux Klan are signs of alarm on behalf of the older ideals.

Hence **Fundame·ntalist**, an adherent of fundamentalism. Also *attrib.* or as *adj.*

1922 *Contemp. Rev.* July 20 The fundamentalist creed. *Ibid.* 21 The Fundamentalists have been fortunate in their non-ministerial leader [*sc.* Mr. Bryan]. 1925 K. Lake *Relig. Yesterday & To-morrow* 60 The most energetic..group, but the least well educated, is the Fundamentalist. *Ibid.* 61 The Fundamentalists have zeal, but it is certainly not according to knowledge. 1926 H. F. Osborn *Evol. & Relig. in Educ.* 12 The fundamentalist movement..sought to re-establish the Biblical literalism of the time of Cromwell, Milton, and the Puritans.

Fundamentum divisionis (fɒndăme·ntǒm diviʒiǒu·nis). *Logic.* Pl. **-menta** (-me·ntă). [L., = foundation or basis of division.] The principle or basis of logical division of a genus into its constituent species.

1849 W. Thomson *Laws of Thought* (ed. 2) 134 The division must be made according to one principle (*fundamentum divisionis*). 1870 W. S. Jevons *Elem. Lessons Logic* xii. 105 The size of the books is in this case the ground, basis, or principle of division, commonly called the *Fundamentum Divisionis*. 1906 H. W. B. Joseph *Introd. Logic* v. 104 The *fundamentum divisionis*, the principle or basis of a division, is that aspect of the genus, in respect of which the species are differentiated.

Fundatrix[2] (fɒndē·triks). *Ent.* Pl. **-atrices.** [Late L. *fundātrix*, fem. of *fundātor* founder.] The 'stem-mother' of Aphidæ, which produces young parthenogenetically.

1907 W. R. Fisher *Forest Protection* (ed. 2) 362 The wingless parthenogenetic ♀, stem-mother or *fundatrix*, hibernates alone on spruce buds. 1923 H. M. Lefroy *Entomol.* 272 These first females are known as fundatrices, or stem-mothers.

Fundi (fɒ·ndi). [Native African name.] A West African grass, *Paspalum exile*, cultivated for its seed, which resembles millet; hungry rice.

1858, 1887 [see Hungry *a.* 4]. 1915 *Nature* XCVI. 350/2 Fundi, *Digitaria exilis*, has been known for some time as a cultivated cereal...It is cooked by being thrown into boiling water or used like porridge.

Fundiform (fɒ·ndifǫ̈rm), *a.* *Anat.* [ad. mod.L. *fundiformis*, f. L. *funda* sling + -form.] Shaped like a sling; in *fundiform ligament* (see quots.).

1889 A. Macalister *Hum. Anat.* Index 761. 1901 Dorland *Med. Dict.* (ed. 2) s.v. *Ligament*, *Fundiform l.*, a portion of the anterior annular ligament of the ankle, forming a loop around the extensor longus digitorum and the peroneus tertius. 1906 A. M. Buchanan *Anat.* I. 481 The fundiform ligament of Retzius.

Funeral, *sb.* Add: **1. c.** *None of your* (*our*, etc.) *funeral*: no affair of yours (ours, etc.); nothing to do with you (us, etc.). *Your* (etc.) *funeral*: your (etc.) affair or concern. orig. *U.S. slang.*

1854 *Oregon Weekly Times* 25 Nov. (Th.) A boy said to an outsider who was making a great ado during some impressive mortuary ceremonies, 'What are you crying about? it's none of your funeral'. 1865–6 *Trans. Ill. Agric. Soc.* VI. 167 As this was 'none of our funeral', of course the party of the other part was provided with all the regalia of the occasion. 1895 *Century Mag.* Sept. 674/1 We don't know for certain it was them, and it's none of our funeral, anyhow. 1877 *Hartford Times* 17 Oct. (Farmer), Oh, that isn't my funeral, I want you to understand. 1908 S. E. White *Riverman* vii. 60 However, it's your funeral. Come on, if you want to. 1917 S. Graham *Priest of the Ideal* i, But although we go into black it is not *our* funeral. 1921 A. S. M. Hutchinson *If Winter Comes* IV. i. 254 However his wife was his funeral, not mine, and I said nothing. 1930 Sayers & Eustace *Documents in the Case* 72 But how he can ever imagine that it will sell...But that's his funeral.

3. (Delete †*Obs.*) Now *U.S.* Also, a funeral service.

1871 Schele de Vere *Americanisms* (1872) 238 This led to the custom, still prevailing in densely-settled districts, and especially among the freedmen of the South, to have *funerals*, i.e. special funeral sermons preached some time after the death of the person. 1905 *N. Y. Even. Post* 9 Mar. 8 An official funeral will be held in the Senate chamber to-morrow at two o'clock, and the body will be taken to Tennessee to-morrow evening. 1922 Marg. B. Houston *Witch-man* xi. 131 The cemetery to which Wilda had fared as much as twice for many of the graves within it, first when the sleeper was laid there and later—sometimes there was the lapse of a year—when his funeral was preached.

Fungation (fɒŋgē·ʃən). *Path.* [f. as Fungate *v.*: see -ation.] The formation of a fungous growth.

1908 *Practitioner* Sept. 395 These palliative operations are performed to prolong life, to prevent fungation, to give relief to pain. 1910 *Ibid.* June 764 Owing to the fungation, this was the most unfavourable of the cases.

Fungicidal (fɒndʒisəi·dăl), *a.* [f. *fungi-*, Fungus + -cide 1 + -al.] Of the nature of or characteristic of a fungicide; fungus-destroying.

1930 *Nature* 13 Dec. 921 The fungicidal power of wood preservatives.

Fungoid, *a.* and *sb.* **B.** *sb.* Add: **b.** *Path.* A fungoid growth. (See A. *adj.* b, and Fungus 2.)

1899 *Westm. Gaz.* 12 Apr. 9/2 He says a fungoid was certainly found in Dr. Bra's cultivations.

Fungoidal (fɒŋgoi·dăl), *a.* [f. Fungoid + -al: cf. -oidal.] = Fungoid A.

1907 W. R. Fisher *Forest Protection* (ed. 2) 427 External injuries of any kind to trees admit the spores of fungi to the inner tissues of the injured tree and thus favour fungoidal attacks.

Fungus, *sb.* **5.** Add: *fungus-eater*, *-flora*, *-hunt*, *-hunter*, *-ring*; *fungus-eating*, *-plagued* adjs.; **fungus-garden** (see quot.); **fungus-gnat**, **-midge** *Ent.*, a fly of the dipterous family *Mycetophilidæ*.

1899 G. H. Carpenter *Insects* 304 *Fungus-Eaters...A considerable number of small Beetles together with the grubs of many Flies and Midges find their sustenance in fungi. *Ibid.* Index 397/1 *Fungus-eating insects. 1892 G. Massee (*title*) British *Fungus-Flora. 1924 J. A. Thomson *Science Old & New* xvi. 88 The *fungus-gardens of the termites are seen at their best in Ceylon, and the characteristic feature is the construction of a maze of chewed wood with labyrinthine passages, on the walls of which the fungi grow. 1884 *Riverside Nat. Hist.* (1888) II. 407 The family *Mycetophilidæ*, commonly called *Fungus Gnats. 1899 Burnand in *Pall Mall Mag.* XVIII. 536 We espied the Professor..evidently enjoying a *fungus-hunt. 1886 P. Robinson *Teetotum Trees* 134 A common object of the country in 'the fall of the year'..is the fungus. And scarcely less familiar, in wooded districts especially, the *fungus-hunter. 1899 G. H. Carpenter *Insects* 256 The *Mycetophilidæ* or *Fungus-midges. 1918 W. Beebe *Jungle Peace* (1919) viii. 178 Light-starved and *fungus-plagued, the shrub and saplings are stunted and weak. 1907 Woodruffe-Peacock *Pasture & Meadow Anal.* 5 The flora of *fungus-rings..should always be most carefully noted the season through.

Funicle. Add: **c.** *Ent.* = Funiculus 4.

1925 A. D. Imms *Entomol.* 14 In some insects, particularly among Hymenoptera, the flagellum is divisible into the ring-joints, the funicle, and the club...The funicle comprises those joints which intervene between the ring-joints and the club, ..or between the latter and the pedicel in cases when the ring-joints are not differentiated.

Funiculaire (fünikülę̈r). [Fr.: see Funicular.] A funicular railway.

1907 *Westm. Gaz.* 9 Oct. 2/1 We never go up anything except by funiculaire. 1927 *Observer* 18 Dec. 9/4 Every attention is paid to the comfort of travellers, even in the funiculaires.

Funicular, *a.* Add: **B.** *sb.* **a.** A funicular polygon (Cent. Dict. 1889). **b.** A funicular railway (Webster 1911).

1911 Lamb in *Encycl. Brit.* XVII. 957/2 The vertices of the funicular will lie on a parabola whose axis is vertical. 1926 H. Bennett tr. *G. Leroux's Adv. Coquette* vi, A number of travellers set down by the funicular gazed from a respectful distance at the actress's enthusiasm.

Funicularize (fiuni·kiŭlărəiz), *v.* [See -ize.] *trans.* To provide with a funicular railway.

1927 R. Capell in *Heritage of Music* 216 The Alps..are now mostly funicularised.

Funiculus. Add: **4. b.** *Ent.* (See quots.)

1826 Kirby & Sp. *Entomol.* xxxiii. III. 389 The Funiculus, a small cartilaginous cord, passing through a minute orifice of the *Postfrænum*, just above the point where the footstalk is fixed, to an opposite hole above it. 1895 D. Sharp *Insects* I. 492 The petiole, besides articulating..with the propodeum by means of certain prominences and notches, is also connected therewith by means of a slender ligament placed on its dorsal aspect and called the funiculus.

Funk, *sb.*[5] In Cuba: Inferior and waste tobacco leaves.

1901 *Chambers's Jrnl.* May 302/1 The remainder of the crops—in the shape of inferior leaves, broken ones, and pieces of vein or rib..—is known as 'funk'..or *desperdicios*, and is serviceable for little else than snuff, bad cigars, and native cigarettes.

Funk, *v.*[2] Add: **1.** Also const. *at*.

1841 *Punch* 13 Nov. 213/2 Funking at the rejection of a clever man,..determining to take prussic acid in the event of being refused..., the student finds his first ordeal approach. 1857 Hood *Pen & Pencil Pictures* 144, I have seen him out with the governor's hounds: he funked at the first hedge. 1859 *Punch* 23 July 34/2 Louis Napoleon, who had gone to war on a pledge that the Austrians should be driven out of Italy, had 'funked' at the Quadrilateral. 1863 Reade *Hard Cash* xxv, I began to funk again at his knowing that;..I was flustered, ye see.

5. funksticks, also *transf.* a coward.

1916 *National Rev.* No. 382. 527 The rising predicted by Bernhardi and feared by all funksticks.

Fu·nk-hole. *Mil. slang.* [f. Funk *sb.*[3]] A dug-out in the trenches. Hence, any place of safety into which one can retreat; employment which is used as a pretext for evading military service.

1900 *Daily News* 20 Nov. 3/2 The Funk Holes which the besieged residents had mined in the river bank. 1914 *Daily Mail* 4 Dec. 8/3, I am sitting in my 'funk hole' lined with straw. 1920 *Blackw. Mag.* May 608/1 Grain-pits that afford excellent ready-made funk-holes. 1928 *Sunday Dispatch* 30 Sept. 2/2 Jim might have stayed! A few hours away from the office wouldn't matter. Lovely funk-holes, offices!

So **Fu·nk-pit.**

1914 *Times* 21 Nov. 6/1 We are very sheltered at the bottom of our funk-pit.

Funkia (fɒ·ŋkiă). [mod.L.; named after the German botanist H. C. *Funck* (1771–1839).] A plant of the genus of liliaceous plants from Japan so named, having racemes of white or pale lilac, drooping, bell-shaped flowers; a plantain-lily.

1841 Loudon *Encycl. Plants* Suppl. 1178. 1883 W. Robinson *Engl. Flower Garden* 132/2 The bold and striking foliage of some of the strongest plain-leaved section of Funkias renders them very effective as edging plants for large beds. 1927 E. H. M. Cox *Evol. Garden* v. 78 Funkias, or Plantain Lilies, are among the best foliage plants of the herbaceous border.

Funniosity (fɒniǫ·sĭti). *jocular.* [f. Funny *a.* + -osity.] Comicality, jocularity; also, something comical, a comicality.

1900 *Westm. Gaz.* 5 July 3/2 There is no end to the freaks and funniosities of the cricket field. 1921 S. Graham *Childr. of Slaves* xiv. 271 The mind stocked with music-hall funniosity and pseudo-cynicism. 1921 — *Europe—Whither Bound?* x. 138 Shylock's cleverness and intellectual assurance was obscured by funniosities.

Funny, *a.* Add: **1. b.** *Funny business*, action (on the part of a clown or actor) intended to excite laughter; hence, jesting, nonsense; also *slang*, fooling or monkeying about; similarly *funny stuff*, *funny dope*. *Funny column*, a newspaper column containing humorous matter or illustrations. orig. *U.S.*

1888 Nye *Baled Hay* 38 There was no funny business in his nature. 1890 *Century Mag.* Dec. 303 She even ventured on the funny column, for it was not Sunday. 1891 E. S. Ellis *Check No. 2134* xiv. 93, I hope we'll get through without any more funny business. 1915 Frost & Dilnot *Crime Club* x, The blue barrel of a revolver showed in the electric light. 'No funny business!' he warned them. 'You guys can't play it on me.' *Ibid.* xii, Especially if you try to put any of the funny dope over on me. 1930 *London Mercury* Feb. 324 He'll be out and about in a fortnight. Till then we will visit him together—and no funny stuff!

c. *sb.* A comic illustration, etc. *U.S.*

1920 C. Sandburg *Smoke & Steel* 33 About the funnies in the papers. 1922 — *Slabs of Sunburnt West* 35 Turning among headlines, date lines, funnies, ads.

Fur, *sb.*[1] Add: **2. b.** *To make the fur fly* (earlier U.S. example).

1834 Crockett *Narr. Life* ii. 11, I knew very well that I was in a devil of a hobble, for my father had been taking a few horns, and was in a good condition to make the fur fly.

9. *fur company*; *fur-trade*, *-trader* (earlier U.S. examples); *fur-farming*, *-hunting*, *-trading*; *fur-sewer*; *fur-bordered*, *-bound*, *-muffled*, *-topped*, *-trimmed*, *-wrapped* adjs.

1903 *Westm. Gaz.* 8 Oct. 4/2 The *fur-bordered, serrated lace collar. 1898 *Ibid.* 18 Nov. 3/2 A *fur-bound coat. 1880 *Scribner's Monthly* May 125/1 Trappers and hunters for the *fur companies would have thought themselves in paradise could they have seen our stores in '74. 1914 J. W. Jones (*title*) *Fur-Farming in Canada. 1923 J. C. Sachs *Furs & Fur Trade* 92 Fur farming..is one of the oldest of occupations. 1920 W. T. Grenfell *Labrador Dr.* xiii. 238 The only trouble with..*fur-hunting is that its very nature limits its supply. 1905 *Westm. Gaz.* 16 Jan. 2/1 Sleighs with *fur-muffled occupants. 1896 Mrs. H. Ward *Sir G. Tressady* xi. 227 Tailoresses and shirtmakers and *fur-sewers. 1928 *Daily Express* 11 Oct. 5/5 Russian boot ..*fur-topped, fleece-lined. 1791 *Laws of Massachusetts* c. 3 (1895) 262 An act for the preservation and encouragement of the *furr trade within the commonwealth. 1807 P. Gass *Jrnl.* 65 This and Hudson's Bay Company..carry on almost the whole of the fur trade in that extensive country. 1831 Peck *Guide Emigrants* 274 They intended to engross the whole fur trade of the west. 1837 *Southern Lit. Messenger* III. 63 The usual route of the *fur-trader. 1840 *Knickerbocker Mag.* XVI. 213 Couriers de Bois, or fur-traders, who had been driven out of their track. 1905 *Daily Chron.* 7 Nov. 4/5 The famous Hudson's Bay Company, which, once merely a *fur-trading body with a vast territory, has now grown into a general dealer. 1908 *Westm. Gaz.* 29 June 4/1 The fur-trading vessels of the Hudson Bay Company. 1898 *Ibid.* 4 Nov. 3/1 The Common Councillors..in their *fur-trimmed robes. 1895 Kipling *2nd Jungle Bk.* 151 He and his master ..hunted together,..*fur-wrapped boy and savage,..yellow brute.

10. fur-bearer, an animal which yields fur, any member of the *Mustelidæ*; **fur-cloth**, **-fever**, **-moth** (see quots.).

1906 E. Ingersoll *Life of Mammals* 162 The *Fur Bearers ..the martens, weasels, badgers, ratels, skunks, otters, and their kin of the family Mustelidæ. 1926 *Spectator* 18 Sept. 409/1 This League is recommending all devices which take fur-bearers alive and unharmed, or kill them instantly. 1928 *Daily Express* 23 June 5/1 *Fur-cloth is specially made to imitate fur, and can be used for all furry animals. 1905 *Pearson's Mag.* July 102/2 Bronchial catarrh, and '*fur fever'..are both caused by inhaling this 'fluff' and dust. 1862 T. W. Harris *Insects injur. Veget.* (ed. 3) 493 Among them [*sc.* destructive moths] may be mentioned..the '*fur-moth (*Tinea pellionella*).

Furane (fiū·rēin). *Chem.* Also **-an.** Abbreviation of *Furfurane.

1906 Muir & Morley *Watts' Dict. Chem.* II. 588/2 Furfurane C_4H_4O, Furane. 1911 Perkin *Org. Chem.* II. 632 Furan, C_4H_4O, is obtained by heating the barium salt of furancarboxylic acid (pyromucic acid) with soda lime.

Furca. Add: **2.** *Ent.* An apodeme or process in the thorax of many insects.

1895 D. Sharp *Insects* I. 103 Entothorax (apophysis or furca). 1910 C. G. Hewitt *House Fly* 9 The theca rests on a triradiate chitinous sclerite—the furca, which consists of a median, slightly convex rod. 1925 A. D. Imms *Entomol.* 47 The endosternites (apophyses of some writers) are commonly represented by the *furcæ*; each furca is a median apodeme, unpaired at its base, with two free distal arms. *Ibid.* 598 The *theca*..articulates distally with a short rod or *furca*.

Furcal (fɒ·ɹkăl), *a.* *Nat. Hist.* [f. L. *furca* fork + -al.] Forked, furcate; esp. *Ent.*, of or pertaining to the furca.

1851 *Trans. Linn. Soc.* XX. 434 Some traces of the entrances into these furcal bones exist in the sternal plates of *Perla*. 1895 D. Sharp *Insects* I. 399 [In Perlidæ] The metasternum..has on each side a furcal slit; similar orifices exist on the other sterna...Newport..says that they

Supplement, p. 3873; Corrigenda, p. 4092; Spurious words, p. 4093; Books quoted, p. 4094

are blind invaginations of the integument; he calls them the sternal or furcal orifices.

Furciferine (fɒɹsi·fĕrəin), *a. Zool.* [f. L. *furcifer* (see Furciferous) + -ine.[1]] Belonging to a group of S. American deer (subgenus *Furcifer*) with forked antlers.

1891 Flower & Lydekker *Mamm.* 329 The Furciferine group includes *Cervus chilensis*.

Furcræa (fɒɹkrī·ă). Also **Four-**, **-crœa**, **-croya**. [mod.L.; named after the French chemist Antoine François de *Fourcroy* (1755–1809).] A plant of the amaryllidaceous genus so named of Mexican desert plants.

1829 Loudon *Encycl. Plants* 246. 1900 L. H. Bailey *Cycl. Amer. Hort.* s.v., As a rule, Furcræas bear fruit not more than once, and then die without producing suckers. 1901 *Westm. Gaz.* 3 July 7/1 Poles of the furcroea aloe for the construction of recreation-rooms and school houses.

Furcula. Add: **2.** *Embryol.* A process from which the epiglottis is developed (see quots.).

1893 A. M. Marshall *Vert. Embryol.* 562 On the fifteenth day..a swelling is present on the floor of the pharynx, opposite the first, second, and third branchial arches; and along the middle of this swelling, or furcula, there runs a longitudinal groove. 1902 A. Keith *Human Embryol.* 249 The furcula..bounds the pulmonary groove; in its anterior part..is developed the epiglottis.

3. *Ent.* A forked appendage at the end of the abdomen in springtails.

1925 A. D. Imms *Entomol.* 216 The majority of Collembola carry a pair of partially fused appendages in relation with the 4th abdominal segment. They constitute the *furcula*, or springing-organ, which enables the insect to take sudden leaps into the air.

Furfura·ceo-, used as combining form of Furfuraceous, meaning 'furfuraceous and ..'.

1887 W. Phillips *Brit. Discomycetes* 253 Cups..furfuraceo-villose, fawn-coloured.

Furfural (fū·ɹfiŭræl). *Chem.* [f. L. *furfur* bran + *al* of *aldehyde*.] = Furfurol. Also called **Furfura·ldehyde**.

1879 *Jrnl. Chem. Soc.* XXXVI. 137 A preparation of glacial acetic acid (99–100 p.c.) which had been observed by the author to give a deep red coloration with aniline.., he finds to contain furfuraldehyde. 1895 *Bloxam's Chem.* (ed. 8) 568 Pyromucic aldehyde, or furfural,..is the aldehyde of furfurane. 1901 *Daily Chron.* 11 May 2/2 In the case of whisky the chief cause of mischief is furfural, from which old matured whisky is free.

Furfurane (fū·ɹfiŭrēⁱn). *Chem.* [ad. G. *furfuran*, f. L. *furfur* bran: see -ane.] A colourless liquid, C_4H_4O, obtained by the distillation of barium pyromucate with soda-lime; = *Furan.

[1877 *Jrnl. Chem. Soc.* II. 745 The author [*sc.* Adolf Baeyer] proposes for the group C_4H_4O (Limpricht's *Tetraphenol*) the name 'furfuran'.] 1895 *Bloxam's Chem.* (ed. 8) 744 Furfurane, C_4H_4O, is found in the first runnings of the distillation of wood-tar.

Furfuryl (fū·ɹfiŭril, -əil). *Chem.* [f. L. *furfur* bran + -yl.] The univalent radical C_4H_3O, of which furfurane is the hydride.

1885 *Jrnl. Chem. Soc.* XLVIII. II. 1144 Reciprocal Transformation of the Pyrroline, Furfuryl, and Thiophene Groupings. 1890 *Bloxam's Chem.* (ed. 7) 513 Furfuryl alcohol.

Furnace, *sb.* **5.** Add: **furnace lines**, spectrum lines of vapour heated to the highest temperature of a furnace. So *furnace spectrum*.

1922 A. S. Eddington in *Encycl. Brit.* XXX. 298/2 The 'furnace lines' of strontium 4607 and calcium 4455. 1925 F. J. M. Stratton *Astronom. Physics* 32 Furnace, Arc, and Spark Spectra.

Furnish, *sb.* Add: **d.** The materials from which paper is manufactured.

1920 Cross & Bevan *Paper-Making* 374 The characters of these sorted rags are taken into account in the composition of the paper-maker's furnish. 1929 Parley in *Penrose's Ann.* XXXI. 99 A good proportion of cotton and/or linen in the furnish of a paper, as well as high chemical purity, are essential for durability.

Furnish, *v.* **10. a. Furnish forth.** Add more recent examples of echoes of Shaks.

1850 Smedley *F. Fairlegh* iv, Clayton had..slain a sufficient number of victims to furnish forth pies for the supply of the whole mess. 1860 Geo. Eliot *Bro. Jacob* ii, What housewife..would not think shame to furnish forth her table with articles that were not home-cooked? 1903 Langbridge *Flame & Flood* xvi, So she would..order..the best that the 'cuiseen'..could furnish forth.

Furnisher. Add: **2.** In textile printing, a revolving brush that supplies the colour.

1899 F. H. Thorp *Industr. Chem.* 495 The color is fed to the print roll from the color box by a revolving cylindrical brush called the 'furnisher', which dips into the color paste.

Furnishing, *vbl. sb.* **1.** *attrib.* (earlier U.S. examples).

1833 *Knickerbocker Mag.* I. 157 Gardiner's magnificent furnishing establishment already totters on its base. 1848 E. Bryant *What I saw in California* i. 14 These I obtained at reasonable rates, of Messrs. Wilson & Clarke, who keep a general furnishing store for these expeditions.

Furniture. Add:

6. *spec.* The mountings of a rifle.

1852 *Household Words* 13 Mar. 582/1 Such close fittings as those of the furniture of guns to the stocks. 1892 Greener *Breech-loader* 14 The furniture of the stock consists of the heel-plate, trigger-guard, &c.

7. b. Applied in the book trade to well-bound volumes and 'standard' sets which serve to fill and adorn the shelves of a private library. (Cf. *furniture-picture* in 10 in Dict.)

1928 *Periodical* No. 143. 25 Its [*sc.* the N.E.D.'s] claims as 'furniture' are not despicable. 1928 *Times Lit. Suppl.* 5 Apr. 260/3 The big 'furniture' books in folio and quarto which long formed the most conspicuous feature of private libraries. 1928 *Publishers' Circular* 6 Oct. 461 Much of it just furniture, and yet there were many very nice items.

10. *furniture-polish* (examples), *-sale*.

1833 J. Neal *Down-Easters* I. 15 Plastering the foot all over with his *furniture polish and wrapping it up. 1870 'Fanny Fern' *Ginger-snaps* 205 That 'furniture-polish man', who looked so much like a clergyman that Betty mistook him for one. 1891 Kipling *Light that Failed* iv. 59 If they want furniture-polish, let them have furniture-polish, so long as they pay for it. 1842 *Knickerbocker Mag.* XX. 468 Of all the different kinds of auctions, the most amusing are *furniture sales.

Hence **Fu·rnitureless** *a.*, having no furniture.

1894 H. Nisbet *Bush Girl's Rom.* 23 That first rough shanty, as yet doorless and windowless as well as furnitureless. 1910 *Daily Chron.* 12 Mar. 7/5 The furnitureless condition of Japanese houses. 1927 *Glasgow Herald* 8 Nov. 11 Marlborough House is still furnitureless, and is a place of ladders and dust-sheets.

Furor. Add: **4.** Sometimes with L. adj. added to define the nature of the 'frenzy', as *furor poeticus*, *furor biographicus*.

1928 *Daily Tel.* 11 Sept. 12/1 Once upon a time Macaulay complained of the furor biographicus or lues Boswelliana which makes biographies an orgy of praise.

Furphy (fū·ɹfi). *Austral. soldiers' slang.* [See quot.] A canard or absurd story.

1916 *Anzac Bk.* 56/1 Furphy was the name of the contractor which was written large upon the rubbish carts that he supplied to the Melbourne camps. The name was transferred to a certain class of news item, which flourished greatly upon all the beaches. 1916 C. J. Dennis *Ginger Mick* 122 Soljerin's me game. That's no furphy.

Furriered (fɒ·riəɹd), *pa. pple.* [-ed [1].] Dressed by a furrier.

1923 *Daily Mail* 2 July 4 This regal looking garment.. Lined and Furriered beautifully. 1927 *Observer* 20 Nov. 20 French fur productions. Furriered from hundreds of perfect pelts. 1929 *Daily News* 5 Oct. 1, 8 Fitch Skins.. furriered in Paris.

Furriery (fɒ·riəri). [f. Furrier + -y [3].]

†1. *pl.* Furs collectively. *Obs.*

1784 King in King & Cook *Voy.* III. vi. vi. 340 No labour can ever be turned to so good account as what is employed upon their furrieries. The animals, therefore, which supply these, come next to be considered. 1799 Tooke *View Russian Empire* III. 51 For smaller furrieries and edgings, the skins of the Marten, the Squirrel, the Ermine, the Rabbit and the Marmotte are the choicest. [1828–32 Webster, *Furriery*, furs in general. *Tooke*.]

2. The art of dressing and making up furs; furrier's work; the trade or business of a furrier.

1920 C. J. Rosenberg *Furs & Furriery* Pref. p. v, There was no work obtainable dealing with the practical side of Furriery. 1929 *Daily News* 5 Oct. 1 A stole which cannot fail to please—the quality and furriery are *sans reproche*. *Ibid.*, The finest points of furriery are embodied in this charming Coat.

Furring, *vbl. sb.* Add:

4. The business of collecting furs, fur-trading.

1849 *Jrnl. Rp. Newfoundland's Voy.* 67 Sixty miles within that bay the Hudson's Bay Company have a furring establishment. *Ibid.*, The settled inhabitants..are supported by the salmon fishery, by furring, and by killing seals.

Furrow, *sb.* **2.** Delete † *Obs.* and add def. and examples: *spec.* (more particularly Water-furrow), the depression lying between two ridges of cultivated land and serving for drainage.

c 1470 [see 1 β]. 1565 Cooper *Thesaurus*, *Porca in agro*, a ridge, or a lande lyinge betweene two furroes wheron the corne groweth. 1573 Tusser *Husb.* (1878) 39 Seed sowen, draw a forrough, the water to draine. [*marg.* Water furrough.] 1733 Tull *Horse-hoeing Husb.* (1733) 251 To lay such wet land up into Ridges, that the Water may run off into the Furrows. 1844 Stephens *Bk. Farm* I. 465 Heavy land is formed into narrow ridges, to allow the rain to flow quickly into the open furrows. 1895 R. H. Wallace *Agriculture* 206 Drainage systems may be put into three classes: (1) Deep, thorough, parallel, furrow, leading, closed, covered, or minor drainage [etc.]. *Ibid.* 217 The water is run on at the ridges, and surplus taken away by the furrows. 1921 K. D. Doyle *Agric. & Irrigation* 25 In porous soils the furrows must be short.

Furrowed, *ppl. a.* Add: in *Masonry* (see quots.).

1904 C. F. Mitchell *Brickwork & Masonry* 128 *Furrowed Work*..This labour, used to accentuate quoins, consists in sinking a draught about the four sides of the face of a stone, leaving the central portion projecting about ⅜ inch, in which a number of vertical grooves about ⅜ inch wide are sunk. 1929 E. G. Warland *Mod. Pract. Masonry* 24 *Furrowed Surfaces*.—Small flutings, from ½ to ⅜ in. wide, are worked vertically or horizontally across the surface.

Fursa (fūᵊ·ɹsa). [Marathi *phursā*.] A small very poisonous viper of arid sandy regions, *Echis carinata*. Known also as *krait* and *kuppur*.

1885 G. C. Whitworth *Anglo-Ind. Dict.*

Furunculosis (fiurɒŋkiŭlōᵘ·sis). *Path.* [mod.L., f. L. *furunculus* Furuncle: see -osis.] The diseased condition that accompanies the appearance of a crop of boils.

1889 *Buck's Handbk. Med. Sci.* VII. 692/1 Furunculosis [of the vulva] occurs as the result of poisoning of the parts by an acrid vaginal discharge. 1908 *Practitioner* June 858 Eczema, with complicating furunculosis. 1924 *Times Trade & Engin. Suppl.* 29 Nov. 246/2 Its potency is such that six doses will clear up most cases of furunculosis or acne.

Fusain. Add:

2. (fiū·zēⁱn). One of the four distinctive bands which together form bituminous coal. Hence **Fu·sainiza·tion**, **Fu·sainized** *pa. pple.* (see quots.).

1883 *Jrnl. Chem. Soc.* XLIV. 941 Fusain is a variety of coal, resembling wood-charcoal in appearance. Some stalks, the interior of which is composed of fusain, are covered with a bark which has been converted into coal. 1918 Stopes & Wheeler *Constit. Coal* 22/2 The two terms 'carbonised wood' and 'mother of coal'..are both open to grave objections...We therefore propose to adopt the Anglicised form of the French word, *fusain*, as is done by Stevenson (1911–13). We suggest also..for the process of forming fusain, *fusainization*, and *fusainized* as the corresponding adjective. 1923 A. R. Warnes *Coal Tar Distill.* (ed. 3) 17 Fusain. The equivalent of 'mother-of-coal', 'mineral charcoal', etc. of various authors. *Ibid.* 23 'Mother-of-coal', 'carbonised wood', or fusain, as it is now called, is the dull charcoal-like substance which is found in practically all coal.

Fuscous, *a.* Add: *Path.* (see quot.).

1924 R. Muir *Pathol.* 45 In the nerve cells of the cortex of the brain..a considerable amount of pigment is met with in senile insanity and allied conditions, this being known as fuscous degeneration.

Fuse, *sb.*[2] **2.** Add: **fuse-plug**, the plug that holds the fuse of a shell.

1928 *Manchester Guardian Weekly* 31 Aug. 178/3 Fuse-plug levees—that is, levees which will blow up automatically when the water reaches the dangerous height.

Fuse, *sb.*[5] *Electr.* [f. Fuse *v.*[2]] In full *safety fuse*: A strip or wire of easily fusible metal inserted in an electric circuit, which melts (or 'blows') and thus interrupts the circuit when the current increases beyond a certain safe strength.

1884 R. Hammond *Electric Light in our Homes* v. 56 Conductor Joined with Fuse. *Ibid.* 58 Showing Safety Fuses in Circuit. 1890 J. W. Urquhart *Electr. Light Fitting* 160 The main object, then, of a safety fuse or cut-out..is to prevent accidental overheating. *Ibid.* 165 [see *b].

b. fuse-block, -board, -box, -carrier, -holder, -plate, -plug, various contrivances for holding a fuse or a number of fuses; **fuse-wire**, wire used to make fuses.

1885 *J. Dredge's Electr. Illum.* II. 325 A fuse box containing six fuses. 1890 J. W. Urquhart *Electr. Light Fitting* 162 The fuse plate may easily be removed and replaced by others. *Ibid.* 165 In such cases it is considered safer to assemble all the fuses upon a fuse board. 1892 F. C. Allsop *Electric-Light Fitting* 57 The reason why lead or lead-tin alloy is preferred for the fuse-wire of a cut-out. 1893 Maycock *Electric Lighting* III. xv. § 220. 384 A S.P. fuse block. *Ibid.* 386 The fuse wire is fitted in what is called a fuse plug. 1894 Salomons *Electr. Lt. Install.* (ed. 7) II. 219 Another improvement..is that of placing under the fuse binding-screw a washer carrying a steady pin, which passes loose into the fuse block. *Ibid.* III. 162 It is almost impossible to remove the fuse-box cover or replace the fuse without removing this box completely. 1899 W. P. Maycock *Electr. Wiring*, etc. 185 The removable fuse-carrier is of porcelain. *Ibid.* 245 The fuse-holders are of porcelain. 1899 H. M. Leaf *Internal Wiring* 85 A guide for determining..the sizes of fuse wires that may be employed for cut-outs. 1914 S. C. Batstone *Electric-Light Fitting* 104 Porcelain Tubular Fuse Carrier.

Fuse, *v.*[2] Add:

2. c. Of an electric light: To be extinguished owing to the melting of a fuse. *colloq.*

1930 *Daily Express* 6 Nov. 2/2 Two minutes before he arrived..the lights in the building fused.

Fuselage (fiū·zelāʒ, -ĕdʒ). *Aeronautics.* [Fr., f. *fuseler* to shape like a spindle, f. *fuseau* spindle: see Fusil [1] and -age.] The body or framework of an aeroplane, so called from its spindle-like shape. It usually contains the engine, crew, tanks, etc.

1909 C. C. Turner *Aerial Navig.* (1910) 318 [Some French Aeronautical Terms]. *Fuselage*.—Fusiform frame. 1909 *Flight* 19 June 366/2 The aeroplane itself was considerably damaged, the *fuselage* which carries the elevating-plane in front..being completely broken. 1913 A. E. Berriman *Aviation* 249 Another French word at present in common use is *fuselage*, meaning the girder-like backbone employed in modern aeroplane design. This member also forms the body of the machine. 1913 *Times* 14 Apr. 4/1 The number of machines which have broken their fuselage—to say nothing of their wings.

Fusi-, combining form of L. *fusus* spindle, used with the meaning 'spindle-shaped'. Also less correctly **fuso-**.

1901 Dorland *Med. Dict* (ed. 2), *Fusocellular*, having spindle-shaped cells. 1921 Beattie & Dickson *Gen. Pathol.* 367 Fusi-spirochætal infections.

Fusion. Add: **3. c.** *Psychol.* A blending together of separate sensations into a new complex experience or qualitative perception.

1892 W. James *Text-bk. Psychol.* 57 The so-called Fusion of Sensations in Hearing. 1903 G. F. Stout *Groundwork Psychol.* 45 They [*sc.* sensations] may combine..like the bitterness, sweetness, and aroma of a cup of coffee...The first of these modes of union is called *fusion* or blending... Fusion is characterised by the absence of any definite order among the constituents of the sensation complex. 1911 E. B. Titchener *Text-bk. Psychol.* II. 351 The classical instance of the qualitative perception is the tonal fusion.

Fuss, *sb.*[2] Add: **4. fuss-box, -pot**, jocular terms for one who fusses, a fusser.

1915 W. J. Locke *Jaffery* x, You thought I was going off my chump, you dear old *fuss-box. But you were wrong. 1922 *Blackw. Mag.* Dec. 708/1 'What a fussbox you are,

Ronnie,' she laughed. 1921 G. O'Donovan *Vocations* i. 16 You *are* a *fuss-pot. First you won't and then you will.

Fusticate, *v.* (at end of Fusty *a.*). Add: Also *intr.* to stay in a close stuffy atmosphere.

1923 Silberrad *Lett. Jean Armiter* iv. 102 'Are you going to stop—' (I feel sure he meant 'fusticating', though he was too polite to say it) 'in here all afternoon?' he asked.

Fusula (fiū·ziŭlă). *Ent.* Pl. **-æ**. [mod.L., incorrectly f. L. *fusus* spindle.] (See quot.)

1909 A. E. Shipley *Arachnida* in *Cambr. Nat. Hist.* IV. 325 These spinnerets..are movable turrets on which are mounted the 'fusulae' or projections where the tubes from the spinning glands open. *Ibid.* 326 In some spiders the fusulae are all much alike, but usually a few very much larger than the rest are noticeable under the microscope, and these are often alluded to as 'spigots'.

Fusuma (fū·suma). [Jap.] A sliding screen, covered with paper, used to separate room from room in a Japanese house.

1886 E. S. Morse *Japanese Homes* 126 The *fusuma* forming the movable partitions between the rooms are covered on both sides with thick paper. 1890 B. H. Chamberlain *Things Japanese* 24 The rooms are divided from each other by opaque paper screens, called *fusuma* or *karakami*, which run in grooves at the top and bottom. 1905 *Westm. Gaz.* 23 Sept. 10/2 Sliding the fusuma, the screen of opaque paper separating the living- from the sleeping-room, Sada entered the chamber.

Fut[2] (fɒt), *int.* [Variant of Phut.]

1. Imitative representation of the noise of a bullet landing, a shell bursting, etc. See Phut.

1898 J. M. Falkner *Moonfleet* ix. 125 There came a flash of fire..and a fut, fut, fut, of bullets in the turf.

2. *To go fut*: to collapse, come to grief; to fail to work or function. *colloq.*

1908 A. S. M. Hutchinson *Once Aboard the Lugger* III. iii. 150 The plans..have all gone fut. 1917 W. J. Locke *Red Planet* xiii, There's a limit to the power of bearing strain. As soon as you feel you're likely to go *fut*, throw it all up and come and see me. *Ibid.* xvi, My head goes *fut* now and then. 1919 Gertrude Page *Veldt Trail* i, The carburetter went *fut* yesterday. 1923 *Daily Mail* 15 May 13 My literary ambitions have gone fut. 1928 L. Robinson *Give a Dog—* II. Plays 416 Did the 'phone really go fut?

Hence **Fut** *v. intr.*, of a bullet, to land with a dull abrupt sound.

1901 *Westm. Gaz.* 3 Jan. 2/1 The bullets..came more thickly now, squealing over our heads and futting on the ground between the horses' hoofs.

Futilitarianism (fiūtilitēᵊ·riăniz'm). [f. Futilitarian + -ism.] Futilitarian policy.

1921 *Glasgow Herald* 3 Feb. 8 To associate the activities of the Church with the Labour Party would be one more example of the Higher Futilitarianism with which ecclesiastics in all ages have been tempted to experiment. 1924 C. E. Montague *Right Place* x. 153 At least for some eager and absorbed hours your true rambler has washed all that futilitarianism out of his soul.

Futon (fū·tǫn). [Jap.] A Japanese bed-quilt.

1886 E. S. Morse *Japanese Homes* 212 The *futons*, or comforters, are..hung over the balcony rail to air. 1891 Chamberlain & Mason *Handbk. Japan* 8 Beds are still rare; but good quilts (*futon*) are laid down on the mats.

Futural (fiū·tiŭrăl), *a. Grammar.* [ad. med.L. *futūrālis* (see Futurality).] Having a future sense.

1906 J. H. Moulton *Gram. N.T. Grk.* I. 120 Futural presents..have no lack of durativity about them.

Future, *a.* **1. b.** *Future life* (examples).

1814 J. Kenrick (*title*) The Necessity of Revelation to teach the Doctrine of a Future Life. 1879 *Psychol. Rev.* I. 335 Those who believe in God and a Future Life.

Futurism (fiū·tiŭriz'm, -tʃər-). [f. Future *a.* + -ism, after It. *futurismo*, F. *futurisme*.] An art-movement, originating in Italy, characterized by violent departure from traditional forms, the avowed aim being to represent the sensation of movement and growth in objects, not their appearance at some particular moment. Also applied to a similar tendency in literature.

1909 *Daily Chron.* 5 May 6/6 'Futurism' is the declaration of the new school of literature grounded by the International Review 'Poesia'. 1915 W. H. Wright *Mod. Painting* 276 Marinetti, a poet, is the spiritual (and monetary) father of Futurism. 1921 Galsworthy *To Let* II. ii, Paul Post—that painter a little in advance of Futurism.

Futurist (fiū·tiŭrist, -tʃər-). [f. prec., after It. *futuristo*, F. *futuriste*.] An adherent of 'futurism' in art or literature. Also *attrib.* and quasi-*adj.*

1911 W. J. Locke *Clementina Wing* xxii. 278 After that they had gone to see the New Futurists. 1914 *Star* 16 Dec. 6/2 Small bullet-proof shields,..painted in cubist patterns in futurist colours. 1915 W. H. Wright *Mod. Painting* 272 The famous Futurist statement that 'a running horse has not four legs, but twenty'. 1916 Boyd Cable *Action Front* 128 Erratic daubs of bright colours laid on after the most approved Futurist style. 1924 C. Hamilton *Prisoners of Hope* 129 The walls..were covered with the raw and confused handiwork of the people who called themselves futurists because they had never been taught how to paint.

Futuristic (fiūtiŭri·stik, -tʃər-), *a.* [f. prec. + -ic.] Having the characteristics of 'futurism'.

1915 W. H. Wright *Mod. Painting* 257 His [*sc.* Gleizes'] well-known L'Homme au Balcon appears to us today almost Futuristic in conception. 1921 *Queen* 10 Sept. 326 Quaint futuristic or jazz embroidery. 1921 Galsworthy *To Let* I. i, What was the use of going in to look at this crazy, futuristic stuff with the view of seeing whether it had any future?

Futurity. Add: **4.** *U.S.* **futurity race**, a race for futurity stakes; **futurity stakes**, stakes to be raced for at some future date, often long after the entries or nominations are made; also, a race so arranged.

1902 *Encycl. Brit.* XXIX. 335/2 The Futurity Stakes, the richest event of the year..is for two-year-olds, and is run at Sheepshead Bay (U.S.).

Fuzzy, *sb. Soldiers' slang.* = *fuzzy-wuzzy* (Fuzzy *a.* 5).

1923 Kipling *Land & Sea Tales* 11 A wounded Sudanese —what our soldiers used to call a 'fuzzy'. 1926 Rose Macaulay *Crewe Train* II. iii, Those infernal fuzzies of yours have upset the lamas.

Fyke, *sb.* (For 1860 read 1848, and add:)

1871 *Game Laws N.Y.* in *Fur, Fin & Feather* (1872) 21 Fykes set in any of the waters surrounding Long Island. 1903 *N.Y. Even. Post* 20 Oct. 3 He stopped up the stream with the exception of one narrow outlet, in which he placed his fyke.

G

G. III. Add: **a.** G. = Grand, in the descriptions of the ranks of various orders, as G.C.I.E. = Grand Commander of the Indian Empire, G.C.M.G. = of St. Michael and St. George, G.B.E. = Grand Cross of the British Empire. G.C. = Grand Chaplain, Chapter, etc. G.O.M. = Grand Old Man (W. E. Gladstone); also *transf.* G.B. (*U.S.*) = grand bounce, i.e. dismissal, rejection. G.O.P., the initial letters of *Grand Old Party*, used to designate the Republican party in the United States. **b.** = General, as G.H.Q. = General Head Quarters. G.O.C. = General Officer Commanding. G. P. = general practitioner (i.e. an ordinary 'medical man'). G.P.I. = general paralysis of the insane. G.P.O. = General Post Office. **c.** = Great, as G.B. = Great Britain; G.B.P. (g.b.p.) = great British public. **d.** Miscellaneous. G.A.T. = Greenwich apparent time; G.M.T. = Greenwich mean time. g.m., humorous substitute for *a.m.* or *p.m.* G.T.T. (*U.S.*) = gone to Texas. See also *Gee-string, *G.P.U., *G string.

a. 1871 *Whitaker's Alm.* 70 Lord Lisgar, G.C.M.G. 1884 *Punch* 23 Feb. 95/2 G.O.M. been looking worn and irritable since Session opened. 1888 *Chicago Times* (Farmer), Bloomington people assert that their city was the birthplace of the G.O.P. a 1889 *A Californian Romance* in Barrère & Leland *Dict. Slang*, I have Been given the G.B. on your account. 1889 *Whitaker's Alm.* 108 The Most Eminent Order of the Indian Empire..Knights Grand Commdrs. G.C.I.E. 1903 A. H. Beavan *Tube, Train*, etc. i. 2 *note*, This is by no means the oldest steam-engine at work in the kingdom, the doyen being one built as far back as 1767...It is said that this G.O.M. is more economical than many of the modern engines. 1904 *Hartford Courant* 30 Nov. 1 Every republican of prominence has been invited, and nearly 1,000 of the G.O.P. will be present. 1909 S. E. White *Rules of Game* I. iii. 19 'I'm mighty sorry, old man', he whispered...'Did you get the G.B.?' 1918 *Whitaker's Alm.* 143 G.B.E., Knights Grand Cross or Dames Grand Cross [of the British Empire].

b. 1883 *Queen's Regul. Army* II. 45 Office of G.O.C. Camp, Colchester. 1887 *Graphic* 30 Apr. 447/2 The ordinary general practitioner—the 'G.P.', as he is familiarly called. 1895 *New Age* II. 328/3 Come with me..into the G.P.O. 1899 *Tit-Bits* 21 Oct. 83/3 The 'Dead Letter' department of the G.P.O. 1915 A. C. Walsh *Diary* 52 We are billeted at Delelle, a small village about 10 miles due south of G.H.Q., at St. Omer. 1926 G. W. Deeping *Sorrell & Son* xxix, 'If I became a G.P.,' he said, 'would you mind?' 1930 *Times Lit. Suppl.* 3 July 542/3 If the G.O.C. could have flown or rather hovered over the scene for ten seconds, the attack would have been countermanded. 1930 *Daily Express* 8 Sept. 1/1 Pathological experiments..have enabled 'G.P.I.' to be diagnosed in its incipient stages. 1931 Sir H. Gough in *Daily Tel.* 23 July 12/6 In a memorandum from G.H.Q. the policy of the Fifth Army was definitely laid down.

c. 1925 G. Frankau *Life—and Erica* xv. § 1 It's no good making the G.B.P. laugh at you. 1928 *Punch* 8 Feb. 150/3 The g.b.p. does like a wedding.

d. 1840 Haliburton *Clockm.* Ser. III. viii. 104 Now it's time for me to cut dirt, and leave the country. I believe I must hang out the G.T.T. sign—Why, what the plague is that? says I. Gone to Texas, said he. 1884 (*title*) G.T.T. Gone to Texas. Letters from our boys, ed. by Thomas Hughes. 1901 'Linesman' *Words Eyewitness* (1902) 246 Merely referring to it as such and such an hour G.M. 1928 W. M. Smart *Sun, Stars & Univ.* iv. 49 The true Greenwich Mean Time (G.M.T.). 1929 S. Lewis *Dodsworth* xxxii, I bet I never went to bed before three g.m. once, the whole way over!

Gabardine. A form of Gaberdine used *spec.* as the name of a dress material of cotton or silk with a wool lining.

1904 *Ladies' Field* 14 May 426/1 Gabardine, a material of flax and cotton, with a wool lining, both gabardine and lining being waterproofed. 1908 *Times* (weekly ed.) 14 Aug. p. iii/2 Gabardine is a material which has many qualities not to be overlooked when it is a question of sporting dresses. 1923 G. C. Denny *Fabrics* 46 Gabardine or gaberdine (wool). A firm material similar to whip cord.

Gabbroid (gæ·broid), *a. Min.* [f. Gabbro + -oid.] Resembling gabbro. Also as *sb.*, any crystalline rock in which the ferro-magnesian minerals predominate.

1905 Chamberlin & Salisbury *Geol.* I. 432 The term *gabbroids* may be used to include the dark crystalline rocks in which the ferromagnesian minerals predominate, as the diorites, gabbros, dolerites, peridotites, etc. *Ibid.*, The granitoids are usually acidic and the gabbroids usually basic.

Gabfest (gæ·bfest). *U.S. slang.* [f. Gab *sb.*[2] + G. *fest* festival.] A gathering for talk; a spell of talking.

1904 *Grand Rapids Evening Press* 30 July 5 The pioneer graduates of Olivet college have decided to hold a 'gabfest' Aug. 17. 1910 W. M. Raine *B. O'Connor* 101 I'll leave you and your jelly fish Scotty to your gabfest.

Gable, *sb.*[1] **4.** Add: **gable-topped** *a.*, topped by a gable, having a gable-shaped top.

1842 *Civil Eng. & Arch. Jrnl.* V. 81/1 Some..architects ..give us a gable-topped and an elliptic bed-topped window alternately. 1903 Ld. R. Gower *Rec. & Remin.* 214 A small gable-topped building. 1923 Collingwood *Rom. Brit.* 86 A gable-topped canopy.

Gaboon (găbū·n). Also **Gabun**. [The name of a French colony in West Africa.] A kind of wood (see quot. 1920). Also *attrib.*, as **Gaboon chocolate**, dika; **Gaboon viper**, *Bitis gabonica*.

1920 A. L. Howard *Timbers of World* 140 Gaboon. *Boswellia Klaineana*...This..useful wood..fills a place of importance which justifies a title which would give it individuality, though it should not be called mahogany. *Ibid.*, Gaboon has been tried for the purpose of making aeroplane propellers. 1928 *Daily Tel.* 29 May 6 Specimens of the green mamba and gaboon viper from West Africa. 1929 *Encycl. Brit.* VII. 882/1 The heart-wood..is known as black ebony,..billet-wood, Gabun, Lagos, Calabar or Niger ebony.

Gad, *sb.*[1] Add: **1. d.** An ear-mark for cattle, usually *fore* or *hind(er) gad*. *U.S.*

1667 *Portsmouth Rec.* (R.I.) 269 A fore gadd one the r[ight ear] The eare marke..is two hinder gads. The eare marke.. is a hinder gadd. 1842 *Ibid.* 386 The ear mark..is a fore gad on the left [ear]. 1845 *Ibid.* 390 The Ear mark of the Creatures of Edward Anthony is a hind Gad on the left ear.

Gad-bush, variant of *God-bush.

Gadget (gæ·dʒĕt). *colloq.* or *slang.* Also occas. **gadjet**. [Origin obscure. First known in use among seafaring men, and said by several correspondents to have been current c 1870, and by a few as far back as the fifties of the nineteenth century, but not found in print before 1886.

One of the most plausible suggestions of etymology is F. *gâchette*, which is or has been applied to various pieces of mechanism, e.g. in a lock and in a gun; it is a dim. of *gâche* staple (of a lock), wall-staple or hook. The possibility of connexion with F. *engager* to engage (one thing with another) has also been suggested; cf. dial. F. *gagée* tool, instrument. Derivation from Gauge is improbable.]

Used as an indefinite or general name for: A comparatively small tool, contrivance, or piece of mechanism, esp. in nautical use.

1886 Robt. Brown *Spunyarn & Spindrift* xxxi. 378 Then the names of all the other things on board a ship! I don't know half of them yet; even the sailors forget at times, and if the exact name of anything they want happens to slip from their memory, they call it a chicken-fixing, or a gadjet, or a gill-guy, or a timmey-noggy, or a wim-wom—just *pro tem.*, you know. 1904 Kipling *Traffics & Discov.*, *Steam Tactics* 179, I telegraphed Mr. Pyecroft a question. 'Not-in-the-least', was the answer. 'Steam gadgets always take him that way.' *Ibid.* 190 You've certainly got the hang of her steamin' gadgets in quick time. 1907 *Motor Boat* 4 July 439/1 There will be no harm in pointing out a few of the requirements of a Whitehead torpedo, which will enable the reader to appreciate the number of 'gadgets' which are involved. 1911 C. E. W. Bean '*Dreadnought*' *of Darling* ii. 30 He had known every stick in their sides and every gadget on their decks. 1915 Kipling *New Army* 39 They have installed decent cooking ranges and gas, and the men have already made themselves all sorts of handy little labour-saving gadgets. 1918 *Glasgow Even. News* 14 Sept. 6 There are a variety of gadjets connected with a motor-car; an aeroplane is replete with them—thermometer, barometer, altimeter, and the pilot only knows what besides. 1919 Blackburn & Newby *All about Aircraft* 100 *Gadget*, any small and ingenious piece of mechanism, such as a gun mounting. 1920 *Blackw. Mag.* Mar. 318/2 Naval ratings, brought up all their days amongst steam, electricity, and hydraulic gadgets. 1922 *Chambers's Jrnl.* 435/2 A fine, new ten-knot steamer.. with all the newest stunts and gadgets. 1923 'B. M. Bower' *Parowan Bonanza* i. 12 Solid ledge of gold...Knock it off in chunks with a single-jack and gadget. 1927 *Glasgow Herald* 18 Aug. 9 Innumerable motor car and wireless gadgets.

b. *transf.* and *gen.* An accessory or adjunct; a knick-knack or gewgaw.

1915 'Bartimeus' *Naval Occas.* 142 Look here, old lady, here's a gadget I got for you—he fumbled with the tissue paper enclosing a little leather case. 1917 *Daily Chron.* 3 Aug. (Weekley) The Prussian assessor [state lawyer] with his monocle and ornamental gadgets. 1922 *Blackw. Mag.* Apr. 421/1, I had to work with concordances, glossaries, all sorts of gadgets. 1925 *Ibid.* Sept. 423 Another waiter offered a selection of 'gadgets',—the appetising morsels of anchovy, stuffed-olive, or pâté.

c. *spec.* in local use. A winch or similar mechanical gear for discharging vessels; also, a craft equipped with such gear.

1899 *Bristol Times & Mirror* 10 June 3/8 The gadget which was used in the discharge of vessels was being towed down the Harbour...The man who was steering the gadget rather lost his head...There was ample room for the gadget to have passed through if it had been steered properly. 1931 *Ibid.* 16 May, Pulley gear was rigged to the stays or spars of the sailing ship over the hold, and the heaving rope passed to the winch drum of the gadget lying alongside.

d. *Glass-making.* A spring-clip used for gripping the foot of a wine or other footed glass when it is being shaped.

1918 P. Marson *Glass & Glass Man.* 83 The servitor has now done his part of the work, and the glass is handed to the workman. It is then cracked off, and the foot caught by a spring clip arrangement attached to a pontil, called a 'gadget'. 1923 H. J. Powell *Glassmaking in England* 43.

Gadi (gā·di), **gaddi** (gɒ·di). Also **gâdi**, **gadhi**, **guddy**, **-ee**. [Marathi *gādī*, Bengali *gadi*, Hind. *gaddī*, lit. cushion.] The cushioned throne of an Indian ruler; *transf.*, the regal position.

1855 H. H. Wilson *Glossary Judicial & Revenue Terms.* 1879 E. Arnold *Lt. Asia* II. 333 The marriage feast was kept, as Sākyas use, The golden gadi set, the carpet spread. 1886 Yule & Burnell *Hobson-Jobson* s.v. *Guddy*, *Guddee*, 'To be placed on the *guddee*' is to succeed to the Kingdom. 1906 *Westm. Gaz.* 6 Sept. 4/3 The Jám died in 1895, whereupon this child was installed on the gâdi of Jamnagar by Colonel Hancock, then 'Agent to the Governor' in Kathiawar. 1923 *Blackw. Mag.* Jan. 10/1 He had had a very narrow escape of being deposed from the *gadi*. 1927 *Times* (weekly ed.) 29 Sept. 346/2 The Nawab of Bhopal succeeded to *gadi* on the death of the Begum his mother.

Gadinine (gæ·dinīn). *Chem.* [irreg. f. mod.L. *gadus* cod + -ine [5].] A ptomaine, $C_7H_{16}NO_2$, formed in the putrefaction of fish and the bacterial cultures of human fæces.

1887 A. M. Brown *Anim. Alkaloids* 41 The chlorohydrate of gadinine crystallizes in colourless needle-shaped prisms. 1888 *Buck's Handbk. Med. Sci.* VI. 63/2 Gadinine..is a base whose chloroplatinate crystallizes in golden-yellow scales.

Gadolinium (gædoli·niɒm). *Chem.* [Discovered by Marignac (1880): see Gadolinite and -ium.] A metallic element found in gadolinite.

1886 *Jrnl. Chem. Soc.* L. 667 Marignac gives the name *Gadolinium* (Gd) to the substance which has hitherto been provisionally distinguished as Yα. 1908 *Ibid.* XCIV. II. 695 Gadolinium sulphide. 1920 *Ibid.* CXVIII. II. 317 The fractional crystallisation of the acetates effects a rapid separation of gadolinium from samarium and didymium.

Gaduol (gæ·diuǫl). [irreg. f. mod.L. *gadus* cod: see -ol.] An alcoholic extract of cod-liver oil.

1901 Dorland *Med. Dict.* 1905 *Jrnl. Soc. Chem. Ind.* XXIV. 301 The Board of General Appraisers overruled the assessment of duty on gaduol and morrhuol at 55 cents per lb., as 'medicinal preparations in the preparation of which alcohol has been used'.

Gaekwar (gai·kwāɹ). Also **Guicowar**, **Gaikwar**. [Marathi *gāekwār*, lit. cowherd.] The title of the native ruler of Baroda in India.

1854 E. Thornton *Gaz. India* I. 266 Baroda,..the capital of the territory of the prince called the Guicowar. 1881 W. W. Hunter *Imp. Gaz. India* I. 451 The Gáekwár of Baroda is entitled to a salute of 21 guns.

Gaertner[1] (gēᵊ·ɹtnəɹ). The name of August *Gaertner*, German bacteriologist (born 1848), used attrib. or in the genitive to designate the *bacillus enteritidis*, found in cows that have died of enteritis or similar forms.

1899 R. Muir & Ritchie *Man. Bacteriol.* (ed. 2) 331 During the last few years, in some epidemics of meat-poisoning, similar bacilli differing slightly from Gaertner's bacillus have been isolated. 1928 *E. O. Jordan & I. S. Falk's Bacteriol. & Immunol.* 444 The term 'Gärtner bacillus' came to be used by some writers..as a general term synonymous with 'paratyphoid bacillus'. 1928 *Daily Express* 11 Aug. 7/1 Death was due to heart failure following infection by the bacillus gaertner from ham purchased in the police canteen. 1930 *Brit. Med. Jrnl.* 22 Mar. 546/1 The patient's serum after operation contained no agglutinins for the organism, isolated, a feature not unusual in Gaertner infections.

Gaertner[2]. The name of G. *Gaertner*, Austrian physician (1855–1921). *Gaertner's phenomenon*, the degree of fullness of the veins of the arm as it is raised to varying heights as indicating the degree of pressure in the right auricle. *Gaertner's tonometer*, an instrument for measuring blood-pressure by means of a compressing ring applied to the finger.

1903 Crile *Blood-Pressure* 310 Gaertner's tonometer..consists of a pneumatic ring about 1 cm. in height and 2½ cm. in diameter. *Ibid.* 324 The Gaertner method. *Ibid.* 354 With the Gaertner tonometer be noted that..the pressure fell once from 120 to 90.

Gaff, *sb.*[2] Add: **3.** *To stand the gaff*, to submit silently to being blamed. Similarly *to give the gaff*. *U.S. slang.*

1903 *McClure's Mag.* Oct. 563 'Good,' they cheer, when you find fault; 'give us the gaff. We deserve it and it does us good.' 1910 W. M. Raine *B. O'Connor* 244 Neil has got to stand the gaff for what he's done. 1921 R. D. Paine *Comr. Rolling Ocean* iv. 66 It was dead white of you to stand the gaff and keep your mouth shut. 1924 W. M. Raine *Troubled Waters* xviii. 194 Just because he shuts his mouth and stands the gaff.

Gaffe (gæf). Also **gaff**. [Fr.] A blunder, an instance of clumsy stupidity, a 'faux-pas', 'bloomer'.

1909 *Pall Mall Gaz.* 12 Apr. 1/1 These two gentlemen, whose weather predictions are still listened to with some deference, have made a bad 'gaffe', to use a popular slang

expression. 1921 *Blackw. Mag.* Jan. 51/1, I should like to see your face, friend Ahmed el-Aoufi, after Raisuli had discovered the 'gaffe' that you had made. 1924 Galsworthy *White Monkey* I. ii, 'He's a bit romantic, of course.' 'Oh! Have I made a gaff?' 'Not a bit; jolly good shot.' 1928 C. Mackenzie *Extremes Meet* 207 Knowing nothing, you might easily make a bad gaffe.

Gag, *sb.*[1] Add: **1. b.** (Earlier U.S. example of modern sense.)

1861 *Congress. Globe* App. 49/1 The Pacific railroad bill, just passed through this House under the 'gag', and in violation of the constitution.

4. gag-bill, a theatrical bill summarizing the sensational episodes of a play; **gag-book**, a book containing a selection of jokes to be used as gags; **gag-man** *U.S.*, a deviser of jokes or comic situations for plays or films.

1885 J. K. Jerome *On the Stage* 147 The old man has got the knack of making out good *gag bills. 1909 B. Williams *Actor's Story* xix. 259 Not having a '*gag' book I had to think how to adapt a scene suitable for my particular line of business. 1928 *Sunday Express* 15 Jan. 4 '*Gag men' have long flourished in America. One of them thought of making the villain sit on a red-hot stove. 1928 *Collier's* 29 Dec. 28/3 'What you need is a smart gag man,' I say.

Gag (gæg), *sb.*[3] *U.S.* [Local name.] A large serranoid fish, *Mycteroperca microlepis*, found off the coasts of the southern United States.

1899 Jordan & Evermann *Fishes Amer.* 1177.

Gag, *v.*[1] **1. b.** Delete *Obs.* exc. *dial.* and add examples.

1908 *Practitioner* Sept. 367 The operation causes a little gagging and retching at first, but the patient soon becomes accustomed to the feeling of the cords in the throat. 1909 R. A. Wason *Happy Hawkins* 296 My heart popped up in my mouth till I'd like to have gagged. 1929 *Nation* (N.Y.) 20 Mar. 331 We offered to go into the World Court in 1926 —but with five reservations. Europe swallowed the first four but gagged at the fifth.

Gaga (gæ·gā), *a. slang.* [? Imitation of idiotic laughter.] Fatuous; doting, exhibiting senile decay; 'dotty'. Also *advb.*

[1905 *Daily Chron.* 18 Mar. 8/6 'Ah, you English,' quoth Mr. De Vries not so long ago, after a round of the London theatres, 'you like to laugh—ga-ga!'..Is not that the pathetic cry of our present drama, 'Ga-ga!']

1921 M. Baring *Passing By* 210 Sir Arthur is quite gaga and took me for George the whole evening. 1926 Edna Ferber *Show Boat* xix. 385 Nola darling, you've just gone gaga, that's all. What do you mean by staying down there in that wretched malarial heat! 1927 *Sunday Express* 13 Mar. 4 The conventional pictures of a young man and a young woman looking 'ga-ga' at each other. 1929 W. J. Locke *Ancestor Jorico* xviii, 'But why did he leave the half-million to his son, in his will?' '*Gaga*, my dear Binkie. Just *gaga*. Senile, if you'd like it better.'

Gaiassa (gəiˌæ·sä). [Arab. *khāyāsah*.] A high-stemmed vessel with lateen sails used on the Nile for freight.

1906 *Westm. Gaz.* 21 Mar. 3/2 One of the most heterodox of boats to European eyes is the 'Gaiassa' of the Nile.

Gaine (gēⁱn). *Electr.* [Fr., = sheath.] A metal tube screwed to a fuse.

1918 *Nature* CII. 218/1 The gaine is a metal tube screwed to the fuse, which enters a cavity in the filling and makes good contact with it. 1922 *Encycl. Brit.* XXX. 121/1 Sometimes the relay element interposed between fuze and main bursting charge is contained in a 'gaine' screwed to the fuse itself.

Gainsborough (gēⁱ·nzbɒrə). [The name of Thomas *Gainsborough* (1727–88), English painter.]

1. A portrait painted by Gainsborough.

1894 W. Armstrong *Gainsborough* 83 As refutations of Sir Joshua we could name many Gainsboroughs which beat the *Blue Boy*. 1903 A. B. Chamberlain *Gainsborough* 132 She [*sc.* Signora Grassi] called her house a 'painted Paradise' because of the Gainsboroughs hanging there.

2. A large broad-brimmed hat of the type worn by women in Gainsborough's portraits.

1878 *Cassell's Fam. Mag.* Aug. 569/2 The..wearers of the Gainsborough, Rembrandt, and beef-eater hats. 1904 *Westm. Gaz.* 12 Aug. 5/1 Extemporised Gainsboroughs.

Gaita (gai·tä). [Sp.] A musical instrument resembling a bagpipe, played in Galicia, Spain. So **Gaitero**, a piper.

1922 *Glasgow Herald* 14 Aug. 4 Within the deep, wide recess of the chimney the son of the house is singing to the accompaniment of the 'gaita'. 1927 *Chambers's Jrnl.* 758/2 Their little *gaitas* (bagpipes) tasselled with the national colours of red and yellow. *Ibid.*, A famous band of *gaiteros*, or pipers.

Gaiter, *sb.*[1] **2.** *U.S.* In full *gaiter-boot*, *-shoe*.

1849 *Rep. U.S. Comm. Patents* (1850) 221 Improvement in Machines for cutting Gaiter Boots. 1849 Willis *Rural Lett.* 230 Dandies strolling and stealing an occasional look at their loose *demi-saison* pantaloons and gaiter-shoes. 1875 Mrs. Stowe *We & Neighbors* x. 106 Looking as if they never had heard of a French hat or a pair of gaiter-boots.

Gaize (gēⁱz). *Geol.* [Fr.] A fine-grained micaceous sandstone found in the Mesozoic rocks of France and England.

1885 Geikie *Text-bk. Geol.* (ed. 2) 832 A porous calcareous and argillaceous sandstone known as *Gaize*, containing a large percentage of silica soluble in alkali.

Gal = Girl. (Earlier U.S. examples.)

1796–1801 Fessenden *Orig. Poems* (1806) 76 *note*, Gal is, in New England, the vulgar pronunciation of the word *girl*. 1834 S. Smith *Sel. Lett. Major Jack Downing* 126 And the gals get on their clean gowns.

Galabeeah (galā·biya). Also **galabeah**, **-biya**, **-beeyeh**, **-bieh**, **gallabi(y)a**. [= Arab. جلابية *jalābiya*, pop. equivalent of جلباب *julbāb*.] A smock-like garment worn by Egyptian natives.

1892 D. A. Cameron *Arabic-Engl. Vocab.* 45 'Galâbiya'. 1900 A. C. Doyle *Green Flag*, etc. 328 Tell them to undo the man's galabeeah. 1916 Sir V. Horsley in *Life* (1919) 321 The small boys..are given the head-dress and a few feet of stuff for a galabea. 1921 *Chambers's Jrnl.* 265/1 A figure in a blue *galabieh* and a white-turbaned tarboosh.

Galactan (gălæ·ktăn). *Chem.* [f. Gr. γαλακτ-, γάλα milk + -an.] A gummy substance which is found in plants during the germinative period and yields galactose on hydrolysis.

1886 *Jrnl. Chem. Soc.* L. 609 This carbohydrate [from the seed of Lupinus luteus] very closely resembles galactin (or adopting Scheibler's nomenclature galactan), obtained by Muntz from the seed of the lucerne. 1912 *Ibid.* CII. II. 657 The hepato-pancreatic juice of *Helix pomatia* hydrolyses all the mannans and galactans which have been investigated.

Galactase (gălæ·ktēⁱs). *Chem.* [f. as prec. + *-ase.] An enzyme which occurs in milk.

1900 *Jrnl. Chem. Soc.* LXXVIII. I. 712 Galactase..is a proteolytic ferment similar to trypsin and is present in the milk of all animals. 1901 J. R. Green *Soluble Ferments* 207.

Galactic, *a.* **2.** Add: *Galactic belt*, *latitude*, *plane*, *zone*: that area in space which includes the Milky Way and the large stars near it. *Galactic system*: that system of stars to which the Milky Way and most of the visible stars belong; distinguished from other island-universes visible to us as nebulæ.

1878 Newcomb *Pop. Astron.* IV. 417 Telescopic stars..are least numerous in the regions most distant from the galactic belt, and grow thicker as we approach it. 1898 C. A. Young *Text-bk. Gen. Astron.* 561 The northern 'galactic pole'.. lies, according to Sir John Herschel, in declination +27°. 1902 *Encycl. Brit.* XXV. 755/2 The rate of increase is as rapid as it would be if the boundary of the universe were two planes parallel to the galactic plane. *Ibid.*, It is a remarkable fact that the condensation towards the galactic zone begins with the brighter stars. 1915 *Oxf. Univ. Gaz.* 19 May 616/2 The ratio of the number of faint stars to bright, though it does not change much with galactic latitude, does nevertheless vary in different parts of the sky. 1928 Jeans *Astron. & Cosmog.* 353 The system of stars bounded by the Milky Way is commonly called the Galactic System.

Galactonic (gælæktǫ·nik), *a. Chem.* [f. Galacto-.] *Galactonic acid*, a crystalline acid, $C_6H_{12}O_7$.

1885 *Jrnl. Chem. Soc.* XLVIII. II. 967 Galactonic acid.. is best prepared by the action of bromine on an aqueous solution of lactose. 1895 *Bloxam's Chem.* (ed. 8) 712 The galactoses yield galactonic and mucic acids.

Galalith (gæ·lăliþ). [Fr. (patented 1902 by the Cie. Française de Galalith); irreg. f. Gr. γάλα milk + λίθος stone.] A proprietary name for a product resembling celluloid made from the casein of milk with the addition of other substances, used as a substitute for horn, celluloid, ivory, etc.

1903 *Jrnl. Soc. Chem. Ind.* XXII. 373/2 Galalith prepared according to Fr. Pat. 292, 705, by the action of alkali-lye on casein. 1922 *Glasgow Herald* 25 Feb. 9 A product, formerly a German monopoly, known as galalith. 1922 *Daily Mail* 13 Nov. 1 A number of curved galalith handles, in all white or antique colour.

Galangin (gălæ·ŋgin). *Chem.* [f. Galanga + -in [1].] A yellow crystalline substance allied to flavone, found in galingale.

1882 *Jrnl. Chem. Soc.* XLII. 209 To separate campheride from the two substances, galangin and alpinin, with which it is mixed.

Galax (gæ·læks). Also **galaxy**. [mod.L., ad. Gr. γαλαξίας.] An evergreen plant, *Galax aphylla*, with white flowers and shining leaves, found in the south-eastern United States.

1898 B. Torrey in *Atlantic Monthly* Apr. 458/2, I could only conjecture the plant to be galax. 1922 Marg. B. Houston *Witch-man* xi, The darkly polished galax leaves.

Gale, *sb.*[3] Add: **1. a.** In restricted use, applied to a wind having a velocity within certain limits (see quot. 1923).

1899 *Westm. Gaz.* 24 Jan. 4/3 A gale is not a gale until it has reached Force 7 on the Beaufort scale, though many people lightly class all heavy winds as gales. 1902 *Daily Chron.* 4 Mar. 5/2 Southerly winds were blowing in all parts of the British Isles yesterday, reaching gale force on the west coast of Ireland. 1909 *Westm. Gaz.* 8 Jan. 7/3 The wind is of intermittent gale force. 1923 Sir N. Shaw *Forecasting Weather* (ed. 2) 456 As a result of the investigation of 1905 we now classify winds with velocity above 75 miles per hour as hurricane winds, those with velocity between 64 and 75 miles per hour as storm winds, and those between 39 and 63 as gales.

2. *U.S.* (Earlier example.)

1838 *Southern Lit. Messenger* IV. 65/2 On the way Wint was in 'a great gale' his spirits high, his hopes buoyant, his gaiety of heart overflowing.

Gale, *sb.*[4] **2.** (Earlier U.S. example.)

1789 Morse *Amer. Geog.* 314 He pays one third or one fourth part in cash..and the rest in gales or instalments, as it is called here.

5. *gale-day* (earlier U.S. example).

1831 *Louisville Public Adv.* 11 July, I was thinking to myself that the gale-day is passed.

Galeanthropy (gælˌiæ·nþrǫpi). [f. Gr. γαλέα cat + ἄνθρωπος man.] A maniacal delusion in which the subject imagines himself to be a cat.

1888 H. Power & Sedgwick *Lex. Med.* 1894 F. P. Foster *Med. Dict.*

Galenobismuthite (gălīnobi·zmǒþəit). *Min.* Also **-utite**. [f. Galena + Bismuth + -ite [1].] A tin-white sulphide of lead and bismuth.

1880 *Jrnl. Chem. Soc.* XXXVIII. 14. 1900 Dana *Text-bk. Min.* 308.

Galician (gāli·þiăn, gāli·ʃiăn), *a.*[1] and *sb.*[1] [f. *Galicia* + -an.] **A.** *adj.* Of or pertaining to Galicia, a province in north-west Spain, or its inhabitants. **B.** *sb.* An inhabitant of Galicia; also, the national language of Galicia.

1750 U. Rhys *Tour through Spain* 28 The Galicians make good Soldiers; and are pleased with the Profession. 1809 tr. *A. de Laborde's View Spain* II. 428 This road is frequented by..a great many Galician workmen. *Ibid.* 456 The Galician who serves either his master, or the public, or in the army, is contented to appear a slave. 1848 *Encycl. Metrop.* (1845) XIX. 438/1 The Galicians, or Galegos as the Spaniards call them, are a grave and sober people. 1847 tr. *Bouterwek's Hist. Span. Lit.* 7 The vulgar idiom spoken by the Galician water-carriers in Madrid. 1927 *Chambers's Jrnl.* 759/1 Her head is the Galician woman's carry-all.

Galician (gāli·ʃiăn), *a.*[2] and *sb.*[2] [f. *Galicia* + -an.] **A.** *adj.* Of or pertaining to Galicia, a (largely Jewish) province of Poland, or its inhabitants. **B.** *sb.* An inhabitant of Galicia.

1835 *Penny Cycl.* III. 131/2 The Galician soil is no where so productive as in the districts of Zloczoff and Stanislawoff. 1918 Montefiore *Lib. Judaism* v. 246 It has been too rashly assumed that the Russian, Polish and Galician 'masses' must be for ever wedded to Orthodox Judaism. 1920 *19th Cent.* Mar. 563 This shabby little plebeian, sprung from some Galician Ghetto. 1927 *Times* (weekly ed.) 16 June 664/4 He took charge of a Red-Cross unit on the Galician front.

Galipeine (gæli·pĭˌīn). *Chem.* Also **galipine**. [f. mod.L. *Galipea*, generic name of the tree producing angustura bark.] An alkaloid, $C_{20}H_{21}NO_3$, obtained from angustura bark. Similarly **Galipideine** (gælipi·dĭˌīn), **Gali·pidine**, **-edine**, the alkaloid $C_{19}H_{19}NO_3$.

1884 *Jrnl. Chem. Soc.* XLVI. 341 In the mother-liquors from which the cusparine was originally precipitated as sulphate or oxalate, another alkaloid is found, to which the authors [*sc.* Koerner and Böhringer] have given the name of galipeine. 1892 *Ibid.* LXII. I. 643 Galipidine, $C_{19}H_{19}NO_3$, crystallises from light petroleum in very light, silky, lustrous plates which are pure white. 1912 *Ibid.* CII. I. 895 Angostura Alkaloids...It was found that mixtures of cusparine and galipine could be separated by conversion into the oxalates.

Galjoen (galyū·n). *S. Afr.* [a. Du. *galjoen* galleon.] A S. African fish, *Dipterodon capensis*.

1900 Gilchrist in *Trans. S. Afr. Phil. Soc.* 221 (Pettman) The *galjeon* [sic] also can readily be supposed to have derived its name from its resemblance in shape to the high built three-decker. 1931 *Times Lit. Suppl.* 16 Apr. 301/2.

Gall, *sb.*[1] Add:

1. b. Phr. *To dip one's pen in gall*: to write with virulence and rancour. (Cf. quot. 1641 in sense 3.)

Probably derived from instances like those in quots. 1601, 1605, where there appears to be a pun on Gall *sb.*[3] (the oak-gall, which is used in the manufacture of ink).

[1601 Shaks. *Twel. N.* III. ii. 52 Let there bee gaulle enough in thy inke, though thou write with a goose-pen, no matter: about it. 1605 *1st Pt. Ieronimo* III. iii. 14 *Ier.* What, is your pen foule? *Hor.* No, Father, cleaner then Lorenzoes soule; Thats dipt in inck made of an enuious gall; Else had my pen no cause to write at all.]

1858 *Illustr. News of World* 30 Oct. 283/1 The men who ..have before now dipped their pens in gall. 1892 *Rev. Reviews* V. 376/1 In the *Contemporary Review* for April an anonymous writer dips his pen in gall in order to depict the German Emperor.

6. esp. the North American plant *Nabalus serpentaria* (*N. Fraseri*), a species of rattlesnake-root.

1857 A. Gray *Man. Bot.* (1860) 238 N[abalus] Fraseri. Lion's foot. Gall-of-the-earth. 1901 C. Mohr *Plant Life Alabama* 755.

8. gall-bitters *U.S.*, a preparation of bitters and gall; **gall-bug** *U.S.*, a genus of bark-lice; **gall-sickness** (*b*), the name [tr. Du. *galziekte*] given in South Africa to diseases of the liver in cattle, sheep, and goats.

1846 Sage *Scenes Rocky Mts.* xvi. 133 Were those laboring under..this disease [*sc.* dyspepsia] to drink *gall-bitters.. thousands..would be restored to perfect soundness. 1837 J. L. Williams *Terr. Florida* 69 *Gall Bug...An insect similar in appearance to the puceron. 1896 R. Wallace *Farming Ind. Cape Col.* 288 Deaths in Cape Colony from *gall-sickness.

Gall, *sb.*[3] **2.** Add: **gall-berry** *U.S.*, the ink-berry (*Ilex glabra*); **gall-bush**, = *gall-berry*; **gall-wasp**, a hymenopterous insect which produces galls, e.g. a cynipid.

1901 C. Mohr *Plant Life Alabama* 816 With *gallberry bushes for the undergrowth. 1835 J. Martin *Gaz. Virginia* 41 An ever-green shrub, called the *gall-bush,..bears a berry which dies a black color like the gall of an oak—and hence its name. 1879 *Encycl. Brit.* X. 44/1 Among the Hymenoptera are the *gall-wasps. 1891 Schlich *Man. Forestry* II. 247 Many gall-wasps attack the Oak. 1925 *Glasgow Herald* 28 June 4 The rose gall-wasp (Rhodites).

Gall, *v.*[1] **6. b.** Add: also, to vent one's 'gall' on (a person). *U.S. colloq.*

1909 R. A. Wason *Happy Hawkins* 288 He was still gallin' on Barbie, but I couldn't help feeling..sorry for him.

Galla (gæ·lā). A member of a group of partially civilized tribes of Hamitic race inhabiting equatorial Africa, allied to the Abyssinians in language and origin. Also *attrib.* or as *adj.*

1875 *Encycl. Brit.* I. 263/2 The next great branch of the Ethiopic race comprehends the Galla, who occupy an immense tract in Eastern Africa...Our knowledge of them is chiefly confined to those Gallas who conquered Abyssinia. 1878 *K. Johnston's Africa* 286 The Somâli and Galla people are as closely related as they are hostilely disposed towards each other. 1892 A. S. White *Devel. Africa* (ed. 2) 101 As agriculturists and herdsmen, and in the industrial arts, the Galla bordering on Abyssinia and the Somâl of the Coast towns are the most advanced. 1895 A. H. Keane *Africa* I. 489 The typical Gallas of Kaffa and surrounding regions are perhaps the finest people in all Africa. *Ibid.* II. 570 The Galla love of roaming. 1920 *Blackw. Mag.* May 678/2 The poor old Galla vendor clucking with rage.

Gallanol (gæ·lănǫl). *Chem.* [f. *Gallo-[2] + An(iline + -ol.] An anilide of gallic acid, used in ointments for skin diseases.

1894 *Jrnl. Soc. Chem. Ind.* XIII. 755/2 The germicidal effect of gallanilide (or gallanol) on the carbuncle bacillus.

Gall-darn'd, variant of *Goldarned.

Galled, *ppl. a.*[2] 3. (Earlier U.S. example.)

1814 J. Taylor *Arator* 196 [Putting manure] on nearly a caput mortuum of a galled and gravelly hill side.

Gallegan (gælʸĕ·găn), *a.* [f. next + -an.] = *Galician *a.*[1] and *sb.*[1]

1922 *Glasgow Herald* 14 Aug. 4 The 'arrival'..of the Gallegans. 1927 *Chambers's Jrnl.* 759/2 The pipers..break off their meal to chant an impromptu couplet in the Gallegan dialect.

Gallego (gălʸĕ·go). [Sp.] = *Galician *sb.*[1]

1811 Sir J. Carr *Spain* 50 The Gallejos (pronounced Gallegos) or Galicians are a remarkably fine athletic race of men. 1846 Thackeray *Cornhill to Cairo* i. Wks. 1898 V. 591 A little..boat, rowed by three ragged gallegos. 1922 *Glasgow Herald* 14 Aug. 4 Undoubtedly the Gallego makes good. 1925 *Chambers's Jrnl.* 705/1 The Gallegos are for the most part miserably poor.

Gallery, *sb.* Add: **3. e.** The part of a Friends' meeting-house occupied by the ministers or elders. *Gallery friend*, a Quaker minister or elder.

1802 W. Matthews *Recorder* I. 121 The galleries of London. 1913 *Jrnl. Friends' Hist. Soc.* Jan. 2 Jane Wigham..., the second wife of John Wigham, Tertius, was also a gallery Friend. 1921 R. M. Jones *Later Per. Quakerism* I. 58 The phrases so characteristic of Molinos, Guyon, Fénelon..were heard everywhere in Quaker 'galleries'.

4. c. The group of spectators at a golf match or other game.

1891 H. G. Hutchinson *Hints on Golf* (ed. 6) 71 If you rise to such heights of golfing powers as to attract a gallery. 1906 *Westm. Gaz.* 21 Sept. 4/2 The novice, who is not familiar with the presence of a 'gallery'.

d. At écarté, the spectators who are betting on either player and are allowed to offer suggestions.

1890 'Berkeley' *Écarté & Euchre* 28 French Écarté. When several persons desire to join in a game of Écarté, it is generally arranged in the following manner. Two of the number sit down to play a game in the usual way,..and the remainder, called 'The Gallery', are allowed to take part in the game to the extent of betting on the player of their choice, and advising him, if necessary. 1897 R. F. Foster *Complete Hoyle* 255 Any person in the gallery is allowed to draw attention to errors in the score, and may advise the player he is backing, or even play out the game for him.

12. b. gallery-play, playing to the gallery (see 4 a); showy play designed to gain the applause of the vulgar; also *fig.*

1899 *Westm. Gaz.* 31 Jan. 7/2 A weak opposition, evidently disposed to indulge in 'gallery' play. *a* 1914 J. E. Raphael *Mod. Rugby Football* 107 'Gallery play' should only be resorted to as a last desperate resource. 1916 Boyd Cable *Action Front* 121 You've..done good work for your first show; don't spoil it with rank gallery play. 1923 Kipling *Land & Sea T.* 21 In the Great War there was very little suspicion, or chance, of gallery-play for the V.C.

Galley, *sb.* **8.** Add: **galley-yarn** = *galley-packet.*

1884 Henley & Stevenson *Admiral Guinea* III. iv, You the one overtaken and denounced; and you spin me a galley yarn like that? 1905 *Daily Chron.* 11 July 3/4 Mr. Baring-Gould has gathered up all the old galley-yarns.

Ga·lley-west, *adv.* *U.S. colloq.* [An alteration of Eng. dial. *colly-west, -weston*: see E.D.D.] *To knock galley-west*: to bring to confusion; to knock out completely, dispose of finally.

1883 'Mark Twain' *Life Mississippi* xxviii. 303 What does Ecclesiastes vii 13 say? Says enough to knock their little game galley-west, don't it? 1884 — *Huck. Finn* xxxvii. 382 Then she grabbed up the basket and slammed it across the house, and knocked the cat galleywest. 1891 Marah E. Ryan *Pagan Alleghanies* xiv. 184 Here you come with your theories of hue and knock my serenity galley-west. 1902 C. C. Munn *Rockhaven* i. 3 Thinkin' I'd set the price high 'nough to knock him galley west. 1926 *Atlantic Monthly* Sept. 391 Nowadays good old-fashioned balance-sheet practice has been knocked galley-west.

Gallin (gæ·lin). *Chem.* [Arbitrarily f. Gallein.] A crystalline dye-stuff, $C_{20}H_{14}O_7$, formed by reducing gallein.

1882 *Jrnl. Chem. Soc.* XLII. 59 By the further reduction of hydrogallein, gallin..is produced.

Gallinipper. (Earlier U.S. example.)

1801 *Port Folio* (Philad.) I. 40/3 These Gallinippers.. With monstrous paunches, and with wings of lace.

Gallio (gæ·lio). The name of a Roman proconsul of Achaia, whose refusal to take action is recorded in Acts xviii. 17 ('And Gallio cared for none of those things'), applied *gen.* to one who is indifferent. Hence **Ga·llio-like** *a.* and *adv.*; **Gallionic** (gælię·nik) *a.*, characteristic of a Gallio, indifferent.

1855 Macaulay *Hist. Eng.* xiii. III. 293 Unhappily, Scotland was ruled, not by pious Josiahs, but by careless Gallios. 1865 *Sk. from Cambridge* 137 (Hoppe) Our prevailing tone is what I should venture to describe as one of quiet good sense, and what fanatics would consider to be only fit for careless Gallios. *Ibid.* 140 A Gallio is generally a pleasant companion. 1884 S. J. Reid *Sydney Smith* x. 240 Gallio-like, he cared for none of these things. 1909 *Westm. Gaz.* 8 Mar. 4/3 Gallio-like bargain. 1920 *Q. Rev.* Oct. 403 Japan seemed Gallionic all the time. 1926 *Glasgow Herald* 20 Mar. 8 The Gallionic attitude of the soldiers along the various lines of the route.

Gallipoli (gæli·pǫli). The name of a town in Italy used to designate the olive oil exported from there, which is used in Turkey-red dyeing.

1842 Francis *Dict. Arts.* 1868 Joynson *Metals* 120 Common rosin, melted with a little gallipoli oil and spirits of turpentine. 1884 W. S. B. McLaren *Spinning* (ed. 2) 45 If..oil is used..it should be the best quality of olive. Gallipoli is the name for the very best.

Gallisin (gæ·lisin). *Chem.* [G., f. *gallisiren*: see Gallize *v.* etym.] An unfermentable carbohydrate, analogous to dextrin, obtained by fermenting commercial glucose and adding absolute alcohol in excess.

1884 *Jrnl. Chem. Soc.* XLVI. 981 The authors [*sc.* C. Schmitt and A. Cobenzl] have succeeded in separating from fermented glucose (prepared from potato-starch) an intensely hygroscopic substance which they have named gallisin. 1900 Sadtler *Hand-bk. Indust. Org. Chem.* (ed. 3) 178 Gallisin is stated to have the composition $C_{12}H_{24}O_{10}$.

Gallo-. 1. Add: **Gallo-Roman** *a.*, belonging to Gaul when it formed part of the Roman Empire; also as *sb.* an inhabitant of Gaul under Roman rule.

1841 T. Arnold *Lect. Mod. Hist.* (1860) 24 Throughout the south of France, the population is predominantly..of Gallo-Roman origin. 1879 Kitchin in *Encycl. Brit.* IX. 528/1 These were also the days of what is called 'the Gallo-Roman empire'. *Ibid.* 528/2 The Visigoths and Gallo-Romans defeated the terrible hordes of Attila at Chalons-sur-Marne.

Gallo-[2] (gæ·lo), also before a vowel **gall-**, combining f. Gallic *a.*[2] in the name of compounds derived from gallic acid or related substances.

1864 Watts *Dict. Chem.*, *Gallamic Acid*..has the composition of acid gallate of ammonium *minus* 1 at. water. 1881 *Jrnl. Chem. Soc.* XL. 267 Pyrogallol on treatment with ammonium carbonate yields two acids,..gallocarboxylic acid ..and pyrogallocarboxylic acid. *Ibid.* 811 Gallacetophenone is obtained on heating pyrogallol with glacial acetic and zinc chloride at 145°. 1882 *Ibid.* XLII. 1290 Pyrogallol is dissolved in pure acetone, and a few drops of phosphorus oxychloride added... The product, $C_9H_{10}O_3$, is crystalline. The author [*sc.* M. Wittenberg] calls it gallacetonin. 1883 *Ibid.* XLIV. 335 Gallanilide is deposited as a crystalline mass when digallic acid is dissolved in aniline. 1883 *Jrnl. Soc. Chem. Ind.* II. 377/1 The gallocyanines are blue or violet colours, obtained by the action of nitrosodimethylaniline on..gallic acid. 1887 *Jrnl. Chem. Soc.* LII. II. 1107 Galloflavin..is obtained by dissolving 50 grams of gallic acid in 875 c.c. of alcohol and 1 litre of water. 1888 *Ibid.* LIV. 949 Gallocyanin..is very sparingly soluble in water. 1902 *Encycl. Brit.* XXVII. 561/2 Gallanilide Blue, Delphine Blue, Gallamine Blue.

Gallop, *sb.* Add: **1. c.** A track designed for the galloping or exercising of horses.

1913 in F. Siltzer *Newmarket* App. 269 Horses not completing the full length of a gallop..must at once walk off the gallop to the nearest Walking Ground. 1927 *Times* 6 July 10/5 Scotland Lodge Estate, 1,009 acres,..including the residence, stud farm, and gallops.

Gallows, *a.* **3. gallows-looking** (earlier U.S. example).

1781 in *Maryland Hist. Mag.* V. 126 He was a tall, slim, gallows looking fellow,..with a gold laced jacket on that he had robbed from some old trooper.

Galoptious, galuptious, varr. Goluptious.

1887 *Judy* 21 Sept. 140/1 Four young ladies represented the galopshus sum of 20,000,000 dollars. 1919 W. De Morgan *Old Madhouse* 69 Galoptious room for a dance, this!

Galpon (gælpō·n). [Local name.] In South America, a building given to the use of labourers on a farm.

1894 *Proc. Zool. Soc.* 305 Behind some wood piled up at the side of the big galpon. 1918 W. H. Hudson *Far Away & Long Ago* xiv. 193 My father went to the *galpon*, the big barnlike building used for storing wood, hides, and horsehair.

Galsworthian (gǫ·lzwǝ̄·ðiăn), *a.* [f. the name of John *Galsworthy* (born 1867), English playwright and novelist: see -ian.] Of, belonging to, or characteristic of Galsworthy; (of a work) in the style of Galsworthy.

1912 *Engl. Rev.* June 494 A grim, almost Galsworthian, unpleasantness. 1928 *Daily Express* 24 May 10/6 A tight-lipped Galsworthian pessimist like the Duke of Wellington or Lord Kitchener.

Galton (gǫ·ltǝn). The name of Sir Francis *Galton* (1822–1911), English scientist and anthropologist. *Galton's law*, the formula proposed by him to account for ancestral heredity, which assigns to each of the parents a contribution of one-fourth to the characters of their offspring. So *Galton's curve*, etc.

1889 A. R. Wallace *Darwinism* 414 Galton's law of 'regression towards mediocrity'. 1903 *Daily Chron.* 31 July 5/2 'Galton's law',..now one of the cardinal principles of biology. 1904 tr. *Weismann's Evol. Theory* II. 206 Galton's curve of frequency of variations. 1907 V. L. Kellogg *Darwinism To-day* 71 Variation..is subject to Galton's law of regression.

Galvanoglyph (gæ·lvănǫglif). [f. Galvano- + Glyph.] = Glyphograph. Hence **Galvano·glyphy.**

1866 *Chambers's Jrnl.* 86 Galvanoglyphy, in which the picture is etched on the varnished surface of a zinc-plate.

Galvayne (gæ·lvėin). The name of Sydney *Galvayne*, a writer on horses. *Galvayne's mark*, a depression on the outer side of the upper corner incisor of a horse. Hence **Ga·lvayne** *v. trans.*, to break in (a horse) by Galvayne's method (see quot. 1905).

1905 S. Galvayne *XXth Cent. Bk. Horse* 23 'Galvayning' is really a scientific utilization of the animal's strength against itself... The 'Galvayne' position is attained by tying the animal's head round with the halter-shank, or the 'Galvayne' strap, to its tail. *Ibid.* 29 Once you have got the horse properly 'Galvayned', watch it carefully for a little while before proceeding further. *Ibid.* 32 If the animal be 'Galvayned' on the 'near' side, the trainer must work on the 'off'. 1911 *Encycl. Brit.* XIII. 725 The method of subduing a colt by 'galvayning' is as good as any. It is a more humane system than 'rareying'. 1908 *Animal Managem.* (W.O.) 43 At ten years 'Galvayne's mark', a depression on the outer side of the upper corner incisor, appears.

Galziekte (gālzī·ktǝ). [Du.] = *gall-sickness*, *Gall *sb.*[1] 8.

1902 *Nature* LXVII. 46/2 Tr[*ypanosoma*] *Theileri*, the cause of the cattle disease known as Galziekte.

Gam (gæm), *sb.*[4] The headman of a village in Assam.

1926 *Blackw. Mag.* Sept. 406 The gam, or headman, put in an appearance. 1927 *Ibid.* Mar. 291/2 Village democracies..using their gams as spokesmen.

Gambia (gæ·mbiă). The name of a British Colony in West Africa, used attrib. to designate forms of trypanosomiasis prevalent there. So **Ga·mbian** *a.*

1905 *Proc. Royal Soc.* LXXIV. 389 These experiments go to show that the two diseases—Gambia Fever and Sleeping Sickness—..are distinct. 1913 Dorland *Med. Dict.* (ed. 7), Gambian horse sickness. 1916 Fantham, etc. *Anim. Parasites* 100 Gambian horse sickness.

Gamble, *sb.*[1] **2.** Add: *On a gamble*, at a venture. *U.S. colloq.*

1924 Mulford *Rustlers' Valley* vi. 68 On a gamble he raised his sombrero.

Gamble, *v.* Add: **1. c.** To speculate recklessly.

1884 *Harper's Weekly* Apr. 26 (Cent. D.) The evil effects of gambling in stocks and provisions.

2. Delete *rare* and add U.S. example:

1930 *Publishers' Weekly* 8 Feb. 706 He would not have gambled his money upon them by adding them to his list.

b. Also (*a*) with *off*, and (*b*) without *away*.

1848 Thackeray *Van. Fair* lxiv, When she got her money she gambled; when she had gambled it she was put to shifts to live. 1869 Tourgee *Toinette* xii, Loyd probably traded her off, perhaps gambled her off, in some drunken spree.

Gambling, *vbl. sb.* **b.** Add: **gambling-joint** *U.S.*, a gambling-den.

1921 Mulford *Bar-20 Three* xxi. 272 I'm going to set fire to that gamblin'-joint an' drive 'em out. 1925 B. Travers *Mischief* v, Who does Captain Dumfoil expect to find running a gambling joint? The Archbishop of Canterbury?

Gambrel. 4. Add: *gambrel joint*; **gambrel-roof, -roofed** *a.* (earlier U.S. examples).

1876 J. Burroughs *Winter-sunshine* iv. 104 A fox struggling with a trap which held him by the hind leg, above the *gambrel-joint! 1765 *Massachusetts Gaz.* 19 Dec. (Th.) A large building with two upright Stories and a *Gambrel Roof. 1834 *Knickerbocker Mag.* III. 428 Built in the ancient Dutch mode, with a high, steep gambrel-roof. 1779 in *Mass. Hist. Soc.* Ser. II. II. 466 The [Indian] Queens Pallace was a *gambril ruft house. 1824 *Microscope* 21 Feb. (Th.) In a gambrel-roof'd house,..She dwelt with a heart void of care.

Game, *sb.* Add:

4. d. *pl.* Athletics as organized in a school or college. Also *attrib.*, as *games master*.

1899 Kipling *Stalky* 66 King and Macrea, fellow house-masters, had borne it in upon him that by games, and games alone, was salvation wrought. 1902 *Daily Chron.* 16 July 7/1 Special games-masters and mistresses. 1903 *Ibid.* 27 Nov. 10/5 A games half-holiday. 1909 *Westm. Gaz.* 22 May 1/2 As a games organizer he was a great success.

e. Thieves' slang. *The game*: thieving, house-breaking; usually in phr. *on the game*.

1839 Brandon *Poverty, Mendicity, & Crime* Gloss. (Farmer) *On the game*, thieving. 1851 Mayhew *Lond. Labour* I. 245 Whether the game got stale, or Peter became honest, is beyond the purport of my communication to settle. 1905 *Daily Chron.* 14 Apr. 6/6 Paolillo pressed me to go out 'on the game'.

f. *The game*: prostitution. *slang.*

1898 *Daily News* 21 July 8/6 The prosecutrix pestered her to 'go on the game', i.e., the streets. 1911 F. Harris *Women of Shakespeare* 194 The phrase of the prostitute to-day on the streets of London is: 'I'm on the game.'

6. f. A person's performance in a particular game; the normal standard of one's play. *To be on* (or *off*) *one's game*: to be in (or out of) form, to be playing well (or badly).

1885 I played a wretched game [see Dict. 6 c]. 1891 H. G. Hutchinson *Golf* 16 What am I doing wrong, Tom? I'm quite off my game. *Ibid.* 32 If you are one of the many golfers who overrate their game. 1895 H. W. W. Wilber-

force *Lawn Tennis* xii. 45 Another thing that may put one's partner off his game is running across and taking his balls. 1904 J. P. Mannock *Billiards Expounded* i. 33 It is wonderful how strength of nerve improves with the strength of one's game. 1920 *Westm. Gaz.* 16 Oct. 2/2 Their disregard of the recognised rules was accentuated by the fact that neither man was on his game.

16. a. (sense 11) *game-drive, -park, -shot.*

1895 Scully *Kafir Stories* 98 These *game-drives were fraught with considerable danger. 1897 J. L. Allen *Choir Invisible* xiii, The great neutral *game-park of the Northern and the Southern Indians. 1927 A. C. Doyle *Case Bk. S. Holmes* 82 The famous *game-shot, sportsman, and man-about-town was a big, swarthy fellow.

b. *game-dealer.*

1876 J. S. Ingram *Centen. Exposition* 691 One of the oldest game-dealers in the West.

17. game-goer, a bid (at bridge) which is likely to secure the score of 'game'; so **game-going** *a.*

1929 Work *Compl. Contract Bridge* i. 6 The dealer's first concern when he picks up his hand is to get his side into a game-going contract if game is in their cards. *Ibid.* 7 Dealer having made a bid that is not a game-goer.

Game-legged, *a.* [f. Game *a.*[2] + Leg *sb.* + -ed[2].] Having a game leg.

1889 A. C. Doyle *Sign of Four* xii. 236 A raw recruit, and a game-legged one at that.

Gametic (gămĕ·tik, -ī·tik), *a.* *Biol.* [f. Gamete + -ic.] Of or pertaining to gametes.

1905 Punnett *Mendelism* 25 The theory of gametic purity can be further tested by deducing from it the results which should follow from crossing the heterozygote with either of the homozygotes. *Ibid.* 64 Gametic coupling. 1909 C. C. Hurst *Exper. in Genetics* (1925) 340 Our knowledge of the behaviour of the accessory chromosome, while rendering it certain that sex is a gametic differentiation [etc.].

Gameto-. Add: **Game·toblast**, any of the bodies produced by the division of a gametospore; **Game·tocyte**, a cell giving rise to conjugating gametes; **Gametoge·nesis, -o·geny, -o·gony**, reproduction through gametes; so **Gametoge·nic, -o·genous** *adjs.*; **Game·toklast** = **gametoblast*; **Game·tophore** *Bot.*, a modified branch or filament bearing gametes; **Game·tospore**, the spore of a sporozoan parasite, as of malaria.

1901 *Practitioner* Mar. 281 *Gametoblast—or *Gametoklast—is Ray Lankester's name for the Sporozoite of Schaudinn-Blanchard. *Ibid.* 272 The *gametocytes have a special form (crescentic). 1922 Punnett *Mendelism* (ed. 6) 124 During the *gametogenesis of the F_1 plant. 1903 *Proc. Royal Soc. Lond.* LXXII. 500 The *gametogenic tissues which are destined to become the reproductive elements. *Note*, The term *gametogenic*, as here proposed, is also intended to include the primary sporogenous tissue of plants. 1903 *E. R. Lankester's Treat. Zool.*, *Protozoa* II. 210 *note*, The gametocytes are termed *gametogenous monots, the formation of the gametes being regarded as a special case of monogony. 1902 *Encycl. Brit.* XXVIII. 139/1 *Gametogeny is the name applied to the formation of the gametes, *i.e.*, of the ova and spermatozoa. 1916 Fantham, etc. *Anim. Parasites* 143 The trophozoites begin to show sexual differentiation instead of forming schizonts, that is, *gametogony commences. 1902 *Encycl. Brit.* XXVIII. 556/1 Since..the sporophore bears sexual cells, they are conveniently termed *gametophores. 1901 *Practitioner* Mar. 281 *Gametospore is Ray Lankester's name for the Oocyste, Ookinet, Copula, or Zygote of Schaudinn-Blanchard.

Gametoid (gæ·mĭtoid), *a.* and *sb.* *Biol.* [f. Gamete + -oid.] **A.** *adj.* Having the form of a gamete. **B.** *sb.* A body resembling a gamete, but having a number of nuclei instead of a single one.

1891 [see Zygotoid in Dict.]. 1903 *Proc. Royal Soc. Lond.* LXXII. 503 These 'gametoid' neoplasms. 1908 *Practitioner* Feb. 226 Nuttall and Graham-Smith...These authors particularly note that neither gametoid cells, nor flagellated forms of this parasite, have been observed.

Gamgee (gæ·mdʒi). The name of S. *Gamgee* (1828–1886) used attrib. in *Gamgee tissue*, or absol., to designate an absorbent cotton-wool for dressing wounds, invented by him.

1906 *Practitioner* Nov. 674 The application of a baked or scorched pad of Gamgee tissue. 1920 *Rose & Carless' Man. Surg.* (ed. 10) 288 Swabs..of absorbent material, such as Gamgee tissue. 1924 *Glasgow Herald* 8 Apr. 10 Strips of emergency field-dressing gamgee.

Gamine (gamīn). [Fr.] A female street Arab or the like. Hence **Gaminerie** (gaminri), the action of a gamine.

1921 *Glasgow Herald* 23 Apr. 4 The 'Coquette' is an unscrupulous milliner's assistant, a regular 'gamine', who plays off a lover against a husband. 1927 *Observer* 25 Sept. 15/3 Miss Gertrude Lawrence..can play the *gamine* and the lady. 1930 *Ibid.* 1 June 15 Amused by the rich *gaminerie* of Miss H.

Gamma. 5. Add: **gamma** or **γ rays**, very penetrating rays not appreciably deflected by a magnetic or electric field, emitted by radium and other radio-active substances. So *gamma irradiation.*

1904 *Daily Chron.* 6 June 4/4 It is probably the 'gamma' rays from radium, similar to Röntgen rays. 1904 E. Rutherford *Radio-Activity* 141 The γ or very penetrating Rays. 1929 *Brit. Med. Jrnl.* 14 Sept. 508 The Effect of Gamma Irradiation on Cell Division. 1930 Buckingham *Matter & Radiation* 31 The longest X-rays have the properties of the shortest ultra-violet rays and the longest Gamma-rays merge into the shortest X-rays.

Gamma (grass), var. Gama grass.

Gammon, *sb.*[1] Add: **5.** *U.S.* = Gambrel 1.

1874 J. C. McCoy *Hist. Sk. Cattle Trade West & South-west* 312 Then comes one or more men and insert a strong gammon of four or more feet in length, in the hocks beneath the hamstrings of the hinder legs. In the middle of the gammon stick a flat iron hook is adjusted.

Gammon, *sb.*[4] **3.** Add: Also in phr. *gammon and spinach* (see Spinach 3).

Gammy, *a.* **3.** Add: Also, disabled through injury or pain.

1893 [in Dict.]. 1913 *Punch* 23 Apr. 331 Gammy thumb! The rest o' the squad ain't got gammy thumbs, has they?

Gampless (gæ·mplės), *a.* [f. Gamp *sb.* 2.] Umbrella-less.

1899 *Westm. Gaz.* 2 Oct. 6/2 To provide 'gampless' seat-holders with umbrellas. 1902 Mary E. Mann *In Summer Shade* ix, Any old gampless woman of the congregation.

Gander, *sb.* **4.** Add: **gander-puller** *U.S.*, one who engages in gander-pulling; **gander-pulling** (earlier example).

1835 *Southern Lit. Messenger* I. 645 Of the most conspicuous '*minora sidera*' the Kentuckian horse drover, the horse jockey, the *ganderpuller might be mentioned. 1818 Fearon *Sk. Amer.* 247 They have also another practice.. called '*gander pulling'. This diversion consists in tying a live gander to a tree or pole, [etc.].

Gandhism (gæ·ndiz'm), **Gandhiism** (gæ·ndi,iz'm). Also *erron.* **Ghand(h)-.** [f. the name of M. K. *Gandhi* (born 1869), Indian nationalist + -ism.] The policy advocated by Gandhi. So **Ga·ndhist** (also *attrib.*), **Ga·ndhiite**, a supporter of Gandhi, an adherent of Gandhism.

1921 *Public Opinion* 2 Dec. 554/3 The inherent selfishness of Ghandi-ism. 1921 *Glasgow Herald* 2 Dec. 8 It is..undesirable..to mention 'Ghandhism' just now in this picturesque Rajput city. *Ibid.* 12 Dec. 9 Protests from some few Gandhists. 1927 *Observer* 7 Aug. 13/5 Such reactionary and barren movements as Gandhiism. 1927 W. E. Collinson *Contemporary Engl.* 85 The policy adopted by the Gandhiites of non-violent coercion. 1928 *Observer* 15 Jan. 4 The general Gandhist idea.

Gandura (gandū·ră). Also **gandoura, -urah, gondourah.** An East African under-garment.

1851 *Illustr. Catal. Gt. Exhib.* IV. I. 1262/2 Gandoura, made of wool and silk. 1902 *Daily Chron.* 12 June 7/5 Wearing only his rich white gandurah. 1927 *Glasgow Herald* 17 Sept. 4 The Cadi in spotless burnous and fine white linen gandoura.

Gang, *sb.*[1] **8. b.** (Additional U.S. example.)

1821 T. Dwight *Trav.* (1823) III. 204, I had an opportunity of seeing in one of the mills..what is called a 'gang of saws'; that is, a sufficient number to convert a log into boards by a single operation.

12. *gang-plough* (earlier U.S. example).

1850 *Cultivator* New Ser. VII. 369 We stand much in need of some good..gang plows.

Gang, *v.*[2] Add:

1. b. To arrange (implements) in gangs. *U.S.*

1900 *Yearbk. U.S. Dept. Agric.* 540 The plows are usually ganged, two to one frame.

2. Also, to go in company *with*.

1928 W. A. White *Masks in Pageant* 348 He was frail [in his boyhood] and never ganged with his fellows.

Gangdom (gæ·ŋdǝm). [f. Gang *sb.*[1] + -dom.] = *Gangland.

1930 *Observer* 19 Oct. 17 A mere commonplace of New York gangdom.

Gange, *v.* **1.** (Earlier U.S. example.)

1854 Shillaber *Mrs. Partington* 245 Ike ganged his hook.

Gangland (gæ·ŋlænd). *U.S.* [f. Gang *sb.*[1] + Land *sb.*] The domain of gangsters.

1928 *Daily Tel.* 28 Aug. 7/5 A bomb, known in gangland parlance as a 'pineapple'. 1930 *Daily News* (N.Y.) 6 Nov. 2/1 A Chicago gangland massacre. 1931 *Daily Express* 28 Apr. 2/1 All crimes attributable either to the gangland chief or his benchmen.

Gang-plank. *U.S.* (Earlier example.)

1846 *Knickerbocker Mag.* XXVII. 469 The last bell rang; the gangplank was drawn in-board; the hawsers were cast off.

Gangsman. Add: **3.** = next.

1923 *Glasgow Herald* 30 Aug. 7 The complete story of the gangsmen and their crimes.

Gangster (gæ·ŋstǝɹ). orig. *U.S.* [f. Gang *sb.*[1] + -ster.]

1. A member of a gang of criminals.

1896 *Columbus* (Ohio) *Dispatch* 10 Apr. 4/2 The gangster may play all sorts of pranks with the ballot box, but in its own good time the latter will get even by kicking the gangster into the gutter. 1911 *N. Y. Evening Post* 17 June 6 A musician, returning to his home, was knocked down and killed by a group of gangsters. 1927 *Daily News* 6 Apr. 7/1 This violence [in Chicago] occurred in spite of an eve of the poll order to round up all the gangsters. 1928 *Daily Express* 31 July 8/2 Finding the three Brighton gangsters guilty of murder.

2. A member of a gang of workmen.

1927 *Daily Express* 20 June 1/5 Gangsters followed with new ballast and new track.

Ganister. Add: Also *attrib.* and *Comb.*

1833–4 J. Phillips *Geol.* in *Encycl. Metrop.* (1845) VI. 587/2 The ganister or calliard rocks of the coal strata. 1855 — *Man. Geol.* 191 Ganister measures. 1890 W. J. Gordon *Foundry* 107 The ganister lining of the converter is replaced by bricks of magnesian limestone. 1902 *Daily Chron.* 12 May 3/1 Ganister crushing.

Ganodont (gæ·nodǫnt). [f. mod.L. *Ganodonta*, f. Gr. γάνος brightness + ὀδόντ-, ὀδούς tooth.] An individual of the *Ganodonta*, a group of extinct Eocene mammals. Also *attrib.* or as *adj.*

1897 *Nat. Science* Sept. 153 The Eocene Ganodonts of the northern hemisphere.

Ganophyllite (gænofi·lǝit). *Min.* [f. Gr. γάνος brightness + φύλλον leaf: see -ite[1].] A brown hydrous silicate of manganese and aluminium.

1892 *Jrnl. Chem. Soc.* LXII. II. 1412.

Ganted, U.S. var. of Gaunted *a.* (made lean).

1887 *Scribner's Mag.* Oct. 475/2 Looks right puny an' ga'nted. 1909 R. A. Wason *Happy Hawkins* 333 His face was pale..an' he was ganted down in weight a little.

Gantry. Add: **2. b.** A structure crossing several railway-tracks to accommodate signals.

1902 *Encycl. Brit.* XXXII. 144/1 In cases where room must be economized, signals are usually placed on narrow overhead bridges or 'gantries' spanning a number of tracks.

Gap, *sb.*[1] Add:

6. d. (*a*) The distance between the upper and lower surfaces or planes of a biplane. (*b*) The distance, measured in the direction of the thrust, between the spiral courses of the blades of an aeroplane propeller.

1909 *Hazell's Annual 1910*, 487/2 Another tailless biplane is the Cody, the main planes of which have..a gap of 9 ft. in the centre. 1915 Dommett *Aeroplanes & Airships* 33 The gap between the planes, which are staggered, is 4 ft. 9 in. 1916 H. Barber *Aeroplane Speaks* 63 There will be..loss of efficiency unless the gap between the top and bottom surfaces is equal to not less than 1½ times the chord. *Ibid.* 125 The smaller the pitch, the less the 'gap'. 1918 Dommett *Dict. Aircraft* 24 *Gap*, the distance between the projections on the vertical axis of the entering edges of an upper and lower wing of a biplane. (American definition.)

9. gap-bridge, a bridge or piece of casting which closes the gap in a gap-bed lathe when not in use; **gap-rope** (see quot.).

1888 *Lockwood's Dict. Mech. Engin.*, *Gap Bridge. 1883 *Man. Seamanship for Boys* 60 Foot-Line or *Gap Rope is a rope's end rove through a block at the bowsprit cap, and bent to an eyelet-hole in the foot of the jib, or to the clew of the jib.

Gap, *v.* Add: **c.** To make a gap or breach in.

1895 in Funk's *Stand. Dict.* 1925 *Brit. Weekly* 5 Mar. 515/3 Demolishing two-thirds of the houses, and 'gapping' and 'loop-holing' the remainder. 1927 *Daily Express* 29 July 1/2 The sowing, 'gapping', 'singling', hoeing, and other processes.

Gape, *sb.* Add: **6.** *attrib.* and *Comb.*: **gape-worm**, the worm which causes the gapes (see 3 a).

1872 L. Wright *Bk. Poultry* 196 The egg of the gape-worm.

Garage (gæ·rāʒ, gæ·rėdʒ), *sb.* [F. *garage*, f. *garer* to shelter.]

1. A building, either private or public, where motor vehicles are housed for storage or repairs and cleaning. Also *attrib.* and *Comb.*

1902 *Daily Mail* 11 Jan. 6/7 The new 'garage' founded by Mr. Harrington Moore, hon. secretary of the Automobile Club...The 'garage', which is situated at the City end of Queen Victoria-street,..has accommodation for eighty cars. 1902 *Times* 1 Mar. 4/3 Motor Garage. 1902 A. C. Harmsworth *Motors & Motor-driving* 65 The simplification of the motor engine and the establishment of *garages*. *Ibid.* 306 In stations or 'garages' where a number of cars are kept. 1909 *Westm. Gaz.* 13 Apr. 4/2 A Midland firm of garage proprietors. *Ibid.* 18 Nov. 5/3 Customers who need garage room for business and private vehicles. 1920 *Ibid.* 1 Apr. 4/2 These charges..having been carefully arranged between the hotel proprietors and garage owners. 1931 *Times Lit. Suppl.* 11 June 459/1 The stable boy..has now become a garage boy.

2. A hangar in which aircraft is kept. (Disused.)

1909 A. Berget *Conquest of Air* II. vii. 280 The construction of *garages*, landing stations and shelters.

3. A canal-siding. *U.S.* (Cf. *Gare *sb.*[5])

1918 Webster Addenda.

Garage (gæ·rāʒ, gæ·rėdʒ), *v.* [f. prec.] *trans.* To place (a motor vehicle) in a garage for storage or repairs; to accommodate (a motor vehicle) at a garage. Also *absol.*

1906 *Daily Chron.* 26 May 3/7 They will garage your car ..,wash it, clean it, adjust it, repair it, keep it always at 'concert pitch'. 1907 (*title*) Where to garage. 1916 *In the Hands of the Huns* 24, I garaged our 45-h.p. Mercédès. 1928 Galsworthy *Swan Song* vii. 55 Having garaged his car, he remembered that he had not lunched.

Garamity, variant of *Gor-amity.

Garamond (gæ·rămǫnd). *Typog.* [f. the name of Claude *Garamond* (died 1561), a French type-founder.] A form of type-body.

1928 *Scholartis Press Catal.* June, Printed by the Westminster Press in 14 point Garamond. 1929 *Encycl. Brit.* XVIII. 509/2 The 'Garamond' type steadily acquired influence. 1931 *Times Lit. Suppl.* 25 June, Suppl. p. i/3 The brilliant Garamond setting for Louys' 'Roi Pausole'. *Ibid.* p. i/4 Jules Meynial shows..a catalogue well printed in hand-set Garamond.

Garbanzo: see Garavance, Calavance.

1891 Humboldt in *U.S. Dept. Agric., Div. Veg. Pathol.* Bulletin 2. 30 (Cent. D. Suppl.) Barley, beans, lentils, and garbanzos grow very well in the fields in the greatest part of the province. 1918 *Chambers's Jrnl.* Jan. 33 The fat Castilian garbanzos. 1925 *Glasgow Herald* 31 July 6 These garbanzos or chichis give the peculiar flavour to soups.

Garcinia (gaɹsi·niă). *Bot.* [mod.L., f. the name of Laurent *Garcin*, French botanist + -ia.] A tree of the genus so named of tropical Asiatic and African guttiferous trees, some species of which furnish gamboge.

1886 *G. Nicholson's Illustr. Dict. Gardening* II. 43/2 Garcinias thrive in a peat and loam compost. 1890 W. J. Gordon *Foundry* 126 The garcinia that yields the gamboge.

Garden, *sb.* Add: **1. c.** (U.S. example.)

1803 *Steele Papers* I. 374 [He] speaks of the Lands found in the neighborhood of the Walnut Hills, as being the Garden of America.

d. *To lead up the garden*: to lead on, entice, mislead. *slang.*

1926 Ethel Mannin *Sounding Brass* I. viii, They're cheats, that's wot women are! Lead you up the garden and then go snivellin' around 'cos wot's natcheral 'as 'appened to 'em. 1931 *Publishers' Circ.* 10 Jan. 25/3 It is a little disconcerting to find that everyone has been 'led up the garden' by what was evidently an entirely innocent misconception.

e. *Garden of Eden*: in attrib. use denoting any place of surpassing beauty or delight or of supreme rural felicity. Similarly *Garden of God.*

1860 Mayne Reid *Odd People* 37 This vast Garden of God [*sc.* the valley of the Amazon] is yet unexplored by man. 1918 Kipling *Land & Sea T.* (1923) 120 Garden-of-Eden picnics for weeks an' weeks.

4. a. *garden-border, -door* (later U.S. example), *-hoe, -hose, -paling, -path, -rail, -rake, -seed* (earlier example), *-soil, -spade, -vegetable.*

1862 'Gail Hamilton' *Country Living & Thinking* 19 They hummed with the bees in the *garden-borders. 1845 Caroline M. Kirkland *Western Clearings* 116 The minister..drew his gentle fiance to the *garden-door, and thence into the garden. 1783 E. Parkman *Diary* 300 *Garden Hoe 1/6. 1881 *Rep. Indian Affairs* 3, I distributed among these people six hundred field and garden hoes. 1883 Nye *Baled Hay* 207 Use benzine..cautiously with whitewash brush and *garden hose. 1813 *Niles' Weekly Reg.* IV. 12/2 A temporary breastwork, composed of rails and *garden pailing. 1863 B. Taylor *H. Thurston* xxxi. 396 Crickets chirped loud among the dying weeds along the garden-palings. 1870 'Fanny Fern' *Ginger-Snaps* 162 The irresolute hand, that could only lead them up and down that narrow *garden-path. 1846 *Knickerbocker Mag.* XXVIII. 144 The Doctor stood looking over the *garden rails when one of the 'seven wise men' of the village passed by. 1858 J. A. Warder *Hedges & Evergreens* 60 A light *garden-rake. 1621 Mourt *Relat. Plant. Plymouth* (1865) 82 This day some *garden Seeds were sowen. 1848 *Cultivator* V. 213, I.. potted it in common *garden soil. 1875 Mrs. Stowe *We & Neighbors* ii. 20 Catnip..which grew in a bit of garden soil back of the house. 1744 in *Maryland Hist. Mag.* XXI. 243, 6 good Well Steeled *Gardin Spades. 1831 Peck *Guide for Emigrants* II. 141 *Garden Vegetables.

5. a. *garden-fruit* (later U.S. example).

1747 *N.H. Probate Rec.* III. 507 Herbs Cabbages and such garden fruits as she shall desire.

6. garden city, a town surrounded by a rural belt, in public ownership and organized for healthy living and for industry within restricted limits; **Garden Colony**, a name given to Natal, on account of the wealth and beauty of its flora; **garden county**, the county (of a state) most resembling a garden; the most fertile and beautiful part; **garden craft**, the management of gardens; **garden lot** *U.S.*, a piece of ground for a garden; **garden patch** *U.S.* = *garden-ground* (b); **garden-room**, a room with a door or window opening out on to a garden; **garden sauce** (**sars, sass**) *U.S.*, garden vegetables; **Garden State** *U.S.*, the state of Kansas; **garden-suburb**, a suburb organized on the same lines as a garden-city; **garden-truck** *U.S.*, market-garden produce.

1903 *Times* 29 Aug. 4/5 The *Garden City Pioneer Company (Limited) has acquired about 4,000 acres of land near Hitchin on which to build the first garden city. 1914 *Scotsman* 6 Oct. 7/2 There are at present in existence a number of schemes such as the First Garden City at Letchworth, and the various garden suburbs which have been successfully started in various parts of the country. 1927 *Daily Tel.* 1 May 9/4 The Federal Capital City of Australia..its splendid design on 'garden city' lines. 1899 Devereux *Side Lights S. A.* 158 The '*Garden Colony' deserves its name, so universal in Durban are its lawns of smooth turf and its banks of blossom and foliage. 1899 *Westm. Gaz.* 18 Dec. 12/1 The hills and valleys of the Garden Colony are all clad in green. 1892 *Vermont Agric. Rep.* XII. 113 This is often called the *Garden County of Vermont. 1892 J. D. Sedding (*title*) *Garden Craft, Old and New. 1904 E. Wharton *Italian Villas* 5 To enjoy and appreciate the Italian garden-craft one must always bear in mind that it is independent of floriculture. 1927 Rohde (*title*) Garden-craft in the Bible, and other Essays. 1646 *Charlestown Land Records* 138 One dwelling hous and a *garden Lott..scituate at the sconce-Poynt. 1875 Mrs. Stowe *We & Neighbors* i. 12 The house itself and the *garden-patch in the rear. 1887 Mary E. Wilkins *Humble Romance* 186 She had taken a fancy lately to a landward window, the one with the poor little garden-patch under it. 1892 Stevenson & Osbourne *Wrecker* xx, There was but one place reserved, the *garden-room, whither Lady Ann had now retired. 1899 W. Robinson *Engl. Flower Garden* (ed. 7) xxxii. 367 Where they give shade or a 'garden room' as part of the house they are a real gain. *Ibid.* 368. 1833 J. Neal *Down-Easters* I. 91, I wanted cabbage or potaters, or most any sort o' *garden sarse. 1869 Bowles *Our New West* xi. 231 A load of grain, pork, or '*garden sass'. 1873 Beadle *Undevel. West* xxiv. 504 The country West does not contain arable land enough to supply garden-sauce to an average population. 1871 Schele de Vere *Americanisms* (1872) 659 Kansas is often called the *Garden State, from the beautiful appearance of rolling prairies and vast cultivated fields which abound in that fertile region. 1883 J. H. Beadle *Western Wilds* xxxviii. 612 The soft blue sky of the Garden State. 1905 *Spectator* 11 Mar. 356/2 The *Garden Suburb Trust. 1913 *Punch* 30 July 105 Gentility in our garden suburb. 1868 B. F. Taylor *Between Gates* 84 A deep bushel basket..filled with '*garden truck'. 1897 R. M. Stuart *Simpkinsville* 152, I s'pose you and Mis' Carroll've been swappin' confidences about garden-truck.

1901 Marah E. Ryan *Montana* i. 29 But I've eaten some pretty good garden truck they've raised.

Garden, *v.* Add:

1. b. *Cricket.* To clear away loose fragments likely to deflect the ball from its course. *slang.*

1897 *Encycl. Sport* I. 226/2 Fragments of grass and turf should be removed...The process of clearing the ground of *débris* is known to cricketers as 'gardening'.

Garden spot. *U.S.* [Garden *sb.* 1.]

1. A piece of garden-ground.

1687 *Plymouth Rec.* 190 From thence we are bounded by goodman Watson's garden spot. 1767 in *Essex Inst. Hist. Coll.* II. 87/1 Agreed with the Rev. Peter Clark to hire his House,..and a garden spot. 1834 H. Brackenridge *Recoll.* v. 42 Gallipolitans did not pretend to cultivate anything more than small garden spots. 1878 Mrs. Stowe *Poganuc P.* xi. 116 Though the snow banks yet lay over the garden-spots, deep and high. 1884 'C. E. Craddock' *In Tenn. Mts.* I. 53 She was welcomed to a chair and a view of the weed-grown 'garden-spot'.

2. A place suggestive of a garden. (Cf. Garden *sb.* 1 c.)

1813 *Niles' Weekly Reg.* IV. 317/2 The Rapids of the Miami may justly be termed the 'garden spot' of the territory. 1856–7 D. D. Owen *Geol. Kentucky* (Bartlett 1859) The unbroken tracts lying towards the heads of the streams are indeed the 'Garden Spots' of the State. 1873 J. H. Beadle *Undevel. West* xxii. 433 Garden spot o' the world, sir, no doubt of it.

Garden-stuff. (Earlier Amer. example.)

c 1644 Winthrop *Lett.* (1869) 460 All sorts of English fruits and garden stuffe prosper very well heere.

Gardner (gā·ɹdnǝɹ). The name of Captain M. W. *Gardner*, used attrib. and absol. to designate a type of machine gun invented by him, which has two to five barrels side by side.

1884 *Illustr. Lond. News* LXXXIV. 222/1 The force was drawn up..with three Gardners on the left and three Gatlings on the right. 1899 *Daily News* 30 Jan. 5/1 The workshops were turning out two Gardiners [*sic*] and two Maxims every month. 1903 A. C. Doyle *Green Flag* 11 Caught in the blast of lead from a Gardner.

Gare (gāɹ), *sb.*[5] [Fr.] **a.** A dock-basin on a river or canal. **b.** A railway station. **c.** A pier, wharf, or the like.

1869 Sir S. Northcote in *Life* (1890) I. 360 Two or three *gares* have been hollowed out, where vessels may lie. 1902 *Encycl. Brit.* XXVII. 708/2 Commander Edwards, R.N., proceeded down the Canal, taking possession of the *gares* and dredgers. 1906 *Daily Chron.* 10 Sept. 5/6 When seen at the gare he was wearing a bowler hat and had a grey beard. 1912 *Q. Rev.* Oct. 315 Gares, or mooring stations, are now provided.

Garibaldi. Add: **1. c.** *Garibaldi biscuit*, a sandwich biscuit containing a paste of currants.

1893 *Army & Navy Co-op. Stores* 8 Biscuits...Garibaldi.. 5½ [per lb.]. 1909 H. G. Wells *Tono-Bungay* III. iii. 276 Instead of offering me a Garibaldi biscuit, she asked me with that faint lisp of hers, to 'have some squashed flies, George'.

Garibaldian (gærĭbǫ·ldiăn, -bæ·l-), *a.* and *sb.* [f. Garibaldi + -an.] **A.** *adj.* Of, pertaining to, or supporting Garibaldi. **B.** *sb.* An adherent of Garibaldi. Also **Gariba·ldist.**

1860 *Universe* 8 Dec. 1/2 The Garibaldian General Türr. 1861 E. Dicey *Cavour* xxiv, The Garibaldian Dictatorship. 1863 *All the Year Round* 2 May 222/1 The Garibaldists are coming! 1867 J. Watts-Russell in Cardella *Life* ix. 49 We shot away at the Garibaldians from some windows. 1892 O'Clery *Making of Italy* 121 The numerous expeditions which followed for the purpose of reinforcing..the Garibaldian army.

Garn (gāɹn), *int.* Cockney pronunciation of *go on!* (see Go *v.* B. 84 j) often used to express disbelief or ridicule of a statement.

1888 Runciman *Chequers* 80 Garn, you farthin' face! 1912 G. B. Shaw *Pygmalion* I, The Note Taker (*whipping out his book*) Heavens! what a sound!..Ah—ah—ah—ow—ow—ow—oo! The Flower Girl (*tickled by the performance, and laughing in spite of herself*) Garn! 1925 *Glasgow Herald* 9 Jan. 8 He complained that if he used such words as 'garn' or 'struth' he was accused of vulgarity, whereas were he capable of imitating the peculiar sounds such as were heard from those north of the Tweed he would be able to move in any society.

Garnett, *v.* Add: Also as *sb*, the machine used for this purpose; **Garnett tooth**, a form of saw-tooth used in Garnett machines.

1884 W. S. B. McLaren *Spinning* (ed. 2) 189 The [machine] for opening the looser waste is called a Garnett. 1892 Nasmith *Students' Cotton Spinning* 132 It is customary to cover the licker-in with a set of teeth...These are called 'Garnett' teeth.

Garo (gā·ro). A member of one of a group of Mongoloid tribes of the Garo Hills, Assam; also, their language.

1880 *Encycl. Brit.* XII. 777/2 The following are the twenty principal dialects of the Tibeto-Burman group:—(1) Cáchári or Bodo, (2) Garo, [etc.]. 1883 *Ibid.* XV. 295/1 Of the aboriginal tribes [of Maimansinh] the most numerous are the Hajongs (24,936) and Gâros (10,997). 1912 A. Gordon *Life A. H. Charteris* 339 The plains at the foot of the mountains—called the Dooars—are peopled by Mechis, Rajbunsis, and Garos.

Garret, *sb.*[1] **4.** Add: *garret chamber, -stairs* (earlier U.S. example).

1657 in *Essex Inst. Hist. Coll.* VII. 39/2 John Norman is to build an house for them..with..one *garret chamber. 1889 Rose T. Cooke *Steadfast* ii. 27 She crept upstairs to the 'garret chamber'. 1868 S. Sewall *Diary* I. 241, I thought of Mr. Oakes's Dream about Mr. Shepard and Mitchell beckening him up the *Garret-Stairs in Harvard College.

Garrigue (garī·g). Also **garigue.** [Fr.] In the south of France, uncultivated land of a calcareous soil overgrown with scrub-oak and pine.

1896 *Smithsonian Rep.* 414 Often upon uncultivated lands, there called the garrigues, are seen long trains of ants forming two continuous lines hurrying in opposite directions, one going away from the nest, the other toward it. 1922 *19th Cent.* Sept. 429 The short-toed lark..was found mainly on the *garrigues*—high, chalky downlands, planted with the universal vines.

Garrison, *sb.* **6.** Add: *garrison duty.*

1813 Southey *Nelson* I. 37 The few who were able to perform garrison duty.

Garrupa: see Grouper.

Garter, *sb.* Add: **7.** *To fly the garter*: see Fly *v.*[1] 4 b.

8. garter-stitch, the simplest stitch in knitting, used in making garters; also called *plain knitting*.

1909 *Daily Chron.* 8 Dec. 9/4 Sixty stitches are loosely cast on, and sixty rows of garter-stitch knitted.

Garth[1]. **2.** For † *Obs.* read *Obs.* exc. *Hist.*

1894 J. C. Atkinson *Old Whitby* 43 There is such a perplexing uncertainty in the words..of all who have taken in hand to write about the Horngarth, as to what the *garth* element of it really was. 1908 W. G. Collingwood *Scand. Brit.* 193 He made his *bær*, a group of buildings, in the *tún*, or homefield, which he manured and mowed for hay, and surrounded with a garth.

Gärtner (gē·ɹtnǝɹ). The name of Karl F. *Gärtner*, Danish anatomist (1785–1827), used to designate certain parts of the anatomy of mammalia distinguished or described by him.

Gärtner's canal, in the female, a tube that is the homologue of the vas deferens. *Gärtner's duct*, a straight canal extending from the parovarium through the broad ligament to the vagina.

1890 Billings *Med. Dict.* 1892 *W. W. Keen & J. W. White's Text-bk. Surg.* 978 Gärtner's duct. 1896 tr. *Boas' Text Bk. Zool.* 491 Gärtner's duct in the Ruminants. 1907 W. Rose & Carless *Man. Surg.* (ed. 6) 218 The main Wolffian duct..occasionally runs down between the layers of the broad ligament close to the uterus, to open in the vagina near the urethral orifice, being then known as Gärtner's duct.

Garua (gărū·ă). [Peruvian Sp.] = *Camanchaca.

1877 E. G. Squier *Peru* 38 We are assured that 'it never rains in Lima'; but the dense permeating mist not infrequently forms itself into minute drops, when it is called *guara* [*sic.*]. 1914 C. R. Enock *Ecuador* 195 The Peruvian coast..receives..a light mist-drizzle, known as *garua*. 1927 Kendrew *Climates Cont.* 313 At Lima..heavy showers are rare, the usual rain being a fine drizzle or a wet mist called Garua.

Gas, *sb.* Add:

3. c. Read: 'a balloon or airship'.

f. In full *asphyxiating gas, poison gas*: highly poisonous or asphyxiating gas, such as chlorine, used in warfare. Also = *tear gas, lachrymatory gas.*

First used in the war of 1914–18 by Germany on April 22, 1915.

1915 D. O. Barnett *Lett.* 28 Apr. 124 You may like to know we've got a way of competing with asphyxiating gas. 1915 *War Illustr.* 8 May 282/1 Germans Held Back by their Own Gas. 1915 *Daily Sketch* 18 Aug. 6/2 'Ware Gas. 1916 *War Illustr.* 7 Oct. 177 As soon as the use of the gas lost its novelty it was deprived of much of its effect.

6. *gas-proof* adj.

1909 *Westm. Gaz.* 17 Feb. 7/2 Experts in the use of gas-proof apparatus. 1928 *Daily Express* 30 Apr. 7 Fortifications..shellproof and gasproof.

7. (in sense *3 f), *gas alarm, bombardment, cloud, war, zone*; **gas alert, attack, bomb** (see quots.); **gas-cell**, a cell containing gas in an airship; **gas-cooker** = *gas-stove*; **gas-filled** *a.*, filled with gas, *spec.* applied to a type of electric light bulb; **gas-fired** *a.*, heated by the combustion of gaseous fuel; **gas gangrene**, earlier *gaseous gangrene*, gangrene in which gas (e.g. hydrogen sulphide) is formed; **gas-helmet** = **gas mask*; **gas-mantle** (see Mantle *sb.* 5 g); **gas mask** (earlier *anti-(poison-)gas mask*) a mask used as a protection against poisonous gas; **gas-oxygen** = *oxy-coal-gas* (see Oxy- 2); **gas shell** (see quot.); **gas-spurt**, little heaps or lumps occurring on the surface of some strata thought to be due to the intermittent escape of gas from decomposing organic matter; **gas thread**, a standard form of screw-thread used on iron and brass tubes; **gas trap**, a trap to prevent sewer gas from coming up a pipe; **gas-turbine**, a turbine which uses for its motive power the gas obtained by burning or exploding a fuel; **gas-valve** (see quot.)

1915 D. O. Barnett *Lett.* 183 There was a false *gas alarm last night. 1918 E. S. Farrow *Dict. Mil. Terms* s.v., When conditions of atmosphere and wind are favorable for a gas attack preparations are made to meet it. This is known as *gas alert...*Gas Attacks*, attacks in which chlorine and other gases are brought up to the trench compressed in steel cylinders...*Gas Bomb*, in trench warfare a bomb containing a bursting charge of high explosive and poisonous gas. 1919 G. K. Rose *2/4th Oxf. & Bucks L. Infty.* 203 Throughout the night of August 7/8..a heavy gas-bombardment was kept up. 1928 C. F. S. Gamble *A Sea Air Station* xix. 334 Above us the *gas-bags were banging

limply down. 1915 *War Illustr.* 25 Sept. 128 A coming *gas-cloud. 1890 *Cassell's Mag.* Mar. 255/1 A New *Gas Cooker. 1907 *Jrnl. Soc. Arts* LV. 596/2 *Gas-filled airships have lately been so improved. 1919 *Conquest* I. 25/3 A modern half-watt gas-filled lamp. 1889 *C. E. Groves & W. Thorp's Chem. Technol.* I. 546 The *gas-fired boiler showed an evaporation of from 8·6 to 9·2 lbs. of water per lb. of coal. 1918 *Nomencl. Dis.* 238 Bacillus œdematis maligni. ..The cause of malignant œdema and some cases of *gas gangrene. 1915 *Punch* 15 Dec. 488/3 Will officers please state how many *Gas Helmets they possess? 1917 P. MacGill *Brown Brethren* vii. 102 A few had pulled their gas helmets down over their heads and faces. 1900 *Jrnl. Soc. Arts* XLVIII. 460/2 The Incandescent *Gas Mantle and its Use. 1909 H. G. Wells *Tono-Bungay* III. i. 219 The cerium and thorium alone were worth the money he extracted for the gas-mantles then in vogue. 1915 *War Illustr.* 4 Sept. 69 French soldiers wearing anti-poison *gas masks and respirators. 1917 *Ibid.* 17 Feb. 15/3 An Austro-Hungarian infantryman with gas-mask. 1904 *Nature* 9 June 132/1 The soapstone can be melted in a *gas-oxygen jet, and very fine fibres are easily drawn out from the clear bead thus obtained. 1915 D. O. Barnett *Lett.* 204 Coming through a district where they'd been using *gas-shells. 1918 E. S. Farrow *Dict. Mil. Terms*, *Gas Shells*, ordinary shells from which the greater part of explosive has been taken and replaced by a poisonous liquid, which, when the shell bursts, turns into a poisonous vapor or gas. 1879 *Encycl. Brit.* X. 294/1 *Gas-spurts. 1882 Geikie *Text-bk. Geol.* 486. 1884 Knight *Dict. Mech.* Suppl., **Gas Trap*, a device to prevent the reflux of gas from the sewer. 1914 N. Davey *Gas Turbine* 11 The constant-pressure, single-fluid *gas turbine. 1884 Knight *Dict. Mech.* Suppl., **Gas Valve*, a stop valve for gas mains. 1931 'Miles' (*title*) The *Gas War of 1940. 1915 *War Illustr.* 8 May 270/2 Most of them [*sc.* Canadians] were sufficiently removed from the deadly *gas zone to escape sudden asphyxiation.

Gas (gæs), *sb.*[2] *U.S.* Colloq. abbrev. of *Gasolene. *To step* or *tread on the gas*, to accelerate a motor engine by pressing down the accelerator-pedal with the foot; *gen.* to put on speed.

1905 Rex Beach *Pardners* v. (1912) 125, I turned the gas into the tug, blowin' for the Wells Street Bridge. 1916 H. L. Wilson *Somewhere in Red Gap* vii. 289 Once she'd tramped on the gas of a ninety-horsepower racer and socked him against a stone wall. 1924 W. M. Raine *Troubled Waters* viii. 81 Next moment she was pushing home the brake and shutting off the gas. 1925 H. L. Foster *Trop. Tramp Tourists* 42 My chauffeur turned off the gas..and lighted a cigarette. 1927 Huntington & Whitney *Builders Amer.* 329 The only question is whether we shall stubbornly keep our foot on the gas until there is a collision. 1927 Meherin *Sandy* lxi, With a suddenness that sickened her he stepped on the gas. 1929 *Times* 6 Nov. 15/4 The time may come when, to speed up the cause, he may tread on the gas with the best of them.

Gas, *v.* Add: **1. c.** To inflate with gas.

1922 *Encycl. Brit.* XXX. 48/2 Airship harbours have facilities for gassing airships with hydrogen.

4. *pass.* **b.** *spec.* To be subjected to a gas attack; usually, to be affected by poison gas used in warfare.

The original wider sense is now felt to be a generalization of this use.

1915 *Times* 7 May 9/4 The men in hospital..who were 'gassed'..on Hill 60. 1915 D. O. Barnett *Lett.* 9 June 168 Young had to go off this morning to a village a few miles back to be gassed. He (and a lot of staff men) were put in a trench and given a dose, with respirators on of course. *Ibid.* 14 June 178 They say that round Wipers the German infantry is rotten..[and] won't advance if there is any fire to hold them up, that is, unless we're gassed out. 1919 G. K. Rose *2/4th Oxf. & Bucks Lt. Infty.* 203 The Colonel,..Regimental Sergeant-Major and many signallers and runners, all found that they were gassed. 1922 *Daily Mail* 11 Nov. 7, 18 Girls 'Gassed'. A number of employees were overcome by fumes ..through a stopper flying from a cylinder of ammonia gas. *Ibid.* 14 Nov. 7 Army Officer Gassed in his Bath...Accidental Death, the result of poisoning by a gas escape from a geyser. *Ibid.* 20 Nov. 7 Residents of Horley, Surrey, complain of being 'gassed' by the fumes released in the breaking up of mustard gas shells at a dump near Gatwick Racecourse, about a mile and a half away.

5. b. orig. *U.S.* (Earlier U.S. examples.)

1855 *Herald of Freedom* (Kansas) 8 Sept. 2/4 (Th.) When it's done 'tis done, without buncomin' and gassin' on't two or three days. 1871 Schele de Vere *Americanisms* (1872) 263 One of the means employed for this purpose is to deliver long speeches, merely to consume time, and for this the expression to *gas*, has, of late, come into use.

6. *intr.* Of a storage battery: To give off gas.

1902 E. J. Wade *Second. Batteries* 332 When once the surfaces of a pure lead anode in an electrolyte of dilute sulphuric acid are peroxidised and gassing. *Ibid.* 335 As a rule the positives commence to gas almost immediately the current passes. 1907 Vicarey *Storage Batteries* 7 The charge must be continued until every cell in the whole battery has become milky or 'gasses freely'.

Gas-bag. Add:

1. b. A balloon or airship. *colloq.* (*depreciatory*).

1877 *Design & Work* III. 602 Science! indeed, to talk of propelling a flaccid gas-bag! 1888 *English Mech.* XLVIII. 224 There was an instance the other day..of the impracticability of gas-bags. 1925 E. Fraser & Gibbons *Soldier & Sailor Words.*

c. A bag inflated or inflatable with gas, constituting the envelope of an airship or a section of it.

1898 *Pearson's Mag.* VI. 611 We have an apparatus that can lift a man up several hundred feet into the air without using any gasbag. 1900 *Black & White Budget* III. 818/1 The framework is sub-divided by sixteen network partitions, in each of which a gas-bag of corresponding shape is inserted. 1912 *Rev. Reviews* XLVI. 61 Inside the frames go the gas-bags, sixteen or so in number.

Gas-light. c. Add: **gaslight paper**, a photographic printing-paper on which the negative is printed out by exposure to gas-light; **gaslight-print**, a print made from a negative by gas-light; so *gas-light printing*.

1906 R. C. Bayley *Complete Photographer* 243 *Gaslight papers, as their name implies, are sufficiently insensitive to be worked in gaslight. 1907 *Westm. Gaz.* 26 Oct. 13/2 The sulphide toning process used so much now to give warm brown tones to bromide prints is equally applicable to *gaslight prints. 1906 R. C. Bayley *Complete Photographer* 245 Incandescent gas is much more powerful than is needed for bromide work, but is an excellent light for *gaslight printing.

Gasolene. Add: *U.S.* The petrol used for motor engines. (See also *Gas *sb.*[2])

1895 [in Dict.]. 1895 *New Rev.* Oct. 390 Thirteen [vehicles] were driven by petroleum (or gasolene) motors. *Ibid.* 392 Of the petroleum vehicle..it may be said that it owes much of its extreme lightness to its modesty in the matter of fuel. A few pints of gasolene or rectified petroleum will suffice it for five or six hours. 1931 *Times Lit. Suppl.* 14 May 381/3 If you must do your own dry-cleaning, use carbon tetrachloride, not the perilous petrol (which Americans call gasolene).

Gasper. Add:

2. Colloq. name (orig. given in jocular depreciation) for a cigarette of a cheap brand.

1914 *Isis* 14 Feb. 5/2 Not only does he prefer the Irish-grown 'gasper' to all others, but he provides them for his Saxon guest. 1916 *Punch* 11 Oct. 261 'D'yer fink Jellicoe gits 'is share?' 'Course not, stoopid. Admirals don't smoke gaspers!' 1921 Mais *Why we should read* 32 Why should one prefer a Corona cigar to a 'gasper'?

Gaspergoo, -gou (gæspǝɹgū·). *U.S.* & *Canada.* Also **gaspar-goo.** [Of obscure origin.] The fresh-water drum-fish.

1810 F. Cuming *Tour* (Pittsburg) 302 A fine dish of gaspar-goo, the best fish I had yet tasted of the produce of the Mississippi. 1831 W. B. Dewees *Lett. fr. Texas* xv. 137 Up the country our rivers abound with various kinds of fish, such as cat, buffalo, perch and gaspergoos. 1909 *Cent. Dict.* Suppl., Gaspergou.

Gassed (gæst), *ppl. a.* [*Gas *v.* 4.] Affected by poison gas.

1915 *Morn. Post* 29 May 7/7 The death of the gassed victims around Ypres. 1918 E. M. Roberts *Flying Fighter* 28 Several thousands of other wounded and gassed men followed us.

Gastero-, gastrozooid (gæst(ĕ)rozō·oid). *Zool.* [f. Gastro- + Zooid.] A nutritive or digestive zooid in certain compound Hydrozoa.

1880 *Encycl. Brit.* XII. 554/2 A central short mouth-bearing person (gastrozooids). 1888 Rolleston & Jackson *Anim. Life* 758 The Gastrozooid, a term applied to the digestive zooid of *Hydrocorallina*.

Gasthaus (ga·sthaus). [G., = Guest house.] A (German) inn.

1833 Sir F. B. Head *Bubbles fr. Brunnen* (1834) 274 At one of these solemn villages the postilion stopped at a 'gasthaus' to bait his horses. 1841 Thackeray *Misc. Ess.* Wks. 1885 XXV. 375 If he has dined at an inn or restaurant, gasthaus, posada, albergo, or what not, invariably inserts into his log-book the bill of fare. 1874 Busk *Tirol* 86 Its principal inn..claims to be not merely a *Gasthaus*, but a *Gasthof*. 1928 *Sunday Express* 11 Mar. 3/3 'This is a gasthaus', he answered,..'and my name is Ludwig.'

Gasthof (ga·sthǫf). [G.] A (German) hotel.

1832 Stocqueler *15 Months' Pilgr. Khuzistan* II. iv. 106 A spacious gasthof, or public house. 1865 'Ouida' *Strathmore* v, A Bohemian Gasthof is about the only place..where you see the doctrine of equality in absolute..practice. 1874 [see *Gasthaus].

Gastric, *a.* Add: **c.** *Gastric mill*: a framework consisting of movable calcareous or chitinous plates in the stomach of certain crustacea.

1897 T. J. Parker & Haswell *Text-bk. Zool.* I. 547 A gastric mill is present in Malacostraca. 1927 Haldane & Huxley *Anim. Biol.* i. 7 Gastric mill, with grinding teeth and straining apparatus.

Gastro-. Add examples of recent terms of surgery, etc. (see quots.).

1901 H. Gadow *Amphibia & Reptiles* 282 The vertebrae of the Reptilia and those of all other Amniota are *gastrocentrous; that is to say the centra or bodies of the vertebrae are formed by the pairs of interventralia, while the basiventralia are reduced. 1896 Maylard *Surg. Alim. Canal* 249 When the junction is with the ileum, it is strictly a *gastro-ileostomy; and when with the colon, a *gastro-colostomy. *Ibid.* 156 *Gastrodiaphany..has received up to the present but a very limited trial. 1904 *Nature* 4 Aug. 316/2 The examination by the Röntgen rays and by so-called gastro-diaphany. 1903 *Lancet* 29 Aug. 591/2 We rapidly considered the relative advantage of pyloroplasty..and *gastro-duodenostomy. 1908 *Practitioner* Sept. 450 The original posterior *gastro-jejunal opening had closed. 1925 *F. Taylor's Pract. Med.* (ed. 13) 427 Gastro-jejunal or jejunal ulcer. 1896 Maylard *Surg. Alim. Canal* 249 The more commonly performed [operation] of *gastro-jejunostomy. 1925 *F. Taylor's Pract. Med.* (ed. 13) 427 Symptoms subsequent to gastro-jejunostomy. 1896 Maylard *Surg. Alim. Canal* 248 Brandt also records a successful case [*sc.* of gastrorrhaphy] under the title of *gastroplication. *Ibid.* 156 The method is especially valuable in delimiting the lesser curvature in gastrectasia and *gastroptosis. 1909 Osler & McCrae *Syst. Med.* V. 608 Gastroptosis, although one of the less frequently recognized of the visceral ptoses, is one of the most important as regards symptomatology. 1906 H. J. Paterson *Gastric Surg.* 53 *Gastrorrhagia, or gastric hæmorrhage. 1906 W. Hale White in *Lancet* 3 Nov. 1189/1 *Gastrostaxis, or oozing of blood from the mucous membrane of the stomach.

Gastroscope (gæ·stroskoup). [f. Gastro- + -scope.] An instrument for inspecting the interior of the stomach during life.

1890 tr. *Urbantschy's Electr. in service of Man* 593 The gastroscope has..a fine channel through which air is forced by means of india-rubber balls, in order to inflate the stomach.

Gat[2] (gæt). *Criminals' slang.* [Short for Gatling.] A revolver or other weapon.

1920 *Bulletin* 22 June 10 Then the Chink out with a gat and cuts loose. 1922 *Short Stories* Feb. 42/2 Swipe his gat', said a harsh voice—and I became conscious of the fact that hands were searching my pockets. 1924 W. M. Raine *Troubled Waters* xix, I'll be in the outer room with a gat.

Gate, *sb.*[1] Add:

6. Phr. *To give* (a person) *the gate*: to dismiss him. So *to get the gate. U.S. slang.*

1924 P. Marks *Plastic Age* 273, I guess his girl has given him the gate. 1928 L. North *Parasites* 62 Anyhow, it would stop me from submitting the same ideas he got the gate for.

c. = *starting-gate.*

1928 *Daily Mail* 25 July 14/1 Drift has hitherto been a disappointment. She is bad at the gate.

8. b. *U.S.* (Earlier example.)

1815 *Niles' Weekly Register* IX. 36/1 The engine drives four saws in separate *gates*.

d. In an internal-combustion engine, an arrangement of slots, in the shape of the letter H, through which the gear-lever is pushed to engage different gears. Also *attrib.*

1906 *Westm. Gaz.* 23 Jan. 4/2 The advantage of the gate change is..its simplicity and certainty. 1906 *Daily Chron.* 14 Nov. 9/3 The 'gate' system of gear changing. 1907 *Westm. Gaz.* 5 Dec. 4/2 The gate-operated change-speed gear system. 1908 *Ibid.* 28 May 4/2 The two motions that an ordinary gate-quadrant necessitates. *Ibid.* 14 Nov. 15/2 Four speeds operated through a gate. 1928 *Daily Express* 11 Oct. 1/2 The gear lever can be shifted through the gate at will according to the road and traffic.

13. Gate City *U.S.*, a city placed at the entrance to a district (applied *spec.* to Atlanta, Keokuk, etc.); **gate-crasher** *colloq.*, orig. *U.S.*, one who attends a private party, reception, or entertainment without an invitation; so **gate-crashing** *vbl. sb.*; also *fig.*; **gate-fine**, a fine imposed for failing to be within the College gates by a certain hour; **gate-leg, gate-legged** *a.*, designating a folding-table with a leg or legs set in a gate-like frame which may be swung back to allow the leaves to be shut down; **gate table** = **gate-leg* table; **gate-valve**, a valve with a sliding gate; **gate-wheel**, (*a*) a wheel operating the gates protecting a level crossing; (*b*) a wheel attached or geared to the spindle of a large gate-valve or to a hydraulic gate to effect its opening and closing.

1866 E. A. Pollard *Southern Hist. War* II. 382 The Battles of Atlanta.—The Fall of 'the *Gate City'. 1871 Schele de Vere *Americanisms* (1872) 663 Keokuk, in Iowa, ..is..poetically called Gate City, since here opens to navigation the largest river of the Union. 1889 *Kansas Times & Star* 28 May, The title so long borne by Keokuk, 'Gate City of the West', finally has been surrendered to Kansas City. 1894 *Congress. Rec.* 8384/2 In the front, where..the enterprising citizens of Atlanta have put that beautiful 'gate city' of the South. 1927 *Daily News* 28 June 5/3 'One-eyed Connolly', the champion American '*gate crasher' (one who gains admittance to big sporting events without payment)...The Committee of the White Rose Ball,..held at the May Fair Hotel last evening, dealt severely with a few cases of '*gate crashing'. 1928 *Manchester Guardian Weekly* 26 Oct. 335/2 There he saw the representatives of the press, to the number of 300, of whom perhaps seventy-five were really newspaper men and women, the others being what the American language calls 'ringers', 'gate-crashers', or 'dead-beads'. 1930 *Morn. Post* 19 Aug. 12/1 A 'Political Gatecrasher'. 1906 *Mag. Fine Arts* Apr. 442/2 A *gate-leg table is perhaps the most convenient for modern small rooms. 1930 *Daily Tel.* 5 Apr. 21/3 Gate-leg and other Dining Tables. 1903 *Connoisseur* V. No. 19. *advt.*, Oak *gate-legged table. 1906 *Mag. Fine Arts* Apr. 443 Spiral-legged *Gate-table. 1884 Knight *Dict. Mech.* Suppl., **Gate Valve*, a valve for water or gas main.

Gatha (gā·ta). [Zend; = Skr. *gāthā* song, verse, stanza.] In the sacred writings of the Parsees, any of the five collections of metrical compositions. Also *attrib.*, esp. with reference to their language. Hence **Gathic** (gā·tik) *a.* [cf. F. *gathique*], of or pertaining to the gathas or the language in which they are written; *sb.* the language itself, being the more archaic form of the Avestic language. Also **Gathaic** (gātā·ik) *a.*

1867 M. Haug *Zand-Pahlavi Gloss.* Introd. p. xliii, The difference of the Gâtha dialect (*gâthik*) from the common Avesta language is shown in the pronouns of the first and second persons. 1878 — *Ess. Parsis* 143 The first Gâtha contains verses, each of which consists of forty-eight syllables. 1891 K. E. Kanga *Avesta Lang.* Pref. p. iv, The examples, both Avestaic and Gâthâic..are such as are actually met with in the sacred writings. 1902 L. H. Mills (*title*) A dictionary of the Gâthic language of the Zend Avesta. 1910 E. C. Sykes *Persia* 21 The entire copies of the Avesta and Gathas are believed to have been destroyed when Alexander burnt one of the palaces of Persepolis.

Gather, *sb.*[1] Add: **1. c.** The action of 'gathering' a ball.

1921 *E. H. D. Sewell's Rugby Football* 64 *plate*, A 'gather' at full-speed..of a well-heeled ball.

Gather, *v.* **4. d.** To pick up (a shot bird).

1892 Greener *Breech-Loader* 225 If a wounded bird struggles in front of you from a companion's gun, drop it if you can. Explain to the first shooter that you did so to save time in gathering it. 1892 *Hurlingham Club Rules* 14 All birds must be gathered by the dog or trapper, and no member shall have the right to gather his own bird.

e. *Wrestling.*
1870 W. Armstrong *Wrestliana* 167 In the second fall, Jameson succeeded in 'gathering' Wright, and it seemed all over with him. *Ibid.* 172 Matthew..'gathered' his man well, and hiped him. 1889 — *Wrestling* 203 Your opponent will merely 'gather' his hold and you are helpless.

16. b. Phr. *To gather up the threads*: to resume the story, argument, or the like.

Gathmann (gā·tmăn). The name of Louis *Gathmann* (born 1843), German-American inventor and engineer, used attrib. to designate certain of his inventions, as **Gathmann gun**, a gun with large bore designed to throw the **Gathmann torpedo shell**, a thin-walled steel shell filled with a high explosive which explodes on impact.
1899 *Westm. Gaz.* 16 Mar. 2/3 We can only hope the American Press has drawn the long bow in its descriptions of the Gathmann gun.

'Gator, U.S. colloq. abbrev. of Alligator.
1844 *Knickerbocker Mag.* XXIII. 407 The 'gator is n't what you may call a han'some critter. 1885 *Milnor* (Dakota) *Teller* 5 June 3/3 He was walking on the banks of the stream when he saw an immense alligator. The 'gator humped himself. 1886 *Outing* (U.S.) Apr. 60/2 The natives often feed their dogs and hogs boiled 'gator meat. 1890 C. W. Butler *Big Game N. Amer.* 563 This is not based upon the dog's love of 'Gator-hunting, but upon the 'Gator's love of dog-hunting. 1907 Searcy *In Austral. Tropics* 245.

Gattine (gæti·n). [Fr.] A disease of the silkworm.
1884 *Encycl. Brit.* XVII. 613/2 Owing to the ravages of *gattine*, the silk industry has greatly declined since 1864.

Gau (gau). [G.] A territorial and administrative division of ancient Germany, including several villages or communities; in the Middle Ages, a larger division, over which, under Frankish rule, was placed a graf.
The word is a frequent final element of place-names, as Breisgau, Oberammergau.
1874 Stubbs *Const. Hist.* § 26 The four [*sc.* marks] were in A.D. 804 made into a Gau, in which the archbishop of Bremen had the royal rights of Heerbann and Blutbann. 1875 *Encycl. Brit.* II. 563/1. 1880 *Ibid.* XII. 70/1 'Landschafts' and 'gaus', ruled over by dukes and counts. 1916 E. G. A. Holmes *Nemesis of Docility* i. 19 The counts.. were supposed to..keep order in their own *gaus* or 'shires'.

Gaudete (gǫdī·ti). [L., 2nd pl. imper. of *gaudēre* to rejoice.] The third Sunday in Advent, so called from the first word of the introit.
1897 *Addis & Arnold's Cath. Dict.*

Gauge, *sb.* 15. Add:
gauge-field *Astron.*, a restricted area of the sky photographed for the purpose of gauging the number and density of the stars in that region; **gauge-work** = *gauged work* (see Gauged 2).
1891 A. M. Clerke in *Smithsonian Inst. Rep.* 107 A photographic *gauge-field on a small scale. 1906 *Daily Chron.* 23 Aug. 2/5 *Gage-work window headings. 1920 *Conquest* Apr. 269/2 These slips of steel..are much used in gauge work for building up bars of any desired thickness.

Gaultherase (gǫ·lþĕrēis). *Chem.* [f. *Gaultherin + *-ase.] An enzyme capable of splitting gaultherin into glucose and oil of wintergreen (methyl salicylate).
1896 *Jrnl. Chem. Soc.* LXX. ii. 540 Schneegans has given the name *betulase* to the ferment obtained by Procter from the bark of *Betula lenta*, but the author [*sc.* E. E. Bourquelot] regards as preferable the name *gaultherase*. 1902 *Encycl. Brit.* XXXI. 763/1 The enzymes which act upon glucosides..emulsin and myrosin..erythrozym, rhamnase, and gaultherase.

Gaultherin (gǫ·lþĕrin). *Chem.* [f. Gaultheria: see -in [1].] A crystalline glucoside found in the bark of the cherry birch (*Betula lenta*).
1844 W. Procter in *Amer. Jrnl. Pharm.* (N.S.) XV. 249. 1853 Ure *Dict. Arts* (ed. 4) I. 842 The fluid which contains the gaultherine has a slight bitterish taste. 1923 *Nature* CXII. 674/2 A new methyl salicylate glucoside, monotropitine...It does not appear to be identical with gaultherine.

Gauly, variant of Golly *int.*
1841 *Knickerbocker Mag.* XVII. 401 It's well my gizzard here..was well hooped in, or by Gauly! 1871 Schele de Vere *Americanisms* (1872) 604 *Gauley, by*, a Yankee oath.

Gaunt, *v.* [f. Gaunt *a.*] *trans.* To make lean.
1887 *Outing* (U.S.) May 115/2 Jim, do you want to gaunt Peg-leg for a race, or will you give him his ration?

Gaussage (gau·sėdʒ). [f. Gauss + -age.] The intensity of a magnetic field expressed in gausses. So **Gaussi·vity**, the intensity of magnetizing force expressed in gausses per square centimetre.
1902 *Encycl. Brit.* XXXIII. 214/1 So μ is the inductivity, and H the gaussivity. 1903 S. J. Barnett *Electromagn. Theory* 273 The unit gaussage is the gaussage which exists between two points when unit work must be done to transfer a unit magnetic pole from one to the other.

Gauze. 3. Add: *gauze-net*; **gauze-ring** = *crape ring* (*Crape 3 b).
1839 *Knickerbocker Mag.* XIII. 213 The usual mode..is to keep them [*sc.* mosquitoes] off by *gauze nets. 1867 Chambers *Descriptive Astron.* vii. viii. 709 As a rule the *gauze ring must not be expected to be seen with any aperture below 4 inches. 1889 Young *Text-bk. Gen. Astron.* § 638.

Gavage (gævā·ʒ). [Fr.] A method of forcible feeding by the use of a force-pump and a tube passed into the stomach.
1889 *Buck's Handbk. Med. Sci.* VIII. 102/2 Dr. Turnier, of Paris, has advocated the method of gavage in infants prematurely born. 1905 Osler *Princ. Med.* (ed. 6) 511 When there is persistent anorexia, gavage may be necessary.

Gavroche (gavroʃ). [Name of a gamin in Victor Hugo's *Les Misérables*.] A street urchin.
1876 *Times* 2 Nov. 4/4 A Norwegian *gavroche* is balancing himself by a miracle of adroitness on the dorsal extremities of the slender shafts. 1882 *Pall Mall Gaz.* 8 Dec. 4/1 'Mo-sieu'..is..pronounced as 'm'sieu' in 1882, or, if one wishes to talk as a real *gavroche*, 'm'seu'. 1921 *Blackw. Mag.* Feb. 251/1 Beneath the demure exterior the Parisian *gavroche* lurked.

Gaw, variant of *Gor* (= God).
1909 H. G. Wells *War in Air* iv. § 3 'Gaw!' said Bert. 'We're going up!'

Gawblimy, variant of *Gorblimy.

Gawkily (gǭ·kili), *adv.* [f. Gawky *a.* + -ly [2].] In a gawky or ungainly manner; like a gawk.
1812 L. M. Hawkins *C'tess & Gertrude* IV. 39 'I suppose you read a great deal then', said Lady Elma gawkily. 1928 *Daily Express* 13 Feb. 3 He is tall and almost gawkily built.

Gawking, *ppl. a.* (Earlier U.S. example.)
1817 *Massachusetts Spy* 2 Apr. (Th.) All with their wives, and some with their gawking offspring.

Gay, *a.* Add: **1. f.** Forward, impertinent, too free in conduct, 'fresh'. *U.S. slang.*
1899 G. Ade *Fables in Slang* (1900) 109 The Copper, perceiving that he had come very near getting Gay with our First Families, apologized for Cutting In. 1901 S. Merwin & H. K. Webster *Calumet K* xii. 226 He got gay one day. I warned him once, and then I threw him off the distributing floor. 1904 W. H. Smith *Promoters* ii. 53 Don't get gay! Say another word, and we'll do you! 1905 F. Hopkinson Smith *At Close Range* 41 See here, young feller. Don't get gay. 1910 W. M. Raine *B. O'Connor* 19 If anybody gets gay, drop him. 1911 J. F. Wilson *Land Claimers* vi. 80 And I wouldn't get gay round her. 1915 P. G. Wodehouse *Something Fresh* iv, The flush on the little man's face deepened. 'Are you trying to get gay with me?' he demanded dangerously.

Gāyatrī (gā·yatrī). [Skr., f. *gā* to sing.] **a.** An ancient twenty-four-syllable metre. **b.** A hymn, etc. composed in this metre; *esp.* the verse of the Rig-veda repeated daily as a prayer by Brahmins.
1843 *Penny Cycl.* XXVI. 177/1 The principal metres used in the hymns of the Vedas are the Jagatī, Gāyatrī, and Trishtup. 1845 *Encycl. Metrop.* XVI. 351/1 His father.., guided by the priest,..pronounces three times the Gâyatrî; 'let us meditate on the adorable light of the Divine Ruler, may it guide our intellects!' 1865 Max Müller *Chips* (1867) I. 19 The famous hymn, the Gâyatrî, which now for more than three thousand years has been the daily prayer of every Brahman. 1886 *Encycl. Brit.* XXI. 275/2 The *gāyatrī*..and other chiefly octosyllabic metres. 1916 Macdonell *Vedic Gram.* 446 Gāyatrī triplets.

Gay-Pay-Oo (gāi,pāi,ū·). Quasi-phonetic representation of *G. P. U.
1927 *Observer* 11 Dec. 21/2 The Gay-Pay-OO, or Political Police. 1928 *Punch* 18 Jan. 57/2 The Gay-Pay-Oo, it seems, is the name of the reorganised Russian Cheka.

Gazabo (găzēi·bo). *U.S. slang.* [var. of Gazebo.] A fellow.
1896 G. Ade *Artie* v. 44 Who does I meet comin' out o' the house but a cheap gazabo that was with her the first time I see her. 1910 W. M. Raine *B. O'Connor* 39 A big gazabo in a red wig held up Frost, the engineer.

Gazania (găzēi·niă). *Bot.* [mod.L., f. the name of Theodore *Gaza* (1398–1478), a Greek scholar.] A plant of the genus so named of South African asteraceous plants, which have showy heads of flowers of yellow or orange rays.
1921 G. Jekyll *Colour Schemes* 63 A few belated Orange Lilies have their colour nearly repeated by the Gazanias next to the path.

Gazpacho (gaþpā·tʃo, gas-). Also **gas-**. [Sp.] A vegetable soup consisting of onions, cucumbers, pimentos, etc., chopped very small with bread and put into a bowl of oil, vinegar, and water.
1845 R. Ford *Hand-bk. Spain* I. 69 In Andalucia, during the summer, a bowl of gazpacho is commonly ready in every house of an evening. 1903 Conrad & Hueffer *Romance* I. iv, He spent his days cooking extraordinary messes,..making substitutes for ethereal gaspachos.

Geanticline (dʒī,æ·ntiklain). *Geol.* [f. Gr. γῆ earth + Anticline.] = Geanticlinal *sb.*
1895 Dana *Man. Geol.* (ed. 4) 389 A mountain range includes all the mountain ridges made over the area and border of a single geanticline. 1915 J. Joly *Surface-Hist. Earth* vii, The first Rocky Mountains geanticline came into existence in closing Carboniferous (early Pennsylvanian) time.

Gear, *sb.* Add: **7. b.** The relation of the diameter of the wheel of a cycle or motor vehicle to the gearing, indicative of speed capacity; hence, loosely, speed. Phr. (*on*) *top gear*, at full speed.
1897 *Encycl. Sport* I. 268/1 The higher the gear, the further the machine travels at each stroke of the pedals. 1902 A. C. Harmsworth *Motors & Motor-Driving* xv. 327 In going uphill the engine is best when kept at its maximum rate of speed; if it drops below this, change to a lower gear at once. 1907 'Ian Hay' *Pip* ix. § 4 (1915) 283 Sometimes slowing through a village or changing gear up a hill. 1912 *Motor Cycle* 6 Apr. 340 A change-speed gear for motor cycles. *Ibid.* 22 June 632/2 Directly I put the machine on top gear after it has run about a mile or so it jumps out of gear by itself. It is also difficult to change into the low gear. 1912 *Motor Manual* 162 Remember to have the lowest gear in when starting the car. 1923 Dommett *Motor Car Mech.* (ed. 2) 185 On the top gear with the dog clutches engaged the speeds are equal. 1930 Hutchinson in *Strand Mag.* May 348/1 Trout retired, top gear, into the distance.

IV. (Chiefly in sense *7 b) *gear-change, -changing, -oil, -shaft, -sleeve, -wheel.*
1902 A. C. Harmsworth *Motors & Motor-Driving* x. 197 We have thus three members, the outside gear wheel, the inside gear wheel, and the pinions. 1904 A. B. F. Young *Complete Motorist* iii. 59 Changes of speed in the car have therefore to be provided for by different sets of gearing, by means of which the gear shaft transmits its motion to the road wheels in different ratios. The usual way of accomplishing this is by means of gear wheels. 1907 *Westm. Gaz.* 11 Nov. 7/2 The gear-shafts can be withdrawn at the ends by simply removing a circular flange. 1908 *Ibid.* 20 Nov. 4/2 It is arranged with divided gear-sleeve to enable short shafts to be used. 1909 *Ibid.* 23 Feb. 4/1 The beginner ..can practise the art of gear-changing on the hill. 1910 *Blackw. Mag.* Nov. 606/1 A black and glutinous compound, which I afterwards learned to recognise as gear-oil. 1912 *Motor Man.* (ed. 14) v. 162 Put the gear lever on to the next speed. *Ibid.* 169 A Method for obtaining a 'Silent' Gear Change. 1925 *Morris Owner's Manual* 10 Get the 'feel' of the gear lever with the engine and car stationary. 1927 *Glasgow Herald* 30 Nov. 11 The new model..will be of the standard selective gearshaft type.

b. **gear-driven** *a.*, driven by means of a toothed wheel or wheels.
1906 *Westm. Gaz.* 26 Mar. 10/2 A gear-driven car. 1906 *Daily Chron.* 14 Nov. 9/3 The water circulates by a gear-driven pump.

Geared, *ppl. a.* Add: **3.** (Earlier example.)
1831 Peck *Guide for Emigr.* iii. 288 Nine ox mills, on the inclined plane, five geared horse-mills.
4. Harnessed.
a 1847 in H. Howe *Hist. Coll. Ohio* 138 We..fixed geared horses to the carriages, and moved for Fort Jefferson.

Gearing, *vbl. sb.* **4.** Add: *gearing-beam, -wheel.*
1835 J. H. Ingraham *South-West* II. 288 Two gearing beams are laid across, for supporting the machinery. 1835 Ure *Philos. Manuf.* 109 Two eighty-horse steam-engines.. are mounted with their great gearing-wheels on the ground floor. 1876 Preece & Sivewright *Telegraphy* 81 Made to revolve by means of the 'gearing' or driving wheels.

Geaster (dʒī,æ·stəɹ). [mod.L., f. Gr. γῆ earth + ἀστήρ star.] An earth-star (see Earth- II).
1887 W. Phillips *Brit. Discomycetes* 213 Splitting into several lobes, like a *Geaster*.

Gebang (dʒībæ·ŋ). [Native name.] In full *gebang palm*: A Malayan fan palm, *Corypha gebanga*; the leaves are used for basket-work and thatching, and the pith of the trunk yields a sago.
1846 Lindley *Veget. Kingd.* 138 Employed..in weaving into baskets and bags the young leaves of the Gebang Palm.

Geckotian (gekōu·ʃiăn), *a.* and *sb.* Also **geccotian**. [f. mod.L. *Geccotidæ*, a family of lizards (see Gecko) + -ian.] **A.** *adj.* Of or relating to the geckos. **B.** *sb.* A gecko. So **Geckoi·dian**; **Ge·cconid**, **Ge·ckonid**, **Ge·cconoid**, **Ge·ckonoid** *a.* and *sb.* [f. mod.L. *Gecconidæ*]; **Ge·ccotid**, **Ge·ckotid** *a.* and *sb.*; **Ge·ccotoid** *a.* and *sb.*
1840 tr. *Cuvier's Anim. Kingd.* 277 The fourth family of the Saurians,—The Geckotians. 1841 *Penny Cycl.* XIX. 407/1 Saurians, consisting of the families of Geckoidians, Agamoidians [etc.]. *Ibid.* XX. 458/1 In the Geckotians.. the teeth are more pointed.

Gedackt (gəda·kt). [G. *gedackt*, old pa. pple. of *decken* to cover.] An organ flue stop having its pipes closed at the top. *Gedacktwork* [G. *gedacktwerk*]: such stops collectively.
1880 *Grove's Dict. Mus.* II. 601/2 In Schulze's organ the Gedact (No. 4) was formed of stopped wood pipes that produced a fuller tone than the usual Stopped Diapason. 1904 *Technol. & Sci. Dict.* (ed. Goodchild & Tweney), *Gedact Work*.., those organ stops belonging to the flue work, which consist of closed pipes.

Gedda (ge·dă). [f. *Gedda* (*Jedda*), in Arabia.] *Gedda gum*, an inferior gum arabic. Hence **Geddic** (ge·dik) *a.*, epithet of an acid derived from gedda gum.
1884 *Jrnl. Chem. Soc.* XLV. 57 The dextrorotatory gums, of which Gedda gum is a type. 1890 *Ibid.* LVIII. 59 Geddic acid.

Gee (dʒī), *sb.*[3] The name of the letter G.
1926 *Even. Standard* 12 July 3/2 If one branch of English society drops its initial aitches, and another branch ignores its terminal gees.

Gee, *v.*[2] [f. Gee *int.*] *trans.* To direct (a draught-animal) by the call of 'gee'. Also *absol.*
1845 E. J. Wakefield *Adv. N. Z.* II. 133 He *geed* the bullocks and ploughed on. 1867 'T. Lackland' *Homespun* II. 194 The regiment is somehow got back, by hawing and geeing, into line. *Ibid.* III. 286 The man..is turning up the sod with the gleaming share..while he 'gees' and 'haws' the yoke of cattle.

Gee, *int.*[2] Chiefly *U.S.* [app. shortening of *Geewhillikins, Gee-whizz.] An exclamation expressing emotion.
1901 S. E. White *Westerners* ii. 21 'Gee Christmas!' ejaculated Billy, and laughed loudly. 1902 *Captain* VII. 40 Gee! I thought the hair would come out of my head. 1905 *Amer. Illustr. Mag.* Apr. 701, 'I guess he's tall and thin and homely and dark, gee,' he yowled explosively. 1909 E. Underhill *Runaway Place* 134 'Gee, I believe you're right!' he exclaimed. 1927 Vachell *Dew of the Sea* etc. 269 But gee! if she is downing you, she offs it.

Geebung. Add: **2.** An old settler in New South Wales. Used *attrib.* ? as a derisory epithet.
1900 H. Lawson *Over Sliprails* 55 A drunken doctor from a geebung town.

Geelbek (gī·lbek). *S. Afr.* [Cape Du., f. Du. *geel* yellow + *bek* beak.] **a.** A wild duck, *Anas flavirostris.*

1875–84 Layard & Sharpe *Birds S. A.* 755 The 'Geelbec' is our commonest Duck, being abundant all over the colony and South Africa generally. 1893 H. A. Bryden *Gun & Camera S. A.* 404.
b. A fish, *Otolithus equidens*, common round the Cape.
1865 *Hardwicke's Science Gossip* 1 Mar. 64/2 Under this name [*sc.* Cape salmon] the 'Geelbeck'..has been eulogized. 1931 *Times Lit. Suppl.* 16 Apr. 301/2.
c. 'The term is also applied abusively to a coloured person' (Pettman).

Gee-string. *U.S.* Also **G-string.** [Of obscure origin.] A string worn by American Indians round the waist and between the legs.
1878 J. H. Beadle *Western Wilds* xvi. 249 Around each boy's waist is the tight 'gee-string', from which a single strip of cloth runs between the limbs from front to back. 1891 *Harper's Mag.* Dec. 36/2 Some of the boys wore only 'G-strings' (as, for some reason, the breech-clout is commonly called on the prairie). 1907 S. E. White *Arizona Nights* I. x. 142 These Yuma Indians..were a peaceful, fine-looking lot, without a thing on but a gee-string. 1913 Mulford *Coming of Cassidy* iv. 67 'It's a G-string an' a medicine-bag',..cried Dad from the harness-shop.

Geewhillikins (dʒī,wi·likinz), *int. U.S.* Also **jewhillikin, -ken, gewhillikins, geewhilikens.** [Of obscure origin; perh. a fanciful substitute for *Jerusalem!*] An exclamation expressing astonishment.
1857 *Knickerbocker Mag.* Nov. L. 435 (Th.) And great Gewhilikins! wasn't the snow peppering down! a 1859 *Traits Amer. Humor* (Bartlett) Jewhilliken, how he could whip a nigger! 1865 E. P. Hingston *Orpheus C. Kerr Papers* ii. 31 Geewhillikins! how the critter did squawk and squeal. a 1871 *Country Merchant* 221 (De Vere) Jewhillikin! There goes a drove of them! 1871 Schele de Vere *Americanisms* (1872) 611 *Jerusalem!*, a favorite New England exclamation...In the West it is, as usual, improved to suit the louder taste of the people, and becomes Jewhillikin. 1884 'Mark Twain' *Huck. Finn* xxxviii. 386 'Geewhillikins', I says, 'but what does the rest of it mean?' 1911 Mary Johnston *Long Roll* xx. 262 Geewhilikins! what was that? That was oil.

Gee-whizz (dʒī,whi·z), *int.* Also **-whiz, -whitz.** [f. *Gee *int.*[2] + Whizz *int.*] An exclamation of delight or surprise.
1888 *Judge* (U.S.) 1 Sept. 334 Geewhitz! 1904 *N. Y. Times* 21 Apr. 9 He appeared in the saloon and shouted: 'Gee whiz! The gas pipes is all leakin'.' 1908 *Westm. Gaz.* 9 May 6/1 'The Raid on Prosperity' is what he calls his statement for the defence, and, gee-whiz!..he goes for the Raiders in a way that is positively refreshing. 1929 S. Anderson in *Mercury Story Bk.* 228 Gee whizz, it was fun.

Geez (gī·ez, gīz). Also **Geëz, Gheez, Giez, Giz.** [Ethiopic.] The ancient language of Abyssinia, still used as a liturgical language; = Ethiopic 2.
1790 J. Bruce *Trav. Source Nile* I. 424 Speaking of the Ethiopic at present, I mean only the Geez language, the language of the Shepherds, and of the books. *Ibid.* 425 The Geez is exceedingly harsh and unharmonious. 1839 *Penny Cycl.* X. 52/2 The ancient Ethiopian, or Geez. 1867 [see Ethiopic 2]. 1883 R. N. Cust *Mod. Langs. Afr.* I. 74 The Written Characters of the old Ethiopic, or Gîz. 1908 *Daily Chron.* 6 Mar. 3/5 Their Bible, which is in Gheez,.. contains all the books of our own Old Testament, except the Book of Esther. 1920 *Blackw. Mag.* May 676/1 A book in the Geez language.

Gegenschein (gē·gənʃain). *Astron.* [G., f. *gegen* opposite + *schein* shining.] = *Counter-glow.
1880 *Amer. Jrnl. Sci.* CXX. 442 The gegenschein is an extremely faint spot of light some 7° in diameter, lying in the zodiacal band. 1888 [see *Counter-glow]. 1901 H. H. Turner *Mod. Astron.* iv. 269.

Geikielite (gī·kilait). *Min.* [f. the name of Sir Archibald *Geikie* (1835–1924), Scottish geologist + -lite.] Magnesium titanate, occurring as brownish or bluish black rolled pebbles.
1892 A. Dick in *Min. Mag.* X. 145 Geikielite, a New Mineral from Ceylon. 1906 *Jrnl. Chem. Soc.* XC. ii. 459 The ferric oxide shown in these analyses is in some cases primary (isomorphously replacing the geikielite molecule).

Geilfine (ge·lfinʹ). *Irish Hist.* [Ir.] A division of the fine containing four males besides the head of the family.
1869 tr. *Anc. Laws Irel.* II. 161 The 'Geilfine'-tribe relationship in the direct line, such as the father, and the son, and the grandson, and the great grandson, and the great great grandson to the fifth generation. 1875 H. S. Maine *Early Hist. Instit.* 211 A Geilfine class may consist of a father and four sons who are not in the same degree. 1876 *Encycl. Brit.* V. 800/1 Sometimes a son succeeded his father, but the rule was that the eldest and most capable member of the *geilfine*..was selected during his lifetime to be his successor. 1882 C. G. Walpole *Hist. Irel.* 9.

Geis (geʃ, gīʃ). Pl. **geasa, geise.** [Ir.] Among the ancient Irish nobility, an obligation of honour.
1899 D. Hyde *Lit. Hist. Irel.* 344 He thought he saw Gradh son of Lir upon the plain, and it was a *geis* (tabu) to him to see that. *Ibid.* 373 Every man who entered the Fenian ranks had four *geasa* (gassa, *i.e.*, tabus) laid upon him. 1928 *Observer* 22 Jan. 5/4 Apparently a man could be either:—(1) Born under a 'geis' prohibiting certain actions on his part, or (2) Laid under 'geis' either at birth or any time during his life, either by divine or human agency.

Geissler (gai·slər). The name of Heinrich *Geissler* (1814–79), German physicist, used attrib. or in the genitive to designate certain apparatus invented by him.
1863 E. Atkinson tr. *Ganot's Physics* § 740. 706 Plücker has found that the light in Geissler's tubes does not depend on the substance of the electrodes. 1875 Knight *Dict. Mech.*, *Geisler-tube*, a sealed tube filled with rarefied gas, through which an electric spark is transmitted by means of platinum connections inserted at each extremity. 1883 *Encycl. Brit.* XVI. 30/2 Geisler's Mercurial Air-Pump. *Ibid.* 31/1 Even a Geisler's stop-cock requires to be lubricated to be absolutely gas-tight. 1885 *Ibid.* XIX. 229/2 The capillary part now called a Geissler's tube, by means of which the luminous intensity of feeble electric discharges was raised sufficiently to allow of spectroscopic investigation. 1896 *Chem. News* 6 Nov. 230/1 Note on Use of Geissler Filter-Pump as an Aspirator. 1901 *Jrnl. Chem. Soc.* LXXX. ii. 74 An Improvement on the Geissler Potash Apparatus. 1930 tr. *R. W. Pohl's Electr. & Magn.* 219 Geissler tubes are being used to an increasing degree in practice for lighting.

Geist (gaist). [G., = spirit: see Ghost *sb.*] Intellectuality, spirituality.
1871 M. Arnold *Friendship's Garl.* 9 France has 'Geist' in her democracy, and Prussia in her education. 1883 *19th Cent.* Aug. 274 So that the heaven to which we must look forward will be a heaven of pure *Geist*.

Gel (dʒel). [The first syllable of *gelatin* used as a word.] A semi-solid colloidal solution. Also *attrib.*
1904 Whetham *Recent Devel. Phys. Sci.* iv. 137 The mass will solidify under certain conditions to form a solid which may be called a gel. 1918 *Nature* CI. 66/1 A very minute amount of electrolyte added to a stable colloidal solution may bring about complete precipitation or flocculation of the sol, the sol separating out in a gelatinous form known as a gel. 1922 *Encycl. Brit.* XXX. 591/1 Gel-products. 1926 *Ibid.* Suppl. I. 785 The Brownian movement affords a criterion of whether protoplasm is in the condition of a sol or a gel. 1930 *Nature* 15 Mar. 432 Structure in very permeable collodion gel films and its significance in filtration problems. 1931 *Oxf. Univ. Gaz.* 17 June 693/2 The equilibria between (*a*) silica gel and water vapour, (*b*) silica gel and alcohol vapour, (*c*) iron oxide gel and alcohol.

Gelada (dʒe·lădă). [Native name.] In full *gelada baboon*: An Abyssinian baboon, *Theropithecus gelada*, characterized by a heavy mane in the adult male, and by a tufted tail.
1878 *Proc. Zool. Soc.* 1 A Family of Gelada Baboons. 1893–4 *Lydekker's Royal Nat. Hist.* I. 125 The aspect of the gelada forcibly suggests a large black poodle dog, with an unusually abundant mane. 1906 *Westm. Gaz.* 27 Aug. 10/2 A fine specimen of the Dusky Gelada.

Gelalæan (dʒelăli·ăn), *a.* Also **Jalalæan.** [Arab. *Jalāl-ad-dīn*.] Of or pertaining to Gelal-ed-Din, 'Glory of the Faith', a title of Malek Shah, Sultan of Khorasan, and reformer of the Persian calendar in 1079.
c 1792 *Encycl. Brit.* (1797) IX. 421/1 Gelalean, or Jellalæan Kalendar. 1838 Sir H. Nicolas *Chronol. Hist.* (ed. 2) 25 The Gelalæan era..March 14. A.D. 1079. 1866 Brande & Cox *Dict. Sci.* etc., *Gelalæan Era*, the era of Yezdegird. 1876 *Encycl. Brit.* V. 717/1 Era of Yezdegird, or Persian or Gelalæan Era.

Gelasian (gĕlēi·ziăn), *a.* [f. *Gelasius* (see below): see -ian.] Of or pertaining to Pope Gelasius I (492–6 A.D.); esp. applied to liturgical books or prayers attributed to him.
a 1773 A. Butler *Feasts, Fasts &c. Cath. Ch.* ii. i. (1839) 57 In the Gelasian liturgy..only five Sundays occur in Advent. 1832 *Archæologia* XXIV. 10 The whole ancient Roman liturgy is comprised in the three books called the Leonine, Gelasian, and Gregorian Sacramentaries. 1915 F. E. Brightman *Engl. Rite* Introd. p. x, [The Leonine Sacramentary] contains much official matter, some of which recurs in the later Gelasian and Gregorian books.

Gelasin[2] (dʒe·lăsin). [f. Gel(atin + *-ase + -in [1].] A preparation of agar-agar.
a 1909 *Buck's Handbk. Med. Sci.* I. 138 (Cent. D. Supp.).

Gelatin. 3. *attrib.* Add: *gelatin film.*
1878 *Design & Work* 26 Jan. 121/2 The gelatin film is then moistened with cold water. 1889 *Judge* (U.S.) 22 June 180/2 The gelatine film..is one two-thousandths of an inch in thickness.

Gelatinase (dʒĕlæ·tinēs). *Chem.* [f. Gelatin + *-ase.] An enzyme which liquefies gelatin, occurring among bacteria, yeasts, etc.
1912 *Jrnl. Chem. Soc.* CII. ii. 283 The Gelatinase of Bacillus prodigiosus..The most active gelatinase preparations are obtained from bouillon cultures of the organism.

Gelatose (dʒe·lătōus). *Chem.* [f. Gelat(in + -ose [2].] An albumose derived from gelatin.
1902 *Jrnl. Soc. Chem. Ind.* 15 Jan. 67/2 A neutral solution of a gelatose. 1903 *Jrnl. Chem. Soc.* LXXXIV. i. 301 Gelatin and various gelatoses have been hydrolysed by boiling with hydrochloric acid of sp. gr. 1·20 for 6 hours.

Gemellion (dʒĕme·liǫn). *Archæol.* Also **gemellione.** [ad. med.L. *gemellio*, f. L. *gemellus* a twin.] One of a pair of basins used for washing the hands before meals, the water being poured over the hands from one basin and caught by the other; hence, any decorative basin.
1889 *Cent. Dict.* 1920 *Proc. Soc. Antiq.* 18 Mar. 131 The enamelled basins known as gemellions.

Geminid. Add:
B. *adj.* Pertaining to or resembling the variable star ζ Geminorum. Also as *sb.*, a variable star of the type of ζ Geminorum.
1899 R. H. Allen *Star-Names* 234 Just north of δ lies the radiant point of the Geminids, visible early in October. 1926 Macpherson *Mod. Astron.* 121.

Gemma. Add:
4. *attrib.* and *Comb.*: **gemma grass** *U.S.* (see Gama grass).
1890 Gunter *Miss Nobody* iv. (1891) 47 The mesa is bare of everything for five hundred yards but gemma grasses.

Gemmule. Add:
2. b. In Darwin's theory of pangenesis, one of the hypothetical units conceived as capable of reproducing the part from which it is thrown off.
1871 Darwin *Desc. Man* I. 280 According to this hypothesis, every unit or cell of the body throws off gemmules or undeveloped atoms, which are transmitted to the offspring of both sexes, and are multiplied by self-division.
c. (See quot.)
1902 *Encycl. Brit.* XXV. 394/2 From the other end of the perikaryon,..there arises a series of one or more short, repeatedly branching filaments, called dendrites...At the ends of the dendrites are small enlargements called gemmules.

-gen. 2. Add: The suffix is also occasionally used in names of tissues from which some particular substance is produced, as *phellogen.*

Gene (dʒīn). *Biol.* Also **gen.** [irreg. f. Gr. γεν- to produce.] = *Factor *sb.* Also *attrib.*
1913 Dorland *Med. Dict.* (ed. 7), *Gen*, the invisible rudiment or transmitted germ of a character...*Gene*, same as *gen.* 1917 T. H. Morgan in *Amer. Nat.* LI. 320 While the linkage relations of genes do not at present have any intermediate bearing on our conception of the nature of genes, they have a very important bearing on the problem of the localization of genes in the germ plasm. 1927 E. B. Ford & J. S. Huxley in *Brit. Jrnl. Exper. Biol.* V. 112 Mendelian Genes. *Ibid.* 130 Such fixed characters..will..be considered as end results of the primary gene-effects upon rates of developmental processes. 1928 *Daily Tel.* 11 Sept. 8/2 Whether X-rays could produce 'gene mutations'. 1930 R. A. Fisher *Genet. The. Nat. Selection* 8 He would certainly have inferred that each organism must receive a definite portion of its genes from each parent.

-geneous (dʒī·nĭ,əs), *suffix* [f. scholastic or mod.L. *-geneus*, as in *heterogeneus, homogeneus* (Gr. ὁμογενής, -γενεο-, f. γένος, γενεο- kind)], as in Allogeneous.

General, *a.* and *sb.* Add:
A. *adj.* **1.** *General health*: the ordinary health of the body as a whole, or of a community.
1819 in Sir A. Clarke *Ess. Dis. Skin.* v. (1821) 97 It does not seem to hurt my general health; my appetite is good. 1870 *Food Jrnl.* 1 Mar. 67 So numerous are the forms which charitable relief assumes, that it would be next to impossible to analyse their separate influence on the general health. 1879 *Man. Artill. Exerc.* iii. 69 Attentions to the comforts of the men will..add to their general health. 1899 Gladstone in *Daily News* 11 May 4/1 Although my general health, to use a well-known phrase, is wonderfully good, I seem indeed ..to fear being kept here too long. 1903 *Westm. Gaz.* 26 Mar. 9/2 His leg wound did not heal well, and this, with his poor general health, greatly depressed him.
2. *General circulation*: (*a*) see quot. 1928; (*b*) 'circulation, as of a newspaper, among readers not confined to a narrow class in business or interests' (Webster). *General head-quarters* (abbrev. G.H.Q.): the head-quarters of the commander-in-chief. *General public*: the people at large. *General quarters*: in the navy, the stationing of all hands, and the making of preparations, as if for an encounter with the enemy; also *attrib.* (as *general-quarter*). *General reserve*: see quot. *General strike*: (*a*) a strike of all the workers of one industry; (*b*) a concerted strike by workmen of all or most of the important trades and occupations of a country with a view to securing some common object by the stoppage of business.
1899 *Q. Jrnl. R. Meteorol. Soc.* XXV. 166 Schemes and discussions concerning the *general circulation of the atmosphere. 1906 *Ibid.* XXXII. 292 In the different theories on the general circulation of the atmosphere it is admitted that the Counter Trades descend below the Zones of calms at latitudes 30°. 1926 Sir N. Shaw *Man. Meteorol.* I. 291 Dove rendered a signal service to the observational representation of the general circulation by producing monthly maps of isotherms of the globe. 1928 D. Brunt *Meteorol.* iv. 26 When we draw charts on which are represented, at a large number of stations, the most frequently occurring wind directions.., we find the movement of the winds of the globe form a system which is much simpler in appearance than might have been expected by one accustomed only to the variability of weather in the British Isles. This system is called the 'general circulation' of the atmosphere. 1914 *Times* 3 Oct. 8/2 The Press Bureau..issued the following descriptive account, which has been communicated by an eye-witness present with *General Headquarters. 1865 *Chambers's Jrnl.* 715/2 Whatever injurious words indeed are spoken whether by his fares..or the *general public, he must be prepared with a fitting counterscoff. 1868 *Cassell's Mag.* III. 28 They wish for the patronage of the general public. 1900 *Westm. Gaz.* 5 Mar. 9/2 On every '*general-quarter' day, in my last ship. 1918 E. S. Farrow *Dict. Mil. Terms*, *General *Reserve*, a reserve retained in the hands of the general officer commanding of the whole force until required. 1810, 1830 *General strike [see Strike *sb.* 9]. 1902 *Encycl. Brit.* XXXIII. 26/1 In 1891 a general strike took place in the German printing trade. 1924 J. F. Bryant *Gandhi & Indianisation* 72 His methods were tinged with the ideas of Passive Resistance and the General Strike. 1926 S. Baldwin in *Parl. Deb.* CXCV. 71, I do not think all the leaders when they assented to ordering a general strike fully realised that they were threatening the basis of ordered government.
2. b. (*b*) *General Post*: also *fig.* a general and rapid exchange or interchange of appointments to office.
[1889 Kate Greenaway *Bk. Games* 63 General Post. One person is selected as 'postman' and blindfolded, the others all take the names of different places, except one, who is

chosen the leader, and has a written list of the places chosen by the players. 1898 Alice B. Gomme *Games for Parlour & Playgr.* 51 An occasional call of 'General Post' by the leader, when all players must change their seats, gives a good chance to the blind man.]

7. c. Various phrases used *attrib.*
1860 *Leisure Hour* 10 May 294 These are the 'general utility' men, as they are sometimes facetiously called by those whose genius is not quite so versatile. 1888 J. C. Harris *Free Joe*, etc. 127 One of the many 'general-utility' men that improved methods enable the high schools and colleges to turn out. 1894 Eliz. Banks *Camp. Curios.* 168 Janie was a sort of general utility maid for everybody. 1906 *Daily Chron.* 25 Jan. 4/7 A Scriptural general knowledge paper. 1909 *Westm. Gaz.* 11 Feb. 3/3 The largest fruit and general produce merchants in New York. *Ibid.* 3 Apr. 16/4 As the president of this excellent club, he spoke of the good trout and general-fish waters it leased on the Surrey Wey. *Ibid.* 28 Aug. 16/4 The Thames is in good condition, and general-fish anglers are promised a continuance of sport. 1911 F. O. Bower *Plant-Life* 58 It served as a general-purposes shoot. 1923 Kipling *Land & Sea T.* 143 A general-utility shed.

B. *sb.* **7. c.** The (title of the) head of the Salvation Army.
1882 *All about Salv. Army* 26 If the General were to be removed by death to-morrow, his successor, without a minute's delay, would step into his position. 1884 W. Booth *General's Lett.* (1890) 18 Go to the crowd of sinners, or spot them individually..because out of them you may make Lieutenants, and Captains, and Majors, and Generals. 1886 — *Orders & Regul. Salv. Army* 165 The General must and will appoint his own successor—each successive General doing the same.

General hospital. [app. after F. *hôpital général*, the name of the hospital founded at Bicêtre, France, in 1656.] **a.** A hospital which does not confine itself to patients suffering from one particular class of disease.
1737 (*title*) The plan and elevation of a new general hospital intended to be erected at Bath for the reception of 150 poor strangers. 1757 A. R. *Curiosities of Paris* iv. 62 General Hospital, is a small Distance from the City...They receive all Kinds of Patients upon Application, such as Women with Child, Foundlings, Orphans, and Lunatics. 1794 *Medical Extracts* II. 62 The air in the lowest ward in the General Hospital. c 1803 *Watering & Sea-Bathing Places* 44 The General Hospital..is open to the sick poor of the United Kingdom,..the inhabitants of Bath alone excepted. 1869 [see General *a.* 2]. 1880 *Encycl. Brit.* XII. 302/1 Hospitals are usually divided into General and Special. In General Hospitals cases of all kinds are admitted in some, whilst in others certain classes are excluded.
b. A military hospital receiving the sick and wounded from field hospitals.
1899 *Daily News* 27 Nov. 5/3 Large hospitals..known as 'general hospitals' (or 'base hospitals'), each accommodating 500 men and 20 officers...A large staff is necessary for the working of each 'general hospital'. 1914 *Times* 30 Oct. 10/1, 3rd Southern General Hospital, Oxford.

Generation. 2. Add: *spec.* the production of steam, gas, electricity.
1886 tr. *Urbanitzky's Electr. in service of Man* 95 The generation of electricity is to be explained by the mere contact of bodies with each other. 1900 *Westm. Gaz.* 7 Mar. 7/1 The generation and distribution expenses for the year. 1901 *Daily News* 6 Mar. 9/2 The cost of generation was £106,000. 1901 *Westm. Gaz.* 14 Nov. 8/3 The generation plant for the first section of the new electric tramways.

Generator. Add: **4.** *Math.* = Generant A. b.
1863 Cayley *Math. Papers* (1892) V. 170 The scroll S (m, n, p) has besides the directrix curves m, n, p or Nodal Director, and the nodal generating lines or Nodal Generator, a remaining nodal curve or Nodal Residue.

Genetic, *a.* Add: **B.** *sb. pl.* **a.** That branch of biology which is concerned with the study of natural development when not complicated by human interference.
1897 L. F. Ward *Outl. Sociol.* 180 But there is a shorter adjective form *telic*, which is preferable to teleological and possesses the advantage of being converted into the name of a science, *telics*, as proposed by Dr. Small. These two words may be conveniently set over against *genetic* and *genetics*.
b. The experimental study of heredity, variation, etc.
1907 *Daily Chron.* 23 Feb. 9/3 The..International Conference on Genetics. 1908 Bateson *Genetics* Pref. Note, The physiology of Heredity and Variation, a study now spoken of as Genetics. 1909 — *Mendel's Princ. Heredity* 369 The Progress of Genetics since the rediscovery of Mendel's papers.
Hence **Gene·ticist**, one who studies or is interested in genetics.
1913 Dorland *Med. Dict.* (ed. 7). 1924 E. W. Macbride *Study Hered.* vii. (1925) 186 This theory..uncritically accepted by many 'geneticists'. 1930 R. A. Fisher *Genet. The. Nat. Selection* 46 The pathological mutations observed by geneticists.

-genic (dʒenik), *suffix* [f. -gen + -ic], forming adjectives with the meaning: 'of, pertaining to, or relating to generation or production'; *spec.* (*a*) generating, producing, as *Carcinogenic, *Epeirogenic, Pathogenic, Pyrogenic; (*b*) generated, produced, originating in, as *Authigenic, *Blastogenic, *Cryptogenic.

Geniculum (dʒĕni·kiŭlǫm). *Anat.* [L., dim. of Genu.] A small genu; an angular knee-like or knot-like structure.
1889 *Buck's Handbk. Med. Sci.* VIII. 131/1 The thalami and geniculums project caudad beyond the intersegmental line. 1926 T. L. Stedman *Med. Dict.* (ed. 9), *Geniculum*. 1. A small genu or angular knee-like structure. 2. A knot-like structure.

Genist (dʒī·nist). [ad. late L. *Genistæ* sb. pl., f. L. *gen-* to be born.] One of a sect of ancient Jews who took no strange wives during the Babylonian captivity, and who therefore claim to be pure-blooded descendants of Abraham. So **Ge·nite.**
1613 Purchas *Pilgrimage* ii. viii. 128 He there nameth.. diuers other sects if they may beare that name: as the Genites or Genists, which stood vpon their stocke and kindred. 1882 Farrar *Early Chr.* II. 342 Even down to the fifth century there seem to be..'Genists', or Jews by race.

Genistein (dʒĕni·ste,in). *Chem.* [f. L. *genista* broom + -in.] A volatile alkaloid derived from the common broom, *Genista tinctoria*, $C_{16}H_{22}N_2$.
1899 *Jrnl. Chem. Soc.* LXXV. 833 This new colouring matter, for which the name *genistein* is proposed, crystallises in long, glistening, colourless needles sparingly soluble in cold alcohol or acetic acid. 1900 *Jrnl. Soc. Chem. Ind.* 31 Dec. 1101/2 Genistein from *Genista tinctoria*.

Genitivally (dʒenitai·văli), *adv.* [f. Genitival + -ly [2].] In the genitive case; as a genitive.
In mod. dicts.

Genitive, *a.* and *sb.* **B.** *sb.* Add: **genitive absolute**, a construction in Greek similar to the Latin ablative absolute.
1882 Goodwin *School Grk. Gram.* 172.

Ge·nitively, *adv.* [f. Genitive *a.* + -ly [2].] As a genitive.
1846 Monier-Williams *Sanscr. Gram.* 161 Dependent Compounds, or Compounds Dependent in Case..Genitively Dependent. Or those in which the relation of the first word to the last is equivalent to that of a genitive.

Genizah (gənī·ză). Pl. **genizoth.** [Heb., lit., a hiding, hiding-place, f. *ganaz* to set aside, hide.] A store-room or repository for damaged, discarded, or heretical books and papers and sacred relics, attached to most synagogues; also, the contents of a genizah.
1903 *Jew. Encycl.* V. 612/1 The term 'genizah' is now applied almost exclusively to the hoard at the old synagogue of Fostat near Cairo. 1926 *Glasgow Herald* 24 Feb. 8 All the old prayer books or torn Bibles are reverently carried to the synagogues, where they are placed in what is called a Genizah. ..In these ancient Genizahs have been found some priceless old MSS.

Genoa. (Earlier U.S. example of *Genoa velvet.*)
1764 in *Maryland Hist. Mag.* X. 41 A handsome Crimson Genoa Velvet Pulpit Cushion,..also, Ten yards of best Crimson Genoa Velvet.

Genotype[1] (dʒe·nŏtəip). *Biol.* [f. Gr. γένος Genus + -type.] The type-species of a genus.
1897 *Science* 23 Apr. 639 Genotype applies to any typical material of the type species of a genus. the material, however, should be, if possible, from the original locality of the species. 1903 *Amer. Jrnl. Sci.* July 1 The original conception of the genus [*sc. Romingeria*] has become obscured... If the original description and figure of Billings be taken as a starting point, the subsequent vicissitudes of this genotype will be appreciated.

Genotype[2] (dʒe·nŏtəip). *Biol.* [irreg. f. *Gene + -o- + -type.] **a.** The combination of genes or hereditary characters possessed by a race or organism. **b.** A race or group of organisms having the same combinations of hereditary characters. Hence **Genoty·pic, -ty·pical** *adjs.*; **Genoty·pically** *adv.*
1910 *Science* 28 Oct. 588 Genotypes or pure lines of Johannsen. 1913 Dorland *Med. Dict.* (ed. 7), *Genotype*, the fundamental hereditary constitution (or combination of genes) of an organism. 1922 *Hereditas* III. 211 The genotypical response of the plant species to the habitat. 1930 R. A. Fisher *Genet. The. Nat. Selection* 9 The genotypes are probably unequally fitted, at least to a slight extent, to their task of survival and reproduction. *Ibid.* 81 A change in the genotypic constitution of the species. 1930 C. Elton *Anim. Ecol.* 48 Nothing is more certain than that the species would very quickly become genotypically pure brown in composition.

-genous (dʒĕnəs), *suffix*, [f. -gen + -ous] = *-genic, as (*a*) Alkaligenous, Calcigenous, Kaligenous, Pathogenous, Pyrogenous 2; (*b*) *Cryptogenous, Pyrogenous 1, Terrigenous.

Genre. Add: **1. b.** A kind or category of literary work characterized by a particular form, style, or purpose.
1843, 1880 [in Dict., sense 1]. 1882 Saintsbury *Hist. Fr. Lit.* 50 A better notion of the *genre* may perhaps be obtained from a short view of the subjects of some of the principal of those Fabliaux whose subjects are capable of description.
2. b. *transf.* of literature.
1931 *Times Lit. Suppl.* 21 May 406/3 The story settles down for a time into the methods of a *genre* novel of Shropshire life.

Genro (dʒe·nrou). [Jap., = old men, f. *gen* root + *ro* old.] The 'elder statesman' of Japan, a body of retired statesmen who are at times informally consulted by the emperor.
1921 *Contemp. Rev.* July 8 Prince Yamagata..continues the most influential member of the *Genro*, or Elder Statesmen. 1922 *Times Lit. Suppl.* 2 Nov., The influence wielded in public affairs by the Genro since the Restoration.

Gent, *sb.* Add to note: Now frequent in tradesmen's notices.
1901 *Daily Chron.* 10 Sept. 9/1 Hair Dresser.—First-class gent's junior wanted. 1921 *Dict. Occup. Terms* (1927) § 920 Hairdresser's assistant; gents' or ladies' hand.

Gentianose (dʒenʃiănōus). *Chem.* [f. Gentian + -ose [2].] A crystalline sweetish compound obtainable from yellow gentian (*Gentiana lutea*).
1898 *Jrnl. Chem. Soc.* LXXIV. i. 597 The gentians contain a soluble ferment, analogous to invertin, which hydrolyses gentianose. 1912 *Ibid.* CII. ii. 1072 The Ferments Capable of Hydrolysing Raffinose and Gentianose.

Gentle, *a.* 8. Add: Freq. in *a gentle hint.*
1896 J. C. Harris *Sister Jane* 32 Taking this as a gentle hint, I went out.

Gentleman. Add: **7. c.** **gentlemen's (-man's) agreement, bargain**, an agreement which is not enforceable at law, and which is only binding as a matter of honour. orig. *U.S.*
1886 in J. K. Winkler *Life T. P. Morgan* (1931) 107 [In 1886..was the first of a series of memorable dinner-table conferences. At them were formulated so-called] gentlemen's agreements. 1930 *Times Lit. Suppl.* 27 Feb. 153/3 By a gentleman's agreement—if one may use such a term when speaking of ruffians who now have not even courage to commend them—rival gangs enjoyed the monopoly of trade in different districts. 1930 *News-Chron.* 5 Dec. 9/1 The arrangement respecting the cinemas was a 'gentleman's bargain'. 1931 *Daily Tel.* 3 Oct. 10/2 Any agreement that is reached should be understood by all three parties not as an emergency political agreement but as a Gentlemen's Agreement.

Genu. Add: Also in certain Latin terms, as **genu recurvatum**, 'backward curvation of the knee-joint' (Dorland 1901); **genu valgum**, knock-knee; **genu varum**, bow-legs.
1887 *Encycl. Brit.* XXII. 691/2 During the last few years ..other deformities, such as knock-knee or *genu valgum* and bow-leg or *genu varum*, have been remedied by operation. 1910 *Practitioner* Mar. 346 Either genu-valgum or genu-varum [resulting] from suppression of growth on one side or the other of the epiphysial line. *Ibid.* 348 Genu-valgum (with genu-recurvatum).

Geoffroy (ʒo·frwa). Name of Isidore *Geoffroy* Saint-Hilaire (1805–61), French zoologist, designating a species of cat, *Felis geoffroii*, of S. America.
1883 *List Anim. Zool. Soc.* (ed. 8) 55.

Geological, *a.* Add: *Geological time*: see quot. 1904. So *geological age, epoch.*
1904 *Technol. & Sci. Dict.* (ed. Goodchild & Tweney), *Geological Time*, a chronological measure (of a somewhat indefinite character) which bears the same kind of relation to the measures of time used in history that the distances of the stellar bodies do to the ordinary standard of terrestrial measurement. 1911 *Jrnl. Chem. Soc.* C. ii. 570 The Measurement of Geological Time.

Geonoma (dʒī,ǫ·nŏmă). *Bot.* [mod.L., f. Gr. γεωνόμος a colonist, in allusion to its rapid propagation.] A tree of the genus of small palms of this name, common in Central America.
1910 *Daily Chron.* 12 Mar. 8/4 Other graceful plants for our rooms are the Latania, the Grevillea, the Kentia, the Geonoma, the Rhapis, and the Dracæna.

George. Add: **6.** Also simply *George!*
1888 A. C. Gunter *Mr. Potter* i, George! isn't it horribly lonely?
7. **George guinea** = sense 4 b.
1905 *Westm. Gaz.* 25 May 7/3 The finding of George guineas.

Georgette (dʒǫɹdʒe·t). [Fr., f. the name of Mme. *Georgette*, a French modiste.] A thin, semi-transparent silk crêpe of fine texture. Also *georgette crêpe.*
1920 *Glasgow Herald* 29 Nov. 15 Silk georgette. 1922 *Daily Mail* 10 Nov. 8 The bride's gown of gold embroidered georgette. 1927 Agnes Miller *Colfax Bk.-Plate* xiii. 161 My negligée..was made of georgette and satin.

Georgia (dʒǭ·ɹdʒiă). [fem. (sc. *colonia* colony, or *civitas* state), f. mod.L. *Georgius* = King George I of England.] The American colony and state of that name, lying between South Carolina and Florida. Used *attrib.* in spec. uses.
1740 in *Coll. S. Carol. Hist. Soc.* IV. 60 Capt. Palmer, with his own and the Georgia Rangers.., made Excursions every day. 1853 F. W. Thomas *J. Randolph*, etc. 85 There I thought..that some Georgia man, as the negroes then called the slave-dealers—for to Georgia many of the negroes were then sold..would leap upon me from the woods.
b. In names of trees and plants.
1810 Michaux *Arbres* I. 16 Long leaved pine,..[or] Georgia Pitch Pine. *Ibid.* 30 Georgia bark tree..nom donné par moi. 1813 H. Muhlenberg *Catal. Plants* 23 Georgia bark, or Downy Pinkneya. 1832 D. J. Browne *Sylva Amer.* 228 The Georgia bark is a low tree, dividing itself into numerous branches. 1859 A. L. Hillhouse tr. *Michaux's Sylva* I. 180 From the properties of its bark, the Pinckneya has taken the name of Georgia Bark. 1889 *Century Mag.* Jan. 462/2 And in time we appeared in every shade from Melton gray to Georgia butternut.

Georgian, *a.*[1] Add:
1. b. Belonging to the reign of George V.
1910 P. Gibbs in *Lady's Realm* July 272 Under the new regime of Georgian England. 1912 (*title*) Georgian Poetry 1911–1912. 1921 R. Lynd in *Anthol. Mod. Verse* Introd. p. xxx, The Georgian poets, like the Lake poets, are re-establishing the claim of familiar experiences to poetical treatment in familiar language. 1927 M. Sadleir *Trollope* 3 To the critical eye of Edwardian and Georgian enlightenment the mid-Victorians have appeared smug and hypocritical and selfish. 1928 *Daily Tel.* 10 Jan. 7/2 With the exception of Froude, most of the Victorian biographers set out with the idea of saying nothing but good in their subjects, the Georgians must needs set out to belittle theirs.

B. *sb.* One belonging to the time of the Georges, kings of England, *spec.* to that of George V.
1921 *Spectator* 28 May 689/1 Both the old and the young, Victorians and Georgians. 1923 'M. Arlen' *These Charming People, Smell in Libr.* 223 Oh, the Georgians, the magnificent young Georgians—mostly dead! 1927 J. Boon (*title*) Victorians, Edwardians and Georgians. The Impressions of a Veteran Journalist extending over Forty Years. 1931 *Book Window* Spring No. 204/1 Mr. G. K. Chesterton and Mr. Hilaire Belloc, late Victorians who are good Georgians.

Geosyncline (dʒī,ǫsi·nklain). *Geol.* = Geosynclinal *sb.*
1895 Dana *Man. Geol.* (ed. 4) 389 A mountain system includes all ranges in a region made in different, more or less independent, geosynclines at the same epoch. 1925 J. Joly *Surface-Hist. Earth* v. 85 The geosyncline wherein the Cordilleras of N. America were cradled extended from the Gulf of Mexico to the Arctic Ocean.

Ger (dʒəɹ). Abbreviation of German *sb.* 1; also *Comb.*, as *gerblighter, gerboy.* So **Germ.**
1916 Boyd Cable *Action Front* 20 The Germs are holding the same trench a little further along. *Ibid.*, The Germ trench. 1919 J. B. Morton *Barber of Putney* xiv. 230 It's about time the Gers had their last fling. *Ibid.* xv. 246 The Gerblighter goes into it [*sc.* a scrap] like a dog what's been licked and bullied. *Ibid.* xviii. 300 At the beginning of this jolly old war the Gerboy cavalry withdrew to Meteren.

Geranial (dʒĕrǣ·niăl). *Chem.* [f. Gerani(um + Al(dehyde.] A strong-smelling, colourless oily aldehyde, forming one of the chief constituents of oil of lemon, oil of orange, etc., and used in perfumery. Also **Geranic** (dʒĕræ·nik) *a.*, denoting an acid produced by the oxidation of geranial; **Geraniene** (dʒĕrǣ·niīn), a terpene prepared by the dehydration of geraniol; **Geraniol** (dʒĕrǣ·niǫl), a fragrant colourless oil occurring in oil of geranium, oil of roses, etc.; **Geranyl** (dʒĕrǣ·nail), the radical of geraniol, as in *geranyl-acetate.*
1871 *Jrnl. Chem. Soc.* XXIV. 261 By repeated fractional distillation of [Indian oil of geranium]..a liquid was obtained..called by the author [*sc.* O. Jacobsen] geraniol. 1891 *Ibid.* LX. i. 323 Geranaldehyde and Geranic Acid. 1896 *Ibid.* LXX. i. 445 This partial synthesis of geranic acid establishes Tiemann's formula for geranaldehyde. 1897 *Ibid.* LXXII. i. 248 Geranyl Chloride. 1901 *Ibid.* LXXX. i. 282 Eucalyptus Oil containing 60 per cent. of Geranyl Acetate. 1923 *Nature* 29 Dec. 952/1 Of active principles, australol, geraniol, citral, and piperitol gave coefficients of 22·5, 21, 19·5, and 13 respectively. 1924 *Times Trade & Engin. Suppl.* 29 Nov. 243/2 Quite a number of changes have taken place among perfumery chemicals, and eugenol (10s. 6d.), geraniol (12s. 6d. to 20s.)..have all advanced.

Gerenuk (ge·renŭk). Also **geranook.** [Native name.] A long-necked gazelle-like antelope of East Africa, *Lithocranius walleri.*
1895 H. G. C. Swayne *17 Trips through Somaliland* 312 The Gerenuk is the commonest and most widely distributed of the Somali Antelopes. 1897–8 Sclater & Oldfield *Bk. Antelopes* III. 229 The Gerenuk. Lithocranius Walleri. Vernacular name:—*Gerenuk* of Somalis. 1920 *Brit. Museum Return* 31.

German, *a.*[2] Add: **4. German band**, an instrumental band of street musicians (properly) of German extraction.
1881 *Punch* 12 Nov. 228/2 More German Bands! for Her Majesty's and Drury Lane! Heavens! we are promised a Cycle of Wagner! 1898 H. G. Hutchinson *Golfing Pilgr.* 25 The German bands of our Margates and our Ramsgates. 1906 E. Kennedy *Wander Pict.* 190 At first I thought it was a Salvation Army band, but it turned out to be an awful German band that was making the town hideous.
b. **German ivy, larch.**
1837 Colman *Rep. Agric. Mass.* (1838) 116 The Larch referred to in the text and there called the German Larch, is the common or White Larch. 1864, 1866 German ivy [see Ivy *sb.* 2]. 1868 *Amer. Naturalist* II. 39 German Ivy, so-called, flowering under peculiar circumstances.
C. *German-American.*
1906 *N. Y. Herald* 5 Mar. 14 Advt., Wanted—Competent chambermaid..German-American preferred.

Germanic (dʒəɹmæ·nik), *a.*[2] *Chem.* [f. Germanium + -ic.] Of, pertaining to, or containing germanium, esp. in the quadrivalent state. So **Germa·n(i)ous** *a.*, of, pertaining to, or containing germanium in the bivalent state.
1895 Bloxam *Chem.* 418 White germanic sulphide, GeS_2 ..germanous oxide, GeO.

Germano-. Add: **Ge·rmanophil(e), -phobe** *adjs.* and *sbs.* (see -phil, -phobe).
1898 *Daily News* 14 Dec. 5/7 M. Barthélémy-St.-Hilaire, 'the only *Germanophile Frenchman then living'. 1906 *Outlook* 15 Sept. 338/2 Those whom the *Deutsche Revue* describes as 'very Germanophil Ministers'. 1911 *Q. Rev.* July 254 The editor of one of the greatest Russian newspapers, who is at one time a strong Germanophil, and at another an equally strong Germanophobe. 1904 *Daily Chron.* 22 Oct. 3/2 In this story he is neither Francophil nor *Germanophobe. 1905 *Ibid.* 10 Jan. 5/5 The Germanophobe attitude of the English Press.

Germarium (dʒəɹmē·riǫm). *Zool.* Pl. **-aria.** [mod.L., f. L. *germen* germ.] In certain invertebrates, the ovary proper, as distinguished from the vitellarium.
1877 Huxley *Anat. Invert.* 178 A single or double *germarium*, having nearly the same structure as the ovary of *Macrostomum*. 1888 Rolleston & Jackson *Anim. Life* 646 The germarium is always single, usually globular or elongate, and even folded on itself.

Germiparity (dʒəɹmipæ·rĭti). *Biol.* [irreg. f. L. *germen* germ + *parĕre* to produce + -ity.] Reproduction by means of germs or germ-cells. Also **Germi·parous** *a.*
1889 Geddes & Thomson *Evol. Sex* 66 The first period of 'germiparity'—from the fourth to the sixth day.

Gerontes (gerǫ·ntīz, dʒ-). *Gr. Antiq.* [mod.L., f. Gr. γέρων old man.] *pl.* Members of the Spartan gerusia.
1738 Chambers *Cycl.* s.v. 1890 *W. Smith's Dict. Gr. & Roman Antiq.* (ed. 3) 914/1.

Gerontine (dʒerǫ·ntin, -tīn). *Chem.* [f. Gr. γέρων old man + -ine [5].] A crystalline base obtained from the liver and kidneys, *spec.* of old dogs.
1891 *Jrnl. Chem. Soc.* LX. i. 588 Gerontine is a strongly basic compound isomeric with cadaverine; it is a heavy, yellowish liquid which resinifies on standing.

Gerrymander, *sb.* *U.S.* Add: Also, one elected by gerrymandering.
1813 *Massachusetts Spy* 12 May (Th.) An official statement of the returns of voters for senators give[s]..eleven gerrymanders.
b. *attrib.*, as *Gerrymander district, law*, etc.
1812 *Boston Gaz.* 23 Nov., Some returns from democratic towns are not made conformable to the Gerrymander law of last February. 1813 *Ibid.* 5 Apr., Essex Gerrymander District Address.

Gerrymander, *v.* (Earlier U.S. examples.)
1813 *Boston Gaz.* 8 Apr. (Th.) When a man has been swindled out of his rights by a villain, he says he has been Gerrymandered. 1813 *Massachusetts Spy* 2 June (Th.) The manner in which they have obtained this majority is by a species of gerrymandering.

Geryonid (dʒərai·ǫnid), *a.* and *sb.* *Zool.* [f. mod. L. *Geryoni(i)dæ*.] **A.** *adj.* Of or pertaining to the Geryoni(i)dæ, a family of craspedote medusæ. **B.** *sb.* An individual of this family. So **Geryo·nidan** *a.*
1871 Allman *Gymnoblastic Hydroids* 43 Geryonidan medusæ. 1888 Rolleston & Jackson *Anim. Life* 754 The hydroid appearance of the larva is much masked in the Geryonids by the early development of mesoglæa. *Ibid.* 755 The Geryonid *Carmaris Goltschii*.

Gestalt (gəʃta·lt). *Psychol.* [G., = form, shape. The introduction of the term is ascribed to Chr. von Ehrenfels, in an article 'Ueber "Gestaltqualitäten"' in *Vierteljahrsschrift für wissenschaftliche Philosophie* XIV. (1890) 249–292.]
A 'shape', 'configuration', or 'structure' which as an object of perception forms a specific whole or unity incapable of expression simply in terms of its parts (e.g. a melody in distinction from the notes that make it up). Chiefly *attrib.* in *gestalt psychology, school, theory*, etc. (after G. *gestalttheorie*, etc.). Hence **Gesta·ltist**, a gestalt psychologist.
1924 tr. K. Koffka in *Psyche* V. 80 Gestalt-Psychology has so far got a number of important answers to its questions. *Ibid.* 81 Gestalt-Theory. *Ibid.* 84 Prof. Wertheimer, in his lectures, has treated personality as a Gestalt. 1925 C. Fox *Educat. Psychol.* 15 The *Gestalt* theory. *Ibid.* 17 The hypothesis of the *gestalt* psychology according to which all mental phenomena are figured or have a structure or pattern. *Ibid.* 182 The *Gestalt* psychologists. 1926 *Encycl. Brit.* Suppl. I. 45/1 The work of the Gestalt school with its stress upon the unity of psychic processes. *Note*, The Gestalt theorists. 1931 Belgion *Human Parrot* i. 15 The Behaviourists and the apostles of *Gestalt*. 1931 *Psyche* July 6 The rise of Gestaltists, hormic psychologists and many other varieties. *Ibid.* 76 The concepts in terms of which we think are like the 'figures' of gestalt psychology.

Gesticulatingly (dʒesti·kiŭlēitiŋli), *adv.* [f. Gesticulating *ppl. a.* + -ly [2].] With gesticulations. Also **Gesti·culatively** *adv.*
1893 F. Adams *New Egypt* 22 Strolling about, noisily and gesticulatingly. 1898 E. P. Evans *Evol. Ethics* vii. 223 He can..express the number of objects lying before him gesticulatively with his fingers.

Gesture, *sb.* Add:
4. b. *transf.* [after F. *geste*; cf. *Beau geste.] A move or course of action undertaken as an expression of feeling, especially of friendly feeling, and with the purpose of eliciting a favourable response from another. Also in trivial use.
1916 *Daily News* 2 Feb. 4/4 The cost of museums and galleries ought to be considered as part of the cost of the war...To shut them is a mean and shabby gesture before the whole world. 1921 George V in *Times* 18 Oct. 10/4 The gift of your Medal of Honour to a British comrade in arms, whose tomb in Westminster Abbey stands for all our best endeavour and hardest sacrifice in the war, is a gesture of friendly sympathy and good will which we will not forget. 1921 *Daily News* 9 Nov., The hope that Sir James Craig might make a generous gesture. *Ibid.* 24 Nov., You cannot quite get that gesture from Mr. Balfour. 1922 *Daily Mail* 9 Nov. 9 So far as the movement against Prohibition is concerned, the victory of Mr. Edwards, Governor of New Jersey, is only a gesture. As Governor he promised to make the State as wet as the Atlantic. *Ibid.* 16 Dec. 9 The United States Cabinet to-day sat..to consider a world gesture which is intended..to assist Europe and to allay discontent at home. 1922 *Westm. Gaz.* 20 Dec., The semi-official gestures of Greece towards a reconciliation with this country. 1929 *Woman's Jrnl.* Feb., The right gesture in jewellery.

Get, *sb.*[1] Add: **1. c.** *Lawn Tennis colloq.* The action of returning a (difficult) ball.
1927 *Daily Tel.* 22 Mar. 15/6 One does not remember seeing Hake play better, and some of his gets were most spectacular. 1927 *Daily Express* 20 June 3/5 Never applaud a difficult 'get' in the middle of a rally.

Get (get), *sb.*[3] Also **gett.** [Aramaic.] Among the Jews, a written 'bill of divorcement' prepared according to a prescribed form; also, the divorce itself.
1892 Zangwill *Childr. Ghetto* I. iv, 'He must give her Gett.' 'Of course!' shouted Sam,..'I divorce her at once!'

Get, *v.* Add: *Etym. note.* The pa. pple. is also used *colloq.* with omission of *have.*
1857 *Quinland* I. Introd. 1 Got an hour to spare—thought I'd just run in and see what you were all about. 1884 [see *Get-out 1]. 1887 Mary E. Wilkins *Humble Romance* 370 What you got there, grandma? 1911 R. D. Saunders *Col. Todhunter* i. 11 Oh, of course, you got to laugh at me. 1911 J. F. Wilson *Land Claimers* ix. 118 But I got several plans, and I need ye.
1. e. *I wish you may get it, Don't you wish you may get it?*: ironical expressions concealing the speaker's doubt of or lack of desire for another's success.
1835–7 Dickens *Sk. Boz, Election for Beadle*, An 'I wish you may get it' sort of expression in his eye. 1837 — *Pickw.* xxvii, 'Won't Mr. Dodson and Fogg be wild if the plaintiff shouldn't get it?' added Mrs. Cluppins...'Well,' said Sam, ..'All I can say is, that I wish you *may* get it.' 1848 Thackeray *Van. Fair* xiii, 'There's one of the greatest men in the kingdom wants some.' 'Does he?' growled the senior. 'Wish he may get it.' 1851 Mayhew *Lond. Labour* I. i. 56 I've heard people say when I've cried 'all a-growing' on a fine-ish day, 'Aye, now summer's a-coming.' I wish you may get it, says I to myself; for I've studied the seasons. 1857 Hughes *Tom Brown* i. ix, Don't you wish you may get it?
5. b. Also with *on* (a person). *U.S. colloq.* Cf. On *prep.* *21 b, d.
1919 *Detect. Story Mag.* 25 Nov. 129 He gave me the slip. ..Maybe it's just as well since I haven't got anything on him yet. 1923 L. J. Vance *Baroque* vii. 42 You haven't got any thing on me. 1926 *Ladies' Home Jrnl.* Nov. 129 There was no competition except the scenery. After all, almost any woman's got it on a mountain.
e. *Racing.* To hold out for, to stay (a specified distance).
1898 A. E. T. Watson *Turf* vii. 148 There are not a few horses that cannot fairly 'get' even five furlongs. 1898 *Daily News* 17 Oct. 3/3 He will..be opposed by plenty of candidates who can get the Cambridgeshire course. 1907 *Daily Chron.* 14 Nov. 3/3 Only a wonder of a horse can 'get' those four miles and a half of ditches and fences.
7. d. To understand (a person or statement); to catch. orig. *U.S. colloq.*
1907 M. C. Harris *Tents of Wickedness* I. iii. 33 'I don't get her,' she murmured, as if Leonora was a telephone number. 1915 H. L. Wilson *Ruggles of Red Gap* viii. (1917) 149 'I want all parties here to get that.' 'Say no more please. It's quite understood.' 1921 R. D. Paine *Comr. Rolling Ocean* vi. 106 'I get you, sir' respectfully answered Judson. 1928 F. N. Hart *Bellamy Trial* v. 166, I have a first-class opportunity..if you get what I mean.
16. c. Also *to get it in the neck*: see *Neck *sb.*[1]
d. *To get one's goat*: see *Goat 3 c.
21. c. To succeed in taking or catching; *esp.* (orig. *U.S.*) to succeed in killing.
1887 F. Francis Jr. *Saddle & Mocassin* viii. 138 They'll get you one of these days, Colonel, when you are driving around in your wagon. 1899 Tarkington *Gentl. Indiana* ix. 160 Wiley,..you don't think they've got him? 1900 Eliz. Glyn *Visits Eliz.* (1906) 19 She did not hit any rabbits, but she got a gardener in the leg. 1901 *Daily Chron.* 7 June 8/4 Jones getting Bland at square-leg. 1907 Mulford *Bar-20* iii. 33 The man..was dead. Buck got him immediately after he had shot Johnny. 1908 *Daily Chron.* 16 Sept. 7/5 This climate is sure to get a white man sooner or later.
d. To exercise, worry, annoy. orig. *U.S. colloq.*
1884 A. E. Sweet & J. A. Knox *On Mexican Mustang Thr. Texas* xxvii. 356 Well, it just gets me, it do! 1890 *Congress. Rec.* 4933/2 That is what gets me; I can not stand that. 1904 W. H. Smith *Promoters* xii. 190, I wish to the Lord he hadn't been so quick about it. That's what gets me. 1914 Gertrude Atherton *Perch of Devil* I. xvii, What do you know about that?..Wouldn't it come and get you? 1926 G. W. Deeping *Sorrell & Son* xxix, 'Do you think he minds?' 'I know he doesn't. But it gets me.'
e. To get hold of, attract; to touch emotionally.
1915 *To-Day* 11 Nov. 50/3 The 'curtain' on that dog walking across the stage and sticking his cold nose into the hand of his lonely master always used to get me. 1928 F. N. Hart *Bellamy Trial* i. 6 It's always interested me more than anything else...Well, don't let it get you. 1929 *Atlantic Monthly* Nov. 579 Cairo doesn't get me, altogether.
f. To get the better of.
1926 *S. P. E. Tract No. XXIV.* 122 *It gets me*, it passes my understanding.
22. b. *spec.* To succeed in 'picking up' (a wireless signal, a broadcasting station).
1917 S. Leacock *Frenzied Fiction* iv. (1919) 53 'Will it take long to get him?' I asked...'He's on the line now,' they said. 1921 *Wireless World* IX. 571/1 To ensure that the signals be picked up if it is at all possible to get them. *Ibid.* 586/2 If it be possible to get the Dutch concerts..with this three-valve set. 1924 *Wireless Ann.* 25 Hello, did you get me? 8 XY standing by. 1925 *Wireless Mag.* Apr. 259/3 'Hush, don't talk!' he said. 'I'm just getting Terra del Fuego.' 1929 W. J. Locke *Jorico* 66 One of these days, he declared, he would be able to get China.
29. b. To succeed in making. *U.S. colloq.*
1891 *Outing* (U.S.) Dec. 246/2 Rum had so far 'got him dead'. 1897 'Mark Twain' *Following Equator* lii. 504 He got me so nervous that I couldn't look at the view. 1927 *Atlantic Monthly* Feb. 148, I love to work, but this God-forsaken country gets me discouraged.
31. Of inanimate objects: To come into existence, be produced.
1894 Eliz. Banks *Camp. Curiosity* 191 Spots of iron-rust got on the linen.

b. (Recent U.S. examples with vbl. sb.)

1884 'Mark Twain' Huck. Finn ii, There was a place on my ankle that got to itching. 1904 W. H. Smith Promoters i. 9 When once an idea gets to going in the world it is liable to be picked up by any one. 1910 W. M. Raine B. O'Connor 12 Don't you think you'd arrive earlier at the end of your run if your choo-choo got to puffing?

c. To get there U.S. (earlier example).

1883 Nye Baled Hay 49 They were high-toned, and they got there.

d. (Earlier examples.) Also, to make speed.

1869 A. K. McClure Rocky Mts. 149 As he yelled to them [sc. his horses] to 'git', his keen silken cracker flashed about their flanks. 1877 Providence Jrnl. (Bartlett) We must do what there is to do, and then we can get up and get. 1907 Ld. C. Beresford in Daily Chron. 21 Nov. 5/1 In other words, as the Americans said, 'That fleet can get.'

33. To get that way (U.S. slang): to get into the condition implied. To get left: see Leave v.[1] 7 d. To get next to (U.S. colloq.): to understand clearly.

1922 C. Sandburg Slabs of Sunburnt West 6 How do you get that way?

35*. **Get around** — = get round (42 a). U.S.

1888 Montreal Herald 21 Feb. (Farmer) He thought some means could be devised of getting around the difficulty.

36*. **Get by** —. To 'get past', evade. U.S. colloq.

1904 S. E. White Blazed Trail Stories ii. v. 199 How he had gotten by the office boy Brown could not conceive.

40. **Get on** —. g. To influence in such a way as to harass or obsess; to become a source of worry to.

1920 Rose Macaulay Potterism iii. ii. 125 But please don't..er..let people worry her—get on her nerves. Ibid. 127 'Never mind Arthur' she said. 'I wouldn't let him get on my mind if I were you, mother.'

h. To get on to: to become aware of, 'get wise to'.

1923 Wodehouse Inimit. Jeeves ix. 97, I knew there wasn't a chance of my being able to work this stage wheeze in London without somebody getting on to it and tipping off the guv'nor. 1925 — Carry on, Jeeves ii. 38 As if they thought you were the greatest thing on earth and wondered that you hadn't got on to it yet yourself.

41. To get over the footlights = to get across (see 50*). orig. U.S.

1915 Munsey's Mag. Aug. 515/1 Shaw was generally considered altogether too wild to stand a chance of getting over the footlights.

50*. **Get across.** See *Across B. 2 b.

1913- [see *Across B. 2 b]. 1923 Silberrad Lett. Jean Armiter vi. 148 Sorry—my fault—one fails to get across. 1928 Observer 1 Apr. 6 His verse..in spite of all the efforts of his friends and admirers..has not really 'got across' eleven years after his death. Ibid. 17 June 8 Something, somehow, fails to get across. For it cannot be denied that the actual story..is a little slow. 1930 Times 24 Mar. 15/5 While he can 'get his words across' as Gilbert intended.

53. **Get along.** b. (Earlier U.S. examples.)

1831 Frances Trollope Dom. Mann. Amer. (1832) I. iii. 32, I was then new to the Western America, and unaccustomed to their mode of 'getting along', as they term it. 1833 C. A. Davis Lett. J. Downing (1834) 34, I wish you'd write me..whether you think I could get along with the business.

54. **Get away.** c. (Earlier example.) Also, to carry off successfully. (b) To get away with it: to succeed in what one tries; to carry off a coup; to escape punishment or retribution; to act with impunity.

1878 J. H. Beadle Western Wilds ii. 41 More'n once the robbers would tackle some gritty man that was handy with his 'barkers', an' he'd get away with two or three of 'em. 1912 Mathewson Pitching in a Pinch xii. 259 Being a great ball-player is the gentle art of getting away with it. 1913 Mulford Coming of Cassidy xiv. 231 'Nobody's goin' to make you cry, an' get away with it', he told her. 1924 A. J. Small Frozen Gold i. 40 One Indian can't fight that bunch of cut-throats and get away with it. 1925 E. Fraser & Gibbons Soldier & Sailor Words, Get away with it, to: To get off a charge. To get a tale believed. Just to scrape through a difficulty. [1928 Observer 25 Mar. 14 Some of the artists may be able, as the phrase goes, to 'get away with the swag'.] 1930 Punch 16 Apr. 442 The whole thing swung along at a brave pace...In brief, Mr. Edgar Wallace has got away with it again. 1930 Pett Ridge Miss Collingwood i. 5 Young men carry a new hat which, in the phrase of the day, might enable them to get away with it.

55. **Get back.** b. To get one's own back: to revenge oneself.

1910 [see Own a. *3 c]. 1912 Shaw Pygmalion iv, Higgins. ..You have wounded me to the heart. Liza...I'm glad. I've got a little of my own back. 1922 Westm. Gaz. 28 Nov., Busby said that he did it to 'get his own back'.

c. To get back at (or on): to retort or retaliate upon. U.S. colloq.

1888 Chicago Inter-Ocean (Farmer) Sam Jones has been coming down rough shod on Kansas City feminity...As the open letter writers in the magazines are getting back at Sam for his fondness for tobacco [etc.]. 1896 G. Ade Artie vi. 51 There's only one way to get back at you people. 1906 Springfield Weekly Republican 14 June 11 If the President had not been vindictively anxious to 'get back' at the packers, he could have accomplished his end effectively. 1907 Daily Chron. 17 Oct. 3/3 You cannot afford to be rude to a journalist. Some day he will get back on you. 1911 E. Ferber Dawn O'Hara vii. 99 Some day we'll have money enough to get back at some people we know.

56*. **Get by.** intr. To be successful in escaping or evading something; to succeed, 'manage'; to 'get away' with. orig. U.S. colloq.

1916 S. P. E. Tract No. XXIV 122 That chap would get by with murder. 1926 Amer. Oxonian July 101 The stipend is barely enough to get by on. 1928 Incomes, etc. Univ. Faculty (Yale Univ.) 109 Barely getting by with no funds to meet an emergency. 1930 F. A. Pottle Stretchers 38 We had to stand general inspection...Our frozen overcoats stood rigidly out like garments stolen from statues...But we got by somehow. 1931 Atlantic Monthly Feb. 235 Some have thought it clever to 'get by' [at college] without work.

57. **Get down.** c. intr. To settle down to (something), e.g. to settle down to work, to compose oneself to sleep.

1903, 1904 to get down to brass tacks [see *Brass sb. 5 b]. 1925 E. Fraser & Gibbons Soldier & Sailor Words, Get down to it: Get on with the job. Also, Go to sleep, lie down on your bed on the floor. 1930 Times Lit. Suppl. 29 May 441/3 He never, so to speak, stripped and got down to it—to contact with..reality.

60. **Get in.** m. trans. To bring in.

1893 Chambers's Jrnl. 1 July 414/2, I fetched water, got in sticks, cleaned boots.

61. **Get in with.** a. To get (a person) in bad: to bring him into disfavour with. Also intr., to bring oneself into disfavour with. slang. orig. U.S.

1928 Observer 19 Feb. 16/2 Young Woodley..prefers poetry to cricket. That, of course, 'gets him in bad' with his house-master. 1928 Sunday Dispatch 22 July 22/3 It will be he who will get in bad with the fans.

62. **Get off.** a. Also, to get off with: to become friendly with one of the other sex, esp. with amorous intentions.

1925 E. Fraser & Gibbons Soldier & Sailor Words, Get off with, to: To make the acquaintance of or 'pick up' with anyone, usually some girl, without the formality of an introduction. 1925 F. Lonsdale Spring Cleaning i. 13 What fun it would be if one of us could get off with him.

h. Also intr. To get married or engaged to be married.

1915 'Berta Ruck' Courtship of Rosamond Fayre iii, 'Miss Urquhart's got off herself.' 'She has and she hasn't. Her chap's always away'.

i. (Earlier U.S. example.)

1849 Yale Lit. Mag. XIV. 187 There is the writing of one who tried to 'get off', as the boys say, something comic on every occasion.

j. To prepare (a person) for a journey.

63. **Get on.** b. Often to get a move on: see *Move sb. 6.

l. With to: To succeed in getting hold of or understanding. U.S.

1895 Century Mag. June 273/2 He..leaned across Phebe's seat, and touched the electric button. 'Little girl had n't got on to it, eh?' the grizzled man remarked pleasantly. 1904 N.Y. Sun 7 Aug. 28 Wise people are getting on to the fact that Eastwood is no ordinary real estate development. 1907 M. C. Harris Tents of Wickedness i. v. 73, I don't understand yet why none of the men got on to it.

64. **Get out.** b. Also, to leave one's office, position, or employment, be dismissed.

1906 P. Keany Get on or get out 3 Get on or get out. Don't be afraid of that phrase. It's the whole of the ten Commandments of Business rolled into five small words. 1911 Punch 1 Nov. 319 Get on or get out! 1913 Daily Mail 13 Feb. 9 Railwaymen to 'get on or get out!'

66. **Get over.** e. = *get across, trans. and intr. (see 50*).

1916 Picture-Play Mag. III. 122 If he works from characters and uses..bits of effective business to 'get his plays over', he [sc. scenario writer] should keep such material in handy files. 1921 H. A. Vachell Blinkers viii. § 3 Mrs. Merrytree, delighted to perceive that she had, in stage parlance, 'got over', held the situation firmly. 1928 Sunday Express 29 Apr. 5/6 Her friendliness 'gets over'. 1928 Daily Express 11 June 13 Of the 600 American films..ten per cent. will turn out to be excellent box-office attractions. Fifty per cent. of the remainder will 'just get over'.

68. **Get through.** c. Also trans., to put through.

1873 'Mark Twain' & Warner Gilded Age xx, The Senator..favored the appropriation and he gave the Colonel ..to understand that he would endeavor to get it through.

d. Also trans., to prepare (a person) for an examination so that he passes.

f. intr. To establish telephonic communications. Also trans., to send or receive (a message) by telephone, esp. after a line has been blocked.

1916 Boyd Cable Action Front 188 The signallers leaped to their instruments, buzzed off the call, and getting through, rattled their messages off. Ibid. 189 They haven't had time since they got my message through. 1929 Lorna Rea Six Mrs. Greenes 257 'Lavinia dear', she began as soon as she got through, 'I want you to help me a little to-night'.

70. **Get together.** b. intr. To meet in friendly conference. Also, to agree. U.S.

1889 Judge (U.S.) 10 Aug. 282/1 Five Men..are to be hanged on the same day. In other words, they will follow Mr. Dana's advice and get together. 1904 Chicago Tribune 9 Aug. 4 The representatives of the unions and of the employers should get together and talk it over. 1904 N.Y. Times 23 Dec. 1 The jury was unable to get together, and the Presiding Justice had ordered them locked up for the night.

d. trans. To cause (a crew) to work together.

1898 Encycl. Sport II. 280/2 As the day of the race.. draws near, the attention of the coach must be given entirely towards getting the crew absolutely together.

VIII. 73. **get-off**, (b) the action of rising from the ground in an aeroplane; **get-on**, one who gets on, one who succeeds; also attrib.; **get-there**, used attrib. to designate action which is likely to achieve success.

1916 H. Barber Aeroplane Speaks 50 The Pilot turns the Aeroplane in order to face the wind and thus secure a quick '*get-off'. 1908 Westm. Gaz. 10 Mar. 14/2 A little weary of this '*get on' gospel being continually dinned in their ears. 1908 Daily Chron. 13 Mar. 4/6 Prophetically numbered by Landor among the 'ons' who are get-ons.' 1900 19th Cent. XLVIII. 800 We American women have nothing like your enterprise and *get-there-ativeness in my country. 1901 Daily Chron. 22 June 10/5 Their style of rowing is peculiarly American..and, like the stroke of the famous Sho-woe-coe-mette crew of 1878, it is certainly the 'get there' style.

Geta (gē·tă). [Jap.] Wooden shoes worn out of doors by the Japanese.

1897 Outing (U.S.) XXX. 214/2 Their wooden geta clattering and slapping their soles as they go. 1904 Daily Chron. 13 June 8/5 Some of the 'geta' worn by little girls are painted in many colours. 1905 Westm. Gaz. 16 Mar. 2/1 The Yorozu are artistic to the stilts of their wooden geta.

Get(-)away (ge·t₁ăwē¹). [Get v. 73.] The action of getting away; spec. (a) the breaking cover of a fox, (b) the start of a race, (c) escape, esp. of thieves, with their booty (often to make one's getaway); also attrib.

1852, 1890 [see Get v. 73]. 1890 R. Boldrewood Miner's Right (1899) 121/1 It's the long good-bye I'm thinking, and no get away this time. 1902 H. L. Wilson Spenders xxxvii. 448 We can go back in style even if we didn't save much more than a get-away stake. 1907 Mulford Bar-20 xv. 166 We'll have to make our get-away plumb sudden or we'll never go. a 1909 'O. Henry' Roads of Destiny x. 165 Long jumps, quick get-aways..had helped Mr. Valentine to become noted as a successful dodger of retribution. 1922 Punch 1 Nov. 423/1 Quickly removing the ball from my toe I crawled under the net and made a get-away in the referee's car. 1923 Motor Cycling 26 Sept. 657/2 No one failed to start, although in general the getaways were not so fast or neat as in the case of the trade riders. 1923 Van Loan Old Man Curry 137 All the burglars at the track will be levelling for the get-away money.

Ge·t-out. U.S. colloq.

1. [Get v. 64.] phr. as or like (all) get-out, used to indicate a high degree of something.

1844 'Jon. Slick' High Life N.Y. II. 170 Me a-settin there as lonesome as git-out. Ibid. 222 Captin Doolittle has got a rale sneezer [sc. a pet squirrel]..as black as git out. 1884 'Mark Twain' Huck. Finn xxxviii, We got to dig in like all git-out. 1887 Century Mag. Feb. 610/1 Dark as all git-out. 1916 H. L. Wilson Somewhere in Red Gap v. 197 When I got into the parlour she had them on, pleased as all get-out. 1926 F. N. Hart Bellamy Trial v. 104 Oh, comical as all get out!

2. [Get 65 d.] An escape from a difficult position, evasion.

1909 Westm. Gaz. 4 June 7/3 I'm entirely in your hands. I have got no get-out. 1928 Daily Express 14 Feb. 3 Everybody..agrees that this story..was what is described as a 'get-out'.

Get-rich-quick, a. U.S. [Get v. 33 and Quick adv.] Characterized by attempts to acquire wealth rapidly. Hence **Get-rich-quickishness.**

1905 Chronicle (San Francisco) in Daily Chron. 9 Oct. 4/5 Californians have a strong tendency to invest in get-rich-quick ventures. 1906 Springfield Weekly Republican 12 July 3 The flaming get-rich-quick advertisements of this plantation company. 1909 Public Ledger (Philadelphia) 24 June 8/6 This business of irresponsible dealers and 'get-rich-quick' land schemes. 1914 Gertrude Atherton Perch of Devil i. x, There was a sort of suppressed get-rich-quickishness in their manner. 1920 Baily's Mag. Jan. 35/2 The get-rich-quick brigade. 1921 R. D. Paine Comr. Rolling Ocean viii. 131 If anything should go wrong with this get-rich-quick scheme of his. 1923 Van Loan Old Man Curry 72 Young friend Solomon called the turn on the get-rich-quick stuff.

Get-toge·ther. [Get v. *70 b.] A meeting, gathering.

1911 Springfield Weekly Republican 9 Feb. 12 It was the biggest get-together the organization has ever held. 1926 Ladies' Home Jrnl. Apr. 24 The newcomer sat down at the table, and the Chief went on to the next object of the get-together.

Get up. Add: 4. Inclination to get up and be active; energy, enterprise. Also get-up-and-get, etc. U.S. colloq.

1873 J. H. Beadle Undevel. West iii. 74 If you..have any 'get up' about you, and can and will work, ther's a show for you in rural Nebraska. 1889 Kansas Times & Star 2 Dec., It's not wealth, nor birth, nor state. But get-up-and-get, that makes cities great. 1909 R. A. Wason Happy Hawkins 147 The' ain't any chance for a man with get-up ..on this place, an' I'm sick of it. 1910 W. M. Raine B. O'Connor 223 When it comes to the get-up-and-hustle, she's there. 1915 P. G. Wodehouse Something Fresh x, He'll make a name for himself one of these days. He's got get-up in him. 1924 W. M. Raine Troubled Waters xxv. 258 That slim little girl you could break in two over your knee has got more git-up-and-dust than any man I know.

Ghaffir (gā·fiə). [Arabic.] A native Egyptian policeman.

1923 Glasgow Herald 19 Feb. 9 The whole distance was guarded..by 'ghaffirs', or watchmen. 1928 Blackw. Mag. Feb. 248/1 A canal watchman, known as a Ghaffir.

Ghap (gæp). Also **ghab.** [Hottentot.] The carrion flower.

1878 Trans. S. A. Phil. Soc. I. i. 24 (Pettman) Here we find stunted Mesembryanthemums, numerous kinds of Euphorbias, the peculiar Ghap (Stapelia) in at least half a dozen varieties.

Gharial, variant of Gavial.

1923 Chambers's Jrnl. Dec. 811/1, I had constant opportunity of seeing and observing the habits of the gharial.

Ghaut, ghat. Add: 4. In full burning ghat. The funeral pyre of the Hindus.

1877 Encycl. Brit. VI. 567/1 To erect cinerators on the burning ghat or ground. 1902 Ibid. XXX. 20/2 A sad procession of boats floated down to the burning ghats. 1901 'Linesman' Words Eyewitness (1902) 288 The second farm, which a night or two later blazed as a burning ghat over the poor sergeant's dead body.

Ghawazee (gāwā·zī). Also **ghow-**. [Arab.; pl. of next.] Egyptian dancing girls.

1836 Lane Mod. Egypt. I. 240 The Ghawázee (or public dancing-girls). Ibid. II. 95 The Ghawazee perform, unveiled, in the public streets, even to amuse the rabble. 1845 Ford Handbk. Spain i. 188 The ghowazee of the Egyptians. 1924 S. Rohmer Grey Face iv, Her hair, which was dressed in the fashion of the dancing girls who pose for ever upon the Egyptian monuments, and which is preserved in life to this day by the ghawâzî of Keneh.

Ghazeeyeh (gazī·ye). Also **ghazie.** [Arab.] An Egyptian dancing girl.

1819 T. Hope Anastasius (1820) I. xv. 301 A knot of ghazie distorted their limbs into as uncouth postures as if they had been frogs themselves. 1877 Encycl. Brit. VII. 727/1.

Gheez, variant of *Geez.

Ghetchoo (ge·tʃu). Also **gheechoo.** An aquatic root-plant, Aponogeton monostachyon.

1858 Simmonds Dict. Trade, Ghetchoo, an Indian name for the Aponogeton monostachyon, the roots of which are nearly as good as potatoes, and as much liked by the natives. 1866 Treas. Bot. I. 530/2 Ghetchoo.

Ghilgai (gi·lgəi). Austral. Also **gilgai.** [Native name.] A saucer-like depression forming a natural reservoir for rain-water.

1898 Morris Austral Eng. s.v., Ghilgais vary from 20 to 100 yards in diameter, and are from five to ten feet deep. 1930 Palmer Men are Human v. 41 They watched the gilgais turn to mud on the blacksoil plains.

Ghilzai (gi·lzəi). Also **Ghilji.** The name of one of the most famous of the tribes of Afghanistan. Also attrib.

1826 tr. Mem. Zehir-ed-din Baber 220 Plundering and beating up the quarters of the Ghiljis. 1842 C. Masson Narr. var. Journeys II. 207 The Ghiljis, although considered, and calling themselves, Afghâns..are undoubtedly a mixed race. 1875 Encycl. Brit. I. 235/1 On the British invasion the Ghilzais showed a rooted hostility to the foreigner. 1930 Blackw. Mag. Aug. 172/2 Information at hand pointed to the Ghilzais from Afghanistan.

Gholam (golā·m). Also **ghulam.** [Arab.] A courier, messenger.

1840 Fraser Koordistan I. i. 21 'What am I to do then, your Excellency?' roared out some Gholaum or Beg. 1882 E. O'Donovan Merv Oasis I. 319 We had with us a gholam, or courier, belonging to the British Legation at Teheran.

Ghoont (gūnt). Also **goont, gunt.** [Hind.] A Himalayan pony.

1625 Purchas Pilgrims i. 438 Heere is the great breed of a small kind of Horse, called Gunts, a true travelling scale-cliffe beast. 1834 tr. Jacquemont's Lett. II. 12 In Cashmere, I shall buy, without regard to price, the best ghounte in Tibet. 1858 Simmonds Dict. Trade, Ghoont, a small sure-footed Indian pony, used in the mountain ranges as a pack or saddle-horse. 1871 Balfour Cycl. India (ed. 2) II. 312/2 During winter the ghoont live on the roots of the stunted bushes, and are very expert at scraping the snow from off them with their fore feet.

Ghoork(h)a, variant forms of Gurkha.

Ghost, sb. Add:

10. c. An impression of a signature made by folding the paper over while the ink is still wet.

1919 Sotheby's Catal. 4–7 Nov. 82 On the back of one 'ghost' there is a note in the Author's hand.

d. An imaginary enemy in sham fights.

1908 Westm. Gaz. 19 Aug. 8/1 The day's work..will culminate in a running battle, in which the 'ghosts' will once more be the enemy.

14. e. **ghost-racket** U.S., 'any event or narrative into which the spiritual or ghostly element enters' (Barrère & Leland); **ghost-soul** = *Co-walker.

a 1889 Chicago Tribune (Barrère & Leland) The most novel *ghost-racket on record has just been worked by a Jersey detective. a 1889 Washington (Pa.) Eagle (ibid.) We have had the tallest ghost-racket here in our town that you ever did audit. 1871 Tylor Prim. Cult. I. 451 The notion of a *ghost-soul animating man while in the body. 1924 W. B. Selbie Psych. Relig. 29 As formulated by Professor Tylor this theory of a quasi-material ghost-soul is to be regarded as the typical and almost universal source of religious ideas and practices.

Ghost, v. Add:

4. To do literary or artistic work for another person. (Cf. Ghost sb. 13.)

1922 Glasgow Herald 11 Oct. 3 'A certain general' for whom he did some 'ghosting'. 1931 Let. to Editor, He is capable of translation, secretarial, or ghosting work.

Ghou·lishness. Ghoulish nature or quality.

1910 H. Walker Lit. Victorian Era ii. vii. 505 Her poetry altogether escapes the taint of ghoulishness. 1928 Weekly Dispatch 24 June 12/4 What is there in poor human nature..that creates this ghoulishness?

Ghurrial, variant of Gavial.

1878 P. S. Robinson In my Indian Garden 83 The ghurial is of a finer breed. 1905 Kynoch Jrnl. July–Sept. 152 On the sandbars Ghurrials in thousands basked in the sun.

Giant, sb. Add:

2. c. The name given by Dr. Hertzsprung in 1905 to the stars belonging to the class of larger diffuse stars, as distinguished from the dwarfs (see *Dwarf sb. 2 b).

1928 Jeans Astron. & Cosmog. 61. 1931 Nature 3 Jan. 16 The theory of Sir Arthur Eddington..does [not] establish the division of ordinary stars into giants and dwarfs.

Giantesque (dʒəiˌănte·sk), a. [f. Giant sb. + -esque, after F. gigantesque.] Having characteristics of a giant, gigantic.

1911 Webster. 1929 Sunday Express 20 Jan. 9 You gloat over their giantesque sins and sorrows.

Gib (dʒib, gib), sb.[5] [Of obscure origin.]

1. A piece of wood or metal employed to keep something else, as e.g. some part of a machine, in place. a. A bolt, pin, or wedge for insertion in a hole, to fasten the adjoining parts more tightly together.

Gib and cotter, gib and key: a two-part contrivance, consisting of a fixed and a movable wedge, used to tighten the strap at the end of a connecting rod.

1794 W. Felton Carriages (1801) II. Gloss., Gib, a small half-round wedge, which keeps the pole from rising. 1838 Civil Eng. & Arch. Jrnl. I. 150/1 The corners were secured by a strong iron strap with a gib and key. 1839 R. S. Robinson Naut. Steam Eng. 78 The rectangular hole for the gib and cutter. 1867 Smyth Sailor's Word-bk. 339 Gib, a forelock. 1880 Encycl. Brit. XIII. 732/1 The pin is sometimes rectangular in section, and tapered or parallel lengthwise. 'Gibs' and 'cottars' are examples of the latter. 1887 D. A. Low Machine Draw. (1892) 49 The gib is provided with horns at its ends to keep it in its place. 1888 Lockwood's Dict. Mech. Engin. 91 The gib and cottar arrangement is that in which the cottar is formed in two parts, whose outer faces are parallel with each other, the requisite taper being given to their inner or sliding faces.

b. A bearing surface to reduce friction, or a wedge to take up wear at a sliding contact.

1873 J. Richards Wood-working Factories 13 Gibs of lignum vitæ will be found to wear well. 1874 Knight Dict. Mech. 650/1 The box has two taper-cheeks a a and two taper-gibs b b adjustable by screws, so as to set up the boxing to the wrist and the cheeks to the guides in the cross-head.

c. (See quot.)

1902 Encycl. Brit. XXX. 402/2 The extractor [in a Maxim gun] is recessed to take a movable plate termed a 'gib', behind which is a spring.

2. Mining. A piece of wood used to support the roof of a coalmine.

1847 in Halliwell. 1879 Miss Jackson Shropsh. Word-bk., Gib, a wooden prop used to support the coal when being holed. 1883 Gresley Gloss. Coal-m., Gib, a short prop of timber by which the coal is supported whilst being holed or undermined.

3. attrib. and Comb.: **gib-head**, a head (of a rod, pin, etc.) with projecting shoulder(s; **gib-headed key** (see quot.).

1854 Ronalds & Richardson Chem. Technol. (ed. 2) I. 152 The opposite ends of the connecting-rods are provided..with *gib-heads. 1887 D. A. Low Machine Draw. (1892) 23 When the point of a key is inaccessible the other end is provided with a gib head. 1888 Lockwood's Dict. Mech. Engin., *Gib-Headed Key, a key having a set-off standing at right angles with the thicker end, for convenience of drawing it back in situations where the use of a drift is not practicable.

Gib (dʒib, gib), v.[3] [f. *Gib sb.[5]] trans. To provide or secure with a gib or gibs. Hence **Gibbed** ppl. a.

1884 Knight Dict. Mech. Suppl., Gibbed Lathe, a lathe, the carriage of which has a bar which grips beneath the overhang of the bed, beneath which it is secured by a wedge known as a gib, to prevent the riding up of the carriage. 1895 Funk's Stand. Dict., Gibbed way, a guiding surface provided with gibs for adjustment.

Gibson (gi·bsən). The name of C. Dana Gibson, an American artist and illustrator of magazines, used attrib. to designate a type of feminine beauty and costume popularized by him (c 1900–10), as Gibson girl, Gibson pleats.

1902 Encycl. Brit. XXVI. 590/1 American men..impart as much importance and humour to his pages as his 'Gibson girls' give radiance. 1904 Daily Chron. 11 Apr. 8/4 The lean-limbed, lantern-jawed American..accompanied by a Gibson girl, who calls him 'poppa'. 1905 Ibid. 1 Mar. 6/6 A Gibson girl..is a lady with a perfect figure and a perfectly-fitting dress..Miss Hardren, a handsome brunette in black, with a black picture hat, criticised the Gibson dress unsparingly. Ibid. 13 Mar. 8/1 Gibson pleats starting from the shoulder line and brought in symmetrical lines to the waist.

Giddy, a. Add: 3. b. Nonsensical, absurd. Also used in meaningless exclamation of surprise My giddy aunt (cf. *Aunt 5).

1919 W. N. P. Barbellion Jrnl. Disappointed Man 268 Oh my giddy aunt! 1924 A. J. Small Frozen Gold iii. 92 The giddy part of it is that our strike isn't up north at all.

Gift, sb. 9. Add: **gift-book** (earlier U.S. example); **gift bookstore** U.S., a bookshop conducted as a 'gift enterprise'; **gift coupon**, a coupon issued with certain commodities, a specified number of which entitles the holder to a free gift; **gift-deed** U.S., a deed of gift; **gift enterprise** U.S. (earlier example); **gift-shop** U.S., a shop dealing in articles suitable for gifts; **gift store** U.S. = gift enterprise; **gift-tree** U.S., a tree on which gifts for distribution are hung; a Christmas tree.

1834 Knickerbocker Mag. III. 113 It is, I believe, your standing *gift-book. 1873 W. Mathews Getting on in World vii. 100 To-day some shrewd Yankee starts a '*gift' bookstore, and immediately all the newspapers in the land are flooded with advertisements of gift enterprises. 1931 Morning Post 18 Feb. 6/5 The '*Gift' Coupon system. 1855 Barnum Life 10 My delighted ancestor..handed to my mother a *gift-deed in my behalf, of five acres of land. 1873 *gift enterprise [see above]. 1918 Carolyn Wells Vicky Van i. 10 Little faddly prize bags or *gift-shop novelties are her stakes. 1872 Talmage Abom. Mod. Society 177 In this class of gambler-makers I also put the '*gift stores'. 1898 H. S. Canfield Maid of Frontier 117 The little church where the *gift-tree festivities were in progress.

Gift-over (gi·ft₁ōuvəɹ). [f. Gift sb. + Over adv.] The act of making over as a gift.

1927 Daily Mail 8 July 7/1 That the gift-over, by which the property might pass away from the children on account of the son's marriage, was void. 1929 Glasgow Herald 8 July 8 The gift-over whereby the estate would go elsewhere than to the children.

Gigantoblast (dʒəigæ·ntəblɑst). [f. Gr. γίγαντο-, γίγας Giant + βλαστός embryo, germ.] A very large nucleated red blood corpuscle.

1908 Practitioner Feb. 241.

Gig-boat. = Gig sb.[2] 2 b.

1836 Knickerbocker Mag. VIII. 283, I took a Seminole Indian..and in a fine gig-boat, started up the St. John's river.

Gigerium (dʒidʒīə·riŏm). [sing. of L. gigeria cooked entrails of poultry.] The gizzard.

1875 Encycl. Brit. III. 726/1 A proventriculus, connected by a narrow neck with the gizzard (gigerium). 1884 Coues N. Amer. Birds (ed. 2) 213 The gizzard, gigerium, or muscular division of the stomach.

Gigglish, a. Delete †Obs. and add:

1900 Elin. Glyn Visits Eliz. 222 [She] got rather gigglish.

Gigolo (dʒi·gəlo). [Fr., formed as masc. correlative of gigole tall thin woman, woman of the streets or public dance-halls.] A professional dancing-partner.

1927 Daily News 21 May 5/4 The audience was delighted with the grannies' dance with gigolos—as lounge lizards are called. 1927 Daily Express 24 Oct. 10/4 The Riviera wakes up...Well-known mannequins, dance partners, gigolos, and barmen..have once more returned to their place in the sun. 1931 Times Lit. Suppl. 9 Apr. 286/2 We are glad of the.. wit that depicts..such a skilfully varied gigolo as Dick Rawdon.

Gila (hī·lă). [The name of a river in New Mexico and Arizona.] In full **gila monster**, a large venomous lizard, Heloderma suspectum.

1890 Chambers's Jrnl. 8 Mar. 158/2 The Gila Monster.. which lives in the valleys and sandy plains of Arizona and Sonora, is called by the native Mexicans Escupion, which means 'Spitter'. 1902 Mulford Bar-20 v. 60, I only had th' main show—Gilas, rattlers an' toads.

Gilbertese (gilbəɹtī·z). [f. Gilbert (see below) + -ese.] The language of the Gilbert Islands in the Mid-Pacific.

1908 H. Bingham (title) A Gilbertese-English Dictionary.

Gilbertian (gilbō·ɹtiăn), a. [f. the name of W. S. Gilbert (1836–1911), librettist of the Gilbert and Sullivan operas + -ian.] Of or pertaining to, resembling or reminiscent of the humour or the 'topsy-turvy' situations characteristic of, the Gilbert and Sullivan operas. Hence **Gilbe·rtianism.**

1887 Graphic 29 Jan. 107 All do their duty, and, to borrow a Gilbertian phrase, 'do it very well'. 1891 Strand Mag. Oct. 331/2 There is a perfect home farm on the Gilbertian land. 1894 P. Fitzgerald Savoy Opera 13 The 'Gilbertian' topic of the English traveller 'turning up his nose' at everything he sees abroad. Ibid. 14 note, A sort of 'Gilbertian humour'. 1901 Westm. Gaz. 26 Aug. 2/1 We are getting absolutely Gilbertian over this question of the handing over of actual cash. 1902 Temple Bar Jan. 36 The Gilbertian Libretto. 1906 Daily Chron. 16 Nov. 6/7 The Gilbertian question whether a Lord Chancellor could bring himself to justice for contempt of his own court..is equalled in the quality of Gilbertianism by the puzzle of Baton Rouge, Indiana. 1918 T. H. Ward Engl. Poets V. 540 His peculiar quality of topsy-turvydom, which has perhaps added the word 'Gilbertian' to the language. 1929 Times 18 July 15/2 A Gilbertian situation arose in which a Government pledged to attack and an Opposition pledged to defend private enterprise simply exchanged roles. 1931 Church Times 25 Sept. 327/2 We are living, indeed, in a Gilbertian world, in a land far 'curiouser' than Alice ever knew!

Gilguy. Add: b. (See quot.) Naval slang.

1886 R. Brown Spunyarn & Spindrift xxxi. 378 Sailors forget at times, and if the exact name of anything they want happens to slip from their memory, they call it a chicken-fixing, or a gadjet, or a gill-guy.

Gill, sb.[1] 5. b. Add: **gill-book**, the lamellate respiratory organ of the king-crab (cf. *lung book); **gill-pore**, a minute opening, which communicates between the gill-pouch and the exterior in an individual of the genus Balanoglossus of worms; **gill-pouch**, (a) any one of the biserial chambers behind the collar in an individual of the genus Balanoglossus of worms; (b) a structure present in the embryonic stages of reptiles, birds, and mammals.

1902 Encycl. Brit. XXV. 521/2 The leaves (some 150 in number) of the *gill-book..correspond to the tooth-like processes of the pectens of Scorpio. Ibid., The gill-books of Limulus. 1902 Encycl. Brit. XXVI. 85/1 Each gill-slit may be said to open into its own..gill-pouch; this in its turn opens to the exterior by a minute *gill-pore. 1888 Rolleston & Jackson Anim. Life 590 New *gill-pouches appear to be constantly added throughout life.

Gill, jill, sb.[4] Add: 1. b. The female of animals of the weasel kind.

1875 G. C. Davies Rambles Sch. Field-Club xxviii. 210 A..'hob', or male ferret, and..a 'jill', or female. 1902 in Cornish Naturalist on Thames 72 The female, or 'Jill', changes her entire coat directly she has young.

Gillenia (dʒili·niă). [mod.L., f. the name of Dr. Arnold Gill, German botanist.] A spiræa-like plant belonging to the genus of this name, esp. G. trifoliata; also the root of this plant, which has properties similar to those of ipecacuanha.

1829 Loudon Encycl. Plants 428. 1874 Garrod & Baxter Mat. Med. (1880) 211. 1901 Robinson Eng. Flower Garden (ed. 8) 575 The Gillenias have a distinct and delicate beauty all their own.

Gillenin (dʒili·nin). [f. *Gillen(ia + -in[1].] The active principle of Gillenia, used in America as a substitute for ipecacuanha.

1890 Billings Med. Dict.

Gillie (gi·li), v. [f. Gillie sb.[1]] intr. To act as gillie. Hence **Gi·llying** vbl. sb.

1905 Daily Chron. 2 Mar. 3/2 Contriving during the long vacation of six months to make enough money—by teaching, gillying or field-labour—to keep himself at the University for another year. 1926 Chambers's Jrnl. Mar. 153/1 Archie usually gillied for me. 1927 Scots Observer 9 Apr. 10/1 Nor is it intended to have classes in game-keeping and ghillie-ing.

Gilsonite (gi·lsənəit). Min. [f. the name of S. H. Gilson + -ite[1].] A very pure form of asphaltum.

1896 Chester Dict. Min., Gilsonite,..the first name applied to the asphalt-like mineral now known as uintahite. 1909 Westm. Gaz. 20 May 9/4 The stock is secured upon certain gilsonite..mines. 1921 Brit. Mus. Return 160 Basalt coated with asphalt, and gilsonite, from Vera Cruz, Mexico.

Gilt, ppl. a. 3. a. Add:

gilt-bronze, -latten; **gilt-edge** a. = gilt-edged; also absol., a gilt-edged security; **gilt tooling** (see Tooling vbl. sb. 2 b); **gilt-toy** (see quot. 1862).

1906 Sir F. Treves Highways & Byw. Dorset iv. 43 A track made of *gilt-bronze moss. 1901 Westm. Gaz. 28 Aug. 7/1 The Demand for *Gilt-Edges. 1905 G. Wilson Ann. Glover Incorp. 24 What is termed a gilt-edge security. 1900 S. R. Gardiner Student's Hist. Eng. 314 *Gilt-latten effigies of Richard Beauchamp. 1930 G. H. Bushnell Librarianship viii. 50 Marking books permanently by *gilt tooling. 1839 Ure Dict. Arts 571 Supposing the articles desired to be gilded be brass or copper buttons, or small articles for *gilt toys, or ornaments of dress. 1851 Illustr. Catal. Gt. Exhib. iii. iii. 629/1 Much of the Birmingham jewellery and gilt toys are produced by means of dies or steel blocks, with impressions of articles to be sunk therein. 1862 Chambers's Encycl. IV. 754/2 Gilt toys, this term is known in trade as a designation for small articles which are gilded, but is chiefly applied to the cheap jewellery which is almost exclusively manufactured at Birmingham.

Gimbaler (dʒi·mbăləɹ). Also **gymbler, jumbler.** [f. Gimbal 4 + -er[1].] One who makes gimbals.

1921 Dict. Occup. Terms (1927) § 328.

Gimbri (gi·mbri). Also **ginbri, gunibry.** A small Moorish guitar played by plucking the strings with a piece of dry palmetto leaf.

1876 Stainer & Barrett Dict. Mus. Terms 214/1 The resonance-body of the Gunibry is made of a bottle-pumpkin cut longwise, and covered with sheep skin. 1903 Westm. Gaz. 18 Feb. 2/3 The slender fanatical singer, Whose fingers were skilled on the gimbri. 1907 Mrs. F. Campbell Shepherd Stars 177 The Gimbri wagged his [head] from side to side.

Gimlety (gi·mlĕti), a. [f. Gimlet sb.[1] + -y[1].] Piercing like a gimlet.

1899 Daily News 3 Jan. 5/6 Small, gimlety eyes. 1919 J. Buchan 39 Steps 13 Small gimlety blue eyes.

Gimp, v.[2] Add:

3. To give a ribbed or corrugated surface to. Hence **Gi·mper**, one who or that which gimps.

1902 Encycl. Brit. XXV. 27/1 A roll or rosette of lead ribbon, which has first been cut to the right breadth.., then ribbed or gimped, and finally coiled into a rosette. 1926 R. W. Hutchinson Wireless 57 Pure lead in the form of a tape..is passed through gimpers, which rib it and sever it into different lengths.

Gim-peg, var. gem-peg (Gem sb. 8 d).

1853 [see Gem sb. 8 d]. 1882 Encycl. Brit. XIV. 299/2 A very important substitute for the gim-peg-socket..is the dial.

Gin, sb.[1] Add: 12. gin-band, -stand, -wright.

1855 Florida Plant. Rec. 518 Received one *Gin band from the Tallahassee R.R. Depot. 1860 Texas Almanac 233 Pumps, gin-bands, window-glass, etc. 1835 J. H. Ingraham South-West II. 288 A broad band, which passes over and turns the cylinder and brush of the *gin-stand alone. 1860 Texas Almanac 303 These Gin-Stands..are especially distinguished for combining great ginning speed with a much improved sample of cotton. 1843 Quitman Let. in Life & Corr. 37 We have few mechanics, except carpenters, masons, and *gin-wrights.

b. **gin-house** (earlier example); **gin-pole** U.S. (see quot.).

1827 A. Sherwood Gaz. Georgia 116 At three or four *gin-houses much of the cotton..was cleaned. 1905 Terms Forestry & Logging 38 *Gin pole, a pole secured by guy ropes, to the top of which tackle for loading logs is fastened.

Gin, sb.[2] 2. b. Add: gin-soaked adj.; **gin-berry** U.S. (see quot.); **gin-crawl** (see *Crawl sb.[1] b).

1839 Z. Leonard Adventures (1904) 170 Here we passed the night without any thing to eat except these *gin berries. 1883 Bird o' Freedom 7 Mar. (Ware) Phil Benjamin was taking his daily constitutional, which consisted in what is called 'a *gin crawl'. 1908 Daily Chron. 31 Oct. 3/5 He used to have a 'pub-up', or a 'gin-crawl' four or five times a week. 1927 [see *Crawl sb.[1] b]. 1899 Daily News 15 Apr. 2/1 Lurid accounts of *gin-soaked Africa. 1908 Daily Chron. 20 Aug. 4/4 The gin-soaked grandmother.

Ginestra (dʒine·stră). [It., = broom.] The broom flower.

1899 Daily News 25 Feb. 5/1 The glorious ginestra, or mountain broom. 1921 Q. Rev. Jan. 52 Thou, Fragrant Ginestra, joyful in the wild, Scatterest thy solitary tufts around.

Ginger, sb. Add: 3. a. (Examples of more recent currency.)

1900 Daily News 19 Feb. 2/2 The Munsters..seem to be as full of ginger as any men I have ever seen. 1908 Westm. Gaz. 12 June 2/2 A County Councillor who advised his Council to do just a little so as to avert the threatened 'ginger' of the Board of Agriculture. 1909 Ibid. 20 Aug. 11/4 You may imagine that when a big section of them are assailed with such 'ginger', to use an Americanism, they reply with scathing effect.

4. c. Gold dust.

1887 Leisure Hour 21/1 Every night the books are balanced before the men leave, and the floor is swept, and should there be a discrepancy, the dust has to be picked over for 'ginger' —such being the technical [word] for the missing morsels.

6. d. attrib. or as adj. applied to an organization (or its members) which provides the 'ginger', spirit, or life of a party or movement.

1923 G. D. H. Cole Workshop Organiz. 37 A 'ginger' organization within the Trade Union movement. 1927 Punch 9 Mar. 269/1 The 'ginger group' of Conservative social reformers.

Ginger-beer. Add: b. Ginger-beer plant, a yeast-bearing bacterium, B. vermiforme.

1892 H. M. Ward (title) The Ginger-Beer Plant and the Organisms. 1902 Encycl. Brit. XXVI. 59/1 Ginger-beer plant, showing yeast (Saccharomyces pyriformis) entangled in the meshes of the bacterium (B[acterium] vermiforme).

Gi·nger-cake. U.S. [Ginger sb. 1.] Gingerbread in the form of a cake.

1831 Peck Guide for Emigrants ii. 152 The Yankees.. tell us of their..ginger-cake. 1863 B. Taylor H. Thurston xviii. 234 Piles of dark, leathery ginger-cakes. 1896 J. C. Harris Sister Jane 351 I'll bet a thrip to a ginger-cake that Mary got you in a corner out there in the garden and asked you to marry her.

Gink (giŋk). U.S. slang. [Of obscure origin.] A fellow.

1911 E. Ferber Dawn O'Hara viii. 121 I'm th' gink you killed off two or three years back. 1920 P. G. Wodehouse Damsel in Distress ii, I'm certain this gink is giving her a raw deal. 1921 R. D. Paine Comr. Rolling Ocean xii. 206 If you are the kind of gink that dotes on shipwreck, you can have my share of it. 1927 Sunday Express 6 Feb. 4 One of America's noblemen, a great pirate, a gink with nerve.

Ginnel[2], variant of Gennel.

Ginner[2]. (Earlier U.S. example.)

1858 Texas Almanac Advt., The liability of injury to the ginner while tending the gin.

So **Ginnery.** (Earlier U.S. example.)

1887 Harper's Mag. Aug. 432/1 Showing them..the ginneries where cotton-seed oil was made.

Ginny, a.[2] Add: 2. Gin-like.

1926 Sylvia T. Warner Lolly Willowes 39 A hot ginny churchyard smell.

Gin-sling. U.S. (Earlier examples.)

1800 Massachusetts Spy July 9 (Th.) Regaling themselves in drinking gin sling and smoking segars. 1834 W. A. Caruthers Kentuckian in N. Y. I. 11 Here waiter!..bring me a gin sling.

Giorgionesque (dʒɔ̆rdʒiŏne·sk), a. [f. Giorgione + -esque.] Resembling the style of the Italian painter, Giorgione Barbarelli (1478–1510).

1906 Westm. Gaz. 19 Dec. 10/3 Mr. Lane's beautiful Giorgionesque half length portrait of a young man. 1929 Daily Tel. 8 Jan. 8/5 The rich, almost Giorgionesque modelling, of the Diana.

Gip (dʒip), v.[2] slang. [Cf. Gyp[1] 2.] trans. To cheat.

1930 Byrne Golden Goat xiii. 106 Dariano had gipped the Greek Government during the war of millions in contracts.

Gip, variant of Gyp[3].

Gipo, gypo (dʒi·po). slang. Also **gippo.** [f. gip-, gyp-, first syllable of Gipsy + -o. Cf. *Gippy.] A gipsy.

1902 Eleanor G. Hayden From Thatched Cott. xi. 95 Daily-oh if Jim ha'n't..left the place fur tramps an' gippoes to walk in. 1903 — Turnpike Trav. xi. 228 The greatest insult that can be offered a gipsy is to mistake him for a tramp, and contrariwise a tramp is roused to fury if saluted as 'gippo' or 'gip'. 1912 Engl. Rev. Oct. 476 He could get some one else, perhaps a half gypo, or a lad, to take my place. 1929 Sunday Disp. 13 Jan. 2/1 He was a gypo...He had been born in a caravan.

Gippo[2] (dʒi·po). Also **gyp(p)o, gypoo.** [Altered form of earlier (dial.) gipper, jipper meat juice, gravy, stew, hence as vb., to baste.

1822 Scott Nigel xxx, He was a dexterous fallow that Derrick. This man Gregory is not fit to jipper a joint with him. 1886 W. H. Long Dict. I. Wight s.v. Jipper, Thee'st lat all the jipper out of the pudden. 1896 Farmer & Henley Slang, Jipper (nautical), gravy. 1900 N. & Q. 9th Ser. V. 295 The chef de cuisine was an old navy pensioner, and his instructions were: 'Mind you jipper them [sc. thrushes] well.' From him I learned to call gravy 'jipper', and bread and dripping 'bread-and-jipper'. 1904 Daily Chron. 22 Aug. 3/7 The mysteries of Irish stew, or 'gipper', as it is mysteriously termed in camp. 1909 H. G. Wells Tono-Bungay ii. iii. 153 The child made no end out of the shavin's. So might you. Powder 'em. They might be anything. Soak 'em in jipper, —Xylo-tobacco!

Grease, fat of any kind, gravy.

1914 Times 23 Dec. 3/2 You take your mess-tin, [and] empty out..the greasy 'gyppo' (that means stew). 1916 Daily Mail 1 Nov. 4/4 'Gipoo' (gravy or grease). 1925 E. Fraser & Gibbons Soldier & Sailor Words, Gippo (also Gypo), gravy. Bacon fat. Butter. Any greasy sauce.

Gippy (dʒi·pi). Army slang. Also **gyppy.** [f. as *Gipo + -y[6].]

1. An Egyptian, esp. a native Egyptian soldier. Also attrib. or as adj., Egyptian.

a 1889 World (Barrère & Leland) Colonel Kitchener will probably stick to his original intention of having only gippies (as they call the Egyptian soldiers here) at Suakim. 1911 in Webster. 1915 Sir V. Horsley in S. Paget Life (1919) iii. ii. 308 The Gippy himself has his points. 1925 E. Fraser & Gibbons Soldier & Sailor Words, Gippy (or Gyppy), a native Egyptian soldier. The name was apparently originally coined in the British Army of Occupation in Egypt about 1884. The 'Gyppie' Army was the common colloquial term for the native force organized by Sir Evelyn Wood and Lord Kitchener, and officered by British officers. Ibid., Gippy Bint, an Egyptian girl.

2. A gipsy.

1913 Chums 13 Dec. 253/2 'What's your name, sonny?'.. 'No idea', answered the gipsy with a soft laugh. 'I'm generally called Gippy in England. I've got other names in France, and Spain, and Italy.'

Gipsy, sb. 6. Add: **gipsy('s) pig**, the hedgehog; **gipsy('s) pork**, the flesh of the hedgehog; **gipsy wagon**, a caravan, used by gipsies, travelling showmen, surveyors, and others (Cent. Dict.).

1928 Sunday Disp. 2 Sept. 3/3 '*Gypsy Pork.' Hedgehogs are succulent this month. September is the month when the '*gypsies' pig' is plump and tender.

Giraffine (dʒiræ·fəin). [f. Giraffe + -ine[1].] A. adj. Like or resembling a giraffe. B. sb. A giraffe-like animal. So **Gira·ffoid** a.

1891 Flower & Lydekker Mammals ix. 332 A gradual diminution..can be traced from the more Giraffoid to the more Bovoid forms. 1901 E. R. Lankester in Proc. Zool. Soc. II. 280 [The skull] showed itself to be that of a Giraffine animal, and not that of a Bovine. 1902 Rep. Brit. Assoc. Adv. Sci. 623 The African Okapi..is a giraffine, horned in the male.

Girba (gi·rbă). [Arab.] A water-vessel made of leather.

1864 J. A. Grant Walk Across Africa 418 We had twenty Seedees, and each required to have two goat-skins, or 'girba', to carry his drinking-water. 1866 Baker Albert Nyanza I. iv. 150 This is the unexceptional rule in African travelling—'fill your girbas before starting'.

Girdle, sb.[1] Add: 1. d. Girdle of Venus (Palmistry): see Venus[1] 9 and quots.

1894 [see Venus[1] 9]. 1900 Ina Oxenford Mod. Palmistry 47 The Girdle of Venus is a half circle, of which one end lies between the first and second fingers, and the other between the third and fourth.

4. g. (Earlier U.S. example.)

1825 J. Lorain Pract. Husb. 63 All of them eventually die, provided the girdle be carefully cut through the sap into the heart-wood of the tree.

Girl, sb. Add: 2. e. A coloured woman. U.S.

1835 J. H. Ingraham South-West II. 242 They always address them [sc. the slaves] as 'boy' and 'girl', to all under forty years of age. 1879 Tourgee Fool's Errand x. 42 You must remember that all colored women are 'girls'.

4. a. girl clerk; girl guide: see *Guide sb. 2 d.

1901 Daily Chron. 29 May 3/6 No redeeming feature of girl-clerk labour. 1902 Ibid. 1 Sept. 3/6 The market is vastly overflooded with incapable girl-clerks, who can just manipulate a machine, at 10s. or 12s. a week. 1908 Westm. Gaz. 17 June 9/3 A girl-clerk does not expect to obtain an engagement without the necessary knowledge of shorthand and typing.

Girl-less (gō·ɹl₁lės), a. [f. Girl sb. + -less.] Without or devoid of a girl or girls.

1903 Daily Chron. 15 Apr. 5/1 If 'Harper's Weekly' may be trusted, the girlless telephone will soon be as familiar as the horseless carriage or the boneless sardine. 1929 Masefield Hawbucks 147 It's a very girl-less neighbourhood.

Girly-girly (gō·ɹli gō·ɹli), a. [See Girly a.] Girlish in an exaggerated or affected manner.

In 1900 Girly-girly was the name of a music-hall song. 1891 Outing (U.S.) Dec. 246/1 They despised dancing as 'girly-girly' and silly. 1900 Lawson On Track 73 She'd.. make a sweet little girly-girly dive for her chair. 1927 Daily Express 20 June 8 Typical girly-girly 'romp' stuff.

Girth, sb.[1] 7. U.S. (Earlier example.)

1821 J. F. Cooper Spy xxxiii. (1831) 384 A heavy piece of lumber lay across the girths of the barn.

Giulio (dʒū·liŏ). Archæol. or Hist. = Julio.

1909 Westm. Gaz. 17 Mar. 5/1 A..purse containing twenty-five giulii.

Giuoco piano (dʒuō·ko pyā·no). Chess. [It., lit. plain game.] A common opening in games of chess.

1876 Encycl. Brit. V. 595/1 The position here arrived at is the same as in the Giuoco Piano opening.

Give, v.: Add: 54. **Give away.** f. Latterly U.S.

1816 U. Brown Jrnl. in Maryland Hist. Mag. XI. 232, I was Just going to pay the Chain carriers & dismiss them, James gave away, Although full 6 feet high & well made. 1833 H. Barnard Ibid. XIII. 305 He spoke about an hour and a half, and gave away on account of a sudden dizziness in his head and failure of voice. 1903 R. T. Ely Stud. Evol. Industrial Soc. 42 The cattle-raising frontier has given away continually to higher stages.

61. **Give on.** b. = *Contango v.

1928 Morning Post 19 Nov., He will approach a fellow-member in the House, and say that he wishes to give on 50 shares.

62. **Give out.** e. (U.S. example.)

1831 E. C. Wines Two Yrs. & Half in Navy II. 52 Our money..gave out.

Gi·ve-away. [f. vbl. phr. to give away (see Give v. 54).]

1. An inadvertent betrayal or revelation of oneself, of plans, etc.

1901 Westm. Gaz. 28 Sept. 2/1 'When I was at Poona in '76—' 'My dear Colonel,' purred Reginald, 'fancy admitting such a thing! Such a give-away for one's age!' 1904 Ibid. 19 May 3/2 When Mr. Chamberlain went on to declare that the Government's amendment and his own had the same idea, the give-away was complete. 1920 Blackw. Mag. Mar. 334/1 This..might..have been a sure 'give-away', as steam at once mingled with the smoke. 1924 Galsworthy White Monkey ii. ix, She also realised the give-away.

2. attrib. applied to prices so low that the goods so sold may be said to be 'given away'.

1905 Westm. Gaz. 13 Sept. 8/1 They are advertising their stock at give-away prices. 1906 Daily Chron. 10 Aug. 3/5 Sold at give-away prices.

Given, ppl. a. 1. b. (Earlier U.S. examples.)

1833 J. Neal Down-Easters I. 59 Ah, but your chriss'n name; your given name? 1842 Knickerbocker Mag. XIX. 557 O, my name's Barker; people call me 'Squire Barker; but Ephraim Barker is my given name.

4. (Modern U.S. examples.)

1837 Knickerbocker Mag. X. 430 Why, his own party are the most violent, given-over, as it were, and low-lived people. 1920 Hunter Trail Drivers Texas I. 211 The Indians had just as soon have these..given-out cattle as any.

Giving, vbl. sb. Add: 5. attrib.: **giving-away price** = give-away price (*Give-away 2).

1924 Sale Catal., Giving-away price, per yard 6d.

Givy (gi·vi), a. dial. and U.S. Also **givey.** [f. Give v. 40.] Inclined to give or relax (see quots.).

1829 Virginia Lit. Museum I. 457 Givy. 'Muggy.' The weather is said to be givy, when there is much moisture in the atmosphere. 1859 Bartlett Dict. Amer. (ed. 2), Givy, a term applied to tobacco leaves, in a certain condition of their preparation for market. 1887 Kentish Gloss. s.v., The ground is said to be givey when the frost breaks up and the roads become soft and rotten. 1889 Farmer Americanisms, Givy, pliable; easy to work; i.e. ready to 'give'.

Glabellad (glăbe·lăd), adv. [f. Glabella + *-ad.] In the direction of the glabella.

1803 J. Barclay New Anat. Nomencl. 165 In the head,.. Glabellad will signify towards the glabellar [aspect]. 1808 — Muscular Motions 471 In the motion glabellad, the two obliqui, resisting one another's rotatory powers, become the motors. 1890 Billings Med. Dict.

Glacialin (glē¹·ʃiălin). [f. Glacial + -in[1].] A food preservative composed of boric acid and glycerin. In full glacialin salt.

1883 Encycl. Brit. XVI. 304/2 Boracic acid and borax are also employed by dairymen, the former being known as glacialine salt. 1895 Army & Navy Co-op. Soc. Price List 15 Sept. 699. 1904 Westm. Gaz. 7 Jan. 7/1 Various preparations of boric acid are in use, the most common of which are glacialin salt and boro-glycerine.

Glacière (gla·siɛ̄r). [Fr., = ice house.] An ice-cave.

1865 G. F. Browne Ice-Caves iv. 46 The upper glacière of the Pré de S. Livres. 1879 Encycl. Brit. X. 270/1 Cases ..occur where ice forms in caverns (glacières) even in warm and comparatively low districts.

Glacieret (glæsiəre·t, glā·s-, glē¹·ʃ-). [f. Glacier + -et.] A small glacier or mass of ice which is revealed by the wastage of névé in unusually dry seasons on the summits of the Cordilleras.

1889 Cent. Dict. s.v., The glacierets are considered by some to be properly denominated glaciers, and by others to be something quite different from true glaciers. 1922 C. S. Wright & R. E. Priestley Glaciology 109 A snow-drift glacier, or glacieret.

Glad, a. Add: 2. d. Gay, fashionable. (Cf. *4 d.) U.S. slang.

1911 L. J. Vance Cynthia 177 He's all there with the glad class, and everything like that.

4. d. Glad clothes or rags: (one's) best or ceremonial clothes; esp. evening dress. Glad eye: see *Eye sb.[1] 5. Glad hand: (the) hand of welcome. orig. U.S.

1905 Daily Chron. 11 Jan. 4/5 Only when starvation stares him in the face will he relinquish his '*glad clothes', as the cowboys call them. 1896 G. Ade Artie i. 4 She meets me at the door, puts out the *glad hand an' says [etc.]. 1905 Washington Post 8 Mar. 6 His return was a signal for the extension of the 'glad hand', for few men in the Senate had as many friends. 1911 H. S. Harrison Queed ii. 14 Mr. Bylash didn't go out to give her the glad hand, and welcome her into our humble coturce. 1930 Time & Tide 11 Oct. 1256 He makes a habit of cutting out glad-hand phrases and smooth generalities. 1904 Daily Chron. 6 Oct. 8/2 Donning an elaborate evening frock—the slangy American girl calls it 'gettin' into her *glad rags'. 1906 N. Munro Daft Days vii, 'There's a big garden-party to be at it.' 'My! I guess I'll put on my best glad rags.' 1908 Springfield Weekly Republ. 23 Apr. 1 The women had striven to outdo each other in the splendor of their costumes, while the men were not behind them in the display of what the college boys call 'glad rags'. 1922 H. B. Hermon-Hodge Up against it in Nigeria v. 76 We all turned out in our glad rags to join in the procession.

Glad, v. Add: 4. intr. [f. phr. glad clothes: see prec.] To dress up.

1916 'B. M. Bower' Phantom Herd ii. 32 Some that.. know cow-science so well they don't have to glad up in cowboy's clothes..to make folks think they're range broke.

Glade, sb.[2] 4. Add: **glade mallow** U.S., a tall malvaceous herb, Napæa dioica.

1857 A. Gray First Lessons Bot. (1866) 194 The Glade Mallow and the Indian Mallow.

Glaistig (gla·stik). Also **glastig, -ick.** [Ir.] A supposed she-devil or hag in the shape of a goat.

1903 Q. Rev. July 24 Fairies, brownies, kelpies and glasticks. 1925 Contemp. Rev. Oct. 537 The water-kelpies, the water-bulls, the mermaids, the glastigs. 1926 Hannan Beautiful Isle of Man xiii. 83 The green glaistig is always represented with masses of long yellow hair.

Glance, sb.[2] b. Add: **glance cobalt** (G. glanzkobold) = Cobaltite.

1868 Dana Min. (ed. 5) 71.

Glance, v.[1] Add: 5. Illustrations of the use with various preps. and advs.

1816 Scott Old Mort. xxxv, A horseman..gave a letter. Claverhouse glanced it over. 1831 Peacock Crotchet Castle xvi. 252 Her eye glanced on something which made her change colour. 1843 Ainsworth Windsor Castle i. iii, The duke..was glancing rather wistfully at them. 1862 G. Macdonald D. Elginbrod ii. xviii, Every now and then glancing up at her from her work. 1865 [Mrs. M. C. Harris] Christine xxx. (1866) 181 Mrs. Sherman and the party..glanced off their cards and chatted. Ibid. 187 She glanced up at the clock. Ibid. xxxiii. 208 He would..open her books, and glance through them for some trace of her in them. 1881 Mrs. J. H. Riddell Senior Partner I. v. 96 He did not glance round as the manager entered. Ibid. III. vi. 139 'No,' she agreed, glancing nervously around her. 1881 Jessie Fothergill Kith & Kin I. ii. 22 She..glanced for a moment into his face. 1893 Conan Doyle Mem. Sherlock Holmes (1894) 147 Glancing very keenly across at me. 1902 R. Machray Night Side of London v. 93 You indulge in pleasant little dreams, or glance away from what may become a tragedy. 1907 Smart Set Jan. 54 Her brother-in-law glanced after her.

8. c. Cricket. To deflect (the ball) with the glance-stroke (see Glance sb.[1] 1 b).

1899 Captain I. 593/1 You had better practise slipping and glancing the ball. 1899 A. Lang in Daily News 22 July 4/2 Men were then less apt to 'glance and glide', like The Brook, and K. S. Ranjitsinhji. 1928 Daily Express 19 Dec. 3/2 White..glancing Ironmonger for three.

Gland[1]. Add: 4. Hist. An acorn-shaped ball of lead, used as a missile.

1852 Burn Naval & Milit. Dict. 183 Gland,..leaden ball for a sling, in the form of an acorn, having frequently devices engraved upon it. 1927 Jessie Mothersole In Roman Scot. xviii. 252 These leaden sling-bullets (called 'glandes' because they were shaped like acorns) were only used up to the close of the first century.

Gland[2]. 3. Add: gland-pit, -tube.

1881 Trans. Obstetr. Soc. Lond. XXII. 48 The lumen of the gland-tubes. 1902 Encycl. Brit. XXV. 394/1 The forms of the several kinds of glands depend on the degree of branching of these gland tubes. 1906 Academy 6 Jan. 8/2 The pre-orbital gland-pit which has been traced in the skulls of Hipparion.

Glareal (glē³·riăl), a. Bot. [f. L. glarea gravel + -al.] Growing on dry exposed soils. (Cf. Glareous b.)

1847 H. C. Watson Cybele Brit. I. 66. 1920 Trans. Cardiff Nat. Soc. LIII. 46.

Glass, sb.[1] Add: 15. d. glass-cased (cf. Glass case), -fronted adjs.

1901 Westm. Gaz. 30 Dec. 2/1 The black marble *glass-cased clock. 1902 Ibid. 8 Feb. 2/1 The glass-cased eatables. Ibid. 11 Aug. 9/1 The great *glass-fronted, gilded coach. 1903 Daily Chron. 26 May 5/5 A glass-fronted touring car.

16. **glass-furnace** (later U.S. example); **glass-paper** (earlier U.S. example); **glass-printing**, (a) 'bronze-printing on gelatin cards', (b) 'the art of printing on glass by the transfer process' (Funk 1895); **glass silk** (see quot.); **glass silkworm**, the cylinder on which glass silk is spun; **glass-wave** (see quot.); **glass-wing**, any butterfly with wings that are wholly or partly transparent.

1880 Harper's Mag. Dec. 63 Since..Pittsburgh's first *glass furnace in 1796 this industry has found in that city.. congenial soil. 1815 Niles' Weekly Reg. IX. 94/2 *Glass paper [was manufactured]. 1884 Knight Dict. Mech. Suppl., *Glass silk, a product obtained by winding fine threads of glass in fusion on rapidly rotating and heated cylinders. 1899 Jrnl. Soc. Arts XLVIII. 64/1 Should they [sc. bubbles] pass into the *glass silk-worms, the continuity of the thread would be broken. a 1909 M. W. Travers Exper. Study Gases 275 (Cent. D. Suppl.) When standing sound-waves are produced in a glass tube two different systems of waves are sometimes observed, the air-waves within the tube, and waves which traverse the walls of the tube. The latter are called *glass-waves.

Gla·ssichord. U.S. [f. Glass sb.[1] 4 + -chord as in harpsichord.] A musical instrument in which the notes are produced by the vibrations of glass.

1835 J. H. Ingraham South-West I. ii. 24 The musical rippling of the eddies—like a glassichord, rapidly run over by light fingers. 1886 Harper's Mag. July 286/1 Turning upon his perch, he [sc. the grig] brings to view his 'glassichord', or shrilling organ.

Glastick, -tig, var. ff. *Glaistig.

Glaswegian (glæswi·dʒiăn, glæz-), a. and sb. [f. Glasgow, ? after Galwegian.] Belonging to or characteristic of, an inhabitant or native of, Glasgow.

1818 Scott Rob Roy xxii, The Glaswegian took him by the hand. 1884 Illustr. Lond. News 12 Jan. 27/1 Any of the ten words..in addition to the Glaswegian four.

Glaze, sb. 3. Add: spec. of maize seed. (Cf. Glaze v.[1] 6, quot. 1889.) U.S.

1863 Rep. Maine Board Agric. 11, I think the crop would be required to be cut before the seed was in full glaze.

Glazed, ppl. a. Add:

5. Of pig-iron: Containing a large quantity of silica, and so made brittle and difficult to puddle; = Glazy a. 2 c.

1884 W. H. Greenwood Steel & Iron iv. (ed. 2) 55 The excess of fuel employed when first blowing in a furnace often results in the metal first tapped being more highly siliceous than that produced in subsequent workings, and under these conditions, the siliceous pig known as glazed or blazed pig often results.

b. Of blister steel: Showing signs of fusion on the surface.

1884 W. H. Greenwood Steel & Iron xviii. (ed. 2) 413 Bars showing signs of fusion upon the surface are described as 'glazed bars', and indicate that the heat of the furnace has been too high.

Glazier. Add: 2. b. Phr. Is your father a glazier?: see quot.

1891 J. M. Dixon Dict. Idiomatic Engl. Phrases 132 Is your father a glazier!—a vulgar expression, signifying, 'Do you suppose that I can see through you?' It is used when a person in front of you obstructs your view.

Gleba (glī·bă). Bot. [mod.L. use of gliba, glæba clod, lump, Glebe.] The fleshy part of certain fungi in which the spores are borne. Hence **Gle·bal** a.

1866 Treas. Bot., Gleba, glebula, the peridium or the fleshy part of certain fungals. 1876 Encycl. Brit. IV. 162/2 The whole mass so enclosed is the gleba. 1900 B. D. Jackson Gloss. Bot. Terms, Gleba, the chambered sporogenous tissue within a sporophore of Phalloideæ.

Glebe, sb. 5. Add: glebe law, lot (U.S.).

1836 Southern Lit. Messenger II. 285 The whole history of the *Glebe Law of 1802—a law the question of whose constitutionality is still undetermined. 1730 in Maryland Hist. Mag. VIII. 157 Mr. John Humphreys..hath Liberty from this Vestry to remove the house he built on the *Glebe Lot in the City of Annapolis.

Glebula (gle·biŭlă, glī·-). Bot. [L. glēbula, glæbula, dim. of *Gleba.] a. = *Gleba. b. pl. The spores of certain fungi.

1866 [see *Gleba]. 1866 Treas. Bot., Glebulæ, little roundish elevations of the thallus of lichens; also the spores of certain fungals.

Glee, sb. 5. glee-book; **glee club** (U.S. example).

1862 O. W. Norton Army Lett. 124, I would rather see two or three pretty girls and a *glee-book..than the whole of them. 1889 Kansas Times & Star 16 July, The Yale *Glee Club gave a concert that was largely attended at the Casino, on Broadway, last night.

Glial (gləi·ăl), a. [f. Glia + -al.] Of or pertaining to glia.

1908 Practitioner Oct. 562 By a new staining method, which stains the neuro-fibril networks but leaves the glia totally unstained, [they] have demonstrated..that the Golgi pericellular nets are glial and not nervous in origin.

Glide, sb. Add:

1. b. Aeronautics. The act of gliding; a flight accomplished by gliding.

1902 Encycl. Brit. XXV. 103/1 He made over 2000 glides safely, using gravity as a motive power. 1909 A. Berget Conquest of Air ii. iii. 175 This descending glide. 1916 H. Barber Aeroplane Speaks (1918) 43 At three thousand feet altitude the Pilot is satisfied that he is now sufficiently high to secure..a long enough glide to earth to enable him to choose and reach a good landing-place.

c. Cricket. A stroke by which the ball is deflected towards long leg by the turned blade of the bat.

1888 Steel & Lyttelton Cricket (Badm.) ii. 67 Fig. 10 shows W. G. Grace attempting the glide..This is a stroke in which W. G. Grace excels. 1897 K. S. Ranjitsinhji in Encycl. Sport I. 228/1 There is no more effective stroke on the leg side than the 'glide' or 'glance'. 1901 C. B. Fry in P. F. Warner Bk. Cricket xiii. 227 His [sc. Ranjitsinhji's] so-called 'glide' strokes.

Glide, v. Add:

1. c. Also spec. Of aeroplanes, gliding machines, etc.: To fly without motor power. Also trans., to traverse in a glider or gliding machine.

1894 To-day 17 Mar. 171/2 He believes that the first principle of scientific flying is the ability to glide evenly along in space. 1910 C. C. Turner Aerial Navig. xx. 252 The best means of becoming proficient in flying is first to learn to glide. 1916 H. Barber Aeroplane Speaks (1918) 53 Then the Aeroplane with noiseless engine glides over the boundary of the Aerodrome. 1931 Times 23 June 17/4 The claim that he was the first man to 'glide' the Channel.

9. Cricket. intr. To make the glide stroke (see prec. 1 c).

1899 A. Lang in Daily News 22 July 4/2 Men were then less apt to 'glance and glide', like The Brook, and K. S. Ranjitsinhji. 1927 T. E. Casson Century of Roundels 17 Ranjitsinhji, when he glides, Stands at the crease in posture cringy.

Glideless (gləi·dlės), a. Phonetics. [-less.] Unaccompanied by a glide (Glide sb. 4).

1908 Sweet Primer Phon. 63 Combinations of stops and vowel-like consonants..are glideless in English.

Glider. Add:

2. Aeronautics. a. A motorless flying machine.

1897 Aeronautical Ann. in Epitome (1910) 118, I made my first trial with a soaring machine in the summer of '95...It is exceedingly difficult to make a glider with one surface only which will sail properly. 1903 Daily Chron. 29 Oct. 6/7 The longitudinal stability of aerial gliders. 1909 H. G. Wells Tono-Bungay iii. i. 208, I was developing a glider into a flyer. 1931 Daily Tel. 6 Jan. 12/4 [He] had a leg and an arm broken when his glider crashed.

b. One who glides or is an expert in gliding.

1910 C. C. Turner Aerial Navig. xx. 253 It will be well to take the experiences of the great gliders in proper order, beginning with Lilienthal.

Supplement, p. 3873; Corrigenda, p. 4092; Spurious words, p. 4093; Books quoted, p. 4094

Gliding, *vbl. sb.* Add:
2. *Aeronautics.* A type of flight which is not dependent on motor power: the action of flying in this way. Also *attrib.*, as *gliding angle, contest, distance, flight*; **gliding-boat,** a hydroplane; **gliding machine** = *GLIDER 2 a.
1898 *Sci. Amer. Suppl.* 22 Jan. 18390 (Cent. D. Suppl.) It was a great deal more difficult to control any gliding-machine on the ground than when the operator was in the air. 1902 *Encycl. Brit.* XXV. Illustr. facing p. 100 Multiple-wing Gliding Machine. *Ibid.* 103/1 Reducing gliding flight to regular practice. 1909 *Engin. Wonders of World* 8/1 A gradient equal to the gliding angle of the aeroplane. 1910 C. C. TURNER *Aerial Navig.* xx. 252 There is no reason why thousands who cannot hope to possess their own motor-driven flying-machine should not enjoy gliding through the air on the simple apparatus that suffices for this sport. *Ibid.* 258 Montgomery..built a full-sized gliding-machine with movable parts. *Ibid.* 312 *Gliding angle*, the angle to the horizontal at which a flying-machine descends when not propelled by an engine. 1910 *Daily Chron.* 12 Mar. 3/3 To establish a gliding school at Hockley, in Essex. 1916 H. BARBER *Aeroplane Speaks* 43 Can I see a good landing-ground within gliding distance? 1922 *Daily Mail* (Continental ed.) 19 Oct., The third day of the gliding contest at Itford Hill, near Lewes, Sussex. 1922 *Westm. Gaz.* 23 Oct., 'Gliding' is no longer an adequate name for the new form of flight which has been discovered.

Glimmer, *v.* Add: **2. d.** *To go glimmering*: to die away, die out, vanish, 'peter out'. *U.S. slang.*
1910 W. M. RAINE *B. O'Connor* 28 My reputation has gone glimmering. 1912 MATHEWSON *Pitching in a Pinch* ix. 194 With the decision, the Pirates' last chance went glimmering.

Glimmery, *a.*[1] Add: **c.** Glimmering. Also *advb.*
1907 *Daily Chron.* 4 Mar. 6/4 The marble bust..glimmery white. 1927 *Blackw. Mag.* Mar. 308/2 A great white wall of snow and rock, all glimmery in the rising sun, rose above us.

Glio- (glai,o), combining form of GLIOMA, designating tumours containing gliomatous tissue and some other element, as *gliomyoma, gliomyxoma, glioneuroma.* (Recent medical dicts.)

Gliomatosis (glaiōumătōu·sis). *Path.* [f. mod.L. *gliomat-*, GLIOMA + -OSIS.] An excessive development of the neuroglia cells of the central nervous system.
1890 BILLINGS *Med. Dict.* 1899 *Allbutt's Syst. Med.* VII. 48 From syringomyelia and central gliomatosis it may be impossible to distinguish the later results of hæmatomyelia. 1910 OSLER & MCCRAE *Syst. Med.* VII. 422 Certain forms of diffuse gliomatosis, often mistaken..for hypertrophies of the brain.

Gliosis (glai,ōu·sis). *Path.* [mod.L., f. Gr. γλία GLIA + -OSIS.] A diseased condition of the neuroglia.
1892 OSLER *Princ. Med.* 849 The condition is now regarded as a gliosis, a development of embryonal neurogliar tissue in which hæmorrhage or degeneration takes place with the formation of cavities. 1899 *Allbutt's Syst. Med.* VII. 172 He [*sc.* Weigert] wholly discards the hypothesis of syringomyelia to which the name spinal gliosis has been applied.

Glissando (glisæ·ndo). [Italianized form of F. *glissant*, gerund and pres. pple. of *glisser* to slide.]
1. *Pianoforte.* Applied to the playing of a rapid succession of notes by sliding the tip or back of the finger over the keys instead of striking each note separately.
1873 H. C. BANISTER *Music* Gloss. 240.
2. *Violin.* 'A rapid slur in violin playing' (Stainer & Barrett 1876).
1926 *Bulletin* 27 Feb. 5 We had another style of glissando from Gerard Hekking, who in the Boulnois 'Hymn to Bacchus', in order to finish a tone lower than the 'cello is tuned to, unscrewed the peg as he played the last notes and slid down on the open string.

Glitterer (gli·tərəɹ). [f. GLITTER *v.* + -ER [1].] One who or that which glitters.
1823 BYRON *Don Juan* XIV. lvii, Fondly the wheeling fire-flies flew around her, Those little glitterers of the London night.

Gloaming. 2. Add: **gloaming sight,** a front sight specially adapted for evening shooting.
1895 *Army & Navy Co-op. Soc. Price List* 15 Sept. 925/1 New gloaming sight for guns and rifles.

Gloat, *sb.*[1] Transfer † *Obs. rare* to sense in Dict., and add:
2. An act of gloating; a look, feeling, or expression of triumphant satisfaction.
1899 KIPLING *Stalky* 13 They spun wildly on their heels, jodelling after the accepted manner of a 'gloat'. 1921 GALSWORTHY *To Let* II. iii, To watch the gloat in his eye. 1927 *Bulletin* 7 Oct. 17/2 Preparing to enjoy a satisfying gloat over some of his critics. 1930 IAN HAY & S. KING-HALL *Middle Watch* xx, She now stood regarding the Admiral's wife with a certain deliberate..insolence of expression. One might almost call it a gloat.

Global, *a.* Add:
2. [After F. *global.*] Pertaining to or embracing the totality of a group of items, categories, or the like.
1892 *Harper's Mag.* Sept. 493/2 Global, with the faculties and tastes of a historian, M. de Vogüé directs his thoughts by preference to man, his life and his destinies. 1927 *Contemp. Rev.* Aug. 241 The essence of the American proposal therefore was its 'global' criterion. 1928 *Times* 1 Oct. 14/1 The proposal for a readjustment of tonnage proportions within the global limits originally proposed by the United States. *Ibid.*, The original French proposal was for global tonnage. 1928 *Daily Tel.* 30 Oct. 10 Countries which do not discriminate between 'schedular' and 'global' taxes. 1928 *Spectator* 17 Nov. 720/2 If a global tonnage for cruisers were agreed upon. 1928 *John o' London's Weekly* 24 Nov. 252/1 Adding figures of commerce and foreign investments ..so as to show to-day's global contacts.

Globe, *sb.* **10. b.** Add: **globe-trot** *v.* [back-formation from *globe-trotter, -trotting*], to go globe-trotting. Also *trans.*
1883 *Manchester Guardian* 6 June 6/1 He drives from London to York..and is amusing; he globetrots and is not amusing. 1903 LD. R. GOWER *Rec. & Remin.* 289 Nothing is easier than to 'globe-trot' round the world. 1928 *Observer* 8 Apr. 5/7 You are never instructed, never globe-trotted.

Globigerinid (glōubidʒerai·nid). *Zool.* [f. GLOBIGERINA + -ID [3].] A rhizopod of the group *Globigerinæ.*
1924 *Glasgow Herald* 28 June 4 The unicellular pelagic Globigerinids and Radiolarians.

Globosite (glōubōu·sait). *Min.* [ad. G. *globosit* (Breithaupt, 1865), f. L. *globōsus* GLOBOSE + -ITE [1].] A fluophosphate of iron, found in globular concretions.
1892 DANA *Syst. Min.* (ed. 6) 849 Globosite..occurring at the Arme Hilfe mine near Hirschberg.

Globularetin (glǫbiūlārī·tin, re·tin). *Chem.* [f. mod.L. *globularia*, after *quercetin.*] A derivative of the decomposition of globularin, used as a diuretic, etc.
1864 WATTS *Dict. Chem.* II. 846 Resolved by [boiling] dilute sulphuric acid into globularetin. 1882 *Jrnl. Chem. Soc.* XLII. 1225 When boiled with dilute acids, globularin yields only one decomposition product, globularetin.

Globularin (glǫ·biūlārin). *Chem.* [ad. G. *globularin*, f. mod.L. *globularia* + -IN [1].] A glucoside occurring in the leaves of *Globularia Alypum.*
1864 WATTS *Dict. Chem.* II. 868. 1882 [see *GLOBULARETIN].

Globulicide (glǫ·biūlisəid), *a.* and *sb.* [f. GLOBULE + -(I)CIDE.] **A.** *adj.* = *GLOBULICIDAL. **B.** *sb.* An agent that destroys blood corpuscles. Hence **Glo·bulici·dal** *a.*, destroying the corpuscles of the blood, especially the red corpuscles.
1901 DORLAND *Med. Dict.* (ed. 2), Globulicide. 1902 *Jrnl. Exper. Med.* VI. 145 These extensive deposits of pigment.. seem..to be referable to a greatly increased globulicidal action of the plasma.

Glochidium (glǫki·diǒm). Pl. **-idia** (i·diā). [mod.L.: see GLOCHIDIATE.]
1. The larva of the pond-mussel. Also *attrib.*
1875 HUXLEY & MARTIN *Elem. Biol.* 110 There is a single adductor muscle and a rudimentary foot, from which one or two long structureless filaments, representing the *byssus* of the sea-mussel, proceed. These byssal filaments become entangled with one another and tend to keep the 'Glochidia' in their places. 1888 ROLLESTON & JACKSON *Anim. Life* 137 This *Glochidium* is eventually set free from the parent. 1930 G. R. DE BEER *Embryol. & Evol.* 44 The Glochidium larva of Unio.
2. *Bot.* (See quot.) (Also **glo·chid.**)
1900 B. D. JACKSON *Gloss. Bot. Terms*, *Glochid, glochidium*.., (1) a barbed hair or bristle; (2) a similar structure on the massulae of certain Cryptogams which act as organs of attachment to a macrospore.

Glockenspiel (glǫ·kenʃpīl, -spīl). [G., lit. bell-play.]
1. A musical instrument consisting of a series of small bells or metal bars which are struck with a hammer; a kind of carillon.
1876 STAINER & BARRETT *Dict. Mus. Terms.* 1892 *Work* 2 July 253/3 The glockenspiel proper consists of a set of eight or more clock bells, mounted on a central spindle, which is inserted in a wooden handle. 1905 *Technol. & Sci. Dict.* (ed. Goodchild & Tweney) 444/1 The Glockenspiel or Carillon is an instrument consisting of plates of steel, played by striking with beaters or by hammers set in motion by an action similar to the pianoforte. 1905 *Daily Chron.* 29 June 3/3 A glockenspiel accompaniment.
2. An organ stop.
1898 STAINER & BARRETT *Dict. Mus. Terms* 202/2.

Glomus (glōu·mǒs). [L., = ball or clue of thread.]
1. *Bot.* = GLOMERULE 1 a.
1832 LINDLEY *Introd. Bot.* 111 Suppose the flowers of a simple umbel to be deprived of their pedicels, and to be seated on a receptacle or enlarged axis, and we have a *capitulum* or head, named *glomus* by some, *glomerulus* by others.
2. *Zool.* In the embryo of lower vertebrates, a coil of blood-vessels projecting into the cœlome in the region of the pronephros.
1909 *Cent. Dict.* Suppl. 529/3 Diagrammatic figure of a tadpole, dissected from the ventral surface to show the glomus, the heart and branchial vessels. 1913 *Cunningham's Text-bk. Anat.* (ed. 4) 1355 The glomus coccygeum is a small body, 2–2·5 mm. in diameter, placed immediately anterior to the tip of the coccyx, upon a branch of the middle sacral artery. *Ibid.*, The glomus develops from the capillary network of the region of the tip of the embryonic tail.
3. *Anat.* 'A fusiform swelling of the carotid plexus found at the junction of the body of the lateral ventricle with the descending horn' (Dorland 1903).

Gloria. Add:
3. A mixture of silk and wool used for dresses, the covering of umbrellas, etc. (Now disused?)
1908 *Daily Chron.* 3 Aug. 4/5 Men abroad carry a grey or tan gloria sunshade.

Glorious, *a.* **3. a.** Add: *spec.* as an epithet of the 'Fourth' (of July). *U.S.*
1847 LONGFELLOW in *Life* (1891) I. 121 We did not celebrate the 'Glorious Fourth' here. 1838 *Knickerbocker Mag.* XI. 315 It was on the anniversary of the 'glorious Fourth'. 1896 *Congress. Rec.* 5422/1 Waving the stars and stripes on the Glorious Fourth.

Glory, *sb.* Add:
9. c. Also = *fog-bow* (FOG *sb.*[2] 6 d).
1842 HOWITT *Rur. & Dom. Life Germany* 452 If the fog is dry, you see not only yourself, but your neighbour; if very damp, only yourself, surrounded by a rainbow-coloured glory. 1884 TAIT *Light* § 167 It seems possible that glories may be due to a cause somewhat analogous to that which produces the spurious rainbows. 1910 C. C. TURNER *Aerial Navig.* 141 Halos round the sun and moon, rainbows, 'glories', or 'aureoles'—the coloured rings seen round the shadow cast by the balloon on the clouds.

Glory-hole. Add:
1. c. The hall of worship used by the Salvation Army.
'So called, originally, from a cellar or underground place of meeting in Brighton' (Barrère & Leland).
18.. *Broadside, The Brighton Glory-Hole* (Barrère & L.) These hoary-headed buffers, And devil-dodging duffers, At the Glory-Hole in Teddy Street they rave. 1887 *Daily News* 24 Oct. (Ware *Passing Engl.*) The 'Glory Hole' Disturbances at Maidstone.
3. a. *Naut.* = LAZARETTO 3.
1897 E. G. CONSTANTINE *Marine Engin.* ix. 108 In the 'glory-hole', which had to be descended to tighten up the inner trunk gland next the crank pit.
b. One or more rooms between decks aft used as sleeping quarters for stewards. Also *fig.*
1839 W. H. LEIGH *Reconnoitering Voy.* ii. 16 The other one was of the dog-fish species, and had nothing in his 'glory hole' worth notice. 1898 *Pearson's Mag.* V. 213/2 They went through every part of her, from the sodden shaft-tunnel, to the glory-hole where the stewards live.
4. A large cavernous opening into a mine; an open quarry.
1911 WEBSTER.
5. *Army slang.* A dug-out.
1925 E. FRASER & GIBBONS *Soldier & Sailor Words, Glory hole*, a colloquial expression for any small billet or dug-out.

Gloss, *v.*[2] Add: **2.** *intr.* To become shiny.

Glosso-. Add: **Glo:sso-labio-laryngeal** *a.*, relating to the tongue, lips, and larynx. **Glosso-pa·latine** *a.*, = PALATO-GLOSSAL. **Glo:sso-pharyngeal** *sb.*, the glosso-pharyngeal nerve or muscle. **Glossophy·tia,** black tongue (Billings 1890).
1908 *Practitioner* June 758 All the usual phenomena of a *glosso-labio-laryngeal paralysis. 1888 *Encycl. Brit.* XXIII. 79/2 The *glosso-palatine arch. 1875 HUXLEY & MARTIN *Elem. Biol.* 182 The trunk of the *glossopharyngeal.

Glossophagine (glǫsǫ·fădʒəin), *a.* [f. mod.L. *Glossophaga* (f. Gr. γλῶσσα tongue + φαγεῖν to eat) + -INE [1].] Belonging to or characteristic of the genus *Glossophaga* of large South American bats.
1891 FLOWER & LYDEKKER *Mammals* 672 The Vampirine and Glossophagine divisions.

Glossopteris (glǫsǫ·ptěris). [f. Gr. γλωσσο-, γλῶσσα tongue + πτερίς fern.] An important genus of fossil ferns. Also *attrib.*
1897 A. C. SEWARD in *Science Progress* VI. 178 The Glossopteris Flora; an extinct flora of a Southern Hemisphere Continent. 1902 *Encycl. Brit.* XXXI. 422/1 Glossopteris frond. *Ibid.*, Associated with *Glossopteris* occurs another fern, *Gangamopteris*. 1912 J. W. GREGORY *Making of Earth* III. x. 184 Glossopteris was a fern or fern-like plant with large blunt leaves, each of which has a prominent midrib.

Glottal, *a.* Add: *Glottal stop*, a sound produced by the sudden opening or shutting of the glottis with an emission of breath or voice.
1888 SWEET *Hist. English Sounds* 1 The Glottal stop is produced by a sudden shutting or opening of the glottis, as in a cough. 1911 W. H. VAN DER SMISSEN *Harrap's Mod. German Gramm.* Introd. p. xiii, The utterance of every German initial vowel, unless wholly unstressed, begins with the 'glottal stop'. 1920 MISS A. WERNER in *Man* XX. 14 We find it replaced by *g, dg, j, z* or the glottal stop, if not dropped altogether.

Gloucester. Add: (Also **Glo'ster, Gloster.**)
b. Also the name of several counties or towns in the United States, used *attrib.*
1764 WASHINGTON *Diaries* I. 200 Grafted also in the 7 Row 43 Gloucester white apple. 1765 *Ibid.* 211 The 7th Row has 25 Graffs of the Gloster white Apple. 1786 *Ibid.* III. 30 Planted..in two and an half rows, 95 of the Gloucester hiccory nut. 1788 *Ibid.* 311 In the other half..were a bushel of the Gloucester Beans. 1810 MICHAUX *Arbres* I. 20 Thick shell bark hickery,..[or] Glocester nut hickery. 1832 D. J. BROWNE *Sylva Amer.* 176 It [*sc.* Thick Shellbark Hickory] is also found in the county of Gloucester in Virginia, under the name of Gloucester Walnut.

Glove, *sb.* **2.** Add: *To take the gloves off* (fig.): to set to in earnest. *To handle with gloves off*: cf. 1 f in Dict. (earlier U.S. example).
1828 *Richmond Enquirer* 20 May 3/4 (Th.) The Baltimore Republican handles Mr. C[lay] with gloves off. 1928 *Daily Express* 21 Mar. 1/1 It is time, Mr. Mayor, that we took the gloves off and showed the County of London Electric Supply Company that we will fight. 1931 *Times Lit. Suppl.* 10 Sept. 669/4 Like Lewis Carroll, who was too polite to 'take the gloves off' in his assault on 'Hiawatha'.

Glover (glɒ·vəɹ). The name of John *Glover* (*c* 1866) used *attrib.* in **Glover tower,** = DENITRIFICATOR.
1898 *Jrnl. Chem. Soc.* XXXIV. 757 Vorster declares the Glover tower to be unsuitable for the denitration of nitrose. 1887 *Encycl. Brit.* XXII. 636/2 The Glover tower..serves to concentrate part of the chamber acid and to supply part of the necessary steam without expense for fuel. 1921 *Dict. Occup. Terms* (1927) § 143 *Glover tower man*, sulphuric acid tower man.

Glow, *sb.* Add: **2. b.** In astronomical and meteorological use, applied to certain appearances of light in the sky. (Earlier in *COUNTER-GLOW.)
1901 *Westm. Gaz.* 20 Feb. 2/1 Brorsen discovered that on a fine dark night a faint glow is visible in that part of the sky opposite the sun. 1902 *Encycl. Brit.* XXV. 735/2 It follows that an observer..should see this portion of the light as a faint glow in the northern horizon.

Glow, *v.*[1] Add:
2. c. To pass *to* or *into* a glowing colour.
1888 MRS. H. WARD *Robt. Elsmere* xi, The stretches of purple heather, glowing into scarlet under the touch of the sun. 1906 E. PHILLPOTTS *Portreeve* II. i, The breath of ocean made visible..glowed into red gold as the sun descended.
5. Also with predic. adj.
1855 KINGSLEY *Westw. Ho!* i, Turning first deadly pale, and then glowing red. 1907 *Smart Set* Jan. 126/2 With cheeks glowing red.

Glucase (gliū·kēs). *Chem.* [f. Gr. γλυκύς sweet + *-ASE.] An enzyme present in blood serum, yeast, etc., having the property of converting maltose into glucose.
1894 *Jrnl. Chem. Soc.* LXVI. I. 258 Glucase which occurs in maize slowly hydrolyses dextrin. 1902 *Encycl. Brit.* XXXI. 763/1 Among those which act on carbohydrates the most important are..glucase or maltase, which produces grape sugar from maltose. 1910 *Practitioner* June 823 The hydrolysis is brought about by means of enzymes, such as ptyalin, amylopsin or amylase, lactase and glucase.

Gluco- (gliū·ko), combining form of GLUCOSE used in the designation of substances derived from or connected with glucose or another carbohydrate.
1879 *Jrnl. Chem. Soc.* XXXVI. 545 For these latter bodies [*sc.* leucelnes], the name glucoproteins has been adopted, on account of their sweet taste. 1884 *Ibid.* XLVI. 1343 When coniferin is oxidised with aqueous chromic acid, it is converted into glucovanillin. 1886 *Ibid.* L. 250 Glucoferulic aldehyde..crystallises in needles containing 2 mols. H_2O. 1889 MORLEY & MUIR *Watts' Dict. Chem.* II. 612/2 Glucodrupose $C_{24}H_{36}O_{16}$, the chief constituent of concretions in pears. *Ibid.* 613/1 Glucolignose..occurs in pine wood. 1890 *Jrnl. Chem. Soc.* LVIII. I. 599 On treatment with hydrogen cyanide, glucoheptose yields glucoctonic acid. 1891 *Ibid.* LX. I. 412 A new glucobiose, which from its properties is doubtless constituted like maltose. 1899 *Ibid.* LXXVI. I. 180 A New Glucoproteid from Blood-serum.

Gluconic (gliukǫ·nik), *a.* [irreg. f. GLUCOSE, after *muconic.*] Derived from glucose. *Gluconic acid*, dextronic acid.
1871 *Jrnl. Chem. Soc.* XXIV. 547 Hlasiwetz..considers gluconic acid to be bibasic. 1902 *Encycl. Brit.* XXVI. 723/2 The optical isomeride of this gulose is obtained by making use of the gluconic acid which is the optical isomeride of that prepared from ordinary glucose.

Glucos-, comb. form of GLUCOSE before vowels, in the designations of derivatives of glucose.
1903 *Jrnl. Chem. Soc.* LXXXIV. I. 74 Brucine *glucosamate. *Ibid.*, When *d*-*glucosamic acid is reduced with phosphorus and iodine, a compound, $C_6H_{13}O_3N$, is formed. 1882 *Coll. Index Trans. Chem. Soc.* 11, *Glucosamine (glycosamine) hydrochloride. 1886 *Jrnl. Chem. Soc.* L. 329 Glucosamine hydrobromide, $C_6H_{13}NO_5$, HBr. 1903 DORLAND *Med. Dict.* (ed. 3), *Glucosamin*,..an amido-derivative of glucose. 1862 MILLER *Elem. Chem., Org.* (ed. 2) iv. § 3. 289 The body which corresponds to the alcohol having the composition $C_{12}H_{10}O_{10}$..Berthelot suggests for it the name of *glucosane*, to indicate its analogy with mannitane. 1887 *Encycl. Brit.* XXII. 624/1 Lævulosan, $C_6H_{10}O_5$, analogous to glucosan.

Glucosazone (gliukōu·sāzōun). *Chem.* [f. *GLUCO- + *OSAZONE.] A compound of phenyl hydrazine and acetic acid.
1895 *Jrnl. Chem. Soc.* LXVIII. II. 407 The Glucosazone from Sumach and from Vallonia. 1902 *Encycl. Brit.* XXVI. 723/1 An osazone was thus obtained which was the stereoisomeride of glucosazone prepared from ordinary fructose.

Glucoso- (gliukōu·so), used as a combining form of GLUCOSE in the designations of acid compounds of glucose with some acids, and their salts.
1864 WATTS *Dict. Chem.* II. 872 *Glucosocitric acid, $C^{42}H^{56}O^{46}$. 1871 *Jrnl. Chem. Soc.* XXIV. 925 Quantitative determinations of the ash (sodium pyrophosphate)..have shown that the substance in question has the composition of disodic *glucoso-phosphate. *Ibid.*, Formed from two molecules of *glucoso-phosphoric acid. 1864 WATTS *Dict. Chem.* II. 859 Glucose dissolves without coloration when triturated with cold oil of vitriol, forming *glucoso-sulphuric acid. *Ibid.* 872 Aqueous *glucosotartaric acid is obtained by decomposing the calcium-salt with excess of oxalic acid. *Ibid.*, *Glucosotartrate of calcium.

Glucosone (gliū·kosōun). *Chem.* [f. *GLUCO- + *OSONE.] The osone of glucose.
1902 *Jrnl. Chem. Soc.* LXXXI. 670 We have fermented solutions of glucosone from dextrose and lævulose with yeast in order to remove these carbohydrates.

Glue, *v.* **3. b.** Delete †*Obs.* and add:
1885 *Spons' Mechanics' Own Bk.* 131 The wood glues well.

Glued, *ppl. a.* Add:
2. *fig.* in **glued-on,** applied to devices, effects, etc. in literature which are carelessly superimposed and not woven into the style or form; **glued-up,** applied to a medley of scenes or incidents with little apparent connexion or unity.
1906 *Westm. Gaz.* 15 Feb. 2/3 What the Americans call a 'glued-up' or nailed-up drama. *Ibid.* 16 Sept. 3/2 To avoid auxiliary complications and eschew 'glued-on' comic relief.

Glue-pot. Add: **b.** *transf.* Applied to wet or muddy ground in which one may 'stick'.
1892 *Daily News* (Morris *Austral Engl.*) The Bishop of Manchester..assures us that no one can possibly understand the difficulties and the troubles of a Colonial..clergyman until he has..struggled through what they used to call 'glue-pots'. 1907 C. B. FRY in *Daily Chron.* 18 July 7/2 The veriest 'glue-pot' of a wicket.

Glut, *sb.*[3] Add: **3. b.** A swarm of caterpillars attacking tobacco-plants. *U.S.*
1849 *Rep. U.S. Comm. Patents, Agric.* (1850) 320 There are every year two 'gluts'..; the first attacking the plants about the time that they are one-third or half grown, the other comes on when the tobacco is ready for cutting.

Glut, *sb.*[6] Add: **4.** (See quot.)
1888 *Lockwood's Dict. Mech. Engin.*, *Glut*, a gun-metal block having a face hollowed out to fit against the bossed-up end of the valve-rod in a knuckle joint, and by which the wear is constantly being taken up, the glut being tightened by a wedge and screw, or by a cottar.

Glut-. Add: **Glutanol,** an astringent made from fibrin and tannic acid. **Glutathi·one** (see quot. 1921). **Gluti·mic** *a.*, derived from gluten and imine; so **Glu·timide.** **Glu·tinol** (see quot. 1908).
1908 *Jrnl. Chem. Soc.* XCIV. I. 40 *Glutinol, $C_{14}H_{28}O$, separates from alcohol in leaflets...*Glutanol..differs from glutinol in being soluble in ether with difficulty. 1921 *Ibid.* CXX. I. 636 A dipeptide of cysteine and glutamic acid, which may be provisionally named *glutathione. 1925 *Glasgow Herald* 5 Dec. 4 The oxygen-transporting and oxygen-liberating power of glutathione. 1879 *Jrnl. Chem. Soc.* XXXVI. 546 Amido-acids of the type $C_nH_{2n-3} = NO_3$: *glutimic acid. 1876 *Ibid.* I. 906 *Glutimide..obtained by heating ammonium glutamate to 185°–190° for six hours in a retort.

Glutæo-, gluteo- (gliuti·o), combining form of GLUTÆUS = pertaining to the glutæal region (and some other part of the body), as *glutæo-femoral* adj.
1890 BILLINGS *Med. Dict.*, *Gluteo-femoral crease*, gluteal fold. 1901 DORLAND *Med. Dict.* (ed. 2), *Gluteofemoral*, pertaining to the buttock and thigh.

Glutenin (gliū·tenin). *Chem.* [f. GLUTEN + -IN [1].] A principle derived from the vegetable glutens.
1898 *Jrnl. Chem. Soc.* LXXIV. II. 628 The value of wheaten flour is closely connected with the composition of the gluten, which should consist of glutenin and gliadin in the proportion of 1 to 3.

Glutoform (gliū·tǫfǭɹm). *Chem.* [f. GLUT(EN + *FORM(ALDEHYDE.] Formaldehyde gelatin.
1901 DORLAND *Med. Dict.* (ed. 2).

Glutted, *ppl. a.*[3] [f. GLUT *sb.*[6] + -ED [2].] Furnished with a glut or wedge (cf. *GLUTTER [2]).
1921 *Dict. Occup. Terms* (1927) § 279 *Glutter's turner-out*, ..pulls glutted wheel..with tongs from furnace, and bowls it along, white hot, to press.

Glutter[2] (glɒ·təɹ). [f. GLUT *sb.*[6] + -ER [1].] One who furnishes metal wheels with gluts.
1881 *Instr. Census Clerks* (1885) 56 Wheel Glutter. 1921 *Dict. Occup. Terms* (1927) § 190 *Glutter*,..a smith who fills up small gaps between V-sections of metal wheels..by hammering red hot steel bar into interstices between sections.

Glycæmia, var. *glycohæmia* (s.v. GLYCO-).

Glycero-. Add: *Glycero-degras* (see quot.), *-gel, -ketose, -phosphine, -sol.*
1897 C. T. DAVIS *Manuf. Leather* 239 To the soft mixture of fats is then added about one-quarter of its weight of glycerine, and intimately incorporated with it, so that the mass is finally of a cream-like condition. This *glycero-degras enables the currier to obtain the same advantages as from lubricating with fat or glycerine alone. 1864 *Jrnl. Chem. Soc.* XVII. 323 A *glycerogel prepared from a hydrate containing 9·35 per cent. of silicic acid. 1902 *Encycl. Brit.* XXVI. 742/2 The isomeric *glyceroketose. 1907 *Westm. Gaz.* 19 Sept. 4/1 The oyster..contains about equal supply of nutritive matter with beef and mutton. Another important constituent is the compound technically named *glycerophosphine. 1864 *Jrnl. Chem. Soc.* XVII. 322 A portion of the silicic acid is dissolved, and a *glycerosol is produced at the same time as the glycerin jelly.

Glycerose (gli·sěrous). [f. GLYCER(INE + -OSE [2].] A syrup, $C_3H_6O_3$, formed by the oxidation of glycerine.
1888 *Jrnl. Chem. Soc.* LIV. 1264 For the preparation of glycerose, the lead glyceroxide is spread in thin layers [etc.]. 1903 DORLAND *Med. Dict.* (ed. 3) s.v., There are two glyceroses, glycerin aldehyd and dioxyacetone.

Glyco-. Add: **Glycofo·rmal,** a solution of glycerine and formaldehyde used as a disinfectant. **Glycopro·teid, -pro·tein** (see quots.).
1898 *Jrnl. Chem. Soc.* LXXIV. II. 349 A solution of formaldehyde in glycerol, which they [*sc.* R. Walther and A. Schlossman] call '*glycoformal'. 1902 *Encycl. Brit.* XXXI. 724/1 *Glycoproteids—a number of proteids, on treatment with acid, yield various sugar-like bodies. 1913 DORLAND *Med. Dict.* (ed. 7), *Glycoprotein*, any one of a class of compound proteins consisting of a compound of protein with a carbohydrate group.

Glycoline (glai·kǒlīn, -əin). *Chem.* [f. GLYCOL + -INE [5].] A crystallizable compound contained in commercial fusel-oil.
1881 *Jrnl. Chem. Soc.* XL. 708 Complete analyses of the alkaloid..which the author [*sc.* A. Etard] proposes provisionally to name glycoline, prove that its formula is $C_6H_{10}N_2$. 1889 MORLEY & MUIR *Watts' Dict. Chem.* II. 618/2 When glycerin is distilled with ammonium chloride a chlorinated compound,.is formed,..and a base 'glycoline'.

Glycoluric (glaikoliū·rik), *a.* *Chem.* [f. GLYCOL + URIC *a.*] *Glycoluric acid*, hydantoic acid.
1884 ROSCOE & SCHORLEMMER *Treat. Chem.* III. 96 Glycoluric Acid..$(NH_2)CO.NH$.

Glycolylurea (glai:koliliuɹī·ā). *Chem.* [f. GLYCOL + -YL + UREA.] A colourless compound formed by the action of alcoholic ammonia on bromacetyl urea; = HYDANTOIN.
1881 tr. *Strecker & Wislicenus' Org. Chem.* 420 Glycolyl urea..$C_3H_4N_2O_2$. 1884 ROSCOE & SCHORLEMMER *Treat. Chem.* III. 96 Glycolyl-urea..was first obtained by Baeyer as a product of decomposition of uric acid and allantoin.

Glycolysis (glaikǫ·lisis). *Med.* [f. GLYCO- + Gr. λύσις dissolution.] The digestion of sugar or its utilization in the living organism.
1895 *Jrnl. Chem. Soc.* LXVIII. II. 361 Glycolysis..is not a vital process, but the blood corpuscles contain substances which possess the power in question. 1904 *Nature* 21 Jan. 287 Their [*sc.* X-rays'] first action is to increase glycolysis.

Glycosid, glycoside, var. GLUCOSIDE.

Glycosine (glai·kǒsīn, -əin). *Chem.* [f. GLUCOSE (cf. GLYCO-) + -INE [5].] A colourless compound formed by the action of glyoxal on ammonia.
1858 *Chem. Gaz.* XVI. 353 Glyoxal..is mixed with about three times its bulk of strong ammonia...The liquid now contains two organic bases—one in the shape of a crystalline precipitate, which I [*sc.* H. Debus] propose to call glycosine, and the other in solution, to which in this paper the name of glyoxaline will be applied. 1877 *Jrnl. Chem. Soc.* I. 299 By acting with ammonia on glyoxal, Debus obtained two bases, glycosine, $C_6H_6N_4$, and glyoxaline, $C_3H_4N_2$.

Glycuronic (glaikiurǫ·nik), *a.* *Chem.* [f. GLYCO- + UR(IC + -ONE + -IC.] *Glycuronic acid*, a monobasic acid, $C_6H_{10}O_7$, derived from glucose. Hence **Gly:curonu·ria,** the presence of glycuronic acid in the urine (Dorland 1913).
1882 *Jrnl. Chem. Soc.* XLII. 952 Urochloralic acid..is decomposed, on boiling with dilute acids, into trichlorethyl alcohol and glycuronic acid. 1902 *Encycl. Brit.* XXXI. 723/2 Glycuronic acid..is closely related to dextrose, and on oxidation yields the same acid, saccharic acid.

Glycyphyllin (glai-, glisifi·lin). *Chem.* [f. mod. L. *glycyphylla* (see below), f. Gr. γλυκύς sweet + φύλλον leaf + -IN [1].] A glucoside extracted from the leaves of *Smilax glycyphylla.*
1881 *Jrnl. Chem. Soc.* XXXIX. 240 Were its identity and distinctiveness established, the term glycyphyllin might perhaps be applied to it.

Glycyrrhetin (glisirī·tin, -re·tin). *Chem.* [f. Gr. γλυκύρριζα LIQUORICE + *-etin.*] A bitter compound, $C_{32}H_{47}O_4N$, formed by the action of acids on glycyrrhizin.
1877 *Jrnl. Chem. Soc.* I. 96 Glycyrretin...This compound ..yields when fused with potash only paroxybenzoic acid.

Glycyrrhizic (glisirai·zik), *a.* *Chem.* [f. Gr. γλυκύρριζα LIQUORICE + -IC.] *Glycyrrhizic acid*, an acid occurring in liquorice root.
1879 *Jrnl. Chem. Soc.* XXXVI. 1040 Glycyrrhizic acid prepared by the action of sulphuretted hydrogen on the lead salt, resembles dried albumin in appearance.

Glyoxaline (glaiǫ·ksālīn, -əin). *Chem.* [f. GLYOXAL + -INE [5].] An organic base formed together with glycosine by the action of strong aqueous ammonia on glyoxal.
1858 [see *GLYCOSINE]. 1876 *Jrnl. Chem. Soc.* I. 913 In preparing glyoxaline by Debus's method, it is advisable to replace the alcohol by a 50 per cent. solution of aldehyde.

Gmina (mī·nă). [Polish.] A local division of the Polish administrative organization.
1885 *Encycl. Brit.* XIX. 311/1 The 'primary cell' of the administrative organization of Poland is the *gmina*. *Ibid.* 311/2 Justice is represented by the *gmina* tribunals. 1905 *Daily Chron.* 19 Sept. 5/4 Voters are divided into three classes. 1.—Landed proprietors. 2.—Members of gmina or cantons who own three to twenty acres. 3.—Urban electors.

Gnat[1]. **3.** Add: *gnat-like* adj. and adv.
1905 *Westm. Gaz.* 1 Feb. 2/3 Drifts gnat-like to the flame. 1915 E. R. LANKESTER *Divers. Naturalist* 216 In early September, golf links..swarm with a large gnat-like fly of reddish-brown body. 1920 *Glasgow Herald* 2 June 10 Those gnat-like journalistic attacks.

Gnathion (nē·þiǫn). *Anat.* [f. Gr. γνάθος jaw.] The most anterior point of the premaxilla; the mental point.
1888 O. THOMAS *Catal. Marsupialia Brit. Mus.* Introd. p. viii, Basal length.—From the 'basion', or lower front edge of the *foramen magnum*, to the 'gnathion'.

Gnathobase (nǣ·þobēs). [f. Gr. γνάθος jaw + BASE *sb.*[1]] A jaw process on the parapodia of arthropods. Hence **Gna:thoba·sic** *a.*
1881 E. R. LANKESTER in *Q. Jrnl. Micr. Sci.* Apr. 348 Of the six endites the proximal is somewhat isolated and pushed towards the middle line...It is a jaw process, and may be spoken of as the 'gnathobase'. 1902 — in *Encycl. Brit.* XXV. 695/1 The five pairs of appendages of the post-oral somites of the head or prosoma thus constituted all primitively carry gnathobasic projections on their coxal joints, which act as hemignaths; in the more specialized forms the mandibular gnathobases cease to develop. 1904 W. T. CALMAN in *Ann. & Mag. Nat. Hist.* Feb. 155 The double series of epipodial lamellæ, the segmentation of the thoracic limbs, the double gnathobasic lobes of the first pair.

Gnatty (næ·ti), *a.* [f. GNAT [1] + -Y [1].] Resembling a gnat; infested with gnats.
1845 J. J. HOOPER *Adv. Simon Suggs* ii. 28 You..gnatty, flop-eared varmint! 1909 *Amat. Photographer* 14 Sept. 252/2 They can venture into the 'gnattiest' woods without suffering any assault.

Gnaur, variant of KNAR.
1869 MASTERS *Veget. Teratol.* 158 The huge gnaurs and burrs met with occasionally on some trees often produce great quantities..of roots. 1900 B. D. JACKSON *Gloss. Bot. Terms*, *Gnaurs*, burrs or knotty excrescences on tree-trunks or roots, probably from clusters of adventitious buds. 1903 F. W. BURBIDGE *Let. to W. T. Thiselton-Dyer* 20 June (MS.), I beg to hand you a 'gnaur' or swollen, arrested branch of a Tulip tree.

Gnoscopine (nǫ·skǒpīn, -əin). *Chem.* [irreg. f. Gr. γιγνώσκειν to know + ὄπιον OPIUM + -INE [5].] An alkaloid derived from opium.
1878 *Jrnl. Chem. Soc.* CXXIV. 987 Gnoscopine, $C_{34}H_{36}N_2O_{11}$, is soluble in 1,500 parts of cold alcohol.

Gnurly, variant of KNURLY, NURLY *a.*
1841 *Knickerbocker Mag.* XVII. 48 A few handsful of little green, gnurly, ligneous fragments, which the Key Westers facetiously term 'fire-wood'.

Go, *sb.* **4.** Add: An attack or bout of some sickness or ailment; a spell of doing something.
1825 J. NEAL *Bro. Jonathan* I. 8 He would rivet his large eyes, for half an hour at a 'go', upon some part of the wall. 1920 *Blackw. Mag.* May 614/2 A bad go of snow-blindness had driven me in to Leh. 1928 GALSWORTHY *Swan Song* v. 45 No second go of measles, Jon.

Go, *v.* Add:
18. b. *To go dry*: to adopt prohibition of intoxicants: see DRY *a.* 11 a. *To go native*: to relapse into savagery or heathenism (cf. *FANTEE b). *To go red*: see *RED *a.* Also with sb., *to go bush*: to take to the 'bush'.
1927 W. E. COLLINSON *Contemp. Engl.* 85 The spread of Bolshevistic propaganda has led to the fear, lest Labour should go red. 1927 M. TERRY *Through a Land of Promise* 41 The English settlers..tried to tame them for domestic purposes. But the greater number had already 'gone bush'. *Ibid.* 85, I decided to 'go bush' down the course of the creek. 1928 L. P. GREENE *Red Idol* 253, I do all the heavy work...That's the only thing that's saved me from going native altogether. 1929 LADY DOR. MILLS *Golden Land* 198 '*Il s'est bougnoulisé!*' (gone native). 1930 *Times Lit. Suppl.* 4 Sept. 694 Religious ceremonies which suggest to him that the new religion of Christianity [in S. America] has, after the fashion of new religions, gone native.
19. b. *To go big*: to be a big success, have a large sale. *U.S. slang.* Cf. *87 f.
1930 *Publishers' Circular* 22 Feb. 186 We have reason to believe that *The Miracle of Peille*..will go big.
c. To be accepted or carried into effect; to have effect or weight; to be valid; to be applicable (*for*). *U.S. colloq.*
1891 *Harper's Mag.* Dec. 104/2 Any other night goes, but not this night. 1893 R. KIPLING *Many Inventions, Matter of Fact* 170 Why don't you leave the English papers alone and cable to New York? Everything goes over there. 1901 S. MERWIN & H. K. WEBSTER *Calumet K* iv. 62 What I said went. 1908 MULFORD *Orphan* xi. 137 'Since it's your last wish, why, it goes,' replied the Sheriff. 1909 S. E. WHITE *Rules of Game* III. x. 191, I want one thing distinctly understood. This Government gang don't go here. This is my property. 1920 B. CRONIN *Timber Wolves* 66 When he's away I carry on. And what I says, has to go.
22. *From the word 'Go'* U.S. colloq. (earlier examples).
1838 *Knickerbocker Mag.* XII. 506 You have perjured yourself, from the word 'go'; you have equivocated from Dan to Beersheba. 1866 *Congress. Globe* 61/2 From the very word 'go' I have been a conservative.
24. c. In fig. phr. *Let it go at that*: let that account, estimate, conclusion, etc., be accepted; let us say no more about it.
1898 E. N. WESTCOTT *David Harum* 306 'Very well', said John, 'we will let it go at that.' 1917 J. FARNOL *Definite Object* ii. 19 Eleven will do as well as any other time; let it go at that. *Ibid.* xxxvi. 312 Somebody tried to kill me, but somebody didn't kill me; here I am, getting stronger every day, so we'll let it go at that.
32. a. *Go fetch!* an order to a dog. **b.** *To go to fetch*: (of a batsman) to run out to hit (the ball).
1928 *Daily Tel.* 26 June 17/1 It was the timidity they displayed in dealing with the slow bowling that was the main cause of the collapse of the tourists. Jupp took four wickets for 37 runs. The batsmen would not go to fetch him, and nearly all of them are free players by inclination and habit.
35. f. To yield, produce (a certain amount).
1816 U. BROWN *Jrnl.* in *Maryland Hist. Mag.* X. 369 None [of the fields] that I saw will go 15 Bushels to the Acre. 1867 *Rep. Iowa Agric. Soc.* (1868) 160 Corn.—On well-manured land..will go seventy-five bushels.
36. b. With personal object: To take on in a wager, game, or offer.
1876 [see Dict., 36]. *a* 1889 *N.Y. Spirit of Times* (Farmer), 'I goes you five dollars, this time,' says Jim. 1908 S. E. WHITE *Blazed Trail* xxiv. 161 'Surely you won't refuse to be my guest here..!' 'Wallace,' said Thorpe, 'I'll go you.' 1909 'O. HENRY' *Options* (1916) 38 'Believe I'll go you', he said, brightening. 'I'll accept the invitation gladly.'
c. *Cards.* To make a call or declaration of.
1876 [see NAPOLEON 4.] *c* 1884, 1898 [see NAP *sb.*[6]] 1932 *Sunday Express* 6 Mar. 13/2 Cries of 'I'll stick' and 'I'll go four'.
46. Go it. c. See also *BALD-HEADED *a.*, STRONG *adv.* Phr. (U.S.) *To go it alone*: to play a lone hand at cards; hence *gen.*, to act without assistance, take the whole responsibility (*Standard Dict.* 1895).
54. Go behind —. (Earlier U.S. examples.)
1839 *Congress. Globe* Mar., App. 279/2, I do not desire to go behind these proofs. 1861 *Ibid.* 705/3 It is a thing settled, an award made..and therefore we cannot go behind it.
58. Go for —. e. (Earlier U.S. examples.)
1838 *Congress. Globe* Apr., App. 312/1, I say that it is a gross, rank, palpable fraud! And I go for the fraud! *c* 1870 'MARK TWAIN' *Sketches* Wks. XIX. 23 A thunder storm came up and the lightning began to 'go for' my house.
61. Go on —. g. *To go on record*: see *RECORD *sb.*
1930 *Publishers' Weekly* 1 Feb. 567 He asked the jury to free the defendant, and thus go on record as opposing the tactics of Mr. Yarrow and his organization. *Ibid.* 570 Alfred McIntyre..has already gone on record in favor of 'fewer and better books'.
62. Go over —. a. *To go over the top* (or *the bags*) (Mil.): to issue from a trench to attack the enemy.
1916 *War Illustrated* 9 Sept. 80/1 Some fellows asked our captain when we were going over the top. 1917 S. MCKENNA *Sonia* ix, This chap shouted out, 'Come on, you men!' and went over the top of the trench like a two-year-old.
63. Go through —. f. (Earlier U.S. examples.)
1865 T. W. KNOX *Camp-fire & Cotton-field* 421 Not being privileged to 'go through' me as they had anticipated, the gentlemanly guerrillas went through the overseer. They took his money, his hat, his pantaloons, and his saddle. 1869 *Baltimore Sun* 13 Nov. (De Vere) He was garroted, and the two robbers went through him before the police could reach the spot. 1875 A. A. HAYES *New Colorado* xi. (1881) 154 The road agents had 'gone through' all the passengers of the stage.
65. Go up —. *To go up the line* (Mil.): to leave the base for the front.
71. Go ahead. (Earlier U.S. examples.) Also, to excel anything else.
1834 CROCKETT *Narr. Life* i. 1, I throw aside all hypocritical and fawning apologies, and, according to my own maxim, just 'go ahead'. 1835 *Knickerbocker Mag.* V. 54 They stimulate in the bosoms of all the desire to advance, —or, 'go ahead'. 1839 *Ibid.* XIV. 175 In this respect, as in every other, we are 'going ahead' with accelerated velocity. 1846 *Ibid.* XXVII. 50 Make yourself perfectly sure you are correct, and then, as the wisdom of the departed Crockett has bequeathed to us, 'Go ahead'. *Ibid.* 408 He declared..that of all the music he ever did hear, that 'a leetle went ahead'.
74. Go back. g. *Bridge.* To redouble. *U.S.*
1907 R. F. FOSTER *Bridge* 16 If either the eldest hand or the pone doubles, it is the privilege of the player who named the trump to double him again, the usual expression being; 'I go back'. *Ibid.* 60 When you go over, never forget the possibility of their going back. 1920 — *Auction made easy* 111 *Going back*, redoubling.
h. *Biol.* To revert *to* an earlier or primitive type.
1930 G. R. DE BEER *Embryol. & Evol.* xv. 104 But does this mean that the abnormal horse with extra fingers has 'gone back' to an ancestral type?
78. Go down. h. *Bridge.* To fail to fulfil one's contract.
1918 BERGHOLT *Royal Auction Bridge, Laws & Princ.* 57 If he calls Four Hearts, as is probable, Z. and A. pass, but Y. doubles; and AB. are bound to go down.
80. Go in. a. Said of a theatre, church, etc. when the audience or congregation enter at a fixed time.
1924 D. H. LAWRENCE *England, my Eng.* 227 And the cinema was just going in, and the queues were tailing down the road to the corner.
81. Go in *for*. a. (Earlier U.S. example.)
1835 A. B. LONGSTREET *Georgia Scenes* (1843) 111 She would..'go in' for Augusta, live or die, hit or miss.
85. Go out. c. Also, to leave one's country for the battlefield.
1917 S. MCKENNA *Sonia* viii, 'Is David going out?.. What's he in?' 'The Midland Fusiliers.'
t. *To go all out for*: see *ALL-OUT 2.
87. Go over. a. = *go over the top* (*62 a).
1919 GALSWORTHY *Saint's Progress* II. i. § 3 Calculating exactly where he meant to put foot and hand for the going over.
f. Of a play, speech, etc.: To be successful in its appeal to the audience; to 'get over', 'get across'. Also *gen.* to have a vogue or success. Also, *to go over big* (cf. *19 b). *U.S. Theatr. slang.*
1927 *Daily Express* 29 Aug. 5 'Little Bits of Love' went over with its accustomed success. 1927 *Amer. Speech* Oct. 21 A comedy that 'goes over big' and is very funny is often referred to as a 'wow'. 1927 *Daily Express* 23 Nov. 13 'Escape' has gone over with a great bang. 1927 *Observer* 4 Dec. 16/5 The 'hard-boiled' New Yorkers seemed impressed. My friends say that 'the message went over big'. 1928 *Publishers' Weekly* 26 May 2175 Sometimes an author writes a first book, and it goes over very big. 1930 *New Statesman* 1 Nov. 115/2 Experienced novelists know that a good trial always goes over big.
†g. *Bridge.* To double. *U.S. Obs.*
1908 J. B. ELWELL *Bridge* 111 *Going over*...The effect of 'over', 'over', etc., is that the value of each trick point is doubled, quadrupled, etc. 1907 R. F. FOSTER *Bridge* 60 If you are reasonably certain of the odd trick, you should go over in order to make it more valuable. *Ibid.* [see *74 g]. 1920 — *Auction made easy* 111 *Going over*, obsolete for doubling.
h. 'To be postponed; as, the bill went over for the session' (Webster, 1911). *U.S.*
88. Go round. g. (Earlier U.S. example.)
1871 BARNUM *Struggles & Triumphs* 259 It [*sc.* a turkey] was a small one, and when it was carved, there was not enough of it to 'go round'.
89. Go through. c. (Earlier U.S. example.)
1889 *Kansas Times & Star* 8 Apr., Kump intimates the deal won't go through.
d. Of goods, etc.: To be accepted, find a market.
1924 *Times Trade & Engin. Suppl.* 29 Nov. 247/1 Some modest lots of miscellaneous cloths have gone through for the smaller markets of the Far East. *Ibid.*, One or two fair lines of white shirtings have gone through, and a good many more are under consideration. *Ibid.* 248/2 Contracts which amount to a fair aggregate are going through for South America.
94. Go up. a. = *To go up the line* (*65).
1914 D. O. BARNETT *Lett.* (1915) 19 The officer asked me whether I wanted to go to the fire trench...Of course I went up, and got in with the machine-gun section.
(*b*) To 'ascend' in ancestry.
1930 J. L. MYRES *Who were the Greeks?* 308 Hecataeus' genealogy went back sixteen generations, and then 'went up to a god'.
VIII. go-as-you-please(**ness,** want of regularity or order; **go-at-it** *a.*, full of dash; **go-fever,** a hectic restlessness or longing for movement; **go-slow** *a.*, characterizing a workmen's policy of deliberate limitation of output, ca'canny; **go-to-sleep** *a.*, idle, inactive.
1889 *Judge* 20 Apr. 21/2 A Western *Go-As-You-Please. 1920 H. G. WELLS *Mr. Britling* I. iv. § 6. 117 Explaining ..to this American..how excellent was the backwardness of Essex and English go-as-you-please. 1927 *Observer* 1 May 15/3 The impromptu quality of the entertainment— its untidy *go-as-you-please-ness. 1904 *Daily Chron.* 27 June 7/2 They are a versatile, well-balanced, *go-at-it side, and they field as if they like it. 1891 KIPLING *Light that Failed* 125 He's as restless as a swallow in autumn...He has the beginnings of the *go-fever upon him. 1900 J. BUCHAN *Half-hearted* vi. 78 There comes a thing called the go-fever, which is not amenable to reason. 1907 N. MUNRO *Daft Days* xxiv, I'd not been twenty minutes in her society before I found out she had the go-fever pretty bad. 1930 *Times* 27 Mar. 19/5 The receipts..showed large decreases ..due to the recent '*go-slow' movement amongst the men. 1909 *Athenæum* 26 June 750/1 Settle down to a *go-to-sleep life, I could not.

Goad-stick. *U.S.* [f. GOAD *sb.*[1] 5.] A stick capable of being used as a goad.
1825 J. NEAL *Bro. Jonathan* I. 159, I fetches it a rap with my goard [*sic*] stick. 1834 S. SMITH *Sel. Lett. Major Jack Downing* 46 A farmer ort to stick to his oxbows and goard sticks. 1839 *Knickerbocker Mag.* XIII. 298 A small man..holding a goad-stick in his hand..entered the room. 1851 J. S. SPRINGER *Forest Life* 97 (Th.) The teamster now arranges every ox..., passing through several evolutions with his goad-stick.

Go-ahead, *a.* Add: (Earlier U.S. example.)
1839 *Knickerbocker Mag.* XIII. 207 A queer sort of a chap he is, too: a real go-ahead sort of a fellow as ever I met with.
B. *sb.* An act of or the spirit of 'going ahead'; (zeal for) progress.
1840 C. F. HOFFMAN *Greyslaer* I. iii. 32 Sarting! he does make a clean go-ahead of it. But when did he come up here to mix in our doings? 1844 G. W. KENDALL *Santa Fé Exped.* II. xix. 362 There is a little 'go-ahead' in a spirited, showy, well-trained Mexican horse. *a* 1861 T. WINTHROP *Canoe & Saddle* xii. 251 It racks my heart to know that I must still demand much go-ahead from you.
Hence **Go-aheadative** *a.* (example); **Go-aheadish** *a.*; **Go-aheadism** (earlier example); **Go-aheadi·vity.**
1838 J. F. COOPER *Home as Found* xxix. 488 Aristabulus, who was filled with goaheadism, would have shortened the delay. 1844 *Knickerbocker Mag.* XXIV. 73 Our state of society in America with..its helter-skelterism and go-aheadivity. 1853 A. BUNN *Old Eng. & New Eng.* I. 109 New York..too 'go-a-headish' to suit our..taste. 1872 *Trans. Dep. Agric. Illinois* 173 This is one among the most enterprising and go-aheadative villages in the county.

Goal, *sb.* **6.** Add: *goal-getter, -getting, -kicker, -scorer*; **goal-mouth,** the space between the goal-posts and under the cross-bar in association football, hockey, etc.; **goal-net,** the net behind the goal-mouth.
1904 *Strand Mag.* XXVII. 341 The saving of which meant every fibre of nerve and muscle strained to go one better than the would-be *goal-getter. 1910 *Westm. Gaz.* 21 Jan. 12/1 The goal-getters for the winners were [etc.]. 1904 *Daily Chron.* 21 Nov. 8/3 Hence we had 'Defence, not Defiance,'..and needless to say *goal-getting did not..enter largely into the argument. 1909 *Bendigonian* 24 Aug. 21/2 The *goal-kickers were: [etc.]. 1899 *Captain* II. 127 Filling the *goal-mouth in the event of a corner-kick against their side. 1908 *Westm. Gaz.* 7 Oct. 4/2 The yawning goal-mouth was not fed with that elusive leather sphere. 1930 *Cambridge Daily News* 24 Sept. 7/1 Snow..found the net during a scrimmage in the goalmouth. 1897 *Windsor Mag.* Dec. 22/1 *Goal-nets..would have had to be pretty strong. 1909 *Daily Chron.* 20 Mar. 8/5 He heads the list of West Ham *goal scorers. 1929 *Evening News* 18 Nov. 13/4 The League's leading goalscorer.

Goalie (gōu·li). *Football.* Also **-ee.** [f. GOAL *sb.* + -IE.] A goal-keeper.
1921 *Oxf. Mag.* 28 Jan. 158/2 C. V. Hill..journeyed to Henley..much to the discomfiture of the opposing goalee. 1926 *Spectator* 24 Apr. 753/1 One can imagine an indignant Cockney ejaculating as he regarded the rotundity of the Red goalee.

Goalless (gōu·l,lěs), *a.* [See -LESS.] Without a goal scored by either side.
1904 *Daily Chron.* 18 Nov. 1/7 At Southall Oxford City played a goalless draw with the local team. 1928 *Daily Tel.* 28 Aug. 9/5 The game..ended in a goalless draw.

Goan (gōu·ăn), *a.* and *sb.* [See -AN.] = next.
1927 J. FURTADO (*title*) A Goan Fiddler. 1927 E. GOSSE *Ibid.* Pref. p. vi, He was..not happy among the Goans.

Goanese (gōuǎnī·z), *a.* and *sb.* [f. GOA [1] + -ESE, after *Japanese*, etc.] **A.** *adj.* Of or belonging to Goa. **B.** *sb.* A native of Goa. Also as *pl.*

Goanese ipecac, a meliaceous shrub, *Naregamia alata*, and its dried root which is used as an emetic.
1851 R. F. BURTON *Goa* v. 91 The Goanese smoke all day, ladies as well as gentlemen. *Ibid.* 93 A Goanese noble. 1909 *Chambers's Jrnl.* Aug. 523/1, A batch of Goanese tailors' shops. 1920 *Ibid.* May 299/2, I was obliged to read the burial service in Latin out of a prayer-book lent me by a Goanese cook.

Goanna (goæ·nă). *Austral.* Also **gohanna.** [Corrupt f. IGUANA.] The lace-lizard, *Hydrosaurus* (*Varanus*) *varius*, or any large lizard. See GUANA.
1891 'R. BOLDREWOOD' *Sydney-Side Saxon* vi. 99 Blast that infernal horse! A goanna started him, and he set to and kicked the front of the buggy in. 1900 H. LAWSON *Over Sliprails* 108 The four little Australians..ate under-done kangaroo..with an occasional treat of oak grubs and gohanna. 1903 *Blackw. Mag.* Apr. 468/2 My tongue was like a gohanna's back. 1923 *Chambers's Jrnl.* Aug. 527/1 Snakes, goannas (guanas), scorpions, and centipedes are numerous.

Go-ashore, *a.* (See GO *v.* VIII; earlier examples.)
1840 R. H. DANA *Bef. Mast* xvi, Go-ashore jackets and trousers [were] got out and brushed. 1846 H. MELVILLE *Typee* vi. (1920) 42 He for one preserved his go-ashore traps for the Spanish Main.

Goat. Add:
2. d. = GOATEE. *U.S.*
1876 J. S. INGRAM *Centennial Exposition* v. 151 The little puckered-mouth, pug-nosed Esquimaux, with his slight sprinkling of a mustache and 'goat'.
e. *Bookbinding.* Short for GOATSKIN.
1927 J. S. HEWITT-BATES *Bookbinding for Schools* 13 Goat or Morocco. *Ibid.* 14 Persians..may be made either from goat or sheep. 1927 *Longman's Class. Cat. Educ. Works* 12 Hand grained goat, gilt edges.
3. b. *To play the* (*giddy*) *goat*: also, to play the fool, behave in an irresponsible manner. Also, *to act the goat.*
1879 H. HARTIGAN *Stray Leaves from Mil. Man's Note Bk.* i, Don't be actin' the goat. 1887 KIPLING *From Sea to Sea* (1900) I. xiv. 162 You'll find some o' the youngsters play the goat a good deal when they come out o' stable. [1901 *Tatler* I. 424/1 The dramatic season began..with the production of..The Giddy Goat..adapted from the French.] 1924 GALSWORTHY *White Monkey* I. v, It's playing the goat for no earthly reason. 1929 PETT RIDGE *Affect. Regards* 61 Haven't I got enough trouble without you acting the goat in this fashion?
c. *To get* (a person's) *goat*: to make (him) angry, annoy, irritate. orig. *U.S. slang.*
1912 C. MATHEWSON *Pitching in a Pinch* ii. 28 Then Lobert..stopped at third with a mocking smile on his face which would have gotten the late Job's goat. 1915 H. L. WILSON *Ruggles of Red Gap* xix. (1917) 345 'You certainly got my goat,' she said in the quaint American fashion, 'telling me little No-no was too fat.' 1917 EMPEY *From Fire Step* 152 There was one gun in particular which used to get our goats. 1924 GALSWORTHY *White Monkey* II. i, That had got the chairman's goat!—Got his goat? What expressions they used nowadays! 1929 PRIESTLEY *Good Comp.* III. i. 474 This is what gets my goat, and you can't blame me.
d. A scapegoat; a guilty party. *U.S. slang.*
1924 WEBSTER Addenda. 1929 *Randolph Enterprise* (Elkins, W. Va.) 26 Sept. 1/2 When told of his mistake he explained that he..thought we were the goat.
4. b. goat-foot [after Gr. αἰγιπόδης, αἰγίπους]: a faun or satyr; the god Pan.
1898 G. MEREDITH *Odes Fr. Hist.* 6 To veil an evil leer, And bid a goatfoot trip it like a fay. 1906 *Daily Chron.* 13 Aug. 4/4 It was the hour of Pan. I could almost think I saw the goat-foot playing his pipes by the brook. 1912 R. BROOKE *Grantchester* Poems (1918) 54 To glimpse a Naiad's reedy head, Or hear the Goat-foot piping low.

Goatee. Also **goaty.** (Earlier U.S. examples.)
1844 D. LEE & FROST *Ten Yrs. Oregon* viii. 102 A few individuals..leave what is called, by some of their politer neighbors, a 'goaty' under the chin. *c* 1845 PAULDING *Noble Exile* 107 A queer little amber-colored goatee.

Gob, *sb.*[1] **1.** (U.S. *fig.* examples.)
1838 *Jonathan's Visit* in *Poor Wills Alm.* 1839, See what a big gob o' plums! 1851 J. J. HOOPER *Widow Rugby's Husb.* 153 If he..is a judge of talent, Smith has got it, and that in great gobs! 1887 *Harper's Mag.* Dec. 35/1 It mought be well tuh do lots and gobs of things I ain't never tried.

Gob (gǫb), *sb.*[5] *U.S. slang.* [Cf. *GOBBY.] A sailor, seaman.
1919 *Let.* in *N.Y. Tribune* 28 Jan., A 'gob' is a new sailor...The term 'gob' was never heard in the United States navy until about six years ago. 1921 R. D. PAINE *Comr. Rolling Ocean* iii. 44, I was feeding the coal to her when most of those..amateur gobs were seasick and useless. *Ibid.* xiv. 241 Here is one Yankee gob..that will be there on the first call. 1925 J. GREGORY *Bab of Backwoods* xvi. 193 Step lively, you gobs! 1927 J. BARBICAN *Confess. Rum-Runner* iv. 47 Now, then, you pie-eyed gob, quit drinking that darned hooch!

Go-back. (See GO *v.* VIII.) Add: **b.** One who goes back. **c.** (See quot. 1904.)
1859 *Rocky Mt. News* (Kas. Terr.) 18 June (Th.) Farewell to the 'go-backs'; they have had their day, and soon will be forgotten. 1904 *N. Y. Evening Post* 30 July 3 Vagrant grass, called by the natives in the West 'go-back', because it has gone back from the breaking-up process that was given by the settlers years ago.

Gobbe (gǫb). [Surinam.] A creeping fabaceous herb, *Voandzeia subterranea*, much cultivated in the tropics for its esculent pods and seeds.
1861 BENTLEY *Man. Bot.* 528.

Gobbet, *sb.* Add: **1. d.** A piece of a literary or musical work 'torn' from its context; *spec.* an extract from a text set for translation or comment.
1912 *Punch* 6 Mar. 173/1 He'll gorge you with gobbets of Homer. 1930 D. L. SAYERS *Strong Poison* 160 Playing the most ghastly tripe, sandwiched in with snacks of Mendelssohn and torn-off gobbets of the 'Unfinished'.

Gobby (gǫ·bi). *slang.* [Said to be f. dial. and vulgar *gob* expectoration + -Y [6].] A coastguardsman.
1890 *Scotsman* 4 Aug. (Farmer) When a meeting takes place the men indulge in a protracted yarn and a draw of the pipe. The session involves a considerable amount of expectoration all round, whereby our friends come to be known as gobbies. 1904 KIPLING *Traffics & Discoveries* 126 Think o' her Number One chasin' the mobilised gobbies round the lower deck flats.

Go-between. 2. Add: Also, something intermediate or falling between two classes. *U.S.*
1861 *Trans. Ill. Agric. Soc.* IV. 374 A stallion, then, should be perfect in that class he is intended to represent, (and we shall drop all those go-betweens). 1871 *Ibid.* VIII. 143 It..fattens a horde of go-betweens.

Goblin[2] (gǫ·blin). *slang.* [app. rhyming slang on *sovrin* = SOVEREIGN.] A pound (twenty shillings).
1887 W. E. HENLEY *Villon's Straight Tip* iii. Poems 1908 II. 231 Your merry goblins soon stravag. 1925 P. G. WODEHOUSE *Carry on, Jeeves* iv. 99 Five hundred o' goblins a year.

God, *sb.* Add: **16. a. god-shelf,** a shelf-like shrine of white wood holding the sacred images in a Shinto household.
1880 ISAB. L. BIRD *Unbeaten Tracks in Japan* II. 359 In nearly all Japanese houses there is a *kami-dana* or god-shelf, on which is a miniature temple in wood, [etc.]. 1903 S. L. GULICK *Evol. Japanese* xxv. 292 There is hardly a house in Japan but has some..of these charms, either nailed on the front door or placed on the god-shelf. 1904 SLADEN *Playing the Game* xii, They are never too poor to have a little light burning on the god-shelf.
b. *God-consciousness, -idea* (= consciousness or conception of God as an object of thought).
1894 G. M. GRANT *Relig. World* ii. 29 The *God-consciousness of Israel expanded under the leadership of a long succession of prophets and psalmists. 1914 F. B. WILSON (*title*) The Man of To-morrow. Human Evolution impelling Man onward to God-Consciousness. 1910 E. S. AMES *Psychol. Relig. Experience* 319 The *God-idea is a teleological idea. 1923 J. B. PRATT *Relig. Consciousness* x. 206 The God-idea which most persons carry around with them and live by. 1924 W. B. SELBIE *Psychol. Relig.* 119 The origin of the god-idea varies with different peoples.
17. b. *God-gifted.*
1863 TENNYSON *Milton*, God-gifted organ-voice of England. 1907 'DICK DONOVAN' *Gold-spinner* I. 1 'God-gifted and beautiful' was Helga Arnold!

God-bush. (Also **gad-.**) A name given in Jamaica to the *Arceuthobium gracile*, a leafless mistletoe.
1851 P. H. GOSSE *Nat. Sojourn Jamaica* 131 But what interests me most in this place is a flourishing Misseltoe, or God-bush, as the negroes call it. 1874 *Treas. Bot.* Suppl., *Gad-bush.* 1914 FAWCETT & RENDLE *Flora Jamaica* III. 88 The members of this family [*sc.* *Loranthaceæ*] are generally known by the popular names, Godbush and Mistletoe.

God-damn. Add: **1.** (Later examples.) Also quasi-*adj.* = accursed, damnable.
1869 *St. James's Mag.* IV. 226 It was the fashion in France, on the stage..to represent the Englishman as habitually saying, 'Godam'. 1908 W. P. DRURY *Tadpole of Archangel* 149 Before I could say 'Goddam',..they would be fired. 1929 ABU NADAAR in *Mercury Story Bk.* 99 It was the utter goddam monotony that was the worst.

Godet (gode, gode·t). Transfer †*Obs.* to the sense in Dict., and add:
2. A triangular piece of stuff inserted in a dress, glove, etc. Also *attrib.*, as *godet skirt.*
1896 *Strand Mag.* July Advt. p. xiv, Costume..consisting of wide Godet Skirt. 1923 *Daily Mail* 10 Apr. 14 Black 'godets' in white kid (or white in black). 1925 *Brit. Weekly* 15 Oct. 59/1 Some of the smartest models have a full centre-piece instead of side godets. 1926 *Queen* 17 Feb. Advt. p. vii, The simple bodice has the new long sleeves and the full godet skirt is finished self binds. 1928 *Daily Mail* 31 July 1/2 The skirt has full godet of lace each side.
3. A roller forming part of the machinery for making artificial-silk filament or thread.
1927 T. WOODHOUSE *Artif. Silk* 41 The group [of filaments] is then passed behind a guide-wire, partly round a roller, usually termed a godet, and often made of glass, [etc.].

Go·-devil. *U.S.*
1. A dynamite-cartridge exploder, used to start a flow in an oil-well.
1896 B. REDWOOD *Petroleum* I. 275 To explode the charge, an iron weight, known as a *go-devil*, was dropped into the well, and, striking the disc, exploded the cap and fired the torpedo. Now, however, a miniature torpedo known as a *go-devil squib*, holding about a quart of nitro-glycerine,..is almost invariably employed. 1919 A. B. THOMPSON *Petrol. Mining* 227 The blow is usually administered to the firing head by a 'go-devil', a piece of cast iron with wings to guide it fairly on the cap of the firing head.
2. A jointed flexible tool for clearing away obstructions in a petroleum pipe-line.
1896 B. REDWOOD *Petroleum* II. 473 To remove obstructions in the pipes..an automatic rotary scraper is forced through...The scraper is known as a 'go-devil'. 1913 V. B. LEWES *Oil Fuel* 90 This automatic scraper, called a 'go-devil', rotates as it passes forward and scrapes the pipe clean from deposits. 1916 A. B. THOMPSON *Oil-Field Development* 548 The 'go-devil' is a tool with cutters that rotate when impelled forward by the pump after insertion in the pipe line.
3. A rough sledge, dray, or wagon for dragging logs, hauling stone, etc.
1905 *Terms Forestry & Logging* 36.
4. A rude plough used for breaking up rough, newly-cleared land; a shovel-plough.
1931 *Walters* (Okla.) *Herald* 19 Feb. 6/4 Farm Implements (Advt.) 1 2-row go-devil. 1931 *Randolph Enterprise* (Elkins, W. Va.) 1 Jan. 1/1 We had to [open the roads]..with.. sleighs, 'Yankee Jumpers' and 'Go Devils'.

Godfatherly, *a.* (at end of GODFATHER *sb.*). Delete †, and add recent example (in *transf.* use).
1928 *Observer* 29 Jan. 17/2 That 'brighter cricket' which Lord Hawke, on behalf of Yorkshire, promises for the coming season. This taking of godfatherly vows for a county team is a picturesque departure, which, we may hope, will have no anti-climax.

Go·d-fea:rer. One who fears (and worships) God.
1926 *Contemp. Rev.* May 597 How easy for such 'god-fearers' to regard antiquity as a guarantee of truth.

Go·dfea:ringly, *adv.* In a God-fearing way.
1899 J. H. RIGG *Oxford High Anglicanism* (ed. 2) 404 If, from point to point, the wise and equitable thing is God-fearingly carried out.

Go·d-forsa:ken, *ppl. a.* Of persons: Depraved, profligate, abandoned. Of places: Desolate, dismal, dreary. Hence **Go·d-forsa:kenness.**
1856, 1886 [see GOD *sb.* 17 b]. 1903 *Westm. Gaz.* 11 Feb. 12/1 Of course, it is not of the same date as Brive. But it has the God-forsakenness, the *misère*, the penetrating sadness, its essentially French charm. 1923 W. P. KER *Art of Poetry* 60 You come with Milton..to the Paradise of Fools in a dry, parched, and god-forsaken land on the outside of the fixed stars.

Godfrey (gǫ·dfri). *U.S.* [Meaningless euphemistic assimilation of *God* to the name *Godfrey.*] An exclamation expressing surprise.
1906 W. CHURCHILL *Coniston* 274 'Godfrey!' exclaimed Ephraim. 1909 J. C. LINCOLN *Keziah Coffin* vii. 104 If ever a craft was steered by guess and by godfrey, 'twas that old hooker of Zach's t'other night. *Ibid.* viii. 124 Oh, my godfreys mighty! 1916 'B. M. BOWER' *Phantom Herd* v. 71 Why my godfrey, man, the stuff's all punch.

Godism (gǫ·diz'm). [See -ISM.] A derisive term for belief in God. Also **Godite** (gǫ·dəit), one who believes in God.
1891 J. M. ROBERTSON *Mod. Humanists* 18 Call his [*sc.* Carlyle's] creed 'Godism', and you limit the confusion of words by separately labelling his confusion of thought. *Ibid.* 37 At the mere sound of that word [*sc.* atheism], the Godite always became rabid. 1909 *Lit. Guide* 1 Aug. 124/1 The *Contemporary Review* permits Mr. G. K. Chesterton to make faces over Meredith's grave, and claim him as a believer in godism.

Godless, *a.* Add:
c. *The Godless* [Russ. *bezbojnik*]: the title of a union (and its press organs) in the Soviet Republic of Russia having for its primary object the suppression of religion.
1927 OLFSHCHUK in *The Anti-Religious* No. 10, The Union of the Godless makes every effort in order to transform the International Union of the Godless into an active staff of class conflict,..and to make the fight with religion in the West a factor in the class struggle of the proletariat with the bourgeoisie. 1930 *Slavonic Rev.* Mar. 518 The Union of the Godless is a semi-State institution...The Union organises special 'cells of the Godless' in factories, villages and units of the Red Army.

God's country. See *COUNTRY 2 b.

Godwinian (gǫdwi·niăn), *a.* [f. the name of William *Godwin* (1756–1836) + -IAN.] Pertaining to or characteristic of Godwin's views on politics, social reform, etc. Also **Go·dwinism,** Godwin's doctrine or ideas.
1805 FESSENDEN *Democracy Unveiled* II. 197 It is to be hoped the good sense of Americans will resist the innovations of these Godwinian schemes. 1892 L. STEPHEN *Hours in Library* (new ed.) III. 79 The Godwinism, indeed, is strongest in the crude poetry of 'Queen Mab'. 1913 H. N. BRAILSFORD *Shelley, Godwin*, etc. 216 The ideal man of the Godwinian conception, who lives by reason.

Go-easy, *a.* [f. vbl. phr. *to go easy*: see GO *v.* 2 b and EASY *adv.* 4.] Easy-going.
1877 *Rep. Vermont Dairym. Assoc.* VIII. 22 The many serious drawbacks which the 'go easy' dairymen of Vermont are compelled to encounter.

Go·-ge:tter. *U.S. colloq.* [f. U.S. vbl. phr. *to go get* + ER [1].] One who goes out to get something; an active, enterprising, pushing person.
1922 P. B. KYNE (*title*) The Go-Getter. A story that tells you how to be one. 1925 *Public Opin.* 9 Oct. 364/3 The Go-Getter goes till he gets what he goes for. 1926 *Ladies' Home Jrnl.* Apr. 24 As I look at the salesmen gathered here,..I see the finest bunch of go-getters in New York City. 1927 P. RUSSELL *Benj. Franklin* 238 The thing which is impossible to the go-getter frequently comes around of its own motion to him who waits. 1930 J. BUCHAN *Castle Gay* iv, He's a go-getter, is Craw.
So **Go·-ge:tting** *ppl. a.*, pushing, enterprising. Hence **Go·-ge:ttingness.**
1928 *Daily Express* 27 June 10/7 Such jobs generally call for..a 'go-getting' attitude to life that the public school boy does not possess. *Ibid.* 5 July 13/7 All of which has somewhat shattered my faith in the 'pep' and 'go-gettingness' of the American reporters. 1929 *New Mag.* July 100 He had none of the crisp and go-getting qualities he liked to see in a young man. 1930 *Books of Month* Sept. 9 A ruthless go-getting adventurer.

Goggle, *sb.* **4.** Add: Now esp. with reference to their use by motorists (cf. next).
1899 JEROME *Three Men on Bummel* xiii, Their goggle-covered eyes, their necks tied up in comforters. 1904 A. B. F. YOUNG *Complete Motorist* xii. (ed. 2) 260 Goggles are, un-

happily, almost a necessity when travelling at any but the lowest speeds. 1908 *Motor Cycle* 12 Feb. 132 A new goggle constructed after the principle of the four-glass goggle.

Go·ggled, *ppl. a.*² [f. GOGGLE *sb.* + -ED².] Equipped with or wearing goggles. (Said esp. of motorists.)

1903 *Westm. Gaz.* 20 July 2/3 These ghastly goggled motor guys. 1908 *Ibid.* 22 Aug. 10/1 The swimmer's head, goggled and capped, emerging from the water. 1909 H. G. WELLS *Tono-Bungay* III. ii. 237 A short figure,..hugely goggled,..and surmounted by a table-land of motoring cap.

Gohanna, var. of *GOANNA.

Going, *vbl. sb.* Add: **4.** A line or route, considered as difficult or easy to follow. Also, advance or progress as helped or hindered by the nature of the ground.

1901 'LINESMAN' *Words by Eyewitness* (1902) 101 A narrow path just above the water-line, overhung with bushes in parts, formed the 'going'. 1925 E. F. NORTON *Fight for Everest, 1924* 114 We made very poor going, descending at a very much slower pace than we had made two years before.

5. b. (Modern U.S. example.)

1866 MRS. WHITNEY *L. Goldthwaite* iv, They watched the long, golden going-down of the sun.

e. *Going off*, start, outset. Cf. GO-OFF.

1845 CAROLINE M. KIRKLAND *Western Clearings* 14 You'd better tell 'em at the first goin' off that you a'n't land-hunters.

f. *Going over*, an overhauling; a talking to. *U.S.*

1884 'MARK TWAIN' *Huck. Finn* iii, I got a good going-over in the morning from old Miss Watson on account of my clothes. 1887 C. B. GEORGE *40 Yrs. on Rail* viii. 150 When Mr. Butler took me in hand he gave me a terrible going over. 1919 H. L. WILSON *Ma Pettengill* x. 286 She wanted to give these here accounts a thorough going-over while the sensation lasted.

6. b. *Going-to-press*: used attrib. to designate the latest items of news in a journal.

1906 *Westm. Gaz.* 24 Apr. 7/3 The following are going-to-press Stock Exchange prices.

Goitred, *a.* Add recent examples.

1890 *Century Dict.* s.v., Goitered antelope, same as dzeren. 1923 *Blackw. Mag.* Aug. 152/1 A gentle frog-like croak proceeded from the goitred throat.

Gol (gǫl). An Indian ravine.

1926 *Blackw. Mag.* Nov. 609/1 The road track crossed the gol near its junction with the Chitral River. 1928 *Daily Tel.* 10 Apr. 6/6 The valley of the Shangtu gol.

Gold¹. Add:

8. c. With reference to the use of gold for coinage and as a standard of value, as *gold currency, standard, value*. Also designating a money of account: Reckoned at its full undepreciated value according to a gold standard.

1776 ADAM SMITH *W. N.* II. ii, The..nominal sum of the gold and silver currency of the country. 1831 *Deb. Congress* 22 Feb. p. cl/2 The present rate (of our gold standard) was the result of information clearly incorrect. 1868 J. LAING *Theory of Business* iv. (ed. 2) 65 Had India possessed a gold currency. 1879 *New York Even. Expr. Alman.* 373 Favoring a gold standard, and condemning the Bland silver bill. 1898 LD. FARRER *Stud. Currency* Pref. p. xviii, The relation between the Gold value of the legal Rupee and the Gold value of Silver. *a* 1909 'O. HENRY' *Roads of Destiny* xxi. 357 It's a great thing to be a citizen of a gold-standard nation, ain't it? 1914 *Rep. Royal Comm. Indian Finance* Comm. 7068 § 50 The system adumbrated by the Committee of 1898, viz., a gold standard based on a gold currency in active circulation such as the system in the United Kingdom is commonly held to be. *Ibid.* § 51 The Indian currency system based on what is now known as the gold exchange standard. 1917 W. F. SPALDING *East. Exch. Currency* ii. 13 The exchange value of the Rupee was satisfactorily maintained between the gold points. 1923 *Westm. Gaz.* 22 Aug., If we take the franc of to-day as having one-quarter of the purchasing power of the pre-war gold franc. 1924 *Times Trade & Eng. Suppl.* 29 Nov. 236/3 Indian commercial opinion is itself divided..as to the possibility and desirability of 'scrapping' the gold exchange standard in favour of an effective gold standard in the ordinary sense of the term. 1926 *Encycl. Brit.* Suppl. I. 776/2 In the final phase people reckoned in gold marks and stipulated for payment in paper marks at the exchange of the day....This competition of the gold mark as a money of account was the final undoing of the paper mark.

9. b. *gold-bearing* (earlier and later examples).

a 1799 M. PARK *Trav. Africa* (ed. 2) 304 Were the gold-bearing streams to be traced to their fountains. *a* 1861 T. WINTHROP *John Brent* i. 8 It was my own fault that I looked for gold-bearing quartz. 1869 *Kansas Pac. Railway Pamphlet* 5 Gold bearing railroad and land grant sinking fund bonds. 1894 *Pop. Sci. Monthly* June 174 The northern rivers and creeks have gold-bearing sand.

e. *gold-rimmed* adj.

1901 'SARAH GRAND' *Babs* xxxix, Mr. Jellybood Tinney adjusted his gold-rimmed pince-nez. 1918 H. G. WELLS *Joan & Peter* v. 82 Mr. Sycamore put his hands together before him and sat with his head a little on one side regarding Lady Charlotte attentively through the gold-rimmed spectacles. 1908 EDITH WHARTON *Hermit* 2 With the appearing of every gold-rimmed face [sc. haloed saints].

10. gold belt *U.S.*, the area over which gold is found; **gold blossom** *U.S.* (see BLOSSOM *sb.* 3 a); **gold-copper**, applied to ore yielding both gold and copper; **gold fever** (earlier examples); **gold-pan** *U.S.*, a pan in which gold is washed; **gold point** *Economics* (see quot. 1925); **gold quartz**, quartz containing gold; also *attrib.*; **gold-washed** *a.*, lightly faced with gold.

1879 *Harper's Mag.* Sept. 508 The "*gold-belt'..consists of a strip of land running..due northeast and southwest across the northern end of the State. 1891 *Harper's Mag.* Aug. 446/2 On the 3d day of December, 1862, a fierce storm swept over the whole gold belt. 1846 SAGE *Scenes Rocky Mts.* (1859) 334 The surface affords large quantities of "*gold blossom'. 1906 *Daily Chron.* 26 Jan. 4/5 A large deposit of *gold-copper ore. 1908 *Westm. Gaz.* 1 July 6/3 There are piles of gold-copper ore. 1849 C. LANMAN *Lett. Alleghany Mts.* i. 15 When the *gold fever commenced I..went to speculating in gold lots. 1877 *Harper's Mag.* Dec. 84/2 The madness of the gold fever was upon every body up there. 1875 JOAQUIN MILLER *First Families of Sierras* i. 9 Men were grandly honest there. They invariably left gold in their *gold-pans from day to day open in the claim. 1901 S. E. WHITE *Claim Jumpers* ii. 27 He and Davidson climbed down shafts,..and worked the gold pan. 1891 G. CLARE *Money-Market Primer* 104 So long as credit is good here, high interest almost invariably leads to a rise of the exchanges, but it is noticeable that, when on the very verge of *gold-point, the upward movement almost as invariably receives a check. 1925 S. E. THOMAS *Elem. Econ.* xxix. 461 We find that the rates at which one currency will exchange for another fluctuate between two limits on each side of the Mint Par, marking the points at which it becomes more profitable to send or to receive gold rather than to send or receive a credit instrument. These theoretical limits are known as the *gold points*. 1930 J. M. KEYNES *Treat. Money* II. 320 The degree of separation of the gold points is a vital factor in the problem of managing a country's currency. *a* 1861 T. WINTHROP *John Brent* i. 6 A few years ago I was working a *gold-quartz mine in California. 1872 RAYMOND *Statist. Mines & Mining* 259 Several small gold-quartz mills worked successfully. 1891 *Century Mag.* Feb. 533 The most notable improvement..in gold-quartz machinery. 1872 E. EGGLESTON *End of World* ix. 65 Pewter watch-seals, *gold-washed.

b. gold-seed, also applied to a variety of rice.

1847 *Rep. U.S. Comm. Patents* (1848) 173 Among the varieties of rice is the gold seed rice.

c. gold-robin *U.S.* (earlier example).

1849 WILLIS *Rural Lett.* i. 19 First came a gold-robin, twittering out his surprise to find strange company in his parlor.

Go·ldarn, *v.* *U.S.* Vulgar perversion of GOD-DAMN. Chiefly in **Golda·rned** *ppl. a.*; also **Golda·sted** (cf. *DODGAST).

1870 BRET HARTE *Sensation Novels, Muck-a-Muck* iv, Dog-gone. *Note*, A euphemism common with the men of the West, and equal to the English 'Od rat it', or 'Gol darn'. 1888 *American Humorist* (Farmer), I've broke my goldarned neck. 1888 *Cincinnati Enquirer* (Farmer) 'That goldasted St. Louis mugwump. 1904 *Told at One Bell* 21 I'll do the gall-darn'd working part. 1907 N. MUNRO *Daft Days* xxxii, Every gol-darned idiot in England. 1910 R. W. SERVICE *Ballads of Cheechako* 50 Goldarn his eyes. 1927 *Observer* 25 Sept. 15/2 That goldarned Britisher ain't the simp and saphead he lets on to be.

Gold brick. *U.S. slang.* [GOLD¹.] Something having only a surface appearance of value; a fraud or sham. Phr. *to sell a gold brick*, to perpetrate a fraud on, 'take in' by a confidence trick. Also *attrib.*, as in *gold brick swindle*.

1887 *Chambers's Jrnl.* 1 Oct. 637/1 A 'gold-brick swindler'. 1889 *Kansas Times & Star* 30 Nov., What's new down at the old union depot shack? Any eruptions, gold bricks being sold or important arrivals? 1901 S. E. WHITE *Westerners* xiii. 94 Bunco men can clean him out in a gambling joint, but who ever heard of their selling him a gold brick? 1911 B. WASHINGTON *My Larger Educ.* 292 In many cases, the diploma that the student carries home at the conclusion of his course is nothing less than a gold brick. 1915 P. G. WODEHOUSE *Something Fresh* vi, Preventing Fate from working off on us any of those gold bricks, coins with strings attached, and unhatched chickens at which Ardent Youth snatches.

Hence **Gold-brick** *v. trans.*, to swindle.

1902 H. L. WILSON *Spenders* xxviii. 328 He'll be gold-bricked if he wears 'em [sc. his whiskers] scrambled that way around this place.

Gold bug. *U.S. slang.* (See GOLD¹ 10.)

1879 *Congress. Rec.* 8 May 1170/2 Fresh raids upon gold bugs will be in regular order. 1886 *Ibid.* 27 Mar. 2846/1 It was before the days of 'gold-bugs' and 'bloated bond-holders'. 1894 *Westm. Gaz.* 3 Dec. 3/1 You had better leave the present occupiers..than encourage the gold-bug who would..exploit the land.

Go·ld-digger. [GOLD¹.]

1. One who digs for gold.

1831 *Deb. Congress* 21 Feb. 770 To remove the gold diggers of every kind and description. 1846 *Ibid.* Ex. doc. 41, p. 449 All along the bottom of the stream and in the heart of the town you see holes scooped out by the gold diggers. 1850 [see GOLD¹ 10]. 1850 W. COLTON *Deck & Port* xiv. 398 But you are not perhaps a gold-digger as I had supposed. 1877 *Harper's Mag.* Dec. 88/2 There was the stream of returning gold-diggers. 1889 K. MUNROE *Golden Days* i. 3 He was better fitted to be a gold-digger than anything else.

2. A girl or woman who attaches herself to a man merely for gain. *U.S. slang.*

1927 *Cleveland Press* 29 Jan. (*headline*), Browning promises to show young bride up as gold digger. 1928 *Observer* 15 Apr. 3/5 Our Daily Chron. 1 Apr. 5/3 Be good and also be a gold digger. 1929 ... Kingman ... with her.

Go·ld-digging. (See GOLD¹ 10, and add) also *U.S. slang* (cf. *GOLD-DIGGER 2). Also phr. *a.*

1927 *Cleveland Press* 29 Jan., The charge of gold-digging is one of the major counts in Browning's case. 1928 *Daily Express* 2 Apr. 6/5 ... 'gold-digging' mother's love affairs without involving her daughter. 1929 *Ibid.* 16 Oct. 10/7 She will go to his house, and (in the American phrase) do a little gold-digging—without, you understand, giving anything in return.

Golden, *a.* Add: **1. b.** *To kill the goose that lays the golden eggs*: see *GOOSE *sb.* 1 d.

2. *Golden State.* (Earlier example.)

1847 *Congress. Rec.* 7 May, App. 246/2 From the hills of the Golden State we will send..cattle of every breed.

10. Golden Bible, the Book of Mormon; **Golden Chersonese,** the Malay Peninsula (ἡ χρυσῆ χερσόνησος); **Golden City** *U.S.*, San Francisco.

a 1847 in H. Howe *Hist. Collect. Ohio* 286 Some months ago I borrowed the *Golden Bible. 1667 MILTON *P. L.* xi. 392 Down to the *golden Chersonese. 1883 ISAB. L. BIRD (*title*) The Golden Chersonese and the way thither. 1871 SCHELE DE VERE *Americanisms* (1872) 665 San Francisco finds compensation..in the high-sounding name, *Golden City, under which it is elsewhere known.

b. golden bell, the genus *Forsythia*; **golden-cup oak** = *golden oak* (a); **golden drop,** the genus *Onosma*, esp. *O. tauricum*; **golden oak** *U.S.* (*a*) the canyon live-oak, *Quercus Chrysolepis*; (*b*) the false foxglove, *Dasystoma virginicum*; **golden pert** (earlier examples); **golden-seal** (earlier examples); **golden-top** *U.S.* (see quot. 1909); **golden willow** = *golden osier*.

1901 W. P. WRIGHT *Dict. Pract. Gard.* I. 349/2 Forsythia. (*Golden Bell.) 1897 B. B. SUDWORTH *Arborescent Flora U.S.* 164 *Quercus chrysolepis*...*Golden-cup Oak (Cal.). 1883 W. ROBINSON *Engl. Fl. Gard.* 199/1 Onosma (*Golden Drop*)..O. tauricum..bears in summer drooping clusters of clear yellow, almond-scented blossoms which have gained for the plant the name of 'Golden Drop'. 1909 *Cent. Dict.* Suppl. s.v. *Live-oak*, An evergreen oak of the Pacific coast,..also called *golden oak, maul oak, and Valparaiso oak. 1928 F. N. HART *Bellamy Trial* i. 2 Nine rows of the golden-oak seats packed with grimly triumphant humanity. 1784 CUTLER in *Mem. Amer. Acad. Arts & Sc.* (1785) I. 403 *Veronica*...*Goldenpert. 1821 W. P. C. BARTON *Flora N. Amer.* I. 71 *Gratiola aurea.* Golden pert. 1851 *Trans. Mich. Agric. Soc.* VI. 179 We have the sarsaparilla, ginsing, *goldenseal, sweet cicily. 1881 MCLEAN *Cape Cod Folks* ii. 38 The golden seal..was served in a diluted state with milk and sugar and taken as a beverage. 1909 *Cent. Dict.* Suppl., *Goldentop, an ornamental grass, *Achyrodes aureum*,..introduced from the Mediterranean region into southern California. 1916 J. B. THOBURN *Hist. Oklahoma* II. 15 The most common wild grass..is the ordinary bunch grass, though bluestem, goldentop and other species are by no means uncommon. 1861 *Trans. Ill. Agric. Soc.* IV. 441 The *Golden Willow has been a favorite with me. 1868 [see WILLOW *sb.* 2 b].

Gold-field. Add examples of attrib. use of the plural. Also **Go·ldfielder,** one who works a gold-field.

1900 *Westm. Gaz.* 12 Mar. 1/2 Taking guarantees that the gold-fields government shall respect the rights of natives. *Ibid.* 23 Oct. 5/3 The gold-fields aspect of the South African problem. 1903 *Ibid.* 28 Jan. 9/1 The coast folk have learned that all the goldfielders were not mere adventurers ready to despoil them at a moment's notice.

Goldilocks. 2. Delete †*Obs.* and add modern examples.

1889 M. WRIGHT in A. Lang *Blue Fairy Bk.* 193 The Story of Pretty Goldilocks. 1930 *Observer* 25 May 15 But why is Mr. Max Montesole in Cassio such a quaint goldilocks?

Go·lding². [f. the surname: see quot. 1798.] A kind of hop. Also *golding hop, vine*.

1798 W. H. MARSHALL *Rur. Econ. S. Counties* I. 183 The 'golding' has, of late years, been in high repute. It is a sub-variety..of the Canterbury; which was raised by a man still living (1790) Mr. Golding, of the Malling quarter of the district [of Maidstone]. 1810 — *Review W. Eng.* 378 There are two [varieties of hops]..in more particular esteem, both with the planter and merchant; the Golding Vine..and the Mathon White. 1900 C. SALTER tr. *E. Gross's Hops* 39 The Goldings are the best class of English red hops. 1902 *Times* 5 Sept. 2/5 The golding hops are reported to be developing slowly.

Goldite (gōu·ldəit). *U.S.* [f. GOLD¹ + -ITE¹. Cf. SILVERITE.] An advocate of a gold standard.

1886 *Congress. Rec.* 24 June 6090/2 It does not frighten me to see Goldites voting to preserve greenbacks. 1896 *Nation* (N.Y.) LXII. 130/2 It is generally assumed that there is a 'goldite' majority in the House. 1896 *Westm. Gaz.* 6 July 3/1 It is probable that the National Committee, which is controlled by Goldites, will select him. 1904 *Ibid.* 27 Oct. 2/3 In some States there were only two sets of electors, these being practically Silverites and Goldites.

Goldless, *a.* Delete *rare* and add examples.

1896 W. RALEIGH *Some Authors, Sir J. Harington* (1923) 246 He belongs, by right of kinship, to the 'threadbare, goldless genealogy' of those who indulge themselves with that most costly dish—speech for its own sake. 1900 *The King* 4 Aug. 135 A goldless gold region.

Gold mine. Add: **b.** *fig.* A source of abundant income or profit.

1882 'THORMANBY' *Famous Racing Men* 81 (Farmer) Mendicant..was destined to prove a gold mine. 1888 FROUDE *Eng. in W. Indies* v. 56 The island was a gold mine to the Assiento Company.

Goldsmith. Add: **2.** (Later example.)

1868 *Amer. Naturalist* II. 189 Each season has furnished me many more Does than Goldsmiths.

3. goldsmith-beetle (earlier examples).

1868 *Amer. Naturalist* II. 186 Among the Beetles of North America very few can bear away the palm for beauty from..the Goldsmith Beetle. 1892 *Ibid.* ... *Rural Agric.* IV. 158 This..goldsmith beetle, is not common enough to do much damage with us.

Hence **Go·ldsmithing** *vbl. sb.* [tr. It. *orefficeria*], the art of a goldsmith.

1898 C. R. ASHBEE (*title*) The Treatises of Benvenuto Cellini on Goldsmithing and Sculpture.

Gold-thread. *U.S.* (See GOLD¹ 10 b.)

1789 MORSE *Amer. Geog.* 53 The gold-thread is of the vine kind, and grows in swamps. 1806, 1830 [see GOLD¹ 10 b]. 1836 D. B. EDWARD *Hist. Texas* ii. 43 Let us look at some of the roots and plants below such as..the gold thread, the devil's-bit [etc.]. 1885 *Outing* (U.S.) Nov. 179/1 The rounded leaves and manner of growth reminded us of the gold-thread we used to find in our youthful rambles. 1890 *Harper's Mag.* Apr. 709/2 There are red and white clover..gold-thread, and violets. 1905 *Springfield Weekly Republican* 19 May 3 In the swamps the goldthread sends its starry greeting to the stars.

Gold-washer. c. *U.S.* (Earlier and later examples.)

1849 T. T. JOHNSON *Sights Gold Region* xvii. 158 We passed on our journey many travellers..all with a gold-washer or gingling-pan of some kind or other. 1889 K. MUNROE *Golden Days* i. 2 On all sides were scattered mining implements, patent gold washers, force pumps [etc.].

Goldy, *a.* Delete '*Obs.* exc. *dial.*', and add modern examples. Define: Gold-like, resembling gold in colour and sheen.

a 1861 T. WINTHROP *John Brent* iii. 33 'I don't think that quartz looks quite so goldy as it did at a distance' said he. 1904 R. BRIDGES *Demeter* 81 Now maids playfully dance o'er enamel'd meadows, And with goldy blossom deck forehead and bosom. 1920 GALSWORTHY *Awakening* 35 There were silver threads in her dark goldy hair.

Golf, *sb.* **b.** Add: **golf-club** (= a society for playing golf: add examples); **golf-croquet,** a form of croquet in which golf strokes are used; **golf-green** = *golf-links*; **golf-links** (examples).

1834 in R. Clark *Golf* (1875) 79 *note*, The Royal and Ancient *Golf Club of St. Andrews. 1890 H. G. HUTCHINSON *Golf* 325 The Royal Liverpool Golf Club. 1920 G. W. DEEPING *Second Youth* xv, To play them at *golf-croquet. 1894 (*title*) *Golf Greens of England and Wales. 1891 H. G. HUTCHINSON (*title*) Famous *Golf Links. 1920 P. G. WODEHOUSE *Damsel in Distress* xv. 174 He seemed to spend all his spare time frolicking with the man on the golf-links.

Hence **Go·lfdom,** the realm of golf. **Go·lfist, Go·lfite,** a golfer, devotee of golf.

1902 *Westm. Gaz.* 21 Mar. 2/3 Tax golfists: What a lot you'll make By fining them each time they swear! 1902 in W. W. Tulloch *Tom Morris* (1907) 290 Tom Morris, King of Golfdom. 1926 *Contemp. Rev.* Nov. 679 Mr. Wodehouse ..pictures..type after type of the creatures that have beset golfdom.

Golgi (gǫ·ldʒi) **appara·tus.** *Cytology.* [Named after the Italian physician Camillo *Golgi*.] An intracellular organ or structure of unknown function surrounding the nucleus. Called also *Golgi bodies, elements, granules, network, rods.*

1919 J. B. GATENBY in *Q. Jrnl. Microsc. Sci.* LXIII. 403 The Golgi rods or grains. *Ibid.* 406 The so-called Golgi apparatus of histologists, known to zoologists as 'Nebenkern' batonettes, chondrioplasts, dictyosomes, etc. *Ibid.* 470 Golgi granules..Golgi elements. 1920 L. DONCASTER *Introd. Cytol.* 23 The so-called 'internal reticular apparatus' of Golgi, often known shortly as the Golgi apparatus. *Ibid.* 24 Golgi network. *Ibid.* 101 Golgi bodies. 1925 E. B. WILSON *Cell* (ed. 3) 50 In many cases the Golgi 'net' is built up from originally separate bodies—lamelliform, rod-like, banana-shaped or the like....These bodies are variously designated as 'batonettes', 'dictyosomes', or Golgi-bodies. 1924 HOGBEN & WINTON *Compar. Physiol.* 197 In the cytoplasm are present granular bodies, of which two sorts are commonly distinguished, namely, the mitochondria and Golgi rods.

Goliath. Add:

2. b. The African giant heron, *Ardea goliath*.

c. A giant frog, *Rana goliath*, found in S. Cameroon.

1906 W. L. SCLATER *Birds S. Africa* IV. 55 Goliath Heron. *Ibid.* 56 The Goliath is found throughout the greater part of Africa.

3. A kind of powerful travelling crane. Also *Goliath crane*.

1888 *Lockwood's Dict. Mech. Engin.* s.v., Goliaths, like travellers, are worked both by hand and by steam power. 1892 E. MARKS *Constr. Cranes* 107 A Goliath supplied to the Government of New South Wales. *Ibid.* 108 The Goliath crane, known also as the Wellington crane. 1892 F. COLYER *Lifting & Pressing Machinery* (ed. 2) 164 'Goliath' Travellers. 1928 *Daily Express* 5 Dec. 13 Floating cranes and land cranes, goliaths and derricks.

Gollop (gǫ·ləp), *v.* *dial.* and *colloq.* Also **gollup.** [? Extended f. GULP, meant to symbolize the sound. But cf. '*Gollop*, a large morsel' (Halliwell).] *trans.* To swallow greedily or hastily.

1881 *Lancs. Gloss.* 1927 in *Brit. Weekly* 14 July 326/4 The Ancient Order of Frothblowers. The 1st Qualification for Membership is that he or she 'should gollop their beer with a zest', three gulps to the pint and 14 to the gallon. 1927 *Observer* 2 Oct. 24 Old dogs..seldom chew, like a young otter, but gollop their bites. 1928 P. G. WODEHOUSE in *Strand Mag.* Dec. 532/1 'Don't gollup your food, Harold', said the second burglar. 1928 'SAPPER' *Female of the Species* i. I saw Captain Drummond engaged in the operation, as he called it, of 'golloping his beer with zest'.

Golly, *int.* orig. *U.S.* (Earlier example.)

1743 *Fitz Argum. agst. Tythes* (De Vere) 'By Golly,' says he, 'he has mauled the parsons'.

Gollywog (gǫ·liwǫg). Also **Golliwogg.** A name invented for a black (male) doll, fantastically dressed, with staring eyes and a shock of fuzzy black hair. Also shortened **Go·lly.**

1895 BERTHA UPTON (*title*) The Adventures of two Dutch Dolls—and a 'Golliwogg'. 1904 *Woman's Life* 7 May 227/1 One of her hobbies is the collecting of those quaint, but unbeautiful, dolls known as Gollywogs. 1925 E. F. NORTON *Fight for Everest, 1924* 104 Every now and then I was struck afresh with the absurdly 'gollywog' appearance of the party.

Golomynka (gǫlǒmi·ŋkă). [ad. Russ. голомянка.] A small, very oily fish, *Comephorus baikalensis*, found in the depths of Lake Baikal.

1924 *Chambers's Jrnl.* Dec. 837/2 The lake [Baikal] contains one of the strangest species of fish yet discovered, the Golomynka.

Gom⁴ (gǫm). *Ireland.* Also **gaum.** [Cf. Ir. *gamal* stupid.] A poor silly fellow.

1834 LOVER *Leg. Irel.* Ser. II. 241 Do you think me sitch a *gom*, all out, as to put me off wid four pence ha'pny. 1837–8 J. KEEGAN *Leg. & Poems* (1907) 114 'By gor, you are no gom,' said Biddy. 1894 E. MCNULTY *Misther O'Ryan* xiv. 150 But, shure, I cudn't kape quiet an' see him standin' there purtindin' to be a gaum. 1928 BYRNE *Destiny Bay* i. § 2. 11 You big, thick-footed, herring-fed Southern gom!

Gomla(h, variant forms of *GUMLAH.

-gon, *suffix.* Add: Also with numeral prefixed, as 16-gon.

1898 tr. *H. Schubert's Math. Ess.* 125 He constructed an inscribed 16-gon.

Gonad. Add: Hence **Gonadial** (gǫnēɪ·diăl), **Gonadic** (gǫnæ·dik) *adjs.*, relating to the gonads. **Gonade·ctomy** [Gr. ἐκτομή excision, with ending assimilated to -TOMY], excision of the gonad or sex-gland.

1902 A. SEDGWICK in *Encycl. Brit.* XXVIII. 138/1 Formation..of gonadial sacs. 1914 GEDDES & THOMSON *Sex* iv. 88 The gonadial glands of internal secretion. 1925 CREW *Anim. Genetics* 194 The operation of gonadectomy (extirpation of the sex-gland). *Ibid.* 198 The animals which were merely castrated failed to develop the secondary gonadic characters which they would presumably have shown otherwise.

Gond (gǫnd). [Hind. (Skr. गोण्ड *gonda* fleshy navel, person having this, Gond).]

1. A member of a Dravidian people, many of them jungle-dwellers, of the Central provinces of India. Also *attrib.*

The native name is *koitor*.

1810 MOXON in G. Smith *S. Hislop* (1888) 38 The Gonds.. live mostly in the hills and jungles. 1854 S. HISLOP *Ibid.* 167 We found the inhabitants to consist of Gonds and Dheds. 1855 *Ibid.* 169 The Gond Raja of Dewagad. 1867 W. D. WHITNEY *Lang. & Study Lang.* ix. 327 The wild Gonds and Khonds of the hilly country of Gondwana. 1924 *Blackw. Mag.* Apr. 545/1 Several Gond women washing clothes. 1925 *Ibid.* Jan. 64/1 The Gond nowadays is becoming civilised and Hinduised.

2. = *GONDI.

1856 R. CALDWELL *Compar. Gramm. Dravidian* 8 The Gōnd or Goand. *Ibid.* 9 The people by whom the Gond and the Ku are spoken.

Gondi (gǫ·ndī). [Hind., f. prec.] The native (Dravidian) language of the Gonds.

The native name is *koiydu*.

1855 S. HISLOP in G. Smith *Life* (1888) 168 Inquired about the Gondi. 1875 R. CALDWELL *Gramm. Dravidian Langs.* (ed. 2) 513 A translation of the Gospels of St. Matthew and St. Mark into Gōndi by the Rev. J. Dawson. 1888 G. SMITH *S. Hislop* iii. 62 Gondi was the tongue of the aborigines in the uplands.

Gondite (gǫ·ndəit). *Geol.* [f. *GOND + -ITE¹.] The name given by Fermor to an Indian rock composed of manganiferous garnet and quartz. *Gondite series*, a series of manganiferous metamorphic rocks belonging to the Dharwar system of the Central Provinces.

1909 L. LEIGH FERMOR *Manganese-Ore Deposits of India* in *Mem. Geol. Survey India* XXXVII. 337 The commonest and most characteristic member of the gondite series, and consequently the one to which the name *gondite* has been given, is one made up of a mixture of manganese-garnet and quartz. 1919 D. N. WADIA *Geol. India* 53, 66.

Gondola. Add: **3.** *U.S.* (Earlier example.)

1767 *Boston Gaz.* 21 Sept. (Th.) Wanted, a sett of good Hands, to load and tend on a Gundalo.

4. *U.S.* (Earlier and later examples.)

1871 SCHELE DE VERE *Americanisms* (1872) 480 *Gondola*. ..The use of the word for a peculiarly shaped railroad-car is not unknown in England. 1906 *Westm. Gaz.* 31 Dec. 7/3 The Central News New York correspondent says..When the driver pulled up a heavy 'gondola', or low goods wagon, it broke loose from the adjacent siding. 1922 TITUS *Timber* iii. 37 Two Indians were loading pulp wood into a gondola on the siding.

b. An elongated car attached to the under side of a dirigible balloon or airship. (G., Du. *gondel*.)

1914 *Evening News* 15 Oct. 1/6 The distance between the gondola carrying the engines and the body of the airship has been very much reduced. 1914 F. T. JANE *All World's Air-craft* 10. 1918 W. E. DOMMETT *Dict. Aircraft* 12. 1930 G. G. JACKSON *World's Aeroplanes* 17 Each ship was given four propellers,..and these were driven by ...

Gondwana (gǫndwā·nă). *Geol.* [Skr. *gondavana*, f. *gonda* *GOND + *vana* forest.] The name given to a great system of Indian rocks, chiefly sandstone and shales, of fluviatile origin, classified into Lower, Middle, and Upper. Also *pl.* short for *Gondwana formation, system, bed, rock*, etc.

1879 MEDLICOTT & BLANFORD *Geol. India* Introd. p. xxviii. The Gondwána beds are distributed in large basins. *Ibid.* xxxii, The plants of the Lower Gondwánas consist of acrogens and gymnogens. 1919 D. N. WADIA *Geol. India* 133 The soil yielded by the weathering of the Upper Gondwanas, as of nearly all Gondwana rocks, is a sandy shallow soil.

Gondwanaland (gǫndwā·nălænd). *Geol.* [f. *GONDWANA + LAND *sb.*] The name given by Suess to a vast continental area of the Mesozoic period, of which remnants are preserved in the Peninsula of India, Australia, S. Africa, and S. America.

1896 W. T. BLANFORD in *Rec. Geol. Survey India* XXIX. 52 The southern continent, of which India formed part, and which is widely known by an Indian name, the Gondwana-land of Suess. 1904 HERTHA SOLLAS tr. *Suess's Face of Earth* I. 596 We call this mass Gondwána-Land, after the ancient Gondwána flora which is common to all its parts. 1919 D. N. WADIA *Geol. India* 204 It was in the early Tertiary, or the end of the Cretaceous, that Gondwanaland, the most prominent feature of the earth's Mesozoic geography, finally broke up, and the Peninsula of India acquired its present restricted form.

Gone, *ppl. a.* Add: **3. b.** With adj. complement, as *gone-soft* (= unstrung). (See GO *v.* 44 a.)

1925 A. S. M. HUTCHINSON *One Increasing Purpose* III. xv, Not a fit man..but a gone-soft and nerve-wracked man.

Goner. *slang.* (See under GONE *ppl. a.*; earlier and later examples.)

1847 DOW, JR. *Patent Serm.* I. 32 (Th.) The old year is not quite a goner. 1854 MARY J. HOLMES *Tempest & Sunshine* v. 211 I'd soon give you up as a goner. 1902 S. E. WHITE *Blazed Trail* xxxvi. 243, I have given notes. When they come due, I'm a goner. 1904 *Omaha Bee* 7 July 4 If he does not win on the second ballot he is a goner. 1930 BAGMAN *Little Flutter* xiii. 153 If it failed he was—if one may be permitted the word in the excitement of the moment—'a goner'.

Gongora (gǫ·ŋgŏră). [mod.L., named after Don Antonio Caballero y *Gongora*, viceroy of New Granada (Colombia).] A plant or flower of the genus of tropical American orchids so named.

1871 B. S. WILLIAMS *Orchid-Grower's Man.* (ed. 4) 183 In the earlier days of Orchid culture one often met with specimens of *Gongoras*, but latterly they seem to have become quite a neglected race. 1910 C. H. CURTIS *Orchids* 188 The Gongoras have a quaintness that is attractive, but the species are of little value except as curiosities.

Gonimoblast (gǫ·nimŏblæst). *Bot.* [f. Gr. γόνιμος productive + -BLAST.] In the Red Algæ (see quot.).

1898 tr. *Strasburger's Text-bk. Bot.* 337 The fertilised egg does not become converted directly into an oospore, but, as a result of fertilisation, numerous branching filaments termed gonimoblasts grow out from the sides of the ventral portion of the carpogonium.

Goniometer. Add:

2. *Radiotelegraphy.* Orig. *radiogoniometer*: A direction-finding apparatus (see quots.).

[1910 *Sci. Amer.* 15 Oct. 299 The Bellini-Tosi radiogoniometer....With this apparatus..it is possible to determine within one or two degrees the direction of a wireless station from which signals are received. 1926 S. O. PEARSON *Dict. Wireless Terms* 62 The two aerials are connected to an instrument called a *radiogoniometer*, which consists of two coils fixed mutually at right angles and a third coil rotatable within the fixed ones.] 1928 G. E. STERLING *Radio Man.* 507 A goniometer, or mutual inductance device, for orienting the course in any desired direction without moving the antennas. 1929 A. F. COLLINS *Aviation* 225.

Gonna (gǫ·nə), dial. (esp. U.S.) or vulgar pronunciation of *going to* (see GO *v.* 47 b).

[Cf. the earlier Sc. *ganna, gaunna*: see Eng. Dial. Dict. s.v. *Go*, quots. 1806, etc.]

1913 MULFORD *Coming of Cassidy* ix. 149 Yo're gonna get a good lickin'. 1929 E. W. SPRINGS *Above Bright Blue Sky* 136, 5684 has a busted cylinder. Gonna put a new one in it.

Gonomere (gǫ·nŏmīəɹ). *Cytology.* [f. GONO- + Gr. μέρος part.] Each of the pronuclei, male and female, of a fertilized ovum considered as persisting components of the nuclei of the cells which arise by cleavage. Hence **Gonome·ric** *a.*, pertaining to gonomeres. **Gonomery** (gǫnǫ·mĕri), division or separate existence of gamete nuclei.

1903 *Amer. Naturalist* July 503 These nuclear halves he [sc. Häcker] designates 'Gonomeres' while the vesicles formed from individual chromosomes (chromosomal vesicles) he calls 'Idiomeres'. 1920 W. E. AGAR *Cytol.* 78 In the germ-track..evidences of gonomery can be found at a much later stage of development than in the somatic cells. *Ibid.*, In the prophase each gonomere forms its chromosomes separately from the other. 1925 E. B. WILSON *Cell* (ed. 3) 433 Out of these observations grew the conception of gonomery, i.e. that the maternal and paternal chromosomes might remain in separate groups throughout life, even though included in a common nuclear membrane. *Ibid.*, Gonomeric groups.

Gony. 2. (Earlier example.)

1839 *Knickerbocker Mag.* XIII. 386 May the 'Goneys' eat me, if he [sc. the whale] dodges us this time.

Goo (gū). *U.S. slang.* [Of obscure origin.] A viscid or sticky substance.

1911 E. FERBER *Dawn O'Hara* iii. 31 You mean to tell me that you woke me..to make me drink that goo?..I'll be sick in a minute.

Goober. *U.S.* (Earlier examples.)

1833 *Rep. U.S. Comm. Patents* (1854) 180 The ground pea of the south, or as it is sometimes called, the goober. 1871 SCHELE DE VERE *Americanisms* (1872) 58 The peanut or earthnut..is called ground-pea or goober..and the adjoining States as Goober peas, so that during the late Civil War a conscript from the so-called 'piney woods' of that State was apt to be nick-named a Goober. 1884 A. E. SWEET & J. A. KNOX *On Mexican Mustang thr. Texas* iii. 45 'Rooster dogs,' says I: 'we use them for hunting tarantulas, and for harvesting goober peas.'

b. *Goober-grabbler* (also simply *Goober*), a Georgian or North Carolinan.

1863 BOUDRYE *Fifth N. Y. Cavalry* (1868) 339 Conscripts ..from Mississippi state and 'Goobers' from Tar river. 1869 *Overland Monthly* III. 129 A Georgian is popularly known in the South as a 'Gouber-grabbler'. 1871 [see above].

Good, *a.*, etc. Add: **A.** *adj.* **1. d.** In mod. use freq. as an intensive with *money*.

1889 *Kansas Times & Star* 22 May, Mr. Hammerslough is putting a lot of good money into it.

f. *Good theatre*: said of a play, situation, dialogue, etc. that is effective on the stage.

1928 *Observer* 11 Mar. 15/2 This is an excellent example of what we mean when we say that a play is 'good theatre'. 1928 *Daily Tel.* 15 May 14/5 The play..is, to use the modern phrase, 'very good theatre'.

g. *That's a good 'un*: used ironically to characterize a statement that is incredibly mendacious or absurdly exaggerated. (Cf. 'I like that'.) *slang.*

1813 PAULDING *J. Bull & Br. Jonathan* v. 26 Now this was a good one, for every body knew [etc.]. 1869 *Punch* 30 Jan. 44 Medical-Attendance, Two-an'-Six! Well, that's a good 'un! Why, I attended on 'im. 1914 *Concise Oxf. Dict.* Addenda s.v., *That's a good 'un* (slang), what a lie. 1920 C. SANDBURG *Smoke & Steel* 45 That's a good one.

h. In the colloq. U.S. phrase *looks* or *listens good* = looks or sounds promising.

1911 R. D. SAUNDERS *Col. Todhunter* iii. 43 It looks good to me, suh. 1916 H. L. WILSON *Somewhere in Red Gap* vi. 252 That listens good to her till she finds she has to give fifty-two dollars for the deck first. 1921 R. D. PAINE *Comr. Rolling Ocean* xii. 215 'Thanks, you look good to us', yelled Judson.

2. c. Also *Your* (*his*) *good lady*, your (his) wife (see LADY *sb.* 7). *Your good self* (or *selves*), a commercial form of polite address or reference.

1923 *Daily Mail* 20 Feb. 3 It is more than probable our next orders will be placed with your good-selves. 1931 *Ch. Times* 8 May 569/3 The kindness and consideration shown by your good self to me.

3. c. *To feel good*: to feel oneself to be in good spirits or health. *U.S. colloq.*

1888 *Texas Siftings* 15 Sept. (Farmer) The saloons are going Saturday afternoons, and the men feel pretty good before they come abroad. 1904 *N. Y. Evening Post* 23 June 3 The Captain himself said, 'I feel good', but he did not look well.

4. d. *Good for you* (*him*, etc.)! : a colloquial expression of approval of something said or done by the person addressed or spoken of.

1924 D. H. LAWRENCE *England, my Eng.* 129 'And did she take it in?' he asked. 'As much as she took anything else.' He stood grinning fixedly. Then he broke into a short laugh. 'Good for *her!*' he exclaimed cryptically. 1925 'DORNFORD YATES' *As Other Men are* 111 'Good for you', she said. 'You've put it uncommonly well.'

9. b. *Be good*, as a jocular exhortation to good behaviour.

1908 S. E. WHITE *Riverman* iii. 29 Well, good-bye, boys... Be good!

13. *A good Press*, a favourable reception in newspapers and journals.

1928 *Observer* 22 Jan. 14/6 The new Measure has not, upon the whole, such a 'good Press' as that which the House of Commons rejected in December. 1928 *Daily Tel.* 14 Feb. 10/3 Mr. Amery..has had a very good Press wherever he has gone. 1928 *Sunday Dispatch* 8 July 22/7 A considerable time has passed since a Scotch boxer received such a good Press in the South.

16. b. *Good for*, (*c*) capable of producing; valid for, etc. orig. *U.S.*

1873 J. H. BEADLE *Undevel. West* xviii. 337 From thirty to forty tons of ore.., good for an average profit of a hundred and fifty dollars per ton. 1901 S. MERWIN & H. K. WEBSTER *Calumet K* vi. 104 'How's it coming out?' he asked. 'Do we know how much we're good for?' 1903 *N. Y. Tribune* 20 Sept., A 50-cent combination ticket good for every amusement on the island.

19. freq. in *a good way* (dial. and U.S. *ways*), a considerable distance. Also *transf.* of time.

1551, 1662 [see WAY *sb.*¹ 8]. 1588, 1594 [WAY *sb.*¹ 23 c]. 1824 P. HORRY *Life of Marion* (1841) 111 Yes, by jing, does he live a good way up! 1862 O. W. NORTON *Army Lett.* 125 That day may be a good way off but still I do not get homesick in the least. 1864 T. L. NICHOLS *Forty Yrs. Amer. Life* I. 250 It's a good way, and you will be out late.

22. Make good. i. To succeed; to achieve success; to satisfy expectations; to fulfil a promise or obligation. orig. *U.S.*

1901 S. MERWIN & H. K. WEBSTER *Calumet K* ii. 20 It'll play the devil with us if we can't make good. 1908 G. H. LORIMER *J. Spurlock* v. 89, I need work and I need it quick. Give me a show and I'll make good. 1909 H. G. WELLS *Tono-Bungay* III. i. 214 They couldn't for a moment 'make good' if the quarter of what they guarantee was demanded of them. 1910 W. M. RAINE *B. O'Connor* 55 All I ask of you is to make good. 1914 GERTRUDE ATHERTON *Perch of Devil* I. 58 Ability and talent make good as always. 1927 *Daily Tel.* 7 Mar. 2 The board consider that the company will now make good.

j. *Poker.* (See quots.)

1882 *Poker; how to play it* 8 When all who wish to play have gone in, the person putting up the ante..can play like the others who have gone in, by 'making good',—that is putting up in addition to the ante as much more as will make him equal in stake to the rest. 1895 'TEMPLAR' *Poker Manual* 4 If he determines to play on, he 'makes good', as the expression is; that is, he adds to his ante as much as will make his total stake equal to that of each of the other players. 1904 R. F. FOSTER *Pract. Poker* 232 Make Good.—Adding enough to the blind or straddle to make it equal to the ante. ... To add sufficient to an ante or bet to meet a raise.

B. *adv.* **a.** Well, properly. Now *U.S.*

1834 CROCKETT *Narr. Life* xii. 86, I...shot him [*sc.* a bear] the third time, which killed him good. 1838 CAROLINE GILMAN *Recoll. Southern Matron* 32 We will behave. We will behave good. 1840 *Southern Lit. Messenger* VI. 386/1 She used to tap her with it on the hands, when she behaved bad, or did not say her lesson good. 1859 BARTLETT *Dict. Amer.* (ed. 2) s.v., English travellers have repeatedly noticed the adverbial use of this word. 'He cannot read good.' 'It does not shoot good.' 1865 in Morison *Hist. U. S.* (1927) II. 318 Columbia!—pretty much all burned; and burned *good*. 1885 W. L. ALDEN *Adv. Jimmy Brown* 90 The bee..lit on Tom's hand and stung him good. 1901 S. E. WHITE *Westerners* xv. 113 He'd have trimmed th' little cuss good. 1904 HARBEN *Georgians* 119, I stayed all day an' looked about good before I traded.

d. *Good and*, as an intensive. *U.S. colloq.*

[1834 C. A. DAVIS *Lett. J. Downing* 6 Don't forgit my face, and the Gineral's face; and let the likenesses be good and natural.] 1889 *Kansas Times & Star* 18 Mar., The shamrock doubtless will be wet often, and the tyrannical lion's tail twisted good and plenty. 1896 G. ADE *Artie* xvi. 146, I was good and sore. 1901 S. MERWIN & H. K. WEBSTER *Calumet K* i. 14 We got the letter the same day the red-headed man came here. His hair was good and red. 1921 R. D. PAINE *Comr. Rolling Ocean* iv. 57 I'll roll out there when I get good and ready. 1926 *Publishers' Weekly* 15 May 1593 That made me good and provoked.

C. *sb.* **8. c.** *goods guard, lift, set, yard*.

1902 *Daily Chron.* 5 Feb. 3/4 Every shunter, and..every *goods guard. 1909 *Westm. Gaz.* 3 Apr. 2/1 Goods guards, platelayers, and signalmen. *Ibid.* 1 Apr. 8/3 He got into the *goods lift with some fifteen other men. 1927 W. E. COLLINSON *Contemporary Engl.* 8 *Goods sets i.e. a set of goods trucks. 1900 *Westm. Gaz.* 20 Jan. 8/3 The dreary *goods-yard which does duty for the entraining station of war-bound troops. 1904 *Ibid.* 27 Feb. 8/2 It must be recognised..that the streets are too valuable and too expensive to be used by private persons as their goods-yards.

D. *Comb.* **1. a.** *good-class*.

1901 *Daily Chron.* 2 Sept. 8/2 Good-class rudd have also been secured in this river. 1909 *Westm. Gaz.* 13 Jan. 12/2 A club..which has a number of good-class players. 1925 E. F. NORTON *Fight for Everest, 1924* 39 He must be a good-class man of some intelligence.

b. *good-intentioned, -mannered*.

Some of these combinations have parallel forms with *well*: e.g. *well-conditioned, -intentioned, -mannered*.

1905 H. G. WELLS *Kipps* II. i. 165 That sinister passion for pedagogy to which the *Good-Intentioned are so fatally liable. 1907 *Daily Chron.* 6 Mar. 3/2 It is all very nice and sentimental, and good intentioned. 1906 *Macm. Mag.* July 695 The librarian, a functionary whom he desired good-looking, good-natured, *good-mannered, and ready of speech.

c. *good-going* (suggested by *easy-going*), *-living, -selling*.

1927 J. ADAMS *Errors in School* iii. 69 If we find that three metals that we have tested all expand when heated, we jump to the easy-going conclusion that all metals expand when heated—which is a *good-going error. 1903 *Westm. Gaz.* 2 Nov. 9/2 The city had a population of ten thousand, all *good-living people. 1909 *Ibid.* 1 Mar. 1/3 A most respectable and good-living man. 1908 *Daily Chron.* 10 Jan. 3/3 Ordinarily 'Edwin Drood' is one of the least '*good-selling' novels of Charles Dickens.

3. good-enough (earlier Sc. and U.S. quots.).

1570 R. BANNATYNE *Mem.* 33 This was a guid aneuch obligatioune that the castle shuld be thair friend. 1618 *Haddington Corr.* 135 Your lordships memorie is good aneuche. 1647 *Stirling Chart. & Corr.* 485 The daik [= dyke] is in good aniogh order. 1856 *Congress. Globe* 53 You will have victims who can answer as 'good enough Morgans' at least until after the election. [See Bartlett *Dict. Amer.*, 1860, s.v. *Morgan*.]

Goo·d-loo·ker. Chiefly *U.S.* [Cf. GOOD-LOOKING *a.*, GOOD LOOKS.] One who has good looks.

1894 *Harper's Mag.* Mar. 498 She's a good-looker.. although they say she's gone off a little lately. 1902 WISTER *Virginian* ii. 26 'She's a good-looker' Hm! Yes, the kind of good looks I'd sooner see in another man's wife than mine. 1920 *Blackw. Mag.* June 786/2 He was a 'goodlooker', tall, blond, gentle-spoken. 1928 *Daily Tel.* 29 May 14/2 Felstead [a horse]..is quite a good looker and is well bred. 1929 PETT RIDGE *Affect. Regards, Oh Solitude* 121 There's a lady coming along...A good looker, if ever there was one.

Goodman. Add: **5.** [After Sp. *hombre bueno*.] An arbitrator. *U.S.*

1836 D. B. EDWARD *Hist. Texas* vii. 161 They shall adopt for a definite resolution the opinion most favorable to the defendant between the Alcaldes and the good-man of the plaintiff.

Goods (gudz), *sb. pl.* Chiefly or orig. *U.S. colloq.* [See GOOD *sb.* 8.]

1. Phr. **a.** *To deliver the goods*: to supply the objects contracted for; hence, to perform the contract undertaken; to do what one has undertaken to do; to supply what has been promised or is expected; hence, to come up to requirements or expectations.

[1781 BURGOYNE *Ld. Manor* III. iii, *Sir John.* Hussy! how came you by all that money? *Peggy.* Perfectly honestly —I sold my mistress and myself for it—it is not necessary to deliver the goods, for his honour is provided with a mistress.] 1879 *Congress. Rec.* 4 Apr. 236/1 There are men in the North who walk around..saying; 'See me,..I will take you to victory.' They cannot deliver the goods. 1880 *Ibid.* 25 May 3758/1, 'I will pledge every vote on our side of the chamber' .. 'You cannot deliver the goods'. 1901 S. MERWIN & H. K. WEBSTER *Calumet K* xi. 198, I told him that..when we paid blackmail it would be to some fellow who'd deliver the goods. 1904 F. LYNDE *Grafters* viii. 120 Of the three justices, one of them was elected on our ticket; another is a personal friend of Judge MacFarlane. The goods will be delivered. 1909 *London Mag.* XXII. 631/1 The New Force Man had delivered the goods as per promise. 1909 H. G. WELLS *War in Air* iv. § 5 As yet he was only in the beginning of the adventure. He had still to deliver the goods and draw the cash. 1911 R. W. CHAMBERS *Common Law* ii. 45 'She certainly is a looker', nodded Annan. 'She can deliver the cultivated goods, too.' 1919 *Economist* 12 July 44/1 To win a few votes at an election a Cabinet Minister declares it to be the policy of the Government to nationalise the railways. He is duly elected, and those who are in favour of nationalisation ask him and his colleagues to deliver the goods. 1922 DK. DEVONSHIRE in *Parlt. Deb., Ho. Lords* 4 Dec. LII. 233, I am convinced that the Irish Government intend..to deliver the goods..in the true spirit of the Act. 1923 SIR J. SIMON in *Parlt. Deb., Ho. Comm.* 16 July CLXVI. 1903 When one is asked to draw up a balance-sheet and to see whether the existing system can 'deliver the goods'.

b. *The goods*: what is supplied or provided; what is expected or required (for a purpose expressed or implied); the real thing; the genuine article.

1812 *Norfolk* (Va.) *Herald* 29 May 314 Federalists call the troops now raising 'a standing army'. They are mistaken in the goods. 1881 A. A. HAYES *New Colorado* vii. 103 When the mariner heard an expert, who was chipping away at the wall with a little hammer, remark, 'That's good goods', this purist stopped both ears. 1904 *Cosmopolitan* May 122 'I'll agree to make it 25 [dollars] at the end of 60 days if you are the goods', said the editor. *a* 1910 'O. HENRY' *Rolling Stones* 240 Take it from me—he's got the goods. 1912 MATHEWSON *Pitching in a Pinch* ii. 33 Now O'Toole is all right if he has the pitching goods. 1918 E. M. ROBERTS *Flying Fighter* 35 Some of the road pickets would want to see our identification papers as dispatch riders, and being unable to produce the goods we were often turned back. 1919 T. K. HOLMES *Man fr. Tall Timber* xvi. 196 Believe me! this Gypsy is all the goods and then some.

2. *The goods*: the stolen articles found on the person of a thief; unmistakable evidence or proof positive of guilt; chiefly in phr., e.g. *to catch with the goods*.

1911 *N. Y. Even. Post* 15 June (Th.) 'We've got you..now, and you're going to yield the stolen goods.' The goods in question were the office of Commissioner of Jurors [etc.]. 1919 *Detective Story Mag.* XXVIII. Nov. 50 Detective Craddock had informed Thubway Tham that, sooner or later, he was going to 'catch him with the goods'. 1921 R. D. PAINE *Comr. Rolling Ocean* xiv. 245 You have caught me with the goods, Wyman. It was my way of getting a slant on you.

b. *To have* or *have got the goods on*: to have the advantage of or superiority over; to have knowledge or information giving one a hold over (another).

1923 'B. M. BOWER' *Parowan Bonanza* xxiii. 270 Bill had a happy half-hour, thinking that he had 'got the goods' on Rayfield and Emmett. 1924 W. M. RAINE *Troubled Waters* xxii. 233 They had the goods on us. We were going to hang—every one of us. 1928 *Observer* 15 July 18/2 'Well, the Old Country sure has the goods on everyone else', said one of them [*sc.* Canadian teachers].

Goody, *sb.*¹ **2.** *U.S.* (Later examples.)

1893 W. K. POST *Harvard Stories* 79 There are many individuals that make up the university population of Cambridge—unofficial members. There are the..goodies. 1902 J. CORBIN *American at Oxford* 12 The scout is in effect a porter, 'goody', and eating-club waiter rolled into one.

Goody (gu·di), *int.* *U.S.* [f. GOOD *a.* + -Y⁶. Cf. *LORDY *int.*] A childish exclamation denoting delight or satisfaction.

1853 B. F. TAYLOR *Jan. & June* (1871) 125 Port's tongue [being] busy the while with..'may I go?' and 'goody! goody!' to a provisional affirmative. 1890 *Harper's Mag.* Mar. 608/1 You're coming home with us?..Yes? Oh, goody! You'll come? 1898 P. L. FORD *Hon. Peter Stirling* 244 'That makes five', said Peter. 'Oh, goody!' said Leonore, 'I mean', she said, correcting herself, 'that that is very kind of you'.

Goodyera (gudyī°·ră, gu·dyərə). [mod.L., named after the botanist John *Goodyer*.] A plant or flower of the genus of small terrestrial orchids so named.

[1821 S. F. GRAY *Nat. Arr. Brit. Plants* II. 208 Creeping goodyer.] 1829 LOUDON *Encycl. Plants* (1839) 754. 1868 B. S. WILLIAMS *Orchid-Grower's Man.* (ed. 3) 142 The dark foliage of the *Goodyeras*. 1921 *Glasgow Herald* 16 July 4 That interesting little orchid called goodyera.

Gooey, *a.* *U.S. slang.* [f. *GOO *sb.* + -EY = -Y¹.] Of a viscid or sticky nature.

1923 H. L. FOSTER *Beachcomber in Orient* i. 9 She..extracted a gooey substance from a tube of tinfoil and smeared it with a stick upon the bowls.

Goof (gūf). *slang.* [app. a use of dial. *goof*, GOFF².] A silly, stupid, or 'daft' person. Hence **Goo·fy** *a.*, stupid, silly.

1923 P. G. WODEHOUSE *Inimit. Jeeves* xvii. 232 He was lying back in an arm-chair with his mouth open and a sort of goofy expression in his eyes. 1925 C. R. COOPER *Lions 'n Tigers* iv. 99 The most idiotic, dunce-like goof that ever struggled about on four legs. 1928 *Daily Express* 26 Sept. 13, 'I have gone completely goofy over Mr. Robey,'..writes one Montreal critic. 1930 IAN HAY & S. KING-HALL *Middle Watch* xviii, Have you stopped to think what is happening to that poor old goof in the day-cabin, right now? 1931 *Observer* 11 Oct. 15 The 'sap' gone 'goofy'.

Google (gū·g'l), *v.* *Cricket.* [Back-formation from *GOOGLY.] *intr.* Of the ball: To have a 'googly' break and swerve. Of the bowler: To bowl a googly or googlies. Hence **Goo·gler,** a googly bowler.

1907 *Badminton Mag.* Sept. 289 The googlies that do not

google. 1909 *Westm. Gaz.* 5 July 7/4 Mr. Lockhart, having 'googled' to no purpose from the 'nursery' end. 1923 *Daily Mail* 9 July 11 In R. H. Bettington they have a googler who might triumph over the best of wickets. 1928 *Daily Tel.* 12 June 19/2 Constantine..was out to a semi-yorker, which also 'googled'. 1930 *Ibid.* 25 Apr. 8/5 Grimmett..can spin the ball and google it.

Googly (gū·gli), *sb.* *Cricket.* Also **googlie.** [?] A ball which breaks from the off, though bowled with apparent leg-break action.

1904 P. F. WARNER *How we recovered Ashes* 106 Bosanquet ..can bowl as badly as anyone in the world, but, when he gets a length, those slow 'googlies', as the Australian papers call them, are apt to paralyse the greatest players. 1909 P. A. VAILE in *Westm. Gaz.* 17 Sept. 14/2 The 'googly' is merely the American service at lawn-tennis introduced into cricket. 1924 N. CARDUS *Days in the Sun* 48 Hirst cultivated the swerve and Bosanquet the 'googly'.

b. *attrib.* or as *adj.*, esp. in *googly bowler, bowling*.

1909 *Westm. Gaz.* 12 June 16/1 The discovery of so capable a 'googlie' bowler as Mr. Lockhart. *Ibid.* 17 Sept. 14/2 One 'googly'-man does not necessarily win Tests. 1911 P. F. WARNER *Bk. Cricket* iii. 62 Mr. Bosanquet has been called the 'Googlie King'. 1921 A. W. MYERS *Twenty Years Lawn Tennis* 9 Fifteen years ago, Brookes mainly employed a 'googly' service. 1924 N. CARDUS *Days in the Sun* 80 Tyldesley..was also one of the first batsmen to master the new 'googly' bowling.

Googly (gū·gli), *a.* Also **-ey.** [Cf. next.]

1. Of eyes: Staring without expression. Hence **Goo·gly-eyed** *a.*

1926 *Spectator* 21 Aug. 287/2 A golliwog hugging in its hideous embrace a googley-eyed Dutch doll. 1927 *Daily Mirror* 10 Dec. 16/1 Others with movable googly eyes in a hand-painted face. 1928 *Daily Express* 20 June 13/6 Strange, googly-eyed goldfish.

2. Disposed to love-making, 'spoony'.

1929 G. W. DEEPING *Roper's Row* x. § 3 She ascribed Mr. George's googly, amorous interest to fatherliness.

Goo-goo (gū·gū), *a.* *slang.* Of the eyes or glances: Amorous, 'spoony'. Also *sb.*, an amorous glance, a 'glad eye'.

1906 N. MUNRO *Daft Days* ix, They made goo-goo-eyes at me when I said the least thing. 1906 *Westm. Gaz.* 22 Sept. 5/2, I don't go round making goo-goo eyes for roses, anyway. 1924 C. HAMILTON *Prisoners of Hope* 101 The women..fling a goo-goo at the band.

Goop (gūp). *slang.* [Cf. *GOOF.] A stupid or fatuous person. Hence **Goo·py** *a.*, fatuous, *esp.* fatuously amorous or 'spoony'.

[1900 G. BURGESS (*title*) Goops, and how to be them, Manual of Manners for Polite Infants, inculcating many Juvenile Virtues, both by Precept and Example.] 1918 *Story-Teller* Feb. 695/2 You rabbit-faced goop! 1925 N. VENNER *Imperfect Impostor* i, Go on, it's a bargain. I'll be the poor goop of this piece. 1926 *Chambers's Jrnl.* Dec. 770/1 The baggage always affects strangers like that... Makes 'em frightfully goopy till they discover her for the cockatrice she is. 1929 'A. BERKELEY' *Wychford Poisoning Case* xx. 250 Oh, ass, dolt, fool, goop and mutt!

Goose, *sb.* Add: **1. d.** (*A*) *gone goose* (see GONE *ppl. a.* 1). *U.S.*

1830 *Massachusetts Spy* 7 July (Th.) You are a gone goose, friend. 1834 C. A. DAVIS *Lett. J. Downing* 26 You must get 'em afore the governor makes his appintments, or it 'll be gone goose with us. 1843 HALIBURTON *Sam Slick in Eng.* xvii. II. 29 You must be up and doin', Sam, or it's gone goose with you.

(*b*) *To kill the goose that laid* or *lays the golden eggs*: to destroy a source of one's wealth by one's own heedless action; to sacrifice future advantage to the greed of the moment. [From the Æsopic fable of the woman who killed for food her goose that laid eggs of gold; Gr. χὴν χρυσοτόκος.]

1887 W. E. NORRIS *Major & Minor* v, If Brian had only known how immensely he had risen in her respect by the not very extraordinary display of talent and ability which he had just made, he would doubtless have hastened to kill the goose that laid the golden eggs by playing classical compositions till he wearied her. 1913 J. H. LONGFORD *Evol. New Japan* vii. 88 The Japanese farmer had killed the geese that laid the golden eggs [*viz.* by exporting his silkworm eggs to Europe instead of producing silk himself]. 1916 GALSWORTHY *Five Tales, A Stoic* (1927) 77 You're getting a thousand a year out of my fees. Mistake to kill the goose that lays the golden eggs. I'll make it twelve hundred. 1921 T. R. ST.-JOHNSTON *Islanders of Pacific* 295 Even an insouciant native hesitates to kill the goose that lays his 'golden eggs', for the tapping of the crown is generally fatal to the palm-tree.

7. a. *goose-breast*.

1891 W. MORRIS in Mackail *Life* (1899) II. 261 Goose-breast colour. 1904 *Daily Chron.* 19 Mar. 8/5 Smoked goose-breasts.

8. goose-shot (later U.S. examples); **goose-trap,** also *U.S.*, a swindle; **goose-yoke** *U.S.*, a yoke to hamper the movements of a goose.

1761 *Essex Inst. Hist. Coll.* XLVIII. 96 To be sold by George Deblois..bird, pigeon, duck, and *goose shot. 1789 *Amer. Museum* V. 580 A major...received a wound in the cheek with a goose shot. 1799 *Aurora* (Philad.) 31 Jan. (Th.) The gulls and *goose-traps that have been sported for some time past all come from the shop in which the Washington Lottery wheels remain undrawn, and where a new goose-trap, the Amuskeag canal, was some time since hammered out. 1842 CAROLINE M. KIRKLAND *Forest Life* I. 120 A variety store, offering for sale every possible article of merchandize, from lace gloves to *goose-yokes, ox-chains [etc.]. 1863 'E. KIRKE' *My Southern Friends* iii. 48 One half of it [*sc.* the building] was sparsely occupied with..fishhooks, log chains, goose yokes, etc. 1879 B. F. TAYLOR *Summer-Savory* xvii. 138 And you find it, the variety store of a hundred years ago, where needles and crowbars, goose yokes and finger-rings, liquorice-stick and leather are to be had for cash or 'dicker'. 1896 J. C. HARRIS *Sister Jane* 2/3 Go show your grandmother how to make a goose-yoke.

Gooseberry. 4. Add: Also applied jocularly to inferior or spurious brands of champagne.

1821 LAMB *Elia* Ser. I. *All Fools' Day*, Fill us a cup of that sparkling gooseberry—we will drink no wise, melancholic port on this day. 1850 THACKERAY *Pendennis* iv, Pen could not but respect Foker's connoisseurship as he pronounced the champagne to be condemned gooseberry. 1893 K. DEIGHTON *Lamb's Ess. Elia* 130 Whether used literally of gooseberry wine, or of champagne, inferior brands of which wine are often spoken of contemptuously as 'gooseberry' [etc.].

7. a. *gooseberry-tart* (earlier U.S. example).

1785 A. ELLICOTT in *Life & Lett.* (1908) 44 Our waiters are now preparing some Goose-Berry Tart.

Goo·se-girl. [After G. *gansemagd*.] A girl employed to tend geese.

1826 *German Popular Stories* II. 1 The Goose-girl. 1906 *Westm. Gaz.* 28 July 12/3 Mr. Randal Charlton has written a fairy-tale, and his heroine is called Mave. Of course she ought to be a Princess, but she is rather of the goose-girl type. *Ibid.* 24 Nov. 7/1 Like all Bohemian geese-girls, she carried a long branch, which served as a wand to drive her flock home.

Goosegog (gu·zgǫg). A widespread local form for *gooseberry*. (Cf. dial. *goose-gob, -bob*.)

1823 MOOR *Suffolk Words*, *Gusegog*, a gooseberry—also gew-gog. *a* 1825 FORBY *Voc. E. Anglia*, *Goose-gog*, a gooseberry; particularly when ripe. 1863 MRS. H. WOOD *William Allair* iv, Green goosegogs. 1916 E. V. LUCAS *Vermilion Box* xcix, Gertie's growing goosegogs for the Ghurkas.

Goo·se-necked, *a.* Shaped like the neck of a goose.

1910 *Westm. Gaz.* 22 Apr. 6/3 Goose-necked and other daffodils.

Goo·se-ste·pper. One who practises the goose-step (used contemptuously of supposed dupes of militarism).

1923 H. L. MENCKEN *Prejudices* Ser. III. 10 The most timorous, sniveling, poltroonish, ignominious mob of serfs and goose-steppers ever gathered under one flag. *Ibid.* 49 The first made them almost incapable of soldierly thought and conduct; the second converted them into cringing goose-steppers. 1928 *Daily Express* 15 Oct. 9 An old topical print showing 'Big Willie' and 'Little Willie' inspecting a parade of goosesteppers.

Goo·se-walk. *Draughts.* (See quots.)

1892 J. LEES *Guide to Draughts* 60 (*Single Corner*) 27–24 here loses, and forms what is known as the 'Old Farmer', or the 'Goose Walk'. 1929 *Encycl. Brit.* VII. 621/1 The trap which White falls into in the above game when playing 27–24 at the 12th move is of very common occurrence, and is known by the quaint designation of the 'Goose Walk'.

Gopher, *sb.*¹ Add: **1. b.** A native or inhabitant of Arkansas or Minnesota.

1845 in C. Cist *Cincinnati Misc.* 240 The inhabitants of.. Arkansas [are called] Gophers. 1873 J. H. BEADLE *Undevel. West* xxxiii. 705 In May, 1859, I first became a 'gopher',—practical Western title of the Minnesotians.

3. b. A native or inhabitant of Florida.

1869 *Overland Monthly* III. 129 On account of the great number of gophers in that State,..a Floridian is called a 'Gopher.'

4. (Earlier examples.)

1837 J. L. WILLIAMS *Territory of Florida* 63 The Bull Snake..is sometimes called the Gopher snake. 1853 BAIRD & GIRARD *Catal. N. Amer. Reptiles* I. 165 Gopher Snake (*Georgia Couperi*).

6. *gopher-burrow*; **gopher man** *U.S. slang* (see quot.); **Gopher State,** Minnesota.

1850 L. H. GARRARD *Wah-To-Yah* x. (1927) 138 The animals..stumbled more than once in the numerous *gopher burrows. 1903 A. ADAMS *Log Cowboy* iv. 42 Officer's horse suddenly struck a Gopher burrow with his front feet. 1926 J. BLACK *You Can't Win* ii. 12 Famous '*gopher men' who tunneled under banks like gophers and carried away their plunder after months of dangerous endeavor.

Gopura (gōu·pura). *India.* Also **-am.** [Skr. *gōpura* city gate, f. *gō* eye + *pura* city.] The great pyramidal tower over the entrance-gate to the precinct of a temple (in S. India).

1862 C. R. MARKHAM *Peru & India* 408 The *gopurams* or towers of the great pagoda. 1895 R. W. FRAZER *Silent Gods, Tailless Tiger* (1896) 24 The iron-studded massive gate beneath the many storied gopura.

Gor-amity (gǫrămai·ti), also **garamity,** negro perversion of *God almighty*.

1834 *West India Sketch Bk.* II. 16 Da kow no hab no tail, Gor-a-mity brush fry [= if a cow has no tail, God Almighty brushes the flies]. 1835 *Tough Yarns, Daddy Davy, The Negro* 158 Gor Amighty send rain,—Gor Amighty send sun: but Gor Amighty send poor nigger too. 1837 *United Service Jrnl.* June 209 Goramity, whar for dem nigger makee me wait? *Ibid.* 211 Tank Garamity,..me hab de felicity to find my massa. 1891 *Strand Mag.* Oct. 77/1 I'm the gorramighty of the *Biddy McDougal*.

Goramy, variant of *GOURAMI.

Gorbli·my. Also **Gaw-, -blimey, -blime.** Vulgar corruption of *God blind me!* (Cf. *BLIMY.) See also quots. 1919, 1925.

1896 A. MORRISON *Child of Jago* i. 16 Cawblimy, not what? 1909 WARE *Passing Engl.*, *Gorblimy* (about 1875). A gutter phrase. 1918 W. J. LOCKE *Rough Road* v. 51 'Gorblime!' said Chipmunk, 'that's the first I 'eard of it.' 1919 *War Terms* in *Athenæum* 8 Aug. 729/1 'Gor-blimey,' a soft service cap. 1925 FRASER & GIBBONS *Sold. & Sailor Words*, *Gorblimey*...An exclamation or adjective of emphasis. A 'Gorblimey' was the common colloquial term for an unwired, floppy, field-service cap worn by a certain type of subaltern in defiance of the Dress Regulations. Lines from a song, popular before the War, ran:—'He wears Gorblimey trousers An' a little Gorblimey 'at.'

Gorbuscha (gǫ·ɹbuʃă). Also **gorbuss, garbusche.** [ad. Russ. горбуша, f. горбъ hump, humpback.] The humpback salmon.

1891 *Fur, Fin & Feather* Mar. 151 The salmon most plentiful in the Alaska waters is known as the humpback or garbusche.

Goree, gori (gǫrī·). Also **gore.** [Chinyanja *goli*.] A forked stick used by the Arabs to fasten slaves together by their necks. Also *gori-stick*.

1891 *Life & Work* May [4] This boy..worked in a gori stick for two years. 1899 WERNER *Captain Locusts* 243 Ulendi and certain men came down..from the Unango country, bringing with them people tied in gori-sticks. 1921 W. P. LIVINGSTONE *Laws of Livingstonia* III. ix. 213 The slaves ..fastened with chains or the gori stick. 1925 *Blackw. Mag.* Aug. 276/2 The young ones already had their necks in the goree.

Gorge, *v.* Add: **6.** *intr.* To become fixed so as to form an obstruction. *U.S.*

1873 J. H. BEADLE *Undevel. West* xxxiv. 738 The ice.. gorged against a bluff bank in a short bend of the stream and dammed the water.

Gorgonzola (gǫɹgǫnzōu·lă). A kind of ewe-milk cheese made at Gorgonzola, a village near Milan, Italy. It is rich and strong, with red and green mould, and apt to be 'lively' with mites.

Gorgonzola Hall, a jocular name for the London Stock Exchange, from the fancied resemblance of its interior marble walls to Gorgonzola cheese. (1887 in Farmer.)

1885 *Times* 8 Oct. 6/6 Specimens of Gorgonzola, Roquefort, Gruyere, Parmesan, Edam, and Gouda cheese. 1896 LONG & BENSON *Cheese* 49 The Gorgonzola process. 1910 *Practitioner* Feb. 211 It has become quite an easy matter to make Gorgonzola, Camembert, Pont l'évêque, Gruyère, anything you like, in Nottinghamshire.

Gori: see *GOREE.

Gorilline (gǫri·ləin), *a.* [f. GORILLA + -INE¹.] Resembling the gorilla, esp. in the skull and face.

1925 A. KEITH *Antiq. Man* (ed. 2) II. 386 Rhodesian man..is far more primitive—more ape-like, more gorilline—than any of modern man's variants, living or extinct.

Gorm (gǭɹm), *v.* *vulgar* or *dial.* Also **gawm.** A vulgar substitute for '(God) damn'.

1850 DICKENS *Dav. Copp.* xxi, Gorm the t'other one. 1883 *Punch* 19 May 230/2 I'm gormed if there was more than six of one and half-a-dozen of the other. 1905 E. PHILLPOTTS *Secret Woman* I. iv, An' coming for to count 'em..be gormed if I didn't find but three! 1910 J. FARNOL *Broad Highway* II. xviii, I'll be gormed if it ain't a'most onnat'ral!

Gormy, variant of GAUMY *a.*

In quots. of painting = coarsely executed, dauby.

1907 W. DE MORGAN *Alice-for-Short* xxxii. 331 'What's his work like though, reely?' 'Footy stuff. Gormy colour. No drawin'!' 1919 — *Old Madhouse* 306, I wish she would trot out her gormy daubs and ask my honest opinion of them.

Go·-round. *U.S.* [GO *v.* 88.]

1. A merry-go-round. Also *attrib.*

1886 *Harper's Mag.* July 172/2 The rink and the go-round opposite the hotel were in full tilt. *Ibid.* 174/1 The rink band opposite..grinding out its go-round music.

2. A round of beating.

1898 E. N. WESTCOTT *David Harum* 13, I had to give him one more go-round..an' after that I didn't have no more trouble with him.

Gorp, var. GAUP, GAWP *v. intr.*, to gape. *dial.*

1928 D. H. LAWRENCE *Rainbow* v. 123 The little crowd at the gate gorps and stretches.

Gorsedd (gǭ·ɹseð). [W., = throne, tribunal, session.] A meeting of Welsh bards and druids; esp. the assembly which meets each day as a preliminary to the eisteddfod.

1794 E. JONES *Welsh Bards* (ed. 2) 60 Note 10 Likewise we held a Gorsedd, Tribunal-meeting, or Supreme Congress of the Bards of the Isle of Britain, according to the ancient form of a Druidical Assembly. 1876 *Programme Wrexham Eisteddvod* 6 The Gorsedd will be held every morning..at 9 o'clock, in a field in Grosvenor Road. 1927 *Daily Express* 27 June 11/7 This circle had already met at a Gorsedd in Thors Cave, Staffordshire. 1928 *Observer* 15 July 11 The early morning sessions of the Gorsedd, with the bards in their multi-coloured robes.

Gosain (gōusā·in). *India.* Also (formerly) **gosaing, gosine, gossein.** [Hindi, etc. *gosāin* (Skr. *gosvāmin* 'lord of cows', f. *go* Cow *sb.*¹).] A Hindu who professes a life of religious mendicancy.

1774 G. BOGLE in C. R. Markham *Tibet* (1876) 124 The Gosains, the trading pilgrims of India, resort hither in great numbers. 1793 W. HODGES *Trav.* 112 A Gosine, or Hindoo Religious. 1813 JAS. FORBES *Orient. Mem.* II. 9 This village belongs exclusively to the Gosaings, or Senassees, a caste of religious Hindoo mendicants. 1826 [HOCKLEY] *Pandurang Hari* I. 97 About five miles from the city I reached the hut of a Gossein. *Note*, A religious mendicant. 1931 *19th Century* Jan. 107 A certain *gosain* or Hindu devotee.

Goschens (gǫ·ʃənz), *sb. pl.* *Hist.* A colloquial name for consols after their conversion from 3 to $2\frac{3}{4}$ per cent by G. J. *Goschen* (chancellor of the exchequer) in 1888 (ultimately to $2\frac{1}{2}$).

1889 *Man of the World* 29 June (Farmer) The nickname Goschens is going out of fashion. The new $2\frac{3}{4}$ stock is now called by the old name. 1891 *Punch* 4 Apr. 161/1 Securities yielding a larger return than $2\frac{3}{4}$ Goschens. 1903 *Westm. Gaz.* 15 Aug. 7/1 For various reasons, chief of which is the multitude of better-paying investments, the public are not buying Goschens.

Gospel, *sb.* Add: **8. a.** *gospel ministry*.

1721 *Jrnls. Ho. Repr. Mass.* III. 187 The first settled and Ordained Minister..that Shall Live and Dye in the Work of a Gospel Ministry. 1831 PECK *Guide for Emigrants* 255 The object is, 'to educate pious, indigent young men for the gospel ministry'.

9. gospel-sharp, a Western U.S. term for a Christian minister of religion.

1872 'MARK TWAIN' *Innoc. at Home* ii. (1882) 268 'What we want is a gospel-sharp. See?' 'A what?' 'Gospel-sharp. Parson.'

Goss (gǫs). The name of W. H. *Goss*, of Stoke-on-Trent, used to designate a kind of crest china invented by him.

1906 *Daily Chron.* 31 Aug. 1/7 The Goss china and porcelain. 1926 M. LEINSTER *Dew on Leaf* II. iii. 176 The jingling piano, the goss china, the gummed shells.

Gotch. b. *Comb.* Add: *gotch-eared* adj.

1905 CLARA DRISCOLL *Girl of La Gloria* iii. 21 The *maveriquer*..usually rode a gotch-eared Mexican pony. 1910 'O. HENRY' *Strictly Business* ix. 97 You are a concentrated, effete, unconditional, short-sleeved, gotch-eared Miss Sally Walker.

Goth. Add: **2. b.** = GOTHICIST.

[*c* 1822 in W. Thornbury *Haunted London* (1880) App. 465 The Modern Goth.] 1849 ALLIES *Jrnl. in France* 142 The cathedral [of Milan] itself..is quite indefensible in the eyes of a thorough-going Goth. 1857 (*title*) A Word to the Goths. 1866 FR. PIUS *Life Fr. Ignatius (Spencer)* xii. 276 The famous Goth [*sc.* Pugin]. 1907 R. A. CRAM *The Gothic Quest* 134 Bentley, in some ways perhaps the greatest of all the new Goths of England.

Gotha (gōu·tă). [A town in Thuringia, Germany.]

1. Short for *Almanach de Gotha.*

1897 'OUIDA' *Massarenes* vii, Contrast the commonplace portraits of to-day's *Gotha* with the exquisite designs of the eighteenth-century Kalendars.

2. A large German aeroplane used in bombing.

1919 *Athenæum* 23 May 360/2. 1920 *Glasgow Herald* 21 Aug. 7 It is now well over two years since the last Gotha visited the Metropolis. 1922 *Encycl. Brit.* XXX. 98/1 On Aug. 12 [1917] a party of nine Gothas made the land near Harwich.

Gothenburg (gǫ·þ-, gōu·tənbǫ̈ɹg). [A seaport town in Sweden (Sw. *Göteborg*).] *Gothenburg system*, a system of control of the liquor traffic adopted in Sweden, Norway, and Finland.

1877 *Harper's Mag.* Dec. 146/2. 1911 *Encycl. Brit.* XVI. 769/2 Sweden and Norway.—In these countries the celebrated 'Gothenburg' or company system is in force together with licensing and local veto.

Gothic, *a.* Add: **1. b.** = MOZARABIC.

1867 tr. *Guéranger's Life St. Cecilia* xviii. 164 The Gothic Church of Spain, whose Liturgy was compiled by St. Leander, Archbishop of Seville. 1874 *Month* Feb. 223 The old Gothic or Mozarabic rite. 1911 E. B. O'REILLY *Heroic Spain* 235 The Christians who were under Moorish rule..kept to the old Gothic ritual.

Go-to-meeting, *a.* orig. *U.S.* (See GO *v.* VIII.)

1796–1801 FESSENDEN *Orig. Poems* (1806) 115 Each scrapes, huzzas, and kicks and bounces, Waves high her go-to-meeting cap. 1815 D. HUMPHREYS *Yankey in Eng.* 29 Changing my old shabby duds, for these new Sabbada close, fit for a go-to-meeting-day. 1825 J. NEAL *Bro. Jonathan* I. 148 His 'go-to-meeting' coat, as they call that in America. 1835–1870 [see GO *v.* VIII].

b. as *sb.* = go-to-meeting clothes.

1839 *Southern Lit. Messenger* V. 65/1 She no more looks at him than if he never put on his Sunday-go-to-meetings at all.

Gouda (gau·dă). A flat round cheese made at Gouda in Holland.

1885 [see *GORGONZOLA]. 1890 JAS. MACDONALD *Stephens' Bk. Farm* IV. 515/2 The *Gouda*, or flat Dutch cheese. 1896 LONG & BENSON *Cheese* 14 The Gouda variety is not unlike Cheddar when it is well manufactured. 1902 J. T. LAW *Grocer's Man.* (ed. 2) 326/1 Derbyshire Cheese...One variety is shaped like Gouda cheese, and known as 'Derby Goudas'. *Ibid.* 429/1 Factory Goudas are usually made of skimmed milk in Friesland.

Gouger. (Earlier U.S. examples.)

1790 *Gazette of U.S.* (N.Y.) 13 Jan. (Th.) Demanding Congress now should settle In words, with Gougers, Creeks, and cattle. *a* 1793 FRENEAU *Poems* (1809) II. 98 (*title*) The Gougers.

Gouging, *vbl. sb.* Add: (Earlier U.S. example.)

1774 P. V. FITHIAN *Jrnl.* (1900) 104 The Cooper..is likely to lose one of his Eyes by that Diabolical Custom of gouging which is in common practise among those who fight here.

2. *Austral.* (See quot.)

1902 *Chambers's Jrnl.* Mar. 171/1 In the 'back blocks' of New South Wales opal is abundant and 'gouging'—the term given to opal-mining—is the chief pursuit of every man on the western side of the Darling River.

Gouging, *ppl. a.* [f. GOUGE *v.* + -ING [2].] That practises gouging.

1796 *Gazette of U.S.* (N.Y.) 10 May (Th.) Brave Abraham ..Dar'd tell them all..That gouging Gunn had challenged him. 1825 PAULDING *J. Bull in Amer.* i. 2, I also fully believed that the people were a bundling, gouging, drinking, spitting impious race.

Goulash (gū·lǫʃ). Also goulasch. [Magyar *gulyás(hús)*, f. *gulyás* herdsman + *hús* meat.]

1. A stew or ragout of steak and vegetables highly seasoned. Often called *Hungarian goulash.*

1900 F. B. & W. H. WORKMAN *Ice World Himálaya* 193 Irish stews and *goulasches*, composed of animal odds and ends. 1906 *Westm. Gaz.* 27 Sept. 5/1 The national Hungarian dishes of Gulyas, or ragout, and Paprikahuhn. 1915 P. G. WODEHOUSE *Something Fresh* viii. § 1, In his hour of affliction it soothed him to read of Hungarian Goulash and Escalloped Brains. 1929 E. LINKLATER *Poet's Pub* i, Sucking-pig, celery, and goulasch.

2. *Contract Bridge.* A re-deal before which each player arranges his cards in suits and order of value.

1927 in E. V. Shepard *Correct Contract Bridge* (1930) 245 When all four players pass, no bid having been made, and the players desire to play a Goulash, the cards shall be redealt by the same dealer...No shuffling of any kind permitted. 1930 *Ibid.* 129 Each player arranges all the cards of a suit in sequence before a goulash deal. 1930 M. KERWIN *Contract Bridge* xv. 47 In goulashes lies the greatest gambling element of Contract.

Gou·ra [2]. Also **gowra.** = GORAH.

1790 tr. *Le Vaillant's Trav.* II. 104 The *goura* is shaped like the bow of a savage Hottentot, it is of the same size. 1801 J. BARROW *Trav. S. Afr.* I. 149 This instrument was called the *goura.* 1902 H. BALFOUR in *Jrnl. Anthropol. Inst.* XXXII. 156 The *goura*, a stringed-wind musical instrument of the Bushmen and Hottentots. 1905 *Rep. Brit. Assoc.* 529 The *goura* of the Bushmen..a bow-like instrument having a piece of flattened quill interposed between one end of the string and its attachment to the bow.

Gourami (gūə·rāmi, guərā·mi). Also **gouramy, goramy.** [Malay *gurāmī.*] A large freshwater nest-building fish, *Osphromenus goramy* or *olfax*, native of China and the Malay Archipelago, reared in ponds in warm countries for food.

1878 F. DAY *Fishes of India* I. 372 At the end of a month numerous fry appear, over which the old gouramies keep watch many days. 1879 *Encycl. Brit.* X. 781/1 Goramy, or Gouramy. 1880 GÜNTHER *Study Fishes* 185 In the first third of the present century, the Javanese Goramy was acclimatised in Mauritius and Guiana. 1905 D. S. JORDAN *Fishes* II. 368 The Gouramis: Osphromenidæ.

Gourbi (gūə·ɹbi). [Arab. dial.] A tent used in Northern Africa.

1895 F. B. & W. H. WORKMAN *Alger. Mem.* 113 In the Province of Constantine the people..live in tents or gourbis made of white or light-coloured canvas. 1908 *Westm. Gaz.* 20 Jan. 2/3, I have watched for thee From my lone gourbi.

Gourd [1]. **7.** Add: *gourd-like* adj.; **gourd fiddle** *U.S.*, a rude fiddle made from a gourd; **gourd-melon,** the tallow or wax gourd (*Benincasa*); **gourd-seed corn, maize** *U.S.*, a variety of Indian corn; **gourd tree** (earlier U.S. example).

1858 D. K. BENNETT *Chronol. N. Carolina* 102 '*Gourd fiddles' were then in vogue, 'puncheon floors', and 'cornstalk bows!' 1927 PEAKE & FLEURE *Priests & Kings* 149 The *gourd-like form of the earliest Moravian wares seems to indicate an eastern origin. 1884 *De Candolle's Orig. Cultivated Pl.* 263 White *Gourd-melon, or Benincasa—*Benincasa hispida.* 1831 PECK *Guide for Emigrants* II. 38 The species of corn called the *gourd seed. 1835 *Knickerbocker Mag.* VI. 173 The rich scenery of forty acres of most luxuriant gourd-seed corn. 1872 EGGLESTON *End of World* viii. 60 The relative merits of 'gourd-seed' and 'flint corn'. 1827 *Western Monthly Rev.* I. 313 *Gourd-seed maize as high as the waist. 1854 R. GLISAN *Jrnl. Army Life* xii. (1874) 161 The palm, mango, bread-tree, *gourd-tree [etc.].

Gouty, *sb.* [app. absol. use of GOUTY *a.*] A kind of snow boot or shoe.

1924 *Tourist* Winter Sports No. 20 Snow Boots..The best 'gouties' as they are called in Switzerland, are the two buckle Canadian variety. 1925 *Nation* 7 Nov. 213/2 For curling, or walking on the rinks, it is necessary to wear rubber snow-shoes, or 'gouties', and these are very handy to slip on over house-shoes.

Government. Add: **7. c.** (Earlier example.)

1877 *Harper's Mag.* Dec. 37/1 On 5000 governments which I hold, I have received $166.

d. The governing body of a college; the administrative council of a town or city. *U.S.*

1787 in B. H. Hall *College Words* (1851) 149 The Government of college met, And Willard ruled the stern debate. 1812 in B. Peirce *Hist. Harvard Univ.* (1833) App. 87 The two Boards, which constitute the college-government. 1837 *Knickerbocker Mag.* IX. 347, I am sorry to inform you, that the government deem it expedient that you should spend a few months in the country. 1851 HALL *College Words* 149 Tutors, who are styled the Government, or the College Government. 1908 *Springfield Weekly Repub.* 10 Sept. 12 The city government held a special meeting last week to act on recommendations of the finance committee.

9. government house (earlier U.S. examples).

1802 ELLICOTT *Jrnl.* 43 The Governor..consented that we should meet at the government house. 1803 in *Ann. 8th Congress* 2 Sess. 1507 A Government house, stables, and garden.

Governorate (gʊ·vəɹnŏrĕt). [f. GOVERNOR + -ATE [1], after *consulate*, etc.]

1. A province or portion of country ruled by a governor, esp. in the Turkish empire; *spec.* each of the six major administrative divisions of Egypt.

1899 *Standard* 8 Apr. 4/2 Suakim will form a separate Governorate. 1900 *Pilot* 1 Sept. 263/1 Samos, the freest of Turkish governorates. 1926 *Blackw. Mag.* Mar. 412/1 Kena..is the Mudirieh, or Governorate town, of the province which embraces Luxor.

2. The residence of a governor.

1930 CHESTERTON *Four Felons* 25 The gardens round the Governorate.

Govy (gʊ·vi), hypocoristic (-Y [6]) f. *governess.*

1903 *Westm. Gaz.* 28 Mar. 2/2 I'm trying to avoid the govy difficulty by sending my girls to classes.

Go-way. [Named from its cry *kway-kway* (cf. Bechuana *maquaai*).] The grey touracou, *Schizorhis concolor*, of S. Africa.

1903 W. L. SCLATER *Birds S. Africa* III. 221 The 'Go-way' bird, as it is generally called by hunters and travellers.

Gowers (gau·əɹz). Name of Sir William R. *Gowers*, English neurologist (1845–1915), used to designate certain diseases or symptoms.

1901 DORLAND *Med. Dict.* (ed. 2) s.v. *Sign, Gowers' sign*, abrupt intermittent oscillation of the iris under the influence of light. 1913 W. BATESON *Mendel's Princ. Heredity* 224 Haemophilia and Gowers' disease are too fatal. 1930 H. S. JENNINGS *Biol. Basis Hum. Nat.* 50.

Gownless (gau·nlės), *a.* [See -LESS.] Not provided with or wearing a gown.

1895 T. HARDY *Jude the Obscure* II. vii. 144 Two devil-may-care young men who proved to be gownless undergraduates. 1901 'LUCAS MALET' *Sir Richard Calmady* IV. i, The picture of those reportedly gownless backs had depressed him abominably.

Goya (goi·ă). A shade of very deep pink (said to have been the favourite colour of the Spanish painter Goya). (In vogue from 1931.)

Goy-blamed, *pa. pple.* *U.S.* = *Gor-blamed* (perversion of *God-blamed*) with vulgar substitution of *oi* for *or.*

1832 J. K. PAULDING *Westward Ho!* I. 172 I'll be goy blamed if I haven't bin trying to catch this squirrel.

G.P.U. See *GAY-PAY-OO and *OGPU.

1925 POPOFF *Tcheka* 238 The third period of the Tcheka dates from February 6, 1922. On this date the Tcheka was 'dissolved'; the 'G.P.U.', however, was immediately set up in its place. 1927 *19th Cent.* Nov. 653 The activities of the Cheka and the G.P.U. (initials of the Secret Police Department).

Grab, *sb.* [2] Add: **1.** Also *fig.* (cf. b). *To have the grab on* (slang): to have great advantage of.

1857 *Trans. Ill. Agric. Soc.* II. 287 Hotel-keepers would not act as if it was the last and only grab. 1873 J. H. BEADLE *Undevel. West* xxi. 429 The railroads, of course, get the first grab, their land is already secured.

b. Also: *Grab and keep*, commercial rapacity and selfishness. *On the grab*, intent on gain.

1905 'GUY THORNE' *Lost Cause* ii, They've nothing to get by it..and that flatters 'em because they're always on the grab in every other way. 1905 *Daily Chron.* 9 May 3/1 The grab-and-keep of towns. 1906 *Ibid.* 21 Mar. 6/4 The grab-and-keep of modern commercialism has starved out the good old system of apprenticeship.

5. b. *Chess.* Applied to a particular class of problems: in full *grab theme.* (See quot. 1913.)

1909 A. C. WHITE *Knights & Bishops* p. iii. 1913 — *Sam Loyd* 357 The Grab Theme...The theme includes, in its broadest sense, all problems where a Black piece is captured on two or more squares...In its narrower sense it is limited to the problems where a particular Black piece is captured on two or more squares by a single White piece or by two White pieces of the same kind. *Ibid.* 359 The Grab by the concerted action of the two White Knights is extremely pretty.

6. grab-bag, game *U.S.* (earlier examples).

1855 M. M. THOMPSON *Doesticks* xvi. 135 [A] young woman wanted me to invest in the '*grab bag'; [I] gave half a dollar, and fished in. 1873 MRS. ELIZ. S. WARD *Trotty's Wedding Tour* 139 A country charity-fair grab-bag. 1846 SAGE *Scenes Rocky Mts.* xxxii. 282 Provided you won't attempt the *grab game on us. 1850 W. MILES *Jrnl.* (1916) 7 The grab game had to be carried out, to get even a spot to lie down.

Grab, *v.* **1.** Add: Phr. *to grab hold of* (cf. HOLD *sb.* [1] 2).

1894 CONAN DOYLE *Mem. Sherlock Holmes, Reigate Squires* 123 The fellows evidently grabbed hold of anything they could get.

Graben (grā·bən). *Geol.* [G., = ditch; also *grabenbruch, -senke.*] A rift-valley.

1902 *Encycl. Brit.* XXV. 362/1 The great African lakes which occupy rift-valleys or *graben* of comparatively recent fracture. 1910 *Ibid.* X. 208/1 Occasionally one or more parallel faults have let down an intervening strip of rock, thereby forming 'fault-valleys' or *Graben* (*Grabensenken*). *Ibid.* 598/1 Occasionally crust-blocks resembling 'graben' and 'horsts' are circumscribed by folds instead of faults; when this is so they have been called respectively 'infolded graben' or 'overfolded horsts'. 1919 *Nature* CIII. 239/1 The structure was shown to be that of a tableland bisected by a great rift-valley (graben).

Graceless, *a.* **1. a.** Add: *Graceless florin* (see quot.).

1870 H. W. HENFREY *Guide to Study Eng. Coins* II. 137 The usual letters D.G., for Dei Gratia, were omitted...This raised a storm of remonstrance against this coinage [of 1849], which at once received the name of the 'godless' or 'graceless florin'.

Gracilis (græ·silis). *Anat.* [L., = slender.] In full *musculus adductor gracilis*: A muscle on the medial side of the thigh, passing from the hip-bone to the tibia. It acts as an adductor of the hips, and a flexor and rotator of the knee.

1727–38 CHAMBERS *Cycl.*, *Gracilis*, in anatomy, a muscle of the leg, thus called from its slender shape. 1858 H. GRAY *Anat.* 281 The *Gracilis* is the most superficial muscle on the inner side of the thigh. 1906 A. M. BUCHANAN *Anat.* I. 444 The gracilis is flat and strap-like in the upper third of the thigh.

Gracility. Add:

2. *fig.* Of literary style: Unornamented simplicity.

1900 WRATISLAW *A. C. Swinburne* 146 The dexterous verses *To a Cat* are in a lighter tune than usual, recalling the gracility of Hugo. 1906 *Academy* 1 Sept. 201/2 Their spontaneity, their *gracility*, to borrow a word from the Latin, is perfect.

Gracing (grē¹·siŋ), *vbl. sb.* [2] *slang.* Also **greycing.** Contracted form of *greyhound racing* (see *GREYHOUND 4).

1928 *Star* 8 June, Gracing at Wimbledon. 1928 *Daily*

Express 20 July 17/5 Greycing...Programmes..for to-night's greyhound racing meetings.

Grad, U.S. abbrev. of GRADUATE *sb.* 1.

1893 W. K. POST *Harvard Stories* p. ix, Reverend grads, from the tales I have heard ye tell, I opine that the undergraduate is still the same.

Grade, *sb.* Add: **4. c.** A class at school in relation to advancement. (Cf. GRADED *ppl. a.* 2.) *U.S.*

1852 *Indiana Hist. Soc. Publ.* III. 619 Qualified to teach in any of the grades, from the primary to the grammar school. 1903 A. B. HART *Actual Govt. Amer. Conditions* 543 Many cities have public kindergartens, which take children of 4 to 5 years of age in hand and teach them simple beginnings. The next division is usually the primary, extending over 3 to 6 years, followed by about 4 years of the grammar school; these two systems taken together are often called simply 'the grades'. 1904 O. H. LANG in *Forum* (U.S.) Oct. 268 Polite conduct and usages might advantageously be taught in the grades and in the high school. 1906 C. A. MCMURRY (*title*) Course of Study in the Eight Grades. 1909 *Springfield Weekly Republican* 18 Feb. 2 In the British isles the classes are designated standards and these are supposed to correspond to our grades.

5. a. (Earlier U.S. examples.)

1807 J. MARSHALL *Life of Washington* V. 213 To talents of the highest grade, he united a patient industry. 1816 U. BROWN *Jrnl.* in *Maryland Hist. Mag.* X. 274 Jack Oaks of the meanest grade. 1818 FEARON *Sk. Amer.* 30 Neither trades are (to use an Americanism) of the first grade. *Ibid.* 191 Because their neighbour's face was (to use their own phrase) a grade darker than their own.

7. (U.S. examples of absol. and attrib. uses.)

1852 *Trans. Mich. Agric. Soc.* III. 142 A few full blood Saxons; the rest are a grade sheep. *Ibid.* 182 My cattle are yet grades, and am getting rid of them as fast as possible. *Ibid.* 184 One good grade sow. 1857 *Ibid.* VIII. 707 The greatest show, however, for number and size, was among the grades and natives. 1867 T. LACKLAND *Homespun* II. 198 Grade cows, that are handsome enough to be of full blood. 1874 *Rep. Vermont Board Agric.* II. 378 The kindness of the cows is as conspicuous in grades as in the pure bred. 1882 *Rep. Maine Board Agric.* XXVI. 168 In every dairy of six cows I would keep not less than two Jerseys, or their grades.

10. b. (Earlier U.S. examples.)

1850 R. GLISAN *Jrnl. Army Life* ii. (1874) 12 The cars are moved on these heavy grades by stationary engines. 1851 C. CIST *Cincinnati* 270 The..property is a suburb..which when its grades shall be completed, will possess no more slope than sufficient properly to drain it.

d. *To make the grade*: to reach the proper standard, to be successful. *U.S.*

1930 *Publishers' Weekly* 5 July 29/1 Can the seasonal bookshop make the grade, and under what conditions?

11. (Earlier example of *at grade.*)

1869 *Congress. Globe* 24 Mar. 252/3 Does not the junction road..cross the streets..at grade?..No, sir; it crosses them above grade in nearly every instance.

12. grade teacher *U.S.*, a teacher in a grade school.

1906 *Springfield Weekly Republican* 12 Apr. 6 The grade teachers attempting little..except setting the class to sing music already familiar. 1909 GENE STRATTON-PORTER *Girl of Limberlost* ix. 165 She gathered..all sorts of natural history specimens and sold them to the grade teachers.

Grade, *v.* [2] Add:

5. (Earlier U.S. example.)

1873 *Rep. Vermont Board Agric.* II. 92 He..thought he should improve the color of his butter by grading his herd with Jersey blood.

8. *intr.* To pass imperceptibly from one grade *into* another. Also with *down, up, off.* (Cf. 3 d.) *To grade up*: to take rank with a higher grade or class (cf. 5). *To grade up with*: to compare with, to be like.

1903 *Harper's Mag.* July 186 The type graded downward into the lower invertebrates. *a* 1909 'O. HENRY' *Roads of Destiny* ix. 155, I never yet see anything on the hoof that he exactly grades up with. 1921 *British Museum Return* 157 Rock-crystal grading into quartzite, from.. Minas Geraes, Brazil. 1922 MULFORD *Black Buttes* xiv. 227 Strikes me funny, though, the way they [*sc.* the new cattle] grade up. 1925 ODELL in E. F. Norton *Fight for Everest, 1924* 292 This granite..frequently graded off into pegmatite. 1927 HALDANE & HUXLEY *Anim. Biol.* ix. 198 The activity grades down from one pole of the egg to the other.

-grade, an adj. suffix repr. L. *-gradus* stepping, walking (f. stem of *gradus* step, *gradīrī* to step, walk), occurring in a few L. compounds, e.g. *retrōgradus* RETROGRADE, *tardigradus* TARDIGRADE. Hence in mod.L. scientific formations, as *digitigradus* DIGITIGRADE, *plantigradus* PLANTIGRADE.

Graded, *ppl. a.* **2.** *Graded school* (earlier U.S. example).

1852 *Indiana Hist. Soc. Publ.* III. 615 Union, or graded schools, for the terms are synonymous, are simply the schools of a given township, village or city, classified and arranged according to the attainments of the pupils.

Grader. 1. a. (Earlier examples.)

1849 *Rep. U.S. Comm. Patents, Agric.* (1850) 257 This grader was to be sworn, as flour inspectors and other agents are. 1867 *Rep. Iowa Agric. Soc.* (1868) 266 The grader selects a portion of the best wheat.

Gradgrind (græ·dgraind). Name of the mill-owner in Dickens's *Hard Times* (1854), 'a man of facts and calculations', used allusively for: One who is hard and cold. Hence **Gra·dgrinding, Gra·dgrindery.**

1855 *Putnam's Mag.* Jan. 76/2 There have not been wanting travelled Gradgrinds to assure us that the song from his lips was a humbug and a sham. 1920 *Glasgow Herald* 14 Aug. 5 A .. metropolis of ant-like industry and social Gradgrindery. 1924 *Ibid.* 18 Apr. 8 A nation of Gradgrinds, immersed in work and money-getting, and denying themselves and their employees any opportunity of recreation. 1925 *Public Opinion* 7 Aug. 122/1 The gradgrinding system. 1927 *United Free Ch. Mission Rec.* Sept. 379/2 These self-appointed Gradgrinds seem to imagine that their actions are pleasing to the Almighty.

Gradient. B. *sb.* Add: **2. b. gradient wind** (see quot. 1918).

1911 W. N. SHAW *Forecasting Weather* 46 The direction of the gradient-wind is along the isobars with the low pressure to the left in the northern hemisphere. 1918 *Meteorol. Gloss.*, *Gradient Wind*, the flow of air which is necessary to balance the pressure-gradient. 1928 SIR N. SHAW *Man. Meteorol.* II. p. xxx, *Gradient wind*, the wind tangential to the isobaric line [etc.].

Grading, *vbl. sb.* **2. a.** (Earlier U.S. example.)

1852 *Trans. Mich. Agric. Soc.* III. 150 Compare the grading of my clip..with that of Joseph Barnard.

Graduate, *sb.* **4.** (Earlier U.S. examples.)

1880 *Harvard Catal.* 190 (*heading*) Graduate department. *Ibid.*, Any Graduate course which is taken by less than three students may be withdrawn at the option of the Instructor. 1880 *Harper's Mag.* July 251/2 The solution of the difficulty lies in..putting the extra studies in the graduate courses.

Graduate, *v.* Add: **7.** *trans.* = GRADE *v.* [2] 4. *U.S.*

1815 D. DRAKE *Cincinnati* ii. 62 When the streets shall be graduated from the Hill to the river shore. 1827 *Western Monthly Rev.* I. 78 In graduating a street,..a piece of iron was dug up at a depth of twenty-five feet below the surface. 1829 R. C. SANDS *Writings* II. 182 She proceeded to the capitol..to hear a debate on graduating and paving Tennessee Avenue. 1832 *Louisville Directory* 116 In addition to these general expenses, are to be considered those of graduating and paving streets.

Hence **Graduating** *ppl. a.* (additional U.S. examples).

1838 *Southern Lit. Messenger* IV. 576/1 Expressing the hope that the graduating class of that day might realize the wish of the reverend ex-president. 1845 *Knickerbocker Mag.* XXV. 182 A great girl..spoke of the degree of Forenoon (A.M.) being conferred upon a graduating gentleman! 1873 J. H. BEADLE *Undevel. West* xx. 381 Every year it sends out a graduating class, who scatter through the Nation.

Graduation. 6. Add: Also *attrib.*

1901 *Daily News* 2 Mar. 4/7 There are only seven signatures of Milton known, the first occurring in the Graduation Book of Cambridge, 1628–9. 1903 *N.Y. Times* 7 Oct. 6 The annual graduation exercises of the schoolship St. Mary's were held last night on board the ship. 1906 MARY E. WILKINS-FREEMAN *By Light of Soul* 217 Maria dressed herself in her graduation gown.

Graft (graft), *sb.* [5] orig. *U.S. slang.* [Origin uncertain. Perhaps a use of GRAFT *sb.* [4] 'work' (cf. *job*); but some authorities connect it with GRAFT *sb.* [1] with the notion of 'excrescence'.]

1. A means of making illicit profit; a shady or dishonest means of making money; thieving, thievery. Also, a business or an organization for making money illicitly.

1889 in J. B. Thoburn *Hist. Oklahoma* (1916) I. xxix. 407 The enterprising individual sold water at so much a drink until he was ousted from his profitable graft. 1896 G. ADE *Artie* i. 3 To the church show—the charity graft. 1903 H. HAPGOOD *Autobiogr. Thief* ii. (1904) 34 In those days.. Moll-buzzing, as well as picking pockets in general, was an easy and lucrative graft. *Ibid.* x. 205 The boy had a much better chance to learn the graft than I had when a kid, for my father was an honest man. *Ibid.*, One [highwayman].. explained a few of his grafts. *Ibid.* 222, I was too sleepy those days to go out of town much on the graft. 1904 *Athenæum* 30 Apr. 560 In New York 'graft' is thieves' patter for stealing. 1904 'O. HENRY' *Cabbages & Kings* v. 90 Mellinger had a graft in this country that was the only thing of its kind in the world. 1928 *Saturday Even. Post* 4 Feb. 35/1 'We had a slick graft' he told me, 'We was taking about two hundred smackers a week.'

2. Dishonest gains or illicit profits made by a person in and through his official position, as by bribery or blackmail, esp. in connexion with politics or municipal business; practices intended to secure these, esp. the improper expenditure or receipt of money.

1901 JOSIAH FLYNT (*title*) The World of Graft. 1903 *Daily Chron.* 21 Oct. 7/2 A Chicago paper has the headline, 'Labour revolts at paying graft'. *Ibid.* 3 Nov. 5/3 Are you ready to support a government of law against a government of 'graft', an administration of the city's resources in the interest of the public and of the public treasury, against their dissipation for the benefit of a favoured few? 1904 *Ibid.* 17 Feb. 3/5 Glimpses are also given of the shady side of American politics, where 'graft' is only another word for plunder. 1904 *Rochester Post Express* 30 May 4 Today the whole state is honeycombed with corruption. Graft is so common as to excite no particular attention. 1905 *Daily Chron.* 13 Sept. 5/2 It is now the turn of the War Department to start a campaign against 'graft' among the officials of the army. 1905 D. G. PHILLIPS *Plum Tree* 31, I saw clearly that graft was the backbone, the whole skeleton of legislative business. 1909 *Westm. Gaz.* 13 Oct. 5/4 Showing how Tammany robs the city, bribes the judges, protects criminals, and generally carries on the game of graft, an Americanism for bribery, corruption, and illicit commission. 1912 THORNTON *Amer. Gloss.*, *Graft*, an illicit commission or profit, particularly in connection with a political job. 1915 *Literary Digest* (N.Y.) 21 Aug. 340/1 There is no evidence that Minister Sullivan received any money or participated in any way in what has come to be known as 'graft'.

Graft (graft), *v.* [4] *U.S. slang.* [f. *GRAFT *sb.* [5]] *intr.* To practise 'graft'; to make money by shady or dishonest means.

1903 H. HAPGOOD *Autobiogr. Thief* ii. (1904) 48, I know some thieves who, although they have grafted for twenty-five years, have not yet 'done time'. 1905 D. G. PHILLIPS *Plum Tree* 61, I don't see how those in politics that don't graft, as they call it, are any better than those that do. Would they get office if they didn't help on the jobs of the grafters?

b. *To graft on to*: to secure by illicit means.

1903 A. ADAMS *Log Cowboy* xiii. 84 He had a card or two up his sleeve by which he expected to graft on to some coin of the realm.

Hence **Gra·fting** *vbl. sb.* and *ppl. a.*

1903 H. HAPGOOD *Autobiogr. Thief* xii. (1904) 290 When I was hard up..I didn't mind taking heavy chances in straight grafting. 1904 GRAFTON *The Treasury* Oct. 8/2 We excel other countries in the phenomenal corruption of our city Governments and Legislatures. The evil system of 'grafting', so called, extends everywhere. 1912 F. J. HASKIN *Amer. Govt.* 71 Large business houses felt the loss from the petty grafting of stamps by office boys. 1921 *Glasgow Herald* 13 June 9 The efforts of professional and grafting Irish agitators.

Grafter [3] (gra·ftəɹ). Chiefly *U.S. colloq.* [f. *GRAFT *sb.* [5] or *v.* [4] + -ER [1].]

1. One who makes money by shady or dishonest means; a thief; a swindler.

1900 *Daily Express* 22 June 5/3 American thieves, hotel robbers, 'bunco steerers', 'grafters', 'con' men, and 'crooks' of every degree. 1901 H. McHUGH *John Henry* 49 No more swell Sandwich Salons for me, where the grafters want to butt in all the while. 1903 H. HAPGOOD *Autobiogr. Thief* ii. (1904) 39 A good personal appearance is part of the capital of a grafter, particularly of a pickpocket. 1903 *Westm. Gaz.* 16 July 10/1 Camp followers, adventurers, and a weird aggregation of grafters. 1907 'O. HENRY' (*title*) The Gentle Grafter. 1916 S. LEACOCK *Ess. & Lit. Stud.* 205 All the world loves a grafter—at least a genial and ingenious grafter —a Robin Hood who plunders an abbot to feed a beggar, an Alfred Jingle, a Scapin, a Raffles.

2. One who practises 'graft', esp. in public life; a politician, official, etc., who misuses his position in order to reap dishonest gain or advantage.

1896 *Columbus* (Ohio) *Dispatch* 20 Apr. 3/8 Most of the 'grafters' have left the town, and not many of them will remain here. 1904 F. LYNDE *Grafters* xxiv. 298 You were to crush the grafters in this railroad struggle—show them up. 1904 *Daily Chron.* 28 Mar. 3/5 Kuropatkin shares with Prince Khilkoff, the Minister of Railways, the distinction of being one of the few high officials who are not called grafters. 1906 U. SINCLAIR *Jungle* xi. 134 The two rival sets of grafters hired halls and set off fireworks and made speeches, to try to get the people interested in the matter. 1914 GERTRUDE ATHERTON *Perch of Devil* I. 58 And although she has her pestilential politicians, her grafters .., yet ability and talent make good as always.

transf. 1920 R. L. ALSAKER *Maintaining Health* 356 Children who are waited upon much become selfish. They soon become grafters, expecting and taking everything and giving nothing.

Grafter [4] (gra·ftəɹ). *slang.* [f. GRAFT *v.* [3] + -ER [1].] One who works; a (hard) worker.

1900 H. LAWSON *On Track* 41 'What are we to do now?' enquired Andy, who was the hardest grafter, but altogether helpless, hopeless, and useless in a crisis like this. 1927 *Glasgow Herald* 19 Mar. 9 The visiting eight are heavy and expert in the tight, and to meet them we have a pack which contains at least three players who are by no means 'grafters'.

Graham (grē¹·əm). [See GRAHAMISM.] Used *attrib.* to designate unbolted wheaten flour, and bread or biscuit prepared from this. Also *absol.* = Graham bread.

1834 *Knickerbocker Mag.* IV. 305 'Hail!' said I, 'thou pure, unadulterated substitute—Graham bread!'. 1834 W. L. GARRISON in *Life* (1885) I. 428 If they are Grahamites we have a fine spring of water in our cellar, and plenty of Graham flour upstairs. 1873 J. H. BEADLE *Undevel. West* xxv. 532 The first meal I was delighted to see our Indian servant bring in what I recognized as an old Yankee acquaintance—'Graham biscuits'. 1874 *Rep. Vermont Board Agric.* II. 509 Large enough to hold the flour, the meal, the rye, the graham, butter. 1877 MRS. E. S. WARD *Story of Avis* 63 Aunt Chloe held it impossible that any woman could make home happy without being able to make good Graham bread. 1896 *Godey's Mag.* Feb. 207/1 When Mr. Dives turns from his recondite menu to nibble at wheaten grits and graham bread.

Grahamite. A follower of Graham. (Earlier examples.)

1834 [see *GRAHAM]. 1839 C. F. BRIGGS *Harry Franco* II. iii. 27 'Have you got the dyspepsia?' asked Mrs. D. 'Ain't you a Grahamite?' asked Mr. D. 1844 G. W. KENDALL *Santa Fé Exped.* II. ix. 97 He gave us..a breakfast in the morning which would have been spurned by a dyspeptic Grahamite. 1864 B. TAYLOR *H. Thurston* iii. 45 They were Grahamites for a year or two—lived on bran bread and turnips, boiled wheat and dried apples.

Hence **Gra·hamitish** *a.*

1837 *Southern Lit. Messenger* III. 105 My desire to devour this *light* food was entirely Grahamitish. 1839 *Knickerbocker Mag.* XIII. 233 'What wonder', exclaims a Grahamitish friend of mine.

Grain, *sb.* [1] Add: **13. d.** Short for *grain-leather* (see 19 in Dict.).

1930 *Daily Tel.* 1 Dec. 15/1 Washable Grain Cape Gloves.

18. a. *grain-barge, -barn, -bin* (U.S. example), *-boat, -box, -chamber, -dealer, -land, -market, -merchant* (later U.S. example), *-room, -trade.*

1902 S. E. WHITE *Blazed Trail* xxix. 204 They were locked through after some delay on account of the *grain barges from Duluth. 1844 *Knickerbocker Mag.* XXIII. 439 Let us drop into the '*grain-barn'. 1879 B. F. TAYLOR *Summer-Savory* xiii. 112 The pulpit, with the architecture of a *grain-bin and two stories high. 1891 KIPLING *Light*

that Failed 122 An Odessa *grain-boat. 1872 *Rep. Vermont Board Agric.* I. 312 A convenient *grain-box and root-cellar are great aids. 1887 H. H. JACKSON *Between Whiles* i. 26 A winding staircase outside led to what had been the *grain-chamber. 1867 *Rep. Iowa Agric. Soc.* (1868) 158 Near the river a portion [of the corn crop is] sold to *grain-dealers where it finds a market at St. Louis. 1817 S. R. BROWN *Western Gaz.* 84 It proves to be excellent *grain land. 1871 SCHELE DE VERE *Americanisms* (1872) 481 *Grain* is used in America as *corn* is in England,..the papers quote therefore daily an account of the *Grain Market. 1870 MEDBERY *Men & Myst. Wall St.* 335 All our great *grain-merchants ..do the same. 1873 J. H. BEADLE *Undevel. West* xxv. 524 The other officials and employes were..in charge of [the] *grain room. 1889 *Kansas Times & Star* 22 June, The new Missouri inspection law..will seriously hurt the *grain trade here.

b. *grain-carrier, -crusher, -grower, -huller, -scourer*; *grain-grinding, -growing* vbl. sbs.; *grain-carrying, -cutting, -growing* (earlier U.S. examples) ppl. adjs.

1908 E. NOBLE (*title*) The *Grain Carriers. 1901 *Daily Chron.* 19 Aug. 5/7 Twenty-nine '*grain-carrying ships, chartered for European ports. 1849 *Rep. U.S. Comm. Patents, Agric.* (1850) 113 Their newly invented horse-powers..their seed sowers and *grain-crushers..do much to expedite the labors of the farm. 1838 H. W. ELLSWORTH *Valley Upper Wabash* v. 47, I have a plan..to introduce the mowing and *grain-cutting machine into this state. 1845 F. DOUGLASS *Life* (1846) 12 The blacksmithing, cartwrighting, coopering..and *grain grinding, were all performed by the slaves. 1863 D. G. MITCHELL *My Farm* 131 A professed *grain-grower. 1927 PEAKE & FLEURE *Peasants & Potters* 22 Grain is a more sustaining diet than whelks and limpets, and the grain-growers had more time and more energy to improve the amenities of their surroundings. 1813 *Niles' Weekly Register* IV. 385/2 The public vigilance and scorn must aid the legal authorities; and so it will, in the *grain-growing states. 1847 H. HOWE *Hist. Collect. Ohio* 123 Cleveland is the great mart of the greatest grain-growing state in the Union. 1857 *Trans. Mich. Agric. Soc.* VIII. 621 Macomb county, as a whole, is not a grain growing county. 1858 J. A. WARDER *Hedges & Evergreens* I. x. 144 Just as..grain-growing prevails, we find the fences are legally considered inclosures for the cattle, or barriers against them. 1867 *Rep. Iowa Agric. Soc.* (1868) 148 The enemies to grain-growing are numerous. 1849 *Rep. U.S. Comm. Patents* (1850) 302 What I claim..is covering..*grain hullers with vulcanized India rubber. 1867 *Rep. Iowa Agric. Soc.* (1868) 470 We are not behind the rest of the world in inventive skill, for we have invented..Kent's *grain scourer.

19. grain-conveyor (see CONVEYER 4 b); **grain-cradle** (examples); **grain-elevator** (see ELEVATOR 3 a, b); **grain-gold** (*a*) (mod. U.S. example); **grain-man,** a dealer in grain; **grain-moth** (earlier U.S. example); **grain split,** the grain-side section of a split skin; **grain-worm,** the larva of a grain-moth.

1910 *Encycl. Brit.* VII. 54/2 The guide rollers, for ordinary *grain conveyors, are fitted to the upper or working side of the band at intervals of about 6 ft. 1845 *Cultivator* New Ser. III. 17 My method is to..cut with a *grain cradle previous to the first frost. 1852 *Trans. Mich. Agric. Soc.* III. 30 Best grain cradle. 1873 'MARK TWAIN' & WARNER *Gilded Age* xxii, Pictures of wharves, crowded with steam boats, and of huge *grain elevators on the bank. 1876 H. E. SCUDDER *Dwellers Five-Sisters Crt.* x. 159 'That is a grain elevator,' said he. 'It is used for storing grain.' 1901 S. MERWIN & H. K. WEBSTER *Calumet K* i. 1 The two million bushel grain elevator. 1905 *Macm. Mag.* Nov. 47 The wheat..is warehoused ready for shipment in grain-elevators, which are large rectangular buildings of great height, consisting of vertical bins, some of which are a hundred feet in depth. 1910 *Encycl. Brit.* VII. 57/1 Pneumatic Grain Elevators have been employed with good effect in loading and unloading grain from ships. 1850 W. COLTON *Deck & Port* xiv. 397 Each has a bag of *grain-gold in his hand, which he must double or lose. 1889 *Kansas Times & Star* 11 July, A former *grain man was appointed..contracting freight agent of the..railway here. 1849 *Rep. U.S. Comm. Patents, Agric.* (1850) 336 Ventilation,..has already been suggested among the remedies for the 'little *grain-moth'. 1897 C. T. DAVIS *Manuf. Leather* (ed. 2) 138 Good '*grain splits'. 1837 H. COLMAN *Rep. Agric. Mass.* (1838) 28 A third cause of the failure of the wheat crop in several places in the county, is the *grain worm.

Grain, *v.* [1] Add:

1. Delete †*Obs.* (Modern example.)

1924 *Glasgow Herald* 12 Nov. 16 Arable ground would grain even faster than it does if the dole-fed masses of the great cities, such as Buenos Aires and Sydney, were to be induced to lend a hand at the plough.

2. c. Also of syrup.

1862 *Trans. Ill. Agric. Soc.* (1865) V. 566 The yield of stalk was enormous but the sirup made from it was quite dark, and refused to grain. 1894 R. WELLS *Toffy & Sweets* 7 When lump or crystallised sugars are boiled to the heat.. of 250 degrees, the sugar is liable to grain, and to turn out a solid mass on the slab. 1906 *Daily Chron.* 31 Oct. 8/5 When the syrup has boiled for fifteen minutes add the chestnuts and stir the mixture until it 'grains' and turns white.

8. *trans.* To feed with grain. *U.S.*

1874 *Rep. Vermont Board Agric.* II. 406 Older sheep should be grained the first of the season, after which they may do without till the first of March. 1883 A. E. BOYD (Dakota) *MS. Letter*, When our horses are not doing any kind of work, we do not grain them, but merely give them hay.

Grain, *v.* [2] Transfer † *Obs.* to sense in Dict. and add: **2.** *trans.* To spear (fish) with a grains.

1892 STEVENSON & OSBOURNE *Wrecker* xii, Something struck me right through the forearm and stuck there. I put my other hand up, and, by George, it was the grain; the beasts had speared me like a porpoise. 'Cap'n!' I cried. ..'They've grained me.'

Graine (grēn). Also **grain.** [Fr.] The eggs or 'seed' of the silkworm.

1835 URE *Philos. Manuf.* II. vi. 230 The eggs or grains of the silk-worm are covered with a liquid, which glues them to the piece of cloth or paper on which the female is made to lay them. 1887 *Encycl. Brit.* XXII. 58/2 The eggs of the silk-worm, called *graine*, are hatched out by artificial heat. *Ibid.* 59/2 The sources of healthy graine became fewer and fewer. 1887 *Colonial & Indian Exhib., Rep. Col. Sect.* 337.

Grainering (grē¹·nəriŋ), *vbl. sb.* [f. GRAINER [1] + -ING [1].] The preparation of hides with a grainer or bate.

1897 C. T. DAVIS *Manuf. Leather* (ed. 2) 153.

Graineur (grɛ̈nör). [F. *graineur*, also *greneur.*] A producer of silkworm eggs.

1913 J. H. LONGFORD *Evol. New Japan* vii. 87 French and Italian graineurs, while eager to buy her raw silk, were still more eager to buy the eggs of her healthy silkworms in order to replenish their own exhausted stock.

Graining, *vbl. sb.* [1] **4.** Add: *graining-block, -gouge.*

1846 SAGE *Scenes Rocky Mts.* (1850) 318 Near this is his '*graining block', planted a slope, for the ease of the operative in preparing his skins for the finishing process in the art of dressing. 1875 SIR T. SEATON *Fret-Cutting* 14. The details of the hair and curls must now be worked out with fine hollow gouges and *graining gouges.

Gram [3] (gram). *Biol.* The name of Dr. C. *Gram* of Copenhagen, used to designate his method of staining bacteria. *Gram-positive, -negative*, adjs. indicating that an organism does, or does not, stain by Gram's method.

1884 *Brit. Med. Jrnl.* 6 Sept. 487/2 Gram's method gives good results with many bacteria. 1907 *Practitioner* Aug. 277 The Boas-Oppler bacillus is Gram-positive, whereas the normal bacillary flora of the large intestine is mainly Gram-negative. 1913 MUIR & RITCHIE *Bacteriol.* (ed. 6) 107 In Gram's method the essential feature is the treating of the tissue, after staining, with a solution of iodine. This solution is spoken of as Gram's solution. *Ibid.* 108 There is great variation in the acidity with which organisms stained by Gram retain the dye when washed with alcohol...Most bacteria are either frankly Gram-positive or Gram-negative. 1925 C. H. BROWNING *Bacteriology* ii. 32 Certain bacteria part with the violet stain and are consequently counterstained red with the fuchsine; these are Gram-negative organisms. Other bacteria retain the violet stain and, since this colour is much more intense than that of the red counterstain, they do not appear stained by the latter; hence such Gram-positive organisms show a blue-black colour.

Grama. (Earlier example.)

1844 J. GREGG *Commerce of Prairies* I. 160 A highly nutritious grass called *grama.*

Grammar, *sb.* Add: **5. c.** The name of a class in certain Jesuit schools or colleges.

1629 WADSWORTH *Pilgr.* iii. 13 Father Lacy, the Reader of Poetry, and Master of the Syntax. Father Henry Bentley and Father Iohn Compton of Grammer. 1667 in *Cath. Rec. Soc. Publ.* III. 63 He was newly entered into grammer. *Ibid.* 60 Answering to hard and intrecat questions publickly in our Refectory even the first week he was in grammer. 1773 in *Mem. Stonyhurst Coll.* (1881) 22 The former Master of Poetry, the latter of Grammar, at Bruges. 1837 J. C. FISHER in *Ushaw Mag.* (1904) Dec. 262–3. 1904 *Ibid.* June 201 On Tuesday, May 17th, Syntax played Grammar.

Grammarian. Add: **2. b.** A member of the class named 'Grammar' in Jesuit schools or colleges.

1705 in *Ushaw Mag.* (1903) Dec. 298. 1837 J. C. FISHER *Ibid.* (1904) Dec. 250 In the cyphering school with the Grammarians and High Fig[ures]. 1904 *Ibid.* Mar. 98.

Grammar-school. 2. *U.S.* (Earlier examples.)

1671 *Doc. & Rec. New Hampshire* I. 312 To sett up a grammer schoole and appointe a master thereof. 1789 MORSE *Amer. Geog.* 175 There is also to be a grammar school. 1838 *Southern Lit. Messenger* IV. 365 From a grammar-school to an academy, and from an academy to a college. 1848 *Indiana Gen. Assembly Doc.* II. 279 Connected with the Institution is a flourishing Grammar School, which serves the double purpose of a Normal School and a Preparatory Department.

Gramme (græm). The name of the Belgian electrician Zénobe Théophile *Gramme* (1826–1901) used attrib. to designate a form of dynamo armature introduced by him in 1870 (*Gramme ring, armature, winding*, etc.).

1885 HIGGS *Magn. & Dyn.-electric Mach.* 255 The inductive actions in the coils of a Gramme ring. *Ibid.*, The ring of the Gramme machine. 1893 HAWKINS & WALLIS *Dynamo* 115 The first or 'Ring' method..is also frequently called the 'Gramme' winding. *Ibid.* 193 In the Gramme-wound ring armature the number of loops and the number of inductors are identical.

Gramophone. Substitute the following def. and add more recent quots. (In quot. 1896 in Dict. the word appears to describe a dictaphone.) An instrument for recording and reproducing vocal, instrumental, and other sounds (invented by Emil Berliner, of Washington, D.C.), *esp.* a reproducing instrument consisting essentially of a turn-table revolving at a constant speed, and capable of carrying disks on which are impressed, in a spiral track, wave-forms corresponding to sound vibrations, to reproduce which a stylus, attached to an acoustic device or electric system, travels along the track.

1906 *Daily Chron.* 26 Nov. 4/7 What's wearing me to skin and bone? My neighbour's grinding gramophone. 1913 B. CLEMENTS-HENRY *Gramophones & Phonographs* 5 The disc machine is known as the 'gramophone', and the cylinder machine as the 'phonograph'. 1921 P. A. SCHOLES *Learning to Listen by Gramophone* Pref. p. xv, The accumulated results of their already large experience of the educational use of the Gramophone. 1928 GALSWORTHY *Swan Song* II. iv. 140 'What is the most pitiable sight in the world?'.. 'Oh! I think—a rich man listening to a bad gramophone.'

b. *attrib.* and *Comb.*, as *gramophone record*; **gramophone-cut,** the form of record-cutting in which the recording stylus vibrates parallel to the surface of the disk.

1888 *English Mechanic* 24 Aug. 588/2 The preparation of Grammophone .. Records. 1913 B. CLEMENTS-HENRY *Gramophones & Phonographs* 4 The so-called 'gramophone-cut'. 1913 G. F. ROWELL *Hints about Gramophone* 11 A gramophone recital. 1924 P. A. SCHOLES *1st Bk. Gramophone Record* Introd. p. vii, Many of the best 'tunes' .. await their enjoyment in the form of Gramophone Records.

Gra·mophone, *v.* [f. the sb.] *trans.* To reproduce by means of the gramophone. Also *fig.* and *absol.*

1908 *Daily Chron.* 8 Apr. 3/7 The Tories are canvassing, 'gramophoning', &c. 1927 *Sunday Express* 28 Aug. 5/2 America's noise was gramophoned everywhere. 1928 *Manch. Guardian Weekly* 10 Aug. 113/4 The perils of a syndicated or grammophoned press.

Gramophonic (græmǫ̆fǫ·nik), *a.* [-IC.] Of, pertaining to, or of the nature of the gramophone.

1905 *Westm. Gaz.* 2 Sept. 9/1 She has what I call a 'gramophonic mind'—that is, she assimilates other people's ideas and then rolls them off as if they were her own. 1915 *Morning Post* 4 Mar. 4/4 A gramophonic reproduction of a tune which was being played in Berlin. 1921 P. A. SCHOLES *Learning to Listen by Gramophone* Pref. p. xiv, The illustrated volume to which this one is, frankly, a gramophonic companion. 1927 *Observer* 24 Apr. 4/3 The National Gramophonic Society..issues the first of its orchestral records.

Hence **Gramopho·nically** *adv.*, in a gramophonic manner, by or on a gramophone.

1911 W. J. LOCKE *Glory of Clementina Wing* xx, A stupendous woolly lamb..which, on something being done to its anatomy, opened its mouth and gramophonically chanted the 'Jewel Song' from Faust. 1913 *Christian* 3 Jan. 10/1 To find..the daily Press..giving voice to facts instead of gramophonically repeating the sentiments uttered by huge vested interests. 1924 SCHOLES *1st Bk. Gramophone Record* 30 The only piece of our great Purcell gramophonically available was the song *Nymphs and Shepherds.*

Gramophonist (gră·mǫ̆fōnist, græ·mǒfounist). [-IST.] One who uses or operates a gramophone.

1907 *Daily Chron.* 12 Dec. 7/4 The gramophonist will redistribute the pearls of wisdom which have fallen from the lips of great Unionist statesmen to crowds of admiring villagers. 1923 *Weekly Dispatch* 4 Feb. 2, I must modestly disclaim being a passionate gramophonist (if that is the word). 1924 SCHOLES *1st Bk. Gramophone Record* 123 The description..will..be thought sufficient by many gramophonists.

Gramophony (grămǫ·fŏni, græ·mǒfouni). [f. GRAMOPHONE, after *telephony.*] The art of the gramophone; gramophone reproduction.

1925 SCHOLES *2nd Bk. Gramophone Record* p. xix, It is one of the regrettable features of gramophony to-day that the songs of Schubert..are not to be obtained. 1927 *Daily Mirror* 10 Dec. 12/3 An impression is rapidly gaining ground that the whole future of gramophony rests with the electrical 'pick-up'.

Gran [2] (græn). *dial.* Short for **granny** or *grandmother.*

1895 CROCKETT *Bog-Myrtle* II. ii, His mother or his 'gran' ..aided and abetted him. 1908 *Westm. Gaz.* 8 Feb. 12/3 People say it was just because Gran lived so vividly that she flickered out like a candle come midsummer. *Ibid.*, The lady who received the Grans.

Grand, *a.* and *sb.* Add:

A. *adj.* **10. b.** *Grand manner*, the style of plastic art suited for noble subjects and vast design. [After F. *grande manière.*] Also *attrib.*

1905 *Daily Chron.* 28 Dec. 3/1 The Royal Academy tradition of the Grand Manner in painting. *Ibid.*, Sculpture groups, illustrating a classical theme, built up on Grand Manner traditions. 1925 F. F. POTTER in *Teacher's World* July Extra No., The boys of Manchester Grammar School were engaged in a project in the grand manner, when they drained, levelled, and turfed their playing fields.

12. Grand Army (of the Republic) *U.S.*, an association of veterans who served in the Union army or navy during the Civil War, formed at Decatur, Illinois, in 1866 (cf. POST *sb.* [3] 2 b); **Grand Canyon** *Geol.*, a proterozoic series between the Archean and the Cambrian in the Colorado, U.S.; **Grand Cordon, Cross** (see CORDON *sb.* 6, CROSS *sb.* 19); **Grand Fleet,** the name during the war-period 1914–16 for the British Battle Fleet operating in the North Sea; **Grand National,** the great steeplechase established in 1839 and run annually at Aintree, Liverpool, in the first week of the flat-racing season; **grand prize,** anglicization of *GRAND PRIX 3; **grand quarter** *Her.*: see quot. and cf. *grand quartering*; **Grand Remonstrance, slam** (see REMONSTRANCE *sb.* 3 b, SLAM *sb.* [2] 2 b); **grand-stand**: also *attrib.* in **grand-stand play** *U.S.*, a way of playing a game with an eye to the applause of the grand stand; *fig.* an act done for effect or to win applause; **grand-stander**

U.S., ? a performer who seeks to impress the grand stand; **grand tactics** *Mil.* [F. *la grande tactique*] (see quot.).

1904 *N.Y. Evening Post* 30 May 2 In every city where a *Grand Army post is located the veterans marched to the cemeteries. 1911 H. S. HARRISON *Queed* xxi. 263 A Grand Army man stood in the press on the sidewalk. 1876 J. W. POWELL *Rep. Geol. Eastern Portion Uinta Mount.* 70 The *Grand Cañon Group rests unconformably upon the crystalline schists. .. Fossils have been found at the base of the Grand Cañon series...Red Creek Quartzite and Grand Cañon schists..are believed to be Eozoic. 1894 C. D. WALCOTT in *14th Rep. U.S. Geol. Survey* II. 503. 1925 JOLY *Surface-Hist. Earth* viii. 131 The third (the Killarney or Grand Canyon) closing pre-Cambrian time. 1914 JELLICOE in *Times* 16 Sept. 8/6 The officers and men of the *Grand Fleet beg that you will convey to their comrades of the British Army their intense admiration for the magnificent fight they have made. 1919 — *Grand Fleet 1914–16* iii. 34 The Grand Fleet may be said to have come into being only at the outbreak of the War, when it was so christened. 1922 *Encycl. Brit.* XXXII. 294/1 Up to the outbreak of war, Rosyth was regarded as the principal base and headquarters for the Grand Fleet. 1839 *Sporting Rev.* Mar. 164 The '*Grand National Steeple Chase. 1866 *Field* 10 Mar. 190/3 Why should he be a favourite for the Grand National? 1880 *Encycl. Brit.* XII. 203/1 The chief event is the Liverpool Grand National, run at Aintree towards the close of the hunting season. It dates from 1839. 1886 *Racing & Steeple-chasing* (Badm. Libr.) 352 Tom Olliver won three Grand Nationals. 1894 SIR J. D. ASTLEY *Fifty Yrs. Life* II. 281, I hoped to be able to pick out the winner of the Grand National when the weights appeared. 1866 *Lond. Gaz.* 26 June 3645/2 Paris Universal Exhibition of 1867...17 *grand prizes, each of the value of 2000f. 1880 *Rep. Paris Univ. Exhib. 1878* II. 365, 100 Grand Prizes and exceptional awards in money. 1896 J. WOODWARD *Her.* II. 102 It may happen that one of the heiresses whose arms are to be quartered, herself bore a quartered coat, in this case the quarter appropriated to her contains her whole bearings..and..is called a *Grand-quarter. 1893 W. K. POST *Harvard Stories* 308 They all hold on to something or clasp their knees tightly—to faint or fall over would be a *grand-stand play. 1904 *Utica Observer* 21 June 6 The ultimatum to the Sultan of Morocco, 'Perdicaris alive or Raisuli dead' was a good one. But telegraphing it to the National Convention at Chicago made it look very much like a grand stand play. 1920 C. H. STAGG *High Speed* vii. 121 The men followed glumly. A car like that, and in the hands of a *grand-stander! That's what he was; that's why he'd got a reputation on the coast. *a* 1903 G. F. R. HENDERSON *Sci. War* vii. (1905) 168 *Grand Tactics, the art of generalship, include those stratagems, manœuvres, and devices by which victories are won, and concern only those officers who may find themselves in independent command.

B. *sb.* **7.** In the game of skat, a bid to play with only the four matadores (knaves) as trumps. Varieties of this are called *solo grand, gucki grand, tournee grand, open grand* (or *grand ouvert*). [G. (a. Fr.) *grand*, formerly *grando* (see quot. 1893).]

[1893 tr. *A. Hertefeld's Skat* 7 In *Grando*, the only trumps are the four knaves. *Ibid.* 46 The basis value is in *Grando Tourné*, 12; in *Grando Solo*, 16; and in *Grande Ouvert*, 24.] 1906 R. F. FOSTER *Skat Manual* 121 This he can do by declaring a Grand.

8. A thousand dollars. *U.S. slang.*

1930 F. L. PACKARD *Jimmie Dale & Blue Envelope Murder* xii, 'Who killed Blotz? Five grand.'..'Does it mean that Blotz was murdered by contract for five thousand dollars?' 1931 ERIC LINKLATER *Juan in America* IV. x. 359 D'you think I'd pay a hundred grand for protection if it wasn't worth it? 1932 *Amer. Mercury* Jan. 16, I don't know how much it is, but I suppose around ten, twelve, fifteen grand.

Grand coup (grañ ku). [Fr.: see COUP *sb.* [3]]

1. A great and important stroke or hit; a bold and successful effort.

1813 BYRON *Let. to Moore* 22 Aug. in Moore *Life* (1832) II. 234, I hope you are going on with your *grand coup*—pray do—or that damned Lucien Buonaparte will beat us all. 1856 C. F. ADAMS in *Life & Wks. J. Adams* I. 352 Justly was it denominated by one who had spent his life in the diplomatic service, a '*grand coup*'. 1883 *Standard* 17 Sept. 5/2 (Stanford) [The police] then make a *grand coup* all at once.

2. *Whist.* The getting rid of a superfluous trump in order to avoid a disadvantageous lead.

1884 'CAVENDISH' *Whist* (ed. 14) 143 Sometimes..a player has a trump too many. To get rid of this trump..is to play the *grand coup.*

Grande dame (grand dam). [Fr.] A great lady; a lady of rank and dignified bearing.

1861 THACKERAY *Philip* i, She had been a great beauty, and was a perfect *grande dame* always. 1865 'OUIDA' *Strathmore* I. ii. 35 Or you've made love to some grande dame because it answered a political purpose. 1886 *Athenæum* 30 Jan. 175/1 The mother's stately grace and fully developed beauty, her noble face and rich yet chastened attire, distinguish her as a *grande dame.*

attrib. 1908 *Daily Chron.* 21 Feb. 3/2 Mrs. Saker, who is an accomplished player of 'grand-dame' parts.

Grande passion (grand pasyoñ). [Fr.] An overmastering love for one of the opposite sex; an engrossing love affair.

1823 BYRON *Juan* XII. lxxvii, And if in fact she takes to a *grande passion*, It is a very serious thing indeed. 1854 'C. BEDE' *Verdant Green* II. xi. 95 Despite the hindrance which the *grande passion* is supposed to bring to the student. 1865 'OUIDA' *Strathmore* I. ii. 30 The perpetual gallantries, the never-ending, ever-changing *grandes passions*..that were characteristic of the Sabreur. 1883 L. OLIPHANT *Altiora Peto* II. xxiii. 72 It was sometimes said of Mrs Clymer..that she was a woman capable of a *grande passion.*

Grande tenue (grand tənü). [Fr.] Full dress; *esp.* full military costume. (See also s.v. *EN.)

1865 'OUIDA' *Strathmore* I. x. 171 The ease of the dressing-gown after the restraint of the *grande tenue.* 1886 *Athenæum* 24 Apr. 560/2 The little soldier..is almost a caricature; the *grande tenue* is so ridiculous as to lose the charm which belongs to grotesqueness.

Grandfather. Add: **4. b.** Short for *grandfather('s) clock* (see 5 in Dict.).

1899 F. J. BRITTEN *Old Clocks & Watches* 309 Some of these primitive 'grandfathers' were exceedingly narrow in the waist. 1906 *Bazaar, Exch. & Mart* Suppl. 3 Oct. 1302/3 Wanted, old grandfathers, brass arched dials. 1909 EDITH RICKERT *Beggar in Heart* 1 The house is so still I can hear grandfather ticking on the stairs with the door shut.

5. grandfather clause *U.S. colloq.*, a clause in the recent constitutions of some Southern states, exempting from suffrage restrictions the descendants of men who voted before the Civil War; **grandfather clock** = *grandfather's clock* (and see *4 b).

1903 *N.Y. Evening Post* 21 Dec. 6 It is proposed [in Maryland] to remodel the Constitution so as to exclude colored men from voting. The usual Southern method is followed, '*grandfather clause' and all. 1906 W. H. FLEMING *Slavery* 44 This proviso was popularly known as the 'Grandfather clause'. 1910 *Encycl. Brit.* VI. 552/2 The long or '*grandfather' clock dates from about the fourth quarter of the 17th century. 1928 J. E. HASWELL *Horology* 74 A typical grandfather clock.

Grandfer, granfer (græ·nfəɹ), dial. shortening of GRANDFATHER.

1874 HARDY *Far fr. Mad. Crowd* viii, Ah, he's his grandfer's own grandson. 1930 *Daily Express* 23 May 10/3 What is good enough for granfer is good enough for us, look'ee.

Grand Guignol (grañ ginyol). [Fr. (= Great Punch), the name of a theatre in Paris.] A dramatic entertainment in which short pieces of a sensational or horrific kind are played successively. Also *transf.* Hence **Grand Guignole·sque** *a.*, **Grand Gui·gnolism.**

1920 H. B. IRVING in *M. Level's Crises* Introd. p. iii, M. Level has given literary expression of a high order to the compact horrors of the Grand Guignol. 1922 *Westm. Gaz.* 1 Dec., Violent eccentricity is on the decrease; I have seen Salons of a much more Grand Guignol character than this one. 1923 *Daily Mail* 12 June 8 'The Drums of Oude' ..is perhaps unequalled as a one-act thriller outside frank Grand Guignolism. 1928 *Daily Tel.* 27 Mar. 6 'The Unknown', a morbid Grand Guignolesque conception rendered tolerable..by the actor's arresting personality.

Grand Marnier (grañ marnye). [Fr.; *grand* great, fine, and *Marnier*-Lapostolle, name of manufacturer.] A French liqueur resembling curaçao.

1905 *Daily Chron.* 28 Apr. 6/7 A publican who supplied Benedictine to several customers who asked for Grand Marnier was fined £5. 1910 *Encycl. Brit.* VII. 636/1 A lighter variety of Curaçoa, made with fine brandy, is known as 'Grand Marnier'. 1924 GALSWORTHY *White Monkey* II. ii, He went to a cupboard and returned with two small glasses of a brown fluid. 'Have a Grand Marnier?'

Grand Monarque (grañ monark). [Fr.] The title given to Louis XIV. Also *transf.*, a supreme and absolute ruler.

[Cf. quot. *a* 1704 s.v. GRAND *a.* 8.] 1716 ADDISON *Freeholder* No. 10. ¶ 6 His Governours of Towns and Provinces, who form'd themselves upon the Example of their *Grand Monarque*, practised Rapine, Violence, Extortion. 1840 BARHAM *Ingol. Leg.* Ser. II. *Black Mousquetaire*, 'Twas the *Grand Monarque's* birthday. 1911 *Encycl. Brit.* XVII. 42/2 Louis was singularly well fitted by his physical and intellectual gifts for the rôle of *Grand Monarque* and he played it to perfection.

Grandmother. Add: **4. grandmother clock,** a clock resembling a grandfather's clock, but with a smaller case.

1927 *Daily Tel.* 6 Dec. 3/7 A grandmother clock with brass dial. 1930 *Aberdeen Press & Jrnl.* 31 May 8/3 The gift to ex-Constable Jamie was a beautiful grandmother clock.

Gra·ndmother, *v.* [f. the sb.] *trans.* To be grandmother to. Hence **Gra·ndmothering** *vbl. sb.* (with reference to excessive and doctrinaire legislation).

1901 H. JAMES *Two Faces* ii. in *The Better Sort* (1903) 42 Do you mean by his idea his proposal that I should grandmother his wife? 1923 *Chambers's Jrnl.* Feb. 102/1 A frail little lady who had grandmothered a hefty brood of men. 1929 *Daily Express* 8 Jan. 8/7 Political power has naturally passed into the hands of people with a passion for grandmothering. *Ibid.* 12 Jan. 8/7, I refuse to believe that Britons are so excessively unmanly as to be driven to this state of grandmothering.

Grand Old Party. *U.S. politics.* [See GRAND *a.* 10 d.]

†1. The Democratic party. *Obs.*

Used without capitals and perhaps not specific.

1879 *Congress. Record* 11 June 1913/1 We are for national politics now. We come back to the grand old party of the North. 1888 *Ibid.* 10 May 3981/1, I am glad that I am a member of that grand old party that assures a better trade to our people, larger wages &c.

2. The Republican party.

1888 *Congress. Record* 1 May 3598/1 Old Farmer: Is this Democratic doings or Republican doings? Collector: O, it is the doings of the G.O.P.,—the grand old party,—the Republican party. 1898 *Ibid.* 7 Jan. 444/1 Has the Grand Old Party (G.O.P.) so called never been corrupt? Has it never had dishonest men in it? 1904 *New York Even. Post* 25 Aug. 6 A close examination of Republican speeches fails to reveal an instance in which the Democracy is portrayed as on a parity with the Grand Old Party.

Grandparental (grændpărẹ·ntăl), *a.* [See -AL.] Of or belonging to a grandparent or grandparents.

1903 *Lancet* 18 Apr. 1081/1 Cases in which the taint was grandparental. 1929 *19th Cent.* Dec. 810 A collateral relative at the level of the grandparental or great-grandparental generation. 1930 R. A. FISHER *Genet. Theory Nat. Selection* 198 The grandparental effect..is subject to somewhat large sampling errors.

Grand Prix (grañ pri). [Fr., = great or chief prize.]

1. (In full *Grand Prix de Paris.*) An international race for three-year-olds established in 1863 and run annually in June at Longchamps, Paris. Hence applied to certain motor-races.

1866 *Field* 10 Mar. 199/3 Some of our English friends, too, are travelled gentlemen, who go to the Grand Prix. 1902 *Encycl. Brit.* XXIX. 336/2 The Grand Prix de Paris, an international race for three-year-olds, run at Longchamps... The first Grand Prix fell to an English horse. 1908 *Westm. Gaz.* 2 Apr. 4/3 The drivers have now definitely been selected for the team of three Austin cars entered for competition in the Grand Prix race. 1922 *Encycl. Brit.* XXXI. 1003/2 In 1911 began a new series of races for the *Grand Prix* of the Automobile Club of France. 1931 *Times* 5 June 4/6 To-day's practice for the Irish Grand Prix Race for motor-cars.

2. *Grand Prix de Rome*, a prize awarded by the French government to French artists, entitling the winners to four years' study in Italy.

1922 *Encycl. Brit.* XXX. 186/1 The institution of the Grand Prix de Rome—the blue ribbon of the architectural student.

3. *gen.* The highest prize awarded for products in some particular line at an exhibition.

Also in anglicized form, *grand prize*: see *GRAND *a.* 12.

1880 *Rep. Paris Univ. Exhib. 1878* II. 425. 1916 *Oxf. Univ. Press Gen. Cat.*, The Twenty-three Grands Prix Awarded to the Oxford University Press At International Exhibitions 1889–1911.

Grand siècle (grañ syękl). [Fr., = great century or age.] The reign of Louis XIV, the classical or 'Augustan' age of literature in France.

1912 G. L. STRACHEY *Landmarks Fr. Lit.* v. 133 While the masterpieces of the *Grand Siècle* served no ulterior purpose..those of the eighteenth century were works of propaganda. 1931 *Times Lit. Suppl.* 5 Feb. 91/1 [M. Brémond] has charmed the world with studies in the religion of France during the *grand siècle.*

Granite. Add:

1. b. *fig.* applied to 'stony', hard-headed, or hard-hearted persons. Often *attrib.* and *Comb.* (cf. *granite-like* in 3 b).

1902 *Daily Chron.* 12 Nov. 5/6 That granite-headed ship-owner, Sir Alfred L. Jones. 1908 *Ibid.* 7 Nov. 4/4 His countenance expressed neither the sweetness and tenderness of the saint nor the granite severity of the prophet. 1916 *Punch* 14 June 398/2, I stole a look at Hercules over my shoulder, but he was granite. 1920 C. JERDAN *Scott. Clerical Stories* viii. 164 Strong-boned, granite-headed, and endowed with all kinds of vitality.

3. c. granite ware (earlier U.S. example).

1876 J. S. INGRAM *Centen. Exposition* 706 Upon the bottom of a granite ware basin.

Granodiorite (grǣnədai·ŏrəit). *Petrol.* [f. *grano-*, taken as combining form of *granite*: cf. GRANOPHYRE.] A granular, igneous rock intermediate between granite and quartz-diorite. Hence **Gra·nodiori·tic** *a.*

1893 W. LINDGREN in *Amer. Jrnl. Sci.* Ser. III. XLVI. 202–3. 1911 *Encycl. Brit.* XXVII. 1/1 Grano-diorite..has been very generally adopted in America for rocks which are intermediate in character between the granites and the diorites. *Ibid.* 1/2 Grano-diorites have been described from California. 1925 H. H. READ, etc. *Geol. Golspie* 34 The Rogart granodioritic magma.

Granolithic, *a.* Add: Also *sb.* = granolithic concrete.

1881 *Specif. Patent P. Stuart* No. 610. 4. 1901 *Guinness Trust, Fulham P. Rd.* 8 The open areas between the blocks ..are paved with granolithic for use as playgrounds. 1905 G. L. SUTCLIFFE *Concrete* (ed. 2) 336 Numerous tests have been made of reinforced Granolithic. 1905 TAYLOR & THOMPSON *Concrete* 1 Granolithic is concrete consisting of Portland cement and fine broken stone or sand troweled to form a wearing surface. 1909 *Pall Mall Gaz.* 12 Apr. 2/2 An inscription in brass letters set in granolithic.

Granth (grʊnt). Also **grantha.** [Hindi *granth* book, code, a. Skr. *grantha* tying, knot, literary composition, book, text, f. *granth, grath* to tie.] The sacred scriptures of the Sikhs, composed by Nānak Shāh and others.

1837 G. R. SIDDONS in *Jrnl. Asiatic Soc. Bengal* VI. I. 480 The Granthas, or sacred books, of the Dadupanthi Sect. 1880 *Encycl. Brit.* XI. 844/2 Nothing in Hindī by Rāmānuja has come down to us; of Rāmānand we have one short poem in the Granth. 1901 *N. Amer. Rev.* Feb. 303 The Sikh still..visits the temple to listen to the reading of the Granth. 1927 *Daily Tel.* 22 Feb. 11/5 Three hundred Sikhs, carrying the Granth Sahib, or Holy Book,..were attacked by infuriated Moslems.

Granulitize (græ·niŭlitaiz), *v.* *Geol.* [f. GRANULITE + -IZE.] **a.** *trans.* To make granulitic. **b.** *intr.* To become granulitic. Hence **Granuliti·za·tion,** conversion into granulite.

1903 GEIKIE *Text-bk. Geol.* (ed. 4) I. 248 Granular (granulitised) quartz. 1930 PEACH & HORNE *Geol. Scotl.* 26 These planes are not accompanied by granulitization. *Ibid.* 28 Within the shear-zones new foliation planes are developed and the minerals are granulitized. *Ibid.* 55 The hornblende does not granulitize though the ends of the crystals may be teased out into fibres.

Granulometric (grænɪu̇lome·trik), *a.* [ad. F. *granulométrique*: see GRANULO- and METRIC.] Pertaining to measurement of the different sizes of grains of sand.

1905 L. C. SABIN *Cement & Concrete* xi. 163 Thus, all of the sands tested had the same 'granulometric' composition. 1905 TAYLOR & THOMPSON *Concrete* ix. 141 Granulometric composition of sand.

Grape, *sb.*[1] Add: **7.** = GRAPE-VINE 2 a.

1865 in *Southern Hist. Soc. Papers* (1877) III. 56 Plenty of 'grape', i.e. rumors afloat of a speedy general exchange.

8. a. *grape-arbour, -cutting, -rot, -seed* (earlier U.S. example). **b.** *grape-culturist, -grower.*

1898 MARG. DELAND *Old Chester Tales* 107 They were sitting in the *grape-arbor with a little table between them. 1900 MARY E. WILKINS *Love of Parson Lord* 64 Poor Love ..repaired of an afternoon to the grape-arbor. 1907 *Chicago Evening Post* 4 May 15 (Advt.) Fine summer home on good lake; grape arbors; garden. 1847 *Rep. U.S. Comm. Patents* (1848) 468, I would strongly urge the *grape culturists..to add brandy to their wine after fermentation. 1768 WASHINGTON *Diaries* I. 267 Planted out *Grape Cuttings. 1847 *Rep. U.S. Comm. Patents* (1848) 469 The landlord to furnish the dwelling house..fruit trees and grape cuttings at his own expense. 1889 *Harper's Mag.* Jan. 261/2 The better class of laboring agriculturists, *grape-growers, and stock-raisers. 1886 *Harper's Mag.* June 44/1 When mildew and *grape-rot first appear. 1786 WASHINGTON *Diaries* III. 36 Tho' the ground was nearly prepared for my *grape Seeds, I could not sow them on acct. of the Weather.

9. grape-berry moth (example); **grape codling** (see quot.); **grape-fruit** has of late been popularized in England, esp. as an hors d'œuvre or a preliminary to a meal; **grape-nuts,** the trade name for a patent preparation of Indian corn in a crisp granular form.

1871 *Trans. Ill. Agric. Soc.* VIII. 158 The *Penthina Vitivorana*, or *Grape-berry moth, called also *Grape-codling. 1851 *Illustr. Catal. Gt. Exhib.* IV. I. 971/2 *Grape-fruit. 1859, 1885 [in Dict.]. 1904 *Daily Chron.* 4 May 10/5 The grape-fruit, which is gradually growing in popularity in England. 1905 *Westm. Gaz.* 4 Mar. 12/3 The grape-fruit grows in bunches (hence its name). 1909 *Daily Chron.* 15 June 4/4 The grape fruit, excellent in salad, and excellent to eat alone, so subtly combining the flavours of orange, lemon, and grape. 1905 CHESTERTON *Heretics* 136 There is more simplicity in the man who eats caviar on impulse than in the man who eats *grape-nuts on principle. 1912 J. H. MOORE *Ethics & Education* ix. 50 And it would be just as scientific to advertise moral principles on bill boards as it is to instil the virtues of 'grape nuts' in this way.

Gra·pe-sho·tted, *a.* [f. GRAPE-SHOT.] Loaded with grape-shot.

1910 JER. HART *Vigilante Girl* xiv. 193 When the Section Lepelletier revolted in Paris he placed grape-shotted cannon at the street angles.

Grape-vine. Add: **1.** (Earlier U.S. examples.)

1654 *Providence* (R. I.) *Rec.* (1893) II. 78 Bounded..on the East-end on the lower side..by the grape Vines. 1765 G. CROGHAN *Jrnl.* 128 A great part of the trees in the bottom are covered with grape vines. 1768 WASHINGTON *Diaries* I. 265 Planting out Grape Vines according to Memorandum. 1815 D. DRAKE *Cincinnati* ii. 70 [The shells] were lying in connexion with grape vines and other vegetables. 1829–32 J. P. KENNEDY *Swallow B.* I. xii. 129 A straggling grape-vine swung across from tree to tree.

3. *attrib.*, as *grape-vine beetle, bridle, juice, land, rope, sphinx, telegraph* (see 2 a), *telegraphic* adj., *wire*.

1867 *Rep. Iowa Agric. Soc.* (1868) 189 The vines have been injured to some extent by the leaf-louse; the *grape-vine beetle has not been seen. 1824 P. HORRY *Life of F. Marion* (1833) 47 You might be sure to see..the fences strung along with starved tackies, in *grape-vine bridles and sheep-skin saddles. 1813 PAULDING *Sc. Fiddle* IV. (1814) 81 He..Foster'd the honours of his head, With *grape-vine juice, and bear's grease too. 1871 SCHELE DE VERE *Americanisms* (1872) 407 The comparatively poor land, on which grapevines grow wild, and which is hence called *Grapevine Land. 1843 R. CARLTON *New Purchase* I. xii. 90 An athletic woman stepped ..into the boat, her little boy at the moment casting loose the *grape vine rope—its fastening. 1886 *Harper's Mag.* June 45/2 Leaf-rollers, the *grape-vine sphinx, and caterpillars..must be caught by hand. 1889 FARMER *Americanisms* s.v., During the Civil War exciting news of battles not fought and victories not won were said to be received by *grape-vine telegraph. 1864 in *Southern Hist. Soc. Papers* (1876) I. 437 Many '*grape-vine' telegraphic reports are afloat in camp. 1907 J. L. GIVEN *Making a Newspaper* xiii. 230 Not often does a telegraph editor..manufacture news, or, in the vernacular, employ the '*grapevine wire'.

Graphite. Add: Used as a solid lubricant for machinery. Hence **Graphited** (græ·fəitėd) *a.*, supplied with graphite as a lubricant.

1906 *Bulletin Imp. Inst.* IV. 358 Graphite is of the greatest value as a lubricant for machinery, especially in cases where the pressure on the bearings is very great and the movement slow, so that lubricating oils are soon pressed out. 1912 ARCHBUTT & DEELEY *Lubrication* (ed. 3) 150 In 1906, Dr. Acheson discovered amongst the products of the electric furnace a highly unctuous, soft, and almost chemically pure graphite, possessing all the properties of an ideal solid lubricant. 1922 *Autocar* 10 Nov. 997 Graphited oilless bushes are freely used.

Graphitize (græ·fitəiz), *v.* [See -IZE.] *trans.* To convert (carbon) into graphite. Hence **Graphitiza·tion,** conversion into graphite.

1910 *Encycl. Brit.* XII. 365/1 Two procedures are adopted: (1) graphitization of moulded carbons; (2) graphitization of anthracite *en masse*. 1912 A. ROGERS *Industr. Chem.* 276 After such a run the granulated coke forming the heating core has been graphitized. *Ibid.* 277 The furnace used for graphitizing small carbon electrodes.

Grappier (græ·piəɹ). [Fr., f. *grappe* (as in *grappes de la chaux*).] A hard lump of unslaked hydraulic limestone used for making cement.

1905 E. C. ECKEL *Cements* 180 After slaking is completed, the lime remains as a fine powder interspersed with lumps (grappiers) of harder material. *Ibid.* 185 Grappier cements are made by grinding finely the lumps of unburned and overburned material which remain when a hydraulic lime is slaked. 1920 B. BLOUNT *Cement* 185 Grappiers, or hard-burned lumps from siliceous hydraulic limes.

Grapple, *sb.* Add: **4. b.** 'A tool with spring jaws which are closed by striking the fish' (Knight *Dict. Mech.* Suppl. 1884).

1872 *Game Laws Maine* in *Fur, Fin & Feather* (1872) 162 No person shall be allowed to take or catch any pickerel with spears, hooks or grapples.

Grass, *sb.*[1] Add: **1. c.** *Between grass and hay* U.S. (see quots.).

1871 SCHELE DE VERE *Americanisms* (1872) 208 The peculiar phrase in which the youth, who is no longer a boy, and not yet a man, is picturesquely said to be between grass and hay. 1891 H. C. BUNNER *Zadoc Pine* 17 He..got a couple of eggs cooked for his private supper....The eggs were, as he told Mr. Bryan, 'kinder 'twixt grass and hay'.

4. b. Also, the young shoots of the carnation.

1836 N. PATERSON *Manse Garden* (1860) 189 The young shoots [of carnations] near the ground which do not run to flower are denominated grass. *Ibid.* 190 Pipings (as the grass shoots taken off and stuck in the ground are called)..will take root. c 1899 *Played Out* 47 Masses of clove carnations, with their own beautiful blue-green leaves, or 'grass', as a carnation grower would term it.

9. *esp.* Ground covered with grass closely mown and rolled, forming a lawn or border in a garden. *Keep off the grass*: a notice frequently posted in a park or garden to which the public are admitted; also used trivially as a warning not to take liberties, encroach, or interfere.

1850 *Punch* 5 Oct. 144/1 The public, who are here and there 'requested to keep off the grass'. 1897 MAUGHAM *Liza of Lambeth* v. 59 'Na then', she said, 'keep off the grass!' [i.e. don't take liberties with me]. 1904 *Daily Chron.* 27 Oct. 4/7 'Now, then, some girl can tell me about grass. What is grass?' The protagonist of the class..gave the definition. 'Please, it's what you got to keep off of.'

12. a. *grass-flat, -ground* (earlier U.S. examples), *-meadow, -seed* (earlier and later U.S. examples), *-spire* (modern U.S. example), *-sward, -tuft.*

1836 S. CUMMINGS *Western Pilot* 49 About a mile and a half below Harls Linnen is *grass flats, channel at either side. 1662 *Conn. Hist. Soc. Coll.* XIV. 515 All his lands.. whether they be meadow, plowe, or *grass grownd, or Swamp Ground. 1679 *Connecticut Probate Rec.* I. 318 My mansion house,..my Grass Ground, and plow Land. 1772 *Carroll Papers* in *Maryland Hist. Mag.* XIV. 279 Frost has mowed and stacked his *grass meadows and stacked it a good Crop. 1837 J. L. WILLIAMS *Terr. of Florida* 54 The St. Johns rises..in the extensive grass meadows. 1654 *Springfield* (Mass.) *Rec.* I. 232 Thomas Stebbins and Benjamin Mun should have the use of the trayninge place.. upon condition..thatt they sow itt with Inglish *grass seed. 1880 *Vermont Agric. Rep.* VI. 32, I cannot recommend the use of oats in connection with grass seed. 1867 T. LACKLAND *Homespun* I. 99 The busy spiders..had spun slenderest ropes of very gossamer, and swung them across from one *grass spire to another. 1865 *Rep. Maine Board Agric.* X. 59 The older the *grass-sward for pasture the better. 1891 KIPLING *Light that Failed* (1900) 8 Maisie was picking *grass-tufts. 1909 *Westm. Gaz.* 11 Dec. 16/1 Only recovering his feet after much floundering in one of the sandy hollows which occur between the grass-tufts.

c. *grass-fed* (modern U.S. examples).

1880 *Vermont Agric. Rep.* VI. 26 Time was when the butchers of Brighton claimed that they could distinguish between the grass-fed beef fattened in this valley, and that from other sections, by its superior quality. 1892 GUNTER *Miss Dividends* (1893) 213 What's champagne muscle to grass-fed muscle, you dainty cut of New York.

13. grass-carpet, a carpet made of dried grass; **grass cow,** a cow for grazing; **grass-frog,** the common frog, *Rana temporaria*; **grass-hook,** an implement for cutting grass; **grass-line** = *grass-rope*; **grass-nut,** the tuberous root of a variety of *Cyperus*; **grass scythe,** a scythe for mowing grass; **grass sickness** (see quot. 1923); **grass-way** = *grass-siding*; **grass-work** (*c*) (see quot.).

1831 T. BUTTRICK *Voy., Trav.* etc. 67 He..conducted me into another neat apartment, spread a handsome *grass carpet on the floor, and..bid me welcome. 1867–9 *Trans. Ill. Agric. Soc.* VII. 422 *Grass cows were in plentiful and indeed excessive supply. 1901 H. GADOW *Amphibia & Reptiles* 253 The habits of the *Grass-frog are essentially terrestrial. 1812 *Niles' Weekly Register* II. 131/1 The purveyor of public supplies advertises for..1000 *grass hooks. 1858 J. A. WARDER *Hedges & Evergreens* 97 Using for the purpose [of pruning] a strong knife about two feet long, or a common grass-hook. 1927 *Blackw. Mag.* May 674/1 She was made fast to a *grass-line astern of the *Malplaquet*. 1835 A. B. LONGSTREET *Georgia Scenes* (1843) 184 He was ..raised upon nothing but *grass-nuts and sweet potatoes. 1573 TUSSER *Husb.* (1878) 37 A brush sithe and *grasse sithe. 1787 WASHINGTON *Diaries* III. 243 Called on my return at French's where I had begun with grass Scythes (a cradle having been found not to answer). 1920 *Glasgow Herald* 9 Sept. 9 The discovery of a bipolar organism in *grass-sickness. 1923 *Daily Mail* 18 June 7 The disease in horses known as grass sickness which first appeared in Forfarshire in the summer of 1909...The principal symptoms are paralysis of the palate and gullet, causing inability to swallow. 1927 *Sunday Express* 17 July 17/5 Sometimes the road was so bad that, dodging between the trees, they left it for the flat *grassway beside it. 1880 *Harper's Mag.* June 31/2 Another operation technically known as '*grass work' consists in the fastening of small glass beads or 'dew-drops' to the artificial blades.

Grasserie (gras'ri). [Fr., f. *gras* fat.] A disease of silkworms.

1888 E. A. BUTLER *Silkworms* 70 Sometimes they become yellow and limp, and soon die of a sort of jaundice, called *grasserie*. 1923 *Nature* 24 Mar. 411/2 Flacherie is of less importance in mulberry worms, while grasserie is stated to cause loss to all species.

Grasshopper. Add:

1. c. *slang.* (*a*) A waiter at a tea-garden (*Slang Dict.* 1874). (*b*) A policeman, 'copper' (Farmer & Henley *Slang* 1893).

(*b*) is an instance of rhyming slang.

1907 *Daily Chron.* 1 Apr. 4/4 The criminal classes always speak of policemen as 'grasshoppers'.

5. *grasshopper season, year* (i.e. when the crops are destroyed by grasshoppers); **grasshopper engine** (earlier U.S. example); **grasshopper Indian** *U.S.* (see quot.).

1853 P. KENNEDY *Blackwater Chron.* v. 60 Like one of the old *grasshopper engines on the railroad. 1831 J. O. PATTIE *Personal Narr. Exped. St. Louis to Pacific* (1833) 100 Here we met a band of the *Grasshopper Indians, who derive their name from gathering grasshoppers, drying them, and pulverizing them. 1881 A. A. HAYES *New Colorado* i. 21 There was hardly any farming in the early times; there were terrible *grasshopper seasons before 1876. 1880 *Scribner's Monthly* July 458/1 Then came 1875 and 1876, which were '*grasshopper years' when no crops of consequence were raised in the whole state.

6. A device for operating the sucker-rods of a series of petroleum wells with a single motor.

1895 GROVES & THORP *Chem. Technol.* II. 163 When a number of contiguous wells, none of which yield largely, are to be pumped, a grasshopper, or sucker-rod movement, is employed.

7. A light vehicle the body of which is suspended by braces to the rear ends of wooden springs. ? *U.S.* (Cent. Dict. Suppl. 1909.)

Gra·sshopper, *v.* [f. the sb.] *intr.* To spring *over*, like a grasshopper.

1873 J. H. BEADLE *Undevel. West* xxxii. 704 When they spar [= push (a steam-boat) with poles] thus on both sides, they are said to 'grasshopper over'.

Grassiness. (U.S. example.)

1787 WASHINGTON *Diaries* III. 199 The harrow was ordered to preceed it once, or as many times as the ground from the clodiness, or grassiness of it, should appear to need it.

Grass land. [GRASS *sb.*[1]] Land producing grass; pasture or grazing land.

1689 *Early Connecticut Probate Rec.* 514 Five acres of grass land at the lower end of the medow. 1697 *Connecticut Colonial Rec.* IV. 212 About one acre of grasse land in the said meddowe. 1765, 1846 [see GRASS *sb.*[1] 12]. 1807 J. BARLOW *Columbiad* v. 300 The conscious flocks..spread thro the grassland. 1848 *Cultivator* New Ser. V. 185 In 1843 I plowed up a piece of grassland which had been pasture two or three years. 1880 *Vermont Agric. Rep.* VI. 29 This pest is now found on nearly all of our grass lands, from which it is not excluded by a healthy vigorous sward. 1918 J. W. BEWS (*title*) The Grasses and Grasslands of South Africa. 1920 *Nature* CV. 408/2 It is too often the case that grassland is left to take care of itself, and that no steps are taken for its improvement.

Grass-plat. (Earlier example.)

1654 E. JOHNSON *Wonder-wrkg. Provid.* vi. 11 Others eying the best Grass-platts and best Situation for Farmes and large accommodations.

Grass-widow. 2. (Earlier U.S. examples.)

1845 J. J. HOOPER *Taking Census* ii. 183 John Green's sister, (the grass widder, as lives with 'em,) she goes to her battling bench. 1854 *Yale Lit. Mag.* XX. 21 [She] was arrayed, as who ever saw a veritable grass widow not arrayed, in a memorable suit of black.

Hence **Grass-widowed** *ppl. a.*, living apart from one's husband. **Grass-widower** (earlier U.S. example).

1862 *Rocky Mt. News* (Denver) 14 June (Th.) David is a bachelor again, or rather a 'grass-widower'. 1926 W. J. LOCKE *Stories Near & Far* 112 She could never resolve the problem whether she would have been happier or unhappier in a grass-widowed state.

Grate, *sb.*[1] **9.** Add: **grate-fire,** a fire in an open grate.

1907 *Daily Chron.* 30 Nov. 4/4 When other reformers insist on our abolishing grate fires altogether. 1909 ELIZ. BANKS *Myst. Frances Farrington* 87 Your utterly useless, but expensive, grate-fire.

Grater[1]. Add: **4.** *U.S.* (See quot.)

1878 MRS. STOWE *Poganuc People* xix. 217 'You can find some of them sweet-flag "graters" if you want.' This was the blossom-bud of the sweet flag, which when young and tender was reckoned a delicacy among omnivorous children.

Graticulate (grăti·kiu̇lėt), *v.* [f. F. *graticuler* (see GRATICULATION) + -ATE[3].] *trans.* To divide (a plan or design) into squares in order to make an accurate enlargement or reduction.

1895 *Funk's Standard Dict.*

Graticule. Add:

2. A measuring scale in the eye-piece of a telescope, microscope, or other optical instrument, for the location of objects in the field of view. Also, the glass disc or plate bearing this scale. Hence **Gra·ticuled** *ppl. a.*, fitted with a graticule.

1914 *Handbk. Artillery Instruments* (H.M. Stationery Office) 42 In front of the eyepiece is fixed..a diaphragm, with spider's web graticules attached to it. 1919 RHEINBERG in *Trans. Opt. Soc.* XX. 277 Generally the graticules are on glass and it is usual to refer to the complete discs or plates with the measuring scales or marks on them, as 'graticules'. *Ibid.* 286 Graticuled binoculars are not used much for peace purposes. 1920 *Nature* CV. 563/1 Such motion being observed by a plate micrometer or 'graticule' in the observing telescope. 1922 *Encycl. Brit.* XXXII. 243/1 Graticuled binoculars. 1924 L. C. MARTIN *Opt. Meas. Instr.* 27 The use of lines engraved on a glass (a graticule) is finding an increasing favour.

Gratin. Add: **b.** *attrib.*

1889 A. B. MARSHALL *Cookery Bk.* 17 Gratin Sauce (for Fish). 1901 C. H. SENN *New Cent. Cook. Bk.* 599 Butter a silver-plated gratin-dish. 1902 *Daily Chron.* 15 Feb. 8/4 Drain and turn into a gratin dish,..cover with fine bread-crumbs.

c. Phr. *au gratin* (o gratæ̃): cooked in this way; also, as *sb.*

1846 SOYER *Cookery* 112 Sole au gratin. *Note*, In France we have silver dishes on purpose for *au gratins*, in which they are dressed and served to table, the gratin adhering to the bottom of the dish. 1889 A. B. MARSHALL *Cookery Bk.* 219 Maccaroni au Gratin. 1901 C. H. SENN *New Cent. Cook. Bk.* 445 Vegetable Marrow au Gratin.

Hence **Gratinate** *v.* [after F. *gratiner*: see -ATE[3]], to cook (food) *au gratin*.

1902 WEBSTER Suppl.

Grattage (gratāʒ). *Med.* [Fr., f. *gratter* to scratch.] The removal of granulations by friction with a stiff brush.

1890 BILLINGS *Med. Dict.*, *Grattage*. 1. Abrasion. 2. Curetting.

Gratters, colloq. (school and university) for *congratulations*: see *-ER 6.

1903 D. F. T. COKE *Sandford of Merton* xiii. 98 'Gratter [*sic*], Sandford', he said, 'on your rowing to-day'. 1906 — *Bending of Twig* xii, Gratters, Marsh, on being monitor. 1920 G. W. DEEPING *Second Youth* xiii, Right-ho! Good luck and gratters!

Grattoir (gratwār). *Archæol.* [Fr., f. *gratter* to scrape, scratch.] A scraping tool of flint; an 'end-scraper'. (Cf. SCRAPER 4 c.)

1887 *Amer. Antiquarian* IX. 341, 4000 grattoirs, blades, knives and saws. 1915 W. J. SOLLAS *Anc. Hunters* (ed. 2) 298 The grattoirs or end scrapers are generally short and rough. *Ibid.* 485 The characteristic keeled grattoir.

Grave, *sb.*[1] **6. grave-post** (earlier U.S. example).

1840 *Southern Lit. Messenger* VI. 191/1 When an Indian dies, it is his family or surname, that is put on his grave-post, or *adjedatigwon*.

Gravel, *sb.* Add: **8. a.** *gravel bar, beach.* **c.** *gravel-strewn* adj.

1821 T. NUTTALL *Jrnl. Trav. Arkansa* vii. 136 Four miles above Dardennes commences the first *gravel-bar, accompanied by very rapid water. 1836 J. HALL *Statistics of West* ii. 41 This enlargement of its bed..renders the depth over some of the shoals..very slight at low water, forming several very shoal sand and gravel bars. 1806 in *Ann. 9th Congress* 2 Sess. 1118 The river becomes more obstructed by rapids, and sand, and *gravel beaches. 1927 KENDREW *Climates of Continents* 241 The rivers, whose beds, dry, wide, and *gravel-strewn in summer, often become filled in a few hours in winter by swollen torrents.

9. gravel-crusher, -crushing *ppl. a., slang* (see quots.); **gravel dumper,** a machine for depositing gravel; **gravel eye** (see quot. 1879); **gravel fly** (see quot.); **gravel iron** (see quot.).

1889 BARRÈRE & LELAND *Dict. Slang*, *Gravel-crusher* (military), a soldier compelled to tramp about a square at defaulter's drill. 1901 *Daily News* 9 Jan. 5/2 The 'gravel-crushers' (as the dismounted service is generically known). 1918 E. S. FARROW *Dict. Mil. Terms*, *Gravel Crushers*, a slang expression equivalent to doughboy or infantry soldier, and the French *fifot*. 1900 *Kynoch Jrnl.* Feb.–Mar. 63/2 Cyclists..act more in conjunction with and as the eyes of their *gravel-crushing comrades. 1856 *Trans. Mich. Agric. Soc.* VII. 334 There are on the road 20 *gravel dumpers. 1855 *Poultry Chron.* III. 9/1 The Suabian Pigeons ..have generally a turned crown, *gravel eye, and clean feet. 1879 L. WRIGHT *Pract. Pigeon-Keeper* 101 An altogether red, gravel, or orange eye is a decided fault. 1837 KIRKBRIDE *Northern Angler* 28 The Spider, or *Gravel-fly ..appears about the middle of April, if the weather be warm. ..It is bred in the gravel. 1900 *Daily News* 22 Sept. 9/3 The '*gravel iron' at present in use on all Hansom cabs.. strikes the ground with great force, causing severe shock or jerk.

Gravel, *v.* Add: **6.** *intr.* = DUST *v.*[1] 3 b.

*1870 BLAINE *Encycl. Rur. Sports* § 2618 Where they [*sc.* partridges] bask at noontide, and where they preen, scratch, and gravel.

7. (See quot.)

1902 CORNISH *Naturalist Thames* 216 In winter the eel-man goes 'gravelling', that is, scooping up gravel from the bottom to deepen any part of the channel.

Gravenstein (grā·vənstəin). [f. *Gravenstein* in Holstein, Germany.] A large variety of apple.

1860 HOGG *Fruit Manual* 10 Gravenstein....Large, round, flattened at the ends, and angular....A very valuable apple. 1863 *Rep. Maine Board Agric.* 205 Gravenstein. This apple is more cosmopolitan than any other within my knowledge. 1873–4 *Rep. Vermont Board Agric.* II. 274 The Gravenstein is without exception the finest flavored fall apple in cultivation.

Graver[2]. [f. GRAVE *v.*[2] + -ER[1].] One who graves vessels.

1868 G. G. CHANNING *Early Recoll. Newport, R. I.* 150, I knew several of the name of Swinburne who were caulkers, gravers, and riggers.

Graves (grāv). [Fr. (pl.), a name for gravelly sandy parts of the Bordeaux country.] A light (usually white) wine produced in the Graves district.

1630 J. TAYLOR (Water P.) *Wks.* Fff 4/1 The French Frontiniacke, Claret, Red nor White, Graues nor High-Country could our hearts delight. 1833 C. REDDING *Mod. Wines* 148 Macau produces seven or eight hundred tuns of red Graves. 1908 E. & A. VIZETELLY *Wines of France* 81 *note*, Cérons..produces a fine white Graves.

Gravette (grăve·t). *Archæol.* [f. *La Gravette*, a site in the Dordogne.] The name for a long narrow knife-shaped flint. Usually *Gravette point*.

1915 SOLLAS *Anc. Hunters* (ed. 2) 302 Still, even at this stage [*sc.* the Upper Aurignacian], a new form of implement came into use. This is a knife-like flake known as the Gravette point. *Ibid.* 485 Gravette-like point from the Upper Magdalenian. 1920 *A. H. Keane's Man.* 12 Finely worked knife-like blades (Châtelperron point, Gravette point). 1921 R. A. S. MACALISTER *Europ. Archaeol.* I. 368 The Gravette point..is a flake having one edge treated with secondary chipping and the other left sharp and untouched. *Ibid.* 369 In some Gravette knives the chipped edge is not straight, but has a kind of hump.

Graveyard. (Earlier U.S. examples.)

1773 P. V. FITHIAN *Jrnl.* (1900) 74 He meant it for a Satire upon the neglect of the people in suffering their Grave-Yard to lie common. 1806 WEEMS *Lett.* II. 344 Constantly walking over the grave yard of Foreigners. 1821 J. F. COOPER *Spy* xiv. (1831) 168 The grave-yard was an enclosure on the grounds of Mr. Wharton.

Gravicembalo (grævi̦tʃe·mbălo), It. corruption of *CLAVICEMBALO.

1858 SIMMONDS *Dict. Trade*, Gravecembalo. 1876 STAINER & BARRETT *Dict. Mus. Terms*. 1899 tr. *O. Bie's Hist. Pianoforte* 133 When Italy decided..to replace the Gravicembalo by the pianoforte.

Gravied (grē·vid), *a.* [f. GRAVY + -ED[2].] Served in or with gravy.

1895 *Funk's Standard Dict.*

Gravitation. 4. Add: **gravitation stamp** = *gravity stamp* (see *GRAVITY 8 b).

1894 T. K. ROSE *Metallurgy Gold* 99 Californian 'gravitation' stamps are in general use..for crushing gold ores. 1914 W. GOWLAND *Non-Ferrous Metals* 200 A modern heavy gravitation stamp.

Gravity. Add: **4. d.** *Specific gravity determination*, ascertaining the specific gravity of certain substances for the purposes of investigation or diagnosis.

1899 CAGNEY tr. *Jaksch's Clin. Diagn.* (ed. 4) vii. 326 The approximate sugar content of the urine..being ascertained by means of a specific gravity determination.

8. b. gravity anomaly (see quot.); **gravity (bucket) conveyor,** a conveyor with buckets which can be tilted and emptied; **gravity-fed** *a.*, supplied with petrol by the action of gravity; **gravity feed,** petrol supply operated by gravity; **gravity organ** (see quot.); **gravity stamp** (see quot.); **gravity wave** (see quot.); **gravity wind,** a wind produced by the downward motion of the air.

1925 J. JOLY *Surface-Hist. Earth* ii. 42 A computed value of the force of gravity for the particular station is arrived at and this is compared with the observed value. If there is a difference this difference is known as 'the *gravity anomaly'. The gravity anomaly gives the local departure from perfect isostasy. It is generally small. The result is expressed in dynes. 1910 *Encycl. Brit.* VII. 56/1 The *gravity or tilting bucket conveyor can be used as a combined elevator and conveyor. 1908 *Westm. Gaz.* 20 Feb. 4/2 The *gravity-fed oil-pump. 1909 *Ibid.* 17 Nov. 5/2 The carburetter is gravity-fed. 1914 *Programme Isle of Man Tourist Trophy Races* 9/1 Either *gravity or pressure feed may be used. 1925 A. W. JUDGE *Carburettors* 142 The three systems of fuel supply used on motor vehicles are as follows: (1) The Gravity Feed. (2) Pressure Feed. (3) Vacuum Feed. 1928 *Motor Manual* (ed. 27) 212 *Gravity feed.*—A system of petrol supply to the carburetter in which the petrol tank is placed well above the carburetter, the petrol flowing by gravity. 1909 *Daily Chron.* 18 Feb. 7/5 A *gravity organ is possessed by all the lower water animals, to enable them to tell when they are standing on their feet or are upside down. ..Similar gravity organs have been discovered in plants by Professor Haberlandt. 1911 *Encycl. Brit.* XX. 239/1 The *gravity stamp is a pestle of 900 lb weight more or less, which is lifted by a revolving cam and falls by the force of gravity...Gravity stamps are especially adapted to the fine crushing of gold ores. 1912 G. O. SMART in *Rand Metallurg. Practice* I. 34 Like other crushing machines, the gravity stamp has a limited range of efficient operation. 1912 H. LAMB in *Proc. 5th Internat. Congress Math.* (1913) II. 284 This [formula] is illustrated in the case of *gravity waves. 1930 SIR N. SHAW *Man. Meteorol.* III. 11 The waves between air and water or between two layers of air are called 'gravity-waves' because the force which controls their behaviour is the force of gravity upon the heap of water or air in the protuberant part of the wave. 1928 *Ibid.* II. 255 Katabatic winds...Such winds are *gravity-winds which pay no attention to isobars until they get into the open where they have time to adjust themselves to the requirements of the earth's rotation.

Grazer[2]. [f. GRAZE *v.*[2] + -ER[1].] An act or instance of grazing; a 'close shave', a 'near thing'.

1850 L. H. GARRARD *Wah-To-Yah* xxiv. (1927) 298 A ball, crashing through both sides of their defense, buried itself in the side of a poor steer...'Well, I'll be darned, if that wasn't a grazer.'

Grazier. Add: **3.** A grazing animal. *U.S.*

1852 *Trans. Mich. Agric. Soc.* III. 138 They [*sc.* Durham heifers] are good graziers and winter well.

Grazing, *vbl. sb.*[1] **3.** *grazing land* (U.S. example).

1789 MORSE *Amer. Geog.* 50 Numerous tracts of fine arable and grazing land intervene between the ridges.

Grease, *sb.* **6.** Add: *grease-free, -laden* adjs.; **grease-band,** a band of pliable stuff (e.g. brown paper) coated with cart-grease mixed with tar and fastened round a tree-trunk to prevent the ascent of flightless moths; hence **grease-band** *v. trans.*, to protect with a grease-band; **grease-bush** *U.S.* (earlier example); **grease-cap** (cf. *GREASER 1 c); **grease-gun** (see quot. 1928); **grease-proof, -tight** *adjs.*, impermeable to grease; **grease-wood** *U.S.* (earlier example); also *attrib.*

1900 DRURY in *Bk. Gard.* 1093 *Grease-bands put round the trees..will prevent the females from ascending. *Ibid.* 1100 As a preventive measure all orchard trees should be *grease-banded in autumn, using Willesden or similar grease-proof paper. 1930 J. COUTTS, etc. *Gardening* 704 The stake supporting the tree must also be grease-banded. 1860 MAYNE REID *Odd People* 321 The 'mezquite' of several species..the *grease-bush (*obione canescens*). 1924 A. W. JUDGE *Mod. Motor Cars* I. 245 Screw-down *grease caps are generally provided, and a turn should be given every time the car is used for more than a few miles...The pivot-pin grease holes should be kept clear, otherwise the grease will leak out past the threads of the screw cap. 1908 *Practitioner* Sept. 488 Cyllin obstetrical lubricant..has the advantage that it is *grease-free. 1923 *Daily Mail* 11 May 12, I liked very much the accessibility of all the greasers on the car. Every one can easily be reached with a *grease gun without any acrobatic feats. 1925 A. W. JUDGE *Mech. Car* 163 A screw plunger grease container (or 'grease-gun'). 1928 *Motor Manual* (ed. 27) 212 Grease gun.—A form of force pump for conveniently supplying grease lubricant to various lubricating points on a car. 1900 *grease-proof [see *grease-band* above]. 1910 *Daily Chron.* 8 Mar. 3/3 Each loaf..is packed and sealed in a paper wrapper, which is grease-proof and germ-proof. 1925 A. W. JUDGE *Mech. Car* 163 The nipples are..*grease-tight and dust-excluding. 1845 J. PALMER *Jrnl.* (1847) 48 (Th.) Wild sage and *greasewood found in plenty. 1928 WILLA CATHER *Death for Abp.* I. i. 18 The wagon train had been going all day through a greasewood plain.

Grease, *v.* **1.** Add: *To grease the fat pig* (or *sow*) (fig.): to give to those who do not want.

[1634 P. SEDDON in *Corr. N. Walworth* etc. (Chetham Soc. 1880) 33 Do not grass a fat sow behind.] 1785 GROSE *Dict. Vulgar T.*, *To grease a fat sow in the arse*, to give to a rich man. 1923 *Daily Mail* 7 Aug. 8/6 These instances of extravagance, which seem to recall the old saying of greasing the fat pig.

Greaser. Add: **1. c.** A device for lubricating the parts of a motor vehicle with grease.

1908 *Westm. Gaz.* 17 Nov. 5/2 Greasers are fitted everywhere necessary. 1923 [see *grease-gun*, *GREASE *sb.* 6]. 1924 A. W. JUDGE *Mod. Motor Cars* I. 245 The shackle pins..should be provided either with screw-down greasers or dust-proof oil cups.

d. (See quot.)

1906 CLAREMONT *Gem-Cutter's Craft* 100 The heavy material among which are the diamonds..is..passed through a machine called the 'greaser', which consists of a shaking table made of five shallow steps..coated with a thick layer of grease, and the diamonds adhere to the grease while the remainder of the gravel is washed away.

Great, *a.*, etc. Add: **A.** *adj.* **20. great corn** *U.S.*, Indian corn, maize; **great father,** Indians' name for the President of the U.S.A.; **great insertion,** the section of St. Luke's Gospel, ix. 51–xviii. 14, which is independent of St. Mark; **Great Lakes** (see *LAKE *sb.*[4] 1 c); **great omission,** St. Mark vi. 45–viii. 26, which is omitted in St. Luke; **Great War,** the war which began on 28 July 1914 with hostilities between Austria-Hungary and Serbia, and ultimately involved the majority of the nations of the world; it was suspended by armistice 11 Nov. 1918.

1750 J. BIRKET *Remarks Voy. N. Amer.* (1916) 36 Abundance of Maze or *Great corn. 1832 FRANCES TROLLOPE *Dom. Mann. Amer.* (1832) I. xx. 314 All the chiefs who.. have come to negociate with their *great father, as they call the President. 1840 *Southern Lit. Messenger* VI. 191/1 The term for the highest magistrate is Kosinan, or our great father. 1844 *Knickerbocker Mag.* XXIII. 115 The whites..had remonstrated with the Indians, representing to them that..they would certainly incur the displeasure of their 'great father' at Washington. 1881 *Harper's Mag.* Apr. 671/1 Spotted Tail has been to the Great Father's house so often that he has learned to tell lies and deceive people. 1911 J. V. BARTLET in *Stud. Synoptic Problem* 336 The part of Luke's Gospel prior to the *Great Insertion. 1927 A. H. MCNEILE *Introd. N. T.* 26 The next non-Marcan block, [Luke] ix. 51–xviii. 14, containing more than 30 per cent. of the Third Gospel, is often called the 'Great Insertion'. 1911 J. C. HAWKINS in *Stud. Synoptic Problem* 61 This well deserves its usual name of St. Luke's '*great omission'. 1924 B. H. STREETER *Four Gospels* 160 Another striking feature in Luke's relation to Mark is his 'Great Omission', so called, of a continuous section of 74 verses, Mk. vi. 45–viii. 26. 1916 (*title*) Australia in the *Great War. 1923 [see *GALLERY *sb.* 12 b]. 1927 *Whitaker's Alm.* 371/1 Monuments...Royal Artillery, (South Africa) The Mall, (Great War) Hyde Park Corner. 1930 STAIR GILLON (*title*) The K.O.S.B. in the Great War.

21. b. Hence *great-grandfatherly, -grandparental* adjs.

1903 *Daily Chron.* 2 Jan. 5/2 Is 1903 to revert to the great-grandfatherly ways of 1803? 1929 *19th Cent.* Dec. 810 A collateral relative at the level of the grandparental or great-grandparental generation.

c. great(-**great**), an ancestor or descendant of 'great (great)' degree. *colloq.*

1905 MRS. H. WARD *Marriage W. Ashe* I. ii. 33 'We—you and I—are a little bit cousins too, aren't we?'..'Was our "great-great" the same person?' he said, laughing. 1907 'Q' *Major Vigoureux* xxii, Your grandfathers and grandmothers, and right back into the greats and great-greats. 1926 W. R. INGE *Lay Thoughts* 181 Its great-great-grand-offspring.

C. *sb.* **1. d.** *A great*, a large part or amount. *No great*, not a great deal, nothing great; *adv.* not much. *U.S. colloq.*

1724 *Essex Inst. Hist. Coll.* XXXVI. 337 Mackey's sloop sunk at Boston, & spoild a great of our English goods. 1854 'O. OPTIC' (W. T. Adams) *In Doors & Out* (1876) 186 I've got consider'ble, but I don't care no great about sellin' it. 1885 A. GRAY *Lett.* (1893) 772 No great to see, except a spick and span new Hotel. 1890 *Harper's Mag.* Apr. 715/1, I wa'n't no great of a boy, an' let little things wear on me. *Ibid.* Dec. 146/2, I hadn't been round no great in New York, an' there ain't no general store there.

Great house. *U.S.* (See GREAT *a.* 20. Earlier U.S. examples.)

1634 *Doc. & Rec. New Hampshire* I. 92 You have at the greate house 9 cowes. 1675 *New Castle Court Rec.* 63 The house and Land known by the name of the greate house wth the blokhouse and kitching. 1760 WASHINGTON *Diaries* I. 143 Running walls for Pallisades to them from the Great House and from the Great House to the Wash House. 1774 P. V. FITHIAN *Jrnl.* (1900) 99 We ran from the School-House round the stable, & Kitchen & Great-House, which Distance is about 70 Rod.

Greatness. Add: **4. d.** (with *pl.*) An embodiment of greatness or eminence.

1905 W. HOLMAN HUNT *Pre-Raph.* I. 353 Carlyle was to me one of the real greatnesses of England.

Great Spirit. [transl. of Ojibway *kitchi manitou*: see MANITOU.] The supreme spirit or deity recognized by the North American Indians.

1805 SIBLEY in *Ann. 9th Congress* 2 Sess. 1076 The Great Spirit placed on an eminence, near this lake, one family of Caddoques. 1812 *Niles' Weekly Register* II. 81/1 We return thanks to the Great Spirit for the many favors he has bestowed upon us. 1855 LONGF. *Hiaw.* i. 96 Listen to the words of warning, From the lips of the Great Spirit. 1869 C. L. BRACE *New West* xi. 140 Their idea of a Great Spirit is undoubtedly a reflex of Christian teachings. 1876 JOAQUIN MILLER *Unwritten Hist.* xix. 264 The Indians said the Great Spirit made this mountain [*sc.* Shasta] first of all.

Grecian, *a.* **1. b.** Add: **Grecian curve** = *Grecian bend*; **Grecian gift** = *Greek gift* (GREEK *a.* 4); **Grecian nose,** one that is straight and continues the line of the forehead; **Grecian slippers,** a trade name for slippers cut low at the side and without a heel; **Grecian splice** *Naut.* (see quot.).

1846 J. G. SAXE *Progress* (1847) 18 'She stoops to conquer' in a '*Grecian curve'. 1830 HOOK *Maxwell* viii, A beautiful girl,—Italian eyes—*Grecian nose. 1883 *Man. Seamanship for Boys* 124 A *Grecian Splice [description follows]. *Ibid.* 125 There is also another way to make a Grecian splice, by making all the yarns into foxes, leaving no heart...This splice is also used for tailing a smaller to a larger size rope, when it has to travel through a block.

Green, *a.* Add: **12. Green cross,** designating a poison gas shell, marked with a green cross, or its contents; **green flash** (see quot. 1925); **green fog** *Photog.* (see quots. and FOG *sb.*[2] 4); **green goods** *pl.*, (*b*) vegetables and fruit, greengroceries; **Green Jackets** *pl.*, a name applied to the Rifle Brigade from the dark green colour of its uniform; **Green Linnets** *pl.* (see quots.); **Green Mountain State,** the state of Vermont, U.S.A.; **green peril,** slang name for absinthe; **green ray** (see quot.).

1918 E. S. FARROW *Dict. Mil. Terms*, *Green Cross Shell, very dangerous asphyxiating shell, first used by the Germans, filled with diphosgene or phosgene. 1928 *Daily Express* 22 May 1/2 An immense steel flask of phosgene, the notorious Green Cross poison gas employed by Germany with such deadly effect during the war. 1912 *Nature* 6 June 351/2 The well-known phenomenon of the *green flash at sunset. 1925 REX CLEMENTS *Gipsy of Horn* 125 For the first time I saw the 'Green Flash', as it is called. Just as the sun is about to sink below the horizon a flash of vivid green seems to leap from it. It only lasts a second and is gone. 1882 W. K. BURTON *A B C Mod. Photogr.* 52 *Green fog makes its appearance only with alkaline pyrogallic development. 1892 WOODBURY *Encycl. Photogr.* 299 Green Fog.—It appears green by reflected, and pink by transmitted light....It is produced by reduced metallic silver in a fine state of division, and also by the gelatine becoming decomposed by prolonged heating in the cooking process. 1921 E. BOK *Autobiog.* 99 A market dealer in *green goods. 1824 in Sir H. Smith *Autobiog.* (1901) I. 3 'Well, I will make you a Rifleman, a *green jacket', says the General. 1927 *Observer* 1 May 19 The Duke [of Connaught] loves the Green Jackets best of all in spite of his other military associations. 1870 BREWER *Dict. Phrase & Fable* 365/2 *Green Linnets, the 39th Foot, so called from the colour of their facings. 1901 'LINESMAN' *Words by Eyewitness* (1902) 191 Dorsets and Middlesex (famous old corps, with famous old *sobriquets*, 'Green Linnets' and 'Die-Hards'). 1925 E. FRASER & GIBBONS *Soldier & Sailor Words* s.v. *Nicknames, Green Linnets, The*: The Dorsetshire Regiment. Through the 1st Battalion, as the 39th Foot. From the green facings. 1905 *Westm. Gaz.* 4 May 12/1 Some statistics..of the growth of the absinthe habit in France seem to justify the alarmists who speak of the beverage as 'the *green peril'. 1908 *Daily Chron.* 21 May 1/5 This taxing of the 'green peril' will no doubt be popular. 1918 *Meteorological Office, Observer's Handbk.* 61 The *Green Ray. When the sun sets under favourable conditions the last glimpse of it is coloured a brilliant green.

b. green dolphin *U.S.*, a plant louse (cf. DOLPHIN 7); **green heron** *U.S.* (earlier example); **green racer,** a variety of the American black-snake; **green-wing** (earlier example).

1849 *Rep. U. S. Comm. Patents, Agric.* (1850) 339 These plants are often smothered with lice, or *green-dolphin, as they are termed. 1855 *Knickerbocker Mag.* XLVI. 222 Night-herons, snowy-herons, *green-herons, and little-herons construct their nests so closely together that four or five hundred of them may be counted upon twenty or thirty cedars. 1870 *Amer. Naturalist* III. 124 *Green Racer (*Boscanion vetustus*). I saw one dead specimen of this snake along Hell Gate River. 1874 J. W. LONG *Wild-Fowl Shooting* 193 The *green-wings are quite tenacious of life.

c. green ash, brier *U.S.* (earlier examples).

1810 MICHAUX *Arbres* I. 34 *Green ash (*Fraxinus viridis*) ..nom donné par moi. 1832 D. J. BROWNE *Sylva Amer.* 160 The Green Ash is more common in the western districts of Pennsylvania, Maryland and Virginia. c 1785 SARAH PEARS *Narrative* (MS.) 4 We had not anything to live on..except ..*greenbrier berreys [etc.]. 1837 PECK *Gaz. Illinois* 1. 10 The undergrowth are..grape vines, dogwood, spice bush, green brier, hazle, etc. 1872 *Amer. Naturalist* Dec. VI. 728 The canes matted with thorny 'green brier'..and mixed with tall stinging nettles.

B. *sb.* **7. b.** *fig.* A greenhorn, simpleton. (Cf. A. 8 d.)

Cf. *Verdant Green*, the name of the hero in the title of the story of Oxford university life by 'Cuthbert Bede'.

1838 DICKENS *O. Twist* xviii, 'Well, well', said the Dodger. ..'That hasn't got anything to do with young Green here.' 1840 G. THOMPSON *Newgate Calendar* 280, I then with my comrade stole from a green twelve shirts..and some stockings. 1841 *Southern Lit. Messenger* VII. 54/2, I knifed a flat-boat Hoozier—took his lucre—Went up the country—rifled twenty *greens*.

17. (in reference to a golf-links) *green committee, -keeping, -man, -record.*

1896 *Rules of St. Andrews* in J. Kerr *Golf-bk. E. Lothian* App. p. xxii, When the *Green Committee consider it necessary, a telegraph board shall be used to give the numbers for starting. 1897 *Outing* (U.S.) XXX. 97/1 Either the secretary, or a member of the green committee,..should be given the authority..for the care of the green. 1908 *Daily Chron.* 20 June 5/5 The science of *greenkeeping has not stood still while the other departments of the game have advanced. 1905 *Westm. Gaz.* 10 Feb. 3/1 The *green-men use various liquids to bring the worms to the top, where they may be swept away and destroyed. 1928 *Daily Express* 3 Jan. 9/2 After the snow had fallen greenmen tried to clear it away by flooding the course with hosepipes. 1902 *Westm. Gaz.* 28 July 4/1 Had Herd not been badly bunkered at the fourteenth hole he would probably have beaten the *green record. 1908 *Ibid.* 22 June 9/4 At the age of sixteen he.. had won a scratch medal and broken a green-record.

Greenacre (grī·nēkəɹ). *Docks slang.* [Said to be f. the name of James *Greenacre*, murderer, hanged in front of Newgate, on 2 May, 1837, when the rope broke.] The falling of a set of goods out of the sling.

1928 *Observer* 22 July 10/7.

Greenbacker. *U.S.* (Earlier example.)

1876 *N. Y. Tribune* Oct. (Bartlett) Steps are being taken.. to secure a union of the greenbackers and the Democrats in a fusion election ticket.

Greener[2] (grī·nəɹ). Applied to rifles made by W. Greener or according to his designs.

1901 *Kynoch Jrnl.* Apr.–May 93/2 Diagrams obtained with a Greener-310 rifle and orthoptic sights. 1902 *Ibid.* Apr.–May 84/1 Of these cartridges the Greener sharpshooter is probably the most popular. 1921 *Outward Bound* June 45/1 Tucking away his valuable Greener under his arm.

Greenery-yallery (grī·nəri yæ·ləri), *a. slang.* [f. GREEN and *yaller*, vulgar pron. of YELLOW, with suffix repeated to produce a jingling compound.] Of, pertaining to, or affecting the colours green and yellow, in accordance with 'aesthetic' style or fashion. Also **Gree·nery** *a.*, greenish.

1880 W. S. GILBERT *Patience* II. 37 A greenery-yallery, Grosvenor Gallery, Foot-in-the-grave young man. 1896 MRS. LYNN LINTON in *Amer. Bookman* III. 131/1 The greenery-yallery school would have found no disciple in him [*sc.* Dickens]. 1896 MRS. H. WARD *Sir G. Tressady* 194 You needn't wear greenery-yallery gowns, you know. 1904 B'NESS VON HUTTEN *Pam* II. iv, If I had watery, greenery, grey eyes.

Green head, greenhead[2]. Add: **4.** A green-headed gadfly, *Tabanus lineola*. *U.S.*

1838 E. FLAGG *Far West* II. 107 (Th.) [My horse was] severely troubled by that terrible insect, so notorious all over the West, the large green-bottle prairie fly, called the 'green-head'. 1888 J. KIRKLAND *McVeys* 18 What can be the matter with that horse?..Is he crazy? Pretty near, I guess, with a greenhead on him somewhere where he can't get at it.

5. A large variety of the striped bass. *U.S.*

1884 GOODE *Nat. Hist. Aquat. Anim.* 425 The Striped Bass...Large sea-going individuals are sometimes known in New England by the names of 'Green-head' and 'Squid-hound'.

6. The mallard. Also *greenhead duck*. *U.S.*

1888 *Century Mag.* Dec. 296/1 One day he succeeded in snaring a greenhead duck.

7. An Australian ant.

1926 *Glasgow Herald* 19 Dec. 6 The greenhead is the most vicious attacker of man.

Green hide, greenhide: see GREEN *a.* 9 c.

Greenness. Add: **2. f.** Of horses: Want of training. (See GREEN *a.* 8 c.)

1900 *Daily Mail* 30 Apr. 4/3 They were due to the greenness of many of the horses, to the fact that they were not acclimatised. 1927 *Ibid.* 30 June 13 The failure of Mrs. Whitburn's colt at Ascot may have been due to greenness.

Greenwell (grī·nwĕl). [f. the name of William *Greenwell* (1820–1918), archæologist and angler.] In full *Greenwell's glory*: A trout fly designed by the Rev. W. Greenwell. Also, a salmon fly of his invention.

1879 W. HENDERSON *Life Angler* xxi. 237, 104 fish [trout], chiefly captured with the 'Greenwell's Glory' fly. *Ibid.* xxii. 251 'The Greenwell' fly did most execution [salmon]. 1899 SIR E. GREY *Fly Fishing* viii. 216 In wet fly fishing for trout I am content with March-browns, Greenwell's glories [etc.]. 1920 SIR H. MAXWELL in F. Francis *Angling* 177 *note*, The Greenwell salmon fly, a favourite on the Tweed. 1928 W. F. R. REYNOLDS *With Fly Only* 65 Perhaps an iron blue or two, and a few Greenwells.

Gree·n-winged, *a.* [GREEN *a.* 11 a.] Having green wings: in spec. names or descriptions of animals.

1849 C. LANMAN *Lett. Alleghany Mts.* ix. 73 The Cherokees relate that there once existed among these mountains a very large bird, which resembled in appearance the green winged hornet. 1861– [see GREEN *a.* 11 a].

Greeting, *vbl. sb.*[1] **b.** Add: **greeting-card,** a card sent to relatives and friends at Christmas (and other festivals).

1907 *Westm. Gaz.* 10 Dec. 12/1 The sending of the Royal greeting-cards is also a very big business. 1909 *Daily Chron.* 21 Jan. 5/6 For that renowned festival [*sc.* St. Patrick's Day] an ever-growing number of Irish greeting-cards has nowadays to be prepared, with shamrocks in the place of St. Valentine's doves and violets.

Grège (grēʒ, ‖grĕʒ), *a.* and *sb.* Also **greige.** [F. *grège* raw (silk).] (Of) a colour between beige and grey.

1927 *Weekly Dispatch* 6 Nov. 10 The newest colours [for stockings]..are a deep peach-beige, light tan, and a soft grège shade something between a fawn and a grey. 1928 *Daily Express* 3 Apr. 5/4 Different shades of beige and greige are most in demand. 1931 *Times* 21 May 19/4 A gown of greige satin.

Grenadin (gre·nădin). Also **-ine.** [Fr.: see GRENADINE[1].]

1. An impure commercial variety of fuchsin or magenta, used as a dye-stuff.

1889 *Cent. Dict.*

2. A French variety of the carnation (see quot. 1910).

1904 R. P. BROTHERSTON *Bk. Carnation* 18 The French Grenadin, truly a biennial, both single and double, with small flowers of a sweet scent, and extraordinarily floriferous. 1910 T. W. SANDERS *Carnations* 45 Grenadin Carnations. A Continental strain of dwarf habit, growing about 1 ft. high, and bearing scarlet or white flowers.

Grenadine[3] (grenădī·n). [ad. F. (*sirop de*) *grenadine*, f. *grenade* GRENADE *sb.*[1]] A syrup made from pomegranates (or other fruit).

1896 WORKMAN *Algerian Mem.* 43 We found syrup of grenadine, or pomegranate with water, a delicious drink. 1906 *Daily Chron.* 21 July 8/5 One of them, prepared from ripe gooseberries, is particularly delicious. It is called grenadine. 1916 W. J. LOCKE *Wonderful Year* i, A bottle of grenadine syrup and water.

Gre·nadine[4]. [Used to render mod.L. specific name *granatina*, after F. *grenadin*.] (See quot.)

1900 A. C. STARK *Birds S. Africa* I. 104 Estrilda granatina. Grenadine Waxbill.

Grenville (gre·nvil). *Geol.* The name of a district in the province of Ontario, Canada, designating a series (in the Laurentian system) of highly altered sediments, mainly limestones.

1863 *Geol. Survey Canada* 43 A single band of limestone which has been termed the Grenville band. *Ibid.* 839 The two inferior limestone bands of the Grenville series. 1908 F. D. ADAMS in *Jrnl. Geol.* XVI. 622 The name 'Grenville series' was restricted to the limestone-bearing portion of Logan's Laurentian. 1925 J. JOLY *Surface-Hist. Earth* viii. 130 Two great sedimentary series are fundamental: the Grenville Series..and the Sudbury.

Grès (grę). [Fr.] Stoneware. *Grès de Flandres*, Cologne ware.

1882 *Hamilton Sale Catal.* No. 950 A Pilgrim's Bottle, of old grès-de-Flandres stone ware. 1902 *Encycl. Brit.* XXXI. 875/1 The influence of the Japanese potters on the production of *grès* in France.

Gretna Green (gretnă grī·n). A village in Dumfriesshire just across the border, where runaway couples from England were married (by a blacksmith) according to Scots law.

1852 *Household Words* V. 199/2 It was my impression Gretna marriages were quite matters of the past. *Ibid.* 201/1 Old Colthard..was the first regular Gretna Green parson. 1863 *Chambers's Encycl.* V. 106/2 The Gretna Green marriages may yet be resorted to by English parties, provided the intended husband comply with this requisite [*sc.* 21 days' residence in Scotland]. 1904 *Daily Chron.* 17 Feb. 7/1 Caroline, Marchioness of Queensberry..was the heroine of a genuine Gretna Green marriage. *Ibid.*, The period of the Gretna Green weddings..extended over almost exactly a century.

Grey, gray, *a.* Add:

7. b. *grey-cheeked, -crowned.*

1893 B. TORREY *Footpath-Way* 94 The evergreens immediately about the house were full of *gray-cheeked thrushes. 1876 *Field & Forest* II. 31, I published a 'Monograph of the Genus Leucosticte, or *Gray-crowned Purple Finches'.

8. grey cloth (see quot.); **grey oak** *U.S.*, the upland willow-oak or blue-jack (*Quercus brevifolia*); **grey oil,** olive oil and lanolin containing mercury; **grey pine** *U.S.* and *Canada*, the scrub or jack pine (*Pinus divaricata*); **grey willow** *U.S.*, the white willow (*Salix alba*).

1930 *Aberdeen Press & Jrnl.* 1 Apr. 8/4 Plain *greycloth —that is, unbleached cloth, or cloth dyed in the piece. 1697 *Boston Town Records* VI. 8 From thence to another wallnut tree and so straight to a *gray oak. 1813 H. MUHLENBERG *Catal. Plants* 87 Upland willow-oak, or gray oak. 1832 D. J. BROWNE *Sylva Amer.* 261 The Gray Oak is found farther north than any other species in America. 1908 *Practitioner* Sept. 467 The use of *grey-oil in subcutaneous injections. 1810 MICHAUX *Arbres* I. 16 *Pinus rupestris*...*Grey pine, denomination donnée..en Canada. 1832 D. J. BROWNE *Sylva Amer.* 240 In Nova Scotia and the state of Maine, where it is rare, it is called Scrub Pine, and in Canada, Gray Pine. 1813 H. MUHLENBERG *Catal. Plants* 91 *Gray willow. 1861 *Trans. Ill. Agric. Soc.* IV. 448 Mr. Overman has the Pennsylvania Gray Willow—the most rapid growing variety he has ever known.

b. grey-bird, (*c*) *U.S.* (see quot.); **grey-cheek** *U.S.*, the grey-cheeked thrush; **grey-fin,** a variety of trout found in the Tweed; **grey-fish,** (*b*) the common dogfish; **grey grub** *U.S.* (see quot.); **grey snipe** *U.S.* (earlier example); **grey wolf,** the common wolf, *Lupus griseus*; also *fig.* (see quot. 1904).

1872 *Amer. Naturalist* July VI. 396 The mountain mockingbird, familiarly known to the settlers as the '*gray bird', is said to have similarly increased. 1893 B. TORREY *Footpath-Way* 17 The *gray-cheek's song bears an ardent resemblance to the Veery's. 1847 STODDART *Angler's Comp.* 210 The *grey-fin or bull-trout smolt. 1923 HERDMAN *Founders Oceanogr.* 310 People..are prejudiced against 'dog-fish', so the [United States] Bureau [of Fisheries] altered the name of the latter to '*gray-fish'. 1876 *Rep. Vermont Board Agric.* III. 567 The larva of this moth [*Agrotis Tessellata*] is sometimes called the *gray grub. 1870 *Game Laws Penn.* in *Fur, Fin & Feather* (1872) 120 No person shall kill, capture, take..any *grey snipe. 1831 PECK *Guide for Emigrants* 162 The large *grey wolf, or *canis lupus* of Linneus, is not very plenty. 1880 *Harper's Mag.* July 171/1 You will find bear and the great gray wolf..in the wilderness. 1904 *Grand Rapids Even. Press* 8 June 4 In plain words, a gray wolf, in Chicago phraseology, is a professional grafter.

B. *sb.* **1. c.** The uniform of the Southern troops in the Civil War. *U.S.*

1866 J. C. GREGG *Life in Army* xviii. 172 They were refused admission..on the ground of their uniform; when if they had been dressed in rebel gray..no doubt they would have met with a warm welcome. 1879 TOURGÉE *Fool's Errand* xxii. 134, I have no..ill-will, towards any one who wore the gray. 1885 FRANCES C. BAYLOR *On Both Sides* II. viii. 429 A military society composed of men who had worn the gray.

4. d. Also, undyed. (Cf. *grey cloth* in A. 8.)

1860 S. JUBB *Hist. Shoddy-Trade* 40 Short Ends were sold to the merchants..in the grey. 1929 *Times* 7 Feb. 9/3 There were thousands of piece goods coming into this country 'in the grey' to be dyed here.

Grey-coat. Add: Also, a Confederate soldier. *U.S.*

1880 *Harper's Mag.* Feb. 478/1 The humor of the war continues to crop out here and there, and is relished equally by the gray-coats, and by those who wore the blue.

Greyhead. Add:

2. b. An old male sperm-whale.

a 1889 C. M. SCAMMON (Cent. D.). 1908 *Westm. Gaz.* 28 Dec. 2/1 The right whale and the grayhead are gone.

Greyhound. 4. Add:

greyhound racing, a sport in which a dummy hare propelled mechanically round a set track is coursed by greyhounds. (Cf. *GRACING.)

The Greyhound Racing Association was founded in 1926.

1927 A. CROXTON SMITH (*title*) Greyhound Racing and Breeding.

Grey squirrel. [GREY *a.* 1 and 8 b.] A common squirrel of the United States (*Sciurus carolinensis*), which has been introduced into Europe in recent times.

[1754 G. EDWARDS *Catesby's Nat. Hist. Carolina* II. 74 Sciurus Virginianus cinereus major. The Grey Fox-Squirrel.] 1781 PENNANT *Hist. Quadrupeds* II. 410 Grey Squirrel... *Sciurus cinereus* L. Inhabits the woods of North America, Peru, and Chili; are very numerous in North America; do incredible damage to the plantations of Mayz. 1804 in *Maryland Hist. Mag.* IV. 9 Squirrels in this neighborhood are of a deep black color..less in size than the grey squirrels of Maryland. 1880 BINGLEY *Anim. Biogr.* II. 37 The Gray Squirrel [*Sciurus cinereus.* Linn.]. 1831 AUDUBON *Ornith.* I. 247 The Grey Squirrel..migrates in prodigious numbers. 1831 PECK *Guide for Emigrants* 164 The gray and fox squirrels often do mischief in the corn fields. 1850 N. KINGSLEY *Diary* 105 In the afternoon went out with a gun for the first time, grey squirrels are quite plenty but too much water to hunt them. 1870 *Game Laws Penn.* in *Fur, Fin & Feather* (1872) 107 No person shall kill any fox squirrel, or grey squirrel between the first day of January and the first day of June.

Greystone, graystone. (Later U.S. examples.)

1868 MISS ALCOTT *Little Women* (1869) II. viii. 120, I sat there trying to sketch the gray-stone lion's head on the wall. 1878 J. H. BEADLE *Western Wilds* 522 A very good greystone stucco front..could be had for three hundred dollars.

Grid. Add:

5. *Wireless Telegr.* The wire spiral or wire gauze auxiliary electrode between the filament and the plate of a 3-electrode valve.

The addition of a second grid constitutes a 'screen grid valve' or tetrode; of a third, a pentode.

1922 *Encycl. Brit.* XXXII. 1024/2 In 1907, Lee de Forest ..added to it [*sc.* the Fleming valve] an additional element in the form of a grid or zig-zag of wire placed between the cylinder and the filament but carried on a separate terminal. 1928 G. E. STERLING *Radio Manual* 111 Thus the grid acts as a valve to regulate the flow of current in the tube. 1930 R. D. BANGAY & O. F. BROWN *Wireless Telegr.* 169 A valve containing an additional fine-meshed grid placed between the anode and the ordinary control grid...This type of valve is known as a screen grid valve.

b. *attrib.* and *Comb.*, as *grid battery, bias, circuit, condenser, control, current, leak, potentiometer, rectification, volt, voltage, wire.*

1923 *Glasgow Herald* 29 Jan. 14 The occasional benefit to be derived from a change of gridleaks and grid condensers. 1923 MARCHANT *Radio Telegr.* Gloss. 127 *Grid Leak*, the resistance connected across the block condenser used for conveying the high frequency currents to the grid of a rectifying valve. 1926 S. O. PEARSON *Dict. Wireless Terms*, *Grid bias*..is the number of volts by which the potential of the grid is above or below that of the negative end of the filament. *Grid circuit*, that part of a valve circuit which is connected between the grid and filament of a three-electrode valve. *Grid condenser*, a condenser usually of fixed capacity, connected in series with the lead which joins the grid circuit to the grid of a three-electrode valve. *Grid current*, the current which passes between the filament and the grid of a three-electrode valve. *Grid potentiometer*, a potentiometer arranged to enable the grid potential or grid bias to be critically adjusted. 1926 F. H. CHAPMAN *Wireless Dict.*, *Grid control*, a system of telephony control in wireless telephony transmission. Grid control involves only one oscillating valve and a microphone transformer. 1928 *Morning Post* 16 Feb. 13/4 A grid battery will, as a rule, last about twelve months.

7. *Television.* In full *grid receiver*: see quots.

1929 SHELDON & GRISEWOOD *Television* 147 The operation of the large grid receiver is controlled by a 2500 wire distributor. *Ibid.* 148 This large grid, formed by a continuous neon tube bent back and forth, is the electro-optical element of the receiving equipment used by the Bell Laboratories for large audiences. 1930 *Daily Express* 30 July 6/2 By dividing the grid-vanes and providing separate plates for the upper and lower grid-vanes.

8. A network of lines used, e.g., for finding places on a map. Also *grid-sheet, -system.*

1918 in *Geog. Jrnl.* LIII. (1919) 33 Doubtless the German was amused at the conservative Briton, who at first preferred to use a 'grid' of squares 1000 yards a side. 1922 *Encycl. Brit.* XXXII. 623/1 For the use of large scale maps in trench warfare..it must be possible to read off at sight the coördinates of any desired point from a 'grid' or network of lines printed on the map...For ease and accuracy of reference the 'grid' should be in squares. 1924 *Times Trade & Engin. Suppl.* 29 Nov. 241 Simplicity of reference is ensured by the use of a novel transparent grid sheet, ruled in squares and numbered to correspond with the grid numbers given in the Gazetteer. The use of this grid sheet enables the most obscure place to be found on the map in a moment. 1925 CLOSE & WINTERBOTHAM *Topogr. Surveying* (ed. 3) 135 Some form of reference grid was found necessary by all combatants in the late war. *Ibid.* 136 To overprint his available maps with the appropriate grid. 1930 G. R. DE BEER *Embryol. & Evol.* iv. 29 The comparison of one adult form with another can be made very instructive by inscribing the shape of one form on a grid-system of Cartesian co-ordinates. *Ibid.* 30 By a harmonious transformation of the grid, the skull of Hyracotherium can be distorted and made to resemble that of the horse. 1931 *Times Lit. Suppl.* 10 Sept. 674/4 This grid, which has the appearance of a transparent chessboard, can be made to appear at the same height as any object in the stereoscope picture.

9. A network of electric lines and connexions.

1926 *Public Opinion* 3 Apr. 331/2 The electrical 'grid' is absolutely necessary in the future just as our railway network has been in the past. 1928 *Daily Tel.* 25 Sept. 11/5 By the employment of transforming and switching stations, high-pressure overhead lines and underground mains, the area will be covered by an electric 'grid'. 1930 *Times Financ. Rev.* 11 Feb. p. xxxiii/1 With transforming stations at the points most suitable for enabling the pool of electricity provided by the 'Grid' to be tapped for distribution throughout the area. 1931 *Times Trade & Engin. Suppl.* 24 Jan. 439/4 It is probable that less than 1 per cent. of the entire population of Great Britain will be outside the range of the grid.

10. A strong open framework of iron fixed to the back of a motor car to hold luggage.

1928 *Evening News* 24 July 4/2 It can be carried on either luggage grid or running board. 1928 *Daily Mail* 25 July 1/5 All straps, loops, etc., which are necessary to fit to the grid of a car.

11. A bicycle. *slang.*

1924 D. H. LAWRENCE *England, my England* 103 Oh, well! I wheel the grid, do I?

12. A football field. Cf. *GRIDIRON *sb.* 3. *U.S.*

1928 *Chicago Tribune* 13 Dec. 25/8 (*headline*) Law..to lead Irish on Grid in 1929.

Gridded (gri·dėd), *pa. pple.* [See *GRID 8.] Covered or inscribed with a grid or network of lines.

1926 *Blackw. Mag.* Dec. 774/2 A white screen, gridded and lettered, covered the wall.

Griddle, *sb.* Add: **2. c.** A griddle-cake. *U.S.*

1845 CAROLINE M. KIRKLAND *Western Clearings* 98 The Scot stares in his turn when the man of Connecticut calls that cake a 'griddle' or a 'slap-jack'. 1858 *Acc. Newport* (De Vere) Shovel-cakes are still to be had by a hungry generation, and the griddles of Mrs. Durfee..shall not want an historian.

4. griddle-spade *U.S.*, a flat-bladed implement used for placing or turning cakes on a griddle.

1879 MRS. WHITNEY *Just How* 28 Keep a knife or griddle-spade in your hand, and raise the cake occasionally.

Gridiron, *sb.* Add: **3.** (Earlier and later examples of U.S. uses: see quots. 1893[1], 1896 in Dict.)

1866 E. A. POLLARD *Southern Hist. War* II. 103 'It was', says a Charleston paper, 'the identical "gridiron" carried from Fort Sumter in 1861.' 1871 SCHELE DE VERE *Americanisms* (1872) 258 Sailors laugh at it good-naturedly, and seeing it [*sc.* the Stars and Stripes] hoisted, say: 'There goes the gridiron'. 1904 *Omaha Bee* 24 Oct. 4 The collapse of a flimsy grandstand at Des Moines is a reminder that the damage to life and limb at a football game is not all on the gridiron. 1926 *Ladies' Home Jrnl.* Nov. 12 Eustis Dullard was, as I say, quite as remarkable on the gridiron as Robert Havens father was on the 'Change.

6. gridiron carrier, an open iron framework fixed on a bicycle to carry parcels (cf. *GRID 10); **gridiron track,** a set of short tracks arranged like a gridiron, used for sorting and shifting railway-carriages (cf. quot. 1892 in sense 3 in Dict.).

1898 *Cycling* 26 Large parcels should be carried on a 'gridiron' carrier..clamped to the head socket.

Grief, *sb.* **1.** (Later U.S. example.)

1861 *Trans. Ill. Agric. Soc.* IV. 448 They [*sc.* silver Poplars] bear grief equal to the Cottonwood.

Griff, *sb.*[6], app. short for *GRIFFIN[4].

1891 NAT. GOULD *Double Event* iv. 22 He's got the straight griff for something.

Griffe (grif). *Arch.* [Fr.: see GRIFF *sb.*[3]] A claw-shaped ornament carved at the angle of the square base of a column; a spur.

1875 *Encycl. Brit.* II. 465/1. 1901 R. STURGIS *Dict. Archit.* II. 323/1 The griffe..is often used for elaborate ornamentation, being carved into vegetable or even animal form. 1905 BOND *Gothic Archit.* 455 Griffes are found in Roman work in a similar position...Pliny describes griffes of lizards and frogs.

Griffin[4]. *slang.* [Origin unascertained.] A tip (in betting, etc.); a signal, hint.

1889 *Cassell's Sat. Jrnl.* Jan. 305/3 Plank yourself at the corner to give the griffin (signal) if you hear or see owt. 1891 J. NEWMAN *Scamping Tricks* 95 When he wanted to give the chaps in the office the straight griffin, he used to say, 'Nelson's my guide'. 1912 A. NEIL LYONS *Clara* xxiv. 265 'This is the Straight Griffin, Fred,' said Mr. Cozenza: 'the absolute straight Tip'.

Grig, *sb.*[3] *U.S.* = GIG *sb.*[4]

1822 J. WOODS *Two Yrs.' Resid. Engl. Prairie* 234 Two men..began fishing..striking the fish with a gig, or grig, like a dungprong, with barbed points.

Gri-gri (gri,gri). Variant of GROO-GROO.

1871 KINGSLEY *At Last* vii. (1892) 138 This [*Desmoncus*] furnishes the gri-gri-canes.

Grike (grəik). *Geol.* Also **gryke.** [north. dial.: see *Eng. Dial. Dict.*] A crack or slit in rock; a ravine in a hill-side.

1902 LD. AVEBURY *Scenery of England* 437 Bare surface of Carboniferous Limestone, near Shap, showing 'grikes' or widened joints. 1919 *Glasgow Herald* 26 Dec. 8 Rock which lay about the 'grike' in the crag face. 1925 *Times Lit. Suppl.* 22 Jan. 50/2 The hill-top platforms with deeply eroded crevices called clints or grykes. *Ibid.*, Lime-loving ferns, such as hart's-tongue, which harbour from the wind in the cracks or grykes.

Grill, *sb.*[4] Add: **2.** *To put on the grill*: to subject (a prisoner) to 'third degree' treatment. *U.S.* (Cf. next.)

1928 *Daily Express* 25 May 10/5 Mr. John Brown..is arrested on a murder charge. He does not sound frank, so he is 'put on the grill'.

Grill, *v.*[2] Add: **1. d.** To subject to severe questioning. *U.S.*

1928 A. G. HAYS *Let Freedom Ring* 289 The three men were grilled about their movements on the day of the..attempted hold-up. 1928 *Daily Express* 25 May 10/5 Detectives mercilessly grilling a prisoner in a shut room.

Grillage. Add: **3.** An arrangement resembling a grill.

1890 *Harper's Mag.* June 142/1 On the bottom shelf lay a grillage of bar soap.

Grille, grill, *sb.* Add:

1. b. A rectangular pattern of small dots impressed on some issues of postage stamps. Also *attrib.*

1898 E. B. EVANS *Stamps & Stamp Coll.* (ed. 2) 27. 1916 F. J. MELVILLE *Postage Stamps* 19 This grille embossing was applied to stamps of the United States between 1867 and 1873. 1929 K. B. STILES *Stamps* v. 78 In the year 1867 there was invented a metal roll with points, and these made grill impressions on certain stamps of the United States. *Ibid.* 81 To count the grill points, examine the reverse side of the stamp.

Grille, grill, *v.* Add:

2. To impress (postage stamps) with a grill.

1916 JOHN N. LUFF in F. J. Melville *Postage Stamps* 19 The variety known as 'grilled all over'. 1929 K. B. STILES *Stamps* v. 81 Only one other country has ever issued grilled stamps...Peru.

Grimm's law: see LAW *sb.*[1] 17 c (*c*).

Grimoire (grimwār). [Fr.; altered f. *grammaire* GRAMMAR.] A magician's manual for invoking demons, etc.

1891 A. E. WAITE *Occult Sciences* 55 The most noticeable feature of the Grimoires..is their utter futility. 1902 *Daily Chron.* 9 July 3/2 A monstrous brood of 'grimoires' and 'clavicles'. 1923 *Blackw. Mag.* Aug. 153/2 The curé's argument almost legitimised the *grimoire* as a commentary on the Bible. 1926 *Chambers's Jrnl.* July 460/1 The *grimoires* of the Middle Ages.

Grimthorpe (gri·mþǭɹp), *v.* [f. the name of Sir Edmund Beckett, first Baron *Grimthorpe*, whose restoration of St. Albans Cathedral aroused fierce criticism and controversy.] *trans.* To restore (an ancient building) with lavish expenditure rather than knowledge and fine taste.

1890 *Antiquary* Jan. 34 To this a keen and well-known Yorkshire ecclesiologist replied: 'Heaven forbid I the building might be grimthorped!' 1892 *Athenæum* 23 July 138/2 St. Albans and other great national fabrics that have been 'Grimthorped'. 1900 *Ibid.* 28 July 129/2 This is indeed grimthorping with a vengeance. 1909 *Daily Chron.* 9 July

6/6 The parish church, which despite of vigorous 'grim-thorping' still shows a trace of its old Norman architecture.

Grin, *v.*[2] Add: **1. f.** Of a coat of paint: To show *through* (an upper coat).

1901 in *N. & Q.* 9th Ser. VIII. 225/2 The priming coat grins through the paint of the sashes.

Grind, *sb.*[1] Add: **1. c.** (See quot. 1889.)

1889 Barrère & Leland *Dict. Slang*, *Grind*,..the ferry-boats at Chesterton, wound across by a winch and chain, 'to go over in the grind'. 1901 *Cambridge Rev.* 14 Nov. 76/1 Trinity Hall..had 50 yards to spare at the Red Grind. 1906 *Westm. Gaz.* 11 June 8/2 Besides Charon's, two other ferries—grinds, with chain from bank to bank.

3. b. *U.S.* (Earlier and later examples.)

1893 W. K. Post *Harvard Stories* 11 Come now, old grind, do take a day off. 1908 R. L. Dunn *W. H. Taft* 210 He was keen to learn and if he had not been so lusty outside of the house, he would have been called a grind.

Grind, *v.*[1] Add: **3.** *U.S.* (Later example.)

1884 Howells *Silas Lapham* ix. 167 That's what grinds me...Why should we wait for them to make the advances?

5. b. *To grind in*: see quot. 1928[2]. Also with *on*.

1888 [in Dict.]. 1895 *Boy's Own Paper* XVII. 350/3 To make the valves fit tight you should grind them in their seating with a little fine emery and oil. 1903 Mechedy *Dict. Motoring* 281 New valves should also be ground on to their seatings. 1924 A. W. Judge *Mod. Motor Cars* III. 297 It is usually necessary to grind in the valves whenever the cylinders are decarbonised. *Ibid.* 298 When all pit marks are absent a final grinding in with metal polish paste can be given. 1928 — *Car Maintenance* 43 After replacing a ground-in valve. 1928 *Motor Manual* (ed. 27) 212 Grinding-in.—A simple method of rendering the valves of an engine gas-tight by grinding them by hand on the seatings with fine emery powder and oil.

d. To scour (a skin) with pumice-stone, in making it into parchment.

1860 C. Tomlinson *Useful Arts Gt. Brit., Parchment Manuf.* 38 The grain side of the skin is next ground, but without the addition of chalk or lime.

9. Also with adv.

1924 Galsworthy *White Monkey* I. iii, A taxicab ground up.

Grindstone. **3.** Add: (Earlier U.S. examples.)

a 1847 in H. Howe *Hist. Collect. Ohio* 121 The stones were of the common grindstone grit. *Ibid.* 126 Near the village is an inexhaustible grindstone quarry which is extensively worked.

Gringo. (Earlier examples.)

1844 J. J. Webb *Memoirs* 19 We..were entertained with hospitality universal among the American residents in New Mexico at that time on the arrival of 'gringos' (strangers). *Ibid.* 136 They wanted their families out of the reach of the barbarous heretics, 'gringoes', when they should come. 1876 *Congress. Record* 30 June 4310/1 Cortina has never failed to rouse the hatred of the Mexican population against the 'gringos'. 1928 Willa Cather *Death comes for Abp.* v. i. 135 Any European, except a Spaniard, was regarded as a gringo.

Grip, *v.*[1] Add: **1. d.** With the hands as obj.: To hold firm in a grip.

1907 *Smart Set* Jan. 32/2 She fell back in the chair and gripped her hands round the arms of it. *Ibid.* Feb. 24/1 He gripped his hands together and put the doubt behind him. 1910 E. Maria Albanesi *Love of Anne Lambart* 112 Anne's two cold hands gripped themselves together.

Griper. Add: **4. b.** A device for gripping.

1846 *Rep. U.S. Comm. Patents* (1847) 57 My fourth improvement relates to the employment of gripers jointed to a chuck or head on the end of a hollow mandrel.

Grippy, *a.* Add: **3.** Capable of holding the attention and interest of a spectator, reader, etc.

1921 *Pall Mall & Globe* 15 Nov. 2/3 With a little cutting-down, 'Wat Tyler' would make an entirely good and grippy little play.

Grist, *sb.*[2] **2. d.** *U.S.* (Earlier and later examples.)

1832 Paulding *Westward Ho!* I. 77 There has been a mighty grist of rain lately up above. 1881 McLean *Cape Cod Folks* xviii. 295 'Grists on 'em, this year!' he said. 'Heaps!' Aunt Patty responded. 1906 *Springfield* (Mass.) *Weekly Republ.* 8 Feb. 9 A good-sized grist of matters was presented in the House last week under suspension of the rules.

Grit, *v.* Add: **4.** (Earlier examples.)

1797 Jefferson *The Anas* 26 Dec. (Th.) Mr. Adams, gritting his teeth, said [etc.]. 1840 *Southern Lit. Messenger* VI. 735/2 The duellist gritted his teeth as he cocked the gun a second time.

b. To utter with gritting of the teeth.

1900 *Daily News* 11 Oct. 3/1 The Boers have gritted it between their teeth, mingling it with sullen curses—for to the veldtsman the name [of J. Chamberlain] is as the name of a thing accursed. 1910 Mulford *Hopalong Cassidy* i. 11 'I'll kill you some day, you whelp' he gritted.

Hence **Gri·tting** *vbl. sb.*

1823 *Massachusetts Spy* 30 Apr. (Th.) The harmony arising from the filing of a saw, or the gritting of teeth. *a* 1849 Poe *Tales & Sketches, Hop-Frog* (1852) 255, I could have sworn that it was the gritting of this vagabond's teeth. 1901 *Daily News* 13 Mar 5/2 The gritting and corroding of tubes. 1908 *Westm. Gaz.* 14 Dec. 11/2 The Borough Council includes no less a sum than £2,000 for snow removal and the gritting of the roads.

Gritful (gri·tfŭl), *a.* [f. Grit *sb.*[1] 5 + -ful.] Full of 'grit'.

1897 *New York Voice* 16 Dec. 4/1 This took 'all of the namby-pamby' out of this rich aristocratic young man, and made him gritful, enduring, self-reliant.

Grittily (gri·tili), *adv.* [f. Gritty *a.*[1] + -ly [2].] With a gritty sound.

1911 D. H. Lawrence *White Peacock* II. i, He marched me ..into the sanded passage of the little inn...As we tramped grittily down the passage, [etc.].

Grizzle, *sb.*[2] Add: **2.** A bout of grumbling or sulking; a peevish mood; a fretful effusion.

1900 *Eng. Dial. Dict.* 1923 Una L. Silberrad *Lett. Jean Armiter* xi. § 2, Opportunity to write a good long letter to make up for the short grizzle of last month.

Grizzler (gri·zlǝɹ). *dial.* or *colloq.* [f. Grizzle *v.*[2] + -er [1].] One who frets or grumbles.

1900 *Eng. Dial. Dict.* s.v. *Grizzle v.*[1] 2, If ever there was a grizzler she's the one. 1910 H. G. Wells *Hist. Mr. Polly* vi. § 7, 'I don't think I could abide a grizzler', said Uncle Pentstemon.

Grizzly bear (see Grizzly *a.* b). Add: Also, the name of an American dance in which the hug and walk of a bear are imitated.

In mod. Dicts.

Grocery. Add: **4. b.** *U.S.* (Earlier and later examples.)

1806 *The Balance* (Hudson, N.Y.) 28 Jan. 31 (Th.) There are 174 licenced groceries in the city of Albany. 1830 *Jeffersonian* (Albany, N.Y.) 30 June (Th.) Wilson told the Sheriff to take the jury to a grocery, that he might treat them. 1872 Eggleston *Hoosier Schoolm.* xi. 99, I must a took a little too much at Welch's grocery.

5. *grocery keeper* (U.S.).

1839 *Indiana Ho. Repres. Jrnl.* 274 An act to be passed repealing the present law granting licence to grocery keepers. 1864 'P. V. Nasby' (D. R. Locke) *Struggles* 112 The grocery-keepers are intimatin' that before long I must begin to pay for my licker. 1888 Bryce *Amer. Commw.* II. II. xliii. 134 Grocery keepers, liquor dealers, insurance, vendors of patents.

Groceteria (grōusėtī·riă). *U.S.* [f. Grocery, after *Cafeteria.] A grocery store in which customers help themselves and pay the cashier as they go out.

1918 Webster Addenda. 1923 *Glasgow Herald* 11 Oct. 5. 1926 *Evening Standard* 12 July 3/2.

Grog, *sb.* **4.** Add: **grog-hole** *U.S.* = Groggery.

1848 *Knickerbocker Mag.* XVIII. 521 He was busy about the village, penetrating every grog-hole and gambling-alley. 1871 *Scribner's Monthly* I. 537 Grog-holes, billiard saloons ..were well patronized.

Groggery. *U.S.* (Earlier examples.)

1822 Quitman *Let.* in *Life & Corr.* 71 Consisting of warehouses, low taverns, groggeries, dens of prostitution, and gaming-houses. 1835 Ingraham *South-West* II. 190 Wretched looking dwellings, occupied as 'groggeries' by free negroes.

Groggily (grǫ·gili), *adv.* [-ly [2].] In a groggy manner; shakily.

1897 Kipling *Capt. Cour.* ii. He stepped, rather groggily ..to the cabin steps. 1927 *Daily Express* 2 May 11/3 The bull staggers groggily like a pugilist who has received a severe body blow.

Grogging (grǫ·giŋ), *vbl. sb.* [-ing [1].] The process of extracting spirits from an empty cask by soaking the interior with hot water (see Grog *v.* 2).

1901 *Daily News* 5 Mar. 7/5 [A wine and spirit merchant] was fined £5 and costs for 'grogging'. 1902 *Daily Chron.* 18 Oct. 8/6 Many casks were found on the defendant's premises undergoing the process of grogging.

Grolier (grolye, grōu·liǝɹ). The name of a famous French book-collector, Jean *Grolier* de Servin, Vicomte d'Aiguisy (1479–1565), used *attrib.* to designate the interlacing geometrical designs which adorn the gorgeous bindings of his books. Also *absol.*, a Grolier binding. Hence **Groliere·sque** *a.* (also *absol.*).

1876 *Encycl. Brit.* IV. 41/2 The Grolier style. 1880 Zaehnsdorf *Bookbinding* p. xix, A centre block of Grolier. *Ibid.* xx, The Grolier bindings were bold. 1889 Quaritch *Facsim. Book-binding* 25 The design is smaller in scale than that of the true Grolieresque. 1893 *Q. Rev.* July 196 The geometrical strapwork patterns known as Grolieresque were introduced into England in the time of Edward VI. *Ibid.* 199 Another small volume in a Grolier binding. 1928 Goldschmidt *Bookbindings* I. 102 The earliest Groliers.

Groom, *v.* Add: **2. b.** *fig.* To prepare as a political candidate. *U.S.*

1889 *Kansas Times & Star* 12 Mar., The Star is grooming Fred Howard, lawyer, for mayor as an independent and a Democrat. 1903 J. Hawthorne *Hawthorne & his Circle* 264 Grover Cleveland was being groomed for his first Presidential term.

Groove, *sb.* **6.** Add: **groove-like** *a.*, wanting in novelty or originality.

1902 *Daily Chron.* 5 July 8/3 There are commendations without end waiting for the linen frock that displays just a little originality, so groove-like is the manifestation of that material as a general rule. 1908 *Westm. Gaz.* 4 June 10/3, I think the modern tendency is too groove-like. Once make a success as a Cockney or a love-sick maiden, and a Cockney or a love-sick maiden you will be to the end of time.

Groove, *v.* Add: **4. b.** *fig.* To settle or be settled *into* (or *in*) a routine of work, habit, etc. Also with *down*.

1866 Conington *Let. to Courthope* 28 June in *Misc. Writ.* I. p. lvi, I am grooving down into work here. 1879 Froude *Cæsar* ii. 10 Morality thus engrained in the national character and grooved into habits of action creates strength, as nothing else creates it. 1922 A. S. M. Hutchinson *This Freedom* I. v, She found Anna grooved in the business of helping her mother in the house.

Grorudite (grōu·rudǝit). *Petrol.* [Named by W. C. Brögger, 1894, from *Grorud*, Oslo, Norway: see -ite [1].] A microgranitic dyke-rock containing prisms of ægirine.

1903 Geikie *Text-bk. Geol.* (ed. 4) 208. 1907 B. N. Peach, etc. *Geol. Structure N.-W. Highl. Scotl.* 449 Professor Brögger's typical Grorudite. 1926 H. H. Read, etc. *Geol. Strath Oykell* 72 The grorudites of the Loch Ailsh mass carry much less ægirine than the type grorudites of Norway.

Gros (gro), *a.* [Fr. (see Gross *a.*).] Occurring in various French designations, as **gros bleu**, a dark blue used to paint china; **gros Colmar**, a variety of grape; **gros Michel**, the West Indian banana.

1882 *Hamilton Sale Catal.* No. 495 A *Gros-bleu and Gold Sevres Coffee-cup and Saucer. 1885 *Encycl. Brit.* XIX. 638/1 The chief colours [of Sèvres porcelain] are *gros bleu*, a very dark blue; *bleu du roi*, [etc.]. 1927 *Daily Express* 8 Apr. 5 The Cape grapes..cost 2s. per pound for either the *gros Colmars or the white Hanapoots. 1927 *Observer* 17 Apr. 7/1 The *Gros Michel..which comes from Jamaica.

Grosgrain (grǭ·sgrein, ‖ grogræ̃n). [Fr., = coarse grain.] Applied to various corded fabrics. Hence **Grosgrained** (grǭ·sgreind) *a.*

1869 [see Grogram 1]. 1905 *Westm. Gaz.* 5 Aug. 10/2 Grosgrain is far better with alpaca than any shiny make of taffeta. 1927 *Daily Express* 14 Mar. 5 Two toned grosgrained ribbon. 1930 *Times* 17 Mar. 15/6 On the black grosgrain ribbon hat is a jewelled pin.

Grotian (grōu·ʃiǎn), *a.* [See -an.] Of or pertaining to the Dutch publicist and statesman Hugo *Grotius* (1583–1645), who founded the modern science of international law and propounded the 'governmental' view of the Atonement. Hence **Gro·tianism**, the views or teaching of Grotius.

1864 Shedd *Hist. Chr. Doctr.* II. 366 The Grotian soteriology. 1920 *Expositor* May 372 Jonathan Edwards the younger, went over to Grotianism, bag and baggage. *Ibid.* 373 Johnson had enunciated views of the doctrine [of the Atonement] which one can only characterize as strongly Grotian.

Grouch (grautʃ), *sb.* *U.S.* [var. of Grutch *sb.*] **1.** Grumbling; a complaint or grumble; a grumbling, sulky mood; a fit of ill temper or sulkiness.

1903 Marg. Deland in *Harper's Bazaar* Oct. 947 No woman who comes down to her breakfast table with what her son frankly calls a 'grouch on' is grouchy to herself alone. 1905 *New York Even. Post* 2 Sept. 4 We need still another breakfast food...one that will take away matutinal grouch. 1906 B'ness von Hutten *What became of Pam* I. ii, You are not going to spoil my birthday with one of your grouches. 1913 Mulford *Coming of Cassidy* iii. 61 Longhorn..felt savage elation at this opportunity to unload quite a cargo of accumulated grouches of various kinds and sizes. 1921 *Chambers's Jrnl.* Jan. 37/1 He was known there as the Englishman whom Providence had a grouch against.

2. A grumbler.

1919 H. L. Wilson *Ma Pettengill* ii. 61 A fifty-five-year-old male grouch..who had been snarling at everyone that came near him ever since the train left New York. 1920 W. H. Porter *Eating to Live Long* 146 We pity poor old Carlyle, a crabbed, grumbling grouch all his life long.

Grouch (grautʃ), *v.* *U.S.* [var. of Grutch *v.*] *intr.* To grumble. Also quasi-*trans.*

1925 H. L. Foster *Trop. Tramp Tourists* 137 The tourists ..all came back to the train at a painfully slow walk,..and grouched all the way home. 1926 J. Black *You Can't Win* viii. 90 'Everything's all right now, ain't it?' 'Oh, sure,' he grouched, 'Everything's all right—just like Denmark.'

Grouchy (grau·tʃi), *a.* *U.S.* [f. *Grouch *sb.* or *v.* + -y [1].] Grumbly, ill-tempered.

1902 *Daily Chron.* 25 Jan. 7/2 Thus we may learn which of them, in the opinion of his fellows, is..the slouchiest, the biggest fusser, the 'grouchiest'. 1903 [see *Grouch *sb.* 1]. *a* 1906 'O. Henry' *Trimmed Lamp* etc. 215 What's the matter, Andy, you are so solemn and grouchy to-night? 1929 C. H. Smith *Bridge of Life* i. 5 My maternal grandfather..was a grouchy, crusty old fellow.

Hence **Grou·chily** *adv.*, **Grou·chiness**.

1907 Mulford *Bar-20* xxiii. 221 His definition, grouchily expressed. 1921 R. D. Paine *Comr. Rolling Ocean* iii. 41 'They are all new to me,' grouchily replied Judson. 1925 Mulford *Cottonwood Gulch* vi. 87 The second bar-tender, whose grouchiness was due to lack of proper sleep.

Ground, *sb.* Add: **2. b.** *To take ground* (without *the*).

1893 Stevenson *Catriona* Summary p. viii, The *Covenant* took ground and sank off the coast of Mull. 1893 'Q' *Delect. Duchy* 285 Miss..Lear heard her brother's boat take ground on the narrow beach.

8. b. *From the ground up*: completely, entirely; 'down to the ground'. *U.S. colloq.*

1895 *Congress. Record* 6 Feb., App. 207/1 There never has been a time that a democratic administration has not been American from the ground up. 1920 W. M. Raine *B. O'Connor* 52 We suited each other from the ground up.

f. *To go to ground*: also said of a dog. Also in other phrases.

1925 *Times* 7 Jan. 5/6 Sticking to their fox, the pace continued good to Chesterton, where he was marked to ground. 1931 *Our Dogs* 23 Oct. 292/2 Working Terrier Dog..goes to ground to fox or badger, and stays.

17. b. *ground-basis, -fact, -quality, -sense.*

1920 Nunn *Education* 156 The function of the self-regarding sentiment is to exercise control over the 'objective' sentiments that form the *ground-basis of the self. 1905 *Spectator* 11 Mar. 353/1 The underlying *ground-fact of Russia, the inadequacy of her food-supply. 1897 T. Hardy *Well-Beloved* II. iii, Avice..had yet possessed a *ground-quality absent from her rivals. *Ibid.* III. vii, Pierston heard a voice below, the accents of a woman. They had a ground quality of familiarity, a superficial articulation of strangeness. 1909 Titchener *Text-bk. Psychol.* I. 116 The sense of smell..is also a *ground-sense:..our own disregard of smell sensations is largely due to our assumption of the upright position.

d. In Aviation, as *ground loops, school, speed.*

1917 *Blackw. Mag.* May 805/2 Our ground speed was now a good deal greater than if we had travelled directly west. 1924 Webster Addenda, *Ground school*, a school giving courses in aërodynamics, map-making, photography, etc., for aviators...*Ground speed*, the horizontal component of the velocity of an aircraft relative to the earth. 1928 C. F. S. Gamble *Story North Sea Air Station* i, If there be no wind ..a very much greater 'ground speed' has to be attained.. before the machine will gain enough flying speed for the wings to take some load off the floats, and eventually enable the machine to 'take-off' from the surface of the sea. *Ibid.* iv, 'Ground-straffing' by low-flying machines. 1928 *Daily Mail* 7 May 6/4 Ground Loops.—Touching the ground and rising again. *Ibid.* 9 Aug. 7/1 Ground engineer of the London Aero Club.

18. ground and lofty *U.S.*, applied to acrobatic feats or performers on the ground and on a rope, etc.; **ground chain** *Naut.* (see quot.); **ground-cloth** (see quot.); **ground frost**, a frost which occurs on the surface of the earth but not in the circumambient air; **ground gripper** *U.S.*, a shoe made so as to give the wearer a secure footing; **ground nester**, a bird, etc. that makes its nest on or in the ground; **ground pin** (later U.S. example); **ground-retted** *ppl. a.*, dew-retted; **ground-sheet**, a waterproof sheet spread on the ground as a protection against damp; **ground-space**, the area of ground occupied by a structure; **ground-stroke** *Lawn Tennis*, a stroke by which the ball is made to strike the ground; **ground wire**, (*b*) a wire used to complete a ground-connexion in a circuit; = *earth-wire* (see *Earth *sb.*[1] B. II).

1796 *Gazette of U.S.* (Philad.) 19 Nov., Advt. (Th.) *Ground and Lofty Tumbling [at the Pantheon, Philadelphia]. 1840 *Southern Lit. Messenger* VI. 386/1 He is an adept in the art of walking on his head, turning somersets, and ground and lofty tumbling generally. 1843 Thurlow Weed *Lett.* (1866) 108 A strolling company of ground and lofty tumblers. 1879 F. R. Stockton *Rudder Grange* xiii. 160 They was havin' it, ground an' lofty. 1907 M. C. Harris *Tents of Wickedness* III. iv. 260 He has resigned his parish, left the ministry and bought a seat on the Stock Exchange. Isn't that ground and lofty tumbling. 1883 *Man. Seamanship for Boys* 195 Q. What is *ground chain? A. A piece of small chain shackled to the anchor shackle,..of sufficient length to come through the hawse pipe when the anchor is high enough for catting. 1919 W. B. Faraday *Gloss. Aeronaut. Terms* 54 *Ground Cloth, a floor covering, usually of canvas, placed on the ground under an envelope to protect it from damage. 1900 *Daily News* 12 Oct. 5/1 Towards night, the thermometer fell briskly, and it seemed probable that a sharp *ground frost would occur. 1927 *Saturday Even. Post* (N.Y.) 24 Dec. 24/3 One day the boys would train on pemmican. The next day they would run in moccasins. Then they would discard the leather *ground-grippers and skip around barefoot. 1875 *Field & Forest* I. 10 Altogether, it was a very neat structure, and looked to me as though the owner was habitually a '*ground-nester'. 1880 *Libr. Univ. Knowl.* (N.Y.) X. 496 Ground-nesters, squatters, and miners. 1843 Frémont *Exped.* 54 Our lodge had been planted, and, on account of the heat, the *ground pins had been taken out, and the lower part slightly raised. 1898 *Daily News* 22 Oct. 9/6 Water and *ground retted flaxes. 1907 *Daily Chron.* 15 Mar. 9/5 *Groundsheet (waterproof). 1928 *Daily Express* 12 May 5/5 Some of the motorists were having tea in the cars, and some had spread groundsheets and cushions on the ground. 1866 *Chambers's Jrnl.* 18 Aug. 521/2 The houses..are large.., with very little accommodation, considering the *ground-space they occupy. 1908 *Westm. Gaz.* 28 Mar. 9/2 All citizens are users or consumers of air, water, ground-space. 1895 Wilberforce *Lawn Tennis* 51 There are two ways in which a *ground-stroke may be taken, namely, at the top of the bound, and again quite late, when the ball is near the ground. 1910 *N. Hawkins' Elect. Dict.*, *Ground Wire. 1922 J. C. Wright *Automotive Repair* II. 208 If the ground wire is disconnected the generator will build up an excessive pressure within itself.

b. ground-bee, a bee that nests in the ground; **ground-flicker**, the genus *Soroplex* of woodpeckers; **ground-hornet** (earlier U.S. example); **ground-mouse**, a field mouse; **ground-robin** (earlier U.S. example); **ground-sparrow** *U.S.* (examples); **ground-spider** (earlier example); **ground worm** (see sense 18 in Dict.; Amer. examples).

1849 C. Brontë *Shirley* xxv, The nest..of some *ground-bees, which had burrowed in the turf under an old cherry-tree. 1884–5 *Riverside Nat. Hist.* (1888) IV. 428 The South American *ground flickers. 1821 Z. Hawley *Tour* 95 (Th.) A nest of *ground hornets, concealed under the logway. 1840 J. Buel *Farmer's Comp.* 99 Moles or *ground-mice cannot penetrate and find a shelter. 1877 Whitman *Specimen Days* (1892) 100 Let me make a list of those [birds] I find here [in New Jersey]. *Ground robins. 1874 B. F. Taylor *World on Wheels*, etc. II. vii. 249 The *ground-sparrows build in its margins. 1882 *Vermont Agric. Rep.* VII. 67 The blue bird, cat bird, wren and ground sparrows are acknowledged beneficial. 1867 *Amer. Naturalist* Oct. I. 410 Some of the *ground spiders carry their eggs in a sack attached to the tip of their abdomen. 1708 *Col. Rec. N. Carolina* I. 682 The Fly, the *ground worme, the house wormes [etc.]. 1770 in *Maryland Hist. Mag.* XII. 362 There are such Quantities of ground wormes, that I am afraid it will be difficult to get our tobacco Plants to stand when favoured with a Season.

c. ground flower, a low-growing field-flower, as the primrose, violet, etc.; **ground-laurel** (earlier example).

1902 *Daily Chron.* 1 Apr. 2/1 At Easter there are but the *ground-flowers. 1928 Cottrell *Singing Gold* I. vi. 50 The cup-like tufts of the little white ground-flower, with the sweetest scent in all Australia. 1867 *Amer. Naturalist* May I. 154 In the books, this plant is known as the 'Epigea repens', but otherwise as the Trailing Arbutus, May Flower, and *Ground Laurel.

Grounder. **3. c.** Add examples (in cricket, baseball, football).

1862 Pycroft *Cricket Tutor* 8 The old bat used to be heavy at the point—very requisite for picking up a Grounder. 1874 H. Chadwick *Base Ball Man.* 20 To be..active in fielding 'grounders'. 1927 *Daily Express* 27 May 13/7 Brown opened the scoring, receiving a fine pass from Dean and sending in a beautiful grounder from eighteen yards.

Ground floor. **b.** (Examples of U.S. phrase.)

1872 Talmage *Abom. Mod. Society* 118 A select number go in on the 'ground floor'. 1901 S. Merwin & Webster *Calumet K* xi. 211 Well then, we'll have to let you in on the ground floor. 1904 'O. Henry' *Cabbages & Kings* xii. 206 Says he's heard of the boom along this coast, and wants to get in on the ground floor.

Ground-hog. **2.** (Earlier examples.)

1789 *Maryland Jrnl.* 13 Nov., Advt. (Th.) A Monack or Ground-Hog, presented [to Peale's Museum] by Mr. Johnston. 1807 P. Gass *Jrnl.* ii. 25 Two of our hunters went out and killed an animal called a prarow, about the size of a ground hog. 1819 E. Dana *Geog. Sk. Western Country* 182 Wild cats, foxes, ground hogs and squirrels, are to be found ranging in the forests bordering on the Mississippi.

Ground-leaf. [Ground *sb.* 17 a.] A leaf, *spec.* of a tobacco plant, growing next to the ground.

1640 in *Maryland Archives* 98 Bad Tobacco shall be judged ground leafes [etc.]. 1655 in *Proc. Council Maryland* 314 Eleven hundred and fiftie pounds of Tobacco in Caske without Ground Leaves. 1671 in *Maryland Archives* II. 290 An Act Prohibiting ground Leaves and Seconds. 1784 J. Smyth *Tour U.S.* II. 136 In stripping they are careful to throw away all the ground leaves, and faulty tobacco. 1849 *Rep. U.S. Comm. Patents, Agric.* (1850) 320 'Ground leaves' are those leaves at the bottom of the plant which become dry on the stalk, and ought to be gathered early in the morning when they will not crumble.

Ground-nut. **2.** (Earlier example.)

1740 in *Coll. Georgia Hist. Soc.* I. 199 We have also.. chincopin nuts..hickory and ground nuts.

Ground-pea. [Ground *sb.* 18 c.] = Ground-nut 2.

1769 [see Ground-nut 2]. 1796–1806 B. Hawkins *Lett.* 271 They made beans, ground peas, cymblins. 1823 S. H. Long *Exped. Rocky Mtns.* I. 200 The squaws..are often necessitated to dig the pomme de terre,..and to scratch the ground pea. 1854 *Florida Plant. Rec.* 115, I have picked 80 bushels of ground peas.

Groundsman, now the form in general use = Ground-man b; also in the sense of: An aerodrome mechanic or attendant whose duties are on 'the ground'.

1923 *Daily Mail* 1 Mar. 10 An open-air meeting of pilots, groundsmen, and mechanics at the Croydon aerodrome.

Ground-squirrel. **1.** (Earlier U.S. example.)

1726 *Braintree Rec.* 115 Whosoever should kill any ground squirrels should have threepence per head.

Groundwork. Add: **5.** *Cricket.* = *ground-fielding* (Ground *sb.* 18).

1905 *Westm. Gaz.* 19 Sept. 3/1 The ground-work was always splendid, and the throwing a joy to behold.

Group, *sb.* Add:

6. group-captain, an officer of the Air Force; **group (life) assurance** or **insurance** (see quot. 1927); **group-marriage**, the union and cohabitation, according to tribal usage, of a group of males with a group of females; hence **group-marriager**, a supporter of the evolutional theory of such marriage; **group-wise** *adv.*, (performed) by groups.

1923 *Daily Mail* 13 Feb. 9 *Group-captain in the Air Force. 1927 B. C. Hoskins *Insurance Lex.* 105 *Group Life Assurance.—Under this contract groups or numbers of lives are assured instead of individuals. 1928 *Daily Mail* 25 July 19/5 Group Insurance came into existence only seventeen years ago and it took seven years for all companies to accumulate as much Group Life Insurance as this one contract. 1880 L. Fison *Kamilaroi & Kurnai* 97 *Group Marriage and Relationship. 1906 N. W. Thomas *Kinship Organization* 126 The course of evolution has been, not as *group-marriagers maintain from group to individual terms of relationship but from terms descriptive of status to terms descriptive of relationship. 1901 E. A. Ross *Social Control* 29 The fittest to survive when the competition is man-wise, may be eliminated when the competition is *group-wise.

b. *Psychol.* Designating mental processes and activities belonging to the members of a group or community as a collective whole; e.g. *group consciousness, life, mind, psychology, spirit, will*; **group person** (see quot. 1915).

1915 E. Barker *Polit. Thought in England* 74 That group of minds, in virtue of the common substance of a uniting idea, is itself a group-mind. *Ibid.* 175 Permanent groups are themselves persons, group-persons, with a group-will of their own. 1916 C. C. J. Webb (*title*) Group Theories of Religion and the Individual. 1920 W. McDougall (*title*) The Group Mind. *Ibid.* 8 Group Psychology has, first, to establish the general principles of group life. *Ibid.* 63 The group spirit, the idea of the group with the sentiment of devotion to the group developed in the minds of all its members. 1924 W. B. Selbie *Psychol. Relig.* 72 The working of the social consciousness or group mind.

Grouse (graus), *sb.*[2] *slang.* [f. Grouse *v.*[2]] A grumble or complaint; a reason for grumbling.

1923 *Pictorial Weekly* CXIX. 127/1 A Transfer 'Grouse'. 1927 *Daily Express* 27 Apr. 3/1 'I cannot understand the point of view of the hanging committee...I have no grouse against them. I am not an Academician, but I do not agree with their choice. *Ibid.* 5 Oct. 3/4 The 'moan' of a Gun Room is the naval version of an Army 'grouse'.

Grouser[3] (grau·sǝɹ). [f. Grouse *v.*[2] + -er [1].] One who grumbles or complains.

1885 J. Brunlees Patterson *Life in Ranks* 120 Impossible to do anything at all entirely to the satisfaction of a certain class of individuals...This..body of men is commonly designated by their..comrades as the 'grousers'. 1928 *Yorks. Post* 10/3 Sir John Maxwell on 'Grousers and Grumblers'.

Growl, *v.*[3] Add: **3.** *intr.* To be dully painful. (Cf. dial. or colloq. *grumble.*)

1774 P. V. Fithian *Jrnl.* (1900) 267 My Jaw continues growling & keeps me uneasy.

Growler. Add:

5. A small iceberg (see quots.).

1912 *Standard* 4 May 7/7 He thought the distinction between icebergs and growlers was that the growler was an iceberg with very little protruding above the water. 1912 *Chambers's Jrnl.* Aug. 552/1 'Growlers,' low-lying fragments scarcely projecting above the sea. 1930 *Ibid.* Apr. 216/2 The object is to hasten 'calving' or splitting of the berg into 'growlers' or smaller pieces.

6. *Electr.* A kind of transformer used to test an armature for short circuits.

If a short circuit exists in the armature coils its presence is indicated by a 'growling' noise.

1922 J. C. Wright *Automotive Repair* II. 73 For making tests showing the general conditions of an armature, an instrument commonly known as a 'growler' is desirable.

Growly (grau·li), *a.* [f. Growl *sb.* or *v.*[3] + -y [1].] Resembling a growl.

1920 Galsworthy *In Chancery* I. vii, Val, uttering a growly sound, followed her.

Growth[1]. **5.** Add: *growth-direction, -measurer, -rate, -ratio*; *growth-controlling, -influencing, -making* ppl. adjs.

1922 *Times Lit. Suppl.* 27 Apr. 279/1 A *growth-controlling principle which he named tethelin. 1916 *Nature* XCVII. 290/2 The word 'tropism', first used to indicate the *growth-direction of plant-members under the influence of some stimulus. 1918 *Ibid.* C. 484/2 The *growth-influencing substance 'Tethelin', which Prof. Robertson had isolated from the anterior lobe of the pituitary body. 1922 *Chambers's Jrnl.* Dec. 875/1 The natives..chew it from boyhood, and attach great importance to it as a *growth-making agent. 1924 J. A. Thomson *Science Old & New* xxxvi. 206 *Growth-measurers (auxanometers). 1930 R. A. Fisher *Genet. The. Nat. Selection* 45 The vital statistics of an organism in relation to its environment provide a means of determining a measure of the relative *growth-rate of the population. 1924 J. S. Huxley in *Nature* CXIV. 895 Constant Differential *Growth-ratios and their Significance.

Grub, *sb.* Add: **7.** *U.S.* (Earlier examples.)

1788 Washington *Diaries* III. 306 At Muddy hole they were..taking up grubs in the winter fallow of No. 4. 1825 J. Lorain *Pract. Husb.* 334 The Yankee farmer first chops the fallen timber, then scalps off the grubs level with the ground. 1839 Caroline M. Kirkland *New Home* xx. 133 Grubs are, in western parlance, the gnarled roots of small trees and shrubs. 1847 in D. Drake *Pioneer Life Kentucky* ii. 34 [He got] his mattock fast under the roots of a grub. 1853 *Trans. Mich. Agric. Soc.* IV. 365 A dense growth of hazel bush, oak grubs and willow.

8. *grub wagon*; **grub-stake** *v.* *U.S.* (earlier example); **grub-staker** *U.S.*, a prospector who is supplied with a grub-stake; **grub-worm** (later examples).

1880 *Harper's Mag.* Feb. 382/1 He even showed some inclination to '*grub-stake' some men. 1881 A. A. Hayes *New Colorado* vii. 107 Here does the whilom *grub-staker and present millionaire purchase his corner lot. 1891 *Fur, Fin & Feather* Mar. 150 They take with them a *grub wagon and ten saddle horses, and expect to be absent four months. 1920 Hunter *Trail Drivers of Texas* 69 We were two miles from the grub wagon. 1849 C. Brontë *Shirley* v, My *grub-worm is always a straitened, struggling, careworn tradesman. 1853 R. Glisan *Jrnl. Army Life* ix. (1874) 106 Lieutenant Garland and myself caught a fine lot of buffalo-fish with grub-worms.

Grubbing, *vbl. sb.*[1] Add: **1.** Also, the roots grubbed up.

1823 W. Faux *Memor. Days* 320 (Th.) To root up the small roots is called grubbing, so as to render the land fit for the plough, and the grubbings are to be burnt.

5. *grubbing-hoe* (earlier U.S. examples).

1727 in *Maryland Hist. Mag.* XVIII. 226 Iron ware..6 Grubbing hoes, 6 weeding hoes. 1781 in *Cal. Virginia St. Papers* I. 596, 200 Broad and grubbing Hoes. 1873 J. H. Beadle *Undevel. West* xi. 192 The best land in the West costs next to nothing, and grubbing hoes but two dollars apiece.

Grueller. Add: **3.** A 'gruelling' race or contest.

1876 *Coursing Calendar* 21 Harpist, in an awful grueller, was nearly always in front. *Ibid.* 97 Gay Lad, after his grueller of this morning, could not run well.

Gruesome, *a.* **1.** Add: *absol.* (with *the*): gruesome subjects, descriptions, etc.

1905 *Daily Chron.* 21 Feb. 3/3 'Death and the Woman' ..is another effort after the gruesome, which fails to move us. 1905 *Westm. Gaz.* 30 Sept. 12/1 Those who like the gruesome will find plenty to interest them in the relics of Gustavus Adolphus.

Gruffle (grʋ·f'l), *v.* *dial.* or *colloq.* [Echoic.] *intr.* To utter or make utterance in a gruff muffled tone. Hence as *sb.*

a 1825 Forby *Voc. E. Anglia*, *Gruffle*, to make a sort of growling noise in the throat. 1928 Sylvia Thompson *Battle of Horizons* II. iii. 50 'Tea', gruffled Charles Graham..'Tea is a woman's meal.' *Ibid.* Epilogue 311 Sir Charles' deep gruffle, Mary's mild exclamation.

Grum, *adv.* [f. the adj.] In a grum tone.

1853 B. F. Taylor *Jan. & June* (1871) 74 The drums beat grummer and grummer 'to quarters'.

Grumly, *adv.* Delete *rare*[−0] and add examples.

1827 J. F. Cooper *Red Rover* iii, 'Any fool knowd it,' returned Scipio grumly. 1854 H. H. Riley *Puddleford* 92 (Th.) Mr. Bird very grumly said he had better hold on. 1880 Cable *Grandissimes* vi. 41 'Um-hum,' he said grumly.

Grunth, var. *Granth.

Grutch, *sb.* **3.** (Modern U.S. example.)

1898 A. Nicholas *Idyl of Wabash* 36 There'd been some old grutch atween him an' Bill.

Gryphitic (grǝifi·tik), *a.* [-ic.] Of or belonging to gryphites or gryphite limestone.

1833–4 J. Phillips *Geol.* in *Encycl. Metrop.* (1845) VI. 621/2 The gryphitic beds of Lincolnshire.

G string. *Mus.* [G 2, String *sb.* 3.] (See quot. 1876.)

1876 Stainer & Barrett *Dict. Mus. Terms*, *G string*, the name of the first string on the double bass, the third on the violoncello, viola, and guitar, and the fourth on the violin. 1884 W. Hoe *Dict. Fiddle* s.v. *Strings*, To preserve strings in good condition they should be kept in a tin box...This prevents the G string from shrinking in the heat of the summer.

¶See also *Gee-string.

Guacin (gwæ·sin). *Chem.* [f. Guaco + -in [1].] A bitter amorphous principle obtained from guaco.

1886 *Buck's Handbk. Med. Sci.* II. 58/1 Guacin, bitter diuretic.

Guaco, variant of *Huaco.

Guaiacinic (gwǝiˌăsi·nik), *a.* *Chem.* [f. Guaiacin + -ic.] *Guaiacinic acid*: an acid, $C_{19}H_{20}O_6$, forming one of the principal constituents of gum guaiacum.

Guaiaconic (gwǝiˌăkǫ·nik), *a.* *Chem.* [f. Guaiacum + -one + -ic.] *Guaiaconic acid*: an amorphous substance, $C_{38}H_{40}O_{10}$, which forms one of the principal constituents of gum guaiacum.

1874 Garrod & Baxter *Mat. Med.* 224 The resin contains guaiaretic acid..about 10 per cent.; guaiaconic acid..about 70 per cent.; with other vegetable matter. 1883 *Jrnl. Chem. Soc.* XLIV. 470 Guaiaconic acid, treated with hydrochloric acid, yields methyl chloride and catechol. 1908 *Practitioner* Feb. 250 The iron..acts, not merely as a carrier of oxygen to the guaiaconic acid, but as a direct oxidizing agent.

Guaiaretic (gwǝiˌări·tik), *a.* *Chem.* [f. Guaia(c + Gr. ῥητίνη resin + -ic.] *Guiaretic acid*, $C_{20}H_{26}O_4$, one of the constituents of gum guaiacum. So **Guaia·retate**, a salt of this acid.

1874 [see Guaiaconic]. 1892 *Photogr. Ann.* II. 73 Guaiaretic Acid,..when freshly prepared, is soluble in alcohol, ether, [etc.]. *Ibid.*, Addition of small quantities of colouring matters..to the guaiaretic acid or guaiaretates.

Guaiasanol (gwǝiˌăsǝ·nǫl). *Pharm.* [f. Guaia(cum + *san* (L. *sānus* sound, *sānāre* to heal) + -ol.] A white crystalline powder used as an anæsthetic and antiseptic.

a 1909 *Buck's Handbk. Med. Sci.* IV. 425 (Cent. D. Suppl.) Guaiasanol..was introduced by E. Einhorn and Hütz as a soluble form of guaiacol. 1913 Dorland *Med. Dict.* (ed. 7), *Guaiasanol*, the hydrochlorid of diethyl-glycocoll-guaiacol.

Guam (gwām). The name of the largest island of the Ladrone group in the Pacific. *To clear, sail for Guam*: to sail 'for some port unknown'.

1881 *Times* 23 June 4/5 Having..docked the steamer.. they cleared out 'for Guam'. 1898 *Westm. Gaz.* 7 Dec. 12/1 Sailed for Guam.

Guanajuatite (gwānăhwā·tǝit). *Min.* [f. *Guanajuato*, an inland state of Mexico + -ite [1].] A bluish-grey bismuth selenide.

1877 *Amer. Jrnl. Sci.* Ser. III. XIII. 319.

Guanapite (gwā·năpǝit). *Min.* [f. the *Guanape* Islands, off the coast of Peru + -ite [1].] A sulphate of potassium and ammonium, found in guano.

1870 C. U. Shepard in *Rural Carolinian* I. 470 (Chester). 1914 *Brit. Mus. Return* 225 Guanapite.

Guanase (gwā·neis). *Chem.* [f. Guan(in + *-ase.] An autolytic ferment which transforms guanin into xanthine.

1904 *Jrnl. Chem. Soc.* LXXXVI. I. 838 Fresh pancreas, when subjected to autolysis, does not yield adenine or guanine, and guanine which is added is transformed into xanthine within 3 days. The enzyme present in pancreas which induces this change is termed Guanase.

Guanay (gwā·ne). [ad. Sp. *guanae.*] = Guano *sb.* 3.

1860 [see Guano *sb.* 3]. 1928 *Glasgow Herald* 28 Mar. 4/2 The Peruvian cormorant or guanay.

Guanche (gwā·ntʃe). Also **Guancho.** [Sp.] One of the aboriginal inhabitants of the Canary Islands, who were absorbed by the Spanish on their conquest of the islands in the fifteenth century.

c 1789 *Encycl. Brit.* (1797) IV. 81/1 The inhabitants are chiefly Spaniards; though there are some of the first people remaining, whom they call *Guanches*, who are somewhat civilized by their intercourse with the Spaniards. 1814 tr. *Humboldt's Trav.* I. 117 Santa Cruz, the Annaza of the Guanches, is a neat town, with a population of 8000 souls. 1876 *Encycl. Brit.* IV. 796/1 Many of the Guanches fell in opposing the Spanish invasion. 1884 A. de Candolle *Orig. Cultiv. Plants* 320 It is not known whether the Guanchos (the Berber people of the Canaries) knew the bean.

Guango (gwæ·ŋgo). [Native name.] A tropical American tree of the bean family, *Pithecolobium saman*, the pods of which are used as cattle fodder.

1871 C. Kingsley *At Last* x. (1892) 205 Getting little or no food but cassava cakes and 'guango' of maize..he stumbled in suddenly on one squatting after another.

Guanido- (gwæ·nido), combining form of Guanidine.

1874 *Jrnl. Chem. Soc.* XXVII. 906 Guanido-dibenzoic acid. 1922 *Ibid.* CXXII. I. 530 Guanidoethyl alcohol.

Guarani (gwarā·ni). Name of one of the two main divisions of the Tupi-Guarani, a wide-spread ethnical and linguistic family of South American Indians; also, the language of this people. Hence **Guara·nian** *a.*

1797 *Encycl. Brit.* XIII. 730/1 The Guaranies resolved to quit their settlements in the neighbourhood of the Portuguese, and to remove into the province of Paraguay. 1875 *Ibid.* I. 702/1 The supposition..that the Guarani tribes are the remnant of a once powerful and united people, is scarcely admissible. 1885 *Ibid.* XVIII. 244/2 The inhabitants of Paraguay are mainly Guaranis or half-breeds with a strong proportion of Guarani blood. 1900 *Fortn. Rev.* Jan. 79 There the women speak nothing but the Guarany language, and the men use only Guarany in talking to them, whereas among themselves the men always speak Spanish.

Guarantee, *sb.* **5.** Add: **guarantee company** = *guarantee society*; **guarantee space** (see quot.).

1909 'O. Henry' *Options* (1916) 11 The cashier had..a bond from a *guarantee company filed with the owners. 1902 Eliz. L. Banks *Autobiog. Newspaper Girl* 207, I took a position on what is known as the '*guarantee space' system, by which means a member of the staff is guaranteed a stipulated sum of money every week, and as much over that amount as he or she can make by writing at ordinary or special space-rates.

Guard, *sb.* Add: **7. d.** Also in *Basket-ball*, the player who prevents the opposing forward from throwing a goal.

1905 *Official Basket Ball Rules* 30 The position of the guard is the most difficult and unsatisfactory place in the team...He is expected to prevent his opponent from throwing a goal, and that without making a foul himself. 1929 *Encycl. Brit.* III. 182/2 The players are divided into three groups, forwards, centres and guards.

e. *U.S.* (See quot.)

1836 *Knickerbocker Mag.* VIII. 689, I have frequently seen horses come running..to seek the spots frequented by the 'guards'—a species of hornet, which catches the flies and protects beasts of all kinds from pain.

16. j. (Earlier example.)

1840 *Knickerbocker Mag.* XV. 287 She pursued her walk on the guards with a young woman who came on board as nurse to one of the lady passengers.

18. *guard rope, wall*; **guard arm** *Boxing*, the arm with which blows are parried; **guard-book**, a book having guards for the reception of additional leaves (see 16 l); **guard-changing**, the action of changing the guard, esp. at St. James's and Buckingham Palace; **guard-lock** (earlier U.S. examples); **guard-strap** (see quot.); **guard-tent** (U.S. example).

1889 Michell *Boxing* (Badm. Libr.) 155 Last of all the defences..comes the device of shielding with the arm. For this the right, the '*guard arm', is most commonly employed. 1903 *Daily Chron.* 18 Nov. 8/6 Book Sewers wanted, used to *guardbooks and scrap-books. 1907 *Westm. Gaz.* 9 Dec. 7/2 He also produced the 'transfer guard-book'. 1904 *Daily Chron.* 30 May 8/2 The minor formalities of *guard-changing are completed. 1907 *Westm. Gaz.* 12 Nov. 9/1 The ceremony of guard-changing in the quadrangle. 1815 *Niles' Weekly Reg.* IX. 44/2 The boat, having entered the *guard lock, went through the new canal. 1821 T. Dwight *Trav.* II. 353 (Th.) [The canal] contains nine locks. The first, after the guard-lock, has a descent of six feet. 1832 *Louisville Directory* 111 The guard lock is 190 feet long in the clear. 1909 *Strand Mag.* XXXVII. 365/2 Falling back to the *guard-rope that held the crowd. 1888 *Lockwood's Dict. Mech. Engin.*, *Guard Strap*, the strips of sheet iron which arch over the tops of the wheels of locomotives, as a protection against injury to the drivers. 1848 E. Bryant *What I saw in California* iv. 52 They were greatly alarmed when brought to the *guard tent, expecting immediate punishment. 1815–16 *Niles' Weekly Reg.* IX. Suppl. 164/2 At the upper end of the canal between it and the breast of the dam, is a *guard wall.

Guardo (gā·ɹdo). *U.S. Naval slang.* [Arbitrarily f. Guard(ship) + -o, simulating Sp. words.] A receiving-ship for enlisted men who are to be drafted to sea-going vessels. Also *attrib.*

a 1846 J. A. Gardner *Recoll.* (1906) 116 A droll old guardo midshipman. 1909 *Cent. Dict.* Suppl., *Guardo-move*, a trick played upon a landsman on a receiving-ship.

Guarnerius (gwaɹni·riǝs). Also **Joseph Guarnerius**; **Guarn(i)eri.** The name of a family of famous Italian violin-makers of Cremona of the seventeenth and eighteenth centuries, used to designate a violin made by a member of this family. (Cf. *Joseph.)

1875 G. Hart *Violin* 96 A 'Joseph Guarnerius' for one hundred and fifty guineas! 1898 H. R. Haweis *Old Violins* 217 It was no more a Guarnerius than a Strad. [1908 *Grove's Dict. Mus.* IV. 284/2 A full-sized Stradivari or Giuseppe Guarnieri.] 1923 *Weekly Dispatch* 18 Feb. 2 A new violin alongside his old Guarnerius.

Guarri (gwa·ri). *S. Afr.* Also **guarry, guerrie, quarri.** [Kaffir *um Gwali.*] Any one of several trees or shrubs of the genus *Euclea*, esp. *E. undulata*, or the allied genus *Royena*; the fruit of these trees or shrubs. Also *attrib.*

1789 W. Paterson *Narr.* 43 The ground is covered with shrubs about four feet high, called by the natives Guerrie, a species of Royena. 1866 *Treas. Bot.* s.v. *Euclea*, The fruit is globular, fleshy, and juicy, sometimes as large as a cherry. Those of many of the species, known by the colonists as Guarry, are eaten. 1897 Du Toit *Rhodesia* 32 Various kinds of sweet grass and small shrubs, varied with very good large bush and trees, as 'quarri', &c. 1913 Pettman *Africanderisms*, *Guarri honey*, a very pale honey in much esteem in the Riversdale District, obtained by the bees from *Royena sp.* *Guarri tea*, this is made by the Hottentots from the leaves of *Euclea lanceolata*.

Guatemalan (gwātǝmā·lăn), *a.* and *sb.* Also formerly **Guatelmalan.** [f. *Guatemala* + -an.] Of or pertaining to (a native or inhabitant of) Guatemala, the most northern republic of Central America, bordering on Mexico. Also **Guatema·lian, Guatema·ltecan** [Sp. *guatemaltecano*].

1831 Jas. Bell *Syst. Geog.* V. 617 The Guatelmalans [*sic*] declared themselves independent. 1877 Boddam-Whetham *Across Central Amer.* 19 The kind-hearted Guatemaltecans have a custom of driving out to the plain to meet expected friends. 1880 *Encycl. Brit.* XI. 240/1 Singing-birds are commonly kept in the Guatemalian houses. 1888 *New Princeton Rev.* May 356 Zaldivar transmitted a series of despatches misrepresenting the situation, and appealing for protection against Guatemalan tyranny. 1902 *Encycl. Brit.* XXIX. 151/1 A Guatemalan company. 1920 *Glasgow Herald* 7 Apr. 10 Ayutla, on the Guatemalan border. 1927 *Blackw. Mag.* Aug. 173/1 This map, the work of a well-known Guatemalan engineer.

Guayavita (gwāyavī·tă). [Sp.] = Bay-berry 3. Also *attrib.*

1924 *Glasgow Herald* 21 June 6 A thirst which neither the succulent cactus, nor the green threads of pendulous lichen, nor the guayavita berries can slake.

Guayule (gwayū·l). [Native name.] An asteraceous plant, *Parthenium argentatum*, found in Mexico and Texas, the sap of which furnishes a substitute for rubber; also, the rubber substitute itself.

1906 *Bull. Imper. Inst.* IV. 114 The Guayule rubber of Mexico. *Ibid.*, The Guayule plant. *Ibid.* 115 The Guayule is found at altitudes ranging from 3,000 to 5,600 feet.

Guazu (gwāsū·, gwā·zū). [Guarani *guaçú* deer.] The South American marsh-deer, *Cariacus paludosus*. Also **Guazapuco, Guazu-bira, Guazu-pita** (see quots.).

1837 *Penny Cycl.* VIII. 361/2 The Guazapuco deer, *Mazama paludosa* of Smith, *Cervus paludosus* of Desmarest and Lichtenstein. *Ibid.*, The Guazu-bira, *Cervus nemorivagus* of Lichtenstein...Locality the same as that of the Guazu-pita. 1871 C. Kingsley *At Last* x, A little brown guazu-pita fawn.

Guazuti (gwāsūtī·, gwazū·ti). [Guarani *guaçutí* deer of the field.] The South American pampas-deer, *Cariacus campestris*.

1837 *Penny Cycl.* VIII. 361/2 The Guazuti of D'Azara. 1855 Dallas *Syst. Nat. Hist.* II. 436.

Gubbio (gu·bio). The name of a city in northern Italy used *attrib.* to designate majolica made there in the sixteenth century, particularly a ruby-lustred majolica made by Giorgio Andreoli.

1885 *Encycl. Brit.* XIX. 626/2 The early Pesaro and Gubbio ware. *Ibid.* 627/2 The pictured wares of Urbino sometimes have the Gubbio lustre colours.

Gubernator. (Earlier modern example.)

1858 O. W. Holmes *Contentment* iv. 24 I'm very sure I should not care To fill our Gubernator's chair.

Gubu (gū·bu). [Kaffir *i Gubu* hollow-sounding thing, e.g. a drum.] A Zulu musical instrument consisting of a calabash attached to a bow, the string of which is struck with a stick, giving a monotonous sound.

1906 Clairmonte *Africander* 189 Their chief instrument, called a *gubu*, which is something like a one-string banjo with an empty gourd for a drum. 1914 D. Fraser *Winning Prim. People* vi. 68 A good gubu has a liquid tone that is most soothing.

Guemal (gē·măl). Also **gemul, guemul, huemul.** [Sp., ad. native name.] A deer of either of two South American species, *Mazama bisulca* and *M. antisiensis*, having the antlers simply forked.

1876 *Encycl. Brit.* V. 623/2 The huemul is found in the territory of Magellan. 1883 *List Anim. Zool. Soc.* 174 Gemul Deer. 1898 *Guide Mammalia Dept. Zool. B. M.* 76 The Peruvian Guemal..from the Peruvian Andes. 1911 Skottsberg *Wilds of Patagonia* 189 The Andine deer, the huemul.

Guesdism (gē·diz'm). [f. the name of Jules *Guesde* (1845–1922), French political leader + -ism.] The principles of socialism and reform through revolution advocated by Guesde. So **Gue·sdist**, a follower of Guesde.

1901 *Daily Chron.* 25 May 5/4 The only true Socialists, the Guesdists.

Guess, *sb.* **1.** Add: *By guess and by God* or *godfrey* (Naval slang): (to steer) at hazard without a set course or without the guidance of landmarks.

1909 [see *Godfrey]. 1931 W. G. Carr (*title*) By Guess and by God.

Guess, *v.* Add: **7. b.** In phr. *To keep* (a person) *guessing*: to keep in a state of uncertainty. *colloq.* (orig. *U.S.*).

1905 *Springfield* (Mass.) *Weekly Republ.* 24 Nov. 1 More doubt is now thrown upon the question whether he will go to Washington at all. The governor seems determined to keep us guessing. [1930 H. Zink *City Bosses of U.S.* 23 Murphy proceeded with considerable caution, sometimes withdrawing from a position, sometimes forcing it, and altogether keeping his opponents guessing what he would do next.]

Guest house. Add: **3.** A house for the reception of paying guests for whom a programme of social intercourse is provided.

1925 *Daily Tel.* 13 May 19/4 For Sale, Guest House, South London.

Guevaristic (gēvări·stik), *a.* [f. Guevarist + -ic.] Characterized by Guevarism.

1883 *Encycl. Brit.* XV. 105/1 Lyly was not the first to appropriate and develop the Guevaristic style.

Guianese (giănī·z), *a.* [f. *Guiana* + -ese.] Of or pertaining to Guiana. So **Guianan** (giā·năn), **Guia·nian** *adjs.* and *sbs.*

1879 J. G. Wood *Waterton's Wand. S. Amer.* Expl. Index 478 The European and Guianan types of the human frame. *Ibid.* 479 The Guianan type of female beauty. 1896 J. Rodway *West Indies & Spanish Main* 44 These were Guianians, who had never before seen a white man. 1901 *Daily Chron.* 17 Dec. 5/2 The Guianese hinterland. 1903 *Ibid.* 28 May 5/1 The Guianese natives. 1931 *New Daily Chron.* (Georgetown B. G.) 24 July 5/6 Although Kid Jack lost the fight, yet the meeting with him must have proved a revelation to the Guianese man.

Guichet (giʃe). [Fr.] A wicket, grating, or hatch, *spec.* one through which tickets are issued.

1848 H. Greville *Diary* (1883) 280 Hundreds of prisoners have been shut up. In the Church of L'Assomption..they are fed through a guichet. 1907 *Westm. Gaz.* 22 July 3/1 The *Bigliettaio*, ducking his gold-braided cap through the guichet, triumphantly gave us a ticket. 1926 C. Barry *Detective's Holiday* 131 The post-mistress herself came to the guichet. 1927 *Brit. Weekly* 7 Apr. 12/2 Most of the time being spent waiting in queues at the various guichets.

Guicowar, variant of *Gaekwar.

Guide, *sb.* Add:

2. d. *Girl Guide*, a member of an organization of girls, established in 1908, corresponding to the Boy Scouts. Also simply *Guide*.

1916 [see *Brownie I. 2]. 1924 Anne D. Sedgwick *Little French Girl* I. v, Alix heard of a Women's Institute, of Boy Scouts and Girl Guides.

12. *guide-face, -frame, -framing, -groove.*

1900 Hasluck *Mod. Eng. Handy-bk.* 59 The *guide-faces may be got up with a file. 1901 P. Marshall *Metal Tools* 41 A rising and falling *guide-frame. 1900 *Engineering Mag.* XIX. 781/1 The *Guide-Framing of Gasholders. 1903 *Brit. & Col. Printer* 19 Nov. 12/2 The ends slide in parallel guide-grooves.

13. guide-board (earlier examples); **guide-line**, (*a*) a line used as a guide, a guiding line; (*b*) = next; **guide-rope**, (*c*) *Aeronautics*, a long rope hung from a balloon or small airship so as to trail along the ground and to preserve altitude automatically by the drag of the rope without loss of ballast or gas; also, one of a number of ropes used to steady an airship before flight; **guide-rope** *v. intr.*, to use a guide-rope; **guide-way** (earlier example); **guide-wheel**, a wheel used to guide a moving structure or vehicle.

1843 *Knickerbocker Mag.* XXII. 430 The *guide board measures out the long miles between him and his evening resting-place. 1851 Alice Cary *Clovernook* 165 A little higher than his head there is a guide-board nailed on this tree—white with black letters. 1785 A. Ellicott in *Life & Lett.* 44 My Brother Joseph at Present runs the *guide Line for the choppers. 1798 in *Deb. Congress 1807–8* (1852) 2740, I shall proceed to the Pearl river, where the guide-line will be corrected. 1802 A. Ellicott *Jrnl.* 178, I..examined the country over which the guide line passed. 1867 *All Year Round* XVIII. 452/1 In hauling in his guide-line, lest it should entangle itself with a factory chimney. 1881 [see Guide *sb.* 12]. 1931 *Times* 27 Aug. 13/6 The coast..serves as a guide-line to their destinations. 1838 Monck Mason *Aeronautica* 23 An incident connected with the use of this *guide-rope. 1848 *Chambers's Jrnl.* 6 May 301/2 Mr. Green as a substitute, uses a long rope, called the 'guide-rope'. 1897 *Strand Mag.* XIII. 227/2 One rope (the guide-rope) is securely tied to this crow-bar, and then thrown on the cliff. 1903 *Ibid.* 27 June 476/2 A Life-saving Kite. The kite carries a guide-rope. 1904 *Pall Mall Mag.* XXXII. 20 One can *guide-rope in the centre of Paris. 1925 *Spectator* 11 Mar. 371/1, I hopped over the trees of the Bois..and guide-roped down the Avenue des Champs Elysées to my door at the corner of the Rue Washington. 1876 J. S. Ingram *Centen. Expos.* ix. 270 Both the upper and lower *guide-ways were adjustable for keeping the saw in line whenever required by the settling of floors. 1885 *Marine Engineer* 1 July 91/2 The *guide-wheel supports the 'bag' of the bucket chain. 1903 *Sci. Amer. Suppl.* 18 Apr. 22214 (Cent. D. Suppl.) The boats are furnished with a hinged device at both ends and provided with guide-wheels to roll on. 1909 *Westm. Gaz.* 21 July 5/2 The pilot must be careful to hold the guide-wheel so as to maintain this position.

Guide, *v.* Add: **1.** Also *refl.*

1865 [Mrs. M. C. Harris] *Christine* iii, Moving cautiously upon the ice..he..lay down, guiding himself by his hands alone. 1888 Mrs. H. Ward *Robt. Elsmere* I. viii. 231 And refusing all help, she guided herself out of the room. 1907 *Smart Set* Mar. 128 He guided himself cautiously with his left arm stretched out against the object of quest.

d. *Physics.* = Conduct *v.* 9 c.

1902 *Encycl. Brit.* XXXIII. 214/2 The use of conductors will now be seen partly. They serve to guide a wave along from place to place without loss, and with a limited amount of energy.

2. b. *refl.* and *absol.*

1816 Scott *Old Mort.* xxxix, He..formed the resolution of guiding himself by the circumstances in which he might discover the object of his quest. 1874 J. W. Draper *Hist. Conflict Relig. & Sci.* 136 He guides himself by past as well as by present impressions.

Guide-booky (gǝi·dbuːki), *a.* [f. Guide-book + -y [1].] Resembling or characteristic of (that of) a guide-book; having the style of a guide-book.

1878 A. Mackennal in D. Macfadyen *Life & Lett.* (1905) 72 This talk is a little guide-booky. 1895 *Academy* 23 Mar. 251/3 The guide-booky lines on p. 222 of the same volume.

Guided (gǝi·dėd), *a.* [f. Guide *sb.* + -ed [2].] Accompanied by a guide, having a guide in charge.

1909 *Daily Chron.* 6 Sept. 4/6 On a guided ascent.

Guidguid (gwi·dgwid). [Probably echoic: cf. Guit-guit.] The barking-bird.

1845 [see Barking *ppl. a.*[1] 2 b].

Guigne, var. Gean. wild cherry.

1899 Lady Strachey *Mem. Highland Lady* 85 Up in the guigne trees showering down that most delicious of fruits. *Ibid.* 95 The Logie guignes could only be tasted at the foot of the trees.

Guild. Add: **guild-socialism**, an economic system by which the profits, resources, and methods of each industry are to be controlled by a council of its members, on the model of mediæval guilds; so **guild socialist**.

1913 C. Booth *Industr. Unrest* 16 The Guild Socialists in England occupy middle ground between Syndicalist and Socialist. *Ibid.* 21 Syndicalism, Guild Socialism, and State Socialism hold no terms with each other. 1919 G. D. H. Cole *Guild Socialism* (1920) 4 The desire of the Guild Socialist is..to convert the Socialist Movement as well as the Trade Union Movement to its point of view. *Ibid.* 5, I do not pretend..that Guild Socialism is the right way for all the peoples of the world to tackle their economic problems.

Guild-hall. Add: (spelt *Guildhall*), *spec.* the hall of the Corporation of the City of London, used for municipal meetings, state banquets, etc.

1598 Stow *Surv.* 217 William Hariot Draper Mayor 1481. gave 40. pound to the making of two louers in the said Guildhal. *c* 1792 *Encycl. Brit.* (1797) X. 243/1 The lord-major elect..is soon after presented to the lord-chancellor..; and on the 9th of November following is sworn into the office of mayor at Guildhall.

Guillaume (gi·lyōum). [Fr., a use of the proper name (= William).] A rabbet-plane.

1885 *Spons' Mechanics' Own Bk.* 378 The ends are.. worked to the gauge marks with an iron guillaume. *Ibid.*, The checks are worked out with fillester and guillaume planes.

Guillotine, *sb.* Add: **3. b.** Also *attrib.*, as *guillotine closure, resolution.*

1909 *Westm. Gaz.* 14 May 2/2 Let it be understood..that the guillotine closure will not be used, however prolonged the sittings may be. 1927 *Daily Express* 10 May 2/7 To introduce the guillotine or kangaroo method of closure. 1927 *Daily Tel.* 10 May 12/3 The Government will bring in a 'guillotine' resolution.

4. guillotine-shears, a form of shearing machine for cutting wrought-iron bars and slabs.

1884 W. H. Greenwood *Steel & Iron* xvi. 348 A form of powerful guillotine shears.

Guimauve (gi·mouv). [Fr.] The common marsh-mallow. Also *attrib.*

1870 Hooker *Student's Flora* 71 Marsh-mallow, Guimauve. 1895 *Army & Navy Co-op. Soc. Price List* 15 Sept. 702 Guimauve Pastilles.

Guimpe (gæ̃p, gimp). [Fr.; cf. Gimp *sb.*[2], Wimple *sb.*] A chemisette coming high up the throat; an under-blouse designed to be worn with a low-necked frock.

1889 *Cent. Dict.* 1909 *Westm. Gaz.* 15 Feb. 5/3 Some of the high corselet bodices permit of nothing more than a small guimpe with sleeves. *Ibid.* 3 June 8/3 The corsage is finished with a guimpe of white spotted net.

Guinea. **I.** Add: **1. Guinea negro** or **nigger**; also *ellipt.*

1823 J. F. Cooper *Pioneers* xxx, One of them Guineas down in the kitchen there. *a* 1856 P. Cartwright *Autobiog.* 192 (De Vere), If he don't get his soul converted God will damn him as quick as he would a Guinea Negro. 1861 Lowell *Biglow P.* Ser. II. i. 183 'Tain't quite hendy to pass off one o' your six-foot Guineas. 1896 J. G. Williams *Ole Plantation* Pref., I remember hearing the old plantation negroes before the war speak of one as a 'Gullah nigger' and another as a 'Guinea nigger'.

b. An Italian or Spanish immigrant, or one of similar appearance. *U.S. slang.*

1911 Webster. 1927 J. Barbican *Confess. Rum-runner* iv. 54 Tell that squint-eyed guinea to throw the mud-hook overboard.

Guinean (gi·niăn), *a.* and *sb.* [f. Guinea + -an.] Of or pertaining to, a native of, Guinea.

1650 Bulwer *Anthropomet.* 112 The Guineans take their meat torne in peeces with the thre midmost fingers. 1875 Newton in *Encycl. Brit.* III. 758/2 Beginning on the West Coast, where the Libyan Subregion stops, we have another Subregion, the 'Guinean', comprising the seaboard from Sierra Leone to somewhere about Angola. 1893 — *Dict. Birds* 350 This 'Guinean' Province occupies what is commonly called the 'West Coast' of Africa.

Guinness (gi·nės). [Family name.] A brand of stout manufactured by the firm of Guinness of Dublin; a bottle or glass of this. Also *Comb.*, as *Guinness-coloured* adj.

1842 Barham *Ingol. Leg.* Ser. II. *Auto-da-fé* II, With a three-corner'd Sandwich, and *soupçon* of 'Guinness's'. 1897 *Sat. Rev.* 2 Jan. 2/1 An Irishman drinking his Guinness with uncharacteristic quietude in a London 'pub'. 1922 G. Saintsbury *Scrap Bk.* 33 You can't see the stones for the Guiness-coloured foam.

Guira (gwǝi·ɹă). [Amer. Sp.; 'Brasiliensibus' (Willughby *Ornith.* 1676).] A South American cuckoo.

1883 *List Anim. Zool. Soc.* 305 Guira Cuckoo. 1904 *Westm. Gaz.* 13 May 12/1 The guira lays blue eggs covered with a network of chalky matter.

Guitar, *sb.* **b.** Add: *guitar-case*.

1848 *Knickerbocker Mag.* XVIII. 225 Mr. Thwackit.. took his guitar-case in one hand and his double barreled fowling-piece in the other.

Gujarati (gŭdgără·ti). Also **Gujarathi, Gurjrati, Guzarat(h)i, Guzerattee.** [Hind., f. *Gujarāt* (Skr. *Gurjarā*).] The language of the natives of Gujarat, Baroda, and adjoining states of India.

The alphabet is of the Nagari type.

1808 R. Drummond (*title*) Illustrations of the Grammatical Parts of the Guzerattee, Mahratta, and English Languages. 1838 *Penny Cycl.* XII. 227/2 Gurjaratti, or Guzerati, spoken in Gujerat, and along the coast as far as Bombay. 1931 *Times Lit. Suppl.* 3 Dec. 983/1 An adept in the Gujarati tongue.

Gulash, gulyas, variants of *Goulash.

Gulch, *sb.*[3] *U.S.* Add: **1.** (Earlier examples.)

1835 E. Wix *Newfoundld. Missionary's Jrnl.* (1836) 19 It might be necessary to make a circuit of fifteen miles, to get round the deep precipitous chasms or 'gulshes' and ravines. *a* 1842 O. Russel *Jrnl.* xiii. (1921) 57 The river runs along the foot of a high range of steep bluffs, intersected by deep ravines and gulches.

2. *gulch-man, -miner*; *gulch-mining* (earlier examples).

1869 A. K. McClure *Rocky Mtns.* 210 (Th.) The unfortunate politician is 'corraled' by the mountaineers, the *gulch-men, or the settlers. *Ibid.* 240 (Th.) As a rule, the most successful *gulch-miners are most improvident. 1869 S. Bowles *Our New West* ix. 186 The other form of mining, known as *gulch-mining or dirt-washing is increasing again. 1878 H. H. Jackson *Bits of Travel at Home* 278 We began to see the dreary traces of that dreariest of all things on the earth's surface, gulch mining.

Gulch, *v.*[3] Add: **3.** *pass.* Of an animal: To have fallen into a gulch.

1906 *Harper's Mag.* Oct. 760 An accident had occurred by the sheep being gulched.

Gul-gul (gʋ·lgʋl). [Hind. *galgal.*] A kind of cement made of oil and pounded sea-shells used to preserve a ship's bottom from worms.

1867 Smyth *Sailor's Word-Bk.*

Gullah (gʋ·lă). *U.S.* Also **Goolah.** [Conjectured to be either a shortening of *Angola*, or from a Liberian group of tribes known as Golas.] Used *attrib.* or *absol.* to designate negroes living on the sea-islands and tide-water coastline of South Carolina and Georgia, and the dialect spoken by them.

1822 in Reed Smith *Gullah* (1926) 7 [In an entry of the Charleston City Council, under the year 1822,..reference is made to] 'Gullah Jack' [and his company of] 'Gullah or Angola Negroes'. 1835 W. G. Simms *Partisan* 224 To their arts the Gullah and the Ebo negroes..added their spells and magic in no stinted quantities. 1838 *Southern Lit. Messenger* IV. 641/1 The etymology of all which terms..is quite as untraceable as that of any terms in the Goolah negro dialect. 1896 J. G. Williams *Ole Plantation* Pref. p. v, The older ones of that set of negroes..speak as pure Gullah as their grandfathers...They seem to have been scarcely affected in their low-country Gullah speech [etc.]. 1908 J. Bennet in *S. Atlantic Quarterly* Oct. 339 The vocabulary of our Gullah patois is..five times as great. *Ibid.*, To some Gullah remains a closed book.

Gully, *sb.*[1] **2.** (Earlier U.S. examples.)

1637 *Rhode Isl. Col. Rec.* I. 28 To run uppon a streight line from a fresh spring being in the Gulley. 1648 *Rec. Providence, R. I.* XV. 21 The South-east corner is bounded with a gully and a white Oake tree.

c. *Cricket.* (See quot. 1921.)

1920 G. L. Jessop in P. F. Warner *Cricket* (Badm. Libr.) 165 The position which has been favoured in recent years by fast bowlers, whenever signs of the wicket bumping have been apparent, namely, 'the gully'. 1921 Warner *My Cricketing Life* xii. 229 He [*sc.* A. O. Jones] was, indeed, quite exceptional as a fieldsman in any position, but especially in the slips and at short third man, or in the 'gully', as it is called nowadays. 1927 *Observer* 19 June 25/1 Macaulay fell to a dazzling left-hand catch high up in the gully by Kidd.

Gulose (giū·lous). *Chem.* [f. first syllable of Glucose by transposition + -ose.] An artificial sugar, $C_6H_{12}O_6$, closely related to glucose, produced by the reduction of gulonic acid, and existing in three forms. So **Gulonic** (giulǫ·nik), *a.* [after *Gulose + *-onic*], designating a colourless acid existing in three isomeric forms.

1891 *Jrnl. Chem. Soc.* LX. I. 667, *l*-Gulose is obtained by reducing a well-cooled solution (10 per cent.) of the lactone in the usual way with sodium amalgam. *Ibid.* 668 Gluconic and gulonic acids have the same structure and similar configuration. 1902 *Encycl. Brit.* XXVI. 723/2 Experiment has shown that the hexaldose obtained from ordinary saccharic acid is not glucose, but an isomeride now known as gulose.

Gulp, *v.* Add: **4.** *trans.* To cause or compel (one) to gulp.

1861 *Trans. Ill. Agric. Soc.* IV. 377 It is bad enough for a sick man..to be thus gulped.

Gum, *sb.*[1] **5.** Add: **gum-ring**, a child's teething-ring.

1856 Cozzens *Sparrowgr. Papers* x. 138 It..sat up rigidly in its mother's lap, twirling its thumbs and cutting its teeth without a gum-ring.

Gum, *sb.*[2] Add: **1. f.** ellipt. for Kauri *gum.*

1887 *Col. & Indian Exhib., Rep. Col. Sect.* 287 The ordinary gum of commerce is the semi-fossilised turpentine of the

[Kauri pine] tree. 1893 *Murray's Handbk. N.Z.* (Morris, s.v. *Kauri-gum*) If they find small pieces of gum sticking to the end of the spear. 1906 *Macm. Mag.* Apr. 478 Not having caught on to the feel of the gum.

g. The viscid or waxy substance which surrounds the filaments of silk in its natural state.

1825 J. Nicholson *Oper. Mech.* 399 The silk being now spun, is put into a boiler filled with hot water, into which is put a small quantity of soap, in order to divest the silk of its gum. 1835 Ure *Philos. Manuf.* vi. 248 Marabout..Being white as it comes from the worm, it takes the purest and most delicate shades of colour at once, without the discharge of its gum. 1887 *Encycl. Brit.* XXII. 61/2 The natural gum of the cocoons which holds the filaments together. *Ibid.* 64/2 It has long been the practice to dye some dark silks 'in the gum'.

h. A mixture, of which gelatine is a main ingredient, from which a hard sweetmeat is made in a mould; a sweetmeat made of this.

1921 *Dict. Occup. Terms* (1927) § 434 *Starch hand* (male), ..*gum boiler*; weighs on scales, or, measures by means of measuring glass, ingredients for gums, mainly gelatine and butter;..pours the mixture, known as 'gum' or 'boil', when boiled, into trays or moulds.

i. The substance whose presence causes a ropy condition in wine.

1888 *Encycl. Brit.* XXIV. 603/2 It sometimes happens that wine becomes viscous and forms threads when poured from the bottle. This mischief, which is caused by the development of a foreign ferment, can be cured by the judicious addition of a solution of tannin, which precipitates the 'gum'.

3. a. *Chagual gum* (see quot.); *Sonora gum*, resin obtained from the creosote-bush; **gum-dammar** (see Dammar); **gum-kino** (see Kino¹ 1).

1830 gum kino [see Kino¹ 1]. 1851 *Illustr. Catal. Gt. Exhib.* iv. 1. 997 Gum kino, from the blue gum-tree, the stringy bark, and other *Eucalypti*. 1868 Watts *Dict. Chem.*, *Sonora Gum*, a kind of lac produced by the puncture of a coccus in *Mimosa cerifera*, a tree growing in Mexico. 1869 A. R. Wallace *Malay Archip.* II. 8 Tortoise-shell, rattan gum-dammer, and other valuable products. 1880 *Encycl. Brit.* XI. 275/2 Chagual gum, a new variety brought from St. Iago de Chili, resembles gum senegal.

5. With various other defining epithets. (For *red, rough, rusty, sugar, swamp, water, white gum*, see the first word.)

1833 C. Sturt *Southern Australia* II. viii. 236 Eucalypti were the general timber on the ranges; one species..resembling strongly the black-butted gum, was remarkable for a scent peculiar to its bark. 1846 J. L. Stokes *Discov. Australia* II. iv. 132 York gum...Abundant in York—on good soil. *Ibid.* xii. 387 The trees, which grew only in the valleys, were small kinds of banksia, wattles, and drooping gums. 1847 Leichhardt *Jrnl.* 6 The prevailing timber trees are Bastard box,..and the Flooded Gum. *Ibid.* 283 On the small flats, the apple-gum grew. 1848 T. L. Mitchell *Trop. Australia* 107 A small group of trees of the yellow gum, a species of eucalyptus growing only on the poor sandy soil near Botany Bay. 1887 *Col. & Indian Exhib., Rep. Col. Sect.* 420 Other noble trees, as the Blue, White, Red, Swamp, Water-rooted and Manna-drooping Gums. 1889 Cider Gum [see Sugar *sb.* 5]. 1930 Billis & Kenyon *Pastures New* viii. 123 The trees were very pretty, being a kind of weeping gum.

8. a. *gum-log* (earlier example), *-top*; *gum-topped* adj.

1836 Crockett *Exploits & Adv. Texas* 82 (Th.) A chap just about as rough hewn as if he had been cut out of a gum log with a broad axe. 1874 *Treas. Bot.* Suppl., Gum-top, *Eucalyptus virgata*. 1887 *Col. & Indian Exhib., Rep. Col. Sect.* 428 The Box trees of the *Eucalyptus* class are the Poplar, Gum-topped, and Stanthorpe.

9. gum-bichromate *Photog.*, designating a process of printing on paper coated with a mixture of pigment, gum-arabic, and potassium bichromate; also designating a print so produced; **gum-boiler**, one who boils certain sweetmeat mixtures; **gum-chewing**, the action of chewing chewing-gum; also *attrib.*; **gum-dextrine** (see quot.); **gum-gallic** *Photog.*, designating a dry-plate collodion process; **gum game** *U.S. slang*, a trick or dodge; **gum-platinum** *Photog.* (see quots.); **gum-shakes** (see Shake *sb.*¹ 9); **gum-shoe**, also *attrib.* and *fig.*; **gum-shoe** *v. intr.* (*colloq. U.S.*), to move or act with stealth as if wearing gum-shoes; **gum silk**, silk from which the natural gum has not been removed; **gum-spear**, a spear used in probing soil for kauri gum; **gum-worker** *Photog.*, one who makes prints by any of the processes, such as the gum-bichromate process, in which gum-arabic is used.

1897 Wall *Dict. Photogr.* (ed. 7) 117 The *Gum-bichromate or Photo-aquatint Process. 1900 *Daily News* 1 Oct. 7/4 A striking profile done in red by the gum-bichromate process. 1919 *Brit. Jrnl. Photogr. Alm.* 252 In the gum-bichromate process, also termed aquatint or photo-aquatint. 1921 *gum boiler [see *1 h]. 1907 *Daily Chron.* 29 July 5/2 The *gum-chewing habit. 1919 *Brit. Jrnl. Photogr. Alm.* 366 *Gum-dextrine mountant. 1878 Abney *Treat. Photogr.* 106 The *gum-gallic process, as introduced by Mr. R. Manners Gordon. 1859 Bartlett *Dict. Amer.* (ed. 2) s.v., This is called 'coming the *gum-game' over the hunter. 1869 *Kansas City Advertiser* 7 May (De Vere) 'You can't come that gum-game over me any more,' says a Kansas man to a squatter. 1872 Eggleston *Hoosier Schoolm.* xiv. 118 Now, looky here...You don't come no gum games over me. 1918 *Photo-Miniature* XV. Mar. (Gloss.), *Gum-Platinum Process—of first making a light print on platinum paper, then coating the print with sensitive gum mixture and reprinting from the same negative. 1919 *Brit. Jrnl. Photogr. Alm.* 252 *Gum-platinum* is a compound process, in which a pale print on platinum paper is coated with the sensitive gum mixture, and a second (pigment) image produced by re-printing under the same negative. 1887 *Col. & Indian Exhib., Rep. Col. Sect.* 427 These are all large trees...—some are a little liable to *gum-shakes. 1907 *Springfield* (Mass.) *Weekly Republ.* 4 Apr. 2 He..was forced to accomplish his ends by main strength rather than by *gum-shoe methods. 1925 J. Gregory *Bab of Backwoods* xxvi, I'm the scout, the gumshoe man. 1927 *Daily Express* 7 Nov. 9/2 The film..has obtained a gum-shoe circulation in Britain. 1930 Winkler *J. Pierpont Morgan* 264 That eminent political gum-shoe artist. 1930 *Publishers' Weekly* 8 Feb. 718 Under the present obscene book law the vice crusader..goes *gum-shoeing around from one bookseller to another. 1885 T. Wardle in *Encycl. Brit.* (1887) XXII. 64/1 Sugar is known to have been used for adulterating and loading *gum silk for a very long time. 1906 *Macm. Mag.* Apr. 478 A green hand of a gummy, that hadn't quite got the trick of it yet, went poking around that very cabbage-tree with his *gum-spear. 1908 *Westm. Gaz.* 3 Oct. 14/2 Some photographers now classify themselves as *gum-workers, oil-workers, and so forth.

Gum, *v.*¹ **6.** *U.S.* (Earlier example.)

1844 *Yale Lit. Mag.* XIV. 189 (Th.) He was speaking of the 'moon hoax', which gummed so many learned philosophers.

Gum, *v.*² *U.S.* (Earlier example.)

1851 C. Cist *Cincinnati* 237 Circular..saws gummed and hammered..restored as good as new.

Gümbelite (gü·mbələit). *Min.* [Named after C. W. *Gümbell* who analysed it: see -ite¹.] A greenish-white silicate of aluminium, iron, and potassium.

1871 *Jrnl. Chem. Soc.* XXIV. 325.

Gumbo. *U.S.* **1. b.** (Earlier examples.)

1805 J. F. Watson in *American Pioneer* (1843) II. 233 Shrimps are much eaten here; also a dish called *gumbo*. This last is made of every eatable substance, and especially of those shrimps which can be caught at any time. 1810 F. Cuming *Sk. Tour* liii. (1904) 339 Gumbo..is made by boiling ocroe until it is tender, and seasoning it with a little bit of fat bacon. 1833 J. Hall *Leg. West* 130 (Th.) [She] resolutely refused, through life to eat gumbo-soup. 1846 Corcoran *Pickings* 58 The judge said he had no doubt but there was great culinary economy in buying a demi-decomposed turkey and converting it into gombo.

3. (Earlier example.)

1880 Cable *Grandissimes* xxviii. 227 Bras-Coupé..mastered the 'gumbo' dialect in a few weeks.

Gumbo box. *U.S.* = Gumby.

1861 [H. Jacobs] *Life Slave Girl* 180 A box, covered with sheepskin, is called the gumbo box.

Gumbo-limbo (gʊ·mbo li·mbo). [? Negro.] Either of two gum-yielding trees, *Simarouba glauca* of Florida, or *Bursera gummifera* of the West Indies.

1837 J. L. Williams *Terr. of Florida* 98 Gum Elemi.—Called by the inhabitants, Gumbo-limbo, is a large spreading tree, with a smooth brown bark. 1890 H. M. Field *Bright Skies* v. 70 Perhaps some old savage..has been punished for his cruelty by being turned into that gumbo-limbo tree. 1924 J. A. Thomson *Science Old & New* v. 27 The gumbolimbo, which exudes fragrant balsam when it is wounded.

Gumbotil (gʊ·mbotil). *Geol.* [Named by G. F. Kay of the Iowa Geological Survey; f. Gumbo 2 a + Till *sb.*²] A very sticky grey to dark-coloured clay.

1931 *Nature* 3 Jan. 7 Gumbotils and the Pleistocene Succession.

Gumlah (gʊ·mla). *India.* Also **gomla(h.** [Hind. *gamlā*.] A water-jar.

1834 H. Caunter *Oriental Ann.* ix. 114, I had seen her as she occasionally repaired to the river to replenish her gumlahs. 1837 T. Bacon *1st Impress. Hindustan* II. xii. 415, I caught sight of the large *gumla* (earthern jar, containing about eighteen gallons) filled with water. 1888 J. Inglis *Tent Life* 285 Encasing his head in a great wide-mouthed *gumla*, or earthen pot.

Gummer² (gʊ·məɹ). [f. Gum *v.*¹ + -er¹.] One who gums (in various technical uses).

1881 *Instr. Census Clerks* (1885) 82 Envelope Maker:..Gummer, Cementer. 1902 *Daily Chron.* 24 July 9/4 Pattern-Card Mounters, Cutters and Gummers wanted. 1905 *Ibid.* 11 Aug. 10/6 Envelope Hand Gummers, also fountain gummers. 1921 *Dict. Occup. Terms* (1927) § 549 *Gummer* (bookbinder's); applies gum to back of books,..also gums edge of illustration pages, etc. for insertion in books.

Gumming, *vbl. sb.* Add:

3. The action of becoming gummy; the thickening of oils by exposure to the atmosphere. **b.** The action of becoming clogged by some gummy substance; also *gumming-up*.

1904 *Technol. & Sci. Dict.* (ed. Goodchild & Tweney), *Gumming of Oils*, a condition of 'drying' oils (such as linseed oil) which have been exposed to the air and have become thick or gummy by absorption of oxygen. 1927 *Daily Express* 15 July 9 The total absence of 'gumming-up' of piston rings.

Gummose (gʊ·mous), *sb. Chem.* [f. L. *gummi* Gum *sb.*² + -ose.] An unfermentable reducing sugar formed by the hydrolysis of mucin.

1903 Dorland *Med. Dict.* (ed. 3).

Gummosis (gʊmōu·sis). *Bot.* [mod.L., f. L. *gummi* Gum *sb.*² 7 + -osis.] The formation of gum in plants by the transformation of tissue; Gumming *vbl. sb.* 2.

1891 *Chambers's Encycl.* VIII. 223 Gummosis, which is similar to canker, is caused by *Gleospora gummifera*. 1908 W. R. Fisher tr. *Gayer's Forstbenutzung* (ed. 2) 155.

Gummy (gʊ·mi), *sb. Austral. colloq.* [f. *Gum *sb.*² 1 f + -y⁶.] A gum-digger.

1906 *Macm. Mag.* Apr. 476 We soon were giving those gummies a hand to get some tucker ready. *Ibid.* 478.

Gum-tree. 2. (Earlier example.)

1832 Peck *Guide Emigr.* II. 156 The very woods and bills shake with the negro song of ''possum up a gum-tree'.

Gun, *sb.* Add:

1. d. Any of various devices for discharging missiles through a tube, as by the expansive force of compressed air; usually with defining word, as *air gun, blow gun, grease gun, pop-gun* (1), *spring-gun* (2) (which see).

3. b. A revolver. *U.S.*

1889 Farmer *Americanisms* 281/2. 1890 *Harper's Mag.* Dec. 160/2 That six-shooter you gave Pete was such a pretty gun I couldn't resist when Pete offered to swap. 1900 *Congress. Record* 17 Dec. 735/2 The order was given to 'Keep your guns in your pockets'. 1902 C. Hyne *Mr. Horrocks Purser* 56 Then he made a great fuss and pulled out a gun. 1913 Mulford *Coming of Cassidy* iii. 62 The man from the Bar-20 used two guns. *Ibid.*, Mr. Cassidy slipped his empty guns in their holsters.

c. *Gun down*: in trap-shooting, with the butt of the gun held below the shooter's elbow.

1903 *Forest & Stream* 24 Jan. 79 (Cent. D. Suppl.) Shooting to begin at 2 P.M. sharp. First cup, 25 birds, handicap, 'gun down'.

5. c. *pl.* = gunnery-lieutenant. *Navy slang.*

1925 E. Fraser & Gibbons *Soldier & Sailor Words*, *Gunnery Jack* (also *Guns*), the Gunnery Lieutenant on board ship.

14. a. *gun-battery, -butt, -cupboard, -detachment, factory* (earlier U.S. examples), *-position, -rack* (later U.S. examples), *-ship* (earlier U.S. example), *-shop, -team, -trial.*

1816 H. Clarke *Hist. War* I. 319/2 The mortar and *gun-batteries of the enemy. 1918 E. S. Farrow *Dict. Mil. Terms*, *Gun Battery*, a defense constructed of earth faced with green sods or fascines, sometimes of gabions filled with earth. 1891 Kipling *Light that Failed* ii, To drag down the slayer till he could be knocked on the head by some avenging *gun-butt. 1896 — *Seven Seas* 64 The snap of a closing lock and the jar of a gun-butt slid. 1892 Greener *Breech-Loader* 180 If..a dust-proof *gun-cupboard, it will last longer. 1860 *Man. Artill. Exerc.* II. 22 The medium 12-pounder requires two *gun detachments. 1918 E. S. Farrow *Dict. Mil. Terms* s.v., The cannoneers assigned to the service of a single gun, formed in double rank, constitute a gun detachment. 1780 in *Cal. Virginia St. Papers* I. 372, The warrant for Six thousand pounds on account of the *Gun Factory. 1812 *Niles' Register* III. 60/2 Messrs. Coggswell and Hosford are erecting a gun factory in Albany. 1902 'Linesman' *Words Eyewitness* (1902) 73 From the *gun-position one could look down upon line upon line of trenches. 1838 J. McDonald *Biogr. Sk. N. Massie* etc. 38 His *gun-rack was examined, and there bung his rifle and his pouch in their usual place. 1885 'C. E. Craddock' *Prophet Gt. Smoky Mtn.* i. 21 There were rude gun-racks on the walls. 1841 Lydia M. Child *Lett. New York* viii. 59 You probably recollect that he built a large *gun-ship for the Turkish Sultan. 1878 J. H. Beadle *Western Wilds* xii. 185 They slept together in that little den back of Joe's *gun-shop 1880 Cable *Grandissimes* xxxix. 308 There was a gathering of boys and vagabonds at the door of a gun-shop. 1908 *Westm. Gaz.* 30 Oct. 3/2 Horses..capable of drawing weight at the pace required in a *gun-team. 1898 *Engineering Mag.* XVI. 112/1 Krupp's *gun-trial grounds.

b. *gun-pulling, -toter, -toting.*

a 1909 'O. Henry' *Roads of Destiny* xvi. 271 The bystanders asserted that it was met by the most beautiful exhibition of lightning *gun-pulling ever witnessed in the Southwest. 1929 *Chicago Tribune* 22 Jan. 1/4 She had been 'held up by regular *gun toters in Chicago' and was not 'afraid of amateurs'. 1906 J. Black *You Can't Win* xiii. 185 But the bullying, *gun-toting, would-be bad men and killers never flourished in Butte.

15. gun-barrel (earlier U.S. example); also *attrib.*, pertaining to or resembling a gun-barrel; **gun-bright** (see quot.); **gun captain**, the captain of the crew of a ship's gun; **gun-case** (earlier U.S. example); **gun-dog**, a dog trained to accompany the 'guns'; **gun-fight** *U.S. colloq.*, a fight with revolvers, a shooting affray; **gun-fighter**, one accustomed to use a revolver; **gun-fire**, *spec.* rapid firing in which each gun acts independently and fires as rapidly as it can be served; also *colloq.*, an early morning cup of tea served out to troops before going on first parade; **gun-fodder** = **cannon-fodder*; **gun-lance**, see Lance *sb.*¹ 2; **gun-layer**, one who aims or lays a gun; **gun-lever** (see quot.); **gun-pit**, (*b*) in a fighting aeroplane, the compartment for a gun and gunner; **gun-plane**, a fighting aeroplane armed with a gun or guns; **gun-pointer** = *gun-layer*; **gun-portion** (see quot.); **gun-power**, number and strength of guns available in any given place or circumstances; **gun-range**, (*a*) the range of a gun's fire; (*b*) a place where gun-firing is practised; **gun-reach** = *gun-range* (*a*); **gun-rest**, also, a wall-fixture for portable fire-arms, a gun-rack; **gun-sighting**, the action of elevating and directing a gun in taking aim; also *attrib.*; **gun-sling**, also, a sling for carrying a portable fire-arm; **gun-tow** = Gun-cotton; **gun-wad** (see quot.); **gun-well**, in a submarine, the sunk compartment for a gun; **gun-worker**, one who works in a gun-foundry.

1747 Franklin *Electr. Exper.* 12 Fix a needle to the end of a suspended *gun-barrel. 1864 S. Hibberd *Rose Bk.* 245 Gun-Barrel Budding. *Ibid.* 246 Bud it there at once just under one of the leaf-rings, 'gun-barrel' fashion. 1904 *Westm. Gaz.* 19 Jan. 10/1 The recent gun-barrel fight in Birmingham. 1918 E. S. Farrow *Dict. Mil. Terms*, *Gun-bright, Dutch rush (*equisetum hyemale*) much used in scouring gun barrels. 1901 *Westm. Gaz.* 27 June 8/1 The *gun captain and layer. 1840 *Knickerbocker Mag.* XVI. 212 The cavalcade with its baggage-ponies, loaded with..*gun-cases, and hampers of provisions. 1907 Teasdale-Buckell *Complete Shot* 150 The *Gun-dog League's Field Trials. 1907 S. E. White *Arizona Nights* II. ii. 252 I'll go yore little old *gunfight to a finish. 1910 Jer. Hart *Vigilante Girl* xxvii. 374 This man Hawke is a *gun-fighter, and as cool and courageous as Tower can be. 1920 Hunter *Trail Drivers of Texas* 217 We found as tough a bunch of outlaws, gun-fighters,..as ever infected a country. 1916 Boyd Cable *Action Front* 210 The gunners..will tell you how they stretched themselves to the call for '*gun-fire'. 1919 *War Slang* in *Athenæum* 18 July 632/2 'Gun fire' for early morning tea. 1925 E. Fraser & Gibbons *Soldier & Sailor Words* s.v., In the War recruits in training always had 'Gun Fire' supplied to them, the work before breakfast being found particularly trying. 1900 *Westm. Gaz.* 9 July 2/1 Exceedingly useful in the capacity of *gun-fodder and stop-gap. 1883 *Fisheries Exhib. Catal.* 199 The old-fashioned, non-explosive *gun-lance. 1906 *Daily Chron.* 13 Aug. 5/7 While carrying out *gunlayers' tests with the six-inch guns. 1928 C. F. S. Gamble *North Sea Air Station* xxii. 404 The gunlayer..got burnt about the hands. 1918 E. S. Farrow *Dict. Mil. Terms*, *Gun-levers, in ordnance, two steel arms on a disappearing carriage which support the gun at one end and the counterweights at the other end. The gun-levers are pivoted near their middle upon a gun-lever axle which rests in bronze bushed axle beds in the top carriage. 1928 C. F. S. Gamble *North Sea Air Station* xii, The German officer..standing in the after *gun-pit. 1915 *Times* 4 Oct. 8/4 Our *gunplanes carried out during the night a bombardment of the German lines. 1904 *Collier's* 16 July 15 As the breech-blocks close with a snap the *gun-pointer bends over his sights. 1818 Farrow *Dict. Mil. Terms*, *Gun-portion,..half of the merlon on each side of the gun, that is to say, 9 feet on one side of the embrasure and 9 feet on the other. 1890 G. S. Clarke *Fortif.* xiii. 176 The actual *gun power of the broadside iron-clads. 1928 *Daily Tel.* 11 Sept. 12/4 A division to-day lacks the tank-power and the gun-power necessary for it to strike as a whole. 1852 tr. *Görgei's My Life in Hung.* I. 398 At the distance of three or four *gun-ranges from the Monostor. *Ibid.* 401 Gun-range distance. 1856 gun-range [see Gun *sb.* 14]. 1904 *Daily Chron.* 21 Nov. 5/2 The gun-range at Brassact, near Antwerp. 1825 Waterton *Wand. S. Amer.* 118 Almost out of *gun reach. 1918 W. Beebe *Jungle Peace* xi, Within gun-reach in front of me. 1925 A. S. M. Hutchinson *One Increasing Purpose* III. xv, Pike-rests...Not *gun-rests; they are too far apart for that. 1905 *Daily Chron.* 5 Apr. 8/5 *Gun-sighting platforms. 1812 *Niles' Weekly Register* II. 131/1 The purveyor of public supplies advertises for..25000 *gun slings. 1849 *Rep. U. S. Comm. Patents* (1850) 506 *Gun-tow or cotton ..seems more promising than gunpowder. 1918 E. S. Farrow *Dict. Mil. Terms*, *Gun-wad, a wad for a gun.. used..to keep the ammunition in place either in a gun-barrel or in a paper or metal shell. 1915 *Illustr. London News* CXLVI. 234/1 The deck of a German submarine with the hatch of the *gun-well open. 1905 *Spectator* 4 Mar. 311/2 A meeting of *gun-workers..held at Birmingham on Monday.

Gun, *v.* Add: **1. c.** *Stock Exchange.* (See quot.)

1870 Medbery *Men & Myst. Wall St.* 136 Gunning a stock, is to use every art to produce a 'break', when it is known that a certain house is heavily supplied, and would be unable to resist an attack.

d. To shoot (a person). *U.S. colloq.*

1898 H. S. Canfield *Maid of Frontier* 83 I'll gun you if you do that again. 1916 H. L. Wilson *Somewhere in Red Gap* i. 35 Wilfred went pasty, indeed, thinking his host was going to gun him. 1923 L. J. Vance *Baroque* xxvii. 178 If you don't want to have your Fiancy gunned up without notice by some wild-eyed wop.

e. (See quot.) *U.S.*

1905 *Terms Forestry & Logging* 39 *Gun*, to aim a tree in felling it. In the case of very large, brittle trees, such as redwood, a sighting device (gunning stick) is used.

2. Freq. *fig.*, to go after or in search of.

1893 W. K. Post *Harvard Stories* 188 That bull Mick Shreedy is gunning for me just at present. 1903 *New York Times* 29 Sept. 1 Others talked of mysterious influences that had been 'gunning' for financiers of prominence. 1922 *Daily Mail* 5 Dec. 9 Observing that the Company's statement is not a denial of the assertion that it is 'gunning' for the Mesopotamian oilfields claimed by the heirs of Abdul Hamid. 1923 L. J. Vance *Baroque* vii. 39 The rest's just knowin' how to wait and somethin' about the kind of game you're gunnin' for.

Guna, *sb.* Add:

2. In the Sankhya philosophy of India, any one of the three dominating principles of nature.

1862 V. Bhikshu *Sankhya-Sára* 6 S'ankara's own definition is in these words: 'The reflecting, that the *gunas*,—goodness, passion, and darkness,—are objects of my perception, [etc.]'. 1875 M. Monier-Williams *Indian Wisdom* 67 *note*, The dominance of one or other of the three Gunas, goodness, passion, or darkness.

Gu·n-house. [Gun *sb.* 1 and 3.] **a.** A house in which fire-arms are kept. **b.** (See Gun *sb.* 15.)

1736 *Boston Town Rec.* XII. 142 The Town would give direction for removing the said Bull-House, and..Joyn the same to the Gun-House in the Common. 1776 *Essex Inst. Hist. Coll.* XLII. 205 We took our Departure from the Gun House in the Training field. 1825 J. Neal *Bro. Jonathan* III. 54 The large doors of a gun-house flew open, with a loud noise.

Gun-lock. (Earlier U.S. examples.)

1651 *Connecticut Public Rec.* I. 217 Hee sould away his tooles, and thereby made himselfe vncapeable of repairing any gun locks. 1672 in *Coll. S. Carolina Hist. Soc.* V. 409 Order⁴ that Capt. Rich⁴ Conant doe seize the Indian..with his gun & all the powder & gun locks wch shall be found in his custody.

Gun-man. 1. Add: Also, a lawless person given to the use of fire-arms. *U.S. colloq.*

1903 *New York Sun* 23 Nov. 1 A notorious outlaw and one of the most expert gun men of the West. 1913 *Industrial Worker* (Spokane, Wash.) 3 July, Last evening one of the gunmen of the A.C.M. Co. came to the jail and tried to get a blacksmith out of here. 1913 'B. M. Bower' *Parowan Bonanza* xxi. 251, I never thought I'd ever have to call in a gun-man to camp on your shadow. 1927 *Observer* 17 Apr. 9/2 A Sinn Fein gunman.

Gun-metal. Add:

2. A fashion colour resembling that of gun-metal, a dull bluish-grey.

1905 *Daily Chron.* 12 July 6/7 Gun-metal coloured taffeta. 1909 *Public Ledger* (Philadelphia) 24 June 5/4 Gun-metal calf. 1923 *Daily Mail* 8 Oct. 1/2 In Gun Metal, Shoe Grey and Black. 1931 *Daily Tel.* 21 May 6/3 A train of gun-metal chiffon.

Gunnarite (gʊ·nărəit). *Min.* [f. the proper name *Gunnar* + -ite¹.] A nickel-iron sulphide occurring with pyrrhotite in Sweden.

1899 E. S. Dana *Dana's Syst. Min.* (ed. 6) App. 31. 1900 *Min. Mag.* Nov. 384 Gunnarite...Probably identical with pentlandite.

Gunner. Add:

1. c. *Master gunner* (read): the chief gunner in charge of ordnance and ammunition, formerly *spec.* an officer under the crown, the name still being retained as an honorary title conferred on distinguished soldiers; also, in modern use, a warrant officer in the Royal Artillery who has charge of the stores and equipment in a fort or other armed place.

1647 Haward *Charges Crown Rev.* 21 Master Gunner of England: Fee, *per diem* 2 s. 6d. 1802 C. James *Mil. Dict.*, *Master gunner*, in a ship of war, an officer appointed to take charge of the artillery and ammunition aboard, and to teach the men the exercise of the great guns. 1876 Voyle & Stevenson *Mil. Dict.* 1880 Tennyson *Revenge* xi, Sink me the ship, Master Gunner. 1904 *Standard* 20 Dec. 5/3 Field Marshal Earl Roberts, V.C., K.G., has been appointed Master Gunner of St. James's Park. 1918 E. S. Farrow *Dict. Mil. Terms*, *Master Gunner*.—..In the United States, an enlisted specialist of the non-commissioned staff Coast Artillery Corps, who is assigned to duty as assistant to the Artillery Engineer in connection with the preparation of charts, maps, drawings, range tables, etc., in a coast defense command.

5. b. One who is a member of the Royal Artillery. *Horse gunner* (read): a member of the Royal Horse Artillery.

1896, 1897 [see Dict.]. 1931 *Geog. Jrnl.* LXXVIII. 121 Two other officers, one a Sapper and one a Gunner—I believe I ought to say one of the Royal Engineers, one of the Royal Artillery.

Gunnera (gʊ·nərā, gʊnī·°rā). *Bot.* [mod.L., f. the name of J. E. *Gunner* (1718–73), Norwegian bishop and botanist + -a 2.] A plant of the genus so called, esp. one of the species *G. manicata*, cultivated for its ornamental foliage; prickly rhubarb.

1829 Loudon *Encycl. Plants* 26. 1930 *Times Lit. Suppl.* 18 Dec. 1079/2 We find bilberry, ling and woody nightshade included, but not guelder-rose nor gunnera.

Gunnery. 6. Add: **gunnery jack** *Navy slang*, a gunnery lieutenant.

1904 Kipling *Traffics & Discov.* 53 The Gunner mops up a heathenish large detail for some hanky-panky in the magazines, an' led 'em off along with our Gunnery Jack. 1908 *Daily Chron.* 5 Oct. 4/6 A smarter man than Gunnery Jack is not to be found in the services.

Gunning, *vbl. sb.* **3.** Delete †*Obs.* and add:

1917 H. Macfall *Germany at Bay* (1918) 210 The enormous gunning and munitionment of the Germans made trench warfare a costly affair for such as had it not.

4. gunning-stick, a device used by lumbermen in guiding the falling of a tree.

1905 [see *Gun *v.* 1 e].

Gunnung (gʊ·nʊŋ). *Austral.* [Native name.] An Australian gum-tree, *Eucalyptus robusta*.

Gunny. b. *gunny-sack* (earlier examples).

1870 Keim *Sheridan's Troopers* xxvii. (1885) 233 She was perched high in the air, astride a pyramid of rations in a gunny sack. 1873 J. H. Beadle *Undevel. West* v. 106 We slept upon the ground with a thickness of gunnysacks under us.

Gu·n-play. *U.S.* [*Gun *sb.* 3 b.] The use of fire-arms; a shooting affray; skill in shooting.

1897 *Indianapolis Typogr. Jrnl.* Jan., The talk of 'gun-plays' at the Federation Convention..is without a germ of truth. 1899 G. Ade *Doc. Horne* vi. 57 So you made good with the gun-play did you. 1904 *New York Evening Post* 7 Nov. 1 The feud has been the cause of several assaults and gunplays in Chinatown. 1913 Mulford *Coming of Cassidy* ii. 30 I've heard so much about Bradley's gun-play that I'm some curious. 1928 *Sunday Dispatch* 22 July 9/3 Other charges of gunplay were made against the officer.

Gunpowder. 4. Add:

gunpowder weed *S. Afr.*, a name for *Silene gallica*, a plant having small, black seeds.

1859–60 W. H. Harvey & Sonder *Flora Capensis* I. 127 (Pettman) *Silene gallica*...This is the Gunpowder-weed of the colonists; its black seeds resembling powder. 1897 H. Edmonds & Marloth *Elem. Bot. S. Afr.* 139.

Gun-stock. Add: **gun-stock deformity**, 'displacement of the forearm following fracture of the humerus' (Cent. D. Suppl. 1909).

Gun-stocker. (Early U.S. example.)

1781 in *Cal. Virginia St. Papers* I. 569 [A] compleat Gun-stocker [has been engaged].

Gunter. Add:

3. *Comb.*, as **gunter iron**, 'one of the bands attached to the topmast which slides upon the lower mast in the gunter rig' (Webster 1911).

Gunyang (gʊ·nyæŋ). *Bot.* [Native name.] The Australian plant *Solanum vescum*; also, the edible fruit of this plant.

1874 *Treas. Bot.* Suppl., Gunyang, *Solanum vescum*, known by this name in Victoria, where the native tribes collect its fruits eagerly as an article of food. 1888 D. Macdonald *Gum Boughs* 222 A dwarfed ti-tree, clinging low about the ground, like the gunyang or kangaroo apple.

Gunyio, variant of Gunyah.

1848 H. W. Haygarth *Bush Life* x. 105 Comfortably sleeping in an adjacent 'gunyio', or camp. *Ibid.* xii. 132 Perhaps the most primitive boat in the world: like the 'gunyio's', or huts, of the aborigines, it is built in a few minutes.

Gup, *sb.* Add: Also in general *slang* or *colloq.* use with the sense: Silly talk, blather.

1883 Mrs. Croker *Pretty Miss Neville* xvi. II. 23 Passing friends..related the local 'gup'. 1924 Galsworthy *White Monkey* II. i, The usual 'gup' over the dividend. 1927 *Punch* 30 Mar. 340/3 Need I give the jury any more of this gup?

Gupta-vidya (gu·ptă vi·dyă). *Theosophy.* [Skr. *gupta* hidden + *vidyā* knowledge, science, learning.] Hidden or secret knowledge.

1888 H. P. Blavatsky *Secr. Doctr.* (ed. 2) I. p. xxxviii.

Gural, variant of Goral.

1919 *Chambers's Jrnl.* 777/1, I hoped to get a gural or two on my way. 1922 *Blackw. Mag.* May 558/2 They reminded me of the Himalayan gural.

Guran (gū·rān). One of a people of Kurdistan; also, the language of this people.

1881 *Encycl. Brit.* XIV. 157/2 The Gurán dialect..which is spoken throughout Ardelán and Kirmánsháhán. *Ibid.* 158/1 *note*, The Guráns have for a long period abandoned nomadic habits.

Gurgeon (gə̄·ɹdʒən). *Gurgeon-stopper*, a tree, *Eugenia buxifolia*, of Florida and the West Indies.

1884 [see Stopper *sb.* 8].

Gurian (gū·riăn). One of a Caucasian race inhabiting Tiflis, closely related to the Georgians.

1876 *Encycl. Brit.* V. 257/2 The Gurians, a small people occupying the strip of land between the Rion and the mountains on the south, which form the frontier between Russia and Turkey. 1905 *Westm. Gaz.* 20 Sept. 2/1 Gurians, Georgians, and Mingrelians. 1906 *Daily Chron.* 9 Aug. 3/1 The Gurians are the..most warlike..of the Georgians.

Gurkha (gū·ɹkă). Also **G(h)oorka, G(h)oorkha, Gourkha, Ghurka.** A member of one of the dominant races of Nepal, India, of Hindu descent and Sanskritic speech, and especially famous for prowess in fighting. Also *attrib.*

1848 Sir J. D. Hooker in *Life* (1918) I. 269 The Goorkha Sepoys are immense fellows, stout and brawny. 1875 *Encycl. Brit.* II. 590/1 The four Ghoorka regiments, enlisted from Nepaul. 1918 L. Huxley *Life Sir J. D. Hooker* I. 254 The Ghurka escort.

Gurrah² (gʊ·rā). *Africa.* Also **gurah.** [Native name.] An earthen jar.

1864 J. A. Grant *Walk Across Africa* 41 With a gourd cup they drew water from their wells and filled it into earthen 'gurahs', similar to those in India. 1895 Mrs. Croker *Village Tales* (1896) 153 He..had been flung in the dust, like a broken gurrah.

Gurry⁴. (Earlier examples.)

1837 H. Colman *Rep. Agric. Mass.* (1838) 101 Animal manures. Fish, Fish oil, Gurry and blubber. 1839 *Knickerbocker Mag.* XIII. 391 [Whaling song] She's gone in her flurry, boys, She'll soon be in 'gurry', boys!

c. The slime of sponges.

1887 [see Sponger 3].

Gushily (gʊ·ʃili), *adv.* [f. Gushy *a.* + -ly².] In a gushy manner, gushingly.

1921 W. De Morgan *Old Man's Youth* xxiii. 211 Our visitor gushily asked what the dear boy was saying.

Gusle (gu·slĕ). Also **gusla, gustlé, guzlā.** [Serbian.] A viol having only one string, used in the Balkans.

1869 Tozer *Highl. Turkey* I. 265 The national instrument ..is the guzla... In shape it is like an elongated pear cut in half, and it is something between a guitar and a violin. 1880 *Grove's Dict. Mus.* I. 642 *Guzla*, a kind of rebab, a bow instrument with one string only, used in Illyria. 1922 D. H. Low *Ball. Marko Kraljević* Introd. p. xxxvi, He then makes ready his gusle which in shape bears a rough resemblance to a mandolin. 1930 *Contemp. Rev.* Feb. 225 The gustlé player is the Serbian equivalent of the Saxon harpist.

So **Gu·slar** (pl. *guslari*), one who plays a gusle.

1908 *Daily Chron.* 29 July 4/4 A blind guslar, playing the gusla. 1922 D. H. Low *Ball. of Marko Kraljević* Introd. p. xxxvi, The bard or guslar is often blind.

Guss (gʊs). *local.* (See quots.)

1883 Gresley *Gloss. Coal-m.*, *Guss* (Bristol Coal-field), a short piece of rope by which a boy draws a tram or sled in a pit. 1928 *Times* 4 Oct. 11/4 The guss is a girdle fitted around the waist of boys who pull coal in 'putts' or sledges in the Somerset mines.

Gust, *v.*² Delete *rare* and add: Also without *up*, to blow in gusts.

1899 J. M. Falkner *Moonfleet* xi, The wind came gusting round the corner. 1927 *Chambers's Jrnl.* 312/2 The wind was gusting.

Gustavian (gʊstē¹·viăn), *a.* [f. the name *Gustavus*: see -ian.] Of or pertaining to the reign of any of the Swedish kings named Gustavus, *spec.* the reigns of Gustavus III and Gustavus IV (1771–1809), one of the greatest periods of Swedish literature.

1884 R. B. Anderson tr. *F. W. Horn's Lit. Scand. North* III. v. 336 The poets of the Gustavian period form two groups according to the prevalence, respectively, of the French and the national element. 1887 *Encycl. Brit.* XXII. 757/1 The excellent lyrical poet Frans Mikael Franzén..and a belated academician Johan David Valerius..fill up the space between the Gustavian period and the domination of romantic ideas from Germany.

Gustiness (gʊ·stinės). [f. Gusty *a.*¹ + -ness.] The condition or quality of being gusty.

1901 *Westm. Gaz.* 20 June 10/1 The everlasting gustiness for which the Maoriland capital is famed. 1920 *Times Lit. Suppl.* 9 Sept. 586/1 From the point of view of construction his stories are..irregular, but for sheer gustiness they are hard to equal. 1927 G. W. Deeping *Kitty* xxv, The gustiness of her impatience.

Gusto. 5. (Later example.)

1836 Mary A. Holley *Texas* iv. 66 Melons of the richest gusto abound everywhere.

Gut, *sb.* Add:

1. d. *pl.* Energy, verve, staying power; courage, force of character. *slang.*

Cf. dial. phr. *to have neither gut nor gall* (1887 in E.D.D.). 1893 Farmer *Slang* s.v., Put your guts into it..= Row the very best you can. He (or it) has no guts in him (or it) = He (or it) is a common rotter. 1900 G. Swift *Somerley* 85 If you have what are, at Cambridge, vulgarly but expressively called 'guts'. 1924 W. M. Raine *Troubled Waters* ii. 22 It's about your size to send a skull-and-crossbones threat through the mail, but I notice you haven't the guts to sign it. 1924 R. Keable *Recompence* i. (1926) 9 Can't you dig me out a chap with some guts, who has learned to rough it? 1929 Priestley *Good Comp.* III. v. 583, I expect I haven't the guts to keep on and keep it up.

8. *gut fat* (earlier U.S. example).

1847 *Rep. U.S. Comm. Patents* (1848) 527 The slaughterers formerly got the gut fat for the whole of the labor thus described.

Gut, *v.* **2. a.** Add: Now freq. used *pass.* and of destruction by fire.

1903 *Westm. Gaz.* 25 Aug. 8/2 The farmhouse and outbuildings were completely gutted.

Gutless (gʊ·tlės), *a.* Delete †*Obs.* and add:

b. Lacking in energy, verve, or determination.

1929 W. J. Locke *Jorico* x, Dr. Chepstow firmly refused to allow the convalescent and..gutless Nicholas to venture a second time.

Gutser (gʊ·tsəɹ). *dial.* and *colloq.* Also **gutzer.** [f. *guts* (see *Gut *sb.* 1 d) + -er¹.] Something which takes away one's spirit.

1919 *War Slang* in *Athenæum* 8 Aug. 728/1 A 'gutser' is the last straw. 1925 E. Fraser & Gibbons *Soldier & Sailor Words*, 'He's before a court martial and looks like coming a gutzer.' 'Gutzer' is pre-war slang, and an old term among Scottish boys for falling flat on the water in diving.

Gutta¹. Add: **3.** A drop-like marking on an insect's wing. In recent Dicts.

Gutta². Add:

1. b. A gutta-percha golf ball, a gutty.

1881 R. Forgan *Golfer's Handbk.* 5 The 'guttas' speedily became popular. *Ibid.* 36 The 'gutta' ball..was still far from perfect. 1905 A. S. Cunningham *Rambles in Scoonie & Wemyss* 99 He and his brother were credited with devising the hand hammering of balls, which led to the ultimate marking of guttas.

2. gutta-jelutong (or **joolatong**), a substitute for rubber obtained from any one of several apocynaceous trees of Malay of the genus *Dyera*, spec. *D. costulata*; **gutta-milk**, the freshly exuded juice of the gutta-percha tree.

1903 *Sci. Amer. Suppl.* 28 Feb. 22707 (Cent. D. Suppl.) Gutta-milk. 1904 *Electr. World & Engin.* 18 June 1150 (Ibid.) Importations of 'gutta-joolatong',..which is used in certain industries as a substitute for india rubber. 1927 C. R. Toothaker *Commercial Raw Materials* 207.

Gutter, *sb.*¹ **8.** Add:

gutter-man (*b*) *Logging*, one who removes underbrush, fallen trees, and other obstacles in making a gutter road; (*c*) one who cleans out the gutters of buildings; **gutter road**, the path or track followed in skidding logs.

1905 *Terms Forestry & Logging* 39 Gutterman...Gutter road. 1921 *Dict. Occup. Terms* (1927) § 970 *Roofman*; *gutterman*; sweeps roofs and removes dirt and other obstruction from guttering, rain pipes, etc., of large buildings.

Gutter, *sb.*² **1.** Add to def.: or animals.

1851 C. Cist *Cincinnati* 280 Here the animal falls into the hands of the gutter who tears out the inside, stripping at the rate of three hogs to the minute.

Gutter-snipe. Add: **2. c.** *U.S.* (See quots.)

1870 Medbery *Men & Myst. Wall St.* 136 Gutter snipes. Curbstone brokers. 1877 Bartlett *Dict. Amer.* (ed. 4), *Gutter-snipes*, a Wall Street term for brokers who do business chiefly on the sidewalk or in the street, and who are not members of the Stock Exchange.

Guttural, *v.* [f. the adj.] *trans.* To utter in guttural tones.

1855 *Knickerbocker Mag.* XLV. 430 The Indian guttural'd out: 'You 'member that little notion me talk to you 'bout?'

Guttus (gʊ·tʊs). *Class. Archæol.* Pl. **-ti.** [L.] A narrow-necked cruet or oil-flask.

1921 *Brit. Museum Return* 61 Guttus of early Italian red-figure style.

Gutty, *sb.* Add: Also *attrib.*

1902 *Daily Chron.* 9 Dec. 9/3 He advised them to select the 'gutty' ball only, as the best ball for golf. 1921 *Glasgow Herald* 16 July 4 Their elusive guttie ba's.

Guv (gʊv). Vulgar abbreviation of Governor 7.

1890 *Punch* 15 Mar. 123/1 Yes, you're right, Guv, this *is* dirty fun and dreary. 1895 *Ibid.* 17 Aug. 77/1 Guv wos in it all the while.

Guvacine (giū·vāsin). *Chem.* [f. Skr. *guvāka* betel-nut tree + -ine⁵.] A monacid alkaloid derived from the areca nut.

1891 *Jrnl. Chem. Soc.* LX. II. 1520 Guvacine, $C_6H_9NO_2$, forms small, lustrous, anhydrous crystals.

Guy, *sb.*¹ **3.** Add: *guy-line*; **guy-rod**, a rod used in place of a guy-rope.

1903 A. Adams *Log Cowboy* x. 152 We took a *guy line from the wagon and snubbed it to a tree. 1928 *Daily Express* 7 Apr. 5/5 Drive in the remaining pegs and attach and true up the remaining guylines. 1903 *Electr. World & Engin.* 31 Oct. 711 (Cent. D. Suppl.) *Guy-rods are 8 ft. × ⅝ in., provided with an eye at one end. 1910 *N. Hawkins' Elect. Dict.*, *Guy Rod Bands*, bands by which a guy rod is attached to a telegraph pole.

Guy, *sb.*² **3. d.** *U.S.* (Earlier and later examples.)

1896 G. Ade *Artie* i. 3 You guys must think I'm a quitter. 1904 *Cincinnati Commercial Tribune* 29 June 4 Mr. Bryan is a hefty guy when it comes to Democratic conventions and the platforms thereof. 1915 H. L. Wilson *Ruggles of Red Gap* v. (1917) 95 Think of the guy's imagination, naming this here chafing dish the *Storm King*! 1929 S. Anderson in *Mercury Story Bk.* 231 The young fellow was a nice guy all right.

Guy, *sb.*³ *U.S.* [f. Guy *v.*³ 2.] A joke.

1887 *Congress. Record* 1022/1 He was a democrat, as he says, for a 'guy'. 1911 J. C. Lincoln *Cap'n Warren's Wards* iii. 37, I was only joking...It's a standing guy, you know.

Guy. Used as an exclamation. *U.S.*

1838 *Knickerbocker Mag.* XII. 297 'Guy!' said he, in a tone which seemed hardly to realize the truth, 'I b'lieve I'm upshot!' *c* 1845 Paulding *Noble Exile* 140 Guy, he's as careful as a city mosquito in the autumn.

Gweeon (gwī·ɒn). *Austral.* [Native name.] An aboriginal stone hatchet.

1898 Morris *Austral Engl.*, *Gweeon*, a stone tomahawk of the aborigines.

Gwely (gwe·li). [Welsh.] The social unit, consisting of four generations of one family, in which the great-grandfather, the head of the group, had proprietary right over its landed property.

Gwentian (gwe·ntiăn), *a.* and *sb.* [f. the name *Gwent* + -ian.] Of or pertaining to Gwent in south-east Wales; also *sb.*, the dialect of this region.

1901 *Daily Chron.* 16 Oct. 3/2 The Gwentian bowmen were famous. 1913 J. M. Jones *Welsh Gram.* 8 Gwentian, the dialect of Gwent and Morgannwg, or South East Wales.

Gym (dʒim). Colloq. abbreviation of Gymnasium: also *attrib.*

1889 Barrère & Leland *Dict. Slang*, *Gymcad* (Royal Military Academy), a gymnasium instructor. 1891 H. Scott Holland in *Mem.* (1921) 198 We had a superb exhibition in the gym. 1907 *Daily Chron.* 27 Nov. 3/3 The 'gym.' practices. 1930 *Daily Express* 6 Sept. 2 Girls' Full Length Gym Stockings. 1930 *Cambridge Daily News* 25 Sept. 3/4 Gym slips should not be washed.

Gymnadenia (dʒimnădī·niă). [mod.L., f. Gr. γυμνός naked, bare + ἀδεν-, ἀδήν gland: see -ia¹.] A terrestrial orchid of the genus of that name, esp. a plant of the cultivated species bearing fragrant purple flowers.

1829 Loudon *Encycl. Plants* 750. 1931 A. C. Chater tr. *S. Undset's Wild Orchid* I. i, I'm so excited to see if anything will come of the gymnadenias I put in here last year.

Gymna·stic, *v.* [f. the noun.] *intr.* To practise gymnastics. In quot. *fig.*

1928 *Hearst's International* Aug. 156/2 You gymnasticked around and made Pickett Boone think you and Mason were on the prod.

Gymnemic (dʒimnī·mik, -ne·mik), *a.* [f. mod.L. *Gymnema*, fr. Gr. γυμνός naked + νῆμα thread + -ic.] Designating an acid occurring in the leaves of *Gymnema sylvestre*, whose leaves, when chewed, temporarily destroy the sense of taste.

1889 *Jrnl. Chem. Soc.* LVI. 723 Gymnemic acid occurs in combination in the leaves of *Gymnema sylvestre*, *G. hirsuta*, and *G. montanum*. 1901 Titchener *Exper. Psychol.* I. II. 104 A saturated alcoholic solution of gymnemic acid.

Gynandro-. Add: **Gyna·ndromorph**, an individual which exhibits gynandromorphism. **Gynandromo·rphic** *a.* = *gynandromorphous*. **Gynandromo·rphy** = *gynandromorphism*.

1894 W. Bateson *Study of Variation* 68 Gynandromorphic insects, in which the characters of the whole or part of one side of the body, wings and antennæ, are male, while those of the other side are female. 1913 — *Mendel's Princ. Heredity* 321 They consist of normal males and gynandromorphs having the characters of the sexes mixed in various degrees.

Gynarchic (dʒəinā·ɹkik, dʒin-), *a.* [f. Gynarchy: see -ic.] Of or pertaining to gynarchy.

1922 *Glasgow Herald* 2 Nov. 5 Gynarchic rule is another peculiarity of some of the Formosan tribes.

Gynee (gəi·nī). [Hindi (related to *go* Cow *sb.*¹).] One of a small variety of cattle bred in Bengal.

1850 F. Parks *Wand. Pilgrim* I. 251 We..are building outhouses to receive some thirty-four dwarf cows and oxen (gynees) which are to be fed up for the table.

Gyniatrics (dʒəi-, dʒiniæ·triks). *Med.* [f. Gr. γυνή woman + ἰατρικός of medical treatment.] The treatment of diseases peculiar to women.

1890 Billings *Med. Dict.*

Gyno-. Add: **Gynoca·rdin**, a glucoside from the seeds of *Gynocardia odorata*; hence **Gynocardi·nic** *a.*, whence **Gynoca·rdinate. Gynopho·bia**, fear of woman. **Gy·nospore**, a female germ-cell.

1904 *Proc. Chem. Soc.* XX. 137 A cyanogenetic glucoside, which the authors [F. B. Power and F. H. Gornall] have isolated in a crystalline state, and designate *gynocardin. 1915 *Jrnl. Chem. Soc.* CVIII. I. 646 Methyl *gynocardinate, $C_{17}H_{33}.CO_2Me$. 1905 *Ibid.* LXXXVII. II. 351 *Gynocardinic acid, $C_{12}H_{19}O_9.CO_2H$. 1886 O. W. Holmes *Mortal Antipathy* xix. 231 If we give it a name, we shall have to apply the term **Gynophobia*, or Fear of Woman. 1886 *Academy* 16 Jan. 37 A man..has become afflicted with gynophobia. 1901 *Practitioner* Mar. 281 *Gynospore is Ray Lankester's name for the Macrogamete of Ross.

Gyp³ (dʒip). *dial.* or *colloq.* Also **jip.** [app. contraction of Gee-up, which is used dial. as sb.] *To give* (a person or thing) *gyp*: to punish, thrash, treat roughly.

1898 B. Kirkby *Lakeland Words.* 1902 Wright *Eng. Dial. Dict.* s.v. *Jip*, Ah'll gi'e tha jip...'Ah gav' it jip Ah can tell tha,' said of beating a carpet soundly with a stick in each hand. 1915 Cable *Between Lines* 19 We'll give 'em gyp if they try it. 1917 P. MacGill *Brown Brethren* xii. 170 A cramp in my guts!..Gawd, it isn't 'arf giving me gyp!

Gyp⁴. Colloq. abbreviation of *Gypsophila.

1928 *Daily Express* 8 Sept. 2/1 The children have taken.. flowers and arranged them with gyp or fern.

Gypsophila (dʒipsǫ·filă). *Bot.* [mod.L., f. Gr. γύψος chalk + φίλος loving.] A plant of the genus so called of silenaceous plants, having small delicate paniculate flowers.

1829 Loudon *Encycl. Plants* 368. 1909 *Daily Mirror* 13 Aug. 7/4 The graceful gypsophila (chalk plant).

Gyratory, *a.* Add: **b.** *spec.* pertaining to a system of directing traffic in one-way lines round a place where several roads meet.

1909 *Westm. Gaz.* 7 Aug. 4/2 The gyratory principle, by which vehicles are directed into circular lines ingeniously devised to avoid intersection. 1926 *Rep. Commissioner Police Metropolis, 1925* 16 Gyratory systems for the circulation of traffic, after years of discussion, reached the point of practical demonstration this year. 1928 *Observer* 5 Feb. 13/7 Now that every week dedicates a new bunch of streets to the Gyratory System.

Gyro (dʒəi·°ro). Colloq. abbreviation of (*a*) Gyroscope, (*b*) *gyro-compass* (see below).

1914 H. Crabtree *Spinning Tops & Gyroscopic Motion* (ed. 2) 77 If the position of the ends *N* and *S* of the gyro [= gyro-compass] are reversed.

b. *Comb.* **gyro-accelerometer** (see quot.); **gyro-car**, a mono-rail carriage which is balanced by means of gyroscopes driven at high speed in opposite directions; **gyro-compass**, a form of gyroscope used as a compass, being continuously driven and thus retaining a fixed direction; **gyro-pilot**, a gyro-compass used to steer a vessel without human agency; **gyroplane**, a type of flying-machine supported by a rapidly rotating screw propeller operating in a horizontal plane.

1930 *Morning Post* 21 July 4 A device styled the *gyro-accelerometer, which measures every movement of a carriage and records it on a chart with decimal accuracy. 1909 *Westm. Gaz.* 8 Nov. 8/3 The *gyro-car, as Herr Scherl calls it, is to make a series of runs..in the Exhibition Hall at the Zoological Gardens. 1909 *Daily Chron.* 11 Nov. 1/6 We waited for the gyro-car to emerge from its shed. 1913 J. H. Poynting *Earth* 98 That very remarkable invention by the brothers Anschütz, termed the *Gyro Compass. 1924 *Glasgow Herald* 9 Jan. 5 A Sperry gyro-compass equipment. 1931 *Times Lit. Suppl.* 22 Jan. 51/3 A speck of dust might cause a gyro compass to 'wander'. 1923 *Westm. Gaz.* 24 Dec., Through the agency of an invention known as the *gyro-pilot apparatus, the Cunard liner Laconia, which reached Liverpool yesterday, steered from New York a straight course without human aid. 1924 *Glasgow Herald* 8 Jan. 7 Gyro-Pilot for Cargo Boats. 1907 *Nature* 5 Dec. 107/1 The *gyroplane of Messrs. Breguet, which revives interest in the attempt to overcome gravity by vertical screw propellers. 1909 *Westm. Gaz.* 25 Feb. 4/2 The Lestage gyro-plane.

Gyropter (dʒəi·°rǫptəɹ). (Disused.) [f. Gyro- + Gr. πτερόν wing; cf. *Helicopter.] A rotary wing of a kind of flying-machine; also, a flying-machine having rotary wings.

1908 *Westm. Gaz.* 14 Aug. 10/2 A new machine, the Gyropter, or rotary-wing flying machine. 1908 *World's Work* Oct. 552 The Gyropter Flying Machine. 1908 *Westm. Gaz.* 5 Nov. 10/2 Two huge gyropters or rotary wings which are really aeroplanes, but have vastly more air-cutting surface than ordinary aeroplanes. 1912 *Yks. Post* 13 Jan. (leader), Mr. Davidson proposes the building of what he calls a gyropter.

Gyroscope. Add: **b.** *spec.* those forms of gyroscope attached to vessels, mono-rail carriages, flying-machines, etc., to maintain equilibrium; and, by retaining a fixed direction, to act as a check on, or substitute for, a mariner's compass, and to keep a torpedo, etc., in a straight course.

1891 *Cassell's Family Mag.* 187/1 A small gyroscope has also been fitted to the ship's sextants, so as to give an invariable line of sight. 1904 *Daily Chron.* 29 Feb. 4/5 The newest torpedoes, we are told, will have a speed of thirty knots for 3,000 yards, and, thanks to the gyroscope, almost perfect accuracy can be relied upon. 1907 *Standard* 23 Mar.,

The experiments showed conclusively that gyroscopes could be designed which would exercise a sensible steadying effect upon even the largest passenger steamers on service.

c. *attrib.* and *Comb.*, as **gyroscope-car, -compass** = *gyro-car, -compass*; **gyroscope governor**, a steam governor in which a gyroscope acts as regulator; **gyroscope top**, a spinning top on the gyroscope principle, which when spinning may be supported by one end of its horizontal axis.

1909 *Westm. Gaz.* 20 Apr. 9/3 The *gyroscope-compass, an invention of Dr. Anschuetz-Kaempfe, of Kiel,..is based upon the familiar principle that a rapidly rotating body tends to keep in the same plane. 1875 Knight *Dict. Mech.*, *Gyroscope-governor. 1880 *Encycl. Brit.* XI. 352/2 Perhaps the most common form of gyroscope is that which has been largely sold under the name of the *gyroscope top.

Gyroscopic. Add: *gyroscopic apparatus* = *Gyroscope b; *gyroscopic compass* = gyro-compass; *gyroscopic precession*, 'the steady motion in which the axis of the top describes a right circular cone about the vertical' (Cent. D. Suppl. 1909); *gyroscopic top* = gyroscope top.

1907 *Standard* 23 Mar., Dr. Schlick's gyroscopic apparatus for steadying ships. 1920 T. W. Chalmers (*title*) The Gyroscopic Compass. 1928 A. L. Rawlings (*title*) Theory of the Gyroscopic Compass and its Deviations.

Gyroscopically (dʒəi·°rǫskǫ·pikăli), *adv.* [f. Gyroscopic: see -ically.] By or with a gyroscope.

1911 *Chambers's Jrnl.* 55/1 The success of the gyroscope in preventing the rolling of ships..would seem to augur well for the gyroscopically controlled aeroplane.

Gyrostat. Add: Also, an instrument for controlling the horizontal direction of a submarine. Hence **Gyrostatic** *a.* in **gyrostatic compass** = **gyro-compass*.

1902 *Encycl. Brit.* XXXII. 578/1. 1922 *Ibid.* XXX. 44/1 A gyrostatic compass.

H

H. Add: **2.** *H girder, iron.*

1888 *Lockwood's Dict. Mech. Engin.*, *H Iron*, rolled wrought-iron bar whose section is that of the letter I. Used extensively for building up engineering structures. 1902 A. C. HARMSWORTH *Motors & Motor Driving* vi. 90 The roof of the house is strengthened at certain points by cross timbers which support two small H girders, and carry iron frames to which are attached pulley blocks.

II. 3. b. *H line*, in a spectrum, one of the lines representing calcium.

1897 SIR W. HUGGINS *Sci. Papers* (1909) 438 The H and K lines have become thin and defined. 1902 *Encycl. Brit.* XXXII. 780/2 The H and K lines of calcium are observed at the highest elevations reached by solar prominences.

III. H. = Head-quarters, henry (*Electr.*). h. = hot; as h. and c. = hot and cold (water). H. and D. (see quots. 1918, 1930). H.A. = Horse Artillery. H.A.C. = Honourable Artillery Company. H.E. = His Eminence, His Excellency, high explosive, horizontal equivalent. H.E.I.C.S. = Honourable East India Company's Service. H.F. = high frequency. HF, H^F, Hf, hf = healthy female(s). HHH = halt (in signalling). HM, H^M, Hm, hm = healthy male(s). H.M.I.(S.) = His Majesty's Inspector of Schools. H.P. = high pressure, hot pressed, hybrid perpetual. H.Q. = Head-quarters. H.T., h.t. = high tension.

1880 *Encycl. Brit.* XIII. 170/2 Table H^MF, comprising all the healthy lives, male and female, included in the observations... Table H^M, comprising the healthy male lives only... Table H^F, comprising the healthy female lives. 1893 W. ROBINSON *Engl. Flower Garden* (ed. 3) 644/2 Gabriel Luizet, General Jacqueminot and many other H.Ps. do not usually bloom after the month of August. 1898 *Westm. Gaz.* 14 Nov. 8/1 With its premiums and its reversionary bonuses, and its Hm tables and its surrender values. 1901 *Daily Chron.* 27 June 3/2 To introduce a very much larger proportion of H.E. shell. 1902 *Encycl. Brit.* XXXII. 151 The H.-P. valves are worked by means of a simple lever from the L.-P. valve-rods. 1903 A. WATKINS *Watkins Man.* 29 A box of one maker's plates marked H & D 100. 1908 E. M. SNEYD-KYNNERSLEY (*title*) H.M.I.: Some passages in the life of one of H.M. Inspectors of Schools. 1910 *Hawkins' Electr. Dict.*, H. The symbol of induction. The Henry. h. An abbreviation for the henry, the practical unit of induction. 1913 *Year-Bk. Wireless Telegr.* 289 To make the current-distribution over the cross-section more uniform for H.F. currents. 1915 D. O. BARNETT *Lett.* 39 After reporting at Brigade H.Q. we went on to our regiments. *Ibid.* 153 H.E. is the shell for attacking, because you blow the defenders out of their trenches. 1918 *Photo-Miniature* XV. Mar. (Gloss.), H. & D. (Hurter and Driffield)—used as a prefix to numbers signifying the speed of plates measured by the system devised by these investigators. Fastest plates, H. & D. 400 to 500. 1923 *Supplt. to Popular Wireless* 13 Oct. 10 'Plug-in' H.F. Transformers. 1924 *Exper. Wireless* Apr. 397/2 The atmospheric band frequencies which penetrate the H.F. filter. 1930 *Sel. Gloss. Motion Picture Technician*, *H and D Curve*, the characteristic curve of a photographic emulsion. 1930 *Morning Post* 17 June 20/7, 4 bed-rooms (h. and c. in each). 1931 *Daily Express* 18 Mar. 13/2 Fuller 100 volt H.T. and G.B. Battery.

Haanepoot (hā·nəpōt). Also **haanepot, haenapod, hanapoot, hanna-poot.** Also corruptly **honey-pot.** [Afrikaans *haanepoot*, f. Du. *haan* cock + *poot* foot.] A South African grape often used for making wine or for raisins.

1801 J. BARROW *Trav.* I. 65 A large white Persian grape, called here the haenapod. 1855 W. R. KING *Campaigning in Kaffirland* (ed. 2) 190 The most deliciously flavoured grapes, one sort, called the 'honey-pot',..of immense size. 1878 T. J. LUCAS *Camp Life* 36 A fine fleshy well-favoured variety called hanne poot. 1887 *Colonial & Indian Exhib., Rep. Col. Sect.* 136 Raisins are made from the Haanepot grape. 1927 *Daily Express* 8 Apr. 5 The Cape grapes..either the gros Colmars or the white Hanapoots.

Haarlem (hā·ɹləm). The name of a town in Holland used *attrib.* in **Haarlem blue**, a variety of blue containing alumina; **Haarlem oil**, 'a proprietary diuretic and stimulant oil' (Dorland 1901).

1885 *Spons' Mech. Own Bk.* 407 Slight differences in the manufacture [of Prussian Blue] cause considerable variation in tint and colour, which leads to the material being known by different names—such as 'Antwerp', 'Berlin', 'Haerlem', 'Chinese' Blue. 1885 *Encycl. Brit.* XVIII. 720/1 Barbados tar, Haarlem oil, Seneca oil, and American oil, all consisting wholly or in large part of crude petroleum, were sold by apothecaries for years before petroleum was obtained by boring. 1906 *Practitioner* Dec. 852 Methyloids.—These are an improved combination of methylene blue, Santal oil, copaiba, Haarlem oil, and cinnamon oil, and are supplied in capsoid form.

Habara (hæ·bărā). Also **habareh.** [Arabic.] A woman's outdoor silk garment.

1851 *Illustr. Catal. Gt. Exhib.* v. II. 1410 Habara veil, in black silk, for females. 1913 *Sunday at Home* Oct. 51/2 A black Egyptian habareh and veil.

Habenal (hăbī·năl), *a.* *Anat.* [f. HABENA + -AL.] = HABENAR.

1889 *Buck's Handbk. Med. Sci.* VIII. 145/1 The habenal sulcus. 1901 DORLAND *Med. Dict.* (ed. 2).

Haboob (habū·b). [Arab. هبوب *habūb* blowing furiously.] A violent and oppressive wind which blows at certain seasons in the Sudan, and which brings with it sand from the desert.

1897 *Daily News* 2 Oct. 2/1 This was a real haboob—a tornado of sand and small stones. *Ibid.* 4/6 A soldier that had been swept into the river by the merciless haboob. 1928 *Blackw. Mag.* Feb. 259 May is the month of 'haboobs'.

Habutai (hābutai·). Also **-aye, -ae.** [Jap.] A fine soft Japanese silk.

1896 BRINKLEY *Jap. Engl. Dict.* 1902 *Encycl. Brit.* XXIX. 725/1 Pictures so elaborate and..accurate as those produced by the *yuzen* process on silk crape or *habutaye*.

Hacienda. Add: Also *attrib.*

1860 *Ure's Dict. Arts* (ed. 5) III. 676 Working it on their own account, or, as it is termed, hacienda account. 1897 *Blackw. Mag.* Nov. 685/2 The pleasant picture of hacienda life in the land of the Aztecs.

Haciendado (asiendā·do). [Sp.] The owner of an hacienda.

1862 MAYNE REID *Tiger Hunter* xix, To the haciendado he hired himself out a part of the year. 1897 *Blackw. Mag.* Nov. 685 The polity of the Mexican haciendado remains unchanged. 1897 *Outing* (U.S.) XXIX. 593/2 The plantation homes of the *haciendados*. 1920 *Glasgow Herald* 22 Sept. 8 The Chilean haciendado.

Haciendero (asiende·ro). [Sp.] A farmer.

1927 *Blackw. Mag.* Nov. 652/2 The rich haciendero had paternally assisted them in times of famine.

Hack, *sb.*[1] Add: **6.** An act of hacking; a hacking blow. Also *fig.*

1873-4 *Rep. Vermont Board Agric.* II. 238, I have a chance to have several hacks at the weeds before the crop is sown. 1898 MARG. DELAND *Old Chester Tales* 244. I get more men in a season, that's why; and when the show's done I get a hack at 'em.

Hack, *sb.*[3] **8.** (Earlier U.S. examples.)

1812 *Boston Gaz.* 10 Sept., Advt. (Th.) Hack Stand. 1835 in *Southern Lit. Messenger* IV. 197/1 My hack-driver..assured [me] that there was no other tavern in the city.

Hackamore. (Earlier example.)

1850 W. R. RYAN *Upper & Lower California* I. 152 He overtook me, mounted on a well saddled horse, and leading another by the hackamore.

Hackia (hæ·kiă). = GUAIAC.

1851 *Illustr. Catal. Gt. Exhib.* IV. I. 983/2 Hackia, lignum vitæ, transverse and vertical sections, from River Demerara. 1858 SIMMONDS *Dict. Trade*, *Hackia*, a wood..used for mill cogs and shafts.

Hacking, *vbl. sb.* Add: **1. c.** [After G. *hackung*; cf. F. *hachement*.] Massage with the edge of the hand.

1890 KELLGREN *Techn. Ling's Syst.* 25 Tapotement means hacking or beating. 1893 A. S. ECCLES *Sciatica* 64 Thorough rubbing, kneading, hacking, and passive movements are practised.

Hackle, *sb.*[2] **3.** Add: Also, the feathers on the saddle of a cock.

1850 D. J. BROWNE *Amer. Poultry Yard* 22 The hackles of the lower part of the back. *Ibid.* 253 In capons..the hackle, the tail feathers, and the spurs grew to a much greater length than in cocks.

Hackling, *vbl. sb.*[1] *attrib.* Add: *hackling house.*

1849 E. CHAMBERLAIN *Indiana Gazetteer* 132 A brick building, erected for a hackling house.

Hackman. *U.S.* (Earlier and later examples.)

1796 *Boston Directory*, passim. 1806 *Repertory* (Boston) 3 Oct. (Th.) Died, in this town, Mr. Daniel Henry, hackman. 1819 *N. Y. Gaz.* in *Massachusetts Spy* 16 June 3/1 The horses were stopt by the hackmen on the stand. 1898 HAMBLEN *Tom Benton's Luck* 56 The line of vociferous hackmen who formed a gauntlet across the exit from the railroad station.

Hackman(n)ite (hæ·kmănəit). *Min.* [Named after Victor *Hackman* of Helsingfors: see -ITE[1] 2 b.] A mineral of the sodalite group found in the rock of the Tawa Valley, Lapland.

1903 *Jrnl. Chem. Soc.* LXXXIV. II. 304 Hackmanite, a new member of the sodalite group.

Hackney-carriage. (Earlier U.S. example.)

1797 *Boston Selectmen* 12 June, The Law regulating Hackney Carriages.

Hadahah (hæ·daha). *S. Afr.* Also **ha-di-da, addada.** [Onomatopœic.] The large brown ibis, *Geronticus hagedash.*

1846 T. ARBOUSSET & DAUMAS *Narr. Tour Cape G. H.* 190 A large ibis of a brown lustre commonly called by onomatopy *addada*. 1907 *African Monthly* Oct. 445 Flocks of 'ha-di-da' grub silently and unconcernedly in close proximity to the camp.

Haddocky (hæ·dəki), *a.* [f. HADDOCK[1] + -Y[1].] Of or pertaining to haddocks.

1922 *Contemp. Rev.* Sept. 365 This haddocky scent..has a savour not unpleasing.

Hades. Add: **2. b.** Used trivially as a substitute for *hell* in imprecations, etc.

1912 A. BENNETT *Matador of Five Towns* ii, What the hades are you waiting there for?

Hadith (hæ·diþ). Also **Hadis, Hadithah,** *pl.* **Hadithat.** [a. Ar. حديث *hadīþ* a tradition.] The body of traditions relating to Mohammed, which now form a supplement to the Koran, called the Sunna.

1880 *Encycl. Brit.* XI. 367/2 Rejecting the *Hadith*, or traditional sayings of Mahomet. 1883 *Ibid.* XVI. 594/2 The traditions of Mohammed, or *Hadith*, the collective body of which constitutes the *Sunna*, or custom. 1922 *Blackw. Mag.* Mar. 375/2, I treasured this like a *hadis*, an authentic tradition of which I was the custodian. 1924 GUILLAUME *Trad. Islam* 15 The hadith literature as we now have it provides us with apostolic precept and example covering the whole duty of man. *Ibid.* 150 Many of the hadith already cited will have shown the good sense, amiability, and liberality of the prophet.

Hadjeen, variant of *HYGEEN.

Hadrome (hæ·drōᵘm). *Bot.* [f. Gr. ἁδρός thick + -OME.] = XYLEM. So **Hadroce·ntric** *a.*, having the xylem surrounded by the phloem; **Ha·dromase,** an enzyme in certain fungi capable of dissolving lignin; **Ha:dromycoˈsis** (see quot. 1917).

1898 tr. *Strasburger's Text-bk. Bot.* 102 Other terms often used to designate the vascular bundles are fibro-vascular bundles and mestome. The vascular portion is also termed the xylem or hadrome. 1900 B. D. JACKSON *Gloss. Bot. Terms*, *Hadrome*, a shortened form of *Hadromestome*,..the xylem or woody portion of a vascular bundle. *Ibid.* (*Add.*), *Hadrocentric Bundle*, having the hadrome in the centre surrounded by the leptome (Haberlandt); *Hadromase*, an enzyme found in *Merulius lacrymans*, Schum., and other Fungi, which attacks the hadrome and destroys its lignified cell-walls (Czapek). 1909 J. R. GREEN *Hist. Bot.* 219 Dealing in more detail with the vascular bundles, to which he [*sc.* Schwendener] gave the name *Mestom*, he renamed the xylem *Hadrom* and the phloem *Leptom*. *Ibid.* 406 Czapek found in 1899 that the nutrition of certain fungi which attack lignified cell walls is materially aided by an enzyme, which he called hadromase, which dissolves the woody constituents. 1917 *Nature* 22 Feb. 500/2 Plants suffering from the choking of their vessels (by fungi) (hadromycosis).

Haeckelian (hekī·liăn), *a.* [f. the name of E. H. *Haeckel* (1834–1919), German biologist: see -IAN.] Of or pertaining to the opinions of Haeckel; also as *sb.*, a believer in Haeckel's theories. So **Haeckelism** (he·kəliz'm), **-i·smus**, the opinions and theories of Haeckel.

1894 *Nat. Sci.* Mar. 162 We are well content to cease from controversy, to let Calcareous sponges, the Gastrula, and ..Haeckelismus take care of themselves. 1897 *Ibid.* Jan. 31 The typical form of the Haeckelian genealogical tree. 1899 E. J. CHAPMAN *Drama of Two Lives, Amphioxus & Ascidian* 88 Thus, hæckelism's wondrous gleam Makes clear, to all, how all arose. 1930 G. R. DE BEER *Embryol. & Evol.* xv. 102 There is then no recapitulation in the Haeckelian sense of accelerated repetition of adult stages.

Hæmolysis (hīmǫ·lisis). [f. Gr. αἱμο- HÆMO- + λύσις dissolution, f. λύειν to loose, dissolve.] The dissolution of (esp. the red) blood corpuscles.

1892 OSLER *Princ. Med.* 725 Increased hæmolysis and dissolution of the hæmoglobin in the blood-serum. 1901 *Jrnl. Chem. Soc.* LXXX. II. 325 Hæmolysis produced by Solanine. 1906 *Practitioner* Nov. 591 The jaundice of the newly born..is dependent upon changes, probably toxic in character, with excessive hæmolysis.

Hence **Hæ·molyse** *v. trans.*, to destroy by hæmolysis; **Hæmolysin** (hīmǫ·lisin, hīmǫləi·sin) [see *LYSIN], a substance in the blood serum of an animal, which causes hæmolysis. **Hæmoly·tic** *a.*, of or pertaining to hæmolysis; **Hæmoly·tically** *adv.*

1897 *Allbutt's Syst. Med.* II. 1044 Pointing to a hæmolytic as well as a simple hæmorrhagic origin for the anæmia. 1902 *Jrnl. Chem. Soc.* LXXXII. II. 464 Hæmolysin of Bacillus Megatherium...In cultures of *B. megatherium* a specific lysin occurs which hæmolyses the corpuscles of guinea-pig, monkey, and man. 1903 *Ibid.* LXXXIV. II. 443 Influence of Cold on the Action of some Hæmolytic Agents. 1908 *Practitioner* Feb. 249 To yield substances which have similar hæmolysing properties to the hæmolytic agent found in tape-worms. 1909 *Jrnl. Chem. Soc.* XCVI. II. 1036 Organs which act hæmolytically. 1920 *Nature* 13 May 347/2 The anti-coagulating and hæmolysing action of sodium nucleinate.

Hæmostat (hī·mostæt). *Surg.* [f. Gr. αἱμο- HÆMO- + στατός, vbl. adj. of ἱστάναι to place.] An instrument or a medicine for checking hæmorrhage.

1913 DORLAND *Med. Dict.* 1930 F. A. POTTLE *Stretchers*

110 The assistant mops it up with a gauze sponge, discovers the point where the blood vessel is severed, and the surgeon clips it with a hæmostat, another variety of pincers with handles like manicure scissors.

Haeremai (hā·ərəmāi). *New Zealand.* Also **haere mai, horomai, haire mai.** [Maori, lit. = come hither.] A Maori term of welcome.

1769 COOK *Voyages* (1773) 342 When they came near enough to be heard, they waved their hands and called out *Horomai*;..these ceremonies we were told were certain signs of their friendly disposition. 1832 H. WILLIAMS *Jrnl.* in H. Carleton *Life* (1874) I. 112 They were very glad to see us, and gave us the usual welcome, '*haere mai!! haere mai!!*' 1845 E. J. WAKEFIELD *Adv. N. Z.* I. 249 No shouts of *haeremai*, so universal a welcome to the stranger, were to be heard. 1883 F. S. RENWICK *Betrayed* 34 (Morris) Haire mai ho! 'tis the welcome song Rings far on the summer air.

Hafiz (hā·fiz). Also 7 **hafis,** 9 **hafeez.** [Arab. حافظ *hāfiz* guardian, keeper, observer.] A Mohammedan who knows the whole of the Koran by heart.

1662 J. DAVIES tr. *Olearius' Voy. Ambass.* 314 [The] Turbants..of their Priests, and particularly, of the Hafis, are white. 1819 T. HOPE *Anastasius* (1820) I. x. 192 Who, to obtain the epithet of hafeez, had learnt his whole koran by heart unto the last stop. 1927 *Blackw. Mag.* May 574/2 A hafiz chanted the Koran for the rest of her soul.

Hafnium (hæ·fniŏm). *Chem.* [f. *Hafnia*, L. name of Copenhagen + -IUM.] A metallic element discovered in 1923. Symbol Hf; atomic number 72.

1923 D. COSTER & G. HEVESY in *Nature* 20 Jan. 79/2.

Haggadah. Add: **2.** The Jewish ritual for the first two nights of the Passover.

[1887 J. JACOBS & WOLF *Catal. Anglo-Jew. Hist. Exhib.* 194 Haggadah Pesach, or Liturgy of the Passover.] 1896 W. H. GREENBURG *Haggadah* 6 Upon the first cup one says the benediction...Upon the second cup one recites the Haggada. 1904 *Daily Chron.* 30 Mar. 7/5 Perhaps the whole genius of the celebration of the Passover may be summed up in the words of the Hagadah: 'In every generation each Israelite shall bethink himself as though he had been delivered from Egypt.'

Haggadically (hægæ·dikăli), *adv.* [f. HAGGADICAL + -LY[2].] As in the haggadah.

1920 OESTERLEY & BOX *Lit. Rabbinical Judaism* 78 The Scriptural lesson..is haggadically developed.

Haggis. Add:

1. d. A mixture, hodge-podge.

1899 *Daily News* 13 Sept. 7/6 They cheerfully go through the curious haggis of social and philanthropic duties served up to them each week. 1928 W. A. J. ARCHBOLD (*title*) Bengal Haggis.

Haikal (hai·kăl). [Coptic.] The central chapel of three forming the sanctuary of a Coptic church. Also *attrib.* in **haikal screen**, a screen, often elaborately carved or decorated, which separates the haikal from the body of the church.

1884 A. J. BUTLER *Anc. Coptic Churches* I. i. 28 The screen of the haikal, instead of aligning with that of the side chapels, projects out three or four feet into the choir. 1902 *Encycl. Brit.* XXVII. 238/1 The central division is called the haikal or sanctuary...Haikal screen and choir screen are often sumptuously carved and inlaid.

Haileybury (hē·libŏri). The name of a school (Haileybury College) in Hertfordshire, orig. owned by the East India Company, used to designate the system of providing civil servants, or the servants themselves, for service in India.

1864 in *Mem. Old Haileybury Coll.* (1894) 95, I trust the new men will be found to furnish persons qualified to sustain the character of the Service..[and] also worthily to fill those high posts of trust..which we now see so happily filled by Haileybury civilians of the old school. 1902 *Encycl. Brit.* XXIX. 451/2 Towards the latter years of the 19th century the last of the old Haileybury civilians, who entered the service as nominees of the East India Company's directors under the system abolished in 1857, were leaving India. 1931 L. S. S. O'MALLEY *Ind. Civil Service* 241 A system of pass examinations, such as the Haileybury entrance examination. 1931 *Times Lit. Suppl.* 18 June 474/3 The modern Civilian is the descendant of the Haileybury students of the early nineteenth century. Whatever the merits or demerits of the Haileybury system, it at least 'led to a tradition of service handed down from generation to generation'.

Hair, *sb.* Add:

8. p. *To get* (a person) *by the short hairs*: to have complete control over.

1899 KIPLING *Stalky* 175 I've got him by the short hairs! 1928 *Blackw. Mag.* Feb. 150/1 Those Chinhwan really did seem to have got the rest of the world by the short hairs. 1930 SAYERS & EUSTACE *Docts. in Case* I. 25 She's evidently got her husband by the short hairs.

9. a. *hair-chain, -mattress, -shaft.* **b.** *hair-slide* (SLIDE *sb.* 6). **c.** *hair-dryer, -waver.*

1907 N. MUNRO *Daft Days* xxx, The lockets are large and strong, and *hair-chains much abound. 1895 *Army & Navy Co-op. Soc. Price List* 15 Sept. 180/1 The Princess Patent *Hair Dryer and Burnisher. 1909 *Install. News* III. 7 This Hair-Dryer works..by means of a small..electric fan. 1909 *Westm. Gaz.* 13 Oct. 7/4 One ounce of hair, which she was drawing through the hair-dryer in her hands. 1931 *Times* 16 Mar. 2/7 Box-springs, *hair mattresses. 1906 *Practitioner* Nov. 692 Complete removal..of the *hair-shaft, together with the root-sheath or papilla. 1924 *Chambers's Jrnl.* 668/2 The process flattens the almost spherical hairshaft and causes it to lean inwards. 1895 *Army & Navy Co-op. Soc. Price List* 15 Sept. (Index) *Hair Slides. 1927 *Glasgow Herald* 6 Oct. 11 Her hair-slide was found some distance from the body. 1895 *Army & Navy Co-op. Soc. Price List* 15 Sept. 180/2 *Hair Wavers (Patent).

10. hair-cut, an act of cutting the hair by a hair-dresser; **hair-raising** *a.*, capable of causing the hair to 'stand on end' through fear or excitement; so **hair-raiser**; **hair-restorer, -seal** (earlier U.S. examples); **hair-slip**, a place on a green hide where the grain has decayed causing the hair to slip; so **hair-slipped** *a.*, marked with decayed places.

1899 *Westm. Gaz.* 5 Dec. 8/1 The trade in Pretoria was kept very busy for about ten days giving the burghers a commando *hair-cut. 1904 *Daily Chron.* 8 Apr. 4/7 The barbers of Bethlehem, Pa., have raised the price of haircuts from sevenpence to tenpence. 1924 ROSE MACAULAY *Orphan Island* xviii. § 2. 241 They were interrupted by Mr. Albert Edward Smith, who had come for a shave and a hair-cut. 1897 *Westm. Gaz.* 16 Nov. 3/2 The writer being put on his mettle merely to throw in what an American has felicitously called "hair-raisers" by the way. 1900 *Daily News* 24 Apr. 7/5 The *hair-raising, long, steep descent of Box Hill. 1902 *Daily Chron.* 16 Sept. 3/4 Marvellous yarns of hair-raising perils. 1928 *Daily Express* 17 Aug. 9/1 There were a few hair-raising mishaps, but nobody was hurt. 1877 *Harper's Mag.* Dec. 109/2 *Hair Restorer. 1844 D. LEE & FROST *Ten Years in Oregon* xx. 224 One eye, which..a *hair seal had scratched out. 1903 FLEMMING *Pract. Tanning* 265 Grading and Classification of Green Calf-Skins...Second, regular No. 1...Scores are allowed in this grade, but there must be no holes, *hair slips or other bad imperfections. *Ibid.*, Third, good No. 2. This term designates those skins that are slightly *hair slipped.

Hair, *v.* Add: **4.** *trans.* To fit hairs to (a fiddle-bow).

1898 HAWEIS *Old Violins* 116 Most violinists prefer to pay a small sum and get their bows haired.

Hairily (hē·rili), *adv.* [f. HAIRY *a.* + -LY[2].] With hair or hairiness.

1925 G. W. DEEPING *Sorrell & Son* xxx, A lone, grim, anthropoid creature, hairily grotesque.

Hair-line. Add: **4.** = *hair-cord* (HAIR *sb.* 10).

1862 *Catal. Internat. Exhib., Brit.* II. No. 4104, Claret, drab, grey, and fancy hairlines.

5. *Typogr.* The thin stroke in a letter form (as distinguished from the stem and the serifs).

1896 T. L. DE VINNE in *Moxon's Mech. Exerc., Printing* 415 No defined width is made for the thin-stroke, which is now called the hair-line.

Hairpin. Add: **2.** A jocular word for: A person. *U.S. slang.*

1879 R. GRANT *Little Tin Gods* 8 That is the kind of hairpin that he is. 1910 W. M. RAINE *B. O'Connor* 214 Collins ain't that kind of a hairpin.

3. In full *hairpin bend*: a sharp bend in a road or course likened to a hairpin in form.

1923 *Motor Cycle* 13 Sept. 373/1 There is only one acute hair-pin bend, but there are several corners. *Ibid.* 374/1 A rather tricky and loose-surfaced left-hand hairpin was the principal feature of Chinnor Hill. 1930 SIR G. MACMUNN *Behind Scenes in many Wars* 235 It would be 230 miles by river round cursed hairpin bends.

Hair-trigger. Add: **b.** *attrib.* Also **Hair-triggered** *a.* (earlier U.S. examples).

1806 *The Balance* 7 Jan. (Th.), I know not whether hair-triggered pistols are in use in Penn. 1841 *Congress. Globe* 4 Aug. 499 App. (Th.) When the bill is reported some hair-trigger gentleman of your party will spring to the floor [and] move the previous question.

Hairy, *a.* Add:

1. d. *Hairy at (about, in) the heel (fetlocks)*: deficient in breeding or manners. So *hairy-heeled* adj., and simple *hairy*, in the same sense. *slang.* Cf. HAIR *sb.* 8 d.

1899 CONAN DOYLE *Duet*, *Rescue* 212, I couldn't stand that chap at any price. A bit too hairy in the fetlocks for my taste. 1905 H. A. VACHELL *The Hill* xii, The Rev. Septimus scowled also, because he had always maintained that any Harrovian could accept defeat like a gentleman...'I always said he was hairy at the heel.' 1906 *Macm. Mag.* Nov. 9, I would join you and cry *Viva Pio Nono!* with the hairiest. 1927 *Blackw. Mag.* Oct. 488/2 He took refuge in..the display..of an honest but slightly hairy heel. 1930 A. E. W. MASON *Dean's Elbow* xi, What would those people say..if they knew? Hairy-heeled, eh?

e. *Hairy ape*: one of a low mental or social type.

[1923 EUGENE O'NEILL (*title*) The Hairy Ape.] 1931 *Times Lit. Suppl.* 1 Oct. 750/3 The submerged tenth, the hairy apes of society.

f. Excited, angry, 'out of temper'.

1914 J. JOYCE *Dubliners, Two Gallants* 54 She doesn't know my name. I was too hairy to tell her that. 1927 W. E. COLLINSON *Contemp. Engl.* 116 He got shirty or hairy.

3. c. **hairy woodpecker** *U.S.*, a common woodpecker (*Picus auduboni* or *P. villosus*) of the eastern parts of North America.

1839 AUDUBON *Ornithol. Biog.* V. 164 The Hairy Woodpecker, *P[icus] villosus*, is a constant resident in our maritime and inland districts from the Texas..to the State of New Hampshire. 1872 COUES *Key N. Amer. Birds* 193. 1880 *Harper's Mag.* Oct. 672/2 *Picus auduboni* is not now recognized as a valid species, but only as a local variety of the hairy woodpecker.

B. *sb.* A heavy artillery draught horse, so called from its hairy fetlocks. *Army slang.*

1899 CONAN DOYLE *Duet*, *Rescue* 215 The hairies—trooper's chargers, you know. 1924 *Blackw. Mag.* Mar. 365/2 We had the bar placed as high as possible and put the old 'hairies' as hard at the jumps as they could travel. 1930 *Even. Standard* 15 Feb. 15/1 Whipping up the lumbering hairies to a desperate canter.

Haitian (hē·tiăn, hai·tiăn), *a.* Also 9 **Haytian.** [f. *Haiti* + -AN.] Of or belonging to the island of Haiti in the West Indies, or to the Republic of Haiti which occupies the western part of that island. Also as *sb.*, a native or inhabitant of Haiti.

1828 J. FRANKLIN *Pres. State Hayti* 6 The partial eulogists of the Haytians go to the length of asserting that they have arrived at a high degree of moral improvement. *Ibid.*, Instances of intelligence have been discovered in the Haytian citizen. 1863 *Chambers's Encycl.* V. 274/1 The inhabitants of the eastern or Spanish portion of Hayti, rising against their Haytian oppressors. 1880 *Encycl. Brit.* XI. 546/1 Haytian Republic.

Haka (hā·kā). *New Zealand.* [Maori.] A kind of dance. Also *haka dance.*

1845 E. J. WAKEFIELD *Adv. N. Z.* I. 98 A *haka* was now performed by about one hundred and fifty men and women. 1872 DOMETT *Ranolf* xv. vi. 19 The *haka*-dances where she shone supreme. 1907 *Macm. Mag.* Sept. 855 The Maoris are a people with grand manners, and the *haka* is an amusement wherewith they beguile for their guests the long dark evening hours.

Haker (hē·kəɹ). [f. HAKE *sb.*[1] + -ER[1].] A fisher or a fishing-boat engaged in catching hake.

1880 *Harper's Mag.* Sept. 498/1 Lying off it [*sc.* the Rock] at night, with only a solitary haker for a consort.

Hakka (hæ·kă). [Chinese (Canton dialect) *hā kà yen* stranger dwelling men.] One of a tribe or race of Chinese dwelling in parts of southern China, particularly in the province of Canton, descendants of immigrants from northern China in the middle ages; also, their dialect.

1879 *Encycl. Brit.* IX. 416/2 Hakkas from the vicinity of Swatow. 1921 *Outward Bound* July 17/1 He converses freely in Hakka, Cantonese, Mandarin [etc.]. 1926 *Blackw. Mag.* Nov. 628/1 The Hakkas, as woodcutters and hunters, had already penetrated into the foothills.

Halal (hălā·l), *v.* Also **hallal.** [f. Ar. حلال *halāl* lawful.] *trans.* To kill (meat) in the manner prescribed by the Mohammedan law. Hence **Halal** *sb.*, lawful food; also *attrib.* and *adj.*

1877 STERNDALE *Seonee* 454 Hālāl. Slaughtered according to religious law. 1879 POLLOK *Sport in Brit. Burmah* I. 142 My Mahouts, when they have got down to halal, or cut the throat of a stag, have had a narrow escape. *Ibid.* 179 The mahouts would not eat the stag as it had not been hallaled, so my Madrass servants and the Burmese had it all to themselves. 1883 E. H. AITKEN *Tribes on my Frontier* 167 To allow Peer Khan to make it halal, by cutting its throat in the name of Allah, and dividing the webs of its feet. 1895 *Daily News* 1 June 5/5 The special 'Halāl' meal, ordained for the I'd [*i.e.* I'd-uz-zuhā Festival] in question, will be provided. 1910 ROOSEVELT in *Scribner's Mag.* Apr. 404/1 Wherever possible the game being hal-lalled in orthodox fashion by the Mahometans.

Halch, *v.* Add: **3. b.** *Cotton-spinning*, etc. (see quots.). Also **halch-band.**

1892 NASMITH *Cotton Spinning* 286 As yarn is always wound off a cop by drawing it upwards,..any such condition of the cop nose results in a number of coils being drawn off simultaneously in an entangled condition. In this case the cop is said to be 'halched', and a good deal of waste is produced when the unwinding takes place. 1901 *N. & Q.* 9th Ser. VIII. 81/1 'Halsh'.—This word is in every-day use in various ways. So far as the cotton trade goes it refers to the band of coloured 'tie yarn' that encircles the 'knot', in addition to the ordinary tie yarn that holds each lea in the knot separately. This is called the 'halsh-band', and when the band is tied the knot is said to be 'halshed'...The 'halsh' is also—in the case of a necktie in the form of a bow, for example—that part in the centre that runs in a vertical or slightly oblique direction, embracing the whole bow... Saddlers also use the word, and possibly it is known in the woollen and worsted industries.

Haldanite (hǭ·ldenəit). *Eccl. Hist.* [f. the name *Haldane* + -ITE[1].] A follower of the brothers James Alexander and Robert Haldane, who in the early nineteenth century led an evangelical movement in Scotland.

1820 *Lonsdale Mag.* Oct. 443/2 Mr. Ewing and Mr. Wardlow separated from the Haldanite connection. *Ibid.*, The Haldanites were also now becoming more strict in their discipline.

Hale, *a.* **3.** Add: Often in phr. *hale and hearty.*

1860 *Leisure Hour* 174/1 As hale and as hearty..as ever. 1863 *Good Words* IV. 295/2 He..was hale and hearty though upwards of a hundred years old. 1899 *Captain* I. 124/2 Dr. Grace is close on fifty-one, hale and hearty. 1928 A. B. CALLOW *Food & Health* 7 In the past many people have been perfectly hale and hearty without having any clear ideas about the science of nutrition.

Half, *sb.* Add: **6. f.** *Golf.* A hole or point which is halved.

1908 BRAID *Advanced Golf* 213 Halves ought rarely to be agreed upon unless the balls are so close to the hole that it is next to impossible for the putts to be missed. 1931 *Daily Tel.* 22 May 18/1 He..secured the necessary 5 for the half and the match.

Half-. Add:

II. i. **half-blast** *Golf*, a shot which is played with half the force of a blast (BLAST *sb.* 8 c); **half-blue**, the 'colours' (see BLUE *sb.* 9) awarded to a player chosen to represent his university in inter-university contests as second choice to a 'full blue', or to any chosen representative in sports or games not recognized by the Blues Committee as sufficiently important for the award of a 'full blue'; also, a competitor who has gained this award; **half-brassy shot** *Golf*, a brassy shot played with a half swing; **half-captain**, in women's colleges in

Oxford, one who has attained a certain degree of proficiency in the management of a boat; so **half-captaincy**; **half-colour**, a badge showing that a stage of proficiency half-way towards getting one's colours has been reached (see *COLOUR *sb.* 6 c); **half-court** *Tennis* and *Rackets*, half the court divided by a line (the *half-court line*) parallel with the side lines; **half-fifteen, -forty** *Tennis* (see quot.); **half hit** *Cricket* (see quot. 1888); **half-iron shot** *Golf*, an iron shot played with a half swing; **half nelson** *Wrestling*, a hold in which one arm is thrust through the corresponding arm of the opponent and the hand placed on the back of his neck; also *fig.* in phr. *to get a half-nelson on*, to hold in a crippling position, gain a complete hold over; hence as *v. trans.* with the sense of this phr.; **half-one** *Golf* (see quot.); **half-pin** *Chess*, that position in which a defending man lies between an attacking man and the defended king and in the line of attack of the attacking piece, but has liberty to move backwards along the line of attack; also, that position in which two defending men lie between the attacking piece and the king so that if either moves the other piece becomes pinned; so **half-pinned** *a.*; **half-pinner**, a half-pin problem; **half-shot** *Golf*, a stroke made with half a swing, intended to carry less far than the full shot; **half-stroke** *Golf* = *half-one*; **half-swing** *Golf*, a swing of half the usual amount of distance; **half-thirty** *Tennis* (see quot. s.v. *half-fifteen*); **half-topped shot** *Golf*, a shot which is partly topped; **half-volley** (*b*) *Lawn Tennis*, a stroke made when the ball has just left the ground; so *half-volleyer.*

1928 *Weekly Dispatch* 24 June 21/6 He played a superb "half-blast" out of a trap to lay the ball one foot from the cup. 1908 *Westm. Gaz.* 29 July 10/4 The *half-blue for billiards. 1909 *Ibid.* 26 Feb. 12/2 For some time players of lacrosse at Oxford have been urging the Blues Committee to grant them the Half-Blue. 1903 *Ibid.* 28 Aug. 3/1 The *half-brassy shot approach. 1928 *Daily Express* 7 May 5/2 She may not go on the river unless she is accompanied by a *half-captain or is one herself. *Half-captaincies may be had either in rowing, canoeing, or punting. 1929 *Evening News* 18 Nov. 13/5 The player who appears in future bowls international trial matches, but who fails to be selected for the English team, is to receive a '*half colour'. 1888 *Encycl. Brit.* XXIII. 182/2 A space bounded by the net, the side line, the *half-court line, and the service line. 1895 H. W. W. WILBERFORCE *Lawn Tennis* 62 The half-court-line dividing the space on each side of the net into two equal parts, called the right and left courts. 1898 *Encycl. Sport* II. 462/2 The half court nearest the dedans is called the 'service side'. *Ibid.*, The half-court line..dividing the court lengthways into practically two equal parts. 1888 *Encycl. Brit.* XXIII. 182/2 *Half-fifteen is one stroke given at the beginning of the second and every subsequent alternate game of a set... *Half-thirty is one stroke given at the beginning of the first game, two strokes at the beginning of the second game; and so on, alternately, in all the subsequent games of a set... *Half-forty is two strokes given at the beginning of the first game, three strokes at the beginning of the second game; and so on, alternately, in all the subsequent games of a set. 1888 A. G. STEEL in *Cricket* (Badm. Libr.) iii. 112 Extra cover-point..may be..placed for *half-hits wide on the on—i.e. about half the distance from the batsman that a deep field would stand. 1928 P. TREVOR in *Daily Tel.* 17 July 17/5 Freeman..had two half-hit fieldsmen. 1895 H. G. HUTCHINSON *Golf* (Badm. Libr.) iv. (ed. 5) 143 The attitude..for the *half-iron stroke. 1905 *Westm. Gaz.* 10 Nov. 4/2 The half-iron shot..cannot be played properly unless turf is taken. 1889 W. ARMSTRONG *Wrestling* (Badm. Libr.) 230 *Half Nelson, Lancashire. 1896 G. ADE *Artie* xvii. 154 This thing got the half-Nelson on me before I know it. 1898 *Encycl. Sport* II. 548/2 The half Nelson and heave. 1901 *Black & White Budget* 30 Nov. 315/1 The half-nelson...You grasp your opponent by the right wrist with your left hand, thrust your right hand quickly under his arm at the same time seizing his neck and pressing his head forward. 1903 P. LONGHURST *Wrestling* 77 The arm that has the half-nelson hold. 1912 *Daily Chron.* 6 Mar., And Radicals in sunshine bask with Delight to see the clever Asquith *Half-Nelson Bonar Law. 1897 *Encycl. Sport* I. 472/2 **Half-one*, a handicap of one stroke at every second hole. 1922 G. HUME & A. C. WHITE *Good Companion Two-Mover* 245 The term "*half-pin" arose in 1915, in correspondence between Comins Mansfield and Murray Marble anent No. 122 D, a surprising example, with six half-pins...Greenwood, the composer of this problem, had published a complete *half-pinner in 1859. 1926 H. WEENINK *Chess Problem* 71 By a Half-pin is understood an arrangement where two Black pieces stand in line in such a way that if either one moves the other becomes pinned by a White piece which has been standing behind both of them waiting to exert its pinning powers. 1928 *Observer* 24 June 25 These three variations are highly complex, the first two illustrating the unpin of the White Q by *half-pinned Black Kt's; the third is a half-pin line combined with Black interference. 1891 H. G. HUTCHINSON *Golf* 26 The principle of the cutting stroke, on the other hand, lies in bringing the head of the iron across that line. It may be applied to a full shot, *half shot, quarter shot, or shortest wrist shot. 1893 — *Golfing* 42 When the distance is less than that for which the three-quarter stroke is used, it is commonly called a half-shot distance. 1897 *Encycl. Sport* I. 461 A *half-stroke or over, both in singles and foursomes, shall count as one. 1891 H. G. HUTCHINSON *Golf* 30 Take pains in all *half-swing shots to bring the club-head well and slowly away from the ball before striking. 1905 *Westm. Gaz.* 23 Aug. 3/1 A lucky *half-topped shot. 1897 *Encycl. Sport* I. 621/2 **Half-volley*, a stroke made the moment the ball leaves the ground. 1912 *Daily News* 11 July 2 A famous *half-volleyer.

n. **half-centre** (see quot.); **half-commission** *attrib.*, working for or based on half commission; **half-compression** *attrib.*, designating a device for lessening the compression of the explosive mixture in an internal-combustion engine; **half-duck** = HALF-BIRD; **half-foot** (see quot.); **half-hose** (see HOSE *sb.* 1 a γ); **half-lattice girder**, one consisting of a single system or row of triangles; **half-lichen**, an ascomycete attaching itself parasitically to an alga and thus simulating a lichenoid association; **half-period** (see quots.); **half-plate** *Photog.* (see PLATE *sb.* 5 c), also *attrib.*; **half-ripper, half-rip saw**, a finer-toothed ripping saw (see RIPPER 2, RIP-SAW *sb.*); **half-sibling**, one of two or more colts having the same father but different mothers; **half-speed shaft**, the cam shaft of a four-stroke cycle internal-combustion engine, which rotates at half the speed of the crank shaft; **half-term**, a period approximately half-way through a school or other term, often made the occasion of a holiday; often *attrib.* as in *half-term holiday*; **half-turning bolt** (see quot.); **half uncial**, writing which combines the characters of uncial and cursive; semi-uncial; also *attrib.*; **half wave**, one-half of a complete wave of electricity, light, or sound; chiefly *attrib.*

1888 *Lockwood's Dict. Mech. Engin.*, *Half-centre*, *half-centre is sometimes used to denote the position of the crank-pin of an engine when midway between the two dead centres or dead points. 1909 *Westm. Gaz.* 16 Feb. 7/4 He became a *half-commission man with a firm of stockbrokers. 1927 *Sunday Express* 13 Mar. 2 A half-commission stockbroker. 1932 *Times* 16 Mar. 18/1 The Half Commission Practice. 1901 *Motor-Car World* II. 317/1 To facilitate starting the engine a *half-compression device is fitted which operates on the exhaust valve through the medium of a second or subsidiary cam attached to the main cam working the exhaust. 1907 *Westm. Gaz.* 11 Nov. 7/2 The simple half-compression gear. 1893 W. J. GORDON *Our Country's Birds* 10 Local and Popular Names...*Half Duck. 1903 *MS. in Red Box* 329 Good sport among the half-duck and mussel-duck which abounded at Tudworth. 1880 SKENE *Celtic Scot.* III. 370 A kind of tenancy called *half-foot, where the possessor of the farm furnished the land and seed corn,..the produce being divided. 1875 KNIGHT *Dict. Mech.*, **Half-lattice Girder*, a form of girder..consisting of horizontal upper and lower bars, and a series of diagonal bars, sloping alternately in opposite directions, and dividing the space between the bars into a series of triangles. 1902 D. H. CAMPBELL *Text-bk. Bot.* 188 *Sphæria lemaneæ* and *Thermutis velutina* are examples of the *Half-lichens. 1904 *Technol. & Sci. Dict.* (ed. Goodchild & Tweney) s.v., The area included in this curve is the first *half period element. *Ibid.*, The effect of the whole wave can be expressed in terms of these half period components. 1925 J. JOLY *Surface-Hist. Earth* Glossary 191 *Half Period*, a term used in the science of radioactivity to denote the period required for one half of the present amount of a substance to be radioactively transformed. 1877 *Design & Work* III. 451/1 *Half-plate portrait lens. 1892 *Photogr. Ann.* II. 58 On your slide you require to get all the view on the half-plate negative. 1903 A. WATKINS *Watkins Man.* 13 Half-plate is the favourite amateur size. 1841 *Penny Cycl.* XX. 476/2 The ripping-saw, *half-ripper, hand-saw..are saws for the use of one person. 1846, 1875 *half-rip saw [see RIP-SAW *sb.*]. 1903 *Biometrika* Nov. 391 The high values, however, found for *half-siblings in the case of the thoroughbreds. 1902 A. C. HARMSWORTH *Motors & Motor-Driving* viii. 152 A crank, operated by a connecting rod from the *half-speed shaft on the engine. 1905 *Technol. & Sci. Dict.* (ed. Goodchild & Tweney) s.v. *Motor Cycles*, The half speed shaft, rotating at one half the speed of the crank shaft. 1888 *Boy's Own Paper* Summer No. 16/2 At *half-term it was Hoskyn's custom to write letters to all the parents with reports of their sons' progress. 1875 KNIGHT *Dict. Mech.*, **Half-turning Bolt*, one with a thread occupying one half of its cylindrical surface. 1885 *Encycl. Brit.* XVIII. 153/2 Examples of *half-uncial writing. 1904 *Technol. & Sci. Dict.* (ed. Goodchild & Tweney), **Half Wave Plate*, a plate of doubly refracting crystal, capable of splitting up a plane polarised ray into two portions, one of which is retarded half a wave length with respect to the other. 1928 *Morning Post* 6 Feb. 3/4 A half wave rectifier.

Half-baked, *a.* **2.** (Earlier U.S. examples.)

1842 CAROLINE M. KIRKLAND *Forest Life* I. 41 It is sometimes a term of reproach with us, in speaking of a silly fellow, that he is not half-baked. 1848 *Congress. Globe* 264 (Th.) Perhaps some of that majority are but half-baked Democrats.

Half-binding. (Earlier U.S. example.)

1821 WEEMS *Letters* III. 325 [Books] in neat half binding, red backs, and corners.

Half-blood. Add: **4.** *attrib.* Half-blooded.

1837 H. COLMAN *Rep. Agric. Mass.* (1838) 52, I have slaughtered two half-blood heifers, which have weighed at four years old over 700 lbs. 1873 J. H. BEADLE *Undevel. West* xxi. 406 A handsome half-blood daughter married to a white man.

Half-breed. 4. *attrib.* Add: **b.** *U.S.* Occupied by or belonging to half-breed Indians.

1855 in S. A. DOUGLAS *Senate Rep.* 12 Mar. (1856) 18 Your purchase of Kansas half-breed lands.

Half-cock, *sb.* Add: **3.** *attrib.* **half-cock stroke** *Cricket*, a stroke begun as a forward stroke but checked half-way, the ball being allowed to hit the bat.

1897 RANJITSINHJI *Jubilee Bk. Cricket* 159 It is best to play a half-cock stroke, which means that the bat is merely held almost stationary somewhere between a back- and a forward-stroke rather over the popping-crease, and the ball

is allowed to hit it. 1909 *Westm. Gaz.* 17 Apr. 16/2 He may occasionally use a half-cock stroke with the left leg well up to the bat.

Half-cocked, *pa. pple.* [See HALF-COCK *sb.* and *v.*] **a.** Of a gun: At half-cock. **b.** *To go off half-cocked*: to speak or act prematurely. *U.S.* **c.** *slang.* Partly intoxicated.

a. 1809 W. IRVING *Knickerb.* IV. ii. (1849) 206 The burghers gazed..as a wary housewife does at a gun, fearful it may go off half-cocked. 1833 [see HALF-COCK *v.*]. b. 1833 *Debates Congr.* 31 Jan. 1521 The gentleman from Maryland has gone off half cocked. 1877 HABBERTON *Jericho Road* xvi. 152 Just like you, always goin' off half-cocked. c. 1830 T. WILSON *Pitman's Pay* (1843) 54 Half-cock'd and canty, hyem we gat. 1886 in *Engl. Dial. Dict.* (Hampshire, Northumb.). 1888 [see COCKED *ppl. a.*].

Half-eagle. *U.S.* (Examples.)

1786 in *Amer. Museum* (1789) II. 182/2 There shall be two gold coins; one..equal to five dollars, to be stamped in like manner [to the eagle], and to be called a half-eagle. 1841 *Congress. Globe* 30 July 269/2 It was an open declaration of war upon the half eagles, the gold currency...This gold, in half eagles, was too good for us. 1852 *Knickerb. Mag.* XL. 323 He was about to contribute a half eagle to the funds.

Ha·lf-ha·rdy, *a.* (See HALF- 1 b and HARDY *a.* 4 b.) Also as *sb.*

1824 LOUDON *Encycl. Gard.* 881 Half-hardy annual border-flowers. 1867 *Field* 4 May 342/1 Half Hardy Annuals. 1898 *Westm. Gaz.* 13 July 3/2 A very full list of plants, hardy and half-hardy. 1904 *Ibid.* 6 May 10/1 The fuchsias, the heliotrope, the geraniums..are half-hardies.

Half horse. *attrib.* *U.S.* [HALF *adv.* 2.] Used in the phr. *half horse and half alligator* (see quots.).

[1809 W. IRVING *Knickerb.* IV. ii. (1820) 360 The backwood-men of Kentucky are styled half man, half horse, and half alligator, by the settlers on the Mississippi.] 1820 J. HALL *Lett. fr. West* (1828) 47 Eight or ten of those 'half-horse and half-alligator' gentry, commonly called Ohio boatmen. 1847 T. B. THORPE *Big Bear of Arkansas* 14 The half horse and half alligator species of men, who are peculiar to 'Old Mississippi'. 1860 *Oregon Argus* 13 Oct. (Th.) These half horse and half alligator sort of politicians are becoming a stench in the nostrils of the American people.

Half joe. *U.S.* [f. HALF II. a + JOE[1].] A Portuguese gold coin, worth 3,200 reis, formerly current in the United States. (Cf. *Half Johannes*, s.v. JOHANNES.)

1777 [see HALF- II. a]. 1782 J. THATCHER *Military Jrnl.* 524 The Baron..divided his purse with me, the whole contents of which were two half joes. 1790 *Massachusetts Spy* 7 Oct., Instead of half-joes or guineas, I have brought some quadrangular stones back with me. 1809 in Horry *Life Marion* (1833) 29 He offered..a half joe a-piece for Marion and me to let the recruits go.

Half-leg. *U.S.* Half the height of a man's leg. In phr. *half-leg deep, high.*

1825 J. NEAL *Bro. Jonathan* I. 112 Natty, makin' his way, through the bushes, half-leg deep. 1829–32 J. P. KENNEDY *Swallow Barn* II. i. 13 The snow was lying about half-leg deep. 1852 *Florida Plant. Rec.* 65, I have a little corn half leg high. 1855 *Ibid.* 133 The spring branch newground [is] knee high, spring branch cut half leg.

Half-mile. *attrib.* [f. HALF- II. a.] Extending to, comprising or covering, half a mile.

1799 *Steele Papers* I. 176 The Purse is one hundred and fifty Dollars the first day 3 ½-mile heats.

Halfpenny. Add: **2.** *Not a halfpenny the worse*; *a bad halfpenny.* (Cf. PENNY *sb.*)

1603 HARSNET *Declar. Egreg. Popish Impostures* 17 Sylvester, Bonifacius, and some other Popes, haue beene errand deuill-coniurers, and yet theyr holinesse not a halfe-peny the worse. 1819 J. H. VAUX *Mem.* II. 154 When a man has been upon any errand, or attempting any object which has proved unsuccessful or impracticable, he will say on his return, It's a bad halfpenny; meaning he has returned as he went. 1850 HAWTHORNE *Scarlet L.* Introd. 22 It was not the first time, nor the second, that I had gone away—as it seemed, permanently—but yet returned, like the bad halfpenny.

3. b. A form of ear-mark on cattle and horses. *U.S.*

Cf. *halfpenny slit*, 'an ear-mark given to pigs or sheep' (*E.D.D.*).

1666 *Portsmouth* (R.I.) *Rec.* 266 A halfpeny from the route [of the ear]. 1667 *Ibid.* 269 A halfpeney out of the right ear. 1702 *Topsfield Rec.* 124 A..horse..[with] a half penny cut out of the right Ear. 1845 *Portsmouth* (R.I.) *Rec.* 387 The Ear Mark of the Creatures of David Baker is two half pennys before the near or left ear.

4. b. (Later U.S. example.)

1908 MENCKEN *Philos. Nietzsche* 284 Reich..has attained the ha penny celebrity he seems to crave in much the same manner.

Half-round, *sb.* Add: **c.** Half the circuit of the course of a game.

1865 MAYNE REID *Croquet* (ed. 2) vi. 72 The turning stake can only be tolled, by a ball that has completed the half-round.

d. A tool having a flat and a rounded side.

1872 *Rep. Vermont Board Agric.* 651 With the aid of half rounds and wedges, the blocks [of granite] are separated from the tables or sheets. 1875 KNIGHT *Dict. Mech.* 1050/1 Files with the larger curvature are known as *full* half-rounds; others as *flat* half-rounds.

Half-shaved, *a.* Drunk. *U.S. slang.*

1818 WEEMS *Letters* III. 225 One night, getting half shaved, he was easily over-persuaded (a common curse of whiskey) to try his luck at All Fours. 1846–52 MRS. WHITCHER *Widow Bedott P.* xxviii. 354 I've seen that man half shaved on cider afore breakfast in the mornin'.

Half shot, *a.* *U.S. colloq.* [f. HALF- 1: see SHOOT *v.* 32 d.] Half drunk.

1837 NEAL *Charcoal Sk.* (1838) 13 Moseying is only to be done when a genman's half shot. 1841 *Southern Lit. Messenger* VII. 763/1 He was already about half shot.

Half-sole, *v.* [See HALF- II. n.] *trans.* To furnish with new half-soles.

1844 in C. Cist *Cincinnati Misc.* 54 My boots..have been twice half-soled, and the uppers wont stand it any longer. *c* 1870 'MARK TWAIN' *Sketches* (1872) 159 Part of the works [of my watch] needed half-soling. 1911 H. S. HARRISON *Queed* xxi. 267 If you're ever in Petersburg and want any half-soling done.

Half-time. Add:

1. d. (See quot., also 3 below.)

1904 A. B. F. YOUNG *Complete Motorist* iv. 118 All six valves are interchangeable and mechanically operated by rods worked from a cam shaft which is geared at half-time from the crank-axle.

3. **half-time shaft** = *half-speed shaft* (see *HALF- II. n).

1904 A. B. F. YOUNG *Complete Motorist* iii. 49 The projecting part of a cam fixed on the half-time shaft. 1908 *Westm. Gaz.* 15 Oct. 4/2 The lubrication of the engine is carried out by a Dubrulle mechanical lubricator, fitted on the dash-board, and operated by an eccentric on the half-time shaft.

Halide (hæ·ləid). *Chem.* [f. HAL(OGEN + -IDE.] = HALOID *sb.*

1927 N. V. SIDGWICK *Electronic Theory Valency* vi. 88 The halides of the elements show a similar differentiation into volatile non-salts and non-volatile salts.

Halifax (hæ·lifæks). [The name of a town in the West Riding of Yorkshire.] *Go to Halifax*: see GO *v.* 30 b. (Now regarded as a euphemism for *hell*.)

In U.S., sometimes with supposed allusion to Halifax, Nova Scotia.

1669 [see GO *v.* 30 b]. 1807 *Deb. Congress* (1852) 11 Dec. 1169 Instead of sending it [*sc.* a ship] where he wished it had gone, to Halifax, or to the bottom. 1875- in *Engl. Dial. Dict.* s.v. 1876 GARFIELD in *Congress. Rec.* 4 Aug. 5185/1 'Go to Halifax' was a substitute for a more impious, but not more opprobrious expression. 1882 *Ibid.* 13 July 6015/1 He told them..that he had no further use for them, and they could go home, ashore, or to Halifax.

b. *Halifax gibbet*: see GIBBET *sb.*[1] 1 c.

Haliotis. Add: Also *attrib.*

1845 E. J. WAKEFIELD *Adv. N. Zealand* I. 241 These hooks..take their name from the *haliotus* [sic]-shell, with pieces of which they are lined. 1931 *Oxf. Univ. Gaz.* 17 June 715/2 Toe-bone with carved face and *haliotis* eyes.

Halitosis (hælitōᵘ·sis). *Med.* [mod.L., f. L. *halitus* breath + -OSIS.] An abnormally odorous condition of the breath; foul breath.

1885 *Buck's Handbk. Med. Sci.* I. 695/2 Toxic halitosis. 1928 A. P. HERBERT in *Punch* 17 Oct. 427/1, I shall become a mere mass of degenerate tissues, and flaccid muscles,..with probably a touch of halitosis and lethargy.

Hall, *sb.* **13.** Add: **hall-bedroom** *U.S.*, a small bedroom opening on to the hall of a house; **hall-bed roomer** *U.S.*, one who sleeps in this; **hall-boy**, a call-boy in the hall of an hotel or the like; **hall-man** (example); **hall-room** *U.S.*, a room at the end of and of the width of a hall; also *v. intr.*, to live in such a room.

1893 KATE D. WIGGIN *Polly Oliver* vii. (1894) 76 Run down and ask Mrs. Howe if she will let us have her *hall-bedroom to-night. 1909 *Chambers's Jrnl.* 386/1 Appreciating the difficulty of making a studio out of a hall-bedroom. 1899 J. L. WILLIAMS *Stolen Story* etc. 230 Like many an other lonely *hall-bed roomer. 1912 L. J. VANCE *Destroying Angel* xx, The *hall-boys said you were busy on the telephone. 1919 T. K. HOLMES *Man fr. Tall Timber* i. 3 'Shucks! why didnt you say H. Harvey Stafford?' interrupted the *hall-man. 1886 S. W. MITCHELL *R. Blake* v. (1895) 39 Miss Darnell had for her own use a like space on the third floor, leaving to Miss Wynne a bed-chamber.. known as a *hall-room. 1906 'O. HENRY' *Four Million* xiv. (1916) 139 The restaurant was next door to the old red brick in which she *hall-roomed. *Ibid.* 140 Schulenberg was to send three meals per diem to Sarah's hall-room.

Hallal, variant of *HALAL.

Hallali (hæ·ləli). A bugle call. Also *fig.*

1885 G. MEREDITH *Diana of Crossways* xvii, He knew enough to blow his huntsman's horn...His hallali rang high. 1898 — *Forest History* xix, Right loud the bugle's hallali elate Rang forth. 1920 *Q. Rev.* July 13 The hallali was sounded in a famous letter to Lord Grey de Wilton, the candidate for Bath, in which Disraeli accused the Ministers of having for five years harassed every trade.

Hallful (hǭ·lful). [f. HALL *sb.* + -FUL.] As many or as much as will fill a hall.

1905 *Daily Chron.* 17 Feb. 3/6 The entertainment of a whole hallful of poor children. 1909 *Westm. Gaz.* 26 Sept. 6/3 What a hallful it was that received him with ringing, rousing, rollicking cheers!

Halling (hæ·liŋ). [Norw., ? from *Hallingdal*.] A Norwegian country-dance in triple rhythm; also, the music for such a dance.

1883 *Grove's Dict. Mus.* III. 609/1. 1924 *Glasgow Herald* 31 May 4 We have no space here to describe the wonderful Halling dance.

Hallstatt (ha·lʃtat). The name of a village in Upper Austria, the site of an ancient necropolis, where rich archæological finds have been made, used *attrib.* to denote a period of transition from bronze to iron, and the type of civilization of that period. So **Hallsta·ttian** *a.*

1900 DENIKER *Races of Man* 315 The so-called 'Hallstattian' period lasted in Central Europe, France, and Northern Italy from the tenth or ninth to the sixth century B.C. The Hallstattian civilisation flourished chiefly in Carinthia, Southern Germany, Switzerland, Bohemia, Silesia, Bosnia, the south-east of France, and Southern Italy. 1905 *Brit. Mus. Guide Antiq. Early Iron Age* 36 The drum-shaped brooch..is also not uncommon in the Hallstatt period. *Ibid.* 39 The Hallstatt stage of culture is well represented at Glasinatz. 1931 *Times Lit. Suppl.* 1 Oct. 753/3 Scanty traces of Hallstatt immigrants.

Hallucinosis (hælūsinōᵘ·sis). *Path.* [f. HALLUCIN(ATION + -OSIS.] The condition of being subject to hallucinations.

1908 *Practitioner* Jan. 9 The acute hallucinosis and paranoidal forms of alcoholic insanity.

Halo- (hælo), combining form of Gr. ἅλς, ἁλός sea, as in **Ha:lobio·tic** *a.*, living in the sea. **Halo·li·mnic** *a.* *Biol.*, living in fresh water but having an affinity with salt water forms. **Ha·lophyte** *Bot.*, a plant which grows in soil impregnated with salt, as on the seashore or in the sea; so **Halophy·tic** *a.*, (*a*) having the character of a halophyte; (*b*) adapted to the growth of halophytes. **Halopla·nkton**, marine plankton.

1927 R. S. LULL *Org. Evol.* v. 70 *Halobiotic or Marine Realm. 1898 J. E. S. MOORE in *Internat. Yr. Bk.* 270 (Cent. D. Suppl.) What we may call *halolimnic organisms. 1898 *Nature* 17 Mar. 476/2 The Halolimnic fauna of Tanganyika. 1904 *Westm. Gaz.* 26 May 5/2 The shells of the halolimnic gasteropods. 1895 OLIVER tr. *Kerner's Nat. Hist. Plants* I. 74 Plants which only flourish abundantly on soils rich in alkaline salts are called *halophytes. The same name has also been applied to plants which only thrive in sea-water. 1903 tr. *Schimper's Plant Geog.* 90 Halophytes can thrive on ordinary soil..without any addition of common salt. 1909 tr. *Warming's Oecol. Plants* 219 A halophyte..is one form of xerophyte. 1895 G. HENSLOW *Plant Struct.* 83 *Halophytic plants, and others yielding ethereal oils. 1909 tr. *Warming's Oecol. Plants* 160 The plankton of salt water may be subdivided into neritic and oceanic *haloplankton. 1927 R. S. LULL *Org. Evol.* iii. 43 Marine or halo-plankton.

Halonate (hæ·lonět), *a.* *Bot.* [f. mod.L. *halōn-*, HALO + -ATE[2].] Surrounded by an outer circle.

1911 CROMBIE & SMITH *Brit. Lichens* II. 359. 1921 ANNIE L. SMITH *Handbk. Brit. Lichens* 102 Spores ellipsoid or oblong..usually with a hyaline mucilaginous epispore (halonate).

Halt, *sb.*[1] Add: **b.** A small railway station without the ordinary accommodation or staff, at which a local train stops.

1910 *Offic. Guide L.N.W.R.* (ed. 15) 410 Rail motor car halts at Wendlebury, Charlton, and Oddington. 1914 *Railway Mag.* Aug. 152/2 The provision of the 'halts' on the new line has been much appreciated locally. 1921 *Dict. Occup. Terms* (1927) § 706 *Halt attendant*; a porter who attends at roadside halt, where there is no proper station staff. [1927 CONAN DOYLE *Case Bk. S. Holmes* 285 Little 'halt-on-demand' station of Shoscombe.]

Halter, *sb.*[1] **3.** **halter-break** *v.* *U.S.* (earlier examples).

1860 HOLLAND *Miss Gilbert's Career* xix. 350 You want to halter-break 'em when they're little and get 'em kind o' wonted to the feel of the harness. 1867 *Rep. Iowa Agric. Soc.* (1868) 117 My colts are halter-broken as soon as foaled.

Halteridium (hælterĭ·diŏm). *Zool.* [mod.L. (Labbé, 1894), f. Gr. ἁλτήρ weight used in leaping.] A protozoon of the genus of this name, parasitic in the red blood corpuscles of birds.

1901 G. M. STERNBERG in *Pop. Sci. Monthly* Feb. 367 (Cent. D. Suppl.) The mosquito..could not transmit the malarial parasite of man or another similar parasite of birds (*halteridium*). 1901 *Practitioner* Mar. 278 One of the malaria-like organisms of birds, namely, halteridium.

Haluka: see *KHALUKAH.

Halutzim (hălū·tsim). Also **haluzim.** [Heb.] Jewish pioneers entering Palestine in order to build up their future national home.

1921 *Daily Mail* 11 Apr. 6/5 The 'Haluzim' are the Jewish pioneers who are flocking into Palestine to help in building up the Jewish National Home. 1933 W. P. LIVINGSTONE *Galilee Doctor* 261 The halutzim, or 'pioneers'.

Ham, *sb.*[1] **3.** Add: *ham-curing, -sandwich*; **ham-fisted** *a.*, having large or clumsy hands; **ham loaf** orig. *U.S.*, a shaped mass of chopped cooked ham intended to be cut into slices.

1907 *Daily Chron.* 23 Oct. 4/4 Spinning, or bread-baking, or *ham-curing. 1928 *Daily Mail* 7 May 6/4 *Ham Fisted.—Applied to pilots who are heavy on controls, or generally clumsy. 1928 *Sunday Express* 24 June 8/3 Two thousand lumber-jacks were in town, ham-fisted great fellows with hair on their chests and pine needles growing out of their ears. 1902 *Encycl. Brit.* XXVI. 558/2 Hamburger steak with onions, veal loaf, *ham loaf, beef loaf. 1907 *Daily Chron.* 23 Sept. 7/5 Veal loaf, ham loaf, beef loaf. 1872 'L. CARROLL' *Through the Looking-glass* vii, I fed him with—with—with *Ham-sandwiches and Hay. 1880 RUSKIN *Fathers have told us* I. *Bible of Amiens* i, If he has bought his ham-sandwich, and is ready for the 'En voiture, messieurs'.

Hamamelis (hæmămī·lis). *Bot.* [mod.L., a. Gr. ἀμαμηλίς medlar.] A shrub of the genus so named, of which the North American species (*H. virginica*) is the witch hazel; also, the proprietary name for a medicinal extract of the leaves and bark of this shrub. So **Hamame·lin** (see quot.).

1890 BILLINGS *Med. Dict.*, *Hamamelin*, name given to a dry powdered extract of hamamelis. 1898 *Rev. Brit. Pharm.* 10 Fresh hamamelis-leaves are macerated in a little more than double their volume of water and alcohol. 1910

Practitioner Jan. 72 The addition of half a drachm of tincture of hamamelis. *Ibid.* June 783 *Hydrastis and Hamamelis.*—These two drugs are sometimes useful adjuncts to the action of ergot. 1911 J. U. LLOYD in *Bulletin Lloyd Libr.* No. 18 (Pharmacy ser. no. 4) 47 The preparation known as distilled hamamelis, or distilled extract of hamamelis, introduced by Pond about the middle of the nineteenth century. 1927 E. H. M. COX *Evol. Garden* xiii. 250 The Hamamelis or Witch Hazels.

Haman (hē·mæn). The name of the chief minister of Ahasuerus who was hanged on the gallows prepared for Mordecai, as related in the Book of Esther, used allusively (phr. *to hang as high as Haman*). So **Hama·nic** *a.*

1644 R. BROWN *Ld. Digbies Designe to betray Abingdon* 7 When their blinded Party shall..see him in his colours, they will at last pity..a Prince that makes use of such a wicked head..: And..may know who is that Haman which blasts Mordecai's petition. 1647 *Mercurius Melanchol.* No. 3. 13 What is honour, but another Haman? This day a companion with a King, on the morrow hanging on the gallowes. 1650 J. TRAPP *Comm. O. T.* Isa. lxi. 2 All Hamans be hanged up at that feast-royal, at the last day especially. 1816 SCOTT *Old Mort.* xxvii, The whig Captain Balfour..swore..that if the garrison was not gi'en ower the morn by daybreak, he would hing up the young lord, poor thing, as high as Haman. 1842 BARHAM *Ingol. Leg.* Ser. II. *Merch. Venice*, I'll hang you, like Haman! 1881 H. ADLER in *19th Cent.* Dec. 813 Prof. Goldwin Smith renews his onslaughts upon Jews and Judaism with an acerbity and virulence which I may be permitted to term Hamanic.

Hamarthritis (hæmaɹþrai·tis). *Path.* [mod. L., a. Gr. ἁμαρθρῖτις.] Gout in all the joints.

1848 DUNGLISON *Med. Lex.* (ed. 7).

Hamartite (hæ·măɹtəit). *Min.* [f. Gr. ἁμαρτία failure, error + -ITE[1].] = *BASTNÄSITE.

1872 DANA *Min.* (ed. 5) App. I. 2.

Hamathionic (hæ·măþəi,ǫ·nik), *a.* *Chem.* [f. Gr. ἅμα together + THIONIC.] Denoting an acid formed by the action of sulphuric acid on euxanthic acid.

1864 WATTS *Dict. Chem.*, Hamathionic acid, $C^{14}H^{16}SO^{15}$.

Hamathite (hē·măþəit). [f. Heb. *Khamāth* Hamath + -ITE[1].] An inhabitant of the ancient Syrian city of Hamath. Also *attrib.*

1611 *Bible* Gen. x. 18 The Arvadite, the Zemarite, and the Hamathite. 1880 *Encycl. Brit.* XII. 26/1 Professor Sayce's view that the Hittites were the authors of the Hamathite hieroglyphics. 1924 D. G. HOGARTH *Kings of Hittites* Introd. (1926) 2 Hamathite territory is..the nearest to Galilee in which any sure evidence of occupation by Hittite civilization..has yet appeared.

Hambergite (hæ·mbəɹgəit). *Min.* [Named (*Hambergit*) after A. *Hamberg*, who discovered it: see -ITE[1].] Hydrous borate of glucinum, occurring in greyish-white orthorhombic crystals.

1890 *Jrnl. Chem. Soc.* LVIII. II. 1078 Hambergite, discovered by A. Hamberg in 1889, and named after him by the author. 1902 H. A. MIERS *Min.* 540 Hambergite.. $Be_2(OH)BO_3$.

Hamburger (hæ·mbɜɹgəɹ). [Ger., f. town-name *Hamburg* + *-er*, ending of toponymic adjs.] *Hamburger steak* = Hamburg steak (see STEAK 2 c). Also, a kind of sausage.

1902 *Encycl. Brit.* XXVI. 558/2 Hamburger steak with onions. 1908 'YESLAH' *Tenderfoot S. Calif.* xiv. 118 Out of date eggs, last year's hamburger and over ripe limburger. 1920 *Chambers's Jrnl.* 348/2 Hamburger steaks and German pot roasts. 1929 E. HEMINGWAY *Farewell to Arms* xv, They had the look of not too freshly ground hamburger steak.

Hame[2]. **b.** Add: *hame-rein.*

1902 *Daily Chron.* 9 July 3/6 Why a tight hame rein should be used on so many builders' and other carts is..a puzzle. 1908 *N. & Q.* 10th Ser. X. 106 At the foot of a hill leading from Blackrock, near Brighton, to Rottingdean is a board with the inscription: 'Please slacken hame-rein on going uphill'.

Hamel (hæ·məl). *S. Afr.* [Du.] A wether.

1871 H. H. DUGMORE *Remin. Albany Settler* 13, 14 (Pettman) A dozen of startled hamels, just separated from a large flock, would be likely to try a driver's legs, and lungs too, in crossing it. 1895 SCULLY *Kafir Stories* 28 Would your father have let me die rather than take a hamel from the flock of a rich, lazy boer, who never counts his sheep?

Hamidian (hæmi·diăn), *a.* [f. the name of Abdul *Hamid* II + -IAN.] Pertaining to or resembling the rule of Abdul Hamid, Sultan of Turkey from 1876–. Hence **Hami·dianism.**

1908 *Westm. Gaz.* 1 Aug. 2/3 Thirty years of wandering in the Hamidian wilderness. 1908 *Daily Chron.* 24 Oct. 4/4 The Hamidian rule. *Ibid.* 18 Dec. 4/4 A reversion to Hamidianism. 1930 *Times Lit. Suppl.* 4 Dec. 1047/3 His spy-system appears to have been Hamidian in its extent and efficiency.

Hamidieh (hæmi·diė). [f. the name of Abdul *Hamid* II + *-ieh* adj. suffix.] A body of Kurdish cavalry formed by the Turks in 1891.

1898 H. A. G. PERCY *Diary Asiatic Turkey* 83 Zekki,.. the reputed founder of the Hamidieh System. 1901 *Westm. Gaz.* 27 Aug. 2/2 The Hamidie Cavalry..defy the Porte by ignoring its commands. 1902 *Encycl. Brit.* XXV. 665/2 A tribal militia force (Hamidieh), consisting of 48 regiments, is formed somewhat on the lines of Cossacks.

Hamite, *sb.*[1] Add: Hence **Ha:miticiza·tion**, the action of becoming Hamitic; **Ha·mitoid** *a.*, resembling the Hamitic type.

1884 *Nature* 17 Apr. 581/1 These peoples should apparently be regarded rather as Negroes affected by Hamitic than as Hamites affected by Negro elements. In other words, they are Negroid rather than Hamitoid. 1924 G. W. MURRAY *Engl.-*

Nubian Dict. Introd., In the case of Nubian, the process of Hamiticization has gone so far that it has borrowed Hamitic personal-endings for its verb, Hamitic case-endings for its noun, and possesses a vocabulary largely Hamitic.

Hamlet[2] (hæ·mlėt). The name of the prince of Denmark who is the hero of Shakespeare's play of this name, in allusive phr. *Hamlet without the Prince* (*of Denmark*): a performance without the chief actor or a proceeding without the central figure.

1902 *Daily Chron.* 22 Apr. 3/1 Of what avail is it to promise 'entirely new scenery' for 'Die Meistersinger', if the part of Hans Sachs is to be practically eliminated from the performance? And yet this 'Hamlet-without-the-Prince' method is consistently pursued season after season at Covent Garden.

Hamlinite (hæ·mlinəit). *Min.* [f. the name of A. C. *Hamlin* (born 1828) + -ITE[1] 2.] A fluophosphate of aluminium and strontium, or aluminium and glucinum.

1890 *Amer. Jrnl. Sci.* Ser. III. XXXIX. 511 On Hamlinite, a new rhombohedral Mineral from the Herderite locality at Stoneham, Me. 1928 H. A. MIERS *Min.* 546 Hamlinite... $Al_3Sr(OH)_7P_2O_7$.

Hammel, variant of HEMEL.

1812 SIR J. SINCLAIR *Syst. Husb. Scot.* I. 21 Small open sheds, or what, in Berwickshire, are called *Hammels* or *Hemmels*, with separate straw-yards attached. 1851 H. STEPHENS *Bk. Farm* (1855) I. 242 The hammels [are occupied] by the two-year-olds, or such as are fattening for the butcher. 1893 FREAM *Youatt's Complete Grazier* (ed. 13) 171 The litter used in hammels is..less by one-third than that required for stall-feeding.

Hammer, *sb.* Add: **2. c.** (See quot.)

1912 *Motor Man.* (ed. 14) ii. 40 The Low-tension Tappet. ..A metal lever, sometimes called a 'hammer' or 'finger', in direct contact with the engine, is pivoted in such a way that it normally touches the inside end of the pin.

7. *hammer-boy, -shed*; **hammer-action**, (*a*) action of or as of a hammer; (*b*) those parts of a piano which compose and control the hammers; **hammer-block**, the steel face of a steam-hammer; **hammer-lock** *Wrestling*, a position in which a wrestler is held with one arm bent behind his back; so **hammer-lock** *v.*; **hammer-price** *Stock Exchange*, the price realized for shares (of a defaulter) closed at the hammer; **hammer-rifle**, a rifle fired by means of a hammer; **hammer-thrower** (see sense 1, note).

1906 *Westm. Gaz.* 22 Mar. 7/2 The explosion, which was probably caused by the *hammer action of the water. 1861 FAIRBAIRN *Iron* 121 The *hammer-block is guided in its vertical descent by two planed guides or projections. 1881 *Instr. Census Clerks* (1885) 42 Forge and *Hammer Boy. 1909 *Westm. Gaz.* 19 Aug. 9/4 There has been a considerable shortage of hammer boys in most of the mining districts. 1897 *Pearson's Mag.* III. 638 *Hammer lock and Nelson on the ground. 1905 *Daily Chron.* 21 Feb. 7/4 The very thought of being '*hammer-locked' should be enough to deter the most confirmed 'disorderly'. 1900 *Westm. Gaz.* 4 June 7/1 He can have the stock closed at the *hammer price. 1901 *Ibid.* 13 May 9/1 The actual dealings in the shares being between £6 and £8 per share and the hammer price £2. 1920 G. BURRARD *Notes on Sporting Rifles* 15 Hammerless ejectors are better than non-ejectors and *hammer rifles. 1890 W. J. GORDON *Foundry* 13 The blast-furnaces that stand near the *hammer-shed. 1899 *Daily News* 18 July 7/2 The *hammer-throwers were out in the morning.

Hammer (hæ·mər), *sb.*[3] (See quot.)

1902 *Encycl. Brit.* XXV. 191/1 The South Devon or South Hams cattle are almost restricted to that southern part of the county of Devon known as the Hams, whence they are also called 'Hammers'.

Hammer, *v.* Add: **3. b.** Of a steam pipe: To make a knocking noise, as when steam is turned on or the flow of water suddenly stopped. (Cf. WATER-HAMMER 2.)

1889 HASLUCK *Model Eng. Handybk.* 108 The pump, owing to its not being filled properly at each stroke, will hammer very much.

Hammerer. 1. Add: As a specific occupation.

1909 *Westm. Gaz.* 8 Feb. 3/1 The man was a 'hammerer'—i.e., a driver of rivets into boilers, &c. 1921 *Dict. Occup. Terms* (1927) § 278 *Hammerer*,..flattens saw blades,..by..striking any curved part with hammer.

Hammerkop (hæ·mərkɒp). *S. Afr.* [Afrikaans; f. Du. *hamer* hammer + *kop* head.] = HAMMER-HEAD 4.

1887 *Encycl. Brit.* XXII. 578/1 It [sc. *Scopus umbretta*].. is the 'Hammerkop' (Hammerhead) of the Cape colonists. 1890 [see HAMMER-HEAD 4].

Hammerman. c. (Later example.)

1880 *Harper's Mag.* Dec. 59 The hammer-man, in a swinging seat, times the turning of his rod of steel to the quick stroke of the hammer.

Hammock[1]. **4.** Add: **hammock chair**, a folding reclining-chair with canvas support for the body, suitable for use in a lounge or garden; **hammock-moth** (see quot.).

1885 *Army & Navy Co-op. Soc. Price List* II. 1478 Portable Hammock Chairs. 1899 *Cambr. Nat. Hist.* VI. 379 The Hammock-moth, *Perophora sanguinolenta*, of the centre of South America, the larva of which constructs its portable habitations out of its own excrement.

Hampshire (hæ·mpʃəɹ). The name of a county in the south of England, designating a breed of sheep; also *Hampshire Down*.

1810 VANCOUVER *Gen. View Agric. Hampshire* 371 The.. common Hampshire ewe will cost from 25s. to 40s. each. 1825 LOUDON *Encycl. Agric.* IV. I. 1123/2 The heath sheep, old Hampshire, or Wilts breeds. 1875 *Encycl. Brit.* I. 392/2 These sheep are now usually classed as Sussex Downs and Hampshire Downs, the former being the most refined type of the class.., and the latter..having a heavier fleece, stronger bone, and somewhat coarser and larger frame. 1886 C. SCOTT *Sheep-farming* 12 The Hampshire Down, though a larger sheep than the Southdown, does not mature so early.

b. *pl.* A Hampshire Regiment.

1904 *Westm. Gaz.* 14 June 8/2 The Hampshires, who mustered ten officers and 484 men.

Hamseen, variant of KHAMSIN.

1923 F. S. MARVIN *Sci. & Civiliz.* 29 Physical contrasts of seasonal and regional fertility are abrupt; solar heat contends with Nile water, sea breeze with scorching 'hamseen'.

Han[1] (hæn). Designating a Chinese dynasty (206 B.C.–220 A.D.) marked by the introduction of Buddhism, the extension of Chinese rule over Mongolia, the revival of letters, and increase of wealth and culture.

1876 *Encycl. Brit.* V. 644/1 Lew Pang was then proclaimed emperor (206 B.C.) under the title of Kaou-te, and the new line was styled the Han dynasty. 1930 *Times Lit. Suppl.* 2 Oct. 774/3 The majority seem to reflect the Han style... Two famous homonymous generals who flourished under the Han dynasty.

Han[2]: see KHAN[2].

1903 *Westm. Gaz.* 10 Feb. 3/1 The *hans* are large, rambling inns, with a courtyard in the middle. 1920 *Q. Rev.* Apr. 395 Four hundred emaciated forms, the remnant of such convoys, are lying in one of the hans.

Hancockite (hæ·nkɒkəit). *Min.* [f. the name of E. P. *Hancock* + -ITE[1].] A member of the epidote group, containing strontium and lead, found in New Jersey, U.S.A.

1900 *Jrnl. Chem. Soc.* LXXVIII. II. 88 Hancockite. This occurs as brownish-red, cellular masses of minute, lath-shaped crystals, which are monoclinic.

Hand, *sb.* Add: **15. b.** *To get the hands*: to receive the applause. *U.S. colloq.*

1927 PRINCE OF WALES in *Even. News* 7 Oct. 6/5 They both do a great deal of hard work for the British Legion. It may be I am more the fellow who travels about and gets the hands.

23. Also, the cards held at any stage of such a game as Poker.

1889 R. GUERNDALE *Poker Bk.* 25 To fill your hand, to improve it by the draw. 1913 A. B. LOUGHER *Poker* 13 The next process is that of drawing to fill the hands.

d. *To declare one's hand* (fig.): to reveal one's circumstances or aims. (Cf. DECLARE *v.* 11.)

1924 D. H. LAWRENCE *England, my England* 241 Upstairs Fanny evaded all the thrusts made by his mother, and did not declare her hand.

29. In hand. k. *Billiards.* Of the cue-ball: Having been retrieved by hand, after being pocketed, and having been placed on any selected spot within the D preliminary to the next stroke.

1876 CRAWLEY *Handy-bk. Games* 131 Your ball being in hand, you must play for the hazard that shall bring the object-ball back to the opposite cushion. 1904 J. P. MANNOCK *Billiards Expounded* v. 228 The cue-ball is 'in hand' with the red ball, presenting a straightaway winning hazard into the right middle pocket.

44. Give (one's) **hand. c.** *To give a hand*: to help a person with one's hand.

1880 *Daily Tel.* 26 Nov., He tried to swim back against the stream, but could not, and, feeling exhausted, he struck out for the Middlesex shore, when a policeman gave him a hand up.

45.* **Put** (one's) **hand. a.** *To put one's hand*: to exert oneself, use one's energies; now always with *to*: to set about, undertake (a piece of work).

1388 WYCLIF *Luke* ix. 62 No man that puttith his hoond to the plouȝ, and biholdynge bacward, is able to the rewme of God. 1430 in *Fenland N. & Q.* (1905) July 222 And yat.. ye wole at yis tyme..putte youre handes and ese us by wey of lone of ye somme of C marc. *c* 1450 *St. Cuthbert* (Surtees) 6056 Þat to bi seruyce puttys þair hands. 1535 COVERDALE *Deut.* xii. 18 All yᵗ thou puttest thine hande vnto. 1631 PRESTON *Effect. Faith* 45 If God himselfe put not his hand to the worke no man is able to believe. 1633 BP. HALL *Hard Texts* Zech. xi. 9, I will not put my hand to redresse it. 1879 M. J. GUEST *Lect. Hist. Eng.* ix. 80 Whatever he put his hand to, be did it 'with all his might'.

b. *To put* (one's) *hand*(*s*) *on*, (†*in*, †*unto*): to lay hands on (see LAY *v.*[1] 21 c); †to do violence to (*Sc. Obs.*); to get hold of, seize (also *fig.*).

1535 COVERDALE *Exod.* xxii. 8 [He] shal sweare) that he hath not put his hande vnto his neighbours good. 1837 C. M. GOODRIDGE *Voy. S. Seas* (1843) 44 [We] got into her with such articles as we could immediately put our hands on. 1842 J. H. NEWMAN *Par. Serm.* VI. viii. 111 Perhaps..we can put our hand, as it were, on a time in our childhood [when etc.]. *Mod.* I have a copy of the book, but cannot put my hand on it.

53. Hands off! Also *attrib.*

1902 *Daily Chron.* 23 Jan. 7/1 A protest must be made against the hands-off policy. 1908 *Times Lit. Suppl.* 3 Sept. 281/3 The hopelessly *doctrinaire* character of the old 'hands-off' individualism.

54. Hands up! Also in *Curling* (see quot.).

1897 *Encycl. Sport* I. 264/1 *Hands up*, the command of the Skip..to stop sweeping.

55. Hand..fist. a. Also *fig.* of the making of money.

1888 'R. BOLDREWOOD' *Robbery under Arms* xxvii, We.. made money hand over fist. 1901 *Daily Chron.* 27 Dec. 3/3 To use a phrase common to the Anglo-Saxon, they have been making money hand-over-fist.

60. h. *Hands down*: with ease, with little or no effort; orig. in the racing phr. *to win hands down*, referring to the jockey dropping his hands and so relaxing his hold on the reins, when victory appears certain.

1867 'PIPS' *Lyrics & Lays* (Calcutta) 155 There were good horses in those days, as he can well recall, But Barker upon Elepoo, hands down, shot by them all. 1913 MRS. H. WARD *Mating of Lydia* II. xii, That I should surrender, hands down, to a lot of trumpery complaints and grievances. 1920 W. B. MONEY *Humours of Parish* 126, I started off in the race in full nigger costume, and won hands down.

61. c. *hand-baggage, luggage.*

1902 *Daily Chron.* 27 Feb. 3/3 The Boer delegates have only brought with them *hand-baggage. 1888 LD. MACNAGHTEN in *Law Rep. Ho. Lords* XIII. 55 Passengers take the lighter articles of luggage—or '*hand-luggage' as it is called,—in the carriage with them. 1908 *Daily Chron.* 8 Jan. 4/4 Glancing furtively at that terrible piece of hand-luggage, a New York Sunday newspaper. 1924 W. J. LOCKE *Coming of Amos* iv, Maxime possessed himself of her hand-luggage.

d. *hand-sled, -sleigh.*

1780 *Heath Papers* 6 [They] hall their wood on *hand sleds. 1843 *Knickerbocker Mag.* XXII. 294 The serjeant's hand-sled, piled with wood. 1871 *Rep. Vermont Board Agric.* IV. 92 Provided with a handsled, the boy would first roll on to it the back log. 1841 G. POWERS *Hist. Sk. Coos* 70 A rude *hand sleigh.

62. b. *hand-fisher*; *hand-sewn* ppl. adj.

1855 'P. PAXTON' *Captain Priest* 147 In the deeper places of such streams must the *handfisher seek his prey. 1887 *Col. & Indian Exhib., Rep. Col. Sect.* 401 A handsome pair of men's *hand-sewn Wellingtons. 1911 *Rep. on Labour & Social Conditions in Germany* III. VI–VII. 101, I could have my boots soled and heeled with this quality of leather, and hand-sewn for 3s. 5d.

63. hand-balancer, an acrobat; **hand-board** *U.S.*, a board in front of a preacher or speaker; **hand-fives**, the usual game of fives as distinguished from bat-fives (see FIVES[2] 1); **hand-note**, a note sent by hand; **hand-pick** *v. trans.*, to pick by hand; also *fig.*; **hand-plate**, (*a*) = *finger-plate*; (*b*) a small plate to pass over the surface of work to be tested; **hand-pollinate** *v. trans.*, to pollinate by hand; **hand-reading** = PALMISTRY; so *hand-reader*.

1927 *Daily Tel.* 30 Aug. 12/6 Masu, the Japanese *hand-balancer and juggler. 1845 A. WILEY in *Indiana Mag. Hist.* XXIII. 165 Behold the..awkward man arise and place his chair before him for his pulpit and *hand-board. 1856 STRICKLAND *Cartwright* xx. 203 They drove a stake down, and nailed a board to it,..and this was my hand board. 1905 *Westm. Gaz.* 17 Mar. 4/1 Our game of *hand-fives is perhaps the closest approach we have to the central type of the games. 1831 *Sutherland Farm Rep.* 72 in *Libr. Usef. Knowl., Husb.* III, A few boys and girls *hand-pick the whole. 1898 *Advance* (Chicago) 3 Mar. 282/1 [Loyola] face to face with individuals, hand-picking souls from the fire. 1907 *Westm. Gaz.* 12 Sept. 5/1 The most expensive of the ordinary coals—'large hand-picked coal'. 1918 *Times* 23 Jan. 6/3 True, there has been a widespread feeling that the Irish Convention was handpicked. 1925 J. GREGORY *Bab of Backwoods* xii. 157 An able-bodied trio, hand-picked by William Badger. 1928 *Daily Express* 11 July 1/2 A handpicked 'National' Assembly for Parliament. 1930 J. G. FREDERICK (*title*) Fifty Hand-Picked Common Stocks. 1900 H. LAWSON *Over Sliprails* 49 Scraping old splashes of paint off the brass and *hand-plate. 1918 *Nature* 15 Aug. 470/2 To *hand-pollinate the flowers of a soft-shelled tree with pollen from a tree of similar character. 1902 *Daily Chron.* 28 Nov. 6/3 S. S.,..'hand reader',..appeared..to answer a charge of pretending to tell fortunes by palmistry. 1867 CRAIG *Palmistry* 31 In obedience to the stern dictates of the *hand-reading art.

Hand, *v.* Add: **4. b.** To give, convey: often with implication of palming-off or imposing. *U.S.*

1901 S. MERWIN & WEBSTER *Calumet K* ii. 21, I told him he ought to give it to somebody else, and he handed me a lot of stuff about my experience. 1909 'O. HENRY' *Options* (1916) 30 I've had it handed to me in the neck, too. 1925 F. LONSDALE *Spring Cleaning* II, You ought to have heard the stuff they have handed over to her about you! 1926 J. BLACK *You Can't Win* vi. 75 You'll..maybe get grabbed off a train and handed thirty days at Colorado Springs.

c. *To hand it to*: to acknowledge the superiority of. *U.S. colloq.*

1916 H. L. WILSON *Somewhere in Red Gap* ix. 371 You got to hand it to New York for shopping. 1923 *Harper's Mag.* Apr. 558 You've got to hand it to that kid... He's stood everything and never squealed a yelp. Some young tough, believe me! 1926 COLE *Blatchington Tangle* xli. 279 'I must hand it to you, sir,' the pseudo-American acknowledged.

Handbook. Add: **c.** A betting book; *handbook man*, a bookmaker. Also *hand-booking*, bookmaking. *U.S.*

1903 *N. Y. Evening Post* 14 Sept., A case where an officer arrested a handbook man. 1904 *N. Y. Times* 13 June 1 The handbooking possibilities on the Derby.

Hand-cart. Add: (Earlier U.S. example.)

1640 *New Haven Col. Rec.* 48 Wheele barrow, hand cart or paddles, or oares.

b. *attrib.* with *emigrant*: an emigrant who crossed the prairies with his goods on a handcart. So **Hand-carter.**

1859 H. WILLARD *Pike's Peak Gold Fever* 21 Quite a number of 'hand carters' were brought in by the stage. 1878 J. H. BEADLE *Western Wilds* xxi. 333 Two divisions of the hand-cart emigrants were on the plains.

Handelian (hændī·liăn), *a.* and *sb.* [f. the name of Georg Friedrich *Handel*, properly *Händel* (1685–1759), German musician + -IAN.] **A.** *adj.* Of, pertaining to, or characteristic of Handel, or his style of composition. **B.** *sb.* One who favours or imitates the style of Handel.

1770 *Priv. Lett. 1st Ld. Malmesbury* I. 205 Tenducci is amazingly improved; in his part the old Handelian songs were left out. 1768 MME. D'ARBLAY *Diary* (1842) IV. IV. 231 The concert was very Handelian. 1808 S. WESLEY *Lett.* (1875) 9 This would nettle the Handelians devilishly. 1825 LAMB *Lett.* (1888) II. 132 My sister's cold is as obstinate as an old Handelian, whom a modern amateur is trying to convert to Mozart-ism. 1865 J. HULLAH *Transition Per. Music* 244 It 'bears so genuine a Handelian impress'. 1885 *Athenæum* 28 Feb. 288/1 Revivals of Handelian oratorio. 1911 LADY GUTHRIE in R. L. ORR *Life Ld. Guthrie* (1923) 258 Those dusky simple souls interpreting the glorious Handelian strains.

Handkerchief. Add: *transf.* Applied to parts of costume made up of squares resembling or suggesting handkerchiefs.

1899 *Daily News* 1 July 4/3 The revival of the handkerchief dress. 1900 *Westm. Gaz.* 9 Aug. 3/2 The handkerchief blouse. 1903 *Daily Chron.* 18 July 8/4 The sleeves are handkerchief ones.

Handle, *sb.* Add: **1. b.** *U.S.* (Earlier and later examples.)

1825 J. NEAL *Bro. Jonathan* I. 107 How they [sc. the Indians] pulled foot, when they seed us commin'. Most off the handle, some o' the tribe, I guess. 1908 MULFORD *Orphan* xxii. 271 He reckoned you would..get good and mad, fly off the handle, and raise h—l generally. 1910 — *Hopalong Cassidy* ix. 63 He'll go off the handle one of these days, for he hates Greasers worse'n I do.

c. *Up to the handle*: thoroughly, completely, up to the hilt. *U.S. colloq.*

1835 A. B. LONGSTREET *Georgia Scenes* 234 We'll all go in for you here up to the handle. 1843 HALIBURTON *Attaché* I. viii. 119 Give me your figgery-four, Squire, I'll go in up to the handle for you. 1855 *Knickerbocker Mag.* XLV. 435 (Th. s.v. *Up*) He was enjoying his trip 'up to the handle'. 1860 *Ibid.* LV. 415 He had for the last few years used a boy and dog as fencing material; he found it 'a good instrution'; they did the thing up to the handle. 1877 HABBERTON *Jericho Road* xi. 101 If he isn't playin' possum right up to the handle, then he is a fool.

d. *To use the long handle* (Cricket): To hit freely and continuously.

1903 WARNER in *Cricket* (ed. H. G. Hutchinson) 71 As a rule the hitting or 'long-handle game', as it has been called, pays best under these circumstances [sc. on a sticky wicket]. 1928 *Daily Express* 20 Dec. 3/2 Ryder set about the bowlers unmercifully, using the long handle.

2. b. A small basket with a handle, in which soft fruit is packed for the market.

1900 *Daily Express* 30 June 5/5 French red currants reached 1s. 3d. a basket or 'handle'.

5. handle-bar, a transverse bar, usually curved, with a handle at each end, connected with the driving- or steering-wheel of a cycle, by which the vehicle is guided by hand; *pl.* the right- and left-hand parts of which this is composed.

1894 *Million* V. 377/1 Pick up your dress with your right hand, take hold of the handle bar with your left. 1898 *Science Siftings* XV. 170/1 Handle-bars in which the drop is greater than four inches below the seat are..dangerous. 1908 *Daily Chron.* 21 Nov. 9/4 One cannot effect this unobserved change when other than handle-bar control is fitted. 1909 *Captain* Aug. 448/2 Home-made Handlebar-grips. 1923 H. L. WILSON *Oh, Doctor!* xxiv. 333 [He] threw a confident leg across the saddle and worshipfully grasped the spreading handle bars.

Handle (hæ·nd'l), *sb.*[2] [f. HANDLE *v.*[1]] The feel of or sensation produced by goods, especially textiles, when handled.

1884 W. S. B. MᶜLAREN *Spinning* (ed. 2) 19 It is not merely the coarseness or fineness of the fibre which guides him, but also the softness and kind 'handle', as it is called. 1898 *Daily News* 7 Mar. 2/1 For softness and beautiful handle they have no equal. 1927 T. WOODHOUSE *Artificial Silk* 2 The handle of many artificial silk articles of commerce compares favourably with that of most of the corresponding textures in the other branches of the textile industry.

Handle, *v.*[3] *S. Afr.* [ad. Du. *handelen*.] *trans.* To trade, barter. Also *absol.*

1850 CUMMING *Hunter's Life S. Afr.* i, The trader inquires of the Boer if he has any fat oxen to handle or barter. *Ibid.*, When 'handling' once begins, it often goes on briskly.

Handler. 2. Add: One who shows the points of dogs at a trial, etc.

1897 [in Dict.]. 1931 *Our Dogs* 23 Oct. 296 Handlers and Breakers. Gun dogs wanted for training or boarding.

Handling, *vbl. sb.* Add: **1. c.** In games, the illegal touching of the ball.

1897 *Encycl. Sport* I. 429/1 *Handling*, or *Hands*, touching the ball with any part of the arm when in play. Only the goal-keeper can do so without a penalty. 'Hands' is given against the offender.

Hand-lining, *vbl. sb.* (See after HAND-LINE; earlier U.S. example.)

1880 *Harper's Mag.* Aug. 341/2 The business of hand-lining for deep-water fish.

Ha·nd-me-down, *sb.* and *a.* *dial.* and *U.S.* [f. the verbal phr. *to hand down* (see HAND *v.* 4 b).] **A.** *sb.* That which is handed down, as an heirloom, a second-hand garment, etc.; also, a ready-made garment. **B.** *adj.* Having been handed down or passed on. = REACH-ME-DOWN. Also *fig.*

1888 *New York World* 5 Mar. (Farmer) A twelve-dollar suit of hand-me-downs. 1889 *Sporting Times* 29 June (Farmer) Trousers..which all over proclaim themselves entitled to the epithet of hand-me-down. 1896 G. ADE *Artie* xviii. 70 They'll be workin' for some Reub that come into town wearin' hand-me-downs. 1897 *Congress. Rec.* 25 Mar. 274/1 These cheap-johns, ready-made, 'hand-me-down' statesmen. 1904 *Boston Herald* 15 Oct. 2 He wears a cheap suit of 'hand-me-down' clothing. 1909 *Daily Chron.* 2 July 7/4 He got it from a lady admirer..and he wanted me to 'ave it as a hand-me-down. 1925 S. LEWIS *Martin Arrowsmith* viii § 2 A dirty old office, with hand-me-down chairs and a lot of second-hand magazines.

Hand-off (hændǫ·f), *v.* *Rugby Football.* [f. HAND *v.* + OFF *adv.*] *intr.* To push off an opponent with the hand. Also *trans.* Hence **Ha·nd-off** *sb.*, the action of pushing off an opponent.

1897 *Encycl. Sport* I. 429 *Handing-off*, pushing off an opponent who endeavours to impede a player running with the ball. 1920 *Times* 8 Nov. 6/2 The wings ran well and were not afraid to 'hand-off'. 1922 *Daily Mail* 8 Dec. 12 A dangerous scoring wing with a powerful hand-off and an elusive swerve. 1923 W. J. A. DAVIES *Rugby Football* 135 Coates..ran with his head half turned to the right..which gave one the impression that he was waiting and was anxious to hand-off some one. 1928 *Observer* 19 Feb. 27/1 [He] has a fine kick, with a strong hand-off.

Hand-out. [f. HAND *v.* + OUT *adv.*]

1. *Tennis.* (See HAND *sb.* 63.)

2. That which is handed out; *spec.* food or alms given to a beggar at the door; also *hand-me-out*. *U.S.*

1887 M. ROBERTS *Western Avernus* 71 'Bummers' is American for beggars, and a 'hand out' is a portion of food handed out to a bummer or a tramp at the door when he is not asked inside. 1896 *Amer. Dial. Notes* I. 418 *Hand-out*, clothes such as a tramp asks for. 1896 G. ADE *Artie* vi. 50, I see barrel-house boys goin' around for hand outs that was more on the level than you was. 1903 *Daily Chron.* 4 Apr. 5/2 The weekly hand-out for the butcher. *a* 1906 'O. HENRY' *Trimmed Lamp*, etc. 29 Pretty soon I was in the free-bed line and doing oral fiction for hand-outs among the food bazaars. 1925 WILLA CATHER *Professor's House* 195 He soon drank up all his wages. When Rapp picked him up there he was living on hand-outs.

b. *attrib.* Serving light refreshments in a handy form.

1928 F. N. HART *Bellamy Trial* viii. 277, I would take a good walk, get a bite to eat at one of the hand-out places in the vicinity of the station.

3. Matter handed out to the newspaper press.

1929 *Literary Digest* (N.Y.) 12 Oct. 7/1 Mr. Shearer told ..how he gave the newspaper men at Geneva 'hand-outs' to help them in preparing their despatches. 1929 *Saturday Even. Post* (N.Y.) 7 Dec. 213/2 We have public-relations experts who do their stuff by means of propaganda in the press and hand-outs to the newspaper boys and girls.

4. The act of handing or dealing out cards. *U.S.*

1904 S. E. WHITE *Blazed Trail Stories* II. iv. 193 I'll turn you fer it. First man that gits a jack in th' hand-out stays.

Hand over hand. c. Add: **hand-over-hand stroke**, a style of swimming in which each arm is alternately brought out of the water from behind and with a circular sweep returned to the water in front. Also as *adv. phr.*

1856 'STONEHENGE' *Brit. Sports* 516/2 The Hand-over Hand style is a very rapid mode of swimming. 1872 H. GURR *Art of Swimming* 25 To Swim Hand-over-hand. 1904 R. THOMAS *Swimming* 139 The hand-over-hand is the most ancient stroke, at all events that is recorded.

Hence **Ha·nd-over-ha·nder.**

1924 R. CLEMENTS *Gipsy of Horn* vi. 104 Sending the royal yards aloft to a rattling hand-over-hander.

Hand over head. Add: **2. b.** *Cricket.* Designating a style of bowling (see OVERHAND *a.* 2).

1899 A. LANG in *Daily News* 22 July 4/2 The modern hand-over-head style.

Handshake (hæ·ndʃēk), *v.* [Back-formation from HAND-SHAKING.] *intr.* To shake hands. So **Ha·ndshaker.**

1898 H. JAMES *Turn of Screw* (1928) 133 We handshook and 'candlestuck', as somebody said, and went to bed. 1905 *Westm. Gaz.* 2 Nov. 12/1 As the line moves forward each hand-shaker is steadily pushed along. 1928 *Daily Express* 28 Aug. 8/3 Hearty handshakers.

Hands-up (hæ·ndz,ɒp), *v.* [f. the order *Hands up!* (see HAND *sb.* 54).] *intr.* To put up the hands in token of surrender. Also *trans.*, to cause to surrender. Hence **Ha·nds-up** *sb.*, the action of putting up the hands (in quot. *attrib.*); **Ha·nds-u·pper**, one who surrenders. Also **Ha·nd-up** *sb.*, one who throws up his hands.

1901 *Contemp. Rev.* Mar. 327 A small patrol..went..to the farm of a 'hands upper', *i.e.*, one who had surrendered his arms. 1901 *Daily Chron.* 12 Nov. 5/4 They regard themselves as quite the aristocrats of the camp, and much superior to the 'hands-uppers', as they have delighted in calling the children of less obstinate patriots. 1901 'LINESMAN' *Words Eyewitness* 239 The refugee camps within the British lines, wherein dwell the hundreds of Dutchmen who have surrendered, or 'hands-upped'. 1902 *Westm. Gaz.* 20 Mar. 7/1 Trooper Long..was grabbed by the throat by a 'hands-up' prisoner, who threw down his rifle. 1902 *Appleton's Ann. Cycl.* 629/2 The Boers who had accepted British sovereignty at various times since the fall of Bloemfontein and Pretoria, contemptuously called 'handups' by the others. 1915 *Observer* 4 Apr. 7/2 We have now a case of 'hands-upping', the first in this war, by a whole unit of Germans. 1923 *Daily Mail* 9 Mar. 10 The Germans after 'hands-upping' Rumania proceeded literally to turn out their pockets. 1928 *Observer* 17 June 7 Those faint-hearted ones who are 'hands-uppers' in regard to aviation.

Handwrite (hæ·nd,rəit). *Sc.* and *U.S.* [f. HAND *sb.* + WRITE *sb.* Cf. HANDWRIT and *hand of writ* or *write* (HAND *sb.* 16 b).] Handwriting.

1617 in Tweedie *Sel. Biog.* (Wodrow Soc. 1847) I. 95, I receaved a letter..whilk albeit it wanted a subscription, yet by the handwrite..I knew to be yours. 1638 RUTHERFORD *Lett.* (1664) 14 His hand write, & his seal. 1688 in Wodrow *Hist. Suff. Ch. Scot.* (1722) II. 633 You..adhered to your preaching Book, and declared the same to be your own Hand-write. 1836 B. TUCKER *Partisan Leader* (N.Y., 1861) 16 (Th.) He has got a paper in the captain's hand-write to show him the way. 1856 W. G. SIMMS *Eutaw* (N.Y.) 429 (Th.) Thar's his name in handwrite! Hyar's a boy that reads this handwrite. 1880 *Antrim Gloss.* 49 Whose hand write is that? 1907 N. MUNRO *Daft Days* xv, She knew she could never sustain the standard of hand-write, spelling, and information Bud had established in her first epistle.

Handwriting. Add: **3.** *attrib.*, as **handwriting expert**, one who makes a study of handwriting in order to determine the authorship of disputed documents, to detect forgeries, etc.

1894 *Strand Mag.* VIII. 293/1 The methods employed by handwriting experts. 1897 *Westm. Gaz.* 2 Dec. 5/1 M. Bertillon, the famous handwriting expert, one of the witnesses at the Dreyfus trial. 1898 *Ibid.* 17 Jan. 7/2 The testimony of hand-writing 'experts'.

Handy, *sb.* Add: **2.** A hand-bier.

1909 *Daily Chron.* 8 June 2/5 Hearses, Handys, Biers, &c. 1922 *Daily Mail* 4 Nov. 10 The charges for licences on motor-hearses and handies.

Handy, *a.* Add: **2. b.** Phr. *Handy to*: conveniently situated for. *dial.* and *U.S.* So *handy for* (general colloq.).

1825 JENNINGS *Observ. Dial. W. Eng.* 133 I've hir'd 'twar handy ta tha zea. 1893 'O. THANET' *Stories of Western Town* 136 It is customary in the Lossing Building to say, 'We are so handy to the cars'.

5. b. Handy-man, (*b*) a sailor.

1899 H. BEGBIE *Handy Man* iii, And the babe sleeps sound in her cot o' nights, and the trader may plot and plan, For under the stars on the rolling deep stands the vigilant Handy Man. 1900 *People* 1 Apr. (Ware) The handy man. High praise for the naval brigade.

Hang, *sb.* Add: **1. b.** Also *Cricket* (see *HANG *v.* 19 b).

1897 K. S. RANJITSINHJI *Jubilee Bk. Cricket* 78 The ideal bowler..should do his best to acquire a command of off-break and leg-break, 'top' and 'hang'.

c. *Metallurgy.* A delay in the descent of the charge in a blast-furnace, due to the formation within the furnace of an arch of ore, coke, and flux.

1908 R. FORSYTHE *Blast Furnace* vi, Repeated hangs may be caused by too much limestone.

Hang, *v.* Add: **6. b.** *fig.* To reduce to, or hold in, a state of indecision or inaction; *esp.* in phr. *to hang a jury*, to prevent (as a juryman) a jury from reaching a verdict (cf. *17 c). *U.S.*

1850 J. WEIR *Lonz Powers* (Phila.) I. 142 [These men] either caused their acquittal or hung the..panel, by refusing to agree to any verdict save that of 'Not Guilty'.

7. b. To tie or hitch up (a horse). (Cf. 28 e.) *U.S.*

1835 *Southern Lit. Messenger* I. 581 Having arrived at Blank, we *hung* our horses, as Virginians always do after riding them. 1843 R. CARLTON *New Purchase* xxvi, While *hanging* Dick to a gate post.

11. c. *Metallurgy.* Of a blast-furnace: To have some part of its charge choked up so that the part beneath falls away.

1878 *Jrnl. Iron & Steel Inst.* XII. 202 When a furnace 'hangs' on one side, a more common occurrence with small old furnaces than with large modern ones, a system prevailed in some works of putting half a pig of lead in above the part that was fast. 1908 R. FORSYTHE *Blast Furnace* 242 When the stock becomes wedged so tightly that it can no longer descend, the furnace is said to 'hang'.

17. c. Of a jury: To fail to agree. (Cf. *6 b and *HUNG *ppl. a.*) *U.S.*

1859 BARTLETT *Dict. Amer.*, *To hang*, to stick fast, come to a stand still; as, the jury hung, and 'the man got a new trial'. 1929 *Randolph Enterprise* (W.Va.) 24 Oct. 5/1 The jury hung up on the case and were discharged.

19. b. To slacken motion perceptibly; *spec.* in *Cricket* (see quots.).

1897 K. S. RANJITSINHJI *Jubilee Bk. Cricket* 77 The ball is made to hug the ground when it pitches, and to rise slowly afterwards, or 'hang', as it is called by cricketers... With some bowlers it either 'hangs' or more often comes fast off the pitch owing to something in their regular action. 1897 *Encycl. Sport* I. 246/1 A ball 'hangs' which rises unexpectedly slowly from the pitch. 1906 JEPHSON in *Cricket* (ed. H. G. Hutchinson) 103 He ran up and delivered the ball, to all appearances, exactly similarly each time; but one found now that the ball was hanging in the air, now that it was on to one surprisingly soon.

c. *To hang to* (see quot.).

1888 *Lockwood's Dict. Mech. Engin.*, *Hang To.*—A term having several applications. A file hangs to its work when it cuts without slip. A saw hangs to, when it feels as though being drawn into the timber. A pattern hangs to the sand when it delivers with difficulty.

28. Hang up. a. Also *absol.* = to hang up the receiver of a telephone at the end of a conversation. *To hang up on*: to break off telephonic communication with.

1928 E. WALLACE *Double* viii, 'Oh, Mr. Staines!..What a dull life yours must be!' And then she hung up on him, and left him feeling like a spanked child. 1928 F. N. HART *Bellamy Trial* iii. 101 He'd hung up, I guess. Anyway he didn't answer.

f. Also, to suspend movement or action; to stop or stay.

1854 *Congress. Globe* App. 108 (Th.) In reading the President's message,..be got befogged, and, in the language of the Kentucky boatman, 'hung up for the night'. 1874 EGGLESTON *Circuit Rider* xvi, You mou't get a place 'bout a mile furder on whar you could hang up for the night.

Hangar. Add, with pronunciation (hæ·ŋəɹ): **b.** A shed for the accommodation of aircraft.

1902 *Daily Chron.* 31 Oct. 5/3 Mr. Santos Dumont..will construct a hangar in the Bois de Boulogne. 1922 *Daily Mail* 6 Nov. 9 He was refused permission to go to the hangar where his aeroplane was lying.

Hangbird. (Earlier examples.)

1794 S. WILLIAMS *Hist. Vermont* 118 Hangbird. *Oriolus ictérus*. 1824 Z. THOMPSON *Gazetteer Vermont* 18 The singing birds are the robin, thrush,..springbird, goldfinch and hangbird. 1831 J. Q. ADAMS *Mem.* (1867) VIII. 426 The oriole of Baltimore is the fiery hang-bird.

Hang-down (hæ·ŋ,daun), *sb.* and *a.* [f. phrase *to hang down* (see HANG *v.* 8).] **A.** *sb.* That which hangs down, *spec.* in certain technical uses. **B.** *adj.* That hangs down.

1888 *Lockwood's Dict. Mech. Engin.*, *Hang Down*, or *Hanger*, a bearing suspended from a roof or beam for the journal of a shaft. 1904 *Technol. & Sci. Dict.* (ed. Goodchild & Tweney), *Hang Down* (Eng.), a frame for suspending a bearing from a roof or beam.—(Foundry), the sling which supports heavy weights in the foundry; the upper ends of the rods of the sling are attached to the travelling crane. 1906 KIPLING *Actions & Reactions* (1909) 212 As Guiseppe [*sic*] unshipped the working mechanism of the organ (it developed a hang-down leg) from its wheels.

Hanger[2]. Add: **2. g.** (See quot.)

1905 CALKINS & HOLDEN *Mod. Advertising* 352 Hangers are printed or lithographed cards of various shapes and sizes, to be hung up in a store.

4. e. A coat- or dress-hanger.

1908 *Daily Chron.* 26 Feb. 8/5 Every coat and every skirt should have a hanger to itself.

6. *Comb.* **hanger-board** (see quot. 1893).

18.. *Electr. Rev.* (U.S.) XII. 8 (Cent. Dict.) Electrical connection between the conducting-wires and lamps must be made through a suitable hanger-board. 1893 SLOANE *Electr. Dict.*, *Hanger Board*, a board containing two terminals, a suspending hook, and a switch, so that an arc lamp can be introduced into a circuit thereby, or can be removed as desired.

Hang-fire (hæ·ŋ,fəiəɹ). [f. phrase *to hang fire* (see HANG *v.* 6).] A delay in the explosion of the charge of a gun or of a blasting charge.

1892 GREENER *Breech-Loader* 170 Nothing is more tantalising to the sportsman than miss-fires; hang-fires, too, are a great nuisance. 1899 *Kynoch Jrnl.* Oct.–Nov. 6/2 Hang fires, soft shots, high pressures, and other defects.

Hanging, *vbl. sb.* Add:

5. b. *Metallurgy* = *HANG *sb.* 1 c.

1878 *Jrnl. Iron & Steel Inst.* XII. 202 The modern system of putting the material round the in-wall and allowing it to roll to the centre, has diminished the heat at the in-wall of the furnace and greatly reduced the hanging and scaffolding.

8. *hanging day* (U.S. example).

1806 *Balance* (Hudson, N.Y.) 11 Nov. 355 (Th.) Next Friday [the newspaper] promises to make its debut. Friday —that's hanging day—but no matter.

Hanging, *ppl. a.* **6.** Add: **hanging bridge**, a suspension-bridge; see also quot. 1875; **hanging-drop** *Med.*, the small drop of culture-medium which hangs from a microscopic cover-glass enclosed in a cell; **hanging lie** *Golf*, the position of a ball when it rests on ground sloping downwards in the direction of play; **hanging shelf**, a suspended shelf. (See also quots.)

1867 SMYTH *Sailor's Word-bk.*, *Hanging-blocks..are sometimes fitted with a long and short leg, and lash over the eyes of the topmast rigging; when under, they are made fast to a strap. 1884 KNIGHT *Dict. Mech.* Suppl., *Hanging Block*, a block through which the top-sail tye is rove, then through the tye-block on the yard, and the standing part made fast to the mast head. 1815 *Niles' Weekly Register* IX. 92/1 The main post-road..crosses the Brandywine on a *hanging bridge. 1875 KNIGHT *Dict. Mech.*, *Hanging-bridge*. 1. A hollow, vertical partition depending from the bottom of a boiler and serving to deflect the flame... 2. *a.* A suspension bridge. *b.* A truss-frame bridge. 1867 SMYTH *Sailor's Word-bk.*, *Hanging-compass, a compass so constructed as to hang with its face downwards. 1897 *Allbutt's Syst. Med.* II. 1148 The blood serum of immunised animals even outside the body, in test-tubes or in the *hanging-drop had a strong action on the bacteria against which the animals had been protected. 1908 *Practitioner* Aug. 264 By observation of hanging-drop preparations from growth in glucose broth. 1909 P. A. VAILE *Mod. Golf* plate 96 The stance and address for a *hanging lie. 1825 J. NEAL *Bro. Jonathan* I. 188 A *hanging shelf..loaded with cheeses; ropes of onions; dried apples, [etc.]. 1893 RIVINGTON *Building Construction* II. 108 *Hanging steps are fixed at one end only. 1904 *Technol. & Sci. Dict.* (ed. Goodchild & Tweney), *Hanging Steps*, stone steps having one end built into a wall. 1875 KNIGHT *Dict. Mech.*, *Hanging-tie, a tie which is supported by strap and collar, dependent from the rafters above. *Ibid.*, *Hanging-tool (Iron-turning), a crooked tool, which partially embraces the rest so as not to be easily displaced.

Ha·ng-o·ver. *U.S.* [HANG *v.* 17.] A thing or person remaining or left over; a remainder or survival.

1894 *Outing* (U.S.) XXIV. 67/2 Then there a few 'hang-overs' who have tried before, and two or three green candidates. 1920 C. SANDBURG *Smoke & Steel* 153 A hangover of summer song. 1930 DENNY *Amer. conquers Brit.* 9 That easily inspired hatred of Germany remained as a hang-over in America long after it had been thrown over by the British.

Hangul (hɒ·ŋgŭl). Also **hungal.** [Kashmiri *hānglu*.] A deer, *Cervus cashmirianus*, related to and perhaps a variety of the red deer.

1869 KINLOCH *Large Game Shooting* 44 Cashmeerie hangul. 1902 *Encycl. Brit.* XXVII. 398/2. 1922 *Blackw. Mag.* Mar. 334/1 The hungal or Kashmir stag, found on the western side of Chamba.

Hanjee, variant of KHANJEE.

1920 *Cornhill Mag.* Oct. 438 The hanjee was taking down his shutters.

Hank, *sb.* Add: **2.** (Later U.S. examples.)

1880 *Harper's Mag.* Sept. 534/2 The ceilings [were] hung with hanks of blue yarn. 1888 *Century Mag.* XXXVI. 768/2 These little silken 'hanks' were sometimes..prettily colored.

4. c. *Wrestling.* In the Cumberland and Westmorland style, a throw made by putting the left leg between the legs of an opponent, catching his left leg, and leaning or pulling backwards. Also *back-hank*.

1870 W. ARMSTRONG *Wrestliana* 44 Robinson lifted him up like a cat lifting a mouse, when, Plaskett immediately put in the hank. 1888 *Encycl. Brit.* XXIV. 690/2 Each man tries to throw his adversary by using the 'buttock',.. the 'crossbuttock',..or the 'back-hank'. 1898 *Encycl. Sport* II. 547/2 The hank, when manipulated by an expert wrestler, becomes one of the hardest and most dangerous falls of all.

Hank, *v.* Add: **1. b.** *Wrestling.* To throw (an opponent) by means of the hank (see *HANK *sb.* 4 c).

1881 *Sportsman's Year-book* 314 The next fall resulted in favour of Pooley, who hanked his adversary. 1894 *Carlisle Patriot* 13 July 7/4 (Cumbld. Gloss. 1899) J— was hanked, S— trying the inside click.

Hanky[1] (hæ·ŋki). Also **handky.** Hypocoristic form (see -Y[6]) of HANDKERCHIEF.

1895 J. DAVIDSON *Earl Lavender* iv. 73 They..sighed, and looked up, and the schoolmaster's wife used her handky. 1902 *Westm. Gaz.* 17 Dec. 8/2 Lovely ladies' hankies in dainty lawn. 1924 E. MARSH *Fabl. La Fontaine* 52 Every occurrence was referred to her; Whether one lost a hanky or a lover.

Hanky[2]. = HANKY-PANKY.

1924 GALSWORTHY *White Monkey* II. iv, On our floor, with Michael outside the door, one would know there couldn't be any hanky.

Hannibal (hæ·nibăl). The name of the famous Carthaginian general, who fought against Rome in the third century B.C. Hence, *allusively*, a great general. (Also, in Shaks., humorously confounded with CANNIBAL.) †*Hannibal eye*, a blind eye.

1585 T. WASHINGTON tr. *Nicholay's Voy.* Ded. ¶ iij b, Were it not that I feare the censure of some politike Hanniball. 1603 SHAKS. *Meas. for M.* II. i. 187 Proue this, thou wicked Hanniball. *a* 1652 BROME *New Acad.* III. ii. Wks. 1873 II. 58, I passe For a brisk youth, but for my Hannibal eye here.

Hence **Hannibalian** (hænibǣ·liăn), **Hannibalic** (-bæ·lik) *adjs.*, of, pertaining to, or characteristic of Hannibal.

1678 J. D. (*title*) The History of Appian..In Two Parts. The First consisting of the Punick..and Hannibalick Wars. 1862 tr. *Mommsen's Hist. Rome* III. vi. II. 189 Thus ended the second Punic, or as the Romans more correctly called it, the Hannibalic, war. 1880 *Encycl. Brit.* XI. 444/2 In the year 202 B.C. the Second Punic, or, more properly, the Hannibalian War was at an end. 1886 H. F. LESTER *Under two Fig Trees* 135 And baby had registered a Hannibalic vow. 1904 T. R. GLOVER *Virgil* v. 101 It was some feeling of this kind that kept so much of Italy loyal to Rome throughout the Hannibalic war.

Hanoum, hanum: see *KHANUM.

Hanukkah, variant of *CHANUKKA.

1931 O. S. RANKIN *Orig. Festival Hanukkah* Pref. p. vi.

Hanuman (hɒnumā·n). Also **hoonoomaun, huniman.** [Hind., Hindi *hanumān* (Skr. *hanumant*, f. *hanumat* large-jawed).] **1.** *Hindu Mythology.* Proper name of a monkey-chief; a semi-divine monkey-like creature, to whom extraordinary powers were attributed in legend.

1814 SOUTHEY in Robberds *Mem. W. Taylor* (1843) II. 427 For the last ten years..Buonaparte..was the God Hanuman —the monkeys, whom he commanded, did the mischief. 1886 *Encycl. Brit.* XXI. 287/1 Hanumān, the monkey general. 1886 YULE & BURNELL *Anglo-Ind. Gloss.* s.v. *Lungoor*, The monkey-god Hunimān.

2. (with small initial) An East Indian monkey, *Semnopithecus entellus*, venerated by the Hindus.

1891 J. L. KIPLING *Beast & Man in India* iii. 65 Of late years the tradesmen who form the bulk of the members of our municipalities have felt that there are too many Hanumāns abroad. 1897 *Q. Rev.* Oct. 395 No visitor to Hindostan ..can have failed to see the Sacred Monkey or Hanuman.

Haoma (hōᵘ·mā). [Zend.] = HOM.

1890 *Ann. Rep. Smithsonian Inst.* 91 On the position of the Haoma in the Avesta of the Parsees.

Haori (hā·ori). [Jap.] A short loose jacket worn in Japan.

1897 LA FARGE *Artist's Lett. from Japan* 274 Women under their umbrellas wore the graceful short overcoat they call *haori*, and tottered over the wet ground on high wooden pattens. 1907 *Daily Chron.* 15 May 3/5 The little ornament on his haori (the gown) was the family crest.

Hapax legomenon (hæ·pæks lėgɒ·mėnɒn). Pl. **hapax legomena.** Also simply **hapax.** [Gr. ἅπαξ λεγόμενον once said.] A word or form of which only one instance is recorded in a literature or an author.

[1654 TRAPP *Minor Prophets* 605 'Tis ἅπαξ λεγόμενον read only here: and hence this variety of interpretations. 1801 MAGEE *Atonement & Sacrifice* 336 [The book of Job's] very great antiquity, and uncommon sublimity of elevation, which has occasioned a greater number of ἅπαξ λεγομενα, and expressions difficult to be understood.] 1882 FARRAR *Early Chr.* I. xi. 236 *note*, The number of the *hapax legomena* is remarkable, and some of them are full of picturesqueness.

Haplo-. Add: **Ha·plopore** (see quots.).

1898 F. A. BATHER in *Rep. Brit. Assoc.* (1899) 917 The simple or irregular haplopores become connected in pairs (diplopores). 1900 — in *E. R. Lankester's Treat. Zool.* III. 41.

b. *Cytology.*

1927 F. A. E. CREW *Org. Inher. Man* 52 If a haplo-IV is mated to a diplo-IV eyeless male, half of the offspring are eyeless. 1928 T. H. MORGAN *Theory Gene* 46 Normal and haplo-IV flies of Drosophila melanogaster.

Haploid (hæ·ploid), *a.* *Biol.* [f. Gr. ἁπλόος single + εἶδος form.] Having a reduced number of the chromosomes characteristic of germ-cells; distinguished from *DIPLOID, etc. So **Ha·ploidy**, the condition of being haploid.

1914 CALKINS *Biol.* 209 The chromatin of the nucleus collects in a thick fibrous mass on one side of the nucleus (synapsis stage) and from it emerge one-half as many chromosomes as are formed at ordinary vegetative divisions (in modern terminology this is called the haploid number). 1919 T. H. MORGAN *Phys. Basis Hered.* 160 An interesting case of triploidy has been reported in the threadworm *Ascaris* (Boveri). Two varieties occur, one with four chromosomes (haploid two), and one with two (haploid one). 1927 HALDANE & HUXLEY *Anim. Biol.* ii. 60. 1930 *Times Lit. Suppl.* 30 Oct. 894/4 The phenomenon of haploidy in plants and animals.

Haplome (hæ·ploᵘm). *Min.* Also **aplome.** [ad. (with accommodation to the Gr.) F. *aplome* (R. J. Haüy, 1801), f. Gr. ἁπλόος simple.] A rare variety of garnet.

1854 DANA *Syst. Min.* II. 192 Aplome has the faces striated parallel to the shorter diagonal.

Happen, *v.* Add: **1. a.** Said of an accident or some serious thing (*spec.* death) happening to a person, with vague subject, *anything, something*.

1829 *Blackw. Mag.* June 719/1 In the event of 'any thing happening to his father', as the modern phrase for the termination of man's mortal career runs. 1862 *Cornhill Mag.* (1863) VIII. 574 Doctor says I shall not last long, so I don't think I shall be removed before anything happens. 1884 G. C. DAVIES *Peter Penniless* x, It isn't a night for any man to be left out in if anything has happened to him. 1885 RIDER HAGGARD *K. Solomon's Mines* ii, I will..arrange that in the event of anything happening to us or to you, that your son shall be suitably provided for.

4. d. (Earlier and other U.S. examples.)

1838 J. F. COOPER *Homeward Bound* viii. 112, I only happened in..to make a first call. 1845 CAROLINE M. KIRKLAND *Western Clearings* 116 He could hardly have 'happened in' at a more fortunate juncture. 1872 E. EGGLESTON *Hoosier Schoolm.* xxxiii, Miss Nancy just happened over at Mrs. Thomson's humble home. 1893 KATE D. WIGGIN *Polly Oliver* ii. (1894) 20 A swarm of horrid insects might happen along and devour the plants. 1901 W. CHURCHILL *Crisis* III. ii. 366, I happened around at Colonel Carvel's this afternoon.

Happening, *vbl. sb.* **2.** Add: Also in *sing.*

1896 CROCKETT *Grey Man* xxviii, I could not find it in my heart to tell him of the happening. 1896 E. PHILLPOTTS in *Black & White* 27 June 824/2 Before the final coorious happening, there was a fire in a croft of auld Applebird's. 1899 *Daily News* 5 Apr. 2/4 Such a happening would almost certainly have had much more serious results had it been a horsed carriage. 1907 *Westm. Gaz.* 30 Dec. 2/2 The Denshawi incident is not viewed by all exactly alike, but it was decidedly a regrettable happening.

Happi-coat (hæ·pikōᵘt). Also **happy-.** [Jap. *happi*.] A loose light coat of thin material worn by women.

1931 E. V. GATENBY in *Studies Eng. Lit.* (Tokyo) XI. Oct. 515 *Happi-Coat*, often misspelt 'happy' coat. 1932 *Sale Catal.*, Japanese silk shantung happi-coat.

Happy, *a.* Add:

4. b. *Happy families*: a game played with a pack of special cards, each card depicting on its face a member of a family of four; it is the aim of each player to make as many complete families as he can. *Happy family*: see FAMILY *sb.* 2 b.

1903 *Cassell's Bk. In-Door Amusem.* 126 Happy Families. This is practically the same game as *Spade the Gardener*, save that it is played with a special pack of cards, manufactured for the purpose. 1918 C. DANE *First the Blade* xxv, An early passion for Happy Families.

Hapteron (hæ·ptĕrɒn). Pl. **-a.** [mod.L., badly f. Gr. ἅπτειν to fasten.] An organ of attachment by which many aquatic plants or marine algæ fasten themselves to rocks.

1900 B. D. JACKSON *Gloss. Bot. Terms*, *Hapteron*, Warming's term for organs of attachment which do not contain vascular tissue, as in Podostomaceae. 1902 *Encycl. Brit.* XXV. 438/2 Attached by hairs and special branches (*haptera*) to rocks. 1909 tr. *E. Warming's Oecol. Plants* 241 Lithophytes require *haptera* by which they can attach themselves to rock, unless the thallus itself adheres closely to this.

Haptic (hæ·ptik), *a.* [ad. Gr. ἁπτικός able to come into contact with, f. ἅπτειν to touch.] Of, pertaining to, or relating to the sense of touch.

1890 BILLINGS *Med. Dict.* 1904 *Amer. Jrnl. Relig. Psychol.* May 33 The scourging, thorns, spear and other tactile or haptic sensations come next.

Haptine (hæ·ptin). *Biol. Chem.* Also **-in.** [f. Gr. ἅπτειν to fasten + -INE[5], -IN[1].] In Ehrlich's theory of immunization, a receptor detached from the parent-cell, circulating freely in the blood-current, and acting as a protection against infection by combining with the foreign substance which would produce it. (Cf. *HAPTOPHORE.)

1902 *Brit. Med. Jrnl.* 12 Apr. 918/1 Every normally functioning cell throws off large numbers of side chains, either as isolated complexes, or in connexion with complement. These side chains are spoken of as haptines (Ehrlich).

Haptophore (hæ·ptofōᵊɹ), *a.* *Biol. Chem.* Also **-phor.** [f. as prec. + -PHORE.] Applied, in Ehrlich's theory of immunization, to that group of atoms in the molecule of a toxin or other substance which enables it to combine with the corresponding receptors of a cell, or to a similar group of atoms in the receptor itself. Also **Haptophoric** (-fǫ·rik), **Haptophorous** (-ǫ·fŏrəs).

1900–4 [see *toxophore*, etc. (TOXO-[2]) and *zymophore* (ZYMO-) in Dict.]. 1902 VAUGHAN & NOVY *Cellular Toxins* (ed. 4) 182 Both the toxophil groups of the cell, and the cytophil groups of the toxin may be designated as haptophorous bodies. 1902 *Brit. Med. Jrnl.* 29 Mar. 785 The atom arrangement, or group in the toxin, which corresponds to the receptor, he [sc. Ehrlich] calls the 'haptophoric group'. 1904 *Ibid.* 10 Sept. 574 Although the toxophoric group may be similar, the haptophor is dissimilar.

Hapu (hā·pu). *New Zealand.* Also **harpu.** [Maori.] A clan or small community.

1857 HURSTHOUSE *New Zealand* I. 162 The 70,000 semi-civilized natives now in New Zealand are divided into some dozen chief tribes, and into numerous sub-tribes and 'Harpu'. 1873 *Jrnls. Ho. Repr.* III. App. G. 7. 87 (Morris) Were not all your hapu present when the money was paid? 1891 *Rep. Australas. Assoc. Advancem. Sci.* III. G. 378 (Morris) Tribes or nations, each of which was divided into hapus, and the hapus into families.

Hapuku (hā·puku). *New Zealand.* Also **hapuka, whapuku.** [Maori.] = COD *sb.*[3] 2 b.

c 1845 in Hursthouse *New Zealand* (1857) I. 217 We've.. lowing herds on every side, Hapuka in every tide. 1855 R. TAYLOR *Te Ika a Maui* 411 *Hapuku*, or *whapuku* commonly called the cod, but a much richer fish in flavor. 1859 A. S. THOMSON *Story N. Zealand* I. 30 The Hapuku is the largest New Zealand salt-water fish.

Harbour, *sb.* **5.** Add: **harbour seal** *U.S.*, the common seal, *Phoca vitulina*.

1883 *Fisheries Exhib. Catal.* (ed. 4) 191 Cast of Harbour Seal.

Hard, *a.* (*sb.*) Add: **1. e.** Of a lawn tennis court: Made of asphalt or other hard material, as distinguished from a grass court.

1895 H. W. W. WILBERFORCE *Lawn Tennis* v. 29 Most people on a dry ground or a 'hard' court use brown leather or buck-skin shoes with thick, smooth, red rubber soles. 1909 *Westm. Gaz.* 30 Mar. 12/3 It is possible to place too much significance on hard-court results, grass conditions in England being so materially different.

f. Of silk: Retaining its natural gum. Also applied to a worker in hard silk.

1875 KNIGHT *Dict. Mech.* 2180/2. 1878 A. BARLOW *Weaving* 395 Before the gum has been boiled off the silk it is said to be hard silk. 1921 *Dict. Occup. Terms* (1927) § 399 *Hard hand* (silk); general term for any worker engaged in treating silk while still hard, *i.e.*, before it is degummed.

g. Of porcelain: Made of hard paste. *Hard paste*: see PASTE *sb.* 3 b, PORCELAIN 1 note.

1814 REES *Cycl.* XXVIII. Dd 4/2 Porcelain made of the best proportions of these two substances..is called hard porcelain. 1832 G. R. PORTER *Porcelain & Glass* iii. 43 This paste is not so cohesive or viscous as that which forms hard porcelain. 1881 *Harper's Mag.* Feb. 368/1 There are now hard or true porcelain manufactories in New York. 1885 *Encycl. Brit.* XIX. 642/1 Bristol porcelain is of interest as being the first hard natural porcelain made in England. 1909 *Chambers's Jrnl.* Nov. 751/1 China manufactured in the eighteenth century was of two kinds—namely, 'hard' paste or true porcelain, and 'soft' paste or artificial china.

h. In many specific collocations, e.g. *hard brass, cheese, glaze, pitch, solder, stock*.

Hard coal: = ANTHRACITE. *Hard rubber*: = EBONITE, VULCANITE. *Hard soap*: see SOAP *sb.*[1] 2.

1824 REES *Cycl.* XXVIII. Ee 2/2 The hard and less fusible glaze of the hard porcelain, which is mostly feldspar. 1836 *Penny Cycl.* V. 409/1 The bricks are now separated for sale; the hard sound stocks are the best, and are worth from 1*l.* 10*s.* to 2*l.* a thousand. 1839 URE *Dict. Arts* II. 1016 The hard glaze of pipeclay ware. *c* 1850 Dow Jr. *Sermons* III. 112 (Bartlett) Since the introduction of hard coal. 1855 J. PHILLIPS *Man. Geol.* 100 'Hard' coal, in which the divisional structures are chiefly derived from the planes of stratification. 1860 hard rubber [see VULCANITE 2]. 1873 SPON *Workshop Rec.* Ser. I. 10 Hard Brass, for Casting. —25 parts copper, 2 zinc, 4·5 tin. *Ibid.* 364, 2 parts of good silver and 1 of ordinary brass pins, well melted, is a good, useful jewellers' hard solder. 1875 KNIGHT *Dict. Mech.*, *Hard Solder*, the solder used for uniting the more infusible metals. 1879 *Spons' Encycl. Industr. Arts* I. 324 Alloys employed for joining metals together are termed 'solders' and they are commonly divided into two classes: hard and soft solders. 1879 *Encycl. Brit.* X. 100/1 If the heat is forced, and the distillation [sc. of coal-tar] continued, a large amount of 'heavy' or 'dead oils' is obtained, and the mass left in the still is 'hard pitch'. 1880 *Ibid.* XII. 840/1 All ordinary samples [of caoutchouc] contain two distinct modifications, viz., the hard or fibrous and the soft or viscous. 1888 *Lockwood's Dict. Mech. Engin.*, *Hard Brass*.—(1) Brass which has not been annealed after drawing or rolling...(2) Hammered brass, and brass which contains a large proportion of tin. *Hard Coke*, oven coke. 1889 RIVINGTON *Building Constr.* II. (ed. 2) 105 Hard Stocks are overburnt bricks, sound but considerably blemished both in form and colour. 1902 *Encycl. Brit.* XXVII. 355/1 A perfect Leicester is perhaps the most attractive of all the so-called 'hard' cheese. 1902 *Young Engineer* I. 104 The art of soldering may be divided into two distinct classes—soft soldering,..and hard soldering, in which the solders are composed of gold, silver, copper, zinc, or brass. 1904 *Technol. & Sci. Dict.* (ed. Goodchild & Tweney) s.v. *Bricks*, Those [bricks] which are less overburnt are termed 'hard stock', and are useful for many building purposes. *Ibid.*, *Hard Paviors*.., malm bricks, over-burnt and slightly blemished in colour, used for paving, coping, etc. 1905 *Daily Chron.* 11 July 5/7 The hard-stone works. 1909 *Practitioner* Feb. 266 The mixture of the cocculus with beer..was kept by brewers' druggists, and sold to brewers under the name of 'multum' or 'hard mixture'. 1909 *Westm. Gaz.* 9 Nov. 12/1 Fine Hard Cure Para Rubber. 1921 *Dict. Occup. Terms* (1927) § 262 *Brazer, brazier*; *hard solderer*; joins together parts of steel, iron, brass or copper articles by brazing or hard soldering. *Ibid.* § 572 *Banker hand, hewer* or *mason*; *hard-stone banker mason*; cuts, and if necessary saws, blocks of stone at 'banker'. 1923 E. W. MARCHANT *Radio Telegr.* v. 61 *Hard Valves.*—The only way in which this can be achieved is by exhausting the air so completely from the bulb that there is nothing but a pure electron discharge. 1930 *Sel. Gloss. Motion Picture Technician*, *Hard*, of a vacuum tube, thoroughly evacuated. *Ibid.*, *Hard lights.* (1) Arc lights. (2) Illumination from arcs, in general. Refers to the sharp shadows cast. 1931 *Times* 16 Mar. 22/4 Chinese hard-stone carvings.

7. *Hard case*: also *attrib.* = hardened, tough.

1928 *Sunday Express* 8 Jan. 4 With memories that go back to the days of 'cracker-hash', 'lobscouse', and hard-case, blue-nose, Nova Scotia mates. 1928 *Sunday Dispatch* 29 July 2 Half a dozen particularly hard-case units of the Flying Squad.

b. Of facts: Incapable of being denied or explained away, 'stubborn'. Also *attrib.*

1887 *Graphic* 29 Jan. 123/1 Hard Facts. 1906 *Daily Chron.* 11 Apr. 3/4 A few more hard-fact letters and less of this soft imagining might have made the body of the book as interesting as the appendix. 1929 G. K. CHESTERTON *Poet & Lunatic* iv, Thank God for hard stones; thank God for hard facts.

11. *Hard case*: applied to a sailing ship on which conditions are rough. *Hard luck*: see LUCK *sb.* 1; also *attrib.* *Hard-lying money*: corruption of *hard line money* (see LINE *sb.*[2] 6); hence (joc.) *hard-liar*.

1920 *Blackw. Mag.* Mar. 322/2 The mate of a Yankee *hard-case. 1924 REX CLEMENTS *Gipsy of Horn* vi. 111 He signed away as Third Mate on a hard-case Yankee barque. 1900 G. ADE *More Fables in Slang* (1902) 18 Her *Hard-luck story. 1906 B'NESS VON HUTTEN *What became of Pam* II. viii, Learning..something of..his hard-luck story. 1919 H. L. WILSON *Ma Pettengill* iv. 109 She said it [sc. the letter] would tell a new hard-luck tale for non-payment of a note. *Ibid.* 134 It was another hard-luck letter. 1916 'TAFFRAIL' (H. T. Dorling) *Pincher Martin* iv. 56 *note*, Men serving in destroyers receive sixpence a day extra pay. It is known as '*hard-lying money'. 1925 E. FRASER & GIBBONS *Soldier & Sailor Words*, *Hard-lying money*, the extra allowance granted to officers and men for service in destroyers and torpedo boats, and as compensation for wear and tear of uniform and clothing, etc. Extended in the War to the crews of motor launches and other auxiliary small craft. (Abolished in 1923.) 1927 *Daily Express* 10 Oct. 3 Sometimes, in recompense for discomforts endured, the crews of drifters draw what is termed 'hard-lying money' (those who receive this are naturally known as '*hard liars').

d. Of wear: Rough or severe and continuous. Cf. *hard-wearing* (*HARD *adv.* 8).

1932 *Sale Catal.*, To stand hard school wear.

14. c. *U.S.* (Earlier examples.)

1840 *Congress. Globe* 13 Feb. 197/3 He had heard..the same arguments preached nine hundred and ninety-nine times over a barrel of hard cider. 1848 *Ibid.* 27 Apr. 688/2 They had charged him [sc. President Harrison] with drinking hard cider.

d. Of X rays: Having great penetrating power.

1902 *Encycl. Brit.* XXVIII. 52/2 If the exhaustion of the bulb is carried further, so that there is a considerable increase in the potential difference between the cathode and anode and therefore in the velocity of the cathode rays, the Röntgen rays have much greater penetrating power and are often called 'hard rays'.

e. Of oil (see SOFT *a.* 23 d).

15. (Earlier U.S. example.)

1838 D. WEBSTER *Private Corr.* (1856) II. 37 Money is very hard, all along the coast, from here [i.e. Washington, D.C.] North.

18. b. *Hard labour*: also *attrib.*

1905 *Daily Chron.* 10 July 5/2 Hard-labour convicts. *Ibid.* 6 Nov. 5/6 Hard-labour prisoners. 1908 *Ibid.* 7 Jan. 4/6.

21. *hard-glazed.*

1928 *Daily Express* 6 Oct. 11/7 A hard-glazed lacquer work upon tin-plate.

22. a. hard fescue (see FESCUE *sb.* 4); **hard wheat**, any wheat having a hard grain rich in gluten; also *attrib.* **b. hard-bread** (U.S. examples).

1835 in J. B. Thoburn *Hist. Oklahoma* vi. (1916) 74 The ration of bread shall be one pound of wheat flour, Indian meal, or *hard bread. 1857 W. CHANDLESS *Visit Salt Lake* ii. 11 What we call rolls, in America are ycleped biscuits, and biscuits in their turn hard bread. 1905 E. COLE *Early Oregon* i. 12 Having no salt junk or hard bread left. 1812 in Davy *Elem. Agric. Chem.* (1813) 133 *Hard wheat always sells at a higher price in the market than soft wheat. *Ibid.*, The flour of hard wheat is in general superior to that made from soft. 1843 *Penny Cycl.* XXVII. 301/2 There are three principal varieties... These are the hard wheats, the soft wheats, and the Polish wheats. 1856 MORTON *Cycl. Agric.* II. 1005 *T*[*riticum*] *vulgare durum*, hard African wheat. 1908 *Westm. Gaz.* 1 July 6/3 The hard-wheat lands of Canada.

B. *sb.* **1.** Delete †*Obs.* (Later examples.)

1795 SHIRREFS *Sale Catal.* 3 (E.D.D.) A plain North-country bard, Who fain would cripple through the hard. 1808 JAMIESON *Dict. Scot. Lang.*, *Hard*, difficulty, hardship. *To come through the hard*, to encounter difficulties, to experience adverse fortune. 1895 G. ROY *Generalship* 73 (E.D.D.) The bits o' bairns run a great risk o' coming through the hard. 1902 *Westm. Gaz.* 10 July 10/1 He had 'come through the hards' himself. 1904 *Daily Chron.* 27 May 3/4 She is a lady who..has given her life to nursing, and has gone through its hards.

c. The state or condition of being hard.

1921 *Dict. Occup. Terms* (1927) § 238 *Sider, hard* (needles); burnishes sides of sewing machine needles in the hard, *i.e.*, after hardening on revolving bob with oil and emery.

8. Tobacco in a cake.

1898 BARTRAM *White-headed Boy* iv. 102 Packages of shag tobacco, lumps of sweetened 'hard'. *Ibid.* 105 Lind me a hand..with this lump o' harrd. 1898 *Daily News* 24 Feb. 3/1 Mr. Atkins..pulled at his pipe until he floated off into dreamland on a whiff of 'hard'.

Hard, *adv.* Add: **1. c.** Very, extremely. *U.S. colloq.*

1850 N. KINGSLEY *Diary* 97 Mr. Hopkins is hard sick. *a* 1906 'O. HENRY' *Trimmed Lamp*, etc. 13 He isn't a millionaire so hard that you could notice it, anyhow.

8. a. *hard-sought*; **b.** *hard-lived, -tried*; **hard-hit**, severely stricken by misfortune, grief, or disaster; **hard-pushed**, in difficulties; **hard run** *U.S.*, in difficulties or want, esp. with regard to money; **hard-wearing** *a.*, able to stand a considerable amount of wear.

1884 G. C. DAVIES *Peter Penniless* xix. 145 *Hard Hit. 1891 MISS BRADDON *Gerard* xxix, You've been hard hit. 1909 H. G. WELLS *Ann Veronica* ix, She saw her aunt in tears, her father white-faced and hard hit. 1921 GALSWORTHY *To Let* II. i, A look of life *hard-lived. 1834 [ASA GREENE] *Perils of Pearl St.* 123 (Bartlett) We began to be *hard pushed. Our credit, however was still fair. 1834 *Debates Congr.* 10 Mar. 848 Men, I say, who, to use the mercantile phrase, are '*hard run' to make ends meet, and only wanting an honorable excuse to fail. 1845 *N. Y. Tribune* 1 Nov. (Bartlett) We knew the Tammany party were hard run; but we did not know it was reduced to the necessity of stealing the principles of Nativism. 1909 JUSSERAND *Lit. Hist. Engl. People* III. 162 His [sc. Shakspere's] most wonderful inventions were not *hard-sought finds. 1906 *Daily Chron.* 1 Oct. 3/2 Its purpose of helping the *hard-tried bookseller. 1909 *Ibid.* 11 June 7/5 Everything possible to be done is achieved in the endeavour to make it *hard-wearing. 1928 *Observer* 1 Apr. 13 [This] Lingerie is amazingly hard-wearing.

Hard-and-fa·stness. The condition of being hard and fast; hard and fast character.

1903 *Daily Chron.* 5 Mar. 3/3 The 'hard-and-fastness' of experience. 1904 *Westm. Gaz.* 18 June 13/2 By denying the hard-and-fastness and asserting the strictly provisional character of the forms or categories.

Hard-boiled, *a.* [f. *to boil hard*, where *hard* is a predicative adj.]

1. Of an egg: Boiled till the white and yolk are solid.

1747 MRS. GLASSE *Cookery* (1784) 71 Chop two or three hard-boiled eggs fine. 1833 MARRYAT *P. Simple* xxv, Hard-boiled eggs..and a smoked mutton-ham. 1846 SOYER *Gastron. Regen.* 445 Prepare a border of hard-boiled eggs.

2. Of a hat: Hard. *U.S.*

1903 A. ADAMS *Log Cowboy* ix. 58 That fellow in front of the drug store over there with the hard boiled hat on.

3. Hardened, callous; hard-headed, shrewd. orig. *U.S.* Hence, of measures, practical.

1919 in F. A. Pottle *Stretchers* (1930) 354 We are too hardboiled to make much of a demonstration. *Ibid.* 358 Two hardboiled Irish sergeants are terrorizing the barrack. 1926 *Publishers' Weekly* 10 July 120/1 Stone..being hard-boiled, waited a few days to notice any appreciable increase in sales. 1926 *Ladies' Home Jrnl.* 26 Aug., The hard-boiled cynic has a shell it [sc. satire] can never penetrate. 1928 *Weekly Dispatch* 3 June 10/3 From its obscure beginning down in the 'tough' section of New York, up through the 'hard-boiled' wards of the great city, into municipal politics and thence into the Governor's chair. 1929 A. CONAN DOYLE *Maracot Deep* vi. 153 The hard-boiled Scanlan actually fell down in a faint. 1931 F. BUCK & E. ANTHONY *Bring 'Em Back Alive* 163 It is all a hard-boiled proposition of not treading on the other fellow's feet for fear he may rise up and poke his big toe in your eye.

Ha·rd-burned, -burnt, *a.* [HARD *adv.* 8 d.] Made hard by intensified firing.

1851 C. CIST *Cincinnati* 214 Walls of hard-burnt brick. 1868 *Rep. U.S. Commissioner Agric.* (1869) 260 Hard-burned terra cotta pipes. 1893 KATE SANBORN *Truthf. Wom. S. California* 45 Half-cylindrical plates of hard-burnt clay.

Harden, *v.* Add: **7.** *To harden off*: to inure (plants) to cold by gradually reducing the temperature of a hot-bed or forcing-house or by increasing the time of exposure to wind and sunlight.

1905 *Terms Forestry & Logging* 13 *Harden off*, to prepare seedlings in the seedbed for transplanting by gradually exposing them to wind and sunlight. 1909 *Daily Chron.* 5 June 9/5 This cool treatment or 'hardening off' process. 1912 *Chambers's Jrnl.* Dec. 848/1 Plants raised in this frame require no hardening off.

Hardener. Add: **b.** *Photog.* Any chemical used in the making of gelatine negatives to prevent the melting or frilling of the film in warm weather.

1930 *Sel. Gloss. Motion Picture Technician*, *Hardener*, solution used to harden photographic emulsion.

Harder (hā·ɹdəɹ). *S. Afr.* Also 8 **harter.** [a. Du. *harder*.] A South African fish of the mullet family, *Mugil capensis*.

1731 tr. *Kolben's Pres. State Cape Good-Hope* II. 193 There is..about the Cape a Sort of Herrings the Cape-Europeans call Harters. 1838 D. MOODIE *Record, Native Tribes S. Africa* 13 We..caught and salted 400 large steen-brass, and about 2,000 harders. 1892 Simmonds *Dict. Trade* (new ed.), *Harder*, a kind of mullet about twelve inches long, caught near the coasts of the Cape colony.

Hardhack. *U.S.* (Earlier and later examples.)
1832 W. D. Williamson *Hist. Maine* I. 116 The Hardhack, a barren bush, usually chooses poor cold ground for its residence and growth. 1880 *Harper's Mag.* Dec. 85 Them mulleins an' hardhacks in the buryin'-ground.

Hard-pan. Add: **1.** (Earlier example.)
1817 T. Dwight *Trav. New Eng.* (1821) I. 374 What is here called hard pan, a very stiff loam, so closely combined, as wholly to prevent the water from passing through it.
3. *attrib.*
1870 J. K. Medbery *Men & Myst. Wall St.* 212 Hard pan is soon reached, and both old world and new are full of hard-pan capitalists. 1889 K. Munroe *Golden Days* xi. 122 To tell the honest hard-pan truth. 1907 R. W. Service *Songs of Sourdough* (1908) 77 When a man gits on his uppers in a hard-pan sort of town.

Hardpeer (hā·ɹdpēəɹ). *S. Afr.* Also anglicized **hard pear.** [Afrikaans; f. Du. *hard* hard + *peer* pear.] A small tree of the Cape, *Olinia cymosa*, having hard wood; also applied to other trees (see quot. 1913).
1851 *Catal. Gt. Exhib.* iv. 1. 951 Pear (hard). 1874 *Treas. Bot.* Suppl. s.v. *Olinia*, The plant grows in rocky thickets and woods at the Cape, where it is known as Hardpeer. 1880 Hard Pear [see Pear *sb.* 3]. 1887 Moloney *Forestry W. Afr.* 354 Hardpeer of the Cape..Shrub 4 to 10 feet high. 1913 Pettman *Africanderisms, Hard Pear.* (1) In Natal this name is given to *Pleurostylia capensis.* (2) In the Cape Colony it is applied to *Strychnos Henningsii.*

Hardshell, *a.* and *sb.* Add: **A.** *adj.* **1.** (U.S. example.) Also applied to the fruit of a nut-tree.
1798 *Spectator* (N.Y.) 7 Nov. 2/5 Hardshell almond trees. 1855 *Knickerbocker Mag.* XLVI. 222 'Hard-shell' clam-catchers.
2. (Earlier example.)
1845 J. J. Hooper *Adv. Simon Suggs* i. 13 He lived with his father, and an old 'hard shell' Baptist preacher.
B. *sb.* **1.** Also *fig.*, a stubborn or unemotional person.
1916 H. L. Wilson *Somewhere in Red Gap* iv. 135 A grouchy old hardshell with white hair and whiskers whirling about his head. 1919 T. K. Holmes *Man fr. Tall Timber* xiii. 156 I've ridden up here from Tall Timber Junction to get acquainted with you hardshells.
2. (Earlier and later examples.)
1845 *Knickerbocker Mag.* XXVI. 285 A 'Hard-Shell' recently turned a 'Soft-Shell' out of church. 1855 *Putnam's Monthly* V. 190 The claim of 'Hard-Shells', touching their familiarity with the Bible. 1872 E. Eggleston *Hoosier Schoolm.* xii, Of course the Hardshells are prodigiously illiterate.

Hardshelled, *a.* **1.** Having a hard shell; = Hardshell A. 1.
1611 [in Dict.]. 1796–1806 B. Hawkins *Lett.* 17 A grove of dwarf hard shelled hickory trees. 1839 C. F. Briggs *Harry Franco* II. i. 2 Close by, was a negro opening hard-shelled clams. 1861 *Trans. Ill. Agric. Soc.* (1865) V. 408 Beetles, or, as they are sometimes called, 'hard-shelled bugs'.
2. *fig.* = Hardshell A. 2. Also, hardened, callous.
1842 J. S. Buckingham *Slave States Amer.* I. 197 The Baptists [in Macon, Georgia] are of the order called here 'Hardshelled Baptists'. 1872 W. Mathews *Getting on in World* xi. 153 There is no man so 'hard-shelled' that his soul cannot be reached by kindness. 1904 *N. Y. Herald* 23 Oct. 16 There are a good many hard shelled Bryan men who intend to vote for Roosevelt. 1909 R. A. Wason *Happy Hawkins* 108 It was a hard-shelled book.

Hard-tack. (Earlier and later U.S. examples.)
1836 *Knickerbocker Mag.* VIII. 203 When I was the size of that monkey there, who knows how to do nothing but gnaw hard tack. 1888 *Century Mag.* XXXVI. 614/1 A little rabbit that kept..nibbling at our bread and hard-tack. 1899 T. Hall *Tales* 108 A meal of raw bacon, hard-tack and cold water.

Hardtail (hā·ɹdˌtēɪl). *U.S.* [f. Hard *a.* + Tail *sb.*[1]] **a.** A carangoid fish, *Caranx chrysos* or *C. pisquetus*, the jurel. **b.** Either of two cyprinoid fishes, *Gila elegans* and *G. robusta*, of the Colorado basin of North America.
1884 Goode *Fisheries U.S.* I. 324 The Jurel—Caranx Pisquetus. This fish, known about Pensacola as the 'Jurel', 'Cojinua', and 'Hard-tail'.

Hardware. **2.** Add: **hardware house, store** *U.S.*, an ironmonger's shop; **hardware paper**, a make of durable wrapping-paper.
1789 *Boston Directory*, Whitwell,..hardware store. 1848 *Ladies Repository* VIII. 281 They..roll them out into long bars, such as you see on sale at hardware houses. 1886 *Harper's Mag.* June 48/1 Wrapping the stem [of the peach-tree]..with strong hardware or sheathing paper.

Hardwood. Add:
1. (Later examples of attrib. use with *land*, etc.)
1840 *Knickerbocker Mag.* XXVIII. 337 Most unexceptional 'hardwood' land. 1867–8 *Trans. Ill. Agric. Soc.* VII. 578 Some elevated ridges..called technically, hard wood ridges..escaped wholly, or in part the effects of the fire. 1903 S. E. White *Forest* viii. 89 The trunks of the hardwood forest.
b. *ellipt.* A hardwood tree.
1908 *Westm. Gaz.* 15 Aug. 15/3 The tender colours of the hardwoods bursting towards summer glory.

Hare, *sb.* **6.** Add: **hare-pocket,** a pocket in a shooting coat, made of a size to hold a hare.
1925 G. Burrard *Big Game Hunting* 281 Two 'hare' or 'poacher' pockets will be found most useful on occasions.

Hare, *v.*[2] [f. Hare *sb.*] *intr.* **a.** To double like a hare. ? *Obs.* **b.** To run or move with great speed. Also with *it.*
1893 Farmer & Henley *Slang, To hare it*, to retrace one's steps; to double back. a 1914 J. E. Raphael *Mod. Rugby Football* (1918) 262 Receiving the ball well inside his own half-way, Palmer commenced to 'hare' for the touch-line. 1917 P. Gibbs *Battles of Somme* 173 There were other trenches ahead, and the men 'hared' off to these. 1923 P. G. Wodehouse *Inimitable Jeeves* xiv. 178, I..hared it rapidly to the spot.

Harem. Add: **2. b.** Applied *spec.* to the family unit of fur seals.
1898 D. S. Jordan *Fur Seals* I. 57 The average size of a harem..is about thirty females to a single bull.

Hare's-foot. Add: **4.** A hare's foot used in applying rouge, etc., to the face. Also *attrib.*
1877 'Haresfoot & Rouge' *How to 'Make-up'* 13 Then with a hare's foot apply a colouring of Rouge to the cheeks. 1888 J. Ker *Hist. Preaching* (ed. 2) 281 A hare's-foot brush to touch the dust of holy statues.

Harewood (hēə·ɹwud). Also **hairwood, airwood** (8 **aire-**); and simply 7 **ayer, ayre.** [ad. dial. G. *aehre, ehre*, or its apparent source Friulian, etc. *ayar, ayer, aire*:—Rom. **acre* = L. *acer* maple.] Stained sycamore wood, used by cabinet-makers.
1664 Evelyn *Sylva* I. x. 28 The Timber [of Maple] is far superiour to Beech for all uses of the Turner...Also for the lightness (under the name Ayer) imploy'd often by those who make Musical-instruments. 1676 Mace *Musick's Mon.* 49 Next, what Wood is Best for the Ribbs. The Air-wood is absolutely the Best. *Ibid.* 64 A Lute made of Ayre. 1723 *Evening Post* 30 May, He has..some fine Aire-wood for furnishing the Insides [of harpsicords]. 1843 Holtzapffel *Turning* etc. I. 107 A variety of sycamore, which is called harewood, is richer in figure and sometimes striped. 1873 Spon *Workshop Rec.* Ser. I. 414/1 Have the veneers ready, which must be air-wood. *Ibid.* 423/2 Hair-wood. 1899 *Daily News* 22 June 8/7 A cabinet..of inlaid satin, hare, and other woods. 1901 *Westm. Gaz.* 9 May 1/3 On satin and harewood banded with rosewood.

Hark, *v.* Add: **2. a.** Also const. *at.*
1888 Fenn *Dick o' the Fens* vii, Hark at him!..young squire ar'n't going to eat any more bacon, 'cause it's cruel to kill the pigs. 1895 'G. Mortimer' *Like Stars that fall* xiii, 'You're so spry, I can't trust you for a grass widow.' 'Hark at him!' laughed Mrs. Larpenti.
4. d. *To hark after*: to go after, to follow.
1899 Tarkington *Gentl. Indiana* vii. 109 Men were running around a corner of the court-house, and the women and children were harking after.

Harka (hā·ɹkä). [Arab.] A body of Moroccan irregular troops.
1903 *Daily Chron.* 18 Sept. 4/6 The regions in the Sahara affected by the recent incursions of the Moorish harkas. 1909 *Ibid.* 26 July 1/5 The harka..consisted of about 15,000 Kabyles. 1925 *Blackw. Mag.* Nov. 624/1 [He] led out a harka to fight in the national cause.

Harl, *sb.*[3] Add: **5.** A composition of lime and gravel or sand; roughcast.
1869 R. L. Stevenson in *Scribner's Mag.* (1899) XXV. 42/1 The houses, white with harl. 1898 J. J. H. Burgess *Tang* ii. 23 The gable was white, for the 'harl' had been picked off in the spring.

Harlequin. **6.** Add: **harlequin (Great) Dane**, a Great Dane having a black and white coat; **harlequin fly**, a fly of the genus *Chironomus*; **harlequin opal** = Harlequin *sb.* 4.
1800 *Harlequin Dane [see Dane 2]. 1909 *Daily Chron.* 28 July 7/1 A black and white or harlequin Great Dane. 1901 Miall & Hammond (*title*) The Structure and Life History of the *Harlequin Fly (*Chironomus*). 1887 *Col. & Indian Exhib., Rep. Col. Sect.* 70 Some specimens are of a rare kind, known as '*Harlequin' opals.

Harley (hā·ɹli). *Harley Street*: name of a street in London associated with eminent physicians and surgeons; hence used allusively for the specialists of the medical profession.
1830 *New Monthly Mag.* II. 220 Harley-street was..in an uproar at these monstrous stipulations.

Harm, *v.* Add: **c.** *intr.* To take harm.
1916 Boyd Cable *Action Front* 224 The men is fresh, too, and won't harm for a bit of exercise.

Harmol (hā·ɹmǫl). *Chem.* [f. Harm(ine + -ol.] A compound formed by the action of fuming hydrochloric acid on harmine. Also **Harmo·lic** *a.*, derived from harmol.
1898 *Jrnl. Chem. Soc.* LXXIV. i. 164.

Harmonic, *a.* and *sb.* Add: **A.** *adj.* **4.** *Harmonic minor mode* or *scale*: see quot. 1884.
1884 Maitland in Grove *Dict. Mus.* IV. 666/2 Harmonic minor is the name applied to that version of the minor scale which contains the minor sixth together with the major seventh, and in which no alteration is made in ascending and descending. 1889 E. Prout *Harmony* (ed. 10) vii. § 171 This form is known as the Harmonic Minor Scale, the other two being called Melodic Minor Scales.
5. b. *Harmonic current*, an alternating current the variations of which, graphically represented, follow a harmonic curve.
1910 *Hawkins' Electr. Dict.* 193/1.
B. *sb.* **4. a.** *Electr.* In an alternating circuit, a component current whose frequency is a multiple of the fundamental; also, a corresponding electromagnetic oscillation.
1894 *Amer. Jrnl. Sci.* CXLVIII. 379 The presence of upper harmonics in an alternating current wave. *Ibid.* 383 For every harmonic of the inducing current we shall have a harmonic electromotive force of the same frequency in the resonant circuit. 1906 A. Russell *Altern. Curr.* II. 126 We generally find a pronounced third harmonic in the potential difference wave of a single phase machine when loaded. 1919 R. Stanley *Wireless Telegr.* II. 164 When the fundamental oscillations in a circuit are accompanied by other subsidiary oscillations the latter are called harmonics.

Harmonization. Add:
1. b. Agreement in colour.
1897 R. Kearton *Nature & Camera* 252 Their wonderful harmonisation with the sand upon which they lay stretched. 1925 R. W. G. Hingston in E. F. Norton *Fight for Everest, 1924* 262 We are attracted by their example of harmonization, the pale grey colour of their fur blending well with the upland soil.

Harmonize, *v.* Add: **3. d.** To form a harmonious combination *with.*
1852 *Art-Jrnl.* Apr. 117/3 If it is necessary that the colours of the different articles of dress should..harmonise with each other. 1862 *Englishwoman's Domestic Mag.* May 60/1 Flowers, and shells, and coloured fabrics that harmonise admirably with themselves and with the tropical scenery among which she lives. 1925 R. W. G. Hingston in E. F. Norton *Fight for Everest, 1924* 265 Then unexpectedly the bird alights, the crimson colour vanishes, the white spots disappear, and the bird again harmonizes with the hill.

Harmonogram (haɹmǫ·nǒgræm). [f. as Harmonograph: see -gram.] A figure or curve drawn by a harmonograph.
1902 A. Williams in *Pearson's Mag.* Apr. 443/1.

Harness, *sb.* Add: **4.** *Double harness*, harness for two draught horses working side by side. *Single harness*, harness for a draught horse working alone. Often *fig.*
1862 *Catal. Internat. Exhib., Brit.* II. No. 4732 Double and single harness, pads, collars, round reins, pole pieces. 1901 'M. Gray' *Four-Leaved Clover* i, And it's about time you went in double harness. I go better in single. To confess the solid truth, I was born an old maid.
6. (Later U.S. example.)
1888 Eggleston in *Century Mag.* XXXVI. 529/2 When Barbara had tied a broken string in the 'harness' of the loom, she resumed her seat on the bench.
9. harness (horse) racing *U.S.*, a race between horses harnessed to vehicles; also **harness race** *U.S.* (Webster, 1909).
1901 *World Almanac* 266 Harness racing. 1909 *Ibid.* 213 Harness horse racing.

Harpings, *sb. pl.* Add: Also 9 **harping.**
1827 Cooper *Red Rover* I. viii. 131 She is too lean in the harping, and too full in the counter, to steer.

Harpoon, *sb.* Add:
2. b. *Med.* A trocar-like surgical instrument for removing small pieces of living tissue for microscopic examination.
1876 Bristowe *Theory Pract. Med.* (1878) 719 The extraction by means of a suitable instrument (harpoon) of fragments of striped muscular tissue. 1897 *Allbutt's Syst. Med.* II. 1057 The harpoon designed..for this purpose produces an unsurgical wound.

Harpuisbosje (hā·ɹpisbǒᵘ·ʃye). *S. Afr.* Also semi-anglicized **harpuis, arpuse,** or **rapuis bush.** [f. Du. *harpuis* resin + *bosje*, dim. of *bos* bush.] A shrub belonging to the genus *Euryops*, e.g. the resin-bush, *E. speciosissimus.*
1815 tr. *Lichtenstein's Trav.* II. 176 A shrub, which grows from two feet to three feet and a half high, called by the colonists *harpuisbosjes*, the rosin tree. 1846 H. H. Methuen *Life in Wilderness* 112 We again were in danger of being burnt; a sea of flame raging on one side of the road, and consuming the resinous *arpuse* bushes with a roaring noise, audible a long way off. [1912 *East London Dispatch* 22 Aug. 5 (Pettman) Mr. Moffatt (Tarka) brought up the question of the noxious *rapuis* which had hitherto baffled their efforts.]

Harrian (hæ·riăn), *a.* and *sb.* Also **Hurrian** (hʊ·riăn). [f. Hittite and Assyrian *Ḫar-ri, Ḫur-ri* + -an.] Name of a people of the Hittite kingdom using a language of a Caucasian type. Hence **Ha·rrianize** *v. trans.*, to make Harrian in form or character.
1928 C. Dawson *Age of Gods* 302 Harrian is practically identical with the language of the people of Mitanni, the most powerful state of North-west Mesopotamia...The dominant element in Mitanni was..Indo-Iranian, in origin, but there is no trace of this in the Harrian language, which is purely Asianic or Caucasian in type. 1929 J. Garstang *Hittite Empire* ii. 34 North of it [*sc.* Assyria]..was Alshe, a Harrian dependency; while..eastern Taurus was apparently wholly in possession of the Harrians, whose seat must probably be sought in Armenia itself, possibly in the neighbourhood of Lake Van. *Note*, Professor Sayce would..identify the Harrians with the Amorites. 1930 *Dublin Rev.* Jan. 9 Hurrian was one of the languages of the eastern part of the Hittite Empire. *Ibid.* 11 Nahmaulel..may be either Hurrianized Semitic, or wholly 'foreign'—*i.e.*, presumably Caucasian or Hurrian. *Ibid.* 13 The Hurrian-speaking people, situated on the line of communications between Babylonia and the West, were probably among the intermediaries by whom Babylonian tradition was introduced into Palestine.

Harris (hæ·ris). The name of a district which together with Lewis forms the largest island of the Outer Hebrides, used attrib. to designate the tweed made in that district.
1894 *Strand Mag.* VIII. 661/2 My tailor tells me that Harris tweed cannot wear out. 1898 *Daily News* 5 July 2/4 The delightful 'Harris', 'Sheland', and 'Sutherland' tweeds that were being shown.

Hart. **2.** Add: **hart's nut** = *hart's truffle.*
1888 *Encycl. Brit.* XXIII. 592/1 The truffle *Elaphomyces variegatus* was till quite recent times used, under the name

of Hart's nut or Lycoperdon nut, on account of its supposed aphrodisiac qualities.

Hartal (hā·ɹtæl, ‖hɒ·ɹtāl). *India.* [Hindi हरताल *hartāl* for हट्टताल *haṭṭāl* lit. 'locking of shops' (Skr. *haṭṭa* shop, *tālaka* lock, bolt).] A day of national mourning in India, during which shops are shut and no business transacted: used as a form of boycott.
1920 *Blackw. Mag.* Apr. 441/1 What I had seen there of the crowds at the Hartal..had made me nervous. 1921 *Q. Rev.* July 54 He proclaimed a universal 'hartal', or cessation from business, as a protest against the Rowlatt legislation. 1922 *Ibid.* Oct. 417 Gandhi was preparing a *Hartal* at Bombay.

Hartebeest. Add: *attrib.* **hartebeest house, hut,** 'a frail structure of "wattle and daub", so called, apparently, because a similar primitive structure was often erected by the earlier hunters' (Pettman).
1818 Latrobe *Jrnl.* 256 A *hartebeest-house, being a roof, put upon a wall about two feet in height. 1863 W. C. Baldwin *Afr. Hunting* i. 16 What is called a hartebeest house, of very tall reeds, stuck close together in a kind of trench dug for them in bundles, and meeting over head. 1873 F. Boyle *To Cape for Diamonds* 242 A colony of Hottentot women had seized possession of our '*hartebeest's hut'.

Harveian (haɹvī·ăn), *a.* [f. the name of William *Harvey* (1578–1657), English physician, discoverer of the circulation of the blood + -an.] Pertaining to or founded in honour of Harvey.
1826 T. L. McKenney *Tour to Lakes* (1827) 298 The Harveynian [*sic*] system of the circulation of the blood. 1880 *Encycl. Brit.* XI. 505/1 Caspar Hoffmann,..admitting the truth of the lesser circulation in the full Harveian sense. *Ibid.* 506/2 The Harveian Orations. 1903 *Lancet* 6 June 1608/1 The Harveian Lectures of the Harveian Society of London. 1928 *Daily Tel.* 15 May 14/3 MSS., books, pictures, and other objects of Harveian interest.

Harvester. **3.** Also **harvesting machine.** (Earlier U.S. examples.)
1836 *U.S. Patents* 28 June, Harvesting machine. 1848 *Ibid.* 21 Nov., Harvester. 1851 Cist *Cinc.* 161 Harvesters and mowing-machines.

Has-been, *sb.* Add: (Later *dial.* and U.S. examples.)
1853 B. F. Taylor *Jan. & June* (1871) 206 Dilapidated 'has-beens', and despised 'used-to-be's'. 1879 Miss Jackson *Shropsh. Word-bk.* 180 'Er's a good owd 'as bin. 1904 *Philad. Even. Telegraph* 9 Nov. 5 Parker and his party are among the has beens. 1905 Tarkington *In Arena* 3 I'll potter along trying to look knowing and secretive, like the rest of the has-beens. 1914 Gertrude Atherton *Perch of Devil* I. 70 The obsolete notions that made most of our relations a sort of premature has-beens.
2. *pl.* Old times. *U.S.*
1904 W. H. Smith *Promoters* v. 91, I met old Bishop Slosher..and just for has-beens I took him to lunch with me.

Hash, *sb.* **3. b.** (Earlier U.S. examples.)
1807 *Massachusetts Spy* 14 Oct. 4/1 This settles all the hash. 1822 [see Settle *v.* 21 b].
6. hash-house *U.S. slang*, a cheap eating-house.
1883 *Daily Tel.* 10 Jan. 5/4 (Farmer) Fifteen-cent restaurants, commonly called hash-houses. 1897 *Outing* (U.S.) XXX. 362/1 It has its swell hotels..and its 'hash-houses'.

Haskinize (hæ·skinəiz), *v.* [f. the name of S. E. *Haskin*, the inventor of the process + -ize.] *trans.* To submit (green timber) to a process by which it becomes hard and durable through the application of heat of over 212° F. under a pressure of 200 pounds to the square inch. So **Ha:skiniza·tion.**
1902 *Specif. Patent S. E. Haskin*, Railway sleepers, polished planks, cabinet panels &c. which had been 'haskinised'. 1908 W. R. Fisher tr. *Gayer's Forest Utiliz.* (ed. 2) 509 The process is termed Haskinisation or Vulcanisation, and has given good results on the Manhattan Railway, New York.

Hasmonean (hæzmonī·ăn), *sb.* and *a.* Also **Ash-, -æan, Asmonean, -æan.** [f. mod.L. *Asmōnæus*, f. Ἀσαμωναῖος (Josephus) = חשמונאי *Ḥashmōnāi*, name of the reputed grandfather of Mattathias.] **A.** *sb.* A member of a Jewish dynasty or family to which the Maccabees belonged. **B.** *adj.* Of or pertaining to this dynasty.
1620 Lodge tr. *Josephus* xiv. xxviii. 381 Thus ended the estate of the Asmoneans, after 120. and sixe yeeres. *Ibid. marg.*, The end of the Asmonæan family. 1832 H. Cotton *Five Bks. Maccabees* 50 Ashmonæan princes. 1834 *Penny Cycl.* II. 485 Asmonæans. 1880 *Encycl. Brit.* XIII. 421/2 A certain priest Mattathias, of the family of the Hasmonæans. 1898 Cheyne in *Expositor* Apr. 273 The Hasmonean priestly dynasty. 1926 E. F. Scott *1st Age Christianity* i. 16 In virtue of his priestly descent the Asmonaean king could also hold the office of high-priest.

Hassidic, Hassidism, var. of Chasidic, Chasidism (see *Chasidim).
1927 *Daily Tel.* 5 Apr. 12/6 The devotees of that particular cult which was known as Hassidism. 1927 *Sunday Express* 10 Apr. 5/7 'The Dybbuk' is all about the Hassidic cult.

Haste, *sb.* **5.** Add: *To make haste slowly*, after L. *festina lente* (Suet. *Aug.* 25).
1831 *Debates Congr.* 4 Feb. 98 Thus far the committee have 'made haste slowly'.

Hasty pudding. (Later U.S. examples.)
1879 B. F. Taylor *Summer-Savory* i. 7 Their green knapsacks are growing plump with rations of samp, hasty-pudding, and Indian bread. 1881 *Harper's Mag.* Jan. 227/1 Cod-fish balls for breakfast on Sunday morning,..and fried hasty-pudding.

Hat, *sb.* Add: **5. a.** *To take off one's hat*: to doff or remove the hat, as a salute or sign of respect. Hence *Hats off to..*, as a command or exhortation.
1868 D. Livingstone *Miss. Trav.* viii. 117 As it was the only hill we had seen since leaving the Bamangwato, we felt inclined to take off our hats to it. 1881 *Harper's Mag.* Jan. 206/1 Over in Greenwood there is a stately monument, to the New York fireman,..before which I take off my hat. 1886 *Ibid.* June 45/2 We should take off our hats to them [*sc.* the 'lady-bugs'] and wish them godspeed. 1923 Ld. Rothermere in *Daily Mail* 22 Jan. 6, I say in all sincerity: 'Hats off to France!'
c. *To hang one's hat*: to take up one's quarters (in a certain place). *To hang one's hat on*: to depend upon. *To talk through one's hat*: to make unsupported or 'wild' assertions. *To throw one's hat into the ring*: to take up a challenge. *Under one's hat*: secret, sub rosa. *My hat!*, a trivial exclamation of surprise. See also *High hat.
1847 *Sporting Life* V. 224/2 Warren threw his hat in the ring. 1881 A. A. Hayes *New Colorado* viii. 118 Why that's *my* preacher. I hang my hat on him every time. 1888 *New York World* 13 May, Dis is only a bluff dey're makin'—see! Dey're talkin' tru deir hats. 1902 Harben *Abner Daniel* 81 All this talk about the devil makin' the bad an' the Lord the good is talk through a hat. 1904 *N. Y. American* 18 July 2 If the Tamany leader expects to hang his hat inside Judge Parker's political headquarters, he must come here voluntarily. 1909 S. E. White *Rules of Game* III. ix. 181 I'll give you another [tip] gratis. It's strictly under your hats, though. 1917 W. J. Locke *Red Planet* xxiv, 'You dashed young idiot,' I cried, 'do you think I'm in the habit of talking through my hat?' 1923 Wodehouse *Inimit. Jeeves* xviii. 249 She kept it under her hat. She meant to spring it on me later on, she said. 1928 *Saturday Even. Post* (N.Y.) 4 Feb. 100/3 I'm not telling anyone else—so, under your hat. 1928 *Observer* 4 Mar. 11/2 Mr. Secretary Hoover has been forced to throw his hat into the ring for the Presidency, but he does not mean to follow it there. 1930 Galsworthy *Roof* iv, *Mr. B.* I suppose you think you never snore. *Mrs. B.* I know I don't. *Mr. B.* My hat!
9, 10. *hat-raising, -trimming*; **hat leather** (see quot.); **hat-pad**, a pad usually of velvet for wiping the dust off or smoothing the nap of a hat; **hat-tip**, the circular piece of stuff used to line the crown of a hat; **hat-tree**, (*b*) *Austral.* (see quot.).
1888 *Lockwood's Dict. Mech. Engin.*, *Hat Leather, the leather ring packing used for hydraulic pistons. 1902 W. W. Jacobs *Lady of Barge, Mixed Prop.*, At the hall he paused, and busied himself with the clothes-brush and *hat-pad. 1905 *Westm. Gaz.* 11 Aug. 7/1 At Trafalgar-square there was much *hat-raising. 1908 *Ibid.* 30 Jan. 12/2 The hat-raising habit. 1921 *Dict. Occup. Terms* (1927) § 549 **Hat tip sizer*, prints hat tip with size before gold leaf or bronze dust is applied by hat tip printer. 1898 Morris *Austral Engl.*, **Hat-tree*, name given to a species of *Sterculia*, the Bottle-trees. 1905 *Daily Chron.* 23 Dec. 6/5 The success of the *hat-trimming competition.

Hat, *v.* Add: **c.** *intr.* To work alone. (Cf. Hatter *sb.* 2.) *Austral.*
1891 *The Age* 25 Nov. 6/7 (Morris) Two old miners have been..hatting for gold amongst the old alluvial gullies. 1900 H. Lawson *On Track* 88 And he 'hatted' and brooded over it till he went ratty.

Hatchel, *sb.* See also *Hetchel *sb.*

Hatchel, *v.* Add: **1. b.** *transf.*
1845 [see *Hetchel *v.*].
2. *fig.* (Earlier U.S. example.)
1800 *Aurora* (Phila.) 20 Oct. (Th.) They have..hatchelled them with prosecutions, fines, and imprisonments.

Hatching, *vbl. sb.*[1] **a.** Add: Also, that which is hatched, a brood.
1905 *Kynoch Jrnl.* Apr.–June 108 The hatchings at the present time are quite up to the average of a good year.

Hatchling (hæ·tʃliŋ). [f. Hatch *sb.*[2] + -ling[1].] A very young fish or bird, usually artificially hatched and not old enough to take care of itself.
1899 *19th Cent.* Sept. 399 The ova hatched out *en route*, and the hatchlings died. 1899 *Field* 16 Sept. 496 This assertion may be verified by throwing some hatchlings into a tank where fish of all sizes are mixed together. It will be seen that the strangers are at once devoured.

Hatch-out (hæ·tʃˌaut). [f. the verbal phr. *to hatch out* (see Hatch *v.*[1] 2).] The action of hatching out; also, the brood hatched out.
1898 *Westm. Gaz.* 13 May 4/1 It only depends upon climatic conditions to ensure a good hatch out. 1908 *Ibid.* 5 June 4/2 While the hatch-out is in progress the number of the fly is marvellous. *Ibid.* 14 Aug. 4/2 Partridges are more faithful to a fixed date for the hatch-out of their eggs than grouse.

Hate, *sb.*[1] Add: **1. c.** In the war of 1914–18, a bombardment, a 'strafe'. *slang.*
A jocular use based upon the German 'Hymn of Hate', which was ridiculed in *Punch* 24 Feb. 1915, p. 150, in the legend of a drawing, 'Study of a Prussian household having its morning hate'.
1915 D. O. Barnett *Lett.* 204 There are some unhealthy spots, 'Suicide Corner', 'Deadman's Alley' and others, where they drop shells regularly, trying to catch our transport at night. We call it the 'Evening Hate'. 1927 E. Thompson *These Men thy Friends* 112 He was watching a spasmodic 'hate' of some violence.

Hateworthy (hē¹·tˌwɒ̄·ɹði), *a.* [f. Hate *sb.*[1] + Worthy *a.*] Worthy of hate, hateful.
1901 A. Symons *Poems* (1907) I. 180, I tremble lest a wrath so just avenge On him a mother so most hate-worthy. 1924 *Public Opinion* 9 May 450/3 There is nothing sinister or hateworthy in Mrs. Carlyle's slowly and deliberately formed judgement.

Hathi (hā·ti). *India.* Also **harti, hatty, hotty, huttee.** [Hind. *hāthī* (also Marathi, etc. *hattī*), f. Skr. *hastin* elephant, f. *hasta* elephant's trunk, hand.] An elephant. Also *attrib.*: **hathi tractor,** a kind of tractor used in the war of 1914–18.
[1826 J. Leyden & Erskine tr. *Mem. Zahir al Din* 315 As for the animals peculiar to Hindustān, one is the elephant, the Hindustānis call it *Hathi*.] 1831 Tyerman & Bennet *Voy. & Trav.* II. 375 Our bearers suddenly set up the cry of 'Huttee! huttee!' 1838 in E. Eden *Up the Country* (1866) I. 269 You are of course aware that we habitually call elephants Hotties. 1860 W. H. Russell *Diary India* I. 392 We came to the Ramgunga, a deep stream, which our elephant waded across...The hathi nearly floated his driver off his neck. 1892 Kipling *Barrack-room Ballads, On Road to Mandalay*, An' the *hathis* pilin' teak. 1922 *Glasgow Herald* 11 Feb. 10 Golden also was the head of the 'hathi' selected for this honour.

Hathor (hā·þǭɹ). Also **Athor.** [ad. Gr. Ἀθώρ, f. Egypt. *Ḥet-Ḥerh* the house above, or *Ḥet-Ḥeru* house of Horus.] The name of an Egyptian divinity, the goddess of love, often represented with the head or ears of a cow, used *attrib.* or *Comb.* to designate a type of column surmounted by a capital on which is carved one or more representations of the head of Hathor. So **Hathoric** (hăþǫ·rik), *a.*
1896 Flinders Petrie *Koptos* 4/2 Below the scene is a frieze of *dad* signs alternating with figures, the lower parts of which are like the Isiac girdle tie, while above they have the human Hathor head, with cows' ears and horns...They seem as if they might be copies of some primitive Hathor idol. 1901 R. Sturgis *Dict. Archit.* I. 854/2 The columns are easily divisible into a few general types, such as the single and the clustered lotus-bud, the campaniform, the palm-capped, and the Hathor-headed. *Ibid.* II. 366/2 *Hathoric*, having to do with the Egyptian goddess Hathor.

Ha·tlessness. [-ness.] Hatless condition.
1881 White *Eng. Without & Within* 271 The hatlessness, the shoelessness, the rags, and the dirt. 1902 *Westm. Gaz.* 17 Oct. 2/3 Hitherto hatlessness was only *de rigueur* in the stalls and the front row of the dress circle. 1924 *Glasgow Herald* 29 May 6 Many people, who advocate hatlessness during the summer months.

Hattic (hæ·tik), *a.* Also **Kh-.** [f. Assyrian and Hittite *Ḫatti* + -ic.] Of or pertaining to the Hatti, sometimes regarded as conterminous with the Hittites, sometimes as a section of them. So **Ha·ttian** *sb.*, one of the race of Hatti. **Ha·ttism,** the social and political system of the Hatti.
[1874 *Trans. Soc. Bibl. Arch.* III. 245 The king of the Khati. 1880 Cheyne in *Encycl. Brit.* XII. 25/1 Hittites, a warlike and powerful nation...In the Egyptian inscriptions they are called the Khita or Kheta; in the Assyrian, the Khatti; in the Hebrew Scriptures, the Khittim.] 1924 Hogarth in *Cambr. Anc. Hist.* II. 253 Boghaz Keui..is the site of the Hattic capital. 1924 — *Kings of Hittites* (1926) 3 The Hittite civilization of Hamath was but an outlier of 'Hattism', advanced southward along a trunk-road. *Ibid.* 8 Have any remains been revealed which manifestly are Cappadocian Hattic, wholly or in part? 1928 C. Dawson *Age of Gods* 302 The official language of the empire has been named by its discoverers Nashili or Kanesian; but since the ruling people have always been known as the Hittites, it seems better to retain the same name for their language and to describe the native Hattic tongue as Old Hittite. 1929 J. Garstang *Hittite Empire* ii. 39 The suggestion of language..would seem to indicate an original movement or series of movements from or affecting the Caucasian area, which at the same time peopled Armenia, northern Mesopotamia, and Elam, and won for the Hattians and other Hittite tribes a footing on the eastern mountains and plateau of Asia Minor. *Ibid.* 40 The Hattians themselves were an inland and not a seafaring people.

Hatty, variant of *Hathi.

Hauchecornite (hǭtʃkǫ·ɹnəit). *Min.* [Named (G. *hauchecornit*) after W. *Hauchecorn*: see -ite[1].] A bronze-coloured sulphide of nickel, bismuth, and antimony.
1893 *Jrnl. Chem. Soc.* LXIV. ii. 418.

Hau-hau (hǭˌhǭ), *v.* [Echoic.] *intr.* To utter the cry of a hyena.
1924 *Other Lands* Jan. 43/1 A hyena went hau-hauing down the path between the tent and the garden.

Haul, *sb.* Add: **1. c.** *Logging.* (See quot.)
1905 *Terms Forestry & Logging* 39 *Haul*, in logging, the distance and route over which teams must go between two given points, as between the yard or skidway and the landing.

Haul, *v.* Add: **1. e.** To transport by cart or other conveyance; to cart, carry.
1787 [see sense 1]. 1814 H. M. Brackenridge *Views of Louisiana* 141 They are sometimes employed in hauling lead from the mines. 1852 *Trans. Mich. Agric. Soc.* III. 179, I haul it [*sc.* manure] out in the fall, spread it and plow it in immediately after. 1880 *Harper's Mag.* Sept. 619/2 In winter I haul logs, and in summer I haul mealers. 1887 *Congress. Rec.* 10 Jan. 484/1 There is not one-tenth part of the risk in hauling dressed beef that there is in hauling live animals. 1918 F. Hackett *Ireland* ii. 46 The more fish was caught..the less any one of them was worth. And when it came to salting them or hauling them, the same curse was in it.
absol. 1883 J. Hay *Bread-winners* vi. 96 You know Clinsty Fore, that hauls for the Safe company?
f. *intr.* With *out, up.* Of bachelor seals: To come out of the water to rest on the hauling-grounds.
1869 *Overland Monthly* III. 39 To ascertain if any elephant-seal had 'hauled up' on the beach. 1902 *Encycl. Brit.* XXXII. 488/1 The young males, or bachelors, haul out to rest and sleep on beaches adjacent to, but distinct from, the breeding-grounds.

Haulabout (hǭ·lăbout). *U.S.* [f. the verbal phrase *to haul about* (see Haul *v.* 1).] A vessel, resembling a barge, used for coaling ships.
1904 *Sci. Amer.* 23 July 63/2 Another type of coaling device which has proved highly successful is what is known as the 'haulabout'.

Haulage. **4.** Add: *haulage-engine.*
1909 *Daily Chron.* 16 Sept. 1/3 A haulage engine..was taking a load of bricks up the steep gradient. *Ibid.* 30 Sept. 1/5 The flood carried away the haulage engine at the entrance of the level.

Hauling. **b.** Add: **hauling-ground,** a place where bachelor seals congregate, distinguished from the rookery or ground occupied by breeding seals.
1898 D. S. Jordan *Fur Seals* I. 36 Adjoining the breeding grounds and an essential part of each rookery are what are known as the 'hauling grounds' of the bachelors, frequented by the young males of the ages of 5 years and under.

Haunch, *sb.*[1] Add: **4. c.** The end of a tenon reduced in width. So **Haunched** *a.*, (of a tenon) having its end reduced in width; **Haunching,** a recess in a style for the end of a tenon.
1885 *Spons' Mech. Own Bk.* 276 The haunched tenon [is used] when the edge of the piece on which the tenon is formed is required to be flush with the end of the piece containing the mortice. 1904 A. C. Passmore *Handbk. Techn. Terms, Haunch*, the wide part left close to the root when part of a tenon is cut away. 1904 *Technol. & Sci. Dict.* (ed. Goodchild & Tweney), *Haunched Tenon*, a tenon cut back in its width to allow for wedging.

Haunk-haunk (hǭŋk,hǭŋk). [Echoic.] The cry of a hyena. Cf. *Hau-hau.
1895 Mrs. Croker *Village Tales* (1896) 208 Another sound that made his heart beat very fast—the 'haunk-haunk' of a hyena.

Haunted. Add: **3. b.** In wider use.
1906 *Daily Chron.* 23 Feb. 3/4 The beauty-haunted eyes of such painters as Gainsborough, Romney, Botticelli. 1906 Rider Haggard *Benita* vii, Staring at the white Benita and at her haunted eyes. 1908 *Westm. Gaz.* 17 Aug. 3/1 He paces the garden in this haunting, haunted fashion. 1910 A. C. Benson *Silent Isle* xv, You become aware that some exquisite haunted quality has slipped away from the later work.
c. *Comb.*, as *haunted-looking* adj.
1883 Ld. R. Gower *My Remin.* II. 26 A low, long, damp, haunted-looking gallery. 1918 Mrs. B. Lowndes *Out of the War?* xx. 257 Haunted-looking eyes.

Hausa (hou·sä). Also **Haussa, Hous(s)a.** [Native name.] A member of a widespread and numerous negroid race of central Soudan, of the Bantu family with some Hamitic mixture; also, their language.
1820 J. G. Jackson (*title*) Account of Timbuctoo and Housa. 1853 E. Norris (*title*) Dialogues and a small Portion of the New Testament, in the English, Arabic, Haussa, and Bornu Languages. 1879 *Encycl. Brit.* X. 59/1 An armed police force, recruited..from the Mahometan tribe of the Houssas. 1926 *Blackw. Mag.* Nov. 666/1 The troops were Hausas—I don't think we had begun to call them 'Waffs' then.

Hausfrau (hau·sfrau). [G.] A housewife. Also **Hau·svrow** [after Du. *huisvrouw*].
1798 in *South Africa a Century Ago* (1901) 157 This, as a careful haus-vrow, devolved on me. 1873 Miss Yonge *Pillars of House* xiii. II. 40 A simple painstaking business-like man, who had married a German hausfrau. 1925 Barrington *Divine Lady* II. xv. 213 Her Majesty Queen Charlotte, the prim German hausfrau. 1930 *Observer* 20 Apr. 8/4 The big German newspapers, cognisant of the power of the hausfrau.

Haustellation (hǫstĕlē¹·ʃən). [f. Haustellate: see -tion.] The action of sucking.
1901 *Practitioner* Mar. 278 If a mosquito be killed on the second day after haustellation.

Haustrum (hǫ·strǒm). *Anat.* [mod. use of L. *haustrum* bucket, scoop.] Each of the small sac-like folds in the terminal division of the colon. Hence **Hau·stral** *a.*
[1890 Billings *Med. Dict.*, *Haustra coli*, sacculi of the colon.] 1903 Dorland *Med. Dict.* (ed. 3), *Haustrum*, the recess made by one of the sacculations of the colon. 1913 *Ibid.* (ed. 7) *Haustral*, pertaining to the haustra of the colon.

Haut-Brion (ǫbrī·ǫn). Also 7 **Hobriant,** 8 **Obryan.** [Fr., f. the name of an estate, Château *Haut-Brion*, in the commune of Pessac, near Bordeaux.] In full *Château Haut-Brion*: A variety of claret.
1670 W. Hughes *Compl. Vineyard* (ed. 2) 65 A sort of Claret called Hobriant-wine, of a deep red colour. 1833 Redding *Wines* 145 The first growth of this noted commune [i.e. Pessac] is Château Haut Brion. 1845 *Encycl. Metrop.* XXV. 1287/2 The following are the principal wines, or those most celebrated in the different countries where the vine has long been cultivated:—France...Bordeaux. Lafitte, red... Haut Brion, ditto. 1851 Redding *Wines* (ed. 3) 174 In 1710, a wine called Obryan claret was sold in London at three shillings the bottle. 1888 *Encycl. Brit.* XXIV. 605/1 Château Haut-Brion, Pessac.

Haute école (otekol). [Fr., = high school.] The more difficult feats of horsemanship. Also *attrib.*
1864 G. A. Sala *Quite Alone* xi. I. 191 She was doing the haute école. 1896 *Strand Mag.* Mar. 334/2 Five other 'artistes'—traperists, *haute école*, and 'bareback' ladies. 1931 *Times Lit. Suppl.* 26 Mar. 247/3 The excellent *haute-école* rider seen at the Kingsway Opera House.

Hautefeuillite (otfö·yəit). *Min.* [Fr., f. the name of P. *Hautefeuille*, a French mineralogist, + -ite[1].] A white or colourless hydrous phosphate of calcium and magnesium.
1896 Chester *Dict. Min.*

Haut monde (omǫ̃nd). [Fr., lit. high world.] The fashionable world: cf. Beau-monde.
1930 *Aberdeen Press & Jrnl.* 22 Apr. 4 The Aberdeen Lido scene which depicts *haut monde* life..at the glorified Aberdeen beach of the future. 1931 *Times Lit. Suppl.* 28 May 429/1 Several ladies of the *haut monde.*

Havana. *Havana cigar* (earlier U.S. quot.).
1802 *Ann. Congress* 31 Mar. 229 The greater part of what we have imported came..in the shape of Havana cigars.
c. ellipt. for *Havana-brown.*
1922 *Daily Mail* 12 Dec. 7 In delightful shades of Saxe, Heliotrope, Dove Grey, or Havana.

Have, *v.* Add: **13. c.** To represent as doing something. *U.S. colloq.*
1928 *Amer. Speech* June 379 William De Morgan, in *Alice for Short*, has the 'toffs' say *daw* and *flaw* for 'door' and 'floor'.
14. *To be had (of)*: to be obtained (from).
1736 *Gentl. Mag.* VI. *title-p.*, Sold by the Booksellers..; of whom may be had compleat setts, or any single Number. 1765 *Art of Cookery* (ed. 9) Index, Advt., Thomson's Works. ..N.B. *The Seasons* may be had alone. c 1810 *Watering & Sea-Bathing Places* Term. Advt. 223 And which may be had of all Booksellers. 1930 *Times Lit. Suppl.* 19 June 513 All these books may be had of any bookseller.
e. *To have it on* (a person): to have the advantage of; to have 'the pull' of or over. *To have nothing on*: to have no advantage of or superiority over. *U.S.*
1909 S. E. White *Rules of Game* v. xxiv, They think they have it on us straight enough. 1922 Titus *Timber* vii. 65 You know he has it on you. There is no use trying to fight the law. 1928 *Daily Express* 19 June 12 Kerensky, who tried to do what Napoleon said no man could do: run a revolution and a war simultaneously. Kerensky thought Napoleon had nothing on him. 1928 *Observer* 22 July 28/3, I have carefully analysed the pre-Olympic performances of Liddell, who won in 1924, and J. W. J. Rinkel, who we hope is going to win this year. Liddell had nothing on Rinkel in preliminaries. 1928 *Daily Express* 27 Aug. 15/3 America's heavy-weight champion of the world has nothing on Great Britain's Prime Minister. 1930 *Publishers' Weekly* 5 July 27 Deciding that the antique hussies of history in spite of their hot reputations have nothing on her.
g. *To have it in for*: to have something unpleasant in store for; to have a grudge against or dislike for (app. modelled on *to be in for*: see In *adv.* 8). *U.S.*
1906 G. Ade *In Pastures New* i. 12, I don't think that any fair-minded American has it in for Great Britain. 1909 S. E. White *Rules of Game* v. xxxvi, I always wondered why he had it in for me...He seemed to have a special..enmity for me. 1917 Empey *From Fire Step* 92 Every time I had to go out in front, it just naturally rained. Old Jupiter Pluvius must have had it in for me. 1927 *Daily Mirror* 10 Dec. 2/1 If it was not for the prejudice of a certain detective-sergeant who has had it in for me since I left the police force, I should be found not guilty.
15. d. *To have on*: to puzzle or deceive intentionally; to chaff, tease; to humbug. orig. *dial.*
1867 Staton *Loominary* 117 It looks as if somebuddy wur havin me on. 1893 Farmer & Henley *Slang, To have on*, to secure a person's interest, attention, sympathy; generally with a view to deceiving him (or her). 1895 M. Mather *Idylls* 46, I were nobbud hevin' her on a bit. 1928 *Daily Express* 31 Aug. 7 Speaking unjudicially and in ordinary language you are 'having him on'.
26 ¶. (Later U.S. examples.)
1816 U. Brown *Jrnl.* in *Maryland Hist. Mag.* X. 282 If this forest had never have been fired it would have been a vast..Timbered country. 1911 J. F. Wilson *Land Claimers* i. 17 'If the fire hadn't have gone out,' he mused.

Havelock. Add: *Havelock cap*, a military cap provided with a Havelock.
1880 *Harper's Mag.* Oct. 399 A poncho and havelock cap comprise the rubber clothing outfit.

Haw, *sb.*[2] **3.** See also *Black haw 1.
1680 in Ray *Hist. Plant.* (1688) II. 1927/2 Rhamnus Prunifolius fructu nigro...The black Haw.

Haw, *int.*[2] and *sb.*[5] *dial.* and *U.S.* A call used to direct a horse or team to turn to the left.
1843 *Knickerbocker Mag.* XXI. 494 He admonishes them with his goad, and ejaculates, 'Haw'. 1843 R. Carlton *New Purchase* xxvi. 239 Whoas, gees and haws. 1856 J. C. Morton *Cycl. Agric.* II. 723/2 Horses—terms used in directing—. ..Cheshire...To left. Haw. 1864 Webster s.v., *Haw, haw here*;—words used by teamsters in guiding their teams.

Haw, *v.*[3] *U.S.* [f. prec.] **a.** *intr.* Of a horse or team: To turn to the left. Also *fig.* (see quot. 1864).
1846 *Knickerbocker Mag.* XXVII. 119 The plough-boy has hardly energy to cry out..'Gee-haw, there I tell you to haw, now'. 1861 *Trans. Ill. Agric. Soc.* IV. 99 They were required to plow lands of about fifteen rods in length, and 'haw' about. 1864 Webster s.v., *To haw and gee*, or *haw and gee about*, to go from one thing to another without good reason; to have no settled purpose; to be irresolute or unstable. (*Colloq.*)
b. *trans.* To direct (a horse, etc.) to turn to the left. Also *fig.*
1864 Webster s.v., *To haw and gee*, or *haw and gee about*, to lead this way and that at will; to lead by the nose; to master or control. (*Colloq.*) 1867 T. Lackland *Homespun* III. 286 His boy astride the old plough-horse, while he 'gees' and 'haws' the yoke of cattle himself.
Hence **Hawing** *vbl. sb.*
1843 R. Carlton *New Purchase* xvi. 119 After performing wonders on the journey from Philadelphia to the West in hawing and geeing. 1867 T. Lackland *Homespun* II. 194 The regiment is somehow got back, by hawing and geeing into line.

Hawaiian (hăwai·yăn), *a.* and *sb.* Also **Hawaian.** [f. *Hawaii* + -an.] **A.** *adj.* Of or pertaining to the island of Hawaii, or to the whole group of the Sandwich Islands in the North Pacific. **B.** *sb.* **1.** A native or inhabitant of Hawaii. **2.** The language of Hawaii, belonging to the Malayo-Polynesian group.
1825 W. Ellis *Jrnl. Tour Hawaii* 205 The account given this evening of the Hawaiian *hades*. 1859 [see Inter- 5]. 1864 W. D. Alexander *Hawaiian Gramm.* 20 What would form a long sentence in English, in Hawaiian is generally broken up into several independent propositions. 1877 T. H. Streets *Nat. Hist. Hawaiian & Fanning Isl.* Pref. 8 The Fanning group, with the exception of the Hawaiian, were the only islands visited in the Pacific. 1913 R. Brooke *Coll. Poems* (1918) 23 And new stars burn into the ancient skies, Over the murmurous soft Hawaian sea. 1921 *Nature* 20 Jan. 673/1 Some broad features of Hawaiian petrology. 1929 C. H. Smith *Bridge of Life* ii. 29 White men, Chinese Japanese, Hawaiians and many others slept in the common dormitory.

Hawbuck. (Earlier U.S. example.)
1787 *Amer. Museum* (1789) II. 484 The grate haw-buks set up a hoss-laf at me.

Haw-haw, *v.* Add: **b.** *trans.* To laugh at.
1862 Thackeray *Philip* xxxi, It's good to see him haw-haw Bickerton. 1922 Z. Grey *To the Last Man* x. 226 Some of the gang haw-hawed him.

Hawk, *sb.*[1] **4. b.** Add: **hawk-cuckoo,** an East Indian cuckoo of the genus *Hierococcyx*, resembling a hawk in appearance; **hawk-eye,** (*a*) *U.S.* (examples); (*b*) a keen eye like that of a hawk.
1901 *Westm. Gaz.* 8 Aug. 8/2 The Zoological Society have lately received..a specimen of the *hawk-cuckoo. 1845 *Olympia Pioneer* (Th.) Corn-crackers, Potsoppers, Hard Heads, *Hawk Eyes, Rackensacks, etc. 186. in F. Moore *Songs of Soldiers* (1864) 114 We have come from the prairies Of the young Hawkeye State. 1901 *Lady's Realm* X. 552/2 The most contemptuous glances of her hawk-eyes.

Hawthorn. **3.** Add: **hawthorn jar,** a jar of hawthorn china.
1905 *Daily Chron.* 18 May 4/6 The enormous sum paid yesterday at Christie's for a 'hawthorn' jar. *Ibid.* 12 Aug. 3/1 The 'hawthorn ginger-jars of old Nanking'.

Hay, *sb.*[1] **5.** Add: **hay-box,** a box filled with hay in which food after being brought to boiling-point in a saucepan is placed to finish cooking; also *attrib.*; **hay-press** *U.S.*, a press for baling hay; **hay-scales** *U.S.*, a public weighing-machine for weighing loads of hay, etc.
1915 *Queen* 13 Nov. 897/2 Boiled beef should be allowed thirty minutes' boiling for a large joint and three to four hours in the *hay-box. 1927 *Daily Express* 6 Aug. 9/4 To feed the personnel of the force by means of new mobile hay-box cookers. 1835 Ingraham *South-West* II. 221 A large building resembling a northern *hay-press. 1872 E. Eggleston *Hoosier Sch.-M.* xxvi. 127 To see his new red barn with its large 'Mormon' hay-press..consumed, was too much for the Hawkins' heart to stand. 1773 *Boston Selectmen* 7 Dec. 204 The Ground on which the '*Hay Scales stands. 1855 M. M. Thompson *Doesticks* v. 34 The writer,.. wearied of..the same unvarying prospect of ox-teams, hay-scales,..took the roving fever. 1893 *Citizen Guide to Brooklyn & Long Island* 8 The old hay-scales stood there, and on its roof was the first fire-bell owned by Brooklyn.

Hay·-foot. *Sc.* [Hay *sb.*[1]] *Hay foot, straw foot*: with right and left foot alternately (at the word of command).
In allusion to the alleged use of hay and straw to enable a stupid recruit to distinguish the right foot from the left.
1898 Macmanus *Bend of Road* 40 Poor fool, he's off, hay foot straw foot, an' small grass grows round his heels till he's there. 1911 R. D. Saunders *Col. Todhunter* vii. 98 You never got in a thousand miles of one of 'em for all your 'heppin' and 'hay-foot' and 'straw-foot' drillin'. 1911 H. S. Harrison *Queed* i. 12 They march like little lambs when I say the word. Hay-foot—straw-foot.

Hay-maker. Add: **3. b.** A swinging blow. *slang* or *colloq.*
1924 *Glasgow Herald* 18 July 10 It was not at all improbable that Eagan would bring over a 'haymaker' and put the Englishman cut. 1925 J. J. Corbett *Roar of Crowd* 87, I deliberately pulled my right back and swung 'haymakers' at Choinyski, intending to miss him.

Hay-making. Add: Also *fig.* and *transf.* The action of 'making hay' (see Hay *sb.*[1] 3).
1882 *Daily News* (Ware) A number of men go into a friend's room, find him absent, and testify to their chagrin by disturbing the arrangements of his furniture. But hay-making of this sort is comparatively harmless and inoffensive. 1924 W. R. Inge *Lay Thoughts* (1926) 193 The hay-making of the profiteer after the war.

Haystack. Add: *To look for a needle in a haystack*: see Needle *sb.* 1 c.

Hazard, *v.* Add: **5. c.** With quoted words as obj.
1881 Mrs. Riddell *Senior Partner* III. xxxiii. 110 'I met Mr. Robert the other day,' hazarded the clerk. 1903 R. Langbridge *Flame & Flood* vii. 108 'Love is so rare in this world,' she hazarded.

Hazel[1]. **4. c.** Add: **hazel-splitter** *U.S.*, a breed of pigs; **hazel-wizard,** a diviner by means of a hazel-twig; a water-finder.
1865–6 *Trans. Ill. Agric. Soc.* VI. 334 [Those] who prefer the active, energetic '*hazel splitters' to the lazy Berkshire. 1843 R. Carlton *New Purchase* lii. 206 We had ceased from digging a well, after finding no water at twenty-five feet, although we had employed a great *hazel-wizzard.

Hazlittian (hæzli·tiăn), *a.* and *sb.* [f. the name of W. *Hazlitt* (1778–1830), English critic + -ian.] Of, pertaining to, or an admirer of Hazlitt.
1930 *Times Lit. Suppl.* 18 Dec. 1082/4 We know that we are in the hands of a true Hazlittian. 1931 *Ibid.* 10 Sept. 669/4 His Hazlittian freedom in misquotation.

Hazzan, variant of *Chazzan.
1891 J. E. H. Thomson *Bks. which influenced Our Lord* 5 The synagogue school, taught by the old *hazzan*. 1905 *Jewish Encycl.* XI. 19/1 The senior hazzan of the Bayswater Synagogue.

He, *pron.* Add: **8.** *spec.* **he-man** *U.S.*, a particularly virile or masterful man. So **he-male.**
1832 Paulding *Westward Ho!* I. 101 A young fellow who could..tree a rackoon with any he man that ever breathed in all out of doors. 1909 Ware *Passing English, He-male*, a full shape of male, and resulting from calling female she-male. 1922 Mulford *Tex* xiv. 207 You're about th' best he-man I've seen since I looked into a looking-glass. 1924 A. J. Small *Frozen Gold* vii, He's such a great big he-male-masculine man. *Ibid.* xiv, That was one real bred-in-the-bone he-fight. 1931 *Autobiog. Lincoln Steffens* I. 406 The rulers of his city, who knew what he knew and knew also what a he man was, held him to be the First Citizen of Pittsburgh. 1931 *Punch* 22 July 60/1 One of their [*sc.* the Americans'] hundred-per-cent he-men.
d. *He Bible*: the first of the two issues of the Bible printed in 1611, so called from its rendering of Ruth iii. 15. 1878 [see She 13].

Head, *sb.* Add: **1. d.** A headache or disordered head, esp. this condition caused by a blow or over-indulgence in liquor; *Path.*, a disorder of the head incident to residents in the tropics.
1889 *St. James's Gaz.* 10 Aug. 3/2 He is decidedly feverish, and, in the pleasing vernacular of the modern youth about town, he has a 'head' on him. 1906 *'Varsity* 17 May 323/3 One has not gone to bed over-night to wake up with a 'head' consequent on over-indulgence in the flowing bowl. 1910 *Practitioner* Jan. 18 When a man begins to worry it is time for him to go home, and that applies if he suffers from the so-called Aden or Burma or Punjaub or Madras head. 1919 *Punch* 22 Jan. 67 *Sailor.* The only time I smoked it [*sc.* opium] was in China, an' for three days I 'ad an 'ead on me like a smoke barrage.
3. c. A postage-stamp: so called from the figure of the sovereign's head. (Cf. *queen's head*, Queen *sb.* 14 b.) *colloq.* or *dial.*
1854 R. S. Surtees *Handley Cross* xix. 147 Take that to the Post, and mind you don't pick the 'ead off. 1859 *Punch* Dec. 243/1 We signed it and sealed it, and put it into a hangvelop, and stuck a *ned* on it, and put it into the Post. 1927 G. Sturt *Small Boy in Sixties* i. 2 One very curious request would sometimes come from a villager; the man or woman asking for 'a head'.
8. q. Of a bicycle frame (see quot. 1904).
1887 Bury & Hillier *Cycling* xiv. (1889) 321 (Badm. Libr.) Beneath the head and between the forks is placed the trouser guard. 1902 *Captain* VII. 82/1 That going from the head to the crank bracket is made duplex. 1904 *Technol. & Sci. Dict.* (ed. Goodchild & Tweney), *Head* (Cycles), the socket or hollow tube through which the tube carrying the front fork runs.
r. Of an explosive shell.
1899 *Kynoch Jrnl.* Oct.–Nov. 17/1 The head [of a shrapnel shell] is attached to the body by means of small rivets.
11. f. *Curling.* (See quot. 1897.)
1828 *Kilmarnock Treat. Curling* (1883) 79 Head (probably a corruption of *heat*,) that portion of the game in which both parties play all their stones once. 1877 *Encycl. Brit.* VI. 713 [Curling Rules.] All matches to be of a certain number of heads. 1897 *Encycl. Sport* I. 264/1 (Curling) *Head*, the portion of the game in which all the players have delivered their stones, and have counted the winning shot or shots.
13. b. The top of a book.
1835 Hannett *Bibliopegia* 26 The book is now taken between the hands and well beaten up at the back and head on a smooth board, to bring the sheets level and square. 1876 *Encycl. Brit.* IV. 43/1 The object of the binder in this operation is to make every page of uniform size, presenting a smooth and equal 'head', 'tail', and 'fore-edge'. 1930 *Godfrey's Catal.* No. 134. 26/1 Folio, old sheep (roughly repaired at head and heel).
35. On..head. e. *To do it on one's head*: to do it with ease. *slang.*
1922 A. A. Milne *Red House Mystery* xvi, Right, old boy. Leave it to me. I can do this on my head. 1923 *Westm. Gaz.* 19 Mar., Mr. Wells, assuming the best Cockney accent, intimated that he could 'do it on is 'ead'.
36. Out of one's head. b. Out of one's mind. *U.S.*
1825 J. Neal *Bro. Jonathan* I. 267 You are out o' your head, I guess. 1878 H. James *Fr. Poets & Novelists* 428 Pathelin pretends to be out of his head. 1902 Jefferson *Quiet Hints Preachers* xiii. 103 If they could not understand what was going on they..might think Christians out of their head.
39*. Head in the air. *To go about with one's head in the air*: to assume a pose of superiority. Hence *Head-in-air*, designating either one who is absent-minded and dreamy or one who is a snob or a 'highbrow', or the actions of such persons.
1897 tr. *Hoffmann's Struwelpeter*, Little Johnnie Head-in-Air. 1903 *Travel* May 7 The Laureate crost over the lawn with the dreamy head-in-air gait that was known through five parishes round. 1906 Rider Haggard *Benita* iv, On the ship I always thought him rather a head-in-air kind of swell, but he was a splendid fellow.
46*. Heads and posts. Leather heads placed on posts for use in cavalry exercises.
1895 *Army & Navy Co-op. Soc. Price List* 15 Sept. 1456 Heads and Posts. For Military Tournaments. 1902 *Encycl. Brit.* XXVI. 156/1 Courses for jumping and 'heads and posts' exercise.
47. Head and shoulders. c. A portrait in which only the head and shoulders are shown.
1902 *Daily Chron.* 7 July 3/5 A head and shoulders portrait of Lady Morshead in white dress and fichu.
d. *Head-and-shoulder target*, a target representing a head and shoulders.
1899 *Westm. Gaz.* 23 Nov. 2/2 A hostile force in entrenchments is represented by rows of 'head and shoulder' targets. 1901 *Ibid.* 11 Sept. 3/1 Not only were there the usual head-and-shoulder dummies, but there were several 'surprise' targets.
52*. Open one's head. To speak. *U.S. slang.*
1885 H. Jackson *Zeph* ii. 44 He never opens his head to nobody. 1895 *Century Mag.* Sept. 674/1 I'm glad you didn't open your head about it. 1898 Marg. Deland *Old Chester Tales* 307 Jones said..that he hardly opened his head for the whole twenty-one miles.
53*. Put a head on. 'To punch or assault another, and figuratively to silence, or shut up another' (Clapin). *U.S. slang.* (Cf. *1 d.)
1869 *Overland Monthly* III. 63 The gentlemanly proprietor of the premises had kindly volunteered to 'put a head' on the man who fired the pistol. 1876 *Scribner's Monthly* Nov. 142/2 Threats, profanely emphasized, 'to put a head on' me! 1911 R. W. Chambers *Common Law* ii. 46 Kelly will put a head on you!
62*. *To put a pistol to one's head*: to commit suicide by shooting.
1854 Thackeray *Newcomes* ix, I'm blowed if I don't put a pistol to my 'ead, and end it, Mrs. G. 1896 A. E. Housman *Shropshire Lad* xliv, And early wise and brave in season [you] Put the pistol to your head.
63. head-ball *Cricket*, a cunningly-bowled ball; **head-cheese** *U.S.*, (earlier and later examples); **head-cover** *Mil.*, protection for the head, *spec.* a shield for protection against gun-fire; *Fortif.* (see quot. 1892); **head-drop**, a disease occurring in Japan, characterized by drooping of the head and paralytic symptoms; **head-feast**, a feast in celebration of successful head-hunting; **head-fold** (see quots.); **head form**, the form of the head, *spec.* in reference to the ratio of its breadth to its length; **head-lamp**, one of the headlights of a motor-car; **head-lock, -looking** (see quots.); **head metal** *Founding*, the head of metal at the upper end of a cylindrical casting (see Deadhead 22); **head-noises** *Path.*, subjective sounds due to defective hearing or deafness or to ear-wax; **head-register** (see quots. and Register *sb.*[1] 8 b); **head-resistance** *Aeronautics*, = *Drift *sb.* 2 e; **head-right** *U.S.*, an inheritable right to land, formerly granted by the state of Texas to the heads of immigrating families; **head-shy** *a.*, **-shyness** (see quots.); **head-stream, -tributary** a head-water stream or tributary.
1902 *Westm. Gaz.* 11 Aug. 7/1 Self-restraint that not even the most tempting '*head-balls' of Lockwood and of Rhodes could overcome. 1841 *Southern Lit. Messenger* VII. 39/2 The animal..may be traced in the stewed chine and souse the *head cheese and sausages. 1891 H. Frederick *Copperhead*, etc. (1894) 255 Reducing what remained of the [pig's] head into small bits, to be seasoned..and then fill other pans as head-cheese. 1892 F. Irwin *Fortification* (ed. 2) 37 Always place *head-cover on wall when firing over the top. 1916 Boyd Cable *Action Front* 229 It's a good foot and a half I have of head-cover. 1890 Billings *Med. Dict.*, **Head-drop*, name given to a form of disease endemic in certain valleys in Japan, and characterized..by a feeling of weight of the head. 1882 De Windt *Equator* 82 These '*Head Feasts' are general among the aboriginal tribes throughout the island of Borneo. 1890 Billings *Med. Dict.*, **Head-fold*, a fold of the blastoderm under the cephalic end of the embryo. 1893 A. M. Marshall *Vertebrate Embryol.* 226 The head of the embryo is lifted up above the yolk-sac by an anterior constriction or head fold. 1927 Peake & Fleure *Peasants & Potters* 128 There can be little doubt that profile and *head-form have subtle..interrelations. 1912 *Motor Manual* (ed. 14) iii. 123 Paraffin *Head-lamps. 1901 Dorland *Med. Dict.* (ed. 2), **Head-lock*, the locking together of the chins in twin labor. 1890 Billings *Med. Dict.*, **Head-locking*, in twin labor, one child being born by the breech, its chin catches upon the chin of the second child presenting by the head. 1888 *Lockwood's Dict. Mech. Engin.* s.v., When the casting is removed from the mould the *head metal is turned off, leaving the actual casting smooth and free from these foreign impurities. 1910 *Practitioner* Feb. 243 Sometimes the *head-noises may be rendered more tolerable even if the hearing cannot be improved. 1890 Billings *Med. Dict.*, **Head-register*, register in which the pitch is raised by shortening the vocal chords; second falsetto in females. 1909 H. Klein *Phono-Vocal Method* 37 The blending of the medium and head registers will be practised upon the same plan. 1901 in C. C. Turner *Aerial Navigation of To-day* (1910) vii. 116 That the *head-resistance of the framing can be brought to a point much below that usually estimated as necessary. 1909 *Westm. Gaz.* 1 July 4/1 Allowing a coefficient of ·3 for the pointed ends, the total head-resistance would be reduced to 3,324 lb. 1828 *Laws of Texas* Nov. (Bartlett, 1860), So much of the vacant lands..shall be surveyed and sectionized..as will be sufficient to satisfy all claims for scrip sold, soldier's claims, and *head-rights. 1898 H. S. Canfield *Maid of Frontier* i. 13 He owned the headright of 160 acres on which his house was built. 1900 M. H. Hayes *Among Horses in Russia* iv. 82 They weren't *head-shy, and liked their manes to be scratched. *Ibid.*, Every horseman knows that '*head-shyness' is one of the worst of vices. 1899 A. H. Keane *Man Past & Present* 190 Northwards..about the Irawadi *head-streams. 1908 *Athenæum* 11 Apr. 456/3 From its head-streams in the glens. 1925 Odell in E. F. Norton *Fight for Everest, 1924* 292 A far-flung *head tributary of the Drakar Chu.

Head (hed). The name of Sir Henry *Head* (born 1861), English neurologist, used *attrib.* to designate certain phenomena observed by him.
1910 *Practitioner* Jan. 119 Some of the headache of pyorrhoea alveolaris may be reflex (*cf.* Head's areas). 1913 Dorland *Med. Dict.* (ed. 7) s.v. *Zone, Head's zones*, areas of cutaneous sensitiveness associated with diseases of the viscera; called also zones of hyperalgesia.

Head, *v.* **6.** (Earlier and later U.S. examples with *out* and *up.*)
1845 *Cultivator* New Ser. II. 252 Wheat headed out not more than knee high. *fig.* 1906 *Springfield* (Mass.) *Weekly Republican* 29 Nov. 3 When important questions are heading up.
13. b. (Earlier example of *head off.*)
1841 J. F. Cooper *Deerslayer* v. 29 But 'head him off', as you say of the deer.

Headband. Add: **1. c.** The band connecting a pair of receivers or ear-phones.
1913 *Work* 17 May 145/3 Double Receivers, with adjustable head-band.

Head-block. Add: **4.** (See quot.)
1905 *Terms Forestry & Logging* 39 *Head block*, the log placed under the front end of the skids in a skidway to raise them to the desired height.

Head-chief. *U.S.* [Head *sb.* 63.] The paramount chief of an Indian tribe.
1837 R. M. Bird *Nick of Woods* I. 236 From the head-chief to the commoner. 1881 *Harper's Mag.* Apr. 670/2 White Eagle, head-chief of the Poncas.

Header. Add: **5. b.** A top layer. *U.S.*
1865–6 *Trans. Ill. Agric. Soc.* VI. 641 Prime Pork—Shall be packed with a header of side cuts, the regular width, three half heads.
9. b. = Heading *vbl. sb.* 11.
1877 Raymond *Mines* 165 The header had reached..a length of 12,259 feet.
11. *Association Football.* A ball which is headed (see Head *v.* 15).
1927 *Daily Express* 20 Apr. 13/2 Trotter gave the home club the lead with a beautiful header, following a free kick well taken by Leach. *Ibid.* 26 Apr. 13/3 A few minutes later Forbes increased the home lead with a clever header.
12. *attrib.* and *Comb.*: **header-board,** a diving-board; **header brick** = Header 5; so **heading brick.**
1913 E. F. Benson *Thorley Weir* i, The nude figure of a boy on the *header-board in the act of springing from it into the water. 1897 Moore *How to Build* vii. 110 A '*header' brick is one laid in the wall so that only its end shows. 1901 *J. Black's Carp. & Build., Scaffolding* 24 Cavities in the brickwork obtained by leaving out 'header' bricks at proper intervals. *Ibid.* 26 A 'heading' brick.

Head flaw. *U.S.* [Head *sb.* 64.] A gust of contrary wind. In quots. *fig.*
1803 Weems *Lett.* II. 280 A head flaw..has taken me all aback again. 1834 Seba Smith *Sel. Lett. Major Jack Downing* 90 A good many head flaws and worriments.

Heading, *vbl. sb.* **7.** (Earlier examples.)
1682 T.A. *Carolina* 6 With this [cedar] they make Heading for their Cask. 1752 J. MacSparran *Amer. Dissected* (1753) 26 Barrel and Hogshead Staves and Heading.

Headlight (he·dləit). orig. *U.S.* Also with hyphen. [Head *sb.* 66.] A powerful light carried on the front of a locomotive or on the mast-head of a vessel; *spec.*, each of two powerful lamps carried on the front of a motor-vehicle.
1862 *U.S. Patent* 3 June, No. 35486. 1891 C. Roberts *Adrift Amer.* iii. 55 The great head-light which forms such a noticeable feature of American engines at night. 1904 A. B. F. Young *Complete Motorist* xii. (ed. 2) 257 On dark nights it is advisable, when driving in the country, to carry on such cars a single head-light of greater power...On very fast cars two of these head-lights should be carried. 1907 *Autocar* 28 Dec. 1067/2 The thief calmly took the large valuable head light off and disappeared. 1929 *Evening News* 18 Nov. 4/4 He had almost reached the high road when the headlights of an automobile swung round a corner.

Head-line. Add: **3. b.** A line fastening the head of a vessel to the shore.
1877 Habberton *Jericho Road* i. 9 The head-line was cast off as the pilot's bell rang.
4. A base-line in surveying.
1656 *Doc. & Rec. New-Hampshire* I. 221 From the said head lyne we measured for the length..6 miles & a halfe. 1704 *N.H. Probate Rec.* I. 514 All my land..up as far as the southern hills, viz. as far as to butt against Andrews head line.

Headliner. Add: One whose name appears in a head-line; a chief personage or performer. *U.S.*
1907 *Chicago Tribune* 8 May 7 The 'Headliners' on the program will be James Whitcomb Riley, George Ade, etc. 1914 *Boston Herald* 23 June 8/4 The headliner at B. F. Keith's.

Head-on, *adv.* and *a.* orig. *U.S.* [Head *sb.* 21 b.] **A.** *adv.* (*hea·d-o·n*). With the head pointed directly towards or running full against or towards something. **B.** *adj.* (*hea·d-on*). Of a collision: Involving the direct meeting of the fronts of two vehicles in the same track, or of the head of a vehicle with an object.
1904 *N.Y. Evening Post* 11 May 2 A head-on collision between north and southbound passenger trains. 1907 *Westm. Gaz.* 16 Sept. 5/2 New York, September 16.—A head-on collision between two passenger trains. 1916 H. Barber *Aeroplane Speaks* 46 Gliding just over the trees and head on to the wind. 1930 *Daily Express* 8 Sept. 1/3 When the vehicles collided head-on.

Headphone (he·dfǒun). [f. Head *sb.* + *phone* of Telephone.] = *ear-phone* (*a*), *Ear *sb.*[1] 16. Also *transf.* a plaited coil of hair covering the ear.

1924 *Work* 7 Mar. 506/1 Electrolite Head-phones. *Ibid.* 28 Mar. 576 We..consider our Headphones a perfect treat. 1926 MRS. A. SIDGWICK *Sack & Sugar* xxi. 250 At present they only had head-phones. 1926 *Mus. Assoc. Proc. 1926–7* 19 Many seem to have the headphones permanently attached to themselves. 1929 *Strand Mag.* Aug. 152 Women whose head-phones appear so appropriate.

Headroom. Transfer †*Sc. Obs.* to sense in Dict., and add: **2.** Room above the head; overhead space.

1851 [see HEAD *sb.* 65 a]. 1876 *Encycl. Brit.* IV. 267/2 Sufficient light, and headroom of at least 48 inches, being provided. 1902 *Eng. Dial. Dict.* s.v. *Head* sb. II, *Head-room*, of ceilings, staircases, etc.: sufficient height overhead. 1908 *Installation News* II. 68/1 Arrangements are being made to provide 15 feet headroom.

Headstock. Add:

1. g. The horizontal end members in the underframe of a railway carriage or truck.

1888 *Lockwood's Dict. Mech. Engin.*, *Headstock*. (2) The end timbers in the under frame of a railway truck. 1928 *Daily Express* 29 Dec. 9/4 The interval between headstocks of coaches should be as small..as practicable for necessary freedom of movement.

h. (See quot.)

1927 T. WOODHOUSE *Artificial Silk* 108 Occasionally both reeds are placed on what is termed a dividing head or headstock. *Ibid.* 112 Fig. 50 illustrates the delivery or headstock end with the weaver's beam partially filled with the sheet of sized and dried threads.

Head water. Add: **1. b.** *ellipt.* = *head-water-mark.*

1908 *Westm. Gaz.* 29 Apr. 6/3 The Thames has risen rapidly during the night, and is now 2 ft. 6 in. above head-water at Windsor.

Headway. Add: **6.** The interval of time or the distance between two consecutive trains, trams, buses, etc., running on the same route and in the same direction. orig. *U.S.*

1895 in *Funk's Standard Dict.* 1930 *Oxford Times* 21 Mar. 17/4 I think Route 2 should have a six-minute headway between 8 a.m. and 10.30 a.m. *Ibid.*, Until the headway was closed to 15 minutes in the morning, and 12 minutes in the afternoon, serious inadequacy existed.

Headwear (he·dweəɹ). [f. HEAD *sb.* + WEAR *sb.*] = HEAD-GEAR 1.

1896 J. C. HARRIS *Sister Jane* 39 Gi' me my bonnet. It's all the head-wear I've got left. 1900 *Daily News* 27 Mar. 4/2 They were most easily classified by their headwear. Caps, bowlers, and felt hats were there in almost equal proportions. 1904 GALLICHAN *Fishing & Trav. Spain* vii. 76 He was much interested in my wife's hat. Such headwear had never been seen in Coria.

Headwork. Add: **1. b.** The practice of carrying loads on the head.

1840 R. H. DANA *Bef. Mast* xiv, For we soon found that ..'head-work' was the only system for California.

3. *pl.* **a.** Apparatus for controlling the flow of water in a river or canal. **b.** (See quot. 1905.)

1891 *Scribner's Mag.* X. 468 The river flowing between firm banks, could be permanently controlled by headworks of masonry. 1903 *Sci. Amer. Suppl.* 10 Jan. 22597 (Cent. D. Suppl.) Headworks can be placed more easily along the banks of smaller streams, or dams built across their beds, raising or controlling the waters. 1905 *Terms Forestry & Logging* 40 *Headworks*, a platform or raft, with windlass or capstan, which is attached to the front of a log raft or boom of logs, for warping, kedging, or winding it through lakes and still water, by hand or horse power.

Heady, *a.* Add: **2.** Also, that affects or turns the head; that turns one giddy.

1898 *Atlantic Monthly* Apr. 501/1 He would sit on a heady scaffold.

Healder (hī·dəɹ). [f. HEALD + -ER¹.] An operative who draws the warp yarn through the eyes of a heald. So **Hea·lding** *vbl. sb.*

1881 *Instr. Census Clerks* (1885) 64 Woollen cloth manufacture... Healder. 1888 R. BEAUMONT *Woollen & Worsted Cloth Manuf.* 138 After healding the work of loom mounting is comparatively simple, the only operation requiring attention being that of sleying.

Health, *sb.* **8.** Add: **health visitor**, an official who visits houses, etc. to inspect health conditions.

1901 [see VISITOR 1 c]. 1905 *Westm. Gaz.* 3 Apr. 12/2 An audience of health visitors, district visitors, charity organisation visitors. 1917 *New Witness* 28 June 202/1 The bare idea that a Health Visitor should attempt to force her way into a Frenchwoman's house would be regarded with horror.

Healthy, *a.* Add: **2. b.** In ironical use.

1903 C. HYNE *Mr. Horrocks Purser*, *Transfer*, I want to impress on them that they'll find it more healthy not to try for more. 1916 BOYD CABLE *Action Front* 179 'Additional artillery support would be useful a—a—a.' 'Sounds healthy, don't it?' said the sergeant reflectively.

4. *healthy-mindedness.*

1906 *Westm. Gaz.* 25 Jan. 12/2 The spirit which animated Japan was chivalry and healthy-mindedness. 1931 *Times Lit. Suppl.* 19 Feb. 122/1 So well supplied is the Victorian era with names standing for stability, sanity and healthy-mindedness.

Heap, *sb.* Add: **5. e.** Also, *to knock all of a heap.*

1898 W. J. LOCKE *Idols* xiii, It knocked the prosecution all of a heap. 1928 *Manch. Guardian Weekly* 7 Sept. 183/3 Its owner's anxiety to knock the critics all of a heap.

f. *A heap sight* (U.S.): see HEAP *sb.* 4 c and SIGHT *sb.*¹ 2, 2 b.

1874 E. EGGLESTON *Circuit Rider* i. 14 He 'lows there was a heap sight more corn. 1888 CABLE *Bonaventure* 49 He's ..a heap sight happier than us. 1906 *Smart Set* June 107/1, I care a heap sight too much for Ummy to let him go through what I know 's comin'.

Heaping, *ppl. a.* *U.S.* [f. HEAP *v.*] Of a spoonful: Heaped. Also *fig.* mounting up.

1838 *Congress. Globe* June 470/2 App., The amount of money..is a very high and heaping price. 1868 MISS ALCOTT *Lit. Women* xi, Amy..took a heaping spoonful, choked.., and left the table precipitately. 1908 *Smart Set* June 25/1 Aunt Natica waddled off..to fetch Thorndyke a heaping portion of the *dulce*.

Hear, *v.* Add: **4. b.** *To hear out*: also, to distinguish (the sounds of something heard).

1922 WOODWORTH *Psychology* x. 230 By careful attention and training we can 'hear out' the separate overtones from the total blend.

7. c. *To hear to*, to listen to, to hear of. *U.S.*

1833 H. BARNARD in *Maryland Hist. Mag.* XIII. 379, I made a move to depart—but they would not hear to that. 1869 MRS. STOWE *Oldtown Folks* xx. 243 She has her own ways and doings, and she won't hear to reason. 1915 E. POOLE *The Harbor* 202 When I tried at last to turn our talk to our affairs at home, at first she would not hear to it.

11. *To hear from*: (also, pregnantly) to receive a reprimand from.

1907 *Munsey's Mag.* Dec. 307/1 If those louts up at the castle neglected to have dinner ready.., they would hear from him...If they didn't [spring at his word] they always heard from him.

Hearsy (hə̄·ɹsi), *a.* [f. HEARSE *sb.* + -Y¹.] Resembling or characteristic of a hearse; funereal.

1901 'ANTHONY HOPE' *Tristram of Blent* v. 57 Mr. Gainsborough was obviously a man who would not waste his chance of a funeral;..it would need startling measures to keep him from a funeral. 'I hate hearsey people', grumbled Harry, as he threw the letter down. 1908 T. HARDY *Dynasts* III. VI. vi. 476 Full-clothed in black, with nodding hearsy plumes.

Heart, *sb.* Add:

1. c. A diseased or disordered heart: often with defining word; as *athletic heart*, simple hypertrophy of the heart with no disease of the valves; *fatty heart* (see FATTY *a.* 5); *smoker's heart* (see 1 b).

1871 DA COSTA in *Amer. Jrnl. Med. Sci.* LXI. 17, I noticed cases of a peculiar form of functional disorder of the heart, to which I gave the name of irritable heart. *a* 1883 FAGGE *Princ. Med.* (1886) II. 41 Rather more than a century ago Haller described the 'hairy' heart as occurring especially in bold and adventurous men. 1888 Smoker's heart [see Dict. 1 b]. 1902 *Daily Chron.* 3 Nov. 8/4 [He] has been forbidden to row again..owing to his having developed 'a heart'. 1908 *Westm. Gaz.* 29 Oct. 14/1 [He] failed to qualify before the Medical Board of the police on the ground that he had an 'athletic heart'.

51. c. *Heart-to-heart*: used to denote conversation, discussion, etc. of real frankness and sincerity; usually *attrib.* but also *absol.* as *sb.*

1902 A. H. LEWIS *Wolfville Days* xi. 152 He don't own no real business to transact; he's out to have a heart-to-heart interview with the great Southwest. 1902 *Daily Chron.* 13 Jan. 3/4 A genius for heart to heart preaching. 1906 *Ibid.* 5 Mar. 6/4 A heart-to-heart discussion of the solar plexus and its part in the emotional economy of man. 1909 S. E. WHITE *Rules of Game* v. xvi. 444 Let's have a heart-to-heart, and find out how we stand. 1918 E. M. ROBERTS *Flying Fighter* 201 After a heart-to-heart talk, I induced him to let me remain in the Flying Service.

55. a. (*a*) *heart-strain*, *-tube*; (*b*) *heart-burst*, *-springs*, *-wound*.

1848 BAILEY *Festus* (ed. 3) 252 Like a horse Put to his *heart-burst speed, sobbing up hill. 1896 A. MORRISON *Child of Jago* xiii. 134 Dicky..had been afflicted to heart-burst by his father's dodging and running. 1903 BEATRICE HARRADEN *Kath. Frensham* xviii. 278 She, with..perseverance, dug a hole in their frozen *heart-springs. 1903 *Westm. Gaz.* 27 May 2/3 The words that seemed as if they rushed From deepest heart-springs out. 1906 *Medical Annual* 241 *Heart-strain in Growing Boys. 1909 *Daily Chron.* 21 Aug. 6/2 Heartstrain and contraction of the joints. 1881 *Trans. Obstetr. Soc. Lond.* XXII. 78 An abnormal amount of tension on the primitive *heart-tube. 1839 BAILEY *Festus* 269 Her *heart-wound. 1902 *Temple Bar Mag.* CXXVI. 111 It rained upon his bleeding heart-wound like balm. 1906 *Westm. Gaz.* 3 Aug. 10/2 The faint, fine smell of new-mown grass Stabs like a heart-wound as I pass.

b. *heart-holding*, *-shaking*, *-sickening*, *-tearing*, *-warming* adjs.

1897 J. L. ALLEN *Choir Invis.* xvi, A universal fellowship with seeding grass and breeding herb and every *heart-holding creature of the woods. 1913 E. F. BENSON *Thorley Weir* iv, Things fairer and more heart-holding. 1907 *Tatler* 22 May 132/2 A *heart-shaking tragedy. 1910 *Daily Chron.* 7 Jan. 6/4 Swiftly and with heart-shaking terror events began to pass judgment. 1920 PRINGLE-PATTISON *Idea of God* 224 Shakespeare gives us the heart-shaking tragedies of *Lear* and *Othello*. 1850 R. G. CUMMING *Hunter's Life S. Afr.* (1902) 151/1 On our return from one of these expeditions we came upon a *heart-sickening sight. 1902 *London Mag.* VIII. 432/2 It was heart-sickening, as his great form with its yellow skin and black stripes, as his blazing eyes, his flashing teeth and his outspread claws rose toward us through the air. 1916 BOYD CABLE *Action Front* 149 Thirty-six solid hours of physical stress and *heart-tearing strain. 1920 *Glasgow Herald* 21 Oct. 6 The latest phases of the heart-tearing Irish tragedy. 1899 *Daily News* 20 Apr. 5/7 They are a *heart-warming cordial.

56. heart-block *Path.* (see quot. 1913); **heart brass**, a brass sepulchral tablet in which a heart is represented (see quot.); **heart-hurry** *Path.*, a form of tachycardia, extreme rapidity of pulse appearing spasmodically and of short duration; **heart-rot**, a disease which causes decay in the heart of a tree; also, a fungous disease of beetroots; **heart-talk**, a heart-to-heart talk.

1913 DORLAND *Med. Dict.* (ed. 7), *Heart-block*, the condition in which the muscular interconnection between the auricle and ventricle..is interrupted, so that the auricle and ventricle beat independently of each other. 1930 C. W. CARTER in *Biochem. Jrnl.* XXIV. 1811 A condition of sinus bradycardia and heart block, which develops in pigeons fed on a diet of polished rice. 1912 WARD *Brasses* 80 *Heart brasses proper fall into two main divisions: (*a*) plain, sometimes inscribed or with scrolls, (*b*) held by hands, usually coming out of a cloud. 1903 *Med. Record* 7 Feb. 204 (Cent. D. Suppl.) The evanescent '*heart-hurry' so frequently produced by the most trivial causes. 1882 *Encycl. Brit.* XIV. 311/2 A far more formidable enemy [of larches] is the disease known as the '*heart-rot'. 1919 W. E. HILEY *Fungal Dis. Common Larch* v. 80 Heart-rot of trees is caused by fungi which grow saprophytically on the dead wood. 1912 HUEFFER *Panel* I. ii. 31, I want a regular—what you might call—*heart-talk with Miss Delamere.

Hearth¹. **4.** Add: **hearth tidy**, a pan for containing the ashes that fall from a fireplace.

1920 *Ironmonger* 18 Dec. 95 Saucepans, hearth tidies, curbs, plate racks.

Hearth-rug. Add: Also *attrib.* (*a*) fireside, domestic; (*b*) resembling a hearth-rug.

1901 *Daily Chron.* 31 July 7/2 Turning the hearthrug favourite into the streets is certainly better than shutting it up, slowly to starve in an unoccupied house. 1902 *Ibid.* 2 Sept. 5/2 The sparrow is far too 'fly' a bird for the hearth-rug-bred cat. 1909 *Westm. Gaz.* 20 July 5/1 The inelegant, cumbrous, and shaggy hearth-rug coats.

Heartwater (hā·ɹtwǭtəɹ). *S. Afr.* [f. HEART *sb.* + WATER *sb.*] A febrile disease of sheep, goats, and more rarely cattle, in South Africa, transmitted by the bont tick.

1903 *Nature* 26 Nov. 91/2. 1905 *Rep. Brit. Assoc.* 282 An old-time supposition that *A*[*mblyomma*] *hebræum* was associated with a disease called 'heartwater', which had practically put a stop to the farming of sheep and angora goats in several south-eastern districts.

Heart-wood. Add: **2.** The Tasmanian ironwood, *Notelæa ligustrina*.

1889 J. H. MAIDEN *Useful Native Plants* 579 The heartwood yields a very peculiar figure; it is a very fair substitute for Lignum-Vitæ. 1902 BOULGER *Wood* 221.

Hearty, *a.* and *sb.* Add: **C.** *sb.* **3.** At some English universities, one who enters heartily into college life and sports; an athletic (as distinguished from an æsthetic) man.

1928 *Daily Express* 8 Mar. 8/2 The traditional breach between what are known, unsatisfactorily, as 'æsthetes' and 'hearties'. 1930 *Times Lit. Suppl.* 24 July 610/4 At English universities undergraduates classify themselves into the mutually exclusive categories of 'aesthetes' and 'hearties'.

Heat, *sb.* Add:

14. a. *heat-absorption*, *-capacity*, *-cloud*, *-evolution*, *-flow*, *-haze*, *-insulation*, *-isolation*, *-loss*, *-mist*, *-radiator* (= RADIATOR 1 b), *-retrogression*, *-test*, *-trap*, *-value*. **b.** *heat-regulating*, *-resisting* adjs.; *heat-producer*. **c.** *heat-hazed*, *-misted* adjs.; also with meaning 'against or from heat', as *heat-isolated*, *-proof* adjs.

1902 *Encycl. Brit.* XXXIII. 280/1 *Heat-evolution is reckoned as positive, *heat-absorption as negative. *Ibid.* 279/2 The *heat-capacity of the water. 1895 KIPLING *2nd Jungle Bk.* 140 When the *heat-cloud sucks the tempest. 1902 *Encycl. Brit.* XXXIII. 297/1 *Heat-flow due to Conduction. 1925 J. JOLY *Surface-Hist. Earth* vi. 104 Steady heat-flow to the surface. 1899 *Daily News* 12 Jan. 6/2 The flat, endless continent, fading away in the *heat-haze. 1901 'LINESMAN' *Words Eyewitness* (1902) 30 The ranks of little kopjes across the river slumbered in the heat-haze. 1913 E. F. BENSON *Thorley Weir* iii, Over all lay a grey *heat-hazed sky. 1902 *Encycl. Brit.* XXXIII. 283/2 Expansion or compression under the condition of *heat-insulation, represented by curves called Adiabatics. *Ibid.* 288/1 If the system is *heat-isolated. *Ibid.*, The difficulty of realizing experimentally the condition of *heat-isolation. 1899 CALLENDAR & BARNES in *Rep. Brit. Assoc.* 626 The external *heat loss is more regular and certain. 1902 *Encycl. Brit.* XXVI. 508/1 The heat-loss can be reduced to a minimum. 1901 H. W. WILSON *With the Flag to Pretoria* I. vi. 91 Indistinct lines of Boer entrenchments, flickering through the *heat-mist. 1894 MRS. DYAN *Man's Keeping* vi. I. 98 The deep *heat-misted valley. 1909 *Daily Chron.* 21 Jan. 4/7 Glasses treated in this manner become *heat-proof, and may last for years. 1920 H. G. WELLS *Outline Hist.* 21 This novel covering of feathers, this new heat-proof contrivance that life had chanced upon. 1865–6 *Trans. Ill. Agric. Soc.* VI. 53 *Heat Radiator [exhibited]. 1904 *Technol. & Sci. Dict.* (ed. Goodchild & Tweney), *Heat Radiator*, a device by which the cooling of the cylinder of a motor cycle or of the condenser of a car is promoted. 1897 *Allbutt's Syst. Med.* II. 26 The paralysis of the *heat-regulating centres. 1904 *Daily Chron.* 29 Nov. 4/5 The heat-regulating mechanism of the body. 1899 *Daily News* 21 July 4/4 A *heat-resisting alloy. 1880 HAUGHTON *Phys. Geogr.* vi. 312 Periods of *heat-retrogression (such as the glacial). 1901 *Kynoch Jrnl.* Feb.–Mar. 57/1 The *Heat-Test of Nitro Explosives. 1906 W. DE MORGAN *Joseph Vance* xviii, I think of the *sole di marzo* blazing on the roses in that Tuscan *heat-trap. 1887 *Chambers's Jrnl.* 24 Sept. 623/1 The exact *heat-value of different kinds of liquid fuel.

d. heat bump, a protuberance on the skin supposed to be due to heat; **heat-centres** *Phys.*, areas in the cerebro-spinal axis which are concerned with the production and dissipation of heat; **heat-energy**, that form of energy which is manifested in heat; **heat equator** = *thermal equator* (see *EQUATOR 3 b); **heat-filter**, a cell containing some liquid, usually water or a saturated solution of alum, used to intercept rays of heat while allowing the passage of rays of light; **heat-tone**, the sum of the heat produced in a chemical action and of the external work performed expressed in heat-units; **heat-weight**, the number obtained by dividing a quantity of heat by the absolute temperature of the body possessing it (Funk 1928).

1907 W. E. COLLINSON *Contemp. Eng.* 57 Spots, which, it is hoped, are *heat-bumps. 1907 *Practitioner* June 771 The action of the *heat-centres being sluggish. 1876 P. G. TAIT *Rec. Adv. Phys. Sci.* 138 We are led to speak of the availability of an amount of *heat-energy. 1893 *Jrnl. Soc. Arts* 8 Sept. 897/1 The practically unavoidable waste of heat energy. 1902 *Encycl. Brit.* XXXIII. 283/2 The whole of its intrinsic heat energy might theoretically be recovered in the form of external work. 1904 *Technol. & Sci. Dict.* (ed. Goodchild & Tweney), *Heat Equator. *c* 1911 M. I. NEWBIGIN *Mod. Geogr.* iv. 87 Those regions of the earth which are directly beneath the vertical rays of the sun are heated most intensely...This belt of high temperature is called the heat equator. *a* 1909 WOODBURY *Encycl. Dict. Photogr.* 367 (Cent. D. Suppl.), I have taken a powerful projection lantern and set it as near to the microscope as the intervening *heat-filter will permit. 1902 H. C. JONES *Physical Chem.* 286 Since we have reactions which evolve heat.., and also reactions in which heat is absorbed.., the *heat tone may be positive or negative.

Heated, *ppl. a.* Add: **1. b.** *Heated term*, the hot season of the year. *U.S.*

1867 *Congress. Globe* 5 July 487/1, I think we could go on now during the heated term..better than..during the cold season. 1873 J. H. BEADLE *Undevel. West* 793 The average of the 'heated term', one day with another, is there recorded at eighty-four degrees.

Heater. **2. a.** (Earlier examples.)

1666 *Essex Inst. Hist. Coll.* XXV. 147 It. boxe Iron & heaters. 1744 FRANKLIN *Acc. Fire-places* 27 You..may..warm the Flat-Irons, heat Heaters [etc.].

f. A triangular structure resembling in form the heater of a box-iron.

1797 J. A. GRAHAM *Pres. State Vermont* 119 There are two arches..with a pier in the centre..with the addition of a heater, or triangular front. 1899 *Cumbld. Gloss.* 379 *Heater bit* is the triangular piece of ground, generally grass-grown, at the junction of three roads; so called because of resemblance to the iron heater in a box-iron.

3. heater-piece *U.S.* (examples).

1859 BARTLETT *Dict. Amer.*, *Heater piece*, a gore or triangular piece of land, so called probably, from a flat iron, the form of which it resembles. 1863 D. G. MITCHELL *My Farm* 243 Waal—kinder like to have a little 'heater' piece, the boys, you see, hoe it out in odd spells.

Heave, *sb.* Add:

1. c. *Wrestling.* A chip performed by bringing the right arm round the opponent's right shoulder preparatory to a throw. *Cornwall heave*, a heave in which a wrestler places one hand in front and one behind his adversary, and falls with him.

1889 W. ARMSTRONG *Wrestling* 224 (Badm. Libr.) The Heave, Cornwall and Devon. *Ibid.* 230 The principal Cornish and Devon chips are..the Back-heave, the Belly-heave, the Heaving-toe. 1898 *Encycl. Sport* II. 548/2 One way to stop the heave is to cross click your man and then ply the crossbuttock.

5. *Comb.*: **heave-gate** *local*, a gate which is opened by being lifted out of the sockets or mortises.

1736 PEGGE *Kenticisms* (E.D.S.) *Heave-gate*, when the rails, with the pales nailed to them, may be taken out of their mortises, and then put in again. 1876 *Surrey Gloss.* 1887 I. R. *Lady's Ranche Life Montana* 27, Instead of gates out here, they generally have bars, which you have to let down,..like the 'heave gates' in Sussex. 1907 'J. HALSHAM' *Lonewood Corner* 149, I perched myself on the heave-gate between the two fields.

Hea·vier-than-ai·r, *attrib. phr.* *Aeronautics.* Designating a flying machine whose weight is greater than the weight of the air which it displaces, and whose lift is not dependent on light gases; also applied to the use of such a machine or machines in flight.

[1879 *Encycl. Brit.* IX. 309/2 Weight, however paradoxical it may appear, is necessary to flight. Everything which flies is vastly heavier than the air.] 1888 tr. *F. Marion's Wonderful Balloon Ascents* ix. 162 To form a 'Free Association for Aerial Navigation by means of Machines heavier than Air'.

[1904 *Chambers's Jrnl.* 699/1 All who have sought to sail the skies divide themselves..into..the 'lighter-than-airites' and the 'heavier-than-airites'.] 1908 H. G. WELLS *War in Air* viii, The most efficient heavier-than-air fliers. 1909 tr. *A. Berget's Conquest of Air* II. ii. 155 Many persons ask aviators why their 'heavier-than-air' apparatus is not provided with parachutes. 1909 *Flight* 19 June 356/1 Any heavier-than-air type of machine. 1909 *Daily Chron.* 9 Sept. 1/6 For a long time Mr. Cody has practised heavier-than-air flying on Laffan's Plain. 1927 C. L. M. BROWN *Conquest of Air* 21 When heavier-than-air flight was an accomplished reality.

Heavily, *adv.* Add:

6. *Comb.*: often equivalent to parasynthetic comb. of the adj., as *heavily-booted*, having heavy boots.

1883 ANNIE THOMAS *Mod. Housewife* 131 Trodden by heavily-booted feet. 1903 LD. R. GOWER *My Remin.* II. 79 A large and heavily-veined nose. 1905 *Daily Chron.* 20 Oct. 8/5 Those heavily-jetted waistbelts. 1907 B'NESS VON HUTTEN *Halo* I. i, Very long, half-closed, heavily-lashed eyes. 1927 CONAN DOYLE *Case Bk. Sherlock Holmes* xi. 293 A strong, heavily-moustached face and angry eyes.

Heaviside (he·visəid). *Physics.* Also erron. **heavyside.** The name of Oliver *Heaviside* used attrib. to denote a layer of the atmosphere which reflects back wireless waves.

1913 *Year-Bk. Wireless Telegr.* 395 The conductivity, and consequently the reflecting power, of the Heaviside layer depends greatly on the presence of local electromotive forces.

Heavy, *a.*¹ (*sb.*) Add: **1. c.** Also of timber: Consisting of large trees. *U.S.*

1843 *Yale Lit. Mag.* VIII. 406 In this patch of 'heavy timber'. 1853 B. F. TAYLOR *Jan. & June* (1871) 232 [The storm] went crashing on, into the heavy timber.

2. *Heavy oil*: = dead oil (see DEAD *a.* D. 2).

1838 [see Dict.]. 1879 *Encycl. Brit.* X. 100/1 The heavy oils are a mixture of naphthalin, phenol (carbolic acid), cresol (cresylic acid), and anthracene, &c. 1913 V. B. LEWES *Oil Fuel* 129 The heavy tar oil, or 'creosote oil' forms a fairly good liquid fuel. The specific gravity is usually in the neighbourhood of 1·1, hence its name of 'heavy-oil', being heavier than water. *Ibid.* 180 Heavy oil engines.

9. b. *Golf.* Of a ball: Lying in sand.

1886 H. HUTCHINSON *Hints Game Golf* 39 When lying 'heavy'..bear in mind that it is better to hit the ball with the iron than to miss it with a spoon.

15. *Heavy face* (*type*): see FACE *sb.* 22.

1891 [see FACE *sb.* 22]. 1898 J. SOUTHWARD *Mod. Printing* I. xxii. 140.

21. Also, ponderously dignified; stern, repressive, unbending: esp. *heavy father*, *heavy uncle*, which are also used as attrib. phrases (= sternly paternal or avuncular). orig. *Theatrical slang.*

1898 RIDER HAGGARD *Doctor Therne* iii, Sir John.. received me in his best 'heavy-father' manner. 1931 *Daily Express* 31 Jan. 5/2 The heavy uncle attitude. 1931 *Times Lit. Suppl.* 13 Aug. 613/4 The Venetian Pantalone becomes the Atellane 'heavy father' Pappus.

30. heavy-wooded pine, a variety of pine.

1858 J. A. WARDER *Hedges & Evergr.* II. 250 *Pinus ponderosa*, or Heavy-wooded Pine, has leaves from nine inches to a foot long.

31. *heavy-scented*; **heavy-faced**, having a heavy face (see FACE *sb.* 22, *HEAVY *a.*¹ 15); **heavy-timbered**, (*a*) thickly furnished with growing trees; (*b*) large-limbed.

1917 F. S. HENRY *Printing for School & Shop* vii. 90 *Heavy-faced types are appropriate in printed matter for the iron and steel industry. 1906 *Westm. Gaz.* 4 Jan. 2/1 The *heavy-scented buds. 1908 *Ibid.* 7 Aug. 3/1 Never was such clover!.. heavy-scented, rich, and generous. 1831 PECK *Guide for Emigrants* II. 40 The wide, level, and *heavy timbered alluvions, are..unhealthy. 1861 WHYTE MELVILLE *Market Harb.* 7 Deep-ribbed, heavy-timbered hounds. 1902 S. E. WHITE *Conjuror's House* iv. 39 The fort itself, a medley of heavy-timbered stockades and square block-houses. 1908 *Westm. Gaz.* 25 Aug. 7/1 A dark, heavy-timbered wood.

B. *sb.* **1. b.** *The heavies*, the heavy artillery.

1908 *Daily Chron.* 6 Aug. 6/4 The excellent firing of the 4·7 guns by the First and Seconds (or, as they are more familiarly called, 'the Heavies'). 1916 BOYD CABLE *Action Front* 113 The Heavies as well as the Field guns were to bombard. 1918 E. M. ROBERTS *Flying Fighter* 57 Soon the field artillery and the 'heavies' woke up again.

2. b. Anything particularly large and weighty of its kind.

1897 *Daily News* 25 Nov. 5/1 Amongst the elephantine heavies is Mandarin, who killed a keeper during his last residence at Olympia. 1908 *Pall Mall Gaz.* 27 Mar. 12/3 Firms..which have specialised in the manufacture of 'heavies' [*sc.* motor vehicles].

c. *pl.* *Racing.* Heavy horseshoes.

1930 *Times* 24 Mar. 4/2 It is almost impossible to tell by watching a horse walk in the parade ring whether he is plated, or whether he is carrying, to use a racing term, 'the heavies'.

5. *pl.* The heavy trades or industries (see HEAVY *a.* 5); also, stocks or shares in such a trade or industry.

1900 *Westm. Gaz.* 26 Jan. 11/1 Hope for the Heavies. 1902 *Daily Chron.* 20 May 3/6 The ratio of working expenses for the past half-year on the North British railways was 49 per cent., compared with 65 per cent., or more, on the four 'heavies'. 1922 *Daily Tel.* 12 June 2/3 The prices of the other comparable 'heavies'—Great Western and London and North-Western—have also gone ahead.

Heavy-weight. Add: **c.** *attrib.* Also as *adj.*, particularly heavy of its kind.

1909 *Westm. Gaz.* 2 Mar. 5/2 In a variety of cloths, serges, and heavy-weight cashmere.

Hebdomadarian (hebdǫmădē·riăn). [f. HEBDOMADARY + -IAN.] = HEBDOMADARY *sb.*

1898 ST. CLAIR BADDELEY *Cotteswold Shrine* 75 At a signal given by the hebdomadarian of the week they returned to the Cloister.

Hebe-. **b.** Add: **Hebephre·nic** *a.* and *sb.*, = *hebephreniac*.

1908 *Practitioner* Jan. 12 The patient may gradually become imbecile and demented—the hebephrenic type. 1915 C. R. PAYNE tr. *O. Pfister's Psych. Method* 542 Dementia praecox (in catatonic, hebephrenic and paranoid forms).

Hebetic (hĭbe·tik), *a.* *Phys.* [ad. Gr. ἡβητικός youthful, f. ἥβη youth.] Of, pertaining to, or occurring at the time of puberty.

1890 BILLINGS *Med. Dict.*

Hebraist. Add: **4.** One who maintains that the New Testament was written in Greek that contained Hebrew idioms.

1859 E. MASSON tr. *Winer's Gram. N. T. Diction* I. i. 25 Various..scholars (the Purists) perseveringly endeavoured to demonstrate that the style of the N. T. entirely reaches the standard of classical Greek purity..while others (the Hebraists) maintained..that it exhibits a..predominant Hebrew tincture. 1906 J. H. MOULTON *Gram. N. T. Greek* (1908) 3 The Hebraist went absurdly far in recognising Semitic influence where none was really operative. 1907 [see PURIST 2].

Hebrid (he·brid), *a.* [ad. *Hebrides*: see next.] = *HEBRIDEAN. Also **He·bridal** *a.*

1748 THOMSON *Cast. Indol.* I. xxx, A shepherd of the Hebrid Isles. 1841 YARRELL *Brit. Fishes* (ed. 2) II. 133 The Hebridal Smelt, *Osmerus Hebridicus*..is at once clearly distinguishable from our long-known and highly-esteemed favourite, the common smelt. *Ibid.* 300 The Hebridal Argentine. *Argentina Hebridica.* 1923 *United Free Ch. Mission Rec.* July 275 From many a Hebrid isle..from plain manses and luxurious mansions these men and women have come.

Hebridean (hĕbrĭ·dĭăn, hebridī·ăn), *a.* and *sb.* Also 6–9 -ian. [f. *Hebrides*, an alteration, said to have originated in an accidental misprint, of L. *Hebudes* (Pliny), Gr. Ἐβουδαι (Ptolemy).] **A.** *adj.* Of or pertaining to the Hebrides, a group of islands off the west coast of Scotland. **B.** *sb.* A native or inhabitant of the Hebrides.

1623 COCKERAM, *Hebridean wave*, the Irish sea. 1632 LITHGOW *Trav.* 494 The desperate courage of these awfull Hebridians. 1641 *Sylvester's Wks.* 331/1 *Hebridian Wave*, the Sea about the Isles Hiberides, to the North from Ireland. 1775 JOHNSON *West. Isl.* 221 Such intelligence the Hebridians probably receive from their transmarine correspondents. 1780 J. JOHNSTONE (*title*) Anecdotes of Olave the Black, King of Man, and the Hebridian Princes of the Somerled Family. 1810 SCOTT *Fam. Lett.* 10 June (1894) I. 181, I intend to take the Hebridian character and scenery ..for my subject. 1828–43 TYTLER *Hist. Scot.* (1864) I. 11 Dugal and other Hebridean chiefs. 1833–4 J. PHILLIPS *Geol.* in *Encycl. Metrop.* VI. 561/1 The Zetland Isles, which are in some measure to be viewed as a prolongation to the Hebridian group. *a* 1856 H. MILLER *Cruise Betsey* vi. (1858) 90 The penetrating powers of a true Hebridean drizzle. 1887 WOODWARD *Geol. Eng. & Wales* (ed. 2) 38 The Lewisian (or Hebridean) group. 1926 *Chambers's Jrnl.* Sept. 577/2 Our comely Hebridean.

Hechima (hetʃī·mă). [Jap.] The sponge-gourd (see SPONGE *sb.*¹ 13 c).

Heck (hek), *int.* *dial.* and *U.S.* Euphemistic alteration of *hell*. (Also *hecky* in dial. use.)

[1865 [J. A. FERGUSON] *Wot Aw seed ut th' Preston Egsibishun* 88 (E.D.D.) Well, aw'll go to ecky, he cried. 1876 J. ALMOND *Bunch of Watercresses* 21 (E.D.D.) Where the hecky could he go to?]

1887 *S. Cheshire Gloss.* s.v., What the heck are yō up to? 1925 *Blackw. Mag.* Oct. 545/1, I couldn't make out what in heck was going on. 1928 M. WALSH *White Rivers Run* ii. § 3 By heck! what a kick he must have in that right of his. 1930 *Daily Express* 23 May 10/3 Does the borough council care? By heck, it doesn't!

Heckelphone (he·kəlfōun). [ad. G. *heckelphon*, f. name of *Heckel*, an instrument-maker of Biberich, after *saxophone*.] A baritone oboe.

1905 *Westm. Gaz.* 14 Dec. 8/2. 1914 C. FORSYTH *Orchestration* 228 Strauss has made use of the Heckelphon in...*Salome*.

Hecte, variant of HEKTE.

Hectic, *a.* Add: **4.** Stirring, exciting, disturbing; characterized by a state of feverish excitement or activity. *colloq.*

1904 KIPLING *Traffics & Discov.* 210 Didn't I say we never met in pup-pup-puris naturalibus, if I may so put it, without a remarkably hectic day ahead of us? 1922 *Westm. Gaz.* 19 Aug., The hectic undulations of the mark. *Ibid.* 7 Nov., Those hectic inconsidered actions which kept the country in a state of crisis for some ten days. 1922 *Daily Mail* 21 Nov. 11 As additional excitements to the hectic finishes one horse was killed and the judge mistook the winner of the Leycester Nursery.

Hectically. Add: **b.** With feverish activity.

1908 *Daily Chron.* 18 May 3/5 So many pictures in the Salons look as if they had been painted hectically a month before the exhibitions opened.

Hectography (hektǫ·grăfi). [f. HECTOGRAPH: see -GRAPHY.] The use of the hectograph.

1889 SKRINE *Mem. Thring* 31 Splice 3 pens together,.. and execute the task..by fraudulent hectography.

Heder, variant of *CHEDAR.

Hedge, *sb.* Add:

5. Also *Stock Exchange* (cf. *HEDGE *v.* 8 c).

1917 A. W. ATWOOD *Exchanges & Speculation* xiv. 196 The local elevator companies..place their hedges as soon as they begin to accumulate supplies of grain.

7 and 9. hedge-wren: **hedge-clause** *U.S.*, a safeguarding clause in a contract; **hedge-fence**, a hedge serving as a fence; **hedge-grown** *a.* (see quots.); **hedge-hop** *v.* *colloq.*, to hop over the hedges in a flying machine, to fly low; **hedge selling** (see 5 above and *HEDGE *v.* 8 c).

1928 *Saturday Even. Post* (N.Y.) 10 Mar. 185/2 In the Wall Street language these are called 'hedge clauses. They signify that if the representations turn out to be wrong the banker shall not be held accountable. 1662 *Portsmouth* (R.I.) *Rec.* 396 The said fence..provided that it be a *hedge fence. 1778 *Essex Inst. Hist. Coll.* LII. 13 Seeing this hedge fence, they might take it to be a breastwork thrown up to annoy them. 1826–44 [see HEDGE *sb.* 7 a]. 1820 KEATS *Fancy* 50 The first *Hedge-grown primrose that hath burst. 1900 *Daily Express* 3 Aug. 2/7 Barley is not so good this year, for it has come up irregularly..; barley of this character is known with us as a 'hedge-grown crop'. 1928 *Daily Express* 21 May 10/3 They can '*hedge-hop' with skill or fly to the greater heights with as much impunity as a man pilot. 1930 J. STEPHENSON *Princ. Commercial Corr.* 151 There was little further change, some *hedge selling and Continental liquidation being well absorbed by month-end trade calling. 1930 *Daily Express* 8 Sept. 2/7 A reaction occurred owing to liquidation, hedge selling, a bearish crop estimate. 1899 *Westm. Gaz.* 21 July 2/3 The swallow does not fear us, the *hedge-wren does not flout us. 1907 *Academy* 9 Feb. 131/2 The hedge-wren..Is out in the open.

10. hedge-cactus *U.S.*, a cactus (*Cereus peruvianus*) grown as a hedge-plant; **hedge-nettle** (later example).

1883 J. H. BEADLE *Western Wilds* xxxvi. 593 There is.. the *hedge cactus, with which Mexicans fence their fields. 1869 JANE G. FULLER *Uncle John's Flower Gatherers* 277 There are several other species of the *Hedge-nettle, some of them without hairs.

Hedge, *v.* Add: **8. c.** To insure against risk of loss by entering into contracts which balance one another. Also *trans.*, to operate in (a commodity) in this way.

1909 I. FISHER *Elimination of Risk* 72 An important method of shifting risks is 'hedging', whereby a dealer, for instance in transporting wheat, may be relieved of the risk of a change of price. 1917 A. W. ATWOOD *Exchanges & Speculation* xiv. 195 Hedging..consists in matching a purchase with a sale, or vice versa; in other words, it consists in making a purchase or sale for future delivery to offset and protect an actual merchandising transaction. *Ibid.* xiv. 197 It makes little difference to an elevator if wheat rises or falls fifty cents a bushel, provided its holdings have been hedged.

Hedgehog. Add: **7. b. hedgehog converter, transformer** *Electr.*, a type of transformer (no longer used) with open magnetic circuit, in which the ends of the iron wire core assume a bristling appearance; **hedgehog wheat**, a race of hardy dwarf wheats, grown in mountainous districts of Europe, having dense short ears and awned glumes.

1902 *Encycl. Brit.* XXVIII. 117/2 The wire..used..to form the core of his '*hedgehog' transformers. 1911 WEBSTER, *Hedgehog wheat. 1921 J. PERCIVAL *Wheat Plant* 307 Club, Dwarf, Cluster or Hedgehog Wheat, *Triticum compactum*.

Hedonal (hī·dǫnăl). *Chem.* [f. Gr. ἡδονή pleasure + -AL.] A white crystalline powder used as a hypnotic remedy.

1905 *Medical Annual* 191 Hedonal has been used by Vargas in the treatment of chorea.

Hedrumite (he·drǔməit). *Petrography.* [f. *Hedrum*, Norway + -ITE¹.] A variety of syenite having a laminated structure caused by the elongated form of the feldspar crystals.

1926 HATCH & WELLS *Petrol. Igneous Rocks* Index 548/2.

Hedychium (hĭdi·kiǒm). [mod.L. (Koenig, 1785), f. Gr. ἡδύς sweet + χιών snow, in allusion to the fragrant snow-white flowers of some species.] A plant of the genus so named of zingiberaceous perennials, natives of tropical Asia, bearing showy white, yellow, or red flowers in a terminal spike; the garland flower. Also, a fibre obtained from a species of this genus.

1911 in WEBSTER. 1920 CROSS & BEVAN *Paper-Making* 171 *Hedychium coronarium*. Hedychium has lately come into prominence as a paper-making fibre.

Heebie-jeebie(s (hī·biˌdʒī·bi(z). *slang.* A form of dance resembling the Blues. Also *fig.*, the 'blues', the 'jim-jams'.

1926 *Bulletin* 13 Dec. 5/5 The latest dance, the 'Heebie-Jeebies' is said to represent the incantations made by Red Indian witch doctors before a human sacrifice. 1927 *Punch* 2 Feb. 116/1 It is interesting to observe that in spite of artificial sunlight, television, winter sports and the heebie-jeebie there are still some stalwarts who stand by the old traditional amusements of the English people. 1927 *Weekly Dispatch* 1 May 8 The Heebie Jeebies is rich in haunch movements. *Ibid.* 3 May 3/7 A terrible girl in the next gallery, painted in the fearsome and fashionable 'pink and putty' manner, had given him what an American present might have called the 'heeby-jeebies'. *Ibid.* 17 Aug. 3/2 Does this work never give you the heeby-jeebies? Does it never depress you?

Heel, *sb.*¹ Add:

1. e. *Heel of Achilles*, *Achilles' heel*: the only vulnerable spot (in allusion to the story of the dipping of Achilles in the river Styx: cf. *tendon of Achilles* s.v. TENDON).

1810 COLERIDGE *Friend* 431 Ireland, that vulnerable heel of the British Achilles! 1864 CARLYLE *Fredk. Gt.* XVII. ii. IV. 522 Hanover,..the Achilles'-heel to invulnerable England. 1930 tr. *L. D. Bronshstein's Life* xxv. 202 By his verbal artifices, he only discloses his own Achilles' heel.

f. *Horsemanship.* Management by the heel, esp. the spurred heel.

1728 CHAMBERS *Cycl.* s.v., This horse understands the Heels well.

7. k. The lower part of the back of a book.

1930 *Godfrey's Catal.* No. 134. 26 Small piece gone from heel, and joint becoming tender.

l, m. (See quots.)

1880 PROF. COPE in C. S. TOMES *Man. Dental Anat.* (1898) 471 Stages in the following modification of parts:—.. (6) In the obliteration of the inner tubercle of the lower sectorial. (7) In the extinction of the heel of the same. 1888 *Lockwood's Dict. Mech. Engin.*, *Heel*, the thick or broad end of a wedge-shaped piece, the broad end of a railway switch for example.

24. c. *To run heel.* Delete † and add:

1923 *Times* 17 Jan. 5/5 The old Melbreak hounds will never run heel.

26. a. heel-breast, in a shoe, the inside edge of the heel, adjoining the waist; so **heel-breaster**, an operator who cuts heel-breasts; also, the tool used; **heel-breasting**, the cutting of heel-breasts; **heel-parer**, one who shapes and trims heel-blanks; **heel-scourer**, one who scours the surface of heels.

1921 *Dict. Occup. Terms* (1927) § 420 *Scourer*..designated according to parts upon which he works, *e.g.* bottom or naumkeag scourer, heel scourer, *heel-breast scourer. 1905 *Westm. Gaz.* 30 Oct. 7/3 The same firm have several other novelties, including an automatic Louis *heel-breaster. The uninitiated may like to know that '*heel-breasting' is the operation of bevelling out the curve on the inside edge of the heel to the familiar half-moon or other shape. 1921 *Dict. Occup. Terms* (1927) § 414 *Heel breaster*; cuts breast on front of heel square. 1881 *Instr. Census Clerks* (1885) 76 *Heel Parer. 1904 *Daily Chron.* 11 June 8/6 Boot Trade. —Wanted good heel parers and *heel scourers.

Heel, *v.*¹ Add:

7. *intr.* To run back on the scent, to run heel.

1898 *Daily News* 5 Oct. 6/6 One or two of the best hounds showed a disposition to heel—i. e.—go back on the line if they chanced to lose it.

Heelaman, -oman, varr. of HIELAMAN.

1848 H. W. HAYGARTH *Bush Life Australia* x. 113 The heeloman is a sort of shield, made of the toughest wood procurable, about three feet in length, and six inches in breadth at the centre, whence it gradually tapers off to a point at either extremity.

Heeled, *ppl. a.* Add: **2.** (Earlier examples.)

1868 *All Year Round* 31 Oct. 491/2 It was the correct thing that the gentleman who was vexed at him should ask in a piquant tone whether he was 'heeled'. 1873 J. H. BEADLE *Undevel. West* xi. 190 As it was my first visit to Washington, I was but poorly 'heeled' for the work.

4. *Heeled bet*: in card games (see quot.).

1923 L. H. DAWSON *Hoyle's Games* 274 A 'heeled Bet' is said to be one in which the counters of the stake are placed diagonally across from one card to another signifying that the punter is playing both cards to win.

Heeler. Add: **6.** A sharp blow with the heels or spurs.

1888 'R. BOLDREWOOD' *Robbery under Arms* xii, He fetches him [*sc.* the horse] such a 'heeler' as gave him something else to think of for a few miles.

Heeler². *colloq.* [f. HEEL *v.*² + -ER¹.] A lurch to one side; also, a boat inclined to lurch.

1894 *Times* 6 Aug. 5/2 The wind came off in hard puffs. Each took a regular heeler as they crossed the mouth of the Medina. 1926 REX CLEMENTS *Stately Southerner* 106 The ship herself was a heeler.

Heel-piece. Add: **1. d.** *Shipbuilding.* An angle-bar joining the heels of a frame across the keel. **e.** *Electr.* The iron bar connecting the soft iron cores in an electro-magnet.

1904 A. C. HOLMS *Pract. Shipbuilding* I. 471 The frame heel pieces are usually fitted when the frames are screwed up ready for riveting. 1904 M. M. KIRKMAN *Telegr. & Telephone* 29 The magnet is constructed of a bar or heel piece of soft iron, into which are screwed two pencil-shaped pieces of iron which form the cores of the magnets.

Heel-plate. Add: **3.** A plate to support the heel of the boot in a metal skate; also, 'a slotted plate fixed on a boot-heel, to which a skate may be locked' (*Funk's Standard Dict.* 1895).

1890 D. ADAMS *Skating* 5 A metal sole and heel-plate screwed on to the boot with ordinary screws, is unquestionably the best and firmest. 1895 G. A. MEAGHER *Figure & Fancy Skating* 19 A perfect skate should be all of one piece. This is effected by welding the toe and heel plates on to the blade itself.

Heemraad (hē·mrād, hī·m-). *Hist.* Pl. **-raden.** Also **-raat, -rad.** [Du., f. *heem* village, home + *raad* council.] A local petty court or council assisting the landdrost in South Africa and also formerly in Holland; also, a member of this council.

1801 J. BARROW *Trav.* I. 12 A civil magistrate called a *Landrost*, who, with his *Hemraaden*, or a council of country burghers, is vested with powers to regulate the police of his district, [etc.]. 1876 *Encycl. Brit.* V. 47/2 Prior to 1827 there existed in the several districts of the colony an institution established by the Dutch called the Board of Landrost and Heemraaden. 1888 THEAL in Fitzpatrick *Transvaal* (1899) 10 The abolition in 1827 of the courts of landdrost and heemraden. 1900 *Westm. Gaz.* 19 Dec. 3/2 Lord Caledon, after our second annexation of the Cape, revived an old kind of elected Councils, named Heemraden, for the government of the inland districts.

Heersian (hīə·ɹsiăn), *a.* *Geol.* [ad. F. *heersien*, f. *Heers*, in Limbourg: see -IAN.] Of or pertaining to a system which is specially developed at Heers, consisting of an upper division of marls and a lower division of sandy beds.

[1886 JUKES-BROWNE *Hist. Geol.* 456 Heersien...These beds are 100 feet thick.] 1903 A. GEIKIE *Text-bk. Geol.* (ed. 4) 1234 Heersian marls and Landenian sands.

Hefner (he·fnəɹ). *Photometry.* Short for the name of H. von *Hefner-Alteneck*, a German physicist, used to designate a unit of light intensity, equal to about ·88 candle-power; also in certain *attrib.* uses, as **Hefner lamp**, an amyl-acetate lamp used to compare light intensities; **Hefner lux, -metre**, a light equal in intensity to one hefner at a distance of one metre.

1902 *Encycl. Brit.* XXX. 235/2 For accurate scientific purposes the best standard is the Hefner-Alteneck or amyl-acetate lamp. 1910 *Ibid.* VIII. 784/2 The weighing beam in the Hefner-Alteneck dynamometer is placed transversely to the belt. 1911 *Ibid.* XXI. 526/2 Various experimental investigations into the properties of the Hefner flame. 1917 *G. Martin's Indust. & Manuf. Chem.* II. 357 *note*, The Hefner candle power is equal to about 0·9 British standard candle.

Heft (heft), *sb.*² Pl. **hefte.** [G.] A number of sheets of paper fastened together to form a book; *spec.* a division of a serial work; a part of a serial publication.

1886 *Athenæum* 9 Oct. 464/1 This treatise forms the fifth *Heft* of the second volume. 1892 *Rev. Reviews* Jan. 58/1 There is another interesting article..in Heft 14 of the *Gartenlaube*.

Heft, *v.*¹ **1.** Also *absol.*

1913 R. W. SERVICE *Rhymes of Rolling Stone* 40 And here they must make the long *portage*, and the boys sweat in the sun; And they heft and pack, and they haul and track, and each must do his trick.

Hefty, *a.* **1.** Add: Now in general colloq. or slang use. Also *advb.*, 'powerfully', exceedingly.

1898 KIPLING *Land & Sea Tales*, *Stalky* (1923) 135 What are we going to do? It's hefty damp here. 1905 *Daily Chron.* 18 Sept. 8/2 When an American girl does that, you can guess there's something 'mighty hefty' weighing her down. 1925 E. F. NORTON *Fight for Everest*, *1924* 39 The bucolic bumpkin with coarse features and slow brain fails no less than the 'hefty' giant. 1930 PRIESTLEY *Angel Pavement* ii. 85 It's a hefty commission all right. 1930 *Diary of Public School Girl* 32 Played in a game with Highlands. Got some good hefty bangs.

Hegemon (hī·dʒĭmǫn, he·-). [a. Gr. ἡγέμων leader.] A leading or paramount power.

1904 *Forum* Jan.–Mar. 347 (Cent. D. Suppl.) The *hegemon* of the western hemisphere is the United States. 1920 *Public Opinion* 2 July 6/1 Japan..asserting her ambition to become hegemon of a far East on which white influence shall be reduced to a vanishing point.

Hegemonist (hĭdʒe·mǫnist). [f. HEGEMONY + -IST.] An advocate of hegemony. Also **Hege·monizer.**

1898 *Pall Mall Gaz.* 12 Feb. 4/1 This Prince Kraft was also, it would seem, the earliest Prussian hegemonist, who has so far, and as such, revealed himself to us. 1921 *Pilgrim* Apr. 273 It does not..follow that the resistance of England to the previous hegemonisers would be condemned.

Hehner (hē·nəɹ). The name of the chemist Otto *Hehner* used attrib. in *Hehner value*, a number indicating the percentage of insoluble fatty acids in an oil or fat.

1915 *G. Martin's Indust. & Manuf. Chem.* I. (ed. 2) 642. 1918 T. H. POPE tr. *Villavecchia's App. Anal. Chem.* I. 382 Insoluble, Fixed Fatty Acid Number. (Hehner Number.)

Heiau (hē·au). [Hawaiian.] A temple.

1825 W. ELLIS *Jrnl. Tour Hawaii* 51 Tamehameha..finished the heiau, dedicated it to his god of war. 1920 *Nature* 15 July 628/1 There are shorter notes on heathen prayers and the ceremonial erecton of the *heiau* or god's house.

Heidelberg (hai·dəlbəɹg, ‖ hai·dəlbɛrχ). The name of a German city used *attrib.* in Archæology to denote a jaw found in the sandpit of Mauer near Heidelberg in 1907, or the type of prehistoric man (*homo heidelbergensis*) indicated by this jaw.

1911 A. KEITH in *Nature* 25 May 414/1 The Heidelberg mandible was found in 1907 embedded in the Mauer sand beds. 1912 W. L. H. DUCKWORTH *Prehistoric Man* 10 The Heidelberg or Mauer jaw. 1927 R. S. LULL *Org. Evol.* xxxviii. 677 The Heidelberg man represents the oldest recorded European race, geologically speaking.

Height, *sb.* Add:

1. c. Of type: The distance from the feet to the face. *Height to paper*, the standard height of type.

1771 LUCKOMBE *Hist. Printing* 243 They [*sc.* imperfections] are seldom exact to the prior sorts, but differ from them, sometimes in thickness, height to paper, or depth of Body. 1824 J. JOHNSON *Typogr.* II. ii. 13 Not only founders of different places, but of the same residence, and even each in particular, often vary in height and depth. 1888 *Encycl. Brit.* XXIII. 698/2 The height of type varies slightly with different founders, the mean being ⅞ in. 1892 A. OLDFIELD *Man. Typogr.* xxii. 164 Each letter should be of exactly the same height to paper; the height of type being 11–12ths of an inch. 1900 H. HART *Cent. Typogr.* 23 Five packets of types of the same face, but cast on a Pica body and Dutch 'height-to-paper', were found at the Oxford Press in 1898.

14. *Height of land*, a watershed or ridge of high land dividing two river basins. *Canadian* and *U.S.*

1785 in G. Sheldon *Hist. Deerfield* (1895) I. 559 They told us they wd travel to the height of land by black river. 1805–9 J. J. HENRY *Camp. agst. Quebec* (1812) 36 On this lake, we obtained a full view of those hills which were then, and are now, called the 'Heighth of land'. 1860 H. Y. HIND *Narr. Canadian Red River Exped.* II. 225 The Vermilion Pass, which was traversed by Dr. Hector presents on the whole the greatest natural facilities for crossing the mountains without the aid of engineering work, as the rise to the height of land is gradual from both sides. 1875 *Encycl. Brit.* II. 201/1 In the north it [*sc.* the watershed] is found in a stretch of country, called the Height of Land, that lies between the White and the Green Mountains, and gives birth to the Connecticut and a number of smaller streams. 1902 *Ibid.* XXXI. 330/2 Beyond the Height-of-Land the Winnipeg and English rivers flow westward to Lake Winnipeg. 1918 H. BINDLOSS *Agatha's Fortune* xxv, It was hardly a range of hills, but rather what prospectors call a 'heighth' of land. 1930 G. L. WOOD *Pacific Basin* 5 Behind the peninsula of California the height of land is a thousand miles from the sea.

19. For †*Obs.* read *Obs.* exc. in literary use.

1820 LAMB *Elia* Ser. I. *South-sea House* (1869) 6 While he held you in converse, you felt strained to the height in the colloquy. 1871 TENNYSON *Last Tournament* 658 For once —ev'n to the height—I honour'd him.

Heik, var. of *HIKE *sb.* and *v.*

Heimin (hē·min). [Jap., f. *hei* common + *min* people.] In Japanese society, the common people, including the peasantry, labourers, and traders.

1875 *Trans. Asiatic Soc. Japan* (1884) III. II. 104. 1904 *Daily Chron.* 30 Mar. 4/5 Of those not Samurai, the heimin, or commoners, the peasantry ranked first.

Heimweh (hai·mvē). [G.] Home-sickness.

1756, 18.. [see HOME-SICKNESS]. 1845 FORD *Handbk. Spain* II. 695 If debarred a hope of return, they [*sc.* the Asturians] pine from Nostalgia or Heimweh. 1904 A. B. F. YOUNG *Complete Motorist* xvi. (ed. 2) 323 That restlessness, as haunting as the *heimweh* that is its opposite.

Heine (hai·nɪ). Also **Heinie, Hiney.** *Canadian* and *U.S. Army slang.* [The German surname *Heine*.] A German (soldier).

1925 E. FRASER & GIBBONS *Soldier & Sailor Words*, *Heine* (or *Hiney*). 1929 E. W. SPRINGS *Above bright blue Sky* 227 'There, you're all right,' the sergeant soothed him. 'Those yellow-bellied Heinies can't kill you. We got ten of 'em this morning.'

Heinesque (haine·sk), *a.* [f. the name of H. *Heine* (1799–1856), German poet + -ESQUE.] Of, pertaining to, or resembling the style of Heine.

1899 *Academy* 24 June 677/1 A grimly tragic vignette of peasant life, with a Heinesque turn at the close. 1907 *Daily Chron.* 2 Aug. 3/3 His Heinesque moods are steeled through with a strong man's virility. 1915–16 *Mus. Assoc. Proc.* 158 Beethoven is never sinister, never even Heinesque, if I may use the word.

Heintzite (hai·ntsəit). *Min.* [ad. G. *heintzit*, f. the name of W. H. *Heintz*, German chemist of Halle: see -ITE¹.] A colourless or white hydrous borate of magnesium and potassium found in monoclinic crystals.

1891 *Jrnl. Chem. Soc.* LX. I. 528 For the new borate, Milch proposes the name of *hintzeite*, after Professor Hintze, of Breslau; whilst Ludecke proposes that of *heintzite*, after Heintz, the discoverer of pinnoite. 1902 H. A. MIERS *Min.* 540.

Hei-tiki (hē·tī·ki). *New Zealand.* [Maori; f. *hei* ornament for the neck + *tiki* creator of man.] A greenstone ornament worn by the Maoris, representing the first man.

1835 W. YATE *Acc. New Zealand* (ed. 2) 151 The *hei-tiki* being taken off the neck, laid down..and then wept and sung over. 1880 *Encycl. Brit.* XIII. 540/1 The hideous breast ornament termed *hei tiki*. 1887 *Col. & Indian Exhib.*, *Rep. Col. Sect.* 74 Heitikis or native deities.

Hejeen, variant of *HYGEEN.

Hekistotherm (hĭki·stǫþə̄ɹm). *Bot.* [f. Gr. ἥκιστος smallest + θέρμη heat.] A plant which needs very little heat, as the arctic and antarctic lichens and mosses. Hence **Hekistothe·rmic** *a.*

1900 B. D. JACKSON *Gloss. Bot. Terms* Addit., Hekistotherm. 1909 GROOM & BALFOUR tr. *Warming's Œcology of Plants* 36 Hekistothermic: plants living beyond the limits of tree-growth, where the annual mean temperature sinks below 0° C.

Hekte (he·ktī). Also **hecte.** [Gr. ἕκτη the sixth (of a stater), fem. (sc. μοῖρα part) of ἕκτος sixth.] A Greek silver coin.

1906 G. F. HILL *Historical Greek Coins* 17 A few specimens of an electrum *hekte*, or sixth of the stater. 1921 *British Museum Return* 79 An electrum hecte with the type of a crouching lion and a hemihecte with the type of a winged monster.

Held, *ppl. a.* Add: Also with adverbs.

c 1611 CHAPMAN *Iliad* XXIV. 275 With held vp hands. 1906 *Westm. Gaz.* 28 Dec. 7/2 A long string of 'held-up' cars.

Helderberg (he·ldəɹbǭɹg). *Geol.* Name of a range of hills in New York State, designating a subdivision of the Lower Devonian (or Upper Silurian) in the eastern U.S. Hence **He·lderbergian** (-bǭɹg-, -bǭɹdʒ-), *a.*

1882 A. GEIKIE *Text-Bk. Geol.* 692 Upper Silurian...III. Lower Helderberg formation. 1899 LAPWORTH *Geol.* 228 The Lower Helderberg Series. 1906 CHAMBERLIN & SALISBURY *Geol.* II. 454 From this intermediate or transitional assemblage the Helderberg fauna seems to have taken its origin. *Ibid.* 455 The capulid shells which abound at some localities in the Helderbergian..faunas.

Helgramite: see HELLGRAMMITE.

1894 *Outing* (U.S.) XXIV. 228/2 Helgramites (purchasable at most any of the tackle stores during the bass season).

Helical, *a.* Add: *Helical gear*, *tube* (see quots.). Also *Comb.*, as *helical-cut* adj.

1888 *Lockwood's Dict. Mech. Engin.*, *Helical Gear*, toothed gear in which the wheel-teeth instead of being at right angles with their faces are set at some other angle therewith. 1904 *Technol. & Sci. Dict.* (ed. Goodchild & Tweney) s.v. *Cycles*, A form of tube known as 'helical', which is formed from a thin steel band or ribbon, wrapped into a form of a tube and brazed at the edges. 1908 *Westm. Gaz.* 28 May 4/2 The live axle is chiefly noticeable for its helical-cut driving pinion. *Ibid.* 18 Nov. 5/1 Several of the wheels have helical-cut teeth.

B. *sb.* = helical gear.

1913 *Lockwood's Dict. Mech. Engin.* (ed. 4) s.v. *Helical Gear Cutting*, Double helicals are cut in the same way if the teeth are staggered and divided at the apex.

Helically, *adv.* Add: Also *Comb.*

1908 *Westm. Gaz.* 14 Nov. 14/2 Helically-cut half-time gear-wheels to ensure silence.

Helico- (he·likǫ), comb. form of Gr. ἕλιξ HELIX, in names of chemical substances occurring in snails.

1914 J. A. MANDEL tr. *Hammarsten & Hedin's Physiol. Chem.* (ed. 7) 174 Another phosphoglycoprotein is helicoproteid, obtained by Hammarsten from the glands of the snail Helix pomatia. 1917 *Jrnl. Chem. Soc.* CXII. I. 421 Helicorubin is thus closely related to hæmoglobin, and acts without doubt in the intestine of the snail as a respiratory pigment.

Helicopter (he·likǫptəɹ). *Aeronautics.* Also in Fr. form. [ad. F. *hélicoptère*, f. Gr. ἕλικος, ἕλιξ spiral, HELIX + πτερόν wing.] A flying machine sustained by one or more lifting screws revolving horizontally. Also *attrib.*

1872 *Aeronaut* Jan. (*Encycl. Brit.*, 1879, IX. 319/2) Helicoptère or Screw-Model, by M. Pénaud. 1887 tr. *J. Verne's Clipper of Clouds* iv, We can look forward to such contrivances..which we can call streophores, helicopters, orthopters..by means of which man will become the master of space. 1908 O. & W. WRIGHT in *Century Mag.* Sept. 641/2 Several years later we began building these hélicoptères for ourselves. 1909 *Westm. Gaz.* 28 Jan. 4/2 Mr. Howard Wright's helicopter, with which flying tests have been satisfactorily carried out, is now *en route* for Italy. *Ibid.* 2 Mar. 4/1 The Gobron engined Breguet helicopter aeroplane. 1927 C. L. M. BROWN *Conquest of Air* 39 The helicopter method of flight.

Hence **He·licopter** *v. intr.*, to fly with or as with a helicopter; **Helico·pterist**, one who uses a helicopter.

1923 *Daily Mail* 12 Feb. 7 M. Raoul de Pescara, the helicopterist. 1926 *Spectator* 10 Apr. 665/1 An albatross, helicoptering over the masthead, signalled the land.

Helio. Add: **b.** = *HELIOGRAPH *sb.* 4 b.

1886 KIPLING *Departm. Ditties*, etc. (1904) 23 All honour unto Bangs, for n'er did Jones thereafter know By word or act official who read off that helio. 1901 'LINESMAN' *Words Eyewitness* (1902) 32 Then another helio, spelt out painfully by the frowning, staring signallers, 'Very hard pressed'.

Helio². [colloq. abbrev. of HELIOTROPE.] = HELIOTROPE 1 d.

1922 *Daily Mail* 22 Nov. 5 Very exceptional value with Blue or Black or Helio border. 1928 *Ibid.* 31 July 1/3 Dainty..Dressing Jackets in Pink, Apple and Helio.

Helio-. Add: **He·lioculture** = *HELIOLITHIC culture. **He:liohy·giene**, exposure to the sun as a hygienic practice. **He:liophyllite** (-fi·ləit, -ǫ·filəit) *Min.*, a yellow or green arsenite and chloride of lead. **He·liopo·lar** *a.*, pertaining to the pole of the sun's rotation. **He:liota·ctic** *a.*, sensitive or responsive to the rays of the sun. **He·liota·xis**, phototaxis due to the rays of the sun. **He:liothe·rapy**, the treatment of disease by exposure to the sun's rays.

1925 J. R. HARRIS *Apollo's Birds* 34 The culture which is now generally called *helioculture. 1930 *New Statesman* 21 June 329/2, I..argued from that evidence that heliotherapy..must yield as an ideal to *heliohygiene. 1896 CHESTER *Dict. Min.*, *Heliophyllite, a foliated var. of ecdemite. 1902 *Science* 7 Feb. 223/2 The vector diagram in *heliopolar coordinates takes the form of a conical surface around the Sun. 1904 *Biol. Bulletin* VI. 253 The mating habits of these highly *heliotactic males and wingless females. 1913 DORLAND *Med. Dict.* (ed. 7), *Heliotaxis. 1890 BILLINGS *Med. Dict.*, *Heliotherapy, treatment of disease by exposure to sunlight. 1903 *Lancet* 11 July 104/1 The fundamental principles and practical applications of heliotherapy and phototherapy. 1921 *Glasgow Herald* 15 July 10 For the information of medical practitioners interested in heliotherapy.

Heliogabalus (hīliogæ·bălǒs). [Latinized f. *Elagabal*, Syro-Phœnician sun-god.] The adopted name of Varius Avitus Bassianus, Roman Emperor A.D. 218–222, famed for folly and profligacy, used allusively. Also **He:liogaba·lian** (-găbē·liăn) *a.*, resembling the character or tastes of Heliogabalus. **He:lioga·balize** *v. intr.*, to act like Heliogabalus.

1589 GREENE *Menaphon* (Arb.) 71 For his dissolute life he seemed another Heliogabalus. 1618 J. TAYLOR (Water P.) *Pennilesse Pilgr.* Wks. (1630) N 3/2 Had I beene a Sardanapalus, or a Heliogabalus, I thinke that..the great trauell ouer the Mountaines had tamed me. 1624 BURTON *Anat. Mel.* I. ii. II. ii. (ed. 2) 63 What Fagos, Epicures, Apitios, Heliogables our times affourd? 1859 *National Mag.* V. 142/1 In California..the Celestials..make a Heliogobalian kind of dish of rats' brains.

Heliograph, *sb.* Add: **4. b.** A message sent by heliograph.

1899 *Pall Mall Mag.* Nov. 319, I have just received a heliograph that the Basutos have bands out through..the valley.

Heliolithic (hīlioli·þik), *a.* [f. HELIO-, after *eolithic*, etc.] Designating the civilization characterized by megaliths and sun-worship.

1915 G. ELLIOT SMITH *Pract. Mummification* 4 The habit of megalithic building and sun-worship (a combination for which it is convenient to use Professor Brockwell's distinctive term 'heliolithic culture'). 1916 *Church Q. Rev.* Jan. 283 The world-wide migration of this 'heliolithic culture'. 1926 J. R. HARRIS *Apollo's Birds* 33 There is no known heliolithic temple in the Thames Valley. 1929 G. W. DEEPING *Roper's Row* xxxvi, But assuredly Ruth belonged to the old heliolithic people. She had something of the south in eyes, hair, temperament.

Heliometer. **1.** Add: Also *attrib.*

1893 D. GILL (*title*) Heliometer Observations for Determination of Stellar Parallax made at the Royal Observatory, Cape of Good Hope. 1905 C. L. POOR in *Astrophysical Jrnl.* XXII. 103 The heliometer measures made in connection with transits of Venus in 1874 and 1882.

So **Heliometry** (hīliǫ·mĕtri), the art or practice of using the heliometer.

Helium. Add: **b.** *attrib.*, as *helium-envelope*, *-spectrum*; **helium star**, a star which exhibits the helium line in its spectrum.

1903 AGNES M. CLERKE *Problems Astrophysics* 93 A *helium-envelope surrounds the sun to a depth of five thousand miles. *Ibid.* 94 Now that the *helium-spectrum has been unravelled. 1904 *Technol. & Sci. Dict.* (ed. Goodchild & Tweney), *Helium Stars*, stars the spectra of which show prominently the lines of the gas helium. 1921 *Discovery* Sept. 236/1 The B or helium stars are on the crest of the evolutionary curve, at the meridian of stellar life.

Hell, *sb.* Add: **4. d.** *A hell of a*—: also, an exceedingly bad, great, loud, etc.

1778 in *S. Curwen's Jrnl. & Lett.* (1864) 227 After ravelling in the heat of the season in a hell of a climate. 1806 WEEMS *Lett.* II. 354 I've had a hell of a time in your service. 1897 'MARK TWAIN' *Following Equator* xxxi, It's a charming town, with a hell of a hotel...It's the worst hotel in Australia. 1910 R. W. SERVICE *Ballads of Cheechako* 133 Lord! it's a hell of a night. 1910 MULFORD *Hopalong Cassidy* xxvi. 176, I got money—helluva lot of money. 1918 M'CUDDEN *Five Yrs. R.F.C.* 232 There was immediately a Hell of a yell. 1920 MULFORD *J. Nelson* xii. 126 You must 'a' had one h—l of a time gettin' out. 1922 — *Black Buttes* ii. 24 He was a hell of a trail-boss, an' he had a hell of an outfit, if you leave it to me!

7. b. Also designating similar receptacles for waste.

1872 *Saddl. Harn. & Carriage Builder's Gaz.* 1 Dec. 207/2 Each smith shop has what is termed the 'hell', and in cutting off a set of tires, if the farmer is not present, the largest half of the end cut off finds its way to the 'hell'. 1886 *Encycl. Brit.* XXI. 345/2 A useful adjunct to the many saw-mills, which produce more waste than can be consumed in raising the necessary steam, is the 'slab-burner' or 'hell'.

10. *To give* (a person) *hell*: to give him 'a bad time'. *Hell's delight*: pandemonium. *Like hell*: recklessly, desperately; extremely, very much: freq. as a mere intensive.

1855 Like hell [in Dict.]. 1863 O. W. NORTON *Army Lett.* 161 We have met the enemy and given them hell. 1918 E. A. MACKINTOSH *War, the Liberator* 141 You swine, I'll give you hell for this. 1918 W. J. LOCKE *Rough Road* xi. 131 Just listen to the hell's delight that's going on over yonder. 1924 D. H. LAWRENCE *England, my England* 206 'And I shall miss thee, Jack'..'Miss you like hell.' 1931 D. L. SAYERS *Five Red Herr.* xxii. 248, I am supposed to have faked an alibi, suborned my friends and played merry hell generally.

b. *Hell-for-leather*: at breakneck speed, orig. used with reference to riding on horseback. Also *attrib.* or as *adj.*

1889 KIPLING *Story of the Gadsbys*, *Valley of the Shadow*, Here, Gaddy, take the *chit* to Bingle and ride hell-for-leather. 1893 — *Many Inventions*, *My Lord the Elephant*, I perceived a gunner-orf'cer in full rig'mentals perusin' down the road, hell-for-leather, wid his mouth open. 1915 D. O. BARNETT *Lett.* 176 The little English plane went humming back, hell-for-leather. 1929 H. W. FREEMAN *Joseph & His Brethren* vi. 48 Charging down hell for leather with your sabres all flashing in the sun. 1930 *Daily Express* 6 Sept. 8/7 That magnificent, hell-for-leather, boiling verse.

11. b. *hell-raiser*; *hell-roaring*, *tearing* adjs.

1928 *Daily Express* 1 June 9 She dislikes the '*hell-raiser that he likes to make the public believe he is. 1920 J. GREGORY *Man to Man* iv, Your *hell-roaring old grand-dad. 1914 W. J. LOCKE *Jaffery* xxi, These *hell-tearing fellows.

Helladic, *a.* Add: **b.** *Archæol.* Denoting a Cycladic culture of southern Greece lasting from about 2600–1200 B.C. Also *absol.*

1921 WACE in *Jrnl. Hellenic Studies* XLI. II. 260 Early Helladic pottery. *Ibid.* 265 With the Third Late Helladic Period Mycenae reached the zenith of its dominion and riches. 1925 V. G. CHILDE *Dawn European Civilization* v. 74 The first metal-using culture therefore is called Early Helladic. 1927 PEAKE & FLEURE *Priests & Kings* 113 The sub-periods range from Early Helladic I to Late Helladic III.

Hellandite (he·lăndəit). *Min.* [f. the name of A. *Helland*, Norwegian scientist: see -ITE¹.] A silicate of calcium and the rare earths, found in pegmatite veins in Norway.

1903 *Jrnl. Chem. Soc.* LXXXIV. II. 657 Both in crystalline form and chemical composition, hellandite is analogous to guarinite. 1924 J. W. MELLOR *Inorg. & Theoret. Chem.* V. 512 Brownish-red hellandite from Lindvikskollan near Kragerö, Norway.

He·ll-bent, *a.* and *adv.* *U.S.* [HELL *sb.* 11 d, BENT *ppl. a.* 3.] 'Fiendishly', doggedly, or recklessly determined (*upon* a certain course). Also *advb.* determinedly, recklessly.

1835 *Knickerbocker Mag.* VI. 12 A large encampment of savages,..'hell-bent on carnage'. 1840 *Pol. Song* (Cent. Dict.), Maine went Hell-bent For Governor Kent. 1904 *Boston Herald* 2 Aug. 6 The Populist Democrats are going 'hell-bent', as the old song says, for Roosevelt. 1910 W. M. RAINE *B. O'Connor* ii. 21, I know your kind—hell-bent to spend what you cash in. 1910 MULFORD *Hopalong Cassidy* xxviii. 184 As soon as we lick this aggregation of trouble-hunters, what's left will ride hell-bent for that valley. 1912 L. J. VANCE *Destroying Angel* ix, Unless you're hell-bent upon sticking around here. 1918 MULFORD *Man fr. Bar-20* xv. 152, I was hell-bent to get down here,..an' now I'm hell-bent to get back again. 1926 B. CRONIN *Red Dawson* vi, Shaw sending the coach hell-bent round the curve of Jumping Lead.

Hellenic, *a.* Add: **2.** *Typog.* Designating a variety of Greek type.

1927 *Greek Printing Types* (Exhib. B.M.) 3 It is thus only natural that the Graeco-Latin founts should now make way for more directly Hellenic styles of type. *Ibid.* 21 Thucydides, Funeral Oration of Pericles (part). Printed with 12-point 'New Hellenic' type.

Hellenotype (hele·nǫtəip). *Photog.* = *ivorytype* (see IVORY 9).

1875 KNIGHT *Dict. Mech.*, *Hellenotype*, a picture in which two finished photographs are used. One is taken very light, the paper made translucent by varnish, tinted on the back, and laid [over] the stronger print, so that there is a combination of effects. 1890 WOODBURY *Encycl. Photogr.* 340.

Hellion, hellyon (he·lyən). *U.S. colloq.* [prob. variant of HALLION, with assimilation to HELL *sb.*] A troublesome or disreputable person; a mischievous child.

1845 J. J. HOOPER *Adv. Simon Suggs* i. 18 The 'oudacious' little hellions! 1857 *Jrnl. Discourses* V. 135/2 We are going to dig a cache..and put all the whining men and women into it...We want to be released from such poor hellyons. 1896 J. C. HARRIS *Sister Jane* 136 If dey ever was a hellian he wuz one. 1906 'O. HENRY' *Four Million* 8 Jawn, did ye ever see a straighter-nosed gang of hellions in the days of your life? 1919 H. L. WILSON *Ma Pettengill* vii. 225 Three children that was known to be hellions.

Supplement, p. 3873; Corrigenda, p. 4092; Spurious words, p. 4093; Books quoted, p. 4094

Helminthosporoid (helminþǫspō·roid), *a. Bot.* [f. mod.L. *Helminthosporium* (f. Gr. ἕλμινς, ἑλμινθ- HELMINTH + σπόρος seed, spore): see -OID.] Of, pertaining to, or resembling the genus *Helminthosporium* of hyphomycetous fungi.

1887 W. PHILLIPS *Brit. Discomycetes* 266 The flocci of some Helminthosporoid fungus.

Helmitol (he·lmitǫl). Trade name of a white crystalline product of citric acid with hexamethylene-tetramine, used as an antiseptic, etc.

1903 *Jrnl. Chem. Soc.* LXXXIV. I. 195 Helmitol..forms colourless crystals. 1905 *Medical Annual* 32 Goldberg compares the actions of urotropin, helmitol, and hetralin. 1908 *Practitioner* Jan. 64 The newer drugs, urotropine, hetraline, helmitol, are useless in gleet.

Helotism. Add: **2.** *Biol.* That form of symbiosis in which one organism bears to another the relation of slave to master; *esp.*, the symbiosis existing in a lichen in which the fungus mycelium is dominant.

1909 GROOM & BALFOUR tr. *Warming's Oecology of Plants* 85 The symbiosis between lichen-fungi and algae is obviously most correctly interpreted as helotism.

Help, *sb.* **3. c.** (Earlier modern U.S. examples.)

1807 C. W. JANSON *Stranger in Amer.* 87, I am Mr —'s *help*. I'd have you know..that I am no *sarvant*. 1815 *Massachusetts Spy* 23 Aug. (Th.) Our lady and gentleman 'hired helps' do not understand who is meant when their master is inquired for. 1818 FEARON *Sk. Amer.* 80 Servants, let me here observe, are called 'helps'. If you call a servant by that name they leave you without notice.

Help, *v.* Add:

6. d. To render assistance in dealing *with*.

1924 ANNE D. SEDGWICK *Little French Girl* I. v, If he sat there..not helping with the water-cans, the baskets of flowers, the scissors, it was because he loved her and wanted to watch her. *Mod.* If you are going to wash up, may I help you with the pots?

Helped (helpt), *ppl. a.* [f. HELP *v.* + -ED[1].] That has been helped, aided, or assisted. Also with advs., as *helped-out*.

1905 *Daily Chron.* 15 May 3/5 The dowagers of to-day, with their helped-out complexions and Venetian red hair. 1910 E. M. ALBANESI *For Love of Anne Lambart* 104 But this is no helped success, this is real.

Helter-skelter. Add: **C.** *sb.* **b.** (Also *helter-skelter lighthouse*.) A high structure, similar in shape to a lighthouse, with an external spiral slide down which pleasure-seekers travel, seated on a mat; common in fairs and pleasure-grounds.

1906 *Westm. Gaz.* 1 June 10/2 The World's Manufacturing Company, examples of whose 'helter-skelter' lighthouses are at Earl's Court, Blackpool, Southport, and other places. 1907 *Daily Chron.* 4 Sept. 2/7 All sorts of fearsome things ..from a helter-skelter..to a smashing saloon and a 'coker nut' alley. 1927 *Sunday Express* 5 June 4 They will travel on the merry-go-rounds... They will go down with the mats on the helter-skelter, and up with the swings.

Helvellaceous (helvelēi·ʃəs), *a. Bot.* [f. mod.L. *Helvellaceæ*, f. generic name *Helvella* (in L. a small pot-herb): see -ACEOUS.] Of, pertaining to, or resembling the *Helvellaceæ*, a family of ascomycetous fungi.

1866 *Treas. Bot.* 671/1, *Leotia*, a genus of the helvellaceous order of pyrenomycetous *Fungi*.

Helvellic (helve·lik), *a.* [f. mod.L. *Helvella*, a genus of ascomycetous fungi: see -IC.] Pertaining to *Helvella* or derived from individuals of this genus. *Helvellic acid*, a highly poisonous acid derived from certain fungi of this genus.

1930 HACKH *Chem. Dict.* 350/2 Helvellic acid, $C_{12}H_{20}O_7$ ..A dibasic, poisonous acid from *Helvella esculenta*.

He-man: see *HE *pron.* 8.

Hemi-. Add:

He:miangioca·rpic, -ca·rpous *adjs.*, applied to the conidiophore of a fungus when the hymenium is for some time covered with a membrane. **Hemibla·stula, Hemicla·stic** *a. Geol.* (see quots.).

1902 *Encycl. Brit.* XXVIII. 558/2 Gymnocarpic and *Hemiangiocarpic:—*Hymenomycetes*. 1900 B. D. JACKSON *Gloss. Bot. Terms*, *Hemiangiocarpous*, when the hymenium of some Fungi is for some time covered with a membrane, the gonidiophore is so termed. 1902 *Encycl. Brit.* XXVIII. 361/1 The Discomycetes and their immediate allies are termed Hemiangiocarpous, because however much their fructifications are closed at first, they ultimately open and expose the layers of asci. 1893 tr. *Weismann's Germ-Plasm* ii. 137 Driesch effected a mechanical separation of the two first segmentation-cells [of the eggs of Sea-urchins], and observed that at first each of them continued to undergo further segmentation.., but that later on the resulting *hemiblastula became completed to form an entire one. 1888 TEALL *Brit. Petrography* 433 *Hemiclastic, a term applied to a rock composed of detrital constituents united by a secondary cement; as, for instance, many quartzites.

Hemianopia (hemiănōu·piă). *Path.* [mod.L., f. HEMI- + Gr. -ωπια sight.] HEMIANOPSIA. Also **Hemiano·psy.**

1891 F. TAYLOR *Man. Pract. Med.* (ed. 2) 161 A transient hemianopia may occur in cerebral hæmorrhage. 1898 *Nature* 13 Jan. 255/1 Hallucinations connected with hemianopia. 1908 *Practitioner* Jan. 15 Attacks of aphasia, monoplegias, hemiplegias, word-blindness, and word-deafness, or hemianopsy. *Ibid.* Oct. 558 Hysterical hemianopia.

Hemidesmus (hemide·smŏs). *Bot.* [mod.L., f. HEMI- + Gr. δεσμός bond, fetter; so named in allusion to the incomplete coherence of the anthers with the stigma.] A plant of the genus so named; *esp.*, a plant of *Hemidesmus indicus*, the root of which is used as a substitute for sarsaparilla; also, a syrup prepared therefrom. Hence **Hemide·smic** *a.* (see quot. 1874).

1846 LINDLEY *Veg. Kingd.* 626 An account of the Hemidesmus has been published by Mr. Bell, *Pharm. Journ.* 3. 239. 1874 GARROD & BAXTER *Mat. Med.* (1880) 311 Hemidesmus Root...It..contains a peculiar volatile, crystallizable substance, with acid properties: this has been called hemidesmic acid. 1898 *Rev. Brit. Pharm.* 4 The retention of hemidesmus is noteworthy, and a tribute to the St. Bartholomew's school of physic.

Hemiplegic, *a.* Add: Also *sb.*, a hemiplegic subject.

1890 *Retrospect Med.* CII. 155 Convalescent hemiplegics.

***Hemlock.** Add: **2.** (Earlier examples.) See also *hemlock spruce* and *h. tree* in 4 below.

1728 *Boston Town Rec.* VIII. 222 That no popler, chestnut, pine, henlock [*sic*]..shall be..exposed to sale. 1729 *Manchester* (Mass.) *Rec.* 176 A hemblock standing 2 feet to the estord of the pine.

4. (U.S.) *hemlock brush, land, swamp, tree, wood*; *hemlock-tanned* adj.; **hemlock balsam** (see quot.); **hemlock pine, spruce(fir),** = sense 2.

1832 D. J. BROWNE *Sylva Amer.* 98 The bark contains a small quantity of resin, commonly called *Hemlock Balsam. 1703 *Manchester* (Mass.) *Rec.* 103 To cut down pine and *hemlock brush. 1873–4 *Rep. Vermont Board Agric.* II. 154 *Hemlock land. 1786 WASHINGTON *Diaries* III. 9 Planted the *Hemlock Pine wch was brought to me by Cornelius McDermot Roe. 1834 *Southern Lit. Messenger* I. 97 Bleak spruce and hemlock pines. 1781–2 JEFFERSON *Notes Virginia* (1787) 39 *Hemlock spruce fir, *Pinus Canadensis*. 1789 MORSE *Amer. Geog.* 247 *Hemlock swamps are interspersed thinly through the country. 1881 *Harper's Mag.* Sept. 583/2 An owl hooted dismally from the hemlock swamp. 1851 C. CIST *Cincinnati* 176 *Hemlock tanned sole. 1679 EVELYN *Sylva* xxii. (ed. 3) 101 The *Hemlock-tree (as they call it in New-England) is a kind of Spruce. 1843 *Knickerbocker Mag.* XXII. 164 The place selected..is often near a clump of hemlock trees. 1826 J. NEAL *Bro. Jonathan* III. 392 Is that a *hemlock wood?

Hemming, *vbl. sb.*[1] Add: **b.** *attrib.*, as **hemming-machine,** (*a*) a machine for hemming material; (*b*) a machine used to turn over the edges of the metal in making the handles of cans and utensils in sheet-metal work; so *hemming-machinist*.

1921 *Dict. Occup. Terms* (1927) § 419 *Hemmer*,..hemming machinist.

Hemp, *sb.* **6. b.** Add: **hemp-brake** (earlier example), also **-braker**; **hemp-fillis** (see *FILLIS); **hemp-hook,** a knife for cutting hemp.

1849 *Rep. U.S. Comm. Patents* (1850) 434 *Hemp-brakes and scutchers. 1847 *Ibid.* (1848) 61 Improvements in *hemp brakers. 1862 *Trans. Ill. Agric. Soc.* (1865) V. 674 The ancient manner of harvesting was by pulling..but this mode has long since been abandoned in favor of the *hemp-hook, as the knife is called.

Hen, *sb.* Add: **1. b.** *Like a hen with one chicken*: indicating extreme solicitude or fussiness about a small matter.

1854 MISS BAKER *Northampt. Gloss.* I. 320 'As busy as a hen with one chick.' Unnecessarily solicitous or active over trifles. 1881 *Oxfordshire Words* (Suppl.) s.v., To be as busy as a hen with one chick is to make a great fuss over a little work. They also say 'as proud as a hen with one chick'. 1904 BENSON *Challoners* x, Karl is devoted to him, just like a beautiful old hen in spectacles with one chicken.

8. hen-fruit *U.S. slang*, eggs.

1873 LELAND *Egypt. Sketch-Bk.* 71 Their 'hen-fruit', as it is elegantly termed in America. 1887 *Boston Guide* (Farmer), If he confines his Hen Fruit to the vintage of '87.

Hen and chickens. Add: **3.** The name of a children's game.

1894 ALICE B. GOMME *Trad. Games Eng. Scotl. & Irel.* I. 201 Hen and Chicken...The game is played in the usual manner of 'Fox and Goose' games. One is chosen to be the Hen, and one to be the Fox. The rest are the Chickens.

Hence, *sb. U.S.* [HENCE *adv.* 3 b and 4 c.] **a.** The other world. **b.** The future.

1883 NYE *Baled Hay* 26 All-wool delaine that was worn by one who is now in the golden hence. 1904 F. LYNDE *Grafters* xviii. 233 Now suppose you hint..that more.. developments may besafely predicted in the immediate hence.

Hendeca-. Add: **b.** *Organic Chem.* Noting the presence of eleven atoms of carbon, as in *hendecato·ic, -ceno·ic, -co·ic* acids, *he·ndecane, hende·cinene, hende·cyl*.

1889 MORLEY & MUIR *Watts' Dict. Chem.* II. 673/1 Hendecane $C_{11}H_{24}$...Formed by the action of HI and phosphorus at 230° upon hendecoic (undecylic) acid. *Ibid.* 673/2 Hendecinene $C_{11}H_{20}$. *Ibid.*, Hendecenoic Acid $C_{11}H_{20}O_2$. *Ibid.*, Hendecoic Acid $C_{11}H_{22}O_2$. *Ibid.* 674/1 Hendecyl Alcohol $C_{11}H_{24}O$. 1891 E. THORPE *Dict. Appl. Chem.* II. 101/2 Hendecatoic acid $C_{11}H_{22}O_2$.

Heneicosane (henəi·kosān). *Chem.* Also **henicosane.** [f. Gr. ἕν-, εἷς one + εἴκοσι twenty + -ANE.] A solid, colourless hydrocarbon, $C_{21}H_{44}$, of the paraffin series. Also **Heneicoseno·ic** *a.*

1889 MORLEY & MUIR *Watts' Dict. Chem.* II. 674/1 Heneicosenoic aldehyde $C_{21}H_{40}O$. 1894 G. M'GOWAN tr. *A. Bernthsen's Org. Chem.* 41 $C_{21}H_{44}$ Heneicosane.

Henna. b. Add: (with reference to dyeing or staining with henna) *henna-dyeing*; *henna-dyed, -haired, -tipped* adjs.

1920 *Chambers's Jrnl.* May 299/1 He..showed a handful of his *henna-dyed beard. 1906 *Daily Chron.* 27 June 6/4 From tight-lacing to *henna-dyeing the frisky matron is a study in successful artifice. 1907 *Ibid.* 31 Dec. 3/1 His American trotting-car and his *henna-haired wife. 1923 *Chambers's Jrnl.* 306/1 Their *henna-tipped fingers are loaded with rings.

Hennaed (he·năd). [f. HENNA + -ED[2].] Dyed or stained with henna.

1924 *Countries of World* II. 1145/1 A slim hand with hennaed nails. 1925 H. V. MORTON *Heart of London* 53 Maud's hennaed hair.

Hennotannic (henotæ·nik), *a. Chem.* [f. HENN(A + -O- + TANNIC.] Designating an acid, a brown resinous compound, contained in commercial henna.

1909 *Cent. Dict.* Suppl.

Henrician, *sb.* Add: **3.** A supporter of the ecclesiastical policy of Henry VIII. Hence **Henricianism** (henri·ʃăniz'm), the ecclesiastical policy of Henry VIII.

1828 E. NARES *Mem. Ld. Burghley* I. iv. 53 The king's supremacy, which, like a true *Henrician*, he was very careful to maintain. 1900 F. W. MAITLAND *Eliz. Gleanings* Collected Papers (1911) III. 159 Calvin had spoken ill of Henricianism. 1903 — in *Camb. Mod. Hist.* II. 555 A Reformed religion, or some northern version of Henricanism [*sic*].

Henri Deux (ãṅri dø̄). [Fr., = Henri II.] Designating the style of Renaissance architecture or art developed in France during the reign of Henri II, king of France 1547–59; *spec.* the purest style of the French Renaissance.

1884 KNIGHT *Dict. Mech.* Suppl. s.v., Henri-Deux Ware (*Faïence d'Oiron*).

Henrietta (henrie·tă). *Disused.* [Female name.] Designating a light-weight woollen dress fabric, sometimes with a silk warp.

1851 *Illustr. Catal. Gt. Exhib.* III. III. 494/2 Henrietta cloths, with silk warp and worsted weft. 1862 *Catal. Internat. Exhib., Brit.* II. No. 4018 Paramatta, or Henrietta Cloth, twill. 1890 *Advt.* (Ann Arbor, Mich., U.S.) 1 Mar., We offer a 46-inch Black Silk Warp Henrietta. 1901 *Daily News* 23 Feb. 6/7 Henrietta cloths, which wear so well and drape so charmingly.

Hen-roost. Add: **b.** *fig.* A source of plunder: in allusion to a political speech referring to 'the robbing of hen-roosts'.

1909 *Westm. Gaz.* 16 Apr. 5/1 Mr. Lloyd George's now historic reference to 'hen-roosts'. 1928 *Britain's Industr. Future* (*Lib. Ind. Inq.*) v. xxix. § 2. 420 Apart from the public hen-roosts which Mr. Churchill has raided, it is impossible for an outsider to estimate what private hen-roosts inside the Treasury he has also helped himself to.

Henry[1] (he·nri). Pl. **henries.** The name of Joseph *Henry* (1797–1878), American physicist, used to designate the unit of inductance, i.e., the inductance in a circuit when the electromotive force is one volt, and the inducing current varies at the rate of one ampere per second. Abbrev. H, h.

1893 SLOANE *Stand. Electr. Dict.* 288 *Henry*, the practical unit of electro-magnetic or magnetic inductance. It is equal to 10^9 C.G.S., or absolute units of inductance. 1926 R. W. HUTCHINSON *Wireless* 75 A coil has an inductance (self inductance) of one henry if a current increasing at the rate of one ampere per second brings on an opposing E.M.F. of one volt.

Henry[2]. The name of Benjamin Tyler *Henry* (1821–98), American inventor, used attrib. to designate parts of a breech-loading magazine rifle subsequently used in the Martini-Henry rifle.

1868 *Rep. to Govt. U.S. Munitions of War* 51 Henry rifle. 1880 *Encycl. Brit.* XI. 282/1 In the Henry action the barrel does not move, but is closed at the breech end by a sliding vertical block. *Ibid.* 282/2 The combination of the Martini breech action with the Henry barrel. *Ibid.* 283/2 Henry rifling. 1902 *Ibid.* XXXII. 242/1 In 1861 the Henry grooving for a cylindrical bullet, a modification of the Whitworth, first appeared.

Hentenian (henti·niăn), *a.* [f. the name of John *Henten* or *Hentenius* (1499–1566), a theologian of the Dominican order at Louvain: see -IAN.] Of or pertaining to Henten, or to the editions of the Vulgate (Louvain 1547, often reprinted) prepared by him. 1911 WEBSTER.

Hentriacontane (hentrəiăkǫ·ntēn). *Chem.* Also **hentricontane, -contan.** [f. Gr. ἕν-, εἷς one + τριάκοντα thirty + -ANE.] A solid hydrocarbon, $C_{31}H_{64}$, of the methane series, occurring in petroleum and beeswax.

1887 *Jrnl. Chem. Soc.* LII. I. 124 The most soluble portion of the extract melting..at 67°, is probably identical with normal hentriacontane, $C_{31}H_{64}$. 1901 *Ibid.* LXXIX. I. 985 This hydrocarbon is identical with Krafft's hentriacontane, $C_{31}H_{64}$.

Heortology (hīǫrtǫ·lŏdʒi). [ad. G. *heortologie*, F. *héortologie*, f. Gr. ἑορτή feast: see -OLOGY.] The science which has for its subject the origin, meaning, growth, and history of the religious feasts and seasons of the Christian year. Hence **Heortolo·gical** *a.*, of or pertaining to heortology; **Heorto·logist,** one who studies heortology.

1900 *Expositor* Nov. 348 We are to regard the statement of the calendars as the conjecture of a heortologist. 1901 J. R. HARRIS in *Soc. Hist. Theology* 31 Oct. 5 The Study of Christian Heortology...The problems that belong to the region of Christian Heortology. 1913 J. R. MCKEE (*title*) The Church's Year, a Handbook of Heortology. 1918 E. BISHOP *Liturg. Hist.* 258 Recalling too how the recent heortologist Dr. Kellner considers that the mention of the feast in the Irish calendars does not prove the celebration of the feast.

Hepat-. Add: **Hepate·ctomy,** excision of a part of the liver.

1910 *Practitioner* Mar. 383 Hepatectomy under these conditions does not appear to add to the gravity of the prognosis.

Hepatico- (hĭpæ·tiko), combining form of HEPATIC, = HEPATO-.

For further examples see medical dicts.

1910 *Practitioner* Mar. 384 The hepatico-cystic confluence. *Ibid.* 385 Vautrin put a drain in the hepatic duct, thus making a hepaticostomy.

Hepatin (he·pătin). *Chem.* [f. HEPAT- + -IN[1].] A protein obtained from the liver.

1874 *Dunglison's Med. Lex.*, *Hepatine*, glycogenic matter. 1886 *Jrnl. Chem. Soc.* L. 1054.

Hepatism (he·pătiz'm). *Path.* [f. HEPAT- + -ISM.] A morbid condition of the body due to a disordered or diseased liver.

1901 DORLAND *Med. Dict.* (ed. 2).

Hepato-. Add further examples. (See also medical dicts.)

1903 *Med. Record* 18 July 84 (Cent. D. Suppl.) A hepatolytic serum. 1906 *Practitioner* Nov. 591 The most enthusiastic hepatogenists. 1910 *Ibid.* Mar. 386 Hepato-cholangiostomy and hepato-cholangio-enterostomy.

Hepialid, Epialid (hi-, ipəi·ălid), *a.* and *sb.* [ad. mod.L. *Hepialidæ, Epialidæ*, f. *Hepialus* (Fabricius 1776), *Epialus*, a. Gr. ἠπίολος moth, misread as *ἠπιαλος, prob. by association with ἠπίαλος nightmare: see -ID[3].] Of or pertaining to (a moth of) the family *Hepialidæ* (ghost-moths or swifts). Also **Hepi·aline, Epi·aline** *a.*; **Hepi·aloid, Epi·aloid** *a.* and *sb.*

1890 *Cent. Dict.*, *Epialid* n. and a. *epialine* a. 1895 *Funk's Stand. Dict.*, *Epialid* a. and n. *epialine* a. *epialoid* a. *Ibid.*, *Ghost-moth*, an epialid moth, especially *Epialus humuli*. *Ibid.*, *Swift*, n...2. An epialid or ghost-moth. 1909 *Cent. Dict.* Suppl., *Epialid, hepialid*. 1931 *Ann. Appl. Biol.* XVIII. 54 The larva of a Hepialid moth, *Oncopera intricata*.

Hepplewhite (he·p'l,hwəit). The name of George *Hepplewhite* (died 1786), who was succeeded by A. *Hepplewhite* and Co., used attrib. to designate an English style of furniture of the latter part of the eighteenth century, characterized by lightness, delicacy, and graceful curves, being an adaptation of current French styles.

1900 *Jrnl. Soc. Arts* 23 Mar. 380/1 Hepplewhite and Sheraton furniture should be studied by designers for *motifs*. 1901 *Connoisseur* Dec. 272/2 Six Heppelwhite arm-chairs. 1903 *Chambers's Jrnl.* 20 June 460/1 Three..ball-and-claw Hepplewhite chairs.

Hepta-. Add:

He·pta(i)cosane *Chem.* [Gr. εἴκοσι twenty], a solid hydrocarbon, $C_{27}H_{56}$, of the paraffin series. **He·ptacron** [Gr. ἄκρον vertex], a solid figure having seven vertices. **Hepta·ctin(e)** *Zool.* [*ACTINE 2], a sponge spicule having seven branches. **Heptade·cane** *Chem.* [Gr. δέκα ten], a colourless solid paraffin found in certain lignites. **Heptahy·drated** *a. Chem.*, containing seven molecules of water. **Heptahy·dric** *a. Chem.*, containing seven hydroxyl groups. **He·ptastyle** *Arch.* [STYLE *sb.*[1]], a form of columniation having seven columns in the end row.

1901 *Jrnl. Chem. Soc.* LXXIX. I. 986 The results of the analysis..indicate that the second hydrocarbon is in all probability *heptacosane, $C_{27}H_{56}$. 1904 R. MELDOLA *Chem. Syn. Vital Products* I. 27 Normal Heptacosane..occurs in beeswax and in tobacco leaf. 1862 CAYLEY *Math. Papers* (1892) V. 42 The derivation of the octacrons from the *heptacrons... The heptacron has more than two tripleural summits. 1889 MORLEY & MUIR *Watts' Dict. Chem.* II. 674/2 *Heptadecane...Occurs in bee's wax. 1895 G. LUNGE *Sulphuric Acid* (ed. 2) II. 22 The anhydrous salt..if protected from the air is changed into *heptahydrated..salt. 1889 MORLEY & MUIR *Watts' Dict. Chem.* II. 675/1 *Heptaicosane $C_{27}H_{56}$. 1843 *Civil Eng. & Arch. Jrnl.* VI. 167/1 The temple of the giants, at Agrigentum (*hepta-style).

Heptane. Add: **He·ptone, He·ptonene,** a liquid hydrocarbon of the valylene series. **He·ptose,** a sugar having in its molecule seven atoms of carbon. **Hepteno·ic** *a.* **He·ptenyl,** the radical, C_7H_{13}, of heptene.

1889 MORLEY & MUIR *Watts' Dict. Chem.* II. 676/1 *Heptenoic acid $C_7H_{12}O_2$...Formed by the dry distillation of turpenylic acid. *Ibid.*, *Heptenyl bromide $C_7H_{13}Br$. ..Heptenyl chloride $C_7H_{13}Cl$. *Ibid.* 680/1 *Heptonene C_7H_{10}. 1890 *Jrnl. Chem. Soc.* LVIII. I. 598 The author [E. Fischer] proposes to employ the terms pentose, *heptose, octose, etc., for the sugars. 1895 BLOXAM *Chem.* (ed. 8) 708 Each glucose may be made to yield a heptose, which, in its turn, may be converted into an octose and a nonose.

Heptarch (he·ptaɹk), *a. Bot.* [f. Gr. ἑπτά seven + ἀρχή beginning, origin: cf. DIARCH, MONARCH, OCTARCH, TETRARCH, TRIARCH.] Arising from seven distinct points of origin, as the woody tissue of a root. 1884 [see OCTARCH].

Heracleid. Add: **c.** A poem describing the exploits of Heracles.

1725 [see THESEAN]. 1904 T. R. GLOVER *Virgil* iii. 75 Poets who have composed a Herakleid, a Theseid, or other poems of the kind.

Herbaceous, *a.* Add: **4.** *Herbaceous border*: a border composed mainly of herbaceous plants.

[1824 LOUDON *Encycl. Gard.* III. II. viii. 867 Creeping rooted Herbaceous Border-Flowers.] 1880 *Encycl. Brit.* XII. 250/1 The herbaceous border should be a distinct compartment, and not less than 10 feet in width, backed up by evergreens. *a* 1900 F. MILES in W. Robinson *English Flower Garden* (ed. 8) iv. 83 And what cannot be done with an herbaceous border edge when that edge is the green Grass? 1909 H. G. WELLS *Tono-Bungay* III. ii. § 1 An ardent rose grower and herbaceous borderer.

Herbarium. Add: Also *attrib.*

1887 MOLONEY *Forestry W. Africa* 319 He compared the available herbarium material of the two plants. 1898 B. TORREY in *Atlantic Monthly* Apr. 461/2 A comparison with herbarium specimens.

Herbartian (həɹbā·ɹtiăn), *a.* and *sb.* [f. the name of J. F. *Herbart* (1776–1841), German philosopher + -IAN.] **A.** *adj.* Of or pertaining to Herbart, or to the system of psychology and teaching originated by him. **B.** *sb.* A disciple or follower of Herbart. Hence **Herba·rtianism,** the doctrines of Herbart.

1886 *Encycl. Brit.* XX. 41/1 The whole Herbartian psychology. *Ibid.* 62/2 This difference between a conflict of presentations to enter consciousness..and that opposition or incompatibility of presentations which is only possible when they are in consciousness has been strangely confused by the Herbartians. 1903 F. H. HAYWARD & M. E. THOMAS (*title*) The Critics of Herbartianism. 1904 CATHERINE I. DODD (*title*) Introduction to the Herbartian Principles of Teaching. 1908 H. G. WELLS *New Worlds for Old* v. § 1. (1912) 91 This change in the circle of ideas (as the Herbartians put it) is the essence of the Socialist project. *Ibid.* x. § 1. 225 The majority of Socialists still fail to grasp completely the Herbartian truth.

Herculid (hɔ̄·ɹkiulid). *Astr.* [f. HERCUL(ES 6 + *-ID[2] b.] A meteor belonging to a shower whose radiant point is in the constellation Hercules.

1906 *Westm. Gaz.* 19 Apr. 12/1 The radiant of the Herculids (due to-morrow or Saturday night) is some distance to the right of that of the Lyrids.

Herd, *sb.*[1] Add:

4. b. *Psychol.* Denoting feelings, actions, thoughts, etc., common to a large company of people; esp. **herd instinct,** the instinctive tendency to think and act as one of a crowd. (Cf. sense 3.)

1908 *Westm. Gaz.* 22 Aug. 16/1 The fundamental assumptions of the Liberal and the Conservative are hostile, and are the outcome of herd tradition. 1919 M. K. BRADLEY *Psychoanal.* 113 Not even abandonment to 'herd enthusiasm' could destroy the terrible loneliness of death. 1921 H. CRICHTON MILLER *New Psychol. & Teacher* 201 The Herd Instinct and the Herd Ideal. 1924 W. B. SELBIE *Psychol. Relig.* 148 Man is a gregarious animal, and even in his civilized condition never quite loses his herd consciousness. 1928 G. B. SHAW *Intell. Woman's Guide Socialism* v. (1929) 11 Our minds are mostly herd minds, with only a scrap of individual mind on top.

Here, *adv.* Add: **5. b.** *Here is where...*, this is the point at which. *U.S. colloq.*

1921 R. D. PAINE *Comr. Rolling Ocean* xii. 203 'It makes me feel sick at my stomach', declared Briscoe. 'Here's where you feel sicker. Great Scott, look at that.' *Ibid.* xiv. 250 Here's where I slip it out to the old gink.

B. as *sb.* (Instances of objective uses.)

1838 DICKENS *O. Twist* xxxv, I—I—ought to have left here before. 1857 — *Dorrit* II. xxxiv, You would rather not leave here till to-morrow morning. *Mod. colloq.* Somewhere between here and London...From here to there.

Heredito- (hĭre·dito), used irreg. as combining form of HEREDITY, as in **Here:dito-syphili·tic** *a.*, pertaining to or suffering from hereditary syphilis; also as *sb.*, one who suffers therefrom.

1869 G. LAWSON *Dis. Eye* (1874) 26 Such changes in the choroid as are often seen in heredito-syphilitic patients.

Hereford (he·rĭfŏɹd). The name of the county town of Herefordshire, a county in the west of England, used to designate a breed of cattle originating there. Also **He·refordshire.**

1834 YOUATT *Cattle* iii. 31 The Herefordshire white-faced breed...The Hereford oxen are considerably larger than the North Devons...The old Herefords were brown or red-brown. 1836 *Penny Cycl.* VI. 379/2 The Herefordshire oxen are best suited to the rich pastures of their native county. 1844 STEPHENS *Bk. Farm* III. 1273 Another breed ..is the Hereford, which has long been famed for its excellent steers. 1862 MORTON *Farmer's Cal.* 578 The Herefords, another leading breed of cattle, characterized by red body and white or mottled face, come almost as early to maturity as the short-horn. 1875 *Encycl. Brit.* I. 388/1 The Hereford is the breed which in England contests most closely with the short-horns for the palm of excellence. 1931 *Times Lit. Suppl.* 20 Aug. 625/3 The fat Herefords that graze lazily in English meadows.

Herem, variant of *CHEREM.

Heresy. 4. Add: *heresy-hunter*.

1765 MACLAINE tr. *Mosheim's Eccl. Hist.* xiii. (1844) I. 344 This new set of heresy-hunters. 1902 *Westm. Gaz.* 7 May 12/1 A proceeding quite in harmony with the usual methods of heresy-hunters. 1906 *Daily Chron.* 16 Oct. 3/3 The heresy-hunter made him his quarry.

Herewith, *adv.* Add: **B.** *adj.* Accompanying.

1917 'CONTACT' *Airman's Outings* p. xii, It was a squadron that possessed..the herewith testimonial.

Hermetism (hɔ̄·ɹmĕtiz'm). [f. HERMET(IC + -ISM.] Hermetic or theosophical philosophy; hermetics. So **Hermeto·logist,** a Hermetist.

1894 G. S. HALL in *Forum* Aug. 719 (Cent. D. Suppl.) Its teachings..make the doctrine of sin as vital as with the most ardent of the old hermetologists. 1897 H. C. BOLTON in *Smithsonian Rep.* (1898) 213 Traditions of the kabala, the mysteries of hermetism, and the practice of transmutation.

1927 *Contemp. Rev.* July 59 M. Valéry's poetics have been accused of hermetism and of preciousness.

Herniation (hɔ̄ɹniē·ʃən). *Path.* [f. HERNIA + -TION.] The formation of a hernia.

1897 *Allbutt's Syst. Med.* III. 712 A series of herniations of the intestinal walls.

Herodotean (hĭrǫdǫtī·ăn), *a.* [f. the name of *Herodotus* (Gr. Ἡρόδοτος), Greek historian of the fifth century B.C. + -AN.] Of, pertaining to, characteristic of, or mentioned by Herodotus.

1857 DUFFERIN *Lett. High Lat.* 54 The Herodotean work of Sturleson. 1872 MINTO *Eng. Prose Lit.* II. vi. 413 A Herodotean knack of giving numerical measures of extent. 1881 *Athenæum* 2 Apr. 456/2 Some of the reports which he received he recounts with Herodotean incredulity. 1883 BRYCE in *Macm. Mag.* May 67/2 This is what I mean by calling him Herodotean. Nothing was too small nor too apparently remote from the main studies of his life to escape him or be without interest for him.

Heroin (hĭrōu·in, he·rǫin). *Pharmacy.* [a. G. *heroin*, f. Gr. ἥρως HERO; said to be so derived because of the inflation of the personality consequent upon taking the drug.] Diacetylmorphine, used as an anodyne and sedative. Also *attrib.*

1898 *Lancet* 3 Dec. 1511/1 A new hypnotic, to which the name of 'heroin' has been given, has been tried in the medical clinic of Professor Gerhardt in Berlin. According to a communication made by Dr. Strube to the *Berliner Klinische Wochenschrift* it is a product of the di-acetic ester of morphia, and it was discovered by Professor Dreser, chief of the chemical department of the Elberfeld Farben Fabriken. 1908 *Practitioner* Apr. 436 Subcutaneous injections of morphia or heroin locally. 1910 *Ibid.* Apr. 542 A sedative may be prescribed...Heroin hydrochloride is the best drug for this purpose. 1920 A. B. BAXTER *Parts Men Play* xviii, She..took to opium cigarettes, and then to heroin. She disappeared one night.

Heronite (he·rənəit). *Petrog.* [f. the name of *Heron* Bay, on the north shore of Lake Superior + -ITE[1].] A dark-coloured igneous aphanitic rock containing radiating groups of orthoclase, ægirite, etc., in a matrix of analcite.

Heroon (hĭrōu·ǫn). *Gr. Antiq.* Pl. **-a.** Also **heroum.** [L., a. Gr. ἡρῷον, f. ἡρῷος of a hero, f. ἥρως HERO.] A sepulchral monument in the form of a small temple; orig. a temple or sanctuary dedicated to a hero, often over his supposed tomb.

1775 R. CHANDLER *Trav. Asia Minor* 111 Searching about, we found..an inscription, which has belonged to an heroum or sepulchre. 1820 T. S. HUGHES *Trav. Sicily* I. 298 The Heroa of Theseus and Pirithous. 1883 A. S. MURRAY *Greek Sculpture* II. 289 The heröon at Gjölbaschi in Lycia. 1904 T. R. GLOVER *Virgil* iv. 89 A hērōon of Aeneas in Ambracia.

Herrengrundite (herəngrʊ·ndəit). *Min.* [ad. G. *herrengrundit*, f. *Herrengrund*, Hungary, its locality: see -ITE[1].] A basic hydrous sulphate of calcium and copper occurring in green tabular crystals.

1881 *Jrnl. Chem. Soc.* XL. 524 Herrengrundite, a New Basic Copper Sulphate. 1892 DANA *Syst. Min.* (ed. 6) 962 Herrengrundite...Occurs with malachite and calcite in a quartz-conglomerate at Herrengrund in Hungary.

Herring. Add: **1. b.** *Fat herring* (*FAT *a.* 2 f).

2. Phrase (local). *Every herring should hang by its own head, gills, tail.*

1818, 1824 [in Dict.]. 1890 HALL CAINE *Bondman* II. ii, Adam, thinking as little of pride, said No, that every herring should hang by its own gills.

Herring-bone, *sb.* Add: **1. b.** *pl.* Small cirrocumulus clouds (cf. *mackerel sky*).

1905 *Westm. Gaz.* 22 Apr. 4/2 The sky was sunny, but mottled in the north-west with 'herring-bones', which prophesied wind.

c. *pl.* The herring-bone-line hatching used to represent mountains on a map.

1900 ELLEN T. FOWLER *Farringdons* v, 'I see. And please what are the mountain-ranges that you are drawing now?' 'These', replied Elisabeth, covering her map with herring-bones, 'are your scruples'.

2. e. *Herring-bone coralline* (see quots.).

1755 J. ELLIS *Ess. towards Nat. Hist. Corallines* 17 Herring-bone Coralline. This Coralline is often found sticking to Oysters as they are brought to the London Market, during the Winter-season. 1850 PRATT *Common Things Sea-side* 258 The Herring-bone Coralline ('Halecium halecinum') which grows on stones and shells, in the deep parts of the sea. 1915 E. RAY LANKESTER *Divers. Naturalist* 97 Very minute jelly-fish,..[which] originate as buds from small branching polyps, one kind of which is common on oyster-shells, and is called 'the herring-bone coralline'.

f. *Skiing.* (See quot.)

1924 *Tourist* Winter Sports No. 12/1 *Herring-bone.* A method of climbing without kick-turns which leaves tracks like the well-known stitch.

Herring-bone, *v.* Add: **3.** To make (a wall, floor, etc.) of herring-bone work. Hence **He·rring-boned** *ppl. a.*

1907 W. DE MORGAN *Alice-for-Short* ix, A 'erring-boned brick floor.

Herringer. Add: **c.** A herring-gull.

1928 E. SELOUS *Thought-Transference in Birds* (1931) 132 The great mass of these gulls were black-headed ones, but a certain number of herringers were intermingled with them.

Herschel. Add: **2.** Optics. *Herschel's fringes*, spectra observed at the line of separation between the totally reflected and the ordinarily reflected light given out by a prism standing on a mirror.

1909 *Jrnl. Chem. Soc.* XCVI. II. 141 Warnerke's Modification of the Herschel Effect and the Preparation of the Substance of the Latent Image.

Hertz (hɔ̄ɹts, ‖hęrts). The name of H. R. *Hertz* (1857–1894), German physicist, used attrib. to denote apparatus used or invented by him in his electrical research (cf. next).

1890 *Nature* Feb. 368 By separating the coats of the jar as far as possible we get a typical Hertz vibrator. 1892 LODGE *Mod. Views Electr.* 361 Hertz waves can get through deal doors and stone walls. 1898 *Science Siftings* XIV. 117/2 A Hertz-wave 'detector'. 1898 *Westm. Gaz.* 12 May 9/2 Experiments in Hertz-wave space telegraphy. 1902 *Encycl. Brit.* XXXIII. 230/2 This aerial being used as a Hertz oscillator or radiator.

Hertzian (hɔ̄·ɹtsiăn), *a.* [f. the name *Hertz* (see prec.) + -IAN.] Of or pertaining to Hertz or to the phenomena discovered by him.

Hertzian telegraphy: wireless telegraphy. *Hertzian waves* (see WAVE *sb.* 5 a).

1890 A. E. BOSTWICK in *Ann. Cycl.* 716/1 (Funk) Trouton ..found that glass absorbs Hertzian vibrations with comparative rapidity. 1900 *Jrnl. Soc. Arts* XLVIII. 788/1 The sensation created in 1897 by Mr. Marconi's application of Hertzian waves. 1900 FAHIE *Wireless Telegr.* 197 Sir William Crookes..was..the first to distinctly foresee the applicability of Hertzian waves to practical telegraphy. 1907 ERSKINE-MURRAY *Handbk. Wireless Telegr.* 36 The transmitter consisted of a Hertzian oscillator placed in the focal line of a parabolic mirror. 1908 J. A. FLEMING *Radiotelegr.* 132 An arrangement of two rods..with a spark gap in the centre constitutes the simplest form of linear radiator or Hertzian Oscillator for the production of damped electro-magnetic waves. 1914 R. STANLEY *Wireless Telegr.* 91 Using a suitable length of spark gap the discharge of this Hertzian open circuit is oscillatory.

Herzegovinian (hɔ̄:ɹtsəgǫvi·niăn), *a.* and *sb.* [f. *Herzegovina*: see -IAN.] Of or pertaining to, a native or inhabitant of Herzegovina, a province to the south of Bosnia, now forming part of Yugoslavia. So **Herzego·vinese** *a.* and *sb.*

1876 *Fraser's Mag.* May 541/2 The Herzgovinese insurgents. 1880 *Encycl. Brit.* XI. 775/1 The Herzegovinian districts of Niksich and Dormitor. *Ibid.* 775/2 Much of the old Slavonic customs..still holds among the Herzegovinian Mussulmans...The Herzegovinians are tall, broad, and darker..than the Bosnians. 1900 DENIKER *Races of Man* 345 The southern [Slav] group..comprises the Herzogovinians, Bosnians, Montenegrins. 1904 MARY E. DURHAM *Through Lands of Serb* 6 These Herzegovinese migrated to Montenegro. 1930 *Jugo Slav Movement* 4 The Herzegovinian Serbs of the Narenta.

Heshvan, variant of *HESVAN.

Hesiodic (hĭsiǫ·dik), *a.* [f. the name of *Hesiod* (Gr. Ἡσίοδος), Greek poet of about the eighth century B.C. + -IC.] Of, pertaining to, or resembling the poetical style of Hesiod, or to the school of poetry which followed him. Also **Hesio·dian** *a.*

1838 *Penny Cycl.* XII. 186/2 Ulrici considers..the story of Prometheus and that of the Five Ages as much altered from their original Hesiodic form. 1847 LEITCH tr. *C. O. Müller's Anc. Art* § 77 The Hesiodic bards come down to about the 40th Ol[ympiad]. 1873 J. DAVIES *Hesiod & Theognis* i. 19 Under one or other of these heads it is easy to group the Hesiodic poems. *Ibid.* ii. 23 The Hesiodian rhapsodists. 1908 A. W. MAIR *Hesiod* Introd. p. xi, The Hesiodic epic is the antithesis of the Homeric.

Hesitate, *v.* Add: **1.** Const. various preps.

a 1849 POE *Tales* (1884) I. 93 At the baptismal font I hesitated for a name. 1856 DE QUINCEY *Opium-Eater* (1896) 216 This ..surgeon saw no reason whatever in the simple practice of opium-eating for hesitating upon a life-insurance proposal. 1860 W. COLLINS *Woman in White* iv, I hesitated about answering it. 1908 *Grand Mag.* Dec. 612/2 I'm only hesitating over the price.

d. *spec.* in *Dancing* (see quot.).

1920 E. SCOTT *All about Latest Dances* 87 The term 'hesitate', as regards the waltz we are now considering, implies merely that you pause, or move in what appears a faltering manner at a given juncture.

3. b. With sentence as quasi-obj.

1816 SCOTT *Old Mort.* xii, 'I am not sure,' hesitated Edith. 1881 MRS. RIDDELL *Senior Partner* xvi, 'It looks awful like the stuff last night,' hesitated Mr. McCullagh.

Hesitation. Add: **3.** In full *hesitation waltz* or *valse*: A variety of waltz, characterized by the *hesitation step* (see quot. 1920). Hence **Hesitation-valse** *v.*

1914 V. CASTLE *Mod. Dancing* 71 It is the Hesitation Waltz. 1919 G. D'EGVILLE *How & what to Dance* (1922) 46 The American 'Hesitation'. 1920 E. SCOTT *All about Latest Dances* 86 As you lift the left foot..from the floor, count a short one, two; and on three drag the other foot along the floor, bringing it over in front of the first foot, which is by this time on the floor...That is the hesitation step. 1926 'LUCAS MALET' *Dogs of Want* v. § 2 For over four hours a mixed multitude..had one-stepped, two-stepped, hesitation-valsed, and fox-trotted. 1927 *Daily Express* 31 Oct. 11/6 The foxtrot, tango, and the hesitation.

Hesped (he·sped). [Heb.] A funeral oration pronounced over the dead at a Jewish memorial service.

1892 ZANGWILL *Childr. Ghetto* I. xiv, Ansell was..listening to a *Hesped* or funeral oration at the German synagogue.

Hesperian. B. *sb.* **2.** (U.S. examples.)

1868 *Rep. U.S. Commissioner Agric.* (1869) 314 The family of skippers, Hesperians, are rather small, thick-bodied butterflies. 1876 *Field & Forest* I. 73 The butterflies came out on June 26th..and in general form and color resemble the skipper or Hesperian.

Hesperid. Add: **2.** *Ent.* (Also **Hesperiid.**) One of the family *Hesperidæ* or *Hesperiidæ* of lepidopterous insects; a Hesperian butterfly; also *attrib.*

1889 in *Cent. Dict.* 1930–1 *Proc. Entom. Soc.* V. 88 Similar observations had been made on African Hesperiids. 1931 *Oxf. Univ. Gaz.* 17 June 704/1 The Hesperid butterfly *Parnara telleri cinhara*.

Hessenbergite (he·sənbɔ̄ɹgəit). *Min.* [ad. G. *hessenbergit*, f. the name of F. *Hessenberg*, German crystallographer: see -ITE[1].] A silicate occurring in crystals of eisenrose.

1868 DANA *Syst. Min.* (ed. 5) 762.

Hessian. B. *sb.* **1.** (Earlier U.S. examples.)

1776 *Jrnls. Congress* (1906) V. 640 The Hessians, and other foreigners, employed by the King of Great Britain. 1846 *Knickerbocker Mag.* XXVII. 559 A Montreal editor [noted] the demise at that city of an old Hessian who was in Burgoyne's army when he surrendered.

Hessonite (he·sǫnəit). *Min.* Also **essonite.** [f. Gr. ἥσσων less + -ITE[1]: so called because it is less hard than some minerals, such as hyacinth, which it resembles.] Cinnamon-stone; a variety of garnet.

1820, 1884 [see ESSONITE]. 1896 *Jrnl. Chem. Soc.* LXX. II. 34 Apatite and Hessonite occur in the pegmatite veins cutting the gneiss about Canaan, Conn. 1914 *Brit. Mus. Return* 227.

Hesvan (he·svăn). Also **Chesvan, Heshvan.** [Heb.] The eighth month of the Jewish ecclesiastical year and the second month of the civil year, corresponding to parts of October and November; formerly called Marchesvan or Bul.

1833 SIR H. NICOLAS *Chronol. Hist.* (1838) 178 Marchesvan, Chesvan, or Bul 29 or 30 Days. 1838 E. H. LINDO *Jewish Cal.* 5 The perfect [year] has 355 days, and is when the months of Hesvan and Kislev have each 30 days. 1876 *Encycl. Brit.* IV. 678/1 The signs + and — are respectively annexed to Hesvan and Kislev to indicate that the former of these months may sometimes require to have one day more, and the latter sometimes one day less, than the number of days shown in the table.

Het, *ppl. a.* **1.** Add to def.: also *transf.*, and for 'Now *dial.*' read 'Now *dial.* and *U.S.*' (with *up*).

1902 G. H. LORIMER *Lett. Self-made Merchant* v. 59 But you mustn't get yourself all 'het up' before you take the plunge. 1918 MULFORD *Man fr. Bar-20* v. 51, I was havin' a cussed bad dream an' was all het up. 1922 TITUS *Timber* xvi. 150 You two are all het up over nothing.

Hetærolite (hetī·rolǝit). *Min.* [f. Gr. ἑταῖρος companion, so called because it is found in association with chalcophanite + -LITE.] A metallic oxide containing zinc and manganese.

1877 G. E. MOORE in *Amer. Jrnl. Sci.* XIV. 423. 1879 *Jrnl. Chem. Soc.* XXXVI. 17 Hetaerolite..occurs in botryoidal radio-fibrous masses.

Hetchel, *sb. dial.* and *U.S.* = HATCHEL *sb.*

1869 MRS. STOWE *Oldtown Folks* xlii. 530 She don' know no more 'bout religion than an old hetchel. 1929 SHELTON *Salt-box House* xvii. 143 Mops were made of corn-husks bound to a handle, the husks having been drawn through a hetchel which shredded them.

Hetchel, *v. dial.* and *U.S.* = HATCHEL *v.*

1845 S. JUDD *Margaret* I. xiii. 100 The clouds hung low, and their floating skirts seemed to be pierced and hetchelled by the trees. 1878 *Harper's Mag.* LVII. 576 She'll hetchel the old woman mortally, I'se afraid. 1897 [see HATCHEL *v.* 2]. 1908 C. H. PARKHURST *Lower than Angels* 18 Mercilessly hetchelled by some prosecuting attorney.

Hetero-. Add:

He:teræsthe·sia (see quot. 1903). **Hetera·nthery** *Bot.*, the condition of having stamens of different lengths on different individuals; so **Hetera·ntherous** *a.* **He:teroa·lbumose,** an albumose closely related to the original albumin from which it is derived; one of the heteroproteoses. **He:terobio·phorid,** in Weismann's theory of heredity, a hypothetical organism in which the biophores are of several different kinds. **Heteroblastic** (*b*) *Bot.*, denoting a plant in which there is a marked difference between the immature and adult forms. **He:terobla·stically** *adv.*, in a heteroblastic manner. **He·teroblasty** *Embryol.* (see quot.). **Hetero·ce·ntric** *a.*, (*a*) centred on others, not self-centred; (*b*) denoting rays of light which, though not parallel, do not meet. **He:terochlamy·deous** *a. Bot.* [Gr. χλαμύς, χλαμυδ- cloak], having a perianth in which the calyx and corolla are of a different colour or texture. **He:terochroma·tic** *a.*, relating to or possessing more than one colour; so **Hetero·chro·matism,** (*a*) variability in the markings and colourings of flowers of the same species; (*b*) (see quot. 1928); **He:terochro·sis** *Ornith.* [Gr. χρῶσις], abnormal coloration. **Heterochthon** (hetěrǫ·kþǫn) [Gr. χθών earth], that element of the fauna of a given region which is not indigenous to the region, but which is due to immigration; so **Hetero·chthonous** *a.*, originating in another region than that in which found (Dorland *Med. Dict.* 1913). **Hetero·coelous** (-sī·ləs), *a.* [Gr. κοῖλος hollow], applied to vertebræ in which the articular facets are saddle-shaped, as in certain birds. **He:terocy·clic** *a.*, (*a*) *Chem.*, pertaining to or containing a ring made up of various kinds of atoms; (*b*) *Bot.* (see quot. 1895). **He:terocytoly·tic** *a.*, causing the dissolution of other cells; also as *sb.* **He:terocytoto·xin,** a cytotoxin which destroys cells obtained from an animal of another species. **He:terody·namous** *a. Biol.*, pertaining or relating to the dominance of certain ancestral characteristics in inheritance; *Heterodynamous determinant*, 'in Weismann's doctrine of germ-plasm, one of the determinants which are the bearers of the hereditary qualities of cells that are different in the two parents' (Cent. D. Suppl.). **He:teroga·mete** *Biol.*, a gamete differing in character or size from that of the opposite sex; contrasted with 'isogamete'; hence **Heterogame·tic** *a.* **He:terogeʼnic** *a.* (see quot.); hence **He:terogeni·city. He:tero-immu·ne** *a.*, immune to the cells or cell-products of an animal of a different species from that from which the immune serum was taken. **He:tero-infe·ction,** infection from an external source (Dorland 1901). **He:tero-inocula·tion,** inoculation from an outside organism (Dorland 1901); so **He:tero-ino·culable** *a.* **He:terokine·sis,** in Weismann's theory of heredity, division of cells which contain dissimilar hereditary tendencies. **He:terolecithal** (-le·sipăl) *a. Embryol.*, having the food-yolk unevenly distributed. **Hetero·ly·sin** *Biol. Chem.*, a substance in the blood of one species of animal which destroys the blood-corpuscles of another species of animal (Dorland 1901). **He:terome·ric** *a. Zool.*, having dissimilar parts; **Hetero·merism** = *HETEROSIS 2. **He:teromo·rphosis** *Biol.*, abnormal shape, size, structure, or position of a part. **He:terone·reid** *a.*, of, pertaining to, or of the character of a heteronereis; also as *sb.*, a heteronereis. **He:terone·reis** *Zool.*, a dimorphic sexual form of certain worms of the genus *Nereis*, so called because originally regarded as a distinct genus; also *attrib.* **He:terophyle·tic** *a.*, of or belonging to different groups, *spec.* in *Biol.*, of different descent but alike in appearance. **He:teropro·teose** *Biol. Chem.*, each of a class of proteoses, formed esp. in the digestion of proteids with gastric juice, the members of the class being named from the kind of proteid from which they are derived, as *heteroalbumose, heterocaseose, heteroglobulose*. **He:terorha·bdic** *a.*, having the gill-filaments of unequal size, as in certain molluscs. **Hetero·spory** *Bot.*, the condition of being heterosporous. **Heterostachyous** (-stæ·kiəs), *a. Bot.* [Gr. στάχυς ear of corn], having bisexual flowers, and the sexes in separate spikes, as in certain species of *Carex*. **He:terosugge·stion** *Psychol.*, suggestion from others, contrasted with *AUTO-SUGGESTION. **He:terosylla·bic** *a. Philol.*, belonging to a different syllable (opp. to *tautosyllabic*). **Hetero·sy·llis,** an asexual stage in certain worms. **He:terotha·llic** *a.*, having zygospores developed from the conjugation of hyphæ of two different strains; so **He:terotha·llism. He·terotope,** a chemical element regarded as occupying a separate place in the periodic table (opposed to *ISOTOPE); hence **He:teroto·pic** *a.*, **He:teroto·pically** *adv.* **He:terotro·phic** *a. Biol.* and *Bot.*, deriving nourishment from without, not self-sustaining. **He·terotype** *a. Biol.*, designating a form of mitosis in which the daughter chromosomes remain united at the ends and form rings, each representing two chromosomes. **He:teroty·pic, -ty·pical** *a.* (*a*) = *heterotype *a.*; (*b*) of or pertaining to heterotype (*sb.*).

1903 MYERS *Hum. Pers.* I. p. xvii, *Heteræsthesia, a form of sensibility decidedly different from any of those which can be referred to the action of the known senses—*e.g.* the perception of a magnetic field, specific sensibilities to running water, crystals, metals (see Metallæsthesia), &c. 1883 THOMPSON tr. *Müller's Fert. Flowers* 508 *Heteranthery (*i.e.* the existence of different forms bearing anthers of different lengths). 1884 *Jrnl. Chem. Soc.* XLVI. 1389 *Heteroalbumose, similar to deuteroalbumose, but insoluble in solutions of sodium chloride. 1893 tr. *A. Weismann's Germ-Plasm* 451 The *hetero-biophorids or unicellular organisms. 1895 VINES *Text-bk. Bot.* 14 In certain cases the embryo produced by the spore differs more or less widely from the adult form, and does not directly develope into it, but bears it as a lateral outgrowth; this mode of embryogeny is indirect or *heteroblastic. 1888 *Nature* 13 Dec. 151/1 Tenontogenous or desmogenous [sesamoids], like the patella, are formed *heteroblastically inside of a tendon. 1898 *Ibid.* 1 Sept. 425/1 Prof. Salensky read a paper on '*Heteroblasty', by which name he designates the origin from different embryonic sources of organs, similar in position and function, in nearly related animals. 1901 DORLAND *Med. Dict.* (ed. 2), *Heterocentric, made up of rays that are neither parallel nor meet in one point. 1904 G. S. HALL *Adolescence* II. 301 When life pivots over from an auto-centric to an hetero-centric basis. 1895 VINES *Text-bk. Bot.* 512 When the calyx and corolla clearly differ from each other in colour, texture, etc., the flower is said to be *heterochlamydeous. 1900 B. D. JACKSON *Gloss. Bot. Terms*, *Heterochromatism, a change in the colouring or marking of petals. 1928 J. T. CUNNINGHAM *Mod. Biol.* 220 Heterochromatism, if we use that term for the power to see the whole length of the spectrum, but inability to distinguish red. 1893 NEWTON *Dict. Birds* s.v., There seems to be a certain correlation of colours in most cases of *Heterochrosis. 1903 *Amer. Nat.* XXXVII. 350 The parasitic worms of the holarctic region are not found with the indigenous (autochthon) mammals or birds, but only with the strangers (*heterochthon) that immigrated at a late period. 1884 COUES *N. Amer. Birds* (ed. 2) 138 Both ends of each vertebra are saddle-shaped,..a condition which may be called *heterocœlous. 1897 T. J. PARKER & HASWELL *Text-bk. Zool.* II. 358 The centrum in sagittal section appears episthocœlous, in horizontal section procœlous. This peculiar form of vertebra is distinguished as heterocœlous. 1895 VINES *Text-bk. Bot.* 500 When the whorls are heteromerous the flowers are said to be *heterocyclic. 1903 *Jrnl. Chem. Soc.* LXXXIV. I. 721 A review of the reactions by which heterocyclic compounds have been obtained from the acylhydrazides and their derivatives. 1908 *Practitioner* Mar. 393 *Heterocytolytic ferments. 1902 *Science* 2 May 697/2 In that they are destructive for the specific cells through which they have been produced, they are termed 'cytotoxins'. The most active are the *heterocytotoxins, produced in alien animals. 1893 tr. *A. Weismann's Germ-Plasm* ix. 265 They ..are *heterodynamous, or, in other words, they tend to impress a somewhat different character on the same part of the body. 1902 BATESON & SAUNDERS *Rep. Evol. Comm. Roy. Soc.* I. 126 Correns proposes the terms 'heterodynamous' and 'homodynamous' to express that an organism is dominant or not dominant in respect of a given character. 1930 R. A. FISHER *Genet. Theory Nat. Selection* 164 Crossing over has been found to occur between the 'sex-chromosomes' in the *heterogametic sex, whether male as in *Lebistes*, or female as in *Platypoecilus*. 1901 DORLAND *Med. Dict.* (ed. 2), *Heterogenic, occurring in the wrong sex, as a beard upon a woman. 1901 *Jrnl. Exper. Med.* VI. 82 A matter of purely facultative, by no means exclusive or obligatory *heterogenicity. 1903 *Lancet* 4 Apr. 944/2 The introduction of the *hetero-immune serum. 1893 tr. *A. Weismann's Germ-Plasm* 34 These kinds of division we may speak of as homœokinesis and *heterokinesis. 1896 E. B. WILSON *Cell* 336 *Heterolecithal..having unequally distributed deutoplasm (includes telolecithal and centrolecithal). 1902 *Encycl. Brit.* XXV. 691/1 Metamerized animals are either homœomeric or *heteromeric. 1902 *heteromerism [see *HETEROSIS 2]. 1897 *Pop. Sci. Monthly* Oct. 797 (Funk) His curious investigations into *heteromorphosis—substitution of one organ by another, transformation of one organ into another. 1901 T. H. MORGAN *Regeneration* 39 Even in tubularia in which heteromorphosis takes place, there is usually a delay of twenty-four hours in the formation of the reversed head. 1896 *Cambr. Nat. Hist.* II. 277 There are then three different kinds of males and of females in this one species [sc. *Nereis*], some being found at the bottom of the sea, as the large *Heteronereid form, while the small Heteronereid swims on the surface. 1902 *Ann. & Mag. Nat. Hist.* Sept. 256 At St. Andrews the cosmopolitan *Nereis pelagica* appears to show a heteronereid condition only in the male. 1875 *Encycl. Brit.* II. 67/1 Another [sexual form] which becomes transformed into a *Heteronereis before the sexual elements are developed. 1880 F. M. BALFOUR *Comp. Embryol.* I. 284 Claparède traced the passage of large asexual examples of the Nereis form into the large Heteronereis form. 1902 *Encycl. Brit.* XXVI. 255/2 If these can be shown to be cases of isomorphism or *heterophyletic, convergent analogy. 1896 *Jrnl. Chem. Soc.* LXX. I. 714 The presence of a deuteroproteose and a *heteroproteose was also detected. 1902 *Encycl. Brit.* XXXI. 720/2 It appears that the hetero-proteose molecule is about five or six times the size of the molecule of proto-proteose. 1903 *Phil. Trans.* Ser. B. CXCV. 154 Homorhabdic gills are those with all the filaments alike; *heterorhabdic gills are those which exhibit the above-mentioned differentiation into principal and ordinary filaments. 1898 *Nat. Science* June 375 Its independent appearance in distinct groups may be compared with the appearance of *heterospory. 1902 *Encycl. Brit.* XXXI. 411/2 There is evidence for the occurrence of heterospory in some strobili referred to *Palæostachya*. 1903 *Amer. Jrnl. Sci.* CLXVI. 452 Where a species with normally gynæcandrous spikes appears as inseparable from others which are truly *heterostachyous. 1920 tr. *Baudouin's Suggestion & Autosuggestion* Gloss., *Autosuggestion*, the subconscious realisation of an idea in more or less complete independence of *heterosuggestion. 1924 W. B. SELBIE *Psych. Relig.* 223 If..on the physical side, the power of auto-suggestion is greatly increased by hetero-suggestion. 1913 J. M. JONES *Welsh Gram.* 72 In N. W[ales] the vowel is medium in *aw, ew, iw* before a vowel, that is the *w* is *heterosyllabic. 1896 *Cambr. Nat. Hist.* II. 278 In some genera [sc. of the family Syllidae]..there occur changes quite similar to those characterising 'Heteronereis'—that is, the posterior segments in which the genital organs exist become altered, so that the worm consists of two distinct regions, and is termed a '*Heterosyllis'. 1906 *Rep. Brit. Assoc.* 751 The *heterothallic species *Mucor Mucedo*. 1921 IRENE MOUNCE in *Brit. Mycol. Soc.* VII. 199 The fruiting of a mycelium of a heterothallic Hymenomycete. *Ibid.* 198 Mlle Bensaude's criteria for determining *heterothallism in her fungus. 1919 SODDY in *Jrnl. Chem. Soc.* CXV. 11 Boyle's practical definition of the element..became replaced by a theoretical conception, to which..I propose to apply the term '*heterotope', meaning the occupant of a separate place in the periodic table of elements. 1901 *Rep. Brit. Assoc.* 820 The root-difference between plants and animals is one of nutrition. Plants are autotrophic, animals *heterotrophic. 1902 *Encycl. Brit.* XXV. 439/1 In the early juvenile phases of their life..many such autotrophic Angiosperms are heterotrophic. 1900 B. D. JACKSON *Gloss. Bot. Terms*, *Heterotype. 1902 *Encycl. Brit.* XXVII. 336/1 The form of division which is thus characterized by the early longitudinal fission of the chromosomes and the formation of more or less regular rings is called the heterotype division. 1908 tr. *Strasburger's Text-bk. Bot.* (ed. 3) 86 The heterotype and homotype nuclear divisions. 1918 BABCOCK & CLAUSEN *Genetics* 617 *Heterotypic Division. 1896 E. B. WILSON *Cell* 60 *Heterotypical mitosis in spermatocytes of the salamander.

Heterodyne (he·terǫdəin). *Wireless Telegr.* and *Telephony.* [f. HETERO- + DYNE.] A name given by Fessenden to a method by which incoming oscillations are combined with other oscillations of a slightly different frequency, so that a 'beat' is set up. Also, short for *h. receiver*, etc. Hence **He·terodyne** *v. trans.*

1908 E. RUHMER *Wireless Telephony* App. 201 One of the most interesting of Professor Fessenden's many inventions is what he has called the 'Heterodyne' receiver. 1922 A. F. COLLINS *Bk. Wireless Telegraph* III. ii. 174 The oscillations set up by the incoming waves from the distant sending stations and those set up by the separate oscillator tube, or heterodyne..have a slightly different frequency. 1923 *Glasgow Herald* 13 Oct. 6 A spark station previously heterodyned by a carrier. 1926 R. W. HUTCHINSON *Wireless* 185 Howls and squeaks result from the 'heterodyning'..of the carrier wave. 1927 *Daily Tel.* 21 June 19/1 No more telegrams need fly from London to Geneva and then on to a station supposed to be heterodyning London. 1931 *B.B.C. Year-book* 442/2 *Heterodyne interference*, interference caused to broadcast reception by the carrier wave of an unwanted station beating with that of the wanted station. *Ibid.*, *Heterodyne reception*, a method of receiving C.W. wireless signals in which use is made of a local oscillator to 'beat' with or 'Heterodyne' the incoming C.W.

fig. 1930 *Mus. Assoc. Proc.* 97 To write atonally in a harmonic form at present is to produce a thought 'heterodyne'.

Heterogeneous, *a.* **4.** Add: In various other technical usages.

1883 *Encycl. Brit.* XV. 693/1 Heterogeneous strain. 1895 *Jrnl. Chem. Soc.* LXVIII. II. 72 Graphical Representation of Heterogeneous System. 1902 *Encycl. Brit.* XXVII. 187/1 Will an isentropic line, which starts from a point of the border-curve on the side of the liquid not far from the critical point, remain throughout its descending course in the heterogeneous region, or will it leave the region on the side of the vapour? *Ibid.* XXVIII. 567/2 In the case of crystal-line fusion it is necessary to distinguish two cases, the Homogeneous and the Heterogeneous. In the first case, the composition of the solid and liquid phases are the same, and the temperature remains constant during the whole process of fusion. In the second case, the solid and liquid phases differ in composition; that of the liquid phase changes continuously, and the temperature does not remain constant during the fusion. *Ibid.* XXIX. 257/1 The nuclear are what Weismann calls 'differentiating' or heterogeneous divisions.

Heterogenite (hetěrǫ·dʒĭnəit). *Min.* [a. G. *heterogenit*, f. Gr. ἑτερογενής HETEROGENEOUS: see -ITE[1].] A hydrated oxide of cobalt, derived from smaltite, occurring in dark brown or black amorphous masses.

1872 *Jrnl. Chem. Soc.* XXV. 991 Heterogenite is a product of the decomposition of smaltine or tin-white cobalt (speisskobalt). 1887 DANA *Man. Min.* (ed. 4) 184 Heterogenite. Black; reniform; contains 78 p.c. cobalt oxide, and 21·33 of water.

Heterogeny. Add: **3. b.** = HETEROGENESIS 3 c.

1889 tr. *A. Weismann's Ess. Hered.* 325 It is also certain that in the *Daphnidæ*, heterogeny may pass into pure parthenogenesis by the non-appearance of the sexual generations. 1893 tr. *A. Weismann's Germ-Plasm* v. 173 That form of alternation of generations which is known as heterogeny.

Heterography. Add: **3.** The writing of one word or phrase when another is meant.

1908 *Daily Chron.* 6 May 4/6 Victims of..heterography. 1913 DORLAND *Med. Dict.* (ed. 7).

Heterologous, *a.* Add: **c.** In wider use (see quots.).

1889 WINGRAVE *T. Dunman's Gloss. Anat.* etc. *Terms*, *Heterologous stimuli*, stimuli which will excite a sensory nerve when applied either to its termination or in its continuity. 1893 tr. *A. Weismann's Germ-Plasm* ix. 266 Homologous determinants and ids co-operate, while heterologous ones do not.

Heteroplasty (he·těroplæsti). [f. HETERO- + -PLASTY.] **a.** *Surg.* A plastic operation in which the graft used is taken from an individual other than the patient. **b.** *Biol.* Abnormal formation of tissue, heteroplasia.

1874 *Engl. Mechanic* 321 The name heteroplasty has been adopted for the operation of taking pieces of skin from amputated limbs, and using them to produce cicatrisation on the bodies of other subjects.

Heterosexual (he:těrose·ksiuăl), *a.* [See HETERO- and SEXUAL.] Pertaining to or characterized by the normal relation of the sexes: opp. to *homosexual*. Also as *sb.*, a heterosexual person. Hence **He:terosexua·lity.** (Sometimes misapplied, as in quot. 1901.)

1901 DORLAND *Med. Dict.* (ed. 2), *Heterosexuality*, abnormal or perverted sexual appetite toward the opposite sex. *a* 1909 *Buck's Handbk. Med. Sci.* V. 134 (Cent. D. Suppl.) Heterosexual. 1920 tr. *Freud's Coll. Papers* (1924) II. 207 To convert a fully developed homosexual into a heterosexual. 1927 *Scots Observer* 1 Oct. 15/3 A certain proportion of people..are as instinctively homosexual as the normal individual is heterosexual.

Heterosis. Add: **2.** *Zool.* Segmentation in which the parts are different.

1902 *Encycl. Brit.* XXV. 691/2 It becomes apparent from this enumeration that there are a good many important elements or 'meromes' in an Arthropod metamere or somite which can become the subject of heteromerism or, to use a more apt word, of 'heterosis'. *Ibid.*, The Fourth Law of metamerism (auto-heterosis of the meromes).

Heterosite (he·tĕrosəit). *Min.* Also erron. **heterozite.** [Badly f. Gr. ἕτερος + -ITE[1].] A variety of triphylite.

1854 DANA *Syst. Min.* (ed. 4) II. 407. 1858 NICOL *Min.* 241 Heterozite...Opaque, or translucent on the edges; vitreous or resinous. 1881 *Jrnl. Chem. Soc.* XL. 550 By alteration of the triphylin are formed: first, blue heterosite, then blackish-green melanchlore, and finally the pseudomorph called pseudotriplite.

Heterotropic, *a.* Add: **2.** *Biol.* (See quot.)

1909 R. H. LOCK *Variation, Heredity, & Evol.* x. (ed. 2) 271 In the case of the male *Protenor* all the chromosomes fuse in pairs except one, which is, of necessity, left over. This odd chromosome is described as the heterotropic chromosome.

Heterozygote (he:tĕrozəi·gout). *Biol.* [f. HETERO- + ZYGOTE.] **a.** A zygote resulting from the fusion of two unlike gametes. **b.** A Mendelian hybrid, containing dominant and recessive characters, and which, therefore, does not breed true. Also *attrib.* or *adj.*, = heterozygous.

1902 BATESON & SAUNDERS *Rep. Evol. Comm. Roy. Soc.* I. 126 The zygote formed by the union of a pair of opposite allelomorphic gametes, we shall call a heterozygote. 1902 W. BATESON *Mendel's Princ. Hered.* 23 This *Aa* is the hybrid or 'mule' form, or as I have elsewhere called it, the heterozygote, as distinguished from *AA* or *aa* the homozygotes. 1906 R. H. LOCK *Variation, Heredity, & Evolution* vii. 186 *Plate*, Cobs born by heterozygote plants pollinated with the recessive. 1930 R. A. FISHER *Genet. Theory Nat. Selection* 8 The heterozygote when mated to either kind of homozygote would produce both heterozygotes and homozygotes.

Hence **Heterozygosis** (-zəigōu·sis), **Heterozygosity** (-zəigǫ·siti), the condition or state of having developed from a heterozygote; development from a heterozygote; **Heterozy·goted** *a.*, produced from a heterozygote; also *absol.*; **Heterozygous** (-zəi·gəs) *a.*, of or pertaining to gametes which contain opposite allelomorphic characters; also, of or pertaining to characters which do not become fixed or constant under continual selection, or to an individual containing such characters.

1902 BATESON & SAUNDERS *Rep. Evol. Comm. Roy. Soc.* I. 130 The determination from statistical study of zygotes must be exceedingly difficult, seeing that both resulting forms may be heterozygous. 1918 BABCOCK & CLAUSEN *Genetics* 233 When..the differences are not great enough to obstruct normal cell division, the degree of stimulation is held to increase directly with the amount or kind of heterozygosis present. 1919 R. C. PUNNETT *Mendelism* (ed. 5) 128 We may leave the blue Andalusian fowl undisturbed in its claim to simple heterozygosity. 1930 R. A. FISHER *Genet. Theory Nat. Selection* 57 The viability and general fitness of the heterozygoted. 1931 SHUMWAY *Gen. Biol.* 159 Heterozygous dominants.

Heubachite (hoi·bāχəit). *Min.* [a. G. *heubachit*, f. the place-name *Heubach*thal in Baden: see -ITE[1].] A hydrated oxide of cobalt and nickel, occurring as an incrustation on barite.

1877 *Jrnl. Chem. Soc.* II. 855.

Heumite (hiū·məit). *Min.* [f. the place-name *Heum* in Norway + -ITE[1].] A dark aphanitic igneous rock resembling nephelinite.

1901 *Jrnl. Chem. Soc.* LXXX. II. 169 Heumite is the name given to a dyke-rock from Heum, consisting of hornblende and felspar, with some biotite, and smaller amounts of nephelite, sodalite, diopside, &c.

Heurism (hiū·riz'm). [f. HEUR(ISTIC + -ISM.] The educational principle or practice of placing a pupil, as far as possible, in the position of a discoverer.

1920 T. P. NUNN *Educ. Data & 1st Princ.* 91 Dr. M. W. Keatinge,..a severe critic of heurism and of the general idea of freedom in education. 1925 C. FOX *Educ. Psychol.* 214.

Heuristic, *a.* Add: *spec.* applied to that method of teaching which places the pupil, as far as possible, in the position of a discoverer. Also **Heuri·stical** *a.*

1848 ROSS *Teacher's Man.* v. 92 The Heuristical method. 1898 H. E. ARMSTRONG *Spec. Rep. Educ. Subjects* II. 389 The Heuristic method of teaching or The art of making children discover things for themselves.

Hevea (hī·viă). *Bot.* [mod.L., f. native name *Hevé*.] A tree of the South American euphorbiaceous genus so called, yielding caoutchouc.

1921 *Outward Bound* May 40 To the right are seen some hevea trees. 1927 *Daily Tel.* 11 May 3/4 The rest would be dug up after the present season, and rubber planted in its stead, as the hevea trees remaining were widely spaced.

Hew, *v.* **B. 1. b.** (Modern U.S. examples.)

a 1861 T. WINTHROP *John Brent* xxviii. 298, I omit the story how I saw a vista in new life, hewed in and took up a 'claim', which I have held good. 1891 *Harper's Mag.* Aug. 431/1 How closely they hewed to the line in this respect is attested by the dying remarks of one of the men hanged.

Hewed (hiūd), *ppl. a.* (under HEW *v.*). (Modern U.S. examples. Also of *hewed-log* in attrib. use.)

1805 D. MCCLURE *Diary* (1899) 14 There was a small church made of hewed logs. 1843 *Amer. Pioneer* II. 148 Two small hewed-log houses had been erected, and several cabins. 1849 *President's Mess. Congress* II. 1089 One hewed-log dwelling,..comfortably furnished cost $351. 1883 E. EGGLESTON *Hoosier School-boy* xvi. 106 There's the old hewed-log house..where we used to live.

Hewgag. *U.S.* (Earlier and later examples.)

1855 *Vermont Free Press* 8 June (Th.) The T.I.N. Horn-et Band, with Sackbut, Psaltery, Dulcimer,..and Hugag, marched next. 1905 TARKINGTON *In Arena* 152 He had *all* the honours..; professors and students all kow-towed and sounded the hew-gag before him.

Hexa-. Add further examples of the chemical use. Also **He·xact** *a.*, having six rays; also as *sb.*, a sponge-spicule having six rays. **Hexactine·llidan** *a.* and *sb.*, = HEXACTINELLID. **He·xamere,** an opening or mesh of the sixth degree of the reticulum of sponges. **Hexa·merism**, the condition of having the organs arranged according to the number six or a multiple of six. **Hexara·dial** *a.*, having six radii. **He·xarch** *a. Bot.*, having six strands; also as *sb.*, a stele having six strands.

1885 Remsen *Org. Chem.* 253 As the final products, *hexachlor-benzene, C_6Cl_6, and *hexa-brom-benzene C_6Br_6 are obtained. 1892 *Jrnl. Soc. Chem. Industry* XI. 599/1 It is usually assumed that the benzene-*hexachlorides are derivatives of the hydrocarbon hexamethylene. 1886 R. von Lendenfeld in *Proc. Zool. Soc.* 590 The Recent Families of Sponges...With *hexact spicules and thimble-shaped chambers. 1887 tr. *F. E. Schulze* in *Challenger Rep., Zool.* XXI. 29 Regular Hexacts are all spicules in which the rays lie at right angles to one another, and are of equal length and similar form. *Ibid.* 37 Certain *Hexactinellidan families have typical and regular *Uncinata*, while in others they are absent. 1913 V. B. Lewes *Oil Fuel* 41 In the Russian oils the more important members belong to the series of hydrocarbons known as naphthenes or *hexahydrides, in which the ratio of carbon to hydrogen is C^nH_{2n}. 1905 *Rep. Brit. Assoc.* Aug.-Sept. 156 Small quantities are decomposed into *hexahydrobenzene and a fatty amine. 1885 *Jrnl. Chem. Soc.* XLVIII. II. 780 The action of acetic anhydride and fused sodium acetate on the *hexahydroxybenzene. 1903 *Science* 17 July 80/2 In some species [of corals] the *hexamerism becomes much obscured in later stages, while in others it is more or less distinctly preserved. 1909 *Practitioner* Dec. 798 The drug is *hexamethylenamine, and it has been experimentally shown that a short time after its administration by the mouth its presence can be demonstrated in the cerebro-spinal fluid. 1907 *Ibid.* Aug. 327 *Helmitol.*—This is a salt built up of citric acid, *hexamethylenetetramine, and formaldehyde. 1900 B. D. Jackson *Gloss. Bot. Terms*, *Hexarch.

Hexagonal. Add:
3. b. *Geom.* and *Cryst.* Having a relation to six angles; as *hexagonal symmetry*, the symmetry of a figure or body which coincides with its original position after rotation about an axis through an angle of 60° (i.e. $\frac{1}{6}$ of the whole circle) or any multiple of this.

1878, 1895 [from sense 3].

Hexagonite (he·ksăgǝnəit). *Min.* [f. Hexagon + -ite 1.] A pink variety of tremolite, containing a small amount of manganese, found in St. Lawrence county, New York.

1876 *Proc. Acad. Nat. Sci. Philad.* 160.

Hexone (he·ksōun). *Chem.* [a. G. *hexon*, f. Gr. ἕξ six + -one.] a. A term applied by Kossel to any one of several bases, as lysin, arginine, and histidine, which contain six atoms of carbon in the molecule. b. A fluid consisting of hydrocarbons, C_6H_8, obtained from certain fats and resins.

1898 *Jrnl. Chem. Soc.* LXXIV. I. 612 The substances into which protamine is changed are called protones; these are, by the prolonged action of pancreatic juice, partially broken up into hexones (lysine, histidine, arginine).

Hexose (he·ksous). *Chem.* [f. Hex- + -ose 2.] Any member of a group of sugars containing six carbon atoms to the molecule. So **Hexo·sazone**, the osazone of a hexose sugar; **He·xoside**, a glucoside derived from a hexose.

1897 Remsen *Org. Chem.* (1903) 182 The monosaccharides, therefore, fall into classes which are called trioses, litroses, pentoses, hexoses, etc.; according to the number of oxygen atoms contained in them. 1899 *Jrnl. Chem. Soc.* LXXVI. II. 339 Hexoses..yield only very small quantities of furfuraldehyde. 1902 *Encycl. Brit.* XXVI. 722/2 A most important step had been taken towards synthesizing the natural hexoses.

Hex-radiate (heks,rē¹·diět), *a.* [f. Gr. ἕξ six + L. *radiatus* rayed, Radiate.] = Hexiradiate.

1883 W. S. Kent in *Fisheries Bahamas* 37 The glass-rope, birds'-nest, and hat sponges share..the circumstance that the silicious spicules of which their skeletons are composed belong..to what is known as the hex-radiate type.

Hiaqua (hai·ăkwă). Also **haiqua, haigua, haikwa, hiagua, hikwa, hiqua, hyaqua, ioqua.** [American Indian.] An ornament or necklace composed of tooth-shells, formerly used as money by the Indians of the north Pacific coast of North America.

1881 Tylor *Anthropol.* xi. 282 The Indians of British Columbia, whose strings of haiqua-shells..serve them..as currency. 1883 T. Winthrop *Canoe & Saddle* vii. 95 Tribes ..among whom hiaqua is plenty as salmon-berries are in the woods.

Hiatal (hai,ē¹·tăl), *a.* [f. Hiat(us + -al.] Of or pertaining to a hiatus or opening.

1923 R. Knox *Radiog. & Radio-Ther.* I. 319 Cardiospasm (Hiatal Oesophagismus).

Hibachi (hibā·tʃi). [Jap., f. *hi* fire + *bachi* bowl, pot.] A pan or brazier in which charcoal is burnt in order to warm the hands or heat a room, or for boiling water for making tea.

1874 *Trans. Asiatic Soc. Japan* II. 132 Boys and girls assemble round the *hibachi*. 1921 *Outward Bound* Apr. 22/1 The little *kimori* was bidden to join the family circle around the *hibachi*.

Hiberno-. Add:
1907 *Daily Chron.* 6 Sept. 3/1 Hiberno-Egyptian. 1908 *Westm. Gaz.* 20 Aug. 5/2 A Hiberno-Romanesque church.

Hibschite (hi·bʃəit). *Min.* [f. name of J. E. *Hibsch* of Tetschen, Bohemia + -ite 1.] An isotropic mineral related to lawsonite.

1907 *Min. Mag.* XIV. 400 Hibschite...The chemical composition, $H_4CaAl_2Si_2O_{10}$, is the same as of the orthorhombic lawsonite.

Hiccoughy, variant of Hiccupy *a.*

1911 J. C. Lincoln *Cap'n Warren's Wards* i. 2 The train slowed down, in a jerky hiccoughy sort of way.

Hiccup, *sb.* Add: c. *attrib.* **hiccup-nut** *S. Afr.*, the seed of an ornamental combretaceous shrub, *Poivrea bracteosa*; also, the plant itself.

1868 Jas. Chapman *Trav.* II. App. 447 The exquisite beads of scarlet flowers of the Hiccup-nut.

Hick, *sb.*1 Delete †*Obs.* and add later U.S. examples.

1916 H. L. Wilson *Somewhere in Red Gap* iii. 113 So I yelled out back to an old hick of a gardener..and he comes running. 1921 R. D. Paine *Comr. Rolling Ocean* vi. 106, I come from a small town and that makes me a hick. My opinions aren't worth much. 1925 *Glasgow Herald* 16 Sept. 4 In the United States the 'Hicks' are still for the most part tenacious of that doctrine which assigns to speculations a 'bearish' or depressing influence on the markets. 1927 *Observer* 1 May 10/2 It is..much easier to write a good play about hicks, boobs, hayseeds, highbrows,..and sentimentalists than about decent English people. 1928 *World's Work* Apr. 628 Broadway humorists, only a few years ago, used to make fun of Long Islanders by calling them 'hicks'. 1929 A. Conan Doyle *Maracot Deep* 18 He could not make these country hicks understand.

attrib. 1927 S. Ertz *Now East, Now West* v. (1931) 74 Whether it's in the U.S.A. or in some hick town in Patagonia.

Hickboo (hi·kbū). *Air Force slang.* Also **hickaboo.** An air raid.

1919 *Athenæum* 23 May 360/2.

Hickory. Add: 3. (Earlier U.S. example.)

1705 Beverley *Hist. Virginia* III. 15 The Kernels of the Hiccories they beat in a Mortar with Water, and make a White Liquor like Milk, whence they call our Milk Hickory.

4. a. Also applied *fig.* to members of various religious sects.

1835 *Southern Lit. Messenger* I. 551 Some years ago a kind of 'Hickory Quaker' as he called himself,..found his way..from one of the middle States to Congress. 1855 *Jrnl. Discourses* II. 322 If there are any Gentiles, or hickory 'Mormons'..write it down. 1859 Bartlett *Dict. Amer.* s.v., A 'hickory Catholic'..is a flexible, yielding one. 1872 E. Eggleston *End of World* xxxix. 249 Any member of your class would do better to marry a good, faithful, honest New Light than to marry a hickory Methodist. 1878 J. H. Beadle *Western Wilds* 534 Among the young, or 'Hickory Mormons', there are about as many men as women.

b. **hickory cloth**, a coarse, heavy, durable cloth made of cotton; **hickory milk**, a white liquor made by pounding the kernels of hickory nuts with water; **hickory shad**, the gizzard-shad (*Dorosoma cepedianum*); also, the fall-herring; **hickory shirt** (earlier examples).

1857 *Jrnl. Discourses* IV. 205 Get some good *hickory cloth, or some buckskins, and let the sisters make dresses and garments that cannot be easily torn. [1705 *hickory milk: see 3 above.] 1775 Romans *Florida* 94 Bears oyl, honey, and hickory milk, are the boast of the [Chicasaw] country. 1819 E. Dana *Geog. Sk. Western Country* 53 Cat fish, perch, pike...*hickory shad. 1871 *Amer. Naturalist* V. 398 The 'Hickory Shad'..were also filled with comminuted Crustacea. 1850 L. H. Garrard *Wah-To-Yah* xii. (1927) 58 *Hickory shirts. *a* 1861 T. Winthrop *Canoe & Saddle* iii. 33 Hickory shirts and woolen blankets are worn instead of skin raiment.

Hidalga (hidæ·lgă). [Sp., the feminine of Hidalgo.] A Spanish lady of the nobility.

1885 *Harper's Mag.* June 55/1 An instep so delicately arched that water may flow beneath it, proclaims her a veritable hidalga.

Hidden, *ppl. a.* Add: 1. b. *The hidden hand*, secret or occult influence, esp. of a malignant character.

1917 *Tit-Bits* LXXI. 511 Hidden Hands. 1927 W. E. Collinson *Contemp. Eng.* 104 Hidden band.

c. *Gram.* *Hidden quantity* (see quot.).

1898 G. M. Lane *Latin Gram.* § 2459 A vowel which stands before two consonants, or a double consonant, belonging to the same word, so that its natural quantity cannot be determined from the scansion of the word, is said to possess Hidden Quantity.

Hide, *v.*1 Add:
1. Further examples of *to hide away.*

1854 W. Collins *Hide & Seek* xxiii. III. 227, I shall find him! I don't care where he's hid away from me. *Ibid.* xxiv. 271 She..hid it away in her bosom. 1891 Clo. Graves *Field of Tares* 109 There was a fresh canvas upon the easel, the tattered one had been carefully hidden away.

2. c. *To hide out*: to go into hiding; to hide from the authorities. *U.S.*

1885 'C. E. Craddock' *Prophet Gt. Smoky Mtn.* ii. 44 Loneliness had made his sensibilities tender and 'hiding out' affected his spirits more than dodging the officers. 1911 R. D. Saunders *Col. Todhunter* i. 19 You got to hide out when that word is delivered, suh.

Hide-and-coop. *U.S.* = Hide-and-seek.

1850 S. Judd *Richard Edney* 128 (Th.) As if religion were a game of hide and coop. 1909 *N. & Q.* 10th Ser. XII. 371/1 In 'hide and coop', each called out from his secret place a faint, long-drawn 'c-o-o-p'. 1909 S. E. White *Rules of Game* III. xxii. 257 We ain't doing any good playing hide and coop. *Ibid.* 258 The herders grinned as the rangers came in sight. They had been 'tagged' in this 'game of hide and coop'.

Hide-and-seek. (Earlier and later U.S. examples of **hide-and-go-seek.**)

1724 *Essex Inst. Hist. Coll.* XXXVI. 333 At night was at Madam Brownes playing hide and goe seek with Olive Parker, Wibird, &c. 1821 J. F. Cooper *Spy* xxxvi. (1831) 405 Since when, we have been playing hide-and-go-seek with the ships. 1908 Roosevelt *Lett. Children* 2 Jan., Do you recollect how we all used to play hide-and-go-seek in the White House?

Hide-out (hai·d,aut). *U.S.* and *Canada.* A hiding-place.

1895 *Century Mag.* Sept. 674/2 Think he was fixin' up for a hide-out, in case he should need one? 1913 A. B. Emerson *R. Fielding at Snow Camp* 174 Meanwhile, the wind shrieked through the forest above their 'hideout'. 1920 B. Cronin *Timber Wolves* 76 'In rough country like this a man could bury himself for years'..'This coast is full of hide-outs, as they call them.'

Hidy-hole (hai·di,houl). *Sc.* and *U.S.* Also **hidey-, hidie-.** [Alteration of *hiding-hole*: see Hiding *vbl. sb.*1 4.] A hiding-place.

1828 Moir *Mansie Wauch* ix, We got James..hauled out of his hidy-hole. 1870 R. Chambers *Pop. Rhymes* 91 He had not been long in his hidy-hole, before the awful Etin came in. 1896 Crockett *Cleg Kelly* iii, Tim Kelly's 'hidie-holes', where he kept the weapons of his craft. 1920 *Glasgow Herald* 6 Dec. 10 The story of the Ballantrae smugglers' 'hidie-hole'. 1923 Silberrad *Lett. Jean Armiter* xiv. § 2 The wood and brushwood in the hidy-hole.

Hien, hsien (hyen, ʃyen). Pl. uninflected. Also **heen.** [Chinese.] An administrative division of a fu or department, or of an independent chow or district; also, the seat of government of such a division. Also *attrib.*

1837 *Penny Cycl.* VII. 77/1 The subordinate cities and districts of each province in the three ranks of Foo, Chow, and Hien, are under the charge of their respective magistrates, who take their rank and titles from the cities they govern. 1901 *Westm. Gaz.* 23 Aug. 8/2 Among the candidates was a man who has the hsien B.A. degree. During the examination it was found that he had some books with him. The examiner at once ordered his expulsion from the hall, but the men from his hsien objected. 1909 *Ibid.* 24 May 8/2 A circular has been sent to all viceroys and governors by the Pekin Cabinet ordering that a stop be put to the old custom of levying benevolences on the governors of hien cities.

Hieratite (hai·ərătəit). *Min.* [f. *Hiera*, ancient name of Vulcano, one of the Lipari Islands + -ite 1.] A fluoride of silicon and potassium, crystallizing in the isometric system, occurring in stalactitic concretions in the crater of Vulcano.

1883 *Jrnl. Chem. Soc.* XLIV. 955.

Hieroglyphism (hai,ĕrǝ·glifiz'm). [f. Hieroglyph(ic + -ism.] The use of hieroglyphics.

1875 *Encycl. Brit.* I. 605/1 The development of hieroglyphism in Egypt.

Higgle (hi·g'l), *sb.* [f. the vb.] The adjusting of prices so that demand and supply are equal.

1908 *Daily Chron.* 5 Dec. 4/6 If they were abolished altogether the 'higgle of the market' would level freights correspondingly down.

Hi·ggledipi·ggledness. The quality or condition of being higgledy-piggledy.

1854 *Punch* 18 Nov. 204/1 That structural higgledipiggledness.

Higgledy-piggledy, *a.* (Earlier U.S. examples.) Also *higgle piggledee* (cf. next).

1662 *Essex Probate Rec.* I. 400 Two higle pigledee Lotts ..10 acres of meadow in ye bareberri meadows. 1676 *Essex Inst. Hist. Coll.* LVI. 300 One-half of a higledee pigledee lot of salt marsh.

Higgle-piggle, *adv.* = Higgledy-piggledy *adv.*

1796–1801 Fessenden *Orig. Poems* (1806) 33 Balance Joe, to Lucy Wiggle, Pho, youre wrong, all higgle-piggle!

Higgler. Add: 2. d. (See quot.)

1930 M. Clark *Home Trade* 176 The term 'higgler' is applied in the Covent Garden market to a dealer who buys his supplies of fruit with a view to selling what he buys at a profit to any buyer, either on that market or on any other; to wholesalers or to retailers.

High, *a.* Add: 1. c. *Typogr.* (See quots.)

1888 *Encycl. Brit.* XXIII. 698/2 Spaces and quadrats were formerly only three-fourths of an inch in height; but, since electrotyping has become so common, they are almost invariably cut high, *i.e.*, up to the shoulder of the type. 1904 *Technol. & Sci. Dict.* (ed. Goodchild & Tweeney), *High*, a term applied to type or blocks which stand out in front of the rest of the type in the forme; *e.g.* new type stands higher than worn type.

3. c. Located upwards on a river.

1816 U. Brown *Jrnl.* in *Maryland Hist. Mag.* XI. 358 Thence up said River 3 Miles to John Rush's where we put up & was kindly treated, he being the highest setler up that River.

4. c. *High breast wheel* (see quots.).

1880 *Encycl. Brit.* XII. 522/2 Overshot and High Breast Wheels. *Ibid.* 523/2 With greater variation of head-water level, a pitch-back or high breast wheel is better. 1888 *Lockwood's Dict. Mech. Engin.* s.v. *Breast Wheel*, When the water flows in at a point above the horizontal line, the wheel is termed high breast, and when at a point below, low breast.

d. (See quot.)

1867 Smyth *Sailor's Word-bk.* s.v. *High*, A gun is said to be laid high when too much elevated.

4. Further examples of specialized meanings.

1895 high jump [see Jump *sb.*1 1 b]. 1897 *Encycl. Sport* I. 50/2 High jumping may be, in special cases, a gift. *Ibid.* 51/2 High kicking is very useful during the off-season. *Ibid.* 53/2 A gentle sprint and two or three small high jumps. 1924 C. W. Mason *Chinese Confessions* xliv. 326 The high-jump and hurdles were my specialities.

6. d. Having a highly developed or complex organization; spec. *Biol.*, phylogenetically advanced or developed; often in the comparative degree, as *the higher algæ, the higher apes.*

[1807 W. Wood *Zoography* I. Pref. p. xii, If we ascend to a higher class of beings, and contemplate the extensive

range of the animal creation. 1836 Lindley *Nat. Syst. Bot.* (ed. 2) 431 Another form of Algæ, one which may be considered a higher degree of developement of the last.] 1848 — *Bot.* (ed. 4) xvi. 323 Plants have no circulation of their fluids analogous to that of blood in the higher animals. 1867 H. Spencer *Princ. Biol.* § 364 Every type that is best adapted to its conditions, which on the average means every higher type, has a rate of multiplication that insures a tendency to predominate. 1870 Rolleston *Anim. Life* 42 Forms of life higher in the scale than themselves. 1875 *Encycl. Brit.* II. 168/1 As man is the highest animal. 1896 tr. *Boas' Text-bk. Zool.* 24 The higher Crustacea. 1902 *Encycl. Brit.* XXVI. 366/1 The first is an amyloin of a 'high', the second an amyloin of a 'low' type. *Ibid.* XXVIII. 343/1 The gorilla and the chimpanzee, the highest members of the apes. *Ibid.*, The embryonic stages of higher forms.

8. b. Of the condition of an animal or of soil: Resulting from over-feeding or from too great an application of manure. Also of a crop: Produced by an over-manured soil.

1834 Youatt *Cattle* xvi. 553 This occurs particularly in young cows after their first calving, and when they are in a somewhat too high condition. 1886 C. Scott *Sheep Farming* 116 Hill ewes are never in too high condition; the danger is all the other way. 1902 *Encycl. Brit.* XXVI. 361/1 It is better not to grow barley after roots fed off by sheep, as this rotation leaves the land..in too 'high' a condition...By taking barley as a second corn crop, the latter following roots fed off, or a 'high' crop, [etc.].

9. b. Of tobacco: Moist. *U.S.*

1849 *Rep. U.S. Comm. Patents, Agric.* (1850) 322 Tobacco should not be too moist, or 'high' as it is termed, when put in the stalk-bulks. 1863 *Trans. Ill. Agric. Soc.* (1865) V. 669 Care must be taken that the tobacco does not imbibe too much moisture, or get too high in case before it is bulked.

10. *High explosive*: see *Explosive *sb.* 2.

e. Of money: Lent out at a high rate of interest; dear. *U.S.*

1899 *Daily News* 31 Mar. 3/5 New York...Higher money.

g. *Naut.* Near the wind: designating a vessel or its head when pointing close to the wind, as in the command *no higher.*

1867 Smyth *Sailor's Word-bk.*, No Higher!

h. Including, containing, or referring to a large percentage.

[1907 *Daily Chron.* 12 Dec. 7/4 At least half the members should be elected on some highish franchise.]

i. In card-playing: *Ace high* (*king high*, etc.): having the ace (king, etc.) as highest card: said of the hand, also *occas.* of the person.

1887 Stuart C. Cumberland *Queen's Highway* 276 Had I a 'flush' with 'king high' some one would be sure to rake in the shekels with 'ace high'.

16. (Earlier examples of *high old* and *high time.*)

1833 C. A. Davis *Lett. J. Downing* (1834) 177 Just ater breakfast yesterday, I and the gineral had a high time [i.e. a heated argument] together. 1869 B. Harte *Luck of Roaring Camp* (1871) 226 These are high old times, ain't they? 1873 J. H. Beadle *Undevel. West* xxiii. 451 Santa Fe De San Francisco—so the old Spaniards named it—is a high old city.

17. f. *High-and-mighty*: also used *absol.*

1924 Galsworthy *White Monkey* II. ii, Mr. Mont's a gent ..no high-and-mighty about *him.*

i. *To be for the high jumps*: see *Jump *sb.*1 7.

21. **high dilution** *Homœopathy*, an extremely diluted medicine; so **high dilutionist**, an advocate of extreme dilution of medicine; **high farming**, the extensive use of fertilizers in land cultivation; **high forest** *U.S.*, a forest composed wholly or chiefly of trees raised from seed; also *attrib.*; **high frequency** *Electr.*, in an alternating current the production of a large number of alternations in a unit of time; often *attrib.*; **high grinding** (see quot.); **high hook** *colloq.* or *slang*, the angler of a party who hooks the largest fish; **high-key** *Photog.* (see quots.); **high mass** (see Mass *sb.*1 3 a, High *a.* 19 b); **high milling**, a process of making flour from grain by a number of successive grindings; **high pole** *U.S.*, a tree from 8 to 12 inches in diameter breast-high; **high spots** *U.S. slang*, the outstanding parts or features of something; *to hit the high spots*, to go to excess or extremes; to rise to a very high level; cf. *High light 2; **high steel**, steel having a relatively high percentage of carbon (Webster 1911); **high step**, a military step in which the feet and knees are raised high; **high wine**, wine containing a high percentage of alcohol.

1906 W. De Morgan *Joseph Vance* xvi, She makes some concession to my feelings on the subject of *High Dilutions, and (at great risk to myself, she says) allows me to have Mother-Tinctures. 1892 *high dilutionist [see Dilution 1st]. 1848 Mill *Pol. Econ.* I. 215 To apply the *high farming of Europe to any American lands. 1931 C. S. Orwin (*title*) High Farming. 1902 Webster Suppl., *High forest. 1905 *Terms Forestry & Logging* 13 High forest. 1891 *Eng. Mechanic* LIII. 469/2 A current of very *high frequency and a very high potential. 1893 high frequency [see Frequency 4 b]. 1896 *McClure's Mag.* VI. 414/2 A high frequency current. 1903 *Daily Chron.* 4 Mar. 7/2 High-frequency electrical apparatus. 1884 Knight *Dict. Mech.* Suppl., **High Grinding*, a process of gradual reduction of the wheat by a succession of partial crushings, alternating with sifting and sorting the product. 1894 *Outing* (U.S.) XXIV. 259/2 F. was *high hook with a five and a half pounder. 1928 *Photo-Miniature* XV. Mar. (Gloss.), **High-Key*, a style of photographic print (portrait or landscape) consisting entirely of light tones, differing little from each other in depth. 1919 *Brit. Jrnl. Photogr. Alm.* 250 Photographs consisting almost entirely of light tones are said to be high-key. 1884 Knight *Dict. Mech.* Suppl. s.v., In *high milling the velocity is low; the grinding surfaces at first remote. 1905 *Terms Forestry & Logging* 13 *High pole. 1910 W. M. Raine *B. O'Connor* 12 Here comes your train a-foggin'—also and likewise hittin' the *high spots. 1926 *Spectator* 11 Sept. 373/1 Chicago was the 'high-spot' of the trip. 1927 *Daily Express* 15 Sept. 9/5 The 'high spot' of the production—cinematic equivalent to the chariot-racing scenes in 'Ben-Hur'. 1928 *Sunday Dispatch* 22 July 13/4 It looks as though the standard of racing is going to hit the high spots. 1889 *Infantry Drill* I. i. 37 The *High Step. 1542 Boorde *Dyetary* x. (1870) 254 *Hyghe wynes, as malmyse, maye be kepte longe. 1871 *Trans. Ill. Agric. Soc.* VIII. 143 The necessity would still exist for converting..corn into beef and pork and highwines. 1884 Knight *Dict. Mech.* Suppl., *High Wines*, crude alcohol of higher proof than singlings.

22. a. *high-cost, -power, -pressure, -price, -quality, -service, -standard, -steam, -tension, -type, -wind*; **high-altitude**, occurring or carried out at high altitudes; **high-angle** *Gunnery*, denoting the low-velocity fire from guns, howitzers, and mortars at a high angle of elevation, usually that above 30°; hence *high-angle gun*, etc.; cf. *Curved fire; **high-flash**, denoting oil whose vapour ignites only at a relatively high temperature; **high-lift** (see quot.); **high-pass** (see quot.); **high-sea(s)**, operating or carried out on the high seas; *High Sea Fleet* = G. *Hochsee Flotte*; **high-velocity**, denoting a gun capable of discharging a projectile with great force and speed; also denoting the projectile so fired; **high-warp**, denoting a manner of weaving or tapestry in which the warp is vertical.

1925 E. F. Norton *Fight for Everest, 1924* 86 [They] were both suffering from very bad *high-altitude throat. *Ibid.* 106 This hateful duty of high-altitude cooking. 1879 *Man. Artill. Exerc.* I. v. 23 *High-angle fire from howitzers and mortars. 1890 G. S. Clarke *Fortification* xiv. 205 Large numbers of high-angle guns which would prove most formidable to ships. 1915 *Pearson's Mag.* XXXIX. 66 High-angle trajectory. 1928 C. F. S. Gamble *North Sea Air Station* ix. 122 The addition of some motor-cars equipped with machine-guns on 'high-angle mountings'. 1931 G. B. Ford *Building Height, Bulk & Form* Title-p., Uneconomic types of Buildings on *High-Cost land. 1899 *Westm. Gaz.* 14 Feb. 4/3 A fourth *high-flash oil. 1904 *Technol. & Sci. Dict.* (ed. Goodchild & Tweeney), *High Flash Point*, oil whose vapour is only ignited at a high temperature. 1921 *Discovery* Apr. 96/2 *High-lift wings are, of course, those that give the highest lift-drift ratio. 1930 *Selected Gloss. Motion Picture Techn.* 13 **High-pass filter*, a filter designed to pass currents of all frequencies above a critical or cut-off frequency and substantially reduce the amplitude of currents of all frequencies below this critical frequency. 1898 *Westm. Gaz.* 28 May 2/1 Modern *high-power guns. 1901 *Kynoch Jrnl.* June-July 108/2 Modern high-power smokeless propellants. 1825 J. Nicholson *Oper. Mech.* 661 The *high-pressure engines. 1872 F. W. Robinson *Wrayford's Ward* III. 207 A high-class, high-priced, high-pressure seminary. 1907 *Westm. Gaz.* 15 Oct. 1/1 The high-pressure life which he led in London. 1928 D. Brunt *Meteor.* iv. 30 These high and low-pressure systems. 1906 *Daily Chron.* 27 Sept. 3/6 The benefits of the *high-price policy which they choose to pursue. 1910 *Westm. Gaz.* 21 Apr. 12/1 Until plenty of *high-quality beet is procurable. 1913 V. B. Lewes *Oil Fuel* 180 High-quality coal-gas. 1907 *Daily Chron.* 9 Oct. 4/6 The German *high-sea fleet. 1931 *Times Lit. Suppl.* 10 Sept. 673/3 A lack of familiarity with the naval idiom can alone account..for calling..the fleet under Cornwallis 'the high seas fleet'. 1892 F. Irwin *Fortif.* (ed. 2) 43 Modern *high-velocity guns. 1898 *Engineering Mag.* XVI. 112/2 These high-velocity bullets. 1875 Knight *Dict. Mech.*, **High-warp Loom*, a tapestry loom in which the warp-frame is vertical and the weaver works standing. 1904 *Technol. & Sci. Dict.* (ed. Goodchild & Tweeney), *High Warp*, tapestry in which the warp takes a vertical position, *e.g.* Gobelins tapestry.

b. *high-banked, -bridged, -hedged, -powered*; **high-coloured**, also *fig.*, exaggerated, forced; as, *a high-coloured description*; **high-horsed** (delete † and add examples); **high-seasoned**, seasoned with a considerable amount of spice and condiments; also *fig.*

1899 *Daily News* 25 Dec. 5/2 A dangerous *high-banked river. 1871 'M. Legrand' *Cambr. Freshm.* 138 A Quixotic gentleman, of ancient lineage, in whose *high-bridged and defiant nose the Indian saw a resemblance to an eagle's beak. 1925 F. M. Ford *No More Parades* 309 There were two girls who kept a tea-shop in Poperinghe...*High coloured. 1904 *Westm. Gaz.* 3 Aug. 2/3 In the shady *high-hedged garden. 1906 Kipling in *Tribune* 15 Jan. 2/3 A high-hedged road. 1900 *Westm. Gaz.* 6 Feb. 3/2 To..ride off *high-horsed on the theory that the battle had to be fought. 1928 *Observer* 22 Jan. 14/5 The high-horsed fanatics of universal Communism. 1903 *Daily Chron.* 1 Aug. 3/7 High-priced, *high-powered cars.

B. *sb.* 1. b. An area of high barometric pressure.

1878 *Pop. Sci. Monthly* July 310 These high and low areas, or 'highs' and 'lows' as they are technically known, travel. 1900 *Yearbk. U.S. Dept. Agric.* 332 (Cent. D. Suppl.) The hot wave..seemed to join forces with the permanent high over the ocean.

c. = High School (School *sb.*1 1 j). *U.S. colloq.*

1928 *Boston Even. Transcript* 30 Mar. 15/7 I'm hardly more than a schoolboy, not so very long out of Dorchester High.

d. A high limit of price.

1928 *Weekly Dispatch* 3 June 7/2 When he buys, they buy; the lot of them can create..a new 'high' in any share which Mr. Durant fancies.

3. Also, the highest card in cutting for deal. *High-low-jack (and the game)*: = All-fours 1. (See quots.)

1680 Cotton *Compl. Gamester* (ed. 2) 79 This Game I conceive is called All-Fours from Highest, Lowest, Jack and Game, which is the Set as some play it. *Ibid.* 80 Sometimes you are highest, lowest, Jack, and Game. 1814 C. Jones *Hoyle's Games Impr.* 170 All-fours..derives its name from the four chances therein, for each of which a point is scored, namely, *high*, the best trump out; *low*, the smallest trump dealt; *jack*, the knave of trumps; *game*, the majority of pips reckoned from such of the following cards as the respective players have in their tricks; viz. every ace is counted as 4; king 3; queen 2; knave 1; and ten for 10. 1818 Todd s.v. *All-fours*, The all-four are high, low, Jack, and the game. 1895 *Funk's Stand. Dict.*, *High-low-jack*. Same as All-fours. 1898 B. Kirkby *Lakeland Words* 72 *High-low*, a card game. High-low, Jack an' t' gam. 1911 R. F. Foster *Compl. Hoyle* 328 As High, Jack, and Game are always counted by the player holding those points at the end of the play, there can be no question about them: but serious disputes sometimes arise as to who played Low...It is even possible, if there is no other trump or counting card in play, for the Jack to be High, Low, Jack, and the Game.

b. Phr. *How is that for high?*: an exclamation inviting admiration; in allusion to the card called the high in the game of high-low-jack. *U.S. colloq.*

1871 Schele de Vere *Americanisms* (1872) 326 The phrase 'How is that for high?' borrowed from a low game known as Old Sledge, where the *high* depends, not on the card itself but on the adversary's hand. Hence the phrase means, What kind of an attempt is that at a great achievement? 1887 F. Francis Jr. *Saddle & Mocassin* xviii. 315 'How's that for high, boys?' concluded the narrator, when he had told his tale. 'That's on top,' declared Black Jack; 'that takes the cake.'

High, *adv.* Add: 2. c. (U.S. example.)

1894 *Vermont Agric. Rep.* XIV. 102 Will a colt do well.. if fed high in winter?

d. Highly, strongly.

1846 Soyer *Cookery* 467 Add the beans, drain quite dry, season rather high.

3. b. Far up towards the source (on a river).

1815 *Niles' Weekly Reg.* IX. 29/1 It will probably be the last of August before Mr. G. Kennedy arrives with the Indians high upon the Missouri and Mississippi.

6. (Later U.S. example.)

1854 Mary J. Holmes *Tempest & Sunshine* xvi. 230, I s'pose I did go on high and swar like a pirate.

10. a. *high-kicking*; **high-keyed** *Mus.*, of a high pitch; also *fig.*

1906 *Daily Chron.* 18 June 6/3 Mr. P. Wilson Steer has several examples of his familiar *high-keyed method, including a not too happy portrait of himself in a grey tweed suit. 1901 *Ibid.* 11 Dec. 6/5 Several dancers of the *high-kicking and other schools.

High altar. [High *a.* 7.] The principal altar of a church.

13.. *Gaw. & Gr. Knt.* 592 So harnayst as he watz he herknez his masse, Offred and honoured at þe heȝe auter. *c* 1460 *Oseney Reg.* 137 Reynolde, By the grace of god Bisshop of Clone,..halowed the Chapell of Saunforde and the high auter. *c* 1553 in *Diary of H. Machyn* (Camd. Soc.) 399 The highe altar table. *a* 1700 Evelyn *Diary* 25 Oct. 1644, On the large high altar is a brazen vessel of admirable invention. *c* 1777 in *Cath. Rec. Soc. Publ.* VIII. 173 He lays buried in our Church at the foot of the High Altar. 1826 [see Altar 2]. 1894 C. M. Church *Chapters Early Hist. Ch. Wells* App. W. 419 High altar dedicated to St. Andrew.

Highball. Add: **high ball, high-ball.**
3. A drink of whisky and soda or other mineral water served with broken ice in a tall glass. *U.S.*

1899 G. Ade *Doc. Horne* ii. 11 Lush..drank two magnificent 'high balls'. 1902 W. P. Eaton & E. M. Underhill *Runaway Place* 128 The pleasant occupation of consuming three chocolate éclairs and a high ball. 1925 H. L. Foster *Trop. Tramp Tourists* 109 The crowd from Ohio..celebrated by drinking several highballs. 1931 Susan Glaspell *Ambrose Holt* xix, 'Never mind tea. I didn't come for tea.' 'Then I'll get you a highball.'

4. A signal to proceed, given to a locomotive driver by waving the hand above the head. Hence, a clear way, a straight course. *U.S.*

1920 Hunter *Trail Drivers of Texas* 68 We had a high ball trail from there on. *Ibid.* 354 Mr. Butler and I told them [*sc.* cowboys]..to strike a high ball to town.

High-binder. 2. (Earlier example.)

1878 *Congress. Rec.* 7 Mar. 1549/1 Refined ladies could no longer submit to be jostled at the church door by the Mongolian chiffonier, or high-binder.

3. Read: One of a number who conspire together to achieve some end in politics, business, etc. Add:

1903 A. H. Lewis *The Boss* 136 He's goin' to take copies of th' accounts that show what th' Chief an' them other high-binders at the top o' Tammany have been doin'. 1908 G. H. Lorimer *J. Spurlock* xii. 324 That's what I do mean—it [*sc.* the railroad]'s been stolen by that Bonsall bunch of high-binders. 1916 H. L. Wilson *Somewhere in Red Gap* i. 21 So I left these two lady highbinders and went on into the retail side of the Family Liquor Store.

High-boy. Add: 3. = Tallboy 2. *U.S.*

1891 *Scribner's Mag.* X. 353 In the top drawer of a high chest of drawers, a 'high boy'. 1902 L. V. Lockwood *Col. Furniture Amer.* 56 The common form of the flat-topped bandy-legged high-boy is made of cherry, maple or walnut. 1909 J. C. Lincoln *Keziah Coffin* i. 10 Removing towels, tablecloths, and the like from the drawers in a tall 'high-boy'.

Highbrow, high-brow (hai·brau), *sb.* and *a. colloq.* orig. *U.S.* [Back-formation from *High-browed *a.* 2.] A. *sb.* A person of superior intellectual attainments or interests: always with derisive implication of conscious superiority to ordinary human standards.

1911 H. S. Harrison *Queed* iv. 41 Who knew but what this little highbrow was the very man they were looking for? 1914 Gertrude Atherton *Perch of Devil* I. 41 I'll be a real high-brow in less than no time. 1921 H. Walpole *Young Enchanted* III. vi. 301 There was the theatre (so much better than the highbrows asserted), there were concerts. 1925 A. P. Herbert *Laughing Ann* 86 I'll be a high-brow, but I'll look hearty, And I won't laugh at the Liberal Party.

B. *adj.* Of, pertaining to, or characteristic of a highbrow; intellectually superior.

1916 S. Leacock in 'O. Henry' *Waifs & Strays* (1917) 161 Shakespeare, except as revived at twenty-five cents a seat with proper alterations in the text, is 'highbrow'. 1917 W. J. Locke *Red Planet* xxiv. 306 She'd die of culture in the mater's highbrow establishment. 1925 *Punch* 22 Apr. 437/2 'The programmes are too highbrow,' I maintained. 'They are hopelessly beyond the intelligence of the mass, at any rate.' 1927 Agatha Christie *Big Four* v, One of our highbrow professors.

So **Hi·ghbrowism**, the condition of being highbrow, intellectual superiority.

1921 *Glasgow Herald* 22 Jan. 4/2 This doctrine is tainted with high-browism. 1923 A. Bennett *Things that have interested me* Ser. II. 207 The audiences were artistic and earnest, with a dash of high-browism. 1930 *Observer* 2 Mar. 15 He will lure them into his theatre with stuff that, while good of its kind, is not suspect of highbrowism.

High-browed (hai·braud), *a.* [f. High *a.* + Brow *sb.*1 + -ed 2.]
1. Having a lofty forehead.

1875 *Brit. Q. Rev.* Apr. 500 One can conjure up a vision of them: the one fair, pale, high-browed. 1891 Flügel *Eng.-German Dict.*

2. = Highbrow *a.* orig. *U.S.*

1908 R. W. Chambers *Firing Line* ix, You were very much amused, I suppose—to see me sitting bras-dessus-bras-dessous with the high-browed and precious. 1909 H. G. Wells *Ann Veronica* vii. 121 Their very furniture had mysteriously a high-browed quality. *Ibid.* viii. 144 Goopes, she was sure, was always high-browed and slow and Socratic. 1916 — *Mr. Britling* II. iv. § 10, I was too high-browed about this war business. 1923 A. Bennett *Things that have interested me* Ser. II. 207 If artistic, earnest, and high-browed women only knew how to dress!

High-dutcher. *U.S.* [f. High *a.* 3 + Dutch *a.* + -er 1.] (See quot. 1889.)

1837 *Knickerbocker Mag.* IX. 289 Give me a satisfactory pair of *high-dutchers*. 1889 Farmer *Amer.*, *High Dutchers*, skates, the blades of which are ornamentally curled in front. ..The Dutch are well known as the best skaters in the world —hence the name as given to a superior kind of skate.

Higher-up. *U.S.* [High *a.* 5.] One occupying a superior position or post.

1916 C. Sandburg *Chicago Poems* 61 Higher-ups among the con men of Jerusalem. 1929 *Literary Digest* 12 Oct. 7/1 He is..insists the New York Telegram—'only the henchman of higher-ups'.

High-flyer. Add: 1. c. A variety of walnut.

1822 *Trans. Lond. Hort. Soc.* IV. 517 The Highflyer Walnut. 1824 Loudon *Encycl. Gardening* 742 Walnut...Highflyer of Thetford, the best variety known. 1866 *Treas. Bot.* 640/2 A variety called the Highflyer Walnut, is considered the best English variety. 1880 *Encycl. Brit.* XII. 278/2.

Highgate (hai·gět). [Name of a ward of London.] *Highgate resin*, copalite.

1815 Aikin *Man. Min.* (ed. 2) 64 Fossil Copal. Highgate Resin. 1883 *Encycl. Brit.* XVI. 428/2.

Hi·gh-grade, *a.* (*sb.*) [High *a.* 22 a.]
A. *adj.* Of a high grade or quality; *spec.* in stock-breeding, of more than three-quarters pure blood. b. Denoting ores rich in metal value; *spec.* in commercial use denoting those which, owing to convenience in situation and transport facilities, can be worked at a large profit.

1890 [see High *a.* 22 a]. 1902 *Daily Chron.* 10 Apr. 7/2 Great Britain is becoming very short of high-grade ores. 1907 *Springfield Republ.* 13 May 3 Advt., Auction sale of high grade household furniture. 1910 *Westm. Gaz.* 4 Jan. 5/2 The high-grade nature of the material and workmanship. 1929 *Daily Express* 7 Nov. 8/4 The high-grade private car.

B. *sb.* (*a*) High-grade stock. (*b*) See quot. 1904 and cf. the vb.

1882 *Rep. Maine Board Agric.* XXVI. 253 High-grades of either breed [Jersey or Guernsey]. 1904 *N.Y. Sun* 14 Aug. 11 One of the pests of gold mining in Colorado is the high grades, which is a polite term for the ore thief. The term high grades comes from the fact that they steal only high grade ore.

Hence **Hi·gh-grade** *v. intr.* and *trans.*, to steal high-grade ore.

1907 *Westm. Gaz.* 6 June 10/1, I had been 'high grading' in the Vindicator mine. 1923 'B. M. Bower' *Parowan Bonanza* vi. 73 He..could not leave his claims and let Al Freeman..'high grade' his gold the minute his back was turned. 1927 *Blackw. Mag.* June 833/1 In Cobalt..'high-grading' was rigorously dealt with.

High-ha·ndedly, *adv.* [f. High-handed *a.* + -ly 2.] In a high-handed manner.

1898 N. Munro *John Splendid* xxi, Seven fugitives of the clan that had come so high-handedly through their neighbourhood. 1927 *Daily Express* 26 Oct. 1/2 High-handedly putting a pistol to the heads of his opponents.

Hi·gh hat, hi·gh-hat. *U.S.* [High *a.* 1.] A tall hat; *fig.* a person of affected superiority. Also *attrib.* or as *adj.*, superior, lofty, 'swell'. Hence **High-hat** *v. intr.*, to assume a superior attitude; *trans.* to treat with an air of superiority.

1899 A. H. Quinn *Pennsylv. Stories* 39 Houston..was under strong suspicion of having worn a high hat out to college that morning. 1924 P. Marks *Plastic Age* 149 Christmas Cove's a nice place; not so high-hat as Bar Harbor. *Ibid.* 196 We're a lot of low-brows pretending to be intellectual high-hats. 1927 *Cleveland Press* 29 Jan., We see no point in assuming a high hat attitude towards what one doesn't know. 1927 *Saturday Even. Post* (N.Y.) 24 Dec. 22/3 What made me so sore..was her thinkin' she could high-hat me. 1929 C. E. Merriam *Chicago* 292 Dever's dignity was mistaken by some for 'high-hatting'. 1930 *Publishers' Weekly* 22 Mar. 1674 The shop is not 'high hat'. 1931 G. B. Stern *Shortest Night* xvi. 263 That hot-tempered young high-hat.

High-headed (stress variable), *a.* *U.S.* [High *a.* 22 b.] Carrying the head high; proud, arrogant.

1837 *Southern Lit. Messenger* III. 86 One of them high-headed Roanoke planters. 1909 R. A. Wason *Happy Hawkins* i. 10 The most obstinate, high-headed, bull-intellected thin-skin 'at ever drew down top wages fer punchin' cows.

Highland. B. *adj.* Add:
2. *Highland cattle*, a breed of small cattle from the Highlands, characterized by thick, shaggy hair and long curved horns set widely apart. *Highland fling* (see Fling *sb.* 4 a). *Highland pony*, one of a breed of ponies originating in the Highlands.

1825 Loudon *Encycl. Agric.* § 6118 Along the eastern coast, north of the Frith of Forth, the Highland cattle are intermixed with various local breeds. 1831 Youatt *Horse* iv. 59 The Highland Pony is far inferior to the galloway. 1834 — *Cattle* iii. 66 The striking peculiarities of the Highland cattle. 1844 H. Stephens *Bk. Farm* III. 1274 The West Highland has long been famed in Scotland as a superior breed of cattle. 1875 *Encycl. Brit.* I. 389/1 The Kyloes or West Highland cattle.

b. Resembling, having the characteristics of, or typical of the people of the Highlands of Scotland.

1871 L. W. M. Lockhart *Fair to See* I. ii, I'm as Highland as—as—anything. 1897 R. M. Fergusson *Village Poet* 172 They'll not jew us—we're no' sae hieland.

Highlander. Add: 1. b. *Arctic Highlander*, one of an Eskimo tribe inhabiting the north of Greenland.

1878 *Encycl. Brit.* VIII. 544/1 The Northernmost Greenlanders—the Arctic Highlanders of Ross.

2. b. Highland cattle.

1787 Marshall *Rural Econ. Norf.* (1795) II. 381 Highlanders, Scotch cattle of the Highland breed. 1825 J. C. Loudon *Encycl. Agric.* § 6122 The other variety of Highland cattle is the Norlands, or North Highlanders. 1834 Youatt *Cattle* iii. 69 There is little or no variety of breeds of cattle in the Hebrides. They are pure West Highlanders. *Ibid.* 79 The character of the Highlander must still be, that he will pay better for his quantity of food than any other breed. 1875 *Encycl. Brit.* I. 389/1 They [*sc.* the Pembrokes] excel the West Highlanders in this respect, that they make good dairy cattle, the cows being peculiarly adapted for cottagers' purposes.

Hi·gh-life, -lifed, *a.* *U.S.* [High *a.* 22 a, b.] Full of life or spirit.

1902 A. D. McFaul *Ike Glidden* ix. 70 Ike told him..to always drive on the bit, because the colt was a high-life fellow. 1861 *Trans. Ill. Agric. Soc.* IV. 376 A long narrow-headed high-lifed brainless animal.

High light, hi·gh-light. [High *a.* 10, Light *sb.* 12.]
1. In painting, photography, and cinematography, any of the brightest parts of a subject or a representation of it; often *pl.*

1668, 1859 [see Light *sb.* 12]. 1892 A. Brothers *Photog.* 335 In a portrait, if well lighted, there should be parts which are brighter than the rest of the face—on the forehead and nose, for instance; they are called *high lights*. 1903 Watkins *Watkins Man.* (ed. 2) 64 The tone D is called the 'high light', for although it is the blackest in the negative it represents white in the original. *Ibid.* 77 It may happen that there is no white part or high light in the subject you are developing. 1913 *Jas. A. Sinclair's Handbk. Photog.* (ed. 2) 226 To clear up high-lights or remove pressure marks from thick bromide papers. 1930 *Sel. Gloss. Motion Picture Technician*, *High light*, object, scene, or picture having low color saturation, that is, containing a large proportion of white. 1931 S. Selden & Sellman *Stage Scenery* 158 In order to give interest to high lights and shadows.

transf. and *fig.* 1855 *Knickerbocker Mag.* XLVI. 40 If we have chosen to speak of the shadows in the fair portrait..we have also neglected to point out the high lights. 1928 K. H. Brown *Father* vi. 61 There were artless scarlet high-lights cut from portions of the little boys' outgrown woolen underwear.

2. *fig.* A 'bright', prominent, or outstanding feature or characteristic. Chiefly *pl.*

Phr. *to hit the high lights*, to go to excess. (Cf. *high spots*, *High *a.* 21.)

1905 A. Adams *Outlet* 275 It was the recognized cattle centre of Montana..but devoid of the high-lights which were a feature of the trail towns. 1922 A. Waugh *Public School Life* i. 16 It would be filled with high lights, with breathless escapades, with impossible heroics. 1923 *Weekly Dispatch* 21 Jan. 11 There is no 'hitting the high lights' when he is not in training. 1927 *Hutchinson's Myst. Story Mag.* IX. Feb. 117 One by one, Dan and I met all the high lights of the town. 1931 *Times Lit. Suppl.* 15 Jan. 34/2 It is not readable in the sense that some modern biographies are readable; it has no 'high lights'. 1931 *Morning Post* 21 Aug. 11/7 These were the highlights of to-day's practice over the course.

High-roller. *U.S. slang.* [High *a.*, ? Roller *sb.*1 15.] One who cuts a dash or spends extravagantly.

1881 *Reinbeck* (Iowa) *Times* 15 Sept. 1/6 California's Speculators who invest large sums are called 'high rollers'. 1903 A. H. Lewis *The Boss* xiv. 184 I'd like to learn how you moral an' social high rollers reconcile yourselves to things. *a* 1909 'O. Henry' *Roads of Destiny* xx. 340 There comes a party of these high-rollers that are always hunting up new places to eat in and poke fun at.

So **High-rolling** *vbl. sb.*

1903 *New York Times* 22 Aug., High rolling with the spoils of their first venture at house looting.

High school: see School *sb.*1 1 j.

Hi·gh-speed, *a.* [High *a.* 22 a.] a. Able or fitted to work or travel at high speed. b. Produced by swift processes or machinery.

High-speed steel, an alloy steel of such toughness and hardness that it can be used for tools cutting so rapidly as to become red-hot.

1873 [see High *a.* 22 a]. 1888 *Lockwood's Dict. Mech. Engin.* s.v., High-speed engines may be considered to embrace any engines making over 200 to 300 revolutions per minute...High-speed belting applies to belts for fans, wood-working machinery, centrifugal pumps, &c., in opposition to those for line and counter, and other slowly driving shafts. *High Speed Bearings*, bearings whose length exceeds their diameter by from four to six times. 1898 *Daily News* 1 Oct. 2/8 A high-speed destroyer. 1904 *Chambers's Jrnl.* 142/1 High-speed tool-steel lathes. 1908 *Daily Chron.* 6 Feb. 3/1 The crude truths that we look for only in the high-speed camera. 1909 *Westm. Gaz.* 11 Mar. 4/2 The high-speed flier of the future. 1912 *Chambers's Jrnl.* June 367/1 Their [*sc.* British makers'] introduction of high-speed steel in 1900.

Highstrikes (hai·straiks). *jocular colloq.*, orig. *dial.* or *vulgar*. Perverted form of Hysterics.

1838 C. Seley *Jacques Strop* ii. 4 Didn't I do the *highstrikes* famously? 1846 D. Corcoran *Pickings* 149 She's one of the dreadfullest cases of the highstrikes I ever did see. 1889 *Pall Mall Mag.* Jan. 82 [Mrs.] Flounce fell into the highstrikes at traipsing the roads after four o'clock. 1914 Gertrude Atherton *Perch of Devil* I. 204 If you don't get us out of this quick I'll have high-strikes.

High-toned, *a.* 3. b. Add: Also, stylish, 'grand', 'swell'. Also used as if pass. of a trans. vb.

1888 A. C. Gunter *Mr. Potter of Texas* IV. xxiii, The Democratic Party thought Sampson Potter a more high-toned name to run for Congress than Sammy Potts. 1917 *War Birds* (1927) 34 He got hightoned by the Colonel and lost his head.

Hi·gh-up, *a.* *colloq.*, orig. *dial.* [f. High *a.* + Up *adv.*2] In a high or elevated position, high above the ground; also *fig.*, of high place or rank.

1868 Atkinson *Cleveland Gloss.* s.v., He's some desput high-up chap. 1899 S. MacManus *In Chimney Corners* 155 There was a lot of high-up folk being entertained. 1899 *Westm. Gaz.* 12 June 1/3 The gilt-edged lies of the high-up men. 1903 W. Le Queux in *Book Lover* May 3/1 In a high-up room in the Rue Lafayette. 1918 Carolyn Wells *Vicky Van* ii. 23 A high-up Publican. 1920 Hunter *Trail Drivers of Texas* 219 Our 'high up' officers were..somewhere in town.

Highveld (hai·velt). [Partial transl. of Du. *hoogveld*, lit. high plain.] The inner plateau of the subcontinent of South Africa, which is from 5,000 to 6,000 feet above sea-level.

1905 J. W. Gregory in *Rep. Brit. Assoc.* 399 The old rocks that form the foundation of the present high veldt of Rhodesia. 1906 Rider Haggard *Benita* v, They were on the Transvaal high-veld. 1907 P. Fitzpatrick *Jock of Bushveld* 223 For perhaps a week the towering bulwarks of the Highveld were visible as we toiled along.

High-water mark. Add: c. *jocular colloq.* A dirty mark showing the limit to which a person has washed.

1899 *Daily News* 31 Jan. 6/4 The high-water mark is plainly visible above a tattered scarf tied loosely round his neck.

Highway. Add: 1. c. In allusion to Matt. xxii. 9, 10, Luke xiv. 23.

1843 H. Bonar *Hymn*, '*Go labour on*' vii, Go forth into the world's highway, Compel the wanderer to come in. 1898 *Daily News* 6 Oct. 6/7 The South London officials of the Salvation Army have..been..gathering together of late from the highways and by-paths of Lambeth those who..are entitled to be ranked as 'Hooligans'. 1908 *Westm. Gaz.* 27 Jan. 1/3 It is highways and hedges work, and we shall need van for van and lecturer for lecturer.

4. *highway robbery.*

18.. (*title*) The Malefactor's Register..with trials for Bigamy, Burglary, Felony, Forgery, Highway-Robbery. 1899 *Daily News* 18 May 10/5 A good highway robbery story.

Higly-pigly, *adv.* Add: Also as *adj.*

1675 *Essex Inst. Hist. Coll.* LVI. 308 A higly pigly lot by fox iland, as it was laid out by order of the town for 3 acres, bounded by a creek.

Hijacker (hai·dʒæ·kəɹ). *U.S. slang.* Also **hi-jacker, highjacker.** An armed person who preys on bootleggers. Hence **Hi·jack** *v. trans.*, to seize (illicit liquor) for profit; **Hi·jacking** *vbl. sb.* and *ppl. a.*

1924 *Daily Mail* 22 Dec. (N.Y. Corresp.), The depredations of these Hi-Jackers have become so serious that it is understood that the skippers of some rum-runners have asked their Governments for protection. The duties of American coastguards are confined to seizing rum-ships; they cannot seize a Hi-Jacking ship unless it has pirated. 1924 F. J. Haskin *Amer. Govt.* (revised ed.) 431 Piracy and hi-jacking have developed as collateral activities of bootlegging and smuggling. 1927 Barbican *Confess. Rum-Runner* xvii, So we landed the cargo as quickly as we could, and took the chance of the cargo being seized or hijacked on shore. 1928 *Hearst's International* Aug. 72/1 Some hi-jacking exploit.

Hike (haik), *sb.* *colloq.* orig. *dial.* and *U.S.* Also †**heik.** [f. next.] A vigorous or laborious walk; a tramp or march; a walking tour or expedition undertaken for exercise or pleasure. *On hike*, on the tramp, hiking.

1865 Susan Hale *Lett.* (1919) 15 I've been engaged this week in a pecunious *heik*; to wit, getting money from the ladies of the Parish to get a new gown for Dr. Hedge. 1868 *Ibid.* 45, I ascended the Grand Pyramid, Lucretia got half-way..and Susie didn't try. It is a fearful heik. *a* 1902 *Scribner's Mag.* (Webster 1902) With every hike there's a few laid out with their hands crossed. 1903 S. E. White *Forest* ii. 18 All other utensils belong to permanent camps, or open-water cruises,—not to 'hikes' in the woods. 1907 R. W. Service *Songs of Sourdough* (1908) 59 And I burrowed a hole in the glowing coal, and I stuffed in Sam McGee. Then I made a hike, for I didn't like to hear him sizzle so. 1907 Rex Beach *Barrier* iv. (1908) 53 He's the feller that killed the gold-commissioner. Of course that put him on the hike again. 1916 H. L. Wilson *Somewhere in Red Gap* ix. 369 What's the matter with him and Lon taking a swift hike down to New York? 1921 *Outward Bound* June 10/1 Chinese Boy Scouts..on 'hike' on the veldt of South Africa. 1921 *Blackw. Mag.* Aug. 262/1 Dempsey had passed the afternoon in a 'limbering-up hike'.

Hike (haik), *v.* *colloq.* orig. *dial.* and *U.S.* Also †**hyke, heik.** [Of obscure origin. Cf. *Hoick *v.*

A possible early example of this word may be seen in the following quot.: 1736 *Applebee's Weekly Jrnl.* 17 July 2/1 Gowing..stood Centry 'till the Cargo amounted to as much as they could conveniently yike off with.]

1. *intr.* orig. To walk or march laboriously or vigorously; to tramp. In recent use, to tramp for pleasure; to go for a long walk, tramp, or walking tour.

1809 S. Wesley *Lett.* (1875) 32 Adieu for the present,—we must Contrive one more Pull at Surry before I hyke over to Staffordshire. 1825 J. Jennings *Observ. Dial. W. Eng.*, *To hike off*, to go away; to go off. Used generally in a bad sense. 1868 Susan Hale *Lett.* (1919) 39 This day we moved over to the Thebes side and were to have done Karnak..but..I was really sick with heiking. *a* 1872 J. M. Bailey *Folks at Danbury* 48 (Th.) You've got to hike around, and fling some style inter your victuals. 1884 *Daily Tel.* 2 Feb. 3/1 (Farmer) We three, not having any regler homes..hike about for a living. 1886 Susan Hale *Lett.* (1919) 157 You see the Churches can't do much, but Mr. Warner is wild to be heiking about. *a* 1902 *Scribner's Mag.* (Webster 1902) It's hike, hike, hike (march) till you stick in the mud, and then you hike back again a little slower than you went. 1904 *Chicago Evening Post* 23 Aug. 7 These girls had hiked up the dizzy trail along the face of Glacier to the summit. 1909 S. E. White *Rules of Game* III. xii, 'I'm going to hike out before breakfast,' said he before turning in, 'so if you'll just show me where the lantern is, I won't bother you in the morning'. *Ibid.* v. viii, No animal in its senses would hike uphill and then down again. 1920 *Contemp. Rev.* Sept. 341 To take stick and pack, and 'hike' away from these cities for hundreds or thousands of miles. 1926 *Glasgow Herald* 25 Aug. 8 Guides in gay girlhood will hike through the hollow. 1927 Conan Doyle *Case-bk. S. Holmes* 149, I told him I was a busy man and could not spend my life hiking round the world in search of Garridebs.

2. *trans.* To force to move or go; to convey forcibly or laboriously; to pull *on, up, over*, etc.; to 'drag' *out*. Also *fig.*

1867 Susan Hale *Lett.* (1919) 32 Our side-saddles were *heiked* on to them. 1869 *Punch* 9 Jan. 8/2 If they finds any sitch thing as a jemmy about yer,..they'll hike yer off to be tried for intendin' to commit a felony. 1870 Verney *Lettice Lisle* xxiii, I'd like to hike out the whole boiling o' um. 1886 Susan Hale *Lett.* (1919) 163 Tuesday he heiked us all forth early in the morning to the lake. 1899 *Strand Mag.* Apr. 454/1 We'll join hands end lay ourselves flat on the rock so thet you can hike your head over, and look all you want to. 1904 *Topeka Capital* 10 June 4 City Center kept the price of ice cream sodas at five cents until the State Sunday School convention struck town, and then the scale was hiked to ten cents. 1915 T. Burke *Nights in Town* 119 Two bare-armed ladies, with skirts hiked up most indelicately behind them. 1921 *Chambers's Jrnl.* Dec. 835/2, I hiked him into a taxicab. 1927 *Blackw. Mag.* July 11/1 We flitted across the road like ghosts in the moonlight, hiking our equipage, and deposited same at the door of a wooden inn. 1929 Pett Ridge *Affect. Regards, On Solitude* 117 Saw where I was paying attention..and then barged in...And apparently managed to hike me out!

absol. *a* 1902 Kipling (Webster 1902) If you persist in heaving and hiking like this.

b. *intr.* for *pass.* To be hitched or pulled *up.*

1890 *Amer. Dialect Notes* I. 61 The curtain hikes or hikes up. 1902 G. H. Lorimer *Lett. Self-made Merchant* ix. 119 We boys who couldn't walk across the floor without feeling that our pants had hiked up till they showed our feet to the knee,..didn't like him.

Hence **Hiker** (hai·kəɹ), one who hikes or goes on a hike; **Hi·king** *vbl. sb.* (also *attrib.*).

1927 *Daily Express* 24 May 3/5 We [of the Camping Club] have 3,000 members...Most of these are solitary 'hikers', who carry all their kit with them. 1930 *Times Lit. Suppl.* 11 Sept. 710/4 A special kind of traveller, belonging to the class of 'hikers'. 1931 *Daily Tel.* 21 Jan. 8/6 'Hikers' Hostels at 1s. a Night. 1931 *Times Lit. Suppl.* 7 May 368/1 The sturdy young 'heroes' who accompanied him on the hiking adventures. 1931 *Daily Tel.* 21 May 16/2 The widespread hiking movement in Germany and other Continental countries.

Hilaria (hilē·riă). [L., neut. pl. of *hilaris* Hilarious.] A Roman festival in honour of Cybele, celebrated at the vernal equinox.

1738 Chambers *Cycl.*, The *Hilaria* were solemnized with great pomp, and rejoicing. 1842 W. Smith *Dict. Gr. & Roman Antiq.* 482/2 The hilaria were..either private or public. Among the former..the day on which a person married, and on which a son was born; among the latter, those days of public rejoicings appointed by a new emperor. 1907 L. R. Farnell *Cults Grk. States* III. 301 The Attis-festival of the Hilaria.

Hill, *sb.* Add:
1. b. *Hill and dale*: also, applied to any markings or groovings likened to hills and dales; *spec.* used *attrib.* to denote that manner of making gramophone records, or the records themselves, in which the undulations are cut in a vertical plane by the recording stylus.

1918 in Webster Addenda. 1929 P. Wilson & G. W. Webb *Mod. Gramophones* ii. 34 This form of record has several advantages over the hill-and-dale cut. 1931 *News Chron.* 20 Mar. 15/2 A graph, whose hills and dales represent maximum and minimum velocity of each of a series of strokes.

3. b. Also, the cluster of plants on level ground. *U.S.*

1884 H. Butterworth *Zigzag Journ. Western States* 42 Jerry was working like a beaver, and only three hills of potatoes to the square now.

d. *Her.* A charge representing a hill, usually vert.

1828 Berry *Encycl. Her.* I. 1889 Elvin *Dict. Her.* p. lii, Three Hills, as in the arms of Brinckman.

e. A nitro-glycerine factory.

1897 *Pearson's Mag.* IV. 250/2 You have now reached the bottom of the 'hill'—all nitro-glycerine factories are called 'hills'. 1921 *Dict. Occup. Terms* (1927) § 149 *Nitroglycerine hillman*, an explosive worker engaged on repetition work in nitroglycerine manufacture.

4. a. *hill-slope*; **hill-set** *a.* (after Matt. v. 14), 'set' or situated on a hill.

1906 *Westm. Gaz.* 16 June 12/2 Brown-roofed, *hill-set villages. 1906 *Macm. Mag.* July 695 Ruler of his tiny hill-set principality. 1907 *Westm. Gaz.* 9 Aug. 2/4 Our hillset house of prayer. 1872 Tennyson *Gareth & Lynette* 181 The damp *hill-slopes. 1908 *Daily Chron.* 14 May 5/4 On the north side of the valley the hill-slopes are fairly open.

c. Also, pertaining to the rearing and tending of sheep in hilly country.

1841 *Penny Cycl.* XXI. 358/1 The average weight of the fleece..is now at least 3lbs. in the hill-sheep, and nearly 4lbs. in the lowland-sheep. 1886 C. Scott *Sheep-farming* 101 Hill farms...Hill stocks should always be fixtures on the farm. *Ibid.* 103 Hill sheep farming. *Ibid.* 116 A successful hill lambing depends very much upon..the condition of the ewes at that period. Hill ewes are never in too high condition. *Ibid.* 123 The science of hill-herding.

f. **hill-climb**, the action of climbing hills, esp. as a test for motor vehicles; so **hill-climbing**, also *attrib.*; **hill-engraver**, in map-making, one who makes the representations of elevations on an engraved plate; so **hill-engraving**; **hill-map**, a map showing elevations; **hill-spur** (see Spur *sb.*1 11).

1905 *Westm. Gaz.* 6 June 4/2 At the *hill-climb on May 27. 1907 *Ibid.* 26 Feb. 4/2 The club will organise competitions, hill-climbs, club-runs, and so on. 1632 Shirley *Hide Parke* IV. (1637) G 2, *Hill climbing white-rose, praise doth not lacke. 1861 [see Dict. 4 e]. 1904 *Peel Guardian & Chron.* 23 Apr., The venue of the hill-climbing contest has not been fixed. 1908 *Westm. Gaz.* 19 Mar. 4/1 Its smooth and faultless running and wonderful hill-climbing abilities. 1900 *Geog. Jrnl.* (R.G.S.) June 589 The employment of *hill-engravers, who are, as already stated, so much required for the completion of the *hill-engraving of the 1-inch map. *Ibid.* 578 Progress of the 1-inch *Hill Map of the United Kingdom. 1871 W. Morris in Mackail *Life* (1899) I. 253, I went about looking for game about the *hill spurs. 1887 Meredith *Ballads & P.* 88 Down the hillspurs.

Hillangsite (hi·lăŋzəit). *Min.* [f. the *Hillång* mine, Dalarne, Sweden + -ite 1.] A variety of amphibole, closely related to dannemorite.

1892 E. S. Dana *Dana's Min.* (ed. 6) 391.

Hi·ll-bi·lly. *U.S.* [f. Hill *sb.* 4 + Billy 1 2.] A rustic mountaineer. Also *attrib.*

1904 Harben *Georgians* ix. 87 Come listen to me, you lazy hill-billies. 1907 *New York Even. Post* (semi-weekly ed.) 31 Jan. 6 The long submerged whites [in Alabama], the 'crackers' and the 'hill-billies'. 1911 *New York Sun* 10 Aug. (Funk) These too were farmers' boys and hillbillies and jayhawkers. 1932 *Radio Times* 15 July 120/3 Hill-Billy songs are the folk-tunes of the American ranches and backwoods.

Hi·ll-cou·ntry. [Hill *sb.* 4.] A district composed of hills or elevated ground.

1582 [see Hill *sb.* 4]. 1816 U. Brown *Jrnl.* in *Maryland Hist. Mag.* X. 283 A handsome hill country in a good state of cultivation. 1865 Mrs. Whitney *Gayworthys* xv. 133 The slow, ponderous vehicle went..creaking on, up into the hill-country. 1875 [see Hill *sb.* 4].

Hilling, *vbl. sb.*2 (Later U.S. examples.)

1814 J. Taylor *Arator* 233 How often he had passed over the land..in fallowing, hilling, cutting off hills, planting, replantings. 1833 B. Silliman *Man. Sugar Cane* 17 It is advisable not to plough deep, especially for the last hoeing or hilling. 1887 *Harper's Mag.* Jan. 306/1 There is a broad hilling up so as to have a slope inward toward the plants as well as away from them.

b. *attrib.* with *hoe.*

1639 *Maryland Archives* 80 A hilling hoe. 1703 *Col. Rec. N. Carolina* I. 579 Two weeding hoes, one hilling hoe. 1785 Washington *Diaries* II. 438 Hilling Hoes helved. 1814 J. Taylor *Arator* 104 The instrument is precisely a hilling-hoe except that three strong square iron prongs are substituted for the blade.

Hill-side. *attrib.* (Earlier U.S. examples.)

1806 in *Ann. 9th Congress* 2 Sess. 1006 Although it imposes a heavy task of hill-side digging. 1849 *Rep. U.S. Comm. Patents* (1850) 280 Improvement in Hill-side ploughs.

Hilo 1 (hi·lo). [Sp., = thread :—L. *filum.*] A small vein of ore.

1860 *Eng. & Foreign Mining Gloss.* (ed. 2) 104.

Hilo 2 (hi·lo). [Hawaiian.] *Hilo grass*, a large and coarse grass, *Paspalum conjugatum.*

1915 W. A. Bryan *Nat. Hist. Hawaii* 208 The well known and generally despised Hilo grass, occurs in moist, heavy soils in the lower zone. 1917 *Nature* 20 Sept. 57/2 In the moister portions of the islands large areas have been occupied by Hilo grass.

Himalayan. 1. Add: **Himalayan Black Bear**, *Ursus torquatus.* **Himalayan Oak.**

1869 A. A. A. Kinloch *Large Game Shooting* I. 49 The Himalayan Black Bear is pretty generally distributed throughout the Himalayas. 1884 *Encycl. Brit.* XVII. 341/1 (Nepal) The Himalayan black bear (*Ursus tibetanus*). 1876 C. F. Gordon Cumming *From Hebrides to Himalayas* II. 143 Of the Himalayan oak there are three varieties, all evergreen. 1880 F. N. Macnamara *Himalayan India* 399 Forest..chiefly composed of pines, Himalayan oak, and rhododendron.

Himalo- (himā·lo), used as combining form of the *Himalayas*, as in *Himalo-Chinese* adj.

1873 Elwes in *Proc. Zool. Soc.* 654 Himalayan or Himalo-Chinese Subregion.

Hinau (hi·nau). Also **hino(u).** [Maori.] An evergreen tree of New Zealand, *Elæocarpus dentatus*; the wood of this tree. Also *attrib.*

1845 E. J. Wakefield *Adv. N.Z.* II. 246 The *totara*, the *mai*, and the *hinau*, were found to work up into very handsome side-boards, tables, and book-shelves. 1859 A. S. Thomson *Story N.Z.* I. 156 The hinau berries are generally steeped for several days in a running stream...Hinau cakes are much esteemed. 1866 *Treas. Bot.*, *Hinau*, or *Hino*, *Elæocarpus Hinau*, the bark of which is used for dyeing in New Zealand. 1883 J. Hector *Handbk. N.Z.* 130 (Morris) Hinau, a small tree about fifty feet high and eighteen inches thick in stem, with brown bark which yields a permanent blue-black dye, used for tanning.

Hinayana (hīnăyā·nă). [Skr., f. *hīna* lesser, little + *yāna* vehicle.] The Buddhism of southern India, distinguished from the northern or Mahayana (Great Vehicle) Buddhism, the difference in doctrine being that the Hinayana Buddhists believe that salvation is confined to a small minority, while the Mahayana sect hold it to be open to all.

1877 T. W. Rhys Davids *Buddhism* viii. 1881 *Encycl. Brit.* XIV. 229/1 These volumes [*sc.* the Kandjur] contain about a dozen works of the oldest school of Buddhism, the Hinayâna.

Hind, *a.* Add: c. *To get on one's hind legs*: see Leg *sb.* 2 c. *To talk the hind legs off a donkey*, etc.: see *Talk *v.*

5. as *sb. pl.* *Hinders* = hind-quarters. *colloq.*

1891 Miss Dowie *Girl in Karp.* xiii. 173 The painter spread his coat upon the hinders of the second horse.

Hind-sight. Add: 1. b. *To knock* (or *kick*) *the hindsight out* or *off*: to dispose of or demolish completely. *U.S. colloq.*

1834 W. A. Carruthers *Kentuckian in N.Y.* I. 21 As sure as you saw the fire at the muzzle of his gun, so sure he knocked the creter's hind sight out. 1850 L. H. Garrard *Wah-To-Yah* xx. (1927) 248 They backed their ears preparatory to kicking the hindsights off the first man that struck them. 1871 E. Eggleston *Hoosier Schoolm.* x. 58 Ef its rendered right, it'll knock the hind sights off of any rheumatiz you ever see. 1892 *Congress. Rec.* 1 Apr. 2843/1 The American producer..can knock the hindsights off the producer anywhere else on the face of the earth.

Hinge, *sb.* Add: 1. d. *transf.* Something resembling a hinge in position or shape.

1902 D. G. Hogarth *Nearer East* 43 This hollow Spine between Ararat and Bingiol may be called the hinge of the west Asian relief.

Hino(u, variant ff. *Hinau.

Hint, *v.* Add: 1. c. With sentence as object.

1843 Dickens *Christmas Carol* iii, 'I'm sure he is very rich, Fred,' hinted Scrooge's niece. 1891 Clo. Graves *Field of Tares* 41, 'I have been a stranger to the neighborhood,' returned the other, 'for years.' 'Many years?' hinted Mr. Brinnilow.

2. b. With other constructions; also *absol.*

1865 *Punch* 21 Jan. 32 If I wos allowed to 'int, Ladies, I shud say, Torse Hup! 1891 Hardy *Group of Noble Dames*, *Barbara Ho. Grebe* 77 Her husband's tutor was found to hint very strongly against such a step. 1894 Du Maurier *Trilby* VII. III. 178 The night above was dark, but 'star-dials hinted of morn'.

Hinterland. Add: Also *transf.*

1919 Bradby *Psycho-anal.* (1920) 75 Unexplored territories full of mystery and danger in the hinterland of their own minds. *Ibid.* 251 The individual who is introduced to the 'hinterland' of his own conscious being.

Hiortdahlite (hyǭ·ɹtdāləit). *Min.* [Named *hiortdahlit*, 1890, after T. *Hiortdahl*, a Norwegian scientist: see -ite 1.] A rare mineral, essentially a silicate of zirconium, of sodium, and calcium, found in pale-yellow triclinic crystals.

1892 E. S. Dana *Dana's Min.* (ed. 6) 377 Hiortdahlite.. occurs sparingly imbedded in feldspar. 1902 H. A. Miers *Min.* 558/3.

Hip, *sb.*1 4. b. Add: **hip-flask**, a flask for intoxicating liquor carried in a hip-pocket; **hip-length** *a.*, denoting a garment which reaches down to the hips; **hip-yoke**, in dressmaking, a shaped piece extending from the waist to the hips, designed to fit the figure closely without gathers.

1923 Eliz. Marbury *My Crystal Ball* lxxi. 352 Let these same people frequent ballrooms..and they will find the *hip flasks in evidence and the consequent conditions a sorry spectacle. 1928 *Sunday Dispatch* 2 Sept. 7/1 [American *loq.*] We have become a people who think 'likker', talk it,

Supplement, p. 3873; Corrigenda, p. 4092; Spurious words, p. 4093; Books quoted, p. 4094

and lead a hip-flask life! 1931 *Daily Express* 18 Mar. 5/3 *Hip-length coats. 1931 *Daily Tel.* 21 May 6/4 Small gathers at each side of the *hip yoke in front.

Hip, *v.*[2] Add: **4.** To carry on the hip. *U.S.*
1824 'A. Singleton' *Lett. fr. South & West* 93 Some mothers here [*sc.* in Kentucky] hip their infants, as do the Sumatrans. 1843 R. Carlton *New Purchase* xx. 191 Still oftener each [log] is hipped and hipping is done by one man ..who adroitly whips up the log on his hip.

Hipe, *sb.*[1] Also **hype**. Add quots. illustrating various kinds of hipes, as *left leg hipe*, *right leg hipe*, *swinging hipe*, etc.
1868 S. Gilpin & J. Robinson *Wrestling* 178 (Cumbld. Gloss.) There are two forms of the hipe, the 'standing' and the 'swinging'; this last consists of a quick swing off the breast once round, or nearly so, and then a turn over the knee inside the thigh. 1888 *Encycl. Brit.* XXIV. 690–1 The 'left leg hipe'..consists in lifting and swinging him [*sc.* one's adversary] round to the right, then striking the inside of his right thigh with the outside of the left thigh, by which he gets off his balance and falls; the 'right leg hipe' is the same action *mutatis mutandis*. 1893 *Carlisle Patriot* 26 May 3/3 (Cumbld. Gloss.) In the third round S—— threw M—— after a tight bout with the inside hipe. In the next tussle J—— passed S—— by means of the outside hipe. 1893 Robinson & Gilpin *Wrestling* 56 Robley..has been credited with being the first introducer of the swinging hype.
So **Hi·per**, one who uses the hipe in wrestling.
1823 W. Litt *Wrestliana* 168 As a hiper, he is certainly the quickest and best on the list.

Hipe (həip), *sb.*[2] *Army slang.* [From the word (*h*)*ipe*, the substitute commonly used for the word *arms* in such commands as 'Slope arms!'] A rifle.
1917 P. MacGill *Brown Brethren* vi. 89 He seemed to have lost all interest in his best friend, his "'ipe'. *Ibid.* xii. 173 The sun's catchin' the sniper's 'ipe. 1927 D. B. Wyndham Lewis *On Straw* 59 Brass-Hats rich and ripe Clicked their heels together, Sloped the Army's hipe.

Hipparaffin (hipæ·răfin). *Chem.* [f. Hip(puric + Paraffin *sb.*] A colourless crystalline compound, $CH_2(NHCOC_6H_5)_2$, formed by the oxidation of hippuric acid or from methylal and benzonitrile; called also *methylene-dibenzamide*.
1879 *Jrnl. Chem. Soc.* XXXVI. 650 Hipparaffin is obtained by the action of lead peroxide on hippuric acid in presence of excess of sulphuric or nitric acid.

Hippeastrum (hipĭæ·strǒm). *Bot.* [mod.L., f. Gr. ἱππεύς horseman, knight + ἄστρον star.] A plant of the tropical American amaryllidaceous genus so named; the knight's star lily.
1899 *Daily News* 16 Mar. 9/2 An immense stand of hippeastrums..carried off the palm in the shape of the society's gold medal. 1908 *Daily Chron.* 15 Apr. 6/3 Rich crimson Hippeastrums.

Hipped, *a.*[1] **2.** (Earlier U.S. example.)
1771 H. Pelham in *Copley-Pelham Lett.* (1914) 122 The Expense is not at all adequate to the looks of a hipped Roof upon the upper House.

Hipped, *a.*[3] *U.S. slang.* [? A use of Hipped *a.*[2]] Fond of, 'bitten with'.
1927 *Daily Express* 24 Oct. 8 'New York', as the manager of one of the largest hotels remarked lately, 'is badly "hipped" on dining in public.' 1927 *Hollis St. Theatre Progr.* (Boston U.S.) 19 Sept., Gloss.

Hippety (hi·pěti). Also **-ity**. Jingling combination of Hip *v.*[1] and Hop *v.*, as in *hippety-hop*, *hippety-hoppety*.
1825 Jennings *Observ. Dial. w. Eng.* 45 *Hippety-hoppety*, *adv.*, in a limping and hobbling manner. 1880 *West Cornwall Gloss.* s.v., 'He goes hippety-hoppety' (walks unevenly). 1886 Elworthy *W. Somerset Word-bk.*, *Hippety-hop*, *hippety-hoppety*.., lame, limping in a very marked manner: applied to both man and beast. 1920 *Cornhill Mag.* Sept. 332 A row of children playing hippety-hop across a broad lawn.

Hippo-. Add: **Hi:ppocoproste·rol**, **Hippome·lanin** *Chem.* (see quots.). **Hippo-fly**, a tabanid gad-fly found in swampy parts of equatorial Africa. **Hippoti·grine** *a.*, of or pertaining to the genus *Hippotigris* of striped African equids, such as the zebra and quagga. **Hippo·tragine** *a.*, of, pertaining to, or having the characters of the genus *Hippotragus* or subfamily *Hippotraginæ* of the family *Bovidæ*.
1897 *Jrnl. Chem. Soc.* LXXII. i. 183 *Hippocoprosterol, $C_{27}H_{54}O$ or $C_{27}H_{52}O$, is obtained from the fæces of the horse. 1907 *Ibid.* XCII. ii. 797 *Hippomelanin, the pigment of melanotic tumours of lymph glands in horses. 1901 *Geog. Jrnl.* (R.G.S.) July 75 The large biting fly called the "hippo" fly was a great annoyance. 1875 *Encycl. Brit.* I. 259/1 Of wild horses the asinine group is characteristic of Asia, and the *hippotigrine of Africa. 1891 Flower & Lydekker *Mammals* 342 *Hippotragine Section.—Includes very large African Antelopes, with long horns.

Hippoboscid (hipǫbǫ·sid), *a.* and *sb.* [f. mod. L. *Hippoboscidæ*, f. Hippo- + Gr. βόσκειν to feed: see -id[2].] Of or pertaining to, a member of, the family *Hippoboscidæ* of blood-sucking dipterous insects parasitic on mammals and birds.
1909 *Cent. Dict.* Suppl. 1920 *Q. Rev.* July 91 Tsetse-flies.. are the nearest living relations of the Hippoboscid family.

Hippomobile (hi·pomoubīl). (*Disused.*) [f. Hippo- + Mobile *a.*] A word used in the early days of motor vehicles for a horse-drawn vehicle. So **Hippomo·bilism**, the use of a hippomobile.
1904 in A. B. F. Young *Complete Motorist* xiii. (ed. 2) 275 A hippo-mobile was despatched. 1904 *Westm. Gaz.* 15 Nov. 4/2 A motor-van..would certainly do the journey more quickly..and presumably such a vehicle will supersede the hippomobile in time. 1905 *Ibid.* 20 June 4/2 How much longer, motorists may be tempted to ask, is such a dangerous mode of locomotion as the hippomobile to be tolerated? 1908 *Daily Chron.* 16 Jan. 4/4 Hippomobilism was out of the question.

Hi·ppodroming, *vbl. sb.* (See Hippodrome *sb.* 2 and *v.*)
1868 H. Woodruff *Trotting Horse Amer.* xxxv. 288 An agreement was entered into by means of which the former and Lancet travelled together, trot for purses and divide the profits. It was a new sort of thing, and was..called 'Hippodroming'.

Hippus (hi·pǒs). *Path.* [mod.L., f. Gr. ἵππος horse.] Tremor of the iris; a morbid condition characterized by rapid contraction and dilatation of the pupil.
1738 Chambers *Cycl.* 1848 Dunglison *Med. Lex.* (ed. 7). 1889 *Buck's Handbk. Med. Sci.* VII. 59/2 Tonic contraction of the pupil of the eye is called *myosis spastica*; clonic contraction *hippus*. 1910 *Allbutt's Syst. Med.* VIII. 536 The following alterations of the pupils are comparatively common in chorea—hippus,..contraction, inequality, and eccentric pupils.

Hirado (hirā·do). Also **-ato**. The name of an island off the west coast of the province of Hizen in Japan used *attrib.* to designate a rich blue-and-white porcelain.
1880 A. W. Franks *Jap. Pottery* 96 The works were established..in accordance with the order of a prince of the Matsu-ura family residing at Hirato. Hence the articles made here are generally called Hirato ware. 1881 Audsley & Bowes *Keramic Art Japan* 154 The productions of this kiln have commonly been called Hirado ware.

Hiragana (hirăgā·nă). Also **-kana**. [Jap., f. *hira* plain + *kana* (*kari-na*) borrowed names.] The cursive form of Japanese writing, consisting of abbreviated forms of common Chinese ideographs.
1863 *Chambers's Encycl.* V. 687/1 The phonetic alphabet, invented about the year 810 A.D., is known as the Hiragana form of character. 1880 *Encycl. Brit.* XIII. 585/1 Each character may be written in either the *katakana* or the *hiragana* style. 1883 I. Taylor *Alphabet* I. 35 The Hirakana syllabary was derived from a cursive form of the Chinese writing called the Tsau or 'grass' character.

Hire, *v.* **2.** Add: Also *absol.*
1877 A. Sewell *Black Beauty* xxxi, He determined to give up keeping a horse, and to hire when he wanted one.
3. b. *To hire out* U.S. (Earlier example.)
1833 C. A. Davis *Lett. J. Downing* (1834) 35, I had hired out here this summer.

Hirmologion (hǝ̄ɹmǫlōu·dʒiǫn). Pl. **-ia**. [med. Gr. εἱρμολόγιον or f. εἱρμός (see next) + λογ-, variant of λεγ- to say.] In the Eastern Church, a book containing eucharistic prayers, hirmoi, etc.
1850 Neale *Eastern Church, Gen. Introd.* I. 890.

Hirmos (hǝ̄·ɹmǫs). Also **hirmus**. Pl. **-moi**, **-mi**. [Gr. εἱρμός series, connexion.] In the hymnology of the Eastern Church, a model stanza forming a pattern for the other stanzas.
1850 Neale *Eastern Church, Gen. Introd.* I. 830 *note*, There are a certain number of *Troparia*..called Hirmoi, on the model of which all other troparia, etc., are formed. *Ibid.* 835 *note*, Here we have the actual hirmos on which the third ode is arranged. 1863 R. F. Littledale *Offices East. Ch.* 214. 1880 *Encycl. Brit.* XII. 580/1 An *ode* is a song or hymn compounded of several similar 'troparia'.. To these is always prefixed a typical or standard 'troparion', called the *hirmus*.

Hirsel, *sb.* Add:
1. c. The ground occupied by a flock of sheep.
1822 Scott *Nigel* xxvi, Being in a strange country, like a poor lamb that has wandered from its ain native hirsel. 1856 Morton *Cycl. Agric.* II. 723/2. 1886 C. Scott *Sheep-farming* 122 He will be able to divide the hill into 'hirsels', and the hirsel again into 'cuts'. 1922 *Glasgow Herald* 16 Dec. 4 There they are fed for days..till the hirsels are green again.

Hirudin (hirŭ·din). *Chem.* [f. L. *hirūdo* leech + -in[1].] The active principle extracted from leeches.
1905 *Jrnl. Chem. Soc.* LXXXVIII. ii. 339 The substance named hirudin separated from leech extract has a very variable activity. 1908 *Practitioner* Apr. 463 Coagulation is prevented by the use of 'hirudin'.

Hislopite (hi·zlǫpəit). *Min.* [f. the name of Rev. S. *Hislop* + -ite[1].] A grass-green variety of calcite from India.
1859 S. Haughton in *Phil. Mag.* Ser. iv. XVII. 16.

Hispa (hi·spă). *Ent.* [mod.L., f. L. *hispidus* bristly, hairy.] A beetle of the genus so named.
1794 Nemnich *Naturgeschichte* III. 165. 1862 T. W. Harris *Insects Injur. Veget.* (ed. 3) 120 The Hispas, little leaf-beetles, forming the family *Hispadæ*. 1889 E. C. Cotes in *Notes Indian Insect Pests* 37 The Bengal Rice Hispa. *Ibid.* 39 The Rice Hispa.

Hispano-. Add: **Hi·spano-Go·thic** *a.*, Spanish and Gothic. **Hi·spanophil**, a lover of Spain and Spanish culture.
1847 tr. *Bouterwek's Hist. Span. Lit.* 4 The nobles, who were of French or Hispano-Gothic origin. [1906 *Daily Chron.* 19 May 3/2 A Hispanofilo to the core.] 1909 *Ibid.* 18 Nov. 1/3 The eighteen-carat gold casket presented to the King of Portugal..is oblong in shape and in the Hispano Gothic style. 1910 *Ibid.* 4 Jan. 3/1 The true Hispanophil with the cult in his veins. 1920 *Glasgow Herald* 25 Nov. 6 All good British Hispanophils.

Hisperic (hispe·rik), *a.* [ad. med. L. *Hisperica* (see def.). Cf. G. *hisperisch*.] Epithet of a variety of mediæval Latin, of which *Hisperica Famina* (probably of the 6th century) is a notable example, characterized by a highly artificial vocabulary of which the use of borrowed words of Hebrew, Greek, and other origin, is a salient feature.
1904 W. P. Ker *Dark Ages* 35 *note*, The 'Hisperic' vocabulary, which is that of Apuleius, Florus, Martianus Capella, exaggerated out of all measure. 1907 *Cambr. Hist. Engl. Lit.* I. 69 The hymn..known as *Altus prosator* contains very marked specimens of Hisperic Latinity. 1931 E. J. Jones *Hist. Educ. Wales* I. 179 Hisperic words are included in the Anglo-Saxon glossaries of the tenth century.

Histamine (hi·stămīn). *Physiol. Chem.* [f. Gr. ἱστός web, tissue + Amine.] A base derived from the intestinal mucous membrane.
1913 *Jrnl. Chem. Soc.* CIV. i. 681 Histamine..is a base which Barger and Dale separated from the intestinal mucous membrane...In minute doses it is fatal to rabbits. 1920 *Nature* 4 Mar. 11/2 A compound of known chemical structure, called 'histamine',..which is able to produce a state of the circulation like that present in wound-shock. 1929 *Times* 28 Oct. 15/3 These products produce what is spoken of as 'histamine poisoning', the substance histamine being the principal toxic agent.

Hister (hi·stəɹ). [mod.L. use of L. *hister* = *histrio* actor.] A beetle of the genus so named of the family *Histeridæ* of clavicorn coleoptera. Also **Hi·sterid** *a.*, belonging to this family; *sb.*, a beetle of this family.
1839 J. O. Westwood *Class. Insects* I. 182 Cadet de Vaux, in his *History of the Mole*, observes that, almost as soon as it is dead, it is attacked by a number of Histers. 1874 J. G. Wood *Insects Abroad* 89 The Giant Hister. 1915 W. A. Bryan *Nat. Hist. Hawaii* 417 The histerid beetles. 1925 A. D. Imms *Text-Bk. Entom.* 483 Hister and its allies frequent dung and carrion.

Histidine (hi·stidīn). *Physiol. Chem.* [ad. G. *histidin*, f. Gr. ἱστίον tissue: see -id[2] and -ine[5].] A crystalline base, $C_6H_9O_2N_3$, formed as a cleavage product of the proteids and protamines.
1896 *Jrnl. Chem. Soc.* LXX. i. 582 The sulphate from.. sturgeon sperm has rather different solubilities in sodium chloride solutions, and the name salmine and sturine are suggested by the two protamines. By decomposing the latter base with sulphuric acid, a new crystalline base was prepared, which is called *histidine*. 1919 *Nature* CIV. 322/2 The diamino-acids lysin, histidin, and arginin.

Histo-. Add: **Histocla·stic** *a.*, destroying or breaking down tissue (Dorland, 1913). **Histo·genous** *a.*, formed by the tissues. **Hi·stogram**, a form of graph employed in statistics. **Hi:stohæmato·genous** *a.*, formed from the tissues and the blood. **Hi:stometa·basis**, a state of complete fossilization which has occurred in such a way that the minute markings of grain and texture are preserved. **Hi:stopatholo·gic**, **-ical** *adjs.*, pertaining to diseased tissues in plants or animals. **Hi:stopatho·logy**, the study of diseased tissues. **Histothe·rapy**, the treatment of disease by the application of animal tissues (Dorland, 1906).
1907 *Practitioner* Sept. 455 The *Histogenous Cells which originate locally as the result of local tissue proliferation. 1903 *Nature* 17 Dec. 149/2 We should like to protest against any such crude process of determining goodness of fit as that of placing a normal curve down on seven or eight blocks forming a "*histogram' and judging the look of the fit. 1927 Carr-Saunders & Jones *Soc. Struct. Eng. & Wales* 210 We believe that we should be led to construct histograms not unlike the above if we could measure in the population at large the distribution of power of resistance to disease, of vivacity, of power of concentration, or of any other physical or mental character. 1907 *Practitioner* Sept. 456 *Histohaematogenous leucocytes. 1892 C. A. White in *Smithsonian Rep.* 264 The term *histometabasis is applied to that condition of fossilization in which an entire exchange of the original substance for another has occurred in such a manner as to retain or reproduce the minute and even the microscopic texture of the original. 1927 R. S. Lull *Org. Evol.* xxv. 412 The resultant fossil retains..not only the external form but the histologic characters (histometabasis,..) of the original structure as well. 1903 *Detroit Med. Jrnl.* Feb. 705 (Cent. D. Suppl.) The *histopathologic states of the finer structures of the labyrinth. 1896 N. Walker tr. P. G. Unna (*title*) The *Histopathology of the Diseases of the Skin. 1908 *Practitioner* Jan. 27 The histo-pathology of the lesions.

Histone (hi·stoun). *Physiol. Chem.* Also **-on**. [ad. G. *histon*, f. Gr. ἱστάναι to stay: see -one.] An albumen derived from the nuclei of cells, having the property of preventing the coagulation of the blood of a living animal.
1885 *Jrnl. Chem. Soc.* XLVIII. i. 572. 1905 C. E. Simon *Physiol. Chem.* (ed. 2) 194 The protamins are decomposed entirely like the albumoses and peptones, while the histons are only affected in part, which coincides with the position which the histons occupy midway between the protamins and the true albumins.

Historical, *a.* Add:
2. d. Related to or connected with history; considered from the historian's point of view; belonging to the past.

Historico-. Add further examples.
1900 W. A. Ellis *Life Wagner* I. 225, I was wafted by the image of a great historico-political event. 1905 *Daily Chron.* 20 June 3/3 Pursuing his fascinating historico-biographic method, which gives to criticism the movement and charm of narrative. 1931 *Times Lit. Suppl.* 26 Mar. 242/2 To study the Alsatian question from a historico-psychological standpoint.

History. Add: **4. c.** *To make history*: to influence or guide the course of history; also, to do something spectacular or worthy of remembrance (see *history-maker*, *-making*, sense 9 in Dict.).
1907 *Edin. Rev.* Jan. 4 The average man is of the Centre; and history in the long run is made by the average man. 1915 Ian Hay *First Hundred Thou.* xx. 311 We shall have a chance of making history over this, old man.

Hit, *v.* Add: **1. c.** *Baseball.* (See quot. 1906.)
1904 R. H. Barbour *Sch. & Coll. Sports, Baseball* 188 *Team batting*. The best-known example of this is what is called the sacrifice hit or 'hit-and-run'. *Ibid.* 191 The 'hit-and-run' play may also be used when there is a man on third and a run is badly needed. 1906 H. Chadwick *Spalding's Base Ball Guide* 134 *Hit and Run*. This is a term applicable to a point of play in the game in which a combination of team work at the bat and brainy base-running is brought into play with telling effect.
4. b. To strike exactly or at the proper point. Usually in phr. *to hit on* so many *cylinders*: (of an internal-combustion engine) to be running properly on so many cylinders; hence, *to be hitting on all four* or *six cylinders*, to be running or working perfectly; *fig.* to be in good trim or form.
1912 C. Mathewson *Pitching in a Pinch* xii. 269 So the best infielder takes time to fit into the infield of a Big League club and have it hit on all four cylinders again. 1928 *Saturday Even. Post* 10 Mar. 127/1 Modern science offers you a natural means to keep you 'hitting on all six'—every minute of the day.
8. c. To occur to (a person); to affect in a particular way, to appear to.
1914 Gertrude Atherton *Perch of Devil* I. xxx. 175 Lucky it hit him to buy the house and send that last five thousand. 1916 'B. M. Bower' *Phantom Herd* v. 68, I wanted to see how it would hit you.
d. *To hit at*: to criticize, make fun of or ridicule (a person or thing).
1843 *Punch* 23 Sept. 131/2 Instead of an outburst of enthusiasm at the line 'Confound their politics', the waltzer is supposed to execute a *pirouette*, which is supposed to hit at our wavering propensities.
11. Freq. in modern U.S. colloquial use in the sense 'to arrive at'; also, to go to (a place), go upon (a course). *To hit the pike, trail*, etc.: to take the road, to travel.
1888 *Detroit Free Press* Oct. (Farmer) Professor Rose, who hit this town last spring, is around calling us a fugitive from justice. 1889 Barrère & Leland *Dict. Slang*, *Hit the flat, to* (cowboys), to go out on the prairies. 1896 G. Ade *Artie* xiv. 127 'A little more weather like this and we'll be hittin' the park,' he observed. 1901 S. E. White *Westerners* i. 7 Thought you wasn't no tenderfoot. Ever hit the trail? 1904 *Hartford Courant* 25 June 6 The..convention, whose delegates were so summarily ordered to hit the pike by the national committee-men. 1907 R. W. Service *Songs of Sourdough* (1908) 65 It lies with thee—the choice is thine, is thine, To hit the ties or drive thy auto-car. 1918 Mulford *Man fr. Bar-20* xiii. 131, I was a rich man until I hit town. 1925 Wodehouse *Carry on, Jeeves* v. 126 Jimmy Mundy.. has come to save New York from itself; to force it—in his picturesque phrase—to hit the trail.
19. (Later U.S. examples.)
1905 Rex Beach *Pardners* i. (1912) 24 We hit for camp on the run. *Ibid.* ii. 48 So me and 'Kink' Martin..hit west. 1916 'B. M. Bower' *Phantom Herd* xiii. 218 When I hit for the land of orange blossoms and singing birds and sunshine.
b. To go, pass. *U.S.*
1911 H. S. Harrison *Queed* vii. 86 I've seen you hit by the window many's the time.
20. *To hit it*. **d.** To travel at speed. *U.S.*
1911 J. C. Lincoln *Cap'n Warren's Wards* iii. 39 They nabbed us for speeding....Said we were hitting it at fifty an hour.
22. Also *hit and miss*.
1897 R. M. Stuart *Simpkinsville* 156 Takin' 'em hit and miss, we wouldn't know the diff'rence hardly.
b. *Hit-and-miss*: used *attrib.* to designate certain contrivances, as **hit-and-miss governor**, a type of governor used in internal combustion engines which causes the engine to miss one or more explosions when the speed is too great.
1902 A. C. Harmsworth *Motors & Motor-Driving* viii. 162 Many of these engines have now the ordinary hit and miss exhaust governor as well.
c. *To hit the hay*, to go to bed. *slang.*
1928 Sinclair Lewis *Man Who Knew Coolidge* i. 128 'Fine', we says; 'you bet; we'll hit the hay at ten.' 1929 Conan Doyle *Maracot Deep* ii. 72 'Well, I am ready to hit the hay', be said, sleepily.
d. *To hit the high spots*: see *High *a.* 21.
25*. **Hit up.** **a.** To force up; to speed up. With *it*: To put on pressure; to make efforts in a certain direction.
1893 W. K. Post *Harvard Stories* 49, I could hear him objurgating Steve Hudson for hitting up the stroke. *Ibid.* 146 When you are doing better than three and a half [miles an hour], you are hitting it up pretty well. 1904 F. Lynde *Grafters* xx. 257 Two days after the Universal's triumph in the Belmount field, the Argus began to 'bit it up' boldly toward the capital. 1912 Mulford & Clay *Buck Peters* iii. 49 Hit her up or you'll be late. 1918 in F. A. Pottle *Stretchers* (1930) 270 Back he went, while we waited. When he got back with his jam, we hit it up again. It seemed miles before we got anywhere.
b. To make or score (runs).
1895 [see Up *adv.*[1] 19 b]. 1899 *Daily News* 9 June 6/7 They were batting all day, and hit up 397 for the loss of seven wickets. 1928 *Evening News* 18 Aug. 10/5 Middlesex hit up 365 in the first day's play.

Hitch, *sb.* Add: **1. c.** A catch in or a turn at wrestling.
1834 H. M. Brackenridge *Recoll.* ix. 94 I'll stan iny mon a hitch in Butler county, if so be he'll clear me o' the la'. 1886 *Harper's Mag.* Mar. 525 How with 'ducking' heads and muffled screams you..saw them scrambling for a 'hitch'.
5. b. A mode of harnessing a horse or team; a vehicle with its horse or team. *U.S.*
1876 *Rep. Vermont Board Agric.* III. 143 If he can go best in one kind of a hitch, and, in that hitch, make the best time ever made by any horse. 1898 *Christian Herald* (N.Y.) 2 Mar. 167/2 Several hitches are a mule and steer together. 1905 *Springfield* (Mass.) *Weekly Republ.* 22 Sept. 12 There were also several other creditable displays, both single and double hitches. 1912 Mulford & Clay *Buck Peters* xxii. 201, I want a hitch of some kind,..something with speed and bottom, and the sooner the better.
8. *Soap-making.* (See quot.)
1885 W. L. Carpenter *Soap & Candles* 167 Practice alone will enable the operator to judge of the completion of this first operation called 'pasting' (French *empâtage*)...The soap is then said to be..in a 'hitch' or 'glue'.
9. *Comb.*: **hitch and kick**, **hitch-kick**, a form of high-kicking or long-jumping; **hitch-knot** = sense 6 b.
1911 Webster, **Hitch and kick*, a form of high kicking in which the kicker springs from, kicks with, and alights on, the same foot. 1931 F. A. M. Webster *Athletes in Action* 155 Numerous men using the '*hitch-kick', or 'mid-air-running' style, have beaten 25ft. 1847 Stoddart *Angler's Comp.* 69 In making large fly-hooks..I bring down the thread and fasten it, with a simple *hitch-knot.

Hitch, *v.* Add: **1. c.** (See quot.)
1888 *Lockwood's Dict. Mech. Engin.* s.v., A cutting tool moving automatically in a tool holder is said to hitch or catch when it is pulled into the work at a depth greater than it is intended to cut.
3. b. (Modern U.S. examples.)
1868 H. Woodruff *Trotting Horse Amer.* iv. 59 When it was found that they began to hitch and hobble, a good let-up would do more to restore the stroke than anything else. 1889 *Century Mag.* 907/2. I do not know what would happen to a man who 'hitched' in his saddle.
4. b. To tramp. Also **hitch-hike** *v.*, to travel by means of 'lifts'; whence *hitch-hiker*.
1931 B. Starke *Touch & Go* xii. 192 Two lads spoke to me, and asked if I were hitching it by myself. *Ibid.* iv. 58, I.. wondered how Dot would ever dare..tell the people there that she had hitch-hiked home. *Ibid.* ix. 133 She told me she had hitched her way down to New Orleans a week before. *Ibid.* iv. 64 We may charge this wicked hitch-hiker the ten cents extra that she deserves for asking for a bath towel.
5, 5. c. (Earlier and other examples of absol. use.)
1844 J. J. Webb *Memoirs* 206 Everything arranged, we hitched up, and started on our route. 1845 J. J. Hooper *Taking Census* i. 151 We rode up..and hitching to the fence, walked into the house. 1856 R. Glisan *Jrnl. Army Life* xxiv. (1874) 337 He left his horse behind, having hitched and gone off from him a short distance when he saw the Indians.

Hitch-, in combs. = *hitching* vbl. sb. (see Hitch *v.*). *U.S.*
1899 G. Ade *Doc. Horne* i. 7, I jumped off my horse and threw him one end of my hitch-rein and pulled him out. 1903 A. Adams *Log Cowboy* xxi. 138 Tying our horses in a group to a hitch-rack in the rear of a saloon. 1906 H. D. Pittman *Belle of Blue Grass C.* xiii. 187 A slim-legged yellow girl..swinging by her arms from a hitch rail.

Hitchcockite (hi·tʃkǫkəit). *Min.* [f. the name of Dr. E. *Hitchcock* of Amherst College + -ite[1].] A variety of plumbogummite.
1856 C. U. Shepard *Report Canton Mine* 11 (Chester). 1892 E. S. Dana *Dana's Min.* (ed. 6) 855.

Hitching, *vbl. sb.* (Examples of U.S. attrib. uses.)
1852 C. A. Bristed *Upper Ten Thousand* 67 [He] pulled a hitching-strap from under the seat, and fastened his off-horse very neatly to a lamp-post. 1871 Mrs. Stowe *Sam Lawson* 58 All the hitchin'-posts was full clean up to the tavern. 1884 Howells *Silas Lapham* xviii. 336 He got the hitching-weight from under the buggy seat and made it fast to the mare's bit. 1920 J. Gregory *Man to Man* ix. 103 A dozen saddle-horses were tied at the hitching-rail. 1926 J. Black *You Can't Win* ix. 108, I..limped outside where I had an old 'swift' tied to a hitching rack.

Hitlerite (hi·tlərəit). [-ite[1].] A follower of Adolf *Hitler*, leader of the National Socialist (*Nazi) party in Germany from 1930. Also *attrib.* So **Hi·tlerism**, the political principles or policy of this party; **Hi·tlerist**, a Hitlerite.
1930 *Times* 26 Sept. 13/2 These Hitlerite outbursts may disturb German Liberals and Socialists. [*Ibid.* 27 Sept. 10/1 The action of the Court was hailed in the Hitler camp as a great tactical success.] 1930 *New Statesman* 1 Nov. 106/1 One may magnify or minimise the role of the Hitlerites, but [etc.]. 1931 P. Wyndham Lewis *Hitler* 4 An exponent..of German National socialism, or Hitlerism. *Ibid.* 32 The militant nationalism of the Hitlerist. 1931 *Times Lit. Suppl.* 16 Apr. 296/2 Hitlerite anti-Semitism.

Hittite (hi·təit). [f. Heb. *Ḥittīm* + -ite[1]. The form *Hittite* occurs first in the Geneva version, 1560, of the Bible. The LXX has Χετταῖοι (identified as children of Heth (Χέτ), Heb. *benē Ḥēth*), the Vulgate *Hethæi*, whence *Ethei* in the Wycliffite versions, G. *Hethiter* (Luther), English *Hethite* (Coverdale, etc.), F. *Héthéen*.] In the Bible (Gen. xv. 20, etc.), one of a Canaanitish tribe of greater or less extent; in modern archæology and philology, a member of a powerful and widespread ancient (non-Semitic) race, variously named *Khita* or *Kheta* in Egyptian, and *Khatti*, *Ḥatti* (see *Hattic) in Hittite and Assyrian, whose history can be traced from *c* 1600 to 1200 B.C. in Asia Minor and northern Syria. **b.** The language of this people, which is regarded by some as Indo-European in structure. Also *attrib.* or *adj.*
1871 tr. *Ewald's Geschichte Volkes Israel* III. 262 Among the petty Hittite (i.e. generally Canaanite), and Aramean kings. 1874 Sayce in *Trans. Soc. Bibl. Archæol.* III. 245 The king of the Hittites or the king of the Khati. 1879 — in *Academy* 16 Aug. 124/1 The sculpture accompanied by inscriptions in Hittite (or Hamathite) characters..discovered at Ibreez in Lycaonia..proves that the Hittites had penetrated through the eastern barrier of Asia Minor formed by the Taurus range. 1880 *Encycl. Brit.* XI. 808/2 The discovery of a new hieroglyphic character in the Hittite inscriptions. *Ibid.* XII. 26/2 Our knowledge of the Hittite language is confined to the proper names mentioned in the Egyptian and Assyrian inscriptions. 1880 [see *Hattic]. 1884 W. Wright *Empire of Hittites* 56 There can be little doubt that the Lycaonian *patois*, which continued to be the vernacular of the people till the days of Paul, was Hittite. 1884 Sayce *Ibid.* 170 The bilingual inscription of Tarkondêmos in cuneiform and Hittite. 1918 Cowley *Hittites* i. (1920) 1 Until forty years ago, or less, the Hittites were still grouped with Hivites and Jebusites as an insignificant Syrian tribe unknown outside the Bible.

Hittorf (hi·tǫɹf). The name of J. W. *Hittorf* (1824–1919), German scientist, used attrib. to denote certain phenomena observed and apparatus invented by him. **Hittorf rays**, rays (chiefly cathode rays) created by the electric discharge in a Hittorf tube; **Hittorf tube**, a highly exhausted glass tube having metallic electrodes nearly touching each other, so as to show the insulating effects of a vacuum; also, a Crookes tube.
1893 Sloane *Stand. Elect. Dict.* 289 *Hittorf's solution*, a solution used as a resistance. It is a solution of cadmium iodide in amylic alcohol. *Ibid.* 466 *Hittorf's resistance*, a high resistance, often a megohm, composed of Hittorf's solution. 1910 *N. Hawkins' Elect. Dict.* 199/1 *Hittorf effect*, the effect produced by Hittorf in his vacuum tube.

Hive, *sb.* **7.** Add: **hive-moth**, a moth of the genus *Galleria*.
1931 *Oxf. Univ. Gaz.* 17 June 703/1 Hive-moth (*Galleria*) at Nairobi.

Hi·ve-off. [f. phr. *to hive off* (see Hive *v.* 5).] An act of hiving off; also *fig.*
1898 *Chambers's Jrnl.* II. 9/1 There was a 'hive-off' comparatively early when the 'New Civil Service Co-operation' set up close by.., and appealed to much the same class of customers.

Hives. Add: **b.** *attrib.*: **hive-syrup**, compound syrup of squills.
1839 *Southern Lit. Messenger* V. 65/2 There's nothing there but a few drops of peppermint,..and some of the patent hive-syrup. 1901 Sollmann *Text-bk. Pharmacol.* 612.

Hizen (hīze·n). The name of a province of Japan used *attrib.* and *ellipt.* to denote a class of porcelains characterized by rich decoration, delicate colouring, and fine workmanship, and including Hirado, Imari, and Nabeshima ware.
1881 Audsley & Bowes *Keramic Art Japan* 144 The old red, blue and gold Hizen. *Ibid.* 145 Old Hizen ware.. includes white porcelain. 1902 *Encycl. Brit.* XXIX. 725/1.

Ho (hōu), *sb.*[4] [Native name, said to be a contraction of *horo* man.] **a.** One of the principal dialects of southern India, belonging to the Kolarian group. **b.** One who speaks this language.
1840 S. R. Tickell in *Jrnl. Asiat. Soc.* IX. ii. 997 The Ho language has no written character. 1860 F. Mason *Burmah* (ed. 2) 131 These Moondas now call themselves Hos. 1871 E. Balfour *Cycl. India* (ed. 2) II. 589/2 A Ho bridegroom buys his bride. 1905 P. Wagner tr. *A. Nottrott's Gram. Kol-Language* 4 The dialect of the Larka-Kols or Hos. 1906 Grierson *Linguistic Surv. India* IV. 116. 1908 Risley *People of India* 94 The Hos of Singhbhum.

Hoadleyism (hōu·dli,iz'm). [f. name of Benjamin *Hoadly* (1676–1761), Bishop of Bangor + -ism.] The opinions or policy characteristic of the latitudinarian clergy of whom Bishop Hoadly was typical.
1863 J. S. Brewer *Engl. Studies* (1881) 300 He may write and preach as much Hoadleyism..as he pleases. 1896 Purcell *Manning* I. 499 Its [*sc.* the Established Church's] Hoadleyism, if I may so speak, which prevailed before the Tractarian movement.

Hoar-frost. Add: **hoar-frost line** (see quot.).
1878 *Encycl. Brit.* VIII. 731/1 A curve which represents the relation between the pressure and volume of the unit mass of steam in contact with water as the temperature changes is called the steam line, and the corresponding curve for aqueous vapour in contact with ice is called the hoar-frost line.

Hoary, *a.* Add: **5. c.** In names of moths and butterflies having a hoary or ashy appearance (see quots.).
1832 J. Rennie *Butterfl. & Moths* 183 The Hoary Double Crescent..frequents ash-trees. *Ibid.* 211 The Hoary Grey. ..Wings ten lines to ten lines and a half; first pair hoary or ashy.

Hob, *sb.*[1] **2. b.** (Later U.S. examples.) Also *to raise hob*. U.S.
1905 Tarkington *In Arena* 23, I believe that idiot's right, he won't lose votes by playing hob with *us*. 1911 J. C. Lincoln *Cap'n Warren's Wards* vi. 88 Theoph's been raising

hob because the Odd Fellows built on to their building. 1916 H. L. Wilson *Somewhere in Red Gap* iii. 120 He looked like one of them silly little critters that play hob with Rip Van Winkle..before he goes to sleep.

Hob, *sb.*[2] Add: **3.** Also, a master tap.
1881 Campin *Mech. Engin.* 49 The taps used for making screw tools and worm wheels are called hobs. 1884 Knight *Dict. Mech.* Suppl., *Hob*, a hardened steel mandrel with a threaded portion which is fluted. 1888 *Lockwood's Dict. Mech. Engin.*, *Hob*, or *Hub*, a master tap.
5. (Earlier American examples.)
1686 S. Sewall *Letter Bk.* 34 The Hobs and blew Linnin received per Foy. 1687 *Ibid.* 64 The remainder in naills, viz: one halfe 10d, one fourth 8d, and one fourth part in 2 and 3d hobbs and 4d naills.

Hob, *v.*[3] Add: Hence **Ho·bber**, one employed in driving hobnails into boots. **Ho·bbing** *vbl. sb.*, the action of hobnailing boots and shoes; **hobbing foot** *local*, a shoemaker's last.
1866 R. Hallam *Wadsley Jack* vii. 36 Thie fooit..weean't skar me—noa, not if it wor a hobbin fooit. 1907 *Daily Chron.* 8 Jan. 6/2 The woman was struck on the head by a shoemaker's 'hobbing foot'. 1921 *Dict. Occup. Terms* (1927) § 429 *Hobber*..drives in hobnails round rims of soles of heavy boots, by hand with a hammer. 1922 Geo. Blair *Haunted Dominie* etc. 43 There's some that skimp the hammerin' upon the hobbin'-feet.

Hob (hǫb), *v.*[4] [f. Hob *sb.*[2] 3.] *trans.* To cut or form by means of a hob or master tap. Hence **Ho·bbing** *vbl. sb.* *Hobbing machine*, a machine in which worm-wheels, spur and spiral gears are cut by means of a hob or master tap.
1892 *Lockwood's Dict. Mech. Engin.* Suppl. 1913 *Ibid.*, *Hobbing Machines*. In these, spur and spiral gears as well as worm wheels are cut by a hob, the same hob serving for each type of gear by altering the angle of inclination of the thread.

Hobble, *sb.* Add: **3.** (Earlier U.S. examples.)
1744 F. Moore *Voy. Georgia* 147 Two horses tied with hobbles. 1797 F. Baily *Jrnl. Tour N. Amer.* (1856) 336 Our horses would seldom or never stray..; however, we always took the precaution of putting hobbles on their feet. 1804 L. Dow *Trav.* Wks. 1806 II. 63 [Crossing a stream] I lost my hobbles.
4. In full *hobble-skirt*: A close-fitting skirt usually confined by a wide band below the knees and above the ankles, fashionable about 1910.
1911 *Smart Set* Mar. 40 A hobble skirt is an awful habit to get into. 1912 *Punch* 3 Apr. 255/1 The continued success of the hobble..has..restricted the use of textile material. 1918 *Wireless World* Oct. 372 A feminine atrocity in a cerise muslin sheath on 'hobble-skirt' lines. 1920 M. Asquith *Autobiog.* I. 221 From the hoop to the hobble is not a more violent change than from the riding-hats of 1894 to the riding-hats of 1917. 1921 C. Torr *Small Talk at Wreyland* Ser. II. 69, I said, 'You don't go in for hobble-skirts, I see.'

Hobble, *v.* **7.** (Earlier U.S. example.)
1804 L. Dow *Trav.* Wks. 1806 II. 62 We..hobbled the fore legs of our horses together.

Hobereau (obro). [Fr.] A country gentleman, squire.
1910 *Sat. Westm. Gaz.* 15 Jan. 6/2 Good citizens, Echevin, bailli, hoberaux. 1923 *Blackw. Mag.* Nov. 647/2 Her father, the local *hobereau*, a solid man.

Hobo. Add: Hence **Ho·bo** *v. trans.*, to work (one's way) in the manner of a hobo; also with *it*. **Ho·bodom**, **Ho·boism**, the realm or world of the hobo.
1906 U. Sinclair *Jungle* xxv. 298 Then he explained how he had spent the last summer, 'hoboing it,' as the phrase was. 1923 H. L. Foster *Beachcomber in Orient* ix. 183 Having hoboed my way thus far, I could afford to travel as a passenger the rest of the way. 1928 *Daily Mail* 9 Aug. 11/4, I sort of hoboed my way out to San Francisco. 1930 *Publishers' Weekly* 31 May 3736/2 Any hobo temporarily sober can find a publisher to place on the market with great éclat an epic of Hobodom, provided that there is sufficient of the hobo atmosphere. 1930 *19th Cent.* June 849 These were the high days of American hoboism.

Hoch (hǫχ), *sb.* [a. G. *hoch*, short for *hoch lebe* long live.] An instance of the ejaculation *Hoch!*; an exclamation of loyal approval; a cheer, hurrah. Hence **Hoch** *v. intr.*, to utter a *hoch* or *hochs*; *trans.* to cheer with cries of *Hoch!*
1907 *Daily Chron.* 13 Sept. 6/6 On the whole it will be prudent for the average Englishman not to attempt a 'Hoch!' in welcoming the Kaiser to London to-day. 1909 *Ibid.* 2 June 5/6 They 'hoched' us on our way, and cheered when they got tired of 'hoching'. 1920 *Chambers's Jrnl.* June 374/2 If Britain had had a million Australian troops, they, the present gathering, would be 'hoch, hoching' in Berlin. 1921 A. S. M. Hutchinson *If Winter Comes* III. i. 148 The 25th anniversary of the Emperor William's accession was 'Hoch'd' throughout the German Empire. *Ibid.*, Such fervent and sincere 'Hochs!' never boomed across the seas of the world.

Hocheur (oʃœ̄r). [Fr., f. *hocher* to nod the head.] The white-nose monkey of Africa, *Cercopithecus nictitans*.
1840 *Cuvier's Anim. Kingd.* 57. 1883 *List. Anim. Zool. Soc.* (ed. 8) 12. 1905 *Westm. Gaz.* 6 Feb. 6/3 A specimen of the Hocheur monkey is among the new inmates of the Monkey House.

Hock, *sb.*[6] Add: (Examples.)
1859 Matsell *Vocabulum* 113 *Hock*, the last card in the box. 1913 Mulford *Coming of Cassidy* vii. 118 In his agitation be exposed the hock card before he realized what he was doing.
b. *From soda to hock*: from the top card to the last in the dealing-box; hence, from beginning to end.
1902 H. L. Wilson *Spenders* v. 49 Young Bines played the deal from soda card to hock. 1918 Mulford *Man fr. Bar-20* ii. 21 You got me beat from soda to hock. *Ibid.* xiii. 134 'Are you in?' 'Every d—d chip; from my hat to my worn-out boots; from soda to hock.' 1925 — *Cottonwood Gulch* xvi. 219 You've got 'em all guessin', from soda to hock. Good for you!

Hock (hǫk), *sb.*[7] *U.S. slang.* [a. Du. *hok* hutch, hovel, prison, (*slang*) credit, debt.] Phr. *In hock*: (*a*) in the act (of gambling); (*b*) in prison; (*c*) in pawn; (*d*) in debt. So occas. *out of hock*.
1859 Matsell *Vocabulum* 113 When one gambler is caught by another, smarter than himself, and is beat, then he is in hock. Men are only caught, or put in hock, on the race-tracks, or on the steamboats down South....Among thieves a man is in hock, when he is in prison...' If the cove should be caught in the hock he won't snickle,' if the fellow should be caught in the act, he would not tell. 1896 G. Ade *Artie* xviii. 169 They go back home and leave all their stuff in hock. 1902 W. N. Harben *Abner Daniel* xxiii, I felt..ef they did git Jimmy out o' hock..without me a-chippin' in, I'd never be able to look at 'em without remorse. 1903 A. H. Lewis *The Boss* 31 Well..even a crook has got to go somewhere. That is,..when he ain't in hock. 1908 G. H. Lorimer *J. Spurlock* vii. 141 He made me feel that I was doing him a favour in consenting to have my evening clothes taken out of hock. 1911 Mulford *Bar-20 Days* xiii. 141, I said pound, not pond. P-O-U-N-D; which means that it's pawned, in hock. 1913 — *Coming of Cassidy* vii. 118 If the four lay under the Queen, Cassidy lost; if not, he either won or was in hock. 1926 J. Black *You Can't Win* xxiv. 390, I was in hock to friends who saved me from a heavy sentence, provided me with work [etc.]. 1929 *Collier's* 5 Jan. 40/4 My cash was gone, and I was in hock for the next three years.
b. *attrib.*: **hock-game** (see quot. 1859); **hock-shop**, a pawnshop.
1859 Matsell *Vocabulum* 113 In a *hock-game, if a man hits a card, he is obliged to let his money lie until it either wins or loses. 1908 G. H. Lorimer *J. Spurlock* iv. 81 When my money was all gone, I wore a path to a cosy little *hock-shop in Sixth Avenue. 1926 J. Black *You Can't Win* xxi. 336 The average thief will walk by the hockshop and look in. The hockshop man..knows he has something 'hot', or crooked.

Hock, *v.*[3] *U.S. slang.* [f. *Hock *sb.*[7]] *trans.* To pawn.
1902 H. L. Wilson *Spenders* xxxiii. 397 The only thing I'll do..is to hock a few blocks of the stock I bought outright. 1904 Lorimer *Old Gorgon Graham* 184 You can hock your overcoat before marriage to buy violets for a girl. 1922 H. L. Foster *Adv. Trop. Tramp* xx. 354 I've just hocked my camera, and all I've got is two dollars.

Hockelty. *slang.* Also **hocly**. = Hock *sb.*[6]
1867 *Bohn's Hand-bk. Games* 336 The last card but one is called hocly, and forms part of the banker's gain. 1895 Manson *Sporting Dict.* 58 (Faro), *Hock* or *Hockelty Card*, the last card remaining in the box, after the deal has been made.

Hoe, *v.* **3.** Add: See also Row *sb.*[1] 6 b, c.

Hoe (hōu), *v.*[2] *U.S.* [f. Hoe-down.] *intr.* To dance or play a hoe-down.
1909 *Cent. Dict.* Suppl.

Hoe-cake. *U.S.* (Earlier examples.)
1774 P. V. Fithian *Jrnl.* (1900) 93 Sup'd on chocolate, & hoe-cake, so called because baked on a hoe before the fire. 1780 W. Fleming *Trav. Amer. Col.* 641, I had lived for a constancy on poor dried buffalo bull beef cured in the smook ..without any addition but a piece of Indian hoe-cake.

Hoed, *ppl. a.* (s.v. Hoe *v.*). (Amer. examples.)
1643 *New Plymouth Laws* 74 By improved lands are understood meddow land, plowed land, and howed lands. 1879 *Scribner's Monthly* Dec. 239/2 The owner has only to give it a year of ordinary cultivation, taking from it..some profitable hoed crop.

Hoe-down. *U.S.* (Earlier and later examples.)
1849 T. T. Johnson *Sights Gold Region* iv. 38 One of our party commenced a regular hoe-down, knocking his shins with heavy boots. 1855 *Knickerbocker Mag.* XLVI. 227 Rude, high-legged reels and 'hoe-downs'. 1919 T. K. Holmes *Man fr. Tall Timber* vii. 84 A medley of old-time hoe-downs and jig music.

Hoel, variant of *Hwyl.

Hœrnesite (hō̈·ɹnězəit). *Min.* Also **hörnesite**. [ad. G. *hörnesit* (1859), f. the name of Dr. M. *Hörnes*, Austrian mineralogist + -ite[1].] A hydrated magnesium arseniate occurring in Hungary.
1868 Dana *Syst. Min.* (ed. 5) 817 Hœrnesite...First distinguished by Kenngott in minerals from the Bannat, Hungary. 1903 *Jrnl. Chem. Soc.* LXXXIV. ii. 655 Crystallised Magnesium Phosphate and Arsenate: Artificial Production of Bobierrite and Hœrnesite.

Hoffman (hǫ·fmæn). The name of Frederick *Hoffman* used *attrib.* and in genitive to designate a form of continuous kiln patented by him in 1865.
1875 *Ure's Dict. Arts* III. 20 Hoffmann's Continuous Kiln. 1879 *Notes on Building Construction* III. 101 Hoffmann's Kiln is used chiefly in brick-manufactories on a large scale, where a great number of bricks is required annually. 1889 C. T. Davis *Manuf. Bricks* (ed. 2) 266 The burning chamber of the Hoffman Kiln. 1892 *P. Benjamin's Mod. Mechanism* 599 The Hoffman Magnetic Separator. 1902 *Encycl. Brit.* XXVI. 630/2 The Hoffmann or ring kiln, made up of a number of compartments arranged in a ring and connected with a central chimney.

Hoffmann (hǫ·fmăn).
1. The name of Friedrich *Hoffmann* (1660–1742), German physician, in *Hoffmann's anodyne*.
1836 Brande *Man. Chem.* (ed. 4) 1087 Hoffman's anodyne liquor. 1878 tr. *von Ziemssen's Cycl. Pract. Med.* XVII. 442 The internal use of ether (Hoffmann's anodyne) may lead to poisoning. 1886 *Buck's Handbk. Med. Sci.* II. 725/2 Compound Spirit of Ether, or Hoffman's Anodyne.
2. The name of Georg von *Hoffmann*, Austrian bacteriologist, in *Hoffmann's bacillus*.
1905 *Allbutt's Syst. Med.* I. 990 A species known as Hoffmann's bacillus, common in the healthy nose and throat. 1912 Osler *Princ. Med.* (ed. 8) 60 Hoffmann's Bacillus, which is also spoken of as pseudo-diphtheria bacillus.
3. The name of Johann *Hoffmann*, German physician, in *Hoffmann's atrophy*, *sign*, *symptom*.
1910 *Osler & Macrae's Syst. Med.* VII. 73 The sensory nerves may also be hypersensitive, and tapping at Valleix's points then calls forth abnormally intense sensations (Hoffmann's symptom).

Hofmann (hōu·fmăn). The name of August Wilhelm von *Hofmann* (1818–92), German chemist, used to designate various dyes, etc.
1871 *Jrnl. Chem. Soc.* XXIV. 406 On Hofmann's Tyrosine Reaction. 1875 *Encycl. Brit.* II. 48/2 Violet colours, such as Hofmann's violet. *Ibid.* V. 548/1 Gay-Lussac and Hofmann's Methods. 1884 *Bleaching, Dyeing, & Calico-printing* 176 This dye [*sc.* violet imperial] is now replaced by the Hofmann violets. 1886 *Buck's Handbk. Med. Sci.* III. 677/2 Iodine Green, Hoffman's [*sic*] Green. 1892 Morley & Muir *Watts' Dict. Chem.* III. 269/2 Methyl-violet occurs in Hofmann's violet. 1902 *Encycl. Brit.* XXVII. 337/2 Staining with Hoffmann's [*sic*] blue or other aniline dyes.

Hog, *sb.*[1] Add: **1. c.** *U.S.* (Earlier and later examples.)
1816 *Mass. Spy* 10 Jan. (Th.) [If a man] can be content with hog and hommany, he can live easier in Ohio. 1888 *Century Mag.* XXXVI. 261/2 Corn-bread and bacon, or, in purer vernacular, 'hog and hominy'.
7. c. A person who behaves in a rude mannerless fashion without respect for the safety or convenience of others; esp. in *road-hog* (Road *sb.* 12).
1906 *Daily Chron.* 2 Feb. 7/3 Showing to the astounded heathens (save the word) the latest game of 'hog-amok'. 1928 *Daily Mail* 25 July 17/4 So far we have met no 'canal hogs'.
10. Also, the distance-line itself, the hog-score.
1824 Mactaggart *Gallovid. Encycl.* 274 Sweeping is not allowed until the stone comes over the 'hogg', unless by the person who played it. 1853 W. Watson *Poems* 63 Stan' back at the hog wi' a besom. 1897 *Encycl. Sport* I. 258 It [*sc.* a stone] must be over the Hog, but must not touch the Stone to be guarded.
11. *Like* or *as a hog on ice*, denoting awkwardness or insecurity. *U.S.*
1894 *Vermont Agric. Rep.* XIV. 124 How would a Hackney look going around the track after old Highland Gray? 'Like a hog on ice.' 1922 C. Sandburg *Slabs of Sunburnt West* 8 Chicago fished from its depths a text: Independent as a hog on ice.
b. (Earlier U.S. example.)
1828 in Curtis *Life D. Webster* (1870) I. 337 [Andrew Jackson] will either go with the party, as they say in New York, or go 'the whole hog', as it is phrased elsewhere.
13. a. **hog-house** (earlier Amer. example); **hog-line** *Curling*, the distance-line (= Hog-score); **hog-tight** *a.*, said of fences which are close enough to prevent swine from forcing their way through; **hog-tooth spar**, a popular name for calcite; **hog-wallow** (earlier U.S. example); **hog-yoke** (later U.S. example).
1638 *Essex Inst. Hist. Coll.* IV. 185/1 Granted to John Abby 5 acres nere to Mr. Throgmorton's *hoghowse. 1904 *Westm. Gaz.* 13 May 3/1 There is no reason in the world why you should not mark out a '*hog' line with whitewash. 1859 Bartlett *Dict. Amer.* s.v., *Hog-tight and horse-high, always used together, of fences that are sufficient to restrain trespassing stock. Maryland. 1879 Tourgee *Fool's Errand* xxx. 194 The split-board paling..was 'horse-high, hog-tight, and bull-strong'. 1885 *Rep. Indian Affairs* 110 All of these tracts are enclosed with hog-tight fences. 1896 Chester *Dict. Min.*, **Hog-tooth spar*, like dog-tooth spar, a popular name for calcite, occurring in acute scalenohedrons. 1829 L. Dow *Omnifarious Law* 51 It becomes a trespass to make a dam for a *hog wallow. 1846–52 Mrs. Whitcher *Widow Bedott P.* x. 99, I ain't so fond o' pork as to eat *hog-yokes.
b. **hog-age** *U.S.*, adolescence.
1893 Farmer & Henley *Slang*, *Hog-age*, the period between boyhood and manhood.
c. **hog-sucker** (example).
1888 Goode *Amer. Fishes* 435 The..'Hog Sucker'.. abounds in most waters from the great lakes southward.

Hog, *v.*[1] Add: **1. a.** Also *absol.*
1860 R. F. Burton *Lake Regions Central Africa* I. 85 They [*sc.* asses] hog and buck till they burst their frail girths.
2. (Earlier U.S. example.)
1803 *Ann. 7th Congress* 2 Sess. 407 He did not..believe that there would be any more danger of the ship's hogging, when lowered down..than when on the stocks.
5. b. *intr.* To behave as a road-hog. Also in *vbl. sb.*
1925 R. J. B. Sellar *Sporting Yarns* 135 As they were hogging it through the country-side with the speedometer hovering over the sixty mark. 1925 *Punch* 22 Apr. 432 'Frightful rate that bike we just passed was going, wasn't it?' 'Yes. They ought to have the man for "hogging".' 1926 *Chambers's Jrnl.* Dec. 875/1 Why don't you sound your hooter before hogging round corners?
c. *trans.* To interfere with in wireless transmission, as by a more powerful instrument. So also *to hog the ether*.
1914 *Pears' Christmas Annual* 21/2 They should be hogged till doomsday,.., if a single ship was on fire! *Ibid.*, The operator heard. He started up as if he had been hogged himself.
9. *trans.* To feed swine on (a crop or crop-covered land). *local U.S.*
1859 H. W. Beecher *Pleasant Talk* 93 Some of the best

farmers in this region hog their corn-lands. *Ibid.* 94 Land being hogged, will be free from cut-worms.

Hogan (hōu·gān). [Navajo.] The rude hut of Navajo and other American Indian tribes of the south-western United States.
1871 *Rep. Indian Affairs* (1872) 379 When a member of a family dies, in most cases they immediately leave their hogan (or wigwam) with the dead body in it. 1904 *New York Even. Post* 2 July 2 The North American Indians in their primitive state, living in the tepees, hogans, sod-lodges and grass houses. 1928 Willa Cather *Death comes for the Archbishop* vii. iii. 217 For his lodging the Bishop was given a solitary hogan.

Hogback. Add: **1. b.** The sunfish. *U.S.*
1832 *Coll. New Hampsh. Hist. Soc.* III. 86 The hogback or sunfish, as some call it, is a very attracting thing. It is about as large as the perch.
c. A trout or other fish with a hog-like back.
1895 *Funk's Stand. Dict.* 1923 *Chambers's Jrnl.* Dec. 791/2 Bill, said the latter, the hog-back run is come.
2. (Earlier U.S. examples of form.)
1840 J. P. Kennedy *Quodlibet* 26 The farm where he now lives at the foot of the Hogback. 1849 *President's Mess. Congress* II. 731 The banks [of a stream]..worn in some places into hog-backs. 1888 *Harper's Mag.* Nov. 860/1, I pushed forward across deep gulches, over high peaks and 'hog-backs'.

Ho·g-ki:lling. [Hog *sb.* 12 b.] The killing of a pig. *Hog-killing time*, a time of special enjoyment. *U.S.*
1879 *Harper's Mag.* Nov. 812/1, I..was as big as a dog at hog-killing. 1903 A. Adams *Log Cowboy* xiii. 83 According to their report the boys had had a hog-killing-time. 1927 Vachell *Dew of Sea* etc. 259 When I ask my friends to have a hog-killing-time with me, I foot all bills.

Hog mane. (Earlier Amer. example.)
1767 *Boston Post-Boy* 12 Oct. (Th.) Strayed or Stolen, a large Brown Horse, Hogg Mein, bob Tail, &c.

Hog-nut. **1.** *U.S.* (Earlier example.)
1810 Michaux *Arbres* I. 21 *Pig nut hickery*...*Hog nut hickery*, plus usité dans quelques cantons de la Pensylvanie.

Ho·g-pen. *U.S.* [Hog *sb.* 13.] A pen or enclosure for swine.
1640 in *Maryland Hist. Mag.* V. 374 The Neck of Land called hog penn Neck. 1663 *Springfield* (Mass.) *Rec.* I. 312 There is granted to Rowland Thomas 6 acres of the low land on hog pen dingle below ye place where hog pen was. 1695 [see Hog *sb.* 13]. 1769 in *Maryland Hist. Mag.* XII. 285 If the bounds of the Hog pen cannot be found. 1837 *Southern Lit. Messenger* III. 238 Cornwallis's cave is converted to a hog-pen. 1874 *Rep. Vermont Board Agric.* II. 512 In said basement I have my hog-pen.
attrib. 1849 *Rep. U.S. Comm. Patents, Agric.* (1850) 122 Leached ashes, hen-house and hog-pen refuse are very valuable fertilizers.

Hog-reeve. *U.S.* (Earlier examples.)
1636 *Boston Town Rec.* II. 13 At this meeting Richard Faireback is chosen for our Hog Reeve. 1663 *Watertown Rec.* I. 79 The hogreiffes..presented a list of thos persons that weare deffective in hogge Fences. 1729 *Suffield Doc. Hist.* 242 Josiah Hale was chosen Hoggreeve for the remainder of the year.

Ho·g-round. *U.S.* (See quot. 1899.)
1835 *Louisville Publ. Adv.* 14 Feb., 8000 lbs bulk pork, hog round..for sale. 1886 *Harper's Mag.* 206/2 Lard, made from hog-round. 1899 B. W. Green *Virginia Word Bk.* 189 Hams, shoulders and middlings have different prices, but when taken altogether at one price, it is so much hog-round.

Hog's-back, variant of Hogback.
1827 J. F. Cooper *Red Rover* i, The hog's back over which the water pitches. 1834–63 [see Hogback 2].

Hog-skin. **1.** (Earlier Amer. example.)
1673 *Essex Inst. Hist. Coll.* L. 27 A meale trough..a hog-skin, a reele.

Ho·g-tie, *sb.* *U.S.* [f. the vb.] The form of securing or fettering produced by 'hog-tying'; a secure hold.
1910 W. M. Raine *B. O'Connor* iv, They sure do hate to turn loose a gringo when they have got the hog-tie on him.

Ho·g-tie, *v.* *U.S.* [Hog *sb.*[1] 1.] *trans.* To secure by tying the four feet, or the hands and feet, together. Also *fig.*, to fetter.
1894 [see Hog *sb.*[1] 13]. 1903 A. Adams *Log Cowboy* xi. 75 We threw him, hog-tied him and rolled him into the water. 1906 A. H. Lewis *Sunset Trail* i, Something wherewith he might hogtie steers when in the course of duty he must rope and throw them. 1907 S. E. White *Arizona Nights* III. xii. 300 With a short piece of hard rope the cow-boy always carries to 'hog-tie' cattle, he lashed her wrists together. 1910 W. M. Raine *B. O'Connor* xx, He's hogtied to the scenery long enough to do my business. 1924 Mulford *Rustlers' Valley* xi. 136 However, just now we got to hog-tie our soarin' spirits. 1926 J. Black *You Can't Win* xvii. 240 When I was caught in a burglary, overpowered, hog-tied, and waiting for the waggon.

Hog-trough. (Later U.S. examples.)
1855 M. M. Thompson *Doesticks* x. 83 After a long search [I] found him wrapped up in the colors, fast asleep with his head in a hog-trough. 1911 *Essex Inst. Hist. Coll.* XLVII. 13 A man who carried a short swarth was said to cut a 'hog-trough'.

Hohere, variant of *Houhere.

Hohmannite (hōu·mănəit). *Min.* [Named (1888) after Th. *Hohmann*, the discoverer: see -ite[1].] A hydrous ferric sulphate of an amaranth-red colour; amarantite.
1888 *Jrnl. Chem. Soc.* LIV. 924 Hohmannite and amarantite have the same composition. 1900 *Dana's Text-bk. Min.* 536 Amarantite. $Fe_2O_3 . 2SO_3 7H_2O$... Hohmannite is the same partially altered.

Hoick (hoik), *v.* *slang* or *colloq.* [Perhaps orig. a local variant of *Hike *v.*]
1. *trans.* To lift up or hoist, often with a jerk or rapid movement. Also *transf.* and *fig.*
1907 Belloc *On Nothing* (1908) 136 Beneath him the sand sloped down until it met the sea...Every now and then Mahmoud would force a son or domestic of his to go down and hoick out a pearl. 1911 *Chambers's Jrnl.* Mar. 146/1 The patient Captain Croucher hoicked her from destruction in the nick of time. 1914 W. J. Locke *Fortunate Youth* i. 20 He hoicked a bit of his shirt-tail from his breeches and proceeded to knot the cornelian heart secure therein. 1918 'Q' *Foe-Farrell* vi, I dashed around to the rear of the cab, collared Farrell, and hoicked him inboard. 1931 C. Mackenzie *Buttercups & Daisies* v, Blackbirds and thrushes hoicking worms out of the moist ground.
2. To force (an aeroplane) to climb up steeply to a higher level. Also *intr.* to jerk oneself *out of*, etc.
1918 McCudden *Five Yrs. R. F. C.* 287 He..hoicked out of the dive with such vim that three wing-tips at once collapsed. 1919 *Glasgow Herald* 19 Dec. 10 The pilot yanks the joystick to hoick her up. 1928 *Daily Mail* 7 May 6/4 Hoiking.—Sweeping suddenly to avoid an obstacle or a dangerous approach to earth.
Hence **Hoick** *sb.* *Rowing*, a jerk at the beginning or end of a stroke.
1898 *Encycl. Sport* II. 297/1 *Hoick*, a jerk with the arms at the beginning or end of the stroke, which prevents a steady leg drive from the stretcher. 1907 *Daily Chron.* 8 Mar. 9/1 Cambridge sacrifice everything to a terrible hoick at the finish.

Hoi polloi (hoi pǫ·loi). [Gr. οἱ πολλοί, lit. 'the many'.] The majority; the masses. Also formerly in *Univ. slang*, candidates for a pass degree.
[1668 Dryden *Dram. Poesie* 65 If by the people you understand the multitude, the οἱ πολλοὶ. 1815 Byron *Let. to Moore* 28 Oct., [They] put on masks, and went on the stage with the οἱ πολλοι.] 1837 J. F. Cooper *Europe* II. 94 After which the *oi polloi* are enrolled as they can find interest. *a* 1856 in *Newsp. & Gen. Reader's Comp.* § 448 The *hoi polloi* [of the Mauritius], as we say at Oxford, are mindless —all blank. *Ibid.* § 1042 Last of all came the *hoi polloi*, many of whom are not troubled with an inconvenient depth of *nous*. 1905 *Daily Chron.* 29 Aug. 4/4 A couple of immense swells..staring stiffly at 'the hoy-polloy'.

Hoist, *sb.* **3.** (Later U.S. example.)
1901 S. Merwin & H. K. Webster *Calumet K* v. 74 Long before she could be worked into the wharf, they had rigged the two hoists.

Hoist, *v.* **1.** Add: In later use freq. without implication of effort or much elevation.
1873 Joaquin Miller *Unwritten Hist.* v. (1876) 73 At last he hoisted his black fat hand to his black thick head. 1881 Ferris in *Harper's Mag.* Jan. 185/2 My mother received.. two umbrellas,..a..red one for me. My schoolmates came to see it, and it was hoisted with greatest care.
d. *fig.* (Additional U.S. example.)
1834 W. A. Carruthers *Kentuckian in N. Y.* I. 98, I thought I would run him into a stand 'fore long, but he hoisted his tail and flung me clean off the trail again.

Hoist-. Add: **hoist-door** (see quot.).
1881 *Harper's Mag.* Mar. 528/1 In the middle of the hall was the 'hoist-door', through which the wheat was hoisted up by a crane and stored in the loft.

Hokee-pokee. [Cf. Hokey-pokey.] (See quot.)
1873 Joaquin Miller *Unwritten Hist.* xiii. (1876) 192 One man..danced a sort of a savage hokee-pokee, and sang.

Hokum (hōu·kəm). orig. *U.S. Theatrical slang.* Also **hocum**. [? A blending of Hocus-pocus and Bunkum.] Speech, action, properties, etc., on the stage, designed to make a sentimental or melodramatic appeal to an audience. Hence *gen.* bunkum.
1922 C. Sandburg *Slabs of Sunburnt West* 25 Hokum—they lap it up. 1926 *New York Times* 29 Aug., This may be groundling comedy, but it is not pure hokum. 1926 *Ladies' Home Jrnl.* Apr. 38 'What they tell is..bold and defiant realism.' 'Bold and defiant hokum, I should call it.' 1927 *Sunday Express* 17 Apr. 4 Channing Pollock believed that in 'The Fool' he had written a work of genius. Even when other people said it was hokum he still went on. 1928 *Publishers' Weekly* 16 June 2440 It is pure hokum to suggest that all authors are always interesting. 1928 *Sunday Dispatch* 15 July 15/1 The Adelphi..was occupied by a Mr. Sam Bernard with a musical play called 'The Belle of Bond Street'—what an outrage that 'Girl' and 'Belle' hokum must have become! 1930 *Publishers' Weekly* 15 Mar. 1559 In spite of the fact that the hokum of it all has been pointed out to them.

Holaspidean (hǫlæspi·dĭăn), *a.* *Zool.* [f. mod.L. *Holaspideæ*, a cohort of Sundevall's scutelliplantar oscines + -an.] Pertaining to or characteristic of the *Holaspideæ*; having a single series of large scutella on the posterior portion of the tarsus.
1885 *Riverside Nat. Hist.* (1888) IV. 485 This peculiarity consists in the holaspidean tarsi, technically making them scutelliplantar, the hind surface of the tarsus being broken up into scutes similar to those covering the front part.

Holbein (hōu·lbəin, hǫ·l-). The name of the German painter Hans *Holbein* (1497–1543), used attrib. to designate a kind of embroidery seen in some of his pictures, as *Holbein stitch*, Italian stitch; so *Holbein work*. Hence **Holbeine·sque** *a.* [see -esque], resembling the work of Holbein.
1882 Caulfeild & Saward *Dict. Needlew.* 252/2 *Holbein Stitch*, also known as Italian Stitch, and used in Holbein Embroidery to cover the outline patterns that form the work. *Ibid.* 253/1 *Holbein Work*..consists of an outline Embroidery executed with great care and exactitude, so that the right and wrong side of the work are alike. 1895 J. A. Gray *At Court of Amir* xxxi, The most skilful of the artists gave an almost Holbeinesque look to his drawings. 1904 *Westm. Gaz.* 14 Nov. 4/2 His fine Holbeinesque drawings.

Hold, *sb.*[1] Add: **14.** (See quot.)
1918 H. Croy *How Motion Pictures are made* vii. 179 If the story demands instantaneous materialization the effect is secured by a photographic means usually known as 'the hold'. It is so called by reason of the fact that all the other characters in such a scene must hold their positions while the trick character is made to materialize.

Hold, *v.* Add: **2. d.** To keep back, detain, delay.
1891 F. H. Smith *Col. Carter* 135 'Where did you get this?' he asked, aghast. 'From the carrier. It [*sc.* a letter] was held for postage.' 1904 *New York Times* 20 Aug. 1 The railroad has issued an order..that trains shall not be held for the.. taking of baggage after the regular time scheduled for stops has expired.
e. To detain in custody, keep under arrest. *U.S.*
1903 *New York Evening Post* 19 Aug., The men were held for felonious assault, and the woman as a witness. 1906 *Springfield* (Mass.) *Weekly Republican* 14 June 1 If the New York insurance officials cannot be held for larceny, they might evidently be held for forgery or perjury. 1922 Titus *Timber* iii. 32 'Why did he arrest you?' 'Oh, I dropped a cigarette out here in summer an' started a fire,..an' he held me under the fire law.'
6. g. Phr. *To hold the stage*: see quots. Also *fig.* (cf. 7).
1889 Barrère & Leland *Dict. Slang*, *Hold the stage, to* (theatrical), is said of an experienced actor who is fully at home on the stage, and always commands the attention of the audience. 1893 Farmer & Henley *Slang*, *To hold the stage*, to have the chief place on the boards and the eye of the audience.
h. *To hold the line*: to retain control of telephonic connexion during a conversation. (Cf. *40 g.)
1915 *Punch* 10 Nov. 390/1 Such are some of the miseries of holding the line.
23. d. To continue fine, to keep from raining. (Cf. 44 i.)
1893 *Chambers's Jrnl.* 10 June 355/2 If the weather holds, we'll both take a trip.
35. **Hold down.** **c.** To remain in (a position or situation); to continue to occupy (a place or post) or succeed in discharging the duties of (one's employment). *U.S. colloq.*
1891 C. Roberts *Adrift in America* 92 Jumping an east bound freight.., I managed to hold it down or keep on it till I got to Alameda. 1896 G. Ade *Artie* xiv. 129 I'll bet that guy up in your place don't know nothin' on earth except how to hold down his measly job. 1902 G. H. Lorimer *Lett. Self-made Merchant* v. 60 The fellow who's got the right stuff in him is holding down his own place with one hand. 1909 S. E. White *Rules of Game* I. iii. 19, I didn't much think you could hold down a job here. You see there's too much doing here. 1913 F. H. Burnett *T. Tembarom* ii, I wonder, if I ever did get his job, if I could hold it down?
40. **Hold on.** **c.** Also in jocular phrases.
1930 'Sapper' *Finger of Fate*, etc. 35 Having to hold on by one's eyebrows whenever one moves gets a bit monotonous after a time.
e. (Earlier examples.)
1846 Caroline M. Kirkland *Western Clearings* 45 'But hold on a little till I tell ye!' interposed Master George. [For 1860 read 1848.]
g. *Telephone.* To keep the line open.
1920 *Punch* 1 Sept. 176/3 'What is your number, please?' ..'Just hold on a minute while I look it up.' 1920 Rose Macaulay *Potterism* III. i. 104 You mustn't ring off yet... Hold on while I tell daddy.
41. **Hold out.** **l.** To keep back; to retain or detain. *U.S.*
1911 H. S. Harrison *Queed* v. 57 Surface, by clever juggling of his books had managed to 'hold out' a large sum of money in the enforced settlement of his affairs. 1916 H. L. Wilson *Somewhere in Red Gap* viii. 345, I wanted to send a postal card to the..Dye Works at Red Gap, for some stuff they had been holding out on me a month. 1921 R. D. Paine *Comr. Rolling Ocean* i. 13 He dumped his wages upon the sitting-room table, holding out only the price of a new pair of shoes.
42. **Hold over.** **c.** *U.S. colloq.* (See quot. 1889.)
1872 'Mark Twain' *Innoc. at Home* 18 (Farmer) You ruther hold over me, pard. I reckon I can't call that hand. 1889 Farmer *Amer.*, *To hold over one* is to have an advantage in some way or other. This particular usage probably comes from poker phraseology. 1889 K. Munroe *Golden Days* xii. 127 Do we hold over Bowers?
44. **Hold up.** **d.** (Later U.S. examples in sense 'keep back, withhold'.)
1889 *Kansas Times & Star* 4 Dec., Major Davenport is holding up the firemen's payroll for November owing to alleged irregularities. 1894 *Vermont Agric. Rep.* XIV. 70 When..a cow holds up her milk there is some disturbing element.
e. Also, to arrest the progress of, obstruct the passage of (*lit.* and *fig.*).
1904 *Philadelphia Even. Telegr.* 15 Nov. 1 Out of the 900 steerage passengers that came over on the Merion, 135 failed to pass the immigration inspectors, and were held up. 1905 *N. Y. Evening Post* 16 Mar. 1 Another landslide has occurred..and nine passenger trains are held up in the mountains. 1906 *N. Y. Herald* 5 Mar. 5 It is thought the Senate Finance Committee will seek to devise new excuses for holding up the investigation of the State Banking Department, which it has succeeded in smothering for five weeks. 1909 H. N. Casson *C. H. McCormick* 146 One bill for $15 was held up for a week because it was not properly drawn.

Hold-all. Add: **2.** *fig.*, esp. with reference to books of the omnibus or encyclopædic kind.

1903 *Daily Chron.* 9 Nov. 3/3 There is a little of everything in the hold-all. 1904 M. Davies (*title*) The Housewife's What's What: a Hold-all of Useful Information for the House.

Hold-back. Add: **2.** (Earlier example.)

1850 *Coll. Hist. Soc.* VI. 220 The hold-backs of his harness gave way, and precipitated his gig upon the horse.

3. The act of holding back. Also *attrib.*, unprogressive.

1852 *Trans. Mich. Agric. Soc.* III. 333 A few specimens of the hold-back and stand-still class. 1888 'Buffalo Bill' *Wild West* 617 There was no brake on the wagon, and the horses were not much on the hold back.

Ho·ld-down. [f. phr. *hold down* (Hold *v.* 35).] A device to prevent material or apparatus from shifting or shaking. Also *attrib.*

1888 *Lockwood's Dict. Mech. Engin.*, *Foundation Bolts*. ..Also termed hold-down bolts.

Holder[1]. Add: **2. b.** *Sports.* The possessor for the time (as the winner) of a championship, cup, etc. which is open to competition.

1873 *Football Ann.* 54 Association Challenge Cup, 1872–73. ..Final Tie. Wanderers (holders) beat Oxford Association by two goals..to none. 1887 *Athletic Jrnl.* 9 Aug. 16 West Manchester (the winners and present holders of the Manchester Cup). 1900 *Field* 7 July 3/3 Hants County Public School Challenge Shield...This annual competition was held on the playgrounds of the holders, Churcher's College, Petersfield, on Thursday in last week. *Ibid.* 14 July 61/1 The holder of the challenge cup, Wadsley, was quite unable to do himself justice. 1928 *Daily Mail* 25 July 14/7 Middlesex, the holders, are..the only county to have won two matches in this group.

Holdfast, *sb.* Add: **4. b.** *Bot.* (*a*) An organ of attachment developed by some algæ; a rhizoid. (*b*) A tendril.

1895 *Funk's Stand. Dict.* 1897 Webster, *Holdfast*,..a conical or branching body, by which a seaweed is attached to its support, and differing from a root in that it is not specially absorbent of moisture. 1900 B. D. Jackson *Gloss. Bot. Terms*, *Holdfasts*, the disclike attachments of Algae. 1901 *Chambers's Jrnl.* Apr. 278/2 Often when all other modes of supply are cut off, these holdfasts will entirely nourish the plant. 1902 *Science* Jan. 59/2 Kelp hold-fasts, of which none grow in the immediate vicinity, were taken in abundance by the dredge.

Holding, *vbl. sb.* Add: **1. d.** *Holding up* (see quot.).

1888 *Lockwood's Dict. Mech. Engin.*, *Holding up*, the maintaining of a firm pressure against the heads of rivets while their closing up is being effected, a holding-up hammer being used for the purpose.

e. *Association Football.* The obstruction of a player by the hand or arm extended from the body.

1866 *Cassell's Illustr. Fam. Paper* 17 Mar. 509/2 'Holding' includes the obstruction of a player by the hands, arms, or body without kicking or throwing.

3. c. *pl.* The cards held by a player.

1929 Work *Compl. Contract Bridge* iv. 38 With such holdings..the rebid should be made.

Holding, *ppl. a.* Add:

1. b. *Holding company*: a trading company which possesses the whole of, or a controlling interest in, the share capital of one or more other companies.

1912 *Q. Rev.* Jan. 195 The Federal Steel Company, which is technically, like the Steel Corporation of to-day, a holding company. 1928 *Britain's Industr. Future* (*Liberal Ind. Inq.*) II. viii. 93 To treat trusts, cartels, combinations, holding companies, and trade associations as inexpedient abnormalities in the economic system. 1928 *Daily Mail* 7 Aug. 18/4 This conservative finance enables the Shell, as a holding company,..to maintain its dividends in times of depression.

3. *holding-down bolt, pin, ring.*

1875 Knight *Dict. Mech.*, *Holding-down Bolt*,..one of twelve or more strong bolts, which are passed from the outside of a steam-vessel through the floor-timbers, sleepers, foundation-plate of the engine, and the bosses on the cylinders, condensers, and side-frames, and are secured by strong nuts. 1892 Greener *Breech-Loader* 19 Every gun provided with a holding-down bolt. *Ibid.* 260 Certain accessories.., such as cords, planks, and holding-down pins. 1899–1900 *Kynoch Jrnl.* Dec.–Jan. 29/2 The cones are secured to ships' decks by holding-down rings.

Hold-over. Add: **d.** Something left over; a remainder or survival. *U.S.*

1904 *Los Angeles Express* 11 Aug. 12 Doing the best it could on crackers and cheese and holdovers. *a* 1909 'O. Henry' *Roads of Destiny* iv. 58 She was a hold-over from the Greek classics. 1929 *Atlantic Monthly* Mar. 298 The little village of Washington in Connecticut, one of the most charming holdovers of the past that state possesses.

Hold-up. Add: **c.** A stoppage or check in the passage or progress of a person or thing; a temporary stoppage of traffic; a cessation, stop. orig. *U.S.*

1837 *Knickerbocker Mag.* X. 439 The wheels of the coach are shod with the preparation of iron slippers, which are essential to a hold-up. 1882 in Putnam *Mem. Publisher* (1915) 289 We don't have hold-ups [*sc.* strikes] in Leadville. 1904 *N. Y. Tribune* 15 May 2 A vote of thanks to the Tribune for its efforts to end the hold-up of the Port Chester Railroad's application for a permit to cross streets in the Bronx. 1907 *Putnam's Monthly* July 482/1 He cursed the luck of the hold-up. 1913 A. B. Emerson *R. Fielding at Snow Camp* 154 We got to sit down and wait for a hold-up [of the storm]. 1918 'Q' *Foe-Farrell* vii. 125 There was a hold-up as we [in a taxi] neared the bridge. 1928 *Daily Express* 14 July 2/1 There had been two or three hold-ups with the points prior to my arrival at 4.50 p.m.

d. *attrib.* = Engaged in, involving, or characterized by forcible stopping and robbing of a person.

1899 *Chicago Tribune* 16 Jan., The holdup gang who shot and killed policeman..Wallner. 1901 *N. Amer. Rev.* Feb. 264 'The hold-up-man' goes abroad after dark to follow his nefarious occupation. 1901 S. E. White *Claim Jumpers* xviii. 220 This is no hold-up country. You can't drive a man off his property with a gun. 1913 E. D. Biggers *Seven Keys to Baldpate* ix. 112 'A corking night,' he muttered humorously, 'for my *debut* in the hold-up business'. 1919 Wodehouse *Damsel in Distress* ii, The sun had..delivered him into the hands of the wind, which was now going through him with the swift thoroughness of the professional hold-up artist.

Hole, *sb.* Add:

4. a. Also *transf.*, in golf, the distance between the teeing-ground and the hole to be played.

1891 *H. G. Hutchinson's Famous Golf Links* 90 Point Garry is a long, hazardous hole. *Ibid.* 156 The third hole (135 yards) is an exact counterpart of the second. 1908 Braid *Advanced Golf* 252 Holes of about 360 to 380 yards.

d. *Eton Fives.* A small square portion of the floor enclosed by the pepper-box and step. Phr. *To be in holes*; hence *attrib.* in *holes innings*.

1897 *Encycl. Sport* I. 399 A, who begins serving, is bound to give C—who is said to be 'in holes'—the sort of service which he prefers. *Ibid.* 400 All alike differ from Eton Courts in having no pepper-box, hole, or step. *Ibid.* 402 In the first innings of a game A (who goes in first) is said to have 'holes innings', *i.e.*, when both A and B have been put out, A will be 'in holes'.

7. b. *In holes*: perforated with holes, worn into holes.

1851 Mayhew *London Labour* II. 470/2, I can't abide this muckydam [*sc.* macadam]..it's sloppy stuff, and goes so bad in holes. 1926 Agatha Christie *Murder of R. Ackroyd* x. 127 He wouldn't even buy new face towels, though I told him the old ones were in holes.

c. Aeronautics. *Hole in the air*: a localized condition of the atmosphere having a downward movement of the air through which a machine tends to drop as if into a hole; later called *air-pocket*.

1916 H. Barber *Aeroplane Speaks* 51 Now the Aeroplane is almost over the river, and the next instant it suddenly drops into a 'hole in the air'. 1917 C. C. Turner *Aircraft of To-day* vi. 98 The terms 'air-pocket' and 'hole in the air' are frequently heard in flying circles.

11. *To make a hole* or *holes in*: to put a bullet into; to shoot. *To make a hole in the water*: see Water *sb.* 6 f. *To be in the hole* U.S.: to be in (financial) difficulties (cf. 3).

1916 *Lit. Digest* (N.Y.) 8 Jan. 87/1 The Wards were in the hole to the extent of close to $800,000.

12. hole-high *a.* (see quot.); **hole-proof** *a.*, that will not wear into holes.

1897 *Encycl. Sport* I. 472/2 A ball is said to be *hole high when it is played on to the putting green from a distance. 1913 *Work* 17 May 102 A..cloth that will not tear—in fact, is *holeproof. 1927 *Glasgow Herald* 4 Feb. 10 Unshrinkable, fadeless, and holeproof.

Hole, *v.*[1] Add: **1. c.** To fire a bullet into.

1847 Trollope *Macdermots* iv, We'll hole him till there ar'nt a bit left in him to hole. 1883 — *Land Leaguers* ii. I. 34 Keep yourself from being holed as they holed Muster Bingham the other day.

7. *To hole up*: (*b*) To go into hiding, retire (*dial.*). (*c*) To lie in wait or in ambush (*U.S. slang*).

1910 Mrs. H. Ward *Canadian Born* ix. 181 I'm a poor old broken-down..miner, who wants to hole-up somewhere, and get comfortable for his old age. 1912 Mulford & Clay *Buck Peters* xxvii. 235 Go slow, Tex: mebby he's holin' up on us, like he did on Buck. 1924 — *Rustlers' Valley* xii. 141 Now you'll mebby have to take to th' hills an' hole up just when I need you most. 1925 — *Cottonwood Gulch* xvi. 218 It would have been only a matter of a few minutes before they would have forced him to abandon the horse and to hole up on the defensive, to make a losing fight.

9. *trans.* To indicate by punching a hole in an allotted space in a card.

1911 *Chambers's Jrnl.* May 335/2 Not only are the old-time data, such as age,..'holed' into the card, but whether you are married or single. *Ibid.* 336/2 In this machine the data 'holed' in every tag can be all or partly recorded on another form.

Holeable (hōu·lăb'l), *a.* *Golf.* Also **holable.** [f. Hole *v.*[1] + -able.] Of a putt: That can be holed (in a certain number of strokes).

1909 *Westm. Gaz.* 30 Apr. 12/2 On the green Taylor failed at a holable putt for 5. *Ibid.* 10 June 12/3 Four holeable putts which he missed. 1927 *Sunday Express* 29 May 21/7 The short eleventh was halved in three, both players missing holeable putts.

Holiday, *sb.* Add: **2. c.** Euphemistically used for: Imprisonment.

1901 *Pall Mall Mag.* Feb. 197 A sentence of a month or two..a little 'holiday' with food and shelter and warmth.

4. a. *holiday camp, ramble, tutor*(*ship*); **holiday-course** [= G. *ferienkurs*, F. *cours de vacances*, etc.], a series of lectures, classes, etc. which is held during a school or college vacation; **holiday-home**, a place where poor or indigent persons are accommodated at little or no cost to themselves for a period of holiday; **holiday task**, homework to be done during the holidays.

1877 R. St. J. Corbet (*title*) 'Holiday Camp: Three Days' Picnic: Story for Boys and Girls. 1931 *Geography* (Geog. Assoc., Manchester) Sept. 221 The advantage of such hostels ..over holiday camps is that they give the user the priceless asset of mobility. 1887 *Girl's Own Paper* 22 Oct. 48/3 A lady who has a large house and grounds would give a lady of small means a '*holiday home'. *a* 1851 Mrs. Sherwood *Boys will be Boys* ii, That part of the country..within the nearer reach of a *holiday ramble. 1875 'Ascott R. Hope' (*title*) *Holiday Task: Magazine of Whitminster Grammar School. 1899 Kipling *Stalky* 180 They have a holiday task ..which..none..will ever look at. 1930 C. Mackenzie *April Fools* vii. 138 I'm reading 'Homes without Hands' for a holiday task. 1900 *Captain* II. 375/1 When Mr. Soames asked the professor to come and be *holiday tutor. *Ibid.*, Open to take a *holiday tutorship.

Holing, *vbl. sb.* Add: **1.** Also, the production of holes, e.g. in garments (cf. Hole *v.*[1] 8).

1910 *Daily Chron.* 14 Mar. 6/4 The Stockings that are actually insured against holing.

c. *Golf.* The action of holing the ball; also *attrib.*, as *holing distance, holing-out putt.*

1875 'Stonehenge' (J. H. Walsh) *Brit. Sports* (ed. 12) 695/1 He who succeeds in holeing in fewer strokes than his opponent wins that hole. 1901 *Scotsman* 11 Sept. 10/1 A nicely-played mashie stroke took his ball within holing distance. 1906 *Westm. Gaz.* 10 Aug. 4/2 The longer holing-out putts.

Holism (hǫ·liz'm, hōu·liz'm). [f. Gr. ὅλος whole + -ism.] A term coined by Gen. J. C. Smuts to designate the tendency in nature to produce wholes (*i.e.* bodies or organisms) from the ordered grouping of unit structures. So **Holi·stic** *a.*, **Holi·stically** *adv.*

1926 J. C. Smuts *Holism & Evol.* 99 The whole-making, holistic tendency, or Holism, operating in and through particular wholes, is seen at all stages of existence. *Ibid.* 127 There is a synthesis which makes the elements or parts act as one or holistically. 1927 *Brit. Weekly* 20 Jan. 418/4 The real entities of the material world must, like organisms, be creative, self-transcending, functional. They must be Holistic unities. 1931 Smuts in *Times* 2 Sept. 7/7 Instead of the animistic, or the mechanistic, or the mathematical universe, we see the genetic, organic, holistic universe.

Holland. **1. b.** Add: *Holland sauce* = *Hollandaise.

1892 *Encycl. Pract. Cookery* II. 387 Dutch or Holland Sauce (à la Hollandaise).

Holland[2] (hǫ·lănd). The name of J. P. *Holland* (1840–1914), the inventor of a class of submarines adopted by the American navy, used as the proper name of the first submarine of this type and afterwards generically.

1899 *Westm. Gaz.* 7 Dec. 2/3 The President of the official Naval Board, and several of its members have signed a statement declaring that their 'Holland' has fulfilled all requirements in her trial trip. 1902 *Encycl. Brit.* XXXII. 576/2 The *Holland*, a smaller boat, having a length of about 59 ft., though begun after the *Plunger*, has already been completed. *Ibid.*, The latest Holland design is shown in Fig. 95. 1906 *Daily Chron.* 8 Sept. 5/3 The original Holland class of submarine.

Hollandaise (hǫlăndē·z, ‖olandęz). [Fr., fem. of *hollandais* Dutch, f. *Hollande* Holland.] *Hollandaise sauce* (see quot. 1907).

1907 Escoffier *Mod. Cookery* 22 Hollandaise Sauce... One and one-half lbs. of butter, the yolks of six eggs, one pinch of mignonette pepper and one-quarter oz. of salt, three tablespoonfuls of good vinegar. *Ibid.* 23 The consistence of sauces whose processes are identical with those of the Hollandaise may be varied at will. 1930 N. Lake *Menus made easy* 268 Hollandaise—yolks of eggs and butter with tarragon and chilli vinegar.

Hollander. Add: **b.** An African colonist of Dutch descent. Also *attrib.*, or as *adj.*, and *Comb.*

1699 *Capt. Cowley's Voy. round Globe* in *Collect. Voy.* (1729) iv. 34 The Village inhabited by the Hodmandods, so called by the Hollanders. 1897 in H. M. Stanley *Thro' S. Africa* v. (1898) 75, I do not blame the Boers so much as I blame the Hollanders and our Jews here. 1899 *Westm. Gaz.* 16 Oct. 7/2 The Boers who have occupied Newcastle consist of both Transvaal and Free State commandos, with 400 Hollanders. 1899 *Daily News* 2 Nov. 5/2 It has not been he, but the 'Hollander', a most unfavourable specimen of the Dutch race, who has been concerned in all the doubtful intrigues.. of the last few years. 1902 *Encycl. Brit.* XXXII. 721/1 The effect of this development was the production of a body of officials in the Transvaal, partly Hollander and German, partly Boer. 1903 Omond *Boers in Eur.* 31 South Africa, big towns and seaports excepted, being Hollander-Boer to the core.

2. *Paper-making.* A beating engine, invented in Holland, for the conversion of the bleached rags into paper-pulp.

1878 *Design & Work* 19 Jan. 88/3 About fifty years after the invention of the 'Hollander'..alkali began to be employed for boiling the rags. 1900 C. F. Cross & Bevan *Paper-Making* (ed. 2) 172 The ordinary form of beater is fitted with a single roll, and the general arrangement of its working parts is that..described..for a 'breaking' engine. This type of beater is known as the Hollander. 1902 *Encycl. Brit.* XXXI. 458/2 One of the various forms of beating engine or 'Holländer'. 1907 C. F. Cross & Bevan *Paper-Making* (ed. 3) 179 The Hollander consists of an oblong trough, with semi-circular ends, with a partition or mid-feather running down the centre so as to form a continuous channel round which the stuff can circulate.

3. A Dutch clinker.

1897 Webster, *Hollander*, 2. A very hard, semi-glazed, green or dark brown brick, which will not absorb water;—called also Dutch clinker. Wagner.

4. (See quot.)

1879 *Encycl. Brit.* IX. 400/2 The largest spars [of timber] are called 'Hollander'.

Holler, *sb.* *dial.* and *U.S.* [Cf. next.] = Hollo *sb.*

1825 Jennings *Obs. Dial. W. Eng.*, Hollar. 1886 Elworthy *W. Somerset Word-bk.* 346 *Holler*,..the cry given when the quarry is seen; the view-halloo. 1896 G. Ade *Artie* xvi. 147, I put up a holler right at the jump.

Holler, *v.* *dial.* and *U.S.* [var. of Hollo *v.*] *intr.* = Hollo *v.*

1699 *Cal. Virginia St. Papers* I. 67 We gott to the River side oppisett to the ffort, and theire hollerd and immediately they answered. 1834 S. Smith *Sel. Lett. Major J. Downing* 37 All hollering 'stooboy'. 1843 R. Carlton *New Purchase* xiv. 101 Provided you knew how 'to holler' within hearing of both. 1852 *N. & Q.* V. 148/2 The village boys..get some halfpence given them for their 'hollering'. 1872 in Tourgee *Invisible Empire* x. (1880) 481 He hollered twice. *Ibid.*, I and my wife hollered and his wife hollered. 1901 S. Merwin & H. K. Webster *Calumet K* viii. 155 'I'll go ahead and clear the track,' said Bannon, 'I'll holler up to you, Max, when we're ready down below.' 1926 J. Black *You Can't Win* iv. 43 Holler before you're hurt; that's my motto.

Holliper, variant of Oliver[2].

Holloo, *v.* (Later U.S. example.)

1816 U. Brown *Jrnl.* in *Maryland Hist. Mag.* XI. 365 [I] thought I should freeze, [and] set to Hollooing.

Hollow, *sb.* Add: **1. d.** (See quot.)

1888 *Lockwood's Dict. Mech. Engin.*, *Hollows*, the inside curves imparted to the otherwise angular parts of castings. They are inserted in order that the crystals of the metal may arrange themselves in the strongest position.

Hollow, *a.* and *adv.* Add:

A. *adj.* **2. c.** (Earlier U.S. example.)

1705 *Essex Inst. Hist. Coll.* XLII. 155 The storm still continuing, so that the seas ranne very high and hollow.

6. Of a race: Feebly contested. Hence of a victory: Obtained against feeble competition.

1876 *Coursing Cal.* 5 The next course was equally hollow, Death's Flight leading, and winning with any amount in hand.

7. hollow-blow (see quot.); **hollow-fronted, -nosed, -pointed** *adjs.*, said of a bullet with a hollow in the point to ensure expansion of the projectile on impact; **hollow-horn** *U.S.*, a disease in cattle which results in the wasting of the core of the horn; **hollow-set**, a smith's gouge for curved work; **hollow spun** (see quot.); **hollow tool**, the lower part of a blacksmith's swage (Lockwood, 1888); **hollow wall**, a wall built with a cavity between its two surfaces either for economy's sake or for the preservation of an even temperature in the building

1888 *Lockwood's Dict. Mech. Engin.*, *Hollow Blows, blows delivered by a hammer upon a substance which is either unsupported, or insufficiently supported by an opposing block. 1899 *Kynoch Jrnl.* Oct.–Nov. 14/2 If the ·577 pure lead *hollow-fronted bullet hit a man he knew it at once. 1825 J. Lorain *Pract. Husb.* 455 The *hollow horn, a disease which seldom fails to attack half-famished cattle. 1867 *Rep. Iowa Agric. Soc.* (1868) 129 Cattle have few diseases in this locality except the 'buck eye' and 'hollow horn'. 1904 'O. Henry' *Heart of West* v. 69, I..talked with Uncle Emsley a while about hollow-horn and cyclones. 1909 *Daily Chron.* 26 June 1/4 The other cartridges..being of nickle steel and *hollow-nosed. 1910 G. Burrard *Notes on Sporting Rifles* 40 A hollow-nosed bullet. 1902 *Encycl. Brit.* XXXII. 244/1 The *hollow-pointed expanding bullet with soft lead nose. 1902–3 *Kynoch Jrnl.* Dec.–Jan. 43/1 Without the mutilation so commonly caused by hollow pointed bullets. 1888 *Lockwood's Dict. Mech. Engin.*, *Hollow Set, a smith's gouge, used for dressing off the circular portions of forged work. 1927 *Daily Tel.* 31 Jan. 5 The concrete posts are *hollow-spun, the concrete being poured into a hollow mould and spun into shape. 1833 Loudon *Encycl. Archit.* § 339 Dearn's Mode of building Fourteen-Inch *hollow walls. 1891 *Notes on Building Constr.* II. 10 The hollow wall is often arranged to begin on the damp-proof course.

B. *adv.* **3.** *hollow-booming* adj.

1906 W. Watson in *Tribune* 15 Jan. 2/4 Toll, thou hollow-booming Bell.

Holluschickie (hǫlǝ·sˌtʃiki), *collect. pl.* Also **hollusohuckie.** [ad. Russ. холостякй *kholostyaki* pl. bachelors.] Young male fur seals.

1880 H. W. Elliott *Seal Isl. Alaska* 45 The 'holluschickie' are the champion swimmers of all the seal-tribe. 1894 R. Kipling *Jungle Bk.* 97 They [*sc.* seals] were called the holluschickie—the bachelors. 1896 — *Seven Seas* 70 But he'll lie down on the killing grounds where the holluschickie go. 1901 *Munsey's Mag.* XXV. 355/1 The holluschickie who have reached the age when they contemplate matrimony. 1929 *Encycl. Brit.* IX. 952/1 The young males or bachelors (*holloschickie*).

Holly. Add: **3. b. holly-blue**, the azure blue butterfly *Polyommatus argiolus.*

1905 *Daily Chron.* 6 Apr. 3/2 The holly-blue often flies on days when there is more hail than sun. 1909 J. H. Kelman & T. Wood *Butterfl. & Moths* 23, I do not know why this pretty butterfly is called the 'Azure' Blue...Sometimes it is called the 'Holly Blue'.

Hollyhock. Add: **2. b. hollyhock disease**, = **hollyhock rust*; also, blight caused by the parasitic fungus *Colletotrichum althææ*; **hollyhock fungus**, a fungus, *Puccinia malvacearum*, parasitic on the hollyhock; **hollyhock rust**, the disease caused by this.

1898 W. Robinson *Engl. Flower Garden* (ed. 6) 389/1 Owing to the *Hollyhock disease it is often a better plan to abandon the named kinds increased from cuttings and resort to seedlings only for stock. 1883 *Ibid.* 13/2 The *Hollyhock Fungus (*Puccinia malvacearum*)..is..destructive to the Hollyhock. 1899 Massee *Text-bk. Plant Dis.* 252 *Hollyhock rust. 1910 T. W. Sanders *Garden Foes* 227 Hollyhock Rust (Puccinia malvacearum). At one time this fungoid disease played great havoc with the hollyhock.

Holmia (hōu·lmiă). *Chem.* [mod.L. *holmia*, f. second syllable of *Stockholm*, name of the capital of Sweden, in the neighbourhood of which yttria-bearing minerals are found.] A rare earth of the yttria group occurring in gadolinite, the oxide of the element holmium.

1880 *Jrnl. Chem. Soc.* XXXVIII. 7 The author [*sc.* J. L. Soret] considers that the new earth, *holmia*, discovered by Clève, is identical with an earth discovered by Delafontaine and Marignac. 1889 Morley & Muir *Watts' Dict. Chem.* II. 457/1.

Holmium (hōu·lmiŏm). *Chem.* [mod.L.] An element of the yttrium-cerium group found in gadolinite.

1880 *Jrnl. Chem. Soc.* XXXVIII. 7 The third metal, holmium, is characterised by the bands λ = 6400 and 5360; it should have an atomic weight less than 108; its oxide seems to be yellow. 1893 *Ibid.* LXIV. II. 467 The holmium oxides were obtained from strongly basic yttrium earths containing a large amount of yttrium oxide. 1910 *Encycl. Brit.* XXII. 910/2 By boiling this solution the earths are precipitated in the order yttrium, holmium and dysprosium, and erbium.

Holo-. Add: **Holobe·nthic** *a.* *Biol.*, living at or near the bottom of the sea during all stages of life. **Holocai·n, -cai·ne** *Pharm.*, a crystalline derivative of phenacetin and paraphenetidine, used as a local anæsthetic. **Ho·locene** *a.* *Geol.*, pertaining to the Human or Recent Period; also *sb.* **Holocho·anoid** *a.* and *sb.*, pertaining to, a member of, the *Holochoanoida*, a group of extinct nautiloidean cephalopods; so **Ho·lochoanoi·dal** *a.* **Holocho·rdate** *a.* *Biol.*, having the chorda or notochord extending the whole length of the body. **Holocla·stic** *a.* *Geol.*, designating clastic rocks of aqueous origin. **Ho·locrine** *a.* *Anat.* [see *Endocrine] (see quot.). **Ho·logoni·dium** *Bot.*, Wallroth's term for the algal soredia. **Holomorph** (hǫ·lomǭrf) *Math.* [Gr. μορφή form], an expression which has or imitates, within a specified region of value, the properties of a corresponding integral expression. **Ho·lomo·rphosis** *Biol.*, the perfect reproduction of a lost member or part. **Holono·mic** *a.* *Mech.*, characterizing constrained systems in which the equations are integral or integrable. **Holopa·rasite** *Bot.*, a plant which is wholly parasitic; hence **Ho·loparasi·tic** *a.* **Ho·lophrase** *Philol.*, a word used instead of a phrase, or to express a combination of ideas; so **Ho·lophrasm** (-fræz'm). **Holophy·tic** *a.*, also *Bot.*, (of a plant) capable of maintaining itself, as distinguished from parasitic or saprophytic. **Ho·lophytism** *Bot.*, the condition of being autotrophic. **Holopla·nkton** *Biol.*, all forms of life, considered collectively, which are aquatic in all stages of life; hence **Ho·loplankto·nic** *a.*, living throughout life at or near the surface of the water. **Holopneu·stic** *a.* *Ent.*, breathing by means of many pairs of open stigmata. **Holosa·prophyte** *Bot.*, a plant which is wholly parasitic; hence **Ho·losaprophy·tic** *a.* **Ho·lotype** *Zool.* = *Cotype.

1902 *Encycl. Brit.* XXXIII. 935 Another hindrance to the extension of many deep-sea species is that they are *holobenthic. 1901 Dorland *Med. Dict.* (ed. 2), *Holocain, a crystalline base nearly allied to phenacetin; its chlorid is a local anesthetic, antiseptic, and is used like cocain. 1904 *Guide Fossil Mamm.* etc. *Brit. Mus.* Geol. Time Scale facing p. xvi, *Holocene...Present Day. 1910 *Encycl. Brit.* XIII. 618/1 The Holocene formations obviously include all the varieties of deposits which are accumulating at the present day. 1914 *Brit. Museum Return* 200 Non-marine shells from..the Holocene of Newquay, Cornwall. 1928 V. G. Childe *Most Anc. East* x. 229 In late quaternary and early holocene times. 1883 *Proc. Boston Soc. Nat. Hist.* XXII. 267 *note*, The first three genera appear to have *holochoanoidal siphons. 1898 Gadow *Class. Vert.* 1 With a central solid axis..extending through the whole length of the body, from head to tail, hence *holochordate. 1913 Dorland *Med. Dict.* (ed. 7), *Holocrine,..wholly secretory: a term applied to glands whose only function is to form a secretion. 1888 *Encycl. Brit.* XXIV. 72/1 *note*, When *w* is *holomorphe in a region except at a point z_1, where it becomes infinite without 1/*w* ceasing to be holomorphe near this, this point is called a pole or an infinity of *w*. 1901 T. H. Morgan *Regeneration* 24 [The case in which] the entire lost part is at once, or later, replaced—*holomorphosis. 1910 *Encycl. Brit.* VIII. 759/1 When *t* does not occur explicitly in the relations the system is said to be *holonomic. 1903 W. R. Fisher tr. *A. F. W. Schimper's Plant-Geog.* 203 *Holo-parasites, which live entirely at the cost of the organic substance of their host. 1902 *Encycl. Brit.* XXV. 439/1 *Holoparasitic Rhizanths. *Ibid.* 439/2 Cytineæ, Balanophoreæ, Orobanchaceæ, Lennoaceæ, are families..which are characteristically holoparasitic. 1899 E. J. Payne *Hist. New World* II. 201 This multiplication of elements denoting personality, in combination with more and more elements denoting Things, tends to the dissolution of the *holophrase. ..The holophrase naturally follows the progression of the mind from point to point. 1914 W. R. M. Lamb *Clio Enthroned* 239 We can regard his periodic structures as a reversion..to the primitive holophrase. 1862 D. Wilson *Preh. Man* xxv. II. 436 *Holophrasms are common in all its [*sc.* the Algonquin] dialects. 1900 B. D. Jackson *Gloss. Bot. Terms*, *Holophytism, the condition of a plant with its growth maintained entirely by its own organs, without any suspicion of saprophytism or parasitism. 1902 *Encycl. Brit.* XXXIII. 936/2 The epiplankton of the open sea.. consists almost entirely of *holoplanktonic forms, and their larvæ. 1892 J. A. Thomson *Outlines Zool.* 266 In adult aërial life, the tracheæ of the body acquire stigmata, and the insect becomes '*holopneustic'. 1900 B. D. Jackson *Gloss. Bot. Terms*, *Holosaprophyte, employed by Johow for a true saprophyte, a plant which is dependent upon humus for its existence. 1902 *Encycl. Brit.* XXV. 439/1 Angiospermous holosaprophytes. 1897 *Science* 23 Apr. 638 (Cent. D. Suppl.) A *holotype..is always a single individual. 1920 *Brit. Museum Return* 111 Freshwater and terrestrial Crustacea (including the holotype of a new species) from Mesopotamia.

Holothuria (hǫlopiū·riă). *Zool.* Pl. -iæ, -ias. A Holothurian (q.v.).

1792 Maria Riddell *Voy. Madeira* 79 These holothuriæ are singularly beautiful when floating on the surface of the water in a clear day. 1816 Tuckey *Narr. Exped. R. Zaire* i. (1818) 11 The holothuria made its first appearance on the 4th instant. 1844 *Chambers's Edin. Jrnl.* 23 Nov. 323/2 It may be of small moment to you, who, mayhap, know nothing of holothurias. 1876 tr. *Beneden's Anim. Parasites* (1883) 5 Dr. Greef..found..a holothuria of a foot in length.

Hols (hǫlz), *sb. pl.* Colloq. (esp. school-children's) abbrev. of *holidays* (Holiday *sb.* 2 b).

1906 Desmond Coke *Bending of a Twig* xix, Where are you going these hols.? 1921 Sylvia Thompson *Rough Crossing* ii. § 8, I may be staying in Oxford in the spring hols. 1931 *Church Times* 25 Sept. 344/4 After next 'hols' it will be a very different little boy who will take the train at Waterloo or Victoria.

Holstein (hǫ·lstain). *U.S.* [The name of a duchy in North Germany.] In full *Holstein-Friesian*: = *Friesian.

1872 *Rep. Vermont Board Agric.* I. 176 The Dutch cattle, or as I believe it is settled they are to be called, the 'Holsteins'. 1876 *Trans. Ill. Dept. Agric.* XIV. 296, S. W. Kingsley spoke in favor of Holsteins for the dairy. 1922 Anne D. Sedgwick *Adrienne Toner* xviii. 166 There's a prize heifer arriving this evening...You must see his herd of Holsteins, Roger. (Frisians were, at that date, still Holsteins.)

Holt[2]. **1.** Add: also *U.S. dial.*

1825 J. Neal *Bro. Jonathan* II. 60 [He cried] 'lay holt there; lay holt, every one o' you', throwing the reins behind him, into the carriage. 1848 Bartlett *Dict. Amer.*, *Holt*, for hold. Ex. 'Death has got holt of him.' *a* 1859 *N. Y. Spirit of the Times* (Bartlett), I tripped him..but he war up before I could get my holt on him. 1898 E. N. Westcott *David Harum* xxii. 199 Of course you've heard the things that some folks say of him, an'..they got some holt on your mind. 1909 R. A. Wason *Happy Hawkins* iv. 52 He'd 'a' been killed that trip if you hadn't taken holt when you did.

Holtz (hǫlts). Name of Wilhelm T. B. *Holtz* (1836–1913), German physicist, used to designate electrical machines invented by him.

1878 *Encycl. Brit.* VIII. 102/2. 1884 Knight *Dict. Mech.* Suppl. s.v. *Electrical Machine.* 1910 *N. Hawkins' Elect. Dict.*, *Holtz Influence Machine*, an electrostatic induction machine. 1928 T. L. Stedman *Pract. Med. Dict.* (ed. 10), *Holtz machine*, a machine with large revolving glass disc, for generating frictional electricity.

Holy, *a.* Add: **3. a.** *The holy souls*, the souls of the faithful departed, the blessed dead.

1849 F. W. Faber *Hymn*, '*O, turn to Jesus, Mother, turn*', Pray for the holy souls that burn this hour Amidst the cleansing flame. 1898 Mortimer *Cath. Faith & Practice* II. xiv. 361 The Intermediate State, where the holy souls are waiting until their purification is accomplished. *Ibid.* 371 The joys and consolations of the holy souls in their preparation for Heaven.

b. *The Holy Name*, the name of Jesus as an object of formal devotion among Catholics, as in the Litany of the Holy Name and the festival of the Holy Name of Jesus.

c 1440 *Thornton MS.* f. 192 Of the vertuz of the haly name of Ihesu. 1720 T. M. tr. *Horstius' Paradise of Soul* (1771) 409 Great are the Honours and Priviledges of the Holy Name, Jesus. 1850 tr. *Horstius' Paradise of Soul* 509 The Worship and Honour of the most Holy Name of Jesus. 1851 *Life A. Gentili* (ed. J. B. Pagani) xi. 196 Singing along the way the Litany of the Holy Name of Jesus. 1884 Addis & Arnold *Cath. Dict.* s.v. *Jesus*, An office of the Holy Name. 1901 G. Tyrrell *Autobiogr.* (1912) I. 94 Two of the boys..would bow their heads at the Holy Name at morning prayers.

4. c. Used trivially: (*a*) with *horror* or the like (orig. *U.S.*), expressing intensity; (*b*) with unfavourable implication of piety or sanctimoniousness. *colloq.* *Holy Joe*: see quots. 1874, 1889. *Holy terror*: a person of exasperating habits or manner.

1837 *Southern Lit. Messenger* III. 668, I have a holy horror of gossips. 1856 S. Mordecai *Virginia* xxxii. (1860) 317 The Virginia Legislature had such a holy horror of banks in 1803, that they refused a charter to the petitioners. 1874 *Slang Dict.*, *Holy Joe*, a sea-term for a parson. 1889 Barrère & Leland *Dict. Slang*, *Holy Joe* (prison and nautical), the chaplain or any religious person. 1893 *Strand Mag.* VI. 105/1 Not excepting even the Dwarf, and he's, generally speaking, a holy terror.

5. Holy laugh *U.S.* (see quots.).

a 1833 H. Barnard in *Maryland Hist. Mag.* XIII. 328 The preacher, in the midst of a fervent prayer, will all of a sudden burst out into a loud boisterous laugh...The most godly of his brethren join with him. This is called the 'Holy Laugh'. 1845 J. J. Hooper *Adv. Simon Suggs* x. 122 Near these last, stood a delicate woman in that hysterical condition in which the nerves are incontrollable, and which is vulgarly.. termed the 'holy laugh'.

b. holy bark, cascara sagrada, = *sacred bark*, Sacred *a.* 7 (Webster 1897); **holy basil**, the common Indian species of basil, *Ocimum sanctum.*

1880 *Encycl. Brit.* XII. 720/2 The worship of the *tulsi* plant, or holy basil, by the Hindus. 1886 Yule & Burnell *Hobson-Jobson*, *Toolsy*, the holy Basil of the Hindus.

Holy cross. **c.** Add: **Holy Cross toad**, a frog of New South Wales, *Notaden bennettii*, so called from a dark cross-shaped marking on the back.

1891 Rose in *Proc. Linnæan Soc., New S. Wales* Ser. II. VI. 265 *Notaden bennettii*, the Catholic frog, or as I have heard it called the 'Holy Cross toad'.

Holy-tide. (Later U.S. example.)

1878 *Harper's Mag.* Apr. 618/1 They have served through victory feasts and holy-tides.

Homatropine (hǫmæ·trŏpin). *Chem.* Also -in. [f. Homo- + Atropine.] A crystalline alkaloid, $C_{16}H_{21}NO_3$, derived from atropine, the mandelic acid ester of tropine.

1880 *Jrnl. Chem. Soc.* XXXVIII. 410 Homatropine aurochloride, $C_{16}H_{21}NO_3$.HCl.AuCl$_3$. 1902 *Encycl. Brit.* XXXI. 662/2 Atropine, hyoscyamine, homatropine, duboisine, daturine, and some other bodies have a paralysing action upon the ends of the motor and secretory nerves.

Hombre (ǫ·mbre). *Western U.S.* [Sp.] A man.

1846 Magoffin *Down Santa Fé Trail* (1926) 93 Not only the children, but..*hombres* (men) swarmed around me like bees. 1851 N. Kingsley *Diary* 172 [I] had a fine sing in the evening with three or four other 'hombres'. 1918 Mulford *Man fr. Bar-20* viii. 79 'Friend of this hombre?' 'Yes; sort of.' 1930 *London Mercury* Feb. 324 'Look here,' said Clytemnestra..'is this *hombre* worth it?' 'If you don't think so, leave him to me.'

Homburg (hǫ·mbǝɹg). [Name of a town in Hesse-Nassau, Prussia.] In full *Homburg hat*: A soft felt hat with narrow brim and crown, which was first worn at Homburg, a fashionable health-resort.

1901 *Sketch* 4 Sept. 254/1 The quiet gentleman in dark clothes and a Homburg hat. 1904 *To-Day* 29 June 256/1 At one time any man who wore a 'Homburg' was popularly supposed to be either an actor or an artist. 1910 *Daily Chron.* 5 Mar. 4/6 You may grasp your Homburg in the hollow of your hand. But how are you to get it on again with grace? 1925 E. Wallace *Valley of Ghosts* xv, He..put his Homburg hat on the table.

Home, *sb.*[1] and *a.* Add: **A.** *sb.* **2.** In U.S. and Canada, freq. used to designate a private house or residence merely as a building.

1882 *Harper's Mag.* Dec. 53/1 A lovely drive,..is bordered with homes, many of which make pretensions to much more than comfort. 1889 *Kansas Times & Star* 6 July, A fine stone-front home at Twenty-seventh and Troost. *Ibid.* 5 Dec., For rent, a fine home at 1223 Broadway. 1929 *Publishers' Weekly* 7 Dec. 2661/1 Then out to see the new Ranh Branch, a stunning private home turned over to the library. 1930 *San Antonio* (*Texas*) *Light* 31 Jan., Wilson wounded Elliott and his wife in a dispute Wednesday at the Elliott home in Mendota.

3. *A home from home*, a place away from home which provides home-like accommodation or amenities.

1906 *Morning Post* 1 Feb. 7/2 To provide them with a 'home from home' while engaged in the studies which fitted them for the positions in life they were destined to fill. 1907 *Daily Chron.* 30 Nov. 3/3 The British man is a clubbable animal, and doesn't mind paying handsomely for his 'home from home'.

9. b. *Lacrosse.* Each of the three players stationed nearest their opponents' goal.

1871 *English Mechanic* 23 June 340/3 Home, who is stationed nearest opponents' goal. 1892 *Lippincott's Monthly Mag.* XLIX. 746 Outside home, and inside home. *Ibid.* 748 To secure the ball in the 'draw-off'..and pass it to the home or attack men. 1897 *Encycl. Sport* I. 607/1 The three *Homes* must be adepts in taking short and hard catches with absolute certainty.

11. e. Used of a match when the team referred to is playing on its own ground. (Cf. *Away *adv.* II.)

1930 *Daily Tel.* 5 Dec. 20/3 Clapton Orient, 'at home' to Luton Town at Highbury.

13*. To home. *dial.* (also *U.S.*) = At home.

1833 J. Neal *Down-Easters* I. 62 When he's to home.. he's match for gab with anybody 't ever you come across. 1839 *Knickerbocker Mag.* XIV. 153, I used to be quite good at reckoning, when I was to home, in the state of New Hampshire. 1868 Veaney *Stone Edge* ii, I'm main sorry Master Broom ain't to home. 1872 Susan Coolidge *What Katy did* xii, 'Tain't every girl would know how to take care of a fat old woman, and make her feel to home.

14. b. In relation to domestic economy.

1902 *Encycl. Brit.* XXV. 686/1 The Home Arts and Industries Association. 1927 Peake & Fleure *Hunters & Artists* 79 *Art mobilier*, which has been translated 'mobiliary art', 'portable art', or 'home art'. 1927 *Daily Express* 26 Feb. 5/2 Women who seek a pleasant paying homecraft. *Ibid.* 23 Mar. 5 Modern Homecraft Notions.

d.

1883 *Peel City Guardian* 15 Sept., Our harbour is once more almost empty, as the Home Fleet are fishing of[f] Douglas. 1903 *Westm. Gaz.* 30 Mar. 2/2 What military stations abroad are now reckoned as Home stations. 1904 *To-Day* 14 Dec. 162/1 The Present Home Fleet is to be called the Channel Fleet. 1906 *Daily Chron.* 24 Oct. 7/4 A distinct fleet will be constituted from the ships in commission in reserve, to be called the 'Home Fleet'. 1927 Warwick Deeping *Kitty* I. § 1. 10 A home-service job with one of the home-service battalions.

Home, *adv.* Add: **7. d.** *To write home about*: to boast of, to 'make a song about'.

1925 Aldous Huxley *Those Barren Leaves*, *F. Chelifer* i. (1927) 96 There is nothing in these virtues *à la* Dickens to 'write home about'. 1930 Marg. Kennedy *Fool of Fam.* xix, I know Each had twenty sons, but they weren't anything to write home about.

8. a. *home-come, -coming* adjs. (Cf. Home-coming *a.* in Dict.)

1898 *Month* Nov. 487 The lowing of the home-coming cattle. 1908 *Westm. Gaz.* 22 Dec. 6/3 Who holds up to her home-come soldier's lips The babe he hath not seen. 1918 W. J. Locke *Rough Road* xix, The home-come warrior.

Home, *v.* Add: **4.** To train (a carrier-pigeon) to fly home.

1928 *Sunday Dispatch* 29 July 22 Leatham (Downpatrick) has achieved what many thought impossible—viz., homing a bird from San Sebastian (Spain), distance over 800 miles, to the Emerald Isle, 300 miles of which, supposing the bird crossed from the northern coast of France, is over water.

Ho·me-co·mer. [Home *adv.* 8 a.] One who comes or returns home: in recent use with special reference to the Isle of Man; so **Ho·me-co·ming.**

1540 Palsgr. *Acolastus* Arg. Cj, The father reioyseth the sonne to be a safe home commer vnto hym. 1637 [in Dict.]. 1926 *Peel City Guardian* 26 June 2/2 The Mayor of Douglas intends to do what he can..to promote a big home-coming of Manx people and their descendants for June of next year. 1927 *Ibid.* 7 May, A meeting of the Executive Committee in connection with the Manx Homecoming movement. *Ibid.* 27 May, The Homecomers will arrive at Montreal during the afternoon of June 2nd. 1930 *Ibid.* 21 June 6/1 The White Star liner, 'Doric', will anchor in Douglas Bay.. with 279 'homecomers' on board.

Home-croft. = Croft *sb.*[1] b. In accordance with a housing scheme for industrial workers, a detached cottage, with land and outbuildings for poultry and other small livestock. Also *attrib.* Hence **Ho·mecrofter, Ho·me-crofting** *vbl. sb.*

1859 [see Home A. 14 c]. 1925 *Public Opinion* 7 Aug. 121/1 The industrial workers to spread out and become home-crofters as well as workers. 1925 *Spectator* 5 Dec. 1018/1 Dr. Hilda Clark, whose work in Vienna was of such immense importance, has also sent us a terse but comprehensive account of the work and its objects. We note the interesting fact that she now calls these Land Settlements 'Home-croft Holdings'. *Ibid.*, We do not think that the word 'homecrofting' had been heard of in Vienna three years ago. 1926 *Ibid.* 24 July 130/1 The land and buildings shall be used in perpetuity as 'homecrofts'.

Home-defe·nce. [See Home *sb.*[1] 14 d.] The defence of one's native country; an armed force designed for this. Also *attrib.*

1642 [see Home *sb.*[1] 14 d]. 1671 J. Ogilby *America* ii. 29 Lest if Carthage should be invaded by a foraign Enemy, it should want People for a Home-defence. 1885 *Marine Engineer* 1 July 89/2 With such a fleet..we could dispense with the Channel Squadron, for home defence. 1904 *Rep. R. Comm. Militia & Volunteers* 26 (Parl. Papers XXX) A home-defence army.

Home-fire. Used, like *hearth*, as symbolic of the home and family life, and especially popular during the war of 1914–18 in phr. *To keep the home-fires burning*: to keep the home going, to 'carry on' at home.

1892 Zangwill *Childr. Ghetto* I. xiii, Happy fathers of happy children, men who warmed their hands at the home-fire of life. *c* 1915 Ivor Novello *Song*, Keep the home-fires burning, While your hearts are yearning. 1928 D. L. Sayers *Bellona Club* iii, Health gone—no money—heroic wife keeping the home fires burning. 1931 Patry Williams *Word of Tomorrow* iv. i, When they were holding the line in France, and he and all the other old gollywogs were keeping the home fires burning, snug and comfortable.

Ho·me-folk, -folks. *colloq.* [Home *sb.*[1] 14 i.] The people at one's home, *i.e.* one's friends, relatives, or neighbours.

1884 'C. E. Craddock' *In Tenn. Mts.* viii. 288 All the home-folks an' everybody that kems hyar to sat and talk. 1907 *Westm. Gaz.* 21 Sept. 6/2 They wander from the home-folks' ken. 1909 *Ibid.* 2 Dec. 2/3 Of home-folk caught by crumbling walls. 1915 H. L. Wilson *Ruggles of Red Gap* v. (1917) 99 Then we tried his home-folks in Boston.

Ho·me-guard. [Home *sb.*[1] 14 a.] **a.** A member of a local volunteer force. *U.S.* **b.** The Territorial Forces of England.

1862 O. W. Norton *Army Lett.* 123 Nothing would make me ready to fight sooner than to hear some home guard abuse McClellan. 1873 'Mark Twain' & Warner *Gilded Age* xviii. 170 He was captain of the home-guards in Hawkeye. 1891 *Century Mag.* Jan. 409 An unexpected musketry fire was opened from the Indiana side by a party of home-guards. 1896 *Congress. Rec.* 25 Apr., App. 298 Before Gen. Burnside came, the mountain men of East Tennessee organized themselves into companies called 'Home Guards'. 1909 *Westm. Gaz.* 7 Jan. 7/3 A movement has been set on foot which has for its object the presentation of colours to the 'Home Guard', as we call the Territorials.

Homeland. Add: **b.** = Home *sb.*[1] 6.

c 1890 C. Bingham *Song*, The Dear Home-Land. 1899 *Daily News* 16 Oct. 7/1 Looking..at the old Homeland through the eyes of Young Australia. 1905 *Daily Chron.* 22 June 6/6 We are here to-night..a body of Canadian business men, chiefly in order that we may learn to know the people of the homeland. 1907 (*title*) The Call of the Homeland: a Collection of English Verse.

Ho·me-life. [Home *sb.*[1] 14 b.] Life at home or in domestic surroundings.

1867 'T. Lackland' *Homespun* I. 39 The sincerest pleasures of the home-life are woven closely in with those of the garden. 1871 [see Home B. 1]. 1879 *Rep. Indian Affairs* 32 The absence of the example of the better home-life of our own people. 1898 T. N. Page *Red Rock* vii. 64 These men were thoroughly enjoying home life.

Home market. [Home B. 3.] The market for goods or produce in the place or country of production.

1776 Adam Smith *W. N.* I. xi. 243 The bounty..may..have occasioned..a greater cheapness of corn in the home-market than what would otherwise have taken place there. 1794 [see Home B. 3]. 1813 *Niles' Weekly Register* IV. 274/1 Then shall the home market still the rage for foreign export. 1843 *Amer. Pioneer* II. 214 Money became plenty, and a cash home-market was established. 1847 C. Lanman *Summer in Wilderness* i. 14 This city is the home market for all the natural productions of a wilderness country. 1892 *Rep. Vermont Board Agric.* XII. 132 Furnishing a home market for their products.

Ho·me-place. *U.S.* [Home *sb.*[1] 14 a.] The place or piece of ground where one's home is situated.

1741 *N. H. Probate Rec.* III. 33, I give unto my Son Samuel Dolloff one part of my home place begining at an Elm Stump. 1816 U. Brown *Jrnl.* in *Maryland Hist. Mag.* X. 283 Jacob Beeson..as well as his wife and daughter Jane (which was all the family now on the home place). 1869 Tourgee *Toinette* (1881) 14 'Well, what's this?' said he, taking the first paper from the file, 'The deed of the home place'.

Home-sick, *a.* (Earlier U.S. example.)

1773 P. V. Fithian *Jrnl.* (1900) 53 Feel very home-sick.

Homestead, *sb.* **3.** *U.S.* (Early example of *homestead law.*)

1866 *Rep. Indian Affairs* 215 Freedmen..allowed to enter three hundred and twenty acres of the same under the homestead law.

4. (Earlier U.S. examples.)

1704 *Rec. Providence, R. I.* VII. 210, I give..my homested place to him. 1712 *Ibid.* 57 That part of my homestead ffarme on the west side of the afores[ai]d River. 1749 *N. H. Probate Rec.* III. 741, I give to my Son..all my Homestead Land.

Homestead, *v.* *U.S.* (Earlier example.)

1879 *Congress. Rec.* 26 Apr. 952/1 To prove their right to pre-empt or 'homestead' their lands.

Homesteading. Add: **2.** The granting of land according to the Homestead Act of Congress, 1862 (see Homestead *sb.* 3). *U.S.* Also, a similar settlement in Canada.

1906 *Daily Chron.* 1 Oct. 4/4 There is no more homesteading—viz., free grants of land—it has to be bought. 1925 *Glasgow Herald* 10 Aug. 4 Homesteading has been a great factor in the agricultural development of Western Canada.

Ho·me-stretch. *U.S.* [Home B. 4, Stretch *sb.* 8.] The return-stretch of a course; *esp.* the stretch of a race-course on which a race finishes. Also *fig.*

1861 *Trans. Ill. Agric. Soc.* IV. 38 On the last home stretch the steam [of the plough] became so low that it required some minutes to get up sufficient to run the furrow through. 1864 *Congress. Globe* 12 Mar. 1069/3 Already we see the slave States..on the home-stretch to become free. 1868 H. Woodruff *Trotting Horse Amer.* xxiv. 207, I passed first one and then the other, and came on the home-stretch with a clear lead. 1878 *Trans. Ill. Dept. Agric.* XIV. 146 Still, a fleet horse who gathers up handsomely on the home-stretch, is not to be sneezed at by any one. 1897 [see Home B. 4]. 1904 Gene Stratton-Porter *Freckles* ix, You couldn't break the heart of me entire quicker than to be taking it from me now, when I'm just on the home-stretch.

Home-town. *U.S.* [Home *sb.*[1] 14 a.] The town in which one's home is, or was originally; one's native town. Also *attrib.*

1912 *Top-Notch Mag.* (U.S.) 1 Aug. 64/2 He was killed in a pool-room row in my home town up the State. 1919 H. L. Wilson *Ma Pettengill* xi. 307 Having got the thanks of the French nation and his home-town paper.

Ho·me-work. [Home *sb.*[1] 14 b.]

1. Work done at home, esp. as distinguished from work done in a shop or factory. Also *attrib.*

1856 [see Home *sb.*[1] 14 b]. 1861 G. Moore *Lost Tribes* xviii. 364 One [apartment] more open and larger is reserved for visitors, or..is used for spinning or other home-work. 1904 *Technol. & Sci. Dict.* (ed. Goodchild & Tweney) s.v. *Home Work*, [It] prohibits home work in a house any inmate of which is suffering from a notifiable infectious disease. 1906 *Daily Chron.* 11 Oct. 6/2 The home-work wages paid in the Upper Kahlgrund district. 1907 *Rep. Sel. Commu. Home Work* 61/1 (Parl. Papers VI) Any instance of sweating in home work in connection with such things as ladies' jackets. 1908 *Franco-Brit. Exhib.*, *Women's Section* 64 Frame of Quilting and Embroidery, lent by Home Work Co-operative Society.

2. Lessons and exercises to be done by a school-child at home.

1889 A. E. Fletcher *Sonnenschein's Encycl. Educ.* (ed. 2) 155/1 Written home-work. 1897 *Teaching & Organisation* (ed. P. A. Barnett) 366 The large amount of home-work which is assigned to pupils for preparation alone in the evening. 1905 *Westm. Gaz.* 28 Jan. 5/2, I think it is a wrong principle altogether to help a child with his home-work.

Hence **Ho·me-wo·rker, -working.**

1902 A. Ballantyne *Home-Work* 98 The home-worker.. has been left outside the protecting pale of the Factory Acts. 1907 *Rep. Sel. Comm. Home Work* 19/1 (Parl. Papers VI) The duty of seeing to the sanitary condition of home workers' premises. 1907 *Daily Chron.* 11 Feb. 4/4 The success of this home-working experiment under leasehold conditions.

Hominid. Add: Also = next.

1920 E. R. Lankester in H. G. Wells *Outline of History* 37/2 If so, it is certainly not chimpanzee nor close to the Apes, but decidedly hominid. 1925 *Glasgow Herald* 25 July 4 That the human race, with all its tentative as well as more or less realised Hominids, arose from an ancestral stock common to it and the Anthropoids.

Hominoid (hǫ·minoid), *sb.* and *a.* [f. mod.L. *Hominidæ* Hominid + -oid.] (An animal) of the form of or resembling the *Hominidæ*.

1927 *Glasgow Herald* 3 Sept. 4/2 The divergence of the Hominoid and the Anthropoid branches. *Ibid.*, The early Hominoids.

Hominy. (Later U.S. examples.)

1856 S. Mordecai *Virginia* xxxi. (1860) 314 Slow as the process of 'beating hominy' is, it was a great resource, as was the eating of it for lack of hoecake. 1888 *Rep. Vermont Board Agric.* X. 30 The refuse of white corn after what is termed the 'hominy' has been removed, is more valuable as a feed for stock than yellow corn.

b. (Additional U.S. examples.)

1711 *Col. Rec. N. Carolina* I. 765 The planter here..dare not allow himself to partake of his own creatures except it be the corn of the country in hominy bread. 1827 J. F. Cooper *Prairie* ii, Others [were engaged] in plying the heavy pestle of a moveable hominy-mortar. *Ibid.* xvi, Giving her a morsel of venison, now and then, or a spoon around his hominy-dish. 1843 R. Carlton *New Purchase* xv. 111 Here were all the vulgar pots, kettles, frying-pans, hominy-block, and the like.

Homo. **b.** Add: *Homo sapiens* (sē·pienz): the human species; man in the latest form as represented by the races of to-day.

1859 J. G. Wood *Illustr. Nat. Hist.* I. 779/1 In this order [*sc.* Bimana] there is but one species, namely Man,—Homo sapiens. 1896 tr. *Boas' Text-bk. Zool.* 536 All Men are usually regarded as one species, *Homo sapiens*, divided into a number of races. 1927 Peake & Fleure *Hunters & Artists* 1 Modern man, Homo sapiens. 1932 *Morn. Post* 6 June 10/5 When homo sapiens first began On earth to assert his sway, A fine old English gentleman Was living out Piltdown way.

Homo-. Add: **Ho·mochlamy·deous** *a.* *Bot.*, having a perianth of which the members are similarly coloured. **Homochro·mosome** *Cytol.*, an ordinary, or typical chromosome as distinguished from an accessory one. **Homo·chromy** *Biol.*, cryptic colouring. **Homocla·dic** *a.* *Anat.*, noting an anastomosis formed between branches of the same artery. **Homocy·clic** *a.* *Chem.*, having a ring-structure in which the ring is composed of carbon atoms only; carbo-cyclic; *sb.* a homocyclic compound. **Ho·modesmo·tic** *a.* *Anat.*, joining two homologous parts of the central nervous system: used in reference to nerve fibres. **Homody·namous** *a.* *Biol.*, having a similar controlling force in respect of hereditary qualities. **Ho·mogomph** *a.* *Zool.*, having similar bristles or spines. **Homola·teral** *a.* (*a*) *Cryst.*, = *homohedral* (s.v. Homo-); (*b*) *Anat.*, being on the same side. **Homole·cithal** *a.* *Embryol.* (see quot.); **Homomo·rphosis**, the replacement of a lost member or part by a like new one. **Homotha·llic** *a.* *Bot.*, having zygospores developed from the conjugation of hyphæ of the same strain; so **Homotha·llism.** **Ho·motypo·sis**, a name given by Karl Pearson to the correlation between undifferentiated sets of serial homologues. **Homozo·ic** *a.* *Geog.*, containing the same animals or species of animals.

1897 Willis *Flowering Plants & Ferns* I. 60 All the leaves of the perianth being alike, it may be termed *homochlamydeous. 1904 *Biol. Bulletin* Dec. 6 *note*, At first I was inclined to adopt Montgomery's terms *homochromosome and heterochromosome to distinguish between the ordinary chromosomes and the accessory. 1899 *Nat. Science* Dec. 396 *Homochromy and other protective adaptations. 1913 Dorland *Med. Dict.* (ed. 7), *Homocladic, formed between twigs of the same artery: said of such an anastomosis. 1903 *Nature* 17 Sept. 475/1 The rings may be either *homocyclic or heterocyclic without the character of the spectra being altered. 1913 Dorland *Med. Dict.* (ed. 7), *Homodesmotic, joining similar parts of the central nervous system. 1878 F. J. Bell tr. *Gegenbaur's Comp. Anat.* 64 The metameres, therefore, are *homodynamous parts; as are..the primitive vertebræ of the vertebrates. 1893 W. N. Parker & H. Rönnfeldt tr. *Weismann's Germ-Plasm* 278 Homodynamous determinants..are those of the homologous determinants which have the special function of impressing *a like character* on any part of the body. 1902 Bateson & Saunders *1st Rep. Evol. Comm. Roy. Soc.* 126 Correns proposes the terms 'heterodynamous' and 'homodynamous' to express that an organism is dominant or not dominant in respect of a given character. 1902 *Ann. & Mag. Nat. Hist.* Sept. 259 A series of *homogomph bristles. 1910 *Practitioner* July 98 Should the lesion be in or close to the red nucleus, the tremor will be on the opposite side of the body, while if any other part of the system be affected the tremor will be *homolateral. 1892 E. L. Mark tr. *Hertwig's Embryol. Man & Mammals* 25 *note*, The translator has been accustomed for several years to use the word *homolecithal instead of alecithal, heterolecithal being employed as a coördinate term to embrace telolecithal and centrolecithal eggs. 1901 T. H. Morgan *Regeneration* 27 When the new part is like that removed, or like a part of that removed, as when a leg or a tail is regenerated in a newt, the process is one of '*homomorphosis'. 1906 *Rep. Brit. Assoc.* 751 The germination of the zygospores of the *homothallic species *Sporodinia.* 1921 Irene Mounce in *Brit. Mycol. Soc.* VII. 199 The mere formation of fruit-bodies by a monosporous mycelium is no clear indication that the fungus is homothallic. *Ibid.* 201 The criterion of fruit-body production is insufficient for determining the question of *homothallism and heterothallism. 1901 K. Pearson in *Phil. Trans.* Ser. A. CXCVII. 294 *Homotyposis denotes not only likeness of the homotypes, but that this likeness has probably definite quantitative limits. 1909 Gadow in *Darwin & Mod. Sci.* (ed. A. C. Seward) 320 Hitherto the marine faunas had been neglected. This was remedied by E. Forbes, who established nine *homozoic zones, based mainly on the study of the mollusca, the determining factors being to a great extent the isotherms of the sea.

Homocentric, *a.* Add: *spec.* in *Optics*, applied to pencils of light which proceed from a single focal point.

1890 Billings *Med. Dict.*, *Homocentric light*, light, all the rays of which proceed from a common point. 1904 *Technol. & Sci. Dict.* (ed. Goodchild & Tweney), *Homocentric*, a term employed in optics to signify that a lens is corrected for radial and tangential astigmatism of oblique pencils of light by the merging of the two focal lines into a single focal point.

Homœan (hǫmī·ăn), *a.* and *sb.* Also **Homoian** (hǫmoi·ăn). [f. mod.L. *Homæus*, f. Gr. ὅμοιος like, similar + -an.] (A person) who holds the doctrine that in the Trinity the Son is like the Father.

1833 J. H. Newman *Arians* iv. iv. 362 Furthering their splitting into the Homœan and Homœusian factions. 1888 *Encycl. Brit.* XXIII. 720/1 He appears to have joined the Homoian party, which took shape and acquired influence before the council of Constantinople in 360. *Ibid.*, The Homoian formula, 'filium similem esse patri suo'. 1896 G. P. Fisher *Hist. Chr. Doctrine* 142 The 'Homœans' would not go a step beyond the affirmation of a 'likeness', —meaning a likeness in will and active energy. 1912 E. W. Brooks in *Eng. Hist. Rev.* Oct. 761 It was of course the Homoeusians, not the Homoeans, who inclined towards the Nicenes.

Homœo-. Add: **Homœa·rchon** = *homœarchy* (s.v. Homœo-). **Homœochromatism** (-krōu·mătiz'm), *Biol.*, similarity of colouring in different species of animals or plants that inhabit the same locality. So **Ho·mœochromatic** *a.* **Ho·mœokine·sis** *Biol.*, nuclear division in which the two daughter-nuclei receive chromosomes of the same kind. **Ho·mœopla·sia** *Biol.*, the assumption under plastic conditions by the tissue of one part of the body of the form of that of another. **Homœo·podal** *a.* *Physiol.*, designating nerve cells which have branches only of one kind. **Ho·mœotherm** *Biol.*, a warm-blooded animal. **Ho·mœothe·rmic** *a.* *Biol.* = *homothermous* (s.v. Homo-).

1896 Lindsay *Lat. Textual Emend.* 50 The homœoteleuton and *homœarchon of these lines has led to omission. 1897 *Nature* 27 May 94/1 Mr. Blandford exhibited and discussed series of *homœochromatic..species of butterflies. 1899 D. Sharp *Camb. Nat. Hist.* VI. 337 It is found that in certain localities the colour of various butterflies more or less agrees, while it differs from that of the same butterflies found in other localities...This phenomenon is now called '*homœochromatism'. 1903 *Athenæum* 24 Oct. 552/1 These..he suggested were probable examples of homœochromatism. 1893 W. N. Parker & H. Rönnfeldt tr. *Weismann's Germ-Plasm* Introd. 34 These kinds of division we may speak of as *homœokinesis and heterokinesis. 1890 Billings *Med. Dict.*, *Homœoplasia, development of a similar or normal tissue; hyperplasia. 1902 *J. M. Baldwin's Dict. Philos. & Psychol.* II. 155/2 When a cell has but a single variety of processes it is called *homoiopodal, as contrasted to heteropodal. 1890 *Smithsonian Rep.* 411 These phenomena, which are numerous and active in animals of the higher class (*homeotherms), are much less so in cold-blooded animals. 1889 Wingrave *T. Dunman's Gloss. Anat.* App., *Homœothermic, of even temperature: applied to warm-blooded animals which maintain the same temperature, irrespective of that of the surrounding medium. 1890 *Smithsonian Rep.* 407 Man, mammals, and birds are called creatures of equable temperature, homeothermic.

Homœomorph. Add: **b.** A species similar to another in general aspect, but dissimilar in detail. Hence **Ho·mœomo·rphic** *a.*, of a similar type or substance. **Ho·mœomo·rphy**, (*a*) see quot. 1899; (*b*) *Mus.*, imitation.

1899 S. Buckman in *Proc. Cotteswold Nat. Field Club* (1901) XIII. 232 What is known as mimicry in the animal kingdom is of course one phase of homœomorphy. *Ibid.* 262 Some of the more remarkable homœomorphs. *Ibid.*, The various *Terebratulæ*, which are really homœomorphous developments. *a* 1909 *Buck's Handbk. Med. Sci.* IV. 660 (Cent. D. Suppl.) Either homœomorphic, i.e., of the same order, or heteromorphic, of different type. 1930 *Music & Lett.* Oct. 395 The phenomenon of homeomorphy is dealt with! In musical language it is termed imitation.

Homœosis (hǫmi,ōu·sis). *Biol.* Also **homoiosis.** [mod. L. *homœosis*, ad. Gr. ὁμοίωσις a becoming like, f. ὅμοιος like.] (See quot. 1909.) So **Homœotic** (hǫmiǫ·tik) *a.*, characterized by homœosis.

1890 Billings *Med. Dict.*, *Homoiosis*, assimilation. 1894 W. Bateson *Study of Variation* 85 For the word 'Metamorphy' I therefore propose to substitute the term Homœosis. *Ibid.*, The distinction between Homœotic Variation and strictly Meristic Variation is sufficiently obvious. 1902 *Encycl. Brit.* XXV. 692/1 Homœosis is the making of a merome into the likeness of one belonging to another metamere, and is the opposite of the process of 'heterosis'. 1909 R. H. Lock *Variation, Heredity, & Evol.* v. 133 Homœosis consists in the assumption by one member of a meristic series of the form or character proper to another member of the same series. 1913 W. Bateson *Mendel's Princ. Heredity* 198 A simple homœosis of the stamens and carpels.

Homogamous, *a.* Add: **c.** *Evolution.* Of or pertaining to assortative mating. So **Homogamy** (*b*) *Evol.*, the interbreeding among individuals having similar characteristics; sexual selection. **Homoga·mic** *a.*

1903 *Biometrika* Nov. 481 If the male class of a given character tends to mate with a female class with generally like character, we have a tendency to *homogamy*. *Ibid.*, The whole range of effect from pure random matings to perfectly homogamous unions within a population is almost but not quite as important as the difference between self and cross fertilization in plants. 1907 *Fabian News* XVII. 55/2 Professor Pearson's theory of homogamic mating.

Homogeneous, *a.* Add:

3. *Math.* *Homogeneous co-ordinates*, a system in which the ratios of the co-ordinates (one more than necessary) are substituted for the co-ordinates themselves, making the equations (all except one) homogeneous.

1882 H. Cox in *Q. Jrnl. Pure & Appl. Math.* XVIII. 178 Homogeneous Coordinates in Imaginary Geometry and their Application to Systems of Forces.

Homoiousion (hǫmoi,ūu·ziǫn, -au·siǫn). *Theol.* [eccl. Gr. ὁμοιούσιον: see Homoiousian and cf. *Homoousion.] *The homoiousion*, the term used to express the doctrine that the Son is of like substance with the Father.

1875, *a* 1901 [see *Homoousion].

Homoousion (hǫmo,au·ziǫn, -au·siǫn). *Theol.* [eccl. Gr. ὁμοούσιον, acc. of ὁμοούσιος, qualifying acc. υἱόν son (as in the Nicene Creed): see Homoousian.] *The homoousion* (τὸ ὁμοούσιον): the term ὁμοούσιος as used, e.g. in the formula promulgated by the Council of Nicæa in 325 A.D., to express the doctrine that the Son is 'of one substance' with the Father (τῷ πατρί); the doctrine itself: opposed to the term ὁμοιούσιος (see *Homoiousion). The nom. form homoousios is also used.

1781 Gibbon *Decl. & F.* xxi, Their [*sc.* the Arians'] patron, Eusebius of Nicomedia,..confessed, that the admission of the *Homoousion*, or Consubstantial,..was incompatible with the principles of their theological system. *Ibid.*, The mysterious *Homoousion*, which either party was free to interpret according to their peculiar tenets. 1833 J. H. Newman *Arians* iv. § 3. 333 The Novatians, as maintaining the Homoousion, were included in the persecution. 1875 *Encycl. Brit.* II. 538/2 At length the tenet of the *Homoiousion* was substituted for that of the *Homoousion* at the Council of Rimini (Ariminum) in 360. *a* 1901 W. Bright *Age of the Fathers* (1903) I. 248 Socrates's statement..places the adoption of the Homoiousion, as a substitute for the Homoousion, at least three years too late. 1910 *Encycl. Brit.* II. 543/2 The opposition to the Homoousios, as a formula..not borne out by Holy Writ. *Ibid.* 825/2 The catch-word Homousios. 1921 C. H. Turner *Catholic & Apostolic* (1931) 120 The very existence of Christianity in any full sense of the term was at stake over the Homoousion. *Ibid.* 130 The confession of belief expressed in the Homoousion was, in his conviction as in ours, the only possible issue of the original premisses of Christian teaching.

Homosexual (hǫmo,se·ksiuăl), *a.* (*sb.*). [irreg. f. Homo- + Sexual.] Pertaining to or characterized by sexual propensity for one's own sex. Also *sb.* one who has such a propensity. Hence **Homosexua·lity** [G. *homosexualität*, Benkert]; **Homose·xualize** *v. trans.*, to make homosexual.

1897 H. Havelock Ellis *Stud. Psychol. Sex* I. 1 Burton's climatic theory of homosexuality. *Note*, 'Homosexual' is a barbarously hybrid word, and I claim no responsibility for it. 1902 *J. M. Baldwin's Dict. Philos. & Psychol.* II. 287/1 A special case is inversion or homosexuality. 1912 E. Paul tr. *A. Moll's Sexual Life of Child* 125 The primary appearance of homosexual inclinations does not prove that these inclinations are congenital. *Ibid.* 127 An adult homosexual who as a child once did some needlework for a joke. 1914 G. B. Shaw in *New Statesman* 14 Nov. 21/2 The forty tolerated homosexual brothels of Berlin. 1921 *Blackw. Mag.* Jan. 134/2 What the nature of the friendship was we cannot say; it may have been homo-sexual, a love which was common among the later Greeks. 1924 H. Havelock Ellis *Stud. Psychol. Sex* II. 115 My homosexualized Patmorean ideal. 1929 R. Graves *Good-Bye to all That* iii. 40 In English preparatory and public schools romance is necessarily homosexual.

Homozygote (hǫmozai·gout). *Biol.* [f. Homo- + Zygote.] A zygote formed by the union of two like gametes. Hence **Ho·mozygo·sis, -zygo·sity**, development from a homozygote. **Homozy·gous** *a.*, of, pertaining to, or derived from a homozygote.

1902 W. Bateson *Mendel's Princ. Heredity* 23 The hybrid, or 'mule' form, or, as I have elsewhere called it, the *heterozygote*, as distinguished from..the *homozygotes*. 1903 — in *Nature* 19 Mar. 463/1 The homozygotes will all have pink eyes. 1904 *Biometrika* Jan. 16 The hybrids produced by pairing a heterozygous waltzing form G'JG'J with a homozygous albino GG will be of two kinds, GG'J and GG'J. 1905 W. Bateson & R. C. Punnett in *2nd Rep. Evol. Com. R. Soc.* 125 Homozygosis of resolved forms. 1906 R. H. Lock *Variation, Heredity, & Evol.* vii. 174 A zygote formed by the conjunction of two like gametes is called a homozygote. 1906 [see *Heterozygote]. 1909 R. H. Lock *Variation, Heredity, & Evol.* viii. (ed. 2) 208 Not one of them was a pure homozygous yellow. 1925 *Jrnl. Bot.* LXIII. 362 There is no known method of proving homozygosity with absolute certainty. 1927 Haldane & Huxley *Anim. Biol.* ii. 67 Homozygote parents. 1930 *Jrnl. Genetics* XXIII. 404 The conclusion..that the Creeper gene in the homozygous conditions acts as a lethal.

Homrai (hǫ·mrǝi). [Nepal.] A large hornbill, *Dichoceros bicornis*, native to India and the Malay Peninsula.

1893 Newton *Dict. Birds.* 1905 *Pall Mall Gaz.* 24 Apr. 6/3 This curious bird (*Dichoceros bicornis*) is also known as 'Homrai'.

Honan (hōunā·n). [Chinese, = south of the river.] The name of a province of N. China, used to designate a variety of silk manufactured there.

1923 *Daily Mail* 24 Apr. 1 Fine quality real Silk Honans, beautifully printed.

Hondu (hǫ·ndu). *Western U.S.* Also **hondoo, -ou.** [Sp. *honda* sling.] The loop at the end of a lasso through which the thong or cord runs. Also *fig.*

1889 Farmer *Amer.* 1916 Titus *I Conquered* x. 122 The hoarse rip of the hard twist coming through its hondu.

1919 H. L. Wilson *Ma Pettengill* ii. 54 Some way when he had got his rope over a job the hondoo wouldn't seem to render. He couldn't cinch anything.

Honduran (hǫndiūˑrăn), *a.* [f. next: see -AN.] Of, pertaining to, or characteristic of Honduras. So **Hondura·nean, -a·nian** *adjs.*

1895 R. H. Savage & A. C. Gunter *His Cuban Sweetheart* II. xii. 166 The Honduranean magnates. *Ibid.* III. xiii. 184 The sunburned neck of the average Honduranean. 1902 R. H. Davis *Captain Macklin* iii, The Honduranian consul. 1926 *Glasgow Herald* 17 June 10 The Honduran steamer Olancho. 1927 *Blackw. Mag.* Aug. 186/1 Living under Honduranian laws..these people, once British, are gradually being forced to give up their birthright.

Honduras (hǫndiūrǽs, hǫndiūˑrăs). The name of a British crown colony (British Honduras), and a self-governing state in Central America, used attrib. to designate various plants native to Honduras and the West Indies, as **Honduras bark**, cascara amarga; **Honduras rubber**, a variety of india-rubber obtained from *Castilloa elastica*; **Honduras sarsaparilla**, a mealy variety of sarsaparilla which is probably furnished by *Sarsaparilla papyracea*.

1866 *Treas. Bot.* s.v. *Smilax*, Honduras Sarsaparilla, the botanical origin of which is not known. 1887 *Colonial & Indian Exhib., Rep. Col. Sect.* 256 'Majoe bitter'..has been lately introduced into medicine in the United States under the name of 'Honduras bark' or 'Casc[ar]a amarga'. 1887 Bentley *Man. Bot.* (ed. 5) 667 West Indian, Carthagena, Nicaragua, Honduras..rubbers.

Honest, *a.* Add: **3. e.** *Honest Injun*: see *INJUN.

4. d. *Honest-to-God, honest-to-goodness*: genuine(ly), real(ly). orig. *U.S. colloq.*

1916 'B. M. Bower' *Phantom Herd* iii. 45 The real honest-to-goodness-twelve-months-in-the-year West. 1918 Bert Hall & J. J. Niles *One Man's War* (1929) 352 The only honest-to-God aviator the Americans have ever produced—Raoul Lufbery! 1921 Galsworthy *To Let* III. v, She was..'honest to God' indifferent to it all. 1924 W. M. Raine *Troubled Waters* xiii. 144 Few will believe it, but it's an honest-to-goodness fact. 1926 Lincoln *Big Mogul* iv. 64 It had been the only honest-to-goodness bathroom in the town. 1929 W. H. Thomson *That Terrier 'Brick'* xiii. 69 Honest-to-goodness, I didn't know that I was doing anything wrong. 1931 *Times Lit. Suppl.* 29 Jan. 76/3 The inevitable 'honest-to-God' hundred-per-cent. American young man.

6. b. Used to emphasize the truth of a statement. orig. *U.S. colloq.*

1876 'Mark Twain' *Tom Sawyer* ix. 100 Tell me, Joe,—*honest*, now, old feller—did I do it, Joe? 1901 S. Merwin & Webster *Calumet K* viii. 160 Max..said to his sister: 'Honest, Hilda, I don't see how he does it.' 1921 R. D. Paine *Comr. Rolling Ocean* vi. 105 He is not so bad as he sounds, honest, Jud. 1928 F. B. Young *My Brother Jonathan* II. iv, If it weren't for the life at Prince's I don't think I could stick it..honest!

Honey, *sb.* Add:

4. b. A colour resembling that of honey.

1923 *Daily Mail* 8 May 14 In Reseda,..Champagne, Honey, Copper.

7. honey-creeper (earlier example); **honey-crop**, the distended abdomen of the honey-ant; **honey-flow**, the secretion of honey or nectar by flowers; **honey-gum** *U.S.*, a beehive made from a block of gum-tree; **honey-sugar**, a solid saccharine substance that separates from honey during granulation; **honey-tree** *U.S.*, **honey-water** (see quots.).

1872 Coues *N. Amer. Birds* 91 The Cærebidæ, or *honey-creepers of the tropics. 1899 D. Sharp *Insects* II. 152 The distension is produced entirely by the overcharging of the *honey-crop. 1904 *Daily Chron.* 14 Sept. 4/5 The *honey-flow has practically ceased, save where heather abounds. 1920 *Chambers's Jrnl.* 406/1 In the height of a honeyflow..it would not be long before [the shell of] the carcass became a store-house of sweetness. 1927 *Daily Express* 1 Sept. 5/2 To make the most of the honey-flow in the heather blossom. 1840 W. G. Simms *Border Beagles* (1855) 317 He squatted on his haunches, with the felicity and grace of a black bear at a *honey-gum. 1842 *Penny Cycl.* XXIII. 235/1 *Honey Sugar contains two kinds of sugar, one resembles grape sugar, and the other is uncrystallizable. 1887 *Encycl. Brit.* XXII. 623 Lowitz's honey sugar is identical with a crystallizable sugar present largely in the juice of the grape. 1831 Mary A. Holley *Texas Lett.* (1833) 42 *Honey trees... Hollow trees, in which the bees deposit their honey are so called. 1840 *Cultivator* VIII. 20 There is a dozen 'honey-trees' to be cut and taken care of. 1861 Bentley *Man. Bot.* 673 The unfermented juice [of *Agave americana*] is called *Aguamiel* or *honey-water.

b. honey-eucalypt, a variety of eucalyptus, *Eucalyptus melliodora*, much sought by bees; **honey-locust** (U.S. examples); **honey-ware** = BADDERLOCKS.

1877 F. von Müller *Botanic Teachings* 15 (Morris) The *Honey-Eucalypt (*Eucalyptus melliodora*). This tree passes by the very unapt vernacular name Yellow Box-tree. 1770 *Carroll Papers* in *Maryland Hist. Mag.* XIII. 72 You may get *Honey Locust Pods at Mrs. Ogles. 1832 D. J. Browne *Sylva Amer.* 162 In different parts of the United States, this species is called indifferently Sweet Locust and Honey Locust. 1858 J. A. Warder *Hedges & Evergreens* 27 Almost every writer and experimenter has condemned the honey-locust as unfit for a hedge plant. 1850 Miss Pratt *Common Things of Sea-side* 121 It is called Badderlocks, or Hen-ware in Scotland, and has also in the Scottish isles the name of *Honey-ware, and in Ireland that of Murlins.

Honeycomb, *sb.* Add:

6. honeycomb coil *Wireless*, an inductance coil wound round spokes so as to give a honeycombed appearance; **honeycomb quartz** (see quot.); **honeycomb radiator**, a motor radiator having hexagonal passages arranged like a honeycomb through which the air-draught passes; **honeycomb weave**, a kind of weave in which a strong contrast of fast and loose interlacings gives the fabric a honeycombed appearance.

1923 *Modern Wireless* July 465 How to choose a *honeycomb coil. 1923 *Popular Wireless Suppl.* 13 Oct. 9 Honeycomb coils are the subject of Letters Patent. 1887 *Colonial & Indian Exhib., Rep. Col. Sect.* 61 *Honeycomb quartz, from Sunny Corner, which is in reality decomposed skeleton nodules of septaria. 1904 A. B. F. Young *Complete Motorist* iii. (ed. 2) 55 The front of the car consists of a water-tank pierced like a honeycomb throughout its whole surface with apertures of equal dimensions; this is known as a *'honeycomb radiator'. 1921 *Discovery* Apr. 97/1 Each engine nacelle..is fitted with a nose honeycomb radiator.

Honey-dew. 3. (Earlier U.S. example.)

1851 C. Cist *Cincinnati* 244 Fine cut chewing, of best honeydew and sweet fine cut cavendish.

Ho·ney-fu·ggle, -fu·gle, *v. U.S. colloq.* Also -fogle, -fackle. [app. f. Honey *sb.* with fanciful ending.]

1. *trans.* **a.** To dupe, deceive, swindle.

1829 *Virginia Literary Museum* I. 458 *Honeyfuggle*, to quiz, to cozen. 1856 *Knickerbocker Mag.* XLVIII. Sept. 286 They go cavorting out, honey-fuggling their consciences. 1888 E. Eggleston in *Century Mag.* XXXVI. 81/2 A-tryin' to honey-fugle the varmint to git 'im to come underneath. 1902 Harben *Abner Daniel* xix, He's been tryin' to honeyfuggle the old man into a trade.

b. To obtain by duplicity or wheedling.

1905 D. G. Phillips *Plum Tree* xxiii, Whatever terms he could honeyfugle out of my conciliation-mad candidate.

2. *intr.* To act in an underhand or indirect way.

1856 *Congress. Globe* 22 July, App. 965 Pardon me for using the word, but Sharp 'honey-fuggled' around me. 1888 *Missouri Republican* 20 Jan. (Farmer) Noonan's companion objected to this honey-fugling by knocking the demonstrative stranger down. 1906 *Nation* (N.Y.) 22 Feb. 149 'Don't honey-fugle', he advised the committee, 'but go to the bottom in any way possible'.

Honey-pot. Add: **3.** A sweet girl.

1929 Vachell *Virgin* iii. 58 What a honeypot she was, whether in or out of breeches and boots.

Honeypot: see *HAANEPOOT.

Honeysuckle. 8. honeysuckle-apple (example).

1878 Mrs. Stowe *Poganuc People* xix. 209 She gathered ..stores of what were called 'honeysuckle apples' that grew upon them [*sc.* azaleas],—fleshy exudations..much valued by children.

Honiton (hǫˑnitən). The name of a town in Devonshire used *attrib.* to designate a type of pillow lace which is made there, consisting of floral sprigs either hand-sewn on to fine net, or joined by bars of other lace-work, as *Honiton appliqué, -braid, -guipure, -lace, -shawl, -silk, -sprig, -work*. Also *absol.* = *Honiton lace*.

1851 *Illustr. Catal. Gt. Exhib.* III. III. 559/1 Honiton guipure mantle. Bridal scarf and rich flounce in Honiton lace. *Ibid.* 560/1 Specimen of lace net..for the application of Brussels and Honiton sprigs. *Ibid.*, Tamboured lace scarf, imitation of Honiton, manufactured in London. 1858 Simmonds *Dict. Trade, Honiton Lace*, a pillow, or cushion, lace made in Devonshire, remarkable for the beauty of its figures and sprigs, which are sewed on to net by the needle. 1882 *Encycl. Brit.* XIV. 188/2 Honiton pillow lace resembles Brussels lace. 1895 *Army & Navy Co-op. Soc. Price List* 15 Sept. 1126 Real Lace Handkerchiefs. Honiton. 1921 *Dict. Occup. Terms* (1927) § 377 Honiton maker, Honiton worker.

Honk, *sb.* Add: **b.** The harsh sound of a motor-horn. Also *v. intr.*, to emit such a sound (said of the horn, the motor vehicle, or the driver); also *transf.*; *trans.*, to utter with such a sound; to cause to make the sound 'honk'; to remove or drive away by the hooting of motor vehicles. orig. *U.S.*

1906 'O. Henry' *Strictly Business* v. 57 The honk of the returned motor car at the door. 1906 — *Four Million* 51 She would honk loudly the word 'Clara'. 1911 R. W. Chambers *Common Law* x. 312 Where now the lonely taxi honks. 1911 H. S. Harrison *Queed* i. 6 Now and then a chauffeur honked by. 1914 R. & E. Shackleton *Four on Tour in Eng.* 83 The [motor] horn was honked suddenly. 1915 *Literary Digest* 4 Sept. 467/1 Nearly a dozen autos may be always seen 'honking' their way through Nome's busy thoroughfares. 1924 *Glasgow Herald* 18 Aug. 8 The thundering and purring and swishing and honk-ing of the road traffic. 1927 *Observer* 28 Aug. 10 In the shadiest lanes we were honked and hooted out of the way. *Ibid.* 18 Sept. 8/3 The leisured stroller..is being 'honked' off the highway. 1928 *Ibid.* 22 Jan. 10/7 'Sunstar'..is feeling fit again and proposes to honk off to Doncaster to-night. 1929 *Times* 2 Jan. 15/5 The car had been honking underneath my office window for some time.

Honker. Add: also, one who imitates the cry of a wild goose.

1891 *Outing* (U.S.) Oct. 43/1 Though a fair 'honker', I cannot successfully imitate the constantly varying note of the snow goose.

Honk-honk, reduplication of *HONK *sb.*

1908 H. G. Wells *War in Air* ii. § 2 A curious, amusing, wheezing sound had got into his 'honk, honk'. *Ibid.* § 4 Honk-honking and emitting weird cries. 1915 T. Burke *Nights in Town* 210 The honk-honk of motors. 1917 *Ideas* 23 Mar. 23/2 With a wild 'honk-honk!'..the motor rounded the corner.

Honky-tonk (hǫˑŋkitǫŋk). *U.S. Negro slang.* Also honkatonk. [Origin unascertained.] A drinking saloon, a gin-mill.

1930 J. W. Johnson *Black Manhattan* 74 There were [in New York circa 1820] gambling-clubs, honky-tonks, and professional clubs. 1930 Mulford *Deputy Sheriff* xiii. 168 'This place ain't no damn' honkatonk, stranger,' reproved the bar-tender...'Folks get throwed outa here sometimes.'

Honoris causa (hǫnōˑris kǭˑzə). [L.: lit. for the sake of honour.] In order to honour or out of respect for a person mentioned; now used chiefly as a description of such university degrees as are conferred upon persons in recognition of certain distinctions or achievements without the customary academic examination.

1611 Coryat *Crudities* 240, I wil once more speake of our most worthy Ambassadour Sr Henry Wotton, *honoris causâ*. 1626–7 in *Crt. & Times Chas. I* (1848) I. 193 His colleagues shall be the Earl of Salisbury, *honoris causâ*, and Sir Richard Western. 1882 *Standard* 19 Dec. 2 (Stanford) Receiving the degree of D.D., *honoris causa*, from the late Dr. Sumner, Archbishop of Canterbury in 1857.

Honour, *sb.* Add:

5. e. Now, in many universities, a course of study or a series of examinations in a subject or group of subjects of a higher or more specialized character than is required for a pass or ordinary degree. (Cf. *honours degree, school* in *10.)

8. a. Also at Bridge (see quot. 1886). Phr. *Honours are even*: often used fig. to denote equality in a contest (real or imaginary).

1886 *Biritch, or Russian Whist* 4 There are five honours, viz.:—Ace, King, Queen, Knave and Ten, if trumps are declared. 1909 W. Dalton *'Saturday' Bridge* 5 Honours consist of ace, king, queen, knave, and ten of the trump suit. When there are no trumps they consist of the four aces. 1920 B. Cronin *Timber Wolves* iii. 62, 'I don't know your name?'..'But then I don't know yours, do I? That makes the honours even, don't you think?'

10. honours board, a board at a school or college on which are inscribed the names of members who have gained honours; **honours degree**, an academical degree with honours or obtained in an honour school; similarly *honours examination*; **honour(s) list**, (*a*) a class list of candidates who have been successful in an examination for honours; (*b*) a list of honours conferred by the Sovereign, as at the New Year; also *fig.*; **honour-roll**, a roll of honour; **honour(s) school**, a course of study designed for those who aim at an honours (as distinguished from a pass) degree (at Oxford University, 'qui honorem ambiunt'); similarly *honour moderations*, colloq. *honour mods*.

1904 *Daily Chron.* 31 Oct. 4/4. I cannot deal here with the wholly false and mischievous qualification of an *'Honours Degree' that the rich women are answerable for. 1884 *Oxf. Univ. Cal.* 1885 p. iii, *Honours Examinations for Women. 1861 *Ibid.* 1862 273 *Honour Lists issued by Moderators. 1931 B. Brown *Talking Pictures* ix. 194 Although their names did not appear upon the 'honours list'. 1911 *Rep. Brit. Assoc.* 219 It has been suggested that if students are not encouraged to come to the university younger the better men should be allowed to enter for *Honour Mods. after six months. 1909 *Daily Chron.* 7 April 3/3 Such is the *honour-roll of these sturdy spirits. 1902 *Encycl. Brit.* XXXIII. 603/2 At Oxford there are now the following 'Final *Honour Schools'.

Honourable, *a.* Add: **2. b.** (The only Lord Mayors and Provosts in the United Kingdom who are entitled to be styled 'Right Honourable' are the Lord Mayors of London, York, and Belfast, and the Lord Provosts of Edinburgh and Glasgow.)

3. *Honourable mention*: see Mention *sb.* 2 e.

1866 *Lond. Gaz.* 26 June 3646/1 Grand prizes and money awards of the total value of 250,000 francs (£10,000), 100 Gold Medals,..5000 Honourable Mentions.

Honved (hǫˑnvĕd). [Magyar, = *hon* home + *véd* defence.] The name given to the Hungarian army in the Revolutionary war of 1848–9, and now used to designate the militia reserve.

1854 E. O. S. *Hungary & its Revolutions* 429 The new army,..namely, the Honveds, National Guards, and Volunteers. 1875 *Encycl. Brit.* II. 604/2 The Hungarian militia, or 'honveds', as they are called.

Hooch (hūtʃ) *U.S. slang.* Also hootch. [Abbreviation of Alaskan *hoochinoo*, a powerful alcoholic drink made by the natives of Alaska (see quots. 1899).] Alcoholic liquor, spirits.

[1899 *Boston* (Mass.) *Jrnl.* 11 Jan. 4/5 Recently the House gave its official sanction to the word by enacting that no whisky, beer or 'hoochinoo' shall be sold in Alaska. *Ibid.*, A mixture of rum and molasses, which has..taken the name of 'hoochinoo'.] 1903 *N.Y. Evening Post* 25 Sept. 3 In this bottle was some of the native spirits called 'hooch', distilled from sugar and graham flour. 1904 Eliz. Robins *Magnetic North* ix. 161 Apart from the question of drinking raised again by the 'hootch',..they were ready to eat the more. 1907 R. W. Service *Songs of Sourdough* (1908) 18 A broken wreck with a craze for 'hooch', and never a cent to my name. 1915 H. L. Wilson *Ruggles of Red Gap* v. (1917) 99 To get out in a hack and get a few shots of hooch under their belts. 1927 *Punch* 20 Apr. 428/3 He knows what the poor want in the great black city of Chicago. They want cash. He knows what the thirsty want. They want hooch. *attrib.* 1927 J. Barbican *Confess. Rum-Runner* xiv. 148 There ain't one block in the city without at least one hooch-hole in it.

Hoochy-koochy: see *HOOTCHY-KOOTCHY.

Hood, *sb.* Add: **5. j.** In cephalopods, arachnids, etc. (see quots.). **k.** The waterproof folding top or cover of a perambulator, motor car, charabanc, etc.; the movable cover of a typewriter or other machine. **l.** A protecting cover, also sometimes acting as a reflector, placed over an arc-lamp. **m.** *Naut.* A structure which protects the steering gear. **n.** *Photog.* (see quot. 1918). **o.** 'That part of a horse blanket which covers the horse's head and neck' (Knight *Dict. Mech.* Suppl. 1884).

j. 1883 *Encycl. Brit.* XVI. 674/1 This part of the external annular lobe of the fore-foot is called the 'hood'. 1888 Rolleston & Jackson *Anim. Life* 456 In *Nautilus*..the fore-foot is divisible into an outer and inner portion. The outer portion..is thickened dorsally where it abuts against the coil of the shell and forms the hood. 1902 *Encycl. Brit.* XXV. 543/2 Movable (hinged) sclerite (so-called hood) overhanging the first pair of appendages. k. 1895 *Army & Navy Co-op. Soc. Price List* 15 Sept. 1172 Perambulators..with..reversible jointed hood. 1904 A. B. F. Young *Complete Motorist* viii. (ed. 2) 198 It is a fine-weather vehicle, but a hood can be supplied for use in wet weather. 1912 *Motor Man.* iii. (ed. 14) 101 Complete protection can be obtained with a hood by fitting side curtains, which can be let down. l. 1913 J. B. Bishop *Panama Gateway* v. vi. 382 The reflecting hood is provided with shading skirts, which prevent the glare of the lamp filament from penetrating into distance along the axis of the canal. m. 1902 *Encycl. Brit.* XXXII. 550/1 Vessels which have a Monkey Forecastle forward,..a small poop or Hood aft to protect the steering gear. n. 1892 *Photogr. Ann.* II. 41 Have two caps for each lens, one to fit the hood and one to fit the other end of the mount. 1918 *Photo-Miniature* XV. Mar. (Gloss.), *Hood, Lens*, the detachable rim of a lens-tube somewhat larger in diameter and carrying the lens-cap. Also any separate device of tubular box- or bellows-form fitted to the lens-tube, to screen the lens from strong light.

Hood-cap. Add: **3.** *Photog.* (See quot.)

1892 *Photogr. Ann.* II. 41 Should the hood cap get lost, by unscrewing the hood the other cap comes in handy for exposing, as it fits the mount.

Hooded, *a.* **2.** Add:

1785 Latham *Gen. Syn. Birds* III. II. 426 Hooded M[erganser]...Size nearly that of a Wigeon. 1875 *Encycl. Brit.* III. 421/1 The Mitred Basilisk occurs in Guiana, the Hooded Basilisk in Amboyna.

Hoodlum. Add: **2. hoodlum wagon** *U.S.* (see quot. 1920).

1919 H. L. Wilson *Ma Pettengill* iii. 79 The hoodlum wagon going back next morning to see what could be salvaged. 1920 Hunter *Trail Drivers of Texas* 299 A second wagon for carrying the extra beds and bringing wood and water into camps...This equipage is called the hoodlum wagon.

Hoodlumism. (Earlier example.)

1875 *Scribner's Monthly* X. 276 The selfish 'Trades Unions' ..have been, I think, the principal cause of Hoodlumism.

Hoodoo, *sb.* Add: **1.** (Earlier examples. Common in recent use.) Also *attrib.*

1881 *Harper's Mag.* Apr. 737/2 I'll tell papa you're a Hoodoo. *Ibid.*, How I should like to see a Hoodoo meeting! *Ibid.* 738/1 The Hoodoo priest.

3. A commotion, upset; also, a disturbing feeling, a presentiment of ill-luck or misfortune.

1919 J. C. Snaith *Love Lane* xxxi, I couldn't move him. He'd got the hoo-doo. 1928 C. F. S. Gamble *North Sea Air Station* xii. 162 On about five successive nights..a Zeppelin would be reported approaching the coast somewhere on our beat. Result—a general 'hoo-doo'.

4. A fantastic rock pinnacle or column of rock formed by erosion or other natural cause, occurring in the Western United States.

1884 H. Butterworth *Zigzag Journ. Western States* 54 There is a region there called Goblin Land, full of lofty stone monuments, the remnants of erosion, called hoodoos. These hoodoos are of almost every variety of shape. They seem to be parts of lost mountains. 1921 *Chambers's Jrnl.* June 373/2 Strange, isolated pillars, the 'hoodoos' stood like vedettes on the heights.

B. *adj.* Unlucky, bringing bad luck.

1889 *Kansas Times & Star* 17 Sept., Joe Bracken took sick Friday, September 13, but says that hoodoo date doesn't discourage him. 1904 *New York Globe* 2 Apr. 1 It is hard to find a crew for a 'hoodoo' ship. *a* 1909 'O. Henry' *Roads of Destiny* vii. 110 He's the hoodoo planet of the heavens. 1922 *Blackw. Mag.* Sept. 321/1 My name is Armstrong—Hoodoo Armstrong. 1926 *Scots Observer* 30 Oct. 21/2 That particular service was hoodoo.

Hence **Hoodoo** *v. trans.*, to render unlucky.

1888 *Judge* (U.S.) 21 July 239/2 A Washington paper.. drops into the following poetry, which is sufficient to hoodoo the organization for the balance of the season.

Hoo·dooism. [f. Hoodoo *sb.*] The practice of hoodoo rites.

1881 *Harper's Mag.* Apr. 737/1 What *is* Hoodooism, anyhow?

Hooey (hūˑi). *U.S. slang.* Humbug.

1924 P. Marks *Plastic Age* 100 My prof's full of hooey. He doesn't know a C theme from an A one. *Ibid.* 160 'Bunk!' he exclaimed. 'Hooey!'

Hoof, *sb.* Add: **1.** *On the hoof*: (of cattle) on their feet, alive.

1830 N. Dana *Mariner's Sk.* 163 (Th.) We generally bought our beef 'on the hoof'. 1879 *Harper's Mag.* Nov. 892/2 Good beef on the hoof was worth four and a quarter cents per pound. 1902 *Encycl. Brit.* XXV. 186/1 The estimated dead weight of the sheep imported on the hoof for slaughter.

5. *hoof-fall, -hold*; **hoof-ail** = *hoof-rot*; **hoof and tongue sickness** = *foot-and-mouth disease*; **hoof-rot**, foot-rot.

1884 *Rep. U.S. Comm. Agric.* 246 An article on the '*Hoof-ail' of cattle. 1867 *Queenstown Free Press* 22 Jan. (Pettman) We have had a great deal of *hoof and tongue sickness amongst our cattle. 1910 J. Farnol *Broad Highway* II. xlvii, Nodding sleepily with every plodding *hoof-fall. 1923 H. Sutcliffe *Wrack o' Doom* ii, The broken lands that gave no *hoof-hold. 1863 H. S. Randall *Pract. Shepherd* ii. 25 Scab and *hoof-rot, those dire scourges of the ovine race.

Hoof, *v.* Add: **1.** (Later U.S. examples.)

1877 Habberton *Jericho Road* i. 7 If we get stuck way up the river, so's we have to lay up all summer, and you have to hoof it in deep water. 1888 'Buffalo Bill' *Wild West* 531, I finally concluded that my prospects were good for 'hoofing' the whole distance. 1910 W. M. Raine *B. O'Connor* iv. 58 He hoofed it back to the cabin.

b. To dance. (Also with *it*.) *slang.*

1927 *Hollis St. Theatre Progr.* (Boston, U.S.) 19 Sept., Gloss. 1928 *Daily Express* 2 July 11/5 Mr. Tommy Nolan proposed to his partner, Miss Anna King. She accepted him, and they planned their wedding and honeymoon while 'hoofing'.

2. b. To dismiss, expel, eject. Usually with *out*.

1893 Farmer *Slang* s.v., To hoof out. 1905 *Daily Chron.* 22 Apr. 9/2 Well, at least we know for certain..that he was hoofed out of the Guards. 1924 Galsworthy *White Monkey* III. viii, A packer we had, who got hoofed for snooping books.

So **Hoo·fer** *U.S. slang*, a dancer.

1928 *Sunday Express* 8 Apr. 5/7 To-morrow Roy Lloyd, who was the hoofer in 'Broadway', takes up the part. 1928 *Daily Express* 2 July 11/5 It is officially announced that the 'hoofers' danced 482 hours.

Hoofless, *a.* Add: **2.** Destitute of cattle.

1827 J. F. Cooper *Prairie* v, They have robbed the squatter of his beasts!..The reptiles have left him as hoofless as a beaver!

Hook, *sb.* Add:

1. b. *pl.* The fingers or hands. *slang.*

a 1842 Maginn *Vidocq Versified* (Farmer) To his clies my hooks I throw in. 1877 *Five Years' Penal Serv.* iv. 259 In a week or two a man can bring his hooks and feelers into full working trim again.

c. A thief. *slang.* (Cf. Hook *v.* 6, Hooker [1] 1.)

1887 W. J. Horsley *Jottings from Jail* i. 23 A hook who is going to be legged. 1890 Anstey *Voces Populi* i. 39 Professional 'Hook' (*to line of Policemen*). So *you're 'ere*, are you? 1901 *Westm. Gaz.* 4 Sept. 4/1 The very same 'hook' was caught..a second time red-handed at another station.

11. (Earlier examples.)

1578 Hakluyt *Voy.* (1600) III. 743 A hooke or headland. 1832 E. C. Wines *Two Years & a Half in Navy* i, We were kept off the hook, waiting either for wind or tide.

13. b. *Boxing.* A short swinging blow with the elbow bent and rigid.

1898 *Daily News* 9 Nov. 8/5 After Smith had put a left hook on the chin the issue was not in doubt. 1910 Driscoll *Ringcraft* 94 It only needs practice to convince anyone that the straight blow will always get there before the swing or the hook. 1929 *Evening News* 18 Nov. 16/4 With a couple of left hooks to the head.

15. d. *To go off the hooks*: to get married. So *to be lifted off the hook*. *local.*

1876 Miss Braddon *J. Haggard's Dau.* x, Some of the young chaps will be wanting her to get married. These here pretty ones go off the books so soon. 1889 A. G. Murdoch *Sc. Readings* Ser. III. 9 She had never been, up till date, lifted off the hook... The offers she had refused in her day were many.

16. (Earlier examples.)

1812 *Boston-Gazette* 23 Nov. (Th.) They forget that Rodgers himself says that he went upon his own hook. 1836 Crockett *Exploits & Adv. Texas* (1837) 13 But now I start anew upon my own hook.

b. *To sling* or *take one's hook*: to go away, be off, decamp. *slang* or *dial.*

1874, 1897 [see Sling *v.*[1] 3 d]. 1886 Mabel Peacock *Tales N. Lincs.* 106 An' soa he teks his hook back agaain to steam-booseyard. 1892 Kipling *Barrack-Room Ball., Loot*, Before you sling your 'ook, at the 'ousetops take a look. 1895 *Punch* 21 Dec. 300/2 The train had already taken its hook into the ..gloom of a tunnel. 1930 *Ibid.* 19 Feb. 203/3 We flung our hats in the air the day they slung their hook.

18. hook-and-ladder *U.S.*, apparatus consisting of ladders and hooks used by firemen; often *attrib.* in *hook-and-ladder company*; **hook gauge**, an instrument consisting of a hook attached to a vernier used for measuring the surface level of water; **hook-ladder**, a ladder with hooks at one end by which it can be suspended; **hook-motion**, in a steam engine, a valve gear reversed by V hooks; **hook needle** (see quot.); **hook-net**, a fishing-net with an L-shaped continuation; **hook plate**, a casting for attachment to a wall, having hooks on which radiator pipes may rest; **hook-pot** (see quots.); **hook stroke** *Cricket*, a stroke made by hitting a short-pitched ball, after it has risen, round to leg with a horizontal swing of the bat; **hook tender** *U.S.*, **-tool** (see quots.); **hook-worm**, any of various nematoid worms, as those of the genera *Ankylostoma* and *Uncinaria*, infesting man and certain animals, so called from the hook-like ribs or spines of the male; also, the disease *ANKYLOSTOMIASIS caused thereby; also *attrib.*, as *hook-worm disease*.

1851 C. Cist *Cincinnati* 168 There are beside, two *hook and ladder companies..and one company of fire guards. 1865 *Chambers's Jrnl.* 29 July 469/2, 18 hook-and-ladder trucks. 1902 *Westm. Gaz.* 11 June 8/1 Other Americans pointed with pride to their hook-and-ladder system, which forms such an important aid to the New York fireman. 1909 *Strand Mag.* Apr. 363 There stood the engines and the 'hook-and-ladder'. 1923 Watts *Luther Nichols* 68 Hook-and-ladder Company 17. 1880 *Encycl. Brit.* XII. 477/2 The *hook gauge used first by Mr. U. Boyden of Boston, in 1840. 1858 Simmonds *Dict. Trade*, *Hook-ladder. 1902 *Daily Chron.* 12 June 9/3 The hook ladder fastening to the windows on each floor is now in almost universal use on the Continent and in America. 1905 *Westm. Gaz.* 17 Oct. 7/1 The escape was rushed up, ladders extended, hook-ladders placed into position. 1875 Knight *Dict. Mech.*, *Hook-motion (Steam-engine), a valve gear having hooks for actuating and reversing. 1884 *Ibid.* Suppl., *Hook Needle (Hydraulic Engineering), a hook-ended needle used in sewing mats for lining river banks or making levees. It is used in making the lock-stitch and also in the hook needle fastening. *Ibid.*, *Hook Net (Fishing), one with an L-shaped continuation forming a sort of pocket. *Ibid.*, *Hook Plate, a supporter for Radiators. 1886 R. Brown *Spunyarn & Spindrift* v, A *hook-pot of tea a-piece. 1896 *Idler* Mar. 173/1 There you'd see them crowding about the doors at meal-times, flourishing their hook-pots. 1897 Ranjitsinhji *Jubilee Bk. Cricket* 175 Batsmen of the old school very much disliked the *hook-stroke on principle. 1908 *Daily Chron.* 15 May 8/2 He began exploiting the full drive and the hook stroke. 1911 C. B. Fry in P. Warner *Bk. Cricket* 226 Ranjitsinhji found almost as little difficulty in making his famous 'hook strokes'. 1905 *Terms Forestry & Logging* 40 *Hook tender*, the foreman of a yarding crew; specifically, one who directs the attaching of the cable to a turn of logs. 1875 Knight *Dict. Mech.*, *Hook-tool (Lathe) *a*, a form of hand-tool used in metal turning, which is of a hook shape, and is supported on a rest below and beyond which it extends...*b.* A wood-turning tool having a bent portion used for bottoming boxes, or lids, or other hollow work. 1903 Dorland *Med. Dict.* (ed. 3), *Hookworm. See *Uncinaria* and *Ankylostoma*. 1909 *Times* 29 Oct. 5/6 A commission of eminent medical men to investigate the hook-worm disease. 1925 E. F. Norton *Fight for Everest, 1924* 352 Porters should be vaccinated, and given suitable treatment for hook-worm.

Hook, *sb.*[2] *local.* Variant of Huck *sb.*[1] Also **hook-bone.** The projecting upper part of the thigh bones of cattle near the hip-joint.

1808 *Compl. Grazier* (ed. 3) 9 The roof [of a bull ought to be] wide, particularly over the chine and hips, or hooks. 1844 H. Stephens *Bk. Farm* II. 161 Between the shoulders and the hook. *Ibid.* III. 1253 The broad hook-bones, with the narrow chest, are not entirely occasioned in cows by calf-breeding. 1858 Flint *Milch Cows* 17 The Ayrshire farmers prefer their dairy bulls..broad at the hook-bones and hips, and full in the flanks. 1900 *Westmoreland Gaz.* 3 Feb., Advt. (E.D.D.) Strayed, two Herdwick ewes; marked red pop near shoulder and near hook.

Hook, *v.* Add: **4. c.** To make (rugs) with a hook: see *HOOKED *a.* 4. *U.S.*

1882 *Harper's Mag.* Dec. 126/1 Cynthy Ann..hooked rugs from early in the morning until late into the night.

8. d. *Boxing.* To strike (one's opponent) a swinging blow with the elbow bent (cf. *Hook *sb.* 13 b). Also *absol.*

1898 *Daily News* 24 Nov. 8/3 Corbett hooked with his right hard on Sharkey's jaw. 1910 Driscoll *Ringcraft* 86 Wild attempts to hook him on his well protected jaw.

e. *Rugby Football.* To secure (the ball) with the foot, as hooker, when it is placed in the scrummage. Also *intr.*

1906 Gallaher & Stead *Complete Rugby Footb.* 110 In Britain it is the custom to hook the ball in the scrum with the outside feet crossing over those on the inside. 1913 E. H. D. Sewell in *Daily Graphic* 24 Mar. 15/1 D. A. Greer..may be of use to Ireland henceforward, especially as 'hooking' is his forte. 1927 Wakefield & Marshall *Rugger* 183 The front row tried trick hooking and foot-up tactics.

13. *To hook Jack*: to play truant. *U.S.* (Cf. *HOOKEY 1.)

1905 J. C. Lincoln *Partners of Tide* iv, The boy 'hooked Jack' for a whole day.

Hook-billed, *a.* (Later U.S. example.)

1881 *Amer. Naturalist* XV. 182 The male [of hump-back salmon] is slab-sided, hook-billed and distorted.

Hooke (huk). The name of R. *Hooke* (1635–1703), mathematician, physicist, and philosopher, used in the genitive to designate his discoveries and inventions. **Hooke's coupling** = *Hooke's universal joint*. **Hooke's gearing**, a gearing for wheels having teeth cut in a helicoid form. **Hooke's law**, the law (*ut tensio sic vis*) that within the limits of elasticity the strain produced by a stress of any one kind is proportional to the stress producing it. **Hooke's (universal) joint**: see Universal *a.* 13.

1829 [see Universal *a.* 13]. 1875 Knight *Dict. Mech.*, Hooke's Gearing. *Ibid.*, Hooke's Joint. 1877 *Encycl. Brit.* VII. 803/2 Hooke's law is that elongation (understood of an elastic solid) is proportional to the force producing it. 1883 *Ibid.* XV. 761/2 *Coupling of Intersecting Axes—Hooke's Universal Joint.*—Intersecting axes are coupled by a contrivance of Hooke's, known as the 'universal joint', which belongs to the class of linkwork. *Ibid.* 762/2 *Double Hooke's Coupling*... Let a_1, a_2, a_3 be the angular velocities of the first, intermediate, and last shaft in this train of two Hooke's couplings. 1887 *Ibid.* XXII. 516/2 The kinematic relations of the moving pieces in a Hooke's joint.

Hooked, *a.* Add: **4.** *Hooked rug*, a rug made on a canvas ground with woollen yarn which is pulled through with a hook. *U.S.*

1882 *Harper's Mag.* Dec. 126/1 Her hooked rugs were in demand now. 1894 H. Wells *Trav. Altruria* 126 Home-made hooked rugs, in rounds and ovals.

Hooker [1]. Add: **3.** Also simply *hooker*; and in many other technical usages.

1881 *Instr. Census Clerks* (1885) 134/2 Hooker (to special trade when stated or determinable). Hooker (Undefined).. Factory Labourer. 1900 *Westm. Gaz.* 16 May 8/1 No one received injuries, the hookers having received warning by the clashing of the cage. 1921 *Dict. Occup. Terms* (1927) § 043 *Onsetter*;..*hooker, hooker-at-shaft*..; stands at bottom of shaft in coal or shale mine to push full tubs on to cage and remove empty ones. *Ibid.* § 943 *Hooker, cloth hooker, piece hooker, hooker-and-lapper.*

4. A cow or ox that 'hooks' (see Hook *v.* 11). *U.S.*

1885 'C. E. Craddock' *Prophet Gt. Smoky Mt.* ii. 48 The red cow jes' hooked down the bars, bein' a turrible hooker. 1902 G. H. Lorimer *Lett. Self-made Merchant* vii. 84 You want to..distinguish between a cow that's a kicker, but whose intentions are good..and a hooker, who is vicious on general principles.

5. *Rugby Football.* The player in the front row of the scrummage on either side who endeavours to obtain the ball by hooking it.

1905 *Daily Chron.* 13 Sept. 7/4 The two front men—called 'hookers'—can get the ball just as well as three. 1906 Gallaher & Stead *Complete Rugby Footb.* 110 Our hookers get their bodies low down and practically horizontal, with their legs stretching well out behind them. 1927 Wakefield & Marshall *Rugger* 166 Some hookers prefer to have the weight on the loose-head side.

b. *Cricket.* One who uses the hook stroke.

1911 P. Warner *Bk. Cricket* 208 He has a lovely shot over extra-cover's head,..and on a slow wicket is a fine puller and hooker.

c. *Golf.* A ball which has been hooked.

1908 *Daily Chron.* 23 May 9/2 The seventeenth tee shot is now played from a new tee, which is some distance to the right of the old one, thus bringing in the old bunker as a hazard to catch a hooker.

Hookey (huˑki). Also **hooky.** [Cf. Hook *sb.* 14, *v.* 6, *v.* *13, and Hooky-crooky.]

1. *To play hookey*: to play truant. *U.S. school slang.*

1848 Bartlett *Dict. Amer.* 1867 'Mark Twain' *Amer. Drolleries* 20 He would not play hookey, even when his sober judgment told him it was the most profitable thing he could do. 1883 E. Eggleston *Hoosier School-boy* ix. 63 They remembered that the geography lesson was a hard one, and so they played 'hookey'. 1904 Harben *Georgians* vii. 77 'I sorter feel like playin' hookey myself,' he admitted. 1908 Mulford *Orphan* xii. 150 I'll play on them, too, when they gets home! Off playing hookey from work when we all of us aches from double shifts.

2. *Blind hookey*, a gambling game at cards, in which a pack is divided into as many packets, placed face downwards, as there are players, the dealer taking one packet and each other player betting that the bottom card of his packet is higher than that of the dealer. Also *fig.* or *transf.*

1840 [see *Blind *a.* 16]. 1852 Mundy *Antipodes* (1857) 201 The process of emigration was formerly—as compared with its present gradual perfection—a very blind-hookey kind of game. 1862 Thackeray *Philip* xxi. II. 100 Victimized by his own uncle..at a game called 'blind hookey'. 1909 Ware *Passing English, Blind Hookey*, a leap in the dark; *e.g.*, 'it's Blind Hookey to attempt it'. 1925 *Blackw. Mag.* Aug. 286/2 It is..the common practice of politicians to play blind hookey with the great interests entrusted to them.

Hookey Walker: see Walker *int.*

Hookless, *a.* Add: **b.** Of a garment: Having no hooks.

1906 *Westm. Gaz.* 25 Sept. 2/1 Blouses, in various stages of hookless decrepitude.

Hookum (hūˑkəm). *India.* Also hukm, hookm. [a. Hind., a. Arabic حكم *ḥukm* f. *ḥakama* (cf. Hakim).] A command, order, or instruction from a person in authority. Also *transf.* (see quot. 1925).

1843 Lady Sale *Jrnl. Disasters Afghanistan* 39 The troops ..instead of receiving *hookm* to enter the city, the Shah almost rudely inquired why they had come! 1860 W. H. Russell *Diary in India* II. 226 We had no hookum from the commissioner or deputy. 1881 R. Kipling *Departm. Ditties* (1888) 7 A Hookum hinting at supervision of *dasturi*. 1895 Mrs. Croker *Village Tales* (1896) 224 His coat was restored to him, with a 'hookum', to say that he was free. 1925 Fraser & Gibbons *Soldier & Sailor Words, Hookum*, a regulation. The correct thing, *e.g.*, 'That's the hookum'. An old Army colloquial term.

Hookum-snivey (huˑkəm sniˑvi). *dial.* and *slang.* Also **hook and snivey (snivvy), hook 'em snivey, hookem snivey, hook um snivey.** [app. orig. *hook and snivey*, prob. f. Hook *sb.* or *v.*] An imposture or deceit; also, a contrivance for undoing the bolt of a door from the outside. Also *attrib.* or *adj.*, deceitful, tricky.

1781 G. Parker *View Soc.* II. 81 He..would stand no Hook and Snivey, or Nix the Buffer. 1802 Mar. Edgeworth *Irish Bulls* 129, I ranged them fair and even with my hookem-snivey. 1823 'J. Bee' *Dict. Turf* 98 Hook and Snivvy —practised by soldiers in quarters, when they obtain grub for *nix*, by connivance with the slavey, or her mistress. 1874 *Slang Dict.* s.v., Sometimes used as an irrelevant answer by street boys. As, 'who did that?'—'Hook um snivey'—actually no one. 1892 S. Hewett *Peas. Sp. Devon* 89, I tellee 'onesty is the best policy. Niver yü be up tü hookem-snivey ways. 1905 E. Phillpotts *Secret Woman* II. xi, An' some lying an' doing all manner of hookem-snivey deeds.

Hook-up (huˑkɒp). orig. *U.S. colloq.* [f. phrase *to hook up*: Hook *v.* 4 b, 5.] A connexion or combination.

1903 A. H. Lewis *The Boss* 116 It'll put us in line for a hook-up with th' reform bunch in th' fight for th' town next year. 1911 H. Quick *Yellowstone N.* vii. 191 The Golden Fountain..had no lawyer against us. It was a funny hook-up. 1927 *Observer* 11 Dec. 16/5 National appeals are possible by wireless when the various American 'Radio Corporations' agree to a 'national hook-up'. 1929 *Literary Digest* 18 May 79/1 These lines are the skeleton of a gigantic aerial hook-up that now seems destined to cover South America.

Hooky, Hookey. *U.S.* (See quots.)

c 1845 Paulding *Noble Exile* 114 By the living Hookey, this is a free country. 1890 Marah E. Ryan *Told in Hills* 323 'A regular cave, by hooky!' said the moral guide from Idaho.

Hooligan (hūˑligăn). [Origin unascertained. The word first appears in print in daily newspaper police court reports in the summer of 1898. Several accounts of the rise of the word, purporting to be based on first-hand evidence, attribute it to a misunderstanding or perversion of *Hooley* or *Hooley's gang*, but no positive confirmation of this has been discovered. The name *Hooligan* figured in a music-hall song of the eighteen-nineties, which described the doings of a rowdy Irish family, and a comic Irish character of the name appeared in a series of adventures in *Funny Folks*.]

A young street rough, a member of a street gang. Also *attrib.*, and *transf.*

1898 *Daily News* 26 July 5/1 It is no wonder..that Hooligan gangs are bred in these vile, miasmatic byways. *Ibid.* 8 Aug. 9/3 The constable said the prisoner belonged to a gang of young roughs, calling themselves 'Hooligans'. 1898 *Daily Tel.* 6 Aug. (Ware) William Lineker, described as a Hooligan, sets upon an inoffensive man. 1898 *Daily Graphic* 30 Aug. 4/4 Mr. White..stated that every Saturday and Sunday nights gangs like the 'Hooligan gang' came to his house, broke the windows, glass, &c., and made disturbances. 1898 *Westm. Gaz.* 15 Sept. 1/2 The Khalifa was, after all, only a sort of Soudanese Hooligan. 1901 *Pall Mall Mag.* Feb. 198 Nobody will claim honesty as a Hooligan virtue.

Hence **Hoo·ligan** *v. intr.*, to act as a hooligan; also *trans.*, to treat (a person) roughly; **Hoo:liganesque** *a.*, like a hooligan; **Hooliga·nic** *a.*, resembling that of hooligans; **Hoo·liganism**, the characteristic behaviour of hooligans, rough horse-play; **Hoo·liganize** *v. intr.*, to act as a hooligan.

These derivatives, with the exception of *hooliganism*, are only occasional, but they are inserted here because of their additional testimony to the currency of *hooligan*.

1898 *Pall Mall Gaz.* 19 Aug. 9/3 Any unauthorized person found trespassing on the aforesaid sphere would be *Hooliganed without further notice. 1899 *Ibid.* 5 Jan. 2/3 The proprietor of Lord Tennyson (in wax) says that it was a certain young man, who, with others,..when called upon to desist, Hooliganed about and threw the late Laureate's head at him. *Ibid.* 1 Feb. 2/3 Larking about in the usual *hooliganesque way. 1902 *Daily Chron.* 20 Sept. 5/6 Stay then your *Hooliganic lark. 1898 *Daily Tel.* 12 Aug. 5/7 *Hooliganism', or youthful ruffianism. 1898 *Daily Graphic* 22 Aug. 14/2 The avalanche of brutality which, under the name of 'Hooliganism'..has cast such a dire slur on the social records of South London. 1900 *19th Cent.* July 90 To strike at the very roots of truancy, juvenile crime, and Hooliganism. 1911 *Catholic Times* 1 Sept., The recent outbreak of hooliganism [in Liverpool]. 1901 *Pall Mall Mag.* Feb. 198 The Hooligan..would *Hooliganise less..if in his ruffianism he risked a cut of it [*sc.* the whip].

Hoon (hūn). *India.* Also hun. [Hindi (Skr. *hūna*).] A gold coin, the pagoda.

1807 F. Buchanan *Journ. Madras* II. 310 Huns, or Pagodas. 1877 J. Dowson *H. M. Elliot's Hist. India* VII. 84 Part of the two *lacs* of *huns* (pagodas) which was the stipulated amount of his annual tribute. 1877 Jas. Grant *Hist. India* I. xxvi. 140/1 The pagoda..was called a *hoon* by the Mohammedans, and a *varaha* by the Hindoos. 1914 *Brit. Mus. Return* 118 Hun.

Hoondi (huˑndi). *Indian.* Also hoondee, hoondy, hundi. [Hind. *hundī* (Skr. *hundikā* bill of exchange).] A negotiable instrument, such as a bill of exchange or promissory note, used by native bankers in India and worded in the vernacular; also, money remitted by such an instrument.

1619 in Foster *Engl. Factories India* (1906) 85 [They advise the dispatch of bills of exchange for rupees] hundies [17,100]. 1680 *Ibid.* 182 The exchange of rup[ees]secaus for hundies. 1810 T. Williamson *East India Vade Mecum* II. 330 Hoondies (i.e. bankers' drafts) would be of no use whatever to them. 1924 J. M. Keynes *Indian Currency & Finance* 197 The *hoondees* they buy and sell to each other.. are chiefly the traders' *hoondees* bearing the shroffs' own endorsements.

Hoonoomaun, variant of *HANUMAN.

Hoop, *sb.*[1] Add:

1. c. A hoop, often with paper stretched over it, through which acrobats or performing animals leap. Phr. (fig.) *To go through the hoop(s)*: to undergo an ordeal or trial. Similarly *to put through the hoop*.

1793 in T. Frost *Circus Life* (1875) 43 Through the Hoop on Fire, fourteen feet high, by Mr. Porter and Mr. Ducrow. 1869 B. Clarke *Crocker* 88 When a rider..has been jumping through paper hoops held up at intervals round the ring. 1875 T. Frost *Circus Life* 185. All aspirant, to saw-dust honours..are required to..hold hoops, balloons, banners, &c. 1914 W. W. Gibson *Borderlands, Hoops* 55 *Merry Andrew.* I missed a hoop This afternoon... I've not missed A hoop since I was six. I'm forty-two. 1919 B. Cable *Old Contempt.* 209 Then Tommy Dodd got hold of his sergeant and 'put him through the hoop'. 1925 E. Fraser & Gibbons *Soldier & Sailor Words, Hoop, through the*: up for punishment. 1926 Galsworthy *Silver Spoon* I. x, Let the papers jump through their hoops as much as they liked. 1930 Marg. Kennedy *Fool of Family* xxvii, Disagreeable thoughts were going to assail him...If he had ever let them get hold of him he would never have got through his hoop. *Ibid.* xxx, 'Let's hide..upstairs..'. 'No use. They'll all come up to look at Henry VIII's bed.' 'Oh, well. Then it's through the hoops.'

2. b. A circular wooden frame in which a cheese is moulded.

[1790 W. H. Marshall *Midl. Counties* I. 349 *note*, The cheese vats of this district are merely 'hoops' of ash, with a boarden bottom.] 1857 *Trans. Ill. Agric. Soc.* II. 181 These vats warm, scald, and work the curd ready for the hoop without being removed. 1877 *Rep. Vermont Board Agric.* IV. 54 Most of the cheese made about here was bought and shipped almost as soon as it was out of the hoops.

c. In a built-up gun, each of the cylindrical forgings which are shrunk upon the tube or jacket.

1902 *Encycl. Brit.* XXIX. 160/2 By the use of wire the full benefit is obtained of the ideal thin coil or hoop. *Ibid.* 162/1 The interior of the jacket and other hoops are bored out in a boring-machine and finished before the exterior of the barrel is fine-turned; and so for any other hoop. *Ibid.* 162/2 The covering hoop [*sc.* of wire guns] is often not allowed any shrinkage.

13. b. hoop-ash (earlier examples); **hoop-pole** (Amer. examples); **hoop-skirt** (earlier U.S. example; also fig.); **hoop-snake** (example); **hoop tension**, 'the circumferential tension in a shell or in any thin concentric element of a thick cylinder subject to radial pressure' (Webster 1911); **hoop-wood (tree)** (later example).

1810 Michaux *Arbres* I. 38 Hackberry tree,..*Hoop ash, sur les bords de l'Ohio, Black elder. 1832 D. J. Browne *Sylva Amer.* 133 On the Ohio it is called Hoop Ash and in Kentucky, Hack Berry. 1645 *Dedham Rec.* 112 Sam Milles hath lib[er]tie to cut 400 lengthes of *hoope poles on the common. 1703 *Suffield Doc. Hist.* 145 Any person, that shall presume..to cut..and carry away hoop-polls, from off any of our commons. 1821 J. F. Cooper *Spy* xxxiv. (1831) 389 Lads who wink when they pull a trigger and form a line like a hoop-pole. 1845 in C. Cist *Cincinnati Misc.* 219, I came to a thick piece of brush, in short, a perfect thicket of hoop-poles. 1885 *Rep. Indian Affairs* 206 They..obtain their living by farming and cutting stave-bolts, hoop-poles, and cord-wood. 1865 Mrs. Stowe *House & Home P.* 159 Look at the *hoop-skirt factories. 1896 *Emporia* (Kans.) *Gaz.* 15 Aug., We have raked the old ash heap of failure.. and found an old human hoop skirt who has failed as a business man. 1906 *Springfield* (Mass.) *Weekly Republ.* 19 July 1 Populism was a 'hoopskirt' article of statesmanship. 1840 *Southern Lit. Messenger* VI. 380/2, I never believed in the existence of *hoop-snakes neither, until I went out into the western country. 1902 *Kynoch Jrnl.* Oct.–Nov. 17/1 Since the ratio of the inner to outer radius is now 1·595, the *hoop tension at the inner surface = 62·8 tons. 1821 J. Fowler *Jrnl.* 21 We get out at our ushal time; at ten miles pased a point of Rocks and a *Hoop wood tree on them.

Hoop, *v.*[2] Add: **4. c.** To cry *up*.

1908 'Yeslah' *Tenderfoot S. Calif.* iv. 42 These Californians who are eternally hooping up the glorious climate.

Hooped, *a.* Add: **3.** Rounded like a hoop.

1852 *Trans. Mich. Agric. Soc.* III. 137 The breeder will do well to seek in his animal a proper form, viz...good, hooped ribs.

Hoop-ee, *int.* (Cf. Hoop *int.* and *WHOOPEE.)

1845 J. J. Hooper *Adv. Simon Suggs* iii. 31 Hoop-ee! *won't* they roll over the floor.

Hoop-la (hūˑplā). [f. Hoop *sb.*[1] + La *int.*] A game in which persons throw rings on to a surface containing a number of articles, the object being to gain any of these as a prize by throwing a ring so as to encircle it completely. Also *attrib.*

1909 *London Mag.* Sept. 26 A new game: Hoop-la! 1910 *Daily Chron.* 14 Jan. 3/5 A showman placed his 'hoopla' near the Promenade at Whitley, Northumberland, and invited the public to throw rings (at so many a penny) for prizes. 1912 A. S. M. Hutchinson *Happy Warrier* v. i. § 2. 279 All Maddox's smaller-fry—coker-nut shies, hoop-la's, Living Mermaid. 1927 *Blackw. Mag.* Sept. 358/2 We ..finally sought refuge from the mob in a 'hoopla' stall, where we tried our luck.

Hoop-la, variant of *HOUP-LA.

Hoopless (hūˑplès), *a.* [f. Hoop *sb.*[1] + -less.] Having no hoop.

1885 A. Munro *Siren Casket* 65 Two hoopless pails.

Hooroosh, variant of *HURROOSH.

1836 *Knickerbocker Mag.* VIII. 208 When they were all free, they began to sky-lark and kick up a hooroosh in all quarters. 1839 Sir J. D. Hooker in *Life* (1918) I. 91 He used ..to start up, take his stick, shout, hooroosh..and scare the poor little snips out of their senses. 1851 H. Melville *Moby Dick* cxx. (1926) 502 What a hooroosh aloft there! 1923 *Chambers's Jrnl.* Jan. 17/2 A wild *hooroush* ensued.

Hoosegow (hūˑgau). *U.S. slang.* [ad. S. Amer. or Mex. Sp. *juzgao* = *juzgado* tribunal:—L. *jūdicātum*, pa. pple. of *jūdicāre* to Judge.] Prison.

1920 *Public Opin.* 560/3 Only the keeper and the kept in the hoosegow knew it. 1927 Barbican *Confess. Rum-Runner* iv. 47, I have had one dose of the hoosegow, and I can tell you I don't want any more.

Hoosh (huʃ), *sb. slang.* [Origin unknown.] A kind of thick soup.

1905 R. F. Scott *Voy. 'Discovery'* I. 445 The cook..proceeded to prepare the ingredients of the *hoosh*, by which term the hot, thick soup that constituted the sledging meal was generally known. 1911 — *Last Exped.* (1923) 374 They had some of Chinaman's undercut in their hoosh yesterday. 1923 *Chambers's Jrnl.* Jan. 73/2 The thick savoury 'hoosh' of pemmican and broken plasmon biscuit.

Hoosh (hūʃ), *int.* An exclamation used in driving animals, etc.; hence as vb.

1874 Hardy *Madding Crowd* x, Saying 'Hoosh!' to the cocks and hens when they go upon your seeds. 1900 *Contemp. Rev.* Oct. 512 A loud 'hoosh' from the Kaffir roused one of the Englishmen. 1908 *Athenæum* 11 Apr. 450/1, I hooshed them, hooshed them all into the shed.

Hoosier (hūˑʒiəɹ). *U.S.* Also hoosher. [Origin unknown.] A nickname for a native of the state of Indiana.

1832 *New Year's Addr.* in *Indiana Democrat*, Ask for our 'hoosiers' good plantations. 1834 *Knickerbocker Mag.* III. 441 They smiled at my inquiry, and said it was among the 'hoosiers' of Indiana. 1835 J. H. Ingraham *South-West* I. ix. 105 The primitive navies..manned..by 'real Kentucks' —'Buck eyes'—'Hooshers' and 'Snorters'. 1860 Emerson *Cond. Life* Wks. (Bohn) II. 335 These Hoosiers and Suckers are really better than the snivelling opposition. 1885 *Outing* (U.S.) VII. Nov. 152/2 Oh, say, papa. Did you notice that young Hoosier and his bride who sat opposite me at breakfast?

b. An inexperienced or awkward person.

1874 J. W. Long *Amer. Wild-fowl* viii. 144 'Greenhorns' and 'hoosiers', as the regular hunters call such fellows.

c. *attrib.* Of or belonging to Indiana. **Hoosier cake** (see quot. 1859).

1839 J. Plumbe *Sk. Iowa* 46 (Th.) The Hoosier State has reason to rejoice in the amount and value of its waters. 1845 *Knickerbocker Mag.* XXV. 374 Three hundred miles of Hoosier mud. 1859 Bartlett *Dict. Amer.*, *Hoosier Cake*, a Western name for a sort of coarse gingerbread, which, say the Kentuckians, is the best bait to catch a hoosier with, the biped being fond of it. 1871 E. Eggleston *Hoosier Schoolm.* Pref., It has been in my mind since I was a Hoosier boy. 1878 J. H. Beadle *Western Wilds* i. 18 No grammar of the 'Hoosier' language has ever been published. 1907 *Chicago Evening Post* 4 May 5 A rose festival will be given by the Indiana Society of Chicago, comprising hoosier business men of the city.

Hence **Hoo·sierdom, -land**, Indiana; **Hoosierina**, a woman or girl of Indiana; **Hoo·sierism**, a peculiarity of Indiana, esp. in speech; **Hoo·sierize** *v. trans.*, to convert into a Hoosier; **Hoosieroon** = *HOOSIER.

1848 *Congress. Globe* 7 Aug., App. 1119 In the West, every political thingumderry..does his little best to produce confusion in *Hoosierdom. 1904 *N. Y. Tribune* 31 July, A flitting visit..to his boyhood home in Hoosierdom. 1843 R. Carlton *New Purchase* xxviii, And what could have deceived our *Hoosierina? 1844 *Yale Lit. Mag.* IX. 264 Twelve young Hoosiers and Hoosierina's. 1843 R. Carlton *New Purchase* ix, Thus the cabin lady kept on doing up her small stock of English into *Hoosierisms and other figures. 1878 J. H. Beadle *Western Wilds* i. 18 The native of Indiana finds..that he must drop some of his 'Hoosierisms'. 1853 J. G. Baldwin *Flush Times Alabama* 7 He was built after the model and structure of Bolingbroke in his youth, *Americanized* and *'Hoosierized* a little. 1848 *Congress. Globe* 25 Apr. 668 Our political lucubrations in *Hoosierland. 1834 *Knickerbocker Mag.* IV. 390 A few remote Kentuckians, or Indiana *Hoosheroons. 1853 *Daily Morn. Herald* (St. Louis) 27 Apr. (Th.) He looks like a Hoosieroon: all he lacks is a chunk of gingerbread in his fist.

Hoot, *sb.*[1] Add: **c.** A sound produced mechanically by a motor-horn or the like.

1904 A. B. F. Young *Complete Motorist* xii. (ed. 2) 258 You should have a connection from the exhaust pipe led into a small reservoir and thence into the horn, so that on turning a tap a prolonged hoot will be emitted. 1927 *Scots Observer* 14 May 17/1 An imperative horn hoot made him turn his head.

Hoot, *sb.*[2] *U.S. colloq.* [Perhaps the same as Hoot *sb.*[1] or *int.* Cf. *Hooter [2].] The smallest amount or particle; a whit or atom. Chiefly with negative and in phrases *to give* (*cart, matter*) *two hoots* (*a hoot*).

1878 J. H. Beadle *Western Wilds* xxxviii. 615, I got onto my reaper and banged down every hoot of it before Monday night. 1921 R. D. Paine *Comr. Rolling Ocean* xii 214, I am glad of that even if he did tell me that as a supercargo I wasn't worth a hoot in hades. 1925 N. Venner *Imperfect Impostor* iv, I can't see this place gives a hoot whether I'm here or not. 1925 E. Fraser & Gibbons *Soldier & Sailor Words* s.v., I don't care two hoots in hell. 1926 A. P. Herbert *She-Shanties* 36 We did not care a hoot. 1927 *Observer* 9 Oct. 13 It doesn't matter two hoots how much Oxford is filmed. 1928 *Saturday Even. Post* (N.Y.) 4 Feb. 84/4, I don't give a hoot what you like to see.

Hootch: see *HOOCH.

Hootchy-kootchy (hūˑtʃi,kūˑtʃi), *sb.* and *a.* Also hootchie-kootchie, hoochy-koochy. [Origin unascertained.] A kind of dance. Also *attrib.* and *Comb.*; and *adj.* = Indecent, 'suggestive'.

1899 *Mr. Dooley in Peace & War, On Diplomacy* 18 He's seen th' hootchy-kootchy an' th' Pammer House barber shop. *Ibid.*, *On Cousin George* 36 Hootchy-kootchy girls dancin' before him. 1905 C. R. Cooper *Lions 'n' Tigers* i. 24 The dancers, the 'hootchie-kootchie' experts, and the comedians. 1925 *Manch. Guardian Wkly.* Aug. 103/4 That hootchy-kootchy sort of intonation. 1928 *Weekly Dispatch* 6 May 15/2 Don't forget to take in the Midway of the Chicago Fair of 1893, with its five hundred glittering lights, its great wheel, and its hootchy-kootchy dancers!

Hooter [1]. Add: **c.** The horn of a motor vehicle.

1908 *Lincoln Rutland & Stamford Merc.* 19 June 5 No hooter was sounded on the car when rounding this dangerous corner.

Hooter [2]. *U.S. colloq.* = *HOOT *sb.*[2]

1839 *Havana* (N.Y.) *Republican* 21 Aug. (Th.) Now the Grampus [*sc.* a vessel] stopt, and didn't buge [= budge] one hooter. 1889 *Commercial* (Cincinnati) 17 Oct., It has not harmed the Republican cause in Ohio a hooter. 1896 *Harper's Mag.* XCII. 784/1 Now I can have all I want, I don't care a hooter! 1900 E. A. Dix *Deacon Bradbury* xii, 'Do you mean that you don't know anything about the matter at all?'..'Not a hooter.'

Hooving, var. *HOVING *vbl. sb.*

Hop, *sb.*[2] Add: **1. c.** *To catch on the hop*: to take unawares in the act. *slang* or *colloq.*

1868 *Broadside Ballad, The Cuizkaleary Cove* (Farmer) For to catch me on the hop..You must wake up very early in the morning. 1872 Blackmore *Maid of Sker* xxv, He caught me on the hop; at a moment of rumours and serious warnings. 1887 *Brit. Med. Jrnl.* 21 May 1103/1 The attendants taking him, as it were, 'on the hop'. 1927 R. A. Freeman *Certain Dr. Thorndyke* I. xi, The police..caught him fairly on the hop with all the stolen property in his possession.

d. That distance which can be or is traversed in a flying machine at one stretch; one stage of a long-distance flight.

1909 *Flight* 3 July 398/1 M. Breguet has a biplane there and has made one or two short 'hops'. 1916 H. G. Wells *Mr. Britling* I. i. § 9 He made now what he felt was quite a good hop. 1927 *Daily News* 7 June 7/1 By flying from New York to Eisleben..in one hop. 1930 *Aberdeen Press & Jrnl.* 20 May 7/3 Her two-and-a-half-day Atlantic 'hop' to Rio de Janeiro.

e. *Long hop* (Cricket): see Long *a.*[1] 18 d.

3. Also *hop, step, and long jump*.

1906 *Westm. Gaz.* 30 Apr. 7/1 The preliminaries of the hurdles, standing high jump, hop-step, and long jumps will also be decided. 1909 *Daily Chron.* 24 Sept. 9/3 The hop-step-and-long-jump handicap.

d. Used advb.

1906 *Smart Set* June 102/1 To go hop, skip and jump over the earth's surface.

e. Hence *hop-step-and-jumper*.

1928 *Observer* 17 June 28/4 The only hop, step, and jumper of quality.

Hop, *v.*[1] Add: **4. c.** To jump on to (a moving vehicle); to obtain (a ride) in this way. *U.S.*

1909 *Springfield* (Mass.) *Weekly Republ.* 18 Mar. 16 Hopping a freight cost Edward Monahan both feet. 1918 in F. A. Pottle *Stretchers* (1930) 214 The other day, I hopped a truck and went 'to the front'. 1929 *Literary Digest* (N.Y.) 30 Nov. 30/2 Boys are predominantly the ones who 'hop' rides on trucks, trains and other vehicles.

6. a. *To hop it*: to be off, go away quickly.

1915 *Scotsman* 13 Jan. 7/3 The Zeppelin kept a few miles in the rear of us, and finally hopped it. 1916 Boyd Cable *Action Front* 186 'Are we going to stick it here?' said one. 'Didn't the sergeant say something about 'opping it?' 1924 M. Newman *Consummation* IV. xviii. 216 J. H. hopped it for all he was worth. A perfect tornado of bombs pursued him. 1930 Thurston *Man in Black Hat* xiii, Your lady must have said her prayers and hopped it.

c. With *off*. To start on a 'hop' in a flying machine.

1930 *Morning Post* 5 Aug. 9/2 Given favourable weather, he will hop off for England to-morrow, his first stage to Bima, taking him across the Timor Sea.

Hope, *sb.*[1] Add:

4. Used ironically for: An expectation which has little or no chance of being fulfilled. *slang.*

1904 Vaile *Mod. Lawn Tennis* (1907) 234 It is quite useless to run in on a high bounding, poor length, diagonal service. You have some 'hope' if it is down the centre. 1915 F. Palmer *My Year of War* 231 'What hopes!' was the current phrase I heard among the men in these trenches. 1929 Priestley *Good Comp.* I. iv. 115 'Well, lads, wot's it yer want?' demanded their hostess. 'Cos if it's steaks and chips and feather beds, you've got a bloody hope.' *Ibid.* II. i. 249 If there was enough money behind to rent His Majesty's Theatre, it could go on better still. It amounted to *that*. 'What a hope!' she concluded bitterly.

b. Also *spec.* a son and heir.

1931 *Times Lit. Suppl.* 4 June 448/4 At the imminent peril of being forcibly married to the odious hope of the rival.. dynasty.

5. hope chest *U.S.*, a chest or box in which a young woman collects articles towards a home of her own in the event of her marriage. (Cf. 'bottom drawer'.)

1920 *New York Tribune* 23 Oct. 15/2 (*heading*) Bride Accused as Burglar Charged With Looting Sister-in-Law's Hope Chest. 1922 Marg. B. Houston *Witch-man* vii. 83 The bedspread that three years before she had laid unfinished in Kaid's hope chest.

Hope, *v.* **3. b.** Add: Used sarcastically in implied protest against an imputation. *colloq.*

Mod. I hope I know how to keep a secret and to tell the truth.

Hopeful, *a.* (*sb.*). **2. b.** Add quot. illustrating use without *young*.

1899 Crowest *Beethoven* 41 He committed this hopeful, only now some nineteen years of age, to the care of an old lawyer friend.

Hopkinsian. (Earlier examples.)

1821 T. Dwight *Trav. New Eng.* (1823) IV. 439 In a few particulars, the Hopkinsians have superadded to the doctrinal part of this system. 1837 *Knickerbocker Mag.* IX. 334 [If] a man is going to settle in a place where one sect prevails largely, particularly the Hopkinsian sect.

Hopper [1]. **2.** (U.S. examples in the sense of 'grasshopper'.)

1873 J. H. Beadle *Undevel. West* iii. 71 All agree that the 'hoppers' are coming and that it will be 'mighty tough on the new settlers'. 1875 *Field & Forest* I. 31 Old residents of this state [*sc.* Minnesota] say that before the 'hoppers visited us one week ago we had..the appearance of the best grain crop ever known in the state. 1885 *Century Mag.* Nov. 29/1, I should think he had enough of 'em..to last him till the 'hoppers come again.

10. e. hopper-boy (examples).

1787 in *Rep. U.S. Comm. Patents* (1850) 574 The other [device], denominated an hopper-boy, so constituted as to spread the meal over the floor of a mill to cool. 1813 *Niles' Weekly Register* V. Add. A. 6/2 Our Hopper-boy was an upright shaft revolving round with an arm.

Hopperdozer (hǫˑpəɹdōzəɹ). *U.S.* [f. Hopper [1] + *dozer* (as in Bull-dozer).] A large shallow pan or canvas frame containing or smeared with some poisonous or glutinous compound, drawn over the ground to destroy locusts; a trap for insects.

1904 W. C. Edgar *Story Grain Wheat* ii. 21 Large areas of wheat are saved by means of a machine termed in America the 'hopperdozer'.

Hoppergrass. *local U.S.* = Grasshopper.

1829 *Virginia Literary Museum* I. 458 *Hoppergrass*. This word is often used in the south for grasshopper. 1892 *Rep. Vermont Board Agric.* XII. 163 Alas! the 'hopper grasses' came and carried it away.

Hopperings (hǫˑpəriŋz), *sb. pl.* [f. Hopper [1] + -ing [1].] Gravel retained in the hopper in gold- or diamond-washing.

1893 *Westm. Gaz.* 29 Apr. 7/3 The yield of diamonds from the hopperings is 6½ carats per 100 loads. 1898 *Daily News* 27 Jan. 9/5 Washed 197 loads from the mine, 3,725 loads lumps and hopperings producing 176 carats.

Hopping, *ppl. a.*[1] **2. hopping-john** (earlier example).

1838 Caroline Gilman *Recoll. Southern Matron* xviii. 124 Before me..was an immense field of *hopping John*. [*Note.* Bacon and rice.]

Hopple, *sb.* **1.** (Earlier examples.)

1641 Best *Farm. Bks.* (Surtees) 80 If an ewe bee kittle on her yower,..the best way is to let her dance in a payre of hopples. 1758 C. F. Post *Jrnl.* in R. Proud *Hist. Pennsylv.* (1798) II. App. 120 Our [two] horses..had been hoppled together; but a person told us, he had cut the hopples. 1820 *Massachusetts Spy* 12 Jan. (Th.) A black man, whose hopples were so carelessly made that he pulled his feet through them. 1823 E. James *Exped. Rocky Mts.* I. 143 He stooped down, and with his knife represented the act of cutting the hopples of horses.

Hop-sack. 2. Add: Also *attrib.*, and in form *hopsac*.

1923 *Daily Mail* 5 July 1 Hopsac suiting...in pretty Heather Mixture grounds. 1930 *Daily Express* 8 Sept. 11/5 Hopsack Tweed.

Hop-toad. *local U.S.* [Hop *sb.*[2] or *v.*[1]] A toad.

1827 *Massachusetts Spy* 28 Nov. (Th.) An inhabitant of the Middle States talks of 'hop-toads',—as if all toads were not hoppers. 1847 *Knickerbocker Mag.* XXIX. 183, I have so often..a tender leaning towards little pigs and hop toads. 1849 Mrs. Stowe *Mayflower* 157 I'd always find him stopping to chase hoptoads, or off after chip-squirrels. 1861 *Knickerbocker Mag.* LVII. 420 Killing flies, or pelting hop-toads. 1913 Gene Stratton-Porter *Laddie* xiii, I like hop-toads, owls, and shitepokes.

Horæ (hōˑrī). [L., pl. of *hora* Hour.] A book of hours (Hour 5, 6).

1875 *Quaritch's Gen. Catal.* Suppl. 51 The earlier editions of Kerver's series of Horæ. 1927 *Observer* 27 Nov. 22/4 An exquisite Flemish Horæ of about 1500.

Horary, *sb.* Add: **2. b.** A timed programme or plan. So **Hora·rium.**

1921 *Ampleforth Jrnl.* Jan. 139 Adapting ourselves to the School horarium we began dinner at 5 p.m. 1922 *Westm. Gaz.* 7 Oct., His scheme of breaking the Germans in 24 hours on a meticulously timed 'horary'.

Horbachite (hǫˑɹbaχəit). *Min.* [ad. G. *horbachit*, f. *Horbach* in the Black Forest + -ite [1].] A dark yellow iron-nickel sulphide related to pyrrhotite.

1874 *Jrnl. Chem. Soc.* XXVII. 34 Horbachite subjected to lixiviation in contact with the air, becomes oxidised.

Hordeiform (hǫˑɹdīˑifǫɹm), *a.* [f. L. *horde(um* + -form.] Of the shape of a barleycorn.

1890 Billings *Med. Dict.*

Hordeolum (hǫɹdīˑǒlǒm). *Path.* [mod.L., dim. of L. *hordeum* barley.] A sty on the eyelid.

[1622 R. Banister *Treat. Dis. Eyes* xiii. E 6 b, Of the wart, or barly corne on the Eye-lidde, commonly called..a Stian, ..in Latin, hordeum, or hordeolum.] 1820 B. Travers *Dis. Eye* 350 Diseases of the Eyelids. Hordeolum. Styes.. should be discharged with the point of a lancet. 1833 W. Lawrence *Dis. Eye* 341 Some hordeola form more quickly, with greater suppuration and no slough. 1886 *Buck's Handbk. Med. Sci.* II. 769/2 The characteristic picture presented by a hordeolum (stye) is a circumscribed tumefaction. 1908 *Practitioner* Feb. 288 Epiphora may be due to..a hordeolum.

Horizontal, *a.* (*sb.*). Add: **3.** Uniform; producing or based on uniformity. *U.S.*

1842 *Congress. Globe* 17 Mar. 331 Was it expected that this committee would send in a horizontal tariff? 1872 *Ibid.* 28 Mar. 2016/2 The horizontal reduction of duties would do incalculable injury. 1890 *Ibid.* 9 May 4392/2 The Democratic bill made a horizontal cut of 20 per cent. 1907 *Daily Chron.* 23 Sept. 5/3 The 'Journal of Commerce' [N.Y.] says that the North German Lloyd Company announced yesterday a practically horizontal cut of 25 dols. on the eastward and westward passages.

b. *Horizontal combine*, a combination of firms engaged in the same stages or types of manufacture.

1927 *Observer* 27 Mar. 5 Looking with a benevolent eye on horizontal combines. 1930 M. Clark *Home Trade* 204 There have been the combinations of one business with one or more of the same type. To this type the term 'horizontal combine' is usually applied.

B. *sb.* **3.** A Tasmanian shrub or tree, *Anodopetalum biglandulosum*, the stem and branches of which are first ascending and then horizontal. Also *attrib.*, as *horizontal scrub*.

1888 R. M. Johnston *Geol. Tasmania* Introd. p. vi. (Morris) The Horizontal is a tall shrub or tree. 1891 *Australasian* 4 Apr. (Ibid.) That stuff as they calls horizontal, a mess of branches and root. 1907 *Blackw. Mag.* Oct. 471/2 These tentacles of horizontal were generally clothed with a thick velvety covering of damp green moss.

4. [= F. *horizontale.*] A prostitute. *slang.*

1909 Ware *Passing English.* 1928 A. Philips *Boy at Bank* v. i, More than ten thousand professional 'horizontals' are light o' loves.

Horizo·ntal, *v.* [f. the adj.] *trans.* To plough in horizontal ridges.

1862 *Trans. Ill. Agric. Soc.* (1865) V. 518 Side-hills were generally 'horizontaled'.

Horme (hǭ·ɹmi). *Psychol.* Also **hormé.** [Jung's a. Gr. ὁρμή impulse.] Vital or purposeful energy. Hence **Ho·rmic** *a.*, of, pertaining to, or characterized by horme.

1915 W. H. B. Stoddart *New Psychiatry* 4 This word 'horme' has a wide signification, applicable to all the instincts. 1920 T. P. Nunn *Education: Data & First Princ.* ii. 21 To this element of drive or urge, whether it occurs in the conscious life of men and the higher animals, or in the unconscious activities of their bodies and the (presumably) unconscious behaviour of lower animals, we propose to give a single name—*horme* (ὁρμή). 1926 McDougall *Outl. Abnormal Psych.* 27 Jung says, 'I postulate a hypothetical fundamental striving which I designate *libido*'; and in a footnote..'This energy may also be designated as hormé. Hormé is a Greek word (ὁρμή)—force, attack, press, impetuosity, violence, urgency, zeal. It is related to Bergson's "élan vital". The concept hormé is an energetic expression for psychological values.' *Ibid.* 121 The vital or hormic energy of B's organism. 1927 *Contemp. Rev.* June 769 A kind of hormic determinism. 1931 R. S. Woodworth *Contemp. Schools Psychol.* 213 Purpose can properly be carried over into abnormal psychology, as has been done by the hormic psycho-pathologists, Freud especially.

Hormogonium (hǭɹmogōᵘ·niŏm). *Bot.* [mod. L.] = Hormogone.

1879 W. G. Farlow *Marine Algæ* (1881) 12 The cells intermediate between two heterocysts escape in the form of a small chain, called a hormogonium.

Hormonal (hǭ·ɹmonăl). [f. next + *-al*, as in *ethal, chloral.*] Peristaltic hormone, a proprietary remedy used to stimulate peristalsis.

1911 tr. A. Henle in *Med. Times* 4 Feb. 81/1 Another new physiological remedy, named peristaltic hormon (Hormonal). *Ibid.* 82/1 The Hormonal injection.

Hormone (hǭ·ɹmoun). *Physiol. Chem.* Also -on. [ad. Gr. ὁρμῶν, pres. pple. of ὁρμᾶν to impel, with assimilation to -one.] A substance formed in one organ and carried by the blood stream to another organ which it stimulates. Hence **Hormonic** (hǫɹmǫ·nik) *a.*

1905 E. H. Starling in *Lancet* 5 Aug. 340/1 These chemical messengers, however, or 'hormones'..as we might call them. 1906 — *Recent Adv. Physiol. Digest.* 75 The first products of digestion act on the pyloric mucous membrane, and produce in this membrane a substance which is absorbed into the blood stream, and carried to all the glands of the stomach, where it acts as a specific excitant of their secretory activity. This substance may be called the gastric secretin or gastric hormone. 1911 *Jrnl. Chem. Soc.* C. ii. 642 When exposed to the action of hormones the leaf of *Aucuba japonica* becomes..black. 1916 Schäfer *Endocrine Organs* 6 The action of an autacoid may therefore be described as hormonic or chalonic, according to the kind of effect it produces. 1928 *Brit. Med. Jrnl.* 18 Feb. 255/1 The functional (hormonic) over-activity of the anterior lobe of the pituitary gland. 1930 R. A. Fisher *Genet. Theory Nat. Sel.* 131 The investigation of the influence of the sex hormones has shown how genetic modifications of the whole species can be made to manifest themselves in one sex only.

Horn, *sb.* Add: **2. f.** (U.S. examples.)

1805 *Baltimore Even. Post* 5 July 2/5 (Th. s.v. *Little*), I am very much afraid I shall come out at the little end of the horn. 1852 in *Jrnl. Discourses* I. 26 We have commenced at the little end of the horn, and by and bye we shall come out at the big end.

3. b. Each of the erect and permanent bony processes, covered with hairy skin, growing on the head of a giraffe; also applied to a smaller protuberance in front of the other two.

1753 *Chambers's Cycl. Suppl.* s.v. *Zurnapa*, Its head is wholly of the make of the stag's, but differs in size, and has two little obtuse horns, which are not more than six fingers breadth long, and are hairy. 1840 *Cuvier's Anim. Kingd.* 138 The Giraffe..Is characterized by conical horns in both sexes, that are always covered with a hairy skin, and never fall...In the middle of the forehead, there is an eminence or third horn, broader and much shorter, but equally articulated by suture. 1879 *Encycl. Brit.* X. 619/2 In captivity it [*sc.* the giraffe] is said to make use of its skin-covered horns as weapons of defence.

6. b. *Horns of consecration*: in Mycenæan art, a pictorial symbol or object, often found together with the double axe and pillar, connected with the Cretan worship of the ox.

1901 A. J. Evans in *Jrnl. Hellenic Studies* XXI. 196 The columns of the Knossian shrine apparently approach the outer edge of the openings, leaving room, however, in front of them for the 'horns of consecration'.

13. b. *To blow one's own horn*: 'to blow one's own trumpet' (see Trumpet *sb.* 3).

1903 A. W. Patterson *Schumann* 167 Surely these side-lights upon the straightforwardness and integrity of the man entirely free him from the calumny of ever being guilty of 'blowing his own horn'.

f. An instrument attached to motor vehicles, etc., which is sounded as a warning signal. Also *attrib.*

1901 *Graphic* LXIV. 268/3 The hideous toot-toot of its horn. 1912 *Motor Manual* v. (ed. 14) 170 Invariably sound the horn before turning. 1914 R. & E. Shackleton *Four on Tour in Eng.* 83 The horn was bonked suddenly.

g. A cone-, funnel-, or trumpet-shaped accessory of a phonograph, gramophone, or loud speaker, which collects or disseminates the sounds recorded or reproduced.

1910 S. R. Bottone *Talking Machines* 62 The horn or trumpet which collects the sounds should be of *papier mâché.* *Ibid.* 63 The operator selects a piece of thin brass triblet tubing that fits precisely the horn-carrier of his phonograph. 1931 B. Brown *Talking Pictures* v. 121 Some of the first horns to be used in sound pictures were of the straight trumpet type. *Ibid.* vii. 156 The writer remembers one case where the horn chamber overhung a street.

19. b. In wider use, any cornu.

1848 Dunglison *Med. Lex.* (ed. 7). 1902 *Encycl. Brit.* XXV. 400/1 The crossed pyramidal tract, that lies on the lateral side of the dorsal horn.

d. In other technical usages.

1888 *Lockwood's Dict. Mech. Engin.*, *Horns*, the curved levers which are pivoted at the side of a planing machine, and which being knocked over by the tappets give the necessary feeds to the tool, and the reversing movement to the table. 1893 Sloane *Electr. Dict.*, *Horns*, the extensions of the pole pieces of a dynamo or motor. 1904 *Technol. & Sci. Dict.* (ed. Goodchild & Tweney), *Horn*,..(2) The tips or corners of the pole pieces of the field magnets of a dynamo or electric motor.

21. b. (Examples.)

1847 Parkman *Oregon Trail* iv. 41 My long heavy rifle encumbered me, and the low sound it made striking the horn of my saddle startled him. *a* 1861 Winthrop *Canoe & Saddle* (1862) 212, I threw Kiale's bridle over his neck, and grasping the horn, swung myself into the saddle.

29. horn-ail *U.S.*, disease of cattle affecting the horns; **horn-blower** *U.S.*, a horn-worm; **horn-bug** *U.S.* (examples); **horn-cell** *Anat.*, one of the ganglion cells of the cornua of the spinal cord; **horn pout** *U.S.* (examples); **horn-ray** (see quot.); **horn-rimmed** *a.*, denoting spectacles having rims made of horn; also, applied to a person wearing such spectacles (called colloq. **horn-rimmers**); **horn-rims**, horn-rimmed spectacles; **horn-worm** *U.S.* (examples).

1845 S. Judd *Margaret* ii. v. 284 Glad you got through with the pock so well..its worse than *horn-ail. 1858 C. L. Flint *Milch Cows*, etc. 271 Idiopathic or common fever commonly called 'horn ail', and often 'tail ail'. 1882 *Rep. Maine Board Agric.* XXVI. 22 They have..had trouble in calving or an attack of the 'horn-ail'. 1849 *Rep. U.S. Comm. Patents, Agric.* (1850) 320 The greater portion of the first glut reappear the same year as *Horn-blowers and breed myriads. 1776 J. Trumbull *McFingal* (Th.) Thought *horn-bugs bullets, or, through fears, Muskitoes took for musqueteers. 1837 *Southern Lit. Messenger* III. 587, I am an unfortunate victim..of every species of insect..the horn-bug, gad fly, dragon-fly [etc.]. 1869 Mrs. Stowe *Oldtown Folks* xxvii. 341 Youre saucy enough to physic a horn-bug. 1902 *Encycl. Brit.* XXV. 400/1 These three tracts agree in being descending tracts coming from nerve-cells on a higher level and in being connected with the ventral *horn-cells by synapses. 1798 *Gaz. U.S.* (Philad.) 3 Aug. (Th.) The company concluded to go, for the sake of seeing a *horn pout—when at last I drew one up—and behold! what was it, but a cat fish! 1832 *Coll. New Hampsh. Hist. Soc.* III. 87 On each side of their body and close to the head is a formidable weapon called a *horn*, and hence the name *Horn-pout.* 1860–70 [see Dict.]. 1877 Howells *Out of the Question* vi. (1882) 134, I suppose you plank horn-pout here. 1910 *Outlook* 9 July 529 On the other side of the pond we met Sam Noyes, who was catching hornpouts. 1898 Morris *Austral English*, **Horn-Ray*, a New Zealand and Australian *Ray*, the fish *Rhinobatus banksii.* 1923 *Westm. Gaz.* 12 Apr., A long-necked youth who was talking to a *horn-rimmed female. 1931 Susan Glaspell *Ambrose Holt* xxii, He wore horn-rimmed glasses. 1927 *Punch* 20 Apr. 424/3 He removed his *horn-rims and began polishing them vigorously. 1784 J. Smyth *Tour U.S.* II. 132 The other [species] is the *horn-worm..of a vivid green colour, with a number of pointed excrescences or feelers, from his head like horns: these devour the [tobacco] leaf. 1849 *Rep. U.S. Comm. Patents, Agric.* (1850) 459 The horn-worm is deposited on the smooth or upper surface of the leaf in an egg by the tobacco fly.

Horn, *v.* Add: **3. b.** *fig.* To push, as an ox with its horns.

1851 J. J. Hooper *Widow Rugby's Husb.* 69 You horned me off to get a chance to get gaming witnesses out of the way. 1881 *Times* (Philad.) 5 June (Th.) Mac Veagh is trying his best to horn Blaine out of the Cabinet herd, just as young buffalo bulls horn out the old ones.

c. *intr.* To push or 'butt' *in with.* *U.S. slang.*

1912 C. Mathewson *Pitching in a Pinch* 213 Many of them try hard to 'horn in' with the men who have made good as Big Leaguers. 1920 Mulford *Rustlers' Valley* xviii. 201 Why did Chet horn in on Baldy's arrest? 1921 — *Bar-20 Three* vii. 88 Reckon I'll horn in on th' faro lay-out. 1923 'B. M. Bower' *Parowan Bonanza* x. 118 If I don't miss my guess, you'll have somebody trying to horn in some how.

Hornblendite (hǭ·ɹnblendeit). *Petrog.* [f. Hornblende + -ite [1].] A granular igneous rock largely or entirely composed of hornblende.

1901 *Jrnl. Chem. Soc.* LXXX. ii. 170 Hornblendite from Brandberget, consisting essentially of hornblende. 1930 Peach & Horne *Geol. Scot.* 26 The ultrabasic rocks (pyroxenites, hornblendites) generally form lenticles.

Horned, *a.* Add: **Horned dace** (see quot. 1896). **Horned helmet,** *Cassis cornuta*, a shell from which cameos are cut. **Horned lizard** = *horned frog.* **Horned pout** = *horn pout* (Horn *sb.* 29). **Horned rattler, rattlesnake,** *Crotalus cerastes*, of the United States and Mexico. **Horned screamer,** a South American bird, *Palamedea cornuta.* **Horned snake, viper,** a venomous snake or viper belonging to the genus Cerastes, having a horny process above each eye.

1785, 1869–73 horned screamer [see Screamer 3 a]. 1837 horned pouts [see Pout *sb.*[1]]. 1844 J. Gregg *Commerce of Prairies* II. 231 Horned frog..horned lizard, as those of earlier times more rationally called it. 1845 S. Judd *Margaret* i. xiv. 119 There were clouds, to her eye, like fishes, the horned pout, with its pearly iridine breast, and iron-brown back. 1860 Mayne Reid *Odd People* 22 The little 'Horned Snake'. 1863 Horned Helmet-shell [see Helmet *sb.* 5]. 1863 Wood *Nat. Hist.* III. 107 The true Cerastes or Horned Viper is a native of Northern Africa. 1867 *Amer. Naturalist* I. May 165 Mr. F. W. Putnam exhibited a singular specimen of the Horned Pout (*Pimelodus atrarius* De Kay) from Lake Champlain. 1876 *Encycl. Brit.* IV. 740/1 The black helmet (*Cassis tuberosa*) of the West Indian seas, the horned helmet (*C. cornuta*) of Madagascar ..are also employed [for cameos]. 1888 *Buck's Handbk. Med. Sci.* VI. 166/1 Crotalus cerastes Hallowell, Horned Rattlesnake, 'Side-winder'. 1896 Jordan & Evermann *Fishes Amer.* i. 222 *Semotilus Atromaculatus*...Horned-dace; Creek-chub.

Hornfels (hǭ·ɹnfels), *sb.* *Petrog.* [G., f. *horn* horn + *fels* rock.] A compact rock composed of quartz, feldspar, mica, etc., formed by the action of an intrusive rock upon shale or other sedimentary rock. So **Ho·rnfels** *v. trans.*, to change to hornfels; **Ho·rnfelsed** (-felst) *ppl. a.*, having been changed to hornfels.

[1854 Dana *Syst. Min.* (ed. 4) II. 246 The Hornfels of the Germans is a massive compound of quartz and feldspar breaking with a smooth flinty fracture.] 1899 *Jrnl. Chem. Soc.* LXXVI. ii. 565 Anal. II is of an adinole or hornfels in contact with the granite. 1901 *Rep. Brit. Assoc.* 634 The Old Red Sandstone is indurated and often hornfelsed to a varying distance from the margin. 1922 *Nature* CIX. 61/1 Hornfelsed green rocks. 1930 Peach & Horne *Geol. Scot.* 69 Cryptocrystalline hornfelses. *Ibid.* 70 The hornfelsing of the orthogneisses.

Hornist. (Earlier U.S. example.)

1836 *Knickerbocker Mag.* VIII. 71 Some evil-disposed citizens having no taste for music went to his honor the Mayor, and lodged grievous complaints against the distinguished *hornist.*

Hornless, *a.* Add: **2.** Without a horn (see *Horn *sb.* 13 g).

1909 *Talking Machine News* Oct. 337 Portable Hornless Machine. 1913 Clements-Henry *Gramophones* ix. 54 Some modern disc machines are hornless, in the sense that the amplifier is combined with the body of the cabinet containing the motor.

Horn spoon.

1. A spoon made of horn (see Horn *sb.* 28).

2. *By the (great) horn spoon*, used as a fanciful oath or formula of asseveration. *U.S.*

1842 *Amer. Nat. Song Bk.* II. 222 in *Amer. Speech* IV. 500 He vow'd by the great horn spoon..He'd give them a licking, and that pretty soon. 1848 Lowell *Biglow P.* Ser. i. v. 16 'I should like to shoot The holl gang, by the gret horn spoon!' sez he. 1853 *Knickerbocker Mag.* XLI. Feb. 115 'By the horn spoons!' repeated the skipper suddenly. 1878 J. H. Beadle *Western Wilds* xii. 186 Swearin' by the great horn spoon of the Ancient Scottish Rites that he could whip any Morgan man. 1897 *Outing* (U.S.) XXX. 380/2 'By the Great Horn Spoon!' the voice shouted; 'here's a chunk of civilization'.

Hornswoggle (hǭ·ɹnswǫg'l), *v.* *U.S. colloq.* [Prob. fanciful.] *trans.* To get the better of; to cheat or swindle; to hoodwink, humbug, bamboozle.

1829 *Virginia Literary Museum* I. 458 *Hornswoggle*, to embarrass irretrievably. 1834 W. A. Carruthers *Kentuckian in New York* I. 61, I wish I may be horn swoggled, if ever I thought [etc.]. 1860 *Oregon Argus* 12 May (Th.) P. F. is going to hornswoggle the Douglas Democrats. 1904 *Boston Herald* 27 June 6 One practical working theory in advertising circles is that the ad's chief function is to hornswoggle the consumer. 1911 H. Quick *Yellowstone N.* iii. 82 If you'll stand by..and see your old father hornswoggled out of his eye-teeth you'll never see a cent of my money. 1927 J. Barbican *Confessions of Rum-Runner* xxiii. 261 I'll be hornswoggled if that goddarned pipe didn't go and wind itself round that old buzzard's gullet just like a snake.

Horny, *a.* Add: **1.** Applied to the hard and glossy grains of the hard wheat.

1888 *Encycl. Brit.* XXIV. 532/1 Wheats of hotter countries have a more solid, rigid straw, the ears short, stout, compact, the glumes provided with long awns or beards, and the seed hard and horny.

7. horny-head, a cyprinoid fish of North America, the river-chub.

1884 [see River-chub, River *sb.* 5]. 1896 Jordan & Evermann *Fishes Amer.* i. 314 Hybopsis,..(Horny-heads).

Horopito (hō·-, hǫrǫpī·to). [Maori.] An aromatic evergreen New Zealand tree, *Drimys axillaris*; = Pepper-tree b.

1847 G. F. Angas *Savage Life* II. 17 A straggling shrub, with bright green shining leaves, resembling those of the nutmeg-tree; and a profusion of rich and delicate blossoms, looking like waxwork...The natives call this plant horopito. 1889 T. Kirk *Forest Flora* plate 2 The horopito, or pepper-tree of the settlers.

Horrid, *adv.* (Later U.S. example.)

1867 Susan Hale *Lett.* (1919) 25 I'm horrid sorry there was such a gap in my letters then.

Hors. Add: **Hors concours** (or konkūr), *adv.*, not competing; hence, without a rival; unequalled.

1884 *Tablet* LXIII. 804 (Stanford) A work such as..would,

were it shown in the Salon, range him Hors Concours. 1931 *Times Lit. Suppl.* 7 May 353/3 Dickens and Wilkie Collins were regarded as *hors-concours*; Trollope, however, be despised.

Hors du jeu (or dü ʒö), *adv.*, lit., out of the game; not 'practical politics'. (app. not in Fr. use.)

1928 *Daily Tel.* 14 Aug. 9/4 Dr. Streit, the unofficial leader of the Royalists..frankly admits that the restoration is hors du jeu for the time being.

Horse, *sb.* Add: **1. f.** colloq. or slang abbreviation of Horse-power.

1931 *Star* 8 May 13/1 Each of them with a few 'horses' in reserve.

4. (Earlier example of the use in quot. 1867.)

1840 R. H. Dana *Bef. Mast* xxii, Though 'a bit of a horse' ..yet he was generally liked by the crew.

7. b. (Later U.S. examples.)

1846 Corcoran *Pickings* 83 One carried his saw slung on his arm, and the other had his 'horse' mounted on his shoulder. 1850 N. Kingsley *Diary* 103 Worked at hewing some sticks for horses to use the Pit Saw.

8. h. A groyne. **i.** 'One of the inclined timbers in a staircase which support the steps' (Cent. D. Suppl.). **j.** In other uses (see quot. 1904).

1852 J. Wiggins *Embanking* (1867) 232 Expensive works ..such as those called 'horses' in Essex, and 'groins' in Sussex and Hants. 1904 *Technol. & Sci. Dict.* (ed. Goodchild & Tweney), *Horse*, the wood backing of a zinc mould, used by plasterers for running mouldings. A wooden finial, etc., forming a core which is to be covered with lead.

14. Also *live horse*: work done and not charged for.

1859 Bartlett *Dict. Amer.*, *Live Horse*, in printers' parlance, work done over and above that included in the week's bill.

17. *To talk horse* (earlier U.S. example). *To play horse with*: to treat roughly or unceremoniously.

1855 Haliburton *Nat. & Hum. Nat.* II. 337 Doctor, I am a borin of you, but the fact is, when I get a goin 'talkin boss', I never know where to stop. 1896 G. Ade *Artie* xvii. 163 Do you think I'm goin' out ridin' with her and have a lot o' cheap skates stoppin' to play horse with her everywhere we go? 1904 W. H. Smith *Promoters* x. 169 You've got to have some well-matured plan..if they try to play horse with you again. 1911 L. J. Vance *Cynthia* x, Why does Madame Savaran insist on coming along to see that he doesn't play horse with her stake in the venture? 1923 — *Baroque* viii. 49 Remember the Wop detective that used to play horse with the Black Handers.

22. b. *To ride the high horse* (examples). *To come off the high horse*: to climb down, become less arrogant.

1809 Malkin *Gil Blas* ii. vii. ¶ 5 Riding the high horse with all the arrogance of greatness. *Ibid.* ix. i. ¶ 2 Do not ride a higher horse than a thousand jockeys of quality whom I could name. 1843 Thackeray *Men's Wives, Ravenswing* i. Misc. 1857 IV. 106 It would be his turn to sneer and bully, and ride the high horse. 1887 G. R. Sims *Mary Jane's Mem.* 116 They were awfully civil, and let Mrs. Master John ride the high horse over them. 1928 *Sunday Express* 15 Jan. 6/4 The cable companies have come off the high horse at last in entering into negotiations with the wireless group.

25. *A horse of another colour* (earlier U.S. example). *Horses for courses*: a theory that each race-horse is suited to a particular race-course, and will do better on that course than on any other. *Horse and horse* (U.S.): equally divided or matched, neck and neck. *The man on the horse* (U.S.): the person in authority.

1798 *Aurora* (Philad.) 27 Aug. (Th.) Whether any of them may be induced..to enter into the pay of King John I. [i.e. President Adams] is 'a horse of another colour'. 1887 *Pall Mall Gaz.* 21 July 1/1 The man on the horse,..to use the picturesque American phrase, is now not Lord Salisbury, but Lord Hartington. 1893 Farmer & Henley *Slang*, Horse and horse. 1898 A. E. T. Watson *Turf* vii. 160 A familiar phrase on the turf is 'horses for courses'. 1908 G. H. Lorimer *J. Spurlock* i. 3 It was horse and horse between the professors. 1929 *Daily Express* 7 Nov. 18/4 Followers of the 'horses for courses' theory.

26. b. *horse-line, -market* (earlier U.S. example), *-marrow, -sausage, -serum, -show, -team.*

1902 J. H. M. Abbott *Tommy Cornstalk* 27 If you have the last couple of hours' 'watch' on the *horse-lines, you see it all. 1817 U. Brown *Jrnl.* in *Maryland Hist. Mag.* XI. 372 This day spent in the *Horse Market trying to sell the two Horses. 1909 *Daily Chron.* 15 Apr. 4/6 The plum pudding and *horse-marrow sauce. 1908 *Ibid.* 17 Jan. 5/3 The *horse-sausage boat. 1909 *Practitioner* Dec. 867 The introduction of such large quantities (200 c.c.) of *horse-serum. 1909 *Westm. Gaz.* 4 Feb. 2/1 During *Horse-Show week. 1817 S. R. Brown *Western Gaz.* 107 [The walls] are.. wide enough on the top to admit a *horse team and waggon. 1856 *Rep. Indian Affairs* 294 At Leech lake and Winnepeg, eight government oxen and two horse teams were employed ploughing during the season.

c. *horse-barn, -blanket, -feed, -pen, -rack, -shed, -stable, -trough* (U.S. examples).

1854 Mary J. Holmes *Tempest & Sunshine* xix. 266 I'd as soon be married in the *horsebarn as there. 1885 *Rep. Indian Affairs* 130 The horse-barn, carpenter-shop, warehouse, and some small buildings. *c* 1820 Sands in *Knickerbocker Mag.* XXIX. 470 But wiser Bill Van Snort, the jockey, ..Spread his *horse-blanket in the manger. 1853 F. W. Thomas *J. Randolph*, etc. 121 Why, you were blind as a horse-blanket—blind as your boat. 1884 'Mark Twain' *Huck. Finn* vi. 40 There was an old horse-blanket nailed against the logs at the far end of the cabin. 1831 Peck *Guide for Emigrants* ii. 147 Rye for *horse feed and distilleries. 1837 H. Colman *Rep. Agric. Mass.* (1838) 14 Oats and corn for horse-feed. 1888 C. D. Ferguson *Exp. Forty-niner* ii. 32 Our horse-feed was likely to run out. 1822 J. Fowler *Jrnl.* 77 By night we head [= had] the *Hors Peen [*sic*] finished, and the Hous with two pens four logs high. 1846 J. W. Webb *Altowan* I. iv. 116 Pointing out a spot for a horse-pen..he was not long in disappearing. 1856 S. Mordecai *Virginia* vi. (1860) 71 On either side of the capitol was a long *horse-rack, for the convenience of the public and to diversify the odor. 1869 *Overland Monthly* III. 11 The impatient horses champ many a mouthful of pine from the horse-rack. 1887 *Harper's Mag.* Jan. 231/2 They alighted at the horse-rack nearest the law-office. 1836 Dunlap *Mem. Water Drinker* (1837) I. 120 He..seated himself upon a bench under..the *horse-shed in front of the house. 1845 S. Judd *Margaret* i. xiii. 91 Portions of the horse-sheds were converted into booths for the sale of liquors. 1854 R. Glisan *Jrnl. Army Life* xii. (1874) 160 All the hotels and public buildings have carriage houses and *horse stables. 1904 Tom Watson *Bethany* i. 8 Among corn-cribs, cow-pens, horse-stables, pig-styes ..and worm-fenced cotton fields. 1840 *Knickerbocker Mag.* XVI. 17 Jeremiah and our hero..went out to perform their morning ablutions at the moss covered *horse-trough at the tavern door. 1867 'T. Lackland' *Homespun* i. 140 There were times..when the horse trough was tight frozen.

d. *horse-bus, -cab, -cart* (earlier and later U.S. examples), *-railway* (U.S.).

1905 *Westm. Gaz.* 14 Dec. 6/3 This applies equally to motor-'buses as to *horse-'buses. 1906 *Ibid.* 31 May 12/1 Ordinary *horse-cab fares. 1907 *Daily Chron.* 3 July 5/2 The immediate doom of the horse cab. 1658 *Boston Town Records* II. 147 Henceforth all *horse-carts shall bee led by the carters with a rayne. 1863 D. G. Mitchell *Sev. Stor.*, *My Farm of Edgewood* 135 An active man with a sharp scythe, a light horse-cart and a Canadian pony. 1863 Whitman *Specimen Days* (1892) 31 At the end of the then *horse railway route on Seventh street. 1878 *Harper's Mag.* Jan. 192 He..thought some hunting grounds might be found near the terminus of the horse-railway.

f. *horse-tender*; *horse-hunting, -maiming* sbs. and adjs.

1848 H. W. Haygarth *Bush Life* vi. 61 Cattle-hunting in Australia is excellent sport..with less speed than in *horse-hunting. 1908 *Daily Chron.* 24 Oct. 1/2 Apart from the horse-hunting we had harness to repair. 1907 *Westm. Gaz.* 6 Sept. 5/1 Another case of *horse-maiming. 1908 *Daily Chron.* 14 Aug. 8/6 Three horse-maiming outrages. 1898 W. J. Locke *Idols* xxiii, The *horse-tender. 1907 *Daily Chron.* 12 Nov. 8/1 He pushed close to the horse-tender, a Somali.

h. *horse-headed* adj.

1910 W. J. Locke *Simon the Jester* xii. 146 The horse-headed Englishman cried '*banco*'.

27. a. horse-bucket (earlier U.S. examples); **horse-doctor** (later U.S. examples); **horse-fiddle** *U.S.* (see quot. 1872); **horse-high** *a. U.S.*, too high for a horse to jump over; **horse-holder,** (*b*) *Mil.*, each of the mounted horse artillery gunners who take charge of the dismounted horses while the gun is in action; **horse lot** *U.S.*, a piece of ground on which horses are pastured; **horse ride,** a road for horse-traffic; **horse-rustler** *Western U.S.*, (*a*) one who looks after horses; (*b*) a horse-thief; **horse's neck** *U.S. slang*, a beverage of ginger ale flavoured with lemon-peel, with or without the addition of whisky; **horse-tooth** *a. U.S.*, designating the 'dent' variety of Indian corn; **horse-trade** *U.S.*, a deal in horses; also *fig.* or *transf.*; hence **horse-trader, -trading; horse-wrangler** *U.S.* (later examples).

1827 J. F. Cooper *Red Rover* II. viii. 134 There was a *horse-bucket kicking about her decks. 1846 *Knickerbocker Mag.* XXVII. 555 Golden Sherry in Green Bottles! Chateau Margaux in a horse-bucket as soon! 1810 Weems *Lett.* III. 11 A collection in which there is not a single Bible..nor Dream-book, nor *Horse Doctors. 1894 *Congress. Rec.* 1 Mar. 2500/1 We found..that he was a veterinary surgeon, called in New England a 'horse doctor'. 1843 *Knickerbocker Mag.* XXI. 46 The clangor of trumpets, the clattering of pans, the grinding of *horse-fiddles. 1872 E. Eggleston *End of World* xlvi. 294 Bill Day had a gigantic watchman's rattle, a hickory spring on a cog-wheel. It is called in the West a horse-fiddle, because it is so unlike either a horse or a fiddle. 1911 H. Quick *Yellowstone N.* viii. 212 In addition to the horse-fiddles and bells and horns Absalom had arranged some private theatricals. 1859, 1880 *horse-high [see *Hog-tight *a.*]. 1837 A. F. Oakes *Madras Horse Artillery* 18 The rear rank are *horse-holders. 1877 *Manual Field Artillery Exerc.* viii. 285 The horse-holders do not dismount. 1901 *Daily News* 19 Mar. 5/6 Whether he should retire or hold his ground at the risk of being unable to find the horse-holders after darkness had set in. 1902 J. H. M. Abbott *Tommy Cornstalk* 35 When cavalry are dismounted for skirmishing, one man of every four—the horse-holder, or number three—is out of action. 1849 *Rep. U.S. Comm. Patents, Agric.* (1850) 144 The man..has..no time to make manure, or to haul out and spread the little that is dropped in his *horse-lot. 1889 *Harper's Mag.* June 123/2 In the horse lot she found her father putting on his coat. 1903 *Daily Chron.* 6 Nov. 3/3 On one side of it there will be a *horse-ride, and on the other..a gravelled walk for foot passengers. 1920 Hunter *Trail Drivers of Texas* 63, I told the cook and *horse rustler to take the wagon and camp it up the river. 1925 J. Metcalfe *Smoking Leg*, etc. 138 A tall young man in a grey suit whose drink was *horse's neck in summer and Burton in the winter. 1872 *Rep. Vermont Board Agric.* I. 53 The *horse-tooth corn of the south and west. 1887 J. Kirkland *Zury* 45 The 'dent' which occurs in the top of each Kernel [of Indian corn] produces a withered appearance and gives it the name of 'horse-tooth' corn. 1846 *Knickerbocker Mag.* XXVIII. 361 He was employed in.. an action brought by a man against another for cheating him in a '*horse-trade'. 1902 A. D. McFaul *Ike Glidden* iii. 22 His self-confidence could not admit of a thought that he could be fooled in a horse trade. 1923 *Daily Mail* 15 June 9 [New York World] We hope that foreign Powers will not be weak enough to consent to such unprincipled horse trade. 1850 L. H. Garrard *Wah-To-Yah* vii. (1927) 99 The unfair *horsetrader might have taken my scalp. 1879 *Scribner's Monthly* Nov. 139/2 Profanity among..the horse traders plying their dextrous art. 1853 J. G. Baldwin *Flush Times Alabama* 273 An enterprising young gentleman..engaged ..in the *horse-trading line. 1902 A. D. McFaul *Ike Glidden* iv. 28 A horse-trading expedition. 1902 Wister *Virginian* x. 109 The foreman of the 76 outfit, and the *horse-wrangler from the Bar Circle-L. 1905 A. Adams *Outlet* ii. 15 Within a week I had made up my outfit, including the horse-wrangler and cook.

c. horse-bean (earlier Amer. example); **horse-mushroom,** a variety of edible mushroom, *Agaricus arvensis*, larger and coarser than the common mushroom, distinguished by its yellow colour when bruised; **horse-nicker,** any of several species of *Guilandina*; also the seed produced by such a tree; **horse poison** (see quot.); **horse-weed** *U.S.* (examples).

1684 I. Mather *Remark. Provid.* (1890) 216 The stone weighed about seven grains, being much in shape of our ordinary *horse-beans. 1866 *Treas. Bot.* s.v., The *horse-mushroom need not be excluded on account of its supposed unwholesomeness. 1890 Blackmore *Kit* xlvii, Mingling with the true Agaric some very fine 'Horse-mushrooms'. 1750 *horse-nicker [see Nicker *sb.*[4]]. 1871 C. Kingsley *At Last* i, The grey horse-nicker-beads of our childhood. 1851 P. H. Gosse *Nat. Sojourn Jamaica* 80 One of the most venomous of plants (*Isotoma longiflora*) commonly called *Horse-poison. 1874 J. W. Long *Amer. Wild-fowl* xxiii. 239 The hunter usually selects a position..amongst the high '*horse-weeds' bordering the field. 1893 B. Torrey *Foot-path-Way* 72 Acres and acres of horseweed. 1901 C. Mohr *Plant Life Alabama* 787 *Leptilon Canadense*,..Horseweed. Canada Fleabane.

Horse-back. Add: **3.** *U.S.* (Earlier example.)

1851 J. S. Springer *Forest Life* 41 The pumpkin Pine is.. found..also on abrupt ridges, called horsebacks.

5. horseback opinion *U.S.*, an opinion given (as) from horseback, without opportunity for full consideration of the question.

1879 *Congress. Rec.* 23 Apr. 728/1, I am not here as a judicial authority or oracle. I can only give a horseback opinion. 1903 A. Adams *Log Cowboy* vi. 72 My sister gives it as a horseback opinion that she'd been engaged to this fellow nearly eight months.

Horse-block. 1. (Earlier Amer. examples.)

1713 *Charlestown Land Rec.* 207 Heatons Seller door & hors block [is] in the high way. 1721 *Bristol* (Va.) *Vestry Bk.* 7 To Mr. Luis Green junr. for a horse-block.

Horse-guard. 4. (Earlier U.S. examples.)

1845 Frémont *Exped.* 10 The morning watch being horse guard for the day. 1846 Sage *Scenes Rocky Mts.* (1859) 212 They prove quite useful as horse-guards. 1849 Parkman *Oregon Trail* iv. 46 To have every man in the camp stand horse-guard in rotation whenever we stop.

b. *U.S.* (See quots.)

1796 B. Hawkins *Lett.* 46 A large flie called the horse guard come at the same season, they..attack and destroy all the flies they meet with. 1837 J. L. Williams *Territory of Florida* 71 Horse Guard, a species of large Hornet that burrows in the sand [and] destroys the flies.

Horsehair. c. Add: **horsehair snake** = *horsehair-worm.*

1897 *Outing* (U.S.) XXX. 434/2 The creature referred to as a mystery is what is termed the 'horsehair snake', in reality, a hairworm.

Horse-head. Add: **4.** *U.S.* The silver moonfish, *Selene argentea.*

1884 Goode *Fish. Industr. U.S.* i. 323.

Horseless, *a.* Add: Applied *spec.* *c* 1895–1910 to automobile vehicles.

1895 [see Dict.]. 1901 *Chambers's Jrnl.* Jan. 14/2 The three great trusts that control the making and using of these horseless machines.

Ho·rse-ma:stership. [See -ship.] Skill in managing horses.

1904 *Westm. Gaz.* 21 Sept. 10/1 Thereupon a trumpeter, who knew something about horse-mastership, instantly sounded the forage-call. Two minutes later every animal was standing quietly in its appointed place. 1925 in E. F. Norton *Fight for Everest, 1924* 365 Unless any other member of the Expedition better fitted by his knowledge of horse-mastership undertakes the care of the mess mules. 1927 *Daily Tel.* 26 Apr. 16/7 The Army in India polo team..has undertaken a very difficult and interesting feat of horse-mastership. The problem to be solved is that of transporting a large stable of ponies from India to America.

Horse-meat. Add: **2.** = Horse-flesh 1.

1868 *All Year Round* 22 Feb. 252/2 Horse-meat is a common..article of food. 1870 *Food Jrnl.* 1 Dec. 620 The almost impossibility of obtaining beef and mutton naturally forced the use of horse-meat upon the people. 1904 *Westm. Gaz.* 23 Dec. 10/1 Every day the purveyors and the consumers of horsemeat increase in numbers. 1910 *Daily Chron.* 14 Jan. 1/5 The price of horse meat was 3½d. a lb.

Horse-mill. (Later U.S. examples.)

1848 E. Bryant *What I saw in California* xxi. 269 The flour consumed by Captain Sutter is ground by a very ordinary horse-mill. 1889 Cable in *Century Mag.* Feb. 520/2 A horse-mill—a long pole on which a man sits, and to which a horse or mule is hitched.

Horse-path. [Horse *sb.* 1.]

1. A path or track for horses; a bridle-path.

The name *Horspath* of a parish in Oxfordshire is recorded (as *Horspadan*) in Domesday Book (1086).

1755 L. Evans *Anal. Map Colonies* 29 Foot or Horse Paths. 1784, 1847 [see Horse *sb.* 26 c]. 1835 R. M. Bird *Hawks of Hawk-Hollow* I. xvi. 216 A view of a horse-path sloping down the hills on the further bank of the river.

2. The track for the horse in a horse-mill.

1835 J. H. Ingraham *South-West* II. 288 On the ground floor is the horse path for drawing the main wheel and counter wheel.

Horse-plum. 2. *U.S.* (Example.)

1827 *Western Monthly Rev.* I. 322 The fruit is of the size of a common horse plum.

Horse-power. Add: **1. c.** With qualifying words (see quots.).

1859 Rankine *Steam Engine* 479 Nominal Horse-power is a conventional mode of describing the dimensions of a steam engine, for the convenience of makers and purchasers of engines, and bears no fixed relation to indicated or to effective horse-power. 1862 — *Civil Engin.* 639 To find the indicated horse-power of the engine. 1881, 1891 [see Dict. 1]. 1888 *Lockwood's Dict. Mech. Engin.*, *Actual Horse-Power*, or *Available H.P.*—Sometimes called Dynametrical H.P. The net useful power given out by an engine. 1888 A. Jamieson *Elem. Manual Steam & Steam Engine* xvii. 130 This nett or effective horse-power is termed Brake Horse-power. 1904 *Technol. & Sci. Dict.* (ed. Goodchild & Tweney), *Brake Horse Power*, B.H.P., the power developed by an engine or motor, which is absorbed by a brake dynamometer: distinguished from the indicated horse power as being the amount of power which the engine can put out for useful purposes. 1904 *Westm. Gaz.* 30 Mar. 10/2 The *Good Hope* and the *Drake*..are of 14,100 tons displacement and 30,000 indicated horse-power. 1908 *Ibid.* 31 Mar. 4/2 A petrol-engine and steam-engine with its boiler, each of which is capable of developing, say, 30-brake-horse-power as a maximum.

4. *attrib.* and *Comb.*: **horse-power hour,** a unit representing the work performed or energy consumed in working at the rate of one horse-power for one hour.

1884 Knight *Dict. Mech.* Suppl., Horse-power Computing Scale...Horse-power Jack...Horse-power Pump...Horse-power Regulator. 1899 J. Perry *Steam Engine* 250 Units of Energy used Commercially. 1 horse-power hour = 1,421 centigrade heat units = 2,558 Fahrenheit heat units = 1,980,000 foot-pounds. 1906 *Westm. Gaz.* 28 June 2/1 An output of 36 cubic feet of oxygen per horse-power hour.

Horse-racer. Add: **2.** *U.S.* (See quot.)

1833 Maria Brooks *Zóphiël* v. note, The ring necked serpent...From the extreme swiftness of its movements, it received from the English settlers the name of horse-racer.

Horse-sense. orig. *U.S.* (Earlier and later U.S. examples.)

1832 Paulding *Westward Ho!* II. 60 He's a man of good strong horse sense. 1845 in C. Cist *Cincinnati Misc.* 190 He..has good *horse sense*,..and often speaks to the point and with effect. 1901 [P. L. Ford] *House Party* 186 He was ..none too nimble with his wits. He did have horse sense, however. 1911 H. S. Harrison *Queed* xviii. 223 A rich vein of horse-sense underlay Byrd's philanthropic enthusiasms.

Ho·rse-stea:ler. (In later use chiefly *U.S.*)

1552, 1600 [see Horse *sb.* 26 f]. 1730 in D. T. Valentine *Manual Corpor. N.Y.* (1864) 677 That one Solomon Jennings hath been a notorious Horse-Stealer for many years past. 1834 W. A. Carruthers *Kentuckian in N.Y.* I. 197 A horse-stealer who has blundered into better fortune is scandalized at his former craft. 1837 W. Irving *Capt. Bonneville* (1895) I. 41 One of the most..predatory tribes of the mountains; horse-stealers of the first order.

Hence **Ho·rse-stea:ling** *sb.* and *a.*; **Ho·rse-steal,** an act of horse-stealing.

1831 Mary A. Holley *Texas Lett.* (1833) 104 A party of Tarankaways was..whipped..for horse stealing. 1837 W. Irving *Capt. Bonneville* (1895) I. 43 This wild, horse-stealing tribe. *Ibid.* 260 A marauding, horse-stealing region. 1845 Frémont *Exped.* 18 A party..had been to the Pawnee villages on a horse-stealing excursion. 1847 in D. Drake *Pioneer Life Kentucky* ii. 23 Captivities and horse-stealings, were the daily topics of conversation. 1850 L. H. Garrard *Wah-To-Yah* xx. (1927) 244 A horse-stealing expedition. 1858 Teresa Viele *Following the Drum* 123 Horse-stealing from the Mexicans is a..branch of their business. 1872 E. Eggleston *Hoosier Schoolm.* vi. 70 The whole region..had the reputation of being infested with thieves, who practiced horse-stealing. 1887 *Harper's Mag.* Sept. 645/2, I was defending a prisoner for horse-stealing. 1901 Marah E. Ryan *Montana* ix. 126 A wholesale horse steal from a ranch.

Ho·rse-thief. A horse-stealer.

1772 D. Taitt in *Trav. Amer. Col.* 541 A very great horse thief. 1800 T. Jefferson *The Anas* 2 Jan. (Th.) Sweezy was arrested (being an old horse thief) and his papers examined. 1857 *Quinland* i. xv. I. 229 They say Jim Wrangle has disclosed a company of horse-thieves, consisting of a dozen persons. 1891 Marah E. Ryan *Told in Hills* ii. v. 61 She intimated yesterday that he might be a horse-thief. 1923 R. Kipling *Land & Sea Tales* 230 Murderers, horse-thieves, and cattle-lifters.

So **Ho·rse-thie:ving** *sb.* and *a.*

1835 R. M. Bird *Hawks of Hawk-hollow* II. xiii. 137 Down you rogue, or I'll indict you for horse-thieving. *a* 1861 T. Winthrop *John Brent* vii. 71 'Supposin' it's..more rattle-snakes, or more horse-thieving, scalpin' Utes.' 1874 R. Glisan *Jrnl. Army Life* xxxii. 463 A band of horse thieving prairie Indians.

Horsewhip, *sb.* (Later U.S. examples.)

1843 *Knickerbocker Mag.* XXII. 56 I'd like to have some on 'em tied to a tree, and have fair play at 'em with this horse-whip. 1856 P. Cartwright *Autobiog.* viii. (1858) 74 They came drunk, and armed with..horse-whips.

Horst (hǭɹst). *Geol.* [G., = heap, mass, cluster, sandbank, etc.] A term introduced by Suess to denote tracts of the earth's surface which have resisted lateral thrust and against which surrounding areas have been pressed and dislocated; also, an area that has become raised above surrounding areas which have been depressed by faulting.

1893 Geikie *Text-bk. Geol.* (ed. 3) 1071 Suess has pointed out various areas of the earth's surface, named by him 'Horsts', which seem to have served this purpose [*sc.* as buttresses] in the general rupture and subsidence of the terrestrial crust. 1908 Avebury *Scenery Eng.* 179. 1910 Lake & Rastall *Text-bk. Geol.* 178 Horst Mountain. This is the reverse of a rift-valley.

Hortal, *a.* Delete *Obs. rare*[−1] and add:

1926 *Nat. Hist. Oxford Distr.* 119 Other hortal plants which have become established are several species of North-American Asters.

Hortensia (hǫɹte·nsiă). [mod.L. (Jussieu), f. *Hortense*, Christian name of the wife of the clock-maker Lepaute (1723–88).] The common hydrangea.

1866 *Treas. Bot.* 1901 *Westm. Gaz.* 7 Mar. 3/1 The Parisians are just now greatly affecting white roses and hortensia. 1906 *Daily Chron.* 9 Feb. 5/1 The bouquet was of artificial hortensias.

Horticulturally (hǫɹtikʊ·ltiŭrăli, -tʃǝr-), *adv.* [See -ly [2].] In the way of horticulture.

1905 E. F. Benson *Image in Sand* xviii, Horticulturally speaking. 1927 *Observer* 27 Nov. 13/3 It is not only horticulturally that the Riviera is making ready.

Hortonite (hǭ·ɹtǝnǝit). *Min.* [prob. f. the name of Dr. William *Horton* + -ite [1].] A steatitic pseudomorph of pyroxene.

1868 Dana *Min.* (ed. 5) 222 Hortonite is..found in Orange Co., N.Y., with chondrodite.

Hortonolite (hǭ·ɹtǝnǝlǝit). *Min.* [f. the name of S. P. *Horton* + -o- + -lite.] A silicate of iron and magnesium.

1869 G. J. Brush in *Amer. Jrnl. Sci. & Arts* Ser. ii. XLVIII. 17 On Hortonolite, a new member of the Chrysolite group. 1877 Dana *Text-bk. Min.* 278 Hortonolite...O'Neil mine, Orange Co., N.Y.

Horus (hō·rǝs). [late L., ad. Gr. Ὧρος, ad. Egyptian *Hor.*] The name of an Egyptian deity, represented in art as having the head of a hawk, used *attrib.* to designate an image of this deity.

1923 *Glasgow Herald* 13 Feb. 8 The horus birds.

Hosanna. **B.** *sb.* Add: *attrib.*: **hosanna Sunday,** Palm Sunday; **hosanna tree,** any tree whose branches are used as palm on Palm Sunday.

1911 *Ch. Times* 13 Apr. 500/1 The Christians of Persia also use a species of willow, which is named there from the 'Hosanna Tree'.

Hose, *sb.* Add: **5. c.** *Golf.* The socket into which the shaft of an iron club is fitted.

1893 H. Hutchinson *Golfing* 21 A method of obviating the trouble of occasionally hitting the ball on the hose of these short-faced clubs.

7. *hose-carriage, -cart, -pipe* (earlier U.S. examples); also **hose-company,** a company in charge of a fire-hose.

1876 J. S. Ingram *Centen. Exposition* v. 140 The weight and bulk of the engine and *hose-carriage. 1865 *Trans. Ill. Agric. Soc.* VI. 320 A large amount of three-inch hose always ready on *hose carts. 1806 *Massachusetts Spy* 21 May (Th.) The efforts of several *hose and fire companies at length prevailed. 1841 C. Cist *Cincinnati* 290 Fire engine and Hose Company. 1860 O. W. Holmes *Prof. Breakf.-t.* iv. 106 More widely known through the Moyamensing Hose-Company, and the Wistar parties. 1835 J. Martin *Gazetteer Virginia* 139 The height of the reservoir, above these streets, ..gives a jet of water by means of *hose pipes, of some 60 to 80 feet elevation.

Hospital, *sb.* **6.** Add: *hospital steward, tent*; **hospital ship,** (*b*) a ship for conveying sick and wounded soldiers to their own country; **hospital train,** a train for conveying wounded soldiers from the front to the base hospitals.

1683 *hospital ship [in Dict.]. 1899 *Westm. Gaz.* 20 Nov. 6/2 The American hospital-ship *Maine.* 1916 Boyd Cable *Action Front* 172 Swinging at top speed down the line to the base and the hospital ship and home. 1856 R. Glisan *Jrnl. Army Life* xxv. (1874) 350 Besides the sick, *hospital steward,..and some three others, there will be no troops. 1812 *Niles' Weekly Register* II. 131/1, 300 *hospital, horsemen's and common tents. 1862 McClellan *Own Story* 458 They are nearly all in hospital-tents and are well provided for. 1874 B. F. Taylor *World on Wheels*, etc. i. xxiv. 162 The saddest train upon which the writer ever took passage was the *Hospital Train, with its maimed and mangled burden. 1916 Boyd Cable *Action Front* 172 That he might be lying warm and comfortable in the soothing ease of a bed in the hospital train.

Hospitality. Add: **1. c.** Applied in conventional phr. to the admission of correspondence, etc. to a newspaper.

1913 *Punch* 16 Apr. 298, I thank you for the hospitality of your columns.

d. *To partake of His* or *Her Majesty's hospitality*: to be in prison. *jocular colloq.*

1894 *Strand Mag.* Sept. 296/2 Partaking of Her Majesty's hospitality, in a building specially erected for gentlemen who need a compulsory holiday.

Hospitalize (hǫ·spitălǝiz), *v.* [f. Hospital *sb.* + -ize.]

1. *trans.* To place or accommodate in a hospital.

1901 *Daily Chron.* 10 Sept. 6/2 The disease was spreading rapidly owing to the people refusing to hospitalise first cases. 1904 *Ibid.* 28 Oct. 8/3 The pauper who is hospitalised in an English casual ward.

2. 'To render (a building) unfit for habitation, by long continued use as a hospital' (Webster 1897).

Hence **Ho:spitaliza·tion,** accommodation in a hospital.

1932 *Nation* (N.Y.) 25 May 604 The activities of the Legion..began with a demand for pensions and hospitalization for those disabled in war service.

Hoss (hǫs), dial. (also U.S.) var. of Horse *sb.*

1. = Horse *sb.* 1 and 25 a.

1849 N. Kingsley *Diary* 88 My supper consisted of beans, old hoss, and hard bread. 1872 J. M. Bailey *Folks in Danbury* 37 (Th.) But this is a hoss of another colour. 1888 F. R. Stockton *Dusantes* 15 'These hosses won't do much at holdin back', he said.

2. *U.S.* = Horse *sb.* 4.

1844 *Yale Lit. Mag.* X. 168 Well, hoss, I reckon I will. 1847 *Knickerbocker Mag.* XXIX. 204 We've sworn to give the first strange old hoss that comes along this road an up-and-down beating. 1847, 1857 [see Dict.]. 1904 Harben *Georgians* xv. 148 'Went back on us, ole boss', Jim said, cordially.

3. *attrib.* = Horse *sb.* 26.

1837 R. M. Bird *Nick of Woods* II. iv. 63, I do [know].. all the parts injacent and outjacent, circumsurrounding the hoss-stump. 1876 Habberton *Jericho Road* xv. 142 Losin' your health when you started with Sam Reeves' hoss-gang. *a* 1909 'O. Henry' *Roads of Destiny* xvi. 263 Amos Colvin and me were thicker than two hoss thieves more than ten years.

Host, *sb.*[4] **2.** Add: Also applied to the wafer before consecration (quots. 1687, 1881).

Hostage, *sb.*[1] Add: **5.** *attrib.*

1905 *Westm. Gaz.* 26 Sept. 8/2 The hostage camps [in the Gaboon]. 1909 *Daily Chron.* 18 Nov. 1/7 The dragging of a man to the hostage house [in the Congo].

Hostile. **B.** *sb.* *U.S.* (Earlier example.)

1855 Barnum *Life* 193 There was a good number of 'hostiles' [Indians] who would not come in.

Hot, *a.* Add: **1. e.** Electrically charged. (Cf. U.S. slang phr. *hot squat*, the electric chair.)

1930 *Sel. Gloss. Motion Pict. Techn.* (Acad. Techn. Bureau Hollywood), *Hot*, electrically charged, particularly when dangerous.

6. d. *transf.* Of a literary work: Licentious. *colloq.*

1892 Milliken *'Arry Ballads* 37 As most of our plays are now cribbed from the French, wy they're all pooty 'ot. 1908 *Daily Chron.* 22 June 6/5 Publishing firms..discovered that money was to be made out of what they called 'the hot novel'.

7. c. Of a ball: Hit or kicked hard, and difficult for the opposite side to deal with.

1882 Pardon *Australians in Eng.* 37 Lockwood gave Murdoch a hot chance at point. *Mod.* A. was caught from a hot return. B. put in a hot shot which the goalkeeper safely negotiated.

8. a. *To get hot*: in a game or pursuit, to come near the discovery of something concealed.

1882 *Cassell's Bk. In-door Amusem.* (ed. 2) 29 The progress of the player is usually announced by assuring him that he is 'very cold', 'cold', 'warmer', 'warm', 'hot', 'very hot', or 'burning', according as he is far from or near to the article to be discovered. 1899 Hornung *Amateur Cracksman* 252 'Not there, not there', said Raffles; 'but you're getting hot. Try the cartridges.' 1931 *Times Lit. Suppl.* 29 Oct. 832/4 He needs it [*sc.* personality] to act quickly and effectively when an appliance fails, or when an investigator gets 'hot'.

b. *Hot canary*, a canary of a brilliant flame colour.

1879 *Encycl. Brit.* IX. 192/2 Birds which have successfully undergone this forcing process [*sc.* with cayenne-pepper], and hence called 'hot canaries'.

f. Of a Treasury bill: Newly issued. *colloq.*

1928 *Evening News* 18 Aug. 11/6 The hot Treasuries were offered at 4 3-16 per cent., without finding buyers. 1929 *Times* 16 Nov. 18/1 The 'hot' Treasury Bills were dealt in at 5 13-32 per cent. 1929 *Observer* 17 Nov. 3/3 'Hot' bills yesterday morning changed hands in very small amounts at 5 5-16 per cent. 1931 J. Greenhill *Money Market* (Westminster Bank Guild III. 106).

g. *Astrol.* Of certain of the signs of the zodiac: Favourable, auspicious.

1819 Jas. Wilson *Dict. Astrol.* 268 Aries..is a vernal, hot, dry, fiery, cardinal,..fortunate, hoarse, bitter sign. 1889 R. Baughan *Influence of Stars* 12 Aries..is a hot and fiery sign, and produces a lean body.

h. Applied to elaborated dance music and playing of the virtuoso kind; also to the performer.

1928 *Gramophone* VI. 300/2 It is not a question of 'hot dance music or 'straight' dance music. 1931 *Radio Times* 30 Oct. 338/1 'Hot' playing, as exemplified in the new American records that Christopher Stone occasionally releases for our entertainment. 1932 *Amer. Speech* VII. 245 Hot negro musician of Chicago. *Ibid.* 247 Hot jazz. 1932 '*H.M.V.*' *Catal.*, Hot rhythm records.

11. a. *To go hot and cold (all over)*: to experience alternate sensations of heat and cold owing to fear.

1928 *Daily Mail* 3 Aug. 10/6 The figures given..as to my earnings..made me go all hot and cold—I wonder what I can have done with all that money!

12. c. hot beef, rhyming slang for 'Stop thief!' e.g. in phr. *to give* (a person) *hot beef*; **hot bricks,** chiefly in phr. *like a cat on hot bricks*, denoting a situation of extreme discomfort and restiveness; **hot cakes** orig. *U.S.*: in phr. *to sell* or *go (off) like hot cakes*, to be disposed of very rapidly; **hot chamber, chisel** (see quots.); **hot cross bun** (see Bun *sb.*[2] 1, Cross-bun); **hot curving machine** (see quot. 1884); **hot dog** *U.S. colloq.*, a hot sausage enclosed as a sandwich in a roll of bread; **hot plate,** (*a*) (examples); (*b*) a portable gas or electric heater on which food is kept hot, or a plate with a cover for the same purpose; (*c*) (see quot. 1884); **hot potato,** in fig. phr. (to drop something) *like a hot potato*; **hot-spot** *Mech.*, a portion of the inlet manifold specially heated from the exhaust; usually *attrib.*; also *transf.*; **hot stuff,** (*a*) a person or thing out of the ordinary run, something of surpassing excellence or merit; sometimes with implication of moral censure; (*b*) extraordinary or extreme conduct; **hot-stuff** *v. Army slang*, to requisition; **hot-tube,** a metal tube heated red-hot used for ignition of the charge in an internal combustion engine; also *attrib.*, as *hot-tube igniter, ignition*; **hot wave** *U.S.*, a progressive movement of an area of relatively high pressure and temperature, a heat wave; **hot wind,** a wind blowing from the interior of a continent and characterized by intense heat, *spec.* this phenomenon in South Australia; **hot-wire** *a.*, denoting instruments the indications of which are based on the expansion of wire when heated.

1879 J. W. Horsley *Jottings from Jail* i. (1887) 19 He followed, giving me *hot beef (calling 'Stop thief'). 1896 A. Morrison *Child of Jago* x, Now he first experienced 'hot beef'—which is the Jago idiom denoting the plight of one harried by the cry 'Stop thief!' 1886 'J. S. Winter' *Army Society* xvi, Lady Mainwaring looked..like a cat on *hot bricks. 1860 O. J. Victor *Hist. Southern Rebellion* (1861) I. 46 Revolvers and patent fire-arms are selling like *hot cakes. 1879 *Congress. Rec.* 15 May 1368/1 Four per cent bonds..go off like hot cakes. 1908 *Daily Chron.* 4 Aug. 3/4 Ice creams at 3d. a time went 'like hot cakes'. 1925 J. Gregory *Bab of Backwoods* xi. 141 So they got the blaze going, bacon sizzling, the frying-pan balanced on the fire, hot-cakes mixed and coffee set to boil. 1888 *Encycl. Brit.* XXIII. 702/2 In large stereotyping foundries, after the flong has been well beaten upon the forme,..it is baked and dried (the forme still underneath) on a long thick iron slab, called a *hot chamber, because it is heated from within by steam. 1889 *N. & Q.* 7th Ser. VII. 151/1 Cold and *hot chisels are used for cutting cold and hot iron (or metal) respectively. 1880 *Engineering* XXIX. 372/2 Nearly every steel rail mill in the United States has the Gustin or some other good *hot curving machine. 1884 Knight *Dict. Mech.* Suppl., *Hot Curving Machine*, a machine for bending laterally a hot-rolled rail to suit a curve of any given radius. 1908 G. H. Lorimer *J. Spurlock* vii. 147, I told the Major that he had undoubtedly got hold of the *hottest dog in the frankfurter can. 1926 *Spectator* 11 Sept. 373/1 The President of the Brooklyn team asked them to his box and gave them hot dogs. 1928 S. Vines *Humours Unreconciled* ii. 35 If one trained on hot dog, pumpkin pie, graham flour, ice cream sundaes. 1851 *Catal. Gt. Exhib.* iii. iii. 643 Emigrant's or cottage stove, suitable for wood or coal, with *hot-plate and oven. 1861 Francatelli *Cook's Guide* Advt. 3 Smoke Jacks, Hot Plates,... Steam Tables, and..other description of.. Cooking Apparatus. 1884 Knight *Dict. Mech.* Suppl., *Hot Plate*, a gas stove for heating copper bits for soldering. 1925 L. Stallings *Plumes* vii. 175 The hot plate..was set upon a bracket next the water closet. 1925 G. L. Hill *Ariel Custer* vii. 99 A gas hot plate with two burners. 1893 Farmer & Henley *Slang* s.v., To drop like a *hot potato. 1927 *Observer* 16 Oct. 27 A *hot-spot carburation system. 1930 *Ibid.* 7 Sept. 6 A certain kind of hot-spot fiction. 1931 *Prospectus Alvis Cars* 2 Efficient Carburation System with special Alvis 'Hot Spot' induction pipe. 1889 *Kansas Times & Star* 14 Nov., 'Miss Middleton's Lover.' Were there room for two words more in that last line, '*Hot Stuff' might be appropriate. *a* 1909 'O. Henry' *Roads of Destiny* xviii. 305 We want to introduce a little hot stuff in the way of campaigning. 1915 T. Burke *Nights in Town* 306 Women screamed. Others cried for help. Some one cried, 'Hot stuff, boys—let 'em 'ave it where it 'urts most!' 1915 Sir H. Wilson *Diary* (1927) I. 249 Here is Sarrail, sitting next to Joffre, to urge a plan about which he knows nothing. And all because he is a Radical-Socialist. Hot stuff. 1920 Wodehouse *Damsel in Distress* x. 124 If I'd known you were such hot stuff,..I'd have got you to give me a stroke or two. 1914 Rosher *In R.N.A.S.* (1916) 36, I at once *hot-stuffed one of his inlet valves and set the men to work changing it. 1896 B. Donkin *Text-bk. Gas Engines* (ed. 2) 87 In all modern Otto engines, *hot-tube ignition is used. 1888 *Encycl. Brit.* XXIII. 805/1 The occasional occurrence of '*hot waves' which sweep over large areas of country, raising the temperature much above its normal height, is one of the most striking and most disagreeable features of the climate of the country. *c* 1790 *Encycl. Brit.* (1797) VI. 402/1 A sign of the approaching *Simoom* or *hot wind. 1804 in *Wellington's Disp.* (1837) III. 180 A desire to give his troops some repose, and not to expose the Europeans to the hot winds in Hindustan. 1833 hot wind [see Dict. 1 a]. 1846 J. L. Stokes *Discov. Australia* II. 243 *note*, During the hot winds we observed the thermometer, in the direct rays of the sun, to be 135°. 1850 R. G. Cumming *Hunter's Life S. Afr.* I. 60 At certain seasons..northerly breezes prevail: these are termed by the colonists 'hot winds'. 1900 W. Stebbing *C. H. Pearson* 89 He revelled in the Victoria hot-wind days which shrivelled up everybody else. 1893 *Jrnl. Soc. Arts* 11 Aug. 845/2 The *hot wire apparatus. 1903 *Phil. Mag.* Ser. vi. VII. (1904) 372 In order to make use of the gilt silver wire as a hot-wire voltmeter. 1923 E. W. Marchant *Radio Telegr. & Teleph.* iv. 44 Other forms of detector for wireless circuits are the electrolytic, the hot wire 'barretter' and the crystal.

Hot (hǫt), *int.* *S. Afr.* [Du.] A call to an ox to turn to the left.

[1785 tr. *Sparrman's Voy.* I. 127 Each ox in particular will pay attention, and go to the right or to the left, merely upon hearing its own name pronounced with a *ote* or a *aar* added to it.] 1870 *Cape Monthly Mag.* I. 194 Literally, I did not know my right hand from my left, when *hot* stood for the one and *haar* for the other,—sounds intelligent enough to the most stupid bullock that ever bore the yoke.

Hot, *v.* Add: **3.** *fig.* or *transf.* with *up.* (*a*) To become 'warm' or unpleasantly excited. (*b*) *pass.* Of an internal combustion engine, a car, etc.: To be 'tuned up'; to have the horse-power increased so as to be capable of higher speeds. Also in *ppl. a.*

1923 Wodehouse *Inimit. Jeeves* x. 108 The atmosphere was consequently more or less hotted up when Cyril..breezed down centre. *Ibid.* xviii. 250 'Things are hotting up.' 'What's happened now?' 1928 *Morning Post* 20 Oct. 10/7 This car..is not in any sense a 'hotted up' Morris six-cylinder.

4. To reprimand severely; to give it (a person) hot.

1920 *Blackw. Mag.* Oct. 473/1 The moment the troops there *did* fall back they would be properly 'hotted'.

Hot, *adv.* **2.** (Later U.S. example.)

1884 'Mark Twain' *Huck. Finn* xv. 126 As soon as I got started I took out after the raft, hot and heavy, right down the tow-head.

Hot air. [See Hot *a.* 12 c.]

1. *attrib.* or as *adj.* (earlier and later examples).

1841 C. Cist *Cincinnati* Advt., Manufacturers of Hot Air Furnaces, Stoves, &c. 1875 Knight *Dict. Mech.*, *Hot-air Engine*, one driven by the heating of a body of air admitted to the cylinder...*Hot-air Furnace*, one in which air is heated for warming houses, or for purposes of drying.

2. *slang* (orig. *U.S.*). Vaporous or boastful talk, 'gas', pretentious or unsubstantial statements or claims; also *attrib.* as in *hot-air artist* or *merchant*, one who indulges in talk of this kind.

1899 G. Ade *Fables in Slang* (1900) 126 They strolled under the Maples, and he talked what is technically known as Hot Air. 1904 Eliz. Robins *Magnetic North* xiii, He has more hot air to offer than muscle. 1904 *N.Y. Even. Post* 14 Sept. 7 A prominent Democratic senator who..will not give out 'hot air' interviews. 1911 H. B. Wright *Barbara Worth* 327 The presence av sich..a hot air merchant..is a disgrace to any..company. 1914 'Ian Hay' *Knt. on Wheels* xviii, 'Brand a friend of yours, Miss Jennings?' 'That hot-air artist?' she replied witheringly. 'I don't think!'

Hot-blooded, *a.* Add: **b.** Warm-blooded: opposed to *cold-blooded.*

1874 J. W. Draper *Hist. Conflict betw. Relig. & Sci.* (1875) 248 The hot-blooded animals could not exist in an atmosphere so laden with carbonic acid.

Hot box. *U.S.* An overheated journal-box, esp. of a railway carriage; also *fig.* or *transf.*

1855 *Knickerbocker Mag.* XLV. 199 They shout orders about 'couplings'..and 'hot-boxes'. 1873 'Mark Twain' & Warner *Gilded Age* xlvi. 419 It seemed as if the train would never reach Baltimore...A hot box had to be cooled at Wilmington. 1883 C. D. Warner *Roundabout Journ.* 3 A real American is not comfortable without a 'hot box' occasionally in the course of a long journey. *a* 1910 in H. Withers *Our Money* (1923) 13 The locomotive was attacked by a malady called 'hot box'. 1910 Jer. Hart *Vigilante Girl* x. 140 If that near hind box was to begin to talk different, I'd pull up and examine it right away. Mebbe I'd save a hot box by doin' it.

Hotchkiss (hǫ·tʃkis). The name of B. B. *Hotchkiss* (1826–85), American inventor, used *attrib.* to designate a kind of machine gun and certain rifles invented by him.

1880 *Encycl. Brit.* XI. 285/1 Hotchkiss Magazine Gun. 1890 *Handbk. 6-pndr. Hotchkiss quick-firing gun* 12 The shell is fitted with..a brass Hotchkiss band. *Ibid.*, The fuze may be either the Nordenfelt or the Hotchkiss, Mark II, pattern. 1890 G. S. Clarke *Fortif.* xiii. 191 Twelve Hotchkiss machine guns. 1899–1900 *Kynoch Jrnl.* Dec.–Jan. 31/2 The Hotchkiss Automatic Gun. 1902 *Encycl. Brit.* XXIX. 166/1 In the Hotchkiss and also in the Skoda systems the mechanism is of the vertical breech block type.

Hotchpot. 4. (Later U.S. example.)

1837 *Southern Lit. Messenger* III. 644 A very hotchpot collection.

Hotel, *sb.* **4.** Add: *hotel bus, clerk* (U.S.), *-keeper, -keeping.*

1878 *Harper's Mag.* Jan. 194 The traveller reaches his stopping-place by *hotel 'bus, carriage, or by the democratic street cars. 1879 B. F. Taylor *Summer-Savory* x. 89 He [*sc.* the hustler] is the man to overwhelm the average *hotel clerk. 1866 Mrs. Whitney *L. Goldthwaite* iv, The *hotel-keeper had a 'capital team'. 1870 'Fanny Fern' *Ginger-snaps* 247 Having then left what, in my opinion, is the perfection of *hotel-keeping. 1884 H. S. Cummings *Dartmouth Coll.* 54 He went to Colorado, and engaged in hotel-keeping at Monument.

Hoteldom (hote·ldǝm). [f. Hotel *sb.* + -dom.] The realm of hotels, hotels collectively.

1904 *Westm. Gaz.* 1 June 9/2 Then our representative turned his attention to hoteldom. 1927 *Glasgow Herald* 28 Mar. 11/1 There is to be an addition to London hoteldom.

Hotelier (otę·lye). [Fr.] The keeper or proprietor of a hotel.

1905 *Westm. Gaz.* 10 Mar. 12/1 Some enterprising hotelier. 1925 G. W. Deeping *Sorrell* xxix, An expert hotelier, the man of detail who must organize the very stair-rods and the bath taps. 1930 *Observer* 20 Apr. 7 That prince of hoteliers, the late M. Ritz.

Hot-foot, *adv.* Add: **2.** *attrib.* or as *adj.* Acting with haste or promptitude.

1904 'O. Henry' *Cabbages & Kings* v. 90 He was private secretary of the late hot-foot president of this grocery and fruit stand that they call a country.

3. *sb.* Prompt or rapid action or movement.

1869 *Congress. Globe* 15 Jan. 389/3 The honorable Senator ..admonished us of the importance of hot-foot in this business, if I may say so, of allowing the testimony to be taken at once. 1915 H. L. Wilson *Ruggles of Red Gap* ii. (1917) 27 We'd better report to her before she does it hot-foot over here.

Hot-foot, *v.* Chiefly *U.S.* [f. prec.] *intr.* To go hot-foot; to make haste. Also with *it.*

1896 G. Ade *Artie* iii. 22, I hot-foots up to the dance. 1900 — *More Fables in Slang* (1902) 159 He..Hot-Footed up to see the Boss. 1904 *New York Sun* 27 Aug. 10 Thousands hot footed to the corner of Broadway. 1911 R. D. Saunders *Col. Todhunter* ii. 34 Great Scott and Maria, you must have hot-footed it away from your vittles, young man! 1928 'S. S. Van Dine' *Greene Murder Case* v, When I told you the police were hot-footing it after a burglar.

2. *trans.* To chase or conduct at a rapid pace.

1903 F. B. Smith *How Paris Amuses Itself* 103 Zuléma discovers her irate father, who, having been hot-footed up hill and down dale by the bloodthirsty *Anglais*, is glad enough to come out of his hiding place.

Hottentot. Add: **1. c.** (In full *Hottentot fish.*) A South African fish, *Cantharus blochii*, found in Table and False Bays; also, in Natal, *Cantharus natalensis.*

1798 tr. *Stavorinus' Voy.* I. 560 The Hottentot-fish, which is like a sea-bream. 1838 J. E. Alexander *Exped.* I. 88 The delicious Roman fish, Hottentot.

3. Hottentot bean tree *S. Afr.*, an old colonial name for the tree *Scotia speciosa*; **Hottentot bonnets** *S. Afr.* (see quot.); **Hottentot fish** (see *1 c); **Hottentot('s) god** *S. Afr.*, a mantis, formerly worshipped by the Hottentots.

1833 S. Kay *Trav. & Res. in Caffraria* 106 The *Hottentot's bean tree. 1848 Bunbury *C. Good Hope* 188 *Disperis Capensis*..is known by the name of the *Hottentot Bonnet, on account of the peculiar shape of its purple and green flowers. 1785 tr. *Sparrman's Voy.* I. 211 A genus of insects (the *mantis*, called by the colonists the **Hottentot's god.*

Houbara (hubā·rā). Also **hobara, hubara, oubara, ubara.** [mod.L., f. Arab. حباري *ḥubārī* bustard.] A bustard of the genus so named, consisting of two species. *Otis houbara* or *Houbara undulata*, native to Northern Africa and Western Asia, and *Otis macqueeni*, native to India and Persia.

1827 Malcolm *Sk. Persia* I. 56 The beautiful speckled Hubara, with his head erect and wings outspread. 1836 *Penny Cycl.* VI. 59/2 Arabs are accustomed to compare the eyes of their most beautiful women to those of the *Oubara.* 1869–73 *Cassell's Bk. Birds* IV. 7 According to Jerdon the Indian Houbara is found throughout the plains of the Punjaub and Upper Scinde. 1878 Newton in *Encycl. Brit.* IV. 579/1. 1883 *List Animals Zool. Soc.* 517 Houbara Bustard. 1925 *Blackw. Mag.* Mar. 339/1 The hobara, or lesser bustard.

Houdan (hū·dǣn). Name of a town in the department of Seine-et-Oise, France, used to designate a breed of domestic fowl characterized by black and white plumage, heavy crest, five toes on each foot, and by its prolific laying.

1885 *Encycl. Brit.* XIX. 645/2 The Houdan is a black and white breed of very similar character [to the Crève-cœur]. 1902 *Ibid.* XXXI. 876/2 A race originated in France by crossing Houdans with Dorkings and Light Brahmas, and known as the Faverolles. 1925 *Glasgow Herald* 16 Jan. 6 During the war I had a houdan who ruled my hen run.

Houghton (hōᵘ·tǝn, hau·tǝn). *U.S.* An American variety of gooseberry having smooth red fruit.

1911 Webster.

Houhere (hou·hīᵊri). *New Zealand.* [Maori, f. *hou* to bind or fasten together + *here* tie.] A tree belonging to the genera *Plagianthus* and *Hoheria*, the ribbon-wood or lace-bark, the bark of which was used for tying.

1883 J. Hector *Handbk. N. Z.* 130 (Morris) Houhere, ribbonwood of Dunedin. 1889 T. Kirk *Forest Flora N. Z.* 87 In one or other of its varied forms the houhere is found in nearly every district in the colony.

Hound, *sb.*[1] **7. a.** Add: *hound-dog, -pup* U.S.

1649 *Dedham* (Mass.) *Rec.* 162 That care be taken that the young *hound doges be in time taught to hunt. 1911 R. D. Saunders *Col. Todhunter* ii. 24 I'm as hungry as a young hound-dog this very minute. 1857 Olmsted *Journ. Texas* (1861) 52 The child..five miles from a neighbor;..[with] *hound-pups and negroes for playmates. 1878 J. H. Beadle *Western Wilds* xxviii. 439 What he wouldn't steal, a hound pup wouldn't pull out of a tan-yard.

b. hound-work, the work done by the hounds in hunting.

1928 *Isis* 14 Nov., Some very pretty houndwork now ensued. 1929 *Morning Post* 30 Dec. 13/1 Fine Exhibition of Hound-work with Moderate Scent.

Hound, *sb.*[2] **2.** *U.S.* (Earlier examples.)

1846 *Rep. U.S. Comm. Patents* (1847) 264 The placing on the rear ends of the extended hounds..the adjustable sway bar. 1854 Bartlett *Pers. Narr. Explor. Texas*, etc. II. xl. 456 Mr. Flotte's large carriage got mired; and in the struggle to extricate, the tongue and hounds were broken.

Houp-la (hū·pˌlā), *int.* Also **hoop-la.** [Cf. F. *houp-là!* hallo!] An exclamation accompanying a quick or sudden movement.

1914 H. Garland *Son of Middle Border* xxiii. 286 We began to slip slowly, smoothly, and with joyous ease down the shining track! Hoopla! we had taken wing. 1917 *Punch* 23 May 340/2 A beam of pleasure, succeeded by a falling of the countenance, then a look of decision, ended in a 'Houp-là' as the Japanese doll descended into the basket. 1925 Ford *No More Parades* i. ii, But..Hoopla! ..He executed with his gloved right thumb in the moonlight a rapid pirouette. 1929 Garstin *Houp La!* xxiv. 308 'Houp la!' Bill sighed, letting his head fall back.

Hour. Add: **1. c.** Used to denote the distance of the sun above the horizon in the morning or afternoon. *U.S.*

1637 *Essex Inst. Hist. Coll.* IX. 66 The keeper..[is] to take the Cattle at the pen at Sun halfe an hour highe. 1683 in *Coll. New Hampsh. Hist. Soc.* VIII. 133 At night, about sun half an hour high. 1762 *Narragansett Hist. Reg.* II. 219 We..got to the Ferry the sun about two hours high at night. 1824 in *Coll. New Hampsh. Hist. Soc.* I. 244 Though the sun was an hour above the horizon, it was now as dark as midnight. 1836 *Knickerbocker Mag.* VIII. 352

The sun is two hours up yet. 1907 M. H. Norris *The Veil* i. 3 The sun was an hour high when he entered a narrow road overgrown with grass.

d. (orig. *hour-mile*.) The distance which can be traversed in an hour.

[*a* 1646 J. Gregory in *Gregorii Posthuma* (1650) 318 One Hour-Mile of a Journie upon Hors, answereth to four English Miles.] 1785 tr. *Sparrman's Voy.* II. 81 This place is situated at the distance of two hours (uurs) from that which we had just quitted. 1798 tr. *Stavorinus' Voy.* I. 58 *note*, A Dutch mile, which they in general call an hour, is about three miles and a half English. 1877 Geikie *Life of Christ* I. 388 Three hours from Jerusalem. 1907 in A. H. Anderson *Reading* Advts. p. xlviii a, Dulverton...4 Hours from London, 1 Hour from Taunton and Exeter.

e. A unit of energy or capacity. *Horse-power hour* (see *Horse-power 4). *Ampère hour*, electricity sufficient to furnish a current of an ampère for an hour.

1919 R. Stanley *Wireless Telegr.* I. 452 A proper check.. of the number of ampere-hours' charge and discharge.

f. A unit of measure of work done.

1900 *Daily News* 10 Jan. 8/3 It should be understood that the tailors' 'hour' is not one of time, but merely the word employed for an unit of calculation.

8. hour-zone, each of the lunes on the earth's surface bounded by two meridians, fifteen degrees apart on the equator, equal to an hour in the standard system of time, within which all places have the same standard time, except where a line has been shifted slightly for local convenience.

1898 *Geogr. Jrnl.* (R. G. S.) XI. 677 The groups of 10 degrees of longitude form naturally the 24 hour-zones into which the circumference of the equator is divided.

Hour-glass. c. Add: *hour-glass aneurism, stomach.*

1880 Barwell *Aneurism* 56 The support of muscular fibres has frequently this effect on the vessel, namely, while fusiform dilation exists to right and left, this little tract is healthy; the condition might be called an hour-glass aneurism. 1907 *Practitioner* June 755 There was an hour-glass stomach, due to old ulceration.

House, *sb.*[1] Add: **1.** β. (Later U.S. dial. examples.)

1825 J. F. Cooper *L. Lincoln* III. vii. 175 'Tis an awful calling, to be beating down the housen of people of the same religion and blood with ourselves. 1845 J. J. Hooper *Daddy Bigg's Scrape* 196 Ef they ondertake to bild housen on the hill-sides,..they'll have to rope 'em to the trees.

2. b. *To bow down* (or *worship*) *in the house of Rimmon* (after 2 Kings v. 18): to pay lip-service to some principle which one does not accept; to sacrifice one's principles for the sake of conformity.

1718 De Foe in W. Lee *Life*, etc. (1869) I. p. xiii, Thus I bow in the House of Rimmon, and must humbly recommend myself to his Lordship's Protection. 1903 Kipling *Five Nations, Rimmon* i, Duly with knees that feign to quake—Bent head and shaded brow—Yet once again, for my father's sake, In Rimmon's House I bow.

2. c. *On the house*: at the expense of the tavern, saloon, etc. orig. *U.S.*

1889 *Kansas City Times & Star* 30 Nov., The first drink Thursday was 'on the house' in the leading saloons.

4. c. Also, in day schools, a division of the school for purposes of discipline and games.

1925 *City of Oxford Sch. Mag.* Mar. 8 Kerry House hold the new cup for the winning House for the first year. *Ibid.* July 33 In the points counting for the House Shield.

g. *House full*: the announcement posted outside a place of entertainment to indicate to the public that there is no room available. Also *transf.*

1914 *Aeroplane* 2 Sept. 211/1 Both Services have practically put up the 'House Full' sign, and have a waiting list yards in length.

7. d. The gelatinous envelope secreted by certain tunicates.

1888 Rolleston & Jackson *Anim. Life* 441 The cells of the anterior region of the body in *Larvacea* are large, and secrete a hyaline gelatinous and sticky substance, which forms the so-called 'house'. 1902 *Encycl. Brit.* XXXIII. 479/2 Lohmann has made a careful study of the mode of formation of this 'House' from certain large ectoderm cells the 'oikoplasts'.

9. b. *Curling.* The space within the outermost circle drawn round the tee.

1884 'J. Strathesk' *More Bits* xiv. (1885) 272 David swept behind the Tee, and 'saw him out o' the house'. 1897 *Encycl. Sport* I. 257/2 All leading stones should be thus concaved, that they may be able to keep their position in the 'house'.

c. Lotto played in the Army as a gambling game with special cards and checks.

1900 *Strand Mag.* Apr. 419/2 When they were not drilling they were playing 'House'. 1917 Empey *From Fire Step* 125 The two most popular games are 'Crown and Anchor' and 'House'. *Ibid.* 126 As soon as the *estaminet* is sufficiently crowded the proprietors of the 'House Game' get busy. 1919 G. K. Rose *2/4th Oxf. & Bucks Lt. Infty.* 200 On the air floated the monotonous enumeration of 'House'. 1923 *Daily Mail* 9 June 7 The game of 'house', or 'box and numbers'.

20. *house-cat* (later U.S. examples).

c 1785 Sarah Pears *Narrative* (MS.) 8 He had not killed anything save a [bear] cub not bigger than a house cat. 1845 Hooper *Taking Census* i. 63 'Twas my old house-cat.

23. house bill, a bill of exchange drawn by a business house on itself; **house-bound** *a.* (example); **house-burnt** *a. U.S.*, designating tobacco spoiled by being hung too thick in the drying-house; so **house-burn** *v. intr.*, to become house-burnt; **house cap**, a school cap made of the colours adopted by a particular house, esp. one awarded for proficiency in games; **house-car** *U.S.* (example); **house-carpenter** (earlier and later U.S. examples); **house-cleaning**, the cleaning of the inside of a house, esp. a thorough cleaning in spring or autumn; **house-dinner**, a dinner given to the staff or the occupants of a school-house, etc.; **house-finch** *U.S.* (see quot.); **house frame** *U.S.*, the frame of a wooden house; **house-furnishing**, the furnishing of a house; also *pl.* in concrete sense; **house-log** *U.S.*, a log suitable for, or used in, the construction of a house; **house-parlourman**, a male servant who does work corresponding to that of a house-parlourmaid; **house-piece** = House-place; **house-pride**, pride in one's house, desire to keep one's house beautiful; so **house-proud** *a.*, proud of one's house, desirous to see it always at its best; **house-raising** *U.S.* (earlier and later examples); **house-work**, the work required to keep a house clean and in order; **house-wrecker** = Housebreaker 2; **house-wren** *U.S.*, the common wren of the United States, nesting about houses and outhouses.

1909 *Daily Chron.* 2 Mar. 3/2 That particular bill of exchange, the '*house bill'—a bill drawn by a firm or company on itself. 1878 *Harper's Mag.* Jan. 277/1 The rains set in furiously, and I was completely *house-bound. 1640 in *Maryland Archives* 98 Bad Tobacco shall be judged ground leafes, Second Crops leafs, notably brused or worm eaten, or leaves *house burnt, sun burnt, [etc.]. 1849 *Rep. Comm. Patents Agric.* (1850) 321 Splitting tobacco is admired by many who contend that it cures brighter..and [is] less likely to *house-burn. *Ibid.* 324 In this crop every leaf was saved, none lost by worms nor by 'house-burning' (that is suffering, or even rotting from being hung too thick). 1899 Kipling in *Windsor Mag.* Dec. 33/1 'S'pose we're collared?' said Beetle, cramming his red and black *house-cap into his pocket. 1907 *Daily Chron.* 15 June 4/7 The pride of a little boy who wins his house cap at school. 1858 *Penn. Rail Road Annual Rept.* 14 The Rolling Stock.. consisted..of..Eight-wheeled *House Cars. 1643 in *Maryland Archives* IV. 212 John Thatcher, *house-carpenter. 1688 [see House *sb.* 23]. 1741 W. Stephens *Jrnl. Proc. Georgia* II. 118 The other was looked on as a master House-Carpenter of repute. 1758 in *Lett. to Washington* II. 365 And all this without one farthing expence (except about nine pence per day to the best house Carpenters). 1855 *Knickerbocker Mag.* XLVI. 222 Beech timber is held in great esteem by ship-builders and house-carpenters. 1869 *Causes Reduct. Tonnage* (1870) 18 House-carpenters in Fall River received thirty-five cents an hour. 1863 B. Taylor *H. Thurston* ii. 26 The first thing..was immediately to summon old Melinda..whose speciality was *house-cleaning. 1871 Mrs. Stowe *Sam Lawson* 61 There's the spring house-cleanin' and the fall house-cleanin' to be seen to. 1881 *Amer. Naturalist* XV. 213 The little *house finch (*Carpodacus frontalis*) is everywhere abundant throughout Southern California and Arizona. 1824 in *Coll. New Hampsh. Hist. Soc.* I. 246 A new two-story *house frame nearly covered..and two barns, were blown down. 1858 *Leslie's Illustr. Weekly* 23 Jan. 127 Goods for Winter Use in the *Housefurnishing Line. 1865 Mrs. Stowe *House & Home P.* 61 That such is not always the case in the real home comes often from the mistakes in the house-furnishing. 1904 *New York Sun* 9 Aug. 8 The feminine preference for garments and house furnishings over locomotives and drop forgings. 1825 *Austin Papers* (1924) II. 1026, I wish you to furnish him with tools to git me a set of *House Logs. 1836 D. B. Edward *Hist. Texas* 68 As house logs or rails, it is considered..durable. 1878 *Rep. Indian Affairs* 65 The timber, as a rule, is not valuable, except for the rails and house-logs, very little of it being suitable for working into lumber. 1887 A. W. Tourgee *Button's Inn* 306 It [*sc.* the trap-door] was hung on wooden bar-hinges set into the chimney at one end, and into the house-logs at the other. 1923 *Daily Mail* 25 Jan. 5 A number of men are becoming *house-parlourmen. 1931 *Morning Post* 10 Aug. 16/6 House-parlourman Required for maisonette. 1920 W. J. Locke *House of Baltazar* ix, Baltazar's bedroom at the southern end, once separated from the *house-piece by a wooden partition reaching to the rafters. 1908 *Daily Chron.* 3 Nov. 4/7 'A Quoi Tient la Superiorité des Anglo-Saxons?' It is in '*house pride.' 1909 *Ibid.* 7 Dec. 1/2 The 'instinct of house-pride' seems almost never entirely wanting in the home studied. 1849 C. Brontë *Shirley* II. vii. 169 You are what you call *house-proud; you like to have everything handsome about you. 1899 *Daily News* 17 Oct. 4/7 It is a bad thing for the mother of a family if she cannot be a little 'house-proud'. 1908 *Daily Chron.* 3 Nov. 4/7 If you have ever heard the word 'house-proud', meaning anyone who would spend money and time on his house to have it nice. 1704 *Essex Inst. Hist. Coll.* VIII. 223, I was at my L[and-] Lords *house raising. 1783 *Maryland Jrnl.* 29 Aug. (Th.) A dispute having arisen..at a house-raising last year. 1843 *American Pioneer* II. 451 The frequent necessity for united effort at house-raisings, log-rollings, corn-huskings, &c. 1857 [see Dict.]. 1927 J. D. Freeman *When West was Young* 415 They would..reach the West in time for a big house-raising which would be given them by the entire neighborhood. 1841 A. Bache *Fire-Screen* 119 Mrs. Gibbs, a woman who sometimes came to assist in doing *house-work, had followed Mrs. Brown into the parlour. 1871 *Rep. Indian Affairs* (1872) 378 While the boys are engaged in out-door work, the girls could be employed in sewing or house-work. 1883 *Ibid.* 247 Housework and sewing. 1896 A. Morrison *Child of Jago* xvii, The old buildings were sold..to the *house-wreckers. 1903 *Westm. Gaz.* 7 Sept. 8/2 The band of the housewrecker. 1831 J. J. Audubon *Ornith. Biog.* I. 427 The *House Wren. *Troglodytes ædon.* 1872 *Amer. Naturalist* VI. May 275 Here the common 'house' wren is bleached and faded, forming the so-called *Troglodytes Parkmanni* differing from the *T. ædon* of the east only in this particular. 1904 Ellen Glasgow *Deliverance* v. i. 442 A half-finished nest which a house-wren had begun to build.

House, *v.*[1] **7.** Add: Also with *up*.

1873 J. H. Beadle *Undevel. West* i. 40 We can house up, you know, and keep warm on the prairie in winter, but we can't house up and keep cool in the timber in the summer.

Housecraft (hau·s,kraft). [f. House *sb.*[1] + Craft *sb.* 12.] The art of managing a house; skill in domestic duties. Also *attrib.*

1910 *Daily Chron.* 1 Mar. 9/1 Ignorance of housecraft is the favourite reproach brought against the modern woman. *Ibid.*, St. Martha's College of Housecraft. 1914 J. Collings *Colon. Rural Britain* I. vi. 116 Among the 'optional' subjects contained in the 'Regulations for the Training of Teachers for Elementary Schools' is that of 'Rural Science' (and 'Housecraft' for girls).

Housekeeping, *sb.* Add: **3.** *attrib.*, as *housekeeping goods.*

1899 *Daily News* 26 June 10/6 There is a satisfactory trade doing in damasks, and house-keeping goods. 1900 *Ibid.* 17 Sept. 2/7 Housekeeping goods and damasks.

House-lot. *U.S.* (Earlier example.)

1636 *Springfield* (Mass.) *Rec.* I. 156 Every inhabitant shall have a convenient proportion for a house lott as we shall see meette for every ones quality and estate.

Housemaid. Add: **d.** A small weight or block used for holding a door open.

1898 *Westm. Gaz.* 19 Nov. 2/2 'Housemaid.'—A metal block or figure, used in a house for keeping a door open... *Dictionary of Hardware.*

House-top. Add: **b.** *fig.* A public place; esp. (with allusion to Luke xii. 3) in phrase *to proclaim, declare,* or *cry on* or *from the house-top(s)*, to make public, to proclaim so that everyone knows. Also *attrib.*

1899 *Westm. Gaz.* 15 Nov. 3/2 The policy of house-top virtue. 1906 J. Jackson tr. *Thoughts of Marcus Aurelius* 35 A man who has done a good deed should be like a horse that has run its race..: in other words, he ought not to proclaim it from the house-tops. 1911 C. G. Robertson *Eng. under Hanoverians* II. iv. 345 To cry on the housetops that it was merry in England before the new industry came up. 1931 L. Birch *Pyramid* xviii. 233 That someone should come forward and cry from the housetops that all friendships that are romantic are not, for that reason, immoral.

Hou·se-warmer. [See *-er[6].] = House-warming 2 b.

1922 H. B. Hermon-Hodge *Up agst. it in Nigeria* v. 81 Next evening I gave a sort of house-warmer in my new shanty on the hill.

Housing, *sb.*[1] Add: **1.** (Mod. examples.)

1847 *Rep. U.S. Comm. Patents* (1848) 168 The tobacco was hardly worth the housing. 1849 *Ibid., Agric.* (1850) 321 This mode is pursued easily by simply splitting..the plant ..before it is cut down for housing. 1930 A. P. Herbert *Water Gipsies* viii, Honest John Raven worked hard and late at the office, and sometimes brought home papers with him, or if not he talked 'housing'.

6. d. Each of the supports of the rollers in a rolling-mill.

1880 *Encycl. Brit.* XIII. 329/2 The 'housings', or stout cast-iron supports for the rollers. 1882 [see Dict.]. 1884 W. H. Greenwood *Steel & Iron* xvi. (ed. 2) 321 The necks or bearings of the rolls are supported upon brasses, in massive cast-iron housings or standards.

7. *housing-question, -scheme*; **housing screw**, a screw by means of which the rollers in a rolling-mill can be adjusted and the width of the bar of metal controlled.

1899 W. T. Stead in *Daily News* 19 July 5/5 Milner had charge of the *Housing Question after the boom was launched. 1918 D. Lloyd George *Slings & Arrows* (1929) 199 Your *housing schemes must, in the majority of cases, be schemes outside the town. 1884 W. H. Greenwood *Steel & Iron* xvi. (ed. 2) 328 The *housing screws are made to revolve in either direction or to remain stationary. 1888 *Lockwood's Dict. Mech. Engin.*, *Housing Screws*, the screws which pass through the caps of rail mill housings for the adjustment of the rolls.

Housing, *sb.*[2] **3.** Add: **housing-strap**, a strap which pulls together the sides of a horse's collar.

1908 *Anim. Managem.* (War Office) 204 The 'housing strap' which brings the sides together, often stretches to such an extent that the collar is not properly closed.

Hova (hōu·vă, hǫ·vá). Also **Ovah.** [Malagasy.] **a.** A member of the dominant race of Madagascar; also, in restricted use, one of the middle class, as distinct from the nobles and the slaves. **b.** The language of this race. Also *attrib.*

1839 *Penny Cycl.* XIV. 259/2 The Ovahs. who inhabit the elevated plains in the interior, are in height rather above the European standard. 1868 Oliver in *Jrnl. Anthrop. Inst.* (Encycl. Brit. XV. 176/1) The Hòvas and other Characteristic Tribes of Madagascar. 1883 *Encycl. Brit.* XV. 171/1 The Hòva, who occupy the central province of Imérina. *Ibid.* 172/2 The majority of Hòva houses are built of layers of the hard red clay of the country. 1887 *Fortn. Rev.* Mar. 435 Only a few months ago French politicians..called the Hovas barbarians.

Hoven, *ppl. a.* Add: Also as *sb.*

1845 S. Judd *Margaret* II. v. 284 Glad you got through with the pock so well...It's worse than horn-ail, hoven, or core. 1877 *Rep. Vermont Dairym. Assoc.* VIII. 107 Hoven in cattle is caused by over-feeding upon succulent food like green clover. 1902 *Phil. Trans.* CXCIX. A. 400 The symptoms of 'hoven' are not unlike those of prussic acid poisoning.

Hovering, *vbl. sb.* Add: **d.** The practice of smuggling.

1907 *Westm. Gaz.* 21 Feb. 5/1 The fraud charged against them was that of taking, hovering, and dealing in saccharin, which was subject to duty. 1908 Atton & Holland *King's Customs* 198 The officers..were directed [in 1727] to make the master enter into a 'hovering bond'.

Hoving (hōu·viŋ), *vbl. sb.* [Hove *v.*[2]] Swelling (of cheese).

1811 [see Hove *v.*[2] 3]. 1858 C. L. Flint *Milch Cows* etc. 265 Heat would make them [*sc.* cheeses] sweat..which extracts the fat, and tends to induce hooving.

Hovite (hōu·vait). *Min.* [f. *Hove*, a suburb of Brighton, its locality + -ite[1].] A soft white mineral composed of aluminium and calcium.

1862 J. H. & G. Gladstone in *Phil. Mag.* Ser. IV. XXIII. 465 If it should bear a distinct name, it may be termed Hovite, from the place where it was first recognized. 1868 Dana *Syst. Min.* (ed. 5) 709.

How, *sb.*[3] **2.** (Examples of U.S. colloq. usage.)

1845 W. G. Simms *Wigwam & Cabin* Ser. I. 7 You joined the army again, and come in with Greene? Was that the how? 1878 J. H. Beadle *Western Wilds* ii. 27 Daddy went off at last, and that was the how of my first trip. 1904 W. H. Smith *Promoters* iii. 74 We get up close to 'em, somehow or some other how. 1916 'B. M. Bower' *Phantom Herd* xvi. 272, I calc'late that's about the how of it.

How, *adv.* (*sb.*[3]). Add:

4. c. *How much*: used in facetiously vulgar requests for the repetition of something not heard or not understood. Also, *How much?* = What? Eh? (Cf. *What price* so-and-so?)

1852 F. E. Smedley *Lewis Arundel* xxxiv, 'Then my answer must mainly depend on the exact height of the principles.' 'On the how much?' inquired Frere, considerably mystified. 1928 'Sapper' *Female of Species* v. 76 'A lounge lizard. A ballroom snake. What matter that his Black Bottom is the best in London.' 'My Gawd! sir,' gasped the other. 'His 'ow much?'

d. *And how!* humorous (and vulgar) U.S. colloq. expression used chiefly as an intensive or ironically.

1932 J. W. Drawbell *Good Time!* xvii. § 3 'How's that for your orders from a typical American woman?' 'You mean it, Peggy?' 'And how!' 'Baby!'

How (hau), colloq. abbreviation of Howitzer.

1915 *Times* 14 Apr. 7 The boom in the distance from one of our 'hows'. 1919 C. P. Thompson *Cocktails* 133 A couple of batteries of heavy Hows.

Howardite (hau·ărdait). *Min.* [f. the name of Edward *Howard*, who demonstrated in 1802 the presence of nickel in meteoric iron: see -ite[1].] A silicate of magnesium and iron found in certain meteorites. So **Howardi·tic** *a.*

1848 *Amer. Jrnl. Sci.* Ser. II. VI. 253 A mineral which though frequent in meteoric stones, has never yet been distinctly recognized, and which in a future paper on American Meteorites, I shall more particularly describe under the name of *Howardite*, after the Hon. Mr. Howard. 1916 *Min. Mag.* XVIII. 36 The angrites, nakhlites, howardites, eucrites, and sherghottites..are richer in lime..than chondritic stones generally.

How-come. *U.S. colloq.* (See quot. 1848.)

1848 Bartlett *Dict. Amer.*, *How-come?* rapidly pronounced huc-cum, in Virginia. Doubtless an English phrase, brought over by the original settlers, and propagated even among the negro slaves. The meaning is, How did what you tell me happen? How came it? 1897 R. M. Stuart *Simpkinsville* 230 She heard Miss Euphemia wonderin' the other day how come the right shoulder of her black silk dress to wear out. 1930 *Saturday Even. Post* (N.Y.) 8 Mar. 12/1 These firms assert blandly to..journalists who ring them up, wishful to know how come, they have nothing against women.

How-come-ye-so, *adj. phr. dial.* or *slang.* Tipsy.

1816 *Monthly Mag.* 1 July 494/2 [Degrees of intoxication.] How came you so. 1824 T. Hook *Sayings & Doings* Ser. I. *Merton* xiii, She used to be—'Lord, how come ye so!' every night. 1827 J. F. Cooper *Red Rover* x, It is quite in reason to believe that your husband was..a little of what I call how-come-ye-so. 1843 *Knickerbocker Mag.* XXII. 366 We were never 'groggy', 'intoxicated',..'how-came-ye-so'..or 'tight', but once.

Howden (hau·dən). The name of James *Howden*, Scottish engineer, used *attrib.* to denote a system of forced draught in which the air supplied to the furnace is warmed by the waste heat from the gases formed by combustion. So **How·denize** *v. trans.*, to equip or furnish with the Howden system.

1901 *Engineer* 29 Mar. 323/3 Years ago we advocated an experiment with the Howden system; a system which has now been fitted with success to boilers generating steam for over 600,000 indicated horse-power. *Ibid.*, Until the water-tube boiler question has been settled, let our ships be fitted with cylindrical boilers of proper design, and, in the case of one or more ships, 'Howdenised'. 1902 *Encycl. Brit.* XXVI. 283/2 Forced draught is not uncommon, the Howden system being that usually adopted.

Howel, *v.* (Earlier U.S. example.)

1846 *Rep. U.S. Comm. Patents* (1847) 339 What I claim therein as new..is the attaching the howeling, crozing, and chamfering cutters.

Howl, *sb.* Add: **1. b.** A noise resembling an animal's howl, heard from wireless receivers, and due usually to low-frequency oscillation.

1921 *Wireless World* 10 Dec. 568/1 Ear-splitting howls associated with valve reception. 1927 *Even. Standard* 10 Dec. 10/4 A 'wireless howl'. 1928 L. S. Palmer *Wireless Princ.* 374 These [*sc.* noises]..are of audible frequency and constitute the typical 'howl' to which low-frequency amplifiers are subject.

Howl, *v.* Add: **4. b.** Of a wireless receiver (see prec.).

1920 *Radio Rev.* Apr. 356 The resistance R_3 and condenser C_3 connected to the grid of the selected valve are increased in value until maximum amplification is obtained without 'howling'. 1921 L. B. Turner *Wireless Telegr.* 149 Internal resistance in the common anode battery provides such retroaction, and is sometimes responsible for the 'howling' of low-frequency amplifiers. 1926 *Westm. Gaz.* 5 Feb., If the 'note' does not change, the interference is due to some external source, probably 'howling' on the part of a neighbour. 1928 L. S. Palmer *Wireless Princ.* 379 Low-frequency howling.

Howler. Add: **1. c.** A howling storm.

1894 Susan Hale *Lett.* (1919) 286 I'm thankful my Robert got off yesterday, for wouldn't this have been a howler to drive in.

Howling, *ppl. a.* Add: **4.** As *adv.* In the highest degree. (Cf. *screamingly*.)

1895 *Century Mag.* Sept. 678/2 It's howling lonesome at the Mule Deer. 1928 *Saturday Even. Post* 4 Feb. 100/4 Glad! You're howling right I'm glad!

Howlite (hau·ləit). *Min.* [f. the name of H. *How*, mineralogist of Nova Scotia + -lite.] A white hydrous borosilicate of calcium occurring in Nova Scotia.

1868 Dana *Syst. Min.* (ed. 5) 598 Howlite...A hydrous borate of lime, similar to bechilite, combined with one-sixth of a silicate, analogous to danburite.

Hsien, var. of *Hien.

Huaca (wā·kă). [Sp. *huaca, guaca*, from Quichua.]

1. The name for the all-pervading spirit thought by the Peruvian Indians to be disseminated through the whole world; also, any material object thought to be the abode of such a spirit. **2.** A prehistoric Peruvian tomb or temple, usually a truncated pyramid of stone, and often of immense size.

1862 D. Wilson *Preh. Man* I. ix. 298 The huacas or tombs of the Incas. 1875 *Encycl. Brit.* II. 452/2 The most interesting remains in Peru are those called *Huacas*; but whether they were forts, or palaces, or tombs, is not as yet clearly ascertained. 1901 Keane & Markham *Central & S. Amer.* I. 208 Of these ruins the largest, as well as the most characteristic, are the truncated pyramids here [*sc.* Peru] called *huacas*, or burying-places. 1902 *Encycl. Brit.* XXV. 380/1 The most prolific source of Peruvian relics is the sepulchres or huacas.

Huaco (wā·ko). Also **guaco.** [See quot.] In Peru, Bolivia, and Chile, ancient pottery and other Indian antiquities.

1931 *Connoisseur* Feb. 95 The term *huaco* is derived from the Indian word, *huaca*, meaning 'a holy place', and refers to the cemeteries and tombs from which, with few exceptions, all the examples of pre-Incaic art are obtained. *Ibid.* 97 The linear decoration of the stirrup *huacos* tend to portray some form of action...In the static *huacos* the legs are almost invariably crossed.

Huantajayite (wāntāhəi·əit). *Min.* [f. *Huantajaya*, Peru, the locality where found + -ite[1].] A variety of sodium chloride, containing a small proportion of silver chloride, found as cubic crystals or as an incrustation.

1877 Dana *Text-bk. Min.* 237 Huantajayite.—Composition 20 NaCl + AgCl. 1912 *Brit. Museum Return* 193.

Huascolite (wā·skələit). *Min.* [f. *Huasco*, Chile + -lite.] A variety of galenite containing some zinc sulphide, found near Huasco and elsewhere.

1868 Dana *Syst. Min.* (ed. 5) 42.

Hub[1]. Add: **3. b.** Phr. (U.S.). *From hub to tire*: completely, entirely. *Up to the hub* (earlier examples).

1800 *Aurora* (Philad.) 23 May (Th.) This is not a half-measure—I like to do things by the lump—and this bill you will allow is up to the hub. Those who are acquainted with the slang language of the American Caucuses will be able to explain what is meant by up to the hub. 1815 D. Humphreys *Yankey in England* 33 I've bin up to the hub, and didn't flinch..nor won't back out now. 1899 E. E. Hale *Lowell & Friends* 161 In the war the magazine was loyal from hub to tire.

5. hub-brake, a brake applied at the hub of a wheel of a vehicle; so **hub-braking**; **hub-plank** *U.S.*, a guard plank running horizontally along the side of a bridge at the height of a wagon-wheel hub.

1904 *Westm. Gaz.* 23 Nov. 6/3 A hub-brake has many points of superiority to a rim-brake. 1909 *Daily Chron.* 20 Mar. 8/5 It combines hand control and hub braking.

Hubara, var. *Houbara.

Hubbard (hǫ·bărd). *U.S.* In full *Hubbard squash*: A winter squash with yellow flesh and dark green rind, 'the chief pie squash of the U.S.' (Webster, 1911).

1924 P. G. Wodehouse *Leave it to Psmith* xiii. § 4. 303 Try to remember sometimes that that thing balanced on your collar is a head, not a hubbard squash. 1925 *Brit. Weekly* 26 Feb. 520/5 It was truly an old-fashioned Thanksgiving dinner. We had..celery, onions, and hubbard squash.

Hubris (hiū·bris). Chiefly *Public School* and *Univ. colloq.* [Engl. pronunc. of Gr. ὕβρις (cf. *Hybris).] Wanton insolence.

1884 *Daily News* 28 Oct. (Ware) Boys of good family, who have always been toadied, and never been checked, who are full of health and high spirits, develop what Academic slang knows as *hubris*, a kind of high-flown insolence.

Hubristically (hiubri·stikăli), *adv.* [See -ly[2].] With hubris; in an insolent manner.

1907 *Athenæum* 19 Oct. 473/1 He was..rather inclined to treat cavalierly, not to say hubristically, the quiet people who [etc.].

Hubshee (hǫ·bʃi), *a.* and *sb.* *India.* Also 7 **Hobsy**, 8 **Hobshy, -ee, Habashi**, 9 **hubshi.** [Pers. حبشي *ḥabshī*, Arab. *ḥabashi*, of or belonging to Habesh or Abyssinia.] **A.** *adj.* Abyssinian, Ethiopian; applied in India also to African negroes.

1698 Fryer *Acc. E. India & P.* 147 They speak of his *Hobsies* after this manner, That with their Swords they are able to cut down Man and Horse. *Ibid.* 168 He being from an *Hobsy Cophir* made a free Denizen. 1757 Grose *Voy. E.-Indies* 238 The Moors are also fond of having Abyssinian slaves. known in India by the name of Hobshee Coffrees. 1888 *Contemp. Rev.* Feb. 167 'Hubshees', who looked, though they were not, Negroes, have in India carved out thrones. 1903 Kipling *Five Nations* 95 Oh Hubshee, carry your shoes in your hand. [1900 Deniker *Races of Man* 437 The term 'Abyssinian' has only a political signification, like that of 'Austrian' for example; it is a corruption of the word 'Hubeshi' ('mixed'), which the Arabs formerly gave in derision to the inhabitants of the Abyssinian plateau united together into a Christian state.]

B. *sb.* **1.** A negro.

1789 *Seir Mutaqherin* III. 36 *note* (Y.), In India Negroes, *Habissinians, Nobis* (*i.e.* Nubians), &c., &c., are promiscuously called *Habashies* or *Habissians*, although the two latter are no Negroes. 1901 Kipling *Kim* vii, I would not appear to her as a *hubshi* (nigger).

2. A Himalayan pony with short curly hair.

1884 Sir J. Hooker in Yule *Hobson-Jobson* s.v., One of my Tibetan ponies had short curly brown hair, and was called ..by my servants..'a Hubshee'. I understood that the name was specific for that description of pony amongst the traders.

Huchen (hū·kən). [G., = a kind of trout.] A large elongated salmonoid fish of the Danube, *Hucho hucho*. So **Hucho** (hū·ko) [mod.L.], **Huck** (hŭk) [anglicization of G. *huch*].

1889 *Cent. Dict.*, Huchen, Hucho, Huck. 1897 *Encycl. Sport* I. 14/1 Mahseer in India, the hucho in Bavaria, the monster trout of the Canadian lakes..are alike taken by the spinning rod. 1903 G. W. Hartley *Wild Sport* iii. 52 In the still pools..swims a fish called in German huchen. 1905 *Westm. Gaz.* 15 Aug. 2/2 The huchen is excellent food.

Huckleberry. Add: phr. *A huckleberry to a persimmon*: see Persimmon 3.

Huddledom (hǫ·d'ldəm). [f. Huddle *sb.* + -dom.] A state or condition of confusion and disorder.

1923 *Glasgow Herald* 24 May 9 The huddledoms of haunting disease, poverty, and overcrowding. *Ibid.* 31 May 6 Into this huddledom..came a youth, David Watt Torrance.

Hudsonian (hǫdsōu·niăn), *a.* [f. the name of an English navigator, Henry *Hudson* (died *c* 1611), discoverer of the bay, river, and strait in North America which bear his name: see -ian.] Of or pertaining to Hudson's Bay and the surrounding land, or to the fauna and flora of that land.

1872 Coues *N. Amer. Birds* 258 Hudsonian or Black-tailed Godwit. *Ibid.* 262 Hudsonian Curlew. 1884 *Ibid.* (ed. 2) 267 P[*arus*] *hudsonicus*...Hudsonian Titmouse.

Huemul, variant of *Guemul.

Huff, *v.* **7.** (Earlier U.S. example.)

1800 *Aurora* (Philad.) 18 Dec. (Th.) The Philadelphia Gazette is buffed at our stating a fact.

Huffle, *v.* Add: **2. c.** Of the wind: To make a sound as of blowing in gusts. Hence **Hu·ffle** *sb.*, a sudden gust of wind, or the noise made by this.

1878 Hardy *Ret. Native* I. iii, The winds do huffle queerer to-night than ever I heard 'em afore. 1889 Baring-Gould, etc. *Songs of West* 9 At the huffle of the gale, Here I toss and cannot sleep. 1891 'Lucas Malet' *Wages of Sin* vi. ii, A huffle of wind, hot with the festering reek of the streets away across the river, fluttered the leaves...The wind huffled again.

Huggable (hǫ·găb'l), *a.* [f. Hug *v.* + -able.] Such as invites hugging.

1898 D. C. Murray *Tales* 205 Eminently kissable little face; eminently huggable little figure. 1908 *Daily Chron.* 5 Nov. 7/5 The 'Teddy' Bear is such a huggable creature that..he almost compels a caress. 1928 L. Rossiter *Sex Age* viii. § 5 Sorry, Jacko. But you do look so huggable tonight.

Hugh, variant of Huh, Ugh.

1826 J. F. Cooper *Last of Mohicans* xviii, 'Hugh!' exclaimed the young Mohican. 1848 — *Bee-hunter* III. iv. 113 Many were the 'hughs'..of admiration that succeeded this display of desperate manhood!

Hug-me-tight (hǫ·g,mi,tait). *U.S.* [f. the phr. *hug me tight*.]

1. A knitted woollen sleeveless wrap worn by women.

1868 Miss Alcott *Lit. Women* (1869) II. v. 68 She..used to..demand..the meaning of a hug-me-tight, or wonder how a little thing..could possibly be a bonnet. 1910 *New York Even. Post* 24 Dec., Suppl. 3 Hug-me-tights and mittens, all knit at home by grandmother. 1924 *Modern Draper* II. 94 Articles, such as spencers, hug-me-tights, etc., which are worn above the undergarment, and under the outer garment.

2. A type of buggy. Also *attrib.*

1901 Harben *Westerfelt* i, I seed 'em takin' a ride in his new hug-me-tight buggy yesterday. 1902 — *Abner Daniel* v, He's got a new buggy—a regular hug-me-tight.

Hugoesque (hiūgoe·sk), *a.* [f. the name of Victor M. *Hugo* (1802–1885), French author + -esque.] Resembling the character or style of V. Hugo. Also subst. with *the*.

1893 Saltus *Mme. Sapphira* 164 That would be mediæval. I mean nothing so Hugoesque. 1904 *Daily Chron.* 3 Mar. 3/2 There is a touch of the Hugoesque in Rodwell.

Hukm: see *Hookum.

Hula (hū·lă). [Hawaiian.] A Hawaiian women's dance. Also **Hu·la-hu·la.**

1892 Stevenson & Osbourne *Wrecker* xvii, I was entertained to a sea-bathe, indiscriminate cocktails, a dinner, a *hula-hula*. 1899 Morrow *Bohem. Paris* 96 *note*, The hula-hula of the Hawaiian women lacks the grace, dash and abandon of the Turkish dance. 1919 F. O'Brien *White Shadows South Seas* 4 Kelly began 'Tome! Tome!' a Hawaiian hula. 1927 E. W. Springs *Nocturne Militaire* 258 They vibrated like a hula dancer's empennage.

Hule (ū·lĭ). Also **ule, ulé, ulli.** [Mexican (*h*)*ule*, Nahuatl *ulli* or *olli* caoutchouc.] **a.** In full (*h*)*ule-tree*: Any one of several Central American trees of the genus *Castilla* yielding rubber, spec. *Castilla elastica*; also, a composite undershrub, *Parthenium argentatum*, yielding rubber. **b.** The crude rubber yielded by these trees. So **Hule·ro, ule·ro**, a collector of rubber.

1846 Lindley *Veget. Kingd.* 271 The tree Ule of Papantla, from which caoutchouc is obtained in that country. 1880 *Encycl. Brit.* XII. 835/2 Torquemada mentions..that an oil was extracted from the 'ulli', or rubber, by heat, possessing soft and lubricous properties...Even at that early date the Spaniards used the juice of the ulé tree to waterproof their cloaks. 1894 *Outing* (U.S.) XXIII. 353/1 Curious tales the huleros tell of carved rocks hidden in those fastnesses. *Ibid.*, This home of the gatherer of *hule*. 1920 *Edin. Rev.* Oct. 356 The garments he wears are splashed with ulli.

Hull, *sb.*[1] **3.** Add: *spec.* The outer case of a carton in which a manufactured article is packed.

1932 *Daily Tel.* 8 Sept. 14 These are carton 'hulls' of the five brands concerned.

Hullite (hǫ·ləit). *Min.* [f. the name of E. *Hull* of Dublin + -ite[1].] A hydrous silicate of iron, magnesium, and aluminium, occurring as a black massive mineral in basalt near Belfast.

1878 *Proc. R. Irish Acad.* III. 161 On Hullite,..a Hydrous Silicate of peculiar composition, from Carnmoney Hill, Co. Antrim.

Hulwa (hǫ·lwa). *East Indies.* Also 7 **helwa, holway.** [a. Urdū and Arab. حلوا *ḥalwā* sweetmeat.] A kind of sweetmeat.

1662 J. Davies tr. *Olearius' Voy. Ambass.* 311 At Tabris, they make a certain Conserve of it [*sc.* duschab], which they call Helwa. 1698 Fryer *Acc. E. India & P.* 358 Every Friday Night, at the Sacrament of *Holway*, (or Wafer made up in Sweetmeats). 1884 *Times* 30 May 8 Provisions ran short and the voyagers had to live on hulwa, a glutinous sweetmeat.

Hum, *sb.*[1] Add: **1. c.** *Path.* An auscultatory murmur (only in phr. *venous hum*).

1866 Aitken *Pract. Med.* II. 58 The venous murmurs or hums, significant of anæmia. 1876, 1891 [see Venous *a.* 2].

Hum, *v.*[1] **3.** Phr. *To make things hum* (earlier and later U.S. examples).

1887 M. Roberts *Western Avernus* iii. 34 The owner of the farm..came home, and, in American parlance, 'fairly made things hum'. 1902 Eliz. Banks *Newspaper Girl* xviii. 205 We took you on this paper to help us make things hum! I understand you made things hum over in England. 1906 *Nation* (N.Y.) 18 Jan. 44 The colleges are making athletic reform hum, as if to make up for lost time. 1914 Gertrude Atherton *Perch of Devil* I. xxx, I want money to spend in Butte,..and make things hum.

Hum (hǫm), *v.*[3] *colloq.* or *slang.* *intr.* To smell disagreeably. Hence **Hum** *sb.*, a disagreeable smell.

1927 W. E. Collinson *Contemp. Engl.* 23 Things didn't smell, but ponged, niffed or hummed. *Ibid.*, An awful pong or hum.

Huma (hu·mă). [Hind., a. Pers. هما *humā* phœnix.] A fabulous bird of the east, said to be a restless wanderer but to bring luck to any person over whom it hovers.

1858 O. W. Holmes *Aut. Breakf.-t.* i, I am like the Huma, the bird that never lights, being always in the cars, as he is always on the wing. 1905 *Spectator* 14 Jan. 47/2 The legendary 'huma' of Eastern tradition.

Human, *a.* (*sb.*). Add: **3. b.** Belonging or relative to man as distinguished from (*a*) the lower animals; (*b*) machinery or the mechanical element; (*c*) mere objects or events.

1847 Youatt *Pig* (Philadelphia) 86 Mr. Heaton, a human surgeon. 1882 Geikie *Text-bk. Geol.* 901 The long succession of Pleistocene ages shaded without abrupt change of any kind into what is termed the Human or Recent Period. *Ibid.* 902 The Human Period is above all distinguished by the presence and influence of man. 1907 R. Herriot (*title*) The Human Element. A Novel. 1909 *Daily Chron.* 28 Oct. 3/4 Mr. Courtney's fascinating and human volume. 1913 *Pall Mall Mag.* July 46/2 You must remember that in regard to the human element, we are..behind Germany. The point is that they have the human element—a large body of pilots, observers, artisans, trained during the last sixteen years. 1915 W. P. Livingstone *Mary Slessor* II. vii. (1926) 46 The human interest of her story. 1919 Fairgrieve & Young (*title*) Human Geographies. 1920 — *British Isles* p. vi, This series of elementary books is just what its name denotes—human. Everywhere the human note is predominant and the relation of man to his environment insisted upon. 1921 B. S. Rowntree (*title*) The Human Factor in Business. 1924 R. M. Ogden tr. *Koffka's Growth of Mind* 16 To bridge the gap between human and animal-psychology. *Mod.* The accident was attributed to failure of the human element, and not to any defect in the machinery.

B. *sb.* (U.S. examples.)

1830 Frances Trollope *Dom. Manners Amer.* I. 70, I expect the sun will rise and set a hundred times before I shall see another human that does not belong to the family. 1898 H. S. Canfield *Maid of Frontier* i. 18 A man could ride from here to forty-mile the other side of Edwardsville and never see a human. 1902 Wister *Virginian* iv. 56 'They are just like humans', the Virginian concluded. 1924 A. J. Small *Frozen Gold* i. 22 Into that trail staggered the two humans.

2. With *the*: (*a*) The human race, humanity; (*b*) That which is human, that which relates to man or humanity.

1841 Mrs. Browning *Lett.* (1897) I. 88, I may say so now—as far as the human may say 'yes' or 'no' of their futurity. 1844 — *Drama of Exile* 2085 While the human in the minor Makes the harmony diviner. 1919 M. K. Bradby *Psycho-analysis* 205 The distinctively animal gives way in order to express the distinctively human.

Humane, *a.* Add: **1. d.** Applied to certain weapons or implements which inflict less pain than others of their kind, *spec.* applied to an implement for the painless slaughtering of cattle.

1904 *Daily Chron.* 24 May 5/3 The doctors style the bullets 'humane'. 1920 *Act* 10 & 11 *Geo. V* c. 43 § (8) (*d*) Any.. butcher..having in his possession..any humane killer for the purpose of such business. 1927 *Daily Express* 6 Aug. 7/3 That the humane killer was a dangerous instrument to those who used it.

Humanitarian, *sb.* and *a.* Add: **A.** *sb.* **4.** One who holds the doctrine that human nature is self-perfectible without divine grace.

1900 *Westm. Gaz.* 21 Aug. 3/2 'Humanitarian' means the theory which holds that humanity is sufficient for itself without the revelation of a superhuman existence.

Humanization. Add: **c.** The preparation of cows' milk to resemble human milk.

1905 F. L. Dodd *Municipal Milk* 14 The humanization adapts the milk to infants' digestive processes.

Humanized, *ppl. a.* Add: **3.** Of cows' milk: Specially prepared to resemble human milk.

1901 *Westm. Gaz.* 19 Oct. 5/3 The Borough Council of Battersea has determined to undertake the supply of sterilised and humanised milk. 1905 *Brit. Med. Jrnl.* 15 Apr. 830/1 The composition..of many of the so-called 'humanized' milks varies widely.

Humanly, *adv.* Add: **1. b.** By men; by human hands or agency.

1908 *Westm. Gaz.* 19 Feb. 12/1 The humanly uninhabitable structure. 1915 E. Ray Lankester *Divers. Naturalist* 291 Humanly cut elephant-bone recently found at Piltdown.

Humanoid (hiū·mănoid), *a.* [f. Human *a.* + -oid.] Of human form, man-like: distinguished from *anthropoid* as being more human in character.

1918 Mrs. D. G. Ritchie *New Warden* xvi, The funk and cunning of the humanoid ape. 1922 *Glasgow Herald* 23 Dec. 4 Then came the separating off of the larger Anthropoid Apes, leaving the main stem humanoid. *Ibid.*, As the humanoid brain grew finer.

Hum-bird. (Later U.S. examples.)

1833 C. A. Davis *Lett. J. Downing* (1834) 6 They both came within a humbird's eye of it. 1889 Farmer *Amer.*, *Hum Bird* or *Hummer*.—Popular names of the humming bird, chiefly the *Trochilus colubris*. 1891 Rose T. Cooke *Huckleberries* 167 (Th.), I never see a humbird fuller o' buzz than little Prudy.

Humboldt (hu·mboult). The name of F. H. Alexander von *Humboldt* (1769–1859) used attrib. or in the genitive to denote a current of the South Pacific Ocean which sweeps northward and westward along the coasts of Chile and Peru (also called the Peruvian current).

1865 *Chambers's Encycl.* VII. 183/1 The cold Current of Peru or Humboldt's current. 1927 Kendrew *Climates Cont.* 306 The cold waters of the Humboldt current.

Humbug, *v.* **2.** (Additional U.S. example.)

1841 R. H. Dana *Bef. Mast* xxxiv, For several days we lay 'humbugging about' in the Horse latitudes, with all sorts of wind and weather.

Humgruffin. Add: Also **humgruffian.**

1825 Paulding *J. Bull in Amer.* iv. 29 Another declared she would not give a pin to save such a rude humgruffian from starvation.

Humhum. *Hist.* Also 7 **hammome, hamaone, hummum,** 8 **hump-hump.** [Origin obscure.] A coarse Indian cotton cloth.

1620 in W. Foster *Eng. Factories India* (1906) 193 Of sahannes and hammomes thiere are but fewe at presant in towne. 1687 *Lond. Gaz.* No. 2269/2, 4172 pieces of Hummums. 1696 J. F. *Merch. Wareho. laid open* 22, I shall begin with a Callico called Hummums. 1745 in J. F. Watson *Ann. Philad.* (1877) I. 191 Quilted humhums, turkettees, grassetts, [etc.]. *a* 1793 Freneau *Poems* (1809) I. 31 Hum-hums are here—and muslins—what you please. 1801 in C. Cist *Cincinnati* (1851) 179 Among other goods..humhums. 1820 *Massachusetts Spy* 5 Jan. (Th.) The bleach rotted linen..or the sleazy humhum. [1894 Alice M. Earle *Costume* (*Amer.*) *Col. Times* 142 *Hum-hum*, a plain coarse-meshed Indian fabric made of cotton, much advertised in the middle of the [18th] century. We read of 'blue Humhums' and 'Hump-humps for Sacks' for sale in various Boston newspapers, from 1750 to 1770.]

Humic, *a.* Add: **2.** *sb. pl.* Humic elements.

1857–8 *Trans. Ill. Agric. Soc.* (1859) III. 410 The soils in this portion of Illinois not only need 'humics', for the successful growth of cereals, but the earth should be kept loose.

Humidor (hiū·midǭr). [f. Humid *a.*, after *cuspidor*.] A box, cabinet, or room in which cigars or tobacco are kept moist; also, any apparatus, such as damp sponges, for keeping cigars, the atmosphere, etc., moist. Also **Hu·midostat** (*Cent. Dict.* Suppl. 1909).

1903 *Sun* (N.Y.) 4 Mar. 6/3 (Funk) A humidor as large as a small cottage occupies most of the ground floor. 1922 *Detective Mag.* Nov. 100 The cigar was soft and fresh from the humidor. 1927 P. Marks *Lord of Himself* 198 Take a cigarette out of that humidor.

Humilific (hiūmili·fik), *a.* (*sb.*). [f. L. *humilis* Humble + -fic.] Humiliating, self-depreciating, that humiliates or tends to humble; also as *sb.*, a humble expression. (Opp. to *honorific*.)

1892 *Spectator* 13 Feb. 244/1 Among the Chinese and Japanese..merely honorific and humilific expressions. 1904 V. V. Banford in *Ideals of Science & Faith* 120 The distinction between honorific and humilific occupations. 1905 Sladen *Playing the Game* I. vii, That conversation..so full of the 'unfortunate mistake' vein, so burdened down with Japanese 'humilifics'.

Hummaul, Hummaum: see Hammal, Hammam.

Hummel, *a.* Add: **1. b.** Applied to a hornless stag. Also *absol.*

1907 *Spectator* 5 Jan. 11/1 For battles [between stags] the 'switch-horn'..is a more efficacious weapon than the head of the 'royal'; and, what is yet more remarkable, the 'hummel' stag—that ungainly beast with no horns at all—is a better fighter than the 'switch-horn'. *Ibid.* 11/2 The supremacy of the 'hummels' and 'switch-horns' in battles with their own kind. 1925 J. Buchan *John Macnab* iv, A hummel, a great fellow of fully twenty stone.

Humming-bird. **b.** Add: **humming-bird fly.**

1926 *Nat. Hist. Oxford Distr.* 260 'Humming bird flies.' These beautiful hairy insects are frequently seen in gardens and woods hovering over flowers.

Hummingly (hǫ·miŋli), *adv.* [See -ly[2].] With a humming sound.

1908 *Daily Chron.* 21 Jan. 6/5 He..endeavours to follow the service and join hummingly in the hymns. 1923 *Daily Mail* 6 Aug. 6 However warm the sun and hummingly populous the air, they [*sc.* the swifts] will go.

Humous (hiū·məs), *a.* [f. Humus + -ous.] Relating to or derived from humus. (Cf. *humus acid* s.v. Humus b.)

1909 tr. *Warming's Oecology of Plants* 195 The weightiest cause of the physiological dryness of the soil probably lies in the presence of free humous acids.

Hump, *sb.*[1] Add: **1. c.** Also, the flesh of the hump of other animals.

1861 Andersson *Okavango River* 130 Rhinoceros hump was..a frequent and favourite dish of mine. 1863 rhinoceros hump [see Rhinoceros 3]. 1909 *Daily Chron.* 5 Jan. 4/7 'Humps have arrived.' So runs the legend in an old-established shop in Green-street, Leicester-square. *Ibid.*, A beef hump. 1913 Pettman *Africanderisms*, *Hump*... A favourite piece with South African housewives for salting.

d. *To live on one's hump*: to be self-sufficient, to do without external resources: with reference to the camel's hump as a reserve of nourishment.

1909 *Westm. Gaz.* 11 Sept. 7/2 During nearly three weeks in this glorious place I have lived on my own hump.

3. b. A walk or tramp with a load on one's back. (Cf. Hump *v.* 2.) *Austral. slang.*

1890 'R. Boldrewood' *Miner's Right* v, We get a fair share of exercise without a twenty-mile hump on Sundays.

4. *hump rib* (earlier U.S. example); **hump speed** (see quot.).

1839 J. K. Townsend *Narr. Rocky Mts.* iii. 164 They.. appeared to be surveying, with the keenness of morning appetite, the fine '*hump ribs' which were roasting before them. 1922 *Encycl. Brit.* XXX. 52/1 Above 4/10 of the minimum flying speed, called the '*hump' speed, the water resistance due to wave-making begins to fall. From the hump speed onwards these hydroplane resistances decrease.

Hump, *sb.*[2] *U.S. colloq.* [f. Hump *v.* 3.] Exertion, effort.

1892 *Harper's Mag.* Feb. 487/2 We do seem to be gittin' a leetle less hump on oursel's than we did then.

Hump, *v.* Add: **1. d.** *transf.* of inanimate things.

1901 'Linesman' *Words by Eyewitness* (1902) 168 With the berg humping its mighty shoulders far behind them.

3. (Later U.S. and other examples.) orig. *U.S. slang.*

1908 G. H. Lorimer *J. Spurlock* i. 9 He..said to the cop on guard, 'One of them Ha'voids [= Harvard students]', and to me, 'Hump yourself'. 1928 'Sapper' *Female of Species* ii, Peter—your Sunbeam, and hump yourself. *Ibid.* xiv, That finger will connect with the trigger and the result will connect with you. So, hump yourself.

b. In extended use.

1905 *Smart Set* Sept. 117/1 You'll have to get this machine to hump it all she knows. 1929 Priestley *Good Companions* 3 As you look down on Bruddersford, you feel..that it is only biding its time, that it will hump its way through somehow.

Humpback, *sb.* (*a.*). Add: **A. 3.** Also = *humpback salmon.

1913 *Chambers's Jrnl.* Oct. 729/1 The 'steel-head', the 'dog-salmon', and the 'humpback'.

B. humpback butterfish, salmon (see next).

1884 Goode *Fish. Industr. U.S.* 477 In economic value the Hump-back Salmon is far inferior to the Quinnat.

Hump-backed, *a.* Add: **hump-backed butterfish**, *Selene setipinnis*; **hump-backed salmon** = Haddo.

1884 Goode *Fish. Industr. U.S.* 323 Woods Holl, Massachusetts, where it [*sc.* the Blunt-nosed Shiner] has a peculiar name, the people there calling it the 'Hump-backed Butterfish'. 1902 *Encycl. Brit.* XXVI. 391/1 The dog-salmon and the humpbacked have no commercial value.

Humped, *ppl. a.* Add: Also *humped-up.*

18.. Roosevelt *Hunting Trips* 110 (Cent. Dict.) The cattle..standing humped up in the bushes. 1906 W. S. Maugham *Bishop's Apron* v. 71 The coachman..sat on his box in a slovenly, humped-up fashion.

Humpty. Add: Also as *sb.*, a low padded cushion seat, a dumpty.

1924 *Drapery Sale Catal.*, Humptys and Cushions. 1926 *Brit. Weekly* 18 Mar. 600/2 The ladies of the village are busy making 'humpties', soft cushion seats to pull up on the rug before the peat fire. 1928 *Daily Express* 23 Jan. 5/2 Home-made Humpty.

Hun, *sb.* Add: **4.** *gen.* A person of uncultured or brutal conduct or character; *esp.* during and since the war of 1914–18 applied, often without animus, to the Germans (or their allies); a German. Also *attrib.*

[The immediate source of the application of *Hun* to the Germans was the speech delivered by Wilhelm II to the German troops about to sail for China on 27 July 1900. See the following quots.:—

1900 *Times* 30 July 5/3 According to the Bremen *Weser Zeitung* the Emperor said [27 July at Bremerhaven]:—'.. No quarter will be given, no prisoners will be taken. Let all who fall into your hands be at your mercy. Just as the Huns a thousand years ago, under the leadership of Etzel (Attila) gained a reputation in virtue of which they still live in historical tradition, so may the name of Germany become known in such a manner in China that no Chinaman will ever again even dare to look askance at a German.' 1900 *Daily News* 20 Nov. 5/3 Herr Bebel [in the Reichstag] dwelt..at some length on the so-called Hun letters, and stigmatized the cruel and barbarous methods of European warfare in China. 1900 *Times* 21 Nov. 5/2 A great portion of the speech of the Socialist leader [Bebel] was devoted to the so-called 'Letters from the Huns' (*Hunnenbriefe*)—epistles from German soldiers in China to their relatives at home giving an account of the cruelties which have been perpetrated by the army of occupation.]

1784–5 in *Navy Rec. Soc.* (1906) XXXI. 55 Andrew Duff, Midshipman. Dead. A drunken Hun. 1861 H. Timrod *Carolina* iv. iii. Shout! let it reach the startled Huns! And roar with all thy festal guns! It is the answer of thy sons, Carolina!

1902 Kipling *Rowers* Poems (1919) II. 58 In sight of Peace ..With a cheated crew, to league anew With the Goth and the shameless Hun! 1914 — in *Queen* 5 Sept. 388/2 Stand up and meet the war. The Hun is at the gate! 1915 E. Candler in *Daily Mail* 5 Apr. 4/3 She [*sc.* a Norfolk girl] told me how the eldest [brother 'at the front'] had held up three 'Huns' in a mill...She used the word 'Hun' quite naturally, with no hint of contempt or bitterness. 1915 *Chambers's Jrnl.* Oct. 664/2 Hun-employment no longer exists in this country. 1916 Boyd Cable *Action Front* 133 Do you suppose our friend the Flighty Hun won't have a peep at us to-morrow morning? 1920 Rose Macaulay *Potterism* II. i. 58 He would have to include among his jingoes and Hun-haters some fighting men too.

b. A flying cadet: see quots. *Air Force slang.*

1916 H. Barber *Aeroplane Speaks* 36 The Aeroplane.. remonstrates..'See the Medical Officer, you young Hun.' 1918 Roberts *Flying Fighter* 333 An aeroplane..was flying over the street, but I don't know what the couple of British Huns in it were trying to do. *Ibid.* 336 Every pilot is a Hun until he has received his wings. 1925 Fraser & Gibbons *Soldier & Sailor Words* s.v., The word 'Hun'..was used.. for a newly-joined young officer qualifying for his 'wings', in consequence of the destructive effect on the instructional aeroplanes which young officers while learning to fly usually had.

Hence **Hu·nland**, Germany; **Hu·nnish** *a.* (see sense *4), whence **Hu·nnishness.**

1916 *Daily Mail* 1 Nov. 4/4 Gott strafe England.., the recognised toast throughout Hunland. 1918 *Punch* 27 Mar. 207/2 The Hunnish conduct of the German officer who egged on the natives. 1920 *Glasgow Herald* 20 Nov. 5 No such sentiments could be admitted in Hunland. 1924 C. J. Tolley *Mod. Golfer* 7 The only piece of Hunnishness we ever encountered at Heidelberg was at the hands of an appalling doctor, who..thought fit to inoculate us against every known disease. 1928 *Manchester Guardian Weekly* 2 Nov. 350/2 Once give the better England clear evidence that Hunnishness is not the sole attribute of the German spirit, and [etc.].

Hun, variant of *Hoon.

Hunch, *sb.* Add:

1. b. A hint, 'tip'. (Cf. next, 2 c.)

1901 H. McHugh *John Henry* 57 The reason it's so good is because I took my hunch from Rud. Kipling's style. 1922 Z. Grey *To the last man* ii. 36 All shootin' arms an' such are at a premium in the Tonto...An' I was givin' you a hunch to come loaded.

4. A premonition or intuitive feeling that something will happen; a presentiment.

1904 S. E. White *Silent Places* xviii. 200 'I hope your hunch is a good one', replied Dick. 1907 R. W. Service *Songs of Sourdough* (1908) 52 Then you've a haunch [*sic*] what the music meant. 1918 E. M. Roberts *Flying Fighter* 62 This particular night Fritz had a hunch that somebody was going to pass the place behind the screen. 1926 Cole *Blatchington Tangle* xiii. 97, I had an awful hunch what it was.

Hunch, *v.* Add: **2. b.** *intr.* To push or lunge forward. *U.S.*

1911 S. E. White *Bobby Orde* xvii. (1916) 196 Bending to his task the pusher at the rear dug his toes in, while the others hunched. 1913 Gene Stratton-Porter *Laddie* v, She sat astride the foot-log, and hunched along with her hands. 1925 Mulford *Cottonwood Gulch* xix. 259 They hunched closer, hugging knees under chin.

c. To nudge (a person) so as to direct attention to something. Also *fig.* *U.S.*

1846–52 Mrs. Whitcher *Widow Bedott P.* xx. 207 She kept a hunchin' Miss Coon and grinnin'. 1884 'Mark Twain' *Huck. Finn* xxv. 246 Then the king he hunched the duke, private. 1906 *Life* 1 Feb. 147 Soon some fellow hunched the Legislature, and then there had to be more or less investigating done.

3. Also without *up.*

1906 U. Sinclair *Jungle* xviii, Hiding his hands in his pockets and hunching his shoulders together. 1906 'K. Howard' *Old Game* II. i. 54 She merely hunched her shoulders, swung on her heel, and marched off.

4. To 'hump', to carry on one's back. *slang.*

1918 W. J. Locke *Rough Road* xix. 236 If you knew what it was to hunch a horrible canvas sausage of kit about.

Hunched, *a.* Add: Also with advs.

1920 *Chambers's Jrnl.* 110/1 A long..sinuous beast that hopped in a series of bunched-up bounds. 1921 Mulford *Bar-20 Three* xxi. 267 He..clawed himself into a saddle.. and rode for safety, hunched over and but half conscious.

Hundi, variant of *Hoondi.

Hundred, *sb.* and *a.* Add:

1. b. (*b*) *Hundred Years' War*, the intermittent war between England and France from 1337 to 1453, arising out of the claim of the English kings to the French crown.

1874 Green *Short Hist. Eng. People* 275 The Hundred Years' War had ended.

2. b. Phrases. *Not a hundred miles from; within a hundred miles of*: near, close to, in or at. *A hundred of bricks*: see *Brick *sb.*[1] 5. *A hundred to one*: a hundred chances to one; hence, an expression indicating very slight probability.

1821 *Kaleidoscope* 27 Feb. 277/3 A sporting gentleman passing by a house, not a hundred miles from —— street. 1825 P. Egan *Anecd. Turf* 270 Within one hundred miles of the great Chancery shop of the kingdom. 1852 *Leisure Hour* I. 52/2 Scandalous transactions said to have transpired between two 'well-known' individuals 'not a hundred miles off'. 1903 'J. M'Govan' *Brought to Bay* 74 This retreat, he admitted, was not a hundred miles from the spot where they were at that moment seated.

c. *A* or *one hundred per cent.*: used adjectivally or adverbially with the meaning 'entire(ly), complete(ly)'. Hence *hundred-per-center, hundred-per-centism.* orig. *U.S.*

1911 H. S. Harrison *Queed* vii. 90 You do more work in twenty-four hours than you're doing now, besides feelin' one hundred per cent. better all the time. 1923 *Westm. Gaz.* 1 Jan., An administrator is 100 per cent. successful only when he gets every individual in the factory..working as enthusiastically as if he were working for himself on his own job. *Ibid.* 9 Feb., Under a hundred per cent. disability. 1926 W. R. Inge *Lay Thoughts* 135 Such detachment would not be possible to a 'hundred per cent. American'. 1928 *Publishers' Weekly* 26 May 2164/2, I have frequently encountered excellent accounting systems which were 100 per cent. useless. 1928 *Observer* 4 Mar. 13/2 Perhaps New York is not the place for the Hundred-per-centers. I certainly never met any. *Ibid.* 8 Apr. 8/2 He is really another victim of hundred-per-centism. 1931 *Times Lit. Suppl.* 29 Jan. 76/3 The inevitable 'honest-to-God' hundred-per-cent. American young man..besieges and wins Valerie's heart.

4. a. (Later U.S. examples.)

1838 *Knickerbocker Mag.* XI. 15 When requested..to say how much flour she should make into bread, at their first baking, she answered..'I suppose about a quarter of a hundred'. 1852 *Trans. Mich. Agric. Soc.* III. 332 To dispose of the compound of acorns, ground nuts and carrion for $2 per hundred. 1861 *Trans. Ill. Agric. Soc.* IV. 373 We want a horse sixteen hands high, that will weigh fifteen hundred.

b. (Later U.S. example.)

1888 *Rep. Vermont Board Agric.* X. 15 At Jericho the average price paid was 86 cents a hundred for milk.

5. b. (Example.)

1815 *Niles' Weekly Register* IX. 72/1 The upper, or most northern county, is divided into nine hundreds.

Hung, *ppl. a.* Add: **3.** *U.S.* Of a jury: (see *Hang *v.* 17 c).

Hungal, variant of *Hangul.

Hungarian, *a.* and *sb.* **A.** *adj.* **1.** Add: *Hungarian blue, bonnet* (see quots.); *Hungarian grass*, the forage-plant *Setaria italica*; Bengal grass.

1824 Loudon *Encycl. Gard.* 49 The variety of grape figured and described by Sickler, in his *Garden Magazine* of 1804, as the *Hungarian blue. 1845 *Encycl. Metrop.* VII. 288/2 The *Hungarian Bonnet, *Pileopsis Ungarica*. 1850 Miss Pratt *Common Things Sea-side* 217 The Torbay night cap or Hungarian bonnet. 1861 *Trans. Ill. Agric. Soc.* IV. 319 *Hungarian grass is a sure preventive. 1883 *Rep. Indian Affairs* 23 About 12 acres were planted with Hungarian grass.

Hunger, *sb.* **4. e.** Add: **hunger bread**, a substitute for bread, made of bark, acorns, or other poor materials, sometimes eaten in times of scarcity, as in Russia; **hunger-cure**, treatment of disease by fasting; **hunger-march**, a march, undertaken usually by unemployed, in order to call attention to their needs and claims; so **hunger-marcher**; **hunger-pain**, pain due to hunger; also *Path.* (see quot.); **hunger-strike**, the action of a person, esp. a prisoner, who refuses food in order to induce another to yield to his demands; so **hunger-strike** *v. intr.*, to go on hunger-strike; **hunger-striker, hunger-striking** *vbl. sb.*; **hunger-swarm**, the swarming of bees due to lack of food.

1906 *Westm. Gaz.* 12 Dec. 7/3 Where *hunger bread is eaten there also is found scurvy and typhoid. 1848 Dunglison *Med. Lex.* (ed. 7), *Hunger-cure. 1908 *Westm. Gaz.* 16 July 10/3 A statement of the purpose of the '*Hunger March'. *Ibid.*, He had no knowledge the '*Hunger Marchers' were coming there that day. 1922 *Ibid.* 29 Dec., Unemployed hunger marchers are persisting in their determination to see the Prime Minister. 1820 *hunger-pain [see Hunger *sb.* 4 a]. 1908 *Practitioner* Dec. 821 This patient gave a history of 'hunger pain' which was so typical that the diagnosis of duodenal ulcer was considered. 1908 *Westm. Gaz.* 18 Mar. 5/1 The Central Prisons Administration has circularised the provincial Governors regarding the so-called '*hunger strikes', which are a characteristic feature of Russian prison life. 1903 H. Chisholm tr. *Leo Deutsch's Sixteen Yrs. in Siberia* 78 Upon these conditions I consented not to prolong my 'hunger-strike'. 1913 Mrs. Pankhurst *My Own Story* (1914) 292 She has *hunger-struck in prison. She submitted herself for more than five weeks to the horrible ordeal of feeding by force. 1916 W. J. Locke *Wonderful Year* xvii. 247 'I've been to prison.' Martin..asked if she hunger-struck. 1922 *Blackw. Mag.* Aug. 146/1 He gave his orders for the release of the *hunger-strikers. 1916 W. J. Locke *Wonderful Year* xxiii. 319 Her duties involved incendiarism, imprisonment, and *hunger-striking. 1870 Pettigrew *Handy Bk. Bees* 150 We have known swarms starved out of their hives. Having made a few pieces of comb, and being without food, no eggs were set in them and the bees, through sheer want, cast themselves on the wide world. These are called '*hunger-swarms'.

Hungry, *a.* **2. a.** Add: *The hungry forties*, the decade beginning in 1840, characterized in England by much distress and poverty.

1905 Mrs. C. Unwin (*title*) The Hungry Forties.

Hunk, *sb.*[1] Add: **3.** = Hunks.

1872 E. Eggleston *End of World* xxiii. 155 It was rather to his credit..that he had..been sent adrift by the old hunk that had tried to make him study Latin.

Hunk, *a.* *U.S.* (Later examples.)

1902 G. H. Lorimer *Lett. Self-made Merchant* viii. 109 Notify father all hunk. Keep it dark from others. 1903 A. H. Lewis *The Boss* xiv. 181 The proposition's all hunk... As to my aid: that depends on whether we come to terms.

Hunkerish (hǫ·ŋkəriʃ), *a.* *U.S.* [f. Hunker *sb.*] Unprogressive.

1905 *Springfield* (Mass.) *Weekly Republ.* 8 Sept. 1 The hunkerish conservatism which Mr. Cannon and the Senate stand for.

Hunkerism (under Hunker *sb.*). *U.S.* (Recent example.)

1906 *Springfield* (Mass.) *Weekly Republ.* 6 Dec. 8 The old republican hunkerism.

Hunky (hǫ·ŋki), *a.* *U.S. slang.* [f. Hunk *sb.*[2] and *a.* + -y[1].] In good condition; safe and sound; all right: = Hunk *a.*

1865 'Artemus Ward' *His Book* (1906) 18, I rewarded him with a approvin smile and said: 'Hunky boy! go it, my gay and festive cuss.' 1878 B. Harte *Man on Beach* 47 She's all hunky, and has an appetite. 1889 K. Munroe *Golden Days* xii. 125 If I'd took good care of that map..we'd been all hunky at this minute. 1907 Mulford *Bar-20* ix. 105 That was all hunky for a while. 1911 E. Ferber *Dawn O'Hara* vii. 89 Rather be hunky and healthy than skinny and sick.

So **Hu·nky-do·ry, Hu·nkido·rum** *adjs.*

1889 Farmer *Amer.*, *Hunkey, Hunkidori.*—Both these strange words stand..for 'superlatively good'. 1906 Neil Munro *Daft Days* xxi, Before one marries it's hunky-dory—it's fairy all the time. 1907 M. C. Harris *Tents of Wickedness* IV. ii. 341 I've had my luncheon, and I feel better already. Oh, it's all hunky-dory.

Hunt, *sb.*[2] Add: **3. b.** *Electr.* and *Mech.* A see-sawing or oscillating movement. (Cf. *Hunt *v.* 7 b.)

1901 *Trans. Amer. Inst. Elect. Engin.* 374 (Cent. D. Suppl.). 1920 *Nature* CV. 46/1 The compass is working two repeaters...The other is a correction repeater;..[the latter] moves backwards and forwards very slightly, and this motion we term the 'hunt'.

Hunt, *v.* Add: **3. b.** (U.S. examples.)

1834 *Visit to Texas* i. 10 An old Tennessean and his wife with their sons were going 'to hunt land'. *Ibid.* xiii. 122 He sometimes sends out three or four men to collect and mark them. This is called hunting cattle. 1891 Marah E. Ryan *Told in Hills* IV. iii. 309 All were sleepy enough to hunt beds early. 1903 A. Adams *Log Cowboy* iii. 38 Flood ..suggested that all hands hunt their blankets and turn in for the night.

7. b. *intr.* To be in a state of instability, to oscillate, to jump backwards and forwards, as a governor when its action is more than is needed to adjust the speed, or as the clutch of an arc-lamp which moves rapidly with variations of current, or as a pair of alternators working in parallel. Also occas. *trans.*

1902 *Encycl. Brit.* XXVIII. 86/1 The 'hunting' or rapid up-and-down movements to which some varieties of clutch mechanism are liable. 1904 *Technol. & Sci. Dict.* (ed. Goodchild & Tweney), *Hunting*, variations of speed of an engine when the governor is not controlling it efficiently. 1905 H. J. Spooner *Motors & Motoring* 58 *footn.*, The tendency of many engines fitted with this valve is to run in jerks..under the action of the governor, or, in other words, the governor hunts. 1922 *Encycl. Brit.* XXX. 42/2 The instrument..continually hunts the apparent vertical.

11. *Hunt up.* (Earlier U.S. example.)

1741 *Coll. S. Carolina Hist. Soc.* IV. 33 The General.. sent out the Indians to hunt up the Spanish horses and cattell.

Huntchak (hǫ·ntʃæk). [Armenian.] An Armenian secret society. So **Hu·ntchakist, Hu·ntchagist**, *pl.* **Huntchaki·sti** *adjs.*, of or pertaining to this society; also as *sb.*, a member of this society.

1899 Mrs. L. M. Elton tr. *Nasarbek's Through the Storm*

Introd. p. xxiii, The Revolutionary Armenian Party..called the Huntchak party. *Ibid.* p. xxv, The Huntchak has made itself the working representative of the political and social aims of Armenia. *Ibid.*, As ardent patriots, the Huntchakists have striven to do their utmost for the good of their own people. 1899 *Westm. Gaz.* 16 June 4/1 The secret agents of the Huntchak. 1902 *Encycl. Brit.* XXV. 636/1 Secret societies, such as the Huntchagist. 1903 *Daily Chron.* 5 Nov. 5/5 The London headquarters of the Huntchakisti.

Hunter. 5. c. Add: **huntor-spider** = sense 3 a.

1867 *Amer. Naturalist* I. Oct. 409 This very large hunter-spider [the tarantula].

Hunting, *vbl. sb.* 3, 3 b. Add: *hunting-camp, -ground, -party, -shirt* (additional U.S. examples); *hunting-shirted* adj.

1805 Lewis in *Ann. 9th Congress* 2 Sess. 1069 [The Algonquins have] establishments on the rivers Winnipie and Rainy Lake, and at their *hunting-camps. 1840 *Knickerbocker Mag.* XVI. 161 We shifted our hunting-camps from place to place, according as we found the game. 1897 *Outing* (U.S.) XXX. 374/2 What will be necessary for the smaller hunting-camp will find its place later on. 1721 *Jrnls. Ho. Repr. Mass.* III. 20 Constantly scouting, hunting and discovering the Rivers, Ponds, Carrying-places and *Hunting-grounds. 1750 G. Croghan *Jrnl.* (1904) 55 The Twightwees..have sent word to the French that if they can find any of their People..on their hunting Ground, that they will make them Prisoners. 1827 J. F. Cooper *Prairie* II. xii. 192 Court-houses are the 'happy hunting-grounds', as a Red-skin would say, for them that are born with gifts no better than such as lie in the tongue. 1805 Sibley in *Ann. 9th Congress* 2 Sess. 1089 Besides these, there are rambling *hunting-parties of them to be met all over Lower Louisiana. 1845 Caroline M. Kirkland *Western Clearings* 3 To pass a night in the woods is a small affair for a hunting-party. 1870 Keim *Sheridan's Troopers* xxvii. (1885) 192 It rarely happens that a hunting-party returns without a fight, or at least, being pursued. c 1805 J. J. Henry *Camp. agst. Quebec* (1812) 15 A deep ash-colored *hunting-shirt. 1835 R. M. Bird *Hawks of Hawk-hollow* I. xix. 247 Two men standing by in green hunting-shirts. 1845 in C. Cist *Cincinnati Misc.* 191 The Hunting Shirt, the emblem of the Revolution, is banished from the national military. 1874 E. Eggleston *Circuit Rider* v. 53 The homespun 'hunting shirt' hangs outside his buckskin breeches. 1835 *Knickerbocker Mag.* I. 310 *Hunting-shirted soldiers.

Hunting, *ppl. a.* b. Add: **hunting-ant, -wasp** (see quots.).

1871 C. Kingsley *At Last* xi. (1892) 224 One of us was stung..by a great hunting-ant. 1916 A. T. de Mattos tr. Fabre (*title*) The Hunting Wasp. 1925 in E. F. Norton *Fight for Everest, 1924* 274 Hunting wasps are common at high altitudes in Tibet. 1928 Hingston *Problems of Instinct* 100 Hunting-wasps, which sting their victims with surgical precision and then drag them off to a nest.

Huntingdonian (hɒntiŋdōᵘ·niăn), *a.* and *sb.* Also erron. **Huntingtonian.** [f. the title of Selina, Countess of *Huntingdon* (1707–91) + -IAN.] Of or pertaining to a religious organization, Calvinistic in doctrine, founded by the Countess of Huntingdon, and called the Countess of Huntingdon's Connexion (occas. the Huntingdon Connexion). Also *sb.*, an adherent of this.

1847 W. Howitt *Homes & Haunts Brit. Poets* II. 21 The Methodist and the Huntingtonian had..become successful rivals.

Hurdle, *sb.* Add: 1. b. Also *pl.*, an athletic event consisting of a hurdle-race.

1887 T. B. Reed *Fifth Form St. Dominics* i. 8 He is certain..to win the mile and the 'hurdles' at the Athletic Sports. 1897 *Isis* 13 Nov. 63/1 Three events..: hundred yards, broad jump, and hurdles. 1905 *The Athlete* Aug. 80/1 R. S. Stromach retained his title in the hurdles. 1930 *Daily Express* 8 Sept. 9/5 In the 80 metres hurdles.

3. *hurdle-maker* (earlier U.S. example).

1786 Washington *Diaries* III. 137 A compleat Wheel right, Waggon builder, and Plow and Hurdle maker.

Hurdle, *v.* Add:

4. *intr.* To run a hurdle-race; to jump over an obstacle, as in a hurdle-race. Also *fig.* Hence **Hu·rdling** *vbl. sb.*; also *attrib.*

1896 G. Ade *Artie* vii. 60 Artie did not know the tune or the words, so he merely whistled it on speculation, and when he came to the doubtful parts he hurdled. 1897 *Encycl. Sport* I. 52/2 Few good sprinters will take to hurdling, as there is little doubt that the mechanical and artificial action necessary in hurdling interferes with speed on the flat. *Ibid.* 53/1 Hurdling and long jumping ability often go together. 1922 R. D. Paine *Comr. Rolling Ocean* xv. 256 He hurdled aboard this True American steamer as soon as he hit New York. 1928 *Daily Mail* 31 July 11/5 When Lord Burghley hurdled easily to victory.

Hurdy-gu·rdyish, *a.* Resembling that of a hurdy-gurdy; also *fig.*

1923 *Daily Mail* 22 June 6 The concertina or harmonium music is too hurdy-gurdyish. 1931 *Observer* 27 Sept. 10 A cheap, hurdy-gurdyish fellow.

Hurl, variant of *herl*, Harl *sb.*¹

1837 H. Colman *Rep. Agric. Mass.* (1838) 128 It grew a foot and a half long, bore seed, and had a tolerable good hurl. 1879 *Scribner's Monthly* Nov. 23/2 The third has..body of peacock hurl.

Hurrah. Add: 4. *attrib.* or *adj.* in various *slang* or *colloq.* uses = shouting hurrah, uproarious, jollificatory; joyous, 'glad'.

1836 *Congress. Globe* 17 Feb., App. 115 [Some have declared] that his election had been brought about by the 'hurrah boys', and those who knew just enough to shout 'hurrah for Jackson!' 1903 *New York Even. Post* 30 Oct. 16 Added to this solid element is the hurrah crowd whose enthusiasm has a venal tone. 1906 N. Munro *Daft Days* xii, 'And what are you doing with your hurrah clothes on?' 'I like to put on my Sunday clothes when I'm writing Charles.' 1909 *Daily Chron.* 20 July 1/2 'Hurrah-boats', as the bluejacket aptly calls excursion steamers. 1925 E. Fraser & Gibbons *Soldier & Sailor Words, Hurrah boats*, a Navy term for the pleasure steamers of touring trippers that go round the Fleet at Naval Reviews, usually cheering as they pass ships. 1928 *Daily Express* 4 Dec. 10/3 'Hurrah boys' are college students.

Hurrian, variant of *Harrian.

Hurricane. Add: 2. c. A space in a forest, etc. devastated or cleared by a hurricane. (Earlier *hurricane ground*: see 3 in Dict.) *U.S.*

1824 *Missouri Intelligencer* 12 Feb. (Th.) Hurricanes are so called from the appearance of the land when stripped by a violent wind. 1833 D. Crockett *Sketches & Eccentr.* vii. (1834) 92, I went by to git a neighbour to drive for us, and off we started for the Harricane.

3. *hurricane season*, **hurricane deck** (earlier U.S. examples); **hurricane roof** = *h. deck*; **hurricane wind**, a wind of greater velocity than 75 miles an hour.

1835 C. J. Latrobe *Rambler in N. Amer.* I. 286 On some of the larger..steamers, there is yet a third deck and range of cabins before you come to the roof, or *hurricane deck. 1849 *Wilmington* (N. C.) *Commercial* 27 Nov. 1/6 Passing obliquely through the *hurricane roof immediately over the ladies' cabin. 1866 A. D. Richardson *Secret Service* 226 Standing upon the hurricane roof,..we caught the first glimpse of each shot. 1882 *Southern Hist. Soc. Papers* X. 478 Almost before you could jump into the water, the flames burst through the hurricane roof. 1742 W. Stephens *Jrnl. Proc. Georgia* II. 18 The two frigates..being apprehensive of the *hurricane season, retired into a safe harbour at Charles-Town. 1923 *hurricane wind [see *Gale *sb.*² 1 a].

Hurry, *sb.* 8. Add: **hurry-call** *U.S.*, a call for immediate help in an emergency.

1901 *Munsey's Mag.* XXIV. 798/1 If it was a hurry call, she would send them to Gilchrist. 1908 G. H. Lorimer *J. Spurlock* i. 11 In answer to a hurry-call from his wife to get rich. 1915 P. G. Wodehouse *Something Fresh* iii, His friends..send in a hurry-call to police headquarters.

Hurrygraph (hɒ·rigrɑf). *U.S.* [f. Hurry *sb.* + -graph.] Something done, produced, or experienced in a hurry; a hurried writing, sketch, or picture.

1851 N. P. Willis (*title*) Hurry-Graphs. 1861 *Independent* 31 July (Bartlett), I must close this hurrygraph, which I have no time to review. 1877 Bartlett *Dict. Americanisms* 305. 1887 Hissey *Holiday on Road* 331 The traveller by rail..notices only its beauty [i.e. of the country] from the 'hurrygraphs' he gets. 1918 *Hist. Amer. Literature* I. iii. 242 Fleeting impressions, 'dashes at life', ephemera, 'hurrygraphs' were his forte.

Hu·rry-up. *U.S. slang.* [f. vbl. phr. *to hurry up*, Hurry *v.* 2.] Used for, involving, or requiring hurry. *Hurry-up wagon*, a police-van.

1893 W. K. Post *Harvard Stories* 118 The manager..told him to send for a hurry-up wagon, and run us all in. 1907 *Putnam's Monthly* July 487/1 A hurry-up telegram. 1916 B. Hall & J. J. Niles *One Man's War* (1929) 191 He had to..wait for some hurry-up repairs.

Hurt, *v.* Add: 3. c. Of an injured limb, etc.: To be the source of pain to (one). (Cf. the corresponding intr. sense 8.)

1850 Smedley *Frank Fairlegh* xxxiv, I gave that [*sc.* the ankle] a twist somehow, and it hurts me dreadfully. 1871 *Two Little Bruces* viii, My arm hurts me most.

Hurt, *ppl. a.* Add: c. Of an inanimate thing: Injured, damaged. *U.S. colloq.*

1930 *Publishers' Weekly* 15 Feb. 863 The annual 'hurt book' sales.

Husband, *sb.* 6. Add: **husbands' boat, train,** etc., means of locomotion run chiefly for the convenience of men wishing to join their wives on holiday, esp. applied to vehicles run on Saturday; **husband's tea** *colloq.*, very weak tea.

1869 *Porcupine* XI. 272/2 Passengers by the '*husbands' boat' are more heavily laden with provisions. 1870 *London Soc.* XVIII. 170 The Husbands' boat can carry lovers too! 1929 *Daily Chron.* 24 July 8/6 The New Palace Steamers announce that their p.s. Koh-i-noor will be making the 'husband's boat' trip to-day as usual. 1874 *Slang Dict.* s.v. *Water-bewitched*, Sometimes very weak tea is called *husband's tea'. 1886 A. Hornblow *Splashes from Paris, Ink-Pot* 163 A special train, the *husband's train, would permit him to arrive at Tréport the same night.

Hush, *sb.*² Add: 3. *attrib.* and *Comb.* (sense 1 b).

1919 H. F. B. Wheeler *War in Underseas* 317 Mighty 'hush' ships which lived and moved..on the surface of great waters. 1920 *Melbourne Argus* 29 May 6 Time seems to have left..no surviving link between the frigate of Trafalgar and the 'hush-boat' of to-day. 1930 *Publishers' Weekly* 31 May 2735/1 Youngsters that are reared on the 'hush plan'.

Hush-hush. Reduplicated form of Hush *int.*, used *attrib.* to denote any object of manufacture, process, plan, or policy, the details or existence of which are kept secret; *occas.* a person engaged in such.

1919 C. P. Thompson *Cocktails* 133 The Flying Tank fixed the job without calling on that elaborate organisation for anything more hush-hush than a couple of batteries of heavy Hows. 1920 *Glasgow Herald* 3 May 8 The dramatic arrival at Baku in July, 1918, of General Dunsterville's 'hush-hush' force after its splendidly adventurous march through Persia. *Ibid.* 12 Aug. 4 Minute accounts of the hush-hush birth of this new monster of war. 1922 *Ibid.* 30 Aug. 9 A 'hush-hush' Bristol monoplane. 1925 E. Fraser & Gibbons *Soldier & Sailor Words, Hush hush crowd*, a familiar name for the *personnel* of the Tank Corps, when first organized in June, 1916, and secretly assembled for training. 1927 A. E. W. Mason *No other Tiger* i, He had never been able to take the hush-hush men seriously. 1927 D. Lloyd George *Slings & Arrows* (1929) 184 That 'hush, hush' policy which prevailed before the war. 1931 *Morn. Post* 5 June 12/4 Italian 'hush hush' car in Irish race.

Hush-hush, *v.* [Reduplicated form of Hush *v.*¹] *trans.* To say 'hush, hush' to; to quiet, silence.

1863 'Ouida' *Held in Bondage* iii. I. 71 Hervey, our Coxwain bush-hushes you. 1883 G. Meredith *Day of Dan. of Hades* viii, Not the pines with the faint airs afloat, Hush-hushing the nested dove. 1928 *Daily Express* 12 June 10/4 She might have done it long ago if she had not been firmly hush-hushed by men.

Husi, variant of *Jusi.

Husk, *sb.*⁴ *U.S.* [f. Husk *v.*¹] A corn-husking.

1796–1808 B. Hawkins *Lett.* 30 Here is the town house, and here they have their husks and dances.

Husk, *v.*¹ Add: Also *transf.* and *fig.*

1878 B. F. Taylor *Between Gates* 182 The rough dresses of the men..out of which they husk themselves. 1910 Mulford *H. Cassidy* xviii. 110 He determined to husk Meeker's body from its immortal soul.

Husk, *v.*² Add: 2. *intr.* Of the voice: To become husky. *U.S.*

1922 Titus *Timber* xxix. 254 Her voice husked for the first time.

Husker. *U.S.* (Earlier example.)

1780 E. Parkman *Diary* 279 Breck was very generous in treating ye huskers with Liquor.

Huskily, *adv.*² *U.S.* [f. *Husky *a.* 1 b.] Strongly, actively.

a 1906 'O. Henry' *Trimmed Lamp* etc. 175 It was the bi-monthly dance, a dress affair in which the members took great pride and bestirred themselves huskily to further and adorn.

Husking, *vbl. sb.*¹ *U.S.* (Earlier example.)

1693 C. Mather *Wond. Invis. World* 142 At another time this Deponent was desired by the Prisoners to come unto an Husking of Corn.

Husky, *sb.*¹ Add: a. Also *attrib.*

1922 *19th Cent.* Feb. 274 As a seamstress the 'husky' woman has no equal.

c. (Earlier examples.)

1886 *Colon. & Indian Exhib.* 75 The original Husky has always been an animal requiring firm treatment. 1892 *Harper's Mag.* Mar. 504/2 The Dogs are of a peculiar breed and are called 'huskies'—undoubtedly a corruption of the word Esquimaux.

Husky (hɒ·ski), *sb.*² *U.S.* [f. *Husky *a.* 1 b.] A strong, stoutly-built person; one whose appearance suggests strength and force.

1884 'Mark Twain' *Huck. Finn* xxix. 305 It was a beautiful time to give the crowd the slip; but that big husky had me by the wrist. 1916 C. Sandburg *Chicago Poems* 60 The real huskies that are doing the work of the world. 1929 W. Heyliger *Builder of Dam* v. 46 You're going to need muscle, and he's a husky.

Husky, *a.* Add: 1. b. Tough and strong (like a corn-husk); big, strong, and vigorous. *U.S.* and *Canadian colloq.*

1889 *Kansas City Times & Star* 1 Apr., Mike Burnett, the husky ex-fire chief. *Ibid.* 16 Oct., Wonderful tales of the big husky fish he caught. 1894 *Outing* XXIV. 447/1 He lit out of the country soon as he got husky enough to travel. 1909 S. E. White *Rules of Game* I. ix. 51 Good food and leisure and heredity gave me a husky build. 1927 G. W. Deeping *Kitty* xi, That thick-set, husky young man. *transf.* 1897 *Outing* (U.S.) XXX. 364/2 A husky run down old Ontario in a gale from the West brought *Nox* into Charlotte harbor.

Hussakite (hɒ·săkəit). *Min.* [f. the name of E. *Hussak* + -ite.¹] Xenotime occurring as prismatic crystals in crystalline rocks.

1901 *Jrnl. Chem. Soc.* LXXX. ii. 395. 1922 W. E. Ford *E. S. Dana's Min.* (ed. 3) 592 Hussakite was a xenotime from Brazil erroneously thought to contain large amounts of SO_3.

Hussar, *sb.* 3. Add: *hussar cap.*

1846 *Knickerbocker Mag.* XXVII. 287 [He had] a smart hussar cap of green chestnut burrs. 1854 B. F. Taylor *Jan. & June* 85 Hens with hussar caps.

Hustle, *sb.* 3. Add: Also with *a.* (Cf. *Move *sb.* 6.) *U.S.*

1902 Harben *Abner Daniel* ii. 19, I..told 'em to git a hustle on the'rse'ves.

Hustle, *v.* Add: 2. d. To obtain by hustle or pushing activity. *U.S. colloq.*

1926 J. Black *You Can't Win* vi. 65 Don't think because you couldn't hustle a can that you ain't entitled to your coffee.

4. (Later U.S. examples.)

1898 H. S. Canfield *Maid of Frontier* 177 I've got a warrant here for his arrest,..and you hustle. 1906 'O. Henry' *Four Million* 62 Do you think I'm going to let you hustle for wages while I philander in the regions of high art? 1908 G. H. Lorimer *J. Spurlock* v. 87, I decided that ..I'd hustle over to the nearest trust company.

Hut (hɒt), *int.* A call to a horse.

1856 *N. & Q.* 2nd Ser. I. 395 When a horse forgets what he is doing, and becomes careless, he is reminded of his duty by a sharp *hut*. 1899 *Pall Mall Mag.* Feb. 262 'Hut, you beast!' he added, as Englishmen do, when the mare nuzzled into his neck.

Hut, *sb.* 4. Add: **hut-circle** *Archæol.*, a circle of earth or stones indicating the circumference of a previously existing hut; **hut-clusters, dwellings** *Archæol.* (see quot.).

1865 *hut-circle [see Dict.]. 1913 *Rep. Brit. Assoc.* 205 The district is rich in prehistoric remains, including some hut circles. 1877 *Encycl. Brit.* VI. 427/1 *Hut dwellings. Of these there are at least two kinds, those in the eastern part of the county resembling the beehive structures and enclosures of Dartmoor, and those in the west, comprising '*hut-clusters', having a central court.

Hut, *v.* 2. (Earlier U.S. example.)

1780 in *Maryland Hist. Mag.* III. 118 When I join'd, the troops were hutting, which they compleated a few days after.

Hutchinson (hɒ·tʃinsən). The name of Jonathan *Hutchinson* (1828–1913), English surgeon and pathologist, used chiefly in the genitive to describe certain diseases or symptoms of disease observed by him. **Hutchinson's disease,** a disease of the choroid coat of the eye, which is characterized by senile degeneration of arteries round the yellow spot. **Hutchinson('s) pupil,** dilatation of one pupil on the side of the lesion in cases of hæmorrhage into the membranes of the brain (Cent. Dict. Suppl.). **Hutchinson's teeth,** upper incisor teeth the cutting edge of which is notched, occurring in children suffering from hereditary syphilis.

1890 Billings *Med. Dict., Hutchinson's teeth*, notched and deformed upper incisor teeth, seen in cases of hereditary syphilis. 1908 *Practitioner* Jan. 5 He had had a fit at school, he had well-marked Hutchinson's teeth.

Hutchinsonite (hɒ·tʃinsənəit). *Min.* [f. the name of Arthur *Hutchinson*, Cambridge mineralogist + -ite¹.] A rare mineral containing sulphur, arsenic, thallium, and lead, etc., found in the dolomite of the Binnenthal, Switzerland.

1907 *Jrnl. Chem. Soc.* XCII. ii. 699. 1929 H. L. Bowman *H. A. Miers' Min.* (ed. 2) 605.

Hutia (hutī·ă). Also **houtia, jutia, utia.** [a. Sp. *hutia*, f. Taino *huti, cuti*.] A West Indian rodent of the genus *Capromys*.

1834 McMurtrie *Cuvier's Anim. Kingd.* 84 The Houtias have four molars every where with flat crowns. 1839 *Penny Cycl.* XV. 509/2 According to Bomare, the Utias is a species of rabbit of the size of a rat, which inhabits the West Indies. 1849 *Sk. Nat. Hist., Mammalia* IV. 106 The utias in a wild state..climb trees with great facility, and..live on vegetables. 1877 *Encycl. Brit.* VI. 680/2 The only peculiar quadruped known in the island [of Cuba] is the *jutia* or *hutia*.

Huttoning (hɒ·təniŋ). [f. the name of R. H. *Hutton* (1840–87) and his uncle Richard, bone-setters + -ing¹.] Forcible manipulation of a dislocated or stiff joint.

1890 Billings *Med. Dict., Huttoning*, forcible manipulation of a joint, as practised by so-called 'bone-setters'.

Huxham (hɒ·ksăm). The name of John *Huxham* (1692–1768), physician, used in the genitive in **Huxham's tincture,** the tincture of cinchona bark devised by and named after him.

1807 *London Chron.* 31 Dec. 5 Freake's Tinct. of Bark.. Ditto Huxham's ditto. 1808 Jane Austen *Lett.* (1884) I. 347, I hope Huxham is a comfort to you; I am glad you are taking it. 1890 Billings *Med. Dict.*

Huxley (hɒ·ksli). The name of T. H. *Huxley* (1825–95), scientist, used in the genitive in **Huxley's layer, membrane,** the layer of cells, having clearly defined nuclei, in the root-sheath of mammalian hair, discovered by him.

1889 *Buck's Handbk. Med. Sci.* VIII. 471/1 Henle's layer is found represented by horny, polygonal, non-nucleated elements at a much lower level than Huxley's layer.

Huzoor (hŭzūᵊ·r). Also 8 huzzoor, huzur. [a. Ar. حضور *huḍūr* presence (employed as a title), f. حضر *ḥaḍara* to be present.] An Indian potentate; often used as a title of respect by natives in speaking to or of superiors, and occas. of Europeans.

1776 *Trial J. Fowke* 17/2 (Stanf.) [They] endeavour to lay their complaints before the Huzzoor. c 1791 *Encycl. Brit.* (1797) VIII. 793 *Huzzoor*, a Hindostan word signifying *The presence*. 1843 C. J. C. Davidson *Diary Trav. in Upper India* I. 77 The huzoor's countenance..is as immovably tranquil as that of Boodh. 1898 *Longm. Mag.* May 80 What pleasure hath this slave in life, save to do the Huzoor's will? 1923 Kipling *Land & Sea Tales* 229 'Huzoor!' said Imam Din, stooping low.

Hwyl (hū·əl). [W.] A fervid outpouring of eloquence; also, the fervour of emotion characteristic of gatherings of Welsh people.

1899 *Daily News* 1 Mar. 7/5 What is termed the Welsh 'hwyl', a form of eloquence which seems to exert remarkable influence on the hearers. 1928 *Observer* 15 July 11/3 The National Eisteddfod is a microcosm of Wales. There you may see preacher and ploughman, collier and clerk, all rubbing shoulders and all under the influence of the intangible and untranslatable 'hwyl' of the Eisteddfod.

Hyacinth. Add: 2. b. **Cape H., Peruvian H., Roman H.** (see quots.).

1760 J. Lee *Introd. Bot.* App. 315 Hyacinth, Peruvian, *Scilla*. 1877 [see Roman *a.* 14 b]. 1880 *Encycl. Brit.* XII. 420/2 The earliest of the hyacinths,..the white Roman hyacinth. *Ibid.*, The Cape hyacinth is *Scilla corymbosa*.

3. b. = *Jacinth 1 c.

1855 *Poultry Chron.* III. 9/1 Those pretty spangled Toys ..known by various names, as Porcelains, Hyacinths, Ermines, &c. 1879 L. Wright *Pigeon Keeper* 208 Victorias are simply Hyacinths of a lighter shade.

Hyalo-. Add: **Hy·alogen** [-gen], an albuminous substance present in cartilage, vitreous humour, etc. **Hy·alopilitic** (-pəili·tik) *a. Geol.* [Gr. πῖλος felt], applied to rocks having a fine glassy crystalline structure resembling felt. **Hy·alosome** *Cytology* [Gr. σῶμα body], a body resembling the nucleole of a cell but staining slightly.

1886 *Jrnl. Chem. Soc.* L. 481 In addition to the *hyalogen present in the walls of hydatid cysts, various other allied substances occur in the animal kingdom. 1909 L. Fletcher *Introd. Study Rocks* 128 Felspar is generally in lath-shaped crystals; if the latter are very minute and felted, the structure has been called pilotaxitic or *hyalopilitic, according as glass is absent or present. 1926 G. W. Tyrrell *Princ. Petrol.* 91. 1889 tr. Waldeyer in *Q. Jrnl. Microsc. Sci.* XXX. 168 *Hyalosome [see *karyosome* s.v. Karyo-].

Hyan (həi·ăn). *local.* Also 8–9 hyon, 9 hyant, hyen. [Origin unascertained.] Symptomatic anthrax or 'black quarter', an infectious blood disease affecting young cattle.

1789 *Trans. Soc. Arts* VII. 73, I..should annually have attempted to rear one hundred [calves], were it not for the disorder called here [*sc.* Scarisbrook] the *Hyon*. 1795 J. Aikin *Manchester* 325 Great numbers of calves having been taken off by a disease here called the *hyon*. 1801 *Sporting Mag.* XVII. 253 Drinks to be given to young calves for striking of the *Hyen*. 1881 Sheldon *Dairy Farming* 63/1 In their first winter, especially in certain localities, calves are extremely liable to the fatal disease of 'hyant', 'speed', 'quarter-evil', or 'black-leg', as it is variously termed.

Hyawa (həi·āwă). Also **haiowa, hayawa, hiawa, hyawai.** [Arawak (Makuchi) *haijawa*. In Du. *hajawa* (1770).] Any of various balsam-bearing trees of Guiana, e.g. *Icica heptaphylla*. Also *attrib.*

1825 Waterton *Wand. S. Amer.* 190 They paint themselves with the Roucou, sweetly perfumed with Hayawa or Accaiari. 1840 Schomburgk *Brit. Guiana* 98 The latter tree [*sc. Amyris ambrosiaca*], called *Haiowa* or *Sepou* by the Indians, is most abundant. 1851 *Illustr. Catal. Gt. Exhib.* IV. I. 980/1 Hyawai gum or incense, from River Demerara. 1866 *Treas. Bot.* s.v. *Icica*. 1887 *Colon. & Indian Exhib., 1886, Rep. Col. Sect.* 295 Hyawa gum..is a fragrant thus-like resin, which is very fragrant when burnt. 1899 Rodway *Guiana Wilds* 208 Then it struck him that a torch would be useful, as he saw a hyawa bush growing near.

Hyawaballi (həiăwăbæ·li). [Arawak (Makuchi) *hyawaballi*, f. *Hyawa + -*balli* resembling.] The zebra wood, *Omphalobium lambertii*.

1851 *Illustr. Catal. Gt. Exhib.* IV. I. 985/1 Transverse and vertical sections of the hyawaballi tree, from the River Demerara. 1887 *Colon. & Indian Exhib., 1886, Rep. Col. Sect.* 451 Hiawa-Balli.

Hybrid, *sb.* and *a.* B. *adj.* Add: 2. b. *Meteorology.* (See quot.) Formerly called *false cirrus*.

1932 *Internat. Atlas Clouds & States of Sky*, Cirrus nothus (Hybrid cirrus). Cirrus proceeding from a cumulonimbus and composed of the debris of the upper frozen parts of these clouds.

Hybris (həi·bris). [a. Gr. ὕβρις. Cf. *Hubris.] Presumption, especially against the gods (after Gr. tragic usage).

1920 *Public Opinion* 27 Aug. 195/2 During one of these the oppressor, possessed of place and power, imagined in his hybris, that he might extend his arm across the ocean. 1929 *Encycl. Brit.* XXII. 53/1 Themis is the servant or companion of Zeus...Her opposite is Hybris (ὕβρις), insolent encroachment upon the rights of others.

Hydathode (həi·dăþōᵘd). *Bot.* [f. Gr. ὕδατ-, ὕδωρ water + ὁδός way, path.] The name given by Haberlandt to an organ, such as a water-pore or water-gland, which extrudes liquid.

1897 Willis *Flower. Pl.* I. 116 Water-pores or hydathodes are openings, resembling stomata, upon leaves or elsewhere, through which the plant excretes water. 1902 Tansley in *Encycl. Brit.* XXV. 411/2 Some hydathodes are active glands, secreting the water they expel from the leaf.

Hydnocarpus (hidnoᵘ,kā·ɹpɒs). *Bot.* [mod.L. (Gaertner, 1788), f. Gr. ὕδνον truffle + καρπός fruit, from the appearance of the fruit of *Hydnocarpus venenata*, which is covered with a brown velvety down.] A plant of the genus *Hydnocarpus* of the family *Pangiaceæ*. Also *attrib.*: **hydnocarpus oil,** a homologue of chaulmoogra oil, used in the treatment of leprosy. Hence **Hydnoca·rpic** *a.*, denoting an acid derived from the fruit of hydnocarpus.

1928 *Daily Express* 20 Feb. 2/1 Hydnocarpus oil is obtained from the dried fruit of the hydnocarpus tree, and it is our aim to plant the tree all over the Empire. 1929 *Encycl. Brit.* XVII. 690/2 Organic chemists isolated from Chaulmoogra oil certain complex fatty acids named hydnocarpic and chaulmoogric acids.

Hydral, *a.* Add:

2. Applied to the vessels and vascular cells in the woody tissue, which convey water or sap.

1900 B. D. Jackson *Gloss. Bot. Terms, Tracheome*, stated by Potonié not to be the tracheal, but the hydral system of the bundle, he therefore names it Hydrome.

Hydrastinine (həidræ·stinin). *Pharmacy.* [f. Hydrastine + -ine⁵.] A synthetic alkaloid derived from hydrastine and used to produce (muscular and) arterial contraction. Also **Hydrasti·nic** *a. Chem.* (see quot. 1887).

1887 *Jrnl. Chem. Soc.* LII. I. 383 [Freund and Will] have examined the base hydrastinine, $C_{11}H_{11}NO_2+H_2O$, obtained together with opianic acid where hydrastine is treated with oxidising agents. *Ibid.* 384 Hydrastinic acid, $C_8H_7NO_4$, is obtained by boiling hydrastine with dilute nitric acid. 1929 *Encycl. Brit.* XI. 961/1 The hydrolytic product, hydrastinine, is an important drug, being used as an internal styptic.

Hydrastis (həidræ·stis). [mod.L.] The plant *Hydrastis canadensis* (see Hydrastine); also, the fluid extract of this, used as a styptic.

1882 Bentley *Man. Bot.* (ed. 4) 425 Hydrastis is..used by the Indians of the Western States of North America. 1908 *Practitioner* Jan. 96 Styptol and hydrastis, which act as vaso-constrictors..are recommended for arresting haemorrhage from the non-pregnant organ.

Hydraulic (həidrǭ·lik), *v.* [Back-formation f. Hydraulicking.] (See quot. 1884.)

1884 Knight *Dict. Mech.* Suppl. s.v. *Hydraulicking*, Most of the water..is used, as is said, to hydraulic, that is, to wash banks of auriferous earth by throwing a stream of water upon them through a hose and pipe. 1904 J. Lynch *3 Yrs. Klondike* 125 Those grounds can only be dredged or hydraulicked.

Hydrazone (həi·drăzōᵘn). *Chem.* [f. Hydraz(ine + -one.] One of a class of organic compounds formed by the action of phenyl hydrazine on a compound such as a ketone or aldehyde containing the CO radical.

1893 *Jrnl. Chem. Soc.* LXIV. I. 461 Bülow's test for hydrazones depends on the formation of a tetrazone and its subsequent reaction with sulphuric acid.

Hydro-. Add: **Hydra·mnios** *Path.*, uterine dropsy. **Hy·dro-aroma·tic** *a. Chem.*, of or pertaining to an aromatic compound to which hydrogen has been added. **Hy·drobio·logy,** aquatic biology. **Hydroca·rpic** *a. Bot.* [Gr. καρπός fruit], of or pertaining to water plants which submerge their flowers after fertilization. **Hy·drocata·lysis** *Chem.*, catalysis in the presence of water; hence **Hy·drocataly·tic** *a.* **Hydrodi·ctyon** [Gr. δίκτυον net: from the appearance of the plant in water] (see quot. 1886). **Hy·droglider,** a form of craft designed to glide on the surface of water. **Hy·drotechno·logist,** one versed in **Hy·drotechny** [Gr. τέχνη art], the technical management or utilization of water.

1848 Dunglison *Med. Lex.* (ed. 7), *Hydramnios. 1906 *Practitioner* Nov. 655 When hydramnios is present, or there is a multiple pregnancy. 1905 A. W. Crossley in *Rep. Brit. Assoc.* 153 *Hydro-Aromatic Substances. 1923 Remsen & Orndorff *Org. Chem.* 328 Hydroaromatic Hydrocarbons. 1929 *Encycl. Brit.* XVII. 1001/2 The modern science of *hydrobiology. 1900 B. D. Jackson *Gloss. Bot. Terms*, *Hydrocarpic. 1902 *Encycl. Brit.* XXVI. 742/1 Fermentation is certainly at bottom a process of *hydrocatalysis. *Ibid.* XXXV. (Index) *Hydrocatalytic action. 1872 H. C. Wood *Fresh-Water Algæ* 93 The *hydrodictyon may be looked upon as an elaborate type of a cell-family. 1886 *Encycl. Brit.* XX. 423/2 The zoospores eventually come to rest,..and arrange themselves so as to form the meshes of a small sac-like net, which is a young Hydrodictyon. 1921 *Glasgow Herald* 23 July 7/2 The idea of using *hydrogliders for passengers and for mail purposes on the lochs in the outlying districts of Scotland. 1927 *Ibid.* 26 July 9 The hydroglider which has been constructed..to accomplish the crossing of the Atlantic from Cherbourg to New York. 1897 *Geogr. Jrnl.* X. 619 As to the physics of running water, *hydrotechnologists have recognized the dependence of velocity on the declivity of the water surface and depth. 1902 *Encycl. Brit.* XXV. 374/2 In Arizona, Mexico, and Peru reservoirs and aqueducts prove that *hydrotechny was understood.

Hydro-aeroplane (həidro,ēᵊ·rŏplēⁱn). *Disused.* [f. Hydro- + *Aeroplane.] An aeroplane designed to alight on and rise from the water.

1909 *Westm. Gaz.* 7 Jan. 4/2 Before the present year expires the hydro-aeroplane will be an accomplished fact. 1914 *Scotsman* 21 Dec. 8/2 A German hydro-aeroplane threw two bombs on Calais this afternoon. 1928 C. F. S. Gamble *North Sea Air Station* i. 39 Up till now it has been necessary ..to use the term 'hydro-aeroplane' when describing a machine that was designed to arise from and alight on the surface of water. Owing to its cumbersome sound it was not popular...The Admiralty decided to use the word 'seaplane'.

Hydrocarbon. Add: b. **hydrocarbon oil,** hydrocarbonaceous oil.

1884 Knight *Dict. Mech.* Suppl. 484/2 Fluid hydrocarbon oils. 1930 *Morn. Post* 18 July 14/3 Hydrocarbon oil used on board life-boats.

Hydro-electric. Add: 3. Producing electricity by utilizing the motive power of water.

1905 *Daily Chron.* 18 Sept. 4/5 Abundant hydro-electric power. 1909 *Westm. Gaz.* 22 Oct. 10/1 The construction of a second large hydro-electric plant. 1920 Rushmore & Lof (*title*) Hydro-Electric Power Stations.

Hydro-electricity. Add: 2. Electricity produced by the application of the motive power of water.

1927 *Observer* 22 May 13/1 The national exhibit of hydro-electricity.

Hydrogel (həi·drŏdʒel). *Chem.* [f. Gr. ὕδρο-water, Hydro- + Gel(atin.] A gelatinous colloidal solution.

1864 T. Graham in *Jrnl. Chem. Soc.* XVII. 321 If I may be allowed to distinguish the liquid and gelatinous hydrates of silicic acid by the irregularly formed terms of *hydrosol* and *hydrogel* of silicic acid. 1895 Bloxam *Chem.* (ed. 8) 123 Colloids..can generally exist in solution (the hydrosol form), but are apt to separate as a jelly (the hydrogel form) from such solutions.

Hydroid, *sb.* Add: 2. *Bot.* A tracheid.

1900 B. D. Jackson *Gloss. Bot. Terms.* 1902 Tansley in *Encycl. Brit.* XXV. 400/2 Such differentiated water-conducting cells we call *hydroids*, the tissue they form *hydrom*. 1929 *Encycl. Brit.* XVIII. 6/1 Dead water-conducting cells (hydroids).

Hydrology (həidrɒ·lŏdʒi). [f. Gr. ὑδρο-, ὕδωρ water + -logy.] The science of treatment by baths and waters. Hence **Hydrolo·gical** *a.*

1913 R. F. Fox (*title*) The Principles and Practice of Medical Hydrology. 1921 *Oxford Index Therap.* 452 It is convenient to consider hydrological treatment from two points of view.

Hydrome (həi·drōᵘm). *Bot.* Also **hydrom.** [f. Gr. ὑδρο-, ὕδωρ water + -*ome* as in *rhizome*, *caulome*, etc.] The water-system of a vascular bundle. (A term proposed instead of Tracheome.)

1900 [see *Hydral]. 1902 [see *Hydroid]. 1929 *Encycl. Brit.* XVIII. 6/1 The hydrom strand is either slightly developed or altogether absent.

Hydrophilous, *a.* Add: b. *Bot.* Denoting those plants which depend upon water or moisture for fertilization or seed dispersal.

1902 *Encycl. Brit.* XXV. 437/1 Dissemination is effected by the agency of water, of air, of animals—and fruits and seeds are therefore grouped in respect of this as hydrophilous, anemophilous, and zooidiophilous.

Hydrophytic (həidrofi·tik), *a.* [f. Hydrophyte + -ic.] Of the nature of a hydrophyte; of or pertaining to a species which grows submerged in water.

1901 *Daily Chron.* 6 Sept. 3/3 Easy and luxurious is by comparison the life of hydrophytic societies. 1926 *Nat. Hist. Oxford Distr.* 83 It [*sc. Elodea canadensis*] has never seeded, and has spread vegetatively as is the case with other alien hydrophytic species.

Hydroplane (həi·drŏplēⁱn), *sb.* [f. Hydro- + Plane *sb.*³]

1. In full, *hydroplane boat, craft*: A light motor-boat designed to skim the surface of the water by means of a flat bottom sloping upwards towards the bow; in vogue from 1907 to 1914.

1907 *Motor Boat* 19 Sept. 182/1 The performance of Mr. Robinson's hydroplane boat. 1909 *Westm. Gaz.* 5 Jan. 4/2 If we have been apathetic towards the aeroplane we have exhibited marked enterprise in regard to the hydroplane.

2. The plane of a submarine enabling it to submerge or rise.

1906 *Chambers's Jrnl.* May 414/1 Boats are fitted with hydroplanes, which are nothing more than submerged kites. 1911 *Encycl. Brit.* XXIV. 921/1 Another technical point in the design of submarines which has frequently been the subject of non-technical discussion is the desirability or otherwise of 'bow-rudders' or 'hydroplanes'. 1929 *Ibid.* XXI. 494/2 Hydroplane guards are fitted to prevent wires catching in the hydroplanes when passing through nets fitted as a defence to entrances to harbours, etc. *Ibid.*, In earlier submarines, a pair of hydroplanes were fitted at the stern, but now a pair is fitted forward and a pair aft.

3. = *Hydro-aeroplane, *Seaplane.

[1911 in Grahame-White & Harper *Aeroplane* 316 These suggested Atlantic aero-hydroplanes would float on the water when at rest.] 1913 W. Churchill in *Parl. Deb.* Ser. v. LV. 1502/1 We have decided to call the naval hydroplane a seaplane, and the ordinary aeroplane or school machine, which we use in the Navy, simply a plane. 1913 *Q. Rev.* Apr. 471 For reconnaissance, the work is better done by hydroplanes costing a few hundreds apiece.

Hence **Hy·droplane** *v. intr.*, to travel in a hydroplane; also, to taxi on water.

1909 *Westm. Gaz.* 5 Jan. 4/3 It is due entirely to its [*Ricochet X*] performances at Southampton that hydroplaning has gained recognition in this country. 1922 *Encycl. Brit.* XXX. 50/2 Hydroplaning efficiency..could be sacrificed for sea-worthiness. 1928 C. F. S. Gamble *North Sea Air Station* i. 32 Having succeeded in making his machine hydroplane on her floats.

Hydroscopic (həidrŏskɒ·pik), *a.* [f. Gr. ὑδρο-water + -σκοπος, σκοπεῖν to view + -ic.] = Hygroscopic.

1908 Sir W. Schlich *Man. Forestry* V. 549 [Charcoal's] composition is as follows:—Carbon 75–80%...Hydroscopic water 6–12%. 1910 *Practitioner* July 135 Pankreon is a non-hydroscopic powder.

Hydrosol (həi·drŏsɒl). *Chem.* [f. Gr. ὑδρο-water + Sol(ution.] A liquid colloidal solution.

1864, 1895 [see *Hydrogel]. 1920 *Nature* CV. 372/2 The lubricating graphite..reduced to particles of colloidal dimensions and sold under the trade-names of 'Aquadag' and 'Hydrosol'.

Hydroxylate (həidrɒ·ksilēⁱt), *v.* [f. Hydroxyl + -ate³.] *trans.* To add a hydroxyl radical to (a substance).

1900 *Rep. Brit. Assoc.* 298 The hydroxylated nucleus of the tribromonaphthol.

Hydroxylic (həidrɒksi·lik), *a.* [Hydroxyl + -ic.] Of or pertaining to the hydroxyl radical OH.

1902 *Encycl. Brit.* XXVI. 725/1 The oxygen therefore ceases to be ketonic and becomes 'hydroxylic'. *Ibid.* XXVIII. 364/2 Four of the oxygen atoms are supposed to be present in hydroxylic form (—OH).

Hygeen, hajeen (hidʒī·n, hădʒī·n). Also 6 hugiun, 8 hyghgeen, 9 hejeen, hadjeen, hag(h)een, hajan. [Arab. هجين *hajīn*, pronounced in Egypt *hagīn* (cf. Syriac *haginā, hugīnā*, Talmudic *hōgnā*). Origin uncertain.] A riding dromedary.

1600 Pory tr. *Leo's Africa* ix. 338 Of camels there are three kinds; whereof the first being called Hugiun [orig. *quarum primi Hugiun nuncupati*] are grosse, and of a tall stature. 1713 *Guardian* No. 124 There has not been a Tyger, Leopard, Elephant or Hyghgeen, for some Years past, in this Nation, but I have taken their particular Dimensions. 1790 J. Bruce *Trav.* IV. 332 If..there was danger, [he] should return..mount a hajan or dromedary, and [etc.]. 1864 J. A. Grant *Walk Across Africa* 419 A 'Hadjeen', or riding camel, is indispensable to comfort. 1865 W. G. Palgrave *Arabia* I. 325 The dromedary is the race-horse of his species, thin, elegant,..light of step, easy of pace,..though yet more often the dromedary enjoys his special title of 'hejeen' or 'dolool'. 1875 hejeen [see *Delout]. 1890 S. W. Baker *Wild Beasts* II. 374 As a general rule, the hygeens are not so powerfully proportioned as those which carry baggage. 1908 *Animal Managem.* (W. O.) 276 The riding camel (..Hagheen, Egypt).

Hygrophilite (həigrɒ·filəit). *Min.* [f. Hygrophilous + -ite.¹] A hydrous silicate of magnesium belonging to the pinite group.

1880 Dana *Min.* App. ii. 1896 *Jrnl. Chem. Soc.* LXX. ii. 432 Hygrophilite, white nodules in a red clay slate from Reuschbach, Rhenish Bavaria.

Hyksos (hi·ksɒs), *sb. pl.* Also **Hykshos.** [a. Gr. ὑκσώς, ad. Egyptian *hik-shasu* = βασιλεῖς ποιμένες.] The shepherd kings of Egypt, a Shemite dynasty which conquered Egypt and ruled c 2000 B.C. Also *attrib.*

1863 *Chambers's Encycl.* V. 493/2 As regards the date of the H[yksho]s dominion, the most conflicting opinions have prevailed. 1899 A. H. Sayce *Early Israel* Introd. p. xxv, A Hyksos Pharaoh and his Hebrew vizier. 1931 J. G. Duncan *Digging up Biblical Hist.* II. 163 Hyksos pottery.

Hymettian (həime·tiăn), *a.* [f. L. *Hymettius* (f. *Hymettus*, Gr. Ὑμηττός) + -an.] Of or belonging to Mount Hymettus in Attica, famous in antiquity for its honey and marble; hence *poet.* honied, sweet (cf. Hyblæan).

1601 Holland *Pliny* xvii. i. I. 499 Foure goodly pillars of Hymettian Marble. 1658 Rowland tr. *Moufet's Theat. Ins.* 908 He that will make a good mixture of wine and honey, must mingle with new Hymettian Honey, old Falernian Wine. 1795 Coleridge *To R. B. Sheridan* 4 Thy temples with Hymettian flow'rets wreath'd.

Hymnarium (himnēᵊ·riɒm). Pl. -ia. [med.L.] = Hymnary.

1924 *Glasgow Herald* 7 June 4 The extensive hymnaria attributed to the famous Bishop of Milan [St. Ambrose].

Hypanthodium (həipænþōᵘ·diɒm). *Bot.* [mod.L., f. Hypo- + Anthodium.] The enlargement of the receptacle beneath the calyx.

1861 Bentley *Man. Bot.* 204 The Hypanthodium.—This kind of inflorescence is but a slight modification of the last [*sc.* the Capitulum, Anthodium, or Head]. 1880 A. Gray *Struct. Bot.* v. (ed. 6) 149 Syconium, the name given to the Fig-fruit, is a sort of inflorescence...It has also been named a Hypanthodium.

Hyper-. IV. Add: **Hy·perbar** *Meteorol.* [*Bar *sb.*⁶], a ridge of high barometric pressure. **Hy·percellula·rity,** the morbid formation of cells. **Hyperchlorhydria** (-klorhəi·driă) *Path.* [Chlorhydr(ic + -ia], excess of chlorhydric (= hydrochloric) acid in the digestive juices; hence **Hyperchlorhy·dric** *a.* **Hyperchloruria** (-kloɹ,iūᵊ·riă) *Path.*, excess of chlorides in the urine. **Hyperchromasia** (-krŏmēⁱ·ziă) *Path.* [Gr. χρωμασία coloration], excess of pigment in the skin. **Hyperda·ctyly** [cf. Dactyl], an excess of toes or fingers. **Hy·per-eute·ctic** *a. Metall.*, denoting steel containing more than 0·90 per cent. of combined carbon. **Hy·perexcita·tion,** a state of morbid excitement. **Hypergeusia** (-giū·ziă) *Path.* [Gr. γεῦσις taste], excessive acuteness of the sense of taste. **Hyperke·ratosed** *a.*, excessively keratosed. **Hy·perkerato·sis** *Path.*, excessive development (*a*) of the horny layer of the skin, (*b*) of the cornea. **Hyperleucocytosis** (-l'ᵊukŏsəitōᵘ·sis) *Path.*, a morbid excess of white corpuscles (leucocytes) in the blood. **Hypermne·sia, Hypermne·sis** *Psychol.*, [Gr. μνῆσις], the state or quality of being hypermnestic. **Hypermnestic** (-mnī·stik) *a.*, having a morbidly retentive memory. **Hypermyotrophy** (-məiɒ·trŏfi) (see quot.). **Hypernephroma** (-nĕfrōᵘ·mă) *Path.*, a tumour of suprarenal origin. **Hyperpe·psia** *Path.* [Gr. πέψις digestion], an excessive secretion of neutral chlorides in the gastric juices. **Hyperphala·ngism, Hyperpha·langy,** the development or state of development of more than the normal number of digital phalanges. **Hyperpho·ria** *Path.*, tendency of the visual axis of one eye above the other. **Hyperpiesis** (-pəi,ī·sis) *Path.* [mod.L.; Gr. πίεσις pressure], over-pressure or high pressure, as a symptom affecting the circulation of the blood; hence **Hyperpiesia** (-pəi,ī·ziă), the state or condition set up by hyperpiesis. **Hy·pertension** *Path.*, a state of excessive tension. **Hyperthe·rmia, Hyperthe·rmy** *Path.* [Gr. θέρμη heat], a state of high bodily temperature. **Hyperthy·roid** *a.*, of or pertaining to excessive secretion of the thyroid glands; hence **Hyperthy·roidism** *Path.*, the state arising from excessive thyroid secretion; Graves' disease. **Hyperto·nic** *a.*, pertaining to, characterized by, or producing excessive contraction. **Hypertonus** (həipɔ̄·ɹtŏnɒs) *Path.*, the state or condition of excessive contraction. **Hy·pervitamino·sis** *Path.* [*Vitamine + -osis], the state arising from an excess of vitamines in the diet.

1926 McAdie *Man & Weather* 98 A ridge of high pressure connected the Atlantic *hyperbar with a north polar anticyclone more or less permanent. 1910 *Practitioner* Apr. 464 Associated with this *hypercellularity there is usually a disappearance of the elastic tissue which is normally present. 1906 *Ibid.* Nov. 691 The paroxysmal crisis of *hyperchlorhydria. *Ibid.* Dec. 830 *Hyperchlorhydric dyspepsia. 1907 *Ibid.* June 827 On forced doses, the *hyperchloruria was increased out of proportion to the salt taken. 1889 *Century Dict.*, *Hyperchromasia. 1908 *Practitioner* Aug. 319 A condition known as hyperchromasia, in contradistinction to achromasia, or leucodermia. 1902 Webster Suppl., *Hyperdactyly. 1927 R. S. Lull *Org. Evol.* xx. 330 As though extra toes over the normal five had been added (hyperdactyly). 1902 *Encycl. Brit.* XXIX. 572/2 They [*sc.* forms of steel] are called *hyper-eutectic or hypo-eutectic..according as their carbon-content is above or below the 0·90 per cent. which the eutectic itself contains. 1900 *Westm. Gaz.* 24 Mar. 3/1 A state of *hyper-excitation and imperfect control. 1880 *Encycl. Brit.* XXIII. 80/2 Increase in the sense of taste is called *hypergeusia*, diminution of it *hypogeusia*, and entire loss *ageusia*. 1909 *Practitioner* Nov. 735 Dry, scaly, and *hyperkeratosed lesions. 1890 Billings *Med. Dict.*, *Hyperkeratosis. 1908 *Practitioner* Jan. 22 In the epidermis there is proliferation of the prickle-cell layer, hyperkeratosis. 1907 *Ibid.* Sept. 438 The hypodermic injection of nucleinate of sodium increases *hyperleucocytosis. 1892 D. H. Tuke's *Dict. Psychol. Med.* I. 602/1 *Hypermnesia*,..over-activity of the memory. 1903 F. W. H. Myers *Hum. Pers.* II. 517 The hypermnesia..seems often to act as a kind of nidus for germs of knowledge borne home from some other quarter. 1902 Webster Suppl., *Hypermnesis. 1915 C. R. Payne tr. *O. Pfister's Psych. Method* 360 Here we see the regression to the infantile, the *hypermnestic performance of the dream. 1908 *Practitioner* Dec. 770 A generalised increase in the muscular tissue of the arteries, to which he [*sc.* Savill] applies the term arterial *hypermyotrophy. 1906 *Ibid.* Dec. 814 A *hypernephroma, occurring in the kidney. 1908 *Ibid.* Apr. 543 Chemically pure sub-nitrate..is equally successful in hypopepsia, apepsia, and *hyperpepsia. 1891 Flower & Lydekker *Mammals* 234 The Ichthyopterygia have been shown..to have gradually acquired their *hyperphalangism as an adaptive character. 1897–8 *Proc. Anat. Soc. Gt. Brit.* (heading) The ossification of the terminal phalanges of mammalian fingers, in relation to *hyperphalangy. 1927 R. S. Lull *Org. Evol.* xx. 330 As a further modification the individual phalangeal bones increase in number (hyperphalangy). 1881 *Amer. Jrnl. Med. Sci.* N.S. CI. 377 A clinical study in the diagnosis and treatment of *hyperphoria. 1901 *Jrnl. Amer. Med. Assoc.* XXXVI. 147 A clinical study of one hundred and fifty cases of hyperphoria. 1925 T. R. Elliott in *Brit. Med. Jrnl.* 19 Dec. 1161/1 Discussion on *Hyperpiesia...I will assume that hyperpiesia..is a condition *sui generis*, manifesting certain discomforts. 1908 *Med. Chron.* XLVII. 337 On *hyperpiesis as compensatory of increased peripheral resistance. 1922 H. Batty Shaw (*title*) Hyperpiesia and Hyperpiesis (Hypertension). 1925 T. R. Elliott in *Brit. Med. Jrnl.* 19 Dec. 1162/1 We could not identify hyperpiesis with any particular physical type of child. 1906 *hypertension [see *hypotension* s.v. *Hypo-]. 1920 L. M. Warfield (*title*) Arteriosclerosis and Hypertension. 1887 A. M. Brown *Anim. Alkaloids* 143 Intoxication by the extractive matters is accompanied by *hyperthermia. 1898 *Nature* 24 Nov. 95 Researches on lesions of the nervous centres produced by *hyperthermy. 1922 L. Berman in *Sunday Times* Apr., To bring to mind an immediate complete image of the *hyperthyroid face, one should think of Shelley. 1918 R. Knox *Radiog. & Radio-Therap.* II. 556 *Hyperthyroidism began to receive recognition. 1927 Haldane & Huxley *Anim. Biol.* viii. 162 The thyroid gland sometimes swells up and produces too much thyroxin...In one hospital the patients in the ward reserved for hyperthyroidism eat twice as much as those in any other ward! 1890 Billings *Med. Dict.*, *Hypertonic. 1908 *Practitioner* Dec. 774 Hypertrophied muscle in a state of hypertonic contraction. 1929 *Encycl. Brit.* IV. 21/2 The intravenous administration of hypertonic solutions. 1908 *Practitioner* Mar. 295 A condition of *hypertonus of the vascular system. 1929 *Biochemical Jrnl.* XXIII. 1114 *Hypervitaminosis and vitamin balance.

Hypergamy (həipɔ̄·ɹgămi). *Anthrop.* [f. Hyper- + *-gamy.] A term first used by W. Coldstream, to denote the custom which forbids the marriage of a woman into a tribe of lower standing than her own. Hence **Hype·rgamous** *a.*, pertaining or relating to hypergamy.

1882 Ibbetson *Punjab Census Rep.* I. 356 They [*sc.* the social rules]..may be referred to two laws which I shall call the laws of *isogamy* and *hypergamy*. 1901 Risley & Gait *Rep. Cens. India* § 701 *Hypergamy*, or 'marrying up' is the custom which..compels [a woman] to marry in a group equal or superior in rank. A hypergamous division, therefore, is a group forming part of a series governed by the foregoing rule. 1909 E. S. Hartland *Prim. Paternity* I. 266 The Brahmans everywhere follow a custom known as *hypergamy*, by which a man may marry or have sexual relations with a woman of lower rank, but no man of lower rank may marry into a caste above his own. 1921 *Nature* 13 Jan. 646/1 Dr. Rivers said that the term 'hypergamy' had been used loosely by both Sir Herbert Risley and Dr. W. Crooke to denote marriage between groups which differ in rank, but for the sake of clearness the term should be confined to those instances in which there was a characteristic difference between the marriage rules for the two sexes. 1929 *Encycl. Brit.* IV. 979/2 The ancient hypergamous rule which allowed a woman to be married to a man of higher class.

Hypernic (həi·pɔ̄nik, həipɔ̄·ɹnik), *a.* [f. Hyper- + *Nic(aragua).*] An extract of Nicaragua or similar woods used by dyers.

1897 C. T. Davis *Manuf. Leather* (ed. 2) 567 Take 10 lbs. hypernic chips...Add the hypernic solution by degrees.

Hyphen *attrib.* = *Hyphenated *a.* 2, q.v.

1916 *Literary Digest* (N.Y.) 1 Jan. 4/1 In the event of the Republicans nominating any man on a hyphen platform or on hyphenated promises.

Hy·phenate, *sb.* [f. *Hyphenated *a.* 2.] A hyphenated person.

1916 *Yorkshire Post* 4 Mar. 6/7 The Hyphenates throughout the country are greatly excited. 1920 *Glasgow Herald* 27 Nov. 6 This political hyphenate or composite is desirous of running a Home Rule for Scotland campaign. 1922 *Contemp. Rev.* Dec. 693 The 'hyphenates'—Irish and Germans, Poles and Russians and Italians—..joined in the condemnation of Wilsonism.

Hyphenated, *a.* Add:

2. Applied to persons (or their activities) whose nationality is designated by a hyphenated form, e.g. *Anglo-American, Irish-American*; hence, to a person whose patriotic allegiance is assumed to be divided. orig. *U.S.*

1893 Farmer & Henley *Slang, Hyphenated American*, a naturalised citizen, as German-Americans, Irish-Americans, and the like. 1900 *Daily News* 15 Aug. 3/1 My opponents were of the hyphenated variety—Dutch-Americans and Irish-Americans predominating. 1904 *Westm. Gaz.* 3 Jan. 3/2 American politics, where men who call themselves Irish-Americans, German-Americans, Dutch-Americans, and so on, are contemptuously referred to as 'hyphenated Americans'. 1907 *Nation* (N.Y.) 7 Nov. 410 Some of these hyphenated American journals. 1915 *Literary Digest* (N.Y.) 4 Sept. 462/1 Hyphenated residents will continue to insist that American newspapers should be strictly neutral.

Hyphening (həi·fəniŋ), *vbl. sb.* [f. Hyphen *v.* + -ing¹.] The action of the vb. Hyphen.

1919 *Concise Oxf. Dict.* p. ix, A consequence of this reformed hyphening is that the presence of a hyphen in such a compound [as *tipsy cake*] assures the reader that the word-stress falls on the first part.

Hyphomycetes (həi:foməisī·tīz), *sb. pl. Bot.* [mod.L., f. Gr. ὑφή web + μύκητες fungi.] A group of *fungi imperfecti* so named.

1879 *Encycl. Brit.* IX. 828/1 The expansion or contraction of the filaments of many *Hyphomycetes* according to the supply of water. 1917 *Jrnl. Bact.* (Baltimore) II. 365 The preparation of hyphomycetes for microscopical examination.

Hypnoid (hi·pnoid), *a.*² [Hypn(osis + -oid.] Of or pertaining to hypnosis. So **Hypnoi·dal** *a.*

1902 W. James *Varieties* 484 In it arise whatever mystical experiences we may have, and our automatisms, sensory or motor; our life in hypnotic and 'hypnoid' conditions. 1921 *Discovery* Nov. 294/1 A similar [half-waking] state can be produced artificially and is called light hypnosis or the hypnoidal state. 1915 C. R. Payne tr. *O. Pfister's Psych. Method* 173 Brewer's supposition that the foundation and condition of hysteria may be the existence of hypnoidal (sleep-like) states. *Ibid.* 241 Silberer, who first investigated this kind of hypnoid hallucinations.

Hypo, *sb.*² Add: *attrib.*, as *hypo-bath, -solution*.

1907 *Westm. Gaz.* 9 Feb. 14/2 A weak hypo-bath. 1908 *Ibid.* 13 June 14/2 A generous allowance of hypo-solution.

Hypo-. II. Add: **Hypabyssal** *a. Geol.* [Abyssal], of or pertaining to rocks intermediate between abyssal forms and extrusive lavas. **Hypobenthos** (-be·nþɒs) *Zool.*, the submarine fauna inhabiting the ocean at a greater depth than 500 fathoms. **Hypochlorhydria** (-klōᵊɹhəi·driă) *Path.*, defective secretion of chlorhydric (= hydrochloric) acid in the digestive juices. **Hypochro·mat** *Path.* [Gr. χρῶμα colour], one whose sense of colour is defective. **Hypochylia** (-kəi·liă) *Path.* [Gr. χυλός Chyle], incomplete digestion. **Hy·po-eute·ctic** *a. Metall.*, denoting steels containing less than 0·90 per cent. of combined carbon. **Hypoge·nesis** *Biol.*, reproduction in which the alternation of generations is suppressed or absent; so **Hy·pogene·tic** *a.* **Hypogeusia** (-giū·ziă) *Path.* [Gr. γεῦσις taste], defective sense of taste. **Hy·poglycæ·mia** *Path.*, a deficiency of sugar in the blood; hence **Hy·poglycæ·mic** *a.* **Hypoi·schium** *Anat.* (see quot.). **Hypoleucocytosis** (-lᵊūkŏsəitōᵘ·sis) *Path.*, a deficiency of leucocytes in the blood. **Hypope·psia** *Path.* [Gr. πέψις digestion], defective secretion of neutral chlorides in the gastric juices. **Hypophala·ngia, -pha·langism,** a deficiency of digital phalanges. **Hypopla·nkton** *Zool.*, the plankton existing on the ocean-bed. **Hyposy·stole** *Path.*, defective contraction of the ventricles of the heart. **Hy·potension** *Path.*, a state of low tension. **Hy·potensor,** a therapeutic which reduces arterial tension. **Hy·pothermal** *a.*, (*c*) pertaining to baths with a temperature below 93° Fahr. **Hypothe·rmia** *Path.* [Gr. θέρμη], a depressed bodily temperature. **Hypothy·roid** *a.*, pertaining or relating to defective thyroid secretion; hence **Hypothy·roidism.** **Hypoto·nia** *Path.*, abnormally low tension; hence **Hypoto·nic** *a.*, pertaining to, characterized by, or producing hypotonia.

1903 Geikie *Text-bk. Geol.* (ed. 4) 197 Dyke-rocks..which may have been injected as dykes and veins at a less distance from the surface (*hypabyssal). 1924 Skerl tr. *A. Wegener's Orig. Continents & Oceans* 135 Hypabyssal igneous rocks. 1902 *Encycl. Brit.* XXXIII. 933/1 This zone..extends from about 500 fathoms to the greatest depths...The darkness is probably absolute...To the fauna which lives in these remarkable circumstances the name **hypobenthos* may be applied. 1901 Dorland *Med. Dict.*, *Hypochlorhydria. 1909 *Practitioner* Dec. 817 The secretion of deficient quantities of gastric juice—anacidity or hypochlorhydria. 1930 *Nature* 22 Nov. 815 The best starting point is the result of some investigations on *hypochromats (colour-blind individuals). 1910 *Practitioner* June 761 'Senile' dyspepsia (essentially a *hypochylia). 1902 *Encycl. Brit.* XXIX. 572/2 They [*sc.* steels] are called hyper-eutectic or *hypo-eutectic according as this excess is cementite or ferrite. *Ibid.* XXVII. 131/1 In some other cases medusoid develops directly from medusoid (*hypogenesis). *Ibid.*, In other cases the medusoid is *hypogenetic, medusoid producing medusoid. 1888 *hypogusia [see *hypergeusia* s.v. *Hyper-]. 1926 *Encycl. Brit.* Suppl. I. 851/1 Mild degrees of *hypoglycaemia. *Ibid.*, *Hypoglycaemic reaction. 1929 *Ibid.* XX. 742/2 The ischia usually meet in a ventral ischial symphysis, from which a cartilage or bone projects backward to support the anterior lip of the cloacal orifice; this is the *hypoischium. 1908 *Practitioner* Mar. 292 A characteristic Roentgen-ray *hypoleucocytosis. 1908 *hypopepsia [see *hyperpepsia* s.v. *Hyper-]. 1905 *Pop. Sci. Monthly* July 195 (Cent. D. Suppl.) A condition of *hypophalangia (two-jointed instead of three-jointed digits). 1902 *Encycl. Brit.* XXXIII. 933/1 It is possible that the plankton immediately over the bottom [*sc.* of the ocean] may prove to be sufficiently distinct to be separately classed as **hypoplankton*. 1903 *Nature* 5 Nov. 23/2 There is evidence that certain forms [*sc.* of the Copepoda] are confined to the bottom, and form part of a true hypoplankton. 1901 *Westm. Gaz.* 24 July 6/3 The nervous depression and the *hyposystole of the heart are less accentuated. 1906 *Practitioner* Dec. 829 The difference between the hard tight pulse of hypertension, and the soft compressible pulse of *hypotension. 1907 *Ibid.* June 846 Sub-normal temperature, feeble pulse, and arterial hypotension. 1926 W. McDougall *Outl. Abnormal Psych.* i. 11 Psychic tension and hypotension. 1908 *Practitioner* Apr. 545 A..welcome addition will be made to the limited class of *hypotensors'. 1906 *Ibid.* Nov. 623 Baths below 93° F. are, therefore, known as *hypo-thermal baths. Baths, with a range of temperature between 93° and 98° F., are subthermal, while above 98° they are called thermal. 1887 A. M. Brown *Anim. Alkal.* 143 Intoxication by animal alkaloids is accompanied by *hypothermia. 1931 *Times Lit. Suppl.* 10 Dec. 1004/2 The 'pyknic' and 'leptosome', or hyper- and *hypo-thyroid of other anthropologists. 1907 *Practitioner* Oct. 547 Undue muscular strain on the ankle, knee, hip, and spine, which, together with *hypotonia, tends to break down the long arch. *Ibid.* June 830 The tissue fluids would become *hypotonic. 1908 *Ibid.* Oct. 560 The lower extremities have been thin, powerless, and extraordinarily hypotonic. 1910 *Ibid.* June 831 Toxins..exercising a hypotonic or relaxing effect on the vessels.

Hyposcope (həi·pŏskōᵘp). *Disused.* [f. Hypo- + -scope, after *periscope*.] A form of periscope for attachment to a rifle or for use as a hand instrument.

1902 *Daily Chron.* 15 July 9/1 The 'Hyposcope' competition—seven shots at 200 yards—the peculiarity of which is that, by an optical contrivance, the marksman, completely under cover, may fire round a corner, so to speak, at an enemy. 1915 *Illustr. London News* 20 Feb. 236/1 A trench-periscope (or, to give it its correct name, a hyposcope)...The Hyposcope is on the principle of the camera-obscura.

Hypostasianism (həi-, hipostēⁱ·ziăniz'm). [f. Hypostasis 5 + -ian + -ism.] The doctrine of an independent personal subsistence of the Divine Word.

1883 *Encycl. Brit.* XVI. 719/1 The doctrine of a hypostatic Logos (hypostasianism).

Hyrcan (hɔ̄·ɹkăn), *a.* and *sb.* Also 6–7 **Hircan.** [ad. L. *Hyrcānus*, a. Gr. Ὑρκανός.] = *Hyrcanian *a.* and *sb.*

Hyrcan tiger, after L. *Hyrcanæ tigres* (Virgil *Æn.* iv. 367).

1584 Rich *Second Tome Simonides* Ci, These Souldiers, like to Hircan Tigers, reuenge them selues on their owne bowelles. 1592 Daniel *Delia* xviii, But yet restore thy fearce and cruell minde, To Hyrcan tygers, and to ruthles Beares. 1605 Shaks. *Macb.* iii. iv. 101 The arm'd Rhinoceros, or th' Hircan tiger. 1620 T. Lodge tr. *Josephus' De Bello Judaico* vii. xxvii, Conspiring with the king of the Hyrcans to passe into Media. 1911 in W. James *Mem. & Studies* xv. 395, I took the Hyrcan tiger by the scruff And tore him piecemeal.

Hyrcanian (hɔɹkēⁱ·niăn), *a.* and *sb.* [f. L. *Hyrcānius* (f. *Hyrcania*) + -an. Cf. prec.]

A. *adj.* Of or belonging to Hyrcania.

1596 Shaks. *Merch. V.* ii. vii. 41 The Hircanion deserts. 1602 — *Ham.* ii. ii. 472 The rugged Pyrrhus like th' Hyrcanian beast. 1671 Milton *P. R.* iii. 317 The Hyrcanian cliffs Of Caucasus. 1777 J. Richardson *Arab. Dict.* 1172 The red Hyrcanian or Tabristan willow. 1820 Shelley *Ode to Liberty* viii, From what Hyrcanian glen or frozen hill,..Didst thou lament the ruin of thy reign? 1824 Carlyle *Love Lett.* (1909) 44 Frightful as the Hyrcanian Tiger. 1885 *Encycl. Brit.* XVIII. 603/1 In 59 [A.D.] the Hyrcanian ambassadors were able to return home.

B. *sb.* A native or inhabitant of Hyrcania.

1838 *Penny Cycl.* XII. 419/2 Josephus..mentions a king of the Hyrcanians in the time of Vespasian. 1885 *Encycl. Brit.* XVIII. 603/1 The Hyrcanians were still independent c. 155 [A.D.].

Hystatite (hi·stătəit). *Min.* [ad. G. *hystatit*, f. Gr. ὕστατος lowest, perh. because its rhombohedron is the lowest of the group.] An ore of titanium related to menaccanite.

1857 Dana *Min.* 241 The hystatite variety [of titanic iron] includes the washingtonite variety of Professor Shepard. 1923 *Nature* 24 Feb. 252/2.

Hysteresis. Add: 2. *Physics.* The time-lag occurring between two associated phenomena and resulting from viscosity or inertia.

1903 *Nature* 17 Dec. 160/2 In the relationship of stress to strain, or twisting couple to twist produced, rocks exhibit a marked *hysteresis*. 1918 T. B. Robertson *Phys. Chem. Proteins* 341 Many of these equilibria..can be approached from either direction, so that they are not 'false' equilibria attributable to the internal molecular friction or hysteresis of the systems.

3. *attrib.* and *Comb.*

1902 *Encycl. Brit.* XXVIII. 120/2 The hysteresis tester of Ewing. 1907 Erskine-Murray *Handbk. Wireless Telegr.* 24 The hysteresis losses in iron placed in so rapidly alternating a field are also very great.

Hysteretic (histəre·tik), *a. Physics.* [f. Gr. ὑστερητικός, f. ὑστερεῖν (see Hysteresis).] Of or pertaining to hysteresis. Hence **Hystere·tically** *adv.*, by means of hysteresis.

1902 *Encycl. Brit.* XXVIII. 120/2 Steinmetz found that the hysteresis loss..varies proportionately to a constant called the *hysteretic constant*. *Ibid.* XXX. 433/1 To annihilate the hysteretic effects of previous magnetization. a 1909 *Electr. World & Engineer* XLIV. 163 (Cent. D. Suppl.) The actual condenser dissipates energy hysteretically in its dielectric.

Hystericky, *a.* (Earlier U.S. example.)

1823 J. F. Cooper *Pilot* II. xiv. 239 In order that the women need not be 'stericky in squalls.

Supplement, p. 3873; Corrigenda, p. 4092; Spurious words, p. 4093; Books quoted, p. 4094

I

I. Add: **I. 2. b. i-mutation, i-umlaut** (also *i/j-mutation*, etc.) *Philology*, the fronting influence of an *i or *j on the vowel of a preceding syllable in one and the same word; also, the result of this.

1870 Marsh *Comp. Gram. A.-S. Lang.* 13 i-umlaut of *ō*: *fōt, fēt(e)*. 1891 Mayhew *OE. Phonol.* 41 In North. and Mercian *oe* = *e*, the *i*-umlaut of *o*. 1908 Wright *Old Eng. Gram.* iii. 28, *A* was the only vowel which underwent i-umlaut in OS. and OHG. *Ibid.* iv. 28 Palatal umlaut, generally called i-umlaut.

III. a. I. = illicit, as I.D.B. = illicit diamond buyer, buying; I.G.B. = illicit gold buyer, buying (all dealings in rough or uncut diamonds or unwrought precious metals being against the law of South Africa unless both buyer and seller hold permits). **b.** = Imperial, as I.M.N.S. = Imperial Military Nursing Service; I.S.O. = Imperial Service Order; I.Y. = Imperial Yeomanry. **c.** = In, in various Latin phrases, as I.D.N. = *in Dei nomine* in the name of God; I.N.J. = *in nomine Jesu* in the name of Jesus; I.P.D. = *in præsentia Dominorum* in the presence of the Lords (of Session). **d.** = Independent, as I.L.P. = Independent Labour Party; I.O.F. = Independent Order of Foresters; I.O.G.T. = Independent Order of Good Templars; I.O.O.F. = Independent Order of Odd Fellows; I.O.S.M. = Independent Order of the Sons of Malta. **e.** = Indian, as I.A. = Indian Army; I.C.S. = Indian Civil Service; I.E. = Indian Empire; I.M.S. = Indian Medical Service; I.S.C. = Indian Staff Corps. **f.** = Institute, as I.B.A. = Institute of British Architects; Institution, as I.C.E. = Institution of Civil Engineers; I.E.E. = Institution of Electrical Engineers; I.Mech.E. = Institution of Mechanical Engineers. **g.** = Intelligence, as (N.) I.D. = (Naval) Intelligence Department; I.P. = Intelligence Police; I.Q. = intelligence quotient. **h.** = Irish, as I.F.S. = Irish Free State; I.R.A. = Irish Republican Army; I.R.B. = Irish Republican Brotherhood, Irish Revolutionary Brotherhood; I.S. = Irish Society. **i.** Miscellaneous. I.C. = inferiority complex; Inspected, Condemned; I.D. = Infantry Drill Regulations; I.G. = Inspector General; I.W.W. = Industrial Workers of the World (a labour organization advocating syndicalism).

a. 1884 Mrs. Carey-Hobson *At Home in Transvaal* II. xlii. 520 'The fellow had money there, with which he turned I.D.B.' 'What's that?'..'Illicit diamond buyer.' 1891 E. Glanville *Fossicker* xxix, They have given an unenviable reputation to three letters of the alphabet—I.D.B., which mean 'Illicit Diamond Buyers', and refer to some of the most cunning and most unscrupulous rascals in creation. 1899 Hornung *Amateur Cracksman* 55 'You know what an I.D.B. is?' 'Illicit Diamond Buyer?' 'Exactly.' 1902 *Encycl. Brit.* XXVI. 565/1 Since 1888 a special Court has been held at Kimberley for trying cases relating to illicit diamond buying ('I.D.B.').

b. 1902 *Encycl. Brit.* XXXI. 340/1 The members of the order have the distinction of adding the letters I.S.O. after their names. 1909 *Whitaker's Alm.* 118 Thos. H. Sanderson Sanderson, G.C.B., K.C.M.G., I.S.O. 1918 E. S. Farrow *Dict. Mil. Terms* p. ix, I.M.N.S.—Imperial Military Nursing Service. *Ibid.* p. x, I.Y.—Imperial Yeomanry.

d. 1899 *Westm. Gaz.* 28 Feb. 2/3 The I.L.P. policy kept a sufficient number of Tory working men from voting to allow the Liberal nominee to slip in. 1924 *Glasgow Herald* 5 Apr. 9 He had had to work on many committees during his time in public life, including committees of branches of the I.L.P. 1926 *Socialist Rev.* Dec. 23 Have I.L.P.ers asked themselves where the movement is going?

e. 1899 *Who's Who* 680/1 Late Colonel C. M. Moberly, I.S.C. 1918 E. S. Farrow *Dict. Mil. Terms* p. ix, I.A.—Indian Army. 1931 *Times Lit. Suppl.* 14 May 390/3 The late Ross Scott, I.C.S. *Ibid.* 18 June 474/3 Paradoxically, the I.C.S. 'bureaucrat' in India is the justification of the popularly elected Minister in England.

f. 1899 *Who's Who* 166/1 Major-General Sir John Ardagh, K.C.I.E. 1894, Assoc. I.C.E.

g. 1918 E. S. Farrow *Dict. Mil. Terms* p. ix, I.D.—Intelligence Department. *Ibid.* p. x, I.P.—Intelligence Police. 1922 Woodworth *Psychol.* xii. 274 Brightness or dullness can also be measured by the *intelligence quotient*, which is employed so frequently that it is customarily abbreviated to 'I.Q.' 1925 E. Fraser & Gibbons *Soldier & Sailor Words*, I: the Service abbreviation for 'Intelligence'. 1931 *Times Lit. Suppl.* 19 Mar. 230/3 Faith, insight and enthusiasm are more important than all the I.Qs in the world.

h. 1929 *Whitaker's Alm.* 546/1 Money Orders. Advice of Payment: 2d. inland (and to I.F.S.). 1932 *Morning Post* 23 Aug. 10/3 A force of 200 men of the I.R.A. have seized Donamon Castle.

i. 1917 B. Hall *One Man's War* (1929) 278 The Government had some trouble in Los Angeles with the I.W.W. 1918 E. S. Farrow *Dict. Mil. Terms* p. ix, I.C.—Inspected, Condemned. I.D.R.—Infantry Drill Regulations. I.G.—Inspector General. I.G.C.—Inspector General of Communications. I.G.F.—Inspector General of Fortifications. I.G.D.—Inspector General's Department. 1919 H. L. Wilson *Ma Pettengill* vii. 212 Even the youngest [girl]..had tenaciously held out for a grown man's pay, which made her something even worse than a Bolshevik; it made her an I.W.W. 1920 Wodehouse *Damsel in Distress* xxi. 251 Regular I.W.W. stuff. 1923 E. A. Ross *Russian Soviet Republ.* 250 The I.W.W. longshoremen of Philadelphia and New York refused to load ships with munitions for Wrangel. 1931 Upton Sinclair *Roman Holiday* xxv, I recognized the I.W.W. lumberjack, the only giant in the crowd.

Iambographic (əiˌæmbogræ·fik), *a.* [f. Iambographer + -ic.] Of, belonging to, or practised in the writing of iambic poetry.

1886 *Amer. Jrnl. Philol.* VII. 378 The melic and iambographic poets.

-iana, *suffix.* See Ana *suffix* and add examples.

1718 [see Shakspeariana]. 1728 J. Smedley (*title*) Gulliveriana: or, a fourth volume of Miscellanies, being a sequel to the three volumes published by Pope and Swift. To which is added, Alexanderiana, etc. 1776 [see *Johnsoniana]. 1800 (*title*) Walpoliana. 1838 (*title*) Railroadiana. A New History of England, or Picturesque..Sketches..Descriptive of the Vicinity of the Railroads. 1879 G. J. Finch-Hatton *Voices through many Years* III. 85 Gladstoniana. *Ibid.* 118 Grevilliana. 1890 *Century Mag.* Aug. 515/2 A number of these 'whaleiana' hang in the 'Captains' Room'. 1898 W. Graham *Last Links* 120 Several writers of Keatsiana follow that most inaccurate of writers,..Leigh Hunt. 1902 *St. Edward's Sch. Chron.* June 231/2 A very interesting collection of what I may perhaps term 'Edwardiana', that is 1st, all printed matter designed for the use of the School. 1929 [see *Boswelliana].

Iapetus (əiˌæ·pĕtŭs). *Astr.* [L., a. Gr. Ἰαπετός, a Titan, father of Prometheus, Atlas, and Epimetheus, regarded in Gr. mythology as the ancestor of mankind.] The eighth satellite of Saturn.

1865 Proctor *Saturn & its System* 52 The satellite discovered by Huygens has received the name of Titan; and the four discovered by Cassini have been called..Tethys, Dione, Rhea, and Japetus. 1880 E. C. Pickering *Dimensions Fixed Stars* 18 The variation of light in Iapetus..is commonly explained in this way. 1886 Asaph Hall in *Rep. Brit. Assoc.* 542 From Hyperion to Iapetus we have a very long interval.

Iapygian (əiˌăpi·dʒiăn), *a.* and *sb.* [f. L. *Iāpygius*, f. *Iāpyx, -ygem*, a son of Dædalus said to have ruled over southern Italy: see -ian.] **A.** *adj.* Of or pertaining to the ancient natives and district of Iapygia, the name given by the Greeks to the peninsula of Apulia in southern Italy. **B.** *sb.* **a.** A native of Iapygia. **b.** The language of the Iapygians.

1773 Langhorne tr. *Denina's Anc. Republics Italy* 26 The Iapygyans and Messapians [lost] fifty thousand infantry. 1864 P. Smith *Hist. World* II. 138 It is here..that we find traces of the Iapygian race, in the peninsula called by the Greeks Messapia. 1880 *Encycl. Brit.* XIII. 443/2 The peninsula which stretches eastward towards Greece was inhabited by a people termed by the Greeks Messapians or Iapygians. 1882 *Ibid.* XIV. 327/1 Inscriptions have been found in considerable numbers, written in a language known as Iapygian or Messapian. 1888 King & Cookson *Sound & Infl. in Gr. & Latin* 30 Of the Iapygian in the extreme south and the Ligurian in the north, very little is known.

Iarfine (ī·ăːfinĭ). *Irish Hist.* [Ir., f. *iar* after + *fine* family.] One of the groups into which the ancient Irish clans were divided. (Cf. *Geilfine, *Indfine.)

1875 Maine *Hist. Inst.* 209 The eldest member of the Iarfine moved into the Indfine.

Iatrochemistry (əiˌætroˌke·mistri). [See Iatro- and Chemistry.] That branch of science which applies chemistry to medicine, as practised by iatro-chemical physicians in the 16–17th c. (cf. Iatro-chemical).

1881 Roscoe & Schorlemmer *Treat. Chem.* III. i. 4. 1904 *Science* 1 July 2/2 It is difficult to realize at the present time how the iatrochemistry developed and flourished as long as it did.

Iatrophysics (əiˌætroˌfi·ziks). [f. Iatro- + Physics.] The theory and practice of the iatrophysical school of medicine.

1890 Billings *Med. Dict.*

Ibanag (ībănā·g). [Native name.] The name of one of the tribes inhabiting northern Luzon in the Philippine Islands; also, the language of this tribe.

1885 *Encycl. Brit.* XVIII. 753/1 The other tribes of the Philippines—the Ilocanes, Pampangos, Pangasinanes, Ibanags or Cagayans,..&c. 1900 F. H. Sawyer *Inhabit. Philippines* 252 The Ibanags inhabit the Babuyanes and Batanes Islands. 1901 *Rep. Philippine Comm.* III. 405 In order to state very briefly how the remaining Philippine languages or dialects are related we select from among them some of the principal ones...These are the Ibanag and Ilocano, of Noul Luzon. 1924 D. P. Barrows *Hist. Philippines* 11 The valley of the Cagayan [is inhabited] by a people commonly called Cagayanes, but whose dialect is Ibanag.

Iberian, *a.* and *sb.* Add: **A.** *adj.* **3.** Pertaining to the Iberians of Britain (cf. *B. *sb.* 3).

1880 *Encycl. Brit.* XII. 605/2 Extreme exponents of the theory do not hesitate to speak of the Iberian ancestors of the people of England. 1907 T. Rice Holmes *Anc. Britain* 65 The race to which they [*sc.* neolithic inhabitants of Britain] belonged is often called the Iberian, though there is no reason to believe that its British representatives belonged to the Iberian rather than to some other branch of the Mediterranean stock.

B. *sb.* **3.** A neolithic inhabitant of Britain, considered as one of a branch of the continental Iberians.

1880 Dawkins *Early Man in Britain* 322 The Silures, identified by Tacitus with the Iberians, were left only in those fastnesses which were subsequently a refuge for the Welsh against the English invaders. 1900 W. A. Dutt *Norfolk* 7 The Iceni..were probably mentally as well as physically superior to the Iberians. 1920 H. F. Henderson *Relig. Scotl.* i. 11 The Iberians absorbed the Celts without serious dilution of their original characteristics.

Ibero- (əibī·ro), combining form of Iberian, with the meaning 'Iberian and'.

1891 Rhys in *Academy* 26 Sept. 268/2, I believe Picts and Iberians to have belonged to one and the same family, which I have ventured to call Ibero-Pictish. 1896 A. H. Keane *Ethnology* 378 *margin*, The Ibero-Berber problem. 1900 Deniker *Races of Man* 285 Tawny white skin, black hair. Short stature, dolichocephalic Ibero-insular. 1920 *Glasgow Herald* 24 Sept. 6 The Ibero-American Republics. 1927 Peake & Fleure *Hunters & Artists* 40 It [*sc.* the Capsian industry] has not yet been found with certainty farther south, and in the coastal area seems to occur in two cultural regions, an eastern or Getulian, and a western or Ibero-Maurusian, each of which displays characteristic differences.

-ibility [F. *-ibilité*, L. *-ibilitātem, -tās*], termination of abstract sbs. from adjs. in -ible.

Ibis. Add: **2.** The name of a fashion shade.

1927 *Daily News* 9 May 2/3 A skirt of satin..in the new pale apricot known as 'ibis'.

3. *attrib.* and *Comb.*, as *ibis-red, -headed* adjs.

1910 *Daily Chron.* 19 Feb. 6/2 Thoth, god of wisdom, was *ibis-headed. 1907 *Westm. Gaz.* 29 Oct. 4/3 A pretty blouse of white lace, so arranged with *ibis-red velvet as to have the effect of a smart little bolero. 1909 *Ibid.* 21 June 5/2 An ibis-red coat and skirt.

Iboga (ibōu·gă). [Congolese.] A shrub (*Tabernanthe iboga*) of Central Africa. Hence **Ibogaine** (ibōu·găˌīn) *Chem.*, an alkaloid obtained from this (see quots.).

1902 *Jrnl. Chem. Soc.* LXXXII. i. 114 Iboga is a plant which grows in French Congo...The active principle, ibogaine, $C_{52}H_{66}O_2N_6$, is present in the bark and wood and particularly in the roots of the plant. 1903 Dorland *Med. Dict.* (ed. 2), *Ibogain*, a poisonous alkaloid from iboga, a plant of the Congo region. It increases blood-pressure and diuresis, raises the bodily temperature, and excites the secretions.

Ibsenism (i·bsənizˈm). [f. the name of Henrik *Ibsen* (1828–1906), Norwegian dramatist and poet + -ism.] The dramatic principles and aims characteristic of the writings of Ibsen and the Ibsenites, which examined and criticized social conventions. So **Ibse·ne, Ibse·nity** *nonce-wds.* (with play on *obscene, obscenity*); **Ibse·nian, Ibseni·stic, I·bsenish, I·bsenitish** *adjs.*, of, pertaining to, or resembling the style or views of Ibsen; **I·bsenite,** an admirer or imitator of Ibsen; **Ibseni·tis,** excessive admiration or copying of Ibsen, viewed as a morbid tendency; **I:bsenoma·nia,** a craze for the writings of Ibsen.

1891 G. B. Shaw (*title*) The Quintessence of Ibsenism. 1891 *Literary World* 30 Jan. 98/1 The battle that raged between the Ibsenites and certain hostile critics of the Doll's House. 1892 *Star* 17 Oct. 1/8 A serious drama, with just a touch of ibsenitis. *Ibid.* 5 Nov. 1/7 A touch of Ibsenitis in a dramatist does not necessarily make a plagiarist. [1892 *National Observer* 17 Dec. 107/1 When the din of political factions is silent, and Ibscenity has faded into a literary curiosity.] 1893 *Ibid.* 7 Jan. 190/2 Her story is amateurish, sentimental, Ibsene. But Ibsenity is in the air. 1893 *Westm. Gaz.* 21 Feb. 9/2 Anybody who is not cured of Ibsenomania after seeing this last play..must be declared incurable. 1893 *Black & White* 25 Feb. 219/2 True Ibsenites have been confirmed in their Ibsenism. 1893 *Graphic* 29 Apr. 467/3 The Ibsenish tendency of the sombre story affected them deeply. 1893 *Illustr. Lond. News* 22 July 106/3 The heroine, with her Ibsenitish tendencies, goes to her self-inflicted death. 1895 tr. *M. Nordau's Degeneration* 524 A drama in which we are shown a really Ibsenian idiot. 1895 Marie Corelli *Sorrows of Satan* xvii, I have finished my discourse..of Ibsenism. 1905 *Daily Chron.* 21 Aug. 4/7 From Ibsenistic drama down to pantomime is not married life the Aunt Sally of the playwright still? 1916 *Everyman* 5 May 54/2 Their passion for the erotic and Ibsene.

Icaco (ikā·ko). [Native name. (In F. the fruit is called *icaque*, the tree *icaquier*.)] A rosaceous shrub or tree, *Chrysobalanus icaco*, a native of the West Indies and Florida: the fruit of which is known as the Coco-plum.

1852 Th. Ross tr. *Humboldt's Trav.* II. xvii. 136 Hedges of bead-trees encircled groups of icacoes laden with fruit. 1887 Moloney *Forestry W. Africa* 347 Icaco or Cocoa Plum of the West Indies.

Icarus (i·kărŭs). *Gr. Myth.* The name of the son of Dædalus, who attempted to fly by means of artificial wings fastened with wax (see Icarian *a.*[1]), used allusively.

[1589 Greene *Menaphon* (Arb.) 53, I feare..in the height of my thoughts soaring too high, to fall with wofull repenting Icarus.] 1591 Shaks. *1 Hen. VI*, iv. vi. 56 Then follow thou thy desp'rate Syre of Creet, Thou Icarus, thy Life to me is sweet. *Ibid.* vii. 16 There di'de My Icarus, my Blossome, in his pride. 1694 D'Urfey *Don Quix.* ii. Ep. Ded. A 1 b, The roving Icarus in Poetry, By you is levell'd, when he soars too high. 1931 *Times Lit. Suppl.* 24 Sept. 714/2 Much that he [*sc.* D'Annunzio] has given is not pure gold, but decorative lumber comparable to the ill-assorted trophies of the Vittoriale from which, an Icarus who has ceased to fly, he makes well-calculated sallies.

Ice, *sb.* Add: **2. c.** (*A big thing*) *on ice*: a good thing. *U.S.* *To cut no ice*: to effect nothing, make no difference. So *not to cut (much, any) ice*. orig. *U.S.* *Straight off the ice*: of food, directly or freshly obtained; hence *fig.*, immediately and without intermission. *To get* (or *find*) *one's ice legs* [after Sea legs]: to acquire facility in the use of one's legs on ice, i.e. for skating.

1889 Farmer *Amer.* 1890 A. C. Gunter *Miss Nobody* xx. 231 In the hall, prominently posted up by a wag, under new memberships, is a notice: For Election. Gussie de P. Van Beekman, *vice* Baron Bassington, of Harrowby Castle, England. On ice! 1896 G. Ade *Artie* xi. 96 But that cuts no ice in our set. 1897 *Scribner's Mag.* Sept. 305/1 And it don't cut no ice with you whether folks call you inconsistent or not. 1904 *Albany Weekly Times* 30 June 4 The czar is to send an ice-breaking boat to the Far East, realizing apparently that his forces haven't been cutting much ice over that way. 1911 R. D. Saunders *Col. Todhunter* viii. 111 We need at least three thousand dollars, and while it's pretty certain old Leslie will raise that amount eventually, that doesn't cut any ice now. 1917 Conan Doyle *His Last Bow* 291 It cuts no ice with a British copper to tell him you're an American citizen. 1922 A. S. M. Hutchinson *This Freedom* iii. vi, I started cross-examining to-day. I gave him three and a half hours of it, straight off the ice, and I'm not through with him yet. 1924 R. Keable *Recompence* i. (1926) 6 You were perfectly honest in feeling that your religion cut no ice. 1927 Agatha Christie *Big Four* iii, How would a Chinaman cut any ice in Russia? 1931 *Daily Express* 21 Sept. 19/4 Among those whom I noticed 'getting their ice legs'.

4. b. = *ice pigeon* (see *8).

1881 Lyell *Pigeons* 81 The smooth-legged chequered or spangled ones are known in this country as Ural ice, while the rough-legged spangled birds are called Siberian ice.

8. ice-arm, an arm or projecting portion of ice; **ice-bicycle,** a bicycle adapted for use on ice; **ice-blindness,** defective sight caused by the exposure of the eyes to the glare of ice; **ice-car,** a refrigerating van adapted for the transport of perishable goods; **ice-cart,** a cart in which ice is conveyed for delivery; **ice-cave,** (*b*) a hollow in the ice at the lower end of a glacier; (*c*) a refrigerating culinary utensil; **ice-chest** *U.S.* (earlier example); **ice-crop,** the yield of ice in a single winter or from a certain place; **ice-dyke,** a narrow crevasse filled with ice columns; **ice-farm,** in India, a place where ice is obtained by allowing water to freeze in specially hollowed out beds, or in shallow earthenware pans; **ice-front,** the border of a glacier; **ice-gorge** *U.S.* (earlier example); **ice-harvest** = **ice-crop*; **ice hockey,** a game developed from field hockey but played on ice; also *attrib.*; **ice-lane,** a narrow track between ice-floes; **ice line** (see quot.); **ice-lobe,** a projection from the continental ice-sheet of the glacial epoch; **ice locomotive** (see quot.); **ice maker** (*b*) = *ice-machine*; **ice-marker** (see quot.); **ice-mould,** a hollow utensil used in shaping ice; **ice-pack,** (*b*) a pack (cf. Pack *sb.*[1] 11) prepared with ice; **ice-pan,** a small slab of floating ice; **ice-piece,** an attachment to the bows of a ship to protect them from ice; **ice pigeon,** a breed of domestic pigeon whose prevailing colour is a pale bluish lavender; **ice pipe,** a tube of ice produced by the action of frost on the surface of water-logged clay; **ice-rink** (see Rink *sb.*[2] 3); **ice-run,** a stretch of ice prepared for tobogganing; also *fig.*: **ice-scape** [after *landscape*], a picture of ice scenery; **ice-scouring,** the action of glacier ice on rock; **ice-shed,** the dividing-line from which the ice of a glacier moves in opposite directions; **ice-spirit,** frost as a nature-spirit; **ice-spoon,** a utensil used in icing cakes; **ice sport,** a sport taking place on ice; **ice-storm** (see quot.); **ice-tongue,** a mass of ice projecting from a glacier or iceberg; **ice-white** *a.*, having a whiteness like that of ice; **ice wool** = *Eis wool.

1928 *Daily Tel.* 4 Sept. 11/5 He..had mistaken the Frederikshaab *ice arm for the Sukkertoppen ice arm. 1897 E. Elliott in *Outing* (U.S.) XXIX. 343/2 *Ice-bicycles, in which a runner is substituted for the front wheel, and the rear wheel is bound with a steel or iron rim, set with sharp teeth. 1885 *Buck's Handbk. Med. Sci.* I. 538/1 Snow- or *ice-blindness, is a variety of nyctalopia. 1909 *Chambers's Jrnl.* Aug. 560/2 In Canada there is also a special *ice-car service for the carriage of butter to Montreal. 1842 *Knickerbocker Mag.* XX. 205 Before an omnibus or hotel or restaurant or *ice-cart had assumed its popular cognomen. 1864 T. L. Nichols *Forty Yrs. Amer. Life* I. 247 Every morning the ice-cart comes round. 1897 *Geog. Jrnl.* (R.G.S.) June 670 The term '*ice-cave'..should especially apply to the hollows in the ice at the lower end of glaciers, whence the glacier waters make their exit. 1911 *Madame* 20 May 318/1 Various forms of iced pudding, which, even if you do not happen to possess one of A. B. Marshall's ice caves, are still quite possible to prepare with very little trouble. 1841 C. Cist *Cincinnati* Advt., Manufacturer of Packing-boxes, *Ice-chests, Trunk and Segar Boxes, &c. 1853 A. Bunn *Old Eng. & New Eng.* I. ii. 31 Content ourselves by observing that the *ice-crop (as it is drolly called)..proved to be a fair average one. 1864 *Chambers's Jrnl.* 100/1 Producing an ice-crop which will pay all expenses and leave a profit. 1905 W. H. Sherzer in *Smithsonian Misc. Coll.* XLVII. 468 *Ice dykes. These consist of narrow crevasses, two to fifteen inches across, completely filled with columnar ice. 1908 *Sci. Amer.* 25 Jan. 58/2 Natural Ice Making in the Tropics—The Peculiar '*Ice Farms' of Hot Bengal. 1905 W. H. Sherzer in *Smithsonian Misc. Coll.* XLVII. 455 One year later the distance of this boulder from the *ice front was found..to be 20 ft. 1862 *Congress. Globe* 2896/1 The island is..below the bend in the Delaware, and hence mainly out of danger from *ice gorges. 1864 *Chambers's Jrnl.* 100/2 The season of the *ice-harvest being short and uncertain. 1904 *Westm. Gaz.* 17 Mar. 2/1 Men with horses were ploughing the ice-harvest of the river. 1883 *Boy's Own Paper* 13 Oct. 30/1 For *ice hockey the ball is from six to seven inches in circumference. 1898 *Daily News* 28 Nov. 8/7 The first ice hockey match at Niagara took place on Saturday. 1907 *Westm. Gaz.* 4 Dec. 7/2 An ice-hockey match at Prince's last night. 1909 *Ibid.* 18 Jan. 12/4 The great ice carnivals, skating championships, and ice-hockey matches. 1928 *Daily Express* 4 Aug. 2/7 The spectacle of ice-hockey in Canada. 1896 Kipling *Seven Seas* 29 Down a cruel *ice-lane, That opened as he sped, We saw dead Henry Hudson Steer, North by West, his dead. 1899 W. Watson *Text-bk. Physics* 267 Such a curve will indicate the pressure corresponding to any temperature to which a mixture of ice and water must be subjected, in order that the two states may be in stable equilibrium. This curve is called the '*ice line'. 1903 *Science* 6 Feb. 224/2 The relation of the Michigan, Saginaw and Huron-Erie *ice-lobes in lower Michigan during the Wisconsin stage of glaciation. 1875 Knight *Dict. Mech.*, '*Ice-locomotive, a traction engine for running on ice. 1927 *Daily Tel.* 11 May 18/3 New patent non-chemical refrigerator and *ice-maker. 1875 Knight *Dict. Mech.*, **Ice-marker*, a species of plow for grooving pond ice. 1864 *Chambers's Jrnl.* 101/1 A continuous current through the cistern containing the *ice-moulds. 1900 *Daily Chron.* 12 Nov. 5/6 The condition of Lord Roberts's daughter is somewhat serious. *Ice-packs have been applied. 1901 *Geog. Jrnl.* (R.G.S.) July 40 The *ice-pans appear to drift capriciously backward and forward, and, without any apparent cause, they will select some unexpected course. 1926 *Blackw. Mag.* July 67/1 An awful journey through a country devoid of human beings, across treacherous moving ice-pans. 1830 N. Dana *Mariner's Sk.* 274 (Th.) A lady on each arm answers precisely the same purpose as the '*ice pieces' on the bows of a Greenland whaler. 1881 Lyell *Pigeons* 81 The *Ice Pigeon. This variety derives its name from its beautiful lavender blue colour, considered by the German fanciers to resemble blue ice. 1904 Van Hise in *Monographs U.S. Geol. Survey* 444 This squirting upward at the various openings produces innumerable *ice pipes. 1886 *Field* 13 Mar. 310/1 Nor is it less strange that so few *ice rinks are found in England. 1930 *Daily Express* 16 Aug. 3/1 By the middle of October there will be at least nine ice-rinks in London alone. 1900 *Daily News* 30 Nov. 5/2 The new *ice-run for tobogganers ..is almost ready for use. 1910 H. G. Wells *Hist. Mr. Polly* vi, Mr. Polly swerved a little from the conversational ice-run upon which he had embarked. 1904 Sir J. D. Hooker in *Life* (1918) II. 457 His landscapes, seascapes and *ice-scapes are most interesting. 1901 *Science* 5 Apr. 552/1 *Ice-scouring during maximum glaciation reached far up the mountain slopes above the trough walls. 1894 J. Geikie *Gt. Ice Age* (ed. 3) 330 The *ice-shed in Scandinavia did not coincide with the water-parting. 1897 Ethel L. Voynich *Gadfly* viii. (1904) 141/2 He might have recalled some splendid and fearful *ice-spirit of the mountains. 1900 *Month* Jan. 85, I took you for that evil thing, the ice-spirit, who freezes the limbs of our people. 1828 *Female Instructor* 507 As the cream sticks to the sides scrape it down with your *ice-spoon. 1901 (*title*) *Ice Sports. 1908 *Daily Chron.* 27 July 4/4 Boating in summer and ice sports in winter. 1886 Geikie *Outl. Geol.* 50 By repeated thawings and regelations the branches and boughs are gradually loaded with ice and snow, and, becoming top-heavy, the trees are liable to fall, even when no wind is blowing. Should one be overthrown it collides against its neighbour, and this in turn falls upon another, until shortly the trees are seen crashing to the ground in all directions. This is what is known in North America as an *ice-storm. 1901 *Westm. Gaz.* 19 Mar. 10/2 This *ice-tongue extends eastwards for a distance of perhaps 500 miles. 1904 *Science* 5 Aug. 188/1 A detailed description of about fifteen Greenland ice tongues. 1928 *Daily Express* 10 Oct. 3/3 Where an *ice-white salmon stream flows through a gorge. 1931 *Daily Tel.* 21 May 6/3 A gown of very heavy ice white satin. 1882 *Ice wool [see Eis wool].

Ice, *v.* **1. a.** *To ice up.* Add: also, to hold fast with ice.

1899 C. J. Cutcliffe Hyne *Further Adv. Capt. Kettle* xii, The boats are frozen on to the chocks...Did you never see a boat iced up before?

Ice-boat. Add: *attrib.*, as *ice-boat sailing*; **ice-boatman,** one who sails an ice-boat or ice-yacht.

1897 E. Elliott in *Outing* (U.S.) XXIX. 342/2 This is the wind *ice-boatmen whistle for. 1909 *Westm. Gaz.* 8 Feb. 9/1 A good ice-boatman thinks nothing of jumping cracks in the ice three, four, or six feet in width. 1901 Mrs. Alec Tweedie in *Ice Sports* 255 *Ice-boat sailing..is a somewhat expensive amusement when a man buys his own boat.

Ice-cream. (Earlier U.S. example.)

1744 *Penn. Mag. Hist. & Biog.* I. 126 Among the rarities ..was some fine ice cream, which, with the strawberries and milk, eat most deliciously.

attrib. 1851 A. O. Hall *Manhattaner in N. Orleans* 46 How the ice cream saloons resound with clattering spoons. 1873 J. H. Beadle *Undevel. West* xxviii. 623 Two months vigorous courting will cost more than that—particularly in the ice cream season. 1879 *Harper's Mag.* Dec. 34/2 You may buy..ice-cream freezers.

Hence **Ice-crea·mer,** an ice-cream vendor.

1901 *Scribner's Mag.* XXIX. 484 Every low-down Neapolitan ice-creamer in the town.

Iced, *ppl. a.* Add: **2.** Of a cake, bun, etc.: Covered with icing. Of preserved fruit: = Glacé.

1858 Simmonds *Dict. Trade*, *Iced*, cakes frosted with sugar. 1866 Mrs. Beeton *Preserves & Confect.* 5 Iced Apples, or Apple Hedgehog...Cover the apples very smoothly all over with the icing. *Ibid.* 89 Iced currants...Lay them to dry on paper, when the sugar will crystallize round each currant. 1891 *Encycl. Cookery* (ed. T. F. Garrett) I. 240/1 Iced cake.

b. *Iced heart, liver* (Path.): chronic inflammation of the serous membrane of these organs accompanied by a fibrinous exudation which resembles the icing on cakes. (Cf. *Icing *vbl. sb.* 4.)

1903 *Med. Record* 14 Feb. 273 (Cent. D. Suppl.).

c. (See quots.) Cf. Frosted *ppl. a.* 3 b.

1829 Loudon *Encycl. Plants* 1100/1 *Iced*..covered with particles like icicles. 1900 B. D. Jackson *Gloss. Bot. Terms*, *Iced*, having a glittering papillose surface, as *Mesembryanthemum crystallinum*.

Iceland[2]. Add: **Iceland falcon,** *Falco islandus*, the white gerfalcon of Iceland. **Iceland gull,** *Larus leucopterus*, the lesser white-winged gull.

1771 *Gentl. Mag.* July 297/1 The Iceland Falcon. 1821 *Mem. Wernerian Nat. Hist. Soc.* (1822) IV. i. 176 Iceland Gull. 1843 Yarrell *Brit. Birds* I. 27 Those specimens obtained from Iceland were called exclusively Iceland Falcons. *Ibid.* III. 461 The Iceland Gull sometimes makes its appearance in winter at the mouth of the Elbe. 1883 *List Anim. Zool. Soc.* (ed. 8) 383 *Hierofalco islandus*...Iceland Falcon. *Ibid.* 534 *Larus leucopterus*,..Iceland Gull.

Icenian (əisī·niăn), *a.* [See -ian.] Of or pertaining to the Iceni, an ancient British tribe inhabiting the district roughly corresponding to modern Norfolk and Suffolk, or to this district; also *spec.* in *Geology*, designating the Norwich Crag of the English Pliocene formation. Also **Ice·nic** *a.*

1757 Dyer *Fleece* iii. 72 This method still Norvicum favours, and the Icenian towns. 1830 *Forby's Voc. E. Anglia*, *Mem.* p. xxxix, With only one more extract I will close what remains to be said respecting the Icenian Glossary. 1870 A. D. Bayne *Hist. East. Engl.* I. 393 Some Icenic names are supposed to remain in several towns of Norfolk and Suffolk. *Ibid.* 395 There are thousands of pits in many places, and these are supposed to have been the foundations of Icenian huts. 1900 F. W. Harmer in *Q. Jrnl. Geol. Soc.* Nov. 734 Aldeburgh...where the Icenian (Norwich Crag) Beds come on. 1900 W. A. Dutt *Norfolk* 39 Some authorities have suggested that that important Icenic settlement was at Caistor. 1921 R. A. S. Macalister *Text-Bk. European Archæol.* I. 158 To this type of flint, or to the supposed industry which it represents, has been given the name *Icenian*.

Icer (əi·səɹ). [f. Ice *v.* + -er[1].] An operative who prepares icing and applies it to the surface of cakes, pastry, etc.

1921 *Dict. Occup. Terms* (1927) § 433.

Ice-water. Add: (Later U.S. examples.)

1829–32 J. P. Kennedy *Swallow Barn* II. xvii. 220 The injured part should be bathed frequently with ice-water. 1846 *Knickerbocker Mag.* XXVIII. 187 They may pour in a large spoonful of that [*sc.* brandy], and then fill it up with ice-water. 1863 Mrs. Whitney *F. Gartney's Girlhood* xxi, With quick, professional instinct Miss Sampson sprang forward seizing, as she did so, an ice-water pitcher from the table. 1889 *Harper's Mag.* Sept. 560/1 Here were found..the huge brown hogsheads for ice-water. 1906 *New York Even. Post* 25 July 4 A glass of ice-water placed before us the moment we sit down to breakfast;..a pitcher of ice-water sent to our bed-rooms.

b. Water produced naturally by the melting of glacier or other ice.

1905 *Westm. Gaz.* 2 Sept. 2/3 He and I are going up to where the icewater tinkles at noon under the blue glacier-ice.

Ichabod (i·kăbǫd). Name given by Eli's daughter-in-law to her son, used as an exclamation of regret, in allusion to 1 Sam. iv. 21 (She named the child Ichabod, saying, 'The glory is departed from Israel').

1901 'A. Hope' *Tristram of Blent* xxi, 'Bring me some cold beef', he commanded, and the waiter brought it with an air that said 'Ichabod' for the Imperium. 1904 'H. S. Merriman' *Last Hope* xxi, 'Ichabod', he said, with a short laugh. 1915 *N. & Q.* 11th Ser. XI. 110/1 At one time the Scriptural name Ichabod was used, presumably with a knowledge of its derivation, with the sense of alas! regretting the good old times.

Hence **Ichabo·dian** *a.*, regretful, lamenting.

1887 *Daily News* 1 Dec. 2/1 Dirges were sung with an Ichabodian refrain.

Ichebo, -u, ichibo, -u, var. ff. Itzebu.

Ichhu, variant of *Ichu.

Ichneumoned (ikniū·mənd), *a.* [f. Ichneumon + -ed[2].] Infested with ichneumon parasites.

1897 W. F. Kirby in *Concise Nat. Hist.* 576 Ichneumoned larvæ generally attain their full growth, and then die.

Ichth(o)-, = Ichthyo-, as in **Ichtha·lbin** *Chem.*, an antiseptic powder prepared from ichthyol and albumen. **I·chthoform** *Chem.*, an antiseptic powder prepared from ichthyol and formaldehyde.

1901 Dorland *Med. Dict.* (ed. 2), Ichtalbin,..Ichthoform. 1915 G. Martin *Indust. & Manuf. Chem.* (ed. 2) I. 614 Ichthyol-Albumen (= Ichthalbine) is obtained by precipitating albumen solution with a solution of ichthyol sulphonic acid. *Ibid.*, Ichthoform is a compound of ichthyol sulphonic acid and formaldehyde.

Ichthyan (i·kþiăn), *a.* [f. Gr. ἰχθύς fish + -an.] Of, relating to, or consisting of fishes.

1855 J. Phillips *Man. Geol.* 289 The 'bone bed' full of reptilian and ichthyan remains.

Ichu (ī·tʃū). Also **ichhu, ychu.** [Quichua.] A wiry grass, *Stipa ichu*, occurring on the cold uplands of Peru and Bolivia, used as fodder and for thatching.

1891 E. B. Clark *Twelve Months in Peru* 136 The coarse *ychu* grass, growing in tufts upon the mountain slopes. 1921 *Glasgow Herald* 23 Apr. 10/1 The great ichu-covered steppes of the plateau. 1925 *Countries of World* VI. 3765/2 The thick ichu grass, however, covers the region in general, a natural pasture.

Icing, *vbl. sb.* Add: **2. b.** Preservation by means of ice; refrigeration with ice.

1883 R. F. Walsh *Irish Fisheries* 17 (Fish. Exhib. Publ.) A rate for fish carrying is then struck; this includes icing.

4. *attrib.*, as **icing heart, liver** = *iced heart, liver* (*Iced *ppl. a.* 2 b); **icing-house,** a building where food is preserved by means of ice.

1886 P. S. Robinson *Valley Tee-totum Trees* 24 Hanging up as two 'sides of pork' in the icing-house. 1901 Dorland *Med. Dict.* (ed. 2) s.v. *Liver*, *Icing-l.*, a liver covered by a thick coat, like icing. 1913 *Ibid.* (ed. 7) s.v. *Heart*, *Icing-h.*, pericarditis which appears postmortem like the icing on a cake.

Iconian (əikōu·niăn), *a.* (*sb.*) [-an.] Of or pertaining to Iconium, one of the towns in Asia Minor in which St. Paul preached, or to the church established there (Acts xiii. 5, xiv. 1–7). **b.** *sb.* A native or inhabitant of Iconium.

1899 W. M. Ramsay in *Expositor* Aug. 112 There were strife and wrangling and jealousy between the Antiochean Church and the Iconian Church about precedence and comparative dignity. 1921 — *First Christ. Cent.* xxv. 168 St. Paul addressed the Iconian audiences in Greek. *Ibid.* 172 The Iconians clung to their Phrygian character as opposed to the Lycaonian.

Iconometer (əikǫnǫ·mɪtəɹ). *Photog.* and *Surveying.* [f. Icono- + -meter.] An optical instrument for ascertaining the size or distance of an object or image (see quots.). Hence **Iconome·tric, -me·trical** *adjs.*, of, pertaining to, or ascertained by iconometry; **Iconome·trically** *adv.*, by means of iconometry. **Icono·metry,** the science or art of determining the sizes and distances of objects by means of an iconometer.

1897 *Ann. Rep. U.S. Coast Survey* June 628 (Funk) Iconometry means the measuring of dimensions of objects from their perspectives..; iconometry is the reverse of perspective drawing. 1918 *Photo-Miniature* XV. Mar. (Gloss.) *Iconometer*, a view-meter of 'direct-vision' pattern, i.e., consisting of an open frame with an eyehole or lens fixed behind it. 1919 *Brit. Jrnl. Photogr. Alm.* 244 A *view-meter*, or *iconometer*, is a separate accessory for ascertaining the picture produced by any given lens and size of plate.

Icono-. Add: **Ico·nodule,** = Iconodulist.

1900 'Odysseus' *Turkey in Europe* 230 The division of Asia representing Iconoclasts and Europe Iconodules is almost without exception. 1901 E. Gosse in *Daily Chron.* 22 Nov. 3/3 The sentiment of the author is vehemently on the side of the Iconodules.

Icos-. Add: **b.** *Chem.* In names of hydrocarbons containing twenty atoms of carbon.

1889 Morley & Muir *Watts' Dict. Chem.* II. 746/1 Icosane $C_{20}H_{42}$...Formed by reduction of the dichloride of heptyl tridecyl ketone with HI and P. *Ibid.*, Icosinene $C_{20}H_{38}$. Eicosylene...Prepared from ozokerit, or the solid paraffin from brown coal. *Ibid.*, Icosonene $C_{20}H_{36}$. Didecene...Obtained from the fraction of the product of the distillation of colophony by removing other unsaturated hydrocarbons...Colourless, non-fluorescent, oil. 1895 *Jrnl. Chem. Soc.* LXVIII. i. 127 Icosenic acid, $C_{20}H_{38}O_2$, is formed when behenolic acid is heated with fused caustic potash at 250–270°. *Ibid.*, The dibromide, when hydrolysed with alcoholic potash, yields icosinic acid, $C_{20}H_{36}O_2$, which melts at 69°.

Ictero- (i·ktĕro), combining form of Gr. ἴκτερος jaundice, as in **Ic:terogene·tic, I:eteroge·nic** *adjs.*, causing jaundice. **I:cterohæmatu·ria,** a disease of sheep caused by minute animal parasites (Dorland 1901). **I:cterophthi·sis,** tuberculosis with jaundice.

1890 Billings *Med. Dict.*, Icterophthisis. 1897 *Allbutt's Syst. Med.* IV. 38 This drug [*sc.* toluylendiamin] is the most notable of all icterogenetic poisons. *Ibid.* 65 A notable feature of the blood disorders caused by these various icterogenetic poisons, is an increased destruction variously manifested.

Id[2] (id). *Psycho-analysis.* [A use of L. *id* it, as a translation of G. *es* (Groddeck *Das Buch vom Es*, 1923).] The inherited instinctive impulses of the individual.

1924 Joan Riviere in *Freud's Coll. Papers* II. 250.

-id[2]. Add: **b.** *Astr.* A termination added to the name of a constellation to form the name of any meteor radiating or appearing to radiate from that constellation, as *Andromedid, *Cepheid, *Coronid, *Herculid, Leonid, Lyraid, Perseid, Quadrantid. See also *Bielid.

Idæan (əidī·ăn), *a.* Also **Idaian.** [f. L. *Idæus*, Gr. Ἰδαῖος (f. *Idā, Idē*, Ἴδη) + -an.] Of, belonging to, or dwelling on Mount Ida, either (*a*) a mountain in Asia Minor near the ancient Troy; or (*b*) the chief mountain in Crete, the birthplace of Zeus.

1590 Spenser *F. Q.* ii. vii. 55 Here eke that famous golden Apple grew,..For which th' Idæan Ladies disagreed. *Ibid.* ii. viii. 6 Like as Cupido on Idæan hill. *a* 1649 Drumm. of Hawth. *Poems* Wks. (1711) 7 Trembling roofs of trees ..Which make Idæan woods in every crook. 1810 Scott *Lady of L.* i. xxvi, Where Ellen's hand had taught to twine The ivy and Idæan vine. 1820 Shelley *Prometh. Unb.* iii. i. 25 Pour forth heaven's wine, Idæan Ganymede, And let it fill the Dædal cups like fire. 1876 Gladstone *Homeric Synchr.* 123 Teucer, son of Scamander and of an Idaian Nymph. 1921 *Public Opinion* 17 June 568/3 The sad dwellers on the Idaean plain.

Idalia (əidā·liă). *Ent.* [mod.L.] An American fritillary, *Argynnis idalia*.

Idalian (əidā·liăn), *a.* [f. L. *Idalius*: see -an.] Of or belonging to the ancient town of Idalium in Cyprus, where Aphrodite was worshipped. **b.** *Geol.* (See quot. 1910.)

1799 Campbell *Pleasures of Hope* ii. 90 Some cottage-home..With peace embosom'd in Idalian bowers! 1832 Tennyson *Œnone* 170 Idalian Aphroditè beautiful. 1910 *Encycl. Brit.* VII. 696/2 The Oligocene consists of grey and white marls (known as the Idalian series), which are distributed all over the island [of Cyprus]. 1928 J. H. Mozley tr. *Statius* I. 187 Golden Venus..on her way from the height of Eryx to the Idalian groves.

Iddat (i·dɒ̆t). *Mohammedan Law.* Also -ut. [Arab. عدة *ciddat* period during which intercourse is unlawful.] The period of chastity required to be observed by a divorced or widowed woman before remarriage, so as to avoid confusion of issue.

1865 N. B. E. Baillie *Digest Moohumm. Law* 21 If a decree were pronounced for a divorce on false testimony with the woman's knowledge, she might lawfully intermarry with another husband after the expiration of her *iddut*.

Iddingsite (i·diŋzəit). *Min.* [f. name of J. P. *Iddings*, American mineralogist + -ite[1].] A silicate of iron, calcium, and magnesium, an alteration-product of olivine.

1893 A. C. Lawson in *Bull. Dept. Geol. Univ. California* I. 31. 1900 H. E. Gregory *Geol. Aroostook Volcanic Area* 181 This alteration product appears somewhat like the iddingsite found in the California teschenite. 1903 Geikie *Text-bk. Geol.* (ed. 4) 105 Iddingsite appears to be closely allied to, if not identical with it [*sc.* bowlingite].

Iddy-umpty (idiˌʌ·mpti). Also **iddy-iddy-umpty.** Conventional verbal representation of the dots and dashes of the Morse code.

1906 *Punch* 24 Jan. 60/3 An 'Iddy Umpty' Idyll. 1914 *Daily Express* 15 Dec. 4/5 To see men practising the 'iddy-umpty', as they call it, with the back of a sheath-knife on the top of an empty tobacco-tin in lieu of a regulation 'dummy-key'. 1924 *Glasgow Herald* 23 June 10 For my sins of commission and of omission—as far as the worship of that fetish 'Iddy-Umpty' was concerned—I became for a time an inmate of the great signalling camp at Swanage. 1925 E. Fraser & Gibbons *Soldier & Sailor Words*, *Iddy* (or *Itty*) *Umpty*, an expression first used in India in teaching the dot-and-dash Morse system to native troops. An 'Iddy Umpty' in that way came to be used as a term for a signaller.

Idea, *sb.* Add: **4.** *Big* or *great idea* (cf. *Big *a.* 7 b and B.). orig. *U.S.*, usually *ironical*.

1928 *Saturday Even. Post* (N.Y.) 12 May 22/1 'Listen, big boy,' he protested,..'what's the big idea in this potato contest?'

12. *idea-monger.*

1909 *Englishwoman* Apr. 305 Ibsen..was not merely an ideamonger, but a dramatist. 1923 *Glasgow Herald* 25 Jan. 4/2 Mr. Wells is a prolific idea-monger.

Idealness. (Later U.S. example.)

1891 S. Lanier in *Independent* (N.Y.) 26 Nov. 6 (Funk) The direct result of these associations in the case of Chaucer ..is to increase the idealness of the poem.

Ideationally (əidīˌēi·ʃənăli), *adv.* [f. Ideational *a.* + -ly[2].] By means of ideation.

1910 R. R. Rusk in *Brit. Jrnl. Psychol.* III. 379 The dissociation of the perceptually excited elements of consciousness from the ideationally excited factors.

Idée fixe (ide fiks). [Fr.] A fixed idea (see Fixed *ppl. a.* 2).

1836 H. Greville *Diary* (1883) 88 The King..has some *idée fixe* about marrying the Duke of Orleans. 1877 L. W. M. Lockhart *Mine is Thine* vii, At all events, the attraction of the heart would require to be something out of the common run if it were to subdue this *idée fixe*. 1928 'Van Dine' *Greene Murder Case* xvii, We're dealing with the persistency of an *idée fixe*.

Idem sonans (əi·dem sōu·nænz). *Law.* [L., lit. = sounding the same.] Identity of sound in pronunciation; the occurrence in a document of a material word or name misspelt but having the sound of the word or name intended. Also *adj.*, homophonous *with*.

1848 Wharton *Law Lex.* s.v., The courts will not interfere in setting aside proceedings on account of the misspelling of names, provided..there is an *idem sonans* between the pronunciation of the right name and that which is inserted in the proceedings; as Lawrance, instead of Lawrence, Reynell for Reynolds, Beniditto for Benedetto. *a* 1856 in *Newsp. & Gen. Reader's Comp.* § 1749 The verb was unluckily *idem sonans* with another word.

Identical, *a.* Add: **2. c.** *Identical points* (see quot.).

1890 Billings *Med. Dict.*, *Identical points*, precisely corresponding points in each retina of a pair of eyes.

B. *absol. pl.* Identical things.

1903 Bp. Gott *Lett.* (1917) 195 Most of the books..worry me with endless and subtle refinements and hair-splitting distinctions between identicals.

Identification. Add:

4. *attrib.*, as *identification card, disc, mark, number, paper*; **identification panel** (see quot.); **identification parade,** a parade of persons from among whom a suspect is to be identified; **identification patch,** a patch attached to a soldier's back to help in identifying his unit when going into action behind a barrage; **identification plate,** the registered number plate of a motor vehicle; **identification signal** (see quot.); **identification tag,** a disc or piece of cardboard giving a soldier's name, religion, rank, and number, in order to establish his identity if killed or wounded.

1908 *Westm. Gaz.* 13 Feb. 5/2 An *identification-card with his photograph on it. 1930 T. B. Bruce *Missing* 13, I burnt all letters and papers..keeping only my *identification disc. 1897 Ethel L. Voynich *Gadfly* iii. i, For you to go there just now, with all your *identification marks, would be to walk into a trap with your eyes open. 1901 *Westm. Gaz.* 24 Apr. 3/2 He found fifteen other bodies, searched them for their identification marks. 1904 *Daily Chron.* 13 Apr. 8/3 The Garage Company lent him their identification mark for that purpose. 1904 *Westm. Gaz.* 30 Aug. 4/3 The identification marks of the cartridges of all the known armies of the world. 1918 E. S. Farrow *Dict. Mil. Terms*, **Identification Panels*, in aëroplane or balloon signalling, panels which are displayed at the sound signal of the aircraft or upon the initiative of the command post. 1903 *Westm. Gaz.* 28 Dec. 7/2, 300 men who had no workmen's *identification papers. 1927 W. E. Collinson *Contemp. Engl.* 78 The shortcomings of the *identification parades at the police station. 1918 E. S. Farrow *Dict. Mil. Terms*, **Identification Patch*, tags placed upon the backs of the men's coats when advancing behind a barrage. 1901 *Motor-Car World* II. 74/1 *Identification-plate. 1906 *Westm. Gaz.* 26 Aug. 8/2 The Commission recommends that identification plates should 'be rigidly fixed in an upright position'. 1909 *Ibid.* 24 June 4/1 Five marks for identification plates. 1918 E. S. Farrow *Dict. Mil. Terms*, **Identification Signals*..which will identify the authority sending the communication..are assigned from division headquarters and each consists of one letter and one numeral. *Ibid.* s.v., An *identification tag by which he can be identified if killed or wounded.

Identify, *v.* Add:

3. To discover, perceive. *colloq.*

1924 D. H. Lawrence *England, my England* 45 After a lapse and a new effort, he identified a pain in his head.

Identity. Add: **7.** *Old identity*: a person well known in a place. *New Zealand.*

The phrase was invented by R. Thatcher in Dunedin, N.Z., in a popular song in 1862.

1879 W. J. Barry *Up & Down* xx. 197 The 'old identities' were beginning to be alive to the situation. 1893 *Auckland Weekly News* 9 Dec. 7 Both these old identities are in possession of all their faculties to a wonderful degree. *Ibid.* 28 Another old identity passed away on Dec. 1 in the person of Mr. Thomas Hunt.

8. *attrib.* with the meaning 'that serves to identify the holder', as *identity card, certificate, disc, paper*.

1900 *Westm. Gaz.* 2 Jan. 3/1 When troops are going on service each man has issued to him what is known as a field dressing and an identity card. 1908 *Daily Chron.* 21 Feb. 4/6 The 'identity papers,' which every man and woman in Prussia must carry about with them. 1909 *Ibid.* 15 June 5/5 Rations for three days, ammunition, field bandages, and identity discs were issued to the men. 1911 *Punch* 15 Mar. 181/1 By the March Army Orders the identity discs issued to officers and men in war time are in future to be issued to the former in peace time. 1915 'Ian Hay' *First Hundred Thousand* vi, It's called an Identity Disc. Every soldier on active service wears one. 1918 *Act 8 Geo. V* c. 64 § 11 Every person who receives, detains or has in his possession any identity certificate, life certificate, or other certificate. 1919 J. B. Morton *Barber of Putney* i, In due course came vaccination and inoculation, and identity discs. 1931 *Times Lit. Suppl.* 1 Jan. 2/2 He..forged an identity card, and procured a pistol.

Ideo-. Add: **I·deopla·stic** *a.*, denoting those physiological processes which are supposed to be moulded or modified by mental impressions or suggestions; also, pertaining to the suggestive function of the imagination; so **I·deopla:sty, Ideo·plasy,** imagination in its suggestive capacity, esp. as modifying certain physiological functions or processes.

1901 *Baldwin's Dict. Philos. & Psychol.* I. 507/2 *Ideoplastic*, applied to the physiological functions considered as liable to modification from suggested ideas (used originally by Durand de Gros). *Ibid.*, *Ideoplasy*, suggestions operative in the production of physiological changes. 1919 Conan Doyle *Vital Message* App. 209 We accept Dr. Geley's statement that they are 'ideoplastic'. 1929 *Encycl. Brit.* I. 51/1 For half a century no perceptible progress was made on the idea thrown out by Durand (1855, 1860) that a clear distinction should be effected between the 'ideoplastic' and hypotaxic phenomena.

Idio-. Add: **I·dioblast** (*b*) *Biol.*, a hypothetical structural unit of living protoplasm. **I:diochro·mosome** *Biol.*, a chromosome having the distinctive characteristic of sex in the germ cells of certain insects. **I·diomere** *Cytology*, 'a vesicle formed from an individual chromosome at the time when the daughter-nuclei are about to reconstitute themselves after karyokinetic cell-division' (Cent. D. Suppl. 1909). **I:diopla·smic** *a. Biol.*, of or belonging to idioplasm.

1893 *Nature* 2 Feb. 315 Hertwig..suggests the employment of the term '"Idioblasts" for the minute elementary particles, which Darwin called 'gemmules' in his hypothesis of pangenesis. 1896 P. C. Mitchell tr. *O. Hertwig's Biol. Probl. of To-Day* 22 Herbert Spencer's physiological units, Darwin's gemmules, De Vries' pangenes, and Hertwig's idioblasts. 1909 *Century Dict.* Suppl., *Idiochromosome. 1903 *Bot. Gaz.* June 443 The nuclear stages in which the *idiomeres (partial nuclei) and gonomeres (double nuclei) appear are closely related. 1902 *Encycl. Brit.* XXXII. 213/1 It may still be admitted that in certain cases a cytoplasmic predetermination arises as a secondary result of *idioplasmic influence.

Idiom. Add: **3. b.** *Mus.* A characteristic mode of expression, or an instance of this.

1921 J. B. McEwen *First Steps Mus. Comp.* 5 To put it in somewhat colloquial terms, the composer of ancient music wrote melody, the composer of modern music writes tunes. It is no part of my purpose to make comparisons between these two idioms. *Ibid.*, An intentional reversion to the contrapuntal idiom. 1927 *Grove's Dict. Music* (ed. 3) II. 537/2 The folk-songs of all nations have been cultivated..for the sake, mainly, of their undoubted freshness and spontaneity of idiom as compared with pseudo-classical models. *Ibid.* 538/1 The study of this melodic music has suggested many harmonic idioms of notable freshness and beauty.

Idiot, *sb.* **4.** Add: **idiot-stitch,** tricot-stitch, the easiest stitch in crochet work.

1882 Caulfeild & Saward *Dict. Needlework*, *Idiot Stitch*, one of the names given to Tricot Stitch.

Idle, *a.* **4.** Freq. in phr. *the idle rich.*

1928 F. N. Hart *Bellamy Trial* i. 15 He's magnificent when he gets started on the idle rich.

5. c. *Electr.* Of a current: Wattless. Of a coil or wire: Carrying no electromotive force.

1894 W. P. Maycock *Electric Lighting & Power Distrib.* i. vi. (ed. 2) 155 Those portions of the wire on an armature, as well as those parts at the end which slip between, but do not cut lines of force, are often called *idle wire*. 1904 R. M. Walmsley *Electricity* ii. vi. 1069 This current..contributes nothing to the power, and is therefore often referred to as the *idle current*. 1904 *Technol. & Sci. Dict.* (ed. Goodchild & Tweney), Idle or Wattless Current. *Ibid.* s.v. *Idle Coil*, In certain forms of armature a coil may at a given instant have no induced electromotive force acting in it; it is then termed an Idle Coil.

d. Of money: Out of circulation.

1931 *Times Lit. Suppl.* 19 Feb. 124/2 It may be thought that saving cannot exceed investment because idle money automatically becomes the basis of bank credit.

8. *idle-minded* adj.

1899 *Westm. Gaz.* 21 Aug. 2/3 The empty-headed and idle minded exist in both sexes.

b. Idle Jack, a Natal name for a South African grass-bird.

1875–84 Layard & Sharpe *Birds S. Afr.* 281 It..will suffer itself to be taken with the hand rather than rise again; for this reason it has acquired the name of *Idle Jack* or *Lazy Dick*. 1893 Newton *Dict. Birds*, *Idle Jack*, a local name given in the Cape Colony for *Sphenæacus africanus*.

Idle, *v.* Add: **2. c.** *To idle over*: of an engine, etc., to rotate or run at a low speed without performing any work.

1931 Nordhoff & Hall *Falcons in France* 98 The mechanics already had the engines warmed up, and propellers were idling over at 330 revolutions.

Ido (ī·do). [In this language, = offspring.] An artificial language, based on *Esperanto, selected by the 'Delegation for the Adoption of an Auxiliary International Language' (founded at Paris in 1901), and made public in 1907. Hence **I·doist,** a student or speaker of Ido.

The official name is 'Linguo Internaciona di la Delegitaro (Sistema Ido)'.

1908 *Daily Chron.* 7 Sept. 7/2 The new language has been named 'Ido', and its inventor [M. de Beaufort, of Geneva] claims that it is easier to learn and is more methodical than Esperanto, its parent. 1916 H. G. Wells *Mr. Britling* i. v. § 10 'There would be no English, no Germans, no Russians. Just Esperantists..Or Idoists,' said Herr Heinrich.

Idolize, *v.* **1.** Add: Also *absol.*

1919 M. K. Bradby *Psycho-anal.* 65 For instance, one person may be prone to jealousy, another to idolise.

Idryl (i·dril, -əil). *Chem.* [f. *Idria* in Austria + -yl.] = *Fluoranthene.

1863 Fownes *Man. Chem.* (ed. 9) 698 Idrialin..is generally associated with a hydrocarbon idryl. 1892 Roscoe & Schorlemmer *Treat. Chem.* III. vi. 523 Fluoranthene, $C_{15}H_{10}$, is found in coal-tar, and is also identical with idryl.

Idumæan (əidiumī·ăn, id-), *sb.* and *a.* Also -ean. [f. L. *Idūmæa*, a. Gr. Ἰδουμαία, f. Heb. *Edōm* Edom + -an.] **A.** *sb.* A member of the race inhabiting Idumæa. **B.** *adj.* Of or belonging to Idumæa or Edom, an ancient kingdom situated between Egypt and Palestine.

1537 *Orig. & Sprynge of Sectes* 55 Idumeans. 1620 Lodge tr. *Josephus' De Bello Judaico* IV. vi, Twenty thousand Idumæans come to Jerusalem. 1737 Whiston *Josephus, Antiq.* xii. viii. § 1 He fell upon the Idumeans, the posterity of Esau, at Acrabattene. 1838 *Penny Cycl.* XII. 437/1 The Idumæans marched to the assistance of Jerusalem when it was besieged by Titus. 1863 *Chambers's Encycl.* V. 343/1 The family was of Idumean descent. *Ibid.* 499/2 The Idumæan, Antipater. 1880 *Encycl. Brit.* XI. 754/1 Herod was the name of a family of Idumæan origin.

Idyllic, *a.* Add: Also used trivially.

1899 *Daily News* 20 June 3/3 He was afraid that idyllic prospect never had any substantial foundation.

Ie (ī·e). [Hawaiian *ie* the plant described below, also the mat made from it; Samoan *ie* a fine mat used as currency by the natives.] In Hawaii and Samoa applied to various climbing screw-pines of the genus *Freycinetia* and their products. Also in reduplicated form **Ie-ie.** (Cf. Kie-kie.)

1883 C. F. Gordon Cumming *Fire Fountains* I. 128 Vines without number, the most notable being one called the *ie*. Note, *Freycinetia scandens*. 1903 R. C. L. Perkins in *Fauna Hawaiiensis* I. 400 All those [birds] that were utilised could readily be caught by a bait of flowers, excepting perhaps the Ou, and this bird probably not less easily on account of its fondness for the ripe Ieie. 1915 W. A. Bryan *Nat. Hist. Hawaii* 211 The ieie, a climbing shrub with many of the habits of its cousin, the lauhala.

If. **6.** Add: Also *if anything.*

1909 P. A. Vaile *Modern Golf* v. 92 If anything, touch the grass first. 1931 Belloc *Hist. Eng.* IV. ii. i. 260 If anything the ritual of King-worship was even more exaggerated in her case than in the case of Henry or of Edward.

Ife[2] (ī·fe). [Angola.] A liliaceous plant, *Cordyline* (*Sansevieria*) *cylindrica*, used as a substitute for hemp.

1866 *Treas. Bot.*, *Ife*, an Indian name for *Sanseviera cylindrica*. 1857 Simmonds *Dict. Trade* Suppl., *Ife*,..a plant useful for its fibre.

Igarape (igarapĕ·). Also **-ipe.** [Brazil.] A tributary stream or water-channel in a forest entered from a main river.

1860 Mayne Reid *Odd People* 38 Travelling can only be done by water, either upon the great rivers, or by the narrow creeks (igaripes) or lagoons. 1890 Agassiz *Geol. Sk.*, *Phys. Hist.* Ser. ii. (1890) 185 We turned..into a narrow stream, which has the character of an Igarapé in its lower course.

Igelströmite (i·gəlströmait). *Min.* [Named, 1878, after L. J. *Igelström*, Swedish mineralogist: see -ite[1].] A silvery-white variety of pyroaurite.

1878 *Min. Mag.* II. 108 Igelstromite..occurs in shrinkage cracks or veins, of an earthy form, and a pure white colour.

Igloowik (i·glŭwik). Also **iglooeak.** [Eskimo *iglovigak*.] An Eskimo snow hut. Cf. Igloo[1].

1909 P. W. Browne *Where the Fishers Go* 26. 1909 *Daily Chron.* 11 Oct. 3/3 The Eskimo..terms his snow-house 'igloowik'; while the shorter word 'igloo'..is the common name of the 'permanent house in the settlements and around the missions'.

Igniter. Add: **c.** An apparatus for igniting the charge of gases in the cylinder of an internal combustion engine. Also *attrib.*

1902 A. C. Harmsworth *Motors & Motor-Driving* viii. 154 The Dawson Ignitor. 1902 *Young Engineer* I. 352/1 It is fired by an electric spark,..between the platinum points of an igniter..or by means of a dynamo-coil..which produces sparks at the igniter. 1904 A. B. F. Young *Complete Motorist* iv. (ed. 2) 96 It is the action of this 'tweaker' upon the igniter wire which causes the rupture of the circuit by which the spark is produced. 1909 *Westm. Gaz.* 11 Nov. 5/2 The special Lodge igniter for aëroplanes.

Ignition. Add: **2. c.** *spec.* The act of starting the combustion of the mixture in the cylinder of an internal combustion engine; also, the mechanism for producing this. Also *attrib.*, as *ignition chamber, device, tube, wire*.

1894 B. Donkin *Text-Bk. Gas, Oil, & Air Engines* i. i. 8 Three methods of ignition are employed. 1. The electric spark. 2. A gas jet constantly burning. 3. A tube maintained at a red heat by a gas burner. *Ibid.* i. viii. 103 Ignition tube. *Ibid.* i. xi. 140 Ignition chamber. *Ibid.* 149 Ignition stroke. 1902 S. R. Bottone (*title*) Ignition Devices for Gas and Petrol Motors. 1902 A. C. Harmsworth *Motors & Motor-Driving* viii. 161 The ignition plugs may be examined to see that they are not coated with oil. 1906 *Daily Chron.* 12 May 3/5 All good cars nowadays have the two independent ignitions, the accumulator and coil, and the magneto driven by a cog-wheel on the engine shaft. 1909 *Westm. Gaz.* 15 June 4/2 When battery ignition is used. 1926 R. W. Hutchinson *Wireless* 54 Some makers label the capacities of accumulators as 'ignition capacity'. 1928 C. F. S. Gamble *Story North Sea Air Station* 55 A piece of tin..had sheared four ignition wires.

Ignorance. Add: **3.** (In full *the time* or *days of ignorance*; tr. Arab. جاهلية *jāhiliyah* state of ignorance, f. جاهل *jāhil* ignorant.) The period of Arabian history previous to the teaching of Mohammed.

1788 Gibbon *Decl. & F.* l. v. 185 Of the time of ignorance which preceded Mahomet, seventeen hundred battles are recorded by tradition. 1895 A. Menzies *Hist. Relig.* 213 The Arabs called the period before Islam the 'time of ignorance'; in that period they considered their race had no history. 1904 Ker *Dark Ages* 14 The student of heroic poetry may admire the temper of the Arabian Dark Ages—'the Ignorance'.

Ignotum per ignotius (ignōu·tŏm pɜɪ ignōu·ʃiŭs). [late L., lit. the unknown through the more unknown.] An attempt to explain what is obscure by something which is more obscure.

a 1461 Lydg. in Ashmole *Theat. Chem. Brit.* (1652) 401 Wyth Golden Resouns in taast moost lykerous Thyng *per Ignotum* prevyd *per Ignocius*. 1584 R. Scot *Discov. Witchcr.* iii. xvii. 67 Confuteth that opinion by a notable reason, called *Petitio principij*, or rather, *Ignotum per ignotius*. *a* 1734 North *Examen* ii. i. § 26 (1740) 28 When he drops his own Authority, and brings Fact to confirm all, the vouching that Fact by his own pure Parole, is a Cheat termed *Ignotum per ignotius*. 1888 *Athenæum* 22 Dec. 843/2 When Arabic names are twisted and mis-copied..the identification of sites resolves itself into a case of 'ignotum per ignotius'. 1931 *Times Lit. Suppl.* 30 July 590/3 [He] even goes so far on one occasion as to explain an Egyptian *chiaoush* as being analogous to an Indian *chobdar*, which to some readers may be a case of *ignotum per ignotius*.

Igorrote (īgǫrōu·te). Also **Igolot(e, Igorot, Ygorrote.** [Native name.] The proper name of one of the tribes of Malayan descent inhabiting the Philippine Islands, applied subsequently to other neighbouring savage tribes; and hence used = wild. Also as *collect. sing.* and *attrib.*

1840 *Penny Cycl.* XVIII. 88/2 The Ygorrotes, who inhabit the mountains east of the Gulf of Lingayen, are distinguished by a peculiar physiognomy and a lighter colour. 1875 F. Jagor *Trav. Philippines* 131 The Ygorrotes are not Christians. 1885 *Encycl. Brit.* XVIII. 753/1 The Igorrotes or Igolotes proper (for the name is by many writers very loosely applied to all the pagan mountain tribes of Luzon) inhabit the districts of Bangued, Lepanto, Tiagan, Bontoc. 1898 D. C. Worcester *Philippine Isl.* 438 One of the Igorrote peoples is believed to be descended from the followers of the Chinese invader Limahong. 1903 Barrows in *Philippine Jrnl. Sci.* Oct. 796 The powerful and numerous Igorot of northern Luzon. 1914 D. C. Worcester *Philippines* I. 343 This once prosperous little Igorot hamlet had been burned by the Spaniards.

Iguana. Add: **2.** A small kind of crocodile found in South African rivers.

1875 Bisset *Sport & War S. Africa* 179 The Iguana, a small kind of crocodile.

Iiwi (īˌī·wi). [Hawaiian.] A Hawaiian bird, *Vestiaria coccinea*, prized for its vermilion plumage used in making native cloaks.

1893 Newton *Dict. Birds*, *Eee-eve*, in modern spelling *Iiwi*, the English rendering by many voyagers of the native name of the beautiful scarlet *Vestiaria coccinea*. 1915 W. A. Bryan *Nat. Hist. Hawaii* 329 The beautiful scarlet iiwi.

Ijolite (ī·yəlait). *Geol.* [f. the name of Lake *Ijo* in Finland + -lite.] An igneous rock, composed essentially of nepheline and pyroxene, first found in the Ijo district of Finland.

1897 A. Harker *Petrology* (ed. 2) 52 The 'ijolite' of Ramsay and Berghell from Finland, a nepheline-pyroxene-rock free from felspar but sometimes rich in garnet. 1903 Geikie *Text-bk. Geol.* (ed. 4) 222.

Ikey (əi·ki), *a.* and *sb. slang* and *dial.* Familiar form of *Ike*, short for *Isaac*, used typically for: A Jew; hence, a Jewish receiver or money-lender; as *adj.* (*a*) Artful, crafty, knowing, smart, 'fly'; (*b*) having a good opinion of oneself, 'stuck-up'.

[1836–7 Dickens *Sk. Boz*, *Tales* x, 'Let me alone,' replied Ikey, 'and I'll ha' vound up..in five seconds.'] 1865 *Slang Dict.*, *Ikey*, a Jew 'fence'. 1870 Leybourne *Song* (Farmer) My name it is ikey Bill, A Whitechapel Covey 'am I. 1881 *Punch* 10 Sept. 110/1 'Arf ikey of course, put-up bizness. 1887 *Kentish Gloss.*, *Ikey*, proud. 1889 Barrère & Leland *Dict. Slang*, *Ikey* (popular), a Jew;..Also said of any one who thinks himself knowing, smart, and has a great opinion of himself. 1892 Chevalier *Little Nipper* (Farmer) Artful little ikey little ways.

Ileo-. Add: **I:leo-si·gmoid** *a.*, relating to the ileum and the sigmoid. **I:leo-si:gmoido·stomy,** excision of the whole colon from the cæcum to the sigmoid.

1903 *Therapeutic Gaz.* 15 Feb. 102 (Cent. D. Suppl.) When a colectomy is impossible because of the site of the lesion.. an anastomosis is indicated, either colo-colic or ileosigmoid. 1908 *Practitioner* Apr. 495 To render ileo-sigmoidostomy a successful operation. *Ibid.* June 818 Some short-circuiting operation such as an ileo-sigmoidostomy would have answered the purpose.

Ilfracombe (i·lfrăkūm). The name of a watering place in North Devon, used *Geol.* to designate certain beds found in that neighbourhood belonging to the Middle Devonian system.

1867 *Q. Jrnl. Geol. Soc.* XXIII. 372 Ilfracombe group. A series of silvery slates and shales, containing several thick bands of limestone. 1879 Geikie in *Encycl. Brit.* X. 370/2 Ilfracombe group. Grey unfossiliferous slates..passing down into calcareous fossiliferous slates and limestones. 1879 *Q. Jrnl. Geol. Soc.* XXXV. 536 The junction of the Morte and Ilfracombe slates with the underlying Hangman grits. 1929 *Encycl. Brit.* VII. 291/1 Above these is a thick succession of grits, slates and limestones, the Ilfracombe beds.

Iliac (i·liæk), *a.*[2] [ad. L. *Iliacus*, a. Gr. Ἰλιακός: see Iliad.] Pertaining or relating to ancient Ilium; Ilian.

1878 Gladstone *Homer* 37 The other epics of the Iliac Cycle differ in their narrative from the Iliad.

Iliacus (ilai·ăkŏs). *Anat.* [mod.L.] The flexor muscle of the thigh, the iliac muscle.

[1738 Chambers *Cycl.*] 1875 *Encycl. Brit.* I. 840/2 The thigh can be bent on the abdomen by the action of the psoas, iliacus, and pectineus, which lie in front of the joint.

Iliahi (īliā·hi). [Hawaiian.] The Hawaiian sandalwood, *Santalum freycinetianum*.

1825 W. Ellis *Jrnl. Tour Hawaii* App. 247.

Ilian (i·liăn, əi·liăn), *a.* (*sb.*) [f. *Ili(um* + -an.] Of or pertaining to ancient Ilium, or to the Græco-Roman city of New Ilium in the Trojan Plain; also as *sb.*, an inhabitant of New Ilium.

1582 Stanyhurst *Æneis* i. (Arb.) 36 Whilst stood the great Ilian empyre. 1626 G. Sandys *Ovid's Met.* xiii. 222 To th Ilian Court I went. 1847 Leitch tr. *C. O. Müller's Anc. Art* 483 Coins of the Ilians. 1869 Tozer *Highl. Turkey* I. 44 The site of the ancient Village of the Ilians. 1876 Gladstone *Homeric Synchr.* 34 He appears as the representation of the Dardanian Branch, with a sidelong jealous eye towards the predominating Ilian House of Priam. 1882 *Jrnl. Hellenic Studies* II. 18 After the victory, he [*sc.*

Alexander] gave substantial proof of gratitude to the Ilian gods and heroes. 1888 *Encycl. Brit.* XXIII. 579/2 The temple of the Ilian Athene. *Ibid.*, It was politic to recall the legend of Roman descent from Æneas. Lucius Scipio and the Ilians were alike eager to do so.

Iliat (i·liät). Also **Ilat, Iliaut, Iliyat.** [Turkish ايلات *ilāt*, pl. of *il* country, wandering pastoral tribe (cf. *rūm-eyli* 'country of the Romans', Rumelia).] One of a group of Turkish nomads scattered throughout Persia.

1840 *Penny Cycl.* XVII. 472/1 The wandering tribes of Persia are comprehended under the general term of *Iliyats* or *Ilat*, and are found in every part of Persia. 1865 *Chambers's Encycl.* VII. 420/2 The nomad or pastoral tribes, or eylats (*eyl*, a clan), often spelt *illyats*, are of four distinct races—Turkomans, Kurds, Lūurs, and Arabs. 1888 *Encycl. Brit.* XXIII. 661/1. 1902 D. G. Hogarth *Nearer East* 160 The nomad 'Iliats' who wander here and there.

Ilima (ilī·mă). [Hawaiian.] A plant of the genus *Sida*, bearing green and yellow flowers.

1910 *Glasgow Herald* 16 Apr. 8 Three magnificent wreaths of ilima, the Hawaiian royal flowers.

Ilk, *a.*[1] **3.** ¶ Add: Also, by further extension, often in trivial use, = kind, sort.

1790 J. Fisher *Poems* 155 Ilk ane a cap an' cloak o' silk Has got, as if she was a lady, An' that indeed, o' nae sma' ilk. 1881 A. Morgan *Shakes. Myth.*, Milton was the enemy of all the ilk. 1897 *Evesham Jrnl.* 23 June (E.D.D.) The horses most famous for marvellous exploits must have blood as well as bone, but only certain districts of the Green Isle can produce this ilk. 1899 *Westm. Gaz.* 29 June 3/2 Two very new hats of quite another 'ilk'. *Ibid.* 6 July 3/2 A coat of this 'ilk' is quite another matter from the coat of the tailor costume.

Ill, *a.* and *sb.* Add: **A.** *adj.* **8. b.** = Sick *a.* 2. esp. *U.S.*

1928 C. F. S. Gamble *Story North Sea Air Station* 244 Before they could be attended they were given too much food and were violently ill as a result. 1929 Conan Doyle *Maracot Deep* 153 The sight was so horrifying that we were all ill.

Ill-. Add: **A. III. 4. ill-favour** *v. trans.*, to treat badly, to be inimical to or hostile towards.

1899 F. J. Crowest *Beethoven* 128 His environment generally throughout his early life ill-favoured the contemplative mood. 1908 *Westm. Gaz.* 21 Aug. 2/1 Fortune ill-favoured them in many skirmishes.

B. ill convenience, conveniency, convenient (Amer. examples).

1737 in J. T. Bunce *Hist. Old St. Martin's, B'ham* (1875) 47 Great *Illconveniences have attended the Ringing of States Days & Holidays at Both Churches. 1773 *Carroll Papers* in *Maryland Hist. Mag.* XIV. 367, I found no ill conveniency from it nor did I feel it. 1777 *Mass. Hist. Soc. Collections* Ser. II. II. 235, I shall be particularly obliged to you if, without putting yourself to any ill convenience, you can procure for me the memorandum. 1653 *Braintree Rec.* 6 Upon consideration of great *ill conveniencyes. 1708 in *Maryland Hist. Mag.* XVII. 218 It might be very *ill convenient on Emergency's not to be able to make an Election under three or four months. 1719 *Ibid.* XVIII. 9 [They] have stopped it [*sc.* a road] up and turned it into Ilconvenient & swampy ground. 1723 in J. T. Bunce *Hist. Old St. Martin's, B'ham* (1875) 44 It appearing to be very ill convenient to the Town..that the Guard should be kept at either of the Markett Crosses.

Illano (ilyā·no). [Native name.] A Moro of the coast tribes of Mindanao in the Philippine Islands. Also **Illa·non, Illa·nun.** Hence **Illano·an** *a.*

1840 *Penny Cycl.* XVIII. 87/1 He was informed that the Illanos from that island [*sc.* Magindanao] had formed a settlement on Burias. 1848 F. S. Marryat *Borneo* 21 Pirate's Bay, so called from its being a favourite resort of the Illanoan pirates. 1898 F. T. Bullen in *Nat. Rev.* Aug. 857 There is yet another small section of the inhabitants of this Archipelago, who were once the terror of the surrounding seas...These have long been known as 'Illanons'.

Illative, *a.* and *sb.* Add: **A.** *adj.* **4.** *Gram.* Denoting the case expressing motion into.

1890 Gatschet *Gram. Klamath Lang.* 483 The suffix marks as well (1) a motion or direction toward an object or into a place or country, as (2) a stay or rest at or in a place, region, country. It is more frequently used in the former sense, and hence I have called the case the illative case.

B. *sb.* **1.** Delete †*Obs.* and add examples.

a 1868 Byington *Gram. Choctaw Lang.* (1870) 54. 1870 F. A. March *Gram. A.-S.* § 481 Causals and illatives are very often omitted.

Illawarra (ilăwǫ·ră). The name of a district in New South Wales, used attrib. to designate certain trees indigenous thereto.

1889 Maiden *Usef. Pl. Australia* 422 *Elæocarpus reticulata*, var. *Kirtoni*, is known as 'Illawarra Ash', or 'Mountain Ash'. *Ibid.* 470 A sample of timber...is a light buff coloured timber, heavy, very hard, tough, durable. In the catalogue it is called 'Illawarra Box'. *Ibid.* 543 *Frenela rhomboidea* ..'Illawarra Mountain Pine'.

Ill effect, ill-effect. [Ill *a.* 5, Effect *sb.* 1.] (Usually in *pl.*) A harmful or deleterious effect, an unpleasant consequence.

1675 in *Isle of Man Charities* (1831) 6 The mean provision of the Clergy in that Isle, and the ill effects which necessarily attend upon the same. 1704 *Hist. Man* xlvii. 195 Envy, and the ill Effects of it. 1767 ill effect [see Ill *a.* 3]. 1845 D. Jerrold's *Shilling Mag.* I. 174 Equal ill effect, either from his liking the Princess too much, or too little. 1884 W. Pye *Surg. Handicraft* 531 One year after the accident he..could go to a ball and dance every dance without any ill effects. 1923 R. Lynd *Blue Lion* xxi. 162 It would be mere perversity to quarrel with these [dishes] because there are no ill-effects from eating them.

Illegitimate, *a.* Add: **2. d.** *Racing.* Applied to steeplechasing and hurdle racing as distinguished from flat-racing.

So called from the fact that before the formation of the Grand National Hunt Committee these forms of racing were not under any rules and were not recognized by any racing tribunal. 1888 *Daily Chron.* 31 Oct. (Farmer) A much smarter performer at the illegitimate game than she was on the flat. 1889 Barrère & Leland *Dict. Slang* s.v., *Illegitimate season*, also called the dead season. 1898 A. E. T. Watson *The Turf* viii. 171 The Jockey Club gave no countenance to 'illegitimate' sport.

Ill health, ill-health. [Ill *a.* 7, Health *sb.* 2.] An unsound, disordered condition of health; that state of health which is characterized by the presence of some disease or by the imperfect functioning of the physical processes.

1732 [see Ill *a.* 8]. 1782 [see Health *sb.* 2]. 1783 Johnson *Let. to Mrs. Montagu* 22 Sept., That I have not written sooner, you may impute to absence, to ill-health, to any thing rather than want of regard. 1811–13 Jane Austen *Mansfield Park* ii, Lady Bertram, in consequence of a little ill-health, and a great deal of indolence, gave up the house in town. 1855 Macaulay *Hist. Eng.* xi. III. 63 Danby.. under the plea of ill health..withdrew from court. 1911 A. C. Benson *Diary* (1926) 220 The pictures of her [*sc.* Mrs. Carlyle] in 1854..are hauntingly terrible—the mixture of ill-health and unhappiness very conspicuous.

Illinium (ili·niǝm). *Chem.* [f. *Illin(ois + -ium.] An element belonging to the group of rare earths, having the atomic number 61.

1926 *Chambers's Jrnl.* 480/2 In honour of the university where it was discovered, the new element has been called Illinium. 1932 E. N. da C. Andrade in *Observer* 18 Oct. 22/4 In 1926 the rare earth 61 was discovered in America, and named Illinium.

Illinoian (ilinoi·ăn), *a.* and *sb.* [f. *Illinois + -an.] **a.** *adj.* Of or pertaining to the State of Illinois; *spec.* in *Geol.* belonging to or constituting a glacial period well represented in Illinois. **b.** *sb.* The Illinoian epoch or deposit.

1899 *Bull. Geol. Soc. Amer.* X. 116 The Illinoian surface ..shows distinct effects of erosion. 1906 Chamberlin & Salisbury *Geol.* III. 391 The identification of the Illinoian drift...The Illinoian is made up of clayey till. 1924 C. Schuchert *Geol.* 654 Third or Illinoian glacial stage.

Illinois (ilinoi·, -oi·z). [Amer. Indian.] The name of a former Indian tribe and of one of the United States, used attrib. as in **Illinois coffee** (see quot.), **Illinois hickory, nut**, the pecan tree and nut.

1863 *Trans. Ill. Agric. Soc.* (1865) V. 865 The Chick-pea has again been heralded as a valuable acquisition upon the prairies under the name of *Illinois coffee. 1785 H. Marshall *Amer. Grove* 69 Pecan or *Illinois Hickory. 1783 W. Fleming in *Trav. Amer. Col.* 666, I was informed the Oiona or *Illinois nut grows near the Falls. 1789 Morse *Amer. Geog.* 54 The Illinois or peccanut is of the walnut kind...The trees which bear this fruit grow principally on the Illinois river. 1817 S. R. Brown *Western Gaz.* 25 The pecan or Illinois nut.

Illinoisan (ilinoi·zăn, -oi·ăn), *sb.* and *a.* [f. *Illinois + -an.] **a.** *sb.* A native or inhabitant of Illinois. **b.** *adj.* Pertaining to Illinois; *spec.* in *Geol.* (cf. *Illinoian).

1836 *Public Ledger* (Philad.) 14 Oct. (Th. 447) The Illinoisans are called Suckers, the inhabitants of Indiana Hooshiers. 1857 *Trans. Ill. Agric. Soc.* II. 63 Illinoisans—men who know their rights and dare maintain them. 1877 Habberton *Jericho Road* x. 97 Small parties of discharged Illinoisans and Indianians had frequently passed through.

So **Illinoi·sian** *sb.* [-ian.]

1885 *Century Mag.* Sept. 793/1 'Pendragon', the work of an Illinoisian, William Young. 1890 Whitman *Goodbye my Fancy* Wks. 1902 VII. 37 Abraham Lincoln, familiar, [is] our own, an Illinoisian.

Illipe, variant of Illupi.

Illiquid, *a.* Add: **b.** Of an asset, investment, etc.: Not easily or readily realizable. Hence **Illiqui·dity**, the character of being illiquid.

1913 *Globe* 24 Oct. 6/4 Is cottage property a safe investment for the Reserve Fund? It is an illiquid asset, and a sudden drain on a fund thus locked up might be very inconvenient. 1927 *Glasgow Herald* 18 Apr. 9 The illiquidity of credit in Japan. 1930 *Times* 26 Mar. 26/7 Slow and illiquid loans and investments.

Ill treatment, ill-treatment. [Ill *a.* 2, Treatment 1. Cf. Ill-treat *v.*] Bad or unfavourable treatment; rough handling; harsh or unsympathetic dealings.

1713 [see Ill *a.* 2]. 1811 A. Graydon *Mem.* 292 In revenge for some real or supposed ill treatment. 1818 *Public Ledger* 8 Apr. 3/2 Alledged ill-treatment during a short confinement in that prison. 1864 Pusey *Lect. Daniel* i. (1876) 21 Who revenge on man their illtreatment at the hand of man. 1879 G. Meredith *Egoist* xxiii, He contemplated her with an air of stiff-backed ill-treatment. 1905 Chesterton *Heretics* 79 A permanent possibility of selfishness arises from the mere fact of having a self, and not from any accidents of education or ill-treatment.

Illuminate, *ppl. a.* and *sb.* **A.** *adj.* **2.** Delete †*Obs.* and add example.

1909 *Westm. Gaz.* 19 May 4/2, I once knew a follower of the Rosy Cross, an illuminate member.

B. *sb. spec. pl.* = Illuminati b.

1906 *Edin. Rev.* July 49 The influence of the German 'illuminates' on the French lodges.

Illuminized (ilü·minaizd), *ppl. a.* [f. Illuminize *v.* + -ed[1].] Initiated (see Illuminize *v.* 2).

1900 *19th Cent.* July 104 A great Masonic meeting which was held in 1786 at Frankfurt—whither the headquarters of illuminised Freemasonry were removed after the famous Congress.

Illusion. 5. (Earlier U.S. example.)

1873 Aldrich *Marjorie Daw*, etc. 14 An emerald-colored illusion dress looped up after the fashion of a Dresden china shepherdess.

Illusional (ilū·zǝnăl), *a.* [f. Illusion *sb.* + -al.] Pertaining to, characterized by, or subject to illusions.

1911 Webster. 1923 *Daily Mail* 1 Mar. 4 On reception into prison he was suspicious, illusional, and confused.

Illusioned (ilū·zǝnd), *ppl. a.* [f. as prec. + -ed[2].] Full of illusions.

1920 *Glasgow Herald* 6 July 6 A fervent but illusioned admirer. 1921 Galsworthy *To Let* iii. vi, Even his love felt tainted, less illusioned, more of the earth.

Illustrate, *v.* **3.** Delete †*Obs.* and add example.

1917 *Mod. Lang. Rev.* XII. 205, I do not desire to illustrate my version of 'the Fause Knight,' but merely to claim that it throws new light on the subject matter of the original ballad.

6 Also *absol.*

1863 O. M. Mitchell *Astron. Bible* 168 The subject is difficult. Permit me to illustrate.

Illustrious, *a.* Add: **3. c.** *Most illustrious*: the special epithet of the Order of St. Patrick.

1882 *Encycl. Brit.* XIV. 123/2 The 'most illustrious' Order of St. Patrick was instituted by George III in 1788.

Illustriousness. Add: **2.** [tr. G. *durchlaucht.*] With possessive adjective as a title of dignity or honour given to German princes.

1929 S. N. D *Sir W. Howard Visct. Stafford* iv. 48 His Electoral Illustriousness, the Prince Palatine of the Rhine.

Ill-wish, *v.* Add: Also *absol.* Hence **Ill-wish** *sb.*, the evil or misfortune wished.

1853 T. Q. Couch in Brand *Pop. Antiq.* (1870) III. 101 The witch's malice, or, as it is termed, 'the ill-wish'. 1899 Baring-Gould *Bk. of West* II. 16 A bard, and after him a saint, might not ill-wish unless he had been refused a just request. *Ibid.*, If he ill-wished unjustly, then it was held that the ill-wish returned on the head of him who had launched it.

Illy, *adv.* For '*dial.*' read '*chiefly U.S.*', and add recent examples.

1903 *Atlantic Monthly* July 116 Which is far better than if it had rushed into illy considered legislation. 1904 Claiborne *Old Virginia* 268 (Th.) I dropped one of my gauntlets, ..which I could illy afford to lose. 1927 C. A. & M. R. Beard *Rise Amer. Civiliz.* II. 213 To meet a crisis of this kind labor was illy prepared.

Illyrian (ili·riăn), *a.* and *sb.* [f. L. *Illyrius*, a. Gr. Ἰλλυριός.]

A. *adj.* **1.** Of or pertaining to the Illyrians or to ancient Illyria (or Illyricum), a country lying east of the Adriatic and at an early period extending northwards to the Danube.

1593 Shaks. *2 Hen. VI*, iv. i. 108 Bargulus the strong Illyrian Pyrate. 1678 J. D. (*title*) The History of Appian, of Alexandria. In Two Parts. The First consisting of the Punick, Syrian, Parthian, Mithridatick, Illyrian, Spanish, and Hannibalick, Wars. 1776 Gibbon *Decl. & F.* I. 27 The provinces of the Danube soon acquired the general appellation of Illyricum, or the Illyrian frontier. 1797 *Encycl. Brit.* (ed. 3) II. 714/2 The Heneti, an Illyrian people. 1880 *Ibid.* XII. 709/1 The Danube..was the limit of the Illyrian tribes towards the north.

b. Of or belonging to Illyria, a former division of Austria-Hungary, since October 30, 1918, forming part of Jugo-Slavia.

Illyrian Provinces, a division, made by Napoleon Bonaparte in 1809, of various Austrian territories lying north and east of the Adriatic, and abolished in 1814–15, after which it was made a nominal kingdom of the Austrian Empire.

1838 *Penny Cycl.* XII. 445/2 Napoleon,..in 1809, gave to several tracts of territory ceded by Austria,..the name of the Illyrian Provinces. 1845 *Encycl. Metrop.* XIII. 1084/2 Meanwhile the war in the Illyrian provinces..received a fresh complication from the secession of Bavaria from the French alliance. *Ibid.* XX. 559/1 The Emperor of Austria rules the Illyrian Kingdom with uncontrolled authority. 1921 *19th Cent.* May 856 The Illyrian provinces..provided a strong bulwark against Austria.

c. In literary use, pertaining to the regions lying along the east coast of the Adriatic.

This corresponds to the literary use of *Illyria*, which was retained even when the name had no political significance.

1853 Tennyson *To E. L.*, Illyrian woodlands, echoing falls Of water.

2. Pertaining to the group of ancient dialects represented by the modern Albanian; also, to a division of the eastern branch of the Slavonic languages.

1824 J. Johnson *Typog.* II. 444 The names to the above letters are in the Illyrian and Servian tongues. 1833 *Penny Cycl.* I. 256/2 The hypothesis of the Albanians being descended from the Illyrians, cannot receive confirmation from comparing it with the old Illyrian tongue. 1928 C. Dawson *Age of Gods* xvi. 375 Our knowledge of the Illyrian languages is so slight.

B. *sb.* **1.** One of an Indo-European people who inhabited ancient Illyria, and who were conquered by the Romans in the third and second centuries B.C.

1584 B. Rich tr. *Herodotus* 62 b, The people Eneti comming of the Illyrians. 1788 Lempriere *Classical Dict.* s.v. *Pausanias*, He accompanied the prince in an expedition against the Illyrians. 1880 *Encycl. Brit.* XII. 709/1 It would not be easy to draw any line of demarcation at this

early time between the Illyrians and their neighbours on the west, south, and east. 1928 C. Dawson *Age of Gods* xiv. 325 The Bronze Age in Eastern Europe. The Thracians and the Illyrians.

2. An inhabitant of the former Austrian kingdom of Illyria.

1836 Col. Wiseman *Lect. Doctr. Cath. Ch.* vii, M. Boraga, an Illyrian, obtained permission of the Bishop to open a new mission among the Indians on the Grand River.

3. A member of the Slavonic race now living in the territory of ancient Illyria; also applied loosely to any people inhabiting this region, without reference to the various political meanings of the name.

1845 *Encycl. Metrop.* XIII. 533/2 Fortunately at this crisis he [*sc.* Leopold] obtained the support of the Illyrians.

4. The language of Illyria, or the group of ancient dialects represented by the modern Albanian; also, a division of the eastern branch of the Slavonic languages, spoken in the same or adjacent districts.

1888 Wright tr. *Brugmann's Comp. Gram.* I. 12 Russian ..Bulgarian and Illyrian. 1912 Skeat *Sci. Etymol.* 127 There is, however, sufficient evidence to show that the Old Illyrian was an independent descendant from the original Indo-germanic stock.

So **Illy·ric** *a.* [ad. L. *Illyricus*, Gr. Ἰλλυρικός], **Illy·rican** *sb.* = *Illyrian *sb.* 4. Hence **I·llyrism**, advocacy of Slovene, Croatian, and Serb nationalism; so **I·llyrist.**

1753 R. Clayton *Jrnl. fr. Cairo to Sinai* 34 We had in our company persons who were acquainted with Arabic, Greek, ..Illyrican, German [etc.]. 1838 *Penny Cycl.* XII. 447/2 Antient Illyria..was inhabited by a people called by the general name of the Illyric nations. 1877 *Encycl. Brit.* VI. 783/2 The so-called Morlacks, or Dalmatians proper, who ..speak a Slavonic dialect usually distinguished as the Illyric. 1910 *Ibid.* VII. 475/2 A nationalist or 'Illyrist' party was formed..to combat Hungarian influences. *Ibid.*, Conflicts between Illyrists and Magyarists.

Ilmenorutile (i·lmĕnoru·til). *Min.* [f. the name of the *Ilmen* Mountains (southern Urals) + -o- + Rutile.] A black ferruginous variety of rutile.

1868 Dana *Min.* (ed. 5) 159. 1929 *Encycl. Brit.* XIX. 774/1 The colour [of rutile] is usually reddish-brown, though ..black in the ferruginous varieties ('nigrive' and 'ilmenorutile').

Ilocano (īlokā·no). [Philippine Sp., f. *Ilocos*, the name of two provinces, lit. 'river men', f. Tagalog *ilog* river.] **a.** A member of a large civilized tribe inhabiting the northern part of Luzon in the Philippine Islands. **b.** The language of this tribe. Also *attrib.* So **Ilo·can** *a.* and *sb.*; **Ilo·ko, Ylo·co.**

1840 *Penny Cycl.* XVIII. 88/2 The other tribes that are numerous, the Pampanga, Zambales, Pangasinan, Ylocos, and Cagayan, inhabit the other plains and lower country. 1885 *Encycl. Brit.* XVIII. 753/1 Other tribes of the Philippines—the Ilocanes, Pampangos, Pangasinanes,..Vicols, &c. 1898 D. C. Worcester *Philippine Isl.* 438 Of these [tribes] the Tagalogs and Ilocanos are the most important. 1900 F. H. Sawyer *Inhab. Philippines* 250 Many converted Tinguianes and Igorrotes who speak the Ilocan dialect. 1901 *Rep. Philippine Comm.* III. 400 The first booklets in Ilocano are in Tagalog characters. 1905 F. W. Atkinson *Philippine Isl.* 238 The Ilocanos, who inhabit the northern province of Ilocos Norte, Ilocos Sur, and Unión, in Luzón. 1914 D. C. Worcester *Philippines* I. 21 *note*, The Ilocanos are one of the eight civilized peoples who collectively make up the Filipinos. 1925 Katherine Mayo *Isles of Fear* 50 Families..of the energetic Ilocano tribe.

Ilsemannite (i·lsmănǝit). *Min.* [Named, 1871, after J. C. *Ilsemann*: see -ite[1].] A dark blue variety of molybdate.

1872 Dana *Min.* App. i. (1880) 7 Ilsemannite is a product of the decomposition of metallic molybdates.

Ilumba (ilū·mbă). [Native name.] An Australian timber-tree, *Eucalyptus tesselaris*.

1889 Maiden *Usef. Pl. Australia* 526.

Im-[3]. *Chem.* Altered form of Am(ide used as a combining form. **Imabe·nzil(e)**, a white crystalline powder obtained by the action of dry ammonia on benzil. **Ima·satin** [Isatin], a yellowish-brown substance formed by boiling an alcoholic solution of isatin in ammonia. **Ime·satin**, a dark yellow compound formed by the action of ammonia on isatin.

1857 Miller *Elem. Chem.* III. 469 Imabenzile. *Ibid.* 536 Imesatin...$C_{16}H_6N_2O_3$...Imasatin...$C_{32}H_{11}N_3O_4$. 1885 *Jrnl. Chem. Soc.* XLVIII. ii. 1067 Imabenzil...is best prepared by pouring a hot concentrated alcoholic solution of benzil into excess of ammonia. 1889 Roscoe & Schorlemmer *Treat. Chem.* III. v. 87 Imesatin, $C_8H_6N_2O$, is formed by the action of ammonia on isatin.

Image, *sb.* Add: **5.** Also applied, with qualification, to mental representations due to any of the senses (not only sight) and to organic sensations.

1897 tr. *Ribot's Psychol. Emotions* 145 In the two following cases the 'olfactory image' only exists in a single instance. 1899 *Amer. Jrnl. Psychol.* Oct. 25 Haptical images, beside being vague and ill defined, offer peculiar difficulties. 1903 *Jrnl. Philos., Psychol. & Sci. Methods* 21 Jan. 38 (Cent. D. Suppl.) I have no doubt, in my own case, of the existence of visual and auditory images...I have no doubt, from the reports of others, of the existence of free kinaesthetic images, verbal or other.

Imaginal, *a.*[2] Add: Also *transf.*

a 1901 Myers *Human Personality* (1903) I. Gloss. p. xviii, *Imaginal*,..metaphorically applied to transcendental faculties shown in rudiment in ordinary life.

Imagist (i·mădʒist). [f. Image *sb.* + -ist.] One of a group of modern poets who stand for liberty in choice of subject matter, who avoid the vague and mystical, and endeavour to attain clarity of expression through the use of precise images. Also *attrib.* Hence **I·magism**, the practices and work of the imagists.

1919 *Hist. Amer. Lit.* II. 266 *note*, *Isle of la Belle Rivière* ..was written in what is now called imagist verse, at the age of thirty. 1922 *Edin. Rev.* July 101 In much of the work of the imagists..we find a more or less conscious, and more or less effective yielding to that influence. 1924 T. Maynard *Our Best Poets* 198 Imagism brings together, with an indulgent catholicism, those who use metre with a brilliant exactness, and those who use only cadence. 1929 Noyes *Ret. Scarecrow* iv. 52 The sharp-edged imagism with which our younger writers are experimenting today. 1931 G. Hughes (*title*) Imagism and the Imagists.

Imago. Add: **c.** *fig.*

1921 *19th Cent.* Feb. 214 Since 1914 every constituent element that has been supposed to go to the making of great men—spacious times, tension, supreme effort, turmoil, battle, revolution—has abounded, but the imago has not emerged.

2. *Psycho-analysis.* (See quot. 1924.)

1909 M. K. Bradby *Psycho-anal.* 59 That web of ideas and emotions which is woven in the course of the child's life round the image of the parent or 'parent imago'. 1924 tr. *Baudouin's Psychoanal. & Aesthetics* 220 *note*, The word 'imago' is taken from the title of a novel by Carl Spitteler. ..It is now current..among psychoanalysts in Great Britain and the United States. The term denotes an interior type, a type moulded upon real persons (in especial upon the father or the mother) and which, from the depths of our subconsciousness, continues to guide our actions, and to stimulate our sympathies and our antipathies.

Imambara (imā·mbārā). Also **imambarah, -barra, -bra, imaum-.** [Hind., f. Arab. Imam + Hind. *bārā* enclosure.] A building in which Mohammedans observe the festival of the Moharram.

1883 *Encycl. Brit.* XV. 49/2 The immense Imāmbāra, or mausoleum of Asaf-ud-daulā [*sc.* at Lucknow]. 1886 Yule & Burnell *Hobson-Jobson*, Imaumbarra. 1907 *Westm. Gaz.* 4 Apr. 10/2 The imambra connected with the Mohammedan morgue at Lucknow.

Imbalance (imbæ·lăns). [f. Im-[2] + Balance *sb.*] Lack of balance, *spec.* between the muscles of the eyes.

1901 Dorland *Med. Dict.* (ed. 2).

Imbauba (imbǭ·bă). A Brazilian tree, the cecropia or trumpet-tree. Also *attrib.*

1909 *Cent. Dict.* Suppl. s.v. *Ant*, *Imbauba ant*, a Brazilian arboreal ant, of the genus *Azteca*, which forms small nests in the interior of plants and is thought to protect them from the attacks of the leaf-cutting ants. 1924 J. A. Thomson *Science Old & New* xi. 62 The Imbauba, or Cecropia tree, of Southern Brazil.

Imbecilic (imbĭsi·lik), *a.* [f. Imbecile *sb.* + -ic.] Characteristic of an imbecile.

1918 D. Flatau *Yellow English* xxxv, Looking round with an imbecilic grin. 1927 *Daily Express* 3 Dec. 4 Courteline ..collected..the most hideous and imbecilic portraits he could find.

Imine (i·min, -ǝin). *Chem.* [Alteration of Amine (cf. Imide).] A derivative of ammonia in which two hydrogen atoms are replaced by a radical or radicals. Also **Imino-** (imai·no), combining form of *Imine.

1883 *Jrnl. Chem. Soc.* XLIV. 910 Imines. 1888 Morley & Muir *Watts' Dict. Chem.* II. 750/2 *Imines*, compounds of divalent hydrocarbon radicles with imidogen. 1907 *Jrnl. Chem. Soc.* XCII. i. 393 Mechanism of the Reaction in the Formation of α-Amino- and Imino-acids. 1908 *Ibid.* XCIV. i. 419 The imino-esters were prepared by a modification of Pinner's method...The velocity of reaction of the free imino-esters in aqueous solution have been determined and the results are tabulated.

Immanental (imăne·ntăl), *a.* Delete *rare* and add examples.

1920 A. S. Pringle-Pattison *Idea of God* 219 This lower pantheism..is common in the popular cults of the East, where the immanental unity of the divine is little more than the idea of a teeming nature. 1921 *Challenge* 18 Feb. 249/2 Sr. Ruggiero sees some of the pitfalls that beset a purely immanental system. 1930 C. J. Wright *Miracle in Hist.* 214 Theism can only abide with the recognition of the immanental activity of God in His universe.

Immanentism (i·mănĕntiz'm). [f. Immanent *a.* + -ism.] Belief in the immanence of the Deity. So **I·mmanentist** *a.*, holding or characterized by this belief.

1907 *Hibbert Jrnl.* July 919 Immanentism..explains away rather than explains that irrational fact of experience which we call evil. 1917 C. C. Martindale *Life Mgr. R. H. Benson* II. 392 To this Immanentist school would thus belong St. Teresa, Dame Juliana of Norwich,..and Francis de Sales. 1918 M. D. Petre *Modernism* x. 207 He has been charged with immanentism. 1930 *Times Lit. Suppl.* 14 Aug. 648/2 Mr. Wright stands for a modern, liberalizing and immanentist theology. 1931 *Ibid.* 22 Oct. 812/2 The pure phenomenology which resolves Being into Becoming by a sheer immanentism.

Immediacy. Add: **4.** *pl.* Immediate needs.

1923 H. G. Wells *Men Like Gods* iii. iv. § 3 The old things and the foul things, customs, delusions, habits,..base immediacies, triumph over us!

Immersal (imɔ̄·ɪsăl). [f. Immerse *v.* + -al.] = Immersion 2.

1901 Greenough & Kittredge *Words & Their Ways* 98 Theological and philosophical studies are also pursued with vigor, and this means an immersal in Latin.

Immigrant. B. *sb.* (Earlier U.S. examples.)

c 1787 R. King in *Life & Corr.* (1894) I. 296 The immigrants from Massachusetts, who settled on Connecticut River. 1789 Morse *Amer. Geog.* 253 There are in this state many immigrants from Scotland, Ireland, Germany.

Immigration. Add: Also *attrib.*

1902 H. Vincent in C. Emanuel *Alien Immigration* (1904) 139 Aliens arriving are carefully schooled by the immigration agents to say that they are going to America. 1903 *U.S. Immigration Laws* in Whelpley *Probl. Immigrant* (1905) 89 To prevent the landing of any such alien from such vessel at any time or place other than that designated by the immigration officers. 1904 F. Bradshaw *Alien Immigration* 121 When the alien has passed the Immigration Department his troubles are not yet over. 1905 *Act 5 Edw. VII* c. 13 § 1 An immigrant shall not be landed in the United Kingdom from an immigrant ship except at a port at which there is an immigration officer appointed under this Act.

2. *collect.* The body of immigrants. *U.S.*

1857 *Trans. Ill. Agric. Soc.* II. 365 The immigration was generally a moral, correct people.

Immobilized (imōu·bilǝizd), *ppl. a.* [f. Immobilize *v.* + -ed[1].] Rendered immobile or stationary.

1910 *Blackw. Mag.* July 8/1 An airship can remain poised and practically immobilised in the air even in a wind. 1923 *Edin. Rev.* Jan. 179 The left and centre of the enemy was held...It was now possible to attempt a decisive attack on an immobilised enemy.

Immolation. Add: **3.** The eucharistic preface in the Gallican liturgy.

[1855 *Anc. Lit. Gallican Ch.* 42 *margin*, The beginning of this Immolatio is probably borrowed from a Roman source.] 1872 Shipley *Gloss. Eccl. Terms.*

Immoral. B *sb.* Add: **2.** An immoral person.

1900 *Pop. Sci. Monthly* LVI. 459 Women..having their finer sensibilities offended through the public intrusion of the immorals of the lower world.

Immoralism (imǫ·răliz'm). [f. Immoral *a.* + -ism.] The reverse or negation of moralism; a system of thought or practice which rejects moral law.

1907 *Athenæum* 23 Mar. 348/1 The system..of Nietzsche, with all its blasphemy and immoralism. 1918 *Hibbert Jrnl.* Apr. 378 The..sickly social idealism..which treated the most healthy immorality so much more harshly than it treated the most unhealthy immoralism. 1930 Streeter *Primitive Church* v. 179 The theoretic basis of Gnostic immoralism was a distinction between the ultimate Good God and the more or less evil Creator of the material universe.

Immortable (imǫ·ɹtăb'l), *a.* [f. Immort(al + -able.] Having the capacity to live after death. So **Immortabi·lity.**

1922 J. Y. Simpson *Man & Attainm. Immort.* xiii. 275 The contention that eternal life..is morally conditioned, that man, in short, is immortable rather than immortal. 1930 S. D. McConnell (*title*) Immortability. An Old Man's Conclusions.

Immortal, *a.* and *sb.* **B.** *sb.* Add: **2. a.** Also, a nickname for the 2nd Battalion, the Duke of Wellington's Regiment.

1925 E. Fraser & Gibbons *Soldier & Sailor Words.*

Immune, *a.* (*sb.*) Add: **1.** Revived as a figurative use of 2: Wholly protected *from* something injurious or distasteful.

1898 Mercier in *Brit. Med. Jrnl.* 3 Sept. 586/1 There is for every insane person a certain sphere of conduct for which be ought to be entirely immune from punishment. 1900 *Daily News* 5 July 3/2 A man whose achievements should render him immune from all mud throwing. 1924 D. H. Lawrence *England, my England* 209 Among the graves, she felt immune from the world.

2. Also: Serving to develop immunity. *Immune body*, the substance developed during immunization which gives the anti-serum its special character; the amboceptor. *Immune proteid*, any proteid serving as a protection against disease, as an antitoxin or bacteriolysin. *Immune serum*, the serum which contains an antibody (see quot. 1907).

1902 Muir & Ritchie *Man. Bacteriol.* (ed. 3) 465 In the case of each anti-serum of this group a special immune-body is developed. 1903 Dorland *Med. Dict.* (ed. 3), *Immunproteid*, a substance formed in the body of animals on the injection of an old bacterial culture by the union of the zymose of the culture with the body albumin. 1907 S. Arrhenius *Immunochemistry* 3 We obtain generally not normal serum but serum containing an antibody, which is 'specific' to the injected body (*i.e.* immune-serum). *Ibid.* 219 If the quantity of immune-body present is not very great. 1921 R. T. Hewlett *Man. Bacteriol.* (ed. 7) 307 The stable constituent of immune serum is known as the 'amboceptor' or 'immune body'.

b. as *sb.* Also, an immune plant.

1909 *Rep. Brit. Assoc.* 764 All extracted immunes should breed true to this feature.

Immunify (imiū·nifai), *v.* [f. Immune *a.* + -ify.] *trans.* To render immune. So **Immunifacient** (imiūnifē·ʃĕnt) *a.*, producing immunity; **Immunifaction** (imiūnifæ·kʃǝn), the action of immunizing.

1901 *Q. Rev.* Apr. 402 The animal has become gradually immunified to the specific poison. 1913 Dorland *Med. Dict.* (ed. 7), *Immunifacient*, producing immunity: said of diseases, such as diphtheria and typhoid, which for a time produce immunity against themselves. *Immunifaction*, immunization.

Immunize, *v.* Add: **2.** To render (a system of aerial communication) immune from interference.

1903 *Daily Chron.* 4 Aug. 5/3 Dr. Nikola Tesla, the electrician, has procured two patents for processes immunising his system of etheric telegraphy from external interference.

Immunizer (i·miunǝizǝɹ). [f. Immunize *v.* + -er[1].] That which renders immune.

1927 *Daily Express* 18 June 9/2 'Immuniser' for Cancer. ..It may well be that chemical and medical research will discover this natural immuniser, which will strengthen resistance to cancer in all individuals.

Immuno- (imiū·no), used as combining form of Immune, in chemical and pathological terms; as **Immunoche·mical** *a.*, of or pertaining to immunochemistry. **Immunoche·mistry**, that branch of chemistry which studies the substances and reactions concerned in immunization. **Immunoto·xin**, any antitoxin. **Immu·notransfu·sion**, a transfusion of blood from one who has been immunized.

1901 Dorland *Med. Dict.* (ed. 2), Immunotoxin. 1907 S. Arrhenius (*title*) Immunochemistry. 1925 C. H. Browning *Immunochem. Stud.* 1 The term 'immunochemistry', used by Arrhenius, suits well this department of research. *Ibid.* 15 The immunochemical properties of serum. 1926 R. T. Hewlett *Man. Bacteriol.* (ed. 8) 101 A method of immunotransfusion for the treatment of septicæmia..which is now on trial.

Immunology (imiunǫ·lŏdʒi). [f. Immune + -ology.] The science which treats of the phenomena and causes of immunity. Hence **Immunolo·gical** *a.*; **Immunolo·gically** *adv.*; **Immuno·logist**, one who studies immunology.

1916 (*title*) The Journal of Immunology. *Ibid.* I. 429 *note*, Presented before the meeting of the American Association of Immunologists, May, 1916. 1921 Kassner & Ecker *Princ. Immunol.* Introd. p. xiii, The history of immunology as a science is distinctly modern. 1925 *Literary Digest* (N.Y.) 27 June 24/2 The hope that..scarlet fever will soon be classed with the companion scourge, diphtheria, as amenable to handling by the modern methods of the immunologist. 1928 J. A. Kolmer in Jordan & Falk *Newer Knowl. Bacteriol. & Immunol.* 1110 The question naturally arises whether or not it is possible for us to aid immunological processes by the administration of drugs. 1929 R. T. Hewlett in *Syst. Bacteriol.* III. 375 Dickson had previously observed that the Nevin cheese strain differed immunologically from other strains with which he was working.

Imp, *sb.* **8.** Add: **imp-pole**, a pole for supporting scaffolding.

1875 Knight *Dict. Mech.*

Imp. Abbreviation of *imperative, imperator, imperatrix, imperfect, imperial, impersonal, imprimatur, imprint, improvement.*

Impact, *sb. attrib.* Add: **impact load**, the pressure caused by the impact of one body against another; **impact screen** (see quot.).

1928 C. F. S. Gamble *North Sea Air Station* Introd. 10 Her two stream-lined gondolas..were designed to be capable of sustaining severe *impact loads when alighting on water. 1909 H. Louis *Dressing of Minerals* 42 The *Impact Screen ..consists of a screen usually of fine mesh and set at a rather steep angle, which receives downward jerks from a cam at the rate of 600 per minute, the screen being thrown upwards again by a spring.

Impact, *v.* Add: **3.** *intr.* To make impact *with*. Hence **Impa·cting** *ppl. a.*

1916 Boyd Cable *Action Front* 95 No ping and smack of impacting lead hailed about them. 1928 'Seamark' *Down River* vi, Something impacted with a soft thud against Lingard's temple.

Impacted, *ppl. a.* Add: *Surg.*, applied to a tooth which remains within the jaw-bone, and to a fracture in which the broken parts are driven together so as to become locked.

1884 T. Bryant *Pract. Surg.* (ed. 4) I. 652 The serious results which may attend purulent inflammation about an impacted wisdom tooth. 1886 *Buck's Handbk. Med. Sci.* III. 234/2 Multiple, comminuted, and impacted fractures. 1929 *Encycl. Brit.* IX. 577/1 An impacted fracture is one in which the broken ends are driven together by the causative violence in such a way as to become locked.

Impaction. Add: *Surg.* (cf. prec.).

1848 Dunglison *Med. Lex.* (ed. 7), *Impaction*, a fracture of the cranium, ribs, or sternum, with depression of some of the fragments and projection of others externally. 1874 Bucknill & Tuke *Man. Psychol. Med.* 767 Impaction in the pharynx..admits of immediate relief. 1884 T. Bryant *Pract. Surg.* (ed. 4) I. 652 The impaction of a lower wisdom tooth. 1890 Billings *Med. Dict.*, *Impaction*, the condition of being wedged in and fixed in position; said of the fœtal head in the pelvis in certain cases, of fæces in a distended bowel, of fragments of a fractured bone, etc.

Impair, *sb.*[2] Add: In Roulette (pronunc. ǣnpēɹ), an odd number, or a number marked 'impair'.

1854 *Bohn's Hand-bk. Games* (1867) 348 (Roulette) The impair wins, when the ball enters a hole numbered impair. 1891 *Hoffmann's Cycl. Card & Table Games* 626 If he places his money on Impair, he bets that the ball will drop into an odd number. 1902 *Encycl. Brit.* XXXII. 304/1 Pair indicates even numbers, impair odd numbers.

Impala (impā·lă, -pæ·lă). Also **impalla(h).** [Zulu *i-mpālaj*. (Cf. Pallah.)] A South African antelope of the genus *Æpyceros*.

1896 Kirby *Haunts Wild Game* 546 Impala of the Swazis and Zulus, Pala of the Basuto. 1900 *Field* 6 Jan. 25/1, I have shot quite a number of impala since, but have not been able to secure a better pair of horns. 1907 Fitzpatrick *Jock of the Bushveld* 302 We sat like statues as the impala walked out from its stall between Teddy's knees. 1931 *Times Lit. Suppl.* 3 Dec. 983/4 Graceful photographs of impalla, eland, and other antelope.

Impale, *v.* Add: **4. c.** *fig.* To transfix (a person) with one's eye. Hence **Impa·ling** *ppl. a.*

1877 *My Mother-in-Law* vi, Mrs. Pinkerton devoted herself to impaling me with her eyes once in a while. 1903 *Critic* XLIII. 349/2 There was an impaling fierceness in his eyes.

Impalement. Add: **5.** The act or fact of being impaled upon rocks, the spikes of a gate, or the like.

1887 *Graphic* 19 Mar. 307/2 His ship was rescued after impalement on a rock. 1921 *Contemp. Rev.* Aug. 272 Do you remember climbing the gate and just avoiding impalement?

Impasto. Add: **2.** *Ceram.* Enamel colours or slip laid on ware so thickly as to stand out in relief from the surface.

1903 Solon *Hist. O.Fr. Faïence* 188.

Impastoed (impa·stoud), *ppl. a.* Encrusted with paste.

1923 *Blackw. Mag.* May 641/2 [He] thrust the point of his palette-knife under an impasto'd mass of paper.

Impedance. Add: Also *attrib.*

1902 Impedance coil [see *Choking *vbl. sb.* or *ppl. a.*]. 1916 *Stand. Rules Amer. Inst. Electr. Engin.* 16 The ratio of the internal impedance drop to the terminal voltage, expressed in per cent, is called the 'per cent impedance drop'.

Impeller. Add examples illustrating technical or mechanical usages.

1904 *Elect. Rev.* 27 Aug. 318 (Cent. D. Suppl.) It [*sc.* the conoidal pump] is somewhat different from the ordinary centrifugal pump, due partially to the widening of the pump chamber to admit a special form of impeller. 1909 *Westm. Gaz.* 30 Nov. 5/1 The full movement on each impeller corresponds to an angle of 90 deg. 1923 *Daily Mail* 13 July 12 Cooling is by the thermo-syphon system assisted by a water impellor.

Imperfection. Add:

4. a. *Printing. pl.* Letters that are wanting in a fount; types cast to make up a deficiency in a fount.

1681–5 Fell *Let. to Marshall* 24 Oct. (MS.) The compositor upon Mr. Junius his lexicon wants several imperfections, that we cannot supply without his Matrices. 1683 Moxon *Mech. Exerc.*, *Printing* 381 When the Founder has not Cast a proportionable number of each sort of Letter, the wanting Letters are called Imperfections, as making the rest of the Fount unperfect. 1771 Luckombe *Hist. Printing* 243 Less occasion to cast imperfections, which often prove very hurtful to a new fount of letter; as they are seldom exact to the prior sorts..: so that, was it not for the eagerness of the Compositor,..many a sort, cast for perfecting, would be returned. 1808 Stower *Printers' Gram.* 56 It should be an invariable rule with master printers to examine imperfections before they go into the hands of the compositor. 1888 Jacobi *Printers' Vocab.*, *Imperfections*, short sorts required to perfect a typefounder's bill for a fount of a certain weight.

b. *Bookbinding.* A surplus or missing sheet of a work.

1683 Moxon *Mech. Exerc.*, *Printing* 348 He doubles or quires up all the other heaps and..writes upon them Imperfections of (the title of the book), and writes on it the signature of the sheet that is wanting. 1835 J. Hannett *Bibliopegia* i. 13 If any sheet is wanting or belongs to another volume, or is a duplicate, the further progress of the work must be suspended, till the imperfection is procured or exchanged. 1888 Jacobi *Printers' Vocab.*, *Imperfections*, sheets required by a binder to make good books imperfect through bad gathering, collating, or spoiled sheets.

Imperial, *a.* and *sb.* Add: **A.** *adj.* **2. c.** Designating certain decorations or orders.

1902 *Encycl. Brit.* XXXI. 340/1 The Imperial Service Order was..instituted on 26th June 1902, to commemorate King Edward's coronation. *Ibid.*, The Imperial Order of the Crown of India is conferred for like purposes as the order of the Indian Empire.

d. Designating a policy or an institution concerned with the development of commerce between the constituent parts of the British Empire.

1902 *Encycl. Brit.* XXVI. 397/2 The foundation of the Imperial Federation League—in 1884. *Ibid.* XXXIII. 393/1 The British Empire League, and the Imperial Trade Defence League endeavour to promote inter-Imperial trade. *Ibid.* 681/2 On 4th July she laid the foundation stone of the Imperial Institute. 1927 *Daily Tel.* 5 Mar. 8/7 Appreciation of the work of the Imperial Economic Committee and the Empire Marketing Board for the development of the market for Dominion produce in Great Britain. 1931 G. C. Tryon (*title*) Short History of Imperial Preference.

7. *imperial pint* (see Pint; examples).

1886 Fagge *Princ. & Pract. Med.* II. 199 Enough fruit stones to fill almost an imperial pint measure. 1901 Christie, etc. *Catal. Wines, Turner-Farley* 12 Three Dozen Imperial Pints of Champagne.

B. *sb.* **5.** A large size of photograph $6\frac{7}{8} \times 9\frac{7}{8}$ inches; also *attrib.* of a frame.

1895 *Army & Navy Co-op. Soc. Price List* 656 Suede leather..photograph frames..Carte de Visite size..Cabinet size..Imperial size.

8. (Earlier U.S. example.)

1841 *Knickerbocker Mag.* XVII. 260 Two wigs, moustaches, an imperial, a gay vest.

9. *pl.* The City Imperial Volunteers who were enlisted for the Boer War of 1899–1902; also, in the war of 1914–18, a familiar name for British troops.

1900 *Daily News* 19 Feb. 2/6 Well done, City Imperials. 1925 E. Fraser & Gibbons *Soldier & Sailor Words.*

Imperialine (impī·riălin). *Chem.* [f. mod.L. *imperialis* (see def.) Imperial *a.* + -ine[5].] A bitter colourless alkaloid found in the bulbs of *Fritillaria imperialis*.

1889 Morley & Muir *Watts' Dict. Chem.* II. 751/1.

Imphee. (Earlier U.S. example.)

1861 *Trans. Ill. Agric. Soc.* IV. 108 When corn and Sorghum have been cut down by frosts, one variety of Imphee beside it has not been injured.

Impinge, *v.* **3.** Delete *Obs.* and add example.

1910 *Practitioner* July 109 The striker's thumb..impinges the skull of his opponent.

Implausibility (implǭzibi·lĭti). Delete †*Obs.* and add example.

1926 Boyd Freeman *Towards the Answer* Introd. 7 Perhaps the thing is an impossibility or an implausibility.

Implementation (i:mplĭmĕntē·ʃǝn). [f. Implement *v.* + -ation.] The action of implementing; fulfilment.

1926 *Spectator* 16 Oct. 627/1 The Irish delegation will seek the implementation of co-equality with the States of the British Commonwealth.

Implode, *v.* **1.** Add: Also *trans.*

1913 J. Murray *Ocean* v. (1928) 97 Only those parts of the structure would be burst inwards ('imploded') into which water could not enter rapidly enough to equalise the pressure on the two sides, say, of an iron plate.

Implore, *v.* **1. c.** Delete *rare* and add examples.

1850 Smedley *Frank Fairlegh* xv, 'Gentlemen, don't ring the bells, pray,' implored the old man. 1887 Marie Corelli *Thelma* iii. ii, 'Let me go with thee!' he implored, in broken accents. 1891 T. Hardy *Group Noble Dames*, *Barbara of Ho. of Grebe* 101 'Oh, take it away—please take it away!' she implored.

2. Later examples; const. *for* (a thing), *of* (a person).

1870 H. Smart *Race for Wife* x, She flopped down on her knees, and implored for mercy. 1904 Lillie T. Meade *Love Triumphant* Prol. ii, I implored of Granny to let us leave the cottage.

Impolder (impǭu·ldǝɹ), *v.* [ad. Du. *inpolderen*: see Im-[1] and Polder[1].] *trans.* To make a polder of; to reclaim from the sea.

1899 *Pall Mall Gaz.* 13 Apr. 4/2 This impoldering and pumping, the raising and keeping of dykes and dams. 1901 *Speaker* 9 Mar. 633/2 It was about this time that Haarlem Mere was impoldered. 1929 *Encycl. Brit.* XI. 648/1 A great part of the Netherlands has now been impoldered. *Ibid.* 648/2 The largest impoldering scheme on record has now been commenced.

Impoof, impoofo (impū·f, impū·fo). Also **empofo, impophoo.** [Zulu *i-mpofu*, f. *mpofu* tawny.] The South African eland, *Oreas canna*.

c 1789 *Encycl. Brit.* (1797) IV. 147/1 The Caffres call this species *empofos* and *poffo*. 1834 *Penny Cycl.* II. 89/1 The Canna,..improperly called *eland* or elk by the Dutch colonists of South Africa, and *impoof* by the Caffres. 1875 *Encycl. Brit.* II. 101/2 The eland or impophoo (*Boselaphus Oreas*) is one of the largest of the antelopes. 1882 *Cassell's Nat. Hist.* III. 21 The hunting of these creatures, known in South Africa as the *Impoofo*.

Impoon (impū·n). Also **impoono.** [Zulu *i-mpunzi*.] = Duiker.

1868 *Chambers's Encycl.* X. 370/1, *Impoon* (*Antilope* or *Cephalopus mergens*),..a small species of antelope, very plentiful in South Africa, in wooded districts.

Importee (impoɹtī·). [f. Import *v.* + -ee.] A person imported from abroad.

1858 Carlyle *Fredk. Gt.* iv. vi. (1872) I. 315 Painter Pesne, a French Immigrant, or Importee. 1888 *Scott. Leader* 19 Sept. 5 It was amongst the 'importees' that the row took place.

Impos., colloq. abbreviation of Impossible.

1924 Galsworthy *White Monkey* i. ix, 'If you're tired we could cut that.' 'My dear! Impos.!'

Imposer. Add: **b.** *Printing.* One who imposes (see Impose *v.* 1 d).

1921 *Dict. Occup. Terms* (1927) § 522 *Stone hand*, imposer; imposes type, which has been set up in page form, in correct position in chase or iron frame, for printing in sheets.

Impossibilist (impǫ·sĭbilist, -pǫsi·b-), *a.* and *sb.* [f. Impossible + -ist.] **a.** *adj.* Of or pertaining to views, especially on social reform, which cannot be put into practice, or to those who hold such views. **b.** *sb.* One who holds such impracticable views. So **Impo·ssibilism**, belief in such views.

1899 G. B. Shaw *Pen Portraits & Rev.* (1932) 218 Two volumes of the translation appeared before the firm paid the penalty of its Impossibilism. 1900 F. Maddison in *Speaker* 3 Mar. 592/1 Even amongst those who were but recently impossibilist politicians saner views are prevailing. 1906 *Westm. Gaz.* 8 Feb. 7/2 We are predicting no impossibilist policy. 1909 *Ibid.* 17 Apr. 16/3 Impossibilists in Labour Politics. 1910 *Daily News* 3 Feb. 4/2 There is no fixed hostility, and no impossibilism of attitude. 1917 Chesterton *Short Hist. Eng.* 76 An idealism akin to impossibilism. 1921 *Public Opinion* 29 July 107/1 In a world largely controlled by fanatics, dreamers, and impossibilists, the one thoroughly practical policy is that of the League of Nations Union.

Impossible, *a.* and *sb.* **B.** *sb.* Add: **2.** With def. article: That which is or seems impossible.

1845 Bailey *Festus* (ed. 2) 291 He only holds Perfections, which are but the impossible To other beings. 1895 C'tess Martinengo-Cesaresco *Liberation of Italy* xix. 394 Garibaldi..had always demanded the impossible of his men. 1904 *Daily Chron.* 6 May 7/5 The history of Christianity.. had been a triumph of the impossible. 1916 Huneker *Ivory, Apes & Peacocks* 34 All three were consumptives..: all three suffered from the nostalgia of the impossible.

Impost, *sb.*[2] **1.** Add *attrib.* examples.

1863 *Archit. Publ. Soc. Dict. Archit.* III. 15/1 The decorative impost, or point at which the ornamental impost mouldings are placed, is frequently below the springing...In some

archways the impost point is ornamental with horizontal mouldings. 1901 Sturgis *Dict. Archit.* II. 464 *Impost Block*, a member which gives direct support to one side of an arch, or to the adjoining parts of two arches.

Impracticality (impræktikæ·lĭti). [f. Impractical *a.* + -ity.] The character of being impractical; impracticableness.

1916 H. Walpole *Dark Forest* i. iv, The Russian character..with its lack of restraint, its idealism, its impracticality. 1926 J. Buchan *Dancing Floor* ii. x, The impracticality of an entrance..at that point.

So **Impra·cticalness.**

1905 *Macm. Mag.* Nov. 55 He was accused of vagueness, impracticalness, generality.

Impress, *v.*[1] Add:

2. c. *Electr.* To create or establish (an electromotive force or difference of potential) in a conductor from some outside source, as a battery, dynamo, or other electric generator.

1902 Webster Suppl. 1929 [see next].

Impressed, *ppl. a.*[1] Add: **2.** *Electr.* Of a current, electromotive force, or pressure: Supplied to a circuit by some outside source; distinguished from *counter*, *active*, or *effective* force, etc.

1902 Webster Suppl. 1929 *Encycl. Brit.* XXII. 408/1 A small current flows into the excited winding sufficient to produce a counter voltage equal to the impressed voltage.

Impression. Add: **7.** In modern use, often implying that the belief or idea is mistaken, esp. in *under the impression*.

1860 Ruskin *Unto this Last* iv. § 66, I believe that many of our merchants are seriously under the impression that it is possible for everybody, somehow, to make a profit in this manner. 1865 — *Sesame* ii. § 86 Generally, we are under an impression that a man's duties are public, and a woman's private. 1867 Hook *Lives Abps.* V. xxi. 356 Under the impression that they had been specially assisted by the saint.

9. impression paper, a paper bearing a design which may be transferred by pressure to some other substance; **impression-stitch**, an imitation of sewed work on the soles of boots and shoes; also *attrib.*

1909 *Daily Chron.* 25 May 9/1 It is invaluable for applying original or other designs which cannot be used with *impression paper. 1884 Knight *Dict. Mech.* Suppl., **Impression Stitch Machine*, a machine for crimping the upper edge of welts of a boot or shoe to give it the appearance of sewed work.

Impressionistic, *a.* Add: **2.** Tending towards or influenced by impressionism; following the methods of the impressionists.

1916 Huneker *Ivory, Apes & Peacocks* 38 Laforgue..was an ardent advocate of the Impressionistic painters. 1921 *Times Lit. Suppl.* 24 Feb. 124/1 The impressionistic reporter who asked Mr. Edison what he considered the chief mark of a truly valuable invention.

Impressionistically (impreʃǝni·stikăli), *adv.* [f. Impressionistic: see -ically.] In an impressionistic manner; from the point of view of an impressionist.

1924 Galsworthy *White Monkey* ii. ii, When you smile, Miss Collins, I see you impressionistically. 1924 *Countries of World* III. 1507/1 Their flowers..painted (impressionistically but with unerring truth of impression) in their frescoes. 1926 W. J. Locke *Old Bridge* i. i, I try to express myself.. impressionistically.

Impressive, *a.* Add: **4.** *Psychol.* Directed inward.

1902 *Encycl. Brit.* XXXII. 65/1 My fear or anger may chance to be *expressive* to another, but they are of necessity *impressive* to me.

Imprimitive, *a.* Transfer †*Obs.* to sense in Dict. and add: **2.** *Math.* Denoting a group whose elements may be divided into sets having an equal number of distinct elements, so that every substitution either changes one set into another or interchanges the elements of a set among themselves. Hence **Imprimiti·vity.**

1888 J. M. Page in *Amer. Jrnl. Math.* X. 298 Now a group X_1f... X_rf in the plane is said to be *imprimitive* when it leaves a family of curves. 1889 Oskar Bolza *Ibid.* XI. 210 If they do form a group Q, this group will be imprimitive with the two systems of imprimitivity $x_1, x_2 \ldots x_r$ and $y_1, y_2 \ldots y_r$. 1902 *Encycl. Brit.* XXIX. 121/1 If O, O′, O″,..is a set of objects in respect of which a group G is transitive, it may be possible to divide the set into a number of subsets, no two of which contain a common object, such that every operation of the group either interchanges the objects of a subset among themselves, or changes them all into the objects of some other subset. When this is the case the group is called *imprimitive* in respect of the set; otherwise the group is called *primitive*.

I·mprinted, *ppl. a.*[2] [f. Imprint *sb.* + -ed[2].] Bearing a bookseller's own imprint (Imprint *sb.* 3).

1926 *Publishers' Weekly* 17 July 181/2 A month before publication 300,000 imprinted postcards had been asked for. 1927 *Ibid.* 25 June 2371 Imprinted brochures are now ready for distribution.

Improperium (imprŏpī·riǒm). Pl. **-ia.** *R. Liturg.* [late L., = reproach.] *pl.* A series of antiphons with responses forming part of the liturgical service of Good Friday, expressing the reproach or sorrowful remonstrance of Christ with the Jewish people; *sing.* one of these antiphons with its response.

1880 *Grove's Dict. Mus.* II. 1/1 The *Improperia* are sung, very softly, and without any accompaniment whatever, by two Antiphonal Choirs. 1884 Addis & Arnold *Cath. Dict.* 405/1 During the adoration the 'Improperia' are sung, each improperium being followed by the Trisagion in Greek and Latin.

Improve, *v.*[2] **2. b.** (Later U.S. example.)

1855 *Jrnl. Discourses* II. 304 (Th.) Go and improve that farm, though I do not deed it to you.

Improvement. Add: **2. b.** (Later U.S. example.)

1878 J. H. Beadle *Western Wilds* 43 (Th.) [The land] was common, an' we owned jist the improvements.

7. *attrib.* and *Comb.*; **improvement lease**, in Australia, a lease granted under the Crown Lands Act of 1895 with conditions of improvement to be made by the lessee.

1900 *Daily News* 16 May 5/3 The new improvement undertakings of the Council. 1909 *Daily Chron.* 30 Apr. 6/4 The improvement values added by enterprise. *Ibid.* 7/7 Housing and improvement schemes. 1909 *Westm. Gaz.* 19 May 2/2 The sale of sites in improvement areas. *Ibid.* 4/1 The trifling amount of improvement-sites which their predecessors have acquired.

Impsonite (i·mpsǝnǝit). *Min.* [-ite[1] 2 b.] (See quot. 1909.)

1909 Dana & Ford *Dana's Syst. Min.* (ed. 6) App. ii. 55 *Impsonite*, an asphalt closely similar to albertite but differing in being almost insoluble in turpentine. Found occurring in veins in shales from Impson valley, Indian Territory. 1925 Ries & Watson *Engineering Geol.* (ed. 3) 585 Impsonite. Oklahoma.

Impubescent (impiube·sĕnt), *a.* [f. Im-[2] + Pubescent.] Not pubescent.

1902 *Proc. Zool. Soc.* I. 186.

Impulse, *sb.* Add: **1. b.** *Basic impulse* (see quot.).

1873 F. T. Roberts *Handbk. Med.* 368 Basic impulse [of the heart] is observed in many cases where a cavity in the apex of the left lung has contracted.

5. impulse charge, the charge of powder which is fired to expel a torpedo from its tube; **impulse tube**, a tube serving to expel a torpedo; **impulse turbine**, a turbine working by the impulse of fluid or air impinging on vanes or the like.

1878 *Cassell's Fam. Mag.* 312/2 Direction is given to the torpedo by means of an iron *impulse-tube built into the vessel. 1885 *Marine Engineer* 1 Sept. 144/2 The fish torpedoes lie side by side. Immediately behind them..are a couple of 'impulse tubes'. 1880 *Encycl. Brit.* XII. 524/1 In some turbines the whole available energy of the water is converted into kinetic energy before the water acts on the moving part of the turbine. Such turbines are termed **Impulse Turbines*. *Ibid.* 532/2 The theory of the impulse turbine does not essentially differ from that of the reaction turbine.

Impulsivity (impǝlsi·vĭti). [f. Impulsive *a.* + -ity.] The character of being impulsive or of acting on impulse; impulsiveness. Hence **Impu·lsivist**, one who acts on impulse.

1891 C. Lombroso *Man of Genius* 348 The psychology peculiar to the epileptic—impulsivity, double personality, childishness. 1895 tr. *M. Nordau's Degeneration* 120 Moral insanity, however, is not present in Verlaine. He sins through irresistible impulse. He is an Impulsivist. 1902 A. F. Chamberlain in *Pop. Sci. Monthly* Mar. 419 (Cent. D. Suppl.) In the execution of many of those acts denominated crimes the offender exhibits the phenomenon of a brief period of violent activity, extreme impulsivity. 1925 *Public Opinion* 24 Apr. 391/2 A man of exceptional ability and yet of a febrile impulsivity.

Impurify, *v.* Delete †*Obs.* and add example.

1904 *Daily Chron.* 19 July 3/7 Impure aeration that..takes place in dirty, fœtid cowsheds impurifies it [*sc.* milk].

Imputed, *ppl. a.* Add: **3.** *Economics.* Estimated, valued in relation to something else. *Imputed price, value* (see quots.).

1911 Webster, *Imputed value*, Econ., the value that a thing has merely for its utility in the production of something else;—called also *derived value*. 1929 *Encycl. Brit.* XXII. 960/2 Imputed price..is an estimate of the amount of money for which a given article or a given quantum of goods could be sold or bought.

Imshi (i·mʃi). *Army slang.* Also **imshee, imshy.** [Local Arabic (Berggren).] Be off, go away, shoo. Also as *vb.*

1916 *Anzac Bk.* 135/2 And the King-of-all-the-Huns said, 'It is enough, Imshee!' *Note*, Imshee is the Arabic for 'go away'. The Australasian Corps, which had so far employed it only to street hawkers in Cairo, used this war-cry on April 25. *Ibid.* 136/1 So they imsheed. 1919 *Athenæum* 28 July 664/2 'Imshy', go away (generally corrupted into something like 'hampshire').

In, *prep.* Add:

12. d. Often dependent upon a superlative or a commendatory epithet: Within the sphere of (a particular class or order of things). *colloq.*

1866 Ruskin *Crown Wild Olive* ii. § 53 The newest and sweetest thing in pinnacles. 1879 [see Thing *sb.* 7]. 1911 W. J. Locke *Glory of Clementina Wing* ii, I may not be the latest thing in dandyism.

39. b. *Nothing, not much, little*, etc. *in it*: little or no difference between competitors or any persons or things that are compared. orig. *Racing slang.*

1914 *Concise Oxf. Dict.* 1927 [see *Much B. 2 h]. 1929 S. E. Thomas *Elem. Econ.* xxix. (ed. 4) 533 While in the course of a year Britain imports considerable quantities of gold, she also exports almost equally large quantities, and on balance there is usually very little in it. *Mod.* Is it nearer to go by Broad Street or High Street? There is not much in it.

In, *adv.* Add: **5. d.** Similarly, in phrases implying incidental distribution, e.g. *in places*.

1905 Excellent in parts [see *Curate 2 b]. 1924 Anne D. Sedgwick *Little French Girl* ii. v, The long iron staircase down the face of the cliff was almost as steep as a fire escape in places. 1924 D. H. Lawrence *England, my England* 121 And I sensed I was a prisoner, for the snow was everywhere deep, and drifted in places.

6. j. Well in. (*a*) *Racing.* Applied to a horse which has been treated leniently by the handicapper. (*b*) In comfortable or easy circumstances. *colloq.* orig. *Austral.* Also, profitably engaged in speculation.

(*a*) 1854 J. Mills *Life Racehorse* xvii. 111 The handicapper..considerately classed me among the middle ones, and awarded 6 st. 12 lb. as my burthen. 'He's well in,' said my owner,..'very well in.' 1894 G. Moore *Esther Waters* xxx, Are the 'orses he backs what you'd call well in? 1898 A. E. T. Watson *Turf* i. 16 A horse which is well in in a little handicap.

(*b*) 1891 [see Well-in]. 1902 Webster Suppl., *Well in*, engaged in a profitable speculation in stocks; said of a speculator whose purchases have risen considerably in value on his hands. Hence, in a general sense, prosperous; well off; well to do. (*Colloq., Australia.*) 1913 M. Roberts *Salt of Sea* 158 If you ain't lucky you're bound to be dishonest, ..if you means to be well in all the time.

k. Of fortune or luck: Favourable. (Cf. Out *adv.* 23.)

1901 A. E. W. Mason *Clementina* i, His luck for the moment was altogether in.

12. a. in-maintenance, maintenance for a person living in a workhouse or the like.

1885 *Encycl. Brit.* XIX. 475/2 Relief given in a workhouse is termed 'in (or indoor) maintenance' relief. 1905 *Daily Chron.* 1 Sept. 2/5 For every £1 spent on out-relief in 1902–3 no less than £7 12s. 4d. was expended on in-maintenance.

b. in-side *Cricket*, the side which is batting; **in-work**, one who has work.

1882 Pardon *Australians in Eng.* 16 Matters are going wrong with the in-side. 1924 Galsworthy *White Monkey* i. xii, The out-of-works and the in-works.

In, *sb.* Add:

2. Ins and outs. b. Those who are constantly entering and leaving the workhouse. Cf. *in-and-out class*, etc. (s.v. In and out 4 in Dict. and below).

1884 *Daily News* 10 Dec. (Ware) There are considerable numbers of paupers..who find the workhouse a convenient retreat on emergency...They are known familiarly as 'the ins-and-outs'. 1896 *Rep. Poor Law Schools Comm.* xi. 71 The fluctuating class of children whose parents frequently discharge themselves from the workhouse and in a few days seek readmission. These cases are known among Poor Law officials as 'ins and outs'. 1905 *Rep. Brit. Assoc.* 467 The 'ins and outs' of Great Britain have characteristics which may be described as nomadic.

In. Latin preposition. Add

in a·ntis. *Class. Arch.* (lit. between antæ). Denoting a building in which the side walls are prolonged beyond the front and the pilasters terminating them are in line with the columns of the façade.

1849 W. Smith *Dict. Gr. & Rom. Antiq.* (ed. 2) 1105/2 There were never more than ten columns in the end portico of a temple; and when there were only two, they were always arranged in that peculiar form called *in antis*. 1875 *Encycl. Brit.* II. 388/2 Temples in Antis, with a portico of two or four columns in front.

in arti·culo mo·rtis, at the point of death.

1596 [see Dict. 21]. 1617 J. Chamberlain in *Crt. & Times Jas. I* (1848) II. 1 The late lord chancellor left this world, being visited *in articulo mortis*, or not full half an hour before. 1825 Scott *Talisman* xxviii, Nor did I mention it save *in articulo mortis*..to yonder reverend hermit. 1929 *Encycl. Brit.* VI. 231/1 Those under discipline were allowed to receive the eucharist when *in articulo mortis*.

in contuma·ciam, applied to sentences given against persons in contempt.

1918 *Wireless World* VI. 156 It was only because they were for the moment beyond reach of the Italian Courts that they were condemned *in contumaciam*. 1923 *Westm. Gaz.* 28 Dec., Several of these verdicts were passed in contumaciam.

in co·rpore, = *in vivo.

1905 [see *in vitro].

in flagra·nte deli·cto in the very act.

[1612 Shelton *Quix.* iii. viii. 190 All was done in *Flagrante*, there was no leisure to giue me torment, the cause was concluded.] 1772 *Junius Lett.* II. lxviii. 314 A person positively charged with feloniously stealing, and taken *in flagrante delicto*, with the stolen goods upon him, is not bailable. 1876 tr. *Beneden's Anim. Parasites* (1883) 2 The sharper passes for an honest man as long as he has not been taken *in flagrante delicto*. 1931 *Times Lit. Suppl.* 19 Mar. 209/1 The conspirators were caught *in flagrante delicto*.

in lo·co (*b*), in the place, locally.

1908 *Practitioner* Jan. 22 Some toxin either generated in loco..or reaching the skin from some distant focus of disease.

in no·mine, in the name (of): applied to (*a*) a motet or antiphon in fugal style, probably so called because originally used of a composition set to a text in which these words occurred, e.g. the Introit, 'In nomine Jesu', the Psalm 'Deus, in nomine tuo'; (*b*) a free fugue in which the answer does not exactly correspond to the subject.

1636 C. Butler *Princ. Music* 91 The *In-nomine's* of Parsons, Taverner, D. Ty, etc. 1876 Stainer & Barrett *Dict. Mus. Terms* s.v., The *in nomines* which exist are chiefly the production of composers of the 16th century.

in re·, in the matter of, referring to, = Re *sb.*[2]

1886 *Athenæum* 20 Nov. 671/2 The alleged 'misrepresentation' *in re* Squeers *v.* Bentley. 1896 Ellen Terry *Lett. to G. B. Shaw* 7 Dec. (1931), What do you mean by saying (in re The Philanderer) it is dull and bestial?

in se·culo, in the world (as opposed to 'in religion').

1932 *N. & Q.* 9 Jan. 24/1 The legal point, the position of a tenant whose co-parcener has entered a religious house but has not yet professed, i.e., is yet *in seculo*, is alone considered.

in sta·tu pupilla·ri: as a pupil or ward; under scholastic discipline; at the universities, designating all who have not the degree of Master.

a 1856 in *Newsp. & Gen. Reader's Comp.* § 571 A young Englishman.. while still in statu pupillari. 1860 *Once a Week* 21 July 95/2, I fully admit that in later years we are all of us apt to grow sentimental about the traditions of our respective schools—I merely deny that we do so whilst we remain *in statu pupillari*. 1862 THACKERAY *Philip* xxxix, Other young women who are kept by over-watchful mothers too much *in statu pupillari*. 1882 *Standard* 25 Dec. 5 (Stanford) Academic and urban magnates, fellows, and tutors have predominated over guests who are *in statu pupillari*. 1903 'SIGMA' *Personalia* 172 One of those dusky potentates *in statu pupillari*, who were nearly always represented at the Master's dinners. 1930 *Sunday Times* 12 Oct. 26/2 The possession of a motor-car makes it easy for a person *in statu pupillari* to spend a large part of his existence elsewhere than in the University.

in u·tero, in the uterus or womb, unborn.

1728 CHAMBERS *Cycl.* s.v. *Generation*, For that Dr. Harvey could never discover any thing of it *in utero*. 1795 W. TURNBULL in *Mem. Med.* IV. 364 (*title*) A Case where the Small-Pox was communicated from the Mother to the Child in Utero. 1862 A. MEADOWS *Man. Midwifery* (1871) 156 The placenta, which..still remains for awhile in utero. 1902 *Encycl. Brit.* XXIX. 259/1 The embryo *in utero*.

in vi·tro, in a glass, within a test-tube: denoting bacterial and other cultures grown in the laboratory.

1901 H. E. DURHAM in *Jrnl. Exper. Med.* V. 355 Serum obtained by immunising with one race did not necessarily give more than a trace of reaction in vitro and none whatever in vivo when tested with another race. 1905 *Rep. Brit. Assoc.* 552 The nature of the substance contained in the serum was discussed. *In vitro* it has little power. *In corpore*,..the amount..necessary..is of no consequence. 1905 *Daily Chron.* 9 Oct. 5/4 Experiments 'in vitro'. 1925 C. H. BROWNING *Immunochem. Studies* 14 These alcoholic extracts possess the property of reacting with heterophile antibody *in vitro*.

in vi·vo, in the living body: denoting cultures and reactions occurring in the living body.

1901 [see prec.]. 1908 *Rep. Brit. Assoc.* 742 Experiments *in vivo* and *vitro* lead to the conclusion that 'Atoxyl'.. combines with the proteins and acts in forms of this combination. 1908 *Practitioner* Mar. 392 Normal leucocytes, exposed in vitro and in vivo to the action of such leucotoxins present in the serum of animals, which have been exposed to Roentgen-rays. 1925 C. H. BROWNING *Immunochem. Studies* 14 They are..practically incapable of generating the antibody *in vivo*.

In-, *pref.*[1] Add: **b.** *Geom.* = INSCRIBED *ppl. a.* 3, as in *in-conic*, *in-hexagon*, *IN-CENTRE, IN-CIRCLE, IN-PARABOLA, IN-POLYGON, etc.

Inactivate (inæ·ktiveɪt), *v.* [f. INACTIVE + -ATE [3].] *trans.* To render inactive. Hence **Inactiva·tion.**

1906 DORLAND *Med. Dict.* (ed. 4), *Inactivation*, the destruction of the activity of a serum by the action of heat or other means. 1913 *Ibid.* (ed. 7), *Inactivate*, to render inactive; to destroy the activity of. 1927 HALDANE & HUXLEY *Anim. Biol.* 189 When unaccustomed proteins enter their system, they [*sc.* the higher animals]..destroy or inactivate them.

Inactive, *a.* Add: **b.** *Chem.* Of isomeric forms of certain crystalline organic compounds: Having no effect or action on, causing no rotation in the plane of, polarized light; optically neutral.

1857 MILLER *Elem. Chem.*, *Org.* 334 It [*sc.* a modification of tartaric acid] has been termed by Pasteur, inactive tartaric acid, in allusion to its want of action upon polarized light. 1889 [see *INACTOSE]. 1920 *Discovery* Nov. 330/2 Pasteur..found the lost inactive acid of Mitscherlich, known as paratartaric or racemic acid.

Inactose (inæ·ktōus). *Chem.* [f. *INACT(IVE b + -OSE [2].] An inactive syrupy sugar derived from cane sugar by treatment with silver nitrate and subsequent heating and evaporation.

1882 *Jrnl. Chem. Soc.* XLII. 490 Inactose may be easily obtained by the action of equal weights of normal sugar and silver nitrate in concentrated solution. 1889 MORLEY & MUIR *Watts' Dict. Chem.* II. 751/1 Inactose... This inactive sugar may be formed by dissolving silver nitrate in a solution of cane-sugar in water.

Inaja (inâdʒā·). [Tupi.] In full *inaja palm*: A tall palm, *Maximiliana regia*, which grows in the Amazon region.

1860 MAYNE REID *Odd People* 82. 1866 *Treas. Bot.* II. 726/1 The Inajá Palm of the Amazon.

In and out, *adv.* **4.** Add: *in and out family*, a family constantly entering and leaving a workhouse; *in-and-out shop* (London colloq.), a shop through which one can walk in and out along a passage, where the goods are hung up for inspection; *in and out work*, work which is not continuous. Cf. *ins and outs* (*IN *sb.* 2 b).

1903 *Westm. Gaz.* 29 Sept. 10/1 If his engagements are only for particular plays—'in and out' work. 1904 *Daily Chron.* 14 June 9/1 One notable 'In and Out' family entered and discharged itself sixty-two times from a London workhouse in one year.

Inanga (ī·naŋā). Also **inaka.** [Maori *inaka*, *inanga*.] **a.** Any of several New Zealand and Tasmanian freshwater fishes of the family *Galaxiidæ*; also, the New Zealand smelt or whitebait, *Retropinna richardsoni*. **b.** 'In Samoa, the fry of a sea fish which makes its appearance at the mouths of rivers for a fortnight in August and is a much-prized delicacy' (Funk's Stand. Dict. 1928).

1845 E. J. WAKEFIELD *Adv. N. Z.* II. 100 This fish is called *hinanga* [sic], and resembles Blackwall white-bait in size and flavour. 1896 *Australasian* 28 Aug. 407/3 (Morris) About the same size as this fish is the 'inaka' much used for bait.

Ina·ngulated, *ppl. a.* *Ent.* [f. IN-[3] + ANGULATED.] Angled inwardly.

1898 *Proc. Zool. Soc.* 17 May 441 The inner stripe more or less strongly inangulated below median vein, the outer stripe zigzag.

Inappositeness (inæ·pǫzitnės). [f. INAPPOSITE + -NESS.] The character or quality of being inapposite.

1893 SALTUS *Madam Sapphira* 50 With an inappositeness which afterward was to occur to Nevius as curious. 1895 W. J. LOCKE *At Gate of Samaria* xii, The words estranged them still further. They were pathetic in their ludicrous inappositeness.

Inaptic (inæ·ptik), *a.* [f. IN-[3] + *APTIC.] (See quot. s.v. *APTIC.)

Inarticulacy (inaɹti·kiŭlăsi). [f. INARTICULATE + -CY.] Inarticulateness.

1921 *Observer* 11 Sept. 10/2 That it has not done so..we must ascribe..to the inarticulacy of the scientist himself. 1927 SADLEIR *Trollope* 41 He has virtually entreated her forgiveness for his inarticulacy.

Inaugural. B. *sb.* (Earlier U.S. examples.)

1832 *Deb. Congress* 5 May 2778, I turn now to the other points in the inaugural. 1841 in T. W. Barnes *Mem. Thurlow Weed* (1884) 91 The inaugural does not meet expectations.

Inaugurate, *v.* **1.** (Later U.S. examples.)

1905 D. G. PHILLIPS *Plum Tree* 380 We stayed there until Scarborough was inaugurated.

Inauguration. 1. (Later U.S. example.)

1905 D. G. PHILLIPS *Plum Tree* 314 It was now less than a month before inauguration.

4. attrib. *Inauguration day.* (U.S. example.)

1893 KATE D. WIGGIN *Polly Oliver* xvii. (1894) 185 As it chances to be a presidential year, we will celebrate Inauguration Day.

Inboard. A. *adv.* (Earlier U.S. examples.)

1830 J. F. COOPER *Water Witch* III. vii, Assured of the position of his enemy, he returned in-board. 1851 H. MELVILLE *Moby Dick* cxxxv. (1926) 562 Two of them clutched the gunwale..and..hurled themselves bodily inboard again.

In-book (i·nbuk). [IN *adv.* 12.] In the London bankers' clearing-house, the account-book in which cheques and bills cleared against his bank are entered by the in-clearer; an in-clearing book.

1884 HOWARTH *Clearing System* iv. 52 The in-clearers take with them the 'in-books' and at once enter the various charges under the headings of the several banks.

Inc., U.S. abbreviation of INCORPORATED.

1909 *Cent. Dict.* Suppl. 1926 *Amer. Speech* July, Advt. 2 Waverley Press, Inc. 1928 *Publishers' Weekly* 16 June 2451/1 The retail business will be known as 'Dutton's, Inc.'.

Incaean (iŋkā,ī·ăn), *a.* = INCAN. Also **Incaic** (iŋkē·ik), **Incarian** (iŋkē·riăn) *adjs.*

1880 CABLE *Grandissimes* iv. 23 Possibly between the two sides of the occipital profile there may have been an Incaean tendency to inequality. 1909 *Cent. Dict.* Suppl., Incaic, Incarian. 1926 *Glasgow Herald* 30 Jan. 8 The ruins of an ancient Incaic village.

Incallosal (inkălǫ·săl), *a.* *Anat.* [f. IN-[3] + *CALLOSAL *a.*] Of the brain: Having no corpus callosum.

1901 DORLAND *Med. Dict.* (ed. 2), *Incallosal*, characterized by absence of the corpus callosum, and usually by consequent idiocy.

Incandescent, *a.* Add: Also *sb.* An incandescent lamp or burner.

1925 C. R. COOPER *Lions 'n' Tigers* v. 143 The great, empty building, where only a few incandescents gleamed dully.

Incarnant (inkā·ɹnănt), *a.* (*sb.*) [f. INCARN *v.* + -ANT [1].] That promotes healing of a wound or granulation; also as *sb.*, a substance or agent which promotes healing.

1901 DORLAND *Med. Dict.*

Incendivity (insendi·viti). [f. the stem of L. *incendĕre* to set on fire, kindle + -IVITY.] The ability of a spark to effect ignition.

1925 H. F. COWARD & R. V. WHEELER *Ignition of Firedamp* 20 The ignition of firedamp by a spark the incendivity of which depends entirely on its capacity component. *Ibid.* 21 An increase in the inductance, or in the applied voltage, increases the incendivity of the flash.

In-centre (i·nsentəɹ). *Geom.* [f. *IN-[1] b + CENTRE *sb.*] The centre of an inscribed circle.

1882 C. SMITH *Conic Sections* (1910) 351 The three external bisectors of the angles of a triangle meet the opposite sides in three points on a straight line which is perpendicular to the join of the in-centre and circum centre. 1904 H. S. HALL & F. H. STEVENS *School Geom.* III. 204 Given the base and vertical angle of a triangle, find the locus of the in-centre.

Inch, *sb.*[1] Add: **2.** *An inch of cold iron* or *steel*, a stab with a sword or dagger. (Cf. INCH *v.* 2, quot. 1868.)

4. d. inch-worm (example).

1881 *Harper's Mag.* Oct. 656/1 A wriggling inch-worm,.. awaiting..an opportunity to measure the length of your nose.

Incidence. 4. Add: *Angle of incidence* (*b*), the angle which the chord of the wing of an aeroplane makes with the relative direction of the undisturbed air current.

1916 H. BARBER *Aeroplane Speaks* 60 The most efficient angle of incidence varies with the thrust at the disposal of the designer, the weight to be carried, and the climb-velocity ratio desired. 1927 C. L. M. BROWN *Conquest of Air* 43 The wings, tilted slightly upward (the measure of this tilt is known as the 'angle of incidence').

Incidental, *a.* Add: **1. d.** *Incidental advertisements* (see quot.).

1931 *Times Lit. Suppl.* 20 Aug. 636/3 'Incidental' advertisements, advertisements..which are printed in a separate gathering from the body of the book and sewn in at either the end or the beginning.

Incidentalist (inside·ntălist). [f. INCIDENTAL + -IST.] One who describes or insists on what is merely incidental and not essential.

1904 *Daily Chron.* 19 Nov. 3/1 Mr. Palmer may be described as an 'incidentalist'. 1924 H. E. FOSDICK *Mod. Use Bible* 163 Folk who insist on that kind of literal inerrancy in ancient documents are not Fundamentalists at all; they are incidentalists.

Incidentality (i:nsidentæ·liti). [f. INCIDENTAL *a.* + -ITY.] The quality of being incidental.

1791 *Ann. 1st Congress* (1834) II. 1942 Hence the incidentality of this authority to the mere existence of Government is inferred.

Inclinometer. Add: **2. b.** An instrument for measuring the inclination to the horizontal of a flying machine.

1913 *Captain* Sept. 1069/2 An inclinometer, to show the angle of ascent or descent. 1917 C. G. TURNER *Aircraft of To-Day* vii. 112 The inclinometer has been largely superseded.

Inclusum (inklū·sǝm). *Zool.* [mod.L.] An individual belonging to a group of bivalve molluscs having the mantle cavity open at the anterior extremity or near the middle only.

1914 *Brit. Mus. Return* 201 The mounting of the amber inclusa in glass cells.

Incohesion (inkohī·ʒən). [f. IN-[3] + COHESION.] Want of cohesion.

1882 H. SPENCER *Princ. Sociol.* v. II. 277 Our own Indian Empire..held together by force in a state of artificial equilibrium, threatens some day to illustrate by its fall the incohesion arising from lack of congruity in components. 1922 *Public Opinion* 17 Mar. 244/2 The interminable vacillation, procrastination and incohesion of the Government at home.

Income, *sb.*[1] **6.** Add:

National income: the income of a nation as a whole, *spec.* the aggregate amount available for distribution among the agents of production.

1878 *Encycl. Brit.* VIII. 258/1 The income tax returns given in the preceding tables furnish important materials for ascertaining, if only approximately, the national income of England. 1925 S. E. THOMAS *Elem. Econ.* xvi. 214 The total of the national income represents not only the reward which flows to land, capital, labour and enterprise: it is also the total available in the hands of all members of the community for purchasing goods and services. 1931 *Times Lit. Suppl.* 19 Feb. 124/2 The national income may be divided into the income (wages, salaries and interest) of the producers of capital and consumable goods respectively.

Income-tax. Add: Also *attrib.*

1878 Income tax returns [see *INCOME *sb.*[1] 6]. 1902 *Encycl. Brit.* XXXIII. 194/2 An Income Tax Code. 1909 *Westm. Gaz.* 24 Sept. 5/3 Returns may be demanded in every income-tax district in which a person may reside. 1927 BOWLEY & STAMP *Nat. Income 1924* 17 'Income-Tax' income exceeds ordinary income under certain heads, since it includes *inter alia* various losses which do not come out in the assessment.

Incoming, *ppl. a.* Add: **e.** Of game: Flying towards the sportsman.

1892 GREENER *Breech-loader* 211 It often happens that incoming and motionless ground game is shot over.

Incompatibility. 1. (Early example of phrase.)

1799 in *Ann. 7th Congress* 2 Sess. 751 Independently of the opinions strongly expressed, there appears to me an *incompatibility of temper*.

Incompensated (inkǫ·mpĕnsēted), *a.* *Path.* [f. IN-[3] + COMPENSATED *ppl. a.*] Lacking compensation. (Cf. COMPENSATION 1 c.) So **I:ncompensa·tion** (Dorland 1901).

a 1909 *Buck's Handbk. Med. Sci.* I. 564 (Cent. D. Suppl.) Any of the organic heart lesions when incompensated may be followed by ascites.

Incompetence. Add:

2. b. *Path.* Inadequacy, insufficiency, lack of adjustment; *spec.* of the valves of the heart when they allow blood to regurgitate.

1876 [see Dict., sense 2]. 1890 F. TAYLOR *Man. Pract. Med.* (1891) 468 Incompetence of the aortic valves gives rise to a murmur during the dilatation of the ventricle. 1901 DORLAND *Med. Dict.* (ed. 2) s.v., *Pyloric i[ncompetence]*, passage of food undigested into the intestine.

Inconquerable, *a.* Delete †*Obs.* and add examples.

1905 *Daily Chron.* 4 Oct. 5/1 An inconquerable penchant to conspiracy. 1921 *Edin. Rev.* July 134 That rather ticklish matter, the government and command of the British Empire Navy..does not present inconquerable obstacles to be overcome.

Inconsciently (inkǫ·nʃiəntli), *adv.* [f. INCONSCIENT *a.* + -LY [2].] Unknowingly.

1913 *Glasgow Herald* 18 Oct. 11/1 They stood, inconsciently perhaps, for some of the priceless intangible things without which the millennium would be a sterile and bitter anti-climax. 1929 R. BRIDGES *Test. Beauty* IV. 621 Held by the inborn love of Beauty inconsciently Of preference to imitate the more beautiful things.

Inco-ordinated, *a.* (Examples.)

1885 F. WARNER *Phys. Expression* 71 Co-ordinated movements and inco-ordinated movements. 1911 W. JAMES *Mem. & Stud.* ix. 218 There was no appearance of general dismay and little of chatter or of inco-ordinated excitement.

Incorporatorship (inkǫ·ɹpǫrētəɹʃip). [INCORPORATOR 2.] The position of an incorporator.

1873 'MARK TWAIN' & WARNER *Gilded Age* xlii, It would be more money in my pocket, in the end, than my brother-in-law will get out of that incorporatorship, fat as it is.

Incorrectitude (inkǫre·ktitiūd). [f. IN-[3] + *CORRECTITUDE.] The state of being in the wrong in one's conduct or behaviour.

1898 *Westm. Gaz.* 4 Oct. 2/2 We are certain that it is not wise to adopt this position of positive incorrectitude. *Ibid.* 10 Nov. 2/3 He is brought round to own the incorrectitude of calling Mr. Gladstone a spider.

Increasing, *ppl. a.* Add: esp. in *law of increasing return(s)*: the observed fact that in certain manufactures and industries the expenditure of labour or capital up to a certain point produces a more than proportionate corresponding return.

1890 A. MARSHALL *Princ. Econ.* IV. xiii. I. 379 While the part which Nature plays in production conforms to the Law of Diminishing Return, the part which man plays conforms to the Law of Increasing Return. 1925 S. E. THOMAS *Elem. Econ.* x. 114 The Law of Increasing Returns..states that the expansion of an industry, in which there is no dearth of the necessary agents of production, tends to be accompanied by increasing returns.

Increment. Add: **4. c.** (See quot.)

1905 *Terms Forestry & Logging* 14 *Increment*, the volume or value of wood produced during a given period by the growth of a tree or of a stand.

6. *attrib.*

1909–10 *Act* 10 *Edw. VII* c. 8 § 2 (1) The increment value of any land shall be deemed to be the amount (if any) by which the site value of the land, on the occasion on which increment value duty is to be collected.., exceeds the original site value of the land as ascertained in accordance with the general provisions of this Part of this Act as to valuation.

Incrustive (inkrʊ·stiv), *a.* *Geol.* [f. INCRUST + -IVE.] Of or pertaining to the crust of the earth or to the formation of a crust.

1892 JAS. GEIKIE in *Rep. Brit. Assoc.* 795 He [*sc.* Prof. A. Winchell] was of opinion that the transmeridional progress of the tidal swell in early incrustive times on our planet would give the forming crust structural characteristics and aptitudes trending from north to south.

Incudal (i·nkiudăl), *a.* [f. L. *incus*, *in·cudem* anvil + -AL.] Of or pertaining to the INCUS. Also **I·ncudate** *a.*, (*a*) having an incus; (*b*) designating a forcipate type of mastax in rotifers in which the mallei are absent.

1890 BILLINGS *Med. Dict.*, Incudal. 1896 M. HARTOG in *Camb. Nat. Hist.* II. 211 In Asplanchnidæ the rami are large and hooked, constituting the 'incudate' mastax.

Incudo- (inkiū·do), before a vowel **incud-,** combining form of INCUS, in terms denoting the association of the incus with another part, as *incudo-ma·lleal*, *incu:do-stape·dial*, *incu:do-tympa·nic* adjs.

1890 BILLINGS *Med. Dict.* 1908 *Practitioner* Jan. 123 The lax membrane resting upon the inner tympanic wall and incudo-stapedial articulation.

Incunabulist (inkiunæ·biŭlist). [f. INCUNABULA + -IST.] One who collects or is interested in incunabula.

1923 S. GASELEE in *Library* Mar. 306 It will be duly recorded in what will some day be the magistral authority for all of us incunabulists. 1928 *Ibid.* Sept. 162 The incunabulist has to stop at the threshold of the year 1501.

In-curl (i·nkɔ̄ɹl). *Curling.* [f. IN *adv.* + CURL *sb.*] = *INTURN *sb.* 4.

1903 *Westm. Gaz.* 31 Jan. 3/1 The secret of the game is to be able to play the 'out-curl or in-curl' as the skip may direct.

Incurve (i·nkɔ̄ɹv), *sb.* *Baseball.* [f. INCURVE *v.*] The bending or curving of a ball inwards (i.e. across the front of the batsman); the course of such a ball; a ball pitched so as to curve to the right.

1906 *Spalding's Base Ball Guide* 112 An In-curve..is a ball which curves in towards the batsman as he stands in his position.

Ind- (ind) = INDO-[2]. **I·ndamine,** one of a series of weak synthetic bases of the type of phenylene blue, the salts of which are unstable blue and green dye-stuffs. **Inda·nthrene,** a resistant dye-stuff resembling natural indigo in its properties. **I·ndazine,** (*a*) = **indazole*; (*b*) a dye $C_{28}H_{22}N_4Cl$, allied to the safranines. **I·ndazole,** a crystalline nitrogenous compound, $C_7H_6N_2$, prepared chiefly from a hydrazine derivative of cinnamic acid. **Indazy·lic** *a.*, of or belonging to indazole. **I·ndene,** an oily hydrocarbon, C_9H_8, obtained by the fractional distillation of coal-tar.

1888 *Jrnl. Chem. Soc.* LIV. 949 *Indamines and Indophenols. 1889 MORLEY & MUIR *Watts' Dict. Chem.* II. 751/2 Indamine hydrochloride. 1903 *Jrnl. Chem. Soc.* LXXXIV. I. 446 Both *indanthrene and its brominated derivative give the same substance, $C_{28}H_{14}O_2N_2$. 1922 *Glasgow Herald* 11 May 8 The discovery of indanthrene blue. *Ibid.*, Colours of the indanthrene series. 1891 *Jrnl. Chem. Soc.* LX. II. 1047 *Indazine, a blue dye obtained by treating nitrosodimethylaniline with diphenylmetaphenylenediamine, is the hydrochloride of a base which has many properties in common with the saffranine bases, but which, like the indulines, is free from oxygen. 1884 *Ibid.* XLVI. 441 *Indazole crystallizes in colourless needles which melt at 146·5°. 1904 *Ibid.* LXXXVI. I. 690 Formation of Indazoles from Nitrated *o*-Methylated Amines. 1903 *Nature* 17 Dec. 167/2 A new mode of formation of the *indazylic derivatives. 1889 *Jrnl. Chem. Soc.* LVI. 984 Synthesis of *Indene-derivatives.

Indefinable, *a.* (*sb.*) **B.** *sb.* Add:

1927 LINDEMANN *Physics in The Mind* 137 Though the so-called physical laws will be in general consistent with reality, there is no certainty that the indefinables employed in their statement..have any fundamental significance beyond their appeal to the mental preferences..of the physicist. *Ibid.* 139 The commonest indefinables used in physics are space and time. 1932 — *Phys. Signif. Quantum Th.* 12 The indefinables upon which all our thought processes depend. *Ibid.* 14 The three indefinables commonly used in physics are length, time, and mass.

Independable (indėpe·ndăb'l), *a.* [f. IN-[3] + DEPENDABLE.] Not dependable; untrustworthy; not to be depended *upon*.

1802 BENTHAM *Let. Dumont* Wks. 1843 X. 388/1 All Frenchmen are independable upon. 1897 *Geog. Jrnl.* Feb. 122 This lady is..capricious, independable, and exacting. 1921 S. GRAHAM *Europe—Whither Bound?* xvii. 210 English action is so sluggish and so independable.

Independence. 3. *Independence Day* (earlier example).

1841 *Knickerbocker Mag.* XVII. 276 The enthusiasm which is annually rekindled..by the return of 'Independence day'.

Independent, *a.* Add: **1. c.** *Independent Day* = prec.

1803 ELIZA S. BOWNE *Girl's Life Eighty Yrs. ago* (1888) 161 We are in expectation of great entertainment on fourth of July—Independent day! as they laugh at us Yankees for calling it. 1840 R. H. DANA *Bef. Mast* xxxi, Monday, July 4th. This was 'independent day' in Boston.

5. b. *Independent Labour Party* (abbrev. *I.L.P.*: see *I. III. d): the title of the political organization founded at Bradford in January 1893 by James Keir Hardie as an offshoot of the Social Democratic Federation, for the support of parliamentary candidates of approved socialistic views.

Indestructible, *a.* Add: Used *subst.* An indestructible thing.

a 1861 T. WINTHROP *Life in Open Air* (1863) 17 My pair of these indestructibles [*sc.* socks] will outlast my last legs. 1880 J. ROSS *Hist. Corea* x. 332 The things used in the evening sacrifice are to be removed,..but spirits and indestructibles may remain.

Indeterminate, *a.* Add: **2. e.** *Indeterminate sentence*, a sentence in a criminal case which leaves the prisoner's release dependent on his conduct and on the probability of his amendment. *Indeterminate vowel*, the 'obscure' vowel (ə), mid-mixed-wide; = SHEVA 2.

1888 KING & COOKSON *Sound & Infl. Greek & Latin* 70 The same indeterminate vowel appears in Sk., where it is called a *svarabhakti* vowel. 1894 LINDSAY *Latin Lang.* 257 The obscure or indeterminate vowel (like the Hebrew sh*va).

Indeterminist. Add: Also *attrib.* = **Indetermini·stic** *a.*, of or pertaining to the doctrine of indeterminism.

1907 W. JAMES *Pragmatism* 117 The chaplet of my days tumbles into a cast of disconnected beads as soon as the thread of inner necessity is drawn out by the preposterous indeterminist doctrine. 1922 A. G. HOGG *Redemption from this World* 243 Bushnell, accepting a very indeterministic type of libertarianism, postulates an unresolved plurality of 'powers' or uncaused causes.

Index, *sb.* **10.** Add: **index board** *U.S.*, a board serving to direct travellers; a guide-post; **index centre** (see quot.); **index number,** a number indicating the relative level of prices at given times and calculated by comparing the wholesale prices of certain staple commodities with the prices of a selected period for which the index number is 100; **index plate,** a perforated disk in a gear-cutting machine, etc. (Knight 1884); **index wheel,** any of several wheels having notches, graduations, or perforations for performing actions at regular intervals or for regulating other machinery.

1850 W. MILES *Jrnl.* (1916) 23 Follow a broad frequented wagon road, directed by *index boards. 1859 *Texas Almanac* 23 It is the duty of each overseer..to put up index-boards at the forks of public roads. 1913 *Lockwood's Dict. Mech. Engin.* App., **Index Centres*, the head, and the tail stock between which work is carried to be pitched or indexed. 1887 *Encycl. Brit.* XXII. 466/1 The only matter connected with price which it is necessary to refer to here is the theory of the *index number. 1893 *Jrnl. Soc. Arts* 3 Feb. 211/2 This total index number..merged all prices high and low in a single figure. 1928 J. W. F. ROWE *Wages in Pract. & Theory* 14 Index numbers based on changes in the nominal weekly rates in these industries afford a general guide to the character of wage fluctuations. 1884 KNIGHT *Dict. Mech.* Suppl., **Index Wheel*. 1. A graduated plate marked in circles of holes, for spacing in the cutting of gears....2. A graduated wheel in an instrument for dividing or measuring angles, or in some forms of calculating instruments. 1902 THORNLEY *Cotton Combing Mach.* 37 The index wheel greatly facilitates the adjustment of the time for action of the various parts that act on the cotton.

Index, *v.* Add: **5.** *Mech.* (See quot.)

1913 *Lockwood's Dict. Mech. Engin.* App., *Indexing*, dividing the circle for pitching, for purposes of milling, fluting, and gear cutting. When a spiral movement is imparted to the work through a lead screw and change gears, and a swivel table, the indexing is universal in character.

Indfine (i·ndfinĕ). *Irish Hist.* [Ir., f. *ind* head + *fine* family.] One of the groups into which the ancient Irish clans were divided: cf. *GEILFINE, *IARFINE.

1875 MAINE *Hist. Inst.* 209 The eldest member of the Iarfine moved into the Indfine; and the eldest member of the Indfine passed out of the organisation altogether.

India. 6. Add: *India cracker* (later U.S. example).

1844 *Knickerbocker Mag.* XXIII. 586 The sound of India-crackers..is already perceptible to the senses of the awakening Manhattanese.

Indian, *a.* and *sb.* Add: **A.** *adj.* **2.** In reference to the endurance of tortures by North American Indians.

1737 WESLEY *Lett.* (1931) I. 225 When He shall have chosen one or more to magnify Him, not with a Stoical or Indian indifference, but blessing and praying for their murderers.

4. b. Indian agent (see *AGENT *sb.* 4 b); **Indian apple** (example); **Indian bed,** a layer of clams arranged on the ground for roasting (cf. *clam-bake* s.v. CLAM *sb.*[2]); **Indian bread** (earlier examples); **Indian currant** (see CORAL-BERRY); **Indian fighter,** a frontiersman experienced in or noted for fighting Indians; **Indian file** (earlier and later examples); **Indian fort** (see quot.); **Indian gift, giver** (later examples); so **Indian giving; Indian-hating,** the hatred against Indians felt by settlers who regarded them not only as enemies but also as agents of the devil (see quot.); **Indian liquor,** adulterated liquor for Indians; **Indian millet** (see MILLET 2 and quot. 1889); **Indian mound,** in the U.S.A., a mound in a plain, believed to have been raised by Indians; **Indian orchard,** an orchard of ungrafted fruit trees; **Indian paint,** the grass *Sanguinaria canadensis*; **Indian paint-brush,** a plant of the genus *Castilleja*; **Indian path** (earlier examples); **Indian peach** (see quot.); **Indian pipe** (-**stem**) (examples); **Indian pipeshank** (see quot.); **Indian Reservation, Reserve** (see RESERVATION 3 b, RESERVE *sb.* 5 b); **Indian rice** (example); **Indian sign(s),** the (usually faint) signs that reveal the presence of Indians; **Indian sugar,** maple sugar; **Indian title,** a title to land acquired from the original Indian owners; **Indian tobacco** (later example); **Indian trade,** trade with the Indians; articles used in the trade; **Indian trader,** one engaged in trade with the Indians (see also quot. 1835); **Indian trail** = *Indian path*; **Indian turnip** (earlier and later examples).

1849 PARKMAN *Oregon Trail* ii. 20 The rich flowers of the *Indian apple. 1848 BARTLETT *Dict. Amer.*, *Indian bed. 1633 *Indian bread [see CASSAVA 2]. 1704 SARAH KNIGHT *Jrnl.* 47 Indian mixt Bred. 1805 D. MCCLURE *Diary* (1899) 91 Some cakes of indian bread. 1825 J. NEAL *Bro. Jonathan* I. 76 Honey comb, new butter, cheese, rye and Indian bread; i.e. a bread, baked in half-peck loaves, made partly of rye meal, and partly of Indian meal. 1859 BARTLETT *Dict. Amer.* (ed. 3), *Coral Berry* (Symphoricarpus vulgaris), the *Indian Currant of Missouri. 1832 *Louisville Directory* 97 The..gallantry..characteristic of the backwoods hunters and *Indian fighters as they were termed in those days. 1847 in H. Howe *Hist. Collect. Ohio* 370 A force of thirty eight Virginians, all of them veteran Indian fighters. 1758 *Essex Inst. Hist. Coll.* XVIII. 179 They march'd in *Indian file. 1775 *Ibid.* L. 123 Cha[s]. Grant at the head of ab[t] 50 men with firelocks, marched in Indian file from the lower Town market place to the parade in the upper town. 1830 *Massachusetts Spy* 28 July (Th.) [They] marched us over gold pits, logs, and brushes, in a style called Indian file. 1871 SCHELE DE VERE *Americanisms* (1872) 25 *Indian forts are inclosures, found in large numbers in New York and Pennsylvania.., occupying high bluff points or headlands, scarped on two or more sides and naturally easy of defence. 1879 B. F. TAYLOR *Summer-Savory* xxvi. 207 She is glad it [*sc.* the check] is an '*Indian gift', that the conductor did not present it to her outright. 1892 H. C. BOLTON in *Jrnl. Amer. Folk-lore* V. 68 If an American child, who has made a small gift to a playmate is indiscreet enough to ask that the gift be returned, he (or she) is immediately accused of being an *Indian-giver, or, as it is commonly pronounced Injun-giver. 1904 *N. Y. Herald* 10 Sept. 5 Later he took the position of the 'Indian giver' and wanted the money back. 1837 W. IRVING *Capt. Bonneville* II. vi. 71 His experience in what is proverbially called '*Indian giving' made him aware that a parting pledge was necessary on his own part. 1871 SCHELE DE VERE *Americanisms* (1872) 25 The term *Indian hating..represents a passion, which is even now a mingled ferocity and fanaticism. 1859 *Nat. Intelligencer* 10 July (Bartlett) A barrel of the 'pure Cincinnati'..is a sufficient basis upon which to manufacture one hundred barrels of 'good *Indian liquor!' 1640, 1764 *Indian millet [see MILLET 2]. 1889 FARMER *Amer.*, Indian millet (*Oryzopsis cuspidata*).—This is a perennial bunch-grass, growing from one to two feet high...It is found through the Rocky Mountain region. 1869 B. HARTE *Luck of Roaring Camp* 186 Cattle and sheep are gathered on *Indian Mounds waiting the fate of their companions whose carcases drift by us. 1859 BARTLETT *Dict. Amer.* (ed. 3), **Indian orchard*, an old orchard of ungrafted apple-trees. 1871 SCHELE DE VERE *Americanisms* (1872) 27. 1853 DARLINGTON *Flora Cestrica* (ed. 3) 13

*Indian Paint. 1923 'B. M. BOWER' *Parowan Bonanza* ii. 21 He plucked a bright red '*Indian paint brush' from beside a rock. 1668 *Plymouth Col. Rec.* 103 A bush which standeth on the southwest syde of an old *Indian path. 1793 W. BENTLEY *Diary* (1907) II. 51 An Indian path was visible through the town from the N.W. corner towards Merimack and the canoes. 1859 BARTLETT *Dict. Amer.* (ed. 3), **Indian peaches*, ungrafted peach trees. 1845–50 MRS. LINCOLN *Lect. Bot.* 164 The stems are scaly, but without leaves, the whole plant is perfectly white, and looks as if made of wax, it is sometimes called *Indian pipe. 1853 DARLINGTON *Flora Cestrica* (ed. 3) 174 *Monotropa uniflora*..Indian Pipe. 1884 'C. E. CRADDOCK' *In Tennessee Mts.* I. 60 The ashy Indian pipes silvered the roots of the trees. 1853 DARLINGTON *Flora Cestrica* (ed. 3) 174 *Spiraea salicifolia* ..*Indian Pipeshank. 1870 *Amer. Naturalist* III. 6 The *Indian Pipestem will be found rarely in low woods. 1859 BARTLETT *Dict. Amer.* (ed. 3), **Indian Reservation* or *Reserve*, a tract of land reserved for the use of Indians. *a* 1843 *Indian Reserve-lands [see RESERVE *sb.* 5 b *attrib.*]. 1871 SCHELE DE VERE *Americanisms* (1872) 409 The Wild Rice (Zizania aquatica)...The Indians of the Northern regions.. depend largely upon..this perennial plant, from whence it is also known as *Indian Rice. 1854 BARTLETT *Pers. Narr. Explor. Texas* etc. I. iv. 95 They had seen '*Indian sign', and pointed out..the well-known Indian signal of a puff of smoke suddenly rising from the earth. 1866 *Rep. Indian Affairs* 188 On the 19th, proceeding again to the Malheur river, but found no fresh Indian signs. 1873 J. H. BEADLE *Undevel. West* xxxiv. 738, I rode around our camp, a circle of about six miles, looking for Indian signs. 1833 C. F. HOFFMAN *Winter in Far West* (1835) I. 225 *Indian sugar, —as that made from the maple-tree is called at the West. 1683 *Groton Rec.* (1880) 83 Consarning our purchis of our *indin titll. 1687 *Col. Rec. N. Carolina* I. 355 He resolved that Inhabitants of the South should hold no longer by Indian Titles, but that he would grant pattents. 1849 *President's Message to Congress* II. 943 The Indian title has been extinguished to but a comparatively small portion of the country within the limits of the territory. 1871 SCHELE DE VERE *Americanisms* (1872) 415 *Indian Tobacco (*Lobelia inflata*), occasionally used instead of tobacco by virtue of its acrid leaves. 1644 *Connecticut Public Rec.* I. 113 The propositions of the Commissioners concerneing a generall *Indean trade (except corne, fishe and venison) is also approued. 1692 in *Maryland Hist. Mag.* XIII. 208 They found him in his store,..having great store of Indian trade therein. 1725 G. CHICKEN in *Trav. Amer. Col.* 119 Employing one John Hewet..in the Indian Trade without my leave or Lycence. 1853 R. GLISAN *Jrnl. Army Life* ix. (1874) 104 His prospects are flattering as the command is large and the Indian trade increasing. 1725 G. CHICKEN in *Trav. Amer. Col.* 98 That David Doway, *Indian Trader, when he was last at his house said that he would take his oath. 1835 LONGSTREET *Georgia Scenes* 281 Indian-traders (a long, cheap, but sometimes excellent kind of gun that Mother Britain used to send hither). 1882 *Rep. Indian Affairs* 5 Sept. 21 The Indians of the reservation have hauled for the Indian trader..271,000 pounds of freight. 1837 W. IRVING *Capt. Bonneville* ii. (1895) 12 They observed *Indian trails along the margin of the stream. 1851 R. GLISAN *Jrnl. Army Life* vi. (1874) 60 Taking an Indian trail, I journeyed along the same for about two miles. 1806 in *Ann. 9th Congress* 2 Sess. 1142 *Indian turnip, wild carrot, wild onion. 1859 BARTLETT *Dict. Amer.* (ed. 3). 1871 SCHELE DE VERE *Americanisms* (1872) 399. 1873 JOAQUIN MILLER *Unwritten Hist.* x. (1876) 152 He [*sc.* winter] cut down the banners of the spring that night, lamb-tongue, Indian turnip and catella.

c. Chess. *Indian problem* (see quots. 1881). Also simply *Indian*.

1846 *Chess Player's Chron.* 96 We now publish the names of those amateurs who have sent us the correct solution of our Indian problem. 1881 LOYD *Chess Strategy* 97 The theme of the Indian problem culminates in a stale-mating position, which White has provided for by preparing an ambush so as to allow the defence a move that may expose him to a discovered mate. *Ibid.* 98 The Indian always turns upon a stalemating position. *Ibid.* 100 The leading feature of the old Indian problem does not consist in the discovered mate, but in the unexpected and apparently useless withdrawal of the two pieces to a remote quarter of the board, the one intersecting the protection of the other so as to allow the adverse King a move.

B. *sb.* **1.** Delete 'Now *rare*' and add examples.

1896 in *Macm. Mag.* Sept. (1906) 820 Purely Indian-raised troops. 1923 *Glasgow Herald* 20 Feb. 6 The possible future absorption by Indians of the bulk of Indian Army commissions and military appointments.

c. A member of one of the native races of Australasia, *esp.* in the Philippine Islands a Christianized native of Malayan stock, distinguished from the Mohammedan and heathen peoples, the Negritos, etc. (Cf. *INDIO.)

1885 *Encycl. Brit.* XVIII. 752/1 Cigars they [*sc.* the Negritos of the Philippines] often smoke with the burning end between the teeth—a practice occasionally observed among the civilized Indians.

7. *Iron Indian* (on a ship).

1908 S. E. WHITE *Riverman* xxvi. 227 [A steamboat] two-storied, with twin smokestacks, an iron Indian on her top. 1911 S. E. WHITE *Bobby Orde* i. (1916) 27 In a moment appeared the *Lucy Belle*,..Bobby could make out..the swaying iron Indian with bent bow.

Indianaite (indiæ·nă,əit). *Min.* [f. *Indiana*, one of the United States of America + -ITE [1].] A white clay found in Indiana; a variety of halloysite.

1875 E. F. COX in *Geol. Surv. Indiana* 15 Owing to the mode of its formation and other features, to be mentioned beyond, I have thought proper to give to this porcelain clay the name of *Indianaite*.

Indian corn. Add: Also *attrib.*

1796 I. WELD *Trav. N. Amer.* (1800) I. 183 Indian corn bread..is a coarse, strong kind of bread, which has something of the taste of that made from oats. 1822 J. WOODS *Engl. Prairie Illinois* 258 Mr. Hamilton had only Indian corn bread, and as we had not been accustomed to it, we did not relish it.

Indianesque (indiăne·sk), *a.* [f. INDIAN *a.* 2.] Of an Indian type.

a 1861 WINTHROP *John Brent* iv. 45 This was the Indianesque Saxon who greeted me. *a* 1861 — *Canoe & Saddle* ii. 14 Indianesque, not fully Indian, was her countenance.

Indianian (indi,ă·niăn), *a.* and *sb.* [f. *Indiana*, one of the United States.] **a.** *adj.* Of or belonging to Indiana. **b.** *sb.* A native or inhabitant of Indiana.

1833 C. F. HOFFMAN *Winter in Far West* (1835) I. 223 The term 'Hooshier'..has now become a *soubriquet*, that bears nothing invidious with it to the ear even of an Indianian. 1863 WHITMAN *Specimen Days* (1892) 48 Some unconscious Indianian or from Ohio or Tennessee. 1877 HABBERTON *Jericho Road* x. 97 Small parties of discharged Illinoisans and Indianians had frequently passed through.

Indianism (i·ndiăniz'm). [-ISM.] Action or policy devoted to the interests of Indians; advocacy of (North American) Indians.

1871 *Rep. Indian Affairs* (1872) 181 We were in our original Indianism. 1887 *Longfellow's Prose Wks.* (Camelot) Introd. p. xiii, Those who stood between the culture of *Hyperion* and *Kavanagh*, and the wild Indianism of Aimard and Cooper. 1923 *Spectator* 29 Sept. 422/1 In India it works out in unrest..an exaggerated sense of Indianism—the nationalistic idea.

Indianization (i:ndiănəizē·ʃən). [f. INDIANIZE *v.* + -ATION.] The process of making Indian in character or composition.

1918 *Pall Mall Gaz.* 29 June 5/2, I do not expect as large an Indianisation of the central Cabinet as of the provincial Cabinets. 1922 *Q. Rev.* July 142 The more rapid Indianisation of the public services. 1924 J. F. BRYANT (*title*) Gandhi and the Indianisation of The Empire. 1928 *Manchester Guardian Weekly* 29 June 513/1 The Indianisation of the Indian army.

Indianologist (indiănǫ·lŏdʒist). [f. INDIAN *sb.* 2.] A student of, or authority on, the American Indian.

1894 *Nation* (N.Y.) 31 May 417/3 His ears, in the view of Indianologists, were a sure mark of aboriginal origin.

Indicate, *v.* **1.** Add: *pass.* Of a course of action: To be pointed out or suggested as desirable or necessary.

1907 *Lancet* 25 May 1462/1 Considering the great analogy which is presented between syphilis and leprosy..it seemed indicated to try on this patient the treatment by large doses of atoxyl. 1920 P. G. WODEHOUSE *Damsel in Distress* xv. 184 Strategy, rather than force, seemed to the curate to be indicated. 1922 W. R. INGE *Lay Thoughts* (1926) 235 Whenever a patient consults a doctor, the latter should always order some drug, even if drugs are not really indicated.

Indication. Add: **2. b.** *Mining.* Something which indicates the presence of valuable ore.

1873 J. H. BEADLE *Undevel. West* xviii. 326 My comrades are off down the mountain side picking at 'indications', and mapping out the 'run of the country rock'. 1877 B. HARTE *Story of a Mine* 394 Luckily the fertile alluvium of these valleys..offered no 'indications' to attract the gold-seekers.

Indicator. Add: **2. c.** A geological clue to the presence of gold.

1905 *Rep. Brit. Assoc.* 399 It was..noticed by Llewellyn that a gold pocket appeared to have been deposited at the point where a thin iron-stained line in the slate met a vein of quartz...Llewellyn called these bands *indicators*.

d. In telegraphic addresses, a code word used to indicate the required method of transmission or delivery.

1922 *P. O. Guide* 76 Telegrams directed to registered addresses can be delivered to subscribers by telephone. In London the indicator 'Phone' denotes telephonic delivery from the Central Telegraph Office.

5. Indicator-cock, -point (see quots.).

1888 *Lockwood's Dict. Mech. Engin.*, **Indicator Cock*, the cock by which a communication is made or broken between the piston of the indicator and the engine cylinder into which it is screwed. 1900 E. BUCKINGHAM *Theory of Thermodynamics* 21 The point representing the instantaneous state of the system is called the *indicator point.

Indigency. Transfer † *Obs.* to senses 1 and 3, and add examples to sense 2.

1906 *Daily Chron.* 25 Sept. 6/7 The Government has set up an Indigency Inquiry Commission. 1924 *Glasgow Herald* 7 Feb. 7 Unemployment and indigency..existed on a scale that was entirely disproportionate to the size of the white population.

Indigent, *a.* (*sb.*) **B.** *sb.* Delete †*Obs.* and add examples.

1903 *Westm. Gaz.* 15 Jan. 6/2 Mr. Chamberlain..gratefully accepted the offer to provide accommodation for the indigents. 1905 *Daily Chron.* 23 Sept. 5/1 The farmers submitted a lengthy list of subjects for redress, including.. settlements for indigents, &c.

Indigo. C. 1. and **2.** *Indigo planter*; indigo weed (earlier examples).

1772 J. HABERSHAM *Lett.* 202 We have had a great quantity of Rain fall, which must hurt the *Indigoe Planters. 1852 *Trans. Mich. Agric. Soc.* III. 197 My timber is generally oak, with some hickory, *indigo weed, tea weed.

Indio (i·ndio). [Sp. and Pg.] A member of one of various native races of America and Australasia in those areas formerly subject to Spain or Portugal; *spec.* (*a*) in Brazil and Mexico, an Indian, distinguished as an *Indio bravo*, if he has retained his independence, and *Indio manso* or *Indio fidele*, if he has come under European domination; (*b*) in the Philippine Islands, a Christianized native of Malayan stock. Also **India·no.**

1836 *Penny Cycl.* V. 365/1 All the aborigines, who lead an independent and roving life, are called in Brazil Indianos bravos, or Gentios, in contradistinction to the Indianos mansos (domesticated Indians), who have settled among, or in the neighbourhood of the Europeans. 1839 *Ibid.* XV. 158/1 The Indios Bravos generally live on the produce of the chase. 1840 *Ibid.* XVIII. 88/1 The mountains [of the Philippines] were occupied by a black race, which..was called by the Spaniards, Negritos or Aetas, while the Malays were called Indios. 1860 MAYNE REID *Odd People* 43 The 'Indios bravos',..a phrase used throughout all Spanish America to distinguish those tribes..who refused obedience to Spanish tyranny, and who preserve..their native independence and freedom. In contradistinction to the 'Indios bravos' are the 'Indios mansos', or 'tame Indians'. *Ibid.* 44 The true son of the forest—the 'Indio bravo'. 1883 *Encycl. Brit.* XVI. 218/2 The great majority of the *Indios fideles*, mestizoes, and creoles still adhere at least outwardly to the Roman Church.

Indirect, *a.* Add:

1. c. *spec.* applied to descent in certain Australian tribes.

1888 *Encycl. Brit.* XXIII. 474/1 In the Australian tribal organization of two phratries, four subphratries, and totem clans, there occurs a peculiar form of descent...The children are born into the subphratry neither of their father nor of their mother, and that descent in such cases is either female or male, according as the subphratry into which the children are born is the companion subphratry of their mother's or of their father's subphratry. In the former case we have what may be called indirect female descent; in the latter, indirect male descent...Descent..is direct in the phratry, indirect in the subphratry.

2. *Indirect evidence*: = circumstantial evidence (CIRCUMSTANTIAL *a.* 1).

1833 T. STARKIE *Pract. Treat. Law Evid.* (ed. 2) I. 17 Indirect or inferential evidence, where an inference is made as to the truth of the disputed fact, not by means of the actual knowledge which any witness had of the fact, but from collateral facts ascertained by competent means. 1865 [see Dict.].

4. *Indirect cell-division*: = KARYOKINESIS. *Indirect damages* (see quot. 1880).

1880 T. E. HOLLAND *Elem. Jurispr.* xiii. 220 'Direct', or 'general', damages are those which are the necessary and immediate consequence of the wrong, while 'indirect', or 'special', damages are sometimes granted in respect of its remoter consequences. 1890 BILLINGS *Med. Dict.*, Indirect cell-division. 1901 DORLAND *Med. Dict.* (ed. 2), *Karyokinesis*, indirect nuclear or cell-division.

5. Of or pertaining to the work and expenses which cannot be apportioned to any particular job or undertaking, pertaining to overhead charges and subsidiary work. (Cf. *DIRECT *a.* 6 f.)

1903 [see *DIRECT *a.* 6 f]. 1922 J. D. HACKETT in *Managem. Engin.* Feb., Indirect or 'non-productive' employees. 1923 *Ibid.* May, *Indirect Labor*, subsidiary work done in connection with the manufacture of a product. 1925 RYALL *Primer of Costing* 49 Labour may be employed in..repairing machinery..or in supervising the direct workers...Such labour is classified as Indirect Labour.

6. *Indirect fire*: (*a*) fire from guns with reduced charges, and from mortars and howitzers, at a low velocity and an angle of elevation not exceeding 15°; (*b*) see quot. 1918.

1879 *Man. Artill. Exerc.* I. 23 Indirect or curved fire from guns or howitzers. *Ibid.* 24 Breaching by indirect fire would, as a rule, be by demolition and not by the formation of regular cuts. 1893 G. PHILIPS *Fortif.* (ed. 5) 25. 1918 E. S. FARROW *Dict. Mil. Terms*, *Indirect Fire*, when the target cannot be seen, and guns are aimed by means of calculations, from map, or by bearings. *Indirect Laying Fire*, when a gun is laid for direction on an aiming point or on aiming points and elevation adjusted by sight clinometer.

7. Designating a process by which wrought or malleable iron is obtained from the ore through the intermediate stage of cast iron.

1875 [see *DIRECT *a.* 6 h]. 1884 W. H. GREENWOOD *Steel & Iron* (ed. 2) xii. 288 By the more modern or indirect processes, cast-iron is first produced by the smelting of iron ores, and the cast-iron so obtained is subsequently subjected to a series of operations by which its conversion into wrought iron is effected.

Individualistically (i:ndividiu,ăli·stikăli), *adv.* [f. INDIVIDUALISTIC: see -ICALLY.] In an individualistic manner; from the individualistic standpoint.

1894 *Review of Rev.* (Amer. ed.) Nov. 537/1 The trumpery decorations of the present-day individualistically arrayed establishment. 1922 A. G. HOGG *Redemption from this World* 245 In India the problem has been conceived individualistically, while by the Hebrews it was..conceived socially. 1925 *Contemp. Rev.* Aug. 234 They find themselves at variance of purpose with other less individualistically inclined.

Individuation. Add: **5. c.** (See quots.)

1900 B. D. JACKSON *Gloss. Bot. Terms*, *Individuation* [symbiosis in which the total aggregate result is wholly different from any of the symbionts]. 1927 HALDANE & HUXLEY *Anim. Biol.* xi. 235 Individuation is the improvement of the separate unit, as seen, for example, in the series Hydra—Earth-worm—Frog—Man.

Indo-[1]. Add: *Indo-Arabian*, *-Arabic*, *-Austral*; **Indo-Abyssinian** *a.*, of or pertaining to both the Dravidians of India and the Hamites of north-east Africa; also as *sb.*, one of these peoples. **Indo-African** *a.*, of or pertaining to India and Africa, *spec.* applied to a supposed former continent now covered by the Indian Ocean. **Indo-Dutch, -French** *adjs.*, relating to the Dutch or French in India; also as *sbs.*, Dutch or French residing in India. **Indo-Iranian, -Iranic** *adjs.*, designating a division of the Indo-European languages comprising the Indian and Iranian branches. **Indo-Malayan** *a.*, pertaining to India and the Malayan islands; *spec.*, denoting a zoo-geographical region comprising Ceylon, the Malay peninsula, and Malayan islands; also **Indo-Malaysian. Indo-Oceanic** *a.*, pertaining to the East Indian islands and the islands of the Pacific Ocean. **Indo-Pacific** *a.*, relating to the Indian Ocean and the adjacent parts of the Pacific Ocean; also, relating to the group of languages, usually called Malayo-Polynesian, spoken in the islands of these waters. **Indo-Saracenic** *a.*, pertaining to the products of mixed Indian and Saracenic origin. **Indo-Scythian, -Scythic** *adjs.*, pertaining to India and Scythia; also as *sb.*

1896 KEANE *Ethnology* viii. 170 Again, what is to be made of the expression '*Indo-Abyssinian', or even 'Abyssinian' at all as an ethnical term. *Ibid.* x. 229 Considerable sections of the *Indo-African Continent..must have persisted far into the tertiary epoch. *Ibid.* xii. 295 It is admitted by all ethnologists that Asia is the original home of the Mongolic division, a fact which harmonises with the view that the vanished Indo-African Continent was the cradle of mankind. 1902 SIR J. D. HOOKER in L. Huxley *Life & Lett.* (1918) II. 390 We talk glibly of Indo-European, Indo-Chinese, Indo-Malayan, *Indo-Arabian, and Indo-Oriental Floras. 1884 *Encycl. Brit.* XVII. 627/1 In Europe, before the introduction of the algorithm or full *Indo-Arabic system with the zero. 1896 KEANE *Ethnology* x. 226 The..possible fusion of Melanochroid Caucasic (South Indian) and Austral Negro blood at a remote epoch in some now perhaps submerged *Indo-Austral region. 1883 P. GARDNER *Types Greek Coins* 210 This is a very interesting invention of the *Indo-Greeks. 1877 PAPILLON *Man. Compar. Philol.* 10 The term *Aryan*..employed..by some in the more restricted sense of '*Indo-Iranian*, i.e. to denote the Asiatic subdivision of the Indo-European family. 1888 KING & COOKSON *Sounds & Infl. Gk. & Lat.* 26 The term 'Aryan' or better 'Arian' is also applied in a more restricted sense to the Indo-Iranian group. 1895 A. MENZIES *Hist. Religion* xxi. 380 How the Indo-Iranian religion was developed in India. 1875 *Encycl. Brit.* II. 696/2 The *Indo-Malayan peninsula and Archipelago. 1896 KEANE *Ethnology* xii. 326 *margin*, *Indo-Oceanic linguistic relations. 1877 *Encycl. Brit.* VII. 280/2 The Oriental or *Indo-Pacific marine region. 1880 *Ibid.* XII. 680/2 The eastward extension of the Indo-Pacific fauna. 1908 SIR H. CRAIK *Impressions of India* ii. 16 Our great grandfathers..attempting no flimsy imitations in the *Indo-Saracenic style. 1841 ELPHINSTONE *Hist. India* I. 474 Coins of the latter nation [*sc.* the Hindus] have been found, bearing nearly the same relation to those of the *Indo-Scythians that theirs did to the coins of the Greeks. 1885 *Encycl. Brit.* XVIII. 101/2 The great Indo-Scythian dominion which extended across the Hindū Kūsh southwards, over Afghanistan and Sind. 1853 HUMPHREYS *Coin-coll. Manual* Index, *Indo-Scythic kings.

Indo-[3] (i·ndo), combining form of *Indus*, a river of north-west India, as in **Indo-Gange·tic** *a.*, of or pertaining to the Indus and the Ganges.

1880 *Encycl. Brit.* XII. 735/2 The Indo-Gangetic Plain covers an area of about 300,000 square miles. 1925 J. JOLY *Surface-Hist. Earth* vii. 126 The vast sedimentary collections of the Indo-Gangetic plain.

Indoaniline (indo,æ·nilīn). *Chem.* [f. INDO-[2] + ANILINE.] Any of a series of artificial blue dyes, derivatives of quinone and aniline, used as substitutes for indigo.

1886 *Jrnl. Chem. Soc.* L. 146 A number of dyes belonging to the safranine, or indophenol and indoaniline groups.

Indologist (indǫ·lŏdʒist). [f. INDOLOGY + -IST.] A student of Indology.

1904 *Archæol. Surv. Ceylon*, *Epigraphia Zeylanica* I. p. vi, The thanks of all Indologists are due to the Ceylon Government. 1928 *Spectator* 7 Apr. 535/1 Indologists at once recognized the importance of this ample..collection of material for their studies. 1929 SIR A. STEIN *Alexander's Track to Indus* xii. 89 M. Sylvain Lévi, the eminent French Indologist.

Inductance. Add: **b.** *attrib.*: **inductance coil,** a coil employed on account of its inductance; *spec.* a wireless tuning coil. Also ellipt. for this.

1902 *Encycl. Brit.* XXXIII. 232/1 The Slaby-Arco arrangement consists at the transmitting end of an inductance coil elevated above the ground. 1906 *Westm. Gaz.* 4 Jan. 10/1 In the present telephonic cables running to France and Ireland the introduction of inductance coils has improved their capacity by at least 100 per cent. 1913 *Wireless World* I. 479 The receiver used is the Fleming Valve with necessary tuning condensers and inductances. 1923 E. W. MARCHANT *Radio Telegr.* 38 The coherer may, in a simple circuit, be conveniently placed across the inductance coil. 1925 P. J. RISDON *Crystal Receivers & Circuits* 9 A fixed inductance is one which is not variable, and is employed in circuits where tuning is performed entirely by condensers. 1926 R. W. HUTCHINSON *Wireless* 77 The sliding inductance consists of a single layer of enamelled copper wire wound on an insulating tube.

Induction. 13. Add: **induction current,** (*a*) an electric current induced in a conducting body; (*b*) a current in a body of water induced by the action of another current flowing in an opposite direction to that of the main current; **induction valve** (earlier U.S. example).

1858 E. ATKINSON tr. *Ganot's Elem. Treat. Physics* (ed. 3) 763 The magnetism of the armatures CC' acting upon the armature *n*, excites *induction currents. 1879 G. B. PRESCOTT *Sp. Telephone* iii. 87 Induction currents are produced in the telephone wire. 1898 *Geog. Jrnl.* May 529 A second sort of reverse current, viz. the induction currents (induced by viscosity), which..flow parallel with and in the opposite sense to the primary ocean currents. 1846 *Rep. U.S. Comm. Patents* (1847) 87 The *induction valve is then closed, and an expansion valve simultaneously opened.

Hence **Indu·ctionless** *a.*

1905 FLEMING in *Proc. Roy. Soc.* LXXIV. 48 A variable section of an inductionless coil through which an alternating current was passing.

Inductor. Add: **4.** *attrib.* and *Comb.*, **inductor alternator,** an alternator having a revolving iron core and stationary field coils and armature; **inductor disk, -plate,** the soft iron plates in a dynamo by means of which the current is induced.

1894 W. P. MAYCOCK *Electric Lighting* II. viii. § 141 (ed. 2) 239 *Kingdon's Inductor Alternator. 1885 HIGGS *Magn. & Dyn.-electr. Mach.* 247 With the *inductor disk making 140 revolutions per minute..a total current of 5,000 ampères is obtained. 1894 W. P. MAYCOCK *Electric Lighting* II. viii. § 141 (ed. 2) 239 The moving part consists of a wheel on which are mounted blocks of soft iron called *inductor-plates.

Indus (i·ndɒs). *Astron.* [L.] = INDIAN *sb.* 5.

1838 *Penny Cycl.* XII. 467/1.

Indusium. Add: **4.** *Anat.* A thin layer of grey matter covering the corpus callosum of the brain; also *indusium gresium*.

1901 DORLAND *Med. Dict.* (ed. 2) 320/2.

Industrial, *a.* and *sb.* Add:

A. *adj.* **c.** Characterized by highly developed industries.

1911 C. G. ROBERTSON *Eng. under Hanoverians* II. iv. 346 Napoleon..failed to see that he fought not with a nation of shopkeepers—a commercial State—but with a nation of capitalists and artisans—an industrial State.

d. Of a quality suitable only for industrial use.

1904 *Technol. & Sci. Dict.* (ed. Goodchild & Tweney), *Industrial Soaps*, a term used to describe that class of soap used for special purposes, such as ox gall soap, which is useful for scouring woollen goods and cleaning carpets, soap for silk dyers, fulling soap, etc. 1904 *Chemist & Druggist* LXV. 852/2 Industrial Alcohol Committee..appointed to inquire into the use of duty-free alcohol for industrial purposes. 1905 *Ibid.* LXVI. 630/2 There is only one way in which the influence of the spirit-duties can be satisfactorily counteracted in favour of industrial alcohol. 1906 *Act* 6 *Edw. VII* c. 20 § 4 The expression 'industrial methylated spirits' means any methylated spirits (other than mineralized methylated spirits) which are intended for use in any art or manufacture within the United Kingdom.

e. In specific uses.

Industrial colony, a colony maintained at public cost for the purpose of providing work for the unemployed and those likely to become a public charge. *Industrial Court*, a court for the settlement of industrial disputes. *Industrial exhibition*, an exhibition of industrial products (Webster 1864). *Industrial fatigue*, fatigue in industrial labour; also *attrib.* *Industrial insurance*, a form of life insurance for the poorer or industrial classes, with premiums payable in small weekly instalments. *Industrial partnership*, that economic system whereby a workman shares in the profits and contributes towards the losses of his firm; sometimes used as equivalent to *profit-sharing*. *Industrial psychology*, psychology as applied to industry, used especially in vocational guidance. *Industrial relations* (see quot. 1923). *Industrial Revolution*, the rapid development in industry owing to the employment of machinery, which took place in England in the late eighteenth and early nineteenth centuries. *Industrial Union*, a union of all workers in an industry irrespective of their craft or occupation. *Industrial Workers of the World*, a labour organization which advocates syndicalism.

1919 *Act* 9 & 10 *Geo. V* c. 69 § 14 This Act may be cited as the *Industrial Courts Act, 1919. 1914 *Rep. Brit. Assoc.* 176 What increase..has occurred in general morbidity in recent years, and to what extent this can be ascribed to *industrial fatigue. 1917 *Rep. Comm. Health Munition Workers* 9 (P. P. Eng. XVI. 1027) The problems..of industrial fatigue are primarily..problems of fatigue in the nervous system. 1922 National Institute of *Industrial Psychology. 1926 C. S. MYERS *Industr. Psychol. Gt. Brit.* i. 11 Industrial Psychology ..covers a wide field. 1923 J. D. HACKETT *Labor Terms* in *Managem. Engin.* May, **Industrial Relations*. 'That body of principle, practice, and law growing out of the interacting human rights, needs, and aspirations of all who are engaged in or dependent upon productive industry.' (L. P. Alford.) 1931 *N. & Q.* 5 Dec. 397/2 The inaugural lecture recently delivered by Professor John Hilton (first Montague Burton Professor of Industrial Relations). 1884 A. TOYNBEE (*title*) Lectures on the *Industrial Revolution in England. 1887 *Encycl. Brit.* XXII. 207/2 We have seen..that the rise of socialism as a new and reasoned theory of society was relative to the industrial revolution and to the ideas proclaimed in the French Revolution. 1911 C. G. ROBERTSON *Eng. under Hanoverians* II. iv. 341 The manufacturer of the Industrial Revolution is the modern master who provides capital, owns his mill or factory,..and creates and maintains a market. 1923 J. D. HACKETT *Labor Terms* in *Managem. Engin.* May, *Industrial Union. 1928 *Britain's Industrial Future* (*Lib. Ind. Inq.*) III. xiv. § 3. 155 The Industrial Unions are a modern development, inspired by the idea of enabling all the workers in an industry, whatever crafts they may pursue, to present a united front against their employers. 1912 *Century Mag.* July 473/1 Counsels of violence were emphatically rejected, despite the opposition of the ideas of the *Industrial Workers of the World.

B. *sb.* **2. b.** A joint-stock industrial enterprise.

1908 *Westm. Gaz.* 20 Jan. 11/1 A Colonial Industrial. The prospectus of the Vryheid (Natal) Railway, Coal, and Iron Company, Limited, has now made its appearance. 1909 *Ibid.* 3 June 13/4 A large falling off is shown in the earnings of that well-known industrial, Wm. Cory and Son.

Industrialization (indɒ·striălaizē·ʃən). [f. INDUSTRIALIZE *v.* + -ATION.] The process of industrializing or fact of being industrialized; also, the conversion of an organization into an industry.

1906 *Westm. Gaz.* 26 Oct. 2/1 A creed..that commends itself to all whom the 'industrialisation' of American politics has revolted. 1911 G. H. MAIR *Eng. Lit.*, *Mod.* ix. 225 If we want a picture of the great fact of modern Scotland, its industrialisation, it is to Galt we must go. 1923 *19th Cent.* Jan. 47 It is easy to obtain an exaggerated idea of the pace at which the industrialisation of the country by means of indigenous agency is taking place. 1928 *Daily Tel.* 20 Mar. 12/6 The present rulers of Russia have staked everything upon the policy of industrialisation under State auspices.

Inedita (ine·dită). [mod.L., neuter pl. of L. *ineditus*, f. *in-* IN-[3] + *editus*, pa. pple. of *edĕre* to give out, EDIT.] Unpublished writings.

1886 *Encycl. Brit.* XXI. 141/1 The luminous exposition of the grammar and the happy choice of the pieces in the chrestomathy..all inedita.

Ineducability (ine:diukăbi·liti). [f. INEDUCABLE + -ITY.] The condition of being ineducable.

1927 CARR-SAUNDERS & JONES *Soc. Struct. Eng. & Wales* 214 The criterion of mental deficiency for adults..is social inefficiency, while for children..it is ineducability.

Inée (inē·). Also **onage, onaye.** [Fr., ad. l'ahouin *ene*, Mpongwe *onai*.] An arrow-poison made from the seed of *Strophanthus hispidus*.

1874 *Treas. Bot.* Suppl., *Onaye* or *onage*..also called Inée and Kombé. 1887 *Encycl. Brit.* XXII. 608/1 The inée or onaye poison of the Gaboon, the kombé poison of equatorial North Africa,..are..derived from members of this genus.

Inelastic, *a.* Add: **2. b.** *Econ.* That does not change greatly under altering conditions; applied chiefly to the demand for commodities, e.g. bread, which remains almost stationary whatever the price. So **I:nelasti·city.**

1913 *Q. Rev.* Oct. 520 The demand for gas is comparatively inelastic. 1925 S. E. THOMAS *Elem. Econ.* iv. 37 Demand is said to be elastic when a rise or fall in the price causes a more than proportionate rise in the amount demanded. On the other hand, demand is said to be inelastic when a fall or rise in price causes relatively little rise or fall in the amount demanded. *Ibid.*, The Elasticity and Inelasticity of Demand. 1929 *Ibid.* (ed. 4) 51 Even in the case of necessaries, the degree of inelasticity may vary considerably.

Inemotivity (i:nėmǫti·viti). [f. IN-[3] + EMOTIVITY.] Lack of emotional sensibility.

1902 JAMES in *Encycl. Brit.* XXXII. 66/1 We must remember that the patient's inemotivity may have been a coordinate result with the anæsthesia of his neural lesions, and not the anæsthesia's mere effect.

Inequable, *a.* Delete *rare* and add examples.

1924 *Glasgow Herald* 21 Nov. 11 The inequable incidence of the regulations. 1926 A. E. ELLIS *Brit. Snails* 31 An important obstacle in the way of fresh-water colonization is the inequable temperature of rivers and lakes.

Inert, *a.* **1. b.** Add: Also Chem. *Inert gases*, those gaseous elements such as helium, argon, neon, krypton, and xenon which are chemically totally inert. Also *ellipt.* as *sb.*

1921 *Glasgow Herald* 3 Feb. 9 The Inerts Committee..is to examine the question of what proportion of inert constituents should be allowed in gas.

Ineuphonious (inyuːfōu·niəs), *a.* [f. IN-[3] + EUPHONIOUS.] Not euphonious.

1921 *Public Opinion* 15 July 62/3 Their own ineuphonious patois..communicates its harshness to the voice itself. 1927 *British Weekly* 14 July 337/3 In spite of the..drawback of a somewhat formless, ineuphonious style.

Inevitable, *a.* Add: In extended use: That cannot fail or is bound to occur, appear, be used, etc.; that is inherent (in) or naturally belongs *to*. Hence *sb.* (with *an* and *pl.*), an evitable fact, event, truth, etc.; a person who is necessarily chosen or employed.

1879 FARRAR *St. Paul* Pref., The English version..only requires the removal of errors which were inevitable to the age in which it was executed. 1888 W. WHITMAN in *Century Mag.* Dec. (1911) 255/1 Grant was one of the inevitables; he always arrived; he was as invincible as a law. 1901 *Westm. Gaz.* 24 Apr. 4/2 Here at length are some true inevitables. 1903 *Ibid.* 28 Aug. 3/2 After the Canadian Arch it was only an 'inevitable' that there should be a rush to the Dominion. 1927 *Observer* 17 July 9/4 A further twenty volumes of Everyman's Library...The 'Areopagitica' was another of the inevitables. 1932 *N. & Q.* 6 Feb. 107/1 Illustrations of French wit;..of the 'inevitable' phrase, that gift to the world past all praise.

Infall. Add: **4.** A falling upon from an outside source; *spec.* of meteorites.

1899 *Edin. Rev.* Oct. 328 The waning atmospheric stock of carbon is reinforced by meteoric infalls.

Infantilism (infæ·ntiliz'm). *Path.* [f. INFANTILE *a.* + -ISM.] The state of being mentally or physically undeveloped; infantile or childish condition. *Psychological infantilism*, a term used to describe the nervous and unstable type of mind.

1895 W. D. MORRISON in *Lombroso's Female Offender* Introd. p. xvi, Sexual peculiarities, such as femininism in men, mascul[in]ism in women, and infantilism in both. 1896 *Nat. Sci.* Sept. 154 Though permanent infantilism may occur, in most instances this is only a transient stage. 1897 tr. *Ribot's Psychol. Emotions* xiii. 422 The formula which, in my opinion, sums up and explains the unstable is this: psychological infantilism. 1904 *Brit. Med. Jrnl.* 15 Oct. 1011/2 A case of pancreatic infantilism. 1923 H. G. BAYNES *Jung's Psychol. Types* Pref. p. xv, The developing child who seeks to adventure beyond the magic circle of the

family encounters..the..inertia and infantilism of his own psychology.

Infantility. Delete †*Obs. rare*$^{-1}$ and add examples.

1919 M. K. Bradby *Psycho-analysis* (1920) 31 In these [*sc.* unreasoned convictions] we shall find his kinship with the primitive and with his own infantility. 1921 *Discovery* May 133/2 Its chief characteristics [*sc.* of the 'Personal Unconscious'] are its infantility and its compensatory character. 1928 *Daily Tel.* 28 Aug. 5/2 With amazing veracity and power, Tolstoy portrays all that infantility of the Russian race.

Infare, *sb.* **2.** (Delete *western*, and insert earlier U.S. examples.) Also *transf.*

1744 J. MacSparran *Diary* (1899) 18 Dr. Hazard and Betty Gardiner went to..Billy Hazard's weding. They are both gone again..to the Infair. 1794 in *Amer. Pioneer* II. 223 An Infair was given to-day by Mason, to a fellow named Kuykendall, who had..run off with Mason's daughter..a few weeks ago. 1847 in H. Howe *Hist. Collect. Ohio* 367 The next day after the wedding the party repaired to the house of the groom to enjoy the infair. 1871 Schele de Vere *Americanisms* (1872) 236 The minister is said to settle, ..a ceremony which..in many churches is made the occasion of much ceremony, called an installation or infare, because resembling an old-fashioned wedding festival. 1873 J. H. Beadle *Undevel. West* xxi. 408 Mrs. Thomson's youngest daughter was married yesterday to a white young man..and we arrived in the middle of the 'infair'.

Inferably (i·nfərăbli), *adv.* [f. Inferable + -ly^{2}.] By inference; = *Inferribly.

1903 *Harvard Psychol. Studies* I. 340 The extent of this differentiation—and inferably the definition of rhythmical synthesis—corresponds to the reported musical aptitudes of the subjects.

Inferiority. Add: **c.** *attrib.*: **inferiority complex,** an unconscious feeling of inferiority to others (see *Complex *sb.* 3), often manifested in self-assertive behaviour; *popularly*, a sense of inferiority.

1916 B. Hall *One Man's War* (1929) 221, I discovered that the British like a person who appears to have an inferiority complex. 1927 Thouless *Control of Mind* 184 The man who finds himself timid and lacking in self-confidence ..suffers from what the psycho-analysts call an 'inferiority complex'. 1931 Sir I. Malcolm *Vacant Thrones* 122 At bottom he [*sc.* Lord Curzon] was a reserved man, with an 'inferiority complex'.

Inferribly (infə̄·rĭbli), *adv.* [f. Inferrible *a.* + -ly^{2}.] By inference. (Cf. *Inferably.)

1905 J. M. Robertson *Did Shaksp. write 'Tit. A.'?* 198 It would inferribly be his latest play, as it has 69 double-endings to 461 lines of blank verse. 1913 — *Baconian Heresy* 18 When they were written we know not..but it was inferribly before 1623.

Infield, in-field, *sb.* **1.** (Later U.S. example.)

1903 *New York Sun* 1 Nov. 10 His car was seen to swerve suddenly and dive through the heavy fence of the infield.

3. (Examples.)

1897 *Encycl. Sport* I. 76/1 Short Stop..is also called upon to back up all the positions of the in-field. 1906 *Spalding's Base Ball Guide* 15 The 'infield' team comprising the three base players and short stop. 1912 C. Mathewson *Pitching in a Pinch* ii. 23 Devoe beat out an infield hit.

In-fielder (i·n,fīːldəɹ). *Baseball.* [f. Infield *sb.* + -er^{1}.] One of the players on the in-field.

1874 Chadwick *Base Ball Man.* 55 A ball..which readily falls into the hands of an in-fielder. 1897 *Encycl. Sport* I. 76/2 Third Baseman..must be more on the alert..than the other in-fielders. 1905 *McClure's Mag.* June 113/2 Hutchinson, an in-fielder, had played in the same league with Johnson.

In-fieldsman (i·n,fīːldzmæ̆n). *Cricket.* [f. In *adv.* + Fieldsman.] One who fields close to the wicket.

1910 *Westm. Gaz.* 19 Mar. 18/1 If the ball got past the in-fieldsmen there were men on the boundary to save the four. 1928 *Daily Tel.* 17 July 17/5 Nor was Freeman the only bowler who had his infieldsman too far away.

Infiltration. Add:

1. d. The gradual penetration of one people into another.

1904 *Westm. Gaz.* 14 Nov. 5/1 In the interior of the Empire the French work of gradual 'infiltration' will proceed by not less efficacious means. 1927 Peake & Fleure *Priests & Kings* 54 As time went on there seems to have been an ever-increasing infiltration of Southern Steppe-folk from the desert. 1930 J. L. Myres *Who were the Greeks?* ii. 55 The southward infiltration of Albanian and Slav into districts formerly Romanized.

4. infiltration vein, a vein produced by deposits from percolating waters.

1902 Webster Suppl.

Infinite, *a.* Add: **1. d.** *Mus.* Applied to a form of musical structure which can be repeated infinitely.

1876 Stainer & Barrett *Dict. Mus. Terms* s.v. *Canon*, The above is also an *infinite* canon, because, anyone having such a remarkable desire as to play it for ever, could do so. 1880 *Grove's Dict. Mus.* s.v. *Canon*, Many canons lead back to the beginning and thus become 'circular' or 'infinite'.

Infinitize (i·nfinitəiz), *v.* [f. Infinite *a.* + -ize.] *trans.* To render infinite. Also in *vbl. sb.*

1913 Evelyn Underhill *Mystic Way* 62 They aspire to infinitise life and to define infinity. 1930 *Monument to St. Augustine* 257 In his account of Kant, Hegel reproaches him with a shallow finitizing, whereas Spinoza represents for him an impracticable infinitizing.

Inflationary (inflē̆·ʃənări), *a.* [f. Inflation + -ary^{1}.] Of, pertaining to, characterized by, or involving (monetary) inflation.

1920 *Glasgow Herald* 21 Aug. 7 The transition from an inflationary to a deflationary period in prices. 1921 *Spectator* 28 May 677/1 The enormous Government loans, with their inflationary influence. 1930 *Time & Tide* 1 Nov. 1356 France is uneasy about the inflationary effects of the gold she has collected.

Inflationism (inflē̆·ʃəniz'm). [f. as prec. + -ism.] The character or fact of being inflated; the policy of inflating the currency.

1920 J. M. Keynes *Econ. Conseq. Peace* 223 The inflationism of the currency systems of Europe has proceeded to extraordinary lengths. 1930 *New Statesman* 9 Aug. 572/2 The book is a tract against inflationism.

In-foal (i·n,fōᵘl), *a.* [attrib. use of phrase *in foal*: see In *prep.* 10 b.] That is in foal.

1929 *Chilean Review* No. 31. 59/1 To prevent joint-ill in foals, these stations feed a teaspoonful of potassium iodide crystals twice per month to each in-foal mare.

Infolio. Add: Also *attrib.*

1897 W. J. Locke *Derelicts* xx, She..took up a great in-folio black-letter.

Inform, *v.* Add: **5.** Const. *about*, *on*.

1775 Sheridan *Rivals* Pref. p. viii, For on subjects on which the mind has been much informed, invention is slow of exerting itself. 1862 G. Macdonald *D. Elginbrod* III. x, Do not hesitate to inform us on all possible subjects. 1880 Disraeli *Endymion* lxi. II. 255 It must be a mind..fairly informed on the questions involved in the wealth of nations. 1888 Mrs. H. Ward *R. Elsmere* xliii, The Frenchman..had been informed about him.

c. With quoted words as object.

1877 *My Mother-in-Law* xii, 'Baby is not very well, Charlie,' Bessie informed me. 1881 Mrs. J. H. Riddell *Senior Partner* xiv. I. 290 'You're out of your mind, Janet,' Mr. McCullagh informed her.

Informative, *a.* Add: **2. b.** *Bridge.* = *Informatory *a.* So **Informatively** *adv.*

1921 A. M. Foster *Auction Bridge* 105 There is an 'informative' double which some English players adopt...It is the double of a bid of one of a suit. 1925 *Ibid.* 53 Thus Z bids 'one No Trumps' and A doubles informatively...The Informative Re-double is never left in. 1931 *Ibid.* (ed. 9) 103 It is no longer an 'informative' double, but a 'business' double with a view to securing penalties.

Informatorily (infǭ·ɹmătərili), *adv. Bridge.* [f. Informatory *a.* + -ly^{2}.] Informatively; in order to give information. Cf. next.

1928 *Observer* 29 Apr. 25 We should be placed in the ridiculous position that a player could not double informatorily, just because he happened to hold the suit that has been called against him. 1928 *Daily Express* 23 July 4 Unless you are prepared for any answer partner may make, do not double informatorily. 1929 W. Buller *Refl. Bridge Player* 178 Do you double two of a suit informatorily?

Informatory, *a.* Add: **b.** Bridge. *Informatory double*, a double which is intended to give information to one's partner, as distinct from a 'business double' which is for the purpose of scoring points. So *informatory pass.*

1926 A. M. Foster & Hervey *Auction Bridge* 82 This Informatory Pass would be made against (say) a Spade bid on such a hand as [etc.]. 1927 *Observer* 3 Apr. 25, I am not greatly in love with these Informatory Doubles. 1929 W. Buller *Refl. Bridge Player* 176 The practice described in America as 'The Informatory Double' is not strictly *set* convention.

Infra (i·nfră), *adv.* [L.] Below, underneath, further on.

1888 *Encycl. Brit.* XXVIII. 702/1 See *infra* in regard to rotary printing. 1888 Rolleston & Jackson *Anim. Life* 459 The cell has been..supposed by various authorities to be muscular, nervous, or composed of connective tissue. See the original authorities, *infra*.

Infra-. Add: **Infra-ba·sal** *a.*, below the basal plates. **Infracali·cular** *a.*, below the calyx. **Infra-Chri·stian** *a.*, lower than Christian. **Infragla·cial** *a.*, subglacial. **Infrali·as** *Geol.*, a stratum lying between the Trias and Lias. **Infra-microsco·pic** *a.*, below the microscopic. **Infra-mole·cular** *a.*, situated within the sphere of molecular influence. **Infra-umbi·lical** *a.*, below the umbilicus.

1894 W. Bateson *Study of Variation* 437 *Sphærocrinus geometricus*: abnormal specimen having the basal plate irregularly six-sided by reason of the flattening of the external angle of an *infra-basal piece. 1896 *Phil. Trans.* Ser. B. CLXXXVII. 165 Buds may form at any part of this extension, but then they are otherwise named—*infracalicular, stolonal, cœnenchymal, etc. 1917 J. Denney *Chr. Doctrine Reconcil.* ii. 51 As an *infra-Christian mode of thinking, it sometimes curiously flawed what was otherwise pure Christian truth. 1920 W. R. Inge *Truth & Falsehood in Relig.* 63 It is not justifiable to take examples of infra-Christian survivals in Christianity, and use them to discredit the religion of Christ. 1894 J. Geikie *Great Ice Age* (ed. 3) 91 All such *infra- or intra-glacial deposits..occur somewhat partially. 1882 A. Geikie *Text-bk. Geol.* 766 The so-called beds of passage in England..are..now known as Rhætic, (sometimes as *Infra-Lias). 1919 A. N. Whitehead *Enq. Princ. Nat. Knowl.* 18 There is good evidence that even the *infra-microscopic equations conform to Newton's laws as a first approximation. *Ibid.*, We may penetrate below the molecule to the electrons and the core which compose it, and thus obtain *infra-molecular equations. 1906 *Practitioner* Dec. 781 A supra-umbilical and *infra-umbilical zone.

Infuse, *v.* **5.** Delete †*Obs.* and add: In wider use, to impregnate, pervade, imbue (*with* some quality, opinion, etc.).

1900 *Westm. Gaz.* 29 Jan. 1/3 The cant with which the political history of the war is infused and suffused. 1928 *Observer* 5 Feb. 11/4 The splendid camaraderie and corporate spirit which infuse a newspaper staff.

Infusorigen (infiusō͡ə·ridʒĕn). *Zool.* [f. Infusori(a + -gen.] A stage in the development of certain *Dicyemida*.

1888 Rolleston & Jackson *Anim. Life* 816 Whitman is inclined to believe that an Infusorigen is an individual equivalent to the Gastrula of the vermiform embryo.

Infusorioid (infiusō͡ə·ri,oid), *a.* [f. Infusori(a + -oid.] Resembling an infusorian.

1853 Henfrey tr. *A. Braun's Rejuvenescence in Nature* 281 The appearance of active, Infusorioid structures, which occur not unfrequently in the interior of decaying cells of green fresh-water Algæ.

Ingenium (indʒī·niə̆m). [L., = mind, intellect.] Turn of mind; genius; talent.

1886 G. Macdonald *What's Mine's Mine* xiii. I. 225 It [*sc.* a poem] will serve to show something of Ian's youthful *ingenium*. 1920 T. P. Nunn *Education* 205 To school a boy in the tradition of one of these ancient occupations is to ensure (if it suits his *ingenium*) that he will throw himself into his work with spirit. 1921 *Glasgow Herald* 28 Nov. 5 His scientific ingenium was as keen as ever.

Ingénue (æ̃nʒenü). [Fr., fem. of *ingénu* Ingenuous.] An artless, innocent girl or young woman; also, the representation of such a character on the stage, or the actress who plays the part. Also as *adj.* Hence **Ingénueism.**

1848 Thackeray *Van. Fair* li, When attacked sometimes Becky had a knack of adopting a demure *ingénue* air, under which she was most dangerous. 1857 G. A. Lawrence *Guy Liv.* xxv, Mars herself could hardly play the *ingénues*, when in mature age. 1883 J. Hawthorne *Dust* viii, Was this lady more or less of a woman of the world than he had imagined? Was there not, after all, something of the *ingénue* about her? 1923 Compton Mackenzie *Seven Ages of Woman* iii, My dear, innocence is a charming and attractive quality; but do not be too *ingénue*. 1930 *Daily Express* 6 Oct. 5/3 French actresses grow in popularity and ingénueism the older they become. 1931 *Times Lit. Suppl.* 5 Mar. 161/4 Her French audiences, still demanding the ingénue, find her enigmatical and disquieting.

Ingerence (i·ndʒĕrĕns). [f. L. *ingerĕre* (see Ingest) + -ence. Cf. F. *ingérence*.] Bearing in upon; intrusion; interference.

[1879 Marq. Salisbury in Lady G. Cecil *Life* (1921) II. 356 This is a considerable advance in the direction of 'ingérence' over anything we did either in the case of Rivers Wilson or Romaine.] 1886 *Spectator* 16 Jan. 79 The status of a protected State excludes, of course, all ingerence in the foreign or domestic affairs of the protecting State. 1920 *Edin. Rev.* July 43 It is astonishing to what extent the ingerence of Belgrade is already tolerated.

Ingersollian (iŋgəɹsǭ·liăn), *a.* [f. the name of the American agnostic, Robert Green *Ingersoll* (1833–99) + -ian.] Imbued with the tenets of R. G. Ingersoll. So **I·ngersollism,** the doctrines or tenets of Ingersoll.

1883 G. R. Wendling (*title*) Ingersollism; from a Secular Point of View. 1892 Stevenson & Osbourne *Wrecker* xi, I don't know if you quite believe in prayer, I'm a bit Ingersollian myself.

Ingin, colloq. U.S. form of Indian. (Cf. *Injun.)

1683 *Groton* (Mass.) *Rec.* (1880) 82 If any Ingins can proue a lagiall [= legal] titall. 1870 B. Harte *Luck of Roaring Camp* 15 They're mighty rough on strangers, and they worship an Ingin baby.

Ingoing, *vbl. sb.* Add: **2.** The sum paid by a tenant or purchaser for fixtures, etc. on taking over business or other premises.

1905 *Daily Chron.* 4 May, Furniture Business..for Sale;.. ingoing about £200. 1925 *Daily Tel.* 13 May 19/3 The principal Fully-Licensed Family and Commercial Hotel... Ingoing £1,300.

Ingoing, *ppl. a.* Add: **2.** Penetrating, thorough.

1928 *Blackw. Mag.* May 645/1 Whether he was quite so ingoing as this would have been is far from sure. 1928 A. C. Butler tr. *Grou's Wks.* Pref., He is very ingoing, and, like every spiritual writer worth his salt, very exacting. 1930 E. C. Butler *Vatican Council* II. xxviii. 244 To this, the most ingoing question in regard to the Council, a sure answer may be given.

Ingot. **3.** Add: **ingot-iron,** a mild steel, containing too little carbon to be hardened or tempered, which has been poured into moulds when fluid; **ingot-metal,** steel or iron which is poured into moulds when fluid; **ingot-pitch,** the pitch or condition in which metal is fit to be cast; **ingot-steel,** steel cast in ingots, containing sufficient carbon to harden and temper; **ingot-teeming** (see Teeming *vbl. sb.*^{2}).

1884 W. H. Greenwood *Steel & Iron* xxi. (ed. 2) 461 The Bessemer process is not adapted to the production of malleable iron, but it yields..'*ingot iron', at a cheap rate. 1902 *Encycl. Brit.* XXVIII. 118/1 For most electro-technical purposes the best magnetic results are given by the employment of forged ingot-iron. 1880 *Ibid.* XIII. 330/1 The ingot after having a hole punched through it (or cast in a thick ring if of molten '*ingot metal'). 1902 *Ibid.* XXIX. 571/1 Slagless or 'Ingot-metal' Series. 1904 *Electrochem. Industry* Mar. 90 (Cent. D. Suppl.) *Ingot-pitch. 1851 *Illustr. Catal. Gt. Exhib.* III. III. 616/1 The metal, when melted, is poured into a mould, and acquires the name of '*ingot steel'. 1902 *Encycl. Brit.* XXIX. 571/2 Half-Hard and High-Carbon Steels, sometimes called 'ingot-steel'. 1917 *Nature* 4 Oct. 92/2 The problem of temperature measurement and the pyrometric control of furnace-casting and *ingot-teeming temperatures in steel manufacture.

Ingrain, *a.* (*sb.*^{2}). **B.** *sb.* Add: **2.** That which is ingrain or inherent.

1899 J. Milne *Rom. Pro-Consul* vi. 49 The natives of the Australian North-West were a fine race physically, and, he judged, had an ingrain of Malay blood. 1918 P. T. Forsyth *This Life & the Next* v. 55 It is the holy as what might be called the ingrain, the tissue, the physiognomy of eternal love.

Inguinally (i·ŋgwinăli), *adv.* [f. Inguinal *a.* + -ly^{2}.] By or in the groin.

1908 *Practitioner* Aug. 255 There are also certain other disadvantages to which the inguinally retained testis is liable.

Inhalant, *a.* Add: Also, caused by or concerned with inhalation.

1875 Huxley & Martin *Elem. Biol.* 105 These 'inhalent' and 'exhalent' currents go on, so long as the animal is alive and the valves are open.

Inhalatorium (inhē̆lătō͡ə·riə̆m). *Med.* Pl. **inhalatoria.** [f. Inhale *v.* after Sanatorium.] A building or room used for the treatment of respiratory complaints by vaporized medicaments.

1906 *Chambers's Jrnl.* 347/2 In the medical institute called the Inhalatorium special rooms are set apart for the use of patients, who sit for half-an-hour at a time breathing an atmosphere charged with the vapour suited to their special complaints. 1912 *World* 7 May 697/1 The inhalatoria and gurgling-rooms.

Inhang (i·nhæŋ). *Naut.* [f. In *adv.* + Hang *v.*] = *tumbling home* (Tumbling *vbl. sb.* b).

1898 T. A. Janvier *Sargasso Sea* xxiii, I..settled myself for the night, being very weary, under the inhang of [the ship's] heavy bulging side.

Inhibition. Add: **4.** *Psychol.* The checking or restraining of a thought or action by the (unconscious) will.

1889 *Harper's Mag.* June 78/1 Some describe it as an inhibition of the higher psychic brain-centres. 1890 W. James *Princ. Psychol.* II. 373 The outward consequences of such inhibitions may be the arrest of discharges from the inhibited regions. 1897 T. Adams *Herbartian Psychol.* 257 It is this work of inhibition that causes the peculiar feeling of effort that marks all voluntary attention as opposed to involuntary.

Inhibitor. Add: **2.** That which inhibits. Also *attrib.*

1922 R. C. Punnett *Mendelism* 69 The inhibitor in poultry has its counterpart in wheat. *Ibid.* 70 It is not unlikely that as time goes on we shall find many more such cases of the action of inhibitor factors. 1930 Field & Weill *Electro-Plating* 81 To prevent this undue attack of the metal in preference to the oxide scale, substances called 'inhibitors' are added to the pickles and dips.

Inhistoricity (i:nhistǭri·sĭti). [In-^{3}.] Lack of historicity.

1930 C. J. Wright *Miracle in History* 8 The main fact that emerges for our study is that all of these hypotheses postulate a large amount of inhistoricity in the narratives.

Inhumorous (inhiū·mǭrəs), *a.* [f. In-^{3} + Humorous.] Not humorous; lacking in humour. So **Inhu·morously** *adv.*

1898 *Contemp. Rev.* Aug. 204 Burne Jones was sincere in his art, not fanatically or inhumourously, but quietly and subtly. 1920 *Blackw. Mag.* Aug. 138/1 Many Englishmen ..allow themselves to be convinced by hearsay that Scotsmen are inhumorously inclined. 1926 W. J. Locke *Old Bridge* II. vi, 'Life is real and life is earnest'—but so is the drivelling existence of the inhumorous ant.

Inio- (i·niǫ), combining form of Inion^{1}, as in **I·nioglabe·llar** *a.*, pertaining to the inion and the glabella.

1803 J. Barclay *New Anat. Nomencl.* 146 If lines be drawn between every two of the different aspects, they will constitute the four following diameters: The Dextro-sinistral, the Corono-basilar, the Inio-glabellar, and the Inantinial. 1903 *Science* 30 Oct. 554/2 An inio-glabellar line can be drawn which will correspond very closely to the lower boundary of the cerebrum.

Initiand (ini·ʃi,ænd). [ad. L. *initiandus*, gerundive of *initiāre* to Initiate.] One who is about to be initiated.

1915 *Edin. Rev.* Jan. 127 The initiands are taken away from human society, often to a mountain, sometimes to a forest.

Initis (in-, ɔinəi·tis). *Path.* [mod.L., f. Gr. ἰνός, ἴς fibre + -itis.] Inflammation of the muscular tissue.

1848 Dunglison *Med. Lex.* (ed. 7), *Initis*, fibrous inflammation. 1890 Billings *Med. Dict.*

Injun (i·ndʒən). Colloquial and dial. U.S. form of Indian *sb.* 2; also *attrib.* (Cf. *Ingin.)

1812 Col. J. Cocke in *Salem Gaz.* 28 Aug. 1/2 The people of Tenessee is antious to have orders commanded out for us to march against the Injuns on the Wabash. 1850 Mayne Reid *Rifle Rangers* iii. (1853) 24 Thur's a mighty grist o' venturin', I heern; beats Injun fightin' all holler. 1868 Mrs. M. J. Carrington *Ab-Sa-Ra-Ka* 83 Better not go *fur*. There is *Injuns* enough lying under wolf skins, or skulking on them cliffs. 1911 R. D. Saunders *Col. Todhunter* vii. 104 But you're sure about it, too, ain't you? She ain't doin' no Injun-givin' in your case?

b. In various allusive uses and phrases. *Honest Injun*: honour bright: perh. orig. an assurance of good faith extracted from Indians. *To play Injun*: to act like an Indian; to avoid being seen or captured.

1876 'Mark Twain' *Tom Sawyer* ii, Ben, I'd like to, honest Injun; but [etc.]. 1887 H. Frederic *Seth's Brother's Wife* II. 160 'Is what you've be'n tellin' me here honest? Don't lie to me.' 'Honest Injun, ..every word.' 1889 Barrère & Leland *Dict. Slang*, *Injun here!* (American) a phrase often used jocosely when a man asserts that he has remained true to his principles. 1890 H. C. Bunner *Short Stories* (1891) 90 'Hope to die—Honest Injun—cross my breast!' said the boy. 1902 S. E. White *Blazed Trail* xix. 140 'Our compact holds now, honest Injin, doesn't it?' asked the boy anxiously. 1904 'Alan Dale' *Wanted: A Cook* 98 But, Archie, this is all true. It is, honest Injun. 1918 Mulford *Man fr. Bar-20* xiv. 149 So they're combin' th' country an' patrollin'. Hereafter an' henceforth I've got to play Injun for all I'm worth.

Injunct, *v.* (Earlier U.S. examples.)

1871 Schele de Vere *Americanisms* (1872) 653 Violent contractions, derived from well-known and well-formed words, like burgled, injuncted, and excurted. 1880 *Christian Advocate* (N.Y.) 11 Mar. (Th.) Stoddards have successfully injuncted Scribners from taking and using subscription lists procured by [them].

Injunctive, *a.* (Later U.S. example.)

1905 *New York Even. Post* 6 Dec. 3 Vice-Chancellor Stevenson refused to make any injunctive order.

Injuria (indʒū͡ə·riă). *Law.* [L.] An invasion of another's rights; an actionable wrong.

1883 *Wharton's Law Lex.* (ed. 7), *Injuria*, injury; a wrongful act done. 1898 *Encycl. Laws Eng.* VI. 485 *Injuria* can only be defined as an infringement of a legal right.

Ink, *sb.*^{1} **4.** Add: **ink-feed,** the duct which carries the ink to the nib of a fountain pen; **ink-jerker** *U.S.*, **-spiller** = *ink-slinger*; **ink-mirror,** a surface of ink used in clairvoyance in place of a crystal.

1907 *Westm. Gaz.* 23 Oct. 11/1 The Patent Spoon-Feed has successfully overcome the *ink-feed difficulty. 1869 J. R. Browne *Apache Country* 299 (Th.) This rattle-brained scribbler, this miserable *ink-jerker. 1905 E. F. Benson *Image in Sand* ii, Abdul had..tried him with the simple experiment of the *ink-mirror, and found him extraordinarily sensitive. 1881 *Punch* 10 Sept. 110/2 To think people ain't got more savvy than what these *inkspillers enjoy.

Inkily (i·ŋkili), *adv.* [f. Inky *a.* + -ly^{2}.] In an inky manner; like ink.

1894 Stevenson & Osbourne *Ebb-Tide* I. vi, The sea.., inkily blue.

Inkle, *v.* **1.** Delete † *Obs.* and add examples. (In later use a back-formation from Inkling 2.)

1901 S. Butler *Erewhon Revisited* 42 People like being deceived, but they also like to have an inkling of their own deception, and you never inkle them. 1903 T. Hardy *Dynasts* I. I. vi, Thou art young, and dost not heed the Cause of things Which some of us have inkled to thee here.

Inkosi (iŋkōᵘ·si). *S. Africa.* Also **enkosi, inkhosi, inkos, inkose(e).** [Zulu *inkosi* lord, master = Bondei, Zegua, Nguru *m-gosi*, Karanga *a-hosi* man, Gogo *mu-gosi* chief.] A chief, lord; also used as a title of respect.

(See also Pettman *Africanderisms* s.v.)

[1827 G. Thomson *Trav. & Adv. S. Afr.* 118 (Pettman) Calling the King *Kousi*, which is not his name, but his title, Kousi signifying king, or principal chief in their language. 1837 Sir J. E. Alexander *Narr. Voy. W. Africa* I. xvi. 395 Great chiefs (*inkosee incoolo*) are assisted by *amapakati*, or counsellors.] 1852 Brown tr. *Arbousset's Tour S. Africa* 423 As if a Zulu Inkhosi could show clemency! 1899 C'tess Anna de Brémont *Son of Africa* xxxii. 251 He was a great Inkosi. 1899 Mitford *John Ames* x. 96 Policeman he want to see Inkose. 1905 *Westm. Gaz.* 8 June 2/1 All the members of the kraals concerned will..form,..with the 'inkosi', his several wives and their brothers and sisters and children and dependent relatives, a formidable audience.

Inlaid, *ppl. a.* Add: **2. b.** Of linoleum: Having a pattern so inwoven that it does not wear off with use.

1908 *Westm. Gaz.* 30 May 7/2 The floors will be covered with Greenwich inlaid linoleum.

Inlaut (i·nlaut). *Philol.* [G.] A medial or internal sound; a sound which occurs in the middle of a word.

1892 G. Dunn in *Classical Rev.* Feb. 1/2 Latin d as inlaut and auslaut frequently represents Indo-Germanic dh.

Inlaying, *vbl. sb.* Add: **3.** *attrib.* **inlaying machine,** a machine used in the manufacture of inlaid linoleum; **inlaying-saw** (see quot.).

1875 Knight *Dict. Mech.*, *Inlaying-saw*, a saw used in piercing stuff for buhl-work. 1908 *Westm. Gaz.* 30 May 7/2 A scheme for increasing the speed at which our inlaying machines are worked.

Inlet. **5.** Add: *inlet-cam, -chamber, -nipple, -pipe.*

1901 Waterhouse *Conduit Wiring* 56 Metal inlet and outlet nipples. 1903 *Architect, Suppl.* 24 Apr. 23/2 A 5-inch pipe is carried from the inlet-chamber to the reservoir. 1907 *Westm. Gaz.* 1 Oct. 7/1 Connecting the nozzle to the inlet-pipe of the balloon, the further supply of gas was added to that already within the envelope. 1908 *Ibid.* 9 Jan. 4/1 The inlet-cam being drawn out of position..the inlet-valves become completely closed.

Inlet, *ppl. a.* Add: **2.** *Needlework.* Ornamented *with* lace, etc. let in or inserted. So **I·nletting** *vbl. sb.*

1901 *Daily Chron.* 31 Aug. 8/3 Flowing skirts inlet with lace. 1904 *Ibid.* 3 May 8/5 The inletting and trimming of a serge or cloth gown with Irish lace is quite usual.

In-lot. **2.** *U.S.* (Examples.)

1790 in *Amer. Pioneer* I. 72 Nathaniel Massie doth bind and oblige himself his heirs, &c., to make over and convey.. one in-lot in said town. 1819 E. Dana *Geog. Sk. Western Country* 74 The in-lots 62½ by 87½ feet each, were sold at public auction. 1837 W. Jenkins *Ohio Gaz.* 109 The regular in-lots are ninety nine feet in front, extending back one hundred and ninety eight feet.

Inmix (inmi·ks), *v.* [f. In *adv.* + Mix *v.*] *trans.* and *intr.* = Immix.

1898 Meredith *Poems, Sage Enamoured* iv, Then shall those noblest of the earth and sun Inmix unlike to waves on savage sea. 1910 — *Celt & Saxon* xvi. 237 Celt and Saxon are much inmixed with us. 1931 Belloc *Ess. Catholic* xvi. 318 It was badly inmixed with motives in no way Catholic.

Inner, *a.* Add: **1. e.** *Printing.* Designating the form containing the side of the sheet which includes the second page.

1808 Stower *Printer's Gram.* vii. 171 Inner Form of the Outer Sheet...Inner Form of the Inner Sheet. 1841 T. C. Hansard *Print. & Type-founding* 89 This united mass is called a *form*; that one which contains the first page being called the *outer form*, the other the *inner*. 1875 Knight *Dict. Mech.*, *Inner-form*, the form beginning with the second page of a sheet usually worked off first. 1892 A. Oldfield *Man. Typog.* vii. 56 Sheet work is arranged in two forms, the outer and inner.

f. *Phonetics.* Denoting a sound articulated in a part of the mouth nearer the throat than that designated by the unqualified term.

1867 Bell *Visible Speech* 62 If the breath within the mouth be compressed behind the articulating organs while an *inner closure* is held, a distinct, and in some cases, a powerfully percussive effect will be produced on the abrupt separation of the organs. 1888 Sweet *Hist. Engl. Sounds* 5 Most of these [point and blade consonants] admit also of 'inner' and 'outer' varieties.

g. *Inner tube*: in a pneumatic tyre, a separate tube, inside the cover, which is inflated with air.

1902 *Encycl. Brit.* XXXIII. 535/1 In most tyres for cycles and motor-cars, an inner tube of indiarubber is made separate from the outer cover. 1902 A. C. Harmsworth *Motors & Motor-Driving* x. 223 Half the number of spare covers and inner tubes are required as compared with the requirements when the wheels are of different sizes. 1904 A. B. F. Young *Complete Motorist* ix. (ed. 2) 250 The piercing of the outer cover and inner tube by a nail or other puncturing agent. 1912 *Motor Manual* iii. (ed. 14) 106 The inner tube has become nipped between one of the security bolts and the cover.

h. *Inner reserve* (Finance): a secret reserve not disclosed in a balance-sheet and due to an under-statement of certain capital assets.

1930 *Daily Express* 16 Aug. 10/1 Former Inner Reserves are now brought from the Assets in which they were hidden and are grouped in an exposed Reserve on the Liability side of the Sheet. 1931 *Ibid.* 31 Jan. 10/2 Would it have been wise to contemplate further inroads for the current year on our inner resources?

3 and **3 b.** Also, *the inner woman.*

1858 Hawthorne *Fr. & It. Jrnls.* (1872) I. 157 To behave as her inner woman prompts. 1892 *Gentlewoman's Bk. Sports* 44 After refreshing the inner woman, I was all for trying the Sandhills again.

6. Various phrases used *attrib.*

1908 *Daily Chron.* 22 Jan. 3/3 You may browse at will among the epistles or the notes, feeling that you are always with informed, inner-circle folk. 1909 *Westm. Gaz.* 14 Apr. 10/2 What colour of glass must be used for the front door and inner-court doors? 1927 J. Adams *Errors in School* 32 An idea does not merely mean the inner-world equivalent of an outside object.

Innervation. Add: **2.** *Anat.* The disposition of the nerve fibres.

1868 W. R. Alger *Friendships of Women* 20 The innervation and nutrition of woman are finer and more complicated than those of man. 1908 *Westm. Gaz.* 8 July 2/1 It has been found that the density of the cutaneous innervation—i.e., the number of sensitive nerve terminations in the unit of surface—is greater in small animals than in large.

3. *Psychol.* = Kinæsthesis. Also *attrib.* (? Disused.)

1898 G. F. Stout *Man. Psychol.* II. vi. I. 192 According to Bain, there is a direct sense of energy put forth which is independent of any results the putting forth of energy may produce. This peculiar modification of sensory consciousness has been called the sense of effort, or the innervation-sense.

Innholder. (Earlier U.S. examples.)

1686 in *Coll. New Hampsh. Hist. Soc.* VIII. 282 The several inn-holders shall give bond. 1769 *Boston Post-boy* 11 Sept. (Th.) Capt. Christopher Turner, a noted Innholder. 1771 *Boston Gaz.* 7 Oct. (Th.) A Vendue at the house of Capt. David Goodridge, Innholder in Fitchburg. 1798 *Act of Assembly Mass.* 27 June (Th.) Any person licensed as an Innholder, Tavernkeeper, Victualler, etc. 1813 *Massachusetts Spy* 23 June (Th.) The house of Morris Marcey, innholder in Honest-town..in the South-East corner Sturbridge.

Innocent, *a.* **5. b.** Add: *Innocent conveyances*, a conveyance by deed, the conveyor being unable to convey a larger estate than he possesses.

All conveyances are now innocent by statute in England and in the United States.

1841 Stephen *Comm. Laws Eng.* I. 508 The other conveyances can, in their nature, pass no more than the grantor might lawfully transfer. For this reason, they have received, by way of distinction from a feoffment, (and others now abolished of the like nature,) the appellation of *innocent* conveyances. 1848 Wharton *Law Lex.*, *Innocent conveyances*, a covenant to stand seised, a bargain and sale, and release, so called, because since they convey the actual possession by construction of law only, they do not confer a larger estate in property than the person conveying possesses.

Innuit (i·niuit). Also **Inuit.** [Eskimo, = 'the people', pl. of *innuk* man.] The native name of the Eskimos.

1850 *Eskimaux & Engl. Voc.* p. vii, If the extent of country be considered, the Innuit or Eskimaux is one of the most widely spread nations on the globe. 1860 Mayne Reid *Odd People* 88 They [*sc.* the Esquimaux] generally call themselves

'Inuit' (pronounced enn-oo-eet), a word which signifies 'men'. 1864 *Spectator* 31 Dec. 1506 The Innuits believe in a supreme Being called Anguta, whose daughter Sidne is the creator and the tutelary deity of the Innuit people. 1864 C. F. Hall *Life with Esquimaux* I. 122 A highly-intelligent Innuit..was boat-steerer. 1895 Kipling *2nd Jungle Bk.* 145 Kadlu was an Inuit—what you call an Esquimau. 1903 Jack London *People of the Abyss* xxvii. 313 In Alaska, along the banks of the Yukon River, near its mouth, live the Innuit folk. 1920 W. T. Grenfell *Labrador Doctor* vii. 140 With the influx of white settlers from Devon and Dorset, Scotland and France the 'Innuits' were driven farther and farther north.

Innutritious, *a.* Add: Also *transf.*

1905 *Sydney Morning Herald* 15 Feb. 4/6 The..teacher is offered for his mental food these innutritious products as the bread of life. 1916 E. V. Lucas *Vermilion Box* cxxv, As a rule I have found that the soldier who sits opposite one on railway journeys is an innutritious person, whether he has been to the front or not.

Ino-. Add: **Inopexia** (-pe·ksiă) *Path.* [Gr. πῆξις fastening], increased coagulability of the blood; hence **Inope·ctic** *a.*; **Ino·scopy** *Med.* [Gr. σκοπεῖν], the examination of the fibres in artificially digested blood, sputum, etc. as a means of diagnosis; **Ino·tropism,** the diminution of muscular contractility; so **Inotro·pic** *a.*

1876 tr. *Wagner's Gen. Pathol.* 543 Increased coagulability of fibrin in the living body, *inopexia, is said to be the cause of the formation of thrombi. 1908 *Practitioner* June 833 The method of '*inoscopy', as it is rather unnecessarily termed, of Jousset and others, in which the fluid is allowed to clot. 1903 *Sci. Amer. Suppl.* 4 July 22992 (Cent. D. Suppl.) The author [*sc.* T. W. Engelmann] describes..as *inotropic such [influences] as lessen or destroy contractibility. 1902 *Encycl. Brit.* XXXI. 733/2 The centrifugal cardiac nerves influence the frequency, the force of contraction, and the conductivity of the excitatory wave (chrono-, *ino-, and dromo-tropism of Engelmann).

Inoculist. (Early U.S. example.)

1776 *Narragansett Hist. Reg.* V. 352 Practitioners and Inoculists may be served with them [*sc.* medicines], if applied for soon.

Inoculum (inǫ·kiŭlə̆m). *Path.* [mod.L., f. the base of Inoculate.] The material or virus used in inoculation.

1913 Dorland *Med. Dict.* (ed. 7). 1925 C. H. Browning *Bacteriology* iii. 47 The needle, charged with the inoculum, is introduced into the tube and..the broth..is now said to have been 'inoculated'. *Ibid.* 48 If living bacteria are present in the inoculum and if broth provides them with pabulum multiplication will soon begin.

Inosituria (ɔino-, inositiū͡ə·riă). *Path.* [mod. L., f. Inosite + -uria.] The presence of inosite in the urine. Also **Inosu·ria.**

1890 Billings *Med. Dict.*, Inosituria..Inosuria. 1899 Cagney tr. *Jaksch's Clin. Diagn.* vii. (ed. 4) 352 Inosituria.— Inosite occurs in small quantity in the urine.

Inpass (i·npɑs). *Rugby Football.* [f. In *adv.* + Pass *sb.*^{2} 12.] A pass by a back to the centre, as distinguished from a pass to the wing.

1909 *Daily Chron.* 25 Feb. 8/4 At other times the London backs overdid finesse, and the inpass to the centre instead of the outpass to the wing never came off.

In-phase (i·nfēiz), *a.* *Electr.* [attrib. use of phrase *in phase*.] Of the same phase.

1916 *Standardization Rules Amer. Inst. Electr. Engin.* 15 The Active or In-Phase Component of the current in a circuit is that component which is in phase with the voltage across the circuit; similarly the active component of the voltage across a circuit is that component which is in phase with the current.

I·n-pla·yer. *Rackets.* [f. In *adv.* 7 d + Player.] The server.

1890 Sir W. Hart-Dyke in J. M. Heathcote *Tennis, Rackets, Fives* 358 In a four-handed match the players took alternately the 'in' and 'out' game, the 'In' players picking up the drops and placing the ball, the 'out' players defending the back of the court.

Input, *sb.* Add: **2.** That which is put or taken in, in various technical usages: especially of electrical apparatus. Also *attrib.*

1893 *Phil. Trans.* Ser. B. CLXXXIII. 228 The pressure in the large systemic veins becomes raised during vagus action, because the quantity of blood which passes from them into the right ventricle (which we may refer to as the 'input' of the heart), in a given time, is diminished. *Ibid.*, The fall in the output of the heart during vagus action is due to the diminution of the input of that organ. 1902 *Encycl. Brit.* XXVII. 574/2 The useful return or 'output' at the terminals of a large machine may amount to as much as 95 per cent. of the mechanical energy which forms the 'input'. 1921 *Wireless World* IX. 201/2 The input terminals..are on the left. 1926 R. W. Hutchinson *Wireless* xi. 186 Care must be taken in arranging..the relative positions of wires, etc. on the input (grid) and output (plate) sides of the valve. 1928 C. F. S. Gamble *Story N. Sea Air Station* xix. 317 A more efficient hull and a higher speed for the same power 'input'. 1928 *Times* 23 Mar. 20/1 A certain input impedance which had the effect of increasing or decreasing the resistance of the tuned circuit. *Ibid.*, The input terminals of the valve. 1929 *Prosp. Mona Copper Co.* 7 In addition to the large ore-bodies above water level waiting attack, the New Discovery Lode will soon add its important quota. The additional plant to deal with an in-put of 600 tons daily would require £20,000. 1931 *Daily Express* 21 Sept. 7/4 An advanced form of band-pass tuning, providing a special selector circuit between the input from the aerial and the first valve of the set.

Inquiration (inkwəirē̆·ʃən). *dial.* [f. Inquire *v.* + -ation.] Inquiry.

1789 Charlotte Smith *Ethelinde* III. 136 If so be you would acquaint me where I may make enquiration after your friends or hern, it would come to the same thing. 1839 C. Clark *J. Noakes* v, If they their inquirations make In winter time, some will Condemn that place as no great shakes. 1850 Dickens *Dav. Copp.* li, A decent woman as spoke to her about..making secret inquiration concerning of me. 1886 Hardy *Mayor Casterbr.* xxxvii, 'Suppose we make inquiration into it, Christopher,' continued Longways; 'and if we find there's really anything in it, drop a letter to them most concerned.'

Inquirendo. Add: **2.** An investigation.

a 1849 Darley in *B. W. Procter* (1877) 286 Confound your prose lunatics who leave you no time for inquirendos upon poetic ones. 1897 Louise I. Guiney (*title*) Patrins, to which is added an Inquirendo into the Wit and Other Good Parts of His Late Majesty King Charles the Second.

In-rigger (i·nrigəɹ). [f. In *adv.* + Rigger^{1} 3.] A boat having the rowlocks formed in the gunwale.

1893 J. H. Clasper in *Westm. Gaz.* 9 Oct. 7/3 The Düsseldorf boat was an in-rigger—for which orders are very seldom given nowadays.

Inro (i·nrǫ). [Jap., f. Chinese *yin* seal + *lung* basket.] An ornamental nest of boxes, connected by a thin cord, made of lacquer, ivory, or the like, in which the seal, perfumes, etc. can be carried, worn by the Japanese at the girdle.

[1872 *Trans. Asiatic Soc. Japan* I. 5 No one is allowed to carry the medicine-case (*inrô*), which is the distinguishing mark of a physician, if he has had only a native doctor for his instructor.] 1891 Gonse *Catal. Oriental Objects of Art* 6 An ivory inro, inlaid with parrots in mother-o'-pearl. 1911 *Connoisseur* Mar. 209/2 Among the *objets d'art* most associated with old Japan are the *inro*, or little medicine cases which the Japanese used invariably to carry about with them.

In-running, *ppl. a.* Add: That runs into a river or the sea.

1931 *Times Lit. Suppl.* 1 Oct. 738/2 'Australian Literature' ..must contribute to the great stream of English literature a new in-running river.

Inscript (inskri·pt), *v.* [f. L. *inscript-*, ppl. stem of *inscrībĕre* to Inscribe; or back-formation from Inscription.] *trans.* To inscribe. Hence **Inscri·pted** *ppl. a.*

1923 *Public Opinion* 16 Feb. 155/3 The statement at the head of this article might usefully be inscripted in all Theological Halls. 1923 *Blackw. Mag.* Feb. 151/1 It does not require inscripted monuments to perpetuate the memory of British deeds.

Inscription. Add: **9.** *Inscription maritime* [Fr.], the French naval system of recruiting; a list of men who may be called to serve in the French navy.

1902 *Encycl. Brit.* XXVII. 499/1 This arrangement is purely for the embodiment of the men of the Inscription Maritime. *Ibid.* XXXI. 103/1 For the purpose of the Inscription Maritime the Newfoundland fisheries were kept up at considerable expense to the nations. 1905 *Westm. Gaz.* 3 Aug. 10/1 A system called 'maritime inscription', which ..furnishes a contingent of about 4,700 naval recruits every year.

Insert, *sb.* Add: (Examples.)

1907 *Installation News* Dec. 1/2 There are three of these loose inserts. One is a pamphlet..; the second is an advance price sheet [etc.]. 1916 'B. M. Bower' *Phantom Herd* xvi. 269 He made all of his 'close-ups', his inserts and sub-titles. 1928 R. B. H. Bell *Life Abundant* 142 This little book would not be complete without an insert on the Art of Prayer.

c. The sheet of paper placed between the rollers of a typing machine.

1922 Marg. B. Houston *Witch-man* xiv. 180 She glanced quickly through the sheets of paper lying there, even at the insert in the typewriter.

Inserted, *ppl. a.* Add: **d.** *Needlework.* Ornamented *with* an insertion of lace, velvet, etc.

1902 *Daily Chron.* 7 June 8/4 Some of the rather flamboyant cloth coats..were inserted with yellow braid lace. 1927 *Observer* 2 Oct. 20/2 The felt is inserted with velvet in various devices.

Inserting, *vbl. sb.* (under Insert *v.*). Add: *spec.* = Insertion 2 b.

1886 *Harper's Mag.* Nov. 836/1 An elaborate trousseau made chiefly of tucks and insertings and edgings.

Insertion. **4.** Add **insertion-joint, -sheet** (see quots.).

1904 *Technol. & Sci. Dict.* (ed. Goodchild & Tweney), **Insertion joint*, a joint in pipes which is made watertight by the use of a ring or washer made of indiarubber or rubber alternating with layers of canvas. 1880 *Encycl. Brit.* XII. 842/1 Packing for the stuffing boxes of steam engines is similarly prepared from strips of rubber and frictioned canvas, as also are the so-called *insertion sheets, in which layers of rubber alternate with canvas or even wire gauze.

Inset, *sb.* Add: **3.** *attrib.* and *Comb.*, as **inset-wall,** a wall made on the inner or landward side of a sea or river embankment and returned into it at each end, for stopping a breach in it.

1900 R. F. Grantham in *Trans. Soc. Engineers* 27 The author determined to form an inset or horseshoe wall round and inside the gap.

Insetter^{3} (i·nsetəɹ). [f. Inset *v.* + -er^{1}.] One who insets sheets.

1891 *Pall Mall Gaz.* 27 Oct. 7/2 Compositors, printers,.. stereotypers, insetters.

Inshoot (i·nʃūt). *Baseball.* [f. In *adv.* + Shoot *sb.*] The act of causing the ball to move rapidly inward, as a ball that is pitched with a curve; a ball which moves thus.

1897 *Encycl. Sport* I. 74/2 A movement of the hand, an elevation of the head by the latter [*sc.* the catcher], lets the pitcher know that this ball is to be an in-shoot, the other an out-curve. 1904 *Sci. Amer.* 16 July 42/3 The right-handed pitcher delivers his 'outshoot' with much greater effect of incurve at the plate than he can accomplish with his 'inshoot'...The speed of the ball for 'outshoot' and 'inshoot' is the same.

Inside, *sb.*, *adj.*, etc. Add: **A.** *sb.* **2. e.** The inner history, the real facts.

1904 W. H. Smith *Promoters* v. 101 I'll give it to you straight, for I happen to know the inside.

5. (See quot. 1927.) *U.S.*

1899 Tarkington *Gentl. Indiana* i. 11 Presently the 'Herald' announced a news connection with Rouen, and with that, and the aid of 'patent insides', began an era of three issues a week. *Ibid.* xiv. 249 We must buy 'plate matter' instead of 'patent insides'. 1927 *Amer. Speech* Feb. 242/1 Only in small country papers does one find 'patent insides'. The country editor frequently buys four pages of his paper already printed, filled with 'features', fiction, and advertising. He has only to fill the four remaining pages with local news and advertising.

B. *adj.* **c.** (Later examples of *inside track* in fig. use.)

1884 Howells *Silas Lapham* xx. 367 I've taken his mills, but I guess I've got the inside track. 1892 *Harper's Mag.* Feb. 440/2 My gentleman friend in our office has the inside track, and got me the pass. 1914 Gertrude Atherton *Perch of Devil* II. xxiv, When a woman knows where she stands, and has the inside track,..the man has no show whatever.

d. *fig.* Coming from 'the inside'; inner; not generally available.

1888 *Daily Inter-Ocean* 20 Feb. (Farmer) A secret service officer..claims to have inside information as to the facts in the case. 1912 C. Mathewson *Pitching in a Pinch* ix. 184 Behind this game is some 'inside' history that has never been writtten. 1923 Dorothy Canfield *Rough-Hewn* xx, The delight of her kind at having any inside information about a violent death or a scandal. 1923 D. L. Sayers *Whose Body?* xiii, 'Peruvian Oil..hasn't paid a dividend for umpteen years.' 'No..but it's going to. I've got inside information.'

e. Special collocations: **inside clinch** (see quot. and cf. Clinch *sb.*); **inside forward,** in association football and hockey, either of the two players, called the inside left or right (see below), of the forward line; **inside gouge, inside-jaw chuck, inside lap** (see quots.); **inside left, right,** in association football and hockey, a player playing between the outside left or right and the centre forward; **inside screw, screw-tool** (see quots.); **inside squatter** *Austral.*, one who lives within the margin of the settlements; **inside-tin** (see quot.); **inside work** *Boxing*, infighting.

1886 *Encycl. Brit.* XXI. 591/2 *Inside Clinch. The end [of a rope] is bent close round the standing part till it forms a circle, when it is securely seized..thus making a running eye. 1897 *Windsor Mag.* Dec. 25/2 Each of the two *inside-forward positions. 1897 *Encycl. Sport* I. 418/1 Try to feed the centre and inside forwards when in your opponent's territory. 1888 *Lockwood's Dict. Mech. Engin.*, **Inside Gouge*, a paring gouge, so called because it is ground on the inside or hollow face. 1884 Knight *Dict. Mech.* Suppl., **Inside-jaw Chuck*, a chuck for holding drills, rods, or pipes. These pass through the chuck, the jaws of which have an inside hold. 1888 *Lockwood's Dict. Mech. Engin.*, **Inside Lap*, exhaust lap. 1904 *Technol. & Sci. Dict.* (ed. Goodchild & Tweney) s.v. *Slide Valve*, The distance *a* which the valve projects beyond the steam port when in the middle position is termed the Outside Lap, and the distance *b* the Inside Lap. 1897 *Encycl. Sport* I. 517/1 This is a comparatively easy task for *inside right, but by no means so for *inside left, who cannot reach out to hit the ball as it is rolled in. 1906 *Westm. Gaz.* 16 Mar. 5/1 Bloomer developed into a forward of exceptional skill in the Inside-right position. 1875 Knight *Dict. Mech.*, **Inside-screw*, a hollow screw; one having its thread on the inside. **Inside screw-tool*, a hook-shaped tool for threading interior surfaces while revolving in a lathe. 1881 A. C. Grant *Bush-life in Queensland* xxxii, Stations were formed for nearly a hundred and fifty miles outside John's run, and he began to regard himself as quite an *inside squatter. 1875 Knight *Dict. Mech.*, **Inside-tin* (*Bookbinding*), a plate laid inside the cover of a book when placed in the standing-press. 1929 *Evening News* 18 Nov. 16/4 Chew..attempted many times to get the better of Watson at *inside work.

C. *adv.* **1. b.** *fig.* In a position to have private information.

1870 *Congress. Globe* 3 Feb. 1022/1, I ask the gentleman from Ohio to name the ships which he says have been sold for a song. The gentleman is inside on all these matters.

3. *Inside of.* (Earlier example.)

1877 *Boston Jrnl.* 27 Apr. (Bartlett) They would pollute the society of Heaven inside of twenty-four hours, if they went there.

D. *prep.* (Later U.S. example.)

1924 A. J. Small *Frozen Gold* i. 39, I hear all about it inside twenty-four hours.

Insider. Add: (Earlier and later U.S. examples.)

1848 W. Armstrong *Stocks* 7 Insiders are those by whom and through whom all transactions are made in and about the Exchange. 1902 H. L. Wilson *Spenders* xxx. 355 Shepler's back of all three [stocks]. The insiders are buying up now, slowly and cautiously, so as not to start any boom prematurely.

2. An inside passenger.

1853 B. F. Taylor *Jan. & June* 170 'No Room For Two!' was the exclamation of some insider, the other morning. 1892 *Harper's Mag.* Jan. 257/1 The exhilarating pace, the smooth roads, and the juxtaposition of the insiders tended, in a high degree, to the promotion of enjoyment.

Insinuate, *v.* **8.** *Law.* Delete † *Obs.*

(Still used in the Commissions issued by the Bishop of Winchester to the Deans of Jersey and Guernsey as his Commissaries.)

Insist, *v.* Add: **3. c.** With quoted words.

1888 Mrs. H. Ward *R. Elsmere* xxxix, 'And rather than try', he insisted, 'you will go on believing [etc.]'. 1906 W. S. Maugham *Bishop's Apron* iv, 'Do you care for me at all?' he insisted.

Insolubilize (insǫ·liŭbĭləiz), *v.* [f. L. *insolūbil-is* Insoluble + -ize.] *trans.* To render insoluble.

1897 *Daily News* 4 Oct. 6/4 The colouring matter remaining attached to the paper, and held there by the insolubilised gum. *a* 1909 *Buck's Handbk. Med. Sci.* VIII. 351 (Cent. D. Suppl.).

Inspan, *v.* Add: **b.** *fig.* or *transf.*

1914 Kipling in *Geog. Jrnl.* Apr. 373 One man, apparently without effort, inspans the human equivalent of 'three blind 'uns and a bolter' and makes them do miracles. 1928 *Sunday Express* 8 July 10/5 There are hundreds of keen young players with the player's eyesight available for this lining business. Is it beyond the wit and the capacity of the Wimbledon authorities to inspan them?

In-spawn (i·n,spǭn), *a.* [attrib. use of the phrase *in spawn* (cf. In *adv.* 10 b).] That is about to spawn.

1908 *Westm. Gaz.* 14 Mar. 11/3 Netting the in-spawn dace. 1923 *Daily Mail* 13 Feb. 12 After the fish was landed it disgorged an in-spawn trout of 2 lb.

Inspect, *v.* Add: **3.** *intr.* To prove on inspection. *U.S.*

1865–6 *Trans. Ill. Agric. Soc.* VI. 638 All Flour that inspects 'Sound' and full weight shall be branded.

Inspection. Add: **1.** (See quots. and cf. *Inspectorship.)

1861 *Act 24 & 25 Vict.* c. 134 § 192 Every Deed or Instrument made or entered into between a Debtor and his Creditors..relating to the Debts or Liabilities of the Debtor, and his Release therefrom, or the Distribution, Inspection, Management, and winding-up of his Estate. 1869 *Act 32 & 33 Vict.* c. 71 § 125 (4) The special resolution, together with the statement of the assets and debts of the debtor, and the name of the trustee appointed, and of the members, if any, of the committee of inspection, shall be presented to the registrar. 1883 *Wharton's Law Lex.* (ed. 7), Inspection, Deed of.

6. *attrib.* and *Comb.* (Additional examples.)

1753 in *Maryland Hist. Mag.* III. 366 Which made me apprehend they intended some Opposition to the Inspection Law. 1773 *Ibid.* II. 358 To compel all the Owners or Makers of Tobacco to send it to certain Inspection Houses whence it cannot be again removed till it is put on Board a Ship. 1903 *Westm. Gaz.* 12 Jan. 7/2 The covering of the electrical inspection box at the Thames-street corner of Bennett's-hill was blown off this morning by the fusing of the wires. 1904 *Technol. & Sci. Dict.* (ed. Goodchild & Tweney), *Inspection Chamber* (Sanitation), a chamber at the junction of drains to allow of inspection. 1907 *Westm. Gaz.* 13 Nov. 8/2 Free access to the valves and inspection-doors of the crank chamber is given. 1908 *Ibid.* 2 Apr. 4/2 There are two large inspection doors in the crank-case. 1908 *Installation News* II. 87/2 The straight through type of inspection box should be inserted in the conduit run at short intervals. 1909 *Daily Chron.* 18 Sept. 1/6 The houses were flooded by water and filth from the sewers through the stone slabs covering the inspection chambers being displaced by the flood.

Inspectorship. Add: **b.** *attrib.*, as **inspectorship deed** (also *deed of inspectorship*), see quots. and cf. *Inspection 1.

1861 *Act 24 & 25 Vict.* c. 134 § 191 As to Trust Deeds for Benefit of Creditors, Composition and Inspectorship Deeds executed by a Debtor. 1883 *Wharton's Law Lex.* (ed. 7), *Inspectorship, Deed of*, an instrument entered into between an insolvent debtor and his creditors, appointing one or more person or persons to inspect and oversee the winding up of such insolvent's affairs on behalf of the creditors. 1902 *Encycl. Brit.* XXX. 151/2 Estates, however, continued to be wound up under deeds of arrangement, whether in the form of an assignment, or composition, or inspectorship deed.

Inspirator. **1.** (Late U. S. example.)

1903 K. M. Abbott *Old Paths New Eng.* 99 The first power-loom was set up by Francis Cabot Lowell, the inspirator of cotton manufacture.

Installation. **2.** Add: *attrib.*

1898 *Engineering Mag.* XVI. 48 The installation cost is a matter of estimate. 1908 *Installation News* II. 56/2 Competent to act as installation inspector. 1921 *Dict. Occup. Terms* § 690 *Installation engineer*.., a technical engineer who interviews prospective consumers and points out advantages of electric light or power and advises them as to installation, etc. *Ibid.* § 692 Installation inspector.

Instalment^{1}. **1. b.** *U.S.* (Earlier example.)

1759 *Essex Inst. Hist. Coll.* XLIX. 2, I went to an Instalment at Stoneham where Mr. John Serls took upon him the pastoral charge of the church.

Instalment^{2}. **3.** Add: *attrib.* (freq. in recent use), as *instalment plan*, etc.

1894 *Vermont Agric. Rep.* XIV. 94 They..sell the horse on the installment plan, getting enough down to pay all the horse is worth, and holding notes for the rest. *a* 1909 'O. Henry' *Roads of Destiny* iii. 47 When they get money they exhibit a strong tendency to spend it..instead of giving it to the instalment man. 1921 R. D. Paine *Comr. Rolling Ocean* xi. 187 'This is still a valuable ship', explained Torrance, 'even if she is floating around the high seas on the installment plan'. 1927 *Saturday Even. Post* (N.Y.) 24 Dec. 28/2 Upon that premise..is based the vast present-day development of installment selling. 1927 W. E. Collinson *Contemp. Engl.* 112 To pay by the instalment system.

Instantaneous, *a.* Add: **1.** *Instantaneous (grip) vice* (see quots.).

1888 *Lockwood's Dict. Mech. Engin.*, *Instantaneous Grip Vice*, or *Sudden Grip Vice*, a vice which is provided with levers, a toggle-joint, and rack, by means of which it is enabled to clasp work without the loss of time involved in turning a screw. 1902 P. Marshall *Metal Working Tools* 28. 1904 *Technol. & Sci. Dict.* (ed. Goodchild & Tweney), *Instantaneous Vice*, a vice in which the grip is obtained by some form of cam or rock.

3. (See quot.)

1904 *Technol. & Sci. Dict.* (ed. Goodchild & Tweney), *Instantaneous value* (Elect.), the value of a current or electromotive force at any given instant.

Instar (i·nstaɹ), *sb. Zool.* [L., = form, figure, likeness.] Any one of the periods of an insect's life between two successive ecdyses.

1895 D. Sharp in *Cambr. Nat. Hist.* V. 158 It may be well to adopt a term suggested by Fischer [*Orthoptera Europæa*, 1853, p. 37], and call the Insect as it appears at hatching the first instar, what it is as it emerges from the first ecdysis the second instar, and so on; in that case the pupa of a Lepidopteron that assumed that condition at the fifth ecdysis would be the sixth instar, and the butterfly itself would be the seventh instar. 1929 *Encycl. Brit.* XII. 12/2 In the parasitic groups hypermetamorphosis..is very frequent, the larvae being hatched in forms very different from that assumed in the final instar.

Instep^{1}. Add: **3. b.** The arched part of a boot or shoe between the heel and the sole.

1826 *Kaleidoscope* VI. 223/2 A boot-jack of this description ..has an equal purchase on the instep and heel. 1913 E. C. Bentley *Trent's Last Case* v, On each [shoe], in the angle between the heel and the instep, he detected a faint trace of red gravel. 1927 E. Bramah *Max Carrados Mysteries* 160 He slyly inserted a nail in the angle of the instep.

Instigatrix. Delete † *Obs.* and add example.

1902 *Dublin Rev.* July 105 Lady Macbeth, the instigatrix of the murder.

Institution. **8.** Add:

1902 *Daily Chron.* 7 May 3/7 Institution life year after year is like pushing a stone uphill. 1905 *Ibid.* 27 Sept. 4/5 To any high-spirited woman, the tyranny of institution life must be almost unbearable.

Institutional, *a.* Add:

1. c. Of religion: Organized into or finding expression through institutions (a church, ordained ministers, ritual). Cf. *Institutionalism (*a*).

1908 F. von Hügel *Myst. Elem. Relig.* p. vi, The Infinite can still find room for the Historical and Institutional elements in Religion. 1924 A. E. J. Rawlinson *Authority & Freedom* vi. 136 The Christianity of history is a sacramental and institutional religion.

d. Of a church: Possessing organizations and societies of a charitable or educational nature in addition to the purely religious work. *U.S.*

1901 *Daily Chron.* 11 Dec. 6/6 Practically the Institutional Church is an ordinary Church organisation plus a university settlement. 1908 *Westm. Gaz.* 24 Aug. 4/2 [He] has charge, in his own city of Atlanta, U.S.A., of what is probably the largest institutional church in the world.

Institutionalism. Add: *spec.*, (*a*) the principles of institutional religion; (*b*) the system of housing people in institutions; the characteristics of life in an institution.

1907 *Daily Chron.* 17 Oct. 8/4 There is nothing of 'institutionalism' about life at the Browning Bethany Homes. 1909 G. Tyrrell *Chr. at Cross Roads* Pref. p. xx, The time has come..for a criticism of categories—of the very ideas of religion, of revelation, of institutionalism, of sacramentalism, of theology, of authority, etc. 1909 *Daily Chron.* 28 Oct. 5/3 The great impediment to success in the work of saving fallen women was the machinery of institutionalism. 1927 *Observer* 21 Aug. 7 The Society has set its face against any tendencies towards 'institutionalism', against any attempt..to take children away from their own homes. 1930 W. R. Inge *Chr. Ethics & Mod. Problems* i. 16 The unquestionable advantages which this fanatical institutionalism confers upon the Church as an organisation.

Institutionalize, *v.* Add: **b.** To house, train, or bring up in an institution; to subject (a person) to institutional life.

1905 J. Burns in *Daily Chron.* 1 Dec. 4/4 He has been 'institutionalised', and I never yet knew the average man survive that pauperising ordeal. 1924 *Glasgow Herald* 24 May 9 The day of the institutionalised boy or girl is past.

Institutionize (institiū·ʃənəiz), *v.* [f. Institution + -ize.] *trans.* To render institutional; to institutionalize.

1903 G. Tyrrell *Church & Future* 61 In regarding the 'institutionising' of Christianity as a corruption..Protestantism seems to me to ignore universal and natural laws. 1911 W. James *Mem. & Studies* xiv. 335 The institutionizing on a large scale of any natural combination of need and motive always tends to run into technicality and to develop a tyrannical Machine.

Instroke. Add: **2.** The stroke in a steam engine which carries the piston away from the crank shaft.

1902 *Encycl. Brit.* XXVIII. 183/2 Suction during an entire outstroke of the piston;..compression during the following instroke.

Instruct, *v.* Add: **3. b.** *spec.* (*a*) To direct (a representative) how to vote, etc. (*b*) To remove (a representative) from office by instructions. *U.S.*

1841 in *Congress. Globe* 186 It is the duty of the elected to carry into effect the will of his constituents, if he is instructed what that will is. 1862 *N. Y. Tribune* 22 Jan. (Bartlett) Mr. Tyler..was in 1836 instructed out of the Senate,..having previously been very strongly sustained by the [Virginia] Legislature.

Instruction. Add: **4. c.** *spec.* Directions given to a representative how he is to vote, etc.

1828 *Richmond Whig* 16 Feb. 1/2 (Th.) We have too much respect for the legislature of Kentucky to suppose that they meant to bind the delegation by an instruction. 1841 *Congress. Globe* 9 June App. 74 (Th.) Instruction is the right of a majority, petition that of a minority, or of a single individual.

Instructive, *a.* Add: **b.** *Finnish Gram.* Applied to the case denoting means.

1890 C. N. E. Eliot *Finnish Gram.* 22 The instructive is formed by simply adding the letter *n* to a root, and expresses the means by which anything is done. 1896 [see Inessive].

Instructor. **b.** *U.S.* (Earlier example.)

1891 *Univ. Chicago Official Bull.* I. 11 Lecturers and teachers..shall be classified as follows...(6) The Instructor.

Instrument, *v.* Add: **2. b.** To supply the mechanism for producing richness and variety of tone in (a pianoforte).

1880 *Grove's Dict. Mus.* II. 723/2 The radical change that took place between 1830 and 1850 in 'instrumenting' the pianoforte, giving it what we may call colour of tone.

Instrumentally, *adv.* Add: **3.** *Gram.* In or by the instrumental case.

1846 Monier-Williams *Sanscr. Gram.* 160 Instrumentally Dependent..those [compounds] in which the relation of the first word (being in the crude) to the last is equivalent to that of an instrumental case.

Insulating, *ppl. a.* Add examples.

1898 Sloane *Elect. Dict.* (ed. 2), *Insulating Tape*, prepared tape used in covering the ends of wire where stripped for making joints. 1910 *Hawkins' Elect. Dict.*, *Insulating sleeve*, a sleeve joint of non-conducting material for splicing two ends of insulated wire. *Ibid.*, *Insulating tube*. 1. An insulating sleeve. 2. A non-conducting tube designed to protect an insulated wire at the point where it runs through a partition or wall.

Insulation. Add: **1.** (Later U.S. example.) Also, an insulated piece of land or rock.

1848 E. Bryant *What I saw in California* xi. 157 The waters surrounding these insulations could be traced between them as far as the eye could reach. 1871 *Scribner's Monthly* II. 7 Their smooth sides, uniform width and height..considered in connection with the courses which had wrought their insulation, excited our wonder and admiration.

Insulator. Add: **c.** One of a set of glass 'stands' to be placed under the legs of a piano.

1895 *Army & Navy Co-op. Soc. Price List* 15 Sept. 1337 Piano Insulator. Cut Glass.

Insulin (i·nsiŭlin). *Pharm.* [f. L. *insula* island + -in.^{1}] A specific for diabetes extracted from the islets of Langerhans in the pancreas of animals.

1922 Banting & Best in *Trans. Roy. Soc. Canada* XVI. v. 27 The Preparation of Pancreatic Extracts containing Insulin. 1923 Banting *Antidiabetic Funct. Pancreas* 64 Insulin is administered from twenty minutes to a half hour before meals. 1930 *Bio-Chemical Jrnl.* XXIV. 1199 Insulin injected subcutaneously.

Insult, *sb.* **2.** Add: freq. in the phr. *to add insult to injury.*

1805 *Ann. 8th Congress* 2 Sess. 1072 It was adding insult to injury, and expenses to both, as it regarded the claimants. 1807 *Ann. 10th Congress* 1 Sess. I. 933 Were the laws of a free and respectable State to be evaded by such shameful expedients as these? This was adding insult to injury. 1853 H. T. Riley tr. *Phædrus* 429 You wanted to revenge the sting of a tiny insect with death; what will you do to yourself who have added insult to injury?

Insurance. Add: **4. e.** The act or system of insuring employed persons against sickness or unemployment, esp. in accordance with the National Insurance Act of 1911 and the Unemployment Insurance Act of 1920, which require certain wage-earners to make weekly payments supplemented by their employers, in return for which they are entitled to State assistance in sickness, unemployment, etc.

1911 *Times* 28 Mar. 10/3 The preparation of the Sickness and Invalidity Insurance Bill. *Ibid.* 5 May 14/3 If he had divided his bill into two—one dealing with unemployment and one with invalidity insurance. *Ibid.* 14/5 The burden imposed by State insurance must necessarily fall on manufacturers. 1911 *Act 1 & 2 Geo. V* c. 55. 337 National Health Insurance. 1912 [see *5]. 1920 *Act 10 & 11 Geo. V* c. 30 § 48 (1) This Act may be cited as the Unemployment Insurance Act, 1920.

5. (sense 4) *insurance agent, man*; (sense *4 e) *insurance act, card, commissioner, committee, stamp.*

1874 B. F. Taylor *World on Wheels*, etc. II. ii. 199 He was an insurance agent—a retired doctor, who growing weary of saving lives with pills, had taken to insuring lives with policies. 1879 *Harper's Mag.* July 215 The insurance men ..would insure the lives of the hands who were at work there. 1911 *Act 1 & 2 Geo. V* c. 55 § 15 The regulations made by the Insurance Commissioners. *Ibid.*, The Insurance Committee for each county or county borough. *Ibid.* § 115 This Act may be cited as the National Insurance Act, 1911. 1912 *Chemist & Druggist* LXXX. 950/2 Cards and stamps for health insurance under the National Insurance Act are now procurable at post offices. 1912 *Punch* 31 July 99/3 Mr. Masterman has laid it down that it is the wife's duty, and not that of the husband, to lick the servants' insurance stamps. 1913 *Ibid.* 15 Jan. 49/1 As the 15th of January approaches, bringing fulfilment of 9d. for 4d. through operation of Insurance Act. *Ibid.* 13 Aug. 148/3 Somebody come to see about an insurance card or something. 1929 J. B. Priestley *Good Companions* I. i. § 4 He..threw an insurance card and some money on the table. 1930 *Morning Post* 7 Aug. 11 The employers at four factories agreed to take upon themselves the charge of the insurance stamp which the men refuse to pay.

Insure, *v.* Add: **4. d.** (Cf. *Insurance 4 e.)

1911 *Act 1 & 2 Geo. V* c. 55 § 1 All persons so insured (in this Act called 'insured persons').

Supplement, p. 3873; Corrigenda, p. 4092; Spurious words, p. 4093; Books quoted, p. 4094

Inswept (i·nswept), *a.* [f. In *adv.* + Swept *ppl. a.*] Of the frame of a motor car: Narrowed at the forward end.
1907 *Westm. Gaz.* 12 Nov. 12/3 The frames will be inswept from the dash. 1908 *Ibid.* 30 Jan. 4/1 The frame..is inswept in front and gracefully upturned in the rear.

Inswinger (i·nswi:ŋəɹ). *Cricket.* [In *adv.*] A ball bowled with a swerve or swing from the off to leg in its flight. So **I·nswing**, the swerve or swing imparted to such a ball. Hence **I·nswi:nging** *ppl. a.*
1920 *Times* 29 May 7/2 He [*sc.* Mr. Robertson-Glasgow] again seemed to rely too much on his 'inswinger' on the leg side, and he would surely do very much better if he could be certain of pitching his inswinging ball on the off stump. 1924 N. Cardus *Days in Sun* 49 Jacques, of Hampshire.. was a bowler commanding an in-swinging flight and an off-break. *Ibid.* 254 Nor would it be accurate to describe this ball as an in-swinger, for the true in-swinger swings from almost the first few yards of its flight through the air. 1927 *Observer* 17 Apr. 17/3 Last year he [*sc.* Mr. Allom] specialised in the 'inswing'.

Intaglio, *sb.* **3.** Add: *intaglio cutter, cylinder, engraver, engraving, impression, worker*; **intaglio printer** (see quot. 1921); **intaglio-type**, a process, resembling the graphotype, by which a design is produced in intaglio on a metallic plate; also the resulting design.
1875 Knight *Dict. Mech.* s.v., Intaglio-type,..intaglio impression. 1876 *Encycl. Brit.* IV. 738/2 Cameo-cutting is an art of much more recent introduction than the sister art of intaglio-engraving. 1885 E. Renton (*title*) Intaglio Engraving: Past and Present. *Ibid.* 13 There are many Intaglio Engravers on Stone now existing in England. 1902 *Encycl. Brit.* XXXII. 17/1 Intaglio Processes. *Ibid.*, An intaglio engraving is one in which the printing surface is sunk below the surrounding portions of the block or plate. 1921 *Dict. Occup. Terms* (1927) § 126 *Intaglio cutter, intaglio worker*, as for engraver, except that intaglio cutter uses stone instead of copper disc. *Ibid.* § 529 *Intaglio printer* ..places metal intaglio cylinder in position in machine, sets roll of paper and adjusts machine for even printing.

Intake, *sb.* **3.** Add: *attrib.*, as *intake crib, tunnel*; **intake man** (see quot. 1921).
1909 *Daily Chron.* 21 Jan. 1/7 A fire which occurred at the construction works of a waterworks intake crib on Lake Michigan. 1909 *Westm. Gaz.* 21 Jan., This new intake tunnel was thrust further out into the lake. 1921 *Dict. Occup. Terms* (1927) § 449 *Intake man*, grain intake man (grain milling); at a signal from men on ship, barge, etc., alongside wharf that suction pipe is inserted in grain, starts air pump, which draws up grain through pipe by suction.

Intaker. Add: **2.** (See quot.)
1921 *Dict. Occup. Terms* (1927) § 368 *Drawer*, drawer-in, ..healder, in-taker,..attaches weaving beam to drawing-in frame, and draws each warp yarn, separately, with a hook, through eye (or loop) of heald, and through dent of reed in loom.

Intangibility. Add: **b.** Inviolability.
1783 C. J. Fox in *Mem. & Corr.* (1853) II. 102, I beg of gentlemen to be aware of the lengths to which their arguments upon the intangibility of this charter may be carried. 1929 *Times* 13 Aug. 10/2 There has been too much talk..of the intangibility of the Young Plan.

Intangible, *a.* Add: **c.** Inviolable.
1929 *Daily Tel.* 8 Aug. 11/2 Acceptance of the Young plan as an intangible and indivisible whole.

Intarsio (intā·rsio). Also **-ia.** [It.] An elaborate form of inlaid work in wood practised in Italy during the Renaissance; = Tarsia. Also *attrib.* So **Intarsiatore** (intā:rsiātō·re), a worker in intarsio; **Intarsiatura** (intā:rsiātū·rā), pl. **-e**, = *Intarsio.
1850 Mrs. Jameson *Leg. Monast. Ord.* (1863) 275 The fine intarsiatura in the Choir of San Francesco di Assisi. 1867 *Ecclesiologist* XXVIII. 216 Hidden under the intarsio pavement. 1868 C. C. Perkins *Ital. Sculptors* 262 A celebrated wood-carver and 'intarsiatore' named Luchino Bianchini.. helped them to carve the presses for the sacristy. *Ibid.*, Luchino Bianchini..made the woodwork about its great portal, as well as the intaglios and intarsiature of the choir at San Lodovico. 1892 Agnes M. Clerke *Fam. Stud. Homer* x. 266 Some rusty dagger-blades..skilfully ornamented in coloured metallic intarsiatura. 1894 *Daily News* 6 Dec. 5/2 Humorous intarsia showing Polyphemus..feeling the backs of the sheep. 1896 *Q. Rev.* Oct. 471 The intarsias of the choir-stalls of S. Maria Maggiori at Bergamo. 1907 *Daily Chron.* 15 Jan. 7/1 A very fine specimen of intarsia inlay. 1913 Mrs. H. Ward *Mating of Lydia* iv. xix, The gleaming reflections on lacquer and intarsia, on ebony or Sèvres. 1919 H. F. Jones *Samuel Butler* II. 67 The seats of the stalls in the church of Santa Maria Maggiori at Bergamo are ornamented with intarsia work.

Integrand (i·ntĭgrænd). *Math.* [ad. L. *integrandus*, gerundive of *integrāre* to make whole.] An expression that is to be integrated.
1897 H. F. Baker *Abel's Theorem* 561 The integrand of the Abelian integral u_r is single-valued on the Riemann surface. 1904 *Physical Rev.* Aug. 101 In this case the first integrand is Poynting's Energy Flow function. 1912 J. Pierpont *Lect. The. Functions* II. 386.

Integraph (i·ntĭgraf). *Math.* [f. Inte(grate + -graph.] An integrating instrument.
1894 *Times* 11 Aug. 11/1 Speaking of variable-line instruments, he said that these could be used to evaluate integrals with any assigned limits, while the other class only integrated round closed curves; they were therefore called integraphs. 1902 *Encycl. Brit.* XXX. 582/1 While an integrator determines the value of a definite integral, hence a mere constant, an integraph gives the value of an indefinite integral, which is a function of *x*.

Integrating, *vbl. sb.* and *ppl. a.* (under Integrate *v.*). Add: *Integrating meter* (see quot.).
1902 *Encycl. Brit.* XXX. 597/1 All the above forms of house meters are called continuously integrating meters, in that the operation of recording or obtaining the time-integral of the current or the power is continuous.

Integration. Add: **3.** *Psychol.* The combining of diverse elements into a complex whole; also, a complex state or combination the elements of which are distinguishable.
1893 J. M. Baldwin *Elem. Psychol.* 36 Integration, therefore, represents a structural change in the direction both of simplicity and of complexity. 1898 G. F. Stout *Man. Psychol.* I. 134 Differentiation and Integration.

Intelligence, *sb.* Add:
7. c. Revived in modern wars (cf. *intelligence man, officer* in *d).
1925 E. Fraser & Gibbons *Soldier & Sailor Words* s.v. *I*, 'Intelligence', *i.e.* information of military value. The use of the word as a military technical term dates from the 16th Century, but in the War of 1914–18 it was used to denote specially the department of the General Staff dealing with information.
d. (sense *7 c) *intelligence man, officer*; **intelligence department**, a department of a state organization or of a military or naval service whose object is to obtain information (esp. by means of secret service officers or a system of spies); **intelligence quotient** *Psychol.*, a number intended to express the ratio of a given person's intelligence to the normal, which is fixed at 100; so **intelligence test.**
1875 *Encycl. Brit.* II. 573/1 The *Intelligence Department [of the Army]..under a Deputy-Adjutant-General. 1895 *Whitaker's Alm.* 230 Naval Intelligence Department. 1930 *Publishers' Weekly* 5 July 11 Those lone daredevils of No Man's Land, the scouts, snipers and *intelligence men. 1885 *Intelligence officer [in Dict.]. 1901 *Westm. Gaz.* 31 Dec. 10/1 You are intelligence officer to the new cavalry brigade. 1914 R. Brooke in *Mem.* (1918) 132 Intelligence Officer in H.M.S. *Vengeance.* 1921 C. Burt *Mental & Scholastic Tests* 151 If a child's mental age be divided by his chronological age, the quotient will state what fraction of ability the child actually possesses...This fraction may be termed ..the child's '*intelligence quotient'. 1922 Woodworth *Psychology* xii. 274 Brightness or dullness can also be measured by the intelligence quotient. 1929 *Encycl. Brit.* VII. 969/1 To arrive at a simple expression for the results of measurements made with the Binet scale, the so-called intelligence quotient..was devised. 1921 C. Burt *Mental & Scholastic Tests* 2 The practical value of *intelligence tests.

Intelligentsia (intelidʒe·ntsiă, intelige·ntsiă). [Russ. интеллигенция, prob. a. Pol. *inteligiencja*, G. *intelligenzia*, etc., ad. L. *intelligentia* Intelligence.] The class of society to which culture, superior intelligence, and advanced political views are attributed.
1914 *Round Table* Dec. 115 The importance and meaning of the so-called *intelligentsia*. 1916 H. G. Wells *Mr. Britling* I. ii. § 10 They are the sort of equivalent of the Russian Intelligentsia, an irresponsible middle class with ideas. 1922 Joad *Highbrows* vi. 224 Those waifs and strays of the intelligentsia who had resolutely refused to participate in the war. 1922 Mrs. A. Sidgwick *Victorian* xxviii, He told me..that he belonged to the Intelligentsia and that he was out to shoot capitalists. 1924 Galsworthy *White Monkey* I. ix, It was not the intelligentsia, but just intellectual society, which was gathered there.

Intendit (inte·ndit). *Roman-Dutch Law.* [L., = he avers.] A document setting out a legal claim and the proofs on which it rests.
1886 Kotzé tr. *S. van Leeuwen's Roman-Dutch Law* II. 444 If the plaintiff on his *intendit*, that is statement of his claim.., fully establishes his case, the defendant..has final judgment pronounced against him.

Inteneration. (Later U.S. example, in fig. use.)
1898 Howells *Open-eyed Conspiracy* xviii, I felt a sort of indecency in beholding his inteneration, for I knew that it came from his heart.

Intense, *a.* Add: **4. c.** Feeling or manifesting intense emotion or seriousness.
1879 Howells *L. Aroostook* xiv, 'Why Miss Blood you are intense!' 'I don't know what you mean by that,' said Lydia. 'You like to take things seriously. You can't bear to think that people are not the least in earnest, even when they least seem so.' 1880 Du Maurier *Eng. Soc. at Home* pl. 49 Fair Æsthetic (suddenly, and in deepest tones, to Smith, who has just been introduced to take her in to Dinner). 'Are you *Intense*?' 1897 H. Havelock Ellis *Stud. Psychol. Sex* I. 88 Miss M., aged 29, the daughter of English parents (both musicians) who were both of what is described as 'intense' temperaments. 1925 *Punch* 6 May 487 *Intense Lady.* 'Tell me—have you ever been psyched?'

Intensionally (inte·nʃənăli), *adv. Logic.* [f. Intension 5 + -al + -ly [2].] By way of intension.
1903 *Nature* 3 Sept. 411/1 A class may be defined either extensionally, by an enumeration of its terms, or intensionally, by the concept which denotes its terms.

Inter. (i·ntəɹ), abbreviation of Intermediate = *intermediate examination* (in arts, etc.), often used in ordinary colloquial speech.
1891–2 *Lond. Univ. Guide* 29 Inter. Arts Honours. *Ibid.* 40 Inter. Science and Prel. Sci. Exams.

Inter-. Add: **2. a.** *inter-availability, -connectedness.*
1920 *Glasgow Herald* 1 July 6 The issue of a circular cancelling the *inter-availability of practically all railway tickets between Scotland and England. 1923 *Ibid.* 27 Jan. 11 The deputation intends..to press for the inter-availability of these tickets on all systems. 1927 *Ibid.* 14 Sept. 9 The 'inter-availability,' as it might be termed, of famous experts as between one part of the Empire and another. 1922 A. G. Hogg *Redemption from this World* vi. 191 We labour hardest to perceive the *interconnectedness of events.
3. a. *interglyph, -mutule.*
1875 *Encycl. Brit.* II. 404/1 The *interglyphs are each one-seventh of the whole tablet or triglyph. 1863–9 *Archit. Publ. Soc. Dict. Archit.* III. 149/1 The temple to Ceres at Pœstum has no mutules or triglyphs. The example at Albano has no *intermutules. 1901 Sturgis *Dict. Archit.*, *Intermutule*, the space between two mutules, as in an architrave.
4. a. *inter-consonantal, -fluvial, -morainic, -nebular, -villous.*
1931 *Amer. Speech* VII. Oct. 19 His *inter-consonantal *n* is perhaps Southern. 1830 *New Monthly Mag.*, *Hist. Reg.* Jan. 6/2 Returning from Bagdad across the *interfluvial country, he took up his quarters at Hillah. 1894 J. Geikie *Great Ice Age* (ed. 3) 593 The *inter-morainic lakes which occupy similar positions at the base of the Alps in North Italy. 1929 Jeans *Universe Around Us* 142 The vast stretches of *internebular space. 1890 Billings *Med. Dict.*, *Intervillous lacunæ*, irregular vascular spaces connected with the maternal blood-vessels, surrounding the fœtal villi in the placenta. 1910 *Practitioner* Jan. 40 The intervillous spaces.
c. *intercameral* (between chambers), *-governmental.*
1929 *Times* 29 Oct. 16/1 Nobody believes that the question will..go to the *intercameral conference before the Special Session ends. 1927 *Glasgow Herald* 20 Jan. 8 When it came to negotiation, agreement could not be obtained by *inter-Governmental intervention. 1928 *Britain's Industrial Future* (*Lib. Ind. Inq.*) I. iii. § 3. 28 The system of inter-governmental debts which the War has left behind.
5. *inter-borough, -caste, -church, -electrode, -library, -plane, -valve.*
1905 *Westm. Gaz.* 8 Nov. 5/1 The officials of the *interborough railways. 1928 *Evening News* 5 May 5/7 The Interborough Company declares that a 7 cent fare will enable them to build better cars and run an adequate service. 1928 *Daily Express* 19 May 9/5 The first inter-borough competition of its kind ever organised in London. 1908 *New Reformer* II. 62 It is a case of *inter-caste and inter-provincial marriage. 1925 E. S. Jones *Christ of Indian Road* xiii. 243 We sat down to an intercaste dinner—a hundred high-caste Hindus, a hundred outcastes, a hundred Indian Christians, a few Mohammedans, and several of us of the West. 1905 *Daily Chron.* 22 Nov. 1/7 At an *inter-Church Conference in New York 17,000,000 Church members of all denominations were represented. 1926 *British Weekly* 22 July 327/1 Dr. Clark has toured the world to build this inter-church, international organisation. 1930 *Daily Express* 9 Sept. 11/1 The new..Valve has a greater effective amplification because its *inter-electrode capacity is lower. 1928 J. A. McMillen (*title*) Selected articles on *interlibrary loans. 1916 H. Barber *Aeroplane Speaks* 96 *Interplane struts..have to keep the lifting surfaces or 'planes' apart. 1920 *Blackw. Mag.* Nov. 565/1 Great lanky beasts with double interplane engines, heavy bombers of freak aspect. 1928 C. F. S. Gamble *Story North Sea Air Station* xii. 195 *note*, These rockets..were affixed to the interplane struts of the machine. 1922 *Wireless World* IX. 120/1 Substitute an *intervalve transformer for your telephone transformer.

Interact, *sb.* Add: *attrib.*
1908 *Daily Chron.* 3 July 3/5 At the 'private' or roofed theatres, the performance of interact music was the rule. 1909 *Morning Leader* 29 May 4/6 At the 'private theatres', such as the Blackfriars, they not only had interacts but interact music.

Interactionism (intəræ·kʃəniz'm). *Philos.* [f. Interaction + -ism.] The theory that in the causal relations between mind and body the causal influence runs in both directions, in sensation from body to mind and in volition from mind to body. So **Intera·ctionist** *sb.*, an adherent of interactionism; *adj.*, of or pertaining to this doctrine.
1902 *Pop. Sci. Monthly* 459 (Cent. D. Suppl.) Interactionism has to maintain, in this concrete form of the 'survival theory', that the mental process as such is an aid to evolution. 1903 C. A. Strong *Why Mind has Body* 5 Whether this interactionist tendency in biology be significant or ephemeral, we need not inquire. *Ibid.* 23 What the interactionist..takes for an action of mind on body is..an action of the brain upon the rest of the body. *Ibid.* 33 Interactionism seems almost to necessitate two juxtaposed realities exchanging influences, and thus to imply a metaphysical dualism.

Inter-allied (intəræ̆ləi·d, -æ·ləid), *a.* [f. Inter- 1 b + Allied.] Existing or constituted between allies or allied forces. So **Inter-ally** (-æ·ləi), *a.*
1920 J. M. Keynes *Econ. Conseq. Peace* 96 *note*, The supreme authority is to be in the hands of an Inter-Allied Rhineland Commission. *Ibid.* 240 The settlement of inter-Ally indebtedness. 1925 A. J. Toynbee *Survey Internat. Affairs 1920–23* 1 The four Treaties..had provided for the establishment of a number of inter-Allied bodies to perform temporary or permanent executive duties.

Intercalarium (intəɹkălē·riŏm). *Zool.* Pl. **-ia.** [mod.L., neut. sing. of L. *intercalārius* Intercalary.] A segment or process occurring between the bases of adjacent neural arches in the vertebral column of certain animals.
1887 *Proc. Zool. Soc.* 31 Intercalaria are absent in the hæmal tube. 1893 *Phil. Trans.* Ser. B. 83 Like the scaphium the intercalarium consists of ascending and horizontal processes united at nearly a right angle.

Interception. Add: **1. b.** Also *attrib.*, as **interception-band**, a band of colour apparent to the eye in a state of repose when a rod is passed across a two-coloured disk.
1903 *Psychol. Rev.* IV. 190 We have a graphic representation of the color-deduction determined by the interception of the pendulum...We are now prepared to continue our identification of these geometrical interception-bands with the bands observed in the illusion.
3. *attrib.*
1886 *Encycl. Brit.* XXI. 713/2 It is frequently desirable not to gather sewage from the whole area into a single main, but to collect the sewage of higher portions of the town by a separate high-level or interception sewer.

Interchanger. Add: **2.** An apparatus for the cooling and liquefaction of gases.
1899 *Nature* 20 July 268/2 An interchanger, to make the cooling effectively self-intensive, must have one end at the higher temperature, where the compressed air enters.

Intercooler (i·ntəɹkūləɹ). [Inter- 2 b.] An apparatus for cooling air between the intervals of compression. So **I·ntercooling** *vbl. sb.*, the process of cooling air by this apparatus.
1900 *Engineering Mag.* XIX. 679 A complete system of jacket water and a very large intercooler are used.

Intercrop (intəɹkrǫ·p), *v.* [Inter- 1.] To raise a crop between rows of another (*trans.* and *intr.*). Hence **Intercro·pping** *vbl. sb.* So **Intercrop** *sb.*, a crop so raised.
1901 W. Robinson *Eng. Flower Garden* (ed. 8) 92 Evidence of the good way in which inter-cropping suits plants in nursery beds.

Interdentally (intəɹde·ntăli), *adv.* [f. Interdental + -ly [2].] In an interdental position; between the teeth.
1910 *Practitioner* Jan. 115 The neck of the tooth..is embraced by a thin shallow flap of gum, continuous interstitially (interdentally) with the gum pad.

Interdepartmentally (intəɹdīpāɹtme·ntăli), *adv.* [f. Interdepartmental + -ly [2].] Between or among departments.
1901 *Westm. Gaz.* 7 June 2/2 This is the bane of Government offices, both departmentally and interdepartmentally. 1906 *Ibid.* 30 Oct. 2/1 But there are strong grounds for believing that the question of the attitude of the Government towards the proposals now before the Berlin Conference has not been made a Cabinet question; in other words, that it has been dealt with interdepartmentally.

Interesting, *ppl. a.* Add: **3.** *To be in an interesting condition, situation, state*: to be pregnant. *Interesting event*: a birth.
1748 Smollett *R. Random* lxix, So that I cannot leave her in such an interesting situation, which I hope will produce something to crown my felicity. 1839 Dickens *Nickleby* xxix, Mrs. Lenville (who, as has been before hinted, was in an interesting state). 1848 Thackeray *Van. Fair* xxvii, Mrs. Bunny's in an interesting situation. 1899 *Westm. Gaz.* 27 June 6/3 'Interesting event' at Peterhof. Another daughter! 1918 W. B. Maxwell *We Forget because we Must* II. iii, I'm afraid I seem to make heavy weather of my interesting condition. 1930 Galsworthy *On Forsyte 'Change* 171 Winifred, beginning to be 'interesting', owing to the approach of a little Dartie, kept her eyes somewhat watchfully on 'Monty'.

Interfere, *v.* Add:
4. c. *Chess.* Of a piece: To obstruct the movements of another piece. (Cf. *Interference 1 b.)
1926 H. Weenink *Chess Problem* 38 It will be noticed that ..Re 6 in turn interferes with the line of force of the Bg 4, shutting off its command of d 7 and c 8.
6. *U.S. Football.* To interpose between the player with the ball and a would-be tackler so as to help the former. *Baseball.* To obstruct a runner between two bases; also, to obstruct a catcher or fielder who is trying to take or throw the ball. (Cf. *Interference 1 c.)
1920 W. Camp *Football without a Coach* 51 The full-back and the right half must interfere for their companion.

Interference. Add:
1. b. *Chess.* Obstruction of the line of force of one piece by another. Also *attrib.*
1881 Loyd in A. C. White *Loyd & his Chess Problems* (1913) 303 There are many forms of interference play which have nothing to do with avoiding stalemate. 1926 H. Weenink *Chess Problem* 39 In both problems there is mutual interference of the black Rook and Bishop.
c. *U.S. Football.* The act of interposing between a runner and a tackler to obstruct the latter (see also quot. 1895). *Baseball.* The act of obstructing a baseball runner between two bases.
1895 G. J. Manson *Sporting Dict.* 61 *Interference*, using the hands or arms in any way to obstruct or hold a player who has got the ball. 1920 W. Camp *Football without a Coach* 59 To amount to anything at all interference must be perfectly timed...On a play between tackle and guard..the interference must reach that point prepared to take care of the tackle, the guard and even the backfield men, too. 1923 Dorothy Canfield *Rough-Hewn* xxv, Where *was* the ball? Sometimes it came straight through and the next minute on the same formation swung outside—and Neale uselessly buried under the interference. 1927 H. G. Salsinger in *Secrets of Baseball* 147 Interference plays, too, are scored as they probably have been made.
2. b. *Wireless.* The intrusion of electrical disturbances which interfere with reception. Also *attrib.*
1902 *Windsor Mag.* May 720/2 Two messages were sent, one in English and one in French. Both were received at the same time on the same wire at Poole..without the least interference. 1913 *Yearbk. Wireless Teleg.* 85 For the purpose of preventing interference with the working of any other wireless telegraph station. 1914 R. Stanley *Wireless Teleg.* 292 Marconi patented an interference preventer which involved the use of two aerials and a rotating machine. ..Undue interference is avoided by the observance of the International Radio Laws.

Interferer. Add: *U.S. Football.* One who interposes between a runner and a tackler.
1923 Dorothy Canfield *Rough-Hewn* xxv, Neale could see Rogers rock a second, undecided, on tip-toe; side-step an interferer; and then shoot his body like a projectile into the play.

Interfering, *ppl. a.* Add: **2.** *Wireless.* That causes interference (see *Interference 2 b).
1914 R. Stanley *Wireless Teleg.* 291 If the International Rules are duly observed an interfering station should be one which considers itself out of range.

Interferometry (i:ntəɹfĭərǫ·mĕtri). [f. Interferometer: see -metry.] The action or art of measuring interference phenomena; the study and use of the interferometer.
1915 C. Barus *Exp. Displacement Interferometer* I. 1 Elliptic interferometry applied to the horizontal pendulum. 1916 — (*title*) The Interferometry of Reversed and Non-Reversed Spectra.

Interiorize (intī·riǝrəiz), *v.* [f. Interior *a.* + -ize.] *trans.* To connect with the soul, as distinguished from the body; also, to locate within the mind.
1906 *Academy* 20 Oct. 392/2 To 'interiorise' the struggle, to place it on the stage of the soul, with eternity for background. 1916 Stanford & Forsyth *Hist. Music* (1925) 329 The second [feature in American life] is the interiorizing and democratic habit-of-mind which partly connotes the term *Americanism.*

Interlocal, *a.* (Example.)
1921 A. C. Pigou *Econ. Welfare* 171 So soon as people become thoroughly familiarised with town-planning, local patriotism and inter-local emulation will make resort to external pressure from the central Government no longer necessary.

Interlock, *sb.* Add: **c.** *Cinematography.* The apparatus used to synchronize sound and action in a talking film.
1931 B. Brown *Talking Pictures* ix. 206 Gaumont coupled the armature of his projector motor to that of his gramophone motor, and using a common power supply, obtained synchronism. To-day we use a similar type of arrangement known as the 'electrical interlock'.

Interlock, *v.* Add: **4.** *Cinematography.* To synchronize the devices for recording or reproducing sound and action in a talking film.
1929 *Photoplay* Apr., *Phased, or interlocked*—all motors of sound and picture recording equipment lined up in readiness to start out in perfect step together. 1931 B. Brown *Talking Pictures* ix. 206 Where we have cameras working in conjunction with sound recorders..there is absolute necessity for both devices to be interlocked or driven together, so that sound and photograph are always exactly in phase. *Ibid.* 207 Due to the interlocking action of the coupled rotors the distributor supplies power to the free motor keeping it up to normal speed.

Interlocutor [1]. Add: **c.** The compère in a troupe of nigger minstrels.
1909 *Cent. Dict.* Suppl.

Interludial (intəɹl(i)ū·diăl), *a.* [f. Interlude *sb.* + -ial.] Of, pertaining to, or of the nature of an interlude.
1884 *Encycl. Brit.* XVII. 94/1 Admitted for interludial purposes in a fabrication styled *intermezzo* that was played between the acts of a serious composition, comedy became [etc.]. 1922 S. Grew *Art of Player-Piano* 75 The interludial figure is extended to lead into a *forte.*

Intermat (intəɹmæ·t), *v.* [Inter- 1 b.] *trans.* and *intr.* To mat together.
1904 *Technol. & Sci. Dict.* (ed. Goodchild & Tweney), *Intermat* (Textile Manufac.), the term applied to the feltin; or shrinking of cloths, the fibres intermatting or felting together. 1927 *Daily Express* 18 Apr. 3/1 As the hair grows, it is worked into a kind of felt by intermatting it.

Intermede. **2.** Now current in alien form *intermède* (æ̃ntɛrmɛd).
1887 *Gentl. Mag.* June 540 The singularly appropriate *intermède* arranged by Beaumarchais for performance between the acts of his 'Eugenie'. 1931 *Times Lit. Suppl.* 6 Aug. 606/2 The inclusion between the first and second acts of an *intermède* of song and dance.

Intermediate, *a.* and *sb.* Add: **A.** *adj.* **f.** *Geol.* = Interlobate.
1883 T. C. Chamberlin in *3rd Ann. Rep. U.S. Geol. Survey 1881–2*, 313 Forming a peculiar morainic type, to which the term *intermediate* or *interlobate moraines* will be applied.
g. *Forestry.* Having the crown shaded at the sides but open to the light at the top.
1905 *Terms Forestry & Logging* 14.

Intermedietto (i:ntəɹmīdi,e·to). *Mus.* [It.] A short interlude or intermezzo.
1876 Stainer & Barrett *Dict. Mus. Terms.*

Intermedio- (intəɹmī·dio), used as combining form of Intermediate *a.*, as **intermedio-lateral** *a.*, intermediate and lateral.
1875 *Encycl. Brit.* I. 866/2 Lockhart Clarke has described an intermedio-lateral group of nerve cells. 1890 Billings *Med. Dict.*, *Intermedio-lateral tract*, a spur-like lateral process of gray substance appearing between anterior and posterior horns in sections of spinal cord. 1906 *Fifth Rept. Carnegie Trust Scotland* 20 Pathology of the intermedio-lateral tract of the Spinal Cord.

Intermont (i·ntəɹmǫnt), *a.* [f. Inter- 4 a + L. *mont-, mons* mountain.] Situated between mountains. So **Intermo·ntane, Intermou·ntain** *adjs.*
1828 Webster, Intermontane. 1901 W. M. Davis in *Science* 8 Mar. 396/1 The erosion of narrow valleys in the floor of the weak-rock intermont peneplains. 1902 *Encycl. Brit.* XXV. 362/2 The intermontane basins and the piedmontese plains that slope eastward from the Rocky Mountains in middle latitudes are treeless. 1903 *Science* 12 June 950/1 The study of the anthropology of the Indian races in this intermountain region. 1911 J. L. Myres *Dawn of History* iv. 91 We are ..concerned..with the intermont plains and upland valleys which sustained the old Medes and Persians. 1920 L. V. Pirrson *Phys. Geol.* (ed. 2) 269 Intermontane Plateaus. 1927 *Glasgow Herald* 21 May 8 This fungus..attacks both the green or Oregon and the blue or Colorado Douglas [fir], as well as the intermountain variety.

Intern. **B.** *sb. U.S.* (Examples.)
1889 *Kansas City T. & Star* 16 Oct., Convalescent women and young nurses are given too much freedom with the internes. 1923 E. F. Wyatt *Invis. Gods* II. v. 85 The older man..became..attached to the young surgical interne.
Hence **Inte·rnship**, the condition of an intern; the period of such condition. *U.S.*
1924 *Scribner's Mag.* Feb. 183/1 My father, who had the practice..told me the story in professional confidence...I was at that time just finishing my internship.

Internal, *a.* and *sb.* Add: **A.** *adj.* **1. d.** *Internal reserve* = inner reserve (*Inner *a.* 1 h).
1931 *Daily Express* 31 Jan. 10/2 By having greater recourse to our internal reserves..we could have shown a higher profit figure for the year.
5. internal combustion *a.*, denoting a type of engine in which the pressure necessary to produce motion is obtained in the engine cylinder by the combustion of inflammable vapour; **internal secretion**: cf. *Endocrine.
1884 H. C. F. Jenkin *Gas- & Caloric-Engines* 105 The *internal combustion engine..is really the forerunner of the gas-engine. 1888 *Brit. Gas & Oil Eng. Pat.* No. 12361 in *D. Clerk's Gas & Oil Eng.* (1896) 515 Hargreaves.—Improvements in internal combustion thermo-motor. 1908 *Westm. Gaz.* 29 Oct. 4/1 Even at this year's show the centre of interest will be an internal-combustion motor. 1902 *Encycl. Brit.* XXVIII. 362/2 The action of the thyroid gland has been made known, and the facts of '*internal secretions' have been in part elucidated. 1910 *Rep. Brit. Assoc.* 627 Starling proposed the name hormones for the internal secretions because of their excitatory properties.

International, *a.* (*sb.*) Add: **c. international code**, a code of signals by which seamen of all nations can hold communication at sea; **international copyright**, copyright that is valid in all countries, now in those subscribing to the Berne convention of 5 Sept., 1887.
1838 *Act 1 & 2 Vict.* c. 59 An Act for securing to Authors, in certain Cases, the Benefit of International Copyright. 1844 *Act 7 & 8 Vict.* c. 12. § 1 Which Act [*sc.* 1 & 2 Vict. c. 59] is herein-after, for the sake of Perspicuity, designated as 'the International Copyright Act'. 1901 *Empire Rev.* May 364 A book is subject to national copyright..and also to international copyright in the several countries admitting that right. 1902 *Encycl. Brit.* XXXII. 624/1 The international code of signals, for use between ships of all nations.
B. *sb.* **c.** *pl.* International bonds.
1909 *Westm. Gaz.* 17 Sept. 12/2 Internationals featureless.
d. *The international* = next.
1912 *Songs for Socialists* (Fabian Soc.) 2 The International.

Internationale (-næʃǝnā·l, || æ̃ntɛrnasyonal). [Fr. (sc. *chanson* song).] A revolutionary hymn composed by Eugene Pottier in 1871 and adopted by French socialists and subsequently by others.
1912 Hyndman *Further Remin.* 124 We all left Paris regretfully, with the strains of 'L'Internationale' ringing in our ears. 1933 *Morn. Post* 30 Mar. 11/3 Communists.. waved red flags and sang the 'Internationale'.

Internationalism. Add: **b.** A system of international control.
1902 *Encycl. Brit.* XXVII. 705/2 The investment..helped ..to save the country from bankruptcy and internationalism.

Internee (intəɹnī·). [f. Intern *v.* + -ee [1].] One who is interned; an interned person.
1918 *Rept. Detenus & Internees Bengal* in *Parlt. Papers* VIII. 106 The cases of the State prisoners and internees. 1920 *Observer* 5 Dec. 13/4 Lorries with military guards.. removed the internees to the camp.

Internist (intɔ̄·ɹnist). *U.S.* = Intern *sb.*
1904 *Science* 29 Apr. 696/1 Many internists ('general physicians') of experience and authority. 1918 *Nation* (N.Y.) Feb. 170/1 A maternity bureau composed of expert obstetricians and competent internists.

Interoceanic, *a.* (Earlier U.S. example.) So **Intero·cean** *a.*
1850 *Clayton-Bulwer Treaty* 19 Apr. 8 Interoceanic communication. 1913 *Chambers's Jrnl.* Jan. 22/2 The isthmus ..became a centre of attraction for interocean transit.

Interplanetary, *a.* Add: Also, existing between planets.
1901 *Daily News* 7 Jan. 5/1 Dreams of inter-planetary communication.

Interplant (intəɹplā·nt), *v.* [Inter- 1.] *trans.* To plant (an area already growing a crop) with a second crop among the first.
1927 *Daily Tel.* 11 May 3/4 Included in the 1,442 acres of rubber were 98 acres which were interplanted with coffee.

Interplical (intəɹplǝi·kăl), *a. Zool.* [f. Inter- 4 a + L. *plica* fold + -al.] Situated between folds.
1900 *Proc. U.S. Nat. Mus.* XXIII. 398 The term interplical ridge has been applied to the summit of the radial convexities of the wing and interplical groove the bottom of the alternating concavities. 1903 *Phil. Trans.* Ser. B. CXCV. 161 The thickened chitin bands, which in the sections at most levels are in contact by those edges directed towards the interplical space, are here divaricated.

Interpolate, *v.* Add: **3. c.** (With the words spoken as object.) To intercalate orally.
1881 Mrs. Riddell *Senior Partner* vii. I. 151 'I have not a word to say against Effie,' began..Robert...'If ye had, ye'd best not say it before me,' interpolated his father. 1908 *Smart Set* June 142/1 'I suppose I may claim some eminence as physicians go.' 'Top notch of the whole bunch, dad!' interpolated Keene.

Interpolator. Add: **2.** A mechanical contrivance for securing correct retransmission from a submarine cable of any consecutive letter-elements having the same sign.
1902 *Encycl. Brit.* XXXIII. 226/2 The special form of curb sender mentioned, termed the 'Interpolator'.

Interpose, *v.* Add: **1. c.** *Chess.* To move (a piece) so as to protect one which is threatened. Also *absol.* of the piece: to move to a position to shield another man.
1761 Hoyle *Ess. Game of Chess* 2, 6 B. The Queen gives Check. W. The Bishop interposes. 1765 Lambe *Hist. Chess* 107 If the B. Bp. instead of retreating, checks your K. you must interpose your Bp. 1808 Sarratt *Chess* I. 49 If he interpose his King's Knight, you must take his Rook with your Queen. 1844 W. Lewis *Chess* 19 Sometimes a piece or pawn, which before was out of play, may be interposed, and force the piece that checks to retire. 1861 *Chambers's Encycl.* II. 799/2 The king..must either move out of check or interpose some one of his subjects, unless the checking piece can be captured. 1876 *Encycl. Brit.* V. 593/1 If..the king, being thus in check, cannot move to another square.. and there is no piece or pawn which can be interposed, and the checking piece or pawn cannot be taken, then it is 'checkmate'.

Interpretation. Add: **5.** *attrib.*: **interpretation clause**, a clause in an Act of Parliament which defines the meaning of certain terms for the purposes of the Act.
1897 *Bouvier's Law Dict.* I. 1107/2.

Interpretess. (Later U.S. example.)
1880 Cable *Grandissimes* xxviii. 225 She went to the don's plantation as interpretess.

Inter-resist (i:ntəɹrĭzi·st), *v.* [Inter- 1.] *intr.* To offer mutual resistance. So **Inter-resi·stance.**
1902 *Encycl. Brit.* XXX. 667/1 Bodies..by this force of mutual impenetrability or inter-resistance cause one another to form a joint mass with a common velocity whenever they collide. *Ibid.* 667/2 Withdraw this foundation of bodies as inter-resisting forces..and the evidence of the third law disappears.

Interrupter. Add: **b.** (Earlier U.S example.)
1851 C. Cist *Cincinnati* 302 It has been represented that Prof. Locke had merely invented a new species of 'electrical interrupter'.
c. *attrib.* **interrupter gear**, a timing device attached to machine-guns in aeroplanes to prevent the discharge of bullets when the propeller is in the line of fire.
1928 C. F. S. Gamble *Story North Sea Air Station* x. 150 The Fökker monoplane, which was equipped with a mechanical interrupter gear.

Intersex (i·ntəɹseks). [Inter- 2 b.] An intermediate sex. Also *attrib.* So **I:ntersexua·lity.**
1911 'Xavier Mayne' (*title*) The Intersexes. 1930 G. R. de Beer *Embryol. & Evol.* iii. 22 Animals which have switched over from a period of development in one sex to a period of development in the other are called intersexes, and a series of degrees of intersexuality can be established from very slight to complete sex-reversal. *Ibid.* ix. 71 The example of intersexuality in the gypsy moth. 1931 *Oxf. Univ. Gaz.* 17 June 699/2 Skin and skull of intersex pig *Sus papuensis* from the New Hebrides.

Intersexual (intəɹse·ksiuăl), *a.* [Inter- 3 a.] Existing between the sexes.
1897 in *Havelock Ellis's Stud. Psychol. Sex* I. 183 This is quite as true of intersexual..love. 1904 G. S. Hall *Adolescence* I. 223 A subtle but potent intersexual influence is among the strongest factors of all adolescent sport.

Intersubjective (i:ntəɹsŏbdʒe·ktiv), *a. Psychol.* [Inter- 4 c.] Existing between two different conscious minds.
1899 J. Ward *Naturalism & Agnosticism* II. 170 It seems to depend upon three elements or conditions which are consequences of intersubjective intercourse. 1925 J. E. Turner *Theory Direct Realism* iv. 44 Intersubjective communication.

Interti·llage. *U.S.* [Inter- 1.] Intercropping. Hence **Interti·lled** *ppl. a.*
1914 *Rep. Brit. Assoc.* 270 The intertilled crop has in many sections largely taken the place of fallow.

Intertrade (i·ntəɹtrēd). [Inter- 2 a.] Reciprocal trade. Also *attrib.*
1915 E. Carpenter *Healing of Nations* xi. 168 Merchants and dealers came in and effected the exchange, and so an intertrade has sprung up. 1929 *Daily Tel.* 15 Jan. 6/4 The variations in the curve of consumer demand are much less than the curve of inter-trade demand.

Interval, *sb.* Add: **8.** *Math.* An aggregate of all numbers between and including two terminal numbers.
1902 *Encycl. Brit.* XXVIII. 545/2 This domain [of a variable] may be an 'interval', *i.e.*, it may consist of two terminal numbers, all the numbers between them and no others.

Intervention. Add: **1. b.** *Law.* The action of one, not originally a party, who intervenes in a suit.
1883 [see Intervener [1]].
Hence **Interve·ntionism**, the principle or policy of intervening, esp. in international affairs; **Interve·ntionist**, also, one who favours a doctrine of intervention; one who favours intervention with the course of a disease on medical grounds (*Cent. Dict.*); also as *adj.*
1915 *Morning Post* 19 Apr. 8/4 Interventionist, and, in some places, neutralist meetings were held yesterday at Milan. 1921 *Glasgow Herald* 22 July 7 M. Tchitcherin sees in this fact another 'interventionist' manœuvre. 1923 *Ibid.* 29 Mar. 5 The methods of interventionism..are contrary to the spirit of cooperation. 1930 *Times Lit. Suppl.* 14 Aug. 648/2 The 'interventionist' conception of miracle has passed out of fashion.

Intimal (i·ntimăl), *a.* [f. Intima + -al.] Of or pertaining to the intima.
1908 *Practitioner* Dec. 771 This observer also describes intimal and adventitial thickening in association with arterial hypermyotrophy.

Intolerant, *a.* Add: **1. b.** *Forestry.* Incapable of enduring heavy shade. *U.S.*
1898 Pinchot *Adirondack Spruce* 5 The Poplar, a tree very intolerant of shade..rapidly takes possession of the soil. *Ibid.* 22 If the intolerant species can get the start, being often rapid of growth, they may hold their position by growing above the other trees about them, as do Tamarack and Pine. 1905 *Terms Forestry & Logging* 14.

Intra (i·ntră), *prep.* [L., = within.] In phr. *intra vires*, within the powers or legal authority (*of* a person, etc.).
1884 *Law Times* LXXVIII. 110 (Stanford) If this were *intra vires*, the other securities which they had accepted were not *bonâ fide* ones. 1930 A. Palmer *Company Secretarial Practice* 185 Excess borrowing *intra vires* of the company but *ultra vires* of the directors may be ratified by ordinary resolution.

Intra-. **1.** Add:
I:ntra-ato·mic, within an atom. **Intracho·rdal**, within the notochord. **I:ntracuta·neous, -de·rmal, -de·rmic, -epide·rmic**, between the layers of the skin. **Intrafi·ssural**, within a fissure of the brain. **Intraga·stric**, occurring or situated within the stomach. **Intragla·cial**, within a glacier. **Intramu·scularly** *adv.*, (by injection) into the muscles. **Intrana·tal**, during birth. **Intrara·cial**, within a race. **Intrase·minal** *Bot.*, occurring or existing within a seed; also, within the seminal fluid. **I:ntravagi·nal** (*b*) *Bot.*, within the sheath of a leaf. **Intrave·rtebral**, within a vertebra; hence **Intrave·rtebrally** *adv.*
Also in many other combinations of obvious meaning (see quots.).
1901 M. H. Fischer in *Jrnl. Exper. Med.* V. 347 Finkelstein has suggested the possibility of the production of a diverticulum from increased *intra-appendicular pressure. 1890 Billings *Med. Dict.*, *Intra-articular, pertaining to the interior of a joint. 1908 *Practitioner* Apr. 516 Intra-articular effusion into both knee-joints. 1904 *Nature* 16 June 151/2 Enormous orbital velocities due to *intra-atomic re-arrangement. 1896 H. Gadow in *Phil. Trans.* Ser. B. CLXXXVII. 10 This 'chordal, intravertebral, or *intra-chordal' cartilage has been almost completely ignored in the various text-books. 1903 Dorland *Med. Dict.* (ed. 3), *Intracutaneous. 1921 E. B. Titchener *Text-Bk. Psychol.* 153 Intracutaneous injection of salt solution. 1901 Dorland *Med. Dict.* (ed. 2), *Intradermal, *intradermic, situated or applied within the skin. 1928 *Daily Tel.* 6 Nov. 7/7 Test for tuberculosis among cattle..the 'double intradermal test'. 1890 Billings *Med. Dict.*, *Intradural, within the dura mater. 1908 *Practitioner* Jan. 84 Subcutaneous injection of the meningococcus into animals fails to produce the disease, intra-dural injection being required. 1910 *Ibid.* June 871 An *intra-epidermic abscess. 1901 Dorland *Med. Dict.* (ed. 2), *Intragastric, situated or occurring within the stomach. 1903 G. Herschell *Man. Intragastric Technique* 107 The intragastric needle-douche..may be described as the application of fine jets of fluid under considerable pressure to the interior of the stomach. 1895 Dana *Man. Geol.* (ed. 4) 958 It was *intraglacial, as now in Greenland. 1909 *Practitioner* Nov. 682 *Intraglandular enucleation..should be performed. 1908 *Ibid.* Jan. 80 Jochmann had convinced himself..that an *intralumbar injection could be trusted to penetrate to the base of brain. 1903 Geikie *Textbk. Geol.* VI. v. (ed. 4) 1342 Drifts in the *intra-morainic and extra-morainic areas. 1909 *Practitioner* Dec. 871 Digalen..can be used by the mouth, by the rectum, intravenously, *intramuscularly, and hypodermically. 1902 *Encycl. Brit.* XXXI. 304/1 The causes of the high death-rate among infants, whether due to ante-natal, *intra-natal, or neo-natal conditions, come under..observation. 1923 G. O'Brien *Ess. Econ. Effects Reform.* iv. 179 It is an institution at once *intranational and international. 1902 *Proc. Zool. Soc.* I. 218 An increasing tendency of *intraperiosteal growth reached a large size. 1903 *Phil. Trans.* Ser. B. CXCV. 210 Ciliated discs are situated on the sides of long spurs or in-growths from the interlamellar (*intraplical) edge of the filament. 1894 *Ibid.* CLXXXV. 765 *Intrapontine Section of the Motor Root. 1903 *Biometrika* Feb. 152 The interracial correlation of the mean numbers of stamens and pistils is very much greater than the mean *intraracial correlation between stamens and pistils. 1906 *Practitioner* Dec. 816 The bleeding is wholly *intrarenal. 1906 Dorland *Med. Dict.* (ed. 4). 1900 I. B. Balfour tr. *K. Goebel's Organ. Plants, Index* II. 677/2 *Intraseminal absorption of endosperm. 1900 B. D. Jackson *Gloss. Bot. Terms*, *Intraseminal development*, the whole development undergone by the embryo during the conversion of the ovule into the ripe seed. 1902 *Nature* 3 Apr. 519/1 Seeds from infected plants are entirely free from disease, thereby proving fairly conclusively the impossibility of intra-seminal sources of infection. 1930 *Ann. Botany* Oct. 772 The germination of the seed is reported as 'intra-seminal'. 1908 *Practitioner* Nov. 699 *Intrastomachic haemorrhage. 1890 Billings *Med. Dict.*, *Intratympanic, within the tympanic cavity. 1908 *Practitioner* Jan. 118 The intratympanic muscles.. become much weakened in their action. 1900 I. B. Balfour tr. *K. Goebel's Organ. Plants* II. 359 *Intravaginal squamules in the axil of the leaf-base. 1896 H. Gadow in *Phil. Trans.* Ser. B. CLXXXVII. 10 One of the last changes of importance in the appearance of *intravertebral cartilage. *Ibid.* 12 In all Amphibia and Amniota each spinal nerve lies intravertibrally, *i.e.* issues behind the dorsal arch of its vertebra.

Intracranially (intrăkrē·niăli), *adv.* [f. Intracranial *a.* + -ly [2].] Within the cranium.
1908 *Practitioner* Aug. 296 Rabbits were inoculated intracranially with the fluid.

Intrad (i·ntræd), *adv. Anat.* [f. Intra- + *-ad.] Within, towards the interior.
1901 Dorland *Med. Dict.* (ed. 2).

Intrada (intrā·dă). *Mus.* [Modified f. It. *intrata*, older form of *entrata* entry, prelude.] An introduction or prelude; = Entrée 3 b.
a 1700 in *Grove's Dict. Mus.* (1883) III. 756/1 [In Purcell's suites, for instance, which date from the last 10 or 20 years of the 17th century, besides the Allemande and Courante.. in one case the group also comprises a] Sarabande, Cebell, Minuet, Riggadoon, Intrade, and March. 1876 Stainer & Barrett *Dict. Mus. Terms.*

Intramurally (-miū·răli), *adv.* [Intra- 1.] Within the walls or boundaries.
1927 *Observer* 5 June 7/2 The University College of the South-West..has developed considerably both intra- and extra-murally.

Intra·nsigeance. [Fr.] = Intransigence.
1899 Mackail *Life W. Morris* II. 291 Socialism..from extreme intransigeance..had swung back to something approaching opportunism.

Intransigeantly (intrǽ·nsidʒăntli), *adv.* [f. F. *intransigeant* (see Intransigent) + -ly [2].] Uncompromisingly.
1921 *Contemp. Rev.* Sept. 331 The peasants are intransigeantly anti-Karlist. 1925 *Glasgow Herald* 17 Mar. 8 The advocates of an intransigeantly nationalist policy.

Intransitable, *a.* (U.S. and later examples.)
1838 'Texian' *Mexico v. Texas* 9 In that singular region of Mexico..there extends..a desert..so utterly devoid of water and vegetation as to be intransitable. 1897 *Geog. Jrnl.* X. 64 A road along the coast would become lost in intransitable gorges of the coast range of mountains.

Intransmissibility (i:ntrǝnsmisibi·lĭti). [f. Intransmissible *a.* + -ity.] The state or quality of being intransmissible.
1913 H. Goudy in *Ess. Legal Hist.* 225 The passive intransmissibility of actions of Debt and Account.

Intransparency (intrǝnspē·rĕnsi, -pæ·r-). [f. Intransparent *a.*: see -ency.] The quality of being opaque; also, an instance of this.
1902 *Encycl. Brit.* XXXI. 570/1 The intransparency caused by a mere infiltration generally clears away in the course of time. *Ibid.*, Centrally placed intransparencies, which cover the pupil, are relatively the most disturbing.

Intravascularly (-væ·skiŭlăli), *adv.* [f. Intravascular *a.* + -ly [2].] Within the vascular system.
1906 *Practitioner* Dec. 754 A powerful anti-human serum may be injected intravascularly in man without necessarily producing the serum disease.

Intrigue, *v.* Add: **5.** *trans.* To excite the curiosity or interest of; to interest so as to puzzle or fascinate. Also *absol.* (A modern gallicism.)
1894 *Month* May 122 The publishers often become so intrigued by these claims of authorship, that we find them at times passing by the matter altogether. 1896 [in Dict., sense 1]. 1900 *Westm. Gaz.* 5 Dec. 2/2 We do agree most heartily, but the observation intrigues us not a little. 1909 H. G. Wells *Ann Veronica* iii. § 7, 'I must confess,' he said, 'the New Woman and the New Girl intrigue me profoundly.' 1918 Quiller Couch *Studies Lit.* Ser. I. 147 These theological poets and preachers of the seventeenth century..were intrigued..by man's lapse from a state of innocence. 1924 W. M. Raine *Troubled Waters* xxi. 225 The conspiracy she proposed intrigued his interest.

Intriguing, *ppl. a.* Add: Also, in sense of prec. Hence **Intri·guingly** *adv.*
1909 *Daily Chron.* 29 Apr. 3/2 A brisk, intriguing, and entertaining story. 1920 *Isis* 27 Oct. 2/1 Edited..by three members of Oriel..with a longish and intriguing introduction by Mr. John Masefield. 1922 *Blackw. Mag.* June 778/2 The line of alders on the far bank was intriguingly punctuated with squatting figures.

Introcision (introsi·ʒən). [f. L. *intrō* inwardly + *-cision* of *incision*.] An incision into the body.
1902 *Encycl. Brit.* XXV. 797/2 Early in life the young girls are subjected to horrible mutilation (introcision), which is in some obscure way associated with quite a different operation, 'the terrible rite' or male introcision, to which young men are subjected.

Introduction. Add: **5. d.** The person to whom one is introduced.
1899 H. G. Wells *When Sleeper Wakes* xv, He bowed condescendingly to his first introduction...This first introduction was the Master Aëronaut.

Introessive (-e·siv), *a. Gram.* [f. L. *intro* within + *esse* to be + -ive.] Designating the case which expresses 'motion into'.
1903 *Amer. Anthropologist* Jan.–Mar. 13 Besides a general locative some of the most frequently occurring are inessive, superessive, introessive, ablative, and terminative.

Introitus (intrō̆·itŏs). *Anat.* [L.] The entrance into a canal or cavity.
1901 Dorland *Med. Dict.* (ed. 2). 1908 *Practitioner* June 807 A retroversion of the uterus..can be effectually treated ..so long as the introitus is intact.

Introspectionism (introspe·kʃəniz'm). *Psychol.* [f. Introspection + -ism.] Introspective psychology (see next).
1922 Woodworth *Psychol.* ii. 21 Without caring to attach ourselves exclusively to either introspectionism or behaviourism. 1931 *Psyche* Jan. 68 Straightforward introspectionism, on the whole, judged by the contents of this book, has very little status in modern psychology.

Introspective, *a.* Add: *Introspective psychology*, psychology based on introspection and on the direct observation of one's own mental states.
1911 Webster. 1931 Woodworth *Contemp. Schools Psychol.* ii. 17 What we do find..is..more precise formulation of the aim of introspective psychology.

Introuvable (æ̃ntruvā·bl), *a.* [Fr.] Unfindable, undiscoverable.
1824 *Edin. Rev.* Mar. 2 We are by no means of opinion that it [*sc.* a correct standard of national prosperity] is really *introuvable*. *a* 1856 in *Newsp. & Gen. Reader's Comp.* § 1436 Give me a mere *annonce* of any thing, that can tell me of your *introuvable* friend. 1895 H. Buxton Forman in *Nicoll & Wise's Lit. Anecd. 19th Cent.* 67 The almost introuvable tract *Prothanasia and other Poems.*

Introversion. Add: **1. b.** *Psychol.* The turning of the thoughts and activities exclusively to that which is within, i.e. to the self and its interests; opp. to *Extraversion.
1916 tr. *Jung's Coll. Papers Anal. Psychol.* 289 In the same way I shall call 'regressive introversion', the opposite pathological phenomenon which we find in dementia præcox, where the subject himself suffers these phantastical transfigurations.

Introvert, *sb.* Add:
2. *Psychol.* A person characterized by introversion (see above): also *attrib.* So **I·ntroverted** *ppl. a.*, said of such a person, or his activities, etc.
1916 tr. *Jung's Coll. Papers Anal. Psychol.* 348 The introverted type is characterised by the fact that his libido is turned towards his own personality to a certain extent. *Ibid.* 349 An Extravert can hardly conceive the necessity which compels the Introvert to conquer the world by means of a system. 1920 *Challenge* 21 May 44/2 All works of the imagination are conceived by men of the introvert type. 1923 T. P. Nunn *Education* 143 An 'introvert' concerned mainly with his own feelings and thoughts. 1924 tr. *Freud's Collected Papers* II. 114 When these [*sc.* dispositional factors] are present in sufficient strength there arises the danger of the libido becoming introverted. 1925 C. Fox *Educat. Psychol.* 254 The introvert abstracts from the object and deals with it by concepts concentrating upon the inner world of thought.

Intrusive, *a.* Add: **B.** *sb.* An intrusive rock.
1895 A. Harker *Petrol. Students* vii. 87 Acid Intrusives. The acid intrusive rocks embrace a considerable range of varieties. 1925 Odell in E. F. Norton *Fight for Everest, 1924* 300 Yet the character of the former [*sc.* the limestone series] may be entirely due to its proximity to the hard crystalline rocks and its alteration brought about by pressure against them, if not also by their igneous intrusives.

Intuited (intiū·itĕd), *ppl. a.* [f. Intuit *v.* + -ed [1].] Arrived at or known by intuition.
1886 A. Weir *Hist. Basis Mod. Europe* (1889) 481 The mathematical sciences..drew their conclusions from intuited figures and series. 1890 W. James *Princ. Psychol.* I. 630 Meanwhile, the specious present, the intuited duration, stands permanent, like the rainbow on the waterfall, with its own quality unchanged by the events that stream through it.

Inturn, *sb.* Add: **4.** *Curling.* A turn inwards of the elbow made in delivering a stone.
1897 *Encycl. Sport* I. 262/1 The inturn is made when the curl is to be toward the right.

Intussusceptum (i:ntŏs,sŏse·ptŏm). *Path.* [mod.L., neut. sing. of *intussusceptus*: see Intussuscept *v.*] A portion of intestine which is invaginated with another portion.
1857 Dunglison *Med. Lex.* s.v. *Intussusceptio*, The introduction of one part of the intestinal canal—*intussusceptum* —into another, which serves it as a sort of vagina or sheath. 1901 Dorland *Med. Dict.* (ed. 2).

Intussuscipiens (i:ntŏs,sŏsi·pienz). *Path.* [mod.L., pres. pple. of *intussuscipere*: cf. prec.] The portion of intestine which invaginates an intussusceptum.
1857 Dunglison *Med. Lex.* s.v. *Intussusceptio*, It is the upper part of the small intestine, which is received into the lower—*intussuscipiens*—when the intussusception is said to be progressive. 1908 *Practitioner* Mar. 367 The ends of the bowel are..reduced through the opening in the intussuscipiens.

Inulase (i·niŭlēs). *Chem.* [f. Inula: see *-ase.] An enzyme which converts inulin into fructose.
1899 J. R. Green *Soluble Ferments* 77 The transformation of inulin into sugar is brought about by the action of an enzyme to which the name *inulase* has been given. The existence of this enzyme was first demonstrated by the writer in 1887, when the germination of the tuber of the artichoke was made a subject of examination.

Inule (i·niŭl). [ad. L. Inula.] A plant of the genus *Inula.*
1858 G. Bentham *Handbk. Brit. Flora* 293 Rigid Inule... Common Inule.

Inundatal (i·nʊndǣtăl), *a. Bot.* [irreg. f. Inundate *v.* + -al.] Growing in areas subject to flooding.
1847 H. C. Watson *Cybele Brit.* I. 65 Inundatal. Plants of places liable to be inundated in wet weather, but often dry in summer. 1926 *Nat. Hist. Oxford Distr.* 88 Paludal flora (including uliginal and inundatal species).

Inundation. Add: **1. b.** *attrib.*: *inundation canal.*
1886 *Encycl. Brit.* XX. 108/2. 1902 *Ibid.* XXIX. 599/1 The 'inundation canals' of the Punjab, which utilize the flood waters in the rivers during the monsoon season, and are dry at other times.

Invalidism. (Later U.S. example.)
1925 H. L. Foster *Trop. Tramp Tourists* 83 A sort of personal pride in his invalidism.

Invalidy (i·nvălĭdi), *a. colloq.* [f. Invalid *sb.* + -y [1].] Of the nature of an invalid.
1894 Mrs. H. Ward *Marcella* III. 9 She's fussy, you know, and invalidy, and has to be wrapped up in shawls. 1912 'R. Dehan' *Between two Thieves* 620 We invaded the Crimea with a weakly, invalidy, or crippled army.

Invar (i·nvaɹ). [Abbreviation of Invariable *a.*] A trade-name for an alloy of nickel and steel in which the coefficient of expansion is negligible. Also *attrib.*
1902 *Encycl. Brit.* XXXIII. 805/2 Guillaume's alloy (*invar*) of nickel (35·7 per cent.) and steel (64·3 per cent.). 1921 *Glasgow Herald* 9 Nov. 11 Concentric brass and 'invar' tubes. 1929 Ratcliffe *Phys. Princ. Wireless* iii. 50 A tuning-fork made of 'invar' metal.

Inventory, *v.* Add: **2.** *intr.* and *trans.* To amount to or be worth (so much) on an inventory.
1902 G. H. Lorimer *Lett. Self-made Merchant* ix. 113 The last time I saw her, she inventoried about $10,000 as she stood. 1905 *Springfield* (Mass.) *Weekly Republ.* 20 Oct. 12 The late Senator Platt left an estate which inventories at $20,880.

Inverse, *sb.* Add:
3. *Rouge et Noir.* The section at the end of the table in which are placed bets wagering that the colour of the card that wins the coup will not be the same as that first dealt for a colour.
1867 *Bohn's Hand-bk. Games* 343 If the player..be determined to try his luck on the inverse, he must place his money on a yellow circle, or rather a collection of circles, situated at the extremity of the table. *Ibid.*, The punters place on the Rouge, the Noir, the Couleur, or the Inverse, the sum they wish to risk.

Inversion. Add: **10.** In full, *sexual inversion*: inversion of the sex instincts.
1896 J. A. Symonds (*title*) A Problem in Modern Ethics, being an Enquiry into the Phenomenon of Sexual Inversion. 1897 H. Havelock Ellis *Stud. Psychol. Sex* I. 139 Another exciting cause of inversion..is disappointment in normal love.

Invert, *sb.* Add: **2.** *Teleg.* An inverted insulator.
1876 Preece & Sivewright *Telegraphy* 224 An effort is at present being made to introduce a form of invert in which the bolt passes nearly to the top of the insulating material.
3. *Psychol.* One whose sex instincts are inverted. (Cf. *Inversion 10; *Inverted 3 c.)
1897 H. Havelock Ellis *Stud. Psychol. Sex* I. 12 Caesar was proud of his physical beauty, and like many modern inverts he was accustomed carefully to shave his skin. *Ibid.* 144 The sexual invert is specially liable to suffer from a high degree of neurasthenia. 1921 R. W. Chambers *Common Law* i. 29 This world is full of pale, enraptured artists;..full of unwashed little inverts.

Invertase (i·nvəɹtēs). *Chem.* [f. Invert *v.* + *-ase.] = Invertin.
1899 J. R. Green *Soluble Ferments* 113 Invertase is said by Mieran to be present in the ripe fruit of the Banana. 1902 *Encycl. Brit.* XXVIII. 556/1 Among the enzymes already extracted from fungi are invertases (yeasts, moulds, etc.), which split cane-sugar, and other complex sugars with hydrolysis into simpler sugars.

Inverted, *ppl. a.* Add: **3. c.** *Psychol.* spec. of the sex instincts.
1897 H. Havelock Ellis *Stud. Psychol. Sex* I. 16 The painter Bazzi seems to have been radically inverted. *Ibid.* 156 Social opinion is most amply adequate to deal with the manifestations of inverted sexuality.

Invertor. Add: **2.** *Anat.* A muscle which turns or rotates inward.
1903 *Lancet* 4 July 56/2 If either the evertor or invertor is out of use the combined action of these muscles..becomes impossible.

Investigational (investigē·ʃənăl), *a.* [f. Investigation + -al.] Of or pertaining to investigation.
1905 *Science* 29 Sept. 387/1 Investigational apparatus of great importance. 1930 *Aberdeen Press & Jrnl.* 4 Sept. 7/3 An unprecedented demand for botanical specialists to fill investigational and advisory posts.

Investment. **5. b.** *attrib.* Add: **investment trust**, a trust whose profits are derived from its holdings of selected investments; also *attrib.*
1924 L. M. Speaker *Investment Trusts* 3 The investment trust in its characteristic form is an institution mainly of British origin. It is essentially a corporation, the business of which consists chiefly of judicious investment of its capital. 1929 *Observer* 17 Nov. 2/3 Among the many high-class securities which have had to be sold to meet the demand for money caused by the depressed conditions have been the junior stocks of the large investment trust companies.

Inviable (invəi·ăb'l), *a.* [f. In-[3] + Viable *a.*[1]] Unable to survive. Hence **Inviabi·lity.**
1929 *Encycl. Brit.* XI. 495/1 In this case the F_2 generation, and the results of back-crossing F_1 to either parent, are usually polymorphic, and may include monstrous or more or less inviable forms. In certain cases, owing to the inviability of most gametic and zygotic combinations, the F_2 consists entirely of types resembling one or other parent fairly closely.

Invisible, *a.* Add: **1. d.** *Invisible exports, imports*: those items which do not appear in returns of exports and imports yet for which payment has to be accepted from or made to a foreign country, such as shipping services, insurance, profits on foreign investments, etc.
1911 C. G. Robertson *Eng. under Hanoverians* II. iv. 344 Prior to the Industrial Revolution the seaborne and carrying trades, with their invisible exports, are an expanding source of wealth, but are not indispensable. 1919 J. A. Todd *Mech. Exchange* xiv. 174 An invisible export is something which enables a country to import goods without paying for them directly by the export of other goods, and conversely, an invisible import is something which makes it necessary for a country to export goods without receiving payment directly in other goods. 1923 *Westm. Gaz.* 24 Feb., Depressed shipping means less insurance, less banking, and a smaller earning in freights—all the things we mean when we speak of our invisible exports.

Invita Minerva (invəi·tă minɔ̄·ɹvă). [L., = 'Minerva (the goddess of wisdom) unwilling'.] When one is not in the vein or mood, without inspiration.
1584 R. Scot *Discov. Witchcr.* XII. iii. 219 It should be vnto them (*Inuita Minerua*) to banket or danse with Minerua. 1626 Bacon *Sylva* § 2,2 That nothing bee done *Inuitâ Mineruâ*, but *Secundum Genium*. *a* 1855 in *Newsp. & Gen. Reader's Comp.* § 509 Haydn never began a symphony *invita Minerva.*

Invite, *v.* **1. a.** Add: *To invite in*: to ask (a person) to come into one's house.
1875 *Harper's Mag.* Aug. 417 She found a house where she was invited in. 1888 Mrs. H. Ward *R. Elsmere* xxii, It was evidently the Squire's purpose to come in, so Robert invited him in. 1899 Adelaide Skeel & W. H. Brearley *King Washington* 37 Being occupied in a nice calculation whether or not her breakfast menu would stand the strain of an extra appetite should Mr. Ettrick..invite the captain in.

Invoice, *sb.* **c.** Add: *invoice clerk, man, porter.*
1921 *Dict. Occup. Terms* (1927) §§ 706, 939.

Involute (i·nvŏl(i)ūt), *v.* [Back-formation from Involuted *a.* 2.] *intr.* To become involute or undergo involution.
a 1909 *Buck's Handbk. Med. Sci.* VII. 782 (Cent. D. Suppl.) A circular scaly pink patch that spreads peripherally with a pinkish border, and clears up or involutes in the central portion. 1910 *Practitioner* July 106 The uterus had involuted normally.

Involutionary (invŏl(i)ū·ʃənări), *a.* [f. Involution + -ary.] Characterized by involution; retrograde.
1920 *Discovery* Nov. 338/2 Our conceptions of psychical.. 'regression'.., the backward or involutionary path of mental processes to more infantile conditions.

Inworker. Add: **2.** One who works on the premises of a shop or factory.
1909 *Fabian News* XX. 75/1 A minimum wage for both inworkers and outworkers.

Io [2] (əi·o). [L., a. Gr. Ἰώ, daughter of the river god Inachus, loved by Zeus.]
1. *Astron.* The innermost satellite of the planet Jupiter.
1866 Lockyer *Guillemin's Heavens* 232. 1929 *Encycl. Brit.* XIII. 190/2.
2. In full *Io moth*: A large moth of North America, *Automeris* or *Hyperchiria Io*, having prominent ocelli on each hind wing.
1889 *Cent. Dict.* 1912 Gene Stratton-Porter *Moths of Limberlost* viii. 207 Mr. Eisen presented me with a pair of Hyperchiria Io...Because the Io was yellow, I wanted it.

Iodipin (əi,ō·dipin). *Pharm.* [ad. G. *Jodipin*, It. *Jodipinia*: f. Iodine + L. *adip-, adeps* fat + -in [1].] A compound of iodine and sesame oil used medicinally.
1901 Dorland *Med. Dict.* (ed. 2). 1908 *Westm. Gaz.* 25 July 16/1 A solution of iodipin in oil.

Iodo-. Add: **a. I:odo-cre·sol**, a compound of iodine and cresol used as a substitute for iodoform. **I:odo-pro·teid**, an iodized proteid. **I:odo-ricino·leate**, a salt containing iodine and a ricinoleate. **I:odospo·ngin**, an iodo-proteid found in sponges. **I:odothy·rin** = Thyro-iodine.
1892 Morley & Muir *Watts' Dict. Chem.* III. 31/2 *Iodo-cresol sulphonic acid. 1907 *Practitioner* June 864 Iodalbin... This is an *iodo-proteid compound containing 21–5 per cent. of iodine. *Ibid.* Dec. 864 Calcium *iodo-ricinoleate is a new salt, containing a large proportion of iodine. 1898 *Jrnl. Chem. Soc.* LXXIV. I. 717 *Iodospongin, an iodised proteid present in ordinary sponge. 1897 *Ibid.* LXXII. II. 330 Effect of Fresh Thyroid and *Iodothyrin on Metabolism. 1929 *Encycl. Brit.* XXII. 173/2 A proteid known as thyreoglobulin, the active principle of which..is known as iodothyrin or thyroiodin.
b. Io·dophile *a.*, readily absorbing or combining with iodine. **Iodophi·lia** *Path.*, a condition of the blood in which the leucocytes readily stain with iodine.
1902 *Encycl. Brit.* XXXII. 817/2 The Myxobolidæ..which have an *iodophile vacuole. 1910 *Practitioner* Jan. 95 The disappearance of the iodophile granules after the crisis seems to depend upon some chemical change taking place in the protoplasm of the cell. *Ibid.* 96 The nuclei..are quite unlike the normal iodophile leucocyte with the sharply defined nucleus. 1902 A. Locke in *Boston Med. Jrnl.* 11 Sept. 290/1 A faint extracellular *iodophilia is present in all individuals. 1910 *Practitioner* Jan. 90 From 1 per cent. to 12 per cent., showed 'faint' iodophilia.

Iodonium (əiˌōdōᵘ·niŏm). *Chem.* [f. IOD(INE + ending of AMMONIUM.] A hypothetical, univalent, basic radical, IH_2, analogous to the radicals ammonium (NH_4) and phosphonium (PH_4).
1894 *Jrnl. Chem. Soc.* LXVI. I. 242 A derivative of the hypothetical base $IH_2 \cdot OH$ (iodonium hydroxide), analogous to hydroxylamine. *Ibid.* 462 The analogy between the iodonium compounds and the salts of the heavy metals also extends to the sulphur compounds of the base. 1927 SIDGWICK *Electronic The. Valency* iv. 67 The well-known iodonium salts.

Iodoso- (əi·ǫdōᵘso), used as combining form of IODOUS to denote the presence of the univalent radical IO.
1894 *Jrnl. Chem. Soc.* LXVI. I. 415 Iodoso- and Iodoxy-compounds.

Iodoxy- (əi·ǫdǫksi). *Chem.* [f. IODO- + OXY(GEN.] An element in names of chemical compounds signifying the presence of the univalent iodoxyl radical IO_2. 1894 [see *IODOSO-].

Ion. Substitute: Either of the products (see ANION, CATION) which appear at the respective poles when a substance is subjected to electrolysis; hence, any of the electrically charged particles which are released by dissociation in an electrolyte; a molecule or atom considered electrically; a gaseous particle electrically charged by the action of Röntgen or other rays, etc. Also *attrib.*
1833 FARADAY in *Phil. Trans.* (1834) CXXIV. 79 Finally, I require a term to express those bodies which can pass to the *electrodes*, or, as they are usually called, the poles...I propose to distinguish these bodies by calling those *anions* which go to the *anode* of the decomposing body; and those passing to the *cathode*, *cations*; and when I have occasion to speak of these together, I shall call them *ions*. 1902 SIR J. J. THOMSON in *Encycl. Brit.* XXVIII. 26/1 We thus regard the conductivity of the gas as due to the presence of electrified particles...These particles we shall call *ions*, but they must not be assumed to be the same as the ions in the electrolysis of solutions. 1904 tr. *W. Nernst's Theoretical Chem.* (ed. 2) 394 If the velocity of the electron is very great, it may produce a relatively large number of positive and negative gas ions. 1909 J. W. JENKINSON *Exper. Embryol.* 136 A physiologically balanced solution is necessary, one in which the electrolytes are in a state of chemical equilibrium with the necessary ion-proteid compounds in the tissues. 1927 SIDGWICK *Electronic The. Valency* 91 In a crystal like calcium carbonate we find the same kind of relation between the calcium ion and the CO_3 ion, but a different one for the constituent atoms of the CO_3 group itself:..and this may be taken as evidence that the calcium and the CO_3 are themselves ions.

-ion, *suffix*², the word ION added to the abbreviated Latin forms of the names of elements and radicals to describe these in their dissociated ionized state, as *cuprion*, *sulphidion*, after ANION, CATION.

Ionamine (əi·ǫnămīn, -əin). *Chem.* [f. Gr. ἴον violet + AMINE.] One of a class of dyestuffs having a special affinity for real and artificial silk.
1922 *Glasgow Herald* 24 Apr. 10 By a suitable choice of cotton dyestuffs and 'ionamines' it is possible to produce by subsequent chemical changes on the fibre a still greater range of shades. 1924 KINGZETT *Chem. Encycl.* (ed. 3) 303 'Ionamines', a new class of dyestuffs of promising value for dyeing artificial acetate silk, etc.

Ione (əi·ōᵘn). *Geol.* The name of a village in California used to designate a formation in the middle division of the Tertiary strata.
1906 CHAMBERLIN & SALISBURY *Geol.* III. 264 Contemporaneous deposits of estuarine, lacustrine, and probably subaërial origin (Ione formation) were being made.

Ionic, *a.*² Add: Also, of or pertaining to ions (*ION 2).
1898 [see Dict.]. 1913 *Q. Rev.* July 122 A knowledge of the total mass of water precipitated by the expansion enabled Mr. Wilson..to estimate the number of ionic nuclei required to form the cloud.
b. *Med.* Pertaining to medication in the form of ions. (Cf. *IONIZATION² 4.)
1910 *Practitioner* Jan. 126 Of ionic treatment I have had no experience.

Ionium (əiˌōᵘ·niŏm). *Chem.* [mod.L., f. *ION 2 + -IUM.] A radioactive element obtained from uranium by disintegration and remarkable for its powerful ionization of the surrounding air.
1907 B. B. BOLTWOOD in *Amer. Jrnl. Sci.* Ser. IV. XXIV. 372 The name 'Ionium' is proposed for this new substance, a name derived from the word 'ion'. This name is believed to be appropriate because of the ionizing action which it possesses in common with the other elements which emit α-radiations. 1912 SODDY *Matter & Energy* ix. 220 It is known that the change of uranium into radium is not direct, but that an intermediate substance, ionium, which does produce radium steadily with the lapse of time, intervenes.

Ionization² (əiˌǫnəizē̆·ʃən). [f. IONIZE *v.*² + -ATION.]
1. The dissociation of molecules into ions in an electrolyte.
1901 B. BLOUNT *Pract. Electro-Chem.* 16 Evidence of complete ionisation is forthcoming only when the solution of sodium chloride is exceedingly dilute. 1907 C. L. VON ENDE tr. *Abegg's Electrolytic Dissoc. Theory* 154 That ionization in non-aqueous solutions is so small, as a rule, essentially because of the great amount of association.
2. The production of ions in a gas.
1898 *Nature* 8 Dec. 142/1 The measurements of the ionisation produced by Röntgen rays in fourteen gases showed that the ionisation was connected with the chemical composition in a very simple manner. 1902 SIR J. J. THOMSON in *Encycl. Brit.* XXVIII. 26/1 The process by which the gas is changed into a conductor we shall call the *ionization* of the gas. 1928 D. BRUNT *Meteorology* x. 99 A lightning discharge..building up its complicated structure piecemeal by progressive ionization, the branching being always away from the positive charge.
3. Dissociation into ions in a solid.
1927 SIDGWICK *Electronic The. Valency* 90 With the simpler inorganic salts, such as sodium chloride, we have direct evidence of ionization in the solid from the phenomenon of residual rays.
4. *Med.* The introduction of therapeutics into the body in the form of ions.
1908 *Practitioner* Oct. 563 Cocaine from the positive pole and salicylate of soda from the negative pole..have been made use of by the new treatment of ionisation. 1917 'CONTACT' *Airman's Outings* 322 The department where they dispense massage and ionisation.
5. *attrib.*
1910 *Practitioner* June 785 The modern zinc mercury ionisation treatment is a very definite way of directly applying powerful drugs to a diseased area. 1919 J. A. CROWTHER *Ions, Electrons*, etc. 9 Ionization theory of gaseous conduction. *Ibid.* 14 The ionization chamber. *Ibid.* 52 Ionization currents with large voltages.

Ionize, *v.*² Read:
1. *intr.* Of an electrolyte: To split up into ions.
1899 *Nature* 30 Nov. 114/1 The only ionising inorganic solvents hitherto found in addition to water are nitric acid and liquefied ammonia. 1901 B. BLOUNT *Pract. Electro-Chem.* 16 Solutions of moderate strength..behave as if a portion of the molecules were ionised and a portion were present as ordinary molecules. 1930 FIELD & WEILL *Electro-Plating* 92 Copper sulphate ionises as follows.
2. *trans.* Of X rays, cathode and other rays, an electric field, etc.: To produce ions in a gas and so make it a conductor. Also *absol.*
1898 [see Dict.]. 1902 *Encycl. Brit.* XXVIII. 26/1 The increase is not sufficient to make the electric field ionize the gas. 1926 *Ibid.* Suppl. II. 146 An ion with a mass equal to that of a molecule of oxygen would not ionise unless its energy were greater than 136,000 volts.
Hence **I·onized** *ppl. a.*; **I·onizing** *vbl. sb.* and *ppl. a.*; **I·onizer**, a device for producing the ionization of a gas or liquid (*Cent. D.* Suppl. 1909).
1902 *Encycl. Brit.* XXVIII. 15/2 Towards the explanation of ionizing power some advance has been made. *Ibid.* 36/1 The ordinary characteristics of discharge through ionized gas. 1919 J. A. CROWTHER *Ions, Electrons*, etc. 28 Then the rate of increase in the number of ions per unit volume of the gas is equal to the number formed per second by the action of the ionizing agent less the number lost by recombination. 1927 A. S. EDDINGTON *Stars & Atoms* 19, I can show you the other method of ionizing atoms by battering of a more mechanical kind.

Ionogen (əi·ǫnŏdʒĕn). *Physics.* [f. ION + -O- + -GEN I.] A compound which produces ions when in solution; an electrolyte.
1906 A. SMITH *Gen. Inorg. Chem.* 321 An ion may be defined as, an atom or group of atoms bearing a positive or negative charge of electricity, and formed through the dissociation of an ionogen by a solvent like water. 1922 J. MILLS *Within the Atom* vi. 66 Quite a large group of chemical compounds will dissociate in this manner and these are known as ionogens or electrolytes.

Ionone (əi·ǒnōᵘn). *Chem.* [f. Gr. ἴον violet + -ONE.] One of a group of hydro-aromatic ketones derived from lemon-grass and having the odour of violets.
1894 *Jrnl. Chem. Soc.* LXVI. I. 82 Ionone..has a characteristic odour resembling that of violets. 1906 *Technol. & Sci. Dict.* (ed. Goodchild & Tweney) 758/1 Ionone is a mixture of two stereoisomers. 1922 SUDBOROUGH *Bernthsen's Org. Chem.* 628 These chemists have synthesised two isomerides of irone, which they term α- and β-ionones.

Ionoplasty (əi·ǫnoplæsti). [f. ION + -O- + -PLASTY.] The electrolytic deposition of metals.
1904 *Jrnl. Phys. Chem.* Nov. 583 Study of thin films of copper obtained by ionoplasty.

Ioqua, variant of *HIAQUA.

Iowan (əi·ǒwăn), *sb.* and *a.* Also formerly Iowaian (from the pronunciation *Ioway* of *Iowa*, which is still heard). [f. *Iowa*, name of one of the United States of America, formerly of a tribe of Indians inhabiting Iowa and Minnesota.] **A.** *sb.* A native or inhabitant of Iowa.
1856 N. H. PARKER *Iowa as it is* 56 Our ferry is busy all hours in passing over the large canvas-backed wagons, densely populated with becoming Iowaians. 1927 *Glasgow Herald* 6 Apr. 12 Iowans..used to console themselves by telling the world..that their largest city had the greatest consumption of ice-cream per head of population.
B. *adj.* Of or pertaining to Iowa; *spec.* in *Geol.*, denoting certain glacial formations occurring in Iowa, or the period in which they were formed.
1894 J. GEIKIE *Gt. Ice Age* (ed. 3) 735 The chief track of the current from the Hudsonian centre was down the Dakotan and central Iowan basins. *Ibid.* 760 The East-Iowan till-sheet..is not usually bordered by any definite terminal moraine. The designation 'East-Iowan formation' is chosen because it has been most carefully worked out by Mr. McGee in north-eastern Iowa. 1906 CHAMBERLIN & SALISBURY *Geol.* III. 391 The Iowan ice invasion is recorded in a thin sheet of till. 1922 E. HUNTINGTON & S. S. VISCHER *Climatic Changes* 165 The Iowan loess deposits.

Ipid (əi·pid). *Entom.* [f. Gr. ἴψ, ἰπ- woodworm + -ID³.] A beetle of the family *Ipidæ*.
1922 W. M. WHEELER *Soc. Life Insects* 40 Schneider-Orelli has found that the females of the Ipid ambrosia beetles carry the fungus in the fore part of the stomach.

Ipiti (i·piti). *S. Africa.* Also epiti, impiti, ip(i)eti. [Kaffir and Zulu *i Puti*.] The smallest of the South African antelopes, *Cephalolophus monticola*.
1836 MARTIN *Hist. S. Afr.* 138 (Pettman s.v. *epiti*) A turban made of the skin of the ipiete, a species of antelope. 1879 ATCHERLEY *Trip to Boerland* 26, I shot a few small buck known as *impiti*..not much larger than a hare. 1905 D. BLACKBURN *Richard Hartley* xiii. 244 The beautiful little ipiti, no bigger than a toy-terrier and quite as sprightly and alert.

Ipoh (ī·po). [Macassar *ipo*.] The upas tree, *Ipo* (*Antiaris*) *toxicaria*. Also, one of various arrow-poisons made from the sap of the upas tree. Also *attrib.*
1901 DORLAND *Med. Dict.* (ed. 2), *Ipoh*, the Malay name of various arrow-poisons. 1902 *Encycl. Brit.* XXX. 494/1 The pure Sâkai..make loin-cloths..from the bark of the *trap* and *Ipoh* trees. 1907 *Q. Rev.* July 190 The poison for their arrows is obtained from the ipoh or upas tree.

Ippiappa, variant of *JIPIJAPA.

Ipsilateral (ipsilæ·tĕrăl), *a.* *Physiol.* Also erron. ipso-. [Badly f. L. *ipse* self + LATERAL.] Belonging to or occuring on the same side.
1913 DORLAND *Med. Dict.* (ed. 7), Ipsolateral. 1930 ECCLES & SHERRINGTON in *Jrnl. Physiol.* LXIX. I Reflex summation in the ipsilateral spinal flexion reflex.

Ipsissima verba (ipsi·simă vɜ̄·ɪbă). [L.] The precise words.
1807 SOUTHEY *Lett.* (1856) II. 40 Last night I was in too much haste to look for the *ipsissima verba* of Fuller. 1834 *Edin. Rev.* Apr. 151 We..shall, therefore,..treat the reader to our author's *ipsissima verba*. 1886 *Athenæum* 13 Nov. 630/1 An assurance that the extracts contain the *ipsissima verba* of the poet would be..valuable. 1931 *Times Lit. Suppl.* 28 May 416/2 An undergraduate named Brauer,..who..seems to have taken down the *ipsissima verba* of Kant with almost impeccable accuracy.

Ipso jure (i·pso dʒūᵊ·ri), *advb. phrase.* [L.] By the operation of the law itself.
1913 *Act* 3 & 4 *Geo. V* c. 20 § 97 The act and warrant of confirmation in favour of the trustee shall ipso jure transfer to and vest in him..the whole property of the debtor.

Iraqi (irā·ki). Also Iraki. [Arab.: f. *Irāq* (see def.) + *-i* adj. suffix.] An inhabitant of Iraq, proclaimed Aug. 23, 1921 as the official name of Mesopotamia, an Asiatic kingdom of Arabs having Bagdad as its capital. Also *attrib.* or *adj.*, belonging to this kingdom or its inhabitants. Hence **Ira·quian.**
1923 *Glasgow Herald* 9 Apr. 10 The Iraqians declare that it took the British all their time to win. 1924 *Blackw. Mag.* Mar. 345/1 The administration is now in the hands of Iraqis, assisted by a mere handful of British advisers. 1927 *Observer* 7 Aug. 13/5 An addition of Iraqi or Syrian territory to the Turkish Republic would constitute a danger to his State. *Ibid.*, The Iraqi movement towards Westernisation.

Irene¹ (əiri·ni). *Astron.* [Female proper name, a. L. *Irene*, ad. Gr. Εἰρήνη (εἰρήνη peace).] A minor planet discovered in 1851.
1875 *Encycl. Brit.* II. 807/1.

Irene² (əi·rīn). *Chem.* [f. *IR(ONE + -ENE.] A hydrocarbon formed by the dehydration of irone.
1894 *Jrnl. Chem. Soc.* LXVI. I. 81 When treated with hydriodic acid and phosphorus, irone loses a molecule of water, and forms irene, $C_{13}H_{18}$, which is a colourless oil boiling at 113–115°.

Iretol (əi·rĕtǫl). *Chem.* [f. *IR(IGENIN + -ET + -OL.] A colourless compound obtained by the action of alkali on irigenin.
1894 *Jrnl. Chem. Soc.* LXVI. I. 48 Iretol, $C_6H_2(OH)_3OMe$ is obtained by adding excess of sulphuric acid to the product obtained by heating irigenin with caustic alkali. *Ibid.* [see *IRIDIC *a.*¹ b].

Irian (əi·riăn), *a.*² and *sb.* [f. the name *Ir*, a son of Miled, legendary ancestor of the Irish Celts.] **a.** *adj.* Belonging to or descended from Ir. **b.** *sb.* One of the race so descended.
1899 D. HYDE *Lit. Hist. Ireland* 59 Each man counting his ancestors through their hundredfold ramifications..and from thence to the founder of their house, who in his turn grafts on to one of the great stems (Eremonian, Eberian, Irian, or Ithian). *Ibid.* 204 All the great races, Eremonians, Eberians, Irians, and Ithians, resorted to it impartially, and it became a real university.

Iridal, *a.* Add: **2.** Of or relating to the iris of the eye. 1901 DORLAND *Med. Dict.* (ed. 2).

Iridectome (əiˌride·ktōᵘm). [f. Gr. ἰριδ-, IRIS + ἐκτομή a cutting out.] A knife used in iridectomy.
1875 KNIGHT *Dict. Mech.*, *Iridectome*, a knife for operations on the eye. 1903 DORLAND *Med. Dict.* (ed. 3).

Iridiagnosis (əiˌridəiăgnō·sis). *Med.* [f. as prec. + DIAGNOSIS.] Identification of a disease by observing the iris of the eye; iris diagnosis.
1923 *Glasgow Herald* 9 Nov. 6 Mr. Thomson..affirmed that the science of iridiagnosis refuted the germ theory as the prime factor in the causation of disease. 1928 *Sunday Express* 8 Apr. 10/7, I had never come across iridiagnosis before.

Iridic, *a.*¹ Add: **b.** Denoting a crystalline acid, $C_9H_{11}O_2 \cdot COO_2H$, obtained by decomposition of iridin.
1894 *Jrnl. Chem. Soc.* LXVI. I. 48 On heating irigenin with concentrated potash, in absence of air, formic acid, iridic acid, and iretol are obtained in molecular proportion.

Iridic (əiri·dik), *a.*² *Anat.* [f. Gr. ἰριδ-, IRIS + -IC.] Of or pertaining to the iris of the eye.

1930 *Nature* 19 July 97 Microscopic examination of the pupil tells us that the inner iridic margin..is really in a state of tremor of small amplitude.

Iridin (əi·ridin). *Pharm.* [f. L. *irid-*, IRIS (5) + -IN¹.] A preparation obtained from the rhizome of *Iris versicolor*.
1880 *Encycl. Brit.* XIII. 276/1 'Iridin', a powerful hepatic stimulant.

Iridium. Add: *Comb.*, as *iridium-pointed* adj.
1908 *Daily Chron.* 27 Feb. 7/3 A gold-iridium-pointed nib.

Irido-. Add: **Iridoplegia** (-plī·dʒiă) [Gr. πληγή stroke], paralysis of the iris.
1901 DORLAND *Med. Dict.* (ed. 2). 1907 *Practitioner* Apr. 519 The cardinal physical signs may be enumerated as iridoplegia, affection of speech, alteration of deep reflexes, and muscular tremors.

Iridocyst (əi·ridosist). *Zool.* [f. Gr. ἰριδ-, IRIS + κύστις bag, cyst.] In certain cephalopods, a cell which produces iridescent colours by diffraction of light.
1893 A. E. SHIPLEY *Zool. Invert.* 220 In addition to the chromatophores, the subepidermal tissues contain other modified connective tissue cells known as *iridocysts*; these cells are so modified as to produce iridescent colors by diffraction of light.

Iridocyte (əi·ridosəit). *Zool.* [f. Gr. ἰριδ-, IRIS + κύτος a hollow, cell.] A refracting substance in the skin of some fishes.
1898 *Proc. Zool. Soc.* 298 Pouchet's term 'iridocyte', applied to plate-like aggregations of the reflecting substance which show some traces of a cellular nature or origin. 1902 *Encycl. Brit.* XXVII. 150/2 Guanin may be present..in a peculiar crystalline form, the crystals being known as 'iridocytes'.

Iridol (əi·ridǫl, i·r-). *Chem.* [f. *IRID(IN + -OL.] A colourless compound prepared by the distillation of iridic acid.
1894 *Jrnl. Chem. Soc.* LXVI. I. 48 Iridol..distils on heating iridic acid at 239°.

Irigenin (əiri·dʒĕnin). *Chem.* [f. *IRI(DIN + -GEN + -IN¹.] A colourless compound, $C_{18}H_{16}O_8$, produced by the action of acids on iridin.
1894 *Jrnl. Chem. Soc.* LXVI. I. 47 Iridin undergoes hydrolysis when heated with dilute sulphuric acid at 80–100°, yielding *d*-glucose and irigenin, $C_{18}H_{16}O_8$.

Iris, *sb.* 7. Add: (sense 4) *iris diagnosis*, *science*; (sense 5) *iris blue*, *green*.
1908 SIR F. TREVES *Cradle of the Deep* x. 57 A West Indian island..rising aloft from an *iris-blue sea. 1921 *Glasgow Herald* 17 Feb. 9 *Iris Diagnosis and its Relation to True Health. *Ibid.*, *Iris science also threw an entirely new light upon the ideas prevailing with reference to germs and infection by bacteria, as well as of vaccine and serum treatment. 1880 *Encycl. Brit.* XIII. 276/2 From the flowers of *Iris florentina* a pigment—the 'verdelis', 'vert d'iris', or *iris-green, formerly used by miniature painters—was prepared by maceration.

Irish, *a.* and *sb.* Add: **A.** *adj.* **2.** *Irish guipure*, *linen*, *poplin*, etc.
1751 [see POPLIN¹]. 1851 *Illustr. Catal. Gt. Exhib.* III. III. 516/1 Dowlas is a strong kind of Irish linen, for shirting. *Ibid.* 561/1 Laces: Royal Irish guipure; Irish appliqué. 1895 *Army & Navy Co-op. Soc. Price List* 15 Sept. 1094 Irish Poplin. *Ibid.* 1099 Irish Lawn...Irish Diapers.
b. *Irish potato*, *setter* (see the sbs.); **Irish deer** (see quot.); **Irish terrier**, one of a breed of terriers somewhat heavier than the fox terrier, having straight wiry hair of a sandy red colour.
1889 NICHOLSON & LYDEKKER *Palæontology* 1341 The *Megacerotine*, which contains only the Irish Deer (*Cervus giganteus*), characterised by its enormous palmated antlers. 1894 R. B. LEE *Hist. Mod. Dogs Gt. Brit. & Irel.* 212 The capabilities of the Irish terrier as a water dog. 1897 *Encycl. Sport* I. 323/1 It is just twenty years since the Irish terrier first obtained recognition in the Kennel Club Stud Book.
c. **Irish American** (see quot. 1874); **Irish articles**, articles of belief drawn up by Archbishop Ussher in 1615; **Irish-Australian** *a.*, belonging to an Irish family which has emigrated to Australia; **Irish bleach**, the method of grass or sun bleaching linen; also, the linen itself; **Irish cross**, a Latin cross with the shaft widening at the base and a circle where the arms intersect the shaft; **Irish Free State** [Ir. *Saorstat Eireann*], the name for Ireland, excluding Ulster, after the treaty signed by Great Britain and Ireland in December, 1921; **Irish green**, Connemara marble; **Irish Guards**, a regiment formed to signalize the bravery of the Irish in the Boer War of 1899–1902; **Irish Ireland** *a.*, designating the movement to arouse the interest of all Irish people in their own country; **Irish point**, a kind of lace made in Ireland; **Irish Scots**, Scots from northern Ireland; **Irish Society**, a society founded in the reign of James I. to have jurisdiction over the new Protestant settlement in Ulster.
1874 *Slang Dict.*, *Irish American*, an Irishman who has been for some time resident in the States; sometimes a man born in America of Irish parents. The Irish American body is a power in the United States. 1875 *Encycl. Brit.* II. 500/2 The earliest recorded event in the history of Argyllshire is the settlement in the 4th or 5th century of a body of Irish Scots, under the leadership of Erc. 1877 *Ibid.* VI. 124/2 The separate estates are still held to be under the paramount jurisdiction of the Irish Society. *Ibid.* 565/1 To this series of confessional documents also belong..the Irish Articles, supposed to have been chiefly composed by Archbishop Ussher in 1615. 1882 CAULFEILD & SAWARD *Dict. Needlework* 272/1 Irish Point can be worked entirely as old Brussels needle point. 1883 *Encycl. Brit.* XV. 529/1 The 'Irish green' of architects is a similar rock from Connemara in western Galway. 1887 M. STOKES *Chr. Art in Ireland* 121 After the ninth and tenth century, the form now known as the Irish Cross..prevailed over the others. 1902 *Encycl. Brit.* XXXIII. 684/1 The Queen..issued an order..for a new regiment of Irish Guards to be constituted. 1904 W. B. YEATS in *Daily Chron.* 18 Mar. 3/4, I went..to tell the Irish of America of what we call the Irish Ireland movement. 1907 *Westm. Gaz.* 17 Sept. 1/3 The..Irish-Australian baronet. 1919 *Brit. Manufacturer* Nov. 27/1 For many years 'Irish Bleach' has held a high reputation. 1922 *Act* 13 *Geo. V* c. 2 An Act to make such provisions as are consequential on or incidental to the establishment of the Irish Free State. 1929 *Encycl. Brit.* XII. 628/1 The Irish Free State, with the status of a British Dominion, came officially into being on January 15, 1922.
B. *sb.* **5.** Temper; passion. *U.S.* and *dial.*
1834 CROCKETT *Narr. Life* iv. 30 Her Irish was up too high to do any thing with her. 1859 BARTLETT *Dict. Amer.* (ed. 3) s.v., My friends say that my Irish is getting up, meaning, I am getting angry. 1877 *Holderness Gloss.*, *Iry*; *Irish*, E. and N., passion; anger; rage; fury. [See *Eng. Dial. Dict.*]

Irishman. Add: **2.** A thorny New Zealand shrub, the tumata-kuru, *Discaria toumatou*.
1860 S. BUTLER in H. F. Jones *Life* (1919) I. 80 A country which has never before been burnt, and on which there is a large quantity of Irishman (the name given to a thorny shrub which, in the back country, attains to a considerable size)... A glorious lurid flare marks the ignition of an Irishman. 1883 [see TUMATA-KURU].
3. *Irishman's promotion*, *rise*: reduced wages.
1889 BARRÈRE & LELAND *Dict. Slang* (1897), Irishman's rise. 1902 C. J. C. HYNE *Mr. Horrocks, Purser* ii. 27 I've a sort of memory that you got Irishman's promotion for a bit of a mistake just recently. 1915 *Truth* 25 Aug. 295/2 The utmost the surveyor might expect from most corporations would be an Irishman's rise.

Irisin (əi·risin). *Chem.* [f. IRIS *sb.* + -IN¹.] A substance obtained from the root-stock of the iris, *Iris pseudacorus*.
1887 *Jrnl. Chem. Soc.* LII. I. 26 The rhizome of the water lily, *Iris pseudacorus*, contains a peculiar carbohydrate, called 'irisin' by the author [*sc.* O. Wallach]. Irisin, $C_6H_{10}O_5 + H_2O$, closely resembles inulin. 1892 MORLEY & MUIR *Watts' Dict. Chem.* III. 50/2.

Irofa (irofa). [Jap., named from the first three syllables *i*, *ro*, *fa* (earlier *ha*).] The Japanese syllabary.
1845 *Encycl. Metrop.* XX. 482/2. 1899 KEANE *Man, Past & Present* 308 The Japanese *Katakana* script, in which modified forms of Chinese ideographs are used phonetically to express 47 syllables (the so-called *I-ro-fa* syllabary).

Iroko (irōᵘ·ko). [Ibo.] A timber tree of West Africa, *Chlorophora excelsa*; also, the timber obtained therefrom.
1909 *Cent. Dict.* Suppl. 1925 *Countries of World* V. 3969/2 The timbers include mahogany, ebony, iroko and many other hard woods.

Iron, *sb.*¹ Add:
1. d. A colour resembling that of iron; iron-grey or iron buff.
1923 *Daily Mail* 24 Apr. 1 In the latest shades of..Iron, Parma, Gardenia.
4. g. *pl.* Iron supports to correct bow-legs, etc.
1884 PYE *Surgical Handicraft* xxv. 319 Wooden splints are..preferable to 'irons'. 1927 W. E. COLLINSON *Contemp. Engl.* 56 We could see..deformities due to rickets or injuries and the remedies e.g. irons to correct bow-legs.
12. iron-bacteria, bacteria which work changes in the iron compounds, especially iron carbonate; **iron buff**, a dye-stuff made of hydrated ferric oxide; also, the colour so produced; **iron-chamber** (see quot.); **Iron City** *U.S.*, Pittsburg; **iron gang**, a gang of prisoners working in irons; **iron loss** *Electr.* (see quots.); **iron-oak** (earlier U.S. examples); **iron player** *Golf*, one who plays (in a specified manner) with the iron; **iron ration** *Navy* and *Army*, (*a*) an emergency ration of tinned food; (*b*) *slang*, a bursting shell; **iron shears**, cutters for shearing iron; **iron shot** *Golf*, a stroke made with the iron; **iron steel** (see quot.).
1909 *Cent. Dict.* Suppl. s.v. *Bacterium*, *Iron-bacteria. 1929 *Encycl. Brit.* II. 908/2 All this mass of molluscs became coated with a ½ to ⅓-inch covering of filamentous iron bacteria. 1902 *Ibid.* XXVII. 564/1 *Iron Buff is produced by impregnating the cotton with a solution of ferrous sulphate. 1875 KNIGHT *Dict. Mech.*, *Iron-chamber..that portion of the puddling-furnace in which the iron is worked. 1842 *Daily Morning Post* (Pittsburgh, Pa.) 10 Sept., The subscriber [John Irons]..informs..the public that he has opened a Temperance Hotel, in fifth Street,..in the house lately occupied by Matthew Patrick, and has hoisted an Iron Sign, 'The *Iron City Hotel'. 1871 SCHELE DE VERE *Americanisms* (1872) 564 Pittsburg, in Pennsylvania, derives, from its enormous iron manufactories, the name of Iron City, by which it is universally known. 1848 H. W. HAYGARTH *Bush Life Australia* iv. 35 Had escaped with one or two others from his '*iron gang'. 1852 MUNDY *Antipodes* (1857) 32 The prisoners here form what is called an iron-gang—or ironed gang. 1904 *Technol. & Sci. Dict.* (ed. Goodchild & Tweney), *Iron Losses. 1910 *Hawkins' Electr. Dict.*, *Iron Core Loss*, the electric losses occurring in armatures and transformers due to hysteresis and eddy currents in the iron of the core. *Ibid.*, *Iron Loss in Transformer*, the electrical loss in a transformer due to hysteresis and eddy currents in its masses of iron. 1801 MICHAUX *Hist. des Chênes* 5 *Chêne gris*. Upland white-oak, *Iron Oak. 1832 D. J. BROWNE *Sylva Amer.* 275 In Maryland and a great part of Virginia..it is called Box White Oak, and sometimes Iron Oak and Post Oak. 1909 *Westm. Gaz.* 22 Feb. 12/2 He was also a most accomplished *iron player. 1876 VOYLE & STEVENSON *Milit. Dict.* Suppl. s.v., The ordinary *iron rations for two days should be 2 lbs. preserved meat and 2 lbs. biscuits, supplemented in such manner as circumstances admit. 1896 FARMER & HENLEY *Slang*, *Iron-rations* (nautical), tinned meat; specifically boiled salt-beef. 1915 'IAN HAY' *First Hundred Thousand* xvi, A haversack, occupied by his 'iron ration'—an emergency meal of the tinned variety, which must never on any account be opened except by order of the C.O. 1918 FARROW *Dict. Milit. Terms* s.v., Fritz is getting his iron rations. 1925 E. FRASER & GIBBONS *Soldier & Sailor Words* s.v., 'Iron rations' was in the War also a colloquial expression in speaking of a hot shell-fire, *e.g.*, 'Jerry is letting them have it, lots of iron rations flying about!' 1884 KNIGHT *Dict. Mech.* Suppl., *Iron Shears, cutters, either hand or machine, for iron. 1909 *Westm. Gaz.* 28 May 12/3 Maxwell..had made a splendid *iron shot. 1884 KNIGHT *Dict. Mech.* Suppl., *Iron Steel, metal composed partly of steel and partly of iron.

Iron, *a.* Add: **3. c.** *Iron hand* (Australian politics): the closure.
[1876 *Victorian Hansard* 20 Jan. XXIII. 2002 They [*sc.* the Government] have dealt with the Opposition with a velvet glove; but the iron hand is beneath, and they shall feel it.] 1884 G. W. RUSDEN *Hist. Australia* III. 406 The *clôture*, or the 'iron hand', as McCulloch's resolution was called, was adopted in Victoria, for one session.
4. c. **iron cap** = IRON HAT 2; **iron cross** [G. *das eiserne kreuz*], a Prussian and Austrian decoration awarded for distinguished services in war; **iron gum**, a large native tree of Queensland, *Eucalyptus raveretiana*; **iron horse** (earlier and later U.S. examples); **iron jubilee**, the seventieth anniversary of an event; **iron law** (of wages), the law or idea that wages tend to sink to the level of mere subsistence; **iron paper** (see quot.); **iron road**, **way**, a railway.
1911 *Chambers's Jrnl.* Mar. 166/1 The indication of a deposit of pyrites is the appearance of an outcrop of oxide of iron more or less honeycombed. This is called the '*iron cap', or in Cornwall 'gossan'. 1873 D. M. P. tr. *A. Wellmer's Anna C'tess zu Stolberg* ii. 56 The *Iron Cross, Class I. and II., adorned his hero breast. 1902 *Encycl. Brit.* XXXI. 340/2 The Austrian Iron Cross, founded by Napoleon I. as king of Italy in 1805,..conferred for personal merit. 1914 *Punch* 11 Nov. 390/2 The Iron Cross. (For German looters.) 1889 MAIDEN *Usef. Pl. Australia* 27 *Iron Gum. 1846 *Congress. Globe* 6 Feb. 323/3 The *iron horse..with the wings of the wind,..vomiting fire and smoke. 1857–8 *Trans. Ill. Agric. Soc.* (1859) III. 347 The iron horse was moving..in various directions, awaking the long dormant echoes of the prairie. 1891 E. S. ELLIS *Check No. 2134* xiv. 95 Led with..drew his iron horse down to a slow walk. 1918 *Essex Inst. Hist. Coll.* LIV. 206 On the supposition that 'iron horses' and those made of flesh and blood could be controlled in much the same manner. 1903 *Westm. Gaz.* 6 Feb. 10/1 Pope Leo XIII. will celebrate..during the present year ..his '*Iron Jubilee' as a priest—he was ordained seventy years ago. 1896 *Dict. Pol. Econ.* II. 568/1 He [*sc.* Lassalle] dwelt on what he called the '*iron' or 'brazen law' (*ehernes Gesetz*) of wages, already laid down by Turgot and Ricardo. 1907 J. S. NICHOLSON in *Cambr. Mod. Hist.* X. 774 Ricardo ..was credited with the 'iron law of wages' on the one side and the theories of the continuous growth of rent and the unearned increment on the other. 1913 *Pitman's Comm. Encycl.* IV. 1662/2 The 'iron law'..of the mere subsistence wage taught that the general rate of wages constantly tends to starvation limit. 1875 KNIGHT *Dict. Mech.*, *Iron-paper, a name given to extremely thin sheet-iron, which has been rolled thinner than the finest tissue-paper. 1838 F. COGHLAN (*title*) The *Iron Road Book and Railway Companion. 1880 *Harper's Mag.* Oct. 722/2 On all the iron roads the freight trains were made up through long months to be concentrated on the lines leading into Chicago. 1868 *Rep. U.S. Commissioner Agric.* (1869) 350 Improved lateral roads, by which products may reach the *iron way.

Iron, *v.* **3.** *fig.* (Additional examples of *iron out*.)
1905 *Springfield* (Mass.) *Weekly Republ.* 31 Mar. 8 The differences between Chairman Flaherty..and Col. William A. Gaston are in a fair way to be amicably ironed out. 1916 'LUCAS MALET' *Dogs of Want* v. § 1 Mr. Harvey-Noakes plays a ripping game.. He has flattened me out,..completely ironed me out. 1929 *Observer* 17 Nov. 3/4 The best practical method of ironing out ups and downs of the business cycle. 1930 *Time & Tide* 28 Mar. 389 The progress of negotiations to 'iron out' differences between Britain, Japan, and America.

Iron-cased, *a.* Add: Also in other uses.
1901 WATERHOUSE *Conduit Wiring* 50 The Simplex iron-cased distributing boards. 1906 *Westm. Gaz.* 29 Aug. 10/1 His tubular iron-cased telephone.

Ironclad, *a.* Add: **1. b.** In electricity (see quots.).
1902 *Encycl. Brit.* XXVII. 584/2 The two-pole ironclad type, so called from the exciting coil being more or less encased by the iron yoke. 1910 *Hawkins' Electr. Dict.*, *Iron-clad Drop*, an annunciator having an iron-clad electromagnet. *Iron-clad Dynamo*, a dynamo having an iron-clad armature. *Ibid.*, *Iron-clad Motor*, a motor provided with an iron-clad armature.
2. *fig.* Also, proof against cold. *U.S.*
1872 *Rep. Vermont Board Agric.* I. 54 Currants and gooseberries are iron clad as regards climate.
3. (Earlier and later examples.)
1866 *Congress. Globe* 14 Feb. 835/1 Traitors never would be troubled with the 'iron-clad oath', for they never would have a chance to take it. 1871 SCHELE DE VERE *Americanisms* (1872) 287. 1873 JOAQUIN MILLER *Unwritten Hist.* xxvi. (1876) 337 Some hard iron-clad oaths and then shot after shot. 1911 H. S. HARRISON *Queed* x. 114 He insisted on doing it after an ironclad schedule.

Irone (əi·rōᵘn). *Chem.* [f. IR(IS + -ONE.] A colourless oil extracted from orris root.
1893 *Specif. Tiemann's Patent* No. 8735. 1894 *Jrnl. Chem. Soc.* LXVI. I. 80 Irone..is an oil which is scarcely soluble in water, readily in alcohol. *Ibid.* 81 [see *IRENE²]. 1922 SUDBOROUGH *Bernthsen's Org. Chem.* 627 Irone—a methyl ketone, $C_{13}H_{20}O$—is the odoriferous principle of the iris root, and also probably of the violet.

Ironer. 1. (Earlier U.S. example.)
1835 J. H. INGRAHAM *South-West* II. 197 The planter..inquired of the girl her capabilities as seamstress, nurse, and ironer.

Ironing, *vbl. sb.* Add: **1.** attrib. *ironing-blanket*, *-board*, *-room*, *-stool*.
1858 SIMMONDS *Dict. Trade*, *Ironing-blanket, a coarse blanket used as a smooth surface by laundresses when ironing linen. *Ironing-board, a tailor's board for pressing cloth on with an iron to smooth the seams, etc.; a laundress's board, covered with flannel, for ironing..dresses; a table. 1876 H. E. SCUDDER *Dwellers Five-Sisters Crt.* iii. 52 Nicholas will have to carry the ironing-board for her. 1894 ELIZ. BANKS *Camp. Curiosity* 195 The one large room..should be divided into..three apartments; wash-house, sorting-room, and *ironing-room. 1906 *Westm. Gaz.* 5 July 2/1 The hooded fireplace of the ironing-room. 1878 MRS. STOWE *Poganuc People* xxv. 268 Will seized her off the *ironing stool and, perching her on his shoulder, danced round the table.
5. *Metallurgy.* (See quot.)
1868 H. BAUERMAN *Metall. Iron* 178 An advantage is claimed for bronzed twyers of not being readily destroyed by 'ironing', that is, of being melted by the imperfectly-fused masses of metallic iron which sometimes adhere to the end of the twyer.

Iron-man. Add: **1. c.** A self-acting spinning mule.
1875 KNIGHT *Dict. Mech.*, *Iron-man* (Cotton-manufacture), a name applied to the self-acting mule invented in 1825 by Roberts, of Manchester, England.

Iron-sand. 1. (Earlier U.S. example.)
1805 D. MCCLURE *Diary* (1899) 29 The soil abounds in iron sand Ore.

Ironweed. (Earlier U.S. example.)
1819 W. FAUX *Memorable Days* (1823) 185 Found ironweed all day, and fine extensive peach orchards.

Iroquoian (irǒkwoi·ăn), *a.* and *sb.* [f. *IROQUOIS + -AN.] = next.
1888 J. C. PILLING (*title*) Bibliography of the Iroquoian Languages. *Ibid.* Pref. p. v, To the Iroquoian perhaps belongs the honor of being the first of our American families of languages to be placed upon record. 1906 *Rep. Brit. Assoc.* 679 The Iroquoian tribes of North America possess a word which exactly expresses this potentiality.

Iroquois (irǒkwoi·). The name of a tribe of North American Indians, sometimes called the Five (later Six) Nations; also *attrib.* or *adj.*
1710 SHAFTESB. *Adv. Author* 179 Historys of Incas or Iroquois, written by Friars and Missionarys. 1756–9 A. BUTLER *Lives Saints* (1821) VI. 230 The saint wrote earnestly to the general of the society, desiring to be employed on a mission to the barbarous Hurons and Iroquois in Canada. 1791 J. LONG (*title*) Voyages and Travels of an Indian Interpreter..to which is added..a List of Words in the Iroquois, Mohegan, Shawanee, and Esquimaux Tongues. 1851 L. H. MORGAN *League of Iroquois* I. i. 7 The place where the Iroquois chiefs assembled. 1923 DOROTHY CANFIELD *Rough-Hewn* i, Neale was silent as an Iroquois. *Ibid.* xxv, His Iroquois mask of insensibility.

Irradiate, *v.* Add: **7.** *trans.* To subject to the action of X rays or similar therapeutic radiations. (Cf. *IRRADIATION 9.)
1903 *Med. Record* 31 Jan. 168 (Cent. D. Suppl.) The patient suffering from malignant disease is irradiated without first submitting to tentative exposures.

Irradiated, *ppl. a.* Add: **3.** Exposed to specific radiations.
1927 [see *ERGOSTEROL]. 1930 E. WATCHORN in *Biochemical Jrnl.* XXIV. II. 1560 Large doses of irradiated ergosterol lead to a decreased retention of calcium in rats.

Irradiation. Add: **9.** Exposure of the body to X rays, etc., for therapeutic purposes.
1903 *Med. Record* 31 Jan. 169 (Cent. D. Suppl.) It seemed to be preferable to extirpate the tumorous portions..before resorting to irradiation. 1913 DORLAND *Med. Dict.* (ed. 7). 1926 *Encycl. Brit.* Suppl. III. 284 It was noticed that some forms of malignant disease disappeared after treatment by irradiation.
b. Exposure to specific radiations. (Cf. *IRRADIATED 3.)
10. *Neurol.* The dispersion of a nervous impulse to parts beyond the normal path of conduction.
1890 BILLINGS *Med. Dict.*, *Irradiation*. 2. Applied by Meynert to the slow transmission of stimuli through the fibrillary network of the gray substance, as distinguished from transmission along regularly medullated nerves. 1901 *Baldwin's Dict. Philos. & Psychol.* I. 575/1 It has been suggested that irradiation..is at the foundation of all or most pleasurable sensations.

Irrationalist. Add: *attrib.* or *adj.*
1897 H. M. CECIL (*title*) Pseudo-Philosophy at the End of the Nineteenth Century, an Irrationalist Trio, Kidd, Drummond, Balfour. 1911 W. JAMES *Mem. & Studies* xv. 392 Listen for a moment to such irrationalist deliverances on his part as these.

Irrationalistic (iræʃənăli·stik), *a.* [f. IRRATIONAL *a.* + -ISTIC.] Characterized by irrationalism; contrary to reason; illogical.
1911 W. JAMES *Mem. & Studies* xv. 400, I spoke a while ago of its being an 'irrationalistic' philosophy in its latest phase. 1912 *Q. Rev.* Oct. 364 This brings us to the fundamental difference between the standpoints of history and science, which the theology called 'irrationalistic' appears to have overlooked. 1920 A. S. PRINGLE-PATTISON *Idea of God* 64, I have dwelt in the latter part of this lecture on the tendency to slip into an anti-intellectualistic, and even irrationalistic, mode of statement in expressing the principle of value.

Irreconciliation. Delete †*Obs.* and add examples.
1906 *Daily Chron.* 1 Oct. 5/6 Where..brotherly love and charity [have long been] enemies sworn to irreconciliation. 1927 *British Weekly* 24 Mar. 639/1 Science has its confusions and irreconciliations no less than religion.

Irredeemable, *a.* **1. b.** (Earlier U.S. example.)
1837 D. WEBSTER *Wks.* I. 374, I abhor paper; that is to say, irredeemable paper, paper that may not be converted into gold or silver at the will of the holder.
Hence **Irredeemabi·lity** (earlier U.S. example).
1791 A. HAMILTON *Wks.* (1886) VIII. 228 The partial irredeemability of the 6 per cent.

Irrepealability. (Earlier U.S. example.)
1802 *Ann. 7th Congress* 1 Sess. 592 The character of irrepealability was not exclusively attached to this law.

Irreption. Delete †*Obs.* and add examples.
1926 FRIEDRICHSEN *Gothic Version of Gospels* 190 Previous to this there had been casual but continued irreptions from the Old Latin. *Ibid.* 249 The Gothic reading could..be explained as a corruption due to the irreption of some parallel or reminiscent passage.

Irrigant (i·rigănt), *a.* and *sb.* [ad. L. *irrigans*, *-ant-*, pres. pple. of *irrigāre* to irrigate.] **a.** *adj.* Serving to irrigate. **b.** *sb.* A canal or ditch for irrigation.
1888 P. V. N. MYERS *Anc. Hist.* I. iii. 57 (Funk) The distribution of the waters of the Tigris and Euphrates was secured in ancient times by..canals and irrigants.

Irrigatable, *a.* [f. IRRIGATE *v.*] = IRRIGABLE *a.*
1836 D. B. EDWARD *Hist. Texas* i. 40 Most of these lands are irrigatable, from the numerous streams which flow down the mountains above them.

Irrigate, *v.* Add: **4.** *intr.* To drink; to take a drink. *U.S. slang.*
1856 G. H. DERBY *Phœnixiana* 204 [He] was invited by the urbane proprietor to irrigate. *c* 1880 in Thornton *Amer. Gloss.* App. 975 'Stranger, do you irrigate?' 'If you mean drink, sir, I do not.' 1905 A. ADAMS *Outlet* xxi. 298 Sponsilier..called every one to the bar to irrigate.
5. *trans.* To cause to percolate.
1901 *Practitioner* Mar. 288 Picro-haematoxylin or other stain can be irrigated through the preparation.

Irrigating, *vbl. sb.* or *ppl. a.* (Examples.)
1866 *Rep. Indian Affairs* 120 The first thing necessary to insure success is an irrigating canal. *Ibid.* 121 After the ground was broken an irrigating ditch was opened. 1877 *Ibid.* 47 The irrigating dam referred to above is to save the waters of a small creek. 1885 *Ibid.* 123 We must have many more miles of irrigating ditches. 1892 [in Dict.].

Irrigation. Add:
2. a. Also, the part which is irrigated.
1928 COTTRELL *Singing Gold* I. i. 11 You could look away over the irrigation to the sandhill.
4. *irrigation ditch*; **irrigation-wheel**, a wheel by means of which land is irrigated.
1870 Gov. HUNT *Own Story* (MS.) 1 *Irrigation ditches were dug for as much of the land as could be covered with water. 1902 O. WISTER *Virginian* vi. 77 One of the irrigation ditches ran under the fence from the hay-field to supply the house with water. 1864 J. A. GRANT *Walk Across Africa* 410 Mr. Aipperly had..made friends with the natives by assisting to put up their *irrigation-wheels.

Isabella. **2.** (U.S. examples of absol. use.)
1846 *Knickerbocker Mag.* XXVII. 419 A snaky looking vine..from which glorious bunches of Catawbas and Isabellas may be gathered. 1853 B. F. TAYLOR *Jan. & June* (1871) 23 A respectable Apple tree..inexperienced in the wiles and ways of Catawbas, Isabellas, and the like.

Isallobar (əisˌæ·lobāɪ). *Meteorol.* [f. Gr. ἴσος equal (Iso-) + ἄλλος other + *BAR *sb.*⁶] A line connecting places at which the barometric pressure has changed by an equal amount during a specified period. Hence **Isalloba·ric** *a.*
1911 N. W. SHAW *Forecasting Weather* 337 Dr. Nils Ekholm, of Stockholm,..uses charts of isallobars—that is of equal pressure differences in a given interval. *Ibid.*, Dr. Ekholm's contention is that the travel of the isallobaric groups is more regular than that of the isobaric groups.

Isallotherm (əisˌæ·lǫþɜ̄m). *Meteorol.* [f. Iso- + Gr. ἄλλος other + θέρμη heat.] A line connecting places at which the temperature has changed by an equal amount during a specified period.

Isanakatabar (əisˌænăkæ·tăbāɪ). *Meteorol.* [f. Iso- + Gr. ἀνά on, upon + κατά down + *BAR *sb.*⁶] A line of equal pressure amplitude.
1920 W. J. S. LOCKYER *South. Hemisphere Surface-Air Circulation* 17 An attempt is made in this portion of the memoir to associate an isanakatabar of a particular value with the track of the centres of the anticyclonic systems. 1926 SIR N. SHAW *Man. Meteorol.* II. 372 Lines of equal range, which are called isanakatabars, or lines of equal up-and-down of pressure.

Isat-. Add: **Isatane** (əi·sătēᵘn), a crystalline compound formed by the reduction of isatin with sodium. **I·satogen**, a complex nitrogenous radical common to isatin and related compounds; hence **Isatoge·nic** *a.* **Isato·ic** *a.*, denoting a monobasic crystalline acid obtained from the oxidation of isatin, etc.
1892 MORLEY & MUIR *Watts' Dict. Chem.* III. 78/2 *Isatane $C_{16}H_{14}N_4O_4$. 1900 *Jrnl. Chem. Soc.* LXXVIII. I. 649 This substance is really present in an unstable compound called isatan. 1892 MORLEY & MUIR *Watts' Dict. Chem.* III. 76/1 *Isatogenic acid is perhaps formed by shaking *o*-nitro-phenyl-propiolic acid with H_2SO_4. 1902 *Jrnl. Chem. Soc.* LXXXII. I. 454 *Isatoic acid..results from the action of hypochlorous acid on phthalimide in the absence of alkali hydroxides.

Isaurian (əisǭ·riăn), *a.* and *sb.* [f. *Isauria* + -AN.] **a.** *adj.* Of or belonging to Isauria, an ancient country in Asia Minor, between Cilicia and Phrygia. **b.** *sb.* A native or inhabitant of Isauria; *spec.* applied to a line of emperors of the East.
1776 GIBBON *Decl. & F.* x. (1782) I. 341 In the heart of the Roman monarchy, the Isaurians long continued a nation of wild barbarians. 1843 *Penny Cycl.* XXVII. 770/1 His warlike countrymen the Isaurians. *Ibid.* 770/2 The increasing power of the brothers and other Isaurian friends of Zeno. 1880 *Encycl. Brit.* XI. 114/2 The emperors of this time were those of the Isaurian, Armenian, and Amorian dynasties. 1904 W. M. RAMSAY *Lett. Seven Churches* xxvii. 399 The Empire of Rome had been..transformed into a Roman-Asiatic Empire, on whose throne sat successively Phrygians, Isaurians, Cappadocians, and Armenians.

Isba (i·zba). Also isbah, izba. [Russ.] A Russian hut or log-house.
1784 KING *Cook's Voy.* III. 374 These houses consist of three distinct sorts, jourts, balagans, and loghouses, called here isbas. 1833 R. PINKERTON *Russia* 24 These simple articles compose the whole..furniture of a Russian izba. 1883 READE in *Harper's Mag.* Jan. 251/1 Her serfs, if they wanted new isbahs—alias log huts—..would get the priests ..to versify their petition. 1892 *Daily News* 22 Jan. 6/7 The meanest Kirghis yourt was more artistically decorated than his grimy, unventilated isba.

Isblink (ī·sblink). [Swedish, f. *is* ice + *blink* gleam.] = ICEBLINK 2.
1880 *Encycl. Brit.* XI. 167/2 If..the sea is shallow, the glacier will protrude for a considerable distance, as in the case of the Isblink.

-ish¹. Add: **4.** Added to names of hours of the day or numbers of years to denote: Round about, somewhere near (prob. after *earlyish*, *lateish*).
1916 'PETER' *Trench Yarns* ix. 110 'What time shall I come?' 'Elevenish,' Sam replied. 1925 B. TRAVERS *Mischief* xiv, I shall be going to Shady Nook at about tenish. 1930 J. B. PRIESTLEY *Angel Pavement* iii. § 1 Eightish then, next Tuesday, eh?

Ishan (ī·ʃān). [Pers., = hill, landmark.] A prehistoric mound in Iraq.
1921 *Blackw. Mag.* June 708/1 They had just moved their home to an ishan or mound only some ten or fifteen minutes from the river. 1927 'FULANAIN' *Haji Rikkan* i. 8 Facing us was a group of the strange mounds or *ishans* which here and there, in the marshes of Southern 'Iraq, stand out high, or seeming high in that vast watery expanse.

Island, *sb.* Add: **1. d.** In specific elliptical uses for some particular island or islands, as the Isle of Wight, the Hebrides, the Pacific Islands.
1811–13 JANE AUSTEN *Mansfield Park* ii, She thinks of nothing but the Isle of Wight, and she calls it *the Island*, as if there were no other island in the world. 1817 KEATS *Lett. to J. H. Reynolds* 17 Apr. (1931), I intend to walk over the Island east—West—North South. 1896 CONRAD *Outcast of the Islands* ii. (1919) 15 There was not a white man in the islands, from Palembang to Ternate, from Ombawa to Palawan, that did not know Captain Tom and his lucky craft. 1901 *N.E.D.* s.v. *Isle*, The Isle of Wight is commonly referred to as 'the island'. 1902 *Captain* VII. 141 We used to gather the niggers in from all round the islands [*sc.* Pacific Islands]. 1930 PALMER *Men are Human* xxiii. 205 He was tormented by sporadic impulses to scrap his responsibilities and go off to the Islands [*sc.* Pacific Islands].
2. (Later U.S. examples.)
1834 *Visit to Texas* iv. 41 These groves are called islands, from the striking resemblance they present to small tracts of land surrounded by water. 1843 *Amer. Pioneer* II. 283 An island of timber. 1853 F. W. THOMAS *John Randolph*, etc. 61 Islands—that is, great clumps of trees, covering sometimes many acres, appearing just like many islands in an out-stretched ocean. 1902 S. E. WHITE *Blazed Trail* ix. 63 The pine there grew thick on isolated 'islands' of not more than an acre or so in extent,—little knolls rising from the level of a marsh.
c. = REFUGE *sb.* 3 c.
1878 *Social Notes* 10 Aug. 358/1 It is only very lately that 'islands'—those necessary havens of refuge—have been placed at the most dangerous portions of the boulevards. 1899 *Daily Tel.* 31 Jan. (Ware) The statue being situated on an 'island', a certain amount of skirmishing was necessary in order to reach it. 1926 MRS. A. SIDGWICK *Sack & Sugar* xi. 131, I took Gerda's arm, and was nearly at the island, when the bus swept round a corner and was on us. 1930 COOPER *Ship of Truth* ii. 178 He stood on an island in the middle and saw the traffic sweep past him.
4. island case, a show-case in a museum or other exhibition, surrounded by unoccupied floor-space; **island-hill**, **-mountain**, a hill or mountain rising out of a plain; **island plot**, **site**, a plot of land or a building site surrounded by streets or open spaces; **island-refuge** = *2 c.
1932 *Museums Jrnl.* June 127 In the vertical *island-cases with different displays on opposite sides. 1839 DE LA BECHE *Rep. Geol. Cornwall*, etc. i. 26 The lower *island-hills of Pawlet and Chedzoy..rise out of the plain near Bridgewater. 1906 *Daily Chron.* 31 Aug. 4/4 They [*sc.* the Malvern Hills] lie precisely north by south, moored like some great *island-mountain to the westward of the central plain of England. 1912 *Rep. Brit. Assoc.* 476 The kopjes and island mountains of the warmer temperate and tropical regions are essentially of similar origin. 1908 *Daily Chron.* 20 Apr. 3/5 On this '*island' plot of land has been erected a building which is certainly an adornment to Great Portland-street. 1922 MUIRHEAD *Lond. & Environs* (ed. 2) 8 A busy street should be crossed only at a point where an '*island-refuge' is provided in the middle. 1907 *Westm. Gaz.* 20 Sept. 10/1 Australia and the Strand '*Island Site'. 1921 E. WALLACE *Law Four Just Men* iv. 116 The third house, that at the end of the island site, was occupied.

Isle of Wight (əiləvˌwəi·t). *Bee-keeping.* The name of the island off the Hampshire coast used *attrib.* to designate a form of microsporidiosis infecting bees.
1908 in Reinheimer *Nutrition & Evol.* (1909) 182 The recent Isle of Wight outbreak, which is a new experience in British apiculture. 1912 *Jrnl. Board Agric.* May 133 Investigations into the nature, history, and symptoms of the Isle of Wight Bee Disease.

Islet. Add: **2.** Also, a small isolated space between the lines in finger-prints.
1921 *Discovery* Oct. 257/2 A dozen guiding marks, consisting of the beginnings of lines, bifurcations and islets.
3. (sense 2 b.)
1927 HALDANE & HUXLEY *Anim. Biol.* xii. 279 Islet cell of human pancreas.

Iso-. Add: **Isano·malous** *a.*, isabnormal. **Isene·rgic**, a graphical curve representing constant energy. **Isepipte·sis** *Ornith.*, an imaginary line connecting points which migrating birds reach at the same time; so **Isepipte·sial** *a.* **Isoagglu·tinate** *v. trans.*, to produce isoagglutination in; also *intr.* and *absol.* **Isoagglutina·tion**, the agglutination of the red corpuscles by isoagglutinins; so **Isoagglu·tinative** *a.* **Isoagglu·tinin**, an agglutinin which acts on the blood of other animals of the same species. **I·sobase** *Geol.*, an imaginary line drawn through areas formerly of equal elevation which have undergone deformation; hence **Isoba·sic** *a.* **Isobiogene·tic** *a.*, applied to foodstuffs which produce an equal amount of nourishment. **Isocœlous** (-sī·ləs) *a.* *Ornith.* [Gr. κοῖλος hollow], denoting that arrangement of intestine in birds in which the second and third loops are closed and left-handed. **Isocy·clic** *a.* *Org. Chem.*, pertaining to or possessing a ring composed of atoms of one element. **Isodi·ctyal** *a.*, having meshes of equal size. **Isodynamoge·nic** *a.* = *isobiogenetic. **Isoele·ctric** *a.*, of or pertaining to equal and opposite charges of electricity; in *isoelectric point*, the point at which a colloid is precipitated by the neutralization of the electric charge of the molecules. **Isoenerge·tic** *a.* = *isobiogenetic. **I·sogyre** *Optics*, any of the lines or curves on interference figures; so **Isogy·ric** *a.* **Isohæmaggluti·nating** *ppl. a.*, producing **Isohæmagglutina·tion**, = *isoagglutination. **Isoha·line**, an imaginary line connecting those points in the ocean having an equal degree of salinity. **I·sohel** *Meteorol.* [Gr. ἥλιος sun], a line connecting points having an equal amount of sunshine; hence **Isohe·lic** *a.* **Isohy·dric** *a.* *Phys. Chem.*, possessing an equal concentration of hydrogen ions. **Isohy·et** [Gr. ὑετός rain], a line connecting places having an equal annual rainfall. **Isolysin** (əisolǝi·sin, əisǫ·lisin) *Biol. Chem.*, a lysin existing in the blood of an animal and possessing the power of destroying the red corpuscles of other animals of the same species; so **Iso·lysis**, the destructive action of an isolysin; **Isoly·tic** *a.* **Isomagne·tic** *a.*, denoting a line connecting places having the same magnetic constants. **Isopho·tic** *a.*, of or pertaining to the emission of an equal quantity of light. **Isophoto·graphy**, natural size photographic reproduction. **I·soplere** *Physics* [Gr. πλήρης full], = *ISOMETRIC *line*. **I·sopleth** *Meteorol.* [Gr. πλῆθος fullness], a line plotting the distribution of a given phenomenon. **Isopsy·chric** *a.* [Gr. ψυχρός cold], of or pertaining to a state in which evaporation and condensation are equal; *sb.*, an isopsychric curve. **Isopy·cnic** *a.* [Gr. πυκνός dense], of or pertaining to equal density; *sb.*, a line connecting points of equal density. **I·soseist** [Gr. σειστός shaken], a line connecting points where an earthquake shock was felt at the same moment. **I·sostere** [Gr. στερεός solid], a line connecting points of equal atmospheric density; so **Isoste·ric** *a.* **Iso·stichous** *a.* *Bot.* [Gr. στίχος row], applied to charas in which the primary and secondary rows of cortical cells are of equal diameter. **Isoto·nic** *a.*, having a uniform tension; having or producing equal tension or osmotic pressure. **I·sovol**, a line drawn through the points where the coal has the same ratio of fixed to volatile carbon.
1900 *Geog. Jrnl.* June 662 Maps of isotherms and *isanomalous lines for January and July. 1927 KENDREW *Climates of Continents* 3 'Isanomalous lines' for any month or for the year are lines drawn through places with the same anomaly. 1902 *Encycl. Brit.* XXXIII. 285/1 The lines of constant energy on the diagram are called *Isenergics. 1875 A. NEWTON in *Encycl. Brit.* III. 768/1 His [*sc.* von Middendorff's] chief object has been to trace what he has termed the *isepipteses...Assuming that the advance is directly across the *isepipteslal lines..the whole course of the migration is thus most accurately made known. 1904 *Alien. & Neurol.* Aug. 386 (Cent. D. Suppl.) The serum from such blood was also *isoagglutinating. 1900 *Science* 28 Nov. 858/1 The *isoagglutinative and isolytic properties of human serums in health and in disease. 1903 DORLAND *Med. Dict.* (ed. 3), *Isoagglutinins. 1907 F. P. GAY in *Jrnl. Med. Research* Dec. 321 (Cent. D. Suppl.) Isoagglutinins occurred only in the sera of pathological states. 1893 R. D. SALISBURY in *Geol. Surv. New Jersey* 321 (Cent. D. Suppl.) *Isobase. 1903 GEIKIE *Text-bk. Geol.* (ed. 4) I. 386 De Geer has traced lines of equal deformation round this centre, and has found that these lines (*isobases*) group themselves in concentric circles. 1924 SKERL tr. *A. Wegener's Orig. Continents & Oceans* 22 The isobase maps of de Geer..show a depression of the central portion of Scandinavia of at least 250 m. 1932 E. G. WOODS *Baltic Region* 121 A glance at such a map with the *isobasic lines indicated shows the late-glacial sea at about its maximum development. 1898 A. DASTRE in *Smithsonian Rep.* 543 Two weights of different aliments for which these numerical values are the same are said to be isodynamogenic, *isobiogenetic, or isoenergetic weights. 1889 GADOW in *Proc. Zool. Soc.* 310 The *Pteroclidæ*..have four loops, which are all closed, left-handed, *i.e.* *isocœlous, and straight. 1904 *Technol. & Sci. Dict.* (ed. Goodchild & Tweney) s.v. *Closed Chain Compounds*, When all the atoms in the ring are alike, the ring is called an *Isocyclic..Ring. 1900 *Proc. Zool. Soc.* 20 Feb. 138 Skeleton consisting of..a dermal *isodictyal network. 1898 *Isodynamogenic [see *isobiogenetic]. 1901 *Rep. Brit. Assoc.* 61 At the *isoelectric point, for a distinct small quantity of barium chloride or acid, the electric movement vanishes and coagulation or precipitation occurs. 1898 *Isoenergetic [see *isobiogenetic]. 1902 MANN & MILLIKAN tr. *P. Drude's The. Optics* 354 The whole field of view is now ..traversed by a black curve, the so-called principal *isogyre. *Ibid.* 352 The loci of those points of the field for which φ is constant are the curves of constant direction of polarization (*isogyric curves). 1907 F. P. GAY in *Jrnl. Med. Res.* Dec. 321 (Cent. D. Suppl.) The *isohemagglutinating power of serum resists heating to 56° C. for thirty minutes. *Ibid.*, Earlier observers of human *isohemagglutination asserted that isoagglutinins occurred only in the sera of pathological states. 1902 *Encycl. Brit.* XXXI. 404/2 South of the Tropic of Capricorn the *isohalines run nearly east and west. 1904 *Technol. & Sci. Dict.* (ed. Goodchild & Tweney), *Isohels (Meteorol.), lines connecting places having the same amount of sunshine. 1931 A. A. MILLER *Climatology* 22 The deviation of sunshine (shown on maps by lines of equal duration known as isohels). 1897 *Geog. Jrnl.* Sept. 306 König..has found sufficient material for a first attempt to draw '*isohelic' lines for Western Europe. 1900 *Speaker* 9 June 283 The *isohydric theorem of Arrhenius. 1902 *Encycl. Brit.* XXVIII. 14/1 The concentration of the hydrogen ions should be the same in each separate solution. Such solutions were called by Arrhenius, 'isohydric'. 1899 *Nature* 21 Dec. 172/2 Isobars and *isohyets indicating monthly and annual distribution of barometric pressure and rainfall. 1931 A. A. MILLER *Climatology* 19 Lines drawn through points having equal rainfall during any given period and known as isohyets. 1901 DORLAND *Med. Dict.* (ed. 2), *Isolysin. *a* 1909 VAUGHAN & NOVY *Cellular Toxins* 129 (Cent. D. Suppl.) *Isolysis. 1903 *Isolytic [see *isoagglutinative]. 1903 *Med. Record* 14 Feb. 247 (Cent. D. Suppl.) The possibility of the formation of isolytic substances was thus established. 1899 *Nature* 6 July 236/2 An opportunity will thus be afforded..to obtain some idea of the accuracy with which the *isomagnetic lines can be determined. 1902 *Encycl. Brit.* XXX. 461/1 Formulæ giving smooth curves of continuous curvature, approximating as closely as possible to the district lines. These smooth curves are called terrestrial isomagnetics. 1931 *Nature* 14 Mar. 418 The *isophotic lines embrace each nucleus with an approach to regularity. 1900 *Ibid.* 24 May 79/2 Microphotography, *Isophotography, Megaphotography. 1899 W. WATSON *Text-bk. Physics* 274 Isometric lines or *isopleres. 1909 *Cent. Dict.* Suppl., *Isopleth. 1911 SHAW *Forecasting Weather* 4 The general name of isopleth is given to a line drawn on a diagram or chart separating the region of values above a certain fixed limit from those below. 1928 — *Man. Meteorol.* II. 283 The juxtaposition of the isopleths for temperature and wind. 1904 *Jrnl. Phys. Chem.* May 344 Since adiabatic expansion is *isopsychric at points on the neutral curve, this curve is the locus of the points of mutual tangency of the adiabatics and isopsychrics. 1895 *Funk's Stand. Dict.*, *Isopycnic. 1928 SIR NAPIER SHAW *Man. Meteor.* II. p. xxi, Surfaces of equal specific volume: the isosteric surfaces of Bjerknes (or of equal density: isopycnic surfaces). 1900 *Rep. Brit. Assoc.* 71 *Isoseist. 1900 BJERKNES in *Monthly Weather Rev.* Oct. (repr.) 3/2 In the atmosphere they [*sc.* the isosteric surfaces] have, approximately, the same course as the isobars; the upper *isosteres surround the whole earth, whereas the lower ones intersect the earth's surface along the *isosteric curves. 1902 *Encycl. Brit.* XXX. 719/2 Charts of 'isosteres', or lines of equal density. 1920 GROVES & BULLOCK-WEBSTER *Brit. Charophyta* I. 74 *Isostichous. 1901 DORLAND *Med. Dict.* (ed. 2), *Isotonic. 1905 POYNTING & THOMSON *Properties of Matter* (ed. 3) 190 A series of solutions can be prepared which are isotonic with each other. 1923 *Glasgow Herald* 11 June 7 The *isovols for the Hutton seam take the form of a series of rings with a common centre to the north-west of Durham. 1928 E. R. LILLEY *Geol. Petroleum & Nat. Gas* 113 The isovols (lines of equal carbon ratio).

Isobar. Add: Also *attrib.*
1927 KENDREW *Climates of Continents* 8 The isobar map of the earth for January.

Isobare (əi·sobɛ̄ᵊɪ). *Phys. Chem.* [f. Iso- + Gr. βάρος weight.] An element having the same atomic weight as another but occupying a separate place in the Periodic Table and having different chemical and spectroscopic properties. Hence **Isoba·ric** *a.*², of equal atomic weight; also *sb.*
1918 A. W. STEWART in *Phil. Mag.* XXVI. 331 These elements [*sc.* mesothorium and radiothorium] differ completely from one another in chemical character; but they all possess the same atomic weight. For this reason the name isobares ..is here suggested for them. 1919 SODDY in *Trans. Chem. Soc.* CXV. 23 We have to take into account in our analysis of matter, not only the heterobaric heterotopes before recognised, but also heterobaric and isobaric isotopes and isobaric heterotopes or isobares. 1919 *Nature* 18 Sept. 61/1 Some of the normal elements exhibit properties which may be explained on the assumption that they are isobarics. 1922 F. W. ASTON *Isotopes* 12 Isobares.

Isobaric, *a.* Add: **B.** *sb.* A line of equal pressure.
1903 *Engineer* 24 July 83/3 The isobarics of evaporation happen to be isothermals.

Isobath (əi·sobæþ). [f. Iso- + Gr. βάθος depth.] A contour equal in depth with other parts of the ocean bottom. Hence **Isoba·thic** *a.*
1903 *Geog. Jrnl.* Aug. 128 Towards the west this wall of limestone does not rise as high above the water, although the adjacent soundings are still so deep that the 100-metre isobathic line approaches to within 200 metres of the shore. 1903 *Nature* 29 Oct. 632 Warm currents follow the trend of deepest isobaths.

Isoclasite (əiso̩klē̆·səit). *Min.* [f. G. *isoklas* (f. Iso- + Gr. κλάσις fracture): see -ITE¹.] A hydrous calcium phosphate occurring in small white crystals. 1872 DANA *Min.* App. I.

Isoetes (əisǫᵘ·ĕtīz). *Bot.* [mod.L., a. L. *isoetes* small houseleek, a. Gr. ἰσοετής equal in years, f. ἴσος equal + ἔτος year.] A plant of the aquatic or semi-aquatic cryptogamic genus so named; a quill-wort.
1886 *Encycl. Brit.* XX. 431/2 A striking instance of the same thing has been observed by Goebel in some species of Isoetes, in which an Isoetes plant was produced on the leaf in place of a sporangium. 1910 *Rep. Brit. Assoc.* 784 The whole axis of the *Isoëtes* plant can be compared with that of *Lepidodendron* or *Pleuromeia*.

Isolate, *v.* **4.** Add: Also *absol.*
1888 MRS. H. WARD *R. Elsmere* xxi, Three cases of diphtheria..I must go for..a nurse, and we must isolate and make a fight for it.

Isolating (əi·sǫlēᵘtiŋ), *ppl. a.* *Philology.* [f. ISOLATE *v.* + -ING².] Designating languages in which each element is an independent word, being neither inflected nor compounded.
1861 MAX MÜLLER *Sci. Lang.* Ser. I. viii. 274 Languages belonging to this first or Radical Stage, have sometimes been called Monosyllabic or Isolating. 1868 — *Sel. Ess. Lang.* etc. (1881) I. 44 We find it repeated again and again in most works on Comparative Philology, that Chinese belongs to the isolating class, the Turanian languages to the combinatory, the Aryan and Semitic to the inflectional. 1885 *Encycl. Brit.* XVIII. 774/2 Such languages, constituting the small minority of human tongues, are wont to be called 'isolating', i.e., using each element by itself, in its integral form.

Isolation. Add: **2.** *Psychol.* (See quot.)
1890–1 C. L. MORGAN *Anim. Life & Intell.* 322 We may call the process by which we select a certain quality, and consider it by itself to the neglect of other qualities, *isolation*.

Isolationism (əisolē̆·ʃəniz'm). [f. ISOLATION + -ISM.] The policy of seeking (political or national) isolation: with special reference to the U.S.A.
1922 *19th Cent.* Nov. 731 Her isolationism..discovered that the strain of a formidable advance against freedom was more than it could bear. 1930 *Headway* June 112/2 Add to this the fact that half the people..who have emigrated to America in the last generation or so are Europeans who have left Europe because they wanted to get away from Europe, and the secret of America's 'isolationism' is very largely explained. 1931 NORMAN ANGELL in *Time & Tide* Suppl. 4 July, However much an instructed minority in America might be in favour of the abandonment of isolationism and a larger co-operation with Europe.

Isolationist. Add: Also *attrib.* or *adj.*
1921 *Glasgow Herald* 21 Apr. 8 Regarding the future policy of the United States...The isolationist attitude..is.. much less obvious. 1930 *New Statesman* 26 Apr. 69/2 When Mr. Hoover signed last year the prospect was good, but the prolonged bickerings in London have stiffened the isolationist sentiment of the interior.

Isolative (əi·sǫlătiv), *a.* *Philol.* [f. ISOLATE *v.* + -IVE.] Of a sound-change: Taking place without reference to neighbouring sounds: opp. to *combinative*.
1888 SWEET *Hist. Engl. Sounds* 17 Isolative changes are those which affect a sound without any reference to its surroundings. *Ibid.* 26 Isolative change of *s* into *ʃ* is regular in Gm initial *s* followed by a cons., as in *schwan*, *stein*.

Isomerization (əisǫmĕrəizē̆·ʃən). *Chem.* [f. ISOMER + -IZATION.] The formation of an isomer.
1902 *Nature* 13 Nov. 48/1 Researches..on the isomerisation of cyclic hydrocarbons and ketones.

Isometric, *a.* Add: **5.** *Isometric line*, a curve showing the relation between pressure and temperature when the volume is constant. Also as *sb.*
1899 W. WATSON *Text Bk. Physics* 274 [Those curves] in which the volume is constant [are called] *isometric lines* or *isopleres*. 1902 *Encycl. Brit.* XXXIII. 283/1 Heating or cooling at constant volume, represented by vertical lines such as Bb, called Isometrics, in which the pressure varies, but no external work is done. *Ibid.* 284/1 Let BE be an isometric through B.
6. Econ. *Isometric standard* (see quot.).
1925 S. E. THOMAS *Elem. Econ.* xxix. 475 As an alternative [to the gold standard] the Cambridge School advocates an 'Isometric Standard', or a managed currency; i.e., a paper pound the value of which is stabilised in terms of its purchasing power in the home market.

Isomorphic, *a.* Add: **3.** *Biol.* Of the same or an analogous form.
1888 *Nature* 20 Dec. 180/1 Dicholophus..has assumed peculiar Raptorial characters isomorphic with those of Gypogeranus, which is a true bird of prey.

Isomorphism. Add: **3.** *Biol.* The condition of having similar appearance or character but different ancestry.

Supplement, p. 3873; Corrigenda, p. 4092; Spurious words, p. 4093; Books quoted, p. 4094

Isonomia (əisonōᵘ·miă). = Isonomy.
1853 Sir E. Creasy *Eng. Const.* 198 There is no part of our constitution so admirable as this equality of civil rights, this *isonomia*, which the philosophers of ancient Greece only hoped to find in democratical government. 1926 *Contemp. Rev.* Oct. 485 It was the *name* 'isonomia' that so commended a democracy.

Isoprene (əi·soprīn). *Chem.* [? f. Iso- + Pr(opyl + -ene.] A hydrocarbon resulting from the dry distillation of rubber.
1860 C. G. Williams in *Proc. Roy. Soc.* X. 516. 1862 Miller *Elem. Chem., Org.* (ed. 2) 591 To the most volatile of these [hydrocarbons] Williams has given the name of Isoprene. 1900 Sadtler *Handbk. Indust. Chem.* (ed. 3) 99 On submitting it [*sc.* caoutchouc] to destructive distillation it yields..isoprene.

Isoscelohedron (əisǫsĭlohī·drǫn, -he·drǫn). *Cryst.* [f. *isoscelo-*, assumed as combining form of Isosceles + Gr. ἕδρα base.] A solid figure each of whose faces is an isosceles triangle.
1895 Story-Maskelyne *Crystallography* § 167 An isoscelohedron..formed..of similar and congruent..isosceles..triangles.

Isostatic, *a.* Add: **b.** Pertaining to, produced or characterized by, isostasy. Hence **Isosta·tically** *adv.*
1901 *Geog. Jrnl.* Nov. 517 The elevation of the land caused an ice-sheet to form gradually over it until the surface was depressed, isostatically, by the weight of accumulated ice and the cooling of the crust itself. 1924 Skerl tr. *A. Wegener's Orig. Continents & Oceans* 23 All such isostatic movements of compensation must lag greatly. *Ibid.* 60 It [*sc.* the map] shows us immediately the mass-defect under mountain chains through which the latter are isostatically compensated. 1925 J. Joly *Surface-Hist. Earth* x. 170 The final buoyancy effect would ultimately force upwards, isostatically, the bent and folded masses. 1927 H. Peake & H. J. Fleure *Apes & Men* 80 There may have been a slight compensating, or as it is called isostatic, uprise in Denmark and other regions around the margin of the ice sheet.

Isotherm. Add: Also *attrib.*
1927 Kendrew *Climates of Continents* 3 A glance at any isotherm map shows that the temperature varies greatly along any parallel of latitude.

Isotope (əi·sǒtōup). *Phys. Chem.* [Coined by Prof. Frederick Soddy, 1913; f. Gr. ἴσος equal (Iso-) + τόπος place. A more appropriate word would have been *homotope*. (*Isotopic* was used by Cohen and Miller in 1904 (*Jrnl. Chem. Soc.* 1624 *note*) to designate similar molecular structures; this use did not gain general currency.)] Each of two or more elements or atoms of an element possessing identical chemical properties and occupying the same position in the periodic table, but having different atomic weights. Hence **Isoto·pic** *a.*; **Isoto·pically** *adv.*; **I·sotopism, I·sotopy,** the fact or condition of being isotopic.
1913 Soddy in *Nature* XCII. 400 The same algebraic sum of the positive and negative charges in the nucleus, when the arithmetical sum is different, gives what I call 'isotopes' or 'isotopic' elements. 1914 — *Chem. Radio-Elements* II. 17 The new data are the isotopism of mesothorium-II and actinium, and of radio-actinium and thorium. 1914 *Rep. Brit. Assoc.* 301 Professor Rutherford..said that the chemical inseparability of certain isotopes was..derived from experiments with small quantities. 1919 Soddy in *Trans. Chem. Soc.* CXV. 18 Its [*sc.* actinium's] definite location in the periodic table, by virtue of its isotopy with mesothorium-2. *Ibid.* 19 Uranium Y, discovered by Antonoff, isotopic with Uranium X. 1922 J. Mills *Within the Atom* iv. 38 Two atomic systems may exist which..are isotopic at the Periodic Table, but differ in the total number of protons in their nuclei. In all chemical combinations or reactions these isotopes are indistinguishable. 1925 J. Joly *Surface-Hist. Earth* ix. 150 *note*, Isotopy is not peculiar to the uranium and thorium groups of elements...Uranium of to-day is known to contain two..radio-active isotopes.

Ispaghul (i·spagūl). Also **ispaghool, ispughol.** [Hind., a. Pers. اسپغول.] A sub-tropical plant, *Plantago Ispaghula*, the seeds of which are used in the manufacture of a mucilaginous drink and for poultices.
a 1815 Roxburgh *Flora Indica* (1820) I. 404 *Ispagool*, the Hindee and Persian name, and that by which it is most generally known in Bengal and on the coast of Coromandel. 1863 Simmonds *Dict. Trade* Suppl. 1874 *Treas. Bot.* Suppl., Ispaghool or Ispughol.

Issue, *sb.* Add: **14. c.** An item or amount of something given out or distributed. orig. *U.S.*
1861 *U.S. Army Regul.* 283 His descriptive list..on which the surgeon shall enter all payments, stoppages, and issues of clothing to him in hospital. 1881 *Rep. Indian Affairs* 10 They agreed to go as soon as the issue of beef..had been made. 1899 T. Hall *Tales* 109 Then our..aching bodies are loaded down with a further issue of ammunition. 1911 H. Quick *Yellowstone N.* xii. 305 'You represent the Elkins interests in the matter of supplying for the issue do you not?' says he. *Ibid.* 321 She hove in sight of the issue. 1919 *War Slang* in *Athenæum* 8 Aug. 727/2 Anything supplied by the Army was an 'issue'.

15. (sense 11) **issue roll** (see quot.); (sense *14 c) *issue boot, cigarette, day, house.*
1927 *Daily Express* 4 Oct. 3 Men..running up and down perpendicular 4-inch steel stairs in *issue boots without arriving in hospital. 1925 Fraser & Gibbons *Soldier & Sailor Words* 129 An '*Issue' cigarette..was a ration cigarette, in contradistinction to one bought at the Canteen. 1874 R. Gliban *Jrnl. Army Life* xxxi. 447 They gave the white physicians much annoyance by coming for medicine only on *issue or ration day. 1878 *Rep. Indian Affairs* 39 Other mechanics are putting up new store and *issue-houses. 1911 H. Quick *Yellowstone N.* xii. 316 The way we..hit the trail f'r the Issue House was a high-class piece o' teamin'. 1886 *Encycl. Brit.* XX. 312/1 The judgment rolls pass through three stages—first, they are plea rolls; then, when the parties join issue, *issue rolls; and lastly,..judgment rolls.

Issue, *v.* Add: **11.** To give things out to (a person); to supply (a person) *with.* (Cf. *Issue *sb.* 14 c.)
1925 T. G. Bruce in E. F. Norton *Fight for Everest, 1924* 344 Every man in the Expedition should be issued with one blanket either in Kalimpong or Phari. 1927 *Daily Tel.* 27 Sept. 8/6 Infantry battalions were issued with two weighted dummies apiece. 1928 *Sunday Express* 18 Mar. 3/2 The extraordinary experience of being twice in a year issued by the same bank with a faulty £1 Treasury note. 1930 F. A. Pottle *Stretchers* 37 Before we were issued our heavy trench shoes.

Istrian (i·striăn), *a.* and *sb.* [f. *Istria*, a peninsula near the head of the Adriatic sea belonging to Austria: see -an.] Of or belonging to, a native or an inhabitant of, Istria.
Istrian stone, a fine limestone resembling marble.
1880 *Encycl. Brit.* XIII. 433/2 The Istrians..were only subdued by the Romans in 177 B.C. after two wars. 1881 Freeman *Venice* 98 The Istrian shore has lost its beauty. 1888 *Encycl. Brit.* XXIV. 149/2 This Istrian stone has for most architectural purposes all the beauty of the finest white marble.

It (it), *sb.* Short for *Italian *vermouth*, in *gin and it*.
1932 Barbara Worsley-Gough *Public Affaires* xiv, As I was sipping my gin-and-it before lunch.

It, *pron.* Add:
1. d. In children's games, the player who takes the part of catching or touching the others. (Cf. He.)
1888 [see *Count *v.* 15 c]. 1923 Kipling *Land & Sea Tales* 279 As the sides are chosen and all submit To the chance of the lot that shall make them 'It'.
e. In emphatic predicative use: The actual or very thing required or expected; that beyond which one cannot go; the *ne plus ultra*; the acme. (In modern use from U.S.)
1900 *Dialect Notes* II. i. 42 Did he know his Greek? I should say so. He was *it*. 1904 F. Lynde *Grafters* xxx. 397 Mrs. Hepzibah..thinks you are It. 1906 *Daily Chron.* 5 Mar. 6/6 There is in America a curious use of the word 'it' conveyed by emphasis. Pre-eminently Roosevelt is 'it'. Next after Roosevelt an American would say 'Shaw is it'. 1915 'Ian Hay' *First Hundred Thousand* xx, You can't go anywhere in London without running up against him. He is It.
f. 'Sex appeal.'
1927 Elinor Glyn *'It' & other Stories* i. 10 He had that nameless charm, with a strong magnetism which can only be called 'It'. 1930 G. B. Stern *Mosaic* III. i. 205 The Viennese composer made his first awed acquaintance with the words pep, kick, body-urge, sex-appeal, a hundred-per-cent. stuff, spin it along, put it over, and It. 1932 *Bystander* 23 Mar. 546 A film star who has proved to producers and film public alike that she is blessed with that undefinable quality called 'It'.
3. f. (Modern literary examples.)
1840 K. H. Digby *Mores Cath.* x. vii. (1847) III. 307/1 In Saxon histories..Thus it says. 1894 tr. *Fouard's St. Paul* xv. (1911) 181/1 From the sequel, as it reads in the Acts, it would seem [etc.]. 1902 H. K. Mann *Lives Popes Early Middle Ages* I. II. 234 *note*, 'In mense Junius Indictione ii,' or x., by mistake it reads in the *Chronicle*. 1927 C. E. Jeffery *One Road to Rome* 20 It says in the guide-book that Archdeacon Manning preached his last sermon as an Anglican in..West Lavington.
g. (More modern examples of *were it not* or *had it not been for, if it were not*, etc. *for*.)
1710 Swift *Jrnl. to Stella* 30 Sept., They may talk of the *you know what*; but, gad, if it had not been for that I should never have been able to get the access I have had. *a* 1732 Gay *Fables* II. xiii, Were it not for this cursed show'r, The park had whil'd away an hour. 1736 Butler *Anal.* II. v, Assistance which they would have had no occasion for, had it not been for their misconduct. 1780 *Mirror* No. 102 The misapplication of the term is so completely ridiculous, as to be beneath contempt, were it not for the mischief that I am convinced has been occasioned by it. 1864 Meredith *Sandra Belloni* xxv, I feel better already, if it weren't for my legs.

Ita. Also **eta, ite.** Ellipt. for *Eta palm, Ita-palm. Also, a drink made from the fermented sap of this tree.
1845 *Encycl. Metrop.* XX. 6/2 The Eta, a smaller kind of this palm, furnishes nuts. 1860 Mayne Reid *Odd People* 360 The *itá* is a true palm-tree, belonging to the genus *mauritia*. 1922 W. E. Roth tr. *R. Schomburgk's Trav. Brit. Guiana* I. 150 A considerable supply of a rarer drink, the Ite.

Italian, *a.* and *sb.* **A.** *adj.* **4.** Add: *Italian clover, nettle, paper, vermouth*; **Italian garden,** a formally laid out garden with statuary and paved walks; **Italian paste,** the paste from which macaroni and vermicelli are made.
1908 *Anim. Management* (War Office) 109 'Valerian', '*Italian' or 'Crimson clover', commonly called 'Trifolium'. [1824 Loudon *Encycl. Gard.* (ed. 2) § 75 The prints..that are to represent paradise are full of clipt hedges, square parterres, straight walks,..marble fountains, and water-works. This may be considered as a poetic assemblage of the component parts of a fine *Italian garden in the seventeenth century.] 1883 W. Robinson *Eng. Flower Garden* p. vi/2 It has been affirmed that none but an Italian garden would have suited South Kensington. 1925 *Daily Tel.* 13 May 19/4 Peacehaven..On main road, close to and overlooking sea and Italian gardens. 1930 *Times Lit. Suppl.* 6 Feb. 108/4 A large variety of *Italian papers. 1851 *Illustr. Catal. Gt. Exhib.* IV. I. 1313 *Italian pastes of various kinds, and samples of vermicelli. 1900 *Punch* 17 Jan. 54/1 I'm dieting myself on *Italian vermouth. 1925 N. Toye & A. H. Adair *Drinks—Long & Short* 12 Three and a half glasses of gin, one and a half of Italian Vermouth.

Italianist (itæ·liănist), *a.* [f. Italian + -ist.] Of, pertaining to, or characterized by Italianism.
1875 Keyes O'Clery *Hist. Ital. Revol.* v. 187 The repeated failures of the leaders of the party of action had now somewhat discouraged their friends and lessened their influence in Italy, and it was some time before they recovered their control over the Italianist movement. 1892 — *Making of Italy* Pref. p. vi, For the details of Custozza and Lissa I have throughout relied upon Italianist sources of information.

Italo-. Add: **I·talophil, -phile** *a.*, friendly to Italy or to what is Italian; *sb.*, one who is Italophile; **I·talophobe,** one affected with **Italopho·bia,** intense dread or fear of Italy.
1906 *Daily Chron.* 28 Mar. 5/4 The appointment of the Italophile reactionary Miushkovitch Ministry. 1920 Buckle *Life Disraeli* V. 130 Protestant and Italophil England rejoiced. 1921 *Contemp. Rev.* Oct. 494 Some Italophobe Germans. 1922 *Ibid.* Sept. 302 The official state of hostility between the Vatican and Italy and the periodical protests against it..maintain in the Catholic masses a feeling of Italophobia. 1927 *Scots Observer* 26 Mar. 12/5 Italy found it easier to buy Ahmed Zogu, turn him into an Italophil.

Itamalic (itămæ·lic), *a.* *Org. Chem.* [f. Ita(conic) + Malic.] Denoting an acid formed from itaconic acid, homologous with malic acid. Hence **Itama·late,** a salt of itamalic acid.
1872 Watts *Dict. Chem.* VI. 761 Itamalic acid crystallises from a syrupy solution in long white interlaced needles. *Ibid.* 762 Ethylic itamalate is a colourless liquid having an agreeable peppery odour.

Itatartaric (ită,taːtæ·rik), *a.* *Org. Chem.* [f. Ita(conic) + Tartaric.] Denoting an acid formed by the action of hypochlorous acid on itaconic acid. Hence **Itata·rtrate,** a salt of itatartaric acid.
1872 Watts *Dict. Chem.* VI. 762 Pure itatartaric acid is amorphous, vitreous, smells like honey when gently heated [etc.]..Calcium itatartrate..forms crystalline masses sparingly soluble in water.

Ite (əit). [The suffix -ite[1] used as an independent word: cf. Ism.] A person or thing that is or may be designated by a sb. in *-ite*.
1852 *Blackw. Mag.* Aug. 260/1 The right honourable gentleman has shown that he is neither a Derby-*ite* nor a Russell-*ite*. Then what *ite* are you? 1906 *Westm. Gaz.* 1 Dec. 9/2 A big factory for explosives, holding dynamite, ballistite, cordite..Heaven knows what 'ites'—sufficient to wreck half the world. 1926 R. W. Hutchinson *Wireless* viii. 138 Most of the 'ites' on the market..are galena subjected to various treatments.

Ite: see *Ita.

Ithel (i·þǝl). Also **ithil.** [Local Arab. أثل.] A species of tamarisk growing in Arabia.
1875 *Encycl. Brit.* II. 236/2 The tamarisk or 'Talh', the southern larch or 'Ithel'. 1881 Lady Anne Blunt *Pilgr. Nejd* I. 84 *note*, The Ithel, a tree grown in every village of Central Arabia. *Ibid.* 85 The roof was of ithel beams. 1924 *Blackw. Mag.* Mar. 351/1 Mackintosh..was watching them from the shelter of a clump of *ithil* bushes.

Ithomiine (iþǫᵘ·mi,əin). *Ent.* [f. mod.L. *Ithomiinæ*, f. Gr. ἰθύς straight + ὦμος shoulder.] One of the *Ithomiinæ*, a subfamily of nymphalid butterflies of tropical America. Also **Itho·miid,** one of the *Ithomiidæ* (the *Ithomiinæ* regarded as a family); also *attrib.* or *adj.*
1930 *Proc. Entom. Soc.* V. 91 An Ithomiine butterfly and its Heliconine mimic taken flying together in NW. Peru.

Itis (əi·tis), *sb.* [The suffix -itis used as an independent word.] A bodily condition, affection, or disease that may be or is described or designated by a word ending in *-itis*.
[1896: cf. Dict. s.v. -itis.] 1909 *Practitioner* Nov. 706 It must be remembered that the complaint referred to [*sc.* mucous colitis] is not, strictly speaking, an *itis* at all.

-itis. Add: In irregular trivial use applied to a state of mind or tendency fancifully regarded as a disease.
1903 Asquith in *Westm. Gaz.* 19 Oct. 5/1 All the people were suffering from a new disease—the disease of fiscalitis. 1906 *Ibid.* 27 Apr. 4/2 Several members of Parliament are suffering from a slight attack of Suffragitis. 1912 *Q. Rev.* Oct 504 Cricket has just suffered from so severe an attack of 'testitis' as to render it highly improbable [etc.].

Ito (īᵘto). A word formed from the initial letters of *Jewish Territorial Organization*, an organization to further territorialism among the Jews. Hence **I·toism, I·toist.**
1906 *Daily Chron.* 22 May 5/2 Mr. Zangwill's Jewish Territorial Organisation, which is more familiarly known from its initial letters as the 'Ito'. 1907 *Ibid.* 14 May 3/3 The Zionists, the Itoists, the Socialist Territorialists.

Ivain (əi·vă,in). *Chem.* [f. mod.L. *Iva*, a genus of North American herbaceous perennials + -in[1].] A bitter resinous compound obtained from plants of the genus *Iva* and *Achillea moschata*.
1892 Morley & Muir *Watts' Dict. Chem.* III. 97/2 Ivain $C_{24}H_{42}O_5$. 1902 Dorland *Med. Dict.* (ed. 2).

Ivi (īᵘvi). Also **eevie.** [Fiji *ivi*, Samoan *ifi*.] The Tahitian chestnut, *Inocarpus edulis*; also, the fruit of this.
1874 *Treas. Bot.* Suppl. 1879 *Encycl. Brit.* IX. 156/2 The ivi or Tahitian chestnut (*Inocarpus edulis*). 1881 C. F. Gordon Cumming *At Home in Fiji* I. 275 A group of eevie

trees appears like one gigantic mass of lovely trailing foliage. 1894 B. Thomson *S. Sea Yarns* 7 He repaired to the mainland to consult a rival oracle named *Na-ivi* (the ivi-tree).

Ivicene (i·visīn), *a.* (*sb.*). [f. *Iviza, Iviça*, one of the Balearic Islands + Sp. *-eño*, -ene.] Of or belonging to Iviza; *spec.* denoting a dog, resembling the greyhound, originating in this island; also as *sb.*
1929 *Morn. Post* 5 Feb. 15/3 The Ivicene Described. *Ibid.*, The Ivicene dog, a breed which has never before been seen in this country.

Ivigtite (i·vigtəit). *Min.* [f. *Ivigt(ut*, Greenland + -ite[1].] A micaceous mineral found in cryolite.
1868 T. D. Rand in *Acad. Nat. Sci. Proc.* 142.

-ivity. Add: In 1895 *-ivity* was chosen as the termination to express a specific quality in a given material, electrical circuit, etc., in contrast to *-ance*, which expresses the measurable quantity of that quality in a given instance.
1895 *Rep. Brit. Assoc.* 197.

Ivoried, *a.* (Modern example.)
1893 Ld. De Tabley *Orpheus in Hades* Poems, Ser. II. (1895) 24 On thy bare and ivoried shoulder.

Ivory. Add: **5. d.** *collect. sing.* and *pl.* The keys of a piano or similar instrument. *colloq.*
1854 Thackeray *Newcomes* vi, It is a wonder how any fingers can move over the jingling ivory so quickly as Miss Cann's.
10. ivory bill (earlier U.S. example); (**vegetable**) **ivory palm** (examples); **ivory plum** *U.S.*, the checker-berry; the creeping snowberry; **ivory wood** *Austral.*, a tree of the staff-tree family, *Siphonodon australe*; also, the timber therefrom.
1872 Coues *N. Amer. Birds* 191 The *ivory-bill and the flicker stand nearly at extremes of the family. 1857 A. Gray *First Less. Bot.* (1866) 136 In the *Ivory Palm it has the hardness as well as the general appearance of ivory. 1871 Kingsley *At Last* viii, The vegetable ivory palm. 1828 J. Neal *R. Dyer* 55 *Ivory-plumbs or clustered bunch-berries. 1887 *Colonial & Indian Exhib. 1886, Rep. Col. Sect.* 429 *Ivory-wood.

Ivy, *sb.* Add: **1. c.** *U.S.* = *poison ivy* (see 2).
1848 Parkman *Oregon Trail* xiii. 205 In the morning Shaw found himself poisoned by ivy.

Ivy-berry. Add: **b.** The checkerberry. *U.S.*
1840 *Southern Lit. Messenger* VI. 518/2 There were the fringed polygala, the buttercup, wild geranium, bunch-plum, ivy-berry.

Ivy-leaf. Add: **b.** *attrib.* = Ivy-leaved.
1909 *Daily Chron.* 5 June 9/5 Ivy-leaf geraniums can be depended on to produce a long succession of blooms.

Ixora (iksōᵊ·rā). *Bot.* [mod.L., ad. *Iswara*, name of a Hindu divinity, = Skr. *īśvará* lord, master, f. *īś* to have, possess: so named because the flowers of this plant are presented as votive offerings in temples.] A rubiaceous plant of the genus of tropical ornamental shrubs or small trees so named, species of which are cultivated as stove flowering shrubs.
1829 Loudon *Encyl. Plants* 100. 1846 Lindley *Veg. Kingd.* 764 The fragrance or beauty..of the Gardenias, Hindsias, Posoquerias, Ixoras,..&c. is unsurpassed. 1871 Kingsley *At Last* vii, The fragrance of the 'white Ixora'.

Iyyar (i·yăɹ). Also **Iyar, Jiar, Jyar, Yiar.** [Heb.] The name of one of the Jewish months, being the eighth of the civil and second of the ecclesiastical year; also called *Zif*.
1737 Whiston *Josephus, Jewish War* v. xi. § 4 The Romans began to raise their banks on the twelfth day of the month Artemisius (Jyar). 1902 *Encycl. Brit.* XXVI. 43/2 In 746 B.C. Calah rebelled, and on the 13th of Iyyar (April), in the following year, Pulu or Pul..seized the throne.

Izba, variant of *Isba.

Iztli (i·stli). Also **itztli, itzli, iztle.** [Nahuatl.] A kind of obsidian used by the Aztecs for knives, arrow-heads, etc.
1883 *Encycl. Brit.* XVI. 216/1.

Izzat (i·zɒt). [Arab. عزة.] Honour, reputation, credit.
1895 Kipling *Day's Work, William the Conqueror* 191 'But I am no goatherd,' said Faiz Ullah. 'It is against my *izzat* (my honour).' 1922 *Blackw. Mag.* Feb. 201/1 *Izzat*, too, generally prescribes that he should be an hour or two late. 1923 Kipling *Land & Sea Tales* 226 It is my *izzat*—my honour.

J

J. Add: **III.** J. = judge, justice: *pl.* JJ. J.A. = Justice of Appeal; J.A.(G.) = Judge Advocate (General); J.C. = Juris-consult, Justice-Clerk. J/A = joint account. J.C.R. = junior common room in the University of Oxford; in some other universities, = joint common room, *i.e.* a common room for both men and women. J.D. = Junior Deacon, Junior Dean. j.n.d. *Psychol.* = just noticeable difference.
1892 *Isis* 8 June 35/2 Only the Pres. of the J.C.R. and the Captain of the Eleven retain their equanimity. 1929 *Encycl. Brit.* VII. 420/1 The just noticeable difference, often called the 'j.n.d.', between the stimuli of two sensations.

Jab, *v.* Add: **d.** *trans.* To give (a person) a stabbing blow with the fist.
1901 R. Fitzsimmons *Phys. Culture & Self-Defense* 114 Jab him, if you can, with your left. 1915 Corri *30 Yrs. Boxing Referee* 38 Time and again he jabbed and patted Smith cleverly on the nose with his left hand.

Jacal (hakā·l). *U.S.* Also **jucal, jackal.** [Mexican Sp., ad. Nahuatl *xacalli*.] A hut constructed of erect poles or stakes filled in with wattle and mud, a type common in Mexico and the south-western United States.
1844 J. J. Webb *Memoirs* 53 In a valley..where the herders had a temporary corrall and jucal made of bushes laid upon poles. *Ibid.* 54 The 'jackal' was full, packed so thick it was impossible to count them. 1854 Bartlett *Pers. Narr. Explor. Texas*, etc. II. xxxvii. 392 The barracks at Fort Fillmore are as yet quite rude, being mere *jackals*. 1894–5 *16th Ann. Rep. Bur. Amer. Ethnol.* 108 This method is known to the Mexicans as '*jacal*', and much used by them. It consists of a row of sticks or thin poles set vertically in the ground and heavily plastered with mud. 1900 R. B. C. Graham *Thirteen Stories* 127 A straw-thatched jacal.

J-acid. *Chem.* A sulphonic acid of dihydroxynaphthalene, which, combined with a diazotized amine, gives dyes that form insoluble lakes with iron, aluminium, or chromium mordants.
1920 *Jrnl. Chem. Soc.* CXVIII. I. 731 The peculiar tinctorial properties of derivatives of *J*-acid. 1929 *Encycl. Brit.* VII. 804/2 J-acid colours. *Ibid.* XVI. 73/2 2-amino-5-naphthol-7-sulphonic acid (J-acid).

Jacinth. Add: **1. e.** A breed of fancy pigeons of a slaty-blue colour.
1854 Meall *Moubray's Poultry* 288 Jacinth,..slaty-blue, and pied on back and wings with white.

Jacitara (dʒæsitā·rā). [Brazil.] In full *Jacitara palm*: A South American palm of the Amazon district, *Desmoncus macroacanthus*.
1860 Mayne Reid *Odd People* 52 The bark of the 'jacitara' palm. 1866 *Treas. Bot.* 396/1.

Jack, *sb.*[1] Add: **2. c.** *Every Jack, not a Jack* (of things): every single, not a single.
1926 Montague *Rough Justice* vi. § 2 Not a Jack window in it but looks bang down the reach. *Ibid.* x. § 2 Till be could get to know every Jack atom there was to be known.
15. e. A contrivance by means of which clocks are wound up when the weight is excessively heavy.
1850 Denison *Clock & Watch-making* 181 The loose jack consists of a frame containing a wheel and pinion with the arbor of the pinion squared to form the winding square.
19. c. Money. *U.S. slang.*
1922 *Short Stories* Feb. 95/2 This Charles was a big bird. ..He had a pile of jack. 1924 P. Marks *Plastic Age* 12 He left us a whale of a lot of jack when he passed out a couple of years ago. 1927 Barbican *Confess. Rum-Runner* xxiii. 260 To do a hold-up in good style you want a gun, but we hadn't enough jack to buy one.
26. *U.S.* (Earlier and later examples.)
1885 *Outing* (U.S.) VII. Oct. 75/1 If you can shoot behind the jack,..Bullock will be glad to paddle you within range of an old buck. 1902 S. E. White *Blazed Trail* viii. 61 They stole about in the evening with a bull's-eye lantern fastened on the head of one of them for a 'jack'.
27. b. *U.S.* (Earlier example.)
1785 Washington *Diaries* II. 458 Dispatched at his own request, the Spaniard who had the charge of my Jack from Spain.
28. *U.S.* (Earlier example.)
1887 *Outing* (U.S.) X. May p. iii/1 The 'jacks' is thicker'n tumble-weeds on the prairie.
b. Horse-flesh which has been salted and washed to deprive it of its peculiar taste. *slang.*
1904 *Daily Chron.* 18 May 8/5 Horseflesh so treated is known as 'Jack', and if it passes through a mincing machine and is mixed with fat, flesh, and spice, it cannot then be distinguished from that of the ox.
33. jack-high *a.* and *adv.* *Bowls*, as far up the green as the jack lies; **jack-hunting** *U.S.* (earlier example); **jack-ladder,** (*b*) = *Jack-chain 2; **jackman,** one who attends to a jack; **jack-pot,** (*a*) (earlier U.S. example); (*b*) *Logging*, an unskilful piece of work; (*c*) *Logging* (see quot. 1905); **jack-shaft, -shafting,** a countershaft, -shafting; **jack-tenter,** a fly-frame tenter (*Dict. Occup. Terms* 1921–7); **jack-wheel** = *15 e.
1886 *Rules of Bowling* 21 All players, while looking on, to stand *jack-high at least, and, unless acting as directors, not within three yards of the jack. 1881 *Harper's Mag.* Oct. 690/2 It is the only way to get venison in that season of the year which intervenes between *Jack-hunting and still-hunting. 1886 *Encycl. Brit.* XXI. 345/1 From the rear end of the mill, at the second story or saw-floor, a '*jack ladder' is constructed of heavy timber. 1929 *Ibid.* XIV. 482/1 An endless spiked conveyor known as a jack ladder. 1921 *Dict. Occup. Terms* (1927) § 089 Craneman,..*jackman..., lifts doors of oven, either by hand or by mechanical means, to facilitate charging and discharging. 1888 *St. Louis Globe Democrat* 27 Feb. (Farmer), I never saw such a big game as that was...They played tremendous *Jack-Pots. 1905 *Terms Forestry & Logging* 40 *Jackpot*,..an irregular pile of logs. 1901 *J. Black's Carp. & Build., Scaffolding* 72 The electric motor..with *jack-shaft and friction drive. 1929 *Encycl. Brit.* XIV. 284/2 The geared jack shaft drive. *Ibid.* XVIII. 392/1 *Jack or counter shafting. 1850 Denison *Clock & Watch-m.* 182 The going part never requires a *jack wheel to wind it up except in very large clocks.
35. Jack Johnson [from the name of a noted negro boxer, whose nickname in America was 'The Big Smoke'] = *Black Maria 2; **Jack Mormon** *U.S.*, a 'Gentile' with Mormon leanings; hence **Jack-Mormonism.**
1914 *Illustr. Lond. News* 10 Oct. 504/1 The German '*Jack Johnson' siege-guns. *Ibid.* 505 The gigantic projectile which on bursting makes the black smoke called 'Jack Johnson'. 1914 *Times* 23 Dec. 3/2 A 'Jack Johnson' burst in a field near us and killed 30 horses. *Ibid.* 24 Dec. 6/5 An occasional 'Jack Johnson' shell. 1915 *Punch* 1 Dec. 442/2 If a blinkin' Jack Johnson didn't blow the 'ole 'ouse out of me 'and! 1927 Empey *From Fire Step* 96 Sometimes whole platoons would disappear, especially when a 'Jack Johnson' plunked into their middle. 1850 *Congress. Globe* 27 June App. 822 He was..a *jack Mormon in religion, and a renegade Democrat in politics. 1854 T. Ford *Hist. Illinois* (1864) 33 The county contained a goodly number of inhabitants in favor of peace...These were stigmatised by the name of Jack Mormons. 1890 *Congress. Rec.* 2 Apr. 2941/2 In our country we have a *genus homo* called 'Jack-Mormon',..a class of individuals who do not belong to the Mormon church,..yet who are ever found doing the bidding of Mormon priests. 1900 *Ibid.* 24 Jan. 1129/2 A Jack Mormon county Attorney ruling the supreme court of Utah. 1870 J. H. Beadle *Life in Utah* 197 From 1850 to 1862, '*jack-Mormonism' ruled at Washington.
36. *Jack o' page*, a wedge driven between the walings and the runners of a trench to tighten up the contact. *Jack the Painter*, a kind of acrid green tea used in the Australian bush. *Jack the Ripper*, popular name for a murderer of women in London (1888–91) who mutilated the bodies of his victims; also *allusively*.
1855 G. C. Mundy *Our Antipodes* (ed. 3) 163 Another notorious ration tea of the bush is called '*Jack the Painter'—a *very* green tea indeed. 1880 G. Walch *Victoria in 1880* 113 (Morris) Special huts had to be provided for them [*sc.* the sundowners], where they enjoyed eleemosynary rations of mutton, damper, and 'Jack the Painter'. 1890 *Pall Mall Gaz.* 7 Mar. 5/1 A *Jack the Ripper outrage at Moscow. 1902 *To-Day* XXXV. 99/2 Now we know 'oo Jack the Ripper was! 1906 *Strand Mag.* Mar. 289/2 A statue of General Booth..defying Jack-the-Ripper to take his money-box. 1909 *Westm. Gaz.* 29 June 5/2 Those mysterious political Jack-the-Rippers designated by the name of the Confederates. 1919 C. P. Thompson *Cocktails* 17 If only the officer would let him have a whack at her over the open sights, he'd do the Jack-the-ripper act on her in half a tick.
37. Jack-salmon (earlier U.S. example).
1871 *Game Laws* (Penn.) in *Fur, Fin & Feather* (1872) 122 The species commonly known as Susquehanna salmon, pike, perch, jack salmon..shall henceforth not be taken.. during their spawning time.
38. Jack-bean *U.S.*, a climbing plant of the genus *Canavali* and its fruit; **Jack-in-the-pulpit** (earlier example); **Jack-oak** (earlier and later examples); **Jack-pine,** a name given to several species of pine, as *Pinus banksiana, P. divaricata, P. murrayana.*
1885 'C. E. Craddock' *Prophet Gt. Smoky Mtn.* xv. 280 The yellow gourds and the purple blooms of the *Jack-bean. 1869 Jane G. Fuller *Uncle John's Flower Gatherers* 36 Water arums (*Jack-in-the-pulpit we called it then). 1816 U. Brown *Jrnl.* in *Maryland Hist. Mag.* X. 266 *Jack Oaks and other Scrub Wood. 1836 D. B. Edward *Hist. Texas* iv. 68 The post-oak and Jack-oak are considered in Texas as every man's property. 1888 *St. Louis Globe Democrat* 20 Jan. (Farmer) The Southern part of Illinois ..is full of sand-hills and jack oak. 1884 *Encycl. Brit.* XVII. 824/1 *Pinus contorta* (black pine, or *jack pine). 1904 *New York Even. Post* 6 May 6 Jack pines are being planted over hundreds of acres. 1925 *Chambers's Jrnl.* June 381/2 Where the jackpine grows low and twisted.

Ja·ckal, *v.* [f. Jackal *sb.*] *intr.* To play the jackal (see the sb. 2), as by performing works of drudgery for another.
c 1900 Dobson *18th Cent. Studies* (1914) 204 Johnson..lost many of the papers lent to him by Percy. Malone, who jackalled for him, lost others. 1900 Kipling in *Daily Mail* 21 Apr. 4/5 For three months she had jackalled behind the army..and in that time had carried over thirteen hundred sick and wounded.

Jack-chain. Add: **2.** *Logging* (see quot.).
1905 *Terms Forestry & Logging* 40 *Jack chain*, an endless spiked chain, which moves logs from one point to another, usually from the mill pond into the sawmill.

Jacker. Add: **b.** *jacker-off, -up*: see quots. 1921.
1881 *Instr. Census Clerks* (1885) 70. 1904 *Westm. Gaz.* 28 Apr. 4/1 It was in the lace factory that the lad was set to work as a 'jacker-off'. 1921 *Dict. Occup. Terms* (1927) § 399 *Jacker-off* (lace), takes off from bobbins, waste lengths of unused threads, and winds them on to large wooden bobbins, using a small winding machine. *Ibid.* 688 *Jacker-up* (lead pencil making), places a number of glued pencils together in a clamp, and screws down clamp to make glueing secure; removes pencils when clamping is complete. 1924 Sir Jas. Marchant *Dr. John Clifford* i. 5 Three-fourths of the children were jackers-off or 'piecers'.

Jacket, *sb.* Add: **1. f.** *To dust* (a person's) *jacket* (earlier U.S. example).
1806 *Balance* 18 Mar. 82 (Th.) Col. Smith will never again way lay Cheetham with a large club, to dust his jacket.
g. That worn by soldiers of the horse artillery; *transf.* (*a*) a soldier of the horse artillery; (*b*) an appointment to the Royal Horse Artillery; *to get, obtain the jacket*, to secure such an appointment.
1898 *Geog. Jrnl.* (R.G.S.) May 556 Lieut. Tanner obtained his 'jacket', and was the *beau ideal* of a horse-artillery officer. 1908 *Westm. Gaz.* 15 Oct. 5/3 Until 1895..a 'jacket'—i.e., a post in the Royal Field Horse Artillery—might be given to an officer of Field Artillery or of Garrison Artillery. 1909 J. R. Ware *Passing Engl.*, *Jacket (Military)*, a soldier who wears a jacket (chiefly cavalry or horse artillery). 1925 Fraser & Gibbons *Soldier & Sailor Words*, *Jacket, to get the*: colloquial for an appointment to the Royal Horse Artillery. In allusion to the R.H.A. uniform jacket, in contradistinction to the tunic of the Royal Artillery.
2. b. See also *dust-jacket* (*Dust *sb.*[1] 8 e).
d. *Ordnance.* An outer coil of wrought iron which is wound round and shrunk upon the steel barrel of a gun to strengthen it.
a 1889 Michaelis tr. *Monthaye's Krupp & De Bange* 24 (Cent. Dict.) The tube, without reinforce, is encircled by a single band or jacket (Mantel, in German), shrunk on. 1902 *Kynoch Jrnl.* III. Apr.–May 79/2 A second gun..having a jacket of cast steel. 1902 *Encycl. Brit.* XXV. 674/1 He made a homogeneous cylindrical jacket by winding a bar of wrought-iron round a mandril slightly smaller than the barrel.

Jacketed, *a.* Add:
2. *Ordnance.* Having a 'jacket' (see *2 d above).
1884 Knight *Dict. Mech.* Suppl., *Jacketed Gun*.., one strengthened by bands fitted or shrunk on to the tube proper. 1901 *Kynoch Jrnl.* II. Aug.–Sept. 127/1 A completely nickel jacketed bullet.

Jack-in-the-box. Add: **7. f.** *Cotton Weaving and Engineering.* Differential motion.
1900 *Engineering Mag.* XIX. 765/1 The compensating gear or Jack-in-the-box, linking the driven wheels. 1904 *Technol. & Sci. Dict.* (ed. Goodchild & Tweney) 161/2.

Jack-knife, *sb.* Add: **1.** (Earlier Amer. examples.)
1711 *Springfield* (Mass.) *Rec.* IX. 39 One Dozen of Jack Knives, at six pence the knife. 1760 *Boston News-Letter* 1 May, Jack-knives, pen-knives, buckles and combs.
3. *attrib.* **jack-knife dive,** a dive in which, on leaving the diving-board, the body assumes the shape of U.
1928 *Radio Times* 11 May 274/2 A..member of the Amateur Diving Association—one of those people whom we have all seen on the news films doing jack-knife and swallow dives from incredible heights. 1929 *Encycl. Brit.* XXI. 666/1 Pike Dive, or American Jack Knife.
Hence **Jack-knife** *v.* (Earlier U.S. examples.)
1806 *Balance* 22 July 228 (Th.) A sailor..Jackknifed (as he termed it) the poor creature [*sc.* a cat] in several places about the head. 1888 *Century Mag.* June 251/2 The practice..of dodging shots, 'jackknifing' under fire.

Ja·ck-leg. *U.S.* [Jack *sb.*[1] The allusion is not clear.] Used *attrib.* (esp. with *lawyer*) and *absol.* as a term of contempt or depreciation.
1853 'P. Paxton' *Stray Yankee in Texas* 137 A sorter jack-leg lawyer. 1888 *Florida Times Union* 11 Feb. (Farmer) The State Bar Association is disposed to draw the line between attorneys and jack-leg lawyers. 1891 *Harper's Mag.* June 160/1 Once I was called a jack-leg and shyster. 1902 Harben *Abner Daniel* ii. 16 The Atlanta jack-leg lawyer is akin to the Tompkins family some way. 1902 A. H. Lewis *Wolfville Days* xvi. 242 A jack-laig doctor.
So **Ja·ck-legged** *a.* *U.S.* = prec.
1839 *Congress. Globe* App. 127 A set of jack-legged, pettifogging lawyers.

Jack-rabbit. *U.S.* (Earlier examples.)
1870 Keim *Sheridan's Troopers* xvii. (1885) 108 The animals were longer than the Jack Rabbit proper. 1870 J. H.

Beadle *Life in Utah* 222 (Th.) The jack-rabbit is about four times as large as the common 'cotton-tail'. 1878 B. F. Taylor *Between Gates* 192 The ears of a Jack Rabbit..shut back like a knife-blade at hearing the wheels.

Jacksonian (dʒæksōᵘ·niăn), *a.* [See -ian.] **1.** Pertaining to or characteristic of Andrew *Jackson* (1767–1845), seventh president of the United States of America, a prominent leader of the Democratic party. Also *sb.*, a follower of Jackson. Hence **Jackso·nianism.**
1831 in Thornton *Amer. Gloss.* 625 The anti-Kemble Jacksonians of the Fourth Ward. 1885 H. C. Lodge *Daniel Webster* (ed. 5) 208 To bring overwhelming defeat to the 'Jacksonian democracy'. 1906 W. Churchill *Coniston* v. 51 He..preached the word of Jacksonian Democracy in all the farmhouses round about. *Ibid.* 57 The conscientious Jacksonians who were misguided enough to believe in such a ticket. 1929 *Encycl. Brit.* I. 156/2 Up to this point Adams's career had been almost uniformly successful, but his presidency (1825–29) was in most respects a failure, owing to the virulent opposition of the Jacksonians. *Ibid.* IV. 585/1 Calhoun,..during the remainder of the Jackson regime, was a severe critic of Jacksonianism.
2. Described by or named after John Hughlings *Jackson* (1834–1911), English physician, in *Jacksonian convulsions, epilepsy.*
1887 *Buck's Handbk. Med. Sci.* V. 199/2 Jacksonian Epilepsy. Convulsive seizures, in the beginning limited to a part of the body, most frequently the fingers of one hand, sometimes one side of the face, or one foot. 1906 *Practitioner* Nov. 689 The 'attacks' might be compared to Jacksonian epilepsy. 1908 *Ibid.* Oct. 558 Jacksonian convulsions. 1929 *Encycl. Brit.* IV. 22/1 Many apparent Jacksonian attacks are manifestations of ordinary epilepsy.

Jacksonism (dʒæ·ksǝniz'm). = *Jacksonianism.
1846 M'Kenney *Mem.* I. ix. 200 His ancient..ally in the cause of Jacksonism.

Jacky. 1. Add: A landsman's nickname for a sailor. *U.S.* 1897 [see Dict.].

Jacobæa (dʒækǒbī·ă). [mod.L., fem. of *Jacobæus* Jacobean.] **1.** *Jacobæa lily*: see Jacobean *a.* 2 b.
2. The ragwort, *Senecio Jacobæa*; also, the purple jacobæa, *Senecio elegans*, a cultivated species from S. Africa. 1884 Miller *Plant-n.*

Jacobean, *a.* Add: **1. b.** In the furniture trade, designating wood of the colour of dark oak, or the colour itself.
1928 *Daily Mail* 31 July 1/2 It can be obtained in Light Brown or Jacobean coloured solid oak. 1930 *Daily Express* 8 Sept. 2 This fine Chest is..finished Jacobean colour.

Jacob's ladder. Add:
5. An elevator consisting of a series of bucket-shaped receptacles fixed upon an endless chain.
1845 G. Dodd *Brit. Manuf.* V. 31 The hops are raised to the boiler by a contrivance something like the buckets of a dredging-machine; it is called a 'Jacob's ladder'. 1853 *Household Words* VII. 491/1 The malt..being precipitated up a curious contrivance called a 'Jacob's ladder'. 1860 Ure *Dict. Arts* II. 589 It [*sc.* the bloom] is squeezed four times before it leaves the rolls and falls upon the Jacob's ladder. 1884 W. H. Greenwood *Steel & Iron* 303 The puddled ball..falling from the bottom shoot of the machine on to a Jacob's ladder or other elevator.

Jacobson (dʒēᵊ·kǝbsǝn). The name of the Danish anatomist Ludwig L. *Jacobson* (1783–1843), used in genitive to designate various organs, as **Jacobson's nerve,** the tympanic nerve; **Jacobson's organ,** an olfactory nerve found in mammals and some reptiles; also **Jacobson's reflex** (see quot. 1913). Similarly **Jacobsonian** (dʒēᵊkǝbsōᵘ·niăn) *a.*
1836–9 *Todd's Cycl. Anat.* II. 495/2 *Ramus tympanicus nervi glosso-pharyngei*; nerve of Jacobson. 1860 H. Gray *Anat.* (ed. 2) 524 The tympanic branch (Jacobson's nerve), arises from the petrous ganglion. 1887 *Encycl. Brit.* XXII. 166/1 In snakes and lizards a second olfactory organ is found embedded between the turbinals and the vomer and is known as 'Jacobson's organ'. 1889 A. Macalister *Text-bk. Hum. Anat.* 634 The Jacobsonian cartilages and the single or septal cartilage. *Ibid.* 635 Jacobsonian Organ. 1893 *H. Morris's Hum. Anat.* 928 Jacobsonian cartilages.—In the septal cartilage above the opening of Stenson's canal there is a small pouch which presents a minute opening below. This is the representative of the Jacobsonian organ. 1913 Dorland *Med. Dict.* (ed 7), *Jacobson's reflex*, a reflex seen in cerebral spastic paralysis of the upper extremities.

Jacqueminot (ʒa·kmino). [Name of General J. F. *Jacqueminot* (1787–1865), of Paris.] In full *Général Jacqueminot*: a scarlet-crimson rose of the hybrid perpetual variety, introduced in 1853.
1863 *Gardeners' Ann.* 13. 1869 S. R. Hole *Bk. Roses* 137 *General Jacqueminot*, a Hybrid China Rose,..forms, with his vigorous branches and fine large purple-crimson flowers, a fine Pillar Rose. 1893 W. Robinson *Engl. Flower Garden* (ed. 3) 644/2 General Jacqueminot and many other H. Ps. [= hybrid perpetuals] do not usually bloom after the month of August. 1908 *Daily Chron.* 10 Mar. 3/2 English roses have ..arrived..and include the beautiful Jacqueminot.

Jacutinga (dʒækutī·ngā). Also **jaco-.** [See quot. 1869.] A gold-bearing iron ore of Brazil.
1869 R. F. Burton *Explor. Highl. Brazil* I. 301 The mysterious Jacutinga. The name is evidently derived from the well-known Penelope called Jácu-tinga (P. Leucoptera) from the white spots upon its crested head and blue-black wings. This substance of iron black, with metallic lustre, sparkles in the sun with silvery mica...The constituents are micaceous iron schist and friable quartz mixed with specular iron, oxide of manganese, and fragments of talc. 1876 *Encycl. Brit.* IV. 224/2 Most gold is afforded by..the rock called Itacolumite... and by certain iron ores known as Itabirite and Jacutinga.

Jade, *sb.*[2] Add: **1. c.** A colour resembling that of jade; jade-green. Also *attrib.*
1921 H. Walpole *Young Enchanted* iv. iv, The faint jade of the fading light. 1926 Leinster *Dew on Leaf* iii. 42 The jade rabbit (moon) nibbles the clouds. 1928 *Manchester Guardian Weekly* 31 Aug. 175/3 A faint breeze blowing in from a North Sea of misty jade.

Jadoo (dʒā·dū). Also **jadu.** [Hind. جادو *jādū* enchantment.] Magic, conjuring. *Comb.* **Ja·doo-wallah** [Wallah], a Hindu conjurer.
1886 Kipling *Plain Tales fr. Hills* (1890) 135 If there was any *jadoo* afoot. 1890 *Q. Rev.* July 244 The Indian conjurers, or Jadoo-walla. 1924 J. A. Tyson *Barge of Haunted Lives* iv. 93 These took me before a jaboowallah [*sic*], who..had performed some of his tricks before me at Rajiid.

J'adoube (ʒadū·b). *Chess. Disused.* [Fr., = I adjust.] An expression used when a player wishes to touch a chessman without making a move.
1822 *Sarratt's Game of Chess* 3 If a player touch one of his adversary's pieces, without saying '*J'adoube*', he may be compelled to take it. 1847 H. Staunton *Chess-Player's Handbk.* 36 A Piece or Pawn touched must be played, unless at the moment of touching it the player say '*J'adoube*', or words to that effect.

Jaeger (yē·gǝɹ). Proprietary name of an all-wool clothing material manufactured originally by Dr. [Gustav] Jaeger's Sanitary Woollen System Co. Ltd.
1891 *Dr. Jaeger's Sanit. Woollen Syst.* Revised Price List 40 Jaeger Corsets. 1893 Kate Sanborn *Truthful Woman S. California* 121, I really suffered during a drive, although encased in the heaviest of Jaeger flannels. 1908 A. S. M. Hutchinson *Once aboard the Lugger* VI. i. (1922) 300 When the Jaeger nightdress fell comfortable about her. 1912 H. Walpole *Prelude to Adventure* viii, Over Bunning's red wrists the brown ends of a Jaeger vest protruded from under the shirt. 1921 Galsworthy *To Let* I. iv, His..feet thrust into Jaeger slippers.

Jaffa (dʒæ·fă). [mod. (Arabic) name of *Joppa*, an ancient seaport of Palestine.] In full *Jaffa orange*: an orange of the kind grown in the gardens east of Joppa.
1897 Sir J. D. Hooker in L. Huxley *Life* (1918) II. 408 Jaffas and Floridas are disappointing. 1909 *Westm. Gaz.* 20 Apr. 7/2 The practice of 'faking' oranges by boiling and greasing them and selling them as Jaffas.

Jag, *sb.*[2] **1. c.** Add: Also, a drinking bout: orig. in phr. *To have* or *fetch a jag*: to have a 'load' of drink, to be drunk. *slang.*
1678 Ray *Prov.* 87 Proverbiall Periphrases of one drunk.. He has a jagg or load. 1905 *Daily Chron.* 12 Dec. 4/7 Many young fellows brought their girls, and one did even worse than that by fetching a complete jag to the festival. 1920 H. C. McNeile *Bull Dog Drummond* iv. § 1 A friend who is sleeping off the effects of what low people call a jag. 1921 E. Wallace *Law Four Just Men* iv. 112 He had been on a jag the night before and had finished up in what he called an opium house. 1928 *Daily Tel.* 9 Oct. 11/3 Twelve additional deaths to-day are attributed to week-end 'jags', which have been traced to 'speak-easies'.

Jagatai (dʒægătā·i). [The native name of Turkestan, f. *Jagatai*, a son of Jenghiz Khan, who inherited it.] The branch of the Turkic group of languages spoken in Turkestan. Also *attrib.* Hence **Jagata·ian, Jagata·ic** *adjs.*, pertaining to Turkestan or the dialects spoken there.
1843 *Penny Cycl.* XXV. 406/1 Jagatái, [spoken] in the greater part of independent Turkistán...The Jagatái language has a valuable literature. 1867 *Chambers's Encycl.* IX. 589/2 The former [*sc.* Eastern Turkish] is mainly represented by the Uigur (Jagatai). *Ibid.* 590/1 The Eastern [Turkish] or Jagataian [literature]. 1929 *Encycl. Brit.* XXII. 920/1 The Uzbeg (Jagatai Turkish) tongue.

Jagged (dʒægd), *a.*[2] *U.S. slang.* [f. *Jag *sb.*[2] 1 c + -ed[2].] Drunk.
1902 *Telegram* (Winnipeg) 20 Aug. 7/4 Miller was pretty well jagged. *a* 1906 'O. Henry' *Trimmed Lamp*, etc. 162 What I want is a masterful man that slugs you when he's jagged, and hugs you when he ain't jagged.

Jaggery. 1. Add: Also applied to any kind of crude sugar.
1839 Ure *Dict. Arts* 1198 This goor [*sc.* crude boiled juice of the sugar cane] is of various qualities; one of which, in most common use for making sugar, is known amongst the English settlers under the name of *jaggery*. 1914 *Scotsman* 26 Sept. 5/2, 58 bags cane Jaggery..; and 55 bags Palmyra Jaggery.

Jahvist. Also in form **Yahvist.**
1898 G. B. Gray in *Expositor* May 347 The Elohist and Yahvist must have copied the Babylonian story. 1912 Macalister *Hist. & Civiliz. Palestine* vii. 92 The traditions set down by the Yahvist and the Elohist.

Jail, *sb.* **2.** Add: *jail-fee* (later U.S. examples); *jail-delivered* adj.; **jail-bleach** (see quot.); **jail-break,** a breaking out of jail.
1888 'C. E. Craddock' *Broomsedge Cove* ii. 29 A man with that singular pallor acquired by years of indoor life, and known as '*jail-bleach'. 1910 Jer. Hart *Vigilante Girl* xix. 266 Hamlin did not yet know of the *jail-break. 1831 Mary A. Holley *Texas Lett.* (1833) 87 Louisiana..is the receptacle of the redundant and *jail-delivered slaves of other countries. 1846 D. Corcoran *Pickings* 60, I shall let you go this time on paying your *jail-fees. 1862 *Game Laws* (Md.) in *Fur, Fin & Feather* (1872) 84 The officer who desired the commitment shall pay the jail fees at the rate of twenty five cents per day.

Jake (dʒēᵘk). *sb.* (*a.*). *U.S. slang.* [prob. the personal name *Jake*, abbrev. of *Jacob*.] A rustic lout: usually *country jake*. Also as *adj.*
1884 'Mark Twain' *Huck. Finn* xx. 194 No, don't you worry—these country jakes won't ever think of that. 1902 Clapin *Dict. Amer.* 242 *Jake*, a rough, uncouth country fellow. 1911 [see *Country 16].
b. *adj.* Excellent, admirable, fine.
1924 P. Marks *Plastic Age* xxii. 247 She assured Hugh that Sanford men looked awfully smooth in their knickers and white flannels; in fact, she said the whole college seemed jake to her.

Jalapinol, -ole (dʒæ·lăpinǫl, -ōᵘl). *Chem.* [f. Jalapin + -ol.] A crystalline substance formed by the hydrolysis of jalapin or jalapic acid. So **Ja·lapinolate,** a salt of jalapinolic acid. **Ja·lapino·lic** *a.*, derived from jalapinol, in *jalapinolic acid*.
1864 Watts tr. *Gmelin's Hand-bk. Chem.* XVI. 402 Jalapinolate of ammonia precipitates aqueous chloride of calcium. *Ibid.* 404 Jalapin and jalapic acid are resolved by contact with mineral acids, slowly at ordinary, more quickly at elevated temperatures, into jalapinol and sugar. *Ibid.* 405 Glucosides of Jalapinolic Acid. 1885 *Jrnl. Chem. Soc.* XLVIII. I. 669 Jalapinole crystallises in needles melting at 63°, and has the properties of an aldehyde.

Jam, *sb.*[1] Add: **1.** Also *spec.* in logging, an accumulation of logs in a river. Also *attrib.*
1873 J. H. Beadle *Undevel. West* 719 (Th.) I saw a 'jam' just above the Copperhead Rapids, near Anoka. 1905 *Terms Forestry & Logging* 40 *Jam, to break a*, to start in motion logs which have been jammed. 1909 S. E. White *Rules of Game* I. xii. 69 'Where's the drive, doctor?' asked the lumberman. 'This is the jam camp,' replied the cook. 'The jam's upstream a mile or so.' 1929 *Encycl. Brit.* XIV. 482/1 A log jam in the Montreal river, Ontario, Canada.
2. *Wireless.* Jamming, or an instance of this.
1914 P. Vaux *Sea-Salt & Cordite* 129, I don't like this wireless jam! 1927 W. E. Collinson *Contemp. Engl.* 113 The trouble caused by jams, atmospherics, and howlings.

Jam, *sb.*[2] **c.** Add: *jam-jar.*
1895 *Army & Navy Co-op. Soc. Price List* 785 [Cut glass] Jam Jar. 1902 Barnes-Grundy *Thames Camp* iv. 67 Jane went on with her jam-jar trap (for wasps).

Jam, *v.*[1] Add:
3. c. Wireless. *trans.* To cause interference with (a signal). Also *intr.* To be affected by such interference caused by the interposition of unwanted signals; freq. in *vbl. sb.*
1914 P. Vaux *Sea-Salt & Cordite* 46 Communications became irregularly jammed. *Ibid.* 47 We'll stop this jamming, wherever it's coming from. 1920 *Discovery* Apr. 116/2 When the reception of a message is thus interfered with by other messages being sent at the same time, the message is said to be 'jammed'. *Ibid.*, The jamming of a message may also be caused by stray ether disturbances in the atmosphere itself. 1923 *Harmsworth's Wireless Encycl.* II. 1226/1 Cutting out the local jamming of a near transmitting station by the careful use of loose coupling. 1926 Spanner *Naviators* 124 The Admiral had answered the Japanese C.-in-C. by sending out jamming signals immediately the British scout had been driven down. 1930 *B.B.C. Year-bk.* 444/1 *Jamming*, interference with wanted wireless signals due to other wireless transmitters.
5. b. *trans.* To apply or put (a brake) *on* violently.
1925 *Morris Owner's Manual* 11 Jambing on the brakes at the last moment.
c. *fig.* 'To push (a bill or measure) through the regular routine of a legislative body by the brute force of a majority controlled by "the machine", without proper consideration or discussion' (Cent. Dict. Suppl.). *U.S.*
1901 *N.Y. Com. Advertiser* 11 Apr. (Cent. D. Suppl.). 1926 *Harper's Mag.* Feb. 342/2 The bills hurriedly jammed through our legislative tribunals each year.

Jam, *v.*[2] Add: **2.** To make into jam.
1905 *Daily Chron.* 2 Dec. 4/4 Apples, pears, plums, berries, &c. (fresh or dried, or jammed, or tinned, or bottled).

Jam (dʒæm), *adv.* and *a.* orig. *U.S.* Also **jamb.** [f. Jam *v.*[1]] **A.** *adv.* **1.** Closely; in close contact or with firm pressure. Often with *up*.
1825 J. Neal *Bro. Jonathan* II. 52 He had been sitting, for two or three hours,..'jam up' in a back seat. 1842 *American Pioneer* I. 184 The next moment the sloop ran jamb against it. 1852 Mrs. Stowe *Uncle Tom's C.* iv, 'It'll stand, if it only keeps jam up agin de wall!' said Mose.
2. Thoroughly, completely, perfectly.
1835 D. Crockett *Col. Crockett's Tour* 192 [Andrew Jackson] went jam up for war; but the cabinet got him down to half heat. 1846 *Congress. Globe* 22 May 852 Their notion is that we go jam up to 54° 40', and the Russians come jam down to the same. 1866 C. H. Smith *Bill Arp* 61 Linton played his part of the programme jam up. 1921 R. Hichens *Spirit of Time* xii, 'Is your passenger list full?' 'Jam full, sir.'
b. With *up*: Close up to, very near.
1874 E. Eggleston *Circuit Rider* xvi. 142 How far you rid her to day?..Jam up fifty miles, and over tough roads.
B. *adj.* Perfect, thorough, 'slap-up'.
1842 *Southern Lit. Messenger* VII. 54/2 Introduced him to the 'jam-up little company' in his command. 1853 *Daily Morning Her.* (St. Louis) 9 May (Th.) Wiggins's tavern was a jam-up house of amusement. 1855 Haliburton *Nature & Human Nature* xxi. II. 261 In Paradise..connubial bliss, I allot, was rael jam up.

Jamaica. Add: Also in names of other plants grown in Jamaica and the West Indies; **Jamaica ginger,** white ginger (see Ginger *sb.* 1); **Jamaica kino** (see Kino[1] 1); **Jamaicaman,** a vessel engaged in the Jamaica trade.
1818 *Public Ledger* LVIII. 4/5, 20 Bags and 10 Casks *Jamaica Ginger. 1870 [see Ginger *sb.* 1]. 1882 *Encycl.*

Brit. XIV. 91/2 Between 1808 and 1820 a substance was met with in French commerce under the name of *Jamaica kino. 1809 *Ann. 10th Congress* 2 Sess. 1037 He recollected a story ..of one of our privateers being beat off by a *Jamaicaman. 1866 *Treas. Bot.* s.v. *Monodora*, *Jamaica or American Nutmegs.

Jamaican (dʒămēⁱ·kăn). *a.* (*sb.*). [f. JAMAICA + -AN.] (A native or inhabitant) of Jamaica.

1771 W. GUTHRIE *New Geogr. Gramm.* (ed. 3) 677 The Jamaicans were undoubtedly very numerous, until reduced by earthquakes. 1902 SIR J. D. HOOKER in L. Huxley *Life* (1918) II. 408 The Jamaicans do not deserve the sacrifice England is making in respect of its fruit trade. 1920 *Glasgow Herald* 4 Sept. 5 A volume of Jamaican studies. 1921 *19th Cent.* Apr. 613 If surplus Jamaican labour could cut the Panama Canal.

Jambone (dʒæ·mbōᵘn). *Euchre.* (See quot.)

1885 *Euchre: how to play it* 41 A Jambone is to play a lone hand with the cards exposed on the table, and to give to that adversary who is entitled to the lead, or whose first play it is, the privilege of calling one of the exposed cards to the first trick played, or if the jambone player has the lead, to call upon him to lead any one of the exposed cards.

Jamboree (dʒæmbŏrī·). Add: **b.** *Euchre.* A lone hand containing the five highest cards.

1886 *Euchre: how to play it* 45 *Jamboree* signifies the combination of the five highest cards, as, for example, the two Bowers, Ace, King, and Queen of trumps in one hand, which entitles the holder to count sixteen points. The holder of such a hand simply announces the fact, as no play is necessary; but should he play the hand as a Jambone, he can count only eight points, whereas he could count sixteen if he announced it as a Jamboree.

c. The name given to the 1920 International Rally of Boy Scouts, and now applied to any large scout rally. Also *attrib.*

1919 *Times* 17 Oct. 9/6 The Council of the Boy Scouts Association announce that a 'Jamboree' will be held at Olympia, for about eight days next August. 1931 *Mag. Univ. Students' Union* Apr. 2 The Jamboree spirit was marvellous.

Jammy (dʒæ·mi), *a.* [f. JAM *sb.*² + -Y¹.] Covered with jam, sticky. Also *fig.*, good, first-rate; easy, 'soft'. Hence **Ja·mminess.**

1895 *Punch* 12 Oct. 180/1 The way as that Sam chewed the rag was just jammy. 1899 KIPLING *Stalky* 228 Jam for the Sixth! Jam for us! Either way it's jammy! 1908 'IAN HAY' *Right Stuff* xi. § 3 We had disposed of grouse sandwiches..and jammy scones. 1915 D. O. BARNETT *Lett.* 170 If I get a 'jammy' one as it is called, I shall be back pretty soon. 1920 *Chambers's Jrnl.* 862/2 She was aroused by the ..jammy caresses of her blue-eyed nephews. 1929 G. W. DEEPING *Roper's Row* xvii. § 1 The midday meal—such as it was—was taken al fresco on the pavement. There was a jamminess about these meals and about the ladies' fingers.

Janapa (dʒæ·năpă). Also -um. = SUNN.

1851 *Illustr. Catal. Gt. Exhib.* IV. I. 882/2 *Crotolaria juncea*..is cultivated in most parts of India for its fibre, which..is called *sun* and *sunnee* in different parts of India, but, in the Madras peninsula, *janapum*. 1866 *Treas. Bot.*, *Janapa*, an Indian name for Sunn Hemp.

Jane² (dʒēⁱn). *Austral.* and *U.S. slang.* [Female Christian name.] A woman.

1916 C. J. DENNIS *Ginger Mick* 79 She's like some fat ole Jane 'oo loves to smile. 1924 P. MARKS *Plastic Age* 149, I met a bunch of janes down at Bar Harbour. 1928 L. NORTH *Parasites* 25 Every guy an' jane there was soused to the gills.

Jan(e)ite (dʒēⁱ·nait). [f. the Christian name of *Jane* Austen (1775–1817), novelist + -ITE¹.] = *AUSTENITE¹.

1896 G. SAINTSBURY *19th Cent. Lit.* 129 It did not apparently occur to this critic that he (or she) was in the first place paying Miss Austen an extraordinarily high compliment—a compliment almost greater than the most enthusiastic 'Janites' have ventured. 1927 *Observer* 5 June 6/3 Clearly he is *not* a Janeite. 1928 *Daily Tel.* 7 Aug. 3/3 The best page of her book by far is her spirited defence of Jane Austen, which will endear her to the 'Jane-ites' for all time.

Janitor. Add: **3.** A caretaker of a building who has charge of the cleaning and heating of it. *Sc.* and *U.S.* Hence **Janitorship** (earlier U.S. example).

1878 B. HARTE *Man on Beach* 76 A desire for rural repose led him to seek the janitorship of the Doemville Academy. 1884 H. BUTTERWORTH *Zigzag Journ. Western States* 50 Although he was employed merely as janitor at Yule [school]. 1890 H. C. BUNNER *Short Sixes* (1891) 75 She resolved to see the janitor in the morning.

Janitrix. (Later U.S. example.)

1878 B. F. TAYLOR *Between Gates* 273 When the janitrix of four score was a babe in arms.

Janizary. **4.** Add: **janizary music** [G. *janitscharenmusik*] = *Turkish music* (TURKISH *a.* 2 b); **janizary pedal**, a pedal attached to some old pianofortes, etc., having an arrangement of drums and cymbals connected with it, by which a sound as of martial music was produced.

1888 F. MOSCHELES tr. *Mendelssohn's Lett. to I. & C. Moscheles* 54 He must have a cradle song with drums and trumpets and *janissary music. 1896 HIPKINS *Pianoforte* 106 Drum and triangle (for Janissary music). 1922 JOAN RIVIERE tr. *Freud's Introd. Lect. Psycho-Anal.* 75 The little bells, shaken violently, begin their familiar janizary music. 1900 *Pall Mall Gaz.* 21 May 4/2 Even Mozart condescended to employ the '*Janissary pedal' in one or two of his sonatas.

Jankers (dʒæ·ŋkəɹz). *Army slang.* In the war of 1914–18, used in expressions for defaulters and their punishment.

1916 J. W. HALL *Kitchener's Mob* 35 The 'jankers' or defaulters' squad was always rather large. 1919 *War Slang* in *Athenæum* 25 July 664/2 The advent of the Royal Navy Division introduced to the Army the sailor's slang word 'jankers', the equivalent of the soldier's 'clink', punishment cells. *Ibid.* 8 Aug. 727/2 When doing C.B. or 'time' he [*sc.* the soldier] was doing 'jankers' or 'Paddy Doyle'. 1925 E. FRASER & GIBBONS *Soldier & Sailor Words*, *Jankers King*, *The*: The Provost Sergeant. *Ibid.*, *Janker's men*: Defaulters.

Jann (dʒăn). Also **jan.** [a. Arab. جان *jānn* demon.] = JINN *sb.*

1777 J. RICHARDSON *Dict. Pers., Arab., & Engl.* I. 667 That race of creatures called by the Arabians *Jan* or *Jinn*. 1891 E. S. HARTLAND *Sci. Fairy Tales* x. 256 Hasan is favoured with the sight of 'ten virgins'... He fell madly in love with the chief damsel, who turns out to be a daughter of a King of the Jann. 1931 E. S. STEVENS *Folk-Tales of Iraq* Pref. p. xiv, Stories in which *jânn*, or fairy-folk, don at will the appearance of birds.

Janus. Add: **c.** Designating materials with a double facing, or things having a two-way action, as *Janus-beaver, -cloth, -cord, -lock*; **Janus colours**, a series of coal-tar colours of a strongly basic character, which dye cotton direct or in an acid bath.

1851 *Illustr. Catal. Gt. Exhib.* III. 486/2 Fur Janus beaver. *Ibid.* v. II. 1468/2 Janus locks. 1875 KNIGHT *Dict. Mech.*, *Janus-cloth*, a fabric having each side dressed, and different colors on the respective sides. Such fabric is used for reversible garments. 1882 CAULFEILD & SAWARD *Dict. Needlework*, *Janus cord*, the material so named is a description of Rep, composed of wool and cotton, made for women's dresses, and being a black material, is peculiarly well suited for mourning. 1902 *Encycl. Brit.* XXVII. 559/1 Janus Colours. These comprise a small series of azo colours of a strongly basic character, which possess the unusual property of dyeing cotton in an acid bath.

Jap. Add: **2.** In full jap-silk, Japanese silk.

1902 *To-Day* 14 May 95/1 Printed Jap silks are lovely. 1905 *Daily Chron.* 13 Jan. 4/4 A flowered 'Jap' silk. 1923 *Daily Mail* 22 Jan. 1 The coat is lined floral jap. 1925 *Queen* 7 Jan. 17 A white Jap silk blouse.

Japan, *sb.* **6.** Add: **Japan camphor** = TUB-*camphor*; **Japan cedar** (see CEDAR 3); **Japan current** = KUROSHIWO; **Japan lacquer (tree)** (cf. LACQUER *sb.* 2 b, 4); **Japan quince** (see *JAPONICA); **Japan rose**, any of several Japanese roses, as *Rosa multiflora*, *R. rugosa*, *R. Ywara* (Webster 1911); also *Camellia japonica*; **Japan stream** = **Japan current*; **Japan varnish (tree)** = *varnish sumach* (VARNISH *sb.*¹ 5); **Japan wax** = *JAPANESE *wax*.

1881 BENTLEY *Bot.* (ed. 4) 642 Commercial camphor is derived entirely from the island of Formosa and Japan,.. the latter [being known] as *Japan or Dutch Camphor. 1852 *Cottage Gard. Dict.* (ed. G. W. Johnson), *Japan Cedar, *Cryptomeria*. 1865 PAGE *Handbk. Geol. Terms* (ed. 2), **Japan Current*, that branch of the equatorial current of the Pacific which trends northward along the Japan coasts. 1885 *Encycl. Brit.* XVIII. 118/2 The Japan current sends many branches into the inland seas and channels of the north-eastern coast of Asia. 1835 W. J. HOOKER *Compan. to Bot. Mag.* I. 268/1 The so much celebrated *Japan lacquer or varnish. 1846 LINDLEY *Veg. Kingd.* 466 The valuable black hard varnish called Japan Lacquer, is obtained from Stagmaria verniciflua in the Indian archipelago. 1880 BESSEY *Bot.* 535. 1884 MILLER *Plant-n.* 241/1 Japan Lacquer, or Varnish Tree. 1880 *Encycl. Brit.* XII. 213/1 Buds form on the roots, and may be used for purposes of propagation, as in the *Japan quince. 1793 B. EDWARDS *Hist. Brit. Col. W. Indies* I. 204 *Camellia japonica*, *Japan Rose. 1789 J. BELKNAP in *M. Cutler's Life*, etc. (1888) II. 252, I have sent for the seeds of the *Japan varnish tree. 1843 *Penny Cycl.* XXVI. 147/2 The Japan varnish of Kæmpfer and Thunberg is Rhus vernix. 1865 J. H. BALFOUR *Biogr. J. Coldstream* ii. 23 An avenue of the *Ailanthus*, or Japan varnish. 1859 *Japan wax [see next]. 1866 *Treas. Bot.* s.v. *Rhus*, The Japan wax, which is occasionally imported into this country. 1887 *Colonial & Indian Exhib.*, 1886, *Rep. Col. Sect.* 275 Myrtle wax..which, like Japan wax, is rather a fat than a true wax.

Japanese, *a.* Add: **2.** In the names of plants, animals, etc. native to, and articles produced in Japan, as *Japanese ape, medlar, paper, wax, wolf*.

Japanese rose, a bush rose (*Rosa rugosa*) with crimson and white flowers succeeded by large orange and red fruits, introduced in 1845.

1727 SCHEUCHZER tr. *Kæmpfer's Hist. Japan* (1906) I. 179 Japanese boil'd Camphire may be had for one single Catti of the true Bornean Camphire. *Ibid.*, The Japanese Camphire-tree. 1822 SHOBERL tr. *Titsingh's Illustr. Japan* 318 Three engravings, printed in colours, on Japanese paper. 1859 L. OLIPHANT *Narr. Earl Elgin's Miss. China & Japan* II. 257 Hitherto the most successful cargo brought to this country from Japan has been one of Japanese wax. Mr. Simmonds, in the *China Telegraph*, gives the following account of Japan wax:—'Rhus succedanea, the species which furnishes the Japan wax, has long been grown in our greenhouses, having been introduced from China nearly a century ago'. 1861 BENTLEY *Man. Bot.* 512 From the fruits of *R[hus] succedaneum*, and probably other species, Japanese Wax is obtained. 1866 *Treas. Bot.* s.v. *Eriobotrya*, The Loquat, or Japanese Medlar. 1877 *Trans. Asiatic Soc. Japan* V. 77 The kites are constructed of Japanese paper which is both thin and strong. 1880 *Encycl. Brit.* XIII. 574/2 *Cryptomeria* (Japanese cedar). 1883 *List Anim. Zool. Soc.* 92 *Macacus speciosus*..Japanese Ape. *Ibid.* 68 *Canis hodophylax*...Japanese Wolf. 1889 tr. *J. J. Rein's Industries of Japan* 391 The porosity of Japanese paper unfits it..for writing on with pen and ink. 1900 *Knowledge* 1 Dec. 285/1 Japanese tissue paper used by dentists. 1904 *Technol. & Sci. Dict.* (ed Goodchild & Tweney), *Japanese Paper*, made from the bark of *Morus papifera sativa*, used for expensive printing. 1905 F. H. COLLINS *Author & Printer* 190/2 *Japanese paper*, hand-made in Japan with vellum surface. Used for proofs of etchings and engravings.

Japanesery (dʒæpănī·zəri). Also in Fr. form **japonaiserie.** [f. JAPANESE + -ERY, after Fr. (cf. CHINOISERIE).] Chiefly *pl.* Japanese ornaments, knick-knacks, etc.; rarely *sing.* Japanese fashion.

1885 *Daily News* 30 Apr. 4/8 The 'Mikado' may even bring in a little agreeable Japanesery. 1894 W. J. LOCKE *At Gate of Samaria* ix, Cheap japaneseries that had lent it the suggestion of artistic atmosphere the girl of eighteen had craved. 1895 CROCKETT *Cleg Kelly* xxvii, The little alcove at the top of the stairs, which was cobwebbed with the latest artistic Japonaiseries of the period. 1902 *Westm. Gaz.* 11 Aug. 12/2 His earlier passion for Gothic art had been succeeded by one for *japonaiseries*. 1906 E. NESBIT *Man & Maid* viii. 179 Bright, picturesque cushions and screens and Japaneseries.

Japanesy (dʒæpănī·zi), *a.* [f. JAPANESE + -Y 6.] Inclining to a Japanese character. Also quasi-*adv.*

1890 B. H. CHAMBERLAIN *Things Japanese* 144 Criticism is not at all a 'Japanesey' thing. 1891 SARAH J. DUNCAN *Amer. Girl Lond.* 55 Her parlour was Japanesy, too, in places. 1897 *Daily News* 9 Jan. 6/2 The walls papered Japanesy. 1901 'C. HOLLAND' *Mousmé* xxiii. 328 He..has referred to..their figures as '*petite*' and Japanesy. 1923 E. F. WYATT *Invis. Gods* I. ii. 17 The Japanesy shadows of the black scrub pine. 1925 *Glasgow Herald* 8 May 10 High-art, Japanesy tenements.

Japanned. Add: **3.** *Japanned leather* (see quot. 1875). *Japanned peacock, peafowl*, a peafowl, *Pavo nigripennis*, with upper-wing coverts of a deep lustrous blue.

1814 in *Proc. Zool. Soc.* (1835) 54 The hens..would not suffer a japanned peacock to touch them. 1851 *Illustr. Catal. Gt. Exhib.* IV. II. 1252/1 Japanned leather, grained calf-skin for boots and shoes, and trimmings. 1856 *J. C. Morton's Cycl. Agric.* II. 698/2 The Japanned pea-fowl, as it ought to be styled, instead of the Japan pea-fowl. 1875 KNIGHT *Dict. Mech.*, *Japanned Leather*, leather treated with several coats of Japan varnish and dried in a stove. 1885 NEWTON in *Encycl. Brit.* XVIII. 443/1 The 'japanned' Peacock, often erroneously named the Japanese or Japan Peacock.

Japano- (dʒæ·păno), used as combining form of JAPANESE, esp. in adjs. meaning 'belonging to Japan (and some other country)'. Also **Ja·panophile**, a lover of Japan or the Japanese.

1904 *Daily Chron.* 10 May 5/2 The Japano-Russian war. 1904 SLADEN *Playing the Game* II. iii, Under the influence of the Japanophile Jevons. 1906 *Daily Chron.* 21 May 7/5 The Japano-Korean treaty. 1910 *Westm. Gaz.* 3 Feb. 3/1 The Japano-Chinese war of 1894–5.

Japonica (dʒăpǫ·nikă). [mod.L., fem. of *Japonicus* pertaining to Japan.] The name given to various ornamental plants originally native to Japan, as the common camellia (*Camellia japonica*), the Japan quince (*Pyrus* or *Cydonia japonica*).

1819 KEATS *Let. to Fanny Keats* 13 Mar., Shade it all round with myrtles and Japonicas. 1851 H. MELVILLE *Moby Dick* xlii. (1926) 187 Though in many natural objects, whiteness refiningly enhances beauty, as in marbles, japonicas, and pearls. 1855 J. E. COOKE *Ellie* 137 One of the amusing jests is the appearance here of that young lady there, with the Japonica in her hair. 1858 TERESA VIELE *Following the Drum* 58 Cape jessamine hedges, japonicas, tea-roses. 1906 'O. HENRY' *Strictly Business* ix. 91 You put me in mind of a japonica in a window.

b. The fruit of the Japanese plant *Zizyphus sinensis*, occas. sold in England as a dessert fruit.

1874 *Treas. Bot.* Suppl. 1881 BENTLEY *Bot.* (ed. 4) 512.

Hence **Japo·nicadom** *U.S.* (see quot. 1859).

1851 A. C. HALL *Manhattaner N. Orleans* 123 The general society of New Orleans is still in a chaotic state, and she has no located, acknowledged empire of Japonicadom. 1859 BARTLETT *Dict. Amer.* (ed. 3), *Japonicadom*, a word invented by N. P. Willis to denote the upper classes of society.

Jar, *sb.*² **2.** Add: *spec.* as a unit of electric capacity (see quots.).

[1889 A. W. POYSER *Magn. & Electr.* xiii. (1895) 139 Harris's unit jar.—This instrument is used for measuring the charge given to a Leyden jar.] 1923 *Harmsworth's Wireless Encycl.* II. 1226/1 *Jar*, a unit of capacity used in the Admiralty service.

Jar, *sb.*⁴ *U.S.* [Of obscure origin.] (See quots.)

1863 H. S. RANDALL *Pract. Shepherd* vii. 73 Those usually short, detached, not very coarse, glistening particles of hair found in the fleece, termed 'jar', are very objectionable. 1878 *Trans. Ill. Dept. Agric.* XIV. 239 The jar is coarse hair invariably found in the wrinkled fleeces.

Jardinière. Add: **2.** *Cookery.* (See quots.) *Jardinière soup*: vegetable soup.

1846 SOYER *Cookery* 40 [Sauces.] Jardinière. 1877 *Cassell's Dict. Cookery* 338/1 Jardinière.—This is a garnish made of cooked vegetables, which gives its name to the dish with which it is served. Thus, fillet of beef à la jardinière, mutton à la jardinière, goose à la jardinière, simply mean fillet of beef, mutton, and goose served with a garnish à la jardinière. *Ibid.*, Jardinière Soup. 1907 ESCOFFIER *Guide Mod. Cookery* 357 Prepare the fillet as directed under 'Filet de Bœuf Jardinière'. Set it on a long dish and surround it with a *Macédoine* garnish. The latter comprises the same ingredients as the '*Jardinière*'. *Ibid.* 512, *Sauté* the *suprêmes* in butter. Dish and surround with small heaps of vegetables, arranged very neatly, as explained in the case of the *Jardinière* garnish.

Jargoneer (dʒāɹgŏnī·ɹ). [f. JARGON *sb.*¹ + -EER.] A jargon-monger.

1913 QUILLER-COUCH *On Art of Writing* (1916) 90 A Jargoneer would have said that 'among the beneficent qualities of sleep its capacity for withdrawing the human consciousness from the contemplation of immediate circumstances may perhaps be accounted not the least remarkable'. 1923 G. H. BONNER in *19th Cent.* Nov. 786 Your true jargoneer must have at least two languages in the same word.

Jaro. *New Zealand slang.* *To give* (a person) *jaro*: to rate, vituperate.

1904 G. B. LANCASTER *Sons o' Men* 42 Cookie'll give yer jaro 'f yer late fur supper.

Jarool (dʒărū·l). Also **jarrool.** [Hind., a. Bengali *jarūl*.] An East Indian tree, *Lagerstrœmia flos-reginæ*, providing excellent timber. Also, the wood itself.

1850 HOOKER *Himal. Jrnls.* (1855) II. 318 Their forests are frequented by timber-cutters, who fell jarool, a magnificent tree with red wood. 1884 MILLER *Plant-n.*, Jarool-wood.

Jaspe (dʒasp), **jaspé** (ʒaˑspe), *a.* *Ceramics.* [orig. F. *jaspé*, pa. pple. of *jasper* to marble.] Resembling jasper; of mottled or variegated appearance.

1851 *Illustr. Catal. Gt. Exhib.* III. III. 500/2 Printed and embroidered 'jaspé' cashmere. 1908 *Ladies' Field* 24 Oct. 318/1 The Ghiberti damask has a *jaspé* ground. 1913 *Weekly Dispatch* 11 Feb. 16 Harmonising shades of Pink, Blue, Mauve, Brown and Green on Cream, Jaspe, Black or Grey backgrounds. 1925 *Brit. Weekly* 14 May 153/1 It is therefore as well to use peaceful tones in plain jaspé repp. 1931 *Daily Express* 23 Sept. 4/1 New clasp in Imitation Jaspe Shell.

Jat¹ (dʒāt). Also 7 **Jutt, Jett,** 8 **Jaut.** [Hindi जाट *Jāt.*] A member of an Indian tribe settled in the Punjab, Sind, and North-West Provinces. Also *attrib.*

1622 in Foster *Engl. Factories Ind.* (1908) II. 90 (There) goeth with the carts 27 Jutts, etc. for their safer passadge. *Ibid.* 111 A Jett whome some tymes you have (app)roved off for trusty. *c* 1791 *Encycl. Brit.* VIII. 529/1 The Jauts, or Jats. 1845 *Encycl. Metrop.* XXIII. 781/2 The Ják'har, Shiyág'hs, and Punyás..are all of Jat origin. 1880 *Encycl. Brit.* XIII. 597/2 Early Ját settlements on the shores of the Persian gulf. 1901 *N. Amer. Rev.* Feb. 301 The Jats are the most important people in the Punjab. 1922 *Blackw. Mag.* June 696/1 No man knew Old For-ever who had not seen him in action with his Jats. 1926 *Ibid.* Dec. 806/2 He found no difficulty in engaging a Jat (camel-driver) who was willing to take his camel in that direction.

Jat² (dʒāt). [Hind. جات *jāt.*] A caste, tribe, sect.

1894 MEG DYAN *Man's Keeping* i. Are they not all one jāt or caste? 1909 MAUD DIVER *Candles in Wind* viii. 80 She's another 'jāt' (*note*, class) from us altogether.

Jataka (dʒā·tăkă). [Skr. जातक *jātaka* engendered by, born under, f. जात *jātā*, pa. pple. of *jan* to produce.] In Buddhist literature, a story of one or other of the former births of the Buddha; also, the name of the Pāli collection of these stories. Also *attrib.*

1861 V. FAUSBÖLL *Five Jātakas* Pref., We.., in the Jātaka, meet with some of the Comical stories that are well known all over Europe under different names. 1876 J. FERGUSSON *Hist. Ind. & East. Archit.* I. 88 Bas-reliefs..representing some scene or legend of the time, and..inscribed..with the title of the jataka or legend. 1876 *Encycl. Brit.* IV. 430/1 *Note*, Jātaka stories..containing..the oldest known versions of many of the nursery songs, and fairy tales, and comic stories, and fables, which are the common property of Europe in the present day. 1895 E. B. COWELL *Jātaka* Pref. p. vii, The Pāli work, entitled 'the Jātaka'..contains 550 Jātakas or Birth-stories. 1902 *Encycl. Brit.* XXVI. 432/1 The *Jātaka* book, a set of verses supposed to have been uttered by the Buddha in some of his previous births.

Jatha (dʒā·tā). [Hind. جتھا *jathā.*] An armed or organized band.

1922 *Glasgow Herald* 9 Sept. 9 There is no waning in Sikh fanaticism, and organised jathas, or companies, come forward unceasingly. A jatha of Sikh women wearing daggers has been formed. 1924 *Ibid.* 31 Mar. 11 A continuous procession of martyr jathas from Amritsar to Jaito.

Jatropha (dʒæ·trŏfă). [mod.L. *Jatropha* (f. Gr. ἰᾶσθαι to heal + τροφή nourishment), a genus of *Euphorbiaceæ* yielding oil and starchy foods.] *Jatropha oil*, a fixed oil expressed from the seeds of *Jatropha Curcas* and *J. multifida*. Hence **Jatro·phic** *a.*, pertaining to or derived from plants of the genus *J.*, especially *J. Curcas* and its seeds. **Ja·trophine**, a poison derived from *J. manihot*.

1851 *Illustr. Catal. Gt. Exhib.* IV. I. 879/2 Jatropha oil. 1867 BLOXAM *Chem.* 486 A deleterious substance, which has been named jatrophine.

Jaune, *a.* Add: **2.** Ceramics. *Jaune antique*: a variegated, crystalline terra-cotta of Wedgwood ware of a rich saffron mixed with black. *Jaune brill(i)ant* (see quots. 1851, 1928). *Jaune jonquille*: a ground colour of Sèvres ware.

1851 WATTS tr. *Gmelin's Hand-bk. Chem.* V. 57 Sulphide of Cadmium.—Found native in the form of Greenockite. Prepared as a pigment known by the name of *Jaune brillant*. 1875 METEYARD *Wedgwood Handbk.* 21 He produced other mixtures which he called 'Holy Door' and 'Jaune Antique'. 1918 N. HEATON *Outl. Paint Technol.* 382 Jaune Brilliant. ..Imitation Naples yellow (mixture of cadmium and white lead). 1929 *Encycl. Brit.* XVIII. 351/2 Turquoise blue.., yellow (*jaune jonquille*), and green grounds made their appearance in 1752, 1753 and 1756.

Jaunty (dʒǭ·nti), *sb.* Also **Jonty.** [Said to be a sailor's corruption of F. GENDARME.] The master-at-arms on board ship.

1904 KIPLING *Traffics & Discov.* 197 'A great many cars thinks they can take this road; but they all come back. We walks after 'em at our convenience.' 'Meanin' that the other jaunty is now pursuin' us on his lily feet?' said Pyecroft. 1904 L. YEXLEY *Greg Time Yarns* 3 The Chief of the Police—the Master-at-Arms—is always referred to as the 'Jonty'. 1927 *Blackw. Mag.* Oct. 457/1 Mounting the rope ladder in that awful sea..proved a bit of a task to the unaccustomed Jonties. 1928 COMMR. DANIEL in *Weekly Dispatch* 27 May 14 The sailor spun a yarn that would make the hardest-hearted jonty (master-at-arms) weep.

Java. Add: **Java bean** (see quot. 1908). **Java canvas**, a loosely-woven linen cloth with an even mesh used in embroidery. **Java lemon** (see quot. 1882²). **Java (ape-)man** = *Pithecanthropus* (see PITHECANTHROPE b). **Java skull**, a skull discovered by Dr. Dubois at Trinil, Java, in 1891–2, referred by him to the Java man.

1878 *Cassell's Fam. Mag.* 494/2 The materials used for these curtains are many—velvet,.., Java canvass, and serges. 1882 CAULFEILD & SAWARD *Dict. Needlework*, *Java canvas*, a close make of canvas, having an appearance of being plaited, and made in many sizes and degrees of fineness. *Ibid.*, *Java canvas work*, this Embroidery is named from the material upon which it is worked, and is used for mats, work cases, music cases. 1882 *Encycl. Brit.* XIV. 439/1 The Java lemon is the fruit of *Citrus javanica*. 1908 *Animal Managem.* (W. O.) 100 'Java' beans, imported from Ceylon, Burmah, and the Dutch Indies are quite unfit for consumption. 1915 A. KEITH *Antiq. Man* 264 In the fronto-malar region of the Java skull all the anthropoid traits are retained. 1931 S. G. B. STUBBS & BLIGH 60 *Cent. Health* 3 Pithecanthropus, the Java ape-man.

ellipt. = Java coffee.

1850 L. H. GARRARD *Wah-To-Yah* xiii. 169 Partaking of the nectar-like Java.

Javelin, *sb.* **4.** Add: **javelin-throwing**, an event in athletic sports.

1902 *Daily Chron.* 7 Apr. 3/1 Professors in a university to teach javelin-throwing. 1906 *Westm. Gaz.* 3 May 10/2 Very pretty was the javelin-throwing, the long thin spear being launched high into the air.

Javelle (ʒave·l). [Personal name.] *Eau de Javelle* (*Water of Javelle, Javelle or Javelle's water*): a solution of sodium or potassium hypochlorite used as an antiseptic, disinfectant, and bleaching agent in photography and laundry work, etc. *Javelle salt*, potassium hypochlorite.

1858 SIMMONDS *Dict. Trade*, *Eau-de-Javelle*, chlorine in solution with water. 1862 *Chambers's Encycl.* III. 746/2 *Eau de Javelle*..when administered to man, is stated to act powerfully on the nervous system. 1875 *Ure's Dict. Arts* I. 787 The chloride of potash is known as Water of Javelle. 1890 BILLINGS *Med. Dict.*, Javelle's water. 1892 A. BROTHERS *Photogr.* 260 As a reducing agent for negatives which are too dense and for removing the last traces of sodium thiosulphate, the following solution, which forms *eau de javelle*, may be used:—Chloride of lime 2 ounces. Potassium carbonate 4 ounces. Water 40 ounces. 1905 tr. *D. Mendeléeff's Princ. Chem.* (ed. 3) I. 498 The products of the metalepsis of alkaline hydrates, NaClO and Ca(ClO)₂, which are present in solutions of 'Javelle salt' and bleaching powder. 1928 *Daily Express* 19 Dec. 5 Javelle water, made by dissolving half a pound of washing soda in a quart of cold water, adding four ounces of bleaching powder.

Jaw, *sb.*¹ Add: **1. b.** The process in invertebrates which is used for the ingestion of food.

1870 NICHOLSON *Man. Zool.* 163 The Medicinal Leech (*Sanguisuga officinalis*)..has its mouth furnished with three crescentic jaws. 1877 HUXLEY *Anat. Invert.* 56 In the Arthropoda, what are usually termed jaws are modified limbs. 1902 *Encycl. Brit.* XXV. 696/1 The jaws of Peripatus are formed by the axis or corm itself.

7. *jaw-bearing, -cutting* adjs.; **jaw-clonus, -jerk**, spasmodic contraction of the muscles of the mouth when a blow is struck on the lower jaw as it hangs down; **jaw-piece**, read †(*a*) = JOWPY; (*b*) (see quot.); **jaw-process** = *GNATHOBASE.

1902 *Encycl. Brit.* XXV. 700/1 The mandibular somite.. is followed by two *jaw-bearing somites (maxillary and labial). 1908 *Practitioner* June 762 A *jaw-clonus is often a distinctive feature [in progressive muscular atrophy]. 1902 P. MARSHALL *Metal Wkg. Tools* 45 Adjustable *Jaw-Cutting Nippers. 1906 DORLAND *Med. Dict.* (ed. 4) s.v. *Reflex*, **Jaw-jerk reflex*, clonic contraction of the inferior maxilla and other muscles of mastication. 1886 WILLIS & CLARK *Cambridge* I. 283 A '*jaw-piece' or triangular piece of wood ..interposed between [the principal] itself and the spars forming the roof. 1902 *Encycl. Brit.* XXV. 697/1 It varies as to the presence or absence of the *jaw-process, and as to the stoutness of the segments of the ramus.

Jaw-bone. Add: **2.** *Army slang*, orig. *Canadian.* Credit. Also *to call one's jawbone*, to live on credit (Farmer & Henley *Slang*).

1862 *Times* 21 Oct. 9/4 Individuals who, in digger's parlance, live on jawbone (credit). 1885 A. S. HILL *From Home to Home* 413 His ready money gone, he has nothing to live on but 'jawbone', *i.e.* credit.

Jaw-cracker. *U.S.* = JAW-BREAKER I.

1840 *Congress. Globe* 5 May 367/1 The gentleman had brought up many hard words, which he said he could scarcely spell, nor pronounce them after he had spelt them. They were in fact what in Virginia they termed 'jaw-crackers'. 1842 *Amer. Pioneer* I. 375, I found in his office a dictionary of jaw-crackers, of new coined words, Greek, Latin, and phrases not used by English readers.

Jawing, *vbl. sb.* **b.** (Earlier U.S. example.)

1843 R. CARLTON *New Purchase* xxi. 204 He was compelled at last to put one hand under his jaw, and partly up his cheek, to support his 'jawing tackle'.

Jay. Add: **3. d.** Also *attrib.* or as *adj.* Backward, dull. *U.S.*

1890 H. C. BUNNER *Short Sixes* (1891) 91 'T ain't neuralogy, you jay pill-box, she's *cooked*! 1914 GERTRUDE ATHERTON *Perch of Devil* I. vii. 39 You're different..from the other men in this jay town.

e. Used *attrib.* = inferior, poor. *U.S.*

[1896 FARMER & HENLEY *Slang*, *Jay*..3. (theatrical), an amateur; a poor actor.] 1900 G. ADE *More Fables in Slang* (1902) 185 They..said it was a Shame to String these Jay Amateurs. 1906 in *Daily Chron.* 3 Nov. 4/6 He far outranks the average jay attorney.

Jay-bird. (Earlier Amer. examples.)

1660 *Dedham* (Mass.) *Rec.* IV. 41 En. Dani Fisher is creditor to the Towne for his sonne catching of Jaybirds. 1829–32 J. P. KENNEDY *Swallow Barn* II. iii. 55 A scream of jay-birds heard at intervals.

Jayhawker. *U.S.* (Earlier examples.)

1860 *Ashtabula Sentinel* 26 Dec. 5/3 By the term 'Jayhawkers' is here [*sc.* in Mound City, Kansas] understood the active fighting abolitionists. 1861 *Proclamation of Gen. James Lane* Oct. (Bartlett) We are soldiers, not thieves or plunderers or jayhawkers. 1862 *New York World* 8 Jan. (Bartlett 1877) This expression [*sc.* Gay Yorker] was afterwards used to designate his [*sc.* Colonel Jennison's] men, and in its various travels naturally underwent many changes, until at last it crystallized into *Jayhawker*.

Jay·-walker. orig. *U.S.* [JAY 3 d.] 'One who crosses a street without observing the traffic regulations for pedestrians' (Funk). Also **Jay·-walking** *vbl. sb.*

1925 *Spectator* 12 Dec. 1080/1 Needless to say, there are few 'jay-walkers' in Miami now. 1927 *Weekly Dispatch* 1 May 8 The police are taking the Jay Walker in hand and teaching him how to cross the streets. 1930 *Bulletin* 23 Jan. 5 He thinks that every kerb should be built about a foot above the pavement, so that 'jay-walkers' can be kept away from the outside edge.

Jazz (dʒæz), *sb.* [Origin unknown: generally said to be Negro.] A kind of ragtime dance (three steps to four musical beats) introduced from the United States to Europe towards the end of 1918. Hence, the kind of music to which this is danced, jazz music; often loosely applied to any kind of syncopated dance music.

1918 *Era* 11 Sept. 21 John Lester's Frisco Five. The Jollities of 'Jazz'. 1919 *Punch* 12 Mar. 193/1 'Whitehall,' says a Society organ, 'has succumbed to the Jazz, the Fox-trot and the Bunny-hug.' 1919 PIERRE *How to Jazz* 7 The Jazz or 1919 Fox-Trot... The Jazz is a three-step dance done to four-beat time. The three steps fall on the first three beats of the bar, the third being prolonged to last two beats, namely, the third and fourth. There are three distinct movements, which may be described as the Straight Jazz, the Side Jazz and the Jazz-Roll. 1921 *Contemp. Rev.* Jan. 53 The frank barbarism began its appeal with nigger minstrels, and has landed us in 'jazz'. 1922 C. ENGEL *Discords Mingled* (1931) 147 Jazz is rag-time, *plus* 'blues', *plus* orchestral polyphony; it is the combination, in the popular music current, of melody, rhythm, harmony, and counterpoint. 1927 *Dancing Times* Apr. 55/2 Jerusalem is given over to jazz.

b. *transf.* and *fig.* Restlessness, excitability.

1923 L. J. VANCE *Baroque* vi. 34 Only about enough heroin to give every man, woman and child in N'York the jazz for a week. 1924 GALSWORTHY *White Monkey* II. iii, With all the jazz there is about, she'd appreciate somebody restful. 1928 JOAN SUTHERLAND *The Knot* xii, 'What is really the matter?' she asked. 'You look extraordinarily queer, and you ought to be full of jazz.'

c. *attrib.* and *Comb.*, as *jazz-dance, -dancing, -music*; **jazz band**, an orchestra trained and accustomed to playing jazz-music.

1917 *Era* 20 Aug. 20 Holborn Empire... Frank Powell and The Magleys and the Jazz Band. 1919 *Times* 14 Jan. 11/3 The effort of the orchestra to convert itself into a jazz band. 1919 *Observer* 16 Mar. 14 4 There has been a good deal of curiosity concerning the origin of the term 'Jazz'. Authorities on Jazz dancing say it is a word used by niggers to denote a scramble. 1919 *Punch* 30 Apr. 333/3 An early bather was seen executing the Jazz-dance on the beach at Ventnor on Easter Monday. 1920 C. SANDBURG *Smoke & Steel* 225 The jazz outfit sweats. 1921 *19th Cent.* Apr. 664 The jazz-dancing young man of to-day. 1922 L'EGVILLE *How and what to dance* 62 There is no Jazz-Dance in the ordinary sense of the word, but there has been evolved..a rolling step known as the Jazz-step. This is performed to Jazz-music, which is nothing more nor less than syncopated 4–4 time. 1922 W. J. LOCKE *Tale of Triona* v. 51 The crash of jazz music welcomed them.

c. *attrib.* and *Comb.*, passing into *adj.*, applied to objects of a grotesque or fantastic design or marked by vivid or riotous colouring.

1919 *Punch* 7 May 357 Jazz stockings are the latest thing. 1922 *Glasgow Herald* 14 Dec. 5 He has some justification for using this jazz language. 1923 *Daily Mail* 5 May 8 Jazz patterns in dress. 1924 *Drapery Sale Catal.*, A French 'Pull-on' Model,..piped with Jazz coloured silks. 1928 *Daily Tel.* 10 Apr. 8/2 Blue, yellow, and green jazz fish. 1926 E. WEEKLEY *Eng. Lang.* 76 The rather jazz-patterned idiom which is now spoken.

Jazz (dʒæz), *v.* [f. prec.]

1. *intr.* To dance to jazz-music. Hence *transf.* to move in a grotesque or fantastic fashion.

1919 *Punch* 23 Apr. 318/1 She did not ask whether I could jazz, mainly, I think, because I had already danced with her. 1921 *Librarian* Nov. 72 The joy of jazzing with ladies of the beauty chorus. 1923 *Daily Mail* 18 Apr. 8 There are a good many present-day books that just give the reader a view of the protagonists jazzing across the pages in a vivid pattern of action, passion or crime.

2. *trans.* **a.** To arrange (a musical composition) as jazz.

1920 E. SCOTT *All about Latest Dances* 76 The nigger bands at home 'jazz' a tune; that is to say, they slur the notes, they syncopate, and each instrument puts in a lot of little fancy bits on its own. 1922 C. SANDBURG *Slabs of Sunburnt West* 6 Listen while they jazz the classics. 1927 *Observer* 20 Feb. 12/2 When Mr. ——..next jazzes the 'Austrian Hymn' or 'Ave Verum'.

b. To arrange (a pattern or scheme of colour) in a vivid or grotesque form. Hence *gen.* to liven or brighten up. Chiefly with *up*.

1921 R. D. PAINE *Comr. Rolling Ocean* viii. 133 Now jazz it up, son, and enjoy yourself. 1923 WODEHOUSE *Inimit. Jeeves* xv. 195 It's rather too late to alter the thing [*sc.* a little fairy play] entirely, but at least I can jazz it up. 1923 *Daily Mail* 27 Mar. 8 My colour scheme is rather fetching, don't you think? X—a famous artist—jazzed it up for me. 1924 GALSWORTHY *White Monkey* II. iii, Winifred had jazzed the Empire foundations of her room with a superstructure more suitable to the age. 1928 JOAN SUTHERLAND *The Knot* viii, I've not the cocktail vice more than the rest of us, but I rather want jazzing up.

Hence **Jazzed** (dʒæzd), **Ja·zzing** *ppl. adjs.*

1920 *Glasgow Herald* 26 Feb. 9 This business woman of 1920 has nothing of the jazzing featherhead about her appearance. 1920 *Chambers's Jrnl.* 617/1 Good jazzing partners were scarce. 1920 E. SCOTT *All about Latest Dances* 75 Certain steps and movements already in practice may be more or less adaptable to 'jazzed' music. 1926 *Bulletin* 9 June 5 Some of our own jazzed thoroughfares. 1929 *Musical Times* Feb. 129 The music is jazzed-up, restless stuff. 1930 *Observer* 7 Sept. 19/1 Jazzed versions of real music.

Jazzer (dʒæ·zəɹ). [f. JAZZ *v.* + -ER¹.] One who jazzes (in various senses).

1922 *Public Opinion* 5 May 418/2 The son of an agricultural labourer has won the second prize as the best jazzer in the village. 1927 *Observer* 20 Feb. 12/2 The jazzer simply says that Mozart couldn't write music fit for the twentieth century to listen to. 1927 *Sunday Express* 23 Oct. 5/4 Letters from jazzers, saying that a critic like myself ought to know that bowler hats are never used for saxophones. 1927 *Musical Times* Nov. 978 In the hands of jazzers, syncopation is a ruthless and mechanical defiance of strict time. 1928 *Observer* 18 Mar. 15/3 Captain Doughtie, about to participate in a new arrangement of the universe, spends his time bleating like a discontented jazzer, 'I wa-ant you!'

Jazzify (dʒæ·zifai), *v.* [See prec. and -FY.] *trans.* = *JAZZ *v.* 2.

1927 *Daily Express* 9 Nov. 9 In 'Hit the Deck,' where British bluejackets kneel down, and, with arms uplifted to heaven, jazzify a negro spiritual. 1928 *Daily Tel.* 28 Feb. 15/1 We had already seen our musical taste jazzified, and our British standards of art and life were being jazzified by foreign films.

Jazzophone (dʒæ·zŏfōᵘn). [f. *JAZZ, after *saxophone*.] An instrument of the saxophone type used in playing jazz-music. Hence **Jazzopho·nic** *a.*

1924 W. J. LOCKE *Coming of Amos* vi. 72 At the top of my voice,..so as to be heard above the jazzaphonic tumult. 1929 *Daily Chron.* 29 Jan. 3 Jazzophones as State Jewels. Negro Band Loses its Outfit. 1930 H. REDWOOD *God in Slums* ix. 86 Mouth organ and jazzophone bands.

Jazzy (dʒæ·zi), *a.* [f. *JAZZ *sb.* + -Y¹.] Of or pertaining to, resembling, or of the nature of jazz.

1924 GALSWORTHY *White Monkey* I. ix, 'Whom do you think to meet him, besides Alison?' 'Nothing jazzy.' *Ibid.* III. iii, The present curtains really are too jazzy. 1925 *Chambers's Jrnl.* 466/2 To sing some jazzy stuff called 'Alexander's Rag Time Band'. 1927 H. WALPOLE in *Daily Express* 11 Apr. 5/3 The upper classes drinking cocktails and dancing eternally to the jazziest of music. 1928 JOAN SUTHERLAND *The Knot* xv, I may be frivolous and modern and jazzy and all the things you clever people hate.

Hence **Ja·zzily** *adv.*

1928 *Gramophone* VI. 300/1 With a musically artistic legato rhythmic swing and not 'jazzily'.

Jean(n)ette (dʒăne·t). Also **jeanet.** [f. JEAN + -ETTE.] Coarse jean.

1786 *Maryland Jrnl.* 14 Apr. (Th.) Jeans; jeanets. 1862 *Catal. Internat. Exhib., Brit.* II. No. 3667 Spinners and manufacturers of jeannettes. 1882 CAULFEILD & SAWARD *Dict. Needlework*, *Jeannette*, a variety of jean, coarser in quality, yet not so closely woven. Some Jeanettes are twilled. 1895 *Army & Navy Co-op. Soc. Price List* 15 Sept. 1103 Dress Linings. Per Yard,..Jeanette..0/6.

Jebel (dʒe·bel). Also **jabal.** [Arab. جبال *jabal*, *jebel* mountain, pl. *jibāl*.] A mountain; frequent in specific names.

[1834 *Penny Cycl.* II. 210/1 The mountainous region in the interior is distinguished by the appellation of Jabal, 'the Hills'.] 1920 *Blackw. Mag.* Nov. 667/1 An almost waterless desert country,—an enormous waste of rocky jebels and broad sandy plains. 1927 *Chambers's Jrnl.* 535/1 A low-lying bank of white mist wound itself round the gaunt jabal.

Jeerga, variant of *JIRGA.

Jefferson (dʒe·fəɹsən). *U.S.* [See JEFFERSONIAN *a.*] Used *attrib.* or *ellipt.* to designate a make of shoe.

1838 *Southern Lit. Messenger* IV. 639/1 Slippers, pumps, bootees, Jefferson shoes. 1843 R. CARLTON *New Purchase* xi. 72 A calf-skin Jefferson.

Jeffersonian, *a.* and *sb.* (Earlier examples.)

1799 *Spectator* (N.Y.) 3 Apr. 1813 *Niles' Weekly Register* IV. Suppl. 65/1 This is true Jeffersonian, Madisonian, democratic economy. 1838 *Democratic Rev.* I. Jan. 145 Jeffersonian republicanism.

Jehoshaphat (dʒĭhǫ·ʃăfæt). A biblical name (2 Sam. viii. 16, etc.) used interjectionally as a mild expletive. Also *jumping Jehoshaphat*.

Jejuno-. Add: esp. in names of diseases or operations involving the jejunum, or the jejunum and some other part of the body.

1890 BILLINGS *Med. Dict.*, *Jejunostomy*, operation of making a permanent opening or fistula in the jejunum. 1906 *Practitioner* Dec. 718 A posterior jejunostomy. 1907 *Ibid.* Aug. 269 The jejuno-jejunal flexure.

Jekyll (dʒe·kil). Name of the hero of R. L. Stevenson's story, 'Strange Case of Dr. Jekyll and Mr. Hyde' (1886), who appears as a benevolent and upright character under the name of *Jekyll* and the opposite under the name of *Hyde*: used allusively in reference to opposite sides of a person's character or to one who leads a double life.

1887 *Puck* (U.S.) XXII. 188 Is that you, Livingston?.. No, m' dearsh, it'sh Doct' Hyde. Mist' Jekyll didn't..g-g' out t' night! 1902 *Daily Chron.* 22 May 3/4 While the left lobe is the Jekyll of the intellect, the right, on occasion at least, is apt to play the part of Hyde. 1905 *Strand Mag.* Apr. 455/2 Meeting a young and winsome feminine counterpart of Dr. Jekyll and Mr. Hyde in real life is a very pleasant, if novel, experience. 1915 'IAN HAY' *1st Hundred Thou.* xiv, When he is good he is very good indeed, and when he is bad he is horrid. He is either Jekyll or Hyde. *Ibid.*, But we encountered surprisingly few Hydes. Nearly all were Jekylls —Jekylls of the most competent and courteous type. 1929 W. J. LOCKE *Ancestor Jorico* xviii. 253 Suppose it pleased him to lead a Jekyll and Hyde sort of life? 1931 *Times Lit. Suppl.* 2 July 522/1 Turner was a case of Jekyll and Hyde in real life and oscillated continuously between the Victorian respectability of Bloomsbury..and the Rabelaisian society of the London Docks.

Jellied, *a.* Add: **3.** Done in jelly.

1907 *Daily Chron.* 6 June 5/5 'Jellied eel! 'Ave a plate; lovally jelly,' shouts a third. 1908 *Ibid.* 6 July 3/4 She.. knows the secrets of jellied eels.

Jelly, *sb.* Add: **1.** Also, a preparation of gelatin and fruit juices in cubes or crystals, from which table-jellies are made.

1895 *Army & Navy Co-op. Soc. Price List* 15 Sept. 76 Granulated jellies (Lemon, Orange..flavours). *Ibid.*, Family Jelly Boxes, containing sufficient..for 12 quarts of Jelly.

c. A table-jelly.

1851 *Illustr. Catal. Gt. Exhib.* III. III. 650/1 Moulds for jellies, cakes, &c. 1916 *Punch* 6 Dec. 394/2 He shook all over like a badly-set jelly. 1930 C. MACKENZIE *April Fools* vii. 152 Mr. Wenlow, balanced like a pale jelly on the edge of a chair in the drawing-room.

2. *Enamel jelly* (see quot. 1901). *Glycerine jelly*, a mixture of gelatine and glycerine used for bougies. *Mineral jelly, petroleum jelly*, vaseline. *Royal jelly*, the special food fed to a larva that is to produce a queen bee.

1817 KIRBY & SPENCE *Entomol.* II. 130 They will select one or more to be educated as queens; which..being fed with royal jelly for not more than two days..will come forth complete queens. 1875 *Encycl. Brit.* III. 494/2 As a proof that any worker egg or young larva not more than three days old may be made to produce a queen, the experimenter has only to supply to such an one a portion of royal jelly. 1887 HILLHOUSE tr. *Strasburger's Handbk. Pract. Bot.* 206 If the hæmatoxylin stain is to be preserved in glycerine or glycerine-jelly. 1895 *Army & Navy Co-op. Soc. Price List* 15 Sept. 718 Wheeler's Glycerine Jelly. 1901 DORLAND *Med. Dict.* s.v. *Jelly*, *Enamel-jelly*, a soft material in a growing tooth between the epithelial investment and the calcifying cells of the young enamel. 1902 *Encycl. Brit.* XXXII. 23/1 Cordite M.D. Its composition is—nitro-glycerine, 30%; gun-cotton, 65%; mineral jelly, 5%. 1922 D. T. DAY *Handbk. Petroleum Industry* II. 360 The official petrolatum of the United States Pharmacopœia, otherwise known as petroleum jelly, or 'Vaseline'. 1926 *Bryologist* XXIX. 56 Take several brushfulls of jelly [= glycerine jelly] from the bottle.

4. **jelly-crystals**, a crystalline powder used in the preparation of table-jellies; **jelly-cube**, a cube of concentrated jelly to which water is added to make a table-jelly; **jelly-leaf**, Queensland hemp (see SIDA); **jelly-powder**, (*a*) an explosive, so called from its resemblance to calf's foot jelly; (*b*) = **jelly-crystals*.

1889 MAIDEN *Usef. Pl. Australia* 203 *Sida rhombifolia*.. 'Queensland Hemp'...'Native Lucerne', is a common name, also "Jelly Leaf". 1884 KNIGHT *Dict. Mech.* Suppl. 511/2 **Jelly Powder*..consists of 94% or 95% of nitro-glycerine and 5% or 6% collodion cotton, so mixed as to assume a gelatinous form. 1895 *Army & Navy Co-op. Soc. Price List* 15 Sept. 26 Table Jelly powder..in packets.

Jellygraph (dʒe·ligrɑf). [f. JELLY *sb.* + -GRAPH.] An appliance used for multiplying copies of writing, etc., of which the essential part is a sheet of jelly. Also *attrib.* Hence **Je·llygraph** *v. trans.*, to copy with a jellygraph.

1900 H. G. WELLS *Love & Mr. Lewisham* xxv. 196 The arrival of a letter of atrociously jellygraphed advices from Messrs. Danks and Wimborne. 1904 *Sat. Rev.* 9 Jan. 40 It is better 'jellygraphing' questions for some one else's form than [etc.]. 1911 A. R. HINKS *Astron.* iv. (1919) 113 A 'jellygraphed' post-card. 1919 *Brit. Jrnl. Photog. Alm.* Index, Jellygraph mixture for enlarging easel.

Jelutong (dʒe·lŭtǫŋ). Also **jolo-, jelo-.** [Malay.] A resin-yielding tree, *Dyera costulata*; also the wood of this tree and the gum which it yields (cf. **gutta-jelutong*).

1885 *Spons' Mechanics' Own Bk.* 264 Jolotong...Well adapted for patterns and mouldings, excellent for carving purposes. 1921 *Punch* CLX. 510/1 Deresinate the jelutong. 1922 *Chambers's Jrnl.* 503/1 Jelotong, gutta percha [etc.].

Jemima (dʒĕmai·mă). [Female Christian name.]

1. A made-up tie.

1899 SOMERVILLE & ROSS *Irish R. M.* v. 97 We indulged in ..'Jemima' ties with diagonal stripes. 1920 *Glasgow Herald* 3 Apr. 4, I have never learned the knack of fixing a dress tie, and I have not the moral courage to wear a jemima.

2. *pl.* Elastic-sided boots.

1902 *M. A. P.* 29 Mar. 323/1, I spoke of Mr. Chamberlain's having fallen from sartorial grace to the extent of wearing 'Jemimas'. 1906 *Westm. Gaz.* 31 Dec. 3/1 A pair of well-preserved 'jemimas'. They are the kind of footgear the immortal Teufelsdröckh himself might have worn, unless he had a weakness for bluchers. 1927 *Glasgow Herald* 24 Aug. 8 The old-fashioned, long obsolete elastic-sided boots, known for some obscure reason as 'Jemimas'.

Jena (yē·nă). [A town in Germany famed for its glassworks.] Used *attrib.* in *Jena glass* [G. *Jenaer glas*], which originated in the experiments of Doctors Abbe and Schott.

1892 *Work* IV. 145/2 The new Schott Jena glass. 1902 *Encycl. Brit.* XXIX. 5/1 Analyses of some of the more interesting of the Jena glasses.

Jennerian (dʒenĭə·riăn), *a.* Of or pertaining to Edward *Jenner* (1749–1823), the discoverer of vaccination.

1827 J. BARON *Life E. Jenner* I. 572 The Royal Jennerian Society for the extermination of the Small-pox. 1908 *Practitioner* June 845, V. Pirquet studied the effects of a second (Jennerian) vaccination shortly after the first.

Jeremiah (dʒerĭmai·ă). The name of a Hebrew prophet (see JEREMIAD), used allusively to denote a person given to lamentation or woeful complaining.

1902 *Daily Chron.* 15 Oct. 3/1 This talk about the ratepayers only came from municipal Jeremiahs. 1905 *Ibid.* 1 Sept. 5/7 The Jeremiahs have been on the rampage; the dismal and the doleful would-be experts (etc.). 1928 *Daily Express* 23 Feb. 3/5 There are always Jeremiahs who go about saying that we have never had such bad times. 1928 *Observer* 22 July 16/3 The Socialists are..bound to be confirmed Jeremiahs by the necessity of their propaganda.

Jeremianic (dʒerĭmaiæ·nik), *a.* [f. *JEREMIAH, after *Messianic*.] Of or pertaining to the prophet Jeremiah or the book of the Old Testament which bears his name.

1880 T. K. CHEYNE in *Encycl. Brit.* XIII. 628/1 Brought into its present form by a captivity prophet, working on a Jeremianic basis. 1889 — *Orig. Psalter* (1891) 151 A group of literary works which we may call Jeremianic. 1921 J. MOFFATT *Approach N. T.* ii. 62 The Jeremianic prediction of the new covenant has been fulfilled in Christianity.

Jerk, *sb.*¹ Add: **2. d.** *Golf.* A stroke in which the club-head 'goes on into the ground, cutting up a fid of the turf and being rather arrested with a jerk in the ground' (H. Hutchinson *Golfing* 1893, p. 36).

1897 *Encycl. Sport* I. 465/2 This stroke is called a 'jerk'.

e. *Physical jerks*, the motions practised in physical training. *To put a jerk in it* (slang): to be smart or vigorous in action.

1919 *War Slang* in *Athenæum* 25 July 664/2 'Physical jerks' dates from war-time, as does also the admonition 'put a jerk in it', which is the equivalent of the ante-bellum 'jump to it'. 1922 N. KENT *Quest M. Harland* II. viii, 'I like to see young people enthusiastic. Put a jerk in it, can't you?' 'A—a *what*?' stammered Anthea, tottering. 'Put a jerk in it,' repeated Roger.

Jerk-line. *U.S.* [f. JERK *v.*¹ 2.] A rope used in place of reins to guide a horse.

1907 S. E. WHITE *Arizona Nights* III. iv. 287, I bet that Sang would get a wiggle on him.., if he had a woman ahold of his jerk line. 1910 JOS. HART *Vigilante Girl* x. 140 This train of animals was driven by a 'jerk line' instead of reins.

Jerkwater (dʒɔ̄·ɹk,wǭ:təɹ). *U.S.* [? f. JERK *v.*¹ Cf. *FRESHWATER 1 b.] Used *attrib.* as a term of depreciation.

1911 H. S. HARRISON *Queed* xviii. 225 The spring found West stronger and more contented with his lot as president of a jerkwater college. 1920 *Bulletin* 22 June 10/1 This Oriental who, with perfect self-possession..descended from the jerkwater train carrying a modern suitcase. 1926 J. BLACK *You Can't Win* xx. 303, I followed the pay-roll aboard the jerkwater train that carried it to the waiting miners.

Jerky, *sb.*¹ *U.S.* (Earlier examples.)

1873 J. H. BEADLE *Undevel. West* xxx. 663 The 'jerky' now runs three times per week from St. George. 1878 — *Western Wilds* 386 (Th.) A little jerky carrying ten passengers.

Jerky, *sb.*² *U.S.* (Earlier example.)

1850 W. COLTON *Three Yrs. California* xxii. 298 A junk of bread, and a piece of the stewed jerky.

Jerry, *sb.* Add: By association with *German*, used in the British army in the later stages of the war of 1914–18 as a humorous designation of the enemy.

1919 J. B. MORTON *Barber of Putney* ii, There was three Jerries waiting for 'im to get tired and chuck it. 1925 E. FRASER & GIBBONS *Soldier & Sailor Words*, *Jerry over*, 'Lights out!' The word passed along the lines at the Front at night on the nearing overhead of an enemy aeroplane. *Jerry up*, a warning call on the approach of a German aeroplane. 1929 E. W. SPRINGS *Above bright blue Sky* 172 If you have many chaps like him, it won't take long to chase Jerry back to the Rhine. 1931 TILSLEY *Other Ranks* 8 The way they referred to the Germans—almost affectionately. Old Fritz, or Old Jerry! Might be an ally!

Jerry, *v.* [Cf. JERRY *a.*, JERRY-BUILT.] *trans.* To put *together* hastily.

1915 *Nation* (N.Y.) 27 May 597/1 Mr. Allen rearranged the corrected material..and jerried together his final report.

Jerry-build, *v.* Add: Also *fig.*

1918 'W. N. P. BARBELLION' *Last Diary* (1920) 36 It is easy to reconcile oneself to man's sorrows by shutting the eyes to them... How many people have been jerry-building their faith and creed all their lives by this method!

Jerry-built, *a.* Add: Also *fig.*

1901 *Daily Chron.* 13 Aug. 3/2 In an age of jerry-built books it is refreshing to come across a volume that has taken forty years to compile. 1903 *Ibid.* 20 Feb. 3/2 Fiction, he said, was now jerry-built.

Jersey². *U.S.* = *New Jersey*, the name of the state situated between Pennsylvania and the Atlantic, used *attrib.* and *Comb.*, as *Jersey girl, justice, militia; Jersey-built, -made* adjs.

1770 *Boston Gaz.* 7 May (Th.) A likely active Jersey girl. 1778 *Maryland Jrnl.* 20 Jan. (Th.) Last week, the Jersey militia took a Prize, and began to unload her. 1778 *Boston Gaz.* 25 Aug. 373 Handy, light, Jersey made waggon. 1806 *Repertory* (Bost.) 10 Oct. (Th.) Our Reverend neighbour in law, to use the Jersey phrase. 1829 R. C. SANDS *Writings* II. 121 Trim Jersey-built wagons. 1903 *New York Tribune* 18 Oct. 8 Even with a faithful judge..'Jersey justice' did not shine so brilliantly as usual.

b. In special uses, as **Jersey blue** (see quot.); **Jersey lightning**, 'apple-jack or peach-brandy; very crude and bad whisky' (*Cent. Dict.*); **Jersey pine**, the scrub pine, *Pinus virginiana*; **Jersey stage**, a stage-coach of the type used in New Jersey; **Jersey sweet(ing)**, a variety of apple; **Jersey tea**, the red-root, *Ceanothus americanus*, the leaves of which were used for tea during the American revolution; **Jersey wagon**, a light carriage formerly used in New Jersey.

1852 *Congress. Globe* 12 Aug., App. 967 (Th.) The term applied to them was '*Jersey Blue', synonymous of truth and fidelity. 1863 *Boston Sat. Herald* 9 Aug. 2/7 *Jersey lightning. 1866 J. C. GREGG *Life in Army* xii. 96 When his brains become addled by too much 'Jersey lightning', he is not fit to drive a decent mule team. 1770 J. R. FORSTER tr. *Kalm's Trav.* I. 334 *Jersey Pine. 1832 D. J. BROWNE *Sylva Amer.* 234 The Jersey pine is sometimes 30 or 40 feet high. 1858 J. A. WARDER *Hedges & Evergreens* II. 246 The Jersey pine is..found on dry soils from New Jersey to Carolina. 1800 WEEMS *Lett.* II. 154 O that I had but a *Jersey stage and a couple of good strong horses! 1876 J. BURROUGHS *Winter Sunshine* vii. 163 With a tree of the *Jersey sweet..in bearing, no man's table need be devoid of luxuries. 1836 *Knickerbocker Mag.* VIII. 58 A green 'Jersey-sweetin'. 1846 in W. H. Emory *Notes Milit. Reconn.* 387 The beautiful white clusters of the *Jersey tea. 1870 *Amer. Naturalist* IV. 583 The Ceanothus, or Jersey tea, is a frequent inhabitant of the prairies. 1818 R. SUTCLIFF *Trav. N. Amer.* (1815) p. xi, *Jersey waggon[s]..are made very light, hung on springs with leather braces, and travel very pleasantly. 1841 *Southern Lit. Messenger* VII. 39/1 Besides the fine carriages already mentioned, muddy Jersey waggons..are all sheltered beneath the majestic pines.

Jerseyman (dʒɔ̄·ɹzimăn). A native or inhabitant of Jersey (the Channel Islands), or of New Jersey, U.S.A.

1825 LOUDON *Encycl. Agric.* IV. I. 1129/2 That evil, which the Jersey-man so much deprecates. 1839 *Southern Lit. Messenger* V. 800/2 A Jerseyman is pre-eminently calculated to make a good traveller. 1873 LELAND *Egypt. Sketch-Bk.* 45 The last number of the *Anglo-American* contains the names of half-a-dozen as veritable Jersey-men as ever drank apple-jack. 1878 *Harper's Mag.* 318/2 'Pretty hard times,' said the Jerseyman; 'but I want three hundred dollars in cash.'

Jesse² (dʒe·si). (With capital or small initial.) *U.S.* Also **jessie, -y.** [perh. derived from a humorous perversion of 'There shall come a *rod* out of the stem of *Jesse*' (Isa. xi. 1, A.V.).] *To give* (a person) *Jesse*, or *particular Jesse*: to treat or handle severely, beat or rate soundly. Similarly *to catch Jesse*.

1844 *Nauvoo Neighbor* 17 Apr. (Th.) When Missouri gave them jesse. 1845 C. MATHEWS *Writ.* I. 243 (Th.) He turned on the woman and gave her Jesse. 1846 D. CORCORAN *Pickings* 126 Threatening to give Miss Martin 'jessy' when she would next meet her. 1847 *Streaks of Squatter Life* 81 Allen was giving him particular jesse. 1856 ALICE CARY *Married* II. iii. 122 Just as soon as I go home I'll give you jessie. 1858 TERESA VIELE *Following the Drum* 172 General Harney..had come down..to administer 'jesse' generally to all delinquents. 1863 *Rocky Mtn. News* (Denver) 2 Apr. (Th.) Wherever we go [after vaccination] we are sure to catch jesse on our sore arm. 1865 A. H. STEVENS *Diary* 29 Sept. (1910) 528 While I thought I was giving you Jesse on hearts, you were giving me fits on spades.

Jet, *sb.*³ Add: **5. c.** In oil-burning boilers or engines, a nozzle which injects oil or petrol into the engine-cylinder or fire-box in a fine spray mixed with air.

1887 *Encycl. Brit.* XXII. 500/2 The oil is injected in the form of a spray..by a steam jet arranged in such a way that air will be drawn into the furnace along with the petroleum. 1901 *Motor-Car World* II. 42/1 Sometimes the jet gets stopped up, causing the engine to cease working. 1904 A. B. F. YOUNG *Complete Motorist* iii. 48 Unless the petrol is very carefully filtered the jet or nozzle is apt to become choked.

Jeté (ʒǝte). [F. *jeté*, pa. pple. (sc. *pas* step) of *jeter* to throw.] A dance-step in which one foot is kicked forwards or backwards while a hop is made with the other foot.

1927 *Dancing Times* Apr. 9 All dancers know that the coupé cannot be done alone, as the position of the foot which is being 'cut-away' depends entirely upon the step which follows the coupé. I am therefore taking the 'coupé-dessous', followed in the first instance by a 'posé', and afterwards the 'coupé-dessous' followed by a 'jeté'.

Jetted (dʒe·ted), *a.*² *Tailoring.* [app. f. JET *v.*²] Of a pocket: Having no flap, but an outside seam on either edge, called the **Jetting.**

1923 *Daily Mail* 23 Apr. 8 The skirt pockets, which are finished in jetted fashion. 1928 *Daily Express* 2 May 8 Your tailor..will cut your lounge jacket with jetted, or flapless, pockets.

Jeune premier (ʒön prǝmye). [Fr., lit. = first young man.] An actor who plays the part of the principal lover or young hero. So **Jeune première** (prǝmyɛ̄r), the performer of the corresponding female part.

1852 *Blackw. Mag.* Nov. 600/2 The *prima donna* and *jeune premiere* of the troop. 1877 *Sat. Rev.* 24 Nov. 662/2 What the *jeune premier* would necessarily be when acting the part of a ruined country gentleman. 1888 *Athenæum* 3 Nov. 588/2 Theology also plays a part, albeit in the form of the *jeune premier*, the handsome curate with Broad Church instead of agnostic views. 1896 MRS. H. WARD *Sir G. Tressady* xiii. 283 Ancoats always seems to me the *jeune premier* in his own play. 1902 *Sat. Rev.* 13 Sept. 329/2 [He] plays him with no more intelligence than would suffice for the part of a quite ordinary jeune premier.

Jeunesse dorée (ʒönes dǫre). [Fr., lit. = gilded youth.] Originally applied in France to the group of fashionable counter-revolutionaries formed after the fall of Robespierre; now *gen.*, young men of wealth and fashion.

1837 CARLYLE *Fr. Rev.* III. VII. ii. 409 Fréron, in his fondness, names them *Jeunesse Dorée*, Golden, or Gilt Youth. 1845 *Encycl. Metrop.* XIII. 374/1 These young men, who were commonly known as the 'Jeunesse dorée', no longer permitted the Jacobins to hold assemblies in the public places. *Ibid.*, The Jeunesse dorée and the Thermidorians had on their side the tradesmen. 1886 *Athenæum* 11 Sept. 329/2 We shall not envy the *jeunesse dorée* of the period these so-called sports. 1888 *N. & Q.* 7th Ser. V. 190/1 *Jeunesse dorée* answers, perhaps, rather to Disraeli's expression of 'curled darlings' than to 'dandy'. 1910 D. SCHWANN *Bk. Bachelor* 47 Mason..received the guests, who were the fine flower of dramatic and critical Bohemia, with a sprinkling of the *jeunesse dorée* of Society and high finance.

Jew, *sb.* Add: **1. c.** *Black Jew* = *FALASHA.

a 1817 T. DWIGHT *Trav. New Eng.*, etc. (1823) III. 174 The black Jews in Hindostan. 1822 *Imperial Mag.* IV. 358 A copy of the Hebrew Pentateuch..found in one of the Black Jews' Synagogues, at Cochin. 1836–9 JULIA C. MAITLAND *Lett. fr. Madras* xviii. (1843) 178, I told him about the first preachers, the Black Jews, the Syrian Christians, &c. 1892 G. M. RAE *Syrian Ch.* ix. 150 These black Jews are converts to the faith from among the people of the land. 1930 H. NORDEN *Africa's Last Empire* 185 The black Jews among whom he works.

2. b. A ship's tailor. *Naut. slang.*

1916 *Chambers's Jrnl.* May 278/2 They [*sc.* ships' tailors] were still known as 'jews'.

Jew, *v.* Add: Also with *down*.

1870 *Congress. Globe* 7 July 5340/1 This bill supposes that Congress..is ready to commence jewing down the pay of its General. 1883 'MARK TWAIN' *Life Mississippi* xliii. 437 There's one thing in this world which a person don't ever try to jew you down on. That's a coffin.

Hence **Jewing** *vbl. sb.* Add: (See quot. and cf. *JEW *sb.* 2 b.) *Naut. slang.*

1916 *Chambers's Jrnl.* May 278/2 The term 'jewing', as sewing is still called.

Jewel, *sb.* **3.** Add: *Jewels of the crown*, a rhetorical phrase for colonies of the British Empire.

1901 P. MANSON in *Daily Mail Year Bk.* 101, 10 or 15 years hence that region [*sc.* West Africa] would be regarded as one of the richest jewels in the crown of England. 1931 *N. & Q.* 5 Sept. 166/2 Those irritations against tyranny and stupidity which lost us those jewels of the Crown [*sc.* the American Colonies].

Jewessy (dʒū·ĕsi), *a.* [f. JEWESS + -Y¹.] Resembling or characteristic of a Jewess.

1930 J. B. PRIESTLEY *Angel Pavement* iv. § 1 And there were two or three [*sc.* girls] worth looking at, the flashy young Jewessy type.

Jewhilliken, variant of *GEEWHILLIKINS.

Jewy (dʒū·i), *a.* *depreciatory.* [f. JEW *sb.* + -Y¹.] Resembling or characteristic of a Jew or the Jews; having the characteristics attributed to the Jewish race.

1904 ELLEN T. FOWLER *Kate of Kate Hall* xvii. 194 They [*sc.* the noses] are as like as two peas, and both, to my mind, a bit Jewy. 1919 'BARBELLION' *Jrnl. Disappointed Man* 154 That mean, Jewy, secretive, petty creature, J. M. W. Turner. 1930 J. B. PRIESTLEY *Angel Pavement* iv. § 4 A neat dark Jewy sort of chap.

Jhoom, jhum, variants of JOOM, JÚM.

1895 W. R. FISHER tr. *R. Hess's Forest Protection* 350 Jhuming, or the thorough burning of branchwood on the soil. *Ibid.* 543 In *jhums*, or cultivations on forest clearings, where the branches and undergrowth are burned. 1927 *Blackw. Mag.* June 816/2 Crops are grown by a simple method known as 'Jhoom'. *Ibid.*, A fresh patch of jungle is then cut down, and the 'Jhooming' process repeated.

Jhula (dʒū·la). *India.* Also **joolah.** [Hind., Hindi *jhūlā* swing, swing-rope.] A rude suspension bridge used in the Himalayas.

1830 COL. A. S. H. MOUNTAIN in *Mem.* (1857) 114 Our chief object in descending to the Sutlej was to swing on a Joolah bridge. 1844 STOCQUELER *Handbk. Brit. India* (1854) 246 The rustic bridge is supplanted..by *jhulas*, formed by ropes stretched across, constituting a species of loose parapet. 1923 *Blackw. Mag.* Aug. 259/2 A *jhula* or swinging rope-bridge.

Jiffy. Add: Also **jiffy-quick** *adv.*, in a jiffy.

1927 *Ladies' Home Jrnl.* Dec. 34/3 A waxed surface that ..you can dust up jiffy-quick promises spick-and-span floors with but little trouble.

Jig, *sb.* Add: **5.** (Earlier examples of *the jig is up*.) Also *the jig is over*.

1777 *Maryland Jrnl.* 17 June (Th.) Mr. John Miller came in and said, 'The jig is over with us.' 1800 *Aurora* (Phila.) 17 Dec. (Th.) As the Baltimore paper says, 'The Jigg's up, Paddy.' 1834 W. A. CARRUTHERS *Kentuckian in N.Y.* II. 210, I began to think the jig was up with me, for she began to look serious.

6. b. (Earlier U.S. example.)

1849 *President's Message to Congress* II. 479 Assay and analysis of the washed metals from the jigs at the Boston and Pittsburg Company's mine.

c. (Earlier U.S. example.)

1846 *Knickerbocker Mag.* XXVII. 513 See that your jigs are in perfect order, for if we do get hold of 'em, our lines and books will have to take it, I guess, for a spell.

e. = TEMPLET¹ 2 b.

1913 *Lockwood's Dict. Mech. Engin.* App., *Jig*, an appliance which locates and holds a piece of work, and guides the tools which operate on it. 1921 *Dict. Occup. Terms* (1927) § 200 *Driller*..may use template or jig to fix position of holes.

f. *Wireless.* (See quot.)

1907 ERSKINE MURRAY *Handbk. Wireless Teleg.* 122, I.. propose to adopt a good old English word..to stand for 'a damped train of electrical oscillations of a frequency of the same order as is employed in wireless telegraphy'; or the corresponding 'oscillatory currents, voltages,..' associated with them... The word chosen is..*jig*. 1908 E. RUHMER *Wireless Telephony* II. x. 128.

8. **jig-box**, a box or sieve for jigging ore; **jig-man**, one who works an ore-dressing jigger; **jig-time** *U.S. colloq.*, in phrases expressing a very short space of time.

1902 *Encycl. Brit.* XXXI. 371/2 The pulsating current is obtained by placing a vertical longitudinal partition, *c*, extending part of the way down to the bottom of the *jig box. 1849 *President's Message to Congress* II. 469 The heavier metals are thrown out to be farther cleansed by the *Jigmen. 1916 H. L. WILSON *Somewhere in Red Gap* vii. 314 Kate has about four more of 'em licked to a standstill in *jigtime. 1922 J. A. DUNN *Man Trap* xviii. 247 If we don't get through on jigtime I'll not ask you for a cent.

Jigamaree. **2.** (Earlier U.S. example.)

1824 *Old Colony Memorial* (Plymouth) 6 Mar. (Th.) O the wonderation, what a nation sight of jiggermarees!

Jigger, *sb.*¹ Add: **1. b.** A light shoe. *U.S.*

1841 *Southern Lit. Messenger* VII. 646/2 He then dressed himself with more than ordinary care, discarding his 'stitch-downs' for his 'jiggers' (his pumps).

5. Other specific applications:

a. Also, a templet or former used to shape the insides of rounded or dome-shaped vessels. **l.** *Wireless.* An oscillation transformer. **m.** *Golf.* A short iron-headed club used for approaching. **n.** A bicycle or small motor vehicle. **o.** A ouija. **p.** (See quot.) *U.S.*

a. 1875 KNIGHT *Dict. Mech.* 1214/2.

l. 1902 *Encycl. Brit.* XXXIII. 230/2 The plugs of the sensitive tube..are joined to the terminals of the secondary circuit S S of a small transformer, called a 'jigger'. 1907 ERSKINE-MURRAY *Handbk. Wireless Teleg.* 43 These receiving transformers, or jiggers, as they are frequently called, are of the same type as Tesla's high frequency transformer. 1913 *Wireless World* I. 10/1 Adjustable transmitting jigger.

m. 1893 H. HUTCHINSON *Golfing* 21 On some links these are a great deal used, under the name of jiggers. 1929 *Encycl. Brit.* X. 504/1 *Jigger*, an iron club with narrow blade, in classification intermediate between a midiron and a mashie. 1931 *Punch* 1 July 717/2 *Fully-equipped Visitor*. This looks a weird sort of hole. What on earth does one take here? *Local Player*. One takes a jigger, if that's all one has.

n. 1897 H. G. WELLS in *Humours of Cycling* 7 'Pretty Jigger!' said the Bounder...'Nice-looking machine you've got.' 1906 BENNETT *Whom God hath joined* I. 12 'So you biked up after me?' said Mark. 'I had to. I borrowed this jigger from the office-boy.' 1930 BRAMAH *Little Flutter* iv. 52 My little jigger is no good for a job like this.

o. 1916 SIR O. LODGE *Raymond* 186 Jigger. (A kind of Ouija.)

p. 1879 *N.Y. Herald* 21 Nov. 8/2 A jigger..is a conical metal cup in which to mix fancy drinks.

7. b. *U.S.* (Earlier example.)

1882 *Congress. Rec.* 19 July 6195/2, I never saw an Irishman or a German who would not give up his dinner before he would his glass of beer, his jigger, or his pipe.

8. (sense 5 b) *jigger-boy*; **jigger-head** (see 5 a); **jigger-knife** = sense 5 h; **jigger machine**, the potter's lathe which carries the former or jigger; **jigger-saw** = JIG-SAW *sb.*

1869 *Good Words* 1 Mar. 172/2 A plaster-of-Paris cast is placed on a disc which a handle-turning '*jigger-boy' causes to revolve. 1921 *Dict. Occup. Terms* (1927) § 043 *Jigger boy*.. attaches or detaches tubs..by placing rope in fork of 'jigger', or double crook, in socket at one side or at end of tubs. 1881 *Harper's Mag.* Feb. 362/2 The plaster mould fits into a metal top called the '*jigger-head'. 1875 KNIGHT *Dict. Mech.*, **Jigger-knife*, a drawing-knife with a blade bent at one end and curved at the other, used by wheelwrights. 1921 *Dict. Occup. Terms* (1927) § 105 *Jiggerer, sanitary*, a jiggerer ..who makes sanitary appliances on *jigger machine. 1888 *Lockwood's Dict. Mech. Engin.*, **Jigger Saw*, or *Jig Saw*.

Jigger, *v.*¹ Add: **2.** orig. and chiefly *pass.* with *up*: To be tired out; hence, to be done for. Also *actively*. *dial.* and *slang*.

1861 C. C. ROBINSON *Dial. Leeds* s.v. *Jigger'd up*, Av tramp'd a matter o' fotty mile to-daay, an' am fair jigger'd up. 1867 SMYTH *Sailor's Word-bk.*, *Jiggered-up*, done up; tired out. 1883 W. C. RUSSELL *Sailor's Lang.* s.v. 1885 BRIERLEY *Ab-o'-th'-Yate Yankeeland* v. (E.D.D.) A generation or two would see it jiggered up if it wurno' for th' fresh blood ut's bein sent into it. 1923 *Daily Mail* 13 June 12 I've 'jiggered' up my Rolls-Royce.

Jigger, *v.*⁴ *Pottery.* [f. JIGGER *sb.*¹] *trans.* To shape with a jigger.

1930 W. H. WARBURTON *Hist. Trade Union Organ.* 208, I will try and get the price you want for this article, but you must remember that this..is being jiggered by a firm in the next town at a much less price.

Jiggerer (dʒi·gərəɹ). [f. JIGGER *sb.*¹ + -ER¹.] One who uses or works with a jigger (in various trades).

1881 *Instr. Census Clerks* (1885) 84 Miners...Loader, Jiggerer, Trammer, Hooker-on. *Ibid.* 88 China, Porcelain, Manufacture...Jigger or Gigger Turner, Jiggerer. 1921 *Dict. Occup. Terms* (1927) § 043 *Jiggerer*.., attaches or detaches tubs, singly or in pairs, to or from endless rope, by placing rope in fork of 'jigger', or double crook. *Ibid.* § 105 *Jiggerer*,..presses bat of clay on top of mould, already revolving on vertical spindle. 1930 W. H. Warburton *Hist. Trade Union Organ.* 205 By this scheme his hollow-ware pressers would employ female assistants in the same way as did his hollow-ware jiggerers and 'jolliers'.

Jiggery-pokery (dʒi·gəri,pōu·kəri). *colloq.* [Cf. Sc. *joukery-pawkery* (see Joukery b).] Deceitful or dishonest 'manipulation'; hocus-pocus, humbug.

1893 *Wiltshire Gloss.* 1926 Spanner *Naviators* 104, I thought, at first, it was some more jiggery-pokery to keep down the expenditure this financial year.

Jigging, *vbl. sb.* Add: **2. b.** (Cf. *Jig *sb.* 6 e.)

1913 *Lockwood's Dict. Mech. Engin.* App., *Jigging*, the practice of tooling work held in jigs, adopted in the interchangeable system, when articles are tooled in quantities.

Jiggoty, variant of Jiggety *a.*

1876 H. E. Scudder *Dwellers Five-Sisters Crt.* ii. 30 Mr. Sinclear appeared and received the jiggoty Miss Pix's welcome in a smiling and well-bred manner.

Jig-saw, *sb.* Add: In full **jig-saw puzzle,** a puzzle formed by cutting into small irregular pieces with a jig-saw, a picture mounted on a sheet of thin wood. So *jig-saw map.* Also *transf.*

1909 *Daily Mirror* 17 Aug. 4/4 A jigsaw map of England. *Ibid.*, These jigsaw geography puzzles should be introduced into all the Council schools in London. 1915 *Morning Post* 6 Apr. 2/4 A kind of verbal jig-saw. 1920 *Punch* 22 Sept. 235/1 The comparatively simple task of piecing together these jigsaws. 1921 *Spectator* 16 Apr. 489/2 Minds, grown weary of other 'jig-saws'. 1926 G. W. Deeping *Sorrell & Son* vii. 68 Kit played a game of his own with the town, treating it as a sort of jig-saw puzzle.

Jimbal, variant of Gimbal 2.

1847 *Knickerbocker Mag.* XXIX. 152 His arms dangling from his shoulder joints, and apparently hung in jimbals, sway to and fro.

Jimber-jawed, *a.* *U.S.* (Earlier example.)

1834 W. A. Carruthers *Kentuckian in N.Y.* I. 195 Some ..pushed out the under jaw like a person who (to use a Southern term) is jimber-jawed.

Jim-crow. **2.** Add: *Jim Crow bill, law, school; Jim Crow car* (earlier examples); **Jim Crow's nose,** *Scybalium jamaicense*, a West Indian parasitic plant of the family *Balanophoraceæ*.

1904 *Nation* (N.Y.) 17 Mar. 202 The *Jim Crow bills now before the Maryland Legislature. 1861 H. Jacobs *Life Slave Girl* xxxv. 265, I was not put into a '*Jim Crow car' on our way to Rockaway. 1887 C. B. George *40 Years on Rail* viii. 160 An educated colored man..found, on going from Boston to Salem, his home, that he must ride in the Jim Crow car. 1904 *Richmond Times-Despatch* 25 May 10 Violating the *Jim Crow law by allowing negroes to ride in the same car with whites. 1903 *New York Sun* 29 Nov. 7 The members of the committee have arranged with the parents of negro children to send them all to the *Jim Crow school, thus entirely separating the white and negro pupils. 1866 *Treas. Bot.*, **Jim Crow's Nose*, a West Indian name for *Phyllocoryne*.

Ji·m-da·ndy, *a.* and *sb.* *U.S. colloq.* [Cf. Dandy *a.* and *sb.*] **a.** *adj.* Remarkably fine or 'swell'. Also *adv.* **b.** *sb.* A superfine person or thing.

1888 *Daily Inter-Ocean* 14 Feb. (Farmer) George C. Ball came upon the floor yesterday arrayed in a jim-dandy suit of clothes. 1902 Harben *Abner Daniel* xxxi, You are a jim-dandy, young man. 1902 Wister *Virginian* xxvii. 346 He must have been a jim-dandy of a boy. 1904 Harben *Georgians* ix. 87 Right thar I baked pies—open-top jim dandies, too. 1914 Gertrude Atherton *Perch of Devil* II. iii, I've got..a jim dandy of a limousine. 1919 H. L. Wilson *Ma Pettengill* iv. 119, I bet you made a jim-dandy good report.

Jim-jam. Add: **3. b.** *pl.* The 'creeps'; the fidgets; a fit of depression.

1904 *Strand Mag.* XXVIII. 770/2 By Gosh, look there. Enough to give a fellow the jim-jams, isn't it? 1923 Oppenheim *Mystery Road* II. xiii, If I begin to think, I get the jim-jams. 1926 Galsworthy *Silver Spoon* I. vi, Who was that old buffer?..he gave me 'the jim-jams'. 1931 C. Mackenzie *Buttercups & Daisies* xiii, I reckon if you put him in the upper circle at Charley's Aunt he'd give half the audience the jim-jams and upset the whole piece.

Jimmies, *sb. pl.* *colloq.* = Jim-jam 3.

1921 A. Mason *Flying Bo'sun* xxvi, 'Riley,' said I, 'you drank to much Scotch last night; be careful that you don't get the Jimmies.'

Jimmy, *sb.*[1] U.S. variant of Jemmy *sb.* 6. Also as *v. trans.*, to open with a jemmy.

1904 G. H. Lorimer *Old Gorgon Graham* viii. 159 You can't break a big merchant with a jimmy and a stick of dynamite. 1905 *New York Even. Post* 22 Dec. 3 The thieves jimmied the front door. 1922 R. Parrish *Case & Girl* xxxii, Finally we jimmied open the back door of this garage.

Jimmy (dʒi·mi), *sb.*[2] *Colonial.* An emigrant settler: app. short for *Jimmy* (or *Jemmy*) *Grant*, rhyming slang for *emigrant*.

1859 H. Kingsley *G. Hamlyn* xxvi, 'What are these men that we are going to see?' 'Why one,' said Lee, 'is a young Jimmy (I beg your pardon, sir, an emigrant).' 1867 *Cassell's Mag.* II. 440/2, I never wanted to leave England... I wasn't like one of these Jemmy Grants. 1878 Aylward *Transvaal of Today* 216 A raw emigrant and still what Natalians call a 'Jimmy'. 1922 Sir W. B. Thomas in *Daily Mail* 11 Dec. 8 With his wife and child he had just come over as a 'Jimmie-grant'.

Jimmy Low. An Australian name for the Red Gum, *Eucalyptus resinifera.*

1887 *Col. & Ind. Exhib. 1886, Rep. Col. Sect.* 428 Jimmy Low is usually a large tree, yielding timber of a rich red colour. 1889 Maiden *Useful Pl. Australia* 508 Other names for it are 'Red Gum', 'Grey gum', 'Hickory', and it perpetuates the memory of an individual by being called 'Jimmy Low'.

Jim(p)son weed (= Jamestown-weed; earlier examples).

1832 in T. H. Benton *Thirty Years' View* (1854) I. 256 An eagle [caught] by a pig under a jimpson weed. 1872 E. Eggleston *End of World* xi. 77 Like a..jimson-weed on the sunny side of a board fence! 1876 'Mark Twain' *Tom Sawyer* 18 She..looked out among the tomato vines and jimpson weeds that constituted the garden.

ellipt. 1842 *American Pioneer* I. 314 She said her principal dressings were made of..the leaves of stramonium, or 'jimson'. 1910 C. Harris *Eve's Husband* xiv. 299 Clumps of sweet jimson and borders of balsam and pinks.

Jingled (dʒi·ŋg'ld), *ppl. a.* *U.S.* [f. Jingle *v.* + -ed[1].] Confused with drink; fuddled.

1908 G. H. Lorimer *J. Spurlock* xii. 315 Old Mrs. Corliss was purple with pleasure at having so plausible a pretext for getting comfortably jingled.

Jink, *sb.*[1] **1.** Add: Used esp. of a tricky turn in Rugby football. So **Jink** *v.* (and in *ppl. a.*).

a 1914 J. E. Raphael *Mod. Rugby Football* (1918) 103 This is a method which..should not be copied by the ordinary performer—except perhaps when 'jinking'. *Ibid.* 122 [Poulton Palmer's] 'jink' is all by itself in modern-day Rugger. 1921 *E. H. D. Sewell's Rugby Footb.* 126 The defender, watching the ball (instead of the attacker's eyes !), moves to *his* left as the dummy pass is made, thus making wider the gap which the attacker widens still further by his jink to the defender's right. 1927 Wakefield & Marshall *Rugger* 93 A curious jinking side-step. 1932 *Daily Tel.* 19 Mar. 17/2, I can see him jinking his way past our mid-field players.

Jinker, *v.* *Australia.* *trans.* To manipulate with a jinker (see Jinker[2]).

1903 R. Bedford *True Eyes* 240 Waiting for a fine day to jinker those trees out of the bush.

Jintawan (dʒintā·wăn). [Malay.] A kind of caoutchouc derived from the *Urceola elastica*; also, the tree itself.

1851 *Illustr. Catal. Gt. Exhib.* IV. I. 877/2 Raw caoutchouc from Assam, Singapore (*Urceola elastica*, the Jintawan of the Malays). 1853 Ure *Dict. Arts* I. 984 The said apparatus may be used also for purifying caoutchouc and jintawan. 1880 *Encycl. Brit.* XII. 817/1 Besides the orange..we have the rambutan,..the jintawan,..and the jambosa.

Jinx (dʒiŋks). *U.S.* Also **jinks, ginks.** [Of obscure origin.] A person or thing that brings bad luck, or exercises an evil influence, esp. in sports; a hoodoo.

1912 C. Mathewson *Pitching in a Pinch* xi. 232 A jinx is something which brings bad luck to a ball-player. 1919 *Oxford Mag.* 7 Mar., Will some one remove the jinx? On Friday, February 28, we lost to Oriel and Merton by 3 goals to nil. On Saturday, March 1, in a well-contested game, we lost to Queen's by 1–0. 1927 Agnes Miller *Colfax Bk.-plate* xiv. 172, I thrust that jinx of a book back into the lowest left-hand drawer. 1928 *Wisconsin Alumni Mag.* Dec. 79 Once realizing that the jinx had been broken,..there was no hesitation.

Jipijapa (hīˑpi,hāˑpā). Also **ippiappa.** [Name of a town in Ecuador.] **a.** The screw-pine *Carludovica palmata*, from the leaves of which Panama hats are made. **b.** A Panama hat. Also *jipijapa hat, plant.*

1858 Simmonds *Dict. Trade* s.v. *Panama-hats*, In Central America where they are made, the palm is called Jipijapa. 1877 *Encycl. Brit.* VI. 155/1 Straw hats, usually known as jipijapa or Panamá hats. 1900 *Jrnl. Soc. Arts* 17 Aug. 744 Jipijapa or Panama hats. 1901 *Amer. Anthrop.* Jan.–Mar. 206 Ecuador is the real home of the hats wrongly designated under the name of 'panama'...Everywhere in Latin America the hat is known under the name of *jipijapa*, in honor of the city where its manufacture was first started. 1908 *Daily Chron.* 7 Feb. 4/6 The Jippi-Jappa plant, known sometimes as 'the broom thatch'.

Jiquilite (hikilīˑte). [Sp. *jiquilete*, ad. Nahuatl *xiuhquilitl*, f. *xihuitl* turquoise + *quilitl* plant.] The native name in Central America for the indigo plant.

1866 *Treas. Bot.* 1880 *Encycl. Brit.* XI. 240/2 The cultivation of indigo (afiil or jiquilite) and cochineal.

Jirga (dʒi·ɹgă). Also **jeerga, jirgah.** [Pushtu.] An assembly or council of the headmen of Afghan tribes.

1843 Lady Sale *Jrnl. Disasters in Afghan.* Vocab. p. xii, *Jeerga.* An assembly or council—a diet. 1894 Meg Dyan *Man's Keeping* I. iv. 75 All large issues had to be referred to his Jeerga. 1906 *Westm. Gaz.* 14 May 3/2 They can, in fact, mobilise as easily as a Pathan jirga—with this difference, that they are disciplined rather more than the Pathan. 1908 *Ibid.* 24 Feb. 7/1 Afridis other than Zakka Khels are collecting at Chora for a jirgah. 1908 J. Morley in *Recoll.* (1917) II. v. iv. 243 Conciliatory management of the jirgas of these wild gentry. 1926 *Chambers's Jrnl.* 293/2 He eyed the elders of Pir Mahommed, assembled in *jirga*.

Jitney (dʒi·tni). *U.S.* [Origin unknown.] **1.** A nickel. *slang.*

1915 *Nation* (N.Y.) 4 Feb. 142/1 The word 'jitney'..is the Jewish slang term for a nickel. *Ibid.* 18 Mar. 304/3 A 'jitney' 'bus derives its name from 'jitney', meaning the smallest coin in circulation in Russia. 1916 *Chambers's Jrnl.* June 400/1 Five cents..is the charge for any distance, and as the colloquial name for this coin is a 'jitney', this form of traffic has become known as 'jitney competition'.

2. In full *jitney bus, omnibus*: an automobile which carries passengers for a small fare, usually five cents. Also, on account of the poor quality of these buses, used to designate anything cheap or ramshackle.

1915 *Nation* (N.Y.) 14 Jan. 50/3 [Letter of 28 Nov. 1914.] This autumn automobiles, mostly of the Ford variety, have begun to run in competition with the street cars in this city [*sc.* Los Angeles]. The newspapers call them 'Jitney 'buses'. 1915 *New York Even. Post* 16 Apr., The jitney wears out the streets and should contribute to their repair. 1915 *Literary Digest* 4 Sept. 462/1 In western Pennsylvania striking traction employees are operating a competing jitney service to bring the company to terms. 1916 H. L. Wilson *Somewhere in Red Gap* ii. 59 He..sells these jitney pianos and phonographs and truck like that. 1919 C'tess von Arnim *Christopher Columbus* xxxi, He had come in the jitney omnibus to the nearest point. 1922 *Public Opinion* 21 Jan. 48/2, I entered into his Jitney and waited for him to start.

Comb. 1923 F. Parsons *Everybody's Business* 215 All the jitney operators on the line.

Jiu-jitsu, -jutsu, variants of *Ju-jitsu.

Jixi (dʒi·ksi). *temporary.* [f. *Jix*, nickname of Joynson-Hicks + -*i*; after *taxi*.] A two-seater taxi-cab licensed in 1926 while Sir William Joynson-Hicks was Home Secretary.

1926 *Westm. Gaz.* 7 Apr., Jixi is the name given by the Westminster Gazette, and now used by everyone, to 2-seater taxicabs. 1926 *Punch* 21 Apr. 438/2 The Home Secretary [*sc.* Joynson-Hicks] explained to Sir F. Meyer that the police have licensed two types of 'Jixi'. 1926 *Sunday at Home* 5 June 514/2, I know there are to be Jixes [*sic*], but that rather sounds like the name of a wasp to me. 1927 *Observer* 3 Apr. 9 The first 'Jixie' or two-seater taxicab will probably be seen on the streets of London at the end of the present week.

Joachimite (dʒōu·ăkimait). *Ch. Hist.* [f. the name of *Joachim*, abbot of Floris (12th cent.) + -ite[1].] A follower of the Italian mystic, Joachim of Floris. Also **Jo·achite**; so **Jo·achism.**

1841 K. H. Digby *Mores Cath.* XI. xiii. (1846) III. 799/2 The execrable book, entitled the eternal Gospel,..whose adherents, termed Joachimites, as it was ascribed to Joachim, were again condemned by the Council of Arles. 1906 G. G. Coulton *St. Francis to Dante* 104 The Pope..insisted on his resignation, partly on account of his Joachism. *Ibid.* 108 A great orator and a great Joachite. 1913 A. G. Ferrers Howell *S. Bernardino of Siena* i. 6 There is no trace of Joachism in S. Francis himself. *Ibid.* 10 They cultivated the Joachite literature. 1926 E. Hutton *Francisc. in England* ix. 141.

Joar[2] (dʒōuˑaɹ). Also **johar.** [a. Hind. جوہر *jauhar*, f. phr. *jauhar karnā* to kill one's self.] (See quot. 1802.)

1802 C. James *Milit. Dict.*, *Joar*, a general massacre of the women and children, which is sometimes performed by the Hindoos, when they find they cannot prevent the enemy from taking the town. 1907 *Westm. Gaz.* 27 Nov. 2/1 Three times has the steep and zigzag road which, under many gateways, leads up to the fortress of Chitor, witnessed the rite known as Johar... The last siege of Chitor, terminated by the greatest of the Johars.

Job, *sb.*[2] Add:

4. b. *Job of work*: a task, piece of work.

1557 in Feuillerat *Revels Q. Mary* (1914) 236 Doinge certen Iobbes of woorke. 1872 A. Trollope *Eustace Diamonds* xix, Arthur did not go on the search, because he had a job of work to do. *Ibid.* lxxii, The barrister who will have the cross-examining of her..will have a job of work on his hand. 1890 [see *Coast *v.* 14]. 1928 M. Walsh *While Rivers Run* xx. 279 'A sound job of work!' boasted Alistair. 'We have arriven.' 1931 Patry Williams *Word of Tomorrow* IV. xvi, Tramps..who wouldn't do an honest job of work not if it was offered them.

c. *On the job*: (a) hard at work, busy; (b) (of a racing horse) out to win and well backed.

1891 *Licensed Victuallers' Gaz.* 23 Jan. (Farmer) Of course, there was a long wrangle over the choice of a referee, for no one cared to occupy that thankless post when the Lambs were on the job. 1892 Milliken *'Arry Ballads* 3 'Arry is fair on the job. 1909 *Post & Paddock* 22 Nov. 1/3 Their denunciations of horses 'not trying', being 'out for an airing', or 'not on the job' on every occasion when their speculations go wrong. 1914 Gertrude Atherton *Perch of Devil* I. iv. 22 She was 'on the job' every minute until the cottage was 'on wheels'. 1922 *N. & Q.* 12th Ser. XI. 206/2 To be 'on the job' is for a horse to be 'busy', to be 'out', *i.e.*, backed and trying.

d. A commission to back a horse.

1907 *Favourite* 16 Nov. 9/2 Elfin Revel was a big starting-price job for the Croxteth Plate. 1911 *Turf* 10 Oct. 1/1, I am not now referring to s.p. jobs.

e. A consignment of goods to be sold cheaply as bargains, a job lot.

1858 *Illustr. News World* I. 257/3 Butchers' meat, the week's gathering, to be sold by the job. 1905 *Daily Chron.* 18 Nov. 3/7 As soon as a girl can do a corset, which is at all passable, even if we have to put it into the 'jobs'—that is, lots for selling cheap—she can earn much more.

7. job-analysis, analysis of the essential factors of a particular piece of work and the necessary qualifications of the workman who is to perform it satisfactorily; **job-buyer,** one who buys job lots; **job-print, -printing** *U.S.*, the printing of small pieces of work, as bandbills, programmes, etc.

1923 J. D. Hackett *Labor Terms* in *Management Engineering* May, **Job Analysis*, the determination of the essential factors in a specific kind of work and of the qualifications of a worker necessary for its competent performance. 1929 *Encycl. Brit.* XIII. 78/2 This 'questionnaire method' has received severe condemnation from scientists and should be used sparingly by investigators in the field of job analysis. 1903 *Daily Chron.* 7 Oct. 10/1 E. H...described as a '*Job buyer'. 1909 *Westm. Gaz.* 22 Oct. 7/4 H. N...job buyer. 1921 Mulford *Bar-20 Three* vi. 77 The little printing-plant at Sandy Bend broke all its hazy precedents, with the result that a hard-riding courier, relaying twice, carried the work of the *job-print toward Mesquite. 1832 *Deb. Congress* 3 May 2767 *Job-printing. 1838 *Southern Lit. Messenger* IV. 230/2 Job printing done at this office, with neatness and despatch. 1846 T. L. MacKenney *Mem.* I. ix. 196 Whose 'reward' was conferred in the job-printing of the government in his paper. 1929 E. W. Howe *Plain People* 122 There was always one source of ready money: job printing.

Job, *sb.*[4] **2.** Add: **Job's cat, turkey** *U.S. jocular*, used as types of patient poverty.

1854 Seba Smith *Way Down East* 184, I should rather be as poor as *Job's cat all the days of my life. 1824 *The Microscope* in *Troy Sentinel* 22 May (Th.) We have seen fit to say 'the patience of *Job's turkey', instead of the common phrase, 'as patient as Job'. 1838 Haliburton *Clockm.* Ser. II. ii. 24 Well, I'm e'en a'most starved, and Captain Jack does look as poor as Job's turkey. 1872 E. Eggleston *Hoosier Schoolmaster* iv. 22 But laws! don't I remember when he was poorer nor Job's turkey?

Jobbing, *vbl. sb.*[2] **4.** Add: **jobbing-house** *U.S.*, a firm engaged in stock-jobbing; also, one which buys goods in bulk and sells them to retail dealers.

1870 J. K. Medbery *Men & Myst. Wall St.* 166 Mr. Fisk's maturity dates with his entrance as partner in a well-known Boston Jobbing-house. 1878 *Harper's Mag.* 760/2 We were all employed in the old jobbing-house down town. 1928 *Publishers' Weekly* 30 June 2596 The service of a well-equipped and completely-stocked jobbing house..is..invaluable to the small bookseller.

Jobless, *a.* Transfer *rare* to sense in Dict. and add: **2.** Out of work, unemployed. Hence **Jo·blessness,** the state of being out of work.

1923 *Public Opinion* 30 Mar. 304/1 He means not the fear of foremen so much as the fear of joblessness. 1923 *Glasgow Herald* 25 Oct. 7 The demand that would ensue for land users would mean jobs for jobless men.

Jo·bmongering, *vbl. sb.* [f. Jobmonger + -ing[1].] The action or practice of a jobmonger.

1901 *Daily Chron.* 18 Dec. 5/1 Has Tammany no synonym? Or what about Job-mongering? 1927 *Glasgow Herald* 24 Mar. 4 The intriguing and jobmongering of the Base.

Jobster (dʒǫ·bstəɹ). [f. Job *sb.*[2] + -ster.] = Jobber[2].

1892 Greener *Breech-loader* 117 If unable to send [a damaged gun] to the makers, avoid advertising jobsters. 1901 *Westm. Gaz.* 7 May 2/2 All the jobsters, speculators, South African financiers, all the coal and steel owners, who in 1899 cheered on the war.

Jock[1]. Add: **1. b.** A Scotch soldier.

1931 Tilsley *Other Ranks* 98 Hundreds of Tommies—or Jocks—and civvies lay dead in the cellars under this cathedral.

Jockey, *sb.* Add: **8. b.** *jockey-back, jockey-leg*: applied to a style of boot.

1909 *Boot Catal.*, Gentleman's Brown Willow Calf Lace, whole golosh, *jockey back. 1862 *Catal. Internat. Exhib., Brit.* II. No. 4658, Skins, kips, fronts, shoe legs, *jockey legs, cordovan, grained calf.

9. jockey-club, name of a well known scent; **jockey-stick** *U.S.* (see quots.); **jockey-weight** (see quot.).

1855 Piesse *Art. Perfumery* 122 *Jockey Club Bouquet. 1859 *Great Republic Mag.* Jan. 70 (Bartlett, ed. 1860, p. 396) I..used cologne, hair oil, and scented my handherchief with 'jockey-club'. 1872 Marietta Holley *My Opinions* (1891) 22 That I should take your jockey club and hair oil, and use 'em all myself. 1895 *Army & Navy Co-op. Soc. Price List* 716/1 A new fragrant Toilet Water in Jockey Club, White Rose, Stephanotis [etc.]. 1888 Eliz. B. Custer *Tenting on Plains* 352 [In driving a prairie schooner] a small hickory stick, about five feet long, called the *jockey-stick, not unlike a rake-handle, is stretched between a pilot [mule] and his mate. 1920 Jer. Hart *Vigilante Girl* x. 140 An iron 'jockey-stick' ran from the near leader's harness to the off leader's bit—this pushed or pulled his head as his mate moved in answer to the 'jerk line'. 1892 *Lockwood's Dict. Mech. Engin.*, **Jockey Weight*, a weight which is slid along a lever, in a weighing or testing machine, for purposes of precise adjustment.

Jockey, *sb.*[2] [f. the vb.] A deal in horses.

1867 'T. Lackland' *Homespun* II. 181 Never did a dicker or a jockey occur, but the profit and the loss were..consoled with sundry social drinks at the bar.

Jockeying, *vbl. sb.* **2.** (Earlier U.S. example.)

1779 *Essex Inst. Hist. Coll.* XLIII. 202 The Makers of Money sent it to their servants to purchase goods and they knew it was to be out of circulation in a few months. It would be called by some 'jockeying'.

Jodhpur (dʒǫ·dpʊ̆r). Also **Jodhpor(e, Jodphor(e, Judhpur, Judphor, -phur.** [Name of a native state in Rajputana, India.] Applied to a kind of riding-breeches reaching to the ankle, used for riding and sports, combining breeches and gaiters in one piece.

1899 G. W. Stevens *In India* (ed. 3) 28 The Jodhpur riding-breeches—breeches and gaiters all in one piece, as full as you like above the knee, fitting tight below it, without a single button or strap—have been taken up..by a London artist, and are on the way to be world-famous. 1925 *Vogue* 1 Sept. 66 Judhpur. 1925 *Illustr. Lond. News* 14 Nov. 968 The trousers are cut on Jodhpur lines, giving complete freedom of movement. 1927 *Daily Express* 14 Nov. 5/2 These ski-ing suits are made with a plain, well-cut coat and jodhpurs or trousers...The jodhpurs are useful as an alternative to breeches. 1928 *Ibid.* 2 May 13 Finding some new jodhpors in his room, [he] could not resist trying them on. 1931 *Times* 7 May 17/5 Princess Elizabeth of York is shown dressed for a ride with her fair curls shining and wearing a yellow jumper pulled down over her jodhpurs.

Joe, *sb.*[1] (Earlier and later U.S. examples.)

1765 *Boston Even. Post* 14 Oct. (Th.) Into the L....rs hands [full] many a Jo We've slily put, that so their tongues might go. a 1793 Freneau *Poems* (1809) I. 53 Three shillings are all the small pence that remain, And to change a half joe would be rather profane.

Joe, *sb.*[2] Add: **1. b.** phr. *Not for Joe*, by no means, not on any account.

[1877 Jos. Chamberlain in Garvin *Chamberlain* (1932) I. 236, I have had seven invitations to public meetings this week...Not for Joseph!] 1926 Galsworthy *Swan Song* II. xiii. 219 Not if he knew it—not for Joe.

c. *pl.* The blues. *Austral.*

1916 C. J. Dennis *Ginger Mick* 27 'E's got the joes reel bad.

Joe-pye weed. *U.S.* Also **joe-pie.** [See below.] A tall purple-flowered weed, *Eupatorium purpureum*, also called *trumpet-weed*.

'Joe Pye was an Indian who used this herb largely in treating cases of typhus fever, Maine' (Farmer). The source of this statement does not appear.

1845–50 Mrs. Lincoln *Lect. Bot.* App. 102/2 Purple thoroughwort, joe-pye. 1866 *Treas. Bot.*, Joe-Pye Weed. 1885 *Outing* (U.S.) VII. Nov. 180/1 Joe-pie-weed flaunts his red umbels in view by the ditch and railroads. 1903 E. C. Waltz *Pa Gladden* vii. 144 In other Septembers the slope ..was lovely with..joepye-weed.

Jo-fired (dʒōu·,faiəɹd), *a.* *U.S. slang.* [Fanciful alteration of *hell-fired*] = All-fired.

1824 *Woodstock* (Vt.) *Observer* 24 Feb. (Th.) Whate'er joe fir'd racket they keep up. 1848 *Stray Subjects* 50 He always know'd B. was a jo-fired fool. 1925 Krapp *Engl. Lang. in America* I. 118.

Jog, *sb.*[2] **2.** (Earlier examples.)

1845 S. Judd *Margaret* I. xiv. 118 Directly on the right of the sun-setting was an apparent jog or break in the line of the woods and hills. 1876 H. E. Scudder *Dwellers Five-Sisters Crt.* iii. 56 The house..was set back from the others in a jog of the court.

Jogee, jogi, variants of Yogi.

1864 J. A. Grant *Walk Across Africa* 317 Like mad 'jogees' or devotees. 1903 *Times Lit. Suppl.* 2 Oct. 279/3 He is rescued, and miraculously healed, and he lives the Jogi life, resisting all temptation. 1922 *Chambers's Jrnl.* 343/2 Other *jogis* there are, with heavy iron rings in their ears.

Joggling, *vbl. sb.*[1] **joggling-table** (example).

1849 *President's Message to Congress* I. 435 It is probable that a set of joggling and sleeping tables will be added to the washing machinery.

Johannes. (Earlier example.)

1758 *Essex Inst. Hist. Coll.* XVIII. 102, I this day delivered one Johannes to Major Gage.

John. Add: **1. c.** Applied variously to: a Chinaman (cf. Chinaman 2), a detective. *slang.*

1873 C. Nordhoff *California* 85 (Th.) I passed out of the Chinese theatre, with a lady and two children. We had to walk through a crowd of Johns. 1873 J. H. Beadle *Undevel. West* xvii. 314 Then come the apologists and claim for 'John' a score of virtues which he does not possess. 1878 — *Western Wilds* 401 The melancholy 'Johns', with glazed caps and black pig-tails, [looked] like a lot of half-drowned crows. 1901 *Westm. Gaz.* 18 Sept. 8/2 'George Johns are sure to visit the old girl to see if anyone has got to her...Brake the cab then shift it again as the John will be sure to tell the porter of that.'..Detective-sergeant Stevens said the word 'Johns' on the paper signified 'detectives'.

John Collins (dʒǫn kǫ·linz). *U.S.* A drink consisting of soda-water, gin, sugar, lemon, and ice. (Cf. *Tom Collins.)

1865 *Australasian* 24 Feb. 8 (Farmer) That most angelic of drinks for a hot climate—a John Collins (a mixture of soda water, gin, sugar, lemon and ice). 1913 R. Brooke *Coll. Poems* (1918) p. lxxxvi, I believe I could do a deal in Real Estate, in the bar, over a John Collins, with a clean-shaven Yankee with a tremulous eyelid and a moist lower lip. 1928 T. M. Healy *Lett. & Leaders* I. x. 142, I bear admiringly in mind...two barmen who..after we had sat up all night.. served me with a 'John Collins' [in U.S.].

Johnny. Add: **1.** (Earlier U.S. example.)

1867 J. M. Crawford *Mosby* 223 There lay one of the enemy dead, with his gun cocked ready to fire at his Johnny; but another Johnny was too quick for him.

b. A policeman. [? Partly from *Johnny Darby*, app. an alteration of Gendarme after Darby 2, *pl.* handcuffs.]

1851 Mayhew *Lond. Labour* (1861) II. 154 The 'Johnnys' on the water are always on the look out. 1886 *Graphic* 30 Jan. 130/1 Constables used to be known as 'Johnny Darbies', said to be a corruption of the French *gensdarmes*, and they are still occasionally called 'Johnnies'.

c. (*a*) = *John 1 c; (*b*) a sepoy; (*c*) a gurkha.

1857 T. B. Gunn *N. Y. Boarding Houses* 275 (Th.) He's seed the Johnnies goin' into that there doorway next block. 1858 *Leisure Hour* 326/1 Sepoys..known as Johnnys. 1889 Kipling *Wee Willie Winkie*, etc. (ed. 5) 95 The Highlander ..turning to a Gurkha, said, 'Hya, Johnny!'

3. *Johnny Crapaud* [i.e. toad]: nickname for a Frenchman. *Johnny Newcome*: (a) = *Johnny Raw*; (b) a new-comer of any kind.

1887 W. C. Russell in *Gentl. Mag.* Feb. 135 Those vessels went armed, too, as befitted the majesty of the bunting under which old Dance had gloriously licked *Johnny Crapeau. 1839 Barham *Ingol. Leg.* Ser. I. *Some Acc. New Play*, Now to young '*Johnny Newcome' she seems to confine hers, Neglecting the poor little dear out at dry-nurse. 1865 Bone *Petroleum & Petrol. Wells* 24 (Th.) The Johnny Newcomes had to fight their way to the bar, and deposit 75 c. for the bit of blue paste-board. 1867 Smyth *Sailor's Word-bk.*, *Johnny Raw*, or *Johnny Newcome*, an inexperienced youngster commencing his career; also applied to landsmen in general. 1896 Farmer & Henley *Slang*, *Johnny Newcome*,..a new-born child.

4. Prefixed to other words to form names of plants, birds, etc., as **Johnny Armstrong** *jocular nautical slang*, hand-power. **Johnny-cock-horse,** *U.S.*, the mantis. **Johnny jumper, Johnny-jump-up** *U.S.*, a name for *Viola tricolor* (the pansy) and *Viola pedata*. **Johnny penguin** = Johnny 2 b. **Johnny Reb** *U.S.*, a Northern name for a 'rebel' or Confederate soldier in the Civil War.

1922 *N. & Q.* 12th Ser. XI. 260/2 **Johnny Armstrong*, the action of 'pulling' or restraining a horse. 1888 *Nature* 26 July 303/2 [The humming-bird] was in the clutches of an insect, which he identified as a mantis, popularly known in those parts as '*Johnny-cock-horse'. 1860 Bartlett *Dict. Amer.*, *Johnny Jump Up and Kiss Me, Johnny Jump up, *Johnny Jumper*, names given to the Heart's Ease, or Violet. 1842 *Knickerbocker Mag.* XIX. 115 Mr. Ketchup had now kissed little Chip and stuck a *johnny-jump-up in his cap. 1858 *Congress. Globe* 19 May 2244/2 You stand here, and with smiling faces spend $60,000 a year for morning-glories and johnny jump-ups. 1904 W. D. Nesbit *Trail to Boyland* 57 The johnny-jump-ups, noddin' soft when I go by. 1930 F. A. Pottle *Stretchers* iii. 48 Under foot the ground teemed with lupine and phlox and those large scentless violets which the natives call 'Johnny-jump-ups'. 1882 *Encycl. Brit.* XIV. 49/1 The *Johnny penguin (*Pygoscelis tæniata*). 1866 J. C. Gregg *Life in Army* xxix. 249 These swaggering '*Johnny Rebs'.

Johnsoniana (dʒǫnsōuniǣ·nă). [f. name of Dr. Samuel *Johnson* (1709–84) + *-iana.] Matters connected with Dr. Johnson.

1776 (*title*) Johnsoniana; or, a Collection of Bon Mots, etc., by Dr. Johnson and others. 1909 *Daily Chron.* 14 Sept. 3/2 [Mr. Reade's] latest compilation of Johnsoniana. 1928 *Daily Tel.* 12 June 17/3 Miss Anna Seward's delightful Johnsoniana.

Johnswort. = *St. John's-wort* (John 5).

1874 *Rep. Vermont Board Agric.* II. 390.

Joie de vivre (ʒwa d vīvr). [Fr., = joy of living.] A feeling of healthy enjoyment of life.

1901 'L. Malet' *Hist. Sir R. Calmady* III. v, The hungry all-compelling *joie de vivre* which is begotten whensoever youth thus seeks and finds youth. 1905 E. F. Benson *Image in Sand* xiii, She had found herself in the very highlands of serenity and *joie de vivre*. 1907 *Westm. Gaz.* 5 Feb. 4/2 The new *joie de vivre* of motoring. 1917 McKenna *Sonia* vi, It was only when the twanging banjos changed to rag-time that the majority of our neighbours sheepishly unbent and put forth an assumption of *joie de vivre*. 1925 A. P. Herbert *Laughing Ann* 82 The simple mind and manly air, Not Brains so much as Breeding, With *joie de vivre* and *savoir faire*, Are constantly succeeding. 1930 *Observer* 13 Apr. 15 The *joie de vivre* of Blackpool Beach.

Join, *v.*[1] Add: **6. b.** Delete †*Obs.*

1882 Stevenson *New Arab. Nts.* I. 95 You join yourselves to persons of condition..for no other purpose than to escape the consequences of your crimes. 1904 Weyman *Abbess of Vlaye* ii, Had I known of what sort they were to whom I was joining myself.

15. d. *absol. To join up*: to enlist in the army.

1916 Boyd Cable *Action Front* 5 Just joined up to get a finger in the fighting? 1924 D. H. Lawrence *England, my Eng.* 40 Egbert went and joined up immediately as a private soldier.

Joint, *sb.* Add: **4. c.** *Bookbinding.* The flexible cloth or leather which forms the hinge of the covers of a book.

1835 J. Hannett *Bibliopegia* 104 The volume being laid upon the table or press, with the head towards the workman and the upper board open, the guard or false end paper must be removed and all other substances cleared out of the joint with the folder. 1861 *Chambers's Encycl.* II. 226/2 Coming to his hands flat and solid, and with its joints well formed. 1904 *Technol. & Sci. Dict.* ((ed. Goodchild & Tweney) 327/1 In whole-bound books the joints are generally formed of the same material (pared down) as the cover.

15. (sense 5) *joint face*; **joint-bolt,** a bolt used to fasten two timbers in a T form; **joint-box,** an iron box surrounding the joint or splice of electric wires and cables; **joint-plane** = sense 5; **joint-vetch,** any plant of the genus *Æschynomene*, so called from its jointed seed-pods.

1844 H. Stephens *Bk. Farm* II. 75 The top bar..swells out in the middle, where it is perforated for the *joint-bolt of the lever. 1884 Knight *Dict. Mech.* Suppl., *Joint Bolt*, a bolt used for fastening two timbers, one end-wise to the other. 1901 *Chambers's Jrnl.* Dec. 845/2 A new form of *joint-box, for forming connections. 1902 *Encycl. Brit.* XXVIII. 77/2 They are connected by bends or joint-boxes. 1855 J. Phillips *Man. Geol.* 44 The cleavage and *joint planes in these beds are not parallel to the general cleavage. 1895 L. Fletcher *Introd. Study Rocks* 51 Joint-planes are distinct from planes of fissility in that they are planes of actual discontinuity of material. 1903 *Nature* 24 Dec. 189/2 The caves depend for their form on the joint-planes in the massive limestone. 1829 Loudon *Encycl. Plants* 1284 *Arthrolobium*..*Joint-Vetch. 1884 Miller *Plant-n.*, *Æschynomene aspera*, Sensitive Joint-Vetch.

Joint, *v.* Add: **1. d.** (Earlier U.S. example.)

1815 *Niles' Weekly Register* IX. 36/1 The power is given by one or two horses, which with a man and a boy can dress and joint..the staves necessary for one hundred barrels.

4. *intr.* To form joints.

1772 *Carroll Papers* in *Maryland Hist. Mag.* XIV. 287, I am apprehensive it will be too thick and Joint if the weather proves warm. 1904 *Topeka Daily Capital* 1 June 8 Wheat has not done well, though it is jointing now.

Jointage (dʒoi·ntedʒ). [f. Joint *sb.* + -age.] = Jointing *vbl. sb.*

1905 *Rep. Brit. Assoc.* 91 Mr. W. L. Sutton..says that the Victoria rock is dense, igneous, and quite massive, with comparatively little jointage.

Jointed, *a.* Add: **2.** *Geol.* Traversed or divided by joints (Joint *sb.* 5).

1821 J. Macculloch *Classif. Rocks* 129 In a few instances, from the extreme shortness of the prisms, the columnar passes to a tabular, or a lamellar and jointed structure. 1835 Sedgwick in *Trans. Geol. Soc.* Ser. II. III. 481 A slaty and jointed structure are..often exhibited together. 1863 Ansted *Great Stone Bk.* 133 The harder kinds of sand-rock are always jointed.

3. *Bot.* Having or appearing to have joints; falling to pieces or separating readily at the joints: as a specific vernacular name (see quots.).

1597 iointed Glassewoort [see Glasswort]. 1793 Martyn *Lang. Bot.* 1821 S. F. Gray *Nat. Arr. Brit. Plants* II. 160 Leaves..knotty, jointed, or smooth. 1839 Lindley *Sch. Bot.* 4 If a stem is swelled at the part where the leaves grow, and capable of being snapped across, or apparently so, it is called *articulated* or *jointed*, as in Stellaria Holostea, and Geraniums. 1843 Babington *Brit. Bot.* 31 *Raphanus Raphanistrum* (L.)..Jointed Charlock. 1913 Pettman *Africanderisms*, Jointed cactus, *Opuntia pusilla*.

Jointer[2]. (Earlier Amer. example.)

1654 *Essex Probate Rec.* I. 198, 2 Joynters...Trussing hoopes.

Joint-grass. (Later U.S. example.)

1835 W. G. Simms *Partisan* 55 Rebellion grows like joint-grass when it once takes root.

Jointist. *U.S.* Add: **2.** An advocate of something qualified as 'joint'.

1906 *New York Even. Post* 18 Sept. 6 Arizona 'jointists' are to form an organization with joint Statehood as the only plank in its platform.

Jointless, *a.* Add: **b.** In one piece; without a seam or joint of any kind.

1909 *Prosp. Rubber-tanned Leather Co.* 2 May, Automobile tyres in seamless and jointless bands. 1921 *Dict. Occup. Terms* (1927) § 571 'Composition' or jointless floors.

Joint-worm. **2.** *U.S.* (Examples.)

1862 *Trans. Ill. Agric. Soc.* (1865) V. 488 The real, veritable 'joint-worm' of Virginia and Maryland. 1862 T. W. Harris *Insects injur. Veget.* (ed. 3) 554 An article on the joint-worm, published at Albany in 'The Cultivator', for October, 1851.

Joker. Add: **4.** A clause unobtrusively inserted in a legislative enactment and affecting its operation in a way not immediately apparent. *U.S.*

1904 *New York Even. Post* 11 May 1 They are all nervous over the possibility that there may be a hitherto unperceived joker in the present bill. 1904 *New York Churchman* 6 Aug. 215 That which..it was sought to obtain surreptitiously by what politicians call a 'joker' in the charter of Greater New York. 1906 *New York Even. Post* 30 Apr. 6 The Malby 'joker' to the Adirondack Reserve bill. 1909 *Westm. Gaz.* 6 Apr. 2/1 It carried more of what are known in Washington as 'little jokers' than the Wilson Act, the McKinley Act, or any other Tariff Act since 1861. 1928 *Daily Express* 17 July 8/2 The surtax was slipped into the Finance Act of 1927 very much as a 'joker' is occasionally insinuated into an American Tariff Act—that is to say, surreptitiously, without anybody except those in the know being aware of the significance of what was happening.

Jokist. (Earlier U.S. example.)

1873 'Mark Twain' & Warner *Gilded Age* xxxvi. 331 And here is The Jokist's Own Treasury.

Jolley (dʒǫ·li). *Pottery.* Also **jolly.** [Of unknown origin.] A variety of jigger (see Jigger *sb.*[1] 5 a). Hence **Jo·lleying** *vbl. sb.*, the act of using a jolley. **Jo·llier**[1], one who makes pottery by means of a jolley.

1881 *Instr. Census Clerks* (1885) 88 Earthenware..manufacture...Jollier. Jolly Maker. 1893 E. A. Barber *Pottery & Porcelain U.S.* (1909) 7 A 'jolly'..consisting of a revolving disk or wheel on which the mould is placed. 1904 *Technol. & Sci. Dict.* (ed. Goodchild & Tweney), *Jolly*, a machine used in the manufacture by machinery of cups, jugs, and hollow ware generally. 1921 *Dict. Occup. Terms* (1927) § 105 *Bowl maker*,..a jollier who makes bowls by jolleying process. *Ibid.*, *Cup maker*, a jollier who makes cups on a single or double cup jolley.

Jo·llier[2]. *U.S.* [f. Jolly *v.* 2 c.] One who 'jollies' others; a jovial or sociable person.

1896 G. Ade *Artie* ix. 78 He's one of the biggest jolliers that ever come over the hills. 1901 S. Merwin & H. K. Webster *Calumet K* i. 12 Oh, he's a good-looking young chap...He's a great jollier. 1905 *New York Even. Post* 12 Oct. 2 He was talkative, and, as the attendants say, 'quite a jollier'.

Jolly, *a.* Add: **13. b.** *ironically.*

1916 Galsworthy *Sheaf* i. 13 'Jolly for my new coat!' I said.

C. jolly-tail, a name given to various New Zealand and Australian fishes of the species *Galaxias*.

1892 Simmonds *Dict. Trade* Suppl., *Jolly-tail*, a small fresh-water fish of Australia (*Galaxias attenuatus*). 1898 Morris *Austral Engl.* s.v., *Galaxias weedoni* is called the Mersey Jolly-tail, and *Galaxias atkinsoni*, the Pieman Jolly-tail.

Jolly (dʒǫ·li), *sb.*[3] The name of the German physicist P. von *Jolly* (1809–1884), used *attrib.* or in genitive to designate appliances devised by him, as *Jolly (spring) balance*, a device for determining specific gravity.

1885 Geikie *Text-bk. Geol.* (ed. 2) 82 Jolly's spring balance is a simple and serviceable instrument. 1929 *Encycl. Brit.* XIII. 136/2 In its usual form the Jolly balance consists of a long, delicate, helical spring suspended by one end in front of a uniformly graduated scale.

Jolly, *sb.*[4] *colloq.* Short for Jollification.

1920 *Spectator* 4 Dec. 740/1 Every age must be allowed an occasional 'jolly'. 1921 Galsworthy *To Let* II. iv, Come and have a 'jolly' with us. 1922 A. Bennett *Lilian* I. iv, I was at a bit of a jolly to-night, and my band's never too legible. 1924 M. Newman *Consummation* IV. xv. 197 Troops fed to the teeth with interminable sandbagging, bottomless mud, relentless routine, broken only by the occasional horror of a 'show' (what Bossy called a 'jolly'), or worse still, a 'strafe'. 1928 'Sapper' *Female of Species* i, The pleasure to be derived from what is sometimes described as an evening's jolly seems to me to be over-rated.

Jolly, *v.* Add: **2. a.** Also with *out.*

1924 Selincourt *Cricket Match* vii. (1928) 219 Their main effort seems not to be jollied out for a depressing total.

c. (Examples with *along.*)

1908 G. H. Lorimer *J. Spurlock* i. 16, I..debated whether it would jolly her along if I opened more beer. *Ibid.* v. 91 Our customers expect the boys to have a little snap and jolly their grub along. 1909 S. E. White *Rules of Game* II. iii. 127 Seems like they try to pay for their entertainment by jollying us along.

3. *trans.* To succeed in raising; to work up. *U.S.*

1921 R. D. Paine *Comr. Rolling Ocean* xii. 206, I can jolly steam enough for a couple of pumps and a dynamo.

Jolt, *sb.* Add: **2. b.** *fig.* A surprise; a shock which disturbs one's mental composure.

1905 D. G. Phillips *Plum Tree* 3 I'd like to give him a jolt. 1924 Lowe-Porter tr. *T. Mann's Buddenbrooks* I. vi. 208 Oh, no! I know they gave you a jolt yesterday—a very, very stimulating jolt.

Jolter, *sb.*[1] (Earlier mod. example.)

1843 *Knickerbocker Mag.* XXI. 39 The traveller has but to express a wish to visit a distant plantation, and his..luggage is placed in the donkeyed jolter.

Jo·ltiness. The condition of being jolty.

1891 'L. Malet' *Wages of Sin* IV. iii, Oh! the joltiness of this conversational road. 1905 *Westm. Gaz.* 9 May 4/2 The existing motor-'buses..with their perpetual pulling up, their joltiness, and malodorousness.

Jon (dʒǫn). Abbreviation of *Jonathan 3.

1931 *Daily Tel.* 21 May 5/1 Jons 10s 6d–12s 6d.

Jonathan. Add:

3. An American variety of dessert apple.

1842 *Catal. Fruits Gard. Hortic. Soc.* (ed. 3) 21 Apples... Jonathan. 1845 A. J. Downing *Fruits Amer.* 113 The Jonathan is a very beautiful dessert apple...The original tree of this new sort is growing on the farm of Mr. Philip Rick, of Kingston, New York. 1924 *Glasgow Herald* 23 Dec. 5 In 1922 the price realised for Jonathans did not pay the cost of packing.

Jong (dʒǫŋ). [Tibetan *rdzoṅ* fortress.] A Tibetan prefecture. Hence **Jo·ngpen,** a prefect.

[1888 *Encycl. Brit.* XXIII. 340/2 At Shigatze the Yarotsanpo receives the Pena-Nyang-chu from a valley to the south-east which contains the towns of Pena-jong and Gyangtse-jong.] 1904 *Times* 11 May 5/1 The Tibetans have strongly fortified the jong. 1904 *Westm. Gaz.* 13 May 9/3 A hot fire was opened from the jong, where the jingals have apparently been recently considerably reinforced. 1904 *Daily Chron.* 21 May 5/4 The collection and equipment of the local levies are conducted by various Jongpen, under the orders of the Lhassa Government. 1921 *Glasgow Herald* 13 July 9 The Jongpen of the district rode out to meet us with a few followers.

Jonsonian (dʒǫnsōu·niăn), *a.* Of, pertaining to, or characteristic of Ben *Jonson* (1574–1637), English dramatist.

1886 J. A. Symonds *Ben Jonson* 153 The most truly Jonsonian of all these places..was the Old Devil Tavern at Temple Bar. 1928 C. J. Sisson *Elis. Dram.* iv. 43 The Jonsonian comedy of humour. 1931 *Times Lit. Suppl.* 21 May 405/1 But the 'laws of dramatic art' have already ceased to look Aristotelian or Jonsonian.

Jonval (ʒǫnval). The name of *Jonval*, French inventor, used *attrib.* or in genitive to designate a turbine invented by him. Hence **Jo·nvaliza·tion.** **Jo·nvalize** *v.*

1873 *Spons' Dict. Engin.* VI. 1930 Jonval's turbine may generally be placed, in the case of moderate or high falls, considerably above the highest back-waters. 1875 Knight *Dict. Mech.* 2656/2 In the Jonval turbine, the water is received above and the discharge is downward. 1880 *Engineering* 26 Mar. 245/3 The motors..consist of three turbines of the Jonval system. 1892 P. Benjamin *Mod. Mech.* 893 All this type of Jonval wheels give high results at 'full gate'. *Ibid.*, This name of 'Jonval' is applied to wheels set with a 'draft tube'.

Jordan (dʒǭ·ɹdăn). The name of a river in Palestine, the crossing of which is used (after Num. xxxiii. 51) in pietistic language to symbolize death.

1772 W. Williams *Hymn*, '*Guide me, O Thou Great Jehovah*', When I tread the Verge of Jordan. 1786 S. Stennett (*hymn*), On Jordan's stormy Banks I stand. 18.. in Barrère & Leland *Dict. Slang* (1889) s.v. *T'other*, And I saw a mighty charret a comin'.., To take us to de odder side of Jordan..Jordan am a hard road to trabble.

Jornada. Add: Also **journada, -ado** (and earlier examples of sense 2).

1844 J. J. Webb *Mem.* 91 Stopping over for a few hours.. to prepare for the journey of 50 miles to the Arkansas, without water, [we] started into the 'journada'. *Ibid.* 119 Whether..to..travel a longer distance and through two Journados. 1846 Sage *Scenes Rocky Mts.* xxi. 173 On leaving the Pischepa, a reach of little more than one *jornada* (day's travel) leads over the mountain range.

Joseph. Add: **4.** A violin made by Joseph Guarnieri del Gesù. (Cf. *Guarnerius.)

1880 *Grove's Dict. Mus.* I. 637/2 The value of a good 'Joseph' now varies from £150 to £400.

5. Phrase. *Not for Joseph*: see *Joe *sb.*[2] 1 b.

Josephinite (dʒōu·zĕfinait). [Named 1892 from *Josephine* county, Oregon: see -ite[1].] An alloy of nickel and iron, Fe_2Ni_5, found in placer deposits in the Josephine and Jackson counties of Oregon.

1892 *Amer. Jrnl. Sci.* CXLIII. 509 Josephinite, a new Nickel-Iron. *Ibid.* 514 The placer gravel, in which josephinite is found.

Josephite (dʒōu·zĕfait). [f. the name *Joseph* (see def.) + -ite[1].] A member of either of two orders of St. Joseph, the Priests of the Mission of St. Joseph (founded *c* 1640), or a teaching institute founded in 1817 by Canon von Crombrugghe.

1846 in *N. French's Wks.* I. Pref. p. lvi, At the end of the street, there is a large building yet occupied as a school, and now held by the Josephites. 1908 C. H. Bowden *Simple Dict. for Catholics*, *Josephites*, a teaching institute founded in 1817 in Belgium for the education of the commercial and industrial classes.

Josh (dʒǫʃ), *sb.* *U.S. slang.* [Cf. Josh *v.*] A piece of banter or badinage; a good-natured or bantering joke. Also as *adj.*, ridiculous.

1896 G. Ade *Artie* iii. 30 That ain't no josh, neither. 1902 O. Wister *Virginian* xvi. 188 What did he say to Trampas after..Trampas put the josh on him? 1904 Eliz. Robins *Magnetic North* viii. 141 Nobody but himself would be the wiser even if it was a josh. *Ibid.* xvi. 276 'Minook's all right. No josh about that,' she said. 1908 G. H. Lorimer *J. Spurlock* iii. 40 First, I sat there chuckling, but by and by I began to forget the josh end of it I had joined [the union] for, and to remember my own grievances against the house. 1909 S. E. White *Rules of Game* III. xiii. 215 Perhaps all this monkey business was one elaborate josh.

Josh, *v.* *U.S. slang.* Add: **2.** *intr.* To indulge in banter or ridicule. Hence **Jo·sher, Jo·shing** *vbl. sb.* and *ppl. a.*

1887 F. Francis Jr. *Saddle & Mocassin* 185 He..liked nothing better than to get into a circle of young cow-punchers, and chin and josh [*note*, chat and joke] with them in his funereal fashion. 1904 *New York Sun* 21 Aug. 10 Others said that Mr. Taggart had turned out to be a josher and a jollier. 1905 *Amer. Illustr. Mag.* Dec. 214, I was jus' joshin', mother, 'cause I'spect all your plans are made. 1908 G. H. Lorimer *J. Spurlock* vi. 113 Quite a josher, Mr. Wilkins was, but always the gentleman. *Ibid.* xi. 296 There was no joshing and making ridiculous the honest Long Island landscape. 1909 R. A. Wason *Happy Hawkins* xxii. 263 Dick was smilin' now..an' makin' funny, joshin' remarks. 1910 'O. Henry' *Strictly Business* xviii. 221 Cut that joshing out...Who do you think you are talking to? 1918 *Liberator* (N.Y.) Oct. 7/2 The neighbors do a little joshing first..Make out your will, Henry? and so on.

Joss. **b.** Add: **joss-man** (see quot.); **joss-pidgin,** a religious ceremony; **joss-pidgin-man,** a minister of religion.

1886 Yule & Burnell *Hobson-Jobson* s.v. *Joss-house*, Joss-house-man or Joss-pidgin-man is a priest, or a missionary. a 1889 *Mary Coe* in Barrère & Leland *Dict. Slang* s.v., Allo tim he make joss-pidgin, Wat you fan-kwei cally 'ligion. a 1889 *The Rebel Pig* Ibid., When dey talkey pig look all-samee like he joss-pidgin-man. 1913 *Chambers's Jrnl.* Aug. 590/2 A missionary is known as a European 'joss-man'. 1926 M. Leinster *Dew on Leaf* iv. 45 He do joss-pidgin.

Josser (dʒǫ·səɹ). *slang.* [f. Joss + -er[1].]

1. A clergyman or minister of religion, 'padre'. *Austral.*

1887 Farrell *How He Died* 22 The reverend josser..hammering the pulpit. 1889 Barrère & Leland *Dict. Slang*, *Josser*,..a priest...Australian slang designated those who ministered in them [*sc.* joss-houses] *jossers*, and then extended this term it had created to mean ministers of any religion.

2. A simpleton, duffer; a soft or silly fellow. Hence, in flippant or contemptuous use, a fellow, (old) chap.

1886 *Broadside Ballad*, '*I took it on*' (Farmer), I took it on, Of course I was a josser. 1890 *Punch* 22 Feb. 85/2 These 'Equality' jossers would spile it; if arf their reforms they can carry. 1894 W. H. Wilkins & Vivian *Green Bay Tree* vii, The josser next me, who had won his money. 1898 *Westm. Gaz.* 1 Dec. 2/1 The Parisian *badaud*—read 'booby', unless the more up-to-date 'josser' be preferred. 1903 Strong & Osbourne *Vailima Mem.* 61 An English midshipman..told me that though he had known and liked Mr. Stevenson all this time, it was only the other day..that it came over him all of a heap—'*he's* the josser that wrote *Treasure Island*'. 1927 *Sunday at Home* 544/1 Go and see the old josser. Queer old bird, mind you, and fussy.

b. *attrib.*

1891 *Daily News* 29 June 2/4 Any 'josser' policeman would be enabled..to pry into their show. 1893 *Standard* 29 Jan. 2 (Farmer) Now suppose we are on the road..and we meet a josser policeman?

Jota (hǭ·ta). A local Spanish dance.

1902 *Encycl. Brit.* XXVII. 374/2 The *Jota* is the national dance of Aragon. 1926 *Contemp. Rev.* July 82 The Spanish seguidillas, jotas, and fandangoes.

Jotter (under Jot *v.*[2]). Add: Also, a small pad or writing book used for jotting down notes, memoranda, etc.; a memorandum book or tablet.

1882 Ogilvie *Imp. Dict.*, *Jotter*,..the book in which notes or memoranda are made. 1915 A. S. Neill *Dominie's Log* xii, Neatness of method and penmanship in copybooks and jotters. 1925 *Dollar Mag.* Mar. 48 All books except exercise books and jotters are supplied by the school.

Jounce, *v.* **2.** (U.S. examples.)

1902 H. L. Wilson *Spenders* xiv. 148 Then I jounced Hank. 1910 *N. Y. Even. Post* 4 Aug. (Th.) The raft was jounced about so severely that it broke its anchorages. 1919 T. K. Holmes *Man fr. Tall Timber* xxiv. 294 Mrs. Lemoyne returned..declaring that she was 'jounced to a jelly'.

Jour[2] (dʒūɹ). *U.S.* Also **jur.** Colloquial abbreviation of Journeyman.

1845 *Knickerbocker Mag.* XXVI. 415 You..discover the 'boss' and two or three 'jours', each seated on a low form. 1859 Bartlett *Dict. Amer.*, *Jour* or *Jur*. 1862–3 E. E. Hale *If, Yes & Perhaps* (1868) 35, I stopped at one or two cabinet-makers, and talked with the 'jours' about work. 1884 'Mark Twain' *Huck. Finn* xix, 'What's your line—mainly?' 'Jour printer, by trade.'

Journey, *sb.* Add: **3. e.** The travelling of a vehicle along a certain route between two fixed points and at a stated time.

1851 *Illustr. Lond. News* 25 Oct. 526/1 If they..obtained ..12 passengers at 2d. each per journey, the profit would be 19s. 3d. per diem. 1878 *Porcupine* XX. 507/2 The conductor ..shouts, 'Journey's end'. 1908 *Daily Chron.* 4 Jan. 1/7 London Motor Bus Strike...The company is determined to insist on the journey system of payment. The men say that this system may mean eighteen hours' work a day. *Ibid.* 7 Jan. 4/7 'Payment by day' and 'payment by journey'. 1909 *Westm. Gaz.* 8 Sept. 2/1 The journey-time to Glasgow is 8½ h.

f. The travelling of a part of the mechanism of a machine backwards or forwards along a fixed path.

1884 W. S. B. McLaren *Spinning* 97 The nip should make about forty journeys each way per minute.

10. c. A set of trams in a colliery.

1883 Gresley *Gloss. Coal-mining*, *Journey*, a train or set of trams all coupled together running upon an engine plane. 1896 Mrs. H. Ward *Sir G. Tressady* xxiv, The 'journey' of trucks. 1901 *Daily Chron.* 8 Nov. 11/3 He was caught by the 'journey' and killed. 1921 *Morn. Post* 29 Nov., A journey of loaded trams. 1921 *Dict. Occup. Terms* (1927) § 043 *Journey rider*,..rides on trams or tubs on haulage planes.

Journeyman. Add: **3. b.** In an electric time circuit, a clock consisting of dial and handwork controlled and actuated by the master-clock of the circuit.

1904 *Technol. & Sci. Dict.* (ed. Goodchild & Tweney), *Indicator Dial*, the 'journeyman' clock, consisting only of a dial and handwork, with electrical fittings. *Ibid.*, *Master Clock*, the timepiece controlling and actuating by electricity a series of dial works, or 'journeymen', at different points in the circuit.

Joy, *sb.* Add: **10. joy-flight,** an aerial joy-ride; so **joy-flying; joy-plank,** a plank leading from the stage to the audience in a theatre, for the use of performers; **joy-stick,** the control-lever of an aeroplane; **joy-wheel,** a form of amusement consisting of a gigantic wheel-shaped erection on which passengers are carried up and down in cars by its revolutions.

1923 *Daily Mail* 7 Aug. 8/2 The '*joy flights' in three-seater Avros, at 5s. a time. 1918 *Daily Express* 3 July 12 Strict regulations were made against joy-flights during the war. 1924 *Illustr. London News* 27 Dec. 1265/2 The picture of the Grand Ballet at Florence in 1616..shows a method which was in vogue here in Revues a year or two ago, and is still continued in the Cabarets; performers leaving the stage by means of steps and '*joy-planks'. 1916 H. Barber *Aeroplane Speaks* 28 When the Aeroplane is on the ground the control lever or '*joy-stick' is lashed fast. 1918 *Blackw. Mag.* Mar. 293 Down go his hands on the joystick in double-quick time. 1911 *Oxford Times* 9 Sept. 10/6 A new form of amusement to Oxford, known as the '*Joy Wheel'. 1925 *Brit. Empire Exhib. Off. Guide* 168 Over the Falls; Joy Wheel; House of Nonsense.

Joy-ride (dʒoi·raid), *sb.* orig. *U.S. colloq.* [f. Joy *sb.* + Ride *sb.*[1]] A pleasure trip in a motor car, aeroplane, etc., often without the permission of the owner of the vehicle. Hence **Joy·-ride** *v.* *intr.*, to go for a joy-ride; *trans.* to convey (as) on a joy-ride; **Joy·-rider,** one who goes on a joy-ride. **Joy·-riding** *vbl. sb.*; also *attrib.*

1909 *New York Even. Post* (semi-weekly ed.) 15 July 2 [The] Acting Mayor vetoed the ordinance passed last week to prevent city officers from taking 'joy rides'. *Ibid.* 2 Sept 8 'This was no haphazard expedition,' he said, 'no intensified Arctic joy ride, undertaken on nerve.' 1910 *N. Y. Even. Post* 13 June (Thornton) Judge Dike remarked that the next joy-rider who was brought before him would be sentenced to Sing Sing. 1911 E. Ferber *Dawn O'Hara* ii. 13 No shrieking midnight joy-riders. 1913 *Aeroplane* 17 Apr. 455/2 The pilots of machines already qualified naturally took no risks of damaging their mounts by 'joy riding'. 1914 H. James *Ivory Tower* I. iii. 71 It's one of Mr. Betterman's [nurses] taking a joy ride in honor of his recovery. 1915 D. O. Barnett *Lett.* 206 We joined forces and captured a motor-ambulance which joy-rided us back here. 1920 W. J. Locke *House of Baltazar* xxi, But, my dear, it'll be joy-riding. 1928 Joad *Diogenes or Future of Leisure* 39 A land fit for stockbrokers and actresses to joy-ride in. 1928 *Evening News* 5 May 5/3 For members of the public who wish to fly there are joy-riding machines.

Juba[3] (hū·ba). Also **jubo.** [Cuban Sp.] Any of several Cuban colubroid snakes, as *Leionotus maculatus, Urothecadumerilii, Dromicus angulifer*.

1877 *Encycl. Brit.* VI. 680/2.

Jubiliza·tion. [f. Jubilize *v.*] = Jubilation.

1909 R. A. Wason *Happy Hawkins* 305 He never curbed his jubilization nor altered the heavy seriousness of his expression.

Judæan, Judean (dʒudī·ăn), *a.* and *sb.* [f. L. *Jūdæus*, a. Gr. Ἰουδαῖος, f. Ἰουδαία, f. Ἰούδας, ad. Heb. *Jehūdah* Judah, name of a son of Jacob.] Of or pertaining to (a native or inhabitant of) Judæa.

In Shaks. *Oth.* v. ii. 347 Fo. 1 has the doubtful reading *Iudean*; the other Fos. and the Qos. have *Indian*.

1831 J. Bell *Syst. Geog.* IV. 206 Judean Mountains. 1852 tr. *I. Pfeiffer's Visit Holy Land* 103 The foreground of the picture is formed by the Judæan mountains. 1880 *Encycl. Brit.* XIII. 410/1 A Judæan, Amos of Tekoa. 1922 A. E. Garvie *Beloved Disciple* x. 210 The Synoptic record is incomplete as regards the Judaean ministry. 1932 *Times Lit. Suppl.* 5 Nov. 853/1 A preliminary survey of Judaean sites.

Judæo-, Judeo- (dʒudī·o), used as combining form of L. *Jūdæus* *Judæan, designating persons or things pertaining to Judæa and hence (more widely) to the Jews, often = Jewish.

1823 *Christian Observer* App. 828/1 The New Testament in German-Hebrew, and Judæo-Polish. 1851 *Illustr. Catal. Gt. Exhib.* III. III. 552/1 Judaeo Spanish, Old Testament. ..Judaeo Arabic, four books of New Testament. 1863 *Chambers's Encycl.* V. 712/2 The number of Judæo-Greek fragments..which have survived. *Ibid.* 721/2 Numerous authors wrote in Hebrew,..and Judæo-German. 1880 *Encycl. Brit.* XIII. 681/2 Jonas Fränkel in 1854 established the Judæo-theological seminary at Breslau. 1899 *Literary Guide* 1 Oct. 146/1 The total abandonment of the Judæo-Christian 'continuity' theory. 1900 Deniker *Races of Man* 424 Particular kinds of jargon, the most common of which is the Judeo-German. 1906 *Westm. Gaz.* 17 Aug. 10/2 The Judæo-Spanish world of the Levant. 1908 *Daily Chron.* 21 Jan. 3/4 A Judæo-Arabian legend of Adam and Eve. 1910 *Westm. Gaz.* 12 Mar. 2/1 'The Judæo-Masonic and Protestant coalition' which now governs France. 1910 *Encycl. Brit.* VI. 494/1 The Clementine literature throws light upon a very obscure phase of Christian development, that of Judaeo-Christianity.

Judo (dʒū·do). Also **jiudo.** [Jap., f. *jiu, jū*, a. Chinese *jeu, jou* soft + Jap. *dō*, ad. Chinese *tao* way.] A modern development of ju-jitsu.

1889 *Trans. & Proc. Japan Soc.* I. 9 It is due to the study of *Jū-do* that the Japanese police..are so skilful in seizing malefactors. 1905 Hancock & Higashi *Complete Kano Jiu-Jitsu* p. xi, *Jiudo* is the term selected by Professor Kano as describing his system more accurately than *jiu-jitsu* does. 1931 E. V. Gatenby in *Studies in Engl. Lit.* (Tokyo) XI. 515 There is at least one jûdô society in London.

Jug, *sb.*[2] **2.** (Earlier U.S. example.)

1815–16 *Niles' Weekly Register* IX. Suppl. 190/1 A full grown villain, who with an accomplice, were shortly after safely lodged in the *jug*.

3. jug and bottle department, the bar of a public house at which alcoholic liquors are sold for consumption off the premises; **jug handle,** the handle of a jug; also *attrib.*, shaped like a jug handle; hence **jug-handled** *a.*, *lit.* placed on one side, as the handle of a jug; *fig.* (*U.S.*) unilateral, one-sided, unbalanced.

1894 G. Moore *Esther Waters* xxx, The public entrance and the *jug and bottle entrance were in a side street. 1909 *Daily Chron.* 31 Mar. 1/3 A 'jug and bottle' department ..does not come within the definition of an open bar. 1932 L. Golding *Magnolia Street* I. ix. § 2 She got her pint from the Jug and Bottle Department. 1846 Sol. Smith *Theatrical Apprent.* 118 Not perceiving the entire justice of this arrangement, it being somewhat on the *jug-handle principle, all on one side. 1900 Elinor Glyn *Visits Eliz.* (1906) 92 She has a jug-handle chignon. 1894 *Advance* (Chicago) 27 Dec. 435/3 It is a little unfortunate that the father of the proposal for an impartial board of arbitrators should also be the author of the *jug-handled compulsory proposition recently laid before the public. 1901 *Standard* 1 June, President McKinley remains opposed to jug-handled or one-sided reciprocity. 1904 *Boston Herald* 28 Sept. 6 The trade between Canada and the United States is..jug-handled.

Jug, *v.*[1] Add: **4.** *intr.* To fish with a bait attached to a floating jug (see Jug *sb.*[2] 3). *U.S.*

1884 Goode *Fishery Industry U.S.* 628 This species, and other of the larger Catfishes, are often caught by 'jugging', the bait being attached to a jug filled with air, which will in time tire out the fish and bring it to the surface.

Juglandic (dʒuglæ·ndik), *a.* [f. L. *jūgland-, -ans* walnut + -ic.] Of or pertaining to trees of the walnut family; in *juglandic acid* (see quot. 1875). So **Juglandin** (dʒū·glændin), a compound obtained from the leaves and green shell of the walnut, used medicinally and as a hair-dye.

1865 Watts *Dict. Chem.*, *Juglandin*, a substance contained in the juice expressed from the green shell of the walnut (*Juglans regia*). 1875 *Ibid.* 2nd Suppl. 709 *Juglandic Acid*, an acid said to be obtained from the bark of *Juglans cinerea*...apparently related to chrysophanic acid. 1887 Bentley *Man. Bot.* (ed. 5) 685 The substance termed *juglandin*..is regarded as a useful remedy in habitual constipation.

Juglone (dʒū·gloun). *Chem.* [f. L. *jūgl(ans* walnut + -one.] = Nucin. Hence **Juglo·nic** *a.*, in *juglonic acid*, an acid formed by the action of nitric acid on juglone.

1878 *Jrnl. Chem. Soc.* XXXIV. 233 Juglone (Nucin). By C. Reischauer...This body, prepared from the green shells of walnuts (*Juglans regia*), has been analysed by the author, who assigns to it the empirical formula, $C_{36}H_{12}O_{10}$. 1887 *Athenæum* 11 June 770/1 The outer coating of walnuts contains a crystalline substance termed nucin or juglone. 1906 *Watts' Dict. Chem.* III. 594/2 Di-nitro-oxy-phthalic acid... Juglonic acid. Formed by oxidation of juglone or its acetyl derivative by boiling with HNO_3.

Jugoslav, Yugo- (yū·goslɑ·v), *a.* and *sb.* Also (after Fr.) **Yougo-.** [Austrian German, f. Serb. jyro-, comb. form of jyr south + Slav.] **A.** *adj.* Of or pertaining to the state of Jugoslavia, proclaimed 30 October 1918, and including the Serbians, Croatians, and Slovenes. **B.** *sb.* An inhabitant of Jugoslavia; a southern Slav.

1881 Mrs. A. O. Brodie tr. *V. Tissot's Unknown Hungary* I. 111 The Yougo-Slaves, or Slaves of the south of Austria. 1916 B. Vosnjak *Jugoslav Nationalism* 11 There have been..three Jugoslav state creations. 1917 Fanny S. Copeland tr. *B. Vosnjak's Bulwark agst. Germany* xv. 250 The unification of the Jugoslavs. 1918 *Geog. Jrnl.* LI. 9 The Slovenes..occupy the most westerly of the Jugo-Slav provinces. 1918 in F. Barac *Croats & Slovenes* (1919) 85 Departmental Chief Rojc is a Jugoslav.

Jugum. Add: **2. a.** *Ent.* A small finger-like projection on the fore-wing of the division *Jugatæ* of lepidopters, which extends under the base of the hind wing holding the two together. **b.** *Zool.* In Brachiopoda, a part of the internal supporting skeleton which joins the bases of the two spiralia.

1888 Rollfston & Jackson *Anim. Life* 693 One valve may have depressions or sinuses to which correspond elevations or juga on the other. 1895 E. Meyrick *Brit. Lepidoptera* 5 A membranous or spine-like process called the *jugum* rises from the dorsum of the forewing near the base. 1911 *Encycl. Brit.* XVI. 466/1 In the most primitive moths a small lobate outgrowth—the jugum..—from the dorsum of the forewing is present.

Juice, *sb.* Add: **1. c.** (*a*) The liquor from the sugar cane; (*b*) this made ready for evaporation.

1697 *Phil. Trans.* XIX. 381 The Juice of the Cane. 1784 P. H. Maty in *New Review* Sept. 194 To..cut the cane,.. to have the juice expressed, and boiled into sugar. 1823 J. Taylor *Wond. Trees*, etc. 59 The season continues. about six weeks, when the juice is found to be too thin and poor to make sugar. 1830 G. R. Porter *Sugar Cane* 17 The cane contains three sorts of juice, one aqueous, another saccharine, and the third mucous.

(*b*) 1839 Ure *Dict. Arts* 1202 Where canes grow on a calcareous marly soil, in a favourable season the saccharine matter gets so thoroughly elaborated, and the glutinous mucilage so completely condensed, that a clear juice and a fine sugar may be obtained without the use of lime. 1887 *Encycl. Brit.* XXII 626/1 Wetzel's pan,..and similar devices for the efficient evaporation of juice..are also in use.

d. Petrol. *To step on the juice*: to accelerate a motor engine. *slang.* (Cf. *Gas *sb.*[2])

1909 *Install. News* III. 52/2 We can at least congratulate ourselves on the fact that we are not faced with a three-penny tax on each gallon of 'juice'. 1918 E. M. Roberts *Flying Fighter* 281 Then I discovered that the tank was nearly empty. That meant that I would have to go in search of 'juice'. 1925 E. Fraser & Gibbons *Soldier & Sailor Words*, *The juice*, airman's slang for the petrol supply of an aeroplane.

e. Electricity, electric current. *slang.*

1903 *Electrical Engin.* 28 Aug. 327/2 The first he asked, a councillor Whose town had got the juice. 1917 *Wireless World* Aug. 345 Our 'juice' we got by tapping off on a couple of our accumulators. 1927 *Chambers's Jrnl.* 10 Dec. 21/1 As the train runs, electricity is manufactured by the action of running. The 'juice' is stored by the batteries, which pass to the lamp-globes a supply automatically regulated...Immediately the train stops, the manufacture of 'juice' stops also. 1929 U. Sinclair *Boston* xxiv. 724 The juice was turned off, and Vanzetti was officially pronounced dead.

2. b. The fluid present in cancerous growths.

1878 *Encycl. Brit.* IV. 801/1 In structure such growths are composed of nucleated cells and free nuclei together with a milky fluid called cancer juice. 1898 P. Manson *Trop. Dis.* xxvi. 407 The juice may be spread out on the cover-glass, fixed, stained and decolourised. 1901 Dorland *Med. Dict.* (ed. 2) s.v. *Juice, Cancer-juice*, a milky juice which may be obtained from cancerous tissue, and containing cancer-cells.

6. juice-canal *Anat.*, a minute channel in the connective tissue regarded as the origin of the lymphatic vessels.

1875 *Encycl. Brit.* I. 850/2 The existence of plasma, or juice, canals..along which, not blood, but the liquor sanguinis is supposed to flow. 1890 Billings *Med. Dict.*, *Juice-canals*, ..stellate, irregular, or branched spaces, communicating with each other by numerous tubular processes, within connective tissues; an origin of lymphatic vessels.

Juicily (dʒū·sili), *adv.* *slang.* [f. Juicy *a.* + -ly[2].] 'Beautifully', excellently.

1916 E. F. Benson *D. Blaize* vi. 118 [He] hit it juicily to square leg. 1927 P. G. Wodehouse in *Sunday Express* 18 Oct. 9 Abstemious cove though I am as a general thing.. on this occasion, I freely admit, I had been doing myself rather juicily.

Juicy, *a.* Add: **2. c.** Excellent, first-rate. (Cf. prec.) *slang.*

1916 E. F. Benson *D. Blaize* vi. 119 It didn't often happen that the first ball of an innings was slogged for six. Juicy hit, too!

Ju-jitsu (dʒūdʒi·tsu, dʒū·dzitsu), *sb.* Also **jui-, jiu-jitsu, -jutsu.** [a. Jap. *jūjutsu*, pronounced (dʒudʒits), f. *jū (Chinese *jeu, jou* soft, yielding) + *jutsu, jutsz* (Chinese *shu, shut, jūe, zūe*) art, science.] A Japanese system of wrestling and physical training characterized by certain special holds or 'tricks'. Also *attrib.*

1891 L. Hearn *Life & Lett.* (1923) II. 175 A building in which jū-jutsu is taught by Mr. Kano. 1893 *Ibid.* IV. 30, I am working out an essay—a philosophical essay on 'Jiu-jutsu. 1895 J. Inouye *Wrestlers & Wrestling* 3 These methods were adopted and extensively practised by *Samurai*, and were finally developed into what is now known as *Jujitsu*. 1904 H. I. Hancock *Phys. Train. Women* 2 From remote antiquity there has existed in Japan a system of bodily training known as *jiu-jitsu*. 1905 *Daily Chron.* 21 Feb. 7/4 Their gymnasium is often visited by ju-jitsu wrestlers. 1915 'Bartimeus' *Tall Ship* iv. § 2 He's frightfully strong, and they say he licked the Japanese ju-jitsu man they had at the School of Physical Training. 1921 *Chambers's Jrnl.* 103/1 A Japanese professor of ju-jitsu. 1925 N. Venner *Imperfect Impostor* xvi, Jos Polkins.. enwrapped him in a benevolent jiu jitsu grip that left him powerless to move.

fig. 1906 R. Whiteing *Ring in New* xxix. 206 To lay him flat on his back by a sort of intellectual jiu-jitsu. 1928 F. Romer *Numbers up!* 11 'Revenge?'..'nothing of the kind. I shall merely practise Moral Jiujitsu.'

Hence **Ju-jitsu** *v. trans.*, to overcome by means of ju-jitsu. **Ju-ji·tsian, Ju-ji·tsuist,** one who teaches or practises ju-jitsu.

1904 Sladen *Playing the Game* II. iv, The wiry little Japanese having Jujitsu'd the three biggest men on the

Russian flag-ship. 1905 H. I. Hancock & Higashi *Complete Kano Jiu-Jitsu* p. v, Those famous *jiu-jitsians*, Hoshino and Tsutsumi. 1905 *Westm. Gaz.* 23 Nov. 4/1 He..issued..a challenge to all jiu-jitsuists of the world. 1908 *Observer* 4 Mar. 15/1 They seem to me to put up no fight at all, and to be very easily ju-jitsued by the Japanese servants.

Julep. 2. *U.S.* (Earlier example.)

1787 *Amer. Museum* I. 215 [An ordinary Virginian] rises about six o'clock. He then drinks a julap made of rum, water, and sugar, but very strong.

Juliet (dʒū·liĕt). [A feminine personal name (F. *Juliette*, It. *Giulietta*), diminutive of *Julia*.]
1. A kind of elastic-sided slipper worn by women.
2. *Juliet cap*, a small network cap, usually adorned with pearls, frequently worn by brides, bridesmaids, and children at weddings, etc.

1909 *Westm. Gaz.* 9 Feb. 8/3 Their Juliet caps were composed of violets. 1930 *Daily Tel.* 7 Apr. 7/6 The 'Juliet' cap idea is to be found in the little theatre hats worn abroad.

Jum: see Joom.

Jumble, *sb.* Add: **1. b.** *collect. sing.* Articles for a jumble-sale; also = jumble-sale. *colloq.*

1931 *Times* 16 Mar. 1/3 Maternity Hospital, holding annual Jumble Sale.—Please deluge us with jumble. 1932 *Daily Tel.* 17 Mar. 1/2 Do please help us with our Easter Jumble on March 18th by sending anything saleable, old or new.

Ju·mble-bead. [Alteration of *jumbee bead* (see *Jumby b), prob. after *mumble*.] The particoloured seed of the jequirity.

1855 Mayne *Expos. Lex.*, *Jumble Beads*, an irreverent name for the seeds of the *Abrus precatorius*, from the purpose they are applied to in forming rosaries. 1887 [see Jequirity].

Jumbo. 1. (U.S. example.)

1846 *Knickerbocker Mag.* XXVII. 511 Take the helm and bear away for that jumbo...And so we walk up to the 'jumbo', an old-time schooner.

Jumby (dʒʊ·mbi). *West Indies.* Also **zumbi, zombi, jumbee, jumbie.** [American Negro, orig. Congolese *zumbi*.] A ghost or evil spirit among American and West Indian negroes.

1871 C. Kingsley *At Last* x, Out of the mud comes up—not jumbies, but—a multitude of small stones. 1875 R. F. Burton *Gorilla Land* II. 124 There was no danger of the Zumbi, or ghost. 1887 W. H. Bentley *Kongo Lang.* App. 505 The fetish Zumbi is supposed to bring good luck with it. It sometimes consists of a bundle of charms, at others it is an image, or even an animal. 1891 J. Evelyn *Baffled Veng.* iv. 60 The 'jumbies' (evil spirits) that haunted the ill-omened spot. 1894 Alice Spinner *Study in Colour* iv. 47 To tremble over the terrible tales of the Jumbi and Duppies, that..terrify belated travellers. 1900 Crockett *Little Anna Mark* xxxvii, 'It is nigh to the hour of the *zombis*!' said Eborra behind me...'And what are the *zombis*?' I asked him..'They are the spirits of the dead,' he answered. 1918 W. Beebe *Jungle Peace* vii. (1919) 138 Sam had formerly been a warden in the Georgetown jail, and rumour had it that he left because he saw 'jumbies' in the court where one hundred and nine men had been hanged.

b. *attrib.*, as **jumby-bead,** (*a*) = **jumby-bean*; (*b*) a prayer-bead; **jumby-bean** = *coral-bean* (Coral *sb.*[1] 9); **jumby-bird,** any bird of ill omen (see quots.); **jumby-tree** = *necklace-tree* (Necklace *sb.* 4 b).

1802 H. Swinburne *Crts. Eur.* (1841) II. 330, I gathered to day a handful of *Jumbee beads. 1871 C. Kingsley *At Last* xvi, The scarlet flowers of the Jumby-bead bush. *Ibid.* xiii, Hedges of dwarf Erythrina, dotted with red jumby beads. *Ibid.*, A large goat-sucker, a Nycteribius, I believe, who goes by the name of *jumby-bird among the English Negros. 1910 Beebe *Search for Wilderness* 136 Greater Anis, or as the natives called them 'Big Witch' or 'Jumbie Birds'. 1923 E. Ingersoll *Birds in Legend*, etc. 168 The 'jumbie-bird', or 'big witch', of the West Indian region..is the dead-black ani, a kind of cuckoo. 1928 M. Summers *Vampire* 265 The occult silk-cotton-tree *(bombax ceiba*, often known as the Devil's tree or *Jumbie tree).

Jumma (dʒʊ·mā). Also **jummah.** [a. Hind. جمع *jama* collection, amount, a. Arab. *jama'* total, aggregate.] 'The total assessment (for land revenue) from any particular estate, or division of country' (Yule). So **Jummabu·ndi** [Pers.-Arab. *jama' bandi*], the settlement of the revenues.

1781 in *5th Rep. Sel. Com. Ho. Comm. E. Ind. Co.* (1812) 8 (Y.) An increase of more than 26 lacks of rupees [was] effected on the former jumma. 1800 *Asiat. Ann. Reg., Proc. Parl.* 38/1 The collections on the current jumma have fallen short 16,875l. 1845 *Encycl. Metrop.* XXI. 672/1 *margin*, Jumma-bundee Customs. 1851 *Illustr. Catal. Gt. Exhib.* iv. i. 926/2 Model of a Jamma Bundi. Collector making the annual jambundi. 1858 J. B. Norton *Topics* 269 When he reached the station he found the magistrate absent on jumabundy.

Jump, *sb.*[1] Add: **5. b.** *Contract Bridge.* (Cf. *Jump *v.* 6 e.)

1928 Work *Contract Bridge* 24 One more trick than would be required in Bridge to justify a raise or jump.

7. *All of a jump*, in a jumpy or nervous state. (*At a*) *full jump* (U.S.), at full speed. *At the jump* (additional example). *For the* (*high*) *jump* (Army slang), up for trial, on the crime sheet. *On the jump*: (*a*) (U.S. example); (*b*) in a nervous state; (*c*) at a great speed.

1825 J. Neal *Bro. Jonathan* II. 291 High! what's the matter with you,—all of a jump! 1854 Mary J. Holmes *Tempest & Sunshine* i. 12 What you ridin' Prince full jump down the pike for? 1870 Keim *Sheridan's Troopers* vi. (1885) 39 The irate quadruped made for our party, coming at a full jump. 1884 'Mark Twain' *Huck. Finn* xviii. 162 My nigger had a monstrous easy time..but Buck's was on the jump most of the time. 1896 G. Ade *Artie* xvi. 147, I put up a holler right at the jump. 1912 F. M. Hueffer *Panel* iii. i. 289 She could see that that elderly gentleman was exceedingly 'on the jump', as nervous as a man well could be. 1912 Mulford & Clay *Buck Peters* xxi. 301 Jake went out of the door on the jump. 1919 *War Terms* in *Athenæum* 1 Aug. 695/2 'He's for the high jump' is a favourite expression meaning that someone is to be charged before his company or commanding officer. *Ibid.* 8 Aug. 727/2 'For the jumps' (up for trial). 1921 Mulford *Bar-20 Three* xviii. 230 Hurrying men pulled thick planks from the pile..and hauled them, on the jump, to windows and doors.

8. with adv. *Jump-down* (Canadian): the confines of civilization. *Jump-off* (U.S.): the place from which a person must jump or take off. *Jump-up* (local Austral.): an escarpment.

1873 J. H. Beadle *Undevel. West* xxiv. 490 In this [bayou] we encountered dangerous whirls and jump-offs. 1884 Phillipps-Wolley *Trottings of Tenderfoot* v. 129 The broad stem of a fallen giant gives you 150 feet of splendid wooden road; but..you find you have been gradually ascending, and now stand on what the Americans would call a 'jump off'. 1885 A. S. Hill *From Home to Home* iii. 63 Brandon..that new city, which in..1881 was what is colonially known as the 'jump-down'. 1909 R. A. Wason *Happy Hawkins* ii. 26 The lantern shed a splash o' light on the shelf, but the jump-off looked like the mouth o' the pit. 1927 M. Terry *Through a Land of Promise* 85 We had been looking at the 'jump-up' marking the extremity of the Barkly Tableland.

9. A robbery.

1796 *Grose's Dict. Vulgar T.* (ed. 3) s.v., The jump, or dining-room jump; a species of robbery effected by ascending a ladder placed by a sham lamp-lighter, against the house intended to be robbed. It is so called, because..the thief..has no means of escaping but that of jumping down. 1901 'Linesman' *Words by Eyewitness* (1902) 293 They are sure to see a 'jump' in everything, even in concessions. *Note*, South African euphemism for a robbery.

Jump, *v.* Add: **1. c.** *To jump out of one's skin*: see Skin *sb.* 5 f.

d. To desert work.

a 1904 S. E. White *Blazed Trail Stories* ii. 30 The men ..would begin to 'jump', would ask for their 'time', and quit.

4. c. *To jump down one's throat* (see Throat *sb.* 3 a). *To jump off* U.S. (see quot. and cf. Jumping *vbl. sb.* b).

1849 Parkman *Oregon Trail* ii. 31 It was resolved..to bid a final adieu to the frontier, or in the phraseology of the region, to 'jump off'.

d. *To jump to it*: to take prompt action; orig. in imper. with reference to a drill movement.

1919 *War Slang* in *Athenæum* 25 July 664/2. 1929 *Morn. Post* 13 July 16 He does not know whether the service will come to his fore- or his back-hand; but he is ready to 'jump to it', whatever happens.

6. b. Also, to leave (a place) suddenly. *U.S.*

1921 R. D. Paine *Comr. Rolling Ocean* xiv. 260, I told you about jumping the town because I had stove up a limousine. 1921 Mulford *Bar-20 Three* vii. 88 I'm admittin' I'm walkin' soft, an' ready to jump th' country right quick.

d. *To jump a bounty* (cf. *bounty-jumper*, Bounty 6). *U.S.*

1884 *Congress. Globe* 28 Mar. 2388/1 The man..'who broke his leg attempting to jump a bounty'.

e. *Contract Bridge. intr.* To bid one more than is necessary. Also *trans.*

1928 Work *Contract Bridge* 33 If the partner jump, it must be with three cards of a suit. *Ibid.* 35 Cases of one No Trump jumped to two, and two of a Major jumped to three. 1929 — *Complete Contract Bridge* i. 7 His proper procedure may be to shift to another declaration, or it may be to jump the original bid.

8. c. *U.S.* (Earlier examples.)

1838 Caroline Gilman *Recoll. Southern Matron* xxx. 211 The boys were ordered to stick close to the dogs, and if they jumped the buck, to catch him. 1839 *Southern Lit. Messenger* V. 377/1, I would go, but I am a going to jump mullet to-night. 1874 J. W. Long *Amer. Wild-Fowl Shooting* 205 The most successful method of hunting ducks is identical with..'jumping them up' along the creeks.

d. To cause to rise as with a jump, or with an abrupt movement.

a 1839 Lady H. Stanhope in *Times Lit. Suppl.* (1910) 20 Jan. 20/3, I used to see the painted Lady H.,..jumped by her footman into her sociable. 1909 P. A. Vaile *Mod. Golf* 92 Many players who at snooker..want to jump a ball make the error of hitting the ball.

9. b. (Earlier example.)

1846 E. H. Smith *Hist. Black Hawk* (Farmer) If, through mistakes, I jumped a man's claim, As soon as I knew it I jumped off again.

c. To rob or take unlawful possession of (an empty house).

1859 *Slang Dict.* s.v., To jump a house, to rob it. 1906 *Westm. Gaz.* 30 July 5/2 There are people who 'jump' houses—quietly take possession of an empty house.

Jump-. Add: **jump-bid** *Contract Bridge*, a bid of one more than is necessary; **jump-shift,** a bid of one more than is necessary in a different suit; so **jump denial, raise, take-out; jump-shot** = **jump-stroke* (b); **jump-stroke** (*b*) *Billiards*, a stroke which causes the ball to jump; **jump-turn** *Skiing* (see quot.).

1928 Work *Contract Bridge* 56 With Ace-King-Queen..make a *jump denial by bidding three. 1932 *Daily Tel.* 8 Oct. 15/5 The term [pre-emptive] is equally applicable to opening bids of Two or more, to *Jump Raises, and to *Jump Take-outs. 1929 Work *Complete Contract Bridge* 112 A *jump-shift;..an unnecessarily high bid in another suit. 1909 P. A. Vaile *Mod. Golf* 92 This shot has its exact counterpart on the billiard table in the useful *jump-shot. 1924 *Ski Terms* in *Tourist* Winter Sports No. 12/1 **Jump turn*, a method of changing direction or stopping.

Jumped, *ppl. a.* Add: **b.** *Jumped-up*: that has risen from a lowly station or an inferior position: often with implication of conceit or arrogance.

1835 'Tom Treddlehoyle' *Bairnsla Ann.* 35 (E.D.D.) A bit ov a jumpt up dress-macker, wot reckons ta be t' biggest beauty it taan. 1895 *Punch* 24 Aug. 93 You jumped-up, cheap, Coventry bagman. 1919 Snaith *Love Lane* xxxiv, Democracy. Between you and me, Gert, it's mainly a name for a lot of jumped-up ignoramuses.

Jumper, *sb.*[1] Add:

1. b. A ticket-inspector. *slang.*

1900 [in Dict., sense 1]. 1906 *Daily Chron.* 24 July 3/7 It was not a fact that unless the 'jumpers'—travelling ticket inspectors—made a certain number of reports they were discharged. 1931 *Aberdeen Even. Express* 4 Apr., It is not at all uncommon for a 'jumper' to find that fifty per cent. of the occupants of a second class compartment have only third class tickets.

c. A fraudulently plural voter. *U.S. slang.*

1903 *N. Y. Tribune* 27 Oct. (Cent. D. Suppl.) There are more 'jumpers' than there were two years ago. These 'jumpers' vote in widely separated parts of the city.

d. One who quits a job. *U.S.*

a 1904 S. E. White *Blazed Trail Stories* ii. 33 Silver Jack ..took one of the 'jumpers' in the cutter with him.

2. b. A convert from Roman Catholicism to Protestantism. *Irish.*

1906 Somerville & Ross *Irish Yesterdays* 75 The cook had called her a 'jumper' (*i.e.* a pervert to Protestantism).

5. b. *Contract Bridge.* One who increases a bid by one more than is necessary.

1929 Work *Complete Contract Bridge* iv. 35 The jumper needs more strength than when an original bid is made by North or East.

6. e. *Iron forging.* (See quot.)

1888 *Lockwood's Dict. Mech. Engin.*, *Jumper*..(1) A smith's hammer..used for dealing blows against the ends of rods laid horizontally for the purpose of jumping them up... (2) The sparks or scintillations which fly off from molten iron in the ladle are also termed jumpers.

f. *Masonry.* = Through-stone[2].

1904 *Technol. & Sci. Dict.* (ed. Goodchild & Tweney).

9. *Aeronautics.* A practice machine which is able to rise a few feet from the ground

1918 Farrow *Dict. Mil. Terms.*

Jumper, *sb.*[2] Add: **3.** A loose-fitting outer garment for female wear resembling a blouse (but not tucked in at the waist) worn with a skirt; a similar garment worn by men usually under the coat. Also, a composite garment for children worn as a protection for the ordinary clothing.

Jumper suit, a jumper and skirt made of the same material, usually wool stockinette.

1909 *Public Ledger* (Philadelphia) 24 June 7/6 One-piece & jumper styles. 1909 *Westm. Gaz.* 7 Aug. 15/2 For smaller girls the jumper still holds its own. 1920 *Punch* 6 Oct. 262/2. 1923 *Daily Mail* 13 Feb. 15 Very effective is the little silk jumper-blouse. 1925 *Times* 29 Dec. 7/6 Sports stockinette jumper suits. 1926 G. W. Deeping *Sorrell & Son* i. § 4 The modiste had received a consignment of silk 'jumpers'. 1930 *Daily Tel.* 1 Dec. 9/3 Jumper-suits of jersey and stockinette.

Jumping, *vbl. sb.* **b.** Add: **jumping-board,** a spring-board; also *fig.*; **jumping-net,** a stout circular net into which one may jump to escape from a burning building; **jumping-off board** = **jumping-board*; **jumping-off place** (earlier U.S. examples); **jumping-pole,** a long pole, like a scout's pole, used in jumping long distances or in making pole-jumps or -vaults.

1878 H. H. Jackson *Trav. at Home* 53 There are public gardens..with little ponds, and boats, and targets, and *jumping-boards. 1909 *Athenæum* 21 Aug. 218/2 A jumping-board for the imagination to spring from. 1902 *Encycl. Brit.* XXVIII. 405/2 The *Jumping Net is made of stout tarred hemp rope. 1914 *Engl. Rev.* Sept. 237 Salonika,..was to be the German *jumping-off board to Asia Minor. 1826 T. Flint *Recoll.* 366 Being, as they phrase it, the *jumping off place it [*sc.* Natchitoche] is the resort of desperate, wicked, and strange creatures. 1828 A. Sherburne *Mem.* xi. (1831) 234 Ilean point was denominated the '*jumping-off place*'. 1834 H. Brackenridge *Recoll.* x. 111, I had no jumping off or jumping up place, like those who prepare their exordium and perorations, and leave the body of the speech to take care of itself. 1836 Crockett *Exploits & Adv. Texas* (1837) 64 Where shall I find words suitable to describe the peculiarities of that unholy spot? 'Tis, in fact, the jumping-off place. 1909 F. Ash *Trip to Mars* xvii. 131 A narrow platform which had been erected as a 'jumping-off place' for fliers. 1903 A. Westcott *Life & Lett. Bp. Westcott* I. 322 The learned professor and canon, with a great *jumping-pole in his hand, leaping from rock to rock.

Jumping, *ppl. a.* Add: **b. jumping-deer** (early and later example); **jumping-jack** *U.S.*, a beetle of the family *Elateridæ*; a click- or spring-beetle; **jumping-shrew** (example).

1832 R. Cox *Adv. Columbia R.* xxix. 319 The *jumping-deer, or chevreuil..frequent the vicinity of the mountains in considerable numbers. 1913 R. Brooke *Coll. Poems* (1918) p. lxxxv, Along the red-gold beach are the tracks of various animals, mostly jumping-deer and caribou. 1861 *Trans. Ill. Agric. Soc.* (1865) V. 416 There is scarcely an individual ..to be found who is unacquainted with the 'Spring-beetles', or as they are often termed '*jumping-Jacks'. 1912 *Rep. Brit. Assoc.* 582 Oriental Tree-Shrews and the African *Jumping-Shrews.

c. jumping-bean, -seed (examples); also **-egg.**

1896 *Chambers's Jrnl.* 18 Apr. 249 A new botanical curiosity..has lately been brought into notice in England under the name of 'A *Jumping Bean'. 1894 *Scientific African* Dec. 28 (Pettman) The so-called *jumping 'eggs' found round Cape Town. 1876 *Field & Forest* II. 53 We have..had the pleasure of examining..these so-called *jumping seeds received from California. 1889 Wesley *Naturalist* III. 22 (Pettman) These are the only jumping seeds of which I had heard until I met with those of Natal.

Junction, *v.* [f. Junction *sb.*] *intr.* To form a junction.

1904 *Electr. Investm.* IV. 771/2 Railway companies whose lines junctioned with each other did not always give either the passenger or goods traffic the advantages that the physical junctions rendered possible. 1909 R. A. Wason *Happy Hawkins* xxvii. Deuced if I ever could see where your trail could have junctioned onto the Clarendon family.

June. 2. Add: *June butter*; **June-berry, -bug** (earlier and later examples); **June-grape** *U.S.* (see quot.); **June grass** (examples); **June week,** at Durham University, the last week of the summer term, Commemoration week.

1810 Michaux *Arbres* I. 32 *June berry. 1832 D. J. Browne *Sylva Amer.* 217 The wood of the June berry is of a pure white. 1836 *Congress. Globe* 5 May 349/2 They hopped upon it, to use a homely phrase, like a duck on a *June-bug. *a* 1853 Dow Jr. *Patent Serm.* III. 282 (Th.) Beating June-bugs from roses is his morning repast. 1895 'C. E. Craddock' *Myst. Witch-Face Mt.*, etc. 237 The beautiful green beetle, here called the 'June-bug'. 1906 W. Churchill *Coniston* xv. 189 June-bugs hummed in at the high windows. 1838 H. Colman *Rep. Agric. Mass.* (1839) 71 *June butter..and September butter..are generally of a superior quality to that made at other seasons. 1873–4 *Rep. Vermont Board Agric.* II. 186 This butter is not what is usually called 'Winter butter', but is equal in flavor and color to 'June butter'. 1821 T. Nuttall *Jrnl. Trav. Arkansa* vii. 137 A species of *Vitis*, called the *June grape from its ripening at that early period, was also nearly in blossom. 1855 *Trans. Mich. Agric. Soc.* VI. 160 A stiff *June grass sod plat. 1877 *Rep. Vermont Board Agric.* IV. 169 The owner found that the hay..which was composed largely of 'June Grass..was badly ergotised. 1889 *Durham Univ. Jrnl.* IX. 1 The end of last term was signalised by what was called by some 'Commemoration' and by others 'the *June Week'. 1900 *Ibid.* XIV. 229 Those who have visited the race-course during the June Week..

June, *v.* *U.S.* [Of obscure origin.] **a.** *intr.* To go in a lively fashion. **b.** *trans.* To drive smartly.

1869 *Overland Monthly* III. 127 A trig, smirk little horse is a 'lace-horse', and he often has to 'june' or 'quill'. 1889 Farmer *Amer.*, *To June* (Texas), to go. 1903 A. Adams *Log Cowboy* xiv. 228 To june a herd of cattle..cross in this manner would have been shameful.

Jungar, variant of Jangar.

Jungle. Add: **2. b.** Also *pl.* Shares in West African concerns. Also *attrib.*

1904 *Daily Chron.* 2 Dec. 1/7 Kaffirs weakened, but Jungles moved upward. 1906 *Ibid.* 9 Feb. 2/3 Jungle shares were..firm. 1908 *Westm. Gaz.* 10 Dec. 15/4 A Jungle Dividend.

3. c. Passing into *adj.* = characteristic of the jungle; savage, untamed.

1908 A. Noyes *W. Morris* 118 Torn by the savage jungle-cries of the elemental passions. 1909 *Daily Chron.* 22 Jan. 3/3 These wild poems of fierce jungle-passion and horror.

Jungli (dʒʊ·ŋgli), *a.* and *sb.* [f. Jungle + -*i*, adj. suffix as in Hindi, etc.] Inhabiting (an inhabitant of) the jungle.

[1880: see Jungly *a.* 2.] 1920 *Blackw. Mag.* Oct. 463/1 Just oneself with half a dozen of one's men and some jungli villagers. 1927 *Chambers's Jrnl.* 138/2 Already he ceases to be jungli. *Note*, Wild and boorish, a clodhopper or uneducated peasant. 1927 *Blackw. Mag.* Mar. 390/1 His crew of two junglis managed to make him understand.

Junimist (ʒū·nimist), *sb.* and *a.* [f. Roum. *Junimea*, f. *junima* youth + -ist.] A member of the Junimea, a Roumanian literary club, founded in 1863, which developed into a political association with progressive conservative views. Also *attrib.* or as *adj.*

1902 *Encycl. Brit.* XXXII. 325/1 M. Teodor Rosetti, a prominent member of the Junimist party. *Ibid.* 328/1 Secret negotiations took place between the Junimists and some of the Conservative ministers. 1906 *Westm. Gaz.* 16 Feb. 5/1 M. Filipescu, a Junimist member.

Junior, *a.* (*sb.*) Add: **5.** *Leather-manuf.* Denoting the split taken from the flesh side of a hide.

1897 C. T. Davis *Manuf. Leather* (ed. 2) 392 All the large hides and sides of patent and enameled leather for harness and carriages are split goods...Three splits are frequently made, the first being taken from the flesh side, and termed 'junior'. *Ibid.* 439 A flat split or 'junior winker' used by harness makers, is taken.

6. *Junior college* U.S., a school providing an advanced course. *Junior high school* U.S., a school intermediate between grammar school and high school; also *attrib.* *Junior school*, (*a*) the lower forms of a public or secondary school; (*b*) the junior division of an elementary school, or a separate school for children between the ages of seven and eleven. *Junior service*, the Army. *Junior stock* (see quot. 1914). *Junior technical school*, a school providing a technical and secondary education for boys.

1929 F. M. McDowell (*title*) The *Junior College. 1924 L. V. Koos (*title*) Administration of Secondary School Units, The Junior High School, The Junior College. 1929 *Encycl. Brit.* VII. 973/2 The end of the junior college period marks the completion of general education of a secondary character and the beginning of university specialization. *a* 1920 A. A. Douglass (*title*) The *Junior High School. 1920 P. A. Boyer *Adjustm. School* 115 The underlying philosophy of the Junior High School movement rests in the attempt to meet the needs, capacities and interests of pupils of the early adolescent period. 1902 *Captain* VII. 221/1 Workington passed out of the *Junior school. 1928 *Hadow Report* & *After* 58 The position in a junior school which receives all its pupils at 7 plus and loses them at 11 plus will be one of some difficulty. 1931 *Education Outlook* June 196/1 It is desirable that the function of the junior school be very clearly realised.., *i.e.* of bridging the gap between the infants' department and the senior school. 1915 E. Wallace *Man who bought London* viii. She had a son in the army, and she bore the *junior service a grudge in consequence. 1914 *H. Halford's Dict. Stock Market Terms* 50 **Junior Stocks*, Ordinary and Deferred Stocks ranking for dividend after Debentures and Preference Stocks. 1932 *Daily Tel.* 8 Oct. 2/4 The current quotations of the junior stocks remove the likelihood of an issue in that form. 1929 *Encycl. Brit.* VII. 988/2 Its lower grades have shown a considerable increase, whether in *junior technical schools, art schools or evening classes. 1931 *Education Outlook* June 183/1 Its pupils [*sc.* of the new senior school] are distinguished from their contemporaries in grammar schools, modern schools, and junior technical schools.

B. *sb.* **d.** *Bridge.* The player on the right of the declarer.

1929 Work *Complete Contract Bridge* Gloss.

Junk, *sb.*[2] Add: **1. e.** Worthless stuff, rubbish. *colloq.*

1913 V. Steer *Romance of Cinema* 30 The life of a film is very short. It is 'first run' to-day and 'junk' a few short weeks hence. 1924 Galsworthy *White Monkey* i. v, His 'junk', however, was not devoid of the taste and luxury which overflows from the greater houses of England.

5. Further attrib. uses of sense 1 d, as *junk-heap, -merchant, -pile*; junk-shop (U.S. example).

1906 *Westm. Gaz.* 26 Oct. 2/1 He [*sc.* Hearst]..took hold of a *junk-heap relic of Pacific-coast journalism called the *Examiner*. 1920 R. L. Alsaker *Eating for Health* 195 You and I have to conform to the laws of nature, or else we are thrown into the junk heap. 1901 *Westm. Gaz.* 8 July 3/2 Twenty tons of unsold copies of a well-known cheap magazine were sold for waste-paper to *junk merchants. 1880 *Harper's Mag.* June 67/1 The *junk pile in the barn is invaded, and the rusty plough abstracted. 1912 J. H. Moore *Ethics & Educ.* 10 They should be sent without sighs or lamentations to the junk-pile. 1881 *Harper's Mag.* Oct. 652/1 An old tin peddler going his regular round of gossip and trade...A sort of peripatetic *junk-shop and circus wagon combined.

Junk, *v.* Add: **2.** To treat as junk; to 'scrap'.

1916 B. Hall *One Man's War* (1929) 196 When he got home his ship was a complete wreck. It will be junked. 1922 Titus *Timber* xxxii. 281 Perhaps he had friends..who are junking their mills now and getting ready to move. 1930 *Time & Tide* 20 Sept. 1164 Jugo-Slavia will not disband a soldier, scrap a gunboat, or junk a gun while Italy menaces her.

Junket, *sb.* Add: **4. b.** An excursion or a tour made at the public cost, esp. by members of Congress, for purposes of inspection or legislative business, but which is made the occasion of providing the participants, and sometimes their families, with a more or less luxurious holiday. *U.S.*

1919 Mencken *Amer. Lang.* 107 A member of Parliament is not afflicted by the numerous bugaboos that menace an American congressman. He knows nothing of *lame ducks, pork barrels, gag-rule, junkets*, [etc.].

Junkman[2]. *U.S.* (Earlier and later examples.)

1880 *Scribner's Monthly* Oct. 862/1 He is..a junkman or a rag-picker. 1927 *Observer* 21 Aug. 19/2 They call him the 'junk' man because he buys..'traded-in' cars for the purpose of scrapping them..The typical American junkman is not interested in Fords.

Jupati (dʒū·-, hū·pāti). [Amer. Sp.] In full *jupati palm*: a Brazilian palm, *Raphia tædigera*, the long leaf-stalks of which are employed as building material, etc. by the natives.

1866 *Treas. Bot.* 960/1.

Jupiter. Add: **1. b.** *Jupiter Pluvius*, Jupiter as the dispenser of rain; hence used trivially in reference to a fall or storm of rain.

1864 Sala *Quite Alone* ii, 'Take my advice, and..borrow somebody else's umbrella..'Are you, too, ready for the wrath of Jupiter Pluvius?'

2. d. *Palmistry.* (See quot.)

1888 Kath. St. Hill *Gram. Palmistry* (1890) 19 First Finger. Called finger of Jupiter. *Ibid.* 24 A good Mount of Jupiter [at the base of the forefinger] will always show a great mind.

Jura (dʒū·rā, ‖ ʒūra). The name of a range of mountains lying on the borders of France and Switzerland, used to designate strata of oolitic limestone found mainly in those mountains.

Lower or *Black Jura* = Lias 2. *Middle* or *Brown Jura* = Dogger[2] 2. *Upper* or *White Jura* = Malm *sb.* 1 a.

1859 Page *Handbk. Geol. Terms* s.v. *Jurassic*, Continental geologists are in the habit of dividing the Jurassic formation into three groups—viz., the 'White (or Upper) Jura', 'Brown (or Middle) Jura', and 'Black (or Lower) Jura'. 1885 Geikie *Text-bk. Geol.* (ed. 2) 804 The German Lower or Black Jura presents many points of resemblance to the English Lias. *Ibid.*, The Dogger or Brown Jura represents the Lower Oolite of England. 1885 Lyell *Elem. Geol.* (ed. 4) 311 The Malm, or white Jura..consists of white limestones and marls.

Juriballi (yūribæ·li). Also **juribali, euri-, yourabali.** [Arawak (Makuchi).] Any of several meliaceous trees, especially *Trichilia moschata*, the bark of which is used as a febrifuge; also, the bark itself.

1846 Lindley *Veget. Kingd.* 462 Juriballi bark, a Demerara product. 1851 *Illustr. Catal. Gt. Exhib.* iv. i. 982/1 Youraballi. 1867 Simmonds *Dict. Trade* Suppl., *Juriballi Bark*..is described as being a potent bitter and astringent, and superior to Peruvian bark in fevers of a typhoid or malignant nature. 1903 *Imperial Inst. Techn. Rep.* 285 The Crabwood and Euriballi would have shown fair results.

Jury, *sb.* **6.** Add: **jury-fixer** *U.S.*, one who bribes or 'gets at' a jury; **jury-woman,** (*b*) a female juror.

1882 *Washington Post* 18 Mar. (Th.) There was an idea abroad that there might be some scope in the proceedings before the Grand Jury for a '*jury fixer'. 1927 *Daily Tel.* 24 May 17/6 Retiring of a mixed jury...The manner in which the recalcitrant *jurywoman is eventually brought round is not altogether convincing.

Jus gentium (dʒʊs dʒe·nʃiǝm). [L.] = *law of nations* (see Law *sb.*[1] 4 c).

1548 Hooper *Declar. Commandm.* iii. 31 They shuld observe the commune lawes vsyd among all people whiche is callid ius gentium. 1682 Evelyn *Let. to Pepys* 19 Sept., The right of passes, and petitions thereupon, were formed upon another part of the *Jus Gentium*, than our pretended dominion of the seas. 1771 *Junius Lett.* lxi. (1772) 285 Any law that contradicts or excludes the common law of England; whether it be *canon, civil, jus gentium*, or *levitical*. 1839 *Penny Cycl.* XIII. 361/2 According to their [*sc.* Roman lawyers'] phraseology,..*jus gentium* consists of those rules of law which are common to all nations. 1856 Bouvier *Law Dict.* (ed. 6) I. 685 Among the Romans by *jus civile* was understood the civil law, in contradistinction to the public law, or *jus gentium*. 1880 *Encycl. Brit.* XIII. 191/1 The ambiguity of the phrase *jus gentium* enabled the early founders of international law to apply the principles of the *jus naturæ* to the conduct of states *inter se* in a way of which there is no example in the Roman law-books.

Jusi (hū·sī). Also **husi, jussi.** [Sp. *jusi*, a. Tagalog *husi*.] A delicate fibrous fabric woven in the Philippine Islands.

1851 *Illustr. Catal. Gt. Exhib.* iv. i. 1344/1 Piece of 'jusi', and a shawl of 'jusi'. *Ibid.*, Pieces of striped jusi dresses. 1902 *Encycl. Brit.* XXXI. 667/1 Beautiful fabrics called 'piña' and 'jusi'.

Jussiæan (dʒʊsi,ī·ăn), **Jussieuan** (dʒʊsiyū·ăn), *a.* [f. mod.L. adj. *Jussiæus*, or its origin, the surname *Jussieu* of two famous French botanists + -an.] Of or pertaining to Bernard (1699–1777) and Antoine Laurent (1748–1836) de Jussieu, or to the natural system of botanical classification organized by them.

1824 Loudon *Encycl. Gardening* 47 All the hardy plants ..arranged in groups, according to the Jussieuean system. 1857 A. Henfrey *Bot.* § 392 The Jussieuan System. 1865 G. Bentham *Brit. Flora* Pref. p. viii, The so-called Linnæan or Jussiæan systems. 1876 *Encycl. Brit.* IV. 81/1 It [*sc.* the Linnean method] was superseded by the Jussiæan method.

Just, *adv.* Add: **1. c.** *Just so*: also, in the required or appropriate manner, according to propriety; also as *adj.* = proper.

1751 Richardson in *Johnson's Rambler* No. 97 ¶ 24 When I courted and married my Lætitia, then a blooming Beauty, every Thing passed just so! 1794 *Massachusetts Spy* 3 Sept. (Th.) A few years ago, every body supposed that if people did not behave just so, they ought to be punished. 1824 A. Singleton *Lett. fr. South & West* 18 (Th.) Their just so garb makes [the Quakers] appear like antediluvians.

d. *Just as good*, frequently used to recommend a substitute for a patent medicine or other branded article.

1920 De Haas *Business Organiz.* 320 There is always a great temptation on the part of middlemen to substitute *just-as-good articles*.

Jutia, variant of *Hutia.

Juvenal (dʒū·vǝnăl), *sb.*[3] Anglicized form of the cognomen of the Roman satirist Decimus Junius *Juvenalis*, used gen. to designate a satirist.

1592 Greene *Groats W. Wit* F 1, With thee I ioyne yong Iuuenall [*sc.* Nashe], that byting Satirist. 1693 Dryden tr. *Juvenal* p. vii, I might find in France, a living Horace and a Juvenal, in the person of the admirable Boileau. 1820 T. G. Wainwright *Ess. & Crit.* (1880) 73 Some fanciful 'juvenal'. 1841 D'Israeli *Amen. Lit.* III. 132 Jonson, the Juvenal of our drama. 1883 E. C. Brewer *Dict. Phrase & Fable* (ed. 15) 469/1 The English Juvenal. John Oldham.. The Juvenal of Painters. William Hogarth. 1902 *Daily Chron.* 20 Feb. 3/2 The art of satire is dead in England... The Juvenals of Fleet-street are no more.

Juvenile, *sb.* Add: **3.** *pl.* Books written for children.

1889 *Publishers' Trade List* (Cent. Dict.) Juveniles, classified in series according to price. 1908 *Daily Chron.* 27 Nov. 3/5 What would John Newbery say if he were to.. see his old shop..filled with this season's 'juveniles'? 1930 *Publishers' Weekly* 5 July 28 We announce 10 juveniles.

Juvenilia (dʒūvĭnĭ·liă), *sb. pl.* [L., neut. pl. of *juvenilis* Juvenile.] Literary or artistic works produced in the author's youth (freq. as a title of such works collected). Also *transf.*

1622 G. Wither (*title*) Ivvenilia: a Collection of those Poemes which were heretofore Imprinted and Written by George Wither. 1633 Donne (*title*) Iuuenilia: or certaine paradoxes and problemes. 1693 Dryden tr. *Juvenal* p. ix, His *Juvenilia*, or Verses written in his Youth. *a* 1849 H. Coleridge *Ess.* (1851) II. 265 Whatever effect these juvenilia may have produced at the time, they are quite worthless now. 1896 *Tennyson's Wks.* 2 Juvenilia. 1929 R. A. Knox in *Sunday Dispatch* 13 Jan. 10/5 Not that I belong to the school which would trace, in these innocent juvenilia of our nation, an anthropological or historical origin.

Juvia (dʒū·-, hū·viă). [Amer. Sp.] The Brazil-nut. Also *attrib.*, as *juvia-nut, -tree.*

1852 Ross tr. *Humboldt's Trav.* II. xxiii. 390 Juvia-trees, which furnish the triangular nuts called in Europe the almonds of the Amazon, or Brazil-nuts. 1858 Baird *Cycl. Nat. Sci.* 69/1 The natives are very fond of this nut, and celebrate the harvest of the *Juvia* with great rejoicings. 1860 Mayne Reid *Odd People* 142 The splendid fruits of the *Bertholletia excelsa*, or juvia-tree, known in Europe as 'Brazil nuts'. 1868 W. Rhind *Veget. Kingd.* 387 The Juvia, Brazil, or Castanha Nut.

Juxta-. Add: **Juxta-arti·cular** *a. Anat.*, situated near an articulation. **Juxta-li·ttoral** *a.*, situated close to the shore. **Juxta-pylo·ric** *a. Anat.*, adjacent to the pylorus. **Juxta-terre·strial** *a.*, situated close to the earth.

1901 Dorland *Med. Dict.* (ed. 2), *Juxta-articular. 1876 *Encycl. Brit.* X. 354/2 The marine life of the period has been abundantly preserved, so far at least as regards the comparatively shallow and *juxta-littoral waters. 1908 *Practitioner* Nov. 692 Pyloric, *juxta-pyloric, or complicated ulcers. 1885 Geikie *Text-bk. Geol.* (ed. 2) 598 These *juxta-terrestrial parts of the ocean.

Juxtaposition. Add: **2.** *Crystallogr.* Contactual union between twin crystals. *Juxtaposition twin*, a twin crystal whose parts extend only to the plane of junction; a contact twin.

1883 *Encycl. Brit.* XVI. 366/1 In aragonite the crystals are partly interpenetrating, and partly merely in juxtaposition. 1910 *Ibid.* VII. 582/2 In these two examples the surface of the union..is a regular surface coinciding with the twin-plane; such twins are called 'juxtaposition-twins'.

Juxtapositive (dʒʊkstăpǫ·zītiv), *a.* *Gram.* [f. Juxtaposit(ion + -ive.] The designation of a case expressing juxtaposition.

1890 Gatschet *Gram. Klamath Lang.* 490 Juxtapositive case in -tana.

K

K. 4. Add: K., Kelvin (see *Kelvin). K.E., kinetic energy. K.H.B. *colloq.* (see quot. 1925). K.O., k.o. = knock(ed) out. K.O.S.B., King's Own Scottish Borderers. K.P. (*U.S.*), kitchen police(man) (see quot. 1930). K.V.A., kva., kilovolt ampère(s. K.W., KW, k.w., kw., kilowatt(s.

1905 Eggar *Mech.* Add. 6 K.E. 36, o. 100 foot-pounds. 1909 C. S. Jackson & W. M. Roberts *First Dynamics* 88 The gain of K.E. equals arithmetically the work done by the forces. 1916 'Taffrail' *Pincher Martin* iv. K.H.B. = King's hard bargain, a term used in connection with a man who is an undesirable character. 1921 *World's Work* Dec. 90/1 The power developed is rated at 88,000 k.w. generated at 7,000 volts. 1922 T. Burke *Lond. Spy* 209 As a youth the ring attracted him...A few k.o.'s put an end to that. 1923 H. Cox *Dogs & I* xxii. 209 The Field Spaniel has received the 'K.O.' and taken the count! 1924 *Cricketer Ann.*, 1923–4 82 The band and pipers of the K.O.S.B.'s. 1925 E. Fraser & Gibbons *Soldier & Sailor Words* 134 *K.H.B.*, *A*: a King's Hard Bargain. A worthless or incorrigible fellow. (Old Service term.) 1927 *Observer* 25 Dec. 12/6 His record..includes a k.o. victory over Paul Berlenbach... Knut Hansen, who k.o. Phil Scott in the first round. 1928 *Daily Express* 25 June 17/7 Young Stanley..was then k.o. by a right swing to the jaw. 1930 H. H. C. Buckley *Great Event* 33 There was a much advertised football match between the K.O.S.B. and the Royal Scots. 1930 F. A. Pottle *Stretchers* 31 A cook or K.P. stands by to see that the dishes are decently scraped before they go into the pail. *Ibid.* 33 Before first call, six or more unfortunates crept out of bed and went on kitchen police...They began their toil before dawn, and it is long after dark before the cooks let them go. 'K.P.' is for good reason the most hated detail in the army. 1931 P. Lewis *Romance Water-Power* 211 The single-phase generators are designed for a continuous output of 6,150 kva. at 225 r.p.m. *Ibid.* 216, 3-phase generators of 6,000 kva., at 167 r.p.m. capacity.

(*b*) *K line*, in a spectrum, a prominent line partly caused by calcium.

1902 [see *H II. 3 b]. 1921 *Discovery* Sept. 227/2 Tin atoms can be made to suit a certain series of 'lines' known as the K series. *Ibid.* 228/1 The K lines of tungsten.

Ka (kā), *sb.* The name given by the ancient Egyptians to a person's second self or double, surviving after death together with the *bai* or soul.

a 1892 Tennyson in A. G. Weld *Glimpses* (1903) 119, I believe that beside our material body we possess an immaterial body, something like what the ancient Egyptians called the Ka. 1905 E. F. Benson *Image in Sand* i, Somebody's Ka—his ghost, you know, or his astral body. 1923 *Glasgow Herald* 22 Feb. 4 The Princess has a Ka, or better self.

Kabaka (kābā·kā). The native title of the ruler of Uganda.

1878 H. M. Stanley *Dark Cont.* I. 189 General jack-of-all-trades for the *Kabaka*. 1925 Mackail *Strachan-Davidson* 90 The choice of an English tutor for the eight-year-old Kabaka of Uganda.

Kabeljou (kā·bǝlyau). Also **cabaljao, kabeljaauw.** [Afrikaans, = Du. *kabeljauw* (see Cabilliau).] A South African sea-fish, *Sciæna aquila*.

1838 J. E. Alexander *Exped. S. Africa* II. 83 We got a great prize in a stranded cabaljao, fifty pounds weight, like a huge salmon. 1906 *East London Dispatch* 26 June (Pettman) The Natal 'Cape salmon'..proves to be our well-known and very common Kabeljaauw, called for briefness 'cob' or 'kob'. 1912 J. T. Cunningham *Reptiles, Amphibia, Fishes*, etc. 277 The name kabeljaauw [= cod].. in South Africa has been transferred to a fish of a very different species,..the maigre, *Sciaena aquila*. 1930 C. L. Biden *Sea-Angling Fishes of the Cape* 109 The kabeljou is often mistaken for the geelbek.

Kabyle (kăbai·l). [Arab. قبائل *qabāil*, pl. of *qabīlah*.] A Berber of Algeria or Tunis. Also, the Berber dialect spoken by the Kabyles.

1818 Pananti *Narr. Resid. Algiers* 181 The Bedouins are divided into many scattered tribes, called *Kabiles*, and vulgarly *Nege*. 1861 *Chambers's Encycl.* II. 44/1 In Algeria, where they [*sc.* Berbers] usually are termed Kabyles, they are yet unconquered by the French. 1875 *Encycl. Brit.* I. 261/2 The Kabyles, or Kabaily, of the Algerian and Tunisian territories. 1882 F. W. Newman *Libyan Voc.* 3 The Libyan language..was but one, according to St. Augustine. Now there are at least four, the Kabail in Algeria, the Shilha in the mountains of Morocco, the Tuarik..beyond the Atlas, and the Ghadamsi at Ghadames. *Ibid.* 38 Kabail verbs and verbals, including adjectives. 1900 A. Wilkin *Among Berbers of Algeria* 178 Cheek by jowl the villages of Frenchmen and Kabyles stand. 1900 *Knowledge* 1 Aug. 173/2 The various Kabyle tribes.

Kach(oh)eri, var. Cutcherry.

1903 *Oxford Mag.* 11 Feb. 208/1 The Kachcheri..is the centre of official life in the province. 1928 *U.P. Ch. Mission. Rec.* Sept. 391/2, I can't have the Kacheri turned into a pawn-shop.

Kackle, variant of Cackle *v.*[2] *Naut.*

1883 *Man. Seamanship for Boys* 128 The cable is then served, or, in Naval language, kackled with 2½-in. rounding, for the distance of 9 ft. from the eye.

Kadiak: see *Kodiak.

‖**Kadin** (kā·din). Also **kadine.** [Turk. قادين *qādin* lady; the form *kadine* is prob. through Fr.] A lady of the Sultan's harem (see quot. 1843).

1843 *Penny Cycl.* XXV. 394/2 The women of the harem are divided into five classes:—1, 'Kádin', or 'wives of the Sultan', in number from four to seven. 1896 *Westm. Gaz.* 16 Sept. 1/3 He seldom notices any woman in his harem except the chief kadine.

Kadir (kā·dǝɹ). *India.* Also **Khadir, -ar.** The alluvial deposit of river-beds; a river-bed. Also *attrib.* applied to river-bed land.

1879 Medlicott & Blanford *Geol. India* xvii. 404 The alluvial plain itself..is composed of *bhángar*, or high land ..and *khádar*, or low land, the low plain through which each river flows. *Ibid.* 405 The Assam valley is a gigantic *khádar* or strath. 1882 W. Theobald *Mason's Burma* I. 4 The delta..of the Ganges, the richest land of Lower Bengal, being composed of *Khadir* land. 1887 J. M. Brown *Shikar Sketches* 247 Pig-sticking in the Kadir, or old bed of the Ganges. 1889 Baden-Powell *Pigsticking* 202 The Cup given by the Meerut Tent Club is called the 'Kadir Cup', after the Kadir or river-bed country in which it is competed for. 1919 D. N. Wadia *Geol. India* 251 The Khadar deposits are, as a rule, confined to the vicinity of the present channels. 1922 *Blackw. Mag.* Oct. 526/2 There is more game and greater variety of game in a kadir country than in any other kind.

Kaffir. 4. Add: **Kaffir Circus** *Stock Exchange slang*, the body of brokers who operate in 'Kaffirs', or the place where they operate.

1899 *Sketch* 19 July 572/1 The Miscellaneous Market has acquired a reputation of closely sympathising with the Kaffir Circus. 1901 C. Duguid *How to read Money Article* 121 The market in which they are dealt in the Stock Exchange is often called the 'Kaffir Circus'. Term does not comprise Rhodesians. 1902 *Encycl. Brit.* XXXII. 865/1 At first.. the 'Kaffre circus', as it was called, was regarded with contempt by the older *habitués* of the Stock Exchange.

Kaffrarian (kæfrē·riăn), *a.* and *sb.* [See -an.] **a.** *adj.* Belonging to Kaffraria, the country of the Kaffirs. **b.** *sb.* A Kaffir.

1883 C. F. Gordon Cumming *Fire Fountains* I. 258 From Crimean winters to Kaffrarian summers. 1884 Friend *Flowers & Folk Lore* 524 The seeds of one kind are called Caffrarian peas by Barrow.

Kahawai (kahawai). Also **kawai.** [Maori.] A fish, *Arripis salar*, the 'salmon' of Australia and New Zealand.

1838 J. S. Polack *New Zealand* I. 322 The *kaháwai*, or colourless salmon. 1870 R. Taylor *Te Ika a Maui* (ed. 2) 623 The Kahawai..is one of the most abundant, and is called mackerel by the settlers. 1927 *Daily Express* 26 Feb. 1 The Duchess returned to the Renown with seventeen 'schnapper' and one 'kahawai'.

Kahili (kahī·li). [Hawaiian.] A brush-like implement.

1883 C. F. Gordon Cumming *Fire Fountains* I. 35 At the door of the mausoleum are placed tall *kahilis*, honorific symbols, which to irreverent foreign eyes are suggestive of gigantic feather-brushes, or rather bottle-brushes. 1915 W. A. Bryan *Nat. Hist. Hawaii* 61 *note*, In the hand is a small kahili with ivory and tortoise shell handle.

Kahuna (kahū·nă). [Hawaiian; variant of an Eastern Pacific word (also *tahuna, tahunga*) = wise man.] A Hawaiian witch-doctor.

1886 H. H. Gowen *Paradise of the Pacific* (1892) 85 The *Kahunas* advised him to stave off the calamity by getting rid of the *white power*. 1915 W. A. Bryan *Nat. Hist. Hawaii* 54 A numerous class of more irregular priests or Kahunas, that were little more than sorcerers. 1920 *Nature* 15 July 628/1.

Kai (kai). *New Zealand.* [Maori.] Food, victuals.

[1838 J. S. Polack *New Zealand* I. 289 There is a much larger variety of this esculent [*sc.* potato] called *kai pakehá*, or white man's food.] 1845 E. J. Wakefield *Adv. N. Zealand* I. 265 The determination of the natives not to move till all the *kai* was exhausted. 1925 E. Fraser & Gibbons *Soldier & Sailor Words* 134 *Kai*, food. (A Maori word, used among the New Zealand troops in the War.) 1927 T. E. Donne *The Maori* 95, I kep in te whare for tree day, but no *kai* (food).

So (in reduplicated form) **Kaikai** (kaikai), food; feasting; a feast.

[1807 J. Savage *Some Acc. New Zealand*, *Vocab.* 75 Kiki ..food.] 1845 E. J. Wakefield *Adv. N. Zealand* I. 29 He explained..that there would be much *kai kai* or feasting. 1894 Stevenson & Osbourne *Ebb Tide* I. iv, There shall be no growling about the kaikai, which will be above allowance. 1901 A. C. Haddon *Head-Hunters* 39 One afternoon some of us went to a feast, or kaikai.

Kainga (kainga). *New Zealand.* [Maori.] A place of residence; a settlement, village.

1838 J. S. Polack *New Zealand* I. 66 These animals were a disgrace to the *kainga*, or village, of which they formed a part. 1845 E. J. Wakefield *Adv. N. Zealand* I. 241 ..full of many native *kaingas* [sic] where the pakeha was unwelcome. 1907 J. Cowan *Tour. New Zealand* 174 There are places for artists, these out-of-the-way *kaingas*.

Kaiser. Add: **Kai·serate, Kai·serdom** = Kaisership; **Kai·serism,** absolutism as exhibited in the rule of the German emperor; **Kaisership** (earlier U.S. example).

1848 Lowell *Fable for Critics* 1626 Two dozen of Italy's exiles who shoot us his Kaisership daily. 1881 R. Adamson *Fichte* 81 Even the shadowy bond which seemed to unite the German States had been dissolved by the Austrian emperor's renunciation of the Kaiserate. 1914 C. Brereton *Who is responsible?* 101 In order to smash and pulverize Kaiserdom and all that it stands for in the world. 1914 T. Roosevelt in *New York Herald* 5 Sept. 8/2 The American people will countenance nothing..that resembles..Kaiserism. 1915 *Morning Post* 13 Feb. 6/7 The Revolutionaries, who declare that 'Kaiserism' is as deadly a form of 'Absolutism' as any that can be encountered. 1920 B. Cronin *Timber Wolves* vii. 121 A more flagrant example of business Kaiserism never happened.

Kajang (kā·dʒæŋ). Also **kedgang, kadjan.** [Malay كاجڠ *kājang*.] A matting made of the leaf of the pandanus palm, used by Malays for roofing and for the awning of a boat.

1848 F. S. Marryat *Borneo* 63 The Malay war-boat..is built of timber at the lower part, the upper is of bamboo, rattan, and kedgang (the dried leaf of the Nepa palm). 1901 A. C. Haddon *Head-Hunters* 299 The roof was covered with *kajangs* from the boats. 1904 E. H. Giglioli tr. *Beccari's Wand. Gt. Forests of Borneo* 223 Sampans have generally a roofing of 'kadjan', a sort of matting made with palm or pandanus leaves. 1922 *Chambers's Jrnl.* 503/1 Under the *kajang* (native rush matting) covering.

Kakke (kæ·ke). [Jap., f. *kyaku, kaku* leg + *ki, ke* illness, disease.] The Japanese name for Beri-beri.

1874 *Boston Med. & Surg. Jrnl.* XC. 361. 1876 *Medical Times & Gaz.* 9 Dec. 659 The 'Kakke' Disease of Japan. 1878 *Trans. Asiatic Soc. Japan* VI. ii. 214, I by no means imply that *Holothuria* has any connection with Kakké. 1906 *Practitioner* Nov. 695 In her previous wars, Japan saw her armies practically prostrate with beri-beri or kakké.

Kakur (kā·kuǝɹ). Also **karkur, khakur.** [Javanese.] The muntjak.

1876 Alex. A. A. Kinloch *Large Game Shooting* ii. 26 The Kakur is one of the smallest Deer, not being much more than eighteen inches in height. 1887 J. M. Brown *Shikar Sketches* 254 The harsh roar of a karkur rang out close to us. 1925 A. G. Arbuthnot in G. Burrard *Big Game Hunting* 141 The flesh of kakur is excellent.

Kala-azar (kāla,azā·ɹ). [Assamese, f. *kālā* black + *āzār* disease.] A virulent infectious malarial fever of oriental tropical countries.

1882 *Rep. Sanitary Commiss. Assam.* 1895 *Brit. Med. Jrnl.* 11 May 1055/1 In many tea-gardens..kala azar carries off the coolies in large numbers. 1897 *Ibid.* 5 June 1434/2 The anæmia met with in kala-azar. 1907 *Allbutt's Syst. Med.* II. ii. 50 The Leishman-Donovan bodies of kala azar.

Kale (kēɪl). *U.S. slang.* Money.

1927 *Daily Express* 23 Sept. 1 Enough 'kale' (prize-fighters' name for money) has been received..to assure the promoters a profit of approximately £100,000.

Kalmuck (kæ·lmʊk). Also 8 **-muc,** 9 **-muk, -myk.** [Russ. Калмыкъ.]
1. A member of a Tatar race living on the Caspian. Also *attrib.* or *adj.*

1783 W. Tooke *Russia* IV. 121 The dwellings of the heathenish and christian Kalmucs. *Ibid.* 125 The Kalmuc hords on the Volga. 1882 Stevenson *New Arab. Nts.*, *Pavil. on Links* vi, His broken nose and high cheekbones gave him somewhat the air of a Kalmuck. 1902 *Encycl. Brit.* XXX. 8/2 Kalmyk, or Kalmuck Steppe, a territory or reservation belonging to the Kalmyks. 1903 Ld. R. Gower *Rec. & Remin.* 430 A man..with a rather Kalmuk-featured face and white curly hair.

b. The language (Ural-Altaic) of this people.

1883 *Encycl. Brit.* XVI. 750/2 The Kalmuk and East Mongolian dialects do not differ much...In Kalmuk..the guttural can only be traced through the lengthening of the syllable.

2. (With small initial letter.) A kind of shaggy cloth, resembling bearskin.

Hence **Kalmu·ckian** *a.*

1727 J. G. Scheuchzer tr. *Kæmpfer's Hist. Japan* I. vi. 90 The Prince of the Calmuckian Tartars.

Kalokagathia (kæ:lokægæ·þiă, kǣ:lo-). [Gr. καλοκαγαθία, f. καλοκάγαθος = καλὸς κἀγαθός for καλὸς καὶ ἀγαθός beautiful and good (the perfect character).] Nobility and goodness of character.

1931 tr. W. Rathenau's *New Soc.* x. 105 The Greeks..adopted as the ideal of..the famous principle of life which they called Kalokagathia. 1932 *Time & Tide* 11 June 773/1 The formal kalokagathia of that incredible character.

Kalsomine (kæ·lsǝmain). Add examples. Also as *vb.*, to distemper with kalsomine, *trans.* and *intr.*; hence **Ka·lsominer, Ka·lsomining** *vbl. sb.* (Cf. *Calcimine.)

Supplement, p. 3873; Corrigenda, p. 4092; Spurious words, p. 4093; Books quoted, p. 4094

1840 *Athenæum* 20 June 502 Kalsomine. 1883 *Harper's Mag.* Mar. 503/2 Paint and kalsomine can not be counted upon. 1888 *Pall Mall Gaz.* 3 Mar. 11/1 Over face, arms, neck,..and bosom she spreads a coat of liquid white... In plain words, she, as it were, kalsomines herself. 1889 *Thompson St. Poker Club* 31 An extensive kalsomining contract. 1891 H. C. Bunner *Zadoc Pine* etc. 166 White kalsomined bedrooms. 1893 Kate Sanborn *Truthf. Woman S. California* 81 Those who feel an unctuous joy in painting the lily, kalsomining the calla, and adding perfumes to the violet. 1904 'O. Henry' *Cabbages & Kings* xiv. 248 Let me kalsomine you a little mental sketch to consider. 1916 H. L. Wilson *Somewhere in Red Gap* iv. 128 He was a painter and grainer and kalsominer and paperhanger. *Ibid.* 135 He..began to paper and paint and grain and kalsomine. 1924 *Spectator* 1 Nov. 640 These walls can be whitewashed or covered with vines on the outside and kalsomined within.

Kamerad (kæ·mĕrăd, ‖kamĕrā·t). [G., a. F. *camarade* Comrade.] Comrade, companion: the exclamation used as an appeal for quarter by a German-speaking soldier on surrendering. Hence jocularly as *vb. intr.*, to say 'kamerad', express one's wish to surrender.

1914 *Illustr. Lond. News* 10 Oct. 497 How the enemy surrenders, saying, 'Kamerad..Pardon!' 1916 Boyd Cable *Action Front* 63 'Nein, nein!' answered Ainsley. 'You kamarade—sie kamarade.' The other, in somewhat voluble gutturals, insisted that Ainsley must 'kamarade', otherwise surrender. 1917 P. Macgill *Brown Brethren* vii. 105 'Kamerad! Kamerad!' they whined, their arms shaking as if stricken with palsy. 1917 *Times Hist. War* XIV. 199/2 Then Gardener shouted to the others..'You're late. Everybody else has Kameraded.' 1928 *Daily News* 21 Sept. 5/2 When our men came down the steps of the dugout the card-players perfunctorily held up their hands and 'Kameraded'. 1923 *Westm. Gaz.* 3 July, Sir W. Joynson-Hicks cried 'Kamerad' at once. He tried to let himself down lightly by saying that he had expected a unanimous acceptance.

Kamik (kæ·mik). Also **kammik.** [Eskimo.] A long boot of sealskin worn by the Eskimos.

1900 *Scribner's Mag.* Sept. 297/1 Seal-skin kammiks, or top boots. 1910 Peary *North Pole* xiv. 128 The *kamiks*, or boots, of sealskin, soled with the heavier skin of the square-flipper seal. 1922 *Chambers's Jrnl.* 425/1 Untying the upper part of his *kamik*, or long boot.

Kämmererite (ke·mĕrĕrəit). *Min.* [ad. G. *kämmererit* (1841), in honour of Dr. A. A. *Kämmerer* of St. Petersburg: see -ite [1].] A reddish variety of penninite containing chromium.

1868 Dana *Min.* (ed. 5) 495. 1879 *Min. Mag.* II. 23 Massive granular Kammererite..in considerable quantity. 1883 *Encycl. Brit.* XVI. 414/1 Kämmererite, with 5 to 8 chromium sesquioxide, is violet-blue or green.

Kana (kā·nă). Also 8 **canna, kanno.** [Jap.] Japanese syllabic writing, the chief varieties of which are *Hiragana and *Katakana.

1727 Scheuchzer tr. *Kæmpfer's Hist. Japan* I. iv. 68 The Names of the Provinces..are only in their *Canna*, or common Writing. *Ibid.* IV. iv. 305 Publish'd in the vulgar characters, call'd *Kanno.* 1873 *Trans. Asiatic Soc. Japan* I. 94 The invention of the Japanese syllable *kana* ten centuries ago. 1878 *Ibid.* (1879) VII. 101 It is supposed that he is responsible for the *kana* readings given by the side of the Chinese text. *Ibid.* 230 The *kana* in the Kozhiki and Nihongi are the earliest examples of the use of Chinese characters by the Japanese as phonetic symbols. 1931 Yardley *Amer. Black Chamber* 194 Every time I..saw this benevolent-faced whiskered old missionary as he puzzled over Japanese words, *kana* and code groups.

Kanarese, variant of *Canarese.

Kanat (kanā·t). Also **kanaut.** [Pers., a. Arab. قناة *qanāt.*] In Persia, an underground channel.

1894 Safar Nameh *Persian Pict.* 81 A kanat which is carrying water to many gardens. 1902 P. M. Sykes *Ten Thous. Miles in Persia* iv. 44 A heavy shower or a sandstorm frequently choking up the *kanāt.* 1902 Earl of Ronaldshay *Sport & Politics under Eastern Sky* 364 Our road took us along the *karez* or *kanat* which brought water from the mountains at the head of the plain.

Kandyan (kæ·ndiăn), *a.* and *sb.* Also **Kandian.** [f. *Kandy, Candy*, in Ceylon.] Belonging to (a native or inhabitant of) Kandy (Candy).

1849 in T. Skinner *Fifty Yrs. Ceylon* (1891) 220 Robberies and bloodshed became familiar to the Kandyan. 1883 J. Ferguson *Ceylon* 129 The Kandyan Buddhist temples. *Ibid.* 138 Of nothing is the elephant so much afraid as of fire, and with nothing will a Kandyan approach a wild elephant so readily. 1891 T. Skinner *Fifty Yrs. Ceylon* 30 My raw untaught Kandians. 1892 C. F. Gordon-Cumming *Two Happy Years in Ceylon* I. 255 Most of the chiefs who attended the reception could talk more or less English, but the ladies were as deficient therein as we were in Kandyan. 1923 J. A. Gibson *Cinnamon & Frangipanni* 23 Some of the real old Kandyan brass.

Kang, variant of Cangue, cang.

1928 H. Lamb *Genghis Khan* 27 Targoutai..commanded that a *kang* be put upon him—a wooden yoke resting on the shoulders and holding the wrists of a captive prisoned at both ends.

Kangaroo, *sb.* Add: **3. g.** Applied to a form of Parliamentary closure by which some amendments are selected for discussion and others excluded.

1913 *Q. Rev.* Apr. 551 The 'kangaroo' or selection by the Chairman of Committee of the amendments to be discussed. 1927 *Daily Express* 10 May 2/7 No attempt will be made by the Government to introduce the guillotine or kangaroo method of closure for some days.

4. b. kangaroo mouse (earlier examples); **kangaroo rat** *U.S.*, a variety of pouched rat; **kangaroo ship** (see quot.).

1867 *Amer. Naturalist* I. 394 They are known in the vernacular as 'Kangaroo' or 'Jumping' Rats and Mice, and are entirely confined to Transmississippian regions. 1876 Joaquin Miller *First Families* xxx. 243 Wood-rats, kangaroo-mice..had gone into winter-quarters under the great logs. 1922 H. Jenkins *John Dene of Toronto* ii. 32 'A "mother",' he explained, 'is a kangaroo-ship, a dry-dock ship for salvage and repair of submarines.'

Kanickanick, etc., = Kinnikinic.

1839 J. K. Townsend *Narr. Rocky Mts.* ii. 146 He smokes the article called *kanikanik*,—a mixture of tobacco and the dried leaves of the poke plant. 1847 C. Lanman *Summer in Wilderness* xiv. 87 A bag of ka-nick-a-nick and tobacco was circulated and a cloud of fragrant smoke ascended to the sky.

Kanjar (kæ·ndʒaɪ). A generic term for certain small gipsy communities which wander about India.

1875 *Encycl. Brit.* III. 508/1 The aboriginal tribes consist of the Bhars, Cherus, Dhāngars, Kanjhārs, Kharwārs, Kols. 1885 *Ibid.* XVIII. 72/1 The Nats and Kanjars wander like gipsies over the country. 1916 R. V. Russell & Hira Lal *Tribes & Castes Central India* III. 333 The Kanjars and Berias are the typical gipsy castes of India.

Kans (kāns). *India.* A common Indian grass, *Saccharum spontaneum*, allied to the sugar-cane.

1874 *E. F. T. Atkinson's Statist. Descr. N.-W. Prov. India* I. 89 The very destructive weed *kāns*..yields a good coarse grass for thatching. 1880 *Encycl. Brit.* XI. 423/1 Agriculturists suffer much from the spread of the *kāns* grass, a noxious weed which overruns the fields and is found to be almost ineradicable.

Kansan (kæ·nzăn), *a.* *Geol.* [f. *Kansas*, one of the United States + -an.] Denoting the second epoch of the glacial period in N. America, the deposits of which are found in Kansas. Also *sb.* (*a*) = *Kansan drift, age, formation*, etc.; (*b*) = next.

1894 J. Geikie *Gt. Ice Age* (ed. 3) 755 The name Kansan formation is selected..as a convenient designation of the outermost drift sheet. 1906 Chamberlin & Salisbury *Geol.* III. 389 The tract where the Illinoian till sheet overlaps the Kansan. *Ibid.* 391 Like the Kansan drift, the Illinoian is made up of clayey till. 1924 C. Schuchert *Geol.* 654 Second or Kansan glacial stage. 1924 Mack Cretcher (*title*) The Kansan.

Kansian (kæ·nziăn). [f. as prec. + -ian.] A native or inhabitant of the State of Kansas.

1878 J. H. Beadle *Western Wilds* ix. 133 Discount sixty per cent when a Kansian talks about snakes. 1879 Whitman *Specimen Days* (1892) 141 We found a train ready and a crowd of hospitable Kansians to take us on to Lawrence.

Kanuck, variant of Canuck.

Kaoliang (kē·o͡ulyæŋ). [Chinese; lit. 'high grain'.] The Indian millet, *Sorghum vulgare.*

1904 *Westm. Gaz.* 5 Sept. 7/1 The kao-ling (millet). 1906 *Offic. Hist. Russo-Jap. War* I. (1909) 56 The advanced guard..erected screens of *kao-liang* and trees at every point. 1923 *Chambers's Jrnl.* 40/2, I found the god of rain..glaring at me from the middle of a parched kaoliang patch. 1928 *Brit. Chem. Abstracts* B. 443 A relatively easy-bleaching soda pulp can be obtained from the stalk of 'Kaoliang'.

Karanteen (kæ·răntīn). *S. Africa.* Also **-ine.** The Natal name of the fish *Sargus cervinus.*

1905 *Natal Mercury Pictorial* 334 (Pettman) The fish pictured to-day is a Karantine. It is a local species, and so far as I know has not been classified. 1930 C. L. Biden *Sea-Angling Fishes of Cape* 62 Mackerel, mullet, sardine, and bamboo-fish (Natal karanteen) are the best lures.

Karez (kă·rez). [Pers. (whence Pushtu) كاريز *kārez.*] In Afghanistan = *Kanat.

1875 *Encycl. Brit.* I. 232/1 The water of the *kārez*, or subterranean canals. 1880 *Ibid.* XIII. 836/2 Irrigation by 'karez' is also largely resorted to. 1920 *Blackw. Mag.* Feb. 246/2 Then I planned a *kareez*, a subterranean water-cut. 1924 *Glasgow Herald* 29 May 9 The Persian husbandmen had even begun to repair and refit their wonderful 'Karezes'.

Karlowitz, variant of *Carlowitz.

1892 W. & A. Gilbey *Price List Wines* 9 Castle Hungarian Claret Karlowitz.

Karst (kāst). The name of a barren limestone plateau between Carniola and the Adriatic, marked by abrupt ridges, caverns, sinks, and underground streams; used in *Phys. Geog.* to designate a region or scenery of similar type.

1894 *Geog. Jrnl.* June 509 The country has to be divided into..the Karst mountains, the slate formation, and the plains. 1895 *Ibid.* Oct. 382 The Karst-forms of the glaciers of the Austrian Alps. 1899 *Ibid.* Apr. 427 Dr. Cvijic..is well known for his useful monograph on the phenomena of the 'Karst'. 1900 *Ibid.* Feb. 174 The lake itself is of the nature of a 'Karst' lake. 1911 *Encycl. Brit.* XV. 683/2 As this structure always, wherever found, gives rise to similar features, a landscape of this character is called a Karst landscape. 1914 G. A. J. Cole *Growth Eur.* xiii. 236 The term *karstland* is applied to this scenic type. 1931 J. B. Scrivenor *Geol. Malaya* 54 The wonderful *karst* scenery of towering limestone hills with perpendicular and overhanging cliffs.

Karyo-. Add: **Karyo·gamy** [Gr. -γαμια marriage], the union or fusion of nuclei. **Ka·ryomere, Karyo·merite** [Gr. μέρος part], a nucleolus which serves as a temporary repository for a chromosome. **Karyo·mitome, Karyo·miton,** the nuclear network or reticulum. **Karyoplasma·tic, -pla·smic** *adjs.*, of or pertaining to the karyoplasm.

1901 G. N. Calkins *Protozoa* 90 Numerous phenomena of plastogamy and *karyogamy. 1920 W. E. Agar *Cytol.* 72 The condition of the gametic nuclei..at the moment of karyogamy or nuclear fusion. *Ibid.* 130 The chromosomes of the spermatogonial telophases do not come into contact at all, but each one forms a separate little nucleus, or *karyomere, by itself. 1889 tr. Waldeyer in *Q. Jrnl. Microsc. Sci.* XXX. 247 The definite segmentation-nucleus..arises by the envelopes (or body) of the *karyo- and spermato-merites. 1902 *Encycl. Brit.* XXV. 392/2 The other part of the *karyomiton* or nuclear net is incapable of being stained. 1920 L. Doncaster *Introd. Study Cytol.* 14 The theory of R. Hertwig that in any species the volume of the nucleus bears a fixed ratio to the volume of the cytoplasm dependent on it. This theory, known as that of the 'karyoplasmatic ratio'. *Ibid.* 16 Hertwig..supposes that the unequal rate of growth of nucleus and cytoplasm brings about a condition of 'karyoplasmatic strain' leading to cell-division. 1924 *E. V. Cowdry's Gen. Cytol.* 351 Hertwig's *karyoplasmic relation hypothesis.

Kasha (kæ·ʃă). Proprietary name (Rodier, Paris) for a soft woollen fabric. Also in various combs. (see quots.).

1923 *Daily Mail* 12 Feb. 15 White Kasha cloth. 1924 *Westm. Gaz.* 30 Sept., The soft consistency of kasha and the ease with which it takes on colour. 1925 *Queen* 27 May 14 The sports suit above is of kasha and printed silk. 1926 *Ibid.* 10 Feb. 13 A kasha jumper in a plain matching shade. *Ibid.* 17 Feb. 10 A modified Inverness coat made by Lelong in the new kasha with the slightly spongy surface—kashatoile. 1928 *Observer* 4 Mar. 20/4 The couturiers..give prominence to jersey, crêpella, Kashatoil, Kashangora, and a host of other materials. 1928 *Daily Express* 27 July 5/3 Kashajouraia..has an openwork drawn-thread design in kasha jersey.

Kashmir (kæ·ʃmɪ͡ə). A more phonetic variant of *Cashmere* (see Cashmere); used *attrib.* Hence **Kashmiri** (kæʃmɪ͡ə·ri), a native of Kashmir, the language of Kashmir; **Kashmi·rian.**

1879 C. F. Gordon Cumming *From Hebrides to Himalayas* II. 309 Kashmerians, Persians, Paharis, Hindus of every possible sect. 1880 *Encycl. Brit.* XIII. 821/2 The language distinct from Turki, Persian, Hindi, and Kashmiri. 1882 *Ibid.* XIV. 498/2 Families of Chinese and Kashmiris. 1887 J. M. Brown *Shikar Sketches* 237 The Kashmir stag—cervus Cashmeriensis. 1891 'L. Malet' *Wages of Sin* v. vii, The Kashmiree beauties. 1925 A. G. Arbuthnot in G. Burrard *Big Game Hunting* 126 A very old Kashmir shikari.

Katabatic (kætăbæ·tik), *a.* *Meteorol.* [ad. Gr. καταβατικός affording a means of descent, f. καταβαίνειν to go down.] Of a wind: Caused by the local gravitation of cold air down a steep slope.

1918 *Meteorological Gloss.* 182 A local cold wind is called Katabatic if it is caused by the gravitation of cold air off high ground. 1930 W. G. Kendrew *Climate* 75.

Katakana (katăkā·nă). [Jap., = side *kana.*] The variety of the Japanese syllabary the characters of which are derived from Chinese ideographs of the corresponding sounds.

1822 tr. *Titsingh's Illustr. Japan* 194 These works, published in the learned language, *Gago*, with the *kata-kana*, or women's letters, have been re-printed expressly for them. 1928 Sansom *Hist. Gram. Jap.* 45 At some period in the development of the script, probably about the time when the *hiragana* and *katakana* syllabaries were contrived.

Katalase, variant of *Catalase.

Ka·tathermo·meter (kætă-). [Gr. κατά down.] A thermometer invented by Dr. Leonard Hill which indicates the cooling and evaporating power of the air. Also shortened to **Kata.**

1915 L. Hill in *Phil. Trans.* Ser. B. CCVII. 185 The kata-thermometer..is an instrument designed primarily for the measurement of its own rate of cooling when its temperature approximates to that of the human body. *Ibid.* 188 The dry-bulb kata. *Ibid.* 191 The kata scale. 1925 T. H. Somervell in E. F. Norton *Fight for Everest, 1924* 356 Records of barometer, katathermometer, etc. 1930 W. G. Kendrew *Climate* 189 The conditions of a perspiring body may be imitated by surrounding the bulb of the katathermometer with wet muslin.

Hence **Ka·tathermome·tric** *a.*

1923 *Med. Res. Council, Spec. Rep.* No. 73. 90 A katathermometric comparison of methods of heating and ventilation.

Kathete (kæ·þīt), anglicized f. *kathetus*, Cathetus.

1912 G. Kapp *Electr.* viii. 210 The well-known Pythagorean axiom that the sum of the squares of the kathetes in a rectangular triangle is equal to the square of the hypotenuse.

Katydid. (Earlier and later examples.) See also *Catydid.

1784 J. F. D. Smyth *Tour U.S.* II. 387 There is a very singular insect in this island [*sc.* Long Island], which I do not remember to have observed in any other part of America. They are named by the inhabitants here *Katy did's*, from their note, which is loud and strong, bearing a striking resemblance to those words. 1828 S. Woodworth *Evening*, And from each thicket, marsh, and tree The cricket, frog, and Katydee With various notes assist the glee. 1870 *Scribner's Monthly* I. 164 The Katydids began to drone on the bark. 1886 *Outing* (U.S.) IX. 106/2 Soon the chiding katydids mingled their voices with the rush of the foaming river. 1909 *Springfield* (Mass.) *Weekly Republ.* 16 Sept. 1 All around the globe people are like katydids, saying he did and he didn't in an endless reiteration.

Kawai, variant of *Kahawai.

Kawaka (kawaka). [Maori.] A New Zealand pinaceous tree, the cypress cedar, *Libocedrus doniana.*

1840 J. S. Polack *New Zealanders* II. 261 The Kawaka grows to the height of thirty feet. 1855 R. Taylor *Te Ika a Maui* 440. 1884 *Encycl. Brit.* XXIV. 469/2.

Kawa-kawa (kawakawa). Also **kauá kaua, kava-kava.** [Maori.] An ornamental shrub, *Macropiper* (*Piper*) *excelsum*, of New Zealand.

1838 J. S. Polack *New Zealand* I. 295 The Kauá kauá, or kává (bitter), of the Friendly Islands. 1850 Jos. Greenwood *Journ. Taupo* 30 A most refreshing light beverage made from the leaves of the Kawa-kawa tree. 1855 R. Taylor *Te Ika a Maui* 437. 1888 *Jrnl. Chem. Soc.* LIV. 1207 Kawa-kawa, or *Macropiper methysticum.* 1895 *Buck's Handbk. Med. Sci.* IX. 564/1 Kava-Kava. 1927 Donne *The Maori* 183 The green leaf of the *kawa-kawa* or pepper tree.

Kazoo, *v.* [f. the sb.] *intr.* To blow with a sound like that of a kazoo.

1909 R. A. Wason *Happy Hawkins* xxvi, The storm that was presently kazooin' along was fierce an' horrible.

Keatsian (kī·tsiăn), *a.* and *sb.* Also **Keatsean.** [f. name of John *Keats*, English poet (1795–1821) + -ian.] Of, pertaining to, or characteristic of Keats or his poetry. **b.** *sb.* An admirer of Keats.

1846 T. Wade *Let. to R. M. Milnes* 26 May (Crewe MS.) A Keats-ian poem. 1891 *Athenæum* 23 May 667/3 A little manuscript book..of some interest to Keatsians. 1900 H. B. Forman in *Keats's Works* III. 112 He [*sc.* Woodhouse] opens with a Keatsian enough punctuation of the first four lines. 1908 T. Watts-Dunton in C. Wells *Joseph & his Brethren* Introd. p. xxviii, A Keatsean exuberance of colour and gorgeousness of description. 1914— in *Keats Letters* (ed. G. C. Williamson) 16 It was the American Keatseans who, as far back as July 16, 1894, erected in Hampstead Parish Church a memorial bust to the poet.

Kebleh, var. Kiblah (Mecca).

1902 M. Roberts *Immortal Youth* i. 1 Ah, yes, to be in London, at the centre of things,..at the kebleh of the universe.

Keebaub, var. Kabob, Cabob. (Cf. *Kibaub.)

a 1861 Winthrop *John Brent* xii. 129 Mr. Clitheroe was like a lamb whom the shepherd intends first to shear close..and at last to cut up into keebaubs.

Keel, *sb.*[1] Add: **3. b.** In aircraft, a vertical fin which extends longitudinally underneath in order to give directional stability. Also *attrib.*

1888 *Peel City Guardian* 22 Sept. 3/3 Connecting the balloon with the arrow-like rod beneath is a keel of the same material as that composing the body of the balloon. 1907 C. Dienstback in *Navigating the Air* Introd. p. xxxix, A multiplicity of 'keels' which might be called 'barbarian' if compared to American moderation. 1915 W. E. Dommett *Aeroplanes & Airships* 96 At the bottom of the metal framework is a V-shaped keel. 1926 H. Barber *Aeroplane Speaks* 70 For such directional stability to exist there must be, in effect, more 'keel-surface' behind the vertical axis than there is in front of it. By keel-surface I mean everything to be seen when looking at an aeroplane from the side of it—the sides of the body, undercarriage, struts, wires, etc. 1922 *Encycl. Brit.* XXX. 54/1 R 27 and R 29..were remarkable for the absence of the keel which had existed in all previous rigid airships and had been looked upon as constituting the real strength of the ship to resist bending and shearing forces. 1929 F. H. & H. F. Colvin *Aircraft Handbk.* (ed. 4) 652 *Keel* (airship)—the assembly of members at the bottom of the hull of a semirigid or rigid airship which provides special strength to resist hogging and sagging and also serves to distribute the effect of concentrated loads along the hull. It may be a simple Gall's chain, as in some semirigids, or a very extensive structure inclosing the corridor, as in most rigids.

Keel-boat. **b.** *U.S.* (Earlier and later examples.)

1801 *Massachusetts Spy* 25 Nov. (Th.), 440 flat-boats, 26 keel boats, and 7 large canoes. 1802 A. Ellicott *Jrnl.* 5 He had two boats ready, one of them flat-bottomed..the other a second hand keel-boat. 1819 W. B. Dewees *Lett. fr. Texas* i. 9, I took water on board a large keel boat at Nashville, Tennessee. 1847 H. Howe *Hist. Collect. Ohio* 143 Auglaize is navigable for keel boats to Wapakoneta. 1853 *Daily Morning Herald* (St. Louis) 23 June (Th.) A well-manned little keel-boat or pierrogue might have accomplished the voyage. 1874 E. Eggleston *Circuit Rider* xxvii. 266 A stranger..reported that he had seen such a man on a keel-boat.

Hence **Keel-boatman** *U.S.*, one who works on a keel-boat.

1839 *Knickerbocker Mag.* XIII. 344 A..keel-boatman..saw a steam-boat gallantly paddling up against the centre current of that 'Father of Rivers'. 1843 *American Pioneer* II. 272 The keel-boatman regarded the flat-boatman and raftsmen with great contempt. 1883 'Mark Twain' *Life Mississippi* iii. 41 The keelboatman became a deck hand, or a mate.

Keeled, *a.* Add: **a.** (Earlier U.S. example.)

1781 *Cal. Virginia St. Papers* I. 493 They [*sc.* light Batteaux] will run over shoals, where a Keel'd Vessel must be carried.

c. *Keeled scraper*, a form of prehistoric flint. (F. *grattoir caréné.*)

1911 W. J. Sollas *Anc. Hunters* viii. 218 Carefully flaked like the snout of the keeled scraper. 1921 M. C. Burkitt *Prehistory* iv. 75 *Keeled scrapers.* This tool..is very common in Middle Aurignacian times. It has a flat under surface, from which the flakes on the upper surface are struck off in a fan-shaped manner.

Keen, *a.* **6.** Add: By an extension of the use in *keen competition*, etc. the commercial use of *keen prices*, etc. has arisen (cf. *Keenly *adv.* 6).

Kee·ner[2]. *Western U.S.* [f. Keen *a.* + -er [1].] One who drives a hard bargain.

1859 Bartlett *Dict. Amer.*, *Keener*, a very shrewd person, one sharp at a bargain, what in England would be called 'a keen hand'. *Western.* 1871 Schele de Vere *Americanisms* (1872) 496 *Keener*, a noun made from the adjective, is a Western term for a sharp man. 'I tell you he is a keener, you can't get on his blind side'.

Keenly, *adv.* Add:

6. *Comm.* At a cut price, cheaply.

1928 *Daily Express* 28 Aug. 7 With advantages like this we can quote more keenly.

Keep, *sb.* Add:

4. f. A strip or block to prevent a piece from moving beyond its proper position.

1833 Loudon *Encycl. Archit.* § 1108 The door-frames..to have keeps (stops) three quarters of an inch thick, and of proper breadth.

7. b. Cricket. *To play* (*for*) *keeps*: to play a defensive game in order to remain at the wicket. orig. *Austral.*

1882 Pardon *Australians in Eng.* 109 They don't 'play for keeps', as the Australians call it. 1904 *Daily Chron.* 9 July 7/3 The last five batsmen are men who do not play 'keeps' if they are to make runs, they make them quickly. *Ibid.* 11 Aug. 7/2 This enabled Ranjitsinhji to play his proper game, after having been obliged to play 'keeps' for so long. 1926 Strudwick *25 Yrs. behind Stumps* 82 England batted all day for 221. 'Playing for keeps', one paper said.

Keep, *v.* Add:

16. d. *To keep wicket* (see Wicket 3). Also *absol.* To act as wicket-keeper.

1887 F. Gale *Game of Cricket* 263. 1920 P. F. Warner *Cricket Remin.* 161 Lockyer 'kept' for the Players on and off between 1854 and 1866. 1931 *N. & Q.* 14 Feb. 121/2 Alfred [Lyttelton], of course, 'kept' for England.

35. (U.S. examples of *to keep school.*)

1847 *Knickerbocker Mag.* XXX. 511 A girl whose education does not qualify her for 'keeping school'. 1849 E. Chamberlain *Indiana Gazetteer* 196 There are in the County..school houses in which schools are kept, a portion of the year, in most of the school districts. 1867 'T. Lackland' *Homespun* II. 264 Mr. John Porringer..'kept' this school, and was in the way of keeping it so long as he lived and liked.

38. b. Of a school: To be held. *U.S.*

1845 *Knickerbocker Mag.* XXVI. 277 One afternoon, when 'school didn't keep', some one got into the house. 1867 'T. Lackland' *Homespun* I. 123 The District School has not 'kept' since the week began.

52. Keep out. c. *intr.* To 'stay outside', hold aloof.

1924 H. H. Asquith in W. R. Inge *Lay Thoughts* (1926) 127 [As Mr. Asquith said in August, 1914], 'if we had kept out we should have been left without a friend in the world'.

57. Keep up. Add: **l.** To continue to maintain a friendship or intimacy; to keep in touch. (Cf. 57 f.)

1916 E. V. Lucas *Vermilion Box* xliii. 45 Two of my oldest friends...Both went straight into the army, but we had kept up.

Keeper. Add: **1. f.** A wicket-keeper.

1868 *J. Lillywhite's Cricketers' Comp.* 49. 1920 P. F. Warner *Cricket* (Badm.) 163 The best 'keeper' in England. 1926 Strudwick *25 Yrs. behind Stumps* 244 There were very few, if any, better keepers than the Notts man.

So **Keeping** *vbl. sb.*

1868 in Bettesworth *Walkers of Southgate* (1900) 291. 1920 P. F. Warner *Cricket Remin.* 156 His [*sc.* Blackham's] keeping to Mr. Spofforth with the 1878 Australian XI. was a revelation.

Keeping-room. (Earlier U.S. example.)

1771 Copley in *Copley-Pelham Lett.* (1914) 141, I forget weither or not there was to be a Closit in the Keeping Room.

Keeshond (kē·shǫnd). Also **-hound.** [Du.] A wolf-coloured dog very popular in Holland.

1927 E. C. Ash *Dogs* I. 159 The keeshond is the well-known Dutch dog, often seen on the barges. 1927 *Daily Express* 15 June 15 The Keeshounds, Dutch dogs,..were shown in this country for the first time. They are about the size of a Chow, grey black in colour, exceedingly strong.

Keewatin (kīwā·tin). *Geol.* [The name of a district in Canada.] A group or series of the Archæan in Canada.

1885 A. C. Lawson in *Ann. Rep. Geol. & Nat. Hist. Surv. Canada* I. 14 cc, The most appropriate name for the series that suggests itself to me is 'Keewatin', the Indian name for the North-west, or the North-west wind, which has been applied to the district within which the rocks occur. 1906 Chamberlin & Salisbury *Geol.* III. 330 The extension of the Kewatin ice-sheet to the southward. 1913 F. D. Adams *Problems Canadian Shield* (1915) 59 The widely extended Keewatin series.

Kee-wee, variant of *Kiwi.

Kehoeite (kīhō͡u·əit). *Min.* [Named after H. *Kehoe* its discoverer: see -ite [1].] Hydrous phosphate of aluminium and zinc, amorphous, and white in colour.

1893 W. P. Headden in *Amer. Jrnl. Sci.* Ser. III. XLVI. 22. 1893 *Jrnl. Chem. Soc.* LXIV. II. 537 Kehoeite, a new Phosphate from Dakota.

Kello·vian, variant of *Callovian.

1838 J. Prestwich *Geol.* II. 9 Kellovian Limestones and Marls.

Kelp[1]. **4.** Add: **kelp-crab,** a spider-crab, *Epialtus productus*, found on the coast of California.

1887 G. B. Goode etc. *Fisheries U.S.* v. II. 637 The kelp crab..is eaten by the Indians.

Ke·lpie[2]. An Australian breed of dogs (see quot.).

1930 Hancock *Australia* xiii. 289 The Australian kelpie, bred from judicious crossing of smooth-haired Scots collie (with a slight strain of fox), and the native dingo.

Kelvin. (ke·lvin). [Named after Sir William Thomson, Lord *Kelvin* (1824–1907).]

1. The kilowatt-hour, the ordinary commercial unit of electric energy.

1892 *Electrician* XXIX. 1 The President of the Board of Trade having cordially approved and Lord Kelvin having acquiesced; after the word 'unit' in the Provisional Orders of this year, the words 'hereinafter called a kelvin' will be introduced. 1911 *Encycl. Brit.* XXVII. 740/1, 3600 kilowatt-seconds or 1 kilowatt-hour is called a 'Board of Trade unit' or a 'kelvin'.

2. The scale of absolute temperature. In full *Kelvin scale.*

Kenai (kī·nəi). *Geol.* [The name of a peninsula in S. Alaska.] A Tertiary series in Alaska.

1906 Chamberlin & Salisbury *Geol.* III. 248 Certain fossiliferous beds of western Greenland seem to be of the same age as the Kenai series. 1924 C. Schuchert *Geol.* 596 Throughout Alaska and extending into British Columbia occurs the wide-spread Kenai formation of continental character.

Kenion, early variant of Canyon.

1846 J. W. Webb *Altowan* I. viii. 216 A ravine on the right deepening into a kenion.

Kenite (kī·nəit). [-ite [1].] A member of a tribe of S. Palestine, perhaps a branch of the Midianites. Also *attrib.*

1535 Coverdale *Gen.* xv. 19 The Kenytes, the Kenizites, the Kydmonites. — *Judg.* iv. 11 Heber the Kenyte. 1876 *Encycl. Brit.* IV. 763/1 The aboriginal Rephaim and three Arab tribes, the Kenites, Kenizzites, and Kadmonites. 1911 *Ibid.* XV. 729/2 Moses himself married into a Kenite family (Judges i. 16).

Kennel, *sb.*[1] **3.** Add: *kennel-companion, -friend; kennel-maid, -work;* **kennel lameness,** a rheumatic disease in hounds.

1876 *Coursing Calendar* 9 Miss Ellen and Hamilla..the pair being *kennel companions. 1889 Gretton *Memory's Harkback* 228 After sufficient time to get acquainted with their new *kennel-friends, they were taken out with the pack. 1841 R. T. Vyner *Notitia Venat.* 45 *Kennel-lameness, or shoulder-lameness, as it is sometimes called. 1885 Dk. Beaufort & M. Morris *Hunting* (Badm.) 112 That mortal scourge which among men is known as rheumatism, and among hounds as kennel lameness. 1930 *Fox-hunting* (Lonsdale Libr.) viii. 108 Through this cause they appear to stiffen up, which is mistaken for kennel lameness. 1907 *Westm. Gaz.* 5 July 9/1 In the lady's service was the prisoner, who occupied the position of *kennel-maid. 1929 *Daily Express* 16 Jan. 5/2 The showing of dogs is skilled work for a kennelmaid. *Ibid.*, *Kennelwork as a career for educated girls.

Keno. (Earlier example.) Also *Comb.*: **keno establishment,** ranch, a gambling-house.

1871 *Figaro* 15 Apr., The police pulled every Keno establishment in the city. 1873 J. H. Beadle *Undevel. West* iv. 95 This game, like keno, has less of the 'cutthroat' about it than the others. 1889 K. Munroe *Golden Days* iv. 40 We'll have a drawin' over in Slim Jim's keno ranch.

b. As an exclamation.

1884 [see Dict.]. 1907 Mulford *Bar-20* xix. 193 He wants to know where th' cards are stacked an' why he can't holler 'Keno'. 1908— *Orphan* vii. 87 Bill turned his head, and one eye closed in an emphatic wink. 'Keno', he replied. 1924 —*Rustler's Valley* vi. 75 'If yo're goin' out to Milt you better take some rupplies..' 'Keno', grunted Matt, departing.

Kenotron (ke·nŏtrǫn). *Electr.* [f. Gr. κενός empty + -τρον, denoting instrument.] A thermionic valve exhausted to a high vacuum, with an incandescent filament as cathode and an anode of tungsten or molybdenum, acting as a rectifier.

1915 I. Langmuir in *Electrician* 21 May 242/1 A kenotron has been built capable of rectifying 250 milliamperes at 180,000 volts. 1919 J. A. Fleming *Thermionic Valve* 74 The result has been the production of what may be called an ideally perfect Fleming Valve, which highly exhausted valve,..has been rechristened a Kenotron. 1920 *Nature* 8 Jan. 462/1. 1926 S. O. Pearson *Dict. Wireless Terms* 113.

Kent, *sb.*[2] (Earlier example.)

1820 Scoresby *Acc. Arctic Reg.* II. 296 The fat of the neck, or what corresponds in other animals with the neck, is called the Kent.

Kent, *v.*[2] (Earlier example.)

1820 Scoresby *Acc. Arctic Reg.* II. 296 By means of it, the fish is turned over or kented.

Kentia (ke·ntiă). *Bot.* [mod.L. (Blume, 1836), f. the surname *Kent*: see -ia [1].] Any of several greenhouse palms, formerly referred to the genus of this name, native to Australia and the East Indies, now referred to other genera, as *Areca, Hedyscepe, Howea*, etc.

[1879 *Encycl. Brit.* IX. 779/2 There are 4 palms, among them the *Kentia* of Fiji.] 1909 *Westm. Gaz.* 8 Jan. 9/2 Over 1,000 Kentia palms from the South Sea Islands. 1923 *Chambers's Jrnl.* 255/1 There are four kinds of kentia palms—the thatch, the curly, the umbrella, and the mountain.

Kentuck, abbreviation of *Kentucky, chiefly used *attrib* or as *sb.* = *Kentuckian.

a. 1789 *Massachusetts Spy* 11 June (Th.) A Kentuck boat of 40 feet long. 1834 W. A. Carruthers *Kentuckian in N.Y.* I. 24 A quid of the real Kentuck twist. 1841 *Southern Lit. Messenger* VII. 53/2 A segment of an old Virginia hoe-cake...In Kentuck phrase 'would not be bad *toe* take.'

b. 1835 J. H. Ingraham *South-West* I. ix. 105 Here are congregated the primitive navies of Indiana, Ohio, and the adjoining States, manned..by 'real Kentucks'. 1851 Lady E. C. E. Stuart Wortley *Trav. U.S.* xxvi. 173 The mammoth cave in dear 'Old Kentuck'.

Kentuckian (kentʊ·kiăn), *a.* and *sb.* Also 8–9 **Kentuckyan.** [f. next.] **a.** *adj.* Of or belonging to Kentucky. **b.** *sb.* An inhabitant or native of Kentucky.

1784 T. Jefferson *Writ.* (1894) III. 401 Should..the Indianians and Kentuckians take themselves off. 1810 *Niles' Weekly Register* III. 396/2 The brave Kentuckyans have done their duty. 1827 J. F. Cooper *Prairie* iii, It is part of the religion of a Kentuckian to fret himself a little at a mischance. 1852 Mrs. Stowe *Uncle Tom's C.* xi, Great, tall, raw-boned Kentuckians, attired in hunting shirts. 1880 Cable *Grandissimes* xii. 75 One of those Kentuckian dealers in corn and tobacco.

Kentucky (kentʊ·ki). Also 8–9 **Kentucke.** [From the name of the river; the original meaning of this is uncertain.] One of the southern United States, lying south of the Ohio River and east of the Mississippi. Used *attrib.*, as *Kentucky cattle, forest, horse, jean, rose, shore;* **Kentucky bluegrass,** *Poa pratensis;* **Kentucky boat,** an ark or flat-boat; **Kentucky clover,** *Trifolium reflexum;* **Kentucky coffee** (bean, tree), mahogany, a tall tree, *Gymnocladus dioica*, the seeds of which are used as a substitute for coffee; **Kentucky flat** = *Kentucky boat;* **Kentucky warbler,** a common warbler of the eastern U.S., *Geothlypis formosa.*

1796 A. Ellicott in *Life & Lett.* (1908) 140 Discovered a *Kentucky boat fast upon a log. 1832 *Louisville Directory* 103 The ark or flat boat, often known as the Kentucky boat. 1858 D. K. Bennett *Chron. N. Carolina* 86 We met 373 head of *Kentucky cattle in one drove. 1785 Washington *Diaries* II. 426 Sowed about a tablespoonful of the Buffalo or *Kentucke Clover. 1857 A. Gray *Man. Bot.* (1860) 109 *Kentucky Coffee-tree. 1859 Bartlett *Dict. Amer.* (ed. 3), *Kentucky Coffee*...A large tree, resembling the locust tree, bearing a pod with berries which are used for coffee. 1829 S. Cummings *Western Pilot* 7 The *Kentucky Flat, or Family boat. 1837 R. M. Bird *Nick of the Woods* I. 216 Thee is in a wild *Kentucky forest. 1881 *Harper's Mag.* Apr. 730/2 The two *Kentucky horses were trotting along the beach. 1835 J. H. Ingraham *South-West* II. 175 Pantaloons of *Kentucky jean. 1843 R. Carlton *New Purchase* xi. 73 A Kentucky-jean vest. 1846 *Knickerbocker Mag.* XXVIII. 38 The *Kentucky rose is not excelled..for the plentitude of its blossoms. 1828 J. Hall *Lett. from West* 141 About sunset we landed our boat on the *Kentucky shore. 1860 S. F. Baird, etc. *Birds N. Amer.* 247 *Oporornis Formosus*, *Kentucky Warbler. 1872 E. Coues *N. Amer. Birds* 106 Kentucky Warbler. Clear olive-green; entire under parts bright yellow.

Kenyte (kī·nəit). *Petrol.* [f. Mt. *Kenya* in British East Africa + -ite [1].] A black volcanic rock, a variety of alkali-trachyte containing anorthoclase.

1900 J. W. Gregory in *Q. Jrnl. Geol. Soc.* May 212 One of the most interesting rocks in this kenyte-series is a black porphyritic pitchstone. *Ibid.* 214 The kenytes are most nearly allied to the pantellerites, but are probably as a rule more basic. 1921 H. G. Ponting *Great White South* 103 A monolith of Kenyte.

Kepler's laws: see Law *sb.*[1] 17 c (*a*).

Ker-. Add: Also **co-, che-.** (Additional examples.)

1836 *Public Ledger* (Phila.) 27 July (Th.) Down I came chewhallop..and overset the chair. 1844 'Jon. Slick' *High Life N.Y.* II. 88 We drew up co-wallop right afore Jase's house. *Ibid.* 154 Ca-smash went the chair. *Ibid.* 183 The curtain cum down ca-chunk. 1854 Mary J. Holmes *Tempest & Sunshine* 2 Then, again, you'll go in co-slush. 1896 E. Glanville *Kloof Yarns* ii. 12, I pitched head first—ker smash—in a sudden fit o' dizziness. 1923 *Public Opinion* 15 June 565/1 With both feet set down kerplunk he closed the interview.

Kerato-. Add: **Kerato·genous** *a.* [*-genous (*a*)], productive of horny tissue. **Ke·ratomala·cia, -a·kia** [Gr. μαλακία softness], morbid softening of the cornea. **Ke·ratoscope** (example).

1901 Dorland *Med. Dict.* (ed. 2), *Keratogenous. 1907 *Practitioner* Dec. 849 The keratogenous and analgesic properties of picric acid, as exhibited in the treatment of burns. 1901 Dorland *Med. Dict.* (ed. 2), *Keratomalacia. 1907 *Ophthalmoscope* Mar. 143 Two cases of keratomalacia. 1923 *Nature* 3 Feb. 163/2 Keratomalacia among rats suffering from deficiency of vitamin A. 1910 H. C. Parker *Handbk. Dis. Eye* 81 The cone is observed by inspection..with an instrument known as the *keratoscope.

Keratophyre (ke·rătŏfəiə). *Petrol.* [f. Kerato- + *-phyre*, designating porphyritic rocks.] A felsite with a large percentage of soda.

1889 F. H. Hatch in *Geol. Mag.* Feb. 71 Soda-felsites or keratophyres. 1900 H. E. Gregory *Geol. of Aroostook Volcanic Area* 163 The group of soda trachytes or keratophyres.

Keratosis (kerătō͡u·sis). *Path.* [f. Kerato- + -osis.] A disease characterized by horny growths.

1887 Jon. Hutchinson (*title*) On Some Examples of Arsenic Keratosis. 1889 *Buck's Handbk. Med. Sci.* VII. 109/2 Keratosis was applied to the condition by Kaposi, who believed it to be due to a transformation from the opaline plaque. 1926 A. M. Carr-Saunders *Eugenics* iii. 54 Keratosis (warts and callosities on the palms and the soles).

Kerb, *sb.* **2. b.** Add: *kerbside; kerb market, stocks* (see *on the kerb* in 2).

1905 *Daily Chron.* 28 Apr. 4/4 The *kerb market in New York reflects in a general way the tone of the stock market. *Ibid.* 11 Nov. 4/7 Fruit from the *kerbside barrow is marvellously cheap nowadays. 1923 *Daily Mail* 21 July 3 The growing tendency of motorists to avail themselves of kerbside pumps. 1930 *Daily Express* 30 July 2/6 *Kerb Stocks.

Kerel (ke·rəl). *S. Africa.* [Du., = Carl *sb.*[1]] A fellow, chap.

1902 J. H. M. Abbott *Tommy Cornstalk* 81 It is that 'kerel' French who is coming.

Kerogen (ke·rŏdʒen). [f. Gr. κηρός wax + -gen.] (See quot. 1906.)

1906 D. R. Steuart *Oil-shales of Lothians* III. 142 *note*, We are indebted to Professor Crum Brown, F.R.S., for suggesting the term Kerogen to express the carbonaceous matter in shale that gives rise to crude oil in distillation. 1913 H. M. Cadell *Story of Forth* 209 Wherever the oil has thus been robbed of its Kerogen, it is, of course, rendered worthless. 1923 *Nature* 17 Mar. 374/1 The marine kerogen shales from the oil-fields of Japan.

Kerosene. **b.** Add:

1891 C. Roberts *Adrift Amer.* 211 An old kerosine tin. 1909 *Westm. Gaz.* 3 Feb. 2/2 A gasolene- or kerosene-engine. 1928 *Manchester Guardian Weekly* 10 Aug. 113/4 Mr. Churchill was deeply chagrined by being compelled to withdraw his proposed kerosene tax.

Kerria (ke·riă). [mod.L.; named in 1816 by A. P. de Candolle after William *Ker*, English botanical collector.] A plant of the genus of rosaceous shrubs of this name, with golden flowers, native of Japan (cf. Corchorus 2). *White Kerria* (see quot. 1900).

1829 Loudon *Encycl. Plants* 454, 1210. 1838 R. Sweet *Brit. Flower Garden* Ser. II. IV. No. 337 Kerria japonica, Japanese Kerria. 1900 *Bk. Gardening* (ed. W. D. Drury) 407 *Rhodotypos kerrioides* (White Kerria). *Ibid.* 465 The double-flowered Kerria (*K. japonica floreplena*) is a favourite wall-shrub. 1904 R. J. Farrer *Garden Asia* 99 The golden wreaths of the bending kerria overhead.

Kerry. Add: **3.** *Kerry blue* (*terrier*), a breed of Irish terrier with a blue-grey coat.

1922 R. Leighton *Complete Bk. Dog* 239 The Kerry Blue Terrier. *Ibid.* 240 Primarily, the Kerry Terrier is a water dog. 1930 E. C. Ash *Pract. Dog Bk.* 150 The history of the Kerry Blue is not easy to obtain.

Keswick (ke·zik). [Name of a town in Cumberland, where the introducer of this apple, John Sander, lived.] In full *Keswick codlin*: A variety of cooking apple.

1813 in *Mem. Caled. Hort. Soc.* (1814) I. 374 The Carlisle and Keswick Codlin Apples. 1826 *Catal. Fruits Gard. Hortic. Soc.* 114 Codlin, Keswick. 1831 H. Ronalds *Sel. Apples* 5 Keswick Codlin. A favourite sauce apple from the North of England. 1922 Mulford & Clay *Buck Peters* xxii. 198 It's Buck as sure as little apples Kesicks.

Keta (kī·tă). Kamchatkan name of the dog-salmon, *Oncorhyncus keta* or *lagocephalus.*

1901 Annette Meakin *Ribbon of Iron* xviii, At Nikolaevsk upwards of a hundred and ninety-three thousand puds of a salmon called 'keta'—*salmo lagocephalus*—are salted annually. 1905 D. S. Jordan *Fishes* II. 73 In Japan *keta* is by far the most abundant species of salmon.

Ketazine (kī·tăzīn). *Chem.* Also **-in.** [f. Ket(one + Az(ote + -ine [1].] Any one of a class of organic compounds obtained by the action of hydrazine on ketones.

1894 *Jrnl. Chem. Soc.* LXVI. I. 348 Transformation of Ketazines into Pyrazolines.

Ketene (kī·tīn). *Chem.* Also **-en.** [f. Ketone + -ene.] A pungent colourless gas obtained by decomposing acetic anhydride with intense heat. Also applied to a group of allied compounds (see quot. 1911).

1907 Wilsmore & Stewart in *Nature* LXXV. 510/1 We would suggest that the body is the parent substance of Staudinger's ketenes. 1907 Wilsmore in *Jrnl. Chem. Soc.* XCI. II. 1939 The keten series. *Ibid.* 1941 Keten has a peculiar penetrating smell. 1911 *Encycl. Brit.* XV. 761/2 Two classes may be distinguished: the aldo-ketenes, including ketene itself,..and the keto-ketenes.

Keto- (kī·to). *Chem.* Used as combining form of Ketone, as *keto-aldehyde, -compound, -hexose;* **Ketoge·nic** *a.* (see quot.).

1891 *Proc. Chem. Soc.* VII. 91 Keto-compounds. 1902 *Encycl. Brit.* XXVI. 721/2 Keto-compounds..are converted by it [*sc.* phenylhydrazine] into hydrazones. 1930 *Sci. Amer.* Nov. 391 This is called a ketogenic diet, because it tends to produce an excessive amount of ketones and their derivatives in the blood.

Kettle. Add: **1. b.** A tea-kettle is sometimes tied by mischievous children to a dog's or cat's tail to frighten the animal. Hence *allusively.*

1928 A. Bennett *Strange Vanguard* xxx. 202 He saw that he had been cast that night for the role of kettle to a dog's tail.

4. d. (See quot.).

1895 M. Pemberton *Impreg. City* ii. 6 A small ship's launch, such as sailors call a kettle.

6. *kettle-lid; kettle-scrubber; kettle-moraine* (example); **kettle-bail** *U.S.*, a dredge used in taking scallops.

1887 G. B. Goode, etc. *Fisheries U.S.* v. II. 571 The dredge for a soft bottom differs from the other in having the 'blade' adjusted to swing in the 'eyes' of the arms in order to prevent its sinking into the mud. This is called the '*kettle-bail' style of dredge. 1903 *Edin. Rev.* Oct. 436 The wobbling of a *kettle-lid. 1894 J. Geikie *Gt. Ice Age* (ed. 3) 745 The great interlobate '*kettle moraine' formed by the combined action of the ice-lobes of Green Bay and Lake Michigan. 1843 Thackeray *Ballads, Peg of Limavaddy* xii, That sweet *kettle-scrubber.

Kettle-bottom. 2. (Earlier U.S. example.)

1838 J. F. Cooper *Homeward Bound* iii. I. 39 The Montauk..was a first-class specimen of the 'kettle-bottom' school of naval architecture.

Kettle-bottomed, *a.* (Earlier U.S. example.)

1838 J. F. Cooper *Homeward Bound* x. I. 249 Joe was presbyterian-built, as we say, kettle-bottomed, and stowed well.

Ke·ttle-man. [Cf. Kettle 6 b.] One who attends to a kettle in sugar-boiling.

1833 B. Silliman *Man. Sugar Cane* 15 The manner in which the hands are distributed during the cutting season is the following..forty hands with knives..six kettle men.

Kettler. Delete † and add: **2.** A colour-mixer's assistant who attends to the boiling of dyestuffs.

1921 *Dict. Occup. Terms* (1927) § 381.

Kettling, variant of Catling.

1869 *Overland Monthly* III. 130 Then there are the delusive 'kettlings' among the 'low down' people...I will simply say that it is fried sausages, minus all the unhealthy and absurd meat which most people insist on stuffing into the intestinal integuments.

Keweenawan (kīwī·nǭ·ăn), *a.* *Geol.* [f. *Keweenaw*, a promontory in Lake Superior + -an.] Designating a division of the Algonkian in the region of Lake Superior, including a body of igneous rock of great thickness and extensive deposits of copper. Also as *sb.*, the Keweenawan series or system.

1893 A. Geikie *Text-bk. Geol.* (ed. 3) 716. 1906 Chamberlin & Salisbury *Geol.* II. 198 The Keweenawan system contains the most extensive deposits of native copper known. 1913 A. P. Coleman *Proterozoic Canad. Shield* (1915) 151 The volcanic eruptions so characteristic of the later Keweenawan.

Keweenawite (kīwī·nǭ·əit). *Min.* [See prec. and -ite [1].] An arsenide of copper and nickel found in Keweenaw county, Michigan.

1903 *Jrnl. Chem. Soc.* LXXXIV. II. 157 Keweenawite, a new mineral.

Key, *sb.*[1] Add: **3.** *To hold the keys of*: to have in one's own control.

1924 D. H. Lawrence *England, my Eng.* 208 She would follow her own way just the same. She would always hold the keys of her own situation.

6. c. *Chess.* (*a*) In full *key move*: The first move in a problem game. (*b*) The whole solution of a problem.

1827 W. Lewis *Chess Problems* Pref., I defer for the present publishing the solutions, that the reader may solve the Problems without being tempted to refer to the key. 1846 *Chess Players' Chron.* 65 Amateurs wanting either time or perseverance to undertake the solution themselves..may obtain the key by addressing a note to the editor. 1878 S. Loyd *Chess Strategy* 201 There is always a great deal of chance in solving a problem, such as hitting upon the key by accident. *Ibid.* 60 Key-moves which threaten an easy mate. 1890 J. Rayner *Chess Problems* 12 A really beautiful problem should be strong all round: it should have an elegant key, brilliant strategy, and pretty mates. 1906 W. De Morgan *Joseph Vance* xxxix, Zukertort's problem..turned on Black's last move having been pawn two squares, and White having the choice of taking across, which was the key-move of the problem. 1922 G. Hume & A. C. White *Good Companion Two-mover* 5 In a two-move problem, White makes the opening move, known as the key-move or Key.

d. The device used to 'key' an advertisement (see *Key *v.* 5). orig. *U.S.*

1905 Calkins & Holden *Mod. Advert.* xi. 266 A variation of the 'key' in advertising is the coupon. 1915 H. W. Hess *Product. Advert.* xiii. 199 Accounts may be opened charging up to each key..(1) number of inquiries,..(2) amount spent on that particular key [etc.].

16. *key-basket* (earlier U.S. example), *-box, -safe.*

1838 Caroline Gilman *Recoll. Southern Matron* xxv. 172 When mama had carefully placed hers in her *key-basket. 1904 F. Lynde *Grafters* xx. 264 Kent found a note in his *key-box at the Clarendon. 1905 *To-Day* 21 June 238/2 There's only one key in the *key-safe, and its the renter's key.

b. passing into *adj.* in sense 'dominant', 'controlling' (cf. 5): as *key-house, -metal, -name, -office, -position, -section;* **key industry,** one which is essential to the carrying on of others (e.g. coal-mining); **key man,** one whose work and position are necessary to the good conduct of an industry (see also *17).

1916 *Economic Jrnl.* XXVI. 24 We are asked to learn one essential lesson from the war, and that is, not to be caught short of any 'Key' industry. 1920 *Discovery* May 142/2 Tungsten has..been called the key-metal of this war. 1921 *Act* 11 & 12 *Geo. V* c. 47 Part 1, Safeguarding of Key Industries. 1923 *Daily Mail* 15 Feb. 9 The important key section of the railway line which, if handed over to French control, would create a wide western outlet from the Ruhr. 1926 D. L. Colvin *Prohib. in U.S.* 509 Occupants of key offices such as the Presidency or the Attorney-Generalship. 1927 W. E. Collinson *Contemp. Engl.* 94 Greek was said to occupy a key-position. 1927 J. Boon *Victorians, Edwardians & Georgians* I. 203 There had been considerable difficulty in getting hold of a key witness. 1927 *Glasgow Herald* 3 Mar. 10 There have lately been several murders of Chinese 'keymen', who did much to prevent the last strike being a more complete success. 1929 *Times* 28 Oct. 15/3 One of the unions, with a small membership of 'key' men. 1930 *New Statesman* 30 Aug. 637/1 The Centre is the great opportunist party,..never missing a chance to capture key-positions in the bureaucracy. 1931 *Daily Express* 16 Oct. 3/2 Bristol is largely the key position in the West. 1931 Lejeune *Cinema* 4 A study of these key-names, unobscured by any commercial considerations of box-office value.

17. key-chain, a chain for securing a key or a number of keys; **key-holder,** (*a*) an electric-lamp holder or socket containing a switch; (*b*) a person who keeps the key or keys of a workshop, factory, etc.; **key-log** *Logging*, a log which is so caught or wedged that a jam is formed and held by it; **key-man,** an operator of telegraph keys (see also *16 b); **key-move** (see *6 c); **key-plate,** (*a*) a keyhole escutcheon; (*b*) in colour-printing from a metal surface, the outline slate answering to a keystone in lithography; **key-seat** *v. trans.*, to supply with a key-seat, make a key-seat in; **key-seater,** a machine for cutting key-seats.

1904 *Westm. Gaz.* 28 July 10/3 He subsequently found his *key-chain on a chair in the bedroom. 1928 *Daily Tel.* 11 May 5/6 Workmen were waiting outside ready to begin work for the day...The *key-holder had not arrived. 1928 *Daily Express* 8 Aug. 9/2 Many keyholders were away for the Bank Holiday. 1868 *key-log [see 16]. 1873 J. H. Beadle *Undevel. West* (Phila.) 719 (Th.) There is generally what is called a 'key-log', and by attaching a rope thereto the whole mass is loosened. 1902 S. E. White *Blazed Trail* xxxii. 211 By pulling out or chopping through certain 'key' logs which locked the whole mass. 1907 *Washington Star* 30 Sept. 9 Some of the leading *keymen are sounding their shibboleth the cry of 'government ownership of the telegraph systems'.

Key, *v.* Add: **2. c.** To cause (glued surfaces) to adhere.

1922 *Encycl. Brit.* XXX. 34/2 Roughing of the surfaces to be glued was adopted to secure keying.

5. To distinguish (an advertisement in a particular periodical) with some device or direction intended to identify answers to it. orig. *U.S.*

1905 Calkins & Holden *Mod. Advert.* xi. 264 The advertiser likes to know which particular mediums pull best. To accomplish this the advertising is 'keyed'. Some form of address is used which can be varied in each magazine. 1907 W. D. Scott *Theory & Pract. Advert.* vi. 79 The return coupon was, then, in the beginning a keying device. 1915 H. W. Hess *Productive Advert.* xiii. 199 The average method of keying is very inadequate and makeshift. 1927 *Daily News* 7 June 5/5 Advertisers who key their advertisements report their best results from the 'Daily News'.

Keyhole. 4. Add: **keyhole nebula,** a nebula in the southern sky with a central dark patch shaped like a keyhole, on the edge of which is the variable star η Argûs; **keyhole saw** (earlier U.S. example); **keyhole urchin,** any sea-urchin having openings resembling keyholes in the test, as the genera *Scutella* and *Mellita.*

1890 A. M. Clerke *Syst. Stars* viii. 116 One of the finest of the southern nebulæ, sometimes named the '*Key-hole Nebula', from the aperture of that shape with which it is centrally perforated. *Ibid.* xviii. 282 Such was the brilliancy of the star [η Argûs] in 1838 as almost to obliterate the 'key-hole'. 1777 *Essex Inst. Hist. Coll.* XLIX. 106 Sold..; *key hole saws, at 2s.

Keyhole, *v.* Add examples (of *intr.* use).

1905 *Kynoch Jrnl.* Oct.–Dec. 172 Some of these weapons ..at any range beyond a hundred yards shot wildly, the bullet invariably keyholing. 1923 Kipling *Land & Sea Tales* 190 The bullet must have ricochetted short of the butt, and it has key-holed, as we say. See!' He pointed to an ugly triangular rip and flap on the canvas target face.

Keystone. Add: **1. d.** *ellipt.* = Keystone State (see 5). *U.S.*

1844 *Congress. Globe* 4 June 662/3 The old Key-stone has never furnished the Union with either President or Vice President. 1868 W. Carleton *Farm Ball., Our Army of the Dead* 5 Mid old Key-stone's rugged riches, which the miner's hand await.

5. (Examples of *Keystone State.*)

[1818 *Niles' Weekly Register* XIV. 23/1 Pennsylvania.. standing as the keystone of the federal arch. 1834 *Congress. Globe* 31 May 408/1 The State of Pennsylvania..was still the key-stone of the Union.] 1836 *Southern Lit. Messenger* II. 277 The little German farmer ..in the Key Stone State. 1904 *N.Y. American* 4 Apr. 4 The Pennsylvania men agreed with the Tammany leader that the Keystone State should send an uninstructed delegation.

b. keystone picture *Cinematography*, a picture in which the sides of the image are not parallel.

1915 J. B. Rathbun *Moving Picture Making* 126 To avoid the keystone picture, the angle of the lens must be sufficiently great to bring in the edges. *Ibid.* 135 This distortion makes what is known as a 'keystone' picture which is due principally to the fact that the top of the screen is nearer the picture than the bottom... With the projector installed at one side of the screen, the keystone effect will be horizontal instead of vertical.

Khadar, -ir, variants of *Kadir.

Khaddar (kæ·dăɹ). [Hindi.] Indian home-spun cloth.

1921 *Glasgow Herald* 27 Dec. 7 This tent will be made of hand-spun 'khadder' [*sic*]. 1925 E. S. Jones *Christ of Indian Road* v. 116 The whole city was dressed in white home-spun khaddar, the sign of the Nationalist.

Khaki, *a.* and *sb.* Add: Hence **Kha·kied** (kā·kid) *pa. pple.*, dressed in khaki; *fig.* possessed by a militant spirit; **Kha·kiism,** militant spirit or policy; **Kha·kiite,** an enthusiast for a war policy; **Kha·kiness** = *khakiism.* (All temporary.)

1900 *Daily Express* 26 June 5 (Cassell's Suppl.) The departure of *khakied troops for the front. 1904 *Westm. Gaz.* 19 Nov. 2/1 The last election, when certainly the confidence-trick was indeed played on a Khakied nation. 1900 *Nat. Rev.* June 535 There is no reason to suppose that Lord Salisbury has, so far, surrendered to *Khakiism. *Ibid.*, The *Khakiites are strenuous and determined. 1900 *Westm. Gaz.* 4 May 2/2 The Portsmouth electors..did not allow themselves to be persuaded out of their Liberalism into *khakiness.

Khalukah (halu·ka). Also **chaluka(h), khaluka.** [Talmudic Heb. חלקה *ḥ*[e]*luqqāh* distribution, f. Heb. חלק *ḥālaq* to distribute.] Contributions or donations sent by Jews for the support of poor Jews in Palestine.

1880 *Encycl. Brit.* XIII. 686/2 Annual contributions (*haluka*) amounting to about £50,000 a year. 1920 *19th Cent.* Oct. 627 Fear has been expressed that Jewry in Palestine..will degenerate into a new form of 'Chalukah'. 1923 W. P. Livingstone *Galilee Doctor* 48 The Jew who followed his native genius, engaged in commerce, and made a success of it, was independent of the khalukah. *Ibid.* 163 The khalukah system had made the country a Jewish poorhouse.

Khanum (kā·nʊm). Also **han(o)um,** [Turk. *khānim*, fem. of *khān* Khan [1].] In Turkey and the East, a lady of rank. Also = madam, Mrs.

1826 tr. *Zehir-ed-din Muhammed Baber's Mem.* 12 The second daughter [of Shir Haji Beg], Kullūk Nigār Khanum, was my mother. 1834 Morier *Ayesha* I. iv. 80 She once made the sign of the cross,..but now she is a *kadūn*—a *khanūm*, a head of a harem. 1884 F. Boyle *Borderland* 315 They have been used by hanoums and princesses. 1928 *Daily Tel.* 30 Oct. 12/6 An unveiled Khanum gets him his number when he uses the telephone. 1929 *Spectator* 21 Aug. 276/1 Closely-veiled figures of Turkish *Khanums.*

Kharif (karī·f). [(Hind. a.) Arab. خريف *kharīf* gathered, autumn, harvest, autumnal rain.]

1. In India, the autumn crop, sown at the beginning of the summer rains.

1882 W. W. Hunter *Ind. Empire* 385 The *kharīf* or autumn harvest. 1886 A. H. Church *Food-grains Ind.* 99 Where indigo is grown in the kharif, barley is its usual accompaniment in the rabi.

2. The rainy season in the Sudan.

1920 *Blackw. Mag.* Nov. 668/1 The gazelle here do not drink from khareef to khareef, a period of very nearly ten months.

Khatun (kā·tūn). Also **kadun.** [Hind., a. Pers.] A lady. Also as a term of address.

1834 [see *Khanum]. 1927 *Daily Express* 16 Sept. 6 What do you think, khatun? 1927 *Blackw. Mag.* Nov. 687/2 My wife and other senior *khatuns. Ibid.* 688/1, I..called out to my servant..to bid the *khatun* come in haste.

Khaya (kē·yă). [mod.L., f. Wolof *khaye.*] A genus of tropical African timber trees closely allied to mahogany. Also, a tree of this genus.

1864 J. A. Grant *Walk Across Africa* 340. 1920 *Nature* 29 July 692/1 The various species of Khaya, the African mahoganies.

Khet (ket). [Hind., Hindi.] In India, a tract of cultivated land.

1878 P. Robinson *In my Indian Garden* 176 In the still air could be heard..from the scattered *khets*, the bark of the prowling fox. 1886 — *Teetotum Trees* 63 In all the swampy jheels and crop-grown khets. 1922 *19th Cent.* Oct. 589 The land is divided by one broad distinction into the khet and the jungle—that is to say, into the cultivated and the wild.

Khilafat (kilā·fat). [Arab. خلافة *khilāfat*, f. *khalīf* successor: see Caliph.] The spiritual headship of Islam, residing in the person of the Turkish Sultan at Constantinople. Used to designate the Moslem anti-British movement in India after the treaty of Sèvres. Hence **Khila·fatist,** a supporter of this agitation.

1923 *Edin. Rev.* Jan. 182 The *Khilāfat*..is the Vice-gerency of the Prophet. 1925 *Contemp. Rev.* Apr. 430 An influential section of the Moslem community, dissociating itself from the Khilafatist section. 1926 *Encycl. Brit.* Suppl. II. 429/2 The 'Khilāfat' agitation. *Ibid.* 431/2 The Khilāfat party.

Khoi-Khoin. [lit. 'men of men'.] The Hottentots' name for themselves.

1880 *Encycl. Brit.* XII. 309/2 The common denomination adopted by themselves was Khoi-Khoin (men of men). 1897 A. J. Butler tr. *Ratzel's Hist. Mankind* II. 247 The Khoi-Khoi (Bushmen and Hottentot) group of languages. 1930 Schapera *Khoisan Peoples S.A.* 5 *note.*

Khorasan (korăsā·n). Also incorrectly **-assan, -assin.** The name of a province in North-eastern Persia, used to designate a kind of Persian carpet or rug.

1922 Kendrick & Tattersall *Hand-Woven Carpets* 179 Of the various kinds of carpets made in this province, one kind is called specifically Khorassan...Khorassan rugs are usually large in size. 1931 *Times* 16 Mar. 22/4 A Khorassin carpet 16 ft. × 7 ft. 1931 C. Tattersall *Carpets of Persia* 39 Mashhad. Much like Khorasans, but with shorter and closer pile. *Ibid.* Pl. xxiii, Khorasan Rug.

Khud. *attrib.* Add: *khud-climbing, -stick.*

1906 *Westm. Gaz.* 13 Aug. 7/1 Killed..in India while khud-climbing. 1925 A. G. Arbuthnot in G. Burrard *Big Game Hunting* 118 Take your telescope, rest it on a rock or on your 'khud stick'. 1928 *Blackw. Mag.* Jan. 25/2 He jabbed his khudstick into the ground.

Kibaub, variant of Cabob, Kabob. (Cf. *Keebaub.)

1839 Mrs. Kirkland *New Home* xiv. 87 She would have made out nobly on kibaubs.

Kibble, *sb.*[3] Add: Also, a small hand-drawn cart on runners used for conveying ore or refuse in a mine. Also *attrib.*, as *kibble filler.* Also **Ki·bbler** [cf. Kibble *v.*[2]].

1881 *Instr. Census Clerks* (1885) 84 Copper Miner...Kibble Filler. 1921 *Dict. Occup. Terms* (1927) §§ 047, 054.

Kibble, *v.*[1] Add: **Ki·bbler, Ki·bblerman.**

1881 Ogilvie (Annandale), *Kibbler*, one who or that which kibbles or cuts, especially a machine for cutting beans and peas for cattle. 1921 *Dict. Occup. Terms* (1927) § 159 *Kibbler, kibblerman*..attends and feeds machine in which he breaks up oil cake into nodular pieces before grinding into meal. 1922 *Glasgow Herald* 21 Feb. 3 Chaff and root cutters, grinding mills, or kibblers.

Kibblings (ki·bliŋz), *sb. pl.* [Corruption of pl. of Capelin.] Pieces of small fish used as bait on the banks of Newfoundland.

1843 in Goode *Fish. Indust. U.S.* (1887) 160 Metal hooks baited with parts of small fish (by us called kiblings). 1859 Bartlett *Dict. Amer.*, Kiblings. 1871 Schele de Vere *Americanisms* (1872) 340 Kibblings.

Kibdelophane (kibde·lŏfēn). *Min.* [ad. G. *kibdelophan*, f. Gr. κίβδηλος adulterated, spurious + -φανης showing, appearing.] A variety of ilmenite.

1882 Watts *Dict. Chem.* III. 446. 1892 E. S. Dana *Dana's Syst. Min.* (ed. 6) 217 Kibdelophane. About 30 p.c. titanium. 1929 H. H. Read *Rutley's Elem. Min.* (ed. 21) 331.

Kiboko (kibō͡u·ko). *Africa.* [Swahili, = hippopotamus.] A sjambok.

1921 *Chambers's Jrnl.* 118/1 One of those who had long ruled them with the *kiboko* (sjambok) in times gone by. 1923 tr. *A. Schweitzer's On Edge of Primeval Forest* iv. 67 A kiboko (or sjambok) of hippopotamus hide.

Kick, *sb.*[1] Add:

1. d. (Earlier and later U.S. examples.)

1839 *Chemung* (N.Y.) *Democrat* 25 Dec. (Th.) So take the hint without a kick, and shut the open door. 1904 F. Lynde *Grafters* xii. 155 To-day he came around and gave me back my opinion, clause for clause as his own. But I have no kick coming. 1910 Mulford *H. Cassidy* viii. 57 'We ain't got no kick, have we?' retorted Cavalry.

2. c. *Archery.* The unsteady motion of an arrow at the beginning of its flight caused by faulty handling of the bow.

1894 C. J. Longman & Walrond *Archery* xx. 343 The effort made by the string when released to regain its central position will cause the arrow to strike against the bow with a 'click', and commence its flight with what is called a 'kick' or unsteady wriggle.

d. *Electr.* A momentary high-voltage discharge in an inductive electric current. *B kick* (see quot. 1928).

1910 *N. Hawkins' Electr. Dict.* 233/1 *Kick*...Any impulsive movement imparted in telegraphy to delicate instrument parts by a discharge from the line...*Kick of Coil*, a discharge taking place from an electromagnet coil. *Kick of Relay*, an impulsive movement imparted to the tongue of a telegraphic relay by an electric discharge from the line. 1928 A. E. Stone *Text Bk. Telegr.* 191 With the non-polarised relays a different method has had to be adopted, in order to eliminate the effects of what is known as the B kick. This term is applied to the break in the continuity of signals received on the non-polarised relays, due to the momentary demagnetisation of their cores when the current in the line is reversed.

e. *fig.* A sharp stimulant effect, e.g. that of strong liquor or pungent seasoning; also, a thrill of excitement, fear, etc. orig. *U.S.*

1903 *Daily Chron.* 16 Jan. 5/1 With cayenne and mustard (to give their food the missing 'kick' [*sc.* of alcohol]). 1926 *Ladies' Home Jrnl.* July 26 That's a good word isn't it? I don't know what it means, but it's got a kick. 1928 *Daily Express* 4 Dec. 10/, I was told I should get a kick out of that journey—and I certainly did. 1929 *Evening News* 18 Nov. 15/6 A cocktail basis with a real kick (42 deg. proof spirit).

6. b. Shoes. *U.S.*

1927 *Amer. Dial. Notes* 453. 1927 *Hollis St. Theatre Prog.* (Boston) 19 Sept., Gloss.

8. *Comb.*: **kick-starter** (see quot. 1916); also **kick-start;** hence **kick-start** *v. trans.*, to start (the engine) thus; **kick-switch** *U.S.* (see quot.); **kick-wheel** *U.S.*, a potter's wheel worked by a foot pedal.

1914 *Motor Cycle* 2 Apr. 138/1, 1912 P. and M., free engine, 2-speed, *kick start. 1928 *Manch. Guard. Weekly* 15 June 474/2 The biggest boy is demonstrating..how to *kick-start an engine. 1913 *Motor Cycle* 26 June 68/1 Douglas, 1913, R, clutch, 2-speed, 'kick' starter. 1916 *Motor Cyclists' A.B.C.* 107 A kick starter is fitted to a machine for the purpose of allowing the engine to be started whilst the rider is in the saddle by a downward kick of a pedal. 1919 C. P. Thompson *Cocktails* 235 She mounted on the kickstarter and stamped on it with resolute vigour. 1918 *Dyke's Automobile & Gasoline Engine Encycl.* (ed. 6) 277/2 The coil is ..usually placed on the dash, with a *kick switch on its face. *Note*, Kick switch means, the switch can be kicked from one side to the other by foot. 1923 E. A. Barber *Pottery & Porcelain U.S.* xii. 250 Such wares..were produced in large quantities by negro men and boys, who employed the old-fashioned '*kick-wheel' in their manufacture.

Kick, *v.*[1] Add: **I. 3. b.** Said also of the ball and of the bowler.

1888 Steel & Lyttelton *Cricket* 152 Spofforth was bowling rather more than medium pace, bringing the ball back a foot or more very quickly from the pitch, sometimes kicking to the height of the batsman's head and at others shooting.

c. *Electr.* (See *Kick *sb.*[1] 2 d.)

1928 A. E. Stone *Text Bk. Telegr.* 142 If during this period the tongue of the relay 'kicks', the local circuit is momentarily broken.

5. c. *intr.* (To be or lie) *kicking about*: i.e. in danger of being kicked or otherwise damaged.

1867 'T. Lackland' *Homespun* I. 80 The..doctor, whose instruments..lie kicking about like ordinary household trumpery.

II. Kick in. *trans.* **a.** To break down (a door, etc.) by kicking against the outer side.

1883 Stevenson *Treas. Isl.* v, Then there followed a great to-do,..furniture thrown over, doors kicked in.

b. To propel (an uncoupled railway car, etc.) by repeatedly thrusting a foot against the ground.

1898 Hamblen *Gen. Manager's Story* 25 A conductor..opened the switch, pulled the coupling pin on the crippled car, and gave his engineer a signal to kick it in. *Ibid.* 35 He wanted to kick the last car in on a spur.

III. 10. kick-and-rush, used to describe football played with more vigour than art.

1906 *Daily Chron.* 26 Nov. 9/2 It was a kick-and-rush game, played badly. 1930 *Daily Express* 9 Sept. 12/5 The football they played was of the kick-and-rush order.

Kicker. Add: **5.** (See quot.)

1886 J. Barrowman *Sc. Mining Terms* 40 *Kicker*, the reversing gear of some direct-acting steam and hydraulic pumps.

6. *Poker.* A high third card retained in the hand with a pair at the draw.

1895 *Poker Man.* 57 Sometimes a player raises on a single pair and a kicker, *i.e.* a high card. 1901 D. A. Curtis *Sci.*

Draw Poker 57 Drawing two cards to a pair and a kicker, the chances of a Full are 6 in 1081.

7. *Lumbering.* A device for throwing or rolling a log in a desired direction. In full *log kicker*.

1922 R. C. Bryant *Lumber* 44 Logs which are elevated into the mill by an endless chain are thrown or rolled upon the deck by means of log kickers of various types. *Ibid.* 46 A type of log kicker designed for rolling logs both ways out of the log slide.

Kicking, *ppl. a.* (Earlier U.S. example of phr.)

1847 C. F. Hoffman *Lett.* 23 Jan. 274, I am most glad to hear that you are alive and kicking.

b. *Cricket.* Of a ball: That rises abruptly from the pitch. Said also causatively of the ground, a bowler, or his bowling: also of lawn tennis service. (See Kick *v.*[1] 3 b.)

1888 [see Dict.]. 1924 F. G. Lowe *Lawn Tennis* 12 The only way to take a fast kicking service is to stand right in [etc.].

Kick-up. Add: 1. b. *transf.* An abrupt rise.

1907 F. W. Lanchester *Aerodynamics* 347 One of the most remarkable results brought out by these experiments is the peculiar 'kick up' in the pressure curve.

2. b. A dance. *U.S.*

1778 *Maryland Hist. Mag.* III. 116 We collected the Girls in the neighbourhood and had a kick up in the Evening. 1796–1801 Fessenden *Orig. Poems* (1806) 30 See what lasses we can pick up For our famous village kick up.

4. = Kick *sb.*[2] 1.

1901 *N.E.D.* s.v. *Kick* sb.[2] 1. 1923 H. J. Powell *Glass-making in Eng.* 22 Feet of goblets, showing hem and kick-up. *Ibid.* 74 Stability had been given by pushing upwards and inwards the base of the bulb to form the familiar 'kick-up' of modern wine-bottles.

5. a. (See quot. 1909.) b. On the Mississippi, a steamboat with paddle-wheel astern. *U.S.*

1909 H. Louis *Dressing of Minerals* 451 In larger mines it is more usual to use cars with fixed sides and to use some form of 'Tippler' or 'Tumbler' for turning the car over and thus emptying out its contents. Tipplers are of two kinds: end tipplers or 'Kick-ups' and side tipplers.

Kicky (ki·ki), *a. Cricket.* [f. Kick *v.*[1] + -y[1].] Causing the ball to 'kick' or rise abruptly from the pitch.

1888 Steel & Lyttelton *Cricket* iii. 150 It is a slow easy wicket he has to bat on, and not a 'caked', 'kicky' one. 1903 *Windsor Mag.* Sept. 393/2 A very kicky wicket generally averages matters somewhat by supplying one dead shooter.

Kid, *sb.*[1] Add: 5. d. A young man, fellow. *U.S. slang.*

1895 *Emporia* (Kan.) *Gazette* 15 Aug. 15 Then we have discovered a kid without a law practice and have decided to run him for attorney general. 1926 J. Black *You Can't Win* iv. 26 I'll tell you what I'll do with you, kid.

6. **kid-brush,** a soft brush used in the process of finishing goatskins; **kid point,** stitching on the backs of gloves.

1897 C. T. Davis *Manuf. Leather* 368 The skins..are then wet over with gum-water and brushed with a very soft brush called a 'kid-brush'.

Kid, *v.*[4] Add: Also *absol.* and with clause.

1879 [in Dict.]. 1916 C. J. Dennis *Ginger Mick* 80, I can see ole Ginger..Grinnin' a bit to kid 'is wound don't pain. 1922 *N. & Q.* 12th Ser. XI. 206/2 A Jockey who has something up his sleeve and sits still on his mount, or by some means deceives those riding against him, is said to be 'kidding'. He may also 'kid' to his horse by his tactics and come with a rush at the finish.

Kidder[1] (see Kid *v.*[4]). Add examples.

1888 *Sporting Life* 15 Dec. (Farmer) The champion kidder. 1891 J. Newman *Scamping Tricks* xi. 88 [He] was a beautiful kidder and could patter sweet and pretty. 1899 G. Ade *Fables in Slang* (1900) 84 They wanted a Swell Name for the Team, so the Side-Show Announcer, who was something of a Kidder and had attended a Unitarian College, gave them Zoroaster and Zendavesta. 1902 H. McHugh *John Henry* 41 'Quit your joshin', John Henry!'..'you're getting to be a worse kidder than Bill McConnell!' 1922 *Weekly Dispatch* 17 Dec. 7 He appeared to me to be..the champion 'kidder'. When I saw him ride it seemed to me that other jockeys did not know what he was about.

Kidney. 5. c. Add: **kidney fern,** an American spleenwort (*Asplenium angustifolium*) with kidney-shaped sori; **kidney-iron ore** = *kidney ore*; **kidney-root,** either of two American plants used for medicinal purposes, (*a*) = *Joe-pye weed; (*b*) an asteraceous shrub, *Baccharis pilularis*; **kidney-worm,** any parasitic worm which infests the kidneys of man or lower animals.

1882 *Econ. Geol. Illinois* II. 164 We find an exposure of over twenty feet of shaly strata, with much *kidney-iron ore.

Kier (kīəɹ), *v.* [f. the sb.] *trans.* To boil in a kier or vat.

1922 *Encycl. Brit.* XXX. 590/2 A uniform process of 'kiering' (boiling under pressure with a lye of caustic soda) was introduced.

Kieve, variant of Keeve.

Kiezer (kī·zəɹ). Also **kieser, keyser, kiesh-eer.** [Du. *kiezer*, f. *kiezen* to Choose.] A member of the electoral college in British Guiana which nominates members for the legislative body (the Court of Policy).

1812 Ld. Bathurst in J. Rodway *Hist. Brit. Guiana* (1893) II. 220 The strong measure of dissolving the existing College of Keysers. 1831 in *Alm. & Local Guide Brit. Guiana* (1832) 170 Whereas on the 7th day of September, 1812, Major-General Carmichael, when administering the Government of the said United Colony of Demerary and Essequebo, did, by a Proclamation by him for that purpose issued, declare the College of Kiezers of the said United Colony to be no longer a distinct and separate institution. 1880 *Encycl. Brit.* XI. 251/2. 1891 J. Rodway *Hist. Brit. Guiana* I. 116 Since..1739, these Burgher Officers had been constituted a College of Kiesheers (electors or choosers) to nominate the representatives of the free planters.

Kike (kaik). *U.S. slang.* (See quots.)

1929 Mencken *Amer. Lang.* 115 Our common terms of disparagement, such as *kike*, *wop*, *yap* and *rube*. 1927 P. Marks *Lord of Himself* 148 'Filthy little kike,' he thought contemptuously. *Ibid.* 159 You told me that this Loshakoff was a great musician, but you told me, too, that he was an ugly little kike. 1931 Slosson *Great Crusade* 306 The talk of 'wops', 'kikes', 'sheenies', 'dagoes'.

Kilch (kilʃ). [German-Swiss *kilch*.] Local name of a small whitefish, *Coregonus hiemalis*, of Lake Constance.

1881 K. Semper *Anim. Life* 320 The little fish of the Lake of Constance known as the Kilch. 1931 J. R. Norman *Hist. Fishes* 175 One of the White-fishes (*Coregonus*), an important food-fish of Lake Constance, known locally as the Kilch.

Kilhig (ki·lhig). *U.S. Logging.* [Origin unknown.] A short stout pole used as a lever or brace to direct the fall of a tree.

1905 *Terms Forestry & Logging* 41. 1913 R. C. Bryant *Logging* 83 Kilhig or sampson...It consists of a pole..either sharpened or armed on one end with a spike.

Kilkenny (kilke·ni). The name of a county, and its capital, in Leinster, Ireland, used *attrib.* in *Kilkenny coal* (= anthracite), *marble*; **Kilkenny cats,** two cats fabled to have fought till only the tails remained, taken as the type of combatants who fight until they annihilate each other.

1852 *Pict. Guide Birmingham* 162 Whatever may be the ultimate fate of the combatants—and it once seemed likely to be that of the *Kilkenny cats. 1859 *Slang Dict.*, *Kilkenny Cat*, a popular simile for a voracious or desperate animal or person. 1901 *Graphic* LXIV. 288/1 The fate of the Kilkenny cats will meanwhile have overtaken the villains. 1909 *Daily Chron.* 21 Sept. 3/5 The election of its kings..was a continual cause of bickering and Kilkenny cat fighting. 1931 *Times Lit. Suppl.* 23 July 578/2 All these excitable disputants have disappeared like the Kilkenny cats through the excess of their own zeal. 1910 *Encycl. Brit.* II. 105/2 Anthracite...Other terms..are, 'stone coal'..or 'blind coal' in Scotland, and '*Kilkenny coal' in Ireland. 1930 F. J. North *Limestones* 145 Black *Kilkenny Marble is widely used.

Kill, *sb.*[1] Add: 3. Also, an animal used as a bait in hunting beasts of prey.

1906 G. F. Abbott *Through India* in *Daily Chron.* 24 Apr. 3/4 The kill was tied in the immediate neighbourhood of these towers.

4. *Lawn Tennis* and *Rackets.* The striking of a ball in such a way that it cannot be returned. (Cf. Kill *v.* 7 a.)

1903 *Westm. Gaz.* 31 Aug. 8/1 Grant put in some mighty 'kills' from the service line. 1906 *Field* 13 Oct. 623/3 Mr. R. F. Doherty was sending down some punishing kills across to Mr. Hough's forehand, which very often scored outright. 1908 *Baily's Mag.* June 483/1 They both of them fairly bombarded the wall, often..bringing off beautifully low 'kills'. 1920 Tilden *Lawn Tennis* 87 The server covers and strives for a kill at once.

Kill, *v.* Add:

6. c. The inf. *to kill* added to express the full extent of an effect produced; as *dressed* (*got up*, etc.) *to kill*, dressed to excess, fascinatingly dressed. *colloq.* (orig. *U.S.*)

1848 Bartlett *Dict. Amer.*, *To kill*, to do anything to kill, is a common vulgarism, and means to do it to the uttermost; to carry it to the fullest extent; as, 'He drives to kill'; 'She dances to kill'. 1862 Lowell *Biglow P.* Ser. II. ii. 62 'T was Concord Bridge a talkin' off to kill With the Stone Spike thet 's druv thru Bunker Hill. *a* 1871 *Country Merchant* (De Vere) When he came down after breakfast, to go over to the Judge's and to press his suit, he was dressed to kill. 1877 *My Mother-in-Law* vii, His wife was there, dressed 'to kill', as he himself said.

7. f. *To kill the goods*: in *Soap-making*, to emulsify the melted fat by a partial saponification.

1885 W. L. Carpenter *Manuf. Soap* 167 The boiling, and the addition of fat and lye, must be continued until a small sample..has a tolerably firm consistence... Practice alone will enable the operator to judge of the completion of this first operation, called 'pasting'. In English phraseology, it is called 'killing the goods' or raw material. 1888 J. Cameron *Soaps & Candles* 82 Saponification, Pasting, or Killing the Goods.

g. *'To kill the sea'* (Naut.), to cause the sea to grow calmer, as by the action of a heavy rainfall upon turbulent waves. *To kill the wind* (Naut.), to reduce wind-velocity, as does a rain-storm on a high wind'. (*Funk's Standard Dict.* 1928.)

8. a. *Leather manuf.* To remove the natural grease from (a hair skin).

1897 C. T. Davis *Manuf. Leather* 496 Before a skin can be colored it must first be tanned and prepared, and all grease removed from the hair so as to make it susceptible to the dye. The latter process is technically designated as 'killing the skin'.

b. To obliterate.

1903 E. L. Shuman *Pract. Journalism* 62 The editor can make room by killing the last paragraphs of the other stories.

c. *Bridge.* (See quot.)

1929 Work *Complete Contract Bridge* Gloss. 240 High cards in a suit are 'killed' when they are led through and captured.

d. *Printing.* To mark or designate (matter) as not to be used; to throw out; to order (type) to be distributed.

Killarney (kilā·ɹni). *Geol.* The name (see quot. 1924) given to a 'revolution' in the Lake Superior country at the close of the Proterozoic era. Hence **Killa·rnean** *a.*

1924 Pirsson *Introd. Geol.* I. 502 The Killarney Revolution. *Ibid.* 508 The Killarney mountains of Ontario. 1924 Schuchert *Text-bk. Geol.* 102 Epi-Proterozoic or Lipalian Interval and peneplanation of continents, Eras: General Terms for Major Divisions, Killarney Revolution. Lake Superior, after Leith, Keweenawan granite. Lake Huron-Michipicoten, after Leith, Killarnean granite. 1925 J. Joly *Surface-Hist. Earth* v. 88.

Killer. Add: 2. Also *killer whale.*

1884 Goode *Fish. Indust. U.S.* 17 The Killer Whales are known the world over by their destructive and savage habits. 1921 E. R. G. R. Evans *South with Scott* v, We saw Sibbald's whale, Rorquals, and many killer whales.

b. A locust-killing wasp. *U.S.*

1868 *Amer. Naturalist* II. 217 The 'killer' had seized one of our August locusts, and was endeavouring to rise from the ground with it.

4. b. A contrivance for killing a large ferocious animal (e.g. a wolf, a shark); also an explosive implement for the painless killing of old horses. (Cf. *humane killer*, *Humane *a.* 1 d.)

1892 J. Murdoch *Ethnol. Results Pt. Barrow Exped.* 259 in *9th Ann. Rep. Bureau Amer. Ethnol.* 1887–88, Whalebone wolf-killers. 1901 *Amer. Anthropologist* Apr.–June 391 Eskimo and Samoan 'Killers'. 1901 *Morn. Leader* 18 Dec. 3/7 The deadly instrument known as 'Greener's Killer', thirty-six of which are to be purchased by the War Office for the painless destruction of old and incapacitated horses, is the invention of the well-known gun manufacturer, Mr. W. W. Greener... The 'killer' consists of a noiseless explosive apparatus resembling a short rifled barrel, which contains a small cartridge with steel-pointed bullet.

Ki·llhag. *U.S.* (*local*). Also -hog. [Origin unknown.] A wooden trap used by hunters.

1848 Bartlett *Dict. Amer.*, *Killhag* (Indian), a wooden trap, used by the hunters in Maine. 1864 *Bradford Times* (De Vere), The first furs were brought into town yesterday, and already a number of killhags have been put up everywhere.

Killick. Add: b. (See quots.)

1916 *Chambers's Jrnl.* May 302/2 'Dipping the killick' means that the badge is removed, and that its wearer has been disrated to A. B. *Note*, A 'killick' is an anchor, which is the badge worn by a leading seaman.

Killickinnick, etc. (Examples of forms.)

c 1805 J. J. Henry *Camp. agst. Quebec* (1812) 223 A half part of Red-willow bark, added to as much of the dried sumach, forms the killekinic. 1867 'Mark Twain' *Amer. Drolleries* 41 The most popular..smoking tobacco is.. Killikinick. 1878 H. H. Jackson *Bits of Travel at Home* 289 Great mats of killikinnick vines (the bear-berry). 1889 K. Munroe *Golden Days* xxvi. 284 Put that in your pipe and smoke it, along with your killikinick.

Killing, *vbl. sb.* Add: *Bridge.* The severe defeat of a contract.

1929 Work *Complete Contract Bridge* viii, Every 'killing' accomplished by a slam venture has been offset by losses many times as great.

b. *killing-place*, *-room*; **killing-bottle,** a bottle containing a poison for killing captured insects, etc.; **killing-circle,** the area within which, at a certain range, the charge of shot from a gun is sufficiently compact to kill the game.

1877 *Encycl. Brit.* VI. 134/2 Beetles when caught may.. be dropped..into what is known as the '*killing bottle', the bottom of which contains cyanide of potassium covered over with a layer of gypsum. 1886 Ld. Walsingham & Payne-Gallwey *Shooting* (Badm.) 94 The charge of a 20-bore is smaller, lighter, and has a less *killing circle than has a 12-bore. 1892 Greener *Breech-loader* 148 For ordinary sporting purposes a gun which shall give its largest killing circle at 30 yards with the first barrel, and at 40 with the second, will be found the most convenient of good shots. 1908 *Westm. Gaz.* 3 Oct. 12/1 In a paddock of nearly thirty thousand acres..it was practically impossible to chance upon this *killing-place. 1906 *Ibid.* 1 June 9/2 The most rigid inspection of the meat after it gets into the *killing-room.

2. The act of killing game; a number of animals killed by sportsmen. = Kill *sb.*[1] 2 and 3.

1896 *Harper's Mag.* Apr. 721/1 When we camped by a good killing of musk-ox. 1931 *Amer. Speech* Oct. 5 Sometimes the hunter found that he could make his best 'killings' at the 'salt licks' or 'salt flats' frequented by the buffalos.

3. The prevention of the evolution of gas in the steel during its manufacture.

1887 J. A. Phillips & Bauerman *Elem. Metallurgy* 330 When the charge has become completely fused..it is left at rest for a period which varies with the carbon temper of the metal. This operation, known as *killing*, is of the utmost importance for the production of sound ingots.

Killy. *U.S.* Short for Killifish.

1871 Schele de Vere *Americanisms* (1872) 67 The Barred Killy. 1898 Hamblen *Gen. Manager's Story* xv. 243 Frank had remained for a bit seated on a stone behind me, watching the 'killies' swimming in the shallow water.

Kilmarnock (kilmā·ɹnǫk). [Name of a town in Scotland.] A Scotch cap resembling a tam-o'-shanter. In full *Kilmarnock bonnet, cowl.*

1822 Ainslie *Pilgr. Land of Burns* 6 The manner in which the whole man was so properly roofed in with the ancient Kilmarnock bonnet. *Ibid.* 31 Flourishing..their 'kilmarnocks' manfully round their heads. 1828 Moir *Mansie Wauch* vi. 53 Gallowses, leather-caps, and Kilmarnock cowls. 1877 Jas. M. Neilson *Poems* 49 He..cover'd the bald pow o' Willie Shakspeare Wi's big blue Kilmarnock. 1902 *Daily*

Chron. 20 Dec. 5/2 The Scottish team of curlers who have departed for Canada wanted to be rigged out with old-style Kilmarnocks.

Ki·ln-drier. [f. Kiln-dry *v.*] An apparatus for kiln-drying meal.

1813 *Niles' Weekly Register* V. Add. A. 13/1 His improved elevator, conveyor, drill, hopperboy and kiln-drier.

Kilo-. Add: *kilo-ampère, -calorie, -erg, -gauss, -hertz, -joule, -maxwell, -parsec, -volt.*

1901 J. A. Fleming *Handbk. Electr. Labor.* I. 68 The standard *kilo-ampere balance. 1927 Haldane & Huxley *Anim. Biol.* iii. 88 *note*, The *kilocalorie of 1,000 calories is the unit of energy which is most useful in human physiology. It is sometimes called the 'Large calorie'. 1910 *N. Hawkins' Electr. Dict.*, **Kilo-erg*, a unit of work, equal to one thousand ergs. *Ibid.*, **Kilo-gauss*, a unit of magnetic flux density, equal to one thousand gausses. 1929 *Daily Express* 11 Jan. 3/6 A national common frequency of 1,040 *kilohertz (288·5 metres). 1893 Sloane *Stand. Electr. Dict.* 317 **Kilojoule*, a compound unit; one thousand joules. 1922 *Encycl. Brit.* XXX. 301/2 The most remote cluster known is distant 67 *kiloparsecs or 200,000 light years. 1924 *Nature* 9 Feb. 206/2 Comparison of its angular diameter with those of the Magellanic Clouds..gives distance 300 to 500 kiloparsecs. 1927 *Glasgow Herald* 8 Dec. 13 *Kilovolt transformers. 1923 R. Knox *Radiogr. & Radio-Therap.* I. i. (ed. 4) 45 The kilovoltmeter for measuring the high-tension current.

Kilocycle (ki·lǫsaik'l). *Electr.* [f. Kilo- + Cycle *sb.*] The quantity of 1000 cycles (see *Cycle *sb.* 10 d), as a unit in measuring the frequency of electrical oscillations. (Abbreviated kc.)

1921 *Wireless Board List Radio Telegr. Waves* 3 Frequency is expressed in 'Kilo-cycles' (K.C.). 1926 S. O. Pearson *Dict. Wireless Terms* 113. 1927 *Daily Tel.* 14 June 5/3 The decision of the B.B.C. to adopt forthwith the kilocycle method of stating frequencies instead of the wave-length method. 1928 G. E. Sterling *Radio Man.* 45 The frequency of 1,000,000 cycles can then be expressed as 1,000 kilocycles or 1 megacycle. 1930 *Radio Times* 15 Aug. 329/2 Under the International Agreements at present in force, broadcasting channels normally are confined to about 9 kilocycles separation.

Kilometric, *a.* Add: *Kilometric guarantee*, a guarantee of gross receipts per kilometre conceded by the Turkish government to railway companies within the Empire.

1902 *Daily Chron.* 24 Jan. 3/3 The revenues to be assigned for the service of the kilometric guarantee have not yet been specified. 1909 *Westm. Gaz.* 16 Dec. 2/1 The Bagdad Railway (with its iniquitous kilometric guarantee). 1909 D. Fraser *Short Cut to India* iii. 39 A heavy kilometric guarantee was provided. *Ibid.* 45 When the kilometric receipts exceed..4500 francs, the whole of the surplus goes to the government.

Kilta (ki·ltā). Also **kilter.** [Obscure.] In India, a kind of wicker basket. Also *attrib.* = made of wicker.

1876 C. F. Gordon Cumming *From Hebrides to Himalayas* II. v. 134 Our provisions were packed..in long native baskets, called *kilters*. 1896 S. J. Stone *In & Beyond Himalayas* 39 The provisions and cooking apparatus were carried in kiltas (wicker baskets covered with leather). 1927 *Blackw. Mag.* Mar. 312/1 A *kilta* carrying-chair, carried on the back of one man.

Kilter (ki·ltəɹ). *Poker.* [prob. var. of dial. Kelter[4], rubbish.] A hand consisting only of cards of low value.

1895 *Poker Man.* 55 Suppose you have an utterly valueless hand dealt you, say for example, deuce, four of hearts, six of clubs, seven of spades and nine of diamonds; this sort of hand is termed a 'kilter'. 1904 R. F. Foster *Pract. Poker* 126 The Southern custom of raising the ante on a kilter, and then standing pat.

Kiltorcan (kiltǭ·ɹkăn), *a. Geol.* [f. *Kiltorkin* in Kilkenny, Ireland.] The designation of an upper division of the Old Red Sandstone in the south of Ireland.

1885 A. Geikie *Text-Bk. Geol.* (ed. 2) 716 In Cork and the south-east of Ireland they are followed by the pale sandstones and shaly flagstones known as the 'Kiltorcan beds'. 1912 Jukes-Browne *Stratigr. Geol.* (ed. 2) 211 The Kiltorcan Beds or Upper Old Red Sandstone of Kilkenny.

Kilty (ki·lti), *sb.* Also -ie. [f. Kilt *sb.* + -y[6].] One who wears a kilt; esp. a nickname for a Highland soldier.

1842 Vedder *Poems, Corse o' Dundee* ix, In double quick time did the kilties career. 1904 *Daily Chron.* 26 Sept. 9/3 The Kilties' may be said to represent Canada by being Scotch. 1927 *Scots Observer* 14 May 16/4 The Kilty piping for money.

Hence *attrib.* and (jocularly) as adj.

1900 Crockett *Anna Mark* xii, Yon's nae lassie! Yon's a kiltie lad. 1927 Vachell *Dew of Sea* etc. 261 She assured him..that he was the 'kiltiest' boy she had ever met.

Kimono. Add: b. A similar robe worn as a dressing-gown or tea-gown by women of Western nations.

1902 *Daily Chron.* 11 Jan. 8/3 Over a soft skirt a silken kimono makes a new looking tea-gown. 1928 F. B. Young *My Bro. Jonathan* II. viii, She was dressed in a blue kimono ..wrapped closely about her figure.

Kinaki (kinaki). *New Zealand.* [Maori.] A relish eaten with plainer food.

c 1870 T. Chapman in W. L. Buller *Birds N.Z.* (1873) 93 Norway rats..by diving for these freshwater pipis, provide a *kinaki* (relish) for their vegetable suppers. 1878 *Trans. N.Z. Inst.* XI. 76 Fifty years back it would have been a poor *hapu* that could not afford a slave or two as a *kinaki*, or relish, on such an occasion.

Kinase (kai·nēs). *Biochem.* [f. Gr. κινεῖν to move + *-ase.] A ferment that activates another ferment.

1902 *Jrnl. Chem. Soc.* LXXXII. II. 615 Kinases of Microbic Origin. 1923 T. R. Parsons *Fund. Bio-Chem.* iii. 32 This enterokinase is an example of the group of substances termed 'kinases', which have the power of activating the mother substances or precursors of enzymes.

Kind, *sb.* Add: 8. b. *The worst kind* used advb. = severely, extremely, very badly. *U.S. vulgar.*

1839 Marryat *Diary Amer.* II. 227 He loves Sal, the worst kind. 1877 Bartlett *Dict. Amer.* (ed. 4), *Worst Kind.* Used in such phrases as, 'I gave him the worst kind of a licking.' Also adverbially; as, 'I licked him the worst kind', *i.e.* in the worst manner possible, most severely. 1892 *Harper's Mag.* Feb. 437/2, I want something to read the worst kind. 1901 Marah E. Ryan *That Girl Montana* xvii. 221 Now that you have got here, I'd hate the worst kind to lose you.

14. d. (Earlier U.S. examples.) Also *kinder sorter* (see Sort *sb.*[2] 8 c).

1796–1801 Fessenden *Orig. Poems* (1806) 81, I kind of love you, Sal—I vow. 1830 *Massachusetts Spy* 6 Jan. 1/5, I was kind of provoked at the way you came up. 1834 C. A. Davis *Lett. Jack Downing* 90 This kinder corner'd me, and made me a little wrathy. 1836 *Public Ledger* (Philad.) 27 July (Th.) She looked a kind o' slantindicular at him, and I think he kissed her. 1844 'Jon. Slick' *High Life N.Y.* II. 213 The chap he kinder eyed me askew. 1855 Haliburton *Nat. & Hum. Nat.* I. vi. 190, I rather kinder sorter guess so, than kinder sorter not so.

Kinderspiel (ki·ndəɹʃpīl). [G.] A dramatic piece performed by children.

1902 *Daily Chron.* 19 Dec. 5/2 An opera..and a kinderspiel are being rehearsed. 1930 *Aberdeen Press & Jrnl.* 28 Feb. 3/2 'Blossom Time', a pretty kinderspiel, was part of a delightful entertainment given..by the Sunday School children.

Kind-hea·rtedly, *adv.* [-ly[2].] In a kind-hearted manner.

1900 H. C. Beeching in *Monthly Rev.* Nov. 91 The brass lectern, which the good sister..kindheartedly uncovered for him.

Kine-[2] (ki·ni), variant (reverting to the Gr. initial κ) of *Cine-, as in *kine camera, kinechrome, kinegraph, kinenegative, kine-variety.*

1899 *Daily Chron.* 31 Aug. 3 (Cass. D. Suppl.), The British Museum authorities have made arrangements for the safe custody of kinenegatives dealing with events of national importance. 1923 *Chambers's Jrnl.* 603/2 The kinegraph registers the short intake of the breath marking his embarrassment. 1924 *Westm. Gaz.* 24 Jan., The Kinechrome method of kinematography in natural colours. 1927 *Bulletin* 12 Aug. 14/2 An enthusiast for the kine camera. 1928 *Daily Express* 28 Mar. 13 He has turned the music-hall into a home of kine-variety.

Kinema (ki·nĭmă, kəinī·mă). Variant of *Cinema with initial *k* from the Greek original.

1914 *Even. News* 29 Sept. 4/5 It was my first step in the path of the kinema actor. 1921 *19th Cent.* Apr. 672 Properly handled, the Kinema could be made to endear the two races to one another. 1925 *Public Opinion* 20 Feb. 181/1 The Kinema is the most intimate and appealing medium for the dissemination of ideas. 1928 *Western Morning News* 28 Dec., The new kinema on the site of the old Post Office at Totnes.

b. *attrib.* and *Comb.*, as *kinema-camera, film, -girl, -producer, projection.* Also **Ki·nemaco:lour,** a proprietary name for a method of producing moving pictures in natural colours by means of revolving colour screens.

1927 *Manchester Guardian Weekly* 2 Dec. Suppl. p. xvi/2 The *kinema-camera. 1909 *Daily Chron.* 3 June 7/2 '*Kinema-color', or animated scenes in nature's actual tints. 1914 *Times* 29 Jan. 4/3 These lectures might perhaps be illustrated by kinemacolour photographs. 1918 H. Croy *How Motion Pictures are Made* 288 By the Kinemacolor process colored motion pictures were made of the Coronation. 1915 *Truth* 6 Oct. 567/1 A levy of 1d. per foot on all imported *kinema film. 1919 Narran (*title*) The *Kinema Girl. 1921 *19th Cent.* Apr. 672 The *Kinema-producers in California. 1916 *Chambers's Jrnl.* 26 Feb. 207/1 [The lamp's] suitability for *kinema projection.

Kinematograph. Add earlier example. Hence **Kinematograph** *v. trans.*, **Ki:nemato·grapher, Ki:nematogra·phical** *a.*, **Kinemato·gra·phically** *adv.*, **Ki:nemato·graphy.** (Variants of the corresponding *Cine- forms: cf. prec.)

1896 *19th Cent.* July 135 The *Kinematograph is already at more than one of them [*sc.* the music-halls], showing a stormy sea, the Thames at Waterloo Bridge, the race for the Derby. 1908 *Daily Chron.* 26 Sept. 7/2 By permission of the Lords of the Admiralty, Mr. Charles Urban during the past five months has enjoyed facilities to *kinematograph the efforts made during this period to salve the Gladiator. 1911 *Chambers's Jrnl.* 412/1 Here, however, the scientific *kinematographer has gone farther. 1900 *Nature* 15 Feb. 384/2 Prof. R. W. Wood will exhibit..the *Kinematographical Demonstration of the Evolutions of Reflected Wave-fronts. 1925 *Daily Mail* 13 Apr. 6/5 One..important thing ..is to get into the hiding-place unobserved by the birds which he happens to be *kinematographically on the track of. 1907 *Westm. Gaz.* 24 Aug. 6/3 Acting, Sir, is mere *kinematography. What we require is something more static, reposeful, and intellectual. 1909 *Chambers's Jrnl.* 271/2 The most important stride in colour-photography, at any rate so far as kinematography is concerned, that has yet been attained.

Kinematoscope. = *Cinematoscope.

1898 *Windsor Mag.* VIII. 113/1, I knew that conjurors were to be obtained there,..and the kinematoscope. 1926 *Encycl. Brit.* Suppl. II. 960/2 This machine was patented in the United States as the Kinematoscope Feb. 5 1861.

Kinesimeter (kainĭsi·mĭtəɹ). [f. Kinesi- + -meter.] An instrument for measuring motor sensations of the skin.

1885 H. H. Donaldson in *Mind* X. 402 This machine was devised by Prof. Stanley Hall, and will be described in a forthcoming paper, under the name of the 'Kinesimeter'. 1901 E. B. Titchener *Exper. Psychol.* I. 145 Arm-rest, designed for use with kinesimeter. 1901 *Baldwin's Dict. Philos. & Psychol.* I. 611/1 *Kinesimeter* (regulated moving point, for exploration of the cutaneous surface).

Kinetite (kəi·nĭtəit). [f. Kineto- + -ite[1].] A kind of explosive (see quot. 1918).

1887 W. Smith in *Jrnl. Soc. Chem. Ind.* 29 Jan. 3/1 The so-called kinetite is virtually one of what Dr. Sprengel terms his 'safety explosives'. 1918 E. de W. S. Colver *High Explosives* 142 Kinetite, an explosive which was considerably used from about 1883 to 1900, consisted of potassium chlorate incorporated with nitrobenzene and gelatinised with collodion cotton and sulphur.

Kineto-. Add: **Kine·togram,** a motion-picture taken by a kinetograph. **Kine·tograph** *v. trans.*, to make a cinematographic record of. **Kineto·grapher** = *Cinematographer. **Kineto·graphy** = *Cinematography. **Kinetonu·cleus** *Biol.*, in trypanosomes, a smaller nucleus, concerned with the locomotor activities of the cell. **Kine·tophone,** an apparatus combining the functions of a kinetoscope (*b*) and a phonograph. **Kine·toplast** *Biol.* [F. *kinétoplaste*] (see quots.). **Kinetosta·tics** *Math.*, the conditions of equilibrium of a system with latent cyclic motions.

1897 *Knowledge* Sept. 217/2 When making the original *kinetograms. *Ibid.* 218/1 Slow movements may be *kinetographed. *Ibid.* 217/2 Reproduced through the labours of 'special' *kinetographers. *Ibid.* 217/1 *Kinetography is based upon the principle of the well-known zoetrope. 1906 H. M. Woodcock *Hæmoflagellates* in *Q. Jrnl. Microsc. Sci.* L. 182 The resulting body, which may be termed the *kinetonucleus, passes into the now rounded trophonucleus. 1906 M. Hartog in *Cambr. Nat. Hist.* I. 120 First division of nucleus into larger (trophic) and smaller (kineto-)nucleus. 1920 W. E. Agar *Cytol.* 193 Trypanosomes, where a darkly staining body ('kinetonucleus') which is in close anatomical relation to the flagellum and therefore apparently concerned with the function of locomotion, is supposed by many to have been derived from the nucleus. 1896 *19th Cent.* July 135 The *Kinetophone is not at the [music-]halls yet, perhaps; but is probably on the way to them. 1925 *Manson's Trop. Dis.* (ed. 8) 636 This composite body is known as the *kinetoplast, and is composed of a minute blepharoplast, or basal body, and a parabasal body. 1926 C. M. Wenyon *Protozool.* I. 116 The name *kinetoplast* is employed here to designate the compound structure consisting of a united parabasal and blepharoplast. Kinetoplasts are typically seen in trypanosomes and allied flagellates. 1902 *Encycl. Brit.* XXVII. 571/1 *margin*, *Kinetostatics.

King, *sb.* Add: 5. *Freemasonry.* (See quot.)

1860 A. G. Mackey *Lexicon Freemasonry* 167 *King*, the second officer in a Royal Arch Chapter.

6. (Earlier U.S. examples of modern use.)

1846 J. G. Saxe *Progress* (1847) 28 How would she strive, in fitting verse, to sing The wondrous Progress of the Printing King! 1848 W. Armstrong *Stocks* 14 The interests on one side are represented by some single individual..who..for a while carries everything before him, and raises or depresses any particular stock or stocks at his..will and pleasure. Such persons are termed..the King of the street. 1886 *Harper's Mag.* July 253/1 The mighty magnate rightly called king by the masses.

12. a. *King-Emperor, -Sovereign.*

1902 *Westm. Gaz.* 27 Feb. 11 The *King-Emperor is honoured among us [*sc.* Americans] because he stands for the great people whom he rules. 1908 Sir H. Johnston *Geo. Grenfell* 448 The Governors-General or heads of departments representing the *King-Sovereign in Africa.

13. **king-carp,** a variety of the carp, *Cyprinus rex cyprinorum*; **King Country,** an extensive region in the N. Island of New Zealand formerly allotted to the Maoris under a king; **king-monkey,** an African horse-tailed monkey, *Colobus polycomus*; **king-mullet,** a bright red West Indian mulloid fish, *Upeneus maculatus*; **king-salmon** (earlier U.S. example).

1908 *Westm. Gaz.* 7 Aug. 10/3 Yesterday a *king carp was hooked by Mr. L. Childs. 1910 *Encycl. Brit.* V. 382/2 The king-carp or mirror-carp, in which the scales are enlarged and reduced in number. 1884 Kerry-Nicholls (*title*) The *King Country; or, Explorations in New Zealand. 1851 P. H. Gosse *Nat. Sojourn Jamaica* 208 There was a pair of *King-mullets (*Upeneus maculatus*). 1881 *Amer. Naturalist* XV. 177 These species [in the North Pacific] may be called the quinnat or *king salmon.

14. **king's** (or **king**) **ball** *U.S.* (see quot. 1851); **king's own** *Naut.* (see quots.); **king's peg,** a drink compounded by pouring champagne upon liqueur brandy; **king's roll,** a roll of employers pledged to employ at least a fixed proportion of ex-service men.

1832 J. Hall *Leg. West* (Philad.) 153 [He] spent..his time in..attending the *king-balls, and playing the fiddle. 1851 A. O. Hall *Manhattaner in N.O.* 122 A king's ball? —Ah, you have not heard. Certain of the youngsters..at every yearly winter's ball of the neighborhood, are presented with bouquets by the ladies, who have been the chosen queens of the festivities then concluding; and each bouquet presentee is crowned the king of the next year's ball. 1830 Marryat *King's Own* iii, Every article supplied to his Majesty's service from the arsenals and dockyards is thickly studded with this mark [*sc.* the broad arrow]; and to be found in possession of any property so marked is a capital offence, as it designates that property to be the '*King's own*. 1898 Ansted *Dict. Sea Terms*, *King's own*...It was one of many names given to the salt beef supplied to the people. 1899 C. J. Cutcliffe Hyne *Further Adv. Captain Kettle* xi, Cranze kept up a steady soak on *king's peg—putting in a good three fingers

of the liqueur brandy before filling up the tumbler with champagne. 1912 L. J. Vance *Destroying Angel* ii, Peter whistled, watching the wine cream over the brandy in the long glass. 'King's peg, eh?' he said, with a lift of disapproving eyebrows. 1919 Haig in *Times* 11 Nov. 10/5, I.. appeal to employers..to give a pledge of their sympathy by enrolling their names on the *King's National Roll under the national scheme for the employment of disabled men. 1920 *Ibid.* 16 Feb. 9/4 The King's Roll. First edition, with 9,500 firms, now in the press.

15. **King Charles's head,** a type of 'fixed idea' or ineluctable obsession, with reference to Mr. Dick in *David Copperfield* (ch. xiv.); **King James('s) version** (chiefly *U.S.*), the Authorized Version of the Bible; also *King James.*

1897 A. Lang *Dickens's D. Copperfield* Introd. p. ix, Mr. Dick is an author from whose failing most professional scribes know that they cannot free themselves. We all have our *King Charles's Head. 1933 *Times Lit. Suppl.* 29 June 436/2 Mr. Leslie seems to find the question of the validity of Anglican Orders rather a King Charles's Head. 1835 *Penny Cycl.* IV. 374/2 The period of *King James's translation. 1931 *Sunday School Times* (Philad.) 22 Aug. 458/1 A good English translation should be in good English idiom, and the old King James was that at least. 1932 T. A. Rickard in *Jrnl. Royal Anthrop. Inst.* LXII. 283 He made 'a serpent of brass', as the King James version says.

King-bird. 3. (Earlier U.S. examples.)

1781 *Narragansett Hist. Reg.* I. 283 Fired at king birds. *a* 1793 Freneau *Poems* (1809) II. 97 Did wasps or king-birds bring dismay—? 1801 *Massachusetts Spy* 25 Nov. 1/2 Just as a parcel of King-birds will pick at a Crow.

Kingdom, *sb.* 4. d. Add: *To come into one's kingdom*: to acquire authority, power, attractiveness, or the like.

1930 L. G. Moberly *Eternal Dustbin* xiv. 194 That woman has come into her kingdom.

Ki·ngklip, short for **kingklipfish,** (-visch). [Du. *koningklipvisch*: see *Klipfish.] A South African sea-fish, *Epinephelus gigas.*

1893 H. A. Bryden *Gun & Camera* xx. 449 For a hot climate, many of the fish in Cape waters furnish excellent eating: the Roman, kingklipvisch, stomneus, steenbras, and klipvisch being among the choicest. 1923 *Nature* 24 Feb. 271/2 The kingklip (in appearance like a ling). 1930 C. L. Biden *Sea-Angling Fishes of the Cape* 2 Angling for.. kabeljou, stockfish, and king klipfish.

King-pin. 2. Add example of literal use, and to definition: The most important person or outstanding personage in a party, organization, etc.

1920 *N. Y. Even. Post* 18 Mar. (Th.) This kingpin of lobbyists is William H. Buckley. 1914 *Chambers's Jrnl.* Jan. 62/1 The cars are mounted on bogie trucks, the connection being by means of a central or 'king-pin'.

King's man. Add:

1. In the United States: One who favoured the English cause at the time of the Revolution.

a 1793 Freneau *Poems* (1809) II. 11 (To a Democratic Editor) Whate'er some angry king's-men say, You play a game that must be won.

4. *pl.* A name for the dramatic company otherwise known as 'the King's Majesty's Servants' under James I.

Earlier, the Lord Chamberlain's company.

1911 *Encycl. Brit.* XXIV. 774/2 James I. on his accession took this company under his patronage as grooms of the chamber, and during the remainder of Shakespeare's connexion with the stage they were 'the King's men'. 1923 E. K. Chambers *Elizab. Stage* II. 218 The King's men gave eight plays at Court..during the winter of 1614–15.

5. A member of King's College, Cambridge.

1803 *Gradus ad Cantabrigiam* 81 Ev'n gloomiest Kingsmen, pleas'd awhile, Grin horribly a ghastly smile. 1852 C. A. Bristed *Five Years in Engl. Univ.* 127 He came out the winner, with the Kingsman and one of our three close at his heels.

Kinit (ki·nit). *Physics.* [f. Gr. κινεῖν to set in motion + the final syllable of *unit.*] A unit of force equal to the force which, acting on a pound for one second, will increase its velocity by one foot per second. Proposed by J. D. Everett (1831–1904).

Kinjal (ki·ndʒal). [a. Pers. خنجر *khanjar* dagger.] A long double-edged dagger worn by Kurds and Caucasians.

1889 J. Abercromby *Eastern Caucasus* 130 At his waist hung a *kinjal* and a long native sabre. 1897 Blackmore *Dariel* viii, His hand was playing with his *kinjal* all the time, for so they call those deadly bits of steel, without which they never think their attire complete. 1924 *Blackw. Mag.* Feb. 149/1 The scar of a Kurdish kinjal.

Kink, *sb.*[1] 2. a. (Earlier U.S. examples.)

1812 T. Jefferson *Let. to J. Adams* 11 June, Adair too had his kink. He believed all the Indians of America to be descended from the Jews. 1838 *Knickerbocker Mag.* XII. 200 All of a sudden he got 'a kink in his head', which came nigh doing him an irreparable injury.

Kinkajou. Add:

2. An American step-dance.

1927 *Bulletin* 22 Sept. 5/5 The Kinkajou's Coming..It is.. a lively variation on the fox-trot. 1928 *Dancing Times* Jan. 643/2 Mr. Casani and Miss José Lennard gave demonstrations of the Yale and also the Kinkajou, to the 'Kinkajou Strut', both dance instructions and dance music having been received over the Atlantic 'phone the previous week.

Kinky, *a.* 1. Add: Also **kinkey.** Also *Comb.*, as *kinky-haired, -headed* adjs.

1844 *Congress. Globe* 6 Jan. App. 42/3 [The negro's] skull is as thick, his hair is as kinkey, his nose as flat..as they were the day he was first introduced. 1848 Major Jones *Sk. Travel* 146 The kinky-headed cuss looked at me sideways. 1923 H. L. Foster *Beachcomber in Orient* x. 229 Some tied their black hair in a knot at the back of the head, others let it fall in kinky disarray about the shoulders. 1925 G. W. Deeping *Sorrell & Son* xxix, The hard-bitten, kinky-haired casualty-sister.

2. (Examples.)

1889 *Sportsman* 2 Jan. (Farmer) The kinky ones and the worthy ones who play hole-and-corner with society. 1929 W. J. Locke *Ancestor Jorico* xix. 263 A fellow ought to know something about the funny kinky ways of ordinary men and women.

Kinnikinic. Add: 9 kinnikanic, -kinnio, kinnekinik, -konik, kinickinick. (Examples.)

1826 T. L. McKenney *Tour to Lakes* (1827) 181 The pipe of an Indian..and a pouch made of the skin of some animal, in which he carries his *kinnikanic*, a kind of fragrant weed that has a leaf like our box wood. 1839 C. A. Murray *Trav. N. Amer.* II. 22 We took out our kinnekinik-bag. 1844 — *Prairie-bird* II. 179 Volumes of *kinnekenik* smoke. 1890 Mrs. Custer *Following the Guidon* viii. 101 Kinnikinnic.. is a mixture of willow bark, sumach leaves, sage leaf, and tobacco, and is thoroughly mingled with marrow from buffalo bones. 1920 *Chambers's Jrnl.* 136/1 The curling wisps of *kinickinick* smoke.

Kinoplasm (kəi·noplæz'm). *Cytol.* [ad. G. *kinoplasma*, F. *kinoplasme*, f. Gr. κινεῖν to set in motion + Plasm.] That portion of the cytoplasm which originates the spindle-fibres (see quots.).

1896 E. B. Wilson *Cell* 108 Strasburger believes that the anterior cytoplasmic region, to which the cilia are attached, consists of 'kinoplasm' (archoplasm). 1901 C. N. Calkins *Protozoa* 274 Kinoplasm is fibrillar in structure and devoted to the formation of the active portions of the cell. 1905 H. Wager in *Rep. Brit. Assoc.* 567 Strasburger considers that the cytoplasm is of two kinds, which he calls kinoplasm and trophoplasm... The kinoplasm is that part of the cytoplasm which is active in the mechanics of cell-division and forms the fibres of the spindle, astral radiations, and such structures as centrosomes and blepharoplasts.

Hence **Kinopla·smic** *a.*, of or pertaining to kinoplasm.

1902 E. B. Wilson *Cell* (ed. 2) 322 The kinoplasmic or archoplasmic fibrillæ of the mitotic figure. 1905 H. Wager in *Rep. Brit. Assoc.* 577 Strasburger considers them [*sc.* blepharoplasts] as kinoplasmic in nature, and thus brings them into relation with his other kinoplasmic structures, the centrosome and spindle.

-kins, *suffix.* Variant of -kin in certain oath-words, as *bodikins, lakens* (see Lakin[2]), *maskins, pit(t)ikins*, and in *babykins, boykins*, etc.

Kinzigite (ki·ntsigəit). *Petrol.* [ad. G. *kinzigit*, f. the *Kinzig* Valley in the Black Forest: see -ite[1].] A crystalline schistose rock composed of garnet, biotite, and plagioclase.

1878 *Jrnl. Chem. Soc.* XXXIV. 208 Garnet-graphite-gneiss was hitherto unknown..being formerly known by the name of Kinzigite. 1882 A. Geikie *Text-bk. Geol.* 125 Kinzigite.

Kiota, obs. var. of Coyote.

1860 *Oregon Argus* 24 Nov. (Th.) You may guess there was but little meat on it when the kiotas left it.

Kiowa (kai·ǒwa). *Geol.* [Name of a tribe of American prairie Indians.] The designation of a formation of the Lower Cretaceous in Kansas.

1895 F. W. Cragin in *Amer. Geol.* XVI. 162 The Kiowa shales. *Ibid.*, The upper part of the Kiowa. 1924 C. Schuchert *Geol.* 541 The Kiowa or Denison fauna.

Kip, *sb.*[6] *U.S.* [Origin unknown.] A unit of load = 1000 lbs. Also *kip foot, inch.*

1914 H. R. Thayer *Struct. Design* II. 87 Shear in Kips. *Note*, 1 Kip = 1000 lbs. Moments in Kip Feet. *Ibid.* 250 Maximum shear 110 kips...Maximum moment 9140 kip in[ches].

Kip, *sb.*[7] *Gymnastics. U.S. colloq.* The feat of mounting the horizontal bar, when hanging by the arms, by swinging the legs forward and upward, then suddenly down again. 1911 Webster.

Kip, *v.*[2] *slang.* [f. Kip *sb.*[3]] *intr.* To go to bed, sleep. Also, to lie *down.*

1889 Barrère & Leland *Dict. Slang*, *Kip, to* (popular and thieves), to sleep or lodge. 1926 *Daily Mail* 1 Nov. 4/4 'Kip' (to sleep, from 'kip-house', a low-class lodging-house). 1919 *War Terms* in *Athenæum* 1 Aug. 695/2 'To kip' is to go to bed—or to what serves for a bed. 1929 Priestley *Good Comp.* I. iv. 116 Yes, we'll have to kip down for an hour or two, Annie. 1931 Tilsley *Other Ranks* 15 They kipped together and ate together.

Kip, *v.*[3] *Gymnastics. U.S. colloq.* [f. *Kip *sb.*[7]] *intr.* To perform the kip.

1911 Webster.

Kiplingese (kipliŋī·z). [See -ese.] The literary style and characteristics of Rudyard Kipling, *raconteur* and poet (1865–). Also **Kipling-e·sque** *a.* [see -esque], resembling Kipling in style. **Ki·plingite** [see -ite[1] 1 b], an admirer of Kipling; as *adj.*, characteristic of Kipling. **Ki·plingize** *v.* [see -ize], *trans.*, to make Kipling-like.

1899 *Daily News* 1 Dec. 8/2 The account of the making of the first axe..is told quite in the heroic style of Kingsley and Morris, flavoured here and there with more than a dash of '*Kiplingese'. 1909 H. G. Wells *Tono-Bungay* IV. iii. § 4 They served me up to the public in turgid degenerate Kiplingese. 1894 '*Sunlight' Year Book* 1895 77 A glance at the adaptation is enough to reveal its *Kiplingesque roll and emphasis. 1899 *Daily News* 11 Apr. 6/1 The remainder of the stories are shorter, and, occasionally, Kiplingesque. 1899 *Westm. Gaz.* 28 June 3/1 Thorpe..is, merely, the primitive Kiplingesque type of man transferred from the battle-field or the plains of India to the Stock Exchange. 1901 *Motor-Car World* Apr. 69 It is *not* the top-notchers who flaunt their powers at every passing horse-driver with a Kiplingesque 'ram-you, damn you' flourish. 1898 *Windsor Mag.* Dec. 131/1 True *Kiplingites. 1899 'G. F. Monkshood' *Kipling* 38, I have never met a woman that was a Kiplingite. *Ibid.* 188 Perhaps the most distinctly Kiplingite piece of prose in the whole book. 1903 *Times Lit. Suppl.* 2 Oct. 277/3 The whole poem..has another claim upon the attention of the reader as an example of *Kiplingized Longfellow.

Kiplingism (ki·pliŋiz'm). [See -ism.]

† 1. *Cambridge Univ. slang.* A sarcastic term for the errors and solecisms alleged to occur in the edition of the 'Codex Bezæ' (1793) by Thomas Kipling, afterwards Dean of Peterborough.

1803 *Gradus ad Cantabrigiam* 81 A Kiplingism; a blunder-buss levelled at poor Priscian's head by the *learned* Dr. Kipling. The opposition wits at Cambridge have composed an epigram of *Kiplingisms*. 1899 'G. F. Monkshood' *Kipling* 15 A 'Kiplingism' was long an expression for a Latin blunder.

2. Views or opinions or style of expression characteristic of Rudyard Kipling (see *Kiplingese).

1898 *Daily News* 7 Oct. 6/3 The manner otherwise may degenerate into sheer mannerism, a Kiplingism of Kipling. 1901 *Speaker* 26 Jan. 469/1 Sportsmen may be divided into two classes—those who care more for the chase than the killing and those who merely make 'bags' and break records. But the latter are not sportsmen..and their method is nothing but Kiplingism out of place. 1920 H. G. Wells *Outl. Hist.* 524/1 The crude Darwinism and the Kiplingism of the later Victorian years.

Kipper, *sb.* Add: 3. A person. Also, a young person, a child. *slang.*

1905 *Daily Chron.* 30 Mar. 4/7 The expression 'giddy kipper', which Mr. Charles Brookfield has introduced to Mr. Justice Darling's notice. 1907 *Punch* 10 Apr. 254/2 Half-a-dozen dreadfully common young bicyclists were commenting on her discomfiture with delighted exclamations of 'Giddy old Kipper', 'Sweet Seventeen', 'Cheero, Maudie—you'll win!' 1923 M. M. Gibb *Hetherington's Affinity* xx. 175 If you're enterprising enough to climb one of the trees christened by usage 'The Kipper's Tree', which hardly needs to be translated into plainer terms.

Ki·pper, *sb.*[2] *Austral.* [ad. aboriginal *kippa.*] A young native who has been initiated and is admitted to the rights of manhood.

1853 H. B. Jones *Adv. Australia* 116 Around us sat 'Kippers', i.e. 'hobbledehoy blacks'. 1885 Mrs. Campbell Praed *Austral. Life* i. 24 A ceremony at which the young men..receive the rank of warriors and are henceforth called *Kippers.*

Kipper, *v.* Add *transf.* and *fig.* examples.

1896 Kipling *Seven Seas, M'Andrews' Hymn* 36 The Leevin' God, That does not kipper souls for sport, or break a life in jest. 1924 *Glasgow Herald* 28 Jan. 10 Oily cotton-waste was picked up at the gates of yards and factories, and our hands were duly kippered over smoking lumps of this stuff.

Ki·pperer. [See -er[1].] One who kippers herrings.

1902 *Nature* 4 Sept. 435/2 The 'kipperer' and the 'gutter' have their peculiar troubles. 1920 *Glasgow Herald* 10 July 6 Joint meetings of fishermen, curers, salesmen, freshers, and kipperers were held at both places. 1930 *Aberdeen Press & Jrnl.* 21 Mar. 6/5 A shed..standing alongside a kippering kiln.., occupied by Mr. David Mackenzie, kipperer.

Kippersol (ki·pəɹsǫl). *S. Africa.* [Corrupt f. Kittisol.] The tree *Cussonia thyrsiflora*, which grows something like an umbrella in shape. Its roots contain much moisture and are chewed to quench thirst.

1893 'R. Iron' *Dream Life* 26 A kippersol tree. *Ibid.* 29 She..cut at the root of a kippersol, and got out a large piece ..and sat down to chew it. Kippersol is like raw quince. *Ibid.* 34 When one has had no food but kippersol juice for two days.

Kirghiz (kiəɹgī·z). Pl. **Kirghiz, Kirghizes.** Also **Kirgis, Kirghis, Khirgese.** A member of a Mongolian people dwelling between the Volga and the Irtisch. Also, the language of this people, a dialect of northern Turkic. Also *attrib.* Hence **Kirghi·zian** (**Kirgisian**) *a.* and *sb.*

1837 De Quincey *Rev. Tartars* Wks. 1854 IV. 162 The murderous attacks of their cruel enemies the Bashkirs and the Kirghises. 1888 *Encycl. Brit.* XXIII. 661/2 Tatar dialects (Kirghizian, Bashkiri, Nogai). 1898 A. J. Butler tr. *Ratzel's Hist. Mankind* III. 326 The Kirghiz women adorn their plaits with beads, shells, and copper buttons. 1921 *19th Cent.* May 871 Kirghizes, Lesghiens, Mingrelians. 1922 *Contemp. Rev.* Sept. 342 The Kirgisian population has retained its nomadic habits. *Ibid.* 347 The Communist Party is expelling the Kirgiz from their land and home. 1924 *Blackw. Mag.* Aug. 256/1 The Russians, who were conscripting young Khirgese men for use on the railway.

Kiri (kī·ri). [Jap.] The paulownia.

1727 Scheuchzer tr. *Kæmpfer's Hist. Japan* I. ix. I. 119 Kiri, is a very large but scarce Tree. 1822 Shoberl tr. *Titsingh's Illustr. Japan* 255 Sometimes this cane is made of the wood of the *kiri*-tree. 1875 F. V. Dickins *Chiushingura* (1880) 97 Cloaking the reality like the varnish on the pillow concealing the common *Kiri* wood it is made of. 1876 *Trans. Asiatic Soc. Japan* V. 9 The second of the Imperial badges is a representation of the leaf and flower of the *kiri*, or *Paulownia Japonica.* 1893 Sir E. Arnold *Adzuma* 106 Why, there's the *fuji* swinging lilac links Of sweetness; and the *kiri*,—sweeter still.

Kirombo (kirǫ·mbo). [Native name.] A bird of Madagascar, *Leptosoma discolor*, with a large crested head.

1891 Sibree in *Ibis* Apr. 224 The natives of the north-west of Madagascar give this bird the name of *Kirǒmbo*. It has the curious habit of hovering in the air and uttering a very loud note, striking its wings against the body as it calls. 1899 A. H. Evans *Birds* 378 Sub-fam. 2. *Leptosomatinae.*—

This contains only *Leptosoma discolor*, the Kirombo or Vorondreo of Madagascar and the Komoro Islands. 1915 J. Sibree *Naturalist in Madagascar* x. 138 The *Vorondreo*, or Kirombo roller.

Kischtimite (ki·ʃtiməit). *Min.* [f. *Kyshtym*, a town and district in the Ural Mountains + -ite[1]; cf. G. *kyschtymit.*] A fluocarbonate of the cerium metals allied to parisite.

1853 *Amer. Jrnl. Sci.* XXXV. 427 Kischtimite, a new mineral..from the gold-washings of the Borsowka river in the district of Kischtim in the Ural Mountains. 1892 E. S. Dana *Dana's Syst. Min.* 291.

Kiskadee (kiskădī·). Also **keskeedie, kiskadie.** [Echoic.] A large tyrant-bird of tropical America, esp. *Pitangus sulphuratus* (and other species of Guiana).

1891 *Timehri* New Ser. V. 61 One of the most common of birds..is a brown and yellow Tyrant-shrike called the keskeedie (*Pitangus sulphuratus*). *Ibid.* 88 The large kiskadee (*Pitangus sulphuratus*)..whose loud, harsh and fierce cry of kis-kis-ki-kadee is to be heard at all times of the day. *Ibid.* 89 A third kiskadie (*Megarhynchus pitangua*) is also often met with. *Ibid.* 90 A fourth kiskadee (*Tyrannus melancholicus*)...A fifth form of kiskadee (*Myiozetetes cayennensis*) is also fairly common about the city [*sc.* Georgetown]. 1922 *Blackw. Mag.* July 16/1 Glorious clumps of bamboo with kiskadees clinging like yellow blossoms to the bending plumes.

Kiskitomas. (Earlier U.S. examples.)

1810 Michaux *Arbres* I. 20 Shell bark bickery, nom le plus en usage...Kiskythomas par les Hollandois du New Jersey. 1832 D. J. Browne *Sylva Amer.* 184 The Dutch settlers..near the city of New York, call it Kisky Thomas Nut. 1836 Dunlap *Mem. Water Drinker* (1837) I. 48 While the rustic jest, or the tale of..wars..mingle with the cracking of the kisskatomasses..and walnuts.

Kisleu (ki·sliū, -lef). Also 4–7 **Casleu,** 6–7 **C(h)isleu, -lev,** 9 **Kis(h)lev, -lew.** [Heb.] The third month of the Jewish civil year and the ninth of the ecclesiastical year, corresponding to parts of November and December.

1382 Wyclif *Zech.* vii. 1 The word of the Lord is maad to Zacharie, in the fourthe day of the nynthe monethe, that is Casleu [*later version* Caslew; 1535 Coverdale Casleu]. 1388 — *Neh.* i. 1 It was doon in the monethe Casleu [1535 Coverdale Chisleu], in the twentithe 3eer. 1611 *Bible* 1 Macc. i. 54 The fifteenth day of the moneth Casleu. 1880 *Encycl. Brit.* XIII. 421/2 Upon the great altar of burnt offering a small altar to Jupiter Capitolinus was erected, on which the first offering was made on 25th Kislev 168.

Kiss-. Add: **kiss-curl,** a curl or ringlet drawn over the forehead, twisted in front of the ear, or grown at the nape of the neck.

1856 *Punch* 29 Nov. 219/1 Those pastry-cook's girl's ornaments called kiss-curls. 1867 H. Spicer *Bound to Please* II. 15 Bob Jessamy..was nursing a kiss curl, though it hung limperer than what it usually did do. 1930 *Daily Express* 8 Sept. 3/6 Any kind of curls from Nell Gwynn ringlets to kiss curls.

Kisser. Add: 2. The mouth. orig. *pugilistic slang.*

1860 *Chambers's Jrnl.* XIII. 348/1 His mouth is his 'potato-trap'..or 'kisser'. 1892 P. H. Emerson *Son of Fens* iv, 'Oh,' he say, and dabbed the wet mittens across my kisser kind of smart.

Kissing, *vbl. sb.* 2. Add: **kissing-bee** *U.S.*, an evening 'mixed party'.

1853 *Turnover: a Tale of N. Hampshire* 6 (Th.) [He was about] to shave and dress for a 'party' or 'kissing-bee'.

Kissing, *ppl. a.* b. Add: **kissing bug** *U.S.*, any one of several species of venomous blood-sucking Hemiptera of the family *Reduviidæ.*

1904 *N. Y. Even. Post* 4 Aug. 1 The doctors were unable to decide whether he had been bitten by a mosquito or a kissing bug. 1909 *Cent. Dict.* Suppl. s.v., The name *kissing-bug* originated in the newspapers in June, 1899, many persons being bitten that summer and often on the lip. 1925 *Manson's Trop. Dis.* (ed. 8) 802.

Kiss-me-quick. 1. (Earlier U.S. example.)

1845 *Knickerbocker Mag.* XXV. 375 Seen from the Bowery, it looks like a barn with a 'kiss-me-quick' hood on.

Kit, *sb.*[1] 3. Add: Also *the whole kit and biling* (*boodle, caboodle*). (Cf. *Caboodle.) *vulgar U.S.*

1869 *Trip to Rocky Mtns.* (De Vere) At one time there was good reason to fear that the whole kit and biling, as our men invariably called our traps, would be swept away. 1895 S. Crane *Red Badge of Courage* i. (1911) 14 Of course it might happen that the hull kit-and-boodle might start and run, if some big fighting came first-off. 1909 Parrish *My Lady of South* ix. 113 Wal, I'm yere now, an' I reckon ther whole kit an' caboodle will know 'bout it afore I leave.

Kit (kit), *sb.*[11] [Maori *kete.*] A basket plaited from flax, used by the Maoris.

1856 E. B. Fitton *New Zealand* 68 *note*, Neatly made baskets, plaited from flax, and known by the name of 'Maori kits'. 1877 *Colonial Experiences* 31 Potatoes were procurable from the Maories in flax kits. 1884 Lady Martin *Our Maoris* 44 My heart is like an old kête (*i.e.*, a coarsely-woven basket). The words go in, but they fall through.

Kitchen, *sb.* Add: 5. a. *kitchen-girl* (later U.S. examples).

1835 J. H. Ingraham *South-West* II. 253 There are some Yankee 'kitchen girls',..who can do more house work, and do it better, than three or four negro servants. 1854 Mary J. Holmes *Tempest & Sunshine* viii. 49 There came to the house where she lived a gentleman and lady, who saw the 'little kitchen girl'.

c. *kitchen cupboard, sink, stove* (U.S. example).

1862 *Trans. Ill. Agric. Soc.* (1865) V. 161 The warm *kitchen cupboard. 1879 *Harper's Mag.* June 134/1 The *kitchen sink. 1845 *Knickerbocker Mag.* XXV. 106 He wished her in the south of France or the *kitchen stove, rather than there.

7. **kitchen cabinet** *U.S.* (*a*) (see quot. 1929); (*b*) a group of friends and personal supporters of President Jackson who were alleged by his opponents to have more influence with him than his official Cabinet; hence, a private or unofficial group of advisers to one holding a political office; **kitchen Dutch,** a mixture of English and Dutch used at the Cape in speaking to servants by those who know Dutch only imperfectly; **kitchen police,** in the U.S. army, enlisted men detailed to help the cook, wash dishes, etc.

1841 Clay in T. H. Benton *Thirty Years' View* (1856) II. 324/1 There is a rumor abroad that a cabal exists—a new sort of *kitchen cabinet—whose object is the dissolution of the regular cabinet. 1860 J. Parton *Andrew Jackson* III. xvi. 183 These were the gentlemen—Lewis, Green, Hill and Kendall—who, at the beginning of the new administration, were supposed to have most of the President's ear and confidence, and were stigmatized by the opposition as the Kitchen Cabinet. 1886 *Congress. Rec.* 9 June 5472/1 The only ones that complain of these rules are the members of the kitchen cabinet...I can appreciate the power and force of the kitchen cabinet. It is an irrepressible Cabinet. 1904 *N. Y. Herald* 14 Sept. 5 The kitchen cabinet is a development of the ascendency of Governor Odell in republican affairs. It consists of the body guard of his closest friends and advisers. 1929 *Encycl. Brit.* XIII. 419/1 *Kitchen cabinet*,..an enclosed dresser, fitted with doors, drawers and special containers...The first American kitchen cabinets were brought out about the beginning of the twentieth century in the Middle West. 1894 Mrs. Barkly *Boers & Basutos* vii. 109 By this time they [*sc.* our two children] could both speak Sesuto and 'Low' or '*Kitchen Dutch' (as it is called in those parts) well. 1930 F. A. Pottle *Stretchers* 33 Before first call, six or more unfortunates crept out of bed and went on *kitchen police.

Kitchenable (ki·tʃĕnăb'l), *a.* [f. Kitchen *sb.* or *v.* + -able.] Suitable for cooking and serving at table.

1905 *Chambers's Jrnl.* Feb. 193/2 There is probably no bird upon our game-list which is more eagerly sought after than the wood-cock...for his kitchenable qualities. 1913 Bolam *Wild Life in Wales* vi. 50 In judging of the probable kitchenable qualities of a bird.

Kitchenette (kitʃĕne·t). orig. *U.S.* [See -ette.] A very small room, alcove, cupboard, or fitting in a house or flat, combining kitchen and pantry. Also *attrib.*

1922 *Glasgow Herald* 28 Apr. 5 The New York business woman..wants her kitchenette and her home cooking, be it ever so simple. 1925 Rinehart *Mystery Lamp* 28 'How many rooms?' 'Two..and a sort of kitchenette'. 1926 F. Kilbourne *Dot & Will, Vacation* (1929) 188 They had a little kitchenette apartment on the North Side. 1930 Joanna Cannan *No Walls of Jasper* iii. 56 She had never thought it ..too much trouble to..bustle away into the kitchenette to make up something nice and tasty for her George.

Kite, *sb.* Add: 3. b. A proposal or suggestion offered or 'thrown out' tentatively in order to 'see how the wind blows'. (Cf. *Ballon d'essai.)

1902 *Nature* 14 Aug. 380/2 A few suggestions have been thrown out by various students which must be regarded more as trial hypotheses than as definite conclusions, indeed they should be looked upon rather as 'Kites'. 1904 *Westm. Gaz.* 5 Aug. 2/2 The new Army scheme..is to be debated on Monday, but whether as a Government proposal or as the private kite of the Minister for War remains wholly obscure.

5. b. A playful term for an aeroplane.

1917 in A. J. L. Scott *Sixty Squad. R.A.F.* (1920) 100 He told me that he had managed to fly his kite back with great difficulty. 1928 *Daily Mail* 7 May 6/4 *A Kite.*—Loosely indicating an unidentified aeroplane.

9. a. **kite bar,** a bar or stripe of an undesirable colour in the plumage of a fancy pigeon.

1876 R. Fulton *Bk. Pigeons* 108 A softer shade of blue, with brown, or what are called by Pouter fanciers 'kite' bars.

b. **kite-boat,** a boat propelled by the pulling force of a kite; **kite-flier, -flying** *lit.* and *fig.* (additional U.S. examples); **kite-flying** also, sending up a 'kite' or *ballon d'essai.*

1903 *Daily Chron.* 9 Nov. 4/5 The *kite-boat seems to add unnecessarily to the horrors of the Channel passage. 1903 *Amer. Inventor* 15 Dec. 276 (Cent. D. Suppl.) S. F. Cody.. crossed the English Channel..in a 'kite-boat', described as a miniature submarine boat weighing four tons, and propelled by a modified box-kite. 1844 *Knickerbocker Mag.* XXIV. 258 The most persevering *kite-flyers that I know of, are the Reformers. 1859 Bartlett *Dict. Amer.*, *Kite-Flier*, a financier who practises the operation of 'kite-flying'. 1848 *Ibid.*, **Kite-Flying*, an expression well-known to mercantile men of limited means, or who are short of cash. 1898 'Anthony Hope' in *Daily News* 4 Apr. 7/1 Principally it [*sc.* the press interview] was said to be used as a means of what might be called kite-flying. 1927 *Daily Tel.* 30 Aug. 8/6 These suggestions are dismissed in British circles as mere 'kite-flying'.

Kite, *v.* Add: 1. To move quickly, rush. Also, to fly away, vanish. *U.S.*

1854 'O. Optic' (W. T. Adams) *In Doors & Out* (1876) 92 You did not use to be fond of 'kiting' round in this manner. 1865 Boudrye *Fifth N. Y. Cavalry* 165 A well directed shell..sent them 'kiting' to the woods again. 1901 G. W. Peck *Peck's Uncle Ike* I. 23 Prices of the goods go up kiting. 1908 R. W. Chambers *Firing Line* xix, If you go kiting off to town.

3. b. (Earlier U.S. example.)

1835 C. F. Briggs *Harry Franco* II. iv. 35 He stuffed half a dozen blank checks into his hat, and said he must go out and kite it to save his credit.

Kite's-foot, kitefoot. 2. (Later U.S. examples.)

1824 P. Horry *Life of F. Marion* xi. (1833) 93 By the time we had got well entrenched in clouds of fragrant kite-foot. 1834 W. A. Carruthers *Kentuckian in N. Y.* I. 24 A quid of real Kentuck twist or Maryland kite-foot.

Kittatinny (ki·tătini). *Geol.* [Name of a range of mountains in New York, etc.] A limestone formation in northern New Jersey.

1905 Chamberlin & Salisbury *Geol.* I. 159 The oldest erosion plain of the Appalachian Mountains..is sometimes called the Kittatinny base-level. 1909 H. B. Kümmel in *Jrnl. Geol.* XVII. 354 The known fauna of the Kittatinny limestone is not extensive.

Ki·ttenishness. [-ness.] Kittenish characteristics or behaviour.

1905 *Smart Set* Sept. 15/1 Monsieur de Latour felt, as well as saw, that Madame de Beauregard, for all her kittenishness, was really a very great lady. 1925 *Chambers's Jrnl.* 610/1 Ages back the American girl abjured all that was in the nature of kittenishness.

Kitty[4]. Add: 2. b. Applied to other kinds of pool or joint fund.

1904 *To-Day* 30 Nov. 578/1 Solo calls only are played with a 'kitty'. 1905 *Daily Chron.* 12 Sept. 4/7 'Kitty wins everything', is the bookmakers' plaint. 1924 T. Rohan *Confess. Dealer* iv. 51 The King of the Knock-Out..counts out banknotes to the tune of £1,000, and places these notes in the bowl or kitty which occupies the centre of the table. The first man to help himself from the kitty is the dealer who bid £100 at the sale. 1928 *Daily Express* 21 Feb. 11/1 The heavy cost of 'Kitty' to a racecourse bookmaker and his employees is not met by the profits on a limited turnover.

3. *Bowls.* The jack.

1909 *Westm. Gaz.* 6 Sept. 4/1 When the bowl goes near the kitty. 1920 G. T. Burrows *Mod. Bowls* i. 12.

Kittydid, variant of Katydid.

1815 R. Sutcliff *Trav. N. Amer.* xiv. (ed. 2) 268, I was entertained with the harmony..of the bull frogs, tree frogs, kittydids.

Kiva (kī·vă). [Native word (Hopi).] A chamber built wholly or partly underground, used by the Pueblo Indians for religious rites, etc.

1895–6 *17th Ann. Rep. Bur. Amer. Ethnol.* 611 A pueblo of the size of Awatobi..would no doubt have several ceremonial chambers or kivas. 1927 W. Cather *Death comes for Archbp.* IV. ii. 132 It was a smothered fire in a clay oven, and had been burning in one of the kivas ever since the pueblo was founded.

Kiwi. Add: 2. A non-flying member of the Air Force. *slang.*

1928 B. Hall *One Man's War* (1929) 289 Visited the Avenue Montaigne Headquarters. It is full of non-flying aviators. The American pilots call them Kiwis. 1925 E. Fraser & Gibbons *Soldier & Sailor Words* 137 *Kiwi*, Air Force slang for a man on ground duty and not qualified for flying service.

Ki-yi, *sb.* Add: Also, a little dog. *U.S.*

1907 Mulford *Bar-20* xi. 129 Yore th' snortingest ki-yi that ever stuck its tail atween its laigs, yu are. 1908 — *Orphan* xiii. 162 Don't hurt Humble's ki-yi and he'll be plumb nice to you.

Kizilbash (ki·zilbāʃ). (Also used as *pl.*) Also 8 -bac; 9 **Kizzil-, -bashi.** [Turkish, = red head.] a. A Persianized Turk of Afghanistan. b. Any colonist of Asia Minor of Turkish or mixed origin.

1727 J. G. Scheuchzer tr. *Kæmpfer's Hist. Japan* I. vi. 88 The *Kisilbacs*, or Noblemen, and great Families, in Persia value themselves mightily upon their being of Turcoman extraction. 1875 *Encycl. Brit.* I. 235/1 The *Kizilbâshes* may be regarded as modern Persians, but more strictly they are Persianised Turks. 1898 A. J. Butler tr. *Ratzel's Hist. Mankind* III. 365 In Persia and Afghanistan the Turks, Kizilbashes, Usbeks, Turcomans, are even more sharply distinguished from the Persians. 1902 *Encycl. Brit.* XXV. 120/1 The Kizzilbashes of Kabul. 1920 *Blackw. Mag.* Jan. 121/2 Hosts of Tartar, and Afghan, Persian and Kizilbash.

Klan, short for Ku-Klux-Klan. Also *Klansman.*

1924 J. M. Mecklin *Ku Klux Klan* i. 3 The modern Klan was organized by William J. Simmons in 1915. *Ibid.* 5 Masked men leaped from their cars clad in Klan regalia. *Ibid.* 6 Public sentiment..seems to have supported the Klansmen.

Klang (klaŋ). [G., = sound.] A musical tone composed of fundamental and overtones; = Clang *sb.* 3. Hence **Kla·ngfarbe** (-fa·ɹbə) [G. *farbe* = colour], musical quality of a note, timbre, 'clang-tint' (see Clang *sb.* 4).

1876 Stainer & Barrett *Dict. Mus. Terms*, *Klangfarbe*, ..quality of sound, *timbre*. 1890 J. Klauser *Septonate* i. 37 (Funk) In music a tone or a *klang* is thought, heard, and treated as a unit.

Klaxon (klæ·ksǝn). [Name of the manufacturing company.] An (electric) motor-horn. Also *klaxon-horn.*

1914 *Autocar* 4 July 44/2 The Klaxon will emit a short, sharp, deep-toned note. 1920 *Motor Man.* xv. (ed. 23) 150 The electrically-operated Klaxon horn. 1922 *Encycl. Brit.* XXXII. 492/2 Acoustic signals have not been generally successful with the exception of the Klaxon horn in aircraft. 1922 *Blackw. Mag.* May 654/2 Have a hand Klaxon fitted to your left hand. Nothing but a Klaxon can make itself heard above the din of the lorries. 1923 *Ibid.* July 22/2 Aeroplanes..sailed against the sky, their klaxons sounding.

Hence **Kla·xon** *v. intr.*, to sound a klaxon; **Kla·xoning** *vbl. sb.*

1922 E. V. Lucas *Genevra's Money* vi. 38 The almost constant clatter and Klaxoning of motor-cars and lorries on the high-roads. 1923 G. Frankau *Ger. Cranston's Lady* ii. Lues,

Klaxoning furiously, slackened pace round the dangerous stone-wall turning.

Klementite (kle·mĕntəit). *Min.* [Named (G. *klementit*) after C. *Klement*, of Brussels: see -ITE¹.] A silicate of aluminium and iron occurring in dark olive-green scales.

1892 E. S. DANA *Dana's Syst. Min.* (ed. 6) 656 Klementite. ..In thin scales in quartz veins at Vielsalm in Belgium. 1914 *Brit. Mus. Return* 225.

Kleptobiosis (kle:ptobəi,ō^u·sis). *Zool.* In quots. clepto-. [f. Gr. κλέπτης thief, κλέπτειν to steal + βίωσις way of life.] The association as neighbours of different species of ants, one of which preys on the booty collected by the other. Hence **Kle:ptobio·tic** *a.*

1910 W. M. WHEELER *Ants* xxiii. 426 *Cleptobiosis*.—Forel ..suggests that this term be restricted to those cases in which small ants establish their nests near or on the nests of larger species and either feed on the refuse food or waylay the workers when they return to their home and compel them to give up their booty. 1923 — *Soc. Life Insects* v. 200 1. Brigandage (Cleptobiosis). 2. Thievery (Lestobiosis). 1928 — *Soc. Insects* 278 Compound nests may be divided into several minor categories, the cleptobiotic, lestobiotic. *Ibid.* 279 Certain small but aggressive species..deserve the name of brigands (cleptobiosis).

Klip (klip), *sb.*¹ *S. Africa.* [Du., = cliff, rock, stone.]

1. A stone, pebble.

1852 C. BARTER *Dorp & Veld* vi. 50 Stooping to set large *klips* (stones) behind the wheel, to prevent the wagon from slipping back.

2. A diamond.

1887 J. W. MATTHEWS *Incwadi Yami* xiii. 186 The natives had not yet acquired a knowledge of the value of diamonds or 'klips' as they were then termed. 1892 J. R. COUPER *Mixed Humanity* vi. 48 Flogged to death for stealing a 'klip' (as the Dutch and many of the Kaffirs call a diamond). 1897 *Pearson's Mag.* July 67/1 Fifteen years on that blathted breakwater, just for being found with a few little klips on you.

Hence **Klip** *v. trans.*, to place a stone behind (a wheel) in order to prevent the vehicle from running backwards.

1878 H. A. ROCHE *On Trek in Transvaal* iv. 91 We crawling into the wagon, the wheels of which were 'klipped', to keep us from running down the hill, trying to nap at intervals, and to get warm if we could.

Klip (klip), *sb.*² *Geol.* Also **klippe.** [G. *klippe* (pl. *klippen*) rock.] A mass of rock carried across others by an overfold and left stranded through the denudation of the rocks which once connected it with its place of origin.

1912 B. WILLIS in *Smithsonian Misc. Coll.* LVI. No. 31. 12 It is well known that some of these isolated masses, those of the Klippes, are 'exotic'. 1914 G. A. J. COLE *Growth Eur.* ix. 164 The outlying remnants of overthrust folds or sheets, since they stand up as cliffy masses on the back of more regular ground, have been styled *Klippen*, from 'Klippe', a cliff. Since a technical term is required, we may call these *klips*, meaning outlying portions of a fold or of an overthrust layer, resting on rocks which are not those on which they were originally laid down. *Klips* are thus strangers in the district where they now occur. *Ibid.* 168 An example of klip-structure that is by this time classical is seen in the Klein and Gross Mythen above Schwyz.

Klipfish (kli·pfiʃ). Also **klippfish, -fisch.** [ad. Da. *klipfisk* (f. *klippe* rock) and G. *klippfisch*, Du. *klipvisch* (f. *klip* rock).] **a.** Codfish split open, salted, and dried. **b.** A large ophidioid fish, *Genypterus blacodes*; the ling of New Zealand. **c.** A blennoid fish of the genus *Clinus*, esp. *C. superciliosus*.

1835 *Penny Cycl.* IV. 273/2 The klip-fish is cut along the back, and the back-bone taken out, after which it is salted down in the bottom of the vessel. 1881 WALPOLE *Rep. Salmon Fisheries* 23 The klipp fish are split and boned before they are salted...Cod are either cured as stock fisch or as klipp fisch. 1930 C. L. BIDEN *Sea-Angling Fishes of the Cape* 158 The most common species of klipfish (*Clinus superciliosus*, one of the few sea fishes giving birth to its young).

Klondyke, -dike (klǫ·ndəik), *sb.*

1. The name of a district in Yukon, N.W. Canada, the scene of a gold-rush in the years following 1896. Hence *fig.*, a mine or quarry of valuable material.

1897 *Athenæum* 9 Oct. 483/3 The rich Klondyke of Malory and Geoffrey of Monmouth had not escaped the eyes of previous prospectors.

2. A card-game played with a single pack of fifty-two, the object being to see how many cards can be built up in sequence and suit on a row of aces. *U.S.*

1908 U. SINCLAIR *Metropolis* vi. 91 The smoking-room, where the stout little Major had gotten a group of young bloods about him to play 'Klondike'. 1908 R. W. CHAMBERS *Firing Line* ii. 20 That kills our four at Bridge...We'll have to play Klondike and Preference now.

3. The name given to a herring fishery off the W. coast of Scotland. (Cf. *KLONDYKE *v.*)

1929 W. KEIR *Herring Trade on Continent 1928*, 16 In the early part of the season the trawlers fished mostly on the 'Klondyke' grounds off the West Coast of Scotland.

Klo·ndyke, *v.* [See prec. 3.] *trans.* To export (fresh herring) by fast steamer to the Continent. Hence **Klo·ndyking** *vbl. sb.*

1923 *Glasgow Herald* 25 Oct. 6 A regular fleet of steamers 'Klondyking' or running the fresh fish direct from the various landing ports to Germany. 1927 J. T. JENKINS *Herring* 132 The 'freshing' export trade, known as 'Klondyking'. *Ibid.* 146 While trawled herring are unsuitable for pickling, they are well adapted for 'Klondyking'—a method of preparing herring for export practically fresh by sprinkling them with salt and ice. 1930 *Aberdeen Press & Jrnl.* 30 Jan. 8 If a boycott was attempted, they would klondyke their supplies into the Dutch and other markets. 1930 *Morning Post* 2 Aug., Reference is made to the quantities of herrings 'klondyked'—which means despatched fresh to the Continent. Those who order catches for this purpose are called 'klondykers'.

Klondyker (klǫ·ndəikəɹ). [f. *KLONDYKE *sb.* + -ER¹.]

1. One who tries his fortune in the Klondyke gold-field.

1904 G. BURGESS & W. IRWIN *Picaroons* 102 The Story of the Returned Klondyker.

2. A dealer who exports fresh herrings from the Scottish fisheries to the Continent. Also, a steamer employed for carrying the fish.

1926 *Glasgow Herald* 19 Dec. 8 The 'Klondykers' are.. the German boats which buy the herring and transport them for sale in Germany. 1930 *Aberdeen Press & Jrnl.* 30 Jan. 8/1 It was pointed out that, if the curers refused to handle the Sunday-caught fish, exporters and klondykers would get supplies at a very cheap rate.

Klooch (klūtʃ). *N.W. Amer.* Also **Klootch.** [Chinook jargon (from Nootka) *klootchman* woman, female.] An Indian woman or girl. Also **Kloo·tchman.**

1907 R. W. SERVICE *Songs of Sourdough* (1908) 75 I've sent my klooch to town, With a haggard face and a ribband of red entwined in her hair of brown. 1920 in *Spectator* 25 Dec. 846/1, I drive to the West where the Kloochmen are best.

Klumene (klū·mīn). *Chem.* [f. *K*, chemical symbol of potassium + L. *lūmen* light + -ENE.] Acetylene (see quot. 1900).

1853 H. WATTS *Gmelin's Hand-bk. Chem.* VIII. 150 The black mass which often passes over with the potassium, in the preparation of that metal from burnt tartar and charcoal.., and appears to be a carbide of potassium, gives off, when immersed in water, a peculiar combustible gas, which is klumene gas. 1900 V. B. LEWES *Acetylene* 63 Edmund Davy, in 1836, named the newly-discovered gas bicarburet of hydrogen..; whilst later the name 'klumene' was bestowed upon it, because it had been derived from a kalium compound—potassium carbide. 1901 *Oxf. Univ. Gaz.* 3 Dec. 204 Olefine and Klumene Compounds. 1902 *Encycl. Brit.* XXV. 35/1 Acetylene, klumene or ethine.

Knackaway, variant of *KNOCKAWAY.

Knall-gas (kna·lgæs). [G., f. *knall* loud sudden sound, detonation + *gas* gas.] A detonating gas (esp. an explosive mixture of hydrogen and oxygen).

1910 *Encycl. Brit.* VI. 28/2 The combustion of 'knallgas' (a mixture of hydrogen and oxygen) to water-vapour. 1924 *Nature* 8 Mar. 373/2 In exploding such mixtures as normal hydrogen-air ($2H_2+O_2+4N_2$) or a $2CO+O_2$ 'knall-gas'. 1927 BONE & TOWNEND *Flame & Combust. Gases* 432 The undiluted 'knall-gas' ($2H_2+O_2$).

Knapsacked (næ·psækt), *a.* [f. KNAPSACK + -ED².] Equipped with a knapsack.

1905 *Westm. Gaz.* 26 Aug. 3/1 The knapsacked mountaineers come and go. 1926 ROSE MACAULAY *Crewe Train* I. i, Knapsacked British walkers.

Knawel. (Later U.S. example.)

1893 B. TORREY *Footpath-Way* 38 Found chickweed and knawel in bloom.

Knead, *v.* Add: **3. b.** To poach (ground).

1868 *Rep. U.S. Comm. Agric.* (1869) 425 [It] also points to the avoidance of kneading wet meadow by the tread of cattle.

Knee, *sb.* Add: **1. b.** A damaged condition of the knee. Cf. *housemaid's knee* (HOUSEMAID c), *tennis-knee* (TENNIS *sb.* 3 b).

1921 *E. H. D. Sewell's Rugby Football* 195 Unfortunately developed a 'knee' and had to retire in his prime.

7. d. *Graphics.* A sharp turn or abrupt change in a plotted curve.

1904 *Physical Rev.* Aug. 114 On the rising curve there is seen to be a more or less well defined 'knee' where the relation of stress to strain undergoes a marked change. 1926 R. W. HUTCHINSON *Wireless* viii. 144 Consider now the parts of the curve where the bending is greatest, *i.e.* the 'knees'.

9. b. Earlier examples of *cypress knee*.

1823 E. JAMES *Rocky Mtn. Exped.* III. 178 The innumerable conic excrescences called knees, which spring up from the roots..give a gloomy and peculiar aspect to the scenery of those cypress swamps. 1826 T. FLINT *Recoll.* 262 (Th.) The innumerable cypress 'knees', as they are called, resembling circular bee-hives, throwing their points above the waters.

12. *knee-buckle* (earlier Amer. example), *-grip*, *-pad*, *trousers* (U.S.).

1761 *Essex Inst. Hist. Coll.* XLVIII. 96 To be sold by George Deblois..a great variety newest fashion shoe and *knee buckles. 1925 E. T. BROWN *Complete Motor-cyclist* 126 The non-essential accessories include a luggage grid, speedometer, leg-shields.., *knee-grips, handle-bar gloves. 1858 J. A. WARDER *Hedges & Evergreens* 71 As it is easier to work on your knees, you will provide thick *knee-pads for them. 1899 T. HALL *Tales* 162 Since she was a little girl in short dresses and he a boy in *knee trousers.

13. knee-board (*b*), in a cotton-yarn winding-machine (see quot.); **knee-breech**, sing. of *knee-breeches*; **knee-crop** *U.S.*, a crop in the cultivation of which the field-workers have to kneel; **knee-hobbling** *vbl. sb.*, fastening an animal's knees with a hobble; **knee-length** *attrib.*, reaching down to the knee; **knee-pipe**, a pipe shaped like a bent knee; **knee-plate** (*b*), an angled plate to connect a beam or girder to the side of a ship; **knee-sprung** *a. Farriery* (see quot.); **knee-stake** *v. trans.*, in *Leather manuf.*, to soften (a skin) by aid of the knee.

1895 R. MARSDEN *Cotton Weaving* 257 The board..generally called the *knee-board, an incorrect name if regard be had to its function. This board is usually covered with flannel, and forms a check upon the too easy delivery of the yarn to the draught of the spindle, thereby securing uniformity of tension in the winding. 1904 *Daily Chron.* 11 Oct. 3/5 Men do not dress now, they merely clothe themselves, and they will not alter this fact by adopting the *knee-breech. 1927 *Observer* 22 May 12 A Blow to the Knee-breech Crusade. 1928 *Saturday Even. Post* (N.Y.) 10 Mar. 170/2 The Mexican..does heavy field work—particularly in the so-called 'stoop crops' and '*knee crops' of vegetable and cantaloupe production. 1908 *Animal Managem.* (W.O.) 150 Grazing should be afforded at every opportunity, and for this purpose *knee-hobbling is the best plan to adopt. 1909 *Daily Chron.* 6 Jan. 7/1 Both sexes wear deerskin breeches and *knee-length coats. 1929 *Evening News* 18 Nov. 2/2 A knee-length coat trimmed with brown ermine. 1905 J. W. AXE *The Horse* I. 74 When the knee is displaced forward in advance of the vertical line it is said to be 'bowed', or the horse 'stands over', '*knee sprung'. 1903 FLEMMING *Pract. Tanning* 51 When in just the right condition, the skins are *knee-staked for the purpose of softening them and to get rid of the stretch.

Knee, *v.* Add: **3. b.** To urge (a horse) on by pressing the knees against its flanks. *U.S.*

1924 MULFORD *Rustlers' Valley* iii. 33 Then he..turned his own animal southward and kneed it forward. 1926 — *Cassidy's Protégé* x. 133 The herder,..kneeing his horse, rode swiftly back and forth several times for a hundred feet each way.

7. To renew the knees of (a garment). *U.S.*

1847 H. HOWE *Hist. Collect. Ohio* 348 After wearing out their woollen pantaloons, [they] were obliged to have them seated and kneed with buckskin.

Knee-high, *a.* Reaching as high as the knees. Freq. in U.S. jocular phrase *knee-high to a grasshopper* (*mosquito*, *duck*, etc.), i.e. very short.

1824 *Microscope* (Albany, N.Y.) 12 June 55/1 (Th.) He has lived with me ever since he was 'knee high to a musquitoe'. 1833 J. NEAL *Down-Easters* I. 78 A bit of a rogue he was too, when he wa'n't more'n knee high to a bumbly-bee. 1841 W. G. SIMMS *Kinsmen* (Philad.) II. 63 (Th.) Ever since I was knee high to a splinter. 1843 [see KNEE *sb.* 12]. 1845 S. JUDD *Margaret* I. xvi. 141 But they an't knee high to a toad to't. 1855 *Florida Plant. Rec.* 132 The cotton in the lower most cut..will avrige knee high. 1878 B. F. TAYLOR *Between Gates* 281 Nearly everything will grow in California. It seldom gets knee-high. 1887 *Harper's Mag.* Oct. 754/2 Their myriads of gray trunks stood knee-high in water. 1899 MARY N. MURFREE *Bushwhackers* iii, One of the men said that he had known Jerry since he was 'knee-high ter a duck'.

Kneeler. 4. Add: *attrib.* in *kneeler chair*.

1909 MARG. B. SAUNDERS *Litany Lane* I. xi, She would follow the Stations of the Cross with a slow dreaminess, and lean longer over her kneeler chair when the services had finished.

Kneeling, *vbl. sb.* **3.** *kneeling-desk* (earlier Amer. example).

1647 in *Maryland Archives* IV. 321 A kneeling desk, & a picture of Paules.

Kneipe (knəi·pə), *sb.* Pl. -en. [G.] A convivial meeting of University students (and the like) at a tavern or restaurant. Hence **Kneip** *v. intr.* [after G. *kneipen*], to indulge in this conviviality.

1864 H. MAYHEW *German Life* II. 243 Youths whose lives are apparently given up to the mere conviviality of '*Kneiping*' or beer-drinking. 1874 J. M. HART *German Univ.* 139 (Cent. D. Suppl.) In whatever other respects the German student may be irregular, he always kneips according to rule. 1924 A. GEIKIE *Long Life's Work* vii. 217 After the meetings during the day, every night a 'Kneipe' at which Zirkel, Lossen, Reusch..and a host of younger men took part.

Kneippism (knəi·piz'm). [See -ISM.] A system of hydrotherapy ('kneippsche kur') advocated by Sebastian Kneipp, Bavarian priest (1821–97), a special feature of which is walking barefoot over dewy grass.

1901 DORLAND *Med. Dict.* (ed. 2).

Knicker². Add: Leg coverings of the knickerbocker type (either closed or open at the knee), worn by women and girls instead of drawers with or without an underskirt or petticoat.

1882 *Queen* 7 Oct. (Cassell), I recommend flannel knickers in preference to flannel petticoats. 1895 *Home Chat* 20 Apr. 176/1 We are really most keen over the construction of these knickers, knowing as we do from experience their great comfort. *Ibid.* 2 Nov. 273/2 The ideal knickers are of black satin, with removable Lanura linings. *Ibid.* 301/2 Serge knickers..for girls from twelve to sixteen. 1926 *Ibid.* 22 May 507 French Knicker made in Grafton's Voile and Grafton's Chiffonelle. Trimmed with lace. Elastic waistband. 1926 *Vogue* Late Nov. p. xxiii, An Original Directoire Knicker of milanese.

c. knicker yarn (see *KNICKERBOCKER 3 c).

1929 *Encycl. Brit.* XXIII. 879/2 'Knicker yarns' are produced by throwing little bits of highly coloured material into the last cylinders of the card so that instead of being broken up by carding they are carried forward as 'knickers' into the spun thread.

Knickerbocker. Add: **3. b.** = *KNICKER².

1887 *Lady's World* Oct. 403 It [*sc.* a peasant's blouse] is girdled at the waist by a leather belt, and falls over the short woollen skirt, which just reaches the knees, where it meets the linen knickerbockers. 1913 B. L. BLACKMORE *ABC of Cutting Garments* 140 In girls' knickerbockers, the back-band is sometimes buttoned to the front band, instead of the whole garment being attached to an under-bodice or to stays.

c. knickerbocker yarn: see quots.

1911 *Encycl. Brit.* XXVIII. 906/2 *Flaked Yarn* has a cloudy appearance imparted to it..(*c*) as in *Knickerbocker Yarn*, by dropping small quantities of dyed fibres into two ..rovings at the spinning machine. 1914 BARKER & MIDGLEY *Anal. Woven Fabrics* 271 *Knickerbocker Goods*.—A fabric in part or entirely made from knickerbocker yarns. *Knickerbocker Yarns*.—Yarns which are spotted or striped, often in several colours...The true knickerbocker yarn is produced by flecking the spotting material on to the carder.

Knife, *sb.* Add: **1. f.** *The knife* used as typical of surgical operations, as *to have a horror of the knife*. Phr. (U.S.) *to go under the knife*: to be operated on.

1880 TENNYSON *In Children's Hospital* i, But they said too of him He was happier using the knife than in trying to save the limb. *Ibid.* vii, My sleep was broken besides with dreams of the dreadful knife.

g. *To get or have one's knife into* (a person): to exhibit a malicious or vindictive spirit towards; persecute unrelentingly.

1892 'J. S. WINTER' *Mere Luck* viii, You have..a general disposition to feel that the whole world has, to use a very modern phrase, 'got its knife into you'. 1911 H. WALPOLE *Mr. Perrin & Mr. Traill* vi. 112 This was to be the beginning of persecution. The Reverend May-Thompson had got his knife into him.

2. a. *knife-back*, *-blade* used *attrib.*; also *knife-blade-like*; *knife-tray* (U.S. example); *knife-featured* (example).

1886 *Harper's Mag.* June 119/2 Between these *knife-back ledges are plots of sea-green grass. 1902 *Daily Chron.* 12 Sept. 3/2 The snowy *knife-blade *arête*. 1911 J. A. THOMSON *Biol. Seasons* i. 44 The knife-blade-like larvæ of the eel. 1895 *Century Mag.* Aug. 638/2 A tall, lanky, sharp-boned, *knife-featured fellow. 1851 C. CIST *Cincinnati* 215 Among the principal articles are..*knife trays.

2. b. knife-bar (earlier U.S. example); **knife-bracelet**, an iron bracelet with a sharp edge, used as a weapon by African natives; **knife-cleaner** (earlier U.S. example); **knife-man**, a skilled workman who uses a knife instead of a spade in delicate parts of archæological excavation; **knife-plait, -pleat** *Needlework*, an overlapping pleat about the width of a table-knife blade; **knife-rest** (*b*) *Mil. slang* (see quot. 1925); **knife-roller**, a (cotton-gin) roller furnished with sharp blades; **knife-switch** *Electr.* (see quot.); **knife-thrower** *U.S. slang*, a waitress.

1867 *Trans. Ill. Agric. Soc.* VII. 312 By the arrangement of its parts the *knife-bar is placed further forward than in most machines. 1898 *Geog. Jrnl.* (R.G.S.) XI. 383 To guard themselves from capture, they wear a very sharp *knife bracelet, when fighting they remove the sheath. 1868 LOUISA M. ALCOTT *Lit. Women* (1869) II. i. 12 A *knife-cleaner that spoilt all the knives. 1901–2 R. C. BOSANQUET in *Ann. Brit. School Athens* VIII. 294 The few picked '*knife-men' who lay or crouched in the trenches cutting through the compost of bones and pottery inch by inch. 1911 WEBSTER, **Knife plait*, a narrow overhanging plait. 1927 *Vogue* 2 Nov. 14 French, *Knife, Box, Accordion, Crystal and Combination Pleats can be made in any size. 1928 *Daily Mail* 31 July 1/2 Well made with smart knife pleats at sides. 1919 *War Terms* in *Athenæum* 15 Aug. 759/1 *Knife-rests, *chevaux de frise*. 1921 BEWSHER *51st Div.* 114 Stooks of cut strands of wire and overturned knife-rests lay everywhere. 1925 E. FRASER & GIBBONS *Soldier & Sailor Words* 138 *Kniferest*, the name at the Front for a portable X-shaped wire-entanglement framework, resembling a knife-rest, used for stopping gaps in wire-entanglements in No Man's Land. 1927 A. KEITH-FALCONER *Oxfordshire Hussars* 215 The two R.E. men with the torpedo at once blew the wire up (it was only one knife-rest thick) and the party crossed the trench. 1929 C. EDMONDS *Subaltern's War* 54 A framework of stakes and barbed wire of the kind which soldiers call a 'knife-rest'. 1896 TAGGART *Cotton Spinning* I. 28 The seed cotton..comes into contact with a *knife roller, formed of a number of knife discs. 1910 *N. Hawkins' Electr. Dict.* 235/1 **Knife switch*, a switch having a movable blade of copper or brass which makes a contact between two parallel contact springs. 1905 *Smart Set* Oct. 31/1 'They got a new *knife-thrower up to the hotel', he announced..(A 'knife-thrower', be it known, is parlance for waitress).

Knife, *v.* Add:

3. *U.S. Football. intr.* (See quots.)

1920 W. CAMP *Football without a Coach* 107 If any of these three center men lunges through—'knifes' through, as it is called—he opens the door on either side of him...The hole that the man in the line has left by knifing through now becomes a yawning cavity. *Ibid.* 116 The first caution to be given a guard on defense is not to knife through.

Knife-edge. 2. b. Add: *esp.* A sharp crest of rock or ice, an arête.

1907 *Westm. Gaz.* 26 Nov. 3/2 The road thereto lies along a 'knife-edge'. 1925 E. F. NORTON *Fight for Everest, 1924* 31 A ridge which begins in a knife-edge of rock worthy of the Chamounix Aiguilles.

3. *Diamond-cutting.* (See quot.)

1909 J. WODISKA *Bk. Precious Stones* 349 *Knife-Edge*. The girdle of a brilliant cut to a sharp edge and polished.

Knifer. Add: **2. a.** (See quot. 1896.) **b.** A ruffian who stabs with a knife. *slang.*

1896 FARMER & HENLEY *Slang*, *Knifer*.., a sharking sponge. 1905 *Times* 11 Dec. 5/2 This is a new move of the hooligans and knifers, who lately committed attacks on enlightened working men.

Knifester (nəi·fstəɹ). [f. KNIFE *sb.* or *v.* + -STER.] One addicted to stabbing with a knife.

1932 F. BUCK & E. ANTHONY *Bring 'em Back Alive* 78 In many of these out-of-the-way districts they cheerfully cut your throat for nothing. There are Hindu knifesters who seem to be striving to preserve their amateur standing.

Knight, *sb.* **12. c.** Add: *Knight of the road*, (*b*) a commercial traveller; (*c*) a tramp.

1889 J. BURNLEY *Rom. Mod. Industry* 317 Customers used to come out miles upon summer evenings to meet the 'knights of the road',..and the old travellers on their part would spend two or three days with some of their clients. 1928 *Sunday Express* 12 Feb. 11/4 Secrets of the Commercial Traveller's Bag. By John S. Banks, for twenty years a 'Knight of the Road'. 1928 *Daily Express* 8 Aug. 3/5 If something of this spirit could be instilled into the regular 'knights of the road', if they could be inspired with some notion of the dignity of work and the shame of almstaking.

Kniphofia (niphō^u·fiă). [mod.L.; named after J. H. *Kniphof* of Erfurt (1704–65): see -IA.] A plant of the African liliaceous genus so named, with tall stems bearing spikes of bright scarlet, red, orange, or yellow flowers; cultivated as a perennial, esp. *K. aloides*; the torch lily; = TRITOMA.

1896 W. ROBINSON *Eng. Flower Garden* (ed. 5) 593/1 The Kniphophias..are among the most striking of autumn flowers. 1900 L. H. BAILEY *Cycl. Amer. Hort.* 859/1 Kniphofias are often classed by dealers as bulbous plants. 1900 W. D. DRURY *Bk. Gardening* 336 In height Kniphofias vary between 3 ft. and 5 ft. 1901 *Cassell's Dict. Gard.* I. 426/2 In dry soils Kniphofias should have plenty of water in summer.

Knit, *sb.* Add: **1. b.** (*a*) The action or process of knitting. (*b*) A style of knitted work.

1924 *Sale Catal.* Artificial Silk Scarves..assorted stripes and fancy knits. 1926 E. K. MIDDLETON *New Knitting* Pref., Left hand knit and left hand purl are simpler and quicker than the old right hand knit.

Knitting, *vbl. sb.* **3.** Add: *knitting bee*, *frolic*, *wire*; **knitting-sheath** (later U.S. example).

1880 *Harper's Mag.* Sept. 508/1 In winter they sometimes had *knitting bees. 1828 FEARON *Sk. Amer.* 223 They are invited to the preacher's house, to partake of a supper..this is termed a *knitting frolic. 1867 'T. LACKLAND' *Homespun* I. 23 A great tear trembles on her cheek as she adjusts her needle in the *knitting sheath she wears. 1849 *Rep. U.S. Comm. Patents* (1850) 491 The needle itself, and thimble will be exhibited in museums with distaffs, spinning-wheels, *knitting-wires [etc.].

Knitwear (ni·twēəɹ). [f. KNIT *ppl. a.* + WEAR *sb.*] Knitted articles of clothing.

1925–6 *Army & Navy Co-op. Soc. Price List* 698 'Braemar' Knitwear for Gentlemen. 1928 *Daily Express* 7 May 4 Two-piece suits, knitwear, leather coats and raincoats.

Knob, *sb.* Add: **1. e.** *With knobs on*: jocular slang phr. indicating the speaker's mock approval or appreciation of something that has been said.

1930 MARG. KENNEDY *Fool of Family* xiii. 129 'I'm waiting for the Marchese Ferdinando Emanuele Maria Bonaventura Donzati.' 'With knobs on', agreed Gemma airily. 'Who's he?' 1931 J. J. FARJEON *House Opposite* ii, 'You are nothing,' said the Indian. 'And so are you, with knobs on!' barked Ben, and slammed the door.

2. (Later U.S. example.)

1895 *Century Mag.* Aug. 621/2 One of the many knobs from which Daniel Boone is said to have looked first over the Blue Grass land.

8. *knob-fronted* adj.; *knob-nosed* adj. (additional examples).

1885 *Encycl. Brit.* XIX. 647/2 The Chinese, *knob-fronted, or swan goose, *Anser cygnoides*. 1839 W. C. HARRIS *Wild Sports S. Africa* xxxix. 350 A friendly tribe of natives, whom, from a peculiarity in the nasal prominence, they dignified with the appellation of '*knob-nosed Kafirs'. 1864 J. A. GRANT *Walk Across Africa* 93 A knob-nosed duck. 1905 *Westm. Gaz.* 2 Oct. 8/2 The knob-nosed lizard (*Lyriocephalus scutatus*) from Ceylon.

Knob, *v.* **1.** (Earlier U.S. example.)

1849 *Rep. U.S. Comm. Patents* (1850) 315 The cards.. hook the cotton from the toothed cylinder and carry it forward without rolling or knobbing it.

Knobby, *a.* Add: **3.** Full of rounded knolls or hills; hilly. *U.S.*

1869 'MARK TWAIN' *Innoc. Abroad* xxvi. (1899) II. 317 It is as knobby with countless little domes as a prison door is with bolt-heads.

Knock, *sb.*¹ Add:

1. b. *To take the knock*: to be hard hit financially. *slang.*

1890 *Globe* 21 Apr. 6/1 (Farmer) A broken backer of horses who has taken, what is known in the language of the turf, as the knock. 1900 E. WELLS *Chestnuts* xxiii. 226 When a prominent backer takes the knock racing, he sometimes has the greatest difficulty to avoid his creditors.

3. *Cricket.* A spell at batting; hence, an innings.

1900 *Captain* III. 200/1 'You play cricket yourself, then?' 'Oh, I have an occasional knock.' *Ibid.* 210/1 'W. G.' advises every batsman to have a knock..before going in. An over or two at the nets loosens your muscles. 1909 *Pearson's Mag.* Aug. 180/1 Crofton's had won the toss and taken first 'knock'. 1927 *Observer* 27 Nov. 28 His knock..included eight boundaries.

4. In a steam or internal combustion engine (see quot. 1904).

1903 *Cassell's Cycl. Mech.* III. 264/1 Locating 'Knock' in Steam Engine. 1904 MECREDY *Dict. Motoring*, *Knock*, a peculiar thumping noise sometimes made by an oil engine, which denotes that something is wrong. It is quite a distinct noise from the regular beat of the engine. 1912 *Motor* 6 Aug. 38/2 Engine knock. 1920 *Cornhill Mag.* Sept. 314 The carbon knock, the ignition knock, and the bearing knock are fairly simple propositions.

5. *Knock for knock agreement* (see quot. 1927).

1906 *Daily Chron.* 26 July 6/6 Mr. Fairbank said that the 'knock for knock' agreement had never paid with the horse vehicles. 1927 B. C. HOSKINS *Insurance Lex.* 127 *Knock for Knock Agreement*.—An arrangement made between Companies..for dealing automatically with collisions between vehicles owned by their respective insureds; each Company undertakes to pay for the damage to its own insured's vehicle irrespective of the question of liability as between the parties in collision. 1928 J. B. WELSON *Dict. Accident Insurance* 362.

Knock, *v.* Add:

2. *To knock a hole*, *gap*, etc. *To knock daylight into* (cf. DAYLIGHT 1 c).

1881 *Punch* 17 Sept. 124/1 Ready at the call of duty to frame a new programme or knock daylight into an old one. 1890 A. CONAN DOYLE *Sign of Four* iv, He knocked a hole ..in the lath and plaster ceiling. 1906 SOMERVILLE & ROSS *Some Irish Yesterdays* 85 You may see him skilfully 'knocking a gap' (*i.e.* unbuilding a wall).

d. To surpass, excel, 'beat'. *U.S.*

1853 *Knickerbocker Mag.* XLII. July 55 (Th.) He 'knocked' all the adjacent male population, native and imported, in the matter of looks.

e. To speak ill or slightingly of, disparage, find fault with, criticize captiously. (Cf. *KNOCKER 1 e.) Also *intr.* *U.S. colloq.*

1901 *N. Y. Com. Advert.* 11 May (Cent. D. Suppl.) The fourth, and a very successful way, is what the Tammany men call 'knockin''. This is to fight Tammany Hall until the organization opens and receives you, paying in return almost anything within reason. 1904 *N. Y. Sun* 4 Aug. 5 'Of course there'll be plenty of cranks to knock this scheme', said he. *a* 1909 'O. HENRY' *Roads of Destiny* xx. 339 Now, quit knocking my profession. 1919 'IAN HAY' *Last Million* iii, A certain licence is permitted to professional grouchers; but 'knocking' the Cause is the one thing that the New Crusaders will not permit. 1928 L. NORTH *Parasites* 217 'There you go again. Always your hammer out—knocking California.' 'I'm not knocking California. It's this bit of California I can't stand—this Hollywood.'

absol. 1896 G. ADE *Artie* xii. 110 He's got to make good with 'em to keep 'em from knockin. 1921 R. D. PAINE *Comr. Rolling Ocean* xiii. 219 You are an earnest young cook, Jud, and far be it from me to knock, but—. 1926 *Spectator* 3 Apr. 635/2 A reputation for 'knocking' is enough to ensure being blackballed for some of the best clubs.

5. b. Of a steam or internal combustion engine: To make a peculiar thumping noise. (Cf. *KNOCK *sb.*¹ 4.)

1904 [see *KNOCKING *vbl. sb.* 1]. 1909 *Motor Cycling* 22 Nov. 32/1 If the engine begins to 'knock', a few vigorous thrusts at the pedals should be given immediately. 1925 R. J. B. SELLAR *Sporting Yarns* 186, I shall have to pull up, old chap. Cylinder's knocking!

6. b. *To knock the end in* or *off*: to spoil the whole affair. *slang.*

1919 *War Slang* in *Athenæum* 8 Aug. 727/2 To 'knock the end in' is to spoil the whole show. 1925 E. FRASER & GIBBONS *Soldier & Sailor Words* 138, *Knock the end off*, to, to spoil anything.

e. Also *to knock all of a heap* (see *HEAP *sb.* 5 e); *to knock silly*: to daze, stupefy (cf. SILLY *a.* 6); *to knock the nonsense*, etc. *out of*.

1895 *Century Mag.* Sept. 690/2 What's the matter with me, anyhow? Seem to be knocked silly with her blamed queer talk. 1931 *Times Lit. Suppl.* 15 Oct. 787/1 The boy returned to Turin, where his royal relatives did their best to get his revolutionary notions knocked out of him.

7. Knock about. b. (Earlier U.S. examples.)

1833 CROCKETT *Sketches & Eccentr.* i. 31 David, collecting his clothes,..began to knock about. 1834 W. G. SIMMS *Guy Rivers* xiv. 315 I've been a matter of some fifteen or twenty years knocking about..in one way or another.

8. Knock down. a. Also, to bring down by a shot.

1824 P. HORRY *Life of F. Marion* xii. (1833) 100 In such a country, where many a family goes without dinner unless the father can knock down a squirrel in the woods.

i. *U.S. slang.* (Earlier examples.)

1860 J. G. HOLLAND *Miss Gilbert's Career* xii. 220 Now, tell a feller, is there any chance to knock down? 1864 T. L. NICHOLS *Forty Yrs. Amer. Life* I. 89 The omnibus-drivers were expected to 'knock down' a certain proportion of the receipts.

k. *pass.* of a ship (see quot.). *U.S.*

1891 PATTERSON *Illustr. Naut. Dict.* 104 *Knocked down*, said of a vessel when, by the force of the wind acting upon her sails and spars, she is careened to such an extent that she does not recover herself.

10. Knock off. g. *pass.* of a ship: To be turned to leeward when struck by the sea on the weather bow.

h. *War slang.* To steal, 'pinch'.

1919 *War Terms* in *Athenæum* 8 Aug. 729/1 A curious term used by a Tommy, in 'explaining' his deficiencies of kit, is 'Someone knocked it off' for 'Someone pinched (or made away with) it'. 1928 E. WALLACE *Gunner* ii, I got him nine months at the London Sessions for knockin' off motor-cars.

i. In *machine-knitting* (see quot.).

1927 T. WOODHOUSE *Artificial Silk* 93 The old loop being thus liberated from the needle, is 'knocked off' by what is termed a knock-over-bit, so that the old loop joins the previously-made loop of the fabric.

12. Knock out. a. Also, (*a*) to stun or kill by a blow; (*b*) to empty (a tobacco pipe) by tapping.

1903 *N. Y. Sun* 2 Dec. 1 Scott's reputation is excellent, and the managers fear that he has been knocked out and robbed.

g. *U.S.* (Early example.)

1835 A. B. LONGSTREET *Georgia Scenes* 187 When the game was up, she soon 'knocked out' and went in quest of cold trails.

h. *trans.* To eliminate, get rid of. *U.S.*

1889 *Kansas City Times & Star* 17 May, By a vote of 11 to 9 the Missouri senate knocked out the legislative reduction of tolls here by the Bell Telephone Company. 1904 *N. Y. Sun* 5 Aug. 4 In power, the Democrats wouldn't knock out protection if they could.

i. *intr.* Of an aeroplane: To break down completely, to *CONK out.

1916 B. HALL *One Man's War* (1929) 212 All of a sudden, she knocked out and I let her sit out in the open and walked on into camp.

16. Knock up. a. *Bootmaking.* To cut or flatten the edges of the upper after its attachment to the insole.

1905 *Westm. Gaz.* 30 Oct. 7/3 A mechanical device for trimming off the surplus material from the lasted boot before it is 'knocked up', and a machine for the 'knocking-up' process itself, the latter guaranteed to 'knock up' between 400 and 500 pairs of boots per week.

d. Also, to prepare (food) quickly. *U.S.*

1868 LOUISA M. ALCOTT *Lit. Women* (1869) II. v. 61 Don't cry, dear, but exert yourself a bit, and knock us up something to eat. 1890 *Harper's Mag.* May 894/2, I jest killed a chicken, and knocked up a few biscuit.

Knock-about, *a.* (*sb.*). **B.** *sb.* Add: **3.** A rough fight. *U.S.*

1903 A. H. LEWIS *The Boss* xxii. 316 But he wouldn't listen; he was all for th' strong-arm, an' th' knock-about!

4. A small pleasure-boat or sailing-yacht. *U.S.*

1904 *N. Y. Evening Post* 21 May 6 There are numerous knockabouts and other small yachts in the Pawcatuck River.

Knockaway (nǫ·kăwei). *U.S.* Also **knackaway.** A corruption of *Anaqua*, a Mexican tree.

Knock-down, *a.* and *sb.* Add: **A.** *adj.* **2.** Also: *knock-down book*, *fee*. *U.S.*

1888 *Harper's Mag.* Nov. 934/2 Bills for knock-down fees are presented for payment to auctioneers every month. *Ibid.* 937/2 The knock-down book records the price, buyer, and all particulars of every sale in the Auction-room.

B. *sb.* **1. b.** = *KNOCK-OUT *sb.* 4. *U.S.*

1843 *Knickerbocker Mag.* XXI. 484 'Tom and Jerry' ushered before a Park audience the scientific Mr. T. Beicher Kay, one of the great knockdowns of foreign celebrity.

2. Also *knock down and drag out*. *U.S.*

1834 W. A. CARRUTHERS *Kentuckian in N. Y.* I. 61 It's what I would call a regular row; I never saw a prettier knock down and drag out in all the days of my life. 1837 R. M. BIRD *Nick of Woods* II. 105 It war a reggelar fair knock-down-and-drag-out, and I lick'd him!

4. The careening of a ship by the force of the wind. (Cf. *KNOCK *v.* 8 k.) *U.S.*

1888 *Scribner's Mag.* May 526/1 Every bit of that water came in through the hatch at the time of the knock-down.

5. An introduction. *U.S. slang.*

1896 G. ADE *Artie* iii. 24 Take me over and gi' me a knock down to the queen in the corner. 1911 L. J. VANCE *Cynthia* v. 61 You would n't take her for the kind you could pick up without a knock-down.

Knocker. Add: **1. e.** (See quot.)

1909 *Washington Post* 20 Feb. 1 The 'Knockers' are an organization of Cincinnati's most prominent business men... The business of the 'Knockers' is to knock hard and effectively all everything tending to hinder the material advancement of the city.

f. One who is addicted to captious criticism, fault-finding, or 'throwing cold water'. (Cf. *KNOCK *v.* 2 e.) *U.S. colloq.*

1911 *Springfield* (Mass.) *Weekly Republican* 27 July, The municipal 'boosters'..have no use for what they call 'knockers', critical citizens who are figuratively credited with using a 'hammer'. 1923 L. R. FREEMAN *Colorado River* 386 Disinterested scientists and engineers read the signs aright, and gave warning. Those of them that were not ignored entirely were just as effectually dismissed as Knockers. 1926 *Spectator* 3 Apr. 635/2 The intense dislike felt in America for what they call 'a knocker' (one who is too free with criticism of his associates). 1928 *Sunday Express* 18 Mar. 5/2 All the knockers were there,..yearning to find fault.

Knockered (nǫ·kəɹd), *a.* [See -ED².] Of a house door: Fitted with a knocker.

1921 *U. F. Ch. Missionary Rec.* May 137/1 We entered by those massive brass-studded and knockered doors. 1928 *Daily Tel.* 24 Apr. 12/7 Knockered front doors and curtained windows.

Knocking, *vbl. sb.* Add: **1.** In a steam or internal combustion engine (cf. *KNOCK *v.* 5 b).

1904 A. B. F. YOUNG *Complete Motorist* ix. (ed. 2) 220 If a knocking noise is heard in the cylinders. 1920 *Conquest* June 309/3 The [compressed] fuel..will be spontaneously ignited before the spark occurs. Motorists recognise the resultant symptoms by the name of 'knocking'. 1928 *Punch* 30 May p. xxi, Carbon causes knocking, and knocking means loss of power.

b. Also with *up* (see quots.).

1879 *Organ Voicing* 9 A knocking-up cup, similar in form to the cone...It is of great substance, and therefore, heavy, that it may the more readily effect its mission, namely, that of 'knocking up' or reducing the wind-hole of the pipe. 1909 T. ELLISTON *Organs* 331, *Knocking up cup*. A tool used by metal hands (metal pipe makers) for rounding off the terminals of metal tubes. It is of considerable substance (brass), and has a kind of handle at the top. 1924 F. G. LOWE *Lawn Tennis* 10 When a new stroke has been learnt ..it is an excellent idea to practise it against a wall until it becomes perfect. This 'knocking up' will also materially improve footwork and quicken up the player.

Knock-kneed, *a.* Add: (Earlier Amer. example.)

1774 *Maryland Hist. Mag.* VI. 41 Charles Blundell, an Englishman,..a very slender made fellow much knock-kneed, with light brown hair very short.

Knock-off. A. *sb.* Add:

2. The act of leaving off one's work or occupation; the signal for doing this. Also *attrib.*, as *knock-off signal*, *time*.

1899 'Knock-off' time [see B. in Dict.]. 1902 *Daily Chron.* 13 June 6/3 Just at that moment the officer in charge gave what is technically known as the 'knock-off', or the signal to discontinue the play of water on the building. *Ibid.*, After the 'knock-off' signal had been given.

Knock-on. In *Rugby Football*, the act of 'knocking-on' the ball (see KNOCK *v.* 11).

1882 *Laws of Rugby Union* 15 A Fair Catch is a catch made direct from a kick or a throw forward, or a knock on by one of the opposite side. 1888 [see KNOCK-]. 1893 in *B. F. Robinson's Rugby Football* (1896) 325 In case of a throw-forward or knock-on, the ball shall be at once brought back to where such infringement took place.

Knock-out, *a.* and *sb.* Add: **A.** *adj.* **c.** Designating a method of deciding an athletic competition or tournament by which the defeated competitors in each round are eliminated.

1897 RANJITSINHJI *Jubilee Bk. Cricket* 281 The first elevens meet in a series of matches, played on the 'knock-out' system. 1904 *Westm. Gaz.* 2 Feb. 8/2 The proposed county tournament on the 'knock-out' principle. 1908 *Captain* XVIII. 334/2 A House competition on the 'knock-out' plan. 1921 *E. H. D. Sewell's Rugby Football* 244 The competition was run on 'knock-out' lines as it is at the present time, the teams which entered being drawn in ties, and those left in after each round being again paired by lot until two only were left in for the final.

d. *Mech.* Designating a device for 'knocking out' or releasing some part; e.g. a 'knock-out key' for releasing a drill from a collet or clutch.

1907 *Install. News* Nov. 6/2 The 'knock-out' principle as applied to junction boxes.

e. *knock-out drops*, a liquid drug of which drops are put into liquor to facilitate robbing the person drinking it. *U.S. slang.*

1896 G. ADE *Artie* xviii. 173 They get out the bottle o' knock-out drops and get ready to do business. 1901 *Daily Chron.* 17 Dec. 5/2 'Knock-out drops' are well known in New York, and are a part of the effective tools in trade of the thug, the thief, and the confidence man. 1903 *N. Y. Sun* 12 Nov. 4 Bowery thieves were using chloral or 'knock-out drops' as an aid in robbing victims.

f. *knock-out man*, one who uses knock-out drops. *U.S. slang.*

1903 *N. Y. Evening Post* 18 Sept. 7 He may be one of the new sort of 'knockout men' discovered this week. 1928 *Saturday Even. Post* (N.Y.) 12 May 90/2 They're murderers and knockout men and they never play a straight game.

B. *sb.* **4.** A person or thing of 'stunning', overwhelming, or surpassing quality. *slang.*

1908 *London Mag.* June 473/2 The tent is a knock-out. 1918 'Q' *Foe-Farrell* xi. 163 The view from the top is a knock-out. 1926 *Ladies' Home Jrnl.* Nov. 13 Only it isn't very exciting for him, and I'm no knock-out to introduce around. 1928 *Saturday Even. Post* (N.Y.) 4 Feb. 118/2, I think he'd be a knock-out as a singer in a cabaret if he could sing.

5. *Sport.* A 'knock-out' competition: see *A. c.

1928 *Observer* 19 Feb. 22/2 That Clare and Caius should have got into the semi-finals of the Rugby 'knock-out' was not unexpected. *Ibid.* 4 Mar. 22 Pembroke..have won the finals..of both the football 'knock-outs'.

6. 'A device for throwing out finished work from a punching or stamping machine' (*Funk's Standard Dict.* 1895).

Kno·ck-up, *a.* and *sb.* **A.** *adj.* Designating a practice or casual game at cricket, fives, etc.

1928 *Weekly Dispatch* 24 June 21/7 All-England Championships Practice. Many of the world-famous players engaged in final 'knock-up' games at Wimbledon yesterday.

B. *sb.* **1.** A 'knock-up' game: see above.

2. In a drawing- or stamping-press, an ejecting-attachment for the lower die (Webster 1911).

Knop, *sb.*¹ Add: **1. b.** A loop or tuft (often of different colour) formed in a strand of yarn for ornament. Also *attrib.* in *knop yarn*. (See quots.)

1904 *Technol. & Sci. Dict.* (ed. Goodchild & Tweney), Knop Yarn. 1914 BARKER & MIDGLEY *Anal. Woven Fabrics* 272 *Knop Yarn*.—A yarn upon which knops or lumps of yarn of one or more colours appear at intervals. 1929 *Encycl. Brit.* XXIII. 879/2 The knop yarn—in which knops are formed at any required intervals on an otherwise level thread by holding one thread tightly and allowing the second thread to run in slackly to form knops of the required size.

Knopite (nǫ·pəit). *Min.* [ad. G. *knopit*; named, 1894, after Prof. A. *Knop*: see -ITE¹.] A variety of perofskite in which the calcium is partly replaced by cerium.

1896 *Min. Mag.* Oct. 158 Minerals at first thought to be perofskite and dysanalyte are here described under the new name knopite, of which two types are distinguished. 1899 DANA *Min.* App. 1. 39 *Knopite*...A mineral closely related to perovskite.., but containing cerium without niobium or tantalum and thus intermediate between it and dysanalyte.

Knopped, *a.* Add: **c.** *Knopped yarn*, yarn ornamented with knops or tufts. See *KNOP *sb.*¹ 1 b.

1911 *Encycl. Brit.* XXVIII. 906/2 *Knopped Yarn* is formed by twisting together several strands, one of which is at intervals delivered in greater lengths than the others, in order to allow a loop to be made.

Knopper (nǫ·pəɹ). [G., = gall-nut; pl. *knoppern*.] A species of oak-gall, used in tanning and dyeing.

1879 *Encycl. Brit.* X. 44/1 The 'knoppern' galls of *Cynips polycera*. 1908 E. T. CONNOLD *Brit. Oak Galls* 143 *Cynips calicis*...'The Knopper Gall'...It occurs principally on *Quercus pedunculata*, but also on *Q. sessiliflora*.

Knot, *sb.*¹ **19.** Add: **knot-catcher** (see quot.); **knot-gall**, a species of oak-gall produced by the cynipid *Andricus noduli*; **knot-head** *U.S.*, the Jewett apple; **knot-hole** (*b*) (example); **knot-horn** = *knot-horn moth*; **knot-writing**, a mnemonic aid consisting of strings in which a number of knots are made.

1927 T. WOODHOUSE *Artificial Silk* 100 The threads or yarn from the cone cheeses are first led up through coils in wires termed *knot catchers. 1894 C. R. STRATON *Adler's Altern. Generations* 34 The *knot gall is found in June on *Q*[*uercus*] *pedunculata*, *Q. sessiliflora*, and *Q. pubescens*. 1908 E. T. CONNOLD *Brit. Oak Galls* 65 The Knot Gall. 1903 *Westm. Gaz.* 31 Dec. 3/2 The little coons..climbed up to the *knot-hole, and scrambled down inside. 1899 D. SHARP in *Cambr. Nat. Hist.* VI. 424 The males frequently have the basal-joint of the antennæ swollen; hence the term '*Knot-horns' applied by collectors to these moths. 1896 A. J. BUTLER tr. *Ratzel's Hist. Mank.* I. 344 In West Australia,—a network of reed serves for a messenger's credentials,—a reminiscence of the once more widely-developed *knot-writing.

Knotted, *a.* Add:

3. c. *Geol.* (See quots. and KNOT *sb.*¹ 17.)

1885 A. GEIKIE *Text-bk. Geol.* (ed. 2) 127 *Knotenschiefer* (Knotted schist) contains little knots or concretions of a dark-green or brown..substance, of a talcose or micaceous nature, imbedded in a finely-laminated matrix of a talc-like or mica-like material. 1920 A. HOLMES *Nomencl. Petrol.*, *Knotted Schist* or *Knotenschiefer*.—See *Spotted Slates*.

Knotter. Add: **3.** With prefixed numeral: A boat or ship that makes (so many) knots an hour.

1908 *Pall Mall Gaz.* 20 Apr. 6/1 Not many of the so-called '30 knotters' could steam at this speed. 1929 'SEAMARK' *Down River* i, Essex noted the stolid little ten knotter ahead.

Know, *v.* Add:

8. b. *I want to know*, = well, well! *U.S. colloq.*

1840 *Knickerbocker Mag.* XVI. 20, 'I want to know!' said the lady; 'precious soul!' 1888 *Harper's Mag.* Sept. 530/1 'Why, Jerod Hopkins!' she said, looking up at him; 'I want to know!' 1911 J. C. LINCOLN *Cap'n Warren's Wards* x. 154 'She said she would be delighted!' 'I want to know!'

11. e. *don't you know?*, a variant of *you know*.

1896 F. C. PHILIPS *Undeserving Woman*, *Good Curtain* 104 'When?' said George. 'I'd like to put the thing right at once, don't you know.' 1897 HALL CAINE *Christian* 367 'Oh, let us, Glo,' cried Betty. 'I'd love it of all things, doncher know!' 1930 'SAPPER' *Finger of Fate*, etc. 225 My wife is such a nervous woman, don't you know.

16. b. *What do you know about that?* = Isn't that amazing? 'Well I never'. *U.S. colloq.*

1914 GERTRUDE ATHERTON *Perch of Devil* I. xvii. 103 What do you know about that?..Wouldn't it come and get you? 1916 'B. M. BOWER' *Phantom Herd* ii. 33 Now what do you know about that, Mig?

Know-. Add: **know-all** *a.*, (claiming to be) omniscient.

1881 TENNYSON *Despair* xvi, *We* have knelt in your know-all chapel. 1906 *Daily Chron.* 30 Aug. 3/4 He..maintains in his know-all manner that the two counties of Wigtown and Kirkcudbright..were integral parts always of the kingdom of Scotland. 1924 G. LAMBTON *Men & Horses* 112 Archer rode for Peck whenever he could, he dined with him, he hunted with him, and that was quite sufficient to make the suspicious and 'know all' brigade say that Archer was in Peck's pocket.

Knowing, *ppl. a.* **5.** (Later U.S. example.)

1905 *Springfield* (Mass.) *Weekly Republ.* 29 Dec. 16 Some of the neighbors were knowing to the event.

Know-nothing, *sb.* **1. a.** (Earlier example.)

1827 J. F. COOPER *Red Rover* ii, The fellow is a know-nothing.

2. (Earlier example.)

1854 *Congress. Globe* 10 July 1667/2 That misguided and proscriptive faction, called 'Native Americans' or 'Know-Nothings'.

Know-nothingism. 2. (Earlier example.)

1854 *Yale Lit. Mag.* XX. 12–16 (Th.) A few thoughts on Know-Nothingism.

Knox dolomite. *Geol.* [Named after *Knox* County, Tennessee.] An Upper Cambrian formation of the Appalachian region.

1906 CHAMBERLIN & SALISBURY *Geol.* II. 179 The Knox dolomite. 1920 A. W. GRABAU *Geol.* I. 597 Synclinal fold of Knox dolomite.

Knuck (nǫk). *U.S.* [Abbrev. of KNUCKLE *sb.*] **1.** *pl.* 'A game of marbles in which the winner shoots at his adversary's knuckles' (Clapin).

1840 *Southern Lit. Messenger* VI. 385 To the game of marbles he devotes much of his leisure time, and is counted a proficient particularly in knucks and five in the ring. 1886 *Harper's Mag.* Dec. 41/2 They were playing 'knucks' together.

2. A knuckle-duster.

1918 C. SANDBURG *Cornhuskers* 88, I slipped my fingers into a set of knucks.

Knuckle, *sb.* Add: **2. b.** *Near the knuckle*: near the permitted limit (in regard to decency).

1909 *Westm. Gaz.* 4 May 2/2 A series of articles entitled 'Crimes of Passion', full of abominable details 'as near the knuckle' as the police would allow. *Ibid.* 6 Sept. 1/3 If a play shows that its author has..a sincere respect for his art, it must be stopped if it goes at all 'near the knuckle'. 1930 W. S. MAUGHAM *Cakes & Ale* 147 What I like about 'er is that she gives you a good laugh. She goes pretty near the knuckle sometimes, but she never jumps over the fence.

6. knuckle ball *Baseball* (see quots.).

1927 *Secrets of Baseball* iii. 37 If you're worrying about when to use a 'knuckle ball'. 1928 G. H. RUTH *Baseball* vi. 79 The knuckle ball is a slow ball, that comes floating up to the plate without rotating. And lacking that rotation to keep it on a line, it wobbles from side to side. 1929 *Encycl. Brit.* III. 163/1 There is what is known as the knuckle ball, in which the knuckles of the pitcher's hand play a prominent part in giving the ball erratic motion.

Knuckle, *v.* Add: **3. b.** To dig (one's hand) into a specified position, knuckles first.

1890 HALL CAINE *Bondman* i, Thrusting his head beneath his chin, he knuckled his left hand under the islander's rib.

6. *Farriery.* With *over*, of the knee or fetlock: ?To project through weakness of the ligaments. Also with *forwards*. (Cf. *knuckle kneed*, KNUCKLE *sb.* 6.)

1877 A. SEWELL *Black Beauty* xl, The knees knuckled over, and the forelegs were very unsteady. 1877 M. H. HAYES *Veterinary Notes* i. 30 'Knuckling over', as a result of hard work, appears to be due to relaxation of the capsular and lateral ligaments [of the fetlock joint]. 1906 J. W. AXE *Horse* IV. 53 The animal knuckles over at the joints. 1907 *Ibid.* V. 298 The movements of the hind-limbs are for a time weak, and the fetlocks knuckle over now and again during progression. 1907 VARNELL *Ibid.* VI. 347 In young horses it is common to meet with a knuckling forwards of the hind fetlocks.

7. *Golf.* To bend the knee inward. Also *absol.*

1909 *Times* 23 Apr. 16/2 An elaborate knuckling of the right knee in putting. *Ibid.*, The 'knuckling' habit in putting has long been exposed as fallacious. 1909 *Westm. Gaz.* 11 May 12/3 You may 'knuckle' if knuckling conduces to comfort, provided that..you get the process over before beginning the actual stroke.

Knuckler. Add: **3.** *Baseball.* A knuckle ball (see *KNUCKLE *sb.* 6).

1928 G. H. RUTH *Baseball* vi. 79 Eddie used to toss 'knucklers' until he had the hitters blue in the face.

Knucklesome (nǫ·k'lsəm), *a.* [See -SOME¹.] Having prominent knuckles. Also *transf.*

1919 W. DE MORGAN *Old Madhouse* xx, That young woman was bony and knucklesome. 1922 C. E. MONTAGUE *Disenchantment* xii. § 3 The twisty valley and knucklesome banks of the Somme.

Knut, jocular variant, often pronounced (kənǫ·t), of *NUT *sb.*³ (a showy or fashionable young man). Hence **Knu·tty** *a.*

1913 MRS. HARKER *Ffolliots of Redmarley* v. (1919) 57 He was..a 'knut' of the nuttiest flavour. 1914 *Scotsman* 5 Oct. 8/1 It is clear that he has once been a 'knut' in spite of his oil-stained khaki service jacket and trousers. 1916 E. V. LUCAS *Vermil. Box* xlix. 52 Among the people staying here is a knut. He must be almost the last of the tribe; but here he is, just as knutty as though the Algies and Berties were still ruling the roast, and not Mars at all. 1919 C. ORR *Glorious Thing* xvii. 212 He was trying to be knutty, he said. 1929 G. STOWELL *Hist. Button Hill* III. § 11. 183 The Knut was an urban and suburban phenomenon of the years 1912 to 1914 inclusive.

Kobu (kō^u·bu). Also **kombu.** [Jap.] A seaweed, *Laminaria japonica*, eaten by the Japanese.

1882 SATOW & HAWES *Japan* (1884) 519 *Kombu*, a broad, thick, and very long species of seaweed, most of which is exported to China.

Kodiak (kǫ·dyæk), also **Kadiak** (kæ·dyæk), name of an island off Alaska, designating a very large brown bear, *Ursus middendorffi*, found there.

1899 R. WARD *Rec. Big Game* (ed. 3) 474 Even more gigantic is the Kadiak [*ed.* 1907 Kodiak] bear (*U*[*rsus*] *arctus middendorfi*) of Kadiak Island, Alaska. 1904 C. R. E. RADCLYFFE *Big Game Shooting in Alaska* 268 The Kodiak brown bear (*Ursus middendorffi*). *Ibid.*, A true Kodiak bear. 1930 *Sat. Even. Post* 13 Dec. 11/2 A Kodiak bear looks as big as an elephant as he ambles..through vegetation that comes only to his stomach.

Koechlinite (kō·x^ylinəit). *Min.* [Named after R. *Koechlin* of Vienna: see -ITE¹.] A native molybdate of bismuth.

1916 W. T. SCHALLER in *U.S. Geol. Surv., Bull.* 610. 14 Koechlinite is clearly a secondary mineral formed in the cavities of the quartz rock by the reaction of different solutions, one containing bismuth and the other molybdenum.

Koelreuteria (kəlroitiə·riă). [mod.L.; named after J. G. *Koelreuter* of Karlsruhe (1733–1806).] A tree of the sapindaceous genus so named, native to China.

1829 LOUDON *Encycl. Plants* 304 Kölreuteria. 1900 L. H. BAILEY *Cycl. Amer. Hort.* 861/1. 1901 *Cassell's Dict. Gard.* I. 463/2. 1920 A. D. WEBSTER *London Trees* 71 The Kœlreuteria is readily propagated by cuttings of either root or branch.

Koenenite (kō·nĕnəit). *Min.* [Named after Adolf von *Koenen*, geologist (1837–1915): see -ITE¹.] An oxychloride of aluminium and magnesium, found in red masses.

1902 *Jrnl. Chem. Soc.* LXXXII. II. 611 Koenenite..was found intimately associated with halite, anhydrite and carnallite, in crevices in the clay of the salt deposits at Volpriehausen, in the Sollinger Wald, Hanover. It is red in colour. 1922 W. E. FORD *E. S. Dana's Text-Bk. Min.* (ed. 3) 401.

Koi (koi). [Jap.] The common carp, *Cyprinus carpio*, found in the rivers of Japan.

1727 J. G. SCHEUCHZER tr. *Kæmpfer's Hist. Japan* I. I. xi. 136 *Koi* is another sort of it [*sc. Mebaar*], which also resembles a Carp. 1877 *Trans. Asiatic Soc. Japan* V. Chart facing 112 Fish Taken: Koi...Cyprinus hæmatopterus. 1892 SIR E. ARNOLD *Japonica* 48 It was the custom formerly, at certain feasts, to crimp the live *Koi*, and to place it, to be eaten raw, before the guests. 1893 — *Adzuma* 41 Shall they boil thee a fat *koi* from the fish-pond? 1904 FARRER *Garden Asia* 273 The koi-fish is a sturdy swimmer.

Koine (koi·nī). [Gr. κοινή, fem. sing. of κοινός common, ordinary.] The common literary language of the Greeks (ἡ κοινὴ διάλεκτος) from the close of classical Attic to the Byzantine era. Also *attrib.* and *transf.*

1913 D. B. DURHAM *Vocab. Menander* 8 The year 600 A.D. is a convenient date at which to divide the Koine from the Greek of the middle ages. 1927 A. H. MCNEILE *Introd. N. T.* 278 Such [constructions] as were rapidly making their way into the *Koine* Greek.

Koklas's (kō^u·klăs). Also **kuklass.** [Nepalese, var. of *pokras*, *pukras*.] Any pheasant of the genus *Pukrasia* of N. India and the Himalayas.

1898 *Ibis* Jan. 39 The Koklass was not uncommon in the forest above Gund. 1922 *Blackw. Mag.* Mar. 323/2 In the woods below a kuklass crowed hoarsely.

Kokowai (kō^u·kowai). [Maori.] Red ochre.

1845 E. J. WAKEFIELD *Adv. N. Zealand* I. 124 A carved post which was painted with *kokowai*, or red ochre. *Ibid.* II. 87 The *kokowai*-painted monuments which I have mentioned. 1878 *Trans. N. Zealand Inst.* XI. 75 *Kokowai* is a kind of pigment, burnt, dried, and mixed with shark-liver oil.

Kol (kō^ul). [Of disputed origin.] A term applied to the aboriginal people of Chota Nagpur, India; also = next.

1847 B. H. HODGSON *Aborig. India* p. ii, The Kól or Dhánger race. 1866 E. T. DALTON in *Jrnl. Asiatic Soc. Bengal* XXXV. II. 154 The present population..are of the race best known to us by the name of 'Kol'. 1896 W. CROOKE *Tribes & Castes* III. 295 Mahadêva, so the story goes, once caught a Kol girl. *Ibid.* 315 Most Kols are ploughmen. 1899 A. H. KEANE *Man Past & Present* xiv. 558 The Kols or Kolarians, who formerly overspread the plains of Bengal. 1903 RISLEY & GAIT *Census of India* I. 282 The Kol language has..two main dialects, Mundari and Ho.

Kolarian (kolē^ə·riăn), *a.* and *sb.* [f. *Kolar*, supposed early form of *KOL, identical with Canarese *kallar* thieves + -IAN.] Applied to a non-Aryan linguistic stock of India belonging to the Munda group.

1866 CAMPBELL in *Jrnl. Asiatic Soc. Bengal* XXXV. II. 28, I propose then to call the northern tribes Kolarian or Coolee Aborigines. 1872 E. T. DALTON *Descr. Ethnol. Bengal* 124 The Kolarian tribes. *Ibid.* 152, I class the Juangs with Kolarians chiefly in consequence of the linguistic affinity. 1899 [see *KOL]. 1928 V. G. CHILDE *Most Anc. East* iii. 52 Early Indian races, particularly the Dravidians, the Kolarians, and even the Veddahs of Ceylon.

Kolinsky (kǫli·nski). [Russ. *kolinski*, f. *Kola*, a district in north-eastern Russia.] The fur of the Siberian mink.

1851 *Illustr. Catal. Gt. Exhib.* III. 803 Skins and Furs. ..Kolinski. 1879 *Encycl. Brit.* IX. 837/2. 1891 H. POLAND *Fur-bearing Anim.* Introd. p. li, Kolinski, undressed. 1928 *Strand Mag.* Aug. 183/1 A Persian lamb coat with a collar of kolinsky.

attrib. 1919 *Queen* 5 July, Advt. 21 Kolinsky coat in the fashionable Sable Colour. 1920 *Ibid.* 1 May, Advt. 14 Furs. ..In Rich Kolinsky Sable. 1923 J. C. SACHS *Furs & Fur Trade* 62 The 'sable' brushes, which are in such request by artists, are generally made of kolinski tails; it is also used for wraps and scarves.

Kollergang (kǫ·ləgæŋ). [G.] A crushing mill with vertical runners used in milling paper-pulp.

1890 A. WATT *Paper-making* 82 For the purpose of crushing the knots of the straw, and other hard particles.., a machine termed the 'kollergang' or 'edge-runner' is sometimes employed. 1894 G. CLAPPERTON *Pract. Paper-making* 203 (Index) Kollergang 'broke'. 1926 R. H. CLAPPERTON *Pract. Paper-making* (ed. 3) 40 The ability of the Scandinavian makers to allow a considerable time for milling the pulp in kollergangs or beaters.

Komatik (kǫmæ·tik). [Native word.] A dog-sledge used by the people of Labrador.

1905 DUNCAN *Dr. Grenfell's Parish* xi. 133 The sick and starving are sought out by dog-team and komatik. 1920 GRENFELL *Labrador Dr.* xi. 199 Sails can sometimes be used with advantage on the komatik as an adjunct. 1920 *Sunday at Home* Nov. 76/2 The mountains, down whose steep sides he has slithered in his komatik.

Kombé (kǫ·mbĕ). [Mang'anja.] An arrow-poison of tropical Africa obtained from the seeds of *Strophanthus kombe*.

1874 *Treas. Bot.* Suppl. 1887 [see *INEE]. 1888 *Buck's Handbk. Med. Sci.* VI. 663/1 Strophanthus (Kombé, Arrow Poison).

Kombu, variant of *KOBU.

Komita(d)ji, variant of *COMITADJI.

Kommers (kǫmĕ·ɹs). Also **commerce, -se.** [G., ad. F. *commerce*, L. *commercium* COMMERCE.] A social gathering of German university students, with beer-drinking and song-singing.

1841 W. HOWITT *Student-life Germany* xvi. 315 In these Commerses, the rule is to drink beer, and this is called a Commers in beer. 1844 LONGF. *Hyperion* II. iv, Come in, come in. You shall see some sport. A fox commerce is on foot, and a regular beer scandal. 1908 MRS. A. SIDGWICK *Home Life Germany* vi. 56 A *Kommers* is a students' festival in which the professors and other senior members of a university take part.

Kommos, variant of COMMOS.

Komodo (komō^u·do). Name of an island in the Malay archipelago, applied to a species of lizard.

1927 *Proc. Zool. Soc.* 256 The interesting feature of the Komodo Monitor, apart from its bulk, lies in its relationship. 1932 *Observer* 9 Oct. 14/5 The dragon in question is a Komodo lizard four feet long hailing from Sunda Island off the Azores.

Kona (kō^u·nă). [Hawaiian.] A stormy south-west wind in the Hawaiian Islands.

1892 STEVENSON & LL. OSBOURNE *Wrecker* Prol., It was blowing a kona, hard.

Konak (konā·k). [Turk. *qonaq*.] A large house, palace, or official residence, in Turkey.

1852 C. T. NEWTON *Trav. & Discov. Levant* vi. (1865) 87 We asked for the Konak, or official residence of the Aga. 1878 S. LANE-POOLE *People of Turkey* ix. 221 When in the interior I had the opportunity of visiting some Konaks worthy of note. 1926 *Spectator* 17 July 88/2 The delicate 'konak' or palace of Prince Milosh Obrenovich.

Kongoni (kǫŋgō^u·ni). [Swahili.] An East African hartebeest.

[1889 J. C. WILLOUGHBY *East Africa & its Big Game* 54 These hartebeest (*swahili Kongoni*) are of the species known as *Cokii*, and..are very plentiful here. 1905 H. A. BRYDEN *Big Game Shooting* II. 114 Coke's hartebeest (*Bubalis cokei*) (*Kongoni* of the Swahilis) is the commonest..of this group in East Africa...Jackson's hartebeest (*Bubalis jacksoni*) is also known to the Swahilis as *Kongoni*.] 1908 WINSTON S. CHURCHILL *My Afr. Journey* i. 9 Herds of red kongoni—the hartebeeste of South Africa. 1923 *Blackw. Mag.* Oct. 450/2 A herd of kongoni.

Konk, variant of CONK, the nose.

1846 *United Service Mag.* May 13 Indignant at the liberty thus taken with his konk.

Konk, variant of *CONK *v.*

1918 E. C. MIDDLETON *Glorious Exploits Air* 20 The latter [*sc.* the engine] 'konked'. Down went the aeroplane. 1918 'RAFBIRD' *Zooms & Spins* 19 I'm flapping from Puddle marsh..—came down there with a konking engine. 1919 *Air Pie* 93 What would you do if your engine 'konked' out at 20,000 feet? 1925 E. FRASER & GIBBONS *Soldier & Sailor Words* 138 *Konked* (*konked out*): An Air Force term used of an aeroplane engine stopped working, failed, or broken down. Also a general expression, meaning 'knocked out', dead.

Konze (kǫ·nzi). Also **konzi.** [Swahili.] An African hartebeest, *Bubalis lichtensteini*, inhabiting the Zambesi and Nyassa regions.

1877 F. C. SELOUS *Hunter's Wanderings Africa* (1881) 303 In the afternoon I went out with my rifle, and shot a konze antelope...The black mark down the front of the face of the hartebeest is..wanting in the konze. 1908 R. LYDEKKER *Game Anim. Africa* 111 The konzi, or Lichtenstein's hartebeest.

Kookama, kukama (kukā·mă). *S. Africa.* Also **kokama, kooksam.** [Sechwana.] The gemsbok.

1850 R. G. CUMMING *Hunter's Life S. Afr.* (1902) 140/2 An old kookama or oryx. 1852 J. E. GRAY *Catal. Mamm. B. Mus.* 105. 1857 LIVINGSTONE *Trav. S. A.* iii. 56 The gemsbuck or kukama. 1885 *Riverside Nat. Hist.* (1888) V. 326.

Koolookamba (kūlukæ·mbă). Also **koolo-, kulu-.** Also in short form **kulu.** [Native name on the Gabun river.] An anthropoid ape of equatorial Africa, *Troglodytes koolookamba*, resembling the chimpanzee.

1860 DU CHAILLU in *Proc. Zool. Soc. Boston* VII. 360 The cry of the Kooloo-Kamba is very different from that of the *Troglodytes calvus* and chimpanzee. 1896 R. L. GARNER *Gorillas & Chimpanzees* 176 The kulu-kamba is..by far the finest representative of his genus. *Ibid.*, A young female kulu.

Kootcha (kū·tʃa). Also **-ar.** A small wild stingless honey-bee of Australia of the genus *Melipona* or *Trigona*.

1884 *Trans. Entom. Soc.* 149 Of these stingless bees of Australia two varieties only have come under my immediate observation,..'Kashi' or 'Keelar' and 'Kootchar' are the names given to them by the natives. *Ibid.* 156 The specimens sent by Mr. Hockings..were (1) two 'Kootchar' queens; (2) numerous 'Kootchar' workers; (3) numerous 'Kootchar' drones;..(7) 'Kootchar' wax and propolis;..(10) 'Kootchar' honey-pots; (11) 'Kootchar' brood;..(13) 'Kootchar' queen-cell. 1899 D. SHARP *Insects* II. 63 The other species, called 'Kootchar', is said to produce a very large number of drones.

Koplik (kǫ·plik). Name of a physician of New York, used to designate spots characteristic of some eruptive diseases.

1908 *Allbutt's Syst. Med.* IV. II. 207 The specks of secretion are easily wiped off, the Koplik spots are not. 1908 *Practitioner* Aug. 326 To..examine the buccal mucosa for the presence of the so-called Koplik's spots. 1925 *F. Taylor's Pract. Med.* (ed. 13) 35 Koplik's spots are of value in diagnosis [of measles], as they rarely occur in other eruptive diseases.

Koradji (kōræ·dgi). *Austral.* Also **coradgee, kiradjee, coradge, korradgee, karáji.** [Native.] A medicine-man.

1845 J. O. BALFOUR *Sk. N. S. W.* 14 The Coradgees, who are their wise men, have, they suppose, the power of healing and foretelling. 1885 MRS. C. PRAED *Austral. Life* 23 The Korradgees or medicine men. 1892 J. FRASER *Aborigines N. S. W.* 63 The 'karáji', or native doctor.

Korean, Corean (kōrī·ăn), *a.* and *sb.* Of or pertaining to (a native or inhabitant of) Korea (Chosen = Jap. *cho sun* land of morning calm), a peninsula and state in Eastern Asia; also applied to the language of Korea, an agglutinative language akin to Japanese.

1727 J. G. SCHEUCHZER tr. *Kæmpfer's Hist. Japan* (1906) I. 104 The Coreans had been subdued. *Ibid.* 123 Encompass'd by the Corean Sea. 1813 *Q. Rev.* Oct. 256 Classes and Families of Languages...Tartarian ..Corean. 1822 SHOBERL tr. *Titsingh's Illustr. Japan* 323 A Corean Fisherman and his Wife. 1899 A. H. KEANE *Man Past & Present* viii. 307 The Koreans possess a true alphabet of 28 letters. *Ibid.*, An adaptation of the Chinese symbols to the phonetic expression of the Korean syllables. 1904 FARRER

Garden Asia 73 The Korean is a lifeless creature. 1903 *Blackw. Mag.* Dec. 726/1 A piece of Korean porcelain.

Hence **Kore·anize** *v. trans.*, to give a Korean character to.

1931 W. F. Sands *Undiplomatic Mem.* 70 Emily, Koreanized as Lady Om, was now reigning sweetly in Seoul.

Korero (korē·ro). *New Zealand.* [Maori.] Talk, conversation; a talk or conference.

1845 E. J. Wakefield *Adv. N. Zealand* I. 78 There were about sixty men assembled, and they proceeded to hold a *korero* or 'talk' on the all-important subject. 1930 B. Guthrie *New Zealand Mem.* 54 After some *korero* and polite speeches the Maoris stood aside.

Korimako (kōᵊr-, korimā·ko). [Maori.] The Zealand bell-bird, *Anthornis melanura.*

1855 R. Taylor *Te Ika a Maui* 75 In the first oven a korimako was cooked. 1872 A. Domett *Ranolf* 202 The *Korimăko*, sweetest bird Of all that are in forest heard. 1873 W. L. Buller *Birds N. Zealand* 94 Certain forest-ranges were famed as Korimako preserves.

Korin (kōᵊ·rin). [W. Afr.] A gazelle, *Gazella rufifrons*, of Senegal.

1852 J. E. Gray *Catal. Mamm. B. Mus.* 60 *Gazella rufifrons*, the Korin. Bay brown. 1897–8 P. L. Sclater & O. Thomas *Bk. Antelopes* III. 65.

Korvort, variant of Cavort *v.*

1909 H. G. Wells *Tono-Bungay* III. iii. § 3 She described the knights of the age of chivalry as 'korvorting about on the off-chance of a dragon'.

Kosh, variant of *Cosh *sb.*3

1925 E. Fraser & Gibbons *Soldier & Sailor Words* 138 *Kosh*: A name for a trench club, or knobkerry, used in trench raids..The usual name for the stick, or bludgeon, carried by London roughs when out for mischief.

Kosin (kōᵊ·sin). *Chem.* Also **koussin, kossin.** [f. *kos(s)o*, Kousso + -in 1.] A bitter principle contained in kousso. So **Kosoto·xin.**

1875 *Jrnl. Chem. Soc.* XXVIII. 468 The koso flowers yield about 3 per cent. of kosin. 1887 *Buck's Handbk. Med. Sci.* IV. 318/2 Kosin..is unquestionably the principal tænicide agent of Koosso. 1894 *Jrnl. Chem. Soc.* LXVI. i. 424 Kosotoxin, $C_{26}H_{34}O_{10}$, a pale yellow powder, which melts at 80°. 1900 *Ibid.* LXXVIII. ii. 38 When a solution of kossin in cold acetic acid or in alcohol is allowed to remain, crystals of kosin separate.

Kossak, variant of Cossack; see *Cossack b.

1845 W. D. Cooley tr. *Parrot's Ascent Mt. Ararat* i. 10 This portion of the empire is traversed by a line of Kossak posts.

Koswite (kǫ·swəit). *Petrol.* [Named from *Koswinsky*, N. Urals: see -ite 1.] A variety of olivine-pyroxenite.

1901 *Jrnl. Chem. Soc.* LXXX. ii. 398 Koswite, a new pyroxenite from the Urals...Associated with olivine-gabbros in the Solikamsk district, near the source of the Kosswa river, is a new type of basic eruptive rock to which the name koswite is given.

Kotschubeite (kǫtʃū·bĭ,əit). *Min.* [f. name of the Russian Count P. *Kochubei* + -ite 1.] A variety of clinochlore containing a percentage of chromium oxide.

1892 E. S. Dana *Dana's Syst. Min.* (ed. 6) 648. 1929 H. L. Bowman *H. A. Miers' Min.* 561 Two very striking chrome-chlorites of a deep rose-red colour..have received the names kämmererite and kotschubeite.

Kow-tow, the more usual form of Kotow.

1864, 1883 [see Kotow]. 1907 *Westm. Gaz.* 12 Nov. 14/1 The degrading custom of high native Ministers of the Crown kowtowing. 1920 *Blackw. Mag.* Aug. 225/1 The conventional bowing or kow-tow position. 1925 E. F. Norton *Fight for Everest, 1924* 35 After much kow-towing.

Kraal. 3. Add: **kraal-town**, a town formed to accommodate the company assembled to view a kraaling of elephants in Ceylon.

1891 *Outing* (U.S.) Dec. 174/1 In less than a week's time a town springs into existence. 'Kraaltown!' with its clubs, hotels, saloons, cafés, and 'chummeries', to say nothing of suburban villas, etc.

Kraft (kraft). [G., = strength, in *kraftpapier* kraft paper, *kraftstoff* soda pulp.] A strong smooth brown wrapping-paper made from unbleached soda pulp. More fully *kraft paper, kraft brown.*

1907 G. Clapperton *Pract. Paper-making* (ed. 2) 37 'Kraft' brown papers. *Ibid.*, No Kraft yet produced in this country combines the crispness and elasticity which form so distinctive a feature of the Kraft papers produced by the best Scandinavian mills. 1914 E. A. Dawe *Paper* 56 Kraft browns may be described as glazed browns, as they are sometimes finished with a glazed surface both sides. A special kind of pulp is used for krafts. 1916 Cross & Bevan *Paper-Making* (ed. 4) 149 The extra strong or 'Kraft' varieties [of soda pulps] are suitable only for brown wrapping papers.

b. **kraft leather**, an imitation leather for book-binding resembling kraft paper in appearance.

1928 *Publishers' Weekly* 9 June 2348 In four styles of binding..handsome kraft leather, gold inlay, $1·50.

Krag-Jörgensen (kræg,yō·rgənsən). A type of rifle introduced in Denmark and Norway and adopted in U.S.A. Abbrev. (colloq.) **Krag** (kræg).

1899 *Scribner's Mag.* XXV. 20/1 Our arms were the regular cavalry carbine, the 'Krag', a splendid weapon, and the revolver. 1901 *Kynoch Jrnl.* Aug.–Sept. 133/2 He has also the latest pattern...Ross straight pull Krag-Jorgensen and many others. 1902 *Encycl. Brit.* XXV. 658/1 The cavalry is armed with the Krag-Jorgensen carbine...The infantry and coast artillery have the Krag-Jorgensen rifle. *Ibid.* XXXII. 654/2 The United States magazine rifle..is upon the Krag-Jörgensen system. 1902 *Munsey's Mag.* XXV. 423/1 Guns—the latest Krag-Jorgensens—are the weapons of the American revenue service.

Kran (krān). [Pers. *qrān.*] A Persian coin and monetary unit.

1882 E. O'Donovan *Merv Oasis* I. 249 The Turcomans.. will accept only the old-fashioned *kran* and *toman.* 1902 *Encycl. Brit.* XXXIII. 513/2 The Indian rupee and the Persian kran are widely circulated through Mesopotamia. 1920 *Brit. Mus. Return* 75 A silver kran of Muzaffar al-Din, Shah of Persia. 1922 *Blackw. Mag.* Mar. 393/1 For two krans an Arab will swear a false oath.

Kraurosis (krǫrōᵊ·sis). *Path.* [mod.L., f. Gr. κραυροῦσθαι to become dry or parched, f. κραῦρος brittle and dry: see -osis.] Shrivelled condition or atrophy (of the vulva). Hence **Krauro·tic** *a.*

1894 *Brit. Med. Jrnl.* 7 Apr., Suppl. 63/1 Kraurosis seems to be a peculiar histological atrophy of the vulvar tissues. *Ibid.*, Carcinomatous nodules were detected in the kraurotic tissue. 1908 *Practitioner* Dec. 782 There had been previous kraurosis of the vulva and part of the vaginal wall.

Krause (krau·zə), the name of Karl Friedrich Theodor *Krause* (1797–1868) used to designate certain anatomical parts (see quots.).

1887 *Buck's Handbk. Med. Sci.* V. 65/2 Krause's membrane or intermediate disk. 1901 Dorland *Med. Dict.* (ed. 2) s.v. *Corpuscle, Krause's corpuscles*, round end-bulbs or nerve-endings in the mucous membrane of the mouth, nose, eyes, and genitals. 1904 Stedman *Dunglison's Med. Dict.* (ed. 23) 609/1 *Krause's disk*, dark line traversing transversely each alternating light band in a muscle fibrilla. 1907 *Practitioner* Dec. 853 The accessory lachrymal glands, or Krause's glands, are small acini, which lie below the conjunctiva between the fornix and the edge of the tarsus.

Krill (kril). [ad. Norw. *kril* very small fry of fish.] A small crustacean on which whales feed.

1911 *Rep. Brit. Assoc.* 124. 1912 *Ibid.* 178 A small red crustacean which appears to be *Meganyctiphanes norvegica* ..This small crustacean forms the 'krill' of the whalers... In all cases these whales [*Balænoptera sibbaldii*] appear to have fed on the 'krill'. 1923 *Chambers's Jrnl.* 111/2 The small crustaceans, called by the whalers 'krill', upon which the finner feeds.

Krimmer (kri·mər). Also **crimmer, krimma.** [G., national or local adj. f. *Krim* Crimea.] A grey or black fur made from the wool of young lambs in or near the Crimea.

1904 *Westm. Gaz.* 28 Jan. 4/2 Chinchilla or krimmer. 1906 *Ibid.* 3 Nov. 13/1 Grey krimmer. 1923 *Ibid.* 26 Jan., A definition of 'crimmer lamb', as a commodity in the fur trade, was agreed upon at Malborough-street yesterday. 1929 *Daily Express* 26 Jan. 5/3 The smarter coats are generally collared with a flat fur. These include astrachan, krimma, and caracul.

Kromesky, -eski (krome·ski, krǫ·meski). Also **crom-, -esqui, -esque.** [ad. Russ. (pl.) кромочки *krómochki*, f. кромá slice.] A croquette made of meat or fish minced, rolled in bacon or calves udder and fried.

1861 Francatelli *Cook's Guide* 120 Kromeskys are made with all kinds of croquet preparations, whether of meat, fish, or shell-fish. 1884 *Girl's Own Paper* May 428/1 A dozen oysters will make a moderate sized dish of kromeskies. 1891 *Encycl. Pract. Cookery* (ed. T. F. Garrett) I. 478/2 Some authorities spell it Cromesquis, some Kromesquis, and others Krosmeskies. 1920 E. Silvester *Sensible Cookery* 54 Kromesques of veal. 1928 *Even. News* 28 Dec. 4/5 Kromeskies of Turkey.

Krugerism (krū·gəriz'm). *Hist.* [f. name of Stephanus Johannes Paulus *Kruger* (1825–1904), president of the Transvaal 1883–1901.] The nationalist (pro-Boer) policy of president Kruger. So **Krugerite** (krū·gərəit), an adherent of this policy.

1896 *Westm. Gaz.* 3 Dec. 5/1 Those who have effusively championed Mr. Chamberlain for what they imagined was his agreement with their Krugerite sympathies. 1897 *Daily News* 25 Jan. 5/6 Krugerites we know, and Rhodesites, but the Schreinerites (politically) all seem to live in London. 1897 *Times* 4 Feb. 3 Pure and unadulterated Krugerism. 1898 C. Rhodes in *Daily News* 4 Apr. 3/1 Only Krugerism will be supported, and Northern development will be damned. 1898 D. Story in *New Cent.* IV. 436 The necessity for maintaining the independence of his [*sc.* the Boer's] state..is the essence of Krugerism. 1900 *Pall Mall Gaz.* 29 Mar. 8/1 There are those who suggest that, perhaps, if the scrutineers had not been Krugerites, Joubert would have been found at the head. 1902 *Westm. Gaz.* 27 Mar. 7/3 Cecil Rhodes..had a cordial hatred for what is known to-day as 'Krugerism'—that pernicious system of government and diplomacy introduced by a foreign gang at Pretoria. 1904 Kipling *Traffics & Discov.* 33 An American citizen has a right to choose his own side in an unpleasantness, and Van Zyl wasn't any Krugerite. 1923 B. Ronan *Forty S. African Years* 183 Rhodes..was recognised as the only leader capable of checking the spread of Krugerism in South Africa.

Krupp (krup, ‖krup). [The name of a family of steel-workers and gun-makers at Essen.] In full *Krupp gun*: a steel cannon made at the Krupp works at Essen in Rhenish Prussia.

1883 *Whitaker's Alm.* 445/1 She is a casemate ship..armed with four 10-in. steel Krupps and one 12-in. Krupp. 1887 *Times* (weekly ed.) 26 Aug. 8/1 The Krupps..are mounted on Vavasseur carriages. 1900 *Daily News* 23 July 5/4 The Bogue Forts are being re-armed by the Chinese with quick-firing Krupps. 1916 Boyd Cable *Action Front* 264 One solitary Krupp dropping in here, and we'd have a pretty-looking mess.

Hence **Krupped** (krupt), **Kru·ppized** *ppl. adjs.* (of steel armour-plate) hardened by the Krupp process.

1899 *Army & Navy Reg.* 3 June, (Cent. D. Suppl.) Owing to the great severity of the ballistic tests, which necessitates the employment of a Kruppized process, it is impossible..to furnish the armor at the prices stipulated by Congress. 1902 *Encycl. Brit.* XXXI. 355/2 An A.P. shot should perforate two calibres of wrought iron, one calibre of Harveyed steel, or ⅘ calibre of Krupped armour.

Kruschen (krū·ʃən). In the catch phr. *that Kruschen feeling* (= a feeling of vigorous health), derived from the advertisements of Kruschen salts, a proprietary medicine.

1925 Rose Macaulay *Casual Comm.* 131 The happy spring when..we are full of that Kruschen feeling. 1926 Mrs. A. Sidgwick *Sack & Sugar* xix. 224 His spirits rose till he looked as if he had that Kruschen feeling. 1928 Dunsterville *Stalky's Remin.* xv. 226 He was very liverish in the early morning and had none of that 'Kruschen feeling' about him.

Kudu: see Koodoo.

Kufic, variant of Cufic.

1906 *Harmsworth Encycl.* VI. 422/3 The Kufic script was in use for coins from the end of the 7th to the 13th century. 1913 H. J. R. Murray *Hist. Chess* 171 The titles being in the Kufic character upon a blue ground.

Kuft, Kuftgari, varr. Koft, Koftgari.

1874 H. H. Cole *Catal. Ind. Art S. Kens. Mus.* 149 Sword Hilt. Iron, damascened with gold.. A very good piece of kuft work. *Ibid.* App. 322 Closely foliated damascening in gold kuft. *Ibid.* 324 Kuft damascening. 1880 *Encycl. Brit.* XIII. 81/2 Damaskeening..in..India..being known..as Kuft work or Kuftgari.

Kuge (kū·ge). [Jap.] The name of the nobility attached to the Emperor of Japan; a court noble.

1727 J. G. Scheuchzer tr. *Kæmpfer's Hist. Japan* I. II. ii. 152 The whole Ecclesiastical Court in general assumes the title of *Kuge*, which signifies as much as Ecclesiastical Lords, and this they do by way of distinction from the *Gege.* 1875 F. V. Dickins tr. *Chiushingura* (1880) 159 They were noble ladies, daughters of *Kugé*, who were peers of the Mikado's creation. 1877 *Trans. Asiatic Soc. Japan* VI. I. 23 The Court, Shōgun and Kugé were alike powerless to restore order.

Ku-Klux Klan. Add: There has been a revival of this society during and since the war of 1914–18. Hence **Ku-Klux-Kla·nism.** (Cf. *Klan.)

1924 J. M. Mecklin *Ku Klux Klan* 9 This period of remarkable expansion [June 1920 to October 1921] was accompanied by a wave of lawlessness and crime which, rightly or wrongly, was associated with the Ku Klux Klan. *Ibid.* 98, I have yet to come in contact with the first trace of Ku Klux Klanism.

Kulak (kū·læk). Also **koo-, kou-.** (*Russ. pl.* **kulaki.**) [Russ. кулакъ fist, tight-fisted person.] In Russia, a well-to-do peasant, farmer, or trader; under the Soviet, a peasant-proprietor who tills his land for his own profit.

[1877 D. M. Wallace *Russia* vii. 159 Not a few industrial villages have thus fallen under the power of the *Kulaki*—literally Fists—as these monopolists are called.] 1886 *Encycl. Brit.* XXI. 84/1 The enrichment of a few 'kulaks' and 'miroyedes'. 1921 *Contemp. Rev.* Jan. 26 'Kulaks'..a nickname for the close-fisted village traders, usurers, and rich peasants. 1925 Sir P. Gibbs *Unchanging Quest* xiv, These peasants think the *Duma* will..kill all the *Koulaks*, or Jewish money lenders. 1931 M. Hindus *Red Bread* iv. 66 Legally, a *koolack* is a man who indulges in some form of exploitation, employs hired help or derives an income from rent or interest or the operation of an agricultural or industrial machine. Actually, however, a *koolack* is a successful farmer as success is measured in Russia.

Hence **Ku·lakism, Ku·lakiza·tion.**

1928 *Illustr. Hist. Russ. Rev.* I. 63 The bourgeoisie from their very nature were bound to oppose the abolition of 'Kulakisation'. 1930 *Aberdeen Press & Jrnl.* 3 Apr. 7/3 The blunders made in the process of collectivism by over-zealous village Soviets, thus necessitating the present pause in the interests of the crop but not of kulakism.

Kultur (kultū·r). [G., ad. L. *cultūra*, or F. *culture* Culture.] Civilization as conceived by the Germans; esp. in a derogatory sense, as involving race-arrogance, militarism, and imperialism.

1914 B. Holland in *Spectator* 31 Oct. 589/1 The idea that the extension of the *Kultur* of a nation can be effected by the extension by arms of its Empire. *Ibid.* 589/2. 1915 *Times* 30 Mar. 6/4 *Kultur*, in fact, has become the exact opposite of 'culture'. 1926 C. H. Herford *Mind of Post-War Germany* v. 22 The stabilizing forces which post-war Germany derived from her inherited Kultur.

attrib. 1918 tr. *W. Gettlich's German Grip on Russia* 46 Liège, Louvain and Kalisz..prove how far the temperament of a 'Kultur nation' is capable of going.

Kulturkampf (kultū·rkampf). [G., f. *kultur* (see prec.) + *kampf* conflict.] The conflict between the Prussian government and the Papacy for the control of schools and church appointments (1872–87).

1879 *Dublin Rev.* Oct. 350 History of the Prussian 'Kulturkampf'. 1896 W. Miller *Balkans* II. v. 205 A regular *Culturkampf* raged for nearly twenty years, in which the Turkish officials were far less adverse than the Greek clergy to the Bulgarian demands. 1902 *Encycl. Brit.* XXXII. 271/2 In Germany, when the Pontificate of Leo XIII. began, a disastrous conflict between the Imperial Government and the Church was in progress. It was called the Kulturkampf, as professing to be undertaken on behalf of civilization and culture. 1926 C. H. Herford *Mind of Post-War Germany* i. 6 The Rhinelands, fervently Catholic, and still acutely mindful of Bismarck's *Kulturkampf.*

Kulu: see *Koolookamba.

Kumquat (kǫ·mkwǫt). 1. See Cumquat.

2. An Australian tree, *Atalantia glauca*, and its fruit.

1889 Maiden *Usef. Plants Australia* 8 *Atalantia glauca*. ..'Native Kumquat', 'Desert Lemon'...New South Wales and Queensland.

Kungu (kǫ·ŋgu). Also **kungo.** [Nyanja *nkungu.*] A fly of the genus *Corethra*, breeding on Lake Nyasa. *Kungu cake*, a cake made from these insects.

1865 D. & C. Livingstone *Narr. Exped. Zambesi* 373 A kungo cake, an inch thick..was offered to us. 1897 Sir H. H. Johnston *Brit. Central Africa* 436 The 'Kungu' fly of Lake Nyasa. 1899 D. Sharp *Insects* II. 467 The kungu cake mentioned by Livingstone as used on Lake Nyassa is made from an Insect which occurs in profusion there, and is compressed into biscuit form. 1902 Sir H. H. Johnston *Uganda Protectorate* I. 413 The kungu fly has a soft little body, scarcely as large as that of a flea, with gauzy wings.

Kunzite (ku·ntsəit). *Min.* [Named after G. F. *Kunz*, of New York: see -ite 1.] A lilac-coloured variety of spodumene, found in California, and prized as a gem.

1903 *Nature* 10 Sept. 460/1 The name of Kunzite has, it is stated, been given to the stone. 1922 W. E. Ford *E. S. Dana's Min.* (ed. 3) 481 Kunzite is a clear lilac-colored variety [of spodumene] found near Pala, San Diego Co., California.

Kuomintang (kuǫminta·ŋ). [lit. 'people's national party'.] The nationalist radical party in China, founded under Sun Yat-sen in August, 1912, after the fall of the Emperor.

1912 J. O. P. Bland *Rec. Events & Pres. Policies China* iv. 107 *note*, In the beginning of September, an arrangement was effected, by the leaders of the T'ung-Meng-hui, to amalgamate with five minor political groups 'for the sake of harmony' under a new name, the Kuo-Min-tang, or National-ist party. 1914 *Times* 1 Jan. Special Suppl. 4/2 Immediately upon the signature of the loan a notable defection took place in the ranks of the Kuo Min tang. 1928 T. F. Millard *China* 39, I remember the assassination of one Sung, a Kuomintang leader.

Kupferschiefer (ku·pfərʃīfər). *Geol.* [G., lit. 'copper slate'.] A bituminous brown or black shale of the Permian series, which is worked in Germany for copper.

1856 Sage *Adv. Text-bk. Geol.* 165 In Germany the dark bituminous-looking schist, known as the *kupfer-schiefer*, has long been mined as an ore of copper. 1879 *Encycl. Brit.* X. 352/1 The Kupfer-schiefer contains numerous fish..and remains of plants. 1896 H. Louis *J. A. Phillips' Ore Deposits* (ed. 2) 399 The strata accompanying the *Kupferschiefer* seam.

Kurd (kōɹd). One of a pastoral and predatory race of Aryan stock, which gives its name to Kurdistan in Asia. Also *attrib.* Hence **Ku·rdish** *a.*, of or pertaining to the Kurds or their language, a dialect belonging to the Iranian group; *sb.* the language itself.

1813 *Q. Rev.* Oct. 257 Languages and Dialects...Median. Zendish. Pehlvish. Persian. Kurdish. *Ibid.* 267 The Kurds speak a corrupt Persian. 1836 T. Skinner *Adv. Journ. Overland to India* v. 69 The wife of the Kurdish traveller. 1867 Whitney *Lang. & Study Lang.* v. (1868) 192 The Persian..with its outliers on the north-west and on the east—as the Armenian, the Kurdish, the Ossetic, and the Afghan. 1875 *Encycl. Brit.* II. 712/1 Kurds..are found principally in the eastern and south-eastern districts [of Asia Minor]. 1882 E. O'Donovan *Merv. Oasis* I. 325 A Kurd encampment. 1899 Mrs. L. M. Elton tr. *Nazarbek's Through the Storm* 204 About thirty Kurdish brigands rushed out of the forest. 1912 *Q. Rev.* Jan. 213 To the Arabian and Albanian questions the new rulers of Turkey have added a Kurdish question. 1924 *Blackw. Mag.* Nov. 583/2 Pursued by volleys of oaths in English, Scots, and Kurdish.

Kuruma (kurū·ma). [Jap.] A jinriksha, rickshaw. Also **Kuruma·ya,** a rickshaw man.

1880 Miss Bird *Japan* (1905) 5 *note*, From *kuruma* naturally comes *kurumaya* for the *kuruma* runner. 1889 Sir E. Arnold *Seas & Lands* (1892) 208 The Kurumas are wheeled sharply round and brought up with a general shout of arrival in front of a Japanese inn. 1891 — *Japonica* (1892) 44 The *Kuruma*-men can trot in safety round every corner. *Ibid.* 62 The Tokio citizens call their little cab *kuruma*, which means 'a wheel', and the coolie who pulls it is termed *kurumaya.* 1894 L. Hearn *Glimpses Unfam. Japan* I. i. 2 The ..charm of Japan..began for me with my first kuruma-ride. ..The jinrikisha, or kuruma, is the most cozy little vehicle imaginable. 1904 Sladen *Playing the Game* II. iv, *Kuruma* is the word the natives always use for a *riksha.* 1904 Farrer *Garden Asia* ii. 12 At dangerous corners the kurumaya howls dolefully to make the people avoid the path. *Ibid.* xxiii. 234 Mr. Desire,..taking us up in the kuruma, proceeds to whirl us home to our friends.

Kurvey (kɒɪvē·), *v. S. Africa.* [f. Du. *karwei* hard work (ad. F. *corvée*): see Kurveyor.] *intr.* To carry goods in an ox wagon. Hence **Kurvey·ing** *vbl. sb.* and *ppl. a.*

1873 *Queenstown Free Press* 8 Aug. (Pettman) For various reasons not a farmer kurveys between either Concordia or Springbok and Port Nolloth. 1884 Hobson *At Home in Transvaal* iii, 'There will be an end to those visits one of these days,' said the merchant, 'and then good-bye to your karweying, Walters.' 1902 *Encycl. Brit.* XXXI. 81/2 'Kurveying' (the conducting of transport by bullock-waggon) in itself constituted a great industry.

Kylindrite: see *Cylindrite.

Kylix (= Cylix). Examples of the *k* spelling.

1892 *Times* 7 Feb. 20/1 An Athenian kylix by Sotades. *Ibid.*, These three beautiful kylixes have the ground a pale cream-colour. 1892 *Pall Mall Gaz.* 7 Sept. 1/3 A kylix purchased by Mr. Murray in Rome last spring. 1905 H. B. Walters *Hist. Anc. Pottery* I. 417 The kylikes of the Epictetan cycle. 1921 G. C. Richards tr. *E. Buschor's Greek Vase-painting* 52 Tall-stemmed kylikes. 1922 *Encycl. Brit.* XXX. 183/2 An Attic *kylix* signed by Pamphaios.

Kynurenic, Kynuric: see Cyn-.

Kyrin, -ine (kəiᵊ·rin). *Physiol. Chem.* [f. Gr. κῦρος authority, validity + -in 1.] Any of a class of basic substances resembling the protamines, obtained by hydrolysis of gelatin, casein, etc.

1906 *Jrnl. Chem. Soc.* XC. i. 777 Kyrines, the intermediate decomposition products of proteids by acids. 1916 *Ibid.* CX. i. 103 The author has examined some kyrines in order to determine whether they differ in toxicity from their parent proteins.

L

L. I. 2. (Earlier examples. See also Ell 2.)

1843 Carlton *New Purchase* xi. 80 On the first floor were two rooms, and connected with a Lilliputian half-story kitchen forming an L as near as possible. 1873 Aldrich *Marj. Daw* etc. 167 Mr. Jaffrey's bedroom was in an L of the building. 1874 *Rep. Vermont Board Agric.* II. 510 To save expense, it is apt to be the case that no cellar is put under the L part of the house.

III. 7. Add:

L. = Liberal (in politics). L.A. (later L.L.A.): see *Literate B. 4. L.C.C. = London County Council. L.R.C. = Labour Representation Committee.

1869 *Whitaker's Almanack* 83/1 *Andover*—Hon. D. F. Fortescue, *L.* 1908 *Daily Chron.* 16 Dec. 1/2 Mr. Mackarness (L., Newbury) asked whether [etc.]. 1883 Chr. Struthers *Admiss. Women Scot. Univ.* 16 In 1877, the Senate of that University [St. Andrews] offered on certain conditions, to attach the title of L.A. to their Higher Certificate...In 1882, we find..the title..changed to L.L.A. 1900 W. Smart *Taxation Land Values* 41 The L.C.C. resolutions. 1907 *Daily Chron.* 3 Sept. 4/7 This is one of the little matters that the L.C.C...might well look into. 1905 *Daily Chron.* 26 Sept. 4/7 A paragraph in the 'Westminster Gazette' about..'the L.R.C. rule on the subject'. 1908 *Westm. Gaz.* 23 Oct. 2/2 The Labour Party (by which we mean the thirty-one members who are commonly known as L.R.C. members).

b. Alphabetic abbreviation of *elevated*, = Elevated Railway. Also *attrib. U.S.* (Cf. *El.)

1899 J. L. Williams *Stolen Story* etc. 23 He was making for the Seventy-second Street 'L' Station. *Ibid.* 189 He took the L train for Cortlandt Street. 1904 *New York Sun* 4 Sept. 7 The owners of express wagons are praying that the L strike will come off.

Laager, *sb.* Add: Also *fig.*

1901 *Daily Tel.* 9 Mar. 11/5 It has been the custom of the Secretary of State to lie in laager, surrounded by his civilian secretaries.

Lab (læb), *sb.*2 *colloq.* [Shortened from Laboratory.]

1885- in colloquial use. 1912 *Chums* 5 Oct. 69/3 They walked along the corridor towards the chemistry lab. 1918 Maubyn *Wartime Ballad* 26 Be sure they say the lab's the place For bold experiment.

Labanism (lēᵊ·bǎniz'm), *sb.* [f. the proper name *Laban*: see Gen. xxix.] (See quot.)

1912 *Hastings' Encycl. Relig. & Ethics* V. 719/1 This apparently happened in Formosa, where 'Labanism'—the practice by which a son-in-law resided with his bride's family for a term of service—also existed.

Labby (læ·bi), *sb.* [Of uncertain origin.] A system in gambling (see quot.).

1901 V. B. *Monte Carlo Anecd.* 93 The idea of the ordinary 'Labby' is to set yourself the task of winning a certain sum, and to so arrange your stakes, that whenever you score a win it will wipe out two previous losses.

Label, *sb.*1 9. Add: *label-cutter.*

1881 *Instr. Census Clerks* (1885) 83 Label Cutter. 1909 *Daily Chron.* 2 Feb. 9/4 Advt., Label Cutter (Female).

Lability. (Earlier and later examples.)

1557 R. Edgeworth *Serm.* Pref. ✠ iij, I euer fearinge the labilitie of my remembraunce, vsed to pen my sermons. 1810 Coleridge in *Lit. Rem.* (1838) III. 353 To the species water continuity and lability are essential. 1903 A. R. Wallace *Man's Place in Universe* xi. 207 Those peculiarities which are essential to life—extreme sensitiveness and lability. 1924 Skerl tr. *Wegener's Orig. Continents* 154 It is perhaps possible to explain the frequently described 'lability' of the geosynclinals by the fact that [etc.].

Labilize (lēᵊ·biləiz), *v.* [f. L. *lābil-is* Labile *a.* + -ize.] *trans.* To render labile or unstable.

1903 *Nature* 26 Feb. 385/2 The *rôle* of the oxygen must have been that of a labilising agent.

Laboratory. 4. Add: **laboratory animal,** any animal (e.g. rat, mouse, monkey) commonly used for experiments in a laboratory.

1899 *Allbutt's Syst. Med.* VI. 517 The so-called 'irritation contracture' observable in the monkey (but not in other laboratory animals).

Labour, *sb.* Add: **2. c.** [After Sp. *labor.*] A former division of land in Texas, containing about 177 acres.

1845 T. J. Green *Texian Exped.* xiii. 212 The valley.. [is] laid off in labours beautifully ditched and highly cultivated.

8. *labour bank* (earlier example); also (in senses 2 and 2 b), *labour-bill, bureau, camp, -class, colony, cost, -employing* adj., *master, movement, power, union, -waste*; **Labor Day** *U.S.*, a legal holiday observed on the first Monday of September; **Labour-Liberal** *a.* and *sb.* (a Member of Parliament) combining Labour and Liberal ideas; **labour-note,** a note indicating value in terms of work; **Labour Party,** a political party specially supporting the interests of labour; esp. in England, the organized party formed in 1906 by a federation of trade unions and advanced political bodies to secure the representation of labour in Parliament.

1832 *Crisis* 28 Apr. 16/1 In Poland-street they had established a *Labour Bank. 1898 *Engineering Mag.* XVI. 26 Every improvement in labour-saving machinery diminishes the proportion which the *labour-bill bears to the cost of the product. 1832 *Crisis* 11 Aug. 90/3 Perhaps the best preliminary mode..will be by the establishment of Equitable Exchange *Labour Bureaus. 1872 *Fourth Ann. Rep. Bureau Stat. Labor* 13 The most important subjects for inquiry by..the Massachusetts Labor Bureau [organized in 1869]. 1893 *Rep. Agencies & Methods Unemployed* 6 (Parl. Papers LXXXII) A detailed account of..labour bureaux and of various organisations dealing with distress. 1895 J. A. Hobson *Probl. Unemployed* 127 Labour Bureaux would thus impart increased fluidity to labour. 1908 *Encycl. Soc. Reform* 998/2 The recent establishment of a system of public employment bureaux called labor bureaux. 1900 *Jrnl. Soc. Arts* 11 May 510/1 Prisoners..might serve their time in..quarries, which would be turned into *labour camps. 1851 C. Cist *Cincinnati* 313 The next great effect will be, the general uprising of the *labor class in agriculture—the tenant farmers at the east. 1888 *Charity Org. Rev.* Jan. 43 The Council would gladly see an experiment made in the form of a *Labour Colony, to which unemployed townspeople might be sent for a time. *Ibid.* June 241 The Dutch Labour Colonies. 1895 J. A. Hobson *Probl. Unemployed* 146 The small experiments in Labour Colonies have never fairly tested the possibilities of effective co-operation. *Ibid.* 69 The *labour cost of distributing a given quantity of goods. 1903 *Westm. Gaz.* 9 July 2/1 The imposition of such duties as will equalise our labour-costs with the labour-costs of our foreign competitors. 1888 *Nation* 5 Apr. 279/3 A legal holiday, called '*Labor Day', has been created in Massachusetts, New York, New Jersey, Colorado, and Oregon. 1910 *World Almanac* 30 An act [of 1893–4] making Labor Day a public holiday in the District of Columbia. 1904 *Daily Chron.* 23 Mar. 3/3 Artistic *labour-employing entertainments. 1905 *Westm. Gaz.* 21 Mar. 2/3 Insecurity of labour-employing capital. 1902 *Ibid.* 26 Feb. 6/3 If he could do that when he was returned as a *Labour Liberal member. 1904 *Daily Chron.* 7 Jan. 5/4 Two English Liberal Members (one Liberal and one Labour-Liberal). 1901 *Daily News* 10 Jan. 9/3 The *labour master..certified him able to do the work. 1921 *Dict. Occup. Terms* (1927) § 731 *Labour master*, engages and discharges casual labour..employed by dock or harbour authority [etc.]. 1870 *Scribner's Monthly* I. 71 The preacher..beats about..in a dissertation on..the '*labor movement'. 1893 L. T. Hobhouse (*title*) The Labour Movement. 1923 J. D. Hackett *Labor Terms* in *Managem. Engineering* May, *Labor Movement*. The organized effort of workmen to better their economic condition by means of trade unionism. 1832 *Crisis* 28 Apr. 12/1 Money was not necessary. *Labour-notes were sufficient. 1894 B. Jones *Co-op. Prod.* I. 89 These labour notes were to supersede the use of metallic coins and ordinary bank notes, and were to become a superior kind of money. 1886 *Labour party [in Dict.]. 1892 Roydhouse (*title*) The Labour Party in New South Wales. 1896 J. Edwards *Labour Ann.* 39 This [of 1895] was the first General Election in which an organized Labour party, independent of either Liberal or Tory, and opposing either or both, has taken part in the United Kingdom. 1905 J. R. Macdonald in W. T. Stead *Coming Men* 222 The Labour Party..will represent trades; it will represent the working class; it will represent a coherent body of fundamental Labour opinion. 1922 *Encycl. Brit.* XXXII. 507/1 The Labour party..included the Independent Labour party and the Fabian Society and one or two smaller Socialist bodies. Locally it was organized in several hundred Local Labour parties. *Ibid.* 884/2 For many years there was a Labor or Socialist Labor national party, which regularly nominated a candidate for the [U.S.] presidency. 1887 S. Moore & Aveling tr. *Marx' Capital* II. vi. I. 145 By *labour-power or capacity for labour is to be understood the aggregate of those mental and physical capabilities existing in a human being, which he exercises whenever he produces a use-value of any description. 1895 J. A. Hobson *Probl. Unemployed* 2 Off-time..implies waste of labour-power. 1866 in J. R. Commons *Hist. Amer. Industrial Soc.* (1910–11) IX. 133 Each member belonging to the National *Labor Union. 1883 J. Hay *Bread-winners* xi. 183 The labor unions have ordered a general strike. 1901 S. Merwin & H. K. Webster *Calumet K* xi. 192 The organization of labor unions is generally democratic. 1895 J. A. Hobson *Probl. Unemployed* 30 The sum of *labour-waste is not complete without an allusion to the lowest class of 'unemployed'.

Labour, *v.* Add: **1. b.** To plough up or excavate by means of bombs or shells.

1915 G. Adam *Behind Scenes at Front* 105 The ground is ..laboured deeply with every form of high explosive, and terrible in its desolation and upheaval.

9. For *Obs.* read *Obs.* exc. *poet.*, and add example.

1872 Tennyson *Gareth & Lynette* 474 But Kay the seneschal, who loved him not, Would hustle and harry him, and labour him Beyond his comrade of the hearth.

Laboured, *ppl. a.* **3.** Add: Also *laboured-at.*

1876 G. M. Hopkins *Poems* (1918) 9 And lily-coloured clothes provide Your spouse not laboured-at nor spun.

Hence **La·bouredly** *adv.*, **La·bouredness.**

1882 *Daily Tel.* 24 Feb. (Cass.) He spoke labouredly and with hesitation. 1930 Mackail *Largeness in Literature* 6 Largeness is..the opposite..of thinness, of tightness, of labouredness.

Labour Exchange. [Labour *sb.* 2 + Exchange *sb.* 1 b.]

1. An establishment for the exchange of the products of labour without the use of money. Also *attrib.* Now only *Hist.*

1832 *Crisis* 28 Apr. 16/1 Mr. B. Warden..stated that they had erected a new school, called a Labour Exchange School. *Ibid.* 25 Aug. 97/3 To investigate the Principles upon which the proposed Equitable Labour Exchange was to be founded. *Ibid.* 6 Oct. 122/1 Labour Exchange notes... Labour Exchange banks. 1875 G. J. Holyoake *Hist. Co-op.* (1906) I. 65 The Labour Exchange was not Mr. Owen's idea, but he adopted it. 1894 B. Jones *Co-op. Prod.* I. 90 The exchange was opened on September 3, 1832, under the title of 'The Equitable Labour Exchange'.

2. An office serving as a means of connexion between workers and employers, esp. one forming part of an organization to assist in the finding of employment.

1869 C. L. Brace *New West* v. 53 One of the remarkable instances of the intelligence and humanity of this new community was the establishment, in 1868, of the 'Labor Exchange'. 1893 *Rep. Agencies & Methods Unemployed* 15 (Parl. Papers LXXXII) Registry offices..for shore labourers having the title of the 'British Labour Exchange'. 1895 J. A. Hobson *Probl. Unemployed* 130 If the Bureaux are to perform effectively the work of Labour Exchanges. 1908 *Encycl. Soc. Reform* 997/2 The first labor exchange was that created by the municipality of Paris in 1887.

3. The finding of employment for workers.

1895 J. A. Hobson *Probl. Unemployed* 128 No system of mere labour-exchange, however well-conducted, would increase the total quantity of employment over a long area of time.

Hence **Labour-exchange** *v. trans.*, to record at a labour exchange.

1911 *Times Lit. Suppl.* 9 Nov. 439/1 What is the use of.. labour-exchanging boys, when there are no vacancies?

Labourism (lēᵊ·bəriz'm). [f. Labour *sb.* 2 b + -ism.] The principles or tenets of the Labour Party in politics; the holding or advocacy of these principles.

1905 *Westm. Gaz.* 13 May 2/2 Mr. Haldane has plied him with Imperialism, Mr. Keir Hardie with Labourism. 1908 *Ibid.* 4 May 9/2 Two years ago many Liberals coquetted with Labourism, and the result gave them a fright. 1924 J. R. Macdonald in *Publ. Opinion* 14 Mar. 248/3 Their Toryisms, Liberalisms and Labourisms.

Labourist (lēᵊ·bərist). [f. Labour *sb.* + -ist.] A supporter of the interests of Labour in politics; an advocate of labourism.

1903 *Handy Notes for Unionist Workers* Aug. 3 The Labourists in Parliament..number over a dozen. 1910 *Daily Chron.* 2 Feb. 1/7 Liberals, Labourists and Nationalists are solid against the veto of the Lords and against Food-Taxes. 1927 *Observer* 5 June 12/3 Six months ago the five seats concerned were represented by two Conservatives, two Labourists, and one Liberal.

Labourite (lēᵊ·bərəit). [f. Labour *sb.* + -ite 1.] = Labourist, often used of members of Parliament representing the Labour Party in Britain, Australia, or other countries.

1903 *Daily Chron.* 19 Dec. 5/5 Free Traders and Free Trade Labourites—40. 1909 T. Hodgkin in *Life & Lett.* 15 Nov. (1917) 326 It is this abominable selfishness of men whether Capitalists or Labourites which seems to wreck all forms of government. 1920 *Blackw. Mag.* June 830/1 The moderate Labourites have reason to remember this. 1923 *National Rev.* Jan. 646 The Labourites were led by Mr. Ramsay Macdonald before the war.

Labrador. *attrib.* Add: **Labrador dog** (retriever, etc.), a breed of dog derived originally from Labrador and Newfoundland, a variety of the Newfoundland dog. Also simply *Labrador.* **Labrador pine, twister** (see quots.).

1852 Mundy *Antipodes* (1857) 7 Some of the Newfoundland dogs in this country are the finest I have ever seen—much larger and handsomer than the true *Labrador dog. 1910 *Encycl. Brit.* VIII. 378/1 The Labrador Newfoundland is a smaller black variety. 1921 *Blackw. Mag.* Dec. 794/1 All the guns had dogs—beautifully trained Labradors. 1803 A. B. Lambert *Descr. Genus Pinus* 7 *Labradore Pine... Habitat in America Septentrionali. 1858 J. A. Warder *Hedges & Evergreens* II. 246 *Pinus Banksiana*, or Labrador Pine, is also a low, scrubby, or straggling tree, rising only five or eight feet. 1877 Minot *Land-Birds & Game-Birds New Eng.* 405 Those very small wiry, compactly feathered, weather-tanned birds [woodcock], who appear in October, and who are called, perhaps locally, *Labrador twisters.

Labradore·scence. *Min.* [f. Labradorite.] The brilliant play of colours exhibited by many specimens of labradorite. Also **Labradore·scent** *a.*

1911 *Encycl. Brit.* XVI. 30/1 This optical effect, known sometimes as 'labradorescence', seems due in some cases to the presence of minute laminæ of certain minerals..arranged parallel to the surface which reflects the colour. *Ibid.* XX. 331/1 The labradorescent orthoclase.

Labradorian (læbrădōᵊ·riăn), *a.* and *sb.* [f. Labrador + -ian.] **a.** *adj.* Of or pertaining to Labrador. Also *Geol.* **b.** *sb.* A native of Labrador.

1888 Prestwich *Geol.* II. 20 Labradorian or Norian group. 1894 Dana *Man. Geol.* (ed. 4) 446 C. H. Hitchcock ..adopts the subdivisions, beginning below: Laurentian, Montalban.., Labradorian, and Huronian. 1907 L. Mott *To Credit of Sea* ii, 'An' you a Labradorian!' Johnson said. *Ibid.* iii, The Labradorian smiled.

Labretifery (lēᵊbrĕti·fĕri). [f. Labret + L. *fer-*, carrying + -y 3.] The practice of wearing labrets.

1884 *Science* 3 Oct. 345/1 Dr. W. H. Dall then read a paper on the use of labrets, its title being 'The geographical distribution of labretifery'. 1905 C. Davenport *Jewellery* v. 89 In Mexico there was a very remarkable civilisation, and labretifery..was practised.

Labyrinth, *sb.* **5.** Add:

labyrinth disc, a disc used in labyrinth packing; **labyrinth packing,** in steam turbines, a form of packing used to prevent steam leaking along the shafts, consisting of a series of metal rings keyed alternately to the shaft and the housing.

1922 *Encycl. Brit.* XXXII. 789/2 The pressure of steam in the blading..tends to thrust the discs apart. It is therefore balanced by an arrangement of 'dummies', or labyrinth discs...To prevent the high pressure steam leaking along the shafts, these are fitted with labyrinth packings.

Lace, *sb.* **9.** Add: **lace-wood** (*a*) *Aust.* = *lace-bark* (*b*); (*b*) the wood of the plane tree (*platanus occidentalis*).

1898 Morris *Austral English* 258/1 Lace-bark, Lacey-bark, or *Lacewood. 1902 Boulger *Wood* 101 The beautiful Lacewood or Honeysuckle wood of North America. 1930 *Morn. Post* 2 Aug. 12/2 The anomaly that Queensland silky oak should be purchased by the United States..and then shipped to this country where it is sold as lace-wood.

Lace, *v.* **4. b.** Add to def.: *spec.* in Book-binding, to fasten the boards on a volume by passing the bands through holes in them. Also with *in.*

1835 Hannett *Bibliopegia* 30 One board is then placed on each side of the volume, even at the head, and marked with a bodkin opposite to the slips intended to be laced in. 1871 *Amer. Encycl. Printing* (ed. Ringwalt) 74 When the boards are affixed to the volume by means of the bands being passed through holes made in the boards, they are said to be laced in.

e. *intr.* Of structures that resemble or suggest lacing: to pass *across* a gap or *about* an object. Also *fig.* To become entwined.

a 1889 G. M. Hopkins *Poems* (1918) 76 Her dearness.. more and more times laces round and round my heart. 1899 H. G. Wells *When Sleeper Wakes* x. 103 The cables and bridges that laced across the aisle were empty. *Ibid.* xxii. 288 A flimsy seeming scaffolding that laced about the great mass of the Council House.

6. (Later example.)

1923 H. G. Wells *Men Like Gods* I. vi. § 3. 89 'Tell me', that engaging phrase, laced his conversation.

Lacer (lēᵊ·sər). [f. Lace *v.* 9.] A liquor serving to 'lace' a beverage.

1854 W. G. Simms *Southward Ho!* iv. 32 A bowl of coffee and a cracker is the initial appetizer, with possibly a tass of brandy in the purple beverage, as a lacer.

Lacerator (læ·sĕrēᵊtər). [a. L. *lacerātor.*] One who lacerates.

1886 Moule *Ep. Ephes.* Introd. 25 Marcion was a ruthless and most uncritical emendator, or rather lacerator, of the Scripture text.

La·chrymating, *ppl. a.* [f. Lachrymate *v.*] Causing lachrymation.

1922 *Encycl. Brit.* XXXII. 110/2 If a sufficient number of lachrymating grenades could be thrown.

Lachrymator (læ·krimēᵊtər). [f. as prec. Cf. med. L. *lacrymātor* one who sheds tears.] Any substance, esp. a gas, which irritates the eyes and causes tears to flow.

1922 *Encycl. Brit.* XXXII. 111/2 The principal bases for lachrymators are iodine and bromine.

Lachrymatory. A. *adj.* Add:

Lachrymatory bomb, gas, shell, a bomb, etc., causing the eyes to water.

1916 *Yorkshire Post* 21 July 5/5 A violent artillery preparation with asphyxiating and lachrymatory shells. 1922 *Encycl. Brit.* XXXII. 111/2 The irritant gases are divided into (*a*) Lachrymatory (affecting the eyes), (*b*) Sternutatory (causing sneezing), (*c*) Vesicatory (blistering).

Laciness (lēᵊ·sinės). [f. Lacy *a.* + -ness.] Lace-like quality or effect.

1903 *Westm. Gaz.* 9 July 4/2 Flowered silk, or embroideries, or chiffon, and laciness.

Lacing, *vbl. sb.* Add:

3. e. *Book-binding* (see quot. and *Lace *v.* 4 e).

1875 Knight *Mech. Dict.* s.v., *Lacing*, securing the book to the sides by carrying the bands or slips through perforations in the boards. 1885 Crane *Bookb. for Amateurs* 76.

4. lacing-liver, a liver misshapen by tight lacing.

1907 *Practitioner* Nov. 646 It [the kidney] was kept in this position by the very pronounced lacing-liver.

Lack, *v.*1 **4.** Add: Also with *for.*

1899 A. Skeel & W. H. Brearley *King Washington* 170 He was one of the many who had lacked for partners. 1906 E. Phillpotts *Portreeve* II. iv. 154 The outward signs that she had marked upon him did not lack for inner causes.

Lackwit. (See Lack *v.*1 7.)

1911 H. S. Harrison *Queed* iv. 42 West..abused himself for a shiftless lackwit who was slated for an unwept grave.

Lactalbumen (læktălbiūᵊ·mĕn). Also **-in.** [f. L. *lact-, lac* milk + Albumen.] An albumen occurring in milk.

1857 Dunglison *Med. Dict.*, *Lactalbumen*, casein. 1910 *Encycl. Brit.* I. 514/2 'Lact-albumin' occurs in all kinds of milk.

Lactase (læ·ktēᵊs). [f. Lact(ose) + *-ase.] An enzyme or ferment which brings about the decomposition of lactose.

1909 *Century Dict.* Suppl. 1910 *Practitioner* June 823 The hydrolysis is brought about by means of enzymes, such as..lactase and glucase. 1911 *Encycl. Brit.* XIX. 923/2 The presence of lactase has been much discussed.

Lactated, *a.* [f. L. *lact-, lac* milk.] Combined with a milk-product.

1896 *Rep. Vermont Board Agric.* XV. 25 This is used in making..lactated food for infants and invalids.

Lacta·tional, *a.* [f. Lactation + -al.] Of, pertaining to, or connected with lactation.

1903 *Med. Record* 28 Feb. 337 (Cent. Suppl.).

Lacto-. Add: **Lacto-vegeta·rian** *a.*, consisting of milk and vegetables.

1907 *Practitioner* June 845 The lacto-vegetarian diet.. lessens auto-intoxication. 1929 *Encycl. Brit.* VII. 359/1 A lacto-vegetarian diet which permits the free use of milk and eggs.

Lad, *sb.*1 Add: **2. c.** *spec.* A stable-groom of any age.

1894 *Strand Mag.* May 554/1 He was a good lad, tinged with the archaic stable-slang of Thessaly.

Ladder, *sb.* **3.** (Add later examples.)

1902 *Daily Chron.* 10 Dec. 9/2 Navigation is provided for by a 'ladder' of four locks, each 260 ft. long by 32 ft. wide. *fig.* 1847 De Smet *Oregon Missions* 31 It was on this occasion he conceived the idea of the Catholic ladder—'a form of instruction which represents on paper the various truths and mysteries of religion in their chronological order'. 1910 *Daily Chron.* 24 Jan. 8/3 Some kind of ladder of subjects..would be a great gain.

b. In knitted garments: An instance, or the result, of the knitted fabric becoming undone in a narrow longitudinal strip. So called from the appearance of the threads.

1875 [see 3]. 1908 *Daily Chron.* 31 Dec. 4/6 Silk tights are fragile things, sadly given to 'ladders' on the least provocation.

6. ladder-back (**chair**), a chair in which the back is formed of horizontal pieces of wood, suggestive of a ladder; **ladder-backed woodpecker** *U.S.*, one of several species of North American woodpeckers having the upper parts barred with black and white; **ladder-proof** *a.*, of knitted fabrics, not liable to ladder; **ladder woodpecker** *U.S.* = *ladder-backed woodpecker.*

1908 *Daily Report* 24 Aug. 8/3 Three *ladder-back chairs, with cherubs and a crown, brought £46. 1923 *Daily Mail* 11 Jan. 11 Let the table be of the gate-leg variety and the chairs of the style known as ladder-backs. 1884 Coues *Key N. Amer. Birds* (ed. 2) 485 Picoides americanus..*Ladder-backed Three-toed Woodpecker. 1927 *Observer* 3 Apr. 25 Celanese cami-bockers...In *Ladder-proof Self Stripe. 1870 *Amer. Naturalist* III. 474 The resident species not found westward were the *Ladder Woodpecker, (*Picus scalaris*), the White-bellied Wren [etc.].

Ladder, *v.* Delete ? *Obs.* and add modern examples. Also, to furnish with a fish ladder.

1901 J. Black *Carp. & Build.*, *Scaffolding* 67 The stack was laddered from the bottom to the top with a series of ladders. 1901 *Chambers's Jrnl.* Sept. 585/2 When Mr. Grant ..laddered the Moriston falls.., the Crown claimed and gained the new fishings. 1923 *Daily Mail* 22 June 5 Having just laddered the spire of Truro Cathedral, he found every crevice crammed with jackdaws' nests.

2. *intr.* Of knitted garments, esp. stockings: To develop ladders as the result of the breaking of a thread. Hence **La·ddering** *vbl. sb.*

1922 *Daily Mail* 14 Nov. 12 Advt., Your stockings cannot ladder. Laddering and damage to stockings..are entirely obviated. 1927 W. Deeping *Doomsday* viii. § 2 At the last moment a stocking had 'laddered'.

La·ddish, *a.* [f. Lad *sb.*1 + -ish.] Of or pertaining to a lad or lads; like a lad. Also **La·ddishness.**

1886 *Wesleyan-Meth. Mag.* 63 Want of sympathy with..the ladishness of lads. 1907 *Daily Chron.* 24 Oct. 8/3 Missing the laddish laugh, the boisterous gaiety, which they had known aforetime.

La-di-da, *v.* Also **lah-de-dah.** [Cf. the sb.] *intr.* To use affected manners or modes of utterance.

1867 Stirling Coyne *Widow Hunt* in *N. & Q.* Ser. IX. VIII. 20/2, I like to la-di-da with the ladies. 1930 B. Turner in *John o' London's Weekly* 15 Mar. 907/3 There is perhaps too much 'lah-de-dahing about' when royalty is concerned.

Ladin (lădī·n). [L. *Latīn-us, -um.*] The Romanic dialect spoken in the Engadine in Switzerland, closely related to Romansch.

1879 *Encycl. Brit.* VIII. 213/2 The language [in the Engadine] is a dialect known as 'Ladin'. 1880 *Ibid.* XI. 205/1 The remainder [of the inhabitants of the Grisons] use the Romansch or the Ladin dialect.

Ladle, *sb.* Add: **1. b.** In Scottish churches: A similar instrument consisting of a wooden box at the end of a long wooden handle used for taking up the collection and communion tokens.

1830 T. Chalmers in *Comm. on Irish Poor* 3369 The elders carrying about what they call a ladle. 1871 Alexander *Johnny Gibb* xi. (1881) 69 The elders seized the ladles ..and perambulated the kirk. 1929 *Life & Work* Oct. 232/2 A ladle preserved in the parish church of Foulis Easter.

Ladle, *v.* Add to def.: also with *up.*

1851 Melville *Moby Dick* cxxxiv. (1926) 550 Stubb was lustily singing out for some one to ladle him up. 1871 W. H. G. Kingston *On Banks of Amazon* (1876) 93 Wooden spoons were served to enable us to ladle up the soup.

Ladro·nism. [Sp. *ladrón* (see Ladrone), a hostile Filipino, an insurgent.] In the Philippine Islands, organized resistance to law or authority among the native population.

1902 *Outlook* (U.S.) LXXII. 298/1 A local police and an insular constabulary system have been created, and ladronism, or organized robbery and brigandage,..has almost disappeared. 1903 *Daily Chron.* 26 Dec. 5/6 Ladronism had also been successfully treated by the Courts.

Lady, *sb.* **4. e.** Add: *Lady Bountiful* (see Bountiful *a.*). *The Old Lady (in or) of Threadneedle Street*, the Bank of England.

1797 *Gillray Caricature* (May 22), Political Ravishment, or The Old Lady of Threadneedle-Street in danger! 1820 *Black Dwarf* 12 Jan. IV. 36 Van went to wheedle—the street of Threadneedle, To get him, poor dog, a loan;.. He ask'd the old lady to cash him a bill. 1850 *Househ. Words* I. 337 (*heading*) The Old Lady in Threadneedle Street. *Ibid.*, Compared with the Old Lady of Threadneedle Street. 1884 *Peel City Guardian* II. No. 26. 2/1 The rest of the 'Old Lady in Threadneedle-street' remained unbroken.

15. c. *lady-laden* (earlier example).

1869 Tennyson *Holy Grail* 346 Where the long Rich galleries, lady-laden, weigh'd the necks Of dragons clinging to the crazy walls.

17. b. lady's delight (earlier examples); **lady's ear-drop** *U.S.*, the common fuchsia.

1841 L. M. Child *Lett. N.Y.* i. 14, I am like the *Lady's Delight, ever prone to take root. 1845–50 Mrs. Lincoln *Lect. Bot.* 68 In some cases it [the calyx] is the most showy part; as in the *Lady's-ear-drop. 1887 Mary E. Wilkins *Humble Romance* 195 He cut lavishly sprays of dioletra, or lady's ear-drop, snowballs, daffodils.

Lady-bug. *dial.* and *U.S.* = Lady-bird.

1787 [see Lady *sb.* 16]. 1844 'Jon. Slick' *High Life N.Y.* II. 30 Like lady bugs round a full blown rose. 1886 *Harper's Mag.* June 45/2 We may discover lady-bugs—small red or yellow and black beetles—among our vines. 1889 Mary E. Bamford *Up & Down Brooks* 49 Very frequently one will find a lady-bug with the spider. 1910 *N.Y. Even. Post* 4 Apr. (Th.) Los Angeles, April 1.—Millions of ladybugs are receiving free transportation..to the melon fields of the Imperial valley.

Lady's finger. 2. a. Delete ? *Obs.* and add modern examples.

1864 'Mark Twain' *Sketches* (1926) 138 'Lady-fingers'.. suggestive of..soft dalliance with pastry, ices, and sparkling Moselle. 1902 *Daily Chron.* 22 Sept. 9/1 [A child] who died from..being fed on 'boiled lady's fingers'. 1906 *Westm. Gaz.* 30 Apr. 10/1 Lady-fingers and ice-cream.

c. (Example of *c.*)

1876 J. Burroughs *Winter Sunshine* vii. 154 Others are indeed lady apples..like the egg-drop and lady-finger.

Lady's-maid, *v.* [See Lady *sb.* 17.] *trans.* To wait on (one) as a lady's maid. Also **Lady's-maiding** *vbl. sb.*

1914 W. De Morgan *Ghost meets Ghost* I. xxxii, Maggie goes with her, to lady's-maid her. 1923 Una L. Silberrad *Lett. Jean Armiter* v. 115 It prevents her suffering under his lady's maiding.

Lady's slipper. 2. (Earlier examples.)

1845–50 Mrs. Lincoln *Lect. Bot.* 101 *note*, The Impatiens of the garden is sometimes called Ladies'-slipper, sometimes Balsamine. 1874 B. F. Taylor *World on Wheels* II. iv. 220 The lady-slippers dance upon the air, while wild Sweet Williams stand admiring by.

Lætare (lĭtēᵊ·rĭ), *sb.* [L., imper. sing. of *lætārī* to rejoice: see quot. 1921.] *attrib.* (with *Sunday*) or *ellipt.* Mid-Lent Sunday.

1886 F. L. Dorsey *Midshipman Bob* 6 We would notify the Catholic neighbours the day before 'Lætare-Sunday' (as we called our Mass-day). 1921 *Spectator* 19 Feb. 243/2 The Fourth Sunday of Lent or Mothering Sunday, called 'Laetare' from the opening word of the Introit.

Lafayette. 1. (Earlier example.)

1843 C. Mathews *Writ.* 266 (Th.) He had caught a small carful of striped bass and Lafayette fish.

Lag. A. *sb.* **4. b.** Add: Also *Angle of lag.*

1895 S. P. Thompson *Electr. & Magn.* II. x. 492 The angle ..by which the current lags behind the impressed volts is termed the *angle of lag.* 1896 Bedell *Princ. Transformer* 68 The negative sign indicates that θ is an angle of lag.

c. A delay in time, *spec.* between fixing a scale of wages and beginning to pay in accordance with it.

1923 *Glasgow Herald* 2 Nov. 12/4 The operation of the 'lag' of two months between the period of ascertainment and the months when the wages based on such ascertainment are paid.

Lagetta. (Modern example.)

1871 Kingsley *At Last* xiii, A bit of veritable natural lace, similar to..the famous lace-bark of the Lagetta-tree.

Lag-fault. *Geol.* [Lag *sb.*1 or *v.*2 + Fault *sb.*] A fault caused by one layer of rock moving more slowly than another.

1902 Ld. Avebury *Scenery Eng.* 212 Besides these great overthrusts there is another type of relative earth movement which is known as a 'lag fault'.

Lagniappe (lanyæ·p). *local U.S.* Also **lanyap, -yappe, lagnappe.** [Louisiana French, ad. Sp. *la ñapa*, in the same sense.] Something given over and above what is purchased, earned, etc., to make good measure or by way of gratuity.

1853 'P. Paxton' *Stray Yankee in Texas* 47 (Th.) A dubious note that he had received as a 'lanyappe'. (*Anglice*, boot

money.) 1883 'Mark Twain' *Life Mississippi* xliv, We picked up one excellent word—a word worth travelling to New Orleans to get; a nice limber, expressive, handy word—'lagniappe'. They pronounce it lanny-*yap*. It is Spanish—so they said. 1884 G. W. Cable *Creoles of Louisiana* xvi. (1885) 114 The pleasant institution of *ñapa*—the petty gratuity added, by the retailer, to anything bought—grew the pleasanter, drawn out into Gallicized *lagnappe*.

Lagoon[1]. 3. Add: *lagoon-brook*.
1871 Kingsley *At Last* xi, Across the Savanna wandered a deep lagoon-brook.

Laicity (lĕi·siti). [f. Laic *a.* + -ity.] The principles of the laity; the rule or influence of the laity; also *attrib.*
1911 Webster, *Laicity*, laicality. 1905 *Brit. Weekly* 19 Mar. 587/3 The text of the document, which is directed against the 'laicity laws,' lies before us. 1928 *Daily Tel.* 30 Oct. 12/3 Accused by his own hotheads of betraying the cause of 'laicity' by acquiescing in these details of the Budget.

Laid, *ppl. a.* c. Add: *laid-back*, *-on*.
1908 *Westm. Gaz.* 23 Dec. 4/1 To get in under the ball you must have a shallow head..or else a very much *laid-back face. 1909 *Ibid.* 30 Apr. 4/2 You can take a laid-back club and loft right over it. 1874 Knight *Dict. Mech.* 1246/1 *Laid-on*, Joinery, a term applied to moldings which are got out in strips and nailed on to the surface of the object. 1906 *Westm. Gaz.* 9 June 16/3 The Valenciennes running around the laid-on tucks surrounding the skirt.

Lairish (lē³·riʃ), *a.* [f. Lair *sb.*[2] + -ish.] Suggestive of an animal's lair.
1927 H. M. Tomlinson *Gallion's Reach* xxxi. § 4 It certainly was lairish, that stench.

Lake, *sb.*[4] 1. c. *The Great Lakes* (examples). In earlier use freq. without the adjective.
1813 *Niles' Weekly Reg.* V. 65/1 The position of the great lakes is..well known to the people of the United States. 1840 J. F. Cooper *Pathfinder* Pref., Incidents that might be supposed characteristic of the Great Lakes. 1902 *Encycl. Brit.* XXXII. 551/1 Plan of Great Lake steamer. 1903 N. S. Shaler *Citizen* 77 Where the territory borders on the sea or the Great Lakes, the authorities have charge of such harbours as are not in the control of the federal authority.

d. *transf.* An area where the atmospheric pressure is lower than in surrounding areas.
1922 Kendrew *Climates of Continents* 15 And between the two banks of high pressure is the Mediterranean 'lake' of low pressure.

5. *lake-bass*, *-herring* (example), *-shore* (earlier examples), *-steamer*, *-trout* (examples).
1795 J. Scott *Gazetteer U.S.* s.v. *Vermont*, A species of fish called *lake bass. 1884 Goode *Fisheries* 424 The White Bass or Striped Lake Bass, *Roccus chrysops*. 1875 *Amer. Naturalist* IX. 135, I received..a collection of deep water 'Siscoes'...Compared with Coregonus most of the species have a more slender form; hence their popular name of '*lake herrings', although their resemblance to the sea herring is quite superficial. 1798 I. Allen *Hist. Vermont* 61 The two Frenchmen were landed..with instructions to follow the *lake shore. 1813 *Niles' Reg.* IV. 159/1 Previous to this period, a great deal of prejudice existed against the lake *shore*, as unhealthy. 1849 *President's Message Congress* II. 731 The sandstone on the lake-shore is..covered by fifteen..feet of sand and clay. 1851 C. Cist *Cincinnati* 319 Hence [arise] their efforts to reach Chicago, by way of the Erie lake shore. 1888 C. D. Ferguson *Exp. Forty-niner* i. 11 It was in the month of September, 1849, when.. I embarked on the *lake-steamer, A. D. Patchen for Chicago. 1840 *Knickerbocker Mag.* XV. 186 If they could..breakfast at Mackinac..on a *lake trout. 1847 C. Lanman *Summer in Wilderness* xxvi. 158 Of the trout, the largest species in Lake Superior is called the lake-trout.

6. **lake-basin** (add:) also, 'the entire area drained by the streams that fall into a lake' (1865 Page *Hand-bk. Geol. Terms*); **lake country** (earlier example); **Lake District** = Lake-land; **lake ridge** (see quot.).
1842 *Amer. Pioneer* I. 211 No where was the pressure or want of money more sensibly felt than in the *lake country. 1835 Wordsw. *Somnambulist* 1 *note*, *Force* is the word used in the *Lake District for Water-fall. 1851 *Art Jrnl.* 1 May 132/2 The scale upon which the scenery of the English Lake district is laid out. 1886 Prestwich *Geol.* I. 267 In the Lake District the planes of cleavage also usually strike about E.N.E. 1870 *Amer. Naturalist* June IV. 199 Above all these Drift deposits..are the '*lake ridges'—embankments of sand, gravel, sticks, leaves, etc., which run imperfectly parallel with the present outlines of the lake margins.

Lake, *v.*[3] Add:
b. *intr.* Of blood: To become lake-coloured through the diffusion of the hæmoglobin.
1903 *Med. Record* 13 June 953 (Cent. Suppl.) In a case of leukæmia, laking was almost complete in a short time.

Laker[1]. 3. (Earlier example.)
1823 J. F. Cooper *Pioneers* xxiv. II. 261, I see a laker there, that has run out of the school. It's seldom one finds such a creater in the shallow waters.

5. One accustomed to sailing on a lake.
1838 J. F. Cooper *Home as Found* II. 75 After fishing a few hours, the old laker [Captain Truck] pulled the skiff up to the Point. 1910 *Blackw. Mag.* Aug. 173/1 He was an experienced 'Laker', but the scene..had completely unmanned him.

Lalang (lā·lăŋ). Also lallang. [Malay.] The name given to a long, coarse grass which grows in some of the East Indian Islands. Also *lalang grass*.
1887 *Encycl. Brit.* XXII. 93/1 There are waste spaces.. covered with coarse lalang grass. 1887 Mrs. Daly *Digging & Squatting* 158 A shake-down..made up of dried lallang—the thick strong grass of the country. 1908 *Westm. Gaz.* 12 Aug. 5/1 The prolific weed known as 'lalang' is the great enemy to rubber-growth.
attrib. 1912 *Chambers's Jrnl.* Feb. 98/1 As I stood in the lalang patch..there passed over my head..all the turmoil of a great city.

Lamb, *sb.* 6. Add: *lamb-chop*.
1865 Mrs. Stowe *House & Home P.* 248 All the edible matters..would form those delicate dishes of *lamb-chop.

7. b. **lamb-tongue** *U.S.* = Lamb's tongue 1.
1876 'Joaquin' Miller *Unwritten Hist.* x. 152 He [winter] cut down the banners of the spring that night, *lamb-tongue, Indian turnip and catella.

Lambardar, variant of Lumberdar.
1855 [see Lumberdar]. 1908 *New Reformer* II. 68 Securing the co-operation of the literate among them and the Lambardars to bring about sanitary reforms, etc.

Lambkill. *U.S.* (See Lamb *sb.* 7 b.)
1832 W. D. Williamson *Hist. Maine* I. 116 The Lambkill..has been called mountain Laurel, Spoonwood, Ivy, and Calico Bush. 1880 Bessey *Bot.* 510 *Kalmia angustifolia*, the Sheep Laurel or Lambkill.

Lamb-wool. [Lamb *sb.* 6] = Lamb's-wool. In quot. used with reference to the pallium.
a 1899 R. W. Dixon *Hist. Ch. Eng.* (1902) V. 206 In the case of Parker..there was no gift of the pall...The lamb-wool was perceived to be not of the essence of the appointment of metropolitans.

Lamby (læ·mi), *a.* [f. Lamb *sb.*] Of the nature of a lamb; woolly like a lamb.
1920 *Blackw. Mag.* Jan. 7/2 North Sea fishermen, fully accoutred in their thick 'lamby' suits.

Lamelloid (lăme·loid), *a.* [f. Lamella + -oid.] Having the form of a lamella or lamellæ.
1904 *Amer. Naturalist* Jan. 31 These transverse processes ..possess regular lamelloid walls, so as to form rather canals than simple foramina for the artery.

Lament, *v.* 2. Add: Also with *over*.
1831 T. L. Peacock *Crotchet Castle* v, He laments bitterly over the inventions of gunpowder, steam, and gas. 1853 Kingsley *Hypatia* xiii, Why should they lament over other things?

Laminaria (læminē³·riă). *Bot.* [mod.L.] (See etym. note to Laminarian *a.*)
1848 Henfrey tr. *Schleiden's Plant* 399 Laminarias. 1860 Hartwig *Sea & Wond.* 321 The region of the great laminaria or tangle forests. 1875 J. H. Balfour in *Encycl. Brit.* I. 508/1 The Laminarias, or large tangles of our coasts. 1883 [see Laminarian *a.*].

La·minative, *a.* [f. as Laminate *v.* + -ive.] Of a laminated texture.
1872 *Fur, Fin & Feather* 131 Its laminative, juicy meat is very delicate and delicious.

Laminectomy (læmine·ktŏmi). [f. Lamina + Gr. ἐκτομ-ή excision + -y.] Excision of one or more of the posterior arches of the vertebræ.
1892 *Medical Ann.* 458 Formerly the operation was called 'trephining'.., but the trephine is now seldom used, and the term 'laminectomy' has been substituted. 1918 *Nomencl. Diseases* 166 Operations on Bones...Laminectomy. 1919 S. Paget *Sir V. Horsley* viii. 126 The operation of laminectomy..had seldom been done.

Lamnid (læ·mnid), *a. Zool.* [f. mod.L. *Lamn-a*: cf. Lamnoid.] Belonging to the *Lamnidæ*, a family of sharks.
1921 *Return Brit. Museum* 147 A collection of teeth of Lamnid sharks.

Lamnoid. A. *adj.* (Add examples.)
1898 D. S. Jordan *Descr. Fish fr. Japan* title-p., The Type of a Distinct Family of Lamnoid Sharks. *Ibid.* 199 A remarkably distinct new genus of lamnoid affinities.

Lamp, *sb.*[1] Add: 4. a. *lamp-bulb*, *-chimney* (examples), *cup*, *-screen*.
1911 *Chambers's Jrnl.* Jan. 78/1 If a thin gold film is deposited on the lower half of the *lamp-bulb. 1846 *Rep. U.S. Comm. Patents* (1847) 276, I also claim the *lamp chimney, formed of glass, with two contractions. 1870 Mrs. Ann S. Stephens *Married in Haste* xv. 85 She unscrewed the lamp-chimney..and polished off a stain of black smoke. 1846 *Rep. U.S. Comm. Patents* (1847) 280 What I do claim as my invention..is the peculiar form which I give to the *lamp cup. 1877 Eliz. Phelps *Story of Avis* 239 The Japanese coloring upon the *lamp-screen.

b. *lamp-locking* (see quots.).
1894 *Labour Comm. Gloss.* 51/2 *Lamp-locking Station*, the place in a mine where the safety-lamps of all the miners are examined and locked by an official. 1905 *Westm. Gaz.* 12 July 7/1, I was in the lamp-locking cabin, which is a short distance from the bottom of the shaft.

5. **lamp-mat**, a mat on which a table-lamp is placed; **lamp-standard**, a post or other strong support for a lamp; **lamp-wick** (earlier example).
1856 *Trans. Mich. Agric. Soc.* VII. 700 Some beautiful *lamp-mats and other worsted and crochet work. 1883 'Mark Twain' *Life Mississippi* xxxviii. 400 Lamp..standing on a gridiron, so to speak, made of high-colored yarns, by the young ladies of the house, and called a lamp-mat. 1908 *Daily Chron.* 5 Aug. 3/5 A motor fire engine..collided with a 'lamp standard. 1845 Mrs. Kirkland *Western Clearings* 135 Miss Teeny had picked up the *lamp-wick with a pin several times.

Lamp, *v.*[1] Add:
4. To transmit (a message) by means of a lamp.
1912 Edgar Wallace *Pte. Selby* xxxi. 280 A message in triple code was 'lamped' from the British Headquarters to the Rochester regiment.

5. *U.S. slang*. To see. (Cf. Lamp *sb.*[1] 2 b.)
1916 H. L. Wilson *Somewhere in Red Gap* v. 198 Stella.. was standing on the centre table by now, so she could lamp herself in the glass over the mantel. 1923 L. J. Vance *Baroque* viii. 50 Nobody even lamped its number.

Lamper-eel. 1. (Earlier example.)
1709 *Coll. N. H. Hist. Soc.* III. 53 Edward Taylor was slain by the Indians at Lamper-eel river.

Lamp-holder. [Lamp *sb.*[1] 4 b.] A device for securing a lamp, esp. an electric bulb.
1889 *Century Dict.* 1892 *Rep. fr. Committees* XVI. 404 All switches,..floor sockets, and lampholders shall have uninflammable bases. 1907 *Installation News* Sept. 14/2 In wiring Electroliers..it is generally found to be impracticable to group wires into the lampholders.

Lamping, *vbl. sb.* Add: 2. The action of providing with lamps.
1891 G. Findlay *Railway* 138 At all stations where the lamping of trains is performed.

Lamplighter. Add: 2. (Earlier example.)
1833 J. Neal *Down-Easters* II. 115 One side is clean, said she,—and it will do for lamplighters.

3. (See also quot.)
1888 Goode *Amer. Fishes* 69 The names 'Bitter Head' and 'Lamplighter' are also ascribed to it [the Strawberry Perch].

Lamprey. b. **lamprey-eel** (earlier examples).
1726 S. Penhallow *Indian Wars* (1824) 31 Next day, they kill'd Edward Taylor near Lamprey-Eel River. 1832 R. Cox *Adv. Columbia River* vii. 85 We got plenty of salmon while we remained here, and some lamprey-eels, the latter of which were oily and very strong. 1844 D. Lee & Frost *Oregon* xv. 156 A fire was struck, some dried salmon and lamprey-eels roasted.

Lamp-shade. [Lamp *sb.*[1] 4 a.] A shade placed over a lamp to soften or intercept the light. Also *Comb.*
1859 G. Measom *Guide N. W. Rly.* 238 The bulb of glass is..cut with scissors, and expands into a decanter, water-jug, wine-glass, or lamp-shade. 1881 *Instr. Census Clerks* (1885) 83 Lamp Shade Maker. 1899 Werner *Capt. Locusts* 212 He removed the burnt matches, set the lamp-shade straight. 1902 Mabel Barnes-Grundy *Thames Camp* 154, A glorified pink and white lamp-shade. 1908 *Stratford-on-Avon Herald* 24 July 7/2 Lamp-shade-like protectors are obtainable cheaply.

Lance, *sb.*[1] Add: 5. b. A slender tapering pole. *U.S.*
1902 *Sci. Amer.* 27 Dec. 459/1 The second truck is loaded with four or five hundred lances of well-seasoned cypress or spruce, each a trifle over fourteen feet in length.

8. **lance-rod**, a form of fishing-rod.
1885 *Outing* Oct. VII. 74/1 He..then untied, and fondly handled the several joints of a lance-rod.

Lanceolated, *a.* (Later example.)
1901 *Chambers's Jrnl.* May 348/2 The under side [of the *phiale*] is occupied by narrow lanceolated leaves.

Lancet. 4. Add: *lancet-pointed* (cf. 4 b).
1888 *Century Mag.* Aug. 585/1 These parts..are all in the Lancet-Pointed (Early English) style.

Lancet, *v.* [f. the sb.] *trans.* To dissect with a lancet. In quot. *fig.*
1927 *Sunday Express* 1 May 9/4 It is our time, lanceted, scalpelled, vivisected,..in the grand manner of Beyle and Balzac.

Land, *sb.* 3. e. Add: (*for*) *land's sake*, *land sakes*, *my land*, etc. *U.S.*
1848 J. F. Cooper *Oak Open.* I. v. 82 Land's sake! I've forgotten all about them barrels! 1854 Mary J. Holmes *Tempest & Sunshine* xvi. 223 For land's sake dont tell Tempest. 1863 Mrs. Whitney *F. Gartney's Girlh.* ii, Land sakes, Miss Faith! I don't know what you mean. 1916 Bennett *Lion's Share* xlv. 350 'My land!' exclaimed Nick. 'If he sees me here he'll think I've come on purpose to talk about him.'

10. a. *land certificate*, *grant*, *improvement*, *lottery*, *market*, *piracy*, *question*, *speculating*, *speculation*, *taxation*, *title*. (Chiefly *U.S.*)
1838 *Indiana Mag. Hist.* XXII. 451 Quintle had settled that he was to pay in land and made an assignment on a *land certificate. 1870 Medbery *Men & Myst. Wall St.* 311 Unusual *land-grants were made to railroad companies. 1873 J. H. Beadle *Undevel. West* xi. 191 The election had weakened the Republican party, and land grants were thought to be among the chief causes. 1849 *Hansard Parl. Deb.* 4 May 1266 An advance of money..under the *Land Improvement Act. 1902 *Encycl. Brit.* XXIX. 554/2 The number and amount of loans..under the Land Improvement Acts from 1847 to 1900. 1909 *Daily Chron.* 14 Sept. 5/6 The other kind of banks are rent charge and land-improvement banks. 1808 T. Ashe *Trav. Amer.* iv. 34 He could purchase a share in a capital house, or he might buy a *land-lottery. 1845 Mrs. Kirkland *Western Clearings* 5 *Standing round*; i.e., watching the *land market for values. 1837 *Southern Lit. Messenger* III. 668 It is positively a nuisance that borders upon *land-piracy. 1830 *Deb. Congress* 26 Feb. 210/1 The final adjustment of the *land question. 1816 U. Brown *Jrnl.* in *Maryland Hist. Mag.* X. 367 Now we shall learn something about *Land Speculating presently. 1809 W. Irving *Knickerb.* II. vii, He was soon permitted to land, and a great *land-speculation ensued. 1843 Carlton *New Purchase* x. 65 Mr. Glenville's partner in certain land speculations. 1794 D. Robertson *Tour Isle of Man* v. 37 Here the oppression of game-laws, *land-taxation, and excise-establishment are utterly unknown. 1883 *Peel City Guardian* 8 Dec. 4/1 Land Taxation. 1909 *Westm. Gaz.* 19 May 12/1 The land-taxation proposals of the Budget would affect them. 1812 *McDonogh Papers* 11 This uncertainty in which their *land titles are placed. 1815 D. Drake *Cincinnati* i. 30 The security of land titles. 1838 *Southern Lit. Messenger* IV. 796 Some partial remuneration was indeed promptly bestowed upon the officers of the revolution, in the form of land-titles and half-pay.

b. *land-claimant*, *-dealer*, *-locator*, *-robber*, *-seeker*, *-speculator*, *trader*; *land-finding*, *-killing*, *-thieving*. (Chiefly *U.S.*)
1798 I. Allen *Hist. Vermont* 27 These severities were used ..to prevent aid being given to the *land claimants of New York. 1873 'Mark Twain' & Warner *Gilded Age* xxxi. 279 Great Injun pacificator and *land-dealer. 1845 Mrs. Kirkland *Western Clearings* 2 A friend..became quite a proficient in the mysteries of *land-finding. 1814 J. Taylor *Arator* 128 If an abundance of labour caused a *land killing agricultural system..Flanders should be a wilderness. 1816 U. Brown *Jrnl.* in *Maryland Hist. Mag.* X. 364 Those present *Land Locaters Surveys will hold good until the former can be Established. 1839 *Congress. Globe* 23 Jan., App. 265 The rifle and his faithful dog were the indispensable companions of the Land locator. 1845 T. J. Green *Texian Exped.* xvii. 319 The old governor came out in the greatest rage..to know what that *land robber meant by insulting him in that manner. 1845 J. J. Hooper *Adv. Simon Suggs* iii. 37 By the time he had ridden half a mile, he overtook the *land-seeker. 1798 I. Allen *Hist. Vermont* 24 Lawyers and *land speculators called on Mr. Allen. 1809 W. Irving *Knickerb.* II. iii, Like all land-speculators, he was much given to dreaming. 1873 'Mark Twain' & Warner *Gilded Age* I. 456 He might have been a 'railroad man', or a politician, or a land-speculator. 1891 *Century Mag.* Feb. 535 The promise..was broken when it became important to conciliate *land-thieving squatters. 1776 in *Coll. Vermont Hist. Soc.* I. 17 The Monopolizing *Land Trader of New York..did present a petition.

c. locative, as *land-growing*.
1911 F. O. Bower *Plant Life on Land* 45 The Fern-plant is structurally a land-growing plant.

11. b. **land moccasin** (see Moccasin 3); **land otter** (example); **land pike**, †an iguana; also *fig.* (U.S.), a hog.
1836 Mrs. Holley *Texas* v. 104 *Land and water moccasin..are the only venomous snakes, besides the rattlers, found in Texas. 1844 D. Lee & Frost *Oregon* vi. 71 Beaver was valued at two dollars per skin,..*land otter at fifty cents. 1687 R. Blome *Isles & Terr. in Amer.* 56 A *Land-Pike is another strange Reptile, so called from its likeness to that Fish; but instead of Fins it hath four Feet. 1841 *Cultivator* VIII. 152, I am anxious that he should soon get rid of his land-pikes and alligators. 1842 *Ibid.* X. 37 Hogs, landpike variety, are so cheap [etc.]. 1856 *Trans. Mich. Agric. Soc.* VII. 716 The Suffolk swine..are of the same descent as the long-nosed, slab sided land pike, so often seen in the highways.

12. **land agency** (earlier example); **land-ark** *U.S.*, a covered wagon; **land board** (*b*) *Austral.*, 'an official board that manages public lands' (Webster 1911); **land-bridge**, a neck of land (generally prehistoric) connecting two land masses; **land-claim**, a claim to the ownership of land; **land-club**, a club formed to protect and advance the interests of agricultural communities (so *land-clubber*); **land company** (earlier examples); **land district** *U.S.*, one of the districts into which a state is divided for matters connected with land; **land-fever**, eager desire for, or excitement about, securing land; **land-girl**, a girl who takes up agricultural work; **land-jobber** (earlier U.S. examples); **land-jobbing** (examples); **land-jumping**, 'jumping' another person's land; **land-legs**, the ability to walk comfortably on land after being at sea; **land-looker** (earlier and later examples); **land mine**, an explosive mine used on land; **land-office** (earlier examples); **land-plane**, an aeroplane designed to take off from and alight on dry land; **land-poor** *a.*, poor through owning much land and being unable easily to support the burden of taxation; **land-scrip** (examples); **land-sealing**, hunting seals on land; **land-slide** (earlier example); **land-trap**, an unfortunate speculation in land; **land-warrant** (earlier example); **land-worker**, one who works on the land; **land-yacht**, a land vehicle similar to a yacht.
1831 Peck *Guide Emigrants* III. 316 Hillsboro'..contains ..a *land agency office by John Tillson, Esq. *a* 1861 Winthrop *John Brent* ix. 98 The great blue *landarks, each roofed with its hood of white canvas stretched on hoops. 1913 *Chambers's Jrnl.* Jan. 63/1 At every meeting of the *Land Board, when the Government allots land available for farmers, there are usually four to six applicants for each block. 1898 Sir W. Turner in *Nature* 13 Jan. 259/1 A 'Neolithic *land bridge' was produced..and a free immigration of Neolithic man with his domestic animals became possible. 1911 J. L. Myres *Dawn Hist.* vii. 138 Some think..that the Hyksos conquest of Egypt may have been a further adventure along this southern land-bridge. 1812 *McDonogh Papers* 12 They therefore, sir, look forward to you, knowing..your knowledge of their *land claims, to have those claims laid before Congress. 1857 D. Braman *Inform. Texas* xiii. 151 The land claims issued by Texas. 1908 *Fabian News* XIX. 42/2 He elaborates his scheme of *land-clubs, and has himself actively taken a part in a land-club campaign. 1909 *Westm. Gaz.* 23 Apr. 4/2 These groups, called 'Land Clubs,' have now federated into a league. 1908 *Fabian News* XIX. 44/1 [A book] Useful to *land-clubbers and the like. 1805 *Ann. 8th Congress* 2 Sess. 1044 Having never thought of purchasing any land from the Georgia *land-companies. 1833 *Knickerbocker Mag.* I. 283 'Look', said an old man..to the agent of the land company. 1820 Quitman *Let.* in *Life & Corr.* 51 It has been divided into two *land-districts, of one of which Mr. Brush is register. 1831 Peck *Guide Emigrants* 257 The State is divided into land districts, which are designated by Congress. 1849 Chamberlain *Indiana Gazetteer* 24 In every land district is a land office where all the public lands belonging to that district are sold. 1840 *Knickerbocker Mag.* XVI. 205 (*heading*) Recollections of the *Land-Fever. 1845 Mrs. Kirkland *Western Clearings* 4 In the days of the land-fever. 1919 'Ian Hay' *Last Million* 81 We have consorted with..Farmers, Hedgers, and *Land Girls. 1923 *Daily Mail* 2 Apr. 7 A few more land-girls have put on their breeches and gaiters, smocks and slouch hats, and gone back to their old war-time tasks. 1777 J. Adams *Wks.* (1850) II. 436 *Landjobbers, speculators in land. 1789 J. Morse *Amer. Geogr.* 261 The governors were many of them land-jobbers. 1808 T. Ashe *Trav. Amer.* x. 90 A few sordid monopolizers called land jobbers. 1833 J. B. Wyeth *Oregon* 35 The New England land-jobbers were in their bargains too hard for the torpid Dutchman. 1816 U. Brown *Jrnl.* in *Maryland Hist. Mag.* X. 346 This Henry is a full Bred Land Jobber..; his *Land Jobbing extends from the Mouth of the Mississippi to Uwchland Township Chester County Pennsylvania. 1845 Dougherty *Light to People Kentucky* 1 It was the case of..the first settlers of Kentucky..against..the famous John Kercheval, of land jobbing memory. 1910 Jer. Hart *Vigilante Girl* iv. 46 His opinion was asked by a street tribunal over a '*land-jumping'. 1871 *City Road Mag.* I. 242/1 If Mr. Goschen has had to get his sea-legs on, Jack finds it as difficult to put on his *land-legs. 1908 *Daily Chron.* 10 June 4/4, I had so thoroughly got my sea-legs in the constant tossing about that I had lost my land legs. 1836 D. Webster *Priv. Corr.* (1857) II. 21, I hope you will leave some faithful '*land-lookers' to explore for you in your absence. 1845 Mrs. Kirkland *Western Clearings* 6 These blunders called into action another class of operators, who became popularly known as 'land-lookers'. 1902 S. E. White *Blazed Trail* xvi. 116 This is the usual method of procedure adopted by landlookers everywhere. 1918 E. A. Mackintosh *War, the Liberator* 134 Two sappers brought up *land mines and laid them. 1681 in *Archives Maryland* (1889) VII. 242 An Act relating to the *Land Office. 1755 Hor. Sharpe *Corr.* (1888) I. 193 Issuing a Commission to Mr. Calvert and Doctor Steuart as Joint Judges of the Land Office. 1923 *Daily Mail* 23 June 5 Among *landplanes there are huge new troop-carriers. 1873 J. H. Beadle *Undevel. West* 781 In the country, the old settlers are '*land-poor'—so rich that they can not pay their taxes. 1888 *Harper's Mag.* Apr. 702/2 He was not only land-poor, but he had no experience in the management of his plantation. 1848 *Indiana Gen. Ass. Doc.* I. 181 Such *land Scrip as had been issued on the Wabash and Erie Canal. 1857 D. Braman *Inform. Texas* xiii. 151 The land claims issued by Texas..are head-right certificates, military certificates, land-scrip. 1862 *Congress. Globe* 10 June 2628/1 There is no railroad company..that has the right to locate land scrip. 1911 *Chambers's Jrnl.* July 475/2 In the *land-sealing..thousands of fur-seals are driven and forced onwards. 1838 *Jeffersonian* (Albany) 10 Mar. (Th.) On the 10th ult., the city of Natchez was thrown into consternation by a *landslide. 1801 *Spirit Farmer's Museum* 205 He bought lands in Boston at the time all their great men got caught in the Georgia *land trap. 1769 *Maryland Hist. Mag.* XII. 285, I think you told me there was some *land warrant due to you. 188. F. H. Stoddard in *Andover Rev.* VII. 154 Only the trades-workers and the *landworkers are specially considered. 1928 *Daily Express* 26 May 9/3 There was shown at Olympia last year a '*land-yacht' that was palatial in its appointments.

Land, *v.* Add: 1. c. To place (aircraft, passengers, goods, etc.) on the ground again; to bring to earth from the air.
1918 H. Barber *Aeroplane Speaks* (ed. 6) 49 I'll guarantee to safely land the fastest machine in a five-acre field. 1931 *Times* 19 Feb. 17/2 There was a difference of opinion as to who should land the flying boat?—Very definitely.

2. e. Also *absol.* and *intr.*, with *on* and *out*.
1912 *Chambers's Jrnl.* June 395/1 After sparring for five minutes, and frustrating every attempt you made to 'land' on him, he would sit down.

8. d. Of aircraft or of persons in aircraft: To alight upon or reach the ground. Also of seaplanes: To return to the water.
1899 H. G. Wells *When Sleeper Wakes* xxiv. 326 On Blackheath no aëroplane had landed. 1908 — *War in Air* ii. § 5 The balloon was bumping as though its occupants were trying to land. 1912 *Q. Rev.* July 246 To be able to start and land is perhaps as important. 1912 *Aeroplane* 12 Dec. 584/2 Each pilot landing at such an aerodrome would pay proper garage fees for the time he stayed. 1930 *Times* 11 Nov. 16/4 She [*sc.* a flying boat] circled the station and then landed in comparatively calm water.

Landaulet. Add: b. A motor-car with a leather hood over the rear seats. Usually *landaulette*. Also *attrib.*
1902 *Car* 5 Nov. 367 Electric Landaulette. 1905 *Daily Chron.* 17 Nov. 8/4 Now the 'landaulette' is the popular car of the moment. 1906 *Ibid.* 15 Sept. 6/2 The cabs would be of the landaulette type.

Landfall. 1. Add: Also, arrival at land after an air-voyage over the water.
In quot. 1909 = landing.
1908 H. G. Wells *War in Air* vi. § 4 New York had arisen out of the blue indistinctness of the landfall. 1909 — *Tono-Bungay* IV. i. § 5. 449, I remember our prolonged dragging landfall. 1922 *Encycl. Brit.* XXX. 42/2 It was imperative that they should make a landfall before the petrol supply ran out. 1928 C. F. S. Gamble *Story North Sea Air Station* ix. 121 The airship L. 3..made her 'landfall' off Ingham.

Land-grabber. (Earlier U.S. example.)
1860 *Richmond Enquirer* 7 Aug. 1/7 (Th.) Is not John Bell an outrageous land-grabber?

Land-hunter. *U.S.* [Land *sb.* 10 b.] One who searches for land to settle on or purchase.
1816 U. Brown *Jrnl.* in *Maryland Hist. Mag.* X. 367 This John Hall was a Land Speculator and a Land Hunter and Informed him of the Vacancy. 1834 *Visit to Texas* xxiii. 214 These persons, commonly called land-hunters, were almost all from the United States, and generally from the South Western States. 1845 Mrs. Kirkland *Western Clearings* 2 To mislead an unpractised land-hunter was a matter of no great difficulty. 1894 [see Land *sb.* 10 b].

Landing, *vbl. sb.* Add: 1. d. Coming to or alighting upon the ground after being in the air.
1912 *Aeroplane* 19 Dec. 621/2 Mr. Bendall..put in large number of straights..making very good flights and landings. 1918 H. Barber *Aeroplane Speaks* (ed. 6) 49 You can.. imagine what a difference that would make where forced landings are concerned! 1923 H. G. Wells *Men like Gods* I. iii. § 4. 37 The aeroplanes made an easy landing.

5. (Later U.S. examples.)
1832 S. Cumings *Western Pilot* 49 There is a pretty good landing at the upper end of the town. 1867 J. N. Edwards *Shelby* etc. xx. 366 The next day the brigade moved to the river near Gaines Landing. 1895 M. A. Jackson *Memoirs* xii. 211 Just before reaching the landing I stopped to look back.

8. *landing-compass*, *-deck*, *-field*, *-ground*, *-tower*, *-wheel* (mostly terms of aerial navigation).
1889 *Practical Rules Deviation of Compass* 5 A careful observer must go on shore with the *landing compass. 1922 *Encycl. Brit.* XXX. 50/1 As no launching- or *landing-deck was available, the seaplane had to be operated from the sea. 1928 *Observer* 17 June 13/4 There are already more than 4,000 air-ports and *landing-fields in the United States. 1912 *Aeroplane* 12 Dec. 584/1 The great deterrent at present is the lack of proper *landing grounds. 1920 *Act 10 & 11 Geo. V* c. 80 § 7 Such order may provide for taking possession of..any aerodrome or landing ground. 1912 Kipling *As Easy as A. B. C.* II. 7 They began turning out traffic lights and locking up *landing-towers. 1911 *Hazell's Ann.* 478/1 Able by placing his hand on the *landing-wheels to stop the progress of the machine along the ground.

Landing-place. Add: 1. c. A place where airships, aeroplanes, etc., can or do land.
1902 *Daily Chron.* 5 Mar. 3/2 As he [M. Dumont] says, there is a lack of landing places in the sea. 1911 *Hazell's Ann.* 486/1 The aviator turned in search of a suitable landing-place. 1930 *Aberdeen Press & Jrnl.* 15 Mar. 8/4 The land..provides a splendid landing place, free from any hills and high trees.

Land-leaguer. Add: Also *U.S.*
1876 J. H. Beadle *Western Wilds* xxviii. 432 In August 1873, I took a flying tour through the new counties in Southern Kansas. It was the year of Grangers, land leaguers and war on the railroads.

Land-line. Add: 2. (Earlier example.)
1878 *Chambers's Jrnl.* Sept. 595/2 The effects of lightning ..are chiefly felt on land-lines.

b. A travel-route by land.
1900 *Jrnl. Soc. Arts* XLVIII. 277/1 Any combined sea and land line to India.

Landlord, *sb.* Add: 4. *Comb.*, as *landlord-made*, *-ridden*.
1845 *D. Jerrold's Shilling Mag.* I. 515 Judge-made law may be bad, but landlord-made law is worse. 1882 A. R. Wallace *Land Nationalisation* (1902) 148 The chronic starvation of Ireland, and the landlord-made deserts of the Highlands. *Ibid.* 126 The evils of landlord-made law. 1908 *Daily Chron.* 26 June 5/7 With an air of detachment, as though he were not addressing a landlord-ridden assembly.

Land-lubbing, *a.* [Irreg. f. Land-lubber.] Land-lubberly.
1885 *Punch* 29 Aug. 100/2 The Judge, a land-lubbing chap in a wig, said [etc.]. 1927 *Daily Express* 4 Oct. 3/3 We landlubbing civilians know less about the Navy than our maiden aunts might be expected to know about alimony.

Landmark, *v.* [f. the sb.] *trans.* To be a landmark or as a landmark to, to provide with a landmark.
1921 J. F. Porte *Sir E. Elgar* 8 It is not necessary here to landmark further successes. 1928 *Sunday Dispatch* 9 Dec. 2/2 Her mother, perhaps the only disinterested figure of all the many who landmarked those ten years, had died.

Landolphia (lændǫ·lfiă). [mod.L., named by P. de Beauvais (1804) after Capt. *Landolphe*, commander of the expedition to Oware, which Beauvais accompanied as botanist.] The name of several species of tropical climbing plants, used as sources of rubber.
[1886 *G. Nicholson's Dict. Gard.* II. 232 *Landolphia*...A genus comprising about sixteen species of stove scandent shrubs.] 1910 *Westm. Gaz.* 20 Apr. 4/1 Landolphias, woody climbers,..yield the African rubbers.

Landscape. 5. *landscape-garden*, also as *vb.*
1891 W. Morris *News fr. Nowhere* iii. (1907) 17 The other day we heard that the philistines were going to landscape-garden it [the place].

Landscaped, *ppl. a.* [f. Landscape *v.*] Treated as a landscape; laid out by landscape-gardening.
1927 *Brit. Weekly* 15 Dec. 283/2 Even factories..frequently have lovely landscaped grounds.

Land-shark. [Land *sb.* 1 and 4.]
1. (See Land *sb.* 12.)
2. *U.S.* A land-grabber.
1840 *Knickerbocker Mag.* XVI. 211 Well! you're a land-shark, then—swallowin' up poor men's farms. 1848 W. Armstrong *Stocks* 37 A hundred thousand dollars..which he very naturally refused to deprive her of for the sake of satisfying certain land sharks. 1873 Eggleston *Myst. Metrop.* xi. 94 Making severe remarks on the subject of land speculators, and particularly of land-sharks. 1894 'O. Henry' *Rolling Stones* (1915) 218 A class of land speculators commonly called land sharks, unscrupulous and greedy.
3. *U.S.* A lean breed of hog.
1849 *Rep. U.S. Comm. Patents* (1850) 107 In the county of Yates, I am not aware that there is the first full-blood breeding animal of any description, unless it be the full blood land-shark hog. 1852 *Trans. Mich. Agric. Soc.* III. 332 Variously known as narragansetts, alligators, land sharks and flea breeders.

Land-ship. [Land *sb.* 11.] a. A wagon or other vehicle serving the same purpose on land as a ship on the sea. b. A ship erected and kept on land for training purposes.
1837 *Penny Mag.* 22 July 276/1 The ox-carts of the Pampas..are quaintly termed by the natives, *barcos de tierra*, i.e., 'land-ships'. 1869 *Cassell's Mag.* Jan. 156/2 In some of the best schools of France and Belgium, it has long been a custom to erect a dry land-ship in the playground. 1907 L. Osbourne *Adventurer* xiv. 172 Is a land-ship feasible—and if it is, will you build it? 1916 *Daily News* 19 Sept. 1/2 The new land-ships or tanks did invaluable work. 1927 *Glasgow Herald* 23 June 7 By ship, aeroplane, balloon, or landship.

Land-side. 2. (Earlier examples.)
1740 *Coll. S. Carol. Hist. Soc.* IV. 128 That party being left to alarm the Spaniards on the Land side. 1789 J. Morse *Amer. Geogr.* 381 On the land side, are two spacious gardens.

3. (Add quotation.)
1849 *Rep. U.S. Comm. Patents* (1850) 148 What I claim as my invention is the construction of the removable land sides with wings..the land sides and shares so constructed being connected by one or more screw bolts.

Landswoman. [Suggested by Landsman.] A woman accustomed to live mainly or entirely on land, or one skilled in land-work.
1837 *Penny Mag.* 14 Oct. 398/1 The scene is presented exactly as it appeared to the eye and imagination of a landswoman. 1891 [See after Landsman]. 1923 *Weekly Dispatch* 1 Apr. 7 Miss Ford might be described as 'the complete landswoman'. She can milk, do anything with horses, and do field tasks.

Land-taxer. [f. Land-tax.] One who believes in, or advocates, the taxing of land-values.
1905 *Westm. Gaz.* 13 Apr. 4/1 The land taxers have an idea that valuable sites are being held back by grasping ground landlords. 1909 *Daily Chron.* 30 Apr. 1/6 As land-taxers, we are thoroughly satisfied that we have got a complete system of land valuation. 1928 *Daily Express* 6 June 2/4 Colonel Wedgwood, the famous Socialist land-taxer.

Land-value. [Land *sb.* 10.] The economic value of land in all respects, especially as a basis for rating or taxation. Freq. in *pl.*
1880 H. George *Progr. & Pov.* VIII. ii. 365 To abolish all taxation save that upon land values. 1896 J. Edwards *Labour Ann.* 51 Sir Geo. Grey introduced in New Zealand in 1878, a tax on land values of ½d in the pound. 1900 W. Smart *Taxation Land Values* 38 Of late years we have heard much of a proposal called the taxation of land values. *attrib.* 1900 W. Smart *Taxation Land Values* 60 The land value assessment. 1900 *Hansard Parl. Deb.* 6 Feb. LXXVIII. 730 Land Values Taxation (Scotland) Bill. 1908 *Westm. Gaz.* 20 Feb. 2/2 The rates charged on the land-value basis. 1909 *Daily Chron.* 30 Apr. 6/4 A large accumulation of land-value increment.

Lane, *sb.* Add: 2. c. In sprinting races: The course marked out for each runner by cords or chalk lines.
1909 *Century Dict.* Suppl. 1911 *Encycl. Brit.* XXIII. 853/2 The course for sprinting races..is marked off in lanes for the individual runners by means of cords stretched upon short iron rods.

6. *lane-side* (modern examples).
1909 *Daily Chron.* 4 Aug. 7/3 The great crane's-bill..is a true lane-side flower. 1923 *Daily Mail* 2 Apr. 6 To see the lanesides in this delicate livery of verdure and bloom.

Langobar·dian, *a.* [f. late L. *Langobardi*.] Of or pertaining to the Langobards.
1925 *Contemp. Rev.* Aug. 212 The people are of Langobardian, French, or even Gothic origin.

Languedocian (læŋgədōᵘ·ʃiăn), *a.* [f. *Languedoc*, the name of an old province in southern France.] Belonging to Languedoc.
1908 *Daily Chron.* 25 May 6/4 He has..found time to write poems in the Languedocian language. 1927 A. L. Maycock *Inquisition* 178 The records of the Languedocian tribunals.

Languisher. (Modern example.)
1896 *Godey's Mag.* Feb. 193/2 A few silly languishers flutter and simper, 'How nice! how lovely!'

Lanikin, *a. rare*[−1]. [Cf. Cheshire dial. *lankin* and *lanniky*.] Lanky.
1862 Borrow *Wales* II. xxvi. 295 He was a tall lanikin figure with a pair of..staring eyes.

La·nkily, *adv.* [f. Lanky *a.*] In a lanky fashion.
1903 Conrad & Hueffer *Romance* i. 37 The second mate was lankily stalking the deck. 1926 Bennett *Lord Raingo* I. xlviii. 215 'Yes, Raingo', said the tall, gaunt old man, striding lankily into the presence [of the minister].

Lansquenet. Add to forms: (sense 2) lambskinnet.
1917 Richardson *Richard Mahony* 9 Even the 'shepherds' beguiled the time with euchre and 'lambskinnet'.

Lantern, *sb.* 9. Add: **lantern-bug**, a light-bearing insect, *Laternaria lucifera*.
1927 Haldane & Huxley *Animal Biol.* xi. 228 Many lantern-bugs have this anterior prolongation of the head.

Lap, *sb.*[1] Add: 4. c. A form of loin-cloth worn by Indians in Guiana.
1769 E. Bancroft *Nat. Hist. Guiana* 273 This is called a lap, and is the ordinary covering of the Negroes also. 1876 C. Barrington Brown *Canoe & Camp Life Brit. Guiana* 34 There were two Indians, whom we had hired, dressed in nature's garb, barring the 'lap'. 1899 Rodway *In Guiana Wilds* 254 It would be different with a party of Indians in nothing but their laps.

7. **lap-board** (earlier example); **lap-iron**, a piece of iron used as a lapstone.
1866 Mrs. Whitney *L. Goldthwaite* vi, On the *lap-board across her knees lies her work. 1902 *Westm. Gaz.* 8 Oct. 6/2 The lapstone and the *lapiron have gone out of existence.

Lap, *sb.*[3] 6. (sense 2) *lap-boarded*; *lap-seam*; (sense 4) *lap-drum*, *-roller* (example), *-tenter*; (sense 5 b) *lap time*. Also **lap-system** (see quot.); **lap-winding**, a system of electrical winding in which each turn is partially overlapped by the next.
1927 *Chambers's Jrnl.* Sept. 597/2 *Lap-boarded houses which overhang the sea. 1902 Thornley *Cotton Combing Machines* 17 The six webs are..drawn by frequent pairs of press rollers to the lap-head, consisting of two pairs of heavily weighted press rollers..and of the *lap drums. 1849 *Rep. U.S. Comm. Patents* (1850) 160, I also claim the combination of burring apparatus..with the calender and *lap rollers. 1905 *Westm. Gaz.* 21 Mar. 5/1 He says the explosion was caused by a crack in the *lap-seam [of the boiler]. 1894 *Labour Commission Gloss.* 51/2 *Lap System*, also called 'trip system', is a system (in the carter's industry) of piece-work, *e.g.*, a driver taking loads of coal a given distance for a stated sum, works under the lap system. 1881 *Instr. Census Clerks* (1885) 68 *Lap Tenter. 1901 *Census* Explanatory Notes, Cotton Lap Tenter. 1909 *Westm. Gaz.* 7 Dec. 5/1 The net *lap times of the Auvergne races of 1905. 1902 *Encycl. Brit.* XXVII. 582/1 By the first, or *lap winding*.., the end of the loop is taken to a commutator sector, and thence starts off again to a third inductor.

Lap, *v.*[1] Add: 2. b. *U.S.* Of a bear: To gather and eat fruits or nuts. Hence *lapping-season*.
1868 *Amer. Naturalist* May II. 122 They climb in order to 'lap', as the hunter says. *Ibid.*, When mast is not plenty, they lap black-gum berries. 1881 *Scribner's Mag.* Oct. 838/2 This is called the lapping season, as he ensconces himself in a tree lap and breaks the limbs to pieces, in gathering nuts and fruits.

Lap, *v.*[2] Add:
9. c. *trans.* Of persons engaged in a race, or their vehicles: To travel over (a distance) as a lap; also simply, to traverse.
1923 *Daily Mail* 24 May 10 The course, 37⅞ miles in length, has to be lapped six times. *Ibid.* 4 June 13 The Leyland expert put up the highest speed of the day when he lapped the 2⅞ miles at an average of 117 miles an hour. 1927 *Daily Express* 2 June 12/4 Major Segrave hopes..to lap the course at a fair speed.

Lapageria (læpădʒi³·riă). [mod.L. named after the French Empress Josephine *Lapagerie* 1763–1814.] The name of a species and genus of tall, hardy, climbing shrubs of the Order *Liliaceæ*.
1886 *Nicholson's Dict. Gard.* II. 234/2 Lapagerias rank amongst the most beautiful greenhouse climbing plants in existence. 1929 *Times* 1 Nov. 19/6 A tiny, pillared stone temple of exquisite proportions bowered in clematis, lapageria, and a climbing yellow rose.

La·p-dog, *v.* [f. the sb.] *trans.* To treat as a lap-dog; to pet.
1926 'Lucas Malet' *Dogs of Want* v. § 4. 131 Why, you know, Suze, you can't deny you've been lap-dogging young Simpson a good deal, now can you?

Lapidarist. Delete †*Obs. rare* and add mod. examples.
1886 *Sci. Amer.* 7 Aug. 84/2 The stone called sapphire by Pliny is now known to lapidarists as lapis lazuli. 1926 C. L. Warr *Principal Caird* iv. 135 He was a slow-working lapidarist, polishing every literary pebble.

Lapidicolous (læpidi·kŏləs), *a.* [f. L. *lapid-*, *lapis* stone + *-col-us* inhabiting + -ous.] Of beetles and other insects: Living under or among stones.
1899 D. Sharp *Insects* II. 205 These blind lapidicolous Carabidae are of extremely minute size, and of most sluggish habits.

Lapith (læ·piþ). *Grk. Mythol.* [f. L. *Lapithæ*, ad. Gr. Λαπίθαι.] One of the Lapithæ, a people of Thessaly, celebrated for their wars with the Centaurs.
1874 C. J. Newton *Græco-Rom. Sculpt. Brit. Mus.* 57 One of the Centaurs..attacked by Lapiths while carrying off Greek women. 1883 A. S. Murray *Grk. Sculpture* II. 55 The Lapiths are youthful, beardless, slim, but firmly knit. 1886 *Exhib. Galleries Brit. Mus.* 77 Sepulchral urn. On the front a Centaur carrying off a female Lapith.

Lapped, *ppl. a.* Add: d. Made to overlap.
1844 in C. Cist *Cincinnati Misc.* 51 A new jail of hewed logs and lapt-shingle roof..was erected within less than two years.

Lapper[2]. 2. (Example.)
1849 *Rep. U.S. Comm. Patents* (1850) 195 The..surfaces of cotton batting that has been merely..spread in a lapper.

Lappet, *sb.* Add:
1. c. A device used in lappet-weaving.
1894 T. W. Fox *Mech. Weaving* XII. 313 Swivel-weaving stands in the same relation to picking that lappets stand to shedding.

6. **lappet-shedding** (see quot.).
1894 T. W. Fox *Mech. Weaving* IX. 250 Lappet shedding is a peculiar system of shedding designed to move whip or warp threads out of their longitudinal positions by bending them until they assume a transverse direction [etc.].

Lap-robe. *U.S.* [Lap *sb.*[1] 5.] A rug or cloth to cover the lap of a person seated in a vehicle.
1875 Mrs. Stowe *We & Neighbors* xxxix. 373 Oh, and he took her to ride in such a stylish carriage, white lynx lap-robe, and all! 1897 R. M. Stuart *Simpkinsville* 94 They step forward to the buggies of such ladies as drive up for quinine and capsules without so much as displacing their linen lap robes. 1901 *Scribner's Mag.* Apr. 418/2 He asked if the other man wouldn't like a silver-mounted harness and a lap-robe thrown in. 1914 Gertr. Atherton *Perch of Devil* I. 121 He smiled..into her..eyes and tucked the lap-robe about her.

Lapse, *sb.* Add: 8. *Comb.* **lapse-rate** (see quot.).
1928 Brunt *Meteorol.* vi. 46 The rate of decrease of temperature with height is called the *lapse-rate*, and the average conditions in the troposphere are specified by a lapse-rate of 3° F. per 1,000 feet.

Lap-streak. (Earlier U.S. example.)
1771 *Boston Gaz.* 11 Mar. Advt. (Th.) Whale-boats and all sorts of Lapstreak Boats.

Lap-weld, *sb.* (See Lap *sb.*[3] 6.)

Lap-weld, *v.* [Lap *sb.*[3] 6.] *trans.* To weld with overlapping edges. Hence **Lap-welded** *ppl. a.*
1848 *Mechanics' Mag.* XLVIII. 287 Advt., Lap-welded iron tubes. 1862 *Catal. Internat. Exhib.* II. xxxi. 1 The shelves inside are made of wrought-iron, lap-welded by a new process. 1913 V. B. Lewes *Oil Fuel* 67 Where the well is not more than a foot in diameter..lap-welded iron or steel tubing is used.

Lap-wheel. [Lap *sb.*[4]] (See quot.)
1874 H. H. Cole *Catal. Ind. Art S. Kens. Mus.* 159 The lap-wheels consist of two circular discs or cakes of lac, with ground korund, coarse or fine, according to the work.

Larboarder, *sb.* [f. Larboard *sb.*] One who is on the larboard side of a boat.
1846 Melville *Typee* (1920) vi. 43 The poor larboarders shipped their oars and commenced pulling us ashore.

Larch. 3. Add: **larch-blister**, a disease, caused by a fungus, which attacks larch trees (*Dasyscypha calycina*).
1895 Schlich *Man. Forestry* IV. 402 The larch-blister or canker..is most prevalent in damp places with moist air and in frosty and cloudy localities.

Lard, *sb.* 2. Add to def.: also, in modern use, any edible swine-fat, and (in commercial use) a fatty preparation containing or resembling lard.

3. Add: *lard-grease*, *-keg*, *-pail*, *-tub*; **lard compound**, a substitute for lard based on cottonseed oil; **lard oil** (earlier example); **lard-stearin**, a preparation of lard.
1904 L. L. Lamborn *Cottonseed Products* 172 The ingredients of *lard-compound are summer white cottonseed-oil and oleo-stearin. 1847 *Rep. U.S. Comm. Patents* (1848) 529 *Lard grease is computed to form eighty per cent of all the fat used in making soap. 1851 C. Cist *Cincinnati* 345 The pork merchants paid me cash for my due bills, payable in barrels and *lard kegs. 1845 in C. Cist *Cincinnati Misc.* 181, I know one *lard oil manufacturer alone, whose capacity of producing lard oil..would require for his year's business 2,000,000 lbs. lard. 1851 C. Cist *Cincinnati* 284 We follow now to the manufacture of lard oil, which is accomplished by divesting the lard of one of its constituent parts—stearine. 1891 *Fur, Fin & Feather* Mar. 195 Two empty *lard pails with their covers..will complete the culinary outfit. 1904 L. L. Lamborn *Cottonseed Products* 173 *Lard-stearin is made in the same general manner as oleo-stearin. 1857 *Quinland* I. i. I. 19 His solicitude in regard to the flour-barrel, *lard-tub, and tea-canister.

La·rder, *v.* [f. Larder *sb.*] *trans.* To store up as in a larder.
1905 Haggard *Gardener's Yr.* July 251 The first wasp which ..paralysed caterpillars and lardered them in key-holes.

Lardine. (Earlier example.)
1884 *Rep. Vermont Board Agric.* VIII. 10 Oliomargarine, butterine, lardine, or any other villainous counterfeit.

Large, *a.* 8. b. (Add further examples.)
The compar. *larger* and superl. *largest* are also used in specific names, as *larger red-crested woodpecker*, *largest red oak*.
1813 Muhlenberg *Catal. Plant.* 92 *Large aspen (*Populus trepida* or *grandidentata*). 1832 D. J. Browne *Sylva Amer.* 255 As it surpasses the aspen in height, we have given it the name of Large Aspen. 1837 *Southern Lit. Messenger* III. 660 There are for sale hats, boots and shoes, India rubber articles..*large bread,..everything on earth. 1876 H. E. Scudder *Dwellers* i. 7 There was a large-bread bakery at Skolas. 1832 D. J. Browne *Sylva Amer.* 226 The Yellow Pavia, or *Large Buckeye is first observed on the Alleghany Mountains in Virginia. 1785 H. Marshall *Amer. Grove* 105 American Plane Tree or *Large Button Wood. 1836 D. B. Edward *Hist. Texas* iv. 66 [He took the names of the shrubs] which he could designate, as the..*Large Elder, the Dwarf Elder. 1845 Mrs. Kirkland *Western Clearings* 154 'You'd ought to begin with *large-hand, Joshuay,' said Master Horner to this youth [instructing him in penmanship]. 1787 W. Sargent in *Mem. Amer. Acad.* IX. 159 *Large Laurel. 1819 E. Dana *Geogr. Sketches* 245 The most valuable forest trees growing..in the adjacent region, viz:..large laurel, tupiloo. 1810 Michaux *Arbres* I. 29 *Large tupelo,..nom le plus général dans les États du sud. 1832 D. J. Browne *Sylva Amer.* 222 It is designated [in Georgia and..East Florida] by the name of Large Tupelo.

15. *large-berried*, *-flowered*, *-framed*, *-fruited*, *-grained*, *-leaved*; **large-mouth** (earlier example).
1785 Washington *Diaries* II. 346 Planted..all the *large berried thorns, with a small berried one in the middle of each clump. 1813 Muhlenberg *Catal. Plants* 53 *Large-flowered Custard Apple. 1846 D. J. Browne *Trees Amer.* 2 Of all the trees..the Large-flowered Magnolia is most remarkable for the..beauty of its flowers. 1868 *Rep. U.S. Commissioner Agric.* (1869) 438 *Large-framed, wide and straight-backed, and deep-bodied, short-horn cows. 1813 Muhlenberg *Catal. Plants* 48 *Large fruited Hawthorn. *Ibid.* 88 Large-fruited Shellbark hickory. 1765 Washington *Diaries* I. 216 Three Pecks of Wheat..very *large graind. 1785 H. Marshall *Amer. Grove* 93 *Large-leaved Virginian Mulberry Tree (*Morus rubra*). 1810 Michaux *Arbres* I. 34 Large leaved magnolia. 1832 D. J. Browne *Sylva Amer.* 212 On account of the resemblance of its leaves to those of the umbrella tree..we have given it the specific name of Large-Leaved Umbrella Tree. 1888 Goode *Amer. Fishes* 55 In the *Large-mouth [Bass] the upper jaw extends far behind the eye.

B. *adv.* 3. (Modern examples.)
1834 Seba Smith *Sel. Lett. Major Jack Downing* 149 Other folks may talk larger and bluster more. 1872 in Tourgee *Invis. Empire* v. (1880) 411 He had just talked large about the Ku-Klux.

C. *sb.* Add: 5. f. *Gentleman at large*: see Gentleman 2 c. k. *Verdict at large*: see Verdict *sb.* 1 c.

La·rgessed, *a.* [f. Largess.] Given as largess.
1910 *B'ham Inst. Mag.* Jan. 256 We will not gaze On death, but with the largessed moments praise.

Lariat. Also larietta, laryette.
1830 C. A. Murray *Trav. N. Amer.* I. 339 Both my laryettes (which were very strong and valuable of their kind) were stolen from my two horses. 1841 *Southern Lit. Messenger* VII. 54/1 Why, that young hatter..'tother evening let a Most noble stallion feel the larietta.

Larixin (læ·riksin). *Chem.* [f. Larix + -in[1].] A special substance found in the bark of the larch. Also *larixi·nic acid*.
1862 *Phil. Trans.* CLII. 53 (*title*) On Larixinic Acid, a crystallizable volatile principle found in the Bark of the Larch Tree. *Ibid.* 57 Perhaps the name *Larixine* would be more appropriate. 1880 Garrod & Baxter *Mat. Med.* 366 [Larch bark] contains *larixin* or *larixinic acid*,..a volatile substance forming crystals which resemble those of benzoic acid.

Lark, *sb.*[1] 3. Add: *lark-crested*.
1849 D. J. Browne *Amer. Poultry Yd.* (1855) 57 Lark-crested fowls are of various colors; pure snow-white, brown with yellow hackles, and black.

Lark, *v.*[2] Etym. note, last line, read: 'which is found a few years earlier (1809)'.

Larkiness (lā·kinės). [f. Larky + -ness.] The quality of being larky; sportiveness.
1905 Chesterton *Heretics* 99 It is hard to see at first sight why so human a thing as leisure and larkiness should always have a religious origin. 1924 Hichens *After Verdict* II. xx. 303 The ball-boys stood ready, looking alert and full of suppressed larkiness.

Larkspur. Add: b. The blue colour characteristic of the larkspur.
1927 *Sunday Express* 27 Feb., Newest Season's colours including..Grey, Cocoa, Larkspur, Fawn. 1927 *Daily Express* 12 Mar. 3/5 Larkspur, a pastel blue slightly inclining to the mauve.

Larky, *a.* (Earlier examples.)
1841 *Punch* 25 Dec. 278/2 The old girl has her two nieces home for the holidays—devilish handsome, larky girls. 1847 *Ibid.* 6 Nov. 178/1 A larky young peer would think it a great joke to be quizzed in *Punch*.
Add: b. *transf.*
1925 *Blackw. Mag.* July 80/2 (*Rugby School*) The 'swells' were allowed to wear 'larky' waistcoats, *i.e.*, waistcoats of various hues often with flowery designs embroidered on them.

Larrigan (læ·rigăn). [Of unknown origin.] A boot made of undressed leather.
1902 *Cleveland Plain Dealer* 21 Dec. (Cent. Suppl.). 1922 *Short Stories* Feb. 128/2 Over six feet in his larrigans.
Hence **Larriganed** *a.*, protected by larrigans.
1922 *Short Stories* Feb. 129/1 [The dogs] clipped fangs at Cherriman's larriganed legs.

Larrikin. Add: Also *transf.*
1901 *Daily Tel.* 8 Mar. 8/7 The larrikins of the Legislature..could not be visited retrospectively with an adequate punishment.

Larva. 2. c. Add: *larva-case*, *-stage*.
1855 J. Phillips *Man. Geol.* 459 Thin tufaceous limestones, sometimes full of the larva-cases of phryganidæ. 1893 Tuckey *Hatschek's Amphioxus* 159 Those stages which form the transition from the development of the embryo.. to the larvae stages which are self-nourishing.

Larvule (lā·ɹviŭl). *Zool.* [f. Larv-a + -ule.] (See quot.)
1895 D. Sharp *Insects* I. 431 Owing to the organization being inferior, the creature in its earlier stages is called a larvule.

Laryngo-. Add:
Laryngometry (-ǫ·mėtri) [-metry], a measuring of the larynx. **Lary·ngophone** (-ofōᵘn) [-phone], a type of telephone having a receiver which is applied to the larynx, and not to the ear.
1899 *Nature* 18 May 72/1 Method for rapidly measuring the dimensions of small objects...Application to pupillometry and to laryngometry. 1927 *Observer* 6 Nov. 19/3 We have a special instrument, the laryngophone, by means of which we can speak to each other in flight.

Lash, *sb.*[1] 5. Add: **lash-rope** *U.S.*, a rope used for lashing a pack or load on a horse or vehicle.
1822 J. Fowler *Jrnl.* 159 We then took the lash Roaps and tyed up the Horses. 1843 *Amer. Pioneer* II. 162 Each horse was provided with..a lash rope to secure the load. 1929 *Collier's* 5 Jan. 33/3 'Wait until I get my lash rope' (i.e., the rope with which he bound his load on his sledge).

Lash, *v.*[1] 6. *absol.* (Add modern examples.)
1877 Anna Sewell *Black Beauty* xx. (1880) 93 The man, fiercely pulling at the head of the forehorse, swore and lashed most brutally. 1891 Doyle *Adv. S. Holmes* viii. (1893) 205 The sudden glare..made it impossible for me to tell what it was at which my friend lashed so savagely.

Lashkar. b. Add: Also in recent use.
1908 *Daily Chron.* 27 Apr. 1/7 General Willcock's columns yesterday searched out the enemy's lashkars two miles to the west of Shabkadr. 1924 *Glasgow Herald* 14 May 9 The tribal revolt is subsiding and the rebel lashkars are melting away.

'Lasses, colloq. abbreviation of Molasses. *U.S.*
1807–8 W. Irving *Salmag.* x. 229 This manufacture is called by the Bostonians *lasses candy*. 1842 *Philad. Spirit of Times* 3 Jan. (Th.) Every puppy that would be keeled over with a smaller of rum and 'lasses turns up his nose at him. 1854 Mary J. Holmes *Tempest & Sunshine* xxii. 317 Get along Jack, pokin' your fingers into the 'lasses cup.

Lasso, *sb.* 3. Add: *lasso-throw*, *-throwing*.
1841 Catlin *N. Amer. Indians* II. 152 A line, with a sort of '*laso throw', came from an awkward hand on the deck. *a* 1861 T. Winthrop *John Brent* ii. 13 Man to them was power, and nothing else,—a *lasso-throwing machine.

Lassoer, Lassoing. (Earlier examples.) Also **La·ssoist**.
1884 W. Shepherd *Prairie Exper.* 40 The *lassoer picks out the unbranded calves, and drags them off to the fire. 1838 'Texian' *Mexico v. Texas* 48 The men were collecting the mules, and when these were driven together, the *lassoing began. 1906 *Daily Chron.* 16 May 5/7 There have been *lassoists before, but never, perhaps, such a master of the art as Will Rogers.

Last, *sb.*[1] 3. Add: *last factory*, *manufactory*.
1837 W. Jenkins *Ohio Gaz.* 158 A *last factory, producing 14,000 lasts..per annum. 1847 H. Howe *Hist. Coll. Ohio* 389, 2 machine shops, 1 last manufactory. *Ibid.* 503 A thriving business town, containing..1 last factory.

Last. A. *adj.*
1. b. Add: Also preceded by an ordinal number to denote how many places from the end of a series a person, object, etc., occurs.
1880 Skene *Celtic Scotl.* III. 122 Dathi the second last of the pagan monarchs of Ireland.

d. Delete †*Obs.*, and add: Also, the final portion of a period of time.
1834 Carruthers *Kentuckian in N.Y.* I. 190 Our parson whines it out like an old woman in the last of pea-time. 1883 *Century Mag.* Oct. 921/2 The snipe usually makes its appearance in New Jersey and New York about the last of March or the first of April. 1888 Goode *Amer. Fishes* 59 Many late spawners are occupied with family cares until the last of July.

f. *Last across*: A game, played by children, which consists in trying who shall be the last to cross the road or street in front of an approaching vehicle. Also *fig.*
1904 F. Young *Compl. Motorist* ix. (ed. 2) 230 If it seems good to them [children] to play at 'last across', you had better go very gingerly in their neighbourhood. 1914 'Ian Hay' *Knt. on Wheels* xi. 108 A frisky calf, encountered by the way, almost wrecked its own prospects of ever becoming veal by an untimely indulgence in the game of 'Come to Mother, or Last Across the Road'. 1928 *Sunday Dispatch* 15 July 11/3 Socialist back-benchers are playing a dangerous game of 'last across' with Mr. Speaker—just seeing how far they can go at question time without being 'named'.

7. *last cry* [tr. F. *le dernier cri*], something in the newest fashion. Cf. *Dernier.
1916 W. J. Locke *Wonderful Yr.* x. 133 A morning coat (last cry of Bond Street).

8. ¶. Also *last sacrament(s)*.

9. c. Delete † *Obs.* and add example.
1918 Galsworthy *Five Tales*, *Indian Summer* i, The last of daylight from without mingled with faint intrusion from the lamp within.

h. (Example.)
1910 'Mark Rutherford' *More Pages fr. Jrnl.* 22, I shall be thankful to see the last of you!

10. b. Delete Now *rare* and add mod. examples.
1926 *Manch. Guard. Weekly* Feb. 104/1 The Government followed up the references to agriculture in it [the King's speech] by launching at long last its land policy. 1927 *Sunday Times* 13 Mar. 13/3 But at long last the confidence of those in France was justified.

Last, *v.*[1] 3. Add: Also with *out*.
1881 Mrs. J. H. Riddell *Senior Partner* III. 56 What would hinder him lasting out to ninety [years] or a hundred even?

Last-ditcher. [See Ditch *sb.*[1] 5.] One who resists to the last extremity.
1909 *Westm. Gaz.* 30 Jan. 2/1 The only part he is likely to take in the Social Revolution is to be what may be called a last-ditcher in the attempt to resist it. 1927 *Daily Express* 19 Nov. 3/1 A constituency which is to be congratulated on a true last ditcher.

Lasting, *vbl. sb.*[3] (Add example.)
1886 *Encycl. Brit.* XXI. 830/2 Lasting is a crucial operation, for, unless the upper is drawn smoothly and equally over the last, leaving neither crease nor wrinkle, the form of the boot will be bad.

Lastly, *adv.* Add: 1. b. As *sb.* (See quot.)
1905 *Ch. Q. Rev.* Jan. 387 The reader feels some of that impatience which besets the hearer of a sermon with half a dozen lastlies.

Lastness. (Add examples.)
a 1665 J. Goodwin *Filled w. the Spirit* (1867) 92 Lastness or worstness in estate or condition. 1927 E. Bramah *Max Carrados Myst.* 72 Your account..is entirely based on the fact that you were the last...There stands the man we want, ..only you and your lastness get between.

Lat.[2] [f. the first syllable of *Latvija* Latvia.] A unit of gold currency established by the state of Latvia in August 1922, with a par value of about 25 to the pound sterling.
1923 *Glasgow Herald* 23 June 10 The last Budget year was closed with a surplus of over 18,000,000 lats gold. 1928 *Daily Express* 29 Aug. 2/5 The Latvian Ministry of Finance has decided to place an order for five-lat silver pieces to the value of 5,000,000 lats with the Royal Mint, London.

Lata. Add: Also *attrib.* and as *adj.*: Affected with lata.
1913 *Q. Rev.* Jan. 135 It was also known to his shipmates that he was 'lâtah'. *Ibid.*, If the stimulus in the Lâtah patient was a current of electricity..no one would think mind had anything to do with it.

Latania (lătē³·niă). Also -nier. [mod.L. f. *latanier* the native (Mauritian) name for the plant.] A small genus of stove palms found in the islands of the Indian Ocean.
1819 E. Dana *Geogr. Sketches* 238 On the..outer margin of the cane, the palmetto, or latania, fill the slope between the cane and the inundated lands. 1868 *Putnam's Mag.* I. 594/1 Here and there..is a 'latanier-hut' with adobe walls and a roof thatched with..palmetto. 1886 *G. Nicholson's Dict. Gard.* II. 236.

Latch, *sb.*[3] Var. of Letch *sb.*[1]

Latch-key. Add: Freq. allusive, with reference to the use of a latchkey by a younger member of a household or a lodger.
1902 *Daily Chron.* 22 Aug. 3/6 At the beginning of the latchkey life everything looks delightful. 1905 *Ibid.* 17 Nov. 1/7 The names of 2,596 workmen in Devonport, known as latch-key voters,..were restored to the occupiers' list.

Latch-string. (Earlier example.)
1857–8 *Trans. Ill. Agric. Soc.* III. 342 It is but another proof of the well known characteristics of the people of the west, that they are always to be found with 'their latch strings out'.

Late, *a.*[1] 2. c. Add: Also of land, on which crops are late in ripening.
1901 *Yearbk. U.S. Dept. Agric.* 436 (Cent. Suppl.) The superfluous water which tended to make the land cold, sour, and 'late' is removed, thus making the soil warmer and earlier.

6. *The late unpleasantness* (U.S.), the Civil War (see Unpleasantness).

Latent, *a.* Add: *Latent partner*, one whose name does not appear as a member of a firm or company.
1913 *Act 3 & 4 Geo. V* c. 20 § 90 Any latent partner of a company whose estates have been sequestrated.

h. *Psychol.* (See quot.)
1901 *J. M. Baldwin's Dict. Philos. & Psychol.* 628/2 *Latent Period*, time elapsing between stimulus and beginning of reaction, especially of a muscle.

La·tentize, *v.* [f. Latent *a.* + -ize.] *trans.* To render latent.
1904 G. S. Hall *Adolescence* I. 266 The relative reduction of the individual involves a latentizing of energy.

-later: see -latry.

Lateralize (læ·tĕrălaiz), *v.* [f. Lateral *a.* + -ize.] *trans.* To move or displace to the side; to render lateral.
1903 *Therapeutic Gaz.* 15 Feb. 74 (Cent. Suppl.).
Hence **La·teralizer**.
1901 *Proc. Zool. Soc.* II. 665 In animals which chew the cud the internal pterygoid acts as a powerful lateraliser of the jaw.

Laterization (læ:tĕraizē³·ʃən). [f. L. *later* brick + -ization.] The hardening which takes place in laterite when it is quarried and dried.
1903 Geikie *Text-bk. Geol.* (ed. 4) I. 169 Laterite...The peculiar kind of alteration exemplified by this rock and by Bauxite has been termed 'Laterisation'.

Latest, *a.* Add: 4. *The latest*, the most recent thing, piece of news, etc.
1889 *Kansas Times & Star* 25 June, The latest the dear girls hereabouts are singing,..is, Will he love you as today?

Latex. 2. *Bot.* Add to def: *spec.* that of rubber-trees.
1909 *Westm. Gaz.* 26 Oct. 9/2 The quantity and quality of the latex obtained from the trees were eminently favourable. 1911 *Encycl. Brit.* XXIII. 798/1 To obtain the rubber, the latex is usually treated in the following manner.

Lath, *sb.* 2. b. (Later example.)
1922 Bennett *Lilian* II. iii, The entire office, thanks to that lath, Millicent, was disorganized.

4. a. *lath-hammer* (modern example). c. *lath-cutting*.
1827 *Western Monthly Rev.* I. 80 A *lath-cutting machine is also in operation which cuts them with great rapidity. 1846 *Rep. U.S. Comm. Patents* (1847) 91 One patent has been granted for improvements in lath-cutting machines. 1901 J. Black *Carp. & Build.*, *Home Handicrafts* 35 The laths are nailed to each stud, or joist...For this purpose the best tool to employ is the professional *lath-hammer.

Lathen (la·þ'n), *v.* [f. Lath *sb.* + -en[5].] *trans.* To furnish with laths.
1818 Fearon *Sk. Amer.* 74 The house is filled in with brick, furrowed off, lathened and plaistered, so as to be as tight and comfortable as a brick house.

Lathering, *vbl. sb.* (Earlier examples in the sense of 'beating'.)
1835 J. P. Kennedy *Horse-Shoe Robinson* I. ii. 25 He shut that up..by giving Huger a most tremenjious lathering. 1843 Carlton *New Purchase* xix. 169 Vain all pelting with clods and stones!—all latherings with long bean poles.

Lathi, common var. of Lathee.

Lathing, *vbl. sb.*[1] 3. **lathing hammer**, **hatchet** (earlier and later examples).
1638 *Maryland Archives* IV. 30, 1. hatchett and lathing hammer. 1730 *Maryland Hist. Mag.* XIX. 185, 6 Lathing Hammers. 1812 *Niles' Weekly Reg.* II. 376/2 Lathing hatchets would be a good substitute for tomahawks, if they cannot be had.

Latin. A. *adj.* Add: 4. b. *Latin-American* (adj.), of or belonging to those countries in Central and South America in which Spanish or Portuguese is the dominant language (and which are often referred to collectively as *Latin America*); also (sb.), an inhabitant of one of these countries.
1903 *Westm. Gaz.* 22 June 11/1 Mexico..the richest district in the richest of the Latin-American countries. 1906 *Ibid.* 17 Apr. 9/1 Colombia..is taking her place with those Latin-American countries [etc.]. 1911 *Q. Rev.* Oct. 456 Serious competition for British merchants doing trade with the Latin-American States. 1912 *Chambers's Jrnl.* June 358/2 The amount of British capital invested in the countries of Latin-America is very great. *Ibid.* Nov. 720/2 An Englishman..soon wishes himself well rid of the cunning, money-grabbing Latin-American.

B. *sb.* 5. **Latin school**, a school in which Latin is taught; a grammar-school. *U.S.*
Cf. G. *Lateinschule*, Da. *Latinskole*, Du. *Latijnsche school*.
1680 *Conn. Probate Rec.* I. 355, I give to the lattin schoole in Hartford £50. 1685 *New Plymouth Laws* 300 That every County Town shall have and maintain a Latine School. 1781 S. Peters *Hist. Conn.* (1829) 148 Elms..surround the centre square, wherein are..the jail, and Latin school. 1849 B. H. Hall *College Words* (1856) 124 [A young man from the country] shall be examined and 'conditioned' in

everything, and yet he shall come out far ahead of his city Latin-school class-mate.

Hence *Latin schoolhouse, schoolmaster.*

1687 *Mass. Prov. Acts* VII. 640 To meet on the Sabbath daye to exercise our duties in the Lattin Schoolhouse. 1701 *Boston Town Rec.* VIII. 8 The building a house for the Lattin Schoolmaster. 1819 *Boston Selectmen's Min.* 13 Oct., The Committee for the Latin schoolhouse.

Latinesque (lætineˈsk), *a.* [f. Latin *a.* and *sb.* + -esque.] Resembling Latin; having a Latin character.

1887 Stedman *Victorian Poets* (ed. 13) 448 Its atmosphere, landscape, and notes of sympathy therewith are so un-English that one must possess the author's latinesque training to feel them adequately. 1903 *Westm. Gaz.* 8 Apr. 2/3 A new language, or a Latinesque language.

Latining, *vbl. sb.* (Modern example.)

1893 Furnivall in *Capgrave's St. Katherine* (E.E.T.S.) p. xxiv *note*, I don't think *Prata* above can be a latining of *Akker*, acre, field.

Latinish, *a.* (Modern example.)

1920 H. G. Wells *Outl. Hist.* 340/2 Neustria, the nucleus of France, speaking a Latinish speech.

Latinism. Add: The influence or authority of the Latin Church. (See Latin *a.* 3.)

1920 *Contemp. Rev.* Oct. 495 The Spanish Court ladies were sheltered..under the vaulted roof of Latinism.

Latinity. Add: **3.** Latin character.

1915 Mrs. H. Fraser *More Ital. Yesterdays* x. 191 But true to their Latinity, they gave their victim no chance of feeling it [*sc.* their mistrust].

Latitudinous, *a.* Add: **2.** = Latitudinal *a.*

1906 *Westm. Gaz.* 5 July 4/2 The race is not straight up to the limit of the earth's atmosphere and back again, but latitudinous.

Lattee, variant of Lathee.

1864 Trevelyan *Compet. Wallah* (1866) 144 Placing a lattee, which is the name for the quarter-staff carried by all Indian peasants, under the defaulter's knee.

Laˈtter-wit. *U.S.* [f. Latter *a.*] Wit which a person thinks of employing after the opportunity for doing so has passed.

1928 *Observer* 15 Apr. 11/2 Speakers may and do take the greatest liberties in 'editing' their own speeches for publication. All who have suffered from latter-wit will realise how great is the temptation thus thrust into the path of mortals.

Lattice, *sb.* Add: **2. c.** *Her.* A charge representing lattice-work.

1828 W. Berry *Encycl. Her.* Gloss., *Lattice*, or *Lettice*, ..is formed of perpendicular and horizontal bars,..and the lattice may be either interlaced, or not. 1889 Elvin *Dict. Her.*, *Lattice, Tirlace*, or *Treilée*, consists of bars crossing one another at right angles, which do not interlace, but are nailed together at the crossings.

d. A part of a spinning machine.

1884 McLaren *Spinning* (ed. 2) 213 The wool is taken from it by a roller which combs it off, and passes it on to an endless lattice, marked 'upper lattice'.

4. *lattice-box, -fence, -ornament.*

1865 'Mark Twain' *Jumping Frog* (1867) 16 Smiley kept the beast in a little *lattice box. 1861 *Trans. Ill. Agric. Soc.* IV. 259 An octagon, for exhibition of fancy articles,.. with a good *lattice fence to keep people from the exhibition tables. 1924 Collingwood *Roman Brit.* 75 Coarse ware with incised *lattice-ornament.

Latvian (læˈtviăn), *a.* and *sb.* [f. *Latvia* (Lett. and Lith. *Latvija*), the Baltic state lying between Lithuania and Esthonia.] **a.** *adj.* Of or pertaining to Latvia or its people; inhabiting Latvia. **b.** *sb.* The language of Latvia; Lettish.

1920 *Contemp. Rev.* Aug. 283 Troops under German command on Latvian territory. 1923 *Daily Mail* 3 Mar. 10 According to the Latvian Telegraph Agency. 1924 J. M. Murry *Voy.* ii. 28 All these new languages. Lithuanian, Latvian, Esthonian, Transcaucasian. 1926 *Spectator* 31 July 176/1 Latvian is certainly not so difficult to learn as Chinese.

Laudanosine (lǭdæˈnǫsin, -əin). *Chem.* [f. Laudan-um + -os(e[2] + -ine[5].] A crystalline alkaloid occurring in opium.

1872 *Pharmaceut. Jrnl.* Ser. iii. II. 549 Laudanosine.. dissolves sparingly in cold, but easily in hot water. 1910 *Practitioner* June 879 This product is made by the oxidation of laudanosine.

Laughy, *a.* (Recent examples.)

1906 B'ness von Hutten *What became of Pam* ii. ix, I suppose you felt teary, but now you must feel laughy. 1913 Mrs. Stratton-Porter *Laddie* vii. (1917) 123 Then father, all laughy and criey, said 'Thank God!'

Launch, *sb.*[1] **2.** (Later example.)

1897 W. Clark Russell *Last Entry* 241 The schooner.. swept in long floating launches down upon the boat.

4. a. Also *transf.* (see quot.).

1857 *Trans. Mich. Agric. Soc.* VIII. 193, I have seen the commencement of railways, and witnessed the 'launch' of the first locomotive.

Launch, *sb.*[2] **2. b.** launch-engine (see quot. 1875).

1875 Knight *Dict. Mech.* s.v., Launch-engines generally consist of a boiler with engines attached thereto, and are used for propelling the launches of large ocean steamers in shallow harbors, etc. 1889 Hasluck *Model Engin. Handybk.* (1900) 69 A double cylinder launch-engine fitted with reversing motion. 1909 *Westm. Gaz.* 23 Mar. 4/3 A very fine launch-engine, fitted with..reversing gear.

Launch, *v.* **5.** Delete † *Obs.* and add mod. example.

1906 *Westm. Gaz.* 26 Nov. 6/2 The payment was refused on the ground that the Deal lifeboat launched to the same wreck.

b. Of an airship or aeroplane: To be launched into the air; to take off.

1899 H. G. Wells *When Sleeper Wakes* xxiv. 327 The aëropile on Blackheath was running down its guides to launch. It lifted clean and rose.

Launder, *v.* Add:

3. *intr.* Of a fabric: To admit of being laundered; to bear laundering without damage to its texture, colour, etc. Used with adverbs.

1909 *Daily Chron.* 22 July 7/5 A single initial..done in satin stitch..is showy, quickly worked and launders well. 1923 *Daily Mail* 19 Feb. 1 Advt., This hard wearing fabric which launders perfectly, can be obtained.

Launˈdering, *vbl. sb.* [f. Launder *v.*] The process of washing and doing up linen, etc.

1894 *To-day* 17 Mar. 182/2 French cambrics..are not to be starched in the laundering, but left soft. 1899 Morrow *Bohemian Paris* 299 Collars—clean ones, too, exceptional in Bohemia, laundering being expensive. 1902 *Daily Chron.* 26 Feb. 7/2 Laundering of embroidery on washable materials is much simpler than when silk is used.

Laundress, *v.* Add: **c.** To serve (a person) as a laundress.

1850 Dickens *Dav. Copp.* xxvi, 'Sir', said Mrs. Crupp,.. 'I have laundressed other young gentlemen besides yourself.'

Laundry. Add:

2. b. Articles (linen, etc.) requiring to be, or that have been, laundered.

1916 W. J. Locke *Wonderful Yr.* iii. 50 The proletariat hung laundry to dry over royal salamanders and proud escutcheons. *Ibid.* v. 67 Women below at the water's edge beat their laundry with lusty arms.

4. *laundry-worker.*

1894 Eliz. Banks *Camp. Curiosity* 196 She did not consider me up to the mark for a *laundry-worker. 1906 *Westm. Gaz.* 21 June 8/1 The attention of laundry-workers is drawn to this.

Laundrying, *vbl. sb.* [f. Laundry *sb.* + -ing[1].] Laundering; laundry-work.

1901 D. Sladen *In Sicily* I. 152 The ditch in which they did their laundrying. 1904 *Daily Chron.* 26 May 6/2 The assistants have to provide and pay for the laundrying of their aprons.

Laurel, *sb.*[1] Add: **2. e.** As the name of a colour = laurel-green.

1923 *Daily Mail* 8 Oct. 5/1 Advt., Navy, Nigger,..Amethyst, Laurel, Wine.

3. Versailles, Wood Laurel (see quots.). See also *Mountain laurel.

1882 *Garden* 25 Feb. 134/3 The *Versailles Laurel (*latifolia*) is a large, robust, and bold foliaged form. 1873 Hemsley *Hardy Trees* etc. 394 *Daphne Laureola*, *Wood Laurel.

5. *laurel-brake, -leaf* (attrib.), *-leaved* (modern example), *-thicket.*

1853 J. P. Kennedy *Blackwater Chron.* vi. 73 A man could walk about for a week,..particularly if he got into a big *laurel-brake. 1857 D. H. Strother *Virginia Illustr.* i. 13 The settlers..speak of it..as an ill-omened region, filled with bears, panthers, impassable laurel-brakes, and dangerous precipices. 1927 Peake & Fleure *Hunters & Artists* 49 The rude Proto-Solutrean examples of the '*laurel-leaf' blades. 1874 Garrod & Baxter *Mat. Med.* 222 The bark of Canella alba, or *Laurel-leaved Canella; growing in the West Indies. 1751 C. Gist *Jrnls.* 60 We travelled thro Rocks and Mountains full of *Laurel Thickets. 1834 *Southern Lit. Messenger* I. 97 The tangled laurel thickets affording them secure refuge from foes.

6. laurel magnolia *U.S.*, the sweet magnolia or sweet bay (*Magnolia Virginiana*); laurel oak *U.S.*, a North American species of oak.

1817 S. R. Brown *Western Gaz.* 145 The *laurel magnolia is the beauty of the forest. 1831 Peck *Guide Emigrants* ii. 52 From the Walnut Hills to Baton Rouge..you begin to discover the ever verdant laurel magnolia, with its beautiful foliage, of the thickness and feeling of leather. 1810 Michaux *Arbres* I. 23 **Laurel oak*,..dénomination secondaire dans les Etats à l'ouest des monts Alléghanys. 1832 D. J. Browne *Sylva Amer.* 271 East of the Alleghanies this species..is called Jack Oak, Black Oak, and sometimes from the form of the leaves, Laurel Oak. 1868 *Rep. U.S. Commissioner Agric.* (1869) 200 The Willow oak (*Quercus phellos*) and the Laurel oak (*Quercus imbricaria*) are two desirable lawn trees. 1882 *Econ. Geol. Illinois* ii. 2 We find pin oak..and sometimes laurel oak associated with the post oak and black jack.

Lava. **4.** Add: *lava-bed* (also *fig.*), *-field* (also *fig.*).

1891 *Century Mag.* Mar. 645 The general direction [of march] was towards the *lava beds of northern California. 1905 *Westm. Gaz.* 12 Aug. 13/1 She lived over a 'lava-bed of raw primeval passions'. 1899 *Geogr. Jrnl.* May 50 The most extensive *lava-field in the island. 1906 *Daily Chron.* 21 May 7/3 The smoking lava fields of discussion. 1909 *Ibid.* 15 Jan. 3/3 The aim of the expedition..was to explore the great lava field lying between the United States border and Adair Bay.

Lavender. **B.** *adj.* Add: **b.** (See quot.)

1897 E. J. Wall *Dict. Photogr.* (ed. 7) 383 *Lavender Rays*, the faintly luminous rays at the extreme end of the visible spectrum are sometimes so called.

Laˈvender, *sb.*[3] [Suggested by Lavender *sb.*[1]] = Laundry I.

1849 Willis *Rural Lett.* xii. 112 And the breachy ox has run over the bleach and lavender of a seven days' wear and washing.

Laver, *sb.*[2] **1. c.** Add: Also, a pool or puddle.

1841 Catlin *N. Amer. Indians* II. 77 Stagnant pools,..in which the buffaloes have been lying...We frequently came to these dirty lavers.

Law, *sb.*[1] Add: **3. a.** (Earlier examples of *law and order.*)

1796 *Deb. Congress* (1849) 1689 A military diploma, expressive of his patriotism and attachment to law and order. 1831 Peck *Guide Emigrants* ii. 71 They had better..compel it [vice] to act under the trammels of law and order.

8. b. (Add quots.)

1875 Jowett *Plato* (ed. 2) III. 63 Young men will take the law into their own hands. 1877 Miss Yonge *Cameos* Ser. iii. vii. 63 Cade took the law into his own hands.

17. c. (*e*) *Meteorology. Buys-Ballot's law* (see quot. 1875).

Enunciated in 1857 by the Dutch meteorologist of that name.

1875 *Encycl. Brit.* III. 29/1 Buys-Ballot's 'Law of the Winds'..may be thus expressed:—The wind neither blows round the space of lowest pressure in circles returning on themselves, nor does it blow directly towards that space; but it takes a direction intermediate, approaching, however, more nearly to the direction and course of circular curves than of radii to a centre. 1902 *Ibid.* XXX. 718 Buys Ballot's law was in the nature of a rule for prediction, and was modified by Buchan. 1928 Brunt *Meteorol.* i. 8 It will be found that in general the wind tends to blow around the isobars, or lines of equal pressure, in the direction laid down by Buys-Ballot's law.

21. a. *law-business, -department, -doings, -ledger, -school, -student, -studies.*

1865 Mrs. Stowe *House & Home P.* 33 But *law-business comes in rather slowly at first. 1849 Chamberlain *Indiana Gazetteer* 45 In the winter of 1838, the institution was chartered as an University, and in 1842, a *law department was established. 1853 J. G. Baldwin *Flush Times Alabama* 47 The writer of these faithful chronicles of *law-doings in the South West. 1844 *Knickerbocker Mag.* XXIII. 194 Opinions on cases which had long been 'settled', and carried to the *law-ledgers. 1837 *Ibid.* X. 379 The morning after my arrival, I called upon..the principal of the *law school. 1893 W. K. Post *Harvard Stories* 128 'You couldn't do that if you were a biographee', reasoned Dane Austin, the law-school man. 1843 *Knickerbocker Mag.* XXII. 497 Some score of *law-students. 1845 Mrs. Kirkland *Western Clearings* 42 George Burnet had just come home after finishing what he called his '*law studies'.

c. *law-honest* (earlier example); also *law-honesty.*

1838 J. F. Cooper *Homeward Bound* xxxiii. 320 Mr. Dodge belonged to a tolerably numerous class, that is quaintly described as being '*law honest', that is to say, he neither committed murder nor petty larceny. 1905 *Daily Chron.* 6 Dec. 7/7 What may be called *law-honesty, the kind of honesty necessary in order to avoid falling into the clutches of the law.

23. law-office (earlier example).

1873 'Mark Twain' & Warner *Gilded Age* xii. 117 In the anteroom of the *law-office where he was writing.

Law-abiding, *a.* (Earlier U.S. examples.)

1839 *Congress. Globe* Dec., App. 14/2 Being a law-loving and law-abiding man, he had voted to preserve the laws. 1855 *Ibid.* 26 Jan. 416/2 The people of Oregon are a law-abiding, honest and gallant people.

Lawful, *a.* **3.** (Modern example.)

1898 Mrs. H. Fraser *Dipl. Wife Japan* xxviii. 270 The Japanese are a profoundly lawful people (if I may use the word in its old sense).

Lawfulness. (Modern example of earlier use.)

1924 B. Williams in *History* Jan. 273 The adventures of ..the N.W. Mounted Police, in bringing half a continent to lawfulness and peace.

Lawn, *sb.*[2] **3.** lawn-cutter, a lawn-mower.

1897 Susan Hale *Lett.* 315 Such a delicious drive..and the lawn-cutters making hay smells.

Lawsy, var. of *laws* Law *int.*

1914 Gertr. Atherton *Perch of Devil* i. 75 'Your room's pretty!'..'mine's pink—but lawsy!'

Laˈwyerish, *a.* [f. Lawyer *sb.*] Befitting a lawyer; like that of a lawyer.

1918 Galsworthy *Five Tales, A Stoic* iii. § 1 His lawyerish mind habitually put two and two together.

Laˈwyerism. [f. Lawyer *sb.*] The influence, or principles, of lawyers.

1915 Oliver *Ordeal by Battle* 221 To fall back on lawyerism was perhaps inevitable in the circumstances; but to think that it was possible to substitute lawyerism for leadership was absurd.

Lay, *sb.*[7] **2.** Delete 'Now *rare*' and add: An oyster- or mussel-bed.

1902 *Westm. Gaz.* 12 June 10/1 The oyster and mussel lays off the foreshore have hitherto been worked on the large scale. 1905 *Country Life* 25 Mar. 400/2 More than 200 fresh oyster 'lays' have now been staked out on the north side of the Witham.

c. A period of lying inactive.

1921 R. D. Paine *Comr. Rolling Ocean* vi. 106 At any rate, they ought to be kept clear of long lays in these tropical ports.

Lay, *a.* **4.** Add: lay-brother (*b*), in Freemasonry, applied to one who is not initiated.

1843 De Quincey *Rosicrucians & Free-Masons* Wks. (1871) XVI. 363 That lay-brothers were admitted for the performance of servile offices is not to be taken as any departure from the general rule.

5. *lay-minded* adj.

1898 S. Evans *Holy Graal* 134 We Englishmen of to-day, a lay-minded folk much misguided of philosophic historians.

Lay, *v.*[1] Add: **7. b.** To place documents containing information on the table (see Table *sb.* 5 b) in order to present the information to the members.

1923 *Westm. Gaz.* 3 Aug., The Premier promised to lay all the correspondence, if M. Poincaré consents. 1924 *Hansard Parl. Deb.* 10 Mar. 1931 His Majesty's Government have been willing to lay the complete records, but objections have been raised [etc.].

9. *fig.* (See quot.)

1927 *Daily Express* 2 June 11/2 'Laying an egg' in Air Force slang means dropping a bomb.

21. f. To apply (the tongue) *to* some kind of utterance.

1893 *Cornhill Mag.* Nov. 516 His voice, though he so often laid it to vehement words, was distinctly pleasant.

26. f. To put forward (a horse) as a subject of betting.

1877 *Porcupine* 10 Mar. XVIII. 790/1 Whether it is as immoral to 'bear the market' as to 'lay the favourite';.. all these are irrelevant issues. 1887 W. B. Gilpin *Set Hunting Stories* vi. 68 They refused to lay him except at odds on. *Ibid.* x. 97 His..plans..'to lay the horse all he could without exciting too much suspicion'. 1901 *Daily Chron.* 24 July 3/2 For the Derby or other important races Davis would lay a horse to the extent of £100,000 in one bet.

43. *To lay low* (see Lie *v.* 18 c).

a 1861 T. Winthrop *John Brent* viii. 86 They may..let their chances slide at cards, but my notion is they're layin' low for bigger hauls. 1907 Mrs. Harris *Tents of Wickedness* iv. iii. 359 He..laid low for the first passer-by, and slugged him.

49. Lay away. c. To place (hides) in vats to undergo the final stage in the process of tanning. Also *intr.* of the hides.

1897 C. T. Davis *Manuf. Leather* (ed. 2) 181 The stock is laid away by being spread out smoothly and upon the bottom of the tanvat, and between each layer there is sprinkled a slight thickness of ground bark. *Ibid.* 383 After the hides have 'laid-away' for a sufficient length of time to extract the tannin partially out of the 'liquor'. 1901 Addyman tr. *Villon's Leather Industry* 139 Time required for Laying Away.—The hides are removed from the pit and put back three times so that the tan may be renewed.

50. Lay by. f. To leave (a field or crop) to grow without further husbandry; to finish off. *U.S.*

1784 J. Smyth *Tour U.S.* II. 127, I was also accustomed to sow a quantity of faulty wheat..in my tobacco grounds, when I gave them the last ploughing, or *laid them by.* 1831 Peck *Guide Emigrants* ii. 154 To use the phrase of the country [Illinois], the corn is then [after suckering, in early July] 'laid by', and the leisure and lazy season of the farmer commences. 1835 J. H. Ingraham *South-West* II. 285 The ploughing generally ceases and the crop is 'laid by' about the last of July. 1867 *Rep. Iowa Agric. Soc.* (1868) 158 The ground should be thoroughly rolled;..then lay by with barshear plow.

51. Lay down. q. Also, to cover (a surface) *with* something.

1893 Doyle *Mem. S. Holmes* (1894) 225 The corridor..was laid down with a kind of creamy linoleum.

s. *intr.* To break down or cease to act; to fail; to retire or withdraw. *U.S.*

1911 H. S. Harrison *Queed* vii. 87 Your body's got to carry your mind around, and if it lays down on you [etc.]. 1921 R. D. Paine *Comr. Rolling Ocean* x. 193 'Any water leaking in?' 'A trickle under the floor, but the bilge pump will take care of it unless she lays down on me.' *Ibid.* xvii. 293 You stand by me and I won't lay down on you. 1927 *Cleveland Press* 4 Feb., Offered him a bribe to 'lay down' on the prosecution of George J. McKay, alleged arch-swindler.

53. Lay in. m. Also, to withdraw from use, render inactive.

1894 *Standard* 25 Apr. 6/5 The effect of the Bill would be, they believed, to lay in one-fifth of all that capital.

54. Lay off. a. (Modern U.S. example.)

1919 H. L. Wilson *Ma Pettengill* ii. 46 She took me up to her little bedroom to lay my things off and then down to the parlour.

f. (Earlier example of *intr.* use.)

1863 Whitman *Specimen Days* (1892) 41 Some of the men are..brushing boots; some laying off, reading, writing.

g. (See quot.)

1901 J. Black *Carp. & Build. Home Handicrafts* 43 What painters term 'laying off', that is to say, going over the work with the brush uncharged with paint and with strokes all in one direction.

h. To dispose of, 'work off'.

1926 J. Black *You Can't Win* x. 130, I was sent out with about seventy-five dollars in silver coin to lay off for paper or gold.

55. Lay on. k. (Earlier example.)

1845 *Punch* 1 Mar. 100/1 Announcing that the water was going to be laid on when it wasn't.

56. Lay out. b. (Earlier U.S. example.)

1820 *Massachusetts Spy* 22 July (Th.), I want to lay out [this candidate] as cold as a wedge.

57. Lay over. c. Also *to lay it over*, to get the better of, take advantage of (a person).

1911 J. F. Wilson *Land Claimers* xiii. 179 He let on as how anybody..could lay it all over you.

d. To turn over.

1873–4 *Rep. Vermont Board Agric.* II. 188 Unless so rainy as to be impracticable, he lays it all over, thus inverting the cock, and replaces the cap.

60. Lay up. m. To put up, erect.

1844 D. Lee & Frost *Oregon* xxii. 289 We..were so successful as to finish laying up the cabin..at the end of two weeks. *Ibid.* 292 Mr. Smith was getting out logs for a house..., and I helped him lay it up.

Lay-away. [f. *lay away* Lay *v.* *49 c.]

1. *attrib.* (with *pit, vat, yard*) Used in the process of 'laying away' hides in tanning.

1897 C. T. Davis *Manuf. Leather* (ed. 2) 181 The usual size of the lay-away vats for sole leather hides is nine feet long, seven feet wide and eight feet deep. *Ibid.* 383 The hides are..conveyed to the yard proper, or 'lay-away' yard, where the tanning process is completed. 1901 Addyman tr. *Villon's Leather Industry* 137 Tan-pits or lay-away pits are large vats, sometimes round, and made of oak, bound with iron.

2. A lay-away vat.

1897 C. T. Davis *Manuf. Leather* (ed. 2) 181 The bark ought not to be shaved too fine for the lay-aways...If the bark is too fine,..the hides..do not come out of the lay-aways fully tanned.

Lay-back. [f. Lay *v.*] The characteristic backward slant or set of a bulldog's nose from its tip to the 'stop'.

1894 R. B. Lee *Mod. Dogs, Non-Sporting* 233 The bones of the lower jaw in specimens [of the bulldog] which have the desired appearance, known as 'upturn' and 'lay back' are found to have the contour of a segment of a circle. 1905 H. St. J. Cooper *Bull-Dogs* 98 This well-known dog..has a grandly shaped head, with small well-carried ears, large underjaw, turn-up and lay-back. 1909 *Ladies' Field* 28 Aug. 511/1 Bulldogs:..a brindle, good layback and under-jaw.

Lay-brotherhood. [f. *lay brother* Lay *a.* 4.] An association of lay brothers.

1909 *Hastings' Encycl. Relig. & Ethics* II. 68/2 Each revival of the extreme emphasis has also led to 'lay-brotherhoods'.

Lay-by. **A.** *sb.* Add: **1. b.** A railway siding.

1906 *Westm. Gaz.* 28 Sept. 7/1 A heavy goods train had left the up-line..and run into a short lay-by.

Layer, *sb.* **1. e.** (Additional examples of layer-out.)

(*a*) 1635 *Essex Inst. Hist. Coll.* IV. 90/1 Overseers and layers out of lots of ground for this presinct of Salem. 1678 *Southampton* (N.Y.) *Rec.* II. 72 John Jessup being one of the layers out of land for the town.

(*b*) 1895 Hardy *Jude Obscure* iv. ii. 248 In the afternoon, when everything was done, and the layers-out had finished their beer, and gone, he sat down in the silent place. 1928 *Observer* 10 June 7/4 Poetry, it is generally known, is dead. ..Our critics are a generation of layers-out.

4. g. In map-making, a layer of colour to indicate relative height. Also *attrib.*

1908 *Westm. Gaz.* 13 Aug. 10/2 Mr. Fisher Unwin has just issued some Ordnance Survey maps...What is known as the 'layer' system has been employed. 1922 *Encycl. Brit.* XXXI. 842/1 The hypsometric, or 'layer' tints, which show the successive altitudes of the terrain. 1924 *Catal. Maps Ordnance Surv.* 4 Relief is shown by means of contours and layers. *Ibid.* 5 Relief is indicated by..layer colouring in shades of brown and green.

5. layer-cake, -pudding, a cake or pudding made in layers. Also *fig.*

1902 *Daily Chron.* 3 May 8/4 Layer cakes can be made in great varieties according to the filling used. 1904 *Buffalo Commercial* 2 June 6 The large unwieldy layer cakes that used to be in favor are no longer seen. 1905 *N. Y. Even. Post* 16 Dec., In the mixing of this literary layer cake most of the humor rose to the top. 1909 *Daily Sketch* 14 Oct. 14/3 Layer pudding.

Layer, *v.* Add: **1.** (Earlier example.)

1799 *Massachusetts Spy* 30 Oct. 4/1 Propagation by layering...Layering being an operation by which a great majority of trees and shrubs may be propagated.

3. To place or insert as a layer.

1906 *Times Lit. Suppl.* 12 Jan. 14/1 Mr. Lee has succeeded in neatly layering fallacies of argument between errors of fact.

Layered, *a.* Add: In map-making (see *Layer *sb.* 4 g).

1924 *Catal. Maps Ordnance Surv.* 6 In the Layered Map the different altitudes are indicated by flat tints of various shades.

Laying, *vbl. sb.* **3.** laying-out mark *Naut.* (see quot.).

1883 *Man. Seamanship Boys* 65 The lower and topsail yards are generally marked with a white band of paint round them,..called laying-out marks.

Layˈmanship. [f. Layman[1].] The condition of being a layman.

1908 *Athenæum* 9 May 566/2 His 'laymanship' grated on their clericalism.

Lay-off. [Lay *v.*[1] 54.] A period during which a workman is temporarily dismissed or allowed to leave his work; that part or season of the year during which activity in a particular business or game is partly or completely suspended; an off-season.

1904 *Minneapolis Times* 8 June 8 The men who have been on for a year get a vacation of ten days. Those who have been working less than a year have to get along with only a five-day layoff. 1909 R. A. Wason *Happy Hawkins* 148 Now take a lay-off if you want to,..then come back here. 1919 T. K. Holmes *Man fr. Tall Timber* vi. 58 At the lay-off,..he had given each man enough money on account to make their vacation..a very wet spell indeed. 1923 *Daily Mail* 10 Sept. 8/5 As a consequence of the 'lay-off' during the summer months it often happens that the muscles of the young player are not sufficiently supple for him to face the rigours of the game.

Lay-out. Add: **2. b.** A scheme, plan, or arrangement; a course of action. *U.S.*

1901 S. E. White *Westerners* xxxi. 292 'I'm sorry that I have this to do, Billy', said Lafond. 'I don't want to. It's none of my lay-out.' 1901 — *Claim Jumpers* i. 17 We won't take any chances on this layout, and that I can tell you. 1904 W. H. Smith *Promoters* ii. 53 There isn't a single move in this whole lay-out that we can't justify by history. 1928 *Saturday Even. Post* 4 Feb. 81/3 Here's the layout. The bonds bear 6 per cent.

c. A number of persons associated in some way; a set, party, 'gang' (of persons). (Often in a depreciatory sense.) *U.S.*

1869 *Overland Monthly* III. 128 Several persons in our 'lay-out' (*i.e.*, our company) in New Mexico 'swapped' good American horses for mustangs. 1878 J. H. Beadle *Western Wilds* xxxiii. 538 It would be astonishin' for that lootenint and his layout to git into the fort without a skrimmage. 1884 'C. E. Craddock' *In Tenn. Mts.* iii. 143 All them Peels, the whole lay-out, war gone down to the Settlement. 1903 A. Adams *Log Cowboy* vii. 47 Surround this layout, lads, and let's examine them more closely. 1904 Harben *Georgians* 203 I'm a-goin' to close in on that Clegg lay-out to-night, an' locate the'r still.

Lay-over. [Lay *v.* 57.]

1. An additional cloth laid above a table-cloth.

1777 *Monthly Rev.* LV. 108 Two servants appeared with a small table.., and laid a cloth and a lay-over upon it, in our English fashion, of the finest damask.

2. A stop or stay in a place. *U.S.*

1873 J. H. Beadle *Undevel. West* xxxv. 756 Two invalids and myself..applied for a 'lay over', unable to go further. 1903 A. Adams *Log Cowboy* viii. 53 Their cattle having grown restless during their enforced lay-over.

3. A transplanted oyster.

1891 *Scribner's Mag.* X. 472 Young oysters so treated are termed 'lay-overs'.

Layˈ-shaft. [prob. f. Lay *v.* 43.] A shaft driven by gearing from the main shaft of an engine, *esp.* the secondary shaft or counter-shaft in the gear-box of a motor-car.

1908 *Westm. Gaz.* 7 May 4/2 The whole of the valve mechanism being contained in a neat, hinged lay-shaft on top of the cylinder heads. 1911 Hayter *Motor-Car Mech. for Beginners* (ed. 4) 45 For the next speed the gear wheel B, is slid into mesh with the wheel marked C on the third or lay shaft, E. 1928 E. T. Brown *New Ford Car* 85 The layshaft is mounted on roller bearings.

Lay-up. [Lay *v.* 60 g.] A period during which a person or thing is (temporarily) out of employment or use, as a ship in winter.

1927 *Daily Mail* 7 Apr. 3/6 During the winter lay-up of these vessels their passenger accommodation has been thoroughly overhauled.

Laywoman. (See after Layman[1].) Add: **2.** A non-professional woman.

1922 *Daily Mail* 11 Nov. 8 The success of this laywoman is a..cheerful omen of good luck for those women who..will hold the position of practising members of the English Bar.

Laze-off. [f. Laze *v.*] A rest from work.

1924 Galsworthy *White Monkey* i. xi, There rose in Bicket something truly national,..resenting work, enjoying a spurt, and a laze-off.

Lazy, *a.* **4.** Add: lazy-daisy, a variety of embroidery stitch; lazy sheet *Naut.*, 'a piece of rope spliced in the clew-thimble' designed to serve in emergencies as a sheet.

1923 *Daily Mail* 10 Mar. 14 The way the '*lazy-daisy' stitch is worked is shown at the side of the sketch. 1927 *Ladies' Home Jrnl.* Dec. 83/2 Solid flowers are made of petals set close together, each a complete lazy-daisy stitch. 1883 *Man. Seamanship Boys* 62 *Q.* What is the use of a *lazy-sheet? *A.* To secure the clew of the sail while you hook or unhook the double sheet.

Laˈzzaronism. [f. Lazzarone.] The condition of being a lazzarone.

1873 Leland *Egypt. Sketch-Bk.* 261 From what depth of slavery, donkey-driving, Neapolitan lazzaronism, Ghettos, or Maltese scum he himself ascended, is not mentioned.

Leach, *sb.*[2] **5.** Add: *leach-tub.*

1845 S. Judd *Margaret* i. iii. 12 Here were a draw shave.., frows, sap buckets, a leach tub.

Leach, *v.*[2] **3. c.** Add: Also *trans.*

1840 Buel *Farmer's Comp.* 74 The wind and the sun dissipate its virtues, and rains leach it and waste its fertilizing powers.

Leached, *ppl. a.* (Earlier example.)

1840 Buel *Farmer's Comp.* 74 *Leached ashes* are in many cases beneficial, particularly within the influence of the marine atmosphere.

Lead, *sb.*[1] **2.** Add: *Yellow lead* (see quot.).

1839 Ure *Dict. Arts* 747 Lead ores...12. Yellow lead. Molybdate of lead.

4. (*cold*) *lead*, bullets.

1809 Fessenden *Pills Poetical* 32 Thus our sporting democrats,..When they can't reason with a Fed, In logick substitute cold lead. 1846 *Knickerbocker Mag.* XXVII. 560 Instead of gold and silver, you took it in cold lead! 1918 C. Sandburg *Cornhuskers* 50 Three riders emptied lead into him.

6. b. Phr. *To swing the lead*: (see quots.). *slang.*

1918 *Twenty-Seconds' Echo* [Army Mag.] 1 June, The Swingers of the Lead. 1918 Farrow *Dict. Milit. Terms*, *Swinging the Lead*, a slang expression among soldiers being the equivalent of telling the tale. 1919 *War Slang* in *Athenæum* 25 July 664/1 'To swing the lead', to malinger, go sick, with the object of escaping an irksome duty. 1927 *Daily Express* 2 Mar. 3/4 He said he had some silly ideas and had been 'swinging the lead' for the purpose of getting a permanent pension.

12. lead-flat (see quot. 1875); lead-glass, a kind of glass which contains lead; lead-glazed, of pottery, etc., covered with a glaze containing lead; lead-glazier, one who glazes (pottery) with lead; lead-line, (*d*) the narrow strip of lead between two pieces of stained glass, a came; also *v.*, to put in the lead-lines in stained glass work; lead-plant *U.S.* (example); lead-poisoning (earlier example); lead region, a region in which lead ores occur.

1875 Knight *Dict. Mech.*, **Lead-flat*, a level roof consisting of sheet-lead laid on boarding and joists. 1907 W. De Morgan *Alice-for-Short* xxv. 259 Charles remembers the lead-flat sunk in the roof. 1930 W. A. Thorpe in *Connoisseur* Oct. 226/2 English *lead-glass was peculiarly apt for cut decoration. 1901 *Daily News* 3 Dec. 3/7 He states that there is no difference now in price between the *lead glazed and leadless glazed ware. 1907 *Installation News* Sept. 12/1 All interiors are of the best English porcelain, lead glazed and fitted with brass connection bars. 1908 *Westm. Gaz.* 23 Nov. 9/3 The deceased came under his notice twelve years ago, when he was a *lead-glazier. 1907 W. De Morgan *Alice-for-Short* xxvii. 283 I'll lend you a hand over the *lead-lines. *Ibid.* xii. 136 It was Pope's man, Buttivant, who lead-lines up all the windows. 1846 in Emory *Military Recons.* 399 The *lead plant, or tea plant..is in some places so abundant as to displace almost every other herb. 1841–2 T. D. Mitchell (*title*) Practical notes on *lead poisoning. 1847 C. Lanman *Summer in Wilderness* vi. 41 The *lead region of the Mississippi occupies not far from one hundred square miles.

Lead, *sb.*[2] **6. a.** Add: Also *fig.*

1869 S. Bowles *Our New West* vii. 136 A quaint old miner of the valley, who, 'prospecting' for society that day, had struck a 'lead' in us.

7. *Theatr.* (Earlier example.)

1865 *Punch* 7 Jan. 5/1 As a general rule an actor who plays the 'lead' ought to aim at becoming a general manager.

11. lead-bars (earlier example); lead-net = Leader 15 b; lead-off (*b*), the initial part of an electric or other conductor; lead-rope, a rope used as a lead for a horse.

1840 *Congress. Globe* 5 Mar. App. 227 The horse broke loose from the coach, taking with him a part of what are now called '*Lead bars'. 1910 *Chambers's Jrnl.* Mar. 192/2 The *lead-net is about fifteen hundred feet long. The salmon strike this. 1897 *Phil. Trans.* B. CLXXXVIII. 7 The development of an opposite after-effect at and near the longitudinal *lead-off. 1846 Sage *Scenes Rocky Mts.* (1859) 46 Holding in one hand the *lead-rope of his horse.

b. Used in the sense of 'leading'.

1869 *Overland Monthly* III. 127 With the Texan driver all oxen are 'steers', and he has his 'wheel-steers', his 'swing-steers', and his 'lead-steers'. 1903 A. Adams *Log Cowboy* ii. 16 Closely followed by several lead cattle, I struck straight for the American shore. 1905 — *Outlet* 284 The lead herd had been sighted in trail formation. 1910 W. M. Raine *B. O'Connor* 189 It was as the man in charge circled round to head the lead cows in that a faint voice carried to him. 1929 *Randolph Enterprise* (W. Va.) 28 Mar. 1/2 Dick Collette played the lead violin and Bryan Gainer, second.

Lead, *v.*[1] Add: **2. f.** To aim in advance of.

1892 Greener *Breech-Loader* 267 Theoretically it is correct to lead a quartering pigeon from five to seven feet.

19. a. (Earlier example.) **b.** Also with *to*.

1847 *Punch* 27 Mar. 126/2 To lead off a list of Expiring Acts with one that is to live till the National Debt is paid off..is a delusion. 1911 *Chambers's Jrnl.* July 463/2 From these [wagons] rubber tubes protected by encircling wire led off to each of the streets.

21. b. Of cattle: To set *out* when driven.

1903 A. Adams *Log Cowboy* xx. 129 The cattle led out as if walking on a wager.

Lead, *v.*[2] Add: **3.** (Later example.)

1842 Lever *J. Hinton* xxv. (1844) 172, I seated myself in the scale..and my saddle being leaded to the required weight, the operation took not a minute.

10. To affect with lead-poisoning.

1878 J. H. Beadle *Western Wilds* xxxv. 581 Great care must be taken by the workmen not to get 'leaded'; that is, not to inhale the fumes from the melted lead, which are very poisonous.

Leaded, *ppl. a.* Add: **d.** Affected by lead-poisoning.

1906 *Daily Chron.* 28 June 6/4 The children of 'leaded' mothers usually die, or if they live they inherit the effects of the poison.

Leader[1]. Add: **8. c.** (Earlier example = Leading article 2 a.)

1851 C. Cist *Cincinnati* 319 These articles [sugar, molasses, coffee, etc.] are the leaders, as they are called, in commercial transactions, with the west.

20. leader-pipe = sense 18.

1868 *Putnam's Mag.* Jan. I. 2 Then, without stay or stopping, My first and last eaves-dropping, By leader-pipe I sped.

Leadered, *pa. pple.* [f. Leader[1] 12.] Treated in a leading article; made the subject of a leader.

1884 *Pall Mall Gaz.* 29 Nov. 3/2 If it [an interview] had been a speech it would have been 'leadered' all round. 1897 *Westm. Gaz.* 25 Sept. 5/2 Seeing that the subject is 'leader-ed' in both papers.

Leaderly, *a.* [f. Leader[1] 1.] Having the character of a leader.

1918 H. G. Wells *In Fourth Yr.* ii. 23 Very rarely has it [the United States] failed to set up very leaderly and distinguished men [as Presidents]. 1927 — *Short Hist. World* 72 They distinguished certain families as leaderly and noble.

Lead-in. [Lead *v.*[1]] The wire, or other conductor, connecting a part of an apparatus which is situated outside with a part which is inside, esp. in (wireless) telephony. Also *attrib.*, as *lead-in wire.*

1913 *Work* 14 June 217/3 Lead in, about 40 ft. insulated. 1913 *Wireless World* June 209/2 A special mast has had to be erected...The 'lead-in' wires fall down to Mr. Brunskill's room. 1914 *Ibid.* 15 Aug. 394/3 If querist cannot take the lead-in as shown. 1923 *Daily Mail* 12 Feb. 13 The lead-in wire should not make too acute an angle with the horizontal wire...Make the last few feet of the lead-in of rubber-covered wire. 1925 *Harmsworth's Wireless Encycl.* II. 1279/1 The lower of the three insulated leads-in on the wall is connected to earth.

Leading, *ppl. a.* **3.** Add: *Leading edge* (see quots.).

1877 W. H. White *Man. Nav. Archit.* 579 When the plane is moved obliquely, its leading edge, corresponding to the forward edge of a rudder, may be regarded as continually entering water which was comparatively little disturbed by the previous motion. 1888 *Lockwood's Dict. Mech. Eng. Terms* (1918), *Leading Edge*, that edge of the blade of a screw propeller which cuts the water, as distinguished from the following edge. 1912 *Aeroplane* 12 Dec. 598/1 Looking over the leading edge of the wings from a constant position the ground disappeared regularly.

Leadish, *a.* (Later example.)

1784 *Maryland Jrnl.* 27 July (Th.) There are two great-coats missing, one of which is a leadish-coloured country cloth.

Lead-pipe. [See Lead *sb.*[1] 10.] Used *attrib.* with *cinch* to denote an absolutely sure hold or complete certainty. *U.S. colloq.*

1904 W. H. Smith *Promoters* v. 102 He was one of the lead-pipe-cinch kind,..and what he once buckled to he never let get away from him. 1911 H. Quick *Yellowstone N.* xi. 288 Oh its a cinch, a timelock, leadpipe cinch! 1926 *Punch* 7 July 17/1 The Office of Works does not borrow money even to back what Americans call a lead-pipe cinch.

Leading article. **2. a.** (Later example.)

1877 W. S. Gilbert *Sorcerer* i, Sir, it is our leading article.

Leaf, *sb.* **9.** Add to def.: and *U.S.*

1886 *Harper's Mag.* July 206/2 Lard, 'made from hog round, say lead, gut, leaf, and trimmings', is..in demand. 1904 L. L. Lamborn *Cottonseed Products* 166 Neutral lard is composed of the fat derived from the leaf of the slaughtered animal.

13. b. A blade (of a propeller).

1846 *Rep. U.S. Comm. Patents* (1847) 253, I also claim the giving to the leaves of said propellers a curved form.

16. a. *leaf-blight, -cell, -point, -rib, -roll, -scorch, -substance.*

1849 *Rep. U.S. Comm. Patents* (1850) 440 During the last summer our seedling pears were for the first time badly affected with '*leaf-blight'. 1857–8 *Trans. Ill. Agric. Soc.* III. 492–3 That terrible and mysterious malady, the leaf blight, attacks the young plants in the seed bed, as well as the older stocks in the nursery. 1875 Huxley & Martin *Elem. Biol.* 49 The terminal *leaf-cell soon attaining its full size and not dividing. 1871 Kingsley *At Last* x, When the curving *leaf-points toss in the breeze. 1895 Kipling *2nd Jungle Bk.* 141 Now the lighting shows each littlest *leaf-rib clear. 1862 *Trans. Ill. Agric. Soc.* (1865) V. 734 The *leaf-rolls found on trees contain eggs. 1931 *Times* 16 Mar. 17/3 Apple *leaf-scorch may also be..caused by a..rainy season dissolving the potash contents of the leaves. 1875 Huxley & Martin *Elem. Biol.* 80 Then come irregularly branched (*stellate*) cells forming the lower half of the *leaf-substance.

b. *leaf-crumpler, -cutter*; *leaf-boring, -cutting*, adjs.

a 1887 Jefferies *Field & Hedgerow* (1889) 115 The coils and turns upon this leaf..are the work of a *leaf-boring larva. 1876 *Rep. Vermont Board Agric.* III. 591 Using the empty cases..of one of the *leaf crumplers. 1875 *Encycl. Brit.* II. 98/1 Corrosive sublimate in powder, sprinkled across their paths, has a deadly effect upon the *leaf-cutters. 1924 J. A. Thomson *Science Old & New* xi. 61 One of the early observers of the leaf-cutter ants. 1875 *Encycl. Brit.* II. 98/1 The *Leaf-cutting Ants (*Œcodoma*) are noted pests of central and tropical America. 1881 *Amer. Naturalist* XV. 100 A New Leaf Cutting Ant. 1924 J. A. Thomson *Science Old & New* v. 30 Leaf-cutting bees.

17. leaf-fat (modern examples); leaf-lard (earlier example); leaf-mosaic, a disease affecting the leaves of tobacco and other plants; leaf-nosed (earlier example); leaf-shedding, a disease attacking pine trees (see quot.); leaf-skin, the membrane enclosing the leaf-fat.

1845 J. J. Hooper *Adv. Simon Suggs* v. 65 They've knocked the *leaf fat outen him tonight, in wads as big as mattock handles. 1904 L. L. Lamborn *Cottonseed Products* 166 In the packing plants the leaf fat is taken from the animal immediately after killing. 1847 *Rep. U.S. Comm. Patents* (1848) 538 The articles thus referred to are put up in these establishments, from the hams..*leaf lard [etc.]. 1902 *Encycl. Brit.* XXVI. 60/2 The juices of tobacco plants affected with the disease known as '*leaf mosaic'. 1870 *Amer. Naturalist* III. 472 A second species..is the *Leaf-nosed Bat (*Macrotus Californicus*) from Fort Yuma. 1891 Schlich *Man. Forestry* II. 302 In many cases a fungus (*Hysterium pinastri*) is present, and may occasion the disease, which is called '*leaf-shedding'. 1816 'A. Singleton' *Lett. fr. South & West* (1824) 75 (Th.) Being born smokers, [the negroes] make pouches of the inner *leafskin of a swine, peeled thin, which is soft, transparent, and tough.

Leaf, *v.* **3. a.** Add: *To leaf through*: To go through (a book) by turning over the leaves.

1929 *Publishers' Weekly* 19 Oct. 1928/2 There are..plenty of people who..like to leaf through a book before buying.

League of Nations. An association of self-governing states, dominions, and colonies created by a covenant forming part I of the Peace Treaty of 1919 'in order to promote international co-operation and to achieve international peace and security'.

1919 *Treaty of Peace* xii. art. 376 Disputes which may arise ..shall be settled as provided by the League of Nations. 1920 *Blackw. Mag.* Feb. 293/2 Leagues of Nations are, we believe, useless.

Leak, *a.* (Later example.)

1777 *Essex Inst. Hist. Coll.* XLII. 319 She is Arrived Leake, with a Ship from England.

Leak, *v.* **1. b.** (Earlier example.)

1834 Seba Smith *Sel. Lett. Major Jack Downing* 58 If it should leak out that I was going.

Leakage. **2.** Add to def.: improper disclosure of information from an office, etc.; unexplained continuous disappearance of something.

1904 A. B. F. Young *Complete Motorist* Index, Leakage of small moneys, during travel, 292–3.

5. *attrib.*, as *leakage conductance, current, path.*

1902 *Encycl. Brit.* XXXIII. 215 Any ordinary telegraph circuit may be made approximately distortionless by adding a certain amount of leakance, or *leakage conductance. 1908 *Installation News* II. 55/2 Providing for the *leakage current a path to earth. 1909 *Ibid.* III. 64/1 The *leakage path to the conduit or earth is now very greatly reduced.

Leakance (lɪ̄ˈkăns). *Electr.* [f. Leak *v.* + -ance.] The passage of electric leakage through an insulator. 1902 [see *Leakage 5].

Lean, *v.*[2] (Later example.)

1711 *Lancaster Rec.* 171 We can get but very little Hay, but shall unavoidably leen our cattell.

Leap, *sb.* Add: **1. d.** Ability or inclination to leap.

a 1861 T. Winthrop *John Brent* xx. 219 Our horses were a part of ourselves. While we could go, they would go. Since the water, they were full of leap again.

Leap, *v.* Add: **6. c.** *Mus.* To pass from one note to another by an interval greater than a degree of the scale. (Cf. Leap *sb.*[1] 7.)

1879 G. A. Macfarren *Counterpoint* iv. 10 After several consecutive 2nds, in melody, it is bad to leap, in the same direction, upward or downward to an accented note. 1889 E. Prout *Harmony* (ed. 10) xiii. § 317 The third of the chord exceptionally leaping, instead of moving as usual by step. *trans.* 1927 C. H. Kitson *Counterpoint for Beginners* 17 A part may not leap any interval greater than an octave.

Leapable (lɪ̄ˈpăb'l), *a.* [f. Leap *v.* + -able.] That can be leaped.

1925 A. S. Alexander *Tramps across Watersheds* 128 Some parts of the precipitous sides approach within leapable distance.

Leap-frog. Add: **3.** *Mil.* (See quot.)

1918 Farrow *Dict. Milit. Terms*, *Leapfrog*, a method of maintaining constant communication with a moving command by using two or more instruments with a single unit, keeping one in operation while another is moving past it to a position in front.

Leap-frog, *v.* Add (*b*). *Mil.* Of detachments or units in an attack: To go in advance of each other by turns as boys do when playing leap-frog.

1925 E. Fraser & Gibbons *Soldier & Sailor Words* s.v., On the first 'wave' capturing its allotted objective,..the second passed through beyond it, or 'leap-frogged' forward, to capture the second objective ahead. 1927 *Daily Tel.* 30 Aug. 8/7 Two pairs of mobile picket groups, moving by long bounds and one pair 'leapfrogging' the other.

Lease (līz), *v.*[4] [f. *leas*, pl. of Lea *sb.*[4]] *trans.* To divide (yarn or thread) into leas.

1884 McLaren *Spinning* 242 The length varies from one to twelve yards, and the forms of making up, leasing, and tying are endless. 1927 T. Woodhouse *Artif. Silk* 67 It is quite possible that all the remaining hanks have already been leased.

Leased, *ppl. a.* (Earlier example.)

1868 *Rep. U.S. Commissioner Agric.* (1869) 130 The land is divided as follows: Tilled land,..leased part of the estate.

Leasehold. **b.** Add: Also *fig.*

1904 *Daily Chron.* 10 Oct. 4/7 The people who want a leasehold marriage. 1908 *Ibid.* 15 June 5/3 They are advocates for leasehold marriage, or, in other words, for free love.

Leaˈsing, *vbl. sb.*[3] [f. Lease *sb.*[4] + -ing[1].] *Attrib.* in leasing reed, in weaving, a reed through which the warp threads pass as they come off the bobbins.

1927 T. Woodhouse *Artif. Silk* 108 The ends of the bobbins are threaded through a leasing reed.

Least, *a.* Add: **1. c.** (Later examples.)

1870 *Amer. Naturalist* III. 234 The Least Fern,..and the Roseate Fern, still breed on our coast. 1893 B. Torrey *Footpath-Way* 9 All our common eastern Massachusetts species were present; the kingbird..and the least flycatcher.

4. (Earlier examples of *to say the least of...*)

1809 *Deb. Congress* 20 Feb. (1853) 422 To say the least of it, the people will perceive..an uncommon coincidence. 1811 *Ibid.* 17 Jan. 603 To say the least of such a measure, is to term it an experiment.

Leather, *sb.* **2.** Add to def.: a stirrup-leather.

1928 Byrne *Destiny Bay* vii. § 2. 314 The shorter your leathers, the less you know about your mount.

d. As the name of a colour.

1923 *Daily Mail* 16 Jan. 1 Advt., Coat frock..Grey, Mole, Leather,..New Brown. 1923 *Ibid.* 31 July 1/3 Advt., Grey, Smoke, Leather and Navy.

5. b. *leather-sealer*; *leather-dressing* (example).

1849 *Rep. U.S. Comm. Patents* (1850) 357, I claim the adjustable scraper..for the purposes and uses of *leather dressing. 1662 *Connect. Rec.* I. 377 The *leather sealers.. shal have allowed unto them for each Dicker of Leather they seale 18d. 1798 I. Allen *Hist. Vermont* 272 Weights and measures, leather sealers &c. are regulated according to law.

d. *leather-aproned, -bottomed.*

1782 Trumbull *M'Fingal* (1785) 92 Each *leather-aproned clown grown wise. 1783 E. Parkman *Diary* 298, 9 black chairs..five *leather bottomed Do. 1892 J. E. Cooke *B. Hallam* 127 A rude oaken table and some leather-bottomed chairs.

6. leather leaf (earlier example); leather medal, a medal made of leather instead of metal, sarcastically suggested as a distinction; Leather Stocking, a North American frontiersman [from a character portrayed by J. F. Cooper]; leather tortoise = *leather-back.*

1870 *Amer. Naturalist* June IV. 217 The *Leather Leaf (*Cassandra calyculata*), and *Andromeda polifolia*, are both worthy of attention. 1837 *Harvardiana* III. 147 (Th.) A *leather medal his reward should be, A leather medal and an LL.D. 1860 *Richmond Enquirer* 20 Apr. 2/5 (Th.) The individual who conceived the leather medal idea [for identifying dogs] deserves a leather medal himself. 1889 *Kansas Times & Star* 5 Dec., A leather medal..awaits the first misguided person this season writing it 'Xmas'. [1823 J. F. Cooper *Pioneers* i. I. 18 His limbs were guarded with long leggings of the same material as the moccasins, which

gartering over the knees of his tarnished buck-skin breeches, had obtained for him, among the settlers, the nick name of *Leather-stocking.] *Ibid.* 11 The Leather-stocking has put his hounds into the hills this clear day. 1831 Mrs. Holley *Texas* v. (1833) 43 The character of Leather Stocking, is not uncommon in Texas...The dress of these hunters is usually of deer-skin. Hence the appropriate name *Leather Stocking.* Their generic name..is *Frontiers-men.* 1848 in D. Drake *Pioneer Life Kentucky* viii. 214 He had nearly all his life been a great hunter—was in fact a large, coarse Leather Stocking. 1909 *Daily Chron.* 1 July 7/3 With most birds, you must make your approach with all the art of a leatherstocking. 1811 *Niles' Weekly Reg.* 19 Oct. I. 119/1 It is a Testudo Cariaria [*sic*] or *Leather Tortoise.

Leathered, *ppl. a.* Add: **b.** Made into, or like, leather.

1797 in Goode etc. *Fisheries of U.S.* v. (1887) II. 435 By walking it [seal-skin] becomes leathered and soft to the foot. 1869 S. Bowles *Our New West* 444 If you bring a liver not entirely leathered and lungs not over half consumed.

Leathern, *a.* **2.** *Comb.* (Later example.)

1875 Holland *Sevenoaks* xii. 158 Blue-jays were screaming among leathern-leaved oaks.

Leathery, *a.* Add: **b.** leathery turtle = *leather back* Leather *sb.* 6.

1875 *Encycl. Brit.* III. 112/1 The 'leathery turtle', which is herbivorous, and yields abundance of oil. 1901 [see Luth].

Leavable (lɪ̄ˈvăb'l), *a.* [f. Leave *v.*[1] + -able.] Admitting of being left.

1923 H. G. Wells *Men Like Gods* i. i. § 2. 10 The affairs of the *Liberal* were just then in a particularly leavable state.

Leave, *sb.*[1] **2. b.** (Later example.)

1916 Bennett *Lion's Share* v. 40 'Mother!' cried Audrey. 'Have you taken leave of your senses?'

Leave, *sb.*[2] *Billiards.* [Leave *v.*[1] 3.] The position in which the balls are left for the next player or stroke.

1901 Broadfoot *Billiards* (Badm. Lib.) 319 Every leave was the result of accident rather than of design. 1903 W. Mitchell *Cue Tips* 6 To place the balls in certain favourable positions upon the table and attempt to make as large a break as possible from the 'leave'. 1904 Mannock *Billiards Expounded* 408 'Individual strokes' are not famous for their 'leaves'. 1905 *Westm. Gaz.* 1 June 9/3 His 'leaves' were often impossible ones for Roberts.

Leave, *v.* Add:

3. e. To allow, permit, let. *U.S. colloq.*

1840 *Southern Lit. Messenger* VI. 508/1 If you ha'n't a mind to go, you can leave it be, it's all one to me. 1863 T. D. Price *MS. Diary* 14 Apr., I left him have colt. *c* 1904 H. R. Martin *Tillie* 113 He says his conscience won't leave him wear grand [*i.e.* worldly dress]. 1910 Jer. Hart *Vigilante Girl* iv. 55 It's all right so long as you don't leave her get loose.

7. d. (Earlier example.)

1883 Nye *Baled Hay* 56 That is where we get left.

13. *To leave it at that*: To proceed no farther with a matter; to refrain from pressing a point.

1900 *Captain* VII. 542/1 We'll leave it at that, then. 1909 H. Walpole *Wooden Horse* iv. 78 She had tried..but she had failed; and now, for many years, she had left it at that. 1916 Bennett *Lion's Share* xxxii. 245 'But if it had happened to be the ebb, sir—'. He left it at that. 1928 Galsworthy *Swan Song* 114 He had looked at her, and left it at that.

b. (Earlier example of *leave go.*)

1776 *Essex Inst. Hist. Coll.* XLIII. 118 Tis said we left go pieces of heavy cannon owing to the cowardice of a body of Connecticut troops.

14. e. Add to def.: freq. in pa. pple. *left over*, remaining, not used up.

1899 Burgin *Bread of Tears* ii. i. 138 The undigested fragments which were left over after the making of the world. 1907 *Smart Set* Mar. 72/1 You can go to the boss for your time—if there's anything left over from your breakage account.

Leave, U.S. var. of *lieve* Lief *adv.*

1840 *Southern Lit. Messenger* VI. 508/1 Never mind,..I'd as leave be here as anywheres else. 1898 Marg. Deland *Old Chester Tales* 80, I would just as leave. 1902 A. D. McFaul *Ike Glidden* xviii. 144, I would 's leave git fired.

Leaver. Add example.

1910 *Westm. Gaz.* 17 Jan. 5/1 Of the entrants and leavers examined, approximately 3 per cent. of the children..suffered from..eye disease.

Leaves, var. of *Lieves *adv.*

1771 Copley in *Copley-Pelham Lett.* 142 If Mr Joy would as leaves wainscott the..room as plaister,..I should prefer it. *Ibid.* 160, I had as leaves Miller should paper as any one else.

Leaving, *vbl. sb.* **3.** Add: *leaving certificate* (additional sense: see quot.); *leaving-off time*, the time of ceasing work; *leaving scholarship.*

1889 *Nation* 7 June 464/1 This sum including the 'leaving' scholarship given by the Clothworkers' Company. 1907 *Westm. Gaz.* 26 Aug. 10/2 It is the usual practice at leaving-off time on Saturdays for the workmen..to cease work at once. 1923 J. D. Hackett *Labor Terms* in *Management Engineering* May, *Leaving Certificate.* A card given to laid-off employees, entitling them to consideration when work is resumed.

Lebanese (lebănīˈz), *sb.* and *a.* [f. *Leban-on* + -ese.] **a.** *sb. pl.* The natives or inhabitants of Lebanon. **b.** *adj.* Of or pertaining to Lebanon or its inhabitants.

1920 *Glasgow Herald* 5 Apr. 6 The Lebanese..have.. dissociated themselves entirely from the action of the Syrian Congress. 1926 *Contemp. Rev.* Feb. 194 A distinguished Lebanese Druse. 1927 *Weekly Times* 25 Aug. 208/3 Many ..Lebanese residing in Egypt became French subjects.

Lection. **2.** Add: Also *attrib.*

1927 A. H. McNeile *Introd. N. T.* 383 It [Codex Bezae] contains certain lection marks which Brightman holds to be Byzantine.

Leˈctorship. [f. Lector + -ship.] The office or post of lector.

1906 *Westm. Gaz.* 24 Mar. 3/2 It is hereby expressly stated that the Lectorship cannot be held for life. 1911 A. Brennan *St. Lawrence of Brindisi* 42 The Lectorship was but the first step in his ascent to the highest dignities of the Order.

Lecture, *sb.* **7.** Add: *lecture-agent, -hall, -lamp, -tour*; lecture-day (later U.S. examples).

1873 'Mark Twain' & Warner *Gilded Age* lviii. 527, I am a business man. I am a *lecture-agent. 1753 *Essex Inst. Hist. Coll.* XXI. 153 The meeting adjourned to the next *Lecture Day. 1779 E. Parkman *Diary* 94 Mr. Badcock has been with me to speak about ye Singing..on proposed Lecture day. 1870 'Fanny Fern' *Ginger-Snaps* 170, I get a comfortable seat in church, or concert-room, or *lecture-hall. 1873 'Mark Twain' & Warner *Gilded Age* xlv. 406 It provided for the erection of certain buildings for the university, dormitories, lecture halls, museums, libraries, [etc.]. 1891 T. C. Hepworth *Bk. Lantern* 270 A *lecture lamp has recently been introduced, which not only comprises a shade light for the lecturer's desk [etc.]. 1897 'Mark Twain' *Following Equator* xv. 160, I had a curiosity to know about that man's *lecture-tour and last moments.

Lecturing, *vbl. sb.* *attrib.* Add:

1897 'Mark Twain' *Following Equator* i. 25 The starting point of this lecturing-trip around the world was Paris.

Lecythid (leˈsipid), *a.* and *sb.* [f. mod.L. *Lecythid-*: see Lecyth.] **a.** *adj.* Belonging to the order *Lecythideæ*. **b.** *sb.* A tree of this order.

1871 Kingsley *At Last* xi, Some other Lecythids, which go by the name of monkey-pots. *Ibid.*, Some other Lecythid tree high overhead.

Led, *ppl. a.* **2.** Add: *led lamp.*

1887 P. McNeill *Blawearie* 84 Will Hood had a 'led' lamp; it soon was kindled.

Ledge, *v.*[2] Add: **3.** To place as on a ledge.

1926 Bennett *Lord Raingo* ii. lxxxvi. 403 She ledged a large photograph of Delphine against the foot of the bed.

Ledger. **A.** *sb.* **8.** Add: *ledger-account* (modern examples), *-keeper, -work*; ledger-pole = sense 2.

1902 G. H. Lorimer *Lett. Self-made Merchant* vi. 77 Some one who keeps separate *ledger accounts for work and for fun. 1903 *Daily Chron.* 5 Jan. 5/5 It would be a bad day for loyalty when people considered loyalty as an item in the ledger account. 1906 *Ibid.* 18 Sept. 3/5 A female *ledger-keeper and accountant in one office worked for 6*s.* a week. 1901 J. Black *Carp. & Build.*, *Scaffolding* 86 A combination of chains, clips, and screw bolts, used for securing a *ledger-pole to standard. 1908 *Westm. Gaz.* 24 Mar. 6/3 He came to Paris, learnt *ledger-work, and obtained a situation in a banking-house.

Lee-boarded, *a.* [f. Lee-board[2].] Fitted with a lee-board.

1903 Kipling *Five Nations* 40 The shallow Baltic Where the bluff, lee-boarded fishing-luggers ride.

Leech, *sb.*[2] **2.** Add: *leech-like* adj.

1905 *Westm. Gaz.* 8 Jan. 3/2 He is prepared to stick to it with almost leech-like tenacity. 1908 *Ibid.* 6 Oct. 10/2 Parasitical and leech-like characteristics.

Leech, *sb.*[3] **b.** Add: leech-lining (see quot.).

1883 *Man. Seamanship Boys* 53 *Q.* What is a goring cloth? *A.* A side cloth of a topsail..or lining of a topsail called by sailmakers the leech lining.

Lee lone, Anglicized var. Lee-lane.

1928 Byrne *Destiny Bay* i. § 19. 128 Will you..leave your cousin Jenico and Miss Ann-Dolly by their lee lone?

Leep (līp), *v.* *Anglo-Indian.* [ad. Urdū (Hindī) *līpna.*] *trans.* To wash with cow-dung and water.

1895 Kipling *2nd Jungle Bk.* 80 The big wicker-chest leeped with cow-dung. 1920 *Blackw. Mag.* Oct. 464/1 As you smell the fresh leeped earth of the picquet floor.

Leery, *a.*[2] Add: **2.** *U.S. slang.* Doubtful, suspicious.

1896 G. Ade *Artie* iii. 29 The old lady's a little leary of me, but I can win her all right. *Ibid.* xii. 105 I'm leary of it. 1909 R. A. Wason *Happy Hawkins* 122, I was rather leery about Jabez. 1928 L. J. Vance *Baroque* vi. 34 If you hadn't..made me leary that maybe you'd tip your friends off.

3. *U.S. slang.* Careful.

1911 H. Quick *Yellowstone N.* xii. 300 But be leery that we don't get stuck for non-performance.

Left, *sb.* Add: **4.** A shot fired at a bird on the left hand; a bird in that direction; a blow dealt with the left hand.

1908 R. H. Benson *Conventionalists* i. iii. 82 On Saturday he had killed three rights and lefts, and had not missed more than one single bird flying alone. 1910 *Blackw. Mag.* Jan. 140/1, I got a right and left with the big gun. 1914 J. H. & A. Lambert *Boxing* (ed. 2) 41 If possible send in a straight left to head. 1930 *Daily Express* 8 Sept. 1/6 Siki fell to a left on the body and was counted out.

Left-handed, *adv.* [f. Left Hand 2.] Towards the left; with the left hand.

1848 *Sporting Life* 1 Jan. 241/2 He also bats left-handed. 1854 in *Eng. Mechanic* 19 Aug. 182/1 It blows in circles from right to left, or, as sailors term it, goes round left-handed. 1909 *Chambers's Jrnl.* Oct. 651/2 The great stag ..swinging left-handed..passed Culworth. 1909 E. H. Miles *Lessons Lawn Tennis* (ed. 3) xv. 79, I do not know why ladies should not beat right-handed men players if the latter were compelled to play left-handed. 1928 *Observer* 19 Feb. 24/4 You leave the Oundle road and turn left-handed for Uppingham. 1929 *Morn. Post* 30 Dec. 13/1 Hounds ran fast through Bushill to Chipping Warden, swinging left-handed past Edgecote House.

Leˈftism. [f. Left *sb.* 2 c + -ism.] The political views or principles of the 'left'.

1920 *Oxford Mag.* 19 Nov. 94/1 Mr. Clutton-Brock has consented to read a paper on 'Left-ism'. 1921 'N. Angell' *Fruits of Victory* v. 165 No sooner does the Left of some party break off and found a new party than it is immediately confronted by its own Leftism. 1927 H. G. Wells in *Sunday Express* 20 Mar. 12/5 Leftism seems everywhere in a majority,..but nowhere is it in effective control.

Leˈftist. [f. as prec.] An adherent of the 'left' in politics.

1924 *Contemp. Rev.* July 20, I would support either a violent reactionary, or extreme Leftist.

Left-over, *a.* and *sb.* [Left *ppl. a.* 2.]

1. *adj.* Remaining over; not used up or disposed of.

1897 R. M. Stuart *Simpkinsville* 65, I did carry a handful of left-over flowers around. 1905 *Westm. Gaz.* 28 Dec. 2/1 If..they find themselves with a left-over stock of life-force. 1907 *Smart Set* Feb. 13/1 She tacitly avoided him, and his left-over moments had still been spent philandering in the company of her less discouraging companion.

2. *sb.* Something remaining over; *esp.* a portion of some article of food left over from a meal.

1897 R. M. Stuart *Simpkinsville* 64, I try to keep the Potter's field a-bloomin' with my left-overs. 1906 *Daily Chron.* 21 Aug. 3/2 Miss Green, who produces the 'Everyday Luncheons'..tries to remember the 'left-overs'. 1927 J. Dowd *Negro in Amer. Life* 98 The mother rushes off to work and often leaves nothing for the children's breakfast except left-overs from the last meal.

b. A survival.

1911 L. Abbott *America in Making* 94 The dread of this Executive power is a curious left-over from Colonial days. 1923 Una L. Silberrad *Lett. Jean Armiter* iv. § 4. 106 Being both middle-aged,..two left-overs from a past time.

Leftwardly, *adv.* = Leftwards *adv.*

1908 Hardy *Dynasts* iii. i. iii. 335 With that in eye he has bundled leftwardly Thomière's division.

Left-wing. [See Left *a.* 3 b.] Used *attrib.* with *leader, party*, etc. Also **Left-winger, -wingism.**

1922 G. D. H. Cole *Workshop Organization* (1923) p. xiv, Many more professed no allegiance to the 'left wing' leaders. 1923 *Ibid.* 17 The rise of 'left-wingism' inside the Trade Union movement. 1923 — *Trade Un. & Munit.* p. i, One of the principal contentions of the 'left-wing' elements in the Trade Union and Socialist movements. 1924 *Glasgow Herald* 5 Apr. 9 The unscrupulous, untiring representative of the leftest of left-wingers.

Leg, *sb.* **2.** Add: *To hang a leg* (see Hang *v.* 4 c). *To show a leg*, to make one's appearance; to get out of bed.

1831 B. Hall *Fragm. Voy. & Trav.* I. 247, I say, Master Doughy, do you mean to relieve the deck to-night? Here it's almost two bells, and you have hardly shewn a leg yet. 1854 'C. Bede' *Verdant Green* ii. vii. 61 He used to sing out, 'You must show a leg, sir!' and..kept on hammering at the door till I did. 1919 *War Slang* in *Athenæum* 18 July 632/2 The sergeant's injunction at reveille to 'show a leg', meaning get up.

c. (Earlier example of phrase.)

1825 J. Neal *Bro. Jonathan* I. 8 As if the Yankee man were determined to leave the..brigadier without a leg to stand upon, as a lawyer would say.

3. b. Leg of mutton, a shell of a shape suggestive of a leg of mutton.

1893 Crockett *Stickit Minister* (1895) 242 The lady teachers..explored with their classes the great shell-heaps for 'rosebuds' and 'legs of mutton'.

14. c. Also, a tongue of clay going down into other strata.

1877 J. Geikie *Great Ice Age* (ed. 2) 378 The men..informed me that it was only a 'leg', and was connected with the stuff at the top—from which they said several such 'legs' had come.

17. leg-chair, a chair on which a person's legs can be stretched out; leg-drive, in rowing, drive imparted by movement of the rower's legs; leg-knife, a knife carried on the leg; leg-rest, a tripod or similar device for supporting an apparatus.

1909 *Westm. Gaz.* 30 Dec. 2/1, I stretched my wearied limbs in the luxurious depth of a *leg-chair. 1928 *Observer* 1 July 30/3 They are lacking in *leg-drive, and their boat does not run evenly between the strokes. 1834 C. F. Hoffman *Winter in West* (1835) II. 75 After I had stuck my *leg-knife into the chine of the other. 1840 — *Greyslaer* I. i. 14 The Scotchman, whose *skene dhu* was imitated by the terrible leg-knife, worn beneath the beaded garters of his companion. 1905 *Westm. Gaz.* 4 Apr. 10/2 Owing to the outer casing and the light folding *leg-rests..it matters not how heated the barrel becomes.

Leg, *v.* **5.** Add: In coursing, of a hound: To seize (a hare) by the leg or legs.

1876 *Coursing Calendar* 149 Birkdale..came round on the outside and legged the hare, which Stolen Moments killed.

7. *Cricket.* To send to leg.

1902 *Westm. Gaz.* 11 July 5/2 The newcomer at once started scoring...Nicholl followed him by legging Hopley to the covered stands. 1903 *Star* 8 July 3/4 His first ball was legged by Ranji for what would really have been 3 with a couple of smart sprinters.

Legal, *a.* Add:

1. e. *Legal cap*, a kind of writing-paper. *U.S.*

1874 [see Cap-paper 3]. 1884 'C. E. Craddock' *In Tenn. Mts.* ii. 115 He replaced the sheet of scrawled legal-cap in his pocket. 1902 Harben *Abner Daniel* 3 Old man Bishop ..was carefully reading a long document written on legal-cap paper.

2. *Legal memory* (see quot.).

1882 *Encycl. Brit.* XIV. 650/1 By the Statute of Westminster the First,..the beginning of the reign of Richard I. was fixed as the date of limitation for such actions. This is the well known 'period of legal memory'.

Legation. **3. b.** (Earlier examples.)

1832–3 *Congress. Deb.* App. 90/2 The proceedings..are not

recorded in the legation. *Ibid.*, The instructions are not in the legation [at London].

Legend, *sb.* Add: **8. b.** Applied to the estimated power, displacement, speed, etc., of a ship or its parts, before construction or testing.

1908 *Westm. Gaz.* 31 July 1/3 A ship..in the Bay would exceed her legend speed by a knot or two. 1921 *Glasgow Herald* 17 Dec. 12 The British Government may construct two new ships, not to exceed 35,000 legend tons each.

Legger [2] (le·gəɹ). [f. Leg *sb.* + -er [1].] (See quot.)

1927 T. Woodhouse *Artif. Silk* 95 In the manufacture of stockings on such frames two machines are used...One of these machines, termed the 'legger', knits the upper and longer part of the stocking, whereas the other machine, termed the 'footer', knits the remainder of the stocking.

Legginette. [f. *leggin* Legging + -ette.] A small legging.

1922 *Daily Mail* 14 Nov. 1 Advt., Sterling Value in Boys' Legginettes. 1923 *Weekly Dispatch* 25 Feb. 15 The small girl..is..tucked cosily into legginettes of wool, velvet, or leather.

Leggy, *a.* Add: Also *transf.*, long-stemmed.

1860 O. W. Holmes *Prof. Breakf.-t.* x. 310 The white meeting-house, and the row of youthful and leggy trees before it.

Leghorn. 1. (Earlier examples.)

1740 *Pennsylv. Gaz.* 22 May 7/2 Leghorn hats. 1742 *Boston News-Letter* 24 June 2/2 Just imported..from London..Leghorn Hats for Women. 1744 *Reading Mercury* 31 Dec. Advt., Leghorn Hats.

Legion. Add: **4. b.** *American Legion*, a national association of ex-service men instituted in 1919. *British Legion*, a similar association founded in 1921 and incorporated by Royal Charter in 1925.

1919 G. S. Wheat *Story Amer. Legion* 8 At that dinner [in Paris, 16 Feb. 1919] the American Legion was born. *Ibid.* 32 That was the crux of the initial success of the Legion. 1921 *Times* 16 May 6/4 The arrangements for uniting various ex-Service men's societies into one big organization were completed..yesterday. The new organization will be known as the British Legion. 1924 *Whitaker's Almanack* 843/1 A Conference of Delegates from the various branches of the British Legion was held..on May 20–22, 1923.

Legionnaire (līdʒənēə·ɹ). [ad. F. *légionnaire*, f. *légion* Legion 1 b.] A member of the American, British, or other, Legion.

1927 *Daily Express* 26 Apr. 1/5 Each legionnaire automatically becomes a member of the branch of the Canadian Legion nearest to the settlement on which he lives. 1927 *Daily Tel.* 14 June 7/2 The American Legion..assembles in Paris in September...The legionnaires will be over two weeks on the Atlantic.

Legitimacy. 2. (Earlier example.)

1812 *Niles' Weekly Reg.* 1 Feb. I. 404/1, I never hear an American citizen speak of the '*legitimacy*' of princes without indignation or pity.

Legitimate, *a.* **2. b.** *L. drama* and absol. (Earlier examples.)

1843 *Knickerbocker Mag.* XXI. 485 Such honors as the grateful hearts of all admirers of the 'true legitimate' can bestow, have been showered upon this son of genius. 1846 *Ibid.* XXVIII. 108 The stage of the Chatham [theatre] being small, the management confines itself solely to legitimate business.

c. (Earlier example.)

1812 *Niles' Weekly Reg.* 1 Feb. I. 404/2 The 'legitimate' sovereigns of Russia, Austria and Prussia.

Le·glessness. [f. Legless *a.* + -ness.] Legless condition.

1902 *19th Cent.* Feb. 254 Sir Richard Calmady's leglessness is never for an instant forgotten. 1911 Shaw *Doctor's Dilemma* Pref. xiv, The leg may mortify—it is always safer to operate—..evolution is towards motors and leglessness.

Leg-pull (le·gpul). [f. the phr. *to pull one's leg*: see Leg *sb.* 2.] The act of imposing on a person; an instance of this. Also **Le·g-puller; Le·g-pulling** *vbl. sb.*

1906 *Westm. Gaz.* 30 June 2/1, I, too, have lived in Australia, where leg-pulling is one of the chief joys of life. 1920 H. C. McNeile *Bull-Dog Drummond* ii. § ii, Of course the thing was a hoax, an elaborate leg-pull. 1924 *Glasgow Herald* 23 July 8/7 We felt sure we were suspected of a leg-pull. 1923 *Motor Cycling* 7 Nov. 2/1 You are a confirmed leg-puller. Just fancy kidding me about the speed of the bus I bought from you.

Leguminoid (līgiū·minoid). [f. L. *legūmin-*, Legumen + -oid.] A leguminous plant.

1926 *Chambers's Jrnl.* 15 May 373/1 It has the power like some 'leguminoids', of attracting the nitrogen in the atmosphere and fixing it in the soil.

Leisurable, *a.* 1. (Modern example.)

1905 'Q' *Shining Ferry* i. 9 Old Nicky Vro, the ferryman, had pulled the same leisurable stroke for forty years now, and was not to be hurried.

Leisure (le·ʒiŭɹ, lī·ʒiŭɹ), *v.* [f. Leisure *sb.*] **a.** *intr.* To have or enjoy leisure. **b.** *trans.* To make leisurely.

1928 E. Blunden *Undertones War* 304 There to tarry in careless ways,..Leisuring after fiery days. 1929 Bridges *Test. Beauty* I. 723 Science comforting man's animal poverty and leisuring his toil.

Lemon, *sb.*[1] Add:

1. b. *slang* (orig. *U.S.*). Something bad or undesirable.

1912 Mathewson *Pitching* x. 220 The papers were mentioning him as the '$11,000 lemon'. 1922 'M. Arlen' *Piracy* I. v, 'What would happen if *we* went on strike?'..no one among them..dreamed of answering. The answer was a lemon. 1927 *Daily Express* 13 Dec. 17/1 Middlesbrough seem to have 'picked a lemon', for the draw gives them South Shields as opponents.

4. Also *Comb.*

1886 C. E. Pascoe *London To-day* i. (ed. 3) 27 Figured lemon-satin curtains.

5. *lemon cordial, pie.*

1836 *Mag. Domestic Econ.* I. 182 *Lemon cordial. 1910 C. Harris *Eve's Husband* 154 Then you ate *lemon pie, pound-cake and boiled custard.

7. **lemon cheese (curd), lemon curd,** a confection prepared from lemons, butter, and eggs; **lemon cling** *U.S.*, a variety of clingstone peach; **lemon drop** (example); **lemon-oil,** an essential oil obtained from lemons; **lemon-verbena** (example).

1854 G. W. Francis *Dict. Pract. Receipts*, *Lemon Cheese Curd. 1891 R. Wells *Flour Confectioner* 101 Lemon Cheese. 1909 *Daily Chron.* 17 Aug. 6/4 Boiling lemon cheese over a gas cooking apparatus. 1847 *Rep. (U.S.) Comm. Patents* (1848) 196 Fifteen specimens..of the *lemon cling..measured over a foot in circumference. 1902 *Farm Field & Fireside* 3 Jan. 460/2 *Lemon Curd.—Half a pound of castor sugar,..two lemons. 1915 *Home Chat* 20 Nov. 322 Cheap Lemon Curd. 1870 Eggleston *Blake's Walking-St.* vi. 41 He had inquired if they had any *lemon-drops in their pockets. 1910 *Chambers's Jrnl.* Feb. 104/1 Sicily is the chief source of exports of *lemon-oil, more generally termed 'essence of lemon'. 1869 C. L. Brace *New West* iii. 37 *Lemonverbenas which are small trees.

Lemurian (lĭmiū·riăn), *a.* [f. Lemur + -ian.] Of, pertaining to, or connected with lemurs; characteristic of lemurs.

1890 *Smithsonian Ann. Rep.* 621 An unsymmetrical face, the nasal overture of a pheleiform type, and lemurian attachment of the under jaw. 1893 Newton *Dict. Birds* 354 The hypothesis of a Lemurian continent was..unnecessary. *Ibid.* 355 Lemurian remains have been found fossil in France—if not in England.

Lemurid (le·miŭrid). [f. mod.L. *Lemurid-æ*.] One of the Lemuridæ.

1884 *American* VIII. 218 True monkeys are scarce, but galagos and certain other lemurids are common.

Lemu·riform, *a.* [f. Lemur + -(i)form.] Resembling the lemurs.

1887 Heilprin *Distrib. Animals* 174 Lemurs or lemuriform insectivores (Adapis, Necrolemur).

Lending, *vbl. sb.* **2. a.** (U.S. example.)

1839 Mrs. Kirkland *New Home* viii. 46 After tea, however, things brightened a little...The bath, the razor, the much needed change of those 'lendings' on which so much of the comfort of life depends, produced their humanizing effect.

Leniment. (Modern example.)

1905 R. Garnett *Shaks.* 96 Shall I have license to attend my lord,..And soothe with opiates and leniments?

Leninism (le·niniz'm). [f. *Lenin* the assumed name of Vladimir Ilyich Ulianov (1870–1924), a leading figure in the Russian Revolution of 1917 + -ism.] The political and economic principles or policy of Lenin and his supporters.

1919 J. L. Garvin *Econ. Foundations of Peace* 384 There was general submission to Leninism. 1921 *Times Lit. Suppl.* 3 Feb. 66/4 The more the world sees of Lenin and Leninism as they really are, the less likely it is to be led away by him and his friends.

Leninist (le·ninist), *a.* and *sb.* [f. *Lenin* (see prec.) + -ist.] **a.** *adj.* Of, pertaining to or characteristic of Lenin or his party. **b.** *sb.* A follower or supporter of Lenin or his doctrines.

a. 1920 *Glasgow Herald* 24 Sept. 8 The C.G.T. has since formally abjured the Leninist creed. 1928 E. W. Dickes tr. *Marcu's Lenin* 116 The Minority Party set up its own offices in Russia, and boycotted the Leninist Central Committee.

b. 1920 *Q. Rev.* Apr. 474 The Socialists and the Leninists. 1928 E. W. Dickes tr. *Marcu's Lenin* 187 The Leninists, as the closer adherents of Ulianov now called themselves.

Leninite (le·ninəit), *a.* [f. *Lenin* (see above) + -ite [1].] = Leninist *a.*

1919 J. L. Garvin *Econ. Foundations of Peace* 371 It is necessary not to underestimate the force of the Leninite system. 1920 *Glasgow Herald* 3 July 6 The Constitution of 1919 which recognised the existence of soviets, though not in the Leninite sense.

Lens. Add: **1. c.** Applied to certain objects which resemble a lens in shape.

1902 *U.S. Geol. Surv., Contrib. Econ. Geol.* 113 The principal mines..have revealed valuable ore bodies of two great types, those which occur as lenses..and those which occur in fracture or fissure zones. 1903 *Sci. Amer.* 5 Sept. 165/2 The steam is conducted into what are termed 'lenses', which resemble a double-convex lens.

3. *lens-board, -mount, -tube; lens-grinder, -holder.*

1892 *Photogr. Ann.* II. 289 The most important feature is the novel and convenient mode of attaching the front *lens board to the baseboard. 1921 *Edin. Rev.* Apr. 391 The foreign *lense-grinder worked more cheaply than the English lense-grinder. 1876 J. Thomson tr. *Tissandier's Hist. Photogr.* 223 The ordinary *lens-holder being removed from the front of the camera. 1892 *Photogr. Ann.* II. 43 Unscrew the back combination and use the front alone *in situ*, thus gaining the length of the *lens mount. 1867 T. Sutton & G. Dawson *Dict. Photogr.* 181 The diaphragms within the *lens-tube entirely prevent the reflection of light.

Lenticle (le·ntik'l). *Geol.* [ad. L. *lenticula*.] = Lenticule.

1898 Marr *Stratigr. Geol.* 35 The lenticles will be wider in a direction at right angles to that of the strike. 1902 *Encycl. Brit.* XXVIII. 654/2 Lenticles or eyes of uncrushed diorite.

Lenticular, *a.* 2. (Add quot.)

1903 *Sci. Amer.* 7 Feb. 98/2 The lenses revolve at a given speed..proportioned to the diameter of the illuminant and the lenticular apparatus.

Lentigerous, *a.* (Example.)

1883 E. R. Lankester in *Encycl. Brit.* XVI. 680/2 The two lines of development of the Molluscan eye..the punctigerous and the lentigerous.

Lentil. Add: **4. b.** *Geol.* A lentil-shaped deposit. Cf. *Lens 1 c.

1903 *Amer. Jrnl. Sci.* May 344 In the southwestern belt there is a line of Devonian limestone lentils.

Leonine, *a.*[1] Add: **2. b.** Applied to a variety of leprosy.

1915 C. A. Mercier *Leper Houses* 13 The four varieties of leprosy—leonine, elephantine, alopecic, and ophidian.

Leopard. Add: **2.** (Modern example.)

1920 *New Statesman* Apr. 20/1 For the moment the public is not likely to get a thorough grounding in economics, nor does the Press leopard show any signs of changing his spots.

6. b. **leopard frog** (see quot.); also called *spring frog* and *grass frog*; **leopard tree,** the Spotted Tree of Queensland (*Flindersia maculosa*).

1901 *Chambers's Encycl.* V. 13/1 Widely distributed in the United States are two forms—the Shad- or *Leopard-frog (*Rana halecina*) and the Wood-frog (*R. sylvatica*). 1889 Maiden *Usef. Pl.* 216 *Flindersia maculosa*...Spotted or *Leopard Tree. 1927 M. M. Bennett *Christison* iv. 50 A seared and contorted leopard-tree.

Lepidopterid (lepidǫ·ptĕrid), *sb.* and *a.* [f. Lepidopter-a + -id [3].] **a.** *sb.* A lepidopterous insect. **b.** *adj.* Belonging to or connected with the Lepidoptera.

1906 J. R. A. Davis *Knuth's Handbk. Flower Pollination* I. 123 Lepidopterid Flowers. These are chiefly visited by Lepidoptera. 1908 *Ibid.* II. 480 Herm. Müller [observed] 7 flies, 2 Hymenoptera, and a Lepidopterid.

Lepidopterology (le:pidǫptĕrǫ·lŏdʒi). [f. Lepidoptera + -ology.] That branch of entomology which deals with the study of Lepidoptera.

1898 *Proc. 4th Intern. Congress Zool.* (1899) 232 An important phenomenon that my studies in Lepidopterology have revealed. 1921 (*title*) Bulletin of the Hill Museum, a Magazine of Lepidopterology.

Hence **Le:pidoptero·logist, Le:pidopterolo·gical.**

1898 *Proc. 4th Intern. Congress Zool.* (1899) 232 England and English-speaking America possess the greatest number of Lepidopterologists. *Ibid.* 337 Matters other than Lepidopterological must be settled by a general committee of Zoologists.

Lepori·cide [2]. *nonce-wd.* [L. *lepori-* + -cide 2.] The killing of a hare.

1914 W. De Morgan *When Ghost meets Ghost* I. xviii. 200, I..went..dreading that I should find Achilles (a dog) awaiting applause for an achievement in—in leporicide, I suppose.

Leproid (le·proid), *a.* [f. Lepr-a + -oid.] Of the form or appearance of lepra; resembling lepra.

1910 *Practitioner* Feb. 245 A 'leproid' disease has been described in rats.

Leprosery (leprǫ·sǝri). [ad. Sp. *leproseria*.] A leper-house.

a 1890 *N.Y. Med. Jrnl.* XL. 275 (Cent.). 1891 J. L. Allen in *Century Mag.* Feb. 592 Mother Marianne would herself have written, but she was called away to the leprosery. 1897 *Dict. Nat. Biog.* XLIX. 218/1 He founded the leprosery of St. Thomas the Martyr.

Leptology. (Modern example in new sense.)

1928 *Amer. Naturalist* June 208 A complete science of the fine structure of matter—leptology—is being built up as a result of modern physical research.

Lesional (lī·ʒənăl), *a.* [f. Lesion + -al.] Pertaining to or connected with a lesion or lesions.

1906 *Practitioner* Dec. 830 In lesional arrhythmia..appetite remains good.

Less, *a.* **4.** (Examples of 'minus' sense.)

1910 *Chambers's Jrnl.* Oct. 661/1 If I borrow £100..I pay my interest, less tax. 1911 *Rep. Labour & Soc. Cond. Germany* III. vi–vii. 20 All meat is sold less the bone. 1930 *Times* 25 Mar. 24/2 A full year's dividend on the Preference shares, less tax, absorbing £16,800.

7. b. (Later examples.)

1654 Gataker *Antinom.* 5 In those words of mine nothing les was intended, then this Autor would..enforce them to speak. 1856 Froude *Hist. Eng.* (1863) II. xi. 298 But Elizabeth meant nothing less than to recall Sidney. 1865 *Daily Tel.* 2 Dec. 7/1 We may rest satisfied that the dispute will end in nothing less than a battle royal. 1895 R. L. Douglas in *Bookman* Oct. 22/2 His policy became nothing less than a series of gigantic blunders.

Lessive. (Earlier example.)

a 1760 Franklin *Wks.* (1836) II. 104 One [way] is, to soak it [*sc.* the grain] all night in a *lessive* or lye.

Lesson, *sb.* **4. b.** Add: *To read* (one) *a lesson*: see Read *v.* 11 b.

Let, *v.*[1] Add: **7. c.** (Earlier U.S. example.)

1844 'Jon. Slick' *High Life N.Y.* II. 140 Arter letting into a few of marm's doughnuts..I turned in till morning.

11. a. (*e*) to convert or combine *into*.

1912 Galsworthy *Inn Tranq.* 14 Inhabiting..two little shops let into one, in a small by street.

20. Insert: **Let drive** (see Drive *v.* 11).

24. Insert: **Let slide** (see Slide *v.* 5 b).

29. Let down. b. Add to definition: to fail in supporting, aiding, or justifying (a person, etc.); to leave in the lurch.

1925 E. F. Norton *Fight for Everest* 217 The oxygen party should not this way be let down by their load failing to arrive at V. 1925 Deeping *Sorrell & Son* xii. § 1. 110, I leave it to you Stephen. I know you'll not let me down. 1927 *Observer* 4 Dec. 16/5 In Europe there is a strong feeling that when America went out of the peace she let Europe down. 1927 *Daily Express* 12 Dec. 2/4 A boy who lets his group down..is made to feel ashamed of himself.

c. *intr.* to diminish. *U.S.*

1926 *Publishers' Weekly* 20 Feb. 563 Sales are increasing instead of letting down.

31. Let in. a. Also *fig.*

1920 E. A. Walcott *Open Door* xiii. 162 Let me in on the game, Tommy. 1923 L. J. Vance *Baroque* vii. 39 I'll let you in on a secret. 1928 Edgar Wallace *Double* xv, He had been 'let in' by acquaintances on the Stock Exchange to several good things.

33. Let on. b. To pretend. *dial.* and *U.S.*

1822 Galt *Provost* xlvii, The provost maun ken nothing about it, or let on that he doesna ken. 1826 Mrs. Royall *Sketches* 58 When they [in W. Va.] would say pretence, they say *lettinon*...'Polly is not mad, she is only lettinon'. 1846 Cross *Disruption* v. 48 She..had the sense to..let on to be just as ill pleased as her mistress. 1876 'Mark Twain' *Old Times* 137 If I wanted to..'let on' to prove what had occurred in the remote past..what an opportunity is here! 1897 R. M. Stuart *Simpkinsville* 31 He let on he didn't know him. 1929 *Randolph Enterprise* (W. Va.) 28 Mar. 1/1 We..found out that Mr. Van let on to take the proposal seriously.

34. Let out. e. Add to def: To slacken; to make longer by slackening.

1877 Anna Sewell *Black Beauty* xxxiii. (1880) 158 When the crupper was let out a hole or two, it all fitted well. 1901 G. W. Peck *Peck's Uncle Ike* II. 89 (Born) The pants ought to be let out a couple of holes on my suspenders.

i. (Earlier example.) Also *refl.* and *intr.*: To free oneself from restraint.

1849 Parkman *Oregon Trail* 427 Let out your horse, man; lay on your whip! 1878 Reade *Woman-hater* I. iii. 51 At the end of the song she did let out for a moment.

35. Let up. b. (Earlier and later examples.)

1787 Washington *Diaries* III. 185 The Plows, after the rain let up, proceeded to finish this part of field No. 5. 1841 J. F. Cooper *Deerslayer* vi, Let up, you painted riptyles—let up! 1857 *San Francisco Call* 21 Feb. (Th.) Our spicy contemporary must 'let up' on us for this error of omission. 1902 Harben *Abner Daniel* 39 'Will you never let up on that?' Alan asked. *Ibid.* 270, I wish you'd let up on that infernal clicking. 1913 Galsworthy *Fugitive* II. 49 The hunt was joined the moment you broke away! It will never let up! 1921 R. D. Paine *Comr. Rolling Ocean* i. 8 If I ever let up or weaken, all I need to think of is poor old Dad.

d. To relax, diminish.

1887 A. T. Pierson *Evangelistic Work* vi. 59 His hand lets up its pressure just as the scale is turning for God.

Let-down, *a.* [Cf. *let-down* sb., Let *v.* 29 j.] Characterized by depression or dejection.

1907 M. C. Harris *Tents of Wickedness* II. vii. 193 The next was one of those 'let-down' mornings which everybody must remember having awakened to.

Lethal (lī·păl), *v.* [f. Lethal *a.*] *trans.* To kill animals painlessly; to lethalize.

1922 *Daily Mail* 7 Dec. 6 Advt., Cat. Dying from internal injuries..: Lethalled. 1925 *Observer* 27 Sept. 13/6 Proper lethalling establishments where cats can be put to sleep free of charge.

Lethargy, *v.* (Modern example.)

1893 F. Thompson *Poems* 75 It grew lethargied with fierce bliss.

Lethed, *a.* (Modern example.)

1895 F. Thompson *Sister Songs* 2 On the dull earth's lethed ear.

Let-in, *ppl. a.* [Let *v.* 31 c.] (See quot.)

1882 Southward *Pract. Printing* (1884) 249 Let-in notes are, as the name indicates, let into the text.

Let-off. [Cf. Let *v.* 32 f.] A release or exemption from punishment.

1854 *Punch* 23 Sept. 114/2 A light let-off that will be for the murderer of more than half-a-million!

Letter, *sb.* Add: **4. d.** (See quot. 1825.) *dial.* and *U.S.*

1825 Jamieson *Suppl.* s.v. *Letter*, a spark on the side of the wick of a candle; so denominated by the superstitious, who believe that the person to whom the spark is opposite will soon receive some intelligence by letter. 1853 B. F. Taylor *Jan. & June* (1871) 221 Two 'letters' are snuffed from the candles. 1854– in *Eng. Dial. Dict.* (Lanc., Yks., Northamp., Warw.).

8. letter-ballot, a ballot in which the papers are sent by post; **letter-blindness,** inability (of the eyes) to recognize letters; **letter-book, -case** (earlier examples); **letter-mark,** a contraction or symbol; **letter-scale,** a scale for weighing letters; **letter-weigher,** a device for weighing letters.

1898 *Engineering Mag.* XVI. 126/1 This resolution..submitted to the Society at large in the form of a *letter-ballot. 1899 *Allbutt's Syst. Med.* VII. 433 In others, not even letters can be recognised (*letter-blindness). 1696 S. Sewall *Letter Book* 166, I find it copied out in my *Letter Book from whence I now took it. 1653 *Boston Town Rec.* X. 39 Some other Bills..are in my Leather *Letter case wch comonly lyes upon my table in that closet. 1907 *Congregational Year Bk.* p. xxix, The following *lettermarks and signs are adopted:—B. (Baptist); C. H. (Countess of Huntingdon's Connexion). 1900 Upward *Eben. Lobb* 307 Be it enough To move the index of a *letter-scale But in the estimation of a hair. 1908 *Westm. Gaz.* 28 Apr. 12/1 Many little conveniences..such as a letter-scale which anyone may use. 1862 *Catal. Internat. Exhib., Brit.* II. No. 5825, Inkstand, pen-tray, blotting-book, book-slide, *letter-weigher.

Let-up. (See Let *v.*[1] 35 c.)

1837 *Congress. Globe* 18 Dec. App. 47/2 There was no let up in the matter: the people had so ordered it, and the gentleman ought to be satisfied. a 1848 *N.Y. Tribune* (Bartlett) There was no let up in the stock market today. 1856–1895 [see Let *v.* 35 c]. 1904 Mary E. Waller *Wood-carver* 72 There is no need to spare the wood. There'll be a let-up [of the cold] soon. 1905 *Boston News Bureau* in *Daily Report* 9 Dec. Suppl. iv/4 There will be no let-up in the demand for copper.

Lev (lev). Pl. **leva(s).** [Bulg. *lev* (pl. *leva*) lion.] The monetary unit of Bulgaria, normally equivalent to the franc.

1908 *Daily Chron.* 31 Oct. 1/6 The East Roumelian tribute amounts to 2,951,000 leva. 1925 *Glasgow Herald* 3 Aug. 8 The Bulgarian Government has paid an indemnity of 200,000 levas. 1928 *Daily Tel.* 16 Oct. 18 The Budget 1927–28 showed a surplus of sixty-five million levs.

Levee, *v.*[1] (Earlier examples.) Also, to shut or keep *off* by means of a levee.

1834 [R. Baird] *Valley Mississippi* xxii. 285 Much has been done to levee or embank the Mississippi River. 1837 J. L. Williams *Terr. Florida* 45 Where there is clay enough in the soil, to form good embankments, the waters might be leveed off. 1849 D. Nason *Jrnl.* 69 The banks are leveed.

Hence **Levee·ing** *vbl. sb.*

1845 *Indiana Senate Jrnl.* 364 An act to authorize the leveeing of Blue river, in Shelby county.

Level, *sb.* Add: **2. b.** *On the level*, (in a) fair, honest, or straightforward (way). Freq. as adv. phrase = honestly speaking. *U.S. colloq.*

(*a*) 1896 G. Ade *Artie* vi. 50, I see barrel-house boys goin around for hand-outs that was more on the level than you are. a 1909 'O. Henry' *Roads of Destiny* ix. 157 Bud acted 'on the level'. 1911 — *Rolling Stones* (1915) 194 Now, am I talking on the level or am I not?

(*b*) 1896 G. Ade *Artie* v. 42 On the level, I'm surprised you ain't on to that. 1920 Wodehouse *Damsel in Distress* viii. 103 But, on the level, George, how do you get this way? 1921 R. D. Paine *Comr. Rolling Ocean* iii. 44 This was no fault of mine, on the level. *Ibid.* ix. 162 Don't mind my fooling, Charlie. On the level, I am awfully disappointed. 1923 L. J. Vance *Baroque* vii. 40 No, on the level: if it hadn't been for luck we'd still be guessin'.

3. d. *Psychol.* Applied to different or varying degrees of intelligence or mental activity conceived of as resting on a physical basis in the mind.

1913 *Q. Rev.* Jan. 123 The brain contains some three thousand million cells...The cells are arranged in different 'levels' each higher in function and in a position of command in regard to the level below it, thus forming a sort of a hierarchy.

Level. A. *adj.* **7. b.** Add: *level head*, a well-balanced person.

1906 'O. Henry' *Four Million* 204 James Williams belonged among the level heads.

9. (Earlier example.) Also *levelest* in the same sense, and similarly *level worst*, etc.

1851 *An Arkansaw Doctor* 87 (Th.) We put our horses out at their level best. 1884 'Mark Twain' *Huck. Finn* xxviii. 270 The old man..was on hand and looking his level pisonest. 1891 *Harper's Mag.* July 208/2 The pony will not do his level worst again. 1898 H. S. Canfield *Maid of Frontier* 97 She told me..that she was goin' to do her levelest to make our little home comfortable.

Level, *v.*[1] **3.** Add: Also *refl.*

1907 *Daily Chron.* 25 May 1/7 Another halfpenny may possibly be put on the loaf before prices level themselves again.

d. To bring to a level pace.

1868 H. Woodruff *Trotting Horse* xx. 180 Very soon..Ripton got levelled, and began to trot in his fine, commanding style.

e. To get rid of, put *away*, by levelling.

1910 Galsworthy in *Nation*, *A Sheaf* (1916) 132 All the natural weaknesses and limitations of the dwellers shall be..levelled away and minimized.

8. *intr.* With *away*: To become level.

1921 Galsworthy *To Let* II. ii. 140 Those two crumpled rose-leaves, Fleur's caprice and Monsieur Profond's snout, would level away if he lay on them industriously.

Level-headedness. [f. *level-headed* Level *a.* 10.] Balance of mind or judgement.

1876 *Rep. Vermont Board Agric.* III. 156 That same steadiness, or, in horse parlance, level-headedness,..is quite as essential on the race track..as any where else. 1896 *Alma Mater* 21 Nov. 43/2 A man whose great characteristic is level-headedness. 1927 *Daily Express* 9 Aug. 8/2 A tribute to the level-headedness of the country which in his puny way he tries to wreck.

Lever, *sb.*[1] **4. b.** Add: *lever bit, clock, lock.*

1834 *Visit to Texas* vi. 60 A horse..having their terrible *lever bits put into his mouth, a moderate pull upon which might break his jaw. 1851 C. Cist *Cincinnati* 217 Marine time-pieces, or patent *lever-clocks. 1841 *Ibid.* Advt., Patent *lever lock Factory. 1851 *Ibid.* 215 McGregor & Lee..manufacture lever locks.

5. lever-wood (earlier examples).

1755 in *Coll. N. H. Hist. Soc.* II. 102 In this meadow, they left a bow made of *lever wood, and several arrows. 1810 Michaux *Arbres* I. 32 *Iron wood*..[ou] *Lever wood*, nom dans..Maine et Vermont. 1832 D. J. Browne *Sylva Amer.* 128 In Vermont, New Hampshire and Maine, it [Ironwood] is called Lever Wood.

Lever, *v.* Add: **1. b.** To make way by leverage.

1883 Baring-Gould *J. Herring* i, When he took his weight off,..the plough levered out of the ground.

2. Also *refl.* with *into*.

1910 *Westm. Gaz.* 24 Mar. 2/3 The Moderates have levered themselves into a position they have no claim to occupy on the Council.

Leveresque (līvĕre·sk), *a.* [f. the name of Charles *Lever* (1806–72), an Irish novelist.] Characteristic of Lever's novels or their style. Also **Le·verish** *a.*

1903 *Westm. Gaz.* 18 Mar. 4/2 There are some good stories, old or new, told in a racy and Leverish style. 1905 *Daily Chron.* 15 June 3/1 Of Anglo-Irish lords, of Leveresque landowners, of eighteenth-century spendthrifts. 1922 *Glasgow Herald* 6 June 3 The Leveresque pictures of Irish life.

Levers' lace. Also **leavers'.** [f. the name of John *Lever*, who effected improvements in lace-making machines in 1813.] Any lace made by a 'Lever' machine.

1909 *Westm. Gaz.* 8 Sept. 9/1 The levers branch of the [lace] trade. 1930 *Times* 29 Mar. 9/6 Dress laces, which are known as leavers' laces.

Leviathan. Add: **4. b.** *Leviathan canvas*: A coarse canvas of open texture.

1901 *Lady's Realm* X. 618/1 You can get this Leviathan canvas in many shades of different colours.

Levitation. 1. (Modern examples.) Also *attrib.*

1902 *Q. Rev.* July 125 Many such victims of levitation [*sc.* deep-sea fishes] have been picked up at sea. 1909 H. G. Wells *Tono Bungay* III. iii. § 4. 364 The invisibility of all the machinery gave an extraordinary effect of independent levitation.

Hence **Levita·tional** *a.*, of or pertaining to levitation.

1903 *Edin. Rev.* Apr. 329 These people sought..for a levitational quality akin to the dormitive quality of opium, but never found it.

Levity. Add: **4.** A saying or expression marked by levity.

1930 E. Blunden in *Nation* 6 Dec., 327/1 *Coleridge*, wonderfully well edited by his grandson (only rivalled by J. D. Campbell), lacks his epigrams and levities.

Levy, *sb.*[2] (Earlier examples.)

1832 Mrs. Trollope *Dom. Mann. Amer.* I. 171 He..drew from thence [his pocket] rather more dollars, half-dollars, levies, and fips, than his dirty little hand could well hold. 1834 *Knickerbocker Mag.* III. 349, I was soon eased on this point by an affirmation..that a *levy* was a coin; corresponding..to a New-York shilling.

Levy, *v.* Add: **1. f.** To impose a levy on (a person). Also *refl.*

1902 *Westm. Gaz.* 17 June 9/1 The members will be levied 1s. yearly to support their candidate. 1921 *Ibid.* 24 May 2/4 When the stoppage ceases the miners will levy themselves in order to meet these promissory notes.

Levyist (le·viist). [f. Levy *sb.*[1] + -ist.] One who imposes, or advocates imposing, a levy.

1923 *Glasgow Herald* 5 Mar. 4 Without the investment of money in any form which the levyist could reach.

Lew, *sb.*[2] **2.** (Examples.)

1825 J. Jennings *Observ. Dial. W. Eng.* 52 *Lew*, shelter; defence from storms or wind. 1863 Wise *New Forest* 193 The labourer still sits under the lew..of the hedge. 1899 Raymond *Men o' Mendip* i. 7 The primroses an' cowslips too be out beautiful in the lew between Black-rocks. 1908 *Westm. Gaz.* 6 Oct. 6/3 One of the most noticeable things about many gardens is..the absence of any protecting hedges or 'lews', as they are called. 1910 *Daily Graphic* 21 July 16/1 Advt., Hop Lews, superior, stout, Rot-proof Canvas Wind Shelters.

Lewis (liū·is), *v.* [f. Lewis *sb.*[1]] *trans.* To fasten by means of, after the manner of, a lewis.

1837 *Civil Engin. & Arch. Jrnl.* I. 72/1 When the stone is broken..it is separated on the bed by a large iron crowbar or gavelock, and this is either lewised or chained, and raised by the large crane or 'gin'. 1882–3 *Proc. Assoc. Municip. Engin.* IX. 88 The only ties are wrought-iron 'lewis' bolts, 'lewised' into the old arch stones and turned down and cemented into the new ones.

Lewis gun (liū·is gʌn). [f. the name of the inventor, Col. Isaac Newton *Lewis* of the U.S. army.] A light, magazine-fed, gas-operated and air-cooled machine gun. Hence **Lewis-gunner.**

1916 Sir D. Haig *Disp.* 19 May in *Nelson's Hist. War* XIV. App., Those..brought a Lewis gun to bear on the enemy's line of resistance. 1917 *War Illustr.* VI. 466 A 'Lewis' gunner. 1917 *Inf. Mach. Gun Co. Training* (Prov.) 7 Lewis guns are not included in the term Machine gun. 1922 *Blackw. Mag.* Aug. 158/1 He issued Lewis guns and bombs.

Lewisian (liū·isiăn), *a.* *Geol.* [f. the name of the island *Lewis* in the Hebrides + -ian.] Of, pertaining to or characteristic of, the island of Lewis.

1879 *Encycl. Brit.* X. 327/2 Murchison proposed to term them the Fundamental or Lewisian Gneiss...Afterwards he called them Laurentian. 1901 *Rep. Brit. Assoc.* 615 In the North-west Highlands, the Lewisian (Archæan) gneiss may be resolved into (1) a fundamental complex [etc.]. 1902 *Encycl. Brit.* XXVIII. 653/2 The Lewisian rocks of north-west Scotland.

Lexic (le·ksik), *a.* [f. Gr. λεξικ-ός pertaining to words: see Lexicon.] = Lexical.

1897–98 *Rep. Bur. Amer. Ethnol.* 832 Primitive languages are essentially structural or morphologic, only incidentally lexic.

Lexiconize (le·ksikǫnəiz), *v.* [f. Lexicon + -ize.] **a.** *intr.* To compile a lexicon. **b.** *trans.* To reduce or make into (the form of) a lexicon.

1892 G. Meredith *Lett.* 3 Jan. II. 444 Your lexiconizing is clever, and I cannot go beyond it. 1908 Galton *Mem. Life* 254 They admit of being so classified or 'lexiconised', that..it would be possible for him to tell..whether a similar set had been already registered.

Ley, var. of Lye *v.*[2] (See quot. 1823.) Hence **Leyed** *ppl. a.* (cf. Lyed *ppl. a.*).

1788 Wm. Biggs *Captivity* 35 Sandy hill cranes boiled in leyed corn. 1823 Long *Exped.* I. 114 Another very acceptable dish was called leyed corn. *Ibid.* 195 They sometimes prepare this hard corn for eating by the process of leying it, or boiling it in a ley of wood ashes for..an hour or two.

Liable, *a.* Add: **3. c.** *U.S.* Likely.

1901 S. Merwin & Webster *Calumet K* xi. 198 He's liable to call our men out to-night, ain't he? 1903 A. Adams *Log Cowboy* vii. 48 These fellows are not liable to need any guns for some time. 1903 *N.Y. Even. Post* 22 Aug., Norman Hunter's new record..is liable to stand unmolested for many years.

Liaison. Add: **2. a.** (Later example.)

1870 *Putnam's Mag.* May 545/2 The knowledge gained from these new sources..has..given new zest to the alleged *liaisons* of the Republic.

4. *Milit.* Close connexion and co-operation between two units on the field of battle. Also *transf.*

1920 G. H. Perris *Battle of Marne* xi. 225 With the I Army pulling north-west, the II Army pulling south-east,..how could anything more than a pretence of liaison be kept up? 1922 *Encycl. Brit.* XXX. 268/1 The artillery support was weak..partly through insufficient liaison with the infantry. *transf.* 1915 *Oxford Mag.* 29 Oct. 18/2 The 'overseer' of the Press..an unrivalled artist in the liaison of departments. 1920 *Q. Rev.* July 138 It acted rather as a *liaison* between the Admiralty and the Press Bureau than as a branch of the latter.

5. *Comb.* **liaison officer,** an officer concerned with the liaison of units; also *transf.*

1915 'Ian Hay' *First Hundred Thous.* xix. § 3 That most efficient body, the French *liaison* officers, who act as connecting-link between the Allied Forces. 1917 *Times* 5 May 8/4 The D.S.O. was conferred on him for conspicuous service while acting as artillery liaison officer with the R.F.C.

Liba·tionary, *a.* [f. Libation.] = Libatory *a.*

1896 W. J. Locke *Study in Shadows* vi. 93 Mme. Popea scattered scraps of stuff about her room, in a kind of libationary joy. 1909 *Westm. Gaz.* 16 Feb. 5/2 The new Empress-Dowager had finished performing the libationary sacrifices to the memory of the late Empress-Dowager.

Liba·tioner. [f. Libation.] One who pours out libations (to a god).

1920 *Return Brit. Museum* 47 Black stone squatting figure of Ser, a divine father and libationer of Amen.

Liberal, *a.* **4. b.** (Earlier examples.)

1827 (*title*) The Liberal Preacher [Boston]. 1828 (*title*) Which Society shall you join, liberal or orthodox? [id.].

Liberian (ləibĭə·riăn), *a.* and *sb.* [f. *Liberia*, the Negro republic on the west coast of Africa, founded in 1822.] **a.** *adj.* Of or pertaining to Liberia. **b.** *sb.* A native or inhabitant of Liberia.

1855 *Wesleyan-Methodist Mag.* I. 307 The Liberians..have acquired lands which no European power could peaceably gain from the natives. 1882 *Encycl. Brit.* XIV. 508/1 The Liberian variety of coffee. *Ibid.* 508/2 The Liberian civilization..is apt to deteriorate. 1906 *Westm. Gaz.* 14 July 13/1 The religious tenets professed, if not practised, by modern Liberians. 1914 Walter H. Page *Life & Lett.* (1925) III. 120 About half the Liberian Cabinet..have asked for an audience with me this week.

Libertarian. 2. Add: Also *adj.*

1906 *Westm. Gaz.* 2 Oct. 2/1 No wonder the libertarian woman rebels.

Libertinous, *a.* (Modern example.)

1906 *Daily Chron.* 14 Aug. 3/2 The tale of a bold bad knight, who made libertinous love to a virtuous young woman.

Li·bertist. [f. Libert-y + -ist.] An advocate of liberty.

1887 *Voice* (N.Y.) Aug. 11 But not for a moment can the radical personal libertist accept such a heresy.

Liberty, *sb.* **10.** Add: **liberty boat** *Naut.*, a boat carrying liberty men; **liberty bond,** one of the interest-bearing bonds of the 'Liberty' loans issued by the U.S. government in 1917–18; **liberty cap** (early examples); **Liberty-loan,** one of the four issues of liberty bonds; **liberty tree** (earlier examples).

1837 *United Service Jrnl.* Aug. 474 They knew..that the *liberty-boat would be on shore for them at that hour. 1901 *Daily Chron.* 16 Nov. 4/3 The destroyer Thorn ran down a liberty boat belonging to H.M.S. Forth, with the loss of three lives. 1921 R. D. Paine *Comr. Rolling Ocean* vii. 114 They had permission to stay ashore for the liberty boat that went off to the ship at nine o'clock in the evening. 1922 *Encycl. Brit.* XXXI. 760/2 The *Liberty Bonds and Victory Notes were issued under authority of the Acts of Congress approved April 24 1917, Sept. 24 1917 [etc.]. 1923 A. L. Benson *New Henry Ford* 188 Liberty bonds were converted into $7,000,000 in cash. 1835 *Mechanics' Mag.* 10 Jan. 256/2 It is wholly at variance with classic authority to place the Pileus or *Liberty Cap on the head of the figure representing Liberty. 1843 L. M. Child *Lett. N.Y.* xl. 287 This age and country, in which liberty-caps abound. 1917 *Nation* (N.Y.) 21 June 723/1 The campaign in behalf of the *Liberty loan..was most efficiently conducted. 1921 Bogart *War Costs* 208 The First Liberty Loan Act of April 24, 1917, authorized a bond issue of $2,000,000,000 and advances to allies of $3,000,000,000. 1922 B. J. Hendrick *Life & Lett. W. H. Page* (1924) II. 273 The American Government finally paid this over-draft out of the proceeds of the first Liberty Loan. 1766 *Boston Select Men* 26 Mar., A House..situate in Newbury Street near *Liberty Tree. 1768 *Boston Rec. Comm.* XVI. 312 The Sons of liberty request all..to assemble..under Liberty Tree on Tuesday.

Liberty (li·bəɹti), *sb.*[2] [The name of a London drapery firm, Messrs. *Liberty* and Co.] Used *attrib.* to designate materials, styles, colours, etc., characteristic of textile fabrics or articles sold by Messrs. Liberty.

1888 Mrs. H. Ward *R. Elsmere* I. II. vii. 173 Bits of Liberty stuffs with the edges still ragged, or cheap morsels of Syrian embroidery. 1888 *Daily News* 23 Apr. 6/4 Her dress was of two kindred shades of almost indescribable colour, belonging to the class now commonly known..as Liberty tints. 1891 *Ibid.* 19 Jan. 3/1 'Liberty styles' are to be had in every large drapery establishment. 1892 'F. Anstey' *Voces Populi* Ser. II. 112 Putting on a turban and a Liberty sash. 1900 *Munsey's Mag.* July 517/2 Tying a brown liberty silk veil over my hair. 1927 H. V. Morton *In Search Eng.* xii. § 1. 211 Young women in Liberty gowns who played the harpsichord.

b. *absol.* A material of the class of soft, usually coloured, silks, satins, etc., sold by Messrs. Liberty.

1903 *Daily Chron.* 19 Sept. 8/4 Soft satin, called in Paris Liberty, is again being employed as a blouse fabric. 1909 *Westm. Gaz.* 1 Oct. 8/4 With pannier draperies over an under-skirt of Liberty.

Libidinal (libi·dinăl), *a.* [f. L. *libidin-*, *libido* lust + -al.] Pertaining to or connected with libido.

1922 J. Riviere tr. *Freud's Introd. Lect. on Psycho-Analysis* 283 For a son, the task consists in releasing his libidinal desires from his mother, in order to employ them in the quest of an external love-object in reality. 1925 tr. *Freud's Collected Papers* IV. 39 He withdraws libidinal interest from his love-objects.

Libido (libəi·do). *Psychol.* [L. *libido*, desire, lust.] (See quots. 1922 and 1926.)

1913 C. G. Jung *Psychoanalysis* in *XVIIth Internat. Congr. Med.* § xii. 66 This infantile fixation, which is understood as an unconscious attachment of the sexual libido to certain infantile phantasies and habits. 1922 tr. *Freud's Group Psychol.* 37 Libido is an expression taken from the theory of the emotions. We call by that name the energy..of those instincts which have to do with all that may be comprised under the word 'love'. 1926 Frances G. H. Coster *Psycho-Analysis* 37 Libido..is now very commonly, though not invariably, used to mean the total life-energy or vital impetus of the individual.

Library [1]. **3.** Add: *library book, committee, company, desk, house, -stamp.*

1863 'Gail Hamilton' *Gala-Days* 146 There was the long service, Sunday school and *library books. 1831 *Congress. Rec.* 7 Feb. 618 It was referred to the *Library Committee. 1765 Franklin *Lett.* Wks. (1905) II. 296 Our *Library Company sends for about twenty pounds sterling worth of books yearly. 1837 W. Jenkins *Ohio Gaz.* 99 The public institutions are a bank, a library company and a mechanics society. 1895 M. A. Jackson *Memoirs* xi. 197 Between them is a *library desk. 1837 W. Jenkins *Ohio Gaz.* 281 The *library house is a handsome brick edifice. 1861 *Catal. Cathedral Libr. Calcutta* App. 120 To stamp the title page and other parts of each volume with the *Library-stamp.

Li·cenceless, *a.* [f. Licence *sb.* 2.] Not possessing a licence.

1906 *Daily Chron.* 22 May 7/7 Six licenseless motorists on the Oxford to Birmingham highway were..discovered. 1923 *Glasgow Herald* 10 Oct. 7/1 Licenceless owners will make themselves liable to prosecution if discovered by the Post Office inspectors.

Lichenification (ləi:kĕnifikē·ʃən). [f. Lichen *sb.* 3.] 'The conversion of an eruption into a form resembling lichen' (Dorland).

1903 *Lancet* 18 July 165/1 In some cases the lesions had flattened and left a state of marked lichenification.

Lick, *sb.* **1.** (Later example.)

1919 H. L. Wilson *Ma Pettengill* vii. 215, I was fool enough to argue with him a bit, trying to see if he didn't have a lick of sense.

2. (Earlier examples of the simple *lick*.)

1750 T. Walker *Jrnl. Exploration* (1888) 51 At the mouth of a Creek..is a Lick, and I believe there was a hundred Buffaloes at it. 1784 J. Smyth *Tour U.S.* I. xviii. 141 Licks are particular places..where the clay or earth is impregnated with saline particles. 1800 B. Hawkins *Sk. Creek Country* 29 Parallel with this, are some licks in post and red oak saplin flats.

6. A turn *of* work. Esp. with negatives. *U.S.*

1868 *Putnam's Mag.* June I. 715/1 The father..cultivated a little patch of corn, and did an occasional 'lick of work' for some well-to-do neighbour. 1883 J. Hay *Bread-winners* xii. 185 There won't be a lick of work done in town the rest of the week. 1902 Harben *Abner Daniel* 94 But all day yesterday an' to-day he hain't worked a lick. 1906 H. D. Pittman *Belle of Blue Grass C.* xv. 224 I'll have to take care of the whole gang, and never get a lick of work out of one of them.

Lick, *v.* **7.** Read: To run or ride...

1886 *Outing* Dec. IX. 198/1 He'd nothin' ter do but ter lick it like blazes, with the little dog a-follerin' along.

8. lick-log (earlier example).

1834 Crockett *Narr. Life* xiii. 89 At any rate, I was determined to stand up to my lick-log, salt or no salt.

Licker. Add: Also in sense 6 of the verb.

1907 *Daily Chron.* 31 July 4/7 The licking his Majesty once suffered..[and] the half-crown the late Queen gave the licker for his pluck. 1908 A. S. M. Hutchinson *Once Aboard the Lugger* vi. viii. 456 Into a chair Bill collapsed...He gasped 'George, this is a licker, a fair licker'.

b. *Licker-in*, the cylinder in a carding-machine which receives the cotton, wool, etc., from the feed-rollers and passes it on to the main cylinder. Also *licker-in roller*.

1849 *Rep. (U.S.) Comm. Patents* (1850) 198, I do not claim a licker-in, nor the first main cylinder as such. 1867 *Ure's Dict. Arts* I. 922 The cotton is delivered by the feed rollers to the licker-in. 1884 McLaren *Spinning* (ed. 2) 84 To assist the process..the licker-in rollers are sometimes made hollow, and steam is allowed to fill them. *Ibid.* 195 B is the licker-in, and A the angle stripper between the licker-in and the doffer.

Lickety-split, *adv.* *U.S.* [Fanciful.] At full speed; headlong. Also *lickety-cut*.

(*a*) 1859 Bartlett *Dict. Amer.* (ed. 2), *Lickety Split*, very fast, headlong; synonymous with the equally elegant phrase 'full chisel'. 'He went lickety split down hill.' *Lickety cut* and *lickety liner* are also used. 1869 Mrs. Stowe *Oldtown Folks* xxviii. 358, I tell you if they didn't whip up an' go lickety-split down that 'ere hill. 1890 Susan Hale *Lett.* 269 This train is fearful wobbly..and we are going lickety-split. 1904 Eliz. Robins *Magnetic North* i. 263 We'll go by Pymeut in an ice boat lickety-split. 1911 R. D. Saunders *Col. Todhunter* ix. 122 You're worse'n a old huntin' dog that goes sky-hootin' off lickety-split after a rabbit.

(*b*) 1859 [see above]. 1885 Eliz. S. Phelps *Old Maid's Paradise* x. 157 So they went and pitched into the old chap, lickety-cut. 1898 E. N. Westcott *D. Harum* 175, I up an' put fer the village lickety-cut.

Lick-spittle. Add: **b.** The practice of toadying.

1914 A. Harrison *Kaiser's War* 112 A social system of formality, lick-spittle, bullying, and brutality.

Lick-spittle, *v.* [f. the sb.] *trans.* To toady to (a person).

1927 *Daily Express* 2 May 12/3 Christ criticised the sins of the Church His mother attended, and got His reward. He did not lickspittle the wealthy.

Lid, *sb.* Add: **1. e.** In various slang or colloq. phrases with *down*, *off*, *on* (see quots.), esp. *to put the lid on*, to bring to a close or climax.

(*a*) 1873 M. F. Mahony *Chron. Fermors* I. xii. 225 What wonder if the lid was constantly getting off her temper. 1904 *Philad. Publ. Ledger* 12 Sept. 16 Commissioner of Police McAdoo..has taken frequent occasion to deny that the 'lid' was off, to use the slang definition of a lax police administration. 1920 W. M. Raine *B. O'Connor* 96 'Playing with the lid off back there, ain't they?' The sheriff's nod indicated the distant faro-table. *Ibid.* 218 I'll back that opinion with the lid off. 1927 R. A. Freeman *A Certain Dr. Thorndyke* II. xviii. 272 'My eye!' exclaimed Miller,..'This puts the lid on it—or rather takes the lid off'.

(*b*) 1915 *Literary Digest* 4 Sept. 467/1 In fact, excepting the ordinary saloons,..the 'lid' is down, secure and tight.

(*c*) 1914 H. A. Vachell *Quinneys'* II. xx. § 2. 288 'Blackmail!' gasped Quinney. 'I prefer to call it a weapon, sir, which you are forcing me, sorely against my will, to use.' 'This puts the lid on.' 1919 *Punch* 28 May 430/2 Miss Stevenson..is outside whistling for me, so I must put the lid on. Yours, Alec. 1922 Mrs. A. Sidgwick *Victorian* ix. 69 'That puts the lid on,' said Jane..'You've done for yourself now.' 1928 T. Gann *Discov. & Adv. Central Amer.* 168 Then came the earthquake, which must fairly have put the lid on, as far as Uk was concerned.

Lie, *sb.*[2] **4.** Add: (See also *Lye *sb.*[2])

5. A period of resting or lying.

1930 Lettice U. Cooper *Ship of Truth* i. 30 Sunday was their one chance of a long lie.

Lie, *v.*[1] Add: **10. d.** (Modern example.)

1876 'Mark Twain' *Tom Sawyer* i. 4 But in spite of her, Tom knew where the wind lay, now.

11. c. Of horses, yachts, etc., in a race: *To lie on*: to keep close to, so as to impede the progress of, a competitor.

1928 *Daily Tel.* 17 July 18/2 Fintra [a yacht] lay on Lanni, and kept her in last place.

16.* Lie about, to lie here and there; to be left lying carelessly or in disorder.

1853 Kingsley *Hypatia* xiii, Why, these poor blackguards lying about are very fair specimens of humanity. 1891 Morris *News fr. Nowhere* v. (1907) 31 Most children, seeing books lying about, manage to read by the time they are four years old. 1892 R. Buchanan *Come Live with Me* xiii. 141 Ye might leave it [*sc.* the poison] lying about, and mischief might happen.

21. Lie down. a. Add to def.: to give up, stop.

1904 W. H. Smith *Promoters* i. 21 When they finally lie down, we'll just say, 'All right, we'll go ahead alone'. 1916 *Lit. Digest* (N.Y.) 8 Jan. 87/1 It is natural enough that the accusation of 'lying down' and quitting has been cast up in turn at each of the participants in the conference.

26. Lie out. f. Of land: To lie fallow or unused.

1849 *Rep. (U.S.) Comm. Patents Agric.* (1850) 402 After the corn crop, do not suffer the land to 'lie out'. No error can be more opposed to good farming.

27. Lie over. d. To suspend travelling; to stop.

1854 Bartlett *Pers. Narr. Texas* etc. II. xlv. 538 We arrived there too late for the morning cars. We had, therefore, to lie over a day.

Liegeful (lī·dʒful), *a.* *rare.* [f. Liege *sb.* + -ful.] Loyal, faithful.

1872 A. de Vere *Leg. St. Patrick* 72 If ye be liegeful, sirs, decree the day. *Ibid.* 155 Pure of heart, and liegeful unto Christ.

Lie-up. [f. Lie *v.* 29 b.] The fact of lying inactive in a place.

1926 *Blackw. Mag.* Dec. 850/2 We settled ourselves down for a happy four months of 'lie-up'.

Lieves, var. of *lieve* Lief *adv.* (Cf. *Leaves.)

1863 'Gail Hamilton' *Gala-Days* 241 We'd just as lieves work out of doors..as not.

Life, *sb.* Add: **3. c.** *Not on your life*, not at all, on no account.

1905 *N. Y. Even. Post.* 19 Aug. 2 The congressman was asked if there had been any gambling during the trip. 'Not on your life', he said. 1927 Vachell *Dew of Sea* etc. 259 Mr. Munro snorted. 'Not on your life...I foot all bills.'

12. *Such is life*, an expression implying acceptance of whatever happens.

1849 N. Kingsley *Diary* 52 For my part [I] could almost wish myself in the same Latitude..but such is life.

16. a. *life-form, -habit.*

1899 R. Smith in *Nat. Science* XIV. 110 Oecological Plant Geography, which considers the *life-forms of species. 1905 *Daily Chron.* 17 Aug. 5/7 Each cell capable of developing into a distinct species of life-form. 1891 C. L. Morgan *Animal Sk.* 214 To watch his *life habits with sympathetic interest.

b. *life-preserving, -saver, -saving* (add quots.).

1849 *Rep. (U.S.) Comm. Patents* (1850) Improved Arrangement of the Sections in a *Life-preserving Hammock. 1903 *Boston Even. Transcript* 20 Aug., According to a decision of the Election Commissioners a City Point *life saver cannot vote. 1877 *Harper's Mag.* Dec. 50/2 The *life-saving car is passing from the vessel to the shore with living freight. *Ibid.*, The life-saving station. 1903 *N. Y. Times* 25 Sept. 14 The plight of the sloop had been signalled at the life-saving station at Sandy Hook.

17. life-company, a life-insurance company; **life-force,** vital energy; **life-gun,** a gun used for sending life-saving apparatus to ships; **life-index, -token** (see quot.).

1907 *Westm. Gaz.* 10 Apr. 10/1 That is sufficient justification for the *life-company amalgamation. 1903 G. B. Shaw *Man & Superman* III. 109 These are the creatures in whom you discover what you call a *Life Force! *Ibid.* 134 This is because the philosopher is in the grip of the Life Force. 1903 *Critic* XLIII. 371/2 It would appear that one Wagner once drifted into life-force worship. 1918 Galsworthy *Five Tales, Indian Summer of a Forsyte* v. 341 Five million people..and all of them at the mercy of that Life-Force. 1910 *Chambers's Jrnl.* Mar. 159/2 The *life-gun which is used by the rescuers for shooting lines to the vessel. 1915 *Hastings' Encycl. Relig. & Ethics* VIII. 44/2 '*Life-token' or '*life-index' is the technical name given to an object the condition of which is in popular belief bound up with that of some person, and indicates his state of health or safety.

Life-and-death, *a.* [See Life *sb.* 1 c.] Involving life and death; vitally important.

1863 *Macmillan's Mag.* IX. 60/2 Leaving the period of her..life-and-death troubles about Religion behind her. 1869 *Porcupine* 4 Dec. 346/3 A child of six years, stricken down by inflammation of the lungs, drawing to the close of his hard life-and-death struggle. 1888 Mrs. H. Ward *R. Elsmere* II. III. xxiii. 226, I go about haunted by the *seriousness*, the life-and-death interest people throw into music. 1895 Kipling *2nd Jungle Bk.* 5 Now all that life-and-death fun was ended. 1908 *Daily Chron.* 14 Aug. 1/7 This life-and-death hunt for the dancing girl takes the play to all sorts of interesting places. 1909 *Westm. Gaz.* 27 Aug. 2/2 Their life-and-death interest in the matter would make them watch the result closely.

Lifelikeness. (Earlier example.)

1842 Poe *Tales, Oval Portrait*, I had found the spell of the picture in an absolute life-likeness of expression.

Life-line. [Life *sb.* + Line *sb.*[2]]

1. a. (See Life *sb.* 17.) **b.** A diver's signalling line.

1877 *Encycl. Brit.* VII. 297/1, *e* is the 'life' or 'signal' line, which is attached to the diver's waist, and by which he makes signals and is hauled to the surface. 1896 *Strand Mag.* XII. 351/1 As the strain of the air-pipe was downward, and that of the life-line upward, I concluded that the pipe must be fast below.

2. *fig.* The line of life: see Line *sb.*[2] 1 g.

1860 Hawthorne *Marble Faun* xxix, If there were one of those friends whose life-line was twisted with your own, I am enough of a fatalist to feel assured that [etc.]. 1905 *Daily Chron.* 13 Feb. 3/1 Every man who has lived so long..and kept the life-line so straight and true as Mr. Holyoake.

Lifer. Add: **3.** One who leads a life of a specified character.

Properly the second element of a compound.

1906 *Daily Chron.* 11 May 6/4 The Gospel did not commend itself to the simple lifers of the country-side, but spread like wildfire among the complex lifers of the Greek cities.

Liferent, *v.* [f. the sb.] *trans.* To assign in liferent.

1890 J. Rankine *Erskine's Princ. Law Scot.* (ed. 18) 218 And money may be liferented, the interest, but not as a rule any bonus, being due to the liferenter.

Life-size, *a.* Add: **b.** As *sb.* The size of life; a life-size portrait or statue.

1851 *Art Jrnl.* 1 Mar. 95/2 A figure of life-size. 1885 W. M. Rossetti in *Encycl. Brit.* XVIII. 681/2 Cato as an emblem of wisdom, and (in life-size) numerous figures of classic worthies, prophets, and sibyls.

Life-sized, *a.* [Life *sb.* 16 c.] = Life-size *a.*

1850 *Art Jrnl.* 1 Mar. 91/2 This is a three-quarter life-sized figure. 1879 Clara E. Clement & Hutton *Artists 19th Cent.* I. 26 'The Birds of America'..was completed in 1839..., containing 448 plates, life-sized and colored. 1885 W. M. Rossetti in *Encycl. Brit.* XVIII. 682/2 In the chapel..is an Adoration of the Magi, a square of 21 feet containing about thirty life-sized figures.

Lifetime. Add: *All in a* (or *one's*) *lifetime*, a phrase implying resignation to whatever happens.

1849 N. Kingsley *Diary* 44 My consolation is that it is all in my lifetime and thus make myself quite contented. *Ibid.* 52 This must count as 'all in my lifetime'.

Life-timer. [f. Lifetime.] One serving a life-sentence. (In quot. *fig.*)

1926 J. Black *You Can't Win* v. 48 Life-timers of society, they were slowly sinking without a straw to grasp at.

Lifey, *a.* (Recent fig. example.)

1910 *Chambers's Jrnl.* Nov. 706/2 Those [sapphires] found in Ceylon, which are lighter in colour and 'lifier' than any of the others.

Lift, *sb.*[2] Add: **5. d.** (Earlier example.) Also, elevation, height.

1829 J. Macauley *Hist. N.Y.* I. 170 This lock [of a canal] has an extent within the gates of one hundred and fourteen feet, with a breadth of thirty—the lift is nine feet. 1848 *Indiana Gen. Ass. Doc.* II. 144 Three lift locks, with an aggregate lift of 17½ feet. 1849 Willis *Rural Lett.* iv. 49 The brook at my feet, and, around me, pines of the tallest lift, by thousands!

e. *Aeronaut.* The upward pressure which the air exerts on an airship or aeroplane; the total weight which an airship or aeroplane can raise (including or excluding its own weight).

1902 *Encycl. Brit.* XXV. 104/1 The sustaining power, or 'lift', which in horizontal flight must be equal to the weight. *Ibid.*, With concave surfaces, angles of 2° to 5° will produce adequate 'lift'. 1910 *Blackw. Mag.* July 4/1 The compartments [of the Zeppelin] contained 351,150 cubic feet of hydrogen, giving a lift of eleven tons. 1927 C. L. M. Brown *Conquest Air* 45 A speed at which the resistance of the air exerts on the wings an upward force or 'lift' greater than the downward pull of gravity.

18. (sense 7) *lift-block, plate, purchase*; (sense 10) *lift-boy*; **lift-battery,** a battery in which the guns are lowered for loading and raised for firing; **lift-drift ratio,** in aerodynamics, the ratio of the lift to the drift or drag of a plane; **lift-hammer** = Helve 2; **lift-lock, -pump** (earlier examples); **lift-valve** (see quot. 1887).

1902 *Encycl. Brit.* XXVIII. 454/2 The first 12-in. guns to be installed were the two in the *lift battery, which was finished in 1895. 1883 *Man. Seamanship Boys* 28 There are..two lift-plates bolted to the cap, with eyes on each side of lower *lift-block to hook to. 1906 *Daily Chron.* 20 Sept. 8/1 As I live at the top of a building..I am very dependent on the *lift-boy. 1918 Barber *Aeroplane Speaks* (ed. 6) 8 The Aeroplane must be slow in order to secure the best possible *lift-drift ratio. 1880 *Encycl. Brit.* XI. 425/2 The *lift or helve hammer..thus came into use. 1832 *Louisville Directory* 111 There is one guard and three *lift locks combined, all of which have their foundation on the rock. 1883 *Lift-plate (see *lift-block* above). 1856 *Trans. Mich. Agric. Soc.* VII. 52 Cowing & Co., Seneca Falls, N.Y. [exhibited] 1 *lift pump for watering stock. 1883 *Man. Seamanship Boys* 217 Lower *lift purchase...Used for squaring or topping lower yards. 1887 *Encycl. Brit.* XXII. 505/1 In many stationary engines *lift or disk valves are used, worked by tappets, cams, or eccentrics. 1887 D. A. Low *Machine Draw.* (1892) 68 Flap valves, which bend or turn upon a hinge; (2) lift valves, which rise perpendicularly to the seat; (3) sliding valves, which move parallel to the seat.

Lift, *v.* **1.** Add: occas., to lower after raising from an elevated position (e.g. quot. 1841).

b. Also with *down*.

1838 Dickens *O. Twist* xxi, Sikes dismounted,..holding Oliver by the hand..and lifting him down directly, bestowed a furious look upon him. 1853 Kingsley *Hypatia* xiii, Lift the old disgraced man down, sir. 1889 Doyle *Sign of Four* viii. (1890) 138 'He acted according to his lights', said Holmes, lifting him [the dog] down from the barrel.

2. d. To raise in price, value, or amount. Also *ellipt.*

1907 *Daily Chron.* 7 Nov. 1/7 Home Rails were lifted all round..several rises being substantial. 1928 *Chambers's Jrnl.* Feb. 99/2 He kept on lifting the betting, merely to increase his plunder. *Ibid.* 115/2 Jackson..opened the pot for a pound. The American..raised it five, and Captain Reginald lifted another five.

3. Add: Of aircraft: To rise off the ground.

1879 *Eng. Mechanic* 4 July 410/3 The small flying model ..only just lifted off the pavement. 1899 H. G. Wells *When Sleeper Wakes* xxiv. 327 The aëropile..was running down its guides to launch. It lifted clean and rose. 1907 *Daily Chron.* 9 Oct. 4/5 She will have to get rid of at least 250 lb. of ballast before she will lift.

f. To rise in the air.

1878 B. F. Taylor *Between Gates* 65 The blue dome of Mount Diablo lifts in the far horizon. *Ibid.* 142 Around you the mountains lift three and four thousand feet above the sea.

g. To come into being; to originate.

1928 *Chambers's Jrnl.* Jan. 3/2 Whatever quarrel—sudden it must have been—had lifted between them came to its crisis.

h. To rise in tone or volume of sound.

1912 Galsworthy *Inn Tranq.* 157 He seemed to enjoy the sounds of conversation lifting round him. 1918 — *Five Tales, Indian Summer* v, The wayward music lifted up again.

11. (Additional examples.)

1906 *Daily Chron.* 12 Sept. 5/7 It was freely said that if we only applied the suspensions would be lifted. 1922 *Encycl. Brit.* XXX. 255/2 The bombardment is 'lifted' from the first line to reënforce that on the second line.

c. (Earlier example.)

1846 *Oregon Spectator* 30 Apr. (Th.) [Mr. W.] is less able to lift my paper now, than at any former time.

Lifter. **2. b.** (*d*). Also *attrib.*

1834 McLaren *Spinning* (ed. 2) 152 The bobbin travels up and down on a lifter plate. *Ibid.* 164 The lifter motion is greatly strengthened.

c. A vessel used for raising sunken craft.

1909 *Westm. Gaz.* 16 July 7/2 The gunboats..have arrived on the spot, as have also the Admiralty tugs and lifters.

Lifting, *ppl. a.* Add: **lifting plough,** one which raises the soil it passes through.

1879 *Scribner's Monthly* Dec. 239/2 A subsoil or lifting plow which stirs and loosens the substratum without bringing it to the surface.

Liftless, *a.* [f. Lift *sb.*[2] 10 + -less.] Not provided with a lift.

1916 W. J. Locke *Wonderful Yr.* xvii. 245 She was living ..on the fifth floor of a liftless block of flats in Wandsworth. 1921 *Spectator* 16 Apr. 484/2 In a liftless household.

Lift-up, *a.* [Lift *v.* 1 b.] Made to lift up.

1917 *Installation News* Jan. 5/1 The Cabinets comprise a substantially constructed stained box, fitted with lift-up lid, lock and key.

Ligan, var. of Lagan. (Modern examples.)

1906 *Westm. Gaz.* 13 June 4/2 These are, says Mr. Clifford, the 'ligan' of history. 1909 *Daily Chron.* 20 Mar. 5/5 The custody of flotsam, jetsam, and ligan.

Light, *sb.* Add: **1. i.** (Later example.)

1910 W. M. Raine *B. O'Connor* 25 Mebbe I'd a-put his light out for good and all.

5. b. *Lights out* (Mil.): The last bugle-call of the day, giving the signal for all lights to be extinguished. Hence in non-military use.

1868 *Queen's Regul. Army* § 845 Between tattoo and reveille no trumpet or bugle is to be sounded,..with the exception of the call 'lights out'. 1905 *Captain* XIII. 42/2 It's off...we aren't allowed to talk after lights-out!

7. d. *To see the light*, to become enlightened or convinced. *U.S.*

1812 *Niles' Weekly Reg.* III. 195/2 It is indispensably necessary that every man should 'see the light'. 1889 *Kansas Times & Star* 14 Oct., Up to a few weeks ago, he was opposed to a revival of navigation on the Missouri, but now he has seen the light and says he's for it strong. 1903 *N.Y. Even. Post* 10 Sept., It is altogether likely that they, too, will see the light before another week has passed.

16. light-change, a change in the light which is received from a variable star; **light cure,** a cure effected by sunlight or artificial light; also *attrib.*; **light-curve,** a graph showing the variations in the light received over a period of time, esp. from a variable star; **light-demander,** one of the class of trees which require a relatively large amount of light for healthy growth; (so *light-demanding* adj.); **light-pressure,** the pressure exerted on bodies by light-waves; **light-stand,** a stand to support a light; **light-valve,** a valve which controls the passage of light.

1902 *Chambers's Jrnl.* Feb. 68/2 There is another variable star..the *light-changes of which show that [etc.]. 1901 *Ibid.* Dec. 844/2 Hospitals..have already obtained apparatus for the *light-cure of lupus. 1903 *Science Siftings* 19 Sept. 324 Among the modern methods of light cure the one longest established is that of keeping small-pox patients in rooms from which the actinic rays of light are shut out. 1904 *Daily Chron.* 11 Apr. 5/3 A lengthy visit to Professor Finsen's light-cure institution. 1904 *Westm. Gaz.* 28 Sept. 1/1 His light-cure treatment of lupus. 1902 Newcomb *Study of Universe* 115 The lower curve is the *light-curve of the star. 1926 H. C. Macpherson *Mod. Astron.* 121 The light-changes of Algol...The star's light-curve. 1891 Schlich *Man. Forestry* II. 307 As regards light-requirement it stands half-way between *light-demanders and shade-bearers. 1910 *Chambers's Jrnl.* Mar. 172/2 The ash, oak, sycamore, elm, alder, birch, are all light-demanders in a greater or less degree. 1891 Schlich *Man. Forestry* II. 318 German foresters seem to consider the Douglas Fir to be a moderately *light-demanding species. 1902 *Encycl. Brit.* Index, *Light-pressure. 1908 *Westm. Gaz.* 23 Oct. 5/3 The 'light-pressure' exerted by the sun. 1926 H. C. Macpherson *Mod. Astron.* 43 Explosions, light-pressure, and gravity. 1866 Mrs. Whitney *L. Goldthwaite* vi, On this little green stood..a round white-pine *light-stand with her work-basket and a few books. 1873 *Routledge's Young Gentl. Mag.* Feb. 173 The new *light-valve, by which a perfect equality of tone is preserved.

Light, *a.* Add: **2. b.** *Lighter-than-air.* Of aircraft: Belonging to the balloon type; that rises in the air by reason of its lesser specific gravity. Also *lighter-than-sea*.

1909 *Westm. Gaz.* 11 June 7/2 The best working 'flying' model airship, whether of the heavier-than-air or the lighter-than-air type. 1910 C. C. Turner *Aerial Navig. Today* Gloss., *Lighter-than-air*, a term used to denote all aerial vessels whose ascensional power is derived from the buoyancy of gas or hot air. 1912 S. F. Walker *Aviation* i. 7 'Lighter than Air' apparatus which we call balloons. 1917 C. C. Turner *Air-craft To-day* vii. 105 Certainly the liner is a lighter-than-sea machine, but only a portion of the liner is in the sea. 1923 Hart & Laidler *Aeronaut. Sci.* 8 A second consequence of Borelli's work was naturally an increased attention to the problem of 'lighter-than-air' flight.

ellipt. 1910 *Blackw. Mag.* Feb. 206/1 Neglecting the lighter than air as a military auxiliary.

7. b. Of lines: Made with a light stroke; thin. Also of type.

1898 J. Southward *Mod. Printing* I. xxii. 140 The first would be called a *light face*, and the second a *heavy face*.

Light, *v.*[1] **5. a.** (See quot.)

1884 J. Quincy *Figures of Past* 180 Soon after sunrise the tide lighted us over the bar.

b. (Earlier examples.) Also *to light in* (to join in a fight) or *into*.

1873 J. H. Beadle *Undevel. West* xxiv. 508 Our mules had broken corral and were lighting out toward Wingate. 1878 — *Western Wilds* ii. 37 She swore at us, an' lit out on the road with a partin' blessin'. *Ibid.* xii. 187 They double-quicked into town and lit in generally. 1881 A. A. Hayes *New Colorado* xi. 149 When them tramps see us a-comin', they knew we was on the skeet, and they just give three cheers, and *lit out*. 1889 K. Munroe *Golden Days* xiv. 156 You've got the levellest head of any man that ever lit into the diggings.

Lighted, *ppl. a.* Add: Also *fig.*

1891 Meredith *One of our Conq.* xxxiii, Her lighted mind punished her thus through her conjuring of Dudley's words.

Lighter, *sb.*[2] Add: Also *lighter-up* (see quot. 1921).

1909 *Westm. Gaz.* 21 Apr. 8/1 Robert Brown, lighter-up [at locomotive shed] slight cut on left eyebrow. 1921 *Dict. Occup. Terms* (1927) § 709 Lighter-up, carries live coals from fire hearth in shed to engine fire box.

Light-faced, *a.* [Light *a.*[1] *7 b.] Of type: Having thin printing-surfaces.

1898 J. Southward *Mod. Printing* I. xxiv. 155 In the case of light-faced letters, they are spoiled for good work after the first time of using. 1917 F. S. Henry *Printing for School & Shop* vii. 90 Dainty, light-faced type.

Lighthouse. b. *lighthouse keeper* (earlier example).

1738 *Massachusetts Prov. Acts* XII. (1904) 513 That the sum of Fifty one Pounds..be paid..for his services as Light House Keeper.

Lighthouseman. [Lighthouse b.] A lighthouse-keeper.

1889 *Athenæum* 23 Feb. 257 Advt., The manners and ways of coastguardsmen, lighthousemen, and other amphibious creatures.

Lighting, *vbl. sb.*[2] **1.** *attrib.* Add:
1885 P. HIGGS *Magneto- & Dynamo-electric Mach.* 183 A greater part of its lighting-power is due to the incandescence of the electrodes. 1928 *Chambers's Jrnl.* Jan. 21/1 An automatic regulator wherewith to make..and supply lighting power to the lamps.

Lightless, *a.* Add: **3.** Not having a light, or lamp; lampless.
1906 *Daily Chron.* 18 May 6/6 His undetected offence of riding a lightless bicycle after dark.

Light-line. = *Light water-line* (see LIGHT *a.*[1] 4).
1894 W. H. WHITE *Man. Naval Archit.* (ed. 3) 47 The displacement of a ship between her light and load lines could be estimated, and would give the true 'dead-weight capability'.

Lightning. 2. Add: Also applied to liquor = *CHAIN-LIGHTNING 2. *U.S.*
1876 'JOAQUIN' MILLER *Unwritten Hist.* viii. 115 In one of the saloons where men were wont to..drink lightning. *Ibid.* xi. 164 All ranged themselves..before the bar, calling out 'cocktail',..'lightning straight',..and so on.

b. *pl.* A grade of jute.
1929 T. WOODHOUSE *Spinning, Weaving* etc. *Flax & Jute* 2.

3. d. Acting with the rapidity of lightning.
1883 'MARK TWAIN' *Life Mississippi* xvi. 200 If one of the boats has a 'lightning' pilot, whose 'partner' is a trifle his inferior.

e. lightning beetle = FIRE-FLY 1; **lightning-box,** a box used in producing stage-lightning; **lightning-bug** (earlier example); **lightning-change,** a rapid change of costume made by an actor or performer; **lightning conductor** (earlier example); **lightning-rod** (*b*) = FULGURITE 1; **lightning strike,** a sudden strike which takes place without any warning; **lightning train** *U.S.* = *lightning express.*
1859 B. JAEGER *N. Amer. Insects* 51 (Cass. Suppl.) Some months since a lady presented me two of these living *lightning beetles. 1855 M. M. THOMPSON *Doesticks* xxvi. 237 The prompter was stretched on the top of a canvas volcano, with the bell-rope in his hand, and his hair full of resin, from the '*lightnin-box'. 1797 *Massachusetts Spy* 30 Aug. 4/1 This country at present has two species of *Lightning Bugs. 1890 *Harper's Mag.* June 51/2 No more '*lightning change' from the sock to the cothurn was ever made in life's drama. 1814 W. BENTLEY *Diary* (1914) IV. 262 The post remained, retained on the side of the steeple by the *Lightning conductors. 1892 KENNEDY *Sporting Sk. S. Amer.* 97 These '*lightning-rods' are caused by lightning passing through the loose sand, and fusing it. 1928 *Times* 3 Mar. 12/4 Six collieries were idle in Northumberland to-day as the result of *lightning strikes. 1928 G. B. SHAW *Intell. Woman's Guide* lxxxiii. (1929) 448 A lightning strike of waitresses in a restaurant. 1874 B. F. TAYLOR *World on Wheels* I. viii. 66 In *lightning trains he [the brakeman] is not given to much humor, but the article is in him.

Lightning (ləi·tniŋ), *v.* [f. LIGHTNING *sb.*] = LIGHTEN *v.*[2] 6. Also *fig.*
1903 *Westm. Gaz.* 15 Nov. 8/2 The two metal balls..thundered and lightninged as they delivered the message. 1926 HALL CAINE in *Strand Mag.* Jan. 20/1 Mr. Gladstone leapt to his feet, whereupon the air of the House thundered and lightninged for a short ten minutes.

Lightningy (ləi·tniŋi), *a.* [f. as prec.] Suggestive of lightning. (In comb. with *thunder.*)
1906 GALSWORTHY *Man of Property* II. ii. 141 They had never seen anyone look so thunder and lightningy as that little June!

Light-weight. A. *sb.* **1.** Add: Also of vehicles, esp. motor-cycles.
1908 *Daily Report* 20 July 9/1 Light-weights of 2 h.p. are quite capable of averaging well over 20 m.p.h.

B. *adj.* Add: Also of cloth, etc.
1902 *Daily Chron.* 8 Nov. 8/3 Every woman who walks much clings to a light-weight Russian blouse. 1903 *Ibid.* 4 July 8/4 A cool alpaca skirt, or one of light-weight cloth. 1904 *Ibid.* 17 Aug. 8/3 The hat..is made of light-weight leather.

Light-weighted, *a.* [f. LIGHT-WEIGHT *sb.*] Of light weight; carrying a light weight.
1867 LOWELL *Study Wind.* (1871) 76 We..see the rather light-weighted great man wheeled round the room..to converse with his guests. 1905 *Westm. Gaz.* 21 Mar. 8/2 The London and Brighton Handicap Steeplechase on Friday may be won by the light-weighted Dam.

Lignilite (li·gniləit). *Geol.* A columnar or cylindrical structure in limestone, due to pressure.
1882 GEIKIE *Text-bk. Geol.* 312 Another illustration of the effects of pressure in producing deformation in rocks, is supplied by the so-called 'lignilites', 'epsomites', or 'stylolites'.

Like. A. *adj.* **9. b.** Add U.S. examples of *like* = *was* or *had like.*
1884 'MARK TWAIN' *Huck. Finn* xxxix. 396 We like to got a hornet's nest, but we didn't. 1888 'C. E. CRADDOCK' *Broomsedge Cove* xviii. 327 That's what like to have happened to me. 1916 B. M. BOWER *Phantom Herd* vi. 100, I like to died a-laughing.

B. *adv.* Add: **1. c.** *Like a book,* in careful language; with care or precision; without hesitation; thoroughly. *U.S. colloq.*
1829 *Massachusetts Spy* 28 Jan. (Th.) You talk like a book, Mr. Bond. 1833 J. NEAL *Down-Easters* 26 An educated and travelled Yankee,..talking like a book, even to his washerwoman. 1839 C. F. BRIGGS *Harry Franco* I. xi. 73 Know him like a book, replied Mr. Lummucks. 1841 *Congress. Globe* 13 Feb. 148/1 Democrats, he knew, would vote for it [sc. the Pre-emption bill] like a book. 1875 [see SPEAK *v.* B. 1 d].

6. e. (Modern U.S. examples.)
a 1859 *Southern Sk.* (Bartlett) The old fellow drank of the brandy like he was used to it. *a* 1880 in Tourgee *Invis. Empire* viii. 451 The coloured people dare not dress themselves and fix up like they thought anything of themselves. 1886 *Harper's Mag.* June 109/2 None of them act like they belonged to the hotel. 1898 H. S. CANFIELD *Maid of Frontier* 100, I sprung from the chair like a man had shot me through the head.

C. *sb.* Add: **1. b.** = LIKENESS.
1876 MORRIS *Æneids* VII. 416 To an ancient woman's like her shape she fashioned.

Like, *v.*[2] **2.** (Later U.S. example.)
1892 J. E. COOKE *B. Hallam* 282 She liked to fainted just now.

Likelihood. 2. c. For '*Obs.* exc. *Sc.*' read '*Now rare* exc. *Sc.*'
1894 G. MEREDITH *Ld. Ormont* xxx, The likelihood is, we shall hear nothing further.

Liker. (Modern examples.)
1871 M. ARNOLD *Let.* 18 Aug. (1895) II. 62, I am one of the true likers of the Continent. 1894 W. C. GANNETT *Blessed be Drudgery* 41 Each of us is ringed about by two circles...The outer circle is the circle of our Likers, the inner is the circle of our Lovers.

Lilacky (ləi·lăki), *a.* [f. LILAC 2.] Of a lilac colour.
1910 *Westm. Gaz.* 19 Feb. 2/2 Walls on walls of lilacky limestone.

Lilium (li·liŏm). [L. *lilium*: see LILY.] A plant (or flower) of the genus *Lilium.*
1902 *Westm. Gaz.* 6 Dec. 10/1 Of all flowers none are affected by frost so much as roses,..violets, and liliums. 1903 *Ibid.* 26 Nov. 12/1 White liliums are fetching 4s. a bunch. 1908 *Daily Chron.* 29 Feb. 9/1 A stock of anemones, ranunculus, gladiolus, and liliums. 1923 *Chambers's Jrnl.* Dec. 786/2 The finest liliums and choice gladioli grow superbly.

Lilt, *v.* **1. b.** Add: Also with *out.*
1916 BENNETT *Lion's Share* xxv. 191 Musa lilted out the delicate, gay phrases of Debussy.

3. (Recent examples.)
1904 KIPLING *Traffics & Discov.* 79 He lilted a little on his feet when he was pleased. *Ibid.* 80 He went to England, and he became a young man, and back he came, lilting a little in his walk.

Lilting, *ppl. a.* Add: Also of one's gait: (sense 3 of v.).
1903 *Longman's Mag.* Jan. 271 Swinging down the street with an easy lilting stride..marched two Englishmen, soldiers both.

Lily. 5. lily-pad (earlier and later examples).
1843 *Knickerbocker Mag.* XXII. 1 Huge moccasin darting away beneath the dense reeds and lily-pads of the swamp. 1875 HOLLAND *Sevenoaks* v. 65 A deer, feeding among the lily-pads. 1888 *Nation* 19 July 57/2 The trout breaking at the edge of the lily-pads.

Lima. (Earlier example of *Lima bean.*)
1831 MRS. HOLLEY *Texas* (1833) xi. 123 He had known winters here so mild, as not to kill the Lima bean.

b. *ellipt.* = Lima bean. *U.S.*
1856 COZZENS *Sparrowgr. Papers* vii. 85 Put the Limas to the right..and as for the rest of the seeds sweep them into the refuse basket. 1862 *Trans. Ill. Agric. Soc.* V. (1865) 785 Pole Beans—Amongst these the Limas deservedly rank the highest.

Limb, *sb.*[1] **2. b.** (Later examples.)
1885 *San Francisco News Letter* (Farmer *Slang* s.v. *Cake*) Between you 'n me, red stockings ain't becomin' to all—ahem—limbs. 1898 MARG. DELAND *Old Chester Tales* 237 But it was she who informed him that he might stay until his 'limb' permitted him to walk. 1902 H. L. WILSON *Spenders* xxxi. 369 One of my maids who slipped on the avenue yesterday and fractured one of her—er—limbs. 1904 *Louisville Courier-Jrnl.* 5 Sept. 1 Her limbs were void of shoes or stockings. 1924 W. M. RAINE *Troubled Waters* i. 12 She dexterously arranged the skirt without being able to conceal some inches of slender limb rising from a well-turned ankle.

4. b. Add to def.: An iron core in a dynamo.
1902 *Encycl. Brit.* XXVII. 584/1 (1) the magnet 'cores' or '*limbs*', carrying the exciting coils whereby the inert iron is converted into an electro-magnet; (2) the *yoke*, which joins the limbs together and conducts the flux between them.

5. limb-wood (see quot.).
1901 J. BLACK *Carp. & Builder, Home Handicr.* 62 [For mosaic work] black is obtained by using ebony or bog oak..green, by..a species of native green oak, known as 'limb wood'.

Limb, *v.* Add: **1. b.** With *off*: To strip (a tree) of limbs.
1889 *Harper's Mag.* Jan. 231/1 It seemed to be built principally of alder poles well limbed off and placed, roughly speaking, side by side.

3. *trans.* To be a limb (or limbs) to; to furnish with limbs.
1909 RAYMOND *Dante* etc. 291 We were like two arms that limb one frame.

Limber, *v.*[1] Add: Also **limbering** *vbl. sb.*, **limbering-up** *adj.*
1921 *Blackw. Mag.* Aug. 262/1 Dempsey had passed the afternoon in a 'limbering-up hike'. 1927 *Dancing Times* Dec. 301/1 Most dance students know that limbering is the basis for every kind of dance work.

Li·mbered, *a.* [f. LIMBER *sb.*[1]] Having a limber.
1920 *Blackw. Mag.* Feb. 279/2, I lent him some men and a limbered waggon.

Li·mberly, *adv.* [f. LIMBER *a.*] In a limber or supple manner.
1891 *Harper's Mag.* Nov. 891/2 His long spare arms swing limberly before a long spare body. *a* 1909 'O. HENRY' *Roads of Destiny* xii. 186 They..slouched limberly over to the railroad eating-house.

Limburger (li·mbɒːgəɹ). [a. Du. and G. *Limburger.*] *attrib.* with *cheese,* or *ellipt.* A soft cheese made in the province of Limburg.
1887 *Harper's Mag.* Mar. 644/1 The obese Teuton delights in 'loud' Limburger and Gruyere.

Lime, *sb.*[1] **1. b.** Add: *Time and lime*: see *TIME *sb.* 9.

3. d. A vat containing a solution of lime for unhairing skins.
1897 C. T. DAVIS *Manuf. Leather* (ed. 2) 331 When sufficiently softened the skins are next placed in the 'limes'...The goat-skins remain in the 'limes' about 14 days.

5. *lime-burning, -cask, -grout, -mortar, -ooze, -sifter, -wagon*; **lime-rock, -sink** (earlier examples).
1860 ABBOTT *South & North* 196 [Slaves] employed..in *lime-burning or fishing. 1865 MRS. STOWE *House & Home P.* 94 Seating himself on a *lime-cask which the plasterers had left. 1875 R. R. BRASH *Eccl. Archit. Irel.* 8 The interior of the walls is filled with small stones and *lime-grout. 1764 *Coll. N. H. Hist. Soc.* IX. 168 Capt. Walker's son came and made my *lime mortar. 1867 J. N. EDWARDS *Shelby* etc. xxix. 498 He..disappeared for a moment beneath *lime ooze, half tanned hides and the smell of a charnel house. 1665 *Rec. of Providence* (R. I.) III. 66 Those *Lime Rocks about Hackletons lime Killne shal be perpetually Common. 1673 *Ibid.* III. 229 To fetch for their use as much lime Rock from the rock..as they please. 1771 in *Maryland Hist. Mag.* XIV. 129 Give my service to Mr. Deards and desire Him to send 1 Coarse *lime sifter. 1837 J. L. WILLIAMS *Terr. Florida* 9 Ponds and *lime sinks are numerous between the..rivers. 1864 B. TAYLOR *H. Thurston* vi. 79 No one ever knew a *lime-wagon or a woodsled to give an inch of road to a lighter vehicle.

Lime, *sb.*[2] **2.** Add: **lime-punch** (earlier example); **lime-squash,** a drink made with the juice of the lime (cf. *lemon-squash*).
1774 P. V. FITHIAN *Journal* (1900) 206 We had after Dinner, Lime Punch and Madaira. 1909 *Daily Chron.* 15 June 4/4 For drinking, lime-squash is superior to lemon squash. *Ibid.* 11 Aug. 1/4 If you want a long cool drink try a lime-squash.

Limehouse (ləi·mhaus), *v.* [f. *Limehouse,* a district in the east of London.] *intr.* To make fiery (political) speeches such as Mr. Lloyd George made at Limehouse in 1909. Also **Li·mehousing** *vbl. sb.*
1913 *Daily Mail* 1 Aug. 5 (heading) Mr. Lloyd George himself again...Limehousing at Carnarvon. 1914 *National Rev.* June 543 Mr. Lloyd George went to Ipswich and Limehoused on the eve of the poll. 1920 *Glasgow Herald* 20 Mar. 7 It is exactly what he used to say in the old Limehouse days, though his Limehousing now is of a different kind.

Lime-juice, *v.* [f. the sb. or f. LIME-JUICER.] *intr.* To make long voyages.
1892 STEVENSON & L. OSBOURNE *Wrecker* xiii, But the *Flying Scud*? a deep-water tramp, who was lime-juicing around between big ports?

Limelight. Add to def.: Much used in theatres to light up important actors and scenes, and so direct attention to them. Hence freq. *fig.*
1906 'O. HENRY' *Four Million* 223 To him one evening in the limelight made up for many dark ones. 1908 *Daily Chron.* 25 Jan. 3/2 The beauty of his person..helped to throw the limelight upon him. 1909 *Ibid.* 11 June 4/4 Many women..are likely to die—unwed...They never got into the limelight. 1909 *Chambers's Jrnl.* Feb. 131/2 They are given a notoriety, a public exhibition in the limelight. 1922 *Blackw. Mag.* Aug. 150/1 He did not..pose in the limelight to the same extent as his respected chief. 1924 GALSWORTHY *Forest* I. i. 15 'You know what we're here for?' 'Limelight on the slave trade, is it?' 1928 *Publishers' Weekly* 9 June 2353 Political portraits of the men who will be in the limelight of the national conventions.

Li·melight, *v.* [f. the sb.] *trans.* To illuminate by lime-light. Usu. *fig.* Also **Li·melighted, -lit** *ppl. a.*; **Li·melighting** *vbl. sb.*
1909 *Daily Chron.* 10 Apr. 4/6 The most limelighted person in Europe this morning is Queen Wilhelmina of Holland. 1909 *Westm. Gaz.* 10 Apr. 2/3 We had sympathised with the beautiful lime-lit heroine. 1917 *Daily Express* 21 Feb. 2/4 Unfeminine modern women go limelighting their way through the world. 1927 *Observer* 10 Apr. 29 This is not an occasion when the interests of motorists can be served by limelighting.

Limerick (li·mərik). [The chief town of the county of Limerick in Ireland.] *attrib.* in *Limerick hook,* a form of fishing-hook with a peculiar bend made originally at Limerick. So *Limerick bend, pattern.*
1828 SIR H. DAVY *Salmonia* 141, I have even made a hook, which..I think, I could boast as equal to the Limerick hooks. 1856 'STONEHENGE' *Brit. Rur. Sports* I. v. ii. 235/1 The round-bend hook is that which is most used in England, the Limerick pattern being chiefly in vogue in Ireland. 1867 F. FRANCIS *Bk. Angling* 410 Hooks are of various forms...We have the Limerick bend, the Carlisle or round bend. 1928 *Chambers's Jrnl.* Jan. 2/2 He..picked out his lure without hesitation—a Number 5, Limerick-bend, double-hooked 'Blue Charm'.

Limestone. c. Add: *limestone cliff* (earlier example), *land* (later example), *pan, rock, sand, soil, water.*
1823 LONG *Exped.* I. 32 It is a perpendicular fissure extending about one hundred and sixty feet into horizontal *limestone cliffs. 1811 *Niles' Weekly Reg.* 12 Oct. 101/1 Our steepest *lime stone lands are very favorable to sheep. 1838 J. HALL *Western States* i. 17 It rests upon a horizontal *limestone pan. 1816 U. BROWN *Jrnl.* in *Maryland Hist. Mag.* X. 270 The Market House built on a *Lime Stone Rock. 1872 EGGLESTON *Hoosier Schoolm.* xi. 95 A brook gurgled among the heaps of bare limestone rocks. 1849 CHAMBERLAIN *Indiana Gazetteer* 159 The soil..is a rich alluvion mixed with a *limestone sand and gravel. *Ibid.* 191 The strip along the river has a *lime-stone soil. 1831 PECK *Guide Emigrants* 233 Those persons who have been unaccustomed to *lime stone water..frequently have eruptions of the skin. 1872 EGGLESTON *End of World* ix. 65 Having..quaffed the hard limestone water.

Liminess (ləi·mĭnės). [f. LIMY *a.*] The quality of being limy.
a 1906 WOODRUFFE-PEACOCK *Thoroughbreds & Grassland* II. 7 *note,* A growing liminess in a clay soil.

Limit, *sb.* Add: **2. g.** In *Poker.* The maximum raise allowed.
1894 WILKINS & VIVIAN *Green bay tree* I. 108 Pimlico had obtained a raise of the limit to £20. 1928 *Chambers's Jrnl.* Feb. 99/2 They lifted the limit on each single rise to five pounds, and proportionately increased the ante to five shillings.

h. The very extreme; the last point or stage; the worst (etc.) imaginable or endurable. *colloq.* Orig. *U.S.* (Apparently a fig. use of *2 g.)
1904 *Montgomery Weekly Advertiser* 26 Aug. 4 We can always depend on Kansas to go the limit in the freak line. *a* 1906 'O. HENRY' *Trimmed Lamp* etc. 211 Whenever this little old town does loosen up and get friendly it goes the limit. 1906 *N. Y. Even. Post* 7 May 1 Desertion is bad enough..but to fire at one's comrades while in the act of turning against them is—well, the limit. 1907 *Westm. Gaz.* 16 Aug. 2/1 They [wages] are low everywhere, perhaps, but at Belfast is what Americans would call 'the limit'. 1913–16 G. B. SHAW *Heartbreak House* I. (1927) 18 Really! your father does seem to be about the limit.

5. limit dog, one shown in a class limited to dogs having certain required qualifications.
1903 *Forest & Stream* 21 Feb. 151 (Cent. Suppl.) Limit dogs was won by St. Elvan. 1909 *Daily Chron.* 11 Feb. 5/6 The first prize for limit dogs over 45 lb.

Limited, *ppl. a.* **2.** Add: *Limited express* or *train* (U.S.): cf. *Limited mail. Limited monarchy* (earlier examples).
1648 SIR R. FILMER (*title*) The Anarchy of a Limited and Mixed Monarchy. 1720 in T. B. HOWELL *State Trials* (1812) XV. 62 The nature of our constitution is that of a limited monarchy. 1777 BURKE *Addr. Brit. Col. Amer.* Wks. 1792 V. 148 England has been great and happy under the present limited Monarchy. 1879 F. R. STOCKTON *Rudder Grange* ix. 93 Time flew like a limited express train. 1890 *Harper's Mag.* Aug. 409/1 Coming up by the limited train, Miss Lee was not favorably impressed. 1904 *Dial* 16 Oct. 238 It is not a book for the limited express.

3. (Later examples.)
1901 S. MERWIN & H. K. WEBSTER *Calumet K* ii. 24, I went out of that building to beat the limited—never thought of the wheelbarrow till I was halfway to the station. 1904 *N. Y. Even. Post* 6 May 2 The Sunset Limited of the Southern Pacific encountered a severe hailstorm.

b. = *limited company* (2 b).
1905 *Westm. Gaz.* 20 Nov. 8/1 Company floaters have gone very fast indeed, some limiteds, it is said, not having sufficient capital. 1907 *Daily Chron.* 26 July 3/4 This is my experience in a West-end house..classed with the Limiteds.

Limousine (limuzī·n). [F., f. *Limousin,* the name of a province of France.] A superior type of motor-car having a closed body and a roof over the driver's seat. Also *attrib.*
1902 A. C. HARMSWORTH *Motors* (Badm. Libr.) 55 With certain kinds of engines, too, it is difficult to adopt any other form of car than the Tonneau, or for the wet weather the Limousine. 1905 *Westm. Gaz.* 22 Nov. 9/2 A touring car..fitted with a brougham or limousine body. 1922 W. J. LOCKE *Tale of Triona* v. 47 Whom she saw drive away in luxurious limousines.

Limpet. b. Add: In recent use esp. of officials alleged to be superfluous but clinging to their offices. Also *attrib.*
1905 *Westm. Gaz.* 9 Mar. 2/2 Lord Spencer..had some pertinent criticisms to make of the Limpet Government. 1922 *Daily Mail* 22 Nov. 8 He is rationing the departments and ejecting the 'limpets'. *Ibid.* 23 Nov. 10 Ministries are multiplying their accumulation of limpets and paying them too well. 1927 CARR-SAUNDERS & JONES *Soc. Struct. Eng. & Wales* 54 After the war, attempts were made to rouse our animosity against 'limpets'.

c. limpet-hammer, a stone tool believed to have been used by prehistoric peoples to knock limpets off rocks.
1885 S. GRIEVE *Gt. Auk* 57 We were puzzling ourselves as to what could be the use of the numerous oblong stones we met with among the [limpet] shells, and..he..informed us they were limpet-hammers. *Ibid.*, Subsequent enquiries have only helped to confirm us in the opinion that the large oblong stones found at Caisteal-nan-Gillean are really limpet-hammers.

Lincoln. 1. Add: **Lincoln red,** the distinctive name of a class of shorthorn cattle.
1923 *Daily Mail* 4 July 10 A Lincoln red shorthorn heifer from Sandringham won a second prize.

Lincrusta (linkrɒ·stă). [f. L. *lin-um* flax + *crusta* rind, bark: after LINOLEUM.] A special type of thick wall-paper.
1882 *Encycl. Brit.* XIV. 676/2 Mr. Walton, the original patentee of linoleum, has adapted a preparation of oxidized oil and cork or other thickening material embossed with patterns for wall decorations under the name of 'Lincrusta Walton'. 1891 *Jrnl. Soc. Chem. Industry* X. 150/2 Improvements in the Manufacture of Linoleum, Lincrusta, Cere-Cloth, and the like. 1921 *Spectator* 9 Apr. 464/1 'Lincrusta' wears so well that it seemed a sin to take it off. 1923 UNA L. SILBERRAD *Lett. Jean Armiter* i. 29 Semi-detached house, lincrusta dadoes, basement kitchen—it would suit him.

Lindworm. Also lindorm. [ad. Da. and Sw. *lindorm.* Cf. *LINGWORM.] A fabulous serpent.
1896 CRAIGIE *Scand. Folk-lore* 439 The lindorm is a favourite monster in Swedish as well as Danish tradition. 1910 F. BOND *Misericords* 63 When a wyvern has no wings, as at Limerick, he is, in heraldry, a lindworm. *Ibid.*, No rigid distinction can be made between the dragon, wyvern, and lindworm.

Line, *sb.*[2] Add:
13. c. *To get a line on,* to acquire information about (a thing), to come to know. So *to give* (one) *a line on. U.S. colloq.*
1903 *N. Y. Sun* 18 Nov. 4 'These dressmakers'..cannot get a line on the styles except at the Horse Show. 1915 *Literary Digest* (N.Y.) 21 Aug. Advt. p. ii, Get the right 'line' on the clothes the best dressed men will wear this fall. 1920 BERNARD CRONIN *Timber Wolves* 138 It ain't over wise to give anyone a line on to what's doing. 1921 R. D. PAINE *Comr. Rolling Ocean* iii. 41 How about these other birds. Give me a line on them. 1927 H. V. MORTON *In Search Eng.* iii. § 6. 53, I don't know a darned thing about England yet,..but I'm getting a line on her, sure enough.

17. b. (Earlier example.) Also ellipt. *the line.*
1779 in *Life & Corr. Joseph Reed* II. (1847) 134 Perhaps we would be as well off with Mason and Dixon's line continued. 1849 F. DOUGLAS *Life* 101 We owe something to the slaver south of the line as well as to those north of it. *a* 1909 'O. HENRY' *Roads of Destiny* xxi. 358 If you had come from below the line, I reckon I would have liked you right smart.

19. *ellipt.* = 'receiving line'. *U.S.*
1903 *N. Y. Tribune* 4 Oct., She has had several years' experience 'behind the line', and will doubtless be of great assistance to Mrs Roosevelt.

22. (Earlier examples.)
1786 *Boston Centinel* 11 Jan. 3/1 A line of stages. 1832 in *Amer. State Papers* (1834) XV. 348 The line of stages connecting Philadelphia and Delaware with the Eastern shore of Maryland and Virginia. 1837 W. JENKINS *Ohio Gaz.* 56 The post office is supplied by daily lines of Coaches from Cincinnati to Dayton.

23. e. (Earlier example.)
1779 E. PARKMAN *Diary* 96 After which I..read Ps. 149, which was sung without reading the lines by the Deacon.

i. The amount which one underwriter (or one company) accepts as his share of the total value of the subject matter covered by insurance.
1931 *Times* 14 Mar. 12/6 Many of those [*sc.* insurance companies] who have written large lines..are known to have been influenced by a desire [etc.].

32. line-camp *U.S.*, a line-rider's tent or cabin; **line-drawn** *a.*, made by line-drawing; **line-engine,** an engine having several cylinders arranged in a straight line; **line-engraver,** one who does line-engraving; **line-fence** *U.S.*, a boundary fence between farms; **line-gale** = *line-storm*; **line-officer** *U.S.*, an officer of the line; **line-rider** *U.S.*, one engaged in line-riding; **line-storm** (earlier example); **line-tub,** a tub in which a whaling line is kept; **line-work,** (also) work as a lineman.
1888 T. ROOSEVELT in *Century Mag.* Mar. 667/2 But some of the men are out in the *line camps, and the ranchman has occasionally to make the round of these. 1903 *Westm. Gaz.* 17 Oct. 4/2 An order of the King in Council was published with two *line-drawn illustrations. 1922 *Encycl. Brit.* XXX. 41/2 A double-acting *line engine with cylinders in tandem. 1879 CLARA E. CLEMENT & HUTTON *Artists 19th Cent.* I. 332 At the age of fourteen he was apprenticed to a *line-engraver. 1874 B. F. TAYLOR *World on Wheels* II. ii. 198 We..propped up the *line fence and shingled the kitchen. 1886 *Harper's Mag.* Dec. 43/1 He jumped his horse over the line fence. 1836 *Knickerbocker Mag.* VII. 17, I must take the oars myself, for that blamed *line gale has kept me in bilboes..a dog's age. 1850 in R. GLISAN *Jrnl. Army Life* (1874) 2 July i. 2 This rank..avails its possessor..in everything except commanding troops when a *line officer is present. 1898 H. S. CANFIELD *Maid of Frontier* 134 The *line riders came in at night, reeking and dusty. 1924 MULFORD *Rustlers' Valley* vii, It was evident that they carefully had planned the murders of the two line riders. 1850 N. KINGSLEY *Diary* 115 A fine day with a strong West wind; rather think the *line storm is over. 1839 *Knickerbocker Mag.* XIII. 382 *Line-tubs, water-kegs, and wafe-poles, were thrown hurriedly into the boats. 1851 MELVILLE *Moby Dick* cxxxiv, Reaching out after the revolving line-tubs, oars, and other floating furniture. 1911 H. QUICK *Yellowstone N.* ii. 32 I'm just through with a summer's *line-work in the West.

Line, *v.*[2] Add: **3. b.** *intr.* To guide or control a boat or canoe from the bank of a river by means of a rope. *U.S.*
1923 L. R. FREEMAN *Colorado R.* 356 The low stage..gave them room to work below instead of lining from a ledge, eighty feet above the water.

8. a. To aim in a direct line *upon* an object.
1884 KNIGHT *Dict. Mech.* Suppl., *Peep Sight,* a form of hind sight for rifles. It has an opening through which the muzzle sight is lined upon the object.

Lineal. B. *sb.* **2.** (Modern example.)
1909 *Hansard's Parl. Deb.* 29 Apr. 515 In the cases of spouses and lineals..I propose to exempt from the new..duties all legacies.

Lineally, *adv.* **3. c.** (Add example.)
1780 E. PARKMAN *Diary* 243 The Congregation sung without reading lineally.

Lined, *ppl. a.*[2] Add: **4.** Brought into line with each other.
1891 *Fur, Fin & Feather* Mar. 190 If he starts ahead..without traveling by lined objects, he will never find his way out.

Lineari·stic (linĭari·stik), *a.* [f. LINEAR *a.* + -ISTIC.] Pertaining to or characterized by a linear quality; of a linearized character.
1908 A. J. EVANS in Marett *Anthropol. & Classics* 41 Many of these signs are linearistic degenerations of animal figures.

Linelet (ləi·nlĕt). [f. LINE *sb.* + -LET.] A faint or indistinct line in a spectrum (revealed only when high dispersion is used).
1889 *Nature* 14 Feb. 370/2 The peculiar arrangement of the leading lines (usually two) and train of linelets in each of the five bands of the CH spectrum is..described in the text.

Linen, *sb.* **4. a.** Add: *linen-closet, -duster, -room.*
1885 W. H. WHITE *M. Rutherford's Deliv.* iii, She cared nothing for the *linen-closet, the spotless bed-hangings,..the true household gods of the respectable women of those days. 1886 C. D. WARNER *Their Pilgr.* xv. (1888) 327 The passengers..appeared to take the matter seriously—a sort of *linen-duster congregation. 1900 ELINOR GLYN *Visits Eliz.* (1906) 13 Aunt Maria..said it was her day for seeing the *linen-room.

5. linen press, a cupboard for linen; **linen-wheel** (later examples).
1852 MRS. STOWE *Uncle Tom's C.* xviii, The store-room, the *linen-presses, the china-closet,..all went under an awful review. 1682 *Connecticut Probate Rec.* I. 357 She shall have..a *linen wheele. 1723 in *Narrag. Hist. Reg.* V. 156, 1 Linen Wheel.

Line-of-battle, used attrib. with *ship*: see *BATTLESHIP.

Line-out. [f. *line out* LINE *v.*[2] 8 b.] In Rugby football: (See quot. 1900.)
1900 *Young Sportsman* (ed. A. E. T. Watson) 284 *Line out,*..the arrangement of forwards opposite to one another when the ball is about to be thrown in from touch. 1931 *Times* 16 Feb. 5/2 Barrington made a clever mark from a knock-on in a line-out, but failed with the kick at goal.

Line-up. [f. LINE *v.* 8 a.] An instance of bringing into line; the assembling of a number of persons in a line or file. Also *fig.*
1889 *Kansas Times & Star* 11 Mar., The line-up of the Kansas City ball club this season. 1904 *Springfield Weekly Republ.* 3 June 1 Thus we have a line-up of corporations against the people. 1911 H. S. HARRISON *Queed* xviii. 224 He studied his trustee list now more purposefully than he had ever pored over his faculty line up. 1928 A. G. HAYS *Let Freedom Ring* 289 The prisoners were brought before witnesses—not in a line-up with others of the same general type but separately.

Linger, *sb.* Add: **2.** *U.S.* (See quot.)
1895 *Nation* (N.Y.) 9 May 358/3 The enervating influence of the climate, giving rise to that which in the southwestern United States is called the 'Texas lingers'.

Linger, *v.* Add: **7. c.** *Hort.* To delay the blooming of (flowers) by artificial means.
1906 *Daily Chron.* 12 Sept. 4/4 If you force, you exhaust the [rose-]tree; it languishes. I prefer to 'linger' it.

Lingerie. Add: **b.** *attrib.*
1905 *Daily Chron.* 13 Mar. 8/1 The lingerie blouse made a most emphatic appearance in Paris..this winter. 1909 *Westm. Gaz.* 22 Feb. 5/2 As to the lingerie gown, its importance in the wardrobe cannot be questioned.

Lingering, *vbl. sb.* Add: **c.** *Hort.* Retarding the time of blooming by artificial means.
1907 *Daily Chron.* 13 Feb. 6/4 Lingering is retardation without frost; it keeps September roses blooming until January.

Linguacious, *a.* **1.** (Later U.S. example.)
1827 J. F. COOPER *Prairie* xi, On the summit, Obed fully expected to encounter Esther, of whose linguacious powers he had too often been furnished with sinister proofs.

Lingually, *adv.* Add: **b.** On the lingual side.
1910 *Practitioner* Jan. 115 Internally (lingually), the neck of the tooth..is embraced by a thin shallow flap of gum.

Lingworm. [ad. ON. *lyngormr* 'heather-worm'. Cf. *LINDWORM.] A fabulous serpent.
1870 MAGNUSSON & MORRIS *Völsunga Saga* xiii, The fashion and the growth of him is even as of other lingworms.

Linin[2]. *Biol.* [f. L. *linum,* Gr. λίν-ον flax (in sense of a fishing-net) + -IN[1].] The substance composing the network which permeates the protoplasmic contents of an animal or vegetable cell.
1893 *Trans. R. Irish Academy* (1895) XXX. 665 The nucleo-hyalo-plasma, which, for brevity, we may call by Schwartz's term adopted by Strasburger, *linin.* 1910 *Encycl. Brit.* VII. 716/2 The chromatin, becoming metabolically active, flows out on to the linin reticulum. 1923 F. O. BOWER *Bot. Living Plant* 531 The resting nucleus of a vegetative cell has a reticulate structure. The network is recognised chiefly by the punctuated appearance of the anastomozing threads. These threads consist of a substance called *linin,* which bears minute granules of *chromatin.*

Link, *sb.*[1] **c.** Add to def.: In modern usage sometimes treated as a singular.
1861 H. B. FARNIE *Fife Coast* 115 The links lying at the house door, is a very famous one in the annals of golf. 1884 *Boy's Own Paper* 26 Jan., Golf requires..a 'links', or 'common'. 1892 *Engl. Illustr. Mag.* Oct. 55/2 Westward Ho! there is a very fine links. 1904 *Daily Chron.* 20 Aug. 9/5 On a suburban links. 1920 WODEHOUSE *Damsel in Distress* x. 122 His first act..had been to ascertain whether there was a links in the neighbourhood.

Link, *sb.*[2] **1.** Add: *To let out the links,* to act with greater freedom.
1868 H. WOODRUFF *Trotting Horse* xxxiv. 282 Lancet..in the third heat, let out the links in such a manner that he trotted it in 2 m. 25½ s.

2. c. (Later example.)
1869 *Overland Monthly* III. 130 It consists of swine's flesh, bread, sage, and other matters..chopped fine, and then squirted out into links from the end of a sausage-gun.

Link, *v.*[1] Add: **3.** *To link up,* to connect, combine, etc.
trans. 1897 *Geog. Jrnl.* IX. 364 The mouth of the valley..which I visited for the purpose of linking up the rough survey Garwood and I made. 1915 H. G. WELLS *Boon* (1920) 164 Here is the sort of thing that I invite the intelligent reader to link up if he can with the very natural phenomenon of [etc.]. 1930 *Times* 15 Mar. 19/4 Our company has always been linked up with the trade to..South America.
intr. 1915 H. G. WELLS *Boon* (1920) 109 Every one with ideas..had to refer to that doctrinal core, had to link up to it. 1925 A. S. M. HUTCHINSON *One Increasing Purpose* I. xxiv. 147 Did I tell you that or has its connection with what you said only linked up in me since we parted?

Linkage. Add: Also *attrib.*
1904 *Brit. & Col. Printer* 10 Mar. 14/2 A linkage system transmits the movement to the slide bars.

Linkedness (li·ŋktnės). [f. LINKED *ppl. a.*] Interconnexion.
1908 E. V. LUCAS *Over Bemerton's* xiv, (heading) The Linkedness of Life is illustrated.

Linking, *vbl. sb.* Add: Also *linking-up.*
1908 *Westm. Gaz.* 19 Nov. 10/4 The process provided for by the [Electricity Supply] bill is known as 'linking-up'. 1909 *Daily Chron.* 19 Feb. 6/5 The increase in the traffic was..the natural result of the linking-up policy adopted.

Linn[2]. (Later U.S. example. Cf. *LYNN.)
1884 C. S. SARGENT *Rep. Forests N. Amer.* 514 A good deal of black cherry, lin, and locust.

Lino[2] (ləi·no), abbrev. of LINOLEUM.
1920 *Glasgow Herald* 10 Apr. 4 The Earl caught the gloves, but the hat fell on the lino. 1926 *Spectator* 7 Aug. 206/1 You dash off to heave linos about for an elderly lady who doesn't know *just* what she wants...To move a piece of lino five yards would make anyone pant.

Lino[3] (ləi·no), abbrev. of LINOTYPE.
1907 *Daily Chron.* 3 Dec. 4/4 He gave me a sketch of his paper. It was set up by 'linos'.

Linocut (ləi·nokɒt). [f. LINO(LEUM) + CUT *sb.*[2]] A design cut in relief on a block of linoleum; a print obtained from this.
1923 *Golden Hind* II. No. 5. Contents, Hadyn Mackey: Linocut, p. 26. 1923 *Times Lit. Suppl.* 22 Nov., A good deal of lively and interesting work in pen-drawing, woodcut, lithograph, linocut. 1928 *Publishers' Weekly* 16 June 2456 The jewel merchants in lino-cuts.

Linography (ləinɒ·grăfi). [f. L. *lin-um,* flax (see LINE *sb.*[1]) + -GRAPHY.] (See quot.)
1888 *Jrnl. Soc. Chem. Industry* VII. 568/1 Linography. This is a name given to photographing on linen or calico, to serve as a basis for painting in oil.

Linotype. Add: *attrib.* as *linotype operator.*
1903 *Stationer, Printer* etc. 1 Aug. 364/2 At present linotype operators work on piece, that is to say, they are paid according to the work they do. 1908 J. S. THOMPSON *Mechanism of Linotype* (ed. 3) Advt., All Linotype Operators and Machinists are invited to call.

Li·notyped, *ppl. a.* [f. LINOTYPE *sb.*] Set up by linotype.
1908 *Westm. Gaz.* 21 Apr., The linotyped calumny of millionaire journalism.

Li·notyper. [f. as prec.] = LINOTYPIST.
1896 *Peterson Mag.* VI. 305/1 Stenographers, typewriters, compositors, and linotypers. 1911 H. S. HARRISON *Queed* vii. 83 The little knot of linotypers and helpers..now listened.

Li·notyping, *vbl. sb.* [f. as prec.] The process of composing by linotype.
1902 *U.S. Census Bulletin* No 242. 73 A new departure in the art of linotyping.

Lint[1]. Add: **3. b.** Raw cotton fibre.
a 1887 in J. C. Harris *Life H. W. Grady* (1890) 107 If New England could grow the cotton plant, without lint, it would make her richest crop; if she held monopoly of cotton lint and seed she would control the commerce of the world.

Linter[1]. Add: **b.** *pl.* The short-staple fibre separated from cotton-seed by the linter.
1904 L. L. LAMBORN *Cottonseed Products* 50 The purpose of delinting is to remove more completely the short fibres which form the 'linters'...The products of delinting are the linters. 1907 *Times Financial Suppl.* 11 Feb. 61/3 'Linters' are largely used in the manufacture of mattresses, batting, carpets, cheap yarns, rope and twine, and in upholstery. 1922 *Daily Mail* 17 Nov. 4 New York Cotton...a total yield, exclusive of linters, of 9,773,000 bales.

Lintling, var. of LINTELLING *vbl. sb.*
1833 LOUDON *Encycl. Archit.* § 1067 The cart-sheds to have a joist..built into the wall at each pillar, and chacked to the lintling beams.

Lion. 11. Add: **lion-head,** a species of goldfish; **lion-hunter** (earlier example); **lion-huntress,** a female 'lion-hunter'; **lion marmoset** = *lion-monkey.*
1928 *Daily Express* 5 July 8 Fancy goldfish can be very expensive...I paid £30 each for a *lionhead and an oranda recently. 1829 R. C. SANDS *Writ.* II. 109 And during the interval..two *lion-hunters..came into the box and introduced themselves. 1850 THACKERAY in *Punch* 24 Aug. 89 The *Lion-Huntress of Belgravia. Being Lady Nimrod's Journal of the Past Season. 1904 DOWDEN *Browning* 93 Miss Mitford, Mrs. Jameson, or some unknown lion-huntress who had thrown her toils. 1906 *Westm. Gaz.* 19 Feb. 12/2 Here may be seen the beautiful *lion marmoset from Brazil.

Lip, *sb.* **6. a.** (*b*) Add: In recent use freq. in terms of phonetics, as *lip-articulation, -opening, rounding.*
1910 *Mod. Lang. Rev.* V. 91 Lip-articulation in connection with tongue-articulation. *Ibid.* 93 The lip-rounding is less energetic; the lip-aperture is wider...The lip-opening is reduced to a narrow central aperture.

c. *Phonetics.* Of sounds: Formed or produced by the lips.
1867 A. M. BELL *Visible Sp.* 61 The 'shut' consonants are sufficiently distinguished..by the four radical varieties 'Back', 'Front', 'Point', 'Lip'. 1877 SWEET *Handbk. Phonetics* 32 Lip. S.G. *w* in '*we*', '*wo*' is an example of a pure lip consonant. N.G. *w* = (v) is a 'lip-teeth' consonant.

Lipase (li·pēɪz). *Chem.* [f. Gr. λίπ-ος fat + *-ASE.] A ferment which brings about the decomposition of fats and oils.
1897 *Year-Bk. Pharm.* 77 The author [E. Gerard] attributes the hydrolysing action to the presence of Hanriot's lipase or an analogous ferment. 1901 *Science* 17 May 767 (Cent. Suppl.) A large number of them [enzymes], such as diastase, lipase, trypsin, etc., etc., have been found in both the vegetable and the animal organism. 1906 *Practitioner* Nov. 584 The real work of fat digestion being, of course, close [? *read* done] by the lipase of the pancreas.

Lipochrome (li·pokroum). [f. Gr. λίπ-ος fat + CHROME.] Any one of a large group of pigments (yellows and reds) widely distributed in the vegetable and animal kingdoms, usually associated with fat. Also *attrib.*
1887 SOLLAS in *Encycl. Brit.* XXII. 420/1 A red pigment of the lipochrome series. 1888 ROLLESTON & JACKSON *Anim. Life* 180 The [blood] plasma contains haemocyanin and a red lutein, or lipochrome. 1924 J. A. THOMSON *Science Old & New* xxxvii. 211 In some trout..the flesh has a pinkish colour, which is due to oily globules tinged with a ruddy fat-pigment or lipochrome.

Lipoid, *a.* Add: Also as *sb.*, any one of a class of organically produced fatty bodies.
1913 *Jrnl. Chem. Soc.* CIV. I. 308 Can Lipoids Act as Antigens?

Lipper, *v.*[3] Hence **Li·ppering** *vbl. sb.*
1904 *Sci. Amer.* Suppl. 5 Mar. 23552 (Cent. Suppl.) Both the deck lipperings and blubber-room lipperings are usually deposited in barrels or tubs.

Lippy, *a.* Add: **2.** *slang.* Impertinent.
1893 W. K. POST *Harvard Stories* 195 Ain't he getting pretty flip? The lippy dude! 1906 *Punch* 4 Apr. 250/3 'Aughty as teetotallers an' as lippy as Passive Resisters.

Lip-read, *v.* [f. *lip-reading* LIP *sb.* 7.] *intr.* To apprehend speech by observing the movements of the lips. Also **Lip-reader.**
1912 *Strand Mag.* Mar. 243 The Experiences of a Lip-reader. 1927 *Daily Express* 12 Dec. 10/7 Only a small proportion of them [the deaf] are expert lip-readers; they seem to think it wonderful when some one else can lip-read fluently and they cannot.

Lipstick (li·pˌstik). Also **lip-stick.** [f. LIP *sb.* + STICK *sb.*[1]] A stick of cosmetic for colouring the lips.
1919 H. L. WILSON *Ma Pettengill* iii. 93 Metta was even using a lip stick! 1924 *Glasgow Herald* 7 July 8/7 Here is a lipstick; there a downy nest Of lamb's wool puffs. 1926 *Spectator* 18 Sept. 435/2 What is the matter with powder, paint and lipstick?

b. A shade of red.
1927 *Daily Express* 14 Mar. 5/3 Lipstick—Pillar-box red renamed.
Hence **Li·pstick** *v.*; **Li·psticked** *a.*
1926 *Ladies' Home Jrnl.* Apr. 24 She..had recently lipsticked a red mouth into startling contrast to her natural pallor. 1928 *Sunday Express* 15 Apr. 15/4 She may be made of wax, with large, liquid eyes, a lipsticked mouth, and real hair.

Liquesce, *v.* Add: Also *fig.*, to merge *into.*
1920 *19th Cent.* Dec. 977 The perpetual tendency of privilege, royal as well as any other, to liquesce into the common stream of humanity.

Liqueur, *v.* Add: **2.** *intr.* with *up.* To partake of a liqueur.
1894 DU MAURIER *Trilby* v. (1895) 237 So our three friends finished their coffee and liqueured up.

Liquid, *a.* **1.** Add: *Liquid fire*: a burning composition made from oils, used in warfare; also *fig.*, alcoholic liquor.
1836 D. B. EDWARD *Hist. Texas* 81 Men are made pale by the dying struggles of liquid fire. 1871 *Eng. Mech.* 21 July 433/1 In 1869, the late J. Nicklès..discovered a composition for a liquid fire. 1915 *Illustr. London News* 13 Mar. 321 The enemy attacking a trench into which they had sent liquid fire. 1916 *War Illustr.* 19 Aug. V. 14/2 The Territorials went through a rain of liquid-fire shells mixed with gas shells.

Liquidation. Add: **4.** The action or fact of partaking of liquor.
1889 GRETTON *Memory's Harkback* 311 As regards *liquidation,* champagne..is now almost as *vin ordinaire.* *a* 1909 'O. HENRY' *Roads of Destiny* vii. 106 His desire for liquidation was expressed so heartily that I went with him to a café..where we had some vile vermouth and bitters.

Liquor, *sb.* **7.** Add: *liquor house, law, licence, -selling, trade.*
Also fuller illustration of *liquor-seller, shop,* etc.
1924 W. M. RAINE *Troubled Waters* ii. 21 The postmistress handed him a letter and two circulars from *liquor houses. 1908 *Daily Chron.* 27 Feb. 4/4 Certain *liquor-law restrictions which had existed under the second Empire. 1889 *Kansas Times & Star* 12 July, For 1889 United States *liquor licenses were issued in prohibition Kansas to 155 persons. 1855 BARNUM *Life* 359 The *liquor seller, the moderate drinker, and the indifferent man. 1877 *Harper's Mag.* Dec. 146/2 A method which practically makes the government the liquor-seller. *Ibid.*, All *liquor-selling is not equally dangerous to the community. 1855 M. M. THOMPSON *Doesticks* xxxi. 276 The great excitement was on the liquor question; it was Noggs and no *liquor shops, or Boggs and a few liquor shops. 1877 HABBERTON *Jericho Road* xix. 167 There was not even a streak of light visible under the door of any liquor-shop in the town. 1855 M. M. THOMPSON *Doesticks* xii. 98 Fire in a *liquor-store—hose burst; brandy 'lying round loose'. 1887 *Nation* 15 Dec. 468/3 To keep a liquor-store in Philadelphia. 1908 *Daily Chron.* 12 May 4/4 Unfortunately for the Labour party they have got entangled with the *liquor trade vote. 1848 J. MARSH (*title*) A discourse on the extent and evils of the Sunday *liquor traffic in cities. 1877 *Harper's Mag.* Dec. 146/2 This work is a compilation of evidence on 'the problem of law as applied to the liquor traffic'.

Li·quordom. (Additional example.)
1918 T. H. WALKER *Principal J. Denney* 119 His hatred of liquordom..sprang from devotion to his Master.

Li·quorize, *v. U.S. colloq.* [f. LIQUOR *sb.*] = LIQUOR *v.* 6.
1839 J. K. TOWNSEND *Narrative* i. 130 Refusing the landlord's polite invitation to 'liquorize', we marched from the house.

Lirate (ləi·rēt), *a.* [f. mod.L. *lira* a groove or furrow in a shell, L. *lira* ridge, furrow.] Of a shell: Grooved, furrowed.
1901 *Proc. Zool. Soc.* II. 357 *Actis calotropis*...A very delicate species, virtuous, delicately spirally lirate.

Liration (ləirēi·ʃən). [f. as prec.] The furrowing, or set of furrows, on a shell.
1904 *Annals & Mag. Nat. Hist.* June 459 Three specimens from off Travancore differ..also in having a spiral liration in the concavity of the whorls near the dentate keel. This liration bears small tubercles connected by short cross-ridges with the dentations of the keel.

List, *sb.*[3] Add: **3.** (Later U.S. example.)
1855 BARNUM *Life* vi. 109 Mallet had agreed..to deliver twelve yards of broadcloth 'lists' to Shepard.

4. c. *U.S.* In agriculture: A strip of ground. (Cf. quot. 1686 in 4.)
1768 WASHINGTON *Diaries* I. 267 Began to cross ground at Muddy hole..having run only a single furrow for a list. 1786 *Ibid.* III. 57 Began at the first to cross the lists in order to plant corn. 1814 J. TAYLOR *Arator* 104 A deep and wide furrow is to be run by a large plough..so as to throw the earth..into this old deep furrow, and to form precisely in it, a neat ridge or list on which to plant the corn. 1833 B. SILLIMAN *Man. Sugar Cane* 20 The cotton beds are shaved down into the alleys, covering the trash, &c. and forming a wide list.

List, *v.*[3] **4.** (Earlier example.)
1770 WASHINGTON *Diaries* I. 374 Finished listing Ground for Corn at Muddy Hole.

Listed, *ppl. a.*[1] (Later example.)
1757 *Essex Inst. Hist. Coll.* XLIV. 341 One of the listed Soldiers in the present Expedition.

2. Included in a list or catalogue.
1907 *Installation News* Jan. 11/1 Conduits have now to be manufactured to exact listed diameters.

b. *Listed securities* (see quot.).
1929 *Encycl. Brit.* XIV. 201/2 *Listed Securities,* securities which have been examined, approved and listed, or admitted for trading, on one of the stock exchanges.

Listed, *ppl. a.*[2] (Earlier example.)
1786 WASHINGTON *Diaries* III. 58 The People had begun to break up the Intervals..between the listed ground.

Listen, *sb.* **2.** (Earlier example.)
1788 'ASPASIA' in *Amer. Museum* IV. 565 Every time the door opens, or a foot is on the stairs, you are on the listen.

Listen, *v.* Add: **2. e.** *To listen in*: to listen to signals, messages, etc., that are telegraphed or telephoned; (in recent use chiefly) to listen to words, music, etc., broadcast by wireless; to use a wireless receiving-set. Also *transf.*
1904 *Elect. World & Engin.* 7 May 875 (Cent. Suppl.) The removal of the operator's plug end of line, or her 'listening in', restores the circuits to their proper condition for subsequent use. 1915 A. F. COLLINS *Bk. Wireless* vii, A boy sitting..at home with..a telephone receiver to his ear listening-in to the news of the world. 1922 *Westm. Gaz.* 25 Oct., In a fortnight or so a million subscribers at 10s. each a year will be 'listening in'. 1928 *Chambers's Jrnl.* Jan. 27/2 None of us could help 'listening in' to the fun that was going on in the kitchen.

4. *intr.* To sound (in a certain way). Freq. with *to* = to strike (one) as. *U.S. colloq.*
1912 MATHEWSON *Pitching* vii. 143 All is fair in love, war, and baseball except stealing signals dishonestly, which listens like another paradox. 1921 R. D. PAINE *Comr. Rolling Ocean* xiv. 250 Here's where I slip it out..to help square the repair bill for my joy-ride. How does it listen to you? 1928 L. J. VANCE *Baroque* xxvii. 174 [It] don't listen reasonable to me.

Listener. Add: **3.** *Listener(-in),* one who listens in (see *LISTEN *v.* 2 e).
1922 *Daily Mail* 21 Nov. 7 The limited service has already established itself in high favour with 'listeners-in'. 1923 *Radio Times* 28 Sept. 12/1 It seems to me that the B.B.C. are mainly catering for the 'listeners' who own expensive sets. 1928 *Collier's* 29 Dec. 45/3 This past season over 68,000 listeners-in wrote us about Collier's Radio Hour—largely in the same vein.

Listening, *vbl. sb.* **b.** Add: **listening-post** (see quot. 1918).
1916 *War Illustr.* V. 69/1 At a listening-post. 1918 FARROW *Dict. Milit. Terms, Listening Posts,* sheltered positions in advance of a defensive line for the purpose of early detection of the enemy's movements. 1928 E. BLUNDEN *Undertones War* xv. 167 The men lying at each listening-post were freezing stiff.

2. *Listening-in* (see *LISTEN *v.* 2 e).
1921 *Wireless World* 10 Dec. 581/1 'Listening in' was indulged in. 1922 *Daily Mail* 23 Nov. 5 Listening-in to U.S.

1927 *Saturday Even. Post* 24 Dec. 80/2 These telephones were connected with a listening-in device concealed behind a picture on the wall.

Lister[2]. **2.** (Earlier examples.)
1682 *Derby Rec.* 8 Dec. 130 The Town have chosen..John Hubbel and Abel Gun listers and rate makers. 1703 *Connect. Col. Rec.* 4. 439 When..any inhabitant..shall refuse..to give in to the listers an account of his..rateable estate.

Listerize, *v.* (Earlier example.)
1888 *19th Cent.* June 846 In this way the patients are 'Listerized', to use a hospital term.

Listing, *ppl. a.*[2] [f. LIST *v.*[5] + -ING[2].] Of a ship: Heeling, inclining to one side.
1923 *Publ. Opinion* 30 Mar. 312/3 Six projectiles struck the listing Iowa.

Lit, *ppl. a.* Add: **b.** *slang.* Slightly drunk.
1922 *Daily Mail* 16 Dec. 10, I am afraid I was rather tight—certainly lit up. 1929 S. ANDERSON in *Mercury Story Bk.* 232 Burt got a little lit up.

Literal, *a.* Add: **7.** *Comb.* **literal-minded** *a.*, having a literal mind; characteristic of one who takes a matter-of-fact or unimaginative view of things. Hence *literal-mindedness.*
1869 *Wesleyan-Methodist Mag.* Jan. 28 An old friend, whom we used to call 'Bacon', because he..was a literal-minded man. 1905 J. L. LOWES in *Publ. Mod. Lang. Assoc. Amer.* XX. 816 A strangely literal-minded, not to say naive, interpretation of the charming fiction of the Prologue. 1927 *Glasgow Herald* 31 Oct. 10 The gentleman married the lady on the strength of her literal-mindedness.

Literary, *a.* Add: **4. b.** *sb.* A literary person.
1923 UNA L. SILBERRAD *Lett. Jean Armiter* vi. § 3. 145 Obstacles..may be a blessing in disguise to half-baked literaries.

Literate. B. *sb.* Add: **4.** (*Lady*) *Literate in Arts,* the title conferred on the holder of a higher certificate for women issued by St. Andrews University. Abbreviated *L.L.A.* (see *L III. 7).
1881 *St. Andrews Univ. Cal.* 203 Any Candidate who passes in four subjects, [etc.]..will receive the title of Literate in Arts (L.L.A.). 1883 E. WOOTON *Guide Degrees* 267 A University certificate conferring..the title of 'Literate in Arts'. 1891 R. F. MURRAY *Scarlet Gown* 122 An L.L.A. is a Lady Literate in Arts. 1901 *Daily Record* 30 July 3 Lady Literates in Arts.

Literation. (Example.)
1918 T. HARDY in T. H. Ward *Engl. Poets* V. 174 His aim in the exact literation of Dorset words is not necessarily to exhibit humour and grotesqueness.

b. The method or style of making letters.
1926 *Times Lit. Suppl.* 10 June 390/2 To sacrifice..the exquisite literation that in the old hands delights us like a poem.

Literatize, *v.* Add: **b.** To invest with literary qualities; to convert into literature.
1910 *N.Y. Even. Post* 15 Jan. 6 That desire to 'literatise' life to which a person of reading and cultivated mental habit is prone.

Lithification. (Earlier example.)
1872 *Amer. Jrnl. Sci.* Dec. 468 Even the former moderate temperature..would be sufficient to produce incipient change—at least lithification, if not metamorphism. In fact, lithification of sediments will probably take place under heavy pressure even at ordinary temperature.

Lithistid, *sb.* (Example.)
1885 J. E. TAYLOR *Brit. Fossils* i. 26 Sections of it show it to belong to the *lithistids.*

Lithograph, *sb.* **1.** (Earlier example of *lithograph city.*)
1839 C. F. BRIGGS *Harry Franco* I. xiii. 90 Augustus had travelled in foreign parts, for he had drummed in Arkansas, and collected in the lithograph cities of the west.

Lithographic, *a.* Add: **1. c.** *Lithographic city, town* = prec.
1837 W. JENKINS *Ohio Gaz.* 147 We believe it never existed except on paper; and that the forest retains undisputed possession of a lithographic city. 1846 J. G. SAXE *Progress* (1847) 11 You deem he puffs some lithographic town In western wilds.

Li·thopone. [LITHO-.] A dry white pigment or paint (see quots.).
1901 G. H. HURST *Dict. Chemicals* 226 *Lithopone,* the name given to a white pigment, consisting of a mixture of zinc sulphide, zinc oxide, and barium sulphate. 1902 *Board of Trade Jrnl.* 6 Feb. 258 The white paint known as 'lithopone', consisting of sulphate of baryta and sulphuretted zinc. 1909 *Westm. Gaz.* 16 Aug. 10/2 The manufacture and sale of..'Lithopone', a product which advantageously takes the place of white lead and white of zinc. 1920 *Contemp. Rev.* Jan. 20 Lithopone..is needed for linoleum. It is needed for white paint.

Lithosis (lipō·sis). *Med.* [ad. Gr. λίθωσις petrifying.] A diseased condition of the lungs caused by small particles of stone; stone-mason's or grinder's disease.
1902 *Encycl. Brit.* XXXI. 513 Lithosis or Stone-mason's Disease.

Litter, *v.* **6. a.** Add: (also with) *over.*
1888 MRS. H. WARD *R. Elsmere* I. iv. I. 90 The house was littered over with stanzas from the opening canto of a great poem on Columbus. 1889 DOYLE *Sign of Four* iii. (1893) 84 The table was littered over with Bunsen burners, test-tubes, and retorts.

Little, *a.* **13.** Add:
Little American (cf. *Little Englander*), **Americanism**; **Little Entente** (see ENTENTE); **little hours,** also, the 'small' hours of the morning; **Little Irelander** (cf. *Little Englander*); **Little Mary,** *colloq.* the stomach; **little people** (see also quot.); **little season,** a fashionable season in London in the early part of the year.
1904 *Philad. Press* 11 Aug. 6 Judge Parker's whole contention is that of the *little American...His little Americanism invites fuller discussion. 1829–32 J. P. KENNEDY *Swallow B.* II. vi. 105 Waiting..in order that they might have the coolness of the '*little hours' for their journey. 1927 *Sunday Times* 13 Feb. 5/1 This may not be pleasing to certain *little Irelanders who wish us to live in complete isolation. 1903 *Punch* 14 Oct. 258/1 And what is the subject of the piece [Barrie's *Little Mary*]? Who is *Little Mary? It is nobody: it is simply a nursery name that the child-doctor invents as a kind of polite equivalent to what children ordinarily allude to as their 'tum-tum'. *Ibid.*, Good-natured British audiences have strong Little Maries. 1905 *Daily Chron.* 8 Nov. 6/5 To wear it over their chest, not to speak of Little Mary, as people all now call their other danger spot. 1923 UNA L. SILBERRAD *Lett. Jean Armiter* iv. 82 Then I get a cold in Little Mary, my vulnerable spot. 1888 'C. E. CRADDOCK' *Broomsedge Cove* ii. 25 Those dim traditional pygmy dwellers in Tennessee,..still vaguely known in rural regions as the '*little people'. 1928 *Daily Tel.* 3 Jan. 1/5 Lady Chamberlain's Tuesday afternoon At Homes at the Foreign Office..were one of the features of the '*little season'.

Little-neck. *U.S.* [A locality in Long Island.] *Little-neck* (*clam*), a young or immature quahaug.
1889 *Century Dict.* 1889 J. HATTON in *People* 17 Dec. 2 (Cass. Suppl.) Regret was expressed that New York did not possess the English sole..but there was good compensation in the little-neck clam and the bass.

Liturgism (li·tɒdʒiz'm). [f. LITURGY + -ISM.] Excessive use of the liturgy.
1926 *Quarterly Register* Feb. 117 With this prevailing liturgism, religion ceased to be an important force in common life.

Live, *a.* Add: **2. b.** *U.S.* (Earlier examples.)
1857 *Knickerbocker Mag.* L. 456 A neighbouring bath-house, kept by a live Yankee of the name of Martin. 1861 *Trans. Ill. Agric. Soc.* IV. 263 Our County Society..numbers among its members most of the '*live farmers*' in the county. 1870 *Scribner's Monthly* I. 71 Quite as likely..the 'advanced' preacher selects a 'live' subject, a theme for the times. 1875 MRS. STOWE *Deacon Pitkin's Farm* ii. 45 She's a little crittur; nothin' to look to, but every bit in her is 'live.

c. Corresponding to actual facts.
1927 CARR-SAUNDERS & JONES *Soc. Struct. Eng. & Wales* 152 The Unemployment figures were obtained by taking an average of the 'live registers' of the employment exchanges in Great Britain.

8. live ash *U.S.*, a variety of the American ash; **live fence** *U.S.*, a hedge; also *live-fencing*; **live weight,** the weight of an animal before being killed; **live wire** (see sense 4), *fig.* a person full of energy. Orig. *U.S.*
1857 *Trans. Mich. Agric. Soc.* VIII. 729 The east half of the county is also heavily timbered, but the sugar-maple..bass wood or *live ash predominate. 1804 J. ROBERTS *Penn. Farmer* 84 When the hedge is full grown, then there is a perfect *live fence. 1814 J. TAYLOR *Arator* 199 Several plants are mentioned in these memoirs as proper for making live fences, but I shall confine my observations to one. 1858 J. A. WARDER *Hedges & Evergr.* I. i. 13 Live-fences, or—as they are commonly called—Hedges, are a means of enclosure that belongs to an advanced state of civilization. 1829 *Massachusetts Spy* 25 Mar. (Th.) Messrs. G. Th. and Son have imported 75,000 hawthorns, for '*live fencing'. 1852 *Trans. Mich. Agric. Soc.* III. 151 Two hundred lambs..weighing some one hundred pounds..*live weight. 1910 W. M. RAINE *B. O'Connor* 35 By this time that *live wire would have finished telephoning all over Southern Arizona. 1915 H. L. WILSON *Ruggles of Red Gap* xii. (1917) 210 Cousin Egbert..remarked that I was 'sure a live wire'. 1922 *Daily Mail* 20 Nov. 10 Sir Arnold [Wilson] is known as a 'live wire'.

c. In attrib. combs.
1903 *Westm. Gaz.* 19 June 5/1 The suspension of the live-cattle trade between Boston and Liverpool. 1905 *Ibid.* 12 Apr. 5/2 So far the Central London Railway has carried 200,000,000 passengers..without a live-rail mishap. 1905 H. J. SPOONER *Motors & Motoring* 67 The other kind of transmission gear referred to is the Live-Axle or Cardan Drive. 1907 *Westm. Gaz.* 9 Nov. 15/2 Two new models both of which..are of the live-axle type.

Live, *v.*[1] **5. b.** Add: Also *to live it* (in a running match).
1908 *Daily Chron.* 14 July 8/1 The Italian, however, could not live it with the gallant finish of the Briton.

12. c. *Where one lives,* at or to the right or vital point. *U.S. slang.*
1860 HOLLAND *Miss Gilbert's Career* xxii. 386 When that little wife of mine says, 'Tom you're a good fellow, God bless you', it goes right in where I live. 1883 J. H. BEADLE *Western Wilds* xxxvii. 602 The Mormons never got a cent of it. This hurt Brigham—right where he lived. 1886 *Century Mag.* Feb. 511/1 If I could only have reached him where he lives, as our slang says.

d. To escape being put out.
1912 MATHEWSON *Pitching* xii. 263 He would probably have scored the run which would have won the game had he lived either on second or third base, for a hit followed.

Liven, *v.* Add: **c.** To render live or active.
1903 *Daily Chron.* 6 Mar. 6/7 There were twelve cables lying there. Only three of them were 'alive', and it was decided to 'liven' the others.

Liver, *sb.*[1] **7.** Add: **liver-blende** *Min.*, a liver-brown variety of blende; **liver-chestnut** (see quot.); **liverman,** a seller of liver.
1912 *Return Brit. Museum* 194 '*Liver-blende' from Broken Hill, New South Wales. 1913 W. BATESON *Mendel's Princ. Heredity* 125 There is a dark type of chestnut, sometimes spoken of as *liver-chestnut, which is actually chocolate. 1905 *Daily Chron.* 6 Apr. 8/1 The inner circle about the *liverman's barrow.

Liverishness. [f. LIVERISH *a.*] Disordered condition of the liver.
1904 *Westm. Gaz.* 5 Oct. 10/1 Ordinary attacks of liverishness or biliousness are swiftly dispersed. 1928 *Daily Express* 14 July 15/7 Yellow, perhaps, suggests liverishness.

Livery, *sb.* **9.** *U.S.* (Examples.)
1888 C. D. FERGUSON *Exp. Forty-niner* i. 15 We placed our horses in a livery on Third Street. 1902 HARBEN *Abner Daniel* 29, I could 'a' gone to a livery an' ordered out a team.
attrib. 1903 A. ADAMS *Log Cowboy* xiii. 81 Long before we reached the Mulberry, a livery rig came down the trail to meet us.

b. A conveyance.
1911 J. C. LINCOLN *Cap'n Warren's Wards* i. 8 Of course I shall share the expense of the livery.

10. *livery horse* (earlier example).
1837 COLMAN *Rep. Agric. Mass.* (1838) 17 The number of stage and livery horses kept in the county cannot fall short of one thousand,..who depend on the purchase of hay.

Lives, *U.S.* var. of *lieve(s)* LIEF *adv.*
1772 in *Copley-Pelham Lett.* 189, I had full as lives have it [the portrait] on a larger [plate]. 1848 LOWELL *Biglow P.* Introd., I'd jest ez lives eat tripe. 1856 A. CARY *Married* 22, I would just as lives stand here as not. 1891 *Harper's Mag.* Oct. 820/1, I will get Provided Usher to watch with me. He'd just as lives.

Livet(t, var. forms of LIBBET[1].
1908 SANGER *Seventy Yrs. a Showman* xiv. 48 We could see the big sticks—'livetts' they were termed—hurtling towards..the prizes.

Liveyere (li·vyīəɹ). Also livyere, liveyer. [f. the phrase *live here.*] (See quot. 1909.)
1901 *Chambers's Jrnl.* Jan. 68/2 The residents along this coast are termed 'livyeres' (live heres), to distinguish them from the nomadic fisherfolk. 1905 DUNCAN *Dr. Grenfell's Parish* i. 12 The shore fishermen of the remoter Newfoundland coasts, the Labrador 'liveyeres', the Indians of the forbidding interior. 1907 D. WALLACE *Long Labrador Trail* xxiii. 273 Even tea and molasses, usually found amongst the 'livyeres' (live-heres) of the coast, were lacking. 1909 *Toilers of Deep* July 176/1 The permanent inhabitants of the Labrador coast, the 'liveyers' are about three thousand in number. 1920 GRENFELL *Labrador Doctor* vii. 144 Leaving only a few hundreds of scattered 'Liveyeres' in possession of the Labrador.

Living, *vbl. sb.* **7. living price** (earlier example).
1834 *Congress. Globe* 3 May 362/2 Mr. Forsyth said that..70 to 76 cents was a very living price for fish oil.

Living, *ppl. a.* Add: **6.** *Living picture,* (*a*) = *Tableau vivant* (TABLEAU 4); (*b*) a motion-picture.
1897 *Knowledge* 1 Sept. 216/2 Kinetography: the production of 'living pictures'. *Ibid.*, Last winter saw the 'living pictures' adopted as the craze of the season for music-halls, bazaars, and variety entertainments generally. 1899 HORWOOD *Living Pict.* 189 A film for projecting a Living Picture is nothing more, after all, than a multiple lantern slide. *Ibid.* 207 The first requirement in the projection, as in the taking, of Living Pictures, is absolute rigidity of the apparatus.

Living-room. [LIVING *vbl. sb.* 7.]
1. An ordinary room in a house, normally occupied by day or night.
1825– [see LIVING *vbl. sb.* 7].
2. *U.S.* A sitting-room; the room usually occupied during the day.
1867 T. LACKLAND *Homespun* I. 139 The joy with which grand parents welcome us in the great living-room. 1879 F. R. STOCKTON *Rudder Grange* i. 7 There was a kitchen, a living room, a parlor and bedrooms. 1902 A. D. MCFAUL *Ike Glidden* iii. 15 The family met in the living-room of the home. 1911 H. S. HARRISON *Queed* xix. 239 Queed..went upstairs to the comfortable living-room.

Livonian (livōu·niăn), *a.* and *sb.* [f. med.L. *Livonia,* Livland, a former Baltic province of Russia.] **a.** *adj.* Of or belonging to Livonia. **b.** *sb.* A native or inhabitant of Livonia.
1757 DYER *Fleece* IV. 139 The Livonian gulph Receives her sails. 1824 J. D. COCHRANE *Narr. Journ. Russia* I. 23 A young Livonian Baron..gave me letters of recommendation to the frontiers of Siberia. 1882 *Encycl. Brit.* XIV. 723/2 [The] plateaus..of Maanhoff and of the Livonian Aa. *Ibid.* 724/1 The Livonians..have nearly all passed away. 1926 *Spectator* 31 July 176/1 If one of their German servants or retainers wanted to marry a Livonian girl the Lutheran priest would seek to stop him.

Lizzie (li·zi). *slang.* [The feminine Christian name.] **a.** A motor-car, esp. a 'Ford'. Also *Tin Lizzie.* **b.** (See quot. 1925.)
a. 1922 *Blackw. Mag.* Jan. 37/2 We then prepared to start for home; but 'Lizzie' had other notions, and refused even to think of starting. *Ibid.* Feb. 253/1 An extra bad pothole put Lizzie's back axle out of action. 1929 *Randolph Enterprise* (W. Va.) 26 Sept. 4/5 Elijah Wees has his tin lizzie in running order again from his calf wreck.
b. 1925 E. FRASER & GIBBONS *Soldier & Sailor Words, Lizzie,* a big gun; also its shell. A term originating at the Dardanelles and suggested by the firing of the big fifteen-inch guns of H.M.S. *Queen Elizabeth.*

Lloyd-Georgian (loidˌdʒǭ·dʒiăn), *a.* and *sb.* [f. the name of David *Lloyd George* (1863–), British politician.] **a.** *adj.* Of, pertaining to or associated with Lloyd-George. **b.** *sb.* A follower or supporter of Lloyd-George or of his policy.
1909 *Daily Graphic* 12 Oct. 6/2 The self-sacrificing Ministerial millionaires..with the Lloyd-Georgian iron entering into their souls. 1928 *Daily Tel.* 25 Sept. 12/2 The kaleidoscopic contortions of Lloyd Georgian politics. 1928 *Daily Express* 25 May 4/3 Asquithians and Lloyd Georgians seemed to be represented in approximately even numbers.

 Supplement, p. 3873; Corrigenda, p. 4092; Spurious words, p. 4093; Books quoted, p. 4094

So **Lloyd-Georgeite** = prec. b. **Lloyd-Georgism**, the political policy or principles of Lloyd-George.

1910 *Blackw. Mag.* Apr. 576/1 If Unionism is only to succeed by its exponents taking to Lloyd-Georgism, then Unionism is doomed. 1921 *Spectator* 19 Mar. 352/1 They must now be counted as Lloyd Georgeites rather than as Unionists.

Lo, *int.* b. Add: Also freq. in mod. use, *Lo and behold* (usually facetious).

1850 DICKENS *D. Copperfield* xxii, What does he do, but, lo, and behold you, he goes into a perfumer's shop. 1854 MISS BAKER *Northampt. Gloss.* I. 400 *Lo and behold!* A frequent exclamation in colloquial narration, expressive of a certain degree of wonder and surprise. 1887 *Century Mag.* Jan. 446/2 Lo an' behold, thar was Lawson at the spring a-werryin' Milly. 1930 J. B. PRIESTLEY *Angel Pavement* ii. § 2 And then—lo and behold—it was there all the time.

Lo, *sb.* *U.S.* [Humorously from Pope's line '*Lo*, the poor Indian', etc., *Essay on Man* I. 99.] An American Indian. Also *Mr.* (and *Mrs.*) *Lo*.

1874 J. C. McCOY *Hist. Sketches* 260 Crossing the plains was an undertaking fraught with great danger; especially as Mr. Lo was decidedly fond of horses. 1881 A. A. HAYES *New Colorado* iii. 40 Colonel Craig..and his men began, not unsuccessfully, the repression and suppression of Mr. Lo. 1890 *Buckskin Mose* vi. 88 This document set forth that the bearer was a good Lo. *Ibid.*, He appeared again at the head of our train, in the company of thirty or forty other Los. 1904 *Minneapolis Times* 12 June 6 The march of civilization has convinced Lo that fighting is not as profitable as it used to be. 1904 *N.Y. Even. Post* 6 Aug., On Florida's shield stands a placid and buxom Mrs. Lo, with fringed skirt falling to the knee.

Load, *sb.* 3. c. Add to def.: The total amount of current being supplied by a dynamo or generating station at any given time of the day. *Base-load*, the lowest value the load attains in the twenty-four hours; *peak-load*, the highest value the load attains in the twenty-four hours; so called because the varying output for one day is often represented by a graph in which the ordinates indicate the load.

1902 SLOANE *Stand. Electr. Dict.*, *Load*, in a dynamo, the amperes of current delivered by it under any given conditions. 1903 *Elect. World & Engin.* 23 May 866 (Cent. Suppl.) It is necessary at times of fall and winter peak loads to operate the steam plants in the three combination sub-station and subsidiary steam plants which the company was operating three years ago. 1928 *Daily Express* 4 June 15/3 We have, in twenty-six years, built up a huge base-load..with an annual output of over 25,000,000 units.

8. **load curve**, a curve showing the varying output or production of power over a period of time; **load factor** (earlier example); **load line** (*b*) = *load curve*.

1893 *Jrnl. Soc. Arts* XLI. 898/1 A curve, the abscissae of which represent time, and the ordinates the rate of expenditure, is called a *load curve. *Ibid.* 569/1 Mr. Crompton has introduced the term '*load-factor' to express generally the extent to which central-station plant is usefully employed. *Ibid.* 898/2 The *load-line for a central station is that to which attention is to be directed.

Load, *v.* Add: 2. c. *refl.* with *up*.

1925 E. F. NORTON *Fight for Everest, 1924* 139 Next day Hazard, the porter and myself,..loading ourselves up with all we could save, evacuated the North Col Camp.

9. a. (Earlier example.)

1870 MEDBERY *Men & Myst. Wall St.* 136 To 'load' one's self with stock is to buy heavily.

Loaded, *ppl. a.* 2. Add: In insurance, of a life (cf. LOAD *v.* 10).

1928 *Daily Express* 10 May 11/6 The application was refused in the first instance, and only afterwards accepted as a 'loaded' life.

Loader. 1. c. Add: (*c*) an appliance for loading a fire-arm; a charger.

1843 CARLTON *New Purchase* I. xvii. 122 A powder horn, and its loader of deer-horn. *Ibid.* xxi. 199 An enormously long duck-gun,..with the appurtenances of horns, pouches, loaders, tomahawks and knives.

Loading, *vbl. sb.* 5. Add: *loading-board, gauge, -tool, -tower, -yard*.

1910 W. M. RAINE *B. O'Connor* 36 The *loading board was lowered and the horses led from the car. 1901 *Yng. Engineer* I. 53 The fire-box may be extended to the full width of the *loading gauge. 1874 J. W. LONG *Amer. Wild-Fowl Shooting* 20, I usually made a practice of reloading as fast as possible between shots, carrying an ammunition-box and *loading-tools with me. 1901 *Chambers's Jrnl.* May 312/1 Steam-cranes and movable *loading-towers..lower the coal into the hold of the vessel. 1909 *Westm. Gaz.* 9 June 11/1 Between them is a *loading yard 200 ft. by 60 ft.

Loaf-cake, *U.S.* [LOAF *sb.*^{1} 2.] A plain cake made in the form of a loaf.

1844 *Knickerbocker Mag.* XXIV. 423 The biscuit would not rise, her loaf-cake was heavy. 1863 MRS. WHITNEY *F. Gartney's Girlh.* xi, Opposite sat her aunt, taking care of her as regarded tea, toast, and plain country loaf-cake. 1878 MRS. STOWE *Poganuc P.* xxii. 248 The company sat about the fire, discussing the nuts, apples and cider which were passed around, reinforced by doughnuts and loaf-cake. 1889 MRS. ROSE T. COOKE *Steadfast* xxii. 243 After a decent refection of loaf-cake and hot flip, she took her place. 1906 *Springfield Weekly Republ.* 29 Mar. 7 Sipping hot tea and tasting a large piece of loaf cake.

Loafer. (Earlier U.S. examples.)

1835 *Knickerbocker Mag.* VI. 63 The late Ben Smith, Loafer. I present an outline sketch of one of that species of the *genus homo*..which Custom has christened with the expressive appellation of Loafer! 1839 *Ibid.* XIII. 39 It was something like going to sea *passenger, idler, loafer*, what you please.

Loafering, *vbl. sb.* (Earlier U.S. example.)

1837 J. D. WHITNEY in *Life* (1909) 19 There is another thing which is a sad enemy to time, namely 'loafering', i.e. visiting one another's rooms without any ostensible purpose, to pass away time.

Loaferism. (Earlier U.S. examples.)

1836 *Knickerbocker Mag.* VIII. 407 There is a moral sublimity in..his calling, but it is not the sublimity of loaferism. 1851 A. O. HALL *Manhattaner* 17 It will long remain..the headquarters of Creole loaferism.

Loafery. Add: b. A place where persons loaf.

1898 *Daily Tel.* 10 Feb., (Ware, *Passing Eng.*) Perhaps 'House of Repose' or 'The Loaferies' would be considered appropriate [as a new title for the Whitechapel Workhouse]. 1903 *Liberty Rev.* July 7 A new trap is set for it—the free loafery at the corner.

Loan, *sb.*^{1} 5. Add: *loan-certificate, -market*; **loan-shark** (see quot. and SHARK *sb.*^{1} 2).

1777 *Boston Town Meeting* 26 May 285 If this could be accomplished, and the Money redeemed by *Loan-*Certificates*, it would operate doubly in favor of the States. 1870 MEDBERY *Men & Myst. Wall St.* 11 Its *loan market holds the keys of trade. 1928 *Daily Tel.* 5 May 9/5 It is hoped by this plan virtually to put out of business the '*loan shark', who exacts usurious rates of interest from the person of small means.

Loan, *v.* Add *fig.* examples.

1904 E. B. HOLT tr. *Münsterberg's Americans* 10 The industrial advance loaned greater importance to manufacturer and merchant. 1928 *Chambers's Jrnl.* Jan. 7/2 Kilbucho, thou hast loaned me great reward—Thy restfulness I know!

Lob, *sb.*^{6} Abbrev. of LOBWORM.

1909 *Westm. Gaz.* 23 Oct. 16/4 In a clouded stream red and brandling worms and the tail-end of a lob often prove very attractive.

Lob, *v.* Add: 4. b. To serve a player with a lobbed ball.

1921 A. W. MYERS *Twenty Yrs. Lawn Tennis* 135 Having discovered the wisdom of lobbing Barrett, Hackett..allowed McLoughlin to kill anything smashable. 1928 *Daily Tel.* 5 June 17/1 As soon as one is certain of not being lobbed.

Lobby, *sb.* 4. **lobby member** *U.S.* (earlier examples).

1819 G. C. VERPLANCK *State Triumvirate* 67 There is a class of men..generally known by the name of Lobby members. 1828 PAULDING *New Mirror Travellers* 174 They [the legislature] are called by way of honorable distinction Lobby-Members, because they form a sort of third estate, or legislature chamber in the lobby.

Lobby, *v.* 2. For *a* 1859 read *a* 1848.

Lobbying, *vbl. sb.* (Earlier example.)

1832 in W. L. Mackenzie *Life Van Buren* 237 (Th.) Perhaps I shall have a case of congressional lobbying, by which I can make it a jaunt of pleasure and profit.

Lobe. 2. **lobe-footed** (earlier example).

1872 COUES *Key N. Amer. Birds* 50 It is elevated in all swimming birds, whether lobe-footed, or partly or wholly web-footed.

Lobelia. b. (Earlier example.)

1849 N. KINGSLEY *Diary* 94 Lobelia is the great cure, but some are against it.

Loblolly. Add: 1. b. *U.S.* A mud-hole.

1899 G. ADE *Doc Horne* i. 6 In those days a mud-hole with this deceptive dry crust on top was called a 'loblolly'. 1903 A. ADAMS *Log Cowboy* xi. 164 His ineffectual struggles caused him to sink farther to the flanks in the loblolly which the tramping of the cattle had caused.

3. (Read) = *loblolly pine*.

1819 E. DANA *Geogr. Sketches* 195 Contiguous to the Florida line, a space, occupying in width from 50 to 60 miles, is timbered with cypress, loblolly, and long and short leafed pine.

Lobo. (Add examples.)

1918 MULFORD *Man fr. Bar-20* ix. 88 What you saw was a bear or a lobo or a cougar come up to see th' fire. *Ibid.* 93 The lobo wolf in the canyon.

Local. A. *adj.* 2. d. Add: *Local room* U.S., the reporters' room in a newspaper establishment.

1903 E. L. SHUMAN *Pract. Journalism* 90 Almost the only open door to the editorial room is through the local room.

4. e. Also *local colouring*.

1854 *Chambers's Jrnl.* 7 Jan. 8/2 Local colouring—*couleur locale*—is a modern expression signifying the accordance.. of the adjuncts in a work of art..with the..subject.

B. *sb.* 1. c. A local editor; a local passenger.

1868 *All Yr. Round* 19 Sept. 351/2 [quoting 'Virginia Enterprize'] We observe that Brier, local of the *News*, has on a new coat. 1887 C. B. GEORGE *40 Yrs. on Rail* ii. 35 Tickets..were at first sold only to through passengers, while the 'locals' had to pay cash.

2. g. A local branch of a trade-union.

1911 MARY W. OVINGTON *Half a Man* 98 Strong organizations in the South, as the bricklayers, send men North with union membership, who easily transfer to New York locals.

Locally, *adv.* 4. Add: *Comb.*

1896 R. S. S. BADEN-POWELL *Matabele Campaign* xix, The locally-born children are as healthy..as you could wish. 1905 *Daily Chron.* 27 Apr. 7/3 Beating the locally-trained Ambition.

Located, *ppl. a.* (Earlier examples of U.S. church use.)

1843 CARLTON *New Purchase* I. x. 68 We discovered that Mr. Parson, like most *located* and *permanent* pastors of a wooden country, received almost literally nothing for ecclesiastical services. 1874 E. EGGLESTON *Circuit-Rider* xxxi. 297 He..was directed to the double-cabin of a located preacher.

Locater (lokēᵊ·təɪ). [f. LOCATE *v.* + -ER^{1}.] One who, or something that, locates; a locator.

1902 F. T. BIDLAKE in *C. T. C. Gaz.* Aug. 359/1 A spicule of flint..pierced my tube, but kindly remained in evidence as a locater. 1921 *Chambers's Jrnl.* 9 Apr. 290/1 A great many mineral-claims..upon which their locaters built high hopes.

Location. Add: 5. (Earlier S. African example.)

1835 D'URBAN in W. M. Macmillan *Bantu, Boer, & Briton* (1929) 128 He may be placed in a location in His Majesty's Colony [The Cape].

c. In the production of motion pictures, an exterior place where a scene is filmed.

1908 H. CROY *How Motion Pictures are Made* 120 The director..has but to turn through the photographs instead of having to go out himself and spend hours looking up suitable locations.

7. The action of discovering, or the ability to discover or determine, the position of a person or thing.

1900 *Geogr. Jrnl.* Oct. XVI. 382 These birds [penguins] must have a wonderful power of location.

Lochlet (lǫχlĕt). [f. LOCH^{1} + -LET.] A little loch.

1925 A. S. ALEXANDER *Tramps across Watersheds* 40 These lochlets with their ancient relics are mostly meadows now.

Lock, *sb.*^{2} Add: 2. b. A rail serving to 'lock' the other rails of a fence. *U.S.*

1887 TOURGEE *Button's Inn* 12 The upward slope back of the house..was divided into fields, separated by high rail-fences with immense 'locks' and 'riders'.

5. Phr. *lock, stock, and barrel.* (Earlier Amer. example.)

1843 HALIBURTON *Attaché* II. 40 Look at the whole thing all through the piece, take it, by and large, stock, lock, and barrel, and it's the dandy.

11. b. *Lock and block* (*system*): a system of railway signalling by which a train does not enter a section of line until the preceding train has left it, the signal being locked at 'danger' and only released when the preceding train leaves the section.

1902 *Encycl. Brit.* XXXIII. 146/2 'Lock-and-block' has been used to a limited extent on a good many lines in England and a half-dozen in America. 1905 *Westm. Gaz.* 12 Jan. 7/2 The failure was partly due to faulty line circuits of the lock and block instruments.

19. (sense 9) *lock-bar, canal, -charge, -cut, -pen, -station, thief, -wall.*

1923 F. L. PACKARD *Four Stragglers* 312 The *lock-bar worked through the side of the pier wall. 1903 *Westm. Gaz.* 2 Jan. 3/1, I imagine that the Panama waterway is to be a *lock canal. 1877 HABBERTON *Jericho Road* ii. 20 Dont you b'leeve she could run the dam at Mount Zion, and dodge paying *lock-charges? 1905 *Westm. Gaz.* 16 Aug. 5/3 Motor boats..probably find their way down *lock-cuts made more difficult and tedious than before. 1908 *Daily Chron.* 30 Apr. 1/2 An assistant lockkeeper..found the body of a child floating in the lock-cut. 1907 *Westm. Gaz.* 20 Aug. 12/1 The *lock-pen..opens and shuts now to let through the *Queen Elizabeth* in solitary state. 1862–3 E. E. HALE *If, Yes & Perhaps* (1868) 16, I would start in the morning to walk to the *lock-station at Brockport on the canal. *Ibid.* 22 At night I walked the deck till one o'clock, with my pipe or without it, to keep guard against the *lock thieves. 1885 E. P. WARREN & CLEVERLY *Wand. 'Beetle'* 61 He ran along the *lock-wall to open his gates when he saw us coming.

20. **lock box**, a delivery letter-box provided with a lock; **lock-chain** (earlier example).

1906 MARY E. WILKINS-FREEMAN *By Light of Soul* 384 She saw one letter slanted across the dusty glass of the box. It was not a *lock box, and she had to ask the postmaster for the letter. 1843 *Amer. Pioneer* II. 121 As few of the emigrant wagons were provided with *lock-chains for the wheels, the downward impetus was checked by a large log.

Lock, *v.* Add: 7. d. (Earlier U.S. examples.)

1839 *Hist. Virgil A. Stewart* (N.Y.) 23 (Th.) They are enemies, and let them lock horns. 1855 *Knickerbocker Mag.* XLVI. 95 As neither of the trains stop at way-stations, I expect nothing more than to see the two lock horns at the corner of my kitchen.

f. In passive, of coursing dogs.

1876 *Coursing Calendar* 20 English Opera and Besika.. ran locked together for some distance.

11. b. Add to def.: To enter a lock *with* (another vessel).

1905 *Daily Chron.* 17 June 9/1 The latest regulation that no small boat should 'lock' with a motor-craft appears to have caused considerable surprise.

c. (Earlier example.)

1833 *Congress. Deb.* 26 Jan. 1396 It will pass very much as boats are locked up and down through a canal.

Lockage. Add: 2. e. The passage (of a vessel) through a lock.

1913 J. B. BISHOP *Panama Gateway* v. iv. 375 The average number of lockages through the..Canal..was 39 per day.

Lock-down. *U.S.* [LOCK *v.* 7.] A strip of wood used for holding a raft of logs together.

1881 T. B. WALKER *Let.* 4 June, A string of logs as customarily made for rafting is when the logs are fastened together by means of poles and 'Lock Downs'.

Locked, *a.*^{2} 2. (Earlier example.)

1819 D. THOMAS *Trav. Western Country* 30 The mill-dams on this stream are locked.

Lock-up. 1. a. Add: Also (earlier) *lock-up time*.

1845 T. J. GREEN *Texian Exped.* xvii. 300 One [of the many difficulties to overcome]..was to elude the vigilance of the officer at lock-up time.

b. Also *attrib.*

1908 *Daily Report* 26 Aug. 5/4 As a promising speculative lock-up holding, the shares are worth buying at the present prices.

2. b. (Earlier example.)

1839 *Knickerbocker Mag.* XIV. 110 Seeing the crowd, he just stepped over..when he was seized, and carried to the 'lock up'.

4. *lock-up prisoner.*

1846 CORCORAN *Pickings* 33 To the right of the column we perceived a prisoner whom we at once knew was above and beyond the ordinary class of lock-up prisoners.

Locku·pable, *a.* [f. as LOCKUP *sb.*] Admitting of being locked up.

1907 *Sat. Rev.* 3 Aug. 138 Half mankind thinks the other half mad—not lockupable..but 'dotty'.

Loco^{2}. (Earlier example.)

1838 QUITMAN *Let.* in *Life & Corr.* 165, I thus claim to be a true Loco and Nullifier.

Loco^{3}. (Earlier example.)

1833 S. BRECK in *Recollections* (1877) App. 274 With the *loco*..he may start from one city in the morning and return again in the evening.

Loco (lōᵘ·ko), *a.* *U.S.* [f. LOCO^{1}. Cf. LOCOED.] Mad, insane, 'queer', off one's head.

1887 *Outing* Apr. X. 7/1 You won't be able to do nuthin' with 'em, sir; they'll go plumb *loco*, that's what they will. 1907 S. E. WHITE *Arizona Nights* I. xi. 176 He looked all right enough, neither drunk nor loco. 1910 MULFORD *Hopalong Cassidy* iv. 38 Are you loco? Do you mean to let th' rest of th' outfit see that?

Locomobile. b. *sb.* (Examples.)

1896 SCHLICH *Man. Forestry* V. 748 The elevator and macerating cylinder are driven by a locomobile *m.* 1900 *Sci. Amer.* 27 Jan. 54/1 The steam carriage which is popularly and commercially known as the 'Locomobile'. *Ibid.* 15 Sept. 165/2 A simple water-indicator for locomobiles. 1903 *Motoring Ann.* 37 A Locomobile and a Holden motor-bicycle. 1905 *Daily Chron.* 6 July 5/1 Tracey, the third American, started in a locomobile. 1915 *Literary Digest* (N.Y.) 21 Aug. 387/2 Goodyear Cord Tires...Adopted for the new Locomobile as standard equipment.

Locomote, *v.* (Earlier example.)

1834 *Knickerbocker Mag.* IV. 20 Who but our author would represent him [a bard], 'locomoting' on a long, dog-trot over the bogs of his neighborhood.

Locomotive, *sb.* 4. Add: *locomotive works.*

1848 *Massachusetts Stat.* 13 Mar., A corporation, by the name of the Boston Locomotive Works, for the purpose of manufacturing locomotive engines.

Locomove, *v.* (Later example.)

1873 LELAND *Egypt. Sketch-Bk.* 88, I only remember one instance when a man who made locomotion his business was unwilling to locomove.

Locum. Add: b. Short for LOCUM-TENENCY.

1903 *Lancet* 9 May Advts. 101/2 Hospital Locum wanted by M.R.C.S., L.R.C.P., for three weeks or less.

Locum tenens. Add: b. The post of a locum tenens; a locum-tenency.

1899 *Lancet* 5 Aug. Advts. 86/2 Locum Tenens or good Assistantship wanted by doubly-qualified man. 1908 A. S. M. HUTCHINSON *Once Aboard Lugger* vi. vi. § 2. 437 There's this locum tenens I was going to take up in the North. I haven't offed that yet—haven't refused it, I mean.

Locum-tenent. Add: b. = LOCUM TENENS.

1899 *Lancet* 19 Aug. 547/1, I met with a serious accident.. in consequence of which I had to engage a locum-tenent. *Ibid.*, This sort of thing should make men very careful as to locum-tenents before engaging them.

Locust, *sb.* 6. Add: **locust-borer** (example); **locust bush** (see quot.); **locust-killer** *U.S.*, a species of wasp; **locust wood**, the wood of the locust-tree.

1838 COLMAN *Rep. Agric. Mass.* (1839) 100 *Locust-Borer. ..[He] washed his locust trees with spirits of turpentine, and in that way..compelled the borer to leave them. 1834 A. PIKE *Sketches* 56 The valley was full of small hills interspersed with mezquite bushes, that is, a kind of prickly green *locust bush, which bears long narrow beans in bunches. 1868 *Amer. Naturalist* June II. 217 [heading] The *Locust Killer. I never saw but one of these wasps. 1874 *Rep. Vermont Board Agric.* II. 777 *Clytus robiniae*. The larvae feed upon *locust wood.

Locustal (lokʊ·stăl), *a.* [f. LOCUST *sb.* + -AL.] Of, pertaining to, or connected with locusts.

1891 *Chambers's Encycl.* VII. 187/1 Temperature may also have something to do with locustal migrations.

Locustarian. (Example.)

1895 *Nature* 5 Dec. 108/1 Mr. Scudder..has given much attention to the sounds made by locustarians.

Lode. 6. Add: **lode-light**, a light said to be seen sometimes above a vein of ore.

1883 *Encycl. Brit.* XVI. 443/1 The appearance of the so-called *lode-lights may be explained by the production of phosphoretted hydrogen. 1894 C. LE N. FOSTER *Ore & Stone Mining* 107 Appearances of flame above mineral veins ..are sufficiently well established to have received a special name 'lode lights' in Cornwall.

Lodenmantle. [G. *lodenmantel* f. *loden* thick woollen cloth.] A thick woollen cloak of a style worn in southern Germany and Austria.

1914 GERTR. ATHERTON *Perch of Devil* II. 354 She..wrapped herself in a dark lodenmantl, a long cape with a hood that she had worn..in Bavaria.

Lodge, *sb.* 15. Add: (sense 7) *lodge-meeting, official, -room*; (sense 10) *lodge-cover, -covering, -fire, -skin, -trail.*

1878 J. H. BEADLE *Western Wilds* ix. 137 The former [*sc.* buffaloes] furnished them with food, clothing, *lodge-covers, bow-strings, and a dozen other conveniences. 1849 PARKMAN *Oregon Trail* 117 The squaws of each lazy warrior had made him a shelter from the sun, by stretching..the corner of a *lodge-covering upon poles. 1837 W. IRVING *Capt. Bonneville* (1895) I. 116 Knots of gamblers will assemble before one of their *lodge fires, early in the evening. 1846 SAGE *Scenes Rocky Mts.* (1859) 87 The chill winds and snows have compelled His children to light the lodge-fires of winter. 1903 C. T. BRADY *Bishop* iii. 47 Most of the Churches have a week-night prayer-meeting, and the other nights are taken up with *lodge meetings. 1909 *Daily Chron.* 30 Dec. 1/4 The fifteen *lodge officials and delegates prosecuted for offences against the Industrial Disputes Act. 1911 J. C. LINCOLN *Cap'n Warren's Wards* vi. 88 I'm more used to *lodge rooms than I am to clubs, I guess. 1846 SAGE *Scenes Rocky Mts.* (1859) 190 Exposed to..a chill storm of rain and sleet, with only a thin *lodge skin to shelter us. 1891 *Century Mag.* Mar. 776 We had already devoured..a small sack made of smoked lodge skin. 1843 FREMONT *Exped.* 115 An extremely good *lodge trail, which issues by the head of this stream. 1846 SAGE *Scenes Rocky Mts.* (1859) 178 A lodge-trail leading to the Platte by way of Sibille's creek.

Lodgement. Add: 1. d. *Mining.* = LODGE *sb.* 13 a.

1886 J. BARROWMAN *Sc. Mining Terms* 43 *Lodgment*, a reservoir or storage place underground for water for convenience of pumping.

5. **lodgement-level** (see quot.).

1877 *Encycl. Brit.* VI. 63/2 Driving a gallery..along the course of the coal seam, which is known as a 'dip head level', and a lower parallel one, in which the water collects, known as a 'lodgment level'. 1886 J. BARROWMAN *Sc. Mining Terms* 43 *Lodgment-level*, a room driven level course at a short distance to the dip of a pit and used for storage of water.

Lodge-pole. *U.S.* (See LODGE *sb.* 15.) *Lodge-pole pine* (see quot. 1905).

1834 A. PIKE *Sketches* 50 (Th.) As it is seldom that [the Comanches] find themselves in a place where they can obtain lodge-poles, they are obliged to carry them wherever they go. 1845 FREMONT *Exped.* 202 Our lodge poles were nearly worn out, and we found here a handsome set, very white, and cleanly scraped. 1855–65 [see LODGE *sb.* 15]. 1859 A. JACKSON *MS. Diary* 4 Cut the top off a small lodge pole pine. 1903 A. ADAMS *Log Cowboy* xxi. 330 He..with The Rebel went back about a mile to a thicket of lodge poles. 1905 *N.Y. Even. Post* 29 Apr., The lodgepole pine, which is known in the Sierras of California as tamarack pine,..bears the common name of 'lodgepole' from the fact that the Indians used its long slender trunks as supports for their wigwams, or lodges. 1922 SCHLICH *Man. Forestry* I. 184 Lodgepole Pine (*P. Murrayana*), a western species.

Lodgepole, *v.* [f. prec.] *trans.* To beat with a lodge-pole. Hence **Lodgepoling** *vbl. sb.*

1850 H. GARRARD *Wah-To-Yah* (1927) ix. 116 Often, indeed, their negligent spouses are lodge-poled (beaten) for such accidents. *Ibid.* x. 131 In the course of which she receives at the hands of her imperious sovereign..no very light lodgepoling.

Lodgerdom (lǫ·dʒəɹdəm). [f. LODGER + -DOM.] Lodgers taken collectively; the world of lodgers; a district in which lodgers are common.

1905 *Daily Chron.* 6 Mar. 4/6 Even dingy Lodgerdom would disclaim the place. 1907 *Ibid.* 23 May 3/3 A very pleasant, humorous-pathetic story of lodgerdom. 1927 *Observer* 14 Aug. 6 With all else of discomfort..that goes with the bondage of..lodgerdom.

Lodging, *vbl. sb.* 8. Add: **lodging-hall** *U.S.*, a lodging-house.

1860 HOLLAND *Miss Gilbert's Career* xii. 208 We left Arthur Blague..sitting on his bed in the lodging-hall at Huckleberry run. *Ibid.* xvi. 293 Cheek was..led to the trunk-room of the lodging-hall.

Lodging-room. (Later U.S. examples.)

1849 *Presid. Mess. Congress* II. 1089 One hewed-log lodging-room for hired men, sixteen feet by eighteen feet, cost $35. 1860 HOLLAND *Miss Gilbert's Career* ix. 142 They..crossed a spongy patch of garden to reach the lodging-room. 1906 *Springfield Republ.* 7 Feb. 2 Lodging Rooms to Let.

Lodicle. (Example.)

1888 *Encycl. Brit.* XXIV. 531/2 s.v. Wheat, Within the pale[a] are two minute, ovate, pointed, white membranous scales called 'lodicles'.

Loft, *sb.* Add: 7. c. *fig.* Elevation, uplift.

1925 *Brit. Weekly* 12 Nov. 159/2 We need more loft in our thinking than our fathers had.

Loft, *v.* Add: 3. b. *transf.* and *fig.*

1883 J. MARTINE *Remin. Haddington* 120 He [*sc.* a goat] was a pawky, ill-contrived beast, and thought nothing of pouting and 'lafting' folk. 1902 BARRIE *Little White Bird* xxiv. 282 We had lofted him out of the story, and did very well without him.

Lofted, *ppl. a.* Add: 2. c. Of a ball: Hit into the air.

1904 *Daily Chron.* 20 Aug. 9/5, I saw a lofted ball..miss the head of a player in front by not more than six inches.

Lofting (lǫ·ftiŋ), *ppl. a.* [f. LOFT *v.* + -ING^{2}.] Of a stroke in golf: That lofts.

1905 *Westm. Gaz.* 25 Aug. 3/1 Why to go for a low-running shot or for a high lofting shot, respectively.

Lofty, *a.* 1. b. Add: Also with *tumbling*.

1786 *Maryland Jrnl.* 22 Oct. Advt. (Th.) Surprizing feats of Lofty Tumbling by a Groupe of Performers from Sadlers Wells.

Log, *sb.*^{1} Add: 1. b. (Additional phrases.)

1850 H. C. WATSON *Camp-fires Revol.* 55 'Bill', said one of the party, to a pale, sickly-looking individual, 'we must keep the log rollin'.' 1874 J. W. LONG *Amer. Wild-Fowl Shooting* 156, I reckon 'somebody's cut the log open' as the saying is out here, from the way they are coming. 1904 'ALAN DALE' *Wanted: A Cook* 207 It was so easy that the inelegant simile of 'rolling off a log' impressed us as being absolutely justifiable.

8. (in sense 'made of logs'): *log barn, barrack, building, causeway, chapel, church, city, college, fence* (earlier example), *heap, hut* (earlier example), *kitchen, meeting-house, pen, pound, prison, room, shanty* (earlier example), *stable, tavern, tenement, trap* (later example), *wall, way* (modern example). Also *log chain* (modern examples).

1845 S. JUDD *Margaret* I. iii. 12 On the east side of the road was a *log barn. 1862 O. W. NORTON *Army Lett.* 64 When we came back we burned all the *log barracks and brush houses at the forts. 1816 U. BROWN *Jrnl.* in *Maryland Hist. Mag.* X. 281, I saw..many very good & 2 Story *log Buildings. 1831 T. BUTTRICK *Trav.* 54 In some places, in low grounds, there would be *log-causeways for a considerable distance. 1872 TOURGEE *Invis. Empire* (1880) x. 473 She was..finally choked with a *log-chain until she was insensible. 1901 S. MERWIN & H. K. WEBSTER *Calumet K* xi. 203, I had a few lengths of log chain handy. 1810 F. ASBURY *Jrnl.* (1821) III. 298 Saturday, at William Adams's *log-chapel I preached to a small assembly. 1849 PARKMAN *Oregon Trail* 25 The *log church and school-houses belonging to the Methodist Shawanoe Mission. 1817 S. R. BROWN *Western Gaz.* 106 Vangeville,—A *log city,..has fifteen or twenty old log houses. 1850 FOOTE *Sk. Virginia* 349 Could we..look into the school of the worthy pastor, then gaining its eminence as 'a *log college'. 1684 I. MATHER *Providences* 167 He hath had five Rods of good *Log-fence thrown down at once. 1764 *Coll. N. H. Hist. Soc.* IX. 154 [I] made log fence around my..orchard. 1803 T. M. HARRIS *Jrnl. Tour* 6 June (1805) 58 [In Virginia] the fields are surrounded by a rough zig-zag log-fence. 1838 J. HALL *Western States* vii. 204 People will not forever..warm themselves by *log-heaps built in great wooden chimnies. 1856 A. CARY *Married* 295 Having made a log-heap fire, Martin put the table-cloth about his shoulders. 1778 J. THATCHER *Military Jrnl.* 153 In the month of December, the troops were employed in erecting *log huts for winter quarters. 1874 E. EGGLESTON *Circuit-Rider* v. 56 The wide old *log-kitchen, with its loom in one corner. 1823 *Baptist Mag.* IV. 74 We have a good *log meeting-house on Salt Creek. 1789 WEEMS *Letters* III. 148, I lodged in a *log-pen. 1829 T. FLINT *George Mason* 20 (Th.) [They] assisted him to raise another smaller cabin, in the language of the country, a log-pen. 1832 *Louisville Directory* 102 The ditch was surmounted by a breast work of log pens filled with the earth obtained from the ditch. 1853 'P. PAXTON' *Stray Yankee in Texas* 118 A fish spear is to him [the old Texan] a groin,..a house no house, but a log-pen. 1737 in *Coll. N. H. Hist. Soc.* VII. 358 A *log pound 30 ft. square, six feet high, with a good gate, and a lock and key. 1845 MRS. KIRKLAND *Western Clearings* 212, I went to prison; nothing but a *log prison. 1902 S. E. WHITE *Conjuror's House* x. 119 Virginia entered a small *log room,..and sat down in a musty red armchair. 1847 H. HOWE *Hist. Coll. Ohio* 492 They fell to work..erecting bark huts and *log shanties. 1834 *Southern Lit. Messenger* I. 120 In the *log stable belonging to Mr. Austin at whose house I lodged, I saw a number of them. 1847 H. HOWE *Hist. Coll. Ohio* 293 Newark..then contained five or six log-cabins and Black's *log tavern. 1874 E. EGGLESTON *Circuit-Rider* xvi. 147 Marton was conducted three miles down the river to a log tavern. 1841 J. F. COOPER *Deerslayer* ii. 13 The furniture was of the strange mixture that it is not uncommon to find in the remotely situated *log-tenements of the interior. 1823 LONG *Exped.* I. 155 This was a *log trap, in which one log is elevated above another at one end. 1840 *Knickerbocker Mag.* XVI. 247, I looked around on the bare *log-walls and ceiling. 1843 CARLTON *New Purchase* I. ix. 60 The interstices of the log-wall were 'chinked'. 1874 B. F. TAYLOR *World on Wheels* II. vii. 245 Ah! there were days when, over the old road, ran the yellow mud-stained coach, laboring up its hills, and pitching along its *log-ways, and lurching in its deep worn tracks.

b. *log-heaving, -mauling, -raising*; *log-hauler, -lumberer.* c. *log-built* ppl.a.

1855 *Knickerbocker Mag.* XLVI. 225 The nuptials were celebrated in the one-story 'ten-by-six' *log-built mansion of the bride's father. 1902 S. E. WHITE *Conjuror's House* ix. 111 Your work here among the Indians is not..You coop them up in your log-built houses. 1920 W. T. GRENFELL *Labrador Doctor* xiii. 233 The *log-hauler would not deliver the goods to the rotary saw. 1823 W. FAUX *Memorable Days Amer.* 180 *Log-heaving, that is, rolling trees together for burning, is done by the neighbours in a body, invited for the purpose. 1909 *Westm. Gaz.* 11 Aug. 5/1 The pulp-maker..is not content, like the *log-lumberer, to remove the grown trees, but takes the young plants as well. 1860 *Oregon Argus* 17 Mar. (Th. s.v. Maul) The judge's style as a stumper is of a heavy, *log-mauling kind. 1864 'E. KIRKE' *Down in Tennessee* iii. 43 In April, 1862, he and his band came upon a party of neighbors collected at a *log raising in Fentress County.

9. **log-basket**, a basket, or similar receptacle, for holding logs by a fire; **log-canoe, -cock** (earlier examples); **log-deck** (see quot.); **log-drive** (see DRIVE *sb.* 3); **log-headed** (modern example); **log-jam**, a jam of logs on a river; also *fig.*; **log-man** (earlier modern example); **log-paddock**, a small field fenced in with logs; **log-rule** (see quot.); **log-running**, the operation of sending logs down a river; **log-scale** (see quot.); **log-slate** (earlier example).

1902 *Westm. Gaz.* 17 Dec. 8/2 A really nice *log-basket in wrought iron. 1758 P. STEVENS in *Travels Amer. Col.* 315, I..set out from Crown Point at ten in the morning accompanied by an officer and ten soldiers, who brought us in two *log canoes. 1853 'P. PAXTON' *Stray Yankee in Texas* 58 (Th.) The *log-cock, with his gaudy head-dress. 1905 *Terms Forestry & Logging*, *Log deck, the platform upon a loading jack. 1904 *N.Y. Even. Post* 3 May 2 The annual *log-drives have begun in the upper Hudson watershed. *a* 1904 S. E. WHITE *Blazed Trail Stories* ii. 25 He started up river for the log-drive. 1926 *Spectator* 24 July 149/1 Anyone..would have been thought *log-headed or obstinate. 1900 *Jrnl. Sch. Geog.* (U.S.) Apr. 153 The breaking of a *log jam or an ice dam on one of our rivers. 1903 *N.Y. Tribune* 27 Sept., They had used dynamite to break up log jams. 1907 *Springfield Weekly Republ.* 14 Feb. 8 The congressional log-jam which held back all legislature for nearly a week was finally broken Thursday afternoon. 1845 MRS. KIRKLAND *Western Clearings* 175 He turned his hand to the plough, and was the 'patient *log-man' of a poverty-stricken household. 1900 H. LAWSON *On Track* 29 He was putting up a two-rail fence along the old *log-paddock on the frontage. 1905 *Terms Forestry & Logging*, *Log rule, A tabular statement of the amount of lumber which can be sawed from logs of given lengths and diameters. 1901 S. E. WHITE *Westerners* xxi. 199 In the *log running Michail Lafond was the man always called upon to skim over the bobbing logs. 1905 *Terms Forestry & Logging*, *Log scale, the contents of a log, or of a number of logs considered collectively. 1834 *Knickerbocker Mag.* III. 83 Adding on the *log-slate another 'ditto' to the long column of them.

Log., **log** (lǫg), *sb.*^{3} and *a.* Abbreviation of LOGARITHM, LOGARITHMIC.

1785 C. HUTTON *Math. Tables* 125 To find the Log. of 2. 1805 NORIE *Epitome Navig.* Expl. Tables p. xv, Thus the log. of 295 is 2·469822. 1858 TODHUNTER *Algebra* 308 Given log 2 find log ·0025. 1869 J. H. SMITH *Elem. Algebra* 331 Log *mn* = *x*+*y*. 1890 G. F. MATTHEWS *Man. Logarithms* 18 How many positive integers are there whose logs, to the base 3 have 6 for a characteristic? 1900 A. C. JOHNSON *How to find Time at Sea* (ed. 4) Pref., The Tables..are.. contracted so that all the logs requisite for working a 'chronometer' are displayed at one view.

1785 C. HUTTON *Math. Tables* 150 To find the log. sine of 1° [etc.]. *Ibid.*, To find the log. tang. of 2° [etc.]. 1805 NORIE *Epitome Navig.* Expl. Tables p. xv, The log. sine of 3 points is 9·744739. The log. tangent of 6 points is 10·382776. 1889 W. M. WALTERS *Ocean Tramp* Advt., The Table of Log Sines, Tangents, &c., has been considerably augmented and simplified. 1890 G. F. MATTHEWS *Man. Logarithms* 49 The logarithm of the sine of A is called the logarithmic sine of A and written log sin A.

Log, *v.*^{1} Add: 1. b. (Later example.) c. To clear *up* or cut over (a certain area) in logging.

1843 *Yale Lit. Mag.* VIII. 332 Squatters, eh! I reckon I'm as reg'lar a settler as ever logged up a clearin. *Ibid.* 406. 1902 S. E. WHITE *Blazed Trail* ii. 5 We own, however, five million on the Cass Branch which we would like to log on contract. *a* 1904 — *Blazed Trail Stories* iii. 46 Suppose you log a knoll which..must grow at least a half million.

4. *Mil.* (Later example.)

1839 C. F. BRIGGS *Harry Franco* I. xix. 194 The captain ordered Mr. Ruffin to log me, and swore he would send me back to the States in irons.

5. b. Add to def.: Also, to travel at (a certain speed) as measured by a log; to 'do'.

1928 *Chambers's Jrnl.* Feb. 116/2 The liner was logging a steady seventeen knots.

8. *Tailoring.* To enter (at a certain price) on a log.

1913 J. CARTER in *Oxford Mag.* 22 May 360/1 A particular garment logged at, say, a total price of 15*s.* 6*d.*..may be given out to a workman at 10*s.* 6*d.* or even less.

Log cabin. *U.S.* [See LOG *sb.*^{1} 9.] A cabin, or small house, built of logs.

1803 F. ASBURY *Jrnl.* (1821) III. 119 Kindness will not make a crowded log cabin, twelve feet by ten, agreeable. 1817 S. R. BROWN *Western Gaz.* 48 There are six families living in log cabins. 1835 *Southern Lit. Messenger* I. 546 Most of the log cabins have been exchanged for neat white cottages. *Ibid.* II. 53 We behold the low log-cabin of a school-house. 1844 D. LEE & FROST *Oregon* xxii. 275 And here we found Mr. Smith, who had laid up the body of a log cabin, about fifteen feet square, and was living in it without floor or roof. 1881 W. M. THAYER (*title*) From Log-cabin to White House: the Story of President Garfield's Life.

attrib. 1840 *Boston Atlas* 11 Sept., Crow,..For the party laid low By the log-cabin boys Of old Tippecanoe. 1840 *Nashville Whig* 17 Aug., They are the representatives of a hardy race of honest log cabin pioneers. 1851 *Congress. Globe* 22 June 92 Mr. Clark of New York said all this log-cabin slang was quite out of date. 1887 [see LOG *sb.*^{1} 9].

Logged, *a.* *U.S.* [f. LOG *sb.*^{1} 1 + -ED^{1}.] Built of logs.

1784 WASHINGTON *Diaries* II. 294 A Logged dwelling house with a punchion Roof. 1834 *Knickerbocker Mag.* III. 32 Immediately on the road, appeared a large rude double logged cabin.

Logged, *ppl. a.* b. Add: Also *logged-off*.

1911 *U.S. Dept. Agric., Farmer's Bulletin* 462, 5 The merchantable timber has been stripped from large areas, leaving what is known as 'logged-off' or 'cut-over' land.

Loggerhead. Add: 2. b. (See quot.)

Known to be older than 1885.

1909 A. C. FOX-DAVIES *Heraldry* 193 The leopard's face.. For some unfathomable reason these charges when they occur in the arms of Shrewsbury are usually referred to locally as 'loggerheads'.

3. b. (See quot.)

1904 *Athenæum* 27 Feb. 280/1 The inkstands..include many of the prototypes of the circular heavy inkstand, still used, and known to many under the old name of 'loggerheads'.

6. b. (*b*) (Later examples.)

1870 *Amer. Naturalist* III. 159, I saw a Loggerhead attack a snake. 1906 *N.Y. Even. Post* 8 Aug. 2 Charleston S. C. pet canaries are being killed by a bird that is known as the 'loggerhead'. A loggerhead strikes at the canaries through the bars of the cage.

Lo·ggia'd, *a.* Provided with loggias.

1903 *Westm. Gaz.* 9 Dec. 3/1 A great loggia'd palace, gaunt, time-stained, damp-eaten.

Lo·gginess. [f. LOGGY *a.* 2.] A state of heaviness or sluggishness.

1924 *Scribner's Mag.* July 88/2 He ate sparingly..rather as insurance against any sensation of logginess.

Logging, *vbl. sb.* 3. Add: *logging-chain, company, establishment, swamp, wheel.*

1910 JER. HART *Vigilante Girl* xxvi. 356 He was carrying in his hand a light *logging-chain which was attached to his ankles. 1903 A. B. HART *Actual Govt.* 326 *Logging companies buy up immense areas of land for timber. 1851 J. S. SPRINGER *Forest Life* 67, I have seldom taxed my judgement as severely on any subject as in judiciously locating a *logging establishment. 1848 BARTLETT *Dict. Amer.*, *Logging swamp, in Maine, the place where pine timber is cut. 1905 *Terms Forestry & Logging*, *Logging wheels. A pair of wheels, usually about 10 feet in diameter, for transporting logs.

Loggy, *a.* Add: 2. (Later example.)

1886 *Outing* Apr. VIII. 58/1 They do very well sailing free but on the wind are loggy.

3. Abounding in logs.

1851 A. O. HALL *Manhattaner* 2 The sandy, boggy, loggy, grassy, and snaggy strips of land.

Log-house. (See LOG *sb.*^{1} 9.)

Add earlier and later examples of mod. sense.

1784 J. SMYTH *Tour U.S.* II. 9 Mr. Edmond Gray.. cleared the ground from the woods, besides constructing temporary habitations (log houses) to reside in. 1806 in *Ann. 9th Congress* 2 Sess. 1113 [He] has built himself some log-houses, and enclosed them with a slight stockade. 1853 J. G. BALDWIN *Flush Times Alabama* 142 A few log houses hastily erected and overcrowded with inmates, alone were to be seen. 1879 TOURGEE *Fool's Err.* vii. 34 This log house had in time given way to a more pretentious structure of brick.

Logian (lǫ·dʒiăn), *a.* [f. *logi-a* LOGION + -AN.] Containing the Logia of Jesus.

1909 V. H. STANTON *Gosp. Hist. Docum.* II. 48 To call the source we are considering simply 'the Logian document' cannot, I think, be open to the same objection. 1911 SIR J. C. HAWKINS in *Stud. Synoptic Probl.* 107 The convenient practice which has grown up of calling it the 'Logian source'. 1921 *Contemp. Rev.* Mar. 263 An expanded form of the original Greek Logian document.

Lo·gily, *adv.* [f. LOGY *a.*] In a dull or heavy manner.

1913 J. LONDON *Son of Sun* viii. § 4. 326 The schooner,.. from the weight of water on her decks, behaved logily.

Loglet (lǫ·glet). [f. LOG *sb.*^{1} + -LET.] A little log.

1914 W. DE MORGAN *When Ghost meets Ghost* II. vi. 504 She brought a couple of young loglets to keep a little life in the fire.

Logorrhea (lǫgǫrī·ă). [f. Gr. λόγο-ς word + ῥοία flow, stream.] Excessive volubility accompanying some forms of insanity.

1902 *J. M. Baldwin's Dict. Philos. & Psychol.* II. 30/1 Logorrhea refers to the excessive flow of words, a common symptom in cases of mania. 1907 *Daily Chron.* 13 Feb. 7/4 In the case of a man suffering from the insanity known as logorrhea the ideas come rapidly tumbling over each other.

Log-roller. 1. (Earlier U.S. example.)

1821 *Pennsylv. Intelligencer* 16 Jan. (Th.) We shall see how the 'log-rollers' will unite their strength.

Log-rolling. Add: 1. (Earlier examples.)

a 1792 MONETTE *Mississippi Valley* (1848) II. 8 The standard dinner dish at log-rollings, house-raisings, and harvest days, was a large pot-pie. 1834 CARRUTHERS *Kentuckian in N.Y.* 25 When we Kentuck boys gits at it, it won't all end like a log rollin, with one or two broken shins and a black eye. 1843 CARLTON *New Purchase* xix. 159 Yet at the very next log-rolling, he proclaimed both Glenville and Carlson to be converts to his 'idee'.

2. Also *attrib.*

1838 QUITMAN *Let.* in *Life & Corr.* 165 Tending to promote combinations and log-rolling schemes. 1860 S. MORDECAI *Virginia* xxx. 303 But the log-rolling system of Virginia has diverted her energies from the completion of any one useful work. 1869 *Atlantic Monthly* Sept. 365/2 The log-rolling lobby generally exerted their powers upon objects which possessed a public character.

Logwood. Add: 3. A decoction or extract of logwood, used for colouring or dyeing.

1880 *Encycl. Brit.* XIII. 80/1 Such an ink is costly..on account of the concentrated condition in which the logwood must be used.

Logy, *a.* Also *Comb.* as *logy-looking*.

1888 MRS. CUSTER *Tenting on Plains* xii. (1893) 226 A more logy-looking animal can hardly be found, than the army mule.

Loin, *sb.* 3. Add: *loin-steak.*

1867 *Rep. Iowa Agric. Soc.* (1868) 127 The reason..is the same that persons have for preferring loin-steaks to those cut from just aft of the horns.

Loiter, *v.* Add: 1. c. To delay action.

1822–56 DE QUINCEY *Confess.* (1902) 156 Even honorable lawyers will not in a case of this nature move at a faster pace: they will all alike loiter upon varied allegations through six months.

2. b. (Later example with *out*.)

1863 LYTTON *Caxtoniana* I. 50 The little lake..on the banks of which I loitered out my schoolboy holidays.

Lollop, *sb.* Add: 2. A trifling inactive person.

1910 H. L. WILSON *Ma Pettengill* iv. 125 Of course the poor lollop had never been able to think under any circumstances.

Londonish (lʊ·ndəniʃ), *a.* [-ISH^{1}.] Pertaining to or characteristic of London; exhibiting features or peculiarities found in London.

1922 *Sketch* 1 Nov. 194/3 A few mellow Cockney vowels to make us feel cosy—Londonish. 1925 DEEPING *Sorrell & Son* vi, I had been getting a little—Londonish—shall we call it. 1927 *Observer* 6 Nov. 9/4 The Cromwell-road is at once the most English and the most Londonish of our thoroughfares.

Londony (lʊ·ndəni), *a.* [-Y^{1}.] Suggestive of London or its characteristics.

1907 D. O'CONNOR *Peter Pan Picture-bk.* 27 They made a chimney out of John's tall hat, which he had been Londony enough to bring with him. 1920 GALSWORTHY *In Chancery* I. x. 88 Rather pale she looked and Londony.

Lone, *a.* Add: 1. b. *fig.* (Earlier example.)

1879 B. F. TAYLOR *Summer-Savory* xv. 122 In fact, in pretty nearly all his plays he had a 'lone hand'.

3. b. *Lone star*, the single star in the arms of Texas, hence called the *Lone Star State*. Also *Lone Star Stater*, a Texan.

1845 *Congress. Globe* 8 Jan. App. 78/3 The 'lone star' has found a place upon the democratic banners. 1848 *Ibid.* 28 July App. 973/1 Texas was then a 'lone star'. She is now one of thirty. 1860 *Ibid.* 5 Dec. 11/3 There is a clog in the way of the lone-star State of Texas in the person of her Governor. 1873 J. H. BEADLE *Undevel. West* 805, I am proud to find him in honor and position among the 'Lone Star Staters'. *a* 1909 'O. HENRY' *Roads of Destiny* xvi. 267 The Lone Star State never yet failed to grant relief [etc.].

6. b. In recent use also in form *lone* (and *lones*).

1902 KIPLING *Just So Stories* 197 They walked in the Wet Wild Woods by their wild lones. *Ibid.* 206 This is the picture of the Cat that Walked by Himself, walking by his wild lone through the Wet Wild Woods. 1908 *Westm. Gaz.* 28 May 2/4 The roads are dusty and dry When you walk 'em all by your lone. 1910 W. M. RAINE *B. O'Connor* 21 But why for do they let a sick man like you travel all by his lone? 1917 W. J. LOCKE *Red Planet* vi. 75 After five minutes on my lones, I felt as if I should go off my head.

Lone-hand, *v.* [See LONE *a.* 1 b.] *intr.* To act singly or without assistance.

1922 Z. GREY *To Last Man* xiii. 276 Queen had evidently left his comrades, had lone-handed it in his last fight, but was now trying to get back to them.

Lonesome, *a.* Add: 1. b. *By* (or *on*) *one's lonesome*, all alone, without company or assistance. (Cf. *LONE *a.* 6 b.)

1908 *Daily Chron.* 13 Aug. 5/7 Then, parting from him,.. I went, all by my lonesome, along the Madeira Walk. 1920 BERNARD CRONIN *Timber Wolves* 125 'When I marry Amelia Peters', says George, 'you can hit the trail on your lonesome'.

Mod. I did it all by my lonesome. You mean to say you lifted that by your lonesome!

Long, *a.*^{1} 1. f. Add: Also *long manure.*

1840 BUEL *Farmer's Comp.* 198 Great economy in dung may be effected by feeding these crops with the long manure of the yards and stables, instead of summer-yarding it.

5. b. *Long purse*, one in which there is plenty of money; *long shillings*, good wages.

1824 P. HORRY *Life F. Marion* iii. (1833) 28 Great Britain, the nation of the longest purse in Europe. 1871 *Scribner's Monthly* II. 551 For longer purses there are hard woods in all combinations. 1902 *Chambers's Jrnl.* June 391/1 A couple of powerful trading concerns engaged in flourishing their long purses in each other's faces. 1910 *Ibid.* Sept. 603/2 There are 'long shillings' to be earned at the docks, but no easy ones; and the work is not only hard but dangerous.

c. *Long suit*, in fig. use: (one's) strong point.

1903 A. ADAMS *Log Cowboy* xiv. 218 Young Pete..assured our foreman that the building of bridges was his long suit. 1916 E. V. LUCAS *Vermilion Box* xxx. 26 You want me to help you to a post as organizer...Because organizing has always been your long suit. 1928 *Chambers's Jrnl.* Jan. 9/2 Patience, he told himself, was his long suit. He had only to wait tactfully for a favourable opportunity.

d. *Long chance*, one involving considerable uncertainty or risk.

1907 S. E. WHITE *Arizona Nights* I. xiii. 191 He's plumb scared at the prospect of suffering anything, and would rather die right off than take long chances. *Ibid.* II. iv. 262 'He's one of those long-chance fellows', surmised Jed.

8. Phr. *The longest day*, etc. (earlier and later examples).

1772–6 J. ANDREWS *Lett.* 340, I shall never get the idea out of my mind the longest day I have to live. 1911 H. S. HARRISON *Queed* xxv. 321 You'd be a marked man to the longest day you lived.

15. *long-period, -run, staple, -tail, -term, -wave.*

1903 AGNES M. CLERKE *Probl. in Astrophysics* 348 The typical *long-period variable is Mira Ceti. 1927 H. C. MACPHERSON *Mod. Astron.* 120 The long-period variables. 1923 P. B. BALLARD *New Examiner* 107 Long-period testing. 1896 KIPLING *Seven Seas* 146 It paid..when we came ..and collared the *long-run trade. 1909 *Westm. Gaz.* 22 Apr. 2/3 Half the week is to be given to 'long-run' plays. 1802 *Steele Papers* I. 341 *Long Staple Cotton is in demand. 1836 O. W. HOLMES *Song Centennial Celebr.* 46 They did not rattle round in gigs, Or dash in *long-tail blues. 1908 *Daily Chron.* 24 July 1/6 The *long-term men, who wore blue cotton overalls marked with the broad arrows, were in the rear. 1909 *Westm. Gaz.* 2 June 5/2 A 2½ per cent., long-term loan. 1909 E. B. TITCHENER *Text-bk. Psychol.* I. 60 Let us take..a chart or projection of the solar spectrum, and let us work through it, from the left or *long-wave to the right or short-wave end. 1928 *Chambers's Jrnl.* Jan. 79/1 Many foreign long-wave stations have also been clearly heard with this set.

16. *long-barrelled, -billed* (earlier examples), *-grained, -leafed, -leaved* (earlier mod. example), *-sleeved* (mod. examples), *-spooned.*

1902 *Daily Chron.* 20 Mar. 3/1 The rests for the *long-barrelled muskets disappeared just at the beginning of the war. 1594 BARNFIELD *Affect. Sheph.* II. ix. (Arb.) 13 Wilt thou set springes..To catch the *long-billd Woodcocke? 1822 J. FOWLER *Jrnl.* 148 We thear for the first time seen the long Billed Bird:..the bill about one foot in length. 1831 PECK *Guide Emigrants* II. 156 The *long grained Virginia corn is chiefly produced. 1819 E. DANA *Geogr. Sketches* 173 The *long leafed pine is a stately tree, from 60 to 80 feet, clear of limbs. 1785 H. MARSHALL *Amer. Grove* 83 *Long-leaved Mountain Magnolia or Cucumber Tree. 1810 MICHAUX *Arbres* I. 16 Long-leaved pine. 1813 MUHLENBERG *Catal. Plant.* 53 Long-leaved Magnolia. 1832 D. J. BROWNE *Sylva Amer.* 228 This invaluable tree is known..by different names...it is called Long-Leaved Pine, Yellow Pine, Pitch Pine and Broom Pine. 1897 R. M. GILCHRIST *Peakland Faggot* 95 Vignettes akin to those one sees on the porcelain faces of old Derbyshire '*long-sleeved clocks'. 1903 G. F. ABBOTT *Tour Macedonia* 221 A long-sleeved black jacket. 1866 J. MACGREGOR '*Rob Roy*' *Baltic* (1867) 286 A long, narrow, light racing-canoe, with a *long-spooned paddle.

18. **long chalk** (see CHALK *sb.* 6 b); **long cross** *Numism.*, a cross the arms of which extend to the outer circle on a coin; **long deal**, in card-playing (see quot.); **long distance** *ellipt.*, a long-distance telephone; **long Forties** *Naut.* (cf. FORTY *sb.* 4); **long green** *U.S. slang*, dollar-notes, money; **long-house** (*b*) (earlier examples); **long-leaf pine** *U.S.*, the yellow or pitch pine (also *long-leafed, -leaved pine*: see 16); **long-pull**, the practice in public-houses of giving over-measure to attract custom; **long-room** (later examples); **long sauce** (see SAUCE *sb.* 4 a); **long-short** (earlier example); **long sight** (see also *SIGHT *sb.* 2 b); **long silk** *attrib.* of cotton, long-stapled; **long song** (see quot.); **long-splice** *Naut.*, a form of splice; also as *vb.*; **long-spur** *Ornith.*, one of several long-clawed fringilline birds, chiefly of the genus *Calcarius*; **long-staple** (earlier example); **long-straws**, the drawing of straws as a game; **long-sweetening** (earlier example); **long-time** (add), extending for a long time into the future; **long-wool** (earlier examples of sense *b*).

1904 STAINER *Oxf. Silver Pennies* (O.H.S.) 50 *Long cross voided, each limb terminating in crescent. 1898 H. S. CANFIELD *Maid of Frontier* 86 It was what is termed a '*long deal' that is, no winning or losing card had slipped from the dealer's carelessly careful hands. 1905 TARKINGTON *In Arena* 128, I had it by the *long distance an hour ago, from your own home. 1928 GAMBLE *Story N. Sea Air Station* 183 The Grand Fleet was ordered to rendezvous in the '*Long Forties'; the Battle Cruiser Fleet to join farther south. 1837 *Knickerbocker Mag.* X. 413 The disturber, known in the west by the name of *long green..was happily beyond their reach. 1896 G. ADE *Artie* ix. 79, I never see him do a stroke of work, but he can always make a flash o' the long green. 1903 A. H. LEWIS *Boss* 174 I'd naturally s'ppose that when you went shy on th' long green, you'd touch th' old gentleman. 1751 C. GIST *Journal* 31 They marched in under French Colours and were conducted into the *Long House. 1753 WASHINGTON *Diaries* I. 50 We met in Council at the *Long House.* 1800 B. HAWKINS *Sk. Creek Country* 60 [On] the uplands to the south are the *long-leaf pine. 1831 PECK *Guide Emigrants* II. 47 Up the Red river..the timber is all pine—the long leaf pine. 1904 T. WATSON *Bethany* (1920) 8 Ours was just a plain house..of timbers torn from the heart of the long-leaf Georgia pine. 1901 *Contemp. Rev.* Mar. 355 The unlettered barmaid..tiring of handling the taps and the *long-pull. 1909 *Daily Chron.* 30 Aug. 5/3 As the law stands magistrates have no power to stop the 'long pull'. 1917 *19th Cent.* Feb. 340 The 'long pull' is one of those practices to which temperance reformers attach an exaggerated importance. 1841 *Knickerbocker Mag.* XVII. 458 In the *long room of the Village Inn. 1870 MEDBERY *Men & Myst. Wall St.* 22 A chamber is provided at the Exchange, where members may bargain with members at any hour throughout the day. This is known as the Long Room. 1840 *Knickerbocker Mag.* XVI. 22 A buxom, rosy-cheeked girl, with a blue-striped *long-short..was busied around the fire-place. 1870 YEATS *Nat. Hist. Comm.* II. (1872) 200 The *long silk cotton of Algeria partakes at the same time of the character of the long silk staple of Georgia, and the short cottons of Egypt. 1856 *Chambers's Jrnl.* 28 June 402/1 An item in those streaming fathoms of verse technically known as '*long songs', in which as many as a hundred favourite ditties are sold for a penny. 1883 *Man. Seamanship Boys* 106 To form a *long-splice with a piece of three and four-strand rope...Unlay the ends of the two ropes to the required distance [etc.]. *Ibid.*, How do you Long-Splice a Three or Four-Strand Rope together? 1898 NELTJE BLANCHAN *Bird Neighbors* 148 The colors of the males, among the several *longspurs, may differ widely. 1899 H. SAUNDERS *Man. Brit. Birds* (ed. 2) 223 The Lapland Bunting or 'Longspur' was first recognised as a visitor to our island by Selby early in 1826. 1843 *Knickerbocker Mag.* XXI. 39 It is here that the most valuable product of our country, the *long staple cotton, is raised in the greatest perfection. 1835 R. M. BIRD *Hawks of Hawk-hollow* I. ii. 33 Shall we sit down here, and play *long-straws for sweethearts? 1724 *Coll. Rec. N. Carolina* II. 132 Let who will go unpaid, Rum, *long Sweet'n alias Mollasses,..must be had. 1927 CARR-SAUNDERS & JONES *Soc. Struct. Eng. & Wales* 228 This is no indictment of the usefulness of *long-time forecasts, because it is in any case impracticable to plan so far ahead. 1857–8 *Trans. Ill. Agric. Soc.* III. 458 The *Longwools attain to greater size and shear a larger fleece. 1867 *Rep. Iowa Agric. Soc.* (1868) 67 The long wools or mutton sheep have not yet established their pre-eminence.

c. **longjohn**, a tropical tree of South America (*Triplaris Americana* L.), belonging to the Buckwheat family.

1910 *Chambers's Jrnl.* Feb. 88/2 Impenetrable jungle, consisting mostly of chinchilla or sand box-trees, with now and then a sand-cocoa or a *longjohn.

d. **long-hop** (also in *Fives*), a ball which a player has ample time to hit after it bounces.

1900 *Young Sportsman* (ed. A. E. T. Watson) 237 s.v. *Fives*, C..must above all avoid so returning it [the ball] that it comes into the middle of the outer court as a long-hop.

Long, *adv.* 7. Add modern example.

1887 MORRIS *Odyss.* XII. 251 As the fisher sits on the headland with a rod that reaches long.

9. a. *long-felt.*

1888 *Rep. Vermont Board Agric.* X. 45 A long felt need of the farmers of Albaugh has been a proper market for their butter.

Longeron (lǫ·ndʒĕrǫn). [Fr.] 'Any long spar running lengthways of a fuselage' (Barber).

1916 BARBER *Aeroplane Speaks* Gloss. 1917 *Blackw. Mag.* Apr. 560/1 A burning shell fragment was lodged on a longeron, half-way between my cockpit and the tail-plane. 1918 'AVION' *Aeroplanes & Aero Engines* 83 *Longeron*, the main fore and aft members of a fuselage.

Long-horn. [LONG *a.*^{1} 1 + HORN *sb.*]

1. A long-horned ox or cow. Also *attrib.* and *transf.* (applied to persons).

1834–79 [see LONG *a.*^{1} 18 b]. 1901 W. A. WHITE *Platt* in *McClure's Mag.* 145 The picture of Tom Platt..standing at the head of a drove of wild-eyed human long-horns, as if to keep them from a stampede. 1903 A. ADAMS *Log Cowboy* xiii. 195 Those old long horns McNulta and Lovell, got us in with the crowd. *Ibid.* xxii. 353 There were lots of old long-horn cowmen living in the town. *Ibid.* 356 Some of those old long-horns didn't think any more of a twenty-dollar gold piece than I do of a white chip.

2. The long-eared owl, *Otus vulgaris*.

1856 [see LONG *a.*^{1} 18 b].

3. A form of bi-plane.

1928 GAMBLE *Story North Sea Air Station* i. 36 The machines were of the 'pusher' type with interconnected front and rear elevators...Popularly they were known as 'Longhorns'.

Longi-. Add: **Longirostrine** *a.* = LONGIROSTRAL.

1896 *Guide Fossil Reptiles & Fishes Brit. Mus.* 6 The Amphicœlian section..embraces..a second longirostrine section.

Long-keeping, *a.* [LONG *adv.* 9 a.] Admitting of being kept for a long time.

1859 *Trans. Mich. Agric. Soc.* (1860) X. 229 That it is impossible to raise winter apples in the South, and that it is necessary to look to the North for a supply of long-keeping varieties. 1873 *Trans. Dep. Agric. Illinois* x. 58 A well known favorite, its long-keeping qualities recommending it wherever it is known.

Long Knife. *U.S.* [LONG *a.*^{1} 1.] A Virginian or other white man (so called by the Indians). Cf. *Big Knife* *BIG *a.* B.

a 1784 D. BOONE in Filson *Kentucky* (1793) 40 The savages now learned the superiority of the long knife, as they call the Virginians, by experience. 1788 W. BIGGS *Captivity* 13 He again asked if I was a Shemolsea (that is a long knife or a Virginian). 1833 T. FLINT *Ind. Wars* 35 The Virginia warriors and the Anglo-American militia in general, were thenceforward designated by the western Indians as the *long-knives*. 1835 CARRUTHERS *Cavaliers of Virginia* II. 17 Did not the long knife slay the chief of our nation? 1848 J. F. COOPER *Oak Open.* I. xi. 168 Until the 'long-knives and leather-stockings' came into the woods, the red man had his way.

b. (See quot.)

1805 L. DOW *Trav. Wks.* 1806 II. 67 But they [the Indians] being afraid of Long-knife, (i.e. Congress) refrained from violence.

Long-liner. [f. LONG-LINE 1.] One who fishes with a long-line.

1909 *Westm. Gaz.* 3 June 14/3 Dog-fish, these terrors to netsmen and long-liners. 1920 W. T. GRENFELL *Labrador Doctor* x. 183 The Hearn long-liners and trawlers, who were just beginning their vast fishery in those waters.

Long-lived, *a.* Add quot.

1927 BOWLEY & STAMP *Nat. Income 1924* 39 Furniture, pictures, motor-cars, and other long-lived assets.

Long nine. *U.S.* [LONG *a.*^{1} 1 + NINE *sb.*] A kind of cheap cigar.

1830 N. DANA *Mariner's Sk.* 213 (Th.) The fourfold row of long-nine-smoking beaux, that are regularly drawn up on Sunday forenoon in Market Square. 1835 *Harvardiana* I. 157 (Th.) He unfolded the wrapper; it contained two long-nine segars. 1844 'JON. SLICK' *High Life N.Y.* II. 223 Nobody ever ketched me a halving a long nine. 1858 [see NINE *sb.* 4 b].

Long-tail. 1. Add: *spec.* a greyhound. Also *attrib.*

1876 *Coursing Calendar* 12 The former Duke of Hamilton ..and others of their day, were followers of the 'long tails' on the very same ground. 1927 *Daily Express* 25 May 12 A little more foresight..might have made 'rag running' a very popular entertainment, commanding as much notice as the sport of long-tail racing. 1930 BILLIS & KENYON *Pastures New* vi. 102 Some high-priced coursing dogs,—longtails as they were called—were brought into the colony.

Lonk (lǫŋk) [a dial. variant of *Lank*, the first syllable of Lancashire: see E.D.D.] A large-sized variety of mountain sheep which originated in Lancashire or Yorkshire.

1863 in W. FREAM *Compl. Grazier* (ed. 3, 1893) 473 If the Lonks be as hardy as they are good, they must be the most valuable sheep for the hills that we have at present. 1911 *Chambers's Jrnl.* Dec. 778/2 The lonk is believed to have come originally from the Yorkshire hills.

Looder, variant of LOWDER.

Look, *sb.* Add:

1. d. A distance which can be covered by a look.

1852 *Knickerbocker Mag.* XL. 548 A heap of logs which they had been getting out on a quarter about a look from a branch near the old field on the Fatio grant.

2. c. Also in pl., esp. in *from* or *by the looks of*.

1883 R. CLELAND *Inchbracken* iv. 28 It micht be e'en a bairn by the looks o' the bun'le. 1923 B. M. BOWER *Parowan Bonanza* v. 54 You're just ahead of a big storm, by the looks, Mr. Rayfield.

Look, *v.* Add: 10. c. *Looks like*, it seems likely. *U.S. colloq.*

1910 W. M. RAINE *B. O'Connor* 55 Your cook, Anderson, kid-napped the child, looks like to me.

22. c. (Examples.)

1879 TOURGEE *Fool's Err.* xliv. 330 There could be nothing looking towards marriage between us. 1903 A. T. HADLEY *Freedom & Responsibility* 15 A series of negotiations rather than discussions, looking toward compromise rather than toward mutual enlightenment. 1904 T. N. PAGE in *McClure's Mag.* 621 The South regarded jealously any teaching of the Negroes which looked toward equality.

33. **Look down.** e. (Earlier examples.)

1812 *Niles' Weekly Reg.* III. 45/2 Volunteer companies.. are rolling to the frontiers, in force sufficient to look down opposition. 1837 *Knickerbocker Mag.* IX. 361 We're a free trader..and are forced to go well armed, to look down all resistance. 1838 J. F. COOPER *Homeward Bound* viii. 108 If the people cannot control and look down peculiarity..one might as well live in a despotism at once.

37. **Look in.** c. [After *Listen in*: *LISTEN *v.* 2 e.] *intr.* To use a wireless receiver adapted for television. *colloq.*

1928 *Daily Sketch* 7 Aug. 11/1 The public..can 'listen-in' or 'look-in' to the transmissions.

45. **Look up.** e. (Earlier example.)

1806 *Steele Papers* I. 461 One cause why it has been so low at this market was the scarsity of salt; our river is now full enough for Boats to run, I think the Article will look up.

Looker. 1. b. Add: *looker-round, -up.*

1901 *Daily Chron.* 4 Dec. 9/2 Advt., Lookers-up (2 experienced); also several boys in beer factory. 1926 W. J. LOCKE *Old Bridge* II. viii. 134 The result is art, conquest,.. whatever it may be, which, if sought, is there for the looker-round to behold.

3. *U.S. colloq.* One who looks well; one deserving admiration on the score of looks.

1904 *Springfield Weekly Republ.* 24 June 7 The country folk would say of the speaker that he is not much of a 'looker', and they are entitled to pass judgment upon one who truly belongs to a plain people. 1909 EDITH RICKERT *Beggar Heart* 207 She isn't much of a looker—my missus has other points than looks. 1914 GERTR. ATHERTON *Perch of Devil* I. 72 She's no fool—and she certainly is a looker. 1920 BERNARD CRONIN *Timber Wolves* 73 Did you notice if she was any kind of a looker? 1923 L. J. VANCE *Baroque* vii. 65 Just because daughter's a swell looker don't make father out an innocent.

Look-in. Add: 2. b. A share of attention.

1916 *Lit. Digest* (N.Y.) 1 Jan. 7/2 Between Colonel Roosevelt and the diplomatic correspondence of this epoch the dictionary business is getting a look-in all right—*New York Morning Telegraph.*

Look-outer. [f. *look out* LOOK *v.* 40.] One who looks out or watches.

1841 J. F. COOPER *Deerslayer* iii. 16 But Hutter is a first-rate look-outer, and can pretty much scent danger as a hound scents the deer.

Look-over, *sb.* [f. LOOK *v.* 19.] An examination, a survey.

1909 R. A. WASON *Happy Hawkins* 183 Then I..took a stroll around to see that no one had been givin' us the look-over.

Look-see (lu·k,sī). *slang.* Also **looksee.** [f. LOOK *sb.* and *v.* + SEE *v.* Perhaps orig. Pidgin-English, as suggested in quots.]

1. A survey, a tour of inspection, a look-round

1883 *Boy's Own Paper* 22 Dec. 185/1, I 'spec she just come here to makee look see how de people get on. 1908 *St. George's Rev.* I. 156 China..opium problem...It was my business to go out there and have what my John would call a 'look-see'. 1919 H. L. WILSON *Ma Pettengill* x. 281 It was our mission this day to have a look-see,..and get a general idea of how many head [of cattle] was already coming down. 1924 *Blackw. Mag.* Sept. 356/2, I did not skip out of bed sudden-like...I sat up, and had a look-see. The ground sheet was crawling with scorpions. 1927 *Observer* 9 Oct. 22 We must be grateful to the B.B.C. for letting us have a 'looksee', as the Chinese say.

2. A telescope or periscope.

1925 E. FRASER & GIBBONS *Soldier & Sailor Words.*

3. Appearance, looks.

1926 MARY LEINSTER *Dew on Leaf* 82, I distrust the look-see of things.

Loom, *sb.*^{1} 6. Add: *loom-room*; **loom-house** (earlier example).

1838 *Southern Lit. Messenger* IV. 405 They always lie about the dairy and *loom-house. 1845 *Knickerbocker Mag.* XXV. 448, I went out to look at the *loom-room.

Loom, *sb.*^{3} 1. (Add transf. example.)

1918 GALSWORTHY *Five Tales, Indian Summer* i, Fields and trees faintly glistened, away to a loom of downs.

Loon^{2}. Add:

1. b. In phrases with *loon's* (see quots.). Also freq. *as crazy as a loon* (in reference to its actions in escaping from danger and its dismal cry), etc. *To hunt the loon* (see quot. 1880).

1834 SEBA SMITH *Major Jack Downing* 110 He begun to sing out like a loon for us to come and take him. 1834 C. A. DAVIS *Lett. J. Downing* 42, I saw through it in a minute, and made it all as strait as a loon's leg. 1840 C. F. HOFFMAN *Greyslaer* I. xi. 129 After tramposing for twenty-four hours on a stretch, with not even a loon's nap at the end of it. 1848 MAJOR JONES *Sk. Trav.* 102 A body what never seed a opery before would swar they was every one either drunk or crazy as loons. 1865 'MARK TWAIN' *Sketches* (1926) 163 Our reserve..came filing down the street as drunk as loons. 1880 *Harper's Mag.* Dec. 31 Miss Lois had been hunting the loon with a hand-net—a Northern way of phrasing the wearing of the willow. 1888 C. D. FERGUSON *Exp. Forty-niner* ix. 121 The next morning Costler was as crazy as a loon..the mountain fever had attacked him.

c. *transf.* A crazy person; a simpleton.

Perhaps influenced by LOONY.

1885 'C. E. CRADDOCK' *Prophet Gt. Smoky Mts.* xii. 230 But ye air a smart man ter that loon, fur..he dunno he air a loon. 1918 C. Sandburg *Cornhuskers, Sea Hold* 99, I am a loon about the sea.

Loop, *sb.*[1] Add:

1. e. *U.S.* The looped portion of a lasso.

1907 S. E. White *Arizona Nights* i. v. 93 Some few whirled the loop, but most cast it with a quick flip.

4. f. Add to def.: also, a similar path described by an aeroplane. (Cf. *Loop *v.* 6.)

1913 *Aeroplane* 25 Sept. 350/2 M. Pégoud succeeded in looping the loop completely. 1914 [see *Looper[1]].

g. A configuration in finger-prints.

1902 *Encycl. Brit.* XXV. 469/1 All impressions may be arranged under one of four types, namely, arches, loops, whorls, composites...Loops may be *ulnar* or *radial*.

6. *loop-head, method, -net, -road, system, way*; **loop-line** (examples of *a*).

1876 J. S. Ingram *Centen. Exposition* ix. 318 These were the larger and most important part of the exhibit, while the rest was made up of..prop nuts, *loop heads, offsets and stay ends. 1881 *Encycl. Brit.* XII. 815/2 In 1877 a *loop line, called the 'Belt', had to be made passing round the city, to connect the various railroads. 1908 *Daily Chron.* 16 May 1/5 The loop-line railway linking up all the railway termini. 1901 Waterhouse *Conduit Wiring* 51 The wiring in this building has been carried out entirely on the '*loop' method, there being no joints in any of the wires or cables. 1869 *Game Laws Ill.* in *Fur, Fin & Feather* (1872) 175 That it shall be unlawful..to take, or catch fish..by means of any seine, gill-net, tramel net, pike-net, or *loop-net. 1909 *Daily Mail* 5 Aug. 5/2 To construct *loop-roads for fast motor traffic round villages. 1901 Waterhouse *Conduit Wiring* 33 The great advantage gained by adopting the '*loop' system is complete metallic connection throughout the circuit. 1929 *Times* 1 Nov. 18/3 Traffic proceeding towards London is being diverted at Hatton cross roads, *via* Cranford-lane to the Bath road and London (A.A. *loop-way)...(A.A. loop-way signs).

Loop, *v.*[1] Add: **5.** (Earlier example.)

1837 Kirkbride *Northern Angler* 3 Loop on the dropper-flies; the tail-fly should also be looped.

6. *To loop the loop*, to perform the feat of circling in a vertical loop on a specially prepared track (see Loop *sb.*[1] 4) or in an aeroplane.

1904 *Daily Chron.* 17 Nov. 6/6 A daring attempt to perform a looping-the-loop feat on a cycle has led to a deplorable accident. 1913 *Aeroplane* 2 Oct. 384/1 M. Pégoud's performance culminated on Saturday by his looping the loop four times. 1914 *Isis* 21 Feb. 15/2 To Mr. Hucks belongs the distinction of being..the first Englishman to fly upside down and 'loop-the-loop'. 1923 *Daily Mail* 18 June 7 An attempt to loop the loop with the world's most powerful single-engined aeroplane.

Loop, *v.*[3] [f. Loop *sb.*[2] Cf. Looped *ppl. a.*[2]] *trans.* To furnish with loopholes.

1846 in *Life & Corr. Quitman* 261 The houses are of stone ..all looped for musketry.

Looper[1]**.** Add: **3.** *Aeron.* One who loops the loop, or has done so; a machine specially adapted for looping the loop.

1914 *Aeroplane* 15 Jan. 63/1 Two more names have been added to the roll of loopers. *Ibid.* 12 Mar. 284/2 Mr. Hucks ..first flew his two-seater, and later on the 'looper' at 700 feet, made one loop.

Looping, *vbl. sb.*[1] (Add quot.)

1922 *Encycl. Brit.* XXX. 32/1 Not until April 1913 do we find vertical banking by Chevillard followed by upside-down flying and looping by Pégoud in Sept. of that year.

Looping, *ppl. a.* Add: Also *looping-caterpillar* = Looper[1] 1.

1875 Huxley & Martin *Elem. Biol.* (1877) 98 The polypes ..are capable of crawling about by a motion similar to that of the looping caterpillar.

Loopist (lū·pist). [f. *Loop *v.* 6 + -ist.] = *Looper[1] 3.

1914 *Aeroplane* 15 Jan. 63/1 One of the latest loopists is M. Galtier, who on January 7th looped the loop at Chateaufort.

Loose. A. *adj.* **1.** Add: Of horses, etc., allowed to run free in travelling or marching.

1843 Fremont *Exped.* 10 A few loose horses, and four oxen..completed the train. 1846 J. W. Webb *Altowan* II. i. 41 The neighing of the loose troops, that ever and anon, broke forward to snatch the opportunity of browsing ere the crowd advanced,..presented a living picture. 1885 *Outing* Oct. VII. 21/2 All drove pack and loose animals before them.

3. (Later example.)

1908 *Animal Managem.* (War Office) 17 The skin..when handled, should feel 'loose' and freely movable over the structures beneath.

9. loose-coupling (see quot.); **loose-cover,** a detachable cover for a chair or couch; **loose head,** in football (see quot. 1927); **loose whale,** a whale which remains beside its harpooned mate and endeavours to defend it.

1925 P. J. Risdon *Crystal Receivers & Circuits* 22 There is another form of coupling, known as *loose-coupling, in which the aerial circuit and receiver couplet are quite separate. 1929 W. Deeping *Roper's Row* xxx. 336 With armchairs refreshed with gay cretonne *loose-covers. 1917 in P. Jones *War Lett.* (1918) 259 We used to spend hours arguing over anything, from free-will to the '*loose-head'. 1927 *Daily Express* 14 June 2/3 The 'loose head' (the system of playing more than three players in the front row of the scrummage). 1903 F. T. Bullen in *Strand Mag.* Nov. 539/1 All through the combat..the whale-fishers will be closely beset by the '*loose' whale.

10. d. loose-footed *a.* (modern examples).

1878 J. H. Beadle *Western Wilds* ii. 38 Every loose-footed man wanted to go. *Ibid.* xxviii. 442 Loose-footed young men erect a cabin, barely habitable in good weather.

Loosen, *v.* Add: **7.** *absol.* with *up*. To loose the purse-strings, to talk freely, etc. *U.S. colloq.*

1921 R. D. Paine *Comr. Rolling Ocean* xi. 187 Somebody will have to loosen up to pay for the damage to my nervous system. 1922 C. Sandburg *Slabs of Sunburnt West* 6 Come across, kick in, loosen up. 1927 Byrd in *Ladies' Home Jrnl.* 114 That is the first time he has ever loosened up.

Loose-end. Add: **4.** A tie with loose ends.

1906 *Daily Chron.* 28 May 11/7 Ties.—Good hands required, indoors, at once, for slipping Oxfords, Derbys and loose-ends.

Loose-leaf, *a.* Of a ledger, note-book, etc.: That has each leaf separate and detachable.

1902 *Accountant* 29 Nov. 1240/1 The difficulty he mentions is partly met by using a 'loose leaf' Ledger. 1904 *Ibid.* 28 May 710/2 The employment of the Card or Loose-Leaf Systems for statistical purposes. 1904 S. S. Dawson *Accountant's Compend.* (ed. 2) 468 Loose Leaf Ledgers consist of ledger sheets ruled in the ordinary way, but devised with the view of retaining within the Ledger 'live' Accounts only. 1907 *Daily Chron.* 6 Dec. 11/4 'Loose-Leaf' notebooks and diaries,..in which pages can be taken out or added at will, have already won a well-deserved popularity. 1917 Twyford *Purchasing & Storing* 409 A copy of every printed form used should be posted on a loose-leaf sheet.

Lop, *v.*[2] Add: **2. b.** *To lop down*, to sit down. *U.S. colloq.*

1839 Mrs. Kirkland *New Home* ii. 17 Jist come in, and take off your things, and lop down, if you're a mind to, while we're a getting supper. 1861 Mrs. Stowe *Pearl Orr's Isl.* i. viii. 67 Ruby said she thought she'd just lop down a few minutes on the old sofa. 1892 F. P. Humphrey *New Eng. Cactus* 34 You'd best lop down on the lounge and get a nap.

4. *lop-brimmed* adj.

1901 S. E. White *Westerners* xvi. 131 His broad hat—straight-brimmed in a lop-brimmed camp—was pushed to one side.

Lope, *sb.* **2.** (Earlier examples.)

1824 P. Horry *Life F. Marion* (1833) 111 He dashed off at a charging lope. 1833 J. Hall *Harpe's Head* 38 (Th.) On the buck came, at an easy lope, until he reached the top of a little knoll.

Loppiness. [f. Loppy *a.*[3]] The quality of being loppy or choppy.

1908 *Daily Chron.* 10 Aug. 1/4 He complained that the loppiness of the water had taken the strength out of him.

Loquence (lōu·kwĕns). *rare.* [ad. late L. *loquentia*: cf. Loquency.] Speaking; talk.

1677 T. Harvey tr. *J. Owen's Epigr.* 109 Thy Tongue is loose, thy Body close; Both ill: With Silence this, with Loquence that doth kill. 1886 R. F. Burton *Arab. Nts.* VIII. 346 When the Princess Miriam beheld Nur al-Din and heard his loquence and verse and speech, she made certain that it was indeed her lord Nur al-Din.

Lord-Mayoralty. Add: **b.** The honour or dignity of having a Lord Mayor.

1907 *Daily Chron.* 7 Sept. 6/2 A Lord Mayoralty was conferred on Bradford yesterday.

Lordship. 6. Insert: A royalty on minerals.

1861 Stephens & Burn *Farm-buildings* 171 The contractor will have Kinpurney quarry, free of lordships, for all the stones necessary. 1886 J. Barrowman *Sc. Mining Terms* 43 *Lordship*, rate per ton or other measure paid to the proprietor of minerals, royalty.

Lordy, *int.* *U.S.* = Lord *sb.* 6 c.

Also *Lordy massy* = *lord-a-mercy* Lord *sb.* 6 b.

1857 *Knickerbocker Mag.* L. 236 O Lordy me Sir! I'm so dreadful afeard you're both on you Dorrites! 1869 Mrs. Stowe *Oldtown Folks* xvi. 175 Lordy massy, what ears young ones has! 1897 R. M. Stuart *Simpkinsville* 155 Lordy, but it all takes my breath away. 1928 *Saturday Even. Post* 12 May 20/3 But seven hundred dollars and his pocket piece back again! Phew! Lordy!

Lorie, variant of Lory.

1848 H. W. Haygarth *Bush Life Australia* xii. 139 The lorie, with his splendid livery of blue and green.

Lorrainer (lǫrē·nəɹ). [f. the name of the French province.] An inhabitant of Lorraine.

1903 F. W. Maitland in *Camb. Mod. Hist.* II. xvi. 574 The Lorrainers were not France. 1918 A. Gray tr. *The Crime* II. ii. 106 Called to the Elysée in place of the Lorrainer of alleged 'nationalist' sympathies.

Lorry (lǫ·ri), *v.* [f. Lorry *sb.*] *trans.* To transport or convey by means of a lorry or lorries.

1920 *Blackw. Mag.* Jan. 125/1 Then they were 'lorried' to the Lys front.

Lose, *v.*[1] **3. f.** Add: Also with *off*.

1874 *Rep. Vermont Board Agric.* II. 717, I think that tin buckets are preferable for catching sap to wooden ones, as they..have no hoops to lose off.

4. c. Modern examples with *in*.

1902 *Chambers's Jrnl.* July 441/2 A bird does not gather speed when sailing in the air, as a falling stone would, neither does it lose in pace. 1913 *Q. Rev.* Oct. 413 As a consequence the work loses in freshness and even in clearness.

d. *To lose out*, to be unsuccessful, to fail. *U.S.*

1889 *Kansas Times & Star* 18 Nov., The reason Republicans lost out at the recent elections..was due to their tinkering with the tariff. 1904 *Charlotte Observer* 4 Oct. 4 News comes from New York that Editor Hearst may lose out in his race for renomination as Congressman. *a* 1909 'O. Henry' *Roads of Destiny* iv. 66, I know you've lost out some by not having me to typewrite 'em. 1911 R. D. Saunders *Col. Todhunter* vii. 101 That's right where you're going to lose out, Tim. 1913 Biggers *Seven Keys to Baldpate* xiii. 165 But it's over, and you've lost out. 1929 *Randolph Enterprise* (W. Va.) 14 Mar. 4/1 Elkins rather lost out in the new deal down at Charleston.

Loser. Add: **4.** *Tennis.* A losing stroke.

1928 *Daily Tel.* 29 May 15/5 Mrs. Watson..was not hitting many actual winners; Fraulein Aussem was making a series of losers.

5. *Bridge.* A losing card.

1918 Bergholt *Royal Auction Bridge* 56 An opponent will be able to make two tricks in that suit before Y has had a chance of discarding his two losers. 1921 Flor. Irwin *Compl. Auction Player* ii. 48 You hold five losers. That is a two-bid, no more.

Loss, *sb.*[1] **4.** Add: *To cut one's loss*(*es*), to cease carrying on a losing transaction.

1912 *Q. Rev.* Jan. 287 It is now made the basis of the argument that England should 'cut her loss', and Ireland be sent adrift. 1927 *Daily Express* 13 July 8/2 The only reasonable thing is for Great Britain to..cut her losses, and bring the whole matter to an end.

Lost, *ppl. a.* **6.** Add: **lost river** *U.S.*, a river which disappears in the ground and re-emerges; **lost rock** *U.S.*, a travelled boulder; **lost salmon** *U.S.*, the hump-back salmon; **lost stone** *U.S.* = *lost rock*.

1843 Carlton *New Purchase* ix. 58 Out come the mole rivers that have burrowed all this time under the earth, and which, when so unexpectedly found are styled out there,—'*lost rivers!' And every district of a dozen miles square has a lost river. 1831 Peck *Guide Emigrants* ii. 136 Scattered over the surface of our prairies are large masses of rock, of granitic formation, roundish in form, usually called by the people **lost rocks*...These stones are denominated *boulders* in mineralogy. 1857 *Trans. Ill. Agric. Soc.* II. 347 Another curiosity is the boulders, or 'lost rocks', as they are frequently called, which are found on the surface of the earth in the middle and northern sections of Illinois. 1881 *Amer. Naturalist* XV. 178 As vernacular names of definite application, the following are on record: Hump-back, gorbuscha, ..*lost salmon. 1819 H. C. McMurtrie *Sk. Louisville* 29 (Th.) [Certain stones] in the Illinois and Missouri territories are denominated *lost-stones, from their being strangers to the soil where they are found.

Lot, *sb.* **6. a.** (Earlier examples of *across* or *cross lots*.)

1846–52 Mrs. Whitcher *Widow Bedott P.* xxii. 236 You see yer uncle and me went hum by the turnpike instid o' gwine cross lots. 1848 Lowell *Two Gunners* 21 Joe looked roun' An' see (across lots in a pond..) A goose. 1853 Brigham Young *Jrnl. Discourses* I. 83 [I dreamed that] I cut one of their throats from ear to ear, saying, 'Go to hell across lots'.

10. lot-jumper *U.S.*, one who appropriates another's lot; **lot-layer** (earlier examples).

1869 *Overland Monthly* III. 63 Then there had been a *lot jumper's fight down at the end of the street. 1889 in J. B. Thoburn *Hist. Oklahoma* (1916) I. xx. 223 Gamblers, liquor dealers,..lot-jumpers. 1636 *Ipswich* (Mass.) *Rec.* 26 Feb., Appointed to assist the *lott Layers in laying out Mr. Dudley's..farmes. 1723 in *Coll. N.H. Hist. Soc.* VII. 349 Town-officers, consisting of a clerk, three selectmen, three lot-layers, and a constable.

Lot, *v.* **3.** (Earlier modern examples.)

1838 Caroline Gilman *Recoll.* vi. 51, I have taken to farming, and lot upon seeing the Carolina seeds come up that you gave me. 1844 *Knickerbocker Mag.* XXIV. 187 Here, everybody knows it, and everybody is lotting upon it.

Louden, *v.* **2.** (Earlier example.)

1891 *Harper's Mag.* Sept. 574/2 'Hum!' loudening her voice.

Loud-speaker, loud speaker. *Wireless Telephony.* [Loud *a.* 1.] Any one of several similar instruments for converting electrical impulses into sounds loud enough to be heard at a distance.

1923 *Daily Mail* 1 Mar. 9 For each concert there will be seating accommodation..for 1,000 people, and to these the concert will be delivered by powerful loud speakers. 1924 *Wireless Weekly* 8 Oct. 745/1 Loud speakers of all kinds are an outstanding feature of the show. 1928 *Morn. Post* 6 Feb. 3/4 The variations in the current would cause a hum..to be emitted by the loud-speaker.

Louisianian (lu,iz-, lu,iziæ·niăn), *a.* and *sb.* [f. *Louisiana* (see def.), named after Louis XIV of France.] **a.** *adj.* Of or pertaining to the State of Louisiana at the mouth of the Mississippi. **b.** *sb.* A native or inhabitant of Louisiana.

1805 *Ann. 8th Congress* 2 Sess. 1614 How different is the condition of the Louisianians. 1835 J. H. Ingraham *South-West* I. ix. 101 Americans; that is to say, Anglo-Americans as distinguished from the Louisianian French. 1854 Gayarré *Hist. Louisiana, Fr.* I. 13 Is not this the very poetry of landscape, of Louisianian landscape?

Lounge, *sb.* Add: **2. b.** = *lounge-coat, suit.*

1904 *Westm. Gaz.* 12 May 12/1 Then comes a technical description of overcoats, frock-coats, morning coats, 'lounges', reefers, 'vests', &c. 1905 *Daily Chron.* 16 Mar. 8/7 Advt., Good coat presser and baister for lounges and morning coats.

3. (Earlier U.S. examples.)

1835 *Southern Lit. Messenger* I. 298 You must have some such delightful *lounges* and chairs as I saw in New York. 1845 *Knickerbocker Mag.* XXV. 446 The hard-bottomed chairs were the same, and the lounge, and the tall mahogany clock.

4. lounge lizard, *slang*, one who spends his time in idling in fashionable society.

1923 *Weekly Dispatch* 28 Jan. 3 In America he is so well known as to have got a special and picturesque nickname, the 'Lounge Lizard'. 1925 Krapp *Engl. Lang. Amer.* I. 117 Who will know a generation hence..that a crape-hanger is a reformer, or a lounge lizard one who suns himself eternally in good society. 1926 *Punch* 17 Nov. 534/1 Formal recognition of those firmly attached appendages of Society, the lounge-lizards.

Loungy (lau·ndʒi), *a.* [f. Lounge *sb.* + -y.] Suggestive of lounges or lounging.

1911 G. K. Chesterton *Innocence Father Brown* v. 124, I mean little, loungy men, who had just enough to live on and had nothing to do but lean about in bar-rooms and bet on horses.

Love, *sb.* **16.** Add: **love-pass** = *love-passage*; **love-passage** (earlier example); **love-seat,** a special form of arm-chair designed for two occupants; **love-veil,** a veil made of love silk (see sense 13).

1872 Hardy *Under Greenwood Tree* i. viii, Good luck attended Dick's *love-passes during the meal. He sat next Fancy. 1845 Mrs. Kirkland *Western Clearings* 106 No one..had ever been able to ascertain whether there had actually been any '*love-passages' between them or not. 1915 Burgess *Antique Furniture* 205 Such settees which closely resemble an adaptation of two single chairs, are commonly called '*love-seats'. 1889 *Harper's Mag.* Oct. 696/1 I'd rip up an' press an' clean ladies' dresses, an' do over their crape an' *love veils.

Leve, *sb.*[2] [Of obscure origin.] One of a set of transverse beams supporting the spits in a smoke-house for the curing of herring.

1865 W. White *E. Eng.* I. 146 These open partitions or racks are called 'loves'. They support the speets, which are sticks or laths, long enough to lie across from one to the other. 1880 E. W. H. Holdsworth in *Encycl. Brit.* IX. 253/1 The smoke-room..having a series of wooden frames reaching from floor to roof, with small transverse beams, called 'loves'. 1895 A. Patterson *Man & Nat. Broads* 44 A savoury bloater, fresh down from the 'loves', is engrossing our own attentions.

Love-feast. 2 and **3.** (Later examples.)

1846 *Indiana Mag. Hist.* XXIII. 394 On Monday, we had a love-feast in the church, which has seldom been exceeded in deep and powerful religious excitement. 1893 Eggleston *Duffels* i. 6 At the love-feast these choruses sat side by side at the table. 1904 *Charleston News & Courier* 1 Sept. 4 There will be a great Democratic love feast in which a thousand Democratic editors will take part.

Lover[1]**. 4.** Add: **lovers' walk** (see quot.).

1906 H. D. Pittman *Belle of Blue Grass C.* ii. 19 A tangle of shrubbery near the gate, through which there was a labyrinthine maze, or 'lover's walk'.

Lovership. (Earlier example, used as a form of address to a lover.)

1837 Mrs. Trollope *Vicar of Wrexhill* (1840) 428 Your lovership must excuse me if I declare that it is my intention to accompany the young lady myself.

Lovey-dovey (lɒ·vidɒ·vi), *sb.* and *a.* [f. Lovey + Dovey.]

1. *sb.* = Lovey.

1819 [see Dovie]. 1904 *Daily Chron.* 26 Mar. 6/5 We will..love one another as much as we can, lovey dovey.

2. *adj.* Fondly affectionate; namby-pamby.

1886 *Harper's Mag.* Dec. 134/1, I would wear gray, which mamma prefers, but which I think looks lovey-dovey. 1900 H. Lawson *On Track* 65 Just as lovey-dovey talk is important to her and nonsense to you.

Loving, *ppl. a.* Add: **4.** *Comb.*, as *loving-hearted, -heartedness, -kind, -kindly* adj.

1903 Hardy *Dynasts* i. i. vi. 33 In its early, lovingkindly days Of gracious purpose. 1909 *Westm. Gaz.* 27 Feb. 4/3 The loving-hearted but hot-tempered musician who was head of the Conservatoire at Naples. 1909 Rupert Brooke *Collected Poems* (1918) 99 Quiet and strange, and loving-kind, you sleep. 1926 *Contemp. Rev.* Feb. 226 It may have been the *sirocco*, which never makes for loving-heartedness.

Low. A. *adj.* Add: **2. h.** Phr. *Low to paper*: Of type, of less than normal height.

1888 *Encycl. Brit.* XXIII. 698/2 Types lower than the ordinary dimension are said to be *low to paper*, and if surrounded by higher types will not give a perfect impression.

7. c. (Example.)

1912 *Chambers's Jrnl.* Aug. 533/1 He may feel that he is the superior in every way of some of the 'low whites' with whom he comes into daily contact.

21. *low-sided, -studded, -vaulted.*

1874 J. W. Long *Amer. Wild-Fowl Shooting* 78 A small, *low-sided boat..might be..dangerous on large waters. 1854 Shillaber *Mrs. Partington* 16 A tall man could not stand erect in the *low-studded room. 1873 Aldrich *Marj. Daw* etc. 155, I passed quickly into the house..and found myself in a long, low-studded bar-room. 1884 [see Studded *ppl. a.* 6]. 1868 *Rep. U.S. Commissioner Agric.* (1869) 303 A *low-vaulted room, receiving light from only one large aperture.

22. *low-branching, -burning, -cut, -trained* (also as pa. pple.).

1879 Tourgee *Fool's Err.* xliv. 326 She did not quite relish the idea of his bursting away through the *low-branching second-growth to follow the pack. 1904 Edith Rickert *Reaper* 8 His mother sat by the *low-burning peat. 1902 *Daily Chron.* 17 Jan. 7/6 Their costly, *low-cut dresses—Court Drawing-Room gowns without their trains. 1868 *Rep. U.S. Commissioner Agric.* (1869) 249 *Low-trained hedges may be necessary where land is limited in area, and high in price. *Ibid.*, Evergreens or shrubs may be formed, trimmed, and low-trained a long time without pleaching.

23. low gear, the gear used for the lowest speed in various machines, esp. in a motor or bicycle; **low maple** *U.S.*, the mountain maple; **low-neck,** a low-necked dress. (Cf. 1 c in Dict.)

1896 F. T. Bidlake *Cycling* 66 High gear for downhill, *low gear for up. 1902 Harmsworth *Motors & Motor-driving* 317 The low gear being used for hill climbing. 1907 C. Wheeler *Bicycles in Making* 80 By moving the gear to the left, the hub is driven by a free-wheel connected with the planet cage...This is the low gear. 1832 D. J. Browne *Sylva Amer.* 102 It is sometimes called *Low Maple, from the dwarfish stature of the tree. 1909 *Englishwoman* Apr. 319 Magazines with 'types of beauty'—in tights, ballet dancers' skirts or *low-necks.

B. *sb.* Add: **3. c.** A low point in price.

1929 *Observer* 17 Nov. 3/4 The sharp rally..carried the weighted average of eight leading industrial stocks up to 149.0 from the new low of 133.0.

Low-brow, lowbrow, *sb.* and *a.* *slang* (orig. *U.S.*). [f. Low *a.* 1, in contrast to *High-brow.]

1. *sb.* One who is not, or does not claim to be, highly intellectual.

1913 Biggers *Seven Keys to Baldpate* i. 21 My stuff is only for low-brows. 1916 H. L. Wilson *Somewhere in Red Gap* ix. 389 Ben...said this powerful play was too powerful for a bunch of low-brows like us. 1927 *Observer* 10 July 15/1 This is not a highbrow's book, nor is it a lowbrow's.

2. *adj.* Not highly, or not pretentiously, intellectual; unrefined, coarse, low-class.

1923 *Spectator* 22 Sept. 391/2 Often the sole reason why he [the man of genius] does not write 'low-brow' is because he cannot. 1927 *Sunday Express* 24 Apr. 2/2 He..picked up two newspapers, one of which is so highbrow that few people read it, and the other so lowbrow that I felt quite nervous. 1928 *Collier's* 10 Nov. 30/1 The doctor who is sufficiently adventurous, or lowbrow, to visit a soda-fountain occasionally.

absol. 1927 *Daily Express* 7 May 9/6 Our aim will be.. to steer a course between the 'highbrow' and the 'lowbrow' in music.

Low-browed, *a.* **1.** (Earlier example.)

1855 J. E. Cooke *Ellie* 71 The man, who was a coarse, low-browed fellow.

Low country. 1. (Modern examples.)

1823 Long *Exped.* I. 38 Here commences the low country, which extends west to the Mississippi. 1829–32 J. P. Kennedy *Swallow B.* I. xxiv. 231 The dew..in the low-country, at this season, falls heavily after night. 1869 Tourgee *Toinette* x. (1881) 114 He came from somewhere down in the low country.

Lowder. Add: Also looder.

1881 *Contemp. Rev.* Aug. 190 The cure for this was to throw a fire-brand down the 'lighting-hole' in the 'looder'.

Low-down, *a.* **b.** (Earlier U.S. examples.)

In quot. 1850 used in the geographical sense.

1850 *Congress. Globe* 25 Apr. 821/1 The 'lowdown' Virginia Democracy had to yield to the western mountain Democracy. 1868 *Putnam's Mag.* I. 704 That wretched caste commonly spoken of as the 'mean whites',..but in my district as the 'low-down people'. 1869 *Overland Monthly* III. 130 There are the delusive 'kettlings', among the 'low-down' people.

Low-downer. *U.S.* (Earlier example.)

1868 *Putnam's Mag.* I. 706/1 When candidates refreshed their adherents by the barrelfull, the low-downer enjoyed his periodical benders without expense.

Lower, *a.* **3.** (Modern example.)

1921 *Chambers's Jrnl.* 30 July 545/1 Appreciation of beauty..is that which most distinguishes the humans from their lowers.

Low-flung, *ppl. a.* *U.S. colloq.* [Low *a.* 22.] Of low character or standing.

1843 *Missouri Reporter* (St. Louis) 11 Apr. (Th.) Here we have a beautiful specimen of the dishonesty and low-flung slang of the clique. 1844 *Knickerbocker Mag.* XXIII. 506 Who wants a parcel of low-flung 'outside barbarians' to go in cahoot with us? 1853 J. G. Baldwin *Flush Times Alabama* 24 He..denounced Jefferson as a low-flung demagogue. 1861 *Oregon Argus* 28 Dec. (Th.) It would be impossible to attempt a controversy with such low-flung dogs.

Low-headed, *a.* [Low *a.* 21.] Of trees: Having a low head of foliage.

1861 *Trans. Ill. Agric. Soc.* IV. 328 Plant dwarf', or dwarfed, low-headed cherries, only. 1868 *Rep. U.S. Commissioner Agric.* (1869) 201 The silk tree (*Albizzia julibrissin*) is a low-headed, spreading tree, possessed of the most graceful foliage.

b. *transf.* Favouring low-headed trees.

1861–2 *Trans. Ill. Agric. Soc.* (1865) V. 205 We have never.. been identified with the ultra low headed orchardists.

Lowland. A. *sb.* Add: **1.** *sing.* (Earlier examples.)

1843 *Knickerbocker Mag.* XXII. 5 Everywhere, in lowland and highland,..nothing is more evident than the..degradation of the negro. 1850 R. Glisan *Jrnl Army Life* (1874) iii. 21 On either side of this lowland of the river, are the boundless prairies.

2. b. *pl.* The Low Countries.

1923 G. B. Harrison *Shakespeare's Fellows* iii. 100 Between his service in the Lowlands and the success of *Every Man in his Humour*, 1598, he had tried acting.

Lowly, *a.* Add: **2. b.** Of a low order of development.

1876 *City-Road Mag.* Jan. 44/2 There can be very little doubt that lowly forms can exist..at temperatures not much below 150° Fahr. 1890 Geikie *Class-bk. Geol.* xv. 222 The progress of life, from its earliest appearance in lowly forms of plant or animal, has been continuous. 1912 *Q. Rev.* Apr. 528 The most conspicuous physical features in Europe..had no existence when these lowly organisms lived and died. 1927 Peake & Fleure *Apes & Men* 13 Birds first appear in the Jurassic system, while traces of lowly mammals have been found from the Trias onwards.

Ltd., abbreviation of Limited (sense 2 b).

Lubber, *sb.* Add: **2. b. lubber grasshopper** (earlier example); **lubber-lift** *v.* (see quot. 1905).

1877 *Field & Forest* II. 160 The '*Lubber' grasshopper [is the] large grasshopper *Romalia microptera*. 1797 *Spirit Farmer's Museum* (1801) 85 Our Democrats begin to muster, Rolling around an anxious eye, Some '*lubber lifting' power to spy. 1905 *Terms Forestry & Logging*, *Lubber lift*, to raise the end of a log by means of a pry, and through the use of weight instead of strength.

Lubfish, variant of Lobfish.

1818 Scott *Rob Roy* ii, Stockfish—Titling—Cropling—Lubfish.

Lubric. 3. Delete †*Obs.* and add quot.

1909 *Jusserand's Lit. Hist. Engl. People* III. 436 Here we have a Bellario, all virtue and sweetness..opposed to a series of lubric and ferocious monsters.

Lubricate, *v.* Add: **2. c.** To grease the palm of; to bribe.

1928 *Daily Express* 12 July 1/1 He made specific charges. One was that taxicab proprietors have to 'lubricate' Scotland-yard before their taxicabs are passed for licensing.

Lubrication. Add: Also *attrib.*

1906 *Westm. Gaz.* 23 July 8/2 Motor-'buses, fitted with the new automatic lubrication appliance. 1907 *Ibid.* 13 Nov. 9/1 The lubrication system..can be regulated to suit all engine speeds.

Lubricational (l(i)ūbrikēⁱ·ʃənăl), *a.* [f. Lubrication + -al.] Of, pertaining to, or for lubrication.

1909 *Westm. Gaz.* 18 Nov. 4/2 An automatic lubricational oil pump is fitted at the end of the cam-shaft.

Lucca (lu·kă). [The name of a city and province in Northern Italy.] *Lucca gum*, a gum exuded by the olive tree. *Lucca oil*, a superior quality of olive oil.

1884 *Encycl. Brit.* XVII. 762/2 A resinous matter called 'olive gum', or Lucca gum, formed by the exuding juice in hot seasons. 1906 *Daily Chron.* 12 Jan. 6/7 Best Lucca oil. 1924 *Countries of World* II. 1377/2 The sesamum seed, used for the best lucca oil and grown in Honan.

Lucky bag. 2. *U.S.* (Earlier example.)

1840 *Southern Lit. Messenger* VI. 233/2 Every man-of-war, you know, has her lucky bag, containing a little of every thing, and something belonging to everybody.

Lucu·llic, *a.* = Lucullian *a.*

1905 J. McCabe tr. *Haeckel's Wonders of Life* xi. 98 The careful choice and preparation of savoury food..was just as important..as it is to-day in royal banquets or the Lucullic dinners of millionaires.

Ludolphian (ludǫ·lfiăn), *a.* [f. the name of Ludolph van Ceulen († 1610) who calculated the ratio to 35 places of decimals.] *Ludolphian number*, the ratio of the circumference of a circle to its diameter.

1905 *Westm. Gaz.* 14 Oct. 3/1 The history of the search for this ratio, the Ludolphian number,..is practically the early history of mathematics itself.

Luffa. *Bot.* [mod.L., ad. Arab. *lūfah*: see Loofah.] A genus of plants of the gourd family.

1884 tr. *De Candolle's Orig. Cultivated Pl.* 271 Angular Luffa—*Luffa acutangula*. *Ibid.* 272 The cultivation of the luffa is not very ancient.

Lug, *sb.*[1] **3.** Add: **lug-pole** (= sense 1).

1773 *Massachusetts Gaz.* 1 Feb. Suppl. (Th.) A defect in the Chimney by Reason of the Wooden Lug-pole burning out. 1848 D. Drake *Life Kentucky* v. 107 The tea kettle swung from a wooden 'lug pole'.

Lug, *sb.*[2] Add: **3. d.** *To put* (or *pile*) *on lugs*, to put on airs. *U.S. slang.*

1889 K. Munroe *Golden Days* xvii. 188 If you notice me.. piling on any lugs..you just bump me down hard. 1896 G. Ade *Artie* vi. 54 The family did n't put on no such lugs in them days. 1905 *Springfield Weekly Republ.* 15 Sept. 12 Dr. Hall puts on no 'lugs', and is not above sitting on a cracker barrel in a country grocery for a chat with old acquaintances.

4. (Earlier example.)

1835 J. Martin *Gazetteer Virginia* 175 An eminent tobacco manufacturer of Richmond has offered the inhabitants of this district to take all of their tobacco, (lugs included) at $10 a hundred.

Luge (lūʒ). [Swiss dialect.] A sledge, of Swiss origin, of the bob-sleigh type.

1905 *Sci. Amer.* Suppl. 15 Apr. 24488 The 'luge' is a small sled peculiar to the Grisons. 1907 *Ladies' Field* 19 Jan. 278 On the ascent the luge flies straight up into the air. 1915 E. R. Lankester *Diversions of Naturalist* 167 The [Swiss] 'luge' or sledge is supported in front by a strong mountaineer who prevents it from 'hurtling' down at breakneck speed. 1919 *Daily Mail* 10 Dec., A pair of winter holiday-makers in Switzerland enjoying a run on a Canadian luge.

Hence **Luge** *v. intr.* to toboggan on a luge. Also **Lu·ging** *vbl. sb.*, **Lu·ger.**

1907 *Ladies' Field* 19 Jan. 278 The gentle art of Luging... Les Avants is the most obvious place from which to luge... Caux is the only other [place] where lugers assemble in force. 1909 *Westm. Gaz.* 26 Jan. 5/2 Les Avants..has one of the finest natural luging courses in Europe. 1927 *Daily Express* 28 Dec. 3/1 Youths..'luged' in a reckless, haphazard style.

Lugger, *sb.*[1] Add: Also in *beef, ship lugger.*

1904 *N. Y. Sun* 5 Aug. 1 It was reported that beef luggers in all the cold storage plants were to be called out. *Ibid.* 11 Aug. 3 The men who are called ship luggers, and who load meat aboard the steamships.

Lukanism (lū·kăniz'm). [f. *Lukan* Lucan *a.* + -ism.] A form of expression characteristic of St. Luke.

1919 S. C. Carpenter *Christianity acc. Luke* 69 *note*, There are in the passage several Lukanisms of style.

Lukanize (lū·kănəiz), *v.* [f. as prec. + -ize.] *trans.* To invest with a Lucan character.

1919 S. C. Carpenter *Christianity acc. Luke* 81 It would no doubt be possible to assert that he determined at all costs ..to Paulinize and Lukanize the Master.

Lull, *sb.*[1] **3.** Add: Also *attrib.*

1904 *Pittsburgh Gaz.* 29 July 4 Construction trains that will be run during the lull hours of the day.

Lulu (lū·lu). *U.S. slang.* [Of obscure origin.] Something superlative or wonderful.

1894 'O. Henry' *Cabbages & Kings* xvii. 301, I smelt a million violets. She was a lulu. I told her I came in a private yacht. 1896 G. Ade *Artie* ix. 76 Mebbe you think I ain't got a lulu of a head on me this morning. 1911 H. Quick *Yellowstone N.* ix. 221 It was a lulu of a Society. 1922 Titus *Timber* iii. 38 *She's* a lulu though!

Lumber, *sb.*[1]

4. Add: (sense 1) *lumber-cellar, -closet, house* (later example); (sense 3), *lumber-ark, -box, -bush, -business, -checker, -cutter, -gang, industry, merchant, raft* (earlier examples), *-sledge, -trade, -vessel*; **lumber baron** *U.S.*, a leading or wealthy timber merchant; **lumber-carrier,** also, a vehicle for carrying lumber; **lumber-headed** *a.* (earlier example); **lumber-king** = *lumber baron*; **lumber-mill** (earlier example); **lumber-port,** a porthole in the bow or stern of a vessel for loading or unloading timber; **lumber town,** one chiefly engaged in the timber trade; **lumber tree,** a tree of importance as lumber.

a 1861 T. Winthrop *Canoe & Saddle* v. 83 It [a river] signifies navigation, in birch-canoe, seventy-four, floating palace, dug-out, or *lumber ark. 1889 Eggleston in *Century Mag.* Mar. 791/2 '*Lumber barons', 'silver kings' and creatures of railroad corporations. 1834 Seba Smith *Sel. Lett. Major Jack Downing* 26, I want you to load up the old *lumber-box..with *bean poles*. 1850 *Knickerbocker Mag.* XXXV. 22 (Th.), I had the misfortune to live in this town four years, my father having a *lumber-bush there. 1792 Belknap *Hist. New Hampshire* III. 211 (Th.) Husbandry is much preferable to the *lumber business. 1856 *Trans. Mich. Agric. Soc.* VII. 827 The lumber business of the Saginaw river and its tributaries has been developed. 1928 *Collier's* 29 Dec. 5/4 On the left were rows of twenty-foot lumber piles, trams laid between them, and electric *lumber carriers rolling on the trams. 1910 *Daily Chron.* 18 Jan. 3/4 A cramped and pokey *lumber-cellar. 1901 S. Merwin & Webster *Calumet K* viii. 141 Max, who to Bannon was merely an unusually capable *lumber-checker, was to Peterson a friend and adviser. 1854 Maria S. Cummins *Lamplighter* v, The former *lumber-closet, now transformed into a really snug and comfortable bed-room. 1775 B. Romans *Florida* 117 [They] planted their baronies in the pine barrens. There let the lords be *lumber cutters! 1904 G. Stratton-Porter *Freckles* 354 He joined one of my *lumber-gangs from the road. 1818 Fessenden *Ladies' Monitor* 38, I would not wish your pedant *lumber-headed. 1806 Weems *Letters* II. 356 T'other day..I found a box in the *lumber house of a Gentleman at Columbia. 1889 *Century Mag.* Feb. 601/2 I've come here to write up the *lumber industry. 1918 *Essex Inst. Hist. Coll.* LIV. 321 Mr. Narcross, of Lowell (the '*lumber-king'), hit the audience 'between wind and water' with a highly valuable array of facts. 1789 *Boston Directory* Dillaway, Samuel, *lumber-merchant. 1830 *Deb. Congress* 11 Mar. 606/2 You will not find, in any other description of mills, such constant, unceasing labor as in our *lumber mills. 1838 *Yale Lit. Mag.* III. 76 He..found that the pirates had knocked out the '*lumber port, with the intention of sinking her [the vessel]. 1837 W. Jenkins *Ohio Gaz.* 62 The Hockhocking river..furnishes..a downward navigation for flat boats and *lumber rafts. 1905 *Westm. Gaz.* 27 Jan. 7/2 A large number of coffins were laid upon a *lumber-sledge. 1880 *Harper's Mag.* Aug. 354/1 A cheerful little *lumber town lying high among the hills. *a* 1904 S. E. White *Blazed Trail Stories* i. 3 The streets..of the lumber town were filled with people. 1816 *Deb. Congress* 30 Jan. (1854) 809 A part of their fisheries and *lumber trade gone..they are called upon by your tax-gatherers. 1840 *Knickerbocker Mag.* XVI. 217 The lumber-trade is a business which will be introduced the moment the resources in pine, of more southerly regions, are exhausted. 1874 *Rep. Vermont Board Agric.* II. 161 The lumber trade of Quebec has been, and still is, very large. 1896 *Ibid.* XV. 81 The pine as a *lumber tree is already a thing of the past. 1835 J. H. Ingraham *South-West* I. iv. 51 These *lumber vessels..are usually loaded with shingles, masts, spars, and boards.

Lumber, *v.*[1] **2.** (Modern U.S. examples in special senses.)

1855 J. E. Cooke *Ellie* 207 Keeping the footman lumberin at the knockers on both sides o' the street. 1890 (*Amer.*) *Dialect Notes* I. 65 'Listen how he lumbers', said of a deep-mouthed dog's barking when he has treed a 'coon or 'possum. 1904 T. Watson *Bethany* (1920) 165 And he himself did not always know what he had on his mind until he pushed back his specs, and began to 'lumber' [= hold forth].

Lumber, *v.*[2] Add: **3. b.** To go over (ground) cutting the timber on it. Hence **Lu·mbered** *ppl. a.*

1900 *Yearbk. U.S. Dep. Agric.* 361 Not infrequently sound trees of a merchantable diameter are carelessly left uncut upon the lumbered area. *Ibid.* 365 The cut-over lands ..which..have been lumbered heavily, not only for timber but also for fuel.

Lu·mbersomeness. [f. Lumbersome *a.*] The quality of being cumbrous or unwieldy.

1877 Meredith *Ess. Comedy* (1918) 58 This treble-Dutch lumbersomeness of the Comic spirit is of itself exclusive of the idea of Comedy.

Lumber-wagon. *U.S.* [Lumber *sb.*[1] 3.] 'A waggon with a plain box upon it, used by farmers for carrying their produce to market' (Bartlett, 1848).

1842 M. Crawford *Jrnl.* 5 Left Buffalo at 11 o'clock in the morning in a lumber waggon on our way to the steam boat. 1849 Willis *Rural Lett.* xix. 165 So over the hills I jolted—three days and nights in springless lumber wagons. 1862 O. W. Norton *Army Lett.* 106 Great covered wagons as large as two of our lumber wagons. 1886 C. D. Warner *Their Pilgr.* xiii. (1888) 288 At this season one meets them [hop-pickers] on all the roads, driving from farm to farm in lumber wagons. 1902 Eliz. Banks *Newspaper Girl* 1 Gathered about the little village station in hard-seated lumber-wagons.

Lumber-yard. *U.S.* [Lumber *sb.*[1] 3.] A timber-yard.

1786 *Maryland Jrnl.* 4 Apr. (Th.) Lumber-yard, at the head of Baltimore Bason. 1818 Fearon *Sk. Amer.* 23 The timber, or (as the term is here) lumber yards, are not on that large and compact scale with which, in England, our friends C— and M— are familiar. 1835 *Southern Lit. Messenger* I. 291 Men of business delighted..in seeing the fine river obstructed by logs and slabs, and every corner wearing the appearance of a lumber-yard. 1851 C. Cist *Cincinnati* 207 Connected with the machinery is a lumber yard.

Lumbrous, *a.* (Earlier example.)

1836 J. Hildreth *Campaigns Rocky Mts.* I. iii. 26 Our lumbrous vessel heavily groped her way through the waters.

Lumen. Add: **2.** A unit of quantity of light.

1902 Webster Suppl. 1916 *Stand. Rules Amer. Inst. Electr. Engineers* § 857 *Lumen*, the unit of luminous flux, equal to the flux emitted in a unit solid angle (steradian) by a point source of one candle-power. 1926 *Encycl. Brit.* II. 409/2 In the United States the standard is the *lumen* or the amount of light that would fall on a surface [? *add* one square foot in area] so placed that all its parts are at a distance of one foot from a light source of one candle power.

Luminarism (lū·minăriz'm). [-ism, after Luminarist.] The art or doctrine of the luminarists.

1903 *Edin. Rev.* Oct. 373 We shall probably hear less of Turner as the pioneer of impressionism, luminarism, and pre-Raphaelitism.

Luminism (lū·miniz'm). [f. L. *lūmin-, lūmen* light + -ism.] = *Luminarism.

1905 *Sat. Rev.* 11 Feb. 174 And now, stated in general terms, what is the principle of Monet's luminism?

Lummox (lɒ·məks). *dial.* and *U.S.* Also **lummux, lommox, lummicks, lommocks,** etc. [Of obscure formation. Goes with the dial. verb *lummock* to move heavily or clumsily.] A large, heavy or clumsy person; an ungainly or stupid lout.

a 1815 Forby *Voc. E. Anglia* s.v., Look o' yin great lummox, lazing and lolloping about. 1854 Miss Baker *Northampt. Gloss.* I. 402 A great fat lommocks. 1854 Dow Jr. *Patent Serm.* IV. 149 (Th.) Man in his original state is little more than a big lummux of a baby. 1857 Holland *Bay Path* 381 (Th.) I hope you'll leave somebody else to home besides this lazy lummox. 1893 W. K. Post *Harvard Stories* 186 Well, don't you be such a lazy lummox. 1919 H. L. Wilson *Ma Pettengill* iii. 92 Oswald is a big fair-haired lummox that sings tenor in the Presbyterian choir. 1927 *Saturday Even. Post* 24 Dec. 83/2 A thoughtful weighing of all aspects would surely convince them that the big lummoxes get their money's worth out of the silliest purchase.

Lump, *sb.*[1] Add: **4. b.** (Earlier example.)

1849 N. Kingsley *Diary* 53 The farther north we get the more our anxiety is increased, as those big lumps are not quite eradicated from our minds yet.

5. d. (Recent example.)

1923 H. G. Wells *Men Like Gods* i. viii. § 6. 143 We shall all be..judged in a lump.

8. *lump-lac, -tobacco*; **lump-sugary** *a.*, suggestive of lump-sugar.

1815 Kirby & Sp. *Entomol.* x. (1818) I. 326 In this country ..it is distinguished by the names..*lump-lac when melted and made into cakes. 1873 *Beeton's Dict. Comm.* s.v. *Lac*, Lump lac is the deposit [of lac] formed into cakes. 1909 *Chambers's Jrnl.* Sept. 585/2 The body has a dry, *lump-sugary appearance. 1851 C. Cist *Cincinnati* 244 Charles Bodmann..manufactures *lump tobacco.

Lump, *sb.*[2] **1.** (Later example.)

1844 *Knickerbocker Mag.* XXIV. 471 We discussed the merits of dun-fish,..lump, halibut,..and trout.

Lump, *v.*[3] **4.** Add: *To lump large*, to bulk large, be imposing or impressive.

b. Of the throat: To have a 'lump' rise in it.

1912 J. London *Son of Sun* vi. § 2. 230 Deacon could not speak. His throat lumped and he nodded his head as he reached for the cards.

5. To do piece-work.

1905 *Westm. Gaz.* 10 Oct. 10/1 He..soon had the squad of irregulars at hard work 'lumping' as heartily as any gang of dock labourers.

Lumpless (lɒ·mplĕs), *a.* [f. Lump *sb.*[3] + -less.] Having no lumps.

1908 *Daily Chron.* 3 Mar. 8/1 As soon as the ingredients are fairly worked into a lumpless, creamy whole, stop beating.

Lumpy, *a.* Add: **1. b.** Also of broken weather.

1928 *Saturday Even. Post* 10 Mar. 8/1 'Had good weather?' 'Lumpy weather all the way.'

2. Applied to a person.

1926 Bennett *Lord Raingo* i. xxxviii. 216 The fair but lumpy young woman silently left the room.

Luna. 3. (Earlier example.)

1869 *Amer. Naturalist* II. 679/2 Luna Moth. 1876 *Field & Forest* II. 72 Mr. Rodgers..gives the history of the Luna moth (*Actias luna*).

Lu·nately, *adv.* [f. Lunate *a.*] In a crescent form.

1872 H. C. Wood *Fresh-Water Algæ* (1874) 109 Cells.. more or less lunately curved.

Lunch, *sb.*[2] **3.** Add: *lunch-bell, -can, -counter, -house, -pail, -room, -stand.*

1875 Mrs. Stowe *We & Neighbors* v. 67 The ringing of the *lunch bell interrupted the conversation. 1897 R. M. Stuart *Simpkinsville* 14 They'd give him biscuits out o' their *lunch-cans. 1887 C. B. George *40 Yrs. on Rail* v. 79 You can have one end of the station for a *lunch-counter, if you want it. 1906 'O. Henry' *Four Million* 223 He would be dining ..at whirlwind lunch counters. 1926 J. Black *You Can't Win* vi. 74, I went back uptown and into a lunch counter. The waiter was idle and talkative. 1846 *Knickerbocker Mag.* XXVIII. 558 The following parody was found inscribed on the newspaper-board of a '*lunch-house' in Saint Louis, Missouri. 1901 S. Merwin & H. K. Webster *Calumet K* xv. 289 They slung their *lunch pails on their arms and ate when and where they could. 1919 *Detective Story Mag.* 25 Nov. 129 He breakfasted at a hole-in-the-wall *lunch room before starting out on his quest. 1887 C. B. George *40 Yrs. on Rail* v. 79 Superintendent Johnson..noticed this *lunch-stand, with its modest, yet appetizing display.

Luncheon. Add: **2. b.** *U.S.* Applied to a late supper.

1903 *Boston Even. Transcript* 3 Oct. 5 At this table, from 9 o'clock until midnight, a bountiful standing luncheon was served continuously.

3. luncheon-car, on a railway train, a restaurant-car where luncheons are provided; also *attrib.*

1907 *Daily Chron.* 31 Dec. 3/6 A luncheon-car train will leave King's-cross each day at half-past one. 1909 *Westm. Gaz.* 8 Sept. 2/1 A new luncheon-car express, starting from King's Cross at 1.5 p.m.

Lunching, *vbl. sb.* [f. Lunch *v.*] The action of taking lunch or (*U.S.*) a late supper.

1920 R. L. Alsaker *Maintaining Health* 271 Lunching before going to bed is a bad habit.

Lu·nchless, *a.* Having had no lunch.

1920 Galsworthy *In Chancery* iii. i. 244 Sitting lunchless in the hall of his hotel.

Lung, *sb.* **7.** Add: **lung book,** a lamellate apparatus serving as a lung (cf. **book-lung*); **lung snail,** a snail having lungs in place of gills.

1892 J. A. Thomson *Outl. Zool.* 251 Scorpions have '*lung-books', and most spiders have both lung-books and tracheæ. 1910 E. R. Lankester *Sci. fr. Easy Chair* xxxi. 291 Fig. 49..*h*, heart connected by four big veins with *b*, the lung-books [*sic*], or air-gills. 1909 *Westm. Gaz.* 26 June 15/2 The land and most of the freshwater snails belong to the *lung snails, the gills being reduced to a mere vestige.

Lunge, *sb.*[2] **2.** (Earlier example.)

1845 J. J. Hooper *Taking Census* i. 155 That was a most unfortunate lunge I made into that hole in the river.

Lunge, *sb.*[3] (Earlier examples.)

1866 *Game Laws Vermont* in *Fur, Fin & Feather* (1872) 62 If any person or persons shall hereafter take..any trout or lunge..he shall pay to the treasurer..the sum of one dollar for each trout or lunge taken. 1867 *Ibid.* 68 No person shall kill or destroy any trout or lunge.

Lungy, *a.* Add: **b.** Coming from the lungs.

1909 *Westm. Gaz.* 21 Apr. 2/1 As the armed companies turned this corner of the narrow road a lungey Oriental cheer..saluted each.

Lunkhead. (Earlier example.)

1884 'Mark Twain' *Huck. Finn* xxii. 207 So the duke said these Arkansaw lunkheads couldn't come up to Shakespeare.

Luringly (l(i)ū·riŋli), *adv.* [f. Luring *ppl. a.* + -ly[2].] In a luring, or enticing, manner.

1897 J. L. Allen *Choir Invisible* xvi, This second image ..drawing always nearer, summoning him more luringly.

Lurk, *sb.*[1] Add: **4.** A lurking-place.

1924 *Chambers's Jrnl.* 20 Sept. 683/2 Why did the old beggar come to this secret lurk in the East End and disguise himself?

Lurkingly, *adv.* (Modern example.)

1906 R. B. Cunninghame Graham *Thirty Tales* (1929) 178 They eyed the women just as a starving dog looks at a butcher's shop, sideways and lurkingly.

Lu·rkingness. [f. Lurking *ppl. a.* + -ness.] Lurking quality.

1912 Galsworthy *Inn Tranq.* 51 The mist..seemed to have in its sheer silence a sort of muttered menace, a shuddery lurkingness.

Lurrier (lɒ·riəɹ). [f. Lurry *v.* + -er[1].] An operative in textile-printing (see quot. 1897).

1897 C. F. S. Rothwell *Print. Textile Fabrics* 34 The lurrier brings the colour required from the colour shop, the pieces and back-greys from the stock room, and also does any odd jobs required by the printer. 1921 *Dict. Occup. Terms* (1927) § 399 *Lurrier*, *lurryman*, colour carrier.

Lusatian (l'usēⁱ·ʃiăn), *a.* and *sb.* [f. med.L. *Lusatia*, the name of two districts (Upper and Lower L.) in Germany.] **a.** *adj.* Of or pertaining to Lusatia, esp. to its Slavonic inhabitants. **b.** A native or inhabitant of Lusatia, esp. a Wend.

1555 Eden *Decades* (Arb.) 318 The Slauon tounge..vsed of..the Bohemians, Lusacians, Silesians, Morauians [etc.]. 1862 Latham *Elem. Comp. Philol.* 766 Lusatian language. 1883 *Encycl. Brit.* XV. 68/1 Laws relating to Upper Lusatia ..must still be submitted to the Lusatian diet at Bautzen. 1887 *Ibid.* XXII. 153/2 The Lusatians are also sometimes called Serbs and Sorbs. 1921 *19th Cent.* May 894 We need only except Lessing, who was a Lusatian.

Lush, *sb.*[2] Add: **1. c.** One addicted to drink.

1899 G. Ade *Doc Horne* i. 1 'My uncle didn't think so,' remarked the lush. *Ibid.* iv. 39 The drinking man, often mentioned as the lush.

Lusher. [f. Lush *v.*[2] 2.] A drinker.

1895 Meredith *Amazing Marriage* xxxi, The suspicion cast on the dreary lusher was the wife's wild shot at her husband.

Lusting, *vbl. sb.* (Modern examples.)

1896 Kipling *Seven Seas* 82 With..the lying, and the lusting, and the drink. 1909 *Westm. Gaz.* 18 Aug. 2/3 Thou art grim with the lusting of gain.

Lutecium (l'utī·ʃiŏm). *Chem.* [mod.L. f. *Lutecia, Lutetia*, the Latin name of Paris + -ium.] A rare metallic element of the rare-earth group, occurring in the minerals gadolinite, euxenite, etc., first discovered and named by Urbain in 1907. It closely resembles ytterbium in properties. Symbol Lu; atomic weight 175; atomic number 71.

[1907 *Comptes Rendus* 4 Nov. CXLV. 759 (heading) Un nouvel élément: le lutécium, résultant du dédoublement de l'ytterbium de Marignac. Note de M. G. Urbain. *Ibid.* 761 Je propose pour cet élément le nom de *lutécium*, Lu, dérivé de l'ancien nom de Paris.] 1911 *Encycl. Brit.* XXVIII. 942/2 In 1907 G. Urbain separated ytterbium into two new elements, neoytterbium and lutecium (atomic weight, 174·0). 1922 *Nature* 17 June 781/1 The oxides of lutecium and ytterbium in a preparation of Urbain's were attached to the anticathode.

Lutetian. Add: **b.** *sb.* *Geol.* An Eocene formation in the Paris area.

1921 *Return Brit. Museum* 149 A shell of *Fusus serratus* from the Lutetian (Middle Eocene) of Seine-et-Oise.

Luxury. Add: **7.** *attrib.*, as *luxury duty, tax, trade.*

1904 *Hansard's Parl. Deb.* 19 Apr. 564 An article of luxury which might very fairly pay a luxury duty...The luxury tax at that time was 6*d.* 1905 *Westm. Gaz.* 9 Jan. 3/1 Their action deprives of employment persons who were..employed in luxury trades.

Lycænid (ləisī·nid), *sb.* and *a.* [ad. mod.L. *Lycænidæ*, f. *Lycæna*, Gr. λύκαινα she-wolf.] **a.** *sb.* A butterfly of the family Lycænidæ. **b.** *adj.* Of or pertaining to the Lycænidæ.

1892 W. L. Distant *Naturalist in Transvaal* 68, I have often mistaken it for a large Lycænid. 1901 E. B. Poulton *Mimicry illustr. Afr. Butterfl.* 2 They thus differ in habits from Lycænids generally. 1923 *Oxf. Univ. Gaz.* 4 June 950/1 A beautiful series of 84 Lycaenid butterflies from the Nicobar Islands.

Lyceal (ləisī·ăl), *a.* [f. Lycée + -al.] Of or pertaining to the French Lycées or similar establishments.

1904 G. S. Hall *Adolescence* I. 345 Marro tabulated the conduct of 3,012 boys in gymnasial and lyceal classes in Italy from eleven to eighteen years of age.

Lyceum. 4. b. *attrib.* (Earlier examples.)

1831 *Massachusetts Stat.* 4 Mar., They are hereby made a corporation, by the name of Lyceum Hall,..for the purpose of affording means ..for the prosecution of literary and scientific studies [etc.]. 1843 Carlton *New Purchase* I. 174 The common school system, and the lyceum system. 1844 *Knickerbocker Mag.* XXIV. 294 The remark of a lyceum lecturer upon matrimony.

Lyddite, *v.* [f. Lyddite *sb.*] *trans.* To destroy, wreck, etc., by the explosion of lyddite.

1906 Mrs. F. Campbell *Dearlove* 78 She was pleased they had not dynamited or lyddited him.

Lye, *sb.* **4.** Add: *lye-cask, -leach.*

1843 Carlton *New Purchase* ix. 63 A *lie-cask, or rather, an inverted pyramidical box to contain ashes. 1847 Halliwell, *Lie-leach. 1854 Mary J. Holmes *Tempest & Sunshine* xv. 202 Now be keerful and not run afoul of the plaguey lye leech!

Lye, *sb.*[2], var. of Lie *sb.*[2] 4.

1855 Ogilvie *Suppl.*, *Lye*, a term employed, in *railway lan.*, to denote the sidings or short offsets from the main line, into which trucks may be run for the purpose of loading or unloading. 1901 *Daily Record* 31 Aug. 3 A boy..was accidentally killed at the lye of South Renfrew Station on Thursday night.

Lying, *ppl. a.*[1] **2.** Add: **lying pipe, shaft** (see quots.).

1861 Sir W. Fairbairn *Iron* 57 Calder Heating Apparatus. ..The apparatus consists of two parallel horizontal pipes... called technically the 'lying pipes'. 1886 J. Barrowman *Sc. Mining Terms* 43 *Lying-pipes*, the horizontal pipes in a lodgment. *Lying-shaft*, the shaft of an engine on the end of which the tumbling crank is fixed.

Lying-in. b. (Recent examples.)

1912 *Q. Rev.* July 60 A slight increase in the ratio of lying-in claims to the number of members...A lying-in benefit of 30*s.*

Lymphatic. A. *adj.* **2.** Add: *lymphatic pump* (see quot.).

1910 *Practitioner* June 857 The mechanism by which a constant circulation of fluid into, and out of, the pleuritic cavity is maintained during health is known as the lymphatic pump.

Lyncher. (Earlier example.)

1836 Crockett *Exploits & Adv. Texas* (1837) 66 There exists, throughout the extreme south, bodies of men who style themselves Lynchers.

Lynchet, variant of Linchet.

Lynching, *vbl. sb.* (Earlier examples. Also *lynching-bee.*)

1836 Crockett *Exploits & Adv. Texas* (1837) 68 This is what we call Lynching in Natchez. 1837 *Southern Lit. Messenger* III. 648 The outrages of the borderers, the frontier law of 'regulation' or 'lynching', which is common to new countries all over the world, are ascribed to slavery. 1903 C. T. Brady *Bishop* ix. 172, I don't join no more lynchin'-bees. 1904 Harben *Georgians* vi. 62 They told me ..they were on the way to have a lynching-bee.

Lynch-like, *a.* [f. *Lynch*: see Lynch law.] Characteristic or suggestive of Judge Lynch.

1837 R. M. Bird *Nick of Woods* I. 221 Since Stackpole, having endured the penalty for stealing him, considered himself as having a legal, Lynch-like right to the animal, which no one could dispute.

Lynch-man. [Cf. next.] One of the early administrators of lynch law.

1811 A. Ellicott *Life & Lett.* (1908) 221 The Lynch-men associated for the purpose of punishing crimes in a summary way without the tedious and technical forms of our courts of justice. *Ibid.* 222, I should not have asserted it as a fact had it not been related to me by Mr. Lynch..together with several other Lynch-men as they are called.

Lynch law. (Earlier example.)

The particulars supplied by Ellicott, together with other evidence, clearly establish the fact that the originator of Lynch law was Captain William Lynch of Pittsylvania in Virginia. According to Ellicott, 'this self-created judicial tribunal was first organised in the state of Virginia about the year 1776'; an article in the *Southern Lit. Messenger* (1836) II. 389 gives the date definitely as 1780.

1811 A. Ellicott *Life & Lett.* (1908) 220 Captain Lynch just mentioned was the author of the Lynch laws so well known and so frequently carried into effect some years ago in the southern States in violation of every principle of justice and jurisprudence.

b. Earlier examples of **Judge Lynch.**

1834 W. G. Simms *Guy Rivers* 70 'Ef the whole country's roused, then Judge Lynch puts on his black cap and the rascal takes a hard ride on a rail, a duck in the pond, and a perfect seasoning of hickories tell there ain't much left of him. 1840 — *Border Beagles* 248 The murmurs began to close with the ominous inquiry after that venerable border magistrate, Judge Lynch.

Ly·nchy, *adv.* [See prec.] In a manner suggestive of lynch law.

1840 Haliburton *Clockm.* Ser. iii. xiv. 202 People began to talk considerable hard and Lynchy about their galls comin' so often to a single man to tell their experience.

Lynn, common U.S. var. of Linn[2].

1787 W. Sargent in *Mem. Amer. Acad.* IX. 158 Lynn,..a light white wood very proper for finishing the inside of dwelling houses. 1808 [see Linn[2]]. 1829 Dana *Geogr. Sketches* 84 Sugar maple, black and white walnut,..lynn, sycamore, cotton wood. 1839 in *Trans. Mich. Agric. Soc.* (1855) VI. 263 The table lands are mostly timbered with the varieties of oak, beech, maple, lynn, hickory. 1849 Chamberlain *Indiana Gazetteer* 170 The other forest trees..are ash, walnut..lynn [etc.].

attrib. 1796 Lynn tree; 1799 Lynn bark (see Linn[2]). 1819 E. Evans *Pedestrious Tour* 299 Here are the lynn tree, gum tree, [etc.]. 1886 *Harper's Mag.* June 58/2 Ropes are made of lynn bark.

Lyse, *v.* [Back-formation from Lysis.] *trans.* To dissolve or liquefy.

1925 C. H. Browning *Bacteriol.* vi. 123 The suspension soon becomes transparent, i.e. it is laked or lysed. 1926 *Encycl. Brit.* I. 302/1 Its inability to lyse dead bacteria.

Lysin. Add: **2.** *Biol. Chem.* A substance having the property of dissolving and destroying a cell, as in infection or immunization. Also as the second element of a compound, as *hæmolysin, leucolysin*, etc.

Lysis. Add: **3.** *Biol. Chem.* Dissolution of a cell by a Lysin (q.v. above). Also as the second element in a compound, as *hæmolysis, leucolysis*, etc.

1902 *Jrnl. Exper. Med.* 17 Mar. 4 That complete agglutination has no effect upon subsequent solution (lysis) of the corpuscles will be shown when treating of the latter phenomena. 1925 C. H. Browning *Bacteriol.* vi. 123 This lysis is the indication of the poisonous action of the toxin on the red blood-corpuscles.

Lytic (li·tik), *a.* *Biol. Chem.* [ad. Gr. λυτικός able to loose.] Pertaining to or producing Lysis (q.v. above).

1902 *Jrnl. Exper. Med.* 17 Mar. 281 Only when the lytic serum is very fresh will solution be effected. 1925 C. H. Browning *Bacteriol.* ix. 214 He concluded that the agent causing this solution or lytic action was a living virus.

M

M. 5. Add: M.I. = Mounted Infantry. M.O. = medical officer.

1903 KIPLING *Five Nations* 164 *M.I.*, Trot out the—M.I. 1917 P. MACGILL *Brown Brethren* ix. 133 If you're not better in the morning, just run down and see the M.O. 1924 *Army Quarterly* Oct. 138 Stop a minute—give this chit to the M.O.

Maa (mā), *v.* [Echoic, in imitation of the sound made by a sheep or goat. Cf. MAE *v.*] *intr.* To bleat. Hence **Maa·ing** *vbl. sb.*

1827 DARLEY *Sylvia* II. i. (1892) 57 It will make me *ma-a* like a he-goat on a rock-top when he misses the beard of his charmer. 1886 J. STEWART *Twa Elders* 147 The boys would maa and bleat. 1928 *Blackw. Mag.* Mar. 324/1 Poor old goat!..His caperings were fantastic, his *maaings* continuous.

Maar (mār). *Geol.* [G. dial., a crater-lake.] A crater formed by an explosion without emission of lava.

[1882 GEIKIE *Text-bk. Geol.* 560 Occasionally, as in some of the Maare of the Eifel, these non-volcanic fragments constitute most of the débris.] 1892 G. K. GILBERT in *Bull. Philos. Soc.* (1895) XII. 251 The maars are of still rarer occurrence, and represent the antithetic phase of volcanism. 1904 *Annals & Mag. Nat. Hist.* Feb. 135 Mr. Dusén is therefore uncertain whether to regard this lake as a very old crater or a 'Maar' formation.

Macaroni. 9. Add: **macaroni cheese**, a savoury of which the principal ingredients are macaroni and cheese.

1889 *Cassell's Pop. Cookery* 190/2 *Macaroni Cheese. 1923 *Mrs. Beeton's Everyday Cookery* xxxv.

Macartney. Add: **b. Macartney rose**, a climbing rose (*Rosa bracteata*) brought from China by Earl Macartney.

1837 [see ROSE *sb.* 3]. 1866 *Treas. Bot.* 990/1. 1886 *Encycl. Brit.* XX. 850/1 The Macartney Rose (*R. bracteata*) is also of Chinese origin.

Maccabean, -æan (mækăbī·ăn), *a.* and *sb.* [f. *MACCABEE + -AN.] **a.** *adj.* Of or pertaining to Judas Maccabeus or the Maccabees. **b.** *sb.* = *MACCABEE.

1833 R. LAWRENCE *Book of Enoch* (ed. 2) 217 Between the period of the captivity, and the rise of the Maccabaean dynasty. 1840 J. H. HOWLETT *Metr. Chronol.* (ed. 3) 16 Under the Maccabaean princes, what did the Jews become? 1890 A. J. CHURCH & SEELEY (*title*) The hammer, a story of Maccabean times. 1920 *Q. Rev.* July 4 His [*sc.* Disraeli's] party reaped the benefit of his Maccabean courage.

Maccabee (mæ·kăbī). [ad. L. *Maccabæ-us*, Gr. Μακκαβαῖος, the epithet of the Jewish patriot Judas.

'The source of the name is uncertain, but it is most natural to connect it with מקב [*maqqāb*], "hammer".' 1883 *Encycl. Brit.* XV. 130/2.]

Jewish Hist. A supporter or successor of Judas Maccabæus, the leader of a religious revolt against Antiochus IV, B.C. 175–164, as recorded in the books of the Maccabees in the Apocrypha.

1375 BARBOUR *Brus* I. 465 Thai was lik to the Machabeys, That, as men in the bibill seys [etc.]. *a* 1420 WYCLIF (heading) Here biginnith the firste book of Machabeies. 1550 *Briefe & Compend. Table, Concord. Bible* title-p., The thirde boke of the Machabees. 1614 RALEGH *Hist. World* I. II. x. § 1. 377 Then Modin the Natiue Citie of the Macchabees. 1702 L'ESTRANGE *Wks. Josephus* 1058 Flavius Josephus, his discourse of the Maccabees. *a* 1845 *Encycl. Metrop.* IX. 643/2 Hence, all who fought under that standard were called Maccabees, or Maccabeans. 1920 H. F. HENDERSON *Relig. Scotl.* i. 16 The patriotism of the Jew, especially in the age of the Maccabees, was an ardent passion that enabled him to overcome enemies four times his number.

attrib. 1865 *Sunday at Home* 194/2 But at length one of the Maccabee princes..subdued them. 1883 *Encycl. Brit.* XV. 131/1 The Vatican [*sc.* MS.] does not contain the Maccabee books.

Mace, *sb.*[1] **5.** Add: **mace-reed** = REED-MACE.

1901 MEREDITH *Reading of Life* etc. 126 A hundred mares, all white! their manes Like *mace-reed of the marshy plains Thick-tufted, wavy.

Mace, *v.*[1] Add: **2.** *Billiards.* To hit with a massé stroke.

1849 MARDON *Billiards* 57 (Plate 13) To mace (or, as the French term it, *masser*) a ball, it is necessary to hold the cue perpendicularly, and it should be grasped more than half-way down.

Macédoine (masedwan). [F., f. *Macédoine* Macedonia.]

1. 'A mixture of various kinds of vegetables, or fruits, or fruit embedded in jelly.' Also *attrib.*

1846 FRANCATELLI *Mod. Cook* 32 White Macedoine of vegetables. *Ibid.*, Garnish of brown Macedoine. 1894 L. HERITAGE *Cassell's New Univ. Cookery Bk.* 67 Soup with Macédoines. *Ibid.* 1127 Macédoine of Fruits. 1895 MARY RONALD *Century Cook Bk.* 378 Macédoine salad.

2. *fig.* A medley or mixture of unrelated things.

1820 H. LUTTRELL *Advice to Julia* 18 Such is the tattle of our beaux. These simple elements compose..The *Macédoine* of London-talk. 1852 MUNDY *Antipodes* (1857) 10 Now for a *macédoine* of advertisements, word for word as entered. 1902 *Springfield Republ.* 23 June (Cent. Suppl.) That strange macedoine of mental and moral qualities—the late Count Gurowski.

Macedonic (mæsĭdǫ·nik), *a.* [ad. L. *Macedonic-us*, Gr. Μακεδονικ-ός Macedonian.] = MACEDONIAN *a.*

1859 E. MASSON tr. *Winer's Gram. N. T. Diction* I. 33 The previously distinct dialects..were blended into a popular spoken language, with a predominance of the Macedonic variety.

Macerator. Add: **c.** A pulping machine. *U.S.*

1912 *Publishers' Circular* 12 Oct. 503 Then the macerator, the greatest consumer of contemporary literature, takes them [*sc.* books] to its bosom.

Machærodont, *a.* Add: Also as *sb.* A machærodont animal.

1889 H. A. NICHOLSON & LYDEKKER *Palæont.* II. 1448 The extinct Machærodonts or Sabre-toothed Tigers.

Macheer (mătʃī·ɹ). *Western U.S.* [Corruptly ad. Sp. *mochila.*] A leather flap attached to a saddle.

a 1861 T. WINTHROP *John Brent* v. 55 Showers shrank his buckskins and soaked the macheers of his saddle to mere pulp. *Ibid.* xx. 222. 1876 JOAQUIN MILLER *Unwritten Hist.* iv. 69 The Prince unfastened his cloak from the macheers behind my saddle. *Ibid.* xv. 209.

Machine, *sb.* **4. b.** Add to def.: A fire-engine (*U.S.*); an aeroplane.

a 1859 *Yankee Notions* (Bartlett) As for the machine, why, she's a pearl of the East. 1871 SCHELE DE VERE *Americanisms* (1872) 325 The particular *machine* in this case is the fire-engine, with its hose, ladder, and other paraphernalia. 1909 A. BERGET *Conquest of Air* 142 Let us consider an aeroplane..turning about a centre..: the circle which the centre of the machine itself describes [etc.]. 1919 BOYD CABLE *Old Contemptibles* viii. 124 He paid more attention now to watching for enemy machines, and never failed..to rush his pilot to a machine and into the air if a German was reported in sight.

9. a. *machine house, -power.*

1808 *Steele Papers* II. 562, I bought them [steelyards] from the store last winter for the use of my *Machine house. 1924 *Army Quarterly* Oct. 38 The replacement of muscle-power by *machine-power is the cardinal fact in every department of material life.

c. *machine-driller, -knitter, -printer*; *machine-knitting, -moulding, -production, -riveting*; *machine-finished* adj.; *machine-mould* vb.

1906 *Westm. Gaz.* 11 Jan. 3/1 The wages of *machine-drillers on the surface are 10s. a day. 1892 GREENER *Breech-loader* 52 The machine-made and *machine-finished gun may be distinguished: First, by [etc.]. 1927 T. WOODHOUSE *Artif. Silk* 83 If a *machine-knitter does not wind the yarns in his own mill, he can have them supplied in the form of bottle bobbins. *Ibid.* 86 In *machine-knitting several courses are formed simultaneously. 1922 *Encycl. Brit.* XXX. 36/1 By 1915-6 cast-iron cylinders were cast from metal patterns and *machine-moulded. 1888 *Lockwood's Dict. Mech. Engin.* (1892) 217 **Machine-moulding*..embraces the moulding of wheels and ordinary work by the aid of special machines. 1909 *Westm. Gaz.* 24 Sept. 8/1 An old man..described as a *machine-printer. 1899 J. A. HOBSON *Ruskin* 217 The 'driving' tendency of modern *machine-production. 1888 *Lockwood's Dict. Mech. Engin.* (1892) 217 **Machine-riveting*, riveting performed by a single application of steady pressure at the same instant upon the tail and head of a rivet.

10. machine-card = CARD *sb.*[2] 10; **machine-hours**, the time during which a machine operates; **machine-oven** *U.S.* (see quot.); **machine-piano**, a mechanical piano; **machine-shed**, a shed in which machines work; **machine-shop** (earlier examples); **machine-work** (modern examples).

1853 *Trans. Mich. Agric. Soc.* IV. 108 Various samples of *machine cards, well got up. 1832 *Louisville Publ. Adv.* 30 Mar., A. C. Brown..has established the manufacture of machine Cards. 1924 EMSLEY *Factory Costing* 81 Dividing these individual oncost totals by the number of *machine hours..gives the machine-hour rate for each class. 1890 *Century Dict.*, **Machine-oven*, a bakers' oven,..or an oven for any other use, fitted with a..mechanical device for aiding the process of baking, or for economizing time or space. 1926 *Proc. Mus. Assoc.* 1926-7 24, I do not want graphophone, *machine-piano, or any other kind of mechanical music. 1900 H. LAWSON *On Track* 132 With a rattling whirring roar the great *machine-shed starts for the day. 1845 *Mass. Statutes* 29 Jan., Abbott Lawrence..and John A. Lowell..are hereby made a corporation by the name of the Lowell *Machine Shop. 1849 CHAMBERLAIN *Indiana Gazetteer* 269 Among the manufactories in Indianapolis are ..two foundries with one of which is a machine shop in which steam engines are made. 1866 MRS. WHITNEY *L. Goldthwaite* i, No *machine-work, but all real dainty finger-craft. 1869 *Overland Monthly* III. 11 Seventy huge, clumsy cotton-hoes rose and fell in thoughtless machine-work.

Machine, *v.* **2.** Add: Also with *in.*

1895 JEANETTE E. DAVIS *Elem. Mod. Dressmaking* (ed. 2) 47 Tacking is not strong enough to hold sleeves well to the armhole for machining-in.

b. *absol.* To manufacture by machinery.

1916 H. G. WELLS *Mr. Britling* 16 They had standardised and machined wholesale, while the British were still making the things one by one.

4. c. To render mechanical; to work out on mechanical principles.

1916 H. G. WELLS *Mr. Britling* 67 What can be ruled about can be machined. 1919 J. L. GARVIN *Econ. Found. Peace* 183 As they drilled under arms or machined their Socialism.

Machine-gun, *sb.* [See MACHINE *sb.* 10.] Add earlier and later examples.

1870 *Jrnl. Royal United Serv. Inst.* XIV. 504 Machine Guns: The 'Gatling Battery'—The Agar and Claxton Guns—The French and Montigny Mitrailleurs. 1875 *Ibid.* (1876) XIX. 421 The particular hypothesis that machine-guns..would prove themselves unrivalled as death-dealing instruments. 1875 KNIGHT *Dict. Mech.* 1454/2 The mitrailleur, or machine-gun..sends a large number of small projectiles independently..to a considerable distance. 1917 *Inf. Mach.-Gun Co. Training* (Prov.) 7 Machine gun—A gun of the Vickers or Maxim type. Lewis guns are not included in the term Machine gun. 1919 BOYD CABLE *Old Contemptibles* ix. 146 The steady postman's-knock *rat-tat-tat* of machine-guns.

b. *attrib.* and *Comb.*

1906 *Westm. Gaz.* 4 Oct. 2/3 Motor-bicycles, those machine-gun terrors of the road. 1909 *Ibid.* 9 Dec. 5/1 Experiments carried out with the machine-gun-fitted aeroplane. 1919 BOYD CABLE *Old Contemptibles* xvi. 255 The rifle and machine-gun fire rose again.

Machine-gun, *v.* [f. the sb.] *trans.* To turn a machine-gun on, to fire at with a machine-gun.

1917 'CONTACT' *Airman's Outings* 185 Other guerilla work is done by craft which..machine-gun whatever worth-while objects they spot. 1918 E. M. ROBERTS *Flying Fighter* 38 Whatever they saw was sure to be machine-gunned. 1930 J. B. PRIESTLEY *Angel Pavement* ii. § 3 They sweep, lash, and machine-gun the streets with rain.

Machine-gunner. [f. *MACHINE-GUN *sb.*] One who operates a machine-gun.

1915 'IAN HAY' *First Hundred Thou.* xix. 279 The machine-gunner is a more or less accepted nuisance by this time. 1919 BOYD CABLE *Old Contemptibles* v. 83 The house..was too fiercely swept..by a tempest of bullets from a couple of machine-gunners.

Machinery. Add: **2. d.** The use of, or work by, machines; machining.

1923 *Daily Mail* 13 June 6 Advt., The castings leave the sand so highly finished that machinery is reduced to a minimum.

3. (Earlier example.)

1877 *Harper's Mag.* Dec. 149/2 There are at present finished four dwelling-houses (three for observers and assistants,) and the machinery house.

Mack (mæk), *sb.*[5] Also **mac.** A common abbreviation of MACKINTOSH 2.

1909 'R. ANDOM' *On Tour with Troddles* 239 'It's a case of macks to-day, you chaps', he observed. 'Raining?' I queried. 1917 EMPEY *From Fire Step* 170 In front of the door stood an officer in a mack (macintosh). 1922 *Glasgow Herald* 17 June 9 Rain..which..snuffed out the flaming hues of the characteristic Ascot under the commonplaces of macs and umbrellas.

Mackereling, *vbl. sb.* (Earlier examples.)

1880 *Harper's Mag.* Sept. 510/1 Among the rest are two of the singular 'porgy steamers' turned to mackereling. 1881 McLEAN *Cape Cod Folks* iii. 62, I was going mackerellin' with ye myself that time.

Mackinaw. Add: **Mackinaw blanket, boat** (earlier examples); **Mackinaw jacket**, a kind of thick jacket; **Mackinaw trout** (earlier example).

1826 T. L. McKENNEY *Tour to Lakes* (1827) 250 The *Mackinac blanket, which is the Indian's house, and great-coat, and bed. 1839 HOFFMAN *Wild Scenes* I. 113 We had Mackinaw-blankets, stretched upon balsam branches, to recline upon. 1846 T. L. McKENNEY *Mem.* I. 21 Mackinac blankets, and strouding, two indispensable articles, were wholly beyond his reach. 1839 *Knickerbocker Mag.* XIII. 211 Our boat was one of the kind locally denominated a *mackinac boat, of light construction, about twenty-eight feet long, and nine broad. 1909 ROOSEVELT in *Westm. Gaz.* 23 Sept. 12/2, I had..a *macinaw jacket for cold, if I had to stay out over-night in the mountains. 1840 *Southern Lit. Messenger* VI. 604/1 The celebrated *Mackinaw trout, so called after the town, near which they are found, is generally caught by the hook, and sometimes weigh ten and twelve pounds.

2. A hat plaited from coarse straw.

1895 *Funk's Stand. Dict.*

Ma·ckintoshed, *a.* [f. MACKINTOSH + -ED[2].] Wearing a mackintosh; protected by a mackintosh.

1919 BOYD CABLE *Old Contemptibles* ii. 25 The door flung open, and a rubber-booted mackintoshed figure stamped in. 1927 *Daily Mail* 30 June 9/4 Mackintoshed enthusiasts occupied them [boats]. 1927 *Observer* 10 July 25/1 The two mackintoshed policemen.

Macle. 1. Add: A flawed diamond (see quot.).

1899 R. DEVEREUX *Side Lights S. Afr.* 142 The commonest kind of flaw is a dark ridge stretching right across the stone, as if it had been severed at some period of its growth and welded together again. Diamonds so marked are called 'maccles'.

Maclock, variant of MUCKLUCK.

Maclura (mǎklū·rǎ). [mod.L. (Nuttall, 1818), f. the name of W. *Maclure*: see MACLUREITE.] The Osage orange or bow-wood. Also *attrib.*

1857 *Trans. Ill. Agric. Soc.* II. 222 A few Maclura hedges are growing. *Ibid.* 302 Mr. Tisdell has two hedges of the maclura growing on his farm. 1858 J. A. WARDER *Hedges & Evergreens* 21 The division of the prairies into twenty-acre lots, by the dense hedges of maclura. *Ibid.* 52 The cost of the maclura hedge.

Maconochie (măkǫ·nŏki). *colloq.* [The name of the makers, *Maconochie* Brothers, of London.] Meat stewed with vegetables and tinned, esp. as supplied to soldiers on active service; a tin of such meat. Also *Maconochie ration.*

1915 P. GIBBS *Soul of War* 70 The last tin of bully beef or Maconochie. 1917 'IAN HAY' *Carrying on* viii. 220 How would a Maconochie apiece suit your boys? 1917 EMPEY *From Fire Step* 43 Dinner consisted of stew..Maconochie rations, and water—plenty of water.

Macrocephaly (-se·făli). [Cf. MACROCEPHALIC, -CEPHALOUS.] The quality of being macrocephalic.

1878 BARTLEY tr. *Topinard's Anthropol.* Index 542 Macrocephaly. 1903 *Science* 30 Oct. 550/1 The evolution of man from microcephaly to macrocephaly. 1908 J. L. MYRES in Marett *Anthropol. & Classics* 148 Woolly hair..could also be superinduced, like macrocephaly, by assiduous curling.

Macrocra·nial, *a.* [f. MACRO- + CRANIAL *a.*] Having a long skull; long-skulled.

1902 *Biometrika* Aug. 462 Dolichocephaly and chamaecephaly in both races are associated with macrocranial characters. 1907 *Practitioner* Aug. 318 The population of the south-west of Scotland, exclusive of Glasgow, is long-headed or macrocranial.

Macula. Add: *Anat.* The (depressed) retinal region of most acute vision; the yellow spot. *Comb.* **macula-ring**, the border of the macula.

1901 *Phil. Trans.* B. CXCIV. 74 Fundus oculi (right eye) of the Lemurine Dourocouli. The macula is present, but the macula ring has disappeared.

Macular, *a.* Add: **b.** *spec.* Of or pertaining to the macula of the eye.

1909 M. GREENWOOD in *Further Adv. Physiol.* (ed. Hill) 397 If there is a good deal of macular pigmentation the mixed light undergoes selective absorption.

Maculature. Delete †*Obs.*⁻⁰ and add:

2. *Engraving.* (See quots.)

1904 *Burlington Mag.* V. 70 One of these [impressions of the Hundred Guilder Plate]..is a 'maculature', an impression on a sheet of ordinary paper passed over the plate to remove the ink. 1914 C. DODGSON *Brit. Mus. Guide Processes Engraving* 52 A maculature is another form of weak impression. A copper plate needs to be inked between each impression. Sometimes a second impression is taken from the plate before re-inking, as a means of extracting the remainder of the ink from the lines. This is called a maculature.

Mad, *sb.*[2] (Earlier and later U.S. examples.)

1871 *New Era* Apr. (De Vere) The Squire's mad riz. 1878 E. B. TUTTLE *Border Tales* 50 A grizzly will stand in the middle of the road, growling and getting his mad up, where there isn't a live creature within forty miles of him. 1916 H. L. WILSON *Somewhere in Red Gap* ii. 57 She kept her mad down better. She set there as nice and sweet as a pet scorpion.

Mad, *a.* **5.** (Later U.S. examples.)

1887 F. FRANCIS Jr. *Saddle & Mocassin* 111 The more he studied it [the bill] the madder he got. 1902 G. H. LORIMER *Lett. Self-made Merchant* xiii. 181, I didn't stop to think, but somehow I was mad in a minute. 1908 ELIZA C. HALL *Aunt Jane of Kentucky* ii. 48 The thing that made me maddest was Silas Petty a-leanin' back in his pew and smilin'.

8. (Additional examples.)

1809 *Massachusetts Spy* 5 July (Th.) He is naturally as mad as a beaver, and will scold like a termagant. 1855 HALIBURTON *Nat. & Hum. Nat.* I. 85, I feel as mad as a meat axe. 1902 HARBEN *Abner Daniel* 54 The Colonel is as mad as a wet hen about the whole thing. 1923 P. G. WODEHOUSE *Inimit. Jeeves* xviii. 249 My uncle will be as mad as a wet hen when he finds out that he has been fooled.

9. mad minute (see quot. 1917); **mad-rabbit** *v. intr.*, to lead an adventurous and stirring life.

1917 EMPEY *From Fire Step* 133 Usually when an Irishman takes over a trench,..he sticks his rifle over the top..and engages in what is known as the '*mad minute'. This consists of firing fifteen shots in a minute. 1919 BOYD CABLE *Old Contemptibles* vi. 95 In one long rolling crash the rifles broke out in the 'mad minute' of fire. 1919 GALSWORTHY *In Chancery* II. vii. 65, I wish I were a gipsy..To go *mad-rabbiting everywhere and see everything.

Mad, *v.* **1.** (Later U.S. examples.)

1872 MARIETTA HOLLEY *My Opinions* (1891) 249 At the same time it madded some of the Republicans. But it didn't me. 1893 'O. THANET' *Stories Western Town* 31, I madded him first; I was a fool. 1916 H. L. WILSON *Somewhere in Red Gap* vi. 268, I think to find him all madded up and mortified; but he's strangely cheerful for one who has suffered. 1924 W. M. RAINE *Troubled Waters* vi. 59 O' course, it ain't that any of them's afraid to mad that crazy gunman, Tait.

Madagascan (mædăgæ·skăn), *a.* and *sb.* [irreg. f. *Madagascar* (see next) + -AN.] **a.** *adj.* Of or pertaining to Madagascar. **b.** *sb.* A native or inhabitant of Madagascar.

1886 *Ibis* 135 The alternative hypothesis..that the Madagascan and Columbian species [of Snipes] have changed. 1890 *Century Dict.*, *Madagascan*, a native or inhabitant of Madagascar.

Madagascar (mædăgæ·skăɹ). The name of the large island off the east coast of Africa, used *attrib.* to denote persons and things (esp. products) of Madagascar, and in special collocations as **Madagascar cat**, the ring-tailed lemur, *Lemur catta*; **Madagascar (clove) nutmeg, manna** (see quots.).

1900 BRYDEN *Anim. S. Afr.* 12 Some of these curious lemurs, which are usually known as '*Madagascar Cats'. 1866 *Treas. Bot.* 28/2 One species, *A*[*gathophyllum*] *aromaticum*, grows in Madagascar...The fruit..encloses a kernel of an acrid caustic taste, known as *Madagascar Clove Nutmegs. 1889 *Century Dict.*, *Dulcitol*..is commercially obtained from an unknown plant in Madagascar, and in the crude state is called **Madagascar manna.*

Madagascarian (mædăgæskē·riăn), *a.* [f. prec. + -AN.] = *MADAGASCAN *a.* Also **Madaga·scarene, Madaga·scrian** *sbs.* = *MADAGASCAN *sb.*

1826 *Radawa: or The Enlightened African* etc. iv. 78 The first order is usually composed of those termed the white Madagascrians. 1860 [C. NORDHOFF] *Boy's Life Aboard Ship* II. xiv. 199 The natives..are mostly black, the descendants of Madagascarenes. 1875 A. NEWTON in *Encycl. Brit.* III. 758/2 Madagascar, the Comoros, and the widely scattered Mascarene Islands constitute a fifth Subregion,.. and for this we may most reasonably use the name 'Madagascarian'. 1895 — *Dict. Birds* 347 Those [genera] belonging to the insular or Madagascarian Subregion.

Madbrain. A. *sb.* Delete †*Obs.* and add modern example.

1876 MEREDITH *Beauch. Career* xxxv. He began to think her lost beyond hope, embarked for good and all with the madbrain.

Madcapery (mæ·dkæpĕri). [f. MADCAP *sb.* + -ERY.] The behaviour of a madcap; mischievous or reckless conduct.

1904 SLADEN *Playing the Game* xii. (1905) 139, I wondered what madcapery Rich had been up to.

Madder, *sb.*[1] **4.** Add: **madder-bleach**, a special method of bleaching cotton; **madder-print**, madder-printed cloth or cotton (*Cent. Dict.* 1890).

190. L. A. OLNEY *Textile Chem. & Dyeing* II. 48 (Cent. Suppl.) In calico printing..where a particularly clear and white ground is desired the *madder-bleach is used.

Made, *ppl. a.* Add: **3. b.** Of bills of exchange: (See quots.)

1868 SEYD *Bullion & Foreign Exch.* 89 The foregoing Foreign Bills of Class a are called *drawn* Bills, being usually negotiated from the Drawer direct to a London Foreign Banker; but where such drafts are made in the Country, and sent up to a correspondent in London, who then negotiates the same with his own Indorsement on them, they are called *made* Bills. *Ibid.* 90 Bills drawn abroad and payable abroad, but negotiated in the United Kingdom, are also *made* Bills.

5. *Comb.* *Made-to-order-ness*, the state or condition of being made to order.

1923 *Glasgow Herald* 8 Nov. 4 There is an air of cynical made-to-order-ness about the second [poem].

9. *made-over* (examples); **made-up** (*e*) of articles of trade, ready-made, not made to measure; (*f*) of stakes, arranged after the original programme of races is drawn up.

1912 R. A. WASON *Friar Tuck* xxx. 208 When Jim came back he was a *made-over man, and everyone asked him if he had religion. 1915 *Lit. Digest* (N.Y.) 21 Aug. 371/2 It isn't a made-over model, reduced in size,..it is a brand new car. 1916 J. E. WELLS *Man. Writings M.E.* 294 A copy, and perhaps a somewhat made-over copy of an earlier text. 1876 *Coursing Calendar* 110 In the *made-up stakes for puppies Mr. Farmer's brace..made a good display. 1895 *New Rev.* June 631 It is an odious fact that this country spends about a million and a half a year in the purchase of made-up clothes from Germany.

Madeleine (mæ·dlēn). Also **madeline.** [F.] A (kind of) small rich cake.

1846 FRANCATELLI *Mod. Cook* 404 Madeleines..are made with the same kind of batter as Genoese cakes, to which currants, dried cherries, candied peel or angelica, may be added. 1895 MARY RONALD *Century Cook Bk.* 477 Madeleines. 1922 *Q. Rev.* July 89 He is in his home in Paris, dipping a *madeleine* into a cup of tea.

Madonna. 4. Madonna lily (earlier example).

1877 ELIZ. S. PHELPS *Story of Avis* ix. 172 An exquisite motion which an artist..would not have wasted..on anything less than a *Madonna lily.

Madrasi (mădræ·si), *a.* and *sb.* Also **Madrassi, -assee.** [Urdū مدرسی *Madrasī*, f. *Madras* the city in southern India.] **a.** *adj.* Of or pertaining to Madras. **b.** *sb.* A native or inhabitant of Madras.

a 1877 H. HARTIGAN *Stray Leaves* Ser. II. (1879) 129 While ruminating, a Madrasi servant came out. 1878 *Chambers's Jrnl.* Feb. 115/1 English, after the rickety fashion of a Madrassee, Sam spoke fairly enough. 1921 *Contemp. Rev.* Sept. 291 'Western civilisation', said an eminent Madrasi the other day, 'has led to war'. 1924 *Blackw. Mag.* Aug. 227/2 The officer commanding..Madrasi Christians, will not admit this.

Madrigalesque (mædrigăle·sk), *a.* [f. MADRIGAL + -ESQUE.] Having the features or characteristics of madrigals.

1924 W. H. HADOW *Music* 99 A pleasant light comedy set to madrigalesque music with a real sense of characterization.

Madrilenian (mædrilī·niăn), *a.* and *sb.* Also **Madrileñan, Madrilenean.** [f. Sp. *Madrileño, -leña* of Madrid.] **a.** *adj.* Of or pertaining to Madrid. **b.** *sb.* A native or inhabitant of Madrid.

1890 *Century Dict.* (adj. and sb.) 1909 *Daily Chron.* 2 July 3/1 A far better opportunity..of seeing the inner life of a Madrilenean family of distinction. 1921 J. B. TREND *Pict. Mod. Spain* 65 Some critics have accused Baroja of distorting the Madrileñan character. 1927 *Chambers's Jrnl.* Sept. 675/2 To talk politics with Madrilenians in the cafés.

Madstone. *U.S.* (Earlier example.)

1834 *Southern Lit. Messenger* I. 182 He had no doubt that he should be able to form a concrete mass by means of beef gall and alkali, which would resemble and equal in virtue the madstone.

Maeterlinckian (mǣtəɹli·ŋkiăn, mā·tǝɹ-), *a.* [f. *Maeterlinck* + -(I)AN.] Of, pertaining to, or having the characteristics of, Maurice Maeterlinck, the Belgian author (1862–) or his writings.

1904 W. L. COURTNEY *Development Maeterlinck* 35 It is hardly a characteristic example of the Maeterlinckian drama. 1905 *Daily Chron.* 25 Sept. 6/4 She lived in a far-off Maeterlinckian age. 1909 *Times Lit. Suppl.* 22 Apr. 150/2 Conflicting with the spirit of mystery and fascinating Maeterlinckian unreality.

Mafficker. (Example.)

1910 *Blackw. Mag.* July 9/2 The 'mafficker' may hereafter come within sight of the enemy.

Mafiaism (māfī·a,iz'm). [f. MAFIA + -ISM.] The doctrines and practices of the Mafia.

1927 *Daily Tel.* 22 Nov. 7 Thuggism meant an end to human life; Mafiaism poisoned every department of it. 1928 *Ibid.* 15 May 13/5 A small bronze statue has been presented to Signor Mori, Prefect of Palermo, in token of gratitude for his great work eradicating Mafiaism from Sicily.

Mag (mæg), *sb.*[5] Abbreviation of MAGNETO. Also *Comb.*, as *mag-generator.*

1920 *Blackw. Mag.* Nov. 562/2 Having wrestled for an hour with the mags., they were eventually induced to give forth reluctant sparks. 1922 *Autocar* 10 Nov. 1039 One of the most interesting of the B.T.H. products is a mag-generator set.

Magazine, *sb.* Add: **6. b.** (Later examples.)

1915 'IAN HAY' *First Hundred Thou.* vii. 77 Pumpherston graciously accepted the charger of cartridges..., rammed it into the magazine, adjusted the sights,..and fired his first shot. 1919 BOYD CABLE *Old Contemptibles* xvii. 277 Carruthers..took a box of cartridges from a niche in the wall, and proceeded to recharge his magazine.

7. (sense 6 b) *magazine-slot*; **magazine-rights** *pl.*, the rights of publishing matter in a magazine.

1909 *Westm. Gaz.* 14 July 11/2 In America '*magazine rights' did not necessarily mean publication by instalments. The term was used to distinguish magazine rights from newspaper syndicate rights. 1923 KIPLING *Land & Sea Tales* 178 The tiny twenty-two cartridge had dropped into the *magazine-slot.

Magazinedom (mægăzī·ndəm). [f. MAGAZINE *sb.* + -DOM.] The world or sphere of magazines.

1890 *Rev. of Reviews* I. 9/1 Such a guide to magazinedom as you propose to establish would be extremely useful. 1902 *Tablet* 22 Sept. 448 It is the very romance of magazinedom.

Magdalenian (mægdălī·niăn), *a.* and *sb.* *Archæol.* Also **madelenian.** [f. MAGDALEN or L. *Magdalēna*, substituted for *Madelaine* (see def.) + -IAN.] **a.** *adj.* Belonging to the palæolithic period represented by remains found at La Madelaine, Dordogne, France. **b.** *sb.* A man or woman of this period.

1885 GEIKIE *Text-bk. Geol.* (ed. 2) 914 Those [deposits] which contain well-finished implements associated with carved bone and ivory, as at the caves of La Madelaine (Périgord), have been called Magdalenian. 1896 A. H. KEANE *Ethnol.* 87 Madelenian or Third Cave Age. 1911 SOLLAS *Anc. Hunters* 323 The Magdalenians were quite capable of making respectable buckles or fibulæ. 1921 *Glasgow Herald* 16 Feb. 13 The Magdalenian people. 1930 *Times Lit. Suppl.* 3 July 547/1 It is not a question of what the Aurignacian or Magdalenian believed, so much as of what his remains declare him to have believed.

Mage. 2. Delete †*Obs.* and add quot.

1877 *Smith & Wace's Dict. Chr. Biog.* I. 477/2 The author of that superstition was Masdec,..a mage, who gathered the credulous around him.

Mageship (mē¹·dʒ,ʃip). [See -SHIP.] The position or function of a mage.

1875 DOWDEN *Shaks. His Mind & Art* i. 37 Prospero must forever have remained somewhat apart and distinguished from other Dukes..by virtue of the enchanted island and the marvellous years of mageship.

Magic, *sb.* Add: **1. d.** *Like magic*: at once, with incredible rapidity. (Cf. LIKE B. 1 b.)

1857 *Knickerbocker Mag.* Jan. XLIX. 98 Broiled chicken and oysters..disappeared from before us like magic.

Magic, *a.* **3.** Add: *Magic stitch* (see quot.).

1901 DAY & BUCKLE *Art in Needlew.* 41 A playful variation upon chain-stitch..is effected by the use of two threads of different colour...The light thread disappears, and comes out again to the left of the dark one...This 'magic stitch', as it has been called,..is to be found in Persian, Indian, and Italian Renaissance work.

Magical, *a.* **3.** (Modern example.)

1915 *Hastings' Encycl. Relig. & Ethics* VIII. 321/1 The famous constituent of the mediaeval magical circle.

Hence also **Magica·lity,** magical power or quality.

1924 W. J. LOCKE *Coming of Amos* iv. 43 An untouched cheque-book of whose magicality he was innocently certain.

Magicianly (mădʒi·ʃănli), *a.* [f. MAGICIAN + -LY[1].] Befitting a magician, such as a magician would have.

1928 *Observer* 1 July 8 Here he is again with two trumps up his magicianly sleeves.

Magico- (mæ·dʒiko). Combining form of MAGICAL with other adjs. as *magico-religious.*

1922 *Nature* 29 Apr. 540/2 The complex and inexorable system of magico-religious *gennas.* 1924 W. B. SELBIE *Psychol. Relig.* 37 It [Mana] belongs to the magico-religious region.

Magistery. 5. = MAGISTERIUM 2.

1899 C. PALLEN *What is Liberalism?* xxxii. 165 The Church alone possesses supreme doctrinal magistery in fact and in right.

Maglemose (mæglǝmō̆u·sǝ). [The Danish place-name *Maglemose* (great moss) near Mullerup on the west coast of Sjælland.] Used *attrib.* to designate an early culture illustrated by articles found at Maglemose.

1915 SOLLAS *Anc. Hunters* (ed. 2) 544 The Maglemose industry is widely distributed around the Baltic. 1921 M. C. BURKITT *Prehistory* xii. 155 These..formed the Maglemose culture along the shores of the Baltic. 1927 PEAKE & FLEURE *Hunters & Artists* 106 It is customary to speak of these as the Maglemose civilization.

Maglemosian (mæglǝmō̆u·siăn), *a.* Also **-ean.** [f. prec. + -IAN.] = prec.

1928 WEBSTER Add. 1921 M. C. BURKITT *Prehistory* xiii. 173 The first culture found is the so-called Maglemosean. 1928 C. DAWSON *Age of Gods* iii. 46 The mixed forms of culture known as the Azilian and the Maglemosian.

Magma. Add: **5. magma-basalt** *Min.* = LIMBURGITE.

1885 GEIKIE *Text-bk. Geol.* (ed. 2) 156 Limburgite (Magma-basalt), composed of crystals of olivine, augite and magnetite in a base more or less vitreous. 1886 *Q. Jrnl. Geol. Soc.* XLII. 92 Basalts passing into Magma-basalts.

Magmatic, *a.* (Add examples.)

1903 GEIKIE *Text-bk. Geol.* (ed. 4) 808 Magmatic Ores. 1908 *Amer. Jrnl. Sci.* July 19 Often the blocks represent the effect of shattering, due to the..unequal heating of the solid rock at magmatic contacts.

Magnalium (mægnē¹·liǝm). [f. MAGN(ESIUM) + AL(UMINIUM) + -IUM.] An alloy of magnesium and aluminium.

1900 *Motor-Car World* I. 90/1 Magnalium is a new alloy of aluminium with from ten to thirty per cent. of its weight of magnesium.

Magnateship (mæ·gnē¹tʃip). [See -SHIP.] The dignity or position of a magnate.

1916 W. J. LOCKE *Wonderful Yr.* i. 4 The vast, original Margett had retired..to county magnateship.

Magnesian, *a.* Add: **2.** Of or pertaining to Magnesia (Manissa), the city in Asia Minor.

1904 W. M. RAMSAY *Lett. Seven Ch.* xiv. 175 Of the seven cities implied in the Magnesian title five may be enumerated with practical certainty.

Magneto, *sb.* Add: *spec.* The ignition apparatus in certain kinds of internal combustion engines.

1904 MECREDY *Dict. Motoring* 164 The wire from the terminal Z on the magneto being connected to the stud T. 1906 *Motor Cycles & how to manage them* (ed. 10) 70 The chain or gear, by which the magneto is connected with the engine.

b. *attrib.* as *magneto ignition.*

1903 *Motoring Ann.* 215 Two-cylinder motor, 8-horse Albion magneto ignition. 1904 MECREDY *Dict. Motoring* 167 Many cars are now fitted with magneto ignition.

Magneto-. Add: *magneto-induced* adj.; **magneto-exploder**, a magneto-electric apparatus for firing an explosive charge.

1869 *Chambers's Jrnl.* Apr. 271/2 A *magneto-exploder.. was shewn, which will fire a fuse, and consequently a cannon. 1908 *Installation News* II. 149/2 Water-tight bells and magneto exploders for blasting purposes. 1871 *Eng. Mechanic* 3 Feb. 480/1 He is referring to a galvanic, and not a *magneto-induced current.

Magneton (mægnī·tǫn). [ad. F. *magneton* (see quot. 1912): after ELECTRON.] A unit of magnetic moment.

Weiss and Bohr give different values to the unit.

[1912 WEISS in *Les Idées Modernes sur la Constitution de la Matière, Conférences Faites en 1912*, (heading) Les Moments Magnétique des Atoms et le Magneton.] 1917 R. W. HUTCHINSON *Adv. Text-bk. Magnetism & Electricity* II. 313 This fundamental magnet he calls the 'magneton'. Calculation shows that iron, nickel and magnetite contain 11, 3, and 7 of these magnetons per molecule respectively. 1927 N. V. SIDGWICK *Electronic Th. Valency* 208 The Bohr magneton..is almost exactly five (4·96) times the Weiss magneton. 1929 *Encycl. Brit.* XIV. 653/2 In 1911 Weiss, from measurements then available, concluded that there was a fundamental unit magneton of which all atomic or molecular moments were multiples.

Magnolia. 2. (See quot. 1903.) Also *magnolia metal.*

Said to be named from the manufacturer's mark.

1903 J. F. BUCHANAN *Foundry Nomencl.* 70 *Magnolia*, a famous anti-friction metal, the principal ingredients of which are: lead, tin, antimony and bismuth.

Magpie. 3. b. (Later examples.)

1917 G. W. E. RUSSELL *Politics & Personalities* IV. ix. 357 The most hideous of all known costumes—the episcopal 'Magpie'—costs £100. *Ibid.* 360 Carrying with his own apostolic hands the sacred appliances of Mitre or Magpie.

Magsman[2] (mæ·gzmæn). [f. MAG *sb.*[4]] A contributor to a magazine.

1890 *Rev. of Reviews* Mar. I. 198/2 Mr. Grant Allen is the most indefatigable of all magsmen. Articles from his pen appear in no fewer than four of the magazines of the month.

Magyar. A. *sb.* Add: **3.** *Dress-making.* A Magyar bodice or blouse.

1912 *Home Chat* 13 Apr. 112/2 Take away the lace insertion, and you get a quite plain little Magyar of white muslin. 1923 *Daily Mail* 19 June 15 A tight-fitting bodice which buttons down the back, the bolero bodice, and cross-over magyar.

B. *adj.* Add: **2.** *Dress-making.* Used as the distinctive epithet of a style of blouse, bodice, etc., in which the sleeves are cut in one piece with the main part of the garment.

1912 AMY J. REEVE *Elem. Dress Pattern-making* 17 The Empire yoke may be cut Magyar style if preferred. *Ibid.* 19 Magyar Blouse. Cut from Blouse Pattern. *Ibid.* 27 Magyar Overall...Magyar Bathing Dress. 1912 *Queen* 4 May 737/2 The bodice arranged on simple Magyar lines. 1922 *Daily Mail* 4 Dec. 1 Advt., Charming Wrap Coat with wide magyar sleeves.

Mahatmism (mā,hæ·tmiz'm). [f. MAHATMA + -ISM.] The principles and practice of the Mahatmas.

1905 J. M. ROBERTSON *Did Shaks. write 'Titus Andronicus'?* 7 The Baconian position..has no more in common with theirs than has Mahatmism with the system of Spencer.

Mah Jong (mā dʒǫ·ŋ). Also **Jongg**, and hyphened **Mah-jong(g.** [Chinese 麻雀 *mā-ch'iao* (Shanghai dial. *-tsiang*) sparrows (f. *ma* hemp + *tsiang* small birds), the name of the game.] An old Chinese game, introduced into Europe and America about 1923, played usually by four persons and resembling certain card games in many respects. The pieces used in the game are known as tiles; they are 136 or 144 in number and are divided into five or six suits. The object of each player is, by picking and discarding tiles, to secure a hand of 14 pieces arranged in certain groups (see quot. 1929).

1923 CHIANG LEE *Mah Jong* 7 Mah Jong, or Mah Tsiong (Sparrows), as it is pronounced in the city of Ning Po where it received its name and modern form, has been in vogue in China as a card game for about eight centuries. 1923 *Daily Mail* 23 June 6 There will be..demonstrations of Mah Jongg, the wonderful Chinese game which threatens to oust Bridge. 1926 *Chambers's Jrnl.* 6 Mar. 213/2 For fifty rupees you can purchase a Mah-jongg set of astonishing workmanship. 1929 *Encycl. Brit.* XIV. 677/1 The player who first succeeds in assembling his four groups and final pair, is said to be Mah Jong.

Hence **Mah Jong** *v. intr.*, to complete one's hand at the game of Mah Jong.

1923 J. BRAY *How to play Mah Jong* 12 Each player in turn draws a tile and discards one in place of this until some player completes his hand; i.e. 'Mah Jongs'. *Ibid.* 21 None of the following tiles in the hand assist so far in Mah Jonging (completing the hand)..and may be discarded.

Mahogany. 7. mahogany birch (early example).

1813 MUHLENBERG *Catal. Plant.* 88 *Betula lenta*..soft birch,..black birch,..sweet birch,..or mahogany birch.

Maid, *v.* Add: **3.** *trans.* To wait on (a person) as a maid.

1929 'R. OKE' *Frolic Wind* v, It was, of course, certainly untrue that she had a fourth to maid her.

Maiden. A. *sb.* Add: **9. b.** Short for 'maiden bed' of strawberries (see B. 5 b).

1928 *Daily Express* 28 May 5/3 The 'runners' are laid from the 'maidens' or last year's [strawberry-]beds.

c. Short for *maiden bell* (see B. *4 f.).

1909 *Daily Chron.* 1 Oct. 7/5 The High Wycombe 'tenor' ..thus issues proudly from the Whitechapel foundry a 'maiden'.

B. *adj.* Add: **4. f.** In Bell-founding: (see quots.)

1901 H. E. BULWER *Gloss. Techn. Terms, Church Bells* 2 *Maiden bell*, a bell that requires no tuning after it comes from the mould. 1910 *Encycl. Brit.* III. 668/1 The metal is then boiled and run molten into the mould... When extricated it ought to be scarcely touched and should hardly require tuning. This is called its maiden state. 1912 H. B. WALTERS *Church Bells Eng.* ii. 47 Sometimes a whole peal used to be turned out so nearly correct that no tuning was needed; such bells were known as a 'maiden peal'.

Maidless (mē¹·dlės), *a.* [f. MAID *sb.* + -LESS.] Not having or without a maid-servant.

1909 *Daily Chron.* 19 Aug. 7/3 The clever housekeeper knows the value of saying to the cook—or family, if maidless—'It is going to be so hot that we'll have cold meals'. 1926 *Public Opinion* 23 Apr. 410/3 The maidless mother is the chief victim of the storm.

Maid of honour. Add: **3.** *U.S.* A bridesmaid. Also *transf.*

1906 MARY WILKINS FREEMAN *Light of Soul* 348 Lily asked Maria to be her maid of honor. She planned to be married in church. 1911 H. S. HARRISON *Queed* xxi. 267 A victoria containing two lovely young girls sponsor and maid of honor for South Carolina.

Mail, *sb.*[3] Add: **2.** Also *U.S.* without article.

1873 J. H. BEADLE *Undevel. West* xxii. 441, I think this office gives us three times as much mail as that at Salt Lake.

b. *U.S.* (Earlier example.)

1873 ALDRICH *Marj. Daw*, etc. 163, I go over to K— for my mail.

4. b. (U.S.) *mail-boat* (earlier example), *-boy, carriage, hack, matter* (later example), *-van, wagon* (earlier example); *mail-carrying* adj.; **mail-box** (example of *b*); **mail-catcher** (earlier example); **mail-contract**, a contract for the conveyance of postal matter; **mail-day**, the day on which mails are dispatched or received; **mail-order**, an order for goods sent to a business house by mail; **mail-order firm, house**, one transacting business mainly by mail; so *mail-order business, catalogue*; **mail-rider, -road** (earlier examples); **mail stage** (later examples); **mail-time**, the time mails take to pass between two places.

1851 A. O. HALL *Manhattaner* 26 Next the dashing cabs from the early *mail-boat that was taking its morning smoke behind the swamp. 1922 MARG. B. HOUSTON *Witch-man* xix. 260 She stopped now at the foot of Little Glory to look in the *mail-box. Always she brought him his mail now. *a* 1861 T. WINTHROP *John Brent* xvii. 196 Jake Shamberlain aint a hog, and his *mail boys aint of the pork kind. 1874 *Congress. Rec.* 15 Apr. 3099/1 Hitherto seven [officers] were known as mail-boys and the others as mail-messengers. 1906 NEIL MUNRO *Daft Days* i, The tune of the mail-boy's song. 1860 HOLLAND *Miss Gilbert's Career* x. 166 The Crampton line of public travel and *mail carriage was only one of the many tributaries to the great trunk lines. 1909 *Westm. Gaz.* 1 June 8/3 The various lines of passenger and *mail-carrying steamers. 1876 *Centennial Exposition* v. 155 Other interesting exhibits were..a model showing the patent *mail-catcher used in the fast mail trains. *a* 1861 T. WINTHROP *John Brent* vi. 61 His ranch is down the valley, towards Pravo. He owns half the United States *mail contract. 1907 CORDINGLEY *Lond. Commerc. Dict.*, **Mail Day*, the day on which a merchant writes his foreign letters, or 'Mails' as he calls them. 1916 HAMMERTON *Argentine* 50 Once a week the exiles from Old England must feel a quickening of the pulse when they see the announcement in good bold letters 'Mail Day' or 'Mail arrived'. *a* 1909 'O. HENRY' *Roads of Destiny* x. 165 One afternoon Jimmy Valentine..climbed out of the *mail-hack. 1906 *Churchman* 10 Nov. 724 All *mail matter for the secretary of the convention should be addressed to [etc.]. 1905 *N. Y. Even. Post* 20 Apr. 6 The generic term '*mail-order' business includes everything from the great Chicago firms which do the business of a high-class modern department store by correspondence, to the solitary operator [etc.]. 1906 S. E. SPARLING *Introd. Business Organiz.* 318 The mail order is based almost exclusively upon circular advertising, and while the mail-order firms employ general publicity, they rely almost exclusively upon circularization in developing and holding the trade. 1919 H. L. WILSON *Ma Pettengill* v. 176 We got down the mail-order catalogue the minute you left that money with us. 1928 *Collier's* 29 Dec. 7/1 Wasn't it my suggestion that marriage be turned over to the mail-order houses? 1801 in C. CIST *Cincinnati* (1841) 177 The *mail-rider..from the upper route. 1846 *Knickerbocker Mag.* XXVII. 52 The mail-rider sank down apparently through the solid ground with his horse and saddle-bags. *a* 1861 T. WINTHROP *John Brent* iii. (1862) 32, I had made my arrangements to start about the first of September, with the Sacramento mailriders. 1818 in Fearon *Sk. Amer.* 430 About three miles from the great *mail road to Cincinnati. 1821 T. NUTTALL *Trav. Arkansas* i. 35 On the morning of the second of October, 1818, I took my departure from Philadelphia in the *mail stage. 1834 *Southern Lit. Messenger* I. 181, I took my seat in the mail stage, and travelled three hundred miles without once going to bed. 1912 *Chambers's Jrnl.* Jan. 5/2 The *mail-time between that town [Villa Rica] and London will be reduced from thirty days to about eighteen. 1909 *Ibid.* June 343/2 *Mail-vans in large numbers ..are now being driven by mechanical power. 1872 EGGLESTON *Hoosier Schoolm.* xvii. 135 You can git on the *mail-wagon that passes there about five o'clock.

Mailabi·lity. *U.S.* [f. MAILABLE *a.*] The quality or fact of being mailable.

1903 in *Publishers' Circular* (Lond.) 3 Mar. 275/3 As the card does not bear on the address side the words 'United States of America', its mailability is not affected by my circular of the 16th ult.

Mailed, *a.* **2.** Add: *mailed fist*, taken as the emblem of superior force or might.

[See quot. 1897 in Dict.] 1898 *19th Cent.* Jan. 164 Japan is a foe who will not be terrified by the mailed fist of Germany. 1898 *Rev. of Reviews* Mar. 214 Prince Henry of the mailed fist has by this time reached his destination.

Mailing, *vbl. sb.*[2] Add: **mailing-list** *U.S.*, a register of addresses to which goods and postal matter are sent.

1909 *Daily Chron.* 12 Oct. 4/5 In the States there are 600,000 farmers on the mailing list. 1928 *Publishers' Weekly* 26 May 2201 It is proposed that the booksellers of the country place in this Clearing House..duplicates of their mailing lists.

Main, *a.* **11.** Add: **main crop**, the chief crop, excluding the early and late varieties or sections; also *attrib.* (usu. with hyphen).

1782 MAWE & ABERCROMBIE *Every Man his own Gardener* (ed. 9) 119 Onions or leeks for the main crop should be sown the beginning or middle of this month. 1859 R. THOMPSON *Gard. Assist.* 249 The main crop of the Long Horn, Altrincham, and other large sorts [of carrots] for winter use, should be sown [etc.]. 1877 HIBBERD *Amateur's Kitchen Gard.* 49 The second early and main crop sorts [of peas]. 1880 *Encycl. Brit.* XII. 286/2 The varieties of the potato are very numerous...Early..Main Crop and Late. 1884 *Sutton's Cult. Veg. & Flowers* 147 Potatoes for main crops should now be got in.

Main (mē¹n), *v.* [f. *main road* (MAIN *a.* 8 b).] *trans.* To convert into a main road.

1927 *Daily Tel.* 7 June 11/3 The widening and 'maining' of the road leading to the Royal Hotel corner.

Maine (mē¹n), *sb.*[2] *U.S.* The name of the State of *Maine* used in *Maine* (*liquor*) *law*, a law forbidding the manufacture or sale of intoxicating liquors; hence applied to similar laws (see quot. 1897).

1855 *Knickerbocker Mag.* XLV. 479 They have the Maine Law down below. 1860 W. L. SARGANT *R. Owen & His Soc. Phil.* xix. 216 Nor had he had recourse to a Maine law. 1864 T. H. NICHOLS *Amer. Life* I. 76 But drunkenness becoming common,..spirits were banished, the apple orchards cut down,..'Maine Laws' were finally passed. 1871 *Scribner's Monthly* I. 673 Its special suggestiveness resides in the fact that it originates with the friends of the Maine law. 1897 *Encycl. Soc. Reform* 1107/1 A prohibitory law was passed in Maine in 1846, and in 1851 a more stringent one, including the provision for the seizure and destruction of intoxicating liquors (known as the 'Maine Law'..) was enacted...Vermont in 1852, New Hampshire in 1855, and Connecticut in 1854, passed the Maine law.

b. *Maine law man*: a prohibitionist.

1858 *Leisure Hour* 3 June 352/2 Upon the extensive mines ..are large numbers of teetotallers and Maine Law men.

Main Street. [MAIN *a.* 8 c.] The name given to the principal street in certain towns, esp. in the United States. Hence used allusively.

The term has become more familiar since the publication of Sinclair Lewis's novel, *Main Street*, in 1920.

1817 S. BROWN *Western Gaz.* 92 Main street presents to the traveller as much wealth, and more beauty than can be found in most of the Atlantic cities. 1843 *Yale Lit. Mag.* VIII. 308 It [Bodkinville] can boast of but one street, which, by way of distinction is called Main street. 1853 B. F. TAYLOR *Jan. & June* (1871) 255 The quivering lightning flutters in at the windows on Maine Street. 1855 *Knickerbocker Mag.* XLVI. 328 Louisville is an imposing, wealthy city. Main-street, in its entire extent would do honor to any metropolis in America. 1916 BOWER *Phantom Herd* i. 5 You'll have to let me weed out some of these Main Street cowboys. 1931 *Times Lit. Suppl.* 9 Apr. 282/3 He dislikes uniformity, mass-control, Main-street and Rotarian ideals.

Maiotic, variant of *MEIOTIC *a.*

Maisonnette. Add: **2.** (Usually in the form *maisonette.*) A part of a residential building which is let separately, distinguished from a flat by not being all on one floor.

1912 *Chambers's Jrnl.* Feb. 144/2 Flats or maisonettes, such as Queen Anne's Mansions, Westminster, London.

Maitiff, variant of MÉTIF.

1805 SIBLEY in *Ann. 9th Congress* 2 Sess. 1081 Some of the women who had been servants in good families..married maitiffs of the country.

Maître d'hôtel. Add: **2.** An hotel manager.

1891 R. H. SAVAGE *My official Wife* iv. 46 The attentive *maître d'hôtel* flew past us and threw open the door of a splendid apartment. 1923 'M. ARLEN' *These Charming People* 85 The agreeable and polished M. Risotto, prince of *maîtres d'hôtels*, chanced by our table.

Maize. Add: **3.** Freq. denoting a colour of cloth or dress-material.

1858 'GEO. ELIOT' *Scenes Cler. Life* 16 Maize is a colour that decidedly did *not* suit his complexion. 1878 *Cassell's Family Mag.* IV. 106/1 Coloured silk braids being let into the indented lines—cardinal on mouse-colour, maize on brown, &c. 1923 *Daily Mail* 15 June 6 Advt., Crepe de Chine..newest shades, including: Pale Pink,..Maize, Lemon.

4. *maize-yellow.*

1897 C. T. DAVIS *Manuf. Leather* (ed. 2) 607 Light ochre yellow, *maize yellow to dark gold ochre yellow.

Majesticalness. (Modern example.)

1905 *Westm. Gaz.* 19 Apr. 1/3 The majesticalness of this master-work of human genius and human sorrows.

Majoli (māyǫ·li). [f. the names of Michael and Thomas *Majoli*, Italian bookbinders of the 15th century.] Used *attrib.* to denote an ornamental style of bookbinding.

1890 *Catal. Exhib. Bk.-bindings Grolier Club* 37 [Book] Brown morocco..Sides decorated with a Maioli design. *c* 1895 W. MATTHEWS *Mod. Bookbinding* 71 (Cent. Suppl.) The principal features of a Maioli design, I claim, are a perfect curve in scrollwork where it is used, a framework of flowing curved lines [etc.].

Major, *sb.*[1] Add: **1. c.** (See quot. 1919.)

1910 R. BLATCHFORD *Life in Army* xvii. (1914) 123 The 'major' meant well. 1919 *War Slang* in *Athenæum* 25 July 664/1 'Major', for Sergeant-major—a polite form of address by an N.C.O. 1925 E. FRASER & GIBBONS *Soldier & Sailor Words.*

Major. A. *adj.* Add: **1. d.** In Bridge. *Major suit*: Spades or hearts, which count more than diamonds or clubs.

1919 R. F. FOSTER *On Auction* 66 The standard for a free bid in a major suit is five cards headed by two sure tricks.

B. *sb.*[2] Add: **6.** *U.S.* In some universities, a subject to which special attention is given during a certain period of study.

1890 in T. W. Goodspeed *Hist. Univ. Chicago* (1916) 142 A subject taken as a major requires eight or ten hours class-room work or lecture work a week. 1891 *Univ. of Chicago Bull.* No. 1. 12 The Major will call for 10, 11, or 12 hours of Class-room work each week, the Minor for 4, 5, or 6 hours of Class-room work each week. 1907 *Columbia Univ. Catal.* Mar., Open only to students taking a major in the Department of English. 1926 [see *MINOR B 10].

Major, *v.* Add: **3.** *U.S.* *intr.* Of a university student: To take, or qualify *in*, a major course of study.

1927 *Brit. Weekly* 1 Sept. 470/2 It is a thesis for the Th.D. degree, for which he has already stood the examination, 'Majoring' in the Greek New Testament at Louisville. 1929 *Publishers' Weekly* 20 July 252 Bulbous-headed adolescents who have majored in English descend in shoals.

Majorcan (mădʒǭ·ɹkăn), *a.* and *sb.* Also 7 **Majorkine.** [f. *Majorca* the name of one of the Balearic Islands + -AN.] **a.** *adj.* Of or pertaining to Majorca. **b.** *sb.* A native or inhabitant of Majorca.

1697 MAUNDRELL *Journ. Aleppo* (ed. 2) 124 We..were very courteously receiv'd by the Guardian, Father Raphael, a Majorkine by Birth. 1848 SABINE tr. *Humboldt's Cosmos* II. 147 One maritime people after another, Phoenicians,.. Majorcans,..and Spaniards, made successive efforts to penetrate onwards in the Atlantic Ocean. 1873 *Gentl. Mag.* Feb. X. 219 The family of Napoleon I. was originally native of that island *i.e.* Majorcan. 1876 C. T. BIDWELL *Balearic Isl.* 105 Myrtle-covered posts, in the use of which the Majorcans display natural skill. *Ibid.* 111 Majorcan carpets and matting cover the floors.

Major-domo. Add: **c.** *U.S.* In south-western states, an overseer on a farm or ranch; also, the water-master or official in charge of irrigation in New Mexico.

1836 EDWARD *Hist. Texas* ix. 291 Having thus glanced at the Major domo, we shall take a peek at his Locum tenens. 1848 E. BRYANT *California* xxix. 352 We inquired for the mayor domo, or overseer. 1902 F. H. NEWELL *Irrigation in U.S.* 107 He is usually known as the 'water master' or 'ditch-rider'; or, in Spanish-speaking communities as majordomo. 1910 JER. HART *Vigilante Girl* xiv. 195 Arthur's chair was taken to the *portal*, where they found the majordomo and a group of *vaqueros* waiting.

Majority. 7. Add: *majority-vote*; **majority calling**, in Bridge, the practice of regarding a call of a greater number of tricks as higher than any other, irrespective of the suit; **majority-Socialist**, one who after the division of the German Socialists acted with the larger party; **majority-verdict**, the verdict of the majority of a jury.

1929 *Portland Club Lett.* § 4 While, at the Portland Club, 'value calling' is invariably played at 'Auction', '*majority calling' is being used at 'Contract'. 1919 J. BUCHAN *Hist. War* XX. 125 The great governing parties, apart from the Conservatives on the extreme right and the Minority Socialists on the extreme left, were the Catholic Centre, the Radicals, the National Liberals, and the *Majority Socialists. 1923 E. A. ROSS *Russian Soviet Republ.* 20 At this time [1918] a Soviet was formed in Berlin, to which members of even the Majority Socialists adhered. 1905 *Westm. Gaz.* 7 Apr. 5/2 The jury..sent in to court to inquire if the parties would accept a *majority verdict. 1909 *Daily Chron.* 11 Nov. 1/6 A majority verdict holds good in French criminal trials. 1927 *Chambers's Jrnl.* 602/2 Now he had the *majority vote.

Majorize, *v.* Add: **3.** *Mus.* To put into a major key.

1927 *Musical Times* Nov. 1040 So monotonous a thing as to majorise every cadence.

Make, *sb.*[2] Add: **8.** *On the make* (earlier U.S. examples).

1873 J. H. BEADLE *Undevel. West* xxi. 402 They're all on the make, and in with these roughs. 1883 J. HAY *Bread-winners* x. 150 You aint on the make, you're fixed.

10. *Bridge.* The declaration (of trumps).

1902 J. B. ELWELL *Bridge* 13 In considering a heart make, the dealer should be influenced by the general strength of his hand and by the number of honours he holds in the trump suit. 1905 R. F. FOSTER *Complete Bridge* 316 The declaration is often called the make.

Make, *v.* **35. b.** (Add example.)

1912 GALSWORTHY *Inn Tranq.* 50 Suddenly the ground grew lumpy and made up-hill.

53. f. *To make do*, to get along, be contented, *with* (something) as an inferior substitute.

1927 *Observer* 28 Aug. 16/4 Up to last Sunday the listener who was content to receive only the programmes from his local station..could make do with a very simple and inefficient form of direct-coupled tuning arrangement.

65. Also *to make it*, to succeed in traversing a certain distance. *U.S.*

1905 REX BEACH *Pardners* ii. (1912) 56 We can't make it over into Mexico without being caught up. 1922 TITUS *Timber* vii. 67 I've been planning to drive into the hardwood for the last week; I can make it to-day and from there I have to go into town.

b. (Later and fig. examples.) *U.S.*

1912 R. A. WASON *Friar Tuck* xxvi. 187 Badger-face tried to raise himself on his elbow, but he couldn't quite make it. 1916 H. L. WILSON *Somewhere in Red Gap* i. 25, I hurried home to get a bite to eat and dress and make the party. 1928 *Publishers' Weekly* 24 Nov. 2184/2 Two books that almost made the Best Seller List are [etc.].

83. Make again. b. *intr.* To regain a former state, to recover.

1909 *Westm. Gaz.* 21 Jan. 12/1 As regards the reef 'making again' with good gold values at the south end of the mine, it is said that the predictions of the new consulting engineer have been entirely realised.

85*. Make back. *intr.* To make one's way back, to return.

1848 H. W. HAYGARTH *Bush Life Australia* vi. 57 The desire of returning to the pastures on which they have been reared..is the most difficult to eradicate of all their bad habits, for they have been known to 'make back' through every obstacle, for hundreds of miles.

Make-. Add: **make-and-break**, used *attrib.* to denote apparatus for automatically making and breaking electrical contacts.

1857 *Chambers's Jrnl.* 22 Aug. 121/1 The transmission of the current having..to be made through a make and break key of metal. 1904 A. B. F. YOUNG *Compl. Motorist* (ed. 2) 197 The time of firing is controlled by a simple 'make-and-break' commutator placed on the half-time shaft. 1920 *Conquest* June 404/1 Make-and-break switch.

Make-do, *a.* [f. *to make do*: see *MAKE *v.* 53 f.] Characterized by makeshift methods.

1923 *Daily Mail* 12 Feb. 4 When..prices steadily mounted to their peak, thousands of careful housewives adopted what was known as a 'make-do' policy.

Maker. Add: **6. b.** *Bridge.* The player who makes the declaration.

1902 J. B. ELWELL *Bridge* 24 When the 'maker' is on your right, you have the advantage that your trumps are over his.

Makeshift. 1. (Later example.)

1848 *N.Y. Mirror* 5 June (Bartlett s.v. *Wire-puller*) Already that city [Philadelphia] is filled with wire-pullers, ..and the whole breed of political make-shifts.

Making, *vbl. sb.*[1] Add: **8. b.** *pl.* Paper and tobacco for making cigarettes. *U.S.*

1907 S. E. WHITE *Arizona Nights* I. ix. 161 'Well', agreed Rogers, 'pass over the "makings" and I will.' *a* 1909 'O. HENRY' *Roads of Destiny* viii. 134 He took out his 'makings' and rolled a cigarette. 1916 BOWER *Phantom Herd* viii. 116 Luck..trailed over to a table and gleaned 'the makings' from among the litter of papers..and rolled himself a much-needed smoke.

Making-up. (Add examples.)

1878 E. C. MADDISON *Specul. Stock Exch.* 15 The process known as 'making-up' settles many bargains before the arrival of the settling-day. Making-up commences on the contango-day and is continued on the ticket-day. 1902 DE VINNE *Practice of Typogr., Correct Comp.* (ed. 2) 171 Notes are a hindrance in composition and making-up.

b. (Earlier example.)

1878 E. C. MADDISON *Specul. Stock Exch.* 13 The prices at which bargains are carried over are called the 'making-up' prices.

Malabar. Insert: **1.** An inhabitant of the Malabar coast.

1582 N. LICHEFIELD tr. *Castanheda's Conq. E. Ind.* 37 b, They asked of the Malabars which went with him what he was? 1723 R. MILLAR *Hist. Propag. Chr.* (1731) II. 148 The Malabars were not to be persuaded. 1867 C. J. BOYLE *Far Away* 72 Started on foot up the gorge, our bags on the shoulders of Malabars, who followed at our heels.

2. The language spoken on the Malabar coast.

1801 SIR T. MUNRO in Gleig *Life* (1830) I. 322 From Miliserum to the Chandergeery river no language is understood but the Malabars of that coast. 1837 T. BACON *First Impress. Hindostan* I. 99 He was compelled to fall back upon his only two words of Malabar.

3. A kind of handkerchief (see quot.).

1882 CAULFEILD & SAWARD *Dict. Needlework* 340 *Malabars*, cotton handkerchiefs, printed in imitation of Indian handkerchiefs, the patterns of which are of a peculiar and distinctive type, and the contrasts of colour brilliant and striking.

4. *attrib.*

1696 OVINGTON *Voy. Suratt* 213 Many of their Women by their usual Custom in these cases..have gain'd the Name of Malabar Quills. 1872 tr. *Let. Xavier* in H. J. Coleridge *Life Xavier* II. 73 Enrico Enriquez..writes and speaks the Malabar tongue very well indeed.

Hence **Malabare·se** *a.* [-ESE], of or pertaining to the Malabar coast or its inhabitants; **Malaba·rian** *a.* and *sb.* **Malaba·ric** *a.* and *sb.*

1709 *Propag. Gosp. East* 17 This place [Tranquebar] is altogether stocked with Malabarian Heathens. *Ibid.* 28, I will set down here..the Malabarick Letters. *Ibid.*, I caused..the Lord's-Prayer..to be put into Malabarick. 1723 R. MILLAR *Hist. Propag. Chr.* (1731) II. 142 The Malabarians have a very regular language. 1808 STOWER *Printer's Gram.* Index, Malabaric alphabet. 1922 *Blackw. Mag.* May 612/1 The Moplahs..are the descendants of Arab fathers and Malabarese mothers.

Malaëra·tion. *Path.* [f. MAL- + AERATION.] Imperfect aëration (of the blood).

1843 R. J. GRAVES *Syst. Clin. Med.* xx. 245 Her countenance exhibits no proof of malaëration of the blood. 1908 *Practitioner* Mar. 321 Such cyanosis may..indicate lack of propelling power in the circulation, with consequent malaëration.

Malamute (mæ·lămiut). Also **malemute.** [The name of a tribe of Eskimos on the Alaskan coast.] An Eskimo dog.

1908 LINA R. McCABE in *St. Nicholas* Mar. 387/2 Few pure malamutes..are now employed in the mail service. 1915 *Lit. Digest* (N.Y.) 4 Sept. 467/1 The first automobile appeared at Nome in the spring of 1904, when malamutes and reindeer beat a quick retreat.

Malappro·priator. [f. MALAPPROPRIATE *v.*] One who malappropriates.

1904 HAZLITT *Book-Collector* xi. 206 Your fellow who writes some objurgatory *caveat* against the malappropriator.

Malariology (mălēˑriǫ·lŏdʒi). [f. MALARIA + -(O)LOGY.] The study of malaria.

1926 *Glasgow Herald* 1 Mar. 11/2 Those medical officers desiring to specialise in malariology. 1930 M. F. BOYD (*title*) An Introduction to Malariology.

Malaxation. Add: **c.** A form of massage.

1887 D. MAGUIRE *Art of Massage* (ed. 4) 46 Malaxation is the same movement [as pétrissage], differing only on account of the flat of the hand being applied with more or less strength before bringing the fingers together to exercise the pétrissage.

Malayic (mălē¹·ik), *a.* Also 8 **Malaic.** [See -IC.] = MALAYAN *adj.*

1723 R. MILLAR *Hist. Propag. Chr.* (1731) II. viii. 321 Sermons...in the Malaic tongue. 1890 BRINTON *Races & Peoples* 230 The Malayic Stock.

Malayo-. (Add examples.)

1876 *Encycl. Brit.* V. 288/1 The Macassars... Their language..belongs to the Malayo-Javanese group. 1887 FEATHERMAN *Soc. Hist. Races Mankind* II. i. 251 The Malayo-Melanesians are the most important branch of the Melanesian stock. 1896 A. H. KEANE *Ethnol.* 331 Semi-cultured and rude Malayo-African populations.

Male. B. *sb.* Add: **4.** *Comb.*: **male impersonator**, a female who personates a male on the stage.

1895 C. D. STUART & PARK *Variety Stage* 222 Serio-comics, sisters, dancers, male impersonators, and ballad and character vocalists. 1903 *Era* 31 Jan. 36/1 Miss Flo Windsor, the Dainty and Realistic Male Impersonator. 1930 *Bulletin* 14 May 5 That popular male impersonator and pantomime principal boy, Miss Nora Delany.

Malease. 1. (Modern example.)

1930 *Times Lit. Suppl.* 4 Dec. 1022/2 Yet her achievement was muted by excess of ardour and by a subtle, fundamental malease.

Maledictive (mælĭdi·ktiv), *a.* [f. L. *maledict-* (see MALEDICTION) + -IVE.] Characterized by cursing; uttering maledictions.

?1834 Sir S. Ferguson *Lays Western Gael* (1865) 54 Daily in their mystic ring They tuned the maledictive stones. 1905 K. Meyer *Cáin Adamnáin* Pref., A poem on the maledictive psalms selected by Adamnan.

Mali, variant of Mallee[1].

Malines (mälī·n), *a.* and *sb.* [The name of a town in Belgium (also called *Mechlin*) where lace is made, used *attrib.* and *ellipt.*]

1. In full *Malines lace* = Mechlin lace.

1831 Carlyle *Sartor Res.* I. iv, To Teufelsdröckh the highest Duchess is respectable..but nowise for her pearl bracelets and Malines laces. 1850 *Harper's Mag.* Aug. 431/2 Another pattern is..embroidered and trimmed with *malines*. 1922 *Queen* 13 Apr. 613/1 This coat..had long sleeves slit up at the wrist, and edged with white net bordered with Malines.

2. A Belgian breed of the domestic fowl.

1909 *Daily Chron.* 17 Nov. 3/5 Malines..form quite a considerable class at the Crystal Palace [Poultry show]. 1910 *Encycl. Poultry* II. 295 The Malines fowl is of the Asiatic type, and is large in size...There are two varieties—the Coucou and the White.

Malkite, variant of Melchite.

1909 Agnes S. Lewis *Codex Climaci Rescriptus* Pref., The Orthodox, or Malkite party, which separated from the great Monophysite Church at the Council of Chalcedon in A.D. 451.

Mallard. 2. c. Add: *mallard call, decoy, duck, -shooting*.

1853 R. Glisan *Jrnl. Army Life* (1874) x. 119 And there die like the wounded mallard duck. 1874 *Ibid.* xxxiii. 493 There is an abundance of game along the coast such as canvas-back duck, mallard duck. 1874 J. W. Long *Amer. Wild-fowl Shooting* xiv. 186 Morning and evening mallard-shooting. *Ibid.* xix. 214 They decoy exceedingly well to mallard decoys, and come readily to the mallard call.

Mallein (mæ·lɪ,in), *v.* [f. the sb.] *trans.* To inoculate for glanders.

1915 *Punch* 4 Aug. 101/2 All mules on joining units will in future be malleined.

Malo-Russian (mē^ilo,rɒ·ʃiăn), *sb.* and *a.* [f. Russ. Малороссія Little Russia, or ad. Малороссіянинъ Little Russian.] **a.** *sb.* A member of the Little Russian race inhabiting the south of Russia; their language. **b.** *adj.* Of or pertaining to the Little Russians, Ruthenian.

1862 [see Ruthenian *sb.* 2]. 1880 Morfill *Russia* 74 The Malo-Russian is very rich in Skazki (national tales) and in songs. *Ibid.* 75 The Malo-Russian philologists. 1923 E. A. Ross *Russian Soviet Republ.* 58 Between Great Russia and the Black Sea live the Ukrainians or Little Russians (Malo-Russians).

Malpais (mal pa,ī·s). *U.S.* [Sp., f. *malo* bad + *pais* country, region.] Rugged or difficult country of volcanic origin.

1844 G. W. Kendall *Santa Fé Exped.* II. 384 We had crossed the *mal pais*, or bad country, as it is called. 1847 Ruxton *Adv. Mexico* xi. 79 The tract of country known as the *Mal Pais*, a most interesting volcanic region. 1896 J. W. Fewkes in *Rep. Smithsonian Inst.* 520 The trail..to cross the rugged malpais of the Mogollones. 1907 S. E. White *Arizona Nights* I. v. 96 Sometimes we skipped..over little gullies, barrancas, and other sorts of malpais. 1918 Mulford *Man fr. Bar-20* xvii. 178 Slipping on the treacherous malpais and loose stones.

Maltese. A. *adj.* 2. Add: **Maltese fever** = *Malta fever* (see Malta).

1902 *Chambers's Jrnl.* Mar. 184/2 'Rock' fever is confined to Gibraltar; although it is probable that the ailment known as Maltese fever, which can be contracted only in Malta,..is closely allied to it.

Maltreater (mæltrī·təɹ). [f. Maltreat *v.* + -er.] One who maltreats or ill-uses.

1906 B'ness von Hutten *What became of Pam* I. ii, Tyrants, idlers, drunkards, maltreaters [of women]. 1915 *Eng. Hist. Rev.* Jan. 168 James Wyatt, the maltreater of Salisbury cathedral.

Mamba (mæ·mbă). [ad. Kaffir *m'namba*.] One or other of the venomous tree snakes of the genus *Dendraspis* found in Africa.

1890 P. Gillmore *Through Gasa Land* 23 The mamba frequently grows to the length of ten or eleven feet...There are two varieties, the green and the brown. 1910 J. Buchan *Prester John* iv. 80 A black mamba might appear out of the tangle. 1921 *Chambers's Jrnl.* 26 Feb. 203/2 It was a mamba snake, eight feet long.

Mammoth. B. *adj.* (Earlier examples.)

Freq. in American use before 1850. The reference in quots. 1802 and 1803 is to a large cheese presented to Jefferson.

1802 *Port Folio* (Philad.) II. 31 (Th.) A baker in this city offers Mammoth bread for sale. 1802 *Balance* (Hudson, N.Y.) 19 Oct. 331 (Th.) No more to do with the subject than the man in the moon has to do with the mammoth cheese. 1803 J. Davis *Trav. U.S.A.* (1909) ix. 360 Its extraordinary dimensions induced some wicked wag of a federalist to call it the Mammoth Cheese. 1813 *Niles' Weekly Reg.* IV. 32/2 The Mammoth bank bill passed the senate this day on a third reading.

Mammy. Add: 2. (Earlier example.)

1837 *Southern Lit. Messenger* III. 744 These too were greeted always by the kind appelatives of 'daddy and mammy'.

Mammy[2]. [Of obscure origin.] Used attrib. in **mammy chair**, a wicker basket or chair used on ships for conveying persons to and from surf-boats on the West African coast.

1909 Decima Moore & Guggisberg *We Two in W. Africa* 16 So I found myself sitting in the 'Mammy chair', an ordinary basket-chair with ropes slung to the arms and back, ..and in a moment I was whisked off the deck, swung over the side at the end of a long derrick, [etc.]. 1920 *Blackw. Mag.* June 848/1 A mammy chair was lowered, and we made the usual undignified ascent to the main deck.

Mampus (mæ·mpəs). *dial.* [Of obscure origin.] A great number, a crowd.

c 1730 *Dorset Voc.* in *N. & Q.* Ser. vi. VIII. 45/1 A mampus, multitude. 1851 *Dorset Gloss.* 6 *Mampus*, a great number. 1880 Hardy *Trumpet-Major* I. ii. 32 The mampus of soldiers that have come upon the down. 1891 — *Tess* I. iii. 33 No doubt a mampus of folk of our own rank will be down here in their carriages as soon as 'tis known.

Man, *sb.*[1] 4. h. (Additional examples of *man to man*.)

1901 E. A. Ross *Social Control* 29 So long as the struggle is man to man..a conscience is a handicap. 1908 *Daily Chron.* 11 Aug. 4/5 Another form of suasion is the 'man-to-man' talk.

7. b. *pl.* A class of lay religious teachers or exhorters that flourished in the Highlands of Scotland. *Sc.*

1865 *Chambers's Jrnl.* 18 Feb. 97/1 The Men are fast fading away. I do not mean the sterner sex..but a remarkable class of religious teachers, who have exerted a prodigious influence upon the social and spiritual life of the Highlands of Scotland for a long series of generations.

18. For *man of the moment*, see *Moment 1 c; **man of destiny**, one looked upon as an instrument in the hands of destiny, esp. applied to Napoleon I; also *attrib.*

1827 Scott *Napoleon* IX. 329 The great plans which the *Man of Destiny had been called upon earth to perform. 1909 *Westm. Gaz.* 26 Aug. 5/1 His man-of-destiny characteristics made him an interesting study to the newspaper correspondents. 1921 Shaw *Back to Methuselah* iv. ii. 176 *Napoleon* [*impressively*] I am the Man of Destiny.

19. d. *man-lifting, -stopping* adjs.

1905 *Science Year Bk.* 97 *Man-lifting kites have been undergoing more successful trials at Aldershot, where men were lifted to heights of over 1,200 feet. 1927 C. L. M. Brown *Conquest of Air* 122 By 1905 Cody had attracted official attention to his man-lifting kites. 1899 *Kynoch Jrnl.* Oct.–Nov. 15/2 The *manstopping powers of the..bullets appear to be considerable at short ranges. 1905 *Ibid.* Apr.–June 96 In connection with the Revolver Competitions..man-stopping bullets are not allowed.

20. **man-hour**, an hour of a man's work; **man-power**, (*a*) the power or agency of man in work; also *attrib.*; (*b*) used as a unit of power or rate of working; (*c*) the number of men available for a purpose, esp. for military service; **man-root** (earlier example); **man-rope knot** (see quot.); **man-size** *attrib.*, of the size of a man; large enough to occupy a man.

1924 Emsley *Factory Costing* 76 The number of productive '*man-hours' in each department during each 'cost period'. 1928 *Daily Express* 19 Mar. 3/2 Fixing an arm to a telephone pole must not take more than three-quarter man-hours. 1862 *man-power [see 19 a in Dict.]. 1893 *Eng. Mechanic* Dec. LVIII. 332/2 Maxim's early trials gave..about 1 lb. per man-power. 1927 Churchill *World Crisis 1916–18* (1927) II. 378 It is not possible to settle the question of man-power without a clear idea of the plan of campaign. 1919 *Brit. Manufacturer* Nov. 25/1 One of these man-power ploughs, adapted for small holdings and for use on terraced land, is driven by a cable. 1925 *Army Quarterly* Jan. 367 The man-power of an average regiment of two battalions. 1926 Bennett *Lord Raingo* xii. 60 Biggest piece of political camouflage ever attempted, the Man-Power Bill is. 1846 Emory *Military Reconn.* 13 The principal growth is the buffalo grass,..and very rarely that wonderful plant, the Ipomea Leptophylla, called by the hunter *man root. 1883 *Man. Seamanship Boys* 121 A double-wall, double-crowned..is used for man-ropes, stopper-knots, &c., also called a *man-rope knot. 1913 R. W. Service *Rhymes of Rolling Stone* 103 The *man-size mountains palisade us round on every side. 1928 *Publishers' Weekly* 16 June 2441 It would seem that since writing is a man-size job, he would have his hands full.

Mana (mā·na). [Maori.] Power in general, authority, prestige; *spec.* supernatural or magical power or influence.

Now freq. used by writers on anthropology or primitive religion.

1855 R. Taylor *Te Ika a Maui* 279 The natives..feel..that with the land, their *mana*, or power, has gone likewise. 1877 R. H. Codrington *Let.* in Max Müller *Hibbert Lect.* (1878) 54 There is a belief in a force altogether distinct from physical power, which acts in all kinds of ways for good and evil, and which it is of the greatest advantage to possess or control. This is Mana. 1909 *Athenæum* 27 Feb. 259/1 Mr. Marett..read before that [International] Congress [of Religions] a paper on the conception of 'mana'. 1920 *Times Lit. Suppl.* 29 Apr. 264/2 Notions of the type of mana or orenda are of 'a nascently philosophic order'.

Comb. 1924 W. B. Selbie *Psychol. Relig.* 208 A fearful cringing before some mysterious mana-charged object.

Manage, *v.* Add: 7. b. With const.

1907 *Smart Set* Mar. 83/1 You're the sly rascal..to manage Mr. Leidermann out of the road so well.

11. b. (Earlier examples.)

1854 Maria L. Charlesworth *Ministering Children* iv. 47 Rose was..wondering how William would manage about getting some logs for Mercy's fire. 1874 'Susan Coolidge' *What Katy did* xi. 181 I've been thinking how we are to manage about the housekeeping. 1895 'Geoff. Mortimer' *Like Stars that fall* viii. 108 'How will you manage about your hair?' 'I shall cut it short, I think.'

Mananosay (mænănō^u·seɪ). *U.S.* Also **maninose**. [Amer. Ind.] (See quot. 1859.)

1859 Bartlett *Dict. Amer.* (ed. 2) 84 The Soft Clam or Mananosay (*Mya arenaria*), obtained from the shores of tidal rivers by digging one or two feet in the loose sand. It has a long, extensible, cartilaginous snout, or proboscis, through which it ejects water: whence it is also called Stem-clam. 1870 *Putnam's Monthly Mag.* (De Vere) Even the toothsome Manonosays [*sic*] squirted water up through the sand what time the tides were out. 1890 *Century Dict.*, *Maninose*, the soft clam *Mya arenaria* [Maryland and Virginia].

Manatee. 3. Add: *manatee-fishing*; **manatee-butter**, the edible oil obtained from the manatee.

1860 Mayne Reid *Odd People* 261 The true season of the manati-fishing is when the waters of the great flood have considerably subsided. *Ibid.* 259 Another valuable commodity obtained from this animal is oil, known in the missions as manati-butter (*mantéca de manati*).

Manchesterian (mæn,tʃesti·ᵊriăn), *a.* and *sb.* [f. Manchester + -ian.] **a.** *adj.* Of or pertaining to Manchester. **b.** *sb.* An inhabitant of Manchester, also one of the Manchester School of politicians.

1821 *Kaleidoscope* 3 July 423/3 Professing myself to be a plain Englishman and a Manchesterian. 1897 *Essays in Liberalism* 70 'Sordid inhuman wretch', 'brutal Manchesterian', are the terms applied to those who demonstrate the national loss of wealth which must result from the substitution of 'Fair' for Free Trade.

Hence **Mancheste·rianism** = Manchesterism.

1897 *Essays in Liberalism* 33 A sneer at Cobden, a contemptuous allusion to Manchesterianism and the 'dismal science'.

Manchu (mæn,tʃū·), *sb.* and *a.* Also **Manchew, Manchoo, Manchou, Manchow, Mantcheou, Mantchoo, Mantchu.** [Manchu, 'pure', the name of a tribe descended from the Nü-chên Tartars.]

A. *sb.* 1. A member of a Tungusic race inhabiting Manchuria, which conquered China in 1644 and was the ruling class until the Revolution in 1912.

1759 *Universal Hist., Mod.* IV. 278 Here the present empire of the eastern Tatars, or Manchews..had its beginning. 1821 Sir G. Staunton tr. *Narr. Chinese Embassy* 152 The Mantchoos and the Mongals bear a great resemblance to each other. 1863 G. Fleming *Trav. Mantchu Tartary* 441 In the palmy days of the Mantchus, some two centuries ago. 1883 S. Wells Williams *Middle Kingd.* I. i. 44 The Manchus are an agricultural or a hunting people. 1891 Rockhill *Land of Lamas* 52 The..Seling Amban..is always a Manchu of high rank.

2. The language of the Manchus.

1822 Sir G. Staunton *Misc. Notes China* 95 Table of Contents of a Chinese and Mantchoo-Tartar Dictionary. 1920 *Contemp. Rev.* Apr. 526 Ferdinand Verbiest..to please Kang-hi had learnt Manchu.

B. *adj.* Of or pertaining to the Manchus, their country (Manchuria), or their language. *Manchu leaf*, a kind of tobacco.

1736 R. Brookes tr. *Du Halde's Hist. China* IV. 90 A great Number of Mantcheou Mandarins. 1771 W. Guthrie *Geogr. Gram.* 534 The Chinese went to war with the Manchew Tartars. 1847 T. T. Meadows *Notes China* 195 The prestige of Manchoo power in war has received a severe shock. 1882 *Encycl. Brit.* XIV. 96/1 Tobacco..grown in the province [Manchuria] being greatly prized throughout the Chinese empire under the name of 'Manchu leaf'.

Manchurian (mæn,tʃū·ᵊriăn), *a.* [f. *Manchuria* (f. prec.) the country of the Manchus, now a dependency of China + -an.] Of or pertaining to Manchuria. **Manchurian crane**, a species of crane (see quot.).

1870 A. Williamson *Jour. N. China* etc. II. 29 Several times we saw the beautiful Manchurian crane, *grus montignesia*, which has perpetuated the name of M. de Montigny, late of Shanghai. 1876 A. R. Wallace *Geogr. Distrib. Anim.* I. 220 Japan and North China, or the Manchurian Sub-region. 1899 J. F. Fraser *Round World on Wheel* xxxi. 395 In five minutes down swooped several Manchurian officers.

Mancunian (mæn,kiū·niăn), *a.* and *sb.* [f. L. *Mancunium* Manchester + -an.] **a.** *adj.* Of or pertaining to Manchester. **b.** *sb.* A native or inhabitant of Manchester.

1904 H. Beswick *Last Karkawber* etc. 134 'Th' Owd Rivvur'—as some old Mancunians dub the Irwell. 1908 *Westm. Gaz.* 22 Oct. 2/3 How strangely provincial—may we even say Mancunian?—is the very recent theory that Mr. Cobden invented Free Trade.

Mandarin[1]. Add: 1. c. *transf.* A person of much importance, a great man. Often used *colloq.* of Government officials, leading politicians, etc.

1907 *National Rev.* Aug. 838 Our Parliamentary Mandarins are ineffably shocked at the impiety of an independent Radical. 1908 *New Age* 6 June 112/2 The chams, lamas, and mandarins of London letters are doubtless devising adjectives for it [a book]. 1918 'Berta Ruck' *Disturbing Charm* II. ix. 234 If you let it get known..that you've got a view like that, you'll have some of the Mandarins snaffling that office of yours for themselves. 1925 E. Fraser & Gibbons *Soldier & Sailor Words* s.v., The Mandarins of the War Office.

4. *mandarin blue.*

1912 *Home Chat* 13 Apr. 112/2 In flamingo red, Mandarin blue or wood-violet mauve linen.

Mandate, *sb.* Add: 4. b. *spec.* A commission issued by the League of Nations authorizing a selected power to administer, control and develop a territory for a specified purpose.

1919 *League of Nations Covenant* Art. xxii, in *Encycl. Brit.* (1926) Suppl. I. 755 The character of the Mandate must differ according to the stage of the development of the people, the geographical situation of the territory [etc.]. 1921 *First Assembly* (ed. O. Brett) 228 Copies of the draft mandates for Palestine, Mesopotamia and Syria were circulated confidentially to the members of the sub-Committee. 1922 H. W. V. Temperley *Second Yr. League* 81 The whole question of Mandates is still a most serious and very largely an unfinished one.

attrib. and *Comb.* 1921 *Spectator* 2 Apr. 419/1 They apparently look upon mandate-making as a kind of old-fashioned diplomacy. 1926 *Encycl. Brit.* Suppl. II. 785/2 The mandate system is a term applied to the conditions set up by the Treaty of Versailles [etc.].

Mandate, *v.* Add: 3. To assign under a mandate (of the League of Nations).

1920 *Glasgow Herald* 7 July 11 The Island of Nauru in the Pacific (which is mandated to the British Empire). 1922 *Times Lit. Suppl.* 23 Nov. 756/3 The result of the late war has been to eliminate Germany from the map, her territories being mandated to the British and other nations.

Hence **Mandated** *ppl. a.*

1919 J. M. Keynes *Econ. Conseq. Peace* 248 The Mandated States should be compelled to adhere to this Union for ten years. 1921 *First Assembly* (ed. O. Brett) 229 The natural resources of the Mandated territory. 1922 *Weekly Dispatch* 5 Nov. 8 We were authorised to raise local native forces to protect the mandated area.

Mandatory. A. *adj.* Add: *spec.* Of powers or states: Concerning which the League of Nations has issued a mandate.

1921 *First Assembly* (ed. O. Brett) 260 The Commission shall examine the annual reports of the Mandatory States and advise the Council as to the execution of the terms of the Mandates.

B. *sb.* Add: *spec.* In recent use, a Power selected by the League of Nations to administer and develop a territory; the territory or state which is assigned thus to a Power.

1919 *League of Nations Covenant* Art. xxii. in *Encycl. Brit.* (1926) Suppl. I. 755 This tutelage should be exercised by them as Mandatories on behalf of the League. *Ibid.*, The wishes of these communities must be a principal consideration in the selection of the Mandatory. 1927 *Daily Express* 24 May 3 A memorandum issued by the Arab Executive (Nationalists)..accuses Great Britain of ignoring the covenant principle to assist mandatories to become self-governing.

Ma·n-folk. *poet.* [Man *sb.*[1]] People, human beings, men.

1875 Morris *Æneids* XII. 825 Let not that manfolk shift their tongue, or cast their garb aside. 1887 — *Odyssey* III. 252 Amid other dwellings of manfolk. *Ibid.* I. 393 Of all that befalleth manfolk dost thou deem it the evillest thing?

Manger (mē^i·ndʒəɹ), *v.*[2] *rare.* [f. the sb.] *trans.* To fasten (an animal) to a manger.

1905 W. Holman Hunt *Pre-Raphaelitism* II. 72 An old ram mangered by a halter.

Mangle, *sb.*[3] b. Add: **mangle-board** [Da. *mangle bræt*], a board with which linen and cotton may be pressed and smoothed.

1895 Eleanor Rowe *Chip-carving* 47 The border..may be seen on a mangle-board from Jutland, dated 1708. 1928 *Daily Express* 22 June 12/6 The exhibits include various examples from Denmark, Sweden, Norway and Holland... Dates on the mangleboards go back as far as 1590.

Mangosteen. Add: 2. b. (See quot.)

1859 Bartlett *Dict. Amer.*, *Mangosteen*. In Barbadoes this name is given to the Jujube (*Ziziphus jujube*).

Manhattanese (mænhætănī·z), *sb.* and *a.* [f. *Manhattan* the name of the island on which the older part of New York is situated.] **a.** *sb.* A native or inhabitant of Manhattan or New York. (See also quot. 1909.) **b.** *adj.* Of or pertaining to New York or its inhabitants.

1842 J. F. Cooper *Wing & Wing* I. 11 Hundreds collected on the spot, which, in Manhattanese parlance, would probably have been called a battery. *Ibid.* 193 This gentleman was an American, and a native Manhattanese; his near relatives, of the same name, still residing in New York. 1844 *Knickerbocker Mag.* XXIII. 586 The sound of India-crackers and the pleasant smell of lobsters is already perceptible to the senses of the awakening Manhattanese. 1875 Whitman in *Gentl. Mag.* Dec. 706, I was Manhattanese, friendly, and proud. 1904 *Forum* Jan.–Mar. 410 (Cent. Suppl.) 'Her Own Way'..brings together a number of highly piquant Manhattanese types of to-day, sketched with captivating drollery. 1909 *Cent. Dict.* Suppl., *Manhattanese*,..1. One who lives upon the island of Manhattan.—2. The characteristic phraseology of a New-Yorker.

Manic (mæ·nik), *a.* [f. Mania: see -ic.] Pertaining to or affected with mania.

189. *Buck's Handbk. Med. Sci.* V. 120 (Cent. Suppl.). 1921 R. Mary Barclay tr. *Kraepelin's Manic Depressive Insanity* 54 The conspicuous contrasts between manic and depressive attacks. *Ibid.* 106 Manic stupor. 1922 Woodworth *Psychol.* xi. 259 In the excited insane condition known as 'mania' or the 'manic state', the patient is excessively distractible.

Comb. 1901 *J. M. Baldwin's Dict. Philos. & Psychol.* II. 393/2 Manic-depressive insanity (mania and melancholia).

Manichæistic (mæniki,i·stik), *a.* [f. as Manichæist: see -istic.] Of the nature of Manichæism.

1924 Sir O. Lodge *Making of Man* ii. 49 A Manichæistic conception of existence can never have been really satisfying.

Manifold. C. *sb.* Add: 4. b. Short for *manifold-paper*.

1897 Bram Stoker *Dracula* xvii. (1912) 241, I began to typewrite from the beginning of the seventh cylinder. I used manifold, and so took three copies of the diary.

Manifolder (mæ·nifō^uldəɹ). [f. Manifold *v.* + -er.] A contrivance for multiplying copies of a document, or the like; also, a person using this.

1909 *Century Dict.* Suppl. 1911 Webster (citing G. H. Putnam).

Manipulate, *v.* Add: 3. b. *Finance.* To cause (stocks) to rise or fall by affecting the market in other ways than those arising out of ordinary business; to influence (the market) in such ways.

1870 Medbery *Men & Myst. Wall St.* 188 The stock..was most admirably manipulated, until it finally touched 152. 1903 S. S. Pratt *Work of Wall St.* 147 A market is rigged when it is manipulated.

Hence **Manipulated** *ppl. a.* Add quot.

1903 S. S. Pratt *Work of Wall St.* 147 A deal is the operation resulting from a secret combination or agreement among Wall Street men to effect a certain purpose, usually of a manipulated character in the market.

Manipulation. 4. Add examples of use in finance.

1903 S. S. Pratt *Work of Wall St.* 258 Manipulation plays an important part in stock speculation. For days and even weeks together the market may be in the hands of the manipulators. 1908 *Westm. Gaz.* 26 Aug. 2/2 The opportunity for market manipulation is obvious.

Manipulative, *a.* (Add examples.)

1909 *Westm. Gaz.* 8 Sept. 11/4 The powerful manipulative interests are watching events closely...In the history of American finance many magnates have passed away, but many have been at hand to catch the manipulative mantle as it fell.

Manipulator. Add: 1. c. One who controls the price of stocks by specially contrived methods.

1903 S. S. Pratt *Work of Wall St.* 256 By false tips and matched orders or wash sales the manipulators endeavored to establish fictitious quotations for their stocks. *Ibid.* 146 A professional may or may not be a manipulator, but a manipulator is always a professional.

Man-jack: see Jack *sb.*[1] 2 c.

Manlessness. Delete † and add: b. Manless condition.

1924 *Public Opinion* 7 Nov. 460/2 We find girls robbed of wholesome excitements..by the loneliness and manlessness of their lives.

Manling. Delete †*Obs.* and add modern examples.

1895 Kipling *2nd Jungle Bk.* 184 A Manling with a knife threw stones at my head. 1922 A. S. M. Hutchinson *This Freedom* 276 Her baby boy, her tiny manling.

Mannequin (mæ·nikin). [ad. F. *mannequin* Manikin.] A woman employed in the show rooms of dress-makers, costumiers, and the like, to wear and show off garments. (*Rarely*, a man similarly employed.)

1902 *Pall Mall Mag.* XXVII. 119 Another salon..ornamented with tall mirrors in which were reflected the slender elegant figures of several mannequins, most of them exceedingly pretty and all arrayed in magnificent dresses. 1919 Max Beerbohm *Seven Men* 11 A midinette who..murdered, or was about to murder, a mannequin. 1925 *Daily Tel.* 13 May 20/7 Advt., A vacancy for..young lady..to be trained as a mannequin and taught show-room duties. 1927 *Daily Express* 21 June 3/7 A parade of male mannequins at the Grande Palais, in Paris.

b. *attrib.* as *mannequin parade*.

1930 *Daily Express* 6 Oct. 13/5 Autumn Mannequin Parades will be held on Tuesday and Wednesday this week.

Hence **Ma·nnequining** *vbl. sb.*, **Ma·nnequinism**, the business of mannequins.

1927 *Sunday Express* 15 May 5/3 'Mannequining is a serious business now', said the head of a mannequin school to me. 1928 *Daily Express* 2 June 4/4 More and more..distinguished women..have recently joined the ranks of teachers of mannequinism.

Mannerize, *v.* (Add example.)

1910 A. C. Benson *Silent Isle* xv. 103 Tennyson..became solemn, mannerised, conscious of responsibility.

Mannose (mæ·nōᵘs). *Chem.* [f. Manna[1] + -ose[2].] = Mannitose.

1902 *Encycl. Brit.* XXVI. 722/2 On oxidation, mannose, like glucose, yields a monobasic acid. 1920 Cross & Bevan *Paper-Making* 58 On diluting and boiling,..dextrose appears to be invariably formed, and in many cases also mannose.

Manœuvrability (mănū·vrăbi·lĭti). [f. Manœuvrable.] Capacity for being manœuvred.

1926 *Public Opinion* 1 Jan. 7/2 The manœuvrability of the 'planes should enable a pilot to get in and out of any field. 1927 *Daily Express* 24 Sept. 8 Much will depend on the skill of the pilots in taking the corner, and also on the manœuvrability of the machines. 1930 C. J. Stewart *Aircraft Instruments* Introd. p. xvii, The manœuvrability and the adequacy of the various control surfaces of an aircraft.

Manœuvrable (mănū·vrăb'l), *a.* [f. Manœuvre *v.* + -able.] Capable of being manœuvred, used esp. of aeroplanes or airships.

1928 Gamble *Story N. Sea Air Station* xiii. 211 It [the aeroplane] was manœuvrable and had a lower landing speed.

Man-of-war. 2. c. (Earlier example.)

1772–6 J. Andrews *Lett.* 392 Partaking of the extreem ill qualities of a soldier as well as that of a man-of-war's man.

Mano·rializa·tion. [f. Manorial *a.* + -ization.] The process of making or becoming manorial.

1907 *Q. Rev.* July 147 Varieties occurred in the process of manorialisation.

Manorship. Delete †*Obs.* and add recent example.

1920 *Public Opinion* 6 Aug. 127/3 Both names..are..deeply associated with the neighbourhood of Old Jordans, its homesteads, and churches and manorships.

Mansard. Add: c. *Comb.* as *mansard-roofed*.

1915 E. Atkinson *Johnny Appleseed* 80 From there he saw the white mansard-roofed mansion.

Mansion-house. b. (Earlier examples of U.S. sense.)

1679 *Conn. Public Rec.* III. 42 He shall build upon his sayd accomodations a good sufficient mansion house. 1745 *Itinerant Observ.* 37 A Negro Quarter, is a number of Huts or Hovels, built at some distance from the Mansion-House. 1812 *Niles' Weekly Reg.* III. 9/2 The majority then retired to the Mansion house. 1837 W. Jenkins *Ohio Gaz.* 162 A large and elegant Mansion house has been erected on the ground with numerous smaller cottages and out buildings. 1844 in C. Cist *Cincinnati Misc.* 68 The mansion house of E. S. Haines..and various single buildings are observable for their fine appearance.

Manslaughter (mæ·nslǭtəɹ), *v. colloq.* [f. the sb.] *trans.* To kill without malice aforethought.

1920 Rose Macaulay *Potterism* III. ii. § 6, I had left the house morally certain that Arthur Gideon had murdered (or anyhow manslaughtered) Oliver Hobart. 1922 A. A. Milne *Red House Myst.* ix. 81 'Murdered him?' 'Well, manslaughtered him, anyway.'

Mantel, *sb.* 3. d. Add: *mantel-clock* (earlier example), *-mirror*; **mantel-place** *southern U.S.* = Mantelpiece.

1870 W. M. Baker *New Timothy* 25 The *mantel-clock strikes six sharp insisting blows as she exclaims. 1865 Mrs. Stowe *House & Home P.* 86 Now come the great *mantel mirrors for four hundred [dollars] more. *a* 1870 W. G. Simms *Last Wager* (De Vere) You have a very singular ornament for your *mantle-place.

Mantic, *sb.* Add: Also in *pl.*

1904 *Amer. Jrnl. Relig. Psychol. & Educ.* May 107 Subjective faith and the specific utterances of faith, offerings, vows, castigations, sacramental acts and objects, mantics, revelations.

Mantistic (mænti·stik), *a.* [f. Gr. μάντις prophet + -istic.] Pertaining to divination or prophecy; prophetic, mantic.

1876 A. Wilder *R. P. Knight's Anc. Art & Myth.* 144 (Cent.) An idea of spiritual or mantistic qualities supposed to be peculiar to the female sex.

Mantle, *sb.* 11. Add: **mantle-cell**, a tapetal cell; **mantle-cloth** (see quot.); **mantle fibre** *Cytol.*, a fibril in the nuclear area of a cell which becomes attached to the chromosomes.

1890 *Century Dict.*, *Mantle-cell*, in cryptogamy, same as tapetal cell. 1882 Caulfeild & Saward *Dict. Needlework* 341 *Mantle cloths*, a term employed in trade to denote every description of cloth suitable for mantles, cloaks, and..exterior clothing. 1910 *Encycl. Brit.* VII. 714/2 Some..become attached to the chromosomes and are termed *mantle fibres'.

Man-trap. *transf.* (Add quots.)

1857 W. Chandless *Visit Salt Lake* II. xi. 330 The planks (of the streets) worn out and broken through, leaving large holes, popularly known as 'man-traps'. 1890 *Century Dict.*, *Man-trap*, anything such as an open hatchway on shipboard, or an insecure building, ladder, etc., likely to become the cause of injury or death to the unwary. [Colloq.]

Man-trap, *v.* [f. the sb.] *trans.* To beset with man-traps.

1913 J. London *Son of Sun* IV. iv. 159 Besides, the runs are all man-trapped—you know, staked pits, poisoned thorns, and the rest.

Manualette (mæniuăle·t). [f. Manual *sb.* + -ette.] A small manual or handbook.

1877 E. J. Mills (*title*) Destructive Distillation: a manualette of the Paraffin, Coal Tar, Rosin Oil, Petroleum, and kindred industries.

Manufacturing, *ppl. a.* (Later examples.)

1881 *Harper's Mag.* Jan. 185/2 Wilmington..is now a manufacturing centre of the first importance. 1892 *Rep. Vermont Board Agric.* XII. 140 As these manufacturing centers increase in size, so do the farm lands in like ratio increase in value.

Manu·ry, *a.* [f. Manure *sb.* 1.] Littered with manure.

1890 E. M. Tabor *Stowe Notes Lett. & Verses* 29 The stable-yard repulsive, muddy and manury.

Manzanita. *U.S.* Also **manzanito.** (Earlier and later examples.)

1848 E. Bryant *California* xviii. 236 We have met occasionally with a reddish berry called by the Californians manzanita (little apple). 1873 Joaquin Miller *Unwritten Hist.* vi. (1876) 90 The rich smell of the burning juniper and manzanita. 1910 Jer. Hart *Vigilante Girl* x. 141 He would..take a pot-shot at a chipmunk or squirrel, or a jack-rabbit scared out of the roadside manzanita. 1918 Mulford *Man fr. Bar-20* xvii. 178 He pushed through matted thickets of oak brush and manzanito by main strength.

attrib. 1869 C. L. Brace *New West* xi. 138 Around her were..dishes of the manzanita seed. *Ibid.* xi. 144 These all had Manzanita apples and acorns, for stores. 1873 Joaquin Miller *Unwritten Hist.* xxxiii. (1876) 427, I have cattle on the manzanita hills above me. 1888 Bret Harte *Drift Redwood Camp* 227 A bent manzanito-bush..flew back against his breast. 1907 S. E. White *Arizona Nights* I. iv. 68 For the next day we planned a bear hunt afoot far up a manzañita cañon.

Maori. Add: 3. *White Maori* (see quot.).

1883 'A Citizen' *Illustr. Guide Dunedin* 169 (Morris) Tungstate of lime occurs plentifully in the Wakatipu district, where from its weight and colour it is called White Maori by the miners.

Maoriland (ma·ōrilænd, mauᵊ·ri-). [f. Maori + Land *sb.*] A recent name for New Zealand. **Ma·orilander**, a white man born in New Zealand.

1881 *Every Boy's Annual* 657/2 Our goose-wing pen bears us lightly down upon the Maori-land. Captain Abel Tasman a Hollander, in 1642 discovered New Zealand. 1884 K. Nicholls (*title*) The King Country, or Explorations in New Zealand. A Narrative of 600 Miles of Travel through Maoriland. 1896 *Melbourne Argus* 22 July 4/8 (Morris) Always something new from Maoriland! 1896 *Melbourne Punch* 9 Apr. 233/2 (Morris) Norman is a pushing young Maorilander. 1915 *Morn. Post* 16 June 9/6 The Maorilanders gave 'Hakas' till their voices failed them.

Map, *sb.*[1] Add: 1. e. *fig.* In recent phrases: *Off the map*: out of existence; into (or in) oblivion or an insignificant position; of no account; obsolete. *On the map*: in an important or prominent position; of some account or importance; in existence (see also quots.).

(*a*) 1904 W. H. Smith *Promoters* ii. 54 When she [Carthage] wouldn't let up, the only thing left was to wipe her off the map. 1911 R. D. Saunders *Col. Todhunter* vii. 99 A good set-to is the best way..to put a stop to quarrelin'. It just wipes the whole thing off the map. 1914 *Grand Mag.* Jan. 429/2 [He] had been so harried by the Federal officers that he had faded off the map. 1922 *Tatler* 6 Sept. 386/1 A man who owns a lot of coaches..said that the big stuff..was off the map as far as he was concerned. 1924 W. M. Raine *Troubled Waters* xiii. 143 'Anything new, Matson?'..'Don't forget we've been off the map 'most three weeks.' 1928 *Weekly Dispatch* 13 May 2/6 Cochineal insects, except for making tinctures to colour jellies, are practically off the map to-day.

(*b*) 1920 P. G. Wodehouse *Damsel in Distress* vii. 93 What I mean to say is, you are on the map. You have a sporting chance. 1924 W. M. Raine *Troubled Waters* xix. 205 Didn't know you knew I was on the map. You're sure honouring me. 1926 Bennett *Lord Raingo* I. xii. 60 Some say if there's two members of the War Cabinet, it isn't Andrew Clyth and Tom Hogarth—its Andrew Clyth and Andrew Clyth..But that isn't so. Tom's on the map all right.

2. (Add quots.)

1781 Cowper *Hope* 607 He draws upon life's map a zig-zag line, That shows how far 'tis safe to follow sin. 1899 W. E. H. Lecky (*title*) The Map of Life.

4. *map-roller*; **map-fire**, artillery-fire in which maps are used for laying the guns.

1922 *Encycl. Brit.* XXX. 252/2 The precision with which '*map fire' could be carried out. 1851 C. Cist *Cincinnati* 245 Shade and *map-rollers, turning in ivory, done in a superior style.

Map, *v.*[1] Add: 3. *intr.* To fall into place on a map or plan.

1893 Harkness & Morley *Theory of Functions* 338 Show that..lines parallel to the axes map into unipartite Cartesians.

Maphrodite, aphetic f. Hermaphrodite *a.* 4 b.

1849 N. Kingsley *Diary* 33 She is to appearance a bark or maphrodite brig. *Ibid.* 35.

Maple. 3. Add: (U.S.) *maple-forest, -leaved* adj., *timber, -timbered* adj.; **maple beer**, a beverage made from maple-sap; **maple candy**, candy obtained from maple-sap; **maple molasses** (examples); **maple swamp**, a swamp in which the maple is the prevailing tree; **maple syrup** (examples).

1832 D. J. Browne *Sylva Amer.* 113 *Maple beer..is also made from the same material by the addition of yeast and the essence of spruce. 1857 D. H. Strother *Virginia Illustr.* I. 23 The table was spread with the best in the house—cold bread and meat..maple beer. 1844 *Knickerbocker Mag.* XXIII. 445 While you are getting over the lock-jaw, I will trail some on this snow to take home to little Sue, who begged me to bring her back some *maple candy. 1840 *Ibid.* XVI. 267 A small and beautiful lake (with)..a rich tract of *maple forest on one side. 1813 Muhlenberg *Catal. Plant.* 32 *Maple-leaved Mealy Tree (*Viburnum acerifolium*). *Ibid.* 48 Maple-leaved Hawthorn. 1798–1801 Fessenden *Orig. Poems* (1806) 133 The lips of my charmer are sweet As a hogshead of *maple molasses. 1832 D. J. Browne *Sylva Amer.* 111 Maple molasses is made by discontinuing the evaporation before the liquid is of sufficient consistence to consolidate by cooling. 1863 'Gail Hamilton' *Gala-Days* 225 A land flowing with maple molasses and sugar. 1667 *Providence* (R. I.) *Rec.* V. 317 Standing on the west Side of a *Maple Swampe. 1789 Morse *Amer. Geog.* 143 One species generally predominating in each soil has originated the descriptive names of..maple, ash and cedar swamps. 1832 D. J. Browne *Sylva Amer.* 106 In the maple swamps of New Jersey and Pennsylvania. 1855 *Knickerbocker Mag.* XLVI. 225 Cutting hoop-poles in the maple swamps. 1882 *Rep. Vermont Board Agric.* VII. 63 A sample of his *maple syrup and sugar. 1885 *Outing* Oct. VII. 77/1 A moment later, all smoking and puffy and swimming in maple sirup, it disappears. 1905 E. E. Calkins & R. Holden *Art Mod. Advertising* 113 Maple-sirup is a product to which justice has never been done. 1854 Mrs. Kirkland *Western Clearings* 3 He had purchased fine farming land and *maple timber. 1849 *Presid. Mess. Congress* II. 631 At 7½ a.m., went over good *maple-timbered land to corner.

Maple sugar. *U.S.* (See Maple 3.)

1720 *Phil. Trans.* XXXI. 27 Maple Sugar is made of the Juice of Upland Maple, or Maple Trees that grow upon the Highlands. 1784 [see Maple 3]. *a* 1800 *Spirit Farmer's Museum* (1801) 235 Maple sugar, we have handy. 1832 D. J. Browne *Sylva Amer.* 112 Maple sugar is made in most of the Northern and Western States, and in Canada. 1851 Alice Cary *Clovernook* 74 Everyday in winter she used to feed them [the bees] maple-sugar if she had it. 1886 *Harper's Mag.* June 92/2 Everybody has eaten maple sugar.

attrib. 1907 *Springfield Weekly Republ.* 9 May 16 The Holyoke canoe club opened the river year with a maple-sugar eat at their club-house.

Maple tree. (American examples.)

1660 *Rec. Warwick R. I.* 322 Bounded by a mapell tree on the Northwest corner. 1700 *Providence* (R. I.) *Rec.* IV. 129 The maple tree is the north east Corner bound. 1810 Michaux *Arbres* I. 28 Red flowering maple,..Swamp maple, ..Soft maple..[ou] Maple tree..dans Pensylvanie, la Virginia, et l'Ohio. 1849 E. Bryant *California* iv. 46 The timber on the creek consists of oak, linden, and some maple trees. 1867 J. N. Edwards *Shelby* etc. xx. 337 To send the blood coursing through his veins like the sap in the maple-trees. 1880 *Rep. Vermont Board Agric.* VI. 112 In this state occasionally an aged maple tree may be found with scars made by an axe in tapping.

Mapling (mē^i·pliŋ), *sb.* [f. Maple.] The markings characteristic of maple wood.

1909 W. Bateson *Mendel's Princ. Heredity* 144 A damasked pattern showing where the mapling would have been if the plant had been a coloured one.

Mar, *v.* 2. b. Add: Also *absol.*

c 1420, 1542 [see Make *v.* 46 b]. 1853 Mrs. Gaskell *Ruth* III. i. 43 For the present she would neither meddle nor mar in Ruth's course of life. 1889 [see Make *v.* 46 b].

Marabou[1]. 3. (Recent attrib. example.)

1929 *Times* 31 Oct. 11/6 An attractive bridge coat..in artificial silk velvet finished with a marabout collar.

Marathon (mæ·răþɒn). [The place-name *Marathon* (Gr. Μαραθών) in Attica. Cf. Marathonian *a.*] In full *Marathon race*, a long-distance foot-race run on the open road.

Introduced in the first revived Olympic Games at Athens in 1896, in memory of the famous Greek runner who is said to have brought the news of the battle of Marathon to Athens.

1896 *Fortn. Rev.* June 950 We now come to the great glory of the Greeks—the victory in the Marathon Race. 1905 *Programme of Olympic Games Athens 1906* 3 Flat Races..e. Marathon Race, 42 kilometres. From Marathon to Athens on the road. 1908 T. A. Cook *Olympic Games* 82 The whole of Hellas seemed concentrated at Athens to see the result of the great Marathon Race in the stadium. 1915 'Bartimeus' *Tall Ship* x. 185 'That was a bit of a Marathon, wasn't it?' He measured the distance across the lawn with a humorous eye.

b. Applied to other long-distance races or competitions calling for endurance.

1908 *Daily Chron.* 5 Nov. 1/2 A competition [in potato-peeling]..under the title of 'The Murphy Marathon' was decided last night at the Cookery Exhibition. 1909 *Ibid.* 4 Mar. 8/4 'The Coaching Marathon' from Hampton Court to Olympia. 1923 *Glasgow Herald* 19 Apr. 6/7 The present wave of 'marathon' or endurance dancing.

Hence **Ma·rathon** *v. intr.* to run as in a Marathon race.

1920 *Chambers's Jrnl.* Aug. 519/2 Do I have to marathon ten miles and back?

Marble, *sb.* Add: 5. c. (See quot.)

1924 *Ski Terms* in *Tourist* Winter Sports No. 12/2 *Marble.* A snow-crust formed by alternate freezing and thawing. Found on Southern slopes.

Marbled, *ppl. a.* 3. Add: **marbled-seal** (see quot.).

1871 *Proc. Zool. Soc.* June 506 Occurrence of the Ringed or Marbled Seal (*Phoca hispida*) on the Coast of Norfolk.

Marbleiza·tion. [f. Marbleize *v.* + -ation.] The state of being or process of becoming veined like marble.

188. *Buck's Handbk. Med. Sci.* I. 463 (Cent. Suppl.) A secondary œdema..accompanied with a more or less distinct marbleization of the superficial veins.

Marbleize, *v.* *U.S.* (Earlier example.)

1874 *Rep. Vermont Board Agric.* II. 736 William Hughes ..about 1854 erected mills (the first in this section), for planing and sawing slate and for..the manufacture and marbleizing of slate mantles.

Marblette (mā·ɹblet). [f. Marble *sb.* + -ette.] A composition made to imitate marble. In quot. *attrib.*

1927 Fannie Hurst *Song of Life* 161 A semi-modern..Apartment-House..with..a flock of perambulators under the stairway in the lower marblette foyer.

Marcel (maɹse·l), *sb.* [The name of the French hairdresser who invented the method.] In full *Marcel wave*, a kind of artificial wave of the hair produced by Marcel's process.

1908 *Smart Set* Sept. 86/1 And when she 'comes to', her Marcelle wave is straight as a shad. *a* 1909 'O. Henry' *Roads of Destiny* 62 Man, what do you suppose she did? Loosened up like a Marcel wave in the surf at Coney. 1926 *Glasgow Herald* 25 Sept. 9 It began to rain...Many a beautiful marcel was sacrificed to save a masterpiece of millinery.

b. *Comb.* as *Marcel-waved, -waver, -waving*.

1923 *Chambers's Jrnl.* Sept. 568/1 She could lie without turning one of her exquisitely marcel-waved hairs. 1925 *Daily Tel.* 13 May 20/5 Advt., Expert Marcel Waver and Manicurist. *Ibid.*, Marcel and water waving.

Marcel (maɹse·l), *v.* [f. as prec.] *trans.* To wave (hair) in the 'marcel' fashion.

1906 B'ness von Hutten *What became of Pam* I. x, A gentleman who *marcelled* heads in an Oxford Street shop. 1928 *Daily Express* 28 Dec. 11/1 Her unbobbed hair is marcelled in broad waves from a high forehead.

Hence **Marce·lled** *ppl. a.*; **Marce·lling** *vbl. sb.*

1909 'O. Henry' *Options* 103 A stone house with an engraving of an idol with marcelled hair, playing a flute, over the door. 1922 F. Courtenay *Physical Beauty* 42 If you want that 'marcelled' look, there are comb sets (mounted on springs) which will give it. 1927 *Daily Express* 14 Oct. 6 Women's heads in the late Roman period..are represented not only with distinct marcelling, but also with elaborate jewellery to emphasise the waves.

March, *sb.*[2] 2. b. Add: **March court, meeting** *U.S.*, a court, or town-meeting, held in March, being the principal one of the year; **March-fly**, a dipterous insect of the family *Bibionidæ*.

1836 *Southern Lit. Messenger* II. 302 But if court day be thus important, how much more so is *March court. 1902 L. O. Howard *Insect Bk.* 119 The *March-flies. 1728 *Boston Rec. Comm.* VIII. 222 If the money appropriated..at the last *march meeting be insufficient..Henry Gibbon will advance and pay what falls short. 1766 J. Adams *Wks.* (1830) II. 188 Major Miller and James Brackit Jr. were heard, since March meeting raving against Deacon Palmer. 1866 Lowell *Biglow P.* Ser. II. xi, Mr. Hosea Biglow's Speech in March meeting.

March, *sb.*[3] 4. Add: *march-shire.*

1917 *Eng. Hist. Rev.* Oct. 483 The Warden..had simply taken over certain duties hitherto discharged by the sheriff in the *March shires.

Marching, *vbl. sb.* d. **marching orders** (earlier example).

1780 *Heath Papers* 93 Put the main army under marching orders.

Ma·rcobru·nner. Also **Markbrunner.** [G., f. *Marcobrunn*, the name of a vineyard in the Rheingau.] A Rhenish wine.

1825 T. Hook *Sayings & Doings* Ser. II. I. 48 Ruydersheimer and Markbrunner. 1833 Redding *Mod. Wines* (1851) 224 Marcobrunner is an excellent wine, of a fine flavour. 1862 Tovey *Wine & Wine Countries* 201 At the Hotel Disch [Cologne], the landlord, pitying his condition, pressed upon him a bottle of his Marcobrunner. 1918 Vachell *Some Happenings* xvi. 280 Let us drink your health in some Marcobrunner.

Marconi (maɹkō^u·ni), *v.* [f. the sb.]

1. *intr.* To send a message by wireless telegraphy.

1912 C. N. & A. M. Williamson *Heather Moon* I. iv, I marconied her an hour after he'd said that he would come to us after London. 1919 *Times* 25 June 13/6 Messages were signalled to the coastguards requesting them to marconi to the Fleet.

2. *trans.* To send by wireless telegraphy.

1922 *Glasgow Herald* 2 Nov. 6/2 These figures represent a code which can be wired, cabled, or marconied anywhere. 1926 Phyllis Bottome *Old Wine* xi. 104 Marconiing the news..across space.

Marco·nigraph, *v.* [f. the sb.] **a.** *trans.* To send or record by means of a marconigraph, or by wireless telegraphy. **b.** *intr.* To send a message by wireless telegraphy. **Marco·nigraphy**, Marconi's system of wireless telegraphy.

1903 *Nature* 23 Apr. 583/1 The history of the series of inventions and discoveries which have culminated in Transatlantic Marconigraphy. 1907 *Daily Chron.* 27 Sept. 5/2 The Lusitania was marconigraphed at 5.30 p.m. yesterday 200 miles west of Fastnet. 1909 Mrs. Stratton-Porter *Girl of Limberlost* xxiv. 453 If..I want you..I'll cable, marconigraph, anything.

Marconist (maɹkō^u·nist). [f. Marconi + -ist.] The operator of a marconigraph.

1900 *Star* 4 Aug. 2 (Cass. Suppl.) Then the Marconists begin to pull the enemy's leg by sending what our Marconist calls 'Rot'.

Marcylite. (Earlier example.)

1852 Marcy *Explor. Red River* (1854) 20 We found specimens of a very rich ore, which Professor Shephard, after a careful analysis, pronounced to be a new species, which he has called Marcylite.

Mardi gras (mardi,gra). [F., lit. 'fat Tuesday'.] Shrove Tuesday; the last day of carnival. In U.S. esp. as celebrated in New Orleans. Also *attrib.*

1848 H. Greville *Diary* (1883) 236 This motley crew..dressed more ludicrously than any masks on a *Mardi-gras*. 1869 *De Bow's Rev.* (New Orleans) Mar. 221 We may remark that the celebration of *Mardi-Gras*—the carnival of Spain and Italy, has come into..favor with the Americans. 1883 'Mark Twain' *Life Mississippi* xlvi. 416 The largest annual event in New Orleans is..the Mardi-Gras festivities. 1899 G. Ade *Fables in Slang* (1900) 148 His Father was too Serious a Man to get out in Mardi Gras Clothes and hammer a Ball from one Red Flag to another. 1909 'O. Henry' *Options* 184 The reception they were going to put up would make the Mardi Gras in New Orleans look like an afternoon tea in Bury St Edmonds with a curate's aunt. 1924 *Blackw. Mag.* Nov. 709/2 There are those to whom Mardi-Gras is yet a religious festival.

Maréchal Niel (maréʃal nīl). Also anglicized **Marshal Niel.** [F., named after Adolphe *Niel* (1802–69, Marshal of France).] A variety of climbing rose.

1867 *Gardeners' Chron.* 19 Jan. 52/2 Maréchal Niel, the best of all the yellows. 1867 T. Rivers *Rose-Amateur's Guide* (ed. 9) 136 The rose to which I allude is Marshal Niel. 1905 *Smart Set* Sept. 157/2 You had a great bowl of Maréchal Niels on the piano.

Margarine. Add later definition (see quot.).

1907 *Act 7 Edw. VII* c. 21 § 13 For the purposes of the Sale of Food and Drugs Act and this Act the expression 'margarine' shall mean any article of food, whether mixed with butter or not, which resembles butter and is not milk-blended butter.

b. *margarine-works*; **margarine-cheese** (see quots.).

1899 *Act 62 & 63 Vict.* c. 51 § 25 The expression 'margarine-cheese' means any substance, whether compound or otherwise, which is prepared in imitation of cheese, and which contains fat not derived from milk. 1902 *Encycl. Brit.* XXV. 93/2 From America cheese has come into the English market, made from skim-milk which has again been provided with fatty matter, generally emulsified margarine—hence the term 'margarine cheese' or 'filled cheese'. 1909 *Chambers's Jrnl.* Jan. 24/1 Margarine works are equipped with cooling machinery.

Hence **Ma·rgarine** *v. trans.* To smear or spread (bread) with margarine.

1918 *Punch* 15 May 315 She knows which side her bread's margarined. 1924 Galsworthy *White Monkey* III. iv. 243 'Well', he said, over their cocoa and margarined bread: 'I must see Mr. Mont, that's certain.'

Margin, *sb.* Add: 2. c. (Earlier examples.)

1848 W. Armstrong *Stocks* 10 The purchaser then hands over this margin to the person with whom he hypothecates the Stock. 1870 Medbery *Men & Myst. Wall St.* 62 Seven per cent a year is generally allowed on all margins advanced by customers. 1880 *Harper's Mag.* Oct. 782/2 All speculated, but they did not speculate on margins.

5. **margin clerk**, one who records dealings in margins (sense 2 c).

1886 *Harper's Mag.* July 213/2 Speculative sales of lard..are also made in the Call Room..the caller of provisions and margin clerk presiding.

Margin, *v.* 4. (Later example.)

1902 H. L. Wilson *Spenders* xxxiv. 408 As the stock fell, the banks requested the brokers to margin up their loans, and the brokers, in turn, requested Percival to margin up his trades.

Marginal. A. *adj.* Add: 4. *Stock-broking.* Pertaining to, of the nature of, margins (sense 2 c).

1870 Medbery *Men & Myst. Wall St.* 59 Nor is there any dissimilarity between the conditions of purchase in complete and in marginal transactions. *Ibid.* 62 The broker..demands of his customer either solid deposit of money or stocks, or marginal deposit of money.

B. *sb.* Add: 2. A marginal feather, bone, plate, etc.

1887 *Proc. Zool. Soc.* 347 This group of feathers...They are best termed marginals (*tectrices marginales*). 1909 *Century Dict.* Suppl. [in various special senses].

Marginally, *adv.* Add to def.: Round or about the margin or edge of anything.

1909 H. G. Wells *Tono-Bungay* III. ii. § 7. 250 Wandering marginally through distinguished gatherings, I would catch the whispers: 'That's Mr. Ponderevo!'

Marian. B. *sb.*[2] Add: 3. An English Catholic of Queen Mary's reign (1553–58).

1899 F. W. Maitland *Collected Papers* (1911) III. 130 Canon MacColl laboured under the misfortune of knowing something about the votes that these Marians gave in Parliament. 1904 W. H. Frere *Hist. Eng. Ch. 1558–1625* ii. 23 The champions of the Marians..were to dispute with the champions of the exiles.

Marine. B. *sb.* Add: 5. b. Applied to a shade of blue.

1923 *Weekly Dispatch* 8 Apr. 12 Advt., Latest designs on ..Saxe, Marine, Grey and Black grounds.

Marione·ttist. [f. Marionette + -ist.] An exhibitor of marionettes.

1924 *Glasgow Herald* 10 May 8 It was here the man of so many quarrels..fought the mock duel with..the marionettist's monkey.

Mark, *sb.*[1] Add: 12. e. *Athletics.* A line drawn to indicate the starting-point. Also in phrases (lit. and fig.) as *to get off the mark*, to start (well); *to toe the mark* (see Toe *v.* 2).

1887 Shearman *Athletics & Football* 65 It requires, however, much skill and practice not to 'take off' before the mark [in jumping]. *Ibid.* 198 Nothing was said until the men got upon their marks. 1905 *Pearson's Mag.* Sept. 290/2 He..beat his field by a yard or two off the mark. 1912 E. H. Ryle *Athletics* 91 This method..assists a runner to keep steady on the mark while awaiting the report of the pistol. 1928 *Observer* 5 Feb. 23/5 When you really wish to get going you have a second, a third and a top speed change which will get the car off the mark, in the old phrase, in an inspiriting manner. 1931 *Oxf. Mail* 29 Aug. 8/3 G. Fisher and L. Rogers were quickly off the mark, 20 runs being scored in the first ten minutes.

13. b. (Earlier examples.)

a 1847 Chalmers (Bartlett 1860) Men..called out to make and leave their mark upon the world. 1854 *Harper's Mag.* Sept. 561/2 There was a time when Jacob made his mark upon the stock-brokers and money-changers of that monetary locality.

15. d. *A soft* or *easy mark*, a person who is easily persuaded or deceived. *U.S. slang.*

1896 G. Ade *Artie* xvi. 150 He was the wise guy and I was the soft mark. *Ibid.* xviii. 173 When that kind of a mark comes in they..get ready to do business. 1904 G. H. Lorimer *Old Gorgon Graham* 288 He was too easy a mark to succeed in Wall Street.

22. *A mark at*, a good hand at.

1881 *Punch* 3 Dec. 263/2 Till my chummy Scholard Mike, who's a mark at A.B.C., Read me Littler's little tale.

Mark, *v.* 2. c. Add: *To mark up*, to mark at a higher price; to raise in price.

1870 *Amer. Naturalist* III. 3 The prices of venison and other game was so far 'marked up' that gold..was charged for salmon. 1902 G. H. Lorimer *Lett. Self-made Merchant* iv. 52 The clerks all knocked off their regular work and started in to mark up prices. 1929 *Even. News* 18 Nov. 15/1 Home rail stocks were marked up all round.

13. Delete 'Now *poet.*' and add later examples.

1833 Disraeli *Cont. Fleming* III. v. (1853) 174, I looked up, and marked the tumultuous waving of many torches. 1849 C. Brontë *Shirley* III. xii. 278 She smiled, well pleased to mark the delight of her pupil. 1860 Thackeray *Four Georges* i, Lift up your glances respectfully, and mark him eyeing Madame de Fontanges. 1893 Kipling *Many Invent.* Pref. *To True Rom.*, The children wise of outer skies Look hitherward and mark A light that shifts.

Marked, *ppl. a.* 1. b. Add: **marked cheque** (see quot.); also *U.S.*, 'a check having on it a private mark of the maker known to his bank' (Webster 1911); **marked transfer**, an endorsed transfer (see quot.).

1907 Cordingley *Lond. Commerc. Dict.*, *Marked Cheque*, a cheque marked by the banker on whom it is drawn, stating that it is 'good' for the amount named upon it. 1901 — *Dict. Stock Exch. Terms* 59 *Marked Transfers.* The company..then issue a fresh Certificate to him for the part unsold, and endorse the Transfer that they hold Certificates to cover the number of shares sold, when the Transfer is said to be 'Marked' or 'Certified'.

Marker. 1. b. Add: One who records prices on the Stock-exchange.

1870 Medbery *Men & Myst. Wall St.* 21 The 'marker' or black-board clerk writes off the prices upon the tablet.

f. (Later examples.)

1907 S. E. White *Arizona Nights* I. viii. 149 In the meantime the marker was engaged in his work. First, with a sharp knife he cut off slanting the upper quarter of one ear (of a calf). 1928 *Collier's* 29 Dec. 6/2 There was a lull in the stream of lumber. The marker turned for a look at the order board.

j. In surveying: A person who makes the marks on trees to indicate boundaries or lines of survey.

1809 in *Ann. 9th Congress* 2 Sess. 974 And to each marker or chain-carrier twenty shillings for every day they shall be employed. 1813 *Steele Papers* II. 702 Two common axemen who may serve as markers.

2. (Add example.)

1911 *Encycl. Brit.* XXI. 468/1 s.v. *Phonograph*, While the wax cylinder is rotating, the point of the marker is angled downwards, and this cuts deeply into the wax.

3. b. A monument, memorial stone, etc., marking a place of special interest.

1906 *Springfield Weekly Republ.* 15 Feb. 16 The committee appointed to investigate the matter of a marker for the Washington elm reported in favor of a granite marker.

4. (Earlier and later examples.)

1888 *Congress. Rec.* 12 Dec. 202/2 The waving of the bloody shirt would not have been a marker. 1904 W. H. Smith *Promoters* xxv. 366 What little I've told you isn't a marker to other things he said.

Market, *sb.* Add: 6. (Later examples.)

1894 *Home Chimes* XVI. 366 The artist had to seek a market elsewhere. 1897 E. H. Cooper *Mr. Blake of Newmarket* xxvi. 255 'I've missed the market!' My friend..explained..that he had not got the best bet against the horse which he might have got.

7. c. The kind or amount of business done in bets.

1886 Earl of Suffolk etc. *Racing & Steeple-Chasing* (Badm. Libr.) v. 85 On arriving at the rails, which separate the private stands' enclosure from the ring, he finds the market well set.

10. a. *market-boat* (earlier example), *boy, people, sloop, wagon*.

1809 W. Irving *Knickerb.* v. i. 158 Escorting some bevy of country cousins, about to depart..in a *market-boat. 1863 Mrs. Whitney *F. Gartney's Girlh.* v, The *market-boys, and the waiters, and the confectioners' parcels. 1695 *Acts & Res. Mass.* (1869) I. 238 Hucksters and traders of the town shall not..buy of the *market people. 1786 *Boston Selectmen* 26 Apr., A Committee to treat with the Fishermen and other Market People for the hire of the Building at the end of the market. 1830 J. F. Cooper *Water Witch* I. xi, The rogues will pass the pennant like innocent market people. 1885 *Outing* Nov. VII. 206/2 A big *market-sloop came along bound west. 1880 *Harper's Mag.* July 264/2 At last the morning *market wagons began moving.

b. **market-basket** (earlier examples); **market gardening**, keeping a market garden; **market house** (U.S. examples); **market hunter**, one who hunts game for the market; so **market-hunting** *vbl. sb.*; **market master** (*U.S.* and *S. Afr.* examples); **market money**, money for buying things in a market (see also quot. under 10 a); **market reporter**, one who records the market rates of goods or stocks; **market shooter**, one who shoots game for the market; **market square**, an open square in which a town market is held; **market-stall** (earlier example); **market-truck** *U.S.*, vegetables cultivated for the market (Bartlett 1859); **market-value** (earlier example); **market work**, add: also, the work connected with selling commodities in a market.

1842 *Knickerbocker Mag.* XIX. 111 Often, her *market-basket on her arm, she would wander frantic through the city. 1864 B. Taylor *H. Thurston* x. 141 The grocer's boy made his appearance with a large market-basket on his arm. 1875 Mrs. Stowe *We & Neighbors* xxxix. 372 A family man with a market-basket on his arm. 1892 *Rep. Vermont Board Agric.* XII. 144 Vegetable raising, or *market gardening, is quite extensive and very profitable. 1653 *Boston Town Rec.* X. 9 A *Market House wilbe more the beneficiall to bring trade to my shops. 1803 in *Ann. 8th Congress* 2 Sess. 1508 A prison, town-house, market-house, assembly room. 1813 *Niles' Week' Reg.* IV. 209/1 After the danger had subsided, and the goods which had been removed in the market-house, &c. had been returned, the child was found. 1815 Drake *Cincinnati* i. 59 A market-house has recently been put up on the river bank. 1827 Drake & Mansf. *Cincinnati* iii. 28 There are in this city, three large Market Houses. 1859 Alice Cary *Country Life* vi. 152 The market-house..was a dismantled canal boat set upon dryland. 1889 *Kansas Times & Star* 21 Nov., A grand market house at last. 1874 J. W. Long *Wild-Fowl Shooting* 185 Blue-winged teal..are much sought for by *market-hunters. 1897 *Outing* XXX. 293/1, I had little dreamed that Michigan would ever so far forget herself as to encourage *market-hunting in preference to sportsman like methods. 1851 C. Cist *Cincinnati* 87 A city treasurer, a marshal, a wharf and three *market masters are elected. 1859 *Queenstown Free Press* 3 Aug. (Pettman), I should advise them to send the market-master ..to visit our market. 1868 *Putnam's Mag.* I. Jan. 40/2 Strawberries are down to ten cents a box..but you didn't leave a cent of *market-money. 1853 B. J. Taylor *Jan. & June* 83 And so, as *Market Reporters have it, 'we have movements to note'. 1897 *Outing* XXX. 293/2 The *market-shooter, with no dogs to take care of, can sneak through the known haunts of the quail. 1836 Edward *Hist. Texas* 148 A block shall be designated for a *market square. 1827 Drake & Mansf. *Cincinnati* vi. 55 The Revenue of the Corporation is derived; From...Rent of *Market-stalls. 1791 *Ann. Congress* II. App. 1993 The rapid increase that has taken place in the *market value of the public securities. 1887 H. H. Jackson *Between Whiles* iv. 226 Donald liked slow cruising and the *market-work best.

Market, *v.* Add: 3. To 'count' or 'trade on'; to take advantage of.

1906 Hardy *Dynasts* II. i. 148 These cloaked visitors of every clime That market on your magnanimity To gain an audience.

Marketing, *vbl. sb.* 2. b. (Earlier example.)

1843 N. Boone *Jrnl.* (1917) 234 Indians visited us throughout the course of the day, bringing in marketing of various kinds.

Marking, *vbl. sb.* 4. Add: *marking brush*; **marking stitch** (earlier example).

1855 M. M. Thompson *Doesticks* xxii. 198 A dry-goods box with a *marking brush sticking out of the top of it. 1882 Foote *Led-Horse Claim* xvii. 228 He..swept, with one stroke of his marking-brush, a black circle around the figures. 1861 Mrs. Stowe *Pearl Orr's Isl.* I. xvii. 152, I was going to begin and teach her some *marking stitches.

Marksman. Add: 2. b. *U.S.* = *Marker 1 j.

1816 U. Brown *Jrnl.* in *Maryland Hist. Mag.* XI. 220 This afternoon hunts up Chain Carriers and an Axman or marksman. *Ibid.* 221.

5. (Earlier example.)

1887 Shearman *Athletics & Football* 57 The starter is helped by a 'marksman', who places the men on the scratch.

Marl, *a.* [Reduced f. Marled *ppl. a.*[2]] Of yarn, etc.: Having two or more colours twisted together so as to produce a mottled effect.

1922 *Daily Mail* 18 Dec. 1 Advt., Knitted sports suit in rich Marl mixtures and plain colours. 1923 *Ibid.* 11 June 1 Advt., The fashionable Knitted Marl Wool. *Ibid.* 18 June 4 Advt., Knitted Wool Costume in the marl effect. 1926 *Illustr. Off. Jrnl. Patents* 20 Oct. 1668 Spinning marl or multi-ply yarns.

Marlberry. *U.S.* (Examples.)

1884 C. S. Sargent *Rep. Forests N. Amer.* 100 *Ardisia Pickeringia* Marlberry-Cherry. 1897 G. B. Sudworth *Arborescent Flora U.S.* 316 *Icacorea paniculata.* Marlberry. 1917 Safford in *Rep. Smithsonian Inst.* 384 In addition to these are the paradise tree or bitterwood; soapberry tree;..marlberry; [etc.].

Marl-burn, *v.* [f. Marl *sb.*[1]] *trans.* To spoil by applying too much marl.

1868 *Rep. U.S. Commissioner Agric.* (1869) 391 The effect would be to 'marl-burn' the soil.

Marler (mā·ɹləɹ). [f. Marl *v.*[2] + -er[1].] A marline-spike.

1929 Masefield *Hawbucks* 15 A strong sheath knife with a marler at the back.

Marline, *sb.* Add: b. Comb. *marline-hitch, -hole.*

1883 *Man. Seamanship Boys* 6 To lash a Hammock up..The number of turns taken is seven, they are passed at equal distance with a *marline hitch. *Ibid.* 38 *Marline holes are worked along the foot.

Marm. [Var. of Ma'am, freq. in U.S. writers.]

1. = Ma'am 1.

1837 R. M. Bird *Nick of Woods* I. 120 Say the word, marm. 1845 Mrs. Kirkland *Western Clearings* 17 'Massy no, marm!' said Jane, with a giggle. *Ibid.* 18 No, Marm; but—this 'ere is something about the team, I guess.

2. = Ma'am 2.

1887 Mary Wilkins *Humble Romance* 107 Marm Lawson was not a duchess; but she was Marm Lawson. The 'Marm' itself was a title.

3. = Ma'am 3.

1865 Susan Hale *Lett.* 16 The silk is seven dollars a yard, and the marm that makes it asks a great deal. 1872 *Congress. Rec.* App. 632/3 It will be seen that in the great race thus far the English and American marms are about 'nip and tuck'.

b. Used for 'mother'. (Also in address.)

1835 J. F. Cooper *Monikins* xii. 155 He could scare one by threatening to tell his *marm* how he behaved. 1838 — *Home as Found* xvi. 263 Who taught you to call me marm! ..Say 'ma' this instant. 1845 S. Judd *Margaret* I. 37 'Has your marm got that done?' asked Martha Madeline. 1848 Bartlett *Dict. Amer.* 220 *Marm*, a corruption of the word *madam* or ma'am, often used in the interior of New England for mother.

4. **Marm-school** = *ma'am-school.*

1902 Clapin *Dict. Amer.*

Hence **Marmsome** *a.* 'madam-like'.

1910 Susan Hale *Lett.* 463 A sort of marmsome housekeeper who waited at table.

Marmite (marmīt). [ad. F. *marmite*: see Marmit.] An earthenware cooking utensil; a stew-pot.

1918 'Berta Ruck' *Disturbing Charm* I. xi. 107 The door into the huge French kitchen stood open, giving a glimpse of marmites, burnished copper pans, crocks, and five-decker cookers.

b. *slang.* A bomb or shell resembling a pot.

1918 E. S. Farrow *Dict. Mil. Terms.*

Marmorization. [f. Marmorize *v.*] The process or fact of being marmorized, or converted into marble.

1903 *Amer. Jrnl. Sci.* Aug. XVI. 144 Marmorization of the limestone is abundant in the region.

Marmoro·sis. [f. L. *marmor*.] = Marmarosis.

1909 W. G. Renwick *Marble & Marble Working* 4 Under the combined influences of heat and strain, limestone undergoes a gradual process known as *marmorosis*.

Marocain (marŏkē^i·n). [f. F. *maroquin*: see Maroquin.] A dress fabric of the crêpe type, having a rough texture, woven from specially twisted silk and wool or cotton. Also *colloq.*, a garment made of marocain.

1922 *Glasgow Herald* 28 June 8/6 For her going away dress the bride had a three-piece suit of grey wool marocain.

Supplement, p. 3873; Corrigenda, p. 4092; Spurious words, p. 4093; Books quoted, p. 4094

1926 *Tatler* 30 Aug. 354/2 An evening frock of black crêpe marocain. 1926 *Brit. Weekly* 24 June 250/5 Most of them are of patterned fabrics—muslins,..marocain, ninon and shantung. 1926 Mrs. A. Sidgwick *Sack & Sugar* xi. 126, I wore an embroidered marocain.

Maroodi (märū·di). Also **maroudi**. [ad. Arowak *marodi*.] A bird of either of two varieties of guan (*Penelope cristata* and *Penelope pupile*) found in British Guiana, sometimes distinguished as the white-headed and the common Maroodi.
1825 Waterton *Wand. S. Amer.* (1879) 117 Here the white-crested Maroudi..is pretty plentiful. 1876 C. Barrington Brown *Canoe & Camp Life Brit. Guiana* 345 Maroodies of two kinds (the common and white-headed).. were also numerous. 1883 E. F. im Thurn *Among Indians of Guiana* 62 Now and then a maroodi (*Penelope*) cried shrilly from among the trees. 1922 *Blackw. Mag.* Apr. 521 A quail and a maroodi rewarded their zeal.

Maroon, *sb.*2 2. (Later example.)
1838 Caroline Gilman *Recoll. Southern Matron* xxxii. 223 Feeling the necessity of refreshment, we alighted for a while beneath a tree by the roadside, for a *maroon*.

Maroon, *v.* Add: 2. b. *transf.* To place or leave in a position from which one cannot get away; said e.g. of floods.
1910 *N. Y. Even. Post* 6 Jan. (Th.) Train No. 4.., due here from Los Angeles on January 1, is marooned in the desert. 1912 *Ibid.* 15 July 1/7 Rescue parties found dazed families.. marooned on roofs. *Ibid.*, The torrent rushed..through the [station] yard,..marooning several hundred passengers.

Marooner. Add: 4. = Maroon *sb.*2 1. *U.S.*
1741 W. Byrd *Westover Papers* 13 (Bartlett 1860) We were told that on the South Shore [in Virginia] dwelt a marooner, who modestly called himself a hermit.

Marquetry, *v.* [f. the sb.] *trans.* To ornament with inlaid work.
1925 *Brit. Weekly* 2 Apr. 10/4 Much of his choicest work was..painted, gilded, marquetried, veneered with other woods.

Marquis. Add: 5. A variety of wheat grown extensively in North America.
1906 C. Saunders in *Dept. Agric.* (Canada) Bull. No. 57. 29 *Chelsea* and *Marquis* are new cross-bred sorts produced at the Central Experimental Farm. 1922 *Encycl. Brit.* XXXII. 74/1 On the average Marquis ripens six days earlier than Red Fife. 1924 J. A. Thomson *Science Old & New* xliii. 253 Marquis is a hard, red spring wheat with excellent milling and baking qualities; it is now the dominant spring wheat in Canada and the United States.

Marquise. Add: 3. b. *Archit.* (See quot. 1891.)
1891 *Adeline's Art Dict.* s.v., The term *marquise* is applied to a light roof which projects from the façade of a building. It is generally placed over a flight of steps. On the outside of theatres marquises of considerable length are not infrequently to be seen. Almost invariably they have a glass roof. 1904 B'ness von Hutten *Pam* v. i. 237 A moment later, she stood in the door, under the little 'marquise'. 1906 'Lucas Malet' *Dogs of Want* i. § 1. 7 [She] stood under the glass marquise, at the top of the flight of steps.

Marquisette (markize·t). [F., dim. of *marquise* Marquise.] A firm diaphanous fabric woven from mercerized cotton; a silk fabric resembling this.
1908 *Tatler* 6 May, Suppl. p. iv, A simple house gown of black marquisette. 1909 *Daily Chron.* 12 Apr. 7/1 The soft marquisettes and satin-faced foulards. 1912 *Home Chat* 6 Apr. 60/1 A shot Marquisette, with wide chêne ribbon border. 1928 *Times* 9 May 11/3 A picture gown of fine gold embroidered marquisette, over peach georgette.

Marriage. 8. Add: *marriage-hall*, *-market* (earlier example).
1924 W. J. Locke *Coming of Amos* xvi. 204 Of the marriage in the bleak *marriage-hall of the Mairie, she remembered little. 1850 *Punch* 3 Aug. 54/2 If..the Duke of Cambridge were permitted to take his coronet into the Home *marriage-market.

Marrow, *sb.*1 5. Add: **marrow-gut** *U.S.* (see quot.); **marrow-stem kale**, a variety of kale having a thick edible stem, cultivated for forage.
1848 E. Bryant *California* vii. 96 An intestinal vessel ..commonly called by hunters the 'marrow-gut' which, anatomically speaking, is the chylo-poetic duct. 1920 *Conquest* Apr. 256/3 In place of grass it is possible to grow crops such as cabbage, vetches, rape, marrowstem kale, mangolds, mixtures of oats, peas, tares, etc.

Marrowfat. Add: 2. *U.S.* A tallow-like substance prepared by boiling down marrow.
1841 Catlin *N. Amer. Indians* I. 116 'Marrow-fat' is collected by the Indians from the buffalo bones which they break to pieces, yielding a prodigious quantity of marrow, which is boiled out and put into buffalo bladders. 1846 Sage *Scenes Rocky Mts.* (1859) 113 Marrow-fat, an article in many respects superior to butter. 1888 *Century Mag.* XXXVI. 198/1 Then he slicked his hair with marrow-fat from a horn.
3. *U.S. slang.* (See quot.)
1903 A. B. Hart *Actual Govt.* 75 The 'marrow-fat' fraud consists in a voter's putting in more than one ballot, while the clerk puts down fictitious names to cover the extra ballots.

Marrowsky (marou·ski). Also **marouski, morowski, mowrowsky**. [Asserted to have been derived from the name of a Polish count, doubtfully identified with Count Joseph Boruwlaski. See *Notes & Queries* Ser. XIII. I. 331, 437, 467.] A variety of slang, or a slip in speaking, characterized by transposition of initial letters, syllables, or parts of two words. Also *marrowsky language*.
1863 Nicholson *Autob. Fast Man*, Fanny King, or as Bill Leach, in the interesting language called Marouski, termed her, Kanny Fing. 1883 Sala *Living Lond.* 491 (Farmer) The vocabulary of Tim Bobbin, Josh Billings,.. and the Marrowsky language.
b. An instance of this.
1923 in *N. & Q.* Ser. XIII. I. 331/2 In my childhood..an old cousin used to entertain me with what we now call spoonerisms, but which she termed morowskis.
Hence **Marrow·skyer**, one who uses Marrowsky language or makes marrowskis in his speech; **Marrow·skying** *vbl. sb.* the intentional or accidental transposition of initial letters, etc.
1912 *Brit. Med. Jrnl.* 22 June 1443 It would be interesting if 'marrowskyers'' blunders could also be classified. *Ibid.*, All actors live in dread of 'marrowskying', that curious transposition of syllables. 1860 *Hotten's Slang Dict.* (ed. 2) s.v. *Medical Greek*, At the London University they have a way of disguising English..which consists in transposing the initials of words... This disagreeable nonsense is often termed *marrowskying*.

Marry, *v.* Add: 1. b. (Further example.)
1920 W. B. Money *Humours of Parish* 142, I was marrying her daughter to a very nice young man.
2. b. With *off*.
1866 *Christine* viii. 44 If the young girls did not mind being ..finally married off to some of her *protégés*, it was all very well. 1894 Violet Hunt *Maiden's Progr.* i. 2, I sincerely hope you will be married off before *I* come on, or I shall have no peace. 1908 *Smart Set* June 14/1 Mr. Hardcastle was insisting upon marrying off Aunt Ella to Señor Dominguez y Aguirra.

Marsa, Mars(e, variants of Mas, Massa.
1890 *Century Mag.* Nov. 65 Suit you, marsa? 1901 B. T. Washington *Up from Slavery* 12, I recall the feeling of sorrow among the slaves when they heard of the death of 'Mars' Billy'. *a* 1909 'O. Henry' *Roads of Destiny* ii. 39 Marse Robert robbing the bank! *Ibid.* xxi. 350 I'm not going back on Mars' Jeff.

Marsh. Add: 1. b. *locally*. A meadow; a stretch of grass land whether swampy or dry.
1787– in English use (see *Eng. Dial. Dict.*). 1852 Mrs. Meredith *My Home in Tasmania* I. 163 (Morris) A marsh here is what would in England be called a meadow, with this difference, that in our marshes, until partially drained, a growth of tea-trees and rushes in some measure encumbers them; but, after a short time, these die off..and a thick sward of verdant grass covers the whole extent.
4. **marsh-hay** *U.S.*, hay made from marsh-grasses.
1839 *Cultivator* VII. 33 The common *marsh hay is no better than the 'bog meadow hay' of the east. 1852 *Trans. Mich. Agric. Soc.* III. 132 They feed well at the straw stack and thrive on marsh hay.
b. **marsh-quail** (earlier example); **marsh tacky** *U.S.*, a small pony bred in marshy districts; **marsh-treader** *U.S.*, an insect of the heteropterous family *Hydrometridæ* or *Limnobatidæ*.
1750 J. Birket *Voy. N. Amer.* 4 Oct. (1916) 32 Killd some Squirrels and some very pretty birds called *Marsh quails something bigger than a field fare. 1838 Caroline Gilman *Recoll. Southern Matron* xix. 131 An accident happening to my horse, I was obliged to hire one of the little animals called '*marsh tackies' to carry me over a creek. 1877 Eliz. S. Phelps *Story of Avis* 432 They are short clean steps, very clear and pleasant for a marsh-tackey's foot. 1908 L. O. Howard *Insect Bk.* 282 The *Marsh Treaders. (Family *Hydrometridæ*.)
c. **marsh grass, pennywort, rosemary** (later U.S. examples).
1837 *Southern Lit. Messenger* III. 738 The driver told us his horses were fed on nothing but hay—and this too made of the *marsh grass. 1868 *Putnam's Mag.* I. May 592/1 Clumps..begin to make their appearance above the reeds and tall marsh-grass. 1904 Mrs. Stratton-Porter *Freckles* 11 It's the price of your life to start through the marsh-grass ..unless you are covered with heavy leather above your knees. 1885 *Outing* Nov. VII. 179/1 All the ground about is carpeted with the light-green leaves of the *marsh-pennywort. 1861 Mrs. Stowe *Pearl Orr's Isl.* I. x. 82 '*Marsh rosemary is a very excellent gargle.' Said Mr. Sewell.

Marshaller. Delete †*Obs.* and add modern example.
1910 *Westm. Gaz.* 11 Apr. 8/3 The marshallers were everywhere, watching and directing.

Marshlander. Add: b. An inhabitant of marshland.
1896 W. A. Dutt *G. Borrow in E. Anglia* v. 46 Farther away the marshlanders have seized upon any slight piece of rising ground.

Marsh-mallow. b. Add: Also *attrib.*
1906 *Amer. Illustr. Mag.* Mar. 562/1 Girls assemble shreds and patches, buttons and marshmallow boxes. 1926 *Hutchinson's Best Story Mag.* Nov. 109/1 Chocolate marshmallow ice cream.

Marten. 2. Add: **baum-marten** [G. *baum* tree], the pine marten or its fur.
1879 *Encycl. Brit.* IX. 838/2 *Marten, Baum*,..Found in Europe and Asia, of fine overhair, but woolly fur, of a brownish colour, approaching that of the American marten. 1906 *Westm. Gaz.* 3 Nov. 13/1 There are many kinds of sable, the Russian, Canadian, the baum-marten, and the stone-marten. 1909 *Daily Chron.* 23 Feb. 7/3 The Hudson Bay sables and the dyed baum marten.
4. *marten-skin* (earlier examples).
1778 *Essex Inst. Hist. Coll.* XLIX. 109 Sold..250 martin skins, at 12s 6d. 1795 A. Ellicott in *Life & Lett.* (1908) 123, I have purchased from the Indians some fine Martin skins to replace your old muff and tippet.

Martin1. 3. **martin-box** *U.S.* (earlier and later examples); **martin-cage**, a cage for holding martins; **martin-house** = *martin-box*.
1853 B. F. Taylor *Jan. & June* 60 A *martin-box of a cottage scuds round the corner of the Meeting House. 1871 Mrs. Stowe *Sam Lawson* 108 Your questions tumbles over each other thick as martins out o' a martin-box. 1844 *Knickerbocker Mag.* XXIII. 442 Like a superannuated old man with a *martin-cage upon his crooked back. 1835 R. M. Bird *Hawks of Hawk-h.* I. iii. 44 Here's..the identical old Folly, with..the pot in the chimney, and the *martin-house on a pole. 1854 Shillaber *Mrs. Partington* 101 He heard Gruff scolding Ike for throwing snowballs at his new Martin-house. 1884 'C. E. Craddock' *In Tenn. Mts.* I. 40 There was a lofty martin-house whence the birds whirled fitfully.

Martin5. Add quots.
1856 P. Thompson *Hist. Boston* 714 A twin-heifer is called a martin, and is said to be incapable of bearing young. 1901–2 *Rep. Kansas State Board Agric.* 211 (Cent. Suppl.) Purebred steer, spayed or martin heifer, two years old and under three.

Marvel, common Eng. and U.S. dial. var. of Marble *sb.*
1727 J. Comer *Diary* (1923) 17 He was playing marvils near the Old North Meeting House. 1848 Bartlett *Dict. Amer.* 221 *Marvel*, a common corrupt pronunciation of *Marble*. 1851 J. J. Hooper *Adv. Simon Suggs* xi, Sometimes..I play marvels. 1867 P. Kennedy *Banks Boro* i. 5 In the season we shot marvels on the road. 1876 'Mark Twain' *Tom Sawyer* ii. 13 Jim, I'll give you a marvel.

Ma·rvelry. *poet.* [f. Marvel *sb.* + -ry.] A marvellous thing.
1874 O'Shaughnessy *Music & Moonlight* 12 And the moon's pallid taper fingers played With all the scarce-seen marvelries that stayed In the strange fitful glimmer.

Marxian (mā·ɪksiān), *a.* and *sb.* [f. the name of Karl *Marx* (1818–83), the German socialist + -ian.]
A. *adj.* Of or pertaining to Karl Marx or his socialistic doctrines.
1896 B. Russell *German Soc. Democracy* 71 The 'honourable' Social Democrats, as they called themselves, the party of thorough-going Marxian Communism. 1902 B. Kidd *Princ. Western Civiliz.* 87 [Spencer] really has in view, like the Marxian socialists, a state of society in which [etc.]. 1918 E. Belfort Bax *Reminisc.* 131 A writer of..polemical essays on the materialist theory of history, on Marxian lines.
B. *sb.* One who holds or supports Marxian views; a follower of Marx.
1896 B. Russell *German Soc. Democracy* 89 Although this programme showed, on the whole, a victory of the Marxians, Marx protested against it. 1918 E. Belfort Bax *Reminisc.* 138 The question of Internationalism was indeed one of the great bones of contention between them and the Marxians. 1923 E. A. Ross *Russian Soviet Republ.* 394 Even though it fell in partly with the program of the extreme Marxians, the expropriation of the landlords and capitalists was not really a thing planned.
Hence **Marxianism** = *Marxism.
1896 B. Russell *German Soc. Democracy* 93 The new philosophy of life which Marxianism had introduced. 1914 A. Harrison *Kaiser's War* 206 Bernstein..re-accepted orthodox Marxianism. 1926 *Spectator* 22 May 871/2 It was Western Europe which gave Marxianism to Russia.

Marxism (mā·ɪksiz'm). [f. *Marx* (see Marxian) + -ism, or ad. F. *Marxisme*, G. *Marxismus*.] The political and economic theories advocated by Karl Marx; the holding of Marxian doctrines.
1908 H. G. Wells *New Worlds for Old* xi. § 4. 251 It seemed to me, that fatalistic Marxism crumbled down to dust. 1920 *Q. Rev.* Apr. 477 M. Millerand..was throwing sops to the Cerberus of unchained Marxism. 1928 *Daily Tel.* 15 May 8/2 That twentieth-century development of Marxism which is the political philosophy of New Russia.

Marxist (mā·ɪksist). [f. as prec. + -ist or ad. F. *Marxiste*, G. *Marxist*.]
1. A follower or disciple of Karl Marx, one holding Marxian opinions.
1886 'Alb' *Living Paris & France* 337 The Marxists or Guesdists form the next considerable revolutionary party. 1908 H. G. Wells *New Worlds for Old* xv. § 3. 350 Those 'class war' ideas of the Marxist that have been superseded in English socialism. 1923 — *Men Like Gods* III. iv. § 3. 291 The Marxist had wasted the forces of revolution for fifty years.
2. *attrib.* or *adj.* = *Marxian *a.*
1908 H. G. Wells *New Worlds for Old* xv. § 3. 350 A community made up wholly of 'Labour' and emotionally democratic, such as the Marxist teaching suggests. 1920 *Q. Rev.* July 204 Only the German Social-Democrats in Austria tried to keep alive their old ideal of an international Marxist brotherhood.

Maryland (mē·rilænd). The name of one of the eastern states of North America (named in 1632 after Queen Henrietta *Maria*) used *attrib.* in **Maryland end, parson** (see quots.); **M. yellow-throat**, a common species of ground warbler (*Geothlypis trichas*). Also *ellipt.* (see quot.).
1859 Bartlett *Dict. Amer.* (ed. 2) **Maryland end*, said of the hock of the ham. The other is the Virginia end. 1811 *Mem. Life Pennsylvania* 93 Mr. I.— seemed in all respects to be what was then called in Pennsylvania a *Maryland parson; that is, one who could accommodate himself to his company. 1808 A. Wilson *Amer. Ornithol.* I. 88 *Maryland Yellowthroat. 1891 J. B. Grant *Our Common Birds* 180 Maryland Yellow-Throat...A shy bird; not given to frequent flights...Song vigorous and rich, but not varied. *ellipt.* 1867 Simmonds *Dict. Trade* Suppl., *Maryland*, a mild kind of tobacco.

Marylander. *U.S.* Also **Marilander.** [f. *Maryland + -er 1.] A native or inhabitant of Maryland; a Maryland ham.
1678 *New Castle Court Rec.* 234 They had gott out of Maryland for old debts due for Cattle sold to the Marylanders. 1744 in *Maryland Hist. Mag.* VI. 227, I never knew a good honest Marylander that was not got by a Merchant. 1755 L. Evans *Anal. Map Colonies* 14 The

Sasquehannocks, after the great Defeat by the Marilanders, were easily exterminated by the Confederates. 1838 J. F. Cooper *Homeward Bound* I. xii. 208 This beef is not indigestible, and here is a real Marylander, in the way of a ham. 1860 O. W. Holmes *Prof. Breakf.-t.* ii. 57, I am a Marylander.
So **Ma·rylandian.**
1750 in *Maryland Hist. Mag.* X. 144 Most of our Marylandians do very well, and they are said to be as good as any, if not the best boys in the house.

Mas. 2. (Later example.)
1882 Morris *Hopes & Fears for Art* (1919) 58 The seat of the village mass-john, or the chest of the yeoman's goodwife.

Mascal, variant of Mescal.
1850 W. R. Ryan *Upper & Lower California* I. 193 The usual beverages, besides water, are wine, *mascal*, and *aguardiente*. 1887 F. Francis Jr. *Saddle & Mocassin* iv. 63 The Mexican..reduced himself to a state of complete intoxication with *mascal*.

Mascot. Add: Also *attrib.*
1898 *Speaker* 31 Dec. 783/2 His mascot snakes that were kept, buried in flannel, in an oblong glass-topped box.

Ma·scotism. [-ism.] = next.
1924 W. J. Locke *Coming of Amos* viii. 94 If there is anything in luck, in mascotism or anti-mascotism, one might have reason to believe that Amos..had the most maleficent of influences.

Mascotry (mæ·skǫtri). [f. Mascot + -ry.] Attachment to or belief in mascots; the use of mascots.
1916 *Ch. Times* 7 Apr. 332/4 Mascotry,..the growing superstition with regard to mascots. 1923 *Sunday at Home* May 504/3 There is a worse aspect of mascotry than mere folly,..for mascotry is, in its essence, simply idolatry.

Masculinism (mæ·skiŭliniz'm). [f. Masculine *a.* + -ism.] Tendency to masculine physical traits in a woman. 1911 Webster.

Masculinist (mæ·skiŭlinist). [f. Masculine *a.* + -ist.] A person of the female sex who adopts or affects masculine characteristics or qualities.
1928 *Daily Express* 11 July 5/3 The suffragists modelled their appearance, their manners, and their education on that of boys and men...They were, in short, thorough-going masculinists.

Masculinization (mæ·skiŭlinəizē·ʃən). [f. next + -ation.] The action of making masculine (sense 6).
1924 *Glasgow Herald* 24 Dec. 4 The masculinisation of woman deprives society of a 'precious asset'. 1927 *19th Cent.* Aug. 266 We find him throwing all his authority against the masculinisation prevalent in our schools.

Masculinize (mæ·skiŭlinəiz), *v.* [f. Masculine *a.* + -ize.] *trans.* To make masculine in form or character.
1912 Moret tr. *A. Moret's Kings & Gods of Egypt* i. 29 She even tried to change the very name she had received at her birth and to masculinise it by omitting the feminine ending. 1927 C. C. Martindale *Relig. World* 19 The first way in which Brahmā could be '*thought*', was, as sufficiently 'masculinised' (Brahmā) to be a god, supreme, yet to that extent specified.
Hence **Ma·sculinized** *ppl. a.*
1927 *Daily Express* 28 Sept. 8/7 The second type of masculinised female is the politically-minded woman.

Masdeu (masdǭ). [See quot. 1833.] A sweet, firm-bodied wine of a dark colour and mellow flavour produced at a vineyard in the South of France.
1851 Redding *Wines* vi. 154 This wine is not a factitious French port from the harbour of Cette...It is a genuine production called Masdeu, from the vineyard which produces it, between Perpignan and Collioure. 1903 *Whitaker's Almanack* 453 Of wines imported in casks the following are the usual measurements: Pipe of Port or Masdeu = 115 gallons, [etc.].

Mash, *sb.*3 2. (Earlier and later examples.)
1883 Nye *Baled Hay* 135 Two Laramie girls on horseback yanking a fly drummer along the street,..because he tried to make a mash on them. *a* 1909 'O. Henry' *Roads of Destiny* iv. 61, I certainly seemed to have a mash on her. 1912 Dorothy Canfield *Squirrel-Cage* III. xxix. 319, I thought it would be fun to tease Paul about the mash you made on old What's-his-name.

Mash, *sb.*5 Eng. and U.S. dial. variant of Marsh *sb.*
1671 *Coll. S. Car. Hist. Soc.* V. 336 About ye rivers mouth & up the river beyond ye mashes. 1840 *Knickerbocker Mag.* XVI. 210, I reckon you won't get nothing for him without you turn him out on the mash. 1843 Carlton *New Purchase* ix. 58 They had been sufficiently fortunate..to learn the nature of 'mash land'. 1876 Walt Whitman *Specimen Days* (1887) 146 The sedgy perfume..reminded me of the 'mash' and south bay of my native island. 1892 P. H. Emerson *Son of Fens* iii. 23, I went back to the sheep. ..I used to drive 'em down to mash along with the cows.

Mash, *v.*4 *U.S.* Var. of Mesh *v.* 3 b.
1849 *Rep. U.S. Comm. Patents* (1850) 155 What I claim as new..is..the shaft H, with the pinions i, mashing into racks II. 1859 Bartlett *Dict. Amer.* (ed. 2) s.v., In machinery, one wheel is said to *mash* into or with another, *i.e.* to 'engage' with it.

Mashie-niblick. *Golf.* An iron club combining the features of the mashie and the niblick.
1909 *Century Dict.* Suppl. 1922 Charlotte Leitch *Golf*, plate 5 (facing p. 64) Mashie niblick, 35 inches, 15½ ounces. 1925 J. M. Barnes *Guide good Golf* iv. 30 The mashie-niblick now enjoys wide popularity among players of all classes.

Mask, *sb.*3 1. b. Add: Also = *Gas-mask.
1915 H. W. Wilson *Great War* IV. 331 A Highlander wearing a mask...An anti-poison gas mask of the more 'fashionable' type. 1918 H. W. Wilson & Hammerton *Great War* XI. 454 French soldiers wearing the masks, fitted with goggles and respirators, that rendered them immune to noxious gases. *Ibid.* 455/2 Special masks were devised for the horses.
4. b. Add to def.: Recently extended to denote the head-skin of any 'big game'.
1894 C. Phillipps-Wolley *Big Game Shooting* (Badm. Libr.) II. xv. 417 Peel off the whole mask from the antlers downwards to the muzzle. 1928 C. S. Stockley *Big Game Shooting* 88 Skins..should..be..hung on a frame to dry, the mask being filled with dry grass or paper.

Mask, *v.*4 Add: 1. c. To provide with a gas-mask.
1916 *War Illustr.* IV. 507 Machine-gun section masked, ready for the enemy. 1918 H. W. Wilson & Hammerton *Great War* XI. 455 French soldier with one of the French army dogs, both masked against enemy gas attack.
2. g. To disguise the real character of or diminish the effect of.
1922 Kendrew *Climates of Continents* 18 The south-east trades..are now at their greatest strength, but sea breezes mask them on the immediate littoral. 1931 *Times* 18 Feb. 6/5 It was this late stroke, masked, into the left corner which defeated the game of Joshua Crane.

Masochist (mæ·zǫkist). [f. as Masochism + -ist.] One who is given to masochism.
1895 tr. *M. Nordau's Degeneration* v. i. 538 Masochists or passivists..clothe themselves in a costume which recalls, by colour and cut, feminine apparel. 1913 Dorland *Med. Dict.* 1915 C. R. Payne tr. *Pfister's Psycho-anal. Method* 78 Very many tormentors of animals are..sadists, consequently also, more or less masochists.

Masochi·stic, *a.* Also **masso-**. [f. prec. + -ic.] Of, pertaining to, or characterized by masochism.
1904 G. S. Hall *Adolescence* II. 112 Women may acquire a Massochistic love of violence and pain for the ideal of pleasure. 1928 *Music & Lett.* July 125 The almost masochistic melancholy of the average fox-trot.

Mason and Dixon. *U.S.* = *Mason and Dixon's line*: see Line *sb.*1 17 b.
1833 C. A. Davis *Lett. J. Downing* (1834) 36 And he tell'd me Georgia would go for me, arter the Gineral, as soon as any north of mason and dickson. 1843 *Knickerbocker Mag.* XXII. 185 The writer, who dwelleth near Mason and Dixon, descants upon the awful climate.

Masonry, *sb.* 3. Add: Also *transf.*
1926 J. Black *You Can't Win* xv. 202 George..took no pains to hide himself, feeling sure that the masonry of the road..would protect him against the common enemy—the law.

Mass, *sb.*2 Add: 4. e. (Earlier example.)
1873 Atkinson tr. *Helmholtz' Lect. Sci. Subj.* Ser. I. 101 Although we are not usually clearly conscious of these beating upper partials, the ear feels their effect as a want of uniformity or a roughness in the mass of tone.
10. *mass-formation*, *-suggestion*; *mass-buying*, *-selling*, *-thinking* vbl. sbs.; **mass-action** (*a*), the action of a mass; (*b*) *Chem.*, esp. in *law of mass action*, the law that the rate at which a chemical substance reacts is a function of its concentration in the medium in which the reaction occurs; **mass production**, the production of articles in large numbers after a standard pattern, chiefly by mechanical means; so *mass-produced* adj.; **mass ray** (see quot.); **mass-spectrograph**, an instrument for comparing the masses of rays or electrically charged particles by means of the deflection produced in them while passing through an electric field; so **mass-spectrum**.
1891 G. McGowan tr. *E. von Meyer's Hist. Chem.* 461 Berthollet..deduced precisely the opposite from his own assumption—that *mass-action comes into play in chemical processes. 1924 W. B. Selbie *Psychol. Relig.* 73 It is not only that mass action has a marked effect upon the will, but that [etc.]. 1929 *Publishers' Weekly* 19 Oct. 1928/1 Our shop, like other small shops, is not geared for mass selling or *mass buying. 1917 Empey *From Fire Step* 242 '*Mass formation*, a close-order formation in which the Germans attack. 1923 *Daily Mail* 22 Jan. 5 All cars made in the United States are not necessarily *mass-produced. 1920 *Teacher's World* 19 May 283/2 Advt., *Mass Production. High Class..Chairs. 1922 G. T. Turner & Wood *Man. Up-to-date Organization* 110 Mass Production is a continuous replica of a standardised master-pattern or design. 1923 J. M. Scott-Maxwell *Costing & Price-fixing* 31 Factories on a mass production basis will have all material most carefully specified, examined, and tested. 1929 *Encycl. Brit.* XVIII. 209/1 Recently they [Positive Rays] have been included in the general term '*Mass Rays' which covers all swiftly moving particles of matter of atomic or molecular size whether charged electrically or not. 1922 F. W. Aston *Isotopes* p. iii, The results obtained by means of the *Mass-spectrograph. 1927 Eddington *Stars & Atoms* 101 It is known from Dr. Aston's researches with the mass-spectrograph that the atoms of other elements have masses which are very closely whole numbers. 1922 F. W. Aston *Isotopes* 55 The actual determination of masses from *mass-spectra is a purely empirical process. 1929 *Encycl. Brit.* XVIII. 301/1 On account of its analogy to optical apparatus the instrument has been called a mass-spectrograph and the spectrum it produces a mass-spectrum. 1924 W. B. Selbie *Psychol. Relig.* 116 We have here to reckon with the influence of *mass suggestion. 1924 *Public Opinion* 30 May 528/3 Our modern saints of co-operative *mass-thinking.

Mass, *sb.*4 Var. of Mas, *Mars(e.
1837 *Southern Lit. Messenger* III. 174 Mass Phil been very uneasy about you.

Massage, *sb.* Add: Also *fig.*
1929 H. Walpole *Hans Frost* II. iii. 143 Then with that by now practised and customary spiritual massage she set to work on herself.

Massage, *v.* Add: Also *transf.*
1924 R. Hichens *After Verdict* III. § 1. 314 Arabs were washing sacks below the dam and massaging them with persistently stamping bare brown feet.

Massecuite (mæskwī·t). [F. = cooked mass.] In sugar-making, the juice of the sugar-cane after concentration by boiling.
1882 *Spons' Encycl. Industr. Arts* 1927 The *masse-cuite* is quickly let out of the pan into a tank. 1886 *Harper's Mag.* June 88/2 After the *masse-cuite* has left the pan, the crystallization is completed by cooling. 1902 *Encycl. Brit.* XXXIII. 48/1 When the massecuite..is in the centrifugals, it is first washed with syrup of low density. 1925 *Chambers's Jrnl.* June 368/2 This dark-looking mass of semi-liquid substance is called masse-cuite.

Massic (mæ·sik). [ad. L. *Massic-us* the name of a mountain in Campania.] An ancient wine produced in Campania. Also *Massic wine*.
1638 Sir T. Hawkins tr. *Horace, Odes* I. i. 19 Some others use Old Massique wines to ply. 1653 tr. *Horace, Odes* I. i. 19 In *Massic* Wines some bouze their time away. 1751 [J. Stirling] tr. *Horace, Ode* I. i. Wks. I. II. 2 Cups of old Massic. 1833 Redding *Wines* 8 The Falernian..grew upon the volcanic Campania near Naples, where also the Massic was produced. 1920 *Punch* 15 Sept. 209, I raise my cup of massic Not to the earlier but the later 'classic'.

Massive, *a.* 3. Add: Also *Zool.* applied to bodies which are compact in structure.
1888 Rolleston & Jackson *Anim. Life* 250 There appear to be two fresh-water Sponges in Great Britain...The former is branched, the latter massive and lobate.
Comb. 1904 *Amer. Jrnl. Sci.* Apr. 263 The lavas extruded in a massive-solid condition.

Massive, *sb.* = Massif.
1900 *Geog. Jrnl.* XVI. 206 Mount Cochrane,..which rises 12,140 feet above sea-level. This powerful massive competes with Mounts San Valentin and San Clemente as to which is the highest of Patagonia.

Massivity (mæsi·viti). [f. Massive + -ity.] The fact or condition of being massive.
1908 W. H. Dawson *Evol. Mod. Germany* 13 Everywhere one sees the worship of massivity, the striving after crude, imposing effects—in the modern monuments, the public buildings, the bridges. 1921 S. Graham *Europe—Whither Bound?* xiv. 186 A mighty stone structure, of great height and massivity.

Mass-John: see Mas 2.

Mass meeting. Orig. *U.S.* (See Mass *sb.*2 10 d.) Also *transf.*
1842 H. Mann *4 July Orat.* (Boston) 64 Mass meetings are held. 1843 *Yale Lit. Mag.* IX. 69 Having been caught at a mass meeting the preceding day, he..said he must go to the West. 1844 *Indiana Mag. Hist.* XXII. 419 A great Whig Mass Meeting and Barbecue. 1851 A. O. Hall *Manhattaner* 4 We steamed..by mass meetings of democratic looking logs and snags. 1867 *Amer. Naturalist* June I. 223 The etymological world holds high carnival, though in this country they are, perhaps, more given to mass-meetings and caucuses. 1878 J. H. Beadle *Western Wilds* xxx. 477 A mass meeting of miners was held June 8, 1859, and a committee appointed to draft a code of laws. 1899 *Pomona* (Cal.) *Progress* 6 Nov., A subscription campaign..was started at a mass meeting of Lordsburg citizens.

Massula (mæ·siŭlă). *Bot.* [L., dim. of *massa*: see Mass *sb.*2] (See quot. 1900.)
1882 Vines tr. *Sachs' Bot.* (ed. 2) 454 In the microsporangia [of *Azolla*] the mucilage looks like a large-celled tissue, and forms from two to eight separate clumps (*Massulæ*), each of which encloses a number of microspores. In some species ..these massulæ have their surfaces covered with hair-like appendages. 1900 B. D. Jackson *Gloss. Bot. Terms*, *Massula*..., (1) the hardened frothy mucilage enclosing a group of microspores in Heterosporous Filicineæ; (2) in Phanerogams, a group of cohering pollen-grains produced by one primary mother-cell, as in Orchideæ.

Massy, Eng. and U.S. dial. var. of Mercy *sb.* 4.
1817 Mrs. A. Royall *Lett. fr. Alabama* (1830) ix. 22 Massy upon me! 1845 Mrs. Kirkland *Western Clearings* 17 Massy no, marm. *Ibid.* 210 O! massy! what a wolf-hunter you be! 1867 Rock *Jim & Nell* cx. (E.D.D.) Law! massy, Jim. 1884 Egerton *Sussex Folk & Ways* 41 'Massy!', she said, 'the girls nowadays don't know naun about work!'

Mast, *sb.*1 3. Add: Recently used in various special senses (see quots.).
1914 R. Stanley *Wireless Telegraphy* xiv. 189 The aerial to be supported by two tubular steel masts each 300 feet high. 1918 Farrow *Dict. Milit. Terms*, *Mast*, in aëronautics, the upright part, usually extending upward from the center of a monoplane for support of controls and guy or truss wires; a vertical upright in the main or supplementary planes. 1921 in E. F. Spanner *About Airships* (1929) 167 An airship working from a mast can be relied upon to leave regularly at scheduled time. 1924 *Harmsworth's Wireless Encycl.* II. 1409 *Mast*. Term used in wireless work to describe generally any structure used to raise and support the aerial wires. 1930 *Observer* 9 Mar. 19/2 R 101 rode at the mast through weather of exceptional severity.

Mast, *sb.*2 4. Add: *mast country*.
1920 *Edin. Rev.* July 120 In the *mast countries, *i.e.*, where the pigs lived mostly in the woods, pigs were good feeders.

Master, *sb.*1 Add: 11. b. Short for *master record*: see *29.
1904 Bottone *Talking Machines* 69 With the master running in the phonograph, the trained ears of the specialists enable them to detect the most minute imperfections. 1908 *Daily Chron.* 29 Oct. 7/1 A special room is devoted to recording, or making the master from which copies are to be taken.
15. b. *The Old Masters* is now the name given to the annual Winter Exhibition of the Royal Academy from the name of the first exhibition (1870) 'Exhibition of the Works of the Old Masters'.
25. b. *master-force*, *-part*.
1919 J. L. Garvin *Econ. Found. Peace* 565 A spiritual and imaginative ideal which has lived..to become as it is now the *master-force in civilised affairs. *Ibid.* 53 He had played the *master-part in stimulating the whole Food Ministry.
29. **master card** (see quot.); **master-locked** *a. pple.*, so locked as to be specially secure; **master record**, in phonographic recording, the wax cylinder or plate on which the sound record is first traced; **master rod**, in a rotary or radial engine, the connecting-rod which embraces the crank pin.
1905 R. F. Foster *Complete Bridge* 316 **Master Card*, the best left in play of any suit which has already been led. 1921 *Glasgow Herald* 19 Dec. 9 When the prison cells..are master-locked they cannot be opened..without a master key. 1904 Bottone *Talking Machines* 68 The different modes that have been adopted to obtain many *replicas* from a good '*master' record. 1929 Allighan *Romance of Talkies* 70 This strip may now..be used as a 'master' record from which prints are taken. 1922 *Encycl. Brit.* XXX. 36/2 Connecting-rods of rotary and radial engines consist usually of one *master rod, ball or roller-bearinged, with the big-end enlarged to form circular lugs to secure wrist pins carrying the plain or auxiliary type of rod of the remaining cylinders.

Mastering, *vbl. sb.* 1. (Add example.)
1911 H. Walpole *Mr. Perrin & Mr. Traill* iv. § 2. 71 There are a good many men in the country who make a pretty good thing out of mastering and aren't so very miserable.

Master-keyed, *ppl. a.* [f. Master-key.] Adapted for operation by a master-key.
19.. H. R. Towne *Locks & Builders' Hardware* 121 (Cent. Suppl.) A series of locks are said to be 'master-keyed' when so constructed that each lock can be operated by its own key, which fits it but no other lock in the series, and also by another key which will operate every lock in the series, this latter being designated as a 'master-key' or 'pass-key'.

Masterless, *a.* Add: 1. c. *transf.* Of unknown authorship or provenance.
1899 A. Lang *Homeric Hymns* 6 The conventional attribution of the Hymns to Homer..is merely the result of the tendency to set down 'masterless' compositions to a well-known name. 1903 R. Proctor in *Library* IV. 397 It has become possible to assign to..Peter von Olpe a small group of books hitherto masterless.

Mast-fed, *a.* [Mast *sb.*2] Fed on mast.
1566 [see Mast *sb.*2 4]. 1843 Carlton *New Purchase* lvi. 246 It was mast fed, i.e. fed on acorns and beech nuts. 1845 in C. Cist *Cincinnati Misc.* 181 It is matter of great surprise to me why the St. Louis merchants do not ship their mast fed, and otherwise inferior lard to the Cincinnati market. 1851 C. Cist *Cincinnati* 284 Much the larger share of this, is..made of mast fed and still-fed hogs.

Masting, *vbl. sb.*1 2. (Earlier example.)
1718 *Jrnls. Ho. Repr. Mass.* II. 109 A Proclamation for ..the Protection of His Majesty's good Subjects in their just Rights..of Logging, masting and Tember.

Masting, *vbl. sb.*2 (Later example.)
1789 Morse *Amer. Geog.* 351 Douglass says that in the year 1733, which was a good masting year..one gentleman salted up 3000 barrels of pork.

Ma·stman. *U.S.* [Mast *sb.*1 1.] (See quot. 1890.)
1839 C. F. Briggs *Harry Franco* I. xxii. 236 All hands call him dismal Jerry, except Mike, the mast man, and he calls him Sergeant Longshanks. 1890 *Century Dict.*, *Mastman*, a seaman stationed at a mast in a man-of-war to keep the ropes clear and in order.

Mastodon. *fig.* (Add quot.)
1851 C. Cist *Cincinnati* 187 There are five other tubs, which in the aggregate, contain as much as the great mastodon just described.

Masurium (mäzūᵊ·riŏm). [f. G. *Masuren* the name of a district in East Prussia + -ium.] An element stated to have been discovered spectroscopically in 1925 in certain platinum ores. Its atomic number is 43.
1925 *Chambers's Jrnl.* Aug. 544/2 From Berlin there comes the news that the same means have been employed to effect the recognition of two other new elements, to which the names *masurium* and *rhenium* have been given, in honour of Germany's eastern and western borderlands. 1926 *Ann. Rep. Progress of Chem.* 1925 XXII. 63 Noddack and Tacke..propose the names '*rhenium*' and '*masurium*'.. for these elements.

Mat, *sb.*1 Add: 1. e. Applied to styles of mat-making, with defining words.
1904 *Technol. & Sci. Dict.* (ed. Goodchild & Tweney) s.v. *Mat*, *Celtic* or *Basket Mat*, a type of weave in which the warp and weft form small squares.
f. Phr. *On the mat*, in army use (see quots.).
1898 *Pearson's Mag.* Oct. 372/2 The sergeant..shouts with military brevity: 'On to the mat, John Smith'. [*ante*, Close to the medical officer's desk is a thick padded carpet about a yard square.] 1919 *War Terms* in *Athenæum* 1 Aug. 695/1 'He's on the mat' means the same [as 'He's for the high jump']; the pre-war orderly room was furnished with a piece of carpet, in the exact centre of which the accused stood. 1925 E. Fraser & Gibbons *Soldier & Sailor Words*, *Mat*, *On the*: up for trial. In trouble.
3. b. A group of persons.
1839 Z. Leonard *Adventures* (1904) 61 Instead of travelling in a close mat as heretofore, we now scattered over a considerable range of country for the purpose of hunting.
8. *mat-house*; **mat-grass** (*c*), an Australian grass used in mat-making (see quot.); **mat-plant**, any low close-growing plant covering the ground like a mat.
1902 Hannan *Textile Fibres* 139 Tussock Grass or *Mat Grass (*Xerotes Longifolia*, Juncaceæ).—The plant is a native of Australia, and belongs to the Rush family. 1898 W. C. Scully *Between Sun & Sand* 18 (Pettman) On either side of it stood respectively, a *mat-house and a square tent. 19.. C. MacMillan *Minnesota Plant Life* ii. (Cent. Suppl.) The *mat-plant, such as a purslane or carpet-weed, adapted to life on a flat plane.

Mat, *sb.*5 Abbrev. of Matinée.
1914 Gertr. Atherton *Perch of Devil* I. viii. 55 Although Mr. Compton won't take me to any balls, there are the movin' pictures and the mats—matinées.

Match, *sb.*1 12. Add: **match-ball**, in lawn tennis, a ball that may decide a match; **match-list**, a list of the competitors in a match; **match-play, player** (add examples of lawn tennis usages); so *match-playing* vbl. sb.; **match-point**, the state of a game when one side or player needs only one more point to win the match; also, the point itself; **match race**, a race run as a competition.
1927 *Daily Express* 5 July 2/1 They..retrieved two successive *match balls in the third set. 1909 *Westm. Gaz.* 12 July 12/3 Heavy courts, black balls, and disorganised *match-lists combined to make last week's tournaments anything but pleasant. 1922 Tilden *Lawn Tennis for Match Players* 31 The keynote of *match play is to destroy your opponent's confidence and break up his game. 1909 E. H. Miles *Lessons Lawn Tennis* (ed. 3) 50 The ideal *match player. *Ibid.*, Hints on *Match-playing. 1921 A. W. Myers *Twenty Yrs. Lawn Tennis* 48 In the end he won the match, Dixon, after lazily reaching *match point some eight or nine times,..retiring at two sets all. 1874 B. F. Taylor *World on Wheels* I. xiv. 105 It [the train] ran a *match race with a train on the Michigan Central.

Match, *sb.*2 5. Add: **match-box** (additional example); **match-pot**, a small vessel for holding matches; **match-stand**, a stand for holding matches.
1905 *Pearson's Mag.* July 103/2 Few fingers are too old and few too tiny to help the *match-box maker. 1856 J. C. Robinson *Invent. Objects Mus. Ornamental Art* 37 Wedgwood *Match-pot...Pair of Match-pots. 1908 E. F. Benson *Blotting Bk.* i, The cigarette boxes and *match-stands were always kept replenished.

Match, *a.* 1. Add: **matchmark**, 'a mark placed on the contiguous separable parts of any device' to facilitate reassembling (Webster 1918); **match-wagon**, on railways, a low auxiliary wagon attached to another which is carrying a projecting load, to prevent mishaps from the freight in the latter projecting beyond the buffers.
1891 *Gt. Western Railway, Rules & Regulations*, The Station Master..must before a crane is attached to a goods train take care that..the necessary match-wagons are provided.

Match, *v.*1 9. b. Add: Also *absol.*
1905 H. G. Wells *Kipps* I. ii. 42 Then came a blessed interval when Kipps was sent abroad 'matching'. This consisted chiefly in supplying unexpected defects in buttons, ribbon, lining and so forth in the dressmaking department.

Matched, *ppl. a.* Add: 3. Applied to orders in the Stock Exchange which provide for buying and selling equal quantities of the same stock, or the like, so as to effect a fictitious sale.
1903 S. S. Pratt *Work of Wall St.* 146 The syndicate may be washing sales through matched orders through curb brokers in order to market watered stock. 1908 [see wash-sale, Wash *sb.* 21]. 1908 *Westm. Gaz.* 26 Aug. 2/2 The governors of the Stock Exchange there [in Wall Street] have appointed a committee to inquire into what is known as 'matched orders'.

Mate, *sb.*2 Add: 1. e. (See quot. and cf. 4 b.)
1904 *Technol. & Sci. Dict.* (ed. Goodchild & Tweney) 384 *Mate*, an assistant or subordinate who assists a more skilled workman.
3. d. *spec.* A point on tramway lines which is cast solid and pairs or 'mates' with the movable tongue or switch on the other rail; an 'open' or 'fixed' point. *Orig. U.S.*
1922 *Glasgow Herald* 3 Oct. 8 The weight of the inserts varies from about 100 to 300 lb., depending on the angle of the crossing or mate.

Mate, *v.*2 1. Delete ?*Obs.* and add later examples.
1874 Swinburne *Bothw.* I. i. 4, I might sleep well and laugh and walk at ease, With none to mate me. 1896 Morris *Poems by Way* (1898) 148 *Fig-tree.* I who am little among trees In honey-making mate the bees.

Mater. 1. (Modern example.)
1905 *Sci. Amer.* 12 Aug. 120/2 The Astrolabe of Regiomontanus...*Mater* is the name given to the large disk divided into degrees.

Mater 2 (mē·təɹ). [f. Mate *v.*2 + -er 1.] One who or something which mates.
1915 E. R. Lankester *Diversions of Naturalist* 183 In the case of simple conjugation the cell individuals which fuse or 'mate' with one another, and may be called 'maters' or 'mating cells'.

Maternity. 3. Add: **maternity-benefit**: see *Benefit 4 d.

Maternize (mătɜ̄·ɹnəiz), *v.* [f. Matern(al *a.* + -ize.] *trans.* To be as a mother to, to 'mother'.
1890 'R. Boldrewood' *Miner's Right* xviii. 177 A very decent kindly widow, who allowed her the free use of her own private parlour, and in every way maternised her.

Matey (mē·ti), *a.* [f. Mate *sb.*2 + -y 1.] Like a mate or mates; friendly and familiar (*with*); sociable, companionable. Hence **Ma·teyness** = *Matiness.
1915 T. Burke *Nights in Town* 50 You are all so—what is the word?—matey, isn't it? Yes, that's the note of the London [music] hall—mateyness. 1920 P. G. Wodehouse *Damsel in Distress* xv. 172 After the game he took me off to his cottage and gave me a drink,..We got extremely matey. 1926 *Contemp. Rev.* June 682 The *British Worker*, an equally deplorable organ produced by *intelligentsia* trying to be 'matey'. 1929 W. Deeping *Roper's Row* xxi. § ii, Elizabeth would..want to be matey with people.

Math 1. (Later poet. example.)
1917 Mother St. Jerome *Garden of Life* 18 You feel as you lie in the math The watching unseen of His eyes.

Maths, colloq. abbreviation of Mathematics.
1927 W. E. Collinson *Contemp. Eng.* 28.

Matinée. Add: 2. *attrib.* and *Comb.*, as **matinée coat, jacket**, a baby's short outer garment; **matinée idol**, a handsome actor of a type supposed to be especially attractive to matinée audiences.
1929 *Treasure Cot Catal.* Nov. 31 Very pretty *Matinee Coat in good quality Crepe-de-chine.

Ma·tiness. [f. *Matey *a.*] Friendly quality or character.
1928 *Even. News* 28 Dec. 8/3 There is the same expansive geniality, the same note of unassumed 'matiness'.

Mating, *vbl. sb.*1 (Modern attrib. example.)
1908 *Westm. Gaz.* 12 Aug. 7/3 Mackenzie ran into a mating net with Gunsberg in a lively game.

Matless (mæ·tlės), *a.* [Mat *sb.* + -less.] Not furnished with a mat or mats.
1880 J. Ross *Hist. Corea* x. 318 The dead body..is not, like the Chinese, put on a matless floor.

Matlo(w (mæ·tlo). *slang.* [Phonetic ad. F. *matelot* sailor.] A sailor.
1904 Kipling *Traffics & Discov.* 58 Simultaneous it hits the Pusser that 'e'd better serve out mess pork for the poor matlow. 1908 *Westm. Gaz.* 31 July 2/1 Evolutions and exercises to keep the modern 'matlow' busy and happy. 1914 F. T. Jane *Navy as Fighting Machine* 112 *Matlo*, name used to describe themselves by British bluejackets. Falling into disuse.

Matri- (mæ·tri, mē·tri), used as the combining form of L. *māter* (*mātr-is*) mother, in various words recently used in connexion with the prominence of women and the importance of female relationship in certain primitive societies. Some examples are given below as main words. Cf. also Matriarch, Matriarchal, etc. in Dict.

Matrical, *a.* 2. Add to def.: and other organic formations.
1903 *Jrnl. R. Microsc. Soc.* Apr. 163 The nutrition of the cartilage is probably effected by impenetration of fluids along the fine bundles of fibres which in this way come to stand out clearly amid the matrical substance.

Matriculability (mătri:kiŭlăbi·liti). [f. Matricul(ate) *v.* + -able + -ity.] Ability or fitness to matriculate.
1927 *Camb. Univ. Reporter* 11 Oct. 142 The name of every candidate for matriculation on November 1 or 2, together with evidence of matriculability..must be sent to the Registry.

Matrilineal (mætrili·nĭăl), *a.* [f. *Matri- + Lineal *a.* 2.] Of, pertaining to, or based on (kinship with) the mother or the female line: recognizing kinship with and descent through females only.
1904 N. W. Thomas in *Man* No. 53. 84 Mr. Hill-Tout argues that totemism originates in a patrilineal just as much as in a matrilineal state of society. 1906 — *Kinship Organisations* 30 Membership of a phratry depends on birth and is taken *directly* from the mother (matrilineal descent) or father (patrilineal descent). 1909 E. S. Hartland *Prim. Paternity* I. 281 The alien position occupied among matrilineal peoples by the father in regard to his children. 1921 *Edin. Rev.* July 163 His discovery of matrilineal institutions in Europe.
Hence **Matrili·neally** *adv.*
1907 *Athenæum* 20 Apr. 477/1 The method of reckoning descent matrilineally.

Matrilinear (mætrili·niăɹ), *a.* [f. *Matri- + Linear *a.*] = *Matrilineal *a.*
1910 *Manch. Guard.* 8 Aug. 5 It is said that they [*i.e.* the Choctaw Indians] were governed by chiefs who succeeded by matrilinear descent. 1913 B. S. Phillpotts *Kindred & Clan* etc. 275 Kindreds organized on matrilinear or on patrilinear lines. 1924 L. A. Waddell *Phœnician Orig. Britons* 122 The Mother Right, or Matri-linear form of succession through the mother, and not through the father.

Matriliny (mæ·trilini). [f. as prec. + -y 3.] The observance of matrilineal descent and kinship.
1906 N. W. Thomas *Kinship Organisations* 12 We may now examine the relation of matriliny to the seat of authority in the family.

Matrilocal (mætrilō·kăl), *a.* [f. *Matri- + Local *a.*] Applied to a system of marriage among certain primitive peoples (see quot. 1906).
1906 N. W. Thomas *Kinship Organisations* 16 In a pure matrilineal community, the husband removes to the wife's local group (matrilocal marriage). 1927 *Contemp. Rev.* July 84 The clan is held together by matrilocal marriage.

Matrix. Add: 6. b. (See quot.)
1919 A. N. Whitehead *Princ. Nat. Knowledge* 133 A 'matrix' is a two-dimensional plane in the four-dimensional geometry of event-particles.
7. b. Applied to precious stones (see quot. 1909).
1909 *Century Dict.* Suppl., *Matrix gem*, an opal, turquoise, ruby, or other gem intimately mixed with the matrix material and cut with it. 1921 *Brit. Mus. Return* 157 A suite of specimens of sapphire..comprising two matrix specimens.

Matt, *a.* Now the usual spelling, esp. in *Photogr.*, of Mat *a.*
1876 *Encycl. Brit.* V. 170/1 Water gilding..is finished either 'matt' or burnished...Matt-work is protected with one or two coats of finish-size. 1892 *Photogr. Ann.* II. 76 The metal separates in a matt grey form. 1928 *Chambers's*

Jrnl. Feb. 102/2 Her hair was not red, but very light and very fine, and with a matt lustre on it.
Comb. 1925 *Morris Owner's Manual* 79 The operation is finished when the valve face has a clean, even, matt-surfaced ring around it.

Matter, *v.* 2. Add example with personal subject.
1909 H. W. C. Newte *Sparrows* xl. 505 With your appearance and talents you should be a great social success with the people who matter.

Matthew Walker. *Naut.* [The name of the originator.] In full *Matthew Walker knot*, a knot 'formed by a half hitch on each strand in the direction of the lay, so that the rope can be continued after the knot is formed' (Smyth *Sailor's Word-bk.* 1867).
[1808 D. Lever *Yng. Sea Officer's Sheet Anchor* 5 Matthew Walker's knot.] 1841 R. H. Dana *Seaman's Man.* vii. 37 A Matthew Walker knot,..Unlay the end of a rope [etc.]. 1860 *All Yr. Round* No. 66. 382 'Which knot?' asked Toby. ..'Matthew Walker, spritsail-sheet, stopper, or shroud?' 1883 *Man. Seamanship Boys* 105 A Matthew Walker knot is used for the standing part of the lanyards of lower rigging.

Mattress 1. Add: 3. b. *U.S.* A bed of sugar-cane. Hence **Ma·ttress** *v. trans.*, to form (sugar-cane) into 'mattresses'.
1833 B. Silliman *Man. Sugar Cane* 12 They are cut near the ground, and carted to the vicinity of the fields where they are to be planted; being formed..into long beds about fifteen feet wide, which are called *mattresses*. 1849 *Rep. U.S. Comm. Patents Agric.* (1850) 423 It was..supposed that the cane was spoiled in the mattress by the continued warm weather after it was mattressed.

Maul, *v.* 1. b. (Earlier example.)
1677 in *Virginia Mag.* (1894) II. 168 (Th.) They were.. commanded to go to work, fall trees, and mawl and toat railes.

Mauler. (Recent example.)
1922 *Daily Mail* 17 Nov. 8 A 'mauler' is a woman who ill uses everything she is shown.
2. *spec.* A rail-splitter. *U.S.*
1788 Washington *Diaries* III. 306 The cutters and maulers had shifted to the East side of the Plantation in order to get Rails.

Maum, variant of Mam 1.
1881 *Harper's Mag.* Apr. 728/2 Maum Dulcie, is my habit ready?

Mauma, Maumer, Maumie, variant forms of *mamma* = Mammy 2.
1835 W. G. Simms *Partisan* 141 You have told me nothing of old mauma. 1838 Caroline Gilman *Recoll. Southern Matron* xv. 101 Who does not remember his youthful Christmas; the reiterated charge to his *maumer* to awaken him first? 1881 *Harper's Mag.* Apr. 737/2 Maumie, how I should like to see a Hoodoo meeting! 1890 *Ibid.* July 232/1 Respectable colored 'maumas', ample of girth, in spotted white aprons. 1895 *Century Mag.* May 155/2 Only a few, a very few, of the faithful old 'maumers' and loyal house- and body-servants remain.

Maund, *sb.*2 1. (Add later example.)
1909 *Chambers's Jrnl.* Oct. 665/2 The import of dyeing materials into Kashmir in one year was: Indigo, fourteen maunds, or one thousand one hundred and twenty pounds.

Mau·ndful. [f. Maund *sb.*1] As much as a maund will hold.
1828 [Carr] *Craven Gloss.* I. 314 *Maund-ful*, a basket full. 1924 *Chambers's Jrnl.* Oct. 673/1 Two maunfuls at a time, the pilchards are tipped out of the baskets in which they are carried from the boats.

Mauritian (mǫri·ʃăn), *a.* and *sb.* [f. Mauritius + -(i)an.] a. *adj.* Of or pertaining to the island of Mauritius. b. *sb.* A native or inhabitant of Mauritius.
1865 *Chambers's Jrnl.* Sept. 546/2 To Mauritians..this droll little Mauritian journal..may very probably appear a most influential exponent of public opinion. 1906 B. Burleigh *Two Campaigns* 60 Fiery Mauritian rum. *Ibid.* 111 The place was under a Mauritian named Hemming. 1926 *Chambers's Jrnl.* Apr. 212/1 The Mauritian Creole is a crafty fellow.

Maverick, *sb.* [Etym. note: read 'Samuel A. Maverick, a civil engineer, who accidentally owned unbranded cattle in Texas from 1845 to 1856.']
1. (Earlier example.)
1869 *Overland Monthly* III. 127 Many of his animals..were taken up by his neighbors, branded and called 'mavericks'.

Maverick, *v.* Add: b. *intr.* To stray like a maverick.
1920 W. M. Raine *B. O'Connor* 203 It hadn't penetrated my think-tank that this was your hacienda when I came mavericking in.

Maw-wormy, *a.* [f. Mawworm 2.] = Mawwormish.
1885 *Entr'acte* 6 June (Ware *Passing Engl.*) Without being mawwormy, I fail to see why a wreath should be presented to any man who makes a business of giving opera.

Maximalism (mæ·ksimăliz'm). [f. Maximal *a.* + -ism, or formed after next.] The policy or revolutionary doctrines of Bolsheviks.
1920 *Glasgow Herald* 11 May 10 Bologna is undoubtedly to-day one of the chief Italian strongholds of Maximalism.

Maximalist (mæ·ksimălist). [f. Maximal *a.* + -ist, or ad. F. *maximaliste*, a translation of Russ. *bol'shévik*: see *Bolshevik.] An alternative name for a Bolshevik; one of the party of Russian socialists which favoured a maximum socialist programme at the Congress held in 1903.
1909 *Westm. Gaz.* 23 Dec. 7/4 He is said to have joined the 'Maximalists' in 1907. 1917 *Times* 4 June 8/4 The 'Maximalists' supported Bleichman. 1917 *19th Cent.* Nov. 1022 Excessive attention has been paid to the leader of the 'Bolsheviki' or Maximalists among the Russian Social Democratic Labour Party, Lenin.

Ma·ximed, *a.* [f. Maxim *sb.*1] Expressed as or in a maxim.
1883 J. C. Van Dyke *Bks. & how to use them* 19 (Cent.) There is another maximed truth in this connection: 'Knowledge is a two-edged sword.'

Maximize, *v.* Add: Hence **Ma·ximized**, **Ma·ximizing** *ppl. adjs.*
1920 A. S. Pringle-Pattison *Idea of God* 356 Eternal, not in the sense of a maximized consciousness of time, but as an apprehension different in type. 1927 N. P. Williams *Ideas of Fall* 395 The maximising and minimising versions of the Fall-Doctrine.

Maxixe (maʃi·ʃə, mæksi·ks). [Pg.] A round dance resembling the two-step but showing more variety of movements.
1918 Webster *Add.* 1925 *Chambers's Jrnl.* July 427/1 They sang..and danced the *maxixe* until cockcrow!

May, *sb.*3 5. c. Add: **May-blossom** *U.S.* = Mayflower 3 b; **May-haw** (example); **May-pop** (earlier example).
1871 *Scribner's Monthly* II. 102 Tenderest of all in yonder woods, where hepatica, and *May blossoms, and Quaker ladies twinkle into life. 1868 *Amer. Naturalist* Oct. II. 468 They [deer] visit the ponds in which the *May-haw grows, the fruit of which is juicy with the flavor of the apple. 1852 *Florida Plant. Rec.* 69 The Voss Place had some grass and *May Pops in the Cotton.

Maya 2 (mā·yă), *sb.* and *a.* Also 9 **Maye.** An (Indian of an) ancient stock or race belonging to Yucatan and Central America; the language of these; also *attrib.* or *adj.* = **Mayan** *a.*
1831 J. Bell *Syst. Geog.* V. 575 The other languages, indicating as many different tribes, are..Maye or Yucatan. 1844 *Ch. of Eng. Mag.* 11 May XVI. 308/2 The Maya name for one of the old possessors. 1845 *Trans. Amer. Ethnol. Soc.* I. 252 *K* has in the Maya a different sound from our *c* before *a*, *o*, *u*. 1875 H. H. Bancroft *Native Races Pacific St.* II. 117 This Maya culture. *Ibid.* 118 Yucatan was occupied in the sixteenth century by the Mayas proper. 1914 T. A. Joyce *Mex. Archæol.* 282 Of the land system among the Maya we know very little. 1921 *19th Cent.* Apr. 606 The monuments of the Mayas..bear witness to an ancient civilisation. 1926 *Blackw. Mag.* Nov. 647/2 This man.. was of pure Maya blood, and was filled..with old Mayan lore and tradition. 1889 Susan Hale *Mexico* viii. (1891) 82 The Mayan legends..tell of nothing but wars and conquests, struggles and defeats.

May-butter. (Later U.S. example.)
c 1805 J. J. Henry *Camp agst. Quebec* (1812) 23 We gave salted pork, and they returned two fresh beaver tails, which when boiled, renewed ideas, imbibed with the May-butter of our own country.

May-duke. (Later U.S. examples.)
1841 *Knickerbocker Mag.* XVII. 154 The air is impregnated with the fragrances..of the blossoming may-dukes. 1874 *Rep. Vermont Board Agric.* II. 359 This variety, and the..May Duke, Late Duke, and other Dukes,..are hardly less hardy than plums.

Mayologist (mäyǫ·lŏdʒist). [f. *Maya 2 + -ologist (see -ology).] A student of Maya antiquities.
1926 *Glasgow Herald* 18 May 9 Mr. Joyce, perhaps the eldest of living Mayologists, has been sent..on a mission of inspection.

Mazuma (măzū·mă). *U.S. slang.* [Yiddish.] Money, cash.
1907 Mulford *Bar-20* viii. 90 When th' mazuma is divided up it won't buy a meal. 1913 — *Coming of Cassidy* xii. 191 'What's this?' he demanded...'Money,' replied Hopalong. 'It's that shiny stuff you buy things with. Spondulix, cash, mazuma.'

Mazut (măzū·t). Also **masut, mazout.** [Russ. f. мазать *mázat'*, to grease.] The residue of Russian petroleum, after the more volatile portions have been lost by evaporation or distilled off, used as lubricating oil and for fuel.
1897 *Chambers's Jrnl.* 19 June 393 Masut, the new substitute for coal. 1907 *Times Engineering Suppl.* 16 Oct. 4/2 Among liquid fuels which may be employed that known as 'masut' will help to supply the increasing demand. 1923 *Countries World* II. 1277/1 'Crude oil'..is refined into benzine, petrol and kerosene, the refuse or 'mazout' being consumed for common fuel and furnaces.
attrib. and *Comb.* 1924 *Blackw. Mag.* Feb. 152/1 They caught the sickly sweet smell of half-burnt 'Mazut' fuel. *Ibid.* 154/2 The steam blast of the Mazut burners in the little craft's furnaces.

Mazzinian (matsī·niăn), *a.* and *sb.* [f. the name of Guiseppe *Mazzini* (1805–72), the Italian patriot + -an.] a. *adj.* Of, pertaining to or supporting Mazzini or his policy. b. *sb.* An adherent of Mazzini. So **Mazzi·nianism. Mazzi·nist** = Mazzinian b.
1853 *Jew of Verona* (1861) Pref. iv, Misrepresentation which had been so assiduously thrown around the recent events by the Mazzinian press. 1875 The O'Clery *Hist. Ital. Revol.* v. 165 The Mazzinian programme was the establishment of a single republic...The literary propaganda of Mazzinianism. *Ibid.* 187 They were no less revolutionists than the Mazzinians. 1928 *Observer* 1 July 7/4 Garibaldian, Mazzinian, and democratic writers. 1860 *Illustr. London News* 7 Jan. 18/3 Even the Mazzinists claim him at times as their own.

Me, *pers. pron.* 5. Add: Freq. in U.S. colloquial usage.
1874 *Rep. Vermont Board Agric.* II. 512 In 1861 I built me a horse barn, twenty-eight by forty. 1916 B. M. Bower *Phantom Herd* iii. 42 I'm going to make me one.

Meach, variant of *Mech *v.*

Meaching, variant of *Meeching *ppl. a.*

Meadow, *sb.* 4. b. Add: **meadow blue**, a small blue butterfly; **meadow-hen** (earlier example); **meadow-lark** (earlier U.S. example).
1925 J. Gregory *Bab of Backwoods* xiii. 163 Where big butterflies and the tiny *meadow-blues fanned him with wings which [etc.]. 1863 'Gail Hamilton' *Gala-Days* 97 You know you didn't scare a little *meadow-hen. 1775 B. Romans *Florida* 114 (Th.) *Meadow larks, fieldfares, rice birds, &c. are very frequently had.
c. **meadow-bouts** *U.S.*, the marsh-marigold; **meadow lily**, a variety of lily common in the eastern United States (Cent. Suppl.); **meadow pea** (example).
1784 Cutler in *Mem. Amer. Acad. Arts & Sci.* (1785) I. 459 *Meadow-bouts. 1896 Henslow *Wild Flowers* 98 Lathyrus pratensis, **Meadow Pea*. This genus resembles vetches, but has fewer leaflets.

Meady 1 (mī·di), *a. poet.* [f. Mead 1 + -y 1.] Resembling or suggestive of mead.
1887 Meredith *Ballads & Poems Tragic Life* 102 Yellow flamed the meady sunset.

Meal, *sb.*1 3. Add: *meal-bag*, *chest*, *-tub*.
1644 *Essex Probate Rec.* I. 46 Too *meal baggs. 1652 in *Mayflower Desc.* x. 40 It[em] in meale baggs 00-04-00. 1738 *N. H. Probate Rec.* II. 622 He knows of no meal Bag that his son had but what he borrowed of him. 1845 J. J. Hooper *Taking Census* ii. 167 Throw a meal-bag, or somethin' else over your head. 1866 Mrs. Whitney *L. Goldthwaite* vi, I don't know whether it was your little freedmen's meal-bags. 1738 *N. H. Probate Rec.* II. 622 The *meal chest he says he knows nothing to the contrary but what it is left where it was when his son died. 1642 *Maryland Archives* IV. 100, 1. wherry 1. *meale tubb. 1680 Dangerfield *Answ. Malice defeated* 8 The strict charge she gave the Maid for the securing the Papers, *alias* Meal-Tub Plot. 1731 Tindal tr. *Rapin's Hist. Eng.* XIV. 240 Sir William Waller..searching Cellier's House, found the Model of the pretended Plot..hid in a Meal-Tub, which gave it the Name of the Meal-Tub Plot. 1847 in Drake *Pion. Life Kentucky* iii. 56 The 'meal-tub plot' excited that [the imagination] of our English forefathers.
b. **meal-dried** *a.* (see quot.).
1896 Schlich *Man. Forestry* V. 500 Bark is said to be air-dried when, on bending, it breaks easily; meal-dried, when it has lost all flexibility and become brittle.

Meal, *sb.*2 4. Add: **meal-ticket**, a ticket entitling a person to a meal.
1871 *Trans. Ill. Agric. Soc.* VIII. 4 All the balance of clerks and assistants..shall be allowed the sum of $3 per day, and *meal tickets.

Meal, *v.*2 1. Add: esp. *U.S.* To take one's meals *at* (a place).
1891 H. C. Bunner *Zadoc Pine* etc. 201 A lodging-house for those who 'mealed' at the hotel. 1918 *Jrnl. Friends' Hist. Soc.* 7 John Lecky..generally arranged to meal at Friends' houses.

Mealie. Add *attrib.* examples; also *Comb.* as **mealie-cob worm**, the caterpillar of *Heliothis armigera* which attacks mealies.
1859 R. J. Mann *Natal* 137 (Pettman) The young mealy-cob is generally preferred to bread. 1911 J. D. F. Gilchrist *S. Afr. Zool.* 150 (Pettman) The Mealie-cob worm..does extensive damage to mealies, peas, tomatoes, and lucerne. 1902 J. H. M. Abbott *Tommy Cornstalk* 28 A few Kaffir transport drivers..are boiling their 'mealie-pap' in three-legged pots.

Mealy, *a.* 4. b. **mealy-bug**, (add) a scale-insect (later example).
1927 *Chambers's Jrnl.* Aug. 502/1 The *mealybug, so called from its white waxy or mealy coating, belongs to the big family of scale insects known as the Coccidae.

Mean, *a.*1 Add: 2. f. *U.S. colloq.* In low spirits or health; poorly, not quite well.
a 1848 Dow Jr. *Patent Serm.* I. 7 (Th.) As mean as a rooster in a thunder shower. 1911 H. S. Harrison *Queed* vii. 90 Mebbe you could do better writing and harder writing if only you didn't feel so mean. 1911 J. F. Wilson *Land Claimers* i. 21 'Feel pretty mean', the packer asked him kindly.
3. a. Of domestic animals or things in general: Poor in quality or condition; comparatively worthless.
1817 in *Trans. Ill. State Hist. Soc.* 1910, 148 Hogs in this Country are the meanest that I have ever seen...I do not believe you ever see half so mean hogs as we have here. 1823 W. Faux *Memor. Days* 219 The horses here are nearly all mean, wild, deformed, half-grown, dwarfish things. 1842 Mrs. Kirkland *Forest Life* I. 140 You've had a pretty mean time, I reckon. *a* 1890 *Philad. Post* (Barrère & Leland) The night was dark and stormy, about as mean a night as was ever experienced in Washington.
5. b. (Later examples.)
(*a*) *a* 1848 Dow Jr. *Patent Serm.* I. 147 (Th.) [One girl] thought me real mean for uttering such sentiments. 1891 Rose T. Cooke *Huckleberries* 14 It would be awful mean of me to leave you here alone.
(*b*) 1861 R. H. Newell *Orpheus C. Kerr Papers* (1866) 35, I see he felt powerful mean, so I walked up to him. He jest hooked to my elbow, and without sayin' another word, we marveled for hum.
B. *adv.*1 (Later U.S. example.)
1861 O. W. Norton *Army Letters* 26 Virginia has acted meaner than South Carolina even.

Mean, *v.*1 Add: 3. b. Of a person: To be of some account or importance, to 'matter' *to* (someone); to be a source of benefit, or an object of regard, affection or love *to* (someone).

1888 Mrs. H. Ward *R. Elsmere* II. III. xxvi. 279 It was only by a great effort that he could turn his thoughts from the Squire, and all that the squire had meant to him during the past year. 1912 *Red Mag.* 1 Mar. 515/1 It came over me how much she meant to me and how hard a wrench it was going to be to live along without her. 1914 *Times Lit. Suppl.* 8 Jan. 12/1 Comprehension of what Lady Gregory has meant to him and to others who worked with her.

Mean (mīn), *v.*⁴ [f. Mean *sb.*² 8.] *trans.* To calculate the mathematical mean of; also with *up*.

1882 W. J. L. Wharton *Hydrographical Surveying* 210 We need not mean up each column of times. *Ibid.* 213 When working several sets, calculate them simultaneously as far as this, and mean the results. *a* 1888 Shortland *Naut. Surveying* (1890) 64 The permanent errors will destroy each other in the results of all..observations so meaned.

Meander, *v.* Add: **4.** To pass or travel deviously along or through (a river, etc.).

1831 J. O. Pattie *Personal Narr.* 13 We crossed the Missouri..and meandered the river as far as Pilcher's fort. 1839 Z. Leonard *Adventures* (1904) 69 We separated, each party to meander the rivers that had been respectively allotted to them. 1839 in *Trans. Mich. Agric. Soc.* VII. (1856) 360 Branches of Swan creek meander this tract in such manner as to facilitate drainage.

Meandroid (miæ·ndroid), *a.* [f. Meander *sb.* + -oid.] Of a winding structure; said of corals: cf. Meandrine.

1902 *Encycl. Brit.* XXV. 462/1 An epitheca surrounds the base of massive or mæandroid forms.

Mea·ningfulness. [f. Meaningful *a.*] The quality of being meaningful.

1919 R. H. Fisher *Outside of Inside* 105 In mystical trance he discerned the meaningfulness of the third heaven. 1922 J. Y. Simpson *Man & Attainm. Immortality* xiv. 320 The exquisite sensitivity of their minds to the meaningfulness of its language.

Meaningless, *a.* (Add example.)

1890 W. James *Psychology* I. xvi. 676 He learned lists of meaningless syllables by heart.

Measle, *sb.* **1.** (Modern example of *sing.*)

1924 Galsworthy *White Monkey* I. iii, Fleur knew how catching the word was; it would run like a measle round the ring.

Measle, *v.* Add: **4.** *fig.* To be full of or teem *with* (objectional things).

1856 C. Reade *Never too late* II. xxv. 245 All this..in thieves' cant, with an oath or a nasty expression at every third word. The sentences measled with them.

Measly, *a.* **4.** (Earlier example.)

1864 Miss Braddon *H. Dunbar* II. xi. 212 The audacity to offer a measly hundred pounds or so for the discovery of a great crime!

Measure, *v.* **2. c.** Add: Also *transf.* esp. in various U.S. slang expressions.

1859 B. Jerrold *Douglas Jerrold* vi. 94 The pig was to be measured for his part. *a* 1890 *N. Y. Mercury* (Barrère & Leland) He had been measured for a funeral sermon three times, he said, and had never used either one of them. 1896 Farmer & Henley *Slang, To have been measured for a new umbrella* (American)—(1) To appear in new but ill-fitting clothes, whence (2) To pursue a policy of doubtful wisdom.

4. b. Add to def.: Also, to be comparable *with*.

1904 Sir G. Parker *Ladder of Swords* vi. 61 Her words for the great cause had measured well with her deeds. 1907 *Smart Set* Mar. 126/2 The dog moved a cat-like step forward, making up the interval, and the man made a mental note that its single stride measured with his.

Measurely, *adv.* (Modern U.S. example.)

1878 J. H. Beadle *Western Wilds* xiv. 222 It is measurely free from winter storms.

Measurer. 1. (Examples of special use.)

1636 *Dedham Rec.* I. 36 We doe order that all high-wayes ..be orderly set out by our measurer. 1641 *New Haven Col. Rec.* I. 51 Bro. Pecke chosen measurer for the towne to fill and strike all the corne. 1706 *Boston Town Rec.* VIII. 37 Allexander Seers, Samuell Bridge,..to serve as Measurers of board, Timber, and Plank. 1827 Drake & Mansf. *Cincinnati* vi. 51 The council have power to appoint..Measurers of wood and coal. 1841 *Advt.* in C. Cist *Cincinnati*, George Warren, Measurer of Stone-work, Birch-work, and Plastering.

Measuring, *vbl. sb.* **4.** Add: *measuring roller.*

1894 T. W. Fox *Mech. Weaving* 377 After warp leaves the beam it passes..under and nearly round a measuring roller.

Meat, *sb.* **3.** Add: Also *local U.S.*, pork.

1845 Mrs. Kirkland *Western Clearings* 93 Venison is not 'meat' to be sure, in our parlance; for we reserve that term for pork, *par excellence*. *c* 1845 Paulding *Madmen All* 196 The term meat in the West is understood to apply solely to salt pork. 1891 *Fur, Fin & Feather* 182 A bearskin is worth $5 to him..besides, he likes the flesh if meat (i.e. pork) is 'skeerse'.

d. *transf.* (Add quots.)

1904 W. H. Smith *Promoters* ii. 40 Thousands of miles of new telegraph lines necessary, and they'll be our meat, every mile of 'em. 1907 S. E. White *Arizona Nights* I. vii. 136 'Whew!' I whistles, 'That's a large order—But I'm your meat.

e. *slang phr.* (Contrasted with Milk 2 a.)

1920 P. G. Wodehouse *Damsel in Distress* iv. 58 I know what's the matter with *you*', he said. 'Someone's been feeding you meat!' The young man bubbled with fury.

5. a. *meat can, -platter, -tin, -trough, -tub* (earlier example), *-vat*; **b.** *meat-eater, -eating* (example), *-freezer, -freezing, -packer, -packing, -rationing.*

1897 *Outing* XXX. 284/1 For active service..the two regiments would need to be supplied with..*meat cans. 1905 *Vegetarian Yr. Bk.* 15, I am now a rabid vegetarian with a score of nasty remarks about *meat-eaters. 1853 *Trans. Mich. Agric. Soc.* IV. 154 The Americans are notoriously a *meat eating people. 1909 *Daily Chron.* 2 Nov. 5/4 Australian globe-trotters, *meat-freezers, financiers. 1908 *Westm. Gaz.* 14 Dec. 2/1 The *meat-freezing works employ over 3,000 men. 1909 *Chambers's Jrnl.* Jan. 23/1 Argentina.. had in 1884 the first meat-freezing works established on the banks of the River Plate. 1906 *Westm. Gaz.* 28 May 7/2 The lard used by *meat-packers is taken from hogs. The sanitary conditions in meat-packing houses. 1910 *Chambers's Jrnl.* June 415/2 The lives of Philip Armour the meat-packer and Andrew Carnegie. 1892 J. J. Flinn *Chicago* 330 *Meat packing is the oldest of Chicago's industries. 1863 'Gail Hamilton' *Gala-Days* 75, I decided upon a *meat-platter. 1918 *Times* 7 Feb. 3/1 Should the currency coupon become the basis of *meat rationing, it is probable that [etc.]. 1889 *Century Mag.* Apr. 909/2 They say that he sometimes fills an old *meat-tin with water in anticipation of a long march. 1902 Eliz. Banks *Newspaper Girl* 64, I would have been capable of going into the street and knocking down any little butcher's boy who refused peaceably to deliver up to me the contents of his wooden *meat-trough. 1779 E. Parkman *Diary* 171 We are unhappily low in ye *Meat Tub. 1846 *Rep. U.S. Comm. Patents* (1847) 310 The mode by which I obtain a vacuum in *meat vat A. for curing meat.

6. meat-block, a block of wood on which meat is cut up; **meat-card,** a card entitling the holder to a ration of meat; **meat-coupon,** a coupon of a meat-card, entitling the holder to buy a certain quantity of meat; **meat fish,** fish for use as food; **meat hog,** a hog intended for food; **meat house,** a house in which meat is hung; **meat-jelly,** a jelly prepared from meat; **meat-knife,** a knife used for cutting up meat; **meat-man,** (also) one engaged in bringing meat to a camp; **meat-oil,** an oil obtained from the flesh of whales; **meat train,** the men and horses, etc., conveying meat to a party.

1838 E. Flagg *Far West* II. 59 Mr. W...was on the stump, in shape of a huge *meat-block at one corner of the market-house. 1870 *Food Jrnl.* 1 Dec. I. 622 The restaurateurs are compelled to ask for their customers' '*meat card'. 1918 *Times* 25 Feb. 9/5 You must not tear off *meat coupons yourself. This duty rests with the retailer. *Ibid.*, Only three coupons each week of a meat card can be used for butcher's meat. 1919 'Ian Hay' *Last Million* 97 'Got any meat coupons?' They shook their heads..'Better have bacon and eggs,' announced Hebe. 'They're not rationed.' 1772–6 J. Andrews *Lett.* 336 Early this morning arriv'd in town eleven carts loaded with *meat fish. 1856 *Florida Plant. Rec.* 169, I do not see but verry few of the shoats that I turned out for *meat hogs this year. 1831 Peck *Guide Emigrants* II. 126 Around it [*sc.* the cabin] are put a *meat or smoke house [etc.]. 1865 Mrs. Stowe *House & Home P.* 248 Those fine, clear *meat-jellies which form a garnish..palatable to the taste. 1865 P. V. Nasby *Struggles* 170 Did they [matrons] not..plunge a *meat-knife into their throbbin buzzums. 1832 R. Cox *Adv. Columbia R.* xxv. 261 The *meat-men did not return until nine this morning..but at eleven the hunters' signal drew us to the shore, and the meat-men were dispatched. 1912 *Chambers's Jrnl.* Mar. 184/2 After the blubber is removed you will obtain an extra output of what is called the *meat-oil. 1845 Frémont *Exped.* 234 The *meat train did not arrive this evening, and I gave Godey leave to kill our little dog.

Meater. Transfer † *Obs.* to sense in Dict. and add: **2.** *rare.* One who eats (butcher's) meat; a meat-eater.

1920 *Contemp. Rev.* Dec. 819 The 'meater' lives at higher pressure and exhausts his energy quicker than the non-meat-eater.

Meatless, *a.* Add: **2. b.** *spec.* Of foods specially prepared or supplied for vegetarians: Containing no butcher's meat.

1909 Senn (*title*) Meatless Fare and Lenten Cookery. 1909 *Daily Chron.* 2 Nov. 7/3 Even that anomaly—to most people—'the meatless meal' is included.

Hence **Mea·tlessness.**

1918 *Punch* 27 Mar. 206/2 If he [our butcher] were removed we should be plunged into absolute meatlessness.

Mebby, variant of May-be.

Meccano (mĭkā·no). The registered trade mark and name of a company, now commonly applied to a set of metal pieces, nuts, bolts, etc., and tools, specially designed for constructing small models of buildings, machines, or other engineering apparatus; any portion of such a set; a toy intended to develop a child's constructive instincts. Hence also *fig.* (as in quot. 1928).

1908 (*title*) Meccano (Mechanics made easy). Manual of Instructions for the whole series of Models. 1924 Selincourt *Cricket Match* iii. 56, I shall make a prison cell of meccano, and pretend you're locked..inside. 1926 Rose Macaulay *Crewe Train* vii, She idled about with toy soldiers, meccano or plasticine or something else ridiculous. 1927 *Sunday at Home* Aug. 675/1 There was meccano in the goldfish bowl. 1928 'Rebecca West' *Strange Necessity* ii. 199 The complete meccano set for the mind that is in The First Men in the Moon.

Mechanic. A. *adj.* Add. **1. c.** *Mechanic shop,* a shop in which some mechanical art is carried on. *U.S.*

1819 E. Dana *Geogr. Sketches* 95 It..contains..two copper and tin manufactories, and a number of other mechanic shops. 1837 W. Jenkins *Ohio Gaz.* 102 There are..10 mechanic shops.

B. *sb.* Add: **1. d.** *pl.* A mechanical system or structure, a mechanism.

1909 *Practitioner* Feb. 198 Operative measures..leave his skeletal mechanics in the condition in which they were before he sustained the injury. 1910 *Ibid.* June 767 The restoration of the normal skeletal mechanics by absolute apposition of the fragments.

Mechanical. A. *adj.* **3. b.** (Add example.)

1921 Bertr. Russell *Analysis of Mind* 46 We may define a movement of an animal's body as 'mechanical' when it proceeds as if only dead matter were involved.

Mechanicalization (mĭkæ·nikălaizē^i·ʃən). [f. Mechanicalize *v.* + -ation.] The action of rendering or fact of being mechanical in character, or in the means of operation.

1922 *Glasgow Herald* 5 Jan. 4/6 A record of experimental progress towards mechanicalisation of wireless telegraphy. 1924 *Army Quarterly* Oct. 40 The second step would spread the mechanicalization to the battalion transport. 1927 *Sunday Times* 6 Mar. 20/3 The real benefits that result from a mechanicalisation of industry.

Mechanicalize, *v.* (Later examples.)

1924 *Army Quarterly* Oct. 37 The ultimate probability of a mechanicalized army. *Ibid.* 39 The first step suggested is that the divisional transport should be mechanicalized.

Mechanism. 2. (Later examples). Also recently used, esp. *Psychol.*, of the means or agency by which mental processes and bodily actions are caused to take place (cf. quot. 1885 in Dict.).

1913 J. S. Haldane *Mechanism, Life & Personality* 9 Descartes, in his writings about the nervous system,..suggested nervous mechanisms. *Ibid.* 58 The real difficulty for the mechanistic theory is that we are forced..to postulate that the germ-plasm is a mechanism of enormous complexity and definiteness, and..that this mechanism..can divide and combine with other similar mechanisms. 1921 H. Crichton Miller *New Psychol. & Teacher* 161 This mental mechanism [the complex] lies at the root of all bias, all injustice, and all inability to think clearly. 1924 *Brit. Weekly* 28 Aug. 471/3 He will see strange recesses in human personality and unsuspected mechanisms fashioning religious beliefs. 1929 K. S. Lashley (*title*) Brain Mechanisms and Intelligence.

6. Delete †*Obs.* and add recent examples.

1902 *J. M. Baldwin's Dict. Philos. & Psychol.* II. 59/1 In biology: mechanism is opposed to vitalism, and in more recent controversy to neo-vitalism. 1925 C. D. Broad *Mind & its Place in Nature* 43 One is never quite sure what is meant by 'Mechanism' and by 'Vitalism'.

Mechanist. 3. Delete †*Obs.* and add recent example.

1925 C. D. Broad *Mind & its Place in Nature* 43 One feels that the disputes between Mechanists and Vitalists are unsatisfactory.

Mechani·stically, *adv.* [f. Mechanistic *a.*] On mechanistic principles.

1925 C. D. Broad *Mind & its Place in Nature* ii. 77 The attempts which have been made..to treat mental phenomena mechanistically.

Mechanization; Mechanized *ppl. a.* (Recent examples.)

1915 A. W. Gough *God's Strong People* 32 A tyranny built on a degradation and mechanization of the personal power. 1918 B. Miall tr. *A. Hamon's Lessons of World-war* 50 The 'mechanization' of individuals lessens their intellectuality. 1928 *Daily Mail* 7 Feb. 7/5 The 'mechanisation' of the army. *Ibid.* 8 Feb. 7/5 The fast two-seater tanks of the mechanised army.

Mechanotropism (me·kănŏ·tropiz'm). [f. Gr. μηχανο-, μηχανή machine + Tropism.] The turning or bending of tendrils or other plant organs in response to contact or other mechanical stimulus.

1929 Sir J. C. Bose *Growth & Tropic Movem. Plants* x. 90 Mechanotropism: Twining of Tendrils. In response to the stimulus of contact a tendril twines round its support.

Med., abbrev. of Medical *sb.* 1.

1851 [see Medic *sb.*]. 1853 *Songs of Yale* 16 (Farmer) Take..Sixteen interesting meds, With dirty hands and towzeled heads. 1899 A. H. Quinn *Pennsylv. Stories* 19 The Meds waited till the visitors were opposite them.

Medal, *sb.* **4.** Add: **medal chief** *U.S.*, an Indian chief who received a medal from the Colonial or U.S. authorities; **medal-ribbon,** the ribbon for attaching a particular medal or for wearing without the medal.

1772 D. Taitt in *Trav. Amer. Col.* 518 [Letter] To the Great and Small *medal chiefs. 1800 B. Hawkins *Sk. Creek Country* 27 He is one of the great medal chiefs. 1813 *Niles' Weekly Reg.* V. 270/2 At this moment a medal chief of the Choctaw nation is soliciting to be employed. 1909 *Westm. Gaz.* 4 Oct. 1/3 The *medal-ribbon which a soldier tore off his tunic.

Medi- (mi·di), sometimes used *Zool.* = Medio-.

1890 *Century Dict.* (citing Coues 1887) *Medicephalic a.* 1903 *Amer. Anthropologist* Oct.–Dec. 627 The meditemporal [*sc.* fissure] consists of a segment in the cephalic region of the lobe, 6 cm. in length. *Ibid.* 631 Fissures of the frontal lobe ..The medifrontal springs from the orbitofrontal.

Medial. A. *adj.* **2.** *Medial line*: delete †*Obs.* and add recent example. Also *medial area.*

1908 T. L. Heath tr. *Euclid's Elements* III. x. 50 A *medial* straight line..is so called because it is a mean proportional between two rational straight lines commensurable in square only. *Ibid.* 54 It is manifest that an area commensurable with a medial area is medial.

Medialization (mī·diălaizē^i·ʃən). [f. next + -ation.] The action of making medial.

1902 *Amer. Anthropologist* Jan.–Mar. 24 A similar medialization is found with *ch, s,* which..are..heard after vowels as *j* and *z* respectively.

Medialize (mī·diălaiz), *v.* [f. Medial *a.* + -ize.] *trans.* To make (a consonant) medial.

1902 *Amer. Anthropologist* Jan.–Mar. 25 The earlier Abenakis may have only partially medialized their consonants after vowels.

Median. A. *adj.* Add: **1. b.** *U.S.* Average.

1928 Henderson & Davie *Incomes & Living Lists of a University* 31 The median amount earned by extra teaching.

B. *sb.* **3.** *Math.* Substitute for def.: A straight line drawn from any vertex of a triangle to the middle point of the opposite side.

1883 W. Thomson in *Encycl. Brit.* XVI. 15/1 If *a, b, c* be the three sides of a triangle and *α, β, γ* the three medians.

Medic. B. *sb.* Delete '*Obs.* exc. as'.

1902 W. Winslow Hall *Applied Religion* i. 22 For ages medics have been laying down rules for the regimen of diseased people.

Medic (mī·dik), *a.*² [ad. L. *Mēdic-us*, Gr. Μηδικός Median.] = Median *a.*²

1888 G. Bertin *Abridged Gram. Lang. Cuneiform Inscr.* 81 Medic Grammar. 1912 H. G. Rawlinson *Bactria* ii. 25 A treaty was made between the rival nations, and ratified by a marriage between the Medic king and a Lydian princess.

Medical. A. *adj.* **1. d.** Add: **medical school,** a department of a college, university, or the like, in which medicine is studied.

1841 *Southern Lit. Messenger* VII. 550/2 We had lighted upon the University, in the act of organizing an extensive Medical School.

Medicine, *sb.*¹ Add: **2. f.** *To take one's medicine,* to submit to something disagreeable.

1894 'O. Henry' *Cabbages & Kings* xvii. 299 You go back and take your medicine like a man. 1897 *Congress. Rec.* 6 May 937/1 He will have to take his medicine, as we took ours in 1894. 1903 *N. Y. Times* 21 Sept., Canada can do nothing—she must take her medicine and make the best of it.

6. a. *medicine chest* (earlier example); **medicine ball,** a stuffed leather ball which is thrown and caught to provide exercise.

1903 W. L. Savage in *Athletics & Outdoor Sports for Women* 49 The illustrations below show two of the methods for passing *medicine balls. 1930 *Bulletin* 13 Feb. 8/2 The Prince of Wales..instead of indulging in..tennis and quoits, preferred to devote the time after tea to throwing the medicine ball. 1758 *Essex Inst. Hist. Coll.* XVIII. 87, I took care of my *Medicine chest and Privet chest. 1777 *Rec. N. H. Comm. Safety* 100 Ordered the R. Genl to pay.. for making 2 Brass Keys for the Medicine Chests.

b. *medicine lodge* (later example); **medicine wolf,** the small prairie wolf; **medicine woman,** an Indian woman dealing in magic.

1901 Giddings *Inductive Sociol.* 207 Religious Societies— ..In North American Indian tribes, they are known as *Medicine Lodges. 1837 W. Irving *Capt. Bonneville* II. xv. 147 This little, whining, feast-smelling animal, is..called among Indians the '*medicine wolf'. *c* 1843 O. Russel *Jrnl.* (1921) 131 The big prairie wolf is two feet high...The least known is little prairie or medicine wolf. 1834 *Knickerbocker Mag.* IV. 372 The mother evinced her sagacity, as a diviner or *medicine woman. 1836 *Ibid.* VIII. 152 It was at the wigwam of an old Indian 'medicine-woman' that I stopped.

Medicined, *ppl. a.* Later example in the sense charmed, bewitched.

1826 T. Flint *F. Berrian* (1834) I. 76 After this dance, it was understood that we were medicined, charmed, or under the pledged protection of their household divinities.

Medick. (Later example.)

1912 W. Somerville *Agriculture* iii. 69 Species standing wide apart, like beans and medick, have no mutual interest in any particular organism.

Medinal (me·dinăl).

A proprietary term for a hypnotic (see quots.) registered in 1908.

1908 *Chemist & Druggist* LXXIII. 443/2 Medinal is the mono-sodium salt of diethylbarbituric acid. 1909 *Practitioner* Feb. 307 Medinal..is a new soluble hypnotic which has been introduced by Messrs. Schering of Berlin. 1922 *Daily Mail* 16 Dec. 7 The verdict was Death from an Overdose of Medinal taken by Misadventure.

Medio (me·dio). [Sp.] A coin of Cuba (see quot. 1859).

1859 R. H. Dana *To Cuba* 47 As there is no coin in Cuba less than the medio, 6¼ cents, the musicians get a good deal or nothing. *a* 1909 'O. Henry' *Roads of Destiny* xxi. 358 I've got one Chili Dollar, two real pieces, and a *medio*.

Mediterranean. B. *sb.* **1. b.** Add:

1760 Washington *Diaries* I. 145 Planted 4 Nuts of the Mediterranean Pine in the Pen.

3. A European racial type found especially in countries bordering on the Mediterranean Sea.

1888 C. Morris *Aryan Race* i. 13 The hair of the Mediterraneans is not so long or so cylindrical in section as in the Mongolians. 1921 *Man* No. 107. 180 The brown dolichocephals called Mediterraneans. 1924 *Public Opinion* 28 Nov. 522/2 The Nordic is tall and fair; the Mediterranean shorter and more slenderly built. 1926 *Contemp. Rev.* Jan. 83 For a Mediterranean the most important is not the essence of a thing, but its presence, its actuality.

Mediterra·neanize, *v.* [f. Mediterranean *a.* + -ize.] *trans.* To make Mediterranean in character. So **Mediterra·neaniza·tion.**

1915 *Nation* (N.Y.) 6 May 485/3 That the Greeks are Mediterraneanized Slavs whose only heritage is a language which Demosthenes could neither have pronounced nor understood. 1921 *19th Cent.* May 894 The ancient Alpine race has been mediterraneanised, latinised, slavonised, and teutonised in Europe, and the Teuton in his turn has undergone mediterraneanisation, latinisation and slavonisation.

Medium. A. *sb.* **9. c.** (Earlier example.)

1777 *Essex Inst. Hist. Coll.* XLII. 319 There cargo is Salt ..37 bales, cases, hhds of mediums [etc.].

Medo- (mī·do), combining form of Mede (L. *Mēdus*, Gr. Μῆδος), used parasynthetically with terms denoting other peoples or countries, esp. *Medo-Persian* adj.

1835 J. B. Robertson tr. *Schlegel's Philos. Hist.* vii. I. 272 The Assyro-Babylonian empire which preceded the Medo-Persian. *Ibid.* 273 The Medo-Persian dynasty. 1869 Rawlinson *Man. Anc. Hist.* II. 9 A revolution in the Medo-Persian capital. 1872 *Lit. World* 28 June V. 405/1 The laws for composing the music of a minuet were..Medo-Persian in their rigidity. 1875 J. Peile in *Encycl. Brit.* I. 604/2 The name for God in Medo-Scythic is *Annap*.

Medullate, *v.* Transfer † *Obs.* to sense in Dict. and add: **2.** *intr.* Of nerve structures: To form or produce a 'medulla'.

1898 *Phil. Trans.* B. CXC. 2 The tract which ascends from the internal geniculate body medullates separately from the other intracerebral systems.

Hence **Medulla·tion,** the action of forming a 'medulla'.

188. *Buck's Handbk. Med. Sci.* II. 319 (Cent. Suppl.).

Medullosean (medulō^u·siăn), *a.* [f. Medullose + -an.] Of a pithy texture.

1914 *Brit. Mus. Return* 219 One Medullosean stem and *Cordaites* from the Coal Measures, Bolton.

Meech, *v.* Also **meach.** Dial. variant of Miche *v.*] (Later examples of sense 2.)

c 1800 Dow *Serm.* I. 203 (Bartlett) When you fall short of the object for which you jump, you go meechin off, like a cat that has missed her mouse. 1832 Seba Smith *Thirty Yrs. out of Senate* (1860) 179 The old man hauled in his horns and meeched off, looking shamed enough. 1902 H. L. Wilson *Spenders* xxxi. 366 I'd hate to have you come meachin' around after that stock has kited.

Meeching, *ppl. a.* Also **meaching, meachin, me(e)chin.** [Dial. var. of *miching* Miche *v.*] Skulking, furtive; mean.

1792 *Massachusetts Spy* 22 Mar. XXI. 1/1 There is a kind of meaching souls in the world. *a* 1800 *Spirit Farmer's Museum* (1801) 287 We observed, however, that he had lantern jaws and a meaching look. 1836 Haliburton *Clockm.* Ser. I. xv. (1837) 140 Father goes up to him, lookin as soft as dough, and as meechin as you please. 1844 'Jon. Slick' *High Life N. Y.* II. 219, I gin her hand a leetle mechin shake. 1848 Bartlett *Dict. Amer.* 222 A person with a downcast look is said to look *meechin*. Used on Long Island. 1872 Marietta Holley *My Opinions* (1891) 311 He looked real meachin, and says he, 'I beg your pardon mom'. 1884 Howells *Silas Lapham* ix. 153 I'm not going to have you do anything that will make you feel meeching afterward.

Meet, *sb.* Add: **2.** *Geom.* A point, line or surface of intersection.

1893 J. W. Russell *Pure Geom.* 156 The meets of opposite sides of a hexagon (six-point) inscribed in a conic are collinear. *Ibid.* 236 Given five points on each of two conics, to construct the conic which passes through the four meets of these conics and also touches a given line.

Meet, *v.* Add: **2. g.** *Naut. To meet her*: in bringing a ship on to a desired course, to turn the helm or rudder in the other direction before the ship reaches the desired course, to prevent it going round too far.

1815 *Falconer's Marine Dict.* 194 A bad steersman..moves it [the helm] so far as to bring it [the ship] to her course again before he offers to stop her, or meet her with it. 1841 R. H. Dana *Seaman's Man.* 183 If the order is..'Ease her!' 'Meet her!' or the like, the man should answer by repeating..the order. 1902 A. B. Lubbock *Round the Horn* 187 Occasionally he says sharply, 'Meet her! Meet her!' and sometimes he jumps to the wheel and gives us his powerful aid in grinding it up or down.

4. Add to def.: To be (formally) introduced to (a person). Mostly in imperative. *U.S.*

1920 Mulford *J. Nelson* vi. 37 'Meet th' Doc, Nelson,' said Dave. Johnny turned. 'Glad to meet you, Doctor.' 1926 A. A. Thomson (*title*) Meet Mr. Huckabee!

12. *Sc.* To *meet in with.* To encounter (a person); = sense 4.

1825 Jamieson, To *Meet in wi'*, to meet with. S. B. 1828 D. M. Moir *Mansie Wauch* xi. 96, I..advised him to take a step in at his leisure to St. Mary's Wynd, where he would meet in with some merchants in scores. 1889 Stevenson *Master of Ballantrae* ix. (1891) 247, I was not always as I am to-day; nor (had I met in with a friend of your description) should I have ever been so.

13. *To meet up with,* to overtake or fall in with. *U.S. colloq.*

1837 Sherwood *Gaz. Georgia* (Provincialisms) *Met up with,* for overtook. 1889 K. Munroe *Golden Days* ix. 96 They'd meet up with you somewheres along Coloma way. 1909 R. A. Wason *Happy Hawkins* 16 If any one was to urge me, I'd be obliged to meet up with a little food. 1916 H. L. Wilson *Somewhere in Red Gap* ix. 376 Ben Sutton had met up with his old friend Jake Berger, also from Nome.

Meeting, *vbl. sb.* **7.** Add: *meeting clothes, coat, -day, gown, hat, time*; **meeting-seed** (see quot. 1851).

1867 T. Lackland *Homespun* I. 63 The '*meetin clothes' of the children are laid away for another week, and the old ones got out again. 1887 Mary E. Wilkins *Humble Romance* 139 An thar was Israel in his *meetin coat, an' me in my best gown. 1644 *Portsmouth* (N.H.) *Rec.* 32 It is.. ordered that the business of such 'metinge dayes shal be specified. 1686 *Sewall's Diary* I. 146 Mr. Moodey exercises at our House being our meeting-day. 1887 Mary E. Wilkins *Humble Romance* 300 Hatty in her *meeting-gown of light-brown delaine, and her white *meeting-hat..was not pretty. 1851 *Knickerbocker Mag.* XXXVIII. 372 (Th.) Some people call it 'caraway' and 'aniseseed', but we call it '*meetin'-seed', 'cause we cal'late it keeps us awake in meetin'. 1889 Rose T. Cooke *Steadfast* xxxix. 414 Mothers of young families distributed fragrant bunches of dried 'meetin' seed' among their flocks. 1639 *New Haven Col. Rec.* 26 On the Lords day in the *meeting time. 1871 Mrs. Stowe *Sam Lawson* 200 We were in disgrace, we boys; and the reason of it was this: we had laughed out in meeting-time.

Meeting-house. 2. (Earlier examples.)

1633 *Dorchester* (Mass.) *Town Rec.* 8 Oct., Their shall be every Mooneday..a generall meeting of the inhabitants of the Plantation att the meeting house. 1634 *Watertown Rec.* 1 The charge of the Meeting House shal be gathered by a Rate justly levied.

3. *meeting-house chamber, ground, land, lot, post, rate, yard* (earlier example).

1647 *Watertown Rec.* 11 A wrighting shall be sett vpon the meting-house-post, to give Warning [etc.]. 1651 *Springfield Rec.* I. 200 The above mentioned bargain about the meeting house chamber. 1656 *Watertown Rec.* 48, 2ly [that] ye give acompt of the meeting howse rate. 1689 *Sewall's Diary* I. 286 Paid 40£..for the Releases of Meetinghouse Ground. 1690 *Ibid.* 334 Mrs. Judith Winthrop's Deed of the Meeting house Land in Boston. 1712 *N. H. Probate Rec.* I. 687 Northerly on the fence by the metinge house yard. 1735 *Ibid.* II. 523, I give to my son..a lot of land lying in the Meeting house lot.

Meg, see *Megger.

Mega-. Add: **Megaphyllous** *a. Bot.* [Gr. φύλλον leaf], having large leaves. **Me·gaseism** [Seism], a major earthquake. So **Megasei·smic** *a.* [Seismic], of or pertaining to a megaseism.

1904 *Science* 21 Oct. 529/1 The pteridophytes..may be disposed according to the prevalent size of their leaves in a series, leading from microphyllous to *megaphyllous types. 1909 D. H. Scott in *Darwin & Mod. Science* 203 A large proportion of the higher plants are microphyllous in comparison with the highly megaphyllous fern-like forms from which they appear to have been derived. 1912 *Rep. Brit. Assoc.* 92 A large group of *megaseisms was followed by a long period of quiescence. 1908 *Ibid.* 69 With *megaseismic movements the crust of the world moves much in the same way as a raft does upon the ocean.

b. *megabar* (see *Bar *sb.* 6 and in Addenda).

1917 McAdie *Princ. Aërography* 30. 1918 *U.S. Monthly Weather Rev.* Feb. 75/1. 1925 Joly *Surface-Hist. Earth* iii. 55 *note*, The megabar is one million dynes per sq. cm. It is nearly one atmosphere.

Megalomaniac, *a.* (Examples).

1899 *Pall Mall Gaz.* 14 Feb. 2/3 A megalomaniac world is always apt to regard a waistcoat-pocket community as a joke. 1929 W. J. Locke *Jorice* 29 They had to attribute the great fortune to the megalomaniac dreams of a dying man.

Megaphone. 2. Add: Also *attrib.*

a 1906 'O. Henry' *Trimmed Lamp* etc. 180 The megaphone man roars out at you to observe the house of his uncle.

Megaphone (me·găfō^un), *v.* [f. the sb.] *intr.* and *trans.* To speak or utter through a megaphone. Hence **Megaphoned, Megaphoning** *ppl. adjs.*

1901 Lehmann *Anni Fugaces* 70 The air grows blue with loud reproaches Hurled at the crews by megaphoning coaches. 1912 J. H. Moore *Ethics & Education* 97 Long ago she [a dog] and her associates were accustomed to megaphone to each other in this way. 1920 *Glasgow Herald* 21 Apr. 8 The captain megaphoned an invitation to come on to the flag deck. 1927 H. G. Wells in *Sunday Express* 2 Oct. 12/7 The impressive gatherings.., the megaphoned and broadcast speeches.

Me·gaphonist. [f. Megaphone 2.] One who speaks through a megaphone.

1906 'O. Henry' *Four Million* 203 'What's eatin you?' demanded the megaphonist.

Megapolis. (Modern example.)

1855 [Pray] *Mem. J. G. Bennet* 450 Capital alone is wanting to make this city in point of influence..the megapolis of the world.

Megascopically, *adv.* Add quot.

1893 H. S. Washington *Volcanoes of Kula Basin* 21 Megascopically it is much more frequent and prominent than either the augite or the olivine.

Megatherium. b. (Later example.)

1908 H. G. Wells *War in Air* v. § 6 They were the weirdest, most destructive and wasteful megatheria in the whole history of mechanical invention.

Megathermic (megăþɜ·ɹmik), *a.* [f. Megatherm + -ic.] Pertaining to, connected with, or consisting of, megatherms.

1903 W. R. Fisher tr. *A. F. W. Schimper's Plant Geog.* 226 The megathermic flora is already perceptibly impoverished.

Megger (me·gəɹ). A registered trade mark introduced about 1903 by Messrs. Evershed & Vignoles Ltd., of London, for apparatus designed for measuring electrical insulation resistance. *Megger test,* a test of insulation resistance made with a megger. So **Meg,** a smaller apparatus for measuring insulation resistance.

1923 *Nature* 13 Jan. 63/2 The 'Meg' insulation tester.., a remarkably light and cheap megger running to 10,000 mgo. which should prove a boon to linemen. 1924 *Harmsworth's Wireless Encycl.* II. 1415 There are few instruments of greater general utility in electrical testing than the one which goes by the name of the 'megger'.

Meiosis. Add: **3.** (Also **maiosis.**) The process of chromosome reduction in germ-cells which are undergoing maturation.

1905 Farmer & Moore in *Q. Jrnl. Micros. Sci.* XLVIII. 489 We propose to apply the terms Maiosis or Maiotic phase to cover the whole series of nuclear changes. 1907 *Rep. Brit. Assoc.* 689 There is reason to believe that a sorting of the chromosomes, analogous to that seen in meiosis, takes place in the third division of the ascus. 1910 *Encycl. Brit.* VII. 719/2 *note* In this paper the authors [J. B. Farmer and J. E. S. Moore] suggest the term 'Meiosis' or 'Meiotic phase' for the nuclear changes accompanying the two maturation divisions in plants and animals.

Meiotic (maiǫ·tik), *a.* Also (sense 2) **maiotic.** [ad. Gr. μειωτικός diminishing (see Meiosis) + -ic.]

1. That represents things as less than they really are; characterized by meiosis or litotes.

1907 *Westm. Gaz.* 17 June 2/2 Is there not..a good deal to be said for the meiotic method [of portraying the Cæsar] preferred by Sir Lawrence Tadema? 1915 *Oxford Mag.* 18 June 38/2 We have occasionally mentioned in mild meiotic terms that the Oxford roads do not wholly satisfy our ideal of perfection.

2. That is characterized by meiosis (sense *3).

1905 [see *Meiosis 3]. 1906 *Nature* 29 Nov. 98/2 In this way a definite phase (termed by some writers the maiotic phase) is intercalated in the cellular life-cycle of the organism. 1907 *Rep. Brit. Assoc.* 689 The chromosomes throughout the meiotic phase are sixteen in number. 1913 Bateson *Mendel's Princ. Heredity* 270 This differentiation must come about at this reduction, or meiotic division, as it is called.

Melampyre (me·læmpəiɹ). [f. mod.L. *Melampyrum*, cow-wheat: see Melampyrin.] = Cow-wheat.

1905 E. Phillpotts *Secret Woman* III. v. 244 While the melampyre's lemon blossoms and the orange stars of the woody loosestrife mingled close at hand.

Melano (mĭlā·no). [f. Gr. μελαν-, μέλας black: after Albino.] An animal distinguished by an abnormal development of black pigment in the epidermis, hair, feathers, etc.; opposed to Albino.

1902 *Annals & Mag. Nat. Hist.* IX. 59 Spotted tiger-cats of the *F. Macrura* group. The small specimen is a melano, but shows indications of the normal spotted condition.

Mêlée. Add: *S. Africa.* Off-colour diamonds of less than two carats weight.

1911 Cohen *Remin. Kimberley* 267 (Pettman) On a certain day I had entrusted him with two or three hundred carats of melée—small stones—to sell. 1920 *Daily Tel.* 22 June 1/2 Stones..of various weights from 1½ carats downwards, and a quantity of melee.

Melezitose. (Later example.)

1924 *Nature* 21 June 904/1 If the manna is produced by the intervention of insects, the interesting point arises whether melezitose occurs in the sap of the larch or is produced by the insect.

Melian (mī·liăn), *a.* and *sb.* Also **Melean.** [f. *Melos* (Gr. Μῆλος) the name of an island in the Ægean Sea + -ian.] **a.** *adj.* Of or pertaining to the island of Melos. **b.** *sb.* An inhabitant of Melos.

1550 T. Nicolls tr. *Thucydides* v. xi, The Meliens..refused to be under the obeissaunce of the Athenyans. 1629 Hobbes tr. *Thucydides* v. 341 Dialogue betweene the Athenians and Melians. 1831 J. Bell *System Geog.* II. 513 Marbles of many varieties are abundant in Greece...Another variety was..the Melian. 1883 *Encycl. Brit.* XV. 841/2 The Melian earth (γῆ Μηλιάς) employed as a pigment by ancient artists, was probably native white-lead. *Ibid.* 842/1 The Athenians.. compelled the Melians to surrender at discretion. 1910 W. James *Mem. & Stud.* (1911) 270 The Meleans say that sooner than be slaves they will appeal to the gods.

Melik, variant of Malik.

1920 *Blackw. Mag.* Nov. 669/1 Each hilla, or village, has its sheik, each group of hillas is under a melik.

Meliorant (mī·liŏrănt). [ad. late L. *meliorantem* pr. pple. of *meliorare*: see Meliorate *v.*] Something that makes better; an improver.

1920 Saintsbury *Notes on Cellar-bk.* 102, I am afraid that the 'whets' of our ancestors were rather stimulants to drinking..than meliorants of appreciation.

Meliorative. Delete † and add recent examples.

1902 *Encycl. Brit.* XXXI. 678/1 The so-called meliorative and pejorative developments in word-meaning. 1916 Swinnerton *Chaste Wife* xvii. § 2. 254 Its note had been meliorative rather than optimistic.

Melismatic. (Recent example.)

1909 C. H. H. Parry *J. S. Bach* 99 A recitative for soprano with a beautiful melismatic close.

Melodeon. 1. (Earlier example.)

1849 *Rep. U.S. Comm. Patents* (1850) 278 Improvement in Melodeons.

Melodicon (mĭlǫ·dikǫn). [ad. Gr. μελῳδικόν neut. of μελῳδικός pertaining to melody, f. μελῳδία: see Melody.] (See quot.) *Psalm melodicon*: see Psalm *sb.* 3.

1876 Stainer & Barrett *Dict. Mus. Terms, Melodicon*, an instrument made of steel bars in different lengths tuned to the diatonic scale, struck with hammers held in the hand.

Melon¹**.** Add: **1. c.** *To cut the melon,* to decide a question.

1911 H. Quick *Yellowstone N.* xii. 308 The O.M. as usual cuts the melon with a word.

d. Abundant profits, spoils, or the like, which are shared by several people. Esp. in phr. *to cut the melon*; cf. *melon-cutting* below.

1909 *N. Y. Even. Post* (semi-weekly ed.) 7 Oct. 2 A purse of $25,000 will be distributed among employees. About 8,000 men will participate in the cutting of the melon. 1928 *Weekly Dispatch* 24 June 6/4 The Union Pacific's portfolio [of outside investments] is one of the biggest potential 'melons' on the American horizon.

4. melon-cutting *vbl. sb.*, chiefly *fig.* in Stock Exchange slang, the dividing up or sharing of spoils, or profits.

1908 *Daily Report* 24 Aug. 2/4 The theory that any prospective melon-cutting will be postponed until next year. 1927 *Sunday Express* 24 July 6/4 As the company distributed some Preference shares only a short while ago we should think it unlikely there will be any further melon cutting yet.

Melopœic (melǫpī·ik), *a.* [f. Melopœia + -ic.] Of, pertaining to, or characterized by melopœia.

1927 *Contemp. Rev.* July 73 Wagner..turned to the melopœic chant, dramatised but not lyricised, for the expression of the words.

Meltonian, *a.* (Example.)

1901 *Edin. Rev.* Jan. 100 The red evening coat in which fox-hunters dine may be traced to the Meltonian dandies.

Mem, *v.* [f. the sb.] *trans.* To note or write down as a memorandum.

1914 W. J. Locke *Jaffery* v, Once having 'mem-ed' an unpleasant thing in my diary, the matter is over.

Mem, var. Ma'am. (Add Sc. and U.S. examples.)

1854 Shillaber *Mrs. Partington* 47 'This is grand weather, mem, for poor people' said Mr. Tigh, the rich neighbor of Mrs. Partington. 1867 *Goodwife at Home* i, Eh! Dear be here, mem, is this you, In sic a byous day? 1876 Ramsay *Scot. Life & Character* (ed. 21) iv. 78 Then I canna engadge wi' ye, mem; for 'deed I wadna gie the crack i' the kirkyard for a' the sermon. 1877 G. Macdonald *Marquis of Lossie* III. ix, But, mem,..I canna lee.

Member, *sb.* **1.** Add: Also *virile member*: see Virile *a.* 3.

4. b. (Recent examples.)

1888 J. Runciman *Chequers* 187 You're a red-hot member! 1891 *Sporting Life* 28 Mar. 3/5 But, warm a member as our hero was, standing in front of a blazing furnace for hours.. was too hot even for Jem's *sanguinary* temperament.

12. member-bank *U.S.*, a bank which holds shares in, and has representation on the board of directors of, a Federal Reserve Bank; see also quot. 1930.

1914 *Federal Reserve Act* § 1 The term '*member bank' shall be held to mean any national bank, state bank, or bank or trust company which has become a member of one of the reserve banks created by this Act. 1923 *Accountants' Handbk.* (ed. E. A. Saliers) 865 § 17, Member banks may rediscount short-time commercial notes with federal reserve banks. 1930 J. M. Keynes *Treatise on Money* I. 9 The typical modern Banking System consists of a Sun, namely the Central Bank, and Planets, which, following American usage, it is convenient to call the Member Banks.

Memberment (me·mbəɹmĕnt). [f. Member *sb.* + -ment.] The arrangement of parts in a body.

18.. *Buck's Handbk. Med. Sci.* VII. 313 (Cent. Suppl.).

Membrana·ceously, *adv.* [f. Membranaceous *a.*] With membranaceous material.

1821 W. P. C. Barton *Flora N. Amer.* I. 14 Stem erect, ..four-sided, membranaceously winged on the angles, smooth, nearly naked.

Memoirist. (Later examples.)

1888 G. W. Cable *Stories of Louisiana* ii. (1889) 48 Carlo was beginning to swear 'fit to raise the dead', writes the memoirist, at the tardiness of the Norman pair. 1907 *Daily Chron.* 11 Jan. 3/2 In almost every section of the volume he advances, as a memoirist, a moralist,..or a translator.., someone whose name deserves to be re-written over a faded tomb. 1914 *N. Y. Times* 31 May, These memoirists are as frankly revealing as any that described the daily life of the Grand Monarch's Court.

Memorandize (memŏræ·ndəiz), *v.* [f. Memorand(um + -ize.] *intr.* To make memoranda.

1881 Whitman *Specimen Days* (1892) 178 Now he is sitting on the limb of an old tree..—seems to be looking at me while I memorandize.

Memorial. A. *adj.* **3 a.** (Later examples.)

1891 S. W. Mitchell in *Century Mag.* Dec. 287/2 The man thus imprisoned within himself recovers by effort a vast amount of memorial property presumed to have been lost. 1920 in *Times Lit. Suppl.* 20 May 320/1 A link of material transmission..which..puts the theory of simple memorial piracy definitely out of court.

Memorist. 2. (Later example, not U.S.)

1920 H. G. Wells *Outl. Hist.* 115/2 Here we have..the medicine-man, the shrine-keeper, and the memorist, developed, with the development of the community.

Memory. Add: **1. c.** *Psychol.* Classified into various special kinds according to the way in which it is manifested, or the bodily process with which it is believed to be connected.

1883 F. Galton *Hum. Faculty* 106 One favourite expedient was to associate the sight memory with the muscular memory. 1897 tr. *T. Ribot's Psychol. Emotions* 153 Others..recall the circumstances *plus* the revived condition of feeling. It is these who have the true 'affective memory'. 1899 *Amer. Jrnl. Psychol.* XI. 7 He found that recollection could be mediated..(1) through visual images, (*a*) successive in time or space, or (*b*) grouped..*plus* motor memory. 1901 *Ibid.* XII. 264 Functional memory, *i.e.* memory connected always with some bodily function.

12. *memory-cell, -image, -process, -sketch*; **memory book** *U.S.*, a blank book in which cuttings from newspapers and the like are pasted for preservation; a scrap-book.

1931 *Publishers' Weekly* 14 Feb. 843/1 Another demand.. is that for inexpensive *memory books used by grammar school children. 1892 C. C. Van Liew & Beyer tr. *T. Ziehen's Introd. Physiol. Psychol.* 156 These numerous sensory cells transmit their excitation further to one other ganglion-cell, a *memory-cell. 1895 Halleck *Psychol. & Psychic Cult.* 106 *Memory images are those which most nearly represent existing things. 1921 B. Russell *Analysis Mind* 207 A memory-image of a particular occurrence. 1897 C. H. Judd tr. *Wundt's Outl. Psychol.* 241 The process that arises under such circumstances is a *memory-process. 1906 *Daily Chron.* 16 Apr. 3/5 Some clever *memory sketches of the Franco-British Exhibition.

Mend, *v.* Add:

5. *To mend up*: delete (? *Obs.*) and add modern examples. *To mend one's fences*: see *Fence *sb.*

1833 Seba Smith *Major J. Downing* lvi. 206 (Born) They've got their clothes pretty much mended up, and they look quite tidy. 1854 Maria Charlesworth *Ministering Children* ii. 19 Mamma is going to give me all Edward's old warm stockings, if I mend them up quite neat!

6. b. Also *to mend up.*

1877 Anna Sewell *Black Beauty* xliv. 217 The farrier said he [a horse] might mend up enough to sell for a few pounds.

10. c. To recover from, get better *of*, grow out *of*.

1881 J. Fothergill *Kith & Kin* III. ii. 43 He had always trusted that the boy would mend of such outlandish indifference.

Mendelian. Add: **B.** *sb.* One who adheres to or supports Mendel's principles of heredity.

1903 K. Pearson in *Phil. Trans.* A. CCIII. 57 If we were 'pure Mendelians' we should for the purpose of character classification make *v* = *w*. 1907 *Nature* 23 May 73/1 It would be regarded as a demonstration of the falsity of the doctrine of gametic purity by everyone who was not a Mendelian.

Mendelianism (mendī·liăniz'm). [f. Mendelian + -ism.] (Adherence to or support of) the law or principles of heredity discovered or propounded by Mendel; *Mendelism.

1903 K. Pearson in *Phil. Trans.* A. CCIII. 54 We reach pure Mendelianism by making our protozygotes 'dominants', our allozygotes 'recessives'. 1906 A. D. Darbishire in *Manch. Mem.* L. No. II. 11 What is the essential feature of that which is called Mendelism by those who believe in it, and Mendelianism by those who do not?

Mendelism (me·ndĕliz'm). *Biol.* [f. the name *Mendel*: see Mendelian + -ism.] The law or principles governing the inheritance of certain characters, especially those classified as dominant and recessive, in the vegetable and animal kingdoms, first discovered and formulated by the Austrian monk, Gregor Johann Mendel; also applied to the scientific study of the inheritance of parental characters which originated with Mendel.

1903 *Science* 20 Mar. 451/2 The breeder wants to preserve the desirable characters or traits and eliminate the undesirable ones, but under the strict interpretation of Mendelism this is difficult. 1905 R. C. Punnett (*title*) Mendelism. 1906 L. H. Bailey *Plant Breeding* (ed. 4) 168 Already so many adjustments have been made of the Mendelian principles that it is becoming difficult to determine what Mendelism is. 1909 *Fabian News* XXI. 92/2 Mendelism, as applied to man, is simple enough in such matters as brown eyes and blue. 1911 R. C. Punnett *Mendelism* (ed. 3) xiii. 140 Mendelism has helped us to realise that specific characters may be but incidental to a species. 1920 *Edin. Rev.* July 135 Mendelism promises to furnish the stock-breeder with better and more certain means of increasing the economic value of his stock. 1927 Haldane & Huxley *Animal Biol.* ii. 62 The comparatively new science called Mendelism.

Mendelist (me·ndĕlist). [f. *Mendel* (see Mendelian) + -ist.] = *Mendelian *sb.*

1910 H. Walker *Lit. Victorian Era* I. iii. 230 There are Mendelists and Mutationists as well as Darwinians.

Mendelize (me·ndĕləiz), *v.* [see -ize.] *intr.* To exhibit or transmit parental characters in conformity with Mendel's law of inheritance; to behave as Mendel's law predicts.

1906 L. H. Bailey *Plant Breeding* (ed. 4) 171 We do not know what plants will Mendelize until we try. 1918 Babcock & Clausen *Genetics Agric.* 286 Those changes in specific factors which result in the appearance of new Mendelizing characters. 1924 E. W. MacBride *Introd. Study Heredity* viii. 212 'Sports'..which breed true when crossed with their like, but which 'mendelize' when crossed with the type.

Mendelssohnian (mendĕlsō^u·niăn), *a.* [f. the name of the German composer Felix *Mendelssohn*-Bartholdy (1809–47) + -ian.] Of, pertaining to, or characteristic of Mendelssohn, or his musical productions.

1900 *Musical Standard* LIX. 283/1 The second movement was rendered with a Mendelssohnian elegance. 1909 H. G. Wells *Ann Veronica* iii. § 4. 60 The organ..was, in its Mendelssohnian way, as glad as ever it could be. 1928 *Observer* 29 Jan. 14/4 A clearly conceived and agreeable piece of music with Mendelssohnian orchestration.

Mending, *vbl. sb.* **1. c.** Add: Also *attrib.*

1863 'Gail Hamilton' *Gala-Days* 41, I find myself in a *mending-basket. 1898 A. Nicholas *Idyl of Wabash* 18 Taking his hose from the mending basket and darning them. 1866 Mrs. Whitney *L. Goldthwaite* viii, What should we do without our *mending-day?

2. a. (Also in *sing.*)

1891 *Harper's Mag.* Sept 579/1 Mrs. Dorset was on the bench in the porch, the basket of mending by her.

Menhaden. b. Add: *menhaden oil-works.*

1882 *Harper's Mag.* Sept. 588/1 A deck-load of brick for a menhaden oil-works had been dumped there.

Mennist (me·nist). *U.S.* [Irreg. f. *Menno* (see Mennonite) + -ist.] = Mennonist, Mennonite. Also *attrib.*

1869 *Atlantic Monthly* Oct. 474/1 The Mennists in many outward circumstances very much resemble the Society of Friends. *Ibid.*, In the interior of the Mennist meeting, a Quaker-like plainness prevails.

Menominee (mĕno·mini). *U.S.* Also **-onee.** [The name of a tribe of North American Indians, and of various places in Michigan and Wisconsin.] Applied *attrib.* to a variety of white-fish found in the Great Lakes (see quot. 1888).

1888 Goode *American Fishes* 490 The Menomonee White-fish, *Coregonus quadrilateralis,* inhabits the Lakes of New England, Upper Great Lakes, and is found northwestward to Alaska. 1902 *Rep. U.S. Fish. Comm.* 653 Table showing, by States, the products of the fisheries of the Great Lakes in 1899..White-fish (Menominee) fresh..White-fish (Menominee) salted.

Menopau·sal, *a.* [f. Menopause + -al.] Of, pertaining to, or connected with the menopause.

1910 *Practitioner* June 787 Permanent cessation of the menses, so long as the ovaries have been conserved, is not associated with so-called 'menopausal' symptoms.

Menshevik (me·nʃĭvik), *sb.* (and *a.*). [ad. Russ. Меньшевикъ *men'shévik*, f. меньшiй *mén'shiy* (predicative меньше *mén'she*), compar. of малый *mál'iy* little. The Russ. pl. Меньшевики *men'sheviki* has been used by some English writers.] A member of the more moderate section of the Russian Socialist Party.

The name was originally given to the less extreme party of Russian Social-Democrats at the Congress in 1903. Cf. *Bolshevik.

1917 *19th Cent.* July 141 The Mensheviki or Minimalists (Moderate Socialists) need organisation. 1917 *New Europe* 6 Dec. 236 It was from this Conference [at Stockholm, 1903] that the cleavage between Bolševiks and Menševiks dates. 1923 E. A. Ross *Russian Soviet Republ.* 323 The imprisonment of the Menshevik members of the Moscow printers' union. 1926 *Contemp. Rev.* Sept. 274 He was an outsider— a 'menshevik' (the 'minority' man).

Menshevism (me·nʃĭviz'm). [f. *Menshev(ik + -ism.] The doctrines and practices of the Mensheviks; a moderate form of socialism.

1920 *Glasgow Herald* 14 May 9 Communism as it is offered to Trans-Caucasia has assumed the form of Menshevism. 1926 *Contemp. Rev.* Sept. 275 Marx would prove it; but that would be 'Menshevism'.

Menshevist (me·nʃĭvist). [f. *Menshev(ik + -ist.] = *Menshevik. Also *attrib.*

1919 *Times Lit. Suppl.* 14 Aug. 432/3 A pleasing description of the Menshevists. 1926 *Contemp. Rev.* Sept. 274 He was known to return in all intricate cases to his menshevist fallacies.

Mental. A. *adj.* Add: **1.** (Further example.)

1897 C. H. Judd tr. *Wundt's Outl. Psychol.* 326 The law of mental growth is as little applicable to all contents of psychical experience as any other psychological law of development.

b. *Mental disease, incapacity,* etc.: In recent use, the more common terms for lunacy, insanity, idiocy, etc. *Mental home, hospital, institution, ward,* etc.: Places where insane or feeble-minded persons are confined, treated or trained. *Mental nurse, specialist,* etc.: A nurse or doctor devoted to the care or study of insane or feeble-minded patients. *Mental case, defective, incapable, patient,* etc.: An insane or feeble-minded person.

(*a*) 1904 *Lancet* 27 Aug. 598/2 Scientific views regarding mental disease have..been undergoing great changes. *Ibid.* 17 Sept. 838/1 Those cases of mental incapacity arising from incipient or oncoming insanity. 1926 *Ibid.* 561/1 'Mental deficiency' is a relative term and difficult, perhaps impossible to define.

(*b*) 1898 *H. Morten's Compl. System Nursing* 249 A year's training in a general hospital, and two years' training in a mental hospital, would be the proper scheme to turn out the best mental nurse. 1908 *Westm. Gaz.* 23 Nov. 9/1 An inmate of a mental home..under a certificate signed by two doctors. 1921 *Times* 2 Aug. 4/5 Nobody to-day requires to be convinced of the need for mental hospitals. 1922 *Lancet* 22 July 209/1 The compulsory detention of an individual..in a mental institution. *Ibid.* 11 Nov. 1048/1 The plaintiff was confined in a mental ward.

(*c*) 1898 [see above]. 1922 *Lancet* 5 Aug. 290/1 The two duties of mental nurses.

(*d*) 1904 *Lancet* 17 Sept. 838/1 The Home Secretary..has at last been impressed with the total inadequacy of the provision made for..mental incapables. 1913 Meynell *Life F. Thompson* 279 Many a time I've asked him to have his bit of lunch in with me and the other 'mental'—O yes, she's a mental case, as I may have told you. 1922 W. R. Inge in *Edin. Rev.* July 34 The Eugenics Education Society.. actively supported the Act for the compulsory segregation of mental defectives. 1922 *Lancet* 21 Oct. 888/1 Public opinion became focussed upon the treatment of mental patients.

c. Short for *mentally defective.*

B. *sb.* **a.** Delete † *Obs.* and add modern example.

1881 *Punch* 3 Dec. 264/2 Oh, worms and gentles, It warms one's 'mentals' More than much whiskey.

c. Short for *mental case, defective, patient,* etc. (colloq.).

1913 [see 1 b (*d*) above].

Mentalistic (mentăli·stik), *a.* [f. Mentalist + -ic.] Pertaining to or connected with mentalism.

1920 A. S. Pringle-Pattison *Idea of God* 191, I feel it to be important..to free the position I am defending from the supposed dependence on the Mentalistic doctrines which have often been used to support it.

Mentality. Add: **3.** Mental character or disposition; outlook; kind or degree of intelligence.

1931 Lewis Watt *Future of Capitalism* ii. 23 It is useless to pretend that there will be anything but hostility between the partners in industry so long as this mentality persists.

Mentally, *adv.* **b.** (Later examples.)

1925 *Brit. Med. Jrnl.* 24 Oct. 727/2 This inquiry was made with the object of comparing the heredity and social conditions of a certain number of insane, mentally defective, and normal persons. *Ibid.* Suppl. 14 Nov. 170/1 Persons whose mental defect arose from or followed brain lesions,.. should not be classed as mentally deficient. 1931 *Municipal Year Bk.* 1068 It is possible to secure unity and continuity of treatment and care for the mentally defective.

Mention, *v.* **1. b.** (Later examples.)

1863 G. Macdonald *David Elginbrod* III. III. ix. 158 He mentioned to Miss Talbot that he had been his guest that night. 1904 Lillie T. Meade *Love Triumphant* II. vi. 153 Once I mentioned to Uncle Henry how much she prayed.

Mento-. **Mento-Meckelian** (also as *sb.*) = the mento-Meckelian bone.

1892 J. A. Thomson *Outl. Zool.* 449 The mento-meckelians seem to arise from two lower labial cartilages.

Mercantile, *a.* **5.** quasi-*sb.* Delete † *Obs.* and add: One engaged in trade or commerce.

1921 *Chambers's Jrnl.* July 440/1 With the exception of the nobility..and of the mercantiles..alpargatas, or string-soled shoes, are the footwear of the Spanish nation.

Mercator (mɜ̄ɹkē^i·tǫɹ). The latinized form of the name of G. Krämer (1512–94), the Flemish cartographer, used *attrib.*; cf. *Mercator's projection* (Projection *sb.* 7 b).

1875 Knight *Dict. Mech., Mercator-chart*, a mode of projection invented by Gerald Mercator, in which the meridians and parallels are straight and parallel lines. The meridians are equidistant, but the distance between the parallels increases from the equator towards either pole.

Mercatorial (mɜɹkătō^ə·riăl), *a.*² [f. prec. + -ial.] Of or pertaining to Mercator's method of projection in cartography; based upon or calculated from (the data furnished by) a Mercator chart.

a 1888 Shortland *Naut. Surveying* (1890) 144 Their Mercatorial meridians will be inclined to each of them respectively about 1'·2. *Ibid.* 346 To reduce a plane sheet to a Mercatorial projection proceed as follows. 1902 *Encycl. Brit.* XXXIII. 99/2 The Mercatorial bearing between two stations is the mean of their reciprocal true bearings.

Merchant. A. *sb.* Add: **1. d.** (U.S. examples.)

1790 *Gazette of U.S.* (Philad.) 13 Oct. (Th.) The word merchant should not be confounded with retailers and shopkeepers. 1809 W. Irving *Knickerb.* vii. ix, If peradventure some straggling merchant of the east should stop at the door, with his cart load of tin ware or wooden bowls, the fiery Peter would issue forth [etc.]. 1818 in *Trans. Ill. State Hist. Soc.* 1910, 162 Dry goods are geting very cheap, the country is full of them; we have more merchants than any thing else. 1871 R. Somers *Southern States since War* 129 Few are able at the end of the year to square accounts with 'the merchant'. 1897 J. L. Allen *Choir Invisible* i, A heavy roll of home-spun linen, which she was taking to town to her aunt's merchant as barter for queen's-ware pitchers.

3. Revived in recent slang: A fellow, person; esp. one who deals or specializes in or practises something; with a defining word, as *speedmerchant.*

Also Sc. dial. *sma' merchant,* applied to a boy.

1886 *Referee* Oct., (Ware, *Passing Engl.*) The success of *Indiana* mainly depends upon the extravagant humours of the chief low-comedy merchant. 1909 Ware *Passing Engl., Merchant* (Theatrical 1882). The theatre coming to be called the 'shop', actors dubbed themselves 'merchants', qualified by their line. 1923 *Daily Mail* 15 Feb. 6 The chauffeur of a motor-car has a rain-blurred wind-screen, and the goggled 'speed-merchant' cannot see so well as usual. 1923 *Motor Cycle* 22 Nov. 783/1 This very afternoon as ever was, a merchant on a huge sidecar outfit made a malicious attempt to ram me at a street corner. 1925 E. Fraser & Gibbons *Soldier & Sailor Words, Merchant,* a fellow. One connected with any special branch of the service. Used with various applications, *e.g.* 'A M.G. merchant'—a Machine Gunner. 1927 *Morn. Post* 10 Sept. 7/4 It is not improbable that he may become a 'speed merchant'. 1929 Doyle *Maracot Deep* 244 Storr, the googlie merchant, had a better showing with four for ninety-six.

4. (Recent example.)

1903 Kipling *Five Nations* 8 The pot-bellied merchant foreboding no wrong With headlight and sidelight he lieth along.

6. a. *merchant shipper.*

1919 *Brit. Manufacturer* Nov. 16/2 Orders may..be distributed by the merchant shipper of this country.

b. merchant prince (earlier example).

1841 L. M. Child *Lett. New York* viii. 53, I sometimes ask whether the age of Commerce is better than the age of War? Whether our '*merchant princes' are a great advance upon feudal chieftains?

Merchanting (mɜ̄·ɹtʃăntiŋ), *ppl. a.* [f. Merchant *v.* + -ing².] Engaged in trade as merchants.

1930 *Observer* 9 Feb. 18/1 The merchanting body itself is in no greatly better case.

Merchant mill. *U.S.* ? *Obs.* [f. Merchant *a.* 1.] A mill engaged in the grinding of grain for the purpose of trade.

1774 P. V. Fithian *Jrnl.* (1900) 111 Mr. Carter's Merchant Mill begins to run to-day—She is calculated to manufacture 25,000 Bushels of Wheat a Year. 1816 U. Brown *Jrnl.* in *Maryland Hist. Mag.* X. 273 He has a Merchant Mill, a Saw Mill, a Carding Mill, all on the Waters of Bath. 1837 W. Jenkins *Ohio Gaz.* 68 The village contains..1 large merchant mill, nearly completed, with four run of stones. 1851 C. Cist *Cincinnati* 194 It proposes to perform in a small compass..the work of a merchant mill.

Merchant tailor. (U.S. examples.)

1818 Fearon *Sk. Amer.* 33 Taylors are numerous: they are denominated, (in conformity with the accustomed vanity of the country), 'Merchant Taylors'. 1841 *Advt.* in C. Cist *Cincinnati*, James Bishop, Merchant Tailor. 1889 *Kansas Times & Star* 13 Nov., Call on Ed. Howe, the artistic merchant tailor,..for first class, well fitted suits.

Mercury, *sb.* **11.** Add: **mercury fulminate,** fulminate of mercury; **mercury (vapour) lamp,** an apparatus consisting essentially of an exhausted glass or quartz tube containing mercury vapour, which produces a special kind of illumination when an electric current is passed through it.

1904 *Kynoch Jrnl.* Oct.–Dec. 199 The flame from the *mercury fulminate..ignites the charge of explosive contained in..the case. 1908 *Illuminating Engineer* Aug. 633/1 When burning under normal conditions the *mercury lamp received 36 per cent. more power. 1908 *Electrical Field* Sept. 241/1 (heading) Mercury-Vapour Lamps. 1909 *Westm. Gaz.* 6 Mar. 3/2 A 'new' process of sterilising milk by exposing it to the ultra-violet rays of a mercury-vapour lamp. 1911 *Encycl. Brit.* 670/1 Many attempts have been made to render the mercury vapour lamp polychromatic.

Meredithian (meridi·þiăn), *a.* and *sb.* Also **-ean.** [f. the proper name *Meredith* + -ian.] **a.** *adj.* Of, pertaining to, or characteristic of George Meredith, Eng. novelist and poet (1828–1909) or his works. **b.** *sb.* An admirer of Meredith.

1891 *Lit. World* 29 May 510/3 [She] swathes her thought in Meredithean phrase. 1892 *Rev. of Reviews* Jan. 95/2 Meredithians owe a debt of gratitude to the publishers. 1908 *New Age* 31 Dec. 210/1 [The novel] is strongly Meredithian in unreality of character, choppy style, [etc.]. 1909 *Daily Chron.* 22 Jan. 3/4 The bookseller, an enthusiastic Meredithian. 1926 *Spectator* 19 June 1046/2 He received a letter in reply which began with this superbly Meredithian sentence.

Merge, *v.* Add: **3. b.** Of firms or trading companies: to combine or amalgamate with one another.

1930 J. B. Priestley *Angel Pavement* ii. § 1, That's the way things are going all the time now,..big combinations—merging away till you don't know where you are.

Merger¹**.** Add: **3.** *Comb.* as **merger company,** the larger of two trading companies which form a merger; so *merger share.*

1928 *Daily Mail* 3 Aug. 18/2 There is no compulsion on the Preference shareholders to accept an offer from the *merger company. *Ibid.* 18/3 The *merger shares issued to ..shareholders may bring in a bigger income than the..Preference shares.

Meridian, *sb.* Add: **1.** (U.S. examples.)

1850 *Congress. Globe* 31 May 1106/2 The funeral..will take place to-morrow at 12 o'clock meridian. *Ibid.* 8 July 1329/3 [An adjournment was moved, to take place] on Thursday, the 1st day of August next, at twelve o'clock, meridian.

6. *transf.* Applied to a structure which resembles or suggests a meridian. (In quot. = *Ctenophore* I.)

1902 *Encycl. Brit.* XXVII. 300/1 This [jelly-fish] possesses eight meridians (costæ) of iridescent paddles in constant vibration, which run from near one pole towards the other.

Meridian (mĕri·diăn), *v.* [f. the sb.] *intr.* Of a celestial body: To reach the meridian.

1902 *Chambers's Jrnl.* Nov. 741/1 By the time the moon meridianed, the weather had decidedly improved and the sea gone down.

Meridianal, variant of Meridional.

1900 *Geog. Jrnl.* XV. 540 The great meridianal systems, *e.g.* the Urals and the Rocky mountains.

Merino. Add: **2.** (Earlier example.)

1820 S. Breck in *Recoll.* (1877) App. iv. 298 She has gone on..bedecking herself in merino shawls.

b. Also, a merino shawl.

1845 M. M. Noah *Gleanings* 16 Thin kid shoes and gloves [are worn by the lady of fashion]; a fine merino over her arm.

4. A variety of potato.

1853 *Trans. Mich. Agric. Soc.* V. 208 A great many varieties of potato are cultivated in Europe and America Some of the more approved kinds are..the Merino [etc.]. 1887 Tourgee *Button's Inn* 178 He picked up the potatoes,—delicate white 'Kidneys',..and coarse red 'Merinoes'.

Meristele (meristī·lī). *Bot.* [f. Gr. μέρος part + στήλη pillar: see Stele.] (See quot.) Hence **Meriste·lic** *a.*

1900 B. D. Jackson *Gloss. Bot. Terms, Meristele*.., a portion of the stele of a monostelic stem received by each leaf. 1902 Tansley in *Encycl. Brit.* XXV. 414/2 Fig. 8.—Meristelic arc of collateral bundles, united by conjunctive.

Meritable, *a.* Delete ? *Obs.* and add recent example.

1927 *Observer* 20 Feb. 13/1, I should still have some meritable pieces left over in case the visitor wished to go to a few matinées.

Meront (me·rǫnt). *Zool.* [f. Mero-¹ + Gr. ὀντ- stem of ὤν pr. pple. of εἶναι to be.] A dividing form in Neosporidia.

1924 Fantham & Porter *Some minute Anim. Parasites* 219 The body protoplasm divides also, and two daughter forms are produced. These dividing forms are known as meronts and schizonts. There are several variations in the ways by which daughter meronts are produced. 1926 *Nature* 2 Mar. 8/1 A minute amoeboid germ or amoebula..emerges from the spore. It..penetrates in or between cells. There ..it commences to multiply, and is termed a meront.

Merozoite (merǫzō^u·ait). *Zool.* [f. Mero-¹ + Gr. ζω-ή life + -ite.] In sporozoans, a spore produced by the process of schizogony.

1901 *Pop. Sci. Monthly* June 192 (Cent. Suppl.) When fully developed, the spores, or as they are technically known, the merozoites, drop off the parent cell and work their way through the fluids of the digestive tract. 1914 Fantham & Porter *Some minute Anim. Parasites* 97 The organism, after attaining its full growth, begins to divide, and rosettes of smaller parasites—the merozoites—are formed.

Mes-, now often used before a vowel for Meso-, as **Me·sarch** *a. Bot.* [Gr. ἀρχή beginning] (see quot. 1900). **Mesaxo·nic** *a. Zool.* [Gr. ἄξων, ἄξον- axis + -ic], having the axis in the centre.

1900 B. D. Jackson *Gloss. Bot. Terms*, *Mesarch,..applied by Solms-Laubach to those bundles in which the protoxylem lies in the interior of the primary strand of the wood. 1902 Tansley in *Encycl. Brit.* XXV. 414/2 Fig. 4.—Typical siphonostele (represented as mesarch) with internal phloem. 1898 A. S. Woodward *Outl. Vertebr. Palæontology* 319 They [Perissodactyla] are all digitigrade quadrupeds, with the axis of both feet passing through the digit No. iii (hence *mesaxonic).

Mesatipellic (mesăti₁pe·lik), *a.* *Anthrop.* [f. Gr. μέσ(σ)ατος midmost (superl. of μέσος middle) + πέλλα a wooden bowl (taken in sense PELVIS) + -IC.] Characterized by an index of the pelvic brim between 90 and 95.

1886 W. TURNER *Rep. Crania* II. (Challenger Rep. XVI.) 40 In the males the same index was at or about 91, so that they were mesatipellic. 1900 *Jrnl. Anthrop. Inst.* 149 Turner is inclined to place Melanesians in the mesatipellic group. 1923 *Proc. Soc. Antiq. Scot.* (1924) LVIII. 34 An index of 93·22 is mesatipellic, and considerably higher than that of the average European male.

Mescal. Add: **3.** The mescal-plant, or the baked head of this.

1831 J. O. PATTIE *Personal Narr.* 63, I afterwards ascertained that it was a vegetable called by the Spanish mascal, (probably maguey). 1873 J. H. BEADLE *Undevel. West* xxviii. 614 He gave me in return..a large roll of *mescal*. 1878 — *Western Wilds* xviii. 288 *Mescal*, also one of their luxuries looks when dried like a mass of soft sole-leather, and tastes much like sugar-cane. 1881 *Amer. Naturalist* XV. 875 The 'mescal' of the Arizona Apaches, that is, the baked head of the *Agave palmeri* and *Agave parryi*. 1891 *Century Mag.* Mar. 653 Along deserts bristling with spines of the cactus, spanish bayonet, mescal and palo verde.

4. *Mescal buttons, heads*, the dried tops of a small cactus (*Lophophora Williamsii*) of Texas and northern Mexico, having intoxicating or narcotic properties.

1885 *Outing* Oct. VII. 24/2 The old and young squaws had cut and dried large packages of 'jerked' beef, and had brought down from the hillsides donkey-loads of mescal heads. 1895 D. W. PRENTISS & MORGAN (*title*) Anhalonium Lewinii (mescal buttons); a study of the drug, with especial reference to its physiological action upon man.

Mescalism (meskæ·liz'm). [f. MESCAL + -ISM.] The practice of taking mescal.

1902 *Amer. Anthropologist* Oct.-Dec. 789/1 Through mescalism one seems almost to 'attain an objective knowledge of one's own personality'.

Mesenchyma. (Earlier example of **Mesenchyme.**)

1884 HYATT in *Proc. Boston Soc. Nat. Hist.* XXIII. 138 The characteristics of the middle layer are so exceedingly primitive that we have called it mesenchyme.

Mesh, *sb.* Add: **3. a.** (Example.)

1901 *U.S. Dept. Agric., Bur. Plant Industry*, Bull. 3. 10 The spikelets (meshes) are two to four grained.

4. b. *In mesh*: Of toothed gearwheels, engaged with each other; also *into mesh*.

1904 A. B. F. YOUNG *Compl. Motorist* 78 When the top gear is engaged, none of the other gears are in mesh, although they rotate. 1905 SLOSS *Bk. Automobile* 207 The gears must be thrown into mesh sharply or not at all. 1907 C. WHEELER *Bicycles in Making* 78 When it [the fulcrum pinion] is in mesh with the hub it locks the pinion wheels. 1912 *Motor Man.* (ed. 14) 75 Thus it is possible to slide different pairs of gearwheels into 'mesh'.

6. *mesh-bag*; **mesh-connection,** a method of arranging the coils in a dynamo (see quot.); so **mesh-connected** *a.*

1920 *Edin. Rev.* Oct. 349 The *mesh-bag in which the Mexican hunters carried their arrow heads. 1902 *Encycl. Brit.* XXVII. 592/1 If the four coils are joined up into a continuous helix,..four wires may be attached to equidistant points...Such a method is known as the **mesh connexion*, and gives a perfectly symmetrical four-phase system of distribution. 1904 R. M. WALMSLEY *Electr. Service of Man* 531 Fig. 519. *Mesh-connected Generator.

Mesh, *v.* **3. b.** (Later examples.) Also, to become engaged with another toothed wheel or part of a mechanism, or, of two wheels or parts, to engage with one another. Cf. MASH *v.*[4]

1907 C. WHEELER *Bicycles in Making* 78 Small pinion wheels..also mesh with what is called a fulcrum pinion... The fulcrum pinion is also provided with teeth by which it can mesh and become part of the hub. 1912 *Motor Man.* (ed. 14) 165 Occasionally the gearwheels will not mesh. 1913 R. KENNEDY *Bk. Motor Car* II. 194 Then..gear wheels which are revolving have to mesh with gear wheels which are stationary.

Meshing, *vbl. sb.* Add to def.: A meshed structure; mesh-work.

1907 *Daily Chron.* 25 Sept. 8/4 Splash I go the dredges, small scoops of steel meshing. 1926 *Brit. Weekly* 26 Aug. 430/2, I had a copper frame constructed with a panel of copper meshing to which the letters were fixed.

Mesmerize, *v.* Add: **d.** With *const.*

1916 BENNETT *Lion's Share* x. 76, 'I can't express to you,' he said, moving towards the dais and mesmerising her to keep by his side, 'I can't express to you' [etc.].

Meso-. **Mesodesm** (add) 'a layer of undifferentiated parenchyma' separating the phloem and the xylem in the tissues of certain plants. **Mesognathy, Mesotarsal** *a.* (examples). **Mesothorium** [THORIUM], an isotope of radium.

1902 *Encycl. Brit.* XXV. 414/2 Fig. 7...Xylem and phloem separated by *mesodesm. 1904 *Biometrika* Mar.–July 214 Profile Angle. *Mesognathy. 1897 T. J. PARKER & HASWELL *Zool.* II. 366 The ankle-joint of the bird is a *meso-tarsal joint. 1907 *Mesothorium [see THORIUM]. 1922 F. W. ASTON *Isotopes* 8 Mesothorium, discovered by Hahn in 1907, was shown to be chemically inseparable from radium by Marckwald and Soddy.

Mesocephal (mesose·făl). [f. pl. MESOCEPHALI.] One who has a mesocephalic skull.

1900 DENIKER *Races of Man* 316 In Sweden and Denmark they were dolichocephals or mesocephals.

Meson[2]. [Sp. *mesón* an inn.] A type of inn in Mexico (see quot. 1894).

1826 T. FLINT *F. Berrian* (1834) I. 129 In occasional stops at the *haciendas* and *mesons* the time passed rapidly. 1847 RUXTON *Adv. Mexico* viii. 52 The meson was better than usual, being the stopping-place of the diligencia to Fresnillo. 1894 MARY J. JACQUES *Texan Ranch Life* 274 At last some one suggested that I wanted a 'meson', a yard with locked-up rooms round its sides, in which Mexicans often board.

Mesorrhiny (me·sŏrəini). *Anthropology.* [f. MESORRHINE + -Y.] The state or quality of being mesorrhine.

1904 *Biometrika* Mar.–July 214 Nasal Index. Mesorrhiny.

Mesostatic (mesostæ·tik), *a.* *Bot.* [f. Gr. μέσο-ς middle + στατικ-ός: see STATIC.] (See quot.)

1905 F. E. CLEMENTS *Research Methods Ecology* Gloss. 319 Mesostatic.., completing the succession under mesophytic conditions.

Mesothermic (mesoþə̄·ɹmik), *a.* *Bot.* [f. MESOTHERM + -IC.] Composed of or containing mesotherms.

1903 W. R. FISHER tr. *A. F. W. Schimper's Plant-Geog.* 236 The most important family of the north temperate zone among the *Polycarpicae*, that of the Ranunculaceæ, is mesothermic and microthermic.

Mesquite, mesquit.[2] Add to forms: **masketo, moscheto, musqueto, mus-, mesquito; musquet, -quit, -kit; muskeete.**

1. (Earlier and later examples.)

1805 LEWIS in *Ann. Congress* 1806–7 (1852) 1083/1 A bean that grows in great plenty on a small tree resembling a willow called masketo. 1838 'TEXIAN' *Mexico v. Texas* 70 Even where a tree appears it is sure to be a mesquite (*Mimosa nilotica*). 1838 C. NEWELL *Hist. Revolution Texas* 147 Live oak,..black walnut, cypress, and musquit prevail. 1881 *Amer. Naturalist* XV. 979 The commonest plant of all the country about Tucson is known locally as the mesquite. 1898 H. S. CANFIELD *Maid of Frontier* 136 It made one abrupt curve around the end of an immense mesquite which had fallen near its edge. *a* 1909 'O. HENRY' *Roads of Destiny* viii. 129 Near the store, scattered among the mesquite and elms, stood the saddled horses of the customers.

b. A thicket of mesquite trees.

1834 A. PIKE *Sketches* 63 We emerged from the broken hills into the mesquito. 1910 W. M. RAINE *B. O'Connor* 224 The Irishman..kept his party in the mesquit till the headlight of an approaching train was visible.

2. (Earlier examples.)

1831 MRS. HOLLEY *Texas Lett.* (1833) vi. 69 The pasturage here...called Muskit grass, (pronounced Muskeet) bears a strong resemblance to the blue grass. 1836 — *Texas* ii. 30 It..affords pasturage of the finest kind, abounding in the nopal and musquit grass. 1844 G. W. KENDALL *Santa Fé Exped.* I. 161 We..were finally fortunate enough to reach a high piece of table-land where the *mesquit* grass was fresh. 1849 *Rep. U. S. Comm. Patents Agric.* (1850) 157, I have said nothing of a grass..'the Muskeete' or more properly 'Mesquit' grass.

3. (Earlier examples.) Also, *mesquite brush, chaparral, grove, pasture, pitch, prairie, root, thicket, timber, twig, valley*.

1805 LEWIS in *Ann. Congress* 1806–7 (1852) 1103/1 Some small cultivated fields, fenced round with small cedar and *moscheto brush. 1834 A. PIKE *Sketches* 56 The valley was..full of small hills interspersed with *mezquito bushes. 1854 BARTLETT *Pers. Narr. Explor. Texas* I. 134 [The grass] grew in tufts about the roots of the *mezquit chapporal. 1867 A. D. RICHARDSON *Beyond Mississippi* xix. 226 Another waiting coach was soon rolling us forward among *mesquite groves. 1885 *Outing* Oct. VII. 24/2 Basket-work, rendered fully waterproof by a coating of either *mesquite or pinon pitch. 1905 A. ADAMS *Outlet* 16 The horses had run idle during the winter in a large *mesquit pasture. 1857 D. BRAMAN *Inform. Texas* i. 22 Good and cheap lands, with plenty of *mesquit prairie for stock range. 1889 *Harper's Mag.* Dec. 119/2 A handful of gnarled and knotted *mesquite roots blazed in the wide fireplace. 1845 T. J. GREEN *Texian Exped.* iv. 32 Dawson selected his position in a *musquit thicket favourable for his rifle shooting. 1903 A. ADAMS *Log Cowboy* iv. 26 Suddenly in the dark we encountered a mesquite thicket into which the lead cattle tore. 1847 A. WISLIZENUS *Tour N. Mexico* (1848) 69 (Stanf.) Our road went mostly through fine *mesquite timber. 1857 D. BRAMAN *Inform. Texas* i. 23 On the prairies are much live oak and mesquit timber. 1831 J. O. PATTIE *Pers. Narr.* 59 We found the river skirted with very wide bottoms, thick set with the *musquito trees. 1910 JEN. HART *Vigilante Girl* xxv. 347 A bunch of dried *mesquite twigs. 1844 G. W. KENDALL *Santa Fé Exped.* II. iv. 108 We encamped..in a little *mesquit valley. 1831 J. O. PATTIE *Pers. Narr.* 83 There is here little timber, beside *musqueto wood, which stands thick. 1846 QUITMAN *Diary* in *Life & Corr.* 239 The steamer purchases musketwood at $2.50 per cord for dry, $2.25 green.

Mess, *sb.* **1. c.** (Earlier and later U.S. examples.)

1697 S. SEWALL *Diary* I. 455 Betty gets her Mother a Mess of English Beans. 1775 B. ROMANS *Florida* 12 (Th.) He told me that his mother had an inclination to eat fish, and he was come to get her a mess. 1842 *Knickerbocker Mag.* XIX. 557 Sally couldn't hardly bring in the pail, she gave such a mess. 1861 O. W. NORTON *Army Lett.* 26 H. and I got enough [potatoes] for a mess, and some parsnips. 1872 *Rep. Vermont Board Agric.* I. 197, I tested their milk by weighing every mess for a month. 1877 *Ibid.* IV. 54 We took off what cream arose on the night's mess, and churned it. 1883 J. C. HARRIS *Nights with Uncle Remus* iii. 30 Brer Rabbit, he hop in, he did, en got 'im a mess er greens, en hop out ag'in.

e. *U.S.* A quantity or number *of* something.

1830 *Massachusetts Spy* 23 June (Th.) We saw yesterday a large mess of early potatoes. 1833 C. A. DAVIS *Lett. J. Downing* (1834) 40 With that, he out with his wallet, and unrolled a mess on 'em. 1854 *Knickerbocker Mag.* XLI. 502 There was wolves in the Holler—an unaccountable mess of 'em. 1872 *Rep. Vermont Board Agric.* I. 634 They will dress a mess of ore to any required per cent.

7. *mess-bag, -basket, -chest* (earlier example), *-cloth, -fire, -man, -pan, -pork* (earlier examples), *pot, table* (earlier and later examples).

1885 *Outing* Oct. VII. 55/1 From some dark corner of the *messbags, or petacas, he unearthed a handful of dried apples. 1839 *Knickerbocker Mag.* XIII. 211 Tell Margaret to prepare the *mess-basket. 1858 VIELE *Following Drum* 15 A camp-kettle, *mess chest, bundle of canvas, and set of tent poles. 1839 C. F. BRIGGS *Harry Franco* I. xxiii. 250 Throwing down my knife..I leaped on to the *messcloth, and gave him a blow in the eye. 1837 W. IRVING *Capt. Bonneville* (1895) I. 24 The various *mess-fires were surrounded by picturesque groups. 1850 GARRARD *Wah-To-Yah* (1927) xii. 162 He..walked to a messfire. 1850 *Punch* 20 July 33/1 *Messman wanted for a Cavalry Regiment. 1920 *Chambers's Jrnl.* May 285/2 Understanding the messman to have come off from the Colon with plenty of oysters. 1813 *Niles' Weekly Reg.* III. 295/2 [List of Military Supplies] *Mess pans. 1846 SAGE *Scenes Rocky Mts.* (1859) 279 A large mess-pan, and a tin-cup and plate for each of its number. 1861 O. W. NORTON *Army Lett.* 35 New knapsacks, canteens..mess pans and a complete outfit. 1832 *Louisville Publ. Adv.* 10 Mar., *Mess and Prime Pork in barrels and half barrels, for sale. 1847 *Rep. U.S. Comm. Patents* (1848) 527 The finest and fattest [hogs] making clear and mess pork. 1857 R. GLISAN *Jrnl. Army Life* (1874) viii. 86, I shall be able to say good bye to the *messpots of Uncle Sam. 1819 QUITMAN *Diary* in *Life & Corr.* 42 Mrs. and Miss Griffith, charmed with our *mess-table, became our boarders. 1895 M. A. JACKSON *Memoirs* xi. 19, I took my meals with him and the staff at their mess table.

Message, *sb.*[1] **4. message stick,** also used in Norway.

1860 *Leisure Hour* 3 May 287/1 To this day the people in Norway are called together for the despatch of public business, in a somewhat similar manner. A bud-stick, or message-stick..is painted and stamped with the royal arms.

Messeigneurs, pl. of MONSEIGNEUR.

Messenger. 7. Add: **messenger cable, wire,** one used to support a power cable or other conductor of electricity; a suspension cable or wire.

1898 E. J. HOUSTON *Dict. Electr. Words*. 1916 *Stand. Rules Amer. Inst. Electr. Engineers* § 778 A messenger wire or cable is a wire or cable running along with and supporting other wires, cables or contact conductors.

Messor. b. *attrib.* **messor ant,** a widely distributed genus of Harvesting Ants.

1924 J. A. THOMSON *Science Old & New* xii. 68 In the case of the Messor ants of the Sahara there are deep and spacious underground galleries, in which food is accumulated for the dry season.

Mess-up, *sb. colloq.* [f. MESS *v.* 5.] = MESS *sb.* 3.

1929 *Star* 21 Aug. 12/3, I am afraid there has been a bit of a mess-up.

Mestang, variant of MUSTANG.

1837 W. IRVING *Capt. Bonneville* xix. II. 28 She was mounted on a mestang or half wild horse, which she managed with a long rope hitched round the under jaw by way of bridle.

Mestizo. b. Add: *mestizo-town.*

1887 L. OLIPHANT *Episodes* (ed. 4) vi. 118 There was absolutely nothing to see in the sleepy little *mestizo* town.

Meta-. I. Add: **Metabiolo·gical** *a.*, that is above or beyond the scope of biology.

1921 G. B. SHAW (*title*) Back to Methuselah. A metabiological Pentateuch.

Metabiosis (metăbəiōu·sis). *Biol.* [mod.L. f. Gr. μετα- META- + βίωσις mode of life, cf. μεταβιοῦν to live after.] The association or relationship that exists between two different organisms when the one can only exist after the other has by its presence prepared a medium for it. So **Metabio·tic** *a.*, relating to, based on or involving metabiosis.

1899 *Knowledge* July 151/2 It [the yeast organism] is dependent upon its predecessor for its particular action—that is to say, we have here a condition of metabiosis. *Ibid.* 152/1 This implies nothing more or less than metabiotic relationships between the different kinds of the bacteria concerned.

Metabolizable (metæ·bŏləizăb'l), *a.* [f. METABOLIZE *v.* + -ABLE.] Capable of being metabolized.

1905 *U. S. Dept. Agric., Animal Ind.* Bull. 74. 7 The metabolizable, available and utilizable energy of the hay.

Metabolon (metæ·bŏlǫn). [ad. Gr. μεταβόλον neut. of μεταβόλος changeable, f. μεταβάλλειν to change.] A radioactive atom produced in the process of radioactive disintegration.

1903 RUTHERFORD & SODDY in *Phil. Mag.* V. 586 It seems advisable to possess a special name for these..atom fragments...We would therefore suggest the term *metabolon* for this purpose. 1904 E. RUTHERFORD *Radio-activity* x. 324 The various metabolons from the radio-elements are distinguished from ordinary matter by their great instability and consequently rapid rate of change.

Metacentral, *a.* Add: **2.** *Biol.* Characterized by a metacentre, or new centre of modification.

1901 P. CHALMERS MITCHELL in *Trans. Linn. Soc., Zool.* VIII. 229 What I term a metacentral condition underlies the conformation of the alimentary tract in the Gruiform assemblage.

Metacentric, *a.* Add: **2.** *Biol.* Derived from or related to a metacentre.

1901 P. CHALMERS MITCHELL in *Trans. Linn. Soc., Zool.* VIII. 213 The Grebes are more apocentric modifications of this metacentric type.

Metagenesis. 1. For 'generation' read 'generations' in both cases.

Metageo·metrician. [f. METAGEOMETRY.] = Metageometer.

1903 *Science* 16 Jan. 106/2 Our metageometricians tried to derive the basic geometrical principles from pure reason but failed.

Metal, *sb.* Add: **11.** (Earlier examples.)

1815 TELFORD in *Life* (1838) App. 474 Over the upper bed or course of metal there is to be binding of gravel. *Ibid.* 483 The metal to be of the best blue or red whin. 1825 *Congress Deb.* 21 Nov. App. 20/1 Nearly the whole extent of road..has been cleared..for receiving the first course of metal, as it is called, meaning the stone broken to a small size, agreeably to the McAdam plan.

13. c. *metal-bushed, -studded.*

1883 *Man. Seamanship Boys* 14 *Spindle* passes through a *metal bushed hole in the partners, up through the centre of the barrel. 1909 *Q. Rev.* Jan. 148 Motor-cars,..having armoured or *metal-studded tires damage the surface.

14. metal age, *Archæol.*, the period or stage of development of the human race in which copper and bronze were used for making weapons and tools; **metal-to-metal** *a.*, applied to a contact or connexion; **metal-works,** a factory where metal is produced.

1927 PEAKE & FLEURE *Hunters & Artists* 112 The dawn of the *Metal Age. 1910 *Daily Chron.* 2 Feb. 5/1 The surface where the wheel had been on the axle showing a bright *metal-to-metal contact. 1922 *Encycl. Brit.* XXX. 36/2 The head of steel being secured to the liner with a plain metal-to-metal joint by bolts from the head to the crank-case. 1908 *Westm. Gaz.* 3 Oct. 10/1 On the hours of work in foundries and *metal-works generally the Committee felt itself still imperfectly informed.

Metallic. A. *adj.* **3. c.** Add: Also of the taste of tea made in a metal tea-pot.

1909 *Chambers's Jrnl.* Nov. 693/1 The objection to metal is simply that there is a danger of giving the tea what is known as a 'metallic' taste.

Metallize, *v.* Add: **1. b.** To coat or cover the surface of (something) with metal.

1929 *Daily News* 16 Jan., Doors, window sashes, wainscotings, panel boards and panelling can be artistically metalized with one metal or another.

Hence also **Me·tallizing** *vbl. sb.*, the process of making metallic.

1911 *Chambers's Jrnl.* Jan. 76/1 By means of a secret process..fruit, flowers, insects..can be converted into metal without any depreciation of the natural beauty. 'Metalliʒing' it is called. *Ibid.* 77/1 The metallising factory is now in full swing.

Metallogeny (metălǫ·dʒĕni). *Geol.* [f. METALLO- + -GENY.] The origin or formation of metallic deposits.

1905 *Nature* 13 Apr. 576/1 On the possible *rôle* of slipping in metallogeny.

Metally, *a.* **1.** (Modern poetic example.)

1887 MEREDITH *Reading of Earth* Poems (1904) II. 202, I can hear a faint crow Of the cock..As down the new shafting of mines, A cry of the metally gnome.

Metamorphic, *a.* Add: **2. b.** as *sb.* A metamorphic rock.

1881 W. KING & ROWNEY *Old Chapter Geol. Rec.* 49 The rocks of the locality are well-bedded metamorphics.

Metamorphose, *v.* Add: **1. b.** *intr.* with *into.*

1927 HALDANE & HUXLEY *Animal Biol.* ix. 180 For example, when the tadpole metamorphoses into the frog, some of its tissues start to dedifferentiate.

Metaphorize, *v.* **b.** (Recent example.)

1909 *N. Y. Even. Post* 27 Nov. 5 However agitated or depressed they may be, they must go on metaphorising.

Metapsychic (metăsəi·kik), *a.* [ad. F. *métapsychique*; cf. *METAPSYCHICS.] = *METAPSYCHICAL.

1905 *Westm. Gaz.* 25 Feb. 10/3 The new President [M. Richet]..suggested the term 'metapsychic sciences' as a substitute for 'modern miracle'. 1923 S. DE BRATH tr. *Richet's Thirty Yrs. Psychical Research* 4 The terms 'supernatural' and 'supernormal' must therefore be rejected along with 'the occult'...I proposed the term Metapsychic which has been unanimously accepted.

Metapsychical (metăsəi·kikăl), *a.* *Psychol.* [f. META- + PSYCHICAL: after METAPHYSICAL.] That is beyond the sphere of ordinary psychology; pertaining to *METAPSYCHICS.

1905 L. I. FINCH (*title*) J. Maxwell's Metapsychical phenomena translated. 1914 T. DE MATTOS tr. *Maeterlinck's Unknown Guest* 50 Nevertheless it may be said that these regions quite lately annexed by metapsychical science are as yet hardly explored.

Metapsychics (metăsəi·kiks), *sb. pl.* [After METAPHYSICS: ad. F. *métapsychique* (see quot. 1905); cf. Polish *metapsychika* (1902 Wykłady Jagiellonski).] A name applied to a science or study of certain phenomena which are 'beyond the scheme of orthodox psychology'.

1905 SIR O. LODGE in *J. Maxwell's Metapsychical Phenomena* Introd. p. xi, To emphasise the fact that these occurrences are at present beyond the scheme of orthodox psychology..Professor Richet has suggested that they be styled 'meta-psychical phenomena', and that the nascent branch of science..be called for the present 'Metapsychics'. 1922 B. MIALL tr. *Maeterlinck's Gt. Secret* 249 The recent researches of Dr. W. Crawford which have made a sensation in the world of metapsychics.

Hence **Metapsy·chism. Metapsy·chist,** a student of metapsychics.

1922 *Glasgow Herald* 27 Oct. 4 Modern spiritualism, under the term Metapsychism, is favourably viewed, because it is more of an inquiry into the things of the spirit. 1922 B. MIALL tr. *Maeterlinck's Gt. Secret* xi. 216 Our occultists, who are now assuming the name of metapsychists. 1928 *Daily Express* 27 June 6/4 What a palpitating problem for the psychologists and the metapsychists!

Metapsychological (me·tăsəikolǫ·dʒikăl), *a.* [f. next.] Of or pertaining to metapsychology.

1922 J. STRACHEY tr. *Freud's Group Psychol.* 63 It is much more difficult to give a clear metapsychological representation of the distinction. 1924 W. B. SELBIE *Psychol. Relig.* 295 These questions..cannot be settled on psychological or even on metapsychological grounds.

Metapsychology (me·tăsəikǫ·lŏdʒi). [f. META- 1 + PSYCHOLOGY.] A name given to speculative inquiry regarding the ultimate nature of the mind and its functions which cannot be studied experimentally.

1909 *Century Dict.* Suppl. 1914 BRILL tr. *Freud's Psychopathology of Everyday Life* 309 We venture to explain in this way the myths of paradise and the fall of man, of God, of good and evil, of immortality and the like—that is, to transform *metaphysics* into *meta-psychology*. 1922 J. STRACHEY tr. *Freud's Group Psychol.* 118 There is some difficulty in giving a representation of such a diversion of aim which will conform to the requirements of metapsychology.

Metastability (metăstæbi·lĭti). [f. as next + STABILITY.] Metastable state or quality.

1928 A. S. EDDINGTON *Stars & Atoms* App. B. 130 The strong solar radiation excites the atoms many thousands of times per second, so that they are quickly released from metastability by upward passages.

Metastable (me·tăstĕb'l), *a.* [irreg. f. Gr. μετα- META- + STABLE *a.*] An epithet applied to a state of unstable equilibrium in liquids, gases, atoms, etc., in which change to a more stable form does not take place spontaneously.

1899 J. WALKER *Introd. Phys. Chem.* xi. 101 A super-cooled liquid may be kept for a very long time without any solid appearing, but as soon as the smallest particle of the substance in the more stable solid phase is introduced, the less stable, or, as it has been called, the metastable phase is transformed into it. 1902 A. FINDLAY tr. *Ostwald's Princ. Inorganic Chem.* 117 The region of supercooling nearest to the melting point is therefore designated as *metastable*, and only the more remote regions, in which solidification takes place spontaneously, are called unstable. 1922 A. SMITS *Theory Allotropy* i. 9 The liquid phase in the pseudo-binary system will also become metastable. 1927 N. V. SIDGWICK *Electronic Theory of Valency* 27 There is also another (metastable) arrangement possible with helium.

Metastasize (metæ·stăsəiz), *v.* *Path.* [f. METASTASIS + -IZE.] *intr.* Of a pain, disease, etc.: To pass from one part or organ to another; to undergo metastasis.

1907 *Jrnl. Med. Research* Nov. 187 (Cent. Suppl.) As might be expected the tendency to metastasize is much greater in certain tumors than in others.

Metate. (Add examples.)

1844 G. W. KENDALL *Santa Fé Exped.* II. vii. 150 They first soak the grain in water..then grind it on a large block of stone, the metate. 1854 BARTLETT *Pers. Narr. Explor. Texas* I. 190 A metate stone on which to grind their corn and wheat. 1886 *Outing* Dec. IX. 224/1 A *metate* is a rude stone mortar, still used by the Mexicans to grind and crush corn, chile, coffee, etc.

Metatrophic (metătrǫ·fik), *a.* *Bot.* and *Biol.* [f. Gr. μετα- META- + τροφικός TROPHIC.] Deriving its nourishment from previously existing or decaying organic matter.

1902 *Encycl. Brit.* XXV. 439/1 On the other hand some Angiosperms are persistently heterotrophic, either as *saprophytes* (metatrophic) or as *parasites* (paratrophic), and this manner of life involves some kind of *symbiosis*. 1923 F. O. BOWER *Bot. Living Plant* 430 On the basis of nutrition Bacteria have been classified into three groups:..(ii) *Metatrophic*, those which cannot live unless they have organic substances at their disposal.

Metempsychosic (metempsikǭu·sik), *a.* [f. METEMPSYCHOS(IS + -IC.] Relating to metempsychosis.

1906 W. J. LOCKE *Morals of M. Ordeyne* xviii. 182, I have bemused myself with gnostic and metempsychosic speculations.

Metencephalic, *a.* Add quot.

1899 *Proc. Zool. Soc.* 1024 The metencephalic fossa of the Pygopodes.

Meteorette (mī·tĭǫret). [-ETTE.] A small meteor.

1876 *Gentl. Mag.* XVI. 552 Specks flitting like meteorettes over the crests of the billows.

Meteorically, *adv.* Add: **b.** With the suddenness of a meteor.

1915 A. S. NEILL *Dominie's Log* xiv, She dons the bridal white, and at once she rises meteorically in the social scale.

Meteori·tically, *adv.* [f. METEORITIC *a.*] After the manner of a meteorite.

1919 MAX BEERBOHM *Seven Men* 5 At the end of Term he settled in—or rather, meteoritically into—London.

Meteorogram (mī·tĭǫrǫgræm). [f. Gr. μετεωρο- METEOR + -GRAM.] The record of meteorological phenomena furnished by a meteorograph; (see also quot. 1923).

1904 *U. S. Monthly Weather Rec.* Mar. 121 (Cent. Suppl.) (1) Instrumental errors, (2) errors in exposure of instruments when comparing with standards, (3) errors in reading from meteorograms, etc. 1923 SIR W. N. SHAW *Forecasting Weather* v. 144 The trace given by a barometer is called a 'barogram', that by a thermometer a 'thermogram', while a trace of either the direction or force of wind is called an 'anemogram'. When two or more of these traces are all combined in one picture..the whole is called a 'meteorogram'.

Meter, *sb.*[3] Add: **1. d.** (In full *exposure meter.*) An apparatus for showing the proper length of photographic exposures in any given light.

1892 *Chemist & Druggist* XL. 670/2 That admirable piece of apparatus, the 'exposure meter'. 1902 *Encycl. Brit.* XXXI. 702/1 Based upon the same principle as these exposure tables, various portable exposure meters have been brought out. 1920 *Sat. Westm. Gaz.* 22 May 16/2 The golden rule is to expose by meter on the holiday, and leave all else to the return home.

Metheglin. (Later Amer. examples.)

1789 MORSE *Amer. Geog.* 197 The perry..is an agreeable liquor, having something of the harshness of claret wine, joined with the sweetness of metheglin. 1826 J. F. COOPER *Prairie* ix, If I had but a cup of metheglin..I should swear this was the strongest meal that was ever placed before the mouth of man. 1839 J. K. TOWNSEND *Narr. Rocky Mts.* v. 203 Among the rest, was some *metheglen* or diluted alcohol sweetened with honey. 1855 'SAM SLICK' *Human Nat.* II. ix. 267 All the friends of the new married couple..did nothing for a whole month, but smoke, drink metheglin, [etc.].

Method, *sb.* **10.** Add: *method-master*.

1923 P. B. BALLARD *New Examiner* viii. 100 Are we to be scared by the maxim of a Victorian method-master?

Methodism. 3. The doctrines and practice of the methodic school of physicians.

1896 SIR T. C. ALLBUTT in *Class. Rev.* X. 346/2 A second school was Methodism, which was satisfied to refer all symptoms and all disease to the variations of the 'strictum' and the 'laxum'; that is, to the restriction or laxity of the secretions and other fluids of the body.

Methodize, *v.* Add: **1. c.** To convert into Methodists.

1846 A. WILEY in *Indiana Mag. Hist.* XXIII. 428 Some disciples who are hard cases, who will be hard to methodize.

Metic. (Add fig. example.)

1921 *Times Lit. Suppl.* 10 Nov. 731/2 The proportion of the horrific in Poe's poetry..is entirely different; he is a metic in the land of shadows.

Meti·culousness. [-NESS.] The quality of being meticulous; meticulosity.

1923 *Sunday at Home* Mar. 382/2 He was measured and cautious in his statements to the point of meticulousness. 1927 *Daily Tel.* 2 Mar. 5/5 Examples..handed down to posterity in paint with a meticulousness that..never fails to charm us.

Metoposcopy. 2. (Modern example.)

c 1886 L. HEARN in G. M. Gould *Concerning L. Hearn* (1908) 87 'Are you not a Greek?' I asked, for there was no mistaking the metoposcopy of that head. Yes; he was from Zante.

Metovum. Substitute for def.: An ovum in its second stage, e. g. a meroblastic ovum after formation of the food-yolk; also called *deutovum* (DEUTO- 2).

Metric, *a.*[2] Add: *metric ton*, the weight of a cubic metre of water.

1924 *Times Trade & Eng. Suppl.* 29 Nov. 238/3 The output of certain important goods has considerably increased:..sugar to 318,987 metric tons, against 270,279.

Me·tricaliza·tion. [-IZATION.] A making metrical in character.

1924 *Glasgow Herald* 13 Nov. 10 The question of the metricalisation of our coinage.

Metrically, *adv.*[2] [f. METRICAL *a.*[2]] With regard to measurement; in metrical terms.

1920 *Glasgow Herald* 14 June 11 The theory of Einstein..had been shown to contain not merely descriptively but exactly and metrically the rate of progression of the perihelion of Mercury.

Metriocephalic (metriosĭfæ·lik), *a.* [f. Gr. μέτριος moderate + κεφαλικός belonging to the head; cf. CEPHALIC *a.*] Having a cephalic index between 72 and 77; applied to a class of skulls which are considered neither DOLICHOCEPHALIC nor BRACHYCEPHALIC.

1884 W. TURNER *Rep. Crania* I. (Challenger Rep. X) 60 The mean of the whole series and of the males was metriocephalic. 1901 *Amer. Anthropologist* Jan.–Mar. 40.

Metrocyte (mī·trŏsəit). *Physiol.* [f. Gr. μητρ-, μήτηρ mother + -CYTE.] A special type of large cell regarded as a mother-cell of the red blood corpuscles.

1908 *Practitioner* Aug. 324 Very important is a cell known as Engel's metrocyte; this is a megaloblast in which the nucleus occupies four-fifths of the cell and is reticular, while the surrounding protoplasm shows polychromatophil degeneration.

Me·tronomiza·tion. [f. METRONOME + -IZATION.] The determining or indicating of the rate at which music should be played.

1923 A. BETTI in *Music & Lett.* Jan. 3 Can the metronomisation of a piece be absolutely exact?

Metronym (mī·trŏnim). [f. Gr. μητρ-, μήτηρ mother + ὄνυμα; or back-formation from METRONYMIC.] A metronymic name.

1904 *Nature* 5 May Suppl. p. xiii/2 The acceptance of metronyms in the genealogies as proofs of female kinship, while patronyms are rejected.

Metronymic. a. *adj.* Add to def.: Also applied to a people or state of society where such a system of naming prevails.

1896 GIDDINGS *Princ. Sociol.* 158 In a metronymic group all relationships are traced through mothers; paternal relationships are ignored. 1903 L. F. WARD *Pure Sociol.* 339 The metronymic family.

Metroscope[2]. (Earlier example.)

1845 in C. Cist *Cincinnati Misc.* 270 A very ingenious instrument, called a Metroscope, which has been lately invented for the purpose of taking the measure of the human head so as to furnish an exact fit of hats.

Metrostyle (me·trŏstəil). [f. Gr. μέτρον measure + STYLE.] A device for regulating the speed of a mechanical piano.

1907 *World* 16 July 140/2 The Model 'K' is a Pianola equipped with the Metrostyle. 1909 H. G. WELLS *Tono-Bungay* I. ii. § 8. 76 There was a different grand piano with a painted lid and a metrostyle pianola.

Hence **Me·trostyle** *v. trans.* and *intr.* To regulate the speed of (a mechanical piano) by a metrostyle; to employ a metrostyle.

1920 E. NEWMAN *Piano-player* 147 The roll [of the piano-player] should be metrostyled by some artist who knows the work thoroughly. *Ibid.* 148 Careful metrostyling would no doubt do away with the necessity for most of the time signs.

Metump line. *U.S.* = TUMP-LINE.

1754 in *Coll. N. H. Hist. Soc.* I. 279 The deponent sold the said Indians two shirts,..and there was next to their skin tied a number of small metump lines, not such as are usually made for tying packs.

Mexican. A. *adj.* **b.** Add: *Mexican cotton, eagle, flycatcher, onion, saddle*; **Mexican hog,** the peccary; **Mexican poppy** (earlier example); **Mexican thistle** (example).

1834 R. BAIRD *Valley Mississippi* xxiv. 304 Cotton is the chief staple, Three kinds are cultivated,—sea island, *Mexican, and green seed. 1836 MRS. HOLLEY *Texas Lett.* v. 100 The *Mexican eagle, which is among the smallest of the aquiline tribe. 1870 *Amer. Naturalist* III. 473 A solitary *Mexican Fly Catcher..gave a specimen of the summer group of migrants. 1821 T. NUTTALL *Trav. Arkansa* ix. 216 The *Sus tajassu* or *Mexican hog is not uncommon some distance higher up Red river. 1836 MRS. HOLLEY *Texas Lett.* v. 95 The Pecari or Mexican hog is even yet occasionally met with on the frontiers, in considerable gangs. 1859 G. A. JACKSON *MS. Diary* 12 Got back with 50 lbs of *Mexican onions. 1846 EMORY *Military Reconn.* 13 We find in the bottoms..*Mexican poppy (*Argemone Mexicana*). 1891 'C. E. CRADDOCK' in *Harper's Mag.* Feb. 367/1 He was a bay horse..with a long stride and an old fashioned *Mexican saddle. 1906 *Blersch's Handbk. Agric. S. Afr.* 144 (Pettman) Mexican poppy or yellow poppy, usually called *Mexican thistle at the Cape.

B. *sb.* Add: **2.** (Earlier examples.)

1827 J. F. COOPER *Prairie* v. 63 A foal that is worth thirty of the brightest Mexicans that bear the face of the King of Spain. 1836 *Knickerbocker Mag.* VIII. 580 The lad could not change the Mexican which I gave him. 1845 J. J. HOOPER *Adv. Simon Suggs* vi. 76 There's an old friend of mine..that's got three or four hamper baskets-full of Mexicans.

3. A variety of sheep.

1879 ISAB. L. BIRD *Lady's Life in Rocky Mts.* x. (1910) 173 The flocks are made up mostly of pure and graded Mexicans.

4. A kind of calico (see quot.).

1920 *Encycl. Brit.* VII. 277 (Cotton) *Mexican* is a plain, heavy grey calico, sometimes heavily sized. The origin of the word is doubtful, and it seems to be an arbitrary term. Mexicans are exported to various markets and also used in the home trade.

Mexicanize, *v.* (Example.)

1897–98 *Ann. Rep. Bureau Amer. Ethnol.* p. xvi, These Indians, now practically Mexicanized.

Mica. 2. Add: *Water mica*, trade name for clear, colourless mica.

1905 *Jrnl. Franklin Instit.* Sept. 200 The clear kind is known to the trade as 'water mica'.

3. *mica-packed*.

1909 *Westm. Gaz.* 9 Mar. 4/3 A new three-point sparking-plug..which has no asbestos or *mica-packed joints.

Mi·cacize, *v.* *Geol.* [irreg. f. MICA + -IZE.] *trans.* Used in passive of a rock, to have mica produced in it from original felspars or the like.

1885 GEIKIE *Text-bk. Geol.* (ed. 2) 573 The Liassic shales become micacised towards the central mountains, the fossils by degrees disappear.

Micate (məi·kĕ't), *v.* [f. MICA + -ATE.] *trans.* To provide (a stove or the like) with a sheet of mica. So **Mi·cated** *ppl. a.* **Mi·cating** *vbl. sb.* and *ppl. a.* **Mica·tion**[2], the action of furnishing with mica.

1917– in trade use.

Micawberish (mikǭ·bərɪʃ), *a.* [f. Wilkins *Micawber*, the name of a character in Dickens's novel 'David Copperfield' + -ISH.] Resembling or suggestive of Micawber and his habit of 'waiting for something to turn up'. So **Micaw·berism.**

1880 HOLLINGSHEAD *Plain Engl.* 2 Undeceived by the Micawberism of one class, or the dazzling brilliancy of the other. 1920 *Glasgow Herald* 19 June 6 He was in a state of what may be described as 'Micawberish embarrassment'. 1926 F. W. CROFTS *Insp. French & Cheyne Mystery* 104 Their idea of watching the house was simply adopted in the Micawberish hope that somehow something might turn up to help them. 1929 *Daily Express* 19 Jan. 8/5, I cannot take refuge in Micawberism.

Miche, variant of *MEECH *v.*

Michigan (mi·ʃigăn). *U.S.* The name of the State lying between Lake Huron and Lake Michigan, used *attrib.*

1855 M. M. THOMSON *Doesticks* xii. 97 [The mother] imparted the gratifying intelligence that one was afflicted with the measles, and the other had the Michigan itch. 1857–8 *Trans. Ill. Agric. Soc.* III. 496 For this purpose [subsoiling] the Michigan double or subsoil plow is used.

Michigander (miʃigæ·ndəɹ). *U.S.* [f. prec.] A native or inhabitant of the State of Michigan.

1848 *Congress. Globe* 27 July App. 1042, I mean the military tail you Democrats are now engaged in dove-tailing on to the great Michigander. 1879 *N. Y. Herald* 19 Apr., Mr. Conger, the eminent Michigander. 1897 *Outing* XXX. 293/1 (Heading) Michi-gander Lawmakers.

Miching: see *MEECHING *ppl. a.*

Mick. For 1882 in 1st quot. read 1872.

Micro. (Earlier example.)

1868 *Rep. U.S. Commissioner Agric.* (1869) 313 The presence of 'micros' is indicated by discolored lines...It may be ascertained whether the 'micro' is at home by holding the leaf up to the light.

Micro-. 2. (Add examples.)

a. 1922 *Encycl. Brit.* XXX. 34/2 Micro-investigation of glued joints proved the value of carefully preparing the timber and glue.

b. 1930 *Times* 29 Mar. 17/1 The metallurgy of steel castings, and the discovery of about 25 micro-constituents of steel.

5. a. *microbar, microhenry.*

1914 *Q. Jrnl. R. Meteor. Soc.* July 187 Bjerknes..used as his unit for atmospheric and hydrostatic pressure the megadyne per square centimetre, which he called the bar, with its submultiples the *microbar, millibar, centibar, and decibar. 1925 P. J. RISDON *Crystal Receivers & Circuits* 19 If two inductance coils, A and B, each of, say, 100 *microhenries, be placed in series in a circuit, the inductance of the circuit will be increased to 200 microhenries.

6. Micro-balance, a special balance for weighing small amounts. **Microbioscope,** a cinematographic apparatus for microscopic objects. **Micro-camera,** a camera for photographing minute details.

1922 F. W. ASTON *Isotopes* 36 These desiderata were obtained by the construction of a simple quartz *micro-balance. 1903 *Nature* 5 Nov. 18/1 Mr. Martin Duncan proved the great possibilities of the Urban Duncan *microbioscope for recording natural history observations in the ordinary way and under the microscope. 1928 *Daily Express* 21 June 12 Modern science has at its disposal 'doctors, chemists, biologists, ultra-violet lamps, *micro-cameras, and spectroscopes'.

Microbe. Add: Also *fig.*

1890 *Daily Tel.* 21 June (Ware *Passing Engl.*) The abdication by the Radical party of its proper functions has an unfortunate tendency to foster what we have called the microbe of sectionalism.

Microbiolo·gic, *a.* *Biol.* [f. MICROBIOLOGY + -IC.] Marked by microbiology; microbiological.

1909 *Westm. Gaz.* 9 Dec. 2/1 He is..reminded of the doctrine of the etiology of infectious diseases before the advent of the microbiologic epoch.

Microbism (məi·krǭbiz'm). [f. MICROBE + -ISM.] Microbial condition.

1904 *Lancet* 18 June 1724/1 The various explanations of 'return' cases were considered, including..the possibility of a relapse of the original disease, of latent microbism, or of missed cases.

Microce·phal. [f. Gr. μικροκέφαλος small headed: see MICROCEPHALOUS.] A microcephalous person.

1902 *Jrnl. Amer. Folk-lore* Apr.–June 121 (Cent. Suppl.).

Microlith. Add: **2.** *Archæol.* A small stone implement.

1908 KENDALL in *Man* No. 53. 103 Palæolithic Microliths... By microliths I mean tiny flakes or other pieces of flint which have been trimmed or used by man at some part of the edge.

Micrology. 2. (Example.)

1914 (*title*) Journal of Micrology.

Micronesian, *a.* and *sb.* (Earlier and later examples.)

1847 J. C. PRICHARD *Researches Phys. Hist. Man* V. 157 A certain difference has been noted between the Micronesians and the Polynesians in general. *Ibid.*, Micronesia, or the Micronesian Archipelago. 1884 W. TURNER *Rep. Crania* I. (Challenger Rep. X.) 82 The islands of the Mikronesian group. 1890 BRINTON *Races & Peoples* 235 Some ethnographers would make the Polynesians and Micronesians a different race from the Malays. 1910 *Blackw. Mag.* Nov. 578/2, I have seen no finer type of Micronesian.

Micronucleus. (Earlier example.)

1888 *Amer. Naturalist* XXII. 255 The micronucleus is a hermaphrodite sexual element, of sole importance in conjugation.

Mi·croscoping, *vbl. sb.* [f. MICROSCOPE *v.*] Examination by microscope.

1919 S. PAGET *Sir V. Horsley* II. i. 143 He..spoke his mind against that sort of pathology which hardly gets beyond the microscoping and exhibiting of diseased organs.

Microseismometer (məi:krosəizmǫ·mĭtəɹ). [f. MICROSEISM + -(O)METER.] An instrument for measuring minute earth tremors. So **Microsei·smoscope,** a device for detecting such tremors.

1886 *Encycl. Brit.* XXI. 629/1 The crossed-link suspension ..has been adopted in the microseismometer sketched in fig. 10. *Ibid.*, This kind of action has..been turned to account as a means of detecting very minute earth-tremors by Rossi, who has devised a micro-seismoscope, consisting of a number of pendulums of various lengths, one or other of which is likely to be set swinging when the ground shakes to and fro repeatedly, through even the minutest range.

Microtome. Add: Also *attrib.*

1930 *Ann. Botany* Oct. 777 It is impossible to cut microtome sections of them.

Mi·crotome, *v.* [f. the sb.] *trans.* To cut in sections with a microtome.

1898 *Phil. Trans.* B. CXC. 95 The following nerves of muscles were microtomed for detection of some fibres.

Microtone (məi·krŏtǭun). *Mus.* [f. Gr. μικρό-ς small + τόνος TONE.] A fraction of a tone.

1920 *Outward Bound* Oct. 77/1 The ancient Greeks also recognised and used these microtones. The Greeks found twenty-four in the octave and the Indians usually recognise twenty-two. 1927 *Observer* 23 Oct. 14 But these microtones (seventy-two in the octave) give quarters of the untempered chromatic semitone.

Microzyme. (Earlier example.)

1870 HUXLEY in *Rep. Brit. Assoc.* p. lxxxv, Sheep-pox and glanders are also dependent for their existence and their propagation upon extremely small living solid particles, to which the title of *microzymes* is applied.

Mid. A. *adj.* Add: **1. f.** (so *mid-Victorianism*).

1923 *Daily Mail* 12 Feb. 13 The artist..had an eccentric taste for mid-Victorianism.

2. Add to def.: *Phonetics.* Of a vowel-sound: Produced with the tongue or some part of it in a middle position between high and low.

1876 [see HIGH *a.* 4 b].

d. mid-brow, *sb.* and *a.* = *middle brow* (*MIDDLE A. 6); **Mid-west** = *Middle West* (*MIDDLE A. 6).

1928 *Sunday Express* 1 July 12/6 Delighting the low-brow, the *mid-brow, and the high-brow with equal facility. 1926 EDNA FERBER *Show Boat* v. 80 To the farmers and villagers of the *Midwest..the show boat meant music, romance, gaiety.

C. *adv.* Add: Also *Comb.*

1876 G. M. HOPKINS *Poems* (1918) 22 Mid-numbered He in three of the thunder-throne!

Midas. Add: **2. b. midas-fly,** one of the *Midaidæ*, a small family of dipterous insects.

1895 COMSTOCK *Man. Insects* 461 The Midas-flies rival the robber-flies in size, and quite closely resemble them in appearance.

Middle. A. *adj.* **6.** Add: **middle article** = MIDDLE B. 12; **middle-brow** (*a*) sb., a person of average or moderate cultural attainments; (*b*) adj., claiming to be or regarded as only moderately intellectual; **Middle East,** the south-western countries of Asia; **Middle Eastern** *a.*, of or pertaining to the Middle East; **middle rail** (*b*), the 'live' central rail of an electric railway; **Middle States** (examples); **middle-weight** (attrib. example); **Middle West** *U.S.*, the central States, in contrast with the West or Far West; (so *Middle Western* adj.); **Middle White,** a Yorkshire breed of pig.

a 1894 C. H. PEARSON in Stebbing *Mem.* (1900) 90 T. L. Sanders created the so-called *middle article—the essay on social topics. 1928 *Observer* 17 June 26 Success is less commonly achieved—perhaps because the standard of '*middle-brow' music and plays is always rather low. 1929 *Daily Express* 7 Jan. 10/4 Sooner or later, after he has found it, the middle brows and the low brows come to hear of it. 1902 MAHAN *Retrospect & Prospect* 237 The *middle East, if I may adopt a term which I have not seen, will some day need its Malta, as well as its Gibraltar. 1909 A. HAMILTON (*title*) Problems of the Middle East. 1913 *Q. Rev.* Jan. 297 The interests of Great Britain and Russia in the Middle East..are in reality irreconcilable. 1903 CHIROL (*title*) The *Middle Eastern Question or some political problems of Indian defence. 1909 A. HAMILTON *Probl. Middle East* p. xi, No study of Middle Eastern politics can avoid encroaching upon those of the Near East and of the Far East. 1905 *Technol. & Sci. Dict.* (ed. Goodchild & Tweney) 401 **Middle Rail*.., a heavy conductor in the form of a rail carried on insulating supports, which is laid between the running rails of an electric railway to supply current to the motors. 1784 WASHINGTON *Diaries* II. 326 The *middle States with the Country immediately back of them. 1798 MORSE *Amer. Gazetteer* (ed. 2) 322/1 *Middle States*, one of the Grand Divisions of the United States (so denominated in reference to the northern and southern States). 1835 *Southern Lit. Messenger* I. 551 Some years ago a kind of 'Hickory Quaker' (as he called himself)..found his way..from one of the Middle States to Congress. 1848 J. F. COOPER *Oak Open.* I. xiii. 193 Who ever heard of the 'tribe' of New England, or..of the 'tribe' of the Middle States? 1857 D. BRAMAN *Inform. Texas* 21 Emigrants from the Eastern, Southern-Atlantic, and Middle States. 1904 *N. Y. Even. Post* 28 Jan. 6 If there was a tariff wall separating New England from the Middle States, and another separating both groups from the Western States. 1909 *Westm. Gaz.* 9 Feb. 12/4 Some fine wrestling has been seen, more especially in the *middle-weight class. 1900 G. ADE *More Fables in Slang* (1902) 23 The Prosperous Farmer lived in an Agricultural Section of the *Middle West. 1917 *Nation* (N. Y.) 17 May 589/2 The personal tour of the Secretary of the Treasury through the Middle West, to speak at public meetings, is a wise arrangement. 1925 L. BROMFIELD *Possession* 27 Eureka Reinforced Corsets came to be worn..by housewives of the Middle West. 1924 *Times Trade & Eng. Suppl.* 29 Nov. 235/2 There is room for more systematic visits by Manchester men to the *Middle Western and Western towns. 1893 L. M. DOUGLAS *Man. Pork Trade* p. xiv. Pl., Small and *Middle White Yorkshire Pigs. 1912 *Jrnl. Bath & West & Southern Counties Soc.* Ser. v. VI. 175 For many years the Middle Whites carried off the highest awards at the fat stock shows.

B. *sb.* Add: **1.** *To knock* (a person) *into the middle of next week*: see WEEK *sb.* 5 d.

b. *Southern U.S.* One of the intervals between rows of cotton.

1847 *Florida Plant. Rec.* 242, 23 [slaves] plowing out middles in brickyard [field]. 1851 *Ibid.* 373 Ploughs runing around cotton and splitting cotton middles. 1907 T. F. HUNT *Forage & Fiber Crops* 352 The field is made up into alternate beds and middles or into 'back' furrows and 'dead' furrows.

1909 *Cent. Dict.* Suppl., *To break out middles*, to open lengthwise with a double mold-board or a scooter-plow the middle of an existing cotton bed. Also *to burst* or *burst out middles*. *Comb.* 1907 T. F. HUNT *Forage & Fiber Crops* 352 By means of a middle 'buster', which is a double moldboard plow.

3. b. The part of a side of bacon which is left when the fore-end and the gammon are removed.

1892 SIMMONDS *Dict. Trade* Suppl., *Middles*,..a name for sides of bacon and pork. 1917 G. J. NICHOLLS *Bacon & Hams* 70 These middles are cured in dry salt. 1923 R. E. DAVIES *Pigs & Bacon Curing* 29 The side may be cut into three parts, comprising the fore end, the middle, and the gammon with corner.

8. c. *colloq.* = *middle-weight sb.* (see A. 6).

1908 *Daily Chron.* 29 Jan. 9/2 In the middles the best bout was that between Carter and Smith.

d. Stock Exchange. = *middle price* (see A. 1 e).

1928 *Morn. Post* 19 Nov., The making-up price..is..presumed to represent the middle of the quotation current at that particular moment.

Middle-a·gedness. [-NESS.] Middle-aged condition.

1924 *Blackw. Mag.* Aug. 225/2 Sandy,..I hope, managed to feel young and sentimental in spite of the chilliness and our middle-agedness.

Middle-class. Hence (also) **Middle-classdom, -classism,** the middle class as a whole; their characteristics, interests, or position. **Middle-classy** *a.*, suggestive of the middle class of society.

1930 *Observer* 14 Sept. 7 The secret of Denmark's somewhat stuffy middle-classdom. 1909 *Working Men's Coll. Jrnl.* Apr. 77 Mr. Lupton..did not think the question before the House was one of aristocracy *v.* middle-classism. 1926 *Glasgow Herald* 21 May 8 Highly respectable, middle-classy railway clerks.

Middleman. Add: **5. c.** One who paddles in the middle of a canoe.

1839 J. K. TOWNSEND *Narr. Rocky Mts.* xv. 355 The middle-men ply their oars; the guides brace themselves against the gunwale of the boat, placing their paddles edge-wise down her sides.

Mi·ddlewoman. [After MIDDLEMAN.] (See quot.)

1909 *Englishwoman* Apr. 231 The middlewoman..saves the home-worker the waste of time often incurred in going to the warehouse for work and in taking the finished work back.

Middling, *sb.* **3. c.** (Earlier examples.)

1770 *Carroll Papers* in *Maryland Hist. Mag.* XIII. 69, 3 Casks of fine Flour, 1 d[o] midlings. 1786 WASHINGTON *Diaries* III. 116 My Corn being out, or nearly so, I was obliged to have middlings and ship stuff mixed for bread.

d. *U.S.* Of timber.

1839 J. F. COOPER *Home as Found* ii, One of my own [trees] out of which the sawyers made a thousand feet of clear stuff, to say nothing of middlings.

4. *U.S.* (Earlier examples. Also in *sing.*)

1777 *Cal. Virginia State Papers* I. 288 Bakin in hams, midlings, shoulders, &c. 1831 PECK *Guide Emigrants* 172 To make bacon of hams, shoulders, and middlings or broad-sides. 1834 CROCKETT *Narr. Life* xi. 79, I got also a large middling of bacon, and killed a fine deer. 1847 *Rep. U.S. Comm. Patents* (1848) 527 The hog thus cut up into shoulders, hams and middlings undergoes further trimming. 1857 D. H. STROTHER *Virginia Illustr.* i. 31 Fried middling and hot coffee were then served round. 1904 ELLEN GLASGOW *Deliverance* 51 She has had to fry the middling in the kitchen, and mother complains so of the smell.

Middling. A. *adj.* **5.** Add: *Middling interest* = middle class. *U.S.*

1857 E. STONE *Life of Howland* vii. 137 He resolved on attempting to arrest this hostility by creating..a correct public sentiment, and by overlaying it with what is..denominated a 'middling interest' influence. *a* 1859 *Connecticut Courant* (Bartlett), Men of the middling interest class are now the best off... They have felt they belonged to the middling interest, and have resolved to stay there, and not cope with the rich.

Midget. Add: **2.** For 1859 read 1848.

4. *attrib.* in sense of weak, puny, as *midget effort*; also **midget golf,** a form of miniature golf, usually played indoors; (so *midget golf course* etc.).

1908 *Daily Chron.* 7 Aug. 4/4 The spiritual intelligences..must..laugh at our serious *midget efforts to comprehend and explain the circumambient infinite. 1930 *Daily Express* 6 Nov. 3/7 Sydney's *Midget Golf Boom. 1930 *Daily Tel.* 1 Dec. 23/6 Advt., An 18-Hole Midget Golf Course Complete.

Midinette (midinet). [F. Perh. orig. a pun f. *midi* mid-day + *dinette* light dinner: cf. 1922 Larousse s.v., les *midinettes* sont celles qui se contentent d'une *dinette à midi*.] A milliner's female assistant, esp. in Paris.

1909 *Westm. Gaz.* 7 Aug. 15/1 The Parisian..is tired of the absurd hat. The midinette and those of her kind have made it impossible. 1919 MAX BEERBOHM *Seven Men* 11 A midinette who..murdered, or was about to murder, a mannequin. 1924 *Blackw. Mag.* Nov. 709/2 Our *midinettes*..again dance four abreast along the boulevards. 1925 *Ibid.* July 92/1 Two *midinettes* who are whispering of their loves. 1930 *Times* 31 Mar. 9/2 He used to see the rooms of the Royal Academy crowded with shop assistants, working girls, midinettes,..tired after their day's work.

Midrib. Add: **2.** (Later example.)

1901 *Chambers's Jrnl.* May 301/2 The leaves are thoroughly dried. In testing their dryness the mid-rib or vein should not be overlooked.

b. A structure similar to the principal rib or vein of a leaf.

1929 V. G. CHILDE *Danube in Prehistory* 126 Kite-shaped daggers with rivet-holes and a rudimentary midrib.

Midshipman. 3. Add: **midshipman's hitch,** a special kind of hitch (see quot. 1886); **midshipman's nuts** (earlier example).

1808 D. LEVER *Yng. Sea Officer's Sheet Anchor* 9 To make a *Midshipman's Hitch. 1886 *Encycl. Brit.* XXI. 591/2 Midshipman's Hitch.—Take two round turns inside the bight, the same as a half-hitch repeated; stop up the end; or let another half-hitch be taken or held by hand. Used for hooking a tackle for a temporary purpose. 1846 MELVILLE *Typee* vi. (1920) 43, I took a double handful of those small, broken, flinty bits of biscuit, which generally go by the name of *midshipman's nuts.

Mid-side. (Later U.S. examples.)

1816 U. BROWN *Jrnl.* in *Maryland Hist. Mag.* XI. 224 [The horse] Cumberland in the Milldam..in Mud and Water, Mid sides and Tail covered. 1822 J. FOWLER *Journal* 157 We comenced Crossing the Crick Early, it being about mid Side deep to the Horses.

Midway. A. *sb.* Add: **3.** *U.S.* An avenue in the middle of, or connecting two portions of, an exhibition or fair. Also *attrib.*

The use originated in the inclusion of the 'Midway Plaisance' of Chicago in the grounds of the exposition held there in 1893.

[1891 *World's Columbian Exposition* Apr., At the junction of the Midway Plaisance with Jackson Park is the site chosen for the Proctor Tower.] 1901 *Pan-Amer. Exposition, Buffalo*, folder, The Midway will have the choicest of the world's amusement novelties. 1903 *N.Y. Even. Post* 17 Oct., Out in the little 'Midway' of tents and booths, where the two-headed baby was on exhibition. 1904 *Ibid.* 22 Sept. 6 Ever since Chicago led the way, the 'Midway' features of our great fairs have threatened more and more to overshadow the mere educational features.

C. *adv.* **1.** Add: Also U.S. with *of*.

c 1805 J. J. HENRY *Camp. agst. Quebec* (1812) 192 About midway of the horn [of the moose]..there is a broad flat part. 1903 *Nation* (N.Y.) 17 Sept. 234 He died midway of his 70th year. 1927 *Saturday Even. Post* 24 Dec. 44/3 She stopped midway of her sentence.

Midyear. 2. (Add example.)

1901 *Yearbk. U.S. Dept. Agric.* 154 To teachers the series of meetings is a series of mid-year institutes.

Miff, *v.* **2.** (Later U.S. examples.)

1880 *Kansas Times & Star* 27 Nov., Dr. G. W. Fitzpatrick ..is badly miffed because he wasn't appointed surveyor of the port. 1904 ELIZ. ROBINS *Magnetic North* I. 252 Don't get mifft, Colonel. 1907 *N.Y. Even. Post* (semi-weekly ed.) 2 Sept. 4 He is a little miffed to find that there are other lawyers in the Cabinet whose advice the President prefers to his own.

Might, *sb.* Add: **7.** *dial.* A considerable quantity or amount.

1834 CARRUTHERS *Kentuckian in N.Y.* I. 28 I'm 'bliged to do a might of business in Baltimore afore I can go on. 1878 J. H. BEADLE *Western Wilds* ii. 29 It took a might of time. *Ibid.* 43 It was a might o' comfort, though, to see 'em 'fore they died. 1903 in *Eng. Dial. Dict.* (Yks., Suffolk).

Migrate, *v.* **1.** (Add example of active use.)

1928 *Sunday Dispatch* 29 July 7/2 The proposals for migrating unemployed workers.

2. c. *fig.* Of inanimate objects, esp. manuscripts: To undergo removal from one place or library to another.

1929 *Times* 13 Nov. 11/1 To collect and circulate..information..respecting manuscripts that have 'migrated' and collections that have been dispersed.

Migration. a. (Add examples and cf. *MIGRATE *v.* 2 c.) *spec.* In electrolysis: The movement of ions between the two electrodes.

1894 tr. *D'Alviella's Migration of Symbols* 82 Is it not the Winged Circle, whose migrations I trace in another chapter? 1907 C. L. VON ENDE tr. *Abegg's Electrolytic Dissoc. Theory* 22 This relationship was..discovered by F. Kohlrausch in 1876, and is called the law of the independent migration of the ions. 1929 *Times* 13 Nov. 11/1 A serious obstacle to the work of archæologists, historians and others ..is the migration of manuscripts.

c. *migration velocity.*

1929 *Encycl. Brit.* VIII. 237/2 The migration velocity of an ion with charge *E* and the frictional constant *P* should be represented by the formula [etc.].

Migrationist. Add: **2.** One who emphasizes the importance of migration in the distribution of species.

1918 L. HUXLEY *Life Sir J. D. Hooker* II. xxxii. 98 Darwin was a migrationist; Forbes and others pushed the extension theory to excess.

Mike (məik), *sb.*[5] *slang.* An abbreviation of MICROPHONE *sb.*

1929 ALLIGHAN *Romance of Talkies* 28 The great problem is to hide the microphone, as, although the 'mike' is small in itself, it is directly attached to a first-stage amplifier,..and the whole piece of apparatus is bulky accordingly. 1929 *Photoplay* Apr., *Mike*—microphone.

Milanese. A. *adj.* Add: **2.** Of articles of clothing: Made of Milanese silk. **Milanese silk,** a finely-woven dress material composed of silk or artificial silk.

1922 *Tatler* 30 Aug. Advts. p. c, Ladies' exceedingly dainty Cami-Knickers, made of best quality Milanese Silk. *Ibid.* p. f, Pure Silk Milanese Vest. 1928 *Daily Tel.* 24 Apr. 2/2 A circular knitting machine..able to produce superior ladder-proof warp-knitted 'milanese' fabric.

B. *sb.* Add: **3.** Milanese silk or articles made of Milanese silk. (An ellipt. use of A.)

1927 *Glasgow Herald* 20 Apr. 10/7 What your supplies and your Milanese may be, you alone may care.

Mild, *sb.*[2] Eng. and U.S. dial. var. of MILE *sb.*[1]

1701 in *Essex Inst. Hist. Coll.* XXXVI. 83 To run the lien of mesuer from Ipswich meting howes..six mields. 1725 in *Lancaster* (Pa.) *Rec.* 231 We traueled to Groten 12 milds. ..We marcht up the riuer about 8 milds. 1777 in J. M. Lincoln *Papers R. Lincoln* (1904) 15 They ware Engaged in Carring gun bots..over land about one mild into Lake George. 1836 *Knickerbocker Mag.* VIII. 352, 'I expect we are a mild and a half from the city.'..'Just about'..answered Whip. 1842 PULMAN *Rustic Sketches* 12 A mild below our town. 1859 HUGHES *Scour. White Horse* vi. 129 All the waay,..and 'tis quite-vour mil'd. 1886 ELWORTHY *W. Som. Word-bk.* 476, I count 'tis up vower mild yer-vrom.

Mile, *sb.*[1] **1. d.** (Add example.)

1852 *Punch* 24 Jan. 42/1 The seven Wonders of a Young Lady..5..wearing shoes that were not 'a mile too big for her'.

5. c. mile-heat, a racing heat of one mile; **mile-post** (earlier and later examples).

1802 *Steele Papers* I. 315 He says there are no regular *mile heats at that turf. 1868 H. WOODRUFF *Trotting Horse* v. 70 You can tell by the way he finishes..whether he will be likely to stand the mile-heat out and to repeat it. 1768 in *Maryland Hist. Mag.* II. 317 As we returned (besides the *Mile Posts) we erected Marks on the Tops of all the High Ridges. 1870 KEIM *Sheridan's Troopers* (1885) vi. 41 At the very extreme point was a plain wooden mile-post painted white.

Mileage. Add: **1. c.** A rate per mile charged for the use of railway vehicles carrying goods or passengers over another company's line.

1873 *Cassell's Mag.* VIII. 400/1 As..the Caledonian Company will receive the fares of the passengers, they will be required to pay for the use of the carriages conveying them; in other words the..Company will be charged 'mileage'.

Miler[2]. Add: **2.** *colloq.* A walk or journey of a specified number of miles.

Properly the second element of a compound.

1856 DICKENS in *Dickens-Collins Lett.* 14 Nov. (1892) 72, I went out this morning for a 12-miler.

Milesian, *a.*[2] and *sb.*[2] (Earlier and later examples.)

1705 M. KENNEDY (*title*) A Chronological Genealogical and Historical Dissertation of the Royal Family of the Stuarts, beginning with Milesius the stock of those they call the Milesian Irish, and of the old Scotish Race. 1840 CARLYLE *Chartism* (ed. 2) iv. 28 The wild Milesian features..salute you on all highways and byways...The English coachman ..lashes the Milesian with his whip. 1921 *Edin. Rev.* Jan. 167 And lastly the Milesians. The Milesian being a literary and honorific cognomen of the Firbolgs' conquerors, the Gaels. 1929 GUEDALLA *Missing Muse* 223 The tourist notes [in the Dail] an almost total absence of Milesian eloquence.

Mi·lestone, *v.* [f. the sb.] *trans.* To mark stages on (a road) by or as by milestones; also *fig.*

1902 J. H. M. ABBOTT *Tommy Cornstalk* 157 And the road was mile-stoned by the parched hides and whitened bones of horses, mules, and oxen. 1921 A. W. MYERS *Twenty Yrs. Lawn Tennis* 36 Mrs. Lambert Chambers could almost mile-stone her career on the Chiswick courts. 1922 *Chambers's Jrnl.* Dec. 861/1 The Overland is milestoned with our bones.

Militancy. (Add recent examples.)

1912 in Mrs. Pankhurst *My own Story* (1914) 258 The leaders..have so often warned the Government that unless the vote were granted to women in response to the mild militancy of the past, a fiercer spirit of revolt would be awakened. 1913 MRS. HARKER *Ffolliots of Redmarley* xii. (1919) 156 Eloquent forgot her militancy.

Militant. A. *adj.* Add: **1. c.** Applied to or adopted as a designation by suffragettes who employed or advocated the use of violence.

1907 MARG. MCMILLAN in *Case Women's Suffrage* 114 The militant Suffragette..wants a Vote and will, if necessary fight for it. 1914 MRS. PANKHURST *My own Story* 37 That visit was one of the contributory causes that led to the founding of our militant suffrage organisation, the Women's Social and Political Union.

B. *sb.* Add: **c.** A 'militant' suffragette.

1909 *Englishwoman* Apr. 323 That bias has been greatly intensified amongst almost all classes of suffragists by the tactics of the militants. 1919 DOLF WYLLARDE *Holiday Husband* x. 132 It has been reported to us that you are an ardent Militant among the Suffragettes.

Mi·litantism. [f. *MILITANT A.] A militant policy.

1919 DOLF WYLLARDE *Holiday Husband* x. 130 She could understand the value of militantism in the hands of leaders who used even the purely hysterical as tools.

Militarization. (Later example.)

1918 B. MIALL tr. *A. Hamon's Lessons of World-war* 108 Industry and science..have undergone a veritable process of militarization, whose consequences are disastrous to the human mind.

Militarize, *v.* (Later example.)

1923 MILIUKOV *Russia To-day & To-morrow* 205 But the climax was reached when the Bolsheviks decided to militarize labor.

Hence **Mi·litarised** *ppl. a.*

1925 *Edin. Rev.* July 28 Appalling slaughter and suffering patiently endured by a militarized people..has disillusioned the Germans.

Milk, *sb.* Add: **2. d.** *To bring a person to his milk*: to bring him to his senses, to compel him to acquiesce or submit. *U.S. colloq.*

1857 HOLLAND *Bay Path* 209 There ain't anything that'll bring you to your milk half so quick as a good double-and-twisted thrashin.

3. b. *The milk in the cocoanut*, a puzzling fact or circumstance, or the explanation of this. *U.S. colloq.*

1853 *Knickerbocker Mag.* XLII. 50 The milk in the cocoa nut was accounted for. 1870 *Congress. Globe* 15 June App. 500/2 This is the secret, this is the 'milk in the cocoanut', this the 'meat in the egg'. 1893 *Congress. Rec.* 28

Feb. 2299/1 Here is the milk in the cocoanut! A frank confession it is.

c. Milk-white colour.

1899 Swinburne *Rosamund* i. i. 2 White I know from red, and dark from bright, And milk from white in hawthorn-flowers: but not Woman from woman.

9. a. (*a*) *milk-biscuit, -loaf*; (*b*) *milk-car, -combine, -company, -pitcher, -supply, -truck, -wagon.*

1771 C. Pelham in *Copley-Pelham Lett.* 109 We found in a Drawer a hoard of *Milk Bisket. 1890 *Century Dict.*, *Milk-car. 1919 J. L. Garvin *Econ. Foundations Peace* 309 Working relations with such a '*milk-combine' as has been projected for Britain. 1855 [Pray] *Mem. J. G. Bennet* 67 There were not less than six joint-stock *milk companies in London. 1910 *Practitioner* June 801 Meals were selected from the following articles mainly:—Crisp toast,..veda-bread, *milk-loaf, scones. 1863 'Gail Hamilton' *Gala-Days* 422 A little boy..upset the *milk-pitcher. 1869 Miss Alcott *Lit. Women* II. xxiv. 356 Taking Teddy's little fist out of the milk-pitcher. 1909 *Westm. Gaz.* 9 Oct. 14/1 He follows on a milk-cart, in deep talk with his crony, the lord of the *milk-supply. 1910 *Daily Chron.* 22 Apr. 1/3 The..express..overran its distance, and ran into a *milk truck. 1911 Edna Ferber *Dawn O'Hara* v. 58, I step out of the road to allow a yellow *milk wagon to rattle past.

b. *milk strainer.*

1868 S. Sewall *Letter Bk.* 33 Five Doz. of *milk strainers of the smaller sort. 1872 *Florida Plant. Rec.* 199 The milk strainer is also in bad repair.

10. **milk-blooded** *a.*, cowardly, spiritless; **milk chicken**, a chicken that has been fed on milk and ground oats; (so *milk-fatted* adj.); **milk-fish** *Austral.* (see quot.); **milk-flour, powder**, preparations of desiccated milk; **milk-ranch**, a ranch producing milk; **milk-room**, a room in a house or dairy in which milk is kept; **milk-route**, a route on which a milk-dealer regularly supplies milk to customers; **milk-shake** *U.S.*, a beverage composed of milk, aerated water, etc., mixed by shaking; **milk-sick, -sickness** *U.S.* (earlier and later examples); **milk sociable** *U.S.*, a sociable at which milk is drunk; **milk-toast** *U.S.*, toast which is softened in milk; **milk-train**, a railway train which carries milk; **milk tube**, also, a milking-tube; **milk-wine**, a beverage obtained from fermented milk; **milk-woman** (modern example).

1910 *Blackw. Mag.* Feb. 183/2 The sooner we give up all this *milk-blooded, blue-spectacled, pacificist talk the better. 1902 *Encycl. Brit.* XXXI. 882/2 Chickens fattened quite young..and known as *petits poussins*, or '*milk chickens'. 1931 *Times* 16 Mar. 1/4 Advt., Chickens, finest milk-fatted.. 2s. 2d. per lb. 1880 J. E. Tenison-Woods in *Trans. Linn. Soc. N.S.W.* V. ii. 128 (Morris) Another species [of Trepang] is the '*milk fish' or 'cotton fish' so called from its power of emitting a white viscid fluid.., which clings to an object like shreds of cotton. 1902 *Chambers's Jrnl.* Mar. 191/1 The *milk-flour is..soluble in water. 1906 *N. Y. Even. Post* 10 Feb. (Cent. Suppl.) *Milk-powder. 1909 *Chambers's Jrnl.* Feb. 143/2 The method..has been found successful in the manufacture of milk-powder. 1917 *Statutory Rules & Orders* No. 1296 § 1 No person shall after the 17th December, 1917, use in the manufacture of chocolate any milk, condensed milk, milk powder, dried milk [etc.]. 1889 Farmer *Americanisms*, *Milk Ranch, a dairy farm. 1838 *Knickerbocker Mag.* XI. 17 There was but a single room, with a *milk-room, as it was called, and a loft over head. 1873–4 *Rep. Vermont Board Agric.* II. 97 After the milk is drawn, set it away..in a good milk-room. 1897 'Mark Twain' *Following Equator* xliv. 464 The vested rights..are frequently the subject of sale or mortgage. Just like a *milk-route. 1890 *Century Dict.*, *Milk shake. 1911 H. S. Harrison *Queed* vii. 85 You ain't feelin good, are you, Doc? You're lookin' white as a milk-shake. 1930 *Chambers's Jrnl.* June 348/1 'Milk-shake,' composed of milk, soda-water, and a small quantity of ice-cream, is a very popular 'soft' drink. 1819 E. Dana *Geogr. Sketches* 43 A peculiar disease among the cattle prevails here, which the people call **milk-sick*. 1846 M'Kenny *Mem.* I. vi. 141 The people..about these parts, were afraid of the *milk-sick*, and never used milk after early spring. 1823 S. H. Long *Exped.* I. 76 They have a disease called *milk sickness. 1877 *Field & Forest* III. 41 The southern slope is..white with *Eupatorium ageratoides*, by some supposed to be the cause of milk sickness. 1907 Neil Munro *Daft Days* vi. 51 Why, great Queen of Sheba! I was only joshing you: it was as calm on that ship as a *milk sociable. 1857 *Knickerbocker Mag.* XLIX. 98 Coffee and *milk-toast, waffles and honey, disappeared.. like magic. 1877 Eliz. S. Phelps *Story Avis* 225 Aunt Chloe thought milk-toast would remedy the difficulty. 1873 J. H. Beadle *Undevel. West* 795 They might have to teach the Texas Central Railroad Company how to run a *milk-train fifty miles. 1886 *Century Mag.* XXXI. Feb. 504/1 Before starting from home by the milk-train that left Willoughby Pastures at 4.05. 1877 *Rep. Vermont Dairym. Assoc.* VIII. 106 In such case the milk must be drawn by means of a catheter, or *milk tube. 1911 M. J. Newbigin *Mod. Geog.* vii. 189 A *milk-wine or koumiss, produced by the fermentation of milk, is the characteristic drink. 1879 Stockton *Rudder Grange* v. 56 She had spent the night in a wooden rocking-chair at the *milk-woman's.

Milk, *v.* Add: 4. d. (Earlier example.)

1860 Prescott *Electrical Invent.* 108 (Farmer) The rapidity and simplicity of the means by which a wire could be milked without being cut, or put out of circuit, struck the whole of the party.

e. *Gambling slang.* (See quot.)

1923 *Daily Mail* 22 Feb. 6 Few players are daring enough to wait for a long run, without 'milking'—that is to say, withdrawing a part of their winnings.

Milk-and-molasses. *U.S.* In fig. use (see quot.).

1833 J. Neal *Down-Easters* I. vii. 96 The people of this country..are of two colors, black and white..or half-and-half sometimes at the south, where they are called milk-and-molasses.

Milking, *vbl. sb.* 4. Add: **milking booster, cell**, a cell connected in parallel with one of the cells in an electric battery or series of cells to restore it to condition by separate charging.

1910 *Encycl. Brit.* I. 129/1 To restore the cell, two methods can be adopted... It may be left in circuit, and a cell in good order put in parallel with it. This acts as a 'milking' cell.

Mi·lksoppery. [f. Milksop.] The characteristics or behaviour of a milksop. So **Mi·lksoppish** *a.*, devoid of manly qualities, effeminate.

1925 *Blackw. Mag.* Apr. 548/2 The drawback..of asserted or insinuated milksoppery. 1928 *Observer* 25 Mar. 9/3 Even he, who is the least milksoppish of mortals, speaks of 'those harrowing years'.

Milky, *a.* 3. b. (Earlier examples.)

1765 Washington *Diaries* I. 210 Note, the [mulberry] Stocks were very Milkey. 1768 *Ibid.* 282 Some [wheat] whose straw and head was green but the grain of full size and Milky. 1789 Morse *Amer. Geog.* 52 About the time that it begins to turn from its milky state and to ripen, they run their canoes into the midst of it.

Mill, *sb.*[1] 1. b. (Add examples.) Also *to have been through the mill*: to have gained experience (of life, etc.).

1818 Scott *Hrt. Midl.* xxviii, Frank here won't hear of our putting her through the mill. 1837 *Knickerbocker Mag.* IX. 356, I had been 'through the mill' of a pre-concerted, artificial revival. 1840 R. H. Dana *Bef. Mast* 50 I've been through the mill. 1848 Lowell *Fable for Critics* To C. F. Briggs, To induce bards to club their resources and buy the balance of every edition, until they have all of them fairly been run through the mill. 1868 H. Woodruff *Trotting Horse* vi. 76 It was thought that they would be ruined for service if they were 'put through the mill'. 1887 *Contemp. Rev.* Jan. 10 Certain persons who have gone through the mill of what is known as our 'higher education'.

4. (Add example.)

1919 *Brit. Manufacturer* Nov. 26/2 In the linen industry a 'mill' means the works where flax is spun into yarns, while a 'factory' means the place of the further evolution of the yarns being woven into cloth.

7. b. *U.S.* A circling movement of cattle. (Cf. Mill *v.*[1] 12.)

1903 A. Adams *Log Cowboy* iv. 27 We soon had a mill going which kept them [cattle] busy and rested our horses.

9. *mill-bag, -brook, -lot, -room* (later example); *mill-cut* adj.

1829–32 J. P. Kennedy *Swallow B.* I. xv. 155 With the large canvass *mill-bags spread out for saddles. 1851 R. Glisan *Jrnl. Army Life* (1874) vi. 58, I..endeavored to throw [it] in a mill-bag style over my saddle. 1642 *Dedham Rec.* 83 Vpon ye East side of the *Milbrooke, next to ye Millpond. 1864 T. L. Nichols *Amer. Life* i. 20 Grist-mills which ground our corn, and saw-mills which supplied our timber, were upon a mill brook. 1925 *Glasgow Herald* 2 Apr. 9 To import into this country a sufficient number of *mill-cut houses to supply the shortage. 1746 *Boston News-Letter* 16 Nov., Seven Acres..to be laid out to the Right of the 30 Acre *Mill-Lot, granted to Thomas Richardson. 1833 B. Silliman *Man. Sugar Cane* 45 The length of the *mill-room A is 64 feet.

10. **mill-carriage**, the movable bench of a circular saw; **mill iron** (modern U.S. examples); **mill log** *U.S.*, a log cut at a saw-mill; **mill privilege, right** *U.S.*, the privilege or right of using water for driving a mill; **mill-run** *U.S.*, the quantity of ore put through a mill; **mill-scale** (earlier example); **mill-seat** *U.S.* (earlier and later examples); **mill-site** *U.S.* = *mill-seat*; **mill-stream** (later U.S. examples); **mill town, village**, a town or village characterized by the presence of mills; **mill-work** (earlier example).

1881 *Harper's Mag.* Sept. 584/1 It [an eel]..leads the captor a ten minutes' dance over logs..and *mill carriages. 1805 Sibley in *Ann. 9th Congress* 2 Sess. 1100 It is only a few years ago that the *mill irons and mill stones were brought down. 1837 W. Jenkins *Ohio Gaz.* 276 Large quantities of iron are here manufactured into hollow ware, mill irons, and other articles. 1849 D. Nason *Jrnl.* 99, I asked the guide if there were any *mill-logs among it. 1734 *N.H. Probate Rec.* II. 508, I also give unto my son.. the one half of my *mill Priviledge on the southerly side of ye River at Lole-End. 1838 Colton *Ind. Delineated* 32 Lost River, Lick and Patolsa creeks are the chief streams, affording in many places good mill privileges. 1852 *Rep. Vermont Board Agric.* XII. 134 Many mill privileges with excellent water power are afforded. *c* 1854 Paulding *Antipathies* 262 There's a man at Jack O'Lantern's that owns land and *mill-rights. 1873 J. H. Beadle *Western Wilds* xxix. 465 This estimate..from the *mill-runs—the only honest test of a mine's capacity. 1880 *Encycl. Brit.* XIII. 357/1 During rolling this film [of oxide] becomes somewhat thick and peels off, forming '*mill-scale'. 1770 Washington *Diaries* I. 365 Mr. Ballendine and myself leveled Doeg Run in order to fix on a *Mill Seat. 1784 J. Filson *Kentucke* 19 The several streams and branches of Salt River afford excellent mill-seats. 1829 S. Cumings *Western Pilot* 11 Little Beaver ..affords a vast number of mill seats, many of which are already improved. 1839 J. F. Cooper *Home as Found* ii, The greater portion are now dealing..in mill-seats, and railroad lines, and other expectations. 1831 Peck *Guide Emigrants* 196 There are but few good *mill sites in the State. 1849 Chamberlain *Indiana Gazetteer* 458 It has some good mill sites on it, but its course in general is not rapid. 1815 Drake *Cincinnati* i. 58 In summer and autumn, it [Licking River] is a moderate *mill-stream. 1840 *Knickerbocker Mag.* XVI. 22 A wooden bridge which crossed a mill-stream. 1902 S. E. White *Blazed Trail* xxi. 155 He arrived out of breath in a typical little *mill town. 1863 Mrs. Whitney *F. Gartney's Girlh.* xxiii, It needs just such a man [as minister] among *mill-villages like these, he says. 1770 Washington *Diaries* I. 381 Ball and his People went about 12 oclock to Framing the *Mill Work.

Mill, *sb.*[5] (U.S. examples.)

1786 in *Amer. Museum* (1789) II. 182 Mills, the lowest money of account, of which one thousand shall be equal to the federal dollar, or money unit. 1794 *Amer. Calendar* 62 Decimal Parts of Cents (or Mills).

Also *attrib.* as *mill-tax*.

1848 *Indiana Hist. Soc. Publ.* III. 514 The former will pay on a mill tax $200. 1853 in *Trans. Mich. Agric. Soc.* VII. (1856) 293 A mill tax is annually levied to purchase books for these libraries. 1903 *Scribner's Monthly* Oct. 486 They support the Universities by a direct mill tax levied upon the assessed valuation of the State.

Mill, *v.*[1] Add: 2. e. *Soap manufacture.*

1902 *Chambers's Jrnl.* Apr. 204/1 When quite hard, this fine soap is milled, or cut into very small shreds, after which it is pressed in moulds into fancy shapes.

12. (Earlier example.) Also *transf.* of persons, and *fig.*

1874 J. McCoy *Hist. Sketches* 101 Drovers consider that the cattle do themselves great injury by running round in a circle, which is termed in cow-boy parlance, 'milling'. 1910 W. M. Raine *B. O'Connor* 227, I expect you were able to make out, even if I did get the letters to milling around wrong. 1911 H. Quick *Yellowstone N.* v. 127 The main thing the matter was that failure o' his a-millin' through his mental facilities. 1919 L. F. Cody *Buffalo Bill* 302 Indians and soldiers milled, the Indians fighting with their knives, the soldiers with their guns. 1927 H. E. Fosdick *Pilgr. to Palestine* 262 We look down upon the throng milling around the Chapel of the Sepulcher.

c. *fig.* To turn *over* in one's mind.

1905 *Smart Set* Oct. 17/1 No,..I ain't buyin' no dishes. I was just kind o' millin' things over to myself. 1921 R. D. Paine *Comr. Rolling Ocean* xvii. 298 Judson, on guard in the cabin, was milling this problem over.

Millable (mi·lăb'l), *a.* [f. Mill *sb.*[1]] Suitable for cutting with a saw-mill.

1924 *Times Trade & Engin. Suppl.* 29 Nov. 250/2 It is proposed..to open up 500,000 acres of farming land and 1,000,000,000 feet of millable bush.

Mille·nnialism. [-ism.] Belief in the coming or the present existence of the millennium.

1906 *Pall Mall Gaz.* 4 Jan. 1 In a spirit of fatuous millennialism the constabulary force..was being reduced.

Millerism. (Earlier example.)

1846–52 Mrs. Whitcher *Widow Bedott P.* (1883) xii. 44 When Millerism was makin' such a noise,..the Wiggletown folks raly thought ther was something in it.

Millet. 2. (Add examples.)

1889 Maiden *Usef. Plants Australia* 97 *Panicum decompositum*,..'Australian Millet', 'Umbrella grass'..One of the most valuable of the Darling Downs (Queensland) grasses. 1896 *Australasian* 14 Mar. 488/5 (Morris) One of the very best of the grasses found in the hot regions of Central Australia is the Australian millet, *Panicum decompositum*.

Milliammeter (milie·mītəɹ). Abbreviation of *milliampère meter*.

1909 *Century Dict.* Suppl. 1922 *Daily Mail* 18 Nov. 10 Advt., Weston Ammeters and Milliammeters.

Mi·lliamp. Abbrev. of Milliampère.

1927 *Sunday Express* 17 Apr. 8/3 Advt., Every milliamp of Electricity is made by the Dynamo.

Milliardaire (mi:liădē·ɹ). [f. Milliard: after Millionaire.] A person possessing a 'milliard of money'.

1926 Herford *Mind of Post-War Germany* vii. 34 The hero, son of a milliardaire, is engaged in manufacturing a gas more powerful than all known fuels.

Millibar (mi·libāɹ). *Meteorol.* [f. Milli- + *Bar *sb.*[6]] A unit of barometric pressure equal to the thousandth part of a 'bar'.

1912 *Barometer Man. for Seamen* (ed. 7) 8 *note*, The unit of pressure employed in such cases..is called the *millibar*. 1915 *Marine Observer's Handbk.* 18 On the other side the graduation is in centibars and millibars and can be read to tenths. 1923 Sir W. N. Shaw *Forecasting Weather* p. xx, The millibar, as representing 1,000 dynes per square centimetre, became the accepted unit of pressure for our own charts.

Millime·tric, *a.* [f. Millimetre.] Of the magnitude of a millimetre; minute.

1909 *Milton Memorial Lect.* 194 Those millimetric distinctions by which human character declines or ascends.

Million. Add: 2. c. A small fish, *Lebistes reticulatus*, native to the Barbadoes, which destroys mosquito larvæ; so called from the rate at which it multiplies.

1914 Fantham & Porter *Some minute Anim. Parasites* 106 The small fish known as 'millions' are also sent from place to place..for use in mosquito destruction. 1923 *Nature* 26 May 718/2 Investigations on the millions fish (*Lebistes reticulatus*). 1924 J. A. Thomson *Science Old & New* li. 302 How are mosquito larvae to be killed off in Indian tanks for drinking-water where the paraffin method is obviously impossible? By introducing little fishes called 'millions' which devour the larvae and do no harm.

3. **million-dollar weed** *U.S.* (see quot.); **millionheiress**, an heiress to a 'million of money'.

1921 *Discovery* Feb. 48/1 The water hyacinth..is a beautiful aquatic plant..but its spread in St. John's River and the enormous sums spent in attempting its suppression have earned it the name of the '*million-dollar weed'. 1919 W. De Morgan *Old Madhouse* 457 His mind took kindly to the interruption of this young man's nuptials with an American *millionheiress of startling beauty.

Millionai·reship. [-ship.] The position of a millionaire.

1901 *Chambers's Jrnl.* Apr. 217/2 The flour industry gave the late Mr. Charles A. Pillsbury the means of millionaireship.

Millpond. b. Add:

The use is anticipated in, and perhaps originally suggested by, the following passages:—

1813 Paulding *J. Bull & Bro. Jonathan* (ed. 2) i. 5 He put himself in a boat, and paddled over the mill-pond to some new lands. *Ibid.* ii. 12 The tenants began to carry their grain to different parts of the great mill-pond.

Mim, *a.* (U.S. example.)

1891 Rose T. Cooke *Huckleberries* 96 She was a mim, soft-spoken woman, but guileful and gliding as a snake.

Mimesis. Add: 3. *Path.* (See quot. 1913.)

1909 *Century Dict.* Suppl. 1913 Dorland *Med. Dict.*, *Mimesis*, the simulation of one disease by another.

Mimosa. 3. *mimosa-bush* (earlier example).

1856 F. Fleming *S. Africa* xii. 364 A broad valley, covered with rich pasturage and dotted with '*mimosa*' bushes, stretched out over several acres.

Mimoseous (mimōu·ʃəs), *a. Bot.* [f. Mimosa + -ous.] Belonging to the sub-order *Mimoseæ* of leguminous shrubs.

c 1866 in L. Huxley *Life Sir J. D. Hooker* (1918) II. xxxii. 107 The Mimoseous tree, of which the pods open and wind spirally outwards.

Mince, *v.* 5. a. Add: Also with *out*.

1862 Mrs. H. Wood *Channings* II. v. 75 'You—are—very—kind—to—take—up—Arthur Channing's cause!' they mince out. 1888 Mrs. H. Ward *R. Elsmere* III. vi. xliii. 255 'Ah—"Reculer pour mieux *faire* sauter!"'—said Sir John, mincing out his pun as though he loved it.

Mincemeat. 2. (Add example.)

1876 *Coursing Calendar* 193 Maniac made mincemeat of Smoker, who was so stiff that he could scarcely raise a gallop.

Mincemeaty, *a.* [f. prec. + -y.] Suggestive of mincemeat.

1870 Ph. Brooks in A. V. G. Allen *Ph. Brooks* (1908) 246 Huxley's new *Lay Sermons*..is like..most books for the people that popularize science. It is patronizing and mincemeaty.

Mincy (mi·nsi), *a. U.S.* [f. Mince *v.* + -y.] Using an affected delicacy or daintiness in one's speech.

1913 Mrs. Stratton-Porter *Laddie* xiii, She didn't stop to be mincy. She shot things at him like a man talking to another man.

Mind, *sb.*[1] 13. a. Add: Also *to have two minds*: to be undecided whether or not *to do* a thing; = *to be in two minds* (11 e).

1888 'R. Boldrewood' *Robbery under Arms* II. xii. 205 We'd two minds to camp on the mountain.

b. (U.S. examples.) Also *I'm* (*a*) *mind to*.

1842 J. S. Buckingham *Slave States* II. xiii. 293 The room *up-starrs* is quite *preparred*, so that your *plunder* may be *toted* there whenever *you've a mind*. ? 1830 Seba Smith *Thirty Yrs. out of Senate* (1860) 87, I s'pose a Governor has a right to flog anybody he's a mind to. 1867 Lowell *Fitz Adam's Story* 496 To him the in-comer, 'Perez, how d' ye do?' 'Jest as I'm mind to, Obed; how do you?'

21. *mind-wandering* (vbl.sb.); *mind-weary* (adj.).

1925 C. Fox *Educ. Psychol.* 335 Simply as a result of *mind-wandering due to extraneous incentives or impulses to some other kinds of activity. 1923 Una L. Silberrad *Lett. Jean Armiter* xiii. § iii. 264 But—I am tired! Foot-weary as well as *mind-weary.

b. **mind-blindness** (see quot.); **mind-child**, an imaginary or 'dream' playmate created by a child; **mind-curist**, one who practises 'mind-cure'; **mind-healing** (earlier example).

1909 *Hastings' Encycl. Relig. & Ethics* II. 710/2 '*Mind-blindness' is an acquired condition in which objects can be seen, but fail to be recognized by the sense of sight. 1928 *Daily Express* 8 Dec. 4 The imaginative child should be dealt with carefully. Foster his little plays and the *mind-child he has created. 1904 *Amer. Jrnl. Relig. Psychol. & Educ.* May 80 That kind of giving up, of relaxation, which the *Mind-Curist, the Christian Scientist, and the Hypnotizer..attempt to bring about. 1883 Mrs. Eddy *Let.* to *Boston Post* 7 Mar., My discovery, in 1866, of the Science of *Mind-healing, since named Christian Science.

Minder. 3. b. Add: Now often used for *machine-minder*.

1888 *Encycl. Brit.* XXIII. 709/2 If he is a machinist, he may superintend or be a 'minder', or he may be a layer-on or taker-off of the sheets.

Mindless. 2. b. Add: Also *that*.

1908 Hardy *Dynasts* III. i. iii. 335 He has bundled leftwardly Thomière's division; mindless that thereby His wing and centre's mutual maintenance Has gone.

Mine, *sb.* 5. Add: *mine-dust, -head, -mouth, -slime, worker*; (sense 3) *mine-warfare*.

1886 J. Barrowman *Sc. Mining Terms* 45 **Mine dust*, the riddlings of calcined ironstone. 1913 *Daily Mail* 16 Mar. 9 The present intention is to send labour squads..to successive *mine-heads. 1886 J. Barrowman *Sc. Mining Terms* 45 **Mine mouth*, the point where a mine leaves the surface of the ground. 1921 *Chambers's Jrnl.* Apr. 262/1 A savage land of rocks and lakes and *mine-slime and active and derelict mine-workings. 1910 *Blackw. Mag.* June 805/2 The immense development of *mine warfare. 1901 *Edin. Rev.* Apr. 496 An agreement..that the *mine-workers should receive an advance of 10 per cent. in their rates of wages. 1928 *Brit. Industr. Fut.* (Lib. Ind. Inq.) iv. 266 The pensioning of older mine-workers.

6. **mine-layer**, a special type of vessel for laying mines; **mine-laying**, the laying of explosive mines in the sea; **mine-sinker**, a device for keeping a mine submerged; **mine-thrower**, [tr. G. *minenwerfer*] a trench-mortar.

1909 *Q. Rev.* Oct. 575 Six second-class cruisers of the Naval Defence Act have been converted into *mine-layers. 1923 Churchill *World Crisis, 1915* 260 The mine-layer *Nousret* had on March 18 thirty-six mines ready for laying. 1911 *Q. Rev.* Oct. 466 The money..is now expended upon a large and increasing fleet of *mine-laying and mine-sweeping ships. 1928 Gamble *Story N. Sea Air Station* xviii. 310 The U. C. boats were of a type designed both for mine-laying and torpedo work. 1926 *Spectator* 21 Aug. 271/1 He..produced 50,000 *minesinkers at a very low cost. 1915 *Illustr. London News* 13 Feb. 204/2 The Germans.. had actually provided..themselves with mortars of this description, the so-called *minen-werfer*—*mine-throwers. 1923 *Daily Mail* 17 Jan. 7 They captured 7 Frenchmen, 15 local policemen, 3 minethrowers, and a machine gun.

Mine, *v.* 2. b. (Later example.)

1921 *Brit. Mus. Return* 138 *Phytomyza albiceps*, mining and ruining the leaves of Cinerarias.

Mineral, *sb.* Add: 4. d. *pl.* = Mineral waters.

1903 *Licensed Traders' Dict.* 1927 *Glasgow Herald* 15 Apr. 11 There will be..supper with ale and minerals at Osborne's Hotel.

Mineral, *a.* 5. Add: **mineral rod**, a divining rod.

1849 C. Lanman *Lett. Alleghany Mts.* Add. 187 Travelling about the country under the guidance of *mineral rods* or dreams in search of mines. 1902 A. D. McFaul *Ike Glidden* xxi. 184 They've sent for Squire Blunt to come up here in the morning, with a mineral rod, to assist them.

Mineralized, *ppl. a.* Add: 2. b. (See quot.).

1906 *Act 6 Edw. VII* c. 20 § 4 (1) The expression 'mineralized methylated spirits' means..spirits which, in addition to being methylated..have mixed with or dissolved in them ..mineral naphtha.

Miney, recent variant of Minty *a.*

Mingle, *v.* 2. Add to def.: To mix or shuffle (playing-cards).

1886 Stevenson *Kidnapped* xxiii, Cluny stopped mingling the cards.

Mingo, variant of Mungo[4].

1875 *Encycl. Brit.* I. 176 Mingo is even a shorter description of fibre, and is made in the same way [as shoddy] from old rags.

Mingy (mi·ndʒi), *a. colloq.* [Perh. f. M(ean *a.* + St)ingy *a.*] Mean, parsimonious, niggardly, stingy.

1928 *Daily Express* 4 July 9/2 She wanted to get rid of the 'mingy old —.' 1929 *Ibid.* 19 Jan. 5/3 After all..it isn't much an ordinary woman wants,..nothing that will cost her husband a penny of money or a moment of discomfort. ..So men needn't be so mingy! 1930 E. V. Lucas *Down Sky* 223 It's dear, but we are not going to be mingy.

Miniature. A. *sb.* Add: 5. d. *Chess.* A problem involving few pieces or moves; *spec.* one in which not more than seven pieces are used [ad. G. *miniatur*].

1903 *Brit. Chess Mag.* 91 It shows the composer's various styles better to give No. 76, which is a four-move 'miniature'. 1907 S. S. Blackburne *Terms & Themes Chess. Probl.* 29 Very light-weight problems are known as 'miniatures'. 1908 E. Wallis (*title*) 777 Chess Miniatures in Three.

Minification (minifikēi·ʃən). [f. Minify *v.* + -ation.] Reduction in the apparent size of an object when viewed through a lens.

1904 *Jrnl. R. Microsc. Soc.* June 281 A magnifying power which exactly balances the ten-fold minification before spoken of.

Minim. B. Add: 8. b. In apothecaries' weight, a unit equal to a grain.

1899 W. H. Molesworth *Pocket-Bk. Usef. Formulæ* (ed. 24) 594, 5760 grains or minims = 1 pound (Apothecary's weight).

Minimalist (mi·nimălist). [f. Minimal + -ist or ad. F. *minimaliste*; a translation of Russ. *men'shévik* *Menshevik.] One of the Russian Mensheviks, the less extreme socialists. Also *attrib.* or as *adj.*

1917 *Times* 23 June 7/1 At the 'All Russia' Congress of the Workmen's and Soldiers' Delegates the 'Minimalist Socialists' have defined their programme. 1917 *19th Cent.* July 141 The Mensheviki or Minimalists (Moderate Socialists) need reorganisation. 1918 *Nelson's Hist. of War* XVIII. 108 The Mensheviki, or Minimalists, were of a saner type. 1922 *Blackw. Mag.* June 820/2 The delegation represented not only Communists, but also Minimalists and the converted intelligentsia.

Minime·tric, *a.* [f. Minimeter.] That measures in (terms of) minims.

1902 *Nature* 13 Nov. 47/1 An application of the minimetric method to the examination of air.

Minimum. 6. Add: *minimum rate, wage.*

1877 Leone Levi *Work & Pay* Index, Minimum wages, limits to, 85. 1908 *New Age* 18 July 223/2 A serious objection to the fixing of a minimum wage in England for employed is that it would be most difficult to make provision for the large number of incompetent, inferior, and slow workers. 1909 *Act 9 Edw. VII* c. 22 § 4 Minimum Rates of Wages... Trade Boards shall, subject to the provisions of this section, fix minimum rates of wages for timework for their trades.

Mining, *vbl. sb.* 3. Add: *mining-captain, -town* (earlier example); **mining-piece, time** (see quots.).

1872 *Rep. Vermont Board Agric.* I. 629 Captain Glonville, who for a year or two had been *mining captain, did not understand his business. 1882 Foote *Led-Horse Claim* iii. 30 West [was] the mining-captain of the Led-Horse. 1893 W. C. Hazlitt *Coinage Europ. Continent* 216 **Mining-pieces*, money of two classes: (i) that coined for mines, and (ii) for the miners. The former are generally of silver, and often of large size and elaborate and artistic design... The latter are usually of copper and of low values. 1882 *Harper's Mag.* May 897/1 The very clocks are set to '*mining-time', half an hour faster than sun time. 1888 *Century Mag.* Dec. 163/2 Teamsters, toiling across the great lava beds, on their way to the mountain *mining-towns, make camp.

Minister, *sb.* Add: 7. (Earlier example.)

1859 Bartlett *Dict. Amer.* (ed. 2) s.v. *Catfish*, It is also called by the name of Horned-pout, Bull-head, Mudpout, Minister, or simply Cat.

8. *Comb.* **minister-tax**, a tax for the support of ministers.

1792 *Massachusetts Spy* 31 May, Their lands are assessed ..as follows..viz.—Town Tax 2s. 5d. 2 q^r. Highway Tax 4s. and 3 q^r. Minister Tax 2s. 11d. 1 q^r.

Minister, *v.* Add: 4. b. To care for or attend to (a person).

1908 A. S. M. Hutchinson *Once Aboard Lugger* iv. ii. § 1. 211 Mr. Marrapit..abed of a chill, prevented Margaret meeting her Bill that afternoon. Her father must be constantly ministered.

Ministeriable (ministīə·riăb'l), *a.* [f. Ministeri(al + -able.] Fit for or admitting of being appointed as a minister of state.

1923 J. A. Spender *Life Sir H. Campbell-Bannerman* II. 127 His test of complete co-operation was that Lord Rosebery should be definitely within the circle of ministeriable ex-Ministers.

Ministrable (mi·nistrăb'l), *a.* (and *sb.*). [ad. F. *ministrable* adj. in same sense: cf. -able.]. (A person) fit or likely to be appointed or become a minister.

1921 *Contemp. Rev.* Mar. 289 The anti-British feeling [in France]..oozes out of declarations by Ministers and Ministrable politicians. 1927 *Blackw. Mag.* Feb. 277/2 Those that are ministrables have done the best for themselves.

Mink. 2. (Add early example.)

1683 Penn *Let.* 16 Aug. in J. F. Watson *Ann. Philad.* (1830) 63 The wild-cat, panther,..fisher, minx, musk-rat.

4. *mink-skin* (earlier examples).

1678 *New Castle Court Rec.* 349, 22 mincq skins great and smal. 1778 *Essex Inst. Hist. Coll.* XLIX. 109 Sold..33 mink skins, at 6s. 6d.

Minnesong (mi·nisɒŋ). [ad. G. *minnesang* f. *minne* love + *sang* Song *sb.*: cf. Minnesinger.] One of the songs of the Minnesingers. Also *collect.*

1838 Longf. *Poets & P. Europe* (1847) 182/2 This is the reason that all the Minnesongs, even the most diversified, seem still to resemble each other. 1907 F. C. Nicholson *Old German Love Songs* p. iii, English works on the subject of the German Minnesong are so scanty in number..that an addition to them can hardly be considered superfluous.

Minnie[2] (mi·ni). *Army slang.* [abbrev. of G. *minenwerfer* trench-mortar.] A German trench-mortar, or its bomb.

1917 Empey *From Fire Step* 36 A German 'Minnie' (trench mortar) had exploded in the next traverse. *Ibid.* 64 Trench mortars started dropping 'Minnies' in our front line. 1927 E. Thompson *These Men thy Friends* 116 A minnie had been established in the enemy line.

Minoan (məinōu·ăn, min-), *a.* and *sb.* [f. L. *Minōs* (Gr. Μίνως) a legendary king of Crete + -an.] a. *adj.* Of or pertaining to ancient Crete, or a distinct period of early Cretan civilization extending from the beginning of the fourth to the middle of the second millennium B.C.

1894 A. J. Evans in *Jrnl. Hellenic Stud.* XIV. 367 At a time when 'Minoan' Crete and Mycenaean Greece had.. evolved independent systems of writing. 1902 H. R. Hall in *Nature* 20 Nov. 58/1 The dominion of the proud Minoan thalassocrats disappeared. 1921 *Spectator* 5 Mar. 293/1 A hanging lamp..with a yellow and orange shade with a sort of Minoan design on it in orange, terracotta, and black. 1927 Peake & Fleure *Priests & Kings* 36 Many successive stages have been found of this civilization, which Evans has appropriately termed Minoan, after Minos the legendary king of Crete.

b. *sb.* An inhabitant of Crete in the Minoan age.

1902 H. R. Hall in *Nature* 20 Nov. 58/1 The hieroglyphics of their tutelary deity may have been used by the Minoans as a sort of heraldic device. 1924 *Countries of World* III. 1514/2 The modern inhabitants are the direct descendants of the Minoans.

Minor. A. *adj.* 2. Add: *Minor loyalty*: adherence to an institution, church, trade union, or the like, which is subordinate to loyalty to one's country or its government. *Minor suit*: diamonds or clubs, in the game of Bridge. *Minor tactics*: the tactics or handling of bodies of troops in the immediate face or expected presence of the enemy.

1875 C. Clery (*title*) Minor Tactics. 1885 A. B. Letts *A. B. C. of Minor Tactics* 59 Minor tactics..come into use not only on the field of battle but also off it. 1919 R. F. Foster *On Auction* 75 No good player ever wants to play one of the minor suits for the trump, unless [etc.]. 1927 Carr-Saunders & Jones *Soc. Struct. Eng. & Wales* 83 To discuss the 'minor loyalties' which such associations create. 1928 H. Rowan-Robinson *Some Aspects of Mechanization* 3 The study of the minor tactics of petrol-driven forces.

B. *sb.* Add: 10. In American universities and colleges, a subsidiary subject of study to which less time is devoted than to a major.

1891 [see *Major B]. 1926 *Amer. Oxonian* July 100 Oxford is a school for specialists. There are no minors, no electives, nothing but majors.

†**Minorate**, *v. Obs.* (Later U.S. example.)

1789 Morse *Amer. Geog.* 212 Their design is by quantity to depreciate the value of their bills; and lands mortgaged for public bills will be redeemed in these minorated bills.

Minority. Add: 2. Modern example of *in minority*.

1920 *Act 10 & 11 Geo. V* c. 64 § 2 A husband of full age, and subject to no legal incapacity, whose wife is in minority, shall be her curator during her minority, but no longer.

5. **minority man**, one who is in a minority or who tries to secure recognition of the claims of minorities; **minority member**, a member appointed on a board, committee, or the like, to represent a minority; **minority movement**, a movement to secure justice or proper representation for minorities; **minority report** (example).

1927 *Observer* 1 May 17/1 It was a curious moment..to choose for legislation calculated..to revive the power of '*minority men' and direct actionists in Britain. 1874 *Porcupine* 31 Jan. 693/2 The city of London has already conceded a *minority member. 1927 *Daily Tel.* 6 Sept. 7/3 He did not agree with the *Minority Movement. 1833 *Congress Deb.* 2 Mar. 1927 A new set of majority and *minority reports are to be launched upon the public.

Mint, *sb.*[1] 6. Add: **mint condition** = *mint state*; **mint state** (*transf.*, also of books and other objects which are sought by collectors).

1902 *Connoisseur* May 67/2 Nothing is more marked in present day stamp collecting than the insistence..upon what is expressively termed a '*mint' condition in unused specimens. 1923 *Punch* 7 Feb. 130 *Auctioneer.* 'Here we have Holbein's portrait of the first earl. A masterpiece. In fact his *chef-d'œuvre*, in mint condition and an acquisition to any gallery.' 1931 *Times Lit. Suppl.* 16 Apr. 305/3 Copies of 'Waverley'..are excessively rare in *mint state.

Mint, *sb.*[2] 3. **mint-julep** (earlier and later examples); **mint-sling** *U.S.*, a drink containing some alcoholic beverage flavoured with mint.

1809 W. Irving *Knickerb.* vii. ii. (1825) 292 The inhabitants ..were notoriously prone to get fuddled and make merry with *mint-julep and apple-toddy. 1813 Paulding *J. Bull & Bro. Jonathan* (ed. 2) xviii. 92 Certain mint juleps, which to say the truth are not bad things. 1853 J. G. Baldwin *Flush Times Alabama* 81 Great was he too at mixing an apple toddy or mint julep. 1870 Mrs. Stephens *Married in Haste* lxxii. 360 Mint-julips, whiskey-smashes, and an assortment of drinks. 1804 *Balance* 15 Mar. 86 (Th.) Three *Mint Slings. 1812 Paulding *J. Bull & Bro. Jonathan* 98 The Yankees abhor horse-racing, cock fighting, and mint-slings. 1829–32 J. P. Kennedy *Swallow B.* I. xi. 110 It is a vulgar error..to appropriate the mint sling to the morning.

Mint, *a. ellipt.* for *in mint condition* (see *Mint *sb.*[1] 6).

1928 *Humphris'* (Norwich) *Catal. No. 149* 13/1 'Mint' signifies As New.

Mint-drop. 2. (Earlier examples.)

1837 *Congress. Globe* 29 Sept. App. 339/3 [The money flowed to Mobile] by the aid of 'the far-famed Specie circular', in 'mint drops' and 'hard currency'. 1840 J. P. Kennedy *Quodlibet* 106 [There's] Specie Circlor and Mint Drops, and the Lord knows what. 1850 H. H. Garland *Life J. Randolph* I. xxxi. 250 Randolph..called the nostrums of this man '*Sloan's mint-drops*'.

Minute, *sb.*[1] Add: 1. d. *transf.* The distance that can be travelled in a minute.

1886 *Taunt's New Map Thames* (ed. 5) Advts. 45 Hotel.. Adjoining the River, 3 minutes from Railway Station. 1907 in A. H. Anderson *Reading* Advts. p. xxvii, Hotel..(1 minute from Railway).

6. *Minute of dissent*, a minute recording a person's disagreement with something.

1888 Kipling *Departmental Ditties* (ed. 3) 25 No longer Brown reverses Smith's appeals, Or Jones records his Minute of Dissent. 1930 *Times* 15 Mar. 7/1 All the members have signed the report, but Lord Ebbisham did so subject to a 'minute of dissent' which is attached to the main report.

7. **minute company**, a company of minute-men; **minute costs**, the costs of production of articles estimated by the number of minutes required for their manufacture; **minute-gun** (earlier example).

1775 *Maryland Hist. Mag.* X. 304 To raise a *Minute Company agreeably to the Resolve of the Convention. 1930 *Times* 8 Mar. 20/2 In Belgium, where the wages are lowest, the minute costs are highest. 1738 W. Stephens *Proc. Georgia* 428 At the Depositing of the Corpse seven *minute Guns were fired.

Minuter. 1. Delete †*Obs.* and add example.

c 1908 *Pitman's How to take Minutes* 14 The minuter must take sufficient notes of the proceedings.

Minuti·ssimic, *a.* [f. L. *minūtissim-us*, superl. of *minūtus*: see Minute *a.* + -ic.] Exceedingly minute.

1888 *Amer. Naturalist* Nov. 1014 Of these minutissimic, yet adult, forms, more than fifteen are Gastropods.

Minxish (mi·ŋksiʃ), *a.* [f. Minx + -ish.] Having the character of a minx; like a minx. Hence **Mi·nxishly** *adv.*

1870 *Porcupine* 12 Feb. XI. 443/3 Through a door, left slightly ajar, he..sees another minxish 'Girl of the Period' waiting the return of her companion. 1919 W. De Morgan *Old Madhouse* xxv. 387, I do *not* believe that Lucy..is half as minxish as she made out. 1927 *Daily Express* 27 Apr. 3/2 The mannequin wore it minxishly, for it was a frock for a minx.

Miny, *a.* Also miney. 1. (Recent example.)

1907 *World* 16 July 113/1 What do you say to mines? No, there's nothing miney about me.

Minyan (mi·niăn), *a.* [f. Gr. Μινύαι, an ancient race of Orchomenus in Greece + -an.] Of or pertaining to the Minyans. So **Minyean** (mini,ī·ăn) [Gr. Μινύειος, adj. f. Μινύαι], *adj.* = *Mintan.

1881 Schliemann in *Jrnl. Hellenic Stud.* II. 152 A wall of unwrought stones..which Professor Sayce holds to be the ancient Minyean city wall. 1912 A. J. B. Wace & M. S. Thompson *Prehist. Thessaly* 21 Minyan Ware. This class of pottery was first found in any quantity by Schliemann at Orchomenos. 1928 C. Dawson *Age Gods* viii. 190 The Greek mainland was conquered by a new people from the north, the bearers of the so-called Minyan culture.

Miohippus (məiohi·pəs). *Palæont.* Also meiohippus. [f. *mio-* in Miocene + Gr. ἵππος horse.] An extinct Miocene ancestor of the horse.

1876 *Times* 7 Dec. (Stanf.), In the recent strata was found the common horse,..in the Meiocene the Meiohippus, or Anchitherium. 1927 Haldane & Huxley *Animal Biol.* xi. 239 Miohippus (*Anchitherium*).

Mir (miɹ). [ad. Russ. миръ *mir* world, village community.] A village community in Russia.

1877 D. M. Wallace *Russia* viii. 179 The Mir is the most peculiar of Russian institutions. 1905 J. H. Rose *Develop. European Nations* xi. 294 The ownership of the soil of Russia by the Mirs, the communes of her myriad villages. 1916 Bechhofer *Russia at Cross-Roads* 71 No period is known in Russian history when the Mir did not exist. 1925 *Contemp. Rev.* Jan. 60 They pointed out that the land-holding peasant..did not cease to be a member of the *mir*.

Mira·ged, *a.* [f. Mirage + -ed[1].] Seen in a mirage; of the nature of a mirage.

1920 *Blackw. Mag.* June 817/2 A dim outline of miraged date palms. 1925 *Chambers's Jrnl.* Aug. 486/2 Framed anew, in mystic space—Miraged dream past all believing—Looms the cradle of a race.

Mired, *ppl. a.* 2. (Recent examples.)

1891 Quiller-Couch *Noughts & Crosses* 207 My mired boots played havoc with the neatly sanded floor. 1897 T. C. De Leon *Novelette Trilogy* (Jealous God v) 127 (Born) Lifting tenderly the mired, limp and senseless form of a shriveled old woman, struck down by them ['bus horses].

Mirifically (məiri·fikăli), *adv.* [f. Mirifical *a.* + -ly.] So as to excite wonder or admiration; wonderfully, superbly.

1922 W. J. Locke *Tale of Triona* v. 49 Into the lounge filled with mirifically vestured fellow-creatures.

Mirliton. Delete †*Obs.* and add example.

1894 Du Maurier *Trilby* I. ii. 155 Taffy and Jeannot and Little Billie made the necessary music on their *mirlitons*.

Mirror, *sb.* 7. c. Add: **mirror-glass** (modern example); **mirror-reading**, the reading of matter as reflected in a mirror; **mirror-scale**, a scale provided with a mirror to assist in obtaining accurate readings.

1876 J. S. Ingram *Centennial Exposition* ix. 287 Inside was an oblong square, formed of *mirror-glass, which reached to the top of the case. 1888 *Encycl. Brit.* XXIV. 436/2 The principle gives an instantaneous solution of the question of the ultimate optical efficiency in the method of '*mirror-reading', as commonly practised in various physical observations. 1901 M. W. Travers *Exper. Study of Gases* vi. 56 The **mirror scale* (Jolly)...The scale is etched on the surface of a strip of glass..., which is then silvered on the second surface.

Mis- (məis-, mis-), *prefix.*[3] Repr. Gr. μισο- (μισ-), the form of Miso- sometimes used before a vowel as in **mi·sarchist**, one who hates or opposes government in any form.

1898 L. F. Ward *Outl. Sociol.* x. 228 These misarchists see the beneficent influences of natural law in the industrial world interfered with.

Misact, *v.* (Recent example.)

1925 *Contemp. Rev.* Nov. 624 The wonderful scene in Pimen's cell..was completely 'mis-acted', if I may use a non-existing word.

Misadventurer (misĕdve·ntiūrəɹ). [f. Misadventure + -er[1].] One who meets with or suffers misadventures; an unfortunate person.

1886 Hardy *Mayor Casterb.* II. xviii. 250 His mood was no longer that of the rebellious, ironical, reckless misadventurer.

Miscast, *v.* Add: 1. b. To cast wrongly or not well.

1926 W. J. Locke *Old Bridges* III. ix. 169 She saw the man that had been her neighbour rise and pick up the piece of bread miscast by the child and put it in his pocket.

4. *Theatr.* In passive, of an actor: To be appointed to take a part for which he is not fitted. Also of a play: To have the parts in it allotted to unsuitable actors.

1927 *Observer* 10 July 15/1 We say that so-and-so was good or adequate or miscast or unhappy in his part. We do not appraise the acting as we appraise the play. *Ibid.* 21 Aug. 9/4 'The Climax'..was brought to England seventeen years ago...It was then admittedly miscast, and it will be interesting to see whether it will now have a greater success.

Miscasting, *vbl. sb.* Add: 3. *Theatr.* The allotting to an actor of a part which does not suit him.

1926 *Spectator* 25 Sept. 470/2 In a long list of characters there is not one case of miscasting. 1927 *Observer* 26 Sept. 13/4 Those instances of what I thought was miscasting have made me long to try my hand at casting a play.

Miscegen. [See under Miscegenation.] (U.S. examples.)

1864 S. S. Cox *Eight Yrs. in Congress* (1865) 354 A very sprightly suffragan of the miscegen stamp... The result would be an average miscegen and a superior patriot.

Miscegenation. (Add Austral. example.)

1927 M. M. Bennett *Christison* ii. 29 'Miscegenation' being official jargon for what Governor Bourke called 'detaining black women by force'.

Mischief, *sb.* 9. c. (Add example.)

1895 *Century Mag.* June 279/2 And there's kindnesses and kindnesses, Mr. Ludovic. There's some that cost like the mischief.

Mischief, *v.* Add: 3. b. To do or work harm; to be mischievous.

1930 H. M. Tomlinson *All Our Yesterdays* I. iv. 43 The children got up and began to mischief with the dangerous ship.

Mi:scomprehe·nding, *ppl. a.* [Mis-[1] 2.] That fails to understand.

1909 *Milton Memorial Lect.* 102 The entirely miscomprehending reader.

Miscontent, *v.* (Recent example.)

1920 M. Hewlett *Light Heart* v. 33 'I have had words come by me,' she said, 'that you are beguiling my Thordis. That miscontents me.'

Miscue·ing, *vbl. sb.* [-ing[1].] The making of a mis-cue.

1929 *Times* 1 Nov. 7/4 At the end of the last of these breaks he missed a difficult *massé* cannon, through partly miscueing.

Mi·scure. [Mis-[1] 4.] Unsuccessful curing or preserving of bacon. So **Miscu·red** *a.*, that has not been properly cured.

Misdraw, *v.* 1. (Modern example.)

1885 *Proc. Soc. Psychical Research* III. 427 There were also 40 diagrams..all misdrawn.

Hence **Misdraw·n** *ppl. a.*, badly or wrongly drawn (up).

1867 Bagehot *Engl. Const.* 268 The practical arguments and the legal disquisitions in America are often like those of trustees carrying out a misdrawn will.

Miserere. 4. (Earlier attrib. example.)

1888 B. Webb *Contin. Ecclesiol.* ii. 39 Four beautiful stalls, with miserere-seats and canopies.

Misery. 6. (Earlier U.S. examples.)

1833 J. Hall *Leg. West* 82 You never seed sich a poor afflicted crittur as I be, with the misery in my tooth. 1839 R. M. Bird *Robin Day* ii. 29 (Th.) Can he cure a misery in the tooth? demanded another.

Misfield, *sb.* [f. the vb.] In Cricket or Rugby football: Failure to gather the ball properly.

1909 *Daily Chron.* 25 Feb. 8/4 Guy's scored after a misfield of a high kick by Batchelor.

Misfire, *sb.* Add: 2. A brick not properly fired.

1923 Una L. Silberrad *Lett. Jean Armiter* vii. § i. 162 It..is built of bricks, misfires or mistakes, those that would not sell.

Misfire, *v.* Add: b. Of an internal combustion engine: To fail to explode the charge, or to explode it at the wrong instant. Frequently said (loosely) of a motor vehicle. (Cf. *to miss fire*: Miss *v.*[1] 5 a.) So **Misfi·ring** *vbl. sb.*

1905 *Motor Cycle* 6 Mar. 218/3 If an engine is back firing, that is, giving explosions in the silencer, it is also mis-firing. Misfiring may result from a defect in the ignition system. 1908 *Westm. Gaz.* 11 Aug. 4/2 So soon as I turned in the other direction the extraordinary mis-firing recommenced. 1925 *Morris Owner's Manual* 44 Want of attention to this precaution may..be the cause of misfiring. 1928 *Cars & Motor-cycles* III. 1244 An engine is said to misfire when the gas in one or more of the cylinders does not ignite.

Misfit, *sb.* Add: Also *attrib.*

1910 *Encycl. Brit.* XIV. 223/2 The advantage of this combination is that..it..lessens the danger of making 'misfit' pig iron, *i.e.* that which, because it is not accurately suited to the process for which it is intended, offers us the dilemma [etc.].

Misgotten, *ppl. a.* 1. (Modern example.)

1903 W. S. Jackson *Nine Pts. Law* vi. 171 Here was he with a trunk-load of misgotten gold wandering haphazard.. over two countries.

Mishit (mi·shit), *sb.* Also erron. miss-. [Mis-[1] 4.] A faulty or bad hit.

1882 Pardon *Australians in Engl.* 25 He made two mishits which fell harmless. 1898 [see Mis-[1] 4]. 1900 *Young Sportsman* (ed. A. E. T. Watson) 161 The right-hander who steps in to drive takes two risks—the risk of a 'miss-hit', and the risk of being stumped.

So **Mishi·t** *v. trans.*, to hit (a ball) faultily.

1930 *Times* 17 Mar. 4/4 Three minutes from the end Craig made his only mistake of the game, miss-hitting a bumping ball.

Misinfo·rmative, *a.* [Mis-[1] 6.] That gives wrong information. So **Misinfo·rmatory** *a.*

1912 *Times Lit. Suppl.* 15 Feb. 64/3 To modify these few misinformative parts of a work which otherwise is..valuable. 1927 *Observer* 3 Apr. 25/3 A so-called Informatory Double that does not contain top card strength is better termed 'misinformatory'.

Misknowing, *vbl. sb.* 2. (Modern example.)

1892 F. S. Ellis *Conc. Shelley* To Rdr., Well would it be for the world if no more was known of any poet's life, except through his works, than is known of Shakespeare's; how greatly should we then be delivered from misknowing!

Mislocation. (Later example.)

1874 L. Bacon *Genesis New Eng. Churches* p. x, Every careless mislocation of words in the structure of a sentence.

Misma·te, *v.* [Mis-[1] 1: back formation from Mismated.] *refl.* To mate or match (oneself) unsuitably.

1891 Hardy *Group Noble Dames* I. iii. 113 No syllable would have been breathed of how I mismated myself for love of you!

Misma·ting, *vbl. sb.* [Mis-[1] 3.] Wrong assorting (of types).

1902 De Vinne *Pract. Typogr., Printing Types* (ed. 2) 236 This difficulty tempts founders to make one set of small capitals serve for two or more distinct faces. An inexpert can seldom detect the mismating.

Misorder, *v.* 1. (Modern example.)

1909 *Daily Chron.* 24 Aug. 4/3 [He] charged the Admiralty with having so misordered the Navy as to expose the nation to the gravest jeopardy every hour.

Misprint, *v.* Add: b. *intr.* Of an animal: To place its feet or leave its several foot-prints in unusual or irregular positions.

1909 Baillie-Grohman *Master of Game* 262 A hind..misprints, that is sometimes the hind foot will be placed beside the fore foot, sometimes inside or in front of it.

Mispronou·ncer. [Mis-[1] 5.] One who pronounces words incorrectly.

1885 *Educat. Times* 1 June 207/1 Warnings more adapted to American mispronouncers than to English.

Mis-recollect, *v.* (Later example.)

1862 *N. Y. Tribune* 21 Mar. (Bartlett) The Senate, if we do not mis-recollect, has twice passed a bill abolishing the franking privilege.

Misruling, *vbl. sb.* (Modern examples.)

1927 *Daily Tel.* 25 Oct. 8/5 If in refereeing I give a flagrant legal mis-ruling..the Rugby Union can send for me and say what they think about me and my mis-ruling.

Miss, *sb.*[1] 7. b. (Examples of *to give a miss* in transf. sense.)

1918 'Berta Ruck' *Disturbing Charm* I. ii. 10 The Professor chose (as he often did) to give lunch a miss. 1930 *Morn. Post* 16 July 8/3 The leek is..among the..vegetables that are too often given a miss.

Miss, *sb.*[2] 5. Earlier and additional examples. Cf. Miss *v.*[2]

1790 N. Webster cited in *Gazette U. S.* 17 Nov. (Th.) The use of Miss for Mistress in this country is a gross impropriety. 1819 *Massachusetts Spy* 12 May (Th.), I concluded he had resolved to marry Miss Spruce, but found upon inquiry that his name was Spruce, and Miss Spruce was his wife. 1839 Mrs. Kirkland *New Home* xxxiv. 280 'Miss Skinner despised every body that lived in log-houses..; didn't she, Miss Briggs?' Mrs. Briggs nodded. 1854 Mary J. Holmes *Tempest & Sunshine* iv. 53 The one that works best this week shall go Saturday and carry Miss Crane some strawberries. 1872 Marietta Holley *My Opinions* (1891) 295 Miss Aster would give up her bedroom to me, or mebby she would make Mr. Aster sleep with one of the boys, and have me sleep with her. 1878 Rose T. Cooke *Happy Dodd* x. (Th.) Mis' Potter sent that. 1888 Powles *Land of Pink Pearl* 154 No married woman, not even excepting the Governor's wife, is ever accorded the title of 'Mrs,' but all ladies, married or single, are called 'Miss' or 'Missey' indiscriminately.

Miss, *v.*[1] Add: 5. c. *ellipt.* Of an internal combustion engine: To miss fire or misfire.

1904 *Peel City Guardian & Chron.* 14 May 3/2 Hargreaves was 'missing' very badly.

9. c. In various recent colloq. phrases, as *to miss the bus*: see *Bus *sb.*[2] 1 b.

1930 *Aberdeen Press & Jrnl.* 3 Sept. 4/5 As a medium for a dull debut, 'A Devil's Disciple' by Bernard Shaw.., to use an Americanism, missed the boat by twenty years. 1931 *Time & Tide* 29 Aug. 1001 There are ten men in the Cabinet... There are three more who, by strange irony of circumstance, have missed the train.

Missable (mi·săb'l), *a.* [f. Miss *v.*[1] + -able.] That can be or is likely to be missed.

1924 *Glasgow Herald* 15 June 11/6 Of course it was not a record, but he holed out everything missable.

Missalist. (Modern example.)

1909 *Daily Chron.* 9 Oct. 4/4 The three brothers Maris might be re-incarnations of the Van Eyck brothers, or the de Limburg missalists.

Miss-and-out. *U.S.* A shooting competition from which a person must retire after one miss.

1903 *Forest & Stream* 21 Feb. 159/3 A miss-and-out was.. shot at live birds.

Missilery (mi·siləri). [f. Missile *sb.* + -ery.] Missiles collectively; a collection of missiles.

1880 *Harper's Mag.* Sept. 506/1 There were in her mainmast eighteen large grape, and sixteen musket-balls, besides smaller missilery in profusion.

Mission, *sb.* 10. Add: *mission-farm, -house* (earlier examples), *-land, -station, style*; also *mission-bred*.

1909 *Times Lit. Suppl.* 7 Jan. 3/2 He makes capital fun of the '*mission-bred Kaffir's misuse of book-learning. *a* 1861 T. Winthrop *John Brent* ii. 16 He had found his early way to California, bought a *mission farm and established himself as a ranchero. 1794 Loskiel *Mission Indians N. Amer.* II. xi. 166 The *mission-house on the Mahony..was..burnt. 1837 W. Irving *Capt. Bonneville* (1895) II. 102 In approaching this deserted mission house from the south, the traveller passes over the mountain of San Juan. *a* 1861 T. Winthrop *John Brent* i. 7 They had been speculating in beef, bread-stuffs, city lots,..*mission lands. 1876 W. Booth in Begbie *Life W. Booth* (1920) I. xxv. 417 What is a *Mission Station? ..It is not a building, or a chapel, or a hall; it is not even a society, but a band of people united together to mission, to attack, to christianize an entire town or neighbourhood. 1911 *N. Y. Even. Post* 1 Mar. 8 The dignified..cement house, often in mission style with attractive tile roof.

b. **mission furniture**, a plain, solid style of furniture said to have been modelled originally on the furniture of the Spanish missions; (also *mission style*); **mission grape**, a variety of grape (originating in the Spanish missions in California) grown in the United States of America.

1904 *N. Y. Times* 9 May 4 Advt., In soft green pottery that will harmonize especially well with *Mission furniture in the favorite green oak. 1910 *Daily Chron.* 24 Jan. 3/5, I have often wondered why the modest designs of the mission furniture are so attractive. 1867 *Rep. Iowa Agric. Soc.* (1868) 205 The *Mission grape is not as much esteemed as formerly. 1888 *Encycl. Brit.* XXIV. 611/1 The variety of grape first planted in that region [California] was known as the 'Mission' grape, and is generally supposed to have been imported from Mexico. 1909 P. A. Wells & Hooper *Mod. Cabinet Work* 257 In America there has been a similar movement, known as 'The *Mission Style,' which is more or less a revival of Gothic and Jacobean forms applied to modern work.

Missional (mi·ʃənăl), *a.* [f. Mission *sb.* + -al.] Relating to or connected with a religious mission; missionary.

1907 W. G. Holmes *Age of Justinian & Theodora* II. 687 Several prelates, whose missional activities brought over whole districts and even nationalities to their creed.

Missionarism (mi·ʃənăriz'm). *rare.* [f. Missionary + -ism.] = Missionizing.

1890 H. S. Holland in S. Paget *Life* II. iv. (1921) 197 If I believe anything at all, I believe, with it, all that missionarism involves.

Missionary, *v.* [f. the sb.] a. *intr.* To act as a missionary. b. *trans.* To act as a missionary towards.

1862 *Independent* 24 Apr. (Bartlett) He [the Rev. Stephen H. Tyng] was always fond of missionarying. 1893 Kate D. Wiggin *Polly Oliver* vii. (1894) 87 Boys hate to be missionaried, and I'm sure I don't blame them.

Missionate, *v.* (Add example.)

1828 *Richmond* (Va.) *Enquirer* 19 Aug. 4/1 (Th.) [Mr. Weed] was next heard of in the southern tier of counties, missionating for the administration.

Missionist (mi·ʃənist). [-ist.] One who does mission work.

1909 Marg. B. Saunders *Litany Lane* I. iii. 34 These were wood-carvers, church artists, metal-workers, window designers, architects, carpenters and missionists.

Mississi·ppian. [-an.] An inhabitant of the State of Mississippi.

1845 Quitman *Let.* in *Life & Corr.* 225 Men..who wish to serve, as Mississippians, under the flag of their own state.

Mississippi plan. The plan of asserting the rule of whites over blacks by force if necessary.

1877 *Congress. Rec.* 9 Jan. 501/1 The plan of intimidation or bull-dozing is frequently spoken of as the 'Mississippi plan'. 1893 *Ibid.* 6 Oct. 2248/1 The Mississippi plan..is acknowledged to be the most efficacious of all known methods for eliminating the 'unwelcome voter'.

Miss-mark. [f. Miss *v.*[1] Cf. Mark *sb.*[1] 7 e.] A person who misses the mark, or fails in a purpose.

1908 Hardy *Dynasts* III. vii. ix. 520 So, as it is, a miss-mark they will dub me.

Missouri (mis-, mizūə·ri). The name of a river and of one of the United States of America.

1. In slang phr. *to come from Missouri*: to believe nothing until it is demonstrated. (Originally *I come from Missouri. You've got to show me.*)

1912 C. McCarthy *Wisconsin Idea* 291 In the words of the current slang phrase, every Wisconsin legislator 'comes from Missouri' and you have to 'show him'.

2. *attrib.* and *Comb.* a. Applied to varieties of animals and plants or to other objects occurring, or used in, or characteristic of, Missouri, as *Missouri antelope, cap, chipmunk, flax, hyacinth, silver-tree, whip.* b. **Missouri compromise**, an arrangement made in 1820 which provided that Missouri should be admitted to the Union as a slave state, but that slavery should not be allowed in any new state lying north of 36° 30'; **Missouri toothpick**, a bowie-knife (cf. Toothpick 4).

1805 Lewis in *Ann. 9th Congress* 2 Sess. 1046 With the addition of the skins of the *Missouri antelope, (called cobri by the inhabitants of Illinois). 1824 *Massachusetts Spy* 4 Feb. (Th.) Randolph appears this winter in a large drap surtout,..and a flat *Missouri fur cap. 1868 *Amer. Naturalist* Dec. II. 530 *Missouri Chipmunk (*Tamias quadrivittatus*). This little Chipmunk I saw in the bare rocky hills of the Mauvaise Territory. 1854 T. H. Benton *Thirty Years* 8/2 This array of names shows the *Missouri compromise to have been a Southern measure. 1865 *Congress. Globe* 20 Feb. App. 70/1 In accordance with this principle he caused the repeal of the Missouri compromise. 1870 *Ibid.* Jan. App. 70/2 The Missouri compromise..had been a sacred compact for thirty years between slavery and freedom. 1887 *Century Mag.* Mar. 692/1 His agency in bringing about the repeal of the Missouri Compromise. 1846 Emory *Military Reconn.* 16 On these hills we found cedar growing, very stunted, *Missouri flax, several varieties of wild currants. 1880 *Encycl. Brit.* XII. 420/1 The *Missouri hyacinth, *Hesperoscordum lacteum*. 1814 F. Pursh *Flora* I. 114 Oleaster, or *Missouri Silver-tree. 1855 *Herald of Freedom* (Lawrence, Kas.) 9 June (Th.) We mistrust that the author of that statement saw a *Missouri toothpick and was frightened out of his wits. 1873 J. H. Beadle *Undevel. West* xxx. 649 They come on down the road, and with their big *Missouri whips would snap off the heads of chickens.

Missourian (mis-, mizūə·rian). [-an.] A native or inhabitant of the State of Missouri.

1820 *Deb. Congress* 26 Jan. 948, I cannot believe that I, or any other man or men, are better capable of governing Missourians than they are of governing themselves. 1850 N. Kingsley *Diary* 158 Several started off the bar to day for home, all Missourians. 1889 K. Munroe *Golden Days* iii. 23–24 The Missourian flung them right and left. 1899 T. Hall *Tales* 279 'The bar ain't here—wish it was,' interrupted a long-nosed Missourian.

Mis-speak, *v.* Add: 3. b. *refl.* To fail to convey the meaning one intends by one's words.

1894 *Congress. Rec.* 19 Jan. 1051/1, I simply wanted to bring that matter out plainly...I believe he misspoke himself.

Misstay, *v.* (Earlier example.)

1849 N. Kingsley *Diary* 88 We misstayed in but 11 feet of water, but the bottom is very muddy and not dangerous.

Mi·ss-stays. [f. as Misstay *v.*] Of a ship: The act or fact of failing to go about.

1878 D. Kemp *Yacht & Boat Sailing* 245 A 'miss-stays' may be the consequence.

Mis-step, *sb.* (Earlier examples.)

a 1800 *Spirit Farmer's Museum* (1801) 205 The Squire.. can sit on the sessions, and fine poor girls for natural missteps. 1837 *Yale Lit. Mag.* III. 8 (Th.) Forgetting the round door block, he made a mis-step.

Mis-step, *v.* (Modern example.)

1869 S. Bowles *Our New West* v. 102 Mules don't mis-step, and even the top-heavy pack jacks..carried their burden and themselves unharmed to the top.

Mist, *sb.*[1] 5. Add: *mist-pale* adj.; **mist-belt**, a tract of country where mist or rain is common.

1905 *Rep. Brit. Assoc.* 594 Passing either east or west of this '*mist-belt' the rainfall rapidly diminishes. 1849 C. Brontë *Shirley* xxix, A phantom abbess or a *mist-pale nun.

Mistake, *sb.* 2. b. Add: Also *In mistake for*.

1906 Galsworthy *Man of Property* I. ii. 39 Old Jolyon.. for the first time in his life gave the driver a sovereign in mistake for a shilling. 1923 *World's Work* May 563/1, I remember looking at him and..expecting that I had been arrested in mistake for him.

Mistake, *v.* Add: 4. c. *To mistake one's man*: to judge incorrectly, or underestimate, the capabilities, character, etc., of the person one has to deal with.

1794 *Massachusetts Spy* 16 Apr. (Th.) If he supposes I am to be frightened by his pompous accusations, he has much mistaken his man. 1804 *Ibid.* 5 Sept. (Th.) It seems that in one instance the General Committee have mistaken their man. 1837 J. Q. Adams in *Congress. Globe* 9 Feb. App. 264/1 Did the gentleman think he could frighten me from my purpose by the threat of a Grand Jury? If that was his object, let me tell him he mistook his man. 1841 *Ibid.* 18 June 75/3 Mr. G. said that he was not to be coughed or cried down; gentlemen mistook their man if they supposed he was to be affected by the machinery of the political party.

Mistify: see Mystify *v.*

Mistify (mi·stifəi), *v.* [f. Mist *sb.*[1] + -fy.] *trans.* To reduce to a mist or fine spray.

1902 *Encycl. Brit.* XXVII. 635/2 The nozzles for 'mistifying' the wash..can be fitted to any length of tubing.

Mistletoe. 1. b. (Earlier U.S. examples.)

1806 in *Ann. 9th Congress* 2 Sess. 1142 Mistletoe, thistle, wild hemp, bulrush. 1819 E. Evans *Pedestrious Tour* 318 In this..country [Louisiana] grows the celebrated plant called mistletoe. 1838 J. Hall *Western States* ii. 28 The mistletoe is seen hanging from the branches of the trees throughout the whole course of the Ohio.

Mistrust, *v.* 3. b. (Add examples.)

1840 Hoffman *Greyslaer* I. x. 109, I mistrust that your Injun friend there..didn't help you much..in finding out old Josie. 1872 Eggleston *End of World* xv. 106, I put the letter there, and I don't doubt your ma mistrusted it, and got a holt on it. 1898 A. Nicholas *Idyl of Wabash* 188 Before early apples were ripe I mistrusted what was keeping him.

Mistrusting, *vbl. sb.* (Recent example.)

1921 *Spectator* 30 Apr. 556/2 Class bitterness and the mistrusting of the employer by the employed.

Mistune, *v.* (Add example.) Hence also **Mistu·ning** *vbl. sb.*

1914 R. Stanley *Text-bk. Wireless Telegr.* 134 Thus we find that in the Telefunken transmitter the circuits are slightly mistuned, the aerial circuit having a free wave length about a per cent. higher than that of the primary circuit, and this mistuning is increased with the closeness of the coupling.

Misuse, *sb.* 2. (Modern example.)

1881 Swinburne *M. Stuart* I. i. 10 The Catholics naked here to all misuse Fall off in numbered force, in means and power.

Misuser[1]. (Recent example.)

1927 *Manch. Guardian Weekly* Oct. 315/2 An exercise in most delicate raillery at the expense of all the misusers of the English language.

Mitchell-grass. *Austral.* The name of several varieties of fodder grass grown in Australia (see quot. 1902).

1883 F. M. Bailey *Synopsis Queensland Flora* 660 (Morris) Used for food by the natives. The most valuable fodder-grass of the colony. True Mitchell-grass. 1886 *Encycl. Brit.* XX. 174/1 The desert drought-resisting Mitchell grass is *Danthonia pectinata*. 1902 *Ibid.* XXXII. 108/2 The 'Mitchell grasses' (*Astrebla pectinata*) and its varieties, viz., the Wheat (*triticoides*), the weeping (*elymoides*), and the curly (*curvifolia*),..have the most extraordinary vitality. 1909 *Chambers's Jrnl.* Dec. 809/2 Mitchell grass is said to be able to survive a rainless period extending over three years. 1927 M. M. Bennett *Christison* v. 55 Curly Mitchell grass shimmered gold and silver.

Mite, *sb.*[2] Add: 6. **mite society**, a society whose object is to collect funds for some charitable purpose by small contributions (see sense 1 c).

1823 *Baptist Mag.* IV. 133, I have also assisted in the organization of two Female Mite Societies. 1863 G. K. Wilder *MS. Diary* 20 Jan., This eve we are intending to go to Mite Society. 1878 *Harper's Mag.* Jan. 203/1 By means of 'mite' societies..sufficient money was raised to inclose it [the grave-yard].

Mitella. 2. (Later example.)

1882 *Harper's Mag.* Nov. 853/2 Why should the starry blossom of the fringed mitella seek the snow-flake as its model?

Mithan. Add to forms: **mithong, mithun.**

1921 *Blackw. Mag.* Feb. 258/2 There was no rice, no water, no fences, no herds of mithun. 1923 *Ibid.* Feb. 186/2 The mithong were once more stalled beneath the houses.

Mithraistic (mipreɪ,i·stik), *a.* [f. Mithraist + -ic[1].] Pertaining to or suggestive of Mithraists or Mithraism.

1920 *Glasgow Herald* 1 May 4 Hymn-writing..ran too much to gloomy terrorism and Mithraistic images of wounds and blood.

Mitochondria (məitokǫ·ndriă). *pl. Biol.* [mod.L. f. Gr. μίτος thread + χονδρίον dim. of χόνδρος cartilage.] Spherical or rod-shaped granules occurring in the cytoplasm of certain cells.

1896 E. B. WILSON *Cell* 418 There is no doubt that at this stage these granules, which are the mitochondria, bear some definite relation to the nucleus. 1911 *Jrnl. Morphology* XXII. 777 Further, there are certainly no filamentous mitochondria (chondriokonts) in the spermatogonia. 1920 DONCASTER *Introd. Cytology* 22 The study of mitochondria is less easy than that of the nuclear constituents of the cell.

Mitochondrial (məitokǫ·ndriăl), *a.* [f. prec. + -AL.] Of or pertaining to mitochondria.

1896 E. B. WILSON *Cell* 419 The distribution of the mitochondrial matter seems to have been equally carried out. *Ibid.*, A cloud of mitochondrial granules. 1920 DONCASTER *Introd. Cytology* 22 The mitochondrial bodies..undergo division.

Mitosome (məi·tosōᵘm). [f. Gr. μίτος a thread + σῶμα body.] (See quot. 1896.)

1896 E. B. WILSON *Cell* 338 *Mitosome*, a body derived from the spindle-fibres of the secondary spermatocytes, giving rise, according to Platner, to the middle-piece and the tail-envelope of the spermatozoön. Equivalent to the Nebenkern of La Valette St. George. (Platner, 1889.) 1911 *Jrnl. Morphology* XXII. 772 Mitosome and cell plate. 1920 DONCASTER *Introd. Cytology* 95 *note*, This mitochondrial mass ('mitosome') constitutes the 'Nebenkern' of some authors.

Mitotically, *adv.* (Example.)

1902 *Science* 21 Mar. 457/1 Just before the separation of egg from periplasm, the nuclei probably all divide once, mitotically.

Mitre, *sb.*² 5. Add: **mitre-gate,** a gate which meets another in a mitre-joint.

1913 J. B. BISHOP *Panama Gateway* v. v. 3:8 It is necessary to..operate six pairs of *mitre-gates, and force them to mitre.

Mitred, *ppl. a.*² (Add examples.)

1786 GOUGH *Sepulchral Mon.* I. p. clxxv, The knight has plated armour, and the lady the mitred headdress. 1906 H. DRUITT *Costume Monum. Brasses* 270 The mitred head-dress without veil.

Mitten. 3. (Add example.)

1923 P. G. WODEHOUSE in *Strand Mag.* Apr. 335, I was reluctantly compelled to hand the misguided blighter the mitten and go to London.

Mix, *v.* 4. Modern examples of *to mix in with.* Also *to mix in*: to join in or begin a fight: so *to mix it.*

1870 JULIE P. SMITH *Widow Goldsmith's Dau.* vi. 69 (Born) Of course they [*sc.* guttersnipes] couldn't expect to mix in with the rich children. 1895 MURAT HALSTEAD *Hundred Bear Stories* 117 Elk killing didn't seem half so great an achievement as it had before the bear had mixed in with the proceedings. 1912 R. A. WASON *Friar Tuck* xxi. 158 'Well, what if he did shoot', sez Slim, 'we wouldn't have to mix in, would we?' 'You know blame well we'd mix in', sez Tank, 'an' you can't tell where it would end.' 1918 E. M. ROBERTS *Flying Fighter* 91 He grew angry and we mixed it. I gave him a black eye, and he came back and apologized to me in the morning. 1924 W. M. RAINE *Troubled Waters* x. 102 One thing led to another, and they both got down from their horses and mixed it.

Mixed, *ppl. a.* Add: 6. b. *Phonetics.* Of a vowel sound: Produced with the tongue in a position intermediate between those required for back and front vowels.

1867 A. M. BELL *Visible Sp.* 72 The 'Mixed' vowels have smaller cavities, the edges of the tongue being raised to the sides of the teeth. 1890 SWEET *Primer Spoken Engl.* 4 In the vowels we distinguish three horizontal positions, or degrees of retraction of the tongue: back, mixed, front. 1911 D. JONES *Pronunc. English* 10 Vowels are .. classed as front, mixed, and back, according to the horizontal position of the highest point of the tongue.

9. (Further examples.)

1848 G. ROBERTS *Diary of Walter Yonge Esq.* 15 *note*, The writer's abhorence of all scenic exhibitions, .. mixt-dancing, &c. was so great. 1906 *Bazaar, Exch. & Mart* 6 July 34/1, I should like a place where mixed bathing is allowed. 1910 *Westm. Gaz.* 20 Apr. 9/4 The paragraphs.. concerning him..arose because their mixed bathing party used to bathe from a private bathing-place.

11. **mixed-celled** *a. Pathol.*, involving or containing cells of more than one kind; **mixed crystal,** a crystal formed of more than one crystalline substance: **mixed income,** an income which is partly earned and partly unearned.

1908 *Practitioner* Feb. 235 Leucocythaemia..may be qualified by such descriptive titles as "mixed-celled leucocythaemia, (the spleno-medullary form)..or lymphocytic leucocythaemia. 1910 *Encycl. Brit.* VII. 591/1 Two or more of these elements may be present together in the same crystal, which is then spoken of as a "mixed crystal" or isomorphous mixture. 1927 BOWLEY & STAMP *Nat. Income 1924* 17 In practice this gives an intermediate figure as the exemption limit for a "mixed income".

Mixer. 1. Add: One who mixes drinks. *U.S.*

1919 T. K. HOLMES *Man fr. Tall Timber* viii. 93 He.. drank several insidious concoctions of the hotel's most famous 'mixer'.

2. b. In talking films, the apparatus which controls the contributions from the various microphones.

1929 ALLIGHAN *Romance of Talkies* 63 The mixer controls also the gain of the amplifiers for the recording machines.

3. Orig. *U.S.* A person in respect of his capacity for mixing with others. Orig. and esp., *A good mixer*: One who mixes readily with others; a sociable person.

1896 G. ADE *Artie* xii. 105 I'm a good mixer. 1903 A. ADAMS *Log Cowboy* xvi. 240 The travel-stained old rascal proved to be a good mixer. 1904 W. H. SMITH *Promoters* xx. 287 He was a most excellent 'mixer', told a story well [etc.]. 1904 *N.Y. Even. Post* 25 Nov. 7 As diplomacy is practised now, the really useful expert is the higher-bred 'mixer'. 1915 H. L. WILSON *Ruggles of Red Gap* v. (1917) 100 Oh, Bill's all right when you get him out with a crowd. ..Bill's really got the makings of one fine little mixer. 1916 J. B. THOBURN *Hist. Oklahoma* III. lxxii. 787 He made up for some of his deficiencies by a genial disposition which made him a 'good mixer'. 1925 W. SOMERSET MAUGHAM in *Good Housekeeping* Sept. 15/2 He was a good mixer, and in three days he knew everyone on the ship. 1931 *Times Lit. Suppl.* 5 Mar. 169/2 No man was less of a 'mixer'.

4. *attrib.* as *mixer-valve.*

1904 *Elect. World & Engin.* 2 Jan. 22 (Cent. Suppl.) *Mixer-valve.

Mix-in, *colloq. U.S.* [f. *to mix in* *MIX *v.* 4.] A fight or 'scrap'.

1912 R. A. WASON *Friar Tuck* xxi. 158 An' what he's achin' for now is a mix-in with the Cross brand outfit.

Mixing, *vbl. sb.* c. (Additional examples.)

1849 *Rep. U.S. Comm. Patents* (1850) 178, I claim the mixing tub and knives as used in making bricks. 1896 TAGGART *Cotton-spinning* I. 50 This lattice is one of a series ..which are so arranged that the cotton can be taken as required to any one of the four mixing stacks or bins shown in the plan.

Mixologist (miksǫ·lŏdʒist). *U.S. slang.* [f. MIX + -(O)LOGIST.] One specially skilled in the mixing of drinks.

1856 *Knickerbocker Mag.* June XLVII. 615 Who ever heard of a man's..calling the barkeeper a mixologist of tipicular fixins? 1870 RAE *Westward by Rail* xv. 201 The most delicate fancy drinks are compounded by skilful mixologists in a style that captivates the public.

Mixture. Add: 3. d. In internal combustion engines: The gas or vaporized oil or spirit mixed with air which forms the material for the explosive charges.

1894 B. DONKIN *Gas, Oil, & Air Engines* i. 6 Sometimes an auxiliary pump is used for compressing the mixture. 1901 *Motor-Car World* Oct. 272/1 A by-pass throttle or 'accelerator' valve, by opening which a full charge of mixture can be admitted at any speed of the engine. 1905 *Motor Cycle* 6 Mar. 218/3 *Mixture*, the term applied generally by motor cyclists to the admixture of petrol vapour with air entering the cylinder of an engine. 1914 W. D. NEWTON *War* iii. 19 Brun shut off mixture, and, slowing down, he swung from the motor-cycle.

Mixy (mi·ksi), *a.* [f. MIX *v.* + -Y¹.] Adapted for mixing.

1929 BRIDGES *Test. of Beauty* II. 343 Nor that the unwholesomeness of mixy pollen..was by the flowers contrived for their own benefit.

Mneme (nī·mi). *Psychol.* [ad. Gr. μνήμη memory.] The capacity which a living substance or organism possesses for retaining after-effects of experience or stimulation undergone by itself or its progenitors.

[1904 RICHARD SEMON (*title*) Die Mneme als erhaltende Prinzip im Wechsel des organischen Geschehens.] 1913 HARTOG *Probl. Life & Reproduction* 275 The mnemic possibilities of an organism may be termed, collectively, its 'mneme'. 1914 L. SIMON tr. *Semon's Mneme* (1921) 12 The capacity for such after-effect of stimulation constitutes what I have called the Mneme. 1920 T. P. NUNN *Educ.* 22 Memory..is conscious mneme just as conation is conscious horme.

Mnemic (nī·mik), *a.* [f. as prec. + -IC.] Pertaining to, of the nature of, or involving mneme.

1908 *Daily Chron.* 3 Sept. 5/7 Alleging the existence of a mnemic factor in the life of plants. 1913 [see above]. 1920 T. P. NUNN *Education* 38 Many writers have ascribed a mnemic origin to certain characteristics of mythology and folklore. 1925 C. FOX *Educ. Psychol.* 143 A mnemic phenomenon is studied by observation or introspection.

Mnemotechnist (nimote·knist). [f. MNEMOTECHNY + -IST.] = MNEMONIST.

1891 *Chambers's Encycl.* VII. 240/2 The mnemotechnist who has a succession of things to be remembered assigns them to a particular room and compels himself to detect some association..between each of them and one of the 'hieroglyphs' which are to serve as memorial links.

Mo (mōᵘ), *sb.*² Colloq. or slang abbrev. of MOMENT. Chiefly in ellipt. phr. *half a mo*: wait for half a moment, *i.e.*, for a short time.

1896 in Ware *Passing Engl.* (1909) 9 In half a mo'—half a mo' Your pluck and perseverance you can show. 1903 SHAW *Man & Superman* II. 70 Straker [*running after him*] Here! Mister! arf a mo! steady on! 1905 H. G. WELLS *Kipps* II. v. 211 Chitterlow hesitated. 'Half a mo', my boy', he said. 1915 'IAN HAY' *First Hundred Thous.* I. vii. 80 'Half a mo'!' replies Wagstaffe.

Moan, *sb.* Add: 3. *Navy slang.* A complaint or grievance; an 'airing' of complaints.

1914 F. T. JANE *Navy as Fighting Machine* 112 *Moan*, nautical term for any complaint about things. 1927 *Daily Express* 5 Oct. 3/4 The midshipmen fling their moanful forms into chairs, and one says:—'Come on, you chaps, let's have a moan!'

Moan, *v.* Add: 3. c. *Navy slang.* (See quot.)

1925 E. FRASER & GIBBONS *Soldier & Sailor Words* 156 *Moan, to*, to complain. To grumble. To be a pessimist. (Navy—equivalent to the Army 'grouse'.)

Mob, *sb.*¹ 6. a. Add: *mob-emotion, -madness, -sensation.*

1901 E. A. ROSS *Social Control* xiii. 147 *Mob-madness leads men captive to the impressions of the moment. 1929 GALSWORTHY in *Story-Teller Mag.* Aug. 597/2 Impervious by nature and by training to *mob-emotion Soames yet was emotionalized. Here was something that was not mere *mob-sensation.

7. **mob man** = MOBSMAN.

1835 *Maryland Hist. Reg.* IX. 160 At every corner you may see large companies of worthies marching to and fro, and a *mob man, as such, cannot be seen.

Mob, *v.*² 1. b. (Add example.)

1863 W. PHILLIPS *Speeches* 58 That man..stood..looking on, while George Thompson was mobbed from this platform.

Mobbish, *a.* (Later example.)

1920 *Q. Rev.* July 166 This mobbish or, as it may be termed, 'synnomic' character of primitive mentality is well known.

Mo·bbishness. [-NESS.] Tendency to mobbism; the practice of acting in groups.

1920 *Q. Rev.* July 166 The savage enjoys no privacy, but is always in some sort of a crowd,..experiencing therefore all those peculiar mental effects which mobbishness brings in its train.

Mobbism. (Earlier U.S. example.)

1794 *Massachusetts Spy* 16 Apr. 3/2 A few days since, we experienced a scene of the most unlicensed mobism.

Mobilizable, *a.* Add: b. Of a cell, molecule, etc.: Capable of becoming mobile.

188. *Buck's Handbk. Med. Sci.* I. 44 (Cent. Suppl.) The hæmal and other mobile or mobilizable cells of the body.

Mobilization. 1. (Add example.)

1930 *Morn. Post* 7 Aug. 11/6 The credit mobilisation in London by the Australian banks to meet Governmental commitments..was approved.

Mocassin. 2. **Moccasin flower** (earlier example).

1680 in Ray *Hist. Plant.* (1688) II. 1926/1 Helleborine flore rotundo luteo, purpureis venis striato. The Mockasine flower.

3. (Earlier examples.)

1784 J. FILSON *Kentucke* 27 The horned and the mockason snakes. 1784 J. SMYTH *Tour U.S.* I. vii. 54 The most noxious, virulent, and deleterious of the species, the rattle, moccasson, and horn-snakes.

Moccasined, *a.* 1. (Earlier examples.)

1829 J. F. COOPER *Wish-ton-wish* (1859) xxiv. 358 The two chiefs left the piazza in the noiseless manner of the moccasined foot. 1845 *Knickerbocker Mag.* XXV. 200 He had seen the tracks of many moccasined feet in the fresh snow beyond.

Mock, *a.* 2. b. Add: **mock narcissus,** one of a number of varieties of narcissus.

1880 *Encycl. Brit.* XII. 257/2 Another group, the Mock Narcissi, with coronets of medium size, includes the fine varieties of N. incomparabilis [etc.].

Mockage. 1. (Modern example.)

1918 A. R. MACEWEN *Hist. Ch. in Scotl.* II. xxvii. 176 In their mockage they termed every thing that repugned to their corrupt affections 'devout imagination'.

Mocker. Add: 1. c. *transf.*

1611 BIBLE *Prov.* xx. 1 Wine *is* a mocker, strong drinke is raging.

Mocker-nut. (Earlier and later examples.)

1810 MICHAUX *Arbres* I. 20 *Mocker nut hickery*..dans N.Y. et N.J. 1832 D. J. BROWNE *Sylva Amer.* 187 In the part of New Jersey which lies on the river Hudson, this species is known by the name of Mockernut Hickory. 1871 *Trans. Ill. Agric. Soc.* VIII. 206 The Mocker nut and Pig-nut hickories are common, but not much valued.

Mocock (mokǫ·k). *U.S.* Also **mocuck.** [American Indian.] (See quot. 1827.)

1827 T. L. MCKENNEY *Tour Lakes* 194 A mocock is a little receptacle of a basket form, and oval, without a handle, made of birch bark, with a top sewed on with *wattap*. 1839 MRS. KIRKLAND *New Home* xx. 138 The Indians bring in immense quantities, slung in panniers or mococks of bark on the sides of their..ponies. 1842 — *Forest Life* II. 285 The mococks or bark panniers in which they brought the sugar to market were pretty objects. 1847 C. LANMAN *Summer in Wilderness* xi. 71 Each of them.. placed before me whole mocucks of maple sugar. 1905 *N.Y. Even. Post* 6 May, An old squaw stopped to offer a small mocock, a birch-bark box, holding perhaps a pound of maple sugar.

Modal. A. *adj.* Add: 6. *Statistics.* Of or pertaining to a mode; that is exhibited by the mode (sense *8 d).

1900 K. PEARSON *Grammar of Sci.* (ed. 2) 383 The *average* value of the character is very frequently taken as determining the type instead of the modal value.

Mode, *sb.* Add: 8. d. *Statistics.* That value of a character or variate for which the frequency is greatest; the longest ordinate in a distribution curve.

1900 K. PEARSON *Grammar of Sci.* (ed. 2) 382 A numerical value for which such a frequency is greatest is termed a *modal* value or *mode.* 1902 *Biometrika* Apr. I. 305 The now established use of the word 'mode' is for that value of an organ or character, at which the frequency of the population per unit of the character or organ is a maximum. 1906 R. H. LOCK *Variation Heredity & Evolution* 89 When dealing with a symmetrical curve the position of the mode is identical with that of the *median.*

Model, *sb.* Add: 7. d. In dressmaking, etc., an article made by a recognized designer; any copy of such an article made by a dressmaker or milliner; also, a motor-car or similar manufacture of a particular design; often with a defining word as *Parisian model, 1924 model.*

1906 *Bazaar, Exch. & Mart* Suppl. 3 Oct. 1308/1 Great bargains in ladies' wearing apparel, new and equal to new. Paris models. 1909 *Westm. Gaz.* 2 Nov. 5/1 The engine of the 20-h.p. model..is of the monobloc order. 1910 *Ibid.* 4 Jan. 5/2 Mr. Huff pays a visit to Europe..to inspect the new models at Olympia. 1912 *Tatler* 9 Oct. Advts. p. vi, Pictured on the previous page are two charming models; the upper [hat] is of black velvet [etc.]. 1922 *Ibid.* 2 Aug. Advts. p. f, Special Show of Sports Models for Scotland. Coat,.. Tweed Skirts,.. Hats. 1924 *Queen* 23 July 28/2, I am perfectly certain that this speed can be very much exceeded on this model when the car has been properly run in. 1927 *Motor Cycling* 7 Dec. 102 Road Tests of 1928 Models. *Ibid.*, The first point which struck us about the machine was the difference from the 1927 models on the score of mechanical silence.

10. b. *Zool.* An insect to which another has a mimetic resemblance.

1877 *Encycl. Brit.* VI. 127/1 Probably this beetle shared in the immunity from attack accorded to its model. 1902 *J. M. Baldwin's Dict. Philos. & Psychol.* II. 80/2 The latter is called the model and the former the mimic. 1907 *Nature* 31 Oct. 673/2 An insect thus resembled by another is spoken of as its 'model', the imitating insect is called a 'mimic'. 1930 R. A. FISHER *Genetical Theory Nat. Selection* 148 The resemblance which is favourable to the mimic will be for the same reason disadvantageous to the model.

15. a. (Further example.)

1909 *Chambers's Jrnl.* Feb. 87/1 It [Kinlochleven] is built on the model-town system.

Model, *v.* Add: 8. To act as a mannequin.

1927 *Cleveland Press* 4 Mar., Vivian..will model Saturday in the shoe section of the Bailey Co...Other models will be Rita Del Mar..and Audrey Clapp.

Modelling, *vbl. sb.* 5. Add: **modelling-stand,** a stand on which clay-modelling or the like is done.

1909 *Chambers's Jrnl.* Sept. 565/2 Lily had laid down his card on the ledge of my *modelling-stand.

Moderantism. (Later example.)

1886 H. MORSE STEPHENS in *Encycl. Brit.* XX. 604/2 In Paris Robespierre determined to increase the pressure of the Terror: no one could accuse him of moderantism.

Moderate. A. *adj.* 3. c. Of prices, charges, etc.: Not excessive, reasonable, low.

1904 *Punch* 6 Apr. p. ii. Advt., Hotel..standing high in its own beautiful park...Moderate tariff or inclusive terms.

Moderate, *v.* 3. b. (Earlier U.S. examples.)

1766 CLAP *Ann. Yale-Coll.* 15 Mr. Andrew moderated at the Commencements. 1778 STILES *Lit. Diary* (1901) II. 311 The first Commencements were private. Rector Pierson moderated and gave Degrees till his Death.

Moderatorial (mǫdĕrătōᵊ·riăl), *a.* [f. MODERATOR + -IAL.] Of, pertaining to or characteristic of a moderator or chairman.

1867 T. LACKLAND *Homespun* II. 155 This moderatorial edict is echoed up in the bell-tower. 1926 *Scots Observer* 13 Nov. 4/4 There was a moderatorial flavour in the eloquence of the evening.

Modern. A. *adj.* Add: 2. g. *Typog.* Applied to a kind of type distinguished, e.g. from antique, by thin serifs and hair lines, and by greater symmetry and precision of cut. Usually *modern-cut* or *-face* (*type*).

1890 JACOBI *Printing* 292 *Modern-face type*, founts of recent date, the reverse of antique or old-faced types. 1894 *Amer. Dict. Printing* 379 *Modern Faces*, These are those kinds of Romans which have been cut since the beginning of the century. 1902 DE VINNE *Pract. Typogr.*, *Title-pages* 234 Of modern-cut types we have many varieties.

Modernism. Add: 3. *Theol.* A tendency or movement, to which attention was first called in the Roman Catholic Church, towards modifying traditional beliefs and doctrines in accordance with the findings of recent criticism and research; any liberalizing movement or all such movements taken collectively.

1907 tr. *Encyclical Let.* ('*Pascendi Gregis*') *of Pius X*, 15 If we..seek to know how the believer, according to Modernism, is marked off from the Philosopher, it must be observed [etc.]. 1908 G. TYRRELL *Medievalism* 23 The most penetrating observer of contemporary Modernism. 1913 A. FAWKES *Stud. Modernism* 373 The name Modernism was given to the present phase of the liberalising movement in the Church of Rome by the *Civiltà Cattolica.* 1915 *Hastings' Encycl. Relig. & Ethics* VIII. 763/1 Modernism is the name given by the papal encyclical which condemned it to a complex of movements within the Roman Communion, all alike inspired by a desire to bring the tradition of Christian belief and practice into closer relation with the intellectual habits and social aspirations of our own time. 1923 *Edin. Rev.* Jan. 62 Between English Modernism and the now discredited Roman Modernism there is a deep cleavage. 1927 H. D. A. MAJOR *Engl. Modernism* 18 In the Roman Church Modernism is opposed to Mediævalism; in the English Church Modernism, as in Holland, is opposed to Traditionalism; in America Modernism is opposed to Fundamentalism.

Modernist. Add: 4. *Theol.* One who inclines to, supports, or advocates 'modernism'; a holder of advanced or liberal religious views.

1907 tr. *Encyclical Let.* ('*Pascendi Gregis*') *of Pius X*, 6 It is one of the cleverest devices of the Modernists (as they are commonly and rightly called) to present their doctrines without order and systematic arrangement. 1920 W. SANDAY *Divine Overruling* 67, I do not disclaim the name of Modernist. The name describes justly what I aim at being. I aim at thinking the thoughts and speaking the language of my own day, and yet at the same time keeping all that is essential in the religion of the past. 1923 *Edin. Rev.* Jan. 62 Roman Modernists took Newman's doctrine of development. 1927 H. D. A. MAJOR *Engl. Modernism* 79 What the Modernist is opposed to is dogma which is false, dogma which is out of date and repels the modern-minded man and woman.

attrib. 1918 MAUDE D. PETRE *Modernism* v. 101 These words are not written in a spirit of hostility to the Catholic modernist position.

Modernistic (mǫdəni·stik), *a.* [f. MODERNIST + -IC.] Advanced or modernist in character; pertaining to or suggestive of modernism; having affinity to or sympathy with what is modern.

1909 *Daily Chron.* 12 June 1/3 'L'Unione' is denounced as reeking with modernistic and kindred ideas opposed to the principles and dogmas of the Roman Church. 1924 A. PRINGLE in *Public Opinion* 17 Oct. 383/1 The New Testament in relation to its own time is essentially and boldly modernistic. 1927 *Sunday Times* 13 Feb. 20/4 The audience liked its florid style as a change from more modernistic music.

Modesty. Add: 3. b. (Recent example.)

1910 *Westm. Gaz.* 21 Mar. 5/3 The 'modesty' and the edge of the sleeves are of golden lace.

Modifica·tional, *a.* [f. MODIFICATION + -AL.] Having the nature of, or arising from, modification. So **Modifica·tionally** *adv.*

1908 *Athenæum* 11 July 47/2 Many of the unfit are only *modificationally* unfit. 1924 J. A. THOMSON in *Glasgow Herald* 19 July 4 When we put aside these parasitic diseases and modificational diseases, there remain those that may be called constitutional.

Modiste. (Earlier example.)

1840 *Knickerbocker Mag.* XV. 387 'Modestes' made frocks and bonnets of the freshest patterns, for the girls.

Modistic (modi·stik), *a.* [f. MODISTE + -IC.] Relating to fashion or fashions.

1907 *Times* 16 Nov. 9/6 The sleeves of this dress show the trend of modistic thought in this direction. 1915 *Queen* 6 Nov. 855/3 The modistic information it contains is of the most enlightening description.

Mœritherium (mīᵊriþī·riŏm). [mod.L. f. Gr. Μοῖρις, the name of a lake in Egypt + θηρίον a wild beast.] A genus of extinct ungulate proboscidian mammals, of which remains have been found in Egypt.

1902 *Encycl. Brit.* XXX. 510/2 Most remarkable is a primitive proboscidean (*Mœritherium*), with a nearly full series of front- and cheek-teeth. 1924 J. A. THOMSON *Science Old & New* xli. 236 Millions of years ago, in the Eocene epoch..there lived in North Africa a primitive hoofed animal called Moeritherium.

Mohawk (mōᵘ·hǭk), *v.* [f. the sb.] *intr.* To masquerade as a Mohawk.

1825 J. NEAL *Bro. Jonathan* I. 227 Does he ever go out a mohawking? Peters alluded to a fashion—when a 'tory' was to be tarred and feathered..the people did it in the disguise of Indians. *Ibid.* 229 Some loitering rascal who has been out a Mohawking, today.

Mohican. A. *adj.* 1. (Earlier example.)

1643 *Rec. Massachusetts Bay* (1853) II. 46 Concerning any advice..about the Nariganset or Mohegen sachems and their people.

Moist, *v.* Add: 3. *intr.* To rain slightly, to drizzle. *U.S.*

1916 H. L. WILSON *Somewhere in Red Gap* iii. 117 It was moisting when we started, and pretty soon it clouded up. *Ibid.* 118 It wasn't moisting any more—it was raining for fair.

Moi·stily, *adv.* [f. MOISTY *a.* + -LY.] Tearfully.

1927 H. V. MORTON *In Search Eng.* x. § 2 Three of those prim, sallow, enthusiastic, middle-aged lovers of England.. were regarding moistily the bare rooms in which Brewster and the 'Pilgrim Fathers' were imprisoned.

Moistly, *adv.* Delete †*Obs.* and add recent examples.

1905 H. G. WELLS *Kipps* II. iii. § 1. 157 The bull really came at them..opened a mouth below his moistly glistening nose, and booed. 1905 E. F. BENSON *Image in Sand* viii. 172 The sobs and gasps of the faithful sounded moistly round him in the darkness. 1906 BARONESS VON HUTTEN *What became of Pam* 78 March had moistly melted into April.

Moisture. 4. Add: *moisture-bearing, -proof* adjs.

1922 KENDREW *Climates of Continents* 290 The rainfall increases steadily towards the east and south. An irregularity is caused by the Appalachians,..within range of the *moisture-bearing winds from both the Gulf and the Atlantic. 1904 *Elect. Rev.* 10 Sept. 420 (Cent. Suppl.) *Moisture-proof. 1909 *Installation News* II. 179 Fittings made in malleable iron, covered with a moisture-proof enamel have been substituted.

Mol, also variant of *MOLE, *sb.*⁷

Molal (mōᵘ·lăl), *a. Chem.* [f. *MOLE *sb.*⁷ + -AL.] Of the concentration of solutions: Estimated in terms of moles or gramme-molecules dissolved in each 1000 grammes of solvent.

1908 *Phys. Rev.* Jan. 55 (Cent. Suppl.) From the molal fluidity of the components of the mixture the molal fluidity was computed by the mixture formula.

Molar, *a.*² Add: 2. Molecular, as in *molar weight.*

Ostwald introduced the word in this sense to avoid seeming to accept the molecular hypothesis.

1902 A. FINDLAY tr. *Ostwald's Princ. Inorg. Chem.* 155 In order to apply one of these methods, *e.g.* the depression of the freezing point, to the determination of the molar weight of a new substance, one first determines the depression which is produced by the solution of a substance whose molar weight is known.

Molasses. 3. Add: *molasses barrel, -cake, candy, cask, -gingerbread, -hogshead, house, -settlings, -tank, tierce.*

1846 CORCORAN *Pickings* 29 Isn't that cotton bale dancing a quadrille with the *molasses barrel? 1864 B. TAYLOR *H. Thurston* i. 19 The distribution of wedges of *molasses-cake. 1809 W. IRVING *Knickerb.* v. ii. 295 Each..he patted on the head..and gave him a penny to buy *molasses candy. 1837 *Southern Lit. Messenger* III. 587, I was.. quietly sucking a lump of molasses candy. 1850 N. KINGSLEY *Diary* 103 [We] are privately enjoying ourselves over a dish of mollasses candy. 1863 MRS. WHITNEY *F. Gartney's Girlh.* v, A pile of roasted peanuts, and one of delicate molasses-candy,..at either end of the board. 1851 A. O. HALL *Manhattaner* 5 It was a modest commercial plain.. with..*molasses casks, and corn sacks. 1864 T. L. NICHOLS *Amer. Life* I. 36 The spectators..ate *molasses-gingerbread. 1863 'GAIL HAMILTON' *Gala-Days* 76 He..came back with a *molasses-hogshead. 1864 *Trans. Ill. Agric. Soc.* V. (1865) 317 A near neighbour of mine..and his two sons, have a neat *molasses house, with an engine to run the crushing mill. 1877 HABBERTON *Jericho Road* iv. 39 [He] mixed *molasses-settlings with brown sugar, to give weight to the latter. 1910 *Chambers's Jrnl.* Feb. 88/2 A few rusty *molasses-tanks. 1851 MELVILLE *Moby Dick* xxii. (1926) 104 Have an eye to the *molasses tierce, Mr. Stubb.

Mole, *sb.*² Add: 6. b. A shade of grey.

1908 *Westm. Gaz.* 29 Aug. 13/2 Mole has always been recognised..as a shade universally harmonious. 1923 *Daily Mail* 16 Jan. 1 Advt., In exquisite shades of Nigger, Cinnamon, Gold, Mole, Silver.

7. b. *mole-blue*; also (sense *6 b) as *mole hat, suit.*

1920 *Chambers's Jrnl.* July 455/1 The fur varies in shade from *mole-blue to hare-brown. 1908 *Westm. Gaz.* 26 Sept. 13/2 How charming with a *mole suit is a *mole hat, massed with roses!

8. **mole ditch,** a drainage course made by a MOLE-PLOUGH; (so *mole-ditching* vbl. sb.); **mole-drainer** = MOLE-PLOUGH.

1871 *Trans. Ill. Agric. Soc.* VIII. 83 The sloughs have all been underdrained with *mole ditches, which furnish abundant stock water in fields Nos. 3, 4 and 5. 1867 *Rep. Iowa Agric. Soc.* (1868) 154 Under-draining by *mole-ditching has been tried. 1857–8 *Trans. Ill. Agric. Soc.* III. (1859) 361 Dragging the *mole drainer all over our lands.

Mole (mōᵘl), *sb.*⁷ *Chem.* Also **mol.** [ad. G. *mol* (W. Ostwald), f. *molekül* MOLECULE.] That weight of a substance of which the number of grammes is the same as the molecular weight.

1902 A. FINDLAY tr. *Ostwald's Princ. Inorg. Chem.* 156 Thus it has been established that when one gram-molecule or mole (the molar or molecular weight of a substance expressed in grams) of any substance is dissolved in a litre or 1000 gm. of water, the solution produced freezes at −1·850°.

Mole, *v.*² 2. Add: *To mole out* (also) to elicit, bring to light.

1924 W. M. RAINE *Troubled Waters* vii. 70 Tait would mole out quite enough evidence against him without any additional data supplied by indiscretion.

b. *intr.* To behave in the manner of a mole.

1856 W. G. SIMMS *Eutaw* 129 How he snaked, and moled, and cooned,..we need not narrate.

Molestive (mole·stiv), *a.* [f. MOLEST *v.* + -IVE.] Tending to annoy one; troublesome.

1905 HOWELLS in *N. Amer. Rev.* Nov. 657, I suppose that the stranger always finds the patriotism of a country molestive.

Mollifyingly (mǫ·lifəiˌiŋli), *adv.* [f. MOLLIFYING *ppl. a.* + -LY².] In a mollifying manner.

1928 *Daily Express* 17 Nov. 8/4 'You understand, of course,' he added mollifyingly, 'that I shall not interfere with your activities in any way.'

Molly, variant of MALLEE¹.

Molly¹. 4. **Molly cotton-tail** (earlier example).

1835 LONGSTREET *Georgia Scenes* 237 The reader must here be informed that when I went into the neighbourhood of which I have been speaking the common appellation of the rabbit was 'Molly Cotton-tail'.

Molly (mǫ·li), *v.* [Formed from MOLLY-CODDLE.] *trans.* = MOLLY-CODDLE *v.*

1907 MRS. HARRIS *Tents of Wickedness* II. ii. 138 Paul hasn't been mollied, and I hope he's a nice fellow.

Molly-cosset (mǫ·likǫsət), *v.* [f. MOLLY¹ + COSSET *v.*] *intr.* To act in a molly-coddling manner.

1909 W. DE MORGAN *It never can happen again* liii, I will molly-cosset over Phoebe and Joan.

Molossic, *a.* (Earlier example.)

1864 BUSHNELL *Work & Play* i. 34 You distinguish..the solemn, religious spondee, the swift trochaic run of eagerness or fear, the heavy molossic tread of grief or sorrow.

Mom (mǫm). U.S. abbreviation of MAMMA.

1911 R. W. CHAMBERS *Common Law* v. 156 City-wearied fathers of youngsters who called their parents 'pop' and 'mom'.

Moment, *sb.* 1. c. Add: *Man of the moment*: one who is of great importance at the time in question.

1871 BROWNING *Pr. Hohenst.-Schw.* Poet. Wks. 1897 II. 297/1 Well, that's my mission, so I serve the world, Figure as "man o' the moment.

Momentaneity (mōᵘmĕntănī·iti). [f. MOMENTANE(OUS *a.* + -ITY: after SPONTANEITY.] Transitory character; momentariness.

1928 D. H. LAWRENCE *Kangaroo* vii. 157 All her high moments would have this Bacchic, weapon-like momentaneity.

Momentaneous, *a.* 1. (Recent example.)

1928 D. H. LAWRENCE *Kangaroo* vii 162 Do I want this curious transparent blood of the antipodes, with its momentaneous feelings?

Momentarily, *adv.* 3. (Later example.)

1899 W. J. LOCKE *White Dove* iii, Sylvester.., having done all that was momentarily possible, was at last able to reflect.

Momentive (mōᵘme·ntiv), *a.* [f. MOMENT(UM) + -IVE.] Pertaining to, or acting in the way of, momentum.

1875 KNIGHT *Dict. Mech.* 2525 *TelodynamicCable*, a means for transmitting power,..in which high speed is employed to give the momentive effect of great mass.

Momie-cloth: see MUMMY-CLOTH.

1882 CAULFEILD & SAWARD *Dict. Needlework* 350 *Momie cloth*..has a cotton warp and woollen weft, or else a silk warp and woollen weft, and has the appearance of very fine Crepe.

Monact, *a.* and *sb.* (Examples.)

1885 tr. *F. E. Schulze* in *Challenger Rep., Zool.* XXI. 29 It seems to me, however, that those spicules, called by Carter 'Clavulæ'..are really monacts. *Ibid.* 37 The derived nature of a monact spicule is in many cases determinable.

Monadnock (mǫnæ·dnǫk). *Geol.* [The name of a mountain in New Hampshire, U.S.A., having this character.] A hill or rocky mass rising above the general level of a peneplain, believed to be a remnant of erosion.

1895 W. M. DAVIS in *Geog. Jrnl.* V. 141, I have fallen into the habit of calling a residual mound of this character, a *monadnock.* 1899 — *Physical Geog.* 190 Several monadnocks are scattered over the Piedmont plain of Virginia.

Monadological (mǫnădolǫ·dʒikăl), *a.* [f. G. *monadologisch*, F. *monadologique*: see -AL.] Of or pertaining to monadology.

1897 tr. *W. Wundt's Outl. Psychol.* 313 Matter is thought of as made up of similar [mental] atoms of a lower order (monistic, or monado-logical spiritualism).

Monandrous, *a.* 2. (Add example.)

1884 A. LANG *Custom & Myth* 261 Among people regulated on the patriarchal or monandrous family system.

Monastic. A. *adj.* Add: 4. *Ceramics.* Applied to a type of glaze.

1909 *Chambers's Jrnl.* Feb. 128/1 Others give a dull effect in artistic shades and are known as 'monastic' glazes.

Mondaine (mondę̄n), *sb.* (and *a.*). [F. *mondaine*, f. *mondain* worldly, ad. L. *mundānus*, f. *mundus* world: cf. MUNDANE.] A woman belonging to the world of fashion.

1908 *Westm. Gaz.* 3 Oct. 13/2 The bold attempt of the milliners to coax mondaines to the smaller hat will be watched with interest. 1912 *Tatler* 23 Oct. Advts. p. vi, Not only have the requirements of the smart mondaine been carefully considered but [etc.]. 1920 *Q. Rev.* July 38 The provocative elegance of the Flavian *mondaines.* 1924 *Public Opinion* 7 Nov. 458/2 She was in point of fact a most accomplished mondaine.

b. *adj.* Attached to things of the world; worldly.

1929 LORNA REA *Six Mrs. Greenes* II. § 2. 58 Lavinia, mondaine, vivid, with a delicate certainty of touch that enabled her [etc.].

Mondanity: variant of MUNDANITY.

1911 MRS. H. WARD *Case of Richard Meynell* xii. 242 With her grey hair, and her plain widow's dress, she threw her sister's charming mondanity into bright relief.

Mondial, *a.* Transfer †*Obs.* to sense in Dict. and add:

2. [ad. mod.F. *mondial.*] Pertaining to, affecting or involving the whole world; world-wide, universal.

[1918 A. GRAY tr. *The Crime* II. iii. 175 While in this question Germany could accept the system *individuel* she could not accept the system *mondial.*] 1919 S. HUDDLESTON *Peacemaking at Paris* i. 10 Chaos threatened, with the black night of a mondial revolution. 1920 *Glasgow Herald* 28 June 8 The codification of mondial commercial laws is also aimed at. 1924 *Blackw. Mag.* Aug. 280/2 They were resolved to create their 'mondial situation', and to strengthen it..against the English.

Monel metal. [f. the name of Ambrose *Monel* who was president of the International Nickel Company in 1905, when that firm introduced the alloy.] An alloy, produced originally from natural ores, containing about 67 per cent. of nickel, 28 to 30 per cent. of copper, and small quantities of other substances, possessing a high tensile strength and great resistance to corrosion.

1920 *Chambers's Jrnl.* May 284/1 Monel metal, consisting of about two-thirds nickel, 28 per cent. copper, and about 5 per cent. of impurities. 1922 *Encycl. Brit.* XXXI. 926/1 The much more expensive Monel metal has been widely pushed and has found considerable practical application. 1927 T. WOODHOUSE *Artif. Silk* 67 The reels..are made with tinned steel discs and monel wires. 1930 FRANCIS CORLING in *Brit. Med. Jrnl.* 8 Feb. 234/1 The screenage..consists of monel metal, brass, aluminium, and wood.

Monenergist, Monenergistic, *a.*: the more correct forms of MONERGIST, MONERGISTIC *a.* (see s.v. MONERGISM).

1915 *Hastings' Encycl. Relig. & Ethics* VIII. 821/2 The Monenergistic or Monothelete controversy seems at first glance to be a mere sequel to the Monophysite conflict. *Ibid.* 822/1 The Monenergists were possessed with the idea that the redemptive activity of the God-man emanated wholly and solely from His divine nature.

Monetarist (mǫ·n-, mɒ·nĭtărist), *a.* [f. MONETARY *a.* + -IST.] Of a monetary character or having a monetary basis.

1911 P. GEDDES & J. A. THOMSON *Sex* x. 239 This order of things—avowedly mechanical, militarist, and monetarist at best,..seems to many of us..the only possible form of industrial civilisation.

Money, *sb.* 5. Add: **black-money** [cf. 1 d] (see quot.).

1897 S. & B. WEBB *Industr. Democr.* I. 313 When any class of work involves special unpleasantness or injury to clothing, '*black money' or 'dirty money' is sometimes stipulated for.

6. e. *In the money*: among the prize-winners in a competition, show, or the like.

1928 *Even. News* 5 May 8/5 Jose..finished in the money. 1928 *Morn. Post* 20 Oct. 6/1 One of them is to-day a full champion, the other three all winners, and 'in the money,' as the fanciers say, whenever shown.

7. a. *money-centre, -hunger, -power, -purse, -till.*

1860 O. W. HOLMES *Prof. Breakf.-t.* iv. 107 A great *money-centre [New York]. 1870 MEDBERY *Men & Myst. Wall St.* 167 The money-centre of America soon became aware of the opening of a new office with 'Fish and Belden brokers' in flaming gilt over the doorway. 1892 STEVENSON & LL. OSBOURNE *Wrecker* vii. 120 Where we could be as happy as the day was long..far from the *money-hunger of the West. *a* 1861 T. WINTHROP *Canoe & Saddle* 12, I..negotiated with him from a sham vantage ground of *money-power. 1834 SEBA SMITH *Lett. J. Downing* 132 Isn't it Mr. Shakespear that says something about 'he that steals my *munny-pus steals trash'? 1878 B. F. TAYLOR *Between Gates* 273 We stood under fig-trees hung with money-purses filled with seeds. 1857 *Quinland* II. ii. I. 289 If the stars were extinguished, it would not disturb him, unless his *money-till were upset.

b. *money-loaner, -loser*; *money-losing* adj.

1903 W. E. CURTIS *True Abraham Lincoln* 131 He advocated a law prohibiting *money-loaners from charging exorbitant rates of interest. 1928 *Weekly Dispatch* 6 May 15 Broadway..turns out some 50 musical comedies a year. Of this half-hundred, some 10 are still-born,..of the remaining 40 about 30 prove to be *money-losers or, at their best, certainly not money-makers. 1870 MEDBERY *Men & Myst. Wall St.* 200 It is the greatest money-making and *money-losing spot on the globe.

8. **money-act,** an act dealing with finance; **money-belt,** a belt designed for carrying money; **money bug** *U.S.*, a person having great wealth or financial power; **money crop** *U.S.*, a crop that is grown for selling and not (mainly) for the grower's consumption; **money-king,** a magnate in finance, a person of great wealth; **money-market** (earlier examples); **money mart,** a place where financial transactions are made; **money-shark,** an avaricious money-dealer.

1729 FRANKLIN *Paper Currency* Wks. (1905) II. 148 The *Money-Acts in every Part [are] punctually enforced. *a* 1861 T. WINTHROP *John Brent* xvi. 191 They got the horses, and our *money belts. 1867 'E. KIRKE' *On Border* vi. 117 With this, he drew from his pocket a leathern money-belt such as is sometimes worn by travellers. 1923 R. POCOCK in *Outward Bound* Mar. 408/2 Among cowboys..one might ..leave one's money-belt full of gold and notes beside the fire. 1898 *People* 20 Mar. 4/4 The happiness or the misery of 3 millions of people wholly dependent on the whims and caprices of, say, half a dozen '*money bugs', as they are called in the States. 1922 *Public Opinion* 11 Aug. 132/2 The profiteering class, money bugs as the Americans call them. 1881 *Harper's Mag.* Oct. 713/1 Cotton is the *money crop. 1887 J. C. HARRIS *Life H. W. Grady*, etc. 109 Whenever the greed for a money crop unbalances the wisdom of husbandry, the money crop is a curse. 1904 T. WATSON *Bethany* (1920) 5 But they never failed to make it their object to produce on the farm the necessary supplies, tobacco or cotton being merely the surplus crop, the 'money' crop. 1841 *Congress. Globe* 9 July App. 160/2 The great *money kings of the age have crossed the Atlantic. 1844 *Knickerbocker Mag.* XXIII. 402 His customer's reputation in the *money-market was unsullied. 1847 *Sporting Life* 25 Dec. V. 220/2 The most casual glance at the statistics of the turf money market for the past season is quite sufficient to corroborate our assertion. 1855 [PRAY] *Mem. J. G. Bennet* 70 He has interfered with the money market. 1870 MEDBERY *Men & Myst. Wall St.* 1 Great *money-marts have arisen and expanded into paramount importance. 1844 *Congress. Globe* 20 Dec. App. 37/2 Banks..managed..by a set of irresponsible *money sharks.

Moneyed, *a.* 4. (Earlier example.)

1859 BARTLETT *Dict. Amer.* (1860), *Moneyed Corporation*, Construed by statute in New York to mean 'every corporation having banking powers, or having the power to make loans upon pledges or deposits, or authorized by law to make insurances'.—*Revised Statutes.*

Money-maker. 1. b. (Later U.S. examples.)

1729 J. COMER *Diary* (1923) 65 This day came up the case of the money makers to trial. 1777 *Rec. N.H. Comm. Safety* 93 Ordered the R. G. to pay Col. Sam'l Folsom nineteen pounds eleven shillings, for himself & 5 others apprehending Money makers. 1778 *Ibid.* 149 Jnº Mac Glauglin, a money maker.

Mongolianize (mǫŋgōᵘ·liănəiz), *v.* [f. MONGOLIAN *a.* + -IZE.] *trans.* To render Mongolian in character or quality.

1923 *Contemp. Rev.* Mar. 299 The Bolshevik, striving originally to make Russia Western, has succeeded merely in Mongolianising her.

Mongolism (mǫ·ŋgǫliz'm). [f. MONGOL + -ISM.] A type of idiocy or mental deficiency accompanied by a physical resemblance to the Mongolian race.

1922 A. F. TREDGOLD *Mental Deficiency* (ed. 4) 246 Dr. A. E. Garrod described five cases of Mongolism in which congenital cardiac lesions were found. 1924 *Psyche* July V. 1 It is, of course, well known that a certain type of mental and physical backwardness has long been described, under the name of 'Mongolism', by physicians specially interested in states of mental deficiency.

Mo·ngrelizing, *vbl. sb.* [-ING¹.] The action of the verb mongrelize.

1922 W. R. INGE in *Edin. Rev.* July 36 Unchecked mongrelising destroys the symmetry of a national type.

Monitor, *sb.* Add: 9. **monitor-lizard** = sense 5; **monitor man** (see quot.).

1870 GILLMORE tr. *Figuier's Reptiles & Birds* 13 In the Crocodiles and *Monitor Lizards..a mutilated part is not renewed. 1929 *Photoplay* Apr., *Monitor man—the person who operates the volume control on talking picture production.

Monitor, *v.* Add: 2. In the taking or reproducing of sound films, to regulate or control (the volume or intensity of sound recorded or produced). So **Monitoring** *vbl. sb.*

1929 ALLIGHAN *Romance of Talkies* 64 During the recording, the mixer operator monitors the record through the light valves, thereby assuring himself that no record is lost. *Ibid.*, Acoustic treatment of the walls of the monitoring room secures the reverberation characteristic of the theatre.

Monkey, *sb.* Add: 16. *monkey-business, -gland, -motion.*

1904 *Brooklyn Standard Union* 26 Oct. 6 A warning to Russia that England will not tolerate any delay or any '*monkey business' whatsoever. 1928 *Passing Show* 23 June 16/1 Just when we are doddering on the brink of the grave he will freshen us up with *monkey glands. 1929 *Encycl. Brit.* XI. 747/2 The grafting into men of testicles from apes (the so-called 'monkey glands') has been practised by Voronoff and others with resulting rejuvenation. 1845 J. J. HOOPER *Adv. Simon Suggs* xii. 143 Then the old feller made *monkey moshins to let me know twas to be a *sham* sale.

17. **monkey-chain** (see quot.); **monkey eagle,** a bird of prey found in the Philippine Islands (*Pithecophaga Jefferyi*); **monkey-jacket** (earlier example); **monkey-shaft** *Austral.*, a small trial shaft; **monkey-shines** (earlier and later examples); **monkey-spoon, -tail** (*b*), **-tuyere** (see quots.); **monkey-wrench** *sb.*, also fig. in phr. *to throw a monkey-wrench into*, to act as an obstruction or hindrance to; **monkey-wrench** *v. trans.*, to turn with a monkey-wrench.

1883 *Man. Seamanship Boys* 16 Q. What are *monkey chains? A. Small chains abaft the ordinary chains, on which are secured the topgallant and royal backstays. 1909 *Westm. Gaz.* 6 Sept. 5/3 The general plumage of the *Monkey Eagle is a rich brown above and creamy white in the under parts. 1830 N. DANA *Mariner's Sk.* 187 (Th.) My wardrobe consisted of a '*monkey' jacket, bought in Gravesend, [etc.]. 1880 G. SUTHERLAND *Tales of Goldfields* 69 They began to think they might be already too deep for it, and a small '*monkey'-shaft was therefore driven upwards from the end of the tunnel. 1847 *Tom Pepper* I. 43 (Th.) Let me catch him cutting up any *monkey shines in this house, and I'll beat him. 1855 M. M. THOMPSON *Doesticks* xxiv. 206 To a person not accustomed to the characteristic monkey-shines of the sable heroes..a continual fund of amusement is afforded. 1894 'O. HENRY' *Rolling Stones* (1910) 122 The cow-punchers, always so sober-faced while engaged in their monkey-shines, relaxed into a grin of approval. 1881 *Harper's Mag.* Mar. 530/1 Each of the eight bearers [at a funeral in 1749] was given a pair of gloves, a *monkey-spoon, and a mourning ring. *Note*, Used for liquor and so called from the figure of a monkey carved in solid on the handle. It had a circular and very shallow bowl. 1841 *Southern Lit. Messenger* VII. 769/2 He would come on deck at nine o'clock every morning and inspect, with the utmost scrutiny, the bright *monkey-tails. 1883 *Man. Seamanship Boys* 202 At the word 'let go', the anchor is freed by a smart pull on the monkey tails, which are lanyards, attached to the end of the lever. 1887 PHILLIPS & BAUERMAN *Elem. Metallurgy* (ed. 2) 209 A row of blank tuyer-openings are built into the furnace above..so that..the wall may be broken through and blast-nozzles introduced. These are generally known in England by the name of *monkey-tuyers.* 1929 ALLIGHAN *Romance of Talkies* 38 The Talkies threw several kinds of *monkey-wrenches into the machinery of production. 1904 HARBEN *Georgians* 267 He..dug down in the road whar his pipe j'ined the main, till he got to it, an' then he *monkey-wrenched it off.

b. **monkey-puzzler** = *monkey-puzzle*

1906 GALSWORTHY *Man of Property* II. iii. 298 In the shade of a *monkey-puzzler or in the lee of some india-rubber plant.

Monkey, *v.* 2. (Earlier example.)

1883 NYE *Baled Hay* 38 The young coyote may come and monkey o'er his grave.

Monmouth. 1. (Later example.)

1777 *Maryland Jrnl.* 22 July (Th.) [He had on a] Monmouth cap and old coarse shoes.

Monobloc (mǫ·nobløk), *a.* Also **-block.** [f. MONO- + BLOCK *sb.*] Applied to a type of internal-combustion engine: Having all the cylinders cast in one piece. (Also *ellipt.* or as *sb.* a monobloc engine.)

1909 *Westm. Gaz.* 2 Nov. 5/1 The engine of the 20-h.p. model..is of the monobloc order. 1922 *Daily Mail* 6 Nov. 4 Advt., The engine is of the monobloc type. 1922 *Encycl. Brit.* XXX. 36/1 The first prominent 'Mono block'..comprised a mild-steel cylinder liner complete with head and valve seats, screwed into an aluminium block.

Monocerous, *a.* (Example.)

1930 *New Statesman* 336/2, I am not sure that Pliny's wealth of detail did not do something to discredit the poor monocerous ungulate.

Monochromasy (mǫnokrōᵘ·măsi). *Psychol.* [ad. L. type *monochrōmasia* (cf. *monochrōmatus*), Gr. μονοχρωμασία (cf. μονοχρώματος of one colour), f. μονο-, MONO- + χρῶμα colour, CHROME.] The form of colour-blindness in which all colours appear the same.

1900 *Stud. Yale Psychol. Lab.* 15 (Cent. Suppl.) Monochromasy. 1913 DORLAND *Med. Dict.*, *Monochromasy*,.. blindness to all colors but one: color-blindness, in which all colors are seen as one color.

Monochromate (mǫnokrōᵘ·mēᵗ). *Psychol.* [ad. L. *monochrōmat-us*, Gr. μονοχρώματ-ος: see prec.] A colour-blind person to whom all colours appear alike.

1902 *J. M. Baldwin's Dict. Philos. & Psychol.* II. 793 Even so late as 1804 König affirmed that the vision of the faint-light 'monochromates' was in quality blue.

Monochromatic, *a.* Add: 3. *Psychol.* Of a person or of vision: Seeing all colours as one colour.

1902 *J. M. Baldwin's Dict. Philos. & Psychol.* II. 793 The sensations of those individuals whom they named 'monochromatic' (in distinction from ordinary vision, which is tetrachromatic..) were dogmatically affirmed to be vision under the form of red or blue or green, it was uncertain which. 1914 G. M. WHIPPLE *Mental & Phys. Tests* (ed. 2) I. 183 An eye might possess *trichromatic, dichromatic* or *monochromatic* (*achromatic*) vision.

Mo·nocle, *v.* [f. MONOCLE *sb.*] *trans.* To provide with a monocle. So **Mo·nocled** *a.*

1922 MARG. B. HOUSTON *Witch-man* xii. 154 Major Coberton monocled his eye. 1926 L. P. GREENE *Major—Diamond Buyer* 18 The monocled one coughed deprecatingly. 1928 *Daily Tel.* 17 July 16/7 The author..here gives us the further adventures of his gay, monocled hero.

Monoclinism (mǫ·noklainiz'm). *Bot.* [f. Gr. μόνο-ς MONO- + κλίνη bed, couch + -ISM.] Monoclinous condition; hermaphrodism.

1904 MCCABE tr. *Haeckel's Wonders of Life* 257 Adaptation to parasitic habits also favours monoclinism.

Monocoque (mǫ·nokǫk). [ad. F. *monocoque*, f. *mono-*, MONO- + *coque* egg-shell.] In aeroplanes: A type of stream-lined fuselage resembling an elongated egg in shape; an aeroplane having such a fuselage. Also *attrib.*

1918 'AVION' *Aeroplanes & Aero Engines* 83 *Monocoque*, a fuselage shaped like an extremely elongated egg, with a blunt rounded nose, and curved sides, i.e. a fully stream-lined fuselage. 1928 GAMBLE *Story N. Sea Air Station* i. 41 The latter was a monoplane...She had a 'monocoque' body.

Monoculture (mǫ·nokɒltiūr). [irreg. f. MONO- + CULTURE.] The cultivation or production of one kind of thing.

1916 *Yorksh. Post* 16 Feb. 4/2. 1925 E. F. ROW tr. *Demangeon's Brit. Empire* 134 This plantation system, this exploiting to the uttermost of a single valuable product, involves the dangers of all monoculture.

Monodactylate (mǫnodæ·ktilēᵗ), *a.* [f. MONODACTYL + -ATE.] = MONODACTYLOUS.

1902 *Encycl. Brit.* XXX. 509/2 It is, however, certain that there is a monodactylate representative of the family [*Proterotheriidæ*].

Monodist. 2. (Recent example.)

1916 C. V. STANFORD & C. FORSYTH *Hist. Mus.* vii. 148 There is no sudden revolution in the method of handling the musical material such as the monodists engineered in 1600.

Mo·nodrome, *a.* [a. F. *monodrome.*] = MONODROMIC.

1904 *Nature* 11 Feb. 359/2 On monodrome functions and transcendental numbers.

Monodromy (mǫnǫ·drŏmi). *Math.* [f. as MONODROMIC + -Y³.] Of a function: The fact or quality of being monodromic.

1903 *Nature* 19 Feb. 382/2 It is pointed out that in the non-Pythagorean geometries devised by Hilbert, Helmholtz's axiom of monodromy is not verified.

Monogamize, *v.* Transfer †*Obs.* to sense defined in Dict. and add: 2. *trans.* To make monogamic in character.

1911 H. S. HARRISON *Queed* xxiii. 297 Since, however, the church and the law allowed him but one [wife], he must more drastically monogamize his heart.

Monologist. Add: Also *attrib.*

1900 W. TUCKWELL *Remin. Oxf.* 67 He retained..the bounteous fund of ever-ready talk, alternating not monologist, seasoned not swamped with allusion, recitation, epigram.

Monomark (mǫ·nomāɹk). [f. MONO- + MARK *sb.*] One of a system of marks, formed by a combination of letters, and sometimes also figures, designed to distinguish or identify articles of property or manufactured goods, and to facilitate communication between persons. Also *transf.*

1925 *Glasgow Herald* 10 July 11 The idea..is to set up an international system whereby firms may be granted a 'monomark', consisting of a combination of symbols. 1925 *Westm. Gaz.* 10 July, The Monomark system was explained by its inventor, Mr. William Morris. 1926 *Glasgow Herald* 27 Feb. 10 The persistency of the Scot's mental monomarks applied also to the vocal expression of them. 1928 *Times* 14 Aug. 7/1 A 'monomark' attached to a dog's collar did not fulfil the requirement of the law.

Monomeric (mǫnome·rik), *a. Zool.* [f. Gr. μονομερ-ής, f. μόνο-ς MONO- + μέρος part + -IC.] Of bodies: Consisting of or having only one segment; monomerous.

1902 *J. M. Baldwin's Dict. Philos. & Psychol.* II. 151 In monomeric muscles the polarization is stronger in the direction from the equator..towards the extremities than in the opposite direction.

Monongahela. (Earlier examples.)

1834 W. G. SIMMS *Guy Rivers* I. 76 Having cleared his throat with the contents of a tumbler of Monongahela which seemed to stand permanently full by his side. 1844 *Knickerbocker Mag.* XXIII. 73 Then is the time to sing 'The sea! The sea!' and to take some Monongahela to still the qualmishness you begin to experience. *c* 1845 PAULDING *Madmen All* 192 May I never taste Monongahela again!

Monophonic, *a.* (Example.)

1920 E. WALKER in F. S. MARVIN *Recent Devel. Europ. Thought* 286 If we exclude some monophonic conceptions that have still their value for us, it [music] is barely five hundred years old.

Monoplane (mǫ·noplēⁱn). [f. MONO- + PLANE *sb.*³] An aeroplane (or glider) having only one 'plane' or set of horizontal supporting surfaces.

1907 *Nature* 5 Dec. 106/2 For running along the ground the monoplane has two wheels. 1910 *Blackw. Mag.* July 4/1 The aeroplane, whether monoplane, biplane, or other. 1911 GRAHAME-WHITE & HARPER *Aeroplane* 17 He [Lilienthal] abandoned the monoplane type of glider in favour of a biplane. 1911 J. DENNY *Letters* (1920) 183, I should never think of comparing him to a wild man on a monoplane like Bacon. 1918 MCCUDDEN *Five Yrs. R.F.C.* 63 Two Taube monoplanes came over St. Omer.

Hence **Mo·noplane** *v. intr.*, to travel or 'fly' in a monoplane.

1909 *Daily Chron.* 27 July 4/7 The seas shall rage as Blériot Shall monoplane o'erhead.

Monopolizable (mǫnǫ·pŏlaizăb'l), *a.* [f. MONOPOLIZE *v.* + -ABLE.] That can be 'monopolized'.

1898 W. J. LOCKE *Idols* xxii. 215 I'm not a monopolisable woman.

Monopoly. 7. Add: *monopoly value.*

1904 J. J. COCKSHOTT *Licensing Act 1904* 4 Justices..are directed by the new Act to attach such conditions to the grant of every new *on*-license as will secure to the public any monopoly value.

Monosaccharide (mǫnosæ·kăraid). *Chem.* [f. MONO- + L. *saccharum* sugar + -IDE.] Any one of the group of sugars having the formula $C_nH_{2n}O_n$, where *n* is not less than 3 or more than 9.

1906 MCGOWAN tr. Meyer *Hist. Chem.* 482 The monosaccharides are now distinguished from the poly-saccharides (cane sugar, starch, cellulose, &c.). 1910 *Practitioner* June 823 The carbohydrates are hydrolysed into monosaccharides —chiefly dextrose, laevulose, and galactose—before they are absorbed. 1916 A. P. MATHEWS *Physiol. Chem.* 18 The monosaccharides are..classified by the number of carbon atoms..they contain.

Monose (mǫ·nōᵘs). *Chem.* [f. MONO- 2 + -OSE².] = prec.

1903 *Jrnl. Chem. Soc.* LXXXIV. I. 713 By the action of alcoholic hydrogen chloride on bioses, hydrolysis occurred and glucosides of the monoses were formed. 1922 *Encycl. Brit.* XXX. 590/1 Ost has demonstrated the production of the biose as octacetate with the monose as pentacetate.

Monotechnic (mǫnote·knik), *a.* [f. MONO- + TECHNIC *a.*: after POLYTECHNIC *a.*] Dealing with or providing instruction in a single technical subject.

1904 *Jrnl. Inst. Elect. Engin.* 25 Feb. XXXIII. 458 Many of the American schools of engineering are practically monotechnic institutes in contradistinction to the polytechnics here. 1904 G. S. HALL *Adolescence* I. 170 Thousands of our youth of late have been diverted from secondary schools to the monotechnic or trade classes.

Monothematic (mǫnoþĭmæ·tik), *a. Mus.* [f. MONO- + THEMATIC *a.*] Having a single or one predominant theme. So **Monothe·matism.**

1907 R. BOUGHTON *Bach* 15 Monothematic music in polyphonic style was bound to result in a fugue. 1886 PRAEGER tr. *Naumann's Hist. Music* 1188 The employment of *leitmotiv*..is nothing but a return to monothematism.

Monotropic, *a.* Add: 3. *Physical Chem.* Of polymorphous substances: That can undergo change of form in one direction only.

1902 A. FINDLAY tr. *Ostwald's Princ. Inorg. Chem.* 255 Substances like iodine monochloride, which can undergo transformation only in one direction, are called *monotropic*, and those which, like sulphur, can change in both directions, *enantiotropic.* 1922 A. SMITS *Theory Allotropy* ii. 59 So-called normal liquids deposit monotropic forms.

Monotropy (mǫnǫ·trŏpi). *Physical Chem.* [f. as prec. + -Y.] Monotropic state or quality; capacity of a substance to undergo change of crystalline form in one direction only.

1902 A. FINDLAY tr. *Ostwald's Princ. Inorg. Chem.* 255 Enantiotropy and Monotropy. 1922 A. SMITS *Theory Allotropy* II. i. 244 In this way the phenomenon of monotropy between these two modifications is explained.

Monovalent, *a.* Add: b. *Cytol.* Of a chromosome: That does not unite with another to form a single chromosome.

1905 *Rep. Brit. Assoc.* 570 Whether each half of the chromosome is to be regarded as a monovalent chromosome is doubtful.

Monozygotic (mǫnozaigǫ·tik), *a.* [f. MONO- + ZYGOTIC *a.*] Of twins or other multiple births, originating in a single zygote or fertilised ovum.

1917 H. H. NEWMAN *Biol. Twins* 3 Such twins, quadruplets, or larger sets of offspring are known as *monozygotic.* 1930 *Nature* 15 Nov. 766 Dizygotic twins are, in these data, on the whole inferior to their brothers and sisters in the physical measurements, but this is certainly not the case with monozygotic twins. 1931 *Times Lit. Suppl.* 19 Feb. 139/4 A so-called monozygotic pair which arises from the splitting of a single fertilized ovum is indeed material of a unique kind.

Monsoonish (mǫnsū·niʃ), *a.* [f. MONSOON + -ISH.] Suggestive of or characteristic of a monsoon.

1890 KIPLING *Plain Tales* (ed. 3) 127 Not a mere hill-shower but a good, tepid, monsoonish downpour.

Monstrous, *a.* 8. b. (U.S. example.)

1848 *Major Jones's Sketches of Travel* (Bartlett 1848) Augustus is a monstrous pretty city.

Montagu's harrier. [Named after G. *Montagu* (1751–1815) who first distinguished the species.] A species of harrier, *Circus cineraceus.*

1880 *Encycl. Brit.* XI. 492/1 This was called by him the Ash-coloured Falcon, but it now generally bears his name, and is known as Montagu's Harrier. 1905 *Spectator* 7 Jan. 12/1 Buzzards were so common that they were known locally as furze kites. Montagu's harrier also probably bred there. 1909 *Westm. Gaz.* 3 July 14/1 Montagu's harrier is not a resident species.

Montana tree. [f. *Montana* the name of one of the northern states of the United States.] A style of saddle used by the Canadian Mounted Police.

1891 *Harper's Mag.* June 7/2 Their saddle is what is known as the Montana tree.

Montanian (mǫntā·niăn). [-IAN.] A native or inhabitant of Montana.

1878 J. H. BEADLE *Western Wilds* xxii. 358 The Montanian was gone before Manson had thought to ask.

Monte¹. (Earlier examples.)

1836 'A RESIDENT OFFICER' *Sk. Metropolis of Spain* etc. (1843) I. 264 *Monte* is one of the most gambling combinations of hazard yet invented. 1844 G. W. KENDALL *Santa Fé Exped.* II. xii. 236 Within a few short steps..a party.. were busily engaged at a game of monte. 1846 J. W. ABERT in Emory *Military Reconn.* 455 The word 'monte' is one of the first a stranger learns.

b. *attrib.* and *Comb.* in sense 'of monte, used in the playing of monte', as *monte blanket, game, table*; **monte-bank,** a monte table; the money in the possession of the banker at monte (so *monte-banker*).

a 1861 T. WINTHROP *Life in Open Air* etc. (1863) 128 A background of mustangs, *monte-banks, and lynch-law. 1855 F. S. MARRYAT *Mts. & Molehills* xiv. 267, I was soon asleep, notwithstanding that the clinkings of the *monte-bankers, and the noise of the crowd below [etc.]. 1898 H. S. CANFIELD *Maid of Frontier* 78 His long and angular shadow fell across the *monte blanket spread flat upon the ground. 1899 T. HALL *Tales* 276 Judge Leander Quinn was lured away from a *monte game with a couple of buck Indians and seated upon his judicial bench in the 'Bird Cage' concert hall. 1873 J. H. BEADLE *Undevel. West* iv. 92 We take our stand near the *monte table, where a considerable crowd gathers. 1889 K. MUNROE *Golden Days* ii. 15 This influx of gold caused monte-tables, and other gambling layouts, to spring up.

Monteith². A special type of coloured cotton handkerchief (see quot.).

1882 CAULFEILD & SAWARD *Dict. Needlework* 350 *Monteiths*, a description of Cotton Handkerchiefs, which are dyed of one uniform colour, but have a pattern of white spots occurring at regular distances...These Goods are known by the name of the manufacturers, at Glasgow.

Monte-jus (mǫntˌʒüs). Also **-juice.** [F. f. *monter* to raise + *jus* juice, liquid.] In the making of sugar, an apparatus for raising the level of the liquid by means of air or steam pressure.

1872 P. SOAMES *Manuf. Sugar* 133 The cane-juice runs along the gutter to the monte-jus C, where it is elevated into the clarifiers, D. 1921 *Dict. Occup. Terms* (1927) § 449 *Montejuice attendant, montejuice boy*: stands by valves of montejus apparatus.

Month¹. 6. Add: **month-clock,** a clock that goes for a month.

1884 F. J. BRITTEN *Watch & Clockmakers' Handbk.* 268 Month Clocks have an intermediate wheel and pinion between the great and centre wheels.

Monthly. B. *sb.* 2. (Earlier example.)

1833 *Knickerbocker Mag.* I. 185 We have articles on Political Economy in the monthlys, the weeklys, and the dailys.

Monument, *sb.* 7. Add: **Monument City** = *MONUMENTAL CITY (see below).

1906 *Springfield Weekly Republ.* 8 Mar. 4 Baltimore has been known for years as the '*Monument City', and some of these monuments are in reality works of art.

Monument, *v.* (Add example.)

1886 H. BUTTERWORTH *Zigzag Journ. Levant* 265 (Funk) Helena and Constantine erected chapels and altars there, and monumented the places of sacred scenes and associations.

Monumental City. *U.S.* [Cf. *Monument City* above.] The city of Baltimore.

1827 *National Gaz.* (Philad.) 20 Nov. 213 The brave sons of Cincinnatus at the festal board in the 'monumental city'. 1837 *Southern Lit. Messenger* III. 657, I was seated in the cars which..were in rapid motion towards the Monumental City. 1853 F. W. THOMAS *J. Randolph* etc. 178 In 'the monumental city' I read law. 1904 *Baltimore American* 5 Dec. 14 Detectives..of the Baltimore force, have been working there during the past week, and it is probable that they will return to the Monumental City to-day.

Monumentalism (mǫniume·ntăliz'm). [f. MONUMENTAL + -ISM.] A monumental style; building on a grand scale.

1902 *Encycl. Brit.* XXVIII. 451/2 The plain lessons of the Crimean War were unheeded, and monumentalism became the ideal of coast defences.

Moocha (mū·tʃă). Also **moochie.** [Kaffir.] A form of loin-cloth or short hide skirt worn by natives of South Africa.

1878 ROCHE *On Trek in Transvaal* 325 (Pettman) A wee little Kaffir boy with nothing upon him but his moochie or tails, drives by a herd of calves. 1885 RIDER HAGGARD *K. Solomon's Mines* x. 153 He slipped off the 'moocha' or girdle round his middle, and stood naked before us. 1923 *Chambers's Jrnl.* Apr. 222/1 Beneath this the native kilt or *moocha* composed of strips of raw hide.

Mooley (mū·li). *U.S.* [A variant of MOILEY, MULEY.] A hornless cow; a cow.

1838 [see MULEY *sb.* 1]. 1867 T. LACKLAND *Homespun* II. 213 They are all so fond of patient 'mooley' too. 1877 *Rep. Vermont Dairym. Assoc.* VIII. 50 He should hope that his next beef might come from a polled cow or mooley.

1902 A. D. McFaul *Ike Glidden* i. 3, I couldn't help laughing at the sight of your Mooley slinking it for the woods with the cans and milk flying.

Moon, *sb.* 5. Add to def.: a moon-shaped mark.
1855 *Poultry Chron.* III. 57 Breast. The best spangled and clearest from tipping with white at the end of the moon. 1865 *Chambers's Encycl.* VII. 535/2 An artificial fly..adorned with two moons from a peacock's tail. 1909 *Chambers's Jrnl.* Sept. 586/2 Chelsea [sc. china]..may be distinguished by spur-marks on the base and greasy-looking discs known as 'moons' in the paste.

8. b. *U.S. colloq.* = Moonshine 4.
1928 *Collier's* 29 Dec. 8/2 Wherever you go in Colorado a bootlegger..says to you 'Mister, this is good stuff. It's Leadville "moon"'. *Ibid.* 8/3 The art of producing sugar 'moon' and aging it in charred casks.

15. a. *moon-rising, -setting.* c. *moon-white.*
1927 *Observer* 11 Sept. 8 A..short interval between successive *moonrisings being favourable for late harvest work. 1905 E. F. Benson *Image in Sand* xviii. The sublimities of the sun-rises and *moon-settings were gone from her. 1891 Wm. Sharp in *Life* (1910) xi. 177 Every now and then there is a gleam of rare *moon-white beauty. 1921 Galsworthy *To Let* III. ii. 240 What more devotional than the eyes and moonwhite horns of a chewing cow in the warm dusk!

16. **moon-down** *U.S.*, (the time of) the setting of the moon; **moon-milk** = 'milk of the moon' [see Milk *sb.* 6]; **moon-moth**, the Luna moth, *Attacus* or *Actias luna.*
a 1877 *N.Y. Tribune* (Florida Corr.)(Bartlett) They landed at Santa Rosa Island, at about a quarter of an hour to *moondown, or 11 o'clock p.m. 1885 *Cassell's Encycl. Dict.*, *Moon-milk. 1868 *Amer. Naturalist* June II. 187 The pale-green, satin-robed *Moon moth (*Attacus luna*). 1870 *Ibid.* Mar. IV. 52 The beautiful pale green Moon-moth (*Actias Luna*).

Moon, *v.* 3. (Earlier example.)
1888 D. Macdonald *Gum Boughs* 182 (Morris) 'Mooning' opossums is a speciality with country boys.

Moo·n-blind, *sb.* [Cf. the adj.] Moon-blindness.
1668 [see Moon-blind *a.* 1]. 1877 R. I. Dodge *Plains Gt. West* (Farmer) There is said to be [a] plains malady, which, however, I cannot vouch for. It is called moon-blind.

Moon-eye. 1. (Later example, of a person.)
1796 *Captivity of Mrs. Johnson* 112 Our jailer, with moon eyes, came to congratulate us.

Moon-eyed, *ppl. a.* Add: 1. (Later U.S. examples.)
1888 'C. E. Craddock' *Broomsedge Cove* vi. 105 Do ye know ennything bout'n a horses eyes? I be sort'n' feard he's moon-eyed or suthin'. 1905 A. Adams *Outlet* 21 Tolleston took the only blind horse in the herd...At the time of his purchase, no one could see anything in the eyeball which would indicate he was moon-eyed.

2. (Later U.S. examples.)
1873 J. H. Beadle *Undevel. West* xxvii. 588 The woman had tolerably good sight, but was 'moon-eyed'. 1873 Joaquin Miller *Unwritten Hist.* v. (1876) 84 There was a little Chinaman, tawny, moon-eyed and silent, sitting by the bed. 1888 'C. E. Craddock' *Broomsedge Cove* iv. 58 Pa'son Donnard..air sorter moon-eyed, ef the truth war knowed.

4. Of feathers: Having moon-shaped markings.
1896 *Yearbk. U.S. Dept. Agric.* 467 The feather markings of the penciled varieties differ greatly from those of the spangled; the latter being commonly called 'moon-eyed' from the round or oval appearance of the spangles.

Mooning, *vbl. sb.* Add: 3. *Leather-manuf.* The shaving of skins with a moon-knife.
1903 *Sci. Amer.* Suppl. 24 Jan. 22629 (Cent. Suppl.) 'Mooning' is performed with a round steel, shaped like a plate, and having the center cut out, and a handle placed across the opening.

4. The condition of being moon-eyed (sense 2). *U.S.*
1885 Howells *Silas Lapham* ii. 49 Her large eyes..were brown; they had the peculiar look of near-sighted eyes which is called mooning.

Moonless, *a.* (Add example.)
1927 H. C. Macpherson *Mod. Astron.* 75 It is by no means improbable that Mars was originally moonless.

Moonrise. Add: The time at which the moon rises. *U.S.*
1877 Bartlett *Dict. Amer.* 1884 'Mark Twain' *Huck. Finn* viii. 63 When it was good and dark, I slid out from shore about moonrise, and paddled over to the Illinois bank.

Moonshine. 4. (Earlier U.S. and attrib. examples.)
1875 E. King *Southern St. N. Amer.* 478 Producing from his pocket a flask of 'moonshine' whiskey, [he] invited us to drink. *Ibid.* 479 Would we have some more 'moonshine?' No? 1886 *Harper's Mag.* June 55/1 Capps knew a hawk from a handsaw when it came to talking about 'moonshine' whiskey. *Ibid.* 58/1 The manufacture of illicit mountain whiskey—'moonshine'—was formerly, as it is now, a considerable source of revenue. 1886 *Century Mag.* XXXI. 432/1 He had a moonshine apparatus over on Sweetwater. 1902 G. H. Lorimer *Lett. Self-made Merchant* xv. 217 [He] ran..a blind tiger in the back room with moonshine whiskey.

Moo·nshine, *v.* *U.S.* [f. sense 4 of the sb.] *intr.* To smuggle or deal in illicit spirit.
1902 Harben *Abner Daniel* 209 We moonshined it together two yeer, though he never knowed my chief hidin'-place.

Moonshiner. (Earlier U.S. examples.)
1877 *N.Y. Even. Post* 16 June (Bartlett 1877) Nelson County, Kentucky, is the home of the Moonshiner; that is, the manufacturer of illicit whiskey...The Moonshiner regards the revenue officer as a being to be extinguished. 1883 *Century Mag.* May 141 How should the careless deputy Marshall..know that the Moonshiners were Union men and Republicans?

Moonshining, *vbl. sb.* (Earlier examples.)
1886 C. D. Warner *Their Pilgr.* (1888) xiii. 288 The poet and the novelist..might..make this season as romantic as vintage-time on the Rhine, or 'moonshining' on the Southern mountains. 1891 'C. E. Craddock' in *Harper's Mag.* Feb. 368/1 He had been suspected of moonshining.

Moo·n-up. Moonrise.
1907 S. E. White *Arizona Nights* I. v. 90 'Didn't git in till moon-up last night', he growled.

Moony, *a.* 4. (Add example.)
1873 J. H. Beadle *Undevel. West* xxvii. 588 The eyes are very weak and 'mooney', or perpetually 'dancing'.

Mooring, *vbl. sb.* 4. Add: *mooring bridle* (examples); **mooring-mast**, a strong upright structure to which airships are moored.
1867 Smyth *Sailor's Wordbk.*, *Mooring bridle, the fasts attached to moorings, one taken into each hawse-hole, or bridle-port. 1919 *R. Aeronaut. Soc. Gloss. Aeronaut. Terms* 58 *Mooring bridle*, a rigging passing between two points from a fitting in the length of which the mooring rope is attached. *Ibid.* 59 *Mooring mast, a mast to the head of which an airship may be moored. 1922 *Encycl. Brit.* XXX. 14/2 High cost of housing [etc.]..were their chief hampering factors, but the wonderful development of the mooring mast, a British device, has improved the position.

Moose¹. Add: Also used *collect.*
1817 S. R. Brown *Western Gaz.* 202 Cabree and moose are plentiful. 1849 Pritts *Mirror of Border Life* 60 Their food was principally the entrails of moose, deer, bears.

b. *moose-hair, -hide* (earlier example), *-meat* (earlier example); **moose elm** (earlier examples); **moose-fly**, a rust-coloured insect of North America, *Haematobia alcis*, troublesome to moose; **moose-maple**, the mountain maple, *Acer spicatum*; **moose shank** (see quot.); **moose tick**, a tick infecting moose; **moose warden** *U.S.*, a person appointed to take care of moose; **moose-wood** (*b*), **-yard** (earlier examples).
1810 Michaux *Arbres* I. 39 Red Elm,..Slippery elm,..[ou] *Moose elm,..dans le haut de l'Etat de New York. 1832 D. J. Browne *Sylva Amer.* 311 This species of elm..bears the name of Red Elm, Slippery Elm and Moose Elm. a 1862 Thoreau *Maine Woods* (1912) 247 They had got a young moose...It was quite tame,..and covered with *moose-flies. 1845 *Knickerbocker Mag.* XXV. 508 His attire..consisted of a hunting-frock of dressed deer-skin..gaily embroidered with dyed *moose-hair and porcupine quills. 1736 J. Gyles *Mem. Captivity* 10 There [we] made Canoes of Moose-Hides. a 1904 S. E. White *Blazed Trail Stories* vi. 104 He had stopped..and was holding aside the screen of 'mouse-maples. 1845 *Knickerbocker Mag.* XXV. 299 They ate the *moose-meat which the Indians had left. 1887 *Harper's Mag.* Feb. 458/2 '*Moose shanks' are made by peeling the skin from the hind legs of the animal. The smaller end is then sewn up to form the toe; and thus a moose-hide stocking is formed. 1870 *Amer. Naturalist* III. 167 We have observed that the young *Moose tick lived nearly a month without food after hatching. 1857 *Game Laws* in *Fur, Fin & Feather* (1872) 155 The Governor..shall appoint one County *Moose warden for each of the Counties. 1832 Williamson *Hist. Maine* I. 117 (Th.) Moose-bush or *Moose-wood, *Dirca palustris*, is not uncommon in the forest. 1800 D. R. D'Erres *Memoirs* 117 The animals are overtaken in their retreats..which is called the *Moose yard. 1839 Hoffman *Wild Scenes* I. 95 (Th.) The sagacious animal, so soon as a heavy storm sets in, commences forming what is called a 'Moose-yard'.

Mop, *v.*² 1. (Add example.)
1927 *Motor Cycling* 7 Dec. 104/2 With a successful chromium plate the finished surface is so hard that it cannot be buffed or mopped.

2. b. To wipe (perspiration, tears, etc.) *from* the face or brow.
1872 R. W. Buchanan *Saint Abe & seven Wives* i. 4 And mopping from his brow the sweat, The boy glanced round with teeth still set. 1892 — *Come live with me* xxii. 239 He mopped the perspiration from his wrinkled brow. 1907 *Smart Set* Apr. 18/2 She..mopped the hot tears from her face.

Mope, *v.* Add: 4. To confine or shut *up* (in a place).
1863 Mrs. Whitney *F. Gartney's Girlh.* xv, The child shouldn't be moped up here, all winter!

Mopiness (mōᵘ·pinės). [f. Mopy *a.* + -ness.] Mopy state or condition.
1927 *Smallholder* 26 Mar. 115/1 Ordinary Diarrhoea [in chicks]. Symptoms. Looseness of the bowels...There may or may not be mopiness but invariably there is inactivity.

Mopping, *vbl. sb.*² Add: Also *mopping-up* (see quot.).
1925 E. Fraser & Gibbons *Soldier & Sailor Words*, *Mopping-up*, the term for the work allotted to special parties of men appointed to follow close in the track of advancing 'waves' of troops, in order to explore and clear the enemy lines and dug-outs of men remaining behind...The Mopping-up method was first adopted at the Battle of Arras in February, 1917.

Mo·pping, *ppl. a.* [f. Mop *v.*² + -ing ².] *Mopping-up*, that mops up (in sense 3 of v.).
1918 Farrow *Dict. Milit. Terms*, *Mopping Up Wave*, the slang expression for the line of troops in assault which bombs out the positions crossed by the preceding lines.

Mora¹. 3. (Earlier example.)
1832 *Encycl. Amer.* XI. 591 The short syllable..is considered as the original unit for the measure of time in the rhythm, and is called a *time*, or *mora.*

Moraine. Add: b. In rock-gardening, a raised border or ridge formed chiefly of stones on which plants are grown. Also *attrib.* as *moraine gardening, plant.*
1910 L. B. Meredith *Rock Gardens* 84 The one essential of the moraine is drainage of the most perfect description. 1914 H. H. Thomas *Rock Gardening* 65 The moraine may be described as a bed or border of varying size, preferably situated on a slight slope, and consisting of broken stone, with which, however, a certain proportion of light, sifted soil is mixed. *Ibid.* 72 Favourite Moraine Plants. 1931 *Times Lit. Suppl.* 16 Apr. 297/2 This is..the cause of most failures and disappointments in moraine gardening.

Moral, *a.* 7. Add: *Moral force, pressure*: Pressure applied to or operating upon the character or conduct of persons through the moral sense. *Moral suasion*: see Suasion.

Morassic (moræ·sik), *a.* [f. Morass + -ic.] Of, pertaining to or having the characteristics of a morass; morassy.
19.. C. MacMillan in *Minn. Bot. Stud., Bulletin* ix. 905 (Cent. Suppl.) All of these morassic formations characterize quiet shores.

Moratorial (mǫrătōᵊ·riăl), *a.* [f. Moratorium + -al.] Pertaining to or payable in respect of a moratorium.
1914 *Economist* 7 Nov. 833/1 On the debts due to them and covered by the moratorium, they are entitled to a moratorial interest of 5 per cent.

Moravian. B. *adj.*² 2. (Earlier example.)
1739 W. Stephens *Proc. Georgia* 393 An heavy Complaint being exhibited against the Moravian Brethern.

Morcellement. Add: b. *Surg.* = Morcellation.
1903 *Phil. Med. Jrnl.* 31 Jan. 199 (Cent. Suppl.) Porcelini suggested morcellement, the danger of which consists in the subsequent necrosis of the stump of the cervix. 1908 *Practitioner* Oct. 608 Vaginal myomectomy, with and without morcellement.

More. C. *adv.* 5. Add: *More'n, mor'n* (U.S. colloq.) = more than; also *ellipt.* = no more than.
1862 Lowell *Biglow P.* Ser. II. Introd., Poems (1912) 278/1 Some other contractions of ours have a vulgar air about them. *More'n* for *more than*, as one of the worst, may stand as a type of such. 1886 *Harper's Mag.* July 323/2 But he (mor'n you and I with all of our might) Could not here always remain. 1885 W. L. Alden *Adv. Jimmy Brown* 203 There was mornascuttleful [*sic*] of big lumps of coal in the yard in the morning. *Ibid.* 142 They say that Squire Meredith and Deacon Willets are mornhalf eaten up by mosquitoes.

Morgan³ (mǭ·rgăn). *U.S.* A breed of horse named after the progenitor, 'Justin Morgan', which was owned by a schoolmaster of the same name, of Randolph, Vermont, in 1795.
1. *attrib.* as *Morgan breed, horse*, etc.
1843 *Knickerbocker Mag.* XXI. 331 The stage generally being able to work its own way, drawn by horses of the Morgan breed. 1850 *Cultivator* VII. 369 We are expecting to have a Morgan horse here from Mr. W. H. Ladd of Richmond Ohio. 1857 *Trans. Ill. Agric. Soc.* II. 93 Many splendid roadsters, of the Morgan..and Bellfounder stock. 1876 *Rep. Vermont Board Agric.* III. 172 You can teach a Morgan colt anything. *Ibid.* 173 This is precisely what the Morgan blood gives. 1883 J. Hay *Bread-winners* v. 77 If you don't want to talk, a train of Morgan horses couldn't make you.
2. A Morgan horse.
1869 C. L. Brace *New West* xiv. 187 Each coach well made and comfortable, with six horses, evidently picked Morgans. 1872 *Rep. Vermont Board Agric.* I. 227 The stock of Black Hawk..bred to smaller Morgans or French. *Ibid.* 213 He believed the Morgan was the result of a cross. 1878 *Ibid.* III. 169 The Morgan is the strongest blooded family of the horses in the country. 1880 *Encycl. Brit.* XII. 204/2 At the present day the leading families [of trotters] are..the Morgans, whose founder was Justin Morgan, foaled 1793, by a horse called True Briton, or Beautiful Bay. 1889 *Century Mag.* Jan. 341/2 He has about the general balance of the French ponies of Canada or perhaps a Morgan, which for practical purposes were the best horses ever developed in America. 1901 S. Merwin & H. K. Webster *Calumet K* iv. 57 She was a tall, clean-limbed sorrel, a Kentucky-bred Morgan. 1906 Winston Churchill *Coniston* 22 The tough little Morgans of that time..have all but disappeared.

Morganiza·tion. [f. Morganize *v.* + -ation.] The fact or process of getting rid of or destroying by secret methods.
1919 J. L. Garvin *Econ. Foundations of Peace* 502 When there were fears about the 'Morganisation' of British vessels, he said that it would be sounder for Britain to nationalise her entire shipping [etc.].

Mormon. Add: 1. (Earlier example.)
1837 Peck *Gaz. Illinois* I. 74 There are..a few Mormons..scattered through the state.

3. **Mormon fly**, a variety of butterfly found on the Mississippi River; **Mormon-weed** (earlier example).
1847 C. Lanman *Summer in Wilderness* v. 34 They are called the *Mormon fly and I was told were found on these rapids alone. 1872 *Trans. Dep. Agric. Ill.* IX. p. ix, Mr. James H. McConnell..has..prosecuted experiments with the Indian Mallow (*Abuthilon Avacennae*) variously known as 'stump weed', 'velvet leaf', 'butter print', '*Mormon weed', etc.

Mormoness (mǭ·rmŏnės). [-ess ¹.] A female Mormon.
a 1861 T. Winthrop *John Brent* (1862) ix. 99 Selecting, perhaps, a Mormoness to kidnap to-night.

Mormonism. (Earlier example.) Also *fig.*
1831 *Niles' Weekly Reg.* 16 July 353/1 Mormonism..a new religion. 1913 E. F. Benson *Thorley Weir* i. 33 'They can't all be serenading me.' 'I cannot imagine why not. A Mormonism of serenading young men is not illegal.'

Mormonite. (Earlier example.)
1831 *Columbian Reporter* (Taunton, Mass.) 24 Aug. 1/5

The Mormonites. We learn from the Painsville Gazette, that this infatuated people are again in motion [etc.].

Morning, *sb.* 9. Add: **morning-girl**, a non-resident maid-servant employed during the early part of the day only; **morning tea**, tea taken in the morning, usually before getting up.
1921 *Dict. Occup. Terms* (1927) § 900 Daily servant,..*morning girl; a non-resident general servant. 1923 Wodehouse *Inimit. Jeeves* xii. 135 Sometimes when Jeeves has brought in my *morning tea and shoved it on the table beside my bed, he drifts silently from the room. 1930 *Times Lit. Suppl.* 25 Dec. 1103/2 Nor does he consider such domestic objects as morning tea, a Japanese bed-jacket,..as too humble for affectionate record.

Moron² (mōᵊ·rǫn). [f. L. *mōrus*, Gr. μωρός stupid.] One of the highest class of feeble-minded; an adult person having an intelligence comparable to that of a normal average child between eight and twelve years of age.
The term was first adopted and given this meaning by the American Association for the Study of the Feeble-minded in 1910.
1912 H. H. Goddart *Kallikak Family* 54 The type of feeblemindedness of which we are speaking is the one to which Deborah belongs, that is, to the high grade, or moron. 1919 — *Hum. Efficiency* (1920) 86 A moron girl of seventeen years of age was recently asked why she committed her first sex offense. 1922 W. R. Inge in *Edin. Rev.* July 48 It is possible that while we are governed by high-grade 'morons' there will be no practical recognition of the dangers which threaten us. 1929 in *Eugenics Rev.* July 86/2 See the happy moron. He doesn't give a damn. I wish I were a moron. My God! perhaps I am!

b. *colloq.* A brutish, stupid, or abnormal person; a degenerate; a fool.
1922 Titus *Timber* iii. 37 So this backwoods moron, even, knew something about his affairs that John Taylor did not know. 1926 *Amer. Speech* I. 188 The term 'moron' is assuming a new meaning in popular usage...It is often used as synonymous with 'brute' or 'degenerate'. 1927 Miller *Colfax Book-Plate* 203 You know I told you how that moron of a Brandon Tower..changed the suit-cases that time we went to Philadelphia?

Morosophist. (Later example.)
1870 K. H. Digby *Halcyon Hours* 255 Morosophists who love to boast Are those of course who scorn the most This holy maid.

Morphallaxis (mǫrfălæ·ksis). *Zool.* [f. Gr. μορφ-ή form + ἄλλαξις exchange.] The process of regeneration of an organism or a part of it by transformation of an existing part and without actual accretion.
1901 T. H. Morgan *Regeneration* 270 Regeneration by means of morphallaxis takes place only in those forms in which the body is not made up of a series of separated parts.

Morphically (mǭ·rfikăli), *adv.* [f. Morphic *a.* + -al + -ly.] In relation to or as regards shape or form; morphologically.
1893 Hyatt in *Proc. Boston Soc. Nat. Hist.* XXVI. 66 *note*, This is morphically a free cell.

Morpho (mǭ·rfo). [mod.L., ad. Gr. Μορφώ, an epithet of Aphrodite.] A large brilliantly-coloured (usually blue) butterfly of South America belonging to the family *Morphidæ.*
1853 A. R. Wallace *Amazon* 14 Butterflies. Among them were..three Morphos, those splendid large metallic-blue butterflies which are always first noticed by travellers in South America. 1863 H. W. Bates *Naturalist Amazons* I. 103 The splendid metallic blue Morphos..are generally confined to the shady alleys of the forest. 1918 W. Beebe *Jungle Peace* (1919) iii. 37 A shining blue wing of a morpho butterfly.

Morphogenic, *a.* (Example.)
1904 *Science* 2 Dec. 749/2 The specific morphogenic factors are connected in some way with specific forms of protoplasm.

Morphomaniac (mǫrfomēᵊ·niæk). [Irreg. f. Morphia + Maniac.] = Morphinomaniac.
1906 Chesterton *Dickens* ii. 41 These great popular leaders..become drunkards; they become demagogues; they become morphomaniacs. 1912 L. J. Vance *Destroying Angel* xii. 165 He's just short of a raving morphomaniac.

Morphotropic (mǫrfotrǫ·pik), *a.* Pertaining to or characterized by morphotropy. **Morpho·tropism** (mǫrfǫ·trŏpiz'm), **Morpho·tropy**, the change in crystalline form which results from the substitution of different atoms or radicles in the chemical molecule of a crystalline substance.
1900 *Rep. Brit. Assoc.* 167 The consideration of facts such as these leads to the conclusion that morphotropy and isomorphism have a common cause, and that this is more likely to be discovered by the crystallographic study of substances showing morphotropic relationships than from the examination merely of materials likely to exhibit isomorphism. 1905 *Amer. Chem. Jrnl.* July 104 (Cent. Suppl.) The chapter on Morphotropism deals with the dependence of the crystal structure on the chemical constitution of the body. 1910 *Encycl. Brit.* VII. 591/1 A striking example of morphotropy is shown by the humite..group of minerals.

Mo·rris chair. [f. the name of William *Morris* (1834–96), poet and craftsman.] A form of easy chair with an adjustable back.
1902 Webster Suppl. 1911 R. W. Chambers *Common Law* xiii. 379 The big sculptor lying in his morris-chair, sometimes irritable, sometimes morose.

Mort, *sb.*¹ 4. (Later example.)
1888 H. James *Letters* 31 July (1920) I. 138 You have become a beautiful myth—a kind of unnatural uncomfortable unburied *mort.*

Mortality. 1. b. (Recent example.)
1887 Rider Haggard *She* xvi. 187 Mortality is weak, and easily broken down by a sense of the companionship that waits upon its end.

Mortician (mǫrti·ʃăn). *U.S.* [f. L. *mort-, mors* death (cf. Mort *sb.*¹) + -ician.] An undertaker.
1923 *Glasgow Herald* 11 Oct. 5 Instancing thirty words among which figure aptronym,..milline, mortician. 1927 *Ibid.* 1 Oct. 10/7 As the jury troop out of their boxes every tread of their heels will mean another call for the mortician. 1927 *Observer* 9 Oct. 15/7 Not long ago we were told that the American undertaker preferred to be known as a 'mortician'. 1930 *Punch* 18 June 696 He passed me on to a mortician... His prices..were huge, but then he was mortician to all the best movie-stars' husbands.

Mortlake. Add: 2. A loop of a river-channel which has been abandoned by the river.
1902 Ld. Avebury *Scenery Eng.* 303 The loop often remains as a dead river-channel or 'Mortlake'. Such loop-lakes are known in America by the special name of 'Ox-bows'.

Mosaic. A. *adj.*¹ 4. Add: *Mosaic disease*: a disease which attacks the leaves of the tobacco and other plants, producing a mosaic appearance on the surface of the leaf. Called also *leaf mosaic* (see *Leaf *sb.* 17) or simply *mosaic.*
1909 *Century Dict.* Suppl. s.v. *Disease*. 1922 *Glasgow Herald* 19 Oct. 5 Endeavouring to have the Destructive Insects and Pests Order extended to imported potatoes infected by leaf curl and mosaic. 1925 *Contemp. Rev.* Dec. 753 Cuba..is finding soil depletion and mosaic disease increasingly serious matters.

5. *Biol.* Of cross-bred organisms: Having characters from both parents existing side by side and not blended.
1902 Bateson & Saunders *Rep. Evol. Comm. Roy. Soc.* I. III. 127 Such a phenomenon may be taken as indicating that the germ-cells may also have been mosaic.

B. *sb.* Add: 3. b. *Biol.* A cross-bred animal or plant which shows different parental characters existing side by side without blending.
1902 Bateson & Saunders *Rep. Evol. Comm. Roy. Soc.* I. I. 23 These mosaics occurred as rarities both on prickly individuals and on smooth ones still more rarely. 1903 *Proc. Zool. Soc.* II. 84 The suggestion that such a pied individual is a mosaic which throws self-colour gametes is not readily applicable to this case.

Moses. 2. b. (Later example.)
1812 *Boston Gaz.* 26 Oct., Suppl., Advt. (Th.) On Saturday was picked up, on Dorchester Flats, a small Moses boat.

Mosey, *v.* 1 and 2. (Later examples.)
1902 Harben *Abner Daniel* 59 Now I must mosey on down-stairs and dance with that Miss Fewclothes from Rome. 1918 *Punch* 27 Mar. 206/1 Her funnel's caked with Cape Horn ice and blistered in the sun, She's moseyed round above a bit, and, poor old ship, she's done.

Mosquito. 2. b. **mosquito-bar** (earlier example); **mosquito-hawk** (later example of *a*); **mosquito-net** (earlier example).
1809 *Deb. Congress* (1853) 2448 Ninety-five *musquito bars at 4½ and 7 dollars each. 1819 *Massachusetts Spy* 22 Sept. (Th.) The Frenchmen call them *moscheto hawks, because they make their appearance when moschetos are most numerous. 1745 *Itinerant Observ.* 13 And this Colony is either not so enervated as their neighbor, or else are poor enough to scorn Umbrellas and *Musketto-Nets, as Jamaican and Carolinean Effeminacies.

Mossy, *a.* 5. (Modern U.S. example.)
1904 *Collier's* 20 Feb. 1 Arthur Lynch's release has the approval of all England except a few peculiarly mossy old Tories.

6. **mossy-backed** *a.* (example); **mossy-cup oak** (earlier example).
1881 *Harper's Mag.* Sept. 640/2 A thorough-bred, *mossy-backed mountaineer..appeared. 1810 Michaux *Arbres* I. 21 (*Quercus olivaeformis*)..*Mossy cup oak, nom donné par moi à cette espèce.

Most. B. *adv.* 4. For '*Obs.* exc. *dial.*' read 'Now *dial.* and *U.S.*'
1775 *Essex Inst. Hist. Coll.* XIII. 198 It is so long since I saw, or heard direct from you that I most forgit you. 1800 *Farmer's Register* (Greensburgh, Pa.) 8 Nov. (Th.) And though he squeez'd me most to death, I could not help it, no, not I. 1803 *Port Folio* (Philad.) III. 97 (Th.) You know how it most makes you blind, in winter, to look on the snow. 1825 J. Neal *Bro. Jonathan* I. 107 Most off the handle, some o' the tribe I guess. 1838 Caroline Gilman *Recollections* xxvii. 189, I worked my fingers most to the bone for them pictures. 1883 'Mark Twain' *Life Mississippi* iii. 26 Then they both got at it at the same time, swelling round and round each other, and punching their fists most into each other's faces. 1887 Tourgee *Button's Inn* 327 Sometimes I 'most forget him. 1901 S. Merwin & H. K. Webster *Calumet K* i. 6, I 'most met my death climbing up just now.

b. With *all, every*, etc.
1770 Washington *Diaries* I. 395 As the Tassels of most all the Corn..was entirely dry. 1772–6 J. Andrews *Lett.* 403, I think it exceeds most every thing of the kind. 1834 C. A. Davis *Lett. J. Downing* 35 Most all these southern folks are good fellows. 1851 *Knickerbocker Mag.* XXXVII. 65 A little of 'most all other agricultural products. 1863 'E. Kirke' *My Southern Friends* i. 18 He's managed to make twenty-five cents or more 'most every day. c 1865 'Mark Twain' *Sketches* Wks. XIX. 28 He was lucky,..he most always come out winner. 1888 *Rep. Vermont Board Agric.* X. 49 You are more sure of a good butter cow in this breed [Jersey] than in most any other. 1892 J. E. Cooke *B. Hallam* 50 'Never argue with women!' adds Kate, 'As if he was not arguing with me all the time 'most!' 1901 S. Merwin & H. K. Webster *Calumet K* i. 5 That's most all we've been doing for ten days. 1904 *N.Y. Sun* 16 Aug. 5 Most everybody in the Twelfth Ward was there.

Most-favoured-nation, see Favoured *ppl. a.*¹

Mot, variant of Motte. *U.S.*

Mote, *sb.*¹ 3. b. Add to def.: or in cotton.
1902 W. Hannan *Textile Fibres* 102 The fragmental portions of cotton seeds carry a tuft of attached fibres on the outer membrane; this is termed a bearded *mote*, and is regarded as an imperfection or impurity.

5. **mote-knife**, a knife in a carding machine for removing motes from textile fibres.
1896 Taggart *Cotton Spinning* I. 132 The cotton is no sooner taken from the feed than it is carried past one or two bars C and D with sharp edges, known as mote knives.

Mote, *sb.*² Add: 3. *Comb.* as *mote-castle.*
1919 *Proc. Soc. Antiq. Scot.* LIII. 42 Such a fortress is well represented in the mote-castles of Dinan, Hastings and Rennes, in the Bayeux tapestry.

Moth, *sb.* Add: 1. f. Trade name of a type of light aeroplane.
1926 J. L. Pritchard *Bk. Aeroplane* 175 The Moth is a biplane with two seats arranged tandem fashion, and fitted with dual control...The wings can be folded back [etc.]. 1928 *Times* 20 Mar. 13/1 He took the moth up to a height and deliberately attempted to get into a spin.
attrib. 1927 *Morn. Post* 19 Aug. 7 She was piloted by Captain C. D. Barnard in her own Moth light aeroplane.

3. *moth-soft* adj.; **moth-ball**, a ball of naphthaline (sometimes mixed with other substances) used to keep away moths (in quot. fig.); **moth-borer**, the larva of the borer moth, *Diatræa saccharalis*, which attacks the sugar-cane; **moth-miller** (earlier example); **moth spot** (see quot.).
1907 'O. Henry' *Heart of West* vi. Wks. (1928) 116 Me and Solly..prepared to shake off our *moth balls and wing our way against the arc-lights of the joyous and tuneful East. 1900 *Nature* 21 June 182/2 A considerable number of the eggs of the *moth borer (which are laid in patches on the leaves of the sugar-cane) are attacked by parasites. 1877 Bartlett *Dict. Amer.* (ed. 4) *Moth-miller. 1876 G. M. Hopkins *Poems* (1918) 20 Or night, still higher, With belled fire and the *moth-soft Milky Way. 1922 F. Courtenay *Physical Beauty* 26 The so-called '*moth spots' brown spots or patches which appear after middle life, are due to this tan pigment.

Mother, *sb.* 13. c. (Add examples.)
1823 De Quincey *Rosicrucians & Free-masons* Wks. 1871 XVI. 361 These orders have *degrees*—many or few according to the constitution of the several mother-lodges. 1883 J. H. Beadle *Western Wilds* xxxiv. 561 What miners call a 'mother lode' is often like a tree in its upward development: below is the main trunk, above the branches diverge. 1907 *Practitioner* Aug. 320 These granules consist of a zymogen, or mother-ferment, which is called *trypsinogen.*

16. **mother cult**, the worship of a mother-goddess; **mother-metal** [after *mother liquor*], the solidified mass of metals or alloy left after some of a metal has been separated out from it by crystallization; **mother's help**, a domestic servant; **mother ship**, also, a ship (or airship) having charge of submarines or aeroplanes; **mother-starter**, a germ culture used as a source for supplies of that culture; **mother tincture**, in Homoeopathy, a pure (undiluted) tincture of a drug.
1909 *Westm. Gaz.* 2 Feb. 5/1 From the trend of recent writings in Hindu literature it is suggested that the *Mother cult has been revived. 1912 Hastings' *Encycl. Relig. & Ethics* V. 7/1 The worship at the famous shrine of Becharāgī in Baroda may be taken as an example of the ritual of the Mother-cult. 1902 *Encycl. Brit.* XXIX. 573/2 By which time so much iron has separated out that the remaining *mother-metal has reached the composition of hardenite. 1881 *Instr. Census Clerks* (1885) 30 *Mother's Help. 1908 A. S. M. Hutchinson *Once Aboard Lugger* I. vii. § 1. 63 You don't understand. She is not exactly my friend; she is my—my employer. I'm a mothers-help. 1909 *Q. Rev.* Oct. 575 Depôt ships for destroyers, *mother-ships for submarines, and oil-supply vessels. 1922 *Encycl. Brit.* XXX. 17/2 Scouts were flown..off the decks of battleships and 'mother' ships. 1926 H. T. Wilkins *Marvels Mod. Mech.* 215 An engineer, aboard the airship, opened the telescopic apparatus which left the aeroplane swaying in space some 60 feet below the mother ship. 1920 W. Clayton *Margarine* 48 The milk is soured by inoculation after pasteurization with suitable quantities of pure cultures, these in turn having been made from a specially-cared-for '*mother-starter'. 1902 *Encycl. Brit.* XXIX. 312/2 Many employ low potencies, *i.e.* *mother tinctures, first, second, sixth dilutions, &c. 1906 W. De Morgan *Joseph Vance* xvi. 149 She makes some concession to my feelings on the subject of High Dilutions, and (at great risk to myself, she says) allows me to have Mother-Tinctures.

b. **mother of floods** (see quot. 1831); **mother of commonwealths, presidents, states**, names for Virginia.
1879 *Congress. Rec.* 10 Jan. 413/2 To pour out the vials of his impotent wrath upon the '*Mother of Commonwealths'. 1831 Peck *Guide Emigrants* II. 24 'The *Mother of Floods', said to be the aboriginal meaning of Missouri. 1850 *Congress. Globe* 13 May App. 563/3 Virginia, the *mother of Presidents, the Old Dominion. 1868 *Ibid.* 17 Dec. 132/2 Virginia, the proud mother of Presidents, become a breeder of slaves for the southern market. 1904 *N.Y. Tribune* 12 June 8 Virginia concluded not to indorse any candidate. The 'Mother of Presidents' is a trifle particular. 1879 *Congress. Rec.* 10 Jan. 414/1 When the '*mother of States' comes, in the weeds of woe, asking [etc.]. *Ibid.*, That grand old commonwealth of Virginia, the mother of States and Statesmen.

Mother, *v.*¹ Add: 2. c. *Mil.* To protect.
1917 'Contact' *Airman's Outings* 185 If, later, a further advance be made, the low-flying contact machines again play their part of mothering the infantry.

Mothercraft (mʌ·ðəɹkrɑft). [f. Mother *sb.*¹ + Craft *sb.*] The 'craft' or business of a mother; a mother's duties in the family.
1914 *Times* 25 Apr. 10/3 The School of Mothercraft. 1917 B. Vaughan *Menace Empty Cradle* 44 How much better it would be to teach them mothercraft. 1926 *Contemp. Rev.* Nov. 667 Lady Erleigh's essay on the teaching of mothercraft is an intrinsic part of the whole theme.
attrib. 1923 *Westm. Gaz.* 19 Oct., A series of mother-craft lectures and demonstrations on the Psychological and Physical Development of the Child..is to begin..next Tuesday afternoon.

Motherment (mʌ·ðəɹmĕnt). [f. Mother *v.* + -ment.] Motherly care or supervision.
1914 W. J. Locke *Fortunate Youth* ii. 26 She never gushed, it is true, over her offspring; but the little Buttons flourished under genuine motherment.

Motherwise (mʌ·ðəɹwaiz), *adv.* [Wise *sb.*¹ II. 3 b.] In the manner of a mother.
1910 W. J. Locke *Simon Jester* xix. 241 With strong shapely arms that had as yet only held me motherwise.

Motile, *a.* Add: 2. *Psychol.* Recalling impressions most readily in terms of motor or kinæsthetic imagery.
1909 *Daily Chron.* 22 Feb. 4/7 Unless you are a microcephalous idiot, you are either Audile, Motile, or Visile.
b. *sb.* A person whose preferred type of imagery is motor or kinaesthetic.
1886 *Mind* XI. 415 This division of men into visuals, audiles, motiles and indifferents..is of great interest and importance. 1909 C. S. Myers *Exper. Psychol.* 147 Those in whom one or other of these three kinds of imagery is especially developed, are sometimes called 'visiles' 'audiles', or 'motiles'.

Motion, *sb.* 15. Add: **motion-rod**, a rod communicating motion; **motion-study**, the study of moving objects, esp. processes in nature, by means of motion pictures.
1908 *Westm. Gaz.* 13 Feb. 4/2 Contained in this box is the damping mechanism, which is connected to the axle by suitable levers and *motion-rods. 1912 *Chambers's Jrnl.* Sept. 571/1 When the latest industrial science known as '*motion study' is applied to fruit-growing.

Motion, *v.* Add: 5. *trans.* To impart motion to.
1929 Bridges *Test. Beauty* I. 667 Wisdom..choosing to be call'd Athena daughter of Zeus Motion'd the marble to her living grace.

Motion picture. [Motion *sb.* 15.] A cinematographic picture or film; a 'moving picture'. Also *attrib.*
[1891 *Leisure Hour* 711/1 A highly composite mechanism which is to be known as the 'kinetograph' or motion-picture.] 1908 *Daily Chron.* 20 Aug. 7/1 Text books must give way to the motion-picture film. 1913 F. A. Talbot *Pract. Cinematogr.* 129 Plate, The first motion-pictures of an opening flower, taken at the Marey Institute. The complete opening of a convolvulus is shown in fifteen pictures. 1915 P. G. Wodehouse *Something Fresh* v. § 1 The maiden in distress..was merely earning the salary paid her by some motion-picture firm. 1916 Bower *Phantom Herd* i. 1 He had..promised..to speak a good word for them to other motion picture companies who might want to hire real Indians. 1921 R. D. Paine *Comr. Rolling Ocean* vii. 112 There were a few stores, a church,..but not a solitary motion-picture theater. 1929 M. R. Werner *Bryan* 264 Between 1916 and 1919 Bryan was engaged in negotiations for a motion picture on the curse of drink, of which he was to be the star.

Motive, *sb.* 7. (Add example.)
1928 *Daily Express* 21 Apr. 6/2 These motives are mounted in various designs on a background of satin.
8. *motive-hunter.*
1905 *Spectator* 28 Jan. 141/1 He is, therefore, a *motive-hunter, seeking on every side for little justifications for his pride.

Motometer. (Later example.)
1907 *Sci. Amer.* 12 Jan. 47/1 Motometers being tested at Automobile Show.

Motor. A. *sb.* Add: 1. c. (Later example.)
1892 K. Pearson *Grammar of Sci.* ix. 435 The chief motor of modern life with all its really great achievements has been sought..in the individualistic instinct.

5. *attrib.* and *Comb.* Further examples; also vessels driven by motors, as *motor-coaster, -craft, -liner, -ship, -sloop.*
1901 *Chambers's Jrnl.* Nov. 764/2 Great things are anticipated of a new method of land culture by means of a motor-plough. 1905 *Motor Traction* 8 June Advts. p. ii, Motor Buses. Motor Lorries. 1908 *Sketch* 11 Sept. 340 We are at last to have a service of motor-omnibuses in London. 1909 *Chambers's Jrnl.* Jan. 60/1 Travellers in enclosed motor-vehicles frequently experience these peculiar sensations. *Ibid.* June 343/2 Large warehouses have their veritable fleets of motor-wagons. 1910 *Ibid.* Aug. 546/2 The 'final dash' [to the Pole]..will be made with the help of motor-sledges. 1915 *Pearson's Mag.* Jan. 25 These trains go up to the nearest railhead and hand over the stores to the motor-lorry trains. *Ibid.*, The motor-trains, although speedy, are likewise noisy. 1924 B. Gilbert *Bly Market* 17 'That Pickard' the Winch dealer who had so benefited by the War that he'd bought a motor-float. 1927 *Daily Express* 12 Aug. 9/7 The new order governing the size and construction of motor-coaches and other heavy motor vehicles is issued to-day. 1929 W. E. Collinson *Spoken English* 86, I once thought of buying a motor-scooter. 1929 *Times* 31 Oct. 13/3 A rail motor-truck arrived from Forrest, bringing food supplies. 1930 *Daily Express* 1 Aug. 9/2 The most modern form of holiday transport—the motor-caravan, or trailer caravan.
1905 *Daily Chron.* 17 June 9/1 The latest regulation that no small boat should 'lock' with a motor-craft appears to have caused considerable surprise. 1928 *Daily Express* 5 Dec. 11/4 It is feared that the London motor-coaster, Wander (82 tons), has been lost, with a crew of five. 1929 *Times* 2 Nov. 10/2 The Tuscan Star..is the first motor-ship ordered by the Blue Star Line. 1931 *Times Lit. Suppl.* 15 Jan. 33/3 M. Knut Stubbendorff..chartered the motor-sloop Isbjörn. 1931 *Even. Standard* 16 Jan. 9/1 The new motor-liner Warwick Castle..sails for Southampton to-morrow.

b. Of, pertaining to or connected with a motor or motor-cars as *motor-chassis, -horn*, etc.; designed for motor-cars or for motoring as *motor-course, -road*, etc.; adapted for wearing while motoring as *motor-bonnet, -coat, -mask, -veil*, etc.
(*a*) 1902 *Pall Mall Mag.* XXVIII. 410/1 Should motor drivers be subject to an examination as to proficiency? 1909 *Chambers's Jrnl.* June 401/1 The predominant sounds..were not those of wheels or whistles or motor-horns, but of the birds who piped their songs. 1911 *Ibid.* Jan. 55/1 Cleaver and Latham dropped into the Mediterranean..because of motor trouble. 1915 *Pearson's Mag.* Jan. 25 Great lines of these old motor-chassis, mounted with a serviceable lorry body, are to be met with on all the roads of France.
(*b*) 1909 C. W. Blundell in *Englishman* 24 Feb., Let them by all means run on their own motor-courses, enjoy each other's stench, [etc.]. 1909 *Westm. Gaz.* 27 Aug. 2/2 Of more dramatic interest is the second part of the Bill, with its proposal for the creation of motor-roads. 1928 *Britain's Industrial Future* (Lib. Ind. Inq.) I. iv. § 5. 45 To build motor-roads through the Midlands. 1928 *Manch. Guard. Weekly* 19 Oct. 301/2 Motor traffic and the urbanisation of large rural stretches are producing a hideous outbreak of advertisement hoardings, petrol pumps..and gaunt new motor-tracks.
(*c*) 1909 *Chambers's Jrnl.* Sept. 561/2 A stray lock..curling over her forehead in the breeze under her dainty motor-cap. 1910 *Blackw. Mag.* Feb. 179/2 It was Mrs. Cargil in travelling-dress, with a purple bonnet and a green motor-veil. *Ibid.* Apr. 480/1 Clad in a composite costume, of which a long leather motor-coat was the least remarkable part. *Ibid.* Nov. 604/2 My wife..had been patiently sitting in the hall wearing a new motor-bonnet. 1916 *War Illustr.* V. 451/3 Our goggles..are shaped like a motor-mask.

c. Instrumental, as *motor-driven; motor-travelling.* Also *motor-traction.*
1904 *Motor Cycle* 6 June 551 A motor-driven roundabout. 1910 C. C. Turner *Aerial Navig. To-day* 266 The perfect carburetter will add immensely to the efficiency of motor-driven air-craft. 1909 *Chambers's Jrnl.* June 342/2 Putting the accidents on railways and on the roads together, motor-travelling included. 1911 *Ibid.* Aug. 532 The Triumph of Motor-Traction.

6. **motor-bandit**, a thief who uses a motor-car; **motordrome**, a course for motor-racing; **motor-gun**, a gun mounted on a motor-vehicle; **motor-mate**, one who attends to the motor of an airship; **motor-school**, a school where the driving of motor-vehicles is taught.
1913 *Punch* 19 Feb. 133/3 On top of all this *Motor Bandit business comes the news that two men have been charged..with breaking into a bakery and stealing a sponge-cake, value one penny. 1928 *Daily Mail* 25 July 9/3 A light iron barrier passed across main roads..would form an effective check against motor-bandits. 1908 *Westm. Gaz.* 4 Aug. 4/3 Mr. Locke-King has spent a large fortune in building this wonderful *motordrome. 1908 H. G. Wells *War in Air* ii. § 2 Near Maidstone they came on a string of eleven *motor-guns. 1928 Gamble *Story N. Sea Air Station* xxii. 411 During the attack, one of the *motor-mates of the amidships gondola raised the black curtain. 1909 *Chambers's Jrnl.* June 342/1 The..is now getting his country grooms trained at a *motor-school.

B. *adj.* Add: 1. (Later example.)
1928 Sir J. C. Bose (*title*) The motor mechanism of plants.
2. (Further examples.)
1905 McDougall *Physiol. Psychol.* 30 The freed energy flows down the axon of the motor neurone and escapes into the muscle with which it is connected. *Ibid.* 35 A sensory neurone may be connected with a considerable number of motor systems.
b. Of memory, impressions, etc.: Based on, connected with or received through the physical movement of parts of the body. (Distinguished from *audile* and *visual.*)
1899 A. G. Whyte tr. *Binet's Psychol. Reasoning* 24 When we think of the ball, this idea must comprise the images of these muscular sensations, as it comprises the images of the sensations of sight and of touch. Such is the motor image. *Ibid.* 25 By making reading and writing proceed together, the two memories, visual and motor, are constrained to associate and to aid one another. 1900 *Amer. Jrnl. Psychol.* Apr. XI. 310 Motor phenomena are now regarded as necessary elements in all mental processes. 1903 *Amer. Naturalist* Mar. XXXVII. 207 To whatever sense the stimulus is given, the impulse has to go to the motor-image-centres, and then to the muscles. 1924 R. M. Ogden tr. *Koffka's Growth of Mind* 64 If our assumption regarding the defective motor-vision of new-born infants is correct, it appears [etc.]. 1925 C. Fox *Educ. Psychol.* 228 Walking is not bringing into use unconscious motor-images.

Motor, *v.* Add: Also, to traverse (a distance) in or by means of a motor-car.
1928 'S. S. Van Dine' *Greene Murder Case* xii. 141 Vance and Ada and I motored the few blocks to 18, Broad Street.

Motorable (mōᵘ·tŏrăb'l), *a.* [f. Motor *sb.* and *v.* + -able.] Of a road or district: Suitable for motor-cars; capable of being travelled over in a motor-car.
1920 A. L. Bagley *Holiday Rambles N. Wales* 178 This is certainly not a motorable road. 1928 *Observer* 15 July 13/1 Their itineraries should not be confined to motorable roads.

Mo·tor-boat. A motor-driven boat or launch.
1902 *New Liberal Rev.* Apr. 440 The paraffin motor..is..impossible in anything but an open motor-boat. 1905 *Country Life* 11 Mar. p. xlvi/2 A fast motor-boat. 1913 E. F. Benson *Thorley Weir* i. 11 If I must go on the river, give me a motor-boat.
Hence **Motor-boat** *v. intr.*, to travel in or by means of a motor-boat. **Motor-boa·tist**, one who uses a motor-boat.
1922 *Contemp. Rev.* Mar. 409 The scenery through which he tramped or motor-boated. 1908 *Westm. Gaz.* 30 Apr. 4/3 A Ducal Motor-boatist..the Duke of Westminster.

Mo·tor-bus. A motor-driven omnibus.
1905 *Motor Traction* 8 June 157/1 There was a sudden awakening..to the possibilities of the motor 'bus and vehicles for the transport of passengers generally. 1907 *Blackw. Mag.* May 602/1 Even the grinding motor-busses..seemed less incongruous than usual. 1909 *Chambers's Jrnl.* Jan. 62/2 The device has been tested on a motor-bus and has proved very satisfactory.
Hence **Mo·tor-bus** *v. intr.*, to travel by motor-bus.
1915 D. O. Barnett *Lett.* 39 We came on from our last stopping place, whither we motor-bused, in a car.

Mo·tor-car, *v.* [f. the sb.] *intr.* To travel by motor-car.
1901 H. H. Munro *Lett.* in *Square Egg* (1927) 52 Travelling with Aunt Tom is more exciting than motorcarring.

Motorcarist (mōᵘ·tǝɹ,kāᵊrist). [-ist.] One who rides in or drives a motor-car; a motorist.
1899 *Motor-Car World* I. 37/2 Many of the disabilities under which motorcarists suffer in England will be removed. 1901 *Rep. Brit. Assoc.* 764 The cyclist and motor-carist travel over the whole of the roads of the country.

Motor-cycle, *sb.* Also -bicycle. [Motor A. 5.] A special form of bicycle having a small motor (usually a petrol one) by which it is propelled.
1894–6 [see Motor A. 5. in Dict.]. 1902 *Motor Cycling* 12 Feb. 23/1, I rode a motor bicycle with the motor in the back wheel. *Ibid.* 24/1 In a year or two motor cycles will be as plentiful as the ordinary cycle is to-day.
attrib. 1919– [see *Combination 9 b].
Hence **Mo·tor-cycle** *v. trans.* and *intr.*, to travel (or traverse) by means of a motor-cycle; to use a motor-cycle. **Motor-cy·cling** *vbl. sb.* **Motor-cy·clist**, one who uses a motor-cycle.
1902 *Motor Cycling* 12 Feb. 24/1 Now that motor cycling has come to stay,..it may not be out of place to say where improvements may be made that will be beneficial to..all those who motor-cycle. *Ibid.* 19 Feb. 32 Motor cyclists will not require palatial club premises. 1926 Rose Macaulay *Crewe Train* II. viii. 154 Denham, motor cycling between Missenden and Amersham, turned suddenly sick and faint.

Motordom (mōᵘ·tǝɹdǝm). [-dom.] The realm or world of motors; motor-vehicles, the people who use them, or those who deal in them considered collectively.
1900 *Captain* III. 225/1 In the world of motordom. 1909 *Westm. Gaz.* 2 Nov. 2/3 There is scarcely a woman in London who has not had to sacrifice the cadences of talk to the Moloch of Motordom. 1916 W. J. Locke *Wonderful Yr.* vi. 84 The debonair waiter..had of late [been] replaced by the chambermaid and Félise when fashionable motordom halted at the Hôtel des Grottes. 1922 *Blackw. Mag.* Sept. 377/2 This road had all the charms of the old English highway before the scarifying era of motordom.

Mo·tored, *ppl. a.* [-ed ¹.] Provided with a motor.
1928 *Daily Express* 17 Nov. 9/3 The Wright brothers completed their motored glider—the first real airplane—in their bicycle shop at Dayton on Nov. 17th 1903.

Mo·toring, *vbl. sb.* (See after Motor in Dict.) Also *attrib.*, as *motoring-cap, -coat.*
1909 *Chambers's Jrnl.* Sept. 588/2 She raised a little gloved hand and patted the hair under a dainty motoring-cap. *Ibid.* Oct. 677/1 Presently the Squire appeared, leaning on Vanessa's arm, she in her Di Vernon motoring-coat.

Motorism (mōᵘ·tŏriz'm). [f. Motor *sb.* + -ism.] The use or prevalence of motor-vehicles.
1930 Cicely Hamilton in *Time & Tide* 24 Jan. 101 The humanitarian associations..have not yet come forward with their corporate rebuke for the death-dealing motorism of the highway.

Motorium (motōᵊ·riŏm). [mod.L., f. *mōtōrius* moving, f. L. *mōt-* stem of *movēre* to move: cf. -ory.] The part of an organism which is concerned with motion. Distinguished from the *sensorium.*
1888 J. Baldwin *Elem. Psychol.* I. v. 47 (Funk) The motorium is the portion of the nervous organism through which self sends messages to the outer world. 1924 R. M. Ogden tr. *Koffka's Growth of Mind* 80 The optical sensorium and motorium can not be regarded as two independent pieces of apparatus, since for many types of performance they constitute a unitary organ.

Motorization (mōᵘtŏraizēᵊ·ʃǝn). [f. *Motorize *v.* + -ation.]
1. *Psychol.* The process of making a presentation motorial in character.
1901 *Amer. Jrnl. Psychol.* Apr. XII. 304 The motorization of an exposed word would suggest another similar in sound.
2. The introduction or use of motors for various purposes; equipment with motors.
1929 H. Rowan-Robinson *Further Aspects of Mechanization* ii. 9 The motorization of infantry and cavalry divisions furnishes..additional strategic mobility. 1930 *Time & Tide* 13 Sept. 1134 The world moves largely on rubber, which alone makes motorization possible.

Motorize (mōᵘ·tŏraiz), *v.* [f. Motor *sb.* + -ize.]
1. *trans. Psychol.* To convert (visual or auditory sensations or images) into motorial presentations;

to apprehend in a motorial manner. Also *absol.* or *intr.*
1901 *Amer. Jrnl. Psychol.* Apr. XII. 308 The word..seems to be motorized as soon as singly presented. *Ibid.* 309 This..has reference to readers who motorize.
2. To provide or furnish with a motor or with motor-cars, as a source of power or a means of transport, travel, etc.
1918 Webster Add. 1922 *Daily Mail* 24 Nov. 6 These machines have gone beyond the stage of motorised pedal cycles and are in all respects real motor-cycles with the handiness of pedal cycles. 1924 *Public Opinion* 8 Aug. 130/3 If one should dream of motorising the entire world on the scale of the United States.
Hence **Mo·torized** *ppl. a.*
1922 [see 2]. 1927 *Glasgow Herald* 5 Apr. 8 Serried ranks of tanks advancing against each other..with motorised artillery bringing up the rear.

Motorless (mōᵘ·tǝlės), *a.* [-less.] Not provided with a motor; performed without the help of a motor: esp. of gliders or flying in gliders.
1931 *Times Lit. Suppl.* 9 Apr. 291/4 Major Pagé..offers here sound material on design, construction and the science of 'motorless flight'.

Mo·tor-minded, *a.* Having a mind in which motor images predominate over visual and auditory ones. (Cf. *Motile *a.*) So **Motor-mi·ndedness.**
1900 *Amer. Jrnl. Psychol.* Apr. XI. 297 Consonants were not thought to be generally more important than vowels for word perception. The relative importance of these elements might depend upon the reader's tendency to be motor or auditory minded. 1902 *J. M. Baldwin's Dict. Philos. & Psychol.* II. 571 Along with these differences should also be noted the varying prominence which visual and auditory and muscular processes occupy in different minds—eye-mindedness, ear-mindedness, motor-mindedness, &c.

Motorphobe (mōᵘ·tŏrfoᵘb). [-phobe.] One who has a morbid dread or hatred of motor-vehicles.
1905 *Automobile Topics* 27 May 448 (Cent. Suppl.) From pillar to post the poor motorist is pushed...The time will come when..the motorphobes will wonder what ever possessed them to act so foolishly. 1911 *Chambers's Jrnl.* Aug. 533/1 A motorphobe was quoted as declaring solemnly in 1906, 'In another ten years there will not be half the autocars on the roads that there are now.'

Motto. 5. (Add examples.)
1835 *Southern Lit. Messenger* I. 358, I only ate..a few macaronies and mottoes..that's all. 1856 Cozzens *Sparrowgr. Papers* iv. 42 And that lady..went home with her pocket well stuffed with mottoes.

Motuca (motū·kă). Also **motuka.** [? The Tupi name.] A Brazilian fly (*Hadaus lepidotus*, Perty) of the family *Tabanidæ.*
1863 H. W. Bates *Naturalist on Amazons* I. 306 In the daytime the Motúca, a much larger and more formidable fly than the mosquito, insisted upon levying his tax of blood. 1927 W. M. McGovern *Jungle Paths & Inca Ruins* 224 Unlike the vampire bat, the motuka inflicted a very painful sting.

Mould, *sb.*³ Add: 6. e. (See quot.)
1842–59 Gwilt *Archit.* Gloss., *Moulds*, among plumbers, are the tables on which they cast their sheets of lead.
13. c. *spec.* The pieces of old horse-shoes welded together as material for a new shoe.
1908 *Animal Managem.* 235 The lump of metal is now known as a 'mould'. The welded end of the mould is then grasped by tongs.
17. *mould-made.*
1928 *Scholartis Press Catal.* June, A full quarto on an unusual grey mould-made paper.

Mould (moᵘld), *sb.*⁶ [f. Mould *sb.*¹] = Mould-board.
1861 *Trans. Ill. Agric. Soc.* IV. 249 The moulds used on this plow will not only be good, but..shown to be the best, that in the nature of things, can ever be made. 1867 *Rep. Iowa Agric. Soc.* (1868) 266 There is no clogging, and the mould and lay are so hardened that they scour readily.

Moulder, *sb.*¹ Add: 1. b. (See quot.)
1894 *Labour Commission* Gloss., *Moulders*, men in the seed-crushing industry who draw the rolled seed from the fixture wherein it is made hot, and..subject it to a slight pressure.

Mouldy (moᵘ·ldi), *sb.* *Navy slang.* A torpedo.
1920 *Blackw. Mag.* Mar. 335/2 A 'mouldy' that was capable of blowing a forty-by-thirty hole in a steel ship's side. 1925 E. Fraser & Gibbons *Soldier & Sailor Words*, *Mouldy*, the universal Navy name for a torpedo. 1928 *Observer* 11 Mar. 17/4 The King of Afghanistan will be given a lesson in torpedo firing and himself discharge a 'mouldy' from one of L22's tubes.

Mouldy, *a.*² Add: 2. b. Thoroughly bad; esp. very tiresome or boring.
1876 [see sense 2 in Dict.] 1916 E. V. Lucas *Vermillion Box* 220, I should be mouldy company for you, I fear, because I can't talk. 1923 Una L. Silberrad *Lett. Jean Armiter* i. 18 'If ever anyone had had a mouldy time, it's you.' 'I haven't', Jean protested. 'It hasn't been mouldy.'
3. *Comb.*, as *mouldy-minded* adj.
1906 Hardy *Dynasts* II. VI. vii. 320 The rawest Dynast..Will..Down-topple to the dust like soldier Saul, And Europe's mouldy-minded oligarchs Be propped anew.

Mound, *sb.*³ 5. Add: **Mound city** *U.S.*, a name for St. Louis, Missouri; **mound region**, a region in which there are many mounds.
1854 Mayne Reid *Hunters' Feast* i. 5 On the western bank of the Mississippi..stands the large town of St. Louis, poetically known as the 'Mound City'. 1859 Bartlett *Dict. Amer.*, *Mound-City*, the city of St. Louis, so-called from the number of artificial mounds that occupied the site on which the city is built. 1873 J. H. Beadle *Undevel. West* i. 38 This is the centre of the '*Mound Region' of Wisconsin—so called from the many Indian mounds scattered about the valley.

Mount, *sb.*² Add: 4. b. *collect.* A supply of riding horses.
1907 S. E. White *Arizona Nights* I. iii. 53 He kept his own mount of horses, took care of them.

Mount, *v.* 8 and 17. (Add examples.)
1930 *Morn. Post.* 19 July 12/6 He just managed to avoid a crash by cutting out to his right and in doing so he mounted the footpath.
1909 'R. Andom' *On Tour with Troddles* 128 Breakfast over, Mac mounted a pipe and sauntered out of the hotel.

Mountain. Add: 3. b. *To make a mountain out of a molehill*: see Molehill 2.
7. e. *mountain-sheltered* adj.
1924 W. J. Locke *Coming of Amos* xiii. 169 A coast of romantic mountain-sheltered creeks.
8. b. and c. (Further examples.)
1881 *Harper's Mag.* Nov. 868/2 They are poor mountain people,..and the sumac crop is a very important source of revenue to them.
1849 Parkman *Oregon Trail* 145 Though aided by the high-bowed 'mountain-saddle' I could scarcely keep my seat on horseback. 1873 J. H. Beadle *Undevel. West* xv. 255 We change from the coach to a 'mountain-wagon'—so called—a street hack with three seats and no springs.

9. **mountain-fever** (earlier and later examples); **mountain-folding**, the formations of mountains by the folding of the earth's crust; **mountain man** (earlier U.S. example); **mountain railway** (*b*), a miniature ascending railway designed for amusement; a scenic railway; **mountain-schooner**, a wagon used in mountainous country; **mountain slide** (earlier example); **mountain spectre**, a reflection (of persons or things) seen under certain conditions on a mountain; **mountain system, tea** (see quots.).
1859 Jackson *Diary* 23 Jan. in Hall *Hist. Colorado* II. App., Niwot is sick, *mountain fever I think. 1878 J. H. Beadle *Western Wilds* xx. 331 He fell from his horse in a paroxysm of that dread disease, mountain fever. 1925 J. Joly *Surface-Hist. of Earth* x. App. 170 The effects of these conditions on *mountain-folding would probably be principally experienced where the geosynclines had forced the continental materials deep into the magma. 1781 *Cal. Virginia State Papers* I. 494 A late pressing application of General Greene for the aid of the *Mountain Men. 1910 *Penny Guide Japan-British Exhib.* 23 *Mountain Railway. The visitor enters the cars which travel slowly round and upward until the top of the mountain range is reached. 1925 Aldous Huxley *Those Barren Leaves, F. Chelifer* iii. (1927) 106 The switchback, the water-shoot and the mountain railway. 1869 C. L. Brace *New West* xiv. 188 It is more than a hundred miles away from the first link with civilization, and yet coaches, wagons, and the stream of '*mountain-schooners' pour into it unceasingly. 1830 *Massachusetts Spy* 25 Aug. (Th.) *Mountain slides. 1880 *Encycl. Brit.* XI. 399/2 *Mountain spectres are caused by reflexion, and often appear accompanied by chromatic halos. 1895 Dana *Man. Geol.* (ed. 4) 389 A *mountain system includes all ranges in a region made in different, more or less independent, geosynclines at the same epoch. 1886 *Harper's Mag.* June 62/1 Another beverage is '*mountain tea' which is made from the sweet scented golden-rod and from winter-green.

c. (Further U.S. examples.)
Mountain boomer (earlier examples); **mountain buffalo**, a variety of buffalo; also, a species of sheep; **mountain fowl**, a large variety of the domestic fowl; **mountain goat** (earlier examples); **mountain jay**, the great-crested or Blue jay; **mountain lion** (earlier example); **mountain plover**, *Podasocys montanus* (see also Plover).
1858 D. K. Bennett *Chronol. N. Carolina* 94 The only inhabitants we saw on these high points were pheasants, cross bills,..and *mountain boomers, a sort of squirrel. 1870 *Amer. Naturalist* IV. 394 Yet the inhabitants are well acquainted with them (*Sciurus Hudsonius*) as game of the mountain tops, under the name of the 'mountain Boomer'. 1868 *Ibid.* Dec. II. 538, I saw no difference in the skulls, indicating a different species, or '*Mountain Buffalo' of the hunters. (The Bighorn is sometimes called so). 1846 Sage *Scenes Rocky Mts.* (1859) 169 A large bird called the *mountain fowl...This bird is rather larger than our domestic hen, and of a grayish brown color. 1841 Catlin *N. Amer. Indians* II. 196 His leggings and shirt were of the *mountain goat skin. 1844 D. Lee & Frost *Oregon* viii. 98 These [moccasins] are of dressed skins of the deer, antelope, mountain-goat, and sheep. 1872 *Amer. Naturalist* July VI. 398 The great-crested, Woodhouse's and the Canada jays were of frequent occurrence in the mountains, the former being familiarly known as the '*mountain jay'. 1859 G. A. Jackson *MS. Diary* 2 Killed a *mountain lion to-day. 1872 *Amer. Naturalist* May VI. 272 The so-called '*mountain' plover was also occasional, and generally seen on the dry prairies far away from the streams and sloughs.

d. (Further U.S. examples.)
Mountain cherry (earlier example); **mountain chestnut oak**, a kind of oak, *Quercus prima monticola*; **mountain crowder**, a variety of pea; **mountain mahogany**, the mahogany birch, *Betula lenta* (see also Mahogany); **mountain maple**, a variety of maple, *Acer montanum* (see also Maple); **mountain sage** (see quot., cf. also Sage *sb.*¹).
1813 Muhlenberg *Catal. Plant.* 48 *Mountain cherry. 1801 Michaux *Histoire des Chênes* 6 *Mountain Chestnut Oak. 1821 T. Nuttall *Trav. Arkansa* i. 42 Much of the *Quercus Prima monticola* (or mountain chestnut oak) presents itself on the mountain. 1849 *Rep. U.S. Comm. Patents, Agric.* (1850) 138 Peas are cultivated for the table, market, stock...The '*mountain crowder' and 'black-eyed' are the most common varieties. 1810 Michaux *Arbres* I. 26 Sweet birch, [ou] *Mountain Mahogany dans Virginia. 1832 D. J. Browne *Sylva Amer.* 118 Wherever it grows in the United States, it is known by the name of Black Birch: its secondary denominations are Mountain Mahogany in Virginia. 1875 *Amer. Naturalist* IX. 201 Much more attractive with its glossy foliage and long feathery seeds, is the mountain mahogany *Cercocarpus ledifolius* Nutt. 1813 Muhlenberg *Catal. Plant. N. Amer.* 95 *Mountain maple or low maple. 1832 D. J. Browne *Sylva Amer.* 102 The mountain maple seldom rises above 20 feet in height, and it often blooms at an elevation less than six feet. 1844 D. Lee & Frost *Oregon* xi. 122 In this way we went on..toiling through immense tracts of *mountain sage, or more properly, wormwood, an ugly shrub from two to six feet high.

Mountain laurel. (See Mountain 9 d.)
1759 [see Mountain 9 d]. 1810 Michaux *Arbres* I. 35 Mountain laurel,..dénomination la plus générale. 1832 D. J. Browne *Sylva Amer.* 191 The Mountain Laurel is a large shrub, which indifferently bears the name Mountain Laurel, Laurel, Ivy, and Calico Tree. 1845 S. Judd *Margaret* I. ii. 8 She got running mosses..and mountain laurel blossoms. 1880 *Harper's Mag.* June 80 The mountain laurel, with its deep green foliage and showy clusters peers above that rocky crag. 1887 [see Mountain 9 d]. 1906 J. A. Harrison *George Washington* 91 The bluish-pink masses of the mountain-laurel.

Mountain sheep. *U.S.* [Mountain 9 d.] A variety of sheep; the big-horn or Rocky Mountain sheep, *Haplocerus laniger.*
1807 P. Gass *Journal* vii. 82 On the top of the highest [bluff] we saw some Mountain sheep, which the natives say are common about the Rocky mountains. *Ibid.* viii. 88 What the French and natives call mountain sheep. 1837 W. Irving *Capt. Bonneville* I. iii. 69 This animal is commonly called the mountain sheep, and is often confounded with another animal, the 'woolly sheep' found more to the northward. 1846 Sage *Scenes Rocky Mts.* (1859) 163 In size the mountain sheep is larger than the domestic animal of that name, and its general appearance is in every respect dissimilar—excepting the head and horns. 1918 Roosevelt in *Maine my State* (1919) 21 When we had a couple of antelope and a yearling mountain sheep.
attrib. 1841 Catlin *N. Amer. Indians* II. 188 Dressed in a beautiful costume of the mountain-sheep skin.

Mountain snow. 3. (Earlier example.)
1888 'C. E. Craddock' *Broomsedge Cove* ix. 159 He mechanically noted..how the blooming 'Mountain snow' brushed his mare's fine coat.

Mounted, *ppl. a.* 3. (Earlier examples of *Mounted infantry.*)
1847 Baker *Ohio* 235 The novel expedient of charging through the British lines with mounted infantry. 1858 Abbé Domenech *Missionary Adv. in Texas & Mexico* vii. 177 To pursue the Indians they put their infantry soldiers on horse-back;..the Indians were once nearly taking prisoners a whole company of mounted infantry (as they are called).

Mounting, *vbl. sb.* 2. a. (Add example.)
1914 Tweney *Dict. Nav. & Milit. Terms* 157 *Mountings*, a term applied to the platforms on which heavy naval guns and guns of position for fortresses are mounted.

Mounty² (mau·nti). *colloq.* [f. Mount(ed *ppl. a.* + -y ⁶.]
1. One of the Royal Canadian Mounted Police.
1924 A. J. Small *Frozen Gold* vi. 139 A sentence that is at once the badge and boast of the Mounted—'the Mounties never come in without their man'. 1927 Grenfell in *Sunday at Home* Nov. 106/2 The Eskimo borrowed the Mounty's gun and shot him. 1928 *Daily Express* 12 Sept. 8 The mysterious disappearance of Mr. Germaine had been practically forgotten by everyone in the district—everyone, that is, except the famous 'Mounties'.
2. (See quot.)
1931 *Shipper* 25 Apr. 112 A detachment of the Camel Corps on the march outside Cairo. These desert 'mounties' keep law and order in Egypt.

Mourner¹. Add: 1. d. (Earlier and later examples.)
1845 J. J. Hooper *Adv. Simon Suggs* x. 121 Having thus deposited his charge among the mourners, he started out, summarily to convert another soul! *Ibid.* 126 'And then', continued Simon, 'I had to go yonder'—pointing to the mourner's seat. 1856 Strickland *Peter Cartwright* xxvi. 403 You must go to the Methodist's despised mourner's bench. 1891 'C. E. Craddock' in *Harper's Mag.* Jan. 214/2 Everybody else war either convicted o' sin, an' at the mourner's bench or else shoutin' saints o' the Lord. 1904 *Charlotte Observer* 27 July 4 In the city police court a motley crowd of prisoners filled the mourners' benches.
e. *U.S.* (See quot.)
1904 *N.Y. Even. Post* 10 Mar. 12 The rush of people to the Tax Department to swear off taxes has set in. Yesterday the 'mourner's line', which ordinarily contains 10 or 15 persons, extended out into the corridor.

Mourning, *vbl. sb.*¹ 5. Add: *mourning-dress*; **mourning granite**, a grey variety of granite; **mourning-piece** (earlier example); **mourning vein**, a vein of mourning granite; **mourning willow**, the weeping willow.
1840 *Knickerbocker Mag.* XVI. 70 A conclusive proof that the *mourning-dress is an empty ordinance of Fashion. 1872 *Rep. Vermont Board Agric.* I. 669 Below this is a layer of gray, or as it has been recently named, *mourning granite. 1843 *Knickerbocker Mag.* XXII. 189 The parlor..was ornamented..among the rest, [with] the indispensable family *mourning-piece. 1872 *Rep. Vermont Board Agric.* I. 662 The other layers most desirable and most valuable are the dark and light *mourning veins. 1813 Muhlenberg *Catal. Plant.* 91 *Mourning Willow.

Mouse, *sb.* 4. d. Add: Also a device used in underground pipe-conduits (see quot.).
1905 *Jrnl. Franklin Inst.* Mar. 185 A fine wire is sometimes drawn through a duct by a conical piece of wood with a thin leather washer filling the duct, and forced ahead by the air pressure at the rear...This piece of wood is termed the 'mouse'.

Mousery (mau·sǝri). [f. Mouse *sb.* + -ery.] A place where mice abound; a colony of mice.
1888 F. A. Lucas in *The Auk* (N.Y.) July (Cass. Suppl.) The disturbance of this populous mousery by the visits of owls.

Mousse. Also, a kind of ice-cream made with whipped cream.

1908 *Daily Chron.* 22 July 7/4 A mousse is nothing more than the addition of whipped cream instead of plain cream when making ices.

Moustick. Add: Also **mustic.** (Later example.)

1887 A. M. Mackay in *Mem.* (1890) 374 These little horrors—ants and mustics—are the plague of my life.

Moustierian, Mousterian (mustiə·riăn), *a.* and *sb.* [ad. F. *moustierien, mousterien* (f. *Moustier*, see def.): cf. -IAN.] **a.** *adj.* Of or pertaining to the Moustier cave in the Dordogne region of France; belonging to the palæolithic period or culture indicated by the remains found there.

1888 T. Wilson in *Smithsonian Rep.* (Nat. Mus.) 614 The Moustierian implements have been found in the river gravels of Europe. 1896 Keane *Ethnol.* 86 Moustierian or First Cave Age. Implements. *Ibid.* 90 K. Moustierian bed, with typical pointed flint. 1912 *Edin. Rev.* Apr. 366 The first discovery of Mousterian man to excite interest was made in 1856 near Düsseldorf. 1920 *Discovery* Apr. 117/1 That implements of Mousterian type should be found in the Boulder Clay. 1927 Sir A. Keith *Rep. Galilee Skull* (Brit. Sch. Archæol. Jerusalem) 53 This is the first time human remains of Mousterian date have been found outside the limits of Europe.

b. *sb.* A Mousterian man or woman.

1912 Marett *Anthropol.* ii. 45 Those were the days of the Mousterians who dined off woolly rhinoceros in Jersey. 1921 M. C. Burkitt *Prehistory* viii. 119 A stage in which the Mousterians and the forerunners of the Upper Palaeolithic folk were living contemporaneously in France. 1928 V. G. Childe *Most Anc. East* ii. 27 The African Mousterian exhibited a distinct superiority.

Moutan (mū·tăn). [See quot. 1840.] The Tree Peony, *Pæonia moutan.*

1840 *Florist's Jrnl.* (1846) I. 36 The moutan (moutan is the Chinese name of the plant, and used by us as the specific distinction,) is only a half-shrubby, and half-hardy species. 1880 *Encycl. Brit.* XII. 258/1 The Moutans or Tree Pæonies are remarkable for their sub-shrubby habit, forming vigorous plants sometimes attaining a height of 6 to 8 feet.

Mouth, *sb.* **21. mouth-board,** a wooden instrument to which the mouth is applied, in order to secure a constant position of the head for observations or experiments; **mouth-breather,** a person who breathes through the mouth; **mouth-breeder,** any of several species of Cichlid or other fish, which protect their eggs or young by carrying them in the mouth; **mouth-root** (earlier example); **mouth-way,** entrance.

1901 E. B. Titchener *Exper. Psychol.* I. ii. 245 Materials. ..Head-rest, with *mouth-board and sighting mark. 1910 *Practitioner* Jan. 69 The child was a *mouth-breather and showed signs of adenoids. 1927 *Sunday at Home* June 609/1 The *mouth-breeder protects her eggs by carrying them about in her mouth. 1764 Cutler in *Mem. Amer. Acad. Arts & Sci.* (1785) I. 457 Goldenthread. *Mouth Root...The roots are astringent, and of a bitterish taste. Chewed in the mouth they cure apthas and cankerous sores. 1920 A. E. W. Mason *Summons* xii. 121 Crossed the road and disappeared into the *mouthway of an alley.

Mouthful. b. Add: Phr., *To say a mouthful*, to make a striking or important statement; to say something noteworthy. *U.S. slang.*

1922 C. Sandburg *Slabs of Sunburnt West* 7 You said a mouthful. 1924 A. J. Small *Frozen Gold* i. 14 A fight, he says—and he don't know what a mouthful he's said. 1929 Doyle *Maracot Deep* vi. 165 He said a mouthful when he asked her to marry him.

Mouthpiece. 3. (Add example.)

1897 J. L. Allen *Choir Invisible* xiii, Her face concealed by a black velvet riding-mask kept in place by a silver mouth-piece held between her teeth.

Move, *sb.* **6.** (Add examples.)

1899 A. H. Quinn *Pennsylv. Stories* 138 Come, get a move on. 1906 *Washington Post* 25 Apr. 20 If Congress doesn't get a move on pretty soon, it may receive a message that the President is in a hurry. 1910 Mulford *Hopalong Cassidy* v. 41 Get them cows going!..Come on, get a move on! 1914 Gertr. Atherton *Perch of Devil* i. 84 It was time to get a move on. 1927 Vachell *Dew of Sea* etc. 267 'Get a move on', admonished Mr. Munro.

8. *Comb.* **move-man** (see quot.).

1903 J. M. Scott-Maxwell *Costing & Price-fixing* 94 Move-men are the men who move the raw material and manufactured parts from the store to the shop, and move all jobs from one machine to another or one department to another.

Move, *v.* Add: **1. g.** To 'drive' (snipe).

1910 *Blackw. Mag.* Jan. 133/2 Moving snipe on a calm day..is not work for an impatient man.

Mover^1. **5.** (Later examples.)

1878 J. H. Beadle *Western Wilds* xx. 327 Reluctantly the 'movers' consented to his remaining for the night. 1889 *Harper's Mag.* Dec. 121/2 A mover's wagon with dingy cover was creeping slowly townward along the white road. 1906 H. D. Pittman *Belle of Blue Grass C.* xviii. 261 The emigrants, or 'movers' were kindly invited to occupy the old log house.

Movie (mū·vi). *U.S.* Also **movy.** [Back-formation from *Moving picture + -ie, -y^6.] A cinematographic or motion picture or film; esp. in plur., motion pictures or the place where these are exhibited; a cinema.

'The word *movie* appears to have come into the folk-tongue out of the gamin life of either New York or Chicago about 1906–1907... By 1908 *movie* began to appear in the reports of social workers and contemporary newspaper accounts.' 1926 *Amer. Speech* Apr. I. 357.

1913 F. A. Talbot *Pract. Cinematogr.* 22 Contrary to general belief, taking the 'movies' is quite as simple as snap-shot photography with a Kodak. 1913 *N.Y. Even. Post* 10 July 5/7 Guiding the wheel-chair through the entrance gate of the outdoor 'movie'. 1913 *Home Chat* 27 Sept. 578/1 The comparatively small towns [in America] have installed 'movies'—as they call them over there—in their schools. 1913–16 G. B. Shaw *Heartbreak House* i. (1927) 26 *Captain Shotover.* You frequent picture palaces. *Mangan.* Perhaps I do. Who told you? *Captain Shotover.* Talk like a man, not like a movy. 1916 B. M. Bower *Phantom Herd* xi. 193 Say, do I get it right that you're in the movies? 1918 C. Sandburg *Corn-huskers, Mem. Proud Boy,* There is drama in that point...Griffith would make a movie of it to fetch sobs. 1919 H. L. Wilson *Ma Pettengill* i. 30 Nothing to do but travel round in Pullman palace cars..., and go to movies, and so forth. 1928 *Collier's* 29 Dec. 27/3 The big attraction..was a sweet offer..to star him in a talking movie.

b. *attrib.* and *Comb.*, as *movie business, camera, film, operator, picture, show, theatre*; **movie-land,** the domain or sphere of motion-pictures and the persons and things connected therewith; **movie-man,** any cinematographic operator, esp. the photographer of a motion-picture; **movie star,** a distinguished or famous film actor or actress.

1916 B. M. Bower *Phantom Herd* v. 71 There's no art for art's sake in the *movie business. 1925 H. L. Foster *Trop. Tramp Tourists* 118 The company's cinema operator had his *movie camera set up in one corner. 1922 *Atlantic Monthly* June 775 Half the *movie films seem almost to have been made for the flapper. 1928 *Daily Express* 16 Mar. 4/2 There are few people..better qualified to explain the mysteries of *movie-land and of the technical side of films. 1915 *Pearson's Mag.* Jan. XXXIX. 80 My first action..was to ask a *movie-man going home with films, to bring me back a blue serge suit. 1916 B. M. Bower *Phantom Herd* xix. 309 The movie-man that run this show for the Convention. 1922 H. L. Foster *Adv. Trop. Tramp* xix. 343 But the good old days, for writers and *movie operators, are rapidly passing from South America. 1916 E. V. Lucas *Vermilion Box* ccxiii, I wish a *movie picture could be taken of him. 1919 E. Hendrick *Chem. in Everyday Life* 75 If he has some free time, he may want to go to a *movie show. 1919 H. L. Wilson *Ma Pettengill* ii. 39 [They saw] how much they were paying their president..quoted beside some *movie star's salary. 1925 *Film Flashes* 13 Nov. 1 It's a long lane that has no *movie theatre.

Movietone (mū·vitoun). The registered name of a system employed in the production of sound films, by which the sound is recorded simultaneously with the photographs either on the same or on another negative film. Used *attrib.* as (and *ellipt.* =) *movietone film.*

1927 *Daily Express* 27 Aug. 1/3 The 'movietone' is an invention with the same technical basis as the 'phonofilm'. 1927 *Glasgow Herald* 12 Oct. 11/1 The movietone has great possibilities once these shortcomings have been remedied. 1928 *Liberty* 11 Aug. 25/2 George Bernard Shaw as he appears in a strip of Movietone film. Note the sound track on the left margin. 1930 *Nature* 19 July 93/1 Fig. 1 is a reproduction of a movietone film of an orchestra and the microphotometric record of the music recorded.

Moving, *vbl. sb.* **5.** Add: **moving day** (earlier examples); **moving-man** *U.S.*, one who removes furniture.

1832 J. F. Watson *Tales Olden Times* 123 'Moving day' was as now the first of May. 1855 *Knickerbocker Mag.* XLV. 565 In the southern part of New Jersey, one who rents or purchases a house or farm usually takes possession of the same on the twenty-fifth day of the present month, which is therefore denominated 'moving-day'. 1922 H. L. Foster *Adv. Trop. Tramp* xii. 179 While he shipped the furniture from the old place, I was to go down to the new one to see that the moving-men stole none of it en route.

Movingness. (Modern example.)

1930 Gwendolen Greene *Two Witnesses* 99 He was touched almost to speechlessness by the movingness of Christ.

Moving picture. [Moving *ppl. a.*] A cinematographic picture or film; also *attrib.*

1899 *Sketch* 22 Nov. 178/1 The most interesting moving-picture..was the photograph of the chief ladies..being received. 1906 'O. Henry' *Four Million* 3 He cursed the moving pictures. 1913 F. A. Talbot *Pract. Cinematogr.* 52 Perhaps the most unnerving and difficult conditions under which moving-pictures can be taken are those pertaining to the filming of wild animal life at close range under natural conditions. 1914 Gertr. Atherton *Perch of Devil* i. 30 Then there's the movin' pictures. Lord, but we have advantages our poor mothers never dreamed of.

attrib. 1909 *Century Dict.* Suppl. s.v. *Picture*, Moving-picture machine. 1914 Gertr. Atherton *Perch of Devil* i. 173 Clark, who accumulates millions as a moving picture show rolls in dimes. 1919 H. L. Wilson *Ma Pettengill* ii. 63 [He] says he's in the moving-picture business. 1928 *Saturday Even. Post* 10 Mar. 160/4 There are so many pretty moving-picture actresses and good-looking girls.

Mowing, *vbl. sb.*^{1} **3.** *mowing ground* (later examples), *land, machine* (earlier example).

1654 *Boston Town Rec.* VI. 17 Twenty accres more or lesse of *mowing ground upon the marsh of Mr. Thomas Weld. 1722 *Essex Inst. Hist. Coll.* XLII. 90 [To pay damages for] digging in any Corne field, orchard, mowing ground, or damnifying any building of the said Davises. 1770 *Ibid.* XI. 31 My little mare had provided for herself, by leaping out of a bare pasture into a lot of mowing ground. 1787 Washington *Diaries* III. 229 The same difference was equally obvious on a piece of mowing grd. not far distant from it. 1640 *Coll. Conn. Hist. Soc.* XIV. 357 One parsell called Swamp, now *mowing land. 1689 *Conn. Probate Rec.* 478 One acre of mowing Land and one acre of plowing Land lyeing in ye Slipe. 1704 *Waterbury Prop. Rec.* 60 No man shal stak horses in the moing land in said feild. 1789 Morse *Amer. Geog.* 215 The best mowing land in Connecticut produces about twice as much clear profit. 1816 *N. Amer. Rev.* III. 428 At the distance of five or six miles it begins to wind gently through large tracts of fine rich mowing land. 1838 H. W. Ellsworth *Valley N. Wabash* v. 47, I have a plan in view..and that is, to introduce the *mowing and grain-cutting machine into this state.

Mow, *v.*^{1} Add: **4.** *Comb.* **mow-land** *U.S.*, land where grass is grown for mowing; so *mow-lot.*

1845 S. Judd *Margaret* ii. i. 214 She saw..women..raking and turning hay among alders and willows that yet flourished in their best *mow-lands. 1874 *Rep. Vermont Board Agric.* II. 411 The breeding of wrinkled sheep is like a farmer who ridges up his level mow-land and seeds the ridges with an inferior grass. 1845 S. Judd *Margaret* ii. viii. 325, I kept him here in the *mow-lot.

Mozo (mō·ᵘpo). [ad. Sp. *mozo*, in the same sense.] *Southern U.S.* A male servant or attendant; a groom; a labourer.

1847 Ruxton *Adv. Mexico* vii. 48, I at length hired a *mozo* to proceed with me as far as Durango. 1904 Conrad *Nostromo* i. viii. 107 But Captain Mitchell's right-hand man.. after looking down critically at the ragged mozo, shook his head. 1923 *Blackw. Mag.* July 46/2 The mozo, the ostler lad,..was a son of the house.

Much. A. *adj.* **2. d.** (Later U.S. examples.)

1889 *Kansas City T. & Star* 13 Dec., For the latter's fall-down, much thanks. 1890 Susan Hale *Lett.* (1919) 253, I have much funny things to tell you.

B. *absol.* **2. h.** Add: *There is nothing* (or *not*) *much in it*: There is no important feature of interest or value in something; there is no marked difference between two things, etc.

1927 *Observer* 18 Dec. 19/3 The first round there was nothing much in it. In the second round Angus..punched Man-field round the ring.

C. *adv.* **1. d.** Add: *Not much*: 'Not likely', far from it, certainly not. *colloq.*

1886 *Harper's Mag.* Dec. 148/1 'Go home?—explain?' he began, more calmly. 'Not much.' 1887 C. B. George *40 Yrs. on Rail* vii. 141 'If I should die in the attempt, I could best of all this group be spared. I'll try it.' 'Not much,' replied the man who at first had suggested it. 1904 *Pittsburgh Gaz.* 31 Oct. 4 Can anyone suppose Russia would apologize in the face of so grave a violation of neutrality? Not much.

Much, *v.* (Later U.S. examples.)

1868 Susan Hale *Lett.* (1919) 60 They all 'muched' me and I was a heroine. 1896 J. C. Harris *Sister Jane* 143 Man wid black beard come 'long, take de chil' in he arms an' much 'im.

Muchan, mucharn, var. ff. Machan.

Mucilage. 1. c. (Earlier example.)

1877 Eliz. S. Phelps *Story of Avis* 369 If he had the mucilage-bottle, and papa's razor and the purple ink,..he would go.

Mucilage (miū·silēdʒ), *v.* [f. prec.] *trans.* To cause to stick or adhere as with mucilage.

1891 Maran E. Ryan *Told in Hills* iii. v. 197 Over it she walked quickly, fully awakened by the thought of the coffee getting a bath of vinegar, or the mail mucilaged together with molasses.

Mucilaginous, *a.* **2.** (Add example.)

1819 E. Dana *Geog. Sketches* 245 Cotton wood, sycamore, ..mucilaginous elm and red elm.

Muck, *sb.*^{1} Add: **1. d.** (Earlier and later examples.)

1849 E. Chamberlain *Indiana Gaz.* 305 The soil is a black muck based on clay. 1852 *Trans. Mich. Agric. Soc.* III. 191 Clay predominates; the balance black sand and muck. 1872 *Rep. Vermont Board Agric.* I. 129 Those farmers having deposits of muck available for use, will find that they have a most excellent material to compost with manure.

e. *U.S.* (See quot.)

1914 Gertr. Atherton *Perch of Devil* i. 148 His..hands were white with 'muck', a mixture of rock-dust and water.

3. b. (Earlier example.)

1882 'F. Anstey' *Vice Versa* xvi. 282 'If you think the tea worth racing like that for, I don't,' said Coggs viciously; 'it's muck.'

4. b. *To make a muck of*, to do (something) badly; to spoil or bungle.

1927 *Sunday Express* 17 Apr. 4 After arranging that the first-night speech should be made by Joseph Greenwald.. she went on and made a muck of it herself.

5. (sense 1 d) *muck bed, land, swamp.*

1874 *Rep. Vermont Board Agric.* II. 533 Do not wantonly destroy a good *muck bed. 1847 *Rep. U.S. Comm. Patents* (1848) 354 They have been planted the present year, on deep *muck lands. 1861 *Trans. Ill. Agric. Soc.* IV. 108 Flat, muck land of the prairies is worthless. 1874 *Rep. Vermont Board Agric.* II. 664 Mr. Douglas..said it was very easy to build a durable road through a *muck-swamp, by simply making heavy ditches each side.

Muck, *v.* **4.** Also, to mix *up.*

1909 H. G. Wells *Tono-Bungay* iii. i. § 4. 216 It's a festering mass of earths and heavy metals... There they are, mucked up together in a sort of rotting sand.

5. b. *To muck in with* (see quot.). *slang.*

1919 *War Terms* in *Athenæum* 1 Aug. 695/2 'To muck in' with anyone is to share rations with him.

Mucker (mʊ·kəɹ), *sb.*^{4} *U.S. university slang.* [f. Muck *v.* + -er^1.] A youthful townsman, as distinct from a member of a college; a young 'townee'.

1893 W. K. Post *Harvard Stories* 75 On the first corner of Harvard Street were stationed three or four small boys (the occasionally useful Cambridge muckers) employed as vedettes. 1895 *Century Mag.* Oct. 943/1 He was careful to suggest to every likely young 'mucker' that he met to come over to the railway watering-tank, where a crowd of tramps were stopping. 1899 A. H. Quinn *Pennsylv. Stories* 168 Del went through his pockets to the great joy of a limited assortment of muckers who were following.

b. A boorish, unrefined person; one who does not 'play the game'; a 'rotter'.

1899 G. Ade *Fables in Slang* (1900) 108 The Fellow had made a Mistake.., they were not Muckers; they were Nice Boys. 1904 *Publ. Ledger* (Philad.) 4 June 6 If a player on the opponent's side happened to make a muff or misplay, cheering by the side benefited was distinctly out of order; it was, in the elegant language of the campus, 'muckerish', and the college which practiced it was composed of 'muckers'. 1905 D. G. Phillips *Plum Tree* 35 He used to class himself and me together as 'us gentlemen', in contrast to 'them muckers', meaning my colleagues. 1919 T. K. Holmes *Man fr. Tall Timber* ii. 20, I haven't the same patience father had with you muckers. Get out! 1921 R. D. Paine *Comr. Rolling Ocean* vi. 99 He grumbles about the food and says the officers are dubs and most of the boys muckers.

Mucker, *v.*^{2} **b.** Add: Also with *away*: To squander.

1928 H. G. Wells *Way World is Going* § ii. 15 The Western Powers of Europe..muckered away an enormous amount of war gear and money in supporting crazy 'white hopes' against the nascent new thing in Russia.

Muckerdom (mʊ·kəɹdəm). [f. *Mucker *sb.*^{4} + -dom.] The world of muckers or 'townees'; muckers collectively. So **Mu·ckerish** *a.*, befitting or characteristic of a mucker. **Mu·ckerishly** *adv.* **Mu·ckerism,** the characteristic conduct of muckers; unsportsmanlike behaviour.

1893 W. K. Post *Harvard Stories* 254 In five minutes all the best talent in muckerdom will be there with tin-cans and stones. 1904 [see *Mucker *sb.*^{4} b.]. 1906 *Outing* Jan. 494/1 This year there was caterwauling and shouting by cadets individually and muckerishly that was so unusual and unpleasant as to make one discredit one's ears. *Ibid.* 494/2 We hope it does not mean an entrance of muckerism into our Army and Navy games.

Muckluck (mʊ·klʊk). Also **mucluc, mukluk.** [Eskimo.] A high boot made of sealskin.

1901 *Pall Mall Mag.* Jan. 56 We stop on our way..and buy a pair of mucklucks or Esquimaux seal boots. They are water-tight, clumsy, evil-smelling, [etc.]. 1904 Eliz. Robins *Magnetic North* i. 51 Nothing like muck-lucks with a wisp of straw inside for this country. *Ibid.* 176 Stretching out his feet, very comfortable in their strawlined mucklucks. 1913 R. W. Service *Rhymes of Rolling Stone* 118 Then it's down to chewing muclucs, to the water you can *eat*, To fish you bolt with nose held in your hand. 1924 *Chambers's Jrnl.* Jan. 41/1 He was habited..in anorak and skin breeches and mukluks.

Mu·ck-raked, *ppl. a.* [-ed^1.] Subjected to muck-raking, or exposure by scandal-mongers.

1910 *N.Y. Even. Post* 10 Dec. 8 Their knowledge of how it feels to be a muck-raked millionaire.

Mu·ck-raker. [-er^1.] A person who uses a muck-rake; one who seeks out and publishes scandals and the like about prominent people, esp. public officials.

1906 *N.Y. Sun* 12 Apr. 8/3 (Funk) The muck-rakers worked merrily for a time in their own bright sunshine, and an unthinking populace applauded their performance. 1911 *Atlantic Monthly* Apr. 433 Municipal muck-rakers have insisted that the ever-increasing cost of municipal government is due to the waste and corruption of city officials.

Mu·ck-raking, *vbl. sb.* [f. Muck-rake *sb.* and *v.* + -ing^1.] The employing of a muck-rake, in fig. senses.

1911 *N.Y. Even. Post* 25 Jan. 14 The same articles brought President Roosevelt to the defence of the Senate, and led him to apply the word 'muck-raking' to the literature of higher exposure. 1912 *Q. Rev.* Jan. 179 The 'big business interests' Republicans..invariably stigmatise such enquiries as 'muck-raking'. 1928 *Publishers' Weekly* 14 July 168 Not muckraking or campaign propaganda.

Muck-up. [f. phr. *to muck up*: *Muck *v.* 4.] A mixing or confusing.

1930 *Daily Express* 9 Sept. 8/7 The muck-up of society.. is almost complete.

Mucky, *a.* **2.** (Additional U.S. examples.)

1840 Hoffman *Greyslaer* i. v. 61 He had laid the logs right down on a piece of deep, mucky soil, made up of old roots, rotten leaves, [etc.]. 1855 *Trans. Mich. Agric. Soc.* VI. 219 New land with a rich, mucky, or vegetable mould. 1874 *Rep. Vermont Board Agric.* II. 548, I have about five acres of mucky meadow that was mostly covered with alders.

Mu·coid, *sb.* [f. the adj.] A viscous substance containing mucin produced from connective tissue.

1902 *Encycl. Brit.* XXXI. 517/1 Some holothurians have the remarkable property of converting their tough, brown, leather-like skin into mucoid within a few hours, on their being brought into air.

Mud, *sb.*^{1} Add: **1. e.** *transf.* A 'mud student' (see 5).

1906 C. G. Grey *Sequel to Story Official Life* 9 Some of the men from across Tweed were very kind to us muds.

4. a. *mud house* (U.S. example), *-hut, -land, -puddle, -shoal*; **c.** *mud-bottomed* adj.

1908 Hardy *Dynasts* iii. vii. iii. 492 Where there is a *mud-bottomed stream, the Lasne. 1846 Emory *Military Reconn.* 81 It was the remains of a three-story *mud house, 60 feet square, pierced for doors and windows. 1801–3 J. Davis *Trav. U.S.* 3, I have entered with equal interest the *mud-hut of the negro, and the log-house of the planter. 1858 Viele *Following Drum* 125 Half-a-dozen mud-huts neatly thatched with straw..presented a study for an artist. 1927 *Daily Tel.* 22 Nov. 14/1 This scheme..involves the reclamation of over 400 acres of *mudland. 1884 'Mark Twain' *Huck. Finn* xxxiv. 327 The nigger kind of smiled around graduly over his face, like when you heave a brick-bat in a *mud-puddle. 1842 *Knickerbocker Mag.* XX. 309 [He] knew a great deal more about the inconveniences of groping about among *mud-shoals in the dark.

5. mud-brick, brick that is made with mud; **mud-flow,** a (hardened) stream of mud, esp. one of volcanic origin; **mud-grappler** *slang*, fist; **mudguarded** *a.*, provided with mudguards; **mud-hook** (earlier examples); **mud-line** (see quot.); **mud-lump** (earlier example); **mud-mask** *sb.*, **-pack,** a preparation used for cleansing the pores and beautifying the skin of the face; so **mud-mask** *v. trans.*, to treat with a mud-mask; **mud-runner** *U.S.*, a horse accustomed to racing on a mud track; **mud-sill** (earlier examples of *a*); **mud-slinging, -throwing** *vbl. sbs.*, (the employment of) calumny, slander or abuse; malevolent gossip; **mud-stick** *U.S.* (see quot.).

1903 *Speaker* 5 Sept. 527/2 The old town being built of *mud-brick had vanished. 19.. *Bulletin Amer. Mus. Nat. Hist.* XVI. 347 (Cent. Suppl.) The largest ejected block that we saw was one on the surface of the *mud-flow between the rivers Blanche and Sèche. 1844 'Jon. Slick' *High Life N.Y.* II. 207, I wish tu goodness my *mud-grappler had been cut off close up to the wrist, afore it hit you that way. 1923 *Daily Mail* 30 July 6 Advt., So well shielded and efficiently *mudguarded that anyone..can ride it in ordinary costume. 1827 J. F. Cooper *Red Rover* (1881) ii. 37 He would..fasten her to the spot with good hempen cables and iron *mud hooks. 1846 *Knickerbocker Mag.* XXVII. 511 Down fore-s'l and jib, and over with the mud-hook. 1913 Sir J. Murray *Ocean* vii. 155 The ocean bacteria..seem to be especially abundant at what has been called the '*mud-line', that is at the position where all minute organic and inorganic particles settle on the bottom, and form mud—the humus of the ocean—in place of sand or gravel. 1868 *Putnam's Mag.* I. 591/2 *Mud-lumps, or more properly Mud-volcanoes, have been known to rise to the height of twenty-five feet. 1928 *Daily Express* 16 June 3/4, I suggested that I should like a *mud-mask. The assistant appeared to be alarmed. *Ibid.* 22 Dec. 3/5 Faces have been massaged and *mud-masked. 1905 *N.Y. Even. Sun* 17 Aug. (Cent. Suppl.) All the races..were won by the product of stallions that in their day were famous *mud runners. 1685 *Boston Town Rec.* VII. 178 The middle of the wall to lie even with northerlie or outward side of the said Simkins *Mudsell in the old Cellar. 1718 *Lancaster Rec.* 183 Ye Neck Bridge..should have 5 Trussells..to brace into ye Posts above ye caps & down into ye Mudsells. 1928 *Daily Express* 14 Mar. 11/3 The vicar..would have closed the place rather than have had the *mud-slinging that had taken place. 1928 *Sunday Express* 27 May 10/1 The social mud-slinging which gives half society its sole virtuous and intellectual amusement. 1874 J. W. Long *Wild-Fowl Shooting* 142 Now, you see this *mud-stick or setting pole...[*note*] Pole with a forked or widened end to prevent its sinking in mud. 1908 Mrs. E. Wharton *Hermit* etc. 289 I'm sick of *mud-throwing, he muttered.

b. mud-cat (additional example); also, an inhabitant of the state of Mississippi; **mud-catfish** (example); **mud duck** *U.S.*, the domestic duck; **mud-eel** (earlier example); **mud sunfish** (see quot.); **mud-swallow,** a cliff-swallow, which builds its nest with mud.

1883 'Mark Twain' *Life Mississippi* liv, He didn't really catch anything but only just one small useless *mud-cat. 1889 Farmer *Americanisms* 376/1 *Mud-cat State*, Mississippi, its inhabitants being sometimes humorously designated *mud-cats.* 1870 *Amer. Naturalist* IV. 386 What we design considering as mud-loving species are nine in number,.. *Mud Cat-fish (*Amiurus De Kayi*). 1903 *Forest & Stream* 27 Feb. 150 (Cent. Suppl.) They are a cross between the mallard and ordinary *mud duck. 1823 Weems *Letters* III. 353 The British..fairly chased our militiamen across Broad River, to the huge amazement of the *mud eels and cats. 1870 *Amer. Naturalist* IV. 102 The *Mud Sunfish (*Ambloplites pomotis*). 1898 Marg. Deland *Old Chester Tales* 181 *Mud-swallows had built their nests in the corners.

Mud-bank. [f. Mud *sb.*^{1} + Bank *sb.*^{1}] A bank of mud in the bottom of the sea or the bed of a river.

1791 Washington *Diaries* IV. 167 Wilmington, unfortunately for it, has a Mud bank—miles below, over which not more than 10 feet water can be brought at common tides. 1816 U. Brown *Jrnl.* in *Maryland Hist. Mag.* XI. 49, I was here in the dark and Mud Banks of the river from 20 to 30 feet high. 1860 Abbott *South & North* 63 Vast reaches of mud-banks were all around.

Mu·d-clerk. *U.S.* [f. Mud *sb.*^{1} + Clerk *sb.*] An assistant to the purser on a passenger boat.

1872 Eggleston *End of World* xxvi. 171 It was natural enough that the 'mud-clerk' on the old steamboat..should take a fancy to the 'striker'. 1876 'Mark Twain' *Old Times* 14 The doctor's and the postmaster's sons became 'mud-clerks'. 1881 *Century Mag.* Nov. 46 A Yankee youth ..who had served..as 'mud clerk' (that is, subordinate purser) on certain packet-boats.

Mudder (mʊ·dəɹ). *U.S. Racing slang.* [f. Mud *sb.*^{1} + -er.] A horse which runs on a mud track; a mud-runner.

1905 *N.Y. Even. Sun* 17 Aug. (Cent. Suppl.) The third horse, Athlone, is by Handsel, a mudder himself and a son of a mudder.

Muddle, *sb.* **4.** Add: *muddle-thoughted* adj.

1905 E. Phillpotts *Secret Woman* iii. v. 250 What a *muddle-thoughted man you be—all in a mare!

Mu·ddly, *a.* [f. Muddle *sb.* + -y^1.] Confused, muddled.

1909 Marg. B. Saunders *Litany Lane* ii. xvii. 227, I gather it from some of the muddly things he said.

Muddy, *a.* Add: **1. c.** As *sb.* The Missouri or Mississippi. Esp. *The Big Muddy.*

1863 *Rocky Mountain News* (Denver) 19 Mar. (Th.) We expect ere long to stand on the banks of the 'Big Muddy' and meet the hominy fed lasses of the Butternut state. 1878 B. F. Taylor *Between Gates* 23 'The Big Muddy', which is the prose for that ancient maiden Missouri. 1884 'Mark Twain' *Huck. Finn* lxvi. 130 When it was daylight, here was the clear Ohio water inshore, sure enough, and outside was the old regular Muddy.

Mud-hole. [f. Mud *sb.*] **1.** A hole containing mud or in which mud collects, esp. as forming a defect or obstacle in a road or highway.

1784 A. Ellicott in *Life & Lett.* 26 The ground [was] covered with Snow which hid the Mud-Holes. 1822 J. Fowler *Journal* 151 We stoped for dinner at a small mud hole. 1846 M'Kenney *Memoirs* I. viii. 185 It was one mud-hole after another. *a* 1856 P. Cartwright *Autobiography* xx. (1858) 299 Just at this moment I thought of a desperate mudhole about a quarter of a mile ahead; it was a long one, and dreadful deep mud, and many wagons had stuck in it. 1862 O. W. Norton *Army Lett.* 118 Eating raw beef without salt and drinking water from mud holes. 1880 *Harper's Mag.* June 80 Swarm of yellow butterflies disgrace their kind as they huddle around the greenish mud-holes. 1889 *Century Mag.* Oct. 956/2 All mudholes of course should be filled promptly at all times, so that no water may stand in the road. 1909 *Chambers's Jrnl.* Nov. 703/1 To prevent mud-holes..the roads are well graded to the centre.

2. An opening or valve at the foot of a boiler for the removal of dirt and sediment; a mud-valve.

1848 W. Templeton *Locomot. Eng.* (ed. 2) 16 The mud holes..are for the purpose of removing the sediment and scale that constantly accumulate at the bottom of the water spaces. 1875 Knight *Dict. Mech.* 1494/1.

Mudlark, *sb.* **1.** (U.S. examples.)

1833 J. Neal *Down-Easters* i. 47, I should like to know.. what upon irth he means by..mud-larks that's made into Virginny-ham. 1869 *Overland Monthly* III. 129 A hog clandestinely killed outside of camp and smuggled in under cover of darkness, was called a 'slow bear'...'Mud-lark' signified the same thing.

Mud turtle. [f. Mud *sb.*^{1} + Turtle.] (See Mud *sb.*^{1} 5 b.)

1796 *Aurora* (Philad.) 17 May (Th.) The crocodile throats of the gentle snappers or mud turtles in the Jersey market. *a* 1800 in *Spirit Farmer's Museum* (1801) 77 Bull frogs would grunt at his fate, And mud turtles pine at his woe. 1843 *Knickerbocker Mag.* XXI. 124 One mud-turtle remained after the rest. 1854–91 [see Mud *sb.*^{1} 5 b].

Mud wasp. *U.S.* A wasp which uses mud in building its nest.

1824 *Old Colony Memorial* (Plymouth) 6 Mar. (Th.) Resembling in shape what we call a mud wasp. 1861 *Trans. Ill. Agric. Soc.* IV. 338 The common black and yellow mud wasp (*Pelopæus lunatus*) belongs to this group. 1881 *Amer. Naturalist* XV. 443 Baron Osten Sacken..records the breeding of *A*[*grypnus*]*ba*] *cephus* and *A. fur* from the nest of a Texan mud-wasp.

Muff, *sb.*^{4} **2.** (Add U.S. example.)

1888 *Outing* May 120/1 Ferguson..reaching second on the hit, through Sweasy's muff of the ball Gould threw to him.

Muff, *v.*^{3} **1.** (Add U.S. example.)

1888 *Outing* May 119/2 On this Start reached third, and in Ferguson's hit to Sweasy, which he muffed, Start scored the tie run.

Muffetee. 2. (Earlier Amer. example.)

1749 *Boston Gaz.* Nov. in Alice M. Earle *Costume Colonial Times* (1894) 165 Men's fine Worsted Gloves and Muffetees.

Muffle, *v.*^{1} **4.** Add: Also with constr.

1853 Mrs. Gore *Dean's Daughter* I. iii. 34 The..Turkey carpets..muffled the rooms and corridors into the silence of the tomb.

Mu·ffledly, *adv.* [-ly^2.] In a muffled manner.

1903 Conrad & Hueffer *Romance* i. iii. 21 The Church clock began muffledly to chime the quarters behind us.

Muffiered (mʊ·flɜɹd), *ppl. a.* [f. Muffler + -ed^1.] Wearing a muffler.

1927 *Daily Express* 13 Mar. 5/1 From the bridge the mufflered figures glanced down at the business men moving across the quayside.

Mug, *sb.*^{1} Add: **2. c.** A silver drinking-vessel offered as a prize.

1890 *Harper's Mag.* Sept. 593/1 When the cruise is done and the mugs have escaped them.

d. *Thinking mug*: The head. *slang.*

1849 C. Lanman *Lett. Alleghany Mts.* i. 15 'Bout four years ago, it came into my thinking mug that there must be plenty of gold in the bed of Coosa creek.

4. mug-hunting (vbl. sb.). = Pot-hunting.

1890 *Harper's Mag.* Sept. 593/1 He may be bitten by the tarantula of matches, be possessed of the fury of mug-hunting.

Mug, *sb.*^{6} **2.** (Earlier example.)

1880 *Punch* 7 Aug. 59/2 *Son* (amused). Oh! no one learns their lessons now, except the regular mugs, and fellows grinding for an Exam.

Mugful (mʊ·gful). [f. Mug *sb.*^{1} + -ful.] The content of a mug.

1927 *Glasgow Herald* 27 Apr. 15 Lost for ten days in the Sahara with only a mugful of water a day. 1929 *Daily Tel.* 8 Jan. 12/1 Water is retailed by the bucket, and a potent brand of sherry by the mugful.

Mugged (mʊgd), *ppl. a.* [f. Mug *v.*^{6}] Huddled together, confined.

1889 H. S. Holland in S. Paget *Mem.* ii. iii. (1921) 181 The Bishop and Holland start for their normal walk..[and] come back refreshed and pleased, conveying silent reproaches to the 'mugged' ones in the boat.

Muggins. 1. (Earlier example.)

1873 Bret Harte *My Otherself* in *Fiddletown* etc. 116 It was my other self who made that cutting and witty remark when J. B. expressed his opinion that I was a Muggins.

2. a. (Earlier example.)

1865 Sophia Jex-Blake in Marg. Todd *Life* (1918) 165 A most ridiculous game of cards called 'Muggins.'

Mu·gwumpish, *a.* [-ish.] Pertaining to or characteristic of a mugwump; professing disinterestedness; pretentiously superior.

1918 F. Hackett *Ireland* ix. 252 This conviction was accompanied..with many mugwumpish strictures such as 'in the main', 'within certain limits', [etc.]. 1923 *Spectator* 22 Sept. 390/1 Racial, intellectual or moral tests may turn out to be not aristocratic at all, but merely mugwumpish.

Mulatto. A. *sb.* **4.** Add: **mulatto-clay** *U.S.*, a dark coloured clay; **mulatto land** (earlier example); **mulattoloam, mould** = *mulatto land*; **mulatto prairie,** a prairie of mulatto soil; **mulatto soil** (later examples).

1788 Jefferson *Tour Amsterdam* etc. Wks. 1854 IX. 386 It has a southern aspect, the soil a barren *mulatto clay, mixed with a good deal of stone, and some slate. 1784 J. Smyth *Tour U.S.* I. 77 There is some very good land on this river...It is what is called *mulattoe land by the planters, from its color. 1837 Williams *Terr. Florida* 82 The surface is covered with a *mulatto or chocolate colored loam. 1838 *Jeffersonian* (Albany) 28 Apr. 88 (Th.) The *mulatto mould of the Colorado does not surpass in fatness the alluvial soil of Red River. 1869 *Overland Monthly* III. 130 Then there is the 'chocolate' prairie, and the '*mulatto', and the 'mezquite'. 1819 E. Dana *Geog. Sketches* 190 Next to this is very often found a skirt of rich pine land, dark *mulatto soil with hickory..characteristic of good land. 1861 *Trans. Ill. Agric. Soc.* IV. 112 He..would not choose the dark prairie mold, but that kind of soil best known in the west as the 'mulatto soil'.

B. *adj.* **1.** (Earlier example.)

1677 *New Castle Court Rec.* 91 The upholding & detayning of this p[laintif]f's molatto servant in Maryland.

Mulattress. (Earlier and later examples.)

1805 in *Amer. Pioneer* II. (1843) 234 The chief of the audience is formed of mulatresses and negresses. 1887 *Harper's Mag.* Mar. 609/1 A handsome, strong-limbed, and light-footed mulattress.

Mule^1. Add:

4. d. A locomotive or tractor (now generally electric) for towing canal-boats. *U.S.*

1903 *Elect. World & Engin.* 14 Nov. 795 (Cent. Suppl.) The 'mule' has two large hooks for the towropes and has also a running board and guard hand rail [etc.]. 1924 *Chambers's Jrnl.* 731/2 These wire ropes are stretched from the ship to motor-tractors running on rails the length of the docks. Electric 'mules' the tractors are called... These mules both guide and propel the ship.

5. a. *mule-back* (later examples), *mule-cart, -colt, -load, meat, -race, -raising, -route, -steak, -trail, -train, -wagon*; (sense 4 a) *mule-room.*

1878 *Harper's Mag.* Jan. 283/2 He put it in his broken English, 'On horse-back or *mule-back, and many times on foot-back'. 1894 'O. Henry' *Cabbages & Kings* i. 16 The mule-back system of transport that prevailed between Coralio and the capital. 1897 R. M. Stuart *Simpkinsville* 15 Many's the time..he's rode into town, mule-back, with her settin up in front of him. 1849 Parkman *Oregon Trail* 107 Our little *mule-cart was but ill-fitted for the passage of so swift a stream. 1856 *Florida Plant. Rec.* 450, 5 [slaves] with ox and Mul[e] Carts raking an hauling in cane leavs. 1867 *Rep. Iowa Agric. Soc.* (1868) 133 The price of a *mule colt was..forty dollars. 1846 Sage *Scenes Rocky Mts.* (1859) 225 Wood too, being two rials (25 cents) per *mule-load. 1862 O. W. Norton *Army Lett.* 59 The rain soaked everything woolen full of water and made our loads almost mule loads. 1846 Sage *Scenes Rocky Mts.* (1859) 307 We ended our fast of nearly seven days' continuance with a feast of *mule meat. 1891 *Century Mag.* Mar. 774 We made our Christmas and New Year's dinner on mule meat. 1888 'C. E. Craddock' *Broomsedge Cove* i. 13 Yes, sir, 'minds me of a slow *mule-race all the time, the law does. 1867 *Rep. Iowa Agric. Soc.* (1868) 133 Robert Grant..mentions the names of several persons who give especial attention to *mule-raising. 1909 *Englishwoman* Apr. 266 The card-room contains the mechanical processes in cotton manufacture, preparatory to the spinning of yarn in the '*mule' room. 1849 C. Lanman *Lett. Alleghany Mts.* viii. 58 The distance from Hubbard's Cabin..in a direct line, is eight miles, but by the ordinary *mule-route it is thirteen. 1854 J. R. Bartlett *Pers. Narr. Explor. Texas*, I. v. 113 We might reach El Paso by..taking an occasional *mule steak. 1891 *Century Mag.* Apr. 902 The Isthmus was then..traversed occasionally..by adventurers in canoes..a part of the distance and thence by a single *mule trail to Panama. 1876 *Congress. Rec.* 19 June 3885/2 Those expeditions are accompanied..by *mule-trains carrying provisions. 1889 K. Munroe *Golden Days* xxv. 267 Endless processions of mule trains. 1910 Jes. Hart *Vigilante Girl* viii. 123 He stood ..looking beyond the moving mass of coaches, freight-wagons and mule-trains. 1849 Parkman *Oregon Trail* 108 Seeing the *mule-wagon wheeling from the track, he began to turn his own team.

b. (Example.)

1925 Penderel-Brodhurst & Layton *Gloss. Engl. Furniture* 112 *Mule Chest*, a chest standing on a plinth in which sometimes three or four drawers were provided.

c. mule-beater, a stick used for beating mules; **mule-deer** (later example); **mule-gate,** the space in a spinning room within which a mule works; **mule-headed** *a.*, stubborn; **mule-killer** (*a*) *U.S.*, a kind of cart; **mule-litter,** a litter borne by mules; **mule-picket,** a peg for tethering a mule; **mule-skinner** (earlier example); **mule-sweep** = *mule-gate*; **mule-whacker** *U.S.*, a mule-driver.

1909 Eliz. Banks *Myst. Fra. Farrington* 123 Pedro took up one of the disused *mule-beaters, and laid it on him thick and fast. 1880 *Scribner's Monthly* May 129/1 For meat we have bacon and generally steaks or roasted ribs of elk, *mule-deer or mountain sheep. 1892 Nasmith *Student's Cotton Spinning* 409 The pillars..are so pitched that they fall into the alleys between the mules and not into the *mule-gate. 1884 'Mark Twain' *Huck. Finn* xxix. 278 That *mule-headed old fool wouldn't give in then! 1849 Parkman *Oregon Trail* 10 A small French cart, of the sort very appropriately called a '*mule-killer', beyond the frontiers. 1852 *Florida Plant. Rec.* 67, I would call the New Waggon another mule killer. 1904 Farrer *Garden Asia* 81 Nor does a *mule-litter hurry upon the road. 1846 E. Bryant *California* viii. (1849) 102 The ground is so hard that it is with difficulty that we can force our *mule-pickets into it. 1870 J. H. Beadle *Life in Utah* 224, I took to the plains..in the capacity of a '*mule-skinner'. 1869 *Overland Monthly* III. 9 Here..is a cotton-gin..and ponderous wooden wheels, and the *mule-sweep underneath. 1873 J. H. Beadle *Undevel. West* iv. 88 For ten hours daily the streets were thronged with motley crowds of railroad men and *mule-whackers. 1888 *Century Mag.* Nov. 159/2 Ah! you called him 'mule-whacker.'

Mule^2. **2.** Delete '*Obs.* exc. *Hist.*' and add examples.

1930 *Daily News* 2 May, She glanced down at her attire: the foolish, gay kimono, the little blue mules. 1930 Mottram *Europa's Beast* ii. 64 Softly, in her blue satin mules, she crossed to the drawers.

Muled, *a.*^{2} [f. Mule^1 4 c + -ed^1.] Of a coin: That is a mule (sense 4 c).

1914 *Brit. Mus. Return* 115 A muled groat of Henry VIII combining an obverse of the third coinage with a reverse of the second.

Muley. B. *adj.* **2. muley saw** (earlier example).

1859 Bartlett *Dict. Amer.* 284 *Muley Saw*...That variety of mill-saw which is not hung in the gate. It is also spelt *mulay, moiley, muhley.*

Muley (miū·li), *a.*^{3} [f. Mule^1 + -y^1.] Intractable, stubborn, mulish.

1922 J. A. Dunn *Man Trap* v. 68, I got another drink into him, and made a fatal error in doing it, for he turned muley.

Muliebrity. (Recent examples.)

1888 Bret Harte *Phyllis of Sierras* ii. i. 169 This tall.. woman..possessed a refined muliebrity superior to mere liberality of contour. 1911 H. G. Wells *New Machiavelli* ii. (ed. 2) 206 She was one of those women who are wanting in—what is the word?—muliebrity. She had courage and initiative.

Mull, *sb.*^{7} Add: Also *attrib.*

1910 *Encycl. Brit.* VII. 277/2 (*Cotton*) The finer kinds, made from Egyptian yarns, are called mull-dhooties.

Mull, *v.*^{5} **2.** (Earlier example.) Also phr. *neither to mull nor to meddle*: not to interfere in any way.

1857 Holland *Bay Path* xvii. 200 'What do you do with them [troubles]?' 'Let 'em mull'. 1881 Mrs. J. H. Riddell *Senior Partner* I. v. 97 Robert put him in possession of his father's views on things in general..and his determination neither to mull nor meddle in the matter.

Mullein. 3. Add: *mullein plant, -stalk, -top, -weed.*

1885 *Outing* Nov. VII. 177/1 The most unpromising looking specimen, like the imaginary beginning of a *mullein plant it seems. 1854 Shillaber *Mrs. Partington* 41 Birds ..approach the spot and twitter upon the *mullein-stalks that grow rankly by the gate. 1878 Mrs. Stowe *Poganuc P.* iii. 30 Bless my soul, if there ain't old Zeph Higgins, looking like a last year's mullen-stalk. 1886 *Harper's Mag.* Nov. 879/2 A vesper song from a *mullein-top. 1846 J. W. Abert in Emory *Military Reconn.* 386 The bluebird was there with his sprightly notes, and the meadow lark, perched on some tall *mullein weed.

Mullet^3. [ad. F. *molet* in same sense.] A piece of wood containing a groove for testing the thickness of the edges of panels, drawer bottoms, and the like, before fitting.

Mullet-head. [?f. Mullet^1.] An American fresh-water fish with a large flat head.

1873 J. H. Beadle *Undevel. West* v. 102 There is a fish called the mullethead, that cannot be intoxicated by any amount of liquor. 1893 Forbes-Mitchell *Great Mutiny* vi. 110 That fish, my son, is called a mullet-head: it has got no brains.

Mullet-headed, *a.* [?f. Mullet^1. Cf. *mull-head* a dull, stupid fellow (E.D.D.).] Stupid, dull.

1884 'Mark Twain' *Huck. Finn* xxxix. 370 They're so confiding and mullet-headed they don't take notice of nothing at all.

Mulley cow. *U.S.* [Cf. Muley, Moiley.] A hornless cow.

1848 Bartlett *Dict. Amer.* 230 *Mulley cow*, a name used for a cow chiefly among children, or by parents when speaking to children. 1869 *Overland Monthly* III. 126 He..was evidently in search of strays, for he asked me if I had seen a red mulley cow. 1885 [see Muley B. 1].

Mulligan (mʊ·ligăn). *U.S.* [Apparently f. a proper name.] A sort of soup made from odds and ends of foods collected and cast into one pot.

1918 C. Sandburg *Cornhuskers* 80 Then they go to the bunk cars and eat mulligan and prune sauce. 1926 J. Black *You Can't Win* vii. 83 There was a grand jungle by a small clean river where they..cooked their mulligans. *Ibid.* xv. 198 He's crazy as a bed bug and the best 'mulligan' maker on the road.

Mullion. b. Add: **mullion structure** *Geol.*, a special conformation of rocks.

1930 Peach & Horne *Geol. Scotl.* 151 The combination of these two systems of folding gives rise to rod or 'mullion' structure.

Mully saw. *U.S.* [Cf. Muley B. 2.] = Muley saw.

1852 *Trans. Mich. Agric. Soc.* III. 487, 1 reaction water wheel and mully saw gearing.

Multi-. 1. Add: **Multispi·cular** *a.* = *multispiculate.*

1902 *Proc. Zool. Soc.* 210 In one of the two specimens [of sponges] in the collection..there are a few multispicular strands in the otherwise very regular unispicular meshwork.

3. *multivoltage.*

1903 *Elect. World & Engin.* 11 Apr. 621 (Cent. Suppl.) With the aid of diagrams he discussed at some length the rheostatic control and the multivoltage systems.

Multicellularity (mʊltiseliulæ·riti). [f. *Multicellular* (Multi- 1 a) + -ity.] Multicellular condition or formation.

1916 W. Trotter *Instincts of Herd* 18 Looked at in this way, multicellularity presents itself as an escape from the rigour of natural selection. 1922 tr. *Freud's Group Psychol.* 83 Biologically this gregariousness is an analogy to multicellularity and as it were a continuation of it.

Multiflora. (Earlier example.)

1829 *Western Monthly Rev.* III. 57 It is literally embowered in vines of the multiflora rose.

Multigraph (mʊ·ltigrɑf). [f. Multi- + -graph.] The registered name of a compact printing machine designed for office use. *Comb.* as *multigraph operator.*

1918 Webster Add. 1920 *Chambers's Jrnl.* July 474/1 The 'Multigraph' is fitted with an automatic paper-feeding device. 1925 *Daily Tel.* 13 May 20/5 Advt., Experienced multigraph operator and stationery buyer required by City firm.

Multimodal (mʊltimōᵘ·dăl), *a.* *Statistics.* [f. L. *multimod-us* (see Multimodous) + -al.] Of a frequency or distribution curve: Having more than one mode or maximum value. Said also of the incidence of features which corresponds to such a curve.

1902 *Nature* 3 July 234/2 The 'multimodal' character of many botanical distributions. 1902 *Biometrika* Aug. 454 The multimodal appearance of short series of crania..may be wholly due to random sampling.

So **Multimo·dalism.**

1902 *Biometrika* Apr. 305–6 Much of the multi-modalism interpreted in the case of flowers as polymorphism..is not true multi-modalism at all.

Multiplane (mʊ·ltiplēᵘn). [f. Multi- 2 + Plane.] An aeroplane or other flying-machine whose chief supporting surfaces are disposed in (two or) more than two horizontal planes.

1909 A. Berget *Conquest of Air* ii. ii. 139 Will the aeroplane be a 'monoplane' or 'multiplane'?

So **Mu·lti-planed** *a.*, having several planes.

1909 *Westm. Gaz.* 23 Mar. 4/2 The multi-planed helicopter has been abandoned for the biplane.

Multiple. A. *adj.* Add: **2. b.** *Multiple shop, -store*: One of several shops of the same kind belonging to the same firm, opened in different localities (cf. *chain-store).

1903 *Accountant* 12 Dec. 1532/2 Stock Accounts for Multiple-Shops. The multiple-shop business is one which requires, probably, more looking after than any other. 1903 Hazelip *Multiple-Shop Accounts* 1 As there is considerable difference in the class of business carried on by multiple-shop firms, there is also a variation of the system of accounts. 1909 *Westm. Gaz.* 10 May 9/4 Some of the multiple shops.. have been retailing at 9s. 4d. sugar which has cost them 14s. 7½d. to buy. 1927 *Daily Tel.* 14 Mar. 4/7 The multiple shops..have reduced their prices in accord with the drop in wholesale prices. 1929 Eric Gill *Art Nonsense* etc. 315 Politics and social guidance are left to..novelists, multiple-store keepers, manufacturers of motor-cars.

3. f. *Multiple switchboard*: a switchboard having connections with all the sections of 'lines' in an exchange.

1902 *Encycl. Brit.* XXXIII. 237/2 With a multiple-switchboard it is impossible for any one operator to know that the line of the person called for is not already occupied.

g. 1910 *Westm. Gaz.* 17 Feb. 5/1 The wearing qualities [of this clutch]..are claimed to be equal to anything in the way of the plate or multiple-disc type.

Multiplet (mʊ·ltiplet). [f. Multiple + -et: after Triplet.] A group of two or more things.

1927 N. V. Sidgwick *Electronic Theory of Valency* 37 The spectra of individual elements..are often very complicated. In particular, the lines tend to occur in close 'multiplets'—sets of 2, 3, or more.

Multiplication. Add: **3. e.** A system of dicing with three dice in which the sum of two dice is multiplied by the third in calculating the total.

1905 *Hoyle's Games* (ed. Fox) 196 Multiplication. Three dice are used, and there are three throws for each player.

Multiply, *adv.* Add: *Multiply-charged*, having several charges (of electricity).

1922 F. W. Aston *Isotopes* 71 These multiply-charged clusters give most reliable values of mass.

Multiradial (mʊltirēᵘ·diăl), *a.* [f. Multi- + Radial *a.*] That has developed from one type along several diverging lines.

1901 P. C. Mitchell in *Trans. Linn. Soc., Zool.* VIII. 266 It is..plain that this apocentricity is multiradial and no guide to affinity. 1902 — in *Encycl. Brit.* XXVIII. 343/2 Multiradial apocentricities lie at the root of many of the phenomena that have been grouped under the designation *Convergence.*

Multirotation (mʊltirotēᵘ·ʃən). *Phys. Chem.* [f. Multi- + Rotation.] A name for *Mutarotation.

1904 J. W. Mellor *Chem. Stat. & Dynam.* 224 The influence of acids upon the rate of multirotation of sugars. 1907 [see *Mutarotation].

Multiverse (mʊ·ltivɜɹs). [f. Universe by substituting Multi- for Uni-.] An alternative suggested for the word Universe in order to indicate the absence of order or of a single ruling and guiding power.

1904 *Daily News* 11 Oct. 3 [Reporting Sir O. Lodge], The only possible alternative was to regard the universe as a result of random chance and capricious disorder, not a cosmos or universe at all, but rather a 'multiverse'. 1906 *Hibbert Jrnl.* Jan. 460 The proposal to run the universe (turned into a multiverse) as a joint-stock enterprise..is essentially irreligious. 1920 Chesterton *New Jerusalem* viii. 163 When I told a distinguished psychologist..that I differed from his view of the universe, he answered, 'Why universe? Why should it not be a multiverse?'

Mu·mchanceness. [f. Mumchance *a.* + -ness.] Silence, reticence.

1920 'Anthony Hope' *Second String* xxi, Perhaps his very mum-chanceness was his saving. Glib protestations would have smacked too strongly of the principal to commend the agent.

Mummy, *sb.*^{2} (Add example of vocative.)

1903 *Punch* 30 Sept. 231 Mummy dear, of course Uncle Jack is coming to meet us by a Circle Train, isn't he?

Mummy Apple: variant of *Mammee Apple*, Mammee.

1905 *Daily Graphic* 16 Jan. 4/4 The mummy-apple, a delicate tree-melon, springs up spontaneously wherever land is cleared. 1911 J. London *Adventure* vii. 85 Mummy apples, which he had regarded as weeds, under her guidance appeared as appetizing breakfast fruit.

Mumpery (mʊ·mpəri). [f. Mump *v.*^{2} + -ery.] Begging.

1913 W. J. Locke *Stella Maris* xiii. 156 The hard-bitten vagabond of the highroad has his or her well-defined means of livelihood. This was a mistress of mumpery.

Mung. (Earlier example.)

1844 *Spirit of Times* (Philad.) 26 Sept. (Th.) Mung news.

Mung^2, variant of Moong.

1884 *De Candolle's Orig. Cultivated Pl.* 346 Green Gram, or Mûng—*Phaseolus mungo*, Linnaeus. 1924 *Nature* 7 June CXIII. 814/1 The great Linnaeus blundered in that he confused the soybean with the mung bean.

Mungofa. (Earlier example.)

1836 Holbrook *N. Amer. Herpetol.* I. 41 *Testudo Polyphemus*—Daudin. Synonymes...Gopher and Mungofa, Vulgo.

Municipalizer (miuni·sipăləizəɹ). [f. Municipalize *v.* + -er.] One who favours municipal control of public services, institutions, and the like; a municipalist.

1908 Shaw *Commonsense of Municipal Trading* p. ix, The most..disinterested of them would..become ardent municipalizers. 1928 *Weekly Dispatch* 24 June 9/3 Within the movement there are (1) prohibitionists,..(2) municipalisers; (3) advocates of State ownership and control.

Munition, *sb.* Add: **2.** (Recent examples.) Also *colloq.*, the production of munitions; munition-work. *Ministry of Munitions*: A special Ministry created in 1915 to control the production and supply of munitions of war, and lasting until 1921. So *Minister of Munitions.*

1915 *Times* 26 May 9/6 The Prime Minister has decided that a new Department shall be created, to be called the Ministry of Munitions. 1915 *Act 5 & 6 Geo. V* c. 54 § 4 If the Minister of Munitions considers it expedient..that any establishment in which munitions work is carried on should be subject to the special provisions [etc.]. 1916 *Blackw. Mag.* Feb. 205/1 There is no need at this time to praise the women working on munitions. 1916 Boyd Cable *Doing their Bit* 12, I asked the Ministry of Munitions to give me an opportunity to see with my own eyes what is being done now. 1917 *Dalton Guardian* 28 Apr. 3/5 He had been sent to munitions, and had not been out to the front. 1924 B. Gilbert *Bly Market* 66, I expect..you'll be leaving the schooling and go to the munitions.

5. *munition-factory, -maker, -making, -work, -worker*; also *munitions work.*

1909 *Westm. Gaz.* 9 Oct. 2/2 In 1895 he visited the chief firearm and *munition factories of France. 1916 *Blackw. Mag.* Feb. 191/1 The scheme was this: that women of leisure should be given three weeks' training in a..munition factory. 1916 *Home Companion* 12 Aug. 16/1 This is my last chat to you, little mother *munition-makers. 1916 Boyd Cable *Doing their Bit* 24 No man or lathe or tool that can be turned to *munition-making is possibly doing anything else. 1918 *Times* 27 Mar. 3/1 These are all chapters in the romance of *munitions work in the Midlands. 1916 Boyd Cable *Doing their Bit* 40 Anything less promising of *munition work it would be hard to find. 1915 *Daily Sketch* 18 Aug. 2 (heading) Badges for the Volunteer *Munition Worker. 1919 J. L. Garvin *Econ. Foundations of Peace* 111 The demobilization of soldiers and the disbanding of munition-workers.

Munition, *v.* Add: **3.** *intr.* To do munition work; to work in a munition factory.

1916 Boyd Cable *Doing their Bit* 23 A man cast for a commission and refused for the ranks a year ago on account of his eyes has 'gone munitioning'.

Munitioneer (miuniʃəniə·ɹ). [f. Munition *sb.* + -eer.] A worker in a munition-factory.

1916 E. V. Lucas *Vermilion Box* 254 In the need for copper there is quite a good price for engraved plates, and theirs have been weeded out for the munitioneers. 1919 *Athenæum* 23 May 360/1 'Trinitrotoluene,' which the munitioneers shortened to T.N.T.

Munitioner. Add: **c.** = *Munitioneer; a maker of ammunition.

1917 *Graphic* 30 June 806 (Illustration) The King with his munitioners.

Munitionette (miuniʃəne·t). *colloq.* [-ette.] A female munition-worker.

1915 *Daily Sketch* 9 Nov. 13/1 (heading), Munitionettes Who Receive Threepence An Hour. 1917 *Daily News* 17 May 3/1 A shell-shop filled with blue-clad, mob-capped cheering munitionettes. 1919 *Punch* 7 May 366/2 Work for the ex-munitionette drawing unemployment pay.

Munitionless (miuni·ʃənlės), *a.* [-less.] Not provided with munitions.

1927 Churchill *World Crisis, 1916–18*, 224 The mastered agony of the munitionless retreat; the slowly regathered forces; the victories of Brusiloff;..has he no share in these?

Munitionment (miuni·ʃənmĕnt). [f. Munition *v.* + -ment.] Provision with or supply of munitions.

1915 H. Belloc in *Land & Water* 29 May 10*/1 If the Austro-German forces under the effect of superior munitionment for the heavy pieces do pierce their opponent's line.

Mural, *a.*^{1} **2.** (Add example.)

1916 H. F. Osborn *Men of Old Stone Age* 316 This art.. is also mural or parietal.., consisting of drawings, engravings, paintings and bas-reliefs on the walls of caverns and grottos.

Murder, *v.* **1. g.** (Later examples.)

1857 J. Hyde Jr. *Mormonism* vii. 181 (Born) These men will fight, lie, rob, murder for Mormonism, if commanded. 1910 *New Mag.* Nov. 224/2 Yes. I am the man who murders for the king.

Murderee (mɜɹdərī·). [f. Murder *v.* + -ee^1.] A person who is murdered.

1928 F. T. Jesse *Trial of S. H. Dougal* 4 The potential murderer has met the born murderee.

Murmur, *sb.* Add: **5.** *Comb.* **murmur-vowel,** a glide vowel.

1910 *Mod. Lang. Rev.* V. 91 The glide or murmur vowel of normally unstressed prefixes.

Murmur, *v.* **3.** Add: Also with *out.*

1837 Dickens *Pickw.* xxviii. 304 Gabriel murmured out something about its being very pretty. 1893 Doyle *Mem. Sh. Holmes* 41 My lips were parted to murmur out some sleepy words of surprise or remonstrance.

Murmuration. 1. (Modern example.)

1908 *Westm. Gaz.* 5 Aug. 2/1 The plaints and murmurations of these Randlords for the grievances which they clamoured to have redressed.

Murrain. A. *sb.* Add: **3. c.** (See quot.)

1875 Knight *Dict. Mech.* 1275/1 In green-salted hides and skins, those weighing..14 to 25 pounds, if plump, [are called] *kip*, but if thin and poor are called *runners* or *murrains.*

Muscarine. Add: Also -in.

1910 *Practitioner* June 824 Putrefactive organisms split up proteins into..ptomaines—neurin, cholin, muscarin, cadaverin, [etc.].

Muscatel. 1. Add: Also an Australian wine.

1867 *Australasian* 9 Feb. 186/1 Australian Wines in the Indian Market...The Muscatel has plenty of body.

Muscle. 4. d. Add: **muscle-banner,** in anthozoans, a retractor muscle of the mesenteries; **muscle-bound** *a.*, having the muscles stiff and enlarged, esp. as a result of too much exercise or training; also *fig.*; **muscle-memory,** 'memory' located in muscles.

1900 G. C. Bourne in *Lankester's Treat. Zool.* ii. *Anthozoa* 11 The mesenteries are provided with well-developed retractor muscles, supported on folds or plaits of the mesogloea, which..form the so-called *muscle banners. The arrangement of the muscle banners of the Alcyonaria is characteristic. 1902 Webster Suppl., *Muscle-bound. 1909 *Westm. Gaz.* 8 June 9/2, I have met many cases where an unintelligent use of such exercises has..so thickened the muscles as to lead to the condition known as being 'muscle-bound'. 1918 *Nation* (N.Y.) 7 Feb. 133/2 There has been a curious sense of leisureliness, of muscle-bound movement. 1915 *Nature* 11 Mar. XCV. 39/1 Some authorities still believe that there is no getting past the assumption of a non-analysable sense of direction...Others again lay too heavy a burden on *muscle-memory.

Muscovade (mʊ·skovēᵘd). [f. Muscovado.] = Muscovado.

1851 Alice Cary *Clovernook* 74 Every day in winter she used to feed them [the bees] maple sugar if she had it—and if not, a little Muscovade in a saucer.

Muse, *v.* Add: **8. b.** To say or murmur meditatively.

1834 A. M. Ravenscliffe *Two Old Men's Tales* xiii. 250 (Born) 'But what can I promise? I who have nothing,' mused she, 'and am now penniless.' 1843 Dickens *Christmas Carol* 32 'You must have been very slow about it, Jacob.' 'Slow!' the Ghost repeated. 'Seven years dead,' mused Scrooge. 'And travelling all the time?' 1881 Mrs. J. H. Riddell *Senior Partner* I. vii. 150 'That's strange,' mused Mr. McCullagh; 'and you getting on for thirty year of age.'

Museum. Add: **4.** *Comb.* **museum-piece,** an article fit to receive a place in a museum; a fine example of anything, esp. of manufactured articles; also *transf.*, a person or object of peculiar or special worth or interest.

1901 *Brit. Chess Mag.* 351 The more stately carved pieces (named for the sake of distinction 'museum-pieces'). 1914 Vachell *Quinney's* ii. xiv. § 2. 198 An elaborately carved Chippendale settee, a museum piece. 1920 W. J. Locke *House of Baltazar* iii. 31 Quong Ho was admitted to be a museum-piece of discretion. 1927 *Observer* 27 Nov. 13/4 In a few years, when the last pantomime has been played, it may be time to put on another in the best old-fashioned style as a museum piece. 1928 Galsworthy *Swan Song* i. xi. 82 The girl and her brother had been museum pieces, two Americans without money to speak of.

Mush, *sb.*^{1} Add: **1.** (Earlier example of *mush and milk.*)

1817 *Essex Inst. Hist. Coll.* 27 Dec. (1866) VIII. 244 They ..gave me a supper of mush and milk.

4. *Wireless Telegr.* (See quot. 1924.)

1924 *Harmsworth's Wireless Encycl.* II. 1456 *Mush.* Term used for the irregular intermediate frequencies set up by an arc transmitter which interfere with the fundamental wave-lengths. 1928 *Observer* 1 July 4/4 In listening to very faint signals from a great distance a limit is put by the 'mush' and statics and other noises brought in from the aerial.

5. *attrib.* and *Comb.*, as *mush-pot* (sense 1); **mush-head,** a person of a yielding disposition; one lacking in firmness; so *mush-headed* adj.; **mush-ice,** water only partly frozen, ice which is not solid; **mush-sugar,** a mixture of syrup and crystals of sugar.

1919 H. L. Wilson *Ma Pettengill* ii. 63, I up and told her flat she could never run a boarding-house and make it pay; that no woman could who hadn't learned to say 'No!' and she was too much of a *mushhead for that. 1924 R. Cullum *Way of Strong* iii. viii. 294 The game isn't worth it, fighting this *mush-headed crowd who have to get other folks to think for 'em. 1815 *Niles' Weekly Reg.* IX. 201/2 You may, by digging down three feet, take a pole sixty feet long and with the strength of your hands run it down the whole length, and find no termination of what is called the *mush ice. 1907 J. London *White Fang* 202 The fall of the year, when the first snows were falling and mush-ice was running in the river. 1847 H. Howe *Hist. Coll. Ohio* 432 Johnny, who wore on his head a tin utensil which answered both as a cap and a *mush pot, filled it with water and quenched the fire. 1867 *Rep. Iowa Agric. Soc.* (1868) 178 When sugar is contemplated, White Imphee is..the best, as all I have made went to thick *mush sugar immediately.

Mush (mʊʃ), *sb.*^{3} [f. *Mush *v.*^{3}] A journey made on foot through snow, driving a dog-sled.

1926 *Glasgow Herald* 8 Mar. 10/7 From Hudson in northern Ontario it is a twelve-day 'mush' for men and dogs over the frozen sub-arctic prairie to the Red Lake district.

Mush (mʊʃ), *v.*^{3} [Apparently f. F. *marchez* or *marchons*, imp. of *marcher* to advance, the command given to the dogs; hence with *on*: cf. *Mush *sb.*^{3}] *intr.* To travel on foot through the snow with a dog-sled; said also of the dogs.

1903 *N.Y. Sun* 22 Nov., His little boat was cut out, and then he started to 'mush' back over the ice. 1904 S. E. White *Silent Places* xvii. 180 'Mush! Mush on!' shouted Sam. The four dogs leaned into their collars. 1906 'O. Henry' *Four Million* 106, I never got off the train since I mushed out of Seattle, and I'm hungry. 1914 R. Cullum *Way of Strong* i. i. 1 Five great sled dogs crouched in their harness.. They were waiting the long familiar command to 'mush'; an order they had not heard since the previous winter. 1927 *Brit. Weekly* 13 Jan. 409/2 They were mushing on to a new strike.

Musher (mʊ·ʃəɹ). [f. *Mush *v.*^{3} + -er^1.] A person who mushes; one who travels through snow on foot with a dog-sled. So **Mu·shing** *vbl. sb.*

1904 *U.S. Geol. Surv.* Prof. Paper No. 20, 14 Traveling by this means is known, in the language of the country [Alaska], as 'mushing', and the traveler is called a 'musher'. *Ibid.* 15 In 'mushing', the best progress is made in relatively cool weather. 1905 Rex Beach *Pardners* iv. (1912) 89 Other 'mushers' were ahead of us at the road-house. 1925 *Chambers's Jrnl.* July 456/2 Those far northern regions are inaccessible..except to the most hardy and expert 'mushers'.

Mushily (mʊ·ʃili), *adv.* [f. Mushy *a.* + -ly^2.] In a soft or mushy manner.

1910 'O. Henry' *Strictly Business* xvi. 187 'A cool hundred,' said Fuzzy thoughtfully and mushily.

Mushiness (mʊ·ʃinės). *colloq.* [f. Mushy *a.* + -ness.] The condition of being soft or pulpy; also *fig.*, sentimental character, weakness, sloppiness.

1890 [see s.v. Mushy *a.*]. 1894 'Mark Rutherford' *Cath. Furze* xiv. 247 Partly this distressing weakness is due to the absence of a clear conviction that we are right;..but frequently it is simple mushiness of character.

Mushroom, *sb.* Add: **3. c.** A spreading cloud (of smoke).

1924 A. J. Small *Frozen Gold* iv. 110 A sudden, abrupt mushroom of smoke spread out above the building on the uprush of air.

6. c. mushroom-headed *a.* (add example); **mushroom sinker,** a mushroom-shaped sinker; **mushroom valve,** (*a*) a type of valve, used in internal combustion engines, having a flat seat; (so *mushroom-valve engine*, etc.); (*b*) a variety of valve used in wireless receiving sets (see quot. 1924).

1875 Pitt-Rivers *Evol. Culture* (1906) 38 We see [in the plate] the *mushroom-headed 'waddy', with its projecting ridge flattened, then [in later stage of development] curved. 1928 Gamble *Story N. Sea Air Station* xx. 358 A large canister buoy was laid down with a *mushroom sinker. 1877 *Design & Work* 7 July 114/3 Exhaust valve, consisting of ordinary *mushroom valve. 1908 *Westm. Gaz.* 27 Oct. 4/2 Designers have taken steps to remove this old-fashioned defect in the mushroom valve system. *Ibid.* 10 Nov. 4/1 The mushroom-valve engine. 1909 R. W. A. Brewer *Motor Car* 30 Mushroom valves are adopted in gas engine practice because this type of valve opens very readily to its full area and shuts just as readily. 1922 *Wireless World* 10 Dec. 578/1 The Mushroom Valve. 1924 *Harmsworth's Wireless Encycl.* II. 1456 *Mushroom valve*, alternative name given to the Cossor R.M.R. and other Cossor valves on account of the shape of the grid and anode, which are fashioned somewhat like a mushroom.

Mushroom, *v.* Add: **2. c.** *intr.* Of fire: To spread outwards.

1903 *N.Y. Sun* 2 Nov. 3 The flames had gone up the stairs to the very top of the house, and had then 'mushroomed' out, as the firemen say. 1911 *Ithaca Jrnl.* 10 Aug., The flames mushroomed from the shaft on all floors above.

Mushy, *a.* Add: **2.** *fig.* Tender, sentimental, insipid, 'wishy-washy'. Also as *adv.*

1870 *Nation* (N.Y.) 3 Feb. 67 (Cent.) The death penalty is disappearing, like some better things, before a kind of mushy and unthinking doubt of its morality and expediency. 1913 Mrs. Stratton-Porter *Laddie* vii. (1917) 135 They formed a circle around Sally and Peter and as mushy as ever they could they sang, 'As sure as the grass grows around the stump, You are my darling sugar lump,' while they danced. 1916 H. L. Wilson *Somewhere in Red Gap* ii. 75 The mushy state I was in. 1922 H. L. Foster *Adv. Trop. Tramp* xiii. 203 Provided that he is not of the 'mushy' disposition, and

calls merely to talk, he finds her an uninspiring conversationalist. 1928 G. B. Shaw *Intell. Woman's Guide* § 84. 458 You may..be a sharp, cynical sort of person; or you may be a nice, mushy, amiable, goodnatured one.

2. *Wireless Telegr.* (see quot. and cf. *Mush *sb.*[1] 4.)

1924 *Harmsworth's Wireless Encycl.* II. 1456 A mushy note is one which is not absolutely definite or clear cut, and so hard to read. It is a note received by the heterodyne method when damped wires or modulated continuous waves are being received.

Music, *sb.* Add: 10. b. Suppleness or resilience.

1901 W. J. Travis *Pract. Golf* (1903) ix. 111 The man with a less rapid swing will get equally as long a ball by using a more supple shaft. The more 'music' there is in the shaft, however, the greater is the liability to slice or pull.

12. *music-case, -rack* (earlier example).

1890 *Cent. Dict.*, *Music-case. 1855 *Knickerbocker Mag.* XLV. 136 You bide behind the *music-rack while Miss Mince passes.

c. (Recent example.)

1909 *Englishwoman* Apr. 294 The festival music-drama as planned, invented, and carried out by Richard Wagner.. was a stupendous thing for one man to have done.

d. **music-hallish** *a.*, suggestive of a music-hall; **music-roll,** a roll, usually of perforated paper, used in mechanical pianos, and similar instruments.

1930 Ivor Brown in *Observer* 30 Mar. 15 The patriotic song of 1900 should have been sung by someone more robust and *music-hallish than the cute and charming Miss Ada-May. 1906 *Bazaar, Exch. & Mart* Suppl. 3 Oct. 1322/1 Kastner's upright grand auto-piano for sale,..played by hand or by *music rolls. *Ibid.*, Music rolls for 65 note piano players, Pianola [etc.]. 1913 *Strand Mag.* Jan. Advts. 13 For all Player-Pianos 'Songola' Music Rolls.

Musical. A. *adj.* 10. Add: **musical arms,** a modification of the game of musical chairs (see quot.); **musical chairs,** a competitive parlour game in which a number of persons walk to music round a smaller number of chairs and each try to secure a seat when the music stops; **musical fright** = *musical chairs*.

1924 D. C. Minter *Children's Parties* etc. x. 137 *Musical arms. This game is played in the same way as Musical Chairs, without, however, using chairs. 1903 May Crommelin *Crimson Lilies* ii. 16 Afterwards the children..clamoured to play round games for two hours, *musical chairs, general post and so forth. 1916 'Peter' *Trench Yarns* 25 We had to get the men through the danger zone by a sort of musical-chairs rush. They came slowly up to the entrance, and then dashed in and round the corner into safety behind the bricks. 1922 B. Gilbert *Tyler of Barnet* xii. 97 The smallest pigling..looked like a child who, playing at musical chairs, finds when the piano stops that there is no seat. 1879 'Prof. Hoffmann' *Drawing-room Amusem.* 24 *Musical Fright.

Musicalize (miū·zikăləiz), *v.* [f. Musical *a.* + -ize.] *trans.* To make musical; to set (a play) to music.

1928 *Sunday Express* 19 Aug. 5/4 He prepared a musicalised version of the..play.

Musicologist (miūzikǫ·lŏdʒist). [ad. F. *musicologiste*: or f. Music + -ologist.] A person who studies music scientifically.

1927 *Observer* 20 Feb. 18/2 The widest co-operation has.. been secured from French, Spanish, German, and other foreign musicologists. 1930 *Music & Lett.* Apr. 138 The distinguished list of English musicologists.

Musicology (miūzikǫ·lŏdʒi). [ad. F. *musicologie*: or f. Music + -ology.] The scientific study of music.

1919 *Proc. Mus. Assoc.* 1918–19 106 The foundations of Musicology are the documents, manuscripts or printed music of past times. 1928 *Music & Lett.* Apr. 108 The most valuable piece of musicology is the treatment of the six motets.

Musketoo·ner. [f. Musketoon + -er [1].] = Musketoon 2.

1925 *Chambers's Jrnl.* June 339/2, I felt a tearing blow above my right hip and I knew that the kneeling musketooner had touched me.

Musking-place. A place where weasels or kindred animals deposit musk.

1920 *Chambers's Jrnl.* May 291/2 The wolves have their calling-posts, the beavers have their castor-signs, the weasels have their musking-places.

Musk-rat. Add: 1. b. (Earlier example.)

1845 in C. Cist *Cincinnati Misc.* 240 The inhabitants of.. Delaware [are called] Muskrats.

3. *musk-rat burrow, skin.*

1870 *Amer. Naturalist* IV. 385 This fish, when the bank was carelessly approached would withdraw to a deserted *muskrat burrow. 1805 Lewis in *Ann. 9th Congress* 2 Sess. 1070 Dressed elk and moose-deer skins, *muskrat skins, and some buffalo robes. 1823 in M'Kenny *Memoirs* I. (1846) App. 296 Furs and other articles..to wit,..2,500 muskrat skins [etc.].

Musquash. 3. **musquash-root** (earlier example); **musquash-weed** (example).

1807 *Massachusetts Spy* 22 July (Th.) Five children were lately poisoned in Scipio (New York) by eating Wild Parsnip or *Musquash Root. 1767 *Massachusetts Gaz.* 21 May (Th.) Persons (especially Children) would do well to beware of this Weed. It is called wild Hemlock by some, and *Musquash Weed by others.

Mu·squashing, *vbl. sb.* [f. Musquash *sb.* + -ing [1].] The hunting of musquashes.

1833 Seba Smith *Major Downing* 31 (Born) This was most capital fun, but it want quite equal to musquashing.

Muss, *sb.*[4] 1. (Earlier and later examples.)

1840 *Daily Pennant* (St. Louis) 23 Aug. (Th.) George R. went to a Dutch ball Saturday night, and got into a little muss, which cost him [at the police court] Two Dollars. 1840 Hoffman *Greyslaer* III. iv. II. 79 That's jist what I told Red Wolfert when he showed signs of kicking up a muss. 1892 J. L. Ford *Dr. Dodd's School* iv. 83 Before I had time to explain about it Pine pitched into me, and then the muss began.

2. (Earlier example.)

1842 *Spirit of Times* (Philad.) 22 Jan. (Th.) I upset my table, spilt my ink, and knocked down my books, making a deuced muss.

Muss, *v.*[2] 1. (Later examples.)

1907 Mulford *Bar-20* v. 47, I paid twenty wheels for that [a hat] eight years ago, and I don't want it mussed none. 1922 Titus *Timber* i. 12 You who're fitted for harder work than any of us, an' now you don't want to muss up your hands!

Hence **Mussed** *ppl. a.* Also *mussed-up*.

1888 *Detroit Free Press* (Farmer) Neither of us got two winks of sleep during the night on the car... We reached Chicago in a mussed up condition. 1909 *Philad. Publ. Ledger* 24 June 7/6 Advt., Lot 3..Some four hundred soiled or mussed waists, in white lawn & lingerie.

Mussel, *sb.* 4. Add: *mussel-opener, -spawn.*

1909 *Daily Chron.* 25 Sept. 7/6 Advt., Oyster and *Mussel Opener (Young) wanted for evenings. 1902 *Chambers's Jrnl.* May 277/2 Some seasons the *mussel-spawn is pretty much in evidence here.

Mussing (mʊ·siŋ), *vbl. sb.* [f. Muss *v.*[2] and *sb.*[4] + -ing [1].] Confusion, trouble.

1846 Corcoran *Pickings* 48 Well, as I aint flush in the financial way, I accept. Let there be no mussing between us.

Mustang. 1. *attrib.* Add: *mustang horse.*

1844 C. A. Murray *Prairie-bird* I. 307 Mounted on an active, spirited little Mustang horse.

2. (Earlier example.)

1847 *Rep. U. S. Comm. Patents* (1848) 198 He speaks of the great mustang grape in very high terms.

Mustard, *sb.* Add: 1. f. In fig. phrases: That which enhances the flavour of anything, or adds piquancy or zest; the best of anything. *U.S. slang.*

1894 'O. Henry' *Cabbages & Kings* vi. 101 I'm not headlined in the bills, but I'm the mustard in the salad dressing just the same. 1903 A. Adams *Log Cowboy* xv. 237 And for fear they were not the proper mustard, he had that dog man sue him in court for the balance, so as to make him prove the pedigree. *a* 1906 'O. Henry' *Trimmed Lamp* etc. 217 Why don't you invite him if he's so much to the mustard? 1922 C. Sandburg *Slabs of Sunburnt West* 7 Kid each other... Tell each other you're all to the mustard.

3. c. **mustard gas,** dichlordiethyl sulphide, a variety of poison gas used in the war of 1914–18.

1917 *Nation* (N. Y.) 15 Nov. 524/2 The Germans have just invented a new and particularly powerful weapon in their so-called 'mustard gas'. 1925 E. Fraser & Gibbons *Soldier & Sailor Words, Mustard Gas*,..a vesicant and poison gas, one effect of which was to blister the mouth, armpits and face, and affect the eyes. 1928 *Daily Mail* 16 Aug. 17/4 Tanks, armoured cars, and mustard-gas shells.

Mustard seed. 3. (Earlier examples.)

1809 Fessenden *Pills Poetical* 8 Her single good gun loaded with mustard seed shot. 1834 *Southern Lit. Messenger* I. 182 He might as well attempt to batter the rock of Gibralter with mustard seed shot as to attack the yellow fever with alkali. 1844 *Knickerbocker Mag.* XXIII. 440 None of the fine mustard-seed or robin, but the heavy duck-shot.

Muster, *sb.*[1] 9. Add: *muster-field, -ground* (earlier example).

1838 B. Drake *Tales* 179 Our sons:..assembling in the '*muster field', divide themselves into armies, and pelt each other with Buckeye balls. 1841 Foote *Texas & Texans* I. 235 The inhabitants..were convened on a *Muster-ground.

Musterer[2] (mʊ·stərəɹ). *Austral.* [f. Muster *v.*[1] (sense 6) + -er [1].] One who musters sheep or cattle.

1899 L. Cockayne in *Glasgow Herald* 22 Aug. (1925) 4, I have never seen it [the kea] attack sheep, nor have I met with anyone—shepherd, musterer, or mountain traveller —who has done so. 1927 *Observer* 25 Sept. 21/3, I had the opportunity of meeting..drovers and musterers on the great Queensland sheep runs.

Mustering, *vbl. sb.* b. (Add example.)

1841 *Southern Lit. Messenger* VII. 768/1 Who should I see..but Mr. Jim Guest himself, in the same spry dress I had seen him in the morning; mustering jacket and trowsers, and tarpaulin hat.

Mustic, variant of Moustick.

Mutant (miū·tănt), *a.* and *sb.* *Biol.* [ad. L. *mutant-em* pr. pple. of *mutāre* to change.] a. *adj.* That is the result of mutation. b. *sb.* A form or species resulting from mutation.

1901 *Rep. Brit. Assoc.* 848 A period in which they do form mutants, to use the terminology of de Vries, which mutants *may* be true to seed. 1903 *Amer. Naturalist* Nov. 742 No forms intermediate between the mutants, or between the mutants and the parent type were found... The mutant forms were really groups of phylogenetic value. 1918 Babcock & Clausen *Genetics Agric.* 286 Hence they breed true in the main but occasionally throw the new combinations of diverse elements which have come to be known as 'mutants'. 1923 *Glasgow Herald* 25 Jan. 10 Race-making was due..to the in-breeding and isolation of similar variants or mutants. 1930 R. A. Fisher *Genetical Theory Nat. Select.* 11 In domestication..not only is the rigour of Natural Selection relaxed so that mutant types can survive..but [etc.].

Mutarotation (miūtărōtē·ʃən). *Physical Chem.* [f. L. *mutā-re* to change + Rotation.] The change in the amount of optical rotation of substances (especially sugars) in solution. Originally called *Birotation.

1907 J. B. Cohen *Org. Chem.* 100 The name was changed from birotation to *multirotation*. As the latter term implies some simple ratio between the original and final values the word *mutarotation* recently adopted by Lowry..is to be preferred. 1916 A. P. Mathews *Physiol. Chem.* 49 The mutarotation of levulose is probably due..to the fact that it exists in solution in two forms.

Mutate, *v.* Add: c. *intr.* To undergo biological mutation.

1926 Carr-Saunders *Eugenics* 43 Genes which were not present in the parent sometimes appear in the offspring. They seem to arise by the transformation of pre-existing genes. Existing genes sometimes 'mutate'.

Mutational (miutē·ʃənăl), *a.* [f. Mutation + -al.] Of or pertaining to mutation.

1904 *Nature* 25 Feb. 386/2 De Vries's 'mutational variations.

Mutationist (miutē·ʃənist). *Biol.* [f. Mutation + -ist.] One who stresses the importance of mutation as a factor in producing new and 'higher' forms or species.

1904 *Science* 10 June 881/2 It might be inferred that Lamarckians and Darwinians are..regarded as believers in adaptiveness as a factor in evolution, and mutationists are necessarily supposed to hold the opposite view. 1909 *Fabian News* XX. 76/1 The mad mutationist who claims that evolution takes place by mutation only. 1911 A. D. Darbishire *Breeding & Mendelian Discov.* 4 The point at issue between the Selectionist..and the Mutationist, is this.

Mutilla (miuti·lă). [Mod.L., the name of the genus.] An insect of the genus *Mutilla*; a solitary ant.

1881 *Harper's Mag.* Dec. 75/1 The grasshopper felt the fangs of the Mutilla at the nape of his neck.

Mutt (mʊt). *slang.* (orig. *U.S.*) [Apparently abbreviated f. *mutton-head* Mutton 8 b.] One who is stupid, ignorant, awkward, blundering, incompetent, or the like; a blockhead, dullard, or fool.

1910 O. Johnson *Varmint* 377 Engaged to that Ver Plank fellow that was hanging around. I think he's a mutt. 1912 R. W. Chambers *Common Law* x. 282 It's going to be hard for her. She can't stand for a mutt—and it's the only sort that will marry her. 1918 E. M. Roberts *Flying Fighter* 107 He opined that it was a shame to send a 'mutt' like me down to a battery to create trouble. 1920 *Blackw. Mag.* Feb. 176/2 The elder brother was a quiet, inoffensive kind of a mutt. 1924 P. G. Wodehouse *Inimit. Jeeves* xiv. 160 The Cynthia affair had jarred the unfortunate mutt to such an extent that [etc.]. 1925 Chesterton *Tales of Long Bow* v. 179, I reckon those mutts didn't get on to what they were selling me.

b. A term of contempt applied to a dog.

1911 R. W. Chambers *Common Law* x. 310 Now fat old women..Arrive to exercise their various dogs; And 'round and 'round the little mutts all run. 1916 H. L. Wilson *Somewhere in Red Gap* vii. 296 They turned out to be mere dogs;..kind of yapping mutts that some parties would poison off. 1927 *Ladies' Home Jrnl.* Dec. 4/1 Be careful the mutt doesn't get into a race with a caterpillar some day, and die of heart collapse.

Mutton. Add: 7. (Recent example.)

1930 *Punch* 28 May 606/3 Both Houses, having dealt with the Whitsuntide holidays, resumed their muttons.

8. b. **mutton-faced** *a.*, having a face suggestive of mutton (as a term of abuse); **mutton-head** (earlier example).

1892 Stevenson & Osbourne *Wrecker* xii. 193 'You —, —, little, *mutton-faced Dutchman, Nares would bawl. 1804 Fessenden *Terrible Tractoration* 159 And couldst thou, pertinacious Bradley, But maul these *mutton heads, most sadly.

Mutualist. 1. Add: Also *attrib.*

1909 F. Lawton *3rd French Republic* xiv. 320 From 1852 onwards, the Mutualist movement extended rapidly.

Mutualistic (miūtiuăli·stik). *Biol.* [f. Mutualist + -ic.] Characterized by mutualism.

1902 Webster Suppl. 1911 J. G. McIntosh *Manuf. Varnishes* III. 291 Giard does not see that the ants are enemies of the cochineal... Their relations are mutualistic and in no way predatory or parentic.

Mux (mʊks), *sb.* *U.S. colloq.* [f. the vb.] A disordered or muddled state; = Muck *sb.*[1] 4.

18.. Eliz. Stoddard *Two Men* iv. 28 (Funk) I knew you would come back. Now we are in a mux. 1890 *Century Dict.*, *Mux*, work performed in an awkward or improper manner; a botch; a mess; as, he made a mux of it.

Mux (mʊks), *v.* *U.S.* and *dial.* [Of obscure formation: cf. Muss *v.*, Muck *v.* and dial. *mucksy* dirty.] = Muck *v.* 4.

1806 *Balance* (Hudson, N. Y.) 26 Aug. 272 (Th.) To do observance, make obliging mention, Wink lovingly, mux chastity away. 1859 Bartlett *Dict. Amer.* (ed. 2) s.v., To *mux* is much used in New England for *muss*; as 'Don't mux my crinoline.' 1867 Blackmore *Lorna Doone* (1869) III. x. 157 By vice of mismanagement on the part of my mother, and Nicholas Snowe, who had thoroughly muxed up everything, being too quick-headed. *a* 1877 J. M. Bailey *They all do it* 22 (Bartlett) Stop muxin' that bread!..you've eaten enough for twenty people. I shan't have you muxing and gauming up the victuals.

Muzziness. (Add example.)

1904 *Athenæum* 7 May 599/2 We lament the muzziness which seems inseparable from the process employed.

Muzzle, *v.*[1] Add: 3. c. *transf.* To close (a fishing-net).

1876 F. Francis *Bk. Angling* xii. (ed. 4) 438 The Esk..is a fine river, and would be finer if the Solway stake nets were only muzzled.

Muzzle, *v.*[1] 9. (Later example.)

1889 'R. Boldrewood' *Robbery under Arms* xxv, Tim and I jumped off..and muzzled him [the constable].

Muzzy, *a.* Add: 3. *Comb.*, as **muzzy-headedness,** a fuddled or intoxicated condition.

1930 Mottram *Europa's Beast* vii. 169 Cocktails were sheer silliness, a short cut to muzzy-headedness.

Myal (məi·ăl), *a.* [f. Gr. μῦς, μυ-ός muscle (see Myo-) + -al.] Associated with a myotome or muscular segment.

1902 *Encycl. Brit.* XXV. 386/2 The ventral roots on the contrary, are myal or segmental in position.

Mygalid (mi·gălid). *Zool.* [f. mod.L. *Mygalidæ* the name of a family of spiders.] A spider of the family *Mygalidæ*.

1920 J. Ritchie *Anim. Life Scotl.* viii. 447 A Bird-Eating Spider (Mygalid)..has appeared in Edinburgh.

Myo-. Add: **Myofi·bril** [Fibril], a muscular fibril. **Myome·trium** [Gr. μήτρα womb], the muscular substance of the uterus. **My·oneme** [Gr. νῆμα thread], a muscular fibril found in certain protozoans.

1903 *Jrnl. R. Microsc. Soc.* Feb. 38 The terminal delicate discs of the *myofibril form a membrane [etc.]. 1907 *Practitioner* Dec. 792 The *myometrium contained many thick-walled blood-vessels. 1903 *Jrnl. R. Microsc. Soc.* Oct. 618 A. Prenant..has begun naturally with the so-called *myonemes of Protozoa. 1914 Fantham & Porter *Some minute Anim. Parasites* 67 This membrane..is traversed by contractile elements known as myonemes.

Myocardiac (məiokā·ɹdiăk), *a.* [f. Myocardium + -ac.] Of or pertaining to the myocardium.

1908 *Practitioner* Oct. 610 As the author says, myocardiac deficiency is the chief indication for the Nauheim treatment.

Myoepithelial (məioˌepiþī·liăl), *a.* [f. Myo- + Epithelial.] Of animal cells: Having the characteristics of muscular cells in addition to being epithelial.

1881 F. M. Balfour *Compar. Embryol.* II. 550 In all the Coelenterata, except the Ctenophora, the contractile elements of the body wall consist of filiform processes of ectodermal or entodermal epithelial cells. The elements provided with these processes, which were first discovered by Kleinenberg, are known as myo-epithelial cells. 1904 *Nature* 3 Mar. 431/1 At certain stages complete continuity could be observed between motor nerve trunk and the protoplasmic body of the myoepithelial cell.

Myoid (məi·oid), *a.* [f. Myo- + -oid.] Resembling a muscle; composed of muscular tissue. As *sb.*, a structural part in the retinal cones and rods.

1857 Dunglison *Med. Lex.*, *Myoid*, an epithet given to tumors composed of fibre cells or muscular fibres of organic life. 1900 R. M. Gunn in *Lancet* 7 July 7/2 The cell-body, traced from the cuticular end, begins as a distinct granular protoplasmic swelling, called the myoid.

Myomatous, *a.* Add: Also, affected with myoma.

1900 *Lancet* 18 Aug. 501/1 There would be found to be about 1,000,000 myomatous women in their present population.

Myomectomy (məiome·ktŏmi). *Surg.* [f. Myoma + Gr. ἐκτομή excision.] The excision of a uterine myoma; myomotomy.

1890 Billings *Nat. Med. Dict.* 1900 *Lancet* 18 Aug. 501/1 Myomectomy should always be done when it was possible to save the uterus. 1908 *Practitioner* Oct. 608 Vaginal myomectomy.

Myriapodal (miriæ·pŏdăl), *a.* [f. Myriapoda + -al.] Of or pertaining to Myriapoda.

1892 *Rep. U.S. Nat. Mus.* 258 Comparatively little can ever be known concerning the probably great abundance of Insect, Arachnid, and Myriapodal life of former geological time.

Myrmeco-. **Myrmecologist** (example).

1901 W. M. Wheeler in *Amer. Naturalist* XXXV. 432 While it thus becomes necessary to review much that is well known to the myrmecologist, I hope [etc.].

Myrtle, *sb.* 5. Add: **myrtle-of-the-river** *U.S.*, a shrub of the Myrtle family (see quot. 1917); **myrtle warbler** = *myrtle bird*.

1917 Safford in *Smithsonian Rep.* 384 The *myrtle-of-the-river..(*Calyptranthes suzygium*) with opposite glossy leaves and clusters of fruit resembling blueberries. 1924 J. A. Thomson *Science Old & New* v. 27 Even the names transport us into a land of pure delight—the paradise tree, the myrtle-of-the-river, the marlberry, and the bois-fidèle. 1893 B. Torrey *Footpath-Way* 95 Not so was it with the *myrtle warblers. 1902 S. E. White *Blazed Trail* xlii. 296 Myrtle and Magnolia warblers, oven birds, peewits.. passed silently or noisily.

Myrtly (mɔ̄·ɹtli), *a.* [f. Myrtle *sb.* + -y [1].] Containing myrtles or redolent of myrtle.

1882 Armstrong *Garland fr. Greece* 135 Every brake And myrtly jungle seemed to undulate With motions of strange beings.

Mysid (mi·sid). [f. mod.L. *Mysidæ* the name of the family.] A member of the family *Mysidæ*; an opossum-shrimp.

1927 J. A. Thomson in *Glasgow Herald* 7 May 4 The somewhat shrimp-like crustaceans called Mysids flex their tails when one taps on the window of the aquarium with a glass rod.

Mystery[1]. 13. Add: *mystery-mongering*; **mystery ship,** an armed and camouflaged merchantman used to destroy submarines in the war of 1914–18; a Q-boat.

1912 Mrs. R. Davids *Buddhism* i. 20 There is no evidence ..that this late recourse to writing was due to any *mystery-mongering or esotericism. 1919 W. De Morgan *Old Madhouse* xvi. 259 He knew well how prone the human mind is to mystery-mongering. 1916 A. Noyes (*title*) *Mystery ships. 1919 *Boy's Own Paper* July 456/1 What a profound sensation has been aroused..by the doings of our British Mystery-Ships, or Q-Boats. 1920 *Pearson's Mag.* Jan. 84/1 These operations were greatly aided by the gallant actions of British 'Q' ships or 'mystery ships'.

Mystificatory, *a.* (Later example.)

1927 C. E. Montague *Right off Map* viii. 68 This mystificatory drug had been working to some effect on the people of Ria's City.

N

N. I. 1. c. (Add example.)

1899 J. G. Millais *Breath fr. Veldt* 55 The birds alighting in the background are represented in their usual N-shaped formation.

II. 1. N.C.O. = Non-commissioned officer; N.G. = No good.

1803–10 *Orderly Bks. of Manx Fencibles* in *Yn Lioar Manninagh* Jan.-Apr. (1890) I. 152 Any party, consisting of 6 men or upwards, must have a N.C.O...appointed to go with them. 1883 *Army Regul.* II. 102 (margin), Report on conviction of N.C.O. by civil power. 1915 *Cornhill Mag.* Mar. 388 Had a chat with my N.C.O.s.

1840 *St. Louis Daily Pennant* 20 June, The bells, boys, and engines tried to get up a fire last night, but it was N.G. 1888 *Cincinnati Weekly Gaz.* 22 Feb. (Farmer) Hill claims ..that he will make the farmers sweat who have been asserting that his claim was N.G. 1904 *N. Y. Times* 14 May 9 The store people sent the check to the bank, and were astonished when it was sent back with the ominous letters 'N.G.' marked across it.

'n, *colloq. U.S.*, reduced form of *than*.

1903 Kate D. Wiggin *Rebecca* i, We've only just started on it,..'it's more'n two hours'. 1910 Mulford *Hopalong Cassidy* ix. 63 He hates Greasers worse'n I do.

Nabatæan (næbătī·ăn), *sb.* and *a.* Also 7– Nabathæan. [f. L. *Nabat(h)æ-us*, Gr. Ναβαταῖ-ος, Ναβαθαῖ-ος (cf. *Nebāṭu* the native name of the country) + -an.] a. *sb.* One of an ancient Arabian people; their language. b. *adj.* Of or pertaining to the Nabatæans.

1601 Holland *Pliny* xii. xx. I. 374 The Troglodyte Nabathæans: who onely of the ancient Nabathæans, there setled and remained. 1875 *Encycl. Brit.* III. 411/2 Two forms of Shemitic writing (the Palmyrenian.., and the Sinaitic or Nabathæan). 1884 *Ibid.* XVII. 160/1 *Nabatæans*, a famous people of ancient Arabia. 1897 *Recent Research in Bible Lands* (ed. H. V. Hilprecht) 146 Between the decline of the Nabatean Empire and the appearance of Muhammad. 1911 *Encycl. Brit.* XXIV. 626/1 The language of this country was Nabataean. 1920 *Public Opinion* 9 July 42/3 Little did the ancient..Nabataeans imagine that a people called Americans would one day wander among the ruins of their proud city.

Nabob. 4. (Earlier example.)

1803 Eliza S. Bowne *Girl's Life 80 Yrs. ago* (1888) 151 Silk nabobs, plaided, colored and white, are much worn, very short waists, hair very plain.

Nacelle. Read †1. *Obs.* and add:

2. The framework containing the engine(s), etc., of an aeroplane or airship.

1909 *Aero* 13 July 117/2 The dirigible..has a screw at either end of the nacelle or cradle. *Ibid.* 27 July 146/2 'Nacelle'..means the metal or wood framework of a dirigible or an aeroplane. 1920 *Blackw. Mag.* Feb. 195/1 The spirit was not entering the tank, but spilling over the sides on to the floor of the nacelle.

Nacreosity (nēˈkriˌǫ·sĭti). [f. Nacreous *a.* + -ity.] The iridescence of nacre, or a quality suggesting this.

1931 *Observer* 27 Sept. 10 Nacreosity is a pearly iridescence.

Nag, *v.* 3. Add: Also *transf.*

1921 *Challenge* 28 Oct. 375/1 He nags his brain into a state of consuming doubt, but dares not arrive at any conclusion.

Nagana (năgā·nă). [Zulu *nakane*.] A disease affecting domesticated animals in South Africa, believed to be caused by trypanosomes introduced by the bite of the tsetse fly; tsetse-fly disease. Also *attrib.*

1895 D. Bruce (*title*) Preliminary Report on the Tsetse Fly-Disease, or Nagana, in Zululand. 1896 *Nature* 16 Apr. 567/1 Nagana pursues a much slower course in cattle than in horses. 1904 *Q. Rev.* July 120 The 'fly districts' where nagana disease is rife. 1925 *Times* 29 Dec. 11/3 It was believed that wild game..formed a permanent reservoir from which tsetses could convey 'nagana' to domestic stock.

Nagged (nægd), *ppl. a.* [-ed [1].] Annoyed, irritated.

1893 Kate D. Wiggin *Polly Oliver* ix. (1894) 100 Existence was wearing a particularly dismal aspect on that afternoon. ..He felt 'nagged', injured, blue, out of sorts with fate.

Naggish (næ·giʃ), *a.*[2] [f. Nag *sb.*[1] + -ish.] Of horses: Suggestive of a nag; small, inferior.

a 1800 *Spirit Farmer's Museum* (1801) 204, I see some here in gay coats, mounted on naggish horses.

Naggy (næ·gi), *a.*[2] [f. Nag *sb.*[1] + -y [1].] Of horses: Inferior in size or quality; naggish.

a 1861 T. Winthrop *John Brent* vii. 68 The little villain's mount was a red roan, a Flat-head horse, rather naggy, but perfectly hardy and wiry.

Naiad. Add: 2. A stage in the development of an insect from the larva; = Nymph 3.

1929 *Encycl. Brit.* VII. 570/2 Dragon-flies..pass through an incomplete metamorphosis and their nymphs or naiads are aquatic.

Nail, *sb.* 13. a. Add: *nail file, polish.*

1922 F. Courtenay *Physical Beauty* 47 When you have shaped the external edge of the nails with a fine pair of scissors, finish with emery or a steel *nail file.

14. a. *nail factory, machine* (earlier example), *mill*; **nail-gall,** a nail-shaped gall produced on the leaves of the lime by the mite *Phytoptus tiliæ*; **nail-plate** (earlier example); **nail-set,** a driving punch for nails; **nail-stubb,** a worn horse-shoe nail; a stub-nail.

1833 H. Barnard in *Maryland Hist. Mag.* XIII. 374, I found my old friend..who took me to see..a *nail factory [etc.]. 1879 *Encycl. Brit.* X. 46/1 The lime-leaf '*nail-galls' of *Phytoptus tiliae* closely resemble the 'trumpet-galls' formed on American vines by a species of Cecidomyia. 1819 E. Dana *Geog. Sk.* 77 Zanesville is..at the falls, whereon various mills are erected..including..an oil mill, *nail machine, and woolen factory. 1849 *Rep. U.S. Comm. Patents, Agric.* (1850) 93 Within its present limits are about fifty cotton factories..seven rolling, slitting, and *nail mills. 1797 *Essex Inst. Hist. Coll.* LIV. 107 Agreed with Mr. Allen to work at eight shillings pr. ton..cutting every kind of rods and dubble for iron hoops or *nail plates. 1927 R. A. Freeman *A Certain Dr. Thorndyke* II. xviii, Carpenters don't fix mouldings on with screws. They use nails and punch them in with a '*nail-set' and stop the holes with putty. 1851 Melville *Moby Dick* cxiii. (1926) 483 Look ye, blacksmith, these are the gathered *nail-stubbs of the steel shoes of racing horses.

b. *nail-driver* (transf. examples).

1823 J. F. Cooper *Pilot* I. viii. 106 The cannon, above which were painted the several quaint names of 'boxer',.. 'exterminator', and 'nail-driver'. 1872 *Life of Bill Hickman* 54 (Th.), I had a nail-driver [*sc.* a horse], very swift, and no end to his bottom.

Nail, *v.* 8. a. (Add example.)

1876 *Coursing Calendar* 303 Napoleon..turned twice, and nailed his hare in a hedge.

Nail-hole. Add: 2. The notch in the blade of a pocket-knife into which the thumb-nail is put to open it.

1839 *Ure's Dict. Arts* I. 380 The small recess called the nail hole, used in opening the knife, is made while it is still hot by means of a chisel.

Nail-rod. 1. b. (Earlier examples.)

1813 *Niles' Weekly Reg.* V. 290/1 Of iron.—..nail rods and nails, implements of husbandry, etc. 1868 *Rep. U.S. Commissioner Agric.* (1869) 433 The most convenient method of destroying the bugs is by using a pair of tongs made of nail-rod.

Nail-tool. (Later U.S. examples.)

1779 in *Narragansett Hist. Reg.* I. 93 Made nails and mended the nail tool. *Ibid.* 97 Made nail tools and hammer.

Naked. A. *adj.* 17. Add: **naked boys,** the meadow saffron or autumn crocus.

1738 Deering *Catal. Plants*, Meadow Saffron flowers in November without Leaves, whence Gardiners call them *Naked Boys*. 1789 G. White *Jrnls.* (1931) 343 *Colchicum autumnale*, naked boys, blows.

Name, *sb.* Add: 1. c. *Stock Exchange.* The ticket bearing the name of the purchaser of stock which is handed over to the selling stockbroker on name-day or ticket-day.

1907 Poley & Gould *Stock Exch.* 178 It is called the ticket or name day because of the passing of tickets or names on that day. 1912 *Q. Rev.* July 98 In order to run the faster in the settling room beneath the Stock Exchange 'passing names'.

15. (in sense 'bearing a name') *name-label, -ribbon*; *name-daughter* (later example); **name-flower,** used with reference to a person, the flower which has the same name as the person; **name-piece, -story,** in a book containing several pieces or stories, that piece or story whose title is given to the whole book; **name-worthy** *a.*, worthy of being named or mentioned.

1891 Stevenson *Lett.* Nov. (1901) II. 241, I shall begin to despair of everything but my *name-daughter. 1907 Quiller-Couch *Major Vigoureux* ii. 20 Glorious trumpet daffodils!..Major [Narcisse] Vigoureux delighted in them. Were they not his *name-flower? 1909 *Daily Chron.* 28 Oct. 4/5 The bride herself held a large white bouquet of her name flowers. 1910 *Westm. Gaz.* 14 Mar. 11/2 Affixing red *name-labels to their seats in the Council Chamber. 1924 *Glasgow Herald* 24 Apr. 4 The *name-piece of the volume is a genealogical..account of this branch of the..family. 1905 *Daily Chron.* 23 Feb. 6/5 *Name-ribbons may have to be changed. 1927 *Observer* 24 Apr. 8/4 There is an air of strain, as if she were attempting—at any rate in the *name-story (the others are nearer her usual vein)—to achieve a high-flown style and atmosphere outside her scope. 1922 *Chambers's Cycl. Eng. Lit.* III. 693/1 *The Growth of Love, Prometheus the Fire-giver* (1883), *Eros & Psyche* (1885), are *nameworthy poems.

Nameable, *a.* 2. (Earlier U.S. example.)

1780 J. Adams 26 *Lett. Revol. Amer.* (1789) 23 The sixth talk is to shew, 'that no person, in America, is of so much influence, power, or credit, that his death, or corruption, by English money, could be of any nameable consequence'.

Name-day. Add:

3. *Stock Exchange.* In the sale of registered securities: That day (of the days over which the settlement extends) on which the seller receives from the buyer a ticket giving the name, address, and other particulars of the person into whose name the securities are to be transferred. Also called *ticket-day*.

1902 *Encycl. Brit.* XXV. 23/2 The second day, when there are three, and the second and third days, when there are four, are the 'ticket days' or 'name days'. 1907 [see *Name *sb.* 1 c].

Nanny (næ·ni). Also nanna. A child's form of address to a nurse; hence, a children's nurse.

1864 *Chambers's Jrnl.* Sept. 506/1 Don't you know I'm a locomotive, and that you should always shunt yourself on to a siding when you hear *me* coming, Nanny? 1901 *Punch* 4 Dec. 405/2 Please, Nanna, don't turn on the dark. 1912 A. Neil Lyons *Clara* i. 3 That little boy was..inured to the coming and going of 'nannies'. 1927 A. P. Herbert *Misleading Cases* xviii. 132 His brothers and sisters, his aged Nanny, and various domestics.

Nap, *sb.*[3] Add: 4. *U.S.* Temper, anger. Cf. Birse *sb.*[1] 2.

1845 J. J. Hooper *Taking Census* i. 155 This information brought our nap right up. 1849 D. Nason *Jrnl.* 112 The bootblack, having got his nap up, came round very cautiously.

Nap, *sb.*[5] 2. Add: *Nap hand*: a 'hand' which will probably take all five tricks in the game of nap; a strong hand. Also *fig.*

1899 *Captain* I. 369/2 He showed me the way to deal myself a 'nap' hand, no matter who shuffled the cards.

c. A tip that a horse is certain to win.

1895 *Starting Price* 30 Mar. 1/2 Our 'Outsider's' nap of Docker for the Hainton Stakes. 1927 *Daily Tel.* 10 May 6 A tip is a tip that a horse may win; a nap relates to a horse that is certain to win.

Nap (næp), *v.*[4] [f. *Nap *sb.*[5] 2 c.] *trans.* To recommend (a horse) as a certain winner.

1927 *Daily Express* 22 June 17/7 Great Chum napped for White City Cup Final.

Napa (næ·pă). Also **nappa.** [The name of a county and town in California, U.S.A.] Leather prepared from sheep- or goat-skin by a special tawing process. Also *attrib.*

1897 C. T. Davis *Manuf. Leather* (ed. 2) 275 The staking machine..can be adjusted to any kind of leather, including napa. 1903 Flemming *Pract. Tanning* 49 The making of Napa leather. The cheapest tannage by which sheepskins are tanned is the Napa tannage, so called because it originated in Napa, Cal. 1921 B. E. Ellis *Gloves & Glove Trade* 58 'Nappa' gloves are made from tawed leathers. 1928 *Daily Sketch* 7 Aug. 14/2 We can buy washable nappa, suède, kid and antelope.

Nape, *sb.*[1] 2. b. (Modern example.)

1884 Goode *Nat. Hist. Aquatic Anim.* 201 George's fish are very fat fish with white 'napes'.

Napkin, *sb.* 4. **napkin-ring** (earlier example).

1686 *Inventory* in *Narragansett Hist. Reg.* III. 105, 18 Napkins & 9 Napkin Rings.

Napoleon. 2. For 'top-boot' read 'long boot'.

3. (Later examples.)

1880 *Harper's Mag.* May 917/1 The artillery is almost entirely the old brass Napoleon. 1897 *Outing* XXX. 80/1 These gun companies were each supplied with one 12-pounder Napoleon gun and one Gatling gun.

4. b. = *Nap *sb.*[5] 2 c.

1895 *Starting Price* 23 Mar. 1/1 With ruinous 'all day wires' and extortionately priced 'Napoleons' we will have nothing to do.

Napoo (năpū), *int.*, *a.* and *v.* Also **napooh.** *colloq.* [Corruption of F. (*il n'y e*)*n a plus* there is no more.] a. *int.* Finished; gone; done for; 'nothing doing'. b. *adj.* Finished; good for nothing; dead; useless. c. *v. trans.* To do for; to finish, kill or destroy.

1915 'Ian Hay' *First Hundred Thou.* 302 You say 'Na pooh!' when you push your plate away after dinner...' Poor Bill got na-poohed by a rifle-grenade yesterday.' 1917 W. J. Locke *Red Planet* xvi. 194 Instinctively I stretched out my hand. He laughed. 'Napoo. You must take it as gripped.' 1919 J. B. Morton *Barber of Putney* xv. 253 'Can't do nothing,' said Curly, ''e's napoo.' *Ibid.* 301 Even if they themselves were na-pooed, they'd hate to think of the lousy Boche living in their home. 1925 N. Venner *Imperfect Impostor* i, If you haven't got a job to do, you're a washout. You might as well be napood right off. 1929 Priestley *Good Comp.* III. ii. 519 She [*sc.* a motor-car] was napoo before I got up to Newcastle.

Nappe (næp). [ad. F. *nappe* (Nape *sb.*[2]) table-cloth.] 1. *Hydraulics.* The sheet of water that falls over a weir or similar surface.

1906 Horton *Weir Experiments* (*U.S. Geol. Surv., Water-Supply* etc. No. 150) 7 The French term 'nappe' suggesting the curved surface of a cloth hanging over the edge of a table, has been fittingly used to designate the overfalling sheet of water. 1923 F. C. Lea *Hydraulics* 81 The sheet of water flowing over a weir or through a notch is generally called the vein, sheet, or nappe.

2. *Geol.* A recumbent fold or anticline of a special character. Also *Comb.*

1927 L. W. Collet *Struct. Alps* 10 According to Haug, a nappe is *a recumbent anticline*.., the reversed limb of which has partly disappeared owing to stretching. 1929 P. G. H. Boswell *Nappe Theory in Alps* 122 The structure of the Romande nappe-mountains is extraordinarily complex.

Nappy (næ·pi), *sb.*[3] Nursery and colloquial name for Napkin.

1927 W. E. Collinson *Contemp. Eng.* 7.

Narcissine (naɹsi·səin), *a.* Add: 2. Resembling, or of the nature of, Narcissus (see next); loving or admiring oneself.

1911 Max Beerbohm *Zuleika Dobson* ii, Yet was there nothing Narcissine in her spirit. Her love for her own image was not cold æstheticism.

Narcissism (naɹsi·siz'm). [ad. G. *Narzissismus*, f. the name of *Narcissus*, a beautiful youth who fell in love with his own reflection in a fountain (Ovid *Metam.* III. 370) + -ism.] Excessive love or admiration of oneself and all that pertains to oneself.

1916 E. Jones tr. *Ferenczi's Contrib. Psycho-Anal.* 198 Auto-erotism and narcissism are thus the omnipotent stages of erotism. 1921 *Nature* 23 June 516 The recent work of the Freud school on narcissism. 1925 *Contemp. Rev.* Nov. 631 The maintenance and dominance..of the individual's Narcissism tends always to regressive behaviour.

Narcissist (naɹsi·sist). [f. as prec. + -ist.] A person affected with narcissism.

1930 B. Russell *Conq. Happiness* I. i. 22 A narcissist,.. inspired by the homage paid to great painters, may become an art student.

Narcissistic (naɹsisi·stik), *a.* [ad. G. *narzissistisch*, or f. as prec. + -istic.] Of or pertaining to narcissism; marked by excessive love of self.

1916 E. Jones tr. *Ferenczi's Contrib. Psycho-Anal.* 174, I was just striving to make clear to a patient her excessive ambition, arising from narcissistic fixation. 1920 B. Low *Psycho-Anal.* 66 The character-reactions which bridge the gulf between the two sets of Narcissistic and Sublimating desires. 1925 *Contemp. Rev.* Nov. 631 Narcissistic emotion unrelated to external reality.

Narcoleptic (nāɹkole·ptik), *a.* [f. Narcolepsy: cf. Epileptic.] Of the nature of narcolepsy.

1904 G. S. Hall *Adolescence* I. 264 Sometimes a sense of fatigue, lassitude, and sleepiness, rarely narcoleptic, may supervene.

Narragansett (nærăgæ·nsĕt). *U.S.* [The name of a tribe of American Indians and of a bay on the east coast of America.]

1. *Narragansett pacer.* (See quot. 1859.)

1809 W. Irving *Knickerb.* IV. iii. (1825) 152 Stoffel Brinkerhoff..made his triumphant entrance into town, riding on a Naraganset pacer. 1835 *Knickerbocker Mag.* V. 303 But a person now jumped out from our row, with the quickness of a Narragansett pacer. 1859 Bartlett *Dict. Amer.*, *Narragansett Pacer*, a breed of Rhode Island horses once very famous; but although we often hear of *Narragansett pacers*, there is now no particular breed so called. 1886 *Harper's Mag.* July 166/2 Colonial aristocracy..perhaps best known for their breed of Narragansett pacers.

2. *ellipt.* a. A Narragansett pacer.

1826 J. F. Cooper *Last of Mohicans* ii, Giving her Narraganset a smart cut of the whip. 1845 S. Judd *Margaret* III. 398 Nimrod..made us a purchase of some beautiful Narragansetts with draught and carriage horses.

b. A hog.

1852 *Trans. Mich. Agric. Soc.* III. 332 Swine—variously known as narragansetts, alligators,..and flea breeders.

Narrow. A. *adj.* 1. c. Add: *narrow axe*, an axe having a short cutting edge.

1641 *Connecticut Public Rec.* I. 444 A broad axe, a narrow axes, wimbell and chessells. 1755 *Lett. to Washington* I. 136 Broadaxes are wanted, narrow axes I have been obliged to order some to be made.

7. *narrow-beamed.*

1927 *Observer* 14 Aug. 7/4 Agile, narrow-beamed cars, with plenty of acceleration and 'safety-first' brake-power, are his ideal.

Narrow, *v.* 1. Add: Also with *down*.

1906 L. J. Vance *Terence O'Rourke* II. ii. 214 Then it narrowed down to a mere contest of endurance.

2. Also with *down* and *in*.

1885 J. Morris *Kotaka* xi. 106 The entire force and volume of the Fuzikawa being here narrowed down to the width of the gorge. 1885 Sir J. W. Dawson *Egypt & Syria* ii. 39 It is just where the broad expanse of alluvium..is narrowed in by that great promontory. 1889 Stevenson *Master of Ballantrae* iv, The family was now so narrowed down (indeed, there were..just the father and the two sons) that it was possible to break the entail.

Nary, *a.* (Earlier examples.)

1821 *Massachusetts Spy* 14 Feb. (Th.) He asked her whether she was most fond of writing prose or poetry. 'Nary one,' says she, 'I writes small hand.' 1834 Seba Smith *Sel. Lett. Major Downing* 28 Nary side couldn't pull up tother.

Nasalism. (Add example.)

1884 *Proc. Roy. Soc. Edin.* (1887) XXXII. 349 The Yankee nasalism is another familiar instance of the same kind.

Nasalizable (nē¹·zăləizăb'l), *a.* [f. Nasalize *v.* + -able.] Capable of being pronounced nasally.

1872 Haldeman *Pennsylvania Dutch* 11 This vowel being nasalisable.

Nascence. (Later example.)

1901 *Science* 21 June 983/1 Formations often disappear through the agency of fires, floods, mankind, etc., in which cases new formations may arise by nascence.

Nascently (næ·sĕntli), *adv.* [f. Nascent *a.* + -ly [2].] In a nascent manner; incipiently.

1930 *Times Lit. Suppl.* 29 Apr. 264/2 Notions of the type of mana or orenda are of 'a nascently philosophic order'.

Nasical, *a.* **Nasically,** *adv.* [See under Nasik.] (Examples.)

1883 *Encycl. Brit.* XV. 215/2 The sum of any number and the 8 numbers 3 from it, diagonally, and in its row and column, is the constant Nasical summation. *Ibid.* 216/1 The n^3 cabelets of this solid square [might] be Nasically filled by the introduction of a new letter t.

Nastic (na·stik), *a.* *Bot.* [ad. Gr. type ναστικ-ός f. νάσσειν to press close, ναστ-ός squeezed together: see -ic.] Applied to movements of plants whose nature is not determined by external stimulus.

1912 tr. *Strasburger's Text-Bk. Bot.* (ed. 4) 300 Nastic movements..are curvatures which bring about a particular position in relation to the plant and not to the direction of the stimulus. 1929 Sir J. C. Bose *Growth & Tropic Movem. Plants* 216.

Nasute (nē¹·ziut), *a.* Add: 3. Having a pronounced proboscis or nose; nose-shaped.

1884 J. Hall in *Geol. Mag.* 560 In other forms, the anterior extremity becomes nasute or rostrate.

Nat (nāt). [Burmese, f. Skt. नाथ *nāthá* lord.] In Burmah, a spirit or demon.

1824 in G. H. Gough *Med. Traveller* (1826) 82 Carved images..are to be seen.., the supposed representatives of different *nats* or demons. 1858 C. T. W. *Six Months in Brit. Burmah* i. 13 The Nats who guard the royal city, palace, and umbrella. 1923 *Blackw. Mag.* Aug. 149/1 We had been talking..of folk-lore, superstitions, witches, djinns, nats, spooks, ghouls and other inventions of primitive man.

b. *Comb.*, as *nat-worship, -worshipper*.

1833 *Let.* in F. Wayland *Mem. A. Judson* (1853) II. 56 The best outward test is to have refrained from rum, *nat-worship, &c. 1910 *Hastings's Encycl. Relig. & Ethics* III. 21/1 The practical everyday religion of the whole of the Burmese peoples is Animism, called generally in Burmese 'Nat-worship'. 1906 Forlong *Faiths of Man* I. 257 s.v. Barmah, *Nat-worshippers. 1923 *Blackw. Mag.* Feb. 183/2 They are all Nat or spirit worshippers.

Natal (nătæ·l), *sb.*[2] The name of a province of the Union of South Africa, used attributively in the names of (varieties of) plants and animals found there, as **Natal lily,** a bulbous flowering plant, *Imantophyllum miniatum*; **Natal mahogany,** a South African timber tree, *Kiggelaria drageana*; **Natal plum,** a flowering plant, *Carissa grandifolia*, of the dog-bane family, whose fruit resembles a plum.

1904 *Amateur Gardener's Diary* 184 *Natal Lily.., half hardy evergreen plants, with showy orange flowers. 1911 *Encycl. Brit.* XVII. 399/1 *Kiggelaria Drageana*..is known as *Natal mahogany. 1911 *Ibid.* XIX. 253/2 The amatungulu or *Natal plum..is one of the few wild plants with edible fruit.

Nation, *sb.*[1] Add: 5. d. (Earlier examples.)

1725 G. Chicken in *Trav. Amer. Col.* 98 John Sharp Indian Trader.., some time before the said Sharp came from the Cherokees, went to one of the Towns in the said Nation. 1740 *Coll. S. Carol. Hist. Soc.* IV. 83, I desire also that you will send me..the Indian presents, with power to distribute them, for much Depends upon the Nations.

9. *Comb.*, **nation-wide,** as wide as a nation; extending over or affecting a whole nation.

1920 *Edin. Rev.* July 110 He derides the idea of a nation-wide Radical Party. 1925 E. S. Jones *Christ of Indian Road* iii. 72 A year ago began a struggle in South India that has had nation-wide consequences.

Nation. A. *adv.* (Later example.)

1884 'Mark Twain' *Huck. Finn* xix, Looky here, Bilgewater,..I'm nation sorry for you, but you ain't the only person that's had troubles like that.

B. *adj.* (Earlier example.)

1765 *Moving Times* (Bartlett 1877) I believe, my friend, you're very right, They'll get a nation profit by 't.

C. *sb.* (U.S. examples.)

1884 'Mark Twain' *Huck. Finn* xiii, Why, how in the nation did they ever git into such a scrape? *Ibid.* xv, Why, what in the nation do you mean? 1892 — *£1,000,000 Banknote* (1893) 26 What in the nation she could find to laugh about, *I* couldn't see, but there it was.

National. A. *adj.* 1. (Later examples.)

1878 Blackley in *19th Cent.* Nov. 834 (art.) National Insurance: A cheap, practical and popular means of abolishing poor rates. 1913 *Q. Rev.* Apr. 510 The labourer has gained something in a pecuniary sense from..national insurance.

5. **national bank** (earlier example).

1838 *Democratic Rev.* Feb. I. 52 That portion of the plan ..which involved a present non-committalism on the question of a National Bank.

B. *sb.* Add: 4. b. (See quot.)

1904 J. Westlake *Internat. Law* I. 3 All the members of a state, whether sovereign, subjects or citizens, are denoted by the convenient term of its nationals.

5. = *Grand National*: see *Grand *a.* 12.

1909 *Westm. Gaz.* 26 Mar. 12/1 A horse that had never run a National. 1924 Galsworthy *Forest* III. i. 73 My brother 's got a horse running in the National next spring— wonder if he'll think of putting me anything on?

Nationali·stically, *adv.* [f. Nationalistic *a.* + -al + -ly [2].] On nationalistic lines.

1913 H. W. Robinson *Relig. Ideas Old Test.* 32 The redemption is differently conceived and nationalistically applied.

Nationalize, *v.* 1. Add: Also *absol.*

1922 *Times Lit. Suppl.* 27 July 483/2 The Turk, still thinking in terms of religions,..suddenly determined to Westernize and nationalize.

Native, *sb.* 4. (Earlier and later examples of phr. *to astonish the natives*.)

1802 W. Irving *Salmagundi* Wks. I. 140 He was determined to astonish the natives a few. *Ibid.* 143 Young gentlemen who come out from Birmingham to astonish the natives. 1901 Marah E. Ryan *Montana* vi. 96 Much of her afternoon was spent there..fashioning a party gown with which to astonish the natives.

b. *To go native*: see *Go *v.* 48 b.

Native, *a.* Add: 12. c. *Native son*, a Californian. *U.S.*

1916 'B. M. Bower' *Phantom Herd* ii. 27 He..backed out of the way of the Native Son who sprawled himself over the table corner.

Nativism. 1. (Earlier example.)

1844 H. Greeley *Amer. Conflict* (1865) I. 168/2 The baleful 'Nativism' which had just broken out in the great cities, ..had alarmed the foreign-born population.

Nativity. 6. (Modern example.)

1880 Skene *Celtic Scot.* III. 221 There are several kinds of nativity or bondage.

Nattier blue. [f. the name of Jean-Marc *Nattier* (1685–1766), a French painter.] A shade of blue much used by Nattier.

[1909 *Westm. Gaz.* 4 May 5/3 We have quoted the painter Nattier for the soft shade of blue he used.] 1912 *Queen* 4 May p. xvii, The bonnet is fashioned of Nattier blue satin. 1918 W. J. Locke *Rough Road* xxi. 261 His own bedroom with the satinwood furniture and nattier blue hangings.

Natural, *sb.* 1. (Later U.S. example.)

1748 in *Maryland Hist. Mag.* VI. 229, I have taken Wife —like a good Christian and am become a Natural of the country or country born as some call themselves.

13. *colloq.* Short for *natural life*.

1925 Wodehouse *Carry on, Jeeves* iii. 59, I didn't want to have England barred to me for the rest of my natural.

Natural, *a.* Add: 19. *Comb.*, as *natural-coloured*.

1927 T. Woodhouse *Artificial Silk* 85 Natural-coloured artificial silk yarns.

Naturalist. Add: 3. c. One who deals in or sells cage animals, pets, dogs, and the like, or stuffed specimens of animals; also, a skilled stuffer and mounter of animals, a taxidermist.

1863 *Cornhill Mag.* Jan. 120 Some of us may have had the misfortune to see some special pet carried off by death, and to have sent it to a 'naturalist,' to be stuffed.

Nature, *sb.* Add: 13. d. *All nature*, everything, every one, 'all creation'. *Like all nature*, completely. *colloq. U.S.*

1819 *Massachusetts Spy* 3 Nov. 3/1 Father and I have just returned from the balloon—all nature was there, and more too. 1825 J. Neal *Bro. Jonathan* II. 93 Hurra for you—that beats all nater! 1840 C. F. Hoffman *Greyslaer* III. xiv. 254 The poor critter would have been sucked under, smashed on the rocky bottom, and dragged off like all natur.

15. *nature-folk, -lover, -loving* (adj.); **nature study,** the study of natural objects and phenomena, esp. as a subject taught in schools.

1927 Peake & Fleure *Peasants & Potters* 8 They had settled down into a routine, as had many *nature-folk the world over before European industrialism touched them in the last century. 1902 *Chambers's Jrnl.* July 426/2 Many an angler and *nature-lover is a veritable 'prisoner of Hope'. 1913 *Engl. Illustr. Mag.* June 254 It is scarcely possible to find a mountain track or woody dell..which has not fascinated and inspired this *nature-loving poet. 1897 Comstock (*title*) Insect Life, an introduction to *nature-study and a guide for teachers, students and others. 1902 *Chambers's Jrnl.* Oct. 683/1 The Nature-study Exhibition which was held at the Botanical Gardens, London, this autumn. 1911 *Q. Rev.* Jan. 113 Nature-study and school gardening have made..remarkable progress of late years.

Naturist. Add: Also *attrib.*

1930 *Observer* 27 Apr. 18/4 They..spent a holiday in a naturist colony on an island in the Seine.

Naught. A. *sb.* 1. d. (Later U.S. example.)

1781 *Essex Inst. Hist. Coll.* XXVI. 115 One of the French Captains..struck him in the head, and called him all to naught.

Naught, *v.* Add: b. To bring to naught; to annihilate.

1913 Evelyn Underhill *Mystic Way* 137 It is the final disestablishment and 'naughting' of the separate will.

Nautic. B. *sb. pl.* Add: Also nautical exercises.

1904 G. S. Hall *Adolescence* II. 259 There was also special training in swimming and nautics, as rowing and sailing.

Navajo (næ·vāho). Also -joe, **Nabajo.** The name of a tribe of American Indians in northern Arizona and New Mexico, used *attrib.* esp. in *Navajo blanket*, a blanket made by the Navajos. b. The language of the Navajos.

a. 1834 A. Pike *Sketches* 90 In the door-way, too, stood an Indian girl with her Nabajo blanket, black, with a red border, and answering for a gown. 1846 Emory *Milit. Reconn.* 38 The cushions were of spotless damask, and the couch covered with a white Navajoe blanket. 1873 J. H. Beadle *Undevel. West* xxvi. 545 My horse, bridle, saddle, lariat, gun (a Spencer) and two Navajo blankets cost me two hundred dollars. 1895 *Congress. Rec.* 17 Jan. 1083/1, I have seen a great many Navajo blankets.

b. 1873 J. H. Beadle *Undevel. West* xxv. 524 John H. Van Order acted as interpreter from English into Spanish, and Jesus Alviso from Spanish into Navajo. Nearly all the employes understood a little Navajo, but not enough to interpret.

Navalist (nē¹·vălist). [f. Naval *a.* + -ist.] One who stresses the importance of having a strong navy.

1920 *Glasgow Herald* 30 Dec. 6/3 Mr. Daniels's rather flamboyant allusions to the American naval programme would be utilised by our domestic navalists. 1927 *Observer* 20 Mar. 16/4 'Neon'..is a good old-fashioned navalist and an obsolete politician.

Navarchy. Add: **3.** Naval power.
1903 Hardy *Dynasts* I. v. i, Those teeth of treble line In jaws of oaken wood Held open by the English navarchy.

Navel, *sb.* **4.** Add: **navel-stone,** a stone that is a navel (sense 2).
1922 A. E. Housman *Last Poems* 50 Mute's the midland navel-stone beside the singing fountain.

Navigable, *a.* **2. b.** (Earlier example.)
1887 *Nature* 13 Jan. 260/1 Captain Renard has recently sent in to the French Academy an account of his experiments with his so-called navigable balloon, *La France*, at Meudon.

Navigable (næ·vigăb'l), *sb. rare.* [f. the adj.] A dirigible balloon.
1888 W. N. Hutchinson in *Cassell's Family Mag.* (1889) 286/2 A small 'Navigable' has been steered against a breeze. 1908 H. G. Wells *War in Air* i. § 4 They started ironclads, they started submarines, they started navigables.

Navigate, *v.* Add: **1. c.** *U.S.* To walk steadily; to keep on one's course.
1904 *N.Y. Sun* 9 Aug. 10 She was so drunk that she could barely navigate. 1930 *Randolph Enterprise* (Elkins, W. Va.) 13 Feb. 1/1 The fellow was..hardly able to navigate as he was carrying a heavy load of Prohibition poison.

6. To manage, direct, sail or 'fly' (a balloon, airship, aeroplane, or the like) in the air.
1784 *Universal Mag.* LXXIV. Pref. p. ii, By imitating the action of..wings, sails, oars, and a rudder..we may be able to navigate a Globe [sc. a balloon] in any direction we please. 1877 *Design & Work* III. 603/1 To build it [an airship] in England, and navigate it to Zanzibar. 1910 *Blackw. Mag.* July 5/1 The pilot of an aeroplane is almost wholly occupied with navigating his craft. 1922 *Encycl. Brit.* XXX. 43/1 Not only had the flying-boats on war service to be navigated but the pilot and observer had also to 'navigate' a bomb to its desired target.

b. To travel or sail through (the air).
1901 *Chambers's Jrnl.* Mar. 207/2 Count Zeppelin's airship,..with a row of seventeen balloons inside, for navigating the air, has also pointed cigar-like ends. 1907 *Cornhill Mag.* May 609 Grotesque and fantastic schemes for navigating the air were put forward. 1927 C. L. M. Brown *Conquest of Air* 8 Stories of wizards and witches who navigated the upper air with the assistance of tubs and broomsticks.

Navigation. Add: **1. d.** The action or practice of travelling through the air by means of aircraft; flying.
1870 *Wonderf. Balloon Ascents* II. ix. 163 The idea of aerial navigation by means of an apparatus heavier than the atmosphere. 1910 *Blackw. Mag.* July 12/2 The safe navigation of the air. 1920 *Act 10 & 11 Geo. V* c. 80 § 2 Limited to aircraft of any special description, or engaged in any special kind of navigation.

2. b. The art or science of directing the movements of aircraft of any kind. More fully *aerial navigation.*
1909 *Chambers's Jrnl.* Oct. 657/2 Devoting their time entirely to the subject of aerial navigation. 1922 *Encycl. Brit.* XXX. 14/1 Aerial navigation, as distinct from piloting with the ground in view, developed tardily everywhere, though first in Britain.

7. a. (Modern example.)
1926 Bennett *Lion's Share* i. 7 Probably the largest yacht that had ever threaded that ticklish navigation.

Navigator. Add: **1. b.** In full *aerial navigator*: One who practises or is experienced in the navigation of aircraft; an airman.
1784 *Universal Mag.* LXXIV. 20/1 But they soon lost sight of our aerial navigators. 1825 [see Navigator 1. transf.].

Navvy, *v.* Add: Also *transf.*
1918 'Berta Ruck' *Disturbing Charm* I. ii. 11 Charging them eight times what my price used to be when I navvied for that paper regularly.

Navy[1]. Add: **5. c.** A navy revolver.
c1875 'Mark Twain' *Sketches* Wks. XIX. 150 She turned on that smirking Spanish fool like a wild cat, and out with a 'navy' and shot him dead in open court. 1881 *Harper's Mag.* Dec. 956/2 Judge put hand under pillow, drew out 'navy' and fired—*through a looking glass.*

6. (Chiefly articles supplied to the navy) *navy bean, biscuit, bread, jacket, officer, -plug, revolver* (earlier example); **navy bullet,** a bullet used with a navy revolver; **navy catapult** (see quot.); **navy register** (example); **navy stroke,** the style of rowing practised in the navy; **navy-yard** (later U.S. examples).
1903 A. Adams *Log Cowboy* xii. 77 Our supply of flour and *navy beans was running rather low. 1867 T. Lackland *Homespun* II. 216 The people not only want the Word, but they want it as hard and dry as a *navy biscuit. 1847 *Rep. U.S. Comm. Patents* (1848) 374 The '*navy bread' is usually made out of the coarser particles of the meal. 1873 Joaquin Miller *Unwritten Hist.* xxvii. (1876) 345 Was it possible that this man..could still live with a *navy bullet through his body fired at two feet distance. 1914 Twenty *Dict. Nav. & Milit. Terms* 161 *Navy *Catapult*, a device for launching hydro-aeroplanes from a ship by means of compressed air. 1864 in *Maryland Hist. Mag.* XXI. 300 He..had on his *navy jacket with bright buttons and pants of the same dark blue. 1841 *Southern Lit. Messenger* VII. 12/1 The report too is current among *Navy officers, and generally believed by them. a1909 'O. Henry' *Roads of Destiny* xxi. 357 It seems that the only maritime aid I am to receive from the United States is some *navy-plug to chew. 1841 *Southern Lit. Messenger* VII. 4/1 Statistics..furnished by the *Navy Register will show that of the three Presidents [etc.]. a1861 T. Winthrop *Canoe & Saddle* 26 This machine ..is called a Six-shooter, an eight-inch *navy revolver. 1904 Kipling *Traffics & Discov.* 143 Aren't they rowing *Navy-stroke yonder? 1842 *Knickerbocker Mag.* XIX. 107 The General landed at the *navy-yard. 1886 *Harper's Mag.* Sept. 619/1 The fact of establishing a navy-yard.

Nay. B. *sb.* **1.** (Earlier U.S. examples of special sense.)
1774 in *Coll. Vermont Hist. Soc.* I. 8 Passed in the affirmative—all yeas, no nays. 1807 *Steele Papers* II. 492 A Bill has passed the H.R. repealing the duty on salt with only 5 nays. 1871 *Trans. Ill. Agric. Soc.* VIII. 5 Mr. Dalton demanded the yeas and nays.

Nay-say, *v.* (Later example in sense 'deny'.)
1910 W. De Morgan *Affair of Dishonour* xxiii. 383 There might have been a rare company of wenches on the terrace for anything he could naysay.

Nazarenism (næ·zărĭniz'm). [f. Nazarene.] The principles, doctrines, or cult, of the Nazarenes.
1923 *Expository Times* Nov. 73/2 Here..the story of Jesus ends, and the story of Nazarenism begins.

Nazi (na·tsi). [Abbrev. of G. *nationalen Sozialisten* National Socialists.] Usually *pl.* or *collect.* The German National-Socialist party or its members. Also *attrib.*
1930 *Times* 19 Sept. 10/1 Herr Hitler, the leader of the victorious National-Socialists (Nazis), has very carefully refrained from saying anything... The authorities..are understood to be watching developments within the Nazi movement. 1931 W. Lewis *Hitler* 16 The Communist helps the police to beat and shoot the Nazis. *Ibid.* 57 The Democrats..have not been able to deal with the Nazi because of his Mastery of the Street.

Neanderthal (nĭæ·ndəɹtāl). [The name of a valley in Rhenish Prussia; see Neanderthaloid.] In common attrib. use with *man, race,* etc.: Of or belonging to the early type of man indicated by the skull found at Neanderthal.
[1864 Huxley in *Nat. Hist. Rev.* July 429 A series which shall lead by insensible gradations from the Neanderthal skull up to the most ordinary forms.] 1908 *Hastings's Encycl. Relig. & Ethics* I. 564/1 The Neanderthal human remains..presented..remarkable peculiarities. 1922 *Encycl. Brit.* XXX. 145/2 Neanderthal man is now revealed as an uncouth race with an enormous flattened head, very prominent eye-brow ridges and a coarse face.
Hence **Nea·ndertha·ler,** a Neanderthal man; **Neandertha·lian** *adj.*
1920 H. G. Wells *Outl. Hist.* ix. § 3 The Tasmanians were not racially Neanderthalers. *Ibid.*, The tremendous advance they display upon their Neanderthalian predecessors.

Neanthropic (nīˌænþrǫ·pik), *a.* [f. Gr. νέ-ος Neo- + Anthropic.] Of or belonging to the second or modern half of the geological period which is marked by the existence of man.
1894 J. W. Dawson *Meeting-place of Geol. & Hist.* i. 27 The modern, or anthropic [period], is..divisible into two sections—the early modern, or *palanthropic*..; and the *neanthropic*, extending onward to the present time. 1928 V. G. Childe *Most Anc. East* ii. 29 Implements which are allied..to those introduced into Europe with the first neanthropic stocks in Aurignacian times.

Neap, *a.* **1.** Add: Also *neap rise* (see quot.).
1888 *Encycl. Brit.* XXIII. 369/2 The height between high-water mark at neap tide and mean low-water mark at spring tide is called the neap rise.

Near, *adv.*[2] Add: **6.** (Later example.)
1929 *Wisconsin Alumni Mag.* Apr. 227 Olin isn't near as bad as I supposed him to be.

13. (Later example.)
1922 Mulford *Tex* xi. 156 He glowed with pride as he realized that he, perhaps, was nearer to Tex Jones than any man in town.

21. Delete †*Obs.* and add recent (chiefly U.S.) examples: as *near-absinthe, -beer, -engagement, -savagery, -seal, -smile, -star, -wool; near-true* adj.
1928 *Daily Express* 27 Apr. 12/4 The aspirant painters.. drink *near-absinthe instead of beer. 1909 *N.Y. Even. Post* (semi-weekly ed.) 23 Aug. 2 The refusal of the Cities Commission to prohibit the sale of imitation beer, commonly known as '*near beer'. 1920 *Nation* (N.Y.) 31 Jan. 136/1 A dozen men..had..been having a drink of near-beer in a café. 1926 *Ladies' Home Jrnl.* Apr. 24 The decision was based on..two broken engagements, one *near-engagement ..and several flirtations. 1912 J. H. Moore *Ethics & Educ.* 109 That state of *near-savagery when any low-browed irresponsible who can get a gun in his hands is allowed to go out and shoot to death everything that has the breath of life in it. 1902 G. H. Lorimer *Lett. Self-made Merchant* xiii. 184 He..examined every hair of his hide, as if he expected to find it *near-seal. 1911 Edna Ferber *Dawn O'Hara* iii. 34 Assuming a *near-smile, she entered the room. 1928 *Sunday Express* 29 Apr. 5/2 They took to America 'A Night Out,' with so many stars and so many *near-stars that [etc.]. 1910 *Century Mag.* Apr. 891 Clothes and the Man. A *near-true story. By Edith Rickert. 1930 *Cambridge Daily News* 25 Sept. 3/2 Never having worn even *near-wool within rubbing distance of my skin.

Near, *a.* Add: **4. d.** Of clothing: That is worn close to the body.
1889 *Harper's Mag.* Aug. 485/1 When his suit of clothes wore out, he used to borrow mine..leaving me in the office alone with..a suit of very 'near' under-wear.

Nearabout, *adv. dial.* Also **nearabouts.** [See Near *adv.* 1 c and Abouts.] Nearly, almost.
a1878 [see Near *adv.* 5 b]. 1907 Quiller-Couch *Major Vigoureux* xxii. 225 The tide bein' nearabouts on the top of the flood.

Near East. [Near *a.* 4.] The south-eastern part of Europe; the Balkan States together with Asia Minor. (Also *Nearer East.*) Hence **Near-Ea·stern** *adj.* **Near-Ea·sterly** *adv.*
1869 *Wesleyan-Meth. Mag.* July (*heading*) Peeps at the Near East. 1891 J. L. Kipling *Beast & Man Ind.* iv. 84 There was once a time when in the nearer East..he [sc. the ass] was held in high honour. 1903 *Q. Rev.* Oct. 514 The history of the Near East teaches us that in that part of the world political knots are not untied but cut. 1906 *Ibid.* Jan. 284 Lord Salisbury and his successor have..skilfully withdrawn England from the Near-Eastern entanglements. 1909 *Daily Chron.* 25 Aug. 3/6 Near-Easterly. Bosnia and Herzegovina have figured recently in European politics. 1910 *Chambers's Jrnl.* Feb. 65/1 That Far East which is so rapidly becoming the Near East. 1915 *War Illustr.* III. 260 (*heading*) Our Day of Crisis in the Near East. 1915 *Boston Globe* 3 Nov. 10/1 The Near Eastern question. 1923 Edith Wharton *Son at Front* 10 Poor little circumscribed Paul Dastrey, whose utmost adventure had been.. an occasional six weeks in the Near East. 1924 *Times Trade & Engin. Suppl.* 29 Nov. 247/1 The Near East has done a fair amount of buying again.

Nearmost, *a.* (Add example.)
1913 E. Harrison Barker *Wayfaring in France* 468 It is almost a shriek when the wind strikes the nearmost crests [sc. of trees].

Near-sighted, *a.* Add: **1. b.** Adapted for short sight.
1926 W. J. Locke *Old Bridge* I. iv. 45 [He] looked at her apologetically through thick, near-sighted pince-nez.

Near-si·ghtedly, *adv.* In a near-sighted manner.
1909 *Daily Chron.* 11 Oct. 7/1 Dr. Shuttleworth blinked near-sightedly throughout the time he was in the witness box.

Neat, *sb.* **2. b.** Add: *neat beast, -beef, cattle* (earlier examples), *leather* (= Neat's leather), *stock.*
1624 *Essex Inst. Hist. Coll.* L. 235 All my Cattell nowe upon the farme..as *neat bests, horse bests, and swine. 1727 *Smithtown Rec.* 82 It is agreed on that the pounder shall have for pounding a horse four pence, for a net best four pence. 1755 in *Lett. to Washington* I. 135 Not under twelve shillings and sixpence per Hundred *Neet Beef. 1619 *Jrnl. Ho. Burg. Virginia* 13 No man without leave from the Governour shall kill any *Neat cattle whatsoever. 1648 *Maryland Archives* IV. 390 Certaine neate-cattle to the number of 27. 1776 *Coll. N.H. Hist. Soc.* IX. 263 Mens *Neat Leather Shoes of the best common sort. 1849 *Rep. U.S. Comm. Patents, Agric.* (1850) 94 It is estimated that there are in this county..fifteen thousand two hundred and eighty five *neat stock. 1868 *Rep. U.S. Commissioner Agric.* (1869) 427 The present winter (1868) he feeds forty-three head of neat stock, equivalent to thirty-four mature animals. 1882 *Rep. Maine Board Agric.* XVI. 265 The way is to fence off such a piece, and allow no neat stock or horses to run in it at any time.

Neb, *sb.* Add: **3. b.** (Example.)
1893 Stevenson *Catriona* xi, I couldna see the nebs of my ten fingers.

d. 'The pole of an ox-cart' (E.D.D.). *Neb ox,* a draught ox.
1710 *N.H. Probate Rec.* I. 650 All my household goods and four Cows, and a yoak of neb Oxen..to be for her own proper use. 1865 'Gail Hamilton' *Skirmishes* v. 7 Men left their oxen standing by the nebs.

Nebularization (ne·biŭlăraizē·ʃən). [f. Nebular *a.* + -ization.] The act or fact of becoming nebular.
1928 T. C. Chamberlin *Two Solar Families* 159 There may be spiralization that is not nebularization.

Nebulium. Add attrib. examples.
It is now believed that the 'nebulium' spectrum is not due to a new element but to some known (terrestrial) element in a special state.
1903 Agnes M. Clerke *Probl. Astrophysics* II. xxviii. 517 The spectrum is purely gaseous, and is dominated visually, with more than the usual emphasis, by the green nebulium line. 1928 A. S. Eddington *Stars & Atoms* 55 A terrestrial atom will be stimulated to give nebulium light.

Necessitated, *ppl. a.* **2.** (Later example.)
1857 A. & M. N. Ward *Husband in Utah* xvii. 194 Mrs. Farrow informed me of several sisters, who having inherited money from Eastern quarters, were immediately assailed by the necessitated priest.

Nece·ssitator. [f. Necessitate *v.* + -or.] = Necessitater.
1903 Hardy *Dynasts* I. vi. iii. 118 O Great Necessitator, heed us now!..Quicken the issue as Thou knowest how.

Neck, *sb.*[1] Add: **1. e.** Phrases. *To get (catch, take) it in the neck*: To be hard hit (by something); to be severely reprimanded or punished. *To speak (talk) through (the back of) one's neck*: To use extravagant or inaccurate words or language.
1892 *Congress. Rec.* 10 Mar. 1946/1 The gentleman says that the farmer gets it. Several Members:—Gets it in the neck. 1901 W. Irwin *Love Sonnets of a Hoodlum, Epilogue*, My hard-luck story, Showing how Vanity is still on deck And Humble Virtue gets it in the neck. 1903 A. Adams *Log Cowboy* xi. 175 Old Nat will get it in the neck this time, if that old girl dallies with him as she did with us. 1908 H. G. Wells *War in Air* ii. § 3 They'll get it in the neck in real earnest one of these days. 1914 D. O. Barnett *Letters* 31 Dec. (1915) 30 You probably don't know what a village looks like when it has caught it in the neck. 1915 'Ian Hay' *First Hundred Thou.* xviii. 263 Most people get it in the neck here, sooner or later. 1923 Wodehouse *Inimit. Jeeves* iii. 30 Something always comes along to give it you in the neck at the very moment when you're feeling most braced about things in general. 1928 H. C. McNeile *Female of Species* x. 169 I'd never forgive myself if one of you took it in the neck.
1904 *Daily Chron.* 1 Sept. 7/4 Next year..we shall see men bowling round the back of their necks as to-day we hear

them 'talking through them'. 1907 *Strand Mag.* June 672/1 We are not slow to tell them they are 'talking through the back of their neck'. 1910 E. W. Hornung *My Lord Duke* 104 He talked through his neck when we missed our shots. 1912 *Chambers's Jrnl.* Jan. 45/2, I wish you wouldn't talk through the back of your neck, Ransome. 1923 [see *Back *sb.*[1] 3 c].

3. e. (Further example.)
1903 A. H. Lewis *Boss* 174 Still I must say you went in up to your neck on sparks and voylets.

15. a. *neck-buckle, -gear, -ribbon, rope, -wear.* **c.** *neck-hold, -line.*
1767 *Essex Inst. Hist. Coll.* LIII. 298, 7 pair silver Sleeve Buttons, together with *Neck-Buckles, etc. 1890 Hardy *Melancholy Hussar* ii. in *3 Notable Stories* 167 His head would probably have been bent..but for his stiff *neck-gear. 1909 *Daily Chron.* 7 May 4/6 We were talking critically of neck-gear. 1905 *Ibid.* 23 Feb. 3/5 By means of a peculiar '*neck-hold' he can render his man unconscious. 1928 *Ibid.* 9 Aug. 13/1 It can relieve the *neckline of the black dinner dress. 1851 Alice Cary *Clovernook* 97 She selected a white muslin which she thought would do if she only had a new *neck-ribbon. 1877 Eliz. S. Phelps *Story of Avis* 371 The baby had pulled down Avis' pink neck-ribbon and her bright hair. 1822 J. Fowler *Jrnl.* 159 In the evening the Indeans [s]tole all the *neck Roaps of our Horses. 1910 *Westm. Gaz.* 15 Apr. 4/1 Similar good results have followed upon the use of looser *neck-wear. 1915 A. B. Reeve *Exploits of Elaine* v. 82 He was selecting his neckwear with a care that had been utterly foreign to him.

Neck, *v.*[1] Add: **4.** To fasten *together* by means of ropes put round the neck.
1857 D. Braman *Inform. Texas* iv. 73 The usual practice of farmers whenever they want work oxen, is to go to the prairie, and neck together, with ropes, as many pair of three and four-year-old steers as they desire.

5. *slang.* To drink.
1929 Masefield *Hawbucks* 135, I do wish..you'd chuck necking Scotch the way you do.

6. *U.S. slang. intr.* Of couples: To clasp one another round the neck; to hug.
1928 *Daily Tel.* 4 Sept. 7/5 High school children..whose favourite pastime is 'necking' in motor-cars in dark roads with the lights turned off.

Necked, *a.* Add: **4.** Caught by the neck.
1907 S. E. White *Arizona Nights* I. viii. 153 'No more necked calves', they announced.

Neck-handkerchief. (Earlier Amer. examples.)
1642 *Maryland Archives* IV. 95, 9 plaine neckcloths and 5 plaine neckhandkercheifes. 1683 *Connecticut Probate Rec.* I. 376 She gave to her gr[and]child..a Neck Handkercheire.

Neck-tie. b. (Earlier and later examples.)
1878 J. H. Beadle *Western Wilds* iii. 46 He had the pleasure of presiding at a 'necktie sociable', where two of the men who had robbed him were hanged. 1882 in *National Geog. Mag.* Aug. (1929) 247 If Found within the Limits of this City after Ten o'Clock p.m. this Night, you will be Invited to attend a Grand Neck-tie Party. 1919 T. K. Holmes *Man fr. Tall Timber* xxxiii. 421 If Larrabee ever comes back to Tall Timber there ought to be a necktie party for him.

Necro-. Add: **necro·phily** = *necrophilism*; **necrophili·stic** *a.*, of, pertaining to or resembling necrophilism.
1897 tr. *Ribot's Psychol. Emotions* 257, I pass over the extreme cases, those of *necrophily, or of sexual erethism. 1927 *Observer* 8 May 6/4 His circumstances and his griefs, and his disease fostered his necrophily. 1924 C. Gray *Surv. Contemp. Mus.* 185 The general public has taken to its great soft heart the *necrophilistic ardours of the *Valse Triste.*

Necromant. (Modern example.)
1887 A. Lang *Myth, Ritual & Relig.* I. 105 The power of Sorcerers and Necromants.

Necromantist. (Modern example.)
1910 *Daily Chron.* 8 Apr. 4/4 A sheaf of conjectures..which have been drawn from the various necromantists.

Necrotize, *v.* Add: **b.** To cause necrosis. Hence **Ne·crotizing** *ppl. a.* (example) and *vbl. sb.*
1902 *U.S. Dept. Agric. Rep., Bur. Animal Industry* 276 (Cent. Suppl.) Dorset and de Schweinitz described the isolation of a necrotizing acid. 1902 *Proc. Zool. Soc.* I. 211 It is assumed..that the whole process of stripping, necrotising, shedding, and renewing has become rhythmical—a feature due to cumulative inheritance.

Nectarivorous (nektări·vŏrəs), *a.* [f. L. *nectar* (Gr. νέκταρ) nectar + *-vor-us* devouring + -ous, after Carnivorous, etc.] Of birds and insects: That feed on the nectar of flowers.
1896 *Smithsonian Rep.* 421 The nectarivorous insects localize their action upon these nectaries.

Necton, variant of *Nekton.

Née (ne), *a.* [F., fem. of pa. pple. of *naître* to be born.] Placed before a married woman's maiden name, and usually italicized.
1835 H. Greville *Diary* 14 May, Afterwards to a party at the Duchesse de Raujan's (*née* Duras). 1848 Thackeray *Van. Fair* xlviii, The interview between Rebecca Crawley, *née* Sharp, and her Imperial Master.

Needful, *a.* **4.** (Later example.)
1831 Scott *Jrnl.* (1890) II. 400 Young Clarkson had already done the needful—that is, had bled and blistered severely.

Needle, *sb.* Add: **3. d.** In gramophones and similar instruments, the small pointed piece of metal, wood, or other material, which receives the vibrations from the record, and transmits them to the sound-box; the stylus used in recording.
1902 *Encycl. Brit.* XXXI. 679/2 The marker..instead of being a stiff needle coming from the centre of the membrane or glass plate, is now a lever. 1911 *Ibid.* XXI. 468/2 There is still a defect to be overcome in the gramophone, and that is the hissing of the needle produced by friction both during recording and..reproduction. 1913 Clements-Henry *Gramophones* 32 It is unadvisable to use any needle twice.

e. A thin tapering pointed piece of metal or other material used to secure fine adjustment in closing apertures as in valves.
1884 Knight *Dict. Mech.* Suppl. 632/2 (s.v. *Needle lubricator*) In order to regulate the supply of oil, a metallic feed-rod (needle) passes through the tube. 1909 *Chambers's Jrnl.* Nov. 698/1 The gas-regulator can be adjusted to the fiftieth part of an inch, with dead centralisation of the needle.

13. b. *needle-painted* (modern example).
1910 *Westm. Gaz.* 2 Feb. 5/4 An exhibition of needle-painted wild flowers of South Africa was opened yesterday.

14. needle-cast, a disease of pine trees believed to be caused by the fungus *Lophodermium pinastre*; **needle contest, fight, match,** etc., a contest, etc., that arouses much interest and excitement; **needle dam, gate, weir,** a dam or sluice consisting of several thin spars which are placed vertically one after the other into a frame; **needle-paper,** a stout black paper commonly used for wrapping up needles, which has been employed for various purposes in photography.
1895 Schlich *Man. Forestry* IV. 408 This sudden shedding of pine needles is the characteristic of the disease so widely spread in Germany, and termed *Schütte*, or *needle-cast. 1922 *Daily Mail* 22 Nov. 11 There is also a '*needle' contest, recently arranged, between two stable-lads. 1909 H. M. Wilson *Irrigation Engineering* 230 Simple flash-board or *needle gates should be used only where the pressure upon them is low. 1923 *Daily Mail* 16 Jan. 9 There will be a '*needle' match in Sheffield if Barnsley beat Swindon and visit the Wednesday. 1909 *Westm. Gaz.* 3 Apr. 14/2 If *needle-paper of the required kind is not available a..substitute can be prepared.

Needle-point. 2. Add: Also *needlepoint lace.*
1882 A. S. Cole in *Encycl. Brit.* XIV. 189/2 A technical peculiarity in making needlepoint lace is that a single thread and needle are alone used to form the pattern.

Needless, *a.* Add: **2. b.** The phrase (*It is*) *needless to say* (or *add,* etc.) is often used parenthetically.
1826 *Kaleidoscope* 31 Jan. VI. 247/3 The Squire was hard hit by this nonchalance, and (as the newspapers say) 'it is needless to add', acted upon Sheridan's suggestion. 1902 Harmsworth *Motors & Motor-Driving* (Badm. Libr.) 122 Needless to say, the shoulder F is thereby raised, and in turn pushes upwards the lifting rod or digger K. 1926 Bennett *Lord Raingo* I. xxxiv. 157 I've thought the thing out pretty carefully—needless to say.

Nefast, *a.* (Later example.)
1887 Stevenson *Let. to W. Archer* Oct. (1899) II. 71 In good case and spirits..after a most nefast experience of despondency.

Negligibility (neglidʒibi·lĭti). [f. Negligible + -ity.] The quality or state of being negligible.
1911 H. Walpole *Mr. Perrin & Mr. Traill* ii. § 3. (1921) 28 [She] had long ago been crushed into a miserable negligibility by her masterful husband. 1913 G. G. Coulton in *Rep. 7th Ann. Meeting Historical Assoc.* 16 The negligibility of French and German grammar questions.

Negotiate, *v.* **4.** (Add examples.)
1909 *Q. Rev.* Oct. 492 Some rival..had 'negotiated'—this we believe to be the sporting phrase—the same 150 miles in forty-seven hours [etc.]. 1922 Titus *Timber* xvi. 151 Pelly negotiated the *cuspidor* safely.

Negritic (nĭgri·tik), *a.* [f. Negro + -itic.] Of or pertaining to Negroes or the Negro race; nigritic.
1926 *Contemp. Rev.* Apr. 529 The one class that had kept itself pure from negritic intermixture.

Negritize (nī·gritəiz), *v.* [Irreg. f. Negro or Nigrit(ic + -ize.] *trans.* To make negro or nigritic in character.
1899 *Smithsonian Rep.* 513 Not one fact is in evidence from which we may conclude that a single neighboring people known to us has been Negritized.

Negro. Add: **2.** *negro-breaker, -breaking, -catcher, holder* (earlier example), *-monger, slavery, -stealer.*
1845 F. Douglass *Life* (1846) 73 Mr. Covey enjoyed the most unbounded reputation for being a first-rate overseer and *Negro-breaker. a1882 — *Life & Times* I. xv (1884) 94 His proficiency in the art of *negro-breaking. 1862 H. W. Halleck *General Order* Jan. (Bartlett) The object of these orders is to prevent any person in the army from acting in the capacity of a *negro-catcher or of a negro-stealer. 1780 J. Jones *Lett.* 47 The *negro holders in general already clamour against the project. 1741 *Col. Rec. Georgia* IV. 678 This exposes them to the Envy and Hatred of our *Negro-Mongers. 1831 Mrs. Holley *Texas Observ.* (1833) 87 The question of *negro slavery..is one of great importance. 1827 *Western Monthly Rev.* I. 69 It will be the refuge of *Negro-stealers and the Elysium of rogues.

6. (Later example.)
1912 *Chambers's Jrnl.* Jan. 23/1 Negro songs have always been popular among us, and deservedly so.

7. negro-car *U.S.*, a railway-carriage for negroes; **negro cloth** (earlier examples); **negro cotton,** a coarse variety of cotton cloth; so **negro shirting**; **negro shoe,** a class of shoe; **negro State,** any of the Southern States of America in which slavery was legal.
1860 Abbott *South & North* 103 He was thrust into the *negro-car and sent out of the State. 1732 *S. Carolina Gaz.* 17 June 4/1 [He] had on a blue *Negro Cloth Frock. *Ibid.* 30 Sept. 4/2 Just imported, white and blue Negro Cloth. 1786 *Maryland Jrnl. & Baltimore Adv.* 26 Sept., Fine and coarse broadcloths; coatings; *Negro cottons. 1803 *Deb. Congress* 10 Jan. 349 Ornaburgs..kerseys, negro cottons, flannel [etc.]. 1818 *Norfolk* (Va.) *Beacon* 19 Dec. 1/4 Negro Cottons. 10 Bales just received. 1835 *Southern Lit. Messenger* I. 260 The fabrics are heavy—*negro shirtings 29 inches wide [etc.]. 1770 *Carroll Papers* in *Maryland Hist. Mag.* XIII. 69, 24 Pair of *negro shoes. 1772 *Ibid.* XIV. 272 Send me as soon as possible 30 sides of Upper and 30 sides of Soal Leather for negro shoes. 1780 *Essex Inst. Hist. Coll.* XIII. 220 You did not carry home contemptible Ideas enough of the *negro States or of this great Braggadocio. 1809 *Deb. Congress* 20 Jan. 1152 The Potomac the boundary—the Negro states by themselves!

Negrodom. (Earlier example.)
1847 *Congress. Globe* 13 Feb. App. 376/1 Our measures have given all that wide region to be the empire of negrodom.

Negrofy, *v.* (Earlier example.)
1788 B. Franklin *Autob.* Writ. 1907 I. 391 Finding he was likely to be negrofied himself, he..grew tir'd of the contest.

Negroish, *a.* (Earlier example.)
1789 Morse *Amer. Geog.* 65 The children, by being brought up, and constantly associating with the negroes..contract a negroish kind of accent and dialect.

Negroism. 1 and **2.** (Earlier examples.)
1847 *Congress. Globe* App. 323/2 He..thanked God that he voted against that Wilmot proviso. It smelt rank of negroism. 1859 Bartlett *Dict. Amer.* p. viii, The term 'Americanisms' ..may then be said to include the following classes of words: ..8. Negroisms.

Negroization (nīˌgroˌəizē·ʃən). [f. Negro + -ization.] A making or becoming negro in character.
1899 tr. *Ratzel's Hist. Mankind* III. 258 From them Rohlfs expects an ever-increasing 'negroisation' of the Libyan series.

Negrophilism. (Earlier examples.)
1846 *Congress. Globe* 18 May 838/1 The gentleman from Ohio.., the advocat of *negro-philism.* 1860 A. B. Longstreet in *U.S. Ann. Treas. Rep.* 475 A man..of more negrophilism than brains.

Negrophobe (nī·grofōᵘb). [f. Negro + -phobe.] One who has a morbid fear and hatred of negroes.
1900 *Spectator* 15 Sept. 329/2 Negrophiles may be, we ourselves think are, wiser as well as better men than negrophobes.

Neighbourhood. Add: **7.** *neighbourhood road, school.*
1885 W. G. Simms *Partisan* 522 A small track, a common wagon or *neighborhood road, wound into the forest. 1860 S. Mordecai *Virginia* xxx. 303 They [railroads] are like neighborhood roads on an extended scale. 1872 *Rep. Indian Affairs* (1872) 180 The Creeks have thirty-two *neighborhood schools. 1887 *Harper's Mag.* Feb. 353/2 There is a neighborhood school where English is taught.

Neighbourize (nē·bərəiz), *v.* [f. Neighbour *sb.* + -ize.] *intr.* To associate with others as neighbours: to act in a neighbourly fashion.
1899 G. B. Burgin *Bread of Tears* I. ii. 43 We thought we'd just neighbourise, and happen in to hear what it says.

Nekton (ne·ktǫn). *Biol.* Also **necton.** [ad. G. *nekton*, f. Gr. *νεκτόν neut. of *νεκτός vbl. adj., swimming, f. νεῖν to swim.] A collective name for all the forms of organic life found at various depths of the ocean or of lakes which possess the power to swim actively, in contrast to Plankton which float or *Benthos which live on the ocean floor.
1895 *Nat. Science* July 31 The *Plankton, Necton*, and *Benthos* form three well-marked communities of organisms. 1902 *Encycl. Brit.* XXXIII. 932/1 The fauna of the sea is divisible into the *plankton*..(generally taken now to include Haeckel's *nekton*, the strong swimmers, such as fish and cephalopods), and the *benthos*. 1913 Sir J. Murray *Ocean* viii. 159 Nekton—animals which can swim against currents.
Hence **Nekto·nic** *a.*
1903 *Amer. Geol.* Apr. 211 It has been asserted..that slowly creeping organisms preceded the planktonic and nektonic forms.

Nelis, Nelies (ne·lis, ne·liz). [F. *Nelis (d'hiver).*] A late-keeping variety of pear; usu. *winter nelis.*
The form *nelies* is due to the use as a plural.
1860 Hogg *Fruit Man.* 222 Winter Nelis...One of the richest flavoured pears. 1927 *Scots Observer* 20 Aug. 2/3 The winter Nelis..get their glow and perfume long after the frost and snow have done their worst with the orchards.

Nelson (ne·lsən). *Wrestling.* [Apparently f. a proper name.] The name of a class of holds in which the arm is passed under the opponent's from behind and the hand applied to his neck, often with words prefixed to indicate the precise form of the hold, as *double nelson*, *Half-Nelson, *(three-)quarter nelson.*
1889 W. Armstrong *Wrestling* (Badm. Libr.) 233 Probably the most dangerous move in Lancashire and Cornwall and Devon wrestling..is what is called the 'Double Nelson'. 1893 *Lippincott's Mag.* Feb. 211 Among the many holds the Nelson is the most popular one with wrestlers, while the half-Nelson and half-watch-lock are next in order. 1900 *Yng. Sportsman* (ed. A. E. T. Watson) 644 The principal chips associated with catch as catch can wrestling are the double Nelson, the half Nelson, the heave, the Lancashire lock, the flying mare and the three-quarter Nelson.

Nelsonian (nelsōᵘ·niăn), *a.* [f. as *Nelsonic + -ian.] Belonging to the time of Nelson.
1913 *Q. Rev.* Apr. 461 We have only to go back to the eighties to find ships..with their..guns still mounted on the Nelsonian trucks worked by handspikes.

Nelsonic (nelsǫ·nik), *a.* [f. the name of Viscount *Nelson* (1758–1805) + -ic.] Pertaining to, relating to, or characteristic of Nelson.
1909 *Daily Chron.* 13 Sept. 3/3 These Nelsonic qualities in Wolfe do not..come out very clearly in the letters. 1922 *Q. Rev.* Apr. 361 Orders of this nature..are always dangerous in the absence of the Nelsonic spirit.

Nemesia (nĭmī·ʒiă). [mod.L. (Vertenet 1803) f. Gr. νεμέσιον used by Dioscurides (IV. 28) to denote an allied plant.] A genus of South African flowering plants comprising several species, of which a few are cultivated as hardy annuals.
1886 *G. Nicholson's Dict. Gard.* II. 433/2. 1927 *Observer* 20 Mar. 24/3 Modern florists and men of science..have made a rainbow out of a single colour (as in the nemesia).

Neo-. 1. a. Add: *Neo-Darwinian* (sb.), *-Darwinism, -Darwinist, -Lamarckian* (sb.), *-paganism, -Pythagorean* (sb.), *-vitalism, -vitalist, -vitalistic* (adj.).
1895 Romanes *Darwin* II. 10 The *Neo-Darwinians strain the teachings of Darwin. 1902 J. M. Baldwin *Development & Evol.* 135 The possible truth of either of the current doctrines of heredity, called *Neo-Darwinism and Neo-Lamarckism respectively. 1895 Romanes *Darwin* II. 28, I am not a *Neo-Darwinist, and so have no desire to make 'natural selection' synonymous with 'natural causation'. 1910 *Contemp. Rev.* Jan. 107 This important factor of direct action, which has been brought so much into prominence by the *Neo-Lamarckians. 1880 McCarthy *Hist. Own Times* IV. 542 Pre-Raphaelitism..has got mixed up with æstheticism, *neo-paganism, and other such fantasies. 1891 *Chambers's Encycl.* VII. 436/2 *Neopythagoreans may be divided into two groups. 1902 *Encycl. Brit.* XXXI. 712/2 These efforts..by their unfortunate designations of Vitalism and *Neo-vitalism give rise to entirely false conceptions. 1899 J. A. Thomson *Science of Life* 9 The rise of a school of '*neovitalists', who have helped to save the science from self-conceit by their emphasis on the partial nature of all physiological analysis. 1902 *Encycl. Brit.* XXXI. 712/2 All the so-called *neo-vitalistic efforts..have nothing to do with the older vitalism.

2. Neopa·llium, the cortical area of the brain which is the organ of associative memory in mammals. **Neote·nic, Neo·tenous** *adjs.* = *neoteinic.* **Neo·teny** = *neoteinia.*
1901 G. Elliott Smith in *Jrnl. Anat. & Phys.* July 431 It is only one of the three histological formations which constitute the true pallium;..we may call it the 'new pallium', or, if the hybrid term be permissible, '*neopallium'. 1922 J. Y. Simpson *Man & Attainm. Immortality* xi. 241 The gradual association of supremacy..with the cortical area or neopallium. 1901 H. Gadow *Amphibia & Reptiles* iii. 64 Not unfrequently typical *neotenic and overgrown specimens occur side by side with others which have completed their metamorphosis. 1930 G. R. de Beer *Embryol. & Evol.* 27 Some animals have become permanently committed to this *neotenous state. 1901 H. Gadow *Amphibia & Reptiles* iii. 65 These cases of *neoteny are therefore instances of more or less complete retardation, or of the retention, of partially larval conditions. 1920 *Conquest* Apr. 278/2 Neoteny..here means the abnormal time-extension of youthful characters.

Neodymium (nīˌodi·miŏm). *Chem.* [f. Neo- + Di)dymium.] A metallic element of the rare-earth group discovered in 1885 by Auer von Welsbach. It is found in the minerals monazite, cerite, albanite, etc., along with cerium, lanthanum, praseodymium, etc. Symbol Nd; atomic weight 144·3; atomic number 60.
1886 W. Crookes in *Nature* 22 July 266/1 According to Dr. Auer, a line in the well-known yellow band, close to the soda line..is a component of the absorption-spectrum of neodymium. 1902 *Encycl. Brit.* XXVI. 709/1 Cleve, while accepting praseodymium as a new element, doubts the individuality of neodymium.

Nepalese (nepǫlī·z), *a.* and *sb.* Also **Nepaulese.** [f. *Nepal* the name of a state on the north-eastern frontier of India + -ese.] **a.** *adj.* Of, pertaining to, or connected with Nepal. **b.** *sb.* A native or inhabitant of Nepal.
The form *Nepali* (*a.* and *sb.*) also occurs in recent use.
1848 Sir J. D. Hooker in *Life* (1918) I. xiii. 251 The Sikkim Rajah, whose territories were once the prey of the Nepalese. *Ibid.* 263 Accepting the invitation of Major Thoresby, the Nepaulese Resident. 1862 Latham *Compar. Philol.* 25 These..are not only clearly Nepalese, but have been referred to a given Nepalese language. 1884 *Encycl. Brit.* XVII. 343/1 In all matters of domestic policy the Nepalese brook no interference. 1910 *Blackw. Mag.* Jan. 119/1 The Nepalese villagers liked them to come and kill off a tiger free of charge.

Nephewdom (ne·viuːdəm). [-dom.] The relationship or position of a nephew.
1924 W. J. Locke *Coming of Amos* ii. 25 There is nothing inherent in mere nephewdom to rake frantic emotional chords.

Nephropexy (nefrǫpe·ksi). *Surg.* [f. Gr. νεφρό-ς kidney + πῆξις fixing. Cf. F. *néphropexie.*] The operation of fixing a movable or floating kidney; nephrorrhaphy.
1900 *Lancet* 11 Aug. 432/1 Fixation of a displaced kidney (nephropexy of Guyon). 1907 *Practitioner* Dec. 786 A left nephropexy was performed.

Nerine (nĭrəi·nĭ). [mod.L. (Herbert 1820) f. L. *Nērinē* (Verg. Ecl. vii. 37), Gr. νηρηίς a water nymph: see Nereid.] A genus of bulbous plants belonging to the family *Amaryllidaceæ*, indigenous to South Africa.
1837 W. Herbert *Amaryllidaceæ* 285, I have no hesitation in saying that it is a Nerine. 1886 *G. Nicholson's Dict. Gard.* II. 446/2 s.v., When in flower, Nerines are amongst the most beautiful of greenhouse bulbous plants. 1923 *Chambers's Jrnl.* Dec. 786/2 The scarlet or rose-red nerine (the Japanese spider lily) appeared next.

Neritic (nĭri·tik), *a.* [f. Nerit(a + -ic.] Of regions or living things in the sea and in lakes: That is near to the shore or found in shallow coastal waters; opposed to *Oceanic.
1895 *Nat. Science* July 31 The second great zone is the Neritic zone which extends from the coast to a depth of about five hundred fathoms. 1902 *Encycl. Brit.* XXXIII. 936/2 There is a great difference between the epiplankton near land and that far out at sea: the former is termed neritic. 1913 Sir J. Murray *Ocean* vii. 136 The neritic area surrounds all continents and islands.

Nerve, *sb.* Add: **8. e.** Phr. *To get on one's nerves*: To (begin to) affect one with irritation, impatience, fear or the like.
1908 H. G. Wells *War in Air* iv. § 5 'This flying gets on one's nerves', he said. *Ibid.* v. § 7 It's getting on my nerves. 1910 *Chambers's Jrnl.* Mar. 155/2 Sometimes I hate this accursed country... It gets on one's nerves at times. 1916 Bennett *Lion's Share* xxii. 156 The house began to get on my nerves. 1918 Galsworthy *Five Tales, Indian Summer* i. 291 Women, somehow..got a little on one's nerves.

11. b. *nerve-racking.*
1906 *Strand Mag.* May 516/2 The motorists found themselves..plunged with a nerve-racking bounce into a deep gulch. 1908 *Westm. Gaz.* 22 Feb. 2/3 The nerve-racking work of the telephone-girls. 1911 Edna Ferber *Dawn O'Hara* v. 71 Why not go where the newspaper work will not be so nerve-racking. 1915 P. G. Wodehouse *Something Fresh* x. § 5 He felt cool and alert,..and, the nerve-racking hours of waiting past, he listened for the starter's gun.

12. nerve-food, a special food designed (or purporting) to strengthen or improve the nerves; **nerve-impulse,** the impulse propagated along a stimulated nerve; **nerve-net** (see quot. 1927); **nerve-patient,** a patient suffering from disordered nerves.
1909 *Chambers's Jrnl.* Dec. 818/2 Preparations of divers kinds which come under the general description of *nerve-foods. 1900 *Nature* 26 July 291/1 The futility of those hypotheses which would explain the passage of the *nerve-impulse as a mere propagated polarisation. 1918 G. H. Parker in *Jrnl. Gen. Physiol.* I. 231 (heading) The Rate of Transmission in the *Nerve Net of Coelenterates. 1927 Haldane & Huxley *Anim. Biol.* xii. 270 A primitive type [of nervous system] known as a nerve-net, in which the sense-organs communicate with a network of nerve-cells branching all over the body, which in their turn communicate with the muscles. 1909 *Chambers's Jrnl.* Dec. 818/1 Every medical practitioner..obtains an increasing number of *nerve-patients year after year.

Nerver (nɔ̄·ɹvəɹ). [f. Nerve *sb.* and *v.* + -er[1].] Something that gives one nerve or courage.
1889 *St. James's Gaz.* 10 Aug. 3/2 His dose..possibly contains cardamums, hydrocyanic acid, and tincture of capsicum; a capital 'nerver' in its way.

Nerviness. Add: **2.** State of being nervous (sense 9).
1921 *Glasgow Herald* 15 June 8 The home men had only to shake off their 'nerviness' to reduce the Australian bowling to trundling of good class.

Nervous, *a.* Add: **9. b.** Shy or apprehensive *of* (doing something).
1928 *Manchester Guardian Weekly* 26 Oct. 335/3 Nervous of attempting train or tramcar with their strange charge.

Nervuration (nɔ̄ɹviurē·ʃən). [f. Nervure + -ation.] The scheme of arrangement of the nervures or veins on the wing of an insect.
1899 D. Sharp *Insects* II. 319 In the aberrant moths of the genus Costina the nervuration is unusually complex.

Nervy, *a.* Add: **2. b.** (Examples.)
1896 G. Ade *Artie* viii. 75, I just received your nervy letter. 1904 Eliz. Robins *Magnetic North* II. 118 Feeling that it is a little 'nervy'..to walk into another man's house uninvited.

5. Having one's nerves disordered; easily excitable, nervous, 'jumpy'.
1906 *Sat. Rev.* 3 Mar. 254 They are very 'nervy' in Russia. 1916 *Daily Mail* 21 Sept. 7 Advt., When you are Weak, Anæmic, 'Nervy', Run-down, [etc.]. 1924 Galsworthy *White Monkey* II. ii, I know he's very nervy, and gets wrong with people.

Nesh, *a.* **1.** (Add example.)
1915 R. C. Thompson *Pilgr. Scrip* 71 The road from the bridge is like an English lane with blackberry hedgerows.. and a nesh track for a morning gallop.

Nest, *sb.* **6.** (Recent example.)
1924 R. Keable *Recompence* iv. (1926) 77 A delightful nest of occasional tables.

Nest, *v.* Add: **2. c.** *U.S. colloq.* To squat. (Cf. *Nester 2.)
1918 Mulford *Man fr. Bar-20* xi. 124 Not satisfied with nestin' on a man's range, you had to start a little herd.

4. b. (Later example, not in pa. pple.)
1925 N. E. Odell in E. F. Norton *Fight for Everest 1924* 362 Two saucepans that nest into one another.

Nester. Add: **1.** (Earlier example.)
1887 *Ibis* 95 It [*Cisticola cursitans*] is both an early and late nester.

2. *U.S.* A squatter on a cattle-range. (Cf. *Nest *v.* 2 c.)
1907 Mulford *Bar-20* xix. 192 Ain't th' Panhandle full of nesters (farmers)? 1918 — *Man fr. Bar-20* iii. 27 He had found the ruins of a burned homestead..and he guessed that it had been used by 'nesters'.

Nesting, *vbl. sb.* **b.** Add: *nesting-call.*
1924 J. A. Thomson *Science Old & New* xxi. 116 The selection is marked by the bird's remaining near the chosen spot and giving the *nesting-call to the mate.

Nestling, *vbl. sb.*[1] **3.** Add: *nestling-ground.*
1871 *Game Laws N.Y.* in *Fur, Fin & Feather* (1872) 19 No person shall kill..any wild pigeon while on its nestling ground or..in any manner disturb such nestling ground.

Net, *sb.*[1] Add: **2. c.** *Lawn Tennis.* = Let *sb.*[1] 2. *colloq.*
1904 J. P. Paret *Lawn Tennis* 344 Net..Also (same as 'let'), a ball that touches the net and goes into the proper court. 1930 D. Mackail *How Amusing* 450 When Clampson served a let..they actually—yes, in the twentieth century and the Centre Court—called it a 'net'.

5. a. *net-man* (earlier example), *-owner, pocket.* **d. net-cord,** the cord which passes along the top of a net and supports it, esp. that supporting a tennis-net; so **net-cord (stroke),** a stroke in lawn tennis in which the ball hits the net-cord; **net-fish** *v.*, to fish with a net; **net-player** *Lawn Tennis*, a player who advances close to the net; **net-practice,** cricket practice with nets.
1844 *net-cord [in Dict.]. 1887 *Boy's Own Paper* 3 Sept. 778/1 If you are tall enough, take it before it descends to the level of the net-cord. 1904 J. P. Paret *Lawn Tennis* 345 *Net-cord Stroke. 1908 A. W. Myers *Complete Lawn Tennis Player* 31 He bounced it on the ground and made a drive at the net, making by accident a splendid net-cord stroke. 1927 *Daily Tel.* 30 Aug. 10/5 A long, anxious game, finished with a net cord and a double fault, was finally taken by Mrs. Chapin. 1891 *Chambers's Encycl.* VIII. 256/1 He may be arrested if he is *net-fishing, but not if he is fishing in another way. 1847 C. Lanman *Summer in Wilderness* xxvi. 160 A false movement of the *net-man will cause the canoe to be swamped. 1901 *Chambers's Jrnl.* Sept. 585/1 The estuary limits..have been fixed more in the interests of the *net-owners than in those of the salmon. 1919 Suzanne Lenglen *Lawn Tennis for Girls* 53 The *net player..has a free hand at the net. 1902 *Chambers's Jrnl.* Jan. 48/2 The younger man..swung the captive ashore in the *net-pocket. 1899 *Captain* I. 378/2 *Net practice is good in moderation, but nothing is so good as practice games.

Net, *a.* Add: **3.** Also as *sb.*
1910 *Gt. Central Rly. Rep.* 11 Feb. 7 Deducting from our receipts of £2,285,430 our expenses of £1,488,474, we have a net of £796,956.

4. *Comb.*, as *net-priced.*
1909 *Daily Chron.* 16 July 3/2 In his new net-priced series.

Net, *v.*[1] Add: **1. a.** To fasten *down* with a net.
1909 H. G. Wells *Tono-Bungay* III. iii. § 4. 363 Practically I contracted my sausage gas-bag by netting it down.

2. a. (Later example.)
1912 Galsworthy *Inn Tranq.* 126 The dusk is falling... Some stars are already netted in the branches of the pines.

4. *trans.* and *absol.* In ball games in which a net is employed: To send (a ball) into the net.
1906 *Peel City Guardian & Chron.* No. 1216 It seemed as if they meant to force the custodian into the net, not net the ball. 1907 *Ibid.* 26 Oct. 5/2 A rush in the goal resulted in Cain netting. 1927 *Daily Express* 20 Apr. 13/2 Scriven netted for Birmingham in the first five minutes. *Ibid.* 22 June 2/2 Raymond, striving for extra speed, netted and outed a succession of returns.

Ne·therla·ndic, *a.* [f. *Netherland* + -ic.] = Netherlandish *a.*
1902 *Encycl. Brit.* XXXI. 294/1 Wienecke is interesting for the sake of his early Netherlandic manner; the incongruity is not unpleasant.

Netherlandish, *a.* Add: **b.** *sb.* The language of the Netherlands; Dutch.
1890 *Chambers's Encycl.* V. 744/2 The origin of new Netherlandish or Dutch is to be found with the *Rederijkers.*

Netted, *ppl. a.* **2.** (Add example.)
1882 *Harper's Mag.* Apr. 697/2 The netted (snow-)shoes are rarely used, the twelve-foot-long boards bent up at the end..being liked better.

Nettle, *sb.*[1] Add: **2. d.** *To cast (throw) one's frock to the nettles* [= Fr. *jeter le froc aux orties*], to renounce a clerical life; also *transf.*
1916 W. J. Locke *Wonderful Year* xviii. 255 He had burned his boats, thrown his cap over the windmills, cast his frock to the nettles. 1918 — *Rough Road* vi. 58 Young parsons..threw their cassocks to the nettles and put on the full..panoply of war.

4. b. nettle-weed, a plant of the nettle family. *U.S.*
1843 Carlton *New Purchase* xix. 159 They gathered a peculiar species of nettle, (called there nettleweed,) which they succeeded in dressing like flax. 1867 T. Lackland *Homespun* I. 18 Their blackened skeletons..overgrown with nettleweeds and long grasses.

Neurastheniac (niūˌræsþī·niæk). [f. Neurasthenia: after Maniac.] A person affected with neurasthenia; = Neurasthenic B.
1904 *Lancet* 18 June 1737/2 The 'neurastheniacs' that present themselves at the clinic for diseases of the nervous system.

Neurastheny. (Example.)
1891 *Smithsonian Rep.* 660 It is frequent that among vagabonds, robbers, thieves, and other criminals..there is a physical and moral neurastheny, a term coined by Benedikt, of Vienna.

Neuro-. Add: **Neurofi·bril,** the supposed conducting element of nerve fibres and nerve cells. Also *Neurofibrilla.*
1900 *Jrnl. Exper. Med.* 1 Oct. V. 21 *note*, In this paper the term *neurofibril is used in a purely morphological sense to describe the fibrils which lie..within the ganglion cells of the cerebral cortex. 1902 *Encycl. Brit.* XXXI. 793/1 In the ganglion cells and their processes there is no known differentiation of neurofibrillæ. 1908 *Practitioner* Oct. 562 A new staining method, which stains the neurofibril networks but leaves the glia totally unstained.

Neurotically (niurǫ·tikăli), *adv.* [f. Neurotic *a.* + -al + -ly[2].] In a neurotic manner; as the result of a nervous disorder.
1919 Mary K. Bradby *Psycho-Analysis & its Place in Life* 78 Many..thrust their qualms into the unconscious and became neurotically deaf, blind or what not.

Neuro·ticism. [f. Neurotic *a.* + -ism.] The state or condition of being neurotic. **Neuro·ticise** *v. trans.*, to render neurotic. Also **Neu·rotize** *v.*
1900 *Daily Chron.* 5 June 4 (Cass. Suppl.) The holiday season has been darkened by the reports of suicides, which suggest..the neuroticism of Paris. 1922 *Glasgow Herald* 5 Oct. 5 It is at least no more forced and is a great deal more cleanly than much of the brilliant neuroticism of recent novels. 1928 *Daily Express* 7 July 8/3 Already there are signs that tennis is making us soft. We are being sentimentalised and neuroticised by it. 19.. *Buck's Handbk. Med. Sci.* VIII. 274 (Cent. Suppl.) Neurotize.

Neutral. A. *adj.* Add: **4. f.** *Comm.* Of fats or oils: Divested of or not possessing any sensible odour.
1898 Lewkowitsch *Anal. Oils*, etc. (ed. 2) 541 'Vegetable butter,' 'Lactine'..is therefore practically neutral cocoa nut oil. 1904 L. L. Lamborn *Cottonseed Products* 166 Neutral lard is composed of the fat derived from the leaf of the slaughtered animal. 1917 *Statutory Rules & Orders* No. 1162 § 7 Choice and Extra Choice Neutral Lard.

B. *sb.* Add: **1. c.** A position of the driving and driven parts in a gear mechanism in which no power is transmitted.
1914 'Ian Hay' *Knt. on Wheels* x. 103, I left the gears in the first speed instead of the neutral. But it's all right now. 1925 *Morris Owner* Jan. 1154/1 Don't lose your head and start the car in gear. Take things quietly, put the lever in neutral, [etc.]. 1926 J. J. Connington *Death at Swaythling Court* xiii. 250 The Colonel slipped his gear into neutral.

4. An electrical conductor whose potential is normally zero, or the same as that of the earth.
1900 *Jrnl. Inst. Electr. Engin.* XXIX. 538 Each of these boards receives from the main generator board five cables, a pair of 'outers' for lighting, a similar pair for power, and a common neutral. 1910 *Installation News* iv. 62/1 We may have to consider a leakage on one of the outers of a three wire system, the neutral of which is earthed.

Neutralist. (Later examples.)
1915 *Morn. Post* 1 Feb. 8/6 A meeting of neutralists, held here to-day, was broken up by Republicans, who shouted 'Long live the war!' 1920 *Glasgow Herald* 26 May 9/2 The Neutralist elements..hate the very idea of celebrating Italy's entrance into the war.

Neutrality. 4 a. (Later example.)
1883 Stallybrass tr. *Grimm's Teut. Mythol.* II. 883 Out of the Goth. fairguni's neutrality unfolded themselves both a male *Fiörgynn* and a female *Fiörgyn.*

Neutralization. Add: **3.** In automobile racing, the fact of controlling the speed of competitors over a section of a course; a section in which speed is controlled.
1905 *Autom. Topics* Europ. Suppl. 27 May 2 (Cent. Suppl.) There are no cities..to require frequent neutralizations.

Neutralize, *v.* Add: **2. c.** *Comm.* To deprive (fat or oil) of its distinctive odour.
1904 L. L. Lamborn *Cottonseed Products* 165 The oil made from sheep fat cannot be neutralized.

5. In automobile racing, to control the speed of competitors over (a section of the course) so that that section has no effect on the result of a race.
1902 *Encycl. Brit.* XXXI. 13/2 Deducting the Swiss portion of the route (which was neutralized), the distance was 615 miles.

Neutralized, *ppl. a.* (Add example.)
1902 *Encycl. Brit.* XXXI. 13/1 A distance (after deducting the neutralized sections) of 328 miles.

Neutralizing, *ppl. a.* **2.** (Add example.)
1904 L. L. Lamborn *Cottonseed Products* 167 This treatment carries the neutralizing process to a higher degree of perfection and improves the texture of the oil.

Neutro-. Neutro·philic *a.* = *Neutrophilous.*
1905 [see *Oxy-]. 1906 *Jrnl. Med. Research* Dec. 486 The invading cells are endothelial cells, neutrophilic and eosinophilic polymorphonuclear leucocytes.

Neutrodyne (niū·trodəin). [f. Neutro- + Dyne.] *Wireless.* The proprietary name of a type of high-frequency amplification circuit; also *attrib.* Hence **Neu·trodyning** *vbl. sb.*
1925 *Bazaar, Exchange & Mart* 14 May 652/2 This coil.. can also be used as a..neutrodyne. 1926 *Glasgow Herald* 8 Mar. 8 A four-valve neutrodyne circuit. *Ibid.* 30 Apr. 12. 1926 R. W. Hutchinson *Wireless* 217 Several methods have been devised for the control of this oscillation; neutrodyning, as it is termed, is one of the best.

Neutron (niū·trǫn). [f. Neutral A 4 c: after *Electron[2] and *Proton.] An electrically neutral particle consisting of an electron and a proton in close association.
1921 *Phil. Mag.* XLII. 597 Such a particle, to which the name *neutron* has been given by Prof. Rutherford, would have novel and important properties.

Never, *adv.* Add: **1. d.** (Later example.)
1926 Bennett *Lord Raingo* II. lxxi. 322 She faintly annoyed him by her ingenuous exclamations: Oh my! Well, I never! Well I never did!

8. never-fail, a person who never fails (one); **never-was,** a person who has never been great, distinguished, useful, or the like, in contrast to a 'has-been'; so **never-waser.**
1850 H. C. Watson *Camp-fires Revol.* 188 Morgan's one of the *never-fails. 1911 J. C. Lincoln *Cap'n Warren's Wards* xv. 238 One of 'em's a used-to-be, and the other's a *never-was. 1913 'B. M. Bower' *Parowan Bonanza* i. 14 'Nope, I'm a never-was', Bill retorted shamelessly. 1915 A. S. Neill *Dominie's Log* xiv. 155 The average married woman is a 'has been' in thought, while not a few are '*never wasers'.

New, *a.* Add: **6. d.** *New ground*, ground which is cultivated for the first time.
1769 Washington *Diaries* I. 333 That piece of New Ground containing 14 Acres next the widow Sheridan's. 1771 *Carroll Papers* in *Maryland Hist. Mag.* XIV. 134 Our new ground tob(acc)o here has been housed 3 or 4 days past. 1852 *Florida Plant Rec.* 62 Now the Crop is all Planted except the Little Peace of New ground that I cleared at the car Place.

8. *New rich*: In recent use, common as a translation of the French *nouveaux riches*, persons who have recently acquired wealth. Also as *adj.* Hence *new poor*, recently impoverished persons.
1886 *Harper's Mag.* Oct. 795/2 There are..the sons of the 'new rich' who are like men drunk with new wine. 1923 'B. M. Bower' *Parowan Bonanza* xiii. 157 You've never seen *me* look New-rich, have you, Bill? 1926 Bennett *Lord Raingo* I. xxxv. 165 He had demonstrated publicly.. that he belonged to the type of the new rich. 1928 Shaw *Intell. Woman's Guide Socialism* 60 In fact the only people who are disgustingly idle are the children of those who have just become rich, the new rich as they are called. 1920 *Punch* 6 Oct. 279 *Exhausted War Profiteer.* 'Deer forests for the "idle rich" be blowed! The "new poor" can 'ave 'em for me.' 1921 *Ibid.* 16 Feb. 134/3 We of the New Poor..cannot afford to neglect any little gratuitous diversion that comes our way.

10. b. *New-face*, a term used at the Clarendon Press, Oxford, to describe *modern face type* (*Modern A. 2 g). *New time*: In the Stock Exchange: Of prices, quoted for the next settling day before the previous settlement is completed.
1900 H. Hart *Cent. Typogr.* 120 These are the first examples of what are called nowadays 'new-face' types. 1927 *Daily Express* 27 Sept. 10/1 The price for 'new time' was about 15s. 6d., compared with a making up price of 14s. *Ibid.* 10/3 The 'new time' price at one time touched the new record of 4½.

New-Englandism. (Earlier example.)
1835 *Southern Lit. Messenger* I. 423 This is a New-Englandism not confined to the vulgar.

Newfoundland. b. (Earlier example.)
1827 *Hallowell* (Maine) *Gaz.* 20 June 3/4 They report to have seen..2 greyhounds, 1 newfoundland, 50 French dogs.

Newfoundla·ndic, *a.* [-ic.] Of or pertaining to the Newfoundland breed of dog.
1871 *Scribner's Monthly* II. 622 While other curs are so common, individuals of the genuine Newfoundlandic stock are very scarce.

New Jersey. The name of one of the eastern states of the United States, used *attrib.* in the names of plants, as **New Jersey pine,** the Jersey or scrub pine, *Pinus inops*; **New Jersey tea,** a shrub of North America, *Ceanothus americanus*, whose leaves are used as a substitute for tea.
1832 D. J. Browne *Sylva Amer.* 234 *New Jersey Pine *Pinus Inops.* 1815 Drake *Cincinnati* ii. 77 *New Jersey tea. 1877 *Rep. Vermont Board Agric.* IV. 159 Riley recommends persons..to plant a small patch of New Jersey Tea (*Ceanothus*)..as a decoy near the strawberry bed.

New light. [Light *sb.* 6 d.]
1. Novel religious views or doctrines (see Light *sb.* 6 d).
1650–1785 [see Light *sb.* 6 d]. 1806 Fessenden *Democracy Unveiled* II. 181 Altho' not bless'd with second sight, Divine inflation, or new light.

b. The religious sect or the doctrines of the 'new lights'.
1750 J. Birket *Voy. N. Amer.* (1916) 4 There is two Presbyterian meeting houses here, one of the Newlight, and one of the old. 1850 Foote *Sk. Virginia* 373 In his discourse he..read a hue and cry, for the arrest of 'the new light'.

2. A person holding 'new lights' or novel (religious) doctrines (cf. Light *sb.* 6 d).
1743 MacSparran *Diary* (1899) 12 Sunday night a young man named Avery and a new light had a Conversation with me. 1757 Woolman *Jrnl.* iv. (1840) 45 Some of our Society and some of the Society called new-lights use some endeavours to instruct those they have in reading. 1781 Sam Peters *Hist. Conn.* 288 (Th.) The new lights maintained that... 1806 Fessenden *Democracy Unveiled* I. 17 There was a gaunt Genevan priest, Mad as our New Lights are at least. 1839 J. F. Cooper *Home as Found* x, Methodism flourishing but little among us since the introduction of the New Lights. 1847 H. Howe *Hist. Coll. Ohio* 371 There are 15 churches, of which the..Newlights..have..one. 1866 Whittier *Marg. Smith's Jrnl.* Wks. 1889 I. 172 Hence you will see in the same neighborhood..New Lights, Brownists, Antinomians, and Socinians. 1872 Eggleston *Hoosier Schoolm.* xv. 121, I don't know whether you're a Hardshell ..or a Campbellite, or a New Light.

b. *transf.* The name of a fish (see quot.).
1884 Goode *Nat. Hist. Aquatic Anim.* 407 The Crappie —*Pomoxys annularis*... Other names are..'New Light' and 'Campbellite' in Kentucky and Indiana.

3. *attrib.* or as *adj.* Belonging to or holding the views of the 'new lights'.
1744 [see Light *sb.* 6 d]. 1751 MacSparran *Diary* (1899) 55, I officiated at Mrs. Lippet's and a New Light woman was at ch[urch]. 1757 E. Wheelock in *Mem.* (1811) 215 He begins to think that new-light ministers (as they are called) are his best friends. 1784 J. Smyth *Tour U.S.* I. xiii. 102 Here I..bad to defend myself against the formidable attacks of a new-light itinerant preacher. 1837 W. Jenkins *Ohio Gaz.* 373 There are in this county..eight christian (or newlight).. and five dunkard churches. 1849 E. Chamberlain *Indiana Gaz.* 175 There are in the county six churches...Christian, (or Cambellite) Old Christian, (or New Light) and Baptists.

b. *transf.* Of other doctrines: Novel, new-fangled.
1833 Wyeth *Oregon* 25 What the new-light Doctrine of Phrenology calls the disposition bump of Inhabitiveness.
Hence **Newli·ghtism,** new-light doctrines.
1845 S. Judd *Margaret* I. vii. 42 The town underwent and survived..Antinomianism, Newlightism, Scotch Presbyterianism.

New Mexican, *a.* and *sb.* [-an.] **a.** *adj.* Of or belonging to New Mexico, a south-western state of the United States. **b.** *sb.* A native or inhabitant of New Mexico.
1834 A. Pike *Sketches* 170 But even the New Mexicans call him a great rascal. 1846 W. H. Emory in *Ann. 30-1 Congress* Ex. Doc. 47 The power he had of letting these people loose on the New Mexicans was the great secret of his arbitrary sway. *Ibid.* 57 Acoma is the most western of the New Mexican towns. 1846 E. Bryant *California* I. 13, I noticed..a large number of New Mexicans, and half-breed Indians.

News, *sb.* **6. b.** Add: *news-item, -print* (earlier example).
1844 *Knickerbocker Mag.* XXIV. 179 *News-items, matters of information, actual discoveries. 1843 *Ibid.* XXII. 283 The *news-prints kept their works and worth before the public eye.

c. newscaster, a person who prepares and arranges the news for a news-reel; **news-girl,** a girl who sells newspapers; **news-print,** printing-paper for newspapers; (see also 6 b); **news-reel,** a cinematographic reel for giving news; **news-stand** (earlier example).
1930 *Observer* 28 Sept. 21 Graham MacNamee, the *newscaster of our American newspaper newsreel, takes the part of an unseen dramatist. 1868 *Putnam's Mag.* Apr. I. 518/1 A few years ago, a *news-girl was as rare a sight as a Dodo. 1870 *Scribner's Monthly* I. 115 Old and young are enlisted in the street-vending service from the gray-haired grandsire ..to the tiny news-girl. 1909 *Westm. Gaz.* 3 June 2/2 The duty of 5 dollars a ton on *news-print. 1920 *Glasgow Herald* 23 July 7 Last year Canada produced an aggregate of 833,802 tons of newsprint. 1926 *Ibid.* 13 Apr. 16 Eighteen new newsprint machines are being installed this year. 1928 *Daily Express* 6 June 3/1 Short-length talking-films of the '*news-reel' type have been presented at this theatre for months. 1929 *Lit. Digest* (N.Y.) 11 May 40/2 International News-reel camera-men, out to snapshot the eruption of Mauna Loa. 1930 *Times* 15 Mar. 8/6 The talking news-reel is a new vehicle of public information and entertainment. 1872 Eggleston *Hoosier Schoolm.* viii. 77 You can buy trap-doors..dirt-cheap at the *news-stand.

New school. The section of the Presbyterian Church of the United States holding more advanced and liberal views, which separated from the rest of that Church early in the nineteenth century. Chiefly *attrib.*
1806 Fessenden *Democracy Unveiled* I. 113 That were not justice in arrears, These New School folks would lack their ears. *Ibid.* II. 35 Among our new-school rights and duties, There's no monopoly of beauties. 1837 W. Jenkins *Ohio Gaz.* 317 The public buildings consist of..two presbyterian churches, one of the old, and one of the new school. 1849 E. Chamberlain *Indiana Gaz.* 281 The other public buildings are..churches..for the Methodists..Old and New School Presbyterians [etc.]. 1857 *Quinland* II. v. I. 306 He [the teacher] is a 'new-school' presbyterian minister. 1887 Peck *Gaz. Illinois* I. 72 McDonough College..is identified with the interests of the 'old school' Presbyterians, as the Illinois college..is with the 'New School' Presbyterians. *transf.* 1837 *Southern Lit. Messenger* III. 107 As I once read medicine..under a disciple of the 'new school' (vulgarly called steam doctors). 1839 J. F. Cooper *Home as Found* xiii, But they evidently inclined to the opinion that the new school of pews was far better than the old.

Newsie (niū·zi). *U.S.* Also **newsy.** [f. News + -ie, -y[6].] = News-boy.
1889 *Kansas Times & Star* 12 Jan., Nearly 900 'newsies' applied for licenses and badges. 1904 *N.Y. Times* 16 July 7 He approached the 'newsy' and offered to buy a paper. 1905 *N.Y. Even. Post* 3 June, As a 'newsie' he had developed through the various stages of the Bowery gamin. 1916 C. Sandburg *Chicago Poems* 42 The newsies are pitching pennies.

Newspaper. b. (Add examples.)
1873 'Gail Hamilton' *Twelve Miles* ii. 30 The religious *newspaper agents bore into your house like worms of the dust. 1907 Mrs. Harris *Tents of Wickedness* IV. i. 335 Another letter from Sarah; it was long and it contained a *newspaper clipping. 1843 Marg. Fuller *Summer on Lakes* 185 Has ever Art found..a richer theme..sketched in the *newspaper column of to-day? 1809 *Ann. 10th Congress* 2 Sess. 1084 Notwithstanding the licentiousness of *newspaper editors, he was against any law for curbing them. 1888 *Harper's Mag.* May 962/2 The phrase '*newspaper English' has come to have a significance which is not flattering to newspapers. 1873 'Mark Twain' & Warner *Gilded Age* xii. 116 The drudgery of the *newspaper-office was too distasteful. 1878 Whitman *Diary* (1904) 55 Visited the Tribune newspaper office. 1812 *Niles' Weekly Reg.* I. 361/1, I..admit your publication to be a newspaper and to be rated at *Newspaper Postage. 1847 H. Howe *Hist. Coll. Ohio* 241 Kenton..now contains..1 *newspaper printing office. 1873 'Mark Twain' & Warner *Gilded Age* xlvi. 429 Not being a *newspaper reporter, he could not see either of them that night. 1893 W. K. Post *Harvard Stories* 31 At a *newspaper-stand he bought all the picture papers. 1873 *Brit. Postal Guide* 1 Jan. 21 Every Head Postmaster is required to keep, for sale to the public..*newspaper wrappers

bearing an impressed halfpenny stamp, and Post Cards. 1879 Postal Reg. (U.S.) 69 The law allows no compensation to postmasters for the sale of postage stamps, stamped-envelopes, newspaper-wrappers, or postal-cards.

Newspapering. (Recent examples.)
1911 Edna Ferber Dawn O'Hara iii. 29, I would fall to thinking of those years of newspapering—of the thrills of them, and the ills of them. Ibid. iv. 49 One year of newspapering counts for two years of ordinary existence.

New-year. Add: 2. New-year-cookie.
1807–8 W. Irving Salmagundi xx. 450 These notable cakes hight new-year-cookies,..originally were impressed on one side with the..countenance of the illustrious Rip.
3. Also with ellipse of day.
1845 Knickerbocker Mag. XXV. 128 Stay away on New-Year's and you stay away all the year. 1873 J. H. Beadle Undevel. West xxxv. 750 If you are coming to California for pleasure, come between New Year's and the Fourth of July. 1909 Springfield Weekly Republ. 4 Nov. 1 The general elections are not now expected until after New Year's.

New-Yorky, a. [-y¹.] Suggestive or characteristic of New York.
1908 Edith Wharton Hermit etc. 150 To be compared to her! to be accused of being 'New-Yorky'!

Next. A. adj. Add: 13. c. To get next to: to become acquainted with; to come to know. Also to put next to: to acquaint (one) with. U.S.
1896 G. Ade Artie viii. 73, I wonder where he got next to that fancy pass about severin friendships. Ibid. xvi. 146 I've been next, I'll tell you those. 1904 Utica Observer 14 June 6 The British people are 'getting next' to Dowie; and as a natural consequence his usefulness among them is about at an end. 1910 W. M. Raine B. O'Connor 225 Mrs. Mackenzie will put you next to the etiquette wrinkles where you are shy.

Nib, sb.¹ 3. (Add example.)
1901 J. Black Carp. & Builder, Slating & Tiling 13 The ordinary pantile..is provided on the underside with a small projection known as a nib.

Nibble, v. Add: 1. e. To produce by nibbling.
1866 Augusta Wilson St. Elmo xxi. (1883) 190 Just see what a hole the pretty little wretch has nibbled in my new Swiss muslin dress.

Nibbled (ni·b'ld), ppl. a. [f. Nibble v. + -ed.] That has been nibbled or cropped (by beasts).
1866 Blackmore Cradock Nowell viii. (1873) 31 Over the nibbled sward..came wandering the lightest foot that ever passed. 1905 J. B. Firth Highways Derbyshire viii. 119 The Dove flows between closely nibbled hill slopes.

Niblick (ni·blik), v. Golf. [f. the sb.] trans. To hit (a ball) with a niblick.
1909 Westm. Gaz. 15 Jan. 4/2 If bunkered..he would have to niblick the ball out sideways.

Nick, v.² Add: 4. (Modern U.S. example of intr. use.)
1876 Rep. Vermont Board Agric. III. 132 There is another strain or peculiarity among these Canadians, that seems to nick well with the Morgans.
8. c. Also, to rob.
1916 H. L. Wilson Somewhere in Red Gap vi. 236 'I did hear that you'd had your pocket picked.'..'That's right...Some lad nicked me for my roll and return ticket.'

Nickel, sb. 3. a. Add: nickel-plated adj.
1884 Encycl. Brit. XVII. 488/2 The manufacture of cooking utensils and other useful articles out of..nickel-plated iron. 1910 Blackw. Mag. Nov. 611/2 The car's ornate nickel-plated radiator.
b. nickelface (see quot.); nickel-iron, a mixture of nickel and iron.
1914 Literary Year-bk. 495 *Nickelface. The coating of an engraved plate or block with a battery-deposited surface of nickel. 1931 Times 17 Feb. 13/3 The meteorite is a solid mass of *nickel-iron nearly 14 ft. long.

Nickel, v. Add: b. To foul (the bore of a gun) with nickel off the bullet-casing; intr., to become fouled. **Nickelling** (b), the fouling of the bore of a gun with nickel; metallic fouling.
1918 Farrow Dict. Mil. Terms 407 Nickeling, in gunnery, metallic fouling caused by a portion of the cupro-nickel of the envelope of the bullet being left on the surface of the bore. 1920 G. Burrard Notes on Sporting Rifles 31 When a barrel has once been nickelled it is always liable to nickel again very quickly. Ibid. 30 Nickelling at first is impossible to detect with the eye.

Nickelodeon (nikəlōᵘ·diən). U.S. [f. Nickel sb. 2: apparently after Melodeon.] A theatre or motion-picture show for which the admission fee is a nickel; a place containing automatic machines to provide amusement, which can be used for a nickel.
1927 Fannie Hurst Song of Life 292 The nickelodeons and the gewgaw shops of the most terrific city in the world. 1930 Time & Tide 27 Sept. 1206 The film was..handed over by the scientists to the 'nickelodeons' of America.

Ni·ck-tailed, a. Having the tail nicked.
1853 J. G. Baldwin Flush Times Alabama 97 The horse, a nick-tailed trotter, Tom had raffled off.

Nicodemite. (Modern example.)
1921 Outward Bound Apr. 29/2 This is no time to play the Nicodemite.

Nidal, a. Delete rare⁻¹ and add: 2. Phys. Of or pertaining to a nidus.
1874 J. H. Aveling in Obstetr. Jrnl. July 210 The membrane thus developed has received a great number of names. ..I have adopted as more appropriate that of nidal decidua. 1904 G. S. Hall Adolescence I. 483 The decidua were nidal.

Nidation (nəidē·ʃən). Phys. [f. Nidus and -ation.] The development of the decidua in the uterus.
1874 J. H. Aveling in Obstetr. Jrnl. July 210 The act of nidation consists of the periodical development of the mucous membrane lining the interior of the body of the uterus.

Nidi·colous, a. Ornith. [f. Nidicolæ (L. nidus nest + col-ĕre to inhabit) the class of birds that are hatched in a helpless state, unable to leave the nest + -ous.] Belonging to the class Nidicolæ; remaining in the nest for a time after being hatched.
1902 Encycl. Brit. XXVI. 257/2 Columbæ.—Pigeons. Nidicolous. 1927 A. L. Thomson Birds ix. 155 Birds may ..be divided into two main types, those having nidifugous or 'nest-quitting' young, and those having nidicolous or 'nest-dwelling' young.

Nidi·fugous, a. Ornith. [f. Nidifugæ (L. nidus nest + fug-ĕre to flee) the class of birds that leave the nest when hatched + -ous.] Belonging to the class Nidifugæ; leaving the nest soon after being hatched.
1902 Encycl. Brit. XXVI. 257/1 Order Colymbiformes. —plantigrade, nidifugous, aquatic. 1927 [see *Nidicolous].

Nid-nod, v. Add: 1. (Later example.)
1913 W. De La Mare Peacock Pie 98 'Won't you look out of your window, Mrs. Gill?' Quoth the Fairy, nidding, nodding in the garden.
b. transf.
1905 Quiller-Couch Shining Ferry x. 125 The spring-cart nid-nodded down the hill towards Troy.

Nidor. (Modern example.)
1913 Blackw. Mag. Feb. 159/2 A nidor was to him an agony impossible to endure.

Niece. 1. c. niece-in-law (modern example).
1908 Will in Daily Chron. 5 Nov. 5/3 £1,000 to his niece-in-law.

Nietzschean (ni·tʃīən), sb. and a. [f. the name of the German philosopher, Friedrich Nietzsche (1844–1900) + -an.] a. sb. A follower, disciple, admirer or imitator of Nietzsche; one who holds or supports Nietzsche's views or principles. b. adj. Of, pertaining to, characteristic of, or suggestive of Nietzsche or his views. Hence **Nietzsche·anism**; **Nietzsche·anite**; **Nie·tzscheism.**
1908 New Age 4 July 193/1 The Nietzschean lady is very frank and not unjust about the Comédie Française. 1908 Times Lit. Suppl. 3 Sept. 258/2 The writer..is an enthusiastic Nietzschean. 1909 Q. Rev. Jan. 197 The Nietzschean idea of the Superman as now current among us. 1914 Scotsman 7 Sept. 7/7 This is an unconscious denial of Nietzscheism. 1914 Times 31 Oct. 7/1 Mistaken Nietzscheanism always tempts to the development of the devil in man. 1915 A. S. Neill Dominie's Log vi. 66, I am just enough of a Nietzschean to protest against teaching children to be meek and lowly. 1926 Galsworthy in Scribner's Mag. Jan. 21/2 The Neo-German conception of the State..may be inverted Nietzscheism.

Nife (nəi·fi). [f. Ni + Fe the chemical symbols for Nickel and Iron.] A shorthand expression proposed by Suess (Das Antlitz der Erde III. ii. 626) for the (supposed) nickel-iron core of the earth.
1909 Sollas tr. Suess' Face of Earth IV. 544 Further, we assume the existence of three zones or envelopes as determining the structure of the earth, namely, the barysphere or the Nife (Ni-Fe), Sima (Si-Mg), and Sal (Si-Al). 1924 tr. A. Wegener's Orig. Continents & Oceans 146.

Niftiness (ni·ftinės). U.S. slang. [f. Nifty a. + -ness.] Smartness, spruceness.
1923 Watts Luther Nichols 27 His fixed purpose was to keep it so or to increase its niftiness.

Nifty, a. (Later examples.)
1900 G. Ade More Fables in Slang (1902) 275 Lutie was just about as Nifty as the Next One. 1916 H. L. Wilson Somewhere in Red Gap v. 213 Hetty..looking so fresh and nifty and feminine.

Nigerian (naidʒi·riăn), sb. and a. [f. Nigeria the name of a state in West Africa + -an.] a. sb. A native or inhabitant of Nigeria. b. adj. Of, pertaining to, or connected with, Nigeria.
1908 Daily Chron. 31 Jan. 3/3 She was accepted as a full-fledged Nigerian. 1923 Blackw. Mag. Apr. 514/2 His early days have gone down in Nigerian history. 1924 Ibid. Sept. 352/1 Therein he offended against some Nigerian law.

Nigger, sb. Add: 1. c. A nigger in the wood-pile (or fence): A private reason or motive for a view, course of action, or the like, which is not divulged. U.S.
1862 Congress. Globe 3 June 2527/1 [These gentlemen] spoke two whole hours..in showing—to borrow an elegant phrase, the paternity of which belongs, I think, to their side of the House,—that there was 'a nigger in the wood-pile'. 1876 Congress. Rec. 4 Aug. 5153/1 If some one should say.. that there was some 'nigger in the wood-pile', some 'cat in the bag', some motive to actuate me. 1897 Ibid. 18 Feb. App. 61/1 Like a great many others ignorant of facts, he finds 'a nigger in the wood pile' when there is neither wood pile nor nigger. 1911 Woodrow Wilson in Outlook 11 Aug. 944 If you go through the schedules you will find some nigger in every wood pile.
1888 Bret Harte Phyllis of Sierras i. iii. 90 There's another Englishman comin' up from 'Frisco to see him to-morrow. Ef he aint scooped up by Jenny Bradley he'll guess there's a nigger in the fence somewhere. 1911 H. Quick Yellowstone N. xi. 286 He's always looking for a nigger in the fence.
d. To work like a nigger: To work very hard.
1909 Chambers's Jrnl. Aug. 559/2 The saying to 'work like a nigger' was not inspired by any coloured gent I have happened on yet. 1915 Barnett Lett. 79 They're keen as mustard, cheerful, plucky, and they work like niggers.
2. d. A dark shade of brown; also nigger-brown.
1914 Lady's Pictorial 4 July, Advt. v, Soft Taffeta Hat.. In Black,..Nigger, Mole, and White. 1915 Home Chat 2 Jan. 11/1 Nigger-brown cloth.
3. b. (Examples.)
1909 S. E. White Rules of Game i. v. 32 When the car had flown back to its starting-point, the 'nigger' rose from obscurity to turn the log half-way round. 1929 Encycl. Brit. XIV. 482/1 A steam or air 'nigger' (mechanically operated steel arms) helps to place the log in the proper position.
5. nigger-breaker, -chaser, dealer, -driver (earlier example), -stealer, -trader.
1845 F. Douglass Life 57 All of this added weight to his reputation as a '*nigger-breaker'. 1921 Mulford Bar-20 Three xvi. 217 Most likely they'll be *nigger-chasers, th' way some folks'll be steppin' lively to get out of th' way. 1853 F. W. Thomas J. Randolph etc. 285 You know Robinson the *nigger-dealer, who has the pen down town. 1833 J. Neal Down Easters I. 70 When the *nigger-drivers falls out among themselves. 1840 R. M. Bird Robin Day 43, I was 'a kidnapper, a Georgeye *nigger-stealer'. 1884 'Mark Twain' Huck. Finn xxxiii. 314 Only I couldn't believe it. Tom Sawyer a nigger-stealer. 1853 F. W. Thomas J. Randolph etc. 285 He's not in favor of these regular *nigger-traders is he? 1884 'Mark Twain' Huck. Finn viii. 60 But I noticed dey wuz a nigger trader roun' de place considerable lately en I begin to get oneasy.
6. nigger boy, -blood.
1825 J. Neal Bro. Jonathan III. 207 Nobody there, I guess, but a nigger boy. 1833 — Down Easters I. 66 If there's a drop o' nigger-blood in 'em, they'll always show it in their temper.
b. nigger dialect, -melody.
1834 Knickerbocker Mag. III. 445 And I would say too, that although mighty smart, and a mighty smart chance, mighty big, and mighty little was excellent 'nigger' dialect, yet it was not so refined, as an orator might use. 1846 Ibid. XXVIII. 244 Captain Marin would give a touch from a sea-song, or a specimen of a 'nigger-melody'.
c. nigger cloth = negro cloth (Negro 7); nigger duck U.S., the black duck (Anas rubripes); nigger engine, the engine which operates a 'nigger' (sense 3); nigger fish (earlier example); nigger-luck, exceptional good luck.
1860 Holland Miss Gilbert's Career iv. 61 You see he sells some of his *nigger cloth for goods. 1876 Fur, Fin & Feather 101 The gray duck..are obliged to tolerate in their society that..tough, shot-resisting thing which is commonly called '*nigger duck'. 1873 J. H. Beadle Undevel. West xxxii. 704 Then oaths, spars, '*nigger-engine' and all the other available machinery was set in operation. 1876 Goode Fishes of Bermudas 60 The red form corresponds to Terranus ouatalibe, and is known as the *Nigger-fish. 1851 R. Glisan Jrnl. Army Life viii. (1874) 90, I occasionally made him a little envious by my *nigger-luck, as he is pleased to term it. 1888 Critic 14 Apr. (Farmer), I am cussed..if any darned rebel can have such nigger luck and enjoy it while I live.

Nigger, v. Add: 1. b. (Earlier examples.)
1830–33 C. A. Davis Lett. J. Downing (1834) 22 He laid sticks across the large logs.., and niggered them off with fire, and then rolled them up in piles. 1843 Carlton New Purchase I. xx. 188 In addition to the 'niggering off', it became necessary, as the cold increased, to chop off logs.
2. To work 'like a nigger'; to toil very hard; quasi-trans. with it.
1857 J. Hyde Mormonism v. 120 (Born) Many of the people express satisfaction in seeing these 'better-dressed fellers' obliged to 'nigger it' as well as themselves.
3. refl. To make (oneself) like a nigger, by blackening the face.
1881 May Crommelin Miss Daisy Dimity I. ii. 21 Jemmy the third, was 'niggering' himself, by adorning his rosy cheeks with black.

Niggerdom. (Earlier examples.)
1862 Congress. Globe 28 Mar. 1414/2 New England, where they hate niggerdom worse than the devil. 1868 Good Words 1 Oct. 603/2 The conquering nigger..caught many of the Aborigines, blacked them over, and sent them off to proclaim the glories of Niggerdom.

Niggerhead. Add: 1. (Later example.)
1910 R. W. Service Ballads of Cheechako 19 And there was the little lone moose trail..By muskeg hollow and nigger-head it wandered endlessly.
b. A species of cactus.
1881 Amer. Naturalist XV. 984 Another species of the family is one commonly called the 'nigger-head' or 'barrel cactus', a Mammalaria.
2. (Earlier example.) Also attrib.
1847 H. Howe Hist. Coll. Ohio 569 It was a saw mill, with a small pair of stones attached, made of boulders, or 'nigger heads', as they are commonly called. 1901 Chambers's Jrnl. Sept. 634/1 He tightened his grip on the reins as he caught the dim outline of a treacherous nigger-head stone.
3. (Earlier example.)
1884 'Mark Twain' Huck. Finn xxi. 194 You borry'd store tobacco and paid back nigger-head.

Nigger's head. Naut. An ornamental knot; = Turk's head 2.
1925 Glasgow Herald 3 Oct. 4 The glittering ship's bell with its pendant of brightly painted niggershead knotting.

Ni·ggering, vbl. sb. [f. Nigger v. + -ing¹.] The action of the verb in various senses.
1843 Carlton New Purchase I. xx. 188 Niggering belongs mainly to very large timber, and pertains rather to the science of log-rolling than of preparing fuel. 1894 'R. Andom' We Three & Troddles xix. 174 'Busking' be it known is the technical term for amateur niggering.

Niggerish, a. (Earlier example.)
1825 J. Neal Bro. Jonathan II. 67 Ye great niggerish lookin', wap-sided haw.

Niggerism. (Add example.)
1873 Porcupine 19 Apr. XV. 38/3 For the occasional dash or suspicion of niggerism in the mangling of the words, common custom and coincidence will quite account.

Niggle, v.² 1. d. (Later example.)
1929 Deeping Roper's Row xxviii. 312 He would niggle at his food.

Ni·ggly, a. [f. Niggle v.² + -ly¹.] Mean, petty, niggling.
1923 A. G. Gardiner Life Sir W. Harcourt I. 24, I think his trees niggly as you would say, and he teaches an odd doctrine about trees. 1924 W. J. Locke Coming of Amos xii. 158 'Of course,' he replied, 'it's a bit niggly—you poor fellows daren't escape it; but still..there's breadth and intelligence—you'd better come over to us.'

Nigh, a. 10. d. Add: nigh-wheeler.
1873 J. H. Beadle Undevel. West v. 98 The writer seated on his 'nigh-wheeler', and wielding a 'big-bellied black-snake' over the backs of six mules. 1887 Tourgee Button's Inn 90 He checked up the nigh wheeler lest he should drink too freely. 1903 A. Adams Log Cowboy ix. 131 The nigh wheeler in Joe Jenk's team..was missing.

Nigh, v. 1 and 3. (Later examples.)
1874 A. de Vere Alexander v. viii, A month shall find us Nighing old Egypt's coast. 1893 — Mediæval Rec. 37 And now Ximena with her daughters twain Nighed to Valencia.

Night, sb. Add: 5. Night out (example). Also an evening (or night) spent in festivities; a 'spree' (cf. Out adv. 15 b).
1908 Sanger Seventy Yrs. a Showman ix. 30 For these people Lansdown Fair was, as they put it, their 'night out'. 1910 Blackw. Mag. Jan. 149/1 Mr. Lloyd-George declined to deliver a speech on the ground that it was 'the Prime Minister's night out'!
13. night-ascent, -attack (earlier example), club, school (earlier mod. examples).
1866 Chambers's Jrnl. Oct. 644/2 One *night-ascent has been made in this way. 1844 Knickerbocker Mag. XXIII. 117, I knew that Indians in a *night attack make signals by imitating the cry of some animal. 1906 Machray Night Side of London i. 21 Finishing up, perhaps, at some *night-club, or in some other den. 1928 F. B. Young My Bro. Jonathan ii. viii. 355 A life of night-clubs and jazz-bands. 1857 J. F. Maguire Rome & its Ruler xxiv. 286 The *Night Schools and the schools of the Christian Brothers. 1878 Harper's Mag. Mar. 605/2 Well, now, suppose we have a night school, and learn to write.
b. night refuge, shelter, -sock, -wrapper.
1911 Rep. Labour & Social Conditions in Germany III. 223 We also had a visit to the Berlin *night refuge. 1912 Q. Rev. July 51 The following figures show the number of persons admitted to *night shelters. 1906 Galsworthy Man of Property iii. iii, She had worn *night-socks up in those high hotels. 1863 Mrs. Whitney F. Gartney's Girlh. ix, As Miss Sampson [a nurse] entered from her father's chamber to put on her *night-wrapper and make ready for her watch.
c. night-herd (later example), -herder (earlier examples), -patrol, police, -watchman (earlier example).
1901 S. E. White Westerners xv. 119 The song that brings back to every Westerner visions of other times when he has sung it, and other places—the *night herd, the camp fire, the trail. 1873 J. H. Beadle Undevel. West v. 98 The '*night-herder' Billy Keyes, and two other drivers..were Gentiles. 1878 — Western Wilds iii. 53 Our 'outfit' numbered..sixteen men including a night-herder. 1864 J. T. Trowbridge Cudjo's Cave xxiii. 201 They discovered some horsemen drawn up before them beside the road. It was the *night-patrol. 1877 Eliz. S. Phelps Story of Avis 153 To recommend to the Faculty a stricter régime of *night police for those boys. 1863 Mrs. Whitney F. Gartney's Girlh. xxviii, A man employed as *night-watchman in Mr. Rushleigh's factory.
d. night-sparrow (add example).
1840 Hoffman Greyslaer i. iv. 43 The timid and delicate note of the *night-sparrow, rising distinctly fine from a clump of maples.
14. night-chain, a chain for securing a door at night; night-herd v., to herd (cattle) by night, to act as a night-herd (see 13 c); night-lark, a person who goes about by night; night-office R. C. Ch., the part of the canonical office performed during the night hours; night-rider, one who rides on horseback by night, esp. U.S., one of a gang that inflicted great damage on tobacco plantations under cover of night; night-riding vbl. sb., the occupation of night-riders; nightstick U.S., a stick carried by policemen at night.
1904 Ellen Glasgow Deliverance 45 He had fastened the *night-chain and shot the heavy bolt. 1903 A. Adams Log Cowboy ii. 11 Forrest *night-herded them using five guards. Ibid. vii. 97 We night herded as usual. 1895 Meredith Amaz. Marr. xxiii, *Night-larks of different classes, both sexes. 1767 A. B. Life Mary of Holy Cross 84 *Night-office. 1909 Marg. B. Saunders Litany Lane i. iii, A small chapel in which the brothers held their short night-office. 1879 Congress. Rec. 1480/1 There was much said..of Kuklux, White Leagues, and *Night Riders..There are..no night riders in the State of Louisiana. 1880 Tourgee Invis. Empire iii. 397 A huge joke which certain pretended ghostly night-riders were playing upon the ignorant freedmen of the south. 1909 N.Y. Even. Post (semi-weekly ed.) 4 Oct. 4 He advises the anti-pool tobacco growers to form liberty leagues for the purpose of waging war against the night riders. 1909 Chambers's Jrnl. Feb. 104/1 *Night riding began as soon as the farmers' associations were organised. 1905 N.Y. Times 15 July (Cent. Suppl.) San Juan Hill and the Gut were under *nightstick law until early this morning. 1906 N.Y. Even. Post 6 Nov. 16 Patrolman Lemon ran in front of the approaching car and rapped loudly on the ground with his nightstick.

Ni·ght-flying, vbl. sb. [f. Night sb. + Flying vbl. sb.] Flying in an aeroplane or other aircraft by night. So **Ni·ght-fly** v.
1907 A. C. Johnson How to Find Time at Sea (ed. 6) 9 Steering by the Stars, for Night Flying, Night Marching and Night Boat-Work. 1917 C. C. Turner Aircraft of To-Day xv. 237 The exercises included..night-flying. 1927 Daily Tel. 31 May 13/2 We night-fly regularly in America. It's the ideal time for flying in the States.

Night-flying, a. (Add example.)
1922 Encycl. Brit. XXX. 88/1 It is necessary to read the personal narratives of night-flying pilots.

Night-hawk. b. (Earlier example.)
1793 W. Bentley Diary (1909) II. 48 We observed a great number of the birds, called here [Charleston, N. H.] night hawks, playing in the air.

Ni·ght-hawk, v. [f. the sb.] intr. To prowl about at night.
1878 Mrs. Stowe Poganuc P. i. 14 Little girls like you must go to bed early. They can't be up 'night-hawkin'', and goin' round in the cold.

Night-li·ner. [f. Night-line + -er¹.] A person who uses a night-line.
1902 Chambers's Jrnl. Jan. 47/1 The night-liner..slipped into the black water like an otter.

Nightmare, sb. 2. b. (Add example.)
1909 Chambers's Jrnl. Feb. 75/2 From tip to tip of its outstretched arms this nightmare of the deep measured 56 feet.

Nights, adv. (Add examples.)
1786 Exchange Advertiser (Boston) 19 Oct. (Th.) Not a flute that has a hole in it, but that is employed very successfully nights. 1861 O. W. Norton Army Lett. 29 To-morrow we do guard duty. It is tiresome work. No sleep nights.

Nighty, sb. (Earlier example.)
1894 Susan Hale Lett. (1919) 286 A blind I opened (thereby drenching me and my nighty) banged and smashed a big pane.

Nihiliani·stic, a. Theol. [f. Nihilian(ism + -istic.] Of, pertaining to, or suggestive of, nihilianism.
1920 Theology Oct. 189 The Nihilianistic tendencies of Western Eucharistic theology.

Nilome·tric, a. [f. Nilometer + -ic.] Of or pertaining to a nilometer, or the measurement of the height of the Nile.
1921 G. A. F. Knight Nile & Jordan ix. 96 The Second Cataract where Nilometric markings with his cartouche are recorded.

Nilotic, a. Add: 2. as sb. = Nilot.
1924 Chambers's Jrnl. Jan. 11/2 The Nilotics are in nearly every case the aggressors.

Nimble, a. 7. nimble Will (earlier and later examples).
1817 S. R. Brown Western Gaz. 109 This is the short, nutritious grass called 'nimble will', which has completely overspred with astonishing celerity, almost every spot of waste or uncultivated ground. 1822 J. Woods Eng. Prairie 292 Nimble-will,..a kind of florin-grass, or running couch-grass. 1863 Trans. Ill. Agric. Soc. (1865) V. 863 The Muhlenbergia diffusa, or Nimble Will, is a common grass, which is rather known as a troublesome weed.

Nine. A. adj. 5. Add: nine-spotted.
1861 Trans. Ill. Agric. Soc. IV. 347, I found numerous specimens of a nine-spotted lady-bird (Coccinella novemnotata, Herbst), under dry cow-dung. 1867 Amer. Naturalist I. 278 The nine-spotted Lady Bug, Coccinella novemnotata.
B. sb. 4. b. (See also *Long nine.)

Nine-holes. Add: 1. c. In the nine-hole(s): in a difficulty. U.S.
1863 'E. Kirke' My Southern Friends 76 He owned [the slave] till he got in the nineholes one day, and sold har to the Gin'ral. 1877 Congress. Rec. 3 Nov. 230 We have put the gentleman in the 'nine-holes', and there we intend to keep him. 1910 Ibid. 12 June 6002/1 This bill..has passed the Senate, and to use a Western expression, it will put me 'in the nine-hole' if I do not get it through.

Ninepenny. A. sb. Add: 2. Ale that costs ninepence a gallon.
1886 Hardy Mayor of Casterbridge xiii, I'm in..a low key with drinking nothing but small table ninepenny this last week or two.

Nineteenth. A. adj. Add: 2. The nineteenth hole: the bar-room in a golf club-house. slang.
1928 Daily Express 3 Jan. 9/2 Most courses have been completely unplayable, except at the nineteenth hole.

Nineteenth-ce·nturyism. The distinctive spirit, outlook, or character of the nineteenth century; a feature or trait suggestive of the nineteenth century.
1846 Tennyson in Ld. Tennyson Mem. (1897) I. 238 They seem to be very clever and full of a noble 19th century-ism (if you will admit such a word). 1891 'Lucas Malet' Wages of Sin v. iii, There is another of your perverted nineteenth-centuryisms.

Ni·netyish (nəi·nti,ish), a. [f. Ninety + -ish¹.] Of, belonging to or characteristic of 'the nineties' of the nineteenth century; resembling or suggestive of what was then current.
1909 Westm. Gaz. 2 Mar. 2/2 Certainly there is nothing ninety-ish about Saturday's figures. 1918 E. Marsh Rupert Brooke 13 He entertained a culte..for the literature that is now called 'ninetyish'—Pater, Wilde and Dowson.

Ninon (ninon). [F.] A light-weight dress fabric made in a plain weave from silk yarns.
1913 W. J. Locke Stella Maris xiii. 160 Dressed in a soft grey ninon gown. 1922 Daily Mail 30 Nov. 8 Wearing a lovely gown of ninon embroidered in crystal and silver.

Nip, sb.¹ Add: 1. c. (For earlier examples see *Freshen v. 3.)
e. Geog. A notch in a coast made by wave-action, forming a low cliff.
1897 Geog. Jrnl. IX. 542 Where the aggradation begins at the shoreline at the foot of the earlier formed 'nip'.
6. (Earlier and later examples.)
1832 J. K. Paulding Westward Ho! I. 172 There we were at rip and tuck [sic], up one tree and down another. 1846 W. T. Porter Quarter Race in Kentucky 16 (Th.) It will be like the old bitch and the rabbit, nip and tack every jump. Ibid. 123 (Th.) Then we'd have it again, nip and chuck. 1909 Parrish My Lady of South xxxii. 331 It was nip and tuck, the surprised troopers..digging in the spurs in a mad endeavor to get between us and our haven.

Nip, v.¹ Add: 2. c. Of the sea: To cut back (a shore) by making nips (sense *1 e).
1897 Geog. Jrnl. IX. 538 The coasts of the counties of Kent and Sussex..form a succession of headlands nipped back by the sea.
5. Also with off.
1902 Chambers's Jrnl. Nov. 742/2 Small establishments for the treatment of manufacturing refuse..are nipped off by a rise in the price of fuel.
12. (Add examples. In quot. 1919 trans.) Also to 'cut in'.
1908 H. G. Wells War in Air v. § 4 She [a ship] had.. nipped in between the Susquehanna and the Kansas City. 1916 Bennett Lion's Share xxii. 158 They crossed over, nipped into the dark porch of the house and rang the bell. 1919 Times Lit. Suppl. 27 Feb. 107/3 'The light-hearted snottie' who nipped in his piquet boat across the knife-edged ram of a fast-travelling cruiser. 1920 Blackw. Mag. Jan. 111/2 Your friend..nips in and takes up the running, and you are out of the hunt.

Nipitytuck. = Nip and tuck, Nip sb.¹ 6.
1901 Harben Westerfelt xvi. 222 Toot drove nipitytuck down the street from the Hawkbill as fast as he could lick it, and them a-gallopin' after 'im.

Nipper, sb.¹ Add: 4. c. (Later examples.)
1876 Centennial Exposition viii. 235 The curious part of this [hardware] exhibit consisted in the police nippers. a 1906 'O. Henry' Trimmed Lamp etc. 120 The detective threw himself upon Brady and with Kohen's aid got the nippers on his wrist.
8. A slight preliminary achievement.
1904 W. H. Smith Promoters v. 99 All he'd done so far was only a sort of 'nipper' for what he had planned ahead.

Nippiness (ni·pinės). [f. Nippy a. + -ness.] Nimbleness, agility.
1923 Una L. Silberrad Lett. Jean Armiter ii. 50 Jethro is smitten with admiration of her agility; 'nippiness' he calls it. 1928 Daily Express 11 July 8/3 His nippiness in racing between wickets.

Nipping, ppl. a. 5. Add: nipping-roller.
1920 Discovery Mar. 88/1 The padded goods are well squeezed through nipping-rollers, and then dried and 'backed'.

Nipple, sb. 4. c. nipple-cactus (example).
1876 Encycl. Brit. IV. 625/2 Mammillaria.—This group.. is called Nipple Cactus.

Nipponian (nipōᵘ·niăn), a. [f. (Dai) Nippon the native name of Japan + -ian.] Of or pertaining to Japan, Japanese. So **Ni·pponism,** the furtherance of Japanese interests.
1909 Daily Chron. 19 Aug. 4/6 The best English account of the conflict from the Nipponian point of view. 1914 Hastings's Encycl. Relig. & Ethics VII. 489/1 The cry of 'Nipponism'..was raised in a somewhat extravagant fashion.

Nippy (ni·pi), sb. [f. the adj.] Introduced in 1924 for a waitress in one of the restaurants of J. Lyons & Co. Ltd. London.
The word is a registered trade mark of the company.
1925 Punch 11 Feb. 167/2, I can't mike up me mind weyver to be a lidy's 'elp or a 'nippy'.

Nit (nit), sb.² U.S. colloq. [Of obscure origin; perh. a corruption of Naught, Nought: cf. *Nitwit.] None; nothing.
1910 'O. Henry' Strictly Business v. 66 'You fool...Why did you do it?' 'The Stuff', explained Thomas briefly. 'You know. But subsequently nit. Not a drop.'

Niton (nəi·tǫn). Chem. [f. L. nit-ēre to shine: after Argon, Neon etc.] The name given by Sir W. Ramsay to 'radium emanation', the first product of the disintegration of radium; now called *Radon.
1912 Bath & Wilts Chron. 12 Mar. 4/2 (reporting Sir W. Ramsay) Solid niton causes the glass or silica tube in which it is necessary to confine it to glow with a brilliant light. 1920 Discovery Apr. 109/2 From the disintegration of radium, helium and a gas known as niton, or radium emanation, are evolved.

Nitrate, sb. 3. Add: nitrate field.
1898 Jrnl. Sch. Geog. (U.S.) Oct. 307 The rich nitrate fields of northern Chile.

Nitre, sb. Add: 1. d. (See quots.)
1882 Rep. Vermont Board Agric. VII. 65 The higher the tree is tapped the more of nitre or malate of lime is found. 1872 Ibid. I. 219 The gritty sediment from maple syrup, commonly termed 'nitre'.
5. nitre-works.
1775 Coll. S. Carol. Hist. Soc. II. 66 If he was assisted with a sufficient sum..he says he could bring the nitre works to a great degree of perfection.

Ni:trifiabi·lity. [f. Nitrifiable + -ity.] Capability of being nitrified.
1884 Jrnl. Chem. Soc. Trans. 651 Evidence of the nitrifiability of rape-cake.

Nitrifier (nəi·trifəiəɹ). [f. Nitrify v. + -er¹.] An agency or organism which nitrifies.
1903 Lancet 6 June 1590/1 The bacterial organisms themselves are..the real nitrogen bringers or nitrifiers.

Nitro-. Add: d. nitro-bacteria, the bacteria in soil which transform nitrites to nitrates in the process of nitrification.

1902 Encycl. Brit. XXVI. 57/2 Certain de-nitrifying bacteria reverse the operations of nitro-bacteria.
e. Recently used in the trade names of various fertilizers which contain nitrogen.
1909 Daily Chron. 8 Jan. 4/4 Nitrolim is superior to nitrate, inasmuch as it is not so soluble...Precisely how the nitrogen of nitrolim is taken up by plants we have yet to learn. 1920 Discovery Mar. 84/2 Cyanamide..a compound of calcium, carbon and nitrogen with some free carbon, which is liberated during the reaction, is known commercially as 'nitrolim'. 1927 Daily Express 7 Dec., To replace Chilean nitrate we shall make..nitrochalk, a rich mixture of nitrogen and calcium...A third synthetic compound to come is nitrophosphate of potassium.

Nitrogen. b. Add: nitrogen-fixing.
1899 F. H. King Irrigation & Drainage 233 The nitrogen-fixing tubercles were already developed. 1902 Encycl. Brit. XXVI. 55/2 A still more inexhaustible supply of nitrogen is made available by the nitrogen-fixing bacteria of the soil.

Nitrogenisa·tion. [f. Nitrogenize v. + -ation.] The process of combining, or fact of combination, with nitrogen.
1903 Lancet 6 June 1590/1 The increased nitrogenisation of the soil by the widened use of phosphatic manures.

Nitroso-. Add: b. nitroso-bacteria, the bacteria in soil which transform ammonium compounds into nitrites.
1902 Encycl. Brit. XXVI. 56/2 The Nitro-bacteria are smaller, finer, and quite different from the nitroso-bacteria, and are incapable of attacking and utilizing ammonium carbonate.

Ni·t-weed. Bot. [f. Nit sb.] The American pine-weed, Hypericum Sarothra.
1853 Darlington Flora Cestrica (ed. 3) 29 Hypericum Sarothra,..Broom Hypericum. Nit-weed. Pine-weed.

Nitwit (ni·twit). [cf. *Nit sb.²] A person of little intelligence.
1928 A. S. W. Rosenbach Books & Bidders 87 Shakespeare's genius was so overwhelming that even the least of the nitwits of his day appreciated him. 1928 Saturday Even. Post 4 Feb. 121/3 He's about the most complete nitwit I ever encountered—but useful..and harmless. 1930 Musical Times Nov. 987 Music..of the type that the nitwits who write..to the Radio Times call dry and highbrow.

Ni·twitted, a. [f. prec. + -ed¹.] Lacking in intelligence.
1931 Observer 6 Dec. 11 Many of the American films are just as shoddy, just as nitwitted.

Nivated (nəivē·tėd), ppl. a. Geol. [f. L. nivāt-us cooled with snow (cf. Nival) + -ed¹.] Produced or affected by nivation.
1899–1900 F. E. Matthes in Rep. U.S. Geol. Surv. ii. 184 A glance at the nivated areas..impresses one strongly with their general smoothness and the wavy outlines of their features...Glaciated forms are seen to shade out into nivated forms.

Nivation (nəivē·ʃən). Geol. [ad. L. type nivātiōn-em, f. nivātus: see prec.] The action of frost causing disintegration of rocks in the neighbourhood of melting snow.
1899–1900 F. E. Matthes in Rep. U.S. Geol. Surv. ii. 183 These névé effects...I shall, for the sake of brevity, speak of as effects of nivation. Ibid. 184 By far the most remarkable example of nivation exists at 2, a large expanse of grass and willows.

Nivellating (ni·vəlētiŋ), ppl. a. [f. F. nivel-er to level + -ate + -ing².] Of apparatus: Designed to afford a level surface.
1898 Sci. Amer. Suppl. 9 Apr. 18570 (Cent. Suppl.) The nivellating table is designed to take the place of the usual forms of nivellating apparatus.

Ni:vellisa·tion. rare. [f. as *Nivellating + -ization.] A making level or equal.
1879 Vigfusson & Powell Icelandic Reader 469 There is a nivellization of all vowels as to their quantities.

Nix¹. Add: 1. c. Phr. Nix on, enough of, have done with, no more of. colloq.
1911 H. Quick Yellowstone N. ii. 24 Nix on the Conversation game, said he. 1914 Emporia (Kansas) Gaz. Jan. 13 So, in the words of the poet, nix on Willyum Allen. 1921 R. D. Paine Comr. Rolling Ocean iv. 62 Camp Stuart at ten o'clock. Nix on that kid stuff.

Nixie. Add: b. Used as an expletive.
1904 Buffalo Express 20 June 4 Nixie. There isn't any field that would hold 37,000,000 men. 1914 Gertr. Atherton Perch of Devil i. 108 They're all right to marry,..but to sacrifice your life for, nixie.

Nixie² (ni·ksi). U.S. Also nixy. [f. Nix¹ 1 b.] = Nix¹ 1 b.
1905 N.Y. Even. Post 8 Feb. 5 What the railway postal clerks most dread is the class of mail they know as 'nixies'.
b. attrib., as nixie clerk, division, man.
1901 Congress. Rec. 1145/6 These poor 'nixie' clerks in the postoffices of this country. 1904 Springfield Republ. 29 Oct. 4 He was made what is known in the office as a 'nixy' clerk..one who looks up mi-directed letters. 1929 Lit. Digest (N.Y.) 5 Oct. 67/1 The similarity in appearance of the letters N.Y. and N.J...is responsible for many letters reaching the 'Nixie' division. Ibid. 68/2 If he will give the 'Nixie' men just a little clue to what he is guessing at, the hard reader..will do the rest.

No., Nº. (Further example.)
1905 Strand Mag. Apr. 376/1 George II..made a present of No. 10 [Downing Street] to his Prime Minister, Sir Robert Walpole, and his successors.

No, a. 3. b. (Earlier examples.)
1829–32 J. P. Kennedy Swallow B. II. xvii. 220 Which.. would produce a cure 'in almost no time'. 1840 Southern Lit. Messenger VI. 508/2 I'll have everything ready for you in no time at all. 1868 G. G. Channing Recoll. Newport 143 The money was..arranged as to facilitate the payments in 'no time', understood in my day, to mean the shortest period.
6. b. (Add examples.)
1842 Amer. Pioneer I. 276 History informs us that since the struggle of 1799–1800, there presided a no-party-president. 1848 in Scribner's Monthly (1879) Nov. 60/1 Hall wanted it a no-party call. 1905 Kynoch Jrnl. Apr.–June 66 The well-known Kapp-Housman test for separating the 'no-load' losses which occur in dynamo machinery.

No-account, a. U.S. Of no account, importance, value, or use; worthless, depraved or insignificant. (See also *No-'count.)
1845 J. J. Hooper Adv. Simon Suggs iii. 39 I'll jist tell you that the land I'm after is a d—d little, no-account quarter section, that nobody would have but me. a 1859 Hidden Path (Bartlett) Grieving after a no-account feller like that. 1881 Record (Philad.) 8 Feb. (Th.) Mitchell, of Oregon, is another of the 'no-account' men. 1898 H. S. Canfield Maid of Frontier 109 It seems to me..that Charlie is gettin mighty no account. 1902 G. H. Lorimer Lett. Self-made Merchant vi. 69 A mailing-clerk so no-account as to be writing personal letters in office hours. 1905 N.Y. Even. Post 23 Dec. 4 What no-account characterless people do in these concerns does not matter so much.
b. As sb. A 'no-account' person.
1922 Mulford Tex v. 62 Yer fired!..Yer a loafin', windy, clumsy, bunglin' no-account. 1924 — Rustlers' Valley x, Th' no-accounts are gettin' restless up Los Altos way.

Noah's Ark. Add: 5. Bot. The moccasin flower, Cypripedium pubescens.
1853 Darlington Flora Cestrica (ed. 3) 316 Cypripedium pubescens...Noah's Ark. Mocasin-flower.

Nobbily, adv. (Example.)
1880 Punch 25 Dec. 299/1 There wasn't a chap in the room so good-looking or nobbily drest.

No·bbiness. [f. Nobby a. + -ness.] Smartness; affected elegance.
1909 N.Y. Even. Post 7 Aug. 2 He unwittingly errs..on the side either of a certain scrubbiness or of an even more unfortunate 'nobbiness'.

Nobility. Add: 1. c. pl. Instances of nobleness of nature.
1921 R. Hichens Spirit of Time iv. 71 He pointed to the nobilities, the self-sacrifice,..the marvellous examples of courage.

No-'count, aphetic form of *No-account.
1853 'P. Paxton' Stray Yankee in Texas 282 (Th.) Yes, Massa, dem no 'count calves done fool me again. 1885 H. Jackson Zeph iii. 82 Ye miserable, mean-spirited, no-'count critter! 1897 R. M. Stuart Simpkinsville 13 A sort o' queer half-luney, no-'count darky. 1902 A. D. McFaul Ike Glidden xviii. 145 It wasn't enough for you sickly, no-'count mother to waste my grub and money in idleness.

Noctuary. (Recent example.)
1910 Chambers's Jrnl. Sept. 594/2 My sceptical friends.. say I kept myself awake on purpose to write this noctuary.

Nodality (nodæ·liti). [f. Nodal + -ity.] Nodal quality; the degree or extent to which lines, roads, or any set of things having a lineal character, approach each other or converge at a point.
1897 Geog. Jrnl. IX. 78 A higher degree of 'nodality', to use Mr. Mackinder's term, is found where several such furrows meet to form a well-marked though by no means deep hollow. 1902 H. J. Mackinder Britain & Brit. Seas xix. 330 A spot upon which more numerous land and water roads converge..may be said to have a higher degree of nodality.

Nodalize (nōᵘ·dăləiz), v. [f. Nodal + -ize.] trans. To make nodal in form or arrangement; to concentrate in a node.
1928 D. H. Lawrence Rainbow xv. 416 For what purpose were the incalculable physical and chemical activities nodalized in this..speck under her microscope?

Nodule. 3. Add: Also attrib. and Comb.
1890 Proc. Roy. Soc. XLVII. 104 The limited growth in pot 1..is coincident with the entire absence of nodule-formation. 1922 Encycl. Brit. XXX. 72/1 The so-called 'nodule' organisms (Pseudomonas radicicola)..which live in symbiosis with the leguminous plants.

Noegenesis (noʊidʒe·nėsis). [f. Gr. νόη-σις Noesis + -genesis.] The process by which new knowledge is generated from experience; the obtaining of knowledge thus. **Noegene·tic** a., of, pertaining to, or concerned with, noegenesis.
1923 C. Spearman Nature of 'Intelligence' 61 'Noegenesis.' Another basal property of the manifestations of all the principles is that they, and they alone, are generative of new items in the field of cognition. If then, it be desired to depict these three principles summarily, taking into account both their noetic and their generative properties, we must compound some such name as 'noegenetic'. 1929 Encycl. Brit. VII. 968/1 Spearman's..formulation of the three noegenetic laws in terms of which he analyses all mental processes.

Nog, sb.² 2. (Earlier examples.)
1851 A. O. Hall Manhattaner 10, I tremble to think of the juleps, and punches, and nogs, and soups. 1881 Tourgee Zouri's Christmas viii, Then he tried to drain the glass, but a part of the foamy nogg remained in it despite his efforts.

Noggin. Add: 1. b. local U.S. A pail or bucket.
1885 'C. E. Craddock' Prophet Gt. Smoky Mts. x. 175 Mirandy Jane, seated on an inverted noggin, listened tamely to the conversation. 1888 — Broomsedge Cove xviii. 324 Isabel sat idle on an inverted noggin.

No-good. U.S. [The phrase no good used as a substantive: see Good C. 5 g.] A person or thing that is valueless.
1924 A. J. Small Frozen Gold i. 14 I'll learn you half-suckled no-goods what it means.

Nohow, adv. Add: 1. b. Earlier U.S. examples. Esp. in phr. no how you (they) can fix it. Cf. Fix v. 14 c.
1833 J. Hall Harpe's Head 91 (Th.) They don't raise such humans in the Old Dominion, no how. 1835 W. G. Simms Partisan 506 It won't be an easy journey, ma'am, no how, I tell you. 1836 Col. Crockett in Texas 125 [They] would have nothing to do with that affair, nohow they could fix it. 1840 Knickerbocker Mag. XVI. 19, I mean my name aint G. Washington Mortimer, no how. 1843 Carlton New Purchase I. xviii. 141, I..couldn't read a chapter in the Bible no how you could fix it.

Noise, sb. 6. b. Also used of persons, esp. in phr. the (or a) big noise: A person of great importance. orig. U.S.
1908 G. H. Lorimer J. Spurlock vii. 153 A lot of people are beginning to think that Teddy's a mere noise. 1911 R. W. Chambers Common Law vi. 169 Well, sister, take it from muh, she thinks she's the big noise in the Great White Alley. 1927 Sunday Express 10 Apr. 8 Blanche Ring does not convey much, perhaps, to the average British audience, but she was a big noise in New York at that time. 1931 Galsworthy Maid in Waiting vi. 42 Saxenden is a big noise behind the scenes in military matters.

Nolition. (Modern example.)
1857 in Appleton's Illustr. Handbk. Amer. Trav. 237 Do not allow..the nolition of your womankind..to prevent you.

Nolle (nǫ·li), sb. U.S. Abbrev. of Nolle prosequi.
1872 Eggleston Hoosier Schoolm. xxxi. 214, I now enter a nolle in his case..and I ask that this court adjourn. 1878 J. H. Beadle Western Wilds xxxi. 507 He had been indicted along with the others, and a nolle entered.

Nolle, v. (Later example.)
1910 Springfield Weekly Republ. 24 Nov. 10 (headline) Case Against Haskell Nolled.

Nolle pros, sb. = *Nolle sb.
1895 Denver Times 5 Mar. 1/3 John Doyle was dismissed on a nolle pros in both cases against him.

Nolle-pros, v. Also nol-pros. (Earlier and later examples.)
1880 G. A. Pierce Zachariah 436 Judge Spalding informed Zach...that the case could be 'nolle prossed' when it came up. 1905 Springfield Weekly Republ. 15 Dec. 2 The court heard petitions for a new trial, and upon these being granted the cases were nol prossed and the brothers set free. 1926 D. L. Colvin Prohibition in U.S. 505 In the two years 14,567 cases were nolle-prossed or dismissed.

Nomadization. Add: b. A making or becoming nomadic in character or nature.
1920 H. G. Wells Outl. Hist. 606/2 What we now call democracy, the boldness of modern scientific inquiry and a universal restlessness, are due to this 'nomadization' of civilization.

Nomadize, v. Add: b. trans. To make nomadic in character.
1902 D. G. Hogarth Nearer East 156 The incomers 'nomadised' the south-east. Ibid. 272 The southern oases ..are the most 'nomadised'.

Nomady (nōᵘ·mădi). [f. Nomad + -y³.] The state, condition, or life, of a nomad.
1919 Max Beerbohm And Even Now (1920) 263 The Bohemian, as tending always to nomady, feels that [etc.].

No man. 2. No man's land. a. (Earlier fig. example.)
1870 H. A. Nicholson Man. Zool. I. 6 Some observers have established an intermediate kingdom, a sort of no-man's-land, for the reception of those debatable organisms.
b. Naut. (Add example.)
1891 H. Patterson Naut. Dict. 128 No Man's Land, a space or article left uncleaned, unpainted, or otherwise uncared for on account of not falling within the limits of the work assigned to individuals of the crew.
c. In various special applications, a piece of land or a district which has no owner.
1876 H. Brooks Natal 234 In 1866..the Government of the colony took possession of 'No-man's-land'. 1902 Chambers's Jrnl. Jan. 34/1 The independent warlike tribes formerly sandwiched in a No Man's Land between Afghanistan and India. 1909 Westm. Gaz. 21 Aug. 14/1 This place has a higher attraction..for it is no-man's-land, eligible for building on, threatened, but as yet unoccupied. 1910 Chambers's Jrnl. Aug. 495/1 These cottages had been built...on ground between two roads, which was a kind of 'no man's land' and rent free.
d. Mil. The terrain between the front lines of armies entrenched opposite one another.
1908 'Ole Luk-oie' Green Curve (1909) 256 Here and there in that wilderness of dead bodies—the dreadful 'No-Man's-Land' between the opposing lines—deserted guns showed up singly or in groups. 1915 G. Adam Behind Scenes at Front 101 Perilous work it is repairing wire in the No Man's Land between trenches.

Nomenclatorial, a. (Add example.)
1897 Nature 19 Aug. 364/1 To distinguish those [references] that relate to habits and biology from those that are systematic and nomenclatorial.

Nomism (nōᵘ·miz'm). [f. Gr. νόμ-ος law + -ism.] (See quot.)
1917 Hastings's Encycl. Relig. & Ethics IX. 380/1 'Nomism' or 'legalism' is the name given to the view that moral conduct consists in the observance of a law or body of laws.

Non-committal, sb. (Earlier U.S. example.)
1833 Congress. Debates 30 Dec. 82 This message was a non-committal. The President does not announce clearly his opinion.
b. adj. (Earlier U.S. examples.)
1829 Lett. Columbus (Boston) 18 The non-committal system prevailed. Ibid. 19 Timid and time-serving partisans—non-committal and fence-men. 1841 Congress. Globe 30 Aug. 404/3 He was so much ashamed of it, that he declares he must remain non-committal.

Non-committalism. (Earlier U.S. examples.)
1838 Democratic Rev. Feb. I. 52 That portion of the plan ..which involved a present non-committalism on the question of a National Bank. 1845 Congress. Globe 11 Jan. App. 295/3 We have had bold messages from the land of abstractions [Virginia]; this is a message from the headquarters of non-committalism.

Non-concur, v. (Later example.)
1820 Massachusetts Spy 23 Dec. (Th.) [The resolve was] nonconcurred by the Senate.
b. intr. To refuse to concur in; to disagree with.
1862 Congress. Globe 9 July 3214/1, I hope the House will non-concur in that amendment of the Senate. 1907 Springfield Weekly Republ. 20 June 1 The Senate has nonconcurred with the House amendments.

Non-concurrence. (Later U.S. example.)
1805 Massachusetts Spy 17 July (Th.) A non-concurrence of the Council in a measure of this sort.

Non-conducting, ppl. a. (Earlier example.)
1751 Franklin Electr. Experiments (1753) 96 If applied to a piece of non-conducting matter, it will do neither.

Non-condu·ctive, a. [Non- 3.] = Nonconducting.
1868 Rep. U.S. Commissioner Agric. (1869) 173 A non-conductive covering of moss, which prevents the soil from being warmed by the..sun.

Non-conductor. (Earlier example.) Also transf.
1751 Franklin Electr. Experiments (1753) 96 The terms conductor and non-conductors may supply their place. 1910 Blackw. Mag. Jan. 43/1 You know how lost and abstracted one feels after being alone on an expedition; one is a non-conductor; one has lost touch.

Non-confo·rmant. [Non- 2.] = Nonconformist.
1654 E. Johnson Wonder-working Provid. vii. 13 Others would have strict search made for non-conformants, and that none of the late silenced ministers might passe into the Ships.

Non-contri·butory, a. [Non- 3.] Not based on or not involving contributions.
1911 Q. Rev. July 198 The provision for old age in our system is non-contributory and wholly paid by the State. 1927 Carr-Saunders & Jones Soc. Struct. Eng. & Wales 156 The non-contributory old-age pension scheme.

Non-co-opera·tion. [Non- 1.] Refusal or failure to co-operate (with the British); used esp. of native Indians. So **Non-co-o·perate** v. intr., to refuse to co-operate; **Non-co-o·perative** a., that practises or advocates non-co-operation; **Non-co-o·perator,** one who practises or advocates non-co-operation.
1920 in J. F. Bryant Gandhi & Indianisation (1924) 84 And adopt the policy of progressive non-violent non-co-operation until the said wrongs are righted. 1921 Daily Tel. 28 Sept. 9/1 The leaflet..asks the Moplahs actively to non-co-operate with the Government. 1922 Telegr. Corr. India (Parl. Papers XVI.) 3 The origins of the non-co-operation movement. 1922 J. T. Gwynn Ind. Politics (1924) 17 A Non-Co-operating politician. Ibid., Non-Co-operative propaganda. 1924 J. F. Bryant Gandhi & Nationalisation 112 The chief civil officer in the area..was to be given seven days to hand over the district to the non-co-operators.

None. C. adv. 3. b. (Later examples.)
1852 J. B. Jones Col. Vanderbomb (Philad.) 198 (Th.) Our adventurers slept none that night. 1906 Advocate of Peace Mar. 52 Has civilization advanced none from the barbaric days of the 5th century?

Non-elastic, a. Add: Also fig.
1910 Daily Chron. 4 Jan. 6/4 It is intelligence of the non-elastic order.

Non-elective, a. [Non- 3.] Not appointed by election.
1909 W. Churchill in Westm. Gaz. 9 Oct. 9/4 The claim of the House of Lords—that is, the claim of a non-elective and unrepresentative Chamber. 1910 Blackw. Mag. Aug. 283/1 The independent opinion of men formed in the comparatively 'dry light' of the non-elective chamber has a value of its own.

None·ntitize, v. [f. Nonentity + -ize.] trans. To make into a nonentity.
1913 R. W. Service Rhymes of Rolling Stone 176 Sober am I nonentitized; drunk am I more than half a god.

None-so-pretty. 1. (Later example.) Also as adj.
1771 in Alice M. Earle Costume (Amer.) Col. Times (1894) 173 None-so-Pretty Tapes. 1772 Ibid., Blue and white, Red and white, Green and white Furniture checks with None-so-Prettys to match.

Nonesuch. 2. b. (Later U.S. examples.)
1822 Mrs. Royall Lett. fr. Alabama li. (1830) 123, I went to hear this none such. 1927 'Sax Rohmer' Moon of Madness 18 He was a poisonously handsome none-such. Ibid. 26 Da Cunha danced perfectly, with all the sensuous grace of a none-such.

Non-flam, a. [Non- 3.] That is not inflammable; as sb., trade-name of a film or a flannelette that does not catch fire readily.
1909 Daily Chron. 27 Feb. 4/7 So far as flannelette is concerned I use no other than 'Non-Flam'. 1927 Daily Tel. 25 Oct. 14 In France from Jan. 1 next no celluloid film may be used unless made from this so-called 'non-flam' film.

Nonic (nōᵘ·nik). Math. [f. L. nōn-us ninth + -ic.] A curve or equation of the ninth degree or order.
1894 Pearson in Phil. Trans. A. CLXXXV. 103 The nonic was proved..to have only three real roots. Ibid. 106 When the outlying parts, which control the nonic at present, are removed.

Non-offi·cial, a. and sb. [Non- 3.] a. adj. That is not official; not pertaining to, proceeding from, or sanctioned by, the relevant authority; not consisting of officials.
1850 Punch Aug. 57/2 We subjoin a specimen of the two styles of reports, the one official, and the other non-official. 1900 Fortn. Rev. Jan. 49 Diplomatists now confess—what the non-official world recognised years ago—that no solution of the difficulty is possible. 1901 Edin. Rev. Apr. 380 To take objection to outside employment of any kind in non-official hours. 1910 Blackw. Mag. Nov. 705/1 The non-official members of the provincial legislatures.
b. sb. A person who is not an official.
1910 Blackw. Mag. Nov. 711/2 There is no definite cleavage between officials and non-officials.

No-no·nsense, a. [The phr. no nonsense (Nonsense 1 c) used as an adj.] That stands no nonsense.
1928 Saturday Even. Post 12 May 25/1 From a no-nonsense business man he has become a romantic.

Non-provided, a. [Non- 3.] Of education or schools: That is not Provided (sense 4 b).
1918 Quiller-Couch Foe-Farrell 44 He..zigzagged off into Education 'Provided' and 'Non-Provided', lunging and floundering with the Church Catechism and the Rate-book. 1921 Act 11 & 12 Geo. V c. 51 § 29 marg., Conditions to be observed in conduct of non-provided schools.

Non-resident, a. Add: 3. U.S. Of land: Owned by a person who does not reside on it.
1849 E. Chamberlain Indiana Gaz. 313 The large amount of non-resident lands has hitherto retarded improvements.

Non-resistant. B. sb. (Earlier example.)
1755 Lett. to Washington I. 91 The fighting Faction in Pennsylª are ready and threaten to put to Death all the Non-resistents—Dunkers, Moravians, Dutch and Quakers.

Non-resi·ster. [Non- 2.] = Non-resistant B.
1851 Quitman in Life & Corr. (1860) II. 147 By the election of Non-resisters to the Convention, a majority of the people have declared against the course of policy on the slavery questions.

Non-ri·gid, a. (and sb.). [Non- 3.] a. adj. Of airships: Belonging to the type which has no framework to support the envelope, and whose shape is maintained solely by the pressure of the gas inside. b. sb. An airship of this type.
1909 Daily Chron. 3 Aug. 1/7 The two non-rigids that are to come from France. 1910 C. C. Turner Aerial Navig. To-day 292 The 'Ville de Paris' is of the non-rigid type. 1910 Blackw. Mag. July 4/2 The non-rigid airship has not at present the range nor the carrying capacity of the rigid type.

Nonsense, sb. 6. Add: nonsense-syllable, a syllable formed by putting a vowel between any two consonants, used in memory experiments and tests.
1909 Titchener Exper. Psychol. Thought-Processes 25 When Ebbinghaus began the experimental study of memory and association, he chose as his materials *nonsense-syllables. 1911 Starch Psychol. xii. 167 The time required to learn ten nonsense syllables. 1925 Ogden tr. Koffka's Growth of Mind 29 Nonsense-syllables in an ordered series.

Nonsense (nǫ·nsĕns), v. [f. the sb.] intr. To talk nonsense.
1909 R. A. Wason Happy Hawkins 67, I nonsensed a while, tryin' to get her to laugh an' cut up, but not her.

Non-skid, sb. and a. [Non- 4.] a. sb. A tyre designed to prevent skidding. b. adj. That is designed not to skid or to prevent skidding. So **Non-ski·dding** ppl. a.
1908 Westm. Gaz. 3 Nov. 4/1 This tyre..acts as an efficient non-skid. 1909 Chambers's Jrnl. June 404/1 A perfect non-skidding wheel. 1920 Motor Cycle 29 July 129/2 Non-skid chains. 1925 Public Opinion 11 Dec. 588/3 We want light-coloured, waterproof, nonskid surfaces.

Non-sla·veholder. [Non- 2.] A person who owns no slaves or employs freemen and not slaves, esp. in a slave state.
1850 Seabrook in Life & Corr. Quitman (1860) II. xiv. 37 A large proportion of the population are non-slaveholders.

Non-sla·veholding, a. [Non- 3.] Of a state: In which slave-holding is not practised or is illegal.
1834 Southern Lit. Messenger I. 85 Whoever has travelled ..in stages and steam-boats in non-slave-holding states must have perceived [etc.]. 1846 McDonogh Papers 88 If the senators..from your state, a non-slaveholding state, would bring forward such a law.

Non-smo·ker. [Non- 2.] A person who does not smoke.
1902 Encycl. Brit. XXXI. 784/1 He was a non-smoker, a vegetarian, and a great advocate of temperance principles. 1910 Chambers's Jrnl. Mar. 182/1 Non-smokers rarely drink liqueur.
b. A compartment in a railway carriage, or other conveyance, provided for persons who do not smoke, or object to smoking. colloq.

Non-smo·king, a. Applied to a compartment in a railway carriage, provided for non-smokers.
1909 Daily Chron. 17 Sept. 4/7 A non-smoking compartment of a train.

Non-stop, a., sb., and adv. [Non- 4.] a. a. Of a train, omnibus, or the like: That travels between two (usually distant) places without stopping at intermediate ones. Also of a journey, etc.: Made without a stop. b. sb. A non-stop train, or omnibus; also, a non-stop run, etc. c. adv. Without a stop or break in the journey, flight, etc.
a. 1903 Work 11 July 364/1 The L. & N. W. Railway long non-stop run..presents no difficulty. 1904 Windsor Mag. Dec. p. ix. Advt., Awards gained for Glasgow to London Non-Stop Trials. 1908 St. George's Rev. I. 279 A 20-h.p. car..had a completely non-stop run. 1923 P. G. Wodehouse Inimit. Jeeves xv. 192, I was fairly tired, having swung a practically non-stop shoe from shortly after dinner till two a.m.
b. 1909 Westm. Gaz. 8 Sept. 2/1 The innovation and growth of 'non-stops' upon the Metropolitan and District electric lines. 1911 Motor Cycle 27 Apr. 428/1 He..has now made six successive non-stops. 1924 Lond. Guide No. 3 152 Certain of the trains are 'non-stops'—i.e. they do not halt at certain stations en route.
c. 1920 'Ixion' Motor Cycle Remin. 15 The beastie [a motor cycle] did the outward journey non-stop. 1927 Daily Tel. 14 June 11/3 The second attempt to fly non-stop to India. 1928 Gamble Story N. Sea Air Station vii. 108 From Yarmouth to Cromer, then Yarmouth to Southwold and back. This was done non-stop.

Non-support. [Non- 1.] Failure of a husband to support his wife.
1909 Daily Chron. 20 Jan. 6/2 The Englishwoman makes a charge of non-support against her husband. Ibid. 23 Jan. 1/6 She charges him with desertion and non-support.

Non-u·nionize, v. [f. Non-union 2 + -ize.] trans. To make non-union in character; to supply with non-union workmen in place of union ones.
1926 Glasgow Herald 26 July 7 A motion was carried condemning the action of those Scottish newspaper proprietors who had non-unionised their offices since the strike.

Non-violent, a. [Non- 3.] That does not employ violence, or professes not to do so; used esp. of political agitations.
1924 J. F. Bryant Gandhi & Nationalisation 109 The 'non-violent movement' had produced more violence in a year and a half than any other movement in India for nearly three quarters of a century.

Noo·dleness. [f. Noodle sb.¹ + -ness.] Foolishness, stupidity.
1931 St. John Ervine in Time & Tide 11 Apr. 435 Arnold Bennett despised such noodleness.

Noon, sb. Add: 6. noon rest (later example).
1873 J. H. Beadle Undevel. West xxviii. 615 We found water enough for our noon rest in the hollowed surface of a rock.
b. noon-basket U.S., a lunch-basket; noon-clear a., as clear as noonday; noon-halt, a halt made in the middle of the day; noon-house, U.S., a house used for rest and meals at midday; noon-mark, a mark which indicates when it is noon; midday; noon-spell U.S., a rest taken in the middle of the day.
1865 Mrs. Whitney Gayworthys vi. 71 Don't you remember what we used to say at school, when we opened our *noon-baskets? 1874 Hardy Far fr. Madding Crowd xxxi, In her *noon-clear sense that she had never loved him she forgot for a moment [etc.]. 1843 Fremont Exped. 15 At our *noon halt, the men were exercised at a target. 1854 Bartlett Pers. Narr. Explor. Texas etc. II. xxxvii. 395 On our return we made a noon halt on the banks of the river. 1845 S. Judd Margaret i. (1874) 101 Several elderly men and women retired to what was called a '*Noon House', a small building..where they ate dinner and had a prayer. 1853 B. F. Taylor Jan. & June (1871) 131 The sun..has reached the *noon-mark on the threshold. 1889 Rose T. Cooke Steadfast xxv. 275 Goodness! tis most noon-mark and I haven't took a step towardst dinner. 1842 Mrs. Kirkland Forest Life I. 41 Nor is there a tree yet planted whose shade may soften, to the rising generation, the fervours of the *noon-spell. 1887 J. Kirkland Zury 18 Wait till noon-spell, then we'll see! 1889 Rose T. Cooke Steadfast ii. 30 Its nigh about noonspell now.

Nooning. Add: 3. c. (See quot.)
1884 W. Shepherd Prairie Exper. 161 Through the heat of the day the sheep do not care to feed or to travel; if full they will lie down, seeking some shade, or drooping their heads under the shadow of each other's bodies. This is called nooning.
4. nooning-place (earlier example).
1849 Parkman Oregon Trail 422 As we approached our nooning-place, we saw five or six buffalo.

Noon-time. (Earlier mod. example.)
1834 Knickerbocker Mag. III. 283 They would sit and read for hours together from the same story book, during 'noon time' and 'play time'.

Nope (nōᵘp), adv. slang. U.S. [Strengthened form of No adv.; cf. Yep.] = No adv. 1.
1888 N.Y. Life 22 May, Cover 3/2 'I suppose you will be a literary man, like your father, when you grow up'. 'Nope', said the little boy..'literary nuthin'! I'm goin' to be a ten-thousand-dollar cook.' 1891 Harper's Mag. Nov. 970/1 The professor, wishing to express negation, made use of the objectionable form 'nope'. 1908 Mulford Orphan ii. 24 Nope, I reckon not—seven husky Apaches are too much for one man to go out of his way to fight. 1923 'B. M. Bower' Parowan Bonanza i. 14 'Nope, I'm a never-was', Bill retorted shamelessly.

Nordic (nǭ·ɹdik), a. and sb. [ad. F. nordique (1898 J. Deniker in L'Anthropologie IX. 127) f. nord North: see -ic.] a. adj. Of, pertaining to or characteristic of the peoples of Northern Europe or of the type to which Deniker assigns these. b. sb. A person of the Nordic type.
a. 1898 Ripley in Pop. Sci. Monthly Oct. 744 A direct physical relationship between the three [peoples], referring them all to a so-called nordic race, is confirmed by the very latest and most competent authority [sc. J. Deniker]. 1921 Contemp. Rev. Jan. 56 All the talk about Nordic supremacy is vanity when we look at the facts in Europe. 1922 Fleure Peoples of Europe 13 The long-headed men around the Baltic ..became, in course of time, what is called the Nordic race.

Supplement, p. 3873; Corrigenda, p. 4092; Spurious words, p. 4093; Books quoted, p. 4094

b. 1921 *Man* No. 107. Dec. 180 The difference between the blond dolicocephals known as Nordics and the brown dolicocephals called Mediterraneans..is really very small. 1924 *Public Opinion* 28 Nov. 522/2 The Nordic is tall and fair; the Mediterranean shorter and more slenderly built. 1928 P. G. Wodehouse *Money for Nothing* ii. 32 Well, all I can say is,..it's no life for a refined Nordic.

Nordicism (nǭ·ɹdisiz'm). [f. *Nordic a. and sb. + -ism.] The state or condition of being Nordic; the characteristics of the Nordics.

1924 Eckenrode *Jefferson Davis* ii. 24 The modernism of the North and the Nordicism of the South came more and more into conflict. 1925 *Nation* (N.Y.) CXX. 516/1 The transition from Aryanism to Nordicism in Germany.

Norfolk. b. Add: **Norfolk blouse**, a blouse made with pleats like a Norfolk jacket.

1887 *Girl's Own Paper* 29 Oct. 75/3 Norfolk blouse with pleats.

Normal. A. *adj.* 2. b. (Add quots.)

1897 *Phil. Trans.* B. CLXXXVIII. 7 Both nerves were removed at the same time and kept in normal saline until required. 1911 *Encycl. Brit.* XXV. 342/2 A 0·9% solution [of sodium chloride in water] forms what is termed normal saline solution.

B. *sb.* Add: 5. A normal variety of anything; an individual or specimen possessing normal characteristics or faculties.

1894 W. Bateson *Study of Variation* 17 For the belief that such races are descended from the putative normal scarcely ever rests on proof. 1901 *Amer. Jrnl. Psychol.* XII. 235 The blind rats learned the original task as well as the normals—all the normals experimented with. 1908 *Daily Chron.* 14 Oct. 4/4 We might divide them into three groups:—Normals, Juveniles and children; and The degenerate.

Normalism (nǭ·ɹmăliz'm). [f. Normal a. + -ism.] The quality or state of being normal.

1891 F. W. Bain *Antichrist* ii. 113 The planing away of all gnarled and knotty characteristics, the reducing each individual to precisely the same external appearance. This is the essence and the consequence of the impulse to normalism.

Normality. Add: *spec.* in Chemistry: The concentration of a solution expressed in gramme-equivalents (per litre).

1903 *Science Abstracts* Aug. VI. 315 Boric acid was agitated in a thermostat at 26° with an excess of aqueous hydrochloric acids of different normalities.

Normalize, *v.* Add: b. *intr.* To become normal.

1923 *Contemp. Rev.* Mar. 366 If a rise in the price of tin should follow on the already normalising price of materials.

Norseller (nǭ·ɹs'ləɹ). [f. Norsel *sb.* and *v.* + -er.] A person who fits nets with norsels.

1921 *Dict. Occup. Terms* (1927) § 398 *Net orseller, norseller*, attaches orsells or norsells (short lines about ten inches long) to top and bottom of fishing net at regular intervals.

North. B. *sb.* 2. c. (Earlier examples.)

1796 Washington *Messages & Papers* (1898) I. 217 The North, in an unrestricted intercourse with the South. 1831 Peck *Guide Emigrants* ii. 81 The result would be more disastrous to the south and west, than the influx of foreign goods was to..the north..in 1816.

North, *v.* Add: 3. *intr.* To go *out of* by turning northwards.

1900 J. Bloundelle-Burton *Seafarers* viii. 76 Neither steamer nor sailing vessel had been seen since they had northed out of the west-wind drift.

North American, *sb.* and *a.* [f. *North America* the name of that part of the continent of America which lies north of and includes Mexico.] a. *sb.* A native or inhabitant of North America, esp. of the United States or Canada.

1766 [see North C. 1 c]. 1783 A. Stokes *Brit. Colonies* 144 The North Americans will refuse them their assistance. 1825 J. Neal *Bro. Jonathan* II. 1 The man of America—the Original North American..the 'Indian' as he is called. *Ibid.* III. 413 The brave North American was dead.

b. *adj.* Of or pertaining to North America or to its inhabitants; belonging to or characteristic of North America, living in North America, etc.

1771 Franklin *Autobiog.* Writ. 1907 I. 312 This was the mother of all the North American subscription libraries, now so numerous. 1775 Burke *Sp. Conc. Amer.* 22 Mar. 12 The export trade to the Colonies consists of three great branches... The African..the West Indian; and the North American. 1776 (*title*) The North-American and the West-Indian Gazetteer. 1783 (*title*) The North-American Calendar. 1837 *Southern Lit. Messenger* III. 695 A declaration of the independence of the North American States. 1880 G. W. Cable *Grandissimes* iv. 23 She had..the nerve of the true North American Indian.

North-bound, *a.* [North A.] Bound for the north; travelling northwards.

1903 Kipling *Five Nations* 115 We gather and wait her coming—The wonderful north-bound train. 1904 Harben *Georgians* 217 The young man was at the seven-o'clock north-bound train when it stopped in the antiquated brick car-shed.

North-easter. Add: 2. A waterproof hat or cap worn in rough weather.

1838 *Yale Lit. Mag.* III. 9 A large tarpaulin North Easter was the covering of my head.

Northea·sternmost, *a.* [f. North-eastern *a.*] Situated furthest to the north-east.

1837 W. Jenkins *Ohio Gaz.* 91 *Brown*, the northeasternmost township of Miami county.

Northen, *a.* (Later U.S. examples.)

1772 D. Taitt in *Trav. Amer. Col.* 541 The Inhabitants of the Tuskigees are a remnant of Northen Indians and speak a different Language from the Creek. 1773 *Carroll Papers* in *Maryland Hist. Mag.* XV. 58 Keep the Boy if the Northen Post be not come in untill Monday.

Norther, *sb.* Add: 1.' (Earlier examples.)

1827 *Western Monthly Rev.* I. 320 We were struck by a gale, that they call a norther. 1831 Mrs. Holley *Texas Observ.* i. (1833) 19 Our voyage..is..not without hazard, on account of the Northers; as they are called.

2. A strong north wind blowing in other parts, esp. on the Pacific sea-board of North America.

1835 J. F. Cooper *Monikins* xiv. 171 It may be even now questioned whether the ship would claw off..with a sending sea, and this heavy norther. 1850 in *Harper's Mag.* (1878) Jan. 279 We met a norther in coming out of the Gulf of California. 1891 *Scribner's Mag.* X. 283 The weather along the Pacific highway has been uniformly pleasant, for northers are infrequent.

Northerner. 1. (Earlier example.)

1831 Peck *Guide Emigrants* ii. 60 Such for beauty and splendor and fragrance, the *Northerners* have never seen.

Northman. Add: 2. *U.S.* = Northerner 1.

1836 *Southern Lit. Messenger* II. 434 From my very heart, northman as I am, I admire and affect this good remnant of olden time. 1837 *Ibid.* III. 337 Between the Virginians and the North-men there was a wide variance.

Northmost, *a.* (Modern example.)

1888 Swinburne *Armada* iii. i, Darker far than the tempests are that sweep the skies of her northmost clime.

North Star State. *U.S.* The state of Minnesota.

1909 *World To-day* Oct. 1108 The North Star State has been the scene of her greatest usefulness. Mrs. Potter commenced her educational work in Minneapolis.

North-west. B. *sb.* Add: 2. A former company which traded in the North-west Territories of Canada.

1837 *Southern Lit. Messenger* III. 59 It was the British Mackinaw Company, we presume (a Company established in rivalry of the 'North-West'). 1846 J. W. Webb *Altowan* II. ii. 102 The idlers and the curious, as well as the friends of those about to depart, were now gathering about the dismantled lodges of the 'North West'. *Note*, Formerly traders, though now merged into the Hudson's Bay Company; but the whole is generally known in the mountains by that name.

C. *adj.* 3. (Earlier examples.)

1805 Lewis in *Ann. 9th Congress* 2 Sess. 1070 Who were introduced, some years since, by the Northwest traders, in order to hunt the country on the lower parts of Red river. 1818 in M'Kenny *Mem.* I. (1846) App. 309 Northwest Company blankets—so called..to measure six feet six inches long. 1823 *Ibid.* 297 How much should a three point northwest blanket weigh, to be good?

North-we·sterly, *adv.* [f. North-west.] = North-westward A.

1888 *Century Mag.* Dec. 291/1 Some two or three miles west or north-westerly of Georgetown. 1879 *Dublin Rev.* Jan. 96 It flows first south-west, then westerly and north-westerly for more than seven hundred miles.

North-western. A. *adj.* Add: 2. Of or belonging to the regions of the United States lying to the North-west of the earlier southern states.

1802 Ellicott *Jrnl.* 17 Cincinnati was at that time the capital of the North western Territory. 1812 *Niles' Weekly Reg.* III. 13/1 General Hull, with the whole North Western army,..has surrendered to the British and Indians. 1835 Ingraham *South-West* I. ix. 106 Produce of all kinds, brought from the 'Upper country', (as the north western states are termed here).

3. **northwestern gun** (see quot.).

1859 *Congress. Globe* 16 Feb. 1069/1 The arms furnished to the Indians are what are called northwestern guns. They are little popguns, with which nothing can be killed but the buffaloes.

Northwe·sternmost, *a.* [f. North-western A.] Situated furthest to the north-west. So **Northwe·stmost** *a.*

1782 in Poyas *Peep into Past* (1853) 223, I give Robert the Northwestmost part of the track of land I now live on. 1837 W. Jenkins *Ohio Gaz.* 487 *York*, the northwesternmost township of Morgan county.

Nor'-wester. Add: 1. b. **norwester coat**, a strong oilskin or waterproof coat worn in rough weather (cf. sense 3).

1689–90 in *Early Long Island Wills* (1897) 46 My will is that my norwester Coat..may be given to Christopher Leaming.

4. A trader of the North-west company (see *Northwest B. 2).

1902 S. E. White *Conjuror's House* xi. 143 The fierce Nor'westers, the traders of Montreal,..Astor himself, had to give way. 1905 Thwaites *Early Western Trav.* XXI. 9 The 'Nor'westers' first occupied the field, sent out their daring 'bourgeois' in all directions, and reaped a rich harvest of pelts.

Nose, *sb.* Add: 8. e. *To hold one's nose*: to compress the nostrils between the fingers in order to avoid perceiving a (bad) smell. Also *fig.*

a 1592 Greene *Jas. IV.* i. ii. (Rtldg.) 193/2 A stiff docket—hold your nose, master. 1830 Coleridge *Table Talk* 8 July (1884) 102 Son of Jacob! thou stinkest foully. See the man in the moon! he is holding his nose at thee at that distance. 1900 *Fortn. Rev.* Jan. 74 Surely there are times when he is forced to hold his nose and shut his eyes to shut out the abominable visions he conjures up for us.

13. Add to def.: Also, the corresponding part of an airship, aeroplane, torpedo, etc.

1899 *Royal Mag.* Jan. 251/1 In the 'nose' of the torpedo. 1899 H. G. Wells *When Sleeper Wakes* xxiv. 320 The nose of the machine jerked upward steeply. 1909 A. Berget *Conquest of Air* i. iv. 74 To hold the balloon with its nose to the wind. 1909 *Chambers's Jrnl.* Mar. 206/1 It [a torpedo] is fired with a fuse at the nose. 1913 Kipling *Diversity of Creatures* (1917) 293 If I gave her too much nose she'd be liable to up-end and flop. 1914 *War Illustr.* I. 406 A British Army biplane that collapsed and fell with its nose in the earth.

18. **nose-cap** (*b*), the metal cap on the nose of a shell which contains the device for setting the time fuse; **nose-nippers, -riders** *pl.*, eye-glasses which are worn on the nose; **nose-paint** *U.S. slang*, intoxicating liquor.

1918 Farrow *Dict. Mil. Terms* 410 *Nose Cap. 1918 *Daily Express* 31 July 7/2 He unearthed the nose-cap of a shell while digging in his allotment. 1922 Galsworthy *Forsyte Saga* I. ii. vi. 190 His wife, in a Paris-model frock and gold *nose-nippers, reproved him. 1881 A. A. Hayes *New Colorado* xi. 158 We saw..a sign, in which the name which I have never encountered elsewhere was given to stimulating beverages. This sign was '*Nose-paint and Lunch'. 1901 S. E. White *Westerners* xv. 120 Frosty, trot out the nose paint. 1875 E. H. Dering *Sherborne* xviii. II. 53 Sir Thomas..put on a pair of those glasses which are popularly known as *nose-riders.

Nose, *v.* 8. c. (Add example.)

1926 Spanner *Naviators* i. 9 The car nosed its way ahead on bottom gear, and at a snail's pace.

8. b. (Further example.)

1925 Wodehouse *Carry on, Jeeves* i. 28 He began to nose about. He pulled out drawer after drawer.

Nose-bag. Add: 1. Also, a bag containing food for persons. *slang.*

1925 Wodehouse *Carry on, Jeeves* vi. 145 Biffy's man came in with the nose-bags and we sat down to lunch.

c. The practice among holiday-makers of taking their own food or refreshments with them. Also *attrib.*, as *nose-bag crowd*.

1908 *Daily Chron.* 4 Aug. 3/4 Neither was it, as one of Messrs. Lyons's managers observed with appreciation, a 'nose-bag' crowd. 1909 *Ibid.* 7 June 5/2 The 'nosebag' grows and flourishes.

3. *colloq.* A gas-mask.

1915 D. O. Barnett *Lett.* 11 May 135 Every one was ready and had their nose-bags on, and the gas had no effect whatever.

Nose-bagger. [f. Nose-bag.] A visitor to a place who brings his own food or refreshments with him.

1931 *Morn. Post* 17 Oct. 12/5 The friendly little South Coast town, where only the 'nose-baggers'..are frowned upon.

Nose-bleed. 2. (Earlier example.)

1848 *Asmodeus* (N.Y.) 73 (Th.) What's the best cure for nose-bleed, doctor?

No·se-dive, *sb.* and *v.* [Nose *sb.* and Dive *sb.* and *v.*] a. *sb.* A sudden or rapid descent made by an aeroplane with the nose first. Also *attrib.*, *transf.*, and *fig.* b. *vb. intr.* To perform a nose-dive. Also *fig.* **No·se-diving** *vbl. sb.*

a. 1915 *War Illustr.* III. 426/2 It is much more probable that the descent would have become a 'nose-dive'. 1916 H. Barber *Aeroplane Speaks* (1918) 89 Pilots indulging in nose-dive spins are..not heard of again. 1920 Rose Macaulay *Potterism* vi. iv. § 3. 241 Of course, if you chuck the *Fact* you take away its last chance. It'll do a nose-dive now!

b. 1916 *War Illustr.* IV. 92/1 The third [aeroplane] nose-dived and disappeared. 1917 E. W. Walters *Heroic Airmen* etc. xii. 102 He was compelled to resort to nose-diving. 1920 *Chambers's Jrnl.* Mar. 208/1 Checking any tendency to nosedive. 1926 *Spectator* 13 Mar. 492/1 We will nose-dive straight into the middle of Mr. Cobham's book. 1931 *Randolph Enterprise* (W. Va.) 5 Feb. 1/1 A flock of chimney swallows, which at twilight give thrilling exhibitions of gliding, circling, nose diving.

Nose-down, *a.* [Cf. next.] Of an aeroplane: Having the nose directed downwards.

1916 H. Barber *Aeroplane Speaks* (1918) 89 [An inclinometer] will indicate a nose-down position by increase in airspeed.

No·se-down, *v.* [f. Nose *sb.* or *v.* + Down *adv.*] *intr.* To direct the nose of an aeroplane in a downward direction.

1916 H. Barber *Aeroplane Speaks* (1918) 87 The pilot, however, prevents such a state of affairs from happening by 'nosing-down'. *Ibid.*, If a sharp turn necessitates banking beyond that angle, he must 'nose-down'.

Noser. Add: 3. A prying or inquisitive person.

a 1909 'O. Henry' *Roads of Destiny* xiii. 207 One of the little brown oily nosers in red trousers slid in to make an inspection.

Nosey, *a.* Add: 3. *slang.* Inquisitive, curious.

1910 H. G. Wells *Hist. Mr. Polly* vi. § 2. 118 One has to be nosy over one's buying.

b. *Nosey Parker*: An inquisitive person. Hence *Nosey-parkering* ppl. a. and vbl. sb.

1912 Compton Mackenzie *Carnival* xxi. 241 'I saw you go off with a fellah.' 'What of it, Mr. Nosy Parker?' 1915 P. G. Wodehouse *Something Fresh* v. § 5 'But Nosey Parker is what *I* call him', she said. 'He minds everybody's business as well as his own.' 1925 Deeping *Sorrell & Son* xxx. § 4 A nasty, acute little man of the Nosey Parker genus. 1920 Vachell *Virgin* xviii. 280 I'm a pestering nosey-parkering, shilly-shallying sort of an idiot, eh? 1930 Priestley *Angel Pavement* iv. 156 That's what takes your time, my boy—doing your bit of nosy-parkering.

No side. *Rugby.* The (announcement of the) conclusion of a game.

1882 [see Side *sb.*1 20 b]. 1900 *Yng. Sportsman* (ed. A. E. T. Watson) 284 *No side*, the form of the referee's announcement that the time allowed for the game..has expired. 1930 *Times* 14 Mar. 7/1 The home team had cleared to midfield when 'no-side' was called.

Nosing, *vbl. sb.* Add: *Comb.*, as **nosing motion** (see quot.); **nosing-peg**, a peg for securing nosing motion.

1884 Knight *Dict. Mech.* Suppl. 636/1 *Nosing Motion.* Refers to appliances for the perfect winding of yarn on the noses of the spindles, by an accelerating motion, to secure tightness of the yarn on the reduced diameter of the upper end of the mule spindle. 1894 C. Vickerman *Woollen Spinning* 326 Many improvements have from time to time been introduced in working the quadrant chain, some in the shape of nosing pegs for depressing the chain.

Nostalgically (nǫstæ·ldʒikăli), *adv.* [f. Nostalgic *a.* + -al + -ly 2.] By or as by home-sickness.

1928 Galsworthy *Swan Song* iii. xi. 298 A long time he sat there, nostalgically bemused, strangely unwilling to move.

Nostoma·niac. [f. Nostomania: after Maniac.] A person affected with nostomania.

1913 R. W. Service *Rhymes of Rolling Stone* 50 The Nostomaniac.

No·strilled, *a.* [-ed 1.] Having the nostrils formed or drawn in a special way.

Properly the second part of a compound.

1909 *Athenæum* 31 July 125/1 The characteristically Irish 'nostrilled' portraits of the four Evangelists.

Not, *adv.* Add: 1. c. With ellipse of dependent clause after certain verbs, as *hope, say, think not*. colloq.

1907 E. Phillips Oppenheim *Secret* ix. 57 'She is coming back, of course!'..'The chambermaid thought not, sir.' 1908 S. E. White *Rules of Game* ii. iii. 128 'The law'll get him some day.' 'I think not', replied Selwyn. 1912 Galsworthy *Inn Tranq.* 220 Is that a British habit? I think not.

Notal (nōu·tăl), *a.*2 [f. Note *sb.*2 + -al.] Of, pertaining to, or employing, notes.

1884 *Encycl. Brit.* XVII. 85/1 The treachery of tradition is exemplified in the loss of the rules for this once generally understood practice of notal inflexion.

Notated, *ppl. a.* [f. as Notate + -ed.] = Noted *ppl. a.* 2.

1922 W. J. Locke *Tale of Triona* xii. 128 He could play, sensitively, by ear—knowledge of notated music he disclaimed.

Notation. 2. (Recent example.)

1929 J. Gallishaw *Twenty Probl. Fiction Writer* 228 The wise writer depends upon recorded observations, and makes notations.

Notational, *a.* Add: b. Of or pertaining to musical notation. **Nota·tionally** *adv.*

1896 *Musical Herald* 1 Feb. 43/1 With regard to *ba*, Mr. McNaught admitted that, notationally, there was something to be said in favour of abolishing the name, but, educationally, it was better to keep it. 1925 P. A. Scholes *Second Bk. Gramophone Record* 162 Under the notational description of 6/8 we get sometimes *two groups* in a bar, sometimes *three groups*.

Nota·tionist. [f. Notation + -ist.] One who uses or advocates a particular style of musical notation.

1896 *Musical Herald* 1 Feb. 41/2 Every singer should be a two-notationist. 1897 *Ibid.* 1 June 188/2 There is no reason why..Sol-faists and staff notationists should not come to a common understanding and agreement. 1928 *Musical Times* July 619 All those brought up on the Staff would benefit by a grounding in Tonic Sol-fa...The dual notationist is, in fact, the best-equipped musician.

Notch, *sb.* 6. Add: **notch-ladder** (see quot.).

1901 *Chambers's Jrnl.* Oct. 657/2 A notable feature of these smaller mines is the notch-ladder system of conveying the ore from the interior to the pit-head. Two masts, notched like bear-poles, form the means of ascent and descent for a more or less continuous chain of *peons*.

Notch, *v.* 3. (Recent fig. example.)

1911 *Chambers's Jrnl.* Oct. 702/1 A speed of one hundred miles an hour has been notched on more than one occasion.

Notcher. Add: Also, an instrument for making notches.

1879 *Organ Voicing* 8 Tools for voicing and tuning...1. The *notchers* of various sizes. Four will suffice.

Note, *sb.*2 Add: 2. c. = Keynote 2.

1909 *Chambers's Jrnl.* May 276/1 Canada takes her 'note' from the seas which wash her eastern shores.

21. (sense 2) *note-singing*; (sense 13) *note-block, -pad*; **note-broker** (see quot. and sense 17); **notehead paper**, business note-paper having a printed heading; **note-holder**, a holder of notes (sense 17) issued by a business company or the like for temporary financing.

1927 R. A. Freeman *Certain Dr. Thorndyke* ii. xiv. Jotting down on a *note-block a few brief memoranda. 1929 *Encycl. Brit.* IV. 233/1 Bill-brokers are practically unknown in the United States; their general analogue is the *note-broker. 1909 *Westm. Gaz.* 20 May 7/2 The..*notehead paper of a London firm of stock, share, and bond dealers. 1927 *Daily Tel.* 21 June 2/3 Shareholders were prepared for unfavourable figures by the necessity for an arrangement regarding ..the rights of the *note-holders. 1922 Bennett *Lilian* i. iv, She repeated the number, even writing it on her *note pad. 1896 *Musical Herald* 1 Feb. 41/1 Thousands of teachers waste time in *note-singing practice. 1908 E. M. Sneyd-Kynnersley *H.M.I.* xxiv. 288 The clergy encouraged note-singing for the sake of their choirs.

Note, *v.* 6. a. (Add example.)

1897 *Musical Herald* 1 June 189/1 They organise vocal music competitions, but they have no sight-singing, and no noting music by ear.

Note-shaver. (Earlier and later examples.)

1816 *Massachusetts Spy* 4 Sept. (Th.) We have too many note-shavers; too many gentlemen. 1905 D. G. Phillips *Plum Tree* 11 But my clients were poor, and poor pay, and slow pay. Nobody was doing well but the note-shavers.

No·te-shaving. *U.S. slang.* [f. prec.] The profession of a note-shaver; the making of an excessive profit on the discounting of notes.

1855 Barnum *Life* 138 Had I termed the deed an extortion or note-shaving..the verdict might have been different—but I had called the act 'usury'. 1902 Harben *Abner Daniel* 38 He began to utilize this capital in 'note shaving', and other methods of turning over money for a handsome profit. 1911 R. D. Saunders *Col. Todhunter* viii. 113 Old Eph Tucker was a note-shaver long before he was a politician, and he's got note-shavin' in his blood bigger'n a mule.

Nothing. A. *sb.* Add: 1. f. as *adv.* or *interj.* Not at all; in no respect. *U.S. colloq.*

1888 [see *Nope *adv.*]. 1898 A. Nicholas *Idyl of Wabash* 175 'My account—nothing!' was her scornful ejaculation. 1899 Tarkington *Gentl. Indiana* i. 10 'But you only wait—' The editor smiled sadly. 'Wait nothing. Don't threaten, man.' 1911 H. Quick *Yellowstone N.* xi. 288 Stop nothing! Federal injunction won't do it. 1922 Marg. B. Houston *Witch-man* xviii. 238 'He could have found it, of course.' ..'Found it, nothing. I saw other things he'd taken.' 1923 E. F. Wyatt *Invis. Gods* ii. iv. 66 'It is disloyal.' 'Disloyal nothing! Babyhood foe!'

g. *Like nothing on earth*: strange, ugly, wretched, etc., in a superlative degree.

1927 W. E. Collinson *Contemp. Eng.* 117 To look or feel like nothing on earth.

6. e. (Earlier example.)

1835 J. F. Cooper *Monikins* xxiv. (1860) 352 In this happy land, there was no registration, no passports, 'no nothin'—as Mr. Poke pointedly expressed it.

10. a. (Modern example.)

1884 'Mark Rutherford' *Deliverance* (ed. 9) iv. 52 She had learned that she was nothing specially to him.

Notice, *v.* Add: 7. *trans.* To write 'a notice' of (something) in a newspaper or the like.

1854 *Punch* 15 July 20/1 The reporter who 'noticed' the diplomatists.

Noticeability. Add: b. The quality, state, or fact of being noticeable.

1927 H. W. Fowler *Mod. Eng. Usage* 638 The reader will perhaps conclude that its noticeability is not a grace.

Noticeable, *a.* 2. (Earlier example.)

1809 *Mem. Amer. Acad.* III. 248 The moon's limb exhibited very little of that rough or serrated appearance, which was so noticeable in 1806.

Notion. Add: 7. (Earlier example of *to take a notion*.)

1801 M. V. H. Dwight *Journ. Ohio* (1912) 4 We at first refused, but I afterwards chang'd my mind, and 'took a notion'..to go.

9. b. (Earlier examples.)

1803 Ashbury *Jrnl.* (1821) III. 106 How would it tell to the South, that priests were among the notions of Yankee traffick? 1815 Humphreys *Yankey in Eng.* 41 Moreover, long sairse and short sairse; consisting of a variety of leetle notions.

c. *notion-peddling, seller.*

1809 W. Irving *Knickerb.* v. i. 342 He swore that he would have nothing more to do with such a squatting, bundling, guessing,..notion-peddling crew. 1839 *Chemung* (N.Y.) *Democrat* 17 Apr. (Th.) A 'notion seller' was offering Yankee clocks, &c.

Notional, *a.* 4. b. (Earlier example.)

1791 *Gaz. of U.S.* 9 Feb. (Th.) If a man is a little odd in his ways, his friends say he is a notional creature, or full of notions... Love is the most notional passion.

Not-out, *a.* Add: b. *sb.* A batsman who is 'not out'.

1882 Pardon *Australians in Eng.* 6 The not-outs resumed their innings at ten minutes past twelve. 188 *Daily Tel.* 27 May, The overnight not outs, returning to their posts. 1894 *Times* 15 Nov. 11/3 The not-outs..resumed their innings.

No trump(s, *phrase. Bridge.* [No *a.* 1, 6.] 1. *ellipt.* A bid, call, or declaration, which provides for the playing of a hand without a trump suit; the play at bridge without trumps. Also *fig.*

1902 *Encycl. Brit.* XXVI. 370/2 With an established black suit of 5 or 6 cards the dealer should declare no-trump if he has another suit protected. 1904 J. B. Elwell *Adv. Bridge* 236 It is the rule at 'no-trump' to return partner's suit with your highest card. 1905 R. F. Foster *Complete Bridge* 59 The risk of calling no trumps and finding the adversaries with a large honour score for aces must be considered. 1910 *Blackw. Mag.* Dec. 809/2 Nine times out of ten it is No Trumps, but sometimes the class element creeps in. 1912 Flor. Irwin *Fine Pts. Auction Bridge* 56 You can either double the two hearts or go to 'two no-trumps'.

2. *attrib.* (Usually in the form *no-trump.*) Applied to a bid, call, etc., providing for 'no trumps', or to a hand at bridge played without trumps.

1902 *Encycl. Brit.* XXVI. 369/2 If in a no-trump hand the partners conjointly hold 3 aces, they score 30 for honours. *Ibid.*, Each trick above 6 counts..12 in a no-trump declaration. 1909 Dalton *Saturday Bridge* 41 This is an undoubted No Trump call for the dealer.

No-tru·mper. [f. prec. + -er.] A no-trump bid, call, etc., or a hand on which such a bid is or can be made.

1901 A. Dunn *Bridge* 29 As the dealer's hand is not worth a single trick, a light 'no-trumper' means absolute ruin. 1904 J. B. Elwell *Adv. Bridge* 37 A six or seven card suit headed by ace, king, and queen, with a guarded king in another suit, will usually succeed as a 'no-trumper'. 1909 Dalton *Saturday Bridge* 42 Both of the hands quoted above are sound No Trumpers.

Noughting, *vbl. sb.* (Modern example.)

1926 A. E. Taylor *Plato* ix. 225 The 'noughting' and remaking of the soul is the great business of life.

Noumenalism (nau·mĕnăliz'm). [f. Noumenal + -ism.] = Noumenism.

1902 *Encycl. Brit.* XXX. 679/2 Fechner regarded every composite body as the appearance of a spirit;..This noumenalism would not do for Lewes.

Noumenalist (nau·mĕnălist). [f. Noumenal + -ist.] A believer in noumenalism; in quot. attrib.

1925 J. E. Turner *Theory Direct Realism* Pref. 8 The term 'Direct' is intended to imply further the complete absence of any representative or noumenalist factors in the process and object of perception.

Nou·nism. [f. Noun + -ism.] (See quot.) So **Nou·nize** *v. trans.*, to make into a noun. **Nou·ny** *a.*, having or using many nouns.

1871 J. Earle *Philol. Eng. Tongue* 190, 2 Henry IV, iv. i. 71 *there* (nounized). 1904 G. S. Hall *Adolescence* II. xvi. 467 Adjectivism, adverbism, and nounism, or marked disposition to multiply one or more of the above classes of words. 1926 H. W. Fowler *Mod. Eng. Usage* 654 It is as an unfailing sign of a nouny abstract style that a cluster of *-ion* words is chiefly to be dreaded.

Nourishable, *a.* Transfer † *Obs.* to sense 1.

2. (Modern example.)

1876 Meredith *Lett.* (1912) I. 269 The dear heart of him so frankly nourishable by flattery that [etc.].

Nourishment. Add: 4. *spec.* The treatment of leather with some substance to keep it soft or pliant.

1897 C. T. Davis *Manuf. Leather* xlii. 596 For the nourishment of fine glacé leather yolk of eggs is..used.

Novele·ttish, *a.* [f. Novelette + -ish.] Pertaining to or characteristic of a novelette.

1911 in Webster. 1921 *Sat. Westm. Gaz.* 10 Sept. 15/2 The blue-eyed make-up of the novelettish débutante. 1929 *Sunday Express* 13 Jan. 4/4 Novelettish stuff.

Novice. Add: 3. d. Applied to animals exhibited at a show or contest, which have not previously (or before a specified date) won a prize of more than a specified (small) amount.

1903 *Forest & Stream* 21 Feb. 151 (Cent. Suppl.) Novice dogs was a large class, 28 in all. First went to Westlake Chancellor, a good dog. 1909 *Westm. Gaz.* 5 June 9/4 Business..began with the judging of novice ponies in single harness. 1909 *Daily Chron.* 19 June 7/6 'Canterbury Belle' headed the list in a fine show of novice hacks.

Novocaine (nōu·vŏkēn). Also -cain. [f. L. *nov-us* new + Co)caine.] A registered trade-name for a synthetic product obtained from coal-tar, used as a local anæsthetic.

1906 *Lancet* 27 Oct. 1160/1 For operations on the perineum and lower limbs, four to six centigrammes of stovaine or one decigramme of novocaine is requisite. 1910 *Practitioner* Feb. 255 For regional anaesthesia novocain has given good results. 1920 *Discovery* Mar. 88/2 Anæsthetics like novocaine and stovaine are derived from coal-tar.

Nuanced (niū·ānst), *ppl. a.* [f. Nuance + -ed.] Possessing or exhibiting delicate gradations in tone, expression, etc.

1920 *Chambers's Jrnl.* June 374/1 His carefully nuanced Bostonian accent.

Nub, *sb.*1 3. (Earlier example.)

1834 Seba Smith *Sel. Lett. Major Downing* 205 That's pretty much like the nub of the business.

Nubbin. (Earlier and later examples.)

1692 in *Maryland Hist. Mag.* XIII. 209 Jones saw him buy one beaver skin..for thirty ears and nubbins of corn. 1838 Drake *Tales & Sketches* 150 A handfull of salt and a few nubbins of corn. 1910 'O. Henry' *Strictly Business* vi. 76 A red nubbin of corn.

Nuclear, *a.* Add: 1. c. *fig.* Central, cardinal.

1922 *Housemaster's Lett.* 91 You will forgive me if I tell you what I consider the nuclear fault underlying all this writing.

Nuclease (niū·klĭ,ēⁱs). [f. Nucle-ic + *-ase.] An enzyme or a group of enzymes which split up nucleic acid into mononucleotids and other products.

1906 *Jrnl. Med. Research* July 163 (Cent. Suppl.) Jones has shown the existence of enzymes in the thymus and adrenal...Sachs found a similar enzyme in the pancreas and called it 'nuclease'.

Nucleated, *a.* 1. Add: Also (*Physics*), having nuclei or points of greater condensation.

1902 C. Barus in *Science* 31 Jan. XV. 177/1 Looking centrally through the receiver containing saturated benzine vapor and nucleated air. 1903 *Nature* 8 Oct. 549/2 The subsidence of the invisible nucleated air.

Nucleation. Delete *rare*—1 and add examples.

1902 C. Barus in *Science* 31 Jan. XV. 177/1 After nucleation the first dense fogs were vaguely annular during the first.. exhaustions. 1903 *Nature* 8 Oct. 548/2 Experiments are described showing different temperatures for the maxima of nucleation and of ionisation.

Nu·cleator. [f. Nucleate *v.* + -or.] A substance or agent that produces nuclei in gases or liquids.

1903 C. Barus in *Nature* 3 Dec. 103/1 Phosphorus as a nucleator suddenly bursts forth into maximum activity at about 13°.

Nudist (niū·dist). [f. Nude + -ist.] An adherent of the cult of the nude; a person who advocates or practises going unclothed. Also *attrib.*

1931 *John O'London's Weekly* 8 Aug. 620/2 The other members of the nudist colony were..entirely normal people. *Ibid.* 620/3 The nudists of France are pursued by the police, by the clergy, by the wit of Parisian cartoonists.

Nugget(t)y, *a.* 3. Add: Also of persons.

1900 H. Lawson *Over Sliprails* 165 Jimmy Nowlett was a nuggety little fellow, hard as cast iron, good-hearted, but very excitable.

Nullification. 2. b. (Earlier examples.)

1799 *Kentucky Resol.* 14 Nov., A Nullification by those

sovereignties, of all unauthorized acts..is the rightful remedy. 1830 *Massachusetts Spy* 22 Sept. (Th.) Nullification nullified. 1832 Clay *Speeches* (1842) 198 The ranks of those who, unfurling the banner of nullification, would place a state upon its sovereignty.

Nullificator. (Earlier example.)

1830 in *Massachusetts Spy* 27 Oct. (Th.) It is to be hoped that, if the Nullificators do move, it will be to Mexico, or beyond the Rocky Mountains.

Nullifier. 1. (Earlier example.)

1830 *Massachusetts Spy* 7 July (Th.) This argument was considered by the nullifiers as overwhelming.

Nullify, *v.* 1. (Earlier absol. example.)

1829–32 J. P. Kennedy *Swallow B.* I. xviii. 186 I'd be glad to know if we couldn't nullify.

Nu·lling, *vbl. sb.*2 [f. Null *v.*2] The making of knurls; knurled work.

1851 C. Cist *Cincinnati* 245 All kinds of turning used by cabinet makers, including nulling of every pattern, furnished at the shortest notice. 1914 Eberlein & McClure *Pract. Bk. Period Furniture* 63 Nulling, made up chiefly of beading, cabling and hollows, is often used to ornament the bulbous legs of Jacobean furniture.

Number, *sb.* Add: 3. e. An item of information. *U.S. slang.*

1903 A. H. Lewis *Boss* 205 That's a nice number to hand a man!

4. Later examples, esp. of fig. use of phrases *to get* (or *take*) *one's number*.

1908 E. F. Benson *Blotting Bk.* i, I saw one policeman trying to take my number. 1912 Mathewson *Pitching* i. 4 'I've got your number now, Matty!' he shouted at me as he drew up at second base. 1918 Car. Wells *Vicky Van* v. 65 'That's enough', said Lowney. 'I've got his number.' 1920 Hard *Raymond Robins' Own Story* 190 To hurt Bolshevism you need at least to get its number. 1921 R. D. Paine *Comr. Rolling Ocean* viii. 129 Do you remember the day before that when he made that crack at you in front of Miss Crozier? I had his number right then.

e. *One's number is up*, one is doomed (to die), one's time is come; one is 'done for'.

1914 *London Opinion* XL. 231/2 The late Patsey Cadogan, who left £100,000 when his number went up. 1915 'Bartimeus' *Tall Ship* i. 11, I think our number's up, old thing. 1922 P. G. Wodehouse *Girl on Boat* xi. 181 Fate had dealt him a knock-out blow; his number was up. 1928 *Daily Tel.* 10 July 10/5 If he..goes to one of certain public houses frequented by these sharks his number is up. 1929 *Mercury Story Bk.* 98 It was about midday that I first realised that his number was up.

5. c. *Number one*, of the finest quality, the best obtainable, first-rate, 'tip-top'.

1655 *Trans. Mich. Agric. Soc.* VI. 495 Wheat first-rate, peas, also, oats number one. 1861 *Trans. Illinois Agric. Soc.* IV. 446 As an ornament it is not number 1. 1872 Eggleston *End of World* xi. 78 This walk seems the shortest, when I'm in superfine, number-one comp'ny. 1872 — *Hoosier Schoolm.* xv. 125 Seems to me it would be number one to have God help you.

6. e. *colloq.* A bedroom in a hotel.

1902 *Chambers's Jrnl.* Nov. 717/1 The ordinary sojourner at a strange hotel will..ask to be accomodated with a 'bed' that night; the bagman..expresses his desire for a 'number'.

19. *Comb.*, as **number-cloth**, the cloth bearing a horse's number in a race; **number-plate**, a plate bearing a number, esp. that on a registered vehicle.

1924 Edgar Wallace *Educated Evans* vi. 131 Catskin was the one horse..that Educated Evans would have recognized without colours and *number-cloth. 1869 *Good Words* 1 Mar. 170/2 The white porcelain *number-plates upon the doors. 1901 *Motor-Car World* Apr. II. 74/1 We greatly fear that the number-plate is coming. 1911 *Chambers's Jrnl.* Dec. 831/1 White light to illumine the number-plate.

Numhead (nɒ·mhed). *U.S.* [After Numskull.] = Numskull. So **Nu·mheaded** *a.*

1876 *Rep. Vermont Board Agric.* III. 624 The opinion too generally prevails that almost any numhead will do for a farm laborer. 1846–52 Mrs. Whitcher *Widow Bedott P.* x. 98 The old coot was so awful numbheaded I couldent beat any thin' into him.

Numidian (niūmi·diăn), *sb.* and *a.* [f. L. *Numidia* the name of a country in North Africa + -an.] a. *sb.* A native or inhabitant of Numidia. b. *adj.* Of or belonging to Numidia. **Numidian crane**, the Demoiselle crane (*Grus virgo*). **Numidian marble**, a variety of marble.

1614 Gorges tr. *Lucan* iv. 156 The vagrant fierce Numidæans. 1627 May tr. *Lucan* iv. G 6 b, The seeming-fledd Numidians they espy'd. 1697 Dryden *Æneid* iv. 57 And fierce Numidians there your Frontiers bound. 1905 T. Hodgkin in *Life & Lett.* (1917) xi. 229, I wish I had come to this Numidian land when I was younger...Our Numidians long held Rome at bay. 1921 *Edin. Rev.* July 105 A Numidian, riding bareback and stirrupless, is throwing a lasso at a wild ass.

1877 *Encycl. Brit.* VI. 546/2 The Numidian or Demoiselle-Crane..distinguished from every other by its long white ear-tufts. 1909 *Chambers's Jrnl.* July 459/1 A marble of beauty and note is the so-called Numidian marble.

Numinous, *a.* (Modern examples.)

1864 R. S. Hawker *Quest of Sangraal* 17 An Orient Cruse, Fulfill'd, and running o'er, with Numynous Light. 1923 J. W. Harvey tr. *R. Otto's Idea of Holy* 194 A liturgy unusually rich in numinous hymns and prayers is that of Yom Kippur.

Nun, *sb.*1 3. c. **nun's thread** (earlier examples).

1691 *Letter Bk. S. Sewall* 118 A pound of very fine Nuns Thred. 1746 in *Maryland Hist. Mag.* XXI. 381, 10 Pounds Whited brown thread. 1 pound nun's thread sorted.

Nuptiality. Add: 4. Tendency towards marriage.

1902 *Encycl. Brit.* XXXI. 839/1 Nuptiality and Fecundity.

Nurled, variant of Knurled.

Nurse, *sb.*1 8. Add: *nurse-companion*.

1908 Beatrice Harraden *Interplay* 210 Dr. Edgar can no doubt find you a nurse-companion.

Nurse, *v.* Add: 6. b. (Example.)

1912 *Chambers's Jrnl.* Jan. 79/1 In shoeing a horse, instead of the horse's hoof being nursed between the legs of the smith, it is held on the head of the upright.

9. b. *Cricket.* (See quot.)

1897 Ranjitsinhji *Bk. Cricket* 244 Batsmen..often refrain from punishing a bowler as severely as they might when they feel at home with his deliveries...This is the meaning of 'nursing' the bowling.

c. (See quot.)

1912 *Q. Rev.* July 103 The 'bull'..becomes a 'stale' bull, and drifts into the position frequently described as 'holding the baby'—that is to say, nursing a stock or share, perhaps for months, in the vague hope of getting rid of it some day at a profit.

Nursery. Add: 8. c. **nursery school**, a school for children between the ages of two and five years.

1891 Michaelis & Moore tr. *Froebel's Lett.* 30 He [Froebel] thinks of christening it '"Nursery School for Little Children' or 'Self-teaching Institution'. 1917 *19th Cent.* June 1310 *First Stage* (5–11) preceded in some cases by the crèche or the nursery school. 1918 *Education Act* § 8 (a), The supply of Nursery Schools for children over two and under five years of age. 1929 *Nebraska Alumnus* June 165 This nursery school which is a comparatively new development in child training..shares honors with the nursery school at Vassar College [etc.].

Nu·rsery-maid, *v.* [f. *nursery-maid*, Nursery 8 a.] *trans.* To tend or look after (a person) as a nursery-maid does a child.

1899 Cutcliffe Hyne *Further Adv. Capt. Kettle* x. 201 'But you know nothing about diving, and you might have an accident...' 'Oh, I'll risk that. You must nursery-maid me a bit.'

Nursing, *vbl. sb.* 2. Add: **nursing-chart**, a chart for recording certain details regarding a patient's condition.

1925 A. S. M. Hutchinson *One Increasing Purpose* i. xi. 66 Conrad Bryne has crossed to the table where lies the nursing-chart and has taken it up and is deep in it.

Nurtural (nǖ·ɹtiurăl), *a.* [f. Nurture + -al.] Of, belonging to, or due to nurture; usually designating characteristics, etc., which can be attributed to training, environment, or the like, and are not natural or inherited.

1889 *Jrnl. Anthrop. Inst.* XIX. 78 The problem of determining purely 'racial characteristics' will be considerably simplified if we can in this way determine what may be described in contradistinction as 'nurtural characteristics'. 1922 W. R. Inge *Outspoken Ess.* Ser. ii. 257 Professor Pearson has tabulated a long list of natural characters, and another long list of nurtural characters.

Nut, *sb.*1 5. a. Add: *For nuts*; for amusement, 'for fun'.

1914 Gertr. Atherton *Perch of Devil* i. 79 Why don't you sink a shaft, just for nuts.

21. **nut-butter**, a substitute for butter obtained from the oil of nuts; **nut-food**, food prepared from nuts; **nut-meat**, the kernel of a nut; **nut-pine** (earlier example).

1907 *nut-butter [see *s.v.* Nucoline]. 1918 C. A. Mitchell *Edible Oils & Fats* ix. 117 Deodorised coconut oil is used in the preparation of both margarine and 'nut butter'. 1905 *Vegetarian Messenger* Apr. 105, I will send any readers who wish for it an address where *nut-foods can be had guaranteed free of pea-nuts. 1913 A. B. Emerson *R. Fielding at Snow Camp* 102 The three boys stuck to their work..until there was a great bowl of *nutmeats. 1845 Fremont *Exped.* 221 In popular language, it might be called the *nut pine.

Nut (nɒt), *sb.*3 *slang.* [Possibly the same as Nut *sb.*1; cf. Nutty *a.* 4: see also *Knut.] A fashionable or showy young man of affected elegance; a 'young blood', fop or masher.

1904 A. Williams in *Sergeant Brue* in *N. & Q.* Ser. xi. VIII. 78/1 I'm one of the nuts, one of the nibs. 1909 *Punch* 24 Mar. 208/3 He's a nut, I can tell you. 1913 *Ibid.* 12 Feb. 115/1 Spring socks will be black and Spring ties a quiet blue. A strike of nuts is expected at any moment. 1920 W. J. Locke *House of Baltazar* xvii. 205 I've a jolly good mind to set him up regardless, like a pre-war nut—with solid silver boot-trees and the rest to correspond.

Nut, *v.* Add: 3. To fix or fasten by means of nuts.

1894 Elliston *Organ Tuning* 54 The rack pillars are sometimes screwed into the upper boards and the rackboards nutted up.

Nut-cake. *U.S.* [Nut *sb.*1 1.] a. A doughnut. b. A cake containing nuts.

a 1800 *Spirit Farmer's Museum* (1801) 235 Heap the nut-cakes, fried in butter. 1823 [see Nut *sb.*1 19]. 1844 *Knickerbocker Mag.* XXIV. 483 Reflection..was interrupted by the appearance..of 'nut-cakes and cider'. 1857 *Quinland* ii. ii. I. 34 By the way, Hepsy, make us some 'nut-cakes', and bring us the cider. 1872 Marietta Holley *My Opinions* (1891) 251 Where is the rich happy woman that wouldn't give a nutcake to a sick beggar? 1889 Rose T. Cooke *Steadfast* xviii. 198 Who ever heerd tell of puttin' a reason and a bit of citron into the middle of a riz nut-cake before 'twas fried?

Nu·t-grass. Add: (and the Australian *Cyperus rotundus*.)

1909 A. H. Davis *New Selection* iv. 36 Nothing but burr and thistle and nut-grass grew.

Nutmeg. 3. (Add example.)

1822 J. Woods *Eng. Prairie* 307 There are many sorts of sweet melons... I have only noticed musk, of a large size; and nutmeg, a smaller one.

5. **nutmeg hickory**, a species of hickory (see quots.).

1810 Michaux *Arbres* I. 21 *Nutmeg hickory nut. 1832 D. J. Browne *Sylva Amer.* 177 This species..bears the name of Nutmeg Hickory from the resemblance of its fruits to that of the nutmeg.

Nutmeggy, *a.* (Add example.)

1928 *Daily Express* 17 Feb. 4 Luscious prunes with a creamy, nutmeggy rice pudding.

Nutrose (niū·trōᵘz). The trade name for caseine sodium, a substance derived from milk used as a nutrient in medicine and bacteriology.

1907 *Practitioner* Nov. 670 Nutrose was found by Brandenburg and Strauss to be absorbed to the extent of 40 per cent. 1910 *Ibid.* Apr. 491 Wasserman's medium consists of swine serum, nutrose and peptone agar.

Nu·t-shelly, *a.* *U.S.* [f. Nutshell 4.] Condensed, brief, concise.

1843 Carlton *New Purchase* II. l. 171 So nut-shelly had all books and subjects become, that all could be even cracked and devoured in infant schools!

Nutter2. [f. Nut *sb.*1 + But)ter.] Trade-name of a substitute for butter made from the oil of nuts; nut-butter.

1906 *Westm. Gaz.* 18 May 4/2 'Nutter', 'Nucoline', and 'Nuttene'—all representing butter made from nuts. 1909 H. G. Wells *Ann Veronica* vii. § 3 Fruitarian refreshments —chestnut sandwiches buttered with nutter, and so forth. 1915 Barnett *Lett.* 127 One [a trench mortar]..fires a cylindrical thing like a Nutter tin.

Nuttiness (nɒ·tinės). [f. Nutty *a.* (senses 2 and 4) + -ness.]

1. Nutty colour, flavour or character.

1866 Blackmore *Cradock Nowell* xv. (1873) 62 In the height of summer [his colour was] a dappled bay; towards the autumnal equinox, a tendency to nuttiness. 1884 *Sat. Rev.* 8 Mar. 321/2 The six essays..have the 'nuttiness' of age about them.

2. Smartness, spruceness, foppishness.

1916 E. V. Lucas *Vermilion Box* 27 All his nuttiness has gone. You remember how his hair used to be swept right back from his forehead with lovely comb marks in it.

Nutting, *vbl. sb.* Add: 1. b. A nutting party.

1880 *Harper's Mag.* Dec. 89/2 The younger people had their..nuttings, and the like.

2. *nutting-expedition, -ground, -party.*

1873 'Mark Twain' & Warner *Gilded Age* xxi. 200 Parties, picnics..nutting-expeditions in the October woods. 1845 Mrs. Kirkland *Western Clearings* 105 Their way onward lay near the nutting ground. *Ibid.* 98 The occasion was a nutting-party—a regularly planned and numerously attended expedition in search of hickory-nuts.

Nuttish, *a.*2 [f. *Nut *sb.*3] Characteristic or suggestive of a nut.

1909 *Punch* 24 Mar. 208/3 He indulged in a variety of eccentricities. I can imagine nothing more nuttish.

Nychthemeral (nikþī·mĕrăl), *a.* [f. Nychthemer(on + -al.] Pertaining to or consisting of a period of twenty-four hours.

1907 *Nature* 17 Jan. 287/2 The regulation of the nychthemeral cycle of temperature and its inversion in the aged.

O

O. Add: 5. c. O.B.E., Order (Officer) of the British Empire; O.M., Order of Merit.

1917 *Illustr. Lond. News* 30 June 759/1 The five classes of the Order [of the British Empire] are:..4. Officers (O.B.E.), 5. Members (M.B.E.). 1923 B. Copplestone in *Cornh. Mag.* June 765 A Captain and an O.B.E. 1903 *Quarterly Ind. Army List* Oct. p. x/2 O.M. Member of the Order of Merit. 1912 *Chambers's Jrnl.* Apr. 216/1 The Right Hon. Field-Marshal Earl Roberts, O.M.

d. O.K. (see also *O.K. *sb.* and *v.*); O.H. *U.S.*, on hand (Hand *sb.* 32 a); O.P. (*e*) observation post (also *O. Pip*); O.S., ordinary seaman; O.T.C., Officers' Training Corps.

1904 *New York Herald* 30 Oct., No small percentage of the articles that eventually find their way back to the 'O.H.' before spend nearly the entire twelvemonth in the 'O.H.' before they are redeemed. 1916 *War Illustr.* 7 Oct. 185/1 A French 'O-Pip' in the Hills. 1918 'Q' *Foe-Farrell* 15, I tucked the Infant into his little O.P., and left him comfy. He won't see anything there to-night. 1914 Tweney *Dict. Nav. & Milit. Terms* 164 *O.S.* Ordinary Seaman; one who has undergone training as a ship's boy, but who is not fully qualified as a seaman. 1909 *Captain* Aug. p. xiv/1 Senior Divisions of the O.T.C. 1922 Joad *Highbrows* i. 55 The 'Boys of the O.T.C.'..was just a right-down straightforward sort of good hearty song.

O, *sb.*1 2. Add: Also *Comb.*

1917 H. H. Richardson *Fort. R. Mahony* iii. iii. 196 He stood o-mouthed and absent-minded.

Oa·fishly, *adv.* [f. Oafish *a.* + -ly 2.] In an oafish or stupid manner.

1908 A. S. M. Hutchinson *Once Aboard Lugger* i. vii. § 1. 60 The driver becomes temporarily idiot—stands us oafishly silent, or perhaps jerks out some stupid words.

Oak. 9. Add: **oak barren** *U.S.* (earlier example); **oak flat** *U.S.*, a level expanse of ground bearing a growth of oaks; **oak-mast** (earlier example); **oak opening** (earlier and later examples); **oak-pruner** *U.S.*, a variety of beetle (see quot.); **oak towel** *Cant* (see quot.); **oak yard** *U.S.*, an enclosure in which oaks are grown.

1811 *Niles' Weekly Reg.* I. 101/2 Our *oak barrens and other wooded plains may be profitably applied to sheep. 1800 B. Hawkins *Sk. Creek Country* 29 *Oak flats, red and post oak, willow leaved hickory..on its left side. 1849 E. Chamberlain *Indiana Gaz.* 381 Beech and oak flats, which are adapted only to grass. *Ibid.* 17 *Oak and beech mast is found in such quantities as to contribute largely both to feeding and fattening hogs. 1833 C. F. Hoffman *Winter in West* (1835) I. 139 At a sudden turning of the path, I came at once upon the '*oak openings'. 1839 Mrs. Kirkland *New Home* xx. 133 The 'grubs' present a most formidable hindrance to all gardening efforts in the 'oak-openings'. 1848 J. F. Cooper *Oak Openings* I. i. 10 Giving their appellation to this particular species of native forest, under the name of 'Oak Openings'. 1882 *Econ. Geol. Illinois* II. vi. 104 There is an intermediate district occupied by oak-openings. 1899 D. Sharp *Insects* ii. 286 *Elaphidion villosum* is called the *oak-pruner in North America. 1889 Farmer *Americanisms*, **Oak towel*, a stout oaken stick. There is an allusion here to 'wiping' or 'dressing one down'. 1835 R. M. Bird *Hawks of Hawk-hollow* II. v. 52 His father..had suddenly checked his horse at the entrance of the little *oak-yard.

Oa·kery. *U.S. rare.* [f. Oak + -ery.] An oak yard.

1838 Caroline Gilman *Recoll. Southern Matron* xxx. 213 Turning suddenly, he bounded over the fence into papa's oakery.

Oa·kiness. [f. Oaky *a.*] The quality of being oaky.

1863 'Gail Hamilton' *Gala-Days* 128 [In] the English Church..there is a general tone of oakiness, solid, substantial, sincere.

Oak land, Oakland. Chiefly *U.S.* [Oak 8.] Land bearing a growth of oak-trees.

1665–70 *Lancaster* (Pa.) *Rec.* 271 There is another peice of upland..sum part pine Land & partly oak Land. *Ibid.*, Sum part of it [is]..oake land. 1737 Wesley *Jrnl.* 2 Dec., The land is of four sorts—pine-barren, oak-land, swamp, and marsh. 1751– [see Oak 8]. 1811 *Niles' Weekly Reg.* I. 302/1 It was a piece of dry oak land. 1837 W. Jenkins *Ohio Gaz.* 187 The soil of Franklin is, what is generally called oak land, being a mixture of clay, sand and gravel. 1849 E. Chamberlain *Indiana Gaz.* 209 The oak land is more extensive than the beech.

Oakum. 3. Add: *oakum loft*.

1814 *Niles' Weekly Reg.* V. 432/1 The fire commenced in the oakum loft.

Oaky, *a.* 2. (Earlier example.)

1800 B. Hawkins *Sk. Creek Country* 62 The good land spreads out for four or five miles on both sides of the creek, with oaky woods.

Oarer (ōᵊ·rəɹ). [f. Oar *v.* + -er 1.] One who uses an oar; a rower.

1924 *Glasgow Herald* 19 July 6 The Bay of Millport resounds with the..shouts of inexpert but enthusiastic 'oarers'.

Oarlock. Add: Also *attrib.* in *oarlock seat*.

1874 J. W. Long *Amer. Wild-Fowl Shooting* 85 Both may row, if two sets of oarlock-seats are provided.

Oarsman. (Earlier example.)

1811 *Niles' Weekly Reg.* I. 245/1 They certainly possess great dexterity as oarsmen.

Oat, *sb.* Add: 4. d. *To feel one's oats*, to feel important, display self-importance. *U.S. slang.*

1843 Haliburton *Attaché* xxiv. II. 157 You know that, and you feel your oats, too, as well as any one. 1871 Barnum *Struggles & Triumphs* 33 My father..installed me as clerk in this country store. Of course I 'felt my oats'. 1897 Flandrau *Harvard Episodes* 85, I suppose he was feeling his oats when he captained his class eleven.

6. *oat-bag, -straw* (earlier examples).

1851 A. O. Hall *Manhattaner* 5 It was a modest commercial plain..with..bits of machinery, and ploughs, and *oat bags, and hay bales. 1849 *Rep. U.S. Comm. Patents, Agric.* (1850) 380 Getting no other food in winter but a scanty supply of *oat-straw. 1859 Alice Cary *Country Life* i. 7 [He] lay..with a bundle of oat-straw for his pillow.

Oat, *v.* *U.S.* (Earlier and later examples.)

1732 B. Lynde *Diary* 9 May (1880) 26 Next morning.. dined at Hampton;..thence to Greenland, where oated, and for 2 horses and drink, 2s. 1741 *Ibid.* 27 Oct. 121 Breakfasted and oated our 3 horses, at Deacon Tucker's. 1855 Barnum *Life* 70 Old 'Bob' was duly oated and watered.

Oath, *sb.* 1. Add:

Under oath, on or upon oath.

1712 [see Under *prep.* 14 b]. 1851 R. Glisan *Jrnl. Army Life* viii. (1874) 83 He was then under oath not to drink for six months.

Oatmeal. 3. Add: *oatmeal mush* U.S., porridge made of oatmeal. Also *ellipt.*

1883 H. P. Spofford in *Harper's Mag.* Aug. 465/1 You've been the means of starving me..on oatmeal mush. 1902 Clapin *Dict. Amer.*

Obbligato. B. *sb.* Also *transf.*

1921 G. Hopkins *City in Foreground* i, He took the easiest way, which was to supply a gentle *obbligato* to the inspired melody of his companion's speech.

Obclude: variant of Occlude.

1894 *Proc. Zool. Soc.* 434 Only about half the iris is visible, and even some part of the lens is obcluded.

Obeisantly, *adv.* (Modern example.)

1902 *Westm. Gaz.* 2 July 2/3, I..came in turn Of him myself obeisantly to learn.

Obe·lial, *a.* [Obeli(on + -al.] Obeliac.

1890 H. Allen *Clin. Study Skull* 52 The parietal foramina lie on the sides and serve as guides to this the obelial portion.

Obeliscoid (ǫbĭli·skoid), *a.* [f. Obelisk + -oid.] Resembling an obelisk in form; obelisk-shaped; obeliscal.

1877 W. R. Cooper *Egypt. Obelisks* v. (1878) 25 An obeliscoid monolith originally erected by Usirtesen. 1901 A. J. Evans in *Jrnl. Hellenic Stud.* XXI. 173 The obeliskoid pillar of the Cretan ring.

Obeyance. (Modern example.)

1921 Mulford *Bar-20 Three* x. 118 The obeyance of the order might possibly be accepted by the crowd as grounds for justification.

Obiter. C. *sb.* Add: b. = *Obiter dictum*.

1927 *Daily Tel.* 19 July 9/2 Lord Justice Scrutton recalled a recent obiter by Mr. Justice Eve to the effect that [etc.].

Obitual. A. *adj.* (Add U.S. example.)

1893 *Nation* (N.Y.) 30 Nov. 406/3 Obitual days constitute an important, distinctive, and ever recurrent feature in the proceedings of our national Legislature.

Object, *sb.* Add: 5. b. *No object*, not a thing aimed at or regarded as important to obtain. Freq. misused of distance, expense, etc., not taken into account or forming no obstacle.

1782 *Morn. Herald* 20 May, Advt., A Gentlewoman..wishes to superintend the family of a single Gentleman or Lady.. and salary will be no object. 1796 *Ann. Congress* (1849) 878 Enjoying..unexampled prosperity,..the expense of completing the frigates could be no object to the country. 1855 *Poultry Chron.* III. 67/2 Where every convenience is obtainable, and expense no object. 1871 *Eng. Mechanic* 20 Jan. 431/1 The colour of the solder is no object, as the joint will be hidden. 1873 J. H. Beadle *Undevel. West* xxxv. 762 With one team to each family (time being no object to such people) it cost them nothing to move. 1886 *Encycl. Brit.* XX. 228/1 Only those travel who travel by necessity, or to whom money is no object. 1891 Mrs. Riddell *Mad Tour* 3 The time when distance was, as the advertisements say, 'no object'. *a* 1909 'O. Henry' *Roads of Destiny* iv. 62 She..gave her *a la carte* to fit me out—money no object. 1930 *Lond. Mercury* Nov. 45 Distance being no object.. scenes in Siam can be..transmitted.

10. **object chart**, a chart for use in object lessons; **object system**, the system of teaching by object-lessons; **object teaching** (examples); **object-white** *Billiards*, the white object-ball.

1871 *Rep. Indian Affairs* (1872) 306 A new and original series of '*object charts' gotten up expressly for the Indians of Oregon by myself. 1869 C. L. Brace *New West* vi. 75 The improvement which we have sought so much to bring before the public in New York..—the '*Object System'—has already been adopted here. 1878 *Harper's Mag.* Mar. 607/2 This school is too large for strictly Kindergarten Teaching; but the 'object system'..was the one adopted. 1860 H. Barnard (*title*), *Object teaching, and Oral Lessons on Social Science and Common Things. 1871 *Rep. Indian Affairs* (1872) 424 The method of object-teaching has been followed as far as practicable with the apparatus at our command. 1924 Mannock *Billiards Expounded* 97 To enable the object-ball to go on to the baulk cushion and return up by the *object-white. 1907 *Westm. Gaz.* 19 June 7/2 He got the red ball against the top cushion,..and..the object-white against the side cushion.

Objectly (ǫ·bdʒĕktli), *adv.* [f. Object *sb.* + -ly 2.] Objectively.

1925 *Blackw. Mag.* Dec. 786/1 He saw himself objectly as a felon with the mark of Cain.

Obligate, *ppl. a.* Add: 2. b. as *sb.* An obligate parasite.

1907 *Med. Record* 3 Aug. 172 (Cent. Suppl.) It is probable that the intestinal bacteria are not essential to healthy life. The chief value of these obligates lies [etc.].

Obligate, *v.* 3. a. and 5. Add: In later use chiefly *dial.* and *U.S. colloq.*

Oblique. B. *sb.* Add: 3. A movement or march in an oblique direction, esp. in a direction making half a right angle with the previous one.

1845 T. J. Green *Texian Exped.* vi. 52 He suddenly makes a 'left-oblique' for the Laredo road.

Obli·teratingly, *adv.* [f. Obliterating + -ly 2.] In an obliterating manner; so as to obliterate.

1904 H. G. Wells *Food of Gods* i. iii. § 1. 56 He scarcely remembers the leap he must have made..so obliteratingly hot and swift did his impressions rush upon him.

Obliterator (ǫbli·tĕreⁱtǝɹ). [ad. L. *oblit(t)erātor* (see Obliterate) one who obliterates.] One who or a thing which obliterates.

1895 Hardy *Jude Obscure* i. i. 7 In place of it a tall new building..had been erected..by a certain obliterator of historic records. 1900 *Pall Mall Gaz.* 18 Apr. 3/2 Fire was an obliterator of evil deeds more sure than any other.

Oblivia·lity. *rare.* [f. Oblivial *a.* + -ity; or f. L. *oblīvi-um* Oblivion + -ality.] Liability to be forgotten.

1905 E. F. Benson *Image in Sand* i. 5 You certainly did not [meet him], or you would remember. Mr. Henderson has absolutely none of the quality of obliviality.

Oblivion. 2. (Add example.)

1912 Galsworthy *Inn Tranq.* 128 Hand-wrought bronze sconces and a band of metal bordering, all blackened with oblivion.

Obliviscible (ǫblivi·sĭb'l), *a.* [f. L. *oblīvīsci* to forget + -ible.] Able or likely to be forgotten.

1905 *N. Y. Times* Sat. Rev. 12 Aug. 526 (Cent. Suppl.) The sonnets he wrote about those poets, so obliviscible, excepting by himself.

Obnoxity (ǫbnǫ·ksĭti). [f. as Obnoxious *a.* + -ity.] An obnoxious, objectionable, or offensive person or thing; an object of aversion.

1930 D. H. Lawrence *Virgin & Gipsy* iii, That widow of a knighted doctor, a harmless person indeed, had become an obnoxity in their lives.

O'Brienism (obrəi·əniz'm). [f. the name of William O'Brien, Irish patriot (1852–1928) + -ism.] The conduct or policy of William O'Brien, esp. in the British Parliament about 1900 and 1901. **O'Bri·enite**, a supporter of William O'Brien.

1889 *Globe* 18 Feb., (heading) O'Brienism. 1900 *Westm. Gaz.* 22 Oct. 2/2 Mr. Redmond accepts..the new situation caused by the triumph of the O'Brienites and the defeat of the Healyites. 1900 *Ibid.* 24 Dec. 3/1 O'Brienism is an equivalent term for constitutional anarchy. 1901 *Scotsman* 11 Mar. 7/5 O'Brienism is being openly resented by the members who are independent of him. 1921 *Q. Rev.* July 241 The realists come from the north, east, and south, the strongholds of Unionism and O'Brienism.

Obscura·ntic, *a.* [f. Obscurant *sb.* and *a.*] Opposed to enquiry or enlightenment. So **Obscura·nticism** = Obscurantism.

1926 *Contemp. Rev.* Nov. 661 The book..is full of warnings which sometimes are obvious and sometimes obscurantic. 1927 *Ibid.* Feb. 208 It would not be a work of truth or of love, but of well-meaning though mischievous obscuranticism.

Obscure, *v.* 1. c. (Earlier U.S. example.)

1788 Franklin *Autob.* Writ. 1907 I. 358, I found his voice distinct till I came near Front Street, when some noise in that street obscur'd it.

Obscu·ringly, *adv.* [-ly 2.] In an obscuring manner; so as to obscure.

1902 *New Liberal Rev.* Aug. 317 The Celtic fringes hang obscuringly over our eyes, as fringes do under be-feathered hats in the Old Kent Road.

Obscurist (ǫbskiū·rist). [f. Obscure *a.* and *v.* + -ist.] = Obscurantist.

1925 *Chambers's Jrnl.* Mar. 196/1 He is no faddist or

eccentric, no obscurist of any kind, but one who catches at charms in human life and paints them.

Obsequent, *a.* Add: **2.** *Geol.* Of streams: Flowing in the opposite direction from the 'consequent' drainage. **b.** as *sb.* An obsequent stream.
1895 W. M. Davis in *Geog. Jrnl.* V. 134, I would suggest that these streams be called *obsequent*, as their direction is opposed to that of the initial consequent streams. *Ibid.* 145 Such obsequents are represented by the Ousel and Ivel farther east. 1902 H. J. Mackinder *Britain & Brit. Seas* 121 The term 'obsequent' has been invented..for the rivers which commenced as scarp torrents...The Little Ouse of East Anglia is also an obsequent.

Observantine. Add: Also *attrib.*
1930 Eale tr. *H. Grisar's Martin Luther* ii. 51 The vicar ..jeopardized the canonical and disciplinary autonomy of the Observantine monasteries entrusted to his care.

Observation. Add: **2.** (Modern example.)
1911 W. J. Locke *Glory of Clementina Wing* xxii. 277 The daily calls to inquire after her health and happiness had grown to be a sacred observation.
10. *observation balloon, post*; **observation car** (earlier example); **observation ward** (see quot.).
1909 *London Mag.* Sept. 35/2 He made numerous ascents in captive *observation balloons. 1914 *Daily Express* 12 Oct. 4/5 The German gunners were enabled to fire with remarkable accuracy, thanks to observation balloons. 1886 C. D. Warner *Their Pilgr.* xvi. (1888) 344 From the Junction to Fabyan's they rode in an *observation car. 1909 *Westm. Gaz.* 17 Sept. 3/1 The way of this little bird is to sit on its *observation post. 1914 *Daily Express* 28 Sept. 4/5 The damage to the cathedral was the inevitable result of the French using the cathedral as an observation post. 1927 W. E. Collinson *Contemp. Engl.* 58 If there is doubt as to the presence of the disease in the patient when in hospital, he may be put in an *observation ward.

Observe, *sb.* Add: **3.** *Sc.* A division of a sermon.
1833 W. L. Mackenzie *Sk. Canada & U.S.* 8, I went to hear Doctor McLeod, a steadfast Presbyterian of the old school. There..the discourse is divided and subdivided into heads and observes in true covenanting fashion.

Observer. Add: **4. b.** *Mil.* One whose duty it is to make observations, esp. in connexion with the firing of artillery; a person carried in an aeroplane, or other aircraft, for similar purposes. *Comb.*, as *observer officer*.
[1854 *Tomlinson's Cycl. Useful Arts* I. 16 Scarcely had the observer reached the height of 3,000 feet, than he observed..a thin vapour.] 1903 *Heavy Artillery Training* (Prov.) 36 If the target is not visible from the guns or ground quite close to them,..two observers are required. 1911 *Chambers's Jrnl.* Aug. 505/1 The military aeroplane must carry at least two men, one..as a pilot, and the other as an observer. 1914 *Field Artillery Training* 325 The observer, having located the position of the target and conveyed the information to the artillery commander..receives from him the signal 'Observe for line'. 1916 H. Barber *Aeroplane Speaks* (1918) 50 Quickly the Observer climbs into his seat in front of the Pilot.
Comb. 1928 Gamble *Story N. Sea Air Station* xiii. 226 During this year [1916] the rank of Observer Officer was created.

Obsessional, *a.* Add: **b.** Characterized or caused by obsession.
1918 E. Jones *Papers on Psycho-Anal.* xi. 244 The patient ..was suffering from a severe obsessional neurosis and was very superstitious. 1928 *Daily Tel.* 24 Apr. 7/1 A form of neurasthenia, which had produced an obsessional insanity.

Obsessionist (ǫbse·ʃənist). [f. Obsession + -ist.] One who is obsessed, or subject to obsession, by a 'fixed idea'.
1921 *Glasgow Herald* 24 June 8/4 The canards of the anti-waste obsessionists. 1928 *Daily Express* 6 Dec. 10/5, I once sat in a train for five hours opposite an obsessionist, who played chess with himself on a miniature board.

Obsessive (ǫbse·siv), *a.* [f. Obsess *v.* + -ive.] Of or pertaining to obsession; liable to obsess; obsessing.
1909 *Westm. Gaz.* 19 Feb. 5/2. 1911 W. James *Mem. & Studies* vii. 159 Obsessive thoughts and delusions, as well as voices, visions, and impulses..fall subject to one mode of treatment. 1925 *Contemp. Rev.* Dec. 757 The danger is that these ideas may become obsessive.

Obsolescence. Add: **1. b.** *spec.* (See quot.)
1930 W. de C. Hutchinson & Lovell *Dict. Legal etc. Terms* 87 *Obsolescence.* Where machinery is lessened in value not by mere usage or lapse of time, but by the fact that improved machinery is being brought into use, then this lessened value is termed obsolescence as distinguished from depreciation.

Obsole·scing, *ppl. a.* [f. Obsolesce *v.* + -ing[2].] That is becoming obsolete.
1916 E. V. Lucas *Cloud & Silver* 71 The Mayor..still clung to the steadily obsolescing topper.

Obsolete, *a.* **2.** (Add example.)
1920 *Act* 10 & 11 *Geo. V* c. 28 § 10 (2), The purchase or redemption..of obsolete or unproductive capital.

Obstinancy. (Later example.)
1894 B. Thomson *Diversions of Prime Minister* xiii. 213 The steadfastness of their followers was obstinancy under the lash of persecution.

Obtundent. **b.** *sb.* (Later example.)
1908 *Text-bk. Operat. Dentistry* (ed. C. N. Johnson) 460 Obtundents. For the purpose of obtunding, many preparations have been advocated and many methods advised.

Obturator. **2. a.** Add: Also, a device used to occlude an instrument, which can be withdrawn when necessary.
19.. *Buck's Med. Handbk.* I. 779 (Cent. Suppl.) Each instrument has its obturator, which is to be used only for the purpose of rounding out the end of the speculum during introduction.

Obverse. **A.** *adj.* Add: **4.** *Logic.* Of a proposition: Obtained from another proposition by the process of obversion.
1870 A. Bain *Logic* I. 110 To each of the four Propositional Forms..there is an obverse form.
B. *sb.* **3.** (Earlier example.)
1870 A. Bain *Logic* I. 110 No men are gods. The obverse is..all men are no-gods.

Obvious, *a.* Add: **4. c.** quasi-sb., *The obvious*: Something which is obvious; a plain or manifest inference, remark, detail, fact, etc.
1903 Kate D. Wiggin *Rebecca* i, Their steadfast gaze..had the effect of looking directly through the obvious to something beyond. 1919 Mary K. Bradby *Psycho-anal. & its Place in Life* xiii. 175 The work of the artist who consciously and deliberately descends to the obvious..is uninteresting.

Occidental, *a.* **2.** Add: Also of, belonging to, or characteristic of, the Western United States.
1823 S. H. Long *Exped. Rocky Mts.* I. 21 The occidental plane tree is, perhaps, the grandest of the American forest trees. 1846 *Knickerbocker Mag.* XXVII. 471 'I. L. of this vicinity', writes an occidental correspondent, 'had carried the knife for a long time'.

Occlude, *v.* **2.** (Add example.)
1909 H. G. Wells *Tono-Bungay* I. ii. § 7. 74 In the middle was the brown coffin end,..half occluded by the vicar's Oxford hood.

Occlusal (ǫklū·săl), *a.* [f. as Occluse *a.* + -al.] Of or pertaining to occlusion of the teeth; also (of parts of the teeth), that come together when the jaws are closed.
1904 V. H. Jackson *Orthodontia* 201 When a broader occlusal surface is required the ends of the metal should be left extending onto the adjoining teeth. 1905 Burchard *Dental Pathol.* (ed. 2) 248 Occlusal wear is very common and occurs largely with men who chew tobacco.

Occlusion. Add: **1. b.** The overlapping position of the upper and lower teeth when the two jaws are brought together.
1902 *Encycl. Brit.* XXVII. 418/2 The age, sex, and health of the patient, the character of the occlusion or bite, and the force exerted in mastication. 1908 G. V. Black *Operat. Dentistry* I. 85 The Relation of the Occlusion to the Localization of Caries.

Occlusor. (Add example.)
1895 Shipley in A. H. Cooke *Molluscs* etc. 476 The most considerable of these muscles are the two occlusors.

Occult, *v.* Add: **c.** *intr.*
1880–82 [see *Occulting* ppl. a.]. 1902 *Encycl. Brit.* XXVI. 464/1 The light occults every ten seconds,..the occultations being actuated by a double valve arrangement.
Hence **Occulted** *ppl. a.* (modern example). **Occu·lter,** an apparatus for occulting lights.
1898 *Engineering Mag.* XVI. 13 Coast lights are divided into five categories: fixed lights, lights of occultation (occulted lights), colored lights, flashing lights, and mixed lights. 1902 *Encycl. Brit.* XXX. 256/1 This light shows, instead of one prolonged flash at intervals of one minute, as would be produced by the apparatus in the absence of a gas occulter, a group of short flashes.

Occultist. Also *attrib.*
1902 *Encycl. Brit.* XXVI. 275/1 Cabalistic, occultist, Indian, and modern spiritualistic ideas and formulas.

Occupation. **7.** Add: **occupation disease,** a disease incidental to or caused by one's occupation; so **occupation neurosis.**
1906 *Daily Chron.* 6 Dec. 2/2 To add to the six diseases already scheduled any others which are discovered to be what are called *occupation diseases. 1908 S. Flexner in *Science* 24 Jan. 128/2 The many causes of occupation disease, so-called,..are at present only slightly understood. 1896 *Nomencl. Diseases* 33 *Occupation-neurosis (spasmodic or neuralgic). 1899 *Allbutt's Syst. Med.* VIII. 7 'Occupation neuroses' such as painter's colic or mercurial tremor.
Hence **Occupational** *a.* (recent examples).
1908 Tatham in *Suppl. to 65th Ann. Rep. Registrar-General* II. p. v, The present volume, which contains the latest available information respecting English occupational mortality. 1919 J. L. Garvin *Econ. Found. Peace* 328 These occupational federations acted independently of each other. 1930 *Times* 24 Mar. 11/1 Legislation should be introduced to bring victims of this occupational disease [silicosis] within the scope of the Workmen's Compensation Act.

Occupa·tionalism. [-ism.] Occupational character or conduct; professionalism.
1927 E. Barker *National Character* iv. § ii. 96 It is true that a new and qualifying factor has been added to the national temper by the growth of occupationalism.

Ocean, *sb.* **4. c.** **ocean-river,** also, a large navigable river.
1908 *Chambers's Jrnl.* Apr. 296/1 This *ocean-river is..a veritable highway of commerce.

Oceana (ōʃiˌēi·nă). The name of Harrington's ideal state, applied by J. A. Froude to the British Maritime Empire.
[1656 J. Harrington (*title*) The Commonwealth of Oceana.] 1886 Froude *Oceana* 395 If Oceana is to be hereafter governed by a federal parliament, such a parliament will grow when the time is ripe for it. 1899 J. Milne *Romance of Pro-Consul* ix. 87 He was being set to the straightening-out of some twist in Oceana, to the healing of a sore which threatened one of her limbs.

Oceaner. Add: **2.** An ocean-going vessel.
1879 Whitman *Specimen Days* (1892) 136 The proud, steady, noiseless cleaving of the grand oceaner down the bay.

Oceanic, *a.* Add: **1. b.** Belonging to or living in those parts of the sea that are remote from the shore.
1879 H. N. Moseley *Notes Naturalist 'Challenger'* 569 The Oceanic Petrels have reduced the science of flight to the condition of a fine art. 1882 — *Anim. Life Ocean Surface* 19 The oceanic animals, notwithstanding their free and unbounded range, do not escape from parasites. 1902 *Encycl. Brit.* XXXIII. 936/2 The majority of the oceanic epiplankton appears to be stenothermal.
4. *Phys. Geog.* Of climate: Exhibiting the feature characteristic of areas where temperature, rainfall, etc., is controlled or influenced by the ocean.
1922 Kendrew *Climates of Continents* xxix. 215 Thus the east of the British Isles has a continental rather than oceanic rainfall régime.

Oceanology. (Example.)
1896 A. H. Markham in *Smithsonian Rep.* 295 This brings us to the equally important question of oceanology, which should comprise a complete knowledge not only of the surface currents in the Arctic seas, but also surface and deep-sea temperatures, [etc.].

Ochre, *sb.* **4.** Add: **ochre-grave** (see quot.); also *attrib.*
1928 Peake & Fleure *Steppe & Sown* 20 In the early type of kurgan are found skeletons..buried in a contracted position, the bones covered with red ochre. These..are now known as the ochre-graves. *Ibid.* 26 The ochre-grave folk.

Ochrous, *a.* (Earlier examples of U.S. form.)
1806 Webster, *Ocherous*,..like or containing ocher. 1828 — s.v., Ocherous matter; an ocherous color. 1868 *Rep. U.S. Comm. Agric.* (1869) 427 The pasture..hardening in some such manner as 'hard-pan' forms in ocherous soil.

Ocotillo (ōukoti·lyo). *U.S.* Also: **ocotilla.** [Mex.-Sp., dim. of *ocote*, ad. Nahuatl *ocotl* pine-tree.]
1. The Californian candlewood, *Fouquieria splendens*, of the south-west States and Mexico, characterized by naked wandlike thorny branches and bright scarlet flowers.
1883 W. H. Bishop in *Harper's Mag.* Mar. 502/2 The ocotilla is simply a wattle of sticks..waiting to be cut down and turned into palings. 1902 Clapin *Dict. Amer.* 1928 *Saturday Even. Post* 10 Mar. 103/3 The desert vegetation continued—creosote bush, greasewood, mesquite, paloverde, ocotillo.
2. *attrib.*, as *ocotilla stick, wattle*; **ocotillo cactus** = sense 1.
1883 W. H. Bishop in *Harper's Mag.* Mar. 491/1 The houses consist of a frame-work of cottonwood or ocotilla wattles. 1883 — *Old Mexico* xxx. 474 High palisades of ocotilla sticks. 1893 H. J. Finck in *Nation* (N.Y.) 7 Sept. 169/3 Walking-sticks made of the porous ocotillo cactus.

Octave, *sb.* **4. b.** *Law of octaves* (earlier example).
1865 J. A. R. Newlands in *Chem. News* 18 Aug. 83/2 This peculiar relationship I propose to provisionally term the 'Law of Octaves'.

Octavic (ǫktæ·vik), *a.* *Math.* [f. L. *octāv-us* eighth + -ic.] Of the eighth degree or order.
1897 *Nature* 11 Nov. 47/1 More general forms of octavic curves with six double points.

Octet. Add: **4.** *Chem.* A group of eight electrons.
1927 N. V. Sidgwick *Electronic Theory of Valency* 100 The octet..is an extremely stable group of electrons.

Octo·pian, *a.* [f. Octopus + -ian.] Suggestive of an octopus; = Octopean *a.* Also **O·ctopine** [-ine[1]] *a.*
1920 C. E. Montague *Disenchantment* i. 11 He had..struck..a crate, from which some octopian beast..had reached out at him. 1914 Chesterton *Flying Inn* 248 The Captain prepared to swing himself on to one of the octopine branches [of a tree].

Oculism (ǫ·kiŭliz'm). [f. L. *ocul-us* eye + -ism: after Oculist.] The business of an oculist; knowledge of defects of vision, diseases of the eye, etc., and the remedies.
1909 W. Booth in Begbie *Life* (1920) II. 433 The gentleman..was a doctor and..he knew something of oculism.

Oculist. Add: **3.** *Comb.* **oculist-stamp** (also *oculist's stamp*), the more usual name among antiquaries for *medicine-stamp*, or *-seal* (Medicine *sb.*[1] 6 a).
1778 *Gentl. Mag.* XLVIII. 509 An inscription on an oculist's stamp. 1851 Simpson in *Monthly Jrnl. Med. Sci.* XII. 42 Above sixty Roman oculist-stamps have been now discovered in different parts of western Europe. 1886 *Guide Exhib. Galleries Brit. Mus.* 200 Roman Implements, such as steelyards and their weights, oculists' stamps, locks and keys.

Odd, *a.* **4. d.** Add to def.: or *odds*.
1930 *Times* 25 Mar. 24/1 The balance-sheet shows a loan from the bankers of the company as at December 31 of £118,413 odds.
8. d. *odd-job* v., to do odd jobs; *odd-jobbing* vbl. sb.; *odd man* (earlier examples); *odd-timer, odd work*.
1897 Voynich *Gadfly* (1904) 76/1, I lived by *odd-jobbing for the blacks on the sugar plantations. *Ibid.* 133/2 As a miner's fag—odd-jobbing with the coolies. 1863 *All Yr. Round* 11 July 472/2 Either can rest occasionally by employing an '*odd man', of whom there are several at each district establishment, ready to do 'odd' work. 1872 *Routledge's Ev. Boy's Ann.* 2 Joe was really only an 'odd man', and that by the job too. 1925 A. S. M. Hutchinson *One Increasing Purpose* I. xviii. 113 She's an *odd-timer on Miss Marr's typist staff.

Oddity. **2.** Add: Rarely in singular.
1853 Maria Cummins *Lamplighter* (1854) 237 But you wished me to become acquainted with your oddity.

Oddlings (ǫ·dliŋz), *sb. pl.* [f. Odd *a.* + -ling[1].] = Oddments.
1900 *Windsor Mag.* XI. 354 A hundred odd bits, that's all—but they are a manufacturer's oddlings.

Odds, *sb.* Add: **4. d.** Phr. *to ask* (or †*beg*) *no odds*, to desire no advantage; to seek no favour. *U.S.*
1806 *Lion & Tarapin* in *Balt. Even. Post* 5 Mar. 2/2 (Th.) No odds he begs Of any beast that walks upon four legs. 1834 *Vermont Free Press* 7 June (Th.) A Varmounter never uses a dog...Give him a gun, and he asks no odds. 1857 H. C. Kimball in B. Young etc. *Jrnl. Discourses* V. 32/2, I ask no odds of them, no more than I do of the dirt I walk on. 1890 *Congress. Rec.* 12 Aug. 8455/1 This industry in South Dakota would ask no odds of Congress.
8. odds-on, as *sb.*, the state of betting when odds are laid.
1928 *Daily Mail* 31 July 11/4 The favourite..started at heavy odds-on.

Ode. **3.** Add: *ode-metre*.
1901 *Academy* 14 Dec. 585/2 That so-called 'irregular' ode-metre which they [Patmore and Henley] use in common.

Odontology. (Later example.)
1911 *Chambers's Jrnl.* June 375/1 The British Medical Association has recently founded a Section of Odontology.

Odoriferent (ōudŏri·fĕrĕnt), *sb.* [f. med.L. *odōriferens*: cf. Odoriferant.] A substance that emits a sweet scent.
1858 Sala *Journey Due North* viii. 130 These boots have a peculiar..odour..of myrrh, frankincense, sandal-wood, benzoin, and other odoriferents.

Odorimetry (ōudŏri·mĕtri). [f. L. *odor, odōri-* Odour + -metry.] The measurement of the intensity of odours.
1898 *Amer. Jrnl. Psychol.* X. 85 Odorimetry..is concerned ..with the measurement of the intensity of smell-stimuli considered as objectively as possible.

Œcological, *a.* (Example.) **Œco·logist,** one who studies or is versed in œcology.
1899 *Nat. Science* July 11 One of the most important oecological studies which has yet appeared in the United States. 1893 *Smithsonian Rep.* 439 Whether with the œcologist, we regard the organism in relation to the world, or with the physiologist as a wonderful complex of vital energies, the two branches have this in common.

Œdemic (īde·mik), *a.* [-ic.] Of the nature of, or marked by, œdema.
1904 *Science* 15 Apr. 633/2 An atmosphere containing one half part per thousand sulphureted hydrogen produces death with cramps and œdemic inflammation of the lungs.

Œno-. Add: **Œnocyte** (ī·nosəit) [-cyte], one of a set of wine-coloured cells which form a constituent of fatty tissue in certain insects. **Œnophil** (ī·nofil) [Gr. -φιλος loving] = *œnophilist*.
1900 Miall & Hammond *Harlequin Fly* 40 Closely associated with the epidermis of the Chironomus-larva are some peculiar cells, named *oenocytes* by Wielowiejski from their colour, which is that of yellow wine. 1930 *New Statesman* 28 June 366/1 Professor Saintsbury, an oenophile who is free from the snobbish contempt his kind affect for whisky.

Oersted (5·ɹsted). *Elect.* [f. the name of H. C. *Oersted* (1777–1851) the Danish physicist.] A unit of magnetic reluctance.
1903 *Elect. World & Engin.* 13 June 1010 (Cent. Suppl.) For practical work..the magnetic reluctance of a cubic centimeter of all non-magnetic materials..is the same as that of an air-pump vacuum. This unit of reluctance is called the 'oersted'.

Of, *prep.* Add: **4. c.** *U.S.* In expressing the time: From or before (a specified hour); = To *prep.* 6 b.
1879 F. R. Stockton *Rudder Grange* i. 10 We ceased to call it a boat at about a quarter of eleven. 1890 Susan Hale *Lett.* (1919) 243 At quarter of four I was taking my bath. 1902 A. D. McFaul *Ike Glidden* vi. 40, I notice by the town clock that it is five minutes of seven. 1904 F. Lynde *Grafters* x. 140 The hands of the clock..pointed to five minutes of the hour.
42. a. (Add example.)
1842 W. Howitt *Rur. & Dom. Life Germany* xvii. 234 Ladies are too much of practical cooks and housewives to be much visible before dinner.
43. b. (Add example.)
1848 Mrs. Anne Jameson in G. Macpherson *Mem.* (1878) 254, I ran to Ireland, of all places in the world.
52. b. (Later examples.)
1867 'E. Kirke' *On Border* iii. 67, I don't forget..how you worked of nights. 1891 Barrie *Little Minister* xl. (1892) 413 So long as women sit up of nights listening for a footstep. 1897 J. L. Allen *Choir Invis.* xvii. (1918) 175 You have holidays of Saturdays. I have not, you see.

Of, U.S. dial. or colloq. var. of Have *v.* 24 c.
1847 Porter *Big Bear* 104 (Farmer) If I hadn't a had on pantalets, I reckon somebody would of knowd whether I gartered above my knees or not. 1854 Mary J. Holmes *Tempest & Sunshine* viii. 115, I don't see why in the old Harry he couldn't of lived. 1916 H. L. Wilson *Somewhere in Red Gap* vii. 317 She must of seen the laugh was on her.

Off. **A.** *adv.* Add: **1. b.** (Later example.)
1902 G. H. Lorimer *Lett. Self-made Merchant* xiv. 203 By the time the real weather comes along everybody has guessed wrong and knocked the market off a cent or two.
e. *ellipt.* Off one's head; deranged, crazy.
1866– in *Eng. Dial. Dict.* (Sc., N. Eng.). 1904 W. H. Smith *Promoters* i. 8 I've sometimes thought you were a trifle visionary, but I never considered you seriously off.
2. c. *fig.* (Further U.S. examples.)
1809 *Ann. Congress* Jan. 1185 Mr. Williams hoped these were not intended to enforce the embargo. If they were, he was entirely off. 1868 H. Woodruff *Trotting Horse* xxxvi. 300 When a trotter wins with great ease,..it is assumed, not that the loser was 'off', but that the winner is greatly superior. 1902 G. H. Lorimer *Lett. Self-made Merchant* xvi. 231, I may be off in sizing this thing up, because it's a little out of my line.
4. d. Off work or duty, as *a day off*; perh. ellipt. use of B. 5 b.
1893 [see *Day 19]. 1895 A. F. Ingram *Work Gt. Cities* iii, Don't attempt to pay a pastoral visit on washing-day; you had better make it your day off. 1916 'Berta Ruck' *Girls at his Billet* xviii, I am sure your auntie..would be quite agreeable to letting us have the afternoon off for the ceremony.
6. (Further example.)
1931 *Daily Express* 21 Sept. 14/4 Japanese bonds were only slightly off.
7. (Later examples.)
a. 1904 W. H. Smith *Promoters* i. 11 Just as surely as you can take that bottle off from the table.
b. 1884 'Mark Twain' *Huck. Finn* vi. 32 I'd borrow two or three dollars off of the judge for him. *a* 1909 'O. Henry' *Roads of Destiny* xviii. 308 A sound like somebody ripping a clapboard off of a barn-roof. 1926 Mulford *Cassidy's Protégé* xi. 137 He's mebby goin' to be useful,..keepin' them fellers' attention on himself, and off of us.
B. *prep.* Add: **1. b.** (Later colloq. examples.) *Off the map*: see *Map *sb.* 1 e; *Off the reel*: see Reel *sb.*[1] 2 b.
1903 A. H. Lewis *Boss* xix. 264 She's off her trolley. She toins sick; an' in a week she croaks. 1930 *Randolph Enterprise* (W. Va.) 2 Oct. 1/2 The..Foot Ball Team..played the team over there off their feet.
5. b. Also, having lost interest in; no longer 'keen on'; averse to. *Off form*: in bad form. *Off one's game*: see *Game *sb.* 6 f.
Transfer 1894 quot. to sense 1 b.
1912 Mathewson *Pitching* vii. 142 The Chicago pitchers were away off form in the series. 1926 Bennett *Lord Raingo* I. x. 45 I'm off all risks for the present. 1929 W. E. Collinson *Spoken Engl.* 72 Did you buy the thoroughbred Alsatian?' No. I'm rather off dogs at present.
C. *adj.* **2. a.** Add: *Off-horse* (later example), *-lead, -leader, -ox, -wheeler*.
1807 *Balance* (Hudson, N.Y.) 25 Aug. 267 (Th.) We behold a clumsy, awkward off ox trying the tricks of a kitten. 1823 J. F. Cooper *Pioneers* iv, I knew just the spot where to touch the off-leader. 1838 H. Colman *Rep. Agric. Mass.* (1839) 124 What is technically termed an 'off' ox in the team. 1888 Mrs. Custer *Tenting on Plains* xii. (1893) 225 The old reliability of a mule-team is the off-wheeler. *a* 1882 F. Douglass *Life & Times* I. xv. (1884) 89 What was meant by the 'in ox' as against the 'off ox',..I could not very easily divine. 1897 *Outing* XXX. 254/1 To take the off-lead and off-wheeler's reins in right hand. *Ibid.*, Take up about six or seven inches of your off-leader's rein. 1898 Kipling *Day's Work, Walking Delegate* 63 Rod, the off-horse of the pair, had been standing with one hip lifted like a tired cow. 1910 Jer. Hart *Vigilante Girl* x. 140 An iron 'jockey-stick' ran from the near leader's harness to the off-leader's bit.
b. Also of a ball or hit on this side.
1895 H. G. Hutchinson *P. Steele* i. 28 This off-ball Peter ..drove..so hard..that [etc.].
4. (Add examples). Also, a day, night, etc., when one does not feel fit, or is not in the mood for something.
1843 *Knickerbocker Mag.* XXII. 325 After an 'off night' when I was allowed to stay in town. 1845 *Punch* 1 Mar. 100/1 As something was necessary for the off-nights, a new drama..was produced. 1875 *All Yr. Round* 3 Apr. 23/1 That estimable lady..had arranged those meetings on the quiet off-evenings. 1908 *Sketch* 11 Sept. 340/2 Rhodes had an 'off-day' and could do nothing. 1913 A. G. Bradley *Other Days* v. 161 On the rare off-days [we] raided such crows and magpies' nests as we could find. 1929 *Star* 21 Aug. 5/1 It was certainly Elder's off-night He was not feeling in the best of form.
b. *Off year*, one in which no prime election normally takes place. Also as adj. *U.S.*
1882 *Congress. Rec.* 14 Dec. 277/2 This was in the off year, and not the Presidential year. 1906 *N. Y. Even. Post* 5 Nov. 4 In this off-year election.
6. Marked or attended by unfavourable conditions.
1870 Medbery *Men & Myst. Wall St.* 137 An 'off' market, is where prices have fallen either in a week, a day, or even an afternoon.

Off, *v.* Add: **1. b.** To withdraw from; to decline or refuse.
1908 A. S. M. Hutchinson *Once Aboard Lugger* vi. vi. § 2. 437 There's this locum tenens I was going to take up in the North. I haven't offed that yet—haven't refused it, I mean.
2. Also quasi-*trans.* with *it*.
1890 *Punch* 28 June 310/2 He found out after they'd off'd it that they didn't own a white mouse among 'em! 1930 J. Buchan *Castle Gay* iv. 72 He has probably offed it abroad.

Off-, *prefix.* Add: **3.** *off-look* (earlier example).
1871 *Scribner's Monthly* II. 398 A little east of our off-look, there projected..a square stupendous tower.
5. *Off-black*: a very dark shade of colour, one that is almost black. *Off-white*: a very light shade of colour, one verging on white.
1930 *Daily Express* 8 Sept. 5 One of the new off-black shades.., a sort of unripe blackberry colour, is used for the third model. 1927 *Daily Mirror* 10 Dec. 16/1 Jumper suits in white, yellow, or what the Paris dressmakers call 'off whites' will see you through.

Offal. **1.** (U.S. examples, used of grain.)
1849 *Rep. U.S. Comm. Patents* (1850) 303 The process of re-grinding the offal of wheat. 1872 T. D. Price *MS. Diary* 9 Jan., Bro. Josiah came for his grist, pays me $1.20 a bu[shel] for it, and I have offal.
2. a. Now *techn.*, *dial.*, and *U.S. local.* (Also later example of pl. use.)
1826 J. F. Cooper *Prairie* xix, Do you see yon birds watching for the offals of the beast they have killed? 1889 Farmer *Americanisms* 397 Whereas in England no one would think of speaking of calf's heart, pig's fry, sheep's kidneys, etc., as dishes of *offal*, in the States such phraseology is not at all unusual.

Offcast. **B.** *sb.* (Earlier U.S. example.)
1845 S. Judd *Margaret* I. xiv. 104 The..suit of..the Sexton ..is known to be an off-cast of the Parson's.

Off colour. **1.** (Earlier and later examples.)
1875 Holland *Sevenoaks* ix. 114 Everybody invited her, and yet everybody, without any definite reason, considered her a little 'off color'. 1901 Bret Harte in *Harper's Mag.* Dec. 66/1 'The Kernel seems a little off color to-day', said the barkeeper. 1911 Webster s.v. *Color*, *Off color*, of questionable taste; not quite proper; improper. *Slang, U.S.*
2. (Earlier examples.)
1860 A. de Barrera *Gems & Jewels* 164 If the manufactured diamond is found to contain a flaw, or what is technically termed 'off-color', its value is proportionately diminished. 1877 *Encycl. Brit.* VII. 166/1 The value being further diminished..when the stones are 'off colour', that is milky or tinted, or imperfect in other respects.

Off-coloured, *a.* (Add examples.)
1904 *Daily Chron.* 18 May 3/4 These were the 'off-coloured', the half-castes, the outcome of white supremacy in a black country. 1913 Pettman *Africanderisms* 317 *Mêlées*, the off-coloured diamonds from two carats down.

Off-drive, *sb.*, see Off D. 3.

O·ff-duty, *a.* [Off *prep.*] Of persons: Not engaged or occupied with their normal work. Of things, actions, etc.: Suggestive of this state.
1904 *Daily Chron.* 23 Dec. 4/4 The off-duty policeman. 1905 Guy Thorne *When it was Dark* 352 The ship..wore a somewhat neglected 'off duty' aspect.

Offen, *prep.* *dial.* (also *U.S.*) Also **off'n.** [var. of *off of*, Off *adv.* 7, by substitution of *on* for *o'*: see O *prep.*[1] and *prep.*[2]] Off from; from off.
1828 Moir *Mansie Wauch* x. 86 'Set down that bottle,' quoth I, wiping the saw-dust affn't with my hand. 1872 Eggleston *End of World* xi. 76 No more craps of corn offen the bottom land. *a* 1909 'O. Henry' *Roads of Destiny* vi. 97 He'd jist light off'n his bronco and hunt a place to camp. 1910 Mulford *Hopalong Cassidy* ix. 64 Johnny chased that Greaser off'n th' ranch.

Offend, *v.* **7.** Add: Also *intr.* with *against*.
1859 Trollope *Bertrams* I. xiii. 279 That..which appears to offend against the spirit of calm recital which I profess.

Offensive, *a.* Add: **1. b.** *Baseball.* (See quot.)
1912 Mathewson *Pitching* vi. 124 Offensive coaching means the handling of base runners, and requires quick and accurate judgment.

Offer, *sb.* Add: **2. c.** An opportunity or 'opening'.
1876 *Coursing Calendar* 302 Napoleon went past Countess in the race to the hare, and..never gave his antagonist an offer.

Offer, *v.* Add: **3. g.** *refl.* To present (oneself) to a person for acceptance or refusal; to put (oneself) forward.
1764 H. Walpole *Otranto* i. (1765) 18 In short, Isabella, since I cannot give you my son [in marriage], I offer you myself. 1893 Mary E. Mann *In Summer Shade* xi. II. 28, I have this evening offered myself to Mary Burne, and she has accepted me.
h. *intr.* To give in or enter one's name as a candidate.
1803 *Steele Papers* I. 405 The Gentlemen who prevailed upon me 'to offer' as they call it, consisted principally of the moderate men of both parties. 1834 Crockett *Narr. Life* x. 72 I was asked to offer for the Legislature in the counties of Lawrence and Heckman.
7. b. With *up*: To put (a part of a structure) in place to see how it looks or whether it fits properly.
Mod. Well, mate, it's no use looking at it, we can't tell without offering it up.

Offering, *vbl. sb.* Add: **2. c.** *U.S.* Something offered for sale.
1903 *Boston Even. Transcript* 29 Aug., On Saturday next the Transcript will print an unusually attractive line of real estate offerings.
3. (Add examples.)
1811 *Steele Papers* II. 658 One of them is a rough offering book. *Ibid.*, This is intended to furnish as a day book all the results which do not and cannot appear on the face of the offering book. 1910 *J. Hastings' Encycl. Relig. & Ethics* III. 704/2 Certain large silver coins of Alfred the Great were popularly known as 'offering-pennies'.

Off-hand. **B.** *adj.* Add: **1. b.** Of dough: Made straight away and not from a preliminary sponge.
1904 *Daily Chron.* 4 Mar. 10/5 Advt., Wanted a foreman for bread and smalls; used to off-hand doughs.
2. b. *Mining.* (See quot.)
1921 *Dict. Occup. Terms* (1927) § 047 Odd worker, off hand man, wage man; general terms for men or boys employed above or below ground and paid by the day.
3. Of a shot: Fired from a gun held in the hand without other support.
1856 R. Glisan *Jrnl. Army Life* xxiv. (1874) 328, I surprised everybody by killing the duck at an off-hand shot.
4. Of an ox, horse, etc.: That goes on the right-hand side; = Off *a.* 2.
1845 F. Douglass *Life* (1846) 58 Covey..told me which was the in-hand ox, and which the off-hand one.

Off-handed, *a.* Add: **b.** *Mining.* = prec. A. 2 b.
1906 *Daily Chron.* 16 Oct. 5/2 The 'off-handed' men.. dispersed into the four seams of the pit.

Off-handedly, *adv.* (Earlier example.)
1886 *19th Cent.* Oct. 541 The newspaper moralisers speak off-handedly of the skilled workman earning his two or three pounds a week.

O·ff-haul. [f. Off- + Haul *v.*] A rope for drawing a boat out from the shore.
1900 *Law Rep.*, App. Cases 405 There is another rope called the 'off-haul', which is..used to haul the boat from the shore to its position in the river...The boat is again taken out by means of the off-haul rope to its former position.

Office, *sb.* **12. a.** *office-boy* (earlier example), *building, -chair* (later example), *-copy* (earlier example), *-desk, -door, duty* (later example), *-hour* (earlier example), *hymn, -rent, -room*; **b.** *office-holder* (earlier example), *-hunter* (earlier and later examples), *-hunting, -mongering, -seeking* (earlier example); **c.** **office-hunger,** eager desire for public office; **office-name,** a nom de plume; **office patient,** *U.S.*, one who visits a doctor at his office or consulting-room.
1846 *Knickerbocker Mag.* XXVII. 457 No songs for you, my sad street-sweeper!..Nor for you, melancholy *office-boy! 1889 *Kansas City T. & Star* 11 Mar., A permit was granted today to the Builders' and Traders' Exchange for a foundation for their new *office building. 1869 Tourgee *Toinette* xl. (1881) 404 The old surgeon laid down his pen.. and turned his *office-chair round toward his visitor. 1836 *Diplom. Corr. Texas* (1908) I. 142 It contains your commission, a letter of credence to the secretary of the United States, and *office copies of them. 1881 *Rep. Indian Affairs* 93 The articles manufactured by the carpenters..were as follows..one *office-desk [etc.]. 1863 'E. Kirke' *Southern Friends* xxiii. 235 A short rap came at the *office door. 1881–5 McLellan *Own Story* 534 He said that he was so much occupied with *office-duty that it was impossible for him to leave. 1818 Fearon *Sk. Amer.* 143 Those dangerous abuses in government, introduced by *office holders, which..threaten ..to become inveterate. 1802 *Steele Papers* I. 326 Services.. wholly performed during the usual *office hour. 1870 in *Congress. Rec.* 27 Feb. (1875) 1891/1 Bait is good, and especially for democratic *office hunger. 1806 *Ann. Congress* Feb. 506 It would be a struggle between *office-hunters and the people. 1845 W. L. Mackenzie *Butler & Hoyt* 75 General Spicer was a keen office-hunter. 1824 *Niles' Weekly Reg.* 20 Mar. 37/2 *Office-hunting. 1889 Farmer *Americanisms* 397 Office-hunting is quite a business with the thousand-and-one 'hangers-on' to the skirts of political parties. 1907 *New Office Hymn Bk.* II. Introd. p. v, The *Office Hymns are the Hymns in the Divine Office. 1895 Roosevelt in Ld. Charnwood *Life* (1923) 250 These men have a gift at *office-mongering, just as other men have a peculiar knack in picking pockets. 1928 *Saturday Even. Post* (Philad.) 12 May 36/3 At least eight different writers..had been offering their comments under that name [= Richard Roe]—'*office names' they are called in the profession. 1897 R. M. Stuart *Simpkinsville* 94 Even the doctors..are wont to receive their '*office patients' in this comfortable fashion. 1808 *Steele Papers* II. 536 No *office Rent is allowed the agent here. 1902 *Chambers's Jrnl.* Apr. 258/2 Under one number alone solicitors, patent agents,..and next-of-kin agents all found *office-room. 1857 W. R. Alger *Oration* 4 July p. iv, Office-holding partisans, *office-seeking demagogues.

Office, *v.* For †*Obs.* read 'Now *rare.*' and add: **6.** *intr.* To have or occupy an office. *U.S.*
1892 *Nation* (N.Y.) 21 Apr. 303/2 An attorney officing in the same building.

Officer, *sb.* Add: **2. e.** A waiter or servant in a hotel. *U.S.*
1886 *Harper's Mag.* Sept. 594/2 What well-trained waiters!—perhaps they were not waiters, for he was passed from one 'officer' to another 'officer' down to his place.
8. officer-bird, the common redwinged marsh-blackbird, *Agelæus phœniceus*, of the United States and Canada.
1902 Clapin *Dict. Amer.*

Officering, *vbl. sb.* (Later example.)
1890 *Century Mag.* Dec. 207 The American system of officering..was superior to that of the English.

O·fficery, *a.* [f. Officer + -y[1].] Resembling an officer; having the character or nature of an officer.
1905 H. G. Wells *Kipps* III. i. § 6. 289 Saw a lot of young officery fellers coming along.

Office-seeker. Chiefly *U.S.* [f. Office *sb.* 12 + Seeker.] One who seeks office; an office-hunter.
1813 *Ann. Congress* Jan. 582 It would augment the office-seekers who, with the friends of the Administration, were continually haunting the Executive. 1845 *Knickerbocker Mag.* XXV. 374 A Friend writing from Washington..gives us this pleasant sketch of a 'Sucker' office-seeker. *a* 1861 T. Winthrop *John Brent* iii. 25 Bullocks are better company than office-seekers. *a* 1892 Whitman *Pr. Wks.* (1892) 259 The members..were..the meanest kind of bawling and blowing office-holders, office-seekers.

Official, *sb.* **2.** (Add examples.)
1745 A. Butler *Lives Saints* I. (1780) 248 In 1219 Berengarius, Bishop of Barcelona,..made him his archdeacon, grand vicar, and official. 1840 J. R. Hope-Scott in R. Ornsby *Mem.* (1884) I. 230 The acts of his vicar-general and official are not revocable.

Official, *a.* **4.** (Later example.)
1903 W. E. Curtis *True Lincoln* 193 It was perfectly natural for the President to select a member of his official family [*sc.* the Cabinet] from a State of such importance.
5. (Earlier U.S. examples.)
1790 *Ann. Congress* 8 Feb. 2169 His official conduct. *Ibid.* 2170 Official transactions. 1791 Jefferson *Ibid.* 18 Feb. 2176 An official paper. 1805 *Ann. 8th Congress* 1038 The official documents upon our tables.

Officialese. (Recent example.)
1927 E. Thompson *These Men thy Friends* 242 'Who are these noble Arabs?' asked Kenrick...' It's officialese for *beastly Buddoos*' explained Edmund Candler.

Officialization (ǫfiʃălaizēi·ʃən). [f. Officialize + -ation.] The rendering or becoming official in form or character.
1907 *Daily Chron.* 9 Nov. 4/4 One fails to detect a craving for any such officialisation.

Officina. Add: **b.** *spec.* A factory where nitrate is prepared from raw material.
1890 W. H. Russell *Visit to Chile* 171 The external aspect of the oficina was not unlike that of a north-country coal or iron mine. 1905 *Chambers's Jrnl.* Mar. 130/2 Each oficina has to depend upon itself as regards the working. 1906 *Westm. Gaz.* 24 May 11/3 At the present rate of production the officina might be counted on lasting between thirty or forty years.

Offing. Add: **3.** *transf.* Distance from an abrupt side of a road.
1843 Carlton *New Purchase* v. 25 The horses..seemed, in order to secure a good offing, to shy off towards the deep valley.

Offish, *a.* (Earlier U.S. example.)
1830–33 C. A. Davis *Lett. J. Downing* (1834) 75 Others are a little offish.

O·ffsaddle, *sb.* [f. the vb.] A break or rest in a journey during which horses are unsaddled.
1900 *Pall Mall Gaz.* 4 Jan. 1/3 The Cape horse..can canter along steadily all day under a burning sun, with an occasional off-saddle. 1908 *Daily Chron.* 10 Nov. 3/5 Off-saddle time.

Off-saddle, *v.* (Earlier examples.) **O·ff-saddling** *vbl. sb.*
1850 R. G. Cumming *Hunter's Life S. Afr.* I. 119 Accordingly we off-saddled, and in a few minutes I was once more asleep. *Ibid.* 129 Having off-saddled our horses, we knee-haltered them. 1926 Rider Haggard *Benita* 106 Directions as to their herding and the off-saddling of the horses.

Offscouring. **2. b.** (Later examples.)
1835 J. P. Kennedy *Horse-Shoe Robinson* I. xiv. 180 Why, you off-scouring,..it is enough to make Old Scratch laugh, to hear you talk about conscience! 1871 *Scribner's Monthly* II. 546 Every Protestant is counted but the off-scouring of decent society.

Offset, *sb.* Add: **3.** (Further example.)
1903 A. Adams *Log Cowboy* iv. 54 The missing cattle.. after following down the fence several miles had encountered an offset, and the angle had held the squad.
d. A bevelled part on a wheel.
1849 *Rep. U.S. Comm. Patents* (1850) 220, I also claim.. a cutter wheel, having bevels or off-sets around its face.
e. *Naut.* A current flowing outwards from the shore.
1902 *Daily Chron.* 30 Aug. 5/6 There was..what maritime men call an offset at the time Holbein was swimming. *Ibid.* 2 Sept. 5/5 He had got the benefit of a good off-set current under him.
5. (Earlier U.S. example.)
1769 *Conn. Col. Rec.* (1885) XIII. 207 A petition..setting forth that the petitioner and petitionee have executions against each other now in the hands of Ezekiel Williams,.. upon which the petitioner prays for an off-set of the same.
7. b. (Examples.)
1873 J. H. Beadle *Undevel. West* xxvi. 555 He then walked along a flat offset five or six feet below the house. 1878 — *Western Wilds* x. 157 About half way up the cliff is a small offset, where grows a beautiful pine.
c. *Mining.* A step-like working or stope.
1872 *Rep. Vermont Board Agric.* I. 627 It consists in taking out the ore in successive offsets or stopes.
10. b. A process, used esp. in lithographic printing, by which a drawing or design is first transferred to a rubber-covered cylinder and thence to the paper. Used *attrib.*
1918 *Pall Mall Gaz.* 29 June 8/5 A Litho Offset Press. 1926 *Encycl. Brit.* III. 220/2 By the off-set method any paper, whether smooth- or rough-surfaced, may be used... Offset seems to be particularly adapted to colour-work. 1928 *Penrose Ann.* 111 The faulty soluble coating in so many classes of so-called offset papers, engenders printing troubles. 1929 *Horse* I. 61 The process employed in reproducing this notable painting is that known as offset.
11. offset-litho operator, a process-engraver using a method akin to the offset method (*10 b).
1921 *Dict. Occup. Terms* (1927) § 526 *Offset-litho operator*, a photographer..who obtains a negative, not reversed in position, with or without using a screen.

Offsetting, *vbl. sb.* and *ppl. a.* (Examples.)
1892 *Smithsonian Rep.* (Nat. Mus.) 225 If the water-colors have been properly applied there is no fear of offsetting on the backs of the sheets. 1908 *Daily Chron.* 24 Aug. 9/7, I was swimming against a strong offsetting tide.

O·ff-shou·lder, *v.* [f. Off- 1 + Shoulder *sb.*] *trans.* To set down from one's shoulder.
1927 *Glasgow Herald* 22 Oct. 4 The rest off-shoulder their loads and sit.

O·ffsider. [f. Off side.] In certain games: A player who is off side.
1927 *Daily Tel.* 21 Feb. 14/1 Nor did the referee have an eagle eye for the offsider.

O·ff-the-map, *a.* [The phr. *off the map*, *Map *sb.*[1] 1 e, used attributively.] Not known or celebrated; obscure.
1915 *War Illustr.* II. 328/1 One of the curious off-the-map incidents of the war was brought to notice the other day.

Ogeechee lime(-tree): see Lime *sb.*[2] 1 b.

Ogling, *vbl. sb.* **b.** Add: **ogling-glass** *U.S. humorous*, a monocle.
1843 *Knickerbocker Mag.* XXII. 111 There he was promenading,..an ogling-glass lifted to his eye.

Ogpu (ǫ·gpu). [f. the initials of the Russ. Объединённое Государственное Политическое Управленіе *Obedinyónnoye Gosudárstvennoye Politítsheskoye Upravléniye* United State Political Administration.] An organization for investigating and combating counter-revolutionary activities in Soviet Russia, which superseded the *Cheka (q.v.) in 1922.
1927 *Daily Tel.* 7 June 10/2 A report from Leningrad states that the Ogpu (Cheka) has officially announced the execution without trial of 'all the active members of a band of incendiaries'. 1927 *Glasgow Herald* 13 June 12/3 The fertile imagination of the Ogpu, or 'State Political Department'. 1928 *Sunday Times* 8 Jan. 11/1 The day has gone by when Ogpu sought to conceal itself.

Ohio (ohəi·o), the name of an American river, a tributary of the Mississippi, and of one of the United States, used attrib. in *Ohio bluebell, buck-eye, sandstone*; **Ohio fever, idea** (see quots.).
1842 Mrs. Kirkland *Forest Life* II. xxxix. 142 A beautiful perennial, here called the *Ohio bluebell, a far larger plant than the one we know by that name. 1810 Michaux *Arbres* I. 38 *Ohio buck eye,..nom donné par moi. 1832 D. J. Browne *Sylva Amer.* 227 It is called Buckeye by the inhabitants,..but..we have denominated it Ohio Buckeye, because it is more abundant on the banks of this river. 1831 T. Buttrick *Trav.* 57 *footnote*, The '*Ohio fever' became a well known expression for this desire to move West. 1835 *Knickerbocker Mag.* V. 274 Such..as some fifteen years since happened to reside in any part of New-England where what was called the 'Ohio fever' prevailed. 1881 *Congress. Rec.* 13 Apr. 276/2 The *Ohio idea is the absolute equality of all men before the law. *Ibid.*, This [is] the democratic 'Ohio idea'. It is the ideal of Ohio democracy. 1881 *Harper's Mag.* Apr. 711/1 Lime stone..and gray *Ohio sandstone are much used in construction.

Oil, *sb.*[1] Add: **2. b.** **white oil,** decolourized petroleum occurring naturally.
1913 V. B. Lewes *Oil Fuel* 38 In some parts of the world small deposits of what are called 'white oil' are..found.
3. f. (Earlier example.)
1861 *Appleton's Ann. Cycl.* 580/1 The oil, when first struck, has..been known to burst forth with great violence.
h. *Oil and vinegar*: said of two elements or factors which do not agree or blend together, or of any two incongruous constituents, with reference to the incompatible characters of oil and vinegar.
1777 Potter *Æschylus, Agam.* 232 Pour thou oil In the same vase and vinegar, in vain Wou'dst thou persuade th' unsocial streams to mix. 1820 Keats in *Life & Lett.* (1931) 250 Men get such different habits that they become as oil and vinegar to one another. 1910 *Blackw. Mag.* Oct. 562/2 We might as well try to blend vinegar and oil, as mix together these two elements in one chamber.
i. *U.S. slang.* Money.
1903 A. H. Lewis *Boss* 121 The sooner we get th' oil, th' sooner we'll begin to light up.
6. a. *oil-butt, -canakin, -car, -cell* (examples), *-district, -drum, -feed, -industry, -ladle, -pan, -region* (earlier example), *-room, -shell, -stove* (earlier examples), *-sump, -supply, -tank* (examples), *-valve, -well* (earlier examples), *-works*; also *oil-engined* adj. **b.** *oil-burning, -cracking, -distributor* (example), *-raising, -retaining*; *oil-broker, -catcher.* **c.** *oil-fed, -harden, -tanned, -tanning.*
1863 *N. H. Almanac* (Philad.) 687/2 A leading Liverpool *oil-broker. 1886 *Marine Engineer* VII. 283/2 The *oil-burning apparatus has been fitted. 1929 *Randolph Enterprise* (W. Va.) 7 Mar. 6/3, I went abroad on an oil burning freighter. 1851 H. Melville *Moby Dick* cxv. (1926) 487 The broad head of an *oil-butt. 1843 L. M. Child *Lett. New York* xl. 285 Children are driving hither and yon, one with a..band-box, or *oil-canakin. 1876 J. S. Ingram *Centen. Exposition* 336 The oil..was loaded by gravity upon *oil cars. 1849 *Rep. U.S. Comm. Patents* (1850) 331 The complete hanger or pillow-block, with or without the *oil-catcher. 1884 *Rep. U.S. Comm. Agric.* 363 When the cellular structure of the rind has completely developed, and the *oil-cells have begun to fill. 1929 *Times* 31 May 9/3 Notable advances are being made in the technology of *oil-cracking processes. 1889 *Century Mag.* Mar. 712/1 The use of these improvised *oil-distributors. 1862 *Sci. Amer.* 22 Feb. 122/1 The *oil district [in Pennsylvania]. 1910 *Chambers's Jrnl.* Nov. 752/1 The apparatus has..demonstrated its value to the oil-district. 1909 *Daily Chron.* 24 July 6/3 Two small *oildrums will be fixed beneath the plank. 1913 *Chambers's Jrnl.* Jan. 31/1 *Oil-engined ships are..being built. 1924 *Times Trade & Engin. Suppl.* 29 Nov. 250/3 The large oil-engined liner. 1886 *Chambers's Jrnl.* 16 Jan. 47/2 A vessel.. propelled entirely by *oil-fed furnaces. 1905 *Westm. Gaz.* 15 Feb. 8/2 It has a horizontal engine,..magneto-electrical ignition, forced *oil-feed, automatic carburation, and other good features. 1904 *Electrochem. Industry* Feb. 51 (Cent. Suppl.) *Oil-harden. 1880 *Harper's Mag.* Dec. 65 The *oil industry has lent a powerful hand to the iron industry of Pittsburgh. 1851 H. Melville *Moby Dick* xx. (1926) 96 This excellent hearted Quakeress..with a long *oil-ladle in one hand. 1908 *Westm. Gaz.* 16 Apr. 4/3 Special *oil-pans are fitted on each end of the throw for scooping up the oil from the base-chamber. 1910 *Chambers's Jrnl.* Nov. 750/1 This engineer, who has made a deep study of *oil-raising methods. 1862 *Census Compendium* 72 The Pennsylvania *oil region. 1907 *Westm. Gaz.* 5 Dec. 4/2 The spring is.. connected to the gear-box by an *oil-retaining universal coupling. 1877 *Harper's Mag.* Dec. 34/2 The three boys in the *oil-room have used, of all grades of oil, twenty gallons less. 1886 *Boy's Own Paper* 2 Oct. 11/3 Disagreeable smells, as if of a steamboat's lower regions, proved this to be the oil-room. 1904 *Sci. Amer.* Suppl. 9 Apr. 23641 (Cent. Suppl.) *Oil-shell. 1865 *U. S. Patent* 17 Jan. No. 45957 *Oil stove. 1880 *Harper's Mag.* Aug. 400 Oil stoves are objectionable because of the unpleasant odor of the fuel. 1923 Deeping *Secret Sanctuary* ix, A man was bending over one of the wings, pouring oil into the *oil-sump. 1909 *Q. Rev.* Oct. 575 Depôt ships for destroyers, mother-ships for submarines, and *oil-supply vessels. 1862 *U. S. Patent* 18 Feb. No. 34,426 *Oil tank. 1880 *Harper's Mag.* Dec. 65 Sheet-iron oil-tanks. 1913 V. B. Lewes *Oil Fuel* 88 Specially constructed oil-tank steamers then convey it to the distributing ports. 1903 L. A. Flemming *Pract. Tanning* 46 Sheep and lambskins *oil-tanned. *Ibid.* 410 *Oil tanning with Turkey-red oil. 1901 *Sketch* 17 July 408/1 Sand dropped into the *oil-valves. 1864 *Appleton's Ann. Cycl.* 668/1 *Oil wells are..sunk in the sandstones of the N.W. Pennsylvania region. 1870 *U.S. Census* I. (1872) 682 Oil well operators. 1882 *Harper's Mag.* Sept. 588/1 A deck-load of brick for a Menhaden *oil-works had been dumped there.
e. **oil-age,** an age in which oil is used extensively, esp. as a source of power; **oil-bath,** (*a*) an apparatus in which oil is used as a medium for heating or cooling; (*b*) in various machines and the like, a receptacle containing lubricating oil through which part of the mechanism moves; also *attrib.*; **oil-belt,** a zone containing oil-fields; †**oil-bucket,** the well of a former make of oil-lamp; **oil-buoy,** a can-buoy having a supply of oil for calming rough water; **oil-burner,** a ship that burns oil for fuel; **oil-calm,** a calm stretch of water as produced by the use of oil; **oil-can,** also (*slang*), a German trench-mortar shell; **oil-coal,** coal from which oil is obtained; **oil-cup, -gilding** (earlier examples); **oil-jacket,** a jacket made of oil-skin; **oil-king,** a magnate in the oil trade; **oil-mixed** *a.*, mixed with oil; **oil-ring,** a ring attached to a revolving shaft or the like for automatic lubrication; **oil-rock,** rock which yields oil; **oil-shale,** shale which yields oil; **oil-slick,** a smooth oily expanse on the surface of water; **oil-soluble** *a.*, that is soluble in oil; **oil-spring** (earlier examples); **oil-station,** a place where motorists can get supplies of oil; **oil-switch,** a switch having the contact points immersed in oil; **oil-tan,** oil-tanned leather or articles made of this; **oil-tanker,** a vessel having special tanks for the conveyance of oil; a vehicle designed for carrying oil; **oil-thrower,** a device whereby centrifugal force is utilized to remove oil.
1911 *Chambers's Jrnl.* July 465/1 That was the beginning of the great *Oil Age. 1838 *Oil-bath [see 6 a]. 1885 *Marine Engineer* 1 Sept. 151/2 The crank shaft at the lowest point of its revolution constantly touches the surface of an oil bath in the closed motion chamber. 1904 *Strand Mag.* Nov. p. vii/1 Advt., Our Oil Bath Cases ensure..protection to the chains. 1904 *Westm. Gaz.* 1 Dec. 8/1 The spark occasioned by the opening of a circuit was damped down by an oil-bath. 1911 *Chambers's Jrnl.* Aug. 559/1 The crank runs in an oil-bath. 1894 *Congress. Rec.* 31 Jan. 1743/2 The great *oil-belt in this country, commencing in New York, running through Pennsylvania, West Virginia, Ohio, and Kentucky. 1901 *Chambers's Jrnl.* Feb. 126/1 The exploitation of..the most prolific oil-belt of the world. 1820 *Boston Selectmen* 26 Jan., Newly invented *oil buckets and lamp burners. 1889 *Century Mag.* Mar. 714/2 A number of these '*oil-buoys' marking the channel can be so fitted. 1921 R. D. Paine *Comr. Rolling Ocean* ix. 160 That ship of his..is an *oil-burner. 1886 *Outing* Dec. 239/1 There they saw an *ile calm, like as if some one had throwed a barrel of ile on the water. 1918 E. A. Mackintosh *War, the Liberator* 156 'Look out, sirr,..*oil can coming over.' Instantly self-preservation reasserted itself. 1873 C. Robinson *N. S. Wales* 52 Deposits of brown cannel *oil coals and oil shales. 1849 *Rep. U.S. Comm. Patents* (1850) 233 The combination of the *oil cup with the axle. 1858 *Hist. Acting Charades* xv. 183 (Born) A gilder living in the village..explained to him the nature of *oil-gilding. 1851 H. Melville *Moby Dick* xlix. (1926) 227 That worthy,..buttoned up in his *oil-jacket. 1898 *Contemp. Rev.* Aug. 236 The Bill..might have suited the English oil dealers; it was too much for the American *Oil Kings. 1912 *Chambers's Jrnl.* Apr. 287/2 *Oil-mixed concrete is best made by mixing the cement, sand, and water to a mortar, adding the oil to the mixture [etc.]. 1904 *Elect. World & Engin.* 23 Apr. 777 (Cent. Suppl.) Bearings of the usual self-oiling type, with two revolving brass *oil rings in each. 1902 *Sci. Amer.* Suppl. 15 Nov. 22469 (Cent. Suppl.) The Spindletop *oil-rock. 1873 *Oil shale [see above]. 1924 *Times Trade & Engin. Suppl.* 29 Nov. 238/4 The railways of Esthonia are using oil shale as fuel on a large scale. 1889 *Century Mag.* Mar. 710/2 It had..formed an *oil-slick thirty feet to windward. 1927 Haldane & Huxley *Animal Biol.* iii. 93 Vitamin A is a fat-like and *oil-soluble substance. 1832 B. Davenport *Gaz. N. Amer.* (1842) 311/1 s.v. *Franklin*, The celebrated *oil springs..rise from the bed of Oil creek [Pa.] and afford an inexhaustible supply of oil. 1839 Z. Leonard *Adventures* (1904) 252 An oil spring, rising out of the earth. 1930 Rose Macaulay *Relations* xix. 274 Signboards it needed..advertisements all along the road,..telling travellers..about the next gas and *oil station [etc.]. 1904 *Trans. Amer. Inst. Elect. Engin.* 13 (Cent. Suppl.) *Oil-switch. 1904 S. E. White *Silent Places* iii. 23, I ain't got but ..five pairs of moccasins in the place! There's plenty of *oil tan. 1920 *Isle of Man Weekly Times* 21 Sept. 3 Kermode's supplied..installations..for..British Admiralty *oil-tankers. 1927 *Daily Express* 20 Sept. 2/4 The goods train consisted mainly of oil-tankers. 1903 *Elect. World & Engin.* 7 Nov. 777/2 Special *oil throwers are provided to prevent the creepage of oil along the shaft.

Oil, *v.* Add: **1. a.** and **b.** (Later examples.)
1851 H. Melville *Moby Dick* xxv. (1926) 140 A king's head is solemnly oiled at his coronation, even as a head of salad. 1895 C. M. Sheldon *His Brother's Keeper* ii. (1896) 39 Have you been greasing your boots with it?..Half a pint wouldn't oil more than one of 'em. 1909 *Daily Chron.* 6 Sept. 3/3 Her craze for the 'psychic'..oils the wheels of the plot.
3. b. *intr.* To take in a supply of oil.
1914 H. H. Fyfe *Real Mexico* 201 Some day vessels will call here..to 'oil' just as they now 'coal'. 1922 *Glasgow Herald* 21 Oct. 11 After that the Renown only stopped to oil.

Oil-bag. **c.** (Later example.)
a 1889 in *Century Mag.* Mar. 710/1 [I] placed two oil-bags, filled with linseed oil, over the bows.

Oil-cloth. **1. b.** (Later examples.)
1876 J. S. Ingram *Centen. Exposition* xii. 404 In the line of floor oil-cloths the display was remarkable for the immense size of the cloths made in a single piece. 1904 Mrs. Stratton-Porter *Freckles* 72 Freckles..covered the [book-]case with oil-cloth.

Oi·l-clothed, *a.* [f. Oilcloth.] Laid or covered with oilcloth. So **Oi·lclothy** *a.*, suggestive of or resembling oilcloth.
1899 Meg Dyan *Hazard Concealing* 328 There came..the tap of light heels on the oil-clothed landing. 1918 Galsworthy *Five Tales, First & Last* iii. 24 He was in a gas-lighted passage, with an oil-clothed floor. 1923 Una L. Silberrad *Lett. Jean Armiter* ix. 202 Everything was slippery and oilclothy.

Oi·ldom. [f. Oil *sb.* + -dom.] The petroleum-producing districts of a country.
1877 Bartlett *Dict. Amer.*, *Oildom*, the petroleum manufacture; the district in Pennsylvania whence petroleum is obtained. 1880 *Harper's Mag.* Dec. 63 Huge shops..send ..iron tanks into the oil regions—to hold the surplus of Oildom.

Oiled, *ppl. a.* Add: **1. c.** (Further example.)
1835 *Southern Lit. Messenger* II. 53 The holes, ycleped windows, covered with oiled paper to keep out the air.
3. Executed in oil-colours.
1903 Ld. Gower *Rec. & Remin.* 246 To make an oiled copy of the framed 'Three Maries' by Carracci.
4. *slang.* Slightly drunk; tipsy.
1916 E. V. Lucas *Vermilion Box* 141 He was, as the slang phrase has it, 'oiled'; which is a condition of alcoholic comfort well on this side of inebriety. 1920 H. C. McNeile *Bull-Dog Drummond* iii. § 3. Both were quite obviously what in the vernacular is known as oiled.
5. *Comb.*, as **oiled-up,** fouled or choked with oil.
1925 *Morris Owner's Manual* 81 Sooty or oiled-up plugs will cause erratic running, loss of power and..increased petrol consumption.

Oiler. Add: **7. a.** A vessel using oil-fuel.
1915 *Chambers's Jrnl.* Oct. 664/1 The word 'oiler', like 'steamer', for oil-driven ships..is coming into use.
b. An oil-engine.
1926 *Chambers's Jrnl.* Dec. 843/1 She—the engine—..is a cold-starter, two stroke 'oiler'.
8. *U.S. slang.* A Mexican. (Cf. Greaser 2.)
1907 S. E. White *Arizona Nights* I. iv. 82 A few oilers livin' near had water holes in the foothills. *Ibid.* III. ii. 282 We're livin' like a lot of Oilers.

Oiling, *vbl. sb.* Add: **3.** The taking of oil on board, esp. for fuel.
1906 *Westm. Gaz.* 27 Feb. 2/1 The difficulties in the way of 'oiling'..at foreign ports.

Oilman. (Later examples.)
1880 *Harper's Mag.* Dec. 65 There are engines and boilers and pumps to be built for the oil men. 1891 *Century Mag.* Mar. 786 The *Plymouth* left Sydney..with a cargo of pork, oilmen's stores, ironmongery.

Oil-nut. **b.** and **c.** (Earlier examples.)
1792 J. Belknap *Hist. New Hampsh.* III. 101 Oil-nut or Butter-nut. The peculiar property of its bark, the extract of which is one of the best cathartics in the *materia medica* [etc.]. 1813 Muhlenberg *Catal. Plants N. Amer.* 96 Oil nut, (*Pyrularia* or *Hamiltonia oleifera*).

Oilstone, *sb.* (Later example.)
1878 *Harper's Mag.* Jan. 204 Under the name of the Arkansas whetstone or Ouachita oil-stone, [novaculite rock] has almost eclipsed its Turkish rivals.

Ointment. *A fly in the ointment*: see *Fly *sb.*[1] 1 e.

O. K. (ōu kēi), *a.*, *sb.*, and *v.* Orig. *U.S.* Also **okay, okeh.** Used as an abbreviation for 'oll korrect', misspelling of 'all correct'.
Alleged instances of O.K. in 1790 and 1828 have no evidence to support them. The earliest occurrence so far noted is in the Boston *Transcript* of 15 April 1840. In this and two examples from April and June the meaning is not clear, but the explanation 'oll korrect' appears on June 18 (see below). The attribution to Gen. Jackson was probably not intended to be taken seriously. Other jocular extensions of the initials follow in the same year. The suggestion that they represent the Choctaw *oke* 'it is' first appears in 1885, and does not accord with the evidence.
A. *adj.* (See O 5 d.)
1840 *Atlas* (Boston) 18 June 2/1 The band rode in a stage, which had a barrel of Hard Cider on the baggage rack, marked with large letters 'O.K.'—*oll korrect.* *Ibid.* 19 Aug. 2/4 These initials, according to Jack Downing, were first used by Gen. Jackson. 'Those papers, Amos [Kendall], are *all correct.* I have marked them O.K.' (oll korrect). The Gen. was never good at spelling. 1844 *Lowell* (Mass.) *Offering* IV. 148 (Th.) She said my bonnet was O.S., instead of O.K. 1844 *Knickerbocker Mag.* XXIII. 393 Look at his feet,..his every thing, in fact—so perfectly O.K.! 1847–1900 [see O 5 d]. 1848 *Knickerbocker Mag.* XXXI. 86 We have it that can't be beat on any land..it is the extra 'O.K.' brand. 1875 Mrs. Stowe *We & Neighbors* xxx. 281 St. John is O.K. about all the particulars of how they managed in the catacombs. 1904 W. H. Smith *Promoters* xxi. 306, I..was so sure that it was O.K. that I sat down and wrote Starleigh I was certain it would be a go. 1908 Mulford *Orphan* xiii. 160 He's an O.K. dog, that's what he is.
B. *sb.* The letters 'O.K.', esp. as written on a document, etc., denoting approval of its contents; an indorsement, approval, or sanction.
1848 Dow, Jr. *Patent Serm.* I. 273 (Th.) [Fortitude] infuses new life into his soul, while hope adds an O.K. to his condition. 1889 *Kansas City T. & Star* 22 Oct., The building department put its O.K. on O.K. Kimball's permit for a frame building. 1896 *Congress. Rec.* 5 Mar. 2507/1 The deputy marshall..would send word to the prosecuting attorney asking for an 'O.K.' 1901 Merwin & Webster *Calumet K* xiv. 273 A formal permit..signed by Porter himself, and bearing the O.K. of the general manager. 1909 S. E. White *Rules of Game* III. xvii. 238 The High Official added his O.K. to the others. 1925 *Dollar Mag.* Dec. 207 To find new and more vivid forms of expression..in the hope that they will, in time, receive the okeh of the reading public. 1931 *North Amer. Rev.* Jan. 15 During the last two years Raskob has..put his okay on every major move.
C. *v. trans.* To mark with the letters 'O.K.', to indicate that it is correct; hence, to approve of, to sanction.
1888 *Missouri Republican* 25 Jan. (Farmer), Please O.K. and hurry return of my account. 1891 *Congress. Rec.* 13 Feb. 2635/2 If those who were to go into the clerical service of the Government were to be 'O.K.'d' by any one except the Civil Service Commission. 1904 *Brooklyn Standard Union* 25 June 6 The inspectors who O.K.'d the rotten hose. 1914 *Munsey's Mag.* Jan. Advt. p. A v/2 Land sold by Association of Farmers Ok-ed by United States Government.

Okapi (ǫkā·pi). [The native name.] A rare ungulate mammal (*Okapia johnstoni*) related to the giraffes, found in the dense forests of West Africa, first discovered in 1900.
1900 Sir H. Johnston in *Proc. Zool. Soc.* 775, I found the Bambuba natives dwelling alongside the dwarfs called it 'Okapi'. 1901 *Chambers's Jrnl.* July 493/1 The native name for this strange beast, which is quite inoffensive, is the *okapi*. 1930 *Punch* 24 Sept. 337/2 A photographer has succeeded in getting a 'close-up' of the shy okapi.

Okay, Okeh, see *O.K.

Okro, okra. For 8 ocra, read 8–9 ocra.
1843 Carlton *New Purchase* xv. 113 Down came..the rye-coffee, and the ocra, and the spices.

Old, *a.* Add: **1. c.** Also *old one, old un*, one's father. *colloq.* *Any old*: see *Any 1 e. So *every old*.
1900 G. Ade *More Fables in Slang* (1902) 205 An Author was sitting at his Desk trying to..grind out Any Old Thing that could be converted into Breakfast Food. 1918 W. J. Locke *Rough Road* iii. 32 Own 'em, sail 'em, navigate 'em, stoke 'em, clean out the boilers,..do every old thing.
3. (Later examples. Also *techn.* and *spec.*)
1839 in *Trans. Mich. Agric. Soc.* (1856) VII. 368 The deposit [of ore]..is mostly of inferior quality, being what is technically known as an old ore. 1841 L. M. Child *Lett. New York* vii. 44 In New-York, as elsewhere, the vending of 'old clo' is a prominent occupation among the Jews. 1854 *Florida Plant. Rec.* 92, I new it would not doe to give all my old corn away and to feed the mules on new corn.
5. b. *old boy, coon, soldier* (example).
1824– [see Soldier *sb.* 2 b]. 1837 *Knickerbocker Mag.* IX. 268, I must relieve the 'old soldier' who has been on post all the dog-watch. 1846 Corcoran *Pickings* 190 'Why are you not a locofoco?' said we...' I live too near the old coon [Harrison] for that.' 1862 *Punch* Feb. 42/2, I guess them sarcy Britishers Won't easy get to leeward Of such an all-fired smart old 'coon As William H. Seward. 1877 Bartlett *Dict. Amer.* (ed. 4) 436 'He's an old coon', is said of one who is very shrewd; often applied to a political manager.
8. a. Also in *old bean, fellow* U.S. (an overseer or 'boss'), *horse* or *hoss* (see Horse *sb.* 4, *Hoss 2), *lady* (a woman, one's wife or mother), *thing, top*.
Freq. *U.S.* in popular names of national heroes or leaders, as *Old Abe, Bullion, Hickory, Ironsides*, etc.: see Bartlett, Farmer, Clapin, and Thornton.
Old Probabilities: see Probability 2 b.
1872 Eggleston *Hoosier Schoolm.* xvii. 134 Here's the old lady and Shocky. 1873 'Mark Twain' & Warner *Gilded Age* xxvii. 245 You make yourself perfectly comfortable, old lady. 1902 S. E. White *Blazed Trail* xxvii. 187 He was intensely loyal to his 'Old Fellows' [= 'bosses' of lumber camps]. 1913 Galsworthy *Fugitive* I. 18 My dear old thing; you mustn't get into fantods like this. 1914 Conrad *Chance* II. i. 244 The old lady's first-rate, sir, thank you. 1915 Wodehouse *Something Fresh* ii. § i, I say, Dickie, old top, I want to see you about something devilish important. 1919 H. L. Wilson *Ma Pettengill* x. 286 All right, Herman, old top! 1920 *Punch* 29 Sept. 255/1 Remorse seized me; I put my arm about her, with—'Tired, old thing?' 1925 Deeping *Sorrell & Son* iv. § iii, Hallo, Bob, old bean.
c. Of things.
1905 *Smart Set* Sept. 117/2 No one else is going to run off with your old car. 1918 E. A. Mackintosh *War, the Liberator* 91, I always wondered if our old barrage could Be half as bloody good As the Staff said it would.
9. b. *The old boy, old smoker* (examples).
Also *old Driver* (Bartlett, 1877), *Poger, Split-foot, Toast, Toaster* (Farmer, 1889). *U.S. slang.*
1802 *Balance* (Hudson, N.Y.) 14 Oct. 317 (Th.) The devil has been nick-named the old boy. 1834 Seba Smith *Sel. Lett. J. Downing* 66 They carry on so like the old smoker. 1854 Mary J. Holmes *Tempest & Sunshine* xv. 203 'Ho Luce,' continued he, 'where the old boy is your mistress?' *Ibid.* xix. 267 No; he may have her and go to the old boy for all of Josh. 1896 J. C. Harris *Sister Jane* 25 Because the Old Boy's done took possession of him.
11. See also Light *sb.* 6 d, School *sb.* 5 b, Tenor *sb.*[1] 1 c.
12. b. *Old country* (earlier example); *Old England* (later example). Also *Old colony* (Massachusetts), *North State* (North Carolina), *South* (the South before the civil war). *Old Dominion*: see *Dominion 2 b.

Supplement, p. 3873; Corrigenda, p. 4092; Spurious words, p. 4093; Books quoted, p. 4094

1796 F. Baily *Jrnl. Tour N. Amer.* (1856) 172 The scenery..so very different from what we had been used to in the old country. 1840 *Southern Lit. Messenger* VI. 241/1 More of Old England is left in the hearts of the Old Dominion than in all the states beside, save [etc.]. *c* 1845 in Bartlett *Dict. Amer.* (1877) 438 W. A. Graham..will be elected governor by the largest majority ever before given..in the Old North State. 1888 *Mississippi Valley Lumberman* May (Farmer), The hospitality and friendliness of the old south. 1889 Farmer *Americanisms* 398 *Old colony*,..the State of Massachusetts. 1903 K. M. Abbott *Old Paths & Leg. N. Eng.* 357 At the very beginning of your pilgrimage through the Old Colony.

D. 2. b. Add: *Old-boyishness, -fogyish* (earlier example), *-liner* (later examples), *old-soldierism* (the conduct of an 'old soldier').

1850 *Punch* 3 Aug. 52/1 There is a jolly-buckism or an old-boyishness about the concern. *a* 1877 *Independent* (Bartlett), He's slow and rather old-fogyish. 1903 *N.Y. Even. Post* 31 Oct. 5 The old-liners quietly backbite him for taking up a 'fanatic' like Johnson. 1908 R. W. Chambers *Firing Line* xxix. 493, I didn't expect any cordiality..but..they classed us with the old-liners. 1911 H. S. Harrison *Queed* xxii. 276, I think old-soldierism is the meanest profession the Lord ever suffered to thrive.

3. *old-countryman, -issue, -line* (examples), *-standard, -year.*

1848 Bartlett *Dict. Amer.*, **Old Countryman*, a native of England, Scotland, Ireland, or Wales. 1879 Tourgee *Fool's Err.* xvii. 87 Robert, who was..an '*old-issue free nigger' (freed before the war). 1856 *Congress. Globe* 9 Jan. 180/3 Have they offered us one of my colleagues, an *old-line Whig? 1889 Farmer *Americanisms* 399 *Old Line State*, Maryland. 1906 *N.Y. Even. Post* 27 Oct. 10 The old-line Democrats. 1908 R. W. Chambers *Firing Line* xxi. 353 I'm in an old-line institution. 1839 J. F. Cooper *Home as Found* x. (1873) 169 That is the First Presbyterian, or the *old standard [church]; a very good house. 1897 R. M. Stuart *Simpkinsville* i. 14 They got him to come to the *old year party one year, jest for the fun of it.

4. old bach *colloq.*, a confirmed bachelor; **Old Baptist, Old Christian (church)** *U.S.*, names of religious denominations; **old-clothes-shop** (later example); **old-out** *a. Typog.* = *old-face*; **old dirt** *Mining* (see Dirt *sb.* 3 c, Washdirt); **old-face** *a. Typog.* (see Face *sb.* 22); so *old-faced* adj.; **Old Glory,** *U.S.*, the 'Stars and Stripes'; **Old Ned** *U.S. slang* (see quot.); **old Orchard** *U.S.*, a blend of whisky originally distilled at Orchard; **old-rich** *a.*, belonging to a family that has long been rich; **old sledge** (later example); **old soldier** *sb. U.S. slang*, the remaining part of a smoked cigar or chewed quid; also, an empty liquor bottle (Webster 1909); **Old Squaw** (examples); **old style** *a. Typog.*, applied to a fount of type modelled on old-faced or antique; **Old Testament** [see Testament *sb.* 5 *a*]; hence **Old Testamentism**, the religious ideas and teaching of the Old Testament; **old thing** *Austral.* (see quot.); **old Thirteen** *U.S.*, the original 'Stars and Stripes', a flag with thirteen stars and thirteen stripes; **old tiger, witch** (see quots.); **old witch-grass,** an American pasture grass, *Panicum capillare.*

1874 J. C. McCoy *Hist. Sketches* 14 Although young, Peryman is what the ladies term an '*Old Bach'. 1845 A. Wiley in *Indiana Mag. Hist.* XXIII. 18, I see nothing awaiting the '*old Baptist' churches but utter annihilation. 1849 E. Chamberlain *Indiana Gaz.* 175 Presbyterians, Methodists, United Brethren, Christian,..*Old Christian, (or new Light) and Baptists. 1851 A. O. Hall *Manhattaner* 6 Groups of *old clo' shops, gaudily set forth with particolored handkerchiefs. 1888 Jacobi *Printers' Vocab.* 90 **Old-cut type*, founts similar to the Caslon old-faced type. 1878 J. H. Beadle *Western Wilds* vii. 107 In places [we] pass hundreds of acres of '*old dirt', which has been washed out and abandoned. 1875 *Caslon's Circular* July, He was supplied..with the complete series of original *old-face founts. 1863 G. Unwin (*title*) Specimens of *Old-faced Series of Type in use at the Gresham Steam Press. 1865 Boudrye *Fifth N.Y. Cavalry* 270 The moment we beheld the *Old Glory, three enthusiastic cheers burst from one and all. 1896 *Congress. Rec.* 25 Apr. 4433/1 The chivalry and comradeship which inheres in every soldier, whether he marched under 'Old Glory' or the Stars and Bars. 1869 *Overland Monthly* III. 129 Southern smoke-cured pork,..in allusion to the famous negro-song, was termed '*Old Ned'. 1810 R. B. Thomas *Farmer's Almanac* Sept., Come, ye lovers of *Old Orchard, let us take a walk into the fields. 1927 *Public Opinion* 18 Feb. 149/1 These mistakes..seem folly to an *old-rich man. *Ibid.* 149/2 The old-rich know these things well enough, but the new-rich never discover them. 1884 'C. E. Craddock' *In Tenn. Mts.* ii. 82 The mingled charms of *Old Sledge and apple-jack had occasioned comment. 1845 T. J. Green *Texian Exped.* xvi. 272, I have known a whole 'medio' bet upon a race; but the most usual bet was an *old soldier. *c* 1871 'Mark Twain' *Sketches* Wks. XIX. 45 A wooden box of sand, sprinkled with cigar stubs and 'old soldiers'. *a* 1877 in Bartlett *Dict. Amer.* (ed. 4) 438 Ladies who swab our sidewalks,..And..Haul off old soldiers lying there at rest. 1848 Bartlett *Dict. Amer.* 240 *Old-wife*, or **Old-squaw*, the popular name of..the long-tailed Duck of Pennant. 1870 *Amer. Naturalist* Mar. 49 The same kind of food that our Coot and Old Squaw live on. 1871 *Amer. Encycl. Printing* (ed. Ringwalt) 321 **Old-Style Letter*, Roman and Italic letter of the design used previous to the present century, but which has been readopted to a great extent during the last few years. 1875 *Caslon's Circular* July, There appeared in the market a modern imitation of the old-face character called Old Style. 1900 Mary Kingsley in *Spectator* 15 Sept. 333/1 Educating the next generation out of *Old Testamentism. 1848 H. W. Haygarth *Bush Life Australia* i. 6 The Traveller's entertainment is confined to the '*old thing', as it is contemptuously called, that is to say, beef and 'damper'. 1853 B. F. Taylor *Jan. & June* (1871) 68 The '*Old Thirteen' were blazing bright—There were only thirteen then! 1876 Joaquin Miller *First Families* xv. 126 The following popular drinks, that is *Old Tiger, Bad Eye. 1881 *Harper's Mag.* Jan. 184/2 The young folks..played at 'prisoner's base' or '*old witch by the wayside'. 1853 Darlington *Flora Cestrica* (ed. 3) 381 *Panicum capillare*..*Old-witch Grass. 1863 *Trans. Ill. Agric. Soc.* (1865) V. 86 *Panicum Capillare*, Old Witch-grass, is found in sandy pastures.

Old age pension. [Old *a.* 2.] A pension paid by the state in certain countries to persons who have reached a specified age and require such assistance. Used *attrib.* with *act, scheme*, etc. **Old age pensioner,** one who receives an old age pension.

1890 *Chambers's Jrnl.* 8 Feb. 88/1 To qualify..the worker must contribute..for an old-age pension for fourteen hundred and ten weeks. 1892 *Q. Rev.* Apr. 507 Old age pensions commence at seventy years of age. 1906 *Chambers's Jrnl.* 10 Mar. 239/1 There are two possible systems for an old-age pension scheme for this country. 1909 *Reformers' Yr.-Bk.* 56 On and from the 1st of January, 1909, Old Age Pensions may be claimed by all persons of 70 years or over, provided that [etc.]. 1912 *Manch. Courier* Illust. Section 1 Sept. 2/2 An old-age pensioner has been admitted to the infirmary..as 'a paying guest'.

Old-fashion, *a.* Delete †*Obs.*

1888 *Rep. Vermont Board Agric.* X. 20, I have made good butter in old fashion shallow pans.

Old-fashioned, *a.* Add: **4.** as *sb.*

1904 *Daily Chron.* 7 Jan. 3/3 She..does not hesitate to lean to the old-fashioned if occasion require.

Old field. (Add examples.)

1839 *Southern Lit. Messenger* V. 113/1 First..no such foreigner has the faintest idea of what an old-field is. 1840 J. Buel *Farmer's Comp.* 159 Part of the farm was in old field, or commons. 1857–8 *Trans. Ill. Agric. Soc.* III. 452 In 1840 I became possessed of the tract of land containing what was called the 'old field'.

b. Old-field birch (examples); **old-field-pine** (earlier examples).

1810 Michaux *Arbres* I. 26 *White birch* [ou] *Old field birch*, (Bouleau des terreins secs.). 1832 D. J. Browne *Sylva Amer.* 123 In the state of Maine,..[the name] Old Field Birch is..employed to distinguish the white birch from the canoe birch. 1796–1806 B. Hawkins *Lett.* 89 The whole grown up with old field pine, some of them a foot and an half diameter. 1818 Nuttall *N. Amer. Plants* II. 223 Old-field Pine (*P. taeda*). 1841 *Southern Lit. Messenger* VII. 452/1 The old-field pine had not intruded so largely on the domain of the ploughman and reaper.

c. *attrib.* as *old-field colt, ground, plum, preacher, school, school-master, scrub.*

1835 *Southern Lit. Messenger* I. 582, I could..only remember that every untrimmed **old field* colt was a regular descendant of Eclipse. 1772 *Carroll Papers* in *Maryland Hist. Mag.* XIV. 278 Our corn..is very good at all the quarters, some of this *old field ground..excepted. 1887 *Harper's Mag.* Sept. 588/2 She been goin' out..between times, and getherin' *old-field plums. 1904 T. Watson *Bethany* (1920) 168 The tremendous emphasis with which *old field preacher uttered the words. 1834 Carruthers *Kentuckian in N.Y.* I. 26 He sold his horse and cart too, and then turned in to keepin an *old-field school. 1853 J. G. Baldwin *Flush Times Alabama* 125 The master of the old field school was one of the regular faculty. 1888 *Century Mag.* XXXVI. 278/1 He attended what is known in some regions of the South as an 'old field school'. 1853 J. G. Baldwin *Flush Times Alabama* 106 He had been an *old-field schoolmaster. 1834 Carruthers *Kentuckian in N.Y.* I. 12, I bet you my horse Talleyrand..against an *old field scrub.

Old land. *dial.* Also **olland, ollunt** (see E.D.D.). Land that has lain in grass for some time, usually two years or more.

1764–1815 A. Young *Annals Agric.* IX. 429 (E.D.D.). 1882 *N. & Q.* Ser. vi. VI. 406/1 It was the land ploughed out of grass (out-land), which was known as olland. 1895 P. H. Emerson *Birds* etc. *Norf. Broadland* 8 Newlays and olluntes close by the marsh farmhouse. 1909 *Eastern Daily Press* 23 Jan. 8/1 Oats also do much better on an olland than on loose land.

b. Land that has been in cultivation for a long time. *U.S.*

1833 B. Silliman *Man. Sugar Cane* 10 Violet cane..prefers old land, and that which is rather dry.

c. *Geog.* Previously existing land, contrasted with land more recently formed. Also *attrib.*

1895 *Geog. Jrnl.* V. 133 The old-land streams that are extended across the new coastal plain by the addition of consequent lower courses. 1897 *Ibid.* IX. 538 For convenience all the land back of this initial shoreline will be called the 'oldland', and all alluvial accumulation built in front of the oldland..will be called 'foreland'.

Old maid. Add: **3. b.** *U.S.* The velvet-leaf or Indian mallow, *Abutilon avicennæ.*

1839 *Southern Lit. Messenger* V. 751/2 A particular spot in his garden was appropriated to the culture of old maids. 1880 *Scribner's Monthly* May 101/1 In my section an annoying weed is *Abutilon*, or velvet-leaf, also called 'old maid'. 1888 *Century Mag.* XXXVI. 896/1 The flower-garden overrun with..four-o'clocks, old-maids, and sunflowers.

Hence **Old-mai·dy** *a.* = *old-maidish.*

1923 Una L. Silberrad *Lett. Jean Armiter* xiii. § ii. 253 She is much nicer and better really than I, in my old-maidy prejudice, used to think.

Old man. Add: **1.** (U.S. examples.)

Also *U.S.* in *old man eloquent*, often applied (after Milton's phrase) to John Quincy Adams, 1767–1848.

1792 Brackenridge *Adv. Capt. Farrago* xiii. 113 You are welcome, Sir, if you wish to stop..though since my old man's time, we don't take in strangers for common. 1840 *Knickerbocker Mag.* XVI. 208 'You must ask the old man', said the lady. 1848 *Congress. Globe* 24 Feb. 388 Let not the grave of the old man eloquent be desecrated by unfriendly remembrances. 1872 Eggleston *Hoosier Schoolm.* iii. 28 My ole man's purty well along in the world. 1901 S. E. White *Claim Jumpers* i. 4 He's been pestering the old man to send him West. Old man doesn't approve.

b. (Earlier and later examples.)

1845 *Knickerbocker Mag.* XXVI. 206 I've known the Old Man come on deck at midnight. 1873 'Mark Twain' & Warner *Gilded Age* iv. 44 The 'old man' was the captain—he is always so, on steamboats and ships.

d. A master, overseer, foreman, or superintendent.

1844 *Knickerbocker Mag.* XXIII. 83 The 'old man' himself came to the door, and looking down at his apprentice, shook his head sorrowfully. 1887 C. B. George *40 Years on Rail* ix. 167 They feel that if they can only lay it before the 'old man' it will be properly dealt with. 1913 Mulford *Coming of Cassidy* xii. 197 'Is there any chance to get a job here?' he asked anxiously. 'You'll have to quiz th' Old Man'.

e. *U.S. local.* Substituted familiarly for 'old Mr. —'.

1843 Carlton *New Purchase* 78 Ole-man Sturgis. 1859 Bartlett *Dict. Amer.* (ed. 2) 301 In the South and West, instead of saying..'Old Mr. Smith', it is customary to say, 'Old man Smith'. 1862 *Let.* in *Congress. Globe* Mar. (1863) 1664/1, I send a few lines to you by old man Jesse Price. 1902 A. D. McFaul *Ike Glidden* xvii. 126 There is old man Spencer who had always been poor.

fig. 1910 W. M. Raine *B. O'Connor* 30 When Old Man Trouble comes knocking at the door. 1919 C. P. Thompson *Cocktails* 252 Why, being officially booked to meet Old Man Death on ground, I had kept the appointment in the air.

4. b. *U.S.* A grizzly bear.

1886 *Outing* Nov. 108/1 Good boy! You've got more sand than I thought you had to tackle the old man on the open plain.

7. Old-man kangaroo = sense 4.

1901 *Chambers's Jrnl.* May 340/2 He knew..the best ground for shooting an old-man kangaroo.

Old-ma·nnish, *a.* [f. Old man + -ish.] Characteristic or suggestive of an old man.

1927 Deeping *Kitty* vii, His affection for that corner of the City of Westminster grew more deep and old-mannish.

Old-school, *a.* [f. Old *a.* + School *sb.*[1] 5 b.]

1. Of or belonging to a party which adheres to conservative views, principles, or modes of life.

1815 *Niles' Weekly Reg.* IX. 120/2 The federal and 'old school' democratic candidate for congress. 1839 J. F. Cooper *Home as Found* xiii. (1873) 218, I could just get a look of our clergyman's wig; for he was an old-school man.

b. *Theol.* Adhering to established or traditional views or interpretation of doctrine.

1837 Peck *Gaz. Illinois* I. 72 McDonough College..is identified with the interests of the 'old school' Presbyterians. 1847 H. Howe *Hist. Coll. Ohio* 274 The first church, the old school Presbyterian,..was built about 1817. 1873 'Mark Twain' & Warner *Gilded Age* vii. 80 Grandmother..was an Old-School Baptist. 1878 J. H. Beadle *Western Wilds* xii. 183 The Old School Baptisses never went nigh the Methodis' meetin' house.

2. Characteristic or suggestive of a former time; old-fashioned, antiquated.

1806 Fessenden *Democracy Unveiled* ii. 61 These bring grave old-school reflections. 1836 Dunlap *Mem. Water Drinker* (1837) I. 13 His grey hair..and..suit of grey broadcloth, gave him an old-school air. 1882 J. W. Dowling (*title*), Old School Medicine and Homoeopathy.

O·ld-timy, -timey, *a.* [Old-time *a.*] Old-fashioned in character.

1879 F. R. Stockton *Rudder Grange* xvii. 206 Things that were apparently so 'old-timey'..that David Dutton did not care to take them with him.

Old wife. 2. (Earlier mod. example.)

1838 J. F. Cooper *Homeward Bound* xii. 157 I've seen a lover who couldn't tell..a canvas-back from an old-wife.

Old woman. Add: **1. b.** (Examples.)

1834 W. G. Simms *Guy Rivers* II. 97 The old woman, by whom we mean..to indicate the spouse of the wayfarer, and mother of the two youths, was busied about the fire. 1839 Mrs. Kirkland *New Home* xv. 96 If my old woman was to stick up that fashion, I'd keep the house so blue she couldn't see to snuff the candle. 1869 Mrs. Stowe *Oldtown Folks* xxxvii. 481 The old woman is just as choice of her boys as if [etc.].

c. *U.S. dial.* A she-bear.

1886 *Outing* Nov. ix. 104/2, I heerd a cracklin', an'..long come the old woman with a cub follerin' behind.

3. old woman's tooth, a small plane used by cabinet-makers.

1907 Eleanor Rowe *Pract. Wood-carving* 7 The router, very similar to the tool called by the joiner an 'old woman's tooth', may occasionally be used.

Old world, *a.* **2.** (Example.)

1877 *Harper's Mag.* Dec. 91/2 This was..a beautiful garden kept in old-world order by a Scotch gardener.

Oleaginously (ǭliˌæ·dʒinəsli), *adv.* [-ly [2].] In an oleaginous or oily manner.

1912 L. J. Vance *Destroying Angel* x. 119 Three doors, in one of which a rotund Chinaman beamed oleaginously. 1913 Deeping *Sincerity* xxxii. 247 His hands were fat, his neck full of red creases, his manner towards women oleaginously gallant.

Oleander. (Later example.)

1880 G. W. Cable *Grandissimes* xxvi. 193 Their long, over-arched avenues of oleander.

Oleaster. Add: **c.** *Comb.* **Oleaster plum** (see quot.).

1885 Balfour *Cycl. India* s.v., *Oleaster Plum*, fruit of the Elæagnus conferta, which abounds in parts of the Tenasserim jungles.

Olefinic (ǭlĕfi·nik), *a. Chem.* [f. Olefine + -ic.] Of, pertaining to, or having the characteristics of the olefines.

1923 *Daily Mail* 15 Feb. 3 Those olefinic and empyreumatic substances which result from the distillation of coal or oil.

Oleo [2] (ǭ·lio). Abbreviation of Oleograph.

1920 Galsworthy *Captures* (1923) 56 Taking up the oleos, he turned his back on the photographs.

Oleum (ǭ·liŏm). [ad. L. *oleum* oil.] A trade name for oil of vitriol; fuming sulphuric acid. Also *attrib.*

1919 E. Hendrick *Chem. in Everyday Life* 61 SO_3 or oleum, as it is called, mixed with 100 per cent. acid, is needed in some chemical operations. 1921 *Dict. Occup. Terms* (1927) § 143 *Oleum man*,..attends to plant in which fuming sulphuric acid is made... *Oleum plant worker.*

Olfactometer (ǫlfækto·mĭtəɹ). [f. L. *olfactus* smelling, smell + -(o)meter.] An instrument for measuring the keenness of the sense of smell or the intensity of odours. Hence **Olfactome·tric** *a.*, of or pertaining to the measurement of smells. **Olfacto·metry,** the measurement of smells.

1890 *Science* 17 Jan. 44 (Cass. Suppl.) Dr. Zwaardemaker, of Utrecht..has constructed an instrument which he calls an olfactometer. 1898 *Amer. Jrnl. Psychol.* X. 86 Both olfactometry and odorimetry are branches of 'olfactology' (to anglicise another word used by Dr. Zwaardemaker). 1901 E. B. Titchener *Exper. Psychol.* I. ii. 119 Olfactometric technique..is..circumstantial and time-taking. 1902 *Encycl. Brit.* XXXI. 746/1 On this principle an olfactometer may be constructed by which the intensities of different odours may be compared.

Oligotropic (ǫligotrǫ·pik), *a. Entom.* [f. Oligo- + Gr. τροπικ-ός Tropic.] Of bees: That visit few kinds of flowers.

1899 *Nat. Science* Nov. 314 He deals chiefly with the flower visits of oligotropic bees. 1919 J. H. Lovell *Flower & Bee* 106 When a species of bee restricts its visits..to a few allied kinds of flowers [it is termed] an oligotropic bee.

Olio. Add: **3. Olio concert,** a variety concert.

1809 S. Breck in *Recoll.* (1877) App. 271 We..rode round to Mr. Brent's,..with whose family we took tea, and afterward accompanied them to an olio concert.

Olive, *sb.*[1] **1. b. American olive** (example).

1813 Muhlenberg *Catal. Plant. N. Amer.* 2 American olive (purple-berried bay).

C. *attrib.* and *Comb.* Add: **a.** *olive industry, spray*; also objective gen. *olive culture, -plucker.* **d.** *olive-backed* (earlier example); also with reference to the shape of an olive, as *olive-headed, -shaped*, adjs. **e. olive-berry** (later example); **olive thrush,** the olive-back.

1870 *Amer. Naturalist* IV. 541 The *Olive-backed Thrush (*Turdus Swainsonii*). 1869 Mrs. Stowe *Oldtown Folks* xvi. 176, I guess our *olive-berries are pretty well beaten off now. 1893 K. Sanborn *S. California* 155 *Olive culture is just now the fad. 1908 *Practitioner* Jan. 62–3 An acorn-headed, or *olive-headed bougie..should be passed in order to diagnose stricture. 1893 K. Sanborn *S. California* 155 Pomona is the head-quarters of the *olive industry. 1907 Edith Rickert *Golden Hawk* 230 A sweet little, pretty little *olive-plucker. 1908 *Practitioner* Sept. 360 The sounds which will best aid are those..having interchangeable *olive-shaped metallic heads. 1864 Lowell *Fireside Trav.* 222 Climbing the sides of the nearer Monticelli in a gray belt of *olive-spray. 1904 S. E. White *Silent Places* i. 4 The white-throats and *olive thrushes called in a language hardly less intelligible.

Olive-branch. 1. b. (Later example.)

1856 R. Glisan *Jrnl. Army Life* xxiv. (1874) 324 The troops..moved up Rogue River..with the olive branch in one hand, and the sword in the other.

Oliverian. B. *adj.* (Later example.)

1806 *Epitome Gunton's Hist. Peterborough Cath.* 41 The painted windows demolished by the Oliverian rabble.

Olivescent (ǫlive·sĕnt), *a.* [f. Olive + -escent.] Of colour: Bordering on or slightly olive.

1900 *Proc. Zool. Soc.* 506 *Kirontisa whiteheadi*...Upperside deep olivescent brown. Fore wing with two paler olivescent marks within.

Olive-yard. (Recent example.)

1929 *Camb. Med. Hist.* VI. xiv. 475 Enclosed vineyards and oliveyards.

Olivine. c. (Add examples.)

1895 Harker *Petrol. for Students* 68 The Tertiary gabbros of the western islands of Scotland..are in general olivine-gabbros. *Ibid.* 178 The Tertiary basaltic rocks of..the north-east of Ireland are olivine-basalts. 1897 Geikie *Anc. Volcanoes Gt. Brit.* I. 151 Eruptive rocks, some of which are olivine-diabases.

Ological. (Earlier example.)

1854 Dickens *Hard Times* i. xv, I hope you may now turn all your ological studies to good account.

Oly-cook. Add: Also **oliekoek, olycoek, -coke.** (Later examples.)

1881 *Harper's Mag.* Mar. 533/1 His favorite city has surpassed all others in..olie koeks, and New Year cookies. 1889 Rose T. Cooke *Steadfast* vi. 78 Refreshing him with hot flip, oly koek, or Indian preserves.

Olympiad. Add: **2.** A modern (quadrennial) celebration of Olympic games. (See *Olympic A. 2.)

1907 *Westm. Gaz.* 1 Aug. 10/3 When the last Olympiad was held at St. Louis, U.S.A., in 1904, it was decided to hold the next in Rome. 1908 *Ibid.* 31 Mar. 8/3 This year's Olympiad. 1908 *Outlook* 18 July 77/1 How are we to regard the Fourth Olympiad of the revived Games?

Olympic. A. *adj.* **2.** *Olympic games.* Add: Revived as a quadrennial international athletic meeting at Athens in 1896 and in various places since then.

1896 *Scribner's Mag.* Apr. 453/1 The revival of the Olympic Games. Restoring the Stadion at Athens. 1896 *Fortn. Rev.* June 944 What was done to persuade Oxford and Cambridge men to compete in the Olympic Games? Practically nothing. 1908 *Westm. Gaz.* 31 Mar. 8/3 There is now some confusion with regard to the International Olympic games.

-oma, -ome, terminal element representing Gr. -ωμα (which forms neuter nouns cognate with verbs) as in δίπλωμα, L. *diploma*, Fr. *diplome*, Diploma. Other examples adapted from Greek words or possible Greek types are *carcinoma, caulome, phyllome, rhizome* (*-oma*), *sarcoma, trichome* (*-oma*), etc. In modern usage the suffix is regarded as signifying a 'formation' or 'growth' of some kind, and hybrids such as *Cementoma are being formed.

Omaresque (ǭmāre·sk), *a.* [f. as next + -esque.] Suggestive of Omar Khayyam or his poetry.

1892 *Academy* 5 Nov. 404/1 In shorter measures there is often an Omaresque effect of thought.

Omarian (ǫmē·riăn), *a.* and *sb.* [f. the name of the Persian mathematician and epigrammatist, Ghiyāthuddīn Abulfath 'Omar bin Ibrāhīm al-Khayyāmī (*c.* 1100) + -ian.] **a.** *adj.* Of or pertaining to Omar Khayyam or his poetry; having the style or character of his poetry. **b.** *sb.* A student or admirer of Omar Khayyam; a member of the Omar Khayyam Club.

1898 *Daily News* 31 Jan. 6/3 To the devout Omarian a reproduction in black-and-white of this early MS. will carry something of the fragrance [etc.]. 1898 *Westm. Gaz.* 22 Feb. 3/4 The next service demanded of Omarian scholarship is an edition in the original Persian. 1901 *Ibid.* 8 Jan. 2/3 Marie's needs are almost Omarian in their simplicity. 1907 *Daily Chron.* 13 Feb. 3/3 Serious Omarians..are willing to do more for their master than merely turn down an empty glass.

Hence **Oma·rianism, O·marism,** admiration or imitation of Omar Khayyam; the doctrines or cult of Omar Khayyam. So **O·marite** = *Omarian *a.*

1897 *Daily Chron.* 9 Dec. 7/2 All more or less imbued with the spirit of what is called 'Omarianism', and all..decorously convivial. 1898 J. H. McCarthy in *Westm. Gaz.* 22 Feb. 3/3 The protest against what may be called Omarism. 1900 *Academy* 21 July 55/2 Mr. Fawcett called Omarism a fad. *Ibid.*, The Omarite message was interpreted: 'Get drunk as often as you can, and stay so long as you can, for there's nothing in life half so profitable.'

Ombro-. Add: **Ombro·philous** *a. Bot.*, adapted to moist conditions or a wet climate. **Ombro·phily,** ombrophilous quality. **Ombropho·bic, Ombro·phobous** *a. Bot.*, adapted to a dry climate or habitat. **Ombro·phoby,** ombrophobic quality.

1900 B. D. Jackson *Gloss. Bot. Terms*, *Ombrophilous*, rain-loving; *Ombrophily*, the condition described; *Ombrophobic*, hating rain; *Ombrophoby*, dislike or impatience of rain. 1903 W. R. Fisher tr. *Schimper's Plant-geog.* 225, 226 Young leaves are as a rule unwettable and ombrophobous; later they become wettable and ombrophilous.

Omdah, Omdeh. Also **omda.** [ad. Arabic *ʿumdah* column, support, trustworthy authority, f. root *ʿmd* to support.] The headman of an Egyptian village.

1907 *Daily Chron.* 20 Aug. 3/7 Village omdehs to be elected by the whole mass of the villagers. 1922 *Q. Rev.* Apr. 428 Omdehs and others who may be tempted to revert to the old ways would be well to reflect. 1924 *Glasgow Herald* 23 Dec. 7 The numerous 'omdas', or village headmen, who were dismissed during the Zaghlulist regime. 1926 *Blackw. Mag.* Apr. 409/1, I was reluctantly compelled to accept the hospitality of the Omdah..for lunch.

-ome: see *-oma.

Omega. 2. Add: Also *from Alpha to Omega*: from beginning to end; from top to toe.

1930 Mackail *How Amusing* 307, I was a gentleman from alpha to omega.

Omelet, omelette, *sb.* Add: **c.** *attrib.*, as *omelette-pan.*

1879 Mrs. Whitney *Just How* 292 Finish beating and mixing the omelette, setting on the omelette-pan when almost ready.

O·melet, O·melette, *v.* [f. Omelet, -te *sb.*] *trans.* To make into an omelet.

1872 Eggleston *End of World* xxiii. 155 The eggs..were not poached, they were not scrambled, they were not omeletted.

Omen, *sb.* **c.** Add: *omen-animal.*

1902 *Man* II. 61 The chapters on the omen-animals and the cult of skulls are of special value.

Omeno·logy. [f. Omen *sb.* + -logy.] The study or science of omens.

1904 *Hastings' Dict. Bible* V. 553/2 Such..occurrences as the lunar eclipse, would serve as a basis for lunar omenology.

Omni-. Omnitemporal (earlier example).

1882 Westcott *Hist. Faith* (1883) xi. 144 The 'eternal' does not in essence express the infinite extension of time but the absence of time, not the omni-temporal but the supra-temporal.

Omnibus. A. *sb.* Add: **2. b.** Short for *Omnibus book*: see *B. 3.

1931 (*title*) The Omnibus of Romance edited by John Grove.

5. *omnibus-driver, office, riding, sleigh, -ticket*; **omnibus man** (earlier example).

1844 *Knickerbocker Mag.* XXIV. 91 His opinions against the omnibus-riding of so many of our idle citizens. 1852 Hale *If, Yes, & Perhaps* (1868) 3 This [sum]..would buy the omnibus tickets. 1854 Maria S. Cummins *Lamplighter* xviii, You know the way from the omnibus-office. 1857 *Christian Misc.* 219/2 We know no class of men who undergo a more severe life of toil, than the omnibus-men and cabmen of London. 1860 *Boston Audit. Ann. Rep.* 323 One covered omnibus sleigh. 1870 'Fanny Fern' *Ginger-Snaps* 304 This honored name, shouted from lungs that would not have disgraced an omnibus-driver.

B. *adj.* Add: **1.** (Earlier examples.) Also *omnibus contribution.*

1842 *Congress. Globe* 5 July App. 661/1 These two articles ..were caught in the omnibus, or drag-net section, which is placed in the rear of the bill. 1850 *Ibid.* 8 May App. 524/1, I am opposed to all omnibus bills, and all amalgamation projects. 1889 *Echo* 16 Nov. (Cass. Suppl.) Each man pays an omnibus contribution of a shilling a week for benefits.

3. Omnibus book, volume, etc., a book or volume (usually containing several works) published at a price designed to place it within the reach of all; often taken to mean 'including miscellaneous subjects'. **Omnibus ticket,** one admitting a number of persons.

1867 *Rep. Iowa Agric. Soc.* (1868) 408 Some..tender hearted friends would take in their settlement [= family] and then proceed to some hole..in the fence and hand his 'omnibus ticket' to some other parent. 1929 *Daily Tel.* 1 Jan. 6/2 It is a day of what the publishers call 'omnibus books', meaning works which carry many and varied passengers. 1928 *Observer* 25 Mar. 8/4 The vogue for the 'omnibus' volume continues. 1928 *Publishers' Circular* 14 July 39/2 The 'Omnibus' Wells. *Ibid.*, 20 Oct. 549/1 Mr. John Murray has..published an 'omnibus' volume.

Omnibus, *v.* Add: **c.** To convey by omnibus.

1863 'Gail Hamilton' *Gala-Days* 121 We were quickly omnibused to the relics of Donegana.

Omni·ficence. [f. Omnific *a.* + -ence.] The fact or quality of being omnific, or of making or doing everything.

1884 Ruskin *Bible of Amiens* ii. § 28 Unwearied in protective friendship, in meekly dextrous omnificence, in latent tutorship.

Omnopon (ǫ·mnǫpǫn). *Med.* Also **omnipon.** [f. L. *omnis* Omni- + Opium.] A preparation of the hydrochlorides of the combined alkaloids derived from opium used medically.

The word is a registered trade-mark.

1910 *Lancet* 15 Oct. 1169/1 Pantopon is known in Great Britain as 'Omnopon', and represents the total alkaloids of opium in the form of hydrochloric salts. 1922 C. T. Campion tr. *Schweitzer's Edge Primeval Forest* v. 92 He is given an injection of omnipon.

Omophagy (ǫmǫ·fădʒi). Anglicized form of Omophagia.

1905 *Athenæum* 16 Sept. 377/3 Such an omophagy certainly formed part of the cult of Dionysus.

Omphali·tis. *Path.* [f. Gr. ὀμφαλός navel + -itis.] Inflammation of the navel.

1897 *Trans. Amer. Pediatric Soc.* IX. 208 Of the remaining cases..one..was due to pyæmia following omphalitis in the newly-born.

On, *prep.*

1. d. (Later examples of phrases.) For *on the air*: see *Air *sb.* 1 c.

1823 S. H. Long *Exped.* I. 69 Being unaccustomed to travelling on foot, they were much fatigued. 1848 J. F. Cooper *Oak Open.* I. xi. 160 The new-fangled and lubberly abomination of saying '*on* a steamboat', or '*on* a ship'. 1877 Bartlett *Dict. Amer.* (ed. 4) 439 'I met him on the cars', or 'on a steamer'. 1886 *Outing* Nov. 156/2 A splendid, all-round course..eminently calculated to try the various points of sailing on, off, and before the wind.

f. (Later example.)

1871 *Scribner's Monthly* II. 630, I believe on my soul, what I suspected before, that you stole that daguerrotype.

g. (*e*) *on time* (see quot.).

1888 Jacobi *Printers' Vocab.* 91 When a man is paid by the hour or week, and not by piece-work, he is said to be 'on time'.

h. *On the job, on the map*: see the sbs.

i. *On deck*: In Baseball, next on the list to bat.

1883 Nye *Baled Hay* 52 An umpire..to decide who is at bat and who is on deck.

6. Also *U.S.* redundantly in *on yesterday.*

1852 *N.Y. Tribune* 9 Jan. (Bartlett) It was the intention to send in the Treasury Report..on yesterday. 1922 H. C. Lodge in *Congress. Rec.* 27 Dec. 942, I took occasion to ask the Secretary of State on yesterday.

d. *On schedule*: according to schedule; *on time* (earlier examples). See also *1 g and Time *sb.* 43.

1848 *Stray Subjects* 30 S'pose you never heard of burying a man on time. 1872 Marietta Holley *My Opinions* (1891) 268 Thursday mornin' found me to the depott in good time. Betsey also was on time. 1927 *Daily Tel.* 1 Mar. 6/4 The material must be finished on time, routed on schedule, and delivered at exactly the psychological moment.

9. *On time*, on credit. See also Fly *sb.*[2] 2, *Level *sb.* 5 c, Trust *sb.* 1 b.

1873 W. Mathews *Getting on in World* xix. 316 Yet we need not expect that the practice of selling goods on time will ever be abandoned.

10 (*b*). *On guard, on the drink, on the feed, on the go, on the lean, on the listen, on the run, on the* (or *a*) *spree*: see (also) the sbs. (*d*) elliptically, as *on mint, on opera*: on guard at the mint, or opera.

1887 *Chambers's Jrnl.* May 317/1 The sergeant 'on Mint' is virtually invested with supreme authority. *Ibid.* Dec. 795/1 The sentries 'on opera' are provided with neither sentry-boxes..nor order-boards.

b. (Later examples.) See also *Active *a.* 4, Duty *sb.* 5 e, Service *sb.*[1]

1849 D. Nason *Jrnl.* 49 There are nearly a hundred slaves on the work. 1889 Farmer *Americanisms* 401/1 *On herd, Off herd*, cowboy's terms for being on or off duty.

c. *To be on it*: to be ready or prepared for, to be skilled in, something. *U.S. colloq.*

1872 'Mark Twain' *Innoc. at Home* ii. (1882) 269 Pard, he was on it! He was on it bigger than an Injun! 1873 Joaquin Miller *Unwritten Hist.* viii. (1876) 116 There will be blood...I hope the Indians are 'on it'..and that they will receive the wretches warmly as they deserve. 1881 A. A. Hayes *New Colorado* v. 77 You bet he could cook. He was just *on it.*

14. b. (Later U.S. example.)

1906 *Harper's Mag.* Feb. 224 Dreamers awake from their lethargy and seem to take a new lease on life.

21. b. *U.S.* Against (a person).

1901 *Munsey's Mag.* XXV. 711/2 Oh, wasn't that one on me! 1905 *Amer. Illustr. Mag.* Dec. 187 He can't prove anything on you, can he? 1906 *Nation* (N.Y.) 6 Dec. 478 The people rejoiced that the laugh was on those whom they consider their natural enemies. 1916 H. L. Wilson *Somewhere in Red Gap* i. 40 'The joke is sure on us', says Ben Sutton, 'but I bear him no grudge.' 1922 Titus *Timber* vii. 72 And if you give up they'll succeed...The laugh will be on you, then. 1927 *Hutchinson's Mystery Story Mag.* Feb. 104 The man offered me his car to search for the woman. But I had nothing on her, and did not accept the offer.

c. *colloq.* Indicating the person who is to pay the bill (*esp.* for a treat of any kind).

1908 Cutcliffe Hyne *Mr. Horrocks, Purser* 78 And now come and have a bit of cheap lunch. We'll consider we've tossed for it, and it's on me. 1908 S. E. White *Riverman* vii. 59 Come in and have a drink on me. 1913 Mulford *Coming of Cassidy* ii. 30 'Here, have another [drink].' 'All right—this is on me. Here's more luck.' 1918 'Ian Hay' *Last Million* vii. 85 'This is on us', Al Thompson hastened to add. 1926 J. Black *You Can't Win* v. 51 'This is on me', she said, returning my money, 'and so is the dinner'.

d. *To have something* (or *nothing*) *on*: to have some (or no) advantage over. (Cf. *Have *v.* 14 e.)

1912 Mathewson *Pitching* x. 220–1 Always have something on him [= the batter] and never let him have anything on you. This is the prescription for a great pitcher. 1913 E. D. Biggers *Seven Keys to Baldpate* xiv. 171 'I can't just get the full meaning of it all.' 'You have nothing on me there...I can't either.' 1928–30 [see Have *v.* 14 e].

27. (Later *U.S.* example.)

1836 Haliburton *Clockm.* Ser. i. viii. (1837) 57 Your factories down east..go ahead on the English a long chalk.

30. *U.S.* In senses where English usage would have another preposition or expression, such as 'at, of, about, regarding, dealing with'.

1849 Mrs. Stowe *Mayflower* 109 'Nothin' so remarkable, as I know on,' said he. 1928 *Publishers' Weekly* 24 Nov. 2182/1 There is no uniform rule on remaindering. 1930 *Ibid.* 8 Mar. 1178 To aid the bookseller..to get all the facts on a book promptly. *Ibid.* 1345 The latest printing on Wells' 'Outline of History'.

On, *adv.* Add: **2.** (Later example.)

1923 H. G. Wells *Men Like Gods* ii. ii. § 2. 176, I have to go on at the Alhambra on September the 2nd.

7. b. Also *bows on, jaws on, nose on.*

1839 *Knickerbocker Mag.* XIII. 378 He offered..to run his boat, 'bows on', against the side of an 'old bull', *Ibid.* 383 He [a whale] came down, at full speed, 'jaws on', with the determination..of doing battle in earnest. 1880– [see Stem *sb.*[1] 2 b]. 1919 C. P. Thompson *Cocktails* 250 It was Neill's plan to gain height and keep nose-on to the stunter's tail.

13. b. (Further example.)

1908 R. W. Chambers *Firing Line* iv. 46 If you and Virginia have nothing better on I'll dine with you to-night.

d. *On* (*to*), possessing knowledge or cognisance regarding (a person, his intentions, etc.); aware of (a fact, etc.). Also *ellipt.*, aware. *U.S.*

1888 *N.Y. Mercury* 21 July (Farmer) A wife poisoner..ought to have for his wife a woman who is on to him, and who can meet his poison advances with a kerosene bath. 1899 A. H. Quinn *Pennsylv. Stories* 115 The class is about on to us, anyhow, and if they find out about this deal [etc.]. 1902 H. L. Wilson *Spenders* xxiv. 282, 'I s'pose you're on', he began; 'the girl's engaged to that Frenchy'. *a* 1906 'O. Henry' *Trimmed Lamp* etc. 118 The lady can wear 'em along with us and nobody 'll be on. 1911 J. C. Lincoln *Cap'n Warren's Wards* xvi. 254 Everybody has been on to that for some time. 1920 Wodehouse *Damsel in Distress* xxi. 248 'So you're on to him, too?' said Billie. 'When did *you* get wise?'

e. *To be on*: To be in favour of, or willing to be a party to, something.

1898 'H. S. Merriman' *Roden's Corner* xiv. 145 'If there is going to be a fight' he said, 'I'm on'. 1913 Wodehouse *Little Nugget* i. i, He understood..that a scene was about to take place in which he was most emphatically not 'on'. 1923 — *Inimitable Jeeves* xiv. 161 This jamboree is slated for Monday week. The question is, Are we on?

B. *adj.* **2.** Add: Also *on-beer.*

1928 *Daily Tel.* 6 Nov. 7/5 Of the forty-four, full licenses are held by thirty-five, the remaining nine being on-beer houses.

On, *v.* [On *adv.*]

1. *intr.* To go on, to move forward.

1840 Hoffman *Greyslaer* iv. iii. II. 194 I'll see the eend of it. So with that, I ups and ons.

2. *To on with*, to place or put on. (Cf. On *adv.* 4 b.)

1843 Carlton *New Purchase* 139 She bethought as how she'd render off her fat; and so she ons with the grate pot.

On and off. b. (Example of transf. use.)

1904 *Westm. Gaz.* 13 Jan. 2/3 The buyer resented this on-and-off policy.

Onbend, U.S. dial. variant of Unbend *v.*

1849 N. Kingsley *Diary* 47 Onbent the mainsail and put the old fore sail in its place.

Once, *adj.* Add:

A. γ. 8–9 *dial.* **oncet,** 9 **onecest, onct.**

1789 Webster *Diss. Engl. Lang.* 111 In the middle states also, many people [say]..*oncet* and *twicet*. This gross impropriety [has]..prevalence among a class of very well educated people; particularly in Philadelphia and Baltimore. 1840 Hoffman *Greyslaer* vi. vii. III. 317, I ups rifle at onct, and hand on trigger to cut the string with a bullet. 1851 Mayne Reid *Scalp Hunters* I. xxi. 291 He *may* shoot well; he did onecest on a time—plum centre. 1859 Bartlett *Dict. Amer.* (ed. 2), *Onst* (pron. *wunst*), once. A common vulgar pronunciation, especially in the West. 1867 A. D. Richardson *Beyond Mississippi* xi. 135 Even some graduates of leading universities habitually use 'oncet' and 'twicet'. 1913 Mulford *Coming of Cassidy* vii. 117, I saw you onct an' I wondered if I was right.

δ. 9 **wonst, wunst, wancet.**

1840 *Crockett Almanac* 2 Davy Crockett got skeered wunst. *Ibid.* 14, I wonst had an old flame. 1923 'B. M. Bower' *Parowan Bonanza* v. 52 Beans.., wancet they've been wrinkled wit' rain water and dried agin.

B. 3. Delete † *Obs.* and add: Now *U.S. dial.*

1902 Clapin *Dict. Amer.* 294 *Once*,..in parts of Pennsylvania settled by the Germans used as an expletive: 'Sit down once', i.e. once for all.

8. c. *Once in* (illit. *and*) *a while* (earlier examples). Also *once and again* (U.S. *local*).

1781 Witherspoon in *Pennsylv. Jrnl.* 23 May 1/3 He will *once in a while*, i.e. *sometimes*, get drunk. [Used in] the middle states. 1859 Bartlett *Dict. Amer.* (ed. 2), *Once and again*, occasionally, sometimes. A Southern phrase, equivalent to 'once in a while'. 1869 Mrs. Stowe *Oldtown Folks* x. 116 If he could come down here once and a while after work-hours.

9. c. (Later example of *the once*).

1924 Anne D. Sedgwick *Little French Girl* i. viii. 74 'He came twice afterwards. You did not know?'..'I didn't know that. I thought it was only the once.'

O·nce-over. *U.S. colloq.* [f. Once *adv.* + Over *prep.*] A single and rapid survey; a cursory examination. Esp. in phr. *to give* (a person) *the once-over.*

1916 H. L. Wilson *Somewhere in Red Gap* v. 202, I got just about the once-over from every brute there, and that was all. 1920 Isabel Ostrander *How Many Cards?* 153 Me and Yost both give him the once-over. 1922 Titus *Timber* xvi. 151 Drop over to California for the winter and maybe give Honolulu the once-over in the spring. 1923 Dorothy Dix in *Baltimore Sun* 5 Apr. 4 If I were a man contemplating matrimony I would give the once over very carefully to the way a girl dressed. 1923 Wodehouse *Inimitable Jeeves* vii. 72 He..gives the patient the once-over..and recommends complete rest. 1927 *Observer* 15 May 21/2 Thousands..to give Europe the 'once-over'.

Oncer (wɒ·nsəɹ). *colloq.* Also **once-er.** [f. Once.] One who attends church only once on a Sunday. Cf. Twicer.

1892 *Rev. of Reviews* V. 41/2 He has a poor opinion of those whom he humourously terms 'once-ers'. 1909 *Daily Chron.* 22 Apr. 4/7 A minister regretted an increasing disposition on the part of the people to become 'oncers'.

Oncost. Add: **2.** (In general use.) Overhead expenses or costs.

1912 J. G. Williamson *Counting-Ho. & Factory Organization* 65 Oncost expenditure, such as wages of foremen, labourers, and general works supplies, etc...is dealt with in the same manner. *Ibid.* 71 Establishment Charges or Oncost is every expense in the Profit and Loss Account other than the prime cost of Productive work. 1921 *Sat. Westm. Gaz.* 22 Jan. 18/2 To keep its machinery busy and pay its very heavy on-costs. 1924 Sir J. Stamp *Current Probl. Finance & Govt.* 18 Such a tabulation..would enable us to determine the position of any particular case,..to test its ratios of oncost and various kinds of unit efficiency by general experience.

Ondatra. (Later example.)

1867 *Amer. Naturalist* Oct. 400 The Musk-rat, or Ondatra (*Fiber zibethicus*), so extensively diffused over North America.

On-drive, *v.* Add: **b.** *absol.* or *intr.* To send the ball to the on.

1930 *Morn. Post* 7 Aug. 13/1 Bryan on-drove and hooked most effectively.

O·n-driving, *a.* [On *adv.*] That drives on.

1927 *Chambers's Jrnl.* Jan. 39/1 Because there was a check, there arose long on-driving shouts from the huntsmen.

One, *numeral a.*, etc. Add: **1. b.** (Further examples.)

1898 H. G. Hutchinson *Golfing Pilgr.* 235 One up and two to play! And the last two holes being halved, the Burscoughs won this never-to-be-forgotten match by one. 1897 *Encycl. Sport* I. 473/1 (Golf) *One off two, one off three* &c. When the opposite side has played two or three strokes more, the other side plays 'one off two' or 'one off three' as the case may be.

d. With ellipse of *glass* or *drink.*

1925 R. J. B. Sellar *Sporting Yarns* 165 'Did I have one over the regulation number last night?' 'Not at all..you were perfectly all right.'

15. b. (Further example.)

1923 Una L. Silberrad *Lett. Jean Armiter* ix. § ii. 203 He'll be awfully bucked to see you; you're quite one of his. Come on, and see him.

c. (*A*) *one for*: a person who likes, admires, practises, supports, etc., (something) in an outstanding degree; a devotee, admirer, or champion of (anything). *colloq.*

1932 Naomi Royde-Smith *Incredible Tale* 91 She was a one for football.

18. b. Also in *pl.*

1901 *Contemp. Rev.* Mar. 316 She ought to blame the ones, and to punish the others.

32. a. *One-act* (example), *-design, -drill, -piece* (example), *-storey* (earlier and fig. example), *-term, -wive* (= 'wife'). **d.** *one-leaved, -minded, -seeded, -storied* (earlier examples). **e.** *one-designer, -lunger, -pounder* (example), *-rater, -reeler.*

1905 *Athenæum* 7 Oct. 477/3 The *one-act trifle which serves as *lever de rideau*. 1902 *Encycl. Brit.* XXXIII. 906/2 What are called *one-design, or restricted classes [of yachts] have latterly become popular. 1928 *Daily Tel.* 11 Sept. 15/6 The second place on this occasion went to an Essex *one-designer. 1849 *Rep. U.S. Comm. Patents* (1850) 457 A *one-drill seeding machine was patented in 1841. 1875 *Amer. Naturalist* IX. 17 The singular *one-leaved ash, *Fraxinus anomala* Torr. 1911 H. Quick *Yellowstone N.* v. 124 The Old Man..was a *one-lunger. 1877 A. Dobson *Prov. Porcelain* 99 (*The Misogynist*) We, bound with him in common care, *One-minded, celibate, Resolved [etc.]. 1928 'S. S. Van Dine' *Greene Murder Case* iii. 44 She wore a black, *one-piece dress. 1845 Mrs. Kirkland *Western Clearings* 27 The *one-pounder..was fired all day by the opposition. 1897 *Outing* XXX. 91/2 The model *one-rater [= a yacht] which Harry D. Quinby..built..is..a mechanical marvel. 1916 'B. M. Bower' *Phantom Herd* v. 69 We've made quite a haul since you left. A bunch of *one-reelers. 1813 Muhlenberg *Catal. Plants N. Amer.* 96 *One-seeded honey locust. 1833 B. Silliman *Man. Sugar Cane* 64 The bagasse houses at Demerara are high *one story buildings. 1858 [see One-horse 2]. 1829–32 J. P. Kennedy *Swallow Barn* II. i. 8 A small *one-storied house. 1845 *Congress. Globe* 13 Jan. App. 122 The North..never had any but *one-term presidents, democratic or federal. 1860 S. Bowles *Our New West* xi. 218 We..took a quiet tea with a *one-wive Mormon.

33. one-catch-all, *U.S.*, a children's outdoor game; **one-cross (tin),** a make of tin-plate of a particular thickness and weight; **one-man** *a.* (earlier example); **one-while,** *U.S.*, for some time.

1876 J. Burroughs *Winter Sunshine* viii. i. 210, I could not only walk upon the grass, but..play '*one catch all' with children, boys, dogs, or sheep upon it. 1890 *Century Dict.*, *One-cross. 1897 Moore *How to build* viii. 120 He is to furnish all tin cellar heating-pipes of best [one cross] tin. 1842 W. C. Preston *Sp. in Senate* Apr. 15 The whole contest between the veto and the assembly..is a contest between 'the *one-man power' on both sides. 1889 Farmer *Americanisms* 402 '*One while*, a long time. 1897 'Mark Twain' *Following Equator* liii. 511 India..knows about those, and will keep them in mind one while.

One, *v.* **1.** (Later example.)

1921 B. Williamson *Supernat. Mysticism* v. 45 The human race was so oned with Adam that all sinned in him.

One berry. Add: **b.** *U.S. local.* (See quot.)

1877 Bartlett *Dict. Amer.* (ed. 4), *One-Berry*, the Indian turnip (*Arisaema triphyllum*), so called in Connecticut.

One-eyed, *a.* Add: **b.** *U.S. slang.* Dishonest.

1833 *Sk. David Crockett* (N.Y.) 24 In the slang of the backwoods, one swore that he would never be one-eyed.

One-horse, *a.* **1.** (Add example.)

1902 *Daily Chron.* 29 Aug. 6/5 In one-horse [long-distance] rides of that kind.

2. (Earlier examples.)

1854 *N.Y. Jrnl. Commerce* (Th.) I'm done with one-horse bedsteads. 1855 *Knickerbocker Mag.* XLVI. 106 In this 'one-horse' town,..as our New-Orleans neighbors designate it.

One-ideadness (wɒ·nˌəidī·ădnės). Also **one-ideaness.** [f. One-idead + -ness.] The fact or state of being one-idead.

1852 *Blackw. Edin. Mag.* Aug. 261/2 His absorbed one-ideadness. 1920 Begbie *William Booth* I. xxii. 365 It was ..this intense singleness of view, this consuming one-ideaness of soul, which made William Booth so successful.

Oner, *sb.* **1.** (Add example.)

1918 Galsworthy *Five Tales, A Stoic* § 2. 94 'Oh! you *said* you were going our way! What one-ers you do tell! Oh!

One-sided, *a.* **2. b.** (Earlier example.)

1813 Muhlenberg *Catal. Plant. N. Amer.* 49 One-sided Hawthorn.

One step, one-step (wɒ·nstep), *sb.* and *v.* [f. One *a.* + Step *sb.*] **a.** *sb.* A fast dance performed to music in quick time by couples, for the most part, simply walking backwards and forwards. **b.** *v. intr.* To dance the one step.

1911 *Home Chat* 7 Oct. 108/1 Camilla is just mad about the 'One-step'. 1914 Mr. & Mrs. V. Castle *Mod. Dancing* 44 Simply *walk* as softly and smoothly as possible, taking a step to every count of the music. This is the One Step, and this is all there is to it. 1916 H. L. Wilson *Somewhere in Red Gap* iv. 172, I caught him..in the deserted library later, while the rest was one-stepping in the..ballroom. 1921 H. Walpole *Young Enchanted* iii. i. 230 Bunny says I one-step better than anyone he's ever known. 1922 *Encycl. Brit.* XXX. 795/2 The one-step is the most energetic of all the modern dances. 1926 'L. Malet' *Dogs of Want* v. § ii. 122 For over four hours a mixed multitude..had one-stepped, two-stepped, hesitation-valsed, and fox-trotted.

One-way, *a.* [f. One *a.* + Way *sb.*]

†**1.** (See One *a.* 33.)

2. a. (See One *a.* 33.)

b. *spec.* Of thoroughfares, along which traffic is permitted only in one direction. Of traffic, passing only in one direction. Also, pertaining to such traffic. **c.** Leading, tending, pointing or developing, in one direction only.

1926 *Glasgow Herald* 11 Sept. 9 A complaint has been heard from shop-keepers against the one-way system in certain streets. 1926 *Rep. Commissioner Police Metropolis 1925* 16 Experiments had already been made for one-way traffic in certain streets. 1928 A. S. Eddington *Nat. Physical World* 90 Why not make at once the hypothesis that 'becoming' is a kind of one-way texture involved fundamentally in the structure of Nature? 1929 W. E. Collinson *Spoken Eng.* 42 We've got to go right round the square and then along a one-way street. 1930 *Aberdeen Press & Jrnl.* 29 Jan. 8/2 France and Japan..are opposed to only a one-way tendency.

Onflowing, *ppl. a.* (Example.)

1905 R. Davey tr. *Serao's Country of Jesus* vi. iv. 167 The rapidly on-flowing waters reflect the azure blue of the sky above.

Onion, *sb.* Add: Forms: β. Also 9 *U.S. dial.* **ineon, ingyon.**

1825 J. Neal *Bro. Jonathan* II. 84 Ingyons are proper good, when ye're sick.

2. Wild onion. (Examples.)

1822 J. Fowler *Jrnl.* 147 Heere the men geathered some wild Ineons. 1848 E. Bryant *California* iii. 35 Large quantities of wild onions were gathered.

5. b. *slang.* Head; in phr. *off one's onion.*

1922 Wodehouse *Girl on Boat* xii. 202 When..she informed him one day that she was engaged.., he went right off his onion. 1928 *Daily Express* 11 Dec. 7/4 After four drops of beer I am properly off my onion.

6. b. A flaming rocket used against hostile aircraft.

1917 *Blackw. Mag.* Apr. 560/1 A line of fiery rectangles shot up...These were 'onions', the flaming rockets which the Boche keeps for..hostile aircraft. 1928 Gamble *Story N. Sea Air Station* xxii. 384 One of the flying-boats..came into a heavy barrage of 'flaming onions'.

8. *onion-bed* (later examples), *-crop, set*; **onion-skin** (*b*), *U.S.*, used for purposes of fraudulent ballot.

1857 *Quinland* i. xiii. I. 184, I spaded up the *onion-bed after supper. 1874 *Rep. Vermont Board Agric.* II. 551 Raked as smooth as an onion bed. 1879 *Congress. Rec.* 23 June, App. 120/1 The *onion crop of South Carolina. 1886 *Harper's Mag.* Oct. 708/2 '*Onion sets'..are produced by sowing the ordinary black seed very thickly on light poor land. 1879 *Congress. Rec.* 23 June, App. 120/1 The term '*onion skin' or 'tissue ballots' had obtained a generic and well-defined meaning synonymous with 'stuffing the ballot-boxes'.

Only, *a.* Forms: Add: 9 *U.S. dial.* **ondly** (in sense 2 b).

1844 *Yale Lit. Mag.* IX. 335 Leftenant Carter's ondly son, A likely youth, nigh twenty-one.

3. (Later example; used *ellipt.*)

1873 J. H. Beadle *Western Wilds* xxvi. 417, I seed it was my first, last and only, and I set old Sally at a gallop for that pint.

O·nly-childism. [f. *only child* Only *a.* 2 b + -ism.] The fact of being an only child.

1927 *Times* 29 Dec. 7/3 They might come to speak, not of drink, but of 'only-childism', as the greatest curse of this country.

Onolatry (ǫnǫ·lătri). [f. Gr. ὄνο-ς ass + λατρεία -latry.] Worship of the ass.

1903 *Jrnl. Amer. Folk-lore* 203 (Cent. Suppl.).

Onomatology. (Example.)

1919 W. De Morgan *Old Madhouse* 324 He therefore endeavoured to bring back the discussion from the onomatologies into which it had strayed.

Ono·matoma·nia. [see Onomato-.] Add: (*b*), a mania for word-making.

1919 Sir W. Osler in *Proc. Class. Assoc.* 28 Within the narrow compass of the primitive cell..onomatomania runs riot.

Onre·stless, *a. U.S. dial.* [= obs. Sc. *onrestles*, E. dial. *unrestless.*] Restless.

1838 Caroline Gilman *Recoll. Southern Matron* vi. 49 Will mistress please to *medjure* out some calomel for Syphax, who is feverish and onrestless? *Ibid.* xxv. 169 He seemed quite onrestless.

O·nrush, *v.* [f. On-[1] + Rush *v.*] *intr.* To rush on.

1875 Morris *Æneids* xii. 652 Saces on his foaming steed.. onrusheth to the place.

On side. Add: Also **on-side.**

2. *Cricket.* **a.** [see On B. *adj.* 1.] **b.** *attrib.* as *on-side play, player, stroke.*

1903 *Westm. Gaz.* 23 June 3/1 In all those on-side strokes ..Fry is a master. 1906 *Daily Chron.* 22 May 9/2 Though particularly adept in on-side play, he has many other splendid strokes. 1909 *Westm. Gaz.* 17 Apr. 16/2 A good back and on-side player..may confidently expect to do well under these conditions.

Ontal (ǫ·ntăl), *a.* [f. Gr. ὤν, ὀντ- being: see Onto-, + -al.] = Ontological.

1902 J. Ward in *Encycl. Brit.* XXXII. 67/1 The former we may call the phenomenal, and the latter the ontal, meaning of 'aspect'. 1930 F. R. Tennant *Phil. Theol.* II. i. § 2. 20 Further investigation of the regularity of Nature..must wait on inquiry as to what the ontal things which underlie phenomena in reality be.

O·n-the-makeness. [f. phr. *on the make*: Make *sb.*[2] 8 + -ness.] The fact or state of being *on the make.*

1923 Galsworthy *Captures* 5 In talking with Steer one never lost consciousness of his keen 'on-the-make-ness'.

On to, onto, *prep.*

β. (U.S. examples.)

1905 Rex Beach *Pardners* i. (1912) 22 Instead of a fortune, we'd sunk onto the only yellow spot in the whole claim. *Ibid.* ii. 48 So me and 'Kink' Martin loaded our kit onto the burros and hit West. 1911 Mulford *Bar-20 Days* xiv. 147 Hanging onto his Colt as if fearing that the other would snatch it and run.

Ontocycle (ǫ·ntosəik'l). Also **-cyclon.** [f. Onto + Cycle.] Development of an individual organism which produces in its later stages forms which resemble those of early stages. **Ontocy·clic** *a.*, of, pertaining to, or exhibiting the features of an ontocycle.

1893 *Proc. Boston Soc. Nat. Hist.* 109 It is proposed to use in this way ontocycle or ontocyclon for the ontogeny, meaning the cycle of the individual. *Ibid.* 110 Man is not completely ontocyclic, but makes a close approach to this in the loss of the hair, teeth, and proportions and shape of the body. 1899 Hyatt *Biol. Lectures* 134 (Cent. Suppl.) The whole cycle of the ontogeny or ontocycle.

Ontogenic (ǫntodʒe·nic), *a.* [f. Ontogeny + -ic.] Of, pertaining to, or marked by ontogeny; ontogenetic.

1893 *Proc. Boston Soc. Nat. Hist.* 98 The product of the evolution of an ancestor into a phylum through successive independent forms or ontogenic cycles.

Onycho·phagist. [See Onygophagist.] One who bites his nails. So **Onycho·phagy** [mod. L. *onychophagia*, F. *-phagie*], the habit of biting one's nails.

1900 *Daily Chron.* 10 July 5 (Cass. Suppl.) 'Onychophagia' is far more frequent in Parisian than in provincial schools. 1907 *Daily News* 4 July 6 If you bite your nails you are an onychophagist. 1905 *Pop. Sci. Monthly* Nov. 607 (Cent. Suppl.) Habits of various kinds, such as onychophagie or finger-nail biting, excessive smoking, [etc.]. 1913 Dorland *Med. Dict.*, Onychophagy.

Onymously (ǫ·nimǝsli), *adv.* [f. Onymous *a.* + -ly [2], after Anonymously.] With the writer's name given or attached.

1889 Sir V. Horsley in *Life* (1919) 86 He anonymously or onymously is not worth powder and shot.

Oo-. Add: **Oocyte** (ǭ·ǒsəit) [-cyte], an immature ovum or egg-cell. **Oogenetic** (example).

1902 *Encycl. Brit.* XXVIII. 139/1 The germ cells..undergo division and give rise to the progametes, which in the case of the female are sometimes called *oöcytes*. 1910 *Ibid.* VII. 718/1 *note*, The whole of the yolk stored by the 'oocyte' ..is handed on to only one of the four resulting cells. 1895 D. Sharp *Insects* I. 500 At the very earliest stage of the embryonic, or oogenetic process.

Oodle (ū·d'l). Also **-lin.** [Of uncertain origin.] In plur., large or unlimited quantities; abundance, 'heaps'.

1869 *Overland Monthly* III. 131 A Texan never has a great quantity of any thing, but he has 'scads' of it, or 'oodles', or 'dead oodles', or 'scadoodles', or 'swads'. 1887 J. C. Harris in *Cent. Mag.* Apr. 846/2 All you lack's the feathers, and we've got oodles of 'em right here. 1892 Jane Barlow *Irish Idylls* iii. 57 A grand young pig, they'll be gettin' oodles o' money on at the fair afore Lent. 1904 Harben *Georgians* 115 An' now *you*, a man with oodlin's an' oodlin's o' pore blood kin..are a helpin' at the job. 1919 H. L. Wilson *Ma Pettengill* iii. 78 It snowed hard. Just oodles of the most perfectly dazzling snow. 1928 *Blackw. Mag.* Jan. 29/2 The explosion drove the pistons apart, and power, oodles of power, was transmitted..to the shaft.

Oogamy. (Examples.)

1894 Vines *Text-bk. Bot.* I. 225 Oogamy. 1898 H. C. Porter tr. *Strasburger's Text-bk. Bot.* 331 A transition from isogamy to oogamy.

Oogo·nial, *a.* [f. Oogonium + -al.] Of or pertaining to an oogonium.

1902 *Science* 21 Mar. 457/1 The protoplasm in contact with the oogonial wall.

Oont (ūnt). *Anglo-Indian.* Also **unt.** [ad. Hindī (and Urdū) ऊंट *ūnṭ* camel.] A camel.

1892 Kipling *Barrack-room Ballads, Oonts* 5 O the oont, O the oont, O the commissariat oont! With 'is silly neck a-bobbin' like a basket full o' snakes. 1894 A. G. Leonard *Camel* 101 The baggage [camel], known as 'Gamal' and 'Unt' respectively in Egypt and India. 1900 *Pall Mall Gaz.* 1 Jan. 1/3 A mule..requires more experience in handling than the bubbling oont of India.

Oorial. Also *attrib.*

1928 V. G. Childe *Most Anc. East* ix. 201 The foot-hills to the north and west are still the haunts of urial sheep.

Ooze, *sb.*[1] Add: **2. b.** Short for *ooze-leather* (see *4).

1929 Marg. B. Houston *Witch-man* vi. 78 A 'gift' volume of Shakespeare, bound in dark blue ooze.

4. ooze-leather = *ooze-calf.*

1918 *Publishers' Weekly* 9 June 2348 In four styles of binding..ooze leather, two colors, green or brown, $2.50.

Ooze (ūz), *sb.*[4] [Prob. f. *oo's*, plur. of *oo*, Sc. form of Wool.] The nap or short fibres that project from yarn.

1892 Nasmith *Cotton Spinning* 373 When thread is intended for lace purposes..it is passed several times through a gas flame at a high speed, so as to burn off the filaments or 'ooze' on its surface and leave it bare. 1909 *Engineer* 1 Oct. 352/1 The term 'gassing' is applied to the process of burning off the ends of fibres or 'ooze' on the different kinds of yarn.

Oozing, *ppl. a.* (Add example.)

1912 Galsworthy *Inn Tranq.* 127 Before the smell of the deserted oozing rooms,..we felt such discomfort that we soon made to go out again.

Op [2], abbreviation of *Opus.

Opacification (ǫpæ·sifikē·ʃǝn). [f. L. *opāc-us* Opaque + -fication. Cf. F. *opacifier*.] The action or process of making or becoming opaque.

1903 *Med. Record* 28 Feb. 333 (Cent. Suppl.) Hyperplasia, degeneration—these are results of mal-nutrition and the essentials of opacification.

Opal. Add: **1. c.** The colour of an opal.

1914 R. Brooke in *Mem.* (1918) p. cxliii, Like an Italian town in silver-point..with a sea and sky of opal and pearl and faint gold around.

4. *opal-field, -seeker.*

1902 *Chambers's Jrnl.* Aug. 496/2 There are few men on the *opal-fields who do not average five pounds per week. *Ibid.* 496/1 At that hour the *opal-seeker must cease his daily toil.

Open, *sb.* **4. b.** (Later examples.)

1846 J. W. Webb *Altowan* I. ii. 42 All openings or natural clearings are called 'opens' by the half-breeds of the Indian country. *Ibid.* viii. 201 They cautiously entered where there seemed no indication of an open. 1880 *Encycl. Brit.* XIII. 602/2 Living in herds of from fifty to one hundred in the grassy 'opens'. 1902 O. Wister *Virginian* xxxii. 407 It lay before us, a great cup of country,—rocks, woods, opens and streams.

5. b. An open competition, tournament or the like; cf. Open *a.* 14.

1930 *Daily Express* 8 Sept. 11/4 Miss Brazier also has played in 'opens'.

Open, *a.* Add: **5.** †Also, formerly, Stretched at full length on the back: see also *wide open*, Wide *adv.* 3 b.

This is app. the meaning in quots. 1526 and 1604.

11. f. *Elect.* Of a switch: Not forming a connexion, off. Of a circuit: Not complete or 'closed'.

1901 *Chambers's Jrnl.* Sept. 617/2 If a new machine, the switches should be left open, the brushes lifted, and the machine allowed to run without load for a little time. 1907 Erskine-Murray *Handbk. Wireless Telegr.* 5 Modern wireless telegraphy is, in general, open circuit telegraphy *i.e.*, telegraphy from one part of a conductor to another without the use of a return wire. 1925 P. J. Risdon *Crystal Receivers & Circuits* 22 It should perhaps be explained here that an aerial circuit is known as an 'open' circuit, and a receiver circuit as a 'closed' circuit.

g. Of a bet in faro: That is made in expectation of a card winning; not coppered.

1913 Mulford *Coming of Cassidy* vii. 116 The player.. placed fifty dollars on the Queen, open, and coppered the deuce.

h. Of a hand at poker: On which betting can begin or has begun.

1913 Mulford *Coming of Cassidy* xi. 182 When the seventh hand was dealt the puncher picked his cards and laughed. 'She's open', he cried, 'for fifty', and shoved out the money.

i. Applied to a method of administering an anaesthetic.

1922 *Encycl. Brit.* XXX. 137/1 The application of the 'open' method to ether inhalation has been brought about by an exceedingly simple adaptation. The liquid ether is applied to a pad of open-wove fabric, such as 'stockinette' ..stretched over a framework mask.

13. (Further example.)

1929 *Even. News* 18 Nov. 13/5 These men did much to prevent the fast open play of Newport from bearing fruit.

14. (Further examples.)

1866 *Rep. Indian Affairs* 213, I have purchased the necessary subsistence for this tribe in open market. 1870 Medbery *Men & Myst. Wall St.* 7 In comparison with the essential advantage of an open mart for the equalization of values. *Ibid.* 18 The stock which has occasioned the default is sold or bought in the open market under the rule. 1877 *Rep. Indian Affairs* 17 Discouraging purchases in open market. 1903 *McClure's Mag.* Feb. 403/2 He had from the Central [railroad] a rebate of from ten cents to forty-five cents a barrel—usually it was twenty-five cents on the open rate for refined oil to the seaboard.

21. *Open book* (fig.), a person who conceals nothing; one whose opinions, thoughts or actions can readily be understood; also in phr. *to read* (one) *like an open book.* *Open letter*, a letter addressed to a particular person or persons but made public by being printed. *Open shop* (*a*) see sense 14; (*b*) see quot. 1923.

1920 Wodehouse *Damsel in Distress* iv. 53 There's no mystery about me. I'm an *open book. 1890 Stevenson (*title*) Father Damien. An *open letter to the Reverend Doctor Hyde of Honolulu. 1894 R. Blatchford (*title*) Three open letters to the Bishop of Manchester. 1917 *Fortn. Rev.* Nov. 748 (*heading*) Problems of Finance: An Open Letter to Lord Milner. 1909 *Daily Chron.* 3 May 1/5 The strike has originated in the intention..to enforce an '*open shop' on the lake boats. 1920 *Act* 10 & 11 *Geo. V* c. 66 § 7 (2) Any person who lawfully keeps open shop for the retailing of poisons. 1923 J. D. Hackett *Labor Terms* in *Management Engineering* May, *Open Shop.* A plant open to those whom the employer wishes to hire, or to all-comers, irrespective of union membership.

22. a. *open-deck, -hearth, -market, -scale, -seam, -web.*

1886 *Harper's Mag.* June 18/2 In vessels of this class it is usual to have an *open-deck battery. 1919 E. Hendrick *Chem. Everyday Life* 99 *Open-hearth steel is made by boiling steel scrap and pig iron..in a shallow container or hearth. 1932 R. McKenna *Speech to Midland Bank* 7 '*Open market operations'..being a technical term for buying and selling bills or securities in the open market with the object of increasing or diminishing the quantity of money. 1902 *Encycl. Brit.* XXXI. 765/2 The patent, No. 1231, for the barless or *open-scale piano, taken out in London in 1888. 1910 *Installation News* Jan. 4/1 The much abused *open-seam conduit and the socket joint conduit. 1873 T. Cargill *Strains Bridge Girders* 63 The lattice, or *open web girder.

b. *open-gaited.*

1872 *Rep. Vermont Board Agric.* I. 206 A good sized, rangy, open-gaited and enduring horse, of a good color. 1894

Ibid. XIV. 97 His sire being Allen, his dam Lady Alice,.. he is a pure open-gaited trotter.

c. open access, a system whereby users of a library have access to the book-shelves; also *attrib.*; **Open Board**, an association formed in cities of the U.S. to transact dealings in options on a small scale, which were forbidden by the Board of Trade; **Open Brethren**, that section of the Plymouth Brethren which has open communion (see COMMUNION 7); so *open-communion* adj.; **open-casting**, the system of open working in mines; **open credit**, in *Finance*, a credit free from restrictions; **open-mindedly** *adv.*, in an open-minded manner; **open note**, a musical note in staff notation having an open loop, *i.e.* a minim or longer note; **open score** *Mus.* (see quots.); **open-shelf** *a.* = *open-access* attrib.

1894 *Library* VI. 344 There is absolutely no novelty about the principle of *open access. 1899 (*title*) Account of the safe-guarded open-access system in public lending libraries. 1906 *Academy* 26 May 492/2 There is not the same need for an extended classification as is found in an open-access library. 1870 MEDBERY *Men & Myst. Wall St.* 26 The consolidation of the Government and the *Open Boards with the old historic Stock Exchange. 1902 G. H. LORIMER *Lett. Self-made Merchant* ix. 113 If she is the daughter of old Job Dashkam, on the open Board, I should say..that she was a fine girl to let some other fellow marry. 1907 *Daily Chron.* 18 May 4/6 The people in question are a division of the so-called Plymouth Brethren, that is to say the '*Open' Brethren. 1909 *Hastings's Encycl. Relig. & Ethics* II. 845/2 The 'Open' Brethren..fraternize freely with other Christians. 1886 J. BARROWMAN *Sc. Mining Terms* 48 **Open-casting*, holing above the seam; working as a quarry. 1794 J. MORSE *Amer. Geog.* (ed. 3) 223 Except those who are styled '*open communion baptists',..they refuse to communicate in the ordinance of the Lord's Supper with other denominations. 1903 *Pitman's Business Man's Guide* 326 **Open credit*. This is the name given to a letter of credit which contains an unconditional request to pay money to another person. 1909 H. G. WELLS *Tono-Bungay* II. iv. § 5. 180 'Your aunt makes Game of people,' was Marion's verdict, and, *open-mindedly, 'I suppose it's all right..for her.' 1903 *Churchman* 10 Oct. 447 The notes are of the *open (or, as our English friends term it, minim or semibreve) style. 189. S. MACPHERSON *Rudiments Mus.* Add. 83 **Open Score*, the voice-parts of a chorus etc., written on separate staves, one above another. 1899 BRIDGES & SAWYER *Course Harmony* ii. 8 There are two methods of writing harmony—viz., in *open score* and *short score*. In open score each voice is written on a separate staff. 1897 *Library Jrnl.* Jan. 44/1 The adoption of the *open-shelf system.

Open, *v.* Add: **16.** (Further examples.)

1864 PARKES *Man. Pract. Hygiene* 107 The windows should open at the top, and in case the wind has a high velocity, means should be taken to distribute it. 1871 L. W. M. LOCKHART *Fair to see* iii. (1872) 51 'A Cameron of Aberlorna!' exclaimed the host, in a tone of unaccountable astonishment, his eyes opening wide upon Bertrand. 1893 MARY E. MANN *In Summer Shade* I. x. 238 Claude's eyes opened slowly upon his brother's face. 1912 *Chambers's Jrnl.* Feb. 82/1 Suddenly the great eye of the lighthouse opened.

22. (Earlier example of sense 'to begin to be sold'.) Also, to begin to speak.

1851 C. CIST *Cincinnati* 296 They [*sc.* strawberries] usually open at 20 to 30 cents per quart. 1926 BENNETT *Lord Raingo* I. xiii. 63, 'I quite agree with you, Clews,' Sam opened immediately.

23. Open out. f. To start business *in* a new line.

1903 *Letters that bring Business* 38 You have recently opened out in the Fancy China and Glass trade.

g. To open the throttle of a motor engine; hence, to accelerate.

1906 O. SEAMAN in *Later Poems fr. Punch* (1909) 194 'Open her out!' my host had said; And on the instant word The mobile monster flew ahead Like a prodigious bird. 1918 'Q' *Foe-Farrell* 105 There was a certain amount of outcry in the rear. But I opened-out down the slope and soon had it well astern.

24. Open up. a. Also *absol.*

1919 *Brit. Manufacturer* Nov. 19/1 An Englishman who intends to open up with the Chinese should..first acquire a working knowledge of the Chinese language.

c. *trans.* To open the throttle of (an engine).

1922 *Encycl. Brit.* XXX. 41/1 At height, however, it [engine of aeroplane] could be fully opened up.

Open-air. 2. (Earlier example.)

1842 W. HOWITT *Rural & Dom. Life Germany* xvii. 237 Those open-air concerts, walks and other amusements.

Open and shut. *U.S. colloq.* A simple operation; a clear issue or inference; a certainty.

1848 *Stray Subjects* 128 [It] beat all the high pressures he ever heerd, jest as easy as open and shet. 1904 W. H. SMITH *Promoters* x. 162 It seems as if it was a dead open and shut that we've got to stay with 'em.

b. as *adj.* Simple, straightforward.

1902 W. N. HARBEN *Abner Daniel* xix. 153, I 'lowed we was going to make an open-and-shut trade that we could be proud of.

Opener. Add: **1.** Also *opener-up*.

1911 *Chambers's Jrnl.* Mar. 149/2 Carl Mauch, another German opener-up of South Africa.

c. *spec.* An implement for opening tins, cases, etc. Cf. *can-opener* *CAN *sb.*[1] 4 and *tin-opener* TIN *sb.* 5.

1906 *Daily Chron.* 15 Aug. 5/2 An ordinary packing-case opener had been used to force the door of the case. 1912 *Chambers's Jrnl.* Feb. 144/1 The man who invented an opener for tins did well.

3. *colloq.* A case or package that is opened by customs officials.

1909 *Chambers's Jrnl.* May 312/1 As the 'openers', the cases challenged by the officer, are landed, they are set aside and opened by an attendant cooper.

4. *Poker.* (*pl.*) Cards on which a player can begin to bet.

1909 R. A. WASON *Happy Hawkins* 114, I didn't hold openers, an' yet if I didn't draw some cards an' see it out, I stood to lose entirely. *Ibid.* 263 It was Dick's deal an' we all held three cards except Jabez who had furnished openers. 1930 MULFORD *J. Nelson* ii. 25 A round or two had been played when Big Tom drew his first openers.

Opening, *vbl. sb.* **3.** (Earlier examples.)

1663 *Rec. Providence*, (R. I.) V. 206 The place commonly called the first opening of the great swampe. 1685 *Ibid.* VIII. 149 A highway shall be and remain from the lane.. Eastward through the place called the second opening of the great swamp.

Opera. Add: **4. c.** Applied to styles of women's underclothing suitable for wearing with evening dress, characterized by low tops and narrow shoulder-straps.

1923 *Daily Mail* 17 Feb. 4 Advt., Ladies' Pure Wool Combinations, in a soft unshrinkable finish, opera tops, ribbon straps. 1923 *Weekly Disp.* 18 Feb. 14 Advt., Pure Wool Opera Combinations. Ribbon shoulder straps.

Operability. [f. OPERABLE *a.* + -ITY.] Capability of being operated on, or of sustaining a surgical operation.

1907 *Med. Ann.* 140 A report..on the Operability of Cerebral Tumours. 1910 *Practitioner* Jan. 84 The question of operability or otherwise is a matter in which surgeons differ considerably. 1925 GILFORD *Tumors & Cancers* 578 Operability of breast cancers.

Operable, *a.* Transfer †*Obs.* to sense b.

a. (Modern example.)

1911 H. S. HARRISON *Queed* xiii. 160 How could this principle be..reduced to an operable law?

(*b*) In surgery, that can be operated on.

1904 *Archives Middlesex Hosp.* III. 163 All cases for operable cancer. 1907 *Med. Ann.* 140 The operable tumours are those in which lasting relief might be expected from operation. 1925 GILFORD *Tumors & Cancers* 578 The effect of the rays on operable cancers of the breast.

Operate, *v.* Add: **4. c.** Also *transf.*, of a gambler, highwayman, etc.

1884 SWEET & KNOX *Through Texas* i. 16 This high-toned and honorable desperado 'operated' in one of the inland cities of Texas two years ago.

d. (Later example.)

1889 *Harper's Mag.* Aug. 448/1 Do you think all men who are what you call operating around are like that?

8. *Surg.* To operate upon. (See sense 4 b.)

1908 *Practitioner* Sept. 423, I know of two cases of pyelitis which were operated in mistake for appendicitis.

Operatic, *a.*[1] Add: **b.** as *sb. pl.* The production or performance of operas.

1907 NEIL MUNRO *Daft Days* xvi, He says he could never die a Christian death if he had to listen to them at their operatics through the wall. 1920 *Punch* 10 Mar. 197/1 (heading), Operatics. 1928 *Daily Express* 6 Nov. 9/3 This is a real event in London's amateur operatics.

Operating, *vbl. sb.* Add: (Recent example.)

1913 C. ROBERTS & R. M. SMITH (*title*) Practical Locomotive Operating.

b. *operating box, control, costs, expenses.*

1918 'Q' *Foe-Farrell* 117, I..found..the *operating box and the gallery, switched on the lights, and shinned down a pillar to the stalls. 1930 *Daily Express* 6 Sept. 5/5 The *operating control' can be readily grasped from the sketch. 1913 C. ROBERTS & R. M. SMITH *Locomotive Operating* 26 *Operating Costs. 1909 *Daily Chron.* 25 Feb. 3/5 At the same time the *operating expenses had gone down.

Operating, *ppl. a.* (Add example.)

1904 *Daily Chron.* 16 July 7/3 The operating company is to take over the tunnel before the end of the month.

Operation. 5. b. (Earlier and later examples.)

1832 *Reg. Debates Congress* IX. II. App. 107/1 The liability to be called upon for large advances, for the above operation,..makes it absolutely necessary that the limit should be strictly attended to. 1848 W. ARMSTRONG *Stocks* 11 We conceive that this operation [*i.e.* betting] is too well understood to need any particular explanation. 1851 C. CIST *Cincinnati* 236 Such is the extent of the operations of this firm. 1889 *Harper's Mag.* Aug. 448/1 One is an operation, and the other is embezzlement. 1911 J. C. LINCOLN *Cap'n Warren's Wards* xi. 178, I judged..that you were well enough acquainted with Wall Street to know that queer operations take place there.

Operational (ǫpĕrē̍·ʃənăl), *a.* [f. OPERATION + -AL.] Of, pertaining to, or connected with, operations of any kind.

1922 *Edin. Rev.* Oct. 212 The development of..air communications..ensuring the maintenance of a large and flourishing constructional and operational aircraft industry. 1927 H. JEFFREYS (*title*) Operational Methods in Mathematical Physics. 1928 GAMBLE *Story N. Sea Air Station* x. 146 They were placed in various groups for disciplinary and operational purposes.

Operative. B. *sb.* Add: **3. b.** (See quot.)

1905 *N.Y. Press* 23 Oct. (Cent. Suppl.) The word 'detective' became so offensive..that it was dropped by some successful [detective] agencies. The word chosen by the Pinkertons to take its place was 'operative'.

Operatory, *a.* (Modern example.)

1908 *Westm. Gaz.* 22 Oct. 2/1 It is probable that the operatory method may be mechanical.

Operette (ǫpĕre·t). Anglicized form of OPERETTA.

1928 *Observer* 15 Apr. 21/2 Few operettes launched on the public nowadays can compare with the delicious music of Pongrác Kacsoh.

Operettist (ǫpĕre·tist). [f. OPERETTA + -IST.] A writer or composer of operettas.

1922 *Blackw. Mag.* June 717/2 There are a mass of Hungarian operettists.

Ophidian. A. *adj.* Add: **2. b.** Applied to a variety of leprosy.

1915 C. A. MERCIER *Leper Houses* 13 The four varieties of leprosy—leonine, elephantine, alopecic, and ophidian.

Ophiology. (Earlier example.)

1817 *Blackw. Edin. Mag.* May 187/1 Reserving the history of the serpent tribes for the article *Ophiology*.

Ophiomorphic, *a.* (Example.)

1909 LD. BALCARRES *Ital. Sculpture* i. 16 In the Celtic art of the North..these ophiomorphic meanderings of line bewilder the eye by their complexity.

Ophthalmophorous, *a.* (Example.)

1896 *Nat. Science* May 340 [G. A. Boulenger] has, too, for the first time, utilised the development or want of an ophthalmophorous shelf to the second suborbital as a family character.

Opinionator. (Recent example.)

1930 *New Statesman* 8 Nov. 147/1, I can only regret that Mr. West devotes so much of his space to Mr. Wells the opinionator instead of to Mr. Wells the artist.

†Opitulation. (Later example.)

1724 R. SUTTON *Let. to Sir T. Parkyns* (1726) 4, I receiv'd such Opitulation from your Dicæology.

Opopanax. 2. (Earlier example.)

1867 *Gardeners' Chron.* 29 June 690/1 New Perfumes.—Opoponax.

Opossuming, *vbl. sb.* [-ING[1].] Opossum-hunting.

1917 H. H. RICHARDSON *R. Mahony* III. iv. 211 There is to be opossuming and a moonlight picnic to-night.

Opotherapy (ǫpoþe·răpi). *Med.* [f. Gr. ὀπός juice + θεραπεία medical treatment, THERAPY.] The treatment of certain (organic) diseases with prepared extracts of glands or organs, or with similar substances; organotherapy.

1898 *Smithsonian Rep.* 696 An entire new method, designated under the name of opotherapy, or treatment by organic extracts. 1902 *Brit. Med. Jrnl.* 12 Apr. 909/1 (art.) Placentophagy and Placental Opotherapy. 1908 *Practitioner* Mar. 412 The many different substances recently utilised in opotherapy.

Opposer. Add: **1. b.** *spec.* One of two Fellows of New College, Oxford, appointed to conduct the entrance examination at Winchester College.

1901 RASHDALL & RAIT *New College* vi. 132 The Warden and Opposers are not to take bribes.

Opposite. A. *adj.* Add: **5. b. opposite number**, the person who has a similar or corresponding position, duty, or the like, to one, usually in another place or arrangement; one's partner, counterpart, or opponent.

1915 'BARTIMEUS' *Tall Ship* iv. (1916) 84 We were 'opposite numbers' at your brother's wedding. 1917 *Times* 7 May 6/2 The establishment of personal contact between Sir William Robertson and his opposite number, General Pétain. 1919 EDGAR WALLACE *Kate, plus Ten* vi. 107 Pick up Mr. Pretherston and don't lose him—you may choose your own opposite number.

B. *sb.* **3.** (Later example.)

1874 SWINBURNE *Bothw.* IV. v. (1882) 397 The task were hard with Knox for opposite To bend the council.

Oppositionary (ǫpǒzi·ʃənări), *a.* [f. OPPOSITION + -ARY[1].] = OPPOSITIONAL 2.

1926 *Contemp. Rev.* Sept. 276 Petrograd ('Leningrad') became the centre of Zinoviev's oppositionary activity.

Oppositious (ǫpǒzi·ʃəs), *a.* [f. OPPOSITE + -OUS.] Inclined to oppose; recalcitrant.

1923 *Blackw. Mag.* Aug. 176/1 He..became oppositious on leaving truly delectable posadas to left and right.

Opposive, *a.* Delete †*Obs.*[—1] and add modern example.

1911 W. DE MORGAN *Likely Story* 107 He had an opposive or lazy disposition.

Oppressingly, *adv.* [-LY[2].] So as to oppress or be oppressive; oppressively.

1925 *Glasgow Herald* 17 May 7/1 That it [the cost] is oppressingly large no one will deny.

Opsonic (ǫpsǫ·nik), *a. Bacteriol.* [f. as next + -IC.] Of, pertaining to, or of the nature of, opsonins; produced by or arising from opsonins; employing opsonins. *Opsonic index*, an index of the amount or proportion of opsonins present in a person's blood.

1903 A. E. WRIGHT & DOUGLAS in *Proc. Royal Soc.* LXXII. 368 The opsonic power of the blood fluids disappears gradually on standing. 1906 *Practitioner* Dec. 750 A doubling of the opsonic index means that the quantity of opsonin present has been increased in a far greater proportion. 1907 *Cornhill Mag.* Jan. 97 Metchnikoff..seems in a measure to have unconsciously anticipated the opsonic theory. 1910 *Edin. Rev.* Oct. 270 The measurement of the varying opsonic power of the blood in different diseases is now..carried out.

Opsonin (ǫ·psonin). *Bacteriol.* [f. Gr. ὄψον cooked meat + -IN[1].] Any of a class of substances present in blood serum which act on the bacteria of certain diseases in such a way as to promote phagocytosis. Hence **Opsoniferous** *a.*, producing an opsonic effect; **Opsonization**, the action of opsonin on bacteria; **Opsonize** *v. trans.*, to prepare (bacteria) for ingestion by phagocytes; to treat with opsonin; **Opsonoid** *a.* (see quot. 1907).

1903 A. E. WRIGHT & DOUGLAS in *Proc. Roy. Soc.* LXXII. 366 We may speak of this as an 'opsonic' effect and we may employ the term 'opsonins' to designate the elements in the blood fluids which produce this effect. 1906 *Practitioner* Dec. 750 We know..that the presence of opsonins is necessary for phagocytosis. 1907 *Jrnl. Med. Research* Oct. 58 (Cent. Suppl.) In accordance with Ehrlich's nomenclature opsonin, the opsoniferous group of which is destroyed or inactivated, may be termed opsonoid. 1907 *Practitioner* Apr. 581 The hungry phagocyte is supposed to have its diet daintily opsonized for it. 1907 *Science* 13 Sept. 346/1 An alkalinity..prevented opsonization.

Optant (ǫ·ptănt). [G. and Da. *optant*, f. L. *optant-*, *optans* pr. pple. of *optāre* to choose.] A person who, when the territory of which he is a citizen changes its sovereignty, chooses between retaining his former citizenship, and accepting a new one.

1914 W. R. PRIOR *N. Sleswick under Prussian Rule* 9 Nearly 40,000 of the Sleswick Danes had become optants.. The peril to which their optant relatives and neighbours were exposed. 1927 *Daily Tel.* 8 Mar. 11/5 This arbitral tribunal pronounced in favour of the Hungarian optants.

Optical, *a.* Add: **2. b.** *spec.* Of radiation: That can be classed as light (see quot.).

1927 N. V. SIDGWICK *Electronic Theory of Valency* 32 X-rays differ from 'optical' radiation—a term used to cover the infra-red, visible and ultra-violet—only in degree, being of much shorter wave-length.

Opticity (ǫpti·sĭti). [ad. F. *opticité* optical quality: see OPTIC and -ITY.] In the brewing and sugar industries: Optical activity; the quality by which, or the extent to which, a solution rotates a beam of polarized light.

1902 *Encycl. Brit.* XXVI. 365/2 There is a direct relationship between the opticity and the cupric reduction exercised by the mixed products of starch conversion.

Opting, *vbl. sb.* [-ING[1].] The action of the verb OPT.

1922 *Glasgow Herald* 13 Apr. 6 The opting of Australia out of the chain..does..impair the symmetry of the Imperial chain plan.

Option. Add: **2. b.** Alternative; *esp.* in phr. *with* (or *without*) *the option* (*of a fine*).

1901 *Chambers's Jrnl.* Sept. 582/2 A third [conviction] should result in imprisonment without the option of a fine. 1914 MRS. PANKHURST *My Own Story* 71 They were given the option of a fine. *Ibid.* 86 Two of the women..were, as 'old offenders', given thirty days without the option of a fine. 1925 WODEHOUSE *Carry on, Jeeves* vii. 159 He will serve a sentence of thirty days in the Second Division without the option of a fine.

4. b. *U.S.* (See quot.)

1882 *Harper's Mag.* May 897/1 The large land-owners have adopted the policy of granting 'options'; that is, signing an agreement that if any person shall uncover a bed of ore on his land, the finder shall be entitled to a certain interest, generally one-third.

6. *option note, price, time.*

1909 D. LLOYD-GEORGE in *Parl. Debates* 29 Apr. 519 'Option notes' will be charged at similar rates, calculated upon the value of the securities to which the option relates. 1865 *Shareholders' Guardian* 8 Nov. 847/2 If at the expiration of the 'option' time the price be the same as the 'option' price, the person who paid the money has the right to buy, sell, or neither, as he thinks proper.

Optional, *sb.* [f. the adj.] An optional subject of study.

1857 *Yale Lit. Mag.* XXII. 291 What was never known before, since the establishment of optionals, the number pursuing the study of Hebrew is nine.

Optionalize, *v.* [f. OPTIONAL + -IZE.] *trans.* To make optional.

1921 J. HARROWER in *Proc. Class. Assoc.* XVIII. 43 Scotland, where the disastrous results of optionalising Greek in the Universities..have had time to manifest themselves.

Optometrical (ǫptǒme·trikăl), *a.* [f. OPTO- + METRICAL.] Of or pertaining to optometry. **Optometrist**, a person who tests eyes for refractive errors. *U.S.*

1903 *Optical Jrnl.* Dec. 810 (Cent. Suppl.) Optometrical. 1904 *Ibid.* 23 June 69 (Cent. Suppl.) One of the points to be thoroughly discussed will be the best name to give those who professionally test eyes for refractive errors... In those States which have laws governing this line of work the term used is 'Optometrist'.

Optophone (ǫ·ptǒfōᵘn). [f. OPTO- + PHONE.] An instrument in which the action of a beam of light on a selenium cell is utilized to represent printed characters audibly and so enable blind persons to read.

1914 *Chambers's Jrnl.* Aug. 542/2 An interesting instrument, 'The Type-Reading Optophone',..was described recently. 1921 *Glasgow Herald* 7 Apr. 9 Greater speed in optophone reading would be attained with practice. 1923 *Westm. Gaz.* 14 June, An optophone..enables a blind man to read an ordinary newspaper by sound.

Opus (ǫ·pŏs, ōᵘ·pŏs), *v.* [f. the sb.] *trans.* To include and number among the works of a composer of music. Abbreviated *Op.*

1900 W. A. ELLIS *Life Wagner* I. 376 This negligence in 'opus-ing' his musical works. 1921 A. B. SMITH in *Music & Lett.* Oct. II. 364 A large class of composers..write pieces solely for the pleasure of opusing them. *Ibid.*, Every piece of his [Gurlitt] is Op.-ed.

Oquassa. (Example.)

1888 GOODE *Amer. Fishes* 93 Tautog, chogset,..oquassa.. are among the best of them.

Or, *conj.*[2] Add: **7.** *Or* is used (chiefly colloq.) between two numeral adjs., as *one or two*, *two or three*, a few, a small number (of).

1535, 1748 [see ONE 2 c]. 1805 WORDSW. *Prelude* VIII. 25 A stall or two is here.

Oraculate, *v. rare.* [f. L. *ōrācul-um* + -ATE.] *trans.* and *intr.* To say or speak oracularly.

1822 MRS. E. NATHAN *Langreath* II. 315, I think I behold you shaking your wise head..as you would oraculate, 'the simple Madelina little suspects' [etc.]. 1919 J. BUCHAN *Mr. Standfast* I. i. 32 He boomed and oraculated and the Misses Wymondham prattled.

Oral. B. *sb.* Add: **b.** Short for *oral examination.*

1876 [G. H. TRIPP] *Student-Life* 18 Do something splendid on the mathematics and the 'orals', and I will wage any thing you will pass clear.

Orange. A. *sb.*[1] Add: **7. a.** *orange leaf, -wood.*

1838 CAROLINE GILMAN *Recoll. Southern Matron* iii. 25 An orange leaf..was laid on every finger bowl. 1877 ELIZ. S. PHELPS *Story of Avis* 408 The splendor slept..upon the green pulses of the orange-leaves. 1880 G. W. CABLE *Grandissimes* ii. 15 Perfumed ad nauseam with orange-leaf tea. 1885 — *Dr. Sevier* liii. 437 He moved his orange-wood staff an inch. 1889 *Harper's Mag.* Dec. 106/2 Strangers ..were detained by eager vendors of flowers and orange-wood walking-sticks.

d. orange(wood)-stick, a stick of orange-wood used for manicuring the nails.

1909 ELIZ. BANKS *Myst. Frances Farrington* 162 Orange-wood manicure sticks. 1910 *Daily Chron.* 23 Apr. 7/3 Dilute peroxide with one-half water and apply under nails with cotton on an orangewood stick. 1911 H. S. HARRISON *Queed* vii. 89 Orange-stick in mouth, he went around like a museum guide. 1922 F. COURTENAY *Physical Beauty* 46 You may use an orange stick..to push back the cuticle from the nails.

B. *adj.* Add: **1. b.** *spec.* Applied to a variety of opal.

1902 *Chambers's Jrnl.* Aug. 494/1 The miners..say, one stroke of the pick may lay bare a seam of 'pin-fire' opal or break in two a rich band of 'orange'.

2. a. orange book, a report of the Ministry of Agriculture and Fisheries dealing with marketing questions and published in orange covers.

1928 *Daily Express* 30 Apr. 7/4 The report is one of the Ministry's famous 'orange' books—those scientific farming pamphlets for the education of English farmers.

Orarion (orē·riǫn). *Eccl.* [late Gr. ὠράριον, ad. L. *orarium* ORARIUM.] = ORARIUM.

1772 J. G. KING *Rites & Cerem. Gk. Ch.* 36 Plate III. represents a deacon officiating in his..Orarion which is a sort of tippet thrown over his left shoulder. 1850 NEALE *Holy East. Ch.* I. 310 The stole was frequently called the orarion in the Western Church. 1907 A. FORTESCUE *Orthod. East. Ch.* 408 Other clerks wear a shorter sticharion and an orarion wound around them.

Oratist (ǫ·rătist). [f. ORATE *v.* + -IST.] One given to orating; a speaker or writer using pompous or bombastic language.

1887 SWINBURNE *Stud. Pr. & Poetry* 134 The orotund oratist of Manhattan.

Oratorial, *a.* **2.** (Recent example.)

1923 *Daily Mail* 8 Aug. 8/1 The very front rank of our oratorial singers.

Oratorship. (Add examples.)

1592 G. HARVEY *Four Lett.* iii, I was supposed not vnmeet for the Oratorship of the vniuersity. 1869 SIR R. C. JEBB in *Life & Lett.* v. 98, I was standing for the Public Oratorship.

Orca (ǭ·ɹkă). [ad. L. *orca*, a kind of whale: see ORC.] In recent use = ORC 1. Also *attrib.*

1866 tr. *Eschricht* in *Rec. Mem. Cetacea* (Ray Soc.) 172 The teeth of the Orcas are of a quite different kind from those of the cachalots. 1906 *Windsor Mag.* Sept. 469/2 A school of killers or orcas had quietly come up. 1908 *Chambers's Jrnl.* Mar. 263/1 The orca gladiator is fond of the colder waters to the south. 1929 *Encycl. Brit.* XXIII. 556/2 Orca or killer whale.

Orchard. 3. Add: *orchard-land.*

1903 *Daily Chron.* 4 Mar. 7/1 In the orchard-land of Normandy the privately distilled liquor is..a recognized medium of exchange.

Orcharding. 2. (Earlier and later examples.)

1654 *Early Connecticut Probate Rec.* 155 One halfe of all my howsing, barnes and orcharding. 1818 *Massachusetts Spy* 25 Feb. 1/2 [A farm] is well proportioned into Mowing, Pasturing, Ploughland, Woodland and Orcharding. 1849 *Rep. U.S. Comm. Patents, Agric.* (1850) 275 From an acre of orcharding of forty trees..one hundred barrels of fruit would be a small crop. 1855 *Poultry Chron.* III. 60/1 He has about a hundred acres of orcharding—pears, apples, cherries, plums, &c. 1863 *Rep. Maine Board Agric.* 142 One acre of orcharding on suitable soil..will produce three times the amount in value of any other crop.

Orchestra. 4. (Add example.)

1903 *Smart Set* IX. 37/1 There would be a modest little dinner at a quiet French restaurant..and an orchestra-chair at the Metropolitan.

Orchestralist (ǭɹke·strălist). [f. ORCHESTRAL + -IST.] A writer of orchestral music; an orchestrator.

1899 CROWEST *Beethoven* 221 The enharmonic change in the first movement..again illustrates the wonderful resources of this king of orchestralists.

Orchestrator (ǭ·ɹkĕstrē̍tǝɹ). [f. ORCHESTRATE + -OR.] One who composes or arranges music for an orchestra.

1907 E. WALKER *Hist. Mus. Eng.* 306 As an orchestrator he [Elgar] is among the very greatest in musical history. 1927 *Observer* 20 Nov. 14/4 Liszt, as an orchestrator, seems to overtop the other.

Orchid. b. (Add examples.)

1884 *Encycl. Brit.* XVII. 818/1 Orchid-lovers have better reasons to support their fancy than had the speculative growers and barterers of tulips. 1893 B. S. WILLIAMS (*title*) The Orchid-Growers' Manual. 1903 *Daily Chron.* 9 Nov. 3/5 One can never tell what the orchid-seed of enterprise may blossom into. 1908 *Westm. Gaz.* 28 May 12/1 The dangers of orchid-hunting.

Orchidean. Add: Also **orchidian.**

1913 C. A. MERCIER *Astrology in Med.* (1914) 4 One eminent physician discovered..the elixir of life in orchidian extract.

Orchidize (ǭ·ɹkidəiz), *v.* [f. ORCHID + -IZE.] *trans.* To make like an orchid.

1918 BENNETT *Pretty Lady* xxxi. 222 In the right environment she would become another being, that was to say, the same being, but orchidised.

Order, *sb.* Add: **4.** (Further example.)

1897 *Rep. Brit. Assoc.* 575 The logarithmic decrement of the receiver is of the same order of magnitude as that of the vibrator.

b. *ellipt.* for *order of magnitude* (see *4).

1903 SIR O. LODGE *Mod. Views on Matter* 7 We are sure that their mass is of the order one-thousandth of the atomic mass of hydrogen. 1912 *Rep. Brit. Assoc.* 398 The change of weight..should have been of the order of 1 in 10^7 per 1° C. 1927 N. V. SIDGWICK *Electronic Theory Valency* 20 The accuracy of spectroscopic measurements (of the order of one in a million) had made it possible to discover very detailed relations among the various lines of a spectrum.

6. c. Later example of *sing.*

1873 ESTCOURT *Anglican Ordinations* i. 4 Holy Order is a Sacrament, requiring a certain matter and form.

8. (Further example.)

1902 *Pall Mall Mag.* XXVIII. 71/1 The King's new Order of Merit would have attracted more attention if the list had appeared alone, and not at the tail of the honours bestowed at the Coronation.

Order of the boot: see *BOOT *sb.*[3] 1 d.

13. d. *Mil.* Equipment, uniform, dress, etc. for some purpose, as *drill order, field-day order, marching order, review order*, etc.

1837 *King's Regul. Army* 32 General Officers are to cause the Troops..to be frequently paraded, and exercised at least once a week in *Heavy* Marching Order. 1860 *Queen's Regul. Army* 150 There is to be only one order for parade, viz:—marching order, when the full equipment of the soldier is to be carried. 1881 *Ibid.* 157 Field-day Order; to be used generally for summer field-days, divisional and brigade drills, [etc.]. *Ibid.*, Drill Order; to be used at ordinary drills, and in riding-schools. 1883 *Ibid.* 265 When the Staff wear the scarlet tunic, officers will appear in 'review order'.

18. (Further example.)

1893 *Times* 13 June 5/6 Mr. M— ruled out of order an amendment relating to the land question.

20. (Further example.)

a 1909 *U.S. Dept. Agric.* Farmers' Bull. No. 60. 4 (Cent. Suppl.) 'Order' or 'case' in tobacco curing means a moist condition in which the tissue will not break.

24. c. Also *a big order.*

1923 H. G. WELLS *Men Like Gods* II. ii. § 2. 174 'You mean to jump this entire Utopian planet?' said Mr. Hunker. 'Big order', said Lord Barralonga. 1923 *Daily Mail* 15 June 11 No surprise need be felt if Mrs. Bendir's colt, despite the big weight, becomes a very big order.

e. *colloq.* A portion or helping of a dish or article of food served in a restaurant.

1906 'O. HENRY' *Four Million* 103 The clatter of steel, the screaming of 'short orders', the cries of the hungering and all the horrid tumult of feeding man. *Ibid.* 248 And all this while she [the waitress] would be performing astounding feats with orders of pork and beans, pot roasts, [etc.]. 1926 *William Feather Mag.* July in *Amer. Sp.* June (1927) 414 'One order of split pea soup', cries the customer...'An order of ham and eggs', says one.

27. In order. c. Appropriate to or befitting the occasion; suitable; called for; also, in fashion, current, common, 'the thing'.

a 1861 T. WINTHROP *John Brent* viii. 85 If the gent has made a remark what teches you, apologies is in order. 1873 ALDRICH *Marj. Daw*, etc. 29 Not that I am pining for news of them, but any gossip of the kind would be in order. 1878 J. H. BEADLE *Western Wilds* xxv. 399 One week sufficed to conclude my business in Oregon, but before leaving a few general notes are in order. 1903 *N.Y. Times* 4 Sept., Good-byes were in order on the Erin last night. 1904 H. H. HORNE *Philos. Educ.* 196 A quotation from Professor James on any subject which his brilliant pen has touched is always in order.

d. *In* (or *on*) *short order* (also *quick order*): without delay, immediately, summarily. *U.S.*

1834 W. G. SIMMS *Guy Rivers* (1841) II. i. 75 Be off now in a hurry, or I shall fire upon you in short order. 1840 C. F. HOFFMAN *Greyslaer* IV. iii. II. 197, I cut out in quick order from the hollow, and made clean tracks for the camp. 1841 *Knickerbocker Mag.* XVII. 27 If you fight that man, he will use you up in short order. 1846–52 MRS. WHITCHER *Widow Bedott P.* xxv. 307 If ever you dew it agin you'll get your walking-ticket on short order. 1861 O. W. NORTON *Army Lett.* 26 A field of potatoes, five acres, was emptied of its contents in short order. 1892 *Outing* Apr. 19/1, I was so comfortable that I went to sleep in short order. 1902 ELIZ. BANKS *Newspaper Girl* 27, I dressed myself in short order. *c* 1904 in Appel *Business Biogr. J. Wanamaker* (1930) 158 The Trust could shut up every factory outside of the Trust in short order.

Order, *v.* **6.** Also with ellipse of *to be.* *U.S.*

1781 WITHERSPOON *Druid* No. 5 These things were ordered delivered to the army. 1799 *Essex Inst. Hist. Coll.* XIII. 61 But the wind growing faint, I ordered the signal taken in. 1816 U. BROWN *Jrnl.* in *Maryland Hist. Mag.* XI. 364 He orders her brought into the yard for me to see. 1873 J. H. BEADLE *Undevel. West* xi. 191 My bill was introduced by Senator Williams of Oregon, read by title, and ordered printed. 1875 J. G. HOLLAND *Sevenoaks* xxiii. 327 He went out,..jumped into Mr. Talbot's waiting coupe, and ordered himself driven home. 1904 *San Francisco Chron.* 24 July 26 They were ordered deported on the same steamer on which they came. 1907 MRS. HARRIS *Tents of Wickedness* II. iii. 144, I can order the horses brought round at ten o'clock.

Orderly. A. *adj.* **5.** Also *orderly box.*

1904 *Daily Chron.* 18 Mar. 6/3 They had..been seen tearing up documents and throwing them into orderly boxes.

Ordinable, *a.* Transfer †*Obs.* to sense in Dict. and add: Capable of being arranged or set in order.

1902 *Encycl. Brit.* XXXI. 281/2 A manifold which can be arranged in order may be called ordinable.

Ordinary, *sb.* Add: **14. c.** (Earlier examples.)

1637 *Essex Inst. Hist. Coll.* IX. 55 Mr. John Holgraue.. hath undertaken to keep an ordinary for the entertainment of strangers. 1650 *Maryland Archives* 294 Wine or other Provisions to bee expended in any Ordinaries within this Province. 1680 *Coll. N.H. Hist. Soc.* XIII. 15 What person soever..shall profane ye Lord's Day..by dining at ordinarys in time of publique worship..shall forfeite 10s. 1704 S. KNIGHT *Jrnl.* 26 We went forward, and arriving at an Ordinary about two mile further, found tolerable accommodation. 1745 *Itinerant Observations* 43 At our arrival at Snow-Hill, I took up Quarters at an Ordinary, and found them very good. *Note.* Or Tavern, Eating-house, or Inn.

16. a. (Recent example.)

1909 *Times Lit. Suppl.* 20 May 185/2 Shakespeare introduces the ordinary, whether in characters or in events, only as a foil to the extraordinary.

c. One of a class of inmates in a poor-house.

1910 *Daily Chron.* 14 Jan. 8/5 The 'ordinaries' (whom we should call able-bodied) were able to roam all over the building.

19. a. *ordinary-keeper* (earlier examples).

1645 *Essex Inst. Hist. Coll.* IX. 136 To provide for a ordinarie keeper. 1662 *Maryland Archives* 447 All Ordinary Keepers debts either upon bill or accompt..shall be allowed due.

Ordinary, *a.* **6.** (Later U.S. example; cf. *ORNERY.)

1800 *Aurora* (Philad.) 1 May (Th.) This ordinary drunken wretch is supposed to be the perpetrator.

Ordinator. 1. (Recent example.)

1929 BRIDGES *Test. Beauty* I. 134 And wouldst thou play Creator and Ordinator of things.

Ordovician, *a.* Add: **b.** *ellipt.* or as *sb.* Ordovician rocks or strata.

1914 *Brit. Mus. Return* 201 Crinoidea from..the Ordovician of Ohio.

Ore[2]. **3. a.** Add: *ore-bucket, -pass, -vein* (example).

1912 *Chambers's Jrnl.* Dec. 784/2 The men..had begun to send the *ore-buckets down empty. 1883 *Encycl. Brit.* XVI. 453/2 E the main lode, H permanent levels, and K *ore-pass reserved amidst the rubbish (*deads*) D. 1906 *Chambers's Jrnl.* Feb. 159/2 A few digs with the shovel laid bare the outcropping of the *ore-vein.

Oregon (ǫ·rigǫn). The name of one of the United States of America, situated on the Pacific sea-board; used attributively in the names of (varieties of) plants and animals found in Oregon, as **Oregon ash**, a species of ash, *Fraxinus oregona*; **Oregon grape**, the evergreen shrub *Berberis aquifolium*, or its berry; **Oregon horse**, a breed of horse originating in Oregon; **Oregon pine**, a species of fir, *Pseudotsuga douglasii* or *taxifolia*.

1874 R. GLISAN *Jrnl. Army Life* xxxiii. 480 Along the streams grow cotton wood..and the *Oregon ash. 1869 S. BOWLES *Our New West* xv. 107 We unexpectedly find the 'Mahonia Holly'...They call it here the '*Oregon grape, for it bears a little berry. 1889 *Century Mag.* Jan. 341/1 A strain of horses early imported into Montana from the West and known as the *Oregon horse. 1845 *Knickerbocker Mag.* XXVI. 166 The *Oregon pine mentioned in..the North-American Review. 1888 *Encycl. Brit.* XXIV. 386/2 The principal timber is yellow and red fir, ordinarily known as 'Oregon pine', which constitutes the bulk of the forests.

Hence **Oregonese** *pl.*, the people of Oregon; **Oregonian** *a.* and *sb.*, belonging to Oregon, (a native or inhabitant) of Oregon; **Oregonly** *adv.*, after the manner of an Oregonian.

1848 E. BRYANT *California* xv. 197, I think the Oregonese had a little the advantage of us in this respect. *a* 1861 T. WINTHROP *John Brent* xxii. 243 Armstrong's opinion was only my own, expressed Oregonly. 1873 J. H. BEADLE *Undevel. West* xxxv. 762 There is a distinctively Oregonian look about all the natives and old residents. *Ibid.* xxxvi. 772 No Oregonian will eat of salmon caught above the mouth of the Willamette. 1880 K. MUNROE *Golden Days* xi. 118 Most of the Oregonians..had sworn the extermination of such Indians as dwelt in the neighbourhood of their new homes.

Orexigenic (oreksidʒe·nik), *a. Med.* [f. Gr. ὄρεξις OREXIS + *-GENIC.] That stimulates the appetite.

1907 *Amer. Jrnl. Clin. Med* Oct. 1252 (Cent. Suppl.) An orexigenic and stomachic action which is not to be lightly esteemed.

Organ, *sb.*[1] **8.** Add: *organ recital.*

1881 *Harper's Mag.* May 814/1 Piano and organ recitals have long been fashionable.

Organal, *a.* **2.** (Recent example.)

1916 C. V. STANFORD & FORSYTH *Hist. Mus.* 128 At this time the organal voice had..become finally fixed in its position above the plain-song.

Organic, *a.* **6. b.** (Earlier examples.)

1849 *Congress. Globe* 25 July App. 46 (Th.) [The origin of a Territorial Government] is not from such people, but from the law of Congress, usually styled the 'organic law', establishing it... The rules that Government has itself prescribed in the 'organic law'. 1857 *Message of Mayor of Washington* 26 May (Bartlett) The powers of the corporation of Washington are only those which are conferred by the organic law, the charter.

Organicism. Add: **1. b.** The doctrine that everything in nature has an organic basis or explanation.

1912 A. TRIDON tr. *Delage & Goldsmith's Theories Evol.* 163 In that respect, organicism is the perfect antithesis of Weismannism. 1928 *Jrnl. Philos. Stud.* Jan. 39 This is the reason why modern organicism, the organic theory of nature, seems so important for modern biology.

Hence **Organicist.** Add: (*b*) One who holds the organic theory of nature. So **Organicistic** *a.*

1912 A. TRIDON tr. *Delage & Goldsmith's Theories Evol.* 164 Roux and the other organicists lay special stress on the factors of individual evolution. 1928 *Jrnl. Philos. Stud.* Jan. 29 That which was common to the organicists, said Delage, was that they regarded..life, the form of the body.. as resulting from the reciprocal play or struggle of all its elements. *Ibid.* 39 The organicistic schema formerly covered the living world, and now covers also the world of the non-living.

Organism. 1. (Add example.)

1926 A. N. WHITEHEAD *Sci. & Mod. World* 112 This doctrine involves the abandonment of the traditional scientific materialism, and the substitution of an alternative doctrine of organism.

Organistic, *a.* Add: **b.** Of or pertaining to an organism; based on organisms.

1910 *Fabian News* XXI. 16/1 He adopts the organistic view of society—that society is a being.

Organistry (ǭ·ɹgănistri). [f. ORGANIST + -RY.] The post of organist.

1890 *Peel City Guard.* 19 July 4/1 He..held the local town hall organistry.

Organity. Transfer †*Obs.* to sense in Dict. and add: **2.** An organized whole or organism.

1929 BRIDGES *Test. Beauty* IV. 801 These perfected unify'd organities..all act in response to external stimulants.

Organizatory, *a.* [f. med.L. *organizat-* ppl. stem of *organizare*, see ORGANIZE *v.* + -ORY.] Of or pertaining to organization.

1921 *Public Opinion* 17 June 560/1 The merely organisatory work of delivering wooden houses and materials to France.

Organotherapy (ǭ:gănoþe·răpi). [f. ORGANO- + THERAPY.] The treatment of disease with organic extracts. So **Organotherapic** *a.*, of or pertaining to organotherapy. **Organotherapeutics** (*pl.*), the study or practice of organotherapy as a branch of medicine.

1899 *Nature* 3 Aug. 316/1 The most successful branch of organotherapy..has been that of the thyroids. 1900 *Lancet* 25 Aug. 610/2 Dr. J. G. Soutar..regarded the subject of organo-therapeutics as one of great importance. 1908 *Practitioner* Sept. 428 All forms of medical treatment of this affection, whether hygienic, dietetic, medicinal, organotherapic, or electrical in nature, are unsatisfactory. 1909 *Athenæum* 17 July 72/2 Since then, organo-therapy has increased apace. 1922 HARROWER (*title*) Practical Organotherapy.

Oribatid (ǫri·bătid), *sb.* and *a.* [f. mod.L. *Oribatidæ* the name of the family.] (A tick) belonging to the family *Oribatidæ*; a beetle-mite.

1875 *Encycl. Brit.* II. 276/1 The Oribatides in general live on vegetable matter. 1914 *Brit. Mus. Return* 170 Thirty-three Oribatid Mites from Hawaii. 1924 *Glasgow Herald* 12 Jan. 4/2 The hard-shelled 'beetle-mites', or Oribatids feed on decaying vegetable matter.

Orielled, *a.* [f. ORIEL + -ED.] Provided with oriels (sense 2).

1905 *Westm. Gaz.* 4 Nov. 6/2 Tawny sunlight works bright wizardries in orielled cloisters.

Orient, *v.* **1. b.** (Add examples.)

1896 *Science* 3 July 11 We are now at a loss to orient the several parts of the cranium. 1926 MULFORD *Cassidy's Protégé* xiii. 170 Hesitating for a moment while he oriented the report, he started toward the edge of the hill-top.

Orientating, *ppl. a.* [-ING[2].] That orientates.

1921 MRS. E. HERMAN *Creative Prayer* 104 For that world of reality..is..Love, and its highway—the great orientating path that gives it coherence—is Christ.

Orificial (ǫrifi·ʃăl), *a.*[2] [f. L. *orifici-um* ORIFICE + -AL.] Of or pertaining to an orifice.

1926 *Chambers's Jrnl.* Feb. 92/2 Then we cut it [*sc.* a potato] in two or in four according to one's orificial ability. 1926 *Spectator* 25 Sept. 473/1 With a fine inconsistency, they belong to societies of so-called 'orificial surgery' and follow strange cults of electrical healing.

Origenian, *a.* (Modern example.)

1879 R. ORNSBY in *Dubl. Rev.* July 64 A fourth branch of the Origenian evidence is prophecy and its fulfilment.

Original. A. *adj.* Add: **1. d.** *Geol.* Of minerals: That have been present in rocks from their first formation.

1882 GEIKIE *Text-bk. Geol.* 61 The same mineral may occur both as an original and as a secondary constituent.

Originist. Transfer †*Obs.* to sense in Dict. and add: **2.** One who holds a particular view of the origin of *e.g.* species or varieties of living things. Properly the second element of a compound.

1927 *Glasgow Herald* 14 July 4/6 Two rival 'schools'—those of the Diffusionists and the Independent Originists—make bid for favour [among anthropologists].

-orium, *suffix.* Add: Now used in America in many, often hybrid, formations, as *barbatorium*, *bobatorium*, *healthatorium*, etc. (see 1925 *Amer. Sp.* I. 38).

Ornamental. B. *sb.* Add: **b.** A tree, shrub, or the like, grown for the sake of its beauty.

1903 *Pop. Sci. Monthly* Jan. 277 It could be done more easily with strawberries, or with some of the common ornamentals that do not reproduce true to seed.

Ornamentalist. (Add example.)

1925 *Daily Tel.* 13 May 20/6 Pastrycooks.—First Hand Required. Must be first-class decorator and ornamentalist.

Ornate, *ppl. a.* Add: **3.** as *sb.* That which is ornate.

1905 *Westm. Gaz.* 12 Jan. 4/2 It was man who first began to cultivate the ornate.

Orneriness, U.S. colloq. form of ORDINARINESS, esp. in the sense 'meanness'.

1899 TARKINGTON *Gentl. Indiana* iv. 45 They..let loose their deviltries just for pure orneriness.

Ornery (ǭ·ɹnəri), *a.* *U.S colloq.* Also **ornary, or'nary.** [Variant of ORDINARY *a.*] Poor in quality; bad; coarse; mean; low; commonplace.

1816 U. BROWN *Jrnl.* in *Maryland Hist. Mag.* X. 369 The Land is old, completely worn out, the farming extremely ornary in general. 1837 *Knickerbocker Mag.* IX. 68 You're all a pack of poor, or'nary common people. *a* 1861 T. WINTHROP *John Brent* vii. 71 Good company betters the orneriest sort of weather. *c* 1865 'MARK TWAIN' *Sketches* Wks. XIX. 29 You'd think he warn't worth a cent but to set around and look ornery. 1875–6 BRET HARTE *Gabriel Conroy* in *Scribner's Monthly* VI. 246 Asking ornery and perfectly ridiculous questions. 1902 G. H. LORIMER *Lett. Self-made Merchant* x. 136 When I began to hint that the people were pretty ornery dressers, he reckoned that he 'would paste me one if I wasn't so young'. 1921 R. D. PAINE *Comr. Rolling Ocean* v. 90 Am I ornery enough to lie to you, after what had happened on deck last night.

Ornithologically, *adv.* (Example.)

1862 *Ibis* 87 The country..is rather poor ornithologically.

Ornithologize, *v.* (Earlier example.)

1872 *Amer. Naturalist* VI. 268 At Topeka..we also tarried for ten days, devoting the time almost exclusively to ornithologizing.

Ornithomorph. [f. Gr. ὀρνιθόμορφ-ος bird-shaped.] A representation of a bird in art.

1913 J. RENDEL HARRIS *Boanerges* ii. 14 There was an ornithomorph, and..several theriomorphs, before the anthropomorph.

Ornithopter. Also **-ptere.** [f. ORNITHO- + Gr. πτέρον feather, wing.] A machine designed to 'fly' by means of wings acting like those of a bird. Also *attrib.*

1908 *Aeronautics* Nov. I. 86 *Ornithoptere* denotes a machine in which the means of sustentation and propulsion consist of beating-wings. 1927 C. L. M. BROWN *Conquest of Air* 75 As early as 1872 he had built an obviously impracticable machine on the 'wing-flapping' or ornithopter principle.

Ornithosaur. (Add example.)

1913 *Q. Jrnl. Geol. Soc.* LXIX. 372 An Ornithosaur from the Wealden Shales of Atherfield (Isle of Wight).

Ornithosaurian. (Examples.)

1888 LYDEKKER *Catal. Fossil Reptilia Brit. Mus.* I. 24 Considerable portion of the skeleton of a large Ornithosaurian..from the Wealden of Brook, Isle of Wight. 1913 *Q. Jrnl. Geol. Soc.* LXIX. 372 The late Rev. W. D. Fox.. discovered..many associated ornithosaurian bones.

Orogenetic (ǫrodʒĕne·tik), *a.* [f. Gr. ὄρος mountain + -GENETIC.] = OROGENIC.

1888 TEALL *Brit. Petrogr.* 441 Orogenetic, that which relates to the formation of mountains. 1897 *Geog. Jrnl.* X. 268 The slope is gentle, indicating an absence of orogenetic activities. 1925 JOLY *Surface-Hist. Earth* i. 24 The orogenetic movements which developed the Appalachians.

Orographical, *a.* (Add example.) So **Orographically** *adv.*

1923 SIR N. SHAW *Forecasting Weather* v. 156 Orographical Rain. Formed in air-currents ascending mountains. 1902 D. G. HOGARTH *Nearer East* 14 Here is a continuous parting of waters, but not, orographically, a continuous mountain range.

Orometry (orǫ·mĕtri). [f. Gr. ὄρος mountain + -μετρία (in comb.) measurement: see -METRY.] The measurement of forms of relief, or the branch of physical geography which deals with this.

1898 *Geog. Jrnl.* XI. 205 As the geoid is treated in geodesy, he treats the *oroid* in orometry.

Orotundity. (Example.)

1922 J. M. MURRY *Probl. Style* 20 Wordsworthians were there to discover the hallmark of genius on his most insignificant orotundities.

Orphaned, *a.* Add: **3.** Of machinery, etc.: Of which spare parts are no longer available.

1920 F. B. SCHOLL *Automobile Owner's Guide* 3 Orphaned cars may run as well and give as good service as anybody could ask for, but when a company fails or discontinues to manufacture a model, the car immediately loses from one-third to one-half of its natural value.

Orseller, variant of *NORSELLER.

Orthaxial, *a.* (Add example.)

1886 *U.S. Commission of Fish & Fisheries* 985 (Cass. Suppl.) The word orthaxial is used to designate the archaic straight type of vertebrate axis which is not bent upwards at its posterior extremity.

Orthic, *a.* Add: **b.** *Math.* (See quot.)

1904 *Science* 19 Aug. 227/2 Orthic Curves; or Algebraic Curves which satisfy Laplace's Equation in Two Dimensions.

Ortho (ǭ·ɹþo), *a.* Abbreviation of ORTHOCHROMATIC. Also ellipt. = *orthochromatic plate.*

1906 *Westm. Gaz.* 17 May 14/2 The..medium ortho is about half the speed of the well-known extra-rapid..orthoplate. 1921 *Glasgow Herald* 27 Apr. 9, I have said something in previous articles about ortho plates.

Orthodiagram (ǭɹþodəi·ăgræm). [f. ORTHO- + DIAGRAM.] A sketch of the outline of an organ, etc., obtained by the use of an orthodiagraph. **Orthodiagraph**, an instrument designed to secure an accurate outline of an internal organ, foreign substance in the body, or the like, by means of Röntgen rays which strike the plate at right angles. **Orthodiagraphic** *a.*, of or pertaining to an orthodiagraph. **Orthodiagraphy**, the use of an orthodiagraph.

1904 *Elect. World & Engin.* 24 Sept. 514 (Cent. Suppl.) A so-called orthodiagraph, an apparatus which serves in connection with Roentgen tubes for determining the exact size of the heart and for locating foreign bodies. 1907 *Practitioner* Apr. 524 By means of orthodiagraphy..the exact size and shape of an organ or tumour can be ascertained. *Ibid.* 525 The orthodiagraphic axis. *Ibid.* 526 Changes in the size of the heart..can be determined by the system..of measuring orthodiagrams which have been taken direct on paper.

Orthodontia (ǭɹþodǫ·ntiă). [mod.L. f. Gr. ὀρθός, ORTHO- + ὀδόντ-, ὀδούς tooth.] The correcting of irregular and faulty positions of the teeth.

1890 BILLINGS *Nat. Med. Dict.* 1908 *Practitioner* Dec. 858 A case showing the importance of moving the roots of the teeth in orthodontia.

Orthodontic (ǭɹþodǫ·ntik), *a.* [f. as prec. + -IC.] Of or pertaining to orthodontia. **Orthodontics** *sb. pl.*, the science or practice of orthodontia. **Orthodontist**, one who studies or practises orthodontia.

1907 *Amer. Text-bk. Prosthetic Dentistry* (ed. C. R. Turner) 450 And in the front of the mouth also..their movement to correct position by orthodontic means is frequently advisable. 1908 *Text-bk. Operat. Dentistry* (ed. C. N. Johnson) 566 Not infrequently, is the orthodontist called upon to diagnose the presence or absence of a permanent successor to a deciduous tooth. 1909 *Let. to J. A. H. Murray* 8 Dec., At the Annual Meeting, held this evening, of the British Society for the Study of Orthodontia, the Committee brought forward a resolution that the word 'Orthodontics' be substituted for 'Orthodontia' in the name of the Society. 1925 *Brit. Med. Jrnl.* 19 Dec. 1183/2 A paper read before the British Society for the Study of Orthodontics.

Orthoform (ǭ·ɹþofǭɹm). [f. ORTHO- + *-form* the terminal part of CHLOROFORM.] A white crystalline powder possessing local analgesic and antiseptic properties; the methyl ester of meta-amido-para-oxy-benzoic acid.

1897 *Westm. Gaz.* 25 Oct. 5/2 A new anæsthetic called Orthoform, the discovery of two German chemists named Einhorn and Hine. 1898 *Brit. Med. Jrnl.* 5 Feb. 361. 1907 *Practitioner* Aug. 294 Orthoform has been highly spoken of in the treatment of ulcers. 1920 *Glasgow Herald* 13 Dec. 11 Various synthetic drugs, such as novocain and orthoform.

Orthogenesis (ǭɹþodʒe·nĕsis). [ad. G. *orthogenesis* (Eimer): see ORTHO- and -GENESIS.] The evolution or development of organic forms along definite lines which are determined by inherent tendencies and for the most part uninfluenced by the environment.

1895 *Nature* 3 Oct. 554/2 Prof. Eimer, of Tübingen, spoke ..on the subject of orthogenesis. 1902 J. M. BALDWIN *Development & Evol.* xii. 161 Eimer..calls the determination secured by this means 'orthogenesis'. 1911 *Encycl. Brit.* XXVII. 912/1 Many successful series,..as they have survived, must inevitably display orthogenesis to some extent. 1927 HALDANE & HUXLEY *Animal Biol.* x. 217 A third theory of evolution has been advanced, called Orthogenesis, or development in straight lines.

Orthogenetic, *a.* [f. prec., see -GENETIC.] Of, pertaining to, or exhibiting, orthogenesis; characterized by orthogenesis or development along straight lines. Hence **Orthogenetically** *adv.*

1903 *Amer. Geol.* Apr. 205 The orthogenetic formation of the chambers exerts an increasing pull upon the chamber of attachment. 1927 HALDANE & HUXLEY *Animal Biol.* xi. 253 The orthogenetic series can be perfectly well explained by natural selection. *Ibid.*, The extinct cephalopod molluscs ..often evolved orthogenetically into the most bizarre forms. 1930 W. R. INGE *Chr. Ethics & Mod. Probl.* i. 13, I shall not maintain that the evolution of Christianity has been..orthogenetic.

Orthograde (ǭ·ɹþogrēᵈd), *a.* [irreg. f. ORTHO- + L. *-gradus* going, walking: see GRADE.] Having, or walking with, the body upright.

1902 A. KEITH in *Jrnl. Anat. & Physiol.* Oct. 18 The Orthograde Primates, into which group fall the gibbon, orang, chimpanzee, gorilla, and man. 1912 — *Human Body* vi. (1920) 82 The orthograde or upright stage of development. 1925 J. LAIRD *Our Minds & their Bodies* 46 An orthograde (or erect) animal, like man.

Orthometric, *a.* (Add example.)

1883 *Encycl. Brit.* XVI. 349/2 All crystals may be divided into 'orthometric' or erect forms and 'clinometric' or inclined forms.

Orthophonic (ǭɹþofǫ·nik), *a.* [f. ORTHOPHONY + -IC.] Of or pertaining to orthophony; reproducing sounds correctly.

1927 *Gramophone* V. 309/2 The gramophone part of it contains an improved form of orthophonic horn. 1927 *Daily Mirror* 10 Dec. 12/1 The Orthophonic horn has been in use with wireless for two or three years.

Orthoplastic (ǭɹþoplæ·stik), *a.* [f. Gr. ὀρθός ORTHO- + πλαστικός PLASTIC.] Of or pertaining to orthoplasy; forming a shield under which germinal variations may arise.

1902 J. M. BALDWIN *Development & Evol.* x. 142 These influences we may call 'orthoplastic' or directive influences.

Orthoplasy (ǭ·ɹþoplăsi). *Biol.* [f. Gr. ὀρθός ORTHO- + πλάσις moulding.] The retention by an organism and its successors of acquired characters until germinal variations arise to continue these; a view of the origin of variations based on this.

1902 J. M. BALDWIN *Dict. Phil. & Psych.* II. 251/1 Orthoplasy..emphasizes natural selection working upon variations in many cases screened and fostered by the presence of individual modifications. 1902 — *Development & Evol.* xiii. 173 The theory of evolution which makes general use of organic selection is called Orthoplasy.

Orthopter[2]. [ad. F. *orthoptère* in same sense.] A form of ornithopter.

1887 tr. *J. Verne's Clipper of Clouds* vii, Orthopters, machines which endeavour to reproduce the natural flight of birds. 1907 *Sci. Amer.* 12 Oct. 258/2 When suspended the orthopter indicated a forward pull of approximately 24 pounds. 1909 *Westm. Gaz.* 23 Mar. 4/1 The compound aeroplane..which combines the orthopter and biplane.

Orthopteran, *a.* (Example.)

1900 *Proc. U.S. Nat. Mus.* XXIII. 393 The Orthopteran genus *Trimerotropis.*

Orthopteroid (ǭɹþǫ·ptĕroid), *a.* (and *sb.*). [f. ORTHOPTERA + -OID.] Resembling or related to the Orthoptera. As *sb.*, an orthopteroid insect.

1887 HEILPRIN *Distrib. Animals* 146 The discovery..of an apparent orthopteroid (Palæoblattina) in the most nearly equivalent deposits of Calvados, France. 1889 NICHOLSON & LYDEKKER *Palæontol.* I. 593 The Orthopteroid section of the *Palæodictyoptera* includes a group of forms representing the modern Cockroaches. 1910 *Encycl. Brit.* XIII. 432/1 Orthopteroid wing-neuration.

Orthostatic (ǭɹþostæ·tik), *a.* [f. ORTHO- + STATIC or ad. Gr. *ὀρθοστατικ-ός; cf. ὀρθοστάτης an upright pillar.] Upright or vertical.

1926 HOGARTH *Kings of Hittites* ii. 29 Ground-courses of orthostatic slabs.

Orthostereoscope. [f. ORTHO- + STEREOSCOPE.] A binocular microscope in which inversion of the image is avoided or corrected. Hence **Orthostereoscopic** *a.*, **Orthostereoscopism.**

1892 *Jrnl. Quekett Microsc. Club.* 46 If orthostereoscopic vision is required the transposition must be corrected. *Ibid.* 52 If the two prisms were joined into one, it would..make a very efficient orthostereoscope. *Ibid.* 53 Orthostereoscopism.

Orygine (ǫ·ridʒəin), *a.* [f. L. *oryg-*, *oryx* ORYX + -INE[1].] Of or pertaining to the genus Oryx, of antelopes.

1898 *Proc. Zool. Soc.* 352 The Addax, I think, is on the whole more an orygine type than a hippotragine.

Osage orange. See ORANGE *sb.*[1] 3.

1817, 1859 [see ORANGE 3]. 1838 H. W. ELLSWORTH *Valley N. Wabash* v. 52 These fences, whose tops are covered with a luxuriant growth of the wild locust hawthorn, or Osage Orange. 1846 D. J. BROWNE *Trees Amer.* 465 *Maclura aurantiaca* The Osage Orange-tree. 1857 *Trans. Ill. Agric. Soc.* II. 23 The practicability of successfully cultivating the Osage Orange plant into a protective hedge. 1870 KEIM *Sheridan's Troopers* xxii. (1885) 159 Everywhere along the stream there was an abundance of box elder, Osage orange, and some locust. 1891 *Harper's Mag.* Sept. 579/2 There was a hedge of Osage Orange on one side of the yard.

Osazone (ōᵘ·săzōᵘn). *Chem.* [Named by E. Fischer (1884), f. -OSE[2] + *AZO- + -ONE, or the common termination of the different substances *fructosazone*, *GLUCOSAZONE, etc.] Any of a class of crystalline compounds obtained from sugars containing a carbonyl group by the action of phenylhydrazine.

1892 E. F. SMITH tr. *Richter's Org. Chem.* 501 In the presence of an excess of phenylhydrazine the hexoses, like all glucoses combine with two molecules of it upon application of heat and form the *osazones*. 1898 J. WADE *Intro. Org. Chem.* 189 Fructose yields..the same compound [as glucose], and the osazone is best made in quantity from invert sugar. 1902 *Encycl. Brit.* XXVI. 722/2 It was necessary to reproduce the hexose from the osazone. 1905 C. E. SIMON *Physiol. Chem.* 67 *Hydrazons*..can be further transformed into *osazons*, which are very characteristic substances and may serve to distinguish the various sugars from each other.

Oscillate, *v.* Add: **1.** (Further example.)

1913 J. A. FLEMING *Wireless Telegr.* 69 The two plates are then connected together suddenly. The charges in them, therefore, begin to oscillate.

c. *loosely.* Of a special medium or apparatus through which oscillations pass: To experience or suffer the passage of oscillations.

1919 PENROSE *Wireless Telegr.* 47 If there is no resistance, radiation, or other losses, the circuit would oscillate for ever. 1928 *Times* 23 Mar. 20/1 If too much retroaction is employed the circuit resistance may become negative when the whole system will begin to oscillate.

d. *spec.* Of a wireless receiver, or (loosely) of its operator: To radiate electro-magnetic waves owing to faulty operation.

1926 *Westm. Gaz.* 3 Feb., Listeners-in who oscillate may find themselves deprived of their licences.

3. (Further example.)

1905 PREECE & SIVEWRIGHT *Telegr.* 462 The spark gap which oscillates the energy.

Oscillating, *ppl. a.* (Add example.)

1925 P. J. RISDON *Crystal Receivers & Circuits* 11 BC will tend to induce in CD an oscillating current which will react on BC.

Oscillation. 1. (Add examples.)

1877 *Encycl. Brit.* VIII. 81/2 The charge of one armature of the condenser passes through a series of oscillations. 1896 *Q. Rev.* Apr. 505 A simple arrangement for producing electrical oscillations of the longitudinal or sonorous type. 1911 *Encycl. Brit.* XXVI. 532/2 The transmitting antenna wire is alternately charged to a high potential and discharged with the production of high frequency oscillations in it. 1932 E. V. APPLETON *Thermionic Vacuum Tubes* 102 Since the applied anode potential is negative no anode current flows unless oscillations are present.

3. Also *Comb.* as *oscillation-hysteresis.*

1932 E. V. APPLETON *Thermionic Vacuum Tubes* 98 The curves..indicate the existence of oscillation-hysteresis.

Oscillator. Add: **2.** Also, a form of wireless transmitter.

1907 *Cornhill Mag.* Mar. 356 Placing his oscillator at the focus of a parabolic mirror. 1924 *Discovery* June 83/2 Some sixty per cent. of the initial electrical energy emitted by the oscillator could be converted into heat.

3. A person who causes or allows a radio receiver to 'oscillate' or radiate electro-magnetic waves.

1927 *Daily Tel.* 1 Mar. 6 Cases where engineers..have succeeded in tracking down oscillators. 1927 *Glasgow Herald* 20 Sept. 8/2 The running-to-earth of offending oscillators.

Oscillatory, *a.* (Add examples.)

1888 TEALL *Brit. Petrogr.* 441 When the faces of two different forms of the same order are alternately developed in a crystal, the result being a fine parallel striation, the combination is said to be oscillatory. 1922 *Encycl. Brit.* XXXII. 1023/2 High frequency oscillatory currents will be set up in this latter circuit under certain conditions.

Oscillogram (ǫsi·logræm). [f. as next + -GRAM.] A record obtained by means of an oscillograph.

1908 E. RUHMER *Wireless Teleph.* II. xiii. 145 Duddell-Arc oscillograms. Two oscillographic records from a singing arc.

Oscillograph (ǫsi·logrɑf). [ad. F. *oscillographe* (1893 Blondel in *Comptes Rendus* CXVI. 502); f. L. *oscill-āre* to oscillate + -GRAPH.] **a.** An instrument similar in principle to the galvanometer designed to record or reveal oscillations and changes in electric currents, esp. when these oscillations are very small and rapid. **b.** An instrument for detecting and measuring the oscillations of buildings, ships, and other structures. **Oscillographic** *a.*, of, pertaining to, or produced by, an oscillograph.

1900 *Nature* 6 Dec. 142/2 The original idea of the oscillograph is due to M. Blondel. 1902 *Encycl. Brit.* XXX. 599/1 The oscillograph in its modern form is a very perfect instrument for the examination of alternating-current phenomena. 1904 C. H. PEABODY *Nav. Archit.* 344 Investigations of the rolling of ships in quiet water and among waves have been made..by aid of instruments known as oscillographs which have slow and quick pendulums, and registring devices. 1908 Oscillographic [see *OSCILLOGRAM]. 1914 R. STANLEY *Text-bk. Wireless Telegr.* 135 These results were obtained by Dr. Fleming in a valuable series of oscillograph records on oscillatory circuits. 1922 *Encycl. Brit.* XXXII. 1024/1 The study of the oscillatory arc by means of the oscillograph..has shown clearly the nature of the operations taking place.

Oscillometer (ǫsilǫ·mĭtǝɹ). [f. L. *oscill-āre* to oscillate + -METER.] A form of oscillograph (sense b) used in ships.

1899 *Sci. Amer.* 29 July 71/2 An interesting gyroscopic device termed the 'oscillometer', has been put on the market by a Milanese firm.

Oscilloscope (ǫsi·loskoᵘp). [f. L. *oscill-āre* to oscillate + -SCOPE.] **a.** An instrument for representing visibly the oscillations of an alternating current. **b.** An instrument for reducing the apparent number of revolutions of parts of machines to enable vibrations and other faults to be detected easily.

1922 *Glasgow Herald* 10 Oct. 6 The Elverson oscilloscope ..is an apparatus for slowing down to the eye, by means of the optical phenomenon known as 'Persistence of Image', any high-speed machinery which it is desired to examine under working conditions. 1923 R. KNOX *Radiogr. & Radiotherapeutics* I. 86 The best method of detecting reverse current is by the use of an oscilloscope tube.

Oscularity (ǫskiŭlæ·rĭti). [ad. L. type *osculāritas*: cf. OSCULAR and -ITY.] Kissing.

1926 W. J. LOCKE *Old Bridge* I. i. 8 Nowadays she was too mature for casual oscularity.

Osirification (osəi:rifikē̍·ʃən). [f. *Osiris* (see OSIRIAN) + -FICATION.] Identification with Osiris. **Osirify** *v. trans.*, to identify with Osiris; to deify. **Osirism**, the cult of Osiris.

1891 *Century Dict.*, Osirify. 1906 PETRIE *Relig. Anc. Egypt* iv. 23 The most renowned was the *Hapi* or Apis bull of Memphis..who was Osirified and became the Osir-hapi. *Ibid.* v. 38 The earliest phase of Osirism that we can identify is in portions of the Book of the Dead. 1912 *Hastings's Encycl. Relig. & Ethics* V. 238/1 In the earliest royal monuments the dance of men in the festival of Osirification of the King is represented.

Osmatic (ǫsmæ·tik), *a.* [f. Gr. ὀσμή smell + -ATIC.] Having the sense of smell (developed). So **Osmatism**, the ability to perceive smells.

1903 *Amer. Anthropologist* Oct.–Dec. 638 The related doctrines that the olfactory organs are large in osmatic, small or absent in anosmatic animals. 1903 *Trans. Linnean Soc., Zool.* Feb. 369 The size of the hippocampal formation does not seem to vary directly..with the degree of osmatism.

Osmium. Add: Also *attrib.*
1907 *Westm. Gaz.* 16 Feb. 14/2 The osmium lamp..was expensive to start with, and could be used only in the pendent position.

Osmogene. (Example.)
1883 R. Haldane *Workshop Receipts* Ser. II. 315/1 Submitting the liquid..to the process of osmosis in an apparatus known as the 'osmogene'.

Osmotic, *a.* Add: In recent use, esp. *osmotic pressure.*
1891 M. M. Pattison Muir tr. *Ostwald's Solutions* 99 This solution produced an osmotic pressure of more than three atmospheres. 1902 *Encycl. Brit.* XXVI. 739/1 If osmotic pressure could be easily measured, a simple method of determining the molecular weight of dissolved substances would be to determine the osmotic pressures they develop. 1906 *Phil. Trans.* A. CCVI. 481 On the Osmotic Pressures of some Concentrated Aqueous Solutions.

Osnaburg. (Later example.)
1918 Hergesheimer *Three Black Pennys* 38 Tobacco and shoes, ozenbrigs and molasses and rum.
b. *attrib.* chiefly in sense 'made of osnaburg'.
1681 *New Castle Court Rec.* 493 Two Remnants of Osnabriggs Linnen. 1758 *Essex Inst. Hist. Coll.* XII. 145 Others very much soaked in their Osombrige Tents. 1772 *Carroll Papers* in *Maryland Hist. Mag.* XIV. 151 Mrs. Darnalls had an Osnabrigs Petticoat stolen from them. 1774 *Maryland Hist. Mag.* VI. 41 John Johnson..had on..a pair of leather breeches and osnabrig trousers. 1824 J. Taylor *Arator* 123 A regular supply of a winter's coat, two oznaburg shirts, a good hat and blanket. 1835 J. H. Ingraham *South-West* I. App. 274 It is put in a wooden frame, with a loose Osnaburg cloth between it and the frame. 1841 *Southern Lit. Messenger* VII. 775/2 Our slaves in the South-West are annually supplied with two cotton Oznaburg shirts. 1863 'E. Kirke' *My Southern Friends* vii. 99 The thin Osnaburg gown.

Osone (ǫ·sǝun). *Chem.* [Named by E. Fischer (1889), f. -ose² + -one, or the common termination of the substances *fructosone*, *Glucosone, etc.] Any of a class of compounds derived from the osazones by digesting these with concentrated hydrochloric acid and so separating the phenylhydrazine; a keto-aldehyde.
1892 E. F. Smith tr. *Richter's Org. Chem.* 501 The osones dissolve readily in water, and have not been obtained free. 1905 C. E. Simon *Physiol. Chem.* 67 On decomposition with fuming hydrochloric acid the osazons then give rise to the formation of *osons*.

Ossicule·ctomy. *Surg.* [f. Ossicul-um + Gr. ἐκτομή excision.] (A surgical operation for) the removal of the small bones of the ear.
1900 *Lancet* 10 Mar. 702/2 An uncomplicated otorrhoea which has resisted all forms of treatment for six months is certainly a case for ossiculectomy. 1908 *Practitioner* Apr. 525 In his experience..the benefit from ossiculectomy had not been permanent.

Ossicusp (ǫ·sikʌsp). [f. L. *ossi-*, *os* bone + *cuspis* point, Cusp.] A bony horn-like appendage on the forehead of the giraffe and okapi.
1902 *Science* 7 Nov. 752/1 [The okapia] is closely related to *Samotherium*, especially in the presence of these suprafrontal ossicusps (conical bony horns). 1907 *Times* 7 Feb. 4/6 The parietal origin of the ossicusps in the former [the giraffe] and their frontal origin in the latter [the okapi].

Ostatki (ǫstæ·tki). Variant of *Astatki.
1913 V. B. Lewes *Oil Fuel* 71 The oil remaining in the retort, called 'Ostatki' in the Russian distilleries and 'Residuum' in America, is used for fuel.

Osteoderm (ǫ·stiodǝ̄ɹm). [f. Osteo- + Dermis.] An inner skin or dermis which has become ossified; a dermal plate of bone.
1898 Gadow *Classif. Vertebrata* 27 *Pygopodidæ.* Pleurodont...Body scaly without osteoderms. 1902 *Proc. Zool. Soc.* I. 208 Exquisite examples of true dermal bones are those ossifications 'within the skin' which in Amphibia and Reptiles are now generally called osteoderms.

Ostial (ǫ·stiăl), *a.* *Anat.* [f. Osti-um + -al.] Of, pertaining to, or having, an ostium or ostia.
1900 Miall & Hammond *Harlequin Fly* 76 All the valves found in the heart of any Chironomus, whether cellular, ostial, or aortic, appear to be derived from the semicircular muscle-cells. 1910 *Practitioner* Jan. 51 The ostial end of the tube dilates to allow of the passage of the mole.

Ostiate (ǫ·sti,e¹t), *a.* [f. Osti-um + -ate².] Provided with ostia.
1897 E. R. Lankester in *Nat. Sci.* Apr. 266 The parapodial jaws and the ostiate heart cannot be supposed to have been *both* developed independently in each group of arthropods.

Ostrakon (ǫ·străkǫn). Also ostracon. Plur. ostraka, -ca. [ad. Gr. ὄστρακον potsherd.] A sherd of pottery or (more rarely) limestone used to receive an inscription or as a common writing material. Used (often in plur.) *esp.* of archaeological finds in Egypt.
1883 *Proc. Soc. Bibl. Archæol.* 6 Mar. V. 84 The British Museum has lately acquired..a considerable number of ostraka or potsherds discovered at Elephantine, Thebes, and other places. *Ibid.* 1 May 119 Two ostraka or slices of limestone formed for the purpose, inscribed with hieratic inscriptions. 1884 *Ibid.* 4 Nov. VI. 16 This ostrakon is a very interesting one. 1900 *Athenæum* 23 June 783/1 The study of Greek ostraca is a comparatively new one. 1921 G. A. F. Knight *Nile & Jordan* 251 The name Bata has been recovered in a hieratic ostrakon. 1930 J. G. Tait (*title*) Greek Ostraca in the Bodleian Library at Oxford and various other collections.

Ostrogoth. Add: **c.** as *adj.* = Ostrogothic.
1920 H. G. Wells *Outl. Hist.* 350/1 The adventurous wanderings that ended at last in the Ostrogoth Kingdom in Italy.

Otectomy (ǫute·ktŏmi). *Surg.* [f. Gr. ὠτ-, οὖς ear + ἐκτομή excision.] = *Ossiculectomy.
1908 *Practitioner* Apr. 528 The performance of otectomy through a post-aural incision has been recommended.

Other. **A.** *adj.* **2.** Add: *The other thing* (colloq.), the contrary, opposite, or reverse.
1929 J. Van Druten *Young Woodley* xii. 241 'You don't believe me?' 'I do not.'..'Then you must do the other thing.'
D. *Comb.* Add: *other-centred* (centred in others), *-mindedness.*
1925 *Inner Life* Ser. II. 219 Love of the large room is characteristic of souls that are other-centred. 1926 *Public Opinion* 30 Apr. 436/3 The habit of..other-mindedness.

Otherist (ʌ·ðǝrist). [f. as Otherism + -ist.] Altruist.
1904 J. Wells *Life James H. Wilson* 400 He was really an *altruist* or other-ist.

O·thertime, *adv.* [Cf. Other-times.] At another time.
1891–2 *Smithsonian Inst., 13th Rep. Bur. Ethnol.* p. lv, The symbolism elsewhere or othertime connected with such ceremonials persisted.

Otherwise. **A.** Add: **c.** After a noun, adjective, or adverb, followed by *or*: equivalent to a noun, adjective, or adverb having an opposite or different meaning.
1895 *Pall Mall Mag.* Jan. 35 The most amusing feature of the case was the conflict of professional evidence as to the merits, or otherwise, of Mr. Whistler's paintings. 1910 *Practitioner* Jan. 84 The question of operability or otherwise is a matter in which surgeons differ considerably.

Otiant, *a.* Add: **b.** *Philol.* Quiescent.
1905 W. H. Cobb *Crit. Syst. Hebr. Metre* 54 Why are most final letters and aleph otiant written without sh'va?

Otosclerosis (ǫutǫsklīǝrōu·sis). *Path.* [f. Oto- + Sclerosis.] A disease characterized by the formation of spongy bone in the bony capsule of the inner ear which impedes the movement of the stapes and causes deafness. So **Otosclero·tic** *a.*, affected by otosclerosis.
1908 *Practitioner* Jan. 115 It is questionable whether pure otosclerosis is really a disease...Otosclerosis is characterised by an insidious progressive deafness. 1912 *Lancet* 9 Nov. 1303/2 As illustrating heredity in otosclerosis, Dr. Gray showed genealogical trees of a number of families many members of which were otosclerotic.

Otter, *sb.* Add: **4. c.** A type of paravane, used esp. by merchant vessels.
[1910 *Blackw. Mag.* June 899/1 We might adapt to naval use those poaching expedients, the 'cross-line' and the 'otter'.] 1919 *Rep. Brit. Assoc.* 273 The Protector Paravanes, or Otters, carry a form of cutter, but no explosive charge whatever. 1920 *Glasgow Herald* 29 July 4 The development of our anti-submarine operations is described..particulars being given of howitzers, smoke apparatus, depth charges,..otters and paravanes.
7. *otter-skin* (later examples); **otter-board,** a fishing-tackle consisting of a board with several hooks attached; **otter-man,** a fisher who uses an otter-line or otter-board; **otter-sheep,** a breed of sheep; **otter-trawl** (example).
1901 *Field* 5 Jan. 19/2 The *otter-board was only employed..upon those lakes where the trout were indifferent to the angler's flies. *Ibid.*, The *otterman must chuckle inwardly when he sees a perspiring and jaded angler..with one or two fish in his basket. 1863 H. S. Randall *Pract. Shepherd* v. 42 A family of them, the *Otter Sheep, so termed from their short, crooked, rickety legs. 1827 in T. L. McKenney *Mem.* (1846) I. 110 His pouch..was a handsomely ornamented *otter-skin that hung on his left side. 1848 Parkman *Oregon Trail* x. 144 The dandy carried a bow and arrows in an otter-skin quiver at his back. 1899 W. C. McIntosh *Resources of Sea* 93 The new *otter-trawls capture more round than flat fishes.

O·ttered, *ppl. a.* [f. Otter *v.* + -ed¹.] That has been fished with otter tackle. So **O·tterer; O·ttering** *vbl. sb.*
1901 *Field* 5 Jan. 19/2 An observant gamekeeper..tells me that he knows well the signs of an ottered lake. *Ibid.* 19/3 Very gradually, may be, the otterers will learn that they are ruining many fine waters by their malpractices. 1907 *Westm. Gaz.* 24 Jan. 2/1 Trout..obtained by the unsportsmanlike method of netting or 'ottering'.

Otto¹. (Later example.)
1908 *Westm. Gaz.* 30 Mar. 10/3 As a scent otto of violets has become increasingly popular each year.

Ottomanism (ǫ·tǒmăniz'm). [f. Ottoman¹ + -ism.] One of the qualities or characteristics (or all these taken collectively) which distinguish the Turks, *esp.* from European races; the promotion of Ottoman interests. So **O·ttomaniza·tion,** a rendering Ottoman or Turkish in character; **O·ttomanizing** *ppl. a.*
1911 *Q. Rev.* July 261 On behalf of an Ottomanism honestly applied to all the Ottoman nationalities. 1912 *Chambers's Jrnl.* Dec. 817/2 If the Young Turks..had tried fraternisation instead of persisting in Ottomanisation, Turkey's credit would have risen immediately. 1920 *Glasgow Herald* 15 July 4 His liberalism earned him the utter hatred of the ottomanising Committee of Union and Progress. 1920 *Contemp. Rev.* Aug. 210 The Young Turks started upon his foolish policy of forcible Ottomanisation.

Oubliable (ū·bliăb'l), *a.* [f. F. *oublier* to forget + -able.] Forgettable; deserving to be forgotten.
1903 Henley *Ess. Fielding* Wks. 1908 III. 36 Fielding's *Theatre*..is none the less essentially oubliable.

Ouch, *int.*¹ (Earlier and later examples.)
1837 J. C. Neal *Charcoal Sk.* 38 'Ouch!' shrieked Dabbs, 'my eye, how it hurts'. 1843 R. Carlton *New Purchase* ii. 9 The tiers becoming all vocal with 'bless my soul's'—'my goodness!'—and vulgar 'ouches!' 1898 Marg. Deland *Old Chester Tales* 205 Katy..stepped into the shallow trench and lay down. 'Ouch—ain't it cold!' she said. 1921 R. D. Paine *Comr. Rolling Ocean* v. 82 Judson heard a grunt of 'Ouch! That's my nose you're pushing against'.

Ought, *sb.*² (Add example of *pl.*)
1908 Bennett *Human Machine* 43 You have a special apparatus within you for dealing with a universe where *oughts* are flagrantly disregarded.

Ouidaesque (wīdā,e·sk), *a.* [f. *Ouida*, the nom-de-plume of the novelist Louise de la Ramée (1839–1908) + -esque.] Characteristic or suggestive of the novels of 'Ouida'; marked by extravagance or lack of restraint.
1909 *Westm. Gaz.* 6 Apr. 4/2 It is the case of the 'Ouidaesque' young man with the big cigar of the motor shows over again. 1914 W. J. Locke *Jaffery* xxi, Like the Ouidaesque hero, who could ride a Derby winner with one hand and stroke a University crew to victory with the other. 1929 *Sunday Express* 20 Jan. 9 The 'dark Odyssey of Gilbert Stroud' is almost Ouidaesque.

Ouija (wī·dʒa). [f. F. *oui* yes + G. *ja* yes.] A board having the letters of the alphabet and other signs used in connexion with a planchette for obtaining messages and answers in spiritualistic séances. Also *ouija-board.*
1904 *Pop. Sci. Monthly* Jan. 195 The various alphabet-using forms of amateur mediumship, such as table tipping, the 'Ouija-board', and certain other devices for making our muscles leaky. 1909 Carrington *Physical Phenom. Spiritualism* 67 The phenomena of table-tipping, of ouija and planchette writing. 1911 W. James *Mem. & Stud.* viii. 189 Most of us reveal such a tendency whenever we handle a ouija-board. 1922 Sir O. Lodge *Raymond Revised* 45 By the use of instruments known as 'planchette' and 'ouija', often employed by beginners. 1928 *Daily Express* 7 Nov. 20 She used a cardboard ouija which she made herself.

Ouranian (auǝrǟ·niăn), *a.* [f. Gr. οὐράνι-ος heavenly + -an.] Of or pertaining to heaven or the upper regions. (Cf. Uranian *a.*¹)
1908 G. G. A. Murray in Marett *Anthropol. & Classics* 68 A great proportion of our anthropological material is already to be found in prehistoric Crete..the stones, the beasts, the pillars, and the ouranian birds.

Out, *adv.* Add: **1. i.** *To go out*: To play the first nine holes in a golf-course (*in* so many strokes).
1909 *Daily Chron.* 7 May 8/4 Out in 36, he came home in a good 37, and made certain of a place.
3. c. *From this out*, henceforth. *U.S.*
1905 Henriette Corkran *Lucie & I* 36 From this out I will think of you as a young *diablesse*.
13. b. (Later example.)
1924 Galsworthy *Forest* I. i. 11 Out with it, Mr. Farrell.
15. b. (Further examples; see also *Night 5.) (*School*) *is out*: has been dismissed.
1849 Mrs. Stowe *Mayflower* 94 But, when 'school was out', James's spirits foamed over as naturally as a tumbler of soda-water. 1916 'Berta Ruck' *Girls at his Billet* x, Wasn't it your evening out? Didn't I see you? 1925 Wodehouse *Carry on, Jeeves* v. 108, I have already visited some of New York's places of interest on my evening out.
i. Phr. *To be out for* (something): To have all one's attention, energies, etc., directed towards securing, effecting, upholding, or doing (something). Similarly, *to be out to* (do something). Orig. *U.S.* Cf. *All-out.
1889 *Kansas City T. & Star* 1 Apr., The Kansas City Art Association..is out this week for more members. 1901 S. Merwin & Webster *Calumet K* i. 13 They're mostly out for results up at the office. Let's see the bill for it. 1905 *Springfield Weekly Republ.* 6 Oct. 12 George D. Eldredge is out strong for Mr. Nutting. 1913 H. Walpole *Fortitude* III. x. 344 She's out for happiness at any cost and you're out for freedom. 1920 W. J. Locke *House of Baltazar* v. 56 These new women are out for the devirilisation of man.
1901 S. E. White *Westerners* xxix. 272 When they are out to have a good time..they want somebody they can have their sort of fun with. 1912 in *N. & Q.* Ser. XI. VI. 409/2 He was manifestly out to do his competitor harm. 1913 H. Walpole *Fortitude* IV. iii. 418 He was 'out' to defend his whole life. 1922 Mrs. Sidgwick *Victorian* xxviii. 211 He told me..that he was out to shoot capitalists.
19. c. (Earlier example.) Frequently after *not.* Cf. *Not-out.
1609 Armin *Two Maids of More-clacke* D 2 b, *Tutch.* What doe you call it when the ball sir bits the stoole? *Filbon.* Why out. 1746 in 'Bat' *Cricket Man.* (1850) 80 Newland..18—not out. 1881 *Sportsman's Year-Bk.* 137 He..has been in 36 times, and 'not out' four times.
e. In pugilistic use: Defeated through failing to rise within the ten seconds allowed after being knocked down. Also *transf.*
1901 R. Fitzsimmons *Phys. Cult. & Self-Defense* 159 Time was up. The champion was out. 1918 *War Birds* (1927) 150 She responded..by hitting him playfully over the head with an empty port bottle...It was a terrific crack and he was out for some time.
26. (Further example.)
1922 *N. & Q.* Ser. XII. XI. 206/2 A horse is said to be 'out' when it is known he is 'on the job'.

27. Also Put *out.*

Out, *sb.* Add: **1.** *Three-* (or *four-*)*out*: a glass holding a third (or fourth) of some measure of liquor.
1835 Dickens *Sk. Boz, Seven Dials*, A couple of ladies,..having imbibed the contents of various 'three-outs' of gin and bitters [etc.].
3. d. Phr. *At* (also *on the*) *outs*: At variance or enmity.
1901 S. Merwin & Webster *Calumet K* xiii. 251 He was still in the mistake of supposing that Peterson and the boss were at outs. 1904 *N. Y. Sun* 24 Aug. 3 She was at outs with her parents because of her marriage, so she went to live with her aunt. *a* 1909 'O. Henry' *Roads of Destiny* vii. 116 One could not remain long at outs with Bad-Luck Kearny. 1922 Zane Grey *To Last Man* i. 22, I reckoned you belonged to the sheep raisers who're on the outs with my father. 1923 Ld. Charnwood *Roosevelt* v. 89 The strong and upright President Cleveland had ended at outs with his party.
4. d. Permission to go out. *U.S.*
1845 S. Judd *Margaret* II. i. 198 She..gave them [*sc.* pupils] their outs.
e. *To make a poor out*: to have little success.
1904 Harben *Georgians* xix. 176 Warren got down on his knees then and actually tried to pray; but he made a pore out.
5. b. *transf.* Something amiss.
1893 K. Sanborn *S. California* 69 Are there no 'outs', no defects in this Pasadena?
7. A way out; a defence, subterfuge or excuse.
1845 M. M. Noah *Gleanings* 148 He slipped the fatal jack of diamonds from the bottom of the pack, and claimed the money then in stake...I at first thought him in jest, and laughed at him for making so bungling an out. 1853 J. G. Baldwin *Flush Times Alabama* 31, I might have made a pretty good *out* of it, if I had thrown myself upon the merits of my case. 1926 J. Black *You Can't Win* vi. 69 If a copper grabs you, you've got an out. You ain't exactly beggin'.

Out, *v.* Add: **1.** (Recent examples.)
a. 1927 Vachell *Dew of the Sea* etc. 269 I'll out 'em both, even if it breaks the contract.
b. 1899 *Daily News* 30 Jan. 6/4 The water flooded high the stoke-holes, outing the fires.
c. 1915 Corri *30 Yrs. Boxing Referee* 221 Lewis..promptly hit him a terrific punch on the point. 'Outed' by bluff!
d. In cricket: To put or declare (a batsman) out.
1899 *Captain* I. 517/1 Never forget that there are other ways of outing a man besides clean bowling him. 1906 *Daily Tel.* 23 Aug. 9/7 Myers went in, but was almost immediately 'outed' under singular circumstances.
e. In lawn-tennis: To send (the ball) outside the court.
1927 *Daily Express* 22 June 2/2 Raymond, striving for extra speed, netted and outed a succession of returns.
f. In passive: (of a woman) to be dishonoured.
1922 Galsworthy *Windows* II. 71 I'll bet you've never realized the life girls who get outed lead.
4. c. Of information, news, etc.: To become known.
1905 Eden Phillpotts *Secret Woman* I. ix. 85 Yet it outed as she'd said 'no' to him.

Out-. Add: **1.** *out-school.*
1927 *Scots Observer* 8 Oct. 11/4 Back this summer from six months in the district in charge of *out-schools.
2. *out-nurse, -porter.*
1909 *Englishwoman* Apr. 269 If she has a baby, it has to be dragged from bed and carried to some *out-nurse. 1902 *Chambers's Jrnl.* Nov. 717/2 'Boots' will select for him that *out-porter who will most briskly wheel his colossal pile of cases. 1927 *Daily Express* 14 July 9/2 Both men were out-porters at Snow Hill Railway Station.
6. *out-path* (earlier and later examples).
1573 T. C[artwright] *Reply Answ. Whitgift* 27 It is our partes to walke in the broade and beaten way, as it were the common caussie of the commaundement, rather then an outpathe of the example. 1897 G. MacDonald *Rampolli* 64 Could I but the outpath follow—Ah, how were my spirit blest!
21. *out-feature.*
1929 Bridges *Test. Beauty* I. 714 True beauty of manhood outfeatureth childish charm.

Out-act, *v.* (Recent example.)
1906 *Westm. Gaz.* 2 June 6/3 The best of Hamlets [is sometimes] outacted by the worst of gravediggers.

Outage (au·tédʒ). [f. Out *adv.* + -age.] The amount or proportion of (electric) lamps or bulbs that go out or cease to supply light.
1903 *Elect. World & Engin.* 18 Apr. 653 (Cent. Suppl.) The lamp hours were 54,187; percentage of lamp outage, 6–10; globes broken, 23.

Ou·tback, *adv.*, *a.* and *sb.* *Austral.* Also out-back. [f. Out *adv.* + Back *adv.*] **a.** *adv.* (see Dict.). **b.** *adj.* Of or pertaining to the Australian back-country. **c.** *sb.* The remote districts or back settlements; the back-country.
a. [1890 in Dict.] 1909 G. H. Frodsham (*title*) The Church Outback. 1919 W. K. Harris *Outback in Australia* (ed. 3) 1 To understand properly what is meant by real hospitality, the traveller must leave the cities and go Outback.
b. 1900 H. Lawson *Over Sliprails* 57 'The Queenslan' rains'..seem to be held responsible..for most of the out-back trouble. 1909 Davis *New Selection* xiv. 135 He'd had enough out-back life..and intended settling down. 1919 W. K. Harris *Outback in Australia* (ed. 3) 2 Of course, you get various opinions of Outback hospitality.
c. 1907 *Gentl. Mag.* July 78 These young dwellers in the Out Back have often no educational opportunities. 1919 W. K. Harris *Outback in Australia* (ed. 3) 1 There is no limit to the hospitality of the far Outback. 1920 B. Cronin *Timber Wolves* 40 Such men are not uncommon in the outback. 1924 A. J. Small *Frozen Gold* i. 25 Here was a man fresh in from the silent brooding whiteness of the great Outback.
Hence **Ou·tbacker.** A dweller or settler in the outback.
1919 W. K. Harris *Outback in Australia* (ed. 3) 3 Another feature in the character of the Outbacker and the Bush-dweller generally..is his honesty. 1927 *Blackw. Mag.* Oct. 461/2 We..lay down..beneath a grove of giant Tasmanian tree-ferns,..the 'old man' fern of outbackers.

Out-blo·ssoming, *vbl. sb.* [Out- 9.] A blossoming out or forth; often *fig.*
1907 *Daily Chron.* 31 July 4/4 'Sunday out' has become a well-nigh universal out-blossoming. 1924 W. B. Selbie *Psychol. Relig.* 178 The religious awakening of adolescence..is..generally an outblossoming of the whole nature into a larger and more wonderful world.

Ou·tblowing, *vbl. sb.* [Out- 9.] A blowing out or outwards. So **Ou·tblowing** *ppl. a.* That blows out.
1909 *Daily Chron.* 31 May 4/4 An intaking and outblowing of the breath between the teeth. 1928 Peake & Fleure *Steppe & Sown* 14 The borders..had acquired their characteristic loess soil..through the outblowing of the winds from the ice sheets over the loose detritus. 1900 *Geog. Jrnl.* XVI. 406 Blowing towards and in upon the polar regions to make good the drain caused by the surface outblowing south-easterly winds.

Out-board. **A.** *adj.* Add: **2.** Of a motor-boat: Having the whole of the engine and driving apparatus attached outside the boat, at the stern. Also of an engine so attached. Hence *outboard motor-boating, -motored, -motorist.*
1928 *Daily Express* 21 Apr. 10/3 The racing 'outboard' boat has given us a fascinating pastime. 1928 *Daily Tel.* 10 July 17/5 Miss Joan Spicer..is one of the best-known of 'outboard-motoristes'. 1928 *Daily Mail* 25 July 17/4 The new pastime of outboard motor-boating. 1929 *Encycl. Brit.* XV. 879/2 As speeds of over 30 m.p.h. can be attained with such craft equipped with outboard motors rated at 8 h.p., outboard motor-boat racing has become extremely popular.

Ou·tboarding, *vbl. sb.* [f. prec. + -ing¹.] Outboard motor-boating.
1928 *Daily Express* 5 Mar. 2/2 A sport comparatively new to the Thames—'outboarding' on fast, flat-bottomed motor-boats, which skim through the water with bows in the air.

Outbreak, *v.* Add: **c.** To break into utterance.
1871 Browning *Balaustion* (1881) 14 They all outbroke In a great joyous laughter with much love.

Outbreathed, *ppl. a.*¹ (Later example.)
1914 R. M. Jones *Spiritual Reformers of 16th & 17th C.* 177 This entire manifested or out-breathed universe is, he says, the expression of the divine desire for holy sport and play.

Outbred, *ppl. a.* [Out- 11.] Bred from parents that are not closely related.
1903 *Biometrika* Feb. 171 Waltzing mice must be crossed with in-bred and out-bred pure-bred albinos and in-bred and out-bred cross-bred albinos.

Outbreeding, *vbl. sb.* [Out- 10.] Breeding from parents that are not closely related.
1902 *Encycl. Brit.* XXV. 372/2 Since the tribes practised far more in-breeding than out-breeding, the tendency was toward forming not only verbal linguistic groups, but biological varieties. 1923 *Glasgow Herald* 25 Jan. 10 In-breeding and Out-breeding.

Out-burn, *v.* **2.** Also, to overcome by burning.
1872 A. C. Steele *Broken Toys* xxviii. II. 206 The flame in her heart would have outburnt the morning fog and wet wind.

Outcast, *sb.*¹ Add: **6.** The increase in the volume of grain due to malting.
1876 *Encycl. Brit.* IV. 269/2 The increase by measure of malt over dry barley, called the 'outcast', is from 3 to 8 per cent.
7. Matter ejected, or cast up to the surface.
1903 *Astrophys. Jrnl.* Sept. 158 (Cent. Suppl.) Miss Clarke's division of the solar outcasts into 'several distinct envelopes'..is somewhat too definite.

Outcaste, *v.* Add: Also *reflex.*
1915 Kipling *New Army in Training* 64 What will be the position..of the young man who has deliberately elected to outcaste himself from this all-embracing brotherhood?

Outclass, *v.* Add: Also *transf.*
1909 *Chambers's Jrnl.* Jan. 61/1 In the process of production..the Americans soon found themselves outclassed. *Ibid.* Sept. 624/1 This results more from outclassing in guns, armour, and machinery than from decay of the metal hulls.

Outcrier. **a.** (Recent example.)
1931 *Tablet* 23 May 673/1 Once more the outcriers have cried out before they are hurt.

Ou·tcropper. [f. Outcrop *sb.* + -er¹.] One who takes coal from an outcropping seam or vein.
1926 *Glasgow Herald* 7 Oct. 8/3 The outcroppers are doing good business for themselves.

Ou·tcross, *v.* [f. the sb.] *trans.* To cross with an unrelated breed or race.
1931 E. B. Ford *Mendelism & Evolution* II. ii. 40 If the now highly inbred stock be outcrossed to ordinary wild-type flies [etc.].

Outcry, *v.* **1. a.** (Modern example.)
1849 Thackeray *Pendennis* xxi, She at once took side with Helen against Doctor Portman, when he outcried at the enormity of Pen's transgressions.

Out-curl. *Curling.* [Out- 7.] = *Out-turn.
1903 *Westm. Gaz.* 31 Jan. 3/1 The secret of the game is to be able to play the 'out-curl or in-curl' as the skip may direct.

Ou·tcurve. [Out- 7.] **1.** A convex curve or prominence.
1902 *Encycl. Brit.* XXVIII. 622/2 It is convenient to employ a specific name for a projection of a coast-line less pronounced than a peninsula, and for an inlet less pronounced than a bay or bight; outcurve and incurve may serve the turn. 1912 Galsworthy *Inn Tranq.* 68 The sharp outcurve of his dark head.
2. *Baseball.* A ball pitched so as to curve away from the batsman; the course of such a ball.
1897 [see *Inshoot]. 1904 R. H. Barbour *School & College Games* 197 There are several curves recognized, such as the out curve, the in curve and the drop curve.

Outdated, *ppl. a.* (Modern examples.)
1909 Belloc *Marie Antoinette* vi. 106 In his outworn, out-dated ambition. 1915 *Literary Digest* (N. Y.) 21 Aug. 370/1 Out-dated principles of motor construction.

Outdoors, *adv.* (Earlier examples.)
1817 S. R. Brown *Western Gaz.* 113 The chimney is sure to be placed out doors. 1832 Paulding *Westward Ho!* I. 92 Can you cut down a tree as big round as all out doors in less time than you can look at it?

Ou·tdrawn, *ppl. a.* [Out- 11.] Drawn out.
1905 E. F. Benson *Image in Sand* i. 8 Bank after bank of out-drawn stops and keyboard coupled to keyboard makes the air thick with tumultuous melody.

Outdrive, *v.* Add: **2. b.** *Golf.* To drive farther than; to overdrive.
1906 *Daily Chron.* 22 May 9/4 MacFarlane, after being outdriven from the tee, played a perfect approach to within a yard of the hole. 1927 *Daily Express* 30 Nov. 3/1, I disliked amazingly to be outdriven.

Outer, *a.* Add: **1. b.** *Printing.* Designating the form containing the side of the sheet which includes the first page.
1808–1892 [see *Inner *a.* 1 e].
B. as *sb.* Add: **b.** *Electr.* In a direct current distribution system, a conductor whose potential is above or below that of the earth.
1900 *Jrnl. Inst. Electr. Engin.* XXIX. 538 Each of these boards receives from the main generator board..a pair of 'outers' for lighting. 1910 *Installation News* IV. 62/1 A leakage on to the conduit on one of the outers of a three-wire system.

Outering, *vbl. sb.* [f. Outer *a.* and *v.* + -ing.] A making outer or external.
1920 A. S. Pringle-Pattison *Idea of God* 193 Sometimes the process is described as a self-externalization or outering of itself on the part of the subject.

Out-fighting, *vbl. sb.* [Out- 2.] Fighting not at close quarters.
1848 *Sporting Life* 5 Feb. 297/2 At out-fighting, Bateman was decidedly the quickest and the best. 1905 *Times* 6 Mar. 4/2 It is probable that this outfighting, before the adversaries close, will be fruitful in important lessons relating to the art of naval war.

Outfit, *sb.* Add: **1.** (Further example.)
1882 *Harper's Mag.* Jan. 169/2 Such a boat costs $65,000, and of this, $10,000 represents 'outfit'.
3. (Earlier examples.) Also, a set of things for any purpose, or a person along with his conveyance, his tools, or the like.
1869 S. Bowles *Our New West* viii. 163 With a mounted escort of about twenty gallant young miners..we made up a grand 'outfit'. 1872 E. B. Tuttle *Boy's Bk. Indians* (1882) 45 Friday had a beautiful set of arrows, bow and quiver, which I desired to purchase...Friday would not sell his 'outfit', as it is called, for money. 1881 *N. Y. Times* 18 Dec. in *N. & Q.* Ser. VI. V. 65/1 *Outfit*, a comprehensive term, variously applied. An expedition of every sort, large or small, is an 'outfit'. So also a haying or a lumbering party, &c. Likewise a person in a buggy, or one pushing a wheelbarrow. Indifferently applied to a party as a whole, or to its means of travel, its subsistence, &c.

Outfit, *v.* Also simply, to provide or supply (a person) *with.*
1924 W. M. Raine *Troubled Waters* xvi. 167, I outfitted some of the boys with guns, you say.
b. (Earlier and later examples.) Also, to secure an outfit or equipment.
1881 *N. Y. Times* 18 Dec. in *N. & Q.* Ser. VI. V. 65/2 To 'outfit' is to fit out for any purpose whatever. 'We outfitted at St. Paul.' 1902 H. L. Wilson *Spenders* xi. 117 The time before I made the strike I outfitted in Grand Bar. 1902 S. E. White *Blazed Trail* xxv. 168 It's a good place to outfit from because we can probably get freight rates direct by boat. 1924 Mulford *Rustlers' Valley* x. 115 Yestiddy was pay-day, an' if they don't outfit now, some of 'em won't have no money after to-night.

Outfitting, *vbl. sb.* (Example.)
1908 *Westm. Gaz.* 24 Apr. 7/4 Until the cold weather and overcoats finally disappear there will be no improvement in outfitting.

Outfla·nker. [-er¹.] One who outflanks.
1920 *Q. Rev.* Jan. 107 As fast as Joffre created a new Army to prolong his left..so fast did the Germans cover their threatened right and seek to outflank their would-be outflankers.

Outflash, *v.* **a.** (Earlier example.)
1832 Browning *Pauline* 841 Do I not..burn to see Thy calm pure truths out-flash The brightest gleams of earth's philosophy.

Ou·tfought, *ppl. a.* [f. Outfight *v.*] Overcome, vanquished.
1892 Stevenson & Osborne *Wrecker* xii, Our out-fought enemy [*sc.* a squall] only a blot upon the leeward sea.

Outgeneral, *v.* Add: Also *transf.*
1910 Driscoll *Ringcraft* 14 He was the better boxer and the stronger man, but was outgeneralled during two-thirds of the bout.

Outgo, *sb.* **2.** Also, a going out or departure.
1930 F. A. Pottle *Stretchers* 15 The outgo was set for Saturday, December 29.

4. (Earlier example.)
1869 S. Bowles *Our New West* i. 26 The great Salt Lake of Utah..has no visible outgo, though richly fed from various quarters.

Outgo, *v.* **1.** (Modern example.)
1905 R. Rodd in *Outlook* 4 Nov. 629/1 So you, dear Frank, were last of those To whom a tender thought outgoes.

Out-grow, *v.* **1.** Add: Also *refl.*
1878 Hardy *Ret. Native* I. iii. (1890) 25 For fear he should outgrow himself and go for a soldier.

Outing, *vbl. sb.* Add: **3.** (Example in pl. form.)
1856 A. M. Lang *MS. Diary* 29 Feb., I only bowled 4 wickets in one outings and got 20 in 2 innings.
4. Also *fig.*
1899 Cutcliffe Hyne *Further Adv. Capt. Kettle* xii. 310 Captain Owen Kettle's week's outing in the daily papers ran its course with due thrills and headlines.

Outlaugh, *v.* **2.** (Modern example.)
1908 Swinburne *Duke of Gandia* i. 32 Her..Whose eyes outlaugh the splendour of the sea.

Outlaw, *sb.* **3.** (Add example.)
1903 *Wide World Mag.* Mar. 546/2 The whole Western country was scoured for the wildest and most vicious 'outlaw' bronchos that could be found.

Outlawed, *ppl. a.* Add: **b.** That has been allowed to run wild.
1907 Mulford *Bar-20* xx. 197 Yu has got about as much show catchin' one of them as a tenderfoot has of bustin' an outlawed cayuse.

Outlet, *sb.* **1.** Also, a market (for goods).
1919 *Brit. Manufacturer* Nov. 28/1 India..is the most important outlet for Lancashire goods.

Outlier. Add: **2. c.** (Further examples.) Also *attrib.*
1885 Burton *Arab. Nts.* (1887) III. 267 They took leave of him and departing to the outliers of the City, flew..to their several abodes. 1928 *Library Assoc. Rec.* Dec. 244 Were the Central Library to recruit the majority of public libraries as outliers, we should still be faced with the fact that there was only one channel of supply. *Ibid.*, The Central Library has wisely recruited several of the larger public libraries..to act as outlier libraries.

Outlive, *v.* Add: **3. b.** To survive *into.*
1902 J. S. Phillimore *Sophocles* Introd. p. xxviii, The new times into which he has outlived.

Ou·t-lot. *U.S.* [Out- 1.] A lot or piece of ground situated on the outside of a township or other area.
1815 D. Drake *Cincinnati* III. 130 In addition to these original owners, several persons have since divided out-lots, or tracts adjoining to the first town plat. 1837 W. Jenkins *Ohio Gaz.* 148 A tract of land on the east side of the town has like-wise been divided into 23 outlots of five acres each. 1851 C. Cist *Cincinnati* 268 Subdivisions..have been made of farms and out-lots of ground. 1873 E. Eggleston *Myst. Metrop.* xv. 134 Dave distributed freely deeds to some valueless outlots.

Outmode (outmoᵘd), *v.* [Out- 18: cf. F. *démoder.*] *trans.* To put out of fashion. (Chiefly in pa. pple.)
1906 Hichens *Call of Blood* ii. 15 He was not wholly emancipated from la petite femme tradition, which will never be outmoded in Paris. 1908 E. V. Lucas *Over Bemerton's* xiv. 143, I had..an ambition at that time someday to be in Paterson myself, not knowing that the book was already outmoded. 1915 T. Burke *Nights in Town* 392 The poor laddie is sadly outmoded, but he doesn't know it. 1924 H. E. Fosdick *Modern Use of Bible* 95 Many of our ways of thinking..are transient..and will soon be..outmoded.

Outmo·ded, *ppl. a.* [Out- 11: cf. F. *démodé.*] No longer in fashion; out-of-date.
1903 *Academy* 17 Jan. 71/1 Jesse Berridge is a poet, not a poetess, to use a somewhat outmoded word. 1919 S. Huddleston *Peacemaking at Paris* i. 19 To dissipate..the clouds of objections..of prejudices of an outmoded diplomacy. 1926 W. J. Locke *Stories near & far* 133 The joined fragments showed an old photograph of a young man, in out-moded raiment.

Outmost, *a.* **1. c.** (Modern example.)
1887 Morris *Odyss.* x. 553 And but little it lacked of the outmost of the helm it lighted on.

Out of, *prep. phr.* **9.** (Add examples.)
1901 'L. Malet' *Sir R. Calmady* v. x. 469 Obviously it was impossible to go back. He must go on rather—out of sight, out of mind. 1912 F. M. Hueffer *Panel* I. iv. 109 You meant to get her out of your head.
10. d. *Out of it.* (Earlier and later examples.)
1880 *Punch* 25 Dec. 299/1, I was out of it, jolly clean out of it. 1916 Galsworthy *Sheaf* I. § 3. 15 She is simply too 'out of it' to know anything.

Out-of-date. Add: **b.** as *sb.*
1928 *Manch. Guard. Weekly* 17 Aug. 132/1 This column ..is apt to specialise in the out-of-date.

Ou·t-of-da·teness. [f. Out-of-date + -ness.] The state or condition of being out-of-date; obsoleteness.
1915 E. Carpenter *Healing of Nations* xvii. 208 Finally ..one realizes the monstrosity and absurdity of the present conflict—its anachronism and out-of-dateness in the existing age of human thought and feeling.

Out-of-doorness. *nonce-wd.* [-ness.] The state of being out-of-doors.
1929 Deeping *Roper's Row* xxiii, Hazzard liked..the play of the wind through his aggressive hair. It gave him a feeling of out-of-doorness and of freedom.

Out-of-work. [Out of 11 b.] A person who is unemployed.
1928 Galsworthy *White Monkey* I. xii, The out-of-works and the in-works.

Out-pass, *v.* **1.** (Modern example.)
1928 J. B. Mozley tr. *Statius* I. 47 Mayst thou outpass the limits of old Nestor's age.

Out-patient. Add: **b.** *pl.* The out-patient department of a hospital.
1910 *Practitioner* July 87 After death..she was recognised as the woman who had previously attended at out-patients.

Ou·t-peeping, *ppl. a.* [Out- 9.] That peeps out.
1908 A. Austin *Sacr. & Prof. Love*, And on out-peeping roots the sun-god shoots The shafts of his golden quiver.

Out-place. (Modern example.)
1911 *Chambers's Jrnl.* Apr. 221/1 It is this longing..that sends the sportsman into the out-places.

Outplace, *v.* [Out- 18.] *trans.* To displace or oust.
1928 *Daily Express* 16 Jan. 5/3 Skirts dipping at one side will outplace in many houses the skirt dipping at the back that was so popular during the winter.

Outpoint, *v.* Add: **3.** In various sports and games, as coursing, boxing, billiards: To score more points than; to defeat on points.
1903 *Westm. Gaz.* 19 Feb. 7/3 In the second ties, Priestlaw ..was out-pointed cleverly by Handsome Creole. *a* 1909 *Spirit of Times* CXXXVI. 416 (Cent. Suppl.) In the tandem class..[the] black geldings Sampson and Sigsbee outpointed their rivals. 1910 Driscoll *Ringcraft* 13 He was outpointed in the vast majority of rounds. 1923 *Daily Mail* 3 Nov. 11 Inman again outpointed Smith in the 16,000 up billiards match at Thurston's yesterday.

Outpost, *v.* Also, to supply with or as with outposts.
1909 'Q' (Quiller-Couch) *Lady Good-for-Nothing* II. xi, Another farm..outposted with cattle.

Outputter².
For *Mod. Newspr.* read 1902 *Spectator* 22 Nov. 784/1.

Out-rai·l, *v.*² *nonce-wd.* [Out- 21.] *trans.* To surpass in respect of a railing.
1870 Ruskin *Crown of Wild Olive* Pref. § 5 The public-house-keeper on the other side of the way presently buys another railing, to out-rail him with.

Outrange, *v.* **1.** (Add example.)
1930 *Times* 15 Mar. 6/1 At full back, Scotland will have.. R. C. Warren, but he may be outranged by J. C. Hubbard.

Outrank, *v.* (Earlier and later examples.)
1842 *Philad. Spirit of Times* 1 Sept. (Th.) It won't be long before he fills the place of some one of the drones and cakes who now outrank him. 1903 *Westm. Gaz.* 26 Aug. 4/1 Barr did not outrank Wringe here as he had done at the start.

Outreach, *v.*¹ Add: **4. b.** *trans.* To present or give.
1872 [R. W. Buchanan] *Saint Abe & Seven Wives* 149 Unto my Widows I outreach my property completely.

Outreaching, *vbl. sb.* (Modern example.)
1902 A. T. Mahan *Retrospect & Prospect* iv. 111 This outreaching of an imperialistic arm by all the greater nations.. constitutes..the motive to a closer union.

Out-relief. Add: **b.** *concr.* A person receiving out-door relief.
1904 *Westm. Gaz.* 22 Apr. 3/2 Still worse is the case of the aged 'out-relief', with his 3s. a week.

Outride, *sb.* Add: **3.** (See quot.)
c 1883 G. M. Hopkins *Poems* (1918) Pref. 5 Two licences are natural to Sprung Rhythm. The one is rests, as in music...The other is *hangers* or *outrides*, that is one, two, or three slack syllables added to a foot and not counting in the nominal scanning.

Outride, *v.* Add: **2. c.** To ride out of or beyond.
1903 Miss J. Weston (tr.) *Sir Gawain at the Grail Castle* 15 In that one night had he outridden Britain and all that country.
5. *trans.* *U.S.* To keep cattle from going beyond (a tract of land) by riding along the boundaries of it.
1874 J. C. McCoy *Hist. Sk.* 375 He does not herd his cattle but designates certain bounds within which the employees permit the stock to range at will. This manner of holding stock is termed 'out riding' the country.

Outrider. Add: **2. b.** *spec.* A fellow of New College, Oxford, accompanying the Warden on an official visitation of the estates of the college.
1901 Rashdall & Rait *New College, Oxf.* 251 The Warden (or Sub-warden) accompanied by a Fellow known as 'Out-rider'..and the Steward, visit the farms on some part of the College estates.
6. *U.S.* A mounted herdsman who prevents cattle from straying beyond a certain limit.
1907 S. E. White *Arizona Nights* I. vi. 117 We saw..the whole herd and the outriders and the mesas far away.
Hence **Outri·dership.**
1901 Rashdall & Rait *New College, Oxf.* 187 The outridership..was claimed by two Fellows,..who both wanted to accompany the Warden on progress.

Outriding, *ppl. a.* Add: Applied to a syllable in poetry: see *Outride *sb.* 3.
c 1883 G. M. Hopkins *Poems* (1918) Pref. 5 These outriding half feet or hangers.

Outrigger. **5.** (Add example.)
1922 *Encycl. Brit.* XXX. 20/2 In the pusher..the controlling surfaces are carried on an open frame ('outriggers') in front, at the rear, or in both positions.

Outroar, *sb.* (Add example.)
1891 Meredith *One of our Conq.* xvii. (1892) 147 As it were, the towering wood-work of the cathedral organ in quake under the emission of its multitudinous outroar.

Out-room. (Recent U.S. examples.)
1865 Mrs. Whitney *Gayworthys* ii. 21 Gersham..ran up and down the out-room staircase. *Ibid.* 28 As she came into the out-room again. 1929 Shelton *Salt-box House* xii. 88 The floors were..sprinkled with white sea sand, that on the 'out-rooms' being swept lightly in fanciful patterns by brooms.

Outset, *sb.* Add: **6.** An outward-flowing current.
1898 *Geog. Jrnl.* XI. 641 There is an outset from the west bay of Portland of nearly 9 hours' duration.

Ou·tshoot, *sb.* Add: **4.** *Baseball.* = *Outcurve 2.
1903 R. H. Barbour *Weatherby's Inning* 230 Then followed an out-shoot and a drop, neither of which did Joe take to.

Outshot, *sb.* **3. b.** (Example.)
1883 R. Haldane *Workshop Receipts* Ser. II. 389/1 Outshots, [consist of] good, strong, and sound rags.

Outside. **A.** *sb.* Add: **3. b.** *spec.* In Klondike, the rest of the world.
1904 J. Lynch *3 Yrs. Klondike* 54 On September 22 the last boat left for the 'outside' *via* the Lakes and Skagway.
6. b. = Outsider 2.
1899 *Captain* II. 186/1, I headed out to the right, [and] saw our outside get it. 1906 *Field* 13 Oct. 610/1 Their outsides showed so crude a conception of passing that [etc.]. 1927 *Observer* 21 Aug. 18/3 The team are young and play attractive football, with a clever set of outsides who combine well.
B. *adj.* Add: **1. b.** *Outside-left, -right*, that member of a team in Association Football or Hockey who plays on the extreme left, or right, of the forward line.
1890 C. W. Alcock *Football, Assoc. Game* 48 The outside-right should not be more than eight or ten yards beyond him. 1900 *Football Who's Who* 134 Cassidy, Joseph, Manchester City (outside left). 1905 A. Gibson & Pickford *Assoc. Football* I. 161 Every one knows Alec Smith. He's the outside left of the Rangers.
2. b. Also of persons.
1911 *Chambers's Jrnl.* Sept. 591/1 Like all outside men, the stranger had some little skill in such matters.
3. (Further examples.)
1922 *N. & Q.* Ser. XII. XI. 206/2 *Outside*, all other enclosures on a racecourse save Tattersall's, which is 'inside'. 1930 *Times* 27 Mar. 19/6 There was again a demand for 'outside' bills.
b. In Klondike: Belonging to or obtained from another part of the world.
1904 J. Lynch *3 Yrs. Klondike* 141 The leader is always a small 'outside' dog, usually of the Scotch collie breed.
6. *An outside chance*: A very unlikely chance.
1909 *Daily Chron.* 11 Jan. 4/6 The chance that the right marriage of poetry and music should come is an outside one.
C. *adv.* Add: **1. b.** *spec.* In Klondike: Abroad.
1904 J. Lynch *3 Yrs. in Klondike* 227, I had some money besides, so I bought the rest of this dust from him, as I am going 'outside'.

Outsider. **1.** Also *attrib.*
1898 J. McCarthy *Gladstone's Life* xxvii. 295 The outsider class..quarrelled with Mr. Gladstone because he was always giving them a surprise.
2. b. *spec.* The outside-right or outside-left of a football or hockey team.
1904 J. L. Jones *Assoc. Football* 27 The outsider is the man who has to do most of the middling.

Ou·tsize, *sb.* and *a.* [f. Out *a.* + Size *sb.*¹] **a.** *sb.* A person or thing larger than the normal; *esp.*, a ready-made garment larger than the standard sizes. **b.** *adj.* Larger than the average, usual, or stock size.
a. 1883–94 [see Out *a.* 5]. 1907 *Westm. Gaz.* 17 Aug. 10/1 The tendency is to stock more and more of what were formerly regarded as 'out-sizes'. 1924 *Mod. Draper* II. 69 With regard to all ladies' underclothing it is necessary to keep a good assortment of outsizes.
b. 1904 H. G. Wells *Food of Gods* I. ii. § 1. 19 He conceived a picture of coops and runs, outsize and still more outsize coops, and runs progressively larger. 1924 *Mod. Draper* II. 69 Outsize garments are preferred without any very fancy trimmings. 1925 *Chambers's Jrnl.* 166/2 You're an out-size chap—d'you think you can carry him?

Ou·tsized, *a.* = *Outsize b.
1880 *Good Words* 46 He was what is sometimes called an 'outsized man'..imposing in appearance. 1895 *Westm. Gaz.* 20 July 2/1 She was a great outsized woman.

Ou·tspeech. [Out- 7.] Frank or candid words; plain language or terms; outspeaking.
1919 W. De Morgan *Old Madhouse* 439 Outspeech would be the safest course as well as the easiest, with this girl.

Outspread, *v.* Add: **3.** *intr.* To spread out, extend itself.
1906 *Westm. Gaz.* 26 June 2/3 Each young branch, outspreading in the sun, Reflects in shadow on the sod below.

Outsta·ndingly, *adv.* [f. Outstanding *ppl. a.* + -ly².] In a notable or outstanding manner; in or to an exceptional degree; remarkably or conspicuously.
1909 *Westm. Gaz.* 18 Jan. 12/2 He is an outstandingly good putter. 1922 A. S. M. Hutchinson *This Freedom* II. ix. 150 There was outstandingly one such day of absorption in delight..for Rosalie. 1928 *Observer* 18 Mar. 23/3 Her Wagner songs are outstandingly fine.

Outstay, *v.* Add: **2. b.** To surpass in endurance.
1876 *Coursing Calendar* 5 Laughter made the early points with Lady Don, but the latter fairly outstayed the dog.

Outstrip (outstri·p), *v.*² [f. Out- 18 + Strip *v.*¹] *trans.* To surpass in stripping; to wear less clothing than.

1868 *Daily News* 18 Aug., The actresses now seek to succeed by 'out-stripping' one another. 1897 W. C. Hazlitt *Four Generations* II. 155 The abridged petticoats of the ladies proceeded to an intolerable pitch; and they tried, as Byron said, to outstrip one another.

Out-thrown, *ppl. a.* (Add example.)
1927 *Month* May 398 The sides of the outthrown headland are too steep to be rushed.

Out-turn. Add: **b.** *spec.* Tea leaves that have been infused.
1878 E. Money *Cultiv. & Manuf. Tea* (ed. 3) 110, I tried again and again, but never could detect that panning caused any difference to either the Tea, the liquor or the out-turn.
c. *Curling.* A turning motion given to a stone which causes it to curve to the left.
1900 *Young Sportsman* (ed. A. E. T. Watson) 200 The in-turn is made when the curl is to be towards the right, the out-turn when it is to the left.

Outvo·ting, *vbl. sb.* [-ing¹.] Defeating by a majority of votes.
1906 *Westm. Gaz.* 14 Feb. 2/1 The out-voting of the Boers by the industrial and urban settlers.

Outwa·ndering, *vbl. sb.* [Out- 9.] A wandering out or outwards.
1880 H. Collins *Heaven opened* II. xiv. 215 God does not mind the out-wanderings of our vagabond imaginations.

Ou·twash. [Out- 7.] The outflow of water escaping from melting ice sheets or glaciers. In quots. *attrib.*
1903 *Bot. Gaz.* Jan. 38 (Cent. Suppl.) These moraines are usually bordered by sand plains on the outwash side. 1908 *Amer. Jrnl. Sci.* Feb. 108 The river terraces of outwash gravel.

Outwork, *v.* **3.** (Add example.)
1876 *Coursing Calendar* 123 Minstrel Boy, on the inside, led for first honours, where he lost his place, and was ultimately outworked.

Outworld, *sb.* Add: **b.** An outlandish place.
1902 J. Buchan *Watcher by Threshold* etc. v. 312 In this savage out-world a man stood for a man.

Outworldish, *a.* (Modern example.)
1880 G. Macdonald *Bk. Strife* 73 A strange auroral bliss, an arctic awe, A new, outworldish joy awoke intense.

Oval. **A.** *adj.*¹ **5. a.** *oval-faced* (example).
1886 Ruskin *Præterita* I. 326 A graceful oval-faced blonde of fifteen.
B. *sb.*¹ **2.** (Add example.)
1927 *Daily Express* 26 Mar. 9/2 The Prince of Wales.. will..open a games oval.

Ovalize (ōᵘ·văloiz), *v.* [f. Oval *a.*¹ + -ize.] *trans.* To make oval in shape. (In quot. *ppl. a.*)
1905 *Sci. Amer.* Suppl. 11 Mar. 24404 (Cent. Suppl.) The work is performed by means of three special machines—a winder, a finishing roller, and an ovalizing press.

Ovational, *a.* (Add example.)
1928 *Music & Lett.* July 235 The ovational ecstasy is not essentially connected with the musical impression.

Oven, *sb.* Add: **3. b.** A small oven-like tomb above the surface of the ground. *U.S.*
1851 E. S. Wortley *Trav. U.S.* xxi. 126 The graves are all elevated. The dead are buried in sepulchral houses, which are termed here 'ovens'. 1879 *Cassell's Techn. Educ.* IV. 267/2 Owing to the damp nature of the ground..there are no graves in the cemeteries, the coffins with the dead are being deposited in tombs or 'ovens' erected above the soil. 1921 *Chambers's Jrnl.* Aug. 511/1 There was no system in the arrangement of the 'ovens'.

Oven-wood. [Oven *sb.* 4.] Firewood prepared for heating an oven.
1794 [see Oven *sb.* 4]. 1838 J. F. Cooper *Homeward Bound* xxv. 362 They will not now serve as oven-wood for want of the oven. 1857 J. G. Holland *Bay Path* 137 You'd better scull your dug-out over the drink again, and go to splittin' oven-wood. 1869 Mrs. Stowe *Oldtown Folks* xxiii. 276 Will you split me that oven-wood or won't you? 1874 B. F. Taylor *World on Wheels* I. ix. 72 A wine-cask ..filled with oven-wood, to wit, wood split axe-helve size. 1929 E. W. Howe *Plain People* 191 His wife asked him one afternoon to get an armful of oven wood; she was baking and wanted wood to heat the oven of the cookstove to best advantage.

Over, *adv.* Add: **2. b.** (*That*) *is someone all over*, is very characteristic of him or her.
1916 Bennett *Lion's Share* xxxii. 237 That's you all over, Mrs. Moncreiff.
6. b. *fig.* To sleep; as in *go, send over.*
1918 Mary & Jane Findlater *Penny Monypenny* II. xxiv. 233 It used to send me over in a few minutes. *Ibid.* III. xi. 341 Just going over, Aunt Deb, my eyes won't keep open a minute longer.
9. b. Until a later time or period; till the next season.
1861 *Trans. Ill. Agric. Soc.* IV. 317 Old bugs live over, and produce eggs the following season. 1883 J. Hay *Bread-winners* xi. 172, I am so glad you resolved to stay over. 1898 A. Nicholas *Idyl of Wabash* 53 We don't want to winter them steers over.
12. (Further example.)
1912 Galsworthy *Eldest Son* I. ii. 14 Draw it mild, my dear chap. We've had the whole thing over twice at least.
c. As a whole; all over. (Cf. Over *prep.* 7 d.)
1927 *Harper's Mag.* Oct. 530 The correlation between scholarship and football eminence, taking the country over, is depressingly low.

Over, *prep.* Add: **1. d.** *Over one's head*: Without consulting or informing the person concerned or affected.
1902 *Chambers's Jrnl.* Nov. 716/2 The traveller..finds himself called upon..to soften and explain away amenities which have been unwisely transmitted by letter, exchanged, as it were, 'over his head'.
6. d. Phr. *To put it over* (a person): see *Put *v.* 23.
7. a. Also *fig.*
1912 F. M. Hueffer *Panel* I. ii. 62 Immediately afterwards, Mrs. Kerr Howe was all over her like a wave with her projects for the New Theatre.
13. b. *To get over*: see *Get *v.* 66 e. *To put over*: see *Put *v.*¹ 49 i.

Over, *sb.*² Add: **2. b.** *Printing.* *pl.* Copies printed or supplied in excess of the required number to allow for wastage.
1901 D. Cockerel *Bookbinding* I. ii. 36 The printers usually keep a number of 'overs' in order to make good such imperfections. 1904 *Let. to Dr. Furnivall* 7 Oct., To whom are we to send..the overs of papers and cards?

Over against: see Over *adv.* 7 b.

Over-all, *adj. phr.* Add: **2.** Pertaining to or affecting the whole of something.
1930 *Daily Express* 6 Sept. 3 The New B P has 'high overall volatility.' All of it evaporates quickly.

Overalled (ōᵘ·vǝrǭld), *a.* [f. Overall *sb.* + -ed².] Wearing, or clad in, overalls.
1908 *Smart Set* June 94/1 The familiar spectacle of half-grown boys and overalled and unshaven men. 1916 C. H. Stagg *High Speed* i. (1920) 2 He could see an overalled boy jump into the air and crack his heels together.

Over-and-over boat. [Over *adv.* 4.] One of a set of boats suspended from a vertically revolving frame.
1910 Sanger *Seventy Years a Showman* (1927) 127 Father was able to add 'riding' or 'Over-and-over' boats..to his peep-show and roundabouts.

Overarm, *a.* Add: **2.** *Swimming.* Applied to a stroke in which one or both arms are lifted out of the water before being advanced; also of a swimmer, that employs an over-arm stroke.
1887 *Encycl. Brit.* XXII. 770/1 Harry Gardener..used the overhand or overarm stroke. 1893 A. Sinclair & W. Henry *Swimming* (Badm. Libr.) 79 The old-fashioned over-arm swimmer lay on the water, with his shoulder-blades at right angles to the surface. 1912 Sachs *Compl. Swimmer* 133 Until the last few years a swimmer who desired to race, first endeavoured to master the over-arm side stroke.
3. *Lawn-tennis.* Of a style of service, in which the racket is swung above the shoulder to hit the ball.
1929 W. E. Collinson *Spoken Eng.* 90 Last time some of your overarm serves were unplayable.

Overbank, *v.* Add: **2.** *trans.* To supply with too many banks.
1930 *Times* 27 Mar. 21/2 The Port of Karachi..is considerably over-banked.

Overbear, *v.* Add: **2. b.** Also *absol.*
1879 Meredith *Egoist* xxxiii, There are times when there is no medicine for us in sages, we want slaves; we scorn to temporize, we must overbear.
4. To bear too much; to produce too much fruit.
1866 *Ret. Agric. Soc. Maine* 40 This third year..the vine will show a great disposition to overbear. 1872 *Rep. Vermont Board Agric.* I. 118 The Bartlett and Louise Bonne de Jersey commence bearing young, and are inclined to over bear.

Overbelie·f. [tr. G. *aberglaube* superstition: *Aberglaube; cf. Over- 18.] Belief in more than is warranted by the evidence or in what cannot be verified.
1900 J. Morley *Cromwell* I. iii. § ii. 51 Faith in the literal construction of the word was pushed to an excess..resembling a true superstition or over-belief. 1902 W. James *Varieties Relig. Exper.* 515 Over-beliefs in various directions are absolutely indispensable. 1920 'W. S. Palmer' *Christianity & Christ* 153 We have these 'over-beliefs'; and we even count men poor who are without them.

Overbid, *v.* Add: **2. c.** *trans.* and *absol.* In *Bridge.* = *Overcall *v.*
1909 A. Dunn *Auction Bridge* 156 When the second player overbids a weak call from the dealer, the fourth player should support his partner to the best of his ability. 1919 R. F. Foster *On Auction* 169 Overbidding a suit just because there are four honours in it is quite unnecessary. *Ibid.* 180 He must not forget that he has already overbid his hand at the start. 1923 *Daily Mail* 6 Oct. 6/4 The partner of the under-bidder..cannot make any further bid unless the opponents double or over-bid.

Overbi·dding, *vbl. sb.* [f. Overbid *v.* + -ing¹.] Bidding above the value of anything, esp. bidding more than is warranted by the cards one holds at bridge.
1913 Flor. Irwin *Fine Pts. Auction Bridge* 85 There is no fault as common in Auction as overbidding. 1929 M. C. Work *Compl. Contract Bridge* iii. 15 This artificial system is apt to cause overbidding.

O·ver-blouse. [Over- 8 c.] A kind of blouse fitting over another garment.
1923 *Daily Mail* 13 Feb. 15 In usefulness no similar garment can compete with the overblouse.

Overblown, *ppl. a.*¹ **2.** (Add example.)
1929 Bridges *Test. Beauty* III. 55 The empty mind may float lightly in the full moonshine of o'erblown affluence.

O·verboil, *sb.* [f. the vb.] Overboiling condition.
1883 Ruskin *Let.* 30 Oct. in *Igdrasil* (June 1890) I. No. 6. 218 And my brains always on the overboil, if I don't mind.

O·verbrim, *sb.* [Over- 5 b.] A trimming on the brim of a hat.
1930 *Morn. Post* 17 June 7 Advt., Picture Hat of black Tulle edged with Crinoline; overbrim of beige Lace.

Overbuy, *v.* Add: **1. b.** To buy goods at a higher (wholesale) price than (another).
1886 Hardy *Mayor Casterbr.* xxvi, We'll under-sell him, and over-buy him, and so snuff him out.

O·ver-call, *sb.* *Bridge.* [Over- 29 b.] A call or bid made against one's own partner.
1917 E. Bergholt *Royal Auction Bridge* 85 Third hand should not carry on the contest further, unless he has some additional reason which his first overcall was not sufficient to proclaim. 1922 Flor. Irwin *Compl. Auction Bridge Player* 65 To bid against your partner, when no one else has bid, is to use the over-call.

Overca·ll, *v.* *Bridge.* [Over- 27.]
1. *trans.* To bid more on (one's hand) than it is worth; to give a higher 'call' than one can win. Also *absol.* or *intr.*
1927 A. H. Pollen '*Neon's*' *Gt. Delusion* Pref. p. xvi, The bright young conjurers of Kingsway have been over-calling their hands. 1930 *Time & Tide* 11 Apr. 463 Conscious that his partner had been overcalling.
2. To bid higher than (a previous bid) or than (an opponent); *esp.* to bid above (one's partner) when no adversary has done so. Also *absol.*
1909 *Strand Mag.* Jan. 71/2 The fourth player will be in a fine position, either to double the forced call or to overcall it. 1917 E. Bergholt *Royal Auction Bridge* 85 Here Y. has two of his partner's suit, but *six* of his own. He is justified in overcalling with One Spade. 1919 R. F. Foster *On Auction* 183 The partner may be called upon to assist.. when the second hand overcalls the dealer. 1922 Flor. Irwin *Compl. Auction Bridge Player* 65 To 'over-call' is to take the bid away from your partner. *Ibid.* 68 Y..had over-called a desirable thing with an undesirable thing. 1929 M. C. Work *Compl. Contract Bridge* ii. 9 He may overcall a No Trump with a suit-bid, or overcall a suit-bid with another suit or No Trump.
3. Of a call or bid: To exceed or surpass (another) in value.
1923 *Daily Mail* 6 Oct. 6/4 Players forget that 4 clubs do not over-call 3 spades.

Overcarefully, *adv.* (Example.)
1865 Dickens *Mut. Fr.* II. xiv, 'The sister', said Bradley, separating his words over-carefully,..'suffers under no reproach'.

Overcarried, *ppl. a.* [f. Overcarry *v.*] That has been carried over (a boundary).
1903 Kipling *5 Nations* 24 And their overcarried spray is a sea—a sea on the landward side.

Overcast, *v.* Add: **11.** *Geol.* (See quot.)
1900 *Geog. Jrnl.* XVI. 462 The longitudinal folds had been steeply tilted, or 'overcast', *i.e.* laid over into more horizontal positions, or fractured, and the parts carried into different oblique directions.

Overcasting, *ppl. a.* (Further example.)
1901 D. Cockerel *Bookbinding* ii. 51 The custom with binders is to overcast the backs of the leaves in sections, and to sew through the overcasting thread.

O·vercheck, *sb.*² [Over- 8.] A second check on cloth; a large check pattern over a smaller and less distinct one; cloth having such a check.
1906 *Daily Chron.* 25 Apr. 8/5 The finely-traced overchecks will be much in evidence. 1923 *Daily Mail* 16 Jan. 1 Advt., Raincoats in All-Wool overcheck and herring-bone effect. *Ibid.*, Brown and White mixtures with indistinct coloured overchecks.

Overclimb, *v.* (Modern example.)
1882 'Ouida' *Bimbi* v. 149 A loggia..all overclimbed by hardy rose-trees.

Overclo·sely, *adv.* [f. Overclose *a.*] Too closely or minutely.
1909 *Westm. Gaz.* 15 Apr. 12/2 The loving parent does well not to examine overclosely into the reasons for this regret.

Overclothe, *v.* Add: **2.** *refl.* To clothe (oneself) to excess.
1906 *Daily Chron.* 11 Dec. 10/5 So over-clothing yourself that you cannot take exercise.

Over-colour, *v.* Add: **b.** To overspread with colour.
1871 Meredith *H. Richmond* xliii, Her cheeks were deliciously overcoloured.

Overcome, *v.* **7.** (Modern example.)
1875 Morris *Æn.* XII. 907 And e'en the hero-gathered stone..O'ercame not all the space betwixt.

O·ver-compou·nd, *v.* [Over- 27.] *trans.* To wind the field magnets of (a dynamo) by both shunt and series coils in such a way that the voltage rises with increasing load. So **O·ver-compou·nding** *vbl. sb.*
1896 S. P. Thompson *Dynamo-Electr. Machinery* (ed. 5) 237 By over-compounding, one can obtain a constant pressure, not at the terminals of the dynamo, but on the mains at some point in the midst of the lamp-network. 1902 *Encycl. Brit.* XXVII. 588/1 If the series-turns are still further increased, the voltage may be made to rise with an increasing load, and the machine is 'over-compounded'.

Over-correct, *v.* Add: **2.** *Surg.* To correct (a deformity, etc.) to an apparently excessive degree so as to allow for subsequent modification of the correction.
Hence **Over-corre·ction**, the correcting of deformities to a point beyond the normal.
1908 *Practitioner* Jan. 114 Dr. Whitman favours tenotomy and over-correction, with the subsequent use of plaster.

Over-cu·t, *v.* [Over- 27.] *trans.* To cut too much of; to fell (forest trees) to an excessive degree.
1906 Schlich *Man. Forestry* (ed. 3) I. 75 Private owners are inclined to favour their own monetary interests to the disadvantage of future generations by overcutting..their forests. 1913 *Q. Rev.* Oct. 446 In the case of private owner-

ship, there is always a danger of the forests being overcut to obtain quick returns.

Hence **Over-cu·tting** *vbl. sb.*

1928 *Daily Tel.* 9 Oct. 9/7 Wasteful over-cutting, forest fire, fungi, insects, and wind combined are rapidly wiping out Canada's available trees.

O·ver-determina·tion. *Psycho-analysis.* [f. next.] The use of one means of expression for two or more different desires or tendencies.

1915 C. R. Payne tr. *Pfister's Psycho-anal. Method* 143 We have often had opportunity..to show these over-determinations.

Over-dete·rmine, *v.* [Over- 27.] *trans.* To fix, define, or determine with more data than are necessary. Hence **Over-dete·rmined** *ppl. a.*, having more determining factors than are required; *spec.* in *Psycho-analysis*, that expresses two or more different desires or tendencies.

1879 *Encycl. Brit.* X. 377/2 The definitions which have not been mentioned are all 'nominal definitions', that is to say, they fix a name for the thing described. Many of them overdetermine a figure. 1915 C. R. Payne tr. *Pfister's Psycho-anal. Method* 143 The neurotic symptom has several determining factors, at least two. Therefore, it is called over-determined.

Overdo, *v.* Add: **9.** To supply *with* (something) in too great a measure.

1926 Bennett *Lion's Share* vii. 52 A raw girl, overdone with money, who could only speak one language.

Overdo·sage. [Over- 29.] The administering or taking of too large a dose (of medicine, drugs, etc.).

1922 *Encycl. Brit.* XXX. 137/2 To find a method of preventing these chloroform deaths, by enquiring into the conditions of overdosage. 1929 Morrin in *Irish Jrnl. Med. Sci.* Apr. 183 Such symptoms were obviously due to overdosage.

Overdraw, *sb.* **2.** (Examples.)

1902 A. D. McFaul *Ike Glidden* xvi. 122 He was prancin'..until he got him hitched inter this new bitin' gear an' overdraw. 1905 *Springfield Weekly Republ.* 8 Sept. 5 Much has been accomplished to abolish the pernicious practice of docking horses, but it is just as important that the abuse of the overdraw check should be corrected.

Overdraw, *v.* Add: **5. b.** To infuse (tea) too long.

1847 Anne Brontë *Agnes Grey* xii, Other thoughts assisted to..impart a relish to the cup of cold, overdrawn tea.

6. (Later example.)

1912 *Chambers's Jrnl.* June 359/1 Perhaps it will be said that the above statements are overdrawn.

Over-draw·er. [f. Overdraw *v.* + -er.] One who overdraws his banking account, or makes an overdraft.

1906 W. De Morgan *J. Vance* xxxvii. 378 Among the overdrawers, C. Vance & Co. was a conspicuous instance, figuring for a good round sum among the Debtors.

Overdrink, *v.* (Modern example of *intr.*)

1904 'J. O. Hobbes' *Vineyard* iv. 55 They over-eat and over-drink, and they try to forget what they really want.

Over-dri·nking, *vbl. sb.* [Over- 29.] Drinking to excess.

1907 *Westm. Gaz.* 29 Oct. 12/1 The publicans are held responsible for the over-drinking of their customers.

Overdrive, *v.* Add: **4.** (Further example.)

1904 A. B. F. Young *Complete Motorist* 188 These conditions are that they should not be overloaded nor overdriven.

5. *Golf.* To drive farther than (an opponent); to outdrive.

1900 *Gentl. Mag.* Feb. 126 If the opponent is a longer driver one is spared the temptation..of pressing to avoid being overdriven.

Hence **O·verdri·ving** *vbl. sb.*

1837 De Quincey *Revolt of Tartars* Wks. 1854 IV. 143 The cattle suffered greatly from over-driving. 1909 *Chambers's Jrnl.* Mar. 203/1 The electrical equipment is provided with suitable automatic devices to prevent over-driving.

Over-dry, *a.* (Modern example.)

1891 Schlich *Man. Forestry* II. 32 Dry Mould..is formed by the decomposition of certain lichens on over-dry soil.

Over-dry, *v.* **b.** (Modern examples.) Hence **Over-dry·ing** *vbl. sb.*

1867 K. A. Digby *Day on Muses' Hill* 146 The subsoil may be overdried. 1888 *Encycl. Brit.* XXIV. 657/1 Over-drying of wool has to be specially guarded against. *Ibid.* 657/2 Unless the wool is spread with great evenness..at points where the hot air escapes freely it may be much over-dried.

Over-dryness. (Modern example.)

1879 *Encycl. Brit.* X. 753/2 In extremely frosty weather ..they acquire so little moisture that then a difficulty arises from their over-dryness.

Overduer (ōvəɹdiū·əɹ). [f. Overdue *a.*] A ship that is overdue.

1905 *Standard* 14 Mar. 11/3 The only alteration in the market rates on overduers were advances of from 20 gs. to 30–35 gs. on the steamer Pilbarra, [etc.].

Over-early, *a.* (Modern example.)

1871 Kingsley *At Last* x, This over-early marriage among the Coolies is a very serious evil.

Overeat, *v.* **1.** (Modern example.)

1904 [see *Overdrink].

Overface, *v.* **1.** (Later example.)

1926 Bennett *Lord Raingo* I. lvii. 254 He scorned them, but in their collectivity they still over-faced him.

Overflow, *sb.* **5.** Add: *overflow sill.*

1902 *Encycl. Brit.* XXXIII. 786/1 The overflow sill or weir should be a masonry structure of rounded vertical section raised a foot or more above the waste-water course.

Overflow, *v.* **3.** (Later example.)

1890 *Forum* Feb. 700 (Born) The fiery lava of passion overflowing the appointed bounds.

Overflowing, *vbl. sb.* Add: **2. b.** *esp.* in phrases, (*full, to fill*) *to overflowing*: more than full, so as to overflow.

1879 R. A. Sterndale *Afghan Knife* xxvi. 167 In the meantime fugitives kept pouring into the house, which was full to overflowing. 1899 Adelaide Skeel & Brearley *King Washington* xii. 75 (Born) The boys..were filled to overflowing with the excitement of the hour. 1920 H. M. Pim *Sk. Hist. Celtic Philos.* v. 62 They might have produced a Tartarus, and filled it to overflowing.

Hence **Overflow·ingness.** (Modern example.)

1883 Meredith *Lett.* II. 349, I have been hearing from Will of your radiant overflowingness.

Overget, *v.* Add: **4.** To prevail upon; to take possession of.

1904 Herbert Morris & Bastert *Tradesman's Price-list* 11 Similarity of appearance so far overgets a customer as to induce him to pass us. 1928 *Sunday Dispatch* 16 Sept. 2/3 The thought to marry Fanny overgot the man, and he set out to see if it could be done.

Overglaze, *sb.* (Earlier example.)

1880 *Harper's Mag.* Nov. 904 The work most familiar to us as taught in America during the last three or four years has all been on the over-glaze.

Overglaze, *a.* (Earlier example.)

1881 *Harper's Mag.* May 835/1 It was..the most extensive and satisfactory exhibit of amateur overglaze decoration made up to that time.

Overgoing, *vbl. sb.* (Modern example in sense 'transgression'.)

1903 Jerome *Tea Table Talk* v. 95, I was very severe upon both the shortcomings and the overgoings of man.

Overgrown, *ppl. a.* **1.** (Later fig. example.)

1907 R. Brooke in *Mem.* (1918) p. xxix, I have already.. got some faith in the real, sometimes overgrown, goodness of all men.

Overhand. **A.** *adv.* Add: **3. b.** *Archery.* (See quot.)

1875 *Encycl. Brit.* II. 378/2 Shooting over-hand is to shoot at the mark over the bow-hand.

B. *adj.* Add: **2. b.** *Swimming.* Applied to a variety of the side-stroke in the performance of which one hand is raised above the water and carried forward.

1878 'Capt. Crawley' *Swimming* etc. 38 There are two styles of Side Swimming, severally known as the side-stroke and the over-hand. 1887 *Encycl. Brit.* XXII. 770/1 The only movements of the side stroke which differ from those of the overhand are those of the left or upper arm or hand.

c. *Lawn-tennis.* Of a stroke, made with the racket above the arm or shoulder.

1889 H. W. W. Wilberforce *Lawn Tennis* 30 The form of service almost universally used is the overhand service. 1904 J. P. Paret *Lawn Tennis* 345.

Over-handed, *a.* Add: **2. b.** *Overhanded knot* = Overhand knot (Overhand B. *adj.* 4).

1883 *Man. Seamanship for Boys* 91 Q. How do you make a reef-knot? A...First make an over-handed knot round the foot of the sail, [etc.].

Overhang, *sb.* (Add examples.)

1908 H. G. Wells *War in Air* v. § 5 The overhang of the gas-chambers intervened. 1919 T. K. Holmes *Man fr. Tall Timber* ix. 101 The two women..lived alone on Paradise Knoll, just under the overhang of its crown.

Overhaul, *v.* **2.** Also *intr.* for passive.

1920 *Westm. Gaz.* 16 June 10/2 So as the selected yacht may have sufficient time to overhaul and arrive in New York by July 13.

Overhead. **B.** *sb.* Add: **2.** *pl.* A grade of flour.

1879 *Encycl. Brit.* IX. 345/2 Flour..Overheads or coarse flour..Fine thirds..Thirds..Bran.

3. That which is above; the firmament.

1911 *Chambers's Jrnl.* Jan. 79/1 It forms a handy guide, philosopher, and friend to the vast unfathomable overhead. 1924 Anne D. Sedgwick *Little French Girl* II. i. 104 He.. heard the wild, monotonous phrase of a missel-thrush ring forth suddenly from overhead.

4. Ellipt. for overhead charges, expenses, etc.

1915 *Literary Digest* (N.Y.) 21 Aug. 360/1 Advt., Her typewriter is standing idle and adding to 'overhead'. 1918 *Nation* (N.Y.) 7 Feb. 162/1 Larger production will decrease overhead and keep the cost down. 1922 *Public Opinion* 629/2 We are able to reduce overheads through the employment of far more automatic machinery. 1928 *Brit. Industrial Future* (Lib. Ind. Inq.) v. xxix. § 1. 418 Whether the call is for less expenditure on overhead or for less turnover. 1929 *Encycl. Brit.* VI. 495/1 *Overhead* consists of every kind of working cost not comprised in one or other of the previous headings.

C. *adj.* Add: **1.** (Further example.)

1921 *Times Lit. Suppl.* 8 Sept. 574/3 Stress is laid on the complete clearance of overhead cover [from teak plantations].

3. Of costs or expenses: Incurred in the production of a batch of articles apart from the prime cost of each (cf. Oncost), or in the upkeep of plant and premises even when no work is being done.

1911 *Century Mag.* May 121/2 An automatic system of employer's liability..would..increase 'overhead charges'. 1911 Werner *Factory Costs* 212 Under such a system most of the usual overhead expenses become direct. 1917 Ficker *Industrial Cost-finding* 11 This illustrates..the importance of segregating the overhead expenses of a factory. 1922 *Westm. Gaz.* 8 Dec., The overhead cost of every factory that is gas-lighted will go up.

4. *Lawn tennis.* Of a stroke, made with the racket above one's head.

1904 J. P. Paret *Lawn Tennis* 345. 1919 Hierons *Lawn Tennis* 61 In overhead volleying there is far too much pat ball.

Overhear, *v.* **3.** Add: Also *absol.*

1913 *Cassell's Mag.* June 2/1 Glancing over his shoulder to make certain that the nurse hadn't overheard.

Overheat, *v.* Add: **2.** *intr.* To become too hot.

1902 Harmsworth *Motors & Motor-driving* (Badm. Libr.) 172 How to tell when a Motor is Overheating. 1908 *Westm. Gaz.* 27 Oct. 4/1 The engine overheated twice,..but this was when the car was taken out without any water in the radiator.

Over-hit, *v.* **b.** (Add example.)

1919 Hierons *Lawn Tennis* 57 The beginner should take care that he does not over-hit the ball.

Overhung, *ppl. a.* Add: **1. b.** = Overhanging *ppl. a.*

1923 H. G. Wells *Men like Gods* II. iii. 206 The gully was ..difficult, he thought, to ascend, but quite practicable downward. It was completely overhung.

3. (Further example.)

1928 Gamble *Story N. Sea Air Station* Introd. 8 Somewhat similar to a Blériot monoplane, except for..the 'overhung' system of mounting the engine.

O·ver-insu·rance. [Over- 29.] Insurance in excess of the real value (esp. of a ship).

1755 N. Magens *Essay on Insurances* 92. 1802 S. Marshall *Treat. Insurance* I. I. iv. § 4. 118 In the case of an over-insurance..the first underwriters on the policy were formerly holden to be answerable, to the extent of the loss, and the subsequent ones discharged. 1813 R. Stevens *Ess. Average* (1835) 204 A return of premium for over-insurance is claimed. 1880 *Encycl. Brit.* XIII. 185/1 When the value proved under an open policy falls short of the sum originally insured, the difference..is technically termed an over-insurance.

O·ver-insu·re, *v.* [Over- 27.] *trans.* To insure for more than the real value.

1910 *Times* 28 June 6/1 An old vessel, trading at a loss, over-insured. 1922 *Blackw. Mag.* Sept. 318/2 Ship and cargo are over-insured about ten times, I suppose?

Overlap, *sb.* Add: Also *fig.*

1931 Sir A. Keith *Place of Prejudice* 19 Head and heart are never quite separated; there is a large overlap in their fields of action.

b. *Overlap fault* (see quot.).

1883 Gresley *Gloss. Coal Mining* 180 *Overlap Fault*, a peculiar kind of fault where a seam is reversed or doubled back over itself.

Overla·pped, *ppl. a.* [-ed.] That overlaps or is overlapped (in various senses).

1839 Ure *Dict. Arts* 962 A section of the Quarrelton coal ..showing the overlapped coal and the double coal. 1898 Saintsbury *Short Hist. Eng. Lit.* viii. ii. (1900) 498 The constant preference of overlapped or enjambed lines for the strict couplet. 1926 J. Adams *Chr. Good Scot.* viii. 126 To neglect or overlook the nobler ideals of the Church, because of its presently divided and overlapped system, is neither politic nor wise.

Over-late. **b.** *adv.* (Modern example.)

1875 Morris *Æn.* vii. 597 And overlate the Gods thou shalt adore.

Overlay, *sb.* **3.** (Add example.)

1886 J. Barrowman *Sc. Mining Terms* 48 *Overlay*, the material above the rock in a quarry; the tirring.

Overlayer. (Later example.)

1917 *19th Cent.* Jan. 132 Faith in God and in a hereafter has been accompanied in history by an overlayer of superstition.

Overlea·ping, *vbl. sb.* [-ing 1.] The action of the verb Overleap.

1904 Edith Rickert *Reaper* 61 Joan panted with the constant overleaping of mossy bogs.

Over-light, *a.* (Later example.)

1908 *Daily Chron.* 21 Apr. 4/4 Now and then he was a trifle ..over-light in his treatment of opponents.

Overling. Delete †*Obs.* and add modern example.

1917 Kipling *Yrs. Between* (1919) 66 But the idle-minded overlings who quibbled while they died, Shall they thrust for high employments as of old?

Overli·p, *v.* [Over- 1.] *trans.* To pass or flow over the lip or brim of (something).

1872 S. Butler *Erewhon* v. 38 The clouds rolled up to the very summit of the pass, though they did not overlip it.

Overlive, *v.* **c.** *refl.* Also, to live too fast or under too high pressure.

1921 Galsworthy *To Let* II. ii. 126 He had only just relapsed, from having overworked, or overlived, himself again.

Over-living, *vbl. sb.* [Over- 29.] Living on too high a standard.

1817 Scott *Let.* 11 Aug. in *Lockhart* (1837) IV. 87 The task of maintaining a poor, rendered effeminate and vicious by over-wages and over-living, and necessarily cast loose upon society.

Overload, *sb.* Add: Also *Overload cut-out.*

1908 *Installation News* II. 38 There is always some novel addition to our Conduit System..in addition to various side issues such as overload cut-outs.

Overlock, *v.* Add: **c.** To secure (the edge of cloth) so as to strengthen it and prevent fraying.

1909 *Public Ledger* (Philad.) 24 June 5/2 Fishnet Lace Curtains, overlocked edge.

Overlo·rding, *ppl. a.* [f. Overlord *v.*] That overlords or domineers.

1910 Galsworthy *Sheaf* (1916) 132 Our dim consciousness of this serene and overlording principle of Equity.

O·ver-lu·sciousness. [Over- 29.] Excessive lusciousness.

1898 Saintsbury *Short Hist. Eng. Lit.* x. i. (1900) 671 A certain over-lusciousness traceable in his [Keats's] earlier work.

Overly, *adv.* **1.** (Add examples.)

1903 Kipling *5 Nations* 21 Yet, caring so, not overly we care To brace and trim for every foolish blast. 1926 J. A. Muller *Stephen Gardiner* ii. 11 The intense, overly conscientious Thomas Bilney. 1929 M. C. Work *Compl. Contract Bridge* v. 111 Overly sanguine or 'bad break' slam tries.

Overman, *sb.* Add: **3. b.** A grade in the U.S. police.

1885 *Encycl. Brit.* XIX. 341/2 The body of the force being termed 'patrol men', with 'overmen' at stations and prisons.

4. [G. *uebermensch.*] = Superman.

1895 tr. *M. Nordau's Degeneration* III. v. 470 The 'bullies' gratefully recognise themselves in Nietzsche's 'over-man'. 1900 *Q. Rev.* July 116 In such old religion he discovers no prophecy of the man that is to be; he reaches forward to some 'overman' beyond it. 1908 H. G. Wells *War in Air* xi. § 5 His mind ran to 'improving the race' and producing the Over-Man. 1915 *Lond. Q. Rev.* Jan. 59 Such a process of superabstraction would involve either an overman or a *deus ex machina*.

Overmast, *v.* (Later example.)

1902 Conrad *Youth* 40 She was certainly over-masted.

Over-mastery. (Modern example.)

1901 T. Shaw *Address* (Edin.) 4 The struggle for Scottish independence against the overmastery of England.

Over-measure, *v.* **a.** (Modern example).

1877 Tennyson *Harold* iv. iii, By St. Edmund I overmeasure him.

Overname, *v.* (Modern example.)

1902 J. H. Skrine *Pastor Agnorum* 31 Twenty faces in three ranks, and, though no face is like another, we could have safely overnamed the varieties before we fronted them.

Overnight. **C.** *adj.* Add: **2.** Borrowed or lent from the afternoon of one day till the morning of the next.

1928 *Daily Mail* 9 Aug. 18/6 Borrowers occasionally paid up to 4½ per cent. for fresh overnight money.

O·ver-note. [f. Over- 2.] A note heard through or above other sounds; an over-tone.

1917 Conrad *Shadow-Line* 204 He..burst into..a loud laugh...It was a provoking, mocking peal, with a hair-raising, screeching over-note of defiance.

Over-old, *a.* (Modern examples.)

1875 Morris *Æn.* viii. 509 My body over-old for deeds begrudged such government. 1883 Ld. R. Gower *Remin.* II. 140 Their children..have a delicate over-old look for their age.

Over-pai·nting, *vbl. sb.* [Over- 8.] The action of the verb overpaint (sense 1).

1928 *Daily Express* 20 Dec. 1/3 The explanation of the over-painting is simple. The sitter..decided to have his sheriff's robes painted over the clothes in Holbein's picture.

Overpass, *v.* **7. b.** (Modern example.)

1905 *Daily Chron.* 24 Oct. 1 The Russian and Austrian agents in Uskub overpass their duties.

Overpitched, *a.* Add: **b.** *Cricket.* That is pitched too far.

1900 *Young Sportsman* (ed. A. E. T. Watson) 147 He has lunged out as far as he can reach, hoping to 'smother' a somewhat overpitched ball.

Overplacement. Add: Also *attrib.*

1890 *Smithsonian Rep.* 72 Torrential or overplacement deposits formed by wash adown slopes.

Overpre·ssing, *ppl. a.* [f. Overpress *v.*] That is too pressing.

1893 *Harper's Mag.* Aug. 335/1 The finding..such a palpable motive as revenge against an overpressing and clamorous creditor tipped the balance.

Overprint, *sb.* Add: **2.** Of a postage-stamp: (See quot. 1913.)

1899 *Captain* I. 421/2 The correct over-print should have been 'Z.C. de peso'. 1907 *Westm. Gaz.* 11 Feb. 7/3 Transvaal C.S.A.R. stamps which were forged in regard to postmarks and over-prints. 1912 *Chambers's Jrnl.* Nov. 750/2 The halfpenny, penny, and threepence are known with the black overprint. 1913 E. B. Evans *Stamps & Stamp Collecting*, s.v. *Overprint*. Some addition to the design or inscriptions, printed or written over a stamp which was already complete and fit for use without any such addition.

Over-print, *v.* Add: **2.** To print (additional matter or another colour) on a surface already bearing printing; to add by a subsequent printing process; used esp. of printing additions on to postage stamps.

1899 *Captain* I. 187/1 The current stamps of Great Britain were overprinted with the company's name. 1912 *Chambers's Jrnl.* Nov. 750/2 In 1903 permission was again granted to firms to overprint the backs of stamps. 1926 C. F. D. Marshall *Brit. Post Office* 54 We now come (1881) to the first stamps overprinted for official use.

3. To print too many copies of.

Over-regulation. [Over- .] Used *attrib.* of a price paid for a commission in addition to the regulation price.

1875 *Encycl. Brit.* II. 575/1 Appointments..were made under the purchase system... Every regimental commission had a fixed regulation price..in addition to which an over-regulation price, which sometimes even exceeded the regulation price, had sprung up.

Over-riches, *sb.* [Over- 29.] Excessive wealth.

1908 *Daily Chron.* 7 Mar. 3/4 Men almost in despair because of their over-riches.

Override, *v.* **6.** Add: Also *absol.*

1864 E. E. Parkes *Man. Pract. Hygiene* 363 Tight and ill-made boots, by which the toes are often distorted and made to override.

Overriding, *vbl. sb.* Add: **overriding commission**, an extra or additional commission.

1894 [in Dict.]. 1906 *Westm. Gaz.* 15 Feb. 11/1 As a rule, the terms of commission, both underwriting and 'overriding' are very liberal.

Over-ripeness. Add: Also *fig.*

1876 Meredith *Beauch. Career* xlvi. (1891) 424 Immense wealth and native obtuseness combine to disfigure us with this aspect of over-ripeness, not to say monstrosity.

Over-ruff, *v.* and *sb.* [Over- 22.] **a.** *vb. trans.* To trump with a higher card than that with which an opponent has already trumped or ruffed; to overtrump. Also *absol.* **b.** *sb.* An act or instance of over-ruffing.

c 1890 *Up to Date Games of Cards* 37 Ruff means to trump a suit second or third hand, when you are rid of that suit: *over-ruff* means to trump above. 1906 *Westm. Gaz.* 13 Oct. 14/1 Putting his partner to an over-ruff in the spade.

Overrun, *sb.* **3.** (Example.)

1902 De Vinne *Pract. Typogr., Correct Composition* (ed. 2) 309 Every paragraph containing an alteration that compels one or more overruns should be re-read.

Overrun, *v.* Add: **9. c.** To overcome or surmount by running fast.

1889 Hasluck *Mod. Engin. Handbk.* 70 Another advantage of high speed is, that it often enables the engine to over-run the resistance.

Overrunning, *vbl. sb.* (Add example.)

1908 *Westm. Gaz.* 3 Apr. 12/1 Over-running in the cricket-field had..brought the doctors..several youthful cases of a rather severe type.

Over-sail, *v.*[3] Add: **2. c.** To project beyond or overhang (a base).

1912 C. E. Power *Engl. Mediæval Archit.* II. 483 In the Decorated period the triple roll base..begins to rise in height, often oversailing the plinth with flat under-side.

So **Oversai·ling** *ppl. a.*

1833 Loudon *Encycl. Archit.* § 459 What is called a Welsh cornice (two or three oversailing (protruding) courses of brickwork). 1880 Blackmore *Mary Anerley* I. xvii. 278 Strong sunshine glared upon the over-saling tiles, and white buckled walls, and cracky lintels.

Oversay, *v.* Transfer *Obs.* to sense a. b. (Modern example.)

1874 Swinburne *Bothw.* II. xvii. (1882) 213 He shall come back, And twice shall oversay the word he said In your own ear, or else unswear it.

c. To exaggerate; overstate.

1900 W. D. Howells in *Scribner's Mag.* Sept. 368/2 This is oversaying it, of course, but the truth is in what I say.

Hence **Over-say·ing** *vbl. sb.*

1916 T. MacDonagh *Literature in Ireland* 46 Latin dispenses with the redundancies, the over-sayings, compressing a phrase into a verb.

O·verscraw·l, *v.* [Over- 8.] *trans.* To scrawl over or on.

1871 Browning *Pr. Hohenst.-Schw.* Poet. Wks. 1897 II. 297/1 Why keep each fool's bequeathment, scratch and blur Which overscrawl and underscore the piece? 1879 Meredith *Egoist* xxix, A yet more instructive passage than the over-scrawled Seventieth, or French Section.

Over-seas, *adv.* Add: **b.** quasi-*sb.*, foreign parts; abroad. Cf. Oversea B.

1919 *Empire Rev.* Munition workers who have come from overseas. 1926 Bennett *Lord Raingo* I. lix. 264 Every traveller from overseas was knocked silly by the spectacle. *Ibid.*, Britons whose secret conceit, compared to the ingenuous self-complacency of overseas, was as Mount Everest to Snowdon.

O·verseas, *a.* Now a common form of Oversea *a.*

1905 *Daily Chron.* 29 Mar. 3/2 The political liberties of these islands were..deeply endangered by the overseas dominion..of Spain. 1908 *Westm. Gaz.* 26 June 9/3 The magnitude of the overseas possessions which we had to defend. 1912 *Chambers's Jrnl.* Nov. 754/1 In athletic prowess we are now far inferior to those overseas descendants of our race. 1920 *Act* 10 & 11 *Geo.* V c. 29 (*title*), An Act to authorise the granting of Credits and the undertaking of Insurances for the purpose of re-establishing Overseas Trade. 1926 Bennett *Lord Raingo* I. xl. 181 Sam was.. well informed of the doings of the ministry, especially in relation to the overseas-press visit.

Overseer, *sb.* Add: **1. d.** One of a number of officials who manage the affairs of Harvard College, Massachusetts, U.S.A.

1643 [J. Eliot] *New Eng. First Fruits* 13 Over the Colledge are twelve Overseers chosen by the generall Court. 1812 in *Proc. Mass. Hist. Soc.* Ser. II. (1890) V. 176 [Harvard Commencement] The Corporation and Overseers arrived at 20 minutes past ten.

O·ver-self. [Over- .] The finer, stronger, or more assertive part of one's nature.

1888 E. Clodd *Story Creation* xi. 223 The terrible mass of wrong-doing can only be lessened and finally removed by suppression of the over-self. 1908 *Daily Chron.* 30 Apr. 3/1 It is the Shakespeare that projected his over-self into two score of masterpieces of poetry and drama that is Shakespeare for us.

Overset, *v.* **3.** (Add example.)

1911 *Chambers's Jrnl.* June 367/1 He passed Rodney's machine, almost oversetting it with the rush of his passage.

Overse·ttingly, *adv.* [f. Oversetting *vbl. sb.* + -ly 2.] In an oversetting or excessive degree.

1908 Rhoda Broughton *Mamma* xvii, Everybody was kind, but not oversettingly so.

Over-sexed (ōvəɹ,se·kst), *a.* [Over- 28 c.] Having sexual characters or qualities in an excessive degree.

1908 A. Noyes *Wm. Morris* 98 A creature so gluttonously over-sexed and selfishly serpentine as Gudrun. 1923 *Daily Mail* 5 Feb. 5 His..terra-cotta-coloured nudes..are repulsive and over-sexed. 1924 *Blackw. Mag.* Nov. 631/2 It [*sc.* the city type of mind] has lost peaceful possession even of its poor, oversexed, desire-distracted body.

Oversha·ken, *ppl. a.* [Over- 27 b.] That has been shaken overmuch.

1889 Gretton *Memory's Harkback* 141 To give rest to his over-shaken elbows.

Overshoe, *sb.* (Earlier example.)

1848 *Ladies' Repository* VIII. 76 She walked out of the parlor into the kitchen, to get her overshoes, (which were warming at the fire).

Overshoot, *v.* Add: **11.** *trans.* To variegate with patches of a different colour (cf. Shoot *v.* 14 b).

1859 Mrs. Stowe *Minister's Wooing* xli. 350 It was a white silk..overshot with little fine dots of silver, so that it shone when you moved it just like frost-work.

Overshroud, *v.* (Modern example.)

1916 A. S. Way tr. *Æn.* III. 113 A night of rain overshrouds the sky.

Oversight, *sb.* Add: **1. c.** Survey, view.

1889 Gretton *Memory's Harkback* 291 You have a closer and more direct oversight of the home, or Herefordshire, view.

2. (Further example.)

1927 *Public Opinion* 329/2 The generous-hearted demand ..is sometimes made in oversight of the fundamental elements of the problem.

Hence also **Oversi·ghted** *ppl. a.*, overlooked.

1857 J. Hyde Junr. *Mormonism* ix. 215 (Born) There is one oversighted contradiction that stares us in the face.

Oversize, *sb.* Add: **2.** *spec.* That which is above a certain size.

1902 *Encycl. Brit.* XXXI. 374/1 It then goes to a screen with eleven holes to the linear inch, and yields a granular undersize and oversize and a fibrous oversize which is drawn off by a suction fan. 1905 *Electrochem. Industry* Mar. 124 (Cent. Suppl.) The oversize, which contains no slime whatever, is delivered directly to four Wilfley concentrating tables.

O·versleep, *sb.* [f. the vb.] Sleeping too long or beyond the time at which one ought to awake.

1903 W. J. Locke *Where Love Is* v. 43 Even the consolation of scolding him for oversleep and a spoiled breakfast was thus denied.

Oversleе·ping, *vbl. sb.* [-ing 1.] The action of the verb Oversleep.

1908 *Westm. Gaz.* 31 Oct. 3/2 What with your smashings, and your over-sleepings, and burning the dinner on Sunday, and all. 1912 *Red Mag.* Mar. 481/1 Oversleeping by the servants was something unheard of. 1912 R. Brooke in *Mem.* (1918) p. lxxii, My cure consists in perpetual over-eating and oversleeping.

O·ver-soul, *v.* [f. the sb.] *trans.* In passive, to be ruled or dominated in respect of the soul.

1916 A. E. (G. W. Russell) *National Being* ii. 13 None of our modern States create in us such an impression of being spiritually oversouled by an ideal as the great States of the ancient world.

Overspee·d, *v.* [Over- 27.] *intr.* To drive a vehicle at a greater speed than is allowed or than it is guaranteed for.

1906 *Westm. Gaz.* 24 Apr. 4/2 The police had been..engaged elsewhere to look out for over-speeding drivers.

Overspin (ōu·vəɹspin), *sb.* [Over- 5.] A turning motion given to a ball in which the upper part turns in the direction of flight.

1927 *Observer* 27 Mar. 28/2 Employing the shot that comes in from right to left with an overspin that produces the maximum of run.

O·verspring, *v.* Add: **2.** To fit with too flexible springs.

1923 *Daily Mail* 12 July 12 The saddle for my weight was over-sprung, and over pot-holes was inclined to bounce on to the frame.

3. To provide with springs which are compressed when the load is added.

Overstay·al. [-al 2.] The fact of overstaying a time.

1927 *Blackw. Mag.* Mar. 290/2 A scarlet-crested letter.. conveyed the severe official censure..for the overstayal of leave.

Overstepping, *vbl. sb.* [f. Overstep *v.*] The action of the verb Overstep; in *Biol.* [G. *weiterschreiten*] development of an animal up to and beyond the final adult stage of its ancestors.

1930 G. R. de Beer *Embryol. & Evolution* 77 Sewertzow's principle of anaboly is a modification of that of 'overstepping'.

Over-stimulate, *v.* (Add example.)

1928 Mrs. A. B. Callow *Food & Health* 24 Condiments.. have the effect of stimulating gastric secretion, but they have the disadvantage that they tend to over-stimulate.

Overstock, *v.* Add: **b.** *spec.* To leave (a cow) unmilked for too long a period.

O·ver-sto·cking. [Over- 8 c.] A legging or stocking worn above an ordinary stocking as a protection from cold, wet, dirt, etc.

1892 Kipling *Lett. Travel* (1920) 6 The driver with red mittens on his hands, felt overstockings that come up to his knees, and, perhaps, a silvery-gray coon-skin coat on his back, walks beside.

Overstrain, *sb.* (Add example.)

1900 J. Muir in *Phil. Trans.* A. CXCIII. 1 (heading) On the Recovery of Iron from Overstrain.

Overstrained, *ppl. a.* (Add example.)

1902 *Encycl. Brit.* XXXIII. 11/2 Complete recovery [of elasticity] may be produced in iron or steel by exposure of

the overstrained specimen for a few minutes to the temperature of boiling water.

Overstride, *v.* **2.** (Modern example.)

1925 *Glasgow Herald* 5 Nov. 11/2 In conception and in achievement it [*sc.* The British Empire Exhibition] overstrode the confines of mere commercial partisanship.

Overstrike, *v.* Add: **3.** *trans.* To strike a fresh design, etc. over a previous one on (a coin). So **Overstru·ck** *ppl. a.*

1905 *Numismatic Chron.* 110 Supposing a sufficient number of overstruck pennies of the same type are available. *Ibid.*, A well-known instance of overstriking coins in modern times occurred in 1804, when..two million Spanish dollars ..were overstruck with new dies in the Boulton presses at Soho, and issued as British currency. 1914 *Brit. Mus. Return* 114 Another [penny] of the same reign showing the ninth type..overstruck on the seventh.

Over-sum, *v.* Delete †*Obs.* and add example.

1929 Bridges *Test. Beauty* IV. 104 The imperativ obligation cannot be over-summ'd.

Oversweeping, *ppl. a.* [f. Oversweep *v.*] That sweeps or passes over.

1907 Katrina Trask *Night & Morning* 6 The oversweeping tide of a great Love.

Overtake (ōu·vəɹtēk), *sb.* [f. the vb.] An act or instance of overtaking.

1903 *Science* 20 Feb. 300/1 The aggregation came about by overtakes in contradistinction to opposed collisions.

Overtake, *v.* Add: **10.** *Bridge.* To take with a higher card a trick which is already one's partner's.

1904 J. B. Elwell *Advanced Bridge* 164 With no re-entry in a hand, overtaking is often the only means of making a suit.

Overtaxing, *vbl. sb.* (Example.)

1877 Tennyson *Harold* I. i, Nay, there be murmurs, for thy brother breaks us With over-taxing.

Overthrow, *sb.* Add: **1. d.** The state of being overthrown.

1903 *Daily Chron.* 12 Sept. 5/1 A dozen great trees were torn up by the roots, and lay in disorderly overthrow.

Overthrow, *v.* Add: **6.** *trans.* To throw farther than is necessary or desired; to throw too far.

1862 *Chambers's Encycl.* III. 320/1 Misconception of this may lead to overthrowing the ball, or throwing it short.

Overthrowal (ōvəɹþrōu·ăl). [f. Overthrow *v.* + -al 2.] The act of overthrowing; subversion, defeat.

1916 W. J. Locke *Wonderful Year* xxiii. 333 Thus came the overthrowal of all Corinna's scheme of values. 1920 — *Ho. Baltazar* xxi. 257 The ultimate object of this gathering was the overthrowal of the Government.

Overthrust, *v.* (Example.)

1901 *Nature* 3 Jan. 234/1 Huge masses of country have been overfolded, fractured, and overthrust, the older being pushed over the newer.

Overtilt, *v.* (Modern example.)

1905 *Westm. Gaz.* 1 Feb. 2/3 Our house tottereth To ruin; because this people with the breath Of pity would overtilt it.

O·ver-ti·mer. [f. Overtime *sb.* + -er 1.] One who works overtime.

1926 Stanley Baldwin *On England* 99 The just and the unjust, the half-timers, the whole-timers and the over-timers.

Overtop, *v.* Add: **1. b.** *intr.* To rise *over*.

1870 Mayne Reid *White Squaw* ix. 33 In the centre of the group was a large building, which..far o'ertopped over the others.

Over-trawl, *v.* [Over- 27.] *trans.* To trawl (a fishing-ground) too much or to depletion. So **Over-traw·ling** *vbl. sb.*

1913 *Q. Rev.* Apr. 444 In 1892 the Trawlers' Society..again protested against over-trawling.

O·ver-trick. [Over B. 2.] *Bridge.* A trick taken in excess of the number called or contracted for. Also *attrib.*

1921 Flor. Irwin *Compl. Auction Player* 15 Each over-trick is worth twice its value below the line. 1927 *Observer* 5 June 19/2 All over-trick bonuses gained by a vulnerable side ..count double. 1929 M. C. Work *Compl. Contract Bridge* i. 2 A trick-score of 20 or 30 plus two overtricks each worth 50.

Overview, *v.* **1.** (Modern example.)

1863 Susan Warner *Old Helmet* xii. (1864) 156 Mrs. Powle's fair face would overview a moral desolation more hopeless and more cheerless [etc.].

Over-vulcaniza·tion. [Over- 29 b.] The fact or state of being over-vulcanized.

1909 *Installation News* III. 48/2 The brittleness of the insulation, caused either by over-vulcanization or a lack of pure rubber in the compound.

Over-vu·lcanize, *v.* [Over- 27 b.] *trans.* To vulcanize (rubber) excessively; to make hard or brittle by vulcanizing.

1922 *Encycl. Brit.* XXX. 35/1 In 1916 some resistance to petrol was introduced by using pure para heavily loaded with mineral matter and rather over-vulcanized.

O·verwalker. [-er 1.] One who walks too much or too far.

1881 Stevenson *Walking Tours* Wks. 1906 II. 426 It is here that your overwalker fails of comprehension.

Overweighted, *ppl. a.* (Add example.)

1927 Bowley & Stamp *Nat. Income 1924* 23 But when we pass from the accidental grouping in the returns, overweighted by banks, to the whole numbers according to the census, the averages are brought up again to the medians.

O·verwei·ghting, *vbl. sb.* [-ing 1.] The act or fact of giving or having too much weight; overloading, overload.

1905 *Westm. Gaz.* 1 Sept. 2/3 The frightful overweighting of the postman because of the flood of pictorial postcards. 1914 R. M. Jones *Spiritual Reformers 16th & 17th Cent.* xv. 289 The Cambridge scholars were much better equipped for their task.., their gravest difficulty being an overweighting of learning.

Overwi·ntering, *vbl. sb.* [-ing 1.] The action of the verb Overwinter. Also *attrib.*

1900 *Yearbk. U.S. Dept. Agric.* 90 The overwintering crop. 1923 *Glasgow Herald* 17 July 7 Preparations [are to be] made for a probable overwintering there next year.

O·ver-wood. [Over- 1 d.] The tall trees in a forest; contrasted with *underwood*.

1904 Schlich *Man. Forestry* (ed. 3) II. 85 The overwood should consist of healthy trees which, if possible, have been raised from seed.

Overwork, *v.* **3.** Add: Also *transf.* and *fig.*

1878 G. M. Hopkins *Poems* (1918) 33 No Atlantic squall overwrought her. 1922 *Times Lit. Suppl.* 12 Oct. 642/2 Gobineau has carefully avoided any such threadbare device as that of the missing heir so overworked by Scott.

Overwrou·ghtness. [-ness.] Overwrought condition.

1923 Deeping *Secret Sanctuary* xxii. He..poured out a glass of white wine for Stretton, sensing the man's overwroughtness, and noticing the tense mouth and the troubled eyes.

Ovesting, *vbl. sb.* [f. *ovest* Ovet + -ing 1.] The action of feeding on mast and acorns.

1906 A. Marshall *R. Baldock* iii. 28 Sometimes a drove of black pigs would cross his path, fussily intent on their ovesting.

Ovibos (ōu·vibɒs). [The generic name of the musk-ox (*ovibos muschatus*), so called because it represents a sub-family intermediate between the sheep (*ovis*) and the ox (*bos*).] A member of the sub-family *Ovibovinæ*; a musk-ox.

1921 Stefansson *Friendly Arctic* 342 We found the ancient and far-decayed skull of a female ovibos. *Ibid.* 582, I shot two ovibos as all we needed out of the fifteen or twenty seen. 1925 *Chambers's Jrnl.* 14 Feb. 167/1 Here..will roam large herds of the domesticated musk-ox or ovibos. 1929 *Encycl. Brit.* II. 306/1 With the ovibos domesticated, the potentialities of the Arctic will be greater. *Ibid.*, Ovibos beef is indistinguishable from ordinary domestic beef.

Ovigenetic (ōu:vidʒĕne·tik), *a.* [f. Ovi-1 + -genetic.] = Ovogenetic.

1908 *Lancet* 23 May 1495/2 The spermatogenic and ovigenetic cells of the sexual glands in higher animals.

Ovoplasm. (Example.)

1904 McCabe tr. *Haeckel's Wonders of Life* 254 The chemical difference between the ovoplasm of the female and the sperm-plasm of the male cell.

Ovovitellin (ōu:vo,vite·lin). [f. Ovo- + Vitellin.] The vitellin found in the yolk of eggs.

1906 *Westm. Gaz.* 29 Aug. 2/2 The hæmoglobin of the blood of the chick is formed by certain cyanic ferruginous compounds which are found associated with ovovitelline.

Ovule. Add: **3.** *Comb.* as *ovule-bearing.*

1915 Sir E. R. Lankester *Diversions Naturalist* 310 Its leaves are 'needles'...But its ovule-bearing flower..does not..have any resemblance to a 'cone'.

Owe, *v.* **2.** Add: *Sporting.* To be under an obligation to give one's opponent in a match (a number of strokes or points) as a handicap.

1904 J. P. Paret *Lawn Tennis* 345 *Owe-fifteen* (*thirty or forty*), a term used in handicap play to indicate that one player must make one (fifteen), two (thirty), or three (forty) points in each game before he begins to score. 1908 *Daily Chron.* 24 Aug. 9/3 Mr. F. Scarf..owing one stroke, beat Mr. R. C. Oppenheimer,..(handicap 15), by 7 holes up and 5 to play.

Owl, *sb.* **7.** Add: **owl-cote**; **owl-car** *U.S.*, a tram-car running during the night; **owl-train** (earlier and later examples); **owl-wise** *a.*, as wise as an owl; **owl-wise** *adv.*, in the manner of an owl.

1889 Farmer *Americanisms*, *Owl-car*, a tram-car plying late into the night. 1904 *N. Y. Even. Post* 7 May 1 The driver of an 'owl car' that rattled eastward on Spring street. 1920 C. Sandburg *Smoke & Steel* 37 The owl car blutters along in a sleep-walk. 1863 'Gail Hamilton' *Gala-Days* 107 For the substantial stone city..turns out to be a miserable little dirty, hutty, smutty, stagnant *owl-cote. 1876 [S. & A. Warner] *Gold of Chickaree* 248 Six miles to drive to the station and must take the morning train. Its not quite an '*owl train'—but comes along, I believe, by eight o'clock. 1910 *N. Y. Even. Post* 22 Dec. 3 The engine of the 'owl train'—for by this term the one leaving New York after midnight is called..went off the track. 1906 Kipling in *Tribune* 16 Jan. 4/4 Jimmy, at my side, rolled his congested eye-balls, *owl-wise. 1916 Deeping *Sincerity* xxxviii, His round, lard-coloured, mildly owl-wise face.

Owly, *a.* (Modern examples.)

1864 O. W. Norton *Army Lett.* 203 Last night I was out all night in the rain..and I feel owly to-day. 1873 Leland *Egypt. Sketch Bk.* 33 Up started a little dark, old, owly, goblin, night-ghoul of a creature.

Own, *a.* **3. c.** Add: *To get one's own back*: To get even with, to revenge oneself or take vengeance *on*.

1910 Driscoll *Ringcraft* 17 He wanted to get his own back, and..he fancied he saw his chance. 1920 'Ixion' *Motor Cycle Remin.* 124 Whenever he met me I was able to get my own back.

4. own-rooted = *own-root*.

1915 M. E. King *Gothic Ruin & Reconstruction* 12 Let the renascent art blunder at first, as it must if it be own-rooted and not parasitic.

Owner. Add: *Navy slang.* The captain of a warship, barge, or other boat. So **Ow·neress**, the captain's wife.

1904 Kipling *Traffics & Discoveries* 49 I'm going to deviate to the owner's comfortable cabin direct. 1916 G. Taylor *With Scott* 213 Scott was invariably known as The Owner, a naval term always applied to the captain of a warship. 1923 *Blackw. Mag.* Apr. 445/2 The Owner and Owneress have a very jolly little cabin.

b. *owner-driver.*

1924 *Morris Owner* Mar. 20/1 A sympathetic understanding of his car and of road-craft by an owner-driver..makes for more pleasurable motoring.

Owning (ōu·niŋ), *ppl. a.* [-ing 2.] That owns property, plant, business interests, etc.

1904 *Electr. Investm.* 7 Dec. 773/1 A set-off against any advantage the owning company may be said to secure in extra traffic by the connection. 1909 *Westm. Gaz.* 19 Jan. 2/1 Of the five owning companies three at least have other routes which are more profitable to them. 1923 Sadleir *Desolate Splendour* 80 Morvane and the literal appellation of its owning family.

Ox. Add: **5. a.** *ox-chain*, *-common* (later examples), *-gad*, *-goad* (later examples), *-mill*, *-sawmill*, *-sled* (earlier examples), *-team* (later examples), *-wagon* (earlier examples); **b.** *ox-driver* (earlier examples).

1835 J. H. Ingraham *South-West* II. 185 A twenty-four pounder, suspended by a heavy *ox chain. 1866 *Rep. Indian Affairs* 202, I also repaired 20 wagons, 15 ox chains, 15 grain cradles. 1662 *Essex Inst. Hist. Coll.* LVI. 300 For 2 *ox commons..about 5 acres second division of meadow. 1727 *N.H. Probate Rec.* II. 309, I give and Bequeath unto my son..my shear of thatch ground on the great ox common. 1746 *Ibid.* III. 368 Half a share of Marsh lying at a place called the Ox Common. 1828 Mrs. Royall *Black Bk.* II. 114 He was one of your right down flat footed *ox-drivers. 1843 *Yale Lit. Mag.* VIII. 332 'Gee Bright!' shouted the stentorian voice of an ox-driver. 1836 *Knickerbocker Mag.* VIII. 681 His father kept a long *ox-gad to whip him with. 1843 *Ibid.* XXI. 125 The ladies requested the loan of Mr. Diddlemas's *ox-goad to knock down chestnut burrs. 1848 E. Bryant *California* iii. 32 The crack of the ox-goad, the whoa-haws,..create a most Babel-like and exciting confusion. 1826 T. Flint *Recoll.* 211 Steam-mills arose in St. Louis, and *ox-mills on the principle of the inclined plain or tread-mill. 1837 Peck *Gaz. Illinois* I. 33 Ox mills on the inclined plane and horse mills by draught, are common throughout..the state. 1817 in *Trans. Ill. State Hist. Soc.* 1910, 150 An inclined Wheel *ox Saw Mill with two saws. 1844 *Knickerbocker Mag.* XXIII. 445 Let us ride..home on the *ox-sled. 1863 H. S. Randall *Pract. Shepherd* xix. 228 And who does not recollect the old-fashioned, lively and merry scene of hauling out hay on an ox-sled. 1842 *Knickerbocker Mag.* XIX. 303 The carriages in the high-way never run over his heavy *ox-team. 1848 E. Bryant *California* i. 14 Ox-teams seem to be esteemed as preferable. 1881 *Rep. Indian Affairs* xxiv, A majority of the heads of families have ox teams. 1831 Peck *Guide Emigrants* II. 135 From twelve to fifteen large *ox waggons are employed..in hauling it [coal] to market. 1857 D. Braman *Inform. Texas* iii. 56 The ox-wagons, the 'peculiar institution' of this country, are hauling away cotton.

6. **ox-beef** (later example); **ox-chip**, a piece of dry ox-dung; **ox-foot oil** = Neat's foot oil; **ox-frame**, a frame for holding oxen while they are being shod; **ox-yard**, also, a yard where oxen are kept.

1878 *Amer. Home Cook Book* 5 *Ox-beef, when it is young, will have a fine open grain, and a good red colour. 1857 W. Chandless *Visit Salt Lake* I. vii. 122 Some one pitched on an old camping-place studded with '*ox-chips'. 1884 *Encycl. Brit.* XVII. 747/1 A large quantity of *ox-foot oil is prepared in and exported from the River Plate region in South America. 1844 *Knickerbocker Mag.* XXIII. 155 A little slab-roofed smithy...An *ox-frame standing by the door, and at one side a shed. 1896 Morris *Mess. March Wind* 14 The straw from the *ox-yard is blowing about.

b. **ox-balm** (earlier example.)

1853 *Trans. Michigan Agric. Soc.* (1854) 130 The plants were very numerous, among which were *oxbalm..and marsh grass.

Ox-bow. Add: **1.** (Recent U.S. examples.)

1834 Seba Smith *Major Downing* 46 A farmer ort to stick to his ox bows and goard sticks. 1846 Sage *Scenes Rocky Mts.* (1859) 50 An extra quantity of ox-bows, axle-trees..as a resource in case of accidents or breakage. 1881 *Rep. Indian Affairs* 398 Ox-bows, 2-inch..doz. 51.

3. *Comb.* (in sense 1) **ox-bow key**, a key for fastening the end of an ox-bow; **ox-bow stirrup**, a stirrup whose shape resembles that of an ox-bow.

1882 *Rep. Indian Affairs* 480 *Ox bow keys, 2 inch. 1907 S. E. White *Arizona Nights* I. i. 5 Uncie Jim sat placidly on his white horse, his thin knees bent to the *ox-bow stirrups, smoking.

Ox cart. [Ox 5.] A cart drawn by an ox or oxen.

1768 Washington *Diaries* I. 287 Began to draw it [wheat] in..with only my Ox Cart. 1785 *Ibid.* II. 441 A good Oxe Cart—2 Oxe yokes. 1801 *Austin Papers* (1924) I. 61, 2 ox Carts, £6 [each]. 1850 W. Colton *Three Years California* iii. 42 The ox-cart of the Californian is quite unique and primitive. 1877 [see Ox *sb.* 5].

Oxford. Add: **1.** *attrib.* **Oxford bags**, trousers, a style of trousers very wide at the ankles; **Oxford blue**, a dark shade of blue; **Oxford ragwort**, a species of ragwort, *Senecio squalidus*.

1875 *All Y. Round* 20 Feb. 444/2 The hues peculiar to the best period of Sèvres were gros-blue, a dark heavy *Oxford blue. 1926 *Nat. Hist. Oxford Distr.* 72 A few brave adventitious plants may be seen on the walls including the ubiquitous *Oxford Ragwort. 1927 *Observer* 1 May 15/2 Crossword puzzles, sweepstakes, *Oxford trousers.

2. *ellipt.* for Oxford mixture, shoe, trousers, etc.

1909 *Public Ledger* (Philad.) 24 June 5/4 Advt., Boys' dependable, well-made Oxfords. 1914 *Glasgow Herald* 7 Sept. 10/2 Glasgow firms manufacture..zephyrs, Oxfords, shirtings, and dress goods. 1924 *Times Trade & Eng. Suppl.* 29 Nov. 235/3 These goods range in price from $12.50 and $14.50 for the low shoes, or Oxfords, to $16.50 for ordinary boots.

Oxfordish (ɒ·ksfōɹdiʃ). [f. Oxford + -ish.] Oxford jargon or slang.

1863 C. Reade *Hard Cash* I. 16 Ploughed is the new Oxfordish for plucked.

Oxfordist, *sb.* Add: (*b*) In modern use, a supporter of Oxford against Cambridge.

1924 *Glasgow Herald* 7 Apr. 11 Next April they will be militant Oxfordists once more.

Oxidase, variant of Oxydase.

1899 J. R. Green *Soluble Ferments* 289 During the last few years the existence of another class of enzymes has been indicated, all of which act by promoting direct oxidation of various substances, including various aromatic compounds and sugar. These have been called *oxidases*.

Oxter, *sb.* Add: Also *Comb.* as **oxter plate** (see quot. 1904).

1885 Paasch *From Keel to Truck* 46. 1904 A. C. Holms *Pract. Shipbuilding* I. 526 The oxter plates are those which take the sternpost, immediately below, or partly on, the transom. 1927 G. F. Leechman *Theory & Practice of Steering* 51 The rotary current applies considerable pressure upon the hull in the vicinity of the oxter plate.

Oxy-acetylene (ɒ:ksi,ăse·tilīn), *a.* [f. Oxy- 2 + Acetylene.] Consisting of, or involving the use of, a mixture of oxygen and acetylene; used *esp.* of instruments and processes employed in cutting and welding metals.

1909 *Westm. Gaz.* 19 Jan. 4/2 A special weldless steel tubing brazed together by an oxy-acetylene process. 1914 Elbourne *Factory Administr.* 249 The account will include such plant as Heating Furnaces, Smithy Hearths,..Sand-blasting, Oxy-acetylene Apparatus, and so on. 1921 *Dict. Occup.-Terms* (1927) § 249 Oxy-acetylene or electric-welders and cutters. 1922 *Encycl. Brit.* XXX. 34/2 Oxy-acetylene welding was often used in joints. 1925 J. R. Partington *Text-bk. Inorg. Chem.* 188 More recently the oxy-acetylene blowpipe has come into use, in which acetylene gas takes the place of hydrogen.

Oxygenated, *ppl. a.* Add: **b.** Treated with oxygen.

1910 'R. Dehan' *Dop Doctor* lxv. 609 The sippers of ether ..take no shame in seeing the oxygenated greyhound win the coursing-match and the oxygenated racehorse run for the Cup!

Oxylith(e) (ɒ·ksiliþ). [ad. F. *oxylithe*, Oxy- 2 + Gr. λίθος stone.] Peroxide of calcium, which gives up some of its oxygen in the presence of water.

[1902 *Edin. Even. News* 28 Jan. 2 Experiments are now in progress with a substance known in the French service as 'oxylithe', which, it is said, gives off chemically pure oxygen by the simple action of water.] 1903 *Westm. Gaz.* 27 Aug. 2/1 To the solid he [M. Robin] gives the name of oxylith. 1924 *Chambers's Jrnl.* Oct. 701/2 The helmet of this appliance..is supplied with a substance called 'oxylithe', which gives off pure oxygen when breathed upon.

Ox yoke. [Ox 5.] A yoke used for draught oxen.

1573–1688 [see Ox 5]. 1785 Washington *Diaries* II. 441 A good Oxe Cart—2 Oxe yokes. 1809 *Austin Papers* (1924) I. 164 One Plough, one Harrow,..and two Ox yokes. 1847 in H. Howe *Hist. Coll. Ohio* 188 Journeys..of 20 or 50 miles, for the sole purpose of having the staple of an ox-yoke mended. 1879 B. F. Taylor *Summer-Savory* xvii. 138 Awkward H's like a pair of leaning bar-posts with one bar, and B's like ox-yoke.

Oxyphilic (ɒksifi·lik), *a.* *Biol.* [f. Oxyphil + -ic.] Staining readily with acid dyes.

1905 C. E. Simon *Physiol. Chem.* (ed. 2) 326 The granules ..according to their affinity for acid, basic or neutral dyes, ..are termed oxyphilic, basophilic, and neutrophilic respectively.

Oxyurid (ɒksi,ū̆ə·rid). *Zool.* [f. Oxyuris.] A thread-worm, a member of the genus *Oxyuris*.

1921 *Brit. Museum Return* 110 *Oxyuris Paronai* v. Linst., and its association with another Oxyurid in the same Host.

Oyster. Add: **1. d.** A reserved or uncommunicative person.

1930 J. B. Priestley *Angel Pavement* vi. 305, I never knew anybody so close, you old oyster you!

5. a. *oyster-house*, *-pie* (later example), *-shoal*, *-shop* (examples), *-stand*, *-stew*, *-supper*.

1835 Longstreet *Georgia Scenes* (1843) 48 Who should he find there but Monsieur Sancric, of *oyster-house memory. 1851 A. O. Hall *Manhattaner* 59 Some of them [mosquitoes] are dainty, and associate only with fat people whose nightmares are based upon turtle steaks and *oyster pies. 1837 J. L. Williams *Terr. Florida* 22 The pass is rapidly filling with *oyster shoals. 1830 O. W. Holmes *Ballad of Oysterman* 28 Now they keep an *oyster-shop for mermaids down below. 1891 *Harper's Mag.* Dec. 44/2 A small oyster shop, whose red balloon in a side street had caught my eye. 1851 A. O. Hall *Manhattaner* 7 *Oyster stands, where dirty mouths and flickering tallow candles grinned ghostly satisfaction. 1846 Corcoran *Pickings* 128 Mrs. Smith was never known to have an *oyster stew of an evening that she did not divide it with Mrs. Jones. 1861 *Maryland Hist. Mag.* V. 314 Advanced two miles, and bivouacked for the night, having a very palatable oyster stew to sleep on. 1835 Longstreet *Georgia Scenes* (1843) 41, I..propose that we go out and take an *oyster supper before we retire to rest. 1856 Mrs. Stowe *Dred* II. 281 He drinks and frolics, and has his oyster-suppers.

c. *oyster-white* (example).

1901 *Sketch* 11 Sept. 303 Her wedding-dress of oyster-white satin.

d. **oyster-knife** (later examples); **oyster piece**, a piece of oyster veneer; **oyster-scow**, a scow engaged in oyster-fishing; **oyster-tongs** (later example); **oyster veneer**, a whorled veneer obtained from small boughs of trees; = *Oystering b.

1843 Carlton *New Purchase* viii. 53 An *oyster knife worn usually in his bosom like a dirk. 1867 Cozzens *Sayings* xvi. 118 The sword was beaten into the oyster-knife. 1925 *Oyster piece [see *Oystering]. 1824 *Nantucket Inquirer* 26 Jan. [Th.] He wore a hat of the new *oyster-scow cut. 1844 *Knickerbocker Mag.* XXIV. 293, I am told of a coalition between two oyster-scows which are covered over with the shell of an ordinary boat. 1891 *Scribner's Mag.* X. 473 An old bottle, a lost anchor, an escaped dredge or a pair of *oyster-tongs will serve. 1914 Eberlein & McClure *Pract. Bk. Period Furniture* 86 When the cabinets were '*oyster' veneered, inlaid with marqueterie or lacquered.

Oyster, *v.* Add: **b.** To feed on oysters; with *up*.

1861 T. Winthrop *C. Dreeme* 156 Boys, I've got a sick man to oyster up.

Oyster bank. Chiefly *U.S.* [Oyster 5 d.] A raised part in the bed of a river or the bottom of the sea where oysters abound.

1612 [see Oyster *sb.* 5 d]. 1623–4 *Jrnl. Ho. Burg. Virginia* 28 We weare forced..to disperse the wholl Collony, some amoungst the Salvadges but most to the Oyster Banks. 1655 *Rec. New Haven* 247 Sending his servants to the oyster bankes to gather oysters. 1744 F. Moore *Voy. Georgia* 105 On the shore were oyster banks, dry at low water. 1802 Ellicott *Jrnl.* (1919) 235 The sound is so full of oyster banks, and shoals, that it is difficult to navigate it, without a pilot. 1831 [see Oyster *sb.* 5 d]. 1836 Edward *Hist. Texas* 17 The lake is difficult to cross, owing to the mud and oyster banks. 1843 *Knickerbocker Mag.* XXI. 174 The Timoleon, which lay on an oyster-bank a mile or two below.

Oyster-boat. Chiefly *U.S.* [Oyster 5 d.] A (special form of) boat used for oyster-fishing, or in oyster cultivation.

1419–1538 [see Oyster 5 d]. 1813 Paulding *Sc. Fiddle* i. 18 The sailors..urg'd in dreams the gallant chase Of oyster-boats far up the bay. 1860 S. Mordecai *Virginia* I. 24 This place was called the Rock Landing, where oyster boats and small craft resorted. 1891 *Scribner's Mag.* X. 472, I will try to describe how the deck of an oyster-boat must be trimmed for its work.

Oyster cellar. *U.S.* [Oyster 5 d.] A shop in a basement where oysters are sold.

1839 C. F. Briggs *Harry Franco* II. iv. 46, I went and satisfied my appetite with a bowl of oyster soup, in an oyster cellar in the vicinity of the Bear Market. 1857 *Quinland* II. 187 An old..dirty-looking building, beneath which was an oyster-cellar and 'rum-hole'. 1872 Talmage *Abom. Mod. Society* 224 Whether you sell it in low oyster cellar or behind the polished counter of a first class hotel. 1889 [see Oyster 5 d].

Oystered (oi·stəɹd), *a.* [f. Oyster *sb.*] Bearing an oyster-shaped or whorled pattern; used of veneer.

1914 Eberlein & McClure *Pract. Bk. Period Furniture* 57 The practise did not obtain conspicuously till the middle or end of the Carolean epoch when the whorled or 'oystered' veneer..came into vogue.

Oystering, *vbl. sb.* Add: **b.** Oyster veneer or work done with this.

1914 Eberlein & McClure *Pract. Bk. Period Furniture* 90 Marqueterie, oystering and lacquer were freely used in their decorations. 1925 Penderel-Brodhurst & Layton *Gloss. Engl. Furniture* 117 The slices are referred to as Oyster-pieces, and the arrangement as Oystering.

Oyster-man. Chiefly *U.S.* [Oyster 5 d.] A man engaged in taking, breeding, or selling oysters.

1552 [see Oyster 5 d]. 1760 Washington *Diaries* I. 108 An Oyster Man, who had lain at my landing. 1830 O. W. Holmes *Ballad of Oysterman* 1 It was a tall young oysterman lived by the riverside. 1855 *Knickerbocker Mag.* XLVI. 222 In the sound, 'hard-shell' clam-catchers, fishermen, and oyster-men steadily ply their different callings. 1879 *Harper's Mag.* June 63/1 The region..is very thickly settled by fishermen and oystermen.

Oyster-plant. *U.S.* [Oyster 5 d.] The salsify.

1824 'A. Singleton' *Lett. fr. South & West* 72 [The Virginians] also..cherish the salsify, or oyster-plant, so called from its flavour when fried. 1841 *Cultivator* VIII. 114 Oyster Plant, or Salsify..after boiling soft, make gravy of flour, butter, etc. and add to them, and really they are rich substitutes for oysters.

Oyster-saloon. *U.S.* [Oyster 5 d.] A shop where oysters are sold or eaten.

1833 *Knickerbocker Mag.* I. 117 To be seen about taverns and oyster saloons. 1851 A. O. Hall *Manhattaner* 9 Its builders..constructed it upon an angular piece of ground.. garnished with oyster saloons. 1891 *Harper's Mag.* Dec. 46/1 The little oyster saloon, close at hand, had seemed to offer the shortest cut to my cousin's relief.

Oyster-shell. **b.** Add: **oyster-shell bark-louse** *U.S.*, an insect, *Aspidiotus conchiformis*, resembling an oyster-shell in shape, which infests apple-trees; **oyster-shell scale** *U.S.*, the scale of the oyster-shell bark-louse.

1877 *Rep. Vermont Board Agric.* IV. 150 Dr. Worcester has also shown me a branch covered with..oyster shell bark-louse. *Ibid.*, The insect is shorter and stouter than that of the oyster shell scale.

Ozonian (ozōu·niăn), *a.* [f. Ozone + -ian.] That employs ozonized air.

1912 *Chambers's Jrnl.* Aug. 557/2 The success of this experiment should lead to the adoption of ozonian ventilation at all underground railways and stations.

P

P. II. Add: P.B.I. = Poor Bloody Infantry; P.C. (also) = postcard [? per cent.; P.O. (also) = postal order; P.R.O. = Public Record Office.

Pace (pāˈsē), adv. [L. abl. sing. of *pax* PEACE by the leave of (a person).] Used chiefly as an ironical or courteous apology for a contradiction or difference of opinion.

Pace-maker. Add: 1. Also, one of the leading runners in a race.

b. *transf.* A workman who sets the rate of working for others.

2. *Phys.* That part of an animal's heart which determines the rate at which it contracts; a piece of tissue in the vena cava of the mammalian heart where the contractions begin.

Pace-making. Add: The act or practice of making or setting the pace for competitors in a race.

Pacey (pāˈsē), a. [f. PACE *sb.*¹ + -Y.] Having pace or speed, fast.

Pacific. A. *adj.* Add: 2. b. = PEACEFUL 4.

3. c. Of, pertaining to, or situated near, the Pacific Ocean. *Pacific slope*, a native or inhabitant of the Pacific slope. *U.S.*

Pacey. Add.

4. *Pacific blockade*: (See quot. 1880.)

Pacificism (-sīˈfīsīz'm). [f. PACIFIC + -ISM.] = PACIFISM.

Pacificist (pāˈsī-fīsīst). [f. as prec. + -IST.] = PACIFIST.

Pacifism (pæˈsīfīz'm). [ad. F. *pacifisme* (see quot. 1901), f. *pacifique* a. + -ISM.

Pacifist (pæˈsīfīst). [f. as prec. + -IST.

Pacing, *ppl. a.* (Add quot.) Also U.S. example of special sense : cf. PACE *sb.* 2.

Pack, *v.*¹ Add: 1. b. (Later examples.)

2. c. Also *intr.* or in pass. of a person : To have finished packing.

d. *transf.* To retire from or go out of action; to stop working; to die. *colloq.*

5. a. (Further examples.) Also of a group of runners in a long-distance race.

Pack, *sb.*² Add: 1. e. (Later example.)

Pack, *v.*² Also, to select or arrange a body of voters, etc., in order to secure (a particular decision or result).

Packer, *sb.* Add (Later example.)

Packet, *sb.* Add: 1. f. A bullet or other missile; *to stop a packet*, to get hit by a bullet or shell. *slang.*

Packeteer (pæketēˈr). [f. PACKET 2 + -EER.]

Packetarian (pæketēˈrĭan). [f. PACKET 2 + -ARIAN.] One of the crew of a packet-boat.

Packing. Add: 1. d. The conveyance of merchandise on pack animals.

3. *packing-house*, *-shed* (examples): *packing-box* (Later example.)

Pack-mule. *U.S.* Add: [PACK *sb.*¹] A mule used for carrying packs.

Packsaddle, *v.* [PACKSADDLE 1] *trans.* To convey on a packsaddle.

Pack train. *U.S.* Add: A train of pack animals.

Paddle, *v.*² Add: 2. b. (Earlier examples.)

Paddler. Add: 2. A child's waterproof knickers or overall.

Paddling, *vbl. sb.* (Add quot.) b.

Paddock. Add: 2. b. To excavate wash-dirt on shallow ground.

Padre. Add: 2. b. A steam excavator.

Padouk. [Variant of PADAUK.]

Padded, *ppl. a.* (Add example.)

Page, *v.*¹ Add: c. To send for, search for, or communicate with (a person) by means of a page; *U.S.*

Pageant. Add: b. In recent use : A spectacular representation (usually in the form of a procession) of scenes or events belonging to the past history of a place.

Pageanteer. In recent usage, one who takes part in a pageant (sense *5* b).

Pageantry. (Modern example.)

Paido-, see PEDO-.

Pail. Add: 1. d. The tin vessel in which a workman carries his mid-day meal from home. *U.S.*

Pain, *sb.*¹ Add: 7. d. Add: pain-point = pain-spot; pain-spot, a small spot on the surface of the skin which is sensible to pain, or whose adequate stimulus is pressure for pain.

Pain-killer. [PAIN *sb.*¹] A substance or medicine for relieving or abolishing pain.

Painless, *a.* Add: b. (Modern example.)

Painstaking, *a.* (Earlier example.)

Paint, *sb.* Add: 2. e. Phr. As *smart* (pretty, etc.) *as paint*: superlatively smart, pretty, etc.

6. *paint-drum, -oil* (earlier example); paint-brush (?), a parasitic plant with brightly-coloured flowers suggestive of paint-brushes (see quot.); paint-stone, a stone used as a source of paint.

Paint (pānt), *sb.*² and *a.* *U.S.* = PINTO.

Painter¹. 4. Add: *painter's brush* (also = *Indian paint-brush* [INDIAN A. 4 b]).

Painter². [painter²] [f. PAINTER 1 + -ISH.] Characteristic or suggestive of painters.

Painting, *vbl. sb.* Add: 1. b. Condition as regards paint.

6. *painting-machine, city.*

Pair, *v.* 1. Add.

Pairing, *vbl. sb.* Add: *pairing-call.*

Pair-oar. Add.

Pair-oared, *a.* = PAIR-OAR attrib.

Pair-royal. a. (Later examples.)

Palace, *sb.* 8. palace-car (earlier examples).

Palais de danse (palɛ̄ dǝ dãs). [F. = dancing hall.] A hall or other building where facilities for dancing are provided.

Palanthropic (pelænθrōˈpik). a. [irreg. f. PALÆO- + ANTHROPIC.] Of or belonging to the earlier part of the geological period which is marked by the existence of man.

Palatal. A. *adj.* 2. (Earlier example.)

Palate, *sb.* b. (Later example.)

Palatinate, *sb.* Add: 1. d. In the University of Durham : A blazer of palatinate purple (see *3* b) assigned as a distinction in sports ; a person who has gained this distinction.

3. b. Applied in Durham to a light shade of purple or lavender used in academical and municipal robes and in some athletic costumes of members of the University.

Palatogram [-GRAM] a record of the use made of the palate in producing a sound.

Palato-graphy [GRAPHY] (see quot.)

Palaver, *v.* Add: 2. c. Business, affair. *slang.*

Pale, *sb.* 8. *pale-board* (modern U.S. example).

Palestine (palestīn). Also *adj.*

Palestinian (palestīnian). a. and *sb.* [f. *Palestine* the modern name of the country on the Eastern shore of the Mediterranean.] a. and *sb.*, pertaining to, or connected with Palestine or its inhabitants. b. A native or inhabitant of Palestine.

Palette. 1. Add: A similar apparatus used by a mosaic worker.

3. (Later example.)

Paliform, *a.* (Earlier example.)

Paling, *vbl. sb.* Add: 2. *paling-fence* (later U.S. examples).

Pall, *sb.*³ b. pall-holder (earlier examples).

Pallet, *sb.*¹ (Modern example.)

Pally, *a.* See *s.v.* PAL in Dict. (Later example.)

Palm, *sb.*¹ Add: 7. c. Add : palm bottom, a hollow or valley in which palms grow; palm squirrel, a species of small squirrel, *Sciurus palmarum*, found in India; palm-stand, a stand for supporting a palm grown in a plant-pot.

Palm, *sb.*² b. palm-reader.

Palm Beach. The name of a sea-side resort in Florida, U.S.A., used *attrib.* esp. in *Palm Beach suit.*

Palmer, *sb.*¹ Add.

Palmerstonian (pāˌmǝrstōˈnian). a. [f. the name of Henry John Temple, Viscount Palmerston, English statesman (1784–1865) + -IAN.] Of, pertaining to, or characteristic of Lord Palmerston. So *-ism* n., a supporter of Lord Palmerston.

Palmette. 1. Also Add.

Palmetto. c. palmetto ground (earlier example), *hat, leaf, tree* (later examples); also in sense 'thatched with palmetto leaves', as *palmetto cabin, house* (earlier example), *hut*; palmetto banner — palmetto flag; Palmetto State (examples).

Palmful, *a.* Whatever John Brent said : 149 They took their water by the throatful, not by the palmful.

Palm-leaf. c. *palm-leaf hat* (later example), *fan.*

Palpate, *v.* Add: *also. or intr.*

Palsied, *ppl. a.* (Modern example.)

Palter, *v.* 1. (Modern example.)

Paludal, *a.* Add: b. fig.

Paludan, *a.* (later example).

Pam, *sb.* b. *pam-flush,* a flush headed by the knave of clubs.

Pampa. 1. Add: 2. *pampas deer* (earlier example); pampas grass; pampas partridge, a species of Tinamou, *Nothura maior*, found in South America.

Pampsychic, variant of Panpsychic (Pan-).

Pampsychism, variant of panpsychism (in quot. attrib.).

Pan-. Comb. 1. (Earlier example.)

Pan-. Add: 7. Pan-psychic a., pertaining to or based on panpsychism. Pan-psychist, one who believes in panpsychism; also attrib. Pan-psy-chi'stic a., connected with or characterized by panpsychism.

Pantelo'logism [TELEOLOGISM] (see quot.)

Panacea. Add: b. (Earlier example.)

Panatrope (pænatrōˈp). An electrical apparatus for the reproduction of gramophone records, consisting of a pick-up, an amplifier and a loud speaker.

Pancake, *sb.* Add: 2. A vertical descent made by an aeroplane in a level position. *slang.*

3. *pancake-roll* *Electr. Engin.* (see quot. 1910).

Pancake, *v.* Add: b. *intr.* Of an aeroplane or the like: To descend vertically while in a (nearly) horizontal position owing to insufficient lift; to stall. Also of persons flying : To descend by causing the aeroplane, etc., to pancake. Hence **Pa·ncaking** *vbl. sb.* (in quot. fig.)

Panchromatic (pænkrōmæˈtik). a. *Photogr.* [f. Gr. παν- PAN- + χρωματ-ικ- relating to colour, CHROMATIC.] Representing all the colours in their proper intensities; equally sensitive to all the colours of the spectrum; orthochromatic. Also *ellipt.,* a panchromatic plate or preparation which renders a plate panchromatic. Hence **Panchro-matism,** panchromatic quality; panchromatic work.

Pandy, *sb.* Add: 2. Also (see quot.)

Pandect. Add: 2. b. In manuscript containing all the books of the bible.

Pandemonic, a. Add: 2. b. (Modern example.)

Pandemonium, *a.* Add: b. A demoniac person; a denizen of Pandemonium.

Pandora. (Earlier example.)

Pan-drop. *Sc.* [PAN *sb.*³ + DROP *sb.* 10 c.] A variety of comfit having the shape of a flattened sphere and flavoured with peppermint.

Pan-Germanist. [f. PAN-GERMAN.] A supporter of Pan-Germanism. So **Pan-German'istic** a., connected with or suggestive of Pan-Germanism.

Panglot (pæˈnglǫt). a. [f. Gr. παν- PAN- + γλωττ- tongue.] Of language.

Panel, *sb.* 4. b. Add: The official list of doctors in a district who accept patients under the

National Health Insurance Act of 1913. *On the panel,* (of a doctor) registered as accepting patients thus; (of a patient) under the care of a 'panel doctor' and hence subject to certain benefits and restrictions.

1913 *French* 30 July 205/1 The proposed Laureate was a medical man and not on panel.

6. *panel-doctor, practitioner,* one who accepts patients under the National Insurance Act; panel-fence (U.S.), a fence constructed in panels or sections (see PANEL *sb.* 8); panel-robbery, the business of a panel-thief; panel stamp, a stamp for decorating the panels in the cover of a book; panel wall, a division between two panels in a coal mine.

Panethenic (pænēθēˈnik). a. [f. as next.] Pertaining to, affecting, or extending over the whole of Greece.

Panic. *sb.* Add: 3. b. Add: panic bolt, a special bolt for a door designed to unfasten easily in emergencies.

Pan-handler (pæˈnhændlǝr). *v.* When he took the cinema in 1883, 1926, he put panic bolts on the wooden door : where there were ordinary slip bolts before.

Panic, *v.* Before 1. etc., and recent example.

Pan, v. Also 7. Add; also *slang.*

Panel, *v.* Add: attrib., as *panning-trough.*

Pannikin, *sb.* b. Head; in slang phr. *off one's pannikin* (Austral.) insane.

called the pan-handle of the East, and the other the pan-handle of the West.

Pan-handle (pæˈnhænd'l), *v. U.S.* [c. next.] *trans.* and *intr.* To beg.

Pan-handler (pæˈnhændlǝr). *U.S. slang.* [f. next.] A beggar.

Panhellenism (pænheˈliniz'm). a. Pertaining to, affecting, or extending over the whole of (Ægina) Greece. So **Panhelle·nic** a.

Panic, *sb.* Add: 5. Also (see quot.)

Pan-sexual. [PAN-] Pertaining to or involving sex in all its forms or manifestations. So **Pan-sexualism,** the view that the sex instinct plays a part in all human thought and activity and is the chief or only source of energy. **Pan-sexualist,** a supporter of pan-sexualism.

pan-sexualism. (In quot. as adj.) **Pan-sexua·lity** = *Pan-sexualism.*

1915 C. R. Payne tr. *Pfister's Psycho-anal. Method* 60 Which..has brought the reproach of 'pansexualism' against psychoanalysis. 1926 W. McDougall *Outl. Abnormal Psych.* i. 20 It has led Freud..., as Janet has said, to construct 'an enormous system of medical philosophy,' the theory of Pan-sexuality. *Ibid.* 131 Freud, in accordance with his pansexualist tendency, expressed the opinion [etc.]. *Ibid.* 314 The dogma that the Œdipus complex is present in all men is the principal instrument of the pansexual theory.

Pant-. Add: **Panta·rchic** *a.*, of or pertaining to a pantarchy.

1883 L. F. Ward *Dynamic Sociol.* I. 466 The cosmopolitan, or pantarchic stage.

Pantalettes, *sb. pl.* (Earlier examples.)

1834 *Knickerbocker Mag.* IV. 117 In the first place, in their blushing girlhood, they assume the pantalettes, or little pantaloons. 1838 *Southern Lit. Messenger* IV. 28/1 Two pretty sisters, in pantalettes, waited on table.

Pantheian (pænþī·ăn), *a.* [f. Pantheum + -ian.] = Pantheic.

1894 Sir G. Birdwood tr. *D'Alviella's Migration of Symbols* ii. 47 The manufacture of pantheian figures.

Pa·ntherishly, *adv.* [f. Pantherish *a.* + -ly.] In a manner suggestive of a panther.

1920 Mulford *J. Nelson* xviii. 202 Johnny, leaping pantherishly aside out of the rolling smoke, held two guns on the paralysed group.

Panties (pæ·ntiz), *pl.* [dim. of Pants.] Pants worn by children or close-fitting knickers worn by women.

1926 Cosmo Hamilton in *Good Housekeeping* July 186 It made me feel as though I ought to be wearing ringlets, panties to my ankles and a large hoop-skirt. 1928 *Weekly Dispatch* 27 May 15/7 Panties for boys and skirts for girls ..are being made *very* short.

Panting, *vbl. sb.*[1] Add: **b.** *spec.* In Shipbuilding: The bulging in and out of the plating of a ship under the force of the waves. Also *attrib.*

1886 Thearle *Mod. Pract. Shipbuilding* I. 112 The measures for preventing panting must necessarily be of such a character as shall stiffen the framing against lateral strains. 1899 Attwood *Theoret. Nav. Archit.* 212 Panting beams and stringers to be fitted at the after end. 1904 A. C. Holms *Pract. Shipbuilding* 105 At the stern, panting stresses are usually unimportant.

Pantings (pæ·ntiŋz), *vbl. sb.*[2] *pl.* [f. Pants.] Material for making pants.

1928 *Sunday Dispatch* 2 Sept. 10 Richard Cœur de Lion was a swagger sort of buck, and liked all his gentlemen to be positively gaudy in the choice of their pantings.

Pantograph. Add: **c.** An insulated flexible or jointed framework used on electric locomotives for collecting and conveying electric current from overhead wires to the motors.

1918 Webster Add. 1920 *Glasgow Herald* 23 Sept. 7 Electric locomotives can..be fitted..with pantograph collectors for the overhead wires.

Pantomi·mish, *a.* [-ish.] Suggestive of a pantomime; pantomimic.

1923 *Glasgow Herald* 3 Feb. 6/6 A few veterans may recall how pantomimish Mr. Gladstone looked when..he borrowed the hat of a colleague.

Pantopon (pæ·ntopǫn). *Med.* [f. Pan- + Opium.] An alternative name for *Omnopon.

1910 *Lancet* 8 Oct. 1104/1 This preparation, pantopon, represents the totality of the alkaloids of opium.

Pantothermal (pæntoþō·ɹmăl), *a.* [f. Panto- + Thermal.] Adapted to bear the heat or cold of any climate.

1906 *Athenæum* 10 Feb. 175/1 A revision of all captures ..appeared to show one species (*hexaptera*) as cosmopolitan and pantothermal.

Pantry. **2.** Add: **pantry-maid,** a maid-servant who has duties in the pantry.

1921 *Dict. Occup. Terms* (1927) § 900. 1928 *Daily Tel.* 5 June 4/7 He had paid her 22s a week as a pantrymaid.

Pants, *sb. pl.* **1. a.** (Earlier examples.)

1842 *Spirit of Times* (Philad.) 29 Aug. (Th.) A red-faced individual in a bottle-green coat and greasy pants. 1843 *Knickerbocker Mag.* XXII. 504 It irks us, however, to encounter in a description of Mr. Legare's dress the term 'pants' instead of pantaloons.

Pap, *sb.*[2] Add: **1.** (U.S. fig. example.)

1841 *Congress. Globe* 29 Jan. App. 300/2 The very new States are nursed from their chrysalis territorial condition into existence upon Federal pap from the Executive spoon.

3. *pap-food.*

1905 *Daily Chron.* 13 May 4/5 Too prolonged use of artificially digested and 'pap-foods' must be avoided.

Pap, *sb.*[3] *U.S.* Abbreviation of Papa[1].

1844 *Knickerbocker Mag.* XXIII. 15 They said, pap wasn't at home. 1854 Mary J. Holmes *Tempest & Sunshine* v. 69 Come here, and shake your old pap's paw. 1898 A. Nicholas *Idyl of Wabash* 53 His pap left him right smart of a lump. 1924 W. M. Raine *Troubled Waters* ii. 24 There can't any of you..run me out the way you did Pap Thomson.

Pap, *v.*[1] Add: **3.** To make into pap.

1927 *Observer* 6 Feb. 14/4 This does not mean papping food for babes; it means speaking intelligibly to grown-ups.

Papa[1]**.** Also *attrib.*

1901 Sarah Grand *Babs* lxxv. 350 So long as he does not assume papa airs with me, I don't mind.

Papacy. Add: **2. b.** Roman Catholic belief.

1914 *Shropsh. Archæol. Soc. Trans.* Ser. iv. IV. 45 Mr. Jermor seems to have been himself suspected of a leaning towards papacy.

Papaia, variant of *papaya*: see Papaw.

1913 Rupert Brooke in E. Marsh *Mem.* (1918) 108 Great squelchy tropical fruits, custard-apples, papaia, pomegranate,..and the rest.

Papality. (Later example in plur.)

1824 Landor *Imag. Conv.* (1891) II. 167 He resisted the authority of the pope, and refuted the doctrine of transubstantiation, with several other papalities.

Paper, *sb.* Add: **1. d.** (Earlier example of *on paper.*)

1788 *Amer. Museum* III. 336/2 The form of their constitution, as it is on paper, admits not of coercion. But necessity introduced it in practice.

10. d. (Earlier example of *paper blockade.*)

1812 *Boston Gaz.* 20 July (Th.) The paper-blockades, which have justly occasioned so much irritation, are now abandoned.

11. b. *paper-keeper.* **c.** *paper-bound* (example).

1901 *Sketch* XXXV. 26/2 The unsold *paper-bound books in Germany are returned to the publisher, who re-binds them. 1927 *Daily Tel.* 3 May 3 In the opinion of the Postmaster-General the *paperkeepers were amply remunerated at the present rates.

12. **paper-backed** *a.*, having a paper back; also (fig.), lacking in strength, feeble; **paper bark swamp,** a swamp in which paper bark trees grow; **paper cable,** an electric cable insulated with paper; **paper-folding,** the making of objects by folding paper; **paper-making wasp** = *paper-wasp*; **paper-mildew** (see quot.).

1888 Kipling *Soldiers Three* (1889) 52 'Push, men!' sez Crook; 'Push, ye *paper-backed beggars!' he sez. 1903 *Work* 14 Mar. 89/3 Handy Method of Binding Paper-Backed Books. 1909 *Chambers's Jrnl.* Sept. 610/2 The man then buys a paper-backed novel for fourpence-halfpenny. 1920 B. Cronin *Timber Wolves* 88 From the *paper-bark swamps came the reverberating boom of frogs. 1902 *Encycl. Brit.* XXXIII. 219/2 Between London and Birmingham a *paper cable 116 miles long..was laid in 1900. 1893 T. S. Row (*title*) Geometric Exercises in *Paper Folding. 1902 *Chambers's Jrnl.* Oct. 661/2 Paper-folding is an occupation which forms a good occasional lesson for older children. 1905 *Westm. Gaz.* 30 Sept. 13/2 Paper folding has long been a favourite amusement in our Kindergartens. 1867 *Amer. Naturalist* I. 140 The odor that arises from the Tarantula killer when she uses her sting..resembles the odor of the *paper-making wasp (Vespa), only much stronger. 1883 *Encycl. Brit.* XVI. 294/1 The *Paper-Mildew (*Ascotricha chartarum*)..grows on damp paper, and therefore is saprophytic in its mode of life.

Paper birch. *U.S.* (See Birch *sb.* 1 b.)

1810 Michaux *Arbres* I. 25 Paper birch (Bouleau à papier). 1832 D. J. Browne *Sylva Amer.* 121 This tree..is known to the Americans also by those denominations, and sometimes by that of Paper Birch.. 1866 [see Paper *sb.* 12]. 1893 B. Torrey *Footpath-way* 25 The dwarf paper birch (trees of no one knows what age, matting the ground). 1903 S. E. White *Forest* xiv. 193 Probably a little further along there would be a point of high land and delightful little paper-birches.

Papia, variant of *papaya*: see Papaw.

1921 *Outward Bound* Feb. 69/1 The natives..kept bringing fresh fruit to our view—mangoes and custard apples and papia.

Papist, *a.* Add: **3.** An imitator or follower of the poet, Alexander Pope. Also *attrib.*

a 1849 H. Coleridge *Ess.* (1851) II. 118 Nor would so many really monotonous jinglers have passed for correct, orthodox Papists. 1901 F. Harrison *Ruskin* ii. 21 Many a prize poem has had worse couplets in the Papist vein than these on Etna.

Papolater (pǟpǫ·lătəɹ). [f. L. *pāpa* pope + *-later*, -latry.] One who practises papolatry.

1913 A. Fortescue *Lesser Eastern Ch.* i. 4 We are Creed-tamperers, Papolaters, gross disturbers of the peace by our shameless way of sending missionaries.

Papoose. **b.** (Earlier examples.)

1815 Drake *Cincinnati* ii. 85 Poppoos root. 1853 Darlington *Flora Cestrica* (ed. 3) 11 Thalictrum-like Caulophyllum. Blue Cohosh. Pappoose-root.

Paprika (pæ·prĭkă). [Hungarian.] A condiment prepared from the fruit of the *Capsicum annuum*; Hungarian red pepper.

1898 Senn *Culinary Encycl.* 70 *Paprika*, Hungarian red pepper. 1902 J. T. Law *Grocer's Manual* 680 Paprika or Hungarian Red Pepper. 1908 *Daily Chron.* 29 Apr. 9/6 Beat together, adding oil every two minutes; paprika to taste. 1918 'Q' *Foe-Farrell* 91 You rubbed a soupçong of garlic into them with three drops of paprika.

Papuan (pæ·piuăn), *a.* and *sb.* [f. *Papua* the name of a large island north of Australia, often called New Guinea + -an.] **a.** *adj.* Of or belonging to Papua; characteristic of Papua and the neighbouring islands. **b.** *sb.* A native or inhabitant of Papua or a person belonging to the racial type which is found there.

1869 A. R. Wallace *Malay Archipelago* xl. II. 445 In stature the Papuan decidedly surpasses the Malay. *Ibid.* 449 These people..are tall and well-made, with Papuan features, and curly hair. 1875 *Encycl. Brit.* III. 739/1 The Papuan Subregion..comprises, besides the large and imperfectly-known island whence its name is derived, three other provinces, which may be named the Timorese, the Celebesian, and the Moluccan. 1876 *Ibid.* V. 790/2 The rite of circumcision..is still kept up..among the Papuans. 1902 *Chambers's Jrnl.* May 287/2 [With] the Negro..he throws in the Papuans and Malays, who have black or olive skins. 1911 *Q. Rev.* July 103 A fusion between the negroid Papuans and a low type of Caucasians.

Papulate (pæ·piulĕt), *a.* [f. L. *papula* + -ate[2] 2.] = Papulated.

1878 Bristowe *Theory & Pract. Med.* 321 Not unfrequently these patches are papulate,..gyrate, or marginate.

Papyro-. Add: **Papyro·grapher,** a writer on papyrus; **Papyrolo·gical** *a.*, pertaining to or dealing with papyrology; **Papyro·logist,** a student of papyrology.

1906 J. H. Moulton *Grammar N. T. Greek* I. 159 In the less educated *papyrographers we find blunders of this kind. 1902 *Encycl. Dict.* Suppl., *Papyrological. 1925 H. S. Jones *Gr.-Engl. Lexicon* Pref. p. viii, Mr. H. Idris Bell..has supplied valuable notes on recent papyrological publications. 1922 *Glasgow Herald* 14 Apr. 5/2 A most helpful Guide prepared..by the well-known *papyrologist Mr. H. I. Bell.

Paquined (pæ·kind), *a.* [f. the name of the outfitters (*Maison*) *Paquin* + -ed[2].] Dressed in the most up-to-date fashion.

1911 H. Quick *Yellowstone N.* i. 1 A fluffy, lacy, paquined girl floated from place to place.

Par, *sb.*[1] **2. c.** (Earlier example.)

1848 W. Armstrong *Stocks* 5 The par value of any stock is that proportion of the capital stock which it represents [etc.].

4. Read: The number of strokes which a scratch player should require for a (hole or) course, calculated from the length of the holes with two putts for each green, and in some cases taking account of difficulties and obstacles in the course. At present the standard of par is higher in U.S.A. than in England, and in general it is definitely higher than *Bogey.

Pará[2]**.** **Pará nut** (also *Pará-nut oil*).

1884 *Encycl. Brit.* XVII. 746/1 Para-nut or *Brasil-nut oil*, yielded by the kernels of *Bertholletia excelsa*, is employed in South America as a food-oil and for soap-making.

Para[3] (pā·rā). [Native name.] The horseshoe-fern of New Zealand, *Marattia fraxinea.*

1867 J. D. Hooker *Handbk. N.Z. Flora* II. 767 Para, *Marattia salicina.* 1906 Cheeseman *Man. N.Z. Flora* 1026. 1921 H. B. Dobbie *N.Z. Ferns* (ed. 2) 374 *Marattia fraxinea*..'Para', 'King Fern', 'Horseshoe Fern'. The largest herbaceous fern in New Zealand.

Para-[1]**.** **1.** **Paramnesia** (example). **Parathy·roid** *a.*, adjacent to the thyroid gland. **Paratro·phic** *a.*, also, that can exist only as a parasite; obligate.

1890 Gould *New Med. Dict.*, *Paramnesia, loss of the memory of the meaning of words spoken or written. 1906 *Jrnl. Med. Research* Dec. 399 (Cent. Suppl.) It has been suggested that paralysis agitans is due to insufficiency of the *parathyroid glandules. 1910 *Encycl. Brit.* III. 164/2 The true parasites..are placed by Fischer in a third biological group, *Paratrophic bacteria.

Parabellum (pærăbe·lǒm). A special make of automatic pistol or machine-gun used in warfare.

1904 *Text Bk. Small Arms* 178 The Borchardt Leuger or 'Parabellum' automatic pistol belongs to Class I. 1924 *Blackw. Mag.* Feb. 157/1 The vessel..carried two old-pattern Maxims and a German Parabellum.

Parabolicalism (pærăbǫ·likăliz'm). [-ism.] Parabolical character; matter which is parabolical.

1854 C. Walton *Notes & Materials Biogr. W. Law* 236 The deeply experienced spiritual man..will be much disappointed..at finding so much deep experience buried in such a huge mass of parabolicalism and idiocratic deformity.

Para·boliza·tion. [f. Parabolize *v.* + -ation.] The action or process of making parabolic in form.

1903 *Sci. Amer.* Suppl. 17 Oct. 23232/3 Draper's method of 'parabolization by measure'.

Parachor (pæ·răkǫɹ). *Chem.* [f. Gr. παρά Para-[1] + χώρα space.] A measure of the molecular volume at temperatures at which different liquids have the same surface tension.

1924 Sugden in *Jrnl. Chem. Soc.* CXXV. 1. 1178 It is proposed to name this quantity *parachor*..to signify comparative volume.

Parachrose. (Earlier example.)

1820 Mohs *Char. Nat. Hist. Syst. Min.* 40 Parachrose-Baryte. *note.* From παράχρωσις, alteration of colour.

Parachute, *v.* (Earlier and later examples of intr. use.) Also, to use a parachute.

1860 Russell *Diary India* II. ix. 174 And thus, with an able-bodied aborigen holding on by my tunic-tails behind, ..I parachuted down. 1910 Shaw *Misalliance* (1925) 46, *Tarleton*...Been up much? *Lina.* Not in an aeroplane. Ive parachuted; but thats child's play. 1930 E. W. Hendy *Wild Exmoor* 245 Meadow-pipits parachuted down to the brink.

Parachutic (pæră∫ū·tik), *a.* [f. Parachute *sb.* + -ic.] Provided with a parachute (sense 2).

1905 *Spectator* 14 Jan. 47/1 A parachutic arboreal serpent is not an impossible animal.

Parade, *sb.* **7.** Add: *parade-horse.*

1894 *Rep. Vermont Board Agric.* XIV. 123 The descendants of Woodbury Morgan..possess that peculiar qualification necessary for the parade horse.

Para·de-ground. *U.S.* [Parade *sb.*] A place where troops parade; = Parade *sb.* 4.

1724 [see Parade *sb.* 7]. 1843 N. Boone *Jrnl.* App. (1917) 237 By one o'clock our command was formed on the parade ground of Fort Gibson. 1846 M'Kenney *Mem.* I. v. 103 The level of the ground, and its freedom from undergrowth, were such as to give it the appearance of a parade ground. 1891 *Century Mag.* Mar. 715 The rats were so numerous that they were common sights on the parade-ground.

transf. 1863 'Gail Hamilton' *Gala-Days* 174 Besides abundance of food and parade ground, these happy fowls have a very agreeable prospect. 1866 Mrs. Whitney *L. Goldthwaite* vi, Clothes-lines like a parade-ground of telegraphs.

Paradisal, *a.* Add: **b.** Of or pertaining to an Oriental pleasure-ground.

1930 *Observer* 16 Feb. 6/3 A strikingly beautiful border, distinctly oriental in style..on which wild animals disport themselves in a paradisal jungle.

Paradise, *sb.* **8.** Add: **paradise crane,** the Blue or Stanley crane, *Tetrapteryx paradisea.*

1906 *Daily Chron.* 8 May 7/4 His consignment..included ..three paradise cranes, five wolves and seven baboons.

Paradoxician (pærădǫksi·∫ăn). [f. Paradox + -ician.] One who deals in paradoxes; a paradoxer.

1909 W. J. Locke *Septimus* xvi. 186 Sypher was not convinced by the airy paradoxician.

Paradoxographical, *a.* (Later example.)

1904 W. H. Stevenson in *Eng. Hist. Rev.* Jan. 139 *note*, He assigns the younger periplus to the Alexandrian or post-Alexandrian times on account of its paradoxographical character.

Paraffin. **4.** Add: **paraffin paper,** paper rendered airtight or waterproof by treatment with paraffin.

1895 *Rep. Vermont Board Agric.* XV. 25 Paraffine paper [is] placed over [the cheese], and a glass cover adjusted.

Paraffiny (pæ·răfini), *a.* [f. Paraffin + -y.] Of, belonging to, or suggestive of paraffin; covered or smeared with paraffin; smelling of paraffin.

1902 Conrad *Youth* (1922) 21 The ascending air was hot, and had a heavy, sooty, paraffiny smell. 1905 *Westm. Gaz.* 7 Jan. 12/3 The dresser would be a very unlikely place to keep a paraffiny funnel.

Paragon, *sb.* **6.** (Later example.)

1839 Ure *Dict. Arts* 801 The black marble of Bergamo is called paragone, from its black colour, like touchstone.

Paragraph, *v.* **3.** Add: Also *fig.* (Cf. Punctuate *v.* 3 b.)

1909 H. G. Wells *Ann Veronica* ix. 168 Ramage looked at her, and then fell into deep reflection as the waiter came to paragraph their talk again.

Pa·ragraphed, *ppl. a.* [f. Paragraph *v.* + -ed[2].] Mentioned or written about in a newspaper paragraph.

1928 *Manch. Guard. Weekly* 17 Aug. 135/2 A new comedy and the first visit to Manchester of a much-paragraphed young actress brought a large and eager audience to the Palace.

Paragraphist. (Earlier *U.S.* examples.)

1790 *Gaz. of U.S.* (Phila.) 27 Nov. (Th.) A paragraphist in the General Advertiser of Thursday last. 1792 T. Jefferson *Writ.* (1895) VI. 108 One of it's principal ministers enlists himself as an anonymous writer or paragraphist.

Paraguay. **1.** (Earlier examples of *Paraguay tea.*)

1793 B. Edwards *Hist. W. Indies* I. App. 476, *Cassine.* Paraguay tea. Carolina. 1825 Loudon *Encycl. Agric.* I. I. 200 Paraguay tea..is used as a substitute for that of China.

2. b. **Paraguay cat,** a small variety of cat indigenous to South America.

1910 *Encycl. Brit.* V. 489/2 One of these breeds is the Paraguay cat, which when adult weighs only about three pounds.

Paraguayan (pærăgwā·ăn), *a.* and *sb.* Also 9 **Paraguarian.** [f. Paraguay + -an.] **a.** *adj.* Of or belonging to Paraguay or its inhabitants; produced in or characteristic of Paraguay. **b.** *sb.* A native or inhabitant of Paraguay.

1840 J. Bell *System Geog.* VI. I. 238 The Paraguarians collected an army of 6,000 men. 1856 C. Kingsley *Misc.* (1859) II. 18 Very interesting also..are..scattered hints as to the qualities of the Paraguayans themselves. 1885 *Encycl. Brit.* XVIII. 244/1 In the Maté.., or Paraguayan tea, Paraguay has a commercial plant of great importance... The dietary staples of the Paraguayans are still..maize and mandioca (the latter the chief ingredient in the excellent *chipa* or Paraguayan bread). 1901 *Chambers's Jrnl.* Sept. 623/2 The Paraguayans are ominously polite. 1902 *Encycl. Brit.* XXXI. 462/1 The Paraguayan dictator..marched an army through Argentine territory. 1912 *Chambers's Jrnl.* Oct. 663/1 The native Paraguayan gets rather more governmental interference at times than is good for him.

Parallel, *v.* **6.** (Modern example.)

1907 *Smart Set* Mar. 52/2 He..recognizes the truth that so easily their paths might have paralleled if events had only favored.

Parallelism. Add: **2.** (Further example.)

1898 A. S. Woodward *Outl. Vertebrate Palæontol.* Introd. p. xxiii, The case of the horses is often cited as suggesting that such a parallelism in evolution may have occurred.

3. b. *Psych.* Short for *psycho-physical parallelism.*

1898 Stout *Man. Psychol.* I. Introd. iii. 54 The hypothesis of parallelism is that to which we are ourselves inclined. 1903 C. A. Strong *Why Mind has Body* I. vii. 126 This is, of all arguments for parallelism, the one most frequently heard.

Parallelist. Add: **3.** *spec.* One who believes in or upholds the doctrine of psycho-physical parallelism in Psychology. Also *attrib.*

1903 C. A. Strong *Why Mind has Body* I. i. 23 The parallelist hypothesis. *Ibid.* I. vii. 126 There can be no question what are the two arguments most commonly appealed to by parallelists in support of their doctrine. 1915 Stout *Man. Psychol.* Introd. iii. (ed. 3) 85 The parallelist must content himself with saying [etc.].

Parallelization. (Add example.)

1892 Nasmith *Cotton Spinning* v. 150 Its result is to effect a much greater parallelisation of the fibres in the carded sliver.

Paralyse, *v.* **2.** (Later examples.) Also with constr.

1871 L. W. H. Lockhart *Fair to See* xxv. (1872) 303 He saw all this, quite paralysed out of the power of surprise or wrath. 1890 *Congress. Rec.* 19 May 4933/1 You boast about what you have done for the American farmer... What audacity! It paralyzes me.

Paralysedly (pæ·rălaizdli), *adv.* [f. Paralysed *ppl. a.* + -ly[2].] In a paralysed manner.

1876 Rhoda Broughton *Joan* I. xxxiii. III. 48 As she so paralysedly sits the door opens softly.

Pa·ralysingly, [f. Paralysing + -ly[2].] In a paralysing manner.

1926 *Socialist Rev.* Dec. 21 The paralysingly stupid 70/- a week shipping or insurance clerk.

Parameter. Add: **3.** An independent variable in terms of which the co-ordinates of a variable point may be expressed.

1873 G. Salmon *Higher Plane Curves* (ed. 2) 29 If the coordinates can be expressed as rational functions of a parameter, the curve has the maximum number of double points.

Paranoid (pæ·rănoid), *a.* [Irreg. f. Paranoia + -oid.] Resembling or characterized by paranoia. So **Paranoi·dal** *a.*

1904 *Brit. Med. Jrnl.* 15 Oct. 972 The collective grouping of hebephrenia, katanoia, and the paranoid forms makes so vast a congeries that it is impossible to perceive any connecting link between the items of the mass. 1907 *Daily Chron.* 13 Feb. 7/4 Both adolescent and paranoid insanity are characterised by delusions of self-importance. 1904 tr. *Kraepelin's Lect. Clin. Psychiatry* 151 Paranoidal forms of Dementia Præcox. 1908 *Practitioner* Jan. 9 Paranoidal forms of alcoholic insanity may..be mistaken for early general paralysis.

Parapet. **4.** Add: *parapet mounting.*

1914 *Illustr. Lond. News* 29 Aug. 332/2 A Hotchkiss machine-gun on a parapet mounting.

Paraphony. Anglicized form of Paraphonia.

1919 H. J. Watt *Found. Music* 157 The term paraphony was used by several later writers, Thrasyllus, Bacchius and Gaudentius. 1924 T. H. Y. Trotter *Music & Mind* 154 The words 'symphony', 'paraphony', and 'diaphony' are used to express more or less complete unity and dissonance.

Hence **Paraphonic** *a.* (later example); **Parapho·nically** *adv.*

1919 H. J. Watt *Found. Music* 156 For the proper flow of simultaneous melodies intervals must either be themselves actually paraphonic or they must be used paraphonically.

Paraphrenia (pærăfrī·niă). *Path.* [mod.L. f. Gr. παρα- Para-[1] 1 + φρήν mind.] A form of insanity.

1890 Billings *Nat. Med. Dict.* 1915 C. R. Payne tr. *Pfister's Psycho-anal. Method* 522 Dementia praecox (schizophrenia according to Bleuler, paraphrenia according to Freud). 1919 R. Mary Barclay tr. *Kraepelin's Dementia Præcox* 308 This circumstance also plays a part for the delimitation from systematized paraphrenia.

Pa·rapsycho·logy. [Para-[1].] The science or study of phenomena which lie outside the sphere of orthodox psychology; = *Metapsychics. So **Parapsycholo·gical** *a.*

1924 *Times Lit. Suppl.* 10 Jan. 27/2 Its inherent merit.. renders the publication a noteworthy and welcome contribution to parapsychological literature. 1929 *Encycl. Brit.* XXI. 246/2 There is..a group of investigators who..dislike the term 'spiritualism', preferring to employ some noncommittal term such as 'metapsychics' or 'parapsychology'.

Parasite, *sb.* **4.** Add: **parasite drag, resistance** *Aeron.*, the drag of all parts of an aircraft other than that induced by the lift or due to the lifting surface.

1918 Webster Add.

Parasitic, *a.* Add: **3. c.** Applied to trades: † (*a*) see quot. 1909; (*b*) non-productive.

1909 *Q. Rev.* Jan. 83 The so-called parasitic trades—that is, trades in which it is alleged that workers who have incomes or maintenances derived from sources other than their wages underbid those who live entirely on their wages. 1926 *Spectator* 19 June 1032/1 Far too much still goes in what we may call parasitic middlemen's profits.

Parasitoid (pæ·răsitoid), *a.* [f. Parasite *sb.* + -oid.] Resembling parasites; used of the parasitic species of *Hymenoptera.* As *sb.*, a parasitoid insect.

1922 W. M. Wheeler *Soc. Life Insects* 46 Recent studies of the parasitic, or as I prefer to call them with O. M. Reuter, the 'parasitoid' Hymenoptera. *Ibid.*, The parasitoids exhibit another peculiarity.

Parasitological, *a.* (Add example.)

1921 H. G. Ponting *Great White South* 125 On the south side..was Dr. Atkinson's parasitological laboratory.

Parasol, *sb.* Add: **2. b.** A type of monoplane having a special arrangement of the wings to facilitate observation of the ground.

1914 *Aeroplane* 29 Jan. 110/1 M. Gilbert has been flying another 'parasol', 60-h.p. *Ibid.*, The 'parasol' monoplane ..has been fitted with a new..Gnome [engine].

3. **parasol fern** *Austral.*, a species of fern, *Gleichenia circinata.*

1902 F. M. Bailey *Queensland Flora* vi. 1938 G[*leichenia*] *circinata*, Parasol Fern.

Parasympathe·tic, *a.* [Para-[1].] Applied to a system of nerve fibres belonging to the visceral or autonomic nervous system, recently distinguished anatomically from the sympathetic nerves by the peculiarities of their course.

1920 W. M. Bayliss *Princ. General Physiol.* (ed. 3) 485 Some writers abroad have used the name [*sc.* autonomic] as applying to that part of the system which is not sympathetic. For this the name 'parasympathetic' is used by some. 1927 Haldane & Huxley *Anim. Biol.* vi. 138 Autonomic or involuntary nervous system..consists of two parts, the sympathetic..and the parasympathetic.

Paratype (pæ·rătəip). *Zool.* [Para-[1] + Type.] Any specimen of a group which is not chosen as the typical specimen.

1893 O. Thomas in *Proc. Zool. Soc.* 242 Since the other specimens mentioned or enumerated..in the original description are of unquestionably great value in a typical sense, they ought also to have a name and might be called 'paratypes' (or side-types). 1914 *Brit. Mus. Return* 171 Two paratypes of a new species of River-crab from Cochin.

Paratyphoid (pærătai·foid). [f. Para-[1] + Typhoid.] A form of enteric fever milder than true typhoid, from which it can be distinguished bacteriologically.

1903 *Med. Record* 9 May 739 (Cent. Suppl.) Bacteriologic study of the blood in thirty cases of clinical typhoid fever, two of which proved to be paratyphoid and one doubtful. 1908 *Practitioner* June 859 Trypanosomiasis and sleeping sickness, typhoid fever, including paratyphoid,..and epidemic dropsy are all adequately described. 1928 *Daily Express* 3 Aug. 9/5 Para-typhoid is not a dangerous fever.

Paravane (pæ·rāvēn). [f. Para-[2] + Vane.] An apparatus, fitted with vanes to keep it at a constant depth, designed to be towed at the bows of a vessel in order to clear its path from mines, cut the moorings of submerged mines, or destroy hostile submarines.

1919 *Rep. Brit. Assoc.* 273 The Paravane has been developed as a weapon to fulfil two purposes:—(1) To attack a submarine. (2) To protect vessels from moored mines. 1920 *Nature* 8 Jan. 487/1 The paravane or otter..proved a very effective weapon against both mines and submarines. 1927 *Daily Express* 7 Oct. 3/4 Paravanes..look like the result of a marriage between a shark and a torpedo.

Parca, variant of *Parka.

Parcel, *sb.* **7. d.** *fig.* A quantity of money won or lost, usually in a bet, in phrases, *to drop a parcel, to win a parcel* (slang).

1923 Wodehouse *Inimitable Jeeves* xii. 131 'But if you haven't dropped a parcel over the race,' I said, 'why are you looking so rattled?' *Ibid.* xiv. 162, I think I can put you in the way of winning a parcel on the Mothers' Sack Race.

B. 1. c. Add: *parcel-genius.*

1898 Saintsbury *Short Hist. Eng. Lit.* (1900) vii. vii. 468 A man who is at least parcel-genius like Suckling.

Parcellary (pā·ɹsĕlări), *a.* [f. Parcel *sb.* + -ary.] Pertaining to, or dealing with things by, sections or divisions; not comprehensive.

1921 *19th Cent.* June 953 A definite understanding..in the matter of communications,..the exchange of goods and commercial treaties whether parcellary, short-termed or renewable.

Parcel post. (Earlier examples.)

1837 *9th Rep. Comm. P.O.* 28 Would it not occasion great delay if you made a parcel-post of it to that extent? 1842 *Rep. Sel. Committee on Postage* (1843) 41 The Banghy post of the East Indies is a parcel post; the maximum of weight appears to be about 15 lb.

Pa·rchmented, *ppl. a.* Add: **b.** Provided with parchment or substance like parchment.

1913 W. Bateson *Mendel's Principles of Heredity* 22 Mendel..regarded the parchmented type [of pea] as a dominant.

Par-cook (pā·ɹkuk), *v.* [After Parboil *v.* 2.] *trans.* To cook partially.

1927 *Daily Express* 17 Nov. 5/2 The chicken was par-cooked and cooled, the stock being set aside for next day.

Pardner, U.S. colloq. variant of Partner.

1854 H. H. Riley *Puddleford* 126 (Th.) Pardners keep clus arter one another. *a* 1861 T. Winthrop *John Brent* vii. 71, I don't mean sech. I mean jolly dogs, like me and my pardener. *Ibid.* xiii. 140 'Pardners for a kerdrill' cried Jake. 1876 Joaquin Miller *First Families* v. 55 That evening Limber Tim..told..what a hero his 'pardner' had become. 1882 D. Pidgeon *Engineer's Holiday* I. xvii. 200 The mine is worked by two 'pardners' who dig and wash by turns. 1907 S. E. White *Arizona Nights* I. xi. 178 It's money I haven't got, and can't get unless I let somebody in as pardner. 1926 *Ladies' Home Jrnl.* Nov. 24 'There', she added as she crouched once more beside her pardner.

Pardon, *sb.*[1] Add: **6. d.** ellipt. for *I beg your pardon* used interrogatively (see 6).

1930 Joanna Cannan *No Walls of Jasper* 277 Julian said, 'That's all nonsense. You're drunk.' 'Pardon?' said Eric.

Pare, *v.*[1] **3. b.** Add: Also *to pare beyond the quick.*

1918 *Nation* (N.Y.) 7 Feb. 133/1 Men will have to work so hard to restore..manufacture, and trade, that liberal effort will perhaps be pared beyond the quick.

Parentalism (pǎre·ntăliz'm). [f. Parental *a.* + -ism.] Parental character or quality.

1878 Blackley in *19th Cent.* Nov. 838 What some folk sneer at under the name of 'parentalism'. 1923 *Daily Mail* 4 Oct. 7/2 The parentalism of our laws, with their mixture of foolish prohibitions and foolish laxities.

Parentelic (pærĕnte·lik), *a.* [f. L. *parentēla* relationship + -ic.] Of or pertaining to relationship based on common ancestry.

1895 Pollock & Maitland *Hist. Eng. Law* (1898) II. 296 In a parentelic scheme my great-nephew, since he springs from my father, is nearer to me than my first cousin.

Parenteral (pǎre·ntərăl), *a.* [f. Gr. παρα-, Para-[1], beside + ἔντερον intestine + -al.] Applied to or injected into the tissues and not introduced into the alimentary canal. So **Pare·nterally** *adv.*

1913 Dorland *Med. Dict.*, *Parenteral*, not through the alimentary canal, *i.e.*, either subcutaneous or intravenous. 1925 C. H. Browning *Bacteriol.* vi. 123 In order to produce harmful effects on the living body toxins must as a rule be

introduced directly into the tissues, 'parenterally' as it is called.

Parfleche. (Earlier examples.)

1849 Parkman *Oregon Trail* 149 Painted cases of *par flèche*, in which dried meat is kept. 1850 L. H. Gerrard *Wah-To-Yah* vii. (1927) 97 With a sole of par-fleche, lapping over on top of the foot.

Parge-work. (Modern example.)

1906 *Essex Rev.* XV. 162 The unique designs in parge-work on its front.

Parging (pā·ɹdʒiŋ), *vbl. sb.* [f. Parge *v.* + -ing[1].] The action of the verb Parge; pargeting; plastering.

1897 Moore *How to Build* iii. 34 The parging or plastering of the inside of the flue is permitted.

Pariahdom. Add: **b.** *transf.* Degraded position.

1897 W. J. Locke *Derelicts* xx. 256 Forgetful of the gaol and his pariahdom. 1909 — *Septimus* 145 Shame, disgrace, social pariahdom.

Pariahism (pā·riăiz'm). [f. Pariah + -ism.] = Pariahdom. So **Pa·riahship.**

1887 *Globe* 22 Oct. 1/4 It is astonishing that any person.. should regard the national uniform as a badge of pariahism. 1920 *Edin. Rev.* Jan. 18 The possibility of intermarriage is the crucial test of equality of consideration; its absence sets a stamp of servility and pariahship on the proscribed caste.

Parian, *a.* Add: **3.** *Parian cement*: (see quot.).

1880 *Encycl. Brit.* XI. 351/2 Parian cement is plaster hardened with water containing 10 per cent. of borax.

Paring, *vbl. sb.* **4.** *paring-bee* (earlier examples).

1850 *Knickerbocker Mag.* XXXV. 24 Give me the real paring-bee reels and jigs before all your waltzes and Spanish dances. 1854 T. D. Price *MS. Diary* 12 Sept., Had a paring bee. 1857 *Quinland* I. 191 Went this evening..with the young people to a paring-bee at Squire Carter's.

Paris. **Paris green,** also aceto-arsenite of copper used as an insecticide.

1876 *Rep. Vermont Board Agric.* III. 570 As remedies against this beetle, Paris green would probably be effectual. 1884 *Rep. U.S. Comm. Agric.* 327 Paris green or Scheele's green..is, on the whole one of the most satisfactory insecticides. 1902 *Encycl. Brit.* XXVIII. 530/2 The best fruit farmers spray fruit trees regularly in the early spring..with quassia and soft soap and paraffin emulsions, and a very few with Paris green only.

Parish, *sb.* **7.** Add: **parish-pump,** used allusively (often attrib.) to denote political speakers and their speeches, or other matters, that are limited in scope, outlook, or knowledge, or of local interest and importance only.

1915 *Truth* 21 Apr. 720/1 They are the last word in parochialism; but the table is the parish pump and the croupier is the beadle. 1923 *Daily Mail* 12 Mar. 5 Parish pump politicians distort every word they [statesmen] utter. 1923 Una L. Silberrad *Lett. Jean Armiter* x. § i. 211 The to-dos we make over our own parish pump matters.

Parish, *v.* Add: **b.** Of a clergyman: To do parish work.

1880 Gott *Lett.* (1918) 132 The growth and gymnastics of the mind, the mind with which one prays and parishes.

Parishionate (pări·∫ənĕt). [f. Parishion(er + -ate[1].] Body of parishioners.

1920 *Tablet* 3 Sept. 363 The archiepiscopal diocese with its parishionate of nearly four million souls.

Parisianize, *v.* Add: Also *refl.*

1916 W. J. Locke *Wonderful Year* xv. 220 The last thing a solid and virtuous citizen of Central France desires to do in Paris is to Parisianize himself.

Parity[1]**.** **7.** Add *parity level, price.*

1907 *Daily Chron.* 3 Oct. 2/1 Opening under the parity level prices continued to lose ground every hour up to the close. 1909 *Westm. Gaz.* 20 May 12/4 The parity price of Amalgamated was 85 3–16.

Park, *sb.* Add: **5. b.** An open space in or near a city, town, etc., where motor (and other) vehicles can be left.

1925 *Times* 14 Apr. 8/5 The Automobile Association..has put forward a scheme for the construction of motor parks below ground.

7. *park-land* (examples); **parkway** (earlier and later examples).

1920 H. G. Wells *Outl. Hist.* 84/2 They were forest and parkland peoples without horses. *Ibid.* 267/2 A slow change in climate..was replacing the swamps and forests and park-lands of South Russia..by steppes. 1887 *Visit to States* [illegible] 1929 *Times* 21 Jan. [illegible] Parkway [illegible] New York City.

Park, *v.* **2. b.** To place or leave (a vehicle) in a park (sense *5 b) or other place.

1906 *N. Y. Even. Post* 29 Nov. 16 The train was parked near the Union Station and was visited by hundreds of townsfolk and countrymen. 1909 R. Clay *By Night* xiv. [illegible]

c. *transf.* To leave or keep (other things and persons) in a suitable place until required. Also *refl.*

[illegible] The children being 'parked' in their own schoolyards. [illegible] *Atlantic Monthly* June 773 High-school girls..'park' their corsets when they go to dances. [illegible] The outer offices, where callers were received and parked till Sir Mallaby could find time for them. [illegible] *Jeeves* ix. 94 The policeman..retrieved a piece of chewing-gum from the underside of a chair, where he had parked it against a rainy day. 1926 *Ladies' Home Jrnl.* Oct. 38 He parked himself beside the Newly Discovered Genius.

d. *intr.* To take up a position in or as in a park; to place a vehicle in a park; to keep a thing or oneself ready in a place; to stay where one is.

1865 O. W. Norton *Army Lett.* 255 The wagons parked behind the stables to wait orders. 1929 *Strand Mag.* Feb. 183 'I want them' persisted the other 'and I guess I'm parking right here until I do get 'em'. 1929 *Minnesota Alumni Weekly* June 619 The new space along with a lot now used for parking will be seeded.

Parka (pā·ɹkă). Also **parca, parkee, parki.** [Aleutian.] An outer garment or jacket with a hood attached, made of skins, worn by Eskimos.

1890 *Century Dict.* 1907 R. W. Service *Songs of Sourdough* (1908) 56 Talk of your cold! through the parka's fold it stabbed like a driven nail. 1920 — *Ballads of Cheechako* 25 My eyes were seared, yet thralled I peered through the parka hood nigh blind. 1922 *19th Cent.* Feb. 269 They changed their drill parkees for coats of caribou fur. 1922 *Chambers's Jrnl.* Feb. 137/1 He had no snowshoes, no parki. 1926 *Spectator* 18 Sept. 408/2 The woodsman of the north.. wears no fur, unless it be a little trimming round the neck of the 'parca'.

Parked, *ppl. a.* [-ed[2].] That has been parked.

1919 C. P. Thompson *Cocktails* 176 The old farm where the V.A.D. drivers were cleaning their parked ambulances.

Parking, *vbl. sb.* Add: **3.** The placing of motor vehicles in a park (sense *5 b). Also *Comb.*, as **parking-place,** a space provided for the parking of (motor) vehicles.

1925 *Act 15 & 16 Geo. V*, c. 71 § 68 (9) In this section the expression 'parking place' means a place where vehicles, or vehicles of any particular class or description, may wait. 1927 *Rep. Commissioner Police Metropolis 1926* 19 The supply of parking places..can never meet the demand.

Parking, variant of Parkin.

1889 R. Wells *Bread & Biscuit Baker's Assist.* 28.

Parkinsonian (pā·ɹkinsōⁿniăn), *a.* and *sb.* [f. *Parkinson* (see below) + -ian.] **a.** *adj.* Of, pertaining to or connected with Parkinsonism. **b.** *sb.* A person suffering from Parkinsonism. So **Pa·rkinsonism,** the group of symptoms and signs occurring in shaking palsy (*paralysis agitans*), a nervous disease described by James Parkinson in 1817; (also called *Parkinson's disease*).

1924 Wimmer *Chronic Epidemic Encephalitis* 33 Chronic encephalitic Parkinsonism. *Ibid.* 48 The following case is of a peculiar interest on account of..the comparatively rapid development of the Parkinsonian syndrome. 1926 *Times* 26 Nov. 11/5 A considerable number [*sc.* who have had sleepy sickness] develop the severe condition known as 'Parkinsonism'. 1927 *Brit. Med. Jrnl.* 24 Sept. 539/1 This state of fatigue..is common to most, if not all, Parkinsonians.

Parliament, *sb.*[1] **9.** **parliament hinge** (example).

1841 C. Cist *Cincinnati* 247 The lighter castings kept in hardware stores—butt and parliament hinges, for example— will be made here.

Pa·rliamentariza·tion. [f. Parliamentary + -ization.] The act or process of becoming parliamentary in character or in means of government.

1924 *Contemp. Rev.* Aug. 256 The book deals..with the progress of the ideas of Parliamentarisation and racial self-determination under the stress of war.

Parliamentary, *a.* **1.** (Further example.)

1918 *Act 8 Geo. V* c. 3 § 1 (1) A Secretary who shall discharge the functions both of a parliamentary secretary to the Board and a parliamentary under-secretary to the Secretary of State.

2. c. (See quot.)

1886 J. Barrowman *Sc. Mining Terms* 49 *Parliamentary pit*, an outlet pit required by statute.

Parlour. **6.** Add: **parlour-girl** *U.S.* = Parlour-maid; **parlour-house,** a house having a parlour; **parlour melodeon** *U.S.*, a kind of parlour organ; **parlour-organ** (examples); **parlour palm,** the aspidistra.

1863 Mrs. Whitney *F. Gartney's Girlh.* iii, The *parlor-girl made her appearance with her mop and tub of hot water, to wash up the silver and china. 1875 Mrs. Stowe *We & Neighbors* xxxiv. 323 Maggie was parlor-girl and waitress, and a good one too. 1924 in A. Henderson & Maddock *Housing Acts* (1930) 431 Appropriate normal rents may be fixed for different classes of houses, *e.g.* *parlour and non-parlour. 1927 F. E. Fremantle *Housing of Nation* 40 At Roehampton the cost of a parlour house rose to £1,750. *a* 1909 'O. Henry' *Roads of Destiny* vii. 107 The natives were panning out enough from the beach sands to buy all [illegible]

Parma (pā·ɹmă). *Geol.* [The name of foothills of the Ural Mountains.] A low frontal fold parallel to a mountain range and marking the dying out of this towards the plain.

1888 *Encycl. Brit.* XXIV. 4/1 From the broad plateaux, or *parmas*, which stretch towards the north-west, it might be conjectured, that the structure is more complicated. 1905 tr. *Suess' Face of Earth* I. 601 We see great folded ranges with gradually flattening undulations [illegible] similar foreland, where they form secondary folds or 'parmas'.

Parnassianism (paɹnæ·siăniz'm). [-ism.] The Parnassian style in French poetry.

1905 *Times* 4 Oct. 6/2 He began to write the sonnets which attracted the attention of the most expert connoisseurs in Parnassianism. 1922 *Freeman* (N.Y.) 26 Apr. 105 Parnassianism means objectivity, impassivity, attention to line and image rather than to colour and music and vague suggestiveness. 1927 *Observer* 11 Sept. 7/3 Parnassianism, Symbolism, and the Ecole Roman have all had their day.

Parœcious, *a.* (Earlier example.)

1882 *Encycl. Brit.* XIV. 718/2 They [the antheridia] are usually seated in the axils of modified leaves (perigonial), sometimes appearing..on special branches of the same plant (parœcious).

Parolein(e (pæ·rǒlǝin). A proprietary name for liquid paraffin.

1895 Martindale *Extra Pharmacop.* (ed. 8) 330 Paroleine, glymol, fluid odourless petroleums..are used similarly. 1908 *Practitioner* Apr. 441 A parolein spray containing a little oil of eucalyptus. *Ibid.* June 794 A nasal spray of menthol and paroleine.

Parousia (pārūⁿziă). *Theol.* [ad. Gr. παρουσία presence, in N.T. (Matth. xxiv. 27, etc.) used as below.] The Second Coming or Advent of the Lord Jesus Christ.

1875 *Expositor* May 385 The feverish expectation of a visible *parousia* was requiring modification. 1895 *Dubl. Rev.* Apr. 334 The date of Our Lord's second coming, the Parousia. 1918 J. H. Leckie *World to Come* ii. 66 The Church has held its belief in the Parousia in varying forms throughout the ages. 1927 A. H. McNeile *Introd. N.T.* 112 At the end of his [St. Paul's] life, the thought of the Parousia..had practically faded from his mind.

Hence **Parou·siama·nia,** excitement or frenzy aroused by the thought of the Parousia.

1904 *Amer. Jrnl. Relig. Psychol. & Educ.* May 40 Men chanted, raved, spoke in unknown tongues, prophesied, gazed up into heaven all day, longed for vision, with a real parusiamania.

Parrot, *sb.* **4.** Add: *parrot-learning, -pie, -shooting*; **parrot disease,** psittacosis.

1908 *Spratt's Parrot Culture* 29 Should a room have become infected with the *parrot disease, which a writer in *The Lancet* has named 'Psittacosis', it will be needful to have it fumigated with sulphur. 1930 *Daily Express* 6 Feb. 11/5 That dread illness, psittacosis, or parrot disease. 1901 Coulton *Publ. Schools & Publ. Needs* 312 We cannot prevent .. mere *parrot-learning, from counting somewhat.. against real culture. 1907 P. Fountain *Rambles Austral. Naturalist* 8 *Parrot-pie is as much esteemed in Australia as rook-pie in England. *Ibid.*, *Parrot-shooting is a favourite sport in Australia.

Pa·rroted, *ppl. a.* [f. Parrot + -ed[2].] That is repeated mechanically in the manner of a parrot.

1927 Sadleir *Trollope* 295 Wherever he appears as..waverer from their parrotted idealisms, Sir Thomas Underwood is Trollope himself.

Parse, *v.* Add: **e.** *transf.* To examine or analyse minutely.

1788 F. Grose *Rules for drawing Caricaturas* 14 When a caricaturist wishes to delineate any face..he may commit it to his memory, by parsing it in his mind (as the school-boys term it). 1860 *Leisure Hour* 9 Aug. 507/2 Let him soak and remove the leather covering, parsing his way, as it were, by minute examination. 1931 *Times Lit. Suppl.* 7 May 353/3 Reade's biographer is confronted with the necessity of, as it were, 'parsing' a character which..does not make sense.

Parsec (pā·ɹsek). *Astr.* [f. Par(allax + Sec(ond.] A unit used in measuring stellar distances which is equal to the distance at which the parallax of a star would be one second.

1913 *Monthly Notices Roy. Astron. Soc.* Mar. LXXIII. 342 *note*, There is need for a name for this unit of distance. ..Professor Turner suggests *Parsec*, which may be taken as an abbreviated form of 'a distance corresponding to a parallax of one second'. 1914 A. S. Eddington *Stellar Movem.* etc. 14. 1921 *Discovery* Feb. 38/1 The farthest limits of the cluster Charlier found to be at a distance of 750 parsecs— roughly corresponding to about 2,000 light-years... The parsec..is equal to nineteen billions of miles. 1927 *Glasgow Herald* 10 Aug. 9/1 We have no observational evidence of such nebulæ at 6000 parsecs distance. 1928 Sir J. H. Jeans *Astron. & Cosmogony* 6 A distance at which the mean radius of the earth's orbit subtends an angle of one second of arc. This distance was..named the 'parsec' by H. H. Turner.

Parseval (pā·ɹsĕvăl). Also **Parsefal.** [The name of the inventor, August von *Parseval.*] A type of non-rigid dirigible airship used in Germany.

1909 *Chambers's Jrnl.* Oct. 660/2 At present the airship fleet consists of three Zeppelins, three Parsefals, and two Gross dirigibles. *Ibid.*, It is of the Parsefal type. 1910 C. C. Turner *Aerial Navig. To-day* 295 The 'Parseval' is a non-rigid balloon with a cubic capacity of 190,000 cubic [illegible]

Parsley. **3.** Add: **parsley-frog,** a genus of frog, *Pelodytes punctatus*, of the family *Pelobatidæ*, found in France, Spain, and Portugal. [illegible]

Parsnip. **3.** Add: **parsnip butterfly,** a species of butterfly (see quot.).

1869 *Amer. Naturalist* June I. 220 Early in the month the Parsnip butterfly (*Papilio Asterias*) may be seen flying over the beds of parsnips.

Parsonify, *v.* (Example of *a.*) Also (*c*), to make into a parson.

1739 J. Thomson *Let.* 12 Jan. in Goodhugh *Libr. Man.* [illegible]

Part, *v.* **3.** Also *to part brass rags*: see *Brass *sb.* 7.

Partake, *v.* **1. b.** Add: Also *absol.*

1844 D. B. Reid *Illustr. Th. & Pract. Ventilation* 181 Nor was any of the members aware..that they had partaken more heartily than usual. 1870 J. P. Smith *Widow Goldsmith's Dau.* ix. 144 (Born) Chris could not touch anything, but the widow partook with..particular relish.

Parthenopean (pā·ɹþĕnǒpī·ăn), *a.* [ad. It. *Partenopea*, f. L. *Parthenopēi-us* belonging to Naples (f. *Parthenopē* Naples) + -an.] Of or belonging to Naples.

1903 Constance Giglioli (*title*) Naples in 1799: An Account of the Revolution and of the Rise and Fall of the Parthenopean Republic. 1921 *Q. Rev.* Apr. 365 The relationship of the Parthenopean Republic to the Mother-Republic of France, could not be safely dealt with in a public print.

Partial, *a.* Add: **3. b.** (*c*) *Partial fractions*: the simpler fractions into which a compound fraction can be resolved.

1816 tr. *Lacroix' Diff. & Integral Calculus* 186 The general method of integrating differentials of the above form, consists in decomposing them into..partial fractions. 1870 Todhunter *Algebra* 400 The decomposition of a fraction into simpler fractions, called partial fractions. 1880 *Encycl. Brit.* XIII. 36/2 Many integrals of the form here considered may be determined by a transformation, without the employment of the method of partial fractions.

Partialist. **3.** (Add example.)

1921 *Hastings's Encycl. Relig. & Ethics* XII. 530/2 The opponents of this [Universalist] doctrine are designated by its adherents as partialists or limitarians.

Participled (pā·ɹtisip'ld), *a.* [f. Participle *sb.* 2 + -ed.] Euphemism for 'damned' or 'confounded'.

1887 *Sat. Rev.* 17 Dec. 815 Thucydides.., by the way, was a participled Tory, like Clarendon, Gibbon, Tacitus, and all the greatest historians.

Particulate, *a.* (Earlier example.)

1871 Burdon-Sanderson in *Q. Jrnl. Microsc. Sci.* XI. 325 It may be supposed either that the germinal substance is universally and equally distributed, *i.e.* dissolved in such liquids, or that it is unequally distributed or particulate.

c. Affecting or limited to certain parts only of a whole.

1920 *Public Opinion* 9 July 26/1 A social body cannot be making more than particulate progress, if it contains a large proportion of members who do not get a fair chance.

Partition, *sb.* **10.** Add: *partition fence*; **Partition treaty** (earlier example).

1639 *Dedham Rec.* 51 That may both be a *partition fence in the same, as also may serve for a course unto a water mill. 1641 *Rec. Mass. Bay* I. 333 It is declared that where farmes ioyne, the partition fence is to bee run betwixt the owners. 1748 *N. H. Probate Rec.* III. 608 [This land is] to be possess'd and enjoy'd by them..as ye partition fence between them now stands. 1858 J. A. Warder *Hedges & Evergreens* 145 To enable an adjoining owner to repair a partition fence. 1712 Swift *Wks.* 1883 IV. 303 The violation of the *Partition Treaty by the French.

Partitional, *a.* (Earlier example.)

1658 *Boston Rec.* II. 145 All partitionall fences..shall be ordered by the select men.

Parti·tionist. [f. Partition *v.* + -ist.] One who advocates partition or dividing.

1921 *Spectator* 4 June 713/2 Partition has come to be reckoned the unforgivable sin by the Sinn Feiners. The worst thing a man can be called is a partitionist.

Partitivity (partiti·vĭti). [f. Partitive + -ity.] Capacity for being divided into parts.

1873 G. Salmon *Higher Plane Curves* (ed. 2) 378 Index, Partitivity of cubics.

Partner, *sb.* Add: **6. b.** *Biol.* Symbiotically associated with another organism.

1924 J. A. Thomson *Science Old & New* xxxiii. 183 The hermit-crab..deliberately seeks a partner-anemone, and puts it on the back of his borrowed house. *Ibid.* xxxix. 227 There are many cases of luminescence due, or probably due, to partner-bacteria.

Partnering (pā·ɹtnəriŋ), *vbl. sb.* [f. Partner *v.* + -ing[1].] Association as partners.

1897 S. & Beatrice Webb *Industr. Democr.* II. 475 *note*, Occasionally the employer has tried to have only one boy-piecer to two spinners. This system, called 'joining' or 'partnering', is always resisted by the union.

Partnership. **4.** Add: **partnership fence,** a boundary fence shared by two owners.

1845 *Indiana Senate Jrnl.* 335 A bill to provide for the dissolving of partnership fences.

Partridge. **5.** Add: **partridge bush** = Partridge-berry b; **partridge plum,** the fruit of the partridge bush; **partridge-vine** (example). [illegible]

Part-timer. [f. *part-time*: Part B + -er.] A person employed only part of his time; a part-time worker.

1927 *Daily Tel.* 3 May 1 (heading) Part-timers employed.

Party, *sb.* **19.** Add: (sense 6) **party government** (earlier example), **manager, -question, -secret, system**; (sense 9) **party call, dress, -going**; [illegible] What are you going to do about the girls' *party dresses? 1901 Marah E. Ryan *That Girl Montana* vii. 99 Presenting herself to his notice in all the glory of her party dress. 1875 Mrs. Stowe *We & Neighbors* iv. 50, I have definitely decided to give up *party-going and all that round of calling. 1869 R. F. D. Palgrave *House of Commons* 22 This system is called *party government. 1895 *Century Mag.* Sept. 793/2 Branches of the State service ..which his own *party managers were seeking to retain for spoils. 1885 A. Crump *Formation Polit. Opin.* 152 The position was now far too grave to be treated as a *party question. 1855 Tennyson *Maud* II. v. iii, And another, a statesman there, betraying His *party-secret, fool, to the press. 1885 *National Rev.* Apr. 173 The people of England must make up their minds whether they will keep the *Party System or the Empire. 1886 E. A. Pankhurst *Wisd. Burke* 87 The Party System of Government.

b. **party line,** a telephonic line shared by a number of subscribers.

1902 *Encycl. Brit.* XXXIII. 237/2 A number of subscribers can be placed upon a single circuit or 'party line', as it is called. 1906 *Daily Chron.* 15 May 8/4 These lines are constructed on what is known as the 'party line system'.

Partyism. (Earlier example.)

1842 *Amer. Pioneer* I. 278 Partyism or love of party is the vibratory motion.

Partyless (pā·ɹtilĕs), *a.* [f. Party 6 + -less.] Not having or not belonging to a political party.

1896 J. G. Woolley in *Voice* (N.Y.) 9 July 2/4 This means ..a reign of straight-out, inexorable, sectless, seminaryless, partyless righteousness in citizenship. 1909 *Westm. Gaz.* 15 Mar. 2/1 In 1901 Francis Ferdinand was practically alone, partyless.

Parvenuess (pā·ɹvĕniuⁱĕs). [-ess.] A female parvenu.

a 1910 'O. Henry' *Rolling Stones* iii. 58 As proud and satisfied as a prince that's abjured a two-hundred-dollar crown for a million-dollar parvenuess.

Pa·schaltide. [f. Paschal + Tide *sb.*] Easter; the week beginning with Easter Sunday.

1894 G. F. X. Griffith *St. Paul & Missions* xv. 349 The octave of Paschal-tide, a rite of Jewish origin.

Pascual, *a.* Add: **b.** as *sb.*, a pascual plant.

1847 H. C. Watson *Cybele Britannica* I. 67 The pratal plants are occasionally pascual plants, as Phleum pratense; the pascuals are in turn ericetals, as Prunella vulgaris. 1926 *Nat. Hist. Oxford Distr.* 92.

Pasear (pa·sear), *sb.* and *v.* *slang.* [See next.] **a.** *sb.* = *Paseo. **b.** *v. intr.* To take a paseo or walk.

1840 R. H. Dana *Bef. Mast* xxviii. (1869) 258 He was going to *pasear* with our captain a little. 1878 Bret Harte *Man on Beach* 112, I was reck'nin' on taking a little *pasear* with you. 1892 Stevenson & Ll. Osbourne *Wrecker* xii. (ed. 2) 192, I tell you, Mr. Dodd, it was a queer thing to see me and the old lady taking a *pasear* in the garden, and the old man scowling at us over the pickets. 1903 Conrad & Hueffer *Romance* III. iii. 141, I just come from taking a pasear that way. 1909 S. E. White *Rules of Game* II. ii, Come, make a pasear. Glad to show you the sights.

Paseo (pāse·o). *slang.* [Sp. *paseo* walk, *pasear* to walk.] A walk taken at a leisurely pace for exercise, amusement, or the like; any trip or outing of a similar nature; also (concretely) a street or promenade.

1840 R. H. Dana *Bef. Mast* xxii. (1869) 181 The theme of ..conversation..in our afternoon's *paseo* upon the beach, was the ship. 1897 'H. S. Merriman' *In Kedar's Tents* xviii. 205 He..proposed to Julia that they should take a 'paseo' in the garden. 1920 *Glasgow Herald* 22 Sept. 8/5 The greater companies..have built model towns, intersected with finely laid-out paseos and plazas, for their employees.

Pash (pæ∫), *sb.*[4] *slang.* Abbreviation of Passion, esp. in phr. *to have a pash for.*

1922 Joad *Highbrows* iii. 102, I have met such a duck of a man. You'll never believe! I've quite a pash for him. 1927 *Daily Express* 5 Oct. 3/4 Some Gun Rooms have..a 'pash' for Tallulah Bankhead, others have a 'pash' for Gertrude Lawrence.

Paspalum (pæ·spălǒm). [mod.L., f. Gr. πάσπαλος a kind of millet.] A fodder-grass of the genus *Paspalum.*

1906 *Chambers's Jrnl.* 24 Feb. 207/2 Paspalum Grass..is a native of South America, and has been known in the United States since 1880, where it is called hairy and flowered paspalum. 1926 *Brit. Weekly* 12 Aug. 392/3 There's a corner of paspalum down there on the creek that would do your two eyes good to see.

Pasquinade, *v.* (Add example.)

1906 *Daily Chron.* 9 May 3/3 In the common and almost legitimate trade of pasquinading it, he was the man who could 'get home' oftenest.

Pass, *sb.*[2] Add: **12. b.** *Tennis.* A service which drops in the pass-court. [illegible]

17. (sense 4) *pass-coach.* [illegible] **pass-court** *Tennis* (see quot.); **pass-duty,** a duty levied on goods entering a territory; **pass line** *Tennis*, the line between the pass-court and the service-court; **pass pawn,** a passed pawn. [illegible] If he fails to do this, a 'fault' is called, or a 'pass' if the ball has gone beyond the *pass line. 1908 *Daily Chron.* 29 Sept. 1/6 Lasker has a *pass pawn, but..a draw appears probable.

Pass, *v.* Add: **5. c.** (Later example.)

1895 *Century Mag.* Sept. 676/1 It was a poor thing for the Bruce boys to do, to try to pass upon him like this.

26. b. Also in Bridge: To make no bid.

1908 R. F. Foster *Auction Bridge* 29 The player on his left must either pass, or make a better declaration, or 'double'. 1929 M. C. Work *Compl. Contract Bridge* 42 South..bids one No Trump: North..passes.

29. c. (Earlier and later examples.)

1870 Medbery *Men & Myst. Wall St.* 137 To 'pass' a dividend... A dividend is said to be passed when the directors vote against declaring it. 1903 *Forum* Oct. 209 Concerns which not only passed dividends but went bankrupt.

57. **Pass over—.** **a.** (Further examples.)

1749 Mrs. Goadby *Apol. Bampfylde-Moore Carew* xx. (1768) 270 Passing over this Ferry they came to Rhode-Island. 1874 J. W. Draper *Hist. Conf. Relig. & Sci.* vi. (1875) 161 The distance passed over in a voyage from Italy to the Gulf of Guinea.

63. **Pass in.** **b.** *intr.* To die.

1904 *N.Y. Even. Jrnl.* 3 May 2, 'I may die' he told friends, 'and I want to breathe American air again before I pass in.'

65. **Pass on.** **c.** *intr.* To die.

1920 Rose Macaulay *Potterism* III. ii. 131 If I have to pass on before Percy, he will be left bereaved indeed. 1923 *Amer. Mag.* June 15/1 The murderer took poison and so the two passed on. 1928 L. North *Parasites* 77 When my dad passed on there was just enough insurance to have let me finish up.

66. **Pass out.** **c.** *intr.* To die. Also, to become unconscious through drinking. *slang.*

1899 *Westm. Gaz.* 6 Mar. 2/1 Another [spirit] who 'passed out' with consumption is heard coughing. 1918 *War Birds* (1927) 97 We..carried him home after he passed out. 1925 E. Fraser & Gibbons *Soldier & Sailor Words.* 1927 *Hutchinson's Mystery-Story Mag.* Feb. IX. 80 First, the name of the dead relative or friend, then when they passed out.

d. *trans.* To undergo (a course of instruction, etc.) successfully.

1920 *Discovery* Mar. 77/2 Airship pilots..are required to pass-out a course in free ballooning, which includes a night flight and a solo flight.

e. To hand out or distribute.

1926 *Publishers' Weekly* 10 July 116 Librarians..are eager and willing to pass out catalogs that have won their confidence. 1927 *Ibid.* 12 Feb. 599 On that day she had passed out 130 books.

67. **Pass over.** **b.** (Modern examples.)

1840 R. H. Dana *Bef. Mast* xxiv. (1869) 207 The night passed over without any trouble. 1878 Stevenson *New Arab. Nts.* (1882) I. 85 The journey passed over without much incident.

h. To convey across; to transport.

1832 N. Wyeth *Jrnl.* 18 June 157 Reached the place for fording the Platte. 19th, Passed over my goods during a severe wind without accident.

i. *intr.* To die.

1909 *Rev. of Reviews* Feb. 123/2 His automatic writing.. came..through the same friend through whom he has constantly communicated ever since he passed over. 1928 *Daily Mail* 7 Aug. 16/5 This doctor was now with my mother, who had recently passed over.

69. **Pass up:** To refuse to have any further dealings with; to give up, abandon, renounce; to omit to secure; to neglect. *U.S.*

1896 G. Ade *Artie* i. 5, I pass him up. *Ibid.* xii. 112 Well, I guess I'll pass up the whole thing. 1906 H. D. Pittman *Belle of Blue Grass C.* vi. 108, 'I know', he continued, 'when I've got enough. I pass this little town up.' 1921 R. D. Paine *Comr. Rolling Ocean* ii. 33 My duty is to stand by the family... That is why I passed up college. 1926 *N.Y. Times Mag.* 13 Aug. 1 He was sent to the U.S. Senate, but on his own terms, having previously passed up the Senatorship rather than take it on the terms of others. 1930 *Publishers' Weekly* 14 June 2907/2 The customers..are passing up the bookstores.

Passable, *a.* Add: **8.** as *sb.* A person or thing that is tolerably or moderately good, efficient, fit, etc.

1908 *Westm. Gaz.* 26 June 2/1 Amongst such offspring there would be a small class of 'desirables', a large class of 'passables', and a small class of 'undesirables'.

Passage, *sb.*

16. **passage-free** *adv.*, free of charge for passage or conveyance.

1928 *Daily Express* 28 Aug. 3/7 She..brings to Canada almost *passage-free any man of good health and physique who is an experienced agriculturist.

Passage-way. (Earlier Amer. examples.) [illegible]

Passalid (pæ·sălid), *a.* *Entom.* [f. mod.L. *Passalidæ* the name of the family.] Of or belonging to the *Passalidæ*, a family of Coleoptera. [illegible] The whole Passalid family lives in rotten tree-stumps.

Pass-by. Add: **3. b.** A place on a plate-rail (tramway) at which vehicles can pass. Also *attrib.*

1797 J. Curr *Coal Viewer* 26 Pass bye plates. Useful for horses going contrary ways and passing each other with

Supplement, p. 3873; Corrigenda, p. 4092; Spurious words, p. 4093; Books quoted, p. 4094

Passenger. Add: 6. (Further example.)

Passe-partout. Add: 2. c. A kind of adhesive tape or paper used for framing photographs and for other purposes.

Passer. Add: 3. b. *spec.* In various trades: A person who examines materials, or manufactures or prepares them, at one of the required quality, workmanship, etc.

Passimeter (pă·simătər). [L. Pass *v.* or Passenger + -meter.] An automatic machine introduced in America about 1913 for supplying railway passengers with tickets, and counting the number of persons who pass through.

Passing, *vbl. sb.* Add: 2. (Further example.)

4. *passing croquet* = *passing-stroke*; *passing door* Mining, an arrangement of doors in a gallery to enable persons to pass while preventing the free passage of air currents.

Passing-by. Add: b. The action of ignoring or neglecting.

Passing-note. (Earlier example.)

Passion. Add: I. e. *b.* Short for passion-play.

Passional, *n.* Add: 2. b. Subject or susceptible to passion.

Passionist. (Earlier example.)

Passion-tide. (Earlier example.)

Passive. A. *adj.* Add: 7. d. In chess.

Passover. Add: b. A path or pass over hills.

Passoverish, *a.* [f. Passover + -ish.] Suggestive of the passover.

Passway (pa·swei). [Pass *sb.*] A means of passing; a passage or gangway. b. = Pass *sb.* 3.

Past, *ppl. a.* C. Add: past-president, *etc.*

Past. A. *prep.* 3. b. Add: past master.

Pastance. (Recent example.)

Pasteboard. 3. c. (Later example.)

Paster. 2. (Later example.)

Patchless (pæ·tʃles), *a.* [f. Patch *sb.*1 + -less.] Not having or exhibiting patches.

Patchwork. 4. (Add example.)

Patchy, *a.* 1. (Earlier example.)

Patent, *a.* 3. Add: *Patent food* a proprietary food preparation.

Patience-dock. 1. (Earlier examples.)

Patina (pa·tinə), *v.* [f. Patina *sb.*] *trans.* To coat or cover with a patina.

Patronage, *sb.* (Later example.)

Patriarch. (Later example.)

Paternalistically, *adv.* (Later example.)

Paternalistic, *a.* (Example.)

a paternalistic Government, with unlimited power of taxation...

Paternalize (pătə·rnăliz'd), *ppl. a.* [f. as Paternalism + -ed + -ed.] Characterized by or subjected to paternalism.

Path. Add: I. d. *transf.* A channel or duct in an organism.

Patriot. Add: 3. *Patriot's day U.S.*, April 19th, the anniversary of the initial skirmishes in the American War of Independence.

Patrol. *sb.* Add: 5. *Scouting for Boys*, a troop consisting of six boys.

Patrol, *v.* Add: +b. To refine (potassium carbonate) in the preparation of pearl-ash.

Patrolled. (Earlier example.)

Patroller. (Earlier example.)

Patron, *sb.* 6. (Later example.)

Patronage. Add: 4. *Rom. Antiq.* The position or duties and rights of a patron (sense 3).

Patronomatic (pătrŏnŏmă·tik), *a.* [f. Gr. πατρο- + ὄνομα] (as a patronymic).

Patter, *v.*1 4. Add: Also *transf.*

Pattern, *sb.* 13. b. *pattern-maker* (earlier example); pattern-shop (example).

Pattress (pæ·tres), *sb.*

Patria-cohalist. (See -ist.) One who advocates or approves of a patriarchal system of society or government.

Paul Pryism. (Later example.)

Pause, *v.*1 Add: b. *trans.* To cause to stop temporarily.

Patriarchist (peι·triarkist). [f. Patriarch 3 b. + -ist.] A supporter of the Patriarch of Constantinople.

Paternalist (pătə·rnălist), *a.* [See -ist.]

Pave, *v.* Add: 1. d. (Further examples.)

Pave. *v.* Add: c. To form a pavement of.

Pavement. *sb.* Add: 1. d. *transf.*

Pavilion, *sb.* Add: b. (Recent example.)

Pawn, *v.* Add: b. *Stock Exchange.* To deposit (stock) with a banker as security.

Paxillose, *a.* (Example.)

Pay, *sb.*1 Add: 1. b. *pay-check*, *-envelope* (examples), *-roll* (earlier examples).

Pay, *v.*1 Add: 1. b. *pay in.* To make (a regular) contributions to a fund.

Pay, *v.*3 Add: b. *Pay in.* To make (a regular) contributions to a fund.

Pea-bird. Add: 2. *U.S.* The black-headed grosbeak, *Zamelodia melanocephala*.

Peabody bird. *U.S.* [See quot. 1897.] The white-throated sparrow, *Zonotrichia albicollis*.

Peace. *sb.* 15. Add: In sense 'held, organized, founded, etc., to promote peace', as *peace conference*, *convention*, *society*; peace-bell, -belt, *etc.*

Peaceful, *a.* Add: Not violating or infringing peace; used *esp.* of methods for effecting purposes for which force, violence, or war, is an alternative more obvious means.

Peacefully, *adv.* (Earlier example.)

Peach. *sb.*1 Add: 1. b. *slang.* Orig. *U.S.* A person or thing of superlative merit; one who or a thing which is very admirable or desirable; a pretty or attractive young woman, *etc.*

Peachy, *a.* Add: 2. *slang.* Pleasant, agreeable, splendid.

Peacocking, *vbl. sb.* Add: 2. (See quot.)

Peak. *sb.*3 5. b. *Electr.* The highest point of a load curve in the course of a day or other period.

Pearl, *sb.*1 17. b. *pearl-making* adj.

Pear. *sb.* 5. Add: pear-apple (a fruit of the prickly pear); pear-blight (earlier example); pear-midge, a dipterous insect [*Diplosis pyrivora*] infesting pear trees; pear-wood (*b.*), the wood of a species of Mimusops reared in Sierra Leone.

Pearl-white. Add: 3. *Typog.*

Pedagogy. (Add example.)

Peat. *sb.*1 17. b. *slang.*

Pecan. *sb.*

Pecking, *vbl. sb.*2 Add: 3. *Comb.* pecking-arm *Weaving*, the oscillating rod in a loom which imparts motion to the shuttle; pecking-cord, the slack cord connecting two pecking-arms.

Pectinary (pe·ktinări), *a.* [ad. L. *pectinarius*] Of or pertaining to pedology.

Pectinate, *a.* + -ory *?*] Exhibiting a pectinate structure.

Peculant (pe·kiŭlănt), *a.* [ad. L. *peculant-em* pres. pple. of *peculari* to embezzle.] That practises embezzlement or peculation.

Peculiative (pe·kiŭlātiv), *a.* [f. Peculate + -ive.] *rare.*

Peculiar, *a.* Add: 3. b. *Typog.* Applied to types not in a fount, that have to be specially cast.

Pedal, *sb.*1 7. Add: *pedal-cap.*

Pedal, *v.* Add: 1. b. To travel or advance by means of pedalling (in quot. fig.).

Pedalization. [f. Pedal *sb.* + -ization.] Employment of the pedals of an organ or piano.

Pedaller. (Add example.)

Pedaneous. Transf. + *Obs.* *rare* to sense defined in Dict. and adj. 2. Applied to games of chess in which one player opposes a second at the same time, going the round of the boards for each move.

Pedanticize (pĕdæ·ntisəiz), *v.* [f. Pedantic + -ize.] *intr.*

Pedestal, *sb.* Add: 1. b. *intr. To place (seat) on a pedestal* to accord an important place to; a lively or deserved position.

Peditis (pedi·tis). [f. L. *ped-, pēs*, foot + -itis.] Inflammation of the pedal bone of a horse, accompanying laminitis.

Pedological (pedŏlŏ·d͡ʒikăl), *a.* [f. Gr. πέδον the ground + -(O)logical.] Of or pertaining to pedology.

Pedology (pĕdɒ·lŏd͡ʒi). [f. Gr. πέδον the ground + -(O)logy.]

Peep-bo. (Earlier example.)

Peeper, *sb.*1

Peevo (pī·vo), *v.* [f. Peevish *a.*] *intr.* To affect with irritation or fretfulness.

Pedrail (pe·dreιl), *sb.* [f. Ped- + Rail.] A form of walking machine (a device which fits over a wheel of a traction engine or other vehicle, provided with a series of broad foot-like supporting surfaces which facilitate progress over difficult ground.

Pedro (pe·dro). *U.S.* The second part of *Sancho-pedro*: the five of trumps in the card games Sancho-pedro and Pedro.

Pedological — [*duplicate entry*]

Peg, *sb.*1 Add: 5. b. *to peg out*. c. *To buy (clothes) of the peg*, to buy them ready-made.

Peg, *v.* Add: 3. *intr.* To question or fret…

Peg-down, *a.* = pegged-down (see next).

Pegged, *ppl. a.* Add: 3. *Cricket*, etc.

Pegging, *vbl. sb.* 1. (Add example.)
1931 *Observer* 11 Jan. 19/1 Mr. Scullin's views about the pegging of wages are unknown.

b. *Level pegging*; even scores; the state of a contest when none of the contestants are securing any advantage over the others.
1927 *Daily Tel.* 5 Mar. 10/4 It was level pegging when the heavy-weights..took the ring. 1928 *Ibid.* 7 Aug. 12/1 Peters equalised, and it was still level pegging when ends were changed.

Peggy, *sb.* Add: 5. **Peggy bag,** a style of woman's hand-bag having side handles and outside pockets; **peggy-stick** = sense 3.
1920 *Scot at Home & Abroad* 5/3 Mirren had a wheen peppermints in her peggy bag. 1922 *Daily Mail* 11 Dec. 13 Advt.

Pek, Peke (pīk), **Pekie** (pī·ki), abbreviations of **Pekingese dog*.
1920 *Chambers's Jrnl.* 21 Feb. 177/2 Adjoining were the kennels where the Pekies lived. 1922 W. J. Locke *Tale Triona* ix. 105 Instead of pulling your weight you think it's your right to sit on a cushion, a passenger—or a Pekie dog —and let other people pull you. 1924 Galsworthy *White Monkey* II. iv, I'll see what I can do, if you'll lend me your Peke for an hour or so to-morrow afternoon. 1926 *Spectator* 22 May 859/2 A young lady of fashion happens to be travelling to-day..with a couple of wardrobe trunks and a fortune in sables, satchels, vanity cases, also a 'Pek'.

Pekin. Add: 3. **Peking man,** a prehistoric type of man, *Sinanthropus pekinensis*, represented by some remains that have been found at Peking.
1926 *Peking Leader* 24 Oct. in *Bull. Peking Soc. Nat. Hist.* 1927–8 II. iv. xvii, The discovery of the two teeth of the 'Peking Man'. 1929 *Times* 30 Dec. 9/4 The Peking man is considered to antedate Neanderthal man, and is held to be nearer the genus *Homo* than the Piltdown and Java types.

Pekin(g)ese (pīkinī·z, pīkiŋī·z), *a.* and *sb.* [f. *Peking* Pekin, the name of the capital of China + -ese.] a. *adj.* Of or pertaining to Peking; applied especially to a breed of dwarf pug-dogs having long silky hair, obtained originally from the Imperial Palace of Peking, and much kept as pets. b. *sb.* A native or inhabitant of Peking; the form of Chinese used in Peking; a Pekingese dog.
1849 *Ann. Propag. Faith* Mar. 104, I have been informed that you speak..Pekinese. 1866 *Leisure Hour* XV. 45/2 (heading) Peking and the Pekingese. 1874 *Ibid.* 5 Sept. 572/1 This event created great consternation among all classes of the Pekingese. 1888 *Peel City Guardian* 14 Apr. 281/5 A singular Pekingese New Year custom is mentioned in the Shen Pao. 1904 F. T. Barton *Toy Dogs* 73 The Pekinese Spaniel. 1906 *Field* 20 Oct. 663/2 Pekingese were forward in strong numbers, the best dog weighing [etc.]. 1920 *19th Cent.* Sept. 384 The Grand Duchess Tatiana carried in her arms her little Pekingese dog. 1922 *Westm. Gaz.* 23 Dec., There were also considerable numbers of ladies' toy and lap dogs, the popular Pekinese predominating so far as numbers were concerned.

Pelagic, *a.* (Add examples.)
1891 J. Murray in *Challenger Rep., Deep-sea Deposits* p. xxix, The Pelagic Deposits are formed in the deep water of the central regions of the great ocean basins, and consist of organic oozes and a reddish clay. 1909 *Chambers's Jrnl.* Dec. 784/1 Three great primary zones are recognised. These are the Pelagic, the Neritic, and the Abysmal zones.

Pellagric (pelæ·grik), *a.* [f. Pellagra + -ic.] Of or pertaining to pellagra; pellagrous.
1909 *Westm. Gaz.* 20 Oct. 4/1 A toxic substance isolated from bad maize injected into animals produced..all the symptoms of pellagric madness.

Pellet, *sb.*¹ Add: 2. c. = Cast *sb.* 19.
1834 Mudie *Brit. Birds* (1841) I. 141 Mice are preferred to birds, the feathers being more untractable than the fur, both in swallowing, and in casting in pellets or quids. 1894 *Yearbk. U.S. Dept. of Agr.* 217 These masses, known as 'pellets' are regurgitated before fresh food is taken. 1905 *Daily News* 5 Jan. 4/3 The brown owl's pellet very rarely contains the remains of shrews.

Pelmanism (pe·lmăniz'm). [f. *Pelman* (coined in 1899), proprietary name of an educational institute + -ism.] The training system of the Pelman Institute. So **Pe·lmanist, Pe·lmanite,** a student of Pelmanism; **Pe·lmanize** *v. intr.* and *trans.*, to practise Pelmanism, to learn or memorize by the methods of Pelmanism or similar methods; also, to train by Pelman methods.
1918 *Q. Rev. Lit. Advt.* Apr. 21 Pelmanism is..the fruit of gradual evolution. 1920 *Pelman Pie* 25 Advt., A very large proportion of its readers are 'Pelmanists'. 1920 *Blackw. Mag.* Nov. 561/2, I fear I must be suffering from what the Pelmanites call 'mind-wandering'. 1921 *Chambers's Jrnl.* Mar. 176/1 In some Oriental way he had Pelmanised his memory. 1922 T. Burke *Lond. Spy* 78 They followed his movements with intent eyes, pelmanizing each gesture, and practising it to themselves. 1924 *Glasgow Herald* 4 Dec. 9 It is in the case of the Speaker himself that the pelmanising process is brought to scientific perfection.

Pelmet (pe·lmĕt). Also **palmette, pelmette.** [Prob. f. F. *palmette*, a conventional palm-leaf design on a cornice.] A valance or narrow pendant border, esp. one used to conceal curtain rods above a window or door.
1821 *Ann. Reg.* (1822) App. to Chron. 331/2 Beneath the cornice, hung a succession of crimson velvet pelmet tracery, each pelmet having embroidered upon it a rose, a thistle, a crown or a harp. 1898 *Army & Navy Co-op. Soc. Price List* No. 67 Index, Pelmettes. 1904 Hasluck *Upholstery* 149 This pelmet is fixed to a wood lath screwed underneath the door casing. 1922 *Daily Tel.* 12 June 20/6 The velvet and silk damask curtains throughout the castle, with pelmets and cornices. 1925 Penderel-Brodhurst & Layton *Gloss. Engl. Furniture* 123 *Pelmet*, a word used by upholsterers and sometimes by art dealers, who prefer the word 'palmette', to denote the horizontal stiff curtain or valance hiding the rod, rings and headings of the hanging curtains decorating a door, window, bed, etc.

Pelt, *sb.*³ (Add example.)
1886 J. Barrowman *Sc. Mining Terms* 50 *Pelt*, coally stone associated with a coal seam.

Pelt, *v.*¹ 3. b. Also of missiles.
1916 B. Cable *Action Front* 210 Maxim and rifle bullets were still pelting from somewhere in half enfilade at long range.

5. (Further example.)
1916 B. Cable *Action Front* 116 A heavy rifle and machine-gun fire which was pelted across from the opposite parts of the British line.

Pelt, *v.*² (Modern example.)
1920 W. T. Grenfell *Labrador Doctor* ix. 176 Then having killed, 'sculped', and 'pelted' the seal, the exciting return to the vessel!

Pelted (pe·ltĕd), *ppl. a.* [f. Pelt *v.*² + -ed¹.] Having the bark stripped off.
1927 *Daily Express* 12 Mar. 5 An attractive arch in pelted oak, placed at the end of a pathway.

Pelter, *sb.*² 1. d. Also, a slow horse. *U.S.*
1896 G. Ade *Artie* i. 4 It's like hitchin' up a four time winner 'longside of a pelter. 1902 Clapin *Dict. Amer.* 303 *Pelter*, in parts of New England, an old, worn-out horse.

Pelter, *v.* Add: 2. *intr.* To run with rapid steps; = Pelt *v.*¹ 7.
1906 W. S. Maugham *Bishop's Apron* xix. 297 The strange spectacle of a comely young woman and an ecclesiastical dignitary..peltering towards the Achilles Statue as fast as they could go. 1923 *Chambers's Jrnl.* Apr. 240/2 Rawlins ..peltered up on deck to recover his composure.

Pelting, *ppl. a.* 1. (Add example.)
1881 *Punch* 3 Sept. 105/2 Monday · Pelting morning, but left London comfortably by the 2.15.

Pelvigraph (pe·lvigraf). [f. Pelvis + -graph.] An instrument for obtaining measurements of the pelvis. **Pelvi·graphy,** the use of the pelvigraph.
1903 J. Clifton Edgar *Pract. Obstetrics* 184 Pelvigraphy. *Ibid.*, The authors [Neumann and Ehrenfest]..employ for this purpose an instrument termed by them a pelvigraph. 1904 *Lancet* 18 June 1728/1 A description is given of pelvigraphy or the method of taking a series of measurements of certain pelvic diameters and thus plotting out the size of the various pelvic planes.

Pen, *sb.*¹ Add: 2. c. *U.S.* = *Bull-pen.
1845 W. G. Simms *Wigwam & Cabin* Ser. II. 93 Laughter ..ceased on my part as I got in sight of the 'pen' in which I was to be kept secure. 1853 F. W. Thomas *J. Randolph* etc. 286 If I had not caught him in Baltimore..and put him in the pen there for debt. I never should have got the money. 1904 *N.Y. Even. Jrnl.* 10 May 2 A panic was caused among the prisoners in the pen of the Ewen Street Police Court jail. 1908 S. E. White *Riverman* xlvii. 353 You could put me in the pen, perhaps—with Heineman's testimony. 1920 W. M. Raine *B. O'Connor* 21, I know your kind —hell-bent to spend what you cash in, and every mother's son of you in the pen..inside of a month.

4. **pen-keeping,** *W. Indies* (see quot.).
1907 *Daily Cons. & Trade Rep.* 19 Oct. 5 (Cent. Suppl.) The rearing of cattle, horses, and mules is an important industry in Jamaica. This is known as '*pen-keeping', the pens varying in size from 200 to 2,000 acres.

Pen, *sb.*² Add: 6. b. *To touch the pen*, of a person unable to write, to put his hand to the pen with which another writes his name for him.
c 1886 C. Nordhoff *Young Man-of-War's Man* i. 8 [He] told me to 'touch the pen', while he ingeniously wrote my name for me.

7. a. *pen-stalk.* c. *pen-nibber.*
1823 *Trans. Soc. Arts* XL. 252 This operation..may be performed still more accurately by the *Pen-nibber here represented. 1902 *Chambers's Jrnl.* Nov. 692/2 He had in everyday use: (1) wash-hand tray..(13) pen-nibber, (14) ruler. 1907 Kate D. Wiggin *New Chron. Rebecca* 91 Last night I dreamed that the river was ink and I kept dipping into it and writing with a *penstalk made of a young pine tree.

8. **pen-scratch stitch,** in embroidery (see quot.).
1928 *Daily Express* 6 July 5/3 Take..the pen-scratch stitch. These short stitches—three vertical, space, one horizontal, space, and so on—make a charming little trimming.

Pen (pen), *sb.*⁵ *U.S.* Abbreviation of Penitentiary B. 7.
1889 Farmer *Americanisms*. 1910 'O. Henry' *Whirligigs* xvii. 202 One year after I got to the pen, my daughter died. 1924 W. M. Raine *Troubled Waters* xxvii. 273 He escaped from the pen four days ago.

Pen, *v.*³ Add: c. *intr.* To use a pen; to write.
1903 Hardy *Dynasts* I. II. ii. 40 He pens in fits, with pallid restlessness.

Penal (pī·năl), *sb. colloq.* [f. the adj.] A term or sentence of penal servitude.
1892 *Daily News* 17 Nov. 6/6, I was speaking to a youth who had undergone two penals..for picking pockets. 1927 W. E. Collinson *Contemp. Eng.* 77 A convict doing penal or doing time..is sometimes called a lag.

Penalty. Add: 2. e. *Bridge*. A number of points added to the opponents' score when the declarer fails to make his contract, or to the declarer's score when his call is doubled and he makes his contract.
1908 R. F. Foster *Auction Bridge* 37, 50 points penalty for each of the two tricks by which the bidder failed.

5. *penalty-bully, stroke, trick*; **penalty area,** the area in front of the goal in a football pitch within which a breach of certain rules involves the award of a penalty kick; **penalty envelope** *U.S.*, an official envelope which must not be used for private correspondence, under penalty of a fine stated on it; **penalty line,** the line bounding the penalty area of a football pitch.
1929 *Daily Express* 7 Nov. 19/1 The full-backs were often guilty of dribbling the ball in their own *penalty area. 1909 *Westm. Gaz.* 12 Oct. 12/2 It is rarely that a *penalty-bully is given in first-class hockey. 1879 *Postal Laws & Regul.* § 147 Requisitions for postage-stamps, stamped-envelopes,.. and official *penalty-envelopes are required to be made upon printed forms. 1903 *N.Y. Times* 29 Aug., The officials of the District Government were not entitled to the use of the mails like other Federal officials who use penalty envelopes. 1929 *Evening News* 18 Nov. 13/3 The *penalty lines and the touch lines were not visible. 1902 *Encycl. Brit.* XXIX. 26/1 A '*penalty stroke' is a stroke added to the score of a side under certain rules, and shall not affect the rotation of play. 1909 *Westm. Gaz.* 20 Mar. 14/2 *Penalty trick scores incurred during the play of a rubber are not irretrievably gone.

Pen-and-inkery. [-ery.] The use of pen and ink; an author's business.
1905 W. De Morgan in A. M. W. Stirling *De Morgan & Wife* 328, I do wish I had paid more attention to them [*sc.* birds, flowers, and trees] in my time—they would come in so useful in these later days of pen-and-inkery.

Pencil, *sb.* 7. b. Add: **pencil-arm,** that arm in a pair of compasses which carries the pencil; **pencil flower** (earlier example).
1895 Eleanor Rowe *Chip-Carving* 9 Do not use the left hand to move the *pencil-arm of the compasses. 1853 Darlington *Flora Cestrica* (ed. 3) 62 *Stylosanthes elatior.* ..*Pencil Flower.

Pencilling, *vbl. sb.* 1. (Add example.)
1913 W. Bateson *Mendel's Principles of Heredity* 42 Pencilling [in fowls] is a dominant to its absence.

Pendant, *sb.* 12. b. (Add example.)
1900 E. Buckingham *Theory of Thermodynamics* 153 We ..must accept it as a new experimental principle, forming a pendant to Carnot's principle.

Pendle¹. Also 8 pendal.
3. (Later Amer. example.)
1701 *Boston Rec.* VIII. 11 Ordered, That no person shall erect or set up any Pentice, jetty or Pendal over any of the streets, lanes or highwayes of this town.

Pendom (pe·ndəm). [f. Pen *sb.*² + -dom.] The world or domain of writing or literature; writers collectively.
1884 Grenville-Murray *High Life in France* 220 The French continue to be..the best versifiers in pendom.

Pendulation (pendiŭlēⁱ·ʃən). [f. L. *pendulus* (see Pendulum) + -ation.] An oscillating motion ascribed to the poles of the earth.
1909 *Westm. Gaz.* 1 May 12/3 According to Professor Simroth, pendulation, which is the periodical oscillation of the earth's axes,..explains nearly every observed fact in the development and distribution of all animals. 1924 tr. *A. Wegener's Orig. Continents & Oceans* 95 Unfortunately, Reibisch clothed his ideas..in the singular straight-jacket of a strict 'pendulation' of the poles in an 'orbit of swings', which is probably false.

Pendulize (pe·ndiŭləiz), *v.* [f. as Pendulous + -ize.] *intr.* To poise oneself or hover in the air; to be pendant.
1869 E. Newman *Illust. Nat. Hist. Brit. Moths* 12 He who has not seen this fairy creature pendulizing over a purple patch of the common bugle..has a delight yet to come.

Pendulum. Add: 1. c. Used of seismological instruments or parts of apparatus which embody some of the principles of the pendulum but are not actually suspended. **Horizontal pendulum,** a nearly horizontal rod carrying a heavy weight supported by thread and designed so as to swing readily in a plane slightly inclined to the horizontal. **Inverted pendulum,** a heavy mass held in position by springs and supported by rods which rest on a bearing vertically beneath its centre of gravity.
1841 J. D. Forbes in *Trans. Roy. Soc. Edin.* XV. 219 The elegant inverted Pendulum or *Noddy* contrived by the late Mr. Hardy, suggested to me a different arrangement. 1896 *Geog. Jrnl.* VII. 252 The duration of the disturbance as recorded by a free horizontal pendulum may be several hours. 1898 G. H. Darwin *Tides* 118 The instrument..is called a horizontal pendulum. 1904 C. E. Dutton *Earthquakes* 76 Here the inverted pendulum has a knob on its staff, which is supported at O upon gimbals. 1908 C. G. Knott *Earthquake Phenomena* 52 In the case of the inverted pendulum the stability is diminished by making the pendulum very long. 1911 *Encycl. Brit.* XXIV. 591/1 In these instruments the same principles are followed as in the construction of horizontal pendulums.

4. b. **pendulum observation,** an observation made with a pendulum; **pendulum position,** *Billiards*, a position of the two object balls beside the cushions on either side of a corner pocket which makes a large number of cannons possible.
1909 *Westm. Gaz.* 14 Sept. 4/1 Complete series of meteorological, magnetic, seismological, tidal, and pendulum observations were taken under great difficulties. 1927 *Daily Express* 26 Apr. 9/4 Reece..made a record break of 1,151, including 568 cannons by what is known as the 'pendulum position'.

Penelopize, *v.* (Earlier example.)
1841 *Congress. Globe* 14 June App. 43/2 Diplomacy was still drawing out its lengthened thread—still weaving its long and dilatory web—still Penelopizing.

Peneplai·ned, *a.* That has been made a peneplain.
1905 Chamberlin & Salisbury *Geol.* I. 85 Fig. 74. A peneplained surface where the elevations are small but steep-sided.

Peneplanation (pīnīplănēⁱ·ʃən). *Geol.* [f. Peneplain + -ation.] The process of forming a peneplain.
1904 *Amer. Geol.* Sept. 162 Several times the staying process has enabled partial peneplanation to take place.

Peneplane, variant of Peneplain.
1908 J. W. Gregory *Geog.* 32 Pene-planes are due to the levelling down of a country by rivers. 1928 V. G. Childe *Most Anc. East* vi. 123 The eastern end of the tilted peneplane of Arabia.

Pengö (pe·ŋgö). [Hungarian, pres. pple. of *peng* to sound]. The monetary unit of Hungary introduced in 1925, having a par value of about 28 to the pound sterling.
1926 *Glasgow Herald* 4 Jan. 12/2 To-day the new Hungarian currency, the pengo, is quoted for the first time. 1927 *Times* 28 Feb. 11/7 The Hungarian Government has assigned a sum of 321,820 pengoes (£11,600) for..a new Hungarian Legation building in London.

Penguin. Add: 2. b. *slang.* (See quots.)
1918 Farrow *Dict. Mil. Terms* 442 *Penguins*, airplanes with wing surface and power so reduced that they cannot leave the ground. 1919 *Athenæum* 11 July 582/2 Members of the W.R.A.F. were called 'Penguins' because they were 'flappers' who did not fly.

Penguinery. Also **penguinry.** (Later example.)
1921 H. G. Ponting *Gt. White South* 55 The Adélie penguinry was but a mile or two away.

Penible, *a.* 2. (Modern example.)
1915 Quiller-Couch *Nicky-Nan* xiii. 164 The steepness of the coombs..was penible to a man of his weight.

Peninsulate, *v.* (Later example.)
1857 *Christian Misc.* 252/2 The rain peninsulates every house with a moat of puddle.

Peninsula·tion. [f. prec.] The process of making into a peninsula. (In quot. *fig.*)
1923 *Outl. Literature* I. x. 194/1 From this peninsulation of the stage several things follow.

Penitent. B. *sb.* 5. **penitent-form** (earlier examples).
1865 *Wesleyan-Meth. Mag.* Nov. 484 She was the first to come to the penitent form. 1881 *Doctr. & Discipl. Salvation Army* § 28 Bring them out to the penitent form before the people, and so test them further, and pledge them publicly.

Pennant¹. Add: 2. c. *U.S.* A flag awarded as a distinction. Also *attrib.*
1888 *Outing* July 362/1 Up to June 1 the Chicago team led in the League pennant race. 1915 *Lit. Digest* (N.Y.) 21 Aug. 360/3 The Cincinnati Reds..have never yet won a pennant. *Ibid.*, The New York Giants..are not often far from the pennant class.

Penner⁴ (pe·nəɹ). [f. Pen *v.*¹ + -er¹.] One who pens cattle.
1904 *Daily News* 2 Dec. 5/1 There are 42 different men in this gang—'penners', 'shacklers', 'hoisters', 'gutters', and so on.

Pennsylvania (pensilvēⁱ·niă). One of the middle Atlantic states of the United States, named after William Penn, the Quaker, in 1681. Used attrib. to denote articles, products, or varieties of plants characteristic of, or growing in Pennsylvania, as *Pennsylvania corn, dwarf mountain maple, fir tree, mountain laurel, wagon, wind flower*; **Pennsylvania Dutch,** a dialect widely used in Pennsylvania, derived from the German (*deutsch*) of a great number of the early settlers, with a considerable admixture of English words; also, the persons using this dialect.
1739 *Col. Rec. Georgia* III. 429 We all were disappointed by..planting the yellow *Pensilvania Corn. 1869 *Atlantic Monthly* Oct. 473 In the county of Lancaster..my neighbors on all sides are *Pennsylvania Dutch. 1872 Haldeman (*title*) Pennsylvania Dutch: a dialect of South German with an infusion of English. 1889 Farmer *Americanisms*, Pennsylvania Dutch. 1785 H. Marshall *Amer. Grove* 2 *Pennsylvania Dwarf Mountain Maple (Acer pennsylvanicum). 1770 Forster tr. *Kalm's Trav.* 69 *Pennsylvania Fir Tree (*Pinus Amer.*). 1785 H. Marshall *Amer. Grove* 127 *Pennsylvania Mountain Laurel (Rhododendrum maximum). 1841 R. Park *Pantology* 462 The *Pennsylvania waggon is remarkable for its great size. 1845 *Knickerbocker Mag.* XXVI. 268 Sometimes twenty Pennsylvania wagons—you remember the Pennsylvania wagons?—would leave the city in one day. 1869 J. G. Fuller *Flower Gatherers* 28 It blooms later, in May and June, and is called the *Pennsylvania Wind Flower.

Pennsylva·nian, *a.* and *sb.* [f. prec. + -an.] a. *adj.* Of or belonging to Pennsylvania; = *Pennsylvania *attrib.* b. *sb.* A native or inhabitant of Pennsylvania.
1744 Franklin (*title*) An Account of..Pennsylvanian Fire places,..With directions for putting them up. 1785 H. Marshall *Amer. Grove* 51 Pennsylvanian Sharp-keyed Ash (Fraxinus pennsylvanica). 1755 *Lett. to Washington* I. 99 The Road upon which the Pennsylvaneans were Employ'd. 1793 J. Barlow *Hasty Pudding* 6 Ev'n in thy native regions, how I blush To hear the Pennsylvanians call thee Mush. 1816 U. Brown *Jrnl.* in *Maryland Hist. Mag.* X. 345, I was once a Pennsylvanian. 1825 *Wesleyan-Meth. Mag.* IV. App. 455/1, I had my first view of the city of Philadelphia..on the Pennsylvanian shore. 1838 *Southern Lit. Messenger* IV. 165/1 Mr. Ingersoll, being a Pennsylvanian, stands impartial between the two extremes of the Union. 1853 A. Bunn *Old Eng. & New Eng.* I. viii. 167 Mr. Nicholas Biddle..issued the notorious Pennsylvanian bonds.

Penny. Add: 2. b. (Earlier Amer. example.)
1842 J. S. Buckingham *Eastern & Western States* II. 113 [The *Log Cabin Advocate*, Baltimore] was one of the class called here 'Penny Papers', though selling for one cent a copy.

12. **penny ante,** the game of poker when the ante is fixed at one penny; **penny farthing,** an early form of bicycle having a large front wheel and a small rear one; **penny pawn** (see quot.); **penny-peeler,** an avaricious or niggardly person; **penny plain** *a.*, plain and unpretentious; so **penny-plainness.**
1894 *Outing* XXIV. 72/1 They play *penny-ante with feverish absorption. 1902 G. H. Lorimer *Lett. Self-made Merchant* xi. 148 He wasn't one of those elders who would ..tell him it was all right to play whist in the parlor if he'd give up penny-ante at the Dutchman's. 1927 'Ixion' *Further Motor Cycle Remin.* 70 On a greasy corner the outfit was probably less stable than the old '*penny-farthing' type of push bike. 1928 *Daily Tel.* 15 May 15/7 The pageant will end with Miss Dorothy Dickson on a 'penny-farthing' bicycle. 1907 *Westm. Gaz.* 16 Dec. 10/1 What are known as '*penny pawns' abound in the district. A broker who keeps one of these can purchase an article of any value from a penny upwards. He is compelled to keep it for only seven full days. 1925 J. Gregory *Bab of Backwoods* xxi. 269 Willoughby, skinflint, *penny-peeler and nickel grabber that he was, smelled a deal and asked them five thousand dollars for ten acres! 1884 Stevenson (*title of essay*) A '*penny plain and twopence coloured. 1920 'O. Douglas' *Penny plain* vi. 60 Having been all her life so very 'twopence coloured' she wants the 'penny plain' for a change... There is no mistake about our 'penny-plainness'—it jumps to the eye!

Pennywinkle, dial. variant of Periwinkle.²

Pension, *sb.* 9. Add: *pension act, law* (example), *money, roll* (later examples).
1839 *Southern Lit. Messenger* V. 314/1 A few tardy *pension acts..are all the tributes their worth has received. 1838 *Ibid.* IV. 766 When the revolutionary *pension-law was enacted, a majority of the war-worn veterans had travelled.. beyond the reach of human reward. 1854 Shillaber *Mrs. Partington* 190 The old lady had presented a check for a quarter's *pension-money. 1828 A. Sherburne *Mem.* xi. (1831) 242 This gentleman..forwarded to me the certificates of the continuation of my name on the *pension roll. 1907 *Westm. Gaz.* 5 Apr. 10/1 Miss Robb..was the posthumous child of Captain Robb,..and was put on the State pension-roll at birth.

Pensionable, *a.* Add: a. and b. (Further examples.)
a. 1920 *Act* 10 & 11 *Geo. V* c. 67 Sched. VIII. 4 This provision shall apply to the pensionable assistants of the petty sessions clerks at Clerk and Belfast.
b. 1908 *Daily Chron.* 9 Jan. 6/7 They will have the ultimate prospect..of appointment to permanent and pensionable establishments of the Protectorate.
c. Related to, connected with, or affecting, a person's pension.
1909 *Westm. Gaz.* 8 Feb. 8/3 The recognition of colour service in the Forces for pensionable purposes. 1920 *Act* 10 & 11 *Geo. V* c. 67 Sched. IX, The allowance awarded..shall in no case exceed two-thirds of his actual pensionable salary.

Pent, *sb.*² Add: b. *transf.* The brim of a bonnet.
1905 Quiller-Couch *Shining Ferry* x. 118 A..pretty damsel of eighteen or twenty, in..a pink sun-bonnet, under the pent of which her dark hair curtained her temples.

Penta-. **Pentalogy** (add example). **Pentalophodont** *a.* (example).
1921 *Times Lit. Suppl.* 10 Feb. 89/2 In form it is a play in five acts; but every act is a complete play in itself,..the whole drama is a *pentalogy. 1883 *Encycl. Brit.* XV. 623/1 Transitional conditions have..been shown..between the latter and what has been called a '*pentalophodont' type.

Pen-tail. [f. Pen *sb.*² + Tail *sb.*] A species and genus of tree-shrew, *Ptilocercus lowii*, which has fringes of long hair on a part of its tail. So **Pen-tailed** *a.*
1883 *Encycl. Brit.* XV. 402/1 Pentail (*Ptilocercus lowii*). 1910 *Ibid.* XIV. 639/2 In the pen-tailed tree-shrew..the fringes of long hair are confined to the terminal third of the tail. 1927 *Glasgow Herald* 14 May 4/2 The probability is that the pen-tail and tupaia represent two successive phases in the evolution of a Lemurid.

Pentamery (pentæ·mĕri). *Bot.* [f. Penta- + Gr. μέρος part + -y.] Pentamerous condition.
1902 *Encycl. Brit.* XXV. 433/2 Whilst in the pentamery and dimery of Dicotyledones there is usually a posterior sepal with a pair of lateral prophylls.

Pentecostal. B. *adj.* Add: b. Resembling the mixture of nationalities in Jerusalem at Pentecost (Acts ii. 9–11); heterogeneous.
1903 Kipling *5 Nations* 90, I have watched them in their tantrums, all that pentecostal crew, French, Italian, Arab, Spaniard, Dutch and Greek, and Russ and Jew.

Pentode (pe·ntoud), *a.* [f. Gr. πέντε five + ὁδός way.] Applied to a five-electrode wireless valve.
1919 [see *Tetrode]. 1928 *Daily Express* 14 Dec. 5 One pentode valve will do the work of two ordinary valves, but it will be a heavy drain on dry batteries.

Penultim, *a.* (Modern example.)
1910 *Sat. Westm. Gaz.* 5 Mar. 6/1 Slowly exhaling thy penultim breath.

Peonage. 1. (Earlier example.)
1844 J. J. Webb *Mem.* 50 The system of Peonage or voluntary servitude was a fixed institution.

Peonism. (Examples.)
1850 D. Webster *Sp.* Wks. 1851 V. 351, I suppose there is no slavery of that description in California now. I understand that *peonism*, a sort of penal servitude, exists there, or rather a sort of voluntary sale of a man and his offspring for debt. 1852 W. W. H. Davis *El Gringo* 231 Another peculiar feature of New Mexico is the system of domestic servitude called peonism, that has existed, and still exists, in all the Spanish American colonies.

Peony. 2. b. Add: *peony-flowered* adj.
1906 *Daily Chron.* 4 Oct. 6/5 A new variety of peony-flowered, or art dahlia.

People, *sb.* 1. e. (Add examples.)
1824 Miss Mitford *Our Village* I. 276 Even the four-footed people who wear iron shoes make wry faces, poor things! at those stones. 1907 *Westm. Gaz.* 20 Sept. 4/2 In compassing the death..of a pike..we are saving the life of as many other people of the stream as he would have eaten had he lived. 1913 E. H. Barker *Wayfaring in France* 278 All the other feathered people in the grove.

Peopling (pī·pliŋ), *ppl. a.* [f. People *v.* + -ing².] Filling or occupying as inhabitants.
1909 L. Binyon *England* etc. 8 Were these dark heavens the unfathomed gulfs of Time, So might we see bright peopling spirits star The memoriless ages.

Pep (pep), *sb. U.S.* [Abbreviation of Pepper *sb.*] Vigour, energy, or spirit.
1915 *Lit. Digest* (N.Y.) 21 Aug. 371/3 See for yourself if you do not get..all of the flexibility, all of the pick-up and all of the 'pep' that is claimed for any other motor built. 1918 *War Birds* (1927) 87 Col. Rees..tried to put pep in the boys by giving a stunting exhibition below five hundred feet. 1919 H. L. Wilson *Ma Pettengill* v. 168 She was taking longer rides and getting her pep back. 1920 *Chambers's Jrnl.* Feb. 113/2, I put more and more 'pep' into my sermon, but to no purpose. 1924 F. G. Lowe *Lawn Tennis* 137 We have not enough 'pep' and go; we are too soft and hit too late. 1928 R. H. B. Bell *Life Abundant* 182 When the mind is sick, the soul lacks spiritual pep.

Pep, *v. U.S.* [f. the sb.] *trans.* With *up.* To fill or inspire with energy and vigour; to put new life into.
1925 H. L. Foster *Trop. Tramp Tourists* 56 'Just leave them to me,' said the Social Manager. 'I'll get them started, and all pepped up, and the rest will be easy.' 1926 Fannie Kilbourne *Dot & Will* (1929) 271 Besides Will and I had stuck at home so much that I couldn't help feeling kind of pepped up at the idea of going to any party again. 1928 *Daily Express* 30 Nov. 19 University athletics are undergoing a strenuous process of 'pepping up,' on strictly scientific lines.

Pe·pful, *a.* [f. *Pep *sb.* + -ful.] Full of pep or vigour.
1923 *Weekly Dispatch* 22 Apr. 5 The film is..an American conception of the novel, with Richard Dix as a 'pep-ful' parson hero.

Pepper, *sb.* 4. (Add example.)
1847 Longf. in *Life* (1891) II. 85 The paper on 'Nine new Poets', by the editor, is full of pepper.

Pepper-and-salt. Add: 1. b. A person wearing a pepper-and-salt suit.
1900 Elinor Glyn *Visits Eliz.* 236 At dinner I sat between Charlie and one of the pepper-and-salts...They are going to shoot partridges to-morrow.

Pepperet (pe·pərĕt). [f. Pepper + -et.] A pepper-pot.
1927 Deeping *Kitty* i, Regency salt-cellars, mustard-pots and pepperets.

Pepperidge. 2. (Earlier example.)
1810 Michaux *Arbres* I. 30 *Peperidge* fréquemment usitée par les Hollandois du New Jersey.

Pepper-pot. 2. b. (Examples.)
1794 *Massachusetts Spy* 13 Mar. (Th.) A wag in my neighbourhood, a lover of pepper pots. 1800 *Aurora* (Philad.) 19 June (Th.) Daniel Dunn of the Leopard Tavern in Lætitia Court, advertises 'Pepperpot of a superior quality at 6 o'clock every evening'. 1825 J. K. Paulding *J. Bull in Amer.* xiv. 231 Whose principal trade consists in the exportation of Toughy and Pepper Pot.

Peppiness (pe·pinĕs). *U.S.* [f. *Peppy *a.* + -ness.] Peppy or energetic quality.
1927 *Observer* 2 Oct. 13/3 The tendency..to add variety and 'peppiness' to dancing..has developed.

Peppy (pe·pi), *a. U.S.* [f. *Pep *sb.* + -y.] Full of pep or vigour; spirited, energetic, forceful.
1926 *Contemp. Rev.* June 720 The 'peppy' American girl expects to be given a drink by her companion at a party. 1926 Fannie Kilbourne *Dot & Will* (1929) 82 She's a peppy, red-headed little woman. 1930 *Observer* 11 May 26 'Select the scenes, keep to the point,' thus his peppy injunction.

Peptase (pe·ptēⁱs). [f. Pept(one) + *-ase.] Any one of a class of enzymes or ferments which convert proteids into peptones and other products.
1902 *Encycl. Brit.* XXVIII. 556/1 Among the enzymes already extracted from fungi are..*peptases*.

Peptic. A. *adj.* 1. (Add example.)
1907 *Practitioner* June 748 Duodenal ulcer, properly called 'peptic' ulcer, may be present in any part of the duodenum.

Per, *prep.* I. 5. b. **per diem** (earlier examples).
1812 *Niles' Weekly Reg.* I. 361/2 The per diem of the members has been raised to four dollars. 1839 *Congress. Globe* 5 Jan. App. 66/1 In that case, had he asked for his mileage and per diem, all would have considered it an insult. 1846 M'Kenney *Mem.* I. ix. 192, I referred to him the making up of my account for my per diem allowance. 1848 *Wilmington* (N.C.) *Commercial* 24 Aug. 214 The per diem will hardly pay a gentleman for soiling his hands with it.

III. 2. Also with ellipse of *head*.
1918 *Liberator* (N.Y.) Oct. 6/2 We have to collect that money by making members at $16·00 per.

Perambulate, *v.* Add: 3. *trans.* To conduct or 'walk' *about*.

1909 Marg. B. Saunders *Litany Lane* III. xxii, The Princess Max, having opened the affair, was being perambulated about as usual.

b. To wheel or convey in or as in a perambulator (sense 3).
1922 J. A. Dunn *Man Trap* i. 9 Jovial of mouth and eyes despite the handicap that reduced him to being perambulated. 1929 P. Gibbs *Hidden City* xi. 50 Four acres of garden in which some neat nursemaids were perambulating the pink-cheeked babies of the well-to-do.

c. To travel on or traverse in a perambulator.
1902 *To-Day* 30 Apr. 8/1 Babies..are not allowed to 'perambulate' the pavement two or three abreast.

Perambulatory, *sb.* (Later example.)
1843 *Knickerbocker Mag.* XXII. 85 Let..the temperance-halls and root-beer perambulatories make answer.

Percentably (pəɹse·ntăbli), *adv.* [f. Per cent + -ably.] By an appreciable percentage.
1928 *Sunday Dispatch* 2 Sept. 10 Men..who are bent on reducing the mouflon population percentably.

Percentage. (Later attrib. examples.)
1910 *Westm. Gaz.* 20 Jan. 12/4 All figures..have shown large percentage increases. 1928 *Brit. Industr. Future* (Lib. Ind. Inq.) v. xxxi. § 4. 444 The choice in particular cases between block grants and percentage grants.

Percental (pəɹse·ntăl), *a.* Also **per cental.** [f. Per cent + -al.] Reckoned by the hundred; stated as a percentage.
1895 *Daily News* 18 Dec. 9/5 In wheat a fair extent of business was put through at ½d per cental decline. 1897 *Geog. Jrnl.* IX. 319 A map showing, by means of six colours distinguishing different percental proportions, the distribution of German-speaking people in the lands of the Hungarian crown.

Perception. Add: 9. *attrib.* as *perception-time*.
1902 *Amer. Jrnl. Psychol.* XIII. 258 The time measured was, therefore, a single perception-time instead of a recognition-time.

Perceptually (pəɹse·ptiuăli), *adv.* [f. Perceptual + -ly².] In a perceptual manner.
1910 R. R. Rusk in *Brit. Jrnl. Psychol.* III. 379 The adult when he works perceptually is not consciously much troubled with associations. 1922 A. G. Hogg *Redemption fr. this World* 197 Thus miracles..render perceptually obvious both the personality and the infinitude of the Divine will.

Perch, *sb.*¹ 3. Add: **perch-hole,** a hole in which perch are found; **perchpike** = *pike-perch* (Pike *sb.*⁴ 3).
1906 *Macmillan's Mag.* June 574 Agatha by the side of the *perch-hole, very erect, with a still more erect fishing-rod, surprised by the..angler. 1884 *Encycl. Brit.* XVII. 772/2 Burbot, pike, *perchpike, and perch are among the fish caught in the lake [Onega].

Perch, *sb.*² 4. Also, a horizontal bar used in softening leather.
1903 H. R. Procter *Princ. Leather Manuf.* 188 'Perching'..[consists] in fixing the skins on a horizontal pole (the 'perch'), and working them with..a tool formed somewhat like a small shovel with a semicircular blade. 1909 H. G. Bennett *Manuf. Leather* 359 In perching the mechanical treatment is less violent, the goods being fixed on a 'perch' —a horizontal pole about 5 feet above the ground—and scraped by means of the 'moon-knife'.

Perching, *vbl. sb.*¹ Also, a process for softening skins in leather-making; cf. *Perch *sb.*² 4. Freq. *attrib.*
1897 C. T. Davis *Manuf. Leather* (ed. 2) 361 There are, however, above the perching room on the fourth floor, two large logwood tanks. *Ibid.* 362, 12 Slocomb perching machines. These perching machines take the place of hand work, as they are far more efficient and speedy. 1903, 1909 [see *Perch *sb.*² 4].

Percussion, *sb.* 5. Add: **percussion lock** (earlier U.S. example).
1829 *Congress. Deb.* Mar. App. p. xlii/2, I have used the percussion locks but little, but believe them admirably well constructed for general use.

Peregrinatory, *a.* (Recent example.)
1906 *Chambers's Jrnl.* Feb. 150/1 One sees in the streets ..peregrinatory makers of sugar puppets.

Perfect, *a.* B. 4. d. *A perfect day*: One that has been thoroughly enjoyed. *colloq.*
1909 Carrie Jacobs-Bond *Song*, When you come to the end of a perfect day.

Perfecto (pəɹfe·kto). *U.S.* [Sp., = perfect.] A make of cigar.
1898 Hamblen *General Manager's Story* 3 The old gentleman..blowing the smoke from his 'perfecto' out into the cool starlight. 1906 'O. Henry' *Four Million* vii. (1916) 77 He always..handed out real perfectos to the delighted boys. 1918 Vachell *Some Happenings* iii. 32 She examined the Perfectos critically and selected one.

Perfector. Add: 2. *Typog.* A press that prints both sides of a sheet in one operation.
1907 *Cambr. Mod. Hist.* Prosp. 92 The press on which they [the plates] are to be put is a *perfector*.

Perfervidly (pəɹfɜ̄·ɹvidli), *adv.* [f. Perfervid *a.* + -ly².] In a perfervid manner.
1906 *Macmillan's Mag.* Oct. 884 The General was gripping de Pellotin's hand perfervidly.

Perfidity. (Modern example.)
1903 J. Kelman *Honour towards God* iii. 22 Instances are only too common in which pagan and Mohammedan honour has shamed the perfidity of so-called Christians.

Perforable, *a.* (Example.)
1926 J. M. Robertson *Mr. Shaw & 'The Maid'* v. 46 The real question is simply whether his shield is perforable.

Pe·rforating, *vbl. sb.* [f. Perforate *v.* + -ing¹.] The action of the verb perforate. (In quot. *attrib.*)
1907 *Daily Chron.* 23 Nov. 5/6 The material used in making bioscope films is very inflammable, and..a fire.. suddenly broke out in the perforating room.

Perform, *v.* Add: 8. *intr.* Of a play, piece of music, etc.: To admit of being performed; to lend itself to performing (in a certain manner).
1928 *Music & Lett.* Oct. 398 It should perform very well and be interesting to play.

Perfume, *sb.* 3. Add: *perfume industry, -yielding* adj.
1908 *Westm. Gaz.* 23 Mar. 5/1 The perfume industry of India will become one of the most important in the world. India possesses hundreds of perfume-yielding plants.

Pergamum (pɜ̄·ɹgămŏm). [L. *Pergamum*, Gr. Πέργαμος.] The name of a city and ancient kingdom in Asia Minor. Hence the adjs. **Pe·rgamene, Pergame·nian** (9 -onian), **Perga·mic,** of or belonging to Pergamum or in the style of a school of sculptors that flourished there in the third and second centuries B.C. Also **Pergame·nian** *sb.*, a native or inhabitant of Pergamum.
a 1823 Culbertson *Lect. Revelation* xvi. (1826) I. 214 Pergamos..together with all that territory over which the Pergamonian princes bore rule, was bequeathed by Attalus ..to the Romans. 1865 Lightfoot *Galatians* 5 The Pergamene prince Attalus the first effectually curbed their power. 1885 *Encycl. Brit.* 527/2 Sculptors were attracted by the wealth of the state.., and thus arose the so-called 'Pergamenian school' in sculpture. The Pergamenian kings appear to have been far more truly Hellenic..than the other Hellenistic sovereigns. 1903 *Westm. Gaz.* 23 Sept. 3/2 Visitors..will be delighted to recognise the Pergamenian type of the so-called 'Dying Alexander'. 1896 *Pall Mall Gaz.* 19 May 3/2 A victorious king..is to be met by a troop of priests, and conducted to the Pergamenic altar. 1904 W. M. Ramsay in *Expositor* June 406 The possibility that Antipas was..'killed among the Pergamenians'.

Pericemental (perisĭme·ntăl), *a.* [f. Peri- 1 a + Cemental *a.*] Of or pertaining to the pericementum. So **Pericementi·tis,** inflammation of the pericementum.
1904 V. H. Jackson *Orthodontia* 199 Opening the bite has been used to advantage in cases of pericemental inflammation. 1908 *Practitioner* Dec. 857 D. M. Paton suggests the use of anti-diphtheritic serum for many dental conditions, e.g., injury, pain after extraction,..pericementitis.

Peridicine (pĕri·diəin), *a.* [f. Peridium + -ine².] Resembling or consisting of a peridium.
1882 *Encycl. Brit.* XIV. 562/1 Thallus thin, often wanting. Apothecia peridicine, without any ostiole.

Peridotic, *a.* (Example.) **Peridotite.** (Earlier example.)
1891 J. Murray in *Challenger Rep., Deep-sea Deposits* 326 Lamellar aggregates, generally large fragments found with older eruptive rock debris, with peridotite fragments. *Ibid.* 374 A constituent of pyroxenic, amphibolic, and peridotic minerals.

Perigraphic (perigræ·fik), *a. Geom.* [f. Gr. περιγραφή outline, circumference (or περιγράφειν to draw a line round) + -ic.] Having a circumference, as a closed curve.
1901 [see *Aperigraphic].

Perikaryon (perikæ·riŏn). *Anat.* [f. Gr. περί round + κάρυον nut, kernel.] The cell-body of a neurone; that part of a nerve-cell which includes the nucleus.
1902 *Encycl. Brit.* XXV. 394/1 From the other end of the perikaryon..there arises a series of one or more short, repeatedly-branching filaments, called *dendrites*.

Period, *sb.* Add: 15. *attrib.* or as *adj.* in sense 'belonging to or characteristic of a particular (past) period' esp. in style or design in architecture, furniture, dress, etc.
1905 (*title*) Borgia: A Period Play. 1906 G. Kobbé *How to appreciate Music* 47 A pianoforte has no business in a 'period' room. If the person is rich enough to afford 'period' rooms, he also can afford a music room. 1908 *Westm. Gaz.* 17 Dec. 4/1 Some of them..may be said to be striving to create a 'period' type of carriage for themselves. 1914 Eberlein & McClure (*title*) The Practical Book of Period Furniture. 1927 *Times* 28 Oct. 17/3 The bride.. wore a period gown of cream chiffon velvet, trimmed with seed pearls. 1927 *Daily Tel.* 1 Nov. 5/3 A 'period' residence, which has gardens overlooking Hyde Park. 1929 *Star* 21 Aug. 15/2 Fashions in 'period rooms'..have come and gone with startling rapidity during the last quarter-century. 1930 *Times* 18 Mar. 10/4 It is a 'period' novel, full of carefully studied local colour.

Periodic, *a.*¹ 2. Add: (Example of *periodic law*.) *Periodic scheme, table* (*Chem.*), a scheme or table of the chemical elements illustrating the periodic law.
1877 H. Watts *Fownes' Man. Chem.* (ed. 12) 265 This relation of the elementary bodies, which is called the 'periodic law', was first pointed out by Newlands in 1864. 1909 Tilden in *Mem. Lect. Chem. Soc.* (1914) II. 145 Hypotheses as to the origin of the elements..seem to be inseparable from the periodic scheme itself. 1919 Soddy in *Jrnl. Chem. Soc.* CXV. 11 The occupant of a separate place in the periodic table of elements.

6. as *sb. pl.* = next.
1920 Mulford *J. Nelson* xvii. 181 That's the worst of them periodics. You can't never tell when they'll start.

Periodical. B. *sb.* Add: 3. *pl. U.S. slang.* Recurring drinking bouts or sprees.
a 1897 *N.Y. Times* (Barrère & Leland) Are you in the book business?..Ma and pa were talking last night about your having your little periodicals. 1902 H. L. Wilson *Spenders* x. 107 They telegraphed the Butte National to wire his description, and the answer was 'tall and drunk'. Well, son, his periodicals wa'n't all.

Periodicity. Add: 1. (Further examples.)
1879 Roscoe & Schorlemmer *Treat. Chem.* II. II. 506 The law of periodicity was..further developed by Meyer and Mendelejeff. 1907 *Westm. Gaz.* 4 Feb. 6/3 Gallium, scandium, and germanium, all subsequently discovered, did fit into the scale of 'periodicity'.

b. The frequency of alternation.
1900 *Jrnl. Soc. Arts* 19 Oct. 848/2 The other carrying about 20 amperes with a periodicity of 60 cycles per second. 1909 *Installation News* III. 105 Prices for alternating currents are suitable for 40–60 periods. For other periodicities add 10 %.

Periodogram (piəriǫ·dǫgræm). *Meteorol.* Also **-graph.** [See -gram and -graph.] A diagram exhibiting or designed to exhibit the periodic occurrence of certain phenomena.
1902 A. Schuster in *Rep. Brit. Assoc.* 518 The curve which connects the intensity with the period..is a curve which ought to have a name, and for want of a better one I have suggested that of 'periodograph'. 1911 N. W. Shaw *Forecasting Weather* 359 A periodogram for the examination of the periodicity of any long series of records.

Periost (pe·riǫst). *Anat.* Anglicized form of Periosteum.
1902 *Proc. Zool. Soc.* I. 212 The periclerium is continuous with the periost of the pedicle portion [of the horn]. 1927 Haldane & Huxley *Animal Biol.* ix. 185 The basal joint ..was removed and a piece of healthy bone with its bone-forming membrane (periost) grafted in from another situation.

Periscope. Add: 4. *Comb.* as **periscope depth** (see quot.).
1928 Gamble *Story N. Sea Air Station* xviii. 309 German submarines, when travelling awash, could reach 'periscope depth' (that is, the depth at which the fully extended periscope just reaches to the surface—normally 45 feet) in 1½ minutes.

Perish, *sb.* Delete *rare*⁻¹ and add: b. *Austral.* (See quot. 1894.)
1894 *Argus* 28 Mar. 5/4 (Morris) When a man (or party) has nearly died through want of water he is said to have 'done a perish'. 1903 R. Bedford *True Eyes* 312 If Xavier Quinn hadn't found this show three months ago ye'd have done a perish.

Perisher. Add: b. = *Perish b.
1903 R. Bedford *True Eyes* 292 Of course that country we went to on the Peak was a shicer. Just's well you didn't come—we near did a perisher there.

Perishing, *ppl. a.* Add: 3. *colloq.* Applied disparagingly to anything: Troublesome, 'beastly'.
1918 W. J. Locke *Rough Road* xix. 231 Mo says he's blistering glad you're out of it and safe in your perishing bed with a Blighty one. 1930 *Punch* 15 Jan. 79 Hold this perishing split-pin.

4. as *adv.* Excessively, perishingly.
1888 Emma Marshall *Bristol Diamonds* ix. 106 It is perishing cold to-day. 1906 *Westm. Gaz.* 26 Feb. 4/2 I'm perishing hungry. I feel as if I should drop.

Perishless (pe·riʃlĕs), *a.* [f. Perish *v.* + -less.] That cannot perish; imperishable.
1885 J. Beveridge *Poets of Clackmannanshire* 144 Wallace of perishless renown. 1915 *Times* 31 Mar. 9/3 The perishless faith of the lover takes their spears of rebellion into its own wounds to hide them.

Peristeronic, *a.* Also, of or suggestive of pigeons.
1928 *Funk's Stand. Dict.* 1931 Joanna Cannan *High Table* 21 A discourse..which Anne and Cecilia punctuated with polite little peristeronic sounds.

Peritomize (pe·ritŏməiz), *v. Surg.* [f. as Peritomy + -ize.] *trans.* To submit to peritomy.
1903 *Lancet* 30 May 1516/1 The cornea recovers its transparency more completely in those cases which have been peritomised.

Perjurous, *a.* (Recent example.)
1926 A. L. Maycock *Inquisition* 110 No Inquisitor..could be certain of exposing a careful conspiracy, backed by plenty of perjurous witnesses.

Perlicity (pəɹli·sĭti). [f. Perli(ti)c + -ity.] Perlitic character or structure.
1895 L. Fletcher *Introd. Study Rocks* 41 Cellularity, porosity, and perlicity are characters which depend on the presence of numerous cavities or cracks throughout the rock-fragment.

Perm (pɜ̄ɹm). *colloq.* Abbreviation of *permanent wave* (*Permanent 1 d). So **Permed** (pɜ̄ɹmd) *ppl. a.*, having a permanent wave (in the hair).
1928 *Daily Express* 17 Mar. 9/5 These girls took their chairs at 7.30 p.m...Three hours later they rose 'permed', as one says in the profession. 1929 Naomi Royde-Smith *Summer Holiday or Gibraltar* 113 The old girl's had a perm. Look at the waves.

Permalloy (pɜ̄·ɹmăloi). [f. Perm(eable *a.* + Alloy.] An alloy of nickel and iron in the proportion of four to one, which is very sensitive to magnetic forces; introduced in 1923.
1924 *Nature* 19 Apr. 583/2 This new permalloy cable will not make existing cables obsolete, but it will divert the direction of much of the world's communication. 1925 *Chambers's Jrnl.* Apr. 220/1 The conductor of this distortionless cable is composed of a special alloy, known as permalloy, of nickel and iron. 1930 *Times* 21 Mar. 10/2 They did not originate the uniform loading with 'permalloy', which has made all unloaded cables antiquated.

Permanent, *a.* Add: 1. (Further example.)
1908 *Westm. Gaz.* 24 Oct. 3/2 Then arose the question of what was meant by a permanent appointment.

d. *permanent wave*, a wave in the hair produced by a special process designed to make it lasting; so *permanent waver, waving*; *permanent way* (attrib. examples).
1925 *Scribner's Mag.* July 20 Advt., You will enjoy your *permanent wave at Nestle's. 1928 *Daily Express* 23 Aug. 3/6 The curling irons and the tentacles of the *permanent waver will be busier than ever in the autumn season. 1906 *Daily Chron.* 31 Jan. 4/5 Instructions had been issued to the *permanent-way staff to adhere..to the regulations. 1908 *Ibid.* 6 Apr. 5/5 Mr. J. Meecham..has just resigned his position as permanent-way inspector. 1909 *Westm. Gaz.* 23 Mar. 5/1 Large quantities of permanent way material are now being sent..from this country.

Permanently, *adv.* (Add example.)
1930 Joanna Cannan *No Walls of Jasper* 192 She stood.. with..the sun in her eyes, and the wind in her permanently-waved hair.

Permansive (pəɹmæ·nsiv), *a. Gram.* [f. L. *permans-um* supine of *permanēre* to remain (see Permanent) + -ive.] Applied to a tense in some Semitic languages which is used to denote a more or less permanent state.
1866 E. Hincks in *Jrnl. R. Asiatic Soc.* Dec. 485 The verbal forms belonging to each conjugation may be divided into two great classes, which I call permansive and mutative. The former denotes continuance in the state which the verb signifies in that conjugation; the latter denotes change into that state.

Permeameter (pɜ̄ɹmĭæ·mĭtəɹ). *Electr.* [f. Permea(bility + -meter.] An instrument for measuring the magnetic permeability of substances.
1902 *Encycl. Brit.* XXVIII. 119/2 Instruments of this kind for determining the flux density corresponding to a given magnetizing force in a complete magnetic circuit..are called permeameters.

Permittance. (Modern example.)
1913 *A Housemaster's Lett.* 124 The wilful misuse of them or the callous permittance of them to go blunt and to rust.

2. *Elect.* = *Permittivity.
1919 H. Ward *Dict. Techn. Terms Wireless Telegr.* (ed. 2) 159 *Permittance*, term denoting Inductive Capacity.

Permitted, *ppl. a.* Add: b. *Permitted hours*: the hours during which the sale of intoxicating liquor is legal.
1927 *Rep. Commissioner Police Metropolis 1926* 24 'Permitted hours.'—The varying hours during which intoxicating liquor may be sold in different licensing areas in the Metropolis continue to give trouble to the Police.

Permittivity (pɜ̄ɹmiti·vĭti). *Elect.* [f. Permit + -ive + -ity.] (See quot. 1926.)
1919 H. Ward *Dict. Techn. Terms Wireless Telegr.* (ed. 2) 159 *Permittivity*, another term for Dielectric Constant. 1926 *Gloss. Electr. Terms* (Brit. Engin. Stand.) 12 *Permittivity*, of a dielectric medium. The ratio of the capacity between two conductors when surrounded by the medium to the capacity in a perfect vacuum.

Permutation. Add: 2. c. *Logic.* A form of immediate inference from a proposition by substituting a contradictory predicate; obversion.
1851 Karslake *Aids Study Logic* I. 64 The third form of Immediate Inference which we have to speak of is, what may be called *Permutation*. 1906 Joseph *Introd. Logic* 214 In Permutation, or (as it has been also called) Obversion, there is no transposition of terms, but the quality of the proposition is changed.

Permute, *v.* 2. (Later example.)
1846 *Proc. Phil. Soc.* III. 1 In certain cases a letter may have been permuted, that is, changed to some kindred letter.

b. *Logic.* To submit to the process of permutation or obversion.
1906 Joseph *Introd. Logic* 215 The process of permuting and then converting is called Conversion by Negation.

Permutit(e. Trade name for various base-changing alumino-silicates employed in the softening of hard water.
1921 *Chambers's Jrnl.* May 352/1 For the removal of iron and manganese and for the destruction of germ-life, manganese permutit is used in place of the sodium permutit. 1918 A. Smith *Introd. Inorg. Chem.* (ed. 3) 724 In the permutite process, the water is simply filtered through sodium silicoaluminate.

Pernoctate, *v.* Delete *Obs.*⁻⁰ and add recent example.
1923 *Blackw. Mag.* Aug. 250/1 Families of Oriental pilgrims, pernoctating within the Church, will squat down in front of the Tomb of Christ.

Perorative (pe·rǫrĕtiv), *a.* [f. Peroration + -ive.] Appropriate to or suggestive of a peroration.
1921 *Glasgow Herald* 29 Oct. 4 Messrs. Hart (said Cleland in a perorative phrase..) are of that class in society who have found their way to philosophy without the aid of regular tuition.

Peroratorical (perǫrătǫ·rikăl), *a.* [f. Perorator after Oratorical *a.*] Characteristic of a peroration; perorational.
1927 C. E. Montague *Right off Map* vi. 56 His voice was taking on the peroratorical note.

Pero·xided, *ppl. a.* [f. Peroxide + -ed¹.] Treated with peroxide (of hydrogen).
1906 B'ness von Hütten *What became of Pam* x. 71 Miss Vesey had highly peroxided hair and a manner of suspicious dignity.

Perpension. (Modern example.)
1890 R. L. Stevenson *Lett.* 13 July, Upon these points perpend, and give me the results of your perpensions.

Perpetualism (pəɹpe·tiuăliz'm). [f. Perpetual + -ism.] Lasting, perpetual, or universal, quality, *spec.* as a special doctrine in political science or religion (see quots.).
1885 *Encycl. Brit.* XIX. 391/1 Cosmopolitanism..and what has been called perpetualism, or the assumption of a system applicable to every social stage, were alike discredited. 1905 *Westm. Gaz.* 31 July 6/7 Perpetualism abolishes both hell and heaven. 1931 *Observer* 8 Nov. 24 The hybridist who can develop even a slight measure of perpetualism in this plant will sweep the horticultural board of its best cups and medals.

Perpetuate, *v.* Also *absol.*
1894 E. Fawcett *New Nero* ii. 26 That soulless and mysterious will-to-live, which for ever creates, protects, and perpetuates, though blindly and dumbly, unconscious that she does either.

Perradial, *a.* Add: b. as *sb.* A perradial organ.
1892 [see *Adradial *sb.*].

Perseverate (pəɹse·vĕreⁱt), *v. Psych.* [f. L. *perseverā-re* to persist, persevere + -ate³.] *intr.* To (tend to) be spontaneously repeated.
1915 *Brit. Jrnl. Psychol.* Mar. VII. 388 Ideas after disappearing from consciousness continue to 'perseverate' unconsciously. *Ibid.* 389 The degree of hindrance which the perseverating effect of a past mental activity causes to a new one of the same kind. 1920 *Discovery* Nov. 338/1 Lower and more fundamental conative tendencies of instinct, emotion, [etc.] working themselves out by their own perseverating, 'determining tendencies'.

Perseveration. Transfer †*Obs.* to sense in Dict. and add: 2. *Psych.* (Tendency towards) the spontaneous repetition of past experiences.
1915 *Brit. Jrnl. Psychol.* Mar. VII. 388 The present paper gives a description of a fairly large set of experiments on Perseveration. 1920 *Discovery* Nov. 337/1 Perseveration occurs especially in the case of exciting emotional experience. 1922 J. Riviere tr. *Freud's Introd. Lect. on Psycho-Anal.* 25 When a member of the House of Commons referred to another as the 'honourable member for Central *Hell*' instead of 'Hull', it was a case of perseveration.

Perseverator (pɜ̄ɹse·vəreⁱtəɹ). [f. Perseverate *v.* + -or.] A person who exhibits perseveration in a marked degree.
1915 *Brit. Jrnl. Psychol.* Mar. VII. 391 The perseverator on the whole tends to be slower than the non-perseverator.

Persimmon. 3. (Earlier U.S. examples.)
1833 J. K. Paulding *Banks of Ohio* (Lond.) I. 140 If the [broad-]horn gets broadside to the current, I wouldn't risk a huckleberry to a persimmon that we don't every soul get treed, and sink to the bottom. 1834 Crockett *Narr. Life* ix. 70 But to do this, and write the warrants too, was at least a huckleberry over my persimmon. 1836 — *Exploits & Adv. Texas* (1837) 1 Still it is a huckleberry above my persimmon to cipher out how it is [etc.]. 1844 *Philad. Spirit of Times* 24 Aug. (Th.) She's a great gal that!..She's a huckleberry above most people's parsimmons.

4. *persimmon beer* (earlier example), *bush*.
1784 J. F. D. Smyth *Tour U.S.* I. xix. 151 Of these they brew a fermented liquor..called *persimmon beer. 1786 Washington *Diaries* III. 102 A parcel of small *Persimmon bushes.

Personal. B. *sb.* 2. c. (Earlier examples.)
1873 F. Hudson *Journalism U.S.* 472 Take the 'personals' of the *Herald* any day, and they will set one to thinking. 1875 J. G. Holland *Sevenoaks* viii. 103 Returning..to look over the papers, his eye was attracted, among the 'personals', to an item [etc.].

Personalia (pɜ̄ɹsənēⁱ·liă), *pl.* [ad. L. *personālia* neut. pl. of *personālis* personal.] Personal matters; personal observations.
1903 'Sigma' (*title*) Personalia. Political, Social and Various. 1909 H. G. Wells *Tono-Bungay* III. ii. § 6. 243 My aunt received these personalia cheerfully. 1920 *Glasgow Herald* 27 Mar. 8 His speech on Wednesday contained some quite superfluous personalia.

Personalistic (pɜ̄ɹsənăli·stik), *a.* [f. Personalist + -ic.] Inclined towards or suggestive of personalism.
1923 *Contemp. Rev.* Feb. 221 It suggests a philosophical reinforcement for the theistic or personalistic tendencies of popular religion.

Personnel. Also *attrib.*
1914 *Illustr. London News* 17 Oct. 540/2 The personnel-car of the Schneider gun-train.

Perspecta·rtigraph. [f. as Perspectograph + L. *arti-s, ars* Art.] A form of Perspectograph.
1904 *Sci. Amer.* 2 Apr. 268/1 The perspectartigraph..was invented with the idea of making it possible to draw in perspective mechanically, with little or no previous instruction.

Pert, *a.* Add: 6. (Further U.S. examples.)
a. 1767–74 P. V. Fithian *Jrnl.* (1900) 241 Ben seems a little more pert today.
b. 1772 *Carroll Papers* in *Maryland Hist. Mag.* XIV. 272 The Corn looks pert & green.
C. *adv.* (Later example.)
1902 Harben *Abner Daniel* 230 Well, I'm glad I won't have to go furder'n Darley... By ridin' peert I can let you out before sundown.

Perthitically (pəɹþi·tikăli), *adv. Geol.* [f. Perthitic *a.* + -al + -ly².] In a manner suggestive of perthite.
1930 Peach & Horne *Geol. Scotl.* 112 The alkali-felspar includes both orthoclase and albite, which may be present separately, perthitically intergrown.

Perturb, *v.* 2. (Modern example of absol. use.)
1902 *Daily Chron.* 23 Apr. 3/3 It is the unexpected that perturbs.

Peruke-maker. (Later example.)
1905 T. Auden *Shrewsbury* viii. 201 Brought up at Manchester as a barber and peruke-maker, he adopted the Jacobite principles.

Peruse, *v.* 5. Add: Also *absol.* or *intr.*
1886 Hardy *Mayor Casterbr.* II. xviii. 254, I have tried to peruse and learn all my life; but the more I try to know the more ignorant I seem. 1909 H. G. Wells *Ann Veronica* i. 25 Her father..appeared not to observe her entry. 'Sit down,' he said, and perused..for some moments.

Pervenche (pɛɹvā·nʃ), *a.* [Fr. *pervenche*, Periwinkle.] A particular shade of light blue, resembling the colour of the flowers of the periwinkle. Also *attrib.*
1899 *Westm. Gaz.* 30 Mar 3/1 Pervenche and navy are the opposite points of the cold tone of blue. 1909 *Daily Chron.* 6 July 4/5 She wore a beautiful dress of blue embroidered net in a shade of pervenche blue. 1923 *Daily Mail* 26 Apr. 9 The Queen wore a gown of pervenche blue.

Pervert, *sb.* Add: 2. *Psych.* One whose instincts have been perverted.
1906 *Jrnl. Abnormal Psychol.* Apr. 28 Subconscious feelings which represent, in embryo, the grosser manifestations of the most abandoned sexual perverts.

Perviability (pɜ̄ɹvĭăbi·lĭti). [f. Perviable + -ity.] The quality or condition of being pervious or permeable; perviousness.
1895 Nipher *Electricity & Magnetism* 372 (Cent. Suppl.) The specific inductive capacity or perviability of the medium.

Pesky, *a.* (Earlier and later examples.)
1830 *Massachusetts Spy* 13 Oct. (Th.) I'm plagued most to death with these ere pesky sore eyes. 1834 S. Smith *Major Downing* 19 They make pesky bad work, triging the wheels of government. 1834 W. G. Simms *Guy Rivers* 384 Why, for that matter, he's neither one thing nor another...A pesky little creature. 1912 Mulford & Clay *Buck Peters* xxii. 201 Now I shall have to stay marooned in this pesky room until Margie returns.

Pestersome (pe·stəɹsŏm), *a.* [f. Pester *v.* and *sb.* + -some.] Annoying, troublesome.
1843 *American Pioneer* II. 439 All innocent enquiries, by infants and children..should be indulged and encouraged, how pestersome soever they may seem.

Pestology (pestǫ·lŏdʒi). [f. L. *pest-is* Pest + -ology.] The scientific study of pests and the methods of dealing with them. Hence **Pesto·logical** *a.*, of or pertaining to pestology; **Pesto·logist,** a student of pestology.
1921 *Glasgow Herald* 26 Nov. 6 The newly formed Institute of Applied Pestology. 1927 *Daily Express* 23 Sept. 3/3 The pestological exhibition and conferences..opened yesterday... There were insect powders, sprays, pastes and—this will show you how far a pestologist goes—automatic firearms. 1927 *Times* 27 Sept. 12/5 An exhibition organized by the College of Pestology..was opened on Thursday.

Pet, *sb.*¹ Add: 2. b. (Further example.)
1922 P. G. Wodehouse *Girl on Boat* iv. 82 Do be a pet and go and talk to Jane Hubbard. I'm sure she must be feeling lonely.

3. d. *pet-vendor*.
1924 *Glasgow Herald* 21 Nov. 10/7 A London pet-vendor has had about 2,500 snakes through his hands within the last few months.

Pet, *v.*¹ Add: b. *U.S. intr.* To indulge in 'petting' (sense *b).

Petal (pe·tăl), *v.* [f. the sb.] *trans.* To provide with petals; to strew with petals.
1907 *Westm. Gaz.* 3 June 2/3 Sigh, little wind.., Winnow the lilacs pink and white, Petal the shining grass.

Petalodic (petălǫ·dik), *a. Bot.* [f. Gr. πεταλώδ-ης leaf-like (cf. Petalody) + -ic.] Exhibiting or marked by petalody.
1913 W. Bateson *Mendel's Princ. Heredity* 198 In the hose-in-hose *Campanula*, which has the sepals petaloid, the well-formed anthers contain plenty of pollen (some may be petalodic).

Petechioid (pĭtī·kiǫid), *a.* [f. Petechia + -oid.] Of the nature of or resembling petechia.
1903 *Lancet* 4 Apr. 947/2 No fresh petechiæ had developed but the 'petechioid' eruption in the groins and round the flanks was more decided.

Peter, *sb.* 7. (Add example.)
1892 Kipling *Barrack-r. Ball., L'Envoi* vi, See the shaking funnels roar, with the Peter at the fore.

Peter, *v.*² 2. (Earlier and later examples.)
1854 H. H. Riley *Puddleford* 84 He hoped this 'spectable meeting warn't going to Peter out. 1926 Spanner *Naviators* 200 Lucky your engine petered out, Sterne.

3. In *pa. pple.*, exhausted.
1869 *Overland Monthly* III. 127 After a long desert journey the oxen become much 'petered'.

Petiotization (petiǫutəizēⁱ·ʃən). [f. *Petiot* the name of the wine-owner who devised the process + -ization.] A process for obtaining a further yield of wine from the residue of grapes from which the juice has been expressed.
1900 Sadtler *Handbk. Industr. Org. Chem.* (ed. 3) 206 Petiotization is a process which..is carried out as follows: The marc from which the juice has been separated as usual by pressure is mixed with a solution of sugar and water and the mixture again fermented, [etc.].

Petit, *a.* 5. Add: *petit four* (see quots.).
1898 Mrs. De Salis *Housewife's Referee* 266 Petits Fours, small fancy biscuits. 1908 C. H. Senn *Dict. Foods* etc. 109 *Petit Fours*, F. is but the generic name for all kinds

Petitionable (peti ʃənǝbl), *a.* [f. PETITION *sb.* + -ABLE.] That allows, justifies, or involves, the making of a petition.

Pet-name, *sb.* [f. *pet-name sb.* 1.] A few suggestions for amending the Bankruptcy Act.

Pet-name, *v.* [f. *pet-name sb.* 1.] *trans.* To give (a person) a pet-name; to call by a pet-name.

Petri dish (peˑtri). The name of the inventor R. J. Petri, German bacteriologist.] A shallow, circular, glass dish with a cover, used in the preparation of bacteriological cultures.

Petrinist (peˑtrinist), *sb.* A follower of St. Peter; a student of Petrine theology.

Pétrissage (petrisaˑʒ). A kneading process used in massage.

Petrogenesis (petrodʒeˑnǝsis), *a.* *Geol.* [f. as prec.] Of or pertaining to petrogeny.

Petrol. 3. *b.* Add: *petrol-box*, *-engine*.

Petrolatum. *a.* petroleum bearing.

Petroleum. [f. *sb.*] *trans.* To treat with petroleum.

Petrolization (petrolaizeiˑʃǝn). [f. PETROLIZE *v.* + -ATION.] The process of covering the surface of stagnant water with a film of petroleum.

Petrolize, *v.* [f.] Add: 3. To cover the surface (of water) with petroleum.

Petronella (petroneˑla). A Scottish country dance introduced by Nathaniel Gow in 1820.

Petter, *sb.* Add: b. *U.S.* One who pets or indulges in petting.

Petting, *vbl. sb.* Add: the vendors of another picture product.

Petting-party, *U.S. slang.* Add:

Petty. B. *sb.* Add: 3. Abbreviation of PETTINESS.

Pewterer. (Later example.)

-pexy (peksi), terminal element repr.

Peyote (peiyoˑte). [Mex.] A species of cactus, *Lophophora williamsii*.

Phase, *sb.* Add: *In phase*, in the same phase; *out of phase*, not in the same phase.

Phase-meter, an instrument for indicating or measuring difference of phase between (alternating) electric currents.

Phased (feizd), *a.* [f. PHASE + -ED.] Adjusted to the same phase.

Ph.D. (piːeitʃdiː). [Abbreviation of *Philosophiæ Doctor*, Doctor of Philosophy.] A Doctor of Philosophy or the degree itself ; also used allusively.

Phenoloid (fiˑnoloid), *a.* [Mex.] A product resembling phenol.

Philosopher. Add: 1. *c.* A member of a class in which philosophy is studied.

Phenolic. Add: Also *Comb.*

Phenologically, *adv.*

Phenomenologically, *adv.*

Phagocytose (fæˑgosaitous), *v.* [f. PHAGOCYTOSIS.]

Phagolysis (fǝgoˑlisis), *sb.*

Phalangeal, *a.* Add: *b.* as PHALANX 3.

Phalangitis (fælændʒaiˑtis), *Path.* [f.]

Phalanstery. Add: (Modern example of fantom.)

Phantom. Add: (Modern example of fantom.)

Philippina. (Earlier and later examples.)

Philippine cane. A species of sugar cane.

Philism (fiˑlizm). The termination of such words as *ANGLOPHILISM*, *NEGROPHILISM*, etc., used as a noun.]

Philo-, combining form.

Philothe rian, *a.* [f. *philo- African* (earlier example).]

Phenoloid (fiˑnoloid). [f. *philo-* and Gr. *ǫ̑ρ. θήρ wild beast*], (a person) that loves wild animals.

Phoo, *int.*

Phonogram. Add: *attrib.* as *phonogram record*.

Phonograph. 3. *c.* Also *attrib.*

Phonometer (fonoˑmitǝ). An instrument for measuring deficiency in the external muscles of the eye.

Phosgene. Add: Also a poison gas in the War of 1914-18.

Phosphorescent. Add:

Phosphatize, *v.* [f. PHOSPHATE *v.* + -IZE.] = PHOSPHATED *v.*

Phosphoric, *a.* [Add fig. example.]

Phosphagogue (foˑsfagog). [ad. Gr. φωσφόρος in same sense.]

Photagogue (fouˑtagog). [ad. Gr. φωταγωγός in same sense.] For the admission of light.

Photian (fouˑʃian), *a.* Of or pertaining to Photius or the schism in which he took a part.

Phobe (foub), *a. Comb.*

Phobian (foubian), *a.* [as PHOBIA + -ISM.] A morbid fear of or aversion to anything.

Phoebe. (Earlier example.)

Phone, *sb.* Add: Also *with a.*

-phone (foun), The termination of GRAMOPHONE, MEGAPHONE, MICROPHONE, TELEPHONE, etc. (repr. Gr. φωνή voice, sound, φῶν- as sounding)

Phonetization (founǝtaizeiˑʃǝn). [f. PHONETICIZE *v.*] Phonetic representation.

Phonetism. (Earlier example.)

Phoney, phony (fouˑni), *a.* *U.S.* [Of uncertain origin; but see quot. 1904.] That has no reference ; sham, false. counterfeit.

Photo-. Add: 1. *Add* *photo-phobia a.*, *fot*, having an aversion to light.

Photo-survey, (see quot.)

Photo. Add: 1. *Add* *photo phitous a.*, *Bot.*, light-loving.

Photo-. Add: 2. *Photo-tube*, *Photo-topography*.

Phonofilm (fouˑnǝfilm). Trade name for a cinematographic film of a talking picture in which the sound is recorded in terms of light simultaneously with the photographs on the edge of the film, and reproduced when the film is exhibited by means of a photo-electric cell and loud-speaking telephones.

Photo-chemic (fouˑtokeˑmik), *a.* [f. PHOTO- + CHEMIC.] = PHOTOCHEMICAL *a.*

Photo-electric, *a.* *a.* (Add example.)

Photo-electron. An electron liberated from a substance by the action of light.

Photogram. Add: 2. A photograph, picture, diagram, or other facsimile transmitted by electric or ordinary telegraphy.

Photographess (fǝtoˑgrafes), *fem.*, after PHOTOGRAPHER.] A female photographer.

Photometer, *v.* [f. the *sb.*] To measure the intensity of (light) by means of a photometer.

Phototelegram (fouˑtotelǝgram), An instrument for recording the intensity of light at different depths in water.

Photon (fouˑton), *Physics.* [f. PHOTO-, after ELECTRON, PHOTON, etc.] A corpuscle or unit particle of light; a light-quantum.

Photo-play, [f. PHOTO- + PLAY.] A cinematographic presentation of a play or drama.

Photora diogram, [f. PHOTO- + RADIOGRAM.] A photograph transmitted by wireless.

Photostat (fouˑtostat). Trade name of an apparatus which makes photographic copies of manuscripts, maps, documents, etc.; a copy made by this. Also *attrib.* Hence *Photostat ic a.*, of, pertaining to, or produced by a photostat.

Photosynthesis (fouˑtosiˑnǝsis), *Bot.* [f. PHOTO- + SYNTHESIS.] The process by which carbon dioxide is converted into carbohydrates by the chlorophyll of plants under the influence of light.

Photo-topography, [f. PHOTO- + TOPOGRAPHY.] So **Photo-topographical** *a.*, pertaining to, or using, photo-topography, a system of surveying in which photogrammetry or photogrammetric surveying is employed in addition to the usual methods.

Phototrope (fouˑtotroup), *sb.* [f. PHOTO- + -trope turning.] A substance whose colour changes under the influence of light. So **Phototro pic** *a.*;

Photo tropy (foutoˑtropi).

Phrase, *sb.* Add: 3. *d. transf.*

Phraselet (freiˑzlet). A short phrase (in music).

Phrasal (freiˑzǝl), *a.* [f. PHRASE *sb.* + -AL.] Of or pertaining to (musical) phrases.

Phthisio- (θiˑsio-, -taiˑsio-), combining form of PHTHISIS, used in various medical terms as, **Phthisiogenesis**, **Phthisiotherapeu tist**, **Phthisiotherapist**, **Phthisiothe rapy.** *Cf.* PHTHISIOLOGY.

Physiogra phically, *adv.* [f. PHYSIOGRAPHICAL *a.* + -LY 2.] From a physiographical point of view.

Physiologue (fiˑziolog), *sb.* [f. PHYSIO- + -LOGUE.]

Physiotherapeutic (fizioθerapiuˑtik), *a.* [f. PHYSIO- + THERAPEUTIC *a.*] Of or pertaining to physiotherapy.

Physiotherapy, the treatment of diseases by natural remedies (e.g. massage, electricity, light, heat, fresh air, etc.) = *PHYSICOTHERAPY*.

Physiqued (fiziˑkt), *a.* Having a physique of a special character.

Physogastrism (faisogæˑstrizm), *Entom.* [f. PHYSO- Gr. φυσα(ω)-, φυστήρ belly + -ISM.]

Physogastric (faisogæˑstrik), *a.*, having the abdomen swollen or enlarged : **Physogastry** = PHYSOGASTRISM.

Phyto-. Add: **Phytophyle**, a plant-loving insect. **Phytoplankton**, collective name for all the floating vegetable life in the sea or in lakes.

Phytologically, *adv.* [f. PHYTOLOGICAL *a.* + -LY 2.] Botanically.

Pianistically, *adv.* [f. PIANISTIC + -AL + -LY 2.] On pianistic lines.

Piano. 3. *b.* (See quot.)

Piano. 3. *b.* (See quot.)

Pianoforte. Add: *b.* Add a pianoforte obstacle, a jump or obstacle in a steeplechase whose shape resembles that of a pianoforte.

Pianola (pianouˑla), [f. PIANO + -OLA.] Rendered by a pianola.

Pianolist (pianouˑlist), *sb.*

Piassaba. Also 8 *peasar.* B. (Earlier examples.)

Pic-3 (pik), *U.S.* Abbreviation of PICATUNE.

Picaroon, *sb.* 1 1. (Later example.)

Picaroon, *sb.* 2 (Later example.)

Picayune. Also *picco, picco-une.*

Pick. *sb.* 8. *c.* To dislodge (salt) from brine-pans after the evaporation of the brine.

Pick-handle (example).

Pianola. (Add example.)

Piano. (Earlier example.)

20. Pick up. *h.* In Golf *ellipt.*, to pick up one's ball.

Pianoforte. Add: a pianoforte steeplechase jump.

Pianola. Rendered by a pianola.

Pianolist (pianouˑlist), *sb.*

Piassaba. B. (Earlier examples.)

Pic-3 (pik), *U.S.* Abbreviation of PICATUNE.

Picaroon.

Pick-a-back, *sb.* (Later example.)

Picket-fence, *U.S.*, a fence made of pickets (sense 2).

Picnic. *sb.* Add: *1. c.* Also, a lively time; made of pickets.

Picnist-fort, *U.S.*

Picketing, *vbl. sb.* Add: 2. *c.* A fence of palisade made of pickets ; picket-work.

Pickelt-rope, *sb.* (PICKET *sb.*1 7.] A rope used to picket a horse, mule, or other beast.

Picket-rope.

Pickle. *sb.* 1 Add: *d.* (Later example.)

Pickle, *v.* 1 Add: *1. c. intr.* To undergo the process of pickling.

Picker. *sb.* 1

Pickelhaube (pikǝlhauˑbǝ), A German spiked helmet.

Picklock. *sb.* 1 Add:

Pick-up, *sb.* Add: *d.* (Example.)

Pickerel frog. *U.S.* The marsh frog, *Rana palustris*, a species of frog common in America.

Picket, *sb.* 1 Add: 1. *c.* Also, a triangular or arrow-shaped mark of tar or paint placed on masonry, used in making measurements.

Picket.

Pickled. *ppl. a.*

Picnic. *sb.* Add:

Picotee.

Picture, *sb.* Add: 2. 1. A exhibition of these or the place where they are exhibited.

Picture, *v.* Add:

Picotee.

Picul.

Pictograph. *sb.* Add:

Pict_redom, sb. [-DOM.] Pictures or moving pictures collectively; the picture or film world.

Pictured_ome, sb. Also **-drome**. = PICTURE + the termination of HIPPODROME, as the common name of a music-hall.] A building in which motion pictures are exhibited; a picture-palace.

Picturisation (piktiūrəĭzē·ʃən). [f. next.] The process of rendering pictorial in character; presentation as or by means of motion pictures.

Picturize (pi·ktiŭrəĭz), v. [f. PICTURE + -IZE.] trans. To visualize or adorn with pictures; to represent cinematographically or pictorially; to pictorialize.

Piddler. (Recent example.)

Pidgin. Add: In extended use. slang.

Pi-dog, variant of PYE-DOG.

Pie, sb.[1] Add: c. Also, to put one's finger into another's pie, to meddle in the affairs of others.
d. To cut a pie: to meddle with a matter. U.S.
e. (Earlier examples.)

f. b. pie-net (U.S. examples); pie-counter (U.S.), a counter at which pies are sold; hence fig., the source of graft or reward; pie-fork (U.S.), a fork for eating pies; pie melon (U.S.), a melon used for pies.

Piece, sb. Add: 1. c. All to pieces : completely, through and through, from beginning to end. U.S.

22. (Later examples.)

Pierrotic (pīerə·tik), a. [f. PIERROT + -IC.] Of or belonging to pierrots.

Piezo-, comb. form. Add: **Piezo-electricity** (pi-zo-). [Piezo-electric phenomena and the stresses that produce them.]

Piff (pif). [Echoic.] To blow (on a pipe).

Piffer (pi·fər). slang. [from the initials of the name of the force + -ER.] A member of the Punjab Irregular Frontier Force.

Piffling, ppl. a. (Further examples.)

Piecrust, sb. Add: having an ornamental edge suggestive of the crust of a pie.

Pied, ppl. a.[1] Add: 12. a. Pig-fever, -pail.

Piedmont (pi·dmŏnt), a. [f. Piedmont in Italy.]

Piedmontese (pidmŏnti·z), a. and sb. [f. Piedmont + -ESE.]

Pie-eyed, a. slang. Intoxicated to such an extent that vision is affected.

Pie-plate, sb.

Pier[1]

Pier[2] a. U.S. applied to a tribe of North American Indians.

Pigeon-hawk. (Earlier examples.)

Pieria, sb. the name of a genus of butterflies. Of or belonging to the genus Pieris; a butterfly of this kind.

Pigment. 3. (Earlier examples.) Also pig-ment-hue.

Pigment, sb.[3] Add: pigment-layer.

Pigment (pi·gmĕnt), v. trans. To colour with or as with pigment. So **Pigmenting** ppl. a.

Pig-nut. 3. (Earlier examples.) Also pig-nut hickory.

Pig-stick (pi·gstik), sb. [f. PIG-STICKING.]

Pig-sticking. 1. Also attrib.

Pigweed. (Earlier U.S. examples.)

Pi-jaw (pai·dgŏ), sb. slang. [PI a.[2] + JAW sb.] A pious lecture or exhortation, esp. one addressed to schoolboys or young persons by their teachers or parents. Hence **Pi·jaw** v., trans., to lecture or exhort.

Pika. (Later examples.)

Pike, sb.[1] a. (Later examples.)

Pigeon-grass (examples).
pigeon-stand, a standing-place from which pigeons are shot.

Pigeon (gŏdgənkə·r). [f. PIGEON sb. + -EER.] A person who keeps or breeds pigeons.

Pigeon-hawk. (Earlier examples.)

Pigeon-toed. (Later example.)

Pigeon-wing. 3. (Later examples.)

Pigeon-wing, v. b. refl. To convey or transport (oneself) by dancing or cutting pigeon-wings.

Piggly-wig·gly, a. [Fanciful.] A grocery-store having goods arranged round a series of passage-ways in an enclosed space.

Pigment. 3. (Earlier examples.)

Pigon-necon. slang. [Where him hyphen of carbon tissue is soaked in a weak solution.]

Piker[1]
Piker[2] b. Austral. A wild ox living out of the herd.

Piking (pai·kin), vbl. sb. [f. PIKE sb.[4] + -ING.]

Piky (pai·ki), a.[2] [f. PIKE sb.[4] + -Y.]

Pikelet (pai·klĕt).

Pilcher (pi·ltʃər). [cf. PILCH sb.]

Pike-pole. (Earlier example.)

Pike, v.[2] Add: 3. U.S. A cautious or timid gambler who makes only small bets; a person who takes no chances; a 'poor sport' or 'poor thing.'

Pike-driver.

Pile, sb.[1] 2. transf. A very strong or powerful hit, stroke, kick, etc., in various games.

Pile-driver. 3.

Pilgrim, sb.

Pilgrimage, sb.

Piling. (Later examples.)

Pill, sb.[1]

Pill-box.

Pillar, sb.

Pillion[1]

Pillion[2] Recently revived for a seat behind the ordinary saddle of a motor-cycle.

Pillion[1] 1. trans. To place on a pillion. Chiefly in pa.

Pillioned, a. [-ED.] Having a pillion.

Pillionist (pi·liŏnist). [f. PILLION + -IST.] A pillion-rider.

Pillow, sb. In the sense of 'pillow-shaped' as pillow-lava, -mound, -muff, -structure; pillow-book, one suitable for reading in bed before going to sleep; pillow-dance (later example); pillow-slip, a pillow-case.

Pillowing.

Pillowy (pi·loĭ). (Early fig. example.)

Pilot, sb. 1. Also, one who controls an aeroplane or other aircraft during flight; now esp. a person duly qualified to do so.

Piloting, vbl. sb. (Further example.)

Pilotless, a. Add: b. Of aeroplanes.

Piltdown. The name of a place in the county of Sussex, England, applied attrib. to fragments of a skull found there.

Pimento. Add: 3. (Later example.)

Pimple-palm, **-tree**. One of various low, spiny palms of the genus Bactris, growing on the forest floor of British Guiana.

Pimple, sb. (Recent example.)

Pimpling, vbl. sb. + -ING.]

Pin, sb.[1] Add: 1. m. A support of an arch.

Pilotage.

Pilotless.

Pilfiltage. Add: 1. (Further examples.)

Pilot-bird.

Pin, sb.[1] Add: 2. c. To spread out (dough or paste) with a rolling-pin.

Pince-nezed, a. [f. PINCE-NEZ.] Wearing pince-nez.

Pincers, sb. pl.

Pinch, sb. Add: 4. Also in a pinch.

c. narrow pinch, a 'close thing'; a 'near shave.'

14. slang. Something easy to accomplish or attain. Also attrib.

15. b. pinch-gut, examples.

Pinch, v.[1] Add: 14. To pinch in : to encroach on, or upon so as to make narrower, restrict or confine.

15. b. (Later examples.)

Pinch-bar. Add: pinch-based-, having the features pinched or emaciated; pinch-fingered, a type of small tongs formerly used to lift a hot ember from one's fire to light a pipe; pinch-fist, type of small parsimonious.

Pinchable (pi·ntʃab'l), a. + -ABLE.] That may be pinched.

Pinch-bug. A species of stag-beetle, found in the southern states of North America.

Pinched, ppl. a. Add: 1. e. Pinched tuck: a narrow tuck; a pin-tuck.

Pinching, vbl. sb. 5. (Add example.)

Pine, sb.[1] Add: pine bark (earlier example), -log, plain, stump, timber (earlier and later examples); pine-butter, a disease of pine trees, Peridermium strobi; pine-chafer, a pine beetle, whose larva lives in pine trees; pine-creeper, the pine-creeping warbler, Sylvia pinus; pine-snake (earlier example); pine straw, -weevil (examples).

Pine board. [PINE sb.[1] 7.] A board of pine-wood.

Pine land. U.S. [PINE sb.[1] 7.] Land on which the pine naturally grows.

Pine-knot. U.S. 1. A knot of pine-wood. 2. Burned as fuel or for illumination.

Pinery. (Earlier example.)

Pink, sb.[2] Add: 2. U.S. A petrol engine : To emit a dull metallic sound at the explosions; to knock.

Pink (pink), v.[4] [f. PINK v.[3]] intr. To come pink.

Pinking.

Pinkie, a.[1] (Earlier example.) Also pinkie-stern schooner.

Ping, sb.[2] [f. GALSWORTHY White Monkey ii. iv. 193 A footman stood.]

Pinkish.

Pink-lander. U.S. [f. prec. + -ER.] A dweller in pine land.

Pine swamp. U.S.

Pink, sb.[1] Add: 2. Cl. a petrol engine to a valuable variety of coal.

Pine-fern, sb.[?] U.S.

Pink-head. Add: 1. c. Applied to a minute spot pattern on cloth.

Pinkiness (pi·nkinĕs). [f. PINKY.]

Pinking.

Pinned, ppl. a. Add: 6. pinned eye (see def.).

Pinner[1] Add: 4. The workman who inserts the pins in the revolving cylinder of a barrel-organ.

Pinning, vbl. sb. Also pinning-out.

Pin oak. U.S. [PIN sb.[1]]

Pinole. (Earlier examples.)
1845 J. GREGG *Comm. Prairies* vii. I. 159 This pod..the Apaches and other tribes of Indians grind into flour to make their favourite *pinole.* 1846 EMORY *Military Reconn.* 85 Pinole is the heart of Indian corn, baked, ground up, and mixed with sugar.

Piñon. (Earlier examples.)
1839 Z. LEONARD *Adventures* (1904) 157 Its top is covered with the pinone tree. 1846 EMORY *Military Reconn.* 18 When we first left camp this morning, we saw several clumps of the pinon.

Pin-point. (Add example.)
1899 *Daily News* 29 July 8/5 A clear Swiss muslin..with a pin-point embroidery on it.

Pin-pointed, *a.* Having a pin-point; fine-pointed; sharp.
1909 *Daily Chron.* 18 Sept. 10/6 The tiny pin-pointed mapping pen.

Pin-prick, *v.* (Later example.) **Pin-pricking** *vbl. sb.* (Later example.)
1909 *Daily Chron.* 15 July 4/6 Every book for the blind is carefully pin-pricked by voluntary workers who can see. 1927 *Daily Express* 5 Dec. 1/4 The move is interpreted..as a step forward to stop the 'pin-pricking' that has been going on between the two countries.

Pin-tailed, *a.* (Earlier example.)
1864 J. A. GRANT *Walk Across Africa* 389 The pin-tailed duck shot past the boat, seeking less busy scenes.

Pinto, *a.* (Earlier and later examples.)
1867 BRET HARTE *Condensed Novels* etc. 259 The devil in the shape of a fleet pinto colt. 1924 MULFORD *Rustlers' Valley* xx. 225 Simultaneously with this he saw a woman riding a pinto pacer, come swinging into town past the gaol.

Piny. (Recent U.S. example.)
1913 MRS. STRATTON-PORTER *Laddie* vi. 165 Her people.. spent much money on the biggest tombstone in the cemetery, and planted pinies and purple phlox on her.

Pioneeˑrdom. [f. PIONEER *sb.* + -DOM.] Pioneers collectively; prevalence of pioneers.
1873 *Porcupine* 13 Sept. 379/2 A..Californian, who had arrived..from the States, close on to the age of pioneerdom.

Piou-piou. [F.] The popular name for the typical French private soldier.
1900 R. WHITEING *Life of Paris* 207 Polin..figures as the common soldier, the pioupiou, with his simple virtues of good-humour and fidelity to the flag. 1909 *Westm. Gaz.* 18 Jan. 12/4 (heading) Books for Piou-piou. What the French soldier is permitted to read. 1930 *Observer* 23 Feb. 12/1 The 'nounous' which it was naturally the chief object of the 'pioupious' of that period to dazzle.

Pip, *sb.*[1] Add: **c.** phr. *To give* (a person) *the pip*: to make (him) feel ill; to disgust. *To have the pip*: to feel out of sorts.
1913 *Punch* 15 Oct. 324/3 [His] later works gave him the pure pip. 1923 'BARTIMEUS' *Seaways* vii. 97 Dining in the mess gives me the holy pip. 1930 PRIESTLEY *Angel Pavement* ix. 440 You give me the pip, Dad, honestly you do.

Pip, *sb.*[2] Add: **5.** A star worn by second lieutenants, lieutenants, and captains, these ranks being distinguished by one, two, and three stars respectively.
1919 *Chambers's Jrnl.* Jan. 43/2 Thomas, his senior by one 'pip' in the battery. 1920 M. A. MÜGGE *War Diary* 222 Pips, ornamental stars indicating officers' ranks; epaulets.
6. *attrib.* as *pip-card* (sense 1).
1903 *Burlington Mag.* Dec. 246/1 He persuaded him..to make the exchange with twelve figure and fourteen pip cards.

Pip, *sb.*[4] The signallers' name for the letter P, used in abbreviations, as *pip emma*, P.M.
1920 *Isis* 20 Oct. 9/2 You leave Carfax at ten o'clock and return from Frilford at five pip emma. 1926 EDGAR WALLACE *Door with Seven Locks* xiii. 125 Tell him I want to raid Gallows Cottage, Gallows Hill, at eleven-fifteen pip-emma. 1927 W. E. COLLINSON *Contemp. Engl.* 98 Other artillery terms which spread were O pip (for 'observation post').

Pip, *v.*[3] Add: **2.** *transf.* To kill, to do for; to fail in an examination. Also *intr.* with *out*, to die.
1908 A. S. M. HUTCHINSON *Once Aboard Lugger* I. i. 31 'I had forgotten. Your examination?' George half turned away. The bitterest moment of a sad day was come. He growled: 'Pipped.' 1912 F. M. HUEFFER *Panel* I. iii. 85, I was..pipped for active service. 1916 E. V. LUCAS *Vermilion Box* 226 Only yesterday poor Hugh Blackstone was pipped right at my side, and he lasted only ten minutes. 1920 ROSE MACAULAY *Potterism* III. i. 110, I think it's simply rotten pipping out. I *like* being alive. 1927 AGATHA CHRISTIE *Big Four* xi, That's my solution—Gilmour Wilson got pipped by mistake.

Pipe, *sb.*[1] Add: **11. a.** (sense 3) *pipe-fitter, -jointer*; (sense 10) *pipe-fill.*
1907 *Daily Chron.* 15 Mar. 6/7 At Oxford this writer bought the finest *pipe-fill he has known. 1897 WEBSTER, *Pipe-fitter. 1910 *Daily Chron.* 31 Jan. 6/5 Arthur Moon, aged 45, a pipe-fitter. 1902 *Encycl. Brit.* XXV. 509/2 A record should be kept of the history of the pipe..with the name of the *pipe-jointer whose work closes the record.
b. **pipe-burial**, a burial in which a pipe (usually of lead) passes from the coffin or tomb to the surface of the ground, to permit of the pouring of libations; **pipe-drain** *v. trans.*, to drain (land) by laying pipes; chiefly in pa. pple.; **pipe-dream**, a groundless hope or day-dream indulged in while smoking; so **pipe-dreamy** *a.*; **pipe-glove**, a flexible pipe-case; **pipe-lighter**, a pocket mechanical apparatus for lighting pipes; **pipe-making**, the making of pipes (in any sense); **pipe-necked** *a.*, having a long slender neck; **pipe-story**, a fantastic or impossible story (cf. **pipe-dream*); **pipe-water**, water conveyed in pipes.
1929 *Antiq. Jrnl.* IX. 1 (heading) A Roman *Pipe-burial from Caerleon, Monmouthshire. 1907 E. A. WOODRUFFE-PEACOCK *Pasture & Meadow Analysis* 4 A soil that has been *pipe drained for wheat-growing. 1930 W. LAWSON in *Jrnl. Ministry Agric.* Nov. 825 There is nothing to indicate ..whether the land is pipe-drained or not. 1902 W. IRWIN *Love Sonnets of Hoodlum* Epil. (Cent. Suppl.) To just one girl I've tuned my sad bazoo [lament], Stringing my *pipe-dream off as it occurred. 1904 B'NESS VON HÜTTEN *Pam* 238 Look at the sea, and tell me if, in your wildest pipe-dream, you ever saw anything lovelier. 1913 E. D. BIGGERS *Seven Keys to Baldpate* xiii. 169 And don't have any pipe-dreams about the law. 1915 *Strand Mag.* June 651 If it is a fizzle..I abandon pipe-dreams of literary triumph. 1910 'O. HENRY' *Whirligigs* i. 12 La Paz is a good sort of a *pipe-dreamy old hole. 1925 *Daily Tel.* 13 May 20/7 Advt., Pouches,..*pipe gloves and cases. 1916 B. CABLE *Action Front* 57 Each man had with him one of those tinder *pipe-lighters which are ignited by the sparks of a little twirled wheel. 1906 *Westm. Gaz.* 8 Aug. 10/1 For *pipe-making.. a large cob is desirable. 1919 J. C. SQUIRE *Birds* 11 *Pipe-necked and stationary and silhouetted, Cormorants stood in a wise, black, equal row. 1904 *N. Y. Times* 16 Oct. (Cent. Suppl.) What appears on its face to be the veriest *pipe-story. 1908 *Westm. Gaz.* 24 Oct. 17/2, I will not live to see *pipe-water squirting down sham rocks under a sham bridge.

Pipe, *v.*[2] Add: **6.** Also with *into.*
1895 *Century Mag.* Sept. 677/1 A kitchen into which water was piped from a spring higher up on the mountain. 1904 A. J. BURDICK *Mystic Mid-Region* 183 When..pure water has been piped into the valley, towns and perhaps cities will spring up in the midst of the dread region.
b. *fig.*
1927 DEEPING *Kitty* xviii, Between the garden and the boat-house a magnificent plane-tree rose, piping from its trunk a great spray of greyish branches.
7. Also, to wash *away* or remove with water from pipes.
1878 J. H. BEADLE *Western Wilds* x. 149 Worked-out mines,..[with] all the soil 'piped' away in search of the 'pay dirt'.
8. *intr.* To smoke a pipe.
1846 M'KENNEY *Mem.* I. iii. 71 These hardy adventurous fellows never rose from their paddles, nor stopped except to '*pipe*'..[for] a period of nineteen hours.

Pipe-lay, *v.* *U.S.* [f. PIPE-LAYING.] *intr.* To lay pipes (PIPE *sb.*[1] 3 b).
1888 *San Francisco Weekly Examiner* 22 Mar. (Farmer) There are not a few who are pipe-laying and marshalling forces for the fray when the conventions meet.

Pipe-layer. b. (Earlier examples.)
1840 *Richmond Enquirer* Nov. (Th.) The profuse use of gold, corruption of the franchise by pipe layers and yarn spinners,..have conspired to elect W. H. Harrison. 1841 *Congress. Globe* Jan. App. 155/1, I was not defeated by voters. I was defeated by 'pipe layers'.

Pipe-laying. (Earlier examples of *b.*)
1841 *Congress. Globe* 3 Aug. App. 279/2 The city of New York was defrauded, by pipe laying, out of her Representatives. 1842 *Ibid.* 8 June App. 496/1 He..compelling the elections to be held on the same day throughout the republic, would prostrate the pipe-laying system.

Pipeman. 1. (Later example.)
1922 *Daily Mail* 7 Nov. 4 Advt., The pipeman's joy.

Piperling (pəiˑpəɹliŋ). [f. (SAND)PIPER + -LING[1].] A young sand-piper.
1899 H. VAN DYKE *Fisherman's Luck* I. 24 But the piperlings could not fly having no feathers.

Pipe-stem. [f. PIPE *sb.*[1] 11 a.] The stem of a tobacco-pipe.
1727 J. COMER *Diary* (1923) 17 [He] fell over a log, the pipe stem ran down his throat and broke. 1755 *Maryland Hist. Mag.* XVIII. 33 He fell down forward, and run the Pipe stem into the Roof of his mouth. 1846 J. W. WEBB *Altowan* I. vi. 168 One of the half-breeds has a piece of an old pipe-stem, which makes tolerable good smoking. 1855 [see PIPE *sb.*[1] 11 a]. 1860 HOLLAND *Miss Gilbert's Career* vii. 115 A great tribulation that will break my life off as short as a pipe-stem. 1876 JOAQUIN MILLER *Unwritten Hist.* xv. 220 He pointed his pipe-stem at Paquita.
b. *Comb.* as **pipe-stem wood** (see quot.).
1813 MUHLENBERG *Catal. Plants N. Amer.* 43 Pipe-stem wood, *Andromeda acuminata.*

Piping, *vbl. sb.*[2] **4.** (Further attrib. example.)
1859 MRS. STOWE *Minister's Wooing* xii. 126 Miss Prissy.. fell..into a discourse on her own particular way of covering piping-cord.
9. (Earlier example.)
1873 J. H. BEADLE *Undevel. West* xv. 267 Lastly was introduced 'piping', and complete hyraulic mining.

Piping, *ppl. a.* **2. b.** **piping plover** (example).
1870 *Amer. Naturalist* III. 231 The Piping Plover is still found along the coast of Maine.

Pipkin. Add: **3.** *Comb.* as *pipkin-shaped.*
1908 ELLEN TERRY *Story of Life* 199 A three-handled cup, pipkin-shaped, standing on three legs.

Piˑpless, *a.* [f. PIP *sb.*[2] + -LESS.] (See quot.)
1926 *Gloss. Electr. Terms* (Brit. Engin. Stand.) 150 *Pipless bulb*, a bulb so manufactured that no sealing-off tip remains on the visible surface of the glass.

Pipperidge. 2. (Later example.)
1869 MRS. STOWE *Oldtown Fireside Stories* (1871) 182 Old Black Hoss was about as close as a nut and as contrairy as a pipperage-tree.

Pipping (piˑpiŋ), *vbl. sb.* [f. PIP *v.*[2] + -ING[1].] The breaking of the egg-shell by a bird when hatching. (In quot. attrib.)
1901 *Chambers's Jrnl.* Nov. 717/1 Gigantic incubators.. literally vomiting forth their flocks of twittering little creatures at pipping-time.

Pip-pip. [Echoic.] **1.** The sound made by a motor- or bicycle-horn.
1905 SHAW *Major Barbara* III. (1907) 292 *Sarah* [touching Lady Britomart's ribs with her finger tips and imitating a bicycle horn] Pip! pip! *a* 1907 *Mr. Punch awheel* 96 'Pip, pip!' resounds in every lane. 1909 *Westm. Gaz.* 15 May 3/2 She had motor-cars with real pip-pips.
2. *slang.* A substitute for Good-bye.
1920 WODEHOUSE *Damsel in Distress* x, 'Well, its worth trying', said Reggie. 'I'll give it a whirl. Toodleoo!' 'Good-bye.' 'Pip-pip.' Reggie withdrew.

Pip-squeak. *slang.* **1.** A contemptuous name for an insignificant person; a petty object. (In quot. 1923, a two-stroke motor-bicycle.)
1910 E. V. LUCAS *Slowcoach* xxiii. 279 'It belongs to one of those measly pip-squeaks,' said Robert. 1923 *Motor Cycling* 21 Nov. 89/1 The owners of sporting four-stroke machines look down on the owners of so-called 'Pip-Squeaks'. 1925 FRASER & GIBBONS *Soldier & Sailor Words.* 1926 *Blackw. Mag.* June 732/2 After all, the luxurious liner which connects this riotous spot with the outer world is only a pip-squeak of a vessel. 1930 SIR G. MACMUNN *Behind Scenes in many Wars* 88 It does not pay in the East to let pip-squeaks beard the mighty.
2. A small type of high velocity shell distinguished by the sound of its flight.
1916 E. V. LUCAS *Vermilion Box* 209 Whatever else there is to grumble at over here, wet, and rats, and Pip-Squeaks and Jack Johnsons,..we do get two things up to sample [etc]. 1916 *Cornh. Mag.* Mar. 395 They're 'pip-squeak' and splinter-proof, of course. 1927 E. THOMPSON *These Men thy Friends* 176 The Turkish guns suddenly sent over a couple of pipsqueaks.

Piracy. Add: **1. b.** *Geol.* The action or process whereby one stream by the enlargement of its basin cuts off or taps the tributaries or head-waters of another.
1905 CHAMBERLIN & SALISBURY *Geol., Processes* I. 161 So extensive has been the adjustment among the streams of the Appalachian Mountains that there is probably no considerable stream in the whole system which has not gained or lost through its own or its neighbors' piracy.

Pirate, *sb.* Add: **3. b.** A stream which 'steals' the head-waters of another stream. (Cf. *PIRACY 1 b.)
1905 CHAMBERLIN & SALISBURY *Geol., Processes* I. 98 The tributary which does the stealing is known as a *pirate.*

Piratedom (paiˑrĕtdəm). [f. PIRATE *sb.* + -DOM.] Pirates collectively; the world of pirates.
1907 FRANCIS CAMPBELL *Shepherd of Stars* 36 The stronghold of ancient piratedom.

Pirl, *v.* **3.** (Example.)
1920 *Chambers's Jrnl.* Christm. No. 837/2 Before the first puffs of blue smoke circled and pirled above the village roofs.

Pirogue. Also 9 **peerog.**
1885 C. A. STEPHENS *Adv. Six Young Men* 123 We..were constantly meeting parties in odd black boats, called 'peerogs', made each from a single large pine log.

Pirouettist (pirᵘeˑtist). [f. PIROUETTE *v.* + -IST.] = PIROUETTER.
1926 W. J. LOCKE *Old Bridge* II. vii. 119 He may chance to be a mechanical jazz pirouettist or a financial oracle.

Piscatorial, *a.* Add: **b.** as *sb.*
1909 *Westm. Gaz.* 2 Jan. 16/2 At a meeting of the City of London Piscatorials this week Mr. Dryden reported [etc.].

Pish, *v.* **2.** (Earlier mod. example.)
1881 *Punch* 10 Sept. 110/1 A angel as ain't *a lah mowed* is a dowdy a shopgirl 'ud pish.

Pishamin. (Earlier Amer. example.)
1766 J. BARTRAM *Jrnl.* (1769) 18 The lower rich ground produceth glidistia, pishamins, cephalanthus, ash, cypress and cornu femina.

Pismirism (piˑzməiriz'm). [f. PISMIRE + -ISM.] Hoarding.
1906 *Daily News* 22 Dec., The mass of money piled up by the late Mr. Sage in the course of a life of parsimonious pismirism.

Pistachio. **3.** Add: **pistachio ice**, ice cream containing pistachio nuts.
1886 C. E. PASCOE *London To-day* iii. (ed. 3) 47 The more aristocratic foreign visitors to London..flocked thither to eat pistachio ices.

Pistilliform (pistiˑlifǭɹm), *a.* [f. L. *pistillum* PISTIL + -FORM.] Having the form of a pistil.
1855 *Eng. Cycl., Nat. Hist.* III. 586 Cells with few lobes at the circumference, internally striated, with a pistilliform axis.

Pistillode (piˑstiləᵘd). *Bot.* [f. L. *pistillum* PISTIL; after STAMINODE: see -ODE.] A rudimentary pistil.
1905 W. E. SAFFORD *Useful Plants of Guam* 259 An imperfect pistil (pistillode) present or lacking.

Pistiloid (piˑstiloid), *a.* *Bot.* [f. PISTIL + -OID.] Resembling a pistil in shape.
1888 HENSLOW *Orig. Floral Struct.* 291 Pistiloid sepals.. have been observed by Mr. Laxton in double flowers of the Garden Pea.

Pistol, *sb.* **2.** Add: **pistol flare, light**, a night-signal or light fired from a special pistol, used by soldiers; a Very light.
1916 B. CABLE *Action Front* 26 'Keep the lights blazing,' Rawbon paused to shout to the man with the *pistol flares. *Ibid.* 62 A pair of *pistol lights flared upwards.

Piston. **4.** Add: **piston-bellows**, bellows in which the current of air is supplied by the action of pistons; **piston-ring**, an elastic metal packing-ring fitted on a piston.
1875 KNIGHT *Dict. Mech.* 1717/1, *b* is a *piston-bellows, formed by boring out the trunks of trees. 1883 A. E. SEATON *Man. Marine Engin.* viii. 134 Fig. 20 shows a *piston-ring pressed out with a corrugated ribbon of steel. 1908 *Westm. Gaz.* 20 Aug. 4/2 The loss of petrol, due to leaky valves and piston-rings, is going on as long as the engine is running.

Pit, *sb.*[1] Add: **1. h.** A place for the inspection, repair, etc., of motor vehicles.
1931 *Star* 8 May 13/1 He..had faltered and had to go to the pits for minor adjustments.
14. **pit-camp**, a group of pit-dwellings; **pit-cave** (see quot. 1921); **pit-gauge**, a rain-gauge sunk into the ground; **pit-head** (attrib. example); **pit-tip**, the mass of waste material deposited near the mouth of a mine or pit; **pit-trap** = sense 1 f.
1909 *Chambers's Jrnl.* Feb. 109/1 Thistles..always grow in the soil where a *pit-camp has been placed. 1921 *Discovery* Feb. 33/1 Still another kind was a combination of the first two, and is known as the '*pit-cave'. This was made by first sinking a pit and then cutting out the tomb in the form of a side-recess from the bottom of the pit. 1928 PEAKE & FLEURE *Steppe & Sown* 21 Catacomb graves, closely resembling the pit-caves that have been found in Euboea. 1902 *Encycl. Brit.* XXX. 701/2 Professor Joseph Henry, about 1850, recommended to the observers of the Smithsonian Institution the use of the '*pit-gauge'. 1928 *Daily Chron.* 9 Aug. 5/4 From September 1 *pit head prices will be raised by 1s. a ton. 1907 *Westm. Gaz.* 13 Apr. 10/1 In the Black Country may be seen birches growing luxuriantly on a *pit-tip. 1895 KIPLING *2nd Jungle Bk.* 20 It was a pointed stick, such as they set in the mouth of a *pit-trap.

Pitch, *sb.*[1] **5.** **pitch-knot** (later example).
1825 J. NEAL *Bro. Jonathan* I. 58 The fire-place, within which two or three lighted pitch knots, a substitute for candles, were burning.

Pitch, *sb.*[2] Add: **11.** (Earlier examples.)
1699 *Rec. of Derby* (Conn.) 207 The laying out of John Pringles pitch upon the good hill. 1746 *Waterbury Prop. Rec.* 106 A ten Acre pitch which his Father bought of Thos Judd of Hartford.
c. *To queer the pitch*: see *QUEER *v.* 2.
26. *pitch-holder* (sense 11).
1909 *Daily Chron.* 18 Nov. 4/7 One 'pitch' which was the envy of every pitchholder in London was for many years at the end of Burlington House.

Pitch, *v.*[1] Add: **20.** Also of a roof or other structure: To slope downwards.
1771 COPLEY in *Copley Pelham Lett.* 137, I should have the Roof to pitch from under the Arkitraves of the Chamber Windows. 1857 *Trans. Ill. Agric. Soc.* III. 538 The roof may pitch both ways, or shed at the ends. 1897 MOORE *How to Build* vii. 94 The floor shall pitch from building to the front of piazza ¼ inch to every foot of width.
c. To drop *down* or descend abruptly (to a lower level).
1851 N. KINGSLEY *Diary* 168 We have come to where the bed rock pitches down suddenly. 1867 T. LACKLAND *Homespun* I. 70 One of these [pastures]..sloping where it does not pitch, down to the rocky bed of the riotous stream. 1876 JOAQUIN MILLER *Unwritten Hist.* vi. 92 Gorge on gorge, canon intersecting canon, pitching down towards the rapid Klamat.

Pitcher[2]. **2.** (Earlier example.)
1858 *N. Y. Tribune* 18 Aug. 7/3 Pidgeon [acting as] Pitcher [at baseball].

Pitch-hole[1]. Add: **b.** *U.S.* A defect in a highway; a pot-hole.
1874 *Rep. Vermont Board Agric.* II. 659 The highways leading to our larger villages,..are frequently so full of pitch-holes or 'cahoos' as to render them totally unfit for travel. 1890 *Harper's Mag.* Oct. 657/2 The highway was frequently interrupted by 'pitch holes'.

Pitching, *vbl. sb.*[1] Add: **7.** (Further example.)
1858 *N. Y. Tribune* 18 Aug. 7/3 The pitching was good on both sides.
8. b. Oscillation of a vehicle similar to the plunging movements of a ship.
1930 *Morn. Post* 21 July 4 Pitching is caused by the front wheels travelling over an obstruction before the rear wheels.
c. *Mining.* = PITCH *sb.*[2] 24 b.
1903 *Copper Handbk.* III. 88 Pitching. The irregular descent of a vein.
12. **pitching-heat** *Brewing*, the heat of the wort when the yeast is added.
1876 *Encycl. Brit.* IV. 275/1 The heat at which the wort is let down into the fermenting tun. This '*pitching heat' varies very much.

Pitching, *ppl. a.* **2.** (Further example.)
1906 *Chambers's Jrnl.* July 537/2 It is worth going some distance to see a *vaquero* sticking to a 'pitching' horse.

Pitch-off. [PITCH *v.*[1] 20.] The inclination or shelving of the bed of the sea.
1895 DANA *Man. Geol.* (ed. 4) 20 At Keeling atoll,..Captain Fitzroy, R.N., found no bottom in 7,200 feet at 2,200 yards from the breakers—which gives a pitch-off exceeding 1 : 0·92.

Pitch-penny. *U.S.* [f. PITCH *v.*[1] 24.] A variety of pitch-and-toss.
1830 S. BRECK in *Recoll.* (1877) ii. 52 We passed a gang of boys who were playing pitch-penny. 1877 ELIZ. S. PHELPS *Story of Avis* 286 Calculating the distance..as he stood playing the game of human pitch-penny with the infant.

Pitch-pine. (Earlier examples.)
1676 *Essex Inst. Hist. Coll.* LVI. 306, 4½ acres of land.. bounded by a pitch pine. 1708 *N. H. Probate Rec.* I. 622 Beginning at a pitch pine tree. 1736 *Boston Town Rec.* XII. 150 To add to the South East Side ten foot, to be built of square pitch Pine Timber.

Pith, *sb.* **8.** Add: **pith-fleck**, a piece of tissue covering a wound in some trees; **pith-tree** (earlier example).
1908 W. R. FISHER *Schlich's Man. Forestry* (ed. 2) V. 125 *Pith-flecks are common in the wood of birch, alder and species of *Prunus* and *Pirus.* 1864 J. A. GRANT *Walk Across Africa* p. xv, Ambadj; native name for the *pith-tree.

Pithecanthropic, *a.* Add: **b.** Of or pertaining to pithecanthropus or ape-man.
1917 *Q. Rev.* July 35 Degeneracy, as seen in idiots, cretins, and certain ethnic groups, due to a reversion to the pithecanthropic element. 1931 SIR A. KEITH *New Discov. Antiq. Man* 293 The greatest number of these [characters] link these ancient Chinamen to the Pithecanthropic type of Java.

Pitiless, *a.* **2.** (Modern example.)
1902 J. S. PHILLIMORE *Sophocles* 192 Where Polyneices on the plain-lands rim Yet lay, a corpse, dog-worried, pitiless.

Pitman. **5.** (Earlier example.)
1813 *Niles' Weekly Reg.* IV. 111/2, I apply the power by means of a connecting rod or rods (or pitman as it is called when applied in saw mills).

Pitot tube (pito). [f. H. *Pitot* (1695–1771), French physicist, who invented or used the tube.] A tube open at both ends and having one part at right angles to the other, used in apparatus for determining the velocity of fluids and in modern anemometers. Also with ellipse of *tube.*
1880 *Encycl. Brit.* XII. 508/1 A Darcy gauge..consists of two Pitot tubes having their mouths at right angles. 1922 *Ibid.* XXX. 28/1 The open-ended tube is usually referred to as a 'pitot' tube.

Pituitrin (pitiūˑitrin). *Phys.* [f. PITUITARY *a.* + -INE[5].] A substance or hormone produced by the pituitary body; a solution containing this used medicinally.
1910 MARTINDALE & WESTCOTT *Extra Pharmacopœia* (ed. 14) 822 Pituitrin is a solution containing the active principles of the Infundibular portion of the pituitary body. 1922 B. HARROW *Glands* 55 We have given the name 'pituitrin' to the hormone (or hormones) present in the posterior lobe of the pituitary... This hormone has not been isolated in the pure state. 1927 HALDANE & HUXLEY *Animal Biol.* viii. 163 The posterior part [of the pituitary gland] produces a hormone, pituitrin, which affects smooth muscle.

Pity, *v.* **3.** (Modern example.)
1862 CHARLOTTE M. YONGE *Countess Kate* xii. 222 Sylvia and Charlie, took it all in, pitied, wondered, and were indignant, with all their hearts.

Pivie, variant of PEAVEY.
1907 *Black Cat* June 24 Mehetabel launched the boat, and running along the logs, piloted it hither and thither..hooked to a pivie.

Pivot, *sb.* **3.** Also, a 'pivotal man' in industry; the centre half-back of a football team.
1919 *Punch* 29 Jan. 76/2 They are keeping all the pivots in this area for one final orgy of demobilisation at some future date. 1928 *Weekly Dispatch* 24 June 21/7 Robert Plenderleith, the East Fife centre half-back, one of the most promising of young pivots in Scotland.
6. b. *pivot man* (later example in special sense).
1918 *Daily Mail* 6 Dec. 3/3 (heading), 12,000 Pivot men.

Pivotal, *a.* (Add examples.)
1918 *Daily Mail* 11 Dec. 5/1 A pivotal man is an essential man in an industry or occupation on which the re-establishment of other industries depends. 1922 *Encycl. Brit.* XXX. 214/2 The release of 'Pivotal Men'..met with much opposition. 1925 *Times* 5 Jan. 4/3 Young's passes..were..much too high to enable Kittermaster, as the pivotal player, to pave the way for a scoring position. 1927 PEAKE & FLEURE *Priests & Kings* 134 A new feature, however, was the use of door-slabs of stone set with pivotal hinges.
b. as *sb.* A pivotal man.
1918 *Daily Mail* 29 Nov. 3/2 Men who are essential to the building up and expansion of trade..are officially described as 'pivotals'.

Pivotalism (piˑvətăliz'm). [f. PIVOTAL *a.* + -ISM.] After the war of 1914–18, the policy of releasing 'pivotal men' (see quot. 1918 above) from active service before others, to facilitate the speedy reorganization of business.
1922 *Encycl. Brit.* XXX. 215/1 Pivotalism..was called 'favouritism'.

Pivoter (piˑvətəɹ). [f. PIVOT *sb.* and *v.* + -ER.] **1.** A workman who makes and fits pivots for watches.
1906 *Daily Chron.* 12 Sept. 1/6 Advt., Watch Maker.— Wanted a good pivoter; hours 9 to 7.
2. *colloq.* A golfer who turns his body as on a pivot when swinging a golf club.
1928 *Observer* 1 July 30/2 One of the most fluent of 'pivoters' puts it in this way: 'The club should be started back low along the ground [etc.].'

Pivoting, *vbl. sb.* (Later example in special sense.)
1921 FLOR. IRWIN *Compl. Auction Player* 2 'Pivoting' is changing partners after every rubber and according to fixed routine.

Placating (plăkēˑtiŋ), *ppl. a.* [f. PLACATE *v.* + -ING[2].] That placates or is intended to placate; conciliatory. Hence **Placaˑtingly** *adv.*
1911 MARY JOHNSTON *Long Roll* xix. 243 Allen took it calmly, made a placating remark or two, and lapsed into a friendly silence. 1922 J. S. FLETCHER *Ravensdene Court* iv. 54 'Ye'll just indulge an old man's fancy?' he said placatingly.

Place, *sb.* **29.** *place-seeker* (example).
1902 *Kynoch Jrnl.* Oct.–Nov. 14/1 The firing point is not crowded with a lot of *place-seekers croaking their grievances.

Place, *v.* Add: **5. e.** To determine who or what a particular person (or thing) is; to assign to a particular class or category; to identify or recognize. *U.S.*
1855 *Knickerbocker Mag.* XLV. 194 Who is our friend?.. And [are] 'K. Y' his initials? If yea, we can't 'place' him. 1886 *Century Mag.* Feb. 512/2 I've seen you before, but I can't place you. 1890 *Harper's Mag.* July 291/2 He had no memory of having ever heard it before... For a while he could not place it. 1904 MRS. CLAY *Belle of Fifties* 79, I observed..a very busy little woman..whose face was familiar to me, but whom I found myself unable to place. 1923 H. G. WELLS *Men Like Gods* I. ii. § 2. 19 For a time Mr. Barnstaple could not place him.
f. *intr.* To secure a place among the first three in a race.
1924 P. MARKS *Plastic Age* 276 He was going to place in the hundred and win the two-twenty or die in the attempt.

Placement. Add: *spec.* in American football, the placing of the ball on the ground for a place-kick.
1911 in WEBSTER.

Placer[2]. **b.** Add: *placer-camp, -working.*
1906 *Outlook* 9 June 773/1 It will bring the historic placer-camps of Caniar and Omenica within reach of the mining capitalist. 1874 RAYMOND *6th Rep. Mines* 299 The amount of gold washed from the bed of creeks and placer-workings.

Plage[3] (plaʒ). [F., shore, beach: see PLAGE[1].] The beach, esp. at a seaside resort.
1907 *Daily Chron.* 5 July 6/3 She once saw the lady walking on the 'plage' with the baron. 1920 W. T. GRENFELL *Labrador Doctor* ii. 18 There were horses to ride also and a beautiful 'plage' to bathe upon. 1926 *Spectator* 28 Aug. 309/1 The holiday-makers stay in town and go to the plage by train for bathing.

Plagiotropous (plēdʒiǫˑtrŏpəs), *a.* *Bot.* [f. PLAGIO- + Gr. τρόπος turning + -OUS.] = PLAGIOTROPIC. So **Plagioˑtropously** *adv.* **Plagioˑtropy**, plagiotropous condition.
1905 J. B. BALFOUR tr. *Goebel's Organogr. Plants* I. 67 Sachs has divided the organs of plants into the orthotropous and the plagiotropous. *Ibid.* 112 In the shade of woods of the natural habitat the plagiotropy..may be more marked. *Ibid.* 113 Sympodial short-systems..growing plagiotropously.

Plague, *sb.* **4. c.** Add: **plague-rat**, a rat believed to spread plague.
1902 *Encycl. Brit.* XXXI. 791/1 Plague-rats have rarely been found in ships sailing from infected ports.

Plague, *v.* Add: **2. b.** Phr. *to plague one's life out*: to tease or annoy a person excessively.
1834 MRS. ANNE MARSH *Two old Men's Tales* II. viii. II. 46 You are so odd that you would plague the life out of a woman that loved you. 1894 VIOLET HUNT *Maiden's Progr.* iii. 17 Moderna..plagues the other children's lives out with making them give her her cues, at all times and seasons.

Plain, *sb.*[1] **10.** Add: *plains guide, malady, tribe.*
1877 R. I. DODGE *Hunting Grounds Gt. West* v. 63 'Old Bridger', the most thorough and justly celebrated of all plains guides. *Ibid.* 67 Another plains malady..is called 'moon-blind'. *Ibid.* xli. 419 The Tonkaways cannot properly be called a plains tribe.

Plain. **A.** *adj.* **8.** Also of an appellation: Without addition.
1828 *Imperial Mag.* X. 589 The doctor, or, as he now chose to designate himself, plain Thomas Beddoes. 1872 HARDY *Under Greenw. Tree* I. ii. 20 'Reub', says he—'a always used to call me plain Reub, poor old heart!'
d. Also of needles: That knit plain stitches.
1881 *Encycl. Brit.* XII. 299/2 The addition consisted of a set of ribbing-needles placed at right angles to Lee's plain needles.
C. c. **plain-cut** *a.*, plain, unadorned, simple; **plain-faced** *a.*, in lawn tennis, applied to a stroke which imparts no spin or swerve to the ball.
1894 STEVENSON & OSBOURNE *Ebb-Tide* I. v, I never could act up to the plain-cut truth, you see; so I pretend. 1928 *Weekly Disp.* 24 June 22/2 Thus what seems a plain-faced stroke is full of guile.

Plain sailing, *sb.* (Earlier example.)
1823 J. F. COOPER *Pilot* I. xii. 152 This is what the lads would call plain sailing..: they are out of employment [etc.].

Plainsman. (Earlier examples.)
1870 KEIM *Sheridan's Troopers* (1885) xi. 66 Such an animal is a treasure in the esteem of a plainsman. 1873 J. H. BEADLE *Undevel. West* vi. 93 Old plainsmen look at each other with a peculiar smile which may mean anything.

Plaiting, *vbl. sb.* **b.** Also *plaiting-down apparatus.*
1927 T. WOODHOUSE *Artif. Silk* 134 The cloth is..passed over the inclined reversible inspecting board.., between a pair of drawing rollers, and finally to the plaiting-down apparatus.

Plaiˑtless, *a.* [f. PLAIT *sb.* + -LESS.] Having no plaits.
1887 HARDY *Woodlanders* III. xv. 315 This solitary and silent girl stood there in the moonlight..clothed in a plaitless gown.

Plan, *v.* **3.** (Absol. examples.) Also with *out.*
1778 CLARA REEVE *Old Engl. Baron* 113 Some are born to plan, others to execute. 1872 'SUSAN COOLIDGE' *What Katy did* xi. 197 Few visitors came to interrupt her, so she could plan out her hours and keep to the plans. 1895 C. M. SHELDON *His Brother's Keeper* v. (1896) 107 When Aunt Royal comes, I mean to plan for something besides all this. 1926 *American Oxonian* July 99 If I were planning on going after a Rhodes Scholarship next year, I should read a great deal on foreign affairs.

Planation (plănēˑʃən). *Geol.* [f. L. *plān-um* PLANE *sb.*[3] + -ATION.] The production of a level surface by the action of glaciers and flowing water.
1877 G. K. GILBERT *Rep. Geol. Henry Mts.* 127 The process of carving away the rock so as to produce an even surface, and at the same time covering it with an alluvial deposit, is the process of planation. 1900 MARR *Sci. Study Scenery* 145 The drainage superimposed by planation, to use Gilbert's expression. 1927 *Glasgow Herald* 28 Mar. 10 When it had been made much more level as a result of 'planation'.

Planchette. **2.** Also *Comb.* as *planchette board, -writer, -writing.*
1914 H. CARRINGTON *Probl. Psych. Research* 371 There can be little doubt that the same force which propels the *planchette board propels the ouija board also. 1920 ROSE MACAULAY *Potterism* III. i. § 4, I am in touch with several very wonderful thought-readers, crystal-gazers, mediums, and *planchette-writers. 1884 F. W. H. MYERS in *Proc. Soc. Psych. Research* Dec. 232 The Spiritualist theory of *Planchette-writing assumes the former of these two hypotheses.

Plane, *sb.*[3] Add: **1. i.** *Aeron.* A flat, light, framework or surface used in aerostatical experiments; the principal supporting surface (or one such surface) in an aeroplane, now made with a slight curve or camber.
1824 *Mechanics' Mag.* 25 Dec. 214/1 The very ingenious proposal lately made, of directing a balloon..by means of an inclined plane, is worthy of much consideration. 1848 *Chambers's Jrnl.* 6 May 301/1 When it attained the highest point, the edge of the plane would be reversed, and the balloon would descend. 1866 WENHAM in *Rep. Aeronautical Soc.* 36 In order to obtain the necessary length of plane..the surfaces may be superposed, or placed in parallel rows, with an interval between them. 1891 S. P. LANGLEY *Experiments in Aerodynamics* 5 We already possess in the steam-engine as now constructed..more than the requisite power to urge a system of rigid planes through the air at a great velocity. 1910 C. C. TURNER *Aerial Navig. Today* 108 The width of a plane in a biplane should never exceed about one-fifth of the length. 1922 *Encycl. Brit.* XXX. 19/2 The term 'wing' is commonly used of the half of a lifting-surface on one side of the aeroplane, the whole surface constituting a 'plane'.

Plane, 'plane (plēⁱn), *sb.*[5] Abbreviation of *AEROPLANE 2.
1909 LLOYD GEORGE in *Daily Chron.* 23 Aug. 1/1, I have not yet crossed the Financial Channel with my Budget 'plane. 1918 *Illust. Lond. News* 27 July 106 An immense array of new 'planes undergoing finishing stages in various completing processes. 1920 *Blackw. Mag.* June 762/1 A plane which came from Palestine. 1929 E. W. SPRINGS *Above bright blue Sky* 15 It's very little harder to learn to fly a plane than to drive a car.

Plane, *v.*[2] Add: **2.** To travel in an aeroplane; to glide.
1909 *Westm. Gaz.* 9 Aug. 5/1 With this apparatus..one will be able to 'plane' to one's heart's content. 1909 *Daily Chron.* 26 Aug. 1/2 The aviator..'planed gracefully to the earth. 1915 *Chambers's Jrnl.* Jan. 54/1, I planed into a rain-cloud yesterday. 1915 *Spectator* 27 Mar. 427/2 After planing down to a thousand feet, [they] dropped five bombs each on the submarines.

Planer-tree. (Earlier examples.)
1810 MICHAUX *Arbres* I. 39 *Planer tree*, nom de la personne à laquelle cette espèce a été consacrée. 1832 D. J. BROWNE *Sylva Amer.* 246 The planer tree is of the second order, and is rarely more than 35 or 40 feet high.

Planet, *sb.*[1] **4.** Add: **planet cage**, the cylindrical holder of planet-pinions; **planet-pinion** = *planet-wheel*; **planet shower**, a local shower; **planet-stirrer** (see quot.).
1908 *Daily Chron.* 14 Nov. 8/6 The provision of ball bearings for the *planet pinions in the Sturmey Archer gears, and roller bearings for the *planet cage in the Armstrong. 1850 MAYNE REID *Rifle Rangers* lvii. (1853) 288 We were treated each day to some five or six hours of a '*planet' shower. 1902 C. SALTER tr. *Georgievics' Chem. Technol. Textile Fibres* 249 Stirring is effected by so-called *planet stirrers *l*, the stirring paddle, in addition to rotating on its own axis, also describing a circular path round the inner wall of the pan.

Planetal, *a.* (Modern example.)
1908 *Hastings's Encycl. Relig. & Ethics* I. 187/1 The planetal series of our days of the week places Sunday before Monday.

Planetesimal (plænėteˑsimăl). [f. PLANET *sb.*[1] + INFINIT)ESIMAL.] One of a great number of meteorites or minute planets, which, according to a hypothesis put forward by T. C. Chamberlin, have formed the bodies of the planets by accretion in a cold state.
1904 *Amer. Geol.* Feb. 97 The new hypothesis claims that the substance of the atmosphere and ocean were originally a part of the planetesimals, and helped to form the earth's mass. 1906 *Athenæum* 18 Aug. 191/2 These diminutive bodies or planetesimals gradually became aggregated..into a few large bodies or planets. 1912 J. W. GREGORY *Making of Earth* I. i. 11 Still smaller than the minor planets are the bodies which are called planetesimals. 1925 *Glasgow Herald* 14 May 6 The separate masses are styled 'planetesimals', or miniature planets.
b. *attrib.* or as *adj.* Of or belonging to planetesimals. **Planetesimal hypothesis, theory**, the hypothesis that the earth and the other planets have been formed from planetesimals.
1904 *Amer. Geol.* Feb. 95 The planetesimal hypothesis.. seems much better to explain both the astronomical and geological phenomena. 1906 *Athenæum* 18 Aug. 191/1 The Planetesimal Theory of the earth's origin. 1927 MACPHERSON *Mod. Astron.* 181 Two American physicists..put forward the 'planetesimal hypothesis' of the development of the Solar System from a spiral nebula. 1928 T. C. CHAMBERLIN *Two Solar Families* 169 Only motions too slow to carry the accretions beyond their mutual control were retained; all higher motions led to planetesimal orbits.

Planetkin (plæˑnėtkin). [f. PLANET *sb.*[1] + -KIN.] A small planet.
1832 CARLYLE *Reminisc.* (1881) I. 44 A temporary fraction of this planetkin, the whole round of which is but a sandgrain in the all.

Planetoˑlogy. [f. PLANET *sb.*[1] + -(O)LOGY.] The scientific study of the planets. Hence **Plaˑnetoloˑgic** *a.*, of or pertaining to planetology; **Planetoˑlogist**, a student of planetology.
1908 P. LOWELL in *Century Mag.* Feb. 505/1 Planetology, however, will give us the clue to this beclouded hothouse state of things. *Ibid.* 505/2 This gives us a most instructive glimpse into one planetologic process.

Plangently (plæˑndʒĕntli), *adv.* [f. PLANGENT + -LY[2].] So as to beat strongly or distressingly on the mind or feelings.
1927 MÉGROZ *Three Sitwells* 9 We are driven inwards because the external reality we have created is plangently ugly. 1928 *Observer* 19 Feb. 9/2 Nothing is here to make us beat the breast. The old matchless rhythms are no less plangently certain.

Planing, *vbl. sb.* **3.** **planing-machine, -mill** (earlier examples).
1805 *U.S. Patents* 1 June, *Planing machine. 1851 C. CIST *Cincinnati* 227 Planing machines..made by B. Bicknell. 1844 *Knickerbocker Mag.* XXIV. 184 The uplifted arm of Labor..meets his eye in the *planing mill.

Plank, *sb.* **7.** Add: *plank-raft*; **plank-buttress**, a root of a tree resembling and acting as a buttress.
1903 W. R. FISHER tr. *Schimper's Plant-Geog.* 305 The *plank-buttress is a peculiarity of trees in a tropical climate with abundant rainfall. 1910 *Westm. Gaz.* 24 Jan. 5/2 People..had to make use of boats or *plank-rafts.

Plank, *v.* **2. b.** (Earlier examples.) Also *absol.*
1824 *Nantucket Inquirer* 19 Apr. (Th.) His guardy was sent for, and he planked the cash. 1830 R. C. SANDS *Writ.* II. 195 Well..Mr. Mansfield can plank five thousand dollars. 1850 W. COTTON *Three Yrs. Calif.* xiii. 196/7, I told them.. the only way to get out of the scrape was to pay up. Dr. S— was the first to plank down.
4. (Earlier and later examples.) Also of meat.
1855 *Baltimore Sun* 30 Apr. (Bartlett) Did you ever eat a planked shad? Then you have something yet to live for. 1891 *Fur, Fin & Feather* Mar. 197 Cook the trout as Jerseymen cook shad—plank them. 1910 [see *PLANKED 2].

Planked, *ppl. a.* Add: **1.** (Later example.)
1873 J. H. BEADLE *Undevel. West* xxxvi. 769 As one result of their smooth planked streets, much attention is given to fine turn-outs.
2. Also of meat.
1910 *Chambers's Jrnl.* July 430/2 In the restaurants the British visitor will invariably be confronted with the possibilities contained in..'planked steak',..and so on.
b. *Hat-making.* That has been felted on a plank.
1845 DODD *Brit. Manufs.* 164 The felted or 'planked' cap is taken to a stove-room and dried.

Planktoˑlogist. [f. PLANKTON + -(O)LOGIST.] A student of planktology.
1911 *Rep. Brit. Assoc.* 422 The Kiel planktologists..have had to seek for another source of food for the zooplankton.

Planograph (plæˑnograf), *sb.* [f. L. *plān-um* PLANE *sb.*[3] + -GRAPH.] A planographic printing block or print.
1931 A. ESDAILE *Student's Man. Bibliog.* 132 *Planograph*, [a class of engraved illustration] in which the design is neither raised nor incised, but is drawn on a flat surface.

Planograph (plæˑnograf), *v.* [f. the sb.] *trans.* To print from plane surfaces; to practise planography.
1928 *Funk's Standard Dict.*

Planographic (plænŏgræˑfik), *a.* [f. as prec. + -GRAPHIC.] Pertaining to, employed in, or produced by, planography.
1897 H. W. SINGER & STRANG *Etching* etc. 121 The relief print has no plate mark, the intaglio print has one quite clear and distinct, the planographic one has a very slight mark. 1914 EMIL H. RICHTER *Prints* 10 The last group to be considered, planographic processes, is based entirely upon chemical and physical action.

Planography. Add: **2.** Printing done with plane surfaces, in contrast to intaglio or relief work.

Planont (plæˑnǫnt). [f. PLANO-[2] + Gr. ὀντ-, stem of ὤν, pres. pple. of εἶναι to be.] A motile stage in some Microsporidia.
1914 FANTHAM & PORTER *Some minute Anim. Parasites* 218 More than one planont can invade any cell in the gut.

Plant, *sb.*[1] Add: **6. c.** *transf.* The workmen employed at a plant.
1922 J. D. HACKETT in *Managem. Engin.* Feb., No more time is lost by having all the plant out on strike for a week than in having a tenth of the force absent for 10 weeks.
10. a. *plant-stand.*
1862 *Catal. Internat. Exhib., Brit.* II. No. 6070, Ornamental wire *plant-stands, model rosery, and verandah.
e. **plant-breeder** (example); also **plant-breeding**; **plant-food** (earlier examples); **plant-house** (*a*), a green-house; (*b*), a building containing industrial plant; **plant-stove**, a hot-house for plants; **plant-wax**, wax obtained from plants.
1908 *Westm. Gaz.* 28 Mar. 6/2 A study of the fundamental principles of *plant-breeding... He describes the *plant-breeder as an explorer into the infinite. 1868 *Rep. U.S. Comm. Agric.* (1869) 396 Such *plant-food as rain-water and the atmosphere supply. 1873 *Rep. Vermont Board Agric.* II. 212 My scientific friend..shows the hay far richer in plant food than the straw. 1880 *Encycl. Brit.* XII. 221/2 *Plant houses must be as far as possible impervious to wet and cold air from the exterior. 1909 *Westm. Gaz.* 6 May 5/3 A plant-house is being erected outside the south wall of the provincial capital. 1880 *Encycl. Brit.* XII. 223/1 In their interior fittings *plant stoves require more care than greenhouses. 1924 J. A. THOMSON *Science Old & New* xviii. 101 There are *plant-waxes as well as animal-waxes; and some of the former, like myrtle-wax and Japanese wax, are commercial products just like beeswax.

Plant, *v.* Add: **1.** Also *absol.*
1893 B. MITFORD *Gun-runner* iv. 34 Along the banks of this [watercourse] the careful Jeremiah had planted and sown. 1896 *Forum* July 515 Our forefathers..came to work, to plant, to reap, where they might worship God with freedom.
c. *Plant out*, also, to set plants or trees at proper intervals in (a piece of ground).
1900 *Year-bk. U.S. Dept. Agric.* 373 Each orchardist will no doubt develop some method of his own in planting out the orchard.
6. a. Also (U.S.) with *to.*
1900 *Year-bk. U.S. Dept. Agric.* 461 Around this central oasis cluster a dozen smaller ones, all planted to the same palms. *Ibid.* 373 The land should be planted to a crop for at least a year or two before setting out the trees.
7. b. Also with personal object.
1930 HUTCHINSON in *Strand Mag.* May 343/1 People try to plant me with all sorts of impossible yarns.
11. *U.S.* To bury.
1867 'MARK TWAIN' *Amer. Drolleries* 107 He died. There was not a dry eye in the crowd when they planted him. 1882 FOOTE *Led-Horse Claim* xvii. 278 Pity they hadn't planted him instead. 1898 H. S. CANFIELD *Maid of Frontier* 186 They planted Chisholm in the little cemetery. 1910 W. M. RAINE *B. O'Connor* 18 Nothing left to do but plant the deceased and collect the insurance. 1910 A. H. DAVIS *Our Selection* xiii. 123 We planted him on his own selection beneath a gum-tree.

Plantable, *a.* (Earlier example.)
1640 *Maryland Archives* I. 97 A Servant at the end of his Service shall have..fifty acres of land, five whereof at least to be plantable.

Plantation. **7.** *plantation-house* (later examples), *-negro* (earlier example).
1831 PECK *Guide Emigrants* II. 55 All the *plantation houses are surrounded with rich and beautiful groves. 1885 *Outing* Nov. 154/1 Katie spent much of the time..taking note of the old-fashioned plantation-houses. 1771 *Carroll Papers* in *Maryland Hist. Mag.* XIV. 135 My people..do not live so well as our House negroes, but full as well as any *Plantation negroes.

Planter. Add: **6. b.** A fraudulent dealer in works of art: cf. PLANT *v.* 9 b.
1906 *Chambers's Jrnl.* May 390/1 The ingenuity of 'planters' has..to be devoted to manufacturing histories relating to old copies [of Italian paintings].
8. (Earlier example.)
1849 *Rep. U.S. Comm. Patents* (1850) 151 Having thus fully described my improved grain and seed planter.

Plantigrady (plæntiˑgrædi). [f. PLANTIGRADE + -Y.] Plantigrade condition.
1903 *Amer. Naturalist* Nov. 733 In some cases a distinct plantigrady has replaced the previous digitigrady.

Plashily (plæˑʃili), *adv.* [f. PLASHY *a.*[2] + -LY[2].] With a plashing noise.
1926 ROSE MACAULAY *Crewe Train* III. i, Going away, going away, going away. The waves plashily said it over.

Plasmolyˑtically, *adv.* [f. PLASMOLYTIC + -AL + -LY[2].] By means of plasmolysis.
1903 *Science* 1 May 706/2 A reduction of temperature gave rise to parthenogenetic spore formation.., as was also the case when water was plasmolytically withdrawn from the cells.

Plasmotomy (plæzmǫˑtŏmi). [f. PLASMO- + Gr. τομία cutting.] A mode of propagation in some sporozoans; budding.
1902 *Encycl. Brit.* XXXII. 817/2 Cohn and Döflein have discovered cases of plasmotomy, in which a kind of protoplasmic bud of ectosarc and endosarc containing some nuclei becomes detached.

Plaster, *sb.* Add: **3. b.** *U.S.* Plaster of Paris used as a top-dressing for soils.
1787 WASHINGTON *Diaries* III. 222 Where the Plaister had been spread the white and red clover was luxuriant. 1816 U. BROWN *Jrnl.* in *Maryland Hist. Mag.* X. 264 A poor Hill Country well watered and adapted to Plaster. 1840 J. BUEL *Farmer's Companion* 213 Districts in which clover and plaster were first introduced..have unquestionably made the most rapid strides in agricultural improvement. 1880 *Harper's Mag.* June 67/2 Another glance detects the.. farmer sowing his load of plaster across the whitening field.
4. **plaster-sick** *a.*, of land, having its fertility impaired by the application of too much plaster of Paris.
1838 H. COLMAN *Rep. Agric. Mass.* (1839) 42 He says he knows nothing of land becoming, as it is termed, *plaster-sick.

Plaster, *v.* **5. c.** Also, to treat (a crop) with plaster of Paris.
1852 *Trans. Mich. Agric. Soc.* III. 171 As soon as the corn came up, it was plastered on the hill. 1860 T. D. PRICE *MS. Diary* 11 June, Finished plastering corn, put 2 barrels of plaster on the corn.

Plastering, *vbl. sb.* Add: **1. d.** The treatment of wines with gypsum.
1900 SADTLER *Handbk. Industr. Org. Chem.* (ed. 3) 205 Of the methods of 'improving' wines, as it is termed, that known as 'plastering' is probably most largely practised.

Plaster of Paris. Add: **b.** *U.S.* Used as a top-dressing for soils.
1787 WASHINGTON *Diaries* III. 222 We rid to the Farm of one Jones, to see the effect of the plaister of Paris, which appeared obviously great. 1810 *Steele Papers* II. 627 Salt can be brought up the river in sufficient quantity, and plaster of paris if necessary to give a good coat of white clover on the soil.

Plastery (plaˑstəri), *sb.* [f. PLASTER *sb.* + -Y[4].] Plastered work; plastering.
1842 *Amer. Pioneer* I. 207 The stone work and plastery was done by major William Rutledge, a soldier of the revolutionary war.

Plastery, *a.* Also, suggestive of plaster; built with plaster.
1862 'GAIL HAMILTON' *Country Living & Thinking* 6 To move from this tumble-down old house..into a..plastery, shingly, stary, new one. 1907 *Daily Chron.* 18 Sept. 4/4 Plastery little red and white cottages and villas set at all angles among cabbage-plots.

Plastic, *sb.*[1] Add: **2.** = PLASTIQUE.
1923 *Blackw. Mag.* June 722/2 In the evenings Roupin constructed in plastic..a complete model of Haidar Pasha.

Plastid, *sb.* **1.** Also *Comb.* as *plastid-colour.*
1913 W. BATESON *Mendel's Princ. Heredity* 98 In the Stock the cream is a plastid-colour, whereas in *Antirrhinum* the ivory is a true sap-colour.

Plastinoid (plæˑstinoid), *a.* *Biol.* [f. PLASTIN + -OID.] Resembling plastin.
1911 *Encycl. Brit.* XXII. 483/2 More often the chromatin is more or less concentrated in a central mass forming a so-called karyosome, consisting of an achromatic plastinoid substance impregnated with chromatin.

Plate, *sb.* Add: **1. d.** *Geol.* An expanse of undisturbed strata.
1904 HERTHA B. C. SOLLAS tr. *Suess' Face of Earth* I. 600 Towards the north [of North America], however, a very extensive 'plate' without folding appears, which stretches nearly to the Arctic archipelago.
4. h. *Wireless Telegr.* The anode of a thermionic valve, originally made in the form of a flat plate, but now usually cylindrical.
[1904 R. M. WALMSLEY *Electr. in Service of Man* vi. 230 Professor Fleming..proved that there was an actual stream of negatively electrified particles passing from the negative leg to the metal plate M.] 1919 J. A. FLEMING *Thermionic Valve* 165 The grid is surrounded by a perforated cylinder which forms one anode, and this again by another unperforated cylinder which forms the plate. 1922 *Encycl. Brit.* XXXII. 1025/1 Around that [the grid] again is a cylinder of sheet nickel called the plate. 1926 R. W. HUTCHINSON *First Course in Wireless* viii. 140 This movement of electrons from filament to plate constitutes an electric current from plate to filament.
i. (See quot.)
1926 *Gloss. Electr. Terms* (Brit. Engin. Stand.) 43 *Condenser*, a piece of apparatus consisting of conducting surfaces (known as the *plates* or electrodes) at a small distance apart and separated by an insulating material.
j. *Baseball.* A flat piece of metal or stone marking the home base; the home base itself.
1891 N. CRANE *Baseball* 79 *Ball*, a pitched ball, which does not pass over the home plate [etc.]. 1902 *Encycl. Brit.* XXVI. 161/2 This corner is marked by a white plate a foot square, sunk level with the ground, and called the home base. *Ibid.* 162/1 When he completes this circuit and crosses the plate without being put out, he scores a run. 1903 R. H. BARBOUR *Weatherby's Inning* vii. 66 'I can't hit them unless he sends them over the plate,' he growled. 1917 C. MATHEWSON *Sec. Base Sloan* 172 Ellis walked to the plate and faced Chase grimly determined to get a hit.
19. a. *plate circuit, current, voltage.*
1919 J. A. FLEMING *Thermionic Valve* 224 In general the external E.M.F. required in the *plate circuit of a very hard valve is 100 volts, or even more, to produce a *plate current of 3 or 4 milliamperes with the grid at zero potential. 1926 R. W. HUTCHINSON *First Course in Wireless* 140 A current in this circuit is spoken of as a 'plate current.' 1922 *Encycl. Brit.* XXXII. 1027/2 The *plate voltage of the oscillating valve is not supplied by a high voltage battery but at most by a few cells.
20. **plate clutch**, a form of clutch in which the engaging surfaces are flat metal plates; **plate metal** (*b*), **pewter**, the hardest variety of pewter, used for plates and dishes; **plate-printer**, a workman who prints from plates; **plate-roll**, a metal roller for rolling plates; **plate-room** (*a*), a room for keeping plate (sense 15); (*b*) = *plate-safe*; **plate-safe** (see quot.); **plate-shy** *a.* *baseball* (see quot. and sense *4 j).
1906 *Daily Chron.* 14 Nov. 9/3 The enormously increased popularity of the multiple disc or '*plate' clutches. 1668–9 in Welch *Hist. Pewterers' Co.* (1902) II. 140 It is..agreed.. that..every person that taketh Hollow-ware of any workman & returneth not him for the same ½ *plate mettle and ½ London Trifles, shall pay unto such workman [etc.]. 1839 URE *Dict. Arts* 952 The *plate pewter has a bright silvery lustre when polished. 1909 *Daily Chron.* 13 Aug. 1/4 Robert Girling Norman, aged 31, a *plate printer. 1861 FAIRBAIRN *Iron* 111 The cylindrical part B, for *plate-rolls should be slightly concave. 1888 *Encycl. Brit.* XXIII. 710/1 The *plate-safe or *plate-room is the repository of the stereo and electro plates. 1931 *N. & Q.* 10 Oct. 262/2 The plate-room..is a strong steel and fireproof apartment. 1912 C. MATHEWSON *Pitching* iv. 90 For a long time, 'Josh' Devore, the Giant's left-fielder was '*plate shy' with left-handers— that is, he stepped away.

Plate, *v.* Add: **6.** To provide (a book) with a book-plate.
1906 [see *PLATING 1 f]. 1930 *Publishers' Weekly* 1 Mar. 1095/2 After the latter book had been punched and plated, one of our catalogers discovered that..it was an exact duplicate of the former.
7. To examine or test the distribution of shot from (a shot-gun) by firing at a pattern plate set at a suitable distance.
1904 *Kynoch Jrnl.* Oct.–Dec. 189 You can plate your gun with your favourite charge. 1932 G. BURRARD *Mod. Shotgun* III. 80 No record of such a thing has ever been noted on any pattern plate since the plating of guns first began.

Plateau. Add: **1. c.** A horizontal portion of a learning curve representing a period of no apparent progress; a stage in learning corresponding to this.
1897 BRYAN & HARTER in *Psychol. Rev.* IV. 51 Just below the ability to understand what is spoken, there is a long discouraging plateau where many give up in despair. 1908 E. J. SWIFT *Mind in Making* 310 By far the greater part of the learning period is spent on plateaus when both teacher and pupil, failing to understand the situation, feel that they are marking time.

Platen, *sb.* **4.** Add: **platen-press** = *platen printing-machine.*
1888 *Encycl. Brit.* XXIII. 704/2 We may say that of platen presses there are the hand-press, the treadle platen press, and the steam or other power-driven press.

Platform, *sb.* Add: **6. c.** Also, a continental shelf (SHELF *sb.*[1] 4 b).
1899 *Geog. Jrnl.* XIII. 285 It has been recognized that the British Isles and adjoining parts of the European continent rise from a submarine platform, generally known as 'the 100-fathom platform', or 'shelf'.
9. b. (Earlier examples.) Also *transf.*
1803 *Massachusetts Spy* 27 Apr. (Th.) 'The platform of Federalism.' [Heading of an article from a late North-carolina paper.] 1837 W. L. GARRISON in *Life* (1885) II. 201 We care not who is found upon this broad platform of our common nature. 1838 *Congress. Globe* 11 Jan. App. 73/1 We wanted no platform on which to stand, save the Constitution of our country. *a* 1909 'O. HENRY' *Roads of Destiny* x. 166 He leaned on the desk and declared his platform to the clerk. He said he had come to Elmore to look for a location to go into business.
c. *platform-maker* (sense 9 b); **platform-car** (earlier example); **platform-scale** (examples).
1843 [E. H. DERBY] *Two Months Abroad* 20/1 By this [device]..diligences and private carriages are in a few moments lifted..and transferred to *platform cars. 1928 *Daily Tel.* 12 June 14/7 To-day the '*platform-makers' of both parties were trying to frame an election programme. 1841 *Advt.* in C. Cist *Cincinnati*, *Platform and Common Scales. 1851 C. CIST *Cincinnati* 227 Factories in which platform scales are made.

Plating, *vbl. sb.* Add: **1. f.** The furnishing of a book with a book-plate.
1906 *Daily Chron.* 10 Aug. 3/2 'Plating'..would appear to be the process of affixing the book-plate to the inside of the first cover.

Platinite[2] (plæˑtinəit). [f. PLATINUM + -ITE[1].] An alloy of steel and nickel.
1929 *Daily Tel.* 8 Jan. 8/6 Three metallic alloys of great importance, invar, elinvar, and platinite.

Platino-iridium, variant of PLATINIRIDIUM.
1888 *Encycl. Brit.* XXIV. 479/1 Platino-iridium.

Platinum. **2. b.** Add: **platinum sponge**, spongy platinum.
1829 W. HENRY *Elem. Exper. Chem.* (ed. 11) II. 533 Then pass up through the mercury a piece of platinum sponge. 1924 *Times Trade & Engin. Suppl.* 29 Nov. 244/4 'Platinum sponge' may be described as being platinum in an amorphous form.

Platituˑdinist. [f. PLATITUDINIZE *v.* + -IST.] A person who utters platitudes; a platitudinizer.
1905 W. J. LOCKE *Usurper* xx. 243 Jasper..was not sorry when the kind-hearted platitudinist had gone.

Platode, *a.* (Example.) Also as *sb.*, a platode worm.
1904 McCABE tr. *Haeckel's Wonders of Life* 232 The platodes or 'flat-worms' (*platthelminthes*). *Ibid.* 258 Sponges, polyps, platodes, tunicates, etc.

Platonesque (plǡtōneˑsk), *a.* [f. Gr. Πλάτων Plato + -ESQUE.] Suggestive of Plato; worthy of Plato.
1929 BRIDGES *Test. Beauty* II. 260 But yet to read the strange riddle of the hiving bees, their altruism and platonesque intelligence.

Platonic. **B.** *sb.* **3.** (Recent example.)
1923 ROSE MACAULAY *Told by Idiot* I. 11 To Vicky a young man *was* a young man, and no platonics about it.

Platonician. (Later example.)
1874 K. H. DIGBY *Temple of Memory* ix. (1875) 331 It was not be for instance, who'd confound The Platonicians, equally profound,.. With the scholastics.

Platoon. **1.** Add: Recently revived in the British army for a unit of infantry forming a fourth part of a company and subdivided into four sections of about eight men each.
1913 *Army Order* No. 323. 16 Sept. § 4 A company will be divided into four platoons, each commanded by a subaltern. ..Each platoon will be sub-divided under regulations to be issued later. 1917 SIR J. M. BARRIE *Old Lady Shows her Medals* 72 You have knitted enough things already to fit up my whole platoon.
2. (Recent example).
1916 *Nash's & Pall Mall Mag.* Apr. 149/2 To Kijige in due time came Mowbray, with his platoon of actors, camera experts,..and porters.
3. *platoon sergeant.*
1915 D. O. BARNETT *Lett.* 41, I like the men awfully, especially my platoon-sergeant.

Platycraˑnial, *a.* [f. PLATY- + CRANIAL *a.*] Having a broad skull; broad-skulled.
1907 *Practitioner* Aug. 318 The people in the north of Scotland are broad-headed or platycranial.

Platymeric (plætimeˑrik), *a.* *Anat.* [f. PLATY- + Gr. μηρός thigh + -IC.] Of the femur: Having the upper part flattened. Also, of a person, having such femora. **Platyˑmery**, platymeric condition.
1897 *Phil. Trans.* B. 143 Some of the femora, especially those from New Zealand, exhibited an antero-posterior compression at the upper end of the shaft. This condition has been termed 'platymery' by M. Manowvrier...This platymeric condition was conspicuously exhibited.

Platysmal (plătiˑzmăl), *a.* [f. PLATYSMA + -AL.] Of or pertaining to the platysma.
1899 *Proc. Zool. Soc.* 316 In *Dasypus villosus* the most important bundle..is probably platysmal in its nature.

Play, *sb.* Add: **5. c.** (Further example.)
1931 F. L. ALLEN *Only Yesterday* viii. 189 The insignificant Gray-Snyder murder trial got a bigger 'play' in the press than the sinking of the *Titanic.*
17. *play-centre, -garden, -hour*, (earlier example), *-leader, -shed, -wrecker*; **play-box**, a box in which children keep toys, books, cakes, etc. at boarding-schools; **play-broker**, a broker who deals with plays; **play-doctor**, a professional improver or toucher-up of plays; **play-method** = **play-way*; **play-pen**, a low enclosure in which a young child may play; **play-pretty**, a toy; **play-run** (see quot.); **play-way**, an educational method which seeks to utilize the intellectual energy released in play; **play-world**, the world imagined by children at play.
1882 F. ANSTEY *Vice Versa* v. 103 Let every boarder go down into the box-room and fetch up his *playbox, just as it is, and open it here before me. 1913 H. WALPOLE *Fortitude* I. iv, The passage was hung with greatcoats and down each side of it were play-boxes. 1929 DEEPING *Roper's Row* xxi, To Ruth Avery, No. 7 Roper's Row was a child's playbox. 1925 *Scribner's Mag.* Sept. 283/2 The great Delando..lifted his keen glance to the *play-broker who sat opposite him. 1929 *Even. News* 9 Jan. 11/2 She is a daughter of Major James Clare, a leading playbroker, who is also a dramatist. 1908 *Westm. Gaz.* 1 Feb. 7/3 Mrs. Humphrey Ward spoke of the practical work of the *play centres. 1914 *Hastings's Encycl. Relig. & Ethics* VII. 363/2 The 'play-centre', where, outside school hours, children who have no playground but the street, are taught organized games. 1928 *Observer* 10 June 6/4 Shakespeare..knew all, and more than all, about the technique of play-writing that is known by the most efficient '*play-doctor' in Broadway, New York. 1926 A. S. NEILL *Dominie Dismissed* xiii. 153 The attraction of a *play-garden school with its charms of social intercourse. 1774 P. V. FITHIAN *Jrnl.* (1900) 125 At the Noon *play-hours Bob & Nelson, the boy who waits on the School, had a fight. 1907 *Westm. Gaz.* 29 Aug. 3/1 A pressing need is for trained *play leaders who know how to play games. 1914 H. C. COOK in *Perse Playbooks, No. 4* 64 A complaint that the *Play method does not 'train the intellect'. 1931 *Daily Express* 21 Sept. 7/5 Advt., Well built *play-pens in best hard-wood. 1916 H. L. WILSON *Somewhere in Red Gap* vii. 314 He keeps on chattering like a child that's found a new *play-pretty. 1915 E. R. LANKESTER *Diversions of Naturalist* 196 The bower-bird of Australia makes a '*play-run' or reception-room in which he places shells and bits of bone to attract the female. 1906 *Macmillan's Mag.* Nov. 19 Rooms for the teachers and for the permanent staff, a covered *play-shed, and all the outside accessories. 1914 H. C. COOK in *Perse Playbooks, No. 4* 52 The boys do not object to learning anything, so long as they may do it in the *Play way. 1917 — *Play Way* 8 The Play Way is not a bunch of contrivances for making scholarly pursuits pleasurable, but the active philosophy of making pleasurable pursuits valuable. 1909 *Daily Chron.* 13 Dec. 3/4 Nature's kingdom is not all a reign of tooth and claw, but a *play-world also. 1924 R. M. OGDEN tr. *Koffka's Growth of Mind* 352 There is another world besides his play-world. 1901 *Chambers's Jrnl.* Aug. 545/2 Organised *play-wreckers, who without uttering a word or an unseemly laugh have succeeded in destroying whatever chance of success a play may have had.

Play, *v.* Add: **2. c.** *To play up*: to become unruly; to rear or buck.
1909 J. SWIRE *Anglo-French Horsemanship* 25 The secret of remaining on a horse when he 'plays up' is to drop the hands, press the heels down, sink well into the saddle [etc.].
5. (Further example.)
1897 KIPLING *Capt. Cour.* 17 The schooner, with a triangular riding-sail on the mainmast, played easily at anchor.
6. Also *to play loose* (see quot.).
1823 G. ROLAND *Art of Fencing* 105 Making the assault and playing loose, in the language of the fencing-room, are synonymous.
23. b. *Play* (*one*) *up*: To make sport with; to tease, annoy, or irritate.
1924 GALSWORTHY *White Monkey* II. iv. 151 Did she choose that he should go away, thinking that she had 'played him up' just out of vanity? 1927 *Daily Express* 10 Dec. 1 The girls thought they had got hold of a soft-hearted fool, and they began to play me up. 1931 *Ibid.* 16 Oct. 9/1 Advt., My Nerves used to play me up terribly.
28. b. To bring (a musical instrument) into suitable condition by playing.
1932 *Times Lit. Suppl.* 4 Feb. 68/3 Messrs. Hill make a computation of the years it takes to 'play up' an instrument.
29. (Earlier example.) Also, to pass (time) in playing.
1674 HEAD *English Rogue* III. xi. 136 Mine Host..causing them [*sc.* the 'fidlers'] to cease their playing..said..If you have played away my Guests, you shall pay their reckoning. 1902 R. MACHRAY *Night Side Lond.* xiii. 196 When you go upstairs, you find more members up here playing the wee sma' 'oors away.
31. Also *intr.*, to be performed.
1869 *Punch* 9 Jan. 10/2 Mr. Burnand's new Burlesque, now playing at the Haymarket, is called *The Frightful Hair.*
36. b. *Play up to.* (Later examples.)
1927 CHESTERTON *Secret Fr. Brown* I. 40 There was some-

thing downright creepy about that little goblin with the yellow hair, that seemed to play up to the impression. 1949 *Times* 15 July 21/5 There were two alternatives for the style of the new building: to play up to the 19th-century Gothic of the existing Library or to continue the character of the square in general.

c. *Play down to*: To lower one's standard, quality, price, etc., to suit the tastes, demands, etc., of (the persons one has to deal with).

1930 *Cambridge Daily News* 24 Sept. 8/1 Let us avoid playing down to the public, lest it ask us for a better article than we can provide.

d. *Play up*: to make the most of; to exploit or trade upon. *U.S.*

1926 *Publishers' Weekly* 22 May 1687/1 Let us play up the habits, the appearance, the likes and dislikes, let us sell authors to our public. 1930 *Ibid.* 8 Feb. 706/2 He plays up the fact that there is smart reading just as there are smart clothes.

e. *Play up* (intr.): To behave manfully or heroically.

a 1910 H. Newbolt *Coll. Poems* 131 Play up! play up! and play the game! 1924 Mallory in E. F. Norton *Fight for Everest 1924* 236 The party has played up wonderfully.

Playa (plaˑyă). *Geol.* [Sp., = shore.] More fully *playa lake*, a lake which exists only in winter, being dried up in summer.

1883 I. C. Russell in *Pop. Sci. Monthly* Jan. XXII. 380 The Spanish word *playa*..has been adopted by geologists as a generic term under which the various desiccated lake-basins may be grouped. 1885 — *Lake Lahontan* (U.S. Geol. Surv., Monogr. XI) 81 Examples of the more permanent playa-lakes..are furnished by Honey Lake and the lakes of the Carson Desert. *Ibid.* 82 Typical examples of playas of broad extent occur in the Lahontan basin.

Play-by-play, *a.* *U.S.* Applied to a running commentary on a game.

1931 F. L. Allen *Only Yesterday* viii. 207 Thousands more sat in warm living-rooms to hear the play-by-play story over the radio.

Played (plēɪd), *ppl. a.* [f. Play *v.* + -ed 2.] That has been played.

a 1877 in *Encycl. Brit.* (ed. 9) VI. 713 If a played stone rolls over, or stops, on its side or top, it shall be put off the ice.

Player-piano. A piano having a mechanical apparatus attached by which it is played automatically.

1911 *Smart Set* Mar. p. I A/2 Advt., The World Famed Angelus' Player-Piano. 1922 S. Grew *Art of Player-Piano* 1 The player-piano, like the pianoforte and the organ, is a musical instrument. 1927 *Scribner's Mag.* Feb. 70/1 The phonograph, the player-piano, the radio, have each been of great value in increasing musical knowledge.

Playing, *vbl. sb.* 2. *playing-place* (later example), -*site*.

1852 Broderip *Leaves fr. Notebk. Naturalist* 152 On visiting the cedar-brushes of the Liverpool range, he [*sc.* Gould] discovered several of these bowers or playing-places. 1912 *Q. Rev.* Apr. 515 Capital expended..on securing..such conveniences as playing-sites.

Play-off. [f. Play *v.* + Off *adv.*] An additional game or match played to decide a draw or tie; a replay. Also *attrib.*

1906 *Liverpool Even. Express* 9 Mar., The play-off resulted in a win. 1909 *Westm. Gaz.* 21 Oct. 1/3 A prize which Mr. Doherty captured..on the 'play-off'. 1915 *Literary Digest* (N.Y.) 21 Aug. 361/1 The race with the Cubs was a tie at the end of the season and a play-off game was necessary to decide the pennant. 1927 *Daily Express* 26 July 13/1 Bobby Jones..also tied for the United States open in 1925, when Willie Macfarlane beat him on the play-off.

Play-room. *U.S.* [Play *sb.* 17.] A room in which children may play.

1838 *Knickerbocker Mag.* XI. 12 One Saturday afternoon when seated with two or three other children in my little play-room. 1865 Mrs. Stowe *House & Home P.* 45 Charlie and Jim..detesting the dingy lonely play-room, used to run the city streets. 1877 *Harper's Mag.* Dec. 60/2 Our nursery-play-room we call it. 1900 E. A. Dix *Deacon Bradbury* 197 You and I've got to get to work again at those evergreens up in the play-room. 1927 *Ladies' Home Jrnl.* Dec. 12/1 Jessica's song and the children's noise, every sound in the play room, broke off short.

Play-spell. *U.S.* [Play *sb.* 17.] A portion of time for play or recreation.

1845 S. Judd *Margaret* II. i. 186 And her own play-spell comes, if indeed her whole life were not a play-spell. 1854 Mary J. Holmes *Tempest & Sunshine* vi. 89 You may have a play spell the rest of the afternoon. 1861 [see Play *sb.* 17]. 1878 Mrs. Stowe *Poganuc People* xix. 209 No school was kept, and even household disciplinarians recognized a reasonably well-behaved child's right to a Saturday afternoon play-spell.

Plaza. (Later examples.)

1884 Sweet & Knox *Through Texas* xxiii. 307 Old Gen. Ignacio Barterra 'cussed' a forty-foot steeple on the old church on the plaza [etc.]. 1891 *Century Mag.* Apr. 907 The house..was a three-story building..fronting on a small plaza. 1907 S. E. White *Arizona Nights* iii. 47 A freight outfit brought him to Tucson and dumped him down on the plaza.

Pleasure, *sb.* 6. Add: *pleasure-brake, craft, -land, park, party* (earlier examples), -*plane*; pleasure-pain, a comprehensive expression for all mental experiences whether pleasurable or the reverse; applied *attrib.* to that quality of such experiences by which they are distinguished as pleasurable or unpleasurable.

1908 *Westm. Gaz.* 12 Aug. 8/3 She was cycling along the Bromley-road when a *pleasure-brake..turned out of a side-street. 1906 Conrad *Mirror of Sea* 38 Their striving for victory..has elevated the sailing of *pleasure craft to the dignity of a fine art. 1927 *Daily Tel.* 13 Sept. 12/2 Thirty years ago Piccadilly had still to establish its claim to be regarded as the centre of *pleasure-land. 1894 Creighton & Titchner tr. *Wundt's Hum. & Anim. Psych.* xiv. 211 As soon as we give up the reference of feeling to a subjective condition of *pleasure-pain..we have no reason for uniting affective states in general in a common class. 1918 *Jrnl. Educ.* Mar. 153/1 A complex is nothing more nor less than what the Herbartians call an apperception mass, with, however, the addition of its pleasure-pain tone. 1929 *Encycl. Brit.* XVIII. 673/2 The course of mental processes is automatically regulated by the '*pleasure-pain principle*'. 1904 Farrer *Garden Asia* 70 Here we may fancy known beings resting in this *pleasure-park of necessity. 1835 *Southern Lit. Messenger* IV. 303/1 We..were passed and met by several vehicles in which *pleasure-parties to and from the Springs..were dashing along the well graded road. 1842 M. Crawford *Jrnl.* 7 At noon 8 couple of Gentlemen and Ladies and band of music came on board for a pleasure party. 1911 *Chambers's Jrnl.* Jan. 57/1 The aspect of the heavens will be wonderfully changed when the *pleasure-plane of the air has arrived.

Pleasure-house. (Later example.)

1904 Farrer *Garden Asia* 106 How few of the many Europeans who visit Japan, ever see the real pleasure-houses of the country!

Plea·ter. [f. Pleat *v.* + -er]. (See quot.)

1921 *Dict. Occup. Terms* (1927) § 428 *Pleater*, pleats or folds material in pleats, by hand or by pleating machine.

Pledge, *sb.* 5. b. (Earlier examples.)

1833 *New Engl. Mag.* (Boston) Aug. 137 The Temperance Pledge. *Ibid.* 141 Has he signed the pledge? 1840 *Southern Lit. Messenger* VI. 325/1, I have signed the pledge, and since it is done I will make a virtue of necessity.

Pledge, *v.* Add: 4. c. To promise solemnly (to do something).

1928 *Sunday Dispatch* 2 Sept. 1/3 On my pledging not to disclose his name..he promptly handed over another cheque for £10,000.

Plenarium (plĭnēᵊ·riŏm). [ad. med.L. *plēnārium* in same sense, f. *plēnārius* complete: cf. Plenary.] A book or manuscript containing a complete set of sacred writings, e.g. all the gospels or all the epistles.

1908 W. G. Collingwood *Scandinavian Britain* 243 Bishop Patrick set forth to Iceland 'with wood for building a church, and a plenarium, and an iron bell'.

Plenary. B. *sb.* Add: 2. Anglicized form of prec.

1909 *Hastings's Encycl. Relig. & Ethics* II. 609/1 There were the select passages for Sunday in the so-called Plenaries, Postils, and Books of the Gospels and the Epistles. 1920 Marg. Deanesly *Lollard Bible* xii. 318 Of the three late fourteenth century English 'plenaries', or gospels and homilies, one is certainly Wycliffite.

Plethorous (ple·þŏrəs), *a.* [f. Plethora + -ous.] = Plethoric 1.

1906 J. P. Barry *At Gates of East* Pref. p. vii, But the book..may do good in a practical way, if it weans the wearied, the plethorous and the valetudinarian from the Cult of the Spas.

Pleuranthous (pluræ·nþəs), *a.* *Bot.* [f. Gr. πλευρόν side + ἄνθος flower + -ous.] Bearing flowers on lateral growths only and not on the central stem.

1897 J. C. Willis *Man. & Dict. Flowering Plants & Ferns* II. 272 The plant..may be (1) a monopodium,..(2) an acranthous sympodium,..(3) a pleuranthous sympodium, where the inflorescences are borne on lateral axes.

Pleurisy. 3. Pleurisy-root (earlier example).

1781–2 Jefferson *Virginia* (1787) 36 Pleurisy root, *Asclepias decumbens*.

Plightage (plai·tĕdʒ). [f. Plight *v.*1 + -age.] The fact or condition of being plighted or betrothed.

1908 Hardy *Dynasts* III. v. iv. 442 These vile tricks, to pluck you from Your nuptial plightage..Make me belch oaths!

Plightful, *a.* Transfer †*Obs.* to sense in Dict. and add: 2. Grievous; fraught with suffering.

1906 Hardy *Dynasts* II. vi. v. 304 The tears that lie about this plightful scene Of heavy travail in a suffering soul.

Plimsolls (pli·msŏlz), *pl.* A kind of rubber-soled canvas shoes.

1927 Deeping *Kitty* xii, These stealthy affairs..made him think of sneaking out in plimsolls and kidding some 'cop'. 1930 W. Pett Ridge *Miss Collingwood* i. 12 She kicked off her plimsolls, and walked about in stockinged feet.

Plinth. 3. *plinth-like* (example).

1905 *Harper's Mag.* July 195/1 Those short, stubbed girls and women..were of plinthlike bigness up and down.

Plinthed (plinþt), *pa. pple.* [f. Plinth + -ed 1.] Provided with a plinth.

1908 *Daily Chron.* 27 Aug. 3/4 The walls..are plinthed in wood to a yard in height.

Plish (pliʃ). [Echoic: after Plash *sb.*2] The sound of a body striking the surface of water; a splashing sound.

1924 A. J. Small *Frozen Gold* 151 The gurgling plish, plish, of the paddle ceased.

Plissé (plise), *a.* [F., pa. pple. of *plisser* to pleat.] Shirred or gathered in small pleats; as *sb.*, pleated material.

1920 *Glasgow Herald* 13 Nov. 4 Plissé is the last word in style, and the latest knitted frocks have wide borders done in ribbed work that spring out into plissés. 1928 *Times* 9 May 10/6 A train of lime green and silver tissue, lined with plissé chiffon.

Plodding, *vbl. sb.* Add: b. The sound of a heavy dull tread; a thudding.

1905 A. C. Benson *Upton Lett.* 284 A pleasant plodding and clinking of horses coming home made itself heard in the yard.

Plop. A. *sb.* Also *Comb.* as *plop-plump*.

1921 *Blackw. Mag.* Feb. 198/2 The sound of the plop-plump of your naked feet in the round shallow pools of muddy water.

B. *adv.* Also *plop-plop*.

a 1904 A. Hope *Dolly Dial.* (1926) 44 Miss Phaeton flicked Rhino, and the groom behind went plop-plop on the seat.

Plop, *v.* Add: b. To set *down* with a plop.

1900 Elinor Glyn *Visits Eliz.* 66, I do hate to see a great hand..plopping a dish down..in the middle, so that one has to look at the next course all the time one is finishing the last one.

Plosh, variant of Plash *sb.*2

1928 E. Blunden *Undert. War* xii. 138 The passer-by hates the plosh of the whizzing fuze-top into the muck.

Plosive (plōᵘ·siv), *a.* and *sb.* [After Explosive.] a. *adj.* = Explosive A 2. b. *sb.* = Explosive B 1.

1909 D. Jones *Pronunc. Engl., Phonetics* 65 When we try to pronounce a breathed plosive, e.g. p, by itself, it is generally followed by a short breathed sound h. *Ibid.*, The explosion of a plosive consonant is formed by the air as it rushes out at the instant when contact is released.

Plot, *sb.* 8. Add: *plot-owner*.

1907 *Daily Chron.* 3 June 3/6 An association of..plot owners has been formed for the purpose of improving their position.

Plot, *v.*1 Add: 3. c. To plan *out* or arrange.

1915 Winifred Holt *Beacon for Blind* xiv. 140 When a proposed party was being plotted out he would say, 'Oh, don't ask the So-and-so's, they are such frumps'.

Plotter. Add: 4. A plot-holder.

1927 *Smallholder* 20 Mar. 106/3 Every plotter should pull his weight, not only for his own sake but for the good of the national cause.

Plotting, *vbl. sb.*1 b. Add: *plotting-sheet*.

1926 *Blackw. Mag.* Dec. 830/2 Thus by degrees there appeared on the plotting-sheet a series of tiny needle-pricked marks, circled in crimson.

Plotty, *a.* Earlier example, reduplicated *plotty-plotty*.

1897 Sarah Grand *Beth Bk.* xl. (1898) 373, I would not write plotty-plotty books either.

Plough, *sb.*1 Add: 5. h. A surgical instrument.

1907 *Practitioner* Oct. 528 By means of Killian's 'plough', or Ballenger's 'swivel-knife',..the cartilage so isolated is completely excised.

Plough, *v.* Add: 9. d. *Plough out*. (Further example.)

1922 *Encycl. Brit.* XXXII. 1023/1 The inductor is in the form of a steel drum with exterior of laminated iron in which longitudinal grooves are ploughed out.

f. *Plough under*: to bury in the soil by ploughing.

1900 *Year-bk. U.S. Dept. Agric.* 379 If crimson clover is grown, it should be plowed under rather early in the spring to get the best results.

Plougher. b. Add: *plougher-up*.

1910 *Blackw. Mag.* Jan. 138/1 The calamities which had invariably befallen the digger or plougher-up of a fort.

Plough-gear. (Later examples.)

1644 *Maryland Archives* IV. 279 The ploughgeare sent of England. 1660 *Essex Probate Rec.* I. 319 One Cart and other Plowgeere. 1854 *Florida Plant. Rec.* 553/1, 27 Pair of Plough gear. 1885 'C. E. Craddock' *Prophet Gt. Smoky Mts.* i. 15 The girl's hand trembled violently as she stepped swiftly to his horse and took off the plough-gear.

Plough-grind, *v.* [f. Plough *sb.*1] *trans.* To grind the steel wires of cotton cards in a special way so that they shall present a suitable edge to the cotton. Plough-grinding *vbl. sb.*; Plough-ground *ppl. a.*

1892 J. Nasmith *Cotton Spinning* 135 The usual solution of the difficulty is found in the formation of a tooth with a chisel or knife edge, which is presented to the action of the cotton. This is usually obtained by what is called 'plough grinding'. 1896 Taggart *Cotton Spinning* I. 176 A is the plough-ground wire, and is formed by grinding the sides away, almost to the bend, by special emery discs.

Plough-horse. Now chiefly *U.S.* A horse used for drawing a plough.

1573 T. Tusser *Five Hundreth Pts. Good Husbandry* xviii, Sedge couers for plow horse, for lightnes of neck. 1818 Scott *Rob Roy* II. xiii. 280 There may be pasture aneugh for plough-horses, and owsen, and forty or fifty cows. 1829–32 J. P. Kennedy *Swallow Barn* I. i. 23 Beneath the sheds, the long face of a plough horse may be seen. 1847 *Rep. U.S. Comm. Patents* (1848) 241 What are the peculiar qualities of this horse as a plough horse? 1880 *Harper's Mag.* Aug. 356/2 The next day the two girls, mounted on the plough horse and mare, followed an old Indian trail. 1911 R. D. Saunders *Col. Todhunter* ix. 118 A wall-eyed plow-horse with his tail full o' cuckle-burs.

Ploughing, *vbl. sb.* Add: 1. d. (See quot.)

1924 *Ski Terms* in *Tourist* Winter Sports No. 12/2 *Ploughing*. Points in, heels wide apart, in a V pointing downwards for slowing down.

Plough-jogger. (Later examples.)

1846–52 Whitcher *Widow Bedott P.* xx. 207, I wanted old Dawson's wife to see't I'd got a pardner rather above a common plow-jogger, such as hern is. 1863 *Trans. Ill. Agric. Soc.* (1865) V. 255 At least the old plow jogger will be mounted on his buggy seat.

Plough-line. [Plough *sb.*1 8.] A cord or rein used to guide and control horses while ploughing.

1797 B. Hawkins *Lett.* 97 You can also order up axes, hoes,..plough lines, [etc.]. 1845 J. J. Hooper *Adv. Simon Suggs* ii. 26 His father..dropping the plough-line..turned his back to that individual. 1895 [see Plough *sb.*1 8].

Plough-stock. [Plough *sb.*1 8.] A handle or stilt of a plough.

1786 Washington *Diaries* III. 5 [I] directed them to get me..scantling for plow stocks. 1810 *Austin Papers* (1924) I. 168, 1 Plough Stock. 1856 *Florida Plant. Rec.* 471 [A slave] gitten out timber for plow stocks.

Plough-tail. Also *attrib.*

1912 *Chambers's Jrnl.* Sept. 564/1 No doubt the chiel thought he cut a dash among the plough-tail lads.

Pluck, *v.* 8. Pluck up. c. Also, to get new courage, to take heart again.

1842 Dickens *Amer. Notes* I. ii. 20 Even those passengers who were most distrustful of themselves plucked up amazingly. 1890 Clark Russell *Marriage at Sea* i, But she had plucked up as she drew towards the close of her letter.

Pluck-up. [f. Pluck *v.*] A pull or tow.

1894 *Pall Mall Mag.* IV. 380 With, maybe, a little lugger hanging on astern to get a 'pluck-up' towards home.

Plud-pludding, variant of *plod-plodding*: see Plodding *vbl. sb.*

1912 Deeping *Sincerity* i, The grinding of wheels and the 'plud-pludding' of drenched horses drifted along the high road.

Plug, *sb.* Add: 2. k. *Min.* A cylindrical mass of rock formed in the crater of a volcano.

1886 A. Geikie *Class-bk. Geol.* 143 Through its centre there has risen a column or plug of lava. 1900 *Q. Jrnl. Geol. Soc.* LVI. 221 Mount Kenya is an ancient much-eroded volcano; the highest peak is formed of the rocks of the central plug. 1930 *Saturday Even. Post* 13 Dec. 50/3 On a wide ledge..stood a rhyolite plug, some ten feet high.

6. b. A steady plodding course. (Cf. Plug *v.* 4.)

1909 *Daily Chron.* 16 Sept. 3/4 The story is of the quiet plug of the prosaic Henry and the meteoric flight of the splendid Len.

c. A book which does not sell well, and becomes bad stock.

1909 *Century Dict.* Suppl. 1928 *Publishers' Circular* 21 July 59/2 Out of the vast number of publications issued, some must, indeed, turn out to be plugs. 1930 *Publishers' Weekly* 15 Mar. 1546/1 The so-called plugs are weeded out ..making room for new titles.

9. plug-contact *Electr.*, contact made by means of plugs; plug-hat, tobacco (earlier examples).

1903 *Rep. Brit. Assoc.* 36 The contacts are an old form of the Cambridge Instrument Company's type of *plug-contact. 1873 Eggleston *Myst. Metrop.* i. 21 If you only mean a nice slick *plug-hat. 1822–3 *Ann. 17th Congress* 1218 *Plug tobacco manufactured at Columbia. 1864 T. L. Nichols *Amer. Life* II. 216 Six matrons..returned triumphantly at sunset with..plug tobacco for their husbands. 1883 E. W. Howe *Country Town* (1926) 159 Most of them chewed plug tobacco.

Plug, *v.* Add: 1. e. (Later example.)

1925 P. J. Risdon *Crystal Receivers & Circuits* 15 A complete set of such coils will thus enable a big range of wave-lengths to be efficiently covered, by plugging in a coil most nearly corresponding to the wave-length required.

2. (Earlier example.)

1875 J. G. Holland *Sevenoaks* iv. 45 Whosomever you be, stop, or I'll plug ye.

4. a. (Further examples.)

1902 G. H. Lorimer *Lett. Self-made Merchant* iii. 37 Jim hadn't been in the office plugging away at the letters for a month before he had the writer's cramp. 1909 R. A. Wason *Happy Hawkins* 66 She just kept the pinto ploggin' away, an' I sensed I was up against some head ridin'. *Ibid.* 207, I plugged along through the cold. 1911 Edna Ferber *Dawn O'Hara* vii. 99 Lots of us are pluggin' an' savin' in the hopes that some day we'll have money enough to get back at some people we know. 1929 J. Buchan *Courts of Morning* II. xiv. 303 He was terrified half out of his senses, but he doggedly plugged along.

5. To prevent (a person) from carrying out a project by anticipating him or depriving him of his opportunity; to block (an action or design).

1880 *Scribner's Mag.* Aug. 492/2 One fisherman 'plugs' another when he puts out from shore and casts in ahead of him. 1896 G. Ade *Artie* xii. 110, I wouldn't like to start in and plug his game.

6. *intr.* Of floating logs: To stick or jam.

1902 S. E. White *Blazed Trail* xlviii. 338 Several times the jam started, but always 'plugged' before the motion had become irresistible.

7. *trans.* To popularize (a song) by having it sung or played many times; to present (something) over and over again.

[1927 *Weekly Dispatch* 23 Oct. 14/4 In the 'introduction' we were plugged with pictures which make excellent propaganda for the efficiency of the American Fire Brigades.] 1927 *Daily Express* 9 Nov. 9/4, I agreed, because I..thought it would encourage them to plug my songs. 1930 *Observer* 18 May 15 He 'plugs' history as musical comedies 'plug' their songs.

Pluggable (plɒ·găb'l), *a.* [f. Plug *v.* + -able.] Suitable for or capable of being plugged.

1930 *Punch* 9 Apr. 414 One good rousing 'pluggable' air, 'The March of the Musketeers'.

Plugged, *ppl. a.* Add: 2. Of coins: Having a portion removed and the space filled with base metal.

1906 *Springfield Weekly Republ.* 6 Dec. 16 He offered a plugged 10-cent piece to Conductor Slattery and refused to produce any good money. 1909 'O. Henry' *Options* (1916) 245 Mr. Minkle told me..you'd never taken in a lead silver dollar or a plugged one.

Plugging, *vbl. sb.* 1. (Later examples.)

1908 *Animal Managem.* 211 Piece by piece the straw is wetted and forced into the body of the collar... This process is termed 'plugging'. 1928 *Observer* 5 Feb. 18/4 The dance teachers argue that if a foxtrot piece can be popularised by 'plugging'..so can a new dance.

Plug-in, *a.* [f. Plug *v.* 1 c.] Designed to plug in.

1923 *Pop. Wireless* Suppl. 13 Oct. 10/1 The type..is known as the plug-in interchangeable high-frequency transformer. 1926 R. W. Hutchinson *Wireless* 187 The aerial inductance L_1 and the reaction coil L_2 are of the plug-in type.

Plum, *v.* Add: 2. b. To fill or stuff *up* (a person) with false information.

1921 *Chambers's Jrnl.* May 323/1 He ain't to know no different but what Jack's got prairie fever. Mind you plum him up stiff. 1927 *Observer* 20 Nov. 26/5 He has recently returned from Upper Silesia..and promptly puts into writing all that his clever German friends have been 'plumming' him up with.

Plumb. B. *adv.* 2. c. (U.S. examples.)

1846 Sol. Smith *Theatr. Apprenticeship* 213 Long before the time arrived..the house was plum, chock full—full to overflowing. *a* 1861 T. Winthrop *John Brent* xxviii. 296 When we got here, I paid their ticket plum through to York out of my own belt. 1901 F. Norris *Octopus* I. iii. 121 'I'll get plumb out of here,' he trumpeted. 'I won't stay here another minute.' 1904 S. E. White *Blazed Trail Stories* II. iii. 165 You must be plumb locoed.

Plumb, *v.* Add: 4. c. To lie in a vertical line (above something).

19.. Buck *Handbk. Med. Sci.* III. 857 (Cent. Suppl.) According to them the centre of gravity plumbs behind the hip, in front of the knee and through the ankle-joint.

Plumbly (plɒ·mli), *adv.* [f. Plumb *a.* + -ly 2.] Vertically downwards.

1931 J. C. Gregory *Sh. Hist. Atomism* 7 The atoms that fell plumbly through the void were still restless.

Plumbous, *a.* 2. (Example.)

1906 *Watts' Dict. Chem.* I. 128 Lead protoxide PbO. (Plumbous oxide, Litharge, Massicot.)

Plume, *sb.* Add: 3. c. Self-satisfaction at some achievement; distinction.

1910 W. De Morgan *Affair of Dishonour* iv. 66 He wanted..to choose his time, as a nobleman might then do.. not only without shame or remorse, but even with some sense of plume or strut.

6. *plume-horned*; plume-fly, a gnat of the genus *Corethra*, having plume-like antennæ.

1915 E. R. Lankester *Diversions of Naturalist* 27 The transparent glass-like larvæ of the 'plume fly' (Corethra) could be seen swimming in the clear water. *Ibid.* 91 Some [animals] occur in fresh waters (larvæ of gnats, notably of the plume-horned gnat Corethra).

Plume, *v.* 4. c. (Later example with *for*.)

1872 'Susan Coolidge' *What Katy did* iv. 49 Dorry began to rather plume himself for fastening them in.

Plumetty (plū·mĕti), *a.* *Her.* [ad. F. *plumeté*: see Plumetis.] (See quot.)

1780 Edmondson *Her.* II. Gloss., When the field is divided into fusils, filled with the ends of feathers, depicted in metal and colour alternately, such field is said to be *Plumetty*. 1923 *Yorksh. Archæol. Jrnl.* XXVII. 156 This is what modern heralds call plumetty.

Plumpening, *vbl. sb.* [f. Plumpen *v.* + ing 1.] The action or process of making or becoming plump.

1926 *Spectator* 1 May 801/2 The plumpening of cherries on lichened wall.

Plumper 1. Add: c. A preparation for making hides plump.

1903 Flemming *Pract. Tanning* 375 Quebracho is not a good plumper, and for this reason some material is necessary to plump the leather.

Plumper 2. Add: 3. b. In extended sense, something uncommonly large of its kind; a whopper. *colloq.*

1881 *Punch* 1 Oct. 155/1 Lovers of England..can hardly do better than help to fill that Purse, which Mr. Punch hopes will prove a 'plumper'.

Plumping (plɒ·mpiŋ), *ppl. a. colloq.* [f. Plump *v.*1 + -ing 2.] Remarkably or strikingly big; 'whacking', 'thumping'.

1903 McNeill *Egregious English* 91 You win by the skin of your teeth or with a plumping majority, as the case may be.

Plum-pudding. Add: d. (See quot.)

1904 *Sci. Amer.* Suppl. 5 Mar. 23551/3 A muscular, fibrous substance known as 'plum pudding' permeates the blubber of the tongue of these two species of whales.

Plum-tree. (Later example.)

1906 U. Sinclair *Jungle* xxvii. 340 Those golden hours when he, too, had a place beneath the shadow of the plum tree.

Plumuleless (plū·miŭl,lĕs), *a.* [f. Plumule + -less.] Having no plumules.

1872 Coues *Key N. Amer. Birds* 223 The plumuleless plumage is generally compact, with thickened, spongy rhachis.

Plunge, *sb.* Add: 1. b. Short for *plunge-bath*.

1896 G. Ade *Artie* i. 4 If they'll put in a punchin'-bag and a plunge they can have my game.

7. plunge-board, a board from which a person may plunge or dive into water; a diving-board.

1908 *Daily Chron.* 15 Feb. 8/5 When a man wants to take a second plunge into the water he has to get out and remount the plunge-board.

Plunge, *v.* Add: 5. (Further example.)

1892 R. Buchanan *Come Live with me* xxiii. 256 Finally ..he plunged out into the darkness and disappeared.

7. d. To come *out of* impetuously, or with a plunging action.

1891 C. Graves *Field Tares* IV. vi. 241 (Born) The Norwich Express plunging out of Liverpool Street Station, exchanges the gas-lighted obscurity..for the frosty brilliance of a snowy morning.

Plunger. Add: 1. c. *U.S.* A type of yacht.

1892 *Outing* Mar. 467/1 Yachting on the Pacific coast dates from about 1869, when the first club, the San Francisco, was organised, though a few small plungers and sloops had long been owned on the bay.

5. plunger-valve, a valve having a plunging action.

1908 *Westm. Gaz.* 2 Jan. 4/1 The crank-case, into the cover of which the cam-shaft and plunger-valves are built.

Plunk, *v.* Add: 2. b. To make a plunking, or plumping noise.

1903 *Cosmopolitan* Sept. 484 Street pianos plunk away unweariedly. 1929 A. Mason *Swansea Dan* 199 The ocean plunked and gubbled as if in a nightmare.

6. *slang.* *U.S.* To shoot.

1891 *Outing* Nov. 138/2, I would plunk the big gobbler I could distinguish from where I lay, and then take chances for another, run or fly. *a* 1909 *Boston Transcript* (Cent. Suppl.) Instead of using old family shot-guns and plunking each other they fought four rounds with bare knuckles.

Plup (plɒp). [Echoic; cf. Plop.] The sound made by a soft plastic body falling on a surface, or by a body falling into a liquid without splashing; an explosive noise of a similar nature, etc.

1911 Rupert Brooke in E. Marsh *Mem.* (1918) p. lxvii, The 'quaint' remarks fall all round one during meal times, with little soft plups like pats of butter. 1926 *Chambers's Jrnl.* Dec. 847/1 The surge of the water down below, and the *plup* of 'escape' above the roof, were but soft sounds.

Plurality. 4 (Earlier example.)

1803 in *Massachusetts Spy* (1804) 18 Jan. (Th.) The public will is sometimes expressed by pluralities instead of majorities.

Pluranimity. [f. L. *plus, plūr-* more, substituted for Un- in Unanimity.] Diversity of opinions.

1907 W. De Morgan *Alice-For-Short* ix. 95 Whatever innate ideas on the subject of oil-painting he possessed, had been disorganised and carefully thrown out of gear by the want of unanimity, or presence of pluranimity, in his instructors.

Plurennial (plurė·niăl), *a.* [f. L. *plus, plūr-* more than one + *annus* year + -al; after Biennial, etc.] Lasting for more than two or three years; occurring once in several years.

1895 W. R. Fisher *Schlich's Man. Forestry* IV. 137 These [generations] may be single or annual, multiple, biennial or plurennial.

Plus. Add: 1. c. *ellipt.* Placed after a round number or a whole number to indicate a smaller or fractional amount more; with a positive amount added; or more, but not less. Also to indicate a slightly higher grade, as *Beta plus* (β +).

1926 *Rep. Consultative Comm. Educ. Adolescent* 185 Raising the school age to 15 plus must lead either to the building of new schools or to the remodelling of existing schools. 1928 *Oxford Mag.* 25 Oct. 40 Till the University finds some benefactor willing to give '£100,000 plus' (to use modern phraseology). 1931 *N. & Q.* 22 Aug. 127/2 If these are classified according to the academic method, from Alpha plus downward.

3. *adj.* (Later examples.)

1928 *Publishers' Weekly* 30 June 2598 The material for the plus sale is always at hand in the book business. 1930 *Publishers' Circular* 2 Aug. 163/2 The whole book business should look on the reprint business as being *plus* business.

3. b. In various games, having an adverse handicap of a number of strokes or points.

1908 A. W. Myers *Compl. Lawn Tennis Player* 117 It will not take him long to discover the kind of decoy that will deliver the 'plus 15.3' men into his clutches. 1909 *Westm. Gaz.* 8 Feb. 12/4 Supposing a plus 3 man is partnered with a steady player whose handicap is 8, the two as a foursome side would be handicapped at 5. *Ibid.* 8 Mar. 12/2 The plus players. 1922 Joanna Cannan *Misty Valley* 203 Isn't it just like you to come up to the club-house..and to send a plus man in to fetch me out? 1927 R. J. B. Sellar *Play!* 32 The newly-joined member..asked if they might have a game together. 'Humph', growled the plus player, 'perhaps. What's your handicap?'

Plus fours (plɒs fōᵊɹs), *pl.* [f. Plus 3 + Four, since, to produce the overhang, four inches is normally added to the length required for ordinary knickerbockers.] A distinctive style of long, wide knickerbockers, or a suit having such knickerbockers, much worn by golfers and often associated with golf. Also *attrib.* in form *plus-four*.

1920 *Isis* 25 Feb. 6/2 [Illustration]..'Plus Fours'. *Ibid.* 12 May 10/2 The desuetude of the traditional grey flannel bags' of the undergraduate...'Plus fours' have succeeded them. 1921 *Ibid.* 1 June p. xii, Knicker (plus four) Suits from 8½ gns. 1922 *Daily Mail* 15 Nov. 5 The plus four suit is not a good type for ski-ing. 1922 Joanna Cannan *Misty Valley* 201 A tall man in plus fours and a yellow waistcoat. 1923 Herd *Golfing Life* 151 The first time I saw a golfer wearing baggy 'plus 4's' I thought he looked like a lassie. 1929 Vachell *Virgin* ix. 154 The Major got himself up 'to kill', wearing a new suit of 'plus fours'.

transf. 1928 *Saturday Even. Post* 10 Mar. 174/3 You can almost visualize the venerable Francis Joseph tweaking away at his plus-four whiskers.

Plus-foured (-fōᵊɹd), *a.* [f. prec. + -ed 2.] Wearing or clad in plus fours.

1927 *Glasgow Herald* 6 Sept. 10/7 Doubtless some have experience..of the plus-foured person.

Plushily (plɒ·ʃili), *adv.* [f. Plushy *a.* + -ly 2.] With plushy material; with plush-covered furniture.

1916 W. J. Locke *Wonderful Year* xiii. 183 The primly and plushily furnished salon.

Plute (plūt). *U.S.* Abbreviation of Plutocrat.

1923 E. F. Wyatt *Invis. Gods* II. iv. 65 'Paul's a plute and a snob..a kind of a cad—proud of using people. 1924 P. Marks *Plastic Age* 97 The tutoring sections were only for the 'plutes' or the athletes, many of whom were subsidized by fraternities.

Pluto (plū·to). *Astr.* [ad. L. *Plūto*, Gr. Πλούτων, the god of the underworld, and brother of Jupiter and Neptune.] A more remote planet than Neptune, discovered in 1930.

1930 *Nature* 19 July 109/2 Harvard Announcement Card, No. 137, gives the following positions of Pluto. 1930 A. G. Whyte *Our World & Us* 83 'Pluto', the latest real planet to be discovered, is about half as big across as the earth, and does its round of the sun in something like 250 years.

Plutocratically (plūtokræ·tikăli), *adv.* [f. Plutocratic + -al + ly 2.] In a plutocratic manner; by plutocratic persons.

1913 W. J. Locke *Stella Maris* xx. 238 Only the splendour ..of plutocratically owned vehicles meets the enraptured vision.

Plutolo·gical, *a.* [f. Plutology + -ic + -al.] Of or pertaining to plutology or the science of wealth.

1920 *Edin. Rev.* July 80 The whole plutological apparatus was developed—banking, investment, partnership, joint stock companies, and even trusts.

Pluvialine, *a.* (Earlier example.)

1872 Coues *Key N. Amer. Birds* 239 The pluvialine and scolopacine birds form the bulk of the division.

Pluviometric, *a.* (Later example.)

1917 McAdie *Princ. Aërography* 218 The term 'pluviometric' was introduced by Angot to indicate the ratio of the mean daily rainfall of a particular month to the mean daily rainfall of the whole year.

Plywood (plai·wud). [f. (*Three-*, etc.) *ply wood*.] Thin boarding made by gluing or cementing two or more layers or plies of wood together with the grain of one layer running at right angles to that of the next (by which method great strength and resistance to warping are secured). Also *attrib.*

1907 *Timber Trades Jrnl.* 13 Apr. 818/2 Advt., Agents for Swedish..wood Goods..Ply Wood (Oak, Birch, Alder etc.). 1920 *Glasgow Herald* 30 Nov. 3 An action..to determine the ownership of about 109 tons of veneer or plywood. 1922 Schlich *Man. Forestry* I. 228 These pines..are also used for butter boxes, plywood, etc. 1925 *Countries of World* VI. 3864/2 One of the most wonderful developments has been the invention of ply-wood, a material of infinite adaptability. 1926 *Glasgow Herald* 1 Oct. 5 The prosperity of the plywood industry.

Pneumatic, *a.* Add: 1. e. Operated by means of compressed air; used esp. of various tools.

1902 *Encycl. Brit.* XXXI. 801/1 Sometimes, when only a small amount of work is to be done, pneumatic tools are brought to heavy pieces of material. *Ibid.* 803/1 The pneumatic jack..is placed below the piece to be lifted, and operates directly. 1911 *Ibid.* XXVII. 40/2 Pneumatic drills are usually worked by little motors having oscillating cylinders, by which the air and exhaust ports are covered and uncovered. 1930 *Daily Express* 9 Sept 8/7 The noise of pneumatic drills has..been found to annoy the patients in a London Hospital.

Pneumatolysis (pniŭmătɒ·lisis, niū-). *Petrol.* [f. Pneumato- + *Lysis.] The emission of hot vapours or gases from igneous magmas or the action of such vapours in decomposing rocks or altering their constituents. Pneu:matoly·tic *a.*, of, pertaining to, or resulting from, pneumatolysis.

1896 J. A. Phillips *Ore Deposits* (ed. 2) I. 129 He uses the word *pneumatolysis* for this action. *Ibid.* 173 There seems no urgent reason for adopting the theory of pneumatolytic, in preference to ordinary hydrothermal action. 1903 *Nature* 26 Feb. 406/1 The greisen is an example of Prof. Vogt's 'pneumatolytic' action in thoroughly acid rocks. 1904 *Smithsonian Rep.* 335 The importance of pneumatolysis in forming ore deposits was emphasized by the discovery..of a number of economically important deposits. 1911 *Encycl. Brit.* XXI. 869/1 The alteration of felspar into kaolin or china clay is also a pneumatolytic process.

Pneumatomachian. b. *adj.* (Example.)

1915 *Hastings's Encycl. Relig. & Ethics* VIII. 225/2 The leading doctrine of the Macedonians is found in the thesis characterized by their opponents as 'Pneumatomachian', viz. that the Holy Ghost is not to be designated Θεός.

Pneumatophore. Add: 3. An apparatus for providing oxygen for respiration.

1904 *Sci. Amer.* Suppl. 27 Feb. 23545/1 In the earlier forms of the pneumatophor, the supply of oxygen was adjustable by the wearer of the apparatus.

Pneumo-. Add: Pneumo-massa·ge, massage of the drum of the ear by means of air-pressure. Pneumotherapeu·tics, -the·rapy = *Pneumatotherapeutics* (see Pneumato-).

1903 *Detroit Med. Jrnl.* Feb. 715 (Cent. Suppl.) *Pneumo-massage. 1910 *Practitioner* Feb. 242 Even if pneumo-massage does not improve the hearing power, it greatly diminishes the subjective noises. 1910 *Encycl. Brit.* I. 270/2 *Pneumotherapeutics, or the treatment of disease by artificially prepared atmospheres. 1903 *Med. Record* 11 July 71 (Cent. Suppl.) *Pneumotherapy is a 'branch of physical and physiological treatment.

Pneumography. Add: c. A method for facilitating X-raying of tissues by the introduction of air.

1929 *Encycl. Brit.* IV. 21/2 It is sometimes difficult to say just where a brain tumour may be. In such cases use may be made of ventriculography or cerebral pneumography.

Pneus (niūz), *pl.* [f. Pneumatic.] Pneumatic tyres.

1902 C. N. & A. M. Williamson *Lightning Conductor* 18 On roads like these of Dieppe it would be soothing to have 'pneus', as they call them. 1907 — in *Strand Mag.* Nov. 500/1 [The car], with heated pneus, topped a commanding hill.

Poach, *v.*2 Add: 9. b. In various games: To enter a partner's portion of the field or court and deprive him of some of his share in the game.

1889 W. M. Brownlee *Lawn Tennis* 167 He need not be profusely apologetic when he poaches unsuccessfully. 1919 Hibbons *Lawn Tennis* 85 With the man on the other side also at the net and indulging in poaching, he is often very difficult to pass with strokes from the back of the court. 1928 *Daily Express* 9 July 13/3 The pretty little Australian girl..would have won if her partner had not 'poached' and put himself out of position.

Poachable (pōᵘ·tʃăb'l), *a.* [f. Poach *v.*2 + -able.] Capable of being poached.

1924 *Public Opinion* 22 Feb. 169/1 The open wood I seldom visited,—all that was poachable having been poached long before.

Poacher 1. Add: poacher-pocket, a large concealed pocket in a coat used by poachers.

1925 G. Burrard *Big Game Hunting* 181 Two 'hare' or 'poacher' pockets will be found most useful on occasions.

Pochette (poʃet). [ad. F. *pochette* dim. of *poche* pocket.] 1. a. A small pocket or fob.

1913 W. De la Mare *Peacock Pie* 55 A watch..He lifted from the book where it was ticking And crammed in his pochette.

b. A pouch or hand-bag of cloth or leather carried by women.

1923 *Weekly Dispatch* 11 Mar., When jewels are worn in the hair the vanity-bag becomes a satin or crêpe pochette, fastened with a buckle of jewels. 1927 *Glasgow Herald* 11 Mar. 10/7 The reticule, vanity bag, under-arm bag, or pochette seems capable of containing almost all the little things that Eve wants here below. 1930 *Daily Tel.* 9 Apr. 9/2 If you will make yourself pochettes to match your hats.

2. A small violin that can be carried in the pocket; a kit.

1890 *Century Dict.*

Pocket, *sb.* Add: 3. a. (Further example.)

1930 *Times* 25 Mar. 24/7 Cash in hand and at bank is £110,575..We are stronger in the pocket by £50,000.

6. (Further example.)

1893 L. M. Douglas *Man. Pork Trade* 89 Exposed portions such as the 'pocket', made by removal of the blade-bone, should be dusted with a mixture of food preservative..and some finely ground sharps or bran.

7. d. A portion of the atmosphere characterized by different physical conditions from surrounding parts, on entering which aircraft are liable to drop.

1919 C. P. Thompson *Cocktails* 46 The suddenly uncontrolled Hun staggered and whirled in a treacherous 'pocket'.

12. a. (Further examples.)

1846 E. Bryant *California* vi. 71 Once a week is as often as the most..fastidious exquisite of the party consults his pocket mirror. 1848 N. R. Forster *Stowe Catal.* 2nd Day, p. 11, Lot 166 *note*, Pocket-comb. 1887 W. S. Gilbert *Ruddigore* (1895) 222 Nearly all are wont to use their pocket-combs in public places. 1920 W. De Morgan *Affair of Dishonour* xiv. 214 Every spruce coxcomb nowadays has his pocket-mirror, to comb his artificial locks out. 1913 *Punch* 17 Sept. 252 Portrait of gentleman using pocket-clipper to trim beard at back of neck.

13. pocket gopher = Gopher *sb.*1; pocket-hunter (see quot.); pocket-size *a.*, of a size suitable for carrying in the pocket; so pocket-sized *a.*

1873 Eggleston *Myst. Metrop.* iv. 37 She would..explain how the *pocket-gophers built their mounds. 1875 *Amer. Naturalist* IX. 150 The foot-hills of the main range, where the pocket gophers..begin to claim the soil. 1906 *Chambers's Jrnl.* Feb. 159/1 They [prospectors] include the '*pocket-hunter' who disdains to search for gold except in the form of pockets. 1907 *Daily Chron.* 14 Aug. 3/1 A new *pocket-sized edition of Mr. Edward Hulme's 'Wild Fruits of the Countryside' is being published. 1909 *Ibid.* 13 Nov. 3/2 They form a serviceable little group of *pocket-size manuals.

Pocket, *v.* Add: 8. c. Of a vein of ore: To form a pocket.

1873 J. H. Beadle *Undevel. West* xviii. 336 A vein.. 'pinching' and 'pocketing' alternately towards the interior. 1878 — *Western Wilds* xxiv. 563 It may 'pocket' suddenly in a chamber the size of a keg.

Pocket-book. 2. (Later example.)

1930 *Publishers' Weekly* 8 Mar. 1182/2 Advt., Tours in Northern Italy..and Switzerland for light luggage and a light pocketbook.

Pocket-handkerchief. (Earlier examples.)

1645 *Essex Inst. Hist. Coll.* L. 326, 3 pocket handkerchiefs. 1738 *Ibid.* XVIII. 99 [I] went off in ye morn[in]g and left my Pocket handkerchief. 1760 Washington *Diaries* I. 126 Pockethandkerchiefs servd the purposes of Table Cloths and Napkins.

Pocket-hole. Add: b. The hole left in a side of bacon when the blade-bone is removed.

1896 L. M. Douglas *Receipt Bk.* 15 The pocket holes are the weakest part of the side, and can only be maintained sweet by dusting into them some powdered antiseptic.

Pocket-picking, *ppl. a.* That picks pockets.

1868 Geo. Eliot *Ess.* (1884) 329 A poor pocket-picking scoundrel, who will steal your loose pence while you are listening round the platform.

Po·cketwards, *adv.* [-wards.] In the direction of one's pocket.

1909 H. G. Wells *Tono-Bungay* III. i. 280 He made a motion pocketwards, that gave us an invincible persuasion that he had a sample upon him.

Pockety, *a.* 1. Also *transf.*

1920 Galsworthy *In Chancery* II. x. 204 The atmosphere of his house was strange and pockety when Jolyon came in and told them of the dog Balthasar's death.

Pock-mark (pɒ·kmāɹk), *v.* [f. *pock-mark* Pock *sb.* 4.] *trans.* To disfigure as with pock-marks.

1908 *Flag, Bk. of Union Jack Club* 39 The floors lower down were pock-marked with splashes of the liquid. 1925 *Scribner's Mag.* Sept. 228/2 The chalky soil was pockmarked with shell craters. 1928 *Daily Express* 17 Apr. 10/2 Petrol pumps that pockmark the English countryside.

Pocosin. Also 7 pocosen. (Earlier examples.)

1681 *New Castle Court Rec.* 504, 74 perches to a Corner marked spannish oake standing neare a pocosen. 1700 *Maryland Hist. Mag.* XIX. 347 At a bounded red oake by a pocoson.

Poddy (pɒ·di). *Austral.* A hand-fed calf.

1927 B. Cronin *Red Dawson* xiii. 194 His whole outfit was five old cows and a coupler poddies. 1930 H. S. Palmer *Men are Human* xxv. 235 He's tame as a poddy calf.

Podger 2 (pɒ·dʒəɹ). [Of unknown origin.] A small lever inserted into a hole in the head of a screw or bolt in order to turn it.

Podginess (pɒ·dʒinĕs). [f. Podgy *a.* + -ness.] Podgy condition.

1924 *Glasgow Herald* 3 Jan. 6 His..ancestor had long subsided into whiskered podginess and flaccid inertia.

Po·dging, *vbl. sb.* [f. Podge *v.* + -ing 1.] The action of the verb Podge; slow and heavy walking.

1884 Ruskin *Bible Amiens* (1886) iv. 98 What with their little lodgings and stodgings and podgings about it [Dover cliff], they have managed to make it look no bigger than a moderate-sized limekiln.

Podiatrist (pŏdai·ătrist). [f. Podo- + Gr. ἰατρός physician + -ist.] One who treats diseases in the hands and feet; a chiropodist. So Podi·atry, chiropody.

1929 E. W. Springs *Above bright blue Sky* 97 I've got to bobble along and see my podiatrist.

Podophyllin. (Earlier example.)

1851 C. Cist *Cincinnati* 211 Jacob S. Merrel..prepares extracts..such as podophyllin.

Poetizing, *vbl. sb.* (Further example.)

1888 F. H. Williams *Atman* (1891) 243 He is probably bilious, but that is no excuse for his threadbare poetizings.

Poetry. 7. Add: poetry-book, a book containing a collection of poems, esp. one used in schools.

1877 Amelia B. Edwards (*title*) A Poetry-Book of Elder Poets. 1881 Stevenson *Virginibus Puerisque* 176 Whether we regard life as a lane leading to a dead wall..or pule in little atheistic poetry-books about its vanity and brevity [etc.]. 1903 A. McNeill *Egregious Engl.* 102 The demand for poetry-books by new writers has practically ceased to exist.

Pogo (pōᵘ·go). [Of doubtful origin.] A hopping or jumping game introduced into England from the Continent about 1921; a pogo-stick. Pogo-stick, a short pole having a cross-piece for the feet and a strong spring attached at the foot, used in the game of pogo. Pogo *v. intr.*, to play at pogo.

1921 *Glasgow Herald* 30 Aug. 7 Pogo, if it catches on, will make us all Spring-Heeled Jacks...To Pogo you place one foot on each step, clutch the top of the pole firmly in both hands, and hop. That is all. 1924 *Punch* 24 Sept. 338 A dozen well-mounted pogo-players...American pogo-sticks are in every way superior to ours.

Pogrom (pŏgrɒ·m), *v.* [f. the sb.] *trans.* To massacre in a pogrom.

1915 *Boston Jrnl.* 1 Feb. 3/2 [The Jews in Galicia] are being..pogromed.

Pogromist (pŏgrɒ·mist). [f. Pogrom + -ist.] An organizer of or a participant in a pogrom.

1907 *Athenæum* 26 Jan. 99 Small wonder that the 'pogromists' laugh at Europe, and now pursue their work without intermission or disguise.

Pogy. Also poggy. (Earlier attrib. examples.)

1857 [see *Chum *sb.*2]. 1864 *Ann. Rep. Agric. Maine* 42 Rock weed, muscle bed and pogy chum will make grass grow. 1880 *Harper's Mag.* Aug. 347/1 The 'pogy' business was the catching of porgies and menhaden for their oil.

Poikilothermal, *a.* (Example.)

1911 J. A. Thomson *Biology of Seasons* IV. 335 In the hibernating animal..the heat-regulating mechanism ceases to act, and the creature is saved..by becoming temporarily cold-blooded (or poikilothermal).

Poilu (pwalü). *colloq.* [F. *poilu* hairy, unshaved.] A French soldier.

1915 G. Adam *Behind Scenes at Front* 183 France has every reason to be proud of her infantry, the 'poilus' as they have been called in this war. 1918 E. M. Roberts *Flying Fighter* 54 We were away north of the French lines, but that made no difference to the poilus, who also were to attend the ceremony. 1926 *Glasgow Herald* 30 Nov. 8 The adventures of two poilus who miss the train that should have brought them back to barracks.

Poinciana (poinsi,ā·nă). [mod.L., f. the name of M. de *Poinci*, Governor of the Antilles in the 17th century.] A genus of tropical leguminous flowering trees, commonly called *flower fence*; a tree of this genus.

1905 *Chambers's Jrnl.* May 367/1 Probably the most beautiful and conspicuous trees [in the Bermudas] are the poincianas, [etc.]. 1908 R. W. Chambers *Firing Line* iii. 36 Those are royal poincianas, if you please. 1908 *Daily Chron.* 29 Aug. 7/4 There are plenty of wild flowering trees!—magnolia, poinciana, china-berry.

Point, *sb.*1 Add: A. 13. (Further example).

1876 *Coursing Calendar* 125 Irish Nell took the early points, and Laconic the latter..which made it a tie.

e. In Boxing. *To beat* or *defeat on points*: to defeat (an adversary) by securing more points in a number of rounds, not by knocking him out. So *to lose* or *win on points*, etc.

1904 *C. B. Fry's Mag.* June 301/1 Aeneas called 'time', and gave a decision..'on points'. 1929 *Daily Express* 7 Nov. 13/5 Young Stribling, the American boxer, defeated Maurice Griselle France, on points in a ten-round..contest. 1929 *Evening News* 18 Nov. 16/4 Rolland..beat Wilhelm Bech on points. 1930 *Cambridge Daily News* 25 Sept. 7/4 Campolo..will probably retire for good..if Sharkey gives him the full count, or if he loses on points.

15. (Further example.)

1906 L. C. Cornford *Defenceless Islands* 98 Prices have dropped six points. A point is the hundredth part of a penny.

19. c. (Later example.)

1920 *Blackw. Mag.* Jan. 108/1 These marshy channels.. are the invariable point of any hunted boar.

d. A stopping-place on a tramway, omnibus, or other route, from which fare-stages are reckoned. *colloq.*

1907 *Westm. Gaz.* 20 July 11/2 The only way to effect this is to revise the 'points', so as to make the journeys shorter, while maintaining useful and popular penny lengths.

e. Any locality or place considered in some special connexion. (Not clearly distinguished from B. 9.)

1903 *N. Y. Even. Post* 19 Aug., The number here is now estimated at 21,000 persons from Eastern points, with fully 35,000 persons in addition from California. 1926 *Publishers' Weekly* 22 May 1684/2 Some of us here get supplies from other points that they know nothing about. *Ibid.* 18 Dec. 2256 The business must be going to distant points—New York, Chicago, etc.

20. b. *Sculpture.* Any one of a series of holes drilled in a piece of marble to the depth to which the material has to be cut away.

1911 A. Toft *Modelling & Sculpture* 254 A good pointer will keep all his 'points' a little 'full', by never allowing the needle to go quite home.

B. 1. d. (Later example.) Also *to a (fine) point*; to a precise form; perfectly.

1888 *Pittsburg Times* 26 Jan. (Farmer) Boiled down to a fine point bondsmen are in demand. 1902 G. H. Lorimer *Lett. Self-made Merchant* xvii. 253 When she was through I knew that I'd been licked—polished right off to a point. 1911 H. S. Harrison *Queed* iv. 45 The *Post*, not to put too fine a point upon it, had for a time run fast to seed.

2. b. Also, any tapering piece *of* land, or *of* rocks, woods, etc., constituting a special feature of this.

1660 *Rec. of Warwick* (R. I.) 370 His point of Meddowe on the south side of Occupessuatuxet Cove. 1682 *Rec. of Providence* (R. I.) XIV. 101 A black Oake tree standing upon a point of Rocks. 1704 *Ibid.* V. 196–7 Neare unto a poynt of land butting on the Salt River. 1741 in *Col. Georgia Hist. Soc.* II. 252 A point of woods which..stretches itself out towards the south-east. 1772 D. Taitt in *Trav. Amer. Col.* 501, I..viewed this Town which Stands upon a point of Land on the North west side of the River. 1837 Irving *Capt. Bonneville* I. xxiv. 237 The whole band soon disappeared behind a point of woods. 1856 Strickland *Peter Cartwright* xxi. 328 We rode two miles, and the point of timber was plain in view.

f. Either of the extensions at the front end of a saddle-tree.

1908 *Animal Managem.* 166 The front arch extends below the side bars; the extension is known as the 'points', and these are intended to help the girths and prevent the saddle from heeling over.

g. The tip of the lower jaw; the spot on which a knock-out blow is dealt.

1901 R. Fitzsimmons *Phys. Cult. & Self-Defense* 159, I saw Fitzsimmons' right hand reach the point of Corbett's jaw. 1915 Corri *30 Yrs. Boxing Referee* 229 There is no sleeping-draught like a punch on the point, and no sleep so sound and dreamless. 1923 *Daily Mail* 16 Feb. 8 He once caught Lewis with a hard right near the point.

h. The leading part of a herd of cattle; esp. in phr. *to ride point*: to ride at the head of a herd on the march in order to direct it. *U.S.*

1916 'B. M. Bower' *Phantom Herd* xiv. 245 You see a herd drifting before a storm, maybe—a blizzard like yesterday, with your pal riding point.

3. e. Also, the tapering extremity of a lightning conductor; a socket connected by wiring to a source of electricity from which an electric lamp is suspended or from which current can be obtained for various purposes.

1766 *Essex Inst. Hist. Coll.* LII. 275 A new Meeting-House building..was struck with Lightning: it had Points and a Conductor as far as the Bellfree. 1775 *Ibid.* XIII. 208 They have a handsome clock, points to the house, a fine walk on the top [etc.]. 1927 W. E. Collinson *Contemp. Engl.* 90 The fixing of wall-plugs or points.

10. b. (Later example.)

1901 H. James *Sacred Fount* 17 Having a reputation for 'point' to keep up, she was always under arms.

C. 6. b. *To lie to point*: (Of game-birds) to remain on the ground until they are pointed; to lie to the dogs.

1903 S. E. White *Forest* x. 122 The birds had proved themselves most uncultivated..by hopping promptly into trees instead of lying to point and then flushing.

D. 14. point-charge, an electric charge regarded as concentrated in a mathematical point; point-event, something conceived of as having a definite position in space and in time but no extent or duration; point-paper (example); point-shooting, shooting game from a fixed point; point-source, a small source of illumination or other radiation regarded as a point; points victory, a victory won on points.

1903 S. J. Barrett *Electro-Magn. Theory* 66 The law of inverse squares..is due to the continuity of the electric displacement.., the flux from a *point-charge being distributed equally in all directions. 1928 Joad *Future of Life* 36 Faced with a universe consisting of ephemeral *point-events, the mind selects from it certain characteristics which have a particular interest for it. 1899 Mackail *Wm. Morris* ii. 44 *Point-paper'—paper, that is, divided into minute spaces, each representing a single knot of the carpet. 1874 J. W. Long *Wild-Fowl Shooting* 71 For *point-shooting, shooting from a blind on shore, or in the edge of the willows from a boat, a few hints may be welcome. 1876 *Fur, Fin & Feather* Sept. 90 We prepared to move out into the clear water onto a log, and there get some point shooting. 1903 *Nature* 1 Jan. 203/1 If the *point-source is in motion, the pan-potential requires Dopplerisation as well as the ordinary potential. 1929 *Daily Express* 7 Nov. 13/2 Jackson's *points victory was about the most easily gained of the night.

Point, *sb.*3 b. Add: *point russe*.

1879 *Sylvia's Embroidery Bk.* 241 The chain stitch and point russe embroidery is worked with red silk. 1882 Caulfeild & Saward *Dict. Needlework* 430/1 Take the darkest shade of wool and work the outside line of the design in Point Russe.

Point, *v.*1 Add: 7. b. *Sculpture.* To mark at a series of points on (a block of stone or marble) the depth to which the initial working or roughing-out is to be done.

1877 Amelia B. Edwards *Thous. Miles up Nile* 423 A recent writer..is of opinion that the Egyptian sculptors did not even 'point' their work beforehand. 1911 A. Toft *Modelling & Sculpture* 254 The appearance of a work when pointed is not pleasing, covered all over with innumerable holes, and little mounds of marble projecting between these holes.

9. c. *trans.* To indicate or state.

1928 *Publishers' Weekly* 12 May 1957 The effect on books by established authors like Galsworthy's 'Silver Spoon' and Ferber's 'Show Boat' could not be as clearly pointed.

17. *U.S.* To turn, guide, or deflect (cattle) in a particular direction.

1903 A. Adams *Log Cowboy* iv. 42 Priest sent Officer to the left and myself to the right to point in the leaders. 1916 'B. M. Bower' *Phantom Herd* xiv, You're trying to point the herd then..we'll say.

Point-bla·nker. [f. Point-blank + -er 1.] A point-blank shot.

1830 J. F. Cooper *Water Witch* II. vii, 'Run in the quoin, and..give her a point-blanker', said the gruff old seaman.

Point-duty. Also *attrib.*

1908 *Daily Chron.* 20 June 1/3 A point-duty constable.. was knocked down..by a taxi-cab.

Pointer. Add: 3. h. (See quot.)

1872 C. H. Eden *My Wife & I in Queensland* 36 Twelve bullocks is the usual number in a team, the two polers and the leaders being steady old stagers; the pair next to the pole are called the 'pointers'.

9. d. The person who lays or points a gun. *U.S.*

1904 *Sci. Amer.* 18 June 475 The turrets are trained by one man, the trainer; and each gun is pointed by another man, the pointer, who fires the gun.

e. A workman who does the ornamental work on the backs of gloves.

1903 *Sci. Amer.* Suppl. 24 Jan. 22629/3 Some make the gloves,..others, called 'pointers', work the ornamental lines on the back. 1921 *Dict. Occup. Terms* (1927) § 411.

f. The person who 'points' a block of marble.

1911 [see *Point *sb.* A 20 b].

11. *U.S.* A herdsman riding at the head of a herd of cattle on the march to keep it going in the desired direction.

1869 *Overland Monthly* III. 126 On the march the mighty herd sometimes strings out miles in length, and then it has 'pointers', who ride abreast of the head of the column, and 'siders', who keep the stragglers out of the chaparral.

Pointful (poi·ntful), *a.* [f. Point *sb.*1 + -ful.] Full of point; apposite, pertinent. So Poi·ntfulness.

1897 *Daily Tel.* 4 Jan. 5/4 Similarly, and with greater pointfulness, it was remarked that the Select Committee.. never consulted any person who was not in full work. 1931 E. Dudley in *Cath. Gaz.* Feb. 71/2 The story—old, even apocryphal, it may be, but certainly typical and pointful—of Queen Victoria [etc.].

Pointing, *vbl. sb.*1 10. Delete † *Obs.*

1902 *Act 2 Edw. VII* c. 29 § 2 Fishing for trout..by what is known as double rod fishing, or cross line fishing, or set lines,..or by striking the fish..or by pointing.

Poi·ntman. [f. Point *sb.*1 and *v.*1 + Man.]

1. *U.S.* = *Pointer 11.

1903 A. Adams *Log Cowboy* iii. 28 Two riders, known as point men rode out and well back from the lead cattle.

2. = Pointsman 2.

1927 *Observer* 20 Nov. 11/3 It..bore a number of legends; on the footboard, 'Step on the gas'; on the bonnet, 'Don't look inside', and 'Pointman, let us pass'.

Poise, *v.* 7. Also, to hover or be poised in readiness *for* (something).

1896 Shelden *Bro. Keeper* iii. (1899) 64 The gravity of events that were evidently poising for a crisis left little room for anything but sober feeling.

Poison, *sb.* 5. Add: poison gas, any poisonous gas used in warfare; often extended to include any gas or vapour causing sneezing, tears, blisters, etc.; poison mask, a gas-mask; poison-thread, a stinging or thread-cell in cœlenterates.

1915 *Listening-Post* 25 Nov. 33/1 Your boss old Kaiser Bill Cant play the game He uses *poison gas Germs and liquid flame. 1919 *Athenæum* 23 May 360/1 'Liquid fire' and 'poison gas',..are offspring of the same ancient instinct that gave us 'war-gear' [etc.]. 1916 *War Illustr.* IV. 91 *Poison Masks for School Children. 1915 E. R. Lankester *Diversions of Naturalist* 92 They were paralysed (by microscopic *poison-threads like those of the sea-anemones).

b. poison-creeper = *poison-ivy*; poison-nut (earlier example of *b*); poison-vine (examples).

1930 Rose Macaulay *Relations* viii. 101 Mind that *poison-creeper. 1849 Balfour *Man. Bot.* § 947 Strychnos Nux-Vomica, the *Poison-nut or Koochla,..supplies the substance called Nux-Vomica. 1785 A. Ellicott in *Life & Lett.* 41 *Poison-Vine is in great abundance. 1802 — *Jrnl.* 212 My journey up the river was disagreeable and painful, being blistered by the rhus radicans, (poison vine,) from head to feet. 1892 Marah E. Ryan *Told in Hills* II. i. 24 Here and there a poison-vine flashed back defiance under its crimson banners.

Poke, *sb.*4 3. poke-weed (earlier example).

1751 *Gentl. Mag.* July 306/2 Tho' the Phytolacca be known to almost every one in *America*, by the name of *pokeweed, ..yet I think it proper..to give a description of it.

Po·ke-berry. *U.S.* [f. Poke *sb.*4 3.] The berry of *Phytolacca decandra* or the plant itself.

1774 P. V. Fithian *Jrnl.* (1900) 169 To day Harry boil'd up a compound of Poke-Berries, Vinegar, Sugar &c to make red Ink or Liquid. 1834 Carruthers *Kentuckian in N. Y.* II. 215 His face looks like it was boiled in poke-berry juice and indigo. 1858– [see Poke *sb.*4 3].

Poker, *sb.*4 (Earlier examples.)

1836 J. Hildreth *Campaigns Rocky Mts.* I. xv. 128 The M— lost some cool hundreds last night at poker. 1842 *Knickerbocker Mag.* XX. 305 Squeezing a great deal of boisterous amusement out of a game of 'poker'.

b. poker-face, a countenance appropriate to a poker-player; a face in which a person's thoughts or feelings are not revealed; a person having such a face; so poker-faced *a.*

1885 *Encycl. Brit.* XIX. 283/2 A good *poker face* is essential; the countenance should not betray the nature of the hand. 1924 Mulford *Rustlers' Valley* x. 123 He glanced around the circle and found poker faces, but there was a light in Baldy's eyes that warmed him. 1927 *Daily Express* 31 Mar. 8/3 They betrayed no emotion...They have all acquired the poker face. The 'photocracy', to use a word coined by my old friend..is poker-faced.

Pokerish, *a.*2 (Earlier examples.)

1827 *Massachusetts Spy* 21 Nov. (Th.) A patriarchal ram, who would fight anything but a pokerish looking ducking gun. 1833 H. Barnard in *Maryland Hist. Mag.* XIII. 352, I feel quite pokerish in this region.

Polar, *a.* Add: 1. Also, pertaining to or connected with the poles of another planet.

1910 *Chambers's Jrnl.* Jan. 7/1 Professor Lowell's explanation is that as the northern summer on Mars draws nigh the northern polar cap begins to melt.

b. *Polar air*, cold air that has come from high latitudes; *Polar front* (see quot.).

1928 D. Brunt *Meteorol.* 73 On account of their difference of origin, the cold and warm air are called '*Polar air' and 'Equatorial air' respectively. *Ibid.* 72 The surface of separation of cold and warm air is known as the *Polar Front.

Polarity. Add: 2. e. The tendency observed in some animals of a severed head-piece to develop a tail or of a severed tail-piece to develop a head; a similar tendency in parts of plants.

1863 J. A. Allman in *Rep. Brit. Assoc.* 392 There is thus manifested in the formative force of the Tubularia-stem a well-marked polarity. 1901 T. H. Morgan *Regeneration* 38 At the end of a piece of an animal from which a head has been cut off a new head develops...Allman was the first to give the name 'polarity' to this phenomenon.

Polarization. Add: 3. b. = *Polarity 2 e.

1893 J. Loeb *Mech. Concept. Life* (1912) 93 Likewise, there are animals every piece of which produces, at either end, that organ toward which it was directed in the normal condition. We may speak in such cases of polarization.

Pole, *sb.*1 Add: 1. b. Phr. *up the pole*: crazed, drunk or tipsy; in a difficulty; at one's wits' end; also (among soldiers), in or into favour with one's superiors; of good report. *slang* and *colloq.*

1896 *Daily News* 1 Apr. 7/6 She remonstrated with the latter, and told him he was 'up a pole'—i.e., in the wrong. 1897 Barrère & Leland *Dict. Slang* II. 137/2 *Pole, up the* (military), thought well of by your superiors [etc.]. 1899 *Daily Mail* 29 Mar. 5/1 When there are nineteen Frenchmen to four Englishmen they were slightly up the pole. 1903 *N. & Q.* Ser. IX. XI. 238/1 'Have a drink, Tom?' 'No, I'm going up the pole.' 1904 *Westm. Gaz.* 19 Mar. 7/2 Plaintiff's definition of the phrase 'up the pole' differed from that of her cousin..who said it meant being drunk. Mrs. Frasier said that it..meant being crazy. 1905 *Daily Chron.* 14 Dec. 6/4 Alec went to football smoker. Came home up the pole at one a.m. 1916 E. V. Lucas *Vermilion Box* 165 It must require an awful lot of pluck...Either pluck or so much panic that one was practically up the pole with it. 1922 *Daily Mail* 20 Dec. 3 Keith came to her, saying he was 'up the pole and in a frightful mess'.

2. e. The inner rail or boundary fence in a racecourse; the position nearest this; esp. in phr. *to have the pole*.

1851 *Fraser's Mag.* XLIII. 657/1 The distance round is calculated at a mile,..for a saddle horse that has the pole, it comes practically to a little less. *footnote*, A horse 'has the pole', means that he has drawn the place nearest the inside boundary-fence of the track. 1868 H. Woodruff *Trotting Horse* xxiv. 206, I had the pole with Kemble Jackson, and soon took the lead. 1902 A. D. McFaul *Ike Glidden* xxii. 198 This stroke apparently gave the friends of the colt more confidence in the result, as drawing the pole was a position in favor of the colt.

5. a. *pole-bridge* (later example), *-fence* (earlier example), *plantation*. b. *pole-jumper* (example).
1850 *Congress. Globe* 29 Jan. 240/1 Now, his colleague must start by the most direct route the 23rd of November, making provision for..contingencies of travel over corduroy roads, *pole bridges, mud turnpikes, etc. 1788 Washington *Diaries* III. 346 All hands were..finishing the *Pole fence round the Barley and Pease in field No. 1. 1908 *Westm. Gaz.* 1 July 8/4 Quite recently Szathmary, the *pole-jumper, broke the Hungarian record. 1888 T. Bright *Pole Plantations & Underwoods* i. 1 A *pole plantation is an assemblage of young trees, the produce of plants that have been inserted in the soil at regular distances, or of the stems formed from such plants after their having been cut for poles.

c. **pole-bean** (examples); **pole-board**, a board attached at the end of a pole for displaying notices, advertisements, etc.; **pole-cure** *v. trans.*, to cure (tobacco) by suspending it on poles; **pole-dab**, **-flounder**, a species of flat-fish; the witch (*Pleuronectes cynoglossus*); **pole-dray**, a dray or cart having a pole, by which it is drawn; **pole-horse** (example); **pole-mule**, a mule harnessed next the pole of a wagon; **pole-rose**, a rose suitable for training on a pole; **pole-wound**, a wound inflicted with a pole.
1857 *Trans. Ill. Agric. Soc.* III. 503 There are many varieties of *pole beans...Pole beans should be planted in warm and rich soil. 1871 Mrs. Stowe *Oldtown F. Stories* 246 There was thick pole-beans quite up to the buttery-door. 1909 *Westm. Gaz.* 29 Dec. 6/4 Others..carrying *pole-boards setting forth all deceased's honours and titles. 1899 *U.S. Dept. Agric.* Rep. 62. 30 The present method of manipulating these tobaccos after they are *pole-cured is quite different from what it was years ago. 1896 J. T. Cunningham *Marketable Marine Fishes* 233 The witch..has been called the *pole dab, *pole flounder, and long flounder by English naturalists. 1848 H. W. Haygarth *Bush Life Australia* v. 49 In some districts..shaft-drays are used; but *pole-drays are found to be more suitable to the nature of the country. 1889 *Harper's Mag.* June 160/2 The leaders sprang upward and onward.., the *pole-horses simultaneously crashing backward and downward. 1862 O. W. Norton *Army Lett.* 106 The driver riding the near *pole mule and guiding his team with one line. 1848 W. Paul *Rose Gard.* 67 Pillar or *Pole Roses. 1908 Hardy *Dynasts* III. iv. vi. 417 Who knows but that we should have been kings too, but for my crooked legs and your running *pole-wound?

Pole, *sb.*[2] Add: 1. (Recent fig. example.)
1916 K. J. Saunders *Adv. Chr. Soul* 68 When God's will is thy heart's pole, Then is Christ thy very soul.
10. **pole-paper** (see quot.); **pole-shoe** = *pole-piece*.
1926 *Gloss. Electr. Terms* (Brit. Engin. Stand.) 120 Pole-paper, pole-finding paper, a porous paper soaked in certain chemicals which undergoes a visible change when moistened and applied to the positive and negative poles of an electric circuit, thus serving to identify them. 1910 Hobart *Dict. Mech. Engin.*, *Pole shoe*, the extended extremity of the usual pole. It is generally a separate piece from the main pole.

Po·le-boat. [f. Pole *sb.*[1] + Boat *sb.*] A boat propelled with a pole or poles.
1827 A. Sherwood *Gaz. Georgia* 22 Cargoes..are thrown into pole boats. 1835 W. G. Simms *Partisan* 245 At this point the river ceased to be navigable even for the common poleboats of the country. 1841 — *Kinsmen* I. xiv. 163 Wherever a pole-boat had made its way, there had the name of Jack Bannister found repeated echoes.

Po·le-boating, *vbl. sb.* [f. prec. + -ing[1].] Travelling or transporting goods, etc., in pole-boats.
1837 A. Sherwood *Gaz. Georgia* (ed. 3) 193 A revolution in the mode and manner of transshipping goods must take place. The slow, tedious and expensive process of pole-boating will be exploded.

Pol. Econ., colloq. abbrev. of *Political Economy*; see Economy 3.
1893 W. K. Post *Harvard Stories* 12, I have not been tutoring you in Pol. Econ.

Poled (pōuld), *a.* [f. Pole *sb.*[1] and *v.* + -ed[2].] 1. Provided with or supported by (a number of) poles.
1864 E. A. Parkes *Man. Pract. Hygiene* I. ix. 287 This is a two-poled tent, with a connecting ridge-pole. *Ibid.* 288 The first is a single poled pyramidal tent, with a second pole to sustain the entrance flap.
2. Stunned by a pole-ax.
1920 *Outward Bound* Nov. 20/2 It caught him fairly above the ear so that he fell like a poled ox.

Poleless (pōu·l,lės), *a.*[2] [f. Pole *sb.*[2] + -less.] Having no magnetic pole.
1902 *Encycl. Brit.* XXVIII. 115/2 If the iron is of such a form that the lines of magnetization are entirely closed lines, the arrangement constitutes a poleless electromagnet.

Polemician (pǫlĭmi·ʃăn). [f. Polemic + -ian.] = Polemist.
1871 Sir J. D. Hooker in *Life* (1918) II. xxxii. 129 What an irony his life is becoming. I call him a polemician.

Poler. Add: 4. b. A boat propelled with a pole or poles.
1925 *Chambers's Jrnl.* Apr. 253/1, I was travelling by 'poler' because no steamer was available.

Polianite (pōu·liănait). *Min.* [f. Gr. πολιαίνεσθαι to become grey + -ite.] Manganese dioxide (MnO_2) occurring in grey metallic crystals; named by Breithaupt 1844.
1849 J. Nicol *Man. Min.* 420 Polianite..acts like pure hyperoxide of manganese. 1850 Dana *Syst. Min.* (ed. 3) 457 *Polianite*, Breit. This mineral is identical in composition with Pyrolusite, being pure superoxyd of manganese.

Police, *sb.* 6. Add: *police-agent*; **police-captain** (example); **police-dog**, a dog employed by the police to track criminals; **police-grip**, a grip or hold used by policemen; **police judge**, also *U.S.*; **police-trap**, an arrangement made by policemen for detecting motorists who are exceeding the speed limit; **police-whistle**, a special kind of loud whistle used by policemen.
1852 E. E. Hale *If, Yes, & Perhaps* (1868) 44, I had told the *police agent he might send it to the St. Nicholas. 1902 *Chambers's Jrnl.* Oct. 674/1 The next grade above is that of sergeant. Above this comes the *police captain. 1908 *Daily Chron.* 28 Aug. 7/2 Most of the principal German towns possess *police dogs. 1911 *Chambers's Jrnl.* Feb. 136/1 What is needed as an ideal police-dog is an animal that can not only track well, but that can attack the criminal. 1910 H. G. Wells *Hist. Mr. Polly* vii. 175 A combination of something romantic called 'Ju-jitsu' and something else still more romantic called the '*Police Grip'. 1889 *Kansas City T. & Star* 4 Apr., *Police Judge Davenport dismissed the case of 'Jim' Pryor for assaulting 'his honor' on election day. 1908 *Westm. Gaz.* 20 Aug. 4/2 The speed on the flat ..being sufficient with most modern cars to meet all requirements of long- or short-distance *police-traps. 1884 Sweet & Knox *Through Texas* iv. 50 He began blowing a *police-whistle.

Policedom. (Earlier example.)
1866 *Chambers's Jrnl.* 22 Sept. 608/1 Of Antoine the imperturbable, when he returned home,..policedom could make nothing.

Policemanish (pǫlī·smănɪʃ), *a.* [f. Policeman + -ish.] Suggestive of a policeman.
1916 Bennett *Lion's Share* iii. 27 The heavy policemanish step of Mr. Cowl was heard on the landing.

Policemanism (pǫlī·smăniz'm). [f. as prec. + ism.] The methods or conduct of policemen.
1891 *Star* 31 Oct. 4/3 Instances of policemanism crop up daily.

Policy, *sb.*[2] 3. *policy-holder* (earlier example.)
1851 C. Cist *Cincinnati* 98 Penn Mutual Life Insurance Co...All the profits [are] divided among the *policy holders every year.

Poling, *vbl. sb.* 3. Add: **poling-boat**, a boat propelled by poling.
1909 *Lady's Realm* Feb. 466/2 The Yukon bank was lined with canoes and poling-boats, barges and river steamers.

Poling (pōu·liŋ), *vbl. sb.*[2] [f. Pole *sb.*[2] + -ing[1].] Arrangement of the poles of an electromagnet.
1903 *Elect. World & Engin.* 21 Nov. 843 (Cent. Suppl.) By this arrangement and a suitable poling of the coils a minimum of mutual induction may be made to take place.

Polishing, *vbl. sb.* b. *pl.* Also, the bran or husks removed from grain by the process of milling or polishing.
1912 *Chambers's Jrnl.* Apr. 237/2 If the birds were fed on the milled rice mixed with the outer husks or 'polishings' which had been removed, the disease did not manifest itself.

Politic. B. *sb.* Add: 3. *pl.* **Politics.** g. Used as a singular noun.
1906 *Daily Chron.* 7 Dec. 6/4 She [Australia] has a politics of her own, and Europe is all the poorer for being out of touch with it. 1931 M. de la Bedoyère *Drift of Democracy* ii. 16 This politics is the vaguest of disciplines.

Poli·ticalized, *ppl. a.* [f. Politicalize *v.*] Made political in character.
1926 *Public Opinion* 13 Aug. 147/3 We are to have a politicalised Civil Service in this country.

Politico-. b. Add: *politico-literary*.
1924 Galsworthy *White Monkey* 73 She..picked out the biggest 'bug', politico-literary, and waited to pin him.

Poli·tico-econo·mic, *a.* [Politico-.] = Politico-economical.
1840 Carlyle *Chartism* x. 97 Paralytic Radicalism..which ..sounds with Philosophic Politico-Economic plummet the deep dark sea of troubles. 1910 *Westm. Gaz.* 17 Jan. 6/3 'The Strength of England': a Politico-Economic History of England from Saxon Times to the Reign of Charles the First.

Politico-economical, *a.* (Earlier example.)
1837 *Democratic Rev.* I. 113 In spite of the plain principles of politico-economical truth.

Polka, *sb.*[1] 3. Add: **polka-dotted** *a.*, bearing a polka-dot pattern.
1928 F. N. Hart *Bellamy Trial* i. 3 He wore a shabby tweed suit, a polka-dotted tie.

Poll, *sb.*[1] 10. Add: **poll-card**, a card supplied to voters at an election by a candidate, indicating how he wishes them to vote.
1908 *Westm. Gaz.* 4 May 2/2 Mr. Amery's final appeal..is going with the *poll-card to every elector.

Pollenizer (pǫ·lĕnəizəɹ). [f. Pollenize + -er.] = *Pollinator.
1903 *Amer. Naturalist* June 382 Müller finds it difficult to explain the origin of the blue coloring by the selective influence of the pollenizers.

Poll-evil. (Later example.)
1873 J. H. Beadle *Undevel. West* xxvi. 565, I..reined up my horse suddenly and again butted him in the back of the head, at the imminent risk of giving us both the poll-evil.

Pollex. Add: b. The movable part of the forceps in some crustaceans.
1904 *Biol. Bull.* Jan. 75 The added structure is however not a true forceps with one movable finger, but a movable piece with two immobile prongs that otherwise resemble the index and pollex of a forceps.

Pollinating (pǫ·lineɪtiŋ), *ppl. a.* [f. Pollinate + -ing[2].] That pollinates.
1911 F. O. Bower *Plant-Life on Land* 69 The very genesis of the forms of flowers, their tints, and scents is in strict accordance with their efficiency as pollinating mechanisms.

Pollinator (pǫ·lineɪtəɹ). [f. Pollinate + -or.] Any insect or other agent that pollinates plants; a pollinizer.
1903 *Amer. Naturalist* June 368 The small concealed flowers of Gaultheria..do not want for pollinators. 1924 *Chambers's Jrnl.* Aug. 501/2 The value of bees as pollinators is appreciated by progressive fruit-growers.

Polly[2] (pǫ·li). Slang abbreviation of *Apollinaris.
1893 G. Egerton *Keynotes* 59 The draught is transformed into lukewarm water, or 'Polly' without the 'dash' in it. 1899 *Westm. Gaz.* 10 June 6/1 The dividend on Polly shares. 1905 *Daily Chron.* 6 Sept. 4/7 'Johnny and Polly' is a common order in Piccadilly. 1908 *Ibid.* 3 July 6/7 Here, miss! a Scotch and 'Polly, please!

Polonaise. Add: 1. d. (See quot. 1895.)
1895 Jeanette E. Davis *Elem. Mod. Dressmaking* (ed. 2) 93 Polonaise, a mixture of silk and cotton, which has the appearance of a soft dull silk with a distinct serge-like twill, is very much used as a skirt-lining for rich materials. 1923 *Daily Mail* 13 Aug. 4 Advt., The lining of the coat is silk Polonaise.

Polonial (pǫlōu·niăl), *a.* [f. Polonia + -al.] = Polish *a.*
1922 *Blackw. Mag.* June 801/2 A very intelligent-looking secretary to the Polonial Embassy to the Vatican assured me [etc.].

Polonian. A. *adj.* Add: 2. Used as the distinctive epithet of a glacial epoch in Europe.
1914 J. Geikie *Antiquity of Man in Europe* ix. 257 The cold conditions that characterised the close of the Tyrolian stage obviously signalled the approach of another glacial epoch—the Third or Polonian.

Poly-. 1. Add: **Polya·ctine**, a sponge-spicule having numerous rays. **Poly-ce·ntral** *a.*, having several centres; polycentric. **Polycratism** = *Polycracy*. **Polycyclic** *a.*, also, having many cycles or circuits. **Polycythæ·mic** *a.*, of or pertaining to polycythæmia. **Polylithic** *a.*, also, containing different kinds of rock. **Polymasty** (-mæ·sti) [Gr. μαστός breast], the condition of having more than two breasts. **Polymicrian** *a.* (delete *nonce-wd.*; earlier example). **Polyneuri·tic** *a.*, pertaining to or connected with polyneuritis. **Po·lysemy**, the fact of having several meanings. **Po·lystely**, polystelic condition. **Polyto·nal** *a.*, of, pertaining to, or having several tones or keys. So **Polytona·lity**. **Polyto·pic** *a.*, of or pertaining to (the independent origin of a species in) several places. **Polyto·pical** *a.*, dealing with numerous topics.
1902 *Encycl. Brit.* XXXII. 813/1 Fig. 5 A, typical *polyactine. 1907 *Nature* 21 Feb. 398/2 There were seven distinct centres of destructive violence, and..the earthquake was a true *polycentral one. 1925 *19th Cent.* July 148 The maximalists, of course, are for *polycratism, provincial rule, insubordination and importation of foreign ideas. 1904 A. Russell *Th. Alternating Currents* I. iii. 68 The importance of this result..is utilised in systems of *polycyclic distribution. 1908 *Practitioner* Apr. 460 The..*polycythaemic quality of the circulating blood. 1908 *Sci. Amer.* Suppl. 25 Jan. 61/1 These crevices and fissures are filled with a *polylithic mass of brown and white 'calcic spar'. 1904 G. S. Hall *Adolescence* I. 421 *Polymasty or supernumerary breasts occurs about once in five hundred persons. 1829 W. Greenfield (*title*) *Polymicrian Lexicon to the New Testament. 1903 *Med. Record* 1 Aug. 177 (Cent. Suppl.) *Polyneuritic. 1908 *Practitioner* Jan. 17 Polyneuritic psychosis..is sometimes.. confounded with general paralysis. 1928 Jespersen *Monosyllabism in English* 26 We now see the reason why *polysemy is found so often in small words to an extent which would not be tolerable in longer words. 1902 *Encycl. Brit.* XXV. 413/2 This is the condition of astely, entirely parallel with *polystely except that the separate strands are usually all or mostly leaf-traces. 1929 W. W. Cobbett *Cyclop. Surv. Chamber Mus.* I. 41/2 In Stravinsky's *Le Sacre du Printemps* there are several instances of a pedal continued with *polytonal effects. 1923 *Proc. Mus. Assoc.* 1922–3 67 We find the principle of *polytonality or atonality superseding the old key system. 1904 *Science* 10 June 885/1 The idea that a species may originate in more than one place.. did not originate with Briquet, but he resuscitated it and christened it the *polytopic theory. 1876 C. A. Cutter *Rules for a Dict. Catal.* (1904) 21 It will be well to have both words,—*polygraphic* denoting (as now) collections of several works by one or many authors, *polytopical* denoting works on many subjects.

Polyarchism (pǫ·li,ɑɹkiz'm). [f. as Polyarchy + -ism.] = Polyarchy.
1914 E. Barker in *Polit. Quarterly* Feb. (1915) 120 This may seem anarchism. Really it is polyarchism. And as for the problem of polyarchism—why..it is likely to be settled by the needs of mere ordered life.

Polyautographic (pǫ·li,ǭtogræ·fik), *a.* [f. Poly- + Autographic.] Of, pertaining to, or practising, polyautography.
1808 *Gentl. Mag.* Mar. 193/2 The plates of stone used in Polyautographic Printing are of a very fine texture.

Polychromed (pǫ·likrōumd), *a.* [f. Polychrome + -ed.] = Polychrome A.
1922 *19th Cent.* May 804 The polychromed wooden statue of St. Paul recalls a work in stone from the hand of Vecchietta.

Po·lychromism. [-ism.] A spotted or marled condition.
1903 *Amer. Naturalist* May 295 (heading) Albinism, partial albinism and polychromism in hag-fishes.

Polyergus (pǫli,ɜ·ɹgǝs). [mod.L., f. Gr. πολύεργος much-working, f. πολύς much + ἔργον work.] A genus of ants; the Slave-making or Amazon ant.

1908 *Westm. Gaz.* 21 Jan. 2/1 The polyergus seems to lose even the faculty of making a nest. 1924 J. A. Thomson *Science Old & New* xiii. 72 Slave-keeping is much more marked among the Amazon Ants, of which the European Polyergus is a good representative.

Polygamical, *a.* Delete † *Obs.* (Later example.)
1914 Chesterton *Flying Inn* 69 Why should you shrink then, ladies, from this great polygamical experiment?

Polyglo·tter. *colloq.* [f. Polyglot.] A person who speaks several languages. **Polyglo·ttery**, polyglot character or condition. **Polyglo·ttically** *adv.* = Polyglottally.
1912 'R. Dehan' *Betw. Two Thieves* 616 That white haired *Polyglotter in the shabby togs,..is a queer kind of chap. 1915 *Singapore Free Press* 14 Jan., If its *polyglottery were all that was wrong with it [an army], it still might be possible to jog along. 1909 W. J. Locke *Simon Jester* vi. 71 Mr. Papadopoulos *polyglottically acknowledged the honour I had conferred upon him.

Polygonation (pǫ·ligonē·ʃən). [f. Polygon, after Triangulation.] Measuring or surveying land by means of polygons as an alternative method to Triangulation.
1900 *Geog. Jrnl.* XVI. 330 Polygonation..an operation that may be easily carried on by the bottom of valleys, at the side of the roads or paths already existent.

Polygrapher. 1. (Modern example.)
1871 L. B. Phillips *Dict. Biog. Ref.* 298 Cunaeus, Peter (*Van der Kun*), Dutch savant and polygrapher; 1586–1638.

Polymelous (pǫlĭ·mĭləs), *a.* [f. Polymely + -ous.] Exhibiting polymely; having supernumerary limbs.
1901 *Amer. Naturalist* Jan. 27 Having found three undescribed polymelous frogs in different American museums, it occurred to me that [etc.].

Polyp. 3. Add: **polyp-tree** = *polyp-stem*.
1915 E. R. Lankester *Diversions of Naturalist* 97 The little jelly-fish are the ripe individuals of the polyps, and produce eggs and sperm which grow to be polyp-trees.

Polyphage. (Modern example.)
1924 *Scribner's Mag.* Aug. 156/2 The animal immediately became popular as a polyphage in hundreds of other newspaper-offices.

Polyphagia. Later example of **polyphagy.**
1907 Schlich *Man. Forestry* IV. 158 Observations are not yet complete regarding the monophagy, or polyphagy of certain insects.

Polyphloisbic (pǫlifloi·sbik), *a.* [f. Gr. πολύφλοισβοι + -ic.] = Polyphloisboian.
1915 R. Brooke in E. Marsh *Mem.* (1918) p. cxxxviii, Will the sea be polyphloisbic and wine-dark and unvintageable?

Polyphylesis (pǫli,fəi·lĭsis). *Biol.* [f. as Polyphyletic, after Genesis, etc.] The polyphyletic origin of species; polygenesis.
1904 *Science* 10 June 885/1 Briquet's polytopic theory.. which the mutation theory and the growing belief in polyphylesis make more probable.

Polypide. Also *attrib.* as *polypide-bud*.
1902 *Encycl. Brit.* XXXI. 827/1 A nucleated layer..which later invaginates to form the inner vesicle of the polypide-bud.

Polypier. Also *transf.*
1904 T. de Mattos tr. *Maeterlinck's Double Garden* 85 All nations have the natural right to pass through this phase of the political evolution of the human polypier.

Polypodous (pǫli·podəs), *a.* [f. Polypod + -ous.] Having many feet or foot-like organs. So **Poly·pody**, polypodous condition.
1898 A. S. Packard *Text-bk. Entom.* 22 It is more probable that the Symphyla were the descendants of these polypodous forms. *Ibid.* 707 Polypody.

Polysaccharide (pǫlisæ·kărəid, -id). *Chem.* [f. Poly- + med.L. *saccharum* sugar + -ide.] Any one of the group of sugars having the formula $n(C_6H_{10}O_5)$, where n is an integer greater than unity.
1902 *Encycl. Brit.* XXXI. 723/2 By further polymerization and loss of water the group of polysaccharids..is produced.

Polytropic, *a.* Add: 3. Of poisons: Affecting more than one kind of tissue.
1901 *Lancet* 16 Mar. 784/1 In the case of 'polytropic' poisons..the chief response—i.e., the chief antitoxin production—might take place in tissues which the clinician could not discover to have been affected.
4. Of bees: Visiting several kinds of flowers.
1919 J. H. Lovell *Flower & Bee* 120 There are also on the wing at the same time 6 species which are polytropic.

Pom (pǫm). Abbreviation of *Pomeranian* (*dog*).
1910 *Bazaar, Exch. & Mart* 10 June 1523. 1918 F. T. Barton *My Bk. Little Dogs* 33 The Pekinese and the Pom are the most popular toy dogs at the present time. 1923 Rose Macaulay *Told by an Idiot* II. 138 Rome..drove elegantly in hansoms, often with an enormous wolf-hound or a couple of poms. 1928 R. Byron *Station* Prel. 12 Mademoiselle Péron..spent such hours as could be spared from the drama, in pacing the hall...Her pom was the permanent inmate of this oil-clothed passage.

Pomace. 4. Add: **pomace-fly**, a dipterous insect of the genus *Drosophila* whose larvæ live in decaying fruit.
1897 Comstock *Insect Life* 185 As these insects are often abundant about pomace in cider-mills and wineries, they have been termed *pomace-flies. 1924 J. A. Thomson *Science Old & New* xxvii. 152 When the pomace-fly, Drosophila, is feeding on fermenting fruit, it must have yeasts to help it.

Pomelo. Also *attrib.* as *pomelo grove*.
1908 R. W. Chambers *Firing Line* v. 54 Is that the pomelo grove?

Pomeranian. b. *sb.* Also, a native or inhabitant of Pomerania.
1870 Ullathorne in E. C. Butler *Vatican Council* (1930) I. 237 A Pomeranian..gave..an interesting and pathetic account of the difficulties of religion in his country.

Pommel (pv·mĕl), *sb.*[2] [ad. F. *paumelle* in same sense.] (See Pommel *sb.* 6 b.)
1839 Ure *Dict. Arts* 377 Pommels are made of different sizes and with grooves of various degrees of fineness...Pommels serve to give grain and pliancy to the skins. 1852, 1875 [see Pommel *sb.* 6 b].

Pommer, variant of Bombard *sb.* 4.

Pommy (pǫ·mi). *colloq. Austral.* [Of obscure origin.] A recent immigrant from Britain.
1916 *Anzac Bk.* 31/2 A Pommy can't go wrong out there if he isn't too lazy to work. 1927 *Weekly Times* 12 May 523/1 They referred to a man going out from this country as a 'Pommy'.

Pomonal (pomōu·năl), *a.* [f. Pomona + -al.] Of or pertaining to fruit-trees; pomonic.
1857 *Trans. Ill. Agric. Soc.* III. 354 We may proudly claim this land..as the favorite seat of horticultural and pomonal progress.

Pomp, *v.*[1] (Modern example.)
1922 Hardy *Late Lyrics & Earlier* 48 And once or twice she has cast me As she pomped along the street Court-clad, ..A glance from her chariot-seat.

Pompadoured, *pa. pple.* [f. Pompadour 5.] Of hair: Dressed or arranged in the Pompadour style.
1908 *London Opinion* 22 Aug. 362/2 She was large, plumply built, with grey hair artfully pompadoured and undulated.

Pompino, variant of Pompano.
1892 Stevenson & Osbourne *Wrecker* xix, There we sat, ..eating pompino and drinking iced champagne.

Pomposity. Add: 2. b. A pompous personage.
1909 *Daily Chron.* 13 Feb. 4/4 Those delightful commonplace people who are so much more interesting..than the Oddities and Pomposities of the human peep-show.

'Pon (pǫn), aphetic form of Upon *prep.*
1557 *Acts Privy Counc. Irel.* (Hist. MSS. Comm.) 39 Suche impositions as the lorde deputie for the tyme beinge shall taxe and set pon them. 1796 Mme D'Arblay *Camilla* iv. 119 Much obliged to him, 'pon honour! 1850 F. E. Smedley *Frank Fairleigh* v, I didn't think you had it in you; 'pon my word, I didn't.

Pond, *sb.* 4. Add: *pond-keeper, -marl*; **pond-bush** (see quot.); **pond-culture**, the keeping of fish in ponds; **pond-snail** (earlier example).
1859 A. L. Hillhouse tr. *Michaux's Sylva* II. 118 The ponds covered with *Laurus aestivalis*, (*pond-bush). 1885 *Encycl. Brit.* XIX. 127/2 *Pond-culture..has been practised for many centuries. 1909 *Westm. Gaz.* 12 Jan. 5/2 The *pondkeeper was unavoidably absent from his post. 1868 *Rep. U.S. Commissioner Agric.* (1869) 369 These accumulate as in the case of the testacea, and like the calcareous *pond marls are both fossil and recent. 1855 Kingsley *Glaucus* 159 A few of the delicate *pond-snails.

Po·nderate, *a.* [f. L. *ponderāt-*, ppl. stem of *ponderāre* to weigh, consider.] Careful; deliberate.
1922 *Times* 7 Oct. 11/2 It is a time for calm and ponderate consideration of the issues involved.

Pond-lily. *U.S.* [f. Pond *sb.* 4.] Any of several species of water-lily.
1778 [see Pond *sb.* 4]. 1827 *Western Monthly Rev.* I. 251 The flowers are large, of a pure white, nearest resembling the northern pond-lily, *nymphea odorata*. 1846 *Knickerbocker Mag.* XXVII. 52 But the liveliest feature is a little mill-pond; and this too is covered all over with pond-lilies and rank grasses. 1873 Aldrich *Marj. Daw* etc. 14 All this splendor goes into that hammock, and sways there like a pond-lily. 1885 *Outing* Nov. 181/2 The pond-lily is a poem in itself.

Pond pine. *U.S.* [f. Pond *sb.* 4.] A species of pine, *Pinus serotina*, growing on wet or marshy ground in the south-eastern parts of the United States.
1810 Michaux *Arbres* I. 17 Pond pine (Pin des mares). 1832 D. J. Browne *Sylva Amer.* 240 The Pond Pine frequently recurs in the maritime parts of the Southern States. 1858 J. A. Warder *Hedges & Evergr.* II. 249 *Pinus serotina*, or Pond Pine, is thirty five or forty feet high. 1883 P. M. Hale *Woods N. Carolina* 39 Pond Pine...This has considerable resemblance to the Pitch Pine.

Pondy, *a.* Add: 2. Belonging to or suggestive of a pond.
1922 *Chambers's Jrnl.* July 440/1 The peculiar 'pondy' smell of the bird [moorhen] does not suggest that it would prove a great delicacy.

Pone[3]. Add: c. *attrib.* as *pone bread*.
a 1785 *Maryland Hist. Mag.* II. 258, I procured some milk and excellent pone bread from a hut. 1833 J. Neal *Down-Easters* I. 47, I should like to know..what upon irth he means by..hoe-cakes an pone bread.

Ponga (pǫ·ŋă). [Native name.] A common species of tree-fern in New Zealand.
1867 J. D. Hooker *Handbk. N. Z. Flora* II. 767 Ponga, *Cyathea dealbata*. 1921 H. B. Dobbie *N.Z. Ferns* (ed. 2) 86 *Cyathea dealbata* (whitish), 'Ponga', 'Silver King'.

Pontic, *a.*[1] 1. (Later example.)
1816 Byron *The Dream* viii, Like to the Pontic monarch of old days, He fed on poisons.

Pontifical. B. *sb.* Add: 7. Short for *pontifical mass*.
1923 Abp. Seton *Memories of many years* 291 The most interesting of my pontificals was in San Nicola *in carcere*.

Pontificate, *sb.* Add: d. An act of pontificating.
1923 Abp. Seton *Memories of many years* 271, I pontificated six times...My last pontificate this year was at midnight on Christmas.

Pontificate, *v.* 2. Read *intr.* for *trans.* and add: (Later example). Also *trans.*, to say or utter in a pontifical manner.
1921 R. Hichens *Spirit of Time* v. 76 Why should I allow this young woman to pontificate about human nature. 1922 A. S. M. Hutchinson *This Freedom* iv. i. 252 All modern teaching, if this new stuff that they pontificate may be called teaching, offers us [etc.].
Hence **Ponti·ficating** *ppl. a.* and *vbl. sb.*
1926 W. J. Locke *Stories Near & Far* 156 Pontifex—Pontifex something..a playful title given him by her mother, for his possible pontificating aims as a young man. 1930 *Radio Times* 17 Jan. 127/2 Nine out of ten people are fond of pontificating.

Pontificial. B. *sb.* 2. (Modern example.)
1920 *Trans. Scot. Ecclesiol. Soc.* 79 We are enabled to do this, as the pontificial or book of offices used by him has been printed.

Pontine (pǫ·ntəin), *a.*[2] [f. L. *Pontus*, Gr. Πόντος, the Black Sea.] = Pontic *a.*[1]
1920 *Q. Rev.* Jan. 244 It would be necessary to guarantee a local autonomy to the Greeks of the Pontine littoral.

Pontoon (pǫntū·n), *sb.*[2] [Appar. corrupted from Vingt-et-un, or Vingt-un.] Soldiers' name for the card game Vingt-et-un.
1925 Fraser & Gibbons *Soldier & Sailor Words*, *Pontoon*, a popular card game, a form of Vingt et Un. 1927 *Daily Express* 26 July 9/5 A ghostly platoon wouldn't frighten me! ..perhaps they'd be playing pontoon.

Pony, variant of Pone[2].
1895 *Poker Manual* 95 It is unusual for any to shuffle except the pony and the dealer.

Pony, *sb.* Add: 4. b. A small ballet-dancer.
1930 *Daily Express* 23 May 10/5 We have what are known in stage parlance as 'ponies'—a troupe of girls, ages ranging from sixteen to twenty-three or four [etc.].
6. **pony beer** (see sense 4); **pony-boy, -man**, a boy or man who has charge of ponies; **pony report** (see quot.); **pony-skin**, the (dressed) hide of a pony, used *attrib.* to denote garments made of this.
a 1910 'O. Henry' *Rolling Stones* xv. 231 Del Delano drank a *pony beer. 1909 *Daily Chron.* 16 Feb. 5/1 Murten ..is employed as a *pony-boy. 1900 *Geog. Jrnl.* XV. 563 Group of Astor *pony-men at Lob jungle. 1909 *Census Bulletin* 216 28 June 67 (Cent. Suppl.) Besides the full reports delivered to large papers are the '*pony' reports—condensations of the full reports, sold at a cheaper rate. 1908 *Daily Chron.* 26 Dec. 3/4 Among the novelties are the *pony-skin suits. 1909 *Ibid.* 2 June 7/5 A stout man, made doubly stout by his pony-skin coat.

Poo·dle-faker. *Anglo-Ind. slang.* A man who lays himself out (temporarily) to cultivate female society. So **Poo·dle-faking** *vbl. sb.*
1928 *Chambers's Jrnl.* Feb. 97/2 You must either make the trip a 'poodle-faker' or confine your attentions to the smoke-room and the bar.

Pooh Bah (pū bā). [The name of a character in W. S. Gilbert's *Mikado*.] A person who holds a large number of offices at the same time.
1888 Powles *Land of Pink Pearl* 77 To the first of these [vacancies] the Governor appointed an English jeweller, named Brown, to the second one of the local 'Pooh Bahs!' named Crawford. 1923 *Westm. Gaz.* 4 May, Pooh-Bah Role for Local Bodies. 1927 M. Terry *Thr. Land of Promise* 44 Although principally protectors of aboriginals, stock inspection, mining wardens' responsibilities and a host of other offices make them a collection of veritable 'Poo-Bahs'.

Pooh-pooh·y, *a.* [f. Pooh-pooh + -y.] Inclined to pooh-pooh.
1876 H. Parry *Diary* in C. L. Graves *H. Parry* (1926) I. 169 Before the performance I met Otto Goldschmidt, and he was rather pooh-poohy about it.

Pool, *sb.*[1] Add: 2. b. A hollow or depressed part near the end of a dish where gravy can collect.
1882 *Hamilton Sale Catal.* No. 936 A Pair of Blue and White Dishes, with sunk pools.

Pool, *sb.*[3] Add: 4. b. Also *auction pool*, the total sum realized when the names of horses in a race, or likely winners in other contests, are sold by auction to those who wish to hold them.
1928 *Funk's Standard Dict.*
8. (sense 4 b) *pool box, seller* (earlier example).
1888 *Outing* July 351/2 Baseball..is free from the demoralizing effect of the *pool box and book-maker, that makes many shun the race-track. 1888 *Outing* May 118/1 John Hatfield is a bookmaker and *poolseller in St. Louis.

Pool, *v.*[2] Also *transf.*
1927 E. Thompson *These Men thy Friends* 245 Hart and Kenrick pooled friends.

Poop, *sb.*[1] 3. Add: **poop-break**, the front of the poop of a ship.
1912 Masefield in *Eng. Rev.* Oct. 353 Under the poop break, sheltering from the rain.

Poop, *sb.*[2] Add: b. The sound of a motor-horn; the report or bang of a gun. Reduplicated *poop-poop*.
1908 K. Grahame *Wind in Willows* vi. 128, I faithfully promise that the very first motor-car I see, poop-poop! off I go in it! 1919 Deeping *Second Youth* xxviii. 240 The faint 'poop-poop' of distant anti-aircraft guns..brought Laverack sharply back to the immediate present.

Poop, *sb.*[4] Abbreviation of Nincompoop.
1919 Deeping *Second Youth* xiii, That young man's a West End poop... And be used to be quite a nice boy.

Poop, *v.*[1] Add: c. To fire a gun. Also, of a gun: To give a loud report; to bang.
1919 *Chambers's Jrnl.* Jan. 43/1 As soon as the artillery opens up, poop off for all you're worth. Let 'em have a hurricane. 1930 R. Pertwee *Pursuit* 59, I arrived about eight last night and the guns were pooping away like mad.

Poor, *a.* 3. (Add U.S. examples.)
1778 *Maryland Jrnl.* 10 Feb. (Th.) [The sheep] are very poor, and appear to have been out all winter. 1878 J. H. Beadle *Western Wilds* 276 They get poor as snakes on such food; but it does keep body and soul together for a while.
10. **poor farm** (example).
1859 *Yale Lit. Mag.* XXIV. 418 (Th.) [He] let both his sisters go to the '*poor-farm'.

Poor-box. (Earlier example of *poor-box*.)
1737 Pope *Epistle to Bolingbroke* 128 The rest, some farm the poor-box, some the pews.

Poor man. 1. Also *attrib.*
1833 J. Banim *Smuggler* I. 70 What have you to do with ..my poor-man sneers at an earl?

Poorshouse (pūə·ɹzhaus). *Sc.* and *U.S.* variant of Poorhouse.
1756 *Bristol Vestry Bk.* (Va.) 164 Ordered That Stephen Dewey..agree in settleing the Terms of the Poors House. 1870 Nicholson *Idylls* 75 (E.D.D.), I was glad to become a wee Puir's-hoose laddie. 1883 Annie S. Swan *Aldersyde* 263, I suppose ye've gotten anither bairn hame. Ye'd better set up a puirshoose at aince. 1899 Ethel F. Heddle *Marget* ii. 10 She, an' her bits o' gear, is to gang to the sale; but she's no' to gang to the puirs-hoose.

Pop, *sb.*[1] Add: 2. c. The opening of a pop- or puppet-valve.
1904 *Elect. World & Engin.* 28 May 1039 (Cent. Suppl.) The construction of these valves embodies a self-adjusting feature which automatically regulates the 'pop' of the valve.
d. A turn (at doing something); an attempt; a 'go'.
1904 Harben *Georgians* 2 Ef I don't whack it to you this pop, old hoss, I'll eat my hat.

Pop (pǫp), *sb.*[6] *U.S.* Abbreviation of *poppa*: see Papa.
1840 *Knickerbocker Mag.* XVI. 207 'Pop!' screamed a white-headed urchin from the house, 'Mam says supper's ready'. c 1904 H. R. Martin *Tillie* 33 Are you feelin' too mean to go help pop? 1911 [see *Mom].

Pop (pǫp), *sb.*[7] Abbreviation of Poppycock.
1924 Galsworthy *White Monkey* II. iv, Nobody pitied her; why, then, should she pity them? Besides, pity was 'pop', as Amabel would say.

Pop, *v.*[1] 3. (Later example of phr. *to pop corn*.)
1873 'Susan Coolidge' *What Katy did* x. 173 'I popped the corn!' cried Philly.
5. (Further example.)
1858 *Punch* 20 Nov. 206 If you will pop on your hats..I'll take you and your friend out for a drive.

Pop-. Add: **pop-beer**, ginger-beer or other aerated water; **pop-eye** (earlier examples); (*b*) a disease of fishes characterized by protrusion of the eyes.
1886 C. D. Warner *Their Pilgr.* ii. (1888) 40 Shooting-galleries, *pop-beer and cigar shops, restaurants, [etc.]. 1828 Mrs. Royall *Black Bk.* II. 377 But the lawyer..is a shrimp in size, a sallow complexion, small face, and little blue *pop eyes. 1885 'C. E. Craddock' *Prophet Gt. Smoky Mts.* ii. 45 He had wide pop-eyes, and long ears, and a rabbit-like aspect. 1901 *Rep. U.S. Fish Comm.* 126 A chromogen from the disease known as 'pop-eye'.

Pope, *sb.*[1] 7. b. Add: **pope's hat**, applied to the head-dress of the Grenadier Guards.
1886 Stevenson *Kidnapped* ii, An old red-faced general on a grey horse at the one end, and at the other the company of Grenadiers, with their Pope's-hats.

Popean, **Popeian**, variant forms of Popian.

Pop-eyed, *a.* *U.S.* [Pop-.] Having bulging or prominent eyes; open-eyed (with amazement, etc.).
1824 Mrs. Royall *Lett. fr. Alabama* (1830) 176 The first countenance I caught was Senator Foot of Connecticut—a handsome middle-sized black pop-eyed Yankee. 1860 [see Pop-]. 1906 *Atlantic Monthly* Oct. 573 The class was open-mouthed, and the professor pop-eyed with wonder. 1921 R. D. Paine *Comr. Rolling Ocean* ix. 152 They are simply pop-eyed to hear all about the speedy apprentice.

Pop-gun. 3. (Later examples.)
1844 *Knickerbocker Mag.* XXIII. 162 To the United States in reference to the pop-gun shots of foreign tourists, might be addressed the warning which Peter Plymley thundered against Bonaparte. 1874 Eggleston *Circuit Rider* ix. 87 He had been flogged in boyhood for shooting pop-gun wads into the face of a portrait of the reigning monarch.

Popian, *a.* Add: b. as *sb.*, an imitator of the poet Alexander Pope.
1851 H. Coleridge *Essays* II. 121 Neither Rogers nor Campbell are Popeans. They belong to another school—the sentimental. 1914 J. A. Roy *Cowper & his poetry* 54 He [Johnson] failed to remark the absence of the Popeian inversions in the seemingly orthodox verse.

Popish (pōu·piʃ), *a.*[2] [f. *Pope*, proper name + -ish.] = Popian *a.*
1825 *Gentl. Mag.* XCV. i. 334 In this *Popish* controversy ..we have some doubt whether he will be permitted to have the last word. 1882 Mrs. Oliphant *Lit. Hist. Eng.* I. 76 The very words of the Popish era still lingered on Cowper's tongue.

Poplar. 3. **poplar-borer** (example).
1884 *Rep. U.S. Comm. Agric.* 383 The *Poplar-Borer.. has been destructive to poplar trees on the shore of Casco Bay.

Poplarism (pǫ·plăriz'm). [f. *Poplar*, the name of a borough in the east of London + -ism.] The policy of giving out-relief on a generous or extravagant scale, practised by the Board of Guardians of Poplar about 1919 and later; any similar policy which lays a heavy burden on rate-payers. Hence **Po·plarist**, one who practises or advocates Poplarism. **Po·plariza·tion**, a making like Poplar; Poplarism. **Po·plarize** *v. trans.*, to make like Poplar; to subject to Poplarism.
1922 *Glasgow Herald* 3 Nov. 8 The hard-headed workers of Yorkshire..have learned the lesson of Poplarism. 1923 *Daily Mail* 31 July 5/3 'Poplarism' was a portent of the changing of the modern state. 1923 Rose Macaulay *Told by Idiot* I. 44 So Poplarised..did she become that she took to speaking of her parental home in Bloomsbury as being in the West End. 1923 *Glasgow Herald* 1 Oct. 8/6 A decision in the opposite sense would simply mean an indefinite continuance of the Highland variety of 'Poplarisation' in the Lewis. 1924 *Ibid.* 7 Apr. 12/4 Mr. Wheatley..had been accused of desiring to 'Poplarise' the British people. 1925 *Ibid.* 6 Mar. 9 Even the cautious prophets..foretell the announcement of a rebuff to the Poplarists to-morrow. 1928 *Daily Tel.* 6 Nov. 12/6 Those..will demand increased subsidies, allowances, and 'Poplarised' social services, to be paid for out of the proceeds of very high taxation.

Poplocracy (pǫplǫ·krăsi). *U.S.* [f. as next.] = *Popocracy. So **Poplocra·tic** *a.*
1895 T. R. Smith in *Voice* (N.Y.) 18 July 5/3 Our fight will be for poplocracy, popular rule...I think no more significant name could be found than the Poplocratic Party.

Popocracy (pǫpǫ·krăsi). *U.S.* [f. Populist, after Democracy, Aristocracy, etc.] The rule or policy of the Populists or People's Party in U.S. So **Popocrat** (pǫ·pokræt), a member or supporter of the People's Party; a Populist. **Popocra·tic** *a.*, of or pertaining to the Popocrats.
1896 *Boston Rec.* 17 Aug. 4/1 It would never do for the popocrats to hear such a story about one of their leaders. 1896 *Boston Jrnl.* 24 Oct. 7/3 (heading) He is ready to support Popocracy. *Ibid.* 31 Oct. 4/3 (heading) Popocratic claims about Iowa. 1896 *N. Amer. Rev.* CLXIII. 744 The threats..of the Popocrats to change..our financial system. 1904 *Omaha Bee* 16 Aug. 4 If it is so important that the people of Nebraska move cautiously in the selection of their chief executive this year, why did not the popocratic conventions discover the fact before?

Popped (pǫpt), *ppl. a.* [f. Pop *v.*[1] + -ed[2].] Of eyes: Bulging; protruding.
1927 *Scribner's Mag.* Apr. 383/2 Prentice's slightly popped blue eyes wandered to the colored folders.

Popper, *sb.* 3. (Later example.)
1911 S. E. White *Bobby Orde* xviii. (1916) 201 The pan.. was replenished with popcorn, Bobby unhooked the long-handled wire popper from its nail..and set to work over the open fire.

Popple, *sb.*[1] b. (Later example.)
1909 S. E. White *Rules of Game* I. xii. 66 The remains of the forest, overgrown with scrub oak and popple thickets, pushed down to the right-of-way.

Popple, *sb.*[3] Add: 3. A series of reports from guns.
1924 *Blackw. Mag.* Feb. 162/1 At last a popple of fire broke out to their right front.

Poppy, *sb.* Add: 4. b. A perfume derived from the poppy.
1905 *Smart Set* Sept. 113/1 Wistaria, oil of cloves, chypre, poppy and crab-apple.
8. **Poppy Day**, the 11th of November, the day on which the Armistice was signed in 1918, commemorated by wearing a Flanders poppy (see *Flanders); **poppy mallow** (example); **poppy oil** (earlier example).
1921 *Daily Mail* 11 Nov. 9/4 To-day..is *Poppy Day. Twenty million red Flanders poppy emblems will be on sale in the streets. 1924 *Ibid.* 9/1 In honour of the Poppy Day collection..the King's wreath will contain poppies. 1870 *Amer. Naturalist* III. 162 The *Poppy mallow..with its purple blossoms and dark green leaves, forms one of the most brilliant figures in the prairie carpet. 1771 in *Copley-Pelham Lett.* 140 Invoice of Merch'ze shipped by Henry.. Bromfield..fine white *Poppy Oil.

Poppy, *a.* Add: b. Applied to eyes.
1907 *Westm. Gaz.* 11 Dec. 12/1 What poppy eyes these Churchills have got. 1915 *Pearson's Mag.* Jan. 106/1 Hair dark and curly; eyes poppy; lips full.

Poppycock. (Earlier and later examples.)
1863–5 Browne *A. Ward his Trav.* 113 You won't be able to find such another pack of poppycock gabblers as the present Congress of the United States. 1904 Harben *Georgians* 275 'Ah, that's all poppycock,' Abner said, lightly. 1920 *Nation* (N.Y.) 7 Feb 174/1 What is the use of poppycock in these serious times?

Popular. B. c. (Earlier example.)
1865 *Punch* 4 Mar. 92/1 Pity poor Lucy! Obliged to go to the Monday Popular with Cousin Bess (from the country) who will do her hair *à la théière*—that is, teapot fashion.

Popularize, *v.* 2. c. Also *absol.*
1923 *Times Lit. Suppl.* 4 Jan. 10/3 True-blue musicians; they knew their facts and..looked at them steadily in order to check their theories, and they did not popularize.

Poral, *a.* (Further example.)
1926 *Jrnl. Bot.* LXIV. 144 The poral outline is much like that of *Pseudonavicella*.

Porcelain. 5. Add: **porcelain-kiln** = *porcelain oven*.
1893 E. A. Barber *Pottery & Porcelain of U.S.* 258 It [hard porcelain] is fired in biscuit at a low temperature, in the second story of the *porcelain-kiln.

Po·rcelained, *a.* [-ed[2].] Covered or lined with porcelain.
1923 *Daily Mail* 2 July 1 Advt., Porcelained Enamelled Iron Baths.

Porcellanic, *a.* Add: b. Characteristic or suggestive of porcelain.
1930 Joanna Cannan *No Walls of Jasper* 29 His tooth brush dropped into its stand with the accustomed porcellanic chink.

Porcupinal (pǫ·ɹkiupəinăl), *a.* [f. Porcupine + -al.] Belonging to or characteristic of a porcupine.
1846 Ford *Gather. Spain* xii. 139 The porcupinal irritability of the tension of the wind.

Porgy. Add: b. *attrib.* and *Comb.* as *porgy boat, chum, steamer*; *porgy-hunting*.
1906 *N. Y. Even. Post* (S. Suppl.) 18 Aug. 1 The '*porgy' boats, dirty, snub-nosed are far removed in standing from their fellows. 1882 *Rep. Maine Board Agric.* XXVI. 109 Following this [application of 'lime ashes'], an application of '*porgie chum' at the rate of one ton to an acre, had produced similar results. 1904 *Scribner's Mag.* May 548 When we cruise about, hooking on to any job we can catch, and at any price we can get for it, that's *porgy hunting. 1880 *Harper's Mag.* Sept. 510/2 Among the rest are two of the singular '*porgy steamers' turned to mackereling.

Pork[1]. Add: 2. b. *U.S.* Federal moneys sought or granted for individual constituencies; (cf. *pork-barrel* below).
1916 *N. Y. Even. Post* 12 May, 'Pork' has hitherto stood for just one process, the parcelling out of Federal moneys for court houses, post offices, and waterways, not by States, but by Congressional districts.
3. *pork-packing* (earlier example), *-raiser, -raising, trade*; **pork-barrel**, *U.S.* a barrel in which pork is kept; also (*fig.*), the Federal treasury viewed as a source of grants for local purposes; **pork house**, a business house trading in pork; **pork king**, a magnate in the pork trade; **pork-knocker**, an independent gold-miner or diamond-seeker in British Guiana.
1831 *Louisville Publ. Adv.* 22 Dec., 2000 *Pork Barrels wanted. 1852 E. E. Hale *If, Yes & Perhaps* (1868) 2 You will have to go to the pork-barrel. 1909 *Chambers's Jrnl.* Mar. 178/2 We had bought ten empty pork-barrels. 1916 *N. Y. Even. Post* 12 May, The River and Harbor bill is the pork barrel par excellence, and the rivers and harbors are manipulated by Federal machinery and not by State machinery. 1926 R. Luce *Congress* 82 Undoubtedly there was once a 'pork-barrel', a metaphorical barrel from which legislators pulled out 'pork' to satisfy the ravenous appetites of greedy constituents. 1831 W. Jenkins *Ohio Gaz.* 171 Eaton contains..four *pork houses. 1847 *Rep. U. S. Comm. Patents* (1848) 527 The hogs are taken into the pork house from the wagons and piled up in rows. 1930 Rose Macaulay *Relations* xv. 222 *Pork king. 1910 Mary B. & W. Beebe *Search for Wilderness* vi. 187 The universal Guianian name for this type of independent miner is '*pork-knocker', the explanation being that by knocking the rocks to pieces, they find just enough gold to procure the pork upon which they live. 1930 *Times* 14 Mar. 5/3 The pork-knockers make a night of it before they go up into the bush. 1867–8 *Trans. Ill. Agric. Soc.* VII. 475 The only reliable statement of the *pork-packing of the West we have any knowledge of. 1839 *Indiana Ho. Rep. Jrnl.* 231 The scarcity..is likely to prove so mischievous to the interests of our *pork raisers and dealers. 1872 *Trans. Dep. Agric. Ill.* 390 Dark, cold, damp Piggeries are a nuisance to any farmer or pork raiser. *Ibid.* 354 He had said that *pork raising stood pre-eminent as a branch of stock raising in our State. 1851 A. O. Hall *Manhattaner* 13 Here, too, is modest beauty from Ohio (papa in the *pork trade).

Pork-pie. 2. Also *pork-pie cap*.
1910 *Blackw. Mag.* Jan. 113/1 In the dreadful mustard-coloured uniform and pork-pie cap which the Government has ordained for these unusually fat servants.

Pornogra·phically, *adv.* [f. Pornographic + -al + -ly[2].] Lewdly.
1921 *Times Lit. Suppl.* 10 Feb. 90/4 She introduced him to a coward, an alienist who was himself mad, a pornographically minded professor.

Porogamous (pǫrǫ·găməs), *a.* *Bot.* [f. as Porogamic + -ous.] = Porogamic. So **Poro·gamy**, porogamic fertilization.
1902 *Encycl. Brit.* XXV. 436/1 The pollen-tube normally reaches the apex of the embryo-sac through the micropyle (*acrogamy* or *porogamy*). 1905 I. B. Balfour tr. *Goebel's Organogr. Plants* II. 615 The micropyle in all *porogamous* plants evidently conducts the pollen-tube.

Porometer (porǫ·mĭtəɹ). [f. Gr. πόρος Pore *sb.*[1] + -meter.] An instrument for measuring the size of pores. Hence **Porome·tric** *a.*, of or pertaining to a porometer.
1911 *Proc. Roy. Soc.* B. LXXXIV. 137 With a view to testing the question we have designed an instrument which we propose to call a porometer. *Ibid.* 139 The porometric method is a direct one. *Ibid.* 140 The porometer..automatically strikes an average of many hundred stomata at each reading.

Poroscope (pǫ·ro-, pōə·rǒskōup). Also **-skop.** [f. Gr. πόρος Pore *sb.*[1] + -scope.] a. An instrument for testing the porosity of bodies. b. An instrument for examining the pores in surfaces or bodies. So **Porosco·pic** *a.*, of, pertaining to, or employing, a poroscope or poroscopy. **Poro·scopy**, the use of a poroscope; a method of identifying finger-prints by detailed examination of the number, shape, and disposition of the pores.
19.. *Buck's Handbk. Med. Sci.* IV. 768 (Cent. Suppl.) For exact determinations the use of a poroskop, or gasometer and manometer, becomes necessary. 1921 *Discovery* Oct. 259/1 Poroscopy..the only method of identification in the

case of very small fragments of (finger-)prints. *Ibid.*, Poroscopic research..is practised by means of large photographic enlargements.

Porpoise, *sb.* Add: 2. A plunging movement made by a sea-plane when travelling on water.
1931 *Times* 21 Aug. 7/1 It [a seaplane] dropped back on to the water and then porpoised again, double the height of the first porpoise.

Porpoise, *v.* [f. the sb.] *intr.* To move or travel in the manner of a porpoise; *spec.* of aircraft, to make a series of bumps or plunges when taking off or landing. So **Po·rpoising** *vbl. sb.*
1909 H. G. Wells *Tono-Bungay* I. iii. 86 'Just as though an old Porpoise like him would ever make money', she said. ..'He'll just porpoise about.' 1920 L. Bairstow *Appl. Aerodynamics* 55 Such phenomena as the depression of the bow due to switching on the engine and 'porpoising' are reproduced in the model. 1925 *Blackw. Mag.* Dec. 838/1 In spite of some fearful bumps, we managed to 'porpoise' over the ridge. 1931 *Times* 26 Sept. 7/5 The Coroner asked..if it was usual for a machine..to porpoise when taking off on a perfectly smooth sea.

Porsonian (pǫɹsōu·niăn), *a.* [f. the name of Richard *Porson* (1759–1808), Greek scholar.] Applied to a fount of Greek type designed by Porson.
1929 *N. & Q.* 13 Apr. CLVI. 267/2 A stronger and more dignified type than the common current Porsonian.

Port, *sb.*[1] 6. a. Add: *port-fog, -officer*.
1923 R. Kipling *Land & Sea Tales* 173 When the *port-fog holds us moored and helpless, a mile from the pier. 1901 *Chambers's Jrnl.* Aug. 522/2 The *port-officer, and one or two Eurasian residents, came to the office in the course of the day to interview us.

Port, *sb.*[3] 6. Add: **port-light** = Port-hole; **portmouth bit** = *port-bit*.
1926 *Chambers's Jrnl.* July 478/2 *Portlights as fitted to deck cabins have some drawbacks. 1908 *Animal Managem.* 140 Before riding in[to water], it is well to remove the *portmouth bit if one is worn.

Port, *sb.*[6] 2. Add: **port-watch** (see quot.).
1883 *Man. Seamanship for Boys* 5 The starboard watch work the starboard side of the deck, and the port watch the port side of the deck.

Portable, *sb.* [f. the adj.] A portable article; an instrument in a portable form.
1883 J. Hay *Bread-winners* xvi. 251 Plenty of portables in them houses, eh! 1926 *Wireless World* 26 May Advts. 16/1 For sale...Portables. 1931 B. Brown *Talking Films* 132 The Western Electric portable for sound-on-film.

Po·rted, *a.*[2] [f. Port *sb.*[7] + -ed[2].] Supplied with port-wine.
1929 Masefield *Hawbucks* 27 We're all dined and ported, thanks.

Porter-house. Add: b. **porter-house steak** (earlier and later examples).
1843 C. Mathews *Writ.* 206 (Th.), I guess I'll take a small porter house steak without the bone. 1909 *N. Y. Even. Post* 13 Sept. (Th.) At Washington Market, the customary price for porterhouse steak to individual purchasers has been 25 cents a pound.
2. *ellipt.* A porter-house steak.
1908 G. H. Lorimer *J. Spurlock* iv. 63 That [dream] in which the waiter is just taking the covers off a double porter-house, medium, with fresh mushrooms on top, [etc.].

Port-hole. Add: 2. c. An aperture in the column of a sea-anemone.
1897 Parker & Haswell *Text-bk. Zool.* I. 188 Many Sea-anemones possess curious organs of offence called *acontia*. These..can be protruded through minute apertures in the column, called 'port-holes' or *cinclides*.

Po·rtia tree. A widely diffused tropical malvaceous tree, *Thespesia populnea*, characterized by entire leaves, and yielding a valuable timber.
1881 J. S. Gamble *Man. Indian Timbers* 43 T[*hespesia*] *populnea* Corr....the Portia or Tulip Tree...A moderate-sized evergreen tree. 1902 G. S. Boulger *Wood* II. 335 Umbrella-tree...Known also as 'Tulip-tree, Portia-tree, Rosewood of Seychelles.

Portièred (portyę·ɹd), *a.* [f. Portière + -ed[1].] Provided with a portière.
1923 F. L. Packard *Four Stragglers* v. 184 She turned her head a little, facing the portièred window beside the fireplace of the living-room in which they stood.

Portmanto·logism. [f. Portmanteau + -(o)logism.] A portmanteau expression.
1887 *Spectator* 9 Apr. 492/2 An allusion to the 'Torrible Zone' which is one of the most beautiful of portmantologisms. 1920 T. Nicklin *Sounds Standard Eng.* 85 Sometimes we may surmise that these constructions are what may be called 'portmantologisms'.

Portolano. Also **portolan.**
1898 *Geog. Jrnl.* XII. 374 Why, for instance,..do we then have, after a Series of World-maps and Mediterranean portolans, a North Europe (Buondelmonte) of fifteenth century.
Comb. 1897 F. A. Bather tr. *A. E. Nordenskiöld's Periplus* 18 The portolan-manufacturer or draughtsman used by preference gaudy and bright colours.

Portrait, *v.* Add: 1. (Recent example.)
1908 *Daily Chron.* 3 Apr. 4/4 If we are not puffed and paragraphed and portraited in the papers.
b. With const., to produce a certain result or bring *into* some state by making portraits.
1926 W. J. Locke *Old Bridge* II. v. 77 She would paint figures from the live model, and make much money; while he would portrait himself into celebrity.

Portrayist (poətrē·ist). [f. Portray *v.* + -ist.] = Portrayer.
1924 *Glasgow Herald* 25 Sept. 4 His considerable skill as portrayist and his narrative genius.

Portugee (pōə·ɹtiŋgī), *a.* and *sb.* Also **Portugué.** [f. Portuguese, regarded as a plural.] = Portuguese *a.* and *sb.*
1834 *N. Y. Mirror* 5 July 5/2 A Portugué breakfast is teasing to the imagination. 1880 *Harper's Mag.* Sept. 505/1 At one place was a 'Portugee' of the Western Islands.

Port-winy, *a.* Also, suggestive of or resembling port-wine. Hence **Port-wi·nily** *adv.*
1910 R. W. Service *Ballads of Cheechako* 54, I smoked and sat as I marvelled at the sky's port-winey glow. 1921 Aldous Huxley *Crome Yellow* ii. 8 There was the dining-room, solidly, port-winily English, with its great mahogany table [etc.].

Posa·daship. [f. Posada + -ship.] The position of the keeper of a posada.
1923 *Blackw. Mag.* Nov. 700/2 The details of how from posadaship she had fallen to this minute eating-house were slurred over.

Pose, *v.*[1] 1. (Modern example.)
1896 Saintsbury *19th Cent. Lit.* (1903) vi. 297 These merits (which were not unchequered) finally posed Mr. Swinburne as the Third Poet of the later English nineteenth century.

Posed (pōuzd), *ppl. a.*[1] Add: c. Assumed as a pose; deliberately adopted or put on.
1909 Marg. B. Saunders *Litany Lane* I. iv, There was also a nun-like acquiescence in her bearing, prim for her thirty-three years, and possibly a trifle posed.

Posh (pǫʃ), *a.* *slang* or *colloq.* [Of obscure origin: cf. *Posh*, 'a dandy' 1897 Barrère & Leland *Dict. Slang* 141/1.] Elegant or fine in appearance; stylish, smart; first-rate, high-class, superb.
1918 *Punch* 25 Sept. 204 Oh, yes, Mater, we had a posh time of it down there. 1923 Wodehouse *Inimitable Jeeves* vii. 72 Practically every posh family in the country has called him in at one time or another. 1925 Deeping *Sorrell & Son* ii, Tips. Don't forget the tips. If a man's obliging —..It's a posh job. 1927 — *Doomsday* xiv. § 1 'You like it.' 'It's the poshest thing I've ever seen, old chap.' 1927 — *Kitty* xxix, I say—that's a posh show. 1927 *Daily Tel.* 24 May 9 It was a club in Ham-yard—not a very posh club. 1929 Priestley *Good Comp.* II. v. 391 I'd like to have..a very cosy car, small but frightfully posh.
Hence **Posh** *v.* (see quot.).
1919 *War Slang* in *Athenæum* 22 Aug. 791/2 To 'posh up' was to make oneself look as smart as possible.

Posish (pozi·ʃ). *orig. U.S.* Also **pozish.** Colloq. abbrev. of Position.
1862 O. W. Norton *Army Lett.* 113 Snorting their impatience to 'get into posish'. 1889 K. Munroe *Golden Days* vii. 69 All we've got to do is to get the cradle in posish. 1914 *Lincoln Daily News* 10 June in *Dial. Notes* IV. 130 What did I tell you about standing—Oh what a pozish! 1927 P. G. Wodehouse *Without the Option* in *Sunday Express* 16 Oct. 9/3 So there you have the posish, and you can see why..remorse gnawed at my vitals.

Position, *sb.* 10. Add: **position mark**, a mark made on a stone or other component part of a structure to indicate the position it is designed to occupy.
1928 G. C. Coulton *Art & Reformation* viii. 145 An inspection..will convince us that the rare marks found otherwise than on the surface are not banker-marks, but *position-marks.

Positive. A. *adj.* Add: 5. c. Functioning for the special purpose required.
1903 *Sci. Amer.* 21 Feb. 134/1 Instead of depending on splash lubrication alone for oiling every part of the engine, positive oil feeds are led to each of the crankshaft bearings.

Possess, *v.* 9. d. Add: Also *ellipt.*, to be very eager (to do something).
1886 *Harper's Mag.* Sept. 582/2 He was possessed to get a cattle ranch out to Colorado.

Possessed, *ppl. a.* Add: 2. d. *Like all possessed*: with great force, vehemence, energy or spirit. *U.S.*
1834 Seba Smith *Major Downing* 18 These Legislaters have been carrying on so like all possest. 1857 *Putnam's Mag.* Jan. 45 (Th.) He'd carry on like all possessed—dance and sing, and tell stories. 1881 *Harper's Mag.* Apr. 644 That old minister..is a-fiddling away like all possessed at the dance.

Posse·ssingly, *adv.* [f. Possessing *ppl. a.* + -ly[2].] So as to possess or captivate (one); fascinatingly.
1927 *Observer* 11 Dec. 10/4 Miss Jenkins's diary..is nothing worth in itself, but how possessingly dramatised by the identity of her correspondent!

Possessionist. (Recent example.)
1922 *Glasgow Herald* 29 Apr. 6/7 The mock possessions and infernal accomplishments, which most of the possessionists of this age pretend to.

Possible. B. *sb.* Add: 1. d. A person who may possibly do something or attain some position; a possible candidate, competitor, winner, member of a team, etc.
1923 *Daily Mail* 3 Mar. 13 C. L. Spackman..and H. J. Still as reserve backs are possibles.
2. Also *Comb.*
1846 J. W. Webb *Altowan* I. iv. 142 Having, by dint of much search in his possible-sack, found a piece of tobacco.

Possum, *v.* Add: 1. b. *trans.* To pretend or feign.
1853 J. G. Baldwin *Flush Times Alabama* 150 All this time I was possuming sleep—as innocent as a lamb.

Post, *sb.*[1] Add: 4. e. A leg of a chair.
1902 Harben *Abner Daniel* 202 Something like a groan escaped Bishop's lips as he lowered the front posts of his chair to the floor.

Post, *sb.*[2] 13. **post-paid, -rider, -village** (earlier examples).
1653 in Ellis *Orig. Lett.* Ser. II. III. 373 *Post payd. 1708 *Boston News-Lett.* 11 Oct. 4/2 Whereas several persons do write upon their Letters Post paid..without ever paying the Postage of the said Letters. 1772 Goldsmith *Life R. Nash* 117 This description..must be sent in a letter post-paid. 1814 *Niles' Weekly Reg.* V. 369/1 Letters to the editor must be post-paid. 1705 *Boston News-Lett.* 19 Nov. 2/2 Strayed ..a sorrel Mare...Whoever can give any true intelligence of her to..the *Post-rider..shall be sufficiently Rewarded. 1837 W. Jenkins *Ohio Gaz.* 165 Dover, a *post village of Wayne county. 1847 H. Howe *Hist. Coll. Ohio* 264 Allensville, Middleton, Oak Hill and Charleston, are small post villages.

Post, *sb.*[3] 2. d. *post-trader* (earlier example).
1873 J. H. Beadle *Undevel. West* xxv. 525 Mr. Lionel Ayres fills the position of Post Trader.

Post, *sb.*[5] 1. Delete † *Obs.*
1906 Sindall *Paper Technology* 21 The 'coucher', who transfers the wet sheet from mould to felt and builds up the pile or 'post' of alternate wet sheets and felts.

Post-. B. 1. b. Add: **Post-Christian** *a.*, of or belonging to the period since the birth of Christ, or since the introduction of Christianity into a particular country. **Post-tussive** *a.* = *post-tussic* (adj.).
1888 Cheyne, etc. *Bible* (Variorum ed.) Pref., The vowel-points merely represent a valuable, but still *post Christian, exegetical tradition. 1909 *Practitioner* Dec. 861 The so-called '*post-tussive suction' obtained by listening over a phthisical cavity in later stages of the disease.

Postable, *a.* (Recent example.)
1926 *Glasgow Herald* 23 Mar. 9/1 The £40 limitation is wholly inadequate for jewellers and others, whose goods, though of 'postable' dimensions, are of considerable value.

Postal, *a.* b. Add: **postal draft** †(*a*), in 1914 the form used at Post Offices for the payment of Navy and Army Separation Allowances, later called *allowance form*; (*b*), a draft or cheque drawn on the Post-Master General, introduced in Jan. 1925 for the payment of National Health Insurance benefits, and later extended to certain Government Departments; **postal trade**, trade in which orders are received and goods dispatched by post; **postal tube**, trade name for a cardboard tube designed to protect documents, plans, etc., during transmission by post.
1929 *Post Office Guide* July 144 Remittances are made by certain Government Departments, etc., by means of *Postal Drafts. 1902 *Encycl. Brit.* XXV. 99/2 What is called in England '*postal trade', and in America 'mail order business', is growing very rapidly.

Postally (pōu·stăli), *adv.* [f. Postal *a.* + -ly[2].] In a postal manner; as far as postal matters are concerned.
1896 *Rep. Exhib. Sheffield Philatelic Soc.* There were two letters postally used in 1768 and 1772. 1930 *Observer* 20 Apr. 15/5 It might..be better to show him our very latest additions to Whitehall—although they occur, postally at least, in that part of it called Charing Cross.

Post and rail, *attrib. phr.* *U.S.* [see Post *sb.*[1] 8 c.] Constructed with posts and rails.
1684 *Connecticut Public Rec.* III. 512 Great parte of my post and rayle fences being fetched and burnt by the sowders. 1765 Washington *Diaries* I. 216 Sowing..19 Bushels in the large cut within the Post and Rail fence. 1786 *Ibid.* III. 30 Post and rail fencing lately erected as yards for my Stud horses. 1837 *Southern Lit. Messenger* III. 317 Arranging the course of a new post-and-rail fence. 1850 H. C. Watson *Camp-Fires Revol.* 43 A party of our men..pulled up a post-and-rail fence. 1880 *Scribner's Mag.* Feb. 507/2 Which is as much of a 'post and rail' fence as we often find in northern New England. 1914 Conrad *Chance* I. ii. 40 She had taken the trouble to climb over two post-and-rail fences only for the fun of being reckless.

Postcard, *sb.* (Later attrib. example.)
1909 *Daily Chron.* 19 Mar. 1/6 There had been strong opposition..to the Sunday concerts, and a postcard poll was taken.

Po·stcard, *v.* [f. the sb.] *trans.* To communicate with or inform by postcard.
1890 *Let. to Dr. Furnivall* 4 Mar., Have postcarded C— that proof is correct. 1910 *Westm. Gaz.* 2 Feb. 5/3 Advt., Patterns ready for sending by return post. Postcard us to-day.

Post-common. (Modern hist. examples.)
1879 T. F. Simmons *Lay Folks Mass Bk.* 307 They were to kneel again during the post-common, as was the English name for the prayer after the communion. 1882 G. H. Forbes *Anc. Irish Missal* 26 *marg.*, This Postcommon is found without any variation in Gerbert p. 294 b.

Poster[2]. 3. Add: *poster-designing, -panel*.
1911 *Encycl. Brit.* XXII. 196/2 Occasionally eminent French painters..have made essays in poster-designing. 1929 *Ibid.* XVIII. 319/2 On the poster panels of to-day, in the United States, may be seen [etc.].

Poster[3] (pōu·stəɹ). *Rugby Football.* [f. Post *sb.*[1] + -er[1].] A ball that passes directly over the top of one of the goal-posts.
1867 *Routledge's Hdbk. Football* 35 If the ball..rises directly over the end of one of the posts, it is called a *poster*, and is no goal. 1930 *Times* 14 Mar. 7/1 He played in three International matches, dropped a goal in two, and scoring [*sic*] a 'poster' in the other.

Postered (pōu·stəɹd), *a.* [f. Poster[2] + -ed[1].] Depicted or described on posters; adorned or disfigured with posters.
1915 Sheila Kaye-Smith *Sussex Gorse* III. § 16. 173 Rye electors were confronted with the postered virtues and vices

of Captain Mackinnon (Radical) and Colonel MacDonald (Conservative). 1927 *Scots Observer* 7 May 9/2 The real blemishes of Glasgow are raw and postered gable-ends, untended waste grounds [etc.].

Posterish (pōu·stəriʃ), *a.* [f. Poster 2 + -ish.] Characteristic or suggestive of posters. So **Po·sterishness.**

1930 *Aberdeen Press & Jrnl.* 25 Apr. 6 Norah Neilson Gray still seems to us to be straying too much towards a sweet but too pretty posterishness in her work. 1931 *Times Lit. Suppl.* 25 June, Suppl. p. vi/3 Several cover-designs achieve posterish attractiveness.

Postero-. Add: *postero-medial*, *-mesial*; also *postero-ventrally* adv.

1901 *Proc. Zool. Soc.* 263 The characteristic features of this cavity..are:—..(3) the characteristic position of its postero-medial wall, as seen from behind. 1907 *Practitioner* June 859 The main fibres pass into the postero-lateral colum of Burdach, and higher in the cord they pass into the postero-mesial column of Goll. 1902 *Proc. Zool. Soc.* I. 89 The blue sides are margined posteroventrally with a black line.

Post-free, *a.* (Earlier and later examples.)

1723 *Boston News-Lett.* 7 Mar., The Publisher..Desires them to send their Accounts Post-Free. 1929 *Times* 1 Nov. 16/6 The post-free price for copies ordered direct from the publisher is 5s. 9d.

Postiche. B. *sb.* Add: **c.** *spec.* A coil of false hair worn as an adornment.

1886 C. E. Pascoe *Lond. To-day* xl. (ed. 3) 345 False tresses have been imported by cart-loads,..and postiches and other mysteries of the toilette have been brought to that perfection to which competition so greatly conduces. 1908 *Westm. Gaz.* 21 Nov. 15/2 The postiches in use must be carefully manipulated to afford the exact size demanded.

Post-impre·ssionism. [f. Post- A 1 b + Impressionism.] The doctrine or methods of the post-impressionists in art; the representation of the individual artist's subjective view of objects or scenes designed to reveal their spiritual significance without strict fidelity to their natural appearance; any movement or group of aims in art which constitutes a revolt against impressionism.

1910 C. J. Holmes *Notes on Post-Impressionist Painters* 11 The tradition of Post-Impressionism,..if any principles so youthful can be called a tradition, is the expression of personal vision. 1910 *Connoisseur* Dec. 315/2 The committee ..wisely diluted the post-impressionism of the pictures in the entrance room by the inclusion of a dozen or more examples by Manet. 1911 C. L. Hind *Post Impressionists* 1 Post Impressionism has been called the heart of painting; it has also been described as an insult to the intelligence.

Post-impre·ssionist. [f. as prec. + Impressionist.] An artist who practises post-impressionism; one who freely distorts the forms of nature in depicting his own subjective view of an object or scene. Also *attrib.* Hence **Post-impressioni·stic** *a.*, belonging to or characteristic of the post-impressionists.

1910 C. J. Holmes *Notes on Post-Impressionist Painters* 10 In setting up sincerity to personal vision as a guiding rule..the Post-Impressionists were really only reverting to the principle which has inspired all the greatest art in the world. 1911 *Athenæum* 28 Jan. 104/3 Post-Impressionist Sculpture. 1913 E. F. Benson *Thorley Weir* v, An outrageous exhibition of Post-Impressionists at one of the London galleries. 1913 *Punch* 16 July 70/1 They grumble at the ladies' skirts, The Post-Impressionistic settings. 1922 C. Bell *Since Cézanne* 81, I can't think why you don't like it: its Post-Impressionist isn't it?

Posting, *vbl. sb.*1 Add: **3. b.** *pl.* Letters, parcels, or other articles which are posted.

1909 *Daily Chron.* 30 Dec. 3/6 During the Christmas week of last year the postings in London alone totalled upwards of 70,000,000.

Postman 1. **1. c.** Add: **postman's knock,** a parlour game in which the participants in turn take the role of postman and deliver letters which are paid for by kisses.

1927 W. E. Collinson *Contemp. Eng.* 12, I was interested to see the kissing-forfeit game of postman's knock under the guise of 'American post'.

Post-mortem. C. *sb.* Add: **2.** *transf.* Discussion of a game of bridge after it is finished.

1922 Manning Foster *Light Side Auction Bridge* 157 The player with the post-mortem habit cannot resist indulging his passion. *Mod.* Let us not have post-mortems, please.

Post-mo·rtem, *v.* [f. Post-mortem *adj.*] *trans.* To subject to a post-mortem examination.

1910 H. G. Wells *Hist. Mr. Polly* iv. 75 You didn't, I suppose, Mr. Polly, think to 'ave your poor dear father *post-mortemed*.

Post-oak. (Earlier examples.)

1782 *Steele Papers* II. 730 Beginning at a small red Oak ..and runing..then east fifty seven chains to a post Oak. 1800 B. Hawkins *Sk. Creek Country* 19 The trees are post oak, white and black oak, pine [etc.].

b. *attrib.* as *post-oak flat, ridge, wood.*

1836 Edward *Hist. Texas* 46 They are protected..by.. post-oak ridges. 1836 Quitman *Let.* in *Life & Corr.* 145 He lies in the post oak woods, to protect himself from the Mexican horse. 1862 *Trans. Ill. Agric. Soc.* (1865) V. 567 That [cane] brought from the post-oak flats and red clay soil along the edge of the timber. 1906 'O. Henry' *Four Million* 58 Joe Larrabee came out of the post-oak-flats of the Middle West.

Post office. 3. post-office bridge (see quot.).

1926 *Gloss. Electr. Terms* (Brit. Engin. Stand.) 95 *Post Office Bridge, P.O. Bridge*, a self-contained combination of resistors connected up for use as a Wheatstone Bridge.

Postpone, *v.* **2.** (Later example.)

1871 Roby *Lat. Gram.* § 1800 II. 351 Most prepositions are prefixed to the substantive; a few are always postponed; others are occasionally but rarely postponed in prose.

Post-primary, *a.* [Post- B 1 b.] Of education or schools: Subsequent to that which is primary.

1926 *Rep. Consult. Com. Educ. Adolescent* 35 It has been the general tendency of the national system of elementary education to throw up experiments in post-primary education. 1927 *Observer* 20 Feb. 14/6 The aims of raising the school age and completing a national system of post-primary education.

Postulator. (Earlier example.)

1863 tr. Luquet *Life Anna Maria Taigi* 2 The undersigned Bishop of Hesebon, Postulator of the suit of the servant of God, Anna Maria Taigi.

Postvocalized (pōustvōu·kǎlaizd), *ppl. a. Philol.* [f. Post- A. 1 a + *vocalized*, f. Vocalize.] Having the vowel after a consonant.

1876 [see Prevocalized].

Po·st-war, *a.* [f. Post- A. 1 b + War *sb.*] Of or belonging to the period after a war (esp. the war of 1914–18).

1908 *Daily Chron.* 16 July 5/1 There has been a reduction of some £2,000,000 since 1904–5 the first post-war year. 1919 *Athenæum* 23 May 360/2 'Bar' and 'millibar' have appeared in the post-war revival of meteorology. 1920 *Motor Cycle* 27 May 601 First post-war records. D. R. O'Donovan ..beats fourteen records. 1920 J. M. Keynes *Econ. Conseq. Peace* 84 Our hypothetical calculations leave us with post-war human requirements, on the basis of a pre-war efficiency of railways and industry. 1928 *Publishers' Weekly* 9 June 2352 Life and love in the post-War world. 1929 W. J. Locke *Jerico* 263 There was still hope for post-war England. 1930 Rose Macaulay *Relations* iv. 57 They're terribly generation-conscious...It seems a post-war disease.

Pot, *sb.*1 Add: **9.** (Earlier example.)

1856 *Knickerbocker Mag.* XLVIII. 619 (Th.) They had hauled down a big pot and intended henceforth to live as jolly as clams.

d. (Earlier examples.)

1880 Hardy *Trumpet-Major* viii, When Festus put on the big pot, as it is classically called, he was quite blinded *ipso facto* to the diverting effect of that mood and manner upon others. 1885 *Punch* 12 Sept. 131/2 Oh, Yorkshire and Lancashire both are big pots. But Cricket's top honours again go to Notts.

14. pot-bunker *Golf*, an artificially constructed pot-shaped bunker; **pot-burial,** a prehistoric form of burial found in Crete (see quot.); **pot-drum** (see quot.); **pot-marigold,** the common marigold, cultivated as a pot-plant; **pot-seine,** a fishing-net having a pot (sense 5 c); **pot-sick** *a.*, also, sick from confinement in a flower-pot; **pot-washings** *pl.*, food removed from pots by washing; **pot-woman,** a woman serving liquor in a bar.

1909 *Westm. Gaz.* 30 Apr. 4/2 Had its original whins been forest-trees we should not now be digging *pot-bunkers. 1921 *Discovery* Feb. 33/1 A simpler form of burial, known as the '*pot-burial', was effected by trussing up the body, placing it under an inverted jar, and then burying it in the earth. 1912 *Hastings's Encycl. Relig. & Ethics* V. 90/1 The *pot-drum is an earthenware vessel headed with a membrane. 1883 *Encycl. Brit.* XV. 544/1 *Calendula officinalis*, L., the *pot-marigold..is the familiar garden plant with large orange-coloured blossoms, and is a native of the meadows of southern Europe. 1903 *Sci. Amer.* 28 Feb. 160/3 The purpose of this contrivance is to provide a *pot-seine to be used with or without scows and adapted to fish only with the tide. 1872 Hardy *Under Greenw. Tree* ii. iii, Every morning I see her eyes mooning out through the panes of glass like a *pot-sick winder-flower. 1912 C. N. Moody *Saints of Formosa* ix. 195 They threatened to..feed her on the *pot-washings with which the pigs are nourished. 1918 *Pall Mall Gaz.* 29 June 5/4 A '*potwoman' at a public house applied for a summons for wages in lieu of notice.

Potato, *sb.* Add: **6. b.** *potato-digger* (earlier example).

1846 *Rep. U.S. Comm. Patents* (1847) 18 A patent has been granted for a potato digger.

7. potato-ball (earlier examples); **potato-chips,** potatoes sliced and fried in fat or oil; **potato-clay,** a variety of clay used by the Hopi Indians in the making of pigments; **potato-hook** (examples); **potato-masher grenade,** a type of German hand-grenade, so called from its shape; **potato onion** (example); **potato rot** (earlier example); **potato set,** a potato or a part of a potato used as seed; **potato vine** (examples); **potato-worm** (earlier example).

1849 *Rep. U.S. Comm. Patents, Agric.* (1850) 198 In 1847, he planted a single *potato-ball or apple; only one seed grew. 1877 *Rep. Vermont Board Agric.* IV. 33 Nature can make potato balls, but she couldn't make the Early Rose. 1878 *Amer. Home Cook Bk.* 67 Fillet steaks with *potato chips. 1893 Kate D. Wiggin *Polly Oliver* vii. (1894) 78 Meanwhile Polly set on the table..some delicate potato chips which had come out of a pasteboard box. 1900 *Rep. Smithsonian Inst.* (Nat. Mus.) 469 Some of the talc-like substance, called *potato-clay..is then produced, and the operator puts a piece about the size of a walnut in his mouth. 1856 *Trans. Mich. Agric. Soc.* VII. 53 D. O. and W. S. Penfield..[exhibited] six Patridge's *potatoe hooks. 1874 *Rep. Vermont Board Agric.* II. 551 Then with axes, potato hooks, and bog hoes, the turf was all peeled off. 1918 in F. A. Pottle *Stretchers* (1930) 266 We saw bushels of *potato-masher grenades, minenwerfer shells, and a machine gun belt of cartridges. 1857–8 *Trans. Ill. Agric. Soc.* III. 507 The *potatoe onion is planted as a potato, and grows in clusters under ground. 1847 *Rep. U.S. Comm. Patents* (1848) 353 Towards the close of the month the atmosphere became sultry..and the cry of '*potato rot' again began to be heard. 1849 *Cultivator* New Ser. VI. 125 On the 16th. April..dropped *potatoe sets in the drills, about nine inches apart. 1777 P. V. Fithian *Jrnl.* (1900) 257, I took a Walk thro' the Pumpkin and *Potatoe Vines. 1870 *Amer. Naturalist* III. 92 The early frosts that nearly killed the potato vines. 1872 *Rep. Vermont Board Agric.* I. 319 The large night-flying moths, which come from..the large larvae, as the *potato-worm and tobacco-worm.

Potato beetle. [Potato *sb.* 7.] An American species of beetle, *Doryphora decemlineata*, injurious to the potato.

1821 [see Potato *sb.* 7]. 1868 *Amer. Naturalist* May 129 The New Potato-beetle..which is so destructive in the West. 1876 *Times* 29 Aug. 6/5 The fact of its surviving in a letter posted at Listowel, Ontario, and delivered at Stranraer, Wigtonshire, N.B., shows that the potato beetle possesses great powers of endurance. 1877 *Rep. Vermont Board Agric.* IV. 109 Thus this Potato-beetle has made a steady progress..until now it has arrived in our midst. 1884 *Rep. U.S. Comm. Agric.* 308 The Colorado Potato-beetle is too well known to need extended comment. 1887 *G. Nicholson's Dict. Gard.* III. 210/1 *Potato Beetle.* This insect, also often called the Colorado Beetle,..was first observed in the Rocky Mountains of America, in the Colorado Region.

Potato bug. *U.S.* [Potato *sb.* 7.] = prec.

1799 Mrs. Drinker *Jrnl.* (1889) 347 They call them here ..the Potato-Bug, being numerous on the potato tops. 1877 *Rep. Vermont Board Agric.* IV. 108 The Colorado Potato-Beetle or Potato-Bug. 1880 *Harper's Mag.* Sept. 543 It is free as yet from flies, mosquitoes, potato-bugs, and the myriad other plagues of the farmer. 1908 *Springfield Weekly Republ.* 3 Sept. 16 Potato bugs on the rails stalled eight trolly cars laden with excursionists.

Potato patch. *U.S.* A piece of ground on which potatoes are grown.

1807–8 Irving *Salmagundi* xvi. 366 Some..enjoy the varied and romantic scenery of..potato patches and log huts. 1839 *Southern Lit. Messenger* V. 375/2 A corn, pea and potato patch rudely inclosed by a worm fence. 1863 Mrs. Whitney *F. Gartney's Girlh.* xxii, A hollow, beyond which were the cornfields and potato-patches. 1871 *Rep. Indian Affairs* (1872) 523 We fought with our entire force..going over our potato patch repeatedly until they disappeared.

Pot-bound, *a.* (Recent fig. example.)

1925 Deeping *Sorrell & Son* (1926) 56 You can get many a good hint from a man who dislikes you if you are not too pot-bound to soak it up.

Pot-cheese. *U.S.* [f. Pot *sb.*1 14.] Cheese made from coagulated milk from which the water is separated by heating in a pot; cottage cheese.

1813 Paulding *J. Bull & Bro. Jonathan* (ed. 2) xxi. 115 Tell me, thou heart of cork,..and brain of pot cheese. 1859 Bartlett *Dict. Amer.* (ed. 2) *Smear case*,..a preparation of milk;..otherwise called Cottage-Cheese. In New York it is called Pot-cheese. 1878 *Rep. Indian Affairs* 19 They learn to milk and make butter and pot-cheese, which they relish highly. 1903 *U.S. Dept. Agric.* Farmer's Bull. No. 166. 12 *Pot cheese*...This simple kind of cheese is also called Dutch cheese, cottage cheese, and Schmierkase.

Potencé, *a.* Also **Potencée.**

1911 *Hastings's Encycl. Relig. & Ethics* IV. 326/1 The potencée form T..is called also the Tau cross, because it reproduces the form of the Greek letter Tau.

Potential. A. *adj.* Add: **5. c.** *Potential temperature*: (see quot.).

1913 Sir N. Shaw *Forecasting Weather* iii. 60 By potential temperature of any specimen of air is meant the temperature which the air would indicate if its pressure were changed to a standard pressure under conditions which allowed of no escape of heat.

Potentialness. (Recent example.)

1930 Gwendolen Greene *Two Witnesses* 135 The turning of potentialness into creative life.

Pot-head. Add: **b.** A connecting unit used where a single electric conductor branches into several.

1904 *Elect. World & Engin.* 5 Mar. 427 (Cent. Suppl.) The cable being provided with a pot-head at this point and spreading from a three-conductor cable to single-conductor cable.

Pot-hole. Add: **1.** (Earlier example.)

1826 T. L. McKenney *Tour Lakes* (1827) 54 It is certain the waters were once, in many places, some fifty feet above their present level: for their action upon the rocks is plainly seen in the pot holes, as the excavations are called, which are made by the action of pebbles upon the rocks.

3. A depression or hollow part forming a defect in the surface of a road or highway.

1909 *Westm. Gaz.* 30 Aug. 1/3 All road engineers are agreed that the uneven surfaces and pot-holes..are practically confined to the districts where the water-cart reigns supreme. 1920 *Motor Cycle* 30 Sept. 384/2 On the outward journey the pot-holes between Edinburgh and Stirling seemed appalling.

Pot-holey, *a.* [f. Pot-hole + -y.] Having many pot-holes.

1921 *Blackw. Mag.* Nov. 641/2 We lurched along over a very pot-holey road.

Pot-holing, *vbl. sb.* [f. Pot-hole + -ing 1.] The making of pot-holes.

1903 *Geog. Jrnl.* XXI. 672 Of this [erosion] Mr. Ball thinks that at least two-thirds is accounted for by the pot-holing action.

Po·t-housey, *a.* [f. Pot-house + -y.] Suggestive of or appropriate to a pot-house.

1872 T. Hardy *Under Greenw. Tree* i. viii, If I strip by myself and not necessary, 'tis rather pot-housey I own.

Po·t-hunt, *v.* [f. Pot-hunter.] *intr.* To hunt for the pot; to be a pot-hunter.

1926 *Chambers's Jrnl.* July 418/1 You..prefer to pot-hunt

—luckily for us, with six hefty Gurkhas and the servants to feed, as well as ourselves!

Potichomanist (pǫtiʃǫ·mǎnist). [f. Potichomania + -ist.] A person who practises potichomania.

1884 *Decorator's Assist.* 122 Potichomanists have found the art capable of greater results than the mere imitation of porcelain vases, by the introduction of glass panels [etc.].

Po·tlatch, *v.* [f. the sb.] *trans.* To give as a gift (to N. American Indians).

1910 R. W. Service *Ballads of Cheechako* 94 The man who potlatched the whiskey and landed me into the hole Was Grubbe,..Grubbe, of the City Patrol.

Pot-making, *vbl. sb.* The making of pots or pottery.

1927 Peake & Fleure *Peasants & Potters* 141 We think that they had picked up the art of agriculture, weaving and *pot-making, etc.

Potman. Add: **4.** In various manufacturing processes: A man who attends to the filling, emptying, firing, etc., of pots.

1874 J. A. Phillips *Elem. Metallurgy* 581 In order to deliverise by the aid of this arrangement, the potman sinks the ladle sideways to the bottom of the kettle. 1921 *Dict. Occup. Terms* (1927) § 143.

Pot-pie. (Earlier and later examples.)

a 1792 J. W. Monette *Mississippi Valley* (1848) II. 8 (Th.) The standard dinner dish at log-rollings, house-raisings, and harvest days, was a large pot-pie, inclosing minced meats, birds or fruits. 1906 *Amer. Illustr. Mag.* Feb. 465/1, I was out huntin' for squirrels to make a potpie out of, for squirrel potpie's just lickin' good.

Pot-shoot, *v.* [Back-formation f. Pot-shot *sb.*1] *intr.* To take a pot-shot. So **Po·t-shooter** (**-shotter**); **Po·t-shooting** *vbl. sb.*

1904 P. Fountain *Gt. North-West* iv. 27 The breech-loader is the weapon of the dandy pot-shotter. 1907 Mulford *Bar-20* xxi. 209 One hundred paces makes fine pot-shooting. 1913 — *Coming of Cassidy* ii. 31 He..resolved that he wouldn't take chances with a man who would pot-shoot. 1921 — *Bar-20 Three* xiv. 166 I'm leavin' town. I ain't got a chance among buildin's again' pot-shooters.

Potteress (pǫ·tərės). [f. Potter *sb.*1 + -ess.] A female potter.

1926 *Blackw. Mag.* Mar. 395/2 He had not only to find a bride but a bride who was a 'potteress'.

Potting, *vbl. sb.*1 Add: **3. c.** *Woollen manufacture.* (See quot.)

1920 J. M. Matthews *Application of Dyestuffs* i. 66 An operation very similar to that of decatizing is known as potting. It is a treatment of woollen goods with steam and hot water for the purpose of producing a particular character of finish.

7. *potting-bench, -shed* (examples), *-soil.*

1874 *Gardeners' Chron.* 17 Jan. 95/3 A movable wooden tray, shaped like the top of a *potting bench..will answer the purpose. *Ibid.*, The manure and compost yard should include a *potting shed if there is room to erect it. 1907 E. Gosse *Father & Son* vii. 181 My Father would..bolt into the verandah, and round the garden into the potting-shed. 1908 *Daily Chron.* 29 Feb. 9/1 This material is in excellent condition for mixing with *potting soil as a fertiliser.

Potty (pǫ·ti), *a.*1 *slang* or *colloq.* [Of obscure origin; cf. Potter *v.*, Pottering *ppl. a.*]

1. Of persons and things: Small, petty, insignificant; esp. *potty little.*

1899 E. Phillpotts *Human Boy* 72 It is such a potty little place, hardly worth calling a wood. 1904 H. B. M. Watson *Hurricane Is.* viii. 111 'Lord, doctor!' he ended with a sneer, 'to think of you sucking up to a potty prince!' 1907 Galsworthy *Country House* iii. iv. 246 We stand on our petty rights here, And our potty dignity there. 1927 G. K. Chesterton *Secret of Father Brown* v, Who would, or could, have killed him up in that potty little place?

b. Easy to manage, accomplish, or deal with; simple, easy, safe.

1899 E. Phillpotts *Human Boy* 127 Ferrars..got regularly muddled over a potty question about Jacob. 1918 E. F. Benson *David Blaize* iv. 70 It was quite certain that Helmsworth would have won had not that ass Blazes.. dropped the 'pottiest' catch ever seen. 1922 *Blackw. Mag.* July 55/2 It's potty on this scaffolding.., no end of cross-pieces to hold on to.

2. Out of one's senses; foolish, crazy; mad *about* or '*gone*' *on* (someone or something).

1921 *Chambers's Jrnl.* July 511/2 Pull yourself together. You'll be going potty if you don't get a move on. 1923 E. V. Lucas *Advisory Ben* xxxix. 206 I'm potty about her. 1930 *Diary Public School Girl* 35 Do you know, I'm frightfully potty on you.

Potty (pǫ·ti), *a.*2 [f. Pot *sb.*1 + -y.] Savouring of the pot.

1901 *Westm. Gaz.* 4 June 3/2 Debauched teetotalers ruin their insides by intemperate potations of potty tea.

Pouch, *sb.* **1. e.** (Earlier example.)

1879 *P.M.G.'s Rep.* 9 The..number of pouches exchanged with these Travelling Post Offices..in 24 hours is now 1090.

Pouch, *v.* **1.** (Later example.)

1910 A. A. Milne *Day's Play* 114, I heard Slip call 'Mine' and he pouched the ball.

Pouf. 2. Also *attrib.*

1906 *Queen* 28 Apr. p. viii/3 A quaint pouf sleeve.

3. b. A low stuffed seat or cushion; a humpty. Also *attrib.*

1894 [see 3]. 1910 *Army & Navy Auxiliary Co-op. Supply Catal.* 314 Pouffe Hassocks. 1925 C. S. Taylor *Upholstery* 96 The pouffe, or floor cushion, is much in favour.

Pouff (pŭf), *int.* and *sb.* [Imitative; cf. Poof.] **a.** *int.* An expression of contempt. **b.** *sb.* An explosive sound.

1905 Elinor Glyn *Viciss. Evangeline* 62 'Pouff!' I said, and I pointed at him. 1908 *Westm. Gaz.* 25 May 5/2, I was riding on the back of the balloon..when suddenly I heard a 'pouff', as if someone had blown a blast from a bellows.

Poulter. 1. b. *Poulter's measure* (recent example).

1900 W. A. Raleigh in *Introd. to Castiglione's Bk. of Courtier* p. xiv, The one-legged poulter's measure is not responsible for all the horrors of this.

Poultice, *v.* Also *absol.*

1861 'Geo. Eliot' *Silas Marner* xvi. 286 Sometimes things come into my head when I am leeching or poulticing.

Pound, *sb.*2 **6.** **pound-master** (earlier examples).

1841 *Knickerbocker Mag.* XVII. 289 The dull brute..ran toward his own pen with such speed that the pound-master struggled in vain to head him off. 1867 in Mrs. Custer *Tenting on Plains* (1889) xvii. 543, I would you were in the humble employment of Hutchins, the pound-master at home.

Pound, *sb.*3 Add: **4. b.** An act of pounding; a journey or voyage accompanied by pounding.

1907 *Daily Chron.* 6 Dec. 6/4 Majestically the Potsdam glided from Rotterdam on her ten days' pound to New York.

Pound, *v.*1 Add: **2. d.** To produce or turn *out* by pounding.

1904 F. Lynde *Grafters* v. 58 He sat down at the typewriter to pound out a letter to the general counsel, resigning his sinecure.

e. To walk upon; to tramp. *U.S. colloq.*

1909 'O. Henry' *Options* (1916) 30 I'm pounding the asphalt for another job. 1923 L. J. Vance *Baroque* vi. 33, I won't get sent back to pound sidewalks for what I'm pulling off tonight.

Poundage 1. Add: **7.** *attrib.* as *poundage system, tax.*

1909 *Daily Chron.* 13 Aug. 4/3 The fairest system is that which the Bill applies in the case of clubs; namely, a *poundage system on the business done. 1909 *Westm. Gaz.* 12 May 2/2 The two resolutions were for a Customs duty on imported beer and for a *poundage-tax on the liquor sold in clubs.

Poundage 2. Add: **2.** The keeping of cattle in a pound or enclosure; an enclosure in which cattle are kept.

1866 *Cycl. Useful Arts* I. 3/2 The slaughterman..only paying for the poundage of his beasts according to the requirements of his business. 1902 *Encycl. Brit.* XXXII. 644/1 The bye-laws usually provide..for the poundage to have floor-space sufficient for each animal.

Pound-cake. (Earlier examples.)

1807 *New Syst. Cookery* (Boston) 218 A good pound cake. 1813 *Niles' Weekly Reg.* IV. 192/1 If ever he lived to see Baltimore, the rooster should be treated with *pound cake.*

Pounding, *vbl. sb.*1 **4.** *pounding-mill* (later example).

1849 C. Lanman *Lett. Alleghany Mts.* i. 17 The vein gold is brought to light by means of what is called a pounding mill.

Pound-keeper. (Earlier examples.)

1641 *Ipswich Rec.* 3 Dec., Mr. Wilson is the Pound keeper. 1681 *Watertown Rec.* II. 3 Benjamin Crispe is to take the charge of the pound to be pound keeper. 1766 *Essex Inst. Hist. Coll.* XXI. 233 Left[enant] John Rowe Pound Keeper this year.

Pour, *v.* **1.** (Further examples.)

1881 Mrs. J. H. Riddell *Senior Partner* II. x. 203 An old, old pug..took no notice of Mr. McCullagh or anything else, till Janey poured him out a saucer of milk. 1909 Eliz. Banks *Myst. Frances Farrington* 54 Pour me some tea, dear, and tell me about your play.

Pout-net. (Later example.)

1859 *Act* 22 & 23 *Vict.* c. lxx. § 14 To kill Salmon in or from the River by means of any Pout Net, Rake Hook, or similar Engine.

Pouty (pau·ti), *a.* *U.S.* [f. Pout *sb.*2 and *v.*1 + -y.] Inclined to pout; displeased; sullen.

1863 'Gail Hamilton' *Gala-Days* 221 They never were tired when anything was to be done, or..peevish, or pouty. 1897 R. M. Stuart *Simpkinsville* 23 This stove's ez dull-eyed and pouty ez any other woman ef she's neglected.

Poverty. 8. poverty-grass (earlier example).

1853 Darlington *Flora Cestrica* (ed. 3) 361 *Aristida dichotoma*...Poverty-Grass.

Powder, *sb.*1 **5. b.** Add: **powder-burn** *v. trans.*, to burn with the hot gas issuing from a fire-arm; **powder-closet,** a small room or closet formerly used for the powdering of hair and wigs; **powder-post beetle,** a species of beetle injurious to timber; **powder-push,** a surgical instrument for applying powder; **powder-room** (*b*) = *powder-closet.*

1846 J. W. Webb *Altowan* I. iv. 125 He might *powder-burn the bear by the nearness of the shot. 1847 in H. Howe *Hist. Coll. Ohio* 99 In this struggle, Lytle..had..his face powder burnt. 1927 *Scribner's Mag.* Feb. 176/2 In the pursuit, the Rangers literally carried out their leader's orders to 'powder-burn' them. 1905 *Pall Mall Mag.* Dec. 746/1 Violante..lay dozing in the *powder closet which opened out of Donna Carlotta's bedroom. 1927 *Daily Express* 12 Dec. 4 Methley Park..has one or two unusual features, however; and among these are some queer old powder closets. 1929 *Encycl. Brit.* XXII. 221/1 The..insects..which do most damage are the death watch beetle..; the *powder-post beetle (*Lyctus* sp.) and the common furniture beetle. 1908 *Practitioner* Nov. 742 The..straight end of the tube is fitted with a spring *powder-push with a double bellows. 1908 'Frank Danby' *Heart of a Child* xv. 250 He liked to see ..his Staffordshire pottery en-niched in the quaint *powder-room, opening out of the drawing-room.

Powder-blue. 1. *sb.* (Earlier example.)

1656 *Essex Probate Rec.* I. 233 Mace and Ribing, starch and poudarblu.

Powder-house. [Powder *sb.*1 5 b.] A building in which gunpowder is stored.

1720 *Jrnls. Ho. Repr. Mass.* II. 288 Daniel Pawning, Keeper of the Powder-House. 1774 [see Powder *sb.*1 5 b]. 1776 *Rec. N.H. Comm. Safety* 45 Received..three thous[d] weight of powder..and lodged the same in the Powder House. 1832 J. F. Watson *Tales Olden Times* 99 The powder house be remembered. 1848 *Knickerbocker Mag.* XVIII. 216 The powder house, the pound, the poor-house and the county-house, are all objects of notice to the traveller.

Comb. 1789 *Boston Town Rec.* X. 183 Foster, Thomas, powder-house-keeper.

Powderize (pau·dəraiz), *v.* [f. Powder *sb.*1 + -ize.] *trans.* To reduce to powder; to pulverize; also, to mix with powder.

1903 *Sci. Amer.* Suppl. 18 Apr. 22818/1 Only one thing can be done to lighten the task, and that is to powderize the soap when the mixed materials are still warm.

Powellize (pau·ĕlaiz), *v.* [f. the name of W. *Powell* who invented the process + -ize.] *trans.* To preserve (timber) by boiling in a solution of sugar. Hence **Pow·ellized** *ppl. a.*; **Pow·ellizing** *vbl. sb.*

1903 *Sci. Amer.* Suppl. 5 Sept. 23139/1 The London city authorities..intend to repave the Strand thoroughfare with 15,000 Powellized blocks. 1913 *Chambers's Jrnl.* Aug. 621/1 Seeing that elm is plentiful and extremely low in price, Powellising should result in its more extended application. *Ibid.*, After being Powellised it becomes a very handsome and hard wood. 1929 *Encycl. Brit.* XXII. 222/1 Extensive tests carried out with Powellized sleepers on Indian railways give good results.

Power, *sb.*1 Add: **6. c.** *The powers that be*: (after *Romans* xiii. 1) the authorities concerned. Also in sing.

[1526 see sense 6]. 1836 T. Raikes *Jrnl.* (1856) II. 344 There is in the masses of this country a great principle of submission to the powers that be. 1909 *Westm. Gaz.* 11 Jan. 12/4 Perhaps next year the powers that be may take a little more trouble to discover the talent that lies outside London. 1930 *Times* 25 Mar. 23/7 One can only express the hope that the Power-that-be in Nanking will realize the desirability for proceeding slowly and gradually.

18. a. *power-absorption, -buzzer, -meter, -stroke* (example), *valve.* **b.** *power-boat, -brake, -vehicle* (example). **c.** *power house* (earlier example), *-plant.* **e.** *power-boating.* **f. power-board,** a switch-board for directing the supply of electric power; **power-factor** (see quot.); **power-rail,** the rail that carries the current for an electric railway.

1902 *Encycl. Brit.* XXVIII. 78/1 The..measurement of the true *power-absorption in the dielectric of cables. 1904 *Elect. Rev.* 17 Sept. 444 (Cent. Suppl.) The *power-board is a handsome marble panel equipped with Weston ammeter and voltmeter arranged for taking readings. 1908 R. W. Chambers *Firing Line* vii. 84 Every day..the swift *power-boats sped northward to the Inlet. 1902 *Encycl. Brit.* XXVI. 340/1 The necessity for prompt and effective application of brakes in an emergency led to the invention of means to operate them with power superior to muscular force. Such brakes are known as *power brakes. 1928 E. Blunden *Undert. of War* xxvi, I think I have the slightest aptitude for understanding the principle of electricity, the mechanism of the 'fullerphone' or '*power buzzer'. 1893 *Jrnl. Soc. Arts* 25 Aug. 867 The ratio between the true watts and the apparent watts is called the '*power-factor* of the circuit. 1881 *Harper's Mag.* Mar. 597/1 He found himself in the end at that '*Power House' of which he had heard..for many a year. 1903 *Science Abstracts* B. VI. 66 *Power Meter*...This is an apparatus, patented by A. F. Nagle, for measuring the i.h.p., or rather the indicated work in a given time, at one end of an engine cylinder. 1909 *Westm. Gaz.* 4 May 4/1 The rigid dirigible..cannot be made to lift the weight of the *power-plant necessary to render it independent of all winds. 1899 *Trans. Amer. Inst. Elect. Engin.* 16 May 220 This rail..is known as the '*power rail', it forming one terminal of the electrical system. 1908 *Westm. Gaz.* 17 Sept. 5/2 Leakage of electric current has been known to occur between the power-rail and the running-rails. 1908 *Westm. Gaz.* 4 June 4/2 The friction of the piston against the cylinder walls during the *power-stroke. 1919 W. D. Owen *Guide to Study of Ionic Valve* 38 *Power valves need to be very hard otherwise the plate voltage would cause a discharge across the space. 1909 *Chambers's Jrnl.* June 341/1 Thompson in Edinburgh introduced the first *power-vehicle running on india-rubber tires.

Power, *v.* Transfer †*Obs.* to sense defined in Dict. and add: **2.** To supply with mechanical power for propulsion.

1899 *Engin. Mag.* Mar. 1011/1 It is in the powering of the two vessels that the great advance in marine engineering is most apparent. 1929 *Chicago Tribune* 31 Jan. 3/8 His plane is a Travelaire, powered with a whirlwind motor. 1930 *Observer* 25 May 17 Finality on the question of motor passenger line powering is far from being reached.

Powerful, *a.* **6.** (Earlier examples.)

1811 Byron in Moore *Life of Byron* I. 249 For a long time I have been restricted to an entire vegetable diet,..so I expect a powerful stock of potatoes, greens, and biscuit. 1822 J. Woods *Eng. Prairie* 346, I also have got some beefs, and a powerful chance of corn.

Pozzy (pǫ·zi). *Army slang.* Also **possy.** **a.** Abbreviation of Position. **b.** Jam.

1916 *Daily Mail* 1 Nov. 4/4 'Pozzy' (jam). 1919 *War Slang* in *Athenæum* 25 July 664/1 'Pozzy', jam, or a gun position. 1925 Fraser & Gibbons *Soldier & Sailor Words* 229 *Possy* (or *Pozzy*): A position. Dug-out. Also jam (pozzy).

Practicable, *a.* **1.** (Further example.)

1921 *Act* 11 & 12 *Geo. V* c. 31 § 17 The person aggrieved.. may apply to the next practicable court of quarter sessions for the country.

Practical. B. *sb.* **2.** (Earlier example.)

a 1737 M. Green *Spleen* 322 That tribe whose practicals decree Small beer the deadliest heresy.

Practice. 12. Add: *practice-crew*; **practice-curve,** a curve showing the relation of practice to progress.

1887 *Century Mag.* XXXIV. 178/2 Freshmen formed a practice crew of their own. 1924 R. M. Ogden tr. *Koffka's Growth of Mind* 262 New configurations are also attributable to these lower centres; as is demonstrated by the fact that the practice-curve improves by leaps.

Prædella, variant of Predella.

1926 *Trans. Scot. Ecclesiol. Soc.* 71 The single step Prædella is semi-circular, and is enclosed by a beautiful tudor rail.

Praedesque (prē·de·sk), *a.* [f. the name of *Praed* (see def.) + -esque.] In the manner or style of W. M. Praed (1802–39), a poet and writer of society verse. So **Prae·dian** *a.*; **Prae·dism,** the style of Praed's poetry.

1865 *Dublin Univ. Mag.* II. 23 The best epigrams and Praedesque verses of the week. 1883 *Century Mag.* Feb. 595/1 Mr. Locker can write Praedesque poems. 1905 Mrs. H. Ward *Marriage of W. Ashe* i. ii. 29 Meanwhile the outer room gathered to hear the recitation of some *vers de société*, fondly believed by their author to be of a very pretty and Praedian make. 1927 *Observer* 15 May 6 What he was thinking of was polite badinage, Praedism, and Horatian levity.

Præmunire, *sb.* **2. b.** (Later hist. example.)

1902 J. Gairdner *Hist. Eng. Ch. 16th Cent.* IV. viii. 141 Any subject henceforth bringing in bulls of excommunication was liable to a praemunire.

Præsidial, variant of Presidial.

1918 C. G. Robertson *Bismarck* v. 185 Bismarck persuaded the King of Bavaria to write to the King of Prussia, inviting him..to take the Imperial Crown and exercise as Emperor his Praesidial rights in the Confederation.

Prairie. Add: Also 9 **parara, praira, praire, prairy.**

1806 *Massachusetts Spy* 16 July 1/5 (quoting *New Engl. Republican*) A venerable Philosopher sitting in the middle of an immense Map, marked with vast praires, huge rivers, and mountains of salt. 1819 Dana *Geog. Sk.* 37 The ore is dug from an open praira. *Ibid.* 108 There are two kinds of praira, the *river* and *upland*. 1822 *Massachusetts Spy* 6 Feb. 4/3 (quoting *Detroit Gaz.*) We passed also a prairy of several miles extent, which is skirted with woodland. 1834 Crockett *Narr. Life* xii. 85 I came to the edge of an open parara, and looking on before my dogs, I saw in and about the biggest bear that ever was seen in America.

b. *prairie country* (examples), *farm, fire* (earlier examples), *flower* (examples), *hay*; **prairie bottom,** a low-lying expanse of prairie land; **prairie-breaking,** the employment of a prairie-breaker; also, an area ploughed or broken by this means; **prairie clover** (earlier example); **prairie-cock** = Prairie-chicken; **prairie-crane,** an American species of crane, *Grus americana* or *mexicana*; **prairie-cricket,** an American species of cricket; **prairie-fox** (examples); **prairie-hare, -lark, mouse** (see quots.); **prairie-pea,** an American species of *Astragalus*; **prairie-plough, -plover** (earlier examples); **prairie-potato** = *prairie-turnip*; **Prairie Provinces** = *Prairie States*; **prairie-rattlesnake, -rose** (earlier examples); **prairie-snake** (example); **Prairie State** (earlier examples); **prairie-wagon** (example).

1823 Long *Exped.* I. 123 Our party encamped..in a.. beautiful and level *prairie bottom. 1867 *Rep. Iowa Agric. Soc.* (1868) 139 On strong prairie-bottom it is liable to get down. 1861 *Trans. Ill. Agric. Soc.* IV. 37 It was found the plows were running..too deep for ordinary *prairie breaking. 1879 *Scribner's Monthly* Nov. 132/2 The aggregate extent of these long narrow black strips of 'prairie breaking'. 1870 *Amer. Naturalist* IV. 581 The *prairie clovers, or turban flowers (*Petalostemum*) are among the most interesting of the leguminose species. 1846 J. W. Webb *Altowan* I. ii. 31 The *prairie cock (a large species of grouse, of a pepper-and-salt colour, and long, pointed tail). 1876 J. Burroughs *Winter Sunshine* v. 115 About this time..the prairie hens or prairie-cocks set up that low musical cooing or crowing. 1806 in *Ann. 9th Congress* 2 Sess. 1136 The quality of the land is supposed superior to that on Red river, until it ascends to the *prairie country. 1848 E. Bryant *California* iii. 34 Our march was..through an undulating prairie-country. 1844 *Yale Lit. Mag.* IX. 328 The discordant croak of the *prairie crane. 1860 Mayne Reid *Odd People* 341 He [the Yamparico] finds a resource, however, in the *prairie cricket, an insect..of the *gryllus* tribe. 1838 H. W. Ellsworth *Valley N. Wabash* v. 49 A late brother of the writer, who had just finished a *prairie farm. 1884 'Mark Twain' *Huck. Finn* vii. 46 Hogs soon went wild in them bottoms after they had got away from the prairie-farms. 1836 Edward *Hist. Texas* 70 The annual *prairie fires. 1851 Alice Cary *Clovernook* 77 I listened to stories of huge lights made by prairie fires. 1836 J. Hall *Stat. West.* iv. 56 The *prairie-flower displays its diversified hues. 1855 R. Glisan *Jrnl. Army Life* (1874) 75 Presented a collection of dried prairie flowers to the Smithsonian Institute. 1887 J. Kirkland *Zury* 10 The 'prairie flowers' (blue gentian). 1846 Sage *Scenes Rocky Mts.* (1859) 297 A *prairie fox,—a creature about twice the size of a large red squirrel. 1876 J. Burroughs *Winter Sunshine* iv. 108 The prairie fox, the cross fox, and the black or silver-grey fox, seem only varieties of the red fox. 1868 *Amer. Naturalist* II. 536 *Prairie Hare (*Lepus Townsendii*). This hare is common east of the Rocky Mountains. 1845 *Cultivator* New Ser. II. 93 Without any kind of..comfort, except what they may gather from a poor supply of *prairie hay. 1878 J. H. Beadle *Western Wilds* xxviii. 433 First rate prairie hay, on which stock will keep fat all winter. 1885 *Encycl. Brit.* XIX 112/2 In North America [pipits] are represented by only two species—*Neocorys spraguii*, the *Prairie-Lark of the north-western plains, and *Anthus ludovicianus*, the American Titlark. 1868 *Amer. Naturalist* II. 534 *Prairie Mouse (*Hesperomys Sonoriensis*). This widely spread Mouse is common at Fort Benton. 1848 E. Bryant *California* ii. 28 I observed, also, a plant producing a fruit of the size of the walnut, called the *prairie-pea. 1870 *Amer. Naturalist* III. 162 One of the earliest flowers is the Prairie-pea (*Astragalus Mexicanus*). 1839 *Cultivator* VII. 33 It may be amusing to eastern readers to hear a description of a '*prairie plow'. 1861 *Trans. Ill. Agric. Soc.* IV. 392 The sod should be broken with a prairie plow. 1868 *Life among Mormons* 7 For the small birds—*prairie plover and meadow larks—it was not necessary to leave the road. 1843 Fremont *Exped.* 107 Six Kansas women, engaged in digging *prairie potatoes (*psoralea esculenta*). 1848 E. Bryant *California* iv. One of them [Indians] presented to me a root or tuber, of an oval shape, about one and one-half-inch in length and an inch in diameter. This root is called the prairie potato. 1924 *Times Trade & Engin. Suppl.* 29 Nov. 237/3 Owing to the reduction in the output [of grain] of the *Prairie Provinces. 1831 T. Buttrick *Trav.* 78 The *prairie rattlesnake, a small but very poisonous reptile frequently..[is] seen in those parts. 1822 J. Woods *Eng. Prairie* 303 But the *prairie-roses, balm..and sassafras-wood..have all powerful scents. 1843 Fremont *Exped.* 12 A large *prairie snake..was occupied in eating the young birds. 1852 Mrs. Stowe *Uncle Tom's Cabin* xlv. 525 Farmers of rich and joyous Ohio, and ye of the wide *prairie states. 1861 O. J. Victor *Hist. Southern Rebellion* I. 166 Illinois, the 'Prairie State', then proved that she was as rich in her patriotism as in her soil and exhaustless resources. 1867 W. H. Dixon *New America* I. iii. 37 We find that our big Concord Coach has been exchanged for a light *prairie waggon.

Prairie-chicken. (Earlier example.)

1847 J. W. Abert in *Exec. Doc. 30th Congress* 1 Sess. IV. 545 During the day we saw flocks of snow larks and several prairie chickens.

Prairied, *a.* (Later example.)

1930 H. N. Spalding *From Youth to Age* 58 The happy cornlands of the prairied West.

Prairie schooner. (Earlier and later examples.)

1847 Th. Weed in Barnes *Mem. Weed* (1884) 129 We found the road..occupied with an almost unbroken line of waggons, drawn generally by two yokes of oxen, bringing wheat to the city. These teams are called 'prairie schooners'. 1910 *Congress. Rec.* 115 The next schooner I had any association with was that venerable and faithful prairie schooner [etc.].

Prairillon. For *a* 1860 read 1846 Sage.

Praise, *sb.* **4.** Add: **praise-leader** *Sc.*, the leader of the singing in a church.

1920 C. Jerdan *Sc. Clerical Stories* xviii. 370 The minister ..looked down over the side of the pulpit and said to the praise-leader, 'Is David ill?'.

Praise, *v.* Add: **3. e.** *absol.* To express approbation; to bestow praise.

1879 *Fortn. Rev.* 1 Apr. 507 So Molière is read or witnessed; we laugh and we praise. 1896 *Forum* Mar. 1 Whether we praise lavishly or venture to blame, two perils threaten us.

Prance. *sb.* Add: **c.** *transf.* Swagger, arrogance.

1927 *Blackw. Mag.* Oct. 536/1 Truly it was just 'prance', and..it was very far from being the only piece of prancing to be met with in Digby's life.

Pra·nceful, *a.* [f. Prance *sb.* + -ful.] Full of prance; spirited; mettled.

1894 Kipling *Jungle Bk.* 64 Don't you envy our pranceful bands?

Praseodymium (prēˑziǫdi·miǝm). *Chem.* [f. Gr. πράσιος leek-green (see Prase) + (Di)dymium.] A metallic element of the rare-earth group discovered (along with *Neodymium q.v.) by Auer von Welsbach in 1885. It resembles neodymium in properties but is distinguished from it by forming leek-green salts. Symbol Pr; atomic weight 141; atomic number 59.

1886 *Nature* 22 July 266/1 It was now seen that in successive fractions the intensities of the other more refrangible lines belonging both to neo- and praseodymium varied greatly from strong to almost obliteration. 1902 [see *Neodymium].

Prawn, *sb.* **c.** Add: *prawn fisherman, -fishing.*

1921 *Chambers's Jrnl.* Sept. 590/1 Numerous are the adverse comments I've heard on the prawn fisherman and his ways. 1924 *Blackw. Mag.* Apr. 489/2 But neither the Lydons nor anybody else could make me enjoy prawn-fishing on that high walk at Galway.

Praw·ning, *vbl. sb.* [f. Prawn *sb.* + -ing 1.] Fishing for salmon with a prawn as bait.

1909 *Westm. Gaz.* 10 May 12/2 Prawning and spinning for salmon has begun on the Hampshire Avon. 1921 *Chambers's Jrnl.* Sept. 590/1 Prawning for salmon is looked down upon by many as being almost a form of poaching.

Pray, *v.* **5. b.** Also *spec.* To make a formal petition.

1754 [see Dict.]. 1920 *Act* 10 & 11 *Geo. V* c. 67 Sched. 1, The Council shall..determine whether to issue the order as prayed for, or to issue the order with such modifications as may appear to be necessary.

Prayer 1. **6. d.** Add: **prayer cylinder** = Prayer-wheel; **prayer-flag,** a flag having prayers inscribed on it; **prayer-gong,** a gong calling persons to prayer; **prayer-machine, -mill** = Prayer-wheel; **prayer-stool,** a stool for kneeling on while praying.

1894 Isabella L. Bishop *Among Tibetans* ii. 46 *Prayer-cylinders which are turned by pulling ropes. 1897 *Geog. Jrnl.* X. 35 A prayer-cylinder revolved by the wind. *Ibid.* 44 Groups of *prayer-flags in memory of the dead are planted beside every village. 1905 E. F. Benson *Image in Sand* ix, I adore theosophy, *prayer-gongs, and letters from the ceiling. 1894 Isabella L. Bishop *Among Tibetans* ii. 46 Then there are *prayer-mills which revolve easily by being brushed by the hand of the passer-by. 1908 *Daily Chron.* 6 Apr. 1/4 As they knelt upon the wooden *prayer stool.. they made no noise.

Prayer-meeting. (Earlier example.)

1823 *Baptist Mag.* IV. 32 It had been the practice of the church to hold weekly prayer-meetings.

Praying, *vbl. sb.* **b.** Add: **praying flag-staff,** cf. *prayer-flag* above.

1877 T. W. R. Davids *Buddhism* 211 Everywhere in Tibet these praying flag-staffs meet the eye.

Praying, *ppl. a.* (Later example.)

1931 F. L. Allen *Only Yesterday* iv. 80 The 'praying Colonels' of Centre College.

Preaching, *vbl. sb.* **3.** *preaching-place* (later examples), *-stand.*

1845 A. Wiley in *Indiana Mag. Hist.* XXIII. 37 Many new neighbors were taken in as preaching places. 1856 Strickland *Peter Cartwright* viii. 85 We took in a new preaching-place at a Mr. Moor's. 1856 Mrs. Stowe *Dred* xxiii. I. 326 The assembly poured in and arranged themselves before the preaching stand.

Preaching-house. (Earlier example.)

1747 Wesley *Jrnl.* (1909–16) III. 321 Mr. J. Richards had just sent his brother word that he had hired a mob to pull down his preaching-house that night.

Pre-adamite. B. *adj.* **1.** (Further example.)

1916 *Nature* 25 May 259/2 For imitation, a pre-Adamite simian character, plays no small part in the ostensible development, mental, moral, and otherwise, of gregarious folk.

Precarial (prĭkē·riǎl), *a.* [f. med.L. *precāria*: see Precary *sb.*] Of, pertaining to, or connected with *precaria*.

1914 *Eng. Hist. Rev.* Jan. 137 It is also highly probable that precarial transactions were instrumental not only in the bringing together of ecclesiastical property, but also in utilizing it by means of dependent farms.

Pre·cast, *ppl. a.* [Pre- A. 1.] Applied to concrete which is cast in blocks before it is used for building.

1927 *Daily Express* 2 Mar. 3/6 The Concrete Products Association was formed yesterday to improve production and maintain a high standard of quality in the use of 'precast' units in building. 1929 *Daily Tel.* 8 Jan. 7/6 A structure composed of seasoned precast blocks was less likely to crack than one of in situ concrete.

Precess, *v.* Transfer †*Obs.* to sense defined in Dict. and add:

2. *intr.* To undergo precession.

1902–3 O. Lodge in *Jrnl. Inst. Elect. Engin.* XXXII. 83 The pull of gravity on a spinning top does not make it topple over, but makes it precess.

Précis, *sb.* **c.** (Add example.)

1908 *Westm. Gaz.* 24 Apr. 1/3 The Society proposes to give information to all inquirers, to publish *précis* articles and leaflets [etc.].

Precision. Add: **3.** *attrib.* Of apparatus (esp. automatic) designed for exact or precise work.

1909 *Westm. Gaz.* 7 Dec. 5/2 They did not know which to marvel at most, the wonderful automatic precision machines, ..or the staff responsible for their working. 1910 *Ibid.* 6 Jan. 4/2 It is only a question of time ere Germany will be in a position to dispense with those wonderful American automatic precision tools.

Precocial (prĭkōu·ʃǎl), *a.* [f. as Precocious + -al.] = Precocious 3.

1897 F. M. Chapman *Bird-life* 67 The young of what are termed 'praecocial' birds are hatched with a covering of downy feathers.

Precocious, *a.* **3.** (Further example.)

1897 Parker & Haswell *Zoology* II. 382 The newly hatched young may be either well covered with down and able to run or swim and to obtain their own food, in which case they are said to be precocious, or [etc.].

Precociously, *adv.* (Add example.)

1893 E. B. Wilson *Biol. Lectures* 13 (Cent. Suppl.) Eggs that admit of complete orientation at the first or second cleavage,..are commonly supposed to reflect precociously the later organization [etc.].

Precoo·l, *v.* [f. Pre- A. 1 + Cool *v.*] *trans.* To cool (material of any kind) before submitting it to some further treatment. So **Precoo·ler, Precoo·ling** *vbl. sb.*

1904 *Phys. Rev.* XIX. 330 From the compressor, the air passes successively through an aftercooler; a separator;..and finally through a precooler charged with broken ice or snow —reaching the liquefier at a temperature of about 2°. 1926 *Spectator* 18 Sept. 412/1 By having a hermetically sealed compartment with the commodity pre-cooled, a low temperature is maintained until the box is opened at destination. *Ibid.*, After the cleaning the pre-cooling takes place.

Predative (pre·dǎtiv), *a.* [f. L. *prædāt-us* pple. of *prædārī* to plunder + -ive.] Suggestive of depredation; predatory.

1930 D. H. Lawrence *Virgin & Gipsy* iii. 50 She [the gipsy-woman] was..just a bit wolfish..'Good-morning, my ladies and gentlemen,' she said, eyeing the girls from her bold, predative eyes.

Predator (pre·dǎtǫɹ). *Zool.* [ad. L. *prædātor* plunderer.] An animal or organism that preys upon another.

1922 W. M. Wheeler *Soc. Life Insects* 46 Species that behave in this manner are not true parasites, but extremely economical predators, because they eventually kill their victims.

Predestiny. (Later example.)

1909 Bridges *Test. Beauty* III. 856 That old Hebrew poet, imagin'd Eve's predestiny to be helpmate and comfort to God's perfect man.

Predictably (prĭdi·ktǎbli), *adv.* [f. Predictable *a.* + -ly 2.] In a manner that can be predicted or foretold.

1914 J. H. Skrine *Pastor Futurus* 88 The Pentecosts come back, as surely though not so predictably as the dawns.

Predictionism (prĭdi·kʃǝniz'm). [f. Prediction + -ism.] Belief in prediction or prophecy.

1919 P. H. Osmond *Myst. Poets Engl. Church* vii. 215 He was a 'crank', dominated by extravagant notions—a victim of Predictionism and credulity.

Pre-empt, *v.* Add: **c.** *Bridge.* To make a pre-emptive bid.

1914 M. C. Work *Auction Developments* 313 It is the exceptional case in which it is advisable to preempt with an original No Trump. 1929 — *Compl. Contract Bridge* i. 2 In Auction a bidder may bid..more than two for the purpose of pre-empting.

Pre-emption. b. (Examples.)

1747 *Baltimore Town Rec.* 21 Mr. Alexander Lawson applied also to enter his Preemption of making out Ground into the water. 1780 W. Fleming in *Trav. Amer. Col.* 631 For preemption of 400 acres..Claimers 339. 1815 Drake *Cincinnati* i. 52 These sales the Government refused to sanction but granted pre-emption to the purchasers. 1847 in Drake *Pioneer Life Kentucky* i. 13 At length they fixed upon a 'settlement and pre-emption' eight miles from Washington. 1887 *Harper's Mag.* June 69/2 The 'claims' and 'pre-emptions' were marked to await the time when the owner could safely take possession.

Pre-emptioner. (Earlier examples.)

1841 *Knickerbocker Mag.* XVII. 278 They amused themselves by calling the exclusives 'squatters', 'prëemptioners', etc. 1841 *Congress. Globe* 26 Jan. App. 368/3 Those who are called pre-emptioners.

Pre-emptive, *a.* Add: **2.** In auction bridge: Applied to a bid which is made higher than ordinary practice requires in order to prevent opponents from bidding and so acquiring information about each other's cards.

1913 Flor. Irwin *Auction High-Lights* 95 A preëmptive opening-bid in a major suit means that the bidder wants no information and wishes to play the hand at his own suit.

Pre-emptively (prĭ,e·mᵖtivli), *adv.* [f. Pre-emptive *a.* + -ly 2.] In a pre-emptive manner.

1918 Bergholt *Royal Auction Bridge* (ed. 2) 148 By declaring 'pre-emptively', up to the full strength of his hand, Z. will no doubt be able to prevent B. from directing A. what to lead.

Preening, *vbl. sb.* (Later example.)

1875 *Encycl. Brit.* III. 728/1 This *Uropygial gland* secretes an oily fluid, which the bird spreads over its feathers by the operation of 'preening'.

Prefectly (prī·fektli), *a.* [f. Prefect *sb.* + -ly 1.] Characteristic of or befitting a prefect.

1927 Josephine Elder *Thomasina Toddy* xxii. 218 Anne recognised them with her most prefectly twitch of the lips.

Prefer, *v.* **7.** (Modern example with *above.*)

1883 G. Moore *Modern Lover* II. vi. 105 There was one place he preferred above all others.

Preferable, *a.* Add: **3.** = Preference 8. *attrib.*

1913 *Act* 3 & 4 *Geo. V* c. 20 § 97 (1) Such preferable securities as existed at the date of the sequestration, and are not null or reducible.

Preference. Add: **7. b.** (Later example.)

1908 R. W. Chambers *Firing Line* ii. 20 That kills our four at Bridge...We'll have to play Klondike and Preference now.

8. preference voting, a system of voting in which the voter indicates by figures (1, 2, 3, etc.) opposite the names of the different candidates the order in which he supports them.

1908 *Westm. Gaz.* 20 Aug. 2/1 The local Labour Party is inclined to boycott preference voting and advocate its members to plump.

Preferential, *a.* Add: **c.** *Preferential voting* = preference voting (*Preference 8).

1908 *Westm. Gaz.* 20 Aug. 2/1 The State of Western Australia..is now attempting..preferential voting in a simple form.

Prefix, *v.* **5.** (Later example.)

1898 C. S. Sherrington in *Phil. Trans.* B. 85 The skin and musculature of the arm of Man are somewhat prefixed as compared with *Macacus*.

Prefi·xally, *adv.* [f. Prefixal + -ly 2.] In the manner of a prefix.

1922 S. Grew *Art of Player-Piano* 86 The shorter note may be affined prefixally to the note after it.

Preforma·tionary, *a.* [f. Preformation + -ary.] Of, pertaining to, or connected with preformation.

1931 *Times Lit. Suppl.* 15 Jan. 36/4 There arose two schools of preformationary thought.

Prefulgence (prĭfʌ·ldʒĕns). [f. as Prefulgent.] Pre-eminent brightness or splendour.

1926 Swinnerton *Chaste Wife* xxiii. 317 Too stupid to understand anything but physical prefulgence or absolute social convention.

Preheat (prīhī·t), *v.* [f. Pre- A. 1 + Heat *v.*] *trans.* To subject to a preliminary heating. So **Prehea·ted** *ppl. a.*; **Prehea·ting** *vbl. sb.*

1898 *Engin. Mag.* XVI. 245 This method of preheating may follow either the regenerative or the recuperative system. 1902 *Encycl. Brit.* XXIX. 582/1 These..are exposed to an enormous extent of brickwork surface, which we will assume for the moment has been highly preheated. 1911 A. Reynolds tr. *C. Dickmann's Basic Open-Hearth Steel Process* vii. 59 The second way of producing a steam-air gas with high hydrogen content, consists in the employment of superheated steam, or preheated air supply.

Prehensorial (prīhĕnsǫ·riǎl), *a.* [f. Prehensorium + -al.] Adapted for prehension or seizing; prehensory.

1903 *Proc. Zool. Soc.* I. 51 One cannot but wonder how the spider maintains a secure hold back downwards, especially when the powerful prehensorial legs of the first and second pairs are released.

Pre-igni·tion. Too early ignition in an internal combustion engine.

1903 *Work* 4 Apr. 138/2 Otherwise detrimental and even dangerous pre ignition will occur. 1908 *Westm. Gaz.* 20 Aug. 4/2 The tendency to pre-ignition. 1922 *Encycl. Brit.* XXX. 40/2 Should this combination of temperature and pressure be attained in operation it is apt..to lead to general overheating of the cylinder and ultimately to pre-ignition.

Preiotation (prīˌaiǫtē·ʃǝn). [f. Pre- A. 2 + Iota + -ation.] The placing of an *iota* or *i* before a vowel. So **Preiotiza·tion**; **Preio·tized** *a.*, having an *iota* prefixed.

1877 A. H. Keane tr. *Hovelacque's Sci. Lang.* 281 The Lithuanian *este* becomes *jeste* in Church Slavonic; and this 'prëiotation', as it is technically called, is a leading feature of all the Slavonic tongues. 1883 Morfill *Slavonic Lit.* i. 18 The difficulty of expressing the præiotised vowels is the same. 1887 — in *Encycl. Brit.* XXII. 148/2 The addition of a *y* sound before vowels is one of the great characteristics of the Slavonic languages, called 'præiotization'.

Prelatial, *a.* Also, that is a prelate.

1886 F. G. Lee *Edward VI* iii. 142 Both as regards what the prelatial preacher said, and what he did not say, it appeared to the Authorities..somewhat inadequate.

Prelim (prĭli·m). *colloq.* Abbreviation of *preliminary* used elliptically (cf. note in Dict. *s.v.* Preliminary A. b). A preliminary practice, contest or examination; a preliminary sheet (usually without signature) in a book.

1901 *Daily News* 1 Apr. 5/6 We arrived at Putney, just in time to see Oxford come out for their 'prelim'. 1902 *Daily Chron.* 19 Dec. 5/2 The English public school boy goes north for months of special tutoring for his 'prelim'. 1927 *Observer* 18 Dec. 4 He tells..about signatures, prelims, endpapers, uncut and unopened pages, issues and imperfections. 1928 L. J. Vance *Baroque* xxvii. 173 A fight that'd make the Dempsey-Carpenteeyay bout look like a cooked prelim. 1928 *Collier's* 18 Aug. 25/2 You're nothin' but a has-been, staggerin' around like some prelim boy.

Prelimen (prĭlai·mǝn). [f. L. *præ* before + *limen* threshold.] A preliminary step.

1898 C. S. Sherrington in *Phil. Trans.* B. 50 The requisite prelimen to the original aim of the inquiry [having been] carried through, the examination of certain spinal reflexes has been proceeded to.

Prelude, *v.* **1. b.** (Further example.)

1915 J. Buchan *Nelson's Hist. War* II. ix. 34 Von Kluck preluded it [an enveloping movement] by a heavy bombardment of Binche and Bray.

Prematura·tion. [f. Premature + -ation.] The fact of making or becoming mature too early.

1909 *Westm. Gaz.* 3 Feb. 2/1 The systems followed in the schools of the leading civilised races of the world make for prematuration.

Premier. B. *sb.* Add: **c.** The Secretary of State. *U.S.*

1905 *Washington Post* 21 Mar. 4 It is considered unlikely that he could be induced to return to the Cabinet, even as premier. 1925 W. H. Smith *Hist. Cabinet U.S.A.* 28 He [the Secretary of State] is frequently spoken of as the 'premier' of the cabinet, but there is no such title or designation known to our laws.

Premiership. Add: **1. b.** The position of Secretary of State. *U.S.*

1928 H. Minor *Story Democr. Party* 69 Madison had cabinet troubles, too. Monroe accepted the premiership in March 1811 [etc.].

Premisal. Delete ? *Obs.* and add example.

1912 C. Mackey in *Cath. Encycl.* XIV. 75/1 With the proper premisals then from one and the other here assumed, we say [etc.].

Premise, *sb.* **5.** *pl.* (Later example.)

1917 *Statutory Rules & Orders* No. 1259, § 4 For the purposes of this Order..'Premises' shall include any van, stand, cart or other vehicle.

Premium. 7. Add: *premium-bearing*; **premium bond,** a bond on which a premium is paid.

1908 *Westm. Gaz.* 29 Aug. 2/2 The Panama and Congo premium-bearing loans are two of the most scandalous pieces of finance which Europe has ever witnessed. 1931 *Star* 8 May 6/3 Every trick—from premium bonds to guessing the number of beans in a bottle—seems to have been tried.

Premiumed, *a.* Add: **b.** That pays a premium.

1927 *Daily Express* 5 July 5/5 The trade may also be entered as a premiumed apprentice or as a beginner at a nominal wage.

Premonitory. B. *sb. pl.* (Earlier example.)

1834 *Knickerbocker Mag.* IV. 307 The premonitories seize me before I have time to run to the doctors for relief.

Premonstration. (Modern example.)

1920 E. H. Begbie *Mirrors of Downing Street* i. 9 His intuitions are amazing. He astonished great soldiers in the war by his premonstrations.

Prep. 2. a. (Earlier example.)

1899 A. H. Quinn *Pennsylv. Stories* 93 The admission of such prep schools was against the constitution.

b. (Example.)

1899 A. H. Quinn *Pennsylv. Stories* 117 He was going to tell those people from the Governor down to the prep in the gallery,..just what the college had done for him.

c. Short for preparatory school.

1924 H. de Selincourt *Cricket Match* v, To know whose call it is..was driven into me at the prep.

Preparation. 10. Add: (sense 8) *preparation sermon.*

1843 *Knickerbocker Mag.* XXI. 261 On the very day of the preparation sermon at Tinnecum, a number of young persons were assembled.

Preparationist (prepǎrē·ʃǝnist). [f. Preparation + -ist.] One who favours naval and military preparedness.

1915 A. L. Lowell in *World's Work* (N.Y.) 719/1.

Preparing, *ppl. a.* (Modern example.)

1865 Eliz. Wetherell *Old Helmet* i. 21 The other figures, the dark walls and ivy, the servants and the preparing collation, were only a rich mosaic of background for those two.

Prepo·nderously, *adv.* [f. Preponderous + -ly 2.] In a preponderous degree; excessively.

1921 *Public Opinion* 5 Aug. 133/1 Is it a city or merely a village preponderously overgrown?

Preprint. Also *attrib.*

1929 E. C. Bingham *Some Defs. Rheology* 1 This paper is issued in preprint form primarily to stimulate discussion.

Pre·printed, *pa. pple.* [f. Preprint + -ed.] Printed in advance; issued as a preprint.

1928 E. D. P. Evans (*title*) Meaning of Minster in Place-Names. (Preprinted from the Philological Society's Transactions, 1925–28, Part I).

Pre-Raphaeli·tically, *adv.* [f. Pre-Raphaelitic + -al + -ly 2.] In a manner suggestive of the Pre-Raphaelites.

1927 *Glasgow Herald* 7 July 4/6 The drabness of Arnold Bennett's pre-Raphaelitically accurate Five Towns.

Pre·-release, *a.* [Pre- B. 2.] Of cinematographic films: Exhibited before the date fixed for the normal 'release'. **b.** as *sb.* A film 'released' before the normal date.

1927 *Glasgow Herald* 15 Nov. 9/7 An amendment..providing that pre-release cinema shows should take place in provincial centres as well as in London was agreed to without a division. 1929 *Sunday Dispatch* 13 Jan. 16/3 We, in London, have been privileged to view many pre-releases.

Prerogatival, *a.* (Recent example.)

1889 F. W. Maitland *Collected Papers* (1911) II. 71 The further back we look..the more closely does it seem connected with prerogatival rights.

Presanctified, *ppl. a.* (Earlier examples.)

1758 *An Important Inquiry* (ed. 2) App. 397 They offer up and shew the people the Sacrament reserved on those two solemn days, which they call the imperfect Mass, or the Mass of the presanctified. *a* 1773 A. Butler *Feasts & Fasts* vi. iv. (1839) 114 This is called the 'Mass of the presanctified mysteries': *Missa præsanctificatorum.*

Presbyteress. 2. (Modern example.)

1901 J. Wordsworth *Ministry of Grace* v. 271 The Virgins, Widows and Presbyteresses have the first place among the women in church.

Prescribe, *v.* **4.** (Modern example.)

1919 Kath. Routledge *Myst. Easter Island* viii. 116 As both the lifeboat and the cutter were carried in the waist of the ship when we were at sea, the space available for 'constitutionals' was prescribed.

Prescripto·rial, *a.* [f. Pre- + Scriptorial.] Existing before the use of writing.

1897 J. W. Powell in *16th Ann. Rep. Bur. Amer. Ethnol.* p. xcvi, The names are associative or symbolic in the vague fashion characteristic of prescriptorial ideation.

Pre-se·nile, *a.* [Pre- B. 1 d.] Occurring before senility.

1903 W. Osler in *Lancet* 22 Aug. 517/2 The patients in the severe cases are men as a rule in the pre-senile stage and they present well-marked cardio-vascular lesions. 1922 R. C. Punnett *Mendelism* 202 Presenile cataract of the eyes.

Present, *a.* **1.** (Further example.)

1832 *Congress. Deb.* 14 June 3530 Mr. C[layton] observed that the gentleman ought to remember that the present company is always excepted.

Presentational, *a.* Add: **b.** Pertaining to presentation (sense 5).

1928 *Daily Tel.* 19 July 18/3 The intelligent theatres of New York..show an admirable sympathy both for good European drama and new forms of presentational art.

Presentative, *a.* Add: **6.** *Comb.* as *presentative-representative.*

1897 H. H. Ellis tr. *Ribot's Psychol. of Emotions* 55 Then pleasure becomes an anticipation, as in the case of the dog when his food is being brought to him; to employ the term used by Herbert Spenser, it is a presentative-representative state.

Presentor. Add: **3.** One who presents or shows.

1853 *Trans. Mich. Agric. Soc.* IV. 155 The presentor is firmly of the belief that the yield would have been fully one hundred bushels more per acre, had it not been for the unprecedented drought.

Preserva·tionist. [f. Preservation + -ist.] A person who advocates the preservation of species from extinction.

1927 *Blackw. Mag.* Sept. 314/1 The excuses made for her [the peregrine falcon] by modern 'Preservationists' are altogether paltry.

Preserve, *sb.* **1.** (Later example).

1839 T. D. Hooker in Huxley *Life of Hooker* (1918) I. 43 That Capt. Ross did not intend to trust me that.. I am sure

Supplement, p. 3873; Corrigenda, p. 4092; Spurious words, p. 4093; Books quoted, p. 4094

from his asking me to tell the quantity of preserves for animals required.

Preserver. Add: **2. c.** = LIFE-PRESERVER 3.
1912 *Chambers's Jrnl.* Sept. 636/1 In the panic which is certain to ensue after a wreck even the handling of this preserver would be awkward in the narrow passages.

Presidential, *a.* Add: **1. b.** *Presidential year*, a year in which a presidential election occurs.
1903 *N. Y. Even. Post* 5 Sept., Every merchant knows that the buying demand is exceedingly sensitive. It is traditionally so in a Presidential year.

Presiding, *ppl. a.* Add: **b. presiding elder,** the elder put over a district in the U.S. Methodist Church; **presiding officer,** the person who has charge of a polling-station at an election.
1831 PECK *Guide for Emigrants* 258 There are three [Methodist] districts, over each of which is a presiding Elder. 1856 STRICKLAND *Peter Cartwright* vi. 12 There were four presiding-elder districts in the Western Conference. 1904 G. H. LORIMER *Lett. Self-made Merchant* 186 The Doc...knew more Scripture when he was 16 than the presiding elder. 1872 *Act* 35 & 36 *Vict.* c. 33 sched. 1. 21 The returning officer shall appoint a presiding officer to preside at each station.

Presidium (pri̇̄si·diəm). [L. *presidium*: see PRESIDIARY.] The presiding body or standing committee in various Communistic organizations.
1924 *Observer* 23 Mar. 13/5 The Presidium of the Union C.E.C. has decided [etc.]. 1926 *Times* 18 Oct. 8/2 The following members were appointed to constitute the presidium. 1927 *9th Congr. Communist Party Gt. Brit.* 65 This Executive Committee [of the Communist International] elects a presidium of some 20 to 30 members.

Press, *sb.*[1] Add: **10. c.** A mechanism in certain larvæ for regulating the size and character of the silk thread which they produce.
1907 *Amer. Naturalist* Sept. 573 In the case of *Apanteles glomeratus* the press is highly developed.

13. e. Also *to read for press.*
1846 DODD *Brit. Manufs.* VI. 57 To read for press—that is, to search for the minutest errors.

h. Phrases. *To have a good* (or *bad*) *press*: to be favourably (or unfavourably) commented on or criticized in current newspapers, journals, etc.
1908 *Times Lit. Suppl.* 26 Mar. 99/1 Mr. Leaf..has not had a good press lately. 1920 *Sat. Rev.* 10 July 26 Mr. Austen Chamberlain has a very bad press. 1928 *Observer* 11 Mar. 20/5 Infantry to-day has an exceedingly 'bad Press'. It is mocked at as obsolete by mechanomaniacs. 1929 *Times Lit. Suppl.* 17 Oct. 810/4 England has always had a 'bad Press' in every country—except, perhaps, in Spain.

15. a. *press-board* (examples).
1861 MRS. STOWE *Pearl Orr's Isl.* I. v. 28 That dignitary sits..looking majestically over the *press-board on her knee. 1896 MRS. HARRIS *Sister Jane* 17 I've got this press-board on my lap.

16. a. press book, a book printed at a private press; **press-matter,** matter printed in a newspaper or journal; **press-roll,** a roll in a paper-making machine bearing upon a couch-roll; **press-stud,** a stud or fastener of which the two parts are made to engage by pressure; **press tool,** a tool to which pressure is applied in operating it; **press-turf,** peat prepared for use as fuel by pressing.
1930 *Publishers' Weekly* 19 Apr. 2116/2 The past five years has seen keen collecting interest in *Press books both early and modern. 1892 STEVENSON & OSBOURNE *Wrecker* iii. 51 Very few youths of your age occupy nearly two columns of *press-matter all to themselves. 1880 J. DUNBAR *Pract. Papermaker* 46 Prove the rolls level and parallel—the bottom couch roll with the *press roll, [etc.]. 1928 *Daily Express* 14 July 5/4 A large case..fastening down the whole length with *press-studs. 1929 *Even. News* 18 Nov. 10/3 Advt., Toolroom Charge Hand, used to the production of small *press tools, drill jigs, etc. 1916 *Nature* 25 May 269/2 The Whitewater Peat Company..manufactured *press-turf for a short time.

b. press-clipping = *press-cutting.*
1920 *Blackw. Mag.* Aug. 143/1 A *press-clipping association.

Press, *v.*[1] **17.** (Later example.)
1811 *Lett. of John Love* (1840) clxxiii. 349 To press after attaining and communicating to others more of the beginnings and pledges of that glorious life.

Pre·ss-agent, *v.* [f. *press agent*: PRESS *sb.*[1] 16 b.] *trans.* To advertise in the manner of or by means of press agents. **Pre·ss-agenting** *vbl. sb.*
1920 TILDEN *Art of Lawn Tennis* 3, I shall be accused of 'press-agenting' my own book by this statement. 1927 SLOSSON *Great Crusade* 271 The same press-agenting which helped make the reputation of a grand-opera star..was also at the service of a pugilist.

Pre·ss-agentry. [f. as prec. + -RY.] The employment or activities of press agents.
1931 F. L. ALLEN *Only Yesterday* viii. 212 A striking demonstration of what press-agentry could do to make a national sensation.

Pressel (pres'l). [f. PRESS *v.*[1]] (See quot.)
1898 E. J. HOUSTON *Dict. Electr. Words* (ed. 4) 424 *Pressel*, a press switch or push connected to the end of a flexible pendant conductor.

Presser. 5. Add: **presser-eye** (*Spinning*), an aperture or eye through which cotton yarn passes before being wound on the spindle.
1892 J. NASMITH *Cotton Spinning* IX. 340 In short, the traveller performs the same function as the flyer eye in the throstle or the presser eye in the roving frame.

Pressing, *vbl. sb.*[1] **3.** *pressing-machine* (earlier example).
1825 *Austin Papers* (1924) I. 1028 We intend to send a gin and probably a *pressing machine.

Press-mark, *v.* [f. the sb.] *trans.* To provide (a book) with a press-mark.
1902 *Cassell's Encycl. Dict.* Suppl. 1915 *Trans. Bibliogr. Soc.* XIV. 5 The Society's library...has been rearranged and re-pressmarked.

Press-room[1]. **2.** (Later example.)
1878 *Rep. Vermont Board Agric.* 79 At the end from the road were the press room and wash room.

Pressure. 10. Add: **pressure-boiler,** a boiler designed to withstand great pressure, for heating liquids above the normal boiling point; so **pressure-flask**; **pressure-flaking,** the flaking of flint tools by applying pressure with a hard point; **pressure-hull,** the hull (or part of the hull) of a submarine which is designed to withstand the pressure of the sea when the vessel is submerged; **pressure line** = *pressure ridge*; **pressure-log,** a form of log which measures the velocity of flowing water by the height to which it rises in a tube.
1891 S. P. SADTLER *Hand-bk. Industr. Org. Chem.* v. 179 Three grammes of substance are placed in a small beaker (preferably of metal), which is placed as one of several in a Soxhlet *pressure-boiler, or the test is carried out in the Lintner *pressure-flask,—and heated to the temperature of boiling water. 1927 PEAKE & FLEURE *Hunters & Artists* 49 The new technique..includes a high finish by the process of *pressure-flaking. 1928 GAMBLE *Story N. Sea Air Station* xxii. 403 The commanding officer,..and 5 ratings were killed, and the *pressure hull pierced, so that the submarine was unable to submerge. 1909 *Daily Chron.* 3 Sept. 1/2 Much of our hard work was lost in circuitous twists around troublesome *pressure lines and high, irregular fields of very old ice. 1894 W. H. WHITE *Man. Naval Archit.* 453 By means of a number of ingenious *pressure-logs, the velocities of the streams at different points were measured by the heights of water in tubes.

Pretend (pri̇te·nd), *sb.* [f. the vb.] Something pretended; pretence. **b.** *adj.* Pretended; feigned.
1904 J. M. BARRIE *Peter Pan* (1928) 70 Now that they know it is pretend they acclaim her greedily. *Ibid.* 97 It is a pretend meal this evening, with nothing whatever on the table.

Pretend, *v.* **15.** (Later example.)
1900 GASQUET *Eve of Reformation* vi. (1905) 178 He.. passes a hint that some of their lives are not so saintly as they pretend.

Prettification (pri:tĭfikēi·ʃən). [f. PRETTIFY *v.* + -ATION.] The fact or process of making pretty; a prettifying.
1920 *Times Lit. Suppl.* 23 Sept. 617/1 Such work is..the counterfeit of romance. It gives us, not a celebration of life, but a prettification of it.

Pretty. B. *sb.* Add: **b.** (Earlier example.)
1736 *Boston News Lett.* in Alice M. Earle *Costume Col. Times* (1894) 180 Children's Silver Peaks & Flowers, Dutch Prettys.

d. Short for *pretty penny* (A. 5 b). *U.S.*
1909 MRS. STRATTON-PORTER *Girl of Limberlost* xxi. 387 I'd give a pretty to know that secret thing you say you don't.

e. *Golf.* The fairway.
1907 *Westm. Gaz.* 13 Sept. 3/1 Often he will get just as far as if he had been lying on the 'pretty'. 1927 *Daily Tel.* 12 Feb. 10/5 When the ball went sailing down the pretty, straight and true, what a satisfaction it was to both of them.

D. b. pretty-by-night *U.S.*, the Four o'clock or Marvel of Peru, *Mirabilis jalapa.*
1872 EGGLESTON *End of World* xxv. 169 She planted some *pretty-by-nights in an old tea-pot. 1890 *Harper's Mag.* Jan. 282/1 Hollyhocks and larkspur and pretty-by-nights blossomed in the door-yard.

Pretty (pri·ti), *v.* [f. the adj.] *refl.* To make (oneself) pretty; to do (oneself) *up.*
1916 H. L. WILSON *Somewhere in Red Gap* ii. 70 All I think is that he's trying to pretty himself up for Nettie.

Pre·tty-pre·ttiness. [f. PRETTY-PRETTY + -NESS.] Pretty-pretty quality or condition.
1926 'LUCAS MALET' *Dogs of Want* i, The coquettish little Cities of the Plain..and their cheap pretty-prettiness of countless hotels. 1931 *Observer* 6 Sept. 6/4 The revulsions into Sunday School pretty-prettiness are equally surprising.

Pretty-pretty. A. *adj.* (Earlier and later examples.)
1877 *Punch* 3 Feb. 47/2 To paint pretty-pretty, to compose namby-pamby, and perpetuate the modish and the monstrous. 1928 J. GALSWORTHY *Swan Song* xi. 82 Nothing pretty-pretty about that memorial—no angels' wings there!

B. *sb.* (Example in sing.)
1929 DEEPING *Roper's Row* xxxv. 401 But that was a monstrous argument to use, mush, the pretty-pretty, a kitten-faced sentimentality.

Preventer. 2. (Further example.)
1920 *Chambers's Jrnl.* Mar. 208/1 A single set of hydrofoils under the bow, known as a preventer, helps to lift the boat when getting up speed, while checking any tendency to nose-dive.

Preventionism (pri̇ve·nʃəniz'm). [f. PREVENTION + -ISM.] A policy of prevention, esp. in making wars. So **Preve·ntionist,** one who favours such a policy.
1918 A. GRAY tr. *The Crime* II. ii. 109 All these questions.. must simultaneously be answered in the affirmative, if the preventionists wish to justify their point of view. *Ibid.* 118 When preventionism suits their purpose, they speak of the right and the duty of the anticipated defence against future attack.

Preventorium (pri̇ventō·riəm). [f. PREVENT *v.*, after SANATORIUM.] An establishment for the care of persons threatened with tuberculosis with a view to preventing the development of the disease.
1918 *Nation* (N.Y.) 7 Feb. 171/2 Tuberculosis..will cost the community many more millions than it would cost to establish preventoria..for all. 1930 *Aberdeen Press & Jrnl.* 21 Oct. 6/1 There are two preventoria in Aberdeen. 1931 *Week-end Rev.* 23 May 777/2 Will any of your readers help in providing funds for the foundation of the first Preventorium?

Preve·rnal, *a.* [PRE- B. 1 d.] Of or belonging to the period before spring; blooming before spring.
1908 *Science* 7 Feb. 207/1 Overtopped by the autumnal, the sublayers are successively those of the serotinal, estival, vernal and prevernal. 1928 *Observer* 26 Feb. 22/2 The impression given by these prevernal flowers.

Pre·-war, *a.* [PRE- B. 2.] That existed, occurred, etc., before a war, esp. before the war of 1914–18.
1908 *Daily Chron.* 24 Apr. 7/3 The Transvaal Government..are thoroughly honest—a great difference from the pre-war days. 1918 *Blighty* 8 May 10/2 You'll find a bottle of whisky somewhere about...Don't waste it, it's pre-war whisky. 1918 'Q' *Foe-Farrell* 216 Folk were a bit more squeamish, if you remember, in those good old pre-War days. 1924 CARUS *Days in Sun* 174 Here again..we had a batsman whose style has been cultivated by observance of pre-war principles. 1928 *Publishers' Weekly* 30 June 2617 The government of France has succeeded in stabilizing the franc at 25·52 to the dollar, approximately one-fifth of its pre-war ratio.

Pre·-war, *adv.* [f. prec.] Before the war of 1914–18.
1920 SIR WM. GOODE *Econ. Cond. Centr. Europe* I. 12 Four million tons of coal were imported annually pre-war, mainly to Petrograd and Baltic ports. 1923 *Westm. Gaz.* 25 Aug., The new tourist hails from districts and from classes which, pre-war, never dreamed of leaving England. 1928 *Daily Tel.* 4 Sept. 9/6 Some time pre-war there was a large contract out for tender from a foreign Government for water tanks.

Prex. (Earlier and later examples.)
1828 *Yankee* (Portland, Maine) 232 (Th.) Our Prex says this: You surely miss [etc.]. 1906 *N. Y. Even. Post* 11 June 6 If the various unpopular 'Prexes' would study the grounds of their unpopularity.

Prexie, prexy (pre·ksi). *U.S.* [f. PREX + -Y.] = PREX.
1905 *N. Y. Even. Post* 1 Sept. 7 Scores of entering classes are lined up in chapel to listen to good advice from the dean or 'Prexie'. 1907 *Washington Star* 30 Sept. 3 Seniors, juniors, sophs and freshies think he's a dandy Prexy. 1929 *Publishers' Weekly* 22 June 2859/1 Professor Charles E. Merriam..has hobnobbed with politicians as well as prexies.

Price, *sb.* Add: **1. f.** *What price—?*: an expression of contempt, esp. for an ambitious project which has failed.

5. *At a price*: at a relatively high cost.
1920 *Blackw. Mag.* Oct. 449/2 La Touche Arms, where the lonely traveller finds food and tent and—at a price—beer. 1929 *Times* 22 July 15/4 Engineering skill would be quite capable of furnishing such facilities, at a price.

14. *price-boom, -level, -wave*; *price-fixing*; **price-cut,** a reduction or cut in price; **price-list** (example); **price-ring,** an association of traders formed to maintain certain prices; **price-slashing** = *price-cutting*; **price-tag** (earlier example).
1928 *Brit. Industr. Future* (Lib. Ind. Inq.) IV. xx. 268 The rapid industrial slump which followed the *price-boom of 1919–20. 1928 *Publishers' Weekly* 30 June 2596 If turnover is secured by *price cuts which decrease the normal profit [etc.]. 1920 *Melbourne Argus* 4 June 6 Competition will reduce prices in time, but *price-fixing..will only arrest the tendency to cheapness. 1927 BOWLEY & STAMP *Nat. Income 1924* 58 On account of the change in *price-level, we should substitute a comparative level of £9,500, [etc.]. 1877 *Rep. Indian Affairs* 8 Calling upon the traders to furnish printed *price lists. 1928 *Brit. Industr. Future* (Lib. Ind. Inq.) II. viii. 97 For probably, the majority of cartels and *price rings fall under the category of Trade Associations..and not under that of Public Companies or Corporations. 1930 *Publishers' Circular* 14 June 793/3 The economic and cultural consequences of reckless *price-slashing. 1881 *Harper's Mag.* Sept. 587/1 Untying a little green *price tag from the handle of the umbrella. 1891 GEO. CLARE *Money-Market Primer* 89 At all times some semblance of agreement is traceable between the respective *price-waves.

Price-current. Also *pl.* **prices-current.**
1815 *Niles' Weekly Reg.* IX. 3/2 This account of the *selling prices* of the several stocks mentioned, is taken from the *public prices current* of the two places. 1839 *Southern Lit. Messenger* V. 38/2 There are no daily papers..no prices current—no reports from the stock market. 1856 *Trans. Mich. Agric. Soc.* VII. 533 A glance at our 'prices current' might suffice to satisfy the most incredulous.

Priceless, *a.* Add: **3.** *slang.* Incredibly or surpassingly amusing, absurd, etc.; 'delightful'.
1907 *Punch* 23 Jan. 59 Lady Bountiful: Oh, dear Miss Smith, *do* send me some of your priceless little sketches for my rummage sale on the 26th. 1915 BARNETT *Lett.* 11 The British regular really is a priceless man.

Prick, *sb.* **21.** Add: **prick-bar,** an iron bar for cleaning fires in steam engines; **prick-shooting,** shooting at the 'prick' or target.
1893 J. M. WHITHAM *Const. Steam Engin.* xii. 724 The *prick-bar has the fire-end turned through 90° and made chisel-pointed. 1801 T. ROBERTS *Engl. Bowman* 241 Of *Prick-shooting..the marks used in this kind of shooting have..consisted either of a small circular piece of white paper,

fixed to a post..; or of a target. 1887 BUTT *Ford's Archery* 138 This prick-shooting next became known as the paper-game.

Prick, *v.* Add: **28. b.** *Prick out*, to come into view as specks or points.
1930 ROSE MACAULAY *Relations* xx. 305 By two o'clock a few stars had pricked out, tiny candles shaking between the drifting gloom of clouds.

Prickle, *sb.*[1] **6. b.** (Earlier example.)
1875 *Encycl. Brit.* I. 897/1 The cells..next in order are polygonal, and not unfrequently possess pointed processes or prickles projecting from them, hence the name, *prickle cells*, employed by Schultze.

9. prickle-cell (earlier example); **prickle-machine,** a machine for pricking cheese.
1875 *Prickle cell [see *6 b]. 1905 *Rep. U.S. Bur. Anim. Industry* 103 The *prickle-machine..has a disk set with long parallel needle-like spikes which make numerous holes through the cheese to let in the air for the growth of mold.

Prickle-pear. (Later example.)
1836 J. HILDRETH *Campaigns Rocky Mts.* I. xvi. 141 It was covered with the prickle-pear.

Prickly, *a.* **3.** Add: **prickly ash** (earlier and later examples); **prickly rhubarb,** a plant of the genus *Gunnera.*
1783 W. FLEMING in *Trav. Amer. Col.* 667 Blue ash, a species of the White Ash..grows to be a large tree, as does the Prickly ash. 1869 J. G. FULLER *Flower Gatherers* 62 It is *Prickly Ash* in every sense of the word, whether you *taste* or *feel* of it. 1900 *Century Bk. Gardening* 98/2 Gunneras are called 'Prickly Rhubarbs', and the big leaves are not unlike those of a large Rhubarb.

Prickly pear. (Earlier example.)
1739 in *Coll. Georgia Hist. Soc.* I. 188 The islands in Georgia are full of the prickly pear shrubs which feed flies.

Pride, *sb.*[1] **5. b. pride of China** (earlier examples).
1785 WASHINGTON *Diaries* II. 383 Next 3 rows of the seed of the Pride of China. 1833 H. BARNARD in *Maryland Hist. Mag.* XIII. 359 Its streets are planted so thick with the Pride of China that its small dark houses are hardly seen.

12. (Modern example.)
1929 *Times* 30 Sept. 12/6 Owing to the dry weather a pride of 16 lions, including females and cubs, concentrated on the Kajiado road.

Pride, *v.* **4.** (Modern example with *for.*)
1850 MRS. CRAIK *Olive* v. 71 How Elspie then prided herself for the continual tutoring which had made the image.. an image of love.

Priest, *sb.* **10. a.** Add: *priest-ruler.*
1920 H. G. WELLS *Outl. Hist.* 94/2 There flourished the first temples and the first *priest-rulers that we know of among mankind.

Priestess. Add. **3.** *Comb.* as *priestess-queen* (after *priest-king*).
1920 H. G. WELLS *Outl. Hist.* 114/1 *note*, The Sumerians allowed much more freedom and authority to women than the Semites. They had *priestess-queens, and one of their great divinities was a goddess, Ishtar.

Prim, *sb.*[2] (U.S. example.)
1784 CUTLER in *Mem. Amer. Acad. Arts & Sci.* (1785) I. 402 *Ligustrum*..Prim. Privet.

Primary. A. *adj.* **4. d.** (Further example.)
1908 A. RUHL *Other Americans* x. 173 In the gymnasium four little primary girls were imitating..the gestures of the elocution teacher, who waved his arms in front of them.

e. *Primary assembly, meeting* (earlier examples), *election* (examples); also *primary caucus.*
1789 *Annual Register* 215/1 *Primary assembly. 1801 *Spirit Farmer's Museum* 61 The Editor of the Gazette of the United States..notices the 'Primary Assemblies' of our towns. 1833 *Knickerbocker Mag.* I. 291 With all his power over the people in their primary assemblies—he seems to lack certain of the gifts of a great practical politician. 1821 *Massachusetts Spy* 11 Apr. 3/3 And this was all the *hocus-pocus* of a *primary caucus. 1789 *Annual Register* 214/2 *Primary election. 1835 *Biogr. Isaac Hill* 54 The freemen of the State were called upon to give at their primary elections, an expression of their opinion. 1847 T. FORD *Hist. Illinois* (1854) 88 Personal politics..were carried from the primary elections into the legislature. 1829 in *Niles' Weekly Reg.* XXXVI. 363/2 The battle is in reality fought in the *primary meetings, and not on the day appointed by law for the election. 1850 in *Life & Corr. Quitman* (1860) II. xiv. 39 These should be chosen by the Legislature, and the people in their primary meetings.

B. *sb.* **6.** (Earlier and later examples.)
a 1861 T. WINTHROP *Life in open Air* etc. (1863) 147 'Boys', said he,..'when I accepted the office of Orator of the Day at our primary, and promised to bring forward our Resolutions in honor of Mr. Wade [etc.]'. 1868 *All Yr. Round* 19 Sept. 351/2 He is 'powerful' in 'primaries', where he votes early and often for his favourite candidates. 1873 'MARK TWAIN' & WARNER *Gilded Age* lix. 530 To.. leave the true source of our political power (the 'primaries') in the hands of saloon-keepers. 1908 *Contemp. Rev.* Apr. 404 Other Western States have passed similar laws for direct primaries. 1915 *World* in *Literary Digest* (N.Y.) 21 Aug. 338/1 The assembled crowd..listened to numerous candidates at the approaching county primaries.

Priming, *vbl. sb.*[1] Add: **5. b.** (See quot.)
1899 *U.S. Dept. Agr.* Rep. 62. 14 The first priming, which means the first four leaves taken from the stalk, also the last priming, which means the last four or six leaves taken from the top of the stalk, are kept separate.

Primitive. B. *sb.* **7.** (Recent example.)
1919 MARY K. BRADBY *Psycho-analysis* 38 The connection between the primitive and the repressed.

Primp (primp), *a.* [f. the vb.] Smart, neat, prim.
1903 *N. Y. Times* 26 Sept. 4 Advt., All-weather coats they are—just as primp, good-fitting and handsome as a man could wish to wear.

Primp, *v.* **1. b.** (Earlier U.S. examples.)
1887 *Harper's Mag.* Mar. 544/1 When you was primping so, I thought all the time it was for Mrs. Rainwater. 1896 MRS. HARRIS *Sister Jane* 160 Mandy had withdrawn to primp a little, as women will do. 1901 HARBEN *Westerfelt* iv. 49 Ef you want to primp up a little an' bresh that hoss-hair off'n yore pants, go in yore room.

Primrosy, *a.* Also *fig.*
1908 E. V. LUCAS *Over Bemerton's* xx, His duty always lies along the primrosiest path.

Primuline (pri·miŭləin). [f. PRIMULA + -INE[5].] A yellow dye-stuff derived from coal-tar. Also *attrib.*
1902 *Encycl. Brit.* XXVII. 559/2 The Primuline Colours are derived from the yellow dye-stuff known as Primuline. 1916 *Yorksh. Post* 24 Mar. 3/2 He discovered the colour known as primuline.

Primus. B. *sb.* Add: **2.** Trade name of a stove burning vaporized paraffin oil.
1907 *Athenæum* 12 Oct. 436/2 Robinson with great efforts made the 'Primus' work, and then burnt the stew with it. 1923 *Blackw. Mag.* May 609/2 The silent primus was lit. 1927 *Scots Observer* 10 Sept. 12/2 The caravan has its ingleneuk with a Primus installed.

Prince, *sb.* **11. prince's pine** (earlier examples.)
1861 MRS. STOWE *Pearl Orr's Isl.* I. v. 32 The prince's pine raised its oriental feather, with a mimic cone on the top. 1869 J. G. FULLER *Flower Gatherers* 156, I like the Indian name, though the more common one is 'Prince's Pine'.

Prince Albert coat. [f. *Prince Albert* (1819–61), Prince Consort of England.] A frock-coat. Also (ellipt.) *Prince Albert.*
1902 CLAPIN *Dict. Amer.* Pref. p. viii, If a Londoner is fortunate enough to cross the Atlantic,..but is unfortunate enough to have to buy a frock-coat..he must call it a 'Prince Albert'. 1906 W. CHURCHILL *Coniston* 279 He wore a flowing Prince Albert coat, which served to dignify a growing portliness. *a* 1909 'O. HENRY' *Roads of Destiny* xx. 337 You remember..the guy in the hammered brass Prince Albert. 1927 *Scribner's Mag.* Feb. 164/1 Antone was dressed for a call, having donned a shiny Prince Albert coat over his collarless shirt.

Principal. A. *adj.* Add: **2. c.** *Principal boy*, the female player who takes the leading male part in a pantomime.
1896 *Pall Mall Mag.* Oct. 302/1 She was still playing principal boy in the pantomime—a gay, gallant Prince, in plumed cap and tights.

Pringling (pri·ŋgliŋ), *ppl. a.* [f. PRINGLE *v.* + -ING[2].] That pringles, or causes a prickly sensation.
1897 A. CONAN DOYLE *Uncle Bernac* i, I..pressed my lips upon the wet and pringling gravel.

Print, *sb.* Add: **11. b.** Also in general use.
1928 *Daily Mail* 25 July 18/5 Prints of the Memorandum and Articles of Association can be inspected at any time.

15. print-meter, an instrument showing the length of time required for printing photographs from negatives; **print-paper,** printing-paper.
1902 *Encycl. Brit.* XXXI. 702/2 A '*Print meter' is also made for showing the exposures in contact-printing on sensitive papers. 1903 E. L. SHUMAN *Pract. Journalism* 13 If *print paper were still made of rags the modern press could not exist.

Print, *v.* **14.** (Example with *out.*)
1909 *Westm. Gaz.* 11 Dec. 18/2 A huge fortune awaits the man who can invent a paper which will print out by gaslight.

Printed, *ppl. a.* **2. b.** Used of a writer.
1893 W. G. COLLINGWOOD *Life Ruskin* I. v. 56 He was undeniably clever, he knew all about minerals and mountains, he was quite an artist; and a printed poet!

Printing, *vbl. sb.* **b.** Also, the total number of copies (of a book) printed at one time; an impression.
1928 *Publishers' Weekly* 26 May 2117 A best selling novel. ..Four large printings were necessary before publication.

d. printing-paper (earlier example).
1811 R. SUTCLIFFE *Trav.* xiv. (1815) 276 The mill..is.. employed in making writing and *printing paper.

Printing-office. (Earlier and later examples.)
1733 FRANKLIN *Poor Richard's Almanac* title-p., Printed and sold by B. Franklin, at the New Printing-Office. 1895 M. A. JACKSON *Mem.* xx. 328 Such a paper..would give us early news..received at the printing office on Sun[day].

Print-shop. Add: **2.** *U.S.* A printing-office or printery.
1921 *Amer. Printer* 5 Nov. (heading) Visit to an old Oxford printshop.

Priorate. Add: **1. c.** The (term of) office of a prioress.
1925 C. S. DURRANT *Flem. Mystics & Eng. Martyrs* I. x. 150 The Priorate of Mother Salome has ever been looked back to as a time when [etc.].

Prism. 7. Add: **prism-binoculars,** binoculars in the construction of which two pairs of triangular prisms are so introduced as to shorten the length of the apparatus and sometimes to improve the stereoscopic effect.
1911 in WEBSTER.

Prismatic, *a.* Add: **3. b.** *Anat.* Of muscles, in which the fibres run in direct lines from origin to insertion.
1902 *Encycl. Brit.* XXV. 395/2 Muscles of the former group are called prismatic or bandlike.

Prisoner[2]. Add: **3. b.** An iron connecting unit securely held in the rim of a fly-wheel.
1897 F. R. HUTTON *Mech. Engin. Power Plants* xvii. 346 A piece of wrought iron may be inserted into a recess in the interior of the rim, and..bolts driven through the rim keep this wrought iron a prisoner...These prisoners may be of sections of an I, or they may be of the shape of an oval link.

Pri·sonful. [-FUL.] The content of a prison.
1922 BENNETT *Lilian* II. ii, Only the malice of a prisonful of women could have seriously asserted her to be older than Felix.

Pritch-awl. (Modern example.)
1912 BITMEAD *Pract. Upholsterer* 12 Pritch-awl...Its use is for making or showing the position of tufts.

Private, *a.* Add: **3.** (Examples of *private life*).
1526 R. WHYTFORD *Martiloge* 131 b., He resygned his crowne, & lyued a holy pryuate lyfe. 1908 *Westm. Gaz.* 17 Aug. 2/1 Against his private life and his personal character there has never been the smallest whisper of accusation.

7. c. *Private company*: (see quot. 1908).
1908 *Companies (Consolidation) Act.* § 121 For the purposes of this Act the expression 'private company' means a company which by its articles—(*a*) Restricts the right to transfer its shares; and (*b*) Limits the number of its members ..to fifty; and (*c*) Prohibits any invitation to the public to subscribe for any shares or debentures of the company. 1928 *Brit. Industr. Future* (Lib. Ind. Inq.) II. vii. 84 The most important existing legal distinction is between Public Companies..and Private Companies.

Privilege, *v.* Add: **1. c.** *trans.* *R. C. Ch.* To make (an altar) privileged.
1844 *Orthodox Jrnl.* 6 Jan. 3/2 The high altar was privileged by Gregory XIII.

d. In *pa. pple.* Entitled *to* (a special right).
1856 MRS. B. G. FERRIS *Mormons at Home* xii. 199 A few who call themselves physicians..are privileged to a seat in this important assemblage.

Privileged, *ppl. a.* Add: **d.** *Eccl.* Applied to certain days (see quot.).
1877 J. D. CHAMBERS *Div. Worship in Eng.* v. 87 The Privileged Sundays, according to the present Anglican Rite, appear, beside the Principal-Double Festivals and their Octaves, to be the First Sunday in Advent, Passion Sunday and Palm Sunday, and Sunday within the Octave of the Ascension. The Privileged Ferials: Ash Wednesday, the Four Days before Easter, the Vigils, Fasts and days of Abstinence above enumerated

Privy-councilship. [-SHIP.] = PRIVY-COUNSELLORSHIP.
1910 *Blackw. Mag.* Sept. 422/1 Even Privy Councilship does not turn nonsense into sound argument.

Prize, *sb.*[1] **4. b.** Add: **prize-roll,** a roll or list of prizewinners.
1912 *Chambers's Jrnl.* May 329/1 A medal can be verified occasionally if the *prize-roll or some other collateral document is extant.

Prize, *sb.*[3] **3. prize-master** (earlier example).
1760 *Essex Inst. Hist. Coll.* XLVII. 125 He put a *Prize Master (as he called him) and three more of his hands on board the sloop.

Prize, *sb.*[4] **3.** Add: **prize-beam,** a beam used in packing tobacco.
1800 W. TATHAM *Cult. & Com. Tobacco* 52 As all tobacco must be in due case when it is put into the hogshead, so must the prize-beam retain its depressed position until two distinct ends are attained, to wit, that of giving a compact consistency to the cake [etc.].

Prize, *v.*[3] Add: **2. b.** To pack (persons) into a narrow space.
1799 BECKFORD in Oliver *Life Beckford* (1932) 269 Assure Lady Heard that she shall not be worn to death with seeing Sights,..nor prysed into rumbling carriages.

Prize-money. Add: (Earlier example.)
1749 *N. H. Probate Rec.* III. 733, I give to Doctor Robert Ratsey all my Waidges, Prize money [etc.].

b. Money awarded as a prize or as prizes.

Prizer[2]. Add: **b.** A prize-winner.
1851 BP. COPLESTON in *Mem.* 188 My delight was not a little heightened, by seeing my horned countrymen of North Devon among the 'prizers'.

Pro. 4. pro forma. (Further example.)
1930 M. CLARK *Home Trade* 100 An order may be received from an unknown person or firm...In such cases a pro forma invoice may be dispatched.

Pro-, *prefix.*[1] Add: **4. b.** *pro-vicariate.*
1881 *Dubl. Rev.* July 173 The districts of Lake Tanganyika, and the Victoria Nyanza have already been created Pro-Vicariates Apostolic.

5. a. *pro-ally, -Boche, -Boer* (earlier example), *-British* (example), *-German.*
1916 *Lit. Digest* (N.Y.) 1 Jan. 3/2 He has been trapt into the nets of those who wove the *pro-Ally newspaper opinion in this country. 1915 *National Rev.* Apr. 169 A *pro-Boche Government would have been bundled out 'neck and crop' last August. 1896 *Daily News* 22 Apr. 5/1 If it were indeed a necessity of the situation to be *pro-Boer or *pro-British..then as Britons we should be for the British, we admit. 1916 *Lit. Digest* (N.Y.) 1 Jan. 3/2 'The psychological equation' of Theodore Roosevelt's personality 'makes him a *pro-German in all that is best in him, and only his temper and his perpetual desire to be with the masses made him a pro-Ally'.

b. *pro-Britisher.*
1927 *Leader* 31 Dec. 517/1 That was unexpected talk to what in Ireland is called a Chamber of Commerce—Chambers whose members are mostly *pro-Britishers and Shoneens.

Pro-, *pref.*[2] Add: **1. Pro-anthro·pos** [Gr. ἄνθρωπος man], a hypothetical primitive type of man. **Pro-a·vian** (*a.* and) *sb.*, (of or belonging to) a hypothetical prehistoric ancestor of birds. **Pro·phyll,** anglicized form of PROPHYLLON.
19.. *Buck's Handbk. Med. Sci.* IV. 40 (Cent. Suppl.) We

may postulate a Tertiary 'precursor', a '*proanthropos', but exhibit one of his bones in the broad light of day we cannot. 1926 G. HEILMANN *Orig. Birds* 193 We must presume that the *Proavian, once having commenced living in trees, had already developed a bind-toe and a specialized hand with a long second digit...The construction of the Proavian skeleton. 1905 I. B. BALFOUR tr. *Goebel's Organogr. Plants* II. 382 *Prophylls are characterized first of all by their position. We find them..usually in pairs at the base of the lateral shoots.

Proambient (proˌæ·mbiĕnt), *a.* [f. PRO-[2] + AMBIENT *a.*] Of a part of a medium: Lying immediately in front of a moving body.
1904 *Sci. Amer.* Suppl. 9 July 23840/1 To the light given forth by the glowing melted surface,..must be added the enormously greater light of proambient air, itself heated by the compression mentioned.

Pro and con. B. *sb. phr.* (Recent example of sing.)
1920 GALSWORTHY *Captures* (1923) 59 The house rocked with pro and con.

Probable. B. *sb.* Add: **b.** Short for a probable candidate, competitor, starter, etc.
1906 *Pall Mall Gaz.* 23 Jan. 2 The last two 'probables' are untried men as far as Parliament is concerned. 1909 *Westm. Gaz.* 28 May 12/3 All probables ran.

Probate, *sb.* Add: **2. c.** Short for *probate judge.*
1863 J. PARTON *Butler in New Orleans* (1864) 213 Major Strong..found at Biloxi a probate of wills, who was also a justice of the peace, to whom he committed the child.

Probationer. Add: **b.** (*c*) *Lord Probationer*, a newly appointed Scottish judge before he has undergone the trial of fitness.
1910 *Pall Mall Gaz.* 26 Apr. 3/5 He appears again in the First Division, and the junior judge reports to the judges of that court the judgments the Lord Probationer has pronounced.

Probatory, *a.* Add: **3.** (See quot.)
1924 P. S. ALLEN in *Library* Mar. 255 The manuscripts are identified in the catalogue by the first words of the second leaf, the 'probatory words'.

Probing, *ppl. a.* (Further example.)
1909 *Daily Chron.* 10 Aug. 7/2 He answered probing, keenly-put questions with dogged determination not to betray himself.

Problemage (prǫ·blĕmĕdʒ). [f. PROBLEM + -AGE.] The state of being a problem.
1928 S. LESLIE *Skull of Swift* ii. 7 As a result certain passages in his life remain contradictory, while others have passed into insoluble problemage.

Proboscis. 6. proboscis-fish, an African species of fish having a long proboscis.
1904 *Nature* 9 June 130/2 The *proboscis-fish (Mormyrus kannume) is chiefly nocturnal, and employs its long snout in probing about among stones for animal food.

Proce·dural, *a.* [f. PROCEDURE + -AL.] Of or pertaining to procedure.
1919 H. A. L. FISHER *Studies in History & Politics* 52 It includes a reform of the civil, penal, and procedural codes. 1920 *Contemp. Rev.* May 755 The Court..has perfect freedom to deal with questions of substantive and procedural (or adjective) law. 1930 G. R. SHERRILL *Crim. Procedure N. Carolina* 136 We are indebted to the Session of 1868–9 for the bulk of the procedural laws under which we now operate.

Procedure. Add: **4.** *attrib.* as *procedure resolution.*
1910 *Daily Chron.* 22 Mar. 1/1 Some of them might find it convenient to stay away when the division on the procedure resolution takes place.

Procellose (prose·lōus). *Chem.* [f. *pro-* of PRODUCT + *CELLOSE.] (See quots.)
1913 *Nature* 30 June 903/1 A new sugar, procellose...Its composition is $C_{18}H_{32}O_{16}$. 1924 F. F. ARMSTRONG *Carbohydrates & Glucosides* 137 Procellose is a by-product obtained in the preparation of cellose from cellulose.

Process, *sb.* Add: **13.** *process-maker, -printer*; **b. process-water,** water that has been employed in and polluted by some industrial process.
1900 *Fortn. Rev.* Jan. 65 Engraving, indeed, as a profession, and as a means of obtaining fame, has entirely died out; the engraver nowadays is a *process-maker. 1901 *Edin. Rev.* Apr. 551 A few..were found ready to submit their work to the uncertainties and vagaries of the *process-printer. 1927–8 *Rep. Water Pollution Res. Bd.* 9 In some factories..alternative methods are employed by which the production of *process water is avoided. 1930 *Min. of Agr. Standing Comm. on River Pollution, Rep. for 1926–7–8* 10 The practicability of treating 'process-water' by means of biological filters.

Processional, *a.* **b.** (Further example.)
1906 H. BEGBIE *Priest* viii. 124 The sound of a heavy step approaching from the processional aisle on the south caught her ear.

Processioner. 4. (Earlier example.)
1731 *Bristol Vestry Bk.* (Va.) 59 Order'd that George Tucker be Prosessioner in the Stead of Robert Tucker junr who is lame and cannott officiate as prosessioner.

Processor (prose·səɹ). [f. PROCESS *sb.* + -OR.] A process engraver or printer.
1909 MARG. B. SAUNDERS *Litany Lane* I. ii, Her tragic face ..was already being 'blocked' for the night's press in many a rushing 'processor's' den.

Procrypsis (prokri·psis). *Zool.* [f. PRO- (cf. PROCRYPTIC) + Gr. κρύψις concealment.] Protective colouring in insects.
1920 G. D. H. CARPENTER *Naturalist on L. Victoria* 196 Procryptic colouring conceals its wearer from danger, causing it to resemble either the general surroundings or some particular part thereof (Special Procrypsis).

Procto·rially, *adv.* [f. PROCTORIAL *a.* + -LY[2].] In a proctorial capacity.
1883 H. S. HOLLAND in *Mem.* (1921) III. iv. 290 You speak of a deeper sense of the power of evil—I have felt it proctorially.

Procumbent, *a.* Add: **3.** Of teeth: Lying along the jaw.
1891 FLOWER & LYDEKKER *Mammals Living & Extinct* 687 In the fore part of the lower jaw are on each side three elongated, compressed, procumbent teeth. 1902 *Encycl. Brit.* XXX. 506/1 In the lower jaw there is a single pair of procumbent incisors, followed by several small teeth representing the canine and early premolars.

Procurator. 2. a. (Modern example.)
1909 B. WARD *Dawn Cath. Revival* I. 55 The procurator [at Douay] was Rev. Gregory Stapleton, who had held that office since 1773.

Procurrent (prokʊ·rĕnt), *a.* [ad. L. *procurrent-*, *procurrens* pres. pple. of *procurrĕre* to run forward.] Applied to a special form of fish's fin: (see quot.).
1902 JORDAN & EVERMANN *Amer. Food & Game Fishes* 538 *Procurrent* (*fin*). With the lower rays inserted progressively farther forward.

Procu·rvature. [PRO-[2] + CURVATURE.] = PROCURVATION.
1903 R. I. POCOCK in *Annals & Mag. Nat. Hist.* Jan. 114 The species described by Keyserling as *Trechona pantherina* appears to me to be the female of *auronitens*, in spite of a less procurvature of the anterior line of eyes.

Prod, *sb.*[1] Add: **2. b.** *spec.* (See quot.)
1888 LOCKWOOD *Dict. Mech. Engin. Terms* 267 The pyramidal or conical points cast on loam and core plates for the retention of the loam are termed prods.

Prodigiosity (prodidʒiˌǫ·siti). [f. PRODIGIOUS (L. *prōdigiōs-us*) + -ITY.] **1.** A person or thing of an enormous size; a monster.
1895 MEREDITH *Amazing Marriage* xxxvi, We're none of us 'fifty feet high, with phosphorous heads', as your friend..says of the prodigiosities.

2. A marvellous quality or performance.
1910 W. J. LOCKE *Simon the Jester* vi. 77 He had fallen in love with her when she had first taken Marseilles captive with the prodigiosities of her horse Sultan.

Produce, *sb.* **6.** *produce broker, trade* (earlier examples).
1851 C. CIST *Cincinnati* 143 Forwarding and Commission merchants and Produce brokers. 1872 *Rep. Vermont Board Agric.* I. 161 B. F. Rugg, who was then engaged largely in the produce trade,..undertook to carry out a plan for controlling the Boston butter market.

Produce, *v.* **1. b.** (Recent examples.)
1905 *Pall Mall Mag.* July 82/1 We don't want a subsidised theatre for the purpose of producing Shakespearian plays. 1918 *Saturday Rev.* 13 July 623 On that day a play was produced at the Strand Theatre called 'The Hidden Hand'. 1925 *Scribner's Mag.* July 10/2 The..opera..is being produced at a cost of approximately $75,000.

Producer. Add: **1. b.** The person who produces or stages a dramatic performance.
1909 *Westm. Gaz.* 30 Apr. 5/2 Mr. L. C.'s appointment as stage manager, or, according to the more modern term, 'producer,' of the theatre. 1928 *Daily Mail* 25 July 16/1 Very few people outside the theatrical business know what a producer is—or care.

Produ·cership. [f. PRODUCER + -SHIP.] The position or function of a producer.
1926 *Spectator* 1 May 796/1 By a judicious system of African producership and land ownership peace has prevailed.

Production. 1. (Recent example).
1896 *Pall Mall Mag.* Dec. 485, I can remember no notable entertainments..beyond a production by Viennese Jews..of a play. 1925 *Scribner's Mag.* July 7/1 Jesse Lynch Williams has been..preparing a play for production in New York in the fall.

Pro-e·thnic, *a.* [PRO-[1] and [2].]
1. (See PRO- *prefix*[2].)
2. Favouring the nations or Gentiles, and not the Jews.
1920 R. HARRIS *Testimonies* II. ii. 13 Propagating by testimonies a Gospel which is at once pro-ethnic and anti-Judaic.
Hence **Pro-e·thnically** *adv.*
1920 R. HARRIS *Testimonies* II. ii. 16 The words are used pro-ethnically.

Prof (prǫf). *colloq.* Also *U.S.* **proff.** Abbreviation of PROFESSOR.
1838 *Yale Lit. Mag.* III. 144 For Profs and Tutors too, Who steer our big canoe, Prepare their lays. 1855 *Ibid.* XX. 188 (Th.) Flashed all their weapons bare,..Skinning from ponies, while All the Profs wondered. 1891 R. F. MURRAY *Scarlet Gown* 69 And neither visits to foreign coasts, Nor tonics, can ever set free Two well-known Profs from the haunting wraith Of the injured Andrew McCrie. 1916 H. L. WILSON *Somewhere in Red Gap* ii. 74 I bet Wilbur thinks the prof is awful old-fashioned, playing with his fingers that way.

Professed, *ppl. a.* **2.** (Later examples.)
1881 *Harper's Mag.* Feb. 437/1 Her father though not a professed member was..a great respecter of religion. 1911 *Act* 1 & 2 *Geo. V* c. 37 § 5 Any sale made in professed exercise of the power conferred on mortgages by the Act of 1881.

Professional, *a.* **4.** (Earlier example.)
1798 *Ann. 5th Congress* 8 Nov. 2741 The solemn air and dictatorial manner of a professional schoolmaster.

B. *sb.* **2.** (Further example.)
1909 *Westm. Gaz.* 24 Mar. 10/2 It is a belief amongst some of the professionals that the bear account is by no means large.

Professionize, *v.* Add: **b.** *trans.* To make into a profession.
1920 *Christian World* 23 Sept. 14/1 They professionised the study and diverted literature from its true and best purpose.

Proficiency. Add: **3.** *Comb.* as **proficiency pay,** increased pay given in respect of proficiency.
1909 *Westm. Gaz.* 24 Apr. 2/3 £450,000 is the charge for the service or proficiency pay of British soldiers.

Profiler (prǫʊfəi·ləɹ). [f. PROFILE *v.* + -ER[1].] A profile machine.
1904 *Elect. World & Engin.* 19 Mar. 58 (Cent. Suppl.). 1927 *Daily Tel.* 11 May 18/3 Advt., Gear Cutters, Profilers, Radials, &c.

Profitability. Delete *rare.*
1924 SIR J. STAMP *Current Probl. in Finance & Govt.* 11, I may venture to say that we have almost reached a limit of profitability along the old lines of deductive reasoning.

Profiteer (prǫfiti·ɹ), *sb.* [f. PROFIT + -EER.] A person who makes excessive profits on the sale of necessary supplies or goods, esp. in time of war.
1913 *Public Opinion* 23 Aug. 172/3 A sermon preached to profiteers is no sermon to the dispossessed. 1914 *Englishwoman* Nov. 94 The tricks of the armament profiteers are fresh in the public mind. 1920 W. J. LOCKE *House of Baltazar* xviii. 218 Baltazar held the mellowed profiteer with his compelling eyes. 1922 *Daily Mail* 11 Nov. 5 And Papa Hodge is the sort of profiteer who almost reconciles one to the prospect of a capital levy.

Profiteer (prǫfiti·ɹ), *v.* [f. next.] *intr.* To practice profiteering; to be a profiteer.
1916 *New Age* 17 Feb. 361/1 The companies are..not only removed from the common temptation to profiteer, but are guaranteed a practically fixed income. 1920 ROSE MACAULAY *Potterism* II. iii, She had merely profiteered out of it all, and had a good time.

Profiteering (prǫfiti·riŋ), *vbl. sb.* [f. PROFIT + -EER + -ING[1].] The action or fact of making excessive profits by selling or providing necessities, esp. in time of war. Also *attrib.*
1814 *Guernsey Star & Gaz.* in *New Age* (1919) 21 Aug. 278/2 The extortionate profiteering that is being practised by the tradesmen in the public market. 1914 *New Age* 27 Aug. 391/2 England is at war upon profiteering. *Ibid.* 15 Oct. 561/2 The profiteering braggadocio..of 'City Man' and his confederates. 1918 *Morn. Post* 29 Jan. 8/2 The only way in which the profiteering powers of the merchants and the coal-owners can be effectively checked. 1919 *Act* 9 & 10 *Geo. V* c. 66 (title) An Act to check Profiteering. *Ibid.* § 8 This Act may be cited as the Profiteering Act, 1919. 1919 J. L. GARVIN *Econ. Foundations Peace* 303 It irritates still more the angry suspicion of 'profiteering'. 1922 W. J. LOCKE *Tale of Triona* vi. 56 'A dog and a rose and a glass of wine,' said she, 'are a woman's due for amusing a man. But a motor-car is profiteering.'

Profiting, *ppl. a.* (Modern example.)
1908 *Daily Chron.* 3 Oct. 5/4 So many profiting interests are concerned that there can be little doubt as to the ultimate formation of a syndicate.

Progamete (progæmī·t). [f. PRO-[2] + GAMETE.] An immature gamete.
1902 [see *OOCYTE].

Proglo·ttidiza·tion. [f. PROGLOTTID + -IZATION.] The fact of being composed of proglottids.
1901 E. R. LANKESTER *Treat. Zool.* IV. 118 The typical 'proglottidisation' is not expressed externally in *Ligula* and *Triaenophorus*, though the genital pores indicate the repetition of the genital organs.

Prognostical, *a.* (Later example.)
1894 H. LATHAM *Service of Angels* 40 Is it prognostical? Is it proleptic?

Program(me. 4. program boy, girl, a boy or girl employed to sell programs at a place of entertainment; **program picture,** a cinematographic film forming part of a program, but not constituting the main feature of it.
1921 *Dict. Occup. Terms* (1927) § 889 *Programme boy, girl, seller. 1905 *Daily Chron.* 13 Feb. 9/3 An interesting story of a medical student's love for a *programme girl..was told. 1928 *Sunday Dispatch* 19 Aug. 14/2 A '*programme' picture is a film which costs from £6,000 to £8,000 or thereabouts, and cannot be called a 'super'.

Progressism (prǫʊ·gresiz'm, prǫg-). [f. PROGRESS + -ISM.] = PROGRESSIONISM.
1921 B. BOSANQUET *Meeting of Extremes in Contemp. Phil.* 206 Men do not, under the influence of such progressism, admit that some one or more climaxes of the finite may have been attained in the past. 1922 W. R. INGE *Outspoken Essays* (2nd Ser.) 26 The 'Progressism' of much modern thought is a poor substitute for this belief in the substantial reality of the eternal values.

Progressive, *a.* Add: **3. e.** Of taxation: (see quot.).
1902 *Encycl. Brit.* XXXIII. 197/2 The question whether the burden of taxation should not be *progressive*—the proportion of the sum taken by the state from the tax-payers increasing with the wealth of the individual. *Ibid.* 199/1 A general system of progressive taxation.

Prohibition. 6. (Further examples.)
1877 *Harper's Mag.* Dec. 146/1 R. Pitman..Prohibition candidate for Governor. *Ibid.* 146/2 He argues..the prohibition system a success. 1886 *Ibid.* June 157/1 The Prohibition amendment was carried by a decisive majority. 1886 *Century Mag.* Mar. 728/2 The prohibition law was strictly enforced. 1909 in *Westm. Gaz.* 19 Aug. 5/4 Already more than half the entire population is living in Prohibition States.

Prohibitionism. (Later example.)
1915 *N. Amer. Rev.* Dec. 948 All the speakers agreed that the bad saloon did more harm to the liquor trade than prohibitionism.

Prohibitory. Add: **3.** *Gram.* = PROHIBITIVE 3.
1925 G. R. DRIVER in *People & Book* (ed. A. S. Peake) 97 Since *lū* and *lā* implied a precative and a prohibitory sense respectively, there was no risk of confusion between these forms.

Projection, *sb.* Add: **8.** (Later fig. example.)
1924 W. B. SELBIE *Psych. Relig.* 224 Psychology does not justify us in regarding prayer as anything but the projection of our desires and aims on something outside of and above ourselves.

10. projection-room, a room designed for the projection of cinematographic pictures.
1926 *Scribner's Mag.* Aug. 164/1 Do you know my schedule?..Back to the stage till 6. Then an hour in my private projection room. 1930 *Aberdeen Press & Jrnl.* 29 Mar. 7/4 A fire occurred in the projection room of the Swan Cinema.

Proje·ctional, *a.* [f. PROJECTION + -AL.] Of, pertaining to, or connected with projection.
1899 *Phil. Trans.* B. CXCI. 298 The large system of fibres just described above is probably both an associational and projectional system.

Projector. Add: **2. b.** (See quot. 1930.) *Comb.* as *projector-man.*
1927 *Observer* 17 Apr. 3 The picture is what is called 'ridden in'—that is, the orchestra work up to an appropriate climax, and at a given bar the projector-man 'makes his throw'. 1930 *Sel. Gloss. Motion Pict. Techn.* (Acad. Tech. Bureau Hollywood) 26/2 *Projector*, machine used to project motion pictures.

Prolapsed, *ppl. a.* Also *fig.*
1926 STANLEY BALDWIN *On England* 111 We see the sentences of the ancients clean run like athletes and fit for their work as compared with the prolapsed and slovenly figures of so much of our own diction.

Prolating (prǫʊ·lĕ·tiŋ), *vbl. sb.* [f. PROLATE *v.* + -ING[1].] Increase or extension.
1919 *Empire Rev.* 256 The loss of wealth, high taxation, the dislocation of trade and industry with their attendant evils, labour unrest and the prolating of unemployment.

Prola·tively, *adv.* [f. PROLATIVE + -LY[2].] As a prolative infinitive.
1888 KENNEDY *Rev. Latin Primer* 163 The Infinitive of a Copulative Verb used Prolatively is followed by a Complement in the Nominative.

Proleta·rianiza·tion. [f. PROLETARIANIZE + -ATION.] A making or becoming proletarian. So **Proleta·rianized** *ppl. a.*; **Proletariza·tion** = *PROLETARIANIZATION.
1918 *Times* 19 Aug. 5/6 We are drifting towards the complete proletarization of the official classes. 1920 *19th Cent.* Sept. 445 If state agriculture in Russia comes to be on a larger scale, will there not be a sort of proletarianisation of the peasants? 1921 tr. *Rathenau's New Society* v. 60 To some of us it is not easy, and to many it is not agreeable to picture to themselves the aspect of a thoroughly proletarianized country.

Proleta·rianly, *adv.* [f. PROLETARIAN + -LY[2].] According to proletarian views.
1931 ST. JOHN ERVINE in *Time & Tide* 3 Oct. 1130 This *rentier* has been unfeeling enough to practice what is capitalistically called virtue, but is proletarianly known as vice; *he has saved money!*

Proliferate, *v.* Add: **1. c.** *transf.* Of human beings.
1926 *Socialist Rev.* Apr. 33 Those who..have neither the time to care for their children's moral well-being, nor the space which is necessary to ensure their physical welfare, proliferate, unchecked.

Proliferation. Add: **1. c.** *transf.* Enlargement or extension.
1920 H. G. WELLS *Outl. Hist.* 507/2 The British and the French were at first the leading peoples in this great proliferation of knowledge.

Prolifically, *adv.* (Fig. example.)
1915 C. S. JONES *Hohenzollerns* 167 He had for many years sought to win the favour of the great Frederick by writing prolifically on agriculture.

Prolong, *sb.* Transfer †*Obs.* to sense in Dict. and add: **2.** A prolongation.
1905 *Electrochem. & Metallurg. Industry* III. 9/1 This product..is a by-product with the European smelters, who use sheet-iron 'prolongs' on the condensers to collect it.

Prom (prǫm). [abbreviation of PROMENADE.] **1.** *U.S.* = *PROMENADE *sb.* 2 b.
1899 A. H. QUINN *Pennsylv. Stories* 170 All you children can get tickets of me for the Senior Prom right now. 1905 *Springfield Weekly Republ.* 7 July 12 The senior 'prom' of the central and technical high schools crowded the armory Friday night. 1914 GERTR. ATHERTON *Perch of Devil* i. 74 The Prom is anything but an exclusive affair. 1926 *Ladies' Home Jrnl.* Nov. 12 Accordingly Janie went to Eustis' prom.

2. *colloq.* Abbreviation of PROMENADE or *Promenade concert.*
1913 H. WALPOLE *Fortitude* II. i, Except for a walk or two and going into the gallery at Covent Garden once or twice and the Proms sometimes [etc.]. 1925 *Glasgow Herald* 18 July 8/7 A scrap of conversation overheard on the 'prom'. 1927 *Morn. Post* 16 Aug., Mozart's Music at the 'Proms'.

Promenade, *sb.* Add: **2. b.** A ball or dance at a school or college. *U.S.*
1905 *N. Y. Herald* 22 Jan. 10 The fair guests invited to the Junior Promenade, the great event of the college year.

4. *promenade deck* (earlier examples).
1838 in *Steamboat Disasters* (1846) 59 The starboard boiler exploded..blowing off the promenade deck above. 1846 *Knickerbocker Mag.* XXVII. 451 Escaping thence, I went abaft, upon the upper or 'promenade' deck.

Promethea (promī·þiă). *Entom.* [L. *Promēthea* fem. of adj. *Promētheus* (f. PROMETHEUS), the specific name of a moth.] An American species of silk-spinning moth.
1909 MRS. STRATTON-PORTER *Girl of Limberlost* xv. 300 He found a splendid Promethea on a lilac in a corner.

Prominence, *sb.* **2. b.** Add: *prominence-line.*
1927 MACPHERSON *Mod. Astron.* 34 They were able to observe the bright prominence-lines in full daylight.

Promise, *v.* **6. b.** (Further example.)
1911 A. W. TILBY *Eng. People Overseas* I. 18 A rich traffic had promised with China and Japan.

Promote, *v.* Add: **2. c.** *spec.* To further the sale of (an article) by advertising. *U.S.*
1930 *Publishers' Weekly* 31 May 2732/2 The books all to be individualized in appearance and fully promoted.

Promotion. Add: **2. c.** *spec.* Encouraging or helping the sale of an article by advertisements. *U.S.*
1928 *Publishers' Weekly* 26 May 2169 Promotion cannot be done without waste...But the idea back of the new mergers is the idea of outlets, of promotion, of selling more goods.

6. promotion-sheet, a record of an employee's services showing his claim to promotion or increased pay.
1909 *Daily Chron.* 23 Mar. 1/4 The manipulation of their promotion sheets, with the object of postponing the payment of justly earned increased salaries, was one of the grievances of the strikers.

Promo·tional, *a.* [f. PROMOTION + -AL.] Of or pertaining to promotion or promoters; relating to advertising.
1922 *Universalist Leader* 13 May 4 Experience has disclosed that emotional contributions are promotional of the very poverty we had felt moved to alleviate. 1926 *Publishers' Weekly* 22 May 1675/1 As a further promotional step the.. Company is displaying a letter commenting on its service. 1927 *Sunday Express* 10 Apr. 16 Jack Gleason..and Tex Rickard..had gained earlier promotional fame by putting on the Gans-Nelson fight in Goldfield.

Promovable (promū·văb'l), *a.* [f. PROMOVE + -ABLE.] That may be promoted.
1920 O'BRIEN *Even. Memories* 216 Two paid magistrates removable and promovable at the caprice of Dublin Castle.

Prompt, *sb.* **2. b.** Add: **prompt-word,** a word spoken by a prompter; (in quot. transf.).
1918 QUILLER-COUCH *Foe-Farrell* 176, I knew..that I must break his fate to him. I even gave him the prompt-word. 'Homelike', I suggested. 'You've hit it', he said.

Prompt. B. *adv.* Add: **b.** Promptly; soon.
1910 W. M. RAINE *B. O'Connor* 23 The reverend gentleman..had this diverting experience so prompt after he was wishing for it.

Prong, *sb.*[2] **2. c.** (Earlier examples of U.S. sense.)
1784 WASHINGTON *Diaries* II. 311 Carpenters Creek, a branch of Jackson's, which is the principal prong of James River. 1837 PECK *Gaz. Illinois* III. 185 It [*sc.* Crawford's Creek] enters the south prong of Bear creek.

Pronged, *a.* (Transf. example.)
1874 T. HARDY *Far fr. Madding Crowd* xi, The indistinct summit of the façade was notched and pronged by chimneys here and there.

Pronograde (prǫʊ·nogrēid), *a.* [f. L. *prōn-us* PRONE + *-gradus* going, walking: see GRADE.] That goes on all fours.
1902 A. KEITH in *Jrnl. Anat. & Physiol.* XXXVII. 19 Three well marked stages are recognized in the evolution of the highest primates—the pronograde stage, the orthograde stage, and finally, the giant stage. 1918 F. WOOD-JONES *Probl. Man's Ancestry* 22 The likeness [to man] still further diminished in the lemurs, and in the general run of pronograde quadrupedal mammals it reached a minimum.

Pronto (prǫ·nto), *adv.* *U.S. slang.* [Sp. *pronto* promptly, f. L. *promptus.*] Quickly; promptly.
1918 H. A. VACHELL *Some Happenings* x. 166, I reckon to cut him outer the herd—pronto. 1926 J. BLACK *You Can't Win* vi. 66 If we was in the city I'd take fifty cents of it purty pronto. 1927 *Bulletin* 4 Oct. 12/3 Advise him to vamoose, pronto. 1927 *Ladies' Home Jrnl.* Dec. 6/3, I reached for the stars pronto, without even turning my head. 1930 DOR. L. SAYERS & R. EUSTACE *Documents in Case* 161 If I don't get there pronto..I shall never hear the last of it.

Pronunciamento. (Earlier example.)
1836 EDWARD *Hist. Texas* viii. 259 It is not..a question of *pronounciamento* [*sic*] in favor of federalism or centralism.

Proof, *sb.* **18. b.** Add: **proof-bar,** a bar of metal which can be withdrawn from the apparatus in which a metallurgical process is going on to show what stage has been reached; **proof-glass** (example); **proof-reader** (earlier example); **proof-reading** (examples); **proof strength** (earlier example).
1888 LOCKWOOD *Dict. Mech. Engin. Terms* 268 *Proof Bar.—The loose bar which is thrust through a hole in the trough which contains steel undergoing the process of cementation, and which is removed from time to time [etc.]. 1848 *Knickerbocker Mag.* XVIII. 380 With what profound deliberation he drew his *proof-glass from the bung-hole of a brandy-pipe. 1855 [PRAY] *Mem. J. G. Bennet* 41 From this post he was transferred to that of a *proof-reader in the printing-house of Wells & Lilly. 1881 M. T. BIGELOW *Handbk. Punctuation* Pref. p. iv. An experience..of nearly fifty years—more than thirty of which have been spent in *proof-reading. 1899 J. H. QUINN *Man. Library Cataloguing* Index 163 Proof-reading and correction. 1811 *Niles' Weekly Reg.* I. 311/1 The same process repeated until the ley has acquired *proof strength.

Prop, *sb.*[1] **4.** Add: **prop-root,** a root of a tree that supports it like a prop.
For 1895 *Westm. Gaz.* 29 Mar. 2/1 *read* 1858 O. W. HOLMES *Deacon's Masterpiece* 49.
1907 FISHER in *Schlich's Man. Forestry* IV. 533 The roots ..that are stretched by the wind are termed anchor-roots, those on the lee side of the tree *prop-roots.

Prop (prǫp), *sb.*[6] Abbreviation of PROPELLER.
1918 E. M. ROBERTS *Flying Fighter* 239, I crashed into a hedge, smashed my prop to bits, and then the machine landed on its nose in the next field.

Propagand (prǫpăgæ·nd), *v.* [f. PROPAGAND or PROPAGANDA.] *intr.* To resort to or use propagandism; to propagandize.
1901 *Westm. Gaz.* 11 Jan. 2/2 Being free to 'propagand' he has not hesitated to do so. 1923 *Ibid.* 16 May, Russia was spending large sums out of her Secret Service in order to propagand in the East against British interests. 1927 C. E. MONTAGUE *Right off the Map* ix. 79 I've heard about you—propaganding all over the place for..universal disarmament.

Propaganda. 2. (Earlier and later examples.)
1800 *Aurora* (Philad.) 17 Apr. (Th.) We have thrown some useful light upon the Illuminati of Connecticut and Massachusetts, and lately upon a similar propaganda in Delaware State. 1920 H. G. WELLS *Outl. Hist.* 565/2 The feverish state of affairs in the Balkans was largely the outcome of the intrigues and propagandas sustained by the German and Slav schemes.

Propaga·nda, *v.* [f. the sb.] *trans.* = PROPAGANDIZE.
1921 J. F. PORTER *Sir Edward Elgar* 10 Elgar..never attempted to propaganda his work.

Propagandist. B. *adj.* (Earlier example.)
1824 D. WEBSTER *Wks.* III. 62 It may be easy to call this resolution Quixotic, the emanation of a crusading or propagandist spirit.

Propassion. (Later example.)
187. MANNING *Glories of Sacred Heart* ix. 266 All the affections and all those pro-passions, as they are called—because the Church never speaks of passions when it speaks of the Sacred Heart [etc.].

Propeller. Add: **3. b.** (Earlier examples.)
1845 *Niles' Weekly Reg.* 25 Oct. 128/1 The propeller Massachusetts left New York on the 15 Spt. 1852 D. S. CURTISS *Western Portraiture* 39 The terrible..catastrophe of the burning of the propeller Phoenix happened.

c. A fire-engine provided with mechanical propelling apparatus.
1905 *Hartford Courant* 2 Feb. 1 The big propellers—the fire engines that furnish their own power.

d. An appliance similar in design and principle to the propeller of a ship fixed to an aeroplane or other flying machine (originally sometimes at the rear but now usually in front).
1871 *Engl. Mech.* 448 Hollow bladed screw propellor. 1877 *Design & Work* 1 Dec. 466/1 My invention of steering balloons by setting the propellers on universal joints. 1897 *Strand Mag.* June 718/2 The method of propulsion was by aërial screw propellers. 1909 *Westm. Gaz.* 2 Dec. 5/1 Many writers have a habit of describing this component as a tractor, simply because the propeller is used to pull the craft forward instead of pushing it. 1916 H. BARBER *Aeroplane Speaks* 119 The 'pitch'..is the distance the propeller advances during one revolution, supposing the air to be solid.

5. *propeller-flutter, -slip, -thrust.*
1916 H. BARBER *Aeroplane Speaks* 125 *Propeller 'flutter', or vibration, may be due to faulty pitch angle, balance, camber, surface area, or to bad mounting. 1909 *Westm. Gaz.* 4 Mar. 4/2 According to some authorities, more than 50 per cent. of the engine-power is lost in what is known as *propeller-slip. *Ibid.* 13 July 7/1 Engine-power and *propeller-thrust are what will render the aerial navigator of the future..completely independent of the elements.

Propertied, *a.* **3.** (Later example.)
1909 M. E. ALBRIGHT *Shakesperian Stage* 147 The Elizabethan stage..was little more than a union of the old *sedes* and *plateæ* of the moralities, or the propertied and unpropertied stages of the interludes.

Property. 8. a. Add: *property-holder* (earlier example); **property-mark,** a mark indicating ownership; **property qualification** (earlier example).
1824 *Ann. 18th Congress* 1 Sess. II. 3129 *Property-holders of the city of Baltimore. 1908 *Hastings's Encycl. Relig. & Ethics* I. 303/2 These *property-marks' occur almost exclusively on weapons used in hunting, which, after being despatched, remain in the bodies of large game'. 1807 *Ann. 10th Congress* 1 Sess. I. 916 The Constitution of the United States requires no *property qualification in the elected.

Propertyless, *a.* (Earlier example.)
1822 W. COBBETT *Cottage Econ.* 107 They were formerly the sons and daughters of small farmers; they are now the progeny of miserable property-less labourers.

Prophet, *sb.* **5. c.** (Earlier example.)
1862 *Times* 31 Dec., Prophets, tipsters and welshers—the parasites of the ring.

Propitiative (propi·ʃi̇ĕtiv), *a.* [f. PROPITIATE *v.* + -IVE.] Tending to propitiate; conciliatory.
1928 *Observer* 19 Feb. 17/2 Where the majority of passengers have to travel in a brutalising congestion, the sight of half-empty 'firsts' next door is not propitiative.

Proposal. Add: **3. c.** An offer or tender.
1914 *Chicago Tribune* 8 May 14 Sealed proposals plainly marked on the outside 'Proposals for coal'..will be received at the Indian Office.

Propose, *v.* **3. e.** (Further examples.)
1854–5 THACKERAY *Newcomes* II. xiii. 127 Perhaps neither of them will propose for her. 1872 ANNA C. STEELE *Broken Toys* II. xxv. 167, I am going to Vere Court tomorrow to propose for Nella Vere.

Proposition. Add: 7. *U.S.* A matter, problem or undertaking that comes before one for solution, accomplishment or other treatment; a task, project or enterprise in respect of ease or difficulty of performing, resulting profit, etc., as *an easy, a tough, a paying proposition.* Used also of persons who have to be dealt with in any way.

1893 *Scribner's Mag.* June 756/1 'Arn't you ashamed to tell me this?' 'Of course I am, but that isn't the proposition just now.' 1896 G. Ade *Artie* xviii. 168 I'm goin' against a tough proposition. 1901 *Tit-Bits* 27 July 416/2 He was a pretty smooth proposition himself. 1902 O. Wister *Virginian* xviii. 214, I saw over in a fenced meadow.. what he was pleased to call 'the proposition'. Proposition in the West does, in fact, mean whatever you at the moment please. *a* 1904 S. E. White *Blazed Trail Stories* viii. 146 'I'm a pretty rank proposition, myself', said he. 1908 Mulford *Orphan* xiv. 178 And I'd rather have him with me in a mix-up than against me. He's the coolest proposition loose in this part of the country at any game. 1911 J. F. Wilson *Land Claimers* xii. 168 The best you can make of it is a pretty hard proposition. 1915 T. Burke *Nights in Town* 19 He is educated..to regard himself as, in the Broadway phrase, a serious proposition. 1925 Mulford *Cottonwood Gulch* vii. 92 Knife fighters are bad propositions.

b. With a defining term.

1902 O. Wister *Virginian* ii. 19 The biggest tobacco proposition for five cents got out yet. 1903 *N.Y. Times* Sat. Rev. 22 Aug., There are a good many stages at which the discipline proposition may present itself. 1909 S. E. White *Rules of Game* III. ix. 181 We're the only two business propositions in this country. 1929 *Daily Express* 7 Nov. 2/5 Every industry I want to nationalise must be a business proposition.

Proprietariat (proprəiẹ̄tē·riăt). *nonce-wd.* [f. Proprietarian, after Proletariat.] The propertied class.

1928 G. B. Shaw *Intel. Woman's Guide Socialism* 223 The Proletariat and the Proprietariat face each other.

Propriety. 7. (Later example.)

1925 Isabel Smith *Marriage in Ceylon* 137 Angela..had felt it would not be 'the thing' to accept hospitality of the man who in a few days' time would be her husband without someone to 'play propriety'.

Proprioceptive (prōᵘpriose·ptiv), *a. Phys.* [f. L. *proprius* own + *-ceptive* of Receptive.] Of nerves or receptive organs: Receiving impulses only from parts of the body itself and not from the external world. So **Pro·prioceptor**, a proprioceptive nerve or organ.

1906 C. S. Sherrington *Integr. Action Nervous Syst.* 130. Reflexes arising from proprio-ceptive organs came therefore to be habitually attached and appended to certain reflexes excited by extero-ceptive organs. *Ibid.*, The activity thus produced in these latter tissues excites in them their receptors, which are *proprio-ceptors.* 1927 Haldane & Huxley *Animal Biol.* i. 24, v. 125.

Propylitization (prōᵘpilǝitǝizēᵗ·ʃǝn). [f. Propylite + -isation.] The formation of propylite by solfataric action in volcanic rocks.

1903 Geikie *Text-bk. Geol.* 812 The solutions..in their progress..necessarily induce chemical and mineralogical changes in the surrounding rocks, which thus undergo various transformations, being sometimes weakened by the removal of certain constituents, as in propylitisation and kaolinisation.

Pro-rate, *v.* (Earlier example.) Hence **Pro-ra·ting** *vbl. sb.*

1860 *Congress. Globe* 21 Dec. 180/1 The amendment..requires this company to pro-rate passenger fare with all railroad companies or lines which terminate either at Alexandria, Washington or Baltimore. 1911 Webner *Factory Costs* 212 On the other hand, there is no possible way of entirely avoiding a prorating or averaging of expense.

Pro-rate, *sb. U.S.* [f. *pro rata.*] A proportional or pro rata share.

1904 F. Lynde *Grafters* vii. 92 A hundred thousand is a pot of money. I take it for granted the Western Pacific will stand its pro-rate?

Prorean (prōᵘ·rĭ,ăn), *a. Anat.* [f. L. *prōra* Prow *sb.*[1] + -an.] (See quot.)

1890 Sir W. Turner in *Jrnl. Anat.* XXV. 130 The most anterior end of the pallium, in such Carnivora as the Dog, has a beak-like form, and has been named the *prorean convolution*; whilst the fissure which forms its posterior boundary, situated in front of and almost parallel to the pre-sylvian fissure, is the *prorean fissure* of Krueg.

Prose, *sb.* 4. a. Also, a dull prosy person. (*colloq.*)

1844 Dickens *Mart. Chuz.* xxxvii, I verily believe you have said that fifty thousand times in my hearing. What a Prose you are.

Prosecuting, *ppl. a.* (U.S. examples.)

1832 *Indiana Ho. Repr. Jrnl.* 42 Duly elected Prosecuting Attorney of the second Judicial Circuit of the State of Indiana. 1872 Eggleston *Hoosier Schoolm.* xxix. 191 The 'prosecuting attorney' (for so the States' attorney is called in Indiana) had been sent for.

Prospect, *sb.* Add: 8. d. A possible or likely purchaser, subscriber, or customer.

1923 H. M. Swetland *Industr. Publishing* 124 Obviously the first step in getting circulation is to list prospects to whom the paper is to be offered. 1926 *Publishers' Weekly* 16 Jan. 161/2 To carry your helpful suggestions to the people who would be logical prospects for you. 1927 Mathilde Ecker *Over Boat-side* 298 If there was possibility of the prospect signing on the dotted line. 1927 *Observer* 27 Nov. 11/1 There are thousands of 'prospects' who simply will not decide about a car until they have seen the new Ford. 1928 *Sunday Express* 12 Feb. 11/3, I made sales to more than half of the 'prospects' he sent me to.

10. c. (Earlier example.)

1852 Whitmore *Diary* 23 July, Worked out my quartz lead prospecting. Found very good prospect.

d. *transf.*

1922 in *Glasgow Herald* 19 Dec. 8, I consider my bull calves excellent prospects for next season's fairs. 1923 'B. M. Bower' *Parowan Bonanza* viii. 95 A prospector is, paradoxically, not a good prospect for a girl.

Prospect, *v.* 6. (Earlier example.)

1851 N. Kingsley *Diary* 167 They say it does not prospect very well.

Prospecting, *vbl. sb.* 2. (Earlier example.)

1850 W. Cotton *Three Years Calif.* xxi. 292 Half their time is consumed in what they call prospecting; that is, looking up new deposits [of gold].

b. (Earlier example.)

1849 *Presid. Mess. Congress* II. 457 It is obvious that the shallow pits now sunk on the vein..can only be regarded..as mere superficial explorations, or 'prospecting diggings' as they are called in the west.

Prospective. A. *adj.* 5. (Further example.)

1906 Quiller-Couch *Fr. Cornish Window* 200 Our Parliamentary Candidate—or Prospective Candidate, as we cautiously call him—has been visiting us.

Prospe·ctusless, *a.* [f. Prospectus + -less.] For which no prospectus has been published.

1898 *Westm. Gaz.* 26 Oct. 8/1 A lesson to those who deal in prospectusless shares. 1928 *Daily Mail* 9 Aug. 18/1 Our references yesterday to statements published by prospectusless companies.

Prosthetic, *a.* Add: 2. b. as *sb. pl.* = Prosthesis 2.

1911 G. H. Wilson *Man. Dental Prosthetics* Pref., This book has been written in response to the oft-repeated request by teachers and members of the dental profession for a concise modern text-book on Dental Prosthetics.

Prosthetist (prǫ·sþĕtist). *Surg.* [f. Prosthetic + -ist.] One who practises prosthesis of limbs, teeth, etc.

190. *Buck's Handbk. Med. Sci.* V. 513 (Cent. Suppl.). 1911 G. H. Wilson *Man. Dental Prosthetics* 455 It is necessary that the patient shall be under the inspection and study of the prosthetist so as to restore the contour and harmonize the associated parts.

Prosy, *a.* 1. (Earlier example.)

1823 Scott *Pref. Mem. Clara Reeve* (Ballantyne's Nov. Libr.) V. p. lxxxvii, Perhaps, to be circumstantial and abundant in minute detail, and in one word, though an unauthorized one, to be somewhat *prosy*, is one mode of securing a certain necessary degree of credulity in hearing a ghost-story.

Protagonism (protæ·gŏniz'm). [f. as Protagonist + -ism.] The action or fact of supporting or championing a cause.

1909 *N.Y. Even. Post* 27 Nov. 6 The principal character ..is gradually drawn into a protagonism of common sense, candour and progress.

Protagonist. 2. Also, a leading player at some game or sport.

1908 A. W. Myers *Compl. Lawn Tennis Player* 25 The prospect of a close match between two protagonists.

Protagorean (protægōrī·ăn), *a.* [f. Gr. Πρωταγόρει-ος adj. (f. Πρωταγόρας, the name of a Greek philosopher of the 5th century B.C.) + -an.] Of or pertaining to Protagoras or his philosophy.

1678 Cudworth *Intell. Syst.* 10 The Protagorean philosophy made all things to consist of a commixture of parts or atoms and local motion. 1845 Maurice *Mor. Philos.* in *Encycl. Metrop.* 614/1 The Protagorean notion of man being the measure of all things..he treats as a silly truism. 1907 *Hibbert Jrnl.* Jan. 439 A Protagorean treatise of the fifth century B.C. 1921 T. R. Glover *Pilgrim* 176 The idea of Christian charity has been perverted..to mean a Protagorean acceptance of the equal value of all opinions.

Protamine. Also -amin.

1902 *Encycl. Brit.* XXXI. 724/1 These Protamins..take up water and yield the bases above referred to.

Protarsal (protā·rsăl), *a. Entom.* [f. Protarsus + -al.] Of or pertaining to the protarsus.

1902 R. I. Pocock in *Proc. Zool. Soc.* II. 391, and leg with superior basal and anterior apical femoral spine, three inferior apical protarsal spines..and one inferior medium tarsal spine.

Protaxis (prōᵘ·tæksis). *Geol.* [f. Proto- 2 b + Axis.] An original or chief axis in a system of folding.

1895 Dana *Man. Geol.* i. 24 The oldest of the mountain ranges in a chain is called the *protaxis*...The other ranges are usually parallel to the protaxis, and may, or may not, have greater height. 1909 F. D. Adams in *Jrnl. Geol.* XVII. 1 The development of the Grenville series in a great tract of the Laurentian Protaxis.

Protect, *v.* Add: 1. Also *absol.*

1894 E. Fawcett *New Nero* ii. 26 Music..was always an expression of..that soulless and mysterious will-to-live, which for ever creates, protects, and perpetuates.

2. (Earlier examples.)

1789 *Ann. 1st Congress* I. 111 [Measures] calculated to encourage the productions of our country, and protect our infant manufactures. 1820 *Ann. 16th Congress* 1 Sess. II. 2308 If American manufactures were duly protected, they create for agriculture an extensive..home market.

Protecting, *ppl. a.* (Earlier examples of *protecting duty.*)

1790 A. Gallatin *Wks.* (1904) I. 304 A system of protecting duties. 1802 *Ann. 7th Congress* 1 Sess. 230 They have probably caused this protecting duty to impede progress. 1820 *Ann. Reg.* 73/2 The American timber being of an inferior quality to that from the Baltic, required a protecting duty.

Protection. 4. (Earlier examples.)

1820 *Ann. 16th Congress* 1 Sess. II. 2308 All wise nations ..have strenuously extended this species of protection to their manufactures. 1820 *Hansard's Parl. Deb.* 26 May 579 But let your lordships consider..what would be the effect..if the existing system of protection were abolished, and a fixed duty..were substituted.

Protective, *a.* 2. (Earlier example.)

1820 *Ann. Reg.* 771/1 The protective or restrictive system.

Protectorist (prote·ktŏrist). *Hist.* [f. Protector *sb.* + -ist.] = Protectorian B.

1913 J. Willcock *Sir H. Vane the Younger* xvi. 275 About half the members of the Commons were Protectorists or supporters of the constitution prescribed in *The Petition and Advice.*

Proteidogenous (prōᵘtī,idǫ·dʒĕnəs), *a.* [f. Proteid[1] + -o- + *-genous.] Producing proteid.

1918 *Times Lit. Suppl.* 2 May 205/2 The proteidogenous molecules whose by-play is supposed to be life.

Proteistic (prōᵘtī,i·stik), *a.* [f. Prote-us + -istic.] Suggestive of Proteus; changing; variable.

1921 *19th Cent.* July 146 The new proteistic shape of the defeated Guelfs swept away the old 'Right'.

Protensity. Delete *rare*⁻⁰.

1924 Stout *Psychol.* II. i. 212 In all sense-presentations we can discern Quality, Intensity, and Protensity or Duration.

Protest, *sb.* 5. Add: *protest mechanism.*

1920 *Challenge* 21 May 45/1 Adler..has shown how this protest mechanism is responsible for neurotic manifestations of another kind.

Protest, *v.* 2. c. Also, to protest against; to make the subject of a protest.

1904 *Brooklyn Eagle* 5 June, Many of the students are much incensed at the judges and will probably protest the decision. 1928 E. G. Mears *Orientals on Pacific Coast* 6 The Peking Foreign Office has regularly protested acts of injustice and violence.

Protestant. B. *adj.* 1. b. Add: **Protestant Episcopalism,** the system of the Protestant Episcopal Church in the U.S.A.

1836 *Southern Lit. Messenger* II. 282 In regard to Protestant Episcopalism in America it may be safely said that, prior to this publication of Dr. Hawks, there were no written memorials extant.

Protisto·logy. *Biol.* [f. Protista + -(o)logy.] The scientific study of the *Protista.*

1906 McCabe tr. *Bölsche's Haeckel, Life & Work* 206 He gives them the name of 'Protists'. To botany and zoology is now added protistology.

Protocol, *sb.* Add: 2. c. The official mark on a roll of papyrus.

1905 W. E. Crum *Catal. Coptic MSS. in Brit. Mus.* 181 Upon the 1st *selis*, above the Coptic text, is part of the protocol in large Kufic characters. 1909 — *Catal. Coptic MSS. in John Rylands Libr.* 164 Parts of an earlier protocol, in large, brown characters, are visible on *recto.*

Protocolar (prōᵘ·tokǫlăı), *a.* [f. Protocol *sb.* + -ar[1].] Of or pertaining to a protocol.

1905 *N.Y. Even. Post* 15 July (Cent. Suppl.) To some extent it is protocolar but one must not for that think it an empty form.

Protology. Transfer *Obs. rare*⁻⁰ to sense defined in Dict. and add: 2. The science of first things.

1899–1900 *21st Ann. Rep. Bur. Amer. Ethnol.* (1903) 138 In the quaint protology, or science of first things, of the Iroquois things are derived from things through transformation and evolution.

Proton. Add: 2. *Chem.* A unit constituent of matter associated with (or consisting of) an invariable charge of positive electricity.

1920 *Nature* 11 Nov. 357/1 The elements may be considered as being composed of these hydrogen nuclei or 'protons' as Sir Ernest Rutherford would have us call them. 1922 J. Mills *Within the Atom* ii. 13 The hydrogen atom is composed of only one proton and one electron. 1923 G. H. Knibbs *Presid. Addr. Austral. Assoc.* 14 A neutral atom consists of K+N protons and K electrons in its nucleus and N electrons in its rings or sheaths. 1925 *Observer* 13 Sept. 9/1 The idea that the atom of matter was composed of electrons and protons. 1927 A. S. Eddington *Stars & Atoms* 99 Most of it [subatomic energy] is inherent in the constitution of the electrons and protons—the elementary negative and positive electric charges—out of which matter is built.

Protonic (protǫ·nik), *a.*[2] *Biol.* [f. Proton + -ic.] Of or pertaining to a proton.

1902 *Trans. Amer. Microsc. Soc.* June 59 The differentiation has gradually extended posteriad from the protonic inception.

Protopathic, *a.* Add: b. Applied to the first form of sensibility exhibited by an area of skin after the nerves leading to it are severed.

1905 Head, Rivers & Sherren in *Brain* Nov. 106 To this form of sensibility we propose to give the name '*protopathic*'. 1912 J. G. McKendrick *Principles of Physiology* xiii. 224 If a sensory nerve to an area of skin is divided, sensibility may return if the ends unite. The sensations that return first have been termed protopathic, and depend on heat, cold, and pain spots. 1920 W. H. R. Rivers *Instinct & Unconscious* iv. 23 Epicritic sensibility may be only a greater perfection of protopathic sensibility.

Prototheme (prōᵘ·topīm). [f. Proto- + Theme.] (See quot.)

1897 W. G. Searle *Onomasticon Anglo-Saxonicum* Introd. p. xii, The Anglo-Saxon personal names may be divided into several classes. 1. The first and chief class consists of names that may be termed dithematic names, as they consist of two elements or themes, mostly monosyllabic, a first element or prototheme, and a second element or deuterotheme.

Prototroch (prōᵘ·totrǫk). [f. Proto- + Gr. τροχός wheel.] The first of three ciliated bands encircling the larva of certain marine annelids.

1897 Masterman in *Q. Jrnl. Microsc. Sci.* XL. 291 There are three prominent ciliated bands, the preoral (or prototroch), the collar-band..and the trunk band.

Prototrophic (prōᵘto,trǫ·fik), *a.* [f. Proto- + Gr. τροφή nourishment + -ic.] Of bacteria: That feed on inorganic substances.

1900 A. C. Jones tr. *Fischer's Struct. Bacteria* vi. 54 These few mineral substances will be found sufficient probably for all bacteria, be they prototrophic, metatrophic or paratrophic. 1902 *Encycl. Brit.* XXVI. 55/1 Since they require no organic food materials..he [Fischer] regards them as primitive forms in this respect, and terms them *Prototrophic.*

Protozoolo·gical, *a.* [f. Protozo-a + -(o)logical.] Of or pertaining to protozoology. So **Protozoo·logist,** a student of protozoology.

1906 *Nature* 29 Nov. 117/2 When the protozoologist has worked out his life-histories and obtained his results, then the medical man steps in and carries off the honey to the medical hive. 1922 *Daily Mail* 17 Nov. 1 Advt., [Coloured pencils] for Botanical, Zoological and Protozoological work. 1925 *Public Opinion* 29 May 519/1 For such a task we should require the services of entomologists, protozoologists, veterinary and medical scientists.

Protracted, *ppl. a.* 1. (Earlier and later examples of *protracted meeting.*)

1835 A. Reed *Journ. N. Amer.* I. 185 (Th.) Mr. Hall advised a protracted meeting for four days. 1837 *Knickerbocker Mag.* X. 443 A divine, who was riding with him,.. to attend a protracted meeting. 1877 Habberton *Jericho Road* 126 A little Methodist Church where one of the daily evening services of a series known as 'protracted meetings' was going on. 1908 Eliza C. Hall *Aunt Jane of Kentucky* i. (1909) 24 We went home feelin' like we'd been through a big protracted meetin' and got religion over again.

Prove, *v.* 12. Prove up. (Earlier examples.)

1867 A. D. Richardson *Beyond Mississippi* xi. 138 He does not see the land again until ready to 'prove up'...Then he revisits his claim. 1878 J. H. Beadle *Western Wilds* ii. 43 My wife proved up on her Cherokee blood.

Provence. Delete the note on *Provence rose*, and quot. 1905.

Provender, *v.* Add: 3. *intr.* To partake of provender; to feed *on* (something).

1819 Keats *Lett.* (1931) II. 376 Infidel Rooks do not provender with Elisha's Ravens. 1891 Clo. Graves *Field of Tares* iv. vi. 241 (Born) Leaving the iron horse provendering on coal and water...we follow the footsteps of the man.

Prover. Add: 3. b. In *Homœopathy*: A healthy person on whom the effect of a drug is tested.

1902 *Encycl. Brit.* XXIX. 312/2 The manifestations of drug action thus produced are carefully recorded, and this record..after being verified by repetition on many 'provers', constitutes the distinguishing feature of the homœopathic materia medica.

Provide·ntialism. [f. Providential + -ism.] Belief in the providence of God.

1927 J. S. Huxley *Religion without Revelation* Pref. 18 The release of God from the anthropomorphic disguise of personality also provides release from that vice which may be termed Providentialism.

Provincial. A. *adj.* 7. b. Delete *erron.* and read: Of roses of Provence.

Provi·ncializa·tion. [f. Provincialize + -ation.] A making or becoming provincial.

1924 *Glasgow Herald* 16 Sept. 7 In a vigorous speech [he] emphasised the provincialisation and Indianisation aspect of the Report.

Provision, *sb.* 10. Add: *provision man, shop, store, trade* (earlier example).

1872 *Boston* (Mass.) *Ordin.* 25 July, The vehicles of market or *provision men. 1875 Mrs. Stowe *We & Neighbors* i. 8 Simons, the provision man at the corner. 1854 Maria S. Cummins *Lamplighter* xv, Willie accompanied them as far as the *provision shop, which was their destination. 1796 *Boston* (Mass.) *Directory* s.v. *Fletcher*, *Provision store. 1875 Mrs. Stowe *We & Neighbors* i. 21 Dinah met their girl in at the provision store. 1830 *Ann. Congress* 429/2 The *provision trade of the West.

Provision, *v.* (Later examples). Also with *up.*

1903 R. Bedford *True Eyes* 48 Why didn't you provision from home? 1928 *Daily Express* 11 Aug. 4/6 The main thing to remember in going to the islands is to provision-up for your stay well ahead.

Provocator (prǫ·vokeɪtəɹ). [ad. L. *prōvocātor* in same sense.] A provoker or challenger.

1918 A. Gray tr. *The Crime* II. ii. 132 If even the creator of the defensive Entente of 1904 was regarded as a dangerous provocator [etc.].

Provost guard. *U.S.* A body of soldiers acting as military police under a provost-marshal; also, the quarters used by these.

1778 *Jrnl. Cont. Congress* X. 74 About thirty [officers] who have been confined in the provost guard and in the most loathsome gaols. 1864 O. W. Norton *Army Lett.* 212 Company K. is provost guard and river patrol. 1881–5 McClellan *Own Story* 69 These..I at once brought to the city and employed as a provost-guard. 1884 Sweet & Knox *Through Texas* xlii. 595 We may be caught by the provost-guard, and put in the bull-pen.

Prude (prūd), *v.* [f. the sb.] *intr.* To play the prude.

1923 Una L. Silberrad *Lett. Jean Armiter* ix. § 1. 194 Girls aren't brought up in cotton wool nowadays as you were. We do as we jolly well like! It's no good preaching and pruding.

Prudential. A. *adj.* 2. Also *prudential committee.*

1823 *Baptist Mag.* IV. 24 Monday evening was assigned for the missionaries to receive the instructions of the Prudential Committee. 1910 *N.Y. Even. Post* 26 Nov. Suppl. 10 During his..25 years as member of the prudential committee, he has missed but one meeting.

Prune, *sb.* 5. Add: *prune-orchard, rancher*; *prune-coloured* adj.; **prune-brandy,** an intoxicating beverage prepared from prunes.

1895 M. Pemberton *Impregn. City* vi. 41 Drink that, and when you've drained the bumper, we'll have some *prune brandy. 1923 *Blackw. Mag.* Oct. 499/2 The foothills..were covered with a shadow over which *prune-coloured clouds hung. 1921 *Chambers's Jrnl.* Mar. 173/1 *Prune-orchards do not need irrigating. *Ibid.* 174/2 With proper pruning and cultivation the *prune-rancher has an assured..living.

Prunes-and-prismy, *a.* [f. *Prunes and prism* (Prune *sb.* 4) + -y.] Using prim and mincing language; suggestive of 'prunes and prism'.

1931 St. John Ervine in *Time & Tide* 4 July, A tougher-minded generation than ours may find it altogether too prunes-and-prismy.

Prussian. A. *adj.* 2. **Prussian blue.** b. Also, the name of a variety of pea.

1824 Loudon *Encycl. Gard.* III. viii. 618 The egg, the Moratto, the Prussian blue, and the Rouncivals,..are all very fine eating peas. 1832 J. Tod *Annals Rajast'han* II. 765, I never saw finer crops of Prussian-blues..cauliflowers, celery, and all that belongs to the kitchen-garden.

Prussianize, *v.* Also *intr.* To act in a manner regarded as typical of Prussians.

1927 'Ixion' *Further Motor Cycle Remin.* 82 The victim [of the practical joke] occupied a minor official position, by dint of which he Prussianized rather too freely.

Prussification (prɒsifikā·ʃǝn). [f. Prussi(an + -fication.] = Prussianization. So **Pru·ssify** *v. trans.* = Prussianize.

1898 *Daily News* 21 Jan. 4/5 The fund for the Prussification of the Polish provinces of the kingdom. 1924 *Contemp. Rev.* Mar. 301 The Russians were trying their hardest to russify, and the Prussians were trying their hardest to prussify their Polish provinces.

Pry, *v.*[2] (Later examples.)

1926 *Harper's Mag.* Feb. 363/1, I stood rooted to the spot and you could not have pried me away. 1927 Susan Ertz *Now East, Now West* ii. 21 He walked about the decks.. hand in hand with Cleve, whenever that friendly child could be pried loose from some new and fascinating acquaintance.

b. *fig.* To get information *out of* a person by inquiry.

1896 C. M. Sheldon *Bro. Keeper* iii. 66 We managed to pry out of him that he had seen you and Eric go down the ladders.

Psammo-. Add: **Psa·mmophile** *a. Bot.* [-phile.] = *Psammophilous.*

1901 C. Mohr *Plant Life Alabama* 131 The slender, wiry culms of this grass..render the species one of the most striking types of psammophile plants.

Psammology (psæm-, sæmǫ·lodʒi). [f. Psammo- + -(o)logy.] The scientific study of sand.

1897 *Geog. Jrnl.* IX. 570, I have devoted many years to the study of psammology.

Pseudo-. 2. Add: **Pseuda·ndry,** the use by a woman of a masculine nom-de-plume. **Pseudogyny** (-ǫ·dʒini) *Entom.*, pseudogynous condition.

1929 H. M. Paull *Literary Ethics* 189 Initialism, asterism, boustrophedon and *pseudandry. 1903 *Jrnl. R. Microsc. Soc.* Apr. 172 E. Wasmann returns with fresh light to a discussion of '*pseudogyny' in Formica sanguinea, etc.

Pseudopod. Add: 4. (See quot.)

1920 E. E. Fournier d'Albe tr. *Schrenck Notzing's Phenom. Materialisation* 25 The recent investigations by W. J. Crawford have shown that white light acts destructively on the pseudopods or psychic projections from the medium's body.

Pseudopodium. Add: 3. *fig.*

1918 S. Butler *Notebooks* 196 My reviewers felt no sense of need to understand me...When the time comes that they want to do so they will throw out a little mental pseudopodium without much difficulty.

Psocid (ps-, sō·sid), *sb.* [f. mod.L. *Psocidæ.*] A member of the family *Psocidæ* of pseudoneuropterous insects.

1901 *Science* 13 Dec. 941/2 He also found the first psocid recorded from New Mexico. 1922 *Entomol. Mag.* May 104 The occurrence of various species of Psocids..inside houses, has been frequently observed.

Psorosis (psǒrōᵘ·sis). [f. as Psora + -osis.] A disease affecting the bark of orange trees.

1896 *U.S. Dept. Agric., Div. Veget. Physiol. & Pathol.* Bull. 8. 30 Psorosis, a disease known in Florida as 'tears' or 'gum disease', is often confounded with foot rot, but is unquestionably quite distinct...Psorosis does not kill the bark entirely.

Psyche (sǝik), *v. colloq.* [f. Psyche *sb.*] *trans.* To subject to psycho-analysis.

1927 W. E. Collinson *Contemp. Engl.* 107. 1928 *Daily Express* 31 Dec. 2/5 While for some patients being 'psyched' may be a step towards being cured, to others it may amount to being infected.

Psychic. B. *sb.* Add: 1. b. That which is psychic; things of the psyche or soul.

1909 *Daily Chron.* 6 Sept. 3/3 Her craze for the 'psychic' ..oils the wheels of the plot. 1920 W. McDougall *Group Mind* 14 Maciver is under the influence of that unfortunate and still prevalent way of thinking of the psychic as identical with the conscious which has given endless trouble in psychology.

Psycho (sǝi·ko), *sb.* and *v. colloq.* Short for *Psycho-analysis and *Psycho-analyse.

1921 Rose Macaulay *Dangerous Ages* v. § 4 Not that insomnia is always a case for psycho, you know. 1925 *Christian World* 4 June 7/2 How many of us spend twenty minutes a day in consciously psychoing themselves?

Psycho-. Add: **Psychasthe·nic** *sb.*, a person suffering from psychasthenia. **Psycho-biolo·gical** *a.*, that is both psychological and biological. **Psycho-bio·logy,** that branch of biology which deals with psychology. **Psycho-bio·tic** *a.*, = **Psycho-biological.* **Psycho-che·mistry,** the investigation of mental states and processes by chemical methods. **Psycho-galva·nic** *a.* (see quot. 1929). **Psycho-mo·ral** *a.*, of or pertaining to the psychological aspect of morality. **Psycho-neu·ral** *a.*, that is both psychical and neural. **Psycho-neurolo·gical** *a.*, of or pertaining to psycho-neurology. **Psychono·mic** *a.*, directing or governing psychic processes. **Psycho-se·xual** *a.*, of or pertaining to the psychical or mental factor of sexuality; so **Psycho-sexua·lity.** **Psycho-te·chnical** *a.*, that is both psychological and technical. **Psycho-vi·talism,** belief in the action or presence of a vital principle in mental processes. **Psycho-vitali·stic** *a.*, pertaining to or based on psycho-vitalism.

1907 *Jrnl. Abnorm. Psychol.* II. 59 Among these *psychasthenics the disturbance of the personality is not total. 1901 *Amer. Jrnl. Psychol.* XII. 206 On the positive side, the experiments must conform to the *psycho-biological character of an animal if sane results are to be obtained. 1928 *Daily Express* 23 Aug. 3/1 The two authors have produced a highly provocative collection of psycho-biological comments [on marriage]. 1902 *Encycl. Brit.* XXXII. 65/2 This connection of vegetal and animal functions remains one of the obscurest in all *psycho-biology. 1926 *Glasgow Herald* 27 Apr. 4/2 It is possible that some kinds of variations or mutations are *psycho-biotic phenomena. 1900 *Amer. Jrnl. Psychol.* XI. 600 The writer takes up..passive and then active sadness, morbid joy, their original mechanism, their psycho-physiology, *psycho-chemistry, psycho-physics, [etc.]. 1915 C. R. Payne tr. *Pfister's Psycho-anal. Meth.* 336 Secretion of tears, sighing, *psychogalvanic phenomena, changes in the pulse, etc. 1929 *Encycl. Brit.* XVIII. 674/2 The term psychogalvanic reflex..was first used by Veraguth to describe the change in electrical properties of the human body (or any living animal body) in response to nocuous (emotional) stimuli. 1890 *Smithsonian Rep.* 1. 663 Dr. Semal advocated a *psycho-moral examination of the delinquent in order to determine his condition, whether he was a confirmed criminal or only a criminal on occasion. 1902 *Encycl. Brit.* XXXII. 69/1 *Psychoneural parallelism is no doubt a well-established generalization. 1921 *Edin. Rev.* Jan. 61 In London the *Psycho-Neurological Society has been formed ..for the study and discussion of problems in psychotherapy. 1902 J. M. Baldwin *Develop. & Evolution* i. 8 Such conditions are '*psychonomic'. This term may be used to denote the entire sphere of phenomena which are in connection with the psychological, but which, nevertheless, are not intrinsic to the series of psychic changes as such. 1909 E. Jones in *Jrnl. Abnorm. Psychol.* IV. 58 Freud's views of the development after polymorphous *psycho-sexual perversity of normal children. 1915 C. R. Payne tr. *Pfister's Psycho-anal. Meth.* 63 We speak, therefore,..of *psycho-sexuality. 1903 *Harvard Psychol. Stud.* I. 654 The science of pedagogy is a *psycho-technical discipline which makes education mechanical. 1927 *Daily Express* 17 June 12 Electrical machinery, levers, mechanical puzzles, and complete paraphernalia for psycho-technical tests. 1924 R. M. Ogden tr. *Koffka's Growth of Mind* 236 Objections to a physiological theory of association no longer force upon us the acceptance of *psycho-vitalism. *Ibid.* 104 If the choice lay between a mechanistic or a (*psycho-)vitalistic explanation, we should feel obliged to choose the latter.

Psycho-a·nalyse, *v.* [f. Psycho- + Analyse *v.*] *trans.* To subject to psycho-analysis. Hence **Psycho-a·nalysed** *ppl. a.*

1923 *Blackw. Mag.* May 645/2 William thought he might have to be psycho-analysed before he would discover the secret of their persistence. 1927 *Daily Express* 8 July 1/4 The world would have known nothing more of him had not the prison doctor recorded how he psycho-analysed this youth before he died. 1928 'Rebecca West' *Strange Necessity* 240 A psycho-analysed person who has made the realization that all persons he dreams of are disguised versions of himself.

Psycho-ana·lysis. [ad. G. *psychoanalyse* (Freud): cf. Psycho- and Analysis.] A therapeutic method for treating certain mental disorders elaborated by Dr. S. Freud of Vienna, which aims at bringing to light and so providing a remedy for complexes or repressed affects which persist in a person's unconscious mind and have harmful effects on his thought and behaviour. b. That branch of psychology which deals with the unconscious mind; depth-psychology.

1906 J. J. Putnam in *Jrnl. Abnormal Psychol.* I. 28 The method of 'psycho-analysis'. 1908 E. Jones *Ibid.* III. 163 Psychoanalysis always reveals a precise cause for the occurrence, shewing that only it and no other could have arisen. 1910 *Amer. Jrnl. Psychol.* XXI. 310 Psychoanalysis..has its point of departure in the principle that the symptoms of these diseases are only the sensory images of particular thought-constellations, impregnated with feeling, which were distasteful to consciousness and therefore repressed, forgotten, but still live on in the unconscious. 1913 *Q. Rev.* Jan. 144 Both the theory and the practice of psycho-analysis are now in the melting-pot of scientific examination. 1918 *Jrnl. Educ.* Mar. 151 Hitherto writers on psychoanalysis have given numerous..hints about its educational possibilities. 1924 W. B. Selbie *Psychol. Relig.* 286 Psycho-analysis is the name given to the process by which the hidden depths of the individual consciousness can be revealed.

Psycho-a·nalyst. Also -ana·lyzist. [f. Psycho- + Analyst, or ad. G. *psychoanalytiker.*] One who practises or is skilled in psycho-analysis.

1918 *Jrnl. Educ.* Mar. 153/1 Dr. Pfister devotes a couple of pages to an exposition of the need for the psychoanalyst to be himself 'free from complexes'. 1920 *Discovery* Mar. 69/2 The psycho-analysts have arrived at the conclusion that repressed material is always unpleasant. 1927 *Saturday Even. Post* 24 Dec. 83/2 Yet this madness..deserves more attention than it gets from psychoanalysts. 1928 *Observer* 19 Feb. 12/6 The evidence..has broken down, but not before psychologists, pedagogues,..psycho-analysists, and doctors ..have written reams.

Psycho-analy·tic, *a.* [ad. G. *psychoanalytisch*: cf. Psycho- and Analytic.] Of, pertaining to, or employing psycho-analysis. So **Psycho-analy·tical** *a.*; **Psycho-analy·tically** *adv.*

1906 *Jrnl. Abnorm. Psychol.* I. 98 The psycho-analytic method which Freud uses for the demonstration of such complexes in hysteria and other conditions is cumbersome. 1908 *Ibid.* III. 209 It would have added greatly to the interest of this question if a psychoanalytical investigation had been resorted to. 1927 *Observer* 17 Apr. 5/1 The psycho-analytic method. 1927 *Ibid.* 12 June 12 The interesting question of whether medical men may treat a patient psycho-analytically was dealt with in Court the other day. 1927 *Daily Express* 20 June 13/4 A Vienna palmist gave a demonstration before the psycho-analytical clinic in Vienna.

Psychogene·tic, *a.* [f. Psychogenesis.] = Psychogenetical. **Psychoge·nic** *a.*, having a mental or psychic cause.

1904 *Jrnl. Phil. Psychol. & Sci. Methods* I. 328 Hume.. had quite unwittingly furnished what..should have been regarded as a logical deduction and justification—rather than the mere psychogenetic description, which it purported to be—of the realistic belief [etc.]. 1915 C. R. Payne tr. *Pfister's Psycho-anal. Meth.* 532 The educator is often unable to tell whether a psychogenic or physiogenic disturbance is present.

Psychographer. Add: b. A psychological critic or biographer.

1912 G. Bradford *Lee the American* App. 269 But the prince of all psychographers is incontestably Sainte-Beuve. 1930 *London Mercury* Feb. 378 He does not attempt a new 'life', but only a new character-study from the point of view of the 'psychographer'.

Psycho·graphist. [f. Psychograph + -ist.] A person who obtains 'spirit-writings'.

1904 *Kansas City Daily Times* 12 July (Cent. Suppl.) Of fifteen clairvoyants..and 'psychographists' whom I have called upon..the majority have informed me that clergymen are their best customers.

Psychology. Add: 2. Character considered from the point of view of psychology; mental or psychological peculiarities.

1913 G. B. Dibblee *Newspaper* 239 Delane's acuteness of judgment as to the psychology of London society was far from being consonant with the verdict of history. 1928 *Daily Tel.* 11 Sept. 10/5 The psychology of the workaday world has impelled him with its disquiet.

Psychoma (ps-, sǝikōᵘ·mă). [f. Psyche + *-oma.] (See quot.)

1904 McCabe tr. *Haeckel's Wonders of Life* xix. 464 It would seek these in psychic forces. On our monistic principles they are not immaterial forces, but based on the general sensation of substance, which we call psychoma, and add to energy and matter as a third attribute of substance.

Psy·cho-neuro·tic, *a.* and *sb.* [f. Psycho- + Neurotic.] a. *adj.* Of, pertaining to, or connected with psycho-neurosis. b. *sb.* A person suffering from psycho-neurosis; one who is mentally diseased.

190. *Buck's Handbk. Med. Sci.* V. 28 (Cent. Suppl.). 1908 *Practitioner* Apr. 519 The Painful Joints of Psycho-neurotics. 1909 E. Jones in *Jrnl. Abnorm. Psychol.* IV. 144 Every psycho-neurotic symptom is to be regarded as the symbolic expression of a submerged mental complex of the nature of a wish. 1923 B. H. Streeter in *Proc. 7th Internat. Congr. Psychol.* 148 But, though a genius is frequently a psycho-neurotic, it would be quite untrue to say that the majority of psycho-neurotics tend towards genius. 1927 *Daily Express* 4 July 10/4 You may become impatient because you do not realise that the person you are dealing with is what is called psycho-neurotic.

Psy·cho-patholo·gic, *a.* [f. Psycho-pathology.] = Psycho-pathological.

1890 *Smithsonian Rep.* 1. 636 One can thus see the links which form the psycho-pathologic chain of human life, at one end of which we may find insanity and at the other criminality.

Psycho-physical, *a.* (Earlier examples of *psycho-physical parallelism*).

1894 J. E. Creighton & Titchener tr. *W. Wundt's Hum. & Anim. Psychol.* 448 The principle of psychophysical parallelism..refers always to a parallelism of elementary physical and psychical processes. 1896 Titchener *Outl. Psychol.* xv. 342 This rule—the principle of 'psychophysical parallelism', as it is termed is..not an explanation of the relation of mind and body.

Psycho-the·rapist. [f. Psycho- + Therapist.] = Psycho-therapeutist.

1923 *Daily Mail* 19 Jan. 7 An earnest warning to nervous persons to avoid spiritualism is given by Dr. W. Stekel, the Viennese neurologist and psycho-therapist. 1924 W. B. Selbie *Psychol. Relig.* 300 Psychotherapists..recognize the great help that may be derived from religious faith.

Psychotic, *a.* Also as *sb.*, a person suffering from psychosis.

1915 C. R. Payne tr. *Pfister's Psycho-anal. Meth.* 318 He also knows plenty of neurotics and psychotics among alcoholics.

Psychrothe·rapy. [f. Gr. ψυχρό-ς cold + Therapy.] The treatment of diseases with cold.

1902 A. A. Eshner tr. *Winternitz's Hydrotherapy* etc. Pref. v, The consideration of other methods of thermotherapy—as also that of psychrotherapy or excessive cold—is thus naturally associated with the study of hydrotherapy.

Psylla (ps-, si·lă). [mod.L. f. Gr. ψύλλα flea.] A genus of insects injurious to plants; an insect of this genus; a plant-louse.

1918 W. A. Davis *Study Indigo Soils Bihar* 8 In 1907, two diseases appeared simultaneously—the so-called 'wilt' disease and the less serious insect pest 'psylla'.

Psyllid (ps-, si·lid), *a.* and *sb.* [f. mod.L. *Psyllidæ* (f. prec.), the name of the family.] a. *adj.* Of or belonging to the family *Psillidæ* of hemipterous insects; caused by one of these. b. *sb.* An insect of this family; a plant-louse.

1913 *Annals & Mag. Nat. Hist.* XI. 308 Giant Psyllid Gall from Syria. 1920 *Nature* 3 June 714/1, I also find a winged termite, a psillid,..some small spiders, etc.

Pte·ridosperm. *Bot.* [f. Pterido- + Sperm.] An extinct, seed-bearing, fern-like plant.

1906 *New Phytologist* V. 234 The history of the Pteridosperms is very different. Though having..the same type of seed, they retained the habit and much of the anatomy of Ferns. 1931 A. C. Seward *Plant Life thr. Ages* ix. 147 Evidence..eventually proved that the great majority of the Carboniferous 'ferns' were seed-bearing plants—pteridosperms.

Pterodactyl. Add: 2. A type of aeroplane.

1930 *Times* 26 Mar. 8/4 With regard to the pterodactyl, the original machine, Mark 1 A, had been modified as a result of trials.

Pterygiate (ptĕri·dʒi,ĕt), *a.* [f. Pterygium + -ate.] Provided with pterygia.

1904 *Annals & Mag. Nat. Hist.* Aug. 108 Rostrum short, pterygiate, nude at apex, indistinctly carinate.

Pub, *sb.* b. *Comb.* as *pub-keeper*; **pub-crawl,** a round of several public houses made by one or more persons; so **pub-crawler, -crawling** *vbl. sb.*

1915 T. Burke *Nights in Town* 273 We did a '*pub-crawl' in Commercial Road and East India Dock Road. 1920 *Daily Chron.* 28 Jan. 4/4 Flush with funds, freed from any and every restraining influence,..these '*pub-crawlers' have captured the illiterate and the unthinking. 1921 F. B. Young *Black Diamond* vii, I bain't goin' to keep you in *pub-crawlin' any longer. 1925 Deeping *Sorrell & Son* vi. Our *pub-keepers rarely visualize the atmosphere of a garden.

Public, *a.* 1. (Further example.)

1928 *Brit. Industr. Future* (Lib. Ind. Inq.) II. vi. 63 In a modern community man services must be run by a Public Concern—meaning by this a form of organisation which..is operated or regulated in the public interest.

b. *Public utilities*, the services or supplies commonly available in large towns such as trams or omnibuses, electricity, gas, water, drainage, etc. Also *attrib.* as *public-utility.*

1915 *Polit. Quarterly* May 106 Now coal mining is a 'public-utility' industry. 1922 *Encycl. Brit.* XXX. 174/1 The State is held to be justified in introducing restrictive legislation for dealing with strikes and lockouts, particularly in the group of industries known as 'public utility' services. 1928 *Daily Chron.* 9 Aug. 7/2 Crops have been destroyed and communications and public utilities have been crippled.

B. *sb.* Add: 5. *U.S.* Short for *public reproof* (at a college).

1837 *Knickerbocker Mag.* IX. 244 Accordingly I was reported to the government..and received a 'public'. *Ibid.*, Publics were very common. 1842 *Ibid.* XIX. 430 Prayers he has cut, to the extent of a 'public'. 1876 [G. H. Tripp] *Student Life* 133 If we make a noise..we shall get publics, if nothing worse.

Publicist. Add: 3. A publicity agent.

1930 *Oxford Times* 4 Apr. 7/4 This is the experience of Sir Charles Higham, the famous publicist, who celebrated his 21st anniversary as an advertising agent in Fleet-street on Wednesday.

Publicity. Add: 2. The business of advertising or making articles, schemes, or persons publicly known.

1904 *Profitable Advertising* July 118 It is of the utmost importance that every advertiser and advertising man know what other advertisers and advertising men are doing. Only in this way can the art of publicity be intelligently developed.

b. *attrib* and *Comb.*, of persons and agencies for securing publicity.

1911 J. C. Lincoln *Cap'n Warren's Wards* xi. 180 He and his friends needed a representative on the press—a *publicity agent, so to speak. 1925 Deeping *Sorrell & Son* xiv, You ought to be a publicity agent, Stephen. 1907 Upton Sinclair *Industr. Republic* 142 He had an army of experts to help him..skilful lobbyists, newspapers and *publicity bureaus. 1928 L. North *Parasites* 270 Much was made by the Zimski *publicity hounds of this one hundred-per-cent Americanism of the little [movie] star. 1922 W. Lippmann *Public Opinion* 345 The development of the *publicity man is a clear sign [etc.]. 1924 D. Lawrence *True Story of Woodrow Wilson* 44 A group of men..arranged a western trip for him and decided to send a *publicity man with him. 1928 *Publishers' Weekly* 16 June 2439 Many 'publicity men' admit frankly that their intention is to sell the author to the public. 1911 R. D. Saunders *Col. Todhunter* ix. 118 This amazing projection of himself..on the *publicity 'screen' of a newspaper's front page appalled Colonel Todhunter. 1927 Floud *Ministry Agric.* 25 There is also a small *publicity section for the issue of information to the Press.

Publicize (pɒ·blisǝiz), *v.* [f. Public + -ize.] *trans.* To bring to the notice of the public; to make generally known; to advertise.

1928 *Weekly Dispatch* 20 May 14/4 Nowadays the potential star has to be managed and publicised. 1932 *New Yorker* 14 May 12/1 A raffle for charity..was heavily publicized some weeks ago.

Public-schoo·lish, *a.* [f. Public school + -ish.] Suggestive of a public school.

1930 *Observer* 22 June 13 Mr. Leslie Mitchell, as the simple Andy, is too public-schoolish in tone and manner.

Publish, *v.* Add: 4. c. *intr.* To come into public circulation; to be published.

1928 *Public Opinion* 6 Apr. 325/1 The newspapers do not publish on Good Friday.

Publishment. (Earlier Amer. example.)

1692 *Acts & Laws Massachusetts Bay* (1724) 17 Whoever shall presume to deface or pull down any such Publishment, posted up in Writing, before the Expiration of the Time, shall be fined..the Sum of Ten Shillings.

Pucka. Now usually **pukka.** c. Also, real, genuine, true.

1919 C. P. Thompson *Cocktails* 240 On the occasion of his first pukka ascent..it was windy weather. 1927 E. Thompson *These Men thy Friends* 187, I believe that's pukka.

Pucker, *sb.* Add: 2. (U.S. examples.)

1825 J. Neal *Bro. Jonathan* I. 202 Edith was in tears; Jotham, powerless with amazement;—Miriam, in a 'plaguy pucker'. 1847 J. S. Robb *Streaks of Squatter Life* 15 (Th.) If I am delayed, Blair and Rives will get in a pucker.

3. **pucker-struck** *a. U.S.*, fond of finery.

1901 Sarah R. M. Greene *Flood-tide* xxxiii. 296, I hope as the years go by your tastes 'll git a little more pucker-struck; she's sech a thing as not bein' pucker-struck enough.

Puckery, *a.* 1. (Earlier example.)

1830 *Massachusetts Spy* 10 Feb. (Th.) I didn't like the set of the shoulders, they were so dreadful puckery.

Pudding, *sb.* Add: 8. c. *slang.* A pudding-shaped bomb.

1919 *War Slang* in *Athenæum* 25 July 664/1 'Pudding *i.e.* our 60 lb. bomb.

11. a. *pudding-shaped* adj. b. *pudding basin, stick* (later examples).

1909 *Westm. Gaz.* 3 June 8/3 A grey straw hat of the inverted *pudding-basin type. 1895 W. Robinson *Eng. Flower Garden* v. 75 A great many delightful plants..in many cases are jammed into *pudding-shaped masses void of form or grace. 1852 Mrs. Stowe *Uncle Tom's C.* xviii. 223 Interrupting her meditations to give..a rap on the head to some of the young operators with the *pudding-stick that lay by her side. 1878 B. F. Taylor *Between Gates* 109 You can get an idea of it by fancying a paddle or a pudding-stick turning into a fiddle.

c. **pudding fender** = sense 4 b.

1883 *Man. Seamanship for Boys* 186 Pudding Fenders are used in the Navy for large boats..and sometimes on lower yards, to take the chafe on the inside part of the quarter yard.

Puddler. Add: 4. **puddlers' ore,** a variety of hæmatite.

1880 *Encycl. Brit.* XIII. 286/1 Softer varieties are known as 'red ochre' and 'puddlers' ore', owing to their use for 'fettling' puddling furnaces and as pigments.

Puddling, *vbl. sb.* 3. b. Add: **puddling-train** (see quot.).

1874 J. A. Phillips *Elem. Metallurgy* 299 Two pairs of rolls..constitute a puddling train, one pair being used for roughing down the bloom, and the other for finishing it into a bar.

Puddy, *a.* (Further example.)

1912 Deeping *Sincerity* ii, Her round, puddy, exquisitely complacent face looked out from between clay-coloured ringlets.

Pudent (piū·dĕnt), *a.* [f. L. *pūdens* pres. pple. of *pūdēre* to make ashamed: cf. Impudent.] Having or showing a sense of shame or decency; modest; delicate.

1908 G. B. Shaw in W. H. Davies *Autob. Super-Tramp* Pref. p. vii, These pudent pages are unstained with the frightful language..of the fictitious proletarians of Mr. Rudyard Kipling and other genteel writers.

Pudgily (pɒ·dʒili), *adv.* [f. Pudgy *a.*[1] + -ly[2].] In a pudgy manner.

1926 *Harper's Mag.* Feb. 351/1 One day she escorted the pudgily tottering six-weeks-old youngsters [*sc.* puppies] on a ramble over the lawn.

Pueblo. 1. (Earlier example of *Pueblo Indian.*)

1845 J. Gregg *Comm. Prairies* I. 132 On the 9th of August about two thousand of the insurgent mob, including the Pueblo Indians, pitched their camp in the suburbs of the capital.

2. (Earlier examples.)

1834 A. Pike *Prose Sk. & Poems* 132 The Pueblos shall mount and prepare to pursue. 1844 J. J. Webb *Mem.* 32 In 1848 I crossed the plains with a pueblo named Antonio.

Puff, *sb.* 9. b. Add: (in sense 2 b) *puff-sleeve*; **puff-billiards,** a game resembling billiards in which a ball is driven about on a table by puffs of air; **puff-shouldered** *a.*, having puffs (sense 2 b) on the shoulders.

1901 *Com. Advertiser* 11 May (Cent. Suppl.) Mrs. —— is said to have invented *puff-billiards. 1899 A. Conan Doyle *Duet* i. 7 A roomful of *puff-shouldered young ladies. 1932 *Woman's Weekly* 19 Mar. 467/1 Little ruched pieces like *puff sleeves and a bustle bow give the frock quaintness and charm.

Puff, *v.* Add: 1. d. Of a fungus: To emit a cloud of powdery spores.

1887 H. E. F. Garnsey tr. *De Bary's Fungi* 89 Many of the Discomycetes have the peculiar habit of 'puffing'..if they are shaken.

Puffet (pɒ·fĕt). [f. Puff *sb.*[5] + -et, or ad. Du. *poffertje.*] A kind of light pastry.

1920 Mrs. L. Seeley *Cook Book* xiv. 366 *Dutch Puffet.* Mix one quart of milk, three eggs..Bake in long tins three-quarters of an hour.

Puffily (pɒ·fĭli), *adv.* [f. Puffy *a.* + -ly[2].] In a puffy manner.

1904 H. G. Wells *Food of Gods* II. ii. 178 He did the rise over by the chalk-pit crest a little puffily.

Puffing, *vbl. sb.* 5. Add: **puffing-hole** (see quot.).

1872 Jukes *Student's Man. Geol.* (ed. 3) 414 The sea sometimes gradually forms a passage for itself in the surface above, and if that be not too lofty, forms a 'blow-hole' or 'puffing-hole', through which spouts of foam and spray are occasionally ejected high into the air.

Pug, *sb.*[2] 9. (Further example.)

1927 *Blackw. Mag.* June 747/1 His hair tied in a knot in a little red cloth or pug, on the top of his head.

Pug, *sb.*[4] Also *Comb.* as *pug-mark.*

1922 *Chambers's Jrnl.* Dec. 860/1, I found a good many pug-marks.

Pu·gginess[2]. [f. Puggy *a.*[1] + -ness.] Squat character; stumpiness.

1910 H. G. Wells *Hist. Mr. Polly* vii. 166 Mr. Hinks.. displayed a freckled fist of extraordinary size and pugginess ..to Mr. Polly's close inspection.

Pu·ggishness. [f. Puggish *a.* + -ness.] Puggish character.

1924 W. J. Locke *Coming of Amos* ii. 13 There is a puggishness about her rebellious nose which would disqualify her in a competition of Classical Beauty.

Pulchritudinous (pɒlkritiū·dinəs), *a. U.S.* [f. L. *pulc(h)ritūdin-*, *pulc(h)ritūdo* beauty + -ous.] Beautiful, graceful, or fine in any way; morally excellent.

1912 L. J. Vance *Destroying Angel* xv. 217, I love my love with a P because he's Perfectly Pulchritudinous and Possesses the Power of Pleasing. 1925 *Times* 13 Dec. 11/6 In an American paper..the Yarmouth councillors were described as 'pulchritudinous'.

Pull, *v.* Add: 7. e. *To pull hemp*: see *Hemp *sb.* 3.

f. *intr.* To exert influence.

1903 C. B. Gilbert in *Forum* Oct. 311 Such committees are exposed to all kinds of influence..all pulling for this or that applicant.

g. *trans.* and *intr.* To attract or secure (support or custom).

1905 Holden & Calkins *Mod. Advert.* xi. 264 The advertiser likes to know which particular mediums pull best. 1929 L. F. Carr *America Challenged* 96 Both Republicans and Democrats have tried to pull the farmer vote by favoring legislation which the Populists had demanded.

h. To draw or fire (a gun or pistol). *U.S.*

1895 *Century Mag.* June 282/1 He repeated it, and I struck him. He pulled a pistol on me. 1901 Merwin & Webster *Calumet K* viii. 139 Every carpenter and laborer knew that Bannon had 'pulled a gun' on Reilly. 1903 S. E. White *Forest* x. 122 The birds had proved themselves most uncultivated and rude persons by hopping promptly into the trees...I had refused to pull pistol on them. *absol.* 1841 J. F. Cooper *Deerslayer* iii, I shall not pull upon a human mortal as steadily..as I pull upon a deer.

8. b. *To pull in* or *to pieces*: In *Bookbinding*, simply, *to pull.*

1901 D. Cockerell *Bookbinding* I. ii. 46 After the volume has been collated it must be 'pulled', that is to say, the sections must be separated, and all plates or maps detached.

9. (Further example).

1904 Harben *Georgians* 22 So you'n the old man are still pullin' agin one another?

15. b. *To pull one's weight*: (also transf.) to perform one's share of work, etc. Also *to pull weight.*

1925 E. F. Norton *Fight for Everest, 1924* 98 No members of the climbing party pulled more weight in the team than these two by their unostentatious unselfish gruelling work. 1927 E. J. P. Benn *Confess. Capitalist* 230 If the office boy is really pulling his weight..he is providing me with 3½d. per week. 1927 *Observer* 22 May 15/1 Mr. E— T—..has never..failed to pull his weight in a production.

19. d. To relate or say, esp. with the intention of deceiving; to palm off.

1923 M. Arlen *Charming People* 176 Don't pull any of that on me, young man,..you was the suspicious character on the premises. 1924 A. J. Small *Frozen Gold* v. 133 He can pull you the whole story. He can tell it well too. *Ibid.* 140 I'd like to know why..you pulled that line of dope to me. 1928 *Collier's* 29 Dec. 25/3 He was forever 'pulling' impromptu stuff that made me laugh as riotously as the audiences.

24. **Pull down.** a. (Further example.)

1865 J. Macgregor *Rob Roy Baltic* (1867) 205 There is the blind that won't pull down or stop up.

25. **Pull in.** b. (Later example.)

1841 *Punch* 17 July 6/2 I'm a boy in a school, with a bag of apples, which..I naturally sell at a penny a-piece, and so look forward to pulling in a considerable quantity of browns.

e. *intr.* Of a locomotive engine or train: To enter a station.

1903 D. G. Phillips *Plum Tree* 91, I didn't know you till you took out your watch with the monogram on the back, just as we were pulling in. 1929 Leacock *Iron Man* 143 That's your train pulling in now.

28. **Pull out.** d. Also of a ship: To sail out of a harbour or port.

1902 C. J. Cutcliffe Hyne *Mr. Horrocks, Purser* 105 We pull out from here next Tuesday.

28*. **Pull over.** To bring a vehicle to a side of the road or street, or to some other place.

1930 *Morn. Post* 12 June 5, I considered that I had not time to pull over to my near side.

28**. **Pull round.** a. *intr.* To recover from sickness or a fainting-fit; to come round.

1891 R. Buchanan *Come Live with Me* 253 The danger's over..and the little one is pulling round. 1896 *Pall Mall Mag.* Sept. 70 He thinks he's going to pull round again: but I'll bet on his not being alive this day week.

b. *trans.* To restore (a person) to health after sickness, etc.; to put into a healthier or better condition. Also *transf.*

1900 *Outrageous Fortune* iv. 37 The excellent nursing I received, combined with my own naturally good constitution, served to quickly pull me round. 1928 *Sunday Express* 29 Apr. 20/1 In the second half Cardiff made a valiant attempt to pull the game round.

30. **Pull together.** b. Also, to restore (a person) to a normal condition.

1906 S. Maugham *Bishop's Apron* viii. 132 Now come and have tea... I know it'll pull you together.

Pull-. 2. **pull-bell** (later example); **pull-boat,** also, a boat containing an engine and suitable mechanism for drawing logs over water; **pull-bone** *U.S.* = Merrythought; **pull-off** (*b*): see quot.

1919 Rose Macaulay *Three Days* 52 How a *pull-bell clangs when it rings! 1903 *Sci. Amer.* 17 Oct. 276/3 In the cypress swamps of Louisiana there are employed what are known as *pull-boats, an evolution from the plan of placing a hoisting engine upon a scow and snaking the logs out of the swamp...The endless-rope pull-boat engines have 44-inch winding drums. *a* 1906 'O. Henry' *Trimmed Lamp* etc. 136 In her mind she could hear the girls shrieking over a *pullbone. 1926 *Gloss. Electr. Terms* (Brit. Engin. Stand.) 133 **Pull-off*, a metal fitting attached to an ear and used on curves for adjusting the position of a trolley-wire in a horizontal plane.

Pull-back. 2. (U.S. example.)

1833 Seba Smith *Major Downing* (1860) 212 (Th.) This ere sickness of the President has been a bad pull-back to us.

Pulled, *ppl. a.* 4. (Earlier example.)

1616 W. Browne *Brit. Past.* II. i. 517 In his flesh pull'd downe As hee had liu'd in a beleaguerd towne.

Puller. Add: 5. Something that attracts custom or business.

1928 *Sunday Dispatch* 15 July 14/3 Next to the Prince of Wales, Shaw is the best box-office puller in the United States.

b. *Puller-in*: (see quot.). *U.S.*

1895 J. L. Ford *Lit. Shop* ix. (1896) 132 The Jewish old-clothing quarter that lies close to the Five Points is near by. The 'pullers-in', as the sidewalk salesmen are termed in the vernacular of the trade, transact business with a ferocity that can be best likened to that of Siberian wolves.

Pullery[2] (pu·lǝri). *Tanning.* [f. Pull *v.* + -ery.] The place in which the wool, hair, bristles, etc. are removed from hides.

1903 L. A. Flemming *Pract. Tanning* 1 The relations between the soaking process and the subsequent processes of the beamhouse or pullery, and the tannery are close.

Pulley, *sb.*[1] 5. Add: **pulley-cone,** a cone grooved and rotating on its axis, forming a set of pulley-wheels of different sizes.

1903 *Harvard Psychol. Stud.* I. 417 A disc..about 50 c. in diameter, rotating on a vertical pivot, was driven by a *pulley-cone underneath mounted on the same spindle.

Pullicate. Also 8 pullcat.

a 1793 Freneau *Poems* (1809) I. 31 Hum-bums are here—and muslins—what you please—Bandanas, baftas, pullcats, Indian teas.

Pulling, *vbl. sb.* 5. Add: *pulling-boat*; **pulling-bar** = Draw-bar.

1892 J. G. A. Meyer *Mod. Locomotive Constr.* 528, Fig. 850 shows the wrought-iron *pulling-bar which connects the tender to the engine. 1912 Quiller-Couch *Hocken & Hunken* xxiii, The penultimate race (randan *pulling-boats) was finishing amid banging of guns and bursts of music.

Pullman. (Earlier and later examples.)

1872 W. F. Butler *Gt. Lone Land* iv. 57 One takes a Pullman..as one takes a Hansom, Pullman and sleeping-car have become synonymous terms. 1924 W. M. Raine *Troubled Waters* vi. 66 McCoy strolled down to the station to inquire about the lower he had reserved in the Pullman.

Pu·ll-on, *a.* [Pull *v.*] Applied to garments (e.g. hats, gloves, jumpers, leggings), that are pulled on and have no fastenings. Also as *sb.*

1921 *Glasgow Herald* 25 May 4/7 The turban..does not hide all the hair as do the pull-on hat..and other popular shapes. 1923 *Daily Mail* 13 Feb. 7 Advt., Washable doeskin gloves..pull-on shape. 1931 *Daily Express* 23 Sept. 11/5 London police on duty in wet weather will be comfortable..in the new water-proof 'pull-ons', which are tailored to look like ordinary trousers.

Pull-over. Add: 4. A knitted or woven garment for the upper part of the body, which is put on over the head.

1925 *Westm. Gaz.* 28 Apr. 3 The vogue of the Pullover has supplanted the waistcoat for golf. 1927 Deeping *Doomsday* v. § 1 He was mostly seen in golfing clothes, grey, very baggy as to the knickers, with a blue and yellow 'pull-over' under the coat. 1927 *Daily Tel.* 8 Mar. 9/3 He had seen boys at preparatory schools wearing a coat, pullover, waistcoat, shirt, and vest when indoors on quite a mild day.

Pulmotor (pɒ·lmotəɹ). [f. Pulmo- + L. *mōtor* (see Motor) with ellipse of one syllable.] An apparatus used in applying artificial respiration.

1913 *Chambers's Jrnl.* Mar. 270/1 Among the emergency devices for succour of humanity..the pulmotor has aroused considerable attention. 1918 Homer Croy *How Motion Pictures are Made* 273 A man supposed to have been drowned was carried in by the rescuers, while a pulmotor was telephoned for. 1928 *Daily Express* 31 Dec. 12/4, I grabbed up my bag and the pulmotor, and was over here in a jiffy.

attrib. 1923 Watts *Luther Nichols* 69 The lady..had to be brought to by the pulmotor-squad.

Pulp, *sb.* 5. a. Add: *pulp-maker.* b. **pulp-stone** (*b*), a stone used like a grindstone for reducing wood to pulp.

1909 *Westm. Gaz.* 11 Aug 5/1 The *pulp-maker is not content to remove the grown trees, but takes the young plants as well. 1901 J. H. Pratt in *Min. Resources of U.S.* (U.S. Geol. Surv.) 789 *Pulpstones differ from grindstones in having a much broader face.

Pulp, *v.* 1. Also, to reduce to pulp by passing *through* something.

1878 *Amer. Home Cook Book* 13 Stew them till soft enough to pulp through a hair sieve or coarse cloth.

Pulped, *ppl. a.* Also *fig.*

1912 Deeping *Sincerity* xxx. 235 He had left a little man pulped behind him in the pleasant, contemplative Georgian house.

Pulperia (pɒlpi·riă). *U.S.* [Sp.] A retail grocery.

1840 R. H. Dana *Bef. Mast* xxviii. (1869) 257 Here he went dead to leeward among the pulperias, gambling-rooms, etc. 1871 H. M. & P. V. N. Myers *Life under Tropics* iii. 21 We were forced by a sudden shower to seek shelter in a way-side pulperia. 1904 Conrad *Nostromo* I. viii. 80 The horseman hammered with the butt of a heavy revolver at the doors of low pulperias.

Pulping, *vbl. sb.* Add: *pulping-machine.*

1875 *Encycl. Brit.* I. 327/1 A premium was offered for machines to perform this kind of work, [pulping of turnips and mangolds for cattle] under the somewhat inappropriate designation of 'pulping-machines'. 1909 *Chambers's Jrnl.* Aug. 518/1 From this pulping-machine it passes to the centrifugal pump.

Pulpit, *sb.* Add: 4. d. A small raised platform from which a person can observe and control the working of machines.

1903 *Elect. World & Engin.* 26 Dec. 1051 (Cent. Suppl.) The operator of the hoisting motor stands in a pulpit above the floor.

5. d. **pulpit-cloth** (later example).

1763 *Maryland Hist. Mag.* X. 40 That there be a Crimson Velvet Cushion and *Pulpit Cloth procured for the Church.

Pulpitis (pɒlpəi·tis). [f. Pulp *sb.* + -itis.] Inflammation of the pulp of a tooth.

1902 *Sci. Amer.* 20 Dec. 441/3 The properties of the leaves ..were first discovered by D. Dalma, who successfully employed them in painful pulpitis.

Pulque. b. Add: *pulque-shop.*

1910 *N.Y. Even. Post* 21 July (Th. s.v. *Spang*) All of the sweet savors of Araby combined could make slight headway against the reek of a pulque shop.

Pulqueria (pulki·riă). *U.S.* [Sp.] A public-house or shop where pulque is sold.

1914 C. J. Cutcliffe Hyne *Firemen Hot* I. 2 By the time these [dollars] had been passed across the grimy counter of a pulqueria..they received [etc.]. 1922 *Outward Bound* Nov. 110/2 In the great pulquerias, or saloons..the gramophone is invariably to be found.

Pulsatance (pɒ·lsătăns). [f. Pulsate + -ance.] (See quot.)

1919 A. Campbell in *Proc. Phys. Soc.* XXXI. 81 In English a name has not yet been found for 2πn, where *n* represents frequency...I would suggest that it might be called '*pulsatance*'.

Pulsation. Add: 4. *attrib.* as *pulsation theory.*

1927 Macpherson *Mod. Astron.* 124 Certainly the pulsation theory of Cepheid variation has had far-reaching results.

Pulse, *sb.*[1] 4. b. (Later example.)

1904 Bottone *Radium* 75 A series of Stokesian 'pulses or explosive ether waves, shot into space.

d. *Physics.* (See quot.)

1899 Jude *Physics Exper. & Theor.* I. 41 Time-integral, like every other physical quantity, must have a proper unit. In the British system this is that of 1 poundal acting for 1 sec., and is called 1 *pulse.*

Pulse, *sb.*[2] 3. Add: *pulse-cake, -oil.*

1884 *Encycl. Brit.* XVII. 381/2 The staple articles of export are pulse (beans), pulse-cake, and pulse-oil.

Pulvino (pʊlvī·no). *Arch.* [It. *pulvino* pillow.] An impost or dosseret.

1907 *Athenæum* 30 Mar. 389/2 The use of a pulvino to enable a thick wall above to be carried on the comparatively slender diameter of the classic column. 1913 T. G. Jackson *Byzant. & Romanesque Archit.* I. iv. 52 Nothing can be more opposed to classic rule than the pulvino.

Pumicate, *v.* (Recent example.)

1925 *Chambers's Jrnl.* Nov. 704/2 When it is thoroughly 'pumicated' the coral is rinsed and put into a second bag.

Pump, *sb.*[1] 6. a. Add: *pump-clip* (example); b. **pump-gun,** a rifle having a tubular magazine and sliding forearm; **pump-hook, -spear** (earlier examples).

1908 H. G. Wells *War in Air* ii. § 3 Bert stared at these over the card of *pump-clips in the pane in the door. 1921 *Edin. Rev.* July 104 The rifle and *pump-gun have largely displaced the skill and patience of other days. 1640 *Maryland Archives* IV. 112 For a *pumphook. 1702 *Essex Inst.*

Hist. Coll. XLII. 161 Inventory of ship...A pumpe Hooke. 1781 *Maryland Hist. Mag.* VI. 312 Invoice of Schooner Nautilus's Materials...1 pump Hook. 1702 *Essex Inst. Hist. Coll.* XLII. 161 Inventory of ship...Two *pump Speares.

Pump, *v.* Add: **6. b.** (Further example.)
1909 *Daily Chron.* 22 Sept. 9/5 My head aches. It pumps and pumps and I can't think.

10. a. Also, to send forth or discharge with a pumping action.
1916 B. Cable *Action Front* 95 [They] set themselves to pump bullets in a covering fire upon the German parapet.

b. In special connections: (see quots.).
1902 *Encycl. Brit.* XXXI. 887/2 Synchronous [electric] motors sometimes cause serious trouble by 'pumping'. 1918 Gamble *Story N. Sea Air Station* xviii. 309 All submarines have a tendency to 'pump' in heavy seas, that is, they tend to move up and down in a vertical plane.

Pumper1. **1. b.** (Example.)
1876 *Coursing Calendar* 261 Dark Rover proved himself a game puppy by going so well after the pumpers he received.

Pumping, *vbl. sb.* (Further example.)
1876 *Coursing Calendar* 192 After an undecided, June Rose led, and then died off to nothing, New Fashion coming in for a pumping.

Pumping, *ppl. a.* Add: **b.** (In sense 12 of vb.)
1876 *Coursing Calendar* 216 Sir Charles left Albatross as though he were standing, and made rings round him in another pumping course.

Pump log. *U.S.* A hollowed log used in the construction of a pump or as a water-pipe.
1816 *N. Amer. Rev.* III. 429 He declared also, that the mill for grinding apples, which is an overshot and is fed by a pump log..would often stop during the day. 1858 D. K. Bennett *Chronol. N. Carolina* 108 He had some men repairing pump-logs, through which water was carried from the mountain side to his hotel. 1879 Stockton *Rudder Grange* xvi. 197 He looked like he'd been drawn through a pump-log.

Punalua (pʊnālū·ă). Also pin-. [Hawaiian.] A system of group marriage. Also *attrib.* Hence **Punalu·an, Punalua·nic** *adjs.*
1860 L. Andrews in L. H. Morgan *Anc. Society* (1877) III. iii. 427 The relationship of pūnalūa is rather amphibious. It arose from the fact that two or more brothers with their wives, or two or more sisters with their husbands, were inclined to possess each other in common. 1877 L. H. Morgan *Anc. Soc.* III. i. 391 Marriage passed from the punaluan through the syndyasmian into the monogamian form. 1904 G. E. Howard *Matrimonial Instit.* I. 135 The phase of punaluan group marriage. 1922 *Nature* 22 Apr. 503/1 The Punalua family leads an even more shadowy existence, merging into a combined polyandry and polygamy.

Punch, *sb.*1 **7.** Add: **punch-marked**, *a.*, of a coin, bearing a punch-mark; **punch-ticket**, a railway or other ticket suitable for punching.
1910 *Hastings's Encycl. Relig. & Ethics* III. 706/1 On account of this chief characteristic, the term '*punch-marked' is commonly applied to this currency. 1887 C. B. George *40 Years on Rail* xi. 227 Many cases have been reported where in *punch-tickets the bits of pasteboard punched out have been saved and carefully glued in the old places. 1890 *Harper's Mag.* May 908/1 A person..who by many punch-tickets builds up the fortunes of the stockholders.

Punch, *sb.*2 Add: **2.** *transf.* Forceful or effective quality esp. in anything spoken or written; vigour, weight, effectiveness.
1911 Edna Ferber *Dawn O'Hara* xvii. 254 It lacks that peculiar and convincing quality poetically known as the punch. 1919 H. L. Wilson *Ma Pettengill* ii. 64 A gripping drama replete with punch. *Ibid.* 75, I believe he now admits frankly that he wrote most of the play, or at least wrote the punch into it. 1921 R. D. Paine *Comr. Rolling Ocean* i. 7 Dad is the kindest, finest man that ever lived, but he lacks the punch. 1922 *Times Lit. Suppl.* 23 Nov. 763/2 His phrase has, as he might say, a punch in it.

3. *Comb.* **punch-bag, ball**, a stuffed bag or ball suspended at a suitable height on which boxers practise punching.
1899 *Science Siftings* 25 Mar. 329/2 A fifteen-minute controversy with an active punch-bag. *Ibid.* Patients whose dignity revolts at the punch-bag. 1927 *Daily Express* 20 July, His trainer..ordered Dempsey not to box, but to use the punch bag and to shadow box. *Ibid.* 22 June 17/5 He is developing his punch in secret, and..he has broken three punch-balls.

Punch, *sb.*3 **4.** Add: *punch room.*
1827 Drake & Mansf. *Cincinnati* iii. 30 A spacious gallery, with commodious lobbies, punch room, etc. 1841 *Southern Lit. Messenger* VII. 764/1 If you won't go home with me, you can take me down to the punch-room.

Punch, *v.*1 **2.** (Later examples.)
1902 O. Wister *Virginian* xv. 167, I was goin' back to punch cattle or fight Indians. 1923 'B. M. Bower' *Parowan Bonanza* xviii. 276 In that case..you'd still be punchin' cows for your dad, most likely.
absol. 1910 W. M. Raine *B. O'Connor* 30 We used to punch together on the Hashknife.

Puncheon1. **6. b.** (Earlier examples.)
1784 Washington *Diaries* II. 294 A logged dwelling with a punchion roof. 1823 Long *Exped.* I. 145 They [Indians] arranged themselves agreeably to their tribes, on puncheon benches. 1838 Drake *Tales & Sk.* 64 They danced merrily over the puncheon floor of their rustic cabins. 1843 Carlton *New Purchase* xxi. 199 Adjoining the bureau was the puncheon table with its white oak legs.

Pu·ncheoned, *a.* [f. Puncheon1 + -ed1.] Covered or laid with puncheons (sense 5).
1843 Carlton *New Purchase* xv. 109 And first, the puncheoned area was separated into two grand parts.

Punchine (pʊ·nʃəin), *a.* [f. Punch *sb.*5 + -ine1.] Of or pertaining to Punch.
1848 Thackeray *Bk. Snobs* xxiii, It was this braggart violence of soul that roused the Punchine wrath against Mr. O'Connell.

Punching, *vbl. sb.* Also, a piece of metal cut out by a punch.
1903 *Elect. World & Engin.* 28 Mar. 532 (Cent. Suppl.) The four-pole pieces are made of laminated steel punchings.

b. *punching-machine* (examples).
1849 *Rep. U.S. Comm. Patents* (1850) 185 Having thus fully described my improved *punching machine. 1878 *Harper's Mag.* Apr. 645/2 The bar then goes to the punching-machine that..bites a hole through the iron.

Punchy (pʊ·nʃi), *a.*3 [f. Punch *sb.*2 + -y.] Full of punch or vigour.
1930 *Observer* 19 Oct. 19 A punchy rhetorical speech on Free Trade.

Punctatim. (Later example).
1931 *N. & Q.* 26 Dec. 461/1 The transcription has been made *verbatim* and *punctatim*.

Punctiliar (pʊŋkti·liăɪ), *a.* [f. Punctilio + -ar1.] Of or pertaining to a point of time.
1906 J. H. Moulton *Gram. N. T. Greek* I. vi. 109 It is seen that the Aorist has a 'punctiliar' action, that is, it regards action as a *point*. [*Note*, I venture to accept from a correspondent this new-coined word to represent the German *punktuell*, the English of which is preoccupied.]

Punctual, *a.* **2.** Delete †*Obs.*
1904 T. Hutchinson in Shelley *Wks.* 174 Verbal alterations are recorded in the footnotes, punctual in the Editor's Notes at the end of this volume.

Punctuation. Add: **4. b.** A kind of tapotement used in massage.
1890 Ostrom *Massage* 23 Punctuation is used upon the head and around the heart.

Puncture, *sb.* **4.** Add: **puncture-vine**, the land caltrops.
1921 *Discovery* Feb. 48/1 California suffers in a different way from a weed which has been introduced from the borders of the Sahara, probably in ballast. This is the Puncture Vine (*Tribulus terrestris*), which produces a number of prostrate stems, some eight feet long.

Puncture, *v.* Add: **1. e.** To interrupt at intervals; = Punctuate *v.* 3 b.
1899 C. M. M. Sheldon *Bro. Keeper* xi. 249 The major..made a rattling speech, punctured with frequent amens and hallelujahs from the rest of the army.

Punditry (pʊ·nditri). [f. Pundit + -ry.] The characteristics of a pundit; opinions or actions befitting a pundit (sense 6); pundits collectively.
1926 T. M. Healy in *Pioneer Ref. Spelling* Apr. 14, I decry the punditry of Civil Service Commissioners in making so-called orthography a test subject. 1927 Sadleir *Trollope* 23 Mid-Victorian punditry suffered in many cases from an extreme form of the inferiority complex.

Pungo, variant of Pungy.
1854 W. G. Simms *Southward Ho* iii. 28 Their most innocent name is 'pungo'—a sort of schooner, hailing mostly from Manhattan and Massachusetts. *Ibid.*, For the better oysters ..the 'pungoes' pay three shillings.

Punify (piū·nifəi), *v.* [f. L. *pūnīre* to punish + -fy.] *trans.* To punish.
1915 *Times* 23 Mar. 12/2 This state which..supported France in the punifying of free Morocco.

Punishable, *a.* Add: **b.** (Further example.)
1909 *Daily Chron.* 29 Nov. 3/1 If a punishable play is produced, the author and the lessee..should be punished.

c. In sense 3 of the verb.
1920 *Blackw. Mag.* July 106/2 The punishable [ball] escaped scot-free.

Punjabi, Punjabee (pʊ̆ndʒā·bi), *sb.* and *a.* Also Panjabi, Punjaubee. [ad. Hindī पंजाबी *Panjābī*, f. *Panjāb* (Pers. *panj* five + *āb* water).]

A. *adj.* Of or belonging to the province of Punjab in India, so called from its five rivers.
1812 W. Carey *Gram. Punjabee Lang.* Pref. p. iv, The Punjabee language is confessedly of mixed origin. 1851 H. B. Edwardes *Year on Punjab Frontier* I. 30 When all your fat Punjabee dogs are panting in vain after the hare. 1864 *Athenæum* 5 Nov. 597/1 To keep our regular troops..at a strength more than sufficient to render utterly harmless all the turbulent elements of Punjaubee Society. 1886 Mrs. Edwardes *Mem. Sir H. B. Edwardes* II. 315 Before landing at Calcutta, a true Punjabee welcome met him. 1921 *Outward Bound* May 27/1 Ever since I was a boy..these Punjabi lyrics have kept haunting me.

B. *sb.* **1.** A native or inhabitant of the Punjab.
1846 *Hist. Punjab* I. ii. 36 In the plains, Patans..are mixed with Jats and Cathis, who compose the bulk of the Punjabis, properly so called. 1878 G. Smith *Life J. Wilson* xvii. 304 Nanuk, the herd-boy, was the Punjabee or Sikh. 1897 *Daily News* 21 Sept. 5/3 The brunt of the attack fell upon the portion of the camp which was held by the 5th Punjabis.

2. The language used in the Punjab.
1838 *Jrnl. Asiatic Soc. Bengal* Aug. 711 The Sikhs..carried their hatred..to such an extent as to substitute a vocabulary for their native Punjābī. 1862 Latham *Elem. Compar. Philol.* 219 The following..gives a rough sketch of the grammatical character of the Punjabi. 1921 *Outward Bound* Dec. 74/1 They spoke only Punjabi, of which at that time I knew but three words, so conversation languished somewhat.

Punk, *sb.*3 Add: **1. b.** Anything worthless; foolish or empty talk; nonsense.
1900 G. Ade *More Fables in Slang* (1902) 212 Well, if they are Right, then I must be Wrong, but to me it is Punk. 1928 L. North *Parasites* 11 They would take the manuscript to the editor and tell him that it was junk—or punk. 1930 *Chambers's Jrnl.* Apr. 217/2 You can cut out any theories about yielding to sudden temptation, or punk of that sort.

3. (Earlier example.)
1880 *Harper's Mag.* Dec. 73 Before the ancestral tablets..incense was consumed, punk or joss-sticks.

Punk (pʊŋk), *a.* *U.S.* [f. Punk *sb.*3]

1. Of timber: Decayed; rotten.
1902 S. E. White *Blazed Trail* ii. 18 Supplies ran low unexpectedly; trees turned out 'punk'. a 1904 — *Blazed Trail Stories* iii. 49, I cull every log, big or little, punk or sound, that ain't sawed square.

2. Devoid of worth or sense; poor in quality; disappointing; nonsensical; 'rotten'.
1896 G. Ade *Artie* iii. 23 And this crowd up there was purty-y-y punk. *Ibid.* xix. 178 They could n't be any punker'n they are now. 1929 W. Heyliger *Builder of Dam* 4, I call this a punk way to spend an Easter vacation.

Punky, *sb.* (Earlier example.)
1840 *Knickerbocker Mag.* XVI. 270 The tortures..inflicted by the gnats (sand-flies, punkies, brulos, for they bear all these appellations).

Punky, *a.* Add: **b.** *transf.* = *Punk *a.*
1886 *Harper's Mag.* Dec. 105/2 George's mother's folk did have a kind of a punky spot somewhere in their heads. 1904 *N. Y. Times* 5 May 8 Written by another man Mr Austin would doubtless find these verses as amusing as the rest of us do—would appreciate their punky pretentiousness.

Punt, *sb.*1 Add: **1. b.** A push with a punt-pole.
1897 *Geog. Jrnl.* IX. 12 Only practice enables one..to guide the raft by means of timely punts at the surrounding rocks with the pole with which one is armed.

Punta (pʊ·ntă). [It. *punta* point.] The narrow upper part of straw grown in Tuscany for plaiting. Also *attrib.*
1929 *Daily Express* 26 Jan. 5/2 Rough straws and picture hats are always popular...These are being shown of open-work tuscan or punta straw.

Puny. A. *adj.* Add: **4. c.** In bad condition or health; physically weak; out of sorts.
1866 C. H. Smith *Bill Arp* 170 Me and him like to have fit, and perhaps would, if I hadn't been puny; but we finally left it all to Josh Billins to arbytrate. 1904 Harben *Georgians* xvii. 163 Little Minnie begun to fail; she got so puny she spit up ever'thing she ate.

Pup, *sb.*1 Add: **2. b.** (See quot.) *U.S.*
1870 Medbery *Men & Myst. Wall St.* 31 Down in the cock-pit the Commodore's 'pups', as the merciless, cacophonic 'street' argot denominates the broker friends of Vanderbilt, are making an ineffective rally.

c. A boy or youth; a 'young blood'. *U.S.*
1903 G. H. Lorimer *Lett. Self-made Merchant* ix. 118 Chauncey's father was the whole village, barring the railroad station and the saloon, and, of course, Chauncey thought that he was something of a pup himself. 1903 A. H. Lewis *Boss* vi. 48 'Here's a pup', cried Big Kennedy, with his hand on my shoulder, 'I want you to look over'.

5. Also, *to buy a pup*, to involve oneself in something which proves unprofitable.
1923 *Westm. Gaz.* 21 Feb., We had not merely 'bought a pup', he said, but a whole litter that suffered from distemper. 1927 Deeping *Kitty* viii, He was not the sort of man to advise a brother officer to buy a pup.

6. pup-tent, a small tent or bivouac.
1930 F. A. Pottle *Stretchers* 49, I suppose everyone has seen a 'pup tent' at some time or other, but he may not have realized that in the army it is shelter for *two* men.

Pupelo. (Earlier example.)
1806 *Salem Register* 7 Apr. (Th.) Do you not deny to the poor labourer the common refreshment of a little toddy, and stint him with a glass of pupelo?

Puppy, *sb.* **6. puppy love** (earlier example).
1834 Carruthers *Kentuckian in N. Y.* I. 175 Oh! it is nothing more than puppy love!

Purchasabi·lity, [f. Purchasable + -ity.] Capability of being bought.
1904 F. Lynde *Grafters* vii. 91 There isn't any doubt about his purchasability.

Purchase, *v.* Add: **6. c.** *absol.*
1850 T. S. Arthur *Golden Grains* 50 He purchased largely and had the goods forwarded before he left the city. 1904 R. M. Williamson *Bits fr. Bookshop* x. 77 The great public libraries where..books are lent out for hire to those who wish to read but cannot purchase.

d. With money or its equivalent as the subject.
1805 M. G. Lewis *Bravo of Venice* II. vi. 214 Will ten thousand sequins purchase your departure from the Republic? 1904 L. Tracy *King of Diamonds* iii. 35 An establishment where threehalfpence would purchase a cup of coffee and a 'doorstep'.

Purchasery (pʊ̄·ɹtʃəsri). [f. Purchase + -ry.] The business of purchasing.
1927 *Daily Express* 15 Dec. 9/6 There is one branch of salery and purchasery which few women ever explore.

Purdah. 1. b. (Further example.)
1928 Galsworthy *Swan Song* II. v. 143 The diagnosis of Kit's malady was soon verified, and Fleur went into purdah.

Pure, *a.* Add: **4.** (Further example.)
1904 *Jrnl. R. Microsc. Soc.* 52 An animal or plant is pure if it produces gametes of only one sort.

B. *sb.* Add: **6.** A genuine person.
1924 W. M. Raine *Troubled Waters* xix. 201 You-all are losing a better man than Missie ever had. He's a pure, Mac is.

D. *Comb.* **a.** *pure-mindedness.* **b.** *pure-breeding.* **e. pure-line**, 'all the descendants arising from a single plant by self-fertilization'.
1903 A. D. Darbishire in *Biometrika* Feb. 171 This does not help us to decide whether the relative inability to transmit whiteness is due to in-breeding or *pure-breeding. 1906 R. H. Lock *Variation Heredity & Evolution* iv. (1909) 118 If we were to carry on this conception to the case of bisexual inheritance, we should find that the different *pure lines would become crossed and confused together. 1891 Meredith *One of our Conq.* III. vii. 135 He might have put a reluctant faith in the *puremindedness of these aspirations, without reverting to her origin.

Pure blood, *a.* and *sb.* **a.** *adj.* Having pure blood; pure-bred. **b.** *sb.* A pure-bred animal. So **Pure-blooded** *a.*
1850 Garrard *Wah-To-Yah* vii. 109 The unfair horse-trader might have taken my scalp for presuming to dictate to him, a..pure-blooded Cheyenne. 1871 *Rep. Indian Affairs* (1872) 247 He is a pure blood Indian without any admixture of white blood. 1882 *Harper's Mag.* May 895/1 The half and quarter breeds..seem to have..greater powers of resistance than the pure-bloods. 1888 *Rep. Vermont Board Agric.* X. 49 Why don't you get some pure blood Holsteins? 1894 *Ibid.* XIV. 166 Having bred pure bloods for almost thirty years. 1903 F. D. Coburn in *13th Bienn. Rep. Kansas State Board Agric.* 63 A quarter of a billion acres of grass, nurturing 10,000,000 head of cattle..can be doubled in value in a single decade, if only pure-blooded sires are used in all the cow herds during this time. Likewise fifty per cent. can be added to the value if pure-bloods only are used in the northern half of this territory.

Purgatory, *sb.* Add: **4. c.** A swamp difficult to cross. Also *attrib.* *local U.S.*
1831 Peck *Guide for Emigrants* III. 308 In the low prairies near the Wabash, are swamps, called by the people *purgatories*, which are almost impassable in the wet season. 1837 — *Gaz. Illinois* III. 146 The eastern part toward the Wabash contains some wet land and purgatory swamps.

Purler. (Further examples.)
1921 H. G. Ponting *Gt. White South* 282 All went well till..on a very slippery surface I came an awful 'purler' on my shoulder. 1929 Masefield *Hawbucks* 209 You seemed to go a fearful purler.

Purparty. (Later example of pourparty.)
1930 Stewart-Brown in *Eng. Hist. Rev.* Jan. 30 To each co-heir was allotted, as a permanent pourparty, a definite manor or castle for a chief seat.

Purple. C. 2 b. purple-finch (later examples).
1876 J. Burroughs *Winter Sunshine* I. 31 Those *purple finches..are they not stealing our berries? 1903 S. E. White *Forest* viii. 91 You will hear..purple finches or some of the pine sparrows warbling high and clear.

Purpose, *v.* **6.** (Modern example.)
1924 W. J. Locke *Coming of Amos* v. 53 What was the use of a stick purposed to beat neither beast nor man?

Pu·rringly, *adv.* [f. Purring + -ly2.] In a purring manner; while purring.
1907 in *Westm. Gaz.* 25 May 6/2 My pussy..walks purringly. 1925 *Glasgow Herald* 18 Aug. 8 Zizi..would purringly allow herself to be stroked and fondled.

Purse, *sb.* Add: **9. b.** The inmost recess of a badger's burrow.
1901 *Kynoch Jrnl.* Apr.–May 83/2 After traversing an infinity of tunnels and passages, the final purse is reached, where the badger spends the greater part of his life together with Mrs. 'Brock' (alias Badger).

11. purse-end *colloq.* = sense 3.
1928 *Sunday Express* 16 Dec. 21/1 A purse end of £800 is more than Johnny need expect to receive in the States for his first fight.

Purse, *v.* **4.** Also with *out*.
1896 Olive Schreiner *Afr. Farm* I. xii. 114 Pursing out his lips, and waving his hand, he solemnly addressed the boy.

Pursuant. A. *sb.* Add: **2.** One who pursues; a pursuer.
1924 W. J. Locke *Coming of Amos* xiii. 163 Amos..ran..followed also at a run by Hamilton, thereby giving..visitors ..the impression of pick-pocket and pursuant.

Pursuit. Add: **11.** *attrib.* and *Comb.* as *pursuit party, race.*
1909 *Daily Chron.* 5 July 1/6 All available attendants were mustered as a pursuit party. 1908 T. A. Cook *Olympic Games* 188 Pursuit Race Three laps (1·807 kilometres) Teams of four to start. First three to count in each heat.

Pus. b. Add: *pus-former.*
1915 W. Osler *Science & War* 35 Of the germs blown into wounds from the soil and clothing and skin the pus-formers are the most numerous and most important.

Push, *sb.*1 Add: **1. d.** *To give* (a person) *the push*: To dismiss from employment.
1930 Priestley *Angel Pavement* ix. 459 They'd be thinking of giving me the push.

e. An impulse or urge.
1924 T. H. Y. Trotter *Music & Mind* 213 Acts of creation and of reproduction arise not from any inner push, but from processes of calculation.

9. Also *attrib.*
1903 R. Bedford *True Eyes* 127 One evening..Billy joined the 'push' session in the Argyle Cut.

Push, *v.* Add: **1. b.** (Further example.)
1930 *Observer* 9 Mar. 15/3 Mr. Henry Kendall, as the gentlemanly host, will have the deuce of a night of it when the people are pushed on to him.

h. (Further examples.)
1930 Joanna Cannan *No Walls of Jasper* 67 I'll be pushing off now. 1930 Rose Macaulay *Relations* xviii. 268 He'll have to push off in a day or so.

k. *Push in*: To cause to give way by pressure from the outside.
1916 B. Cable *Action Front* 182 Do you think there's any chance of them pushing in the line and rushing this house?

13. Also with *off*.
1873 *Punch* 26 Apr. 178/2 Why do not the managers imitate another class of persons who push off drugs by means of puffing.

Push-. Add: **a.** *push-net, -nipple, -plane.* **b. push-car** (example); **push-cart** (*b*), **-chair**, a form of child's perambulator; **push-cyclist**, a rider of a push-cycle; **push-foot** = *push-pedal*; **push-through** (*b*), an instrument for cleaning the bore of a rifle (cf. *pull-through*).
1883 Nye *Baled Hay* 225 A section-crew..riding down that mountain on a *push-car. 1909 *Daily Chron.* 10 Dec. 5/4 She ran into the..street, and there found the *push-cart, and saw the man hurrying away with the baby. 1921 *Sunday at Home* Feb. 257/2 Up the hill she struggled...She was throwing her weight against a small *push-chair, with a carpet seat. 1923 *Motor Cycling* 5 Dec. 147/1, I presume by 'cyclists' '*push-cyclists' are meant. 1927 *Daily Express* 27 Dec. 3/7 A push-cyclist..writes to protest against being forced to show a red light behind. 1900 G. D. Hiscox *Horseless Vehicles* ii. 37 The movement..was made by a *push-foot connection from a three-throw crank shaft. 1920 W. T. Grenfell *Labrador Doctor* i. 7 The shrimp fishermen used *push-nets in the channels at low tide. 1903 *Engin. Rev.* Jan. 14 (Cent. Suppl.) In the case of the *push-nipple type of boiler the rule would be as follows. 1928 V. G. Childe *Most Anc. East* iii. 54 A steep-ended scraper or *push-plane. 1920 G. Burrard *Notes on Sporting Rifles* 68 Greener's '*push through' is an excellent invention for all ultra small bores.

Pu·sh-bike. *colloq.* [f. Push- + *Bike *sb.*2] An ordinary or push-bicycle. Hence **Pu·sh-biking** *vbl. sb.*
1913 'Ian Hay' *Happy-go-lucky* xiv. 180 Luckily I had the old push-bike with me, and I managed to find my way down here. 1920 *Isis* 3 Nov. 3/1 Self-advertisement, or the man who rides a push-bike with both hands in his trouser pockets. 1921 *Chambers's Jrnl.* Sept. 614/1 The smallness of the fee ..hardly compensated for the insult of being taken for the owner of a 'push-bike'. 1926 *Punch* 8 Dec. 643/1 Music, Greek Plays, 'push-biking' tours—All figure in his pages.

Pusher. Add: **1.** (Further example.)
1909 *Daily Chron.* 12 Oct. 4/6 It is a very difficult matter for an agent to canvass in a legitimate manner, as these special 'pushers' have told such glowing yarns [etc.].

3. (See quot. 1916.)
1916 H. Barber *Aeroplane Speaks* (1918) 141 *Pusher*, an aeroplane of which the propeller is mounted behind the main lifting surface. 1922 *Encycl. Brit.* XXX. 20/2 The first biplanes..were of the 'propeller' type, colloquially 'pushers'; almost all monoplanes were 'tractors'.

Push-push (pʊ·ʃpʊʃ). [f. Push *v.*] A rude carriage impelled by coolies, used by travellers in some parts of India.
1907 *Westm. Gaz.* 13 Dec. 12/1 Hitherto the only means of conveyance for travellers in this delightful part of India has been the 'push-push'. 1921 *United Free Ch. Mission Rec.* June 187/2 All rode wherever they went..if they did not care to hire the 'push-push' an unwieldy machine like a long bathing-coach on four wheels.

Pusiform (pʊ·sifɔ̄ɹm), *a.* [f. Pus + -form.] Having the form of pus; pus-like.
1906 *Practitioner* Nov. 637 All experience of this group of organisms points to all of them producing, in some circumstances, a pusiform fluid.

Pussy, *sb.* **6. a.** (Earlier example.)
1842 *American Pioneer* I. 182, I walked up very carelessly among the soldiers..and concluded they could never fight with us. They appeared to me to be too pussy.

Pu·ssyfoot, *sb.* [f. the nickname '*Pussyfoot*' of an American prohibition lecturer, W. E. Johnson (1862–), given to him on account of his stealthy methods when a magistrate (cf. next).] An advocate or supporter of prohibition; also *attrib.* and allusively.
1919 *Punch* 23 July 86 *Gloomy Policeman.* 'You've had enough. Better go home.' *Reveller*...'Shurr-up—Pussyfoot!' 1920 H. C. McNeile *Bull Dog Drummond* vi. § 1 We are all confirmed Pussy-foots, and have been consuming non-alcoholic beer. 1921 E. Gosse *Bks. on Table* 194 His cheery book [*Notes on a Cellar-Book*] is remarkable for nothing more than for its magnificent refusal to be browbeaten by any Pussyfoot, whether American or native. 1921 T. Burke *Outer Circle* 169 The tea arrived, a viscid, leathery fluid of Pussyfoot vintage. 1924 *Blackw. Mag.* Jan. 135/2 Even those whom he dislikes, even puritans and 'pussyfoots', he treats with a light-handed contempt.

Pu·ssy-foot, *v.* *U.S.* [f. Pussy *sb.* + Foot *sb.*] *intr.* To tread softly or lightly to avoid being noticed; to proceed warily; to conceal one's opinions or plans.
1905 *Atlanta Constitution* 20 Mar. 3 Vice-President Charles Warren Fairbanks is pussy-footing it around Washington. 1918 C. Sandburg *Cornhuskers* 73 Who pussyfoots from desk to desk with a speaking forefinger? 1919 H. L. Wilson *Ma Pettengill* vii. 224 He didn't go back at all till the middle of the night, when he pussy-footed in and got his things out, and disappeared. 1928 *Observer* 5 Feb. 18/1 While most papers are still 'pussy-footing' on the Presidency they called their editors together and afterwards announced a unanimous decision. 1931 E. Thompson *Farewell to India* 203 Trying to coax a horse to wait while I pussy-footed up to him.

Pu·ssyfooter. [f. *Pussyfoot *v.* and *sb.* + -er1.] **a.** One who pussyfoots (in any sense of the verb). **b.** An advocate or supporter of prohibition. So **Pu·ssyfooting** *ppl. a.* and *vbl. sb.* **Pu·ssyfootism.**
1921 *Q. Rev.* Jan. 100 The tyranny that could ensue from the Pussy-footing of Canada is too terrible to contemplate. 1923 *Daily Mail* 23 July 7 In Tudor England people sang the music they liked, and read the books they liked. They had real freedom, and there was no pussyfootism. 1927 *Saturday Even. Post* 24 Dec. 9/1 A good politician is a natural-born pussy-footer. 1928 *Daily Express* 28 Dec. 8/3 The pussyfooters..have given a weary and blasé world a new game to play. 1928 *Collier's* 29 Dec. 38/1 The wrappings which..the pussy-footing politicians impose upon a candidate.

Pussy-willow. (Earlier examples.)
1869 J. G. Fuller *Flower Gatherers* 52 The aments appear before the leaves, and are covered with hairs so soft and silken that children often call them Pussy-Willows. 1878 Mrs. Stowe *Poganuc People* xvii. 182 Then the pussy-willows threw out their soft catkins.

Put, *sb.*1 Add: **3.** Also simply *put*.
1805 L. Dow *Trav. Wks.* 1806 II. 70 Here the family either as a put or for convenience, were guilty of improprieties.

5. *attrib.* as *put option*.
1881 *Guide Oper. Stocks* 15 A Put Option should be obtained when a decline in the market is expected to take place.

Put, *v.*1 Add: **23. d.** Also with *over*. Cf. sense 49 below.
1919 H. L. Wilson *Ma Pettengill* iv. 136 It occurred to him that he could put it all over Ben in another way that would cut him to the heart.

24*. *To put it across* (a person). **a.** To visit with retribution or punishment; to get even with.
1918 D. Valentine *Man with Clubfoot* xxi. 309 When you ..put it across 'der Stelze'..you settled a long outstanding account we had against him. 1928 *Daily Mail* 6 Aug. 14/6 You are a master of mob tactics, but we will put it across you yet.

b. To impose upon; to deceive or delude.
1915 E. Wallace *Man who Bought London* iv, He won't half put it across you people. 1927 *Observer* 27 Mar. 6/4 It would be difficult for a greedy, hysterical, shameless, half-insane revivalist..to 'put it across' ever-increasing audiences. 1928 *Daily Express* 26 May 13/4 Volumes have been written as to how Mother Cuckoo manages to 'put it across' certain inoffensive countryside birds.

27. d. Also *to put* (a person) *through it*: To subject to some ordeal, cross-examination, etc.
1922 A. A. Milne *Red House Myst.* vi. 50 Everybody else is bundled off except me, and I get put through it by that inspector as if I knew all about it. 1923 *Daily Mail* 25 Apr. 10, I intended to put him through it in no uncertain fashion.

35*. Put across. To execute successfully; to establish or carry; = *Put over* (sense *49 i).
1925 H. L. Foster *Trop. Tramp Tourists* 9 And, gentlemen, we'll put it across! We'll do it by working! 1926 D. L. Colvin *Prohibition in U.S.* 434 Wet propagandists asserted that prohibition had been 'put across' against the will of the majority. 1927 *Observer* 6 Nov. 15/1 It will be notorious among managers that this producer is good at putting strong stuff across.

38. Put away. g. Also, to kill. *colloq.*
1847 Anne Brontë *Agnes Grey* xiv, A reward, I should have greatly valued..were he [*sc.* a dog] not now in danger of being 'put away'.

42. Put forth. g. (*b*) (Recent example.)
1924 Rose Macaulay *Orphan Island* xx. 262 Like some lovely fruit that puts forth, ripens, and tumbles, over-mellow, to the ground.

44. Put in. j. (Further example.)
1922 *N. & Q.* Ser. XII. XI. 207/1 A horse which does not 'put all in' is one which does not do its best—a slug, lazy horse, a rogue.

45. Put off. h. (Further example.)
1928 *Observer* 19 Feb. 6/3 The prefatory note, with its apparently exaggerated claim, rather put me off.

47. Put out. c. Also, in pugilistic use, to 'knock out' (Knock *v.* 12).
1910 Driscoll *Ringcraft* 84, I have..not infrequently put opponents 'out' with a blow on the neck.

49. Put over. i. To carry out or represent successfully; to secure appreciation for (a play, cinematographic film, etc.); to make popular. Also *refl.* (Cf. *to get over*: *Get *v.* 66 e.)
1914 Gertr. Atherton *Perch of Devil* II. 293 You don't go into any business..and put it over without running the risk of being shot. 1928 *Daily Express* 18 Apr. 11/2 'Is it true that you wanted a star name to put the play over?' was then asked. 1928 *Weekly Dispatch* 24 June 8/4 Mr. Hayes's humour is not at all easy to 'put over' mechanically [*sc.* on gramophone records]. 1928 *Daily Express* 11 July 9/3 On the screen you..are fascinated by the extraordinary way in which he 'puts himself over'. 1931 F. L. Allen *Only Yesterday* viii. 213 The president emeritus of Harvard had had no professional talent to put over his funeral in a big way.

j. *To put..over*: To impose (something false or deceptive) *on* a person. Also, to pass off, succeed in carrying out.
1916 H. L. Wilson *Somewhere in Red Gap* i. 19 Funny, the way the little man tried to put it over on us, letting on he was just puzzled—not really bothered, as he plainly was. 1921 R. D. Paine *Comr. Rolling Ocean* viii. 130 Who calls it a crime to put one over on the Custom House flatties? 1924 W. M. Raine *Troubled Waters* xix. 209 What are you trying to put over on me? Why don't you go to Mac and ask him? 1928 A. S. W. Rosenbach *Books & Bidders* 117 One of the greatest hoaxes ever planned was put over by a French forger.

50. Put through. c. (Example.)
1916 B. Cable *Action Front* 86 Ask to be put through to the inquiry office.

53. Put up. a. (*d*). (Earlier example.)
1852 *Punch* 11 Dec. 257/1 The entertainments this week have been of a slight and desultory character, the management being..glad to 'put up' anything they could get.

u. To look upon, regard or interpret (something) in a particular way.
1895 *Century Mag.* Sept. 674/2 And Jack says to himself, 'Well,..I done what I could! What is to be will be.' That's about the way I put it up.

54. b. *To put one next to*: see *Next A. 13 c; *to put one wise*: see Wise *a.* 3 b.

Put, *ppl. a.* For *to stay put* see Stay *v.*1 6 b.

Put-. Add: **put-in** *U.S.*, something feigned or pretended.
1902 Harben *Abner Daniel* 301 This ain't no put-in o' mine, gracious knows!

Pu·t-and-take. A gambling game played with a six-sided top.
1922 *Daily Mail* 5 June, A youth was summoned at Hull yesterday for playing 'put and take' in the recreation ground.

Putrid, *a.* Add: **3. b.** *slang.* Of poor or bad quality; worthless, 'beastly', 'rotten'.
1903 Mrs. Everard Cotes *Those Delightful Americans* 104 Last night at billiards you first said your luck was 'rotten', and then you got excited and declared it was 'putrid'. 1913 'Ian Hay' *Right Stuff* vi, He seems to have perfectly putrid notions about some things.

Putty, *sb.* Add: **5. e.** A former type of golf ball made of some material other than gutta-percha.
1891 R. Forgan *Golfer's Handbk.* 39 The 'putty' being the popular name for the 'Eclipse'. 1900 *Yng. Sportsman* (ed. A. E. T. Watson) 293 Several kinds of composition balls, known generically as 'putties' in contradistinction to the 'gutties' or gutta-percha balls..have failed to take the place of those made of the raw material.

6. putty-face, a putty-coloured face; **putty-hearted** *a.*, lacking in courage, cowardly.
1927 May Sinclair *Hist. Anth. Waring* xvii. 88 Charlie, in spite of his *putty face, was handsome in a heavy way. 1885 Stevenson *Prince Otto* II. i, A springless, *putty-hearted, cowering coward!

Puzzle, *sb.* **4.** Add: *puzzle-box.*
1908 Marg. F. Washburn *Animal Mind* x. 232 The dropping off of useless movements is further illustrated in those experiments where animals are required to work some kind of mechanism. This may be called briefly the *puzzle-box method. 1924 R. M. Ogden tr. *Koffka's Growth of Mind* 181 The puzzle-box tests of Thorndike.

Pycno-. Add: **Pycnomo·rphous** *a.*, *Biol.* = *Pycnomorphic.*
1899 L. F. Barker *New Syst. Constituent Neurones* 123 Nissl consequently designates the extremely darkly stained cells as '*pyknomorphous* cells, or cells in which the stainable portions are arranged relatively most closely (πυκνός).

Pyelo-. Add: **Py·elogram**, a diagram of a pelvis.
1923 R. Knox *Radiog. & Radio-Therapeutics* I. 388 Pyelogram showing pelvis and ureter.

Pygmy. C. Add: **pygmy-flint**, a type of microlith.
1907 T. Rice Holmes *Anc. Britain* 82 Of all stone implements the most curious are the tiny objects which are known as 'pygmy flints'. 1930 F. Elgee *Early Man in N.E. Yorksh.* v. 28 Pygmy-flints are usually found on sandy soils. *Ibid.* 31 The pygmy-flint men lived by hunting and fishing.

Pygo-. Add: **Pygo·podine** *a.* = *Pygopodous.* **Pygosty·lous** *a.*, of, pertaining to, or resembling, a pygostyle.
1904 *Amer. Naturalist* Jan. 13 Drawings of the bones of *pygopodine birds. 1903 *Ibid.* 61 A *flat*, horizontally compressed, *pygostylous mass.

Pyjamas, *sb. pl.* Add: Now sometimes *sing.*
1932 *Barker's Spring Catal.*, This Ideal Pyjama is made of a very soft washing cotton.

b. Add: **pyjama-party**, a party at which those present are dressed in pyjamas; also **pyjama-and-bottle party.**
1910 *Westm. Gaz.* 13 Apr. 5/3 Some entertaining details are published in New York..concerning a pyjama party held a couple of days ago at the residence of..a well-known member of Chicago society. 1928 *Sunday Dispatch* 5 Aug. 15/2 Mention was made of the splendid work of Mrs. X—Y— for her pyjama-and-bottle party.

Pylon. Add: **2.** A structure used to mark out the course round which aeroplanes fly.
1909 *Westm. Gaz.* 16 Oct. 9/3 After a successful round of the course his aeroplane came to earth near the second pylon on the south side. 1913 *Everyday Phr. explained* 11 The modern meaning of Pylon is the erection, with flag on top, which, on aviation grounds, marks out the course, outside of which aviators must keep during competitions.

3. A structure for supporting power cables.
1923 E. Shanks *Richest Man* iii. 52 Half a mile up the mountain, a cable, a thin black line, traversed the crystal air, borne up on pylons. 1931 *John O' London's Weekly* 23 May 214/3 The pylons which have lately been spreading over the Downs have something to do with his decision.

Pyo-. Add: **Pyorrhœ·ic** *a.*, of, pertaining to, or affected with pyorrhœa.
1910 *Practitioner* Jan. 121 This is the condition of a pyorrhoeic mouth.

Pyramid, *sb.* Add: **5.** (Further example.)
1932 *New Yorker* 14 May 22/1 The bankers who were setting up the biggest financial pyramids of yesterday are replaced by other steel-nerved bankers today.

8. c. A wedge formation of players formerly adopted in American football to carry the ball towards the opponents' goal.
1899 A. H. Quinn *Pennsyl. Stories* 25 It was Penn's ball. The pyramid started with the cheers of ten thousand back of it.

Pyramid, *v.* Add: **b.** *trans.* *Stock Exchange.* To increase (the amount of stock one holds) by selling at favourable times and applying all the proceeds to the purchase of more stock. *U.S.*
1902 G. H. Lorimer *Lett. Self-made Merchant* v. 64 He'd invent a scheme for speculating in wheat and go on pyramiding his purchases till he'd made the best that Cheops did look like a five-cent plate of ice-cream. 1927 P. Marks *Lord of Himself* 23 He pyramided his winnings and piled gold on gold..and finally saw himself a millionaire three times over.

c. *intr.* To stake all one possesses *on* a venture.
1922 *Chambers's Jrnl.* May 349/2 Harrison and I were satisfied, and we pyramided on it.

Pyro-. 1. Add: **pyro-ele·ctrolyte**, a non-conducting substance which is made a conductor by heat. **Py·rophile** [Gr. -φιλος loving], a person who believes that the interior of the earth is a molten or gaseous mass. **Py·rosphere**, the (supposed) intensely hot interior of the earth.
1902 *Trans. Amer. Inst. Elect. Engin.* 3 Jan. 77 (Cent. Suppl.) *Pyro-electrolyte. 1902 *Nature* 27 Nov. 91/2 The theory of the '*pyrophiles' is dangerous to humanity. 1900 *Geog. Jrnl.* XV. 88 A coloured diagram showing an ideal section of the Earth on the hypothesis that within the solid lithosphere lies a *pyrosphere of intensely high temperature.

Pyrophoric, *a.* Add: **b.** Used as a source of fire.
1910 *Chambers's Jrnl.* Apr. 271/1 The spark given by the friction of the small file rubbing over the pellet of pyrophoric alloy is much longer [etc.].

Pyxie (pi·ksi). *local U.S.* [Shortened f. *Pyxidanthera.*] A flowering evergreen shrub, *Pyxidanthera barbulata*, growing in eastern parts of the U.S. Also *pyxie moss.*
1882 *Harper's Mag.* June 65 Among her [Nature's] treasures is the delicate pyxie..a little prostrate trailing evergreen...Its locality is confined to New Jersey and the Carolinas. 1925 *Scribner's Mag.* July 35/1 The predominant vegetation..consists of..innumerable clusters of oval-leaved *diapensia lapponica* in rounded clumps like red pin-cushions (closely resembling what is called pixy-moss).

Q

Q. I. 3. Also *Q in a corner*.
1813 *Stranger* (N.Y.) 23 Oct. 136 in *N. & Q.* Ser. x. IX. 407/1, I once more spied my favourite chair, where I sat like Q. in a corner.

II. 3. as *adj.*: Pertaining to or connected with the quartering, feeding, equipping, etc. of soldiers.
1924 *Times Lit. Suppl.* 13 Nov. 734/3 General Ironside..devotes himself almost entirely to the 'Q' side, of which the most important factor was the problem of clothing. 1930 H. Belloc *Wolsey* v. 126 It was certainly he who did all the 'Q' work, to him all the letters were addressed; he gave the orders, bought provisions, organised transport, [etc.].

Q-boat, Q-ship. In the war of 1914–18, a merchant-ship fitted with concealed guns and manned by a naval crew disguised as ordinary seamen designed to decoy and destroy enemy submarines. Also ellipt. *Q.*
1919 *Boy's Own Paper* July 457/1 These Q-boats were apparently innocent tramps and trawlers. 1920 *Blackw. Mag.* Mar. 325/1 They had complied with the regulations that dictated that no uniform must be shown aboard sailing 'Q's'. 1920 *Glasgow Herald* 4 May 4 Mr. Chatterton had exceptional opportunities for collecting information about the work of the Q-ships. 1928 Compton Mackenzie *Extremes Meet* 16 He might perhaps have been given a Q-ship for these waters.

Quack, U.S. variant of Quick *sb.*2
1840 J. Buel *Farmer's Comp.* 144 To clean the ground of the roots of foul plants, as dock, quack, etc. *Ibid.* 232 Many species of the *festuca* and *agrostis* genera, particularly the *A. stricta*, of which our quack or witch-grass is a variety. 1872 *Rep. Vermont Board Agric.* I. 289 He who sets out to subdue a piece of quack must resolve on no half-way measures. 1909 *N. Y. Even. Post* (semi-weekly ed.) 11 Mar. 5 In conquering the quack he did the one thing that could have enabled him to get a crop from that unfertilized soil.
So *quack-grass.*
1840 J. Buel *Farmer's Comp.* 123 Some troublesome perennials, as Canada thistles, wild onions, quack grass, daisies, etc.

Quack, *v.*1 **3.** (Further example.)
1925 *Scribner's Mag.* Oct. 385/1 Time..has not obliterated the love of being quacked.

Quacky, *a.*1 (Earlier example.)
1836 *Southern Lit. Messenger* II. 327 The critical department of this work..is in our opinion decidedly quacky.

Quadrangle, *sb.* Add: **2. b.** *Palmistry.* (See quot.)
1883 Frith & Heron-Allen *Chiromancy* 138 The Quadrangle is that part of the human hand comprised between the line of the Head and the line of the Heart, and between the line of Fate and the line of Apollo.

Quadrangular, *a.* (Later *Comb.* example.)
1854 *Poultry Chron.* I. 431 It is a spacious, quadrangular-shaped house, built of a greyish stone.

Quadrant, *sb.*1 Add: **5. b.** The horizontal quadrant-shaped tiller to which the chains or ropes for controlling the rudder of a ship are attached.
1923 *Glasgow Herald* 3 Feb. 8/7 The modern helm, or its equivalent, the quadrant, is placed out-board.

6. quadrant-roller, a roller designed to move round the quarter of a circle.
1862 *Catal. Internat. Exhib.* II. x. 35 The gates are of peculiar construction hanging on pivots without the support of *Quadrant rollers.

Quadri-. 1. Add: **quadripa·schal**, including four passovers; **quadrivo·ltine** [It. *volta* time, turn], (of a silkworm) producing four broods in the year; as *sb*, a quadrivoltine silkworm.
1883 Schaff *Hist. Chr. Church* (ed. 2) I. § 16. 130 Three theories [of the length of Christ's public ministry]..designated as the bipaschal, tripaschal and *quadripaschal schemes, according to the number of Passovers. 1888 E. A. Butler *Silkworms* iv. 69 Most of the other species produce two, three, four, six, or even eight broods per annum, and in the commercial world are, for that reason, distinguished as 'bivoltins', 'trevoltins', '*quadrivoltins', etc.

Quadrille, *v.*2 (Recent example.) Also *transf.*
1903 Ld. Gower *Rec. & Rem.* 59 Teaching us how to quadrille and how to valse. 1905 W. H. Hunt *Pre-Raphaelitism* I. ii. 24, I..rejoiced with the happy birds quadrilling around the sentinel trees.

Quadringenary (kwɒdrindʒī·nări). [f. L. *quadringēnārius* of four hundred each, f. *quadringenti* four hundred.] A four-hundredth anniversary or the celebration of this; = Quater-centenary.
1905 *Times* 5 July 8/2 Another record of the quadringenary has been the starting of a fund.

Quadringentenary (-dʒentī·nări, -dʒe̍ntī·nări), *a.* [f. as prec. with ending of Centenary.] That has lasted four hundred years.
1903 *Saturday Rev.* 17 Oct. 482 What serious contribution can the reader limited to fifteen minutes..make..to the settlement of controversies now of quadringentenary prescription?

Quadringentennial (-dʒente·niăl), *a.* [f. L. *quadringenti* four hundred + *annus* year + -al.] Of or pertaining to a four-hundredth anniversary.
1901 *Westm. Gaz.* 8 Nov. 3/2 One rather wonders what Botticelli..would make of his quadringentennial boom.

Quadrivial. A. *adj.* **2.** (Modern examples.)
1886 S. S. Laurie *Rise & Constit. Universities* 61 Practically under the name of dialectic, logic was a quadrivial study. 1912 *Hastings's Encycl. Relig. & Ethics* V. 172/2 The 'trivial' arts were Grammar, Rhetoric, and Dialectics. ..The 'quadrivial' arts were Geometry, Arithmetic, Astronomy, and Music.

Quadroon. 2. Add: *quadroon ball.*
1805 J. F. Watson in *Amer. Pioneer* II. (1843) 236 The colored women have..their weekly balls, (called quartroon balls) at which none but white gentlemen attend. 1880 G. W. Cable *Grandissimes* iii. 19, I saw the same old man, at a quadroon ball a few years ago.

Quadrumvirate. (Recent example.)
1923 *Contemp. Rev.* Feb. 151 He formed a quadrumvirate..to whom he entrusted full powers.

Quadrupedal. A. *adj.* Add: **1. b.** Of a person: On hands and knees.
1914 Chesterton *Wisdom of Father Brown* 249 Seeing him just quadrupedal in the grass, the priest raised his eyebrows rather sadly.

Quadruplet. Add: **2. b.** *Mus.* A group of four notes to be played in the time of three.
1873 H. C. Banister *Music* 13 Other irregularities..such as four notes for three, termed a Quadruplet.

Quadruply, *sb.* (Later example.)
1876 W. Hector *Judic. Rec.* 130 The practice..of multiplying pleading,—such as answers, replies, duplies, triplies, quadruplies, and an infinite number under other titles.

Quag, *sb.* (Earlier fig. example.) Also *transf.*
1842 I. Taylor *Anc. Christianity* II. 480 Thoughtless thousands of the people are thus beguiled into the filthiest quags of 'abominable idolatry'. 1904 *Daily Chron.* 18 May 3/4 Her clothes were a quag of blood.

Quaggery (kwæ·gəri). [f. Quag *sb.* + -ery.] A bog or marsh.
1843 Carlton *New Purchase* xlvi. 117 Two rods above and one below, the quaggery required a pole to touch its bottom some fifteen feet long.

Quahaug. (Earlier examples.)
1781 S. Peters *Hist. Conn.* (1829) 197 The oysters, clams, quauhogs, lobsters, crabs, and fish, are innumerable. 1809 Irving *Knickerb.* I. 359 Beads manufactured from the Quahaug or wilk; a shell-fish formerly abounding on our coasts.

Quail, *sb.* **5.** Add: *quail-bagger, -bagging, shot, -time, track, -trap.*
1879 *Harper's Mag.* Oct. 703 The..advice offered by a circle of *quail-baggers and other by-standers. *Ibid.*, The conclusion that a *quail-bagging expedition was regarded as an event of considerable importance. c 1865 'Mark Twain' *Sk.* Wks. XIX. 31 He got the frog out..and filled him full of *quail shot. 1897 *Outing* XXX. 94/2 Ever since last *quail-time I have been casting rather dubious glances at a certain old gun. 1842 *Yale Lit. Mag.* VIII. 96, I can't always decipher *quail tracks. 1855 *Trans. Mich. Agric. Soc.* VI. 495 One acre of quail track corn planted on muck land. 1807–8 Irving *Salmagundi* xv. 345 He was particularly adroit in making our *quail-traps. 1845 Mrs. Kirkland *Western Clearings* 120 Nobody..pulled the shingles off his roof to make fishing-lights or quail-traps.

Quake, *v.*1 **4.** Add: **quake-grass** = Quaking-grass.
1909 *Daily Chron.* 25 June 7/2 We used to call 'em 'quake grass', and 'cats' tail'.

Quaker. 3. Add: **Quaker city** *U.S.*, Philadelphia; **quaker-ladies** (examples); **quaker-meeting** (earlier and later examples).
1903 *Critic* Aug. 190 Sketches of Philadelphia life and society by a New York woman who..does not find the *Quaker city so 'slow' as it is generally represented. 1871 *Scribner's Monthly* II. 102 In yonder woods, where hepatica, and May-blossoms, and *Quaker-ladies twinkle into life. 1878 *Harper's Mag.* Apr. 778/3 How could she climb down and gather 'Quaker ladies', or climb up for columbine among the rocks? 1724 *Essex Inst. Hist. Coll.* XXXVI. 332 *Quaker meeting at night. 1797 *Steele Papers* II. 773 Indian and negro rights are fine things to talk about in a quaker meeting, or in the house of Reprs. 1848 J. F. Cooper *Oak Open.* II. i. 9 The silence resembled that of a Quaker meeting.

Quakeress. (Earlier example.)
1721 *N. E. Hist. & Gen. Reg.* (1876) XXX. 61 [Baptism of] John Reynolds, the little child of John Reynolds, his wife a Quakeress, not consenting.

Quakerish, *a.* **b.** (Earlier example.)
1743 in F. Chase *Hist. Dartmouth Coll.* (1891) i. 5 [He] made a great show of sanctity, by means whereof he was under advantage to propagate his Quakerish notions.

Quaking asp. *U.S.* Also **quakenasp.** The American aspen, *Populus tremuloides.* Also *attrib.*
α. 1822 J. Fowler *Jrnl.* 143 The timber on the mountains here is pitch pine, spruce, pine, hemlock, and quakenasp. 1905 *N. Y. Even. Post* 2 Sept., I have seen quakenasp groves on the summer range, where you could walk miles and miles through these bluebells.
β. 1845 Fremont *Exped.* 112 Quaking-asp (*populus tremuloides*) was mixed with the cottonwood. 1878 J. H. Beadle *Western Wilds* xi. 168 The town is in a grove of quaking asp, and was in no danger. 1886 *Leslie's Pop. Monthly* Dec. 683/2 The dying leaves of the 'quakin' asp' trees. 1902 O. Wister *Virginian* iv. 55 They took us along the bed up to the head of the gully, and through a thicket of quaking asps.

Qualified, *ppl. a.* Add: **5. b.** Euphemism for 'bloody', 'damned', etc. *slang.*
1890 Kipling *Plain Tales* (ed. 3) 131 He was..told not to make a qualified fool of himself.

Qualifier. 1. (Add example.)
1909 *Daily Chron.* 7 May 8/4 Out in 36, he came home in a good 37, and..made certain of a place among the qualifiers.

Qualify, *v.* **6.** (Recent example.)
1913 *Act 3 & 4 Geo. V* c. 20 § 47 Where injury can be qualified by the other creditors..in respect thereof.

Qualimeter (kwǫli·mĭtəɹ). [f. L. *quālis* of what kind + -meter.] (See quot. 1918.)
1911 Bauer in *Arch. Roentgen Ray* Jan. 305 Whether the Roentgen Qualimeter, as we may call it, has all the requisites ..is a question which I must leave for others than myself to decide. 1918 R. Knox *Radiogr. & Radio-Therapeutics* I. 89 The Bauer Qualimeter is an instrument for determining the degree of hardness of the X-ray tube...It is a static electrometer and condenser which indicates automatically the potential of the cathode, and hence the quality of the X-rays.

Quality. Add: **10. d.** The 'hardness' or penetrating power of X rays.
1911 *Arch. Roentgen Ray* Jan. 305 The ordinary means..only measures the quality of the rays at the moment of observation.

Qualmless (kwā·m-, kwǭ·mlės), *a.* [f. Qualm *sb.* + -less.] Having or feeling no qualms.
1905 *Westm. Gaz.* 4 Mar. 5/2 Picture of Ronald absolutely qualmless facing charging rhinoceros. 1927 Deeping *Kitty* xix, Any qualms that she may have suffered in the beginning disappeared...By the end of January she was qualmless.

Quank (kwɒŋk). [Imitative.] (See quot.)
1921 *Chambers's Jrnl.* Mar. 178/1 He could even hear the nasal laugh of the zebra, the resonant 'Quank' of the gnus, the rattle of horn against horn as the bucks made play.

Quant, *sb.* Add: Also *quant-pole.*
1901 *Academy* 26 Oct. 389/1 There..lay a large family-boat immovable...A quant-pole stood rigidly upright beside it.

Quant (kwɒnt), *sb.*2 Used for *Quantum 5.
1926 G. N. Lewis in *Nature* 18 Dec. 874/1 It would seem inappropriate to speak of one of these hypothetical entities as a particle of light, a corpuscle of light, a light quantum or a light quant, if we are to assume that it spends only a minute fraction of its existence as a carrier of radiant energy.

Quantimeter (kwɒnti·mĭtəɹ). [f. L. *quant-us* how great + -meter.] An instrument for showing the quantity of X rays administered to a person.
1915 R. Knox *Radiography* etc. 288 The division of the scale has been calibrated to agree with the Kienböck quantimeter.

Quantity. 13. Add: *quantity output, production.*
1919 *Brit. Manufacturer* Nov. 42/1 Quantity output may mean cheap production, but the manufacture of more modest quantities need not be much inferior in this respect. *Ibid.*, An immense home market..has encouraged him to undertake big quantity production.

Quantization (kwɒntəizē·ʃən). [f. next + -ation.] The fact or process of quantizing.
1921 C. G. Darwin in *Rep. Brit. Assoc.* 473 The quantisation consists in fixing half of these by a certain rule in terms of the quantum.

Quantize (kwǫ·ntəiz), *v.* [f. *Quant(um + -ize.] *trans.* To apply quantum mechanics or the quantum theory to; to measure (energy) in quanta. Hence **Qua·ntizing** *vbl. sb.*
1921 C. G. Darwin in *Rep. Brit. Assoc.* 474 Possible chances of development might lie in the direction of discovering a method of quantising non-periodic processes. 1927 Sidgwick *Electronic Th. Valency* 18 This quantizing of the energy of the rotating electron..was a bold assumption, guess, or inspiration, which was justified by the agreement of the results with the observed facts. *Ibid.* 25 It follows that just as we must quantize the angular momentum of the electron in the ellipse, so we must quantize that of the rotation (precession) of the ellipse itself.

Quantum. Add: **5.** *Physics.* A discrete unit quantity of energy, proportional to the frequency of radiation, emitted from or absorbed by an atom.
1910 *Science Abstracts* A. XIII. 556 The absorption of the corresponding light-quantum. 1911 *Ibid.* XIV. 1178 The new hypothesis involves the emission of energy in quantums only. 1912 *Month. Not. Roy. Astron. Soc.* LXXII. Suppl. 730 Thus at any stage in the radiation of the charged atom the number of quanta present is proportional to the cube root of the emitted wave-length. 1913 *Rep. Brit. Assoc.* 382 The exchange of energy..can only take place by finite

jumps, no quantity less than a quantum being ever transferred to the medium or taken from it. 1913 N. Bohr in *Phil. Mag.* XXVI. July 2 Planck's constant, or as it is often called the elementary quantum of action. 1922 J. Mills *Within the Atom* xi. 148 The scientific world has quite unanimously accepted it to be a fact that energy is emitted in quanta.

b. *attrib.* and *Comb.*, as *quantum energy, number, property*, etc.; **quantum dynamics, mechanics, physics**, dynamics, mechanics, or physics revised to take account of quanta; **quantum hypothesis, theory**, a hypothesis or theory put forward by M. Planck in 1900, which accounts for certain atomic phenomena by assuming or showing that energy (heat, light, etc.) is emitted from atoms only in quanta; **quantum jump**, the change in the orbit of an electron in an atom accompanying the loss or gain of a quantum of energy.

1927 Sidgwick *Electronic Th. Valency* 34 *note*, This principle of Bohr's..was originally derived from a 'correspondence' between the results of classical and *quantum dynamics. 1921 *Discovery* Sept. 227/2 Provided that the incident and exciting radiation is..of an electron of the corresponding *quantum energy. 1927 Sidgwick *Electronic Th. Valency* 18 The second assumption is that the electron radiates energy..only when it passes in a '*quantum jump' from one of these stationary states to another of smaller energy. *Ibid.* 19 As the energy of the orbit increases, the frequency of rotation changes (with hydrogen it is inversely proportional to the cube of the *quantum number). 1927 A. S. Eddington *Stars & Atoms* 68 The property here referred to (the *quantum property) is the deepest mystery of light. 1931 H. Johnston tr. *Planck's Universe in light of Mod. Physics* 22 The Principle of Relativity..has proved itself a reliable and eloquent guide in the new regions of *Quantum Physics. 1911 *Science Abstracts* A. XIV. 1702 The *quanta theory of Planck and Einstein must be modified considerably to give a quantitative interpretation of the results obtained. 1912 *Rep. Brit. Assoc.* 415 A *quantum theory which implies a definite change of energy only when an electron enters or leaves the atom. 1914 J. H. Jeans *Rep. Radiation & Quantum Th.* i. 1 The quantum-theory..had its origin in an attempt to account for the spectrum of black-body radiation. 1925 Deeping *Sorrell & Son* xxix, The marvels of science,..'wireless', or the latest aeroplane, or the bending of light, or the quantum theory.

Quarantine, *sb.* 2. Also, a period of seclusion or isolation after exposure to infection from a contagious disease.

1913–14 *Wellcome's Nurse's Diary* 209 Isolation required after exposure to: Asiatic Cholera..12 days' quarantine. 1922 *Nursing Mirror* 132 Period of Quarantine required after the Latest Exposure to Infection... Measles..16 days.

Quarantine, *v.* 3. To go into quarantine.

1928 *Daily News* 7 Aug. 7/3 The Mauretania..is expected to 'quarantine' at New York at 10 a.m. to-morrow.

Quarrel, *v.* 2. Add: Also with *over*.

1870 Mayne Reid *White Squaw* xxviii. 100 Ere long they [the wolves] could be seen skulking through the enclosure and quarrelling over the corpses upon the plain. 1883 G. Moore *Mod. Lover* I. xii. 244 Here a group of Cupids quarrelled over some masks and arrows.

Quarry, *sb.*[1] 4. Delete † *Obs.* and add modern example.

1884 T. Speedy *Sport* xix. 360 We have not above half-a-dozen times seen the peregrine in the act of making a quarry.

Quart, *sb.*[3] 2. Add: *Quart minor*, the sequence of ten, nine, eight, seven.

1885 *Encycl. Brit.* XIX. 114/2 A quart minor is good against a tierce major.

Quarter, *sb.* Add: 7. d. *U.S* The fourth part of a mile; a quarter-mile race.

1827 J. F. Cooper *Prairie* iv. 94 His camp is but a short quarter from us. 1868 H. Woodruff *Trotting Horse* vii. 84 What's the use of a horse going a quarter fast? 1878 J. H. Beadle *Western Wilds* ii. 31 It was weeks before I could walk a quarter. 1899 A. H. Quinn *Pennylv. Stories* 196 I've run the quarter for three years and won a first and second in it, as you know.

9. b. (Earlier example.)

1783 *Maryland Gaz.* 5 Sept. 3/3 Price half a dollar to grown people and a quarter to children.

c. A quarter of a pound; five shillings.

1902 J. Greenwood *Pris. in Dock* ix. 198 Not only did I have to pay to get 'em out, I lost a quarter as well.

15. c. (Earlier examples.)

1745 *Itinerant Observ.* 37 The negroes..have a pretty deal of Liberty in their Quarters, as they are called. 1760 Washington *Diaries* I. 131 Began Plowing the Field by the Stable and Quarter for Oats and Clover. 1774 P. V. Fithian *Jrnl.* (1900) 237 A little Farm-House, or [a] Quarter for Negroes.

27. *quarter-armed, quarter-hourly* adjs.

1881 F. Day *Fishes Gt. Britain* I. 239 *Gasterosteus gymnurus*...The *quarter-armed or smooth-tailed stickleback. 1929 J. Owen *Shepherd & Child* iv. 46 It took him an hour and a half by the striking of the church clock, which had a *quarter-hourly chime.

30. **quarter-ball** *Billiards*, a ball that strikes another so that a quarter of the one overlaps a quarter of the other; **quarter-pole** (earlier example); **quarter-post** *U.S.*, a post marking a quarter-section of land; **quarter-racing** *U.S.*, the holding of quarter-races; **quarter-section** (earlier examples); **quarter-stake** *U.S.*, a stake marking a quarter-section of land.

1873 J. Bennett *Billiards* 34 If the half of one overlaps the half of the other, it is a half ball; and so on for a *quarter ball. Anything less than a quarter ball is called a fine ball. 1868 H. Woodruff *Trotting Horse* xxxi. 259 At the *quarter-pole she had recovered her stroke. 1849 *Presid. Mess. Congress* II. 508 After descending the precipice, the descent was gradual till we came to the *quarter-post, which is in a cedar swamp. 1784 Smyth *Tour in U.S.* I. 22 In the southern part of the colony and in North Carolina, they are much attached to *Quarter racing. 1889 *Harper's Mag.* Sept. 554/1 Foot-racing for the men and quarter-racing for the horses. 1806 in *Ann. 9th Congress* 2 Sess. 1032 The public lands are now sold in sections, half sections, and *quarter sections. 1822 J. Woods *Eng. Prairie* 262 Mr. Collins, who lived near, also offered me his land; it was a quarter-section that is, a hundred and sixty acres. 1845 Mrs. Kirkland *Western Clearings* 2 Section and *quarter-stakes, eighties and forties, and fractions, are plain enough when one is habituated to them.

Quarter, *v.* 8. a. (Later fig. example.)

1824 Car. Bowles in *Corr. Southey* (1881) 48, I keep quartering, or trying to quarter, for a yard or so, and then down goes the wheel into the old groove. I cannot keep out of blank verse.

Quarter-blood, *sb.* and *a.* *U.S.* (A person) whose blood is Indian or Negro to the extent of one quarter; (one) born of a half-breed and a white.

1845 *Knickerbocker Mag.* XXV. 236 Of this description was a quarter-blood [Indian], of great beauty. 1873 J. H. Beadle *Undevel. West* xix. 355 He had four children, only quarter-blood, but differing very much in shade. 1878 — *Western Wilds* ii. 26 The straight black hair, and nose just aquiline enough to give piquancy to the countenance, indicated the quarter-blood.

Quarter-breed, *sb.* *U.S.* The offspring of a half-breed and a white; a quarter-blood.

1880 *Harper's Mag.* Dec. 31 All four were of mixed blood their mother having been a beautiful French quarter-breed.

Qua·rter-deck, *v.* [f. the sb.] *intr.* To walk up and down as on a quarter-deck.

1901 E. F. Benson *Luck of Vails* xviii. 207 He continued quarter-decking about the room for a few times in silence, and his annoyance subsided. 1913 Mrs. H. Ward *Coryston Family* viii. 164 The quarter-decking began again; and Lester waited patiently on a slowly subsiding frenzy.

Quarterer. Add: Also a quartering bird (sense 10 d of Quarter *v.*).

1892 Greener *Breech-Loader* 209 When the shooter facing No. 2 trap gets a quarterer to the left from No. 5.

Quarter-horse. *U.S.* A horse specially trained to run quarter-mile races.

1845 T. J. Green *Texian Exped.* x. 136 Nausea which caused me to break for the door like a quarter-horse to relieve my distress. 1853 B. F. Taylor *Jan. & June* (1871) 61 One meets six-rail fences..plunging along like quarter horses. 1887 *Outing* May 115/1 You would not think him a quarter-horse for he looks like a clumsy sleepy old plug. 1907 S. E. White *Arizona Nights* I. 11 A quarter hoss couldn't have beat me to that shack.

Quarter-jack. Add: 3. *colloq.* or *slang.* = Quarter-master 2.

1920 Sir G. MacMunn *Behind Scenes in many Wars* 300 Fresh caviare..annoyed our men when they got a ration of it and complained of 'that black jam, what the quarter-jack had said was fish'.

Quartermaster. Add: 2. b. **Quartermaster-captain**, an officer in the U.S. army with the rank of captain having duties similar to those of a quartermaster.

1907 *N. Y. Even. Post* (semi-weekly ed.) 13 May 6 The person enjoying the title of quartermaster captain (a rank that causes our British cousins to smile).

Qua·rtermistress. [f. Quartermaster.] An officer in the W.A.A.C. having the duties of a quartermaster.

1917 *Times* 13 Aug. 3/1 The W.A.A.C. will be controlled by a Chief Controller, and the following appointments are authorized:—..Quarter mistress Class I. Attached to Depôt. 2 roses.

Quartic. a. *adj.* (Example.)

1905 R. W. H. T. Hudson (*title*) Kummer's Quartic Surface.

Quartz. 2. b. *quartz-mill* (example).

1908 *Chambers's Jrnl.* Sept. 640/2 Natthey, who had started a little quartz-mill on his claim.

Quassia. 3. quassia cup (example).

1867 Aug. J. E. Wilson *Vashti* xxiv, I have been forced to drink out of quassia-cups until my whole being has imbibed the bitter.

Quater-centenary. Delete *rare* and add examples.

1906 *Athenæum* 30 June 788/1 An excuse for the present work [*sc.* a biography of Geo. Buchanan] is afforded by the quatercentenary of the great Humanist, who was born in February, 1506. 1906 *Daily Chron.* 25 Sept. 4/4 That is why the Quatercentenary of the University [of Aberdeen] has created an unparalleled amount of interest in the north, and is attracting guests and graduates from every corner of the civilised world.

Quaternate, *a.* (Add example.)

1908 *Scott's Autumn List, Lady Beauclerc and Socialism* is the title of the last book of the Rev. H. T. Perfect's quaternate work on Lady Beauclerc's life.

Quaternion. 1. (Further example.)

1815 Scott *Guy M.* xlii, A species of florid elocution which often became ridiculous from his misarranging the triads and quaternions with which he loaded his sentences.

Quattrocentism (kwattro,tʃe·ntiz'm). [f. Quattrocento + -ism.] The fifteenth century style in Italian art.

1905 W. H. Hunt *Pre-Raphaelitism* II. xiii. 367 It was pointed out to them that our pictures had never attempted quattrocentism.

Quaver, *sb.* 1. Also *Comb.*

1727–41 Chambers *Cycl.* s.v. *Rest*, The quaver-rest of common time.

Quaverous (kwē·vərəs), *a.* [f. Quaver *v.* + -ous.] Tremulous, quavering.

1919 J. F. Bridge *Westm. Pilgrim* 146, I can still see two of these old gentlemen..with hardly a quaverous note to mark their years, valiantly voicing 'I saw lovely Phillis'.

Quawk (kwǭk), *sb.* *U.S.* [Imitative: cf. Quawk *v.* and Squawk.]

1. The cry of a duck or night-heron; = Quack *sb.*[2]

1863 'Gail Hamilton' *Gala-Days* 73 For the heavy booming of cannon rose the 'quauk!' of ducks. 1895 F. M. Chapman *Handbk. Birds* (1909) 137 Occasionally they utter a loud, hoarse quawk, the origin of their common name.

2. The black-crowned night-heron or qua-bird.

1867 *Amer. Naturalist* I. 343 The species was the Night-heron or Quawk (*Nyctiardea Gardeni*). 1877 Whitman *Specimen Days* (1892) 100 Quawks. [In a list of New Jersey birds.] 1895 F. M. Chapman *Handbk. Birds* (1909) 136 Black-crowned Night Heron: Quawk.

Quay, *sb.* b. *quay-side* (examples).

1903 *Westm. Gaz.* 31 Dec. 5/3 He saw another man climbing up the quay-side ladder. 1905 *Daily Chron.* 5 May 6/4 He had been working on the quay-side. 1910 *Gt. Central Railway Rep.* 11 Feb. 10 The Company..possessed considerable quay-side property at Hull. 1923 *Daily Mail* 11 July 7 At Grimsby and Immingham dockers and quayside workers resumed.

Queasy. (Later example of queazy.)

1912 Galsworthy *Inn Tranq.* 187, I would think, Sirs, that you should rather blame the queazy state of Pranza's stomach.

6. **queasy-stomached** *a.* (later example).

1802 Gifford tr. *Juvenal* vi. 292 Why waste the wine and cakes The queasy-stomach'd guest, at parting, takes?

Queek (kwīk), *v.* [Imitative.] Of an owl: To screech.

1921 J. Galsworthy *To Let* III. viii. 282 An owl flew, queeking, queeking; a bat flitted by.

Queen, *sb.* Add: 3. b. *Queen Elizabeth's bone*, the gentleman's or cramp bone in a leg of mutton.

1846 *Knickerbocker Mag.* XXVII. 17 From the knuckle-bone to the last joint of the queue, from the Pope's Eye, to Queen Elizabeth's Bone, each preferable and available slice ..was apparent to his practised eye.

6. b. *Queen of the West*, the city of Cincinnati.

1840 *Knickerbocker Mag.* XVI. 157 In this way we glided in our broad-horn past Cincinnati, the 'Queen of the West' as she is now called.

9. d. = Queen-post.

1842 *Civil Engin. & Arch. Jrnl.* V. 361/2 The blocks..being supported by the queens.

13. **queen city (of the west)**, Cincinnati; **queen city of the plains and peaks**, Denver; **queen city of the Pacific**, San Francisco; **queen-fish** (earlier example).

1844 in C. Cist *Cincinnati Misc.* 9 [Cincinnati] is now familiarly called the *Queen City of the West. 1854 Mary J. Holmes *Tempest & Sunshine* xvii. 239 Faster and faster sped the train..until at last the Queen City with its numerous spires was left behind. 1879 Whitman *Specimen Days* (1892) 147 So much for my feeling toward the *Queen city of the plains and peaks. 1880 *Harper's Mag.* Dec. 70 Local prejudice..and proverbial procrastination..unite to keep 'China-town' practically a sealed book to the better-class denizens of the *Queen City of the Pacific. 1884 Goode *Nat. Hist. Usef. Aquatic. Anim.* 380 The Queen-fish—Seriphus politus. This species is known as 'King-fish' or '*Queen-fish'. It ranges from Tomales Bay southward.

14. b. **queen's gray**, a kind of grey cloth; **queen's stuff** (later example); **queen's taste** (in phr. *to the* or *a queen's taste*, to perfection).

1845 in C. Cist *Cincinnati Misc.* 138 Their dresses were chiefly of silk, of various colors, and some of them were of good old fashioned *Queen's gray. 1845 S. Judd *Margaret* II. xi. 358 Rose had on..a *queens-stuff habit of the same colour. 1902 Harben *Abner Daniel* xxxiii. 279 You worked 'im to a *queen's taste—as fine as split milk. 1904 W. H. Smith *Promoters* v. 101 So the old man set it up on him to the Queen's taste. 1911 R. D. Saunders *Col. Todhunter* ix. 126 It's the best and truest thing I ever saw in my life! They've got you finished off to the Queen's taste.

c. **queen's lace**, the wild carrot.

1906 Mary E. W. Freeman *By Light of Soul* 52 She walked slowly between the fields, which were white and gold with queen's lace and golden rod.

Queen Anne. Add: c. **Queen Anne's lace**, the wild carrot.

1930 F. A. Pottle *Stretchers* 204 The fields, which should be clothed with grain, are rioting with the delicate blooms of Queen Anne's lace, with chicory, and centaurea.

Queen-A·nnish, *a.* [-ish.] Suggestive of or designed in a Queen Anne style.

1926 *Spectator* 24 July 134/2 Gradually Queen Annish cornices began to creep in.

Queer, *a.*[2] (Later examples.)

1877 Habberton *Jericho Road* xvi. 151 'Let's..give him fifty [dollars] to send her', 'Fifty queer?' asked Mr. Lodge. 'No, fifty straight', said the little man. *Ibid.* xxii. 203, I wouldn't have a man shove queer money for me after he knew what it was. 1890 *Buckskin Mose* ii. 34 At the same time he pulled out of his pocket a lot of 'queer' or counterfeit bills.

b. (Later example.)

1890 *Buckskin Mose* ii. 36 If I had been detected in 'shoving the queer',..they wouldn't have cared one red cent.

c. *On the queer*: not quite honest or straight.

1909 R. A. Wason *Happy Hawkins* 277 Dick may have been on the queer all right, but he was smooth enough to hide it.

Queer, *v.* Add: 1. (Later example.)

1854 W. Harcourt in Gardiner *Life W. Harcourt* I. (1923) 76, I hear he does this to queer the Britishers.

2. *esp.* in phr. *to queer the* (or *one's*) *pitch*: (now usu. fig.).

1875 Frost *Circus Life* xvi. 278 The spot they select for their performance is their 'pitch', and any interruption of their feats, such as an accident, or the interference of a policeman, is said to 'queer the pitch'. 1891 *Morn. Advertiser* 27 Mar. (Farmer) His pitch being queered he marched to another point, but here he found the police in possession. 1905 *Pall Mall Mag.* Aug. 176/1 'Twas easy for Saul Adams to queer my pitch. 1912 *Chambers's Jrnl.* Dec. 795/2 All branches of the administration work sensibly and effectively so long as you do not 'queer the pitch' by creating exceptions.

b. To make (persons) queer.

1895 *Century Mag.* Sept. 676/1 Something has queered the whole crowd.

Quench, *v.* 1. (Modern example with *out*.)

1863 E. Wetherell *Old Helmet* (1864) I. xi. 230 In Africa they sit in the darkness of centuries, till almost the spark of humanity is quenched out.

d. *Electr.* To prevent (a spark) occurring at the gap when an electric circuit is broken; also, to reduce or damp (oscillations) in a circuit.

1913 *Chambers's Jrnl.* Mar. 232/2 The oscillatory current in the aerial, and therefore the wave-train radiated, continue long after the spark has been quenched. 1923 E. W. Marchant *Radio Telegr. & Teleph.* 34 The oscillation in the oscillating circuit is then suddenly quenched. 1926 *Gloss. Electr. Terms* (Brit. Engin. Stand.) 190 *To quench*, to extinguish completely the spark in a spark gap at the instant when the energy in the primary circuit first becomes zero.

Quenched, *ppl. a.* (Recent example.)

1913 *Chambers's Jrnl.* Mar. 232/2 In this system the spark dies away very rapidly, and for that reason is called a 'quenched spark'.

Quenching, *ppl. a.* (Recent example.)

1923 *Mod. Wireless* I. 260 The..'quenching' oscillation ..effectively checks the radio-frequency oscillation.

Querl, *v.* *trans.* (Example.)

1840 J. F. Cooper *Pathfinder* xiii. 184 One of his hands coiled a rope against the sun, and he called it *querling* a rope, too, when I asked him what he was about.

Querulist. (Recent example.)

1929 C. E. Montague *Disenchantment* iv. 55 The querulist of the book took it hard, I remember, that more kind words did not come to the men.

Questing, *vbl. sb.* (Later example.)

1923 Sadleir *Desolate Splendour* 72 The weary questing of a stranger mind seek teaching or enlightenment.

Que·stingly, *adv.* [-ly [2].] In a questing manner.

1926 Rex Clements *Stately Southerner* 89, I..looked questingly right and left.

Question, *v.* 5. b. (Modern example.)

1879 Meredith *Egoist* xlvii, At the game of Chess it is the dishonour of our adversary when we are stale-mated: but in life..such a winning of the game questions our sentiments.

Questionee. Delete *rare*[−1] and add earlier and later examples.

1838 Carlyle *Lett. to Mill &c.* (1923) lix. 164 Your answer is according to your question, and your questionee,—'as the fool thinks the bell clinks'. 1905 *Grand Mag.* Feb. 131 The ..questionee does not overlook the fact that [etc.].

Questionnaire (kestionɛr, kwe·styənɛ̄ə). [F. *questionnaire*, f. *questionner* to ask questions, f. *question* Question.] A series of questions submitted or sent to persons to be answered usually for the purpose of obtaining precise information on special points, esp. in statistical investigations; a questionary.

1901 E. B. Titchener *Exper. Psychol.* I. 1. 197 The questionary or 'questionnaire' is a series of questions bearing upon the matter to be investigated. 1908 *Circ. 1st Internat. Moral Educ. Congress* 2 Reports based on widely-circulated Questionnaires will be prepared. 1922 *Times* 3 June 8/1 A period of unusual tension and anxiety in Downing-street followed the dispatch of the questionnaire to the Irish leaders. 1924 W. B. Selbie *Psychol. Relig.* 4 A careful study of the phenomena of religious experience derived mainly from biographies, introspection, and a systematic use of the questionnaire.

b. *attrib.* as *questionnaire-method*.

1924 R. M. Ogden tr. *Koffka's Growth of Mind* ii. 45 With the aid of Hall's questionnaire-method, one of his students has collected a large mass of material concerning children's play.

Questionous (kwe·styənəs). [f. Question *sb.* + -ous.] Given to asking questions; inquisitive.

1893 Bridges *Humours of Court* II. i. 914 Of late you are grown questionous and prying.

Queue, *v.* Add: 1. b. To follow or track (a person's steps, etc.).

1906 Hardy *Dynasts* II. v. i. 254 Perhaps within this very house and hour, Under an innocent mask of Love or Hope, Some enemy queues my ways to coffin me.

2. b. To form *up* in a queue; to take one's place in a queue.

3. *trans.* To arrange (persons) in or as in queues.

1928 *Daily Express* 8 Oct. 1/1 The foot and mounted police..had queued the concourse into twisting lines of people.

Queueing-up. [f. *Queue *v.* 2 b.] The forming of a queue (of persons).

1927 *Brit. Weekly* 21 Apr. 55/3 When the public-houses opened their doors in the evening there was no queuing-up.

Qui·bblingly, *adv.* (Recent example.)

1901 W. J. Craig *King Lear* 117 *note*, Perhaps 'roarer' in *Tempest* I. i. 18, quibblingly applied to the raging waters.

Quick. C. *adv.* 3. a. Add: *quick-drying, -loading*.

1913 V. B. Lewes *Oil Fuel* 91 Explosions..from leakages of volatile spirit used in making up anti-fouling and *quick-drying paint..led to extended investigations being made. 1874 J. W. Long *Wild-Fowl Shooting* 37 A *quick-loading [powder] flask, i.e., one having a large feed-hole to the charger, should also be used.

D. **quick-cake**, a cake that can be prepared and baked in a short time; **quick-change** *attrib.* (also transf.); **quick-change** *v. intr.*, to perform a 'quick-change'; *trans.*, to change quickly; **quick-lunch**, a lunch designed to be served and eaten quickly; a snack; also *attrib.*; **quick-minded** *a.*, having an alert and ready mind; quick-witted; **quick-seller**, an article, esp. a book, that sells quickly; **quick-trick**, in bridge, a card that should take a trick in the first or second round of the suit; an ace or a king.

1925 J. Gregory *Bab of Backwoods* ii. 18 I've got..a pan of chicken already frying and..I'll stir up a *quick-cake for him. 1905 *Daily Chron.* 13 Mar. 5/7 Mr. Balfour's.. Ministry may reasonably be dubbed the '*Quick-change Ministry'. 1906 *Daily Chron.* 12 Nov. 6/4 He *quick-changed with the deftness and speed of a Fregoli. 1928 *Collier's* 18 Aug. 18/3 We had to quick-change our hats, put on badges [etc.]. 1903 *N. Y. Even. Post* 24 Sept. 8 The *quick lunch man a few blocks away from the grocery store. 1907 S. E. White *Arizona Nights* xvi. 231 It's only when he scratches up a measly one-grain quick-lunch that he calls up the hens. 1919 H. L. Wilson *Ma Pettengill* ii. 47, I wondered how he'd come to confer himself on the cashier of a quick-lunch place. 1905 E. Phillpotts *Secret Woman* I. i. 13 She was a girl of soothing curves and soothing voice, *quick-minded under her great composure. 1908 *Daily Chron.* 24 Aug. 1/3 They say they never met such a quick-minded man. 1926 *Ironmonger* Suppl. 16 Jan. 50 Advt., Dealers who stocked early are now enjoying the profits from this *quick-seller. 1927 M. C. Work *Contract Bridge* iii. 58 Two *quick tricks..is the minimum strength with which a Contract denial should be made.

Quick, *v.*[4] [cf. Quicken *v.* 4 b.] *trans.* To coat with an amalgam of mercury.

1873 E. Spon *Workshop Receipts* I. 308/1 A little of this solution is poured into a basin, and with a brush dipped therein they stroke over the surface of the metal to be gilt, which immediately becomes quicked.

Quicken, *v.* 5. b. Add: Also, to make (a slope) steeper.

1838 *Civil Eng. & Arch. Jrnl.* I. 376/2 Retaining walls, or quickening the slopes, might perhaps get over the difficulty.

Qui·cklike, *adv.* [f. Quick A + -like.] In a quick manner; quickly.

1913 Mrs. Stratton-Porter *Laddie* viii, He..looked down the hole I showed him and he cried out quicklike.

Quick-step, *v.* [f. the sb.] quasi-*trans.* with *it*. To march in quick time.

1906 *Daily Chron.* 27 Aug. 4/4 They quick-step it up and down the asphalted front at Hythe.

Quid, *sb.*[3] Add: 2. The pellet or cast of an owl or hawk.

1834 Mudie *Brit. Birds* (1841) I. 141 Mice are preferred to birds, the feathers being more untractable than the fur, both in swallowing and in casting in pellets or quids.

Qui·dlet. Diminutive of Quid *sb.*[2]

1911 L. Tracy *Sylvia's Chauffeur* v, [He] handed Dale a fiver—five golden quidlets, if you please!

Quiescence. Also, the action of making quiet or calm.

1859 Trollope *Bertrams* viii. 71 He had been useful as a great oil-jar, from whence oil for the quiescence of troubled waters might ever and anon be forthcoming.

Quiet, *sb.* Add: 4. c. *On the quiet* (also *quiet-like*): in an unobtrusive or underhand manner; secretly, covertly.

1903 *Westm. Gaz.* 4 July 2/2 They comed and ask me to go and do it for them, on the quiet-like. 1903 A. H. Lewis *Boss* 59 They've put out a lot of money on the quiet among my own people. *a* 1909 'O. Henry' *Roads of Destiny* xviii. 308 He dealt out money on the quiet to his lieutenants.

Quieten, *v.* 1. Add: Also with *down*.

1902 Cutcliffe Hyne *Mr. Horrocks, Purser* 37 Mr. Horrocks had given the wink to the chief steward to go and quieten down the Second-Class passengers. 1908 G. A. Birmingham *Spanish Gold* xxi. 296 We got them quietened down after a bit.

Quie·tening, *ppl. a.* [-ing [2].] That produces quietness or becomes quiet.

1905 *Daily Chron.* 25 Mar. 7/3 The presence of a large addition of police has had a quietening effect on the.. operatives on strike. 1907 *Smart Set* Apr. 26/1 (Born) The sheltering, homely realities, that..gave tangibility to her quietening thoughts.

Quieter. Add: b. The silencer of an internal combustion engine.

1888 Wilson & Grey *Mod. Printing Machinery* 454 The noise caused by the escape of the exhaust gases is greatly minimised by the adoption of the 'quieter' which Messrs. Crossley fix to the end of the pipes.

Quietist. 2. (Further example.)

1923 Deeping *Secret Sanctuary* xxiii, In love he had become a Quietist.

Quiff[1] (kwif). Also quif. [Of obscure origin: cf. Coif.] A curl or lock of hair worn on the forehead, esp. by soldiers.

1902 Farmer & Henley *Slang* V. 350/1 *Quiff* (military), a small flat curl on the temple. 1908 *Daily Chron.* 29 Feb. 7/1 A typical youth of the streets, with a 'quiff' brushed into a curl low down on the forehead. 1925 H. G. Wells *Christina Alberta's Father* II. iii. 224 He had..highly oiled and entirely subjugated sandy hair with an army 'quif' on the forehead.

Quiff[2], U.S. and dial. variant of Whiff *sb.*[1]

1. A puff or whiff of tobacco smoke.

1840 *Southern Lit. Messenger* VI. 447/2 A quiff would now and again ascend and hang like a tropical cloud over the hemisphere of his cranium.

2. A puff or blast of wind.

1912 Masefield *Dauber* v. 268 She came within two shakes of turning top, Or stripping all her shroud-screws, that first quiff.

Quill, *sb.*[1] Add: 2. (Later example.)

1833 Loudon *Encycl. Archit.* § 1975 There are several sorts of quills or sprouts which throw the water up or down, into a variety of forms.

8. a. *quill-machine, -work*.

1846 Dodd *Brit. Manufs.* VI. 182 Sail-making. The *quill machines, ..have a considerable number of quills arranged in a row, and made to rotate rapidly. 1843 *Knickerbocker Mag.* XXII. 164 The Indians prepare it in bark, curiously ornamented with *quill work and beads. 1850 L. H. Garrard *Wah-To-Yah* vi. 93 Their robes, leg-gins, and skin dresses, glittering with beads and porcupine quillwork.

Quilt, *sb.*[1] Add: 1. d. A piece of cloth or other suitable material placed over the frames in a bee-hive.

1904 J. R. G. Digges *Irish Bee Guide* 50 Sheet and Quilts are required upon the frames or supers to preserve heat; to prevent draught; and to keep the bees from ascending into the roof... The quilts should be of felt, carpet, or other warm material. 1920 H. Geary *Bee-keeper's Vade-Mecum* 172 Having placed the sticks in position cover with the calico quilts.

Quilting, *vbl. sb.*[1] 3. (U.S. examples.)

1768 *Essex Inst. Hist. Coll.* XVI. 260 Quilting at my house. 1825 J. Neal *Bro. Jonathan* I. 58 She returned however to the quilting and Peters..to the study of Mr. Harwood. 1851 Alice Cary *Clovernook* 72 There was no big meeting that she was not at, and no quilting that she didn't help to get up.

4. **quilting frame** (examples); **quilting-match** *U.S.* = *quilting-party*; **quilting party** (earlier example).

1854 Mary J. Holmes *Tempest & Sunshine* xx. 274 Said she, 'Mighty good opinion Mr. *Quilting-frames has of me (alluding to Mr. Miller's height); glad I know his mind. 1891 *Harper's Mag.* Oct. 824/1 The quilting frames were hung there also. 1837 *Southern Lit. Messenger* III. 297 Arrayed like the cover produced by the united efforts of a *quilting match. 1835 *Knickerbocker Mag.* VI. 180 It so happened, that there was a great *quilting-party invited to Tecumseh-Place, which assembled all the principal young people of the county.

Quince[2] (kwins). [f. L. *quinque* five.] Used for Quintet.

1907 J. H. McCarthy *Needles & Pins* xxii. 245 So here were a quince of vagabonds transmuted into a flying post.

Quincunx (kwi·nkɒŋks), *v.* [f. the sb.] *trans.* To put in quincunx arrangement.

1847 *Simmonds' Colonial Mag.* June 165 Some [say] that the bushes are not near enough together, and that I ought to quincunx them.

Quinnat. (Later examples.)

1881 *Amer. Naturalist* XV. 178 Only the quinnat has been noticed south of San Francisco. 1888 Goode *Amer. Fishes* 93 Tautog, chogset,..quinnat..are among the best of them.

Quinol. (Add example.)

1892 *Photogr. Ann.* II. 47 For greater density use it combined with the ordinary quinol developer, or in a combined solution.

Quinquennial (kwinkwe·niăl), *sb.* [f. Quinquennium + -al.] A fifth anniversary.

1903 *Westm. Gaz.* 14 Jan. 5/2 This year is our quinquennial.

Quinte·ssenced, *a.* [f. Quintessence + -ed[1].] Reduced to its quintessence; quintessential.

1898 Saintsbury *Sh. Hist. Eng. Lit.* VII. vii. 467 Its charms ..consist in extreme strangeness, in quintessenced or preternatural art.

Quip, *v.* Add: 1. b. To bring *into* a specified state by quipping.

1907 *Daily Chron.* 18 July 4/4 They must at least be brought to understand that the deepest feelings of humanity cannot be quipped into vulgarity.

2. (Recent example.)

1908 *Smart Set* June 50 Audrey in her blithesome way Would quip and jest with roguish glee.

Qui·ppishness. [-ness.] Witty or quippish quality.

1909 Bennett *Literary Taste* vi. 31 Charles Lamb's essay on *Dream Children*..enlivened by a certain quippishness concerning the children.

Quire, *sb.*[1] 3. **quire-wise** (example).

1882 J. Southward *Pract. Printing* (1884) 112 Folio sheets are sometimes required to be..folded within each other, or quirewise.

Quirinal (kwi·rinăl). [It. *il Quirinale*, the name of the royal palace on the Quirinal hill (L. *collis Quirinālis*).] The Italian monarchy or government, *esp.* as opposed to the Vatican.

1920 *Glasgow Herald* 24 Sept. 11 In recent years there has been a marked improvement in the relations between the Vatican and the Quirinal. 1922 *Contemp. Rev.* Nov. 583 The complete accord which exists in practice between the Vatican and the Quirinal.

Quiring, *vbl. sb.*[1] [f. Quire *v.*[1] + -ing[1].] Signatures indicating arrangement in quires.

1922 *J. & J. Leighton's Catal. Old & Interesting Bks.* N.S. III. 209 Without printed quiring, &c., but original MS. signatures remain.

Quiring, *vbl. sb.*[2]: see Choir *v.*

1910 R. Brooke *Coll. Poems* (1918) 67 And such a light, and such a quiring, And such a radiant ecstasy there, They'll know not if it's fire, or dew, [etc.].

Quirk, *sb.* 5. Delete † *Obs. rare*[−1] and add recent example.

1928 Galsworthy *Swan Song* II. x. 188 That indefinable look of a damned soul..awakened within Soames .. the queerest little quirk of sympathy.

Quirk (kwɜ̄ɹk), *sb.*[2] *slang*. [Of unknown origin.] A beginner or apprentice in the Air Service.

1916 *Daily Chron.* 13 Oct. 4/5 The quirk becomes used to the handling of the craft..until..the instructor allows him to fly the machine himself. 1928 Gamble *Story N. Sea Air Station* ix. 133 The pilot, a very harmless, innocent 'quirk', hardly fledged, straight from Chingford.

Quirk, variant of Quirt.

1870 Keim *Sheridan's Troopers* (1885) xx. 139 While belabouring the poor brute with the heavy end of a quirk.

Quirl, variant of Querl. (Examples.)

1854 B. F. Taylor *Jan. & June* 23 [The grape vine's] aspirations were manifested in the display of divers mermaidish-looking ringlets, with two or three dainty 'quirls' therein. 1883 *Century Mag.* Apr. 899/1 All conceivable twists, quirls, and crookednesses. 1889 Rose T. Cooke *Steadfast* xv. 162 A hundred resolute little quirls above the low forehead.

Quirt, *sb.* (Earlier example.)

1845 *Amer. Rev.* Feb. 127/2 The 'quirt', with its long heavy lash of knotted raw-hide.

Quit, *sb.*[2] Add: 2. (See quot.)

1923 J. D. Hackett *Labor Terms* in *Managem. Engineering* May, *Quit*, a voluntary separation from work by an individual worker, usually without notice of intention.

Quite, *adv.* Add: 3. d. *colloq.* Expressing appreciation of or agreement with a statement. Freq. *Quite so*.

1892 Conan Doyle *Adventures of Sherlock Holmes* x, 'This maid Alice, as I understand, deposes that she..put on a bonnet, and went out.' 'Quite so. And she was afterwards seen walking into Hyde Park.' 1896 [see So *adv.* 5 b.] 1924 Galsworthy *White Monkey* II. ii, 'I don't hold with it, myself.' 'No, quite!'

4. d. (Earlier example.)

1865 Locker *Lond. Lyrics* (1872) 96 All that sort of thing, of which Dear Hawthorne's 'quite' the best describer.

Quitter, *sb.*[1] 2. (Later example.)

1900 *Times* 2 Oct. 13/4 He examined the mare and found it suffering from a bad quitter which was discharging matter.

Quitter, *v.*[2] a. (Modern U.S. example.)

1871 Mrs. Stowe *Sam Lawson* 156 An old tom-turkey, that'll strut and gobble and quitter, and drag his wings on the ground.

Qui·tting-time. *U.S.* The time when work is stopped for the day.

1850 F. C. Watson *Camp-Fires Revol.* 111 Every day, he'd come into the work shop, about quitting time, and follow me up to the house. 1888 J. Kirkland *McVeys* 203 Once more Strafford sought Phil at the shop at 'quitting-time', after the latter had got in and cleaned his engine.

Quiz, *v.* Also *transf.* To examine (things).

1906 Hardy *Dynasts* II. II. vi. 199 Better quiz evils with too strained an eye Than have them leap from disregarded lairs.

Quoin, *sb.* 4. Add: **quoin-shaft**, a quoin in the form of a shaft or pillar; **quoin-wedge** = sense 2 b.

1875 R. R. Brash *Eccl. Archit. Ireland* 39/2 The quoin shafts are a feature peculiar to a class of churches in this country which seem to be of nearly one age. 1923 D. H. Lawrence tr. *Verga's Mastro-don Gesualdo* I. iv. 71 We want more man-power—a crane!—or tie a pulley-wheel up there to the beam of the roof—then a quoin-wedge underneath [etc.].

Quoit, *v.* 1. (Modern example.)

1871 L. Lockhart *Fair to See* II. xi. 15 The quoiters quoited.

Quotatious (kwotēɪ·ʃəs), *a.* [f. Quotation + -ous.] Fond of using quotations; quotative.

1903 *Daily Chron.* 10 Apr. 3/2 The myriad quotations of that most 'quotatious' of authors.

R

R. Add: I. 1. b. *r-less*, also of speech, in which the letter *r* is not pronounced.

1902 H. L. Wilson *Spenders* xxiv. 277 Her speech bore just a hint of the soft r-less drawl of the South.

II. 2. R.A. (also) = Royal Artillery. R.C. (Example.) R.M.A. = Royal Marine Artillery. R.N.A.S. = Royal Naval Air Service. R.N.R. = Royal Naval Reserve.

1837 *United Service Jrnl.* May 143/2 Lieut. Howgill, R.A. 1713 Dodd in *Life Bp. Challoner* (1909) I. ii. 15 R. C. Chaplain to an English regiment. 1931 *Times Lit. Suppl.* 19 Feb. 126/3 From his first day to his last at Woolwich he 'loathed' the R.M.A. 1919 C. P. Thompson *Cocktails* 186 They had not seen each other since Perris left the destroyer to adorn the R.N.A.S. with his decorative person. 1902 C. J. Cutcliffe Hyne *Mr. Horrocks, Purser* 85 What's the use of being R.N.R. if you don't let people know it?

Rabanna (răbæ·nă). [Malagasy.] A fabric woven from raffia.

1883 *Encycl. Brit.* XV. 172/2 The chief articles of export being.., rôfia palm cloths (rabànnas) and fibre.

Rabat (răbæ·t), *v.* [f. F. *rabattre* to lower.] *trans.* In descriptive or projective geometry, to revolve (a plane) round its line of intersection with another or the horizontal plane until the two planes coincide. So **Raba·tting** *vbl. sb.*; **Raba·tment**.

1885 *Encycl. Brit.* XIX 801/1 In rabatting the plane π_3 its trace OB with the plane π_2 will come to the position OD. 1908 L. N. G. Filon *Projective Geom.* i. 7 If..we rabat the figure 2 upon the plane a_3 we obtain a new figure 3 in the plane a_1. *Ibid.* 10. § 12. Locus of vertex of projection during rabatment.

Rabbi, *sb.* 2. b. (Modern example.)

1855 Macaulay *Hist. Eng.* xi. (1899) I. 703 One of the great Presbyterian Rabbies..might well doubt whether..he should be a gainer by a comprehension.

Rabbinic. B. *sb.* Also *pl.*

1905 *Jewish Encycl.* XI. 93/2 In 1892 Schechter was elected reader in rabbinics [at Cambridge].

Rabbinism. 2. (Recent example.)

1920 *Missionary Rec.* Apr. 78/2 Here he is more independent, refusing responsibility for not a few of his hero's 'rabbinisms'.

Rabbit, *sb.*[1] Add: 2. e. A poor performer at any game, esp. cricket, golf, or tennis. *slang*.

1906 *Westm. Gaz.* 8 May 1/3 Nearly every eleven has a 'rabbit' or two at the end. 1908 A. W. Myers *Compl. Lawn Tennis Player* 184 There was no draw at all, the manager..merely selecting the four semi-finalists and filling in the gaps with the other players, most of them 'rabbits'. 1926 F. G. Lowe *Lawn Tennis Guide* 13 Even the humblest 'rabbit' will find Lawn Tennis a wonderful hobby and relaxation if he follows and plays it keenly. 1927 *Daily Express* 2 Mar. 3/7 The championships are getting on famously. A great elimination of 'rabbits' took place on Monday and yesterday.

3. a. *rabbit-farm, -fur, -trap*.

1900 J. K. Jerome *Three Men on Bummel* v. 106 A man starting a *rabbit farm with twelve selected rabbits..must, at the end of three years, be in receipt of an income of two thousand a year. 1873 *Pract. Mag.* I. 282 *Rabbit Fur as a substitute for Wool and Cotton. 1856 C. Patmore *Angel in Ho.* II. Prol. 3 But she turn'd pale, for now the beast Found stock-still in the *rabbit-trap,..Unglobed himself.

b. *rabbit-farmer, -farming*.

1900 J. K. Jerome *Three Men on Bummel* v. 106 We did not start *rabbit farming...I have never met a *rabbit farmer myself worth two thousand a year.

c. *rabbit-faced*; *rabbit-proof* adjs.

1905 E. F. Benson *Image in Sand* i, He was a *rabbit-faced little man. 1832 *Planting* 26 (in *Libr. Usef. Kn., Husb.* III) The fence of a forest-tree nursery requires to be *rabbit-proof.

4. **rabbit-foot** (*b*), the foot of a rabbit carried, esp by American negroes, to bring luck; **rabbit-hawk**, the North American red-tailed or hen-hawk; **rabbit-hearted** *a.*, cowardly; **rabbit-punch**, a punch on the back of the neck; **rabbit-rat** (example).

1902 Harben *Abner Daniel* 309 Pole worked the *rabbit-foot on them back there. *a* 1909 'O. Henry' *Roads of Destiny* vi. 101 'It's passed the Senate,' said Lonny... 'That's lucky,' said the pale man. 'Do you carry a rabbit's foot?' 1880 G. W. Cable *Grandissimes* vii. 43 A great *rabbit-hawk sat alone in the top of a lofty pecan-tree. 1904 'O. Henry' *Heart of West* 64 The other eye noticed a rabbit-hawk sitting on a dead limb in a water-elm. 1920 *Chambers's Jrnl.* Dec. 812/1 '*Rabbit-hearted' is an expression commonly used. 1913 Corri *30 Years Boxing Referee* 175 The occipital punch is well described by its other name, the '*rabbit-punch', derived from the way in which a gamekeeper puts a rabbit out of pain. 1879 A. R. Wallace *Australasia* iii. 55 The Peramelidæ, or bandicoots and *rabbit-rats, are small animals with sharp nose and long claws, allied to the kangaroos.

Rabbitry. (Example in sense *2 e.) Also, the play or performance of 'rabbits' in any game.

1930 *Observer* 25 May 16 The rabbitry..is faithful to the definition of the game [*sc.* of golf] as 'pedestrianism round the margin of the links'. 1932 A. Marshall *Mr. Jim* v. 44 Her two younger girls..were made welcome at these [tennis] parties, so that Mrs. Gurdon's rabbitry should not be put to shame.

Rabbity, *a.* (Further examples.)

1925 M. R. James *Warning to Curious* 141 This young man..was rather a rabbity anæmic subject. 1928 *Daily Express* 21 Aug. 4 Tennis enthusiasts are generally enthusiasts over dancing as well, be they Wimbledon 'stars' or the rabbitiest rabbits of the public courts.

Rabble, *sb.*[1] 5. Add: *rabble-rouser*.

1843 Carlton *New Purchase* xxii. 211 Nothing surpasses the munificent promises of a genuine rabble-rouser, just before an election. 1926 *Even. Standard* 12 July 3/2 You need not be a Tammany politician to know the meaning of boodle, gerrymander, carpet-bagger, wirepuller, rabble-rouser.

Rabble, *sb.*[2] Add: 4. *Comb.*, as **rabble-arm** = sense 3.

1905 *Electrochem. & Metall. Industry* May 194/1 The upper four hearths are provided with two rabble-arms each, the sixth and seventh with three rabble-arms, in order to increase the stirring and discharge rather on one side of the furnace.

Rabble, *v.*[2] Add: 2. b. To go *off* as a rabble.

a 1861 T. Winthrop *John Brent* ix. 93 He dismissed his audience with an Amen, and an injunction to keep closer to the train..and not be 'rabbling off to catch grasshoppers'.

Rabbling, *vbl. sb.*[1] (Further example.)

1818 Scott *Rob Roy* xxvii, Nane were keener against it [the Union] than the Glasgow folk, wi' their rabblings and their risings, and their mobs, as they ca' them now-a-days.

Rabelaisian. A. *adj.* (Earlier example.)

1817 Lady Morgan *France* (1818) II. 273 He talked of recovery,..and still emitted some of those sparks of Rabelaisian humour, attributed to him by contemporary wits.

Rabelaisianism. Also, a Rabelaisian feature or characteristic.

1922 *Times Lit. Suppl.* 5 Jan. 9/1 His [Balzac's] mere Rabelaisianisms sometimes bring a later accent into what should be a very simple atmosphere.

Race, *sb.*[1] Add: 8. (Earlier examples.)

e. 1833 Loudon *Encycl. Archit.* § 944 The back wall of the barn is to be sunk sufficiently deep for the wheel of the thrashing-mill and the race (horse-course) from it.

g. 1834–6 Barlow in *Encycl. Metrop.* (1845) VIII. 88/2 The wheel is fixed in what is called a race, formed of stonework, agreeing with the curvature of the wheel.

11. a. *race-ground* (earlier example), *-rider* (later example), *-track*; b. **race-goer**, a frequenter of race-meetings; so **race-going** *vbl. sb.*; **race-mark**, a mark attached to pigeons before a particular race; so **race-mark** *v. trans.*, to supply (pigeons) with race-marks; **race-path**, (*a*) a race-track; (*b*) the channel along which water flows to a mill-wheel; **race-plate**, (*b*) a grooved plate through which matrices pass in a type-setting machine (Webster 1911); **race-trough**, a plank with raised edges along which goods are passed in loading or unloading ships or wagons.

1898 A. E. T. Watson *Turf* 210 If I had to propound a rule for the guidance of a young *race-goer who was determined to bet, I should say [etc.]. 1905 *Westm. Gaz.* 31 Aug. 8/3 The Great Central is..catering for the wants of race-goers. 1929 Susan Ertz *Galaxy* xv. 332 He had always been so busy with his..shooting, his *race-going, and latterly his horses. 1727 *Maryland Hist. Mag.* VII. 400 This Vestry resolve to meet on Thursday..at the *race ground near the Bensons. 1890 *Homing News* 3 Jan. 14/3 Advt., He is not certain about the *race marks. 1928 *Sunday Dispatch* 8 July 22/3 Birds competing in the..race from Marennes,..will be *racemarked at No. 5 platform. 1837 *Knickerbocker Mag.* X. 413 The only *race-path known in this new settlement was that on which the husband and wife contended for the prize of domestic comfort. 1853 F. W. Thomas *J. Randolph* etc. 84 Along the devious narrow race-path to the mill-dam. 1827 J. F. Cooper *Prairie* xxiii, She is no great *race-rider. 1866 'P. V. Nasby' *Struggles* 255 The *race track is plowed up and in cotton. 1897 *Outing* XXX. 88/2 The half-mile track..is not only used for training purposes, but is used also as a race-track. 1842 T. Carlyle in *Cornhill Mag.* (1922) Oct. 496 A huge high pier of wood..lowered down upon us a long *race-trough of wood, by the side of which at due distances some four men stationing themselves [etc.].

Race, *sb.*[2] Add: 11. *race-conflict, -culture, -feeling, -quarrel, -sense, -suicide, -type*; *race-conscious* adj.

1880 Tourgee *Invis. Empire* xii. 513 Any one who asked the support of colored men as against a Democratic nominee was precipitating a *race-conflict. 1927 *Observer* 5 June 5/3 Frenchmen are not so *race-conscious as either Englishmen or Americans. 1909 C. W. Saleeby (*title*) Parenthood and *Race Culture. An Outline of Eugenics. 1907 Mrs. Harris *Tents of Wickedness* IV. iii. 358 There's a large negro vote here. *Race feeling runs higher than in any part of the state. 1931 F. L. Allen *Only Yesterday* iii. 68 If a white man stood up for a Negro in a *race quarrel, he might be kidnapped and beaten up. 1909 *Cent. Dict.* Suppl. *Race-sense. 1901 E. A. Ross in *Ann. Amer. Acad. Pol. & Soc. Sci.* July 88 For a case like this I can find no words so apt as '*race suicide'. 1927 Peake & Fleure *Priests & Kings* 181 '*Race-type' in a general sense is a very difficult matter to define.

Race, *v.*[1] Add: 2. (Further example.)

1901 *Oxford Mag.* 24 Apr. 290/1 [The Oxford crew] never allowing their opponents to increase their lead, but never attempting to race up alongside.

Race, *v.*[3] 1. Read: Now *techn.* and *dial.*

1884 *Upton-on-Severn Gloss.*, *Race, v.*, Pron. of rase, to scratch or abrade.

Race-about. [f. Race *v.*[1] + About *adv.*] A type of sailing-yacht.

1905 *St. Nicholas* Aug. 865 There were other prizes, of course: the much-coveted silver cup,..pennants for the raceabouts and halfraters, and a first money prize of twenty-five dollars for the fishermen's sloops.

Ra·ce-coursey, *a.* [f. Race-course + -y[1]]. Suggestive of or like a race-course.

1923 *Chambers's Jrnl.* Dec. 776/2 The eighth hole..is well adapted for the purpose, being of a long, flat, race-coursey make-up.

Race-horse. 1. (Earlier attrib. examples.)

1845 W. G. Simms *Wigwam & Cabin* I. 32 He had the sanguine, the race-horse temperament. 1848 E. Bryant *California* xxiv. 319 We..were soon on the road again, travelling at racehorse speed. 1868 H. Woodruff *Trotting Horse* ii. 47, I do not undertake to disparage the method pursued by the race-horse men.

Racemic, *a.* Add: *Racemic compound*, an optically inactive combinaton of dextro-rotatory and lævo-rotatory isomers in equal molecular proportions.

1897 *Proc. Chem. Soc.* 3 June 135 Those which closely resemble the corresponding active compounds are called *pseudoracemic*, the name racemic compound being reserved for those of the other group.

Racemism (ræ·səmiz'm). *Chem.* [f. Racemic + -ism.] An optically inactive condition produced by the combination of dextro- and lævo-rotatory isomers. So **Racemiza·tion**, the production of this condition. **Ra·cemise**, *v. trans.*, to make optically inactive through racemism. **Ra·cemised** *ppl. a.* **Ra·cemoid** *a.*, exhibiting racemism.

1896 *Proc. Chem. Soc.* 23 Apr. 97 The ethereal salts..were examined for racemoid compounds, but the quantity found was not sufficient to account for the low activity. *Ibid.*, Some other explanation of the difference of activity of the ethereal salts..must be found than the supposition that the mineral acids cause racemisation. *Ibid.*, In examining.. for the presence of racemised salt by converting it into zinc lactate. 1904 *Science* 5 Aug. 178/2 In the cases of some double nuclei (as the camphor group) racemism appears to be impossible, owing to the peculiar molecular structure.

Racemous, *a.* (Later example.)

1821 W. P. C. Barton *Flora N. Amer.* I. 79 In this case, the floriferous ramuli must be considered as racemous branches.

Raceway. Add: 1. (Earlier example.)

1837 *Knickerbocker Mag.* IX. 254, I was jerked out with great spite, and, with an imprecation, thrown into the raceway.

3. A metal pipe enclosing electric wiring inside a building.

1897 Moore *How to Build* iv. 58 Conduits or raceways for carrying wires through the house should be of iron or other metal.

4. A passage or groove along which types are moved in a type-setting machine.

1898 *Inland Printer* Nov. 178/1 This machine will select the type, place them in a raceway and move them along until a line is set up.

Rachill, variant of Ratchel.

Racial, *sb.* [f. the adj.] A member of a particular race.

1922 *Contemp. Rev.* Aug. 159 When he thinks of the problems of African or Indian racials in the West Indies, he doubtless does not think of them only as they emerge in the West Indies.

Racialism (rē·ʃăliz'm). [f. Racial *a.* + -ism.] Tendency to racial feeling; antagonism between different races of men.

1907 *Daily Chron.* 2 Jan. 6/3 The two principal planks in the party platform are opposition to all racialism and co-operation with the Government. 1910 *Westm. Gaz.* 11 Apr. 10/3 In the country districts [of South Africa] the death of Racialism is most apparent. 1919 J. L. Garvin *Econ. Found. Peace* 198 Liberty and racialism had to break up its bases. 1925 E. S. Jones *Christ of Indian Road* ii. 67 Amid the racial clash and bitterness there stands one who is the Son of man. Racialism withers at his touch.

Racialist (rē·ʃălist). [f. Racial *a.* + -ist.] One who fosters racialism.

1930 *Observer* 22 June 13/4 Some of its characters said things that were calculated to make the blood of headstrong racialists boil.

Racialization (rē·ʃăləizē·ʃən). [f. Racial *a.* + -ization.] The process of making or becoming racial in outlook or sympathies. So **Ra·cialize** *v. trans.*

Raciology (rē̆sio̅·lŏdʒi), *sb.* [f. RACE *sb.*2 + -(O)LOGY.] The scientific study of races of men.

Rack, *sb.*1 Add: **3 e.** *To stand (or come) up to the rack*: to face or bear the consequences of what one has undertaken; to take one's share of hard work or responsibility. *U.S.*

Rack-rent, *sb.* Add: **b.** (Later example.)

Racoon. *b.* Add: **b.** raccoon-cap1 a cap made from the dressed skin of the racoon; racoon-oyster (earlier examples).

Back-bone. (Later example.)

Racker2. (Later examples.)

Racket, *sb.*3 Now usually, any scheme or procedure which aims at obtaining money or effecting other objects by unusual, illegal, and often violent, means; a distinctive form of organized crime in Chicago and other large cities of the U.S.A.

Racket. (Later example.)

Racketeer (rækĕtī·r), *v.* *U.S.* [f. the *sb.*] *trans.* To subject to racketeering.

Racketeering, *vbl. sb.* *U.S.* [f. "RACKET *sb.*3 + -ING.]** The business of racketeers; a system of organized crime directed chiefly to extorting money from business firms by intimidation, violence, or other illegal methods.

Racking, *vbl. sb.*1 Masonry. An arrangement of stones or bricks in successive steps.

Rack-out, *v.* [f. RACK *sb.*4 5.] Designed to rack out.

Rack-pin.

Racoon. *b.* F. Scott *Tom Cringle's Log*

Rad, *a.*2 (Further example.)

Raddled *ppl. a.*2 (Further example.)

Radial, *a.* Add: **2 d.** *Radial velocity*, the velocity of a star along the line of sight of an observer.

radial engine, a type of internal combustion engine having its cylinders arranged like radii of a circle.

B. *sb.* Add: **6.** Short for *radial engine.*

Radiant. B. I. **1.** Also, a substance or body emitting other forms of radiation.

Radiate, *v.* Add: **1.** *spec.* To transmit electro-magnetic waves ; to use a wireless transmitter.

Radiation. Add: **2 b.** The emission of Röntgen or X rays, the rays characteristic of radio-active substances ; radio-active concr., radio-active or X rays.

c. *radiation pressure*, pressure accompanying the incidence of light or other radiations on a surface.

d. *radiation pressure*

Radiator. Add: **b.** (Earlier example.)

Radio-., used in combinations with, or used in wireless telegraphy or telephony.

Radioactinium.

Radical. (Later example.)

Radifuous (radifu-ŏs), *a.* [irreg. f. "RADIO- + L. *-fer* producing + -OUS.] Containing or yielding radium.

Radio (rē̄·dio̅), *sb.* The initial element of "RADIO-TELEGRAPH, "RADIO-TELEGRAPHY, "RADIO-TELEGRAM, "RADIO-TELE-PHONY etc.

Radio-, as comb. form, the first element of the many words in the following section.

Radio-activate, *v.* [next + -ATE.] *trans.* To render radio-active.

Radio-active (rē̄·dio̅-æ·ktiv), *a.* [f. RADIO- + ACTIVE *a.*] Of substances: Undergoing spontaneous atomic disintegration with (or without) the emission of rays capable of penetrating opaque bodies and affecting a photographic plate, and having certain electrical properties.

Radio-activate*, *adv.*

Radio-activity (rē̄·dio̅-æktī·viti), *sb.* [f. RADIO- + ACTIVITY.] The property possessed by a group of elements (radium, polonium, thorium, uranium, etc.) and their salts of emitting corpuscles and rays of a special character.

Radio-element. A radio-active element.

Radio-telegram. A message sent by wireless telegraphy.

Radiogen (rē̄·dio̅dʒen), *sb.* An apparatus for obtaining radium emanation dissolved in water or another liquid.

Radiogram1. (Later examples.)

Radiogram2 (rē̄·dio̅græm), *sb.* [RADIO- + TELEGRAM.] Wireless telegram. Also *attrib.* Hence **Radio-gram·matic**, **Radio·grammed**, *ppl. a.*

Radio-te·lephone (-te·lefōn). [RADIO- + TELEPHONE.] Wireless telephone. Also *attrib.* Hence **Radio-te·lephony**, wireless telephony.

Radiograph, *sb.* [RADIO- 2 b.] = "RADIO-TELEGRAM.

Radio·graphic, *a.*2 [RADIO- 2 b.] = "RADIO-TELEGRAPHIC.

Radio-therapeu·tic, *a.* [f. RADIO- 2 + THERAPEUTIC.] Of, pertaining to, or employing, radio-therapy.

Radio-the·rapy, the treatment of diseases with X rays, the rays from radio-active substances, or other forms of radiation.

Radiography. Add: **b.** The study of radio-activity.

Radish. Add: **b.** (Later example.)

Radium (rē̄·dio̅m), *sb.* [L. RADIUS ray ; -IUM.] A rare metallic element, now regarded as the most important of the radio-active group, discovered in pitchblende by Mme. and M. Curie and M. Bémont, in 1898.

Radiolo·gical, *a.* [RADIO- 2 + -(O)LOGICAL.] Of or pertaining to radiology.

Radiolo·gist, a student of radiology.

Radio·logy (rē̄·dio̅·lŏdʒi), *sb.* [RADIO- + -LOGY.] One of the spines or prickles on the skin of the sea-urchin.

Radiometer. Add: **3.** An instrument for determining the amount of X rays administered to a patient.

Radionize (rē̄·dio̅naiz), *v.*

Radiophone (rē̄·dio̅fōn). [RADIO- 2 b.] A wireless station sending out signals in fog which enable ships to determine their position.

Radiophone. (Later example.)

Radon (rē̄·dŏn), *sb.* [f. RADIUM, and the termination of XENON, NEON, ARGON, etc.] A gaseous radio-active element arising from the disintegration of radium, discovered by Dorn in 1900 and originally named NITON. It is the heaviest of the inert gases; symbol Rn; atomic weight 222; atomic number 86.

Rafale (raf·al), *sb.* [F.] *Mil.* A gust of wind. A series of bursts of fire ; a roll of drums.

Raff, *sb.*1 Add: **3 b.** *spec.* Ore which requires re-crushing.

Raffe, *sb.*

Raffia (ræ·fia), *sb.* Add: **2.** Now extensively employed in handicrafts for making baskets, hats, mats, and similar articles.

Raffia. *b.* Comb. as *raffia-embroidered*, *-fibre*, *-work-bag*; raffia-grass = sense 2.

Raffle, *sb.*1 Add: **3 b.** The hopper is continuously charged.

Raffle. (Later example.)

Rafter1. (Later examples.)

Rafting, *vbl. sb.* (Further example.)

Rag, *sb.*1 **1.** *phr.* *To take the rag off (the back)*: to take the palm ; to surpass everybody or everyone. *U.S.*

Ragging, *vbl. sb.*3 Add: **3.** The process of removing foreign matter from the face of a grind-stone.

Rag-book, a book for children of which the pages are made of unterable cloth.

Raggling, *vbl. sb.*

Raggy (ræ·gi), *a.*2 *slang*.

Raglan. (Earlier and later examples.)

Rag-rhythm. = RAG-TIME.

Rag-time. (Earlier and later examples.)

Rag-wheel. (Later example.)

Rag-baby. A doll made of rags.

Rag-bag. (Add example.) Also *attrib.*

Rag carpet. *U.S.* A carpet or rug made by weaving small pieces of cloth on a warp of canvas or other material.

Ragelessness (Further example.)

Rager (rē̄·dʒə(r)), *sb.*

Ragesome (rē̄·dʒsəm), *a.*

Ragged (ræg·d), *ppl. a.*1

Raggen (ræ·gən), *sb.*

Ragging. (Later example.)

Railless (rē̄·lles), *a.* [RAIL *sb.*2 + -LESS.] Having no rail.

Railman (rē̄·lmæn), *sb.* [RAIL *sb.*2 + MAN.] A man employed on a railway ; a railway man.

Rail-motor. Applied *attrib.* to a self-propelled railway coach or car designed for driving from either end, introduced in 1905.

Railroad, *v.* Add: **b.** *To go in when it rains*, to take measures for one's own safety ; to envisage pending providence ; to save oneself from danger ; to shift for oneself. *U.S.*

Railboard, *v.* [f. RAIL *sb.*2 IV. 9.]

Railroad, *v.* **b.** C. B. GEORGE 40 *Years on Rail*

Rail timber. [RAIL *sb.*2] Timber suitable for making rails.

Railway, *sb.* Add: **3 a.** *railway junction*, *switch*.

Railway, *v.* Add: **b.** To provide with a railway.

Railwaydom (rē̄·lwedəm), *sb.* [RAILWAY + -DOM.] Railways considered collectively ; the railway world.

Rain, *sb.*1 Add: **b.** (Later example.)

Rain-proof, *a.* and *sb.* [f. RAIN *sb.*1 + PROOF *a.* 1 b.] *a. adj.* Impervious to rain. A rain-proof garment ; a rain-coat. Hence **Rain-proofed**, *a.*, rendered impervious to rain ; **Rain-proofing**, a manufacturer of rain-proof fabrics.

Raining-piece. Add: **b.** The portion of the hammer of a striking clock by which it is raised to strike a stroke.

Raise, *v.*1 Add: **12 b.** L, which raises later the numbers of each bank-note. **13.** (Further example.)

Raising (rē̄·ziŋ), *vbl. sb.*1 Like, or suggestive of raisin. In quot. *Comb.*

Rake, *v.*1 Add: **9 b.** *Rake down* (esp. *U.S.*): to win.

Raked (rē̄·kt), *ppl. a.*

Raker, *sb.*3 (Further example.)

Baker3 (Further example.)

Raking, *vbl. sb.*1

Rakily (rē̄·kili), *adv.* [f. RAKISH *a.* + -LY 2.] In a rakish manner.

Raking, *vbl. sb.*[1] Add: 1. *a.* Also *fig.*, refuse.

Rake-off, *U.S.* [f. RAKE *v.*] Profit or commission.

Raliance. (Earlier example.)

Railler, *sb.*[1] (Earlier example.)

Rally, *sb.*[1] Add: 1. *d.* *transf.* A renewed effort for victory in any contest.

3. **b.** (Later examples.) Also, a mass-meeting for any purpose.

Rallier. (Earlier example.)

Rally, *v.*[2] (Earlier example.)

Ram, *sb.*[1] Add: 5. *a.* Of a ship: To advance or make *its* way by ramming.

Ramage (710–1890), a printer of Philadelphia, used *attrib.* to denote a printing-press, or any part *of this*, designed by Ramage.

Rambling (*rɑˈmbliŋ*), [f. RAMBLE + -AGE.]

Rambling, *vbl. sb.*[1] Add. *Also Comb.* as *rambling-club*.

Rambo (*rɑˈmbəʊ*). A variety of apple grown in the U.S.A.

Rambunctions (*rambɒˈŋkʃənz*), a. *U.S.* [app. an alteration of RAMBUSTIOUS, RUMBUSTIOUS. So **Rambunc'tiousness.**

Ramie. Add: Also *ramié*.

Range, *sb.*[1] Add: 9. (Earlier examples.)

Range-block, *-clearer*, *-clearing*, *-indicator*, *-taker*.

Rampa (*rɑ́mpə*), *v.* 1. *spec.* On railways:

Rampa (*closely*), *adv.* [f. RAMPACIOUS + -LY.]

Rampage, *v.* Add: 3. *trans.* To rampage about or over (a place).

Rampart, *sb.* Add: (Later example.)

Ramping, *vbl. sb.*[1] (Earlier example.)

Ramrod. Also, a symbol of stiffness or formality.

Ra·mshackleness. [f. RAMSHACKLE + -NESS.] Ramshackle character or state.

Ramshackry (*rɑ́mˈʃækri*), a. *nonce-wd.*

Ram's-horn. 1. (Later examples.)

Ram·sage, variant of RENEGUE *v.*

Ranch, *v.*[1] Add: To let land for grazing.

Rancho (*rɑ́ntʃəʊ*). (Earlier example.)

Ranching, *vbl. sb.* (Earlier examples.)

Ranchero. (Earlier example.)

Ra·ndy-da·ndy. Redupl. form of RANDY *sb.*

Range, *sb.*[2] (Earlier examples.)

16. *a.* Comb.: *range-beds*, *-rider*.

b. *range-block*, *-clearer*, *-clearing*, *-indicator*, *-taker*.

Rangeless (*rɑ́ndʒlɪs*), a. Of a range: That has no range.

Ranger, *sb.*[1] (Earlier examples.)

Ranginess (*rɑ́ndʒɪnɪs*), [f. RANGY + -NESS.] Rangy quality; capacity for ranging.

Rangland, variant of WRANGLED *ppl. a.*

Rangy, a. 1. *a.* (Earlier example.) Also of persons.

Rani·d (*rɑ́nɪd*), *a.* (and *sb.*), [f. mod.L. *Ranidæ*, f. L. *rāna* frog.] Belonging to the family *Ranidæ* or genus *Rana*.

Rank, *sb.*[1] Add: 1. *a.* A row of public vehicles waiting to be hired, or the place where these stand; a cab-rank.

Rank, *sb.*[4]. (Earlier and later examples.)

Ra·nk-and-file, a. [f. *rank* and *file*: RANK *sb.*[1] 5 *b.*] Belonging to the rank and file; privates; ordinary.

Ranker. 3. Also *transf.*

Ranking, *vbl. sb.*[1] Also *transf.*

Ranking, *ppl. a.* Add: *b.* *U.S.* That takes precedence; leading, foremost.

Rankle, *v.*[1] (Earlier example.)

Ransom, *sb.* 2. (Earlier example.)

Ranter. Add: 4. Comb., as *ranter-like*.

Rap, *v.*[1] Add: 1. *c.* To speak of unfavourably; to criticize adversely. *U.S.*

Raper (*rɑ́pə*). [f. RAPE *v.*[2] + -ER.] One who rapes or ravishes.

Raphaelite. (Example.) So **Ra·phaelitism**, **-RAPHAELISM.**

Rapid, *a.* (Later examples.) Also *fig.*

Rapier. Add: *b.* *attrib.*: *rapier-mounted* adj.

Rapilli. (Later example.)

Raploch, *sb.* and *a.* (Earlier examples.)

Rapped, *ppl. a.* (Later examples.)

Rapper. (Later examples.)

Rapping, *vbl. sb.*[1] Also *transf.*

Rapscallion. (Later example.)

Rapscallionism; the conduct or condition of rapscallions.

Rapt, *ppl. a.* Add: 1. (Later example.)

Rapture, *sb.* Add: *b.* *intr.* To take delight in some rapturous manner.

Rare. (Later examples.)

Rare, *a.*[1] Add: *b.* *rare-bred*, *-feathered* adjs.

Rarefy, *v.* 2. *b.* Also *absol.* or *intr.*

Rat, *sb.*[1] Add: 1. *c.* Naut. rare. A strand in a rope.

Rat-catcher. Add: 2. *slang*. Unconventional.

Ratchel 1. (Later example of **rachill**.)

Ratchet, *sb.* Add: *b.* *ratchet--drill*; *-maker*.

Rate, *v.*[1] Add: rate-cutting, a lowering of rates or charges.

Rater[1].

Rath, *a.* (Earlier example.)

Rathskeller (*rɑ́tskelə*). [G. *raths-keller* town-hall cellar.] A beer-saloon or restaurant in a basement.

Ratification. (Earlier example of *ratification meeting*.)

Ratification-ist. One who favours ratification (of something).

Ratine (*rɑ́tiːn*). [F., cf. RATTEEN.] A dress fabric of rough, open texture resembling sponge-cloth.

3. *attrib.*, as *rating area*.

Ration, *sb.* Add: 3. *c.*

Ration, *v.* Add: 1. *b.*

ration-beef (earlier example), *-book*, *rum*, *-sugar*, *tea*.

Rationalization. Add: 1. (Further examples.)

Rationalize, *v.* Add: 1. *c.* To apply rationalization to (industry).

Ratine. a. (Later example.)

Ratoon, *v.* Add: *b.* *trans.* To cut down (plants) to induce them to send up new shoots. So **Ra·tooned** *ppl. a.*

Ratoo·ner. [f. prec. + -ER.] A plant that ratoons.

Rat-tail. 5. Also in the sense of RAT-TAILED *a.* 2.

Rattan, *sb.* Add: *c.* *rattan screen.*

Rattan, *sb.*[2] Add: *rattan--tree*.

Ratta·nning, *vbl. sb.* [f. RATTAN *sb.*[2] + -ING.] Chastisement with rattan sticks.

Ra·tten, *v.* Add: (Later example.)

Rat-tat. Add: *b.* (Later example.)

Rat-tat-tat, *v.* (Later example.)

Rattle, *sb.*[1] Add: 4. *b.* (Further examples.)

e. A crisp crackling sound made by some kinds of paper when handled; the quality in paper which produces this.

Rattle-weed (earlier example.)

Rattling, *vbl. sb.* Add: (Further examples.)

Rattle. Also. (Later examples.)

Razz (*raz*), *sb.* [Short for *RAZZBERRY.*] Disapproval expressed by hissing or booing directed against an actor or other person.

Razz, *v.* (U.S.)

Razzle-dazzle. 2. *slang*. [Variant of *RAZZBERRY.*]

Reactor (*riˈæktə*). [f. RE-ACT *v.*[2] + -OR, after ACTOR.] An animal or organism that reacts.

Read, *v.* (Further examples.)

Readership. Add: 3. *Comb.*, as *reader-paper*.

Real, *a.* and *sb.*[3] Add: 10. *Real school* (trSt.), *etc.*

Real-estate, *attrib.* *U.S.* [See ESTATE 10.]

Realm. 2. (Further examples.)

Realtor (*riːəltə*). *U.S.* A real-estate agent or broker (*spec.* one who is a member or affiliated member of the National Association of Real Estate Boards).

Ream, *v.*[2] (Later examples.)

Reamed, *ppl. a.* [f. REAM *v.*[2] + -ED[2].]

Reamer. Add: 1. *b.* A person who analyses designs in textile fabrics for the purpose of reproducing them.

Re-arrange. (Earlier example.)

Rea·rwardness. [f. REARWARD sb. + -NESS.] The state of being in the rear or in arrears.

Reason·ded, ppl. a. [Later example.]

Reason. sb.1 23. Add: r. *reason-wrought* adj.

Reason, v. Add: 6. b. [Later example.]

Rebate, sb. [Further attrib. example.] Also *Comb.*

Rebato. [b. (Modern example of rabato.)]

Rebel, v. 2. [Modern fig. example.]

Re-bid (rī-). v. [RE-5 a.] trans. and intr.

Rebo·untiin, d. [REBOANT + -IC.] = REBOANT.

Reboard, v. [Modern example.]

Rebound, sb. 3. Add: d. Also *on the rebound.*

Re-broadcast, sb. [f. the vb.] The action or fact of broadcasting matter again; also, matter that is broadcast again.

Re-broa·dcast v. [RE-5 a.]

Rebu·kcaivelly, adv. [f. REBUKE v. + -ATIVE + -LY 2.]

Rebu·rgeoning, vbl. sb. [f. REBURGEON v. + -ING 1.]

Recalcitrant. B. sb. [Further example.]

Recall. [Later example.]

Recall, v. 8. Add: e. attrib., as *recall signal.*

Recap, v.

Reca·pitalize (rī-). v. [RE-5 a.] trans. To capitalize again. So **Reca·pitaliza·tion.**

Recapitulation.

Recast, v. 1. [Modern example.]

Recce, sb. [Further attrib. example.]

Rece·ivable, a. [RECEIVE v. + -ABLE.] That has received or is drawn back.

Receivable, a. [Later example.]

Receive, v. 4. [Further example.]

Recei·ver. 1. Add: 2. d. An official having charge of the equipment and maintenance of the Metropolitan Police.

Recidivist. Also *attrib. or adj.*

Recipience. Add: b. 5 as sb. A recipient of condition.

Recipiency. [Later example.]

Reciprocator. Add: b. *spec.* A double-acting steam engine.

Recitation. [Later examples.]

Receiving, ppl. a. Add: b. 2. b. Applied to a *receiving-house* (later example), *receiving-set, -station.*

Reception. Add: 6. c. The receiving of wireless messages; the method by which or the efficiency with which signals, messages, etc. are received.

Receptionist. Add: 2. A person employed by a surgeon, dentist, photographer, etc., to receive consultants or clients.

Recession. Add: 3. Add: b. *Biol.* Applied to a character possessed by one parent which is not visibly inherited by offspring when the other parent possesses the contrary dominant character. Also as sb., a recessive character.

Recessiveness. [f. *RECESSIVE a.* + -NESS.]

Recommend, v. 5b. [Earlier and later examples.]

Recommendation. Add: 7. Something that is recommended; (in quot. 'investments').

Recommission (rī-). v. [RE-5 a.]

Recommit, v. [Later example.]

Recompense, v. [Modern example.]

Reconcilable, a. Add: 5 as sb. A reconcilable person.

Reconcile, v. 5. b. [Later example.]

Reconcilingly, adv. [f. RECONCILING ppl. a. + -LY 2.] In a reconciling manner.

Recondi·tion (rī-). v. [RE-5 a.] trans. To restore to a proper, habitable, or usable condition; to repair or rehabilitate. So **Recondi·tioning** vbl. sb.

Reconnoi·tringly, adv. [f. RECONNOITRING ppl. a. + -LY 2.] In a reconnoitring manner.

Reconsti·tuted, ppl. a. [RECONSTITUTE v. + -ED 1.]

Reconstruct, v. Add: 3. *U.S.* To win over or reconcile to the Federal system of government.

Reconstruction. Add: 1. c. (See quot.)

Reconstructional, a. [RECONSTRUCTION + -AL.] Of or pertaining to reconstruction; reconstructionary.

Recount, sb. [Modern example.]

Recoup, v. 3. b. Also *absol.* or *intr.*

Recovered, ppl. a. [Further example.]

Receptor. Add: 4. *attrib.*, as *receptor cell, group, organ, system.*

Recapitalization. [Another example.]

Recoil, sb. 4. a. Add: (sense 2) *recoil action.*

Recommend, v. [Earlier and later examples.]

Record-breaker, *-smasher, -smashing.*

Recoverer. 1. [Later example.]

Recovery. Add: 10. *attrib.*, as *recovery school* (sense 2).

Recrement. 2. b. (Recent example.)

Recumbency. [Modern example.]

Recruital. 1. [Modern example.]

Recruiter, (rĭcrū·tĭ). slang. [f. RECRUIT v. + -EE.] = RECRUIT sb. 1.

Recruiting, vbl. sb. Add: *recruiting-market, -office, station.*

Recrui·tship [-SHIP.] The position of a recruit.

Rect, a. Add: 4. *fig.* Upright.

Rectally (rĕ·ktǎli), adv. [f. RECTAL + -LY 2.] In a rectal manner; through the rectum.

Rectification. 7. Transformation of an alternating electric current.

Rectified, pa. pple. [f. RECTIFY v.] Of tulips

Rector. Add: 3. d. *R.C.Ch.* A head parish priest.

Rectress. Add: 3. The wife of a Rector.

Recumbent. A. adj. 1. b. [Further example.]

Recuperator. Add: 3. An agency that restores a person's health.

Recurrent. II. 4. a. Add: 3. [Further example.]

Recurringly, adv. [f. RECURRING ppl. a. + -LY 2.] In a recurring manner; repeatedly.

Red. A. adj. Add: 3. [Later example.]

Reduction. [Earlier example.]

Redactor. [Later example.]

Red-cross, v. [f. the sb.] trans. To mark with a red-cross.

Reduction. Add: 10. c. *Cytol.* The process by which the number of chromosomes in reproductive cells is halved. Also *attrib.*

Reductive. B. adj. [Modern example.]

Red-eye. Add: 4. (Earlier and later examples.)

Reed. sb.1 Add: 12. b. The thin concentric layers of wood as shown in a longitudinal section.

Red-horn, a fog-horn in which the sound is produced by a current of air blowing on a reed (sense 14), usually a knife-like instrument used in tuning a reed-organ; a tuning-knife; reed-mark (see quot.), reed-marked d., of cloth, having the warp threads lying unevenly.

Reed, v. Add: 4. *Weaving.* To pass (warp threads) through the splits of a reed.

Reeded, ppl. a. Add: b. Of wood: having a specified kind of reed (sense 12 b).

Reediness. [Further example.]

Reedon court, sb. Also *attrib.*

Reedling. [Later example.]

Reef. sb.1 Add: 1. [Further example.]

Reefy, a. [f. REEF sb.1 + -Y.]

Reefable, a. [f. REEF v.1 + -ABLE.] Capable of being reefed.

Reefing, vbl. sb. Add: *reefing-wheel.*

Red-water. 3. Also *red-water ordeal.*

Reemer. [Cf. REAMER.] A workman employed in reaming.

Re-encounter, sb. b. [Later example.]

Re-enforce. [Accommodating which re-enforces.]

Re-enlist, v. [f. RE-ENLIST v. + -ER 1.] A person who enlists again.

Re-entrance. Add: b. *Electr.* Of an armature winding, the act or condition of returning upon itself. So **Re-e·ntrancy.**

Re-entrant. A. adj. Also *Electr.* (see quot.)

Re-entry. 2. b. Card of re-entry (also in bridge). To re-entry card.

Re-export, v. [f. RE-EXPORT sb. + -ER 1.] One who re-exports.

Re-export. Add: 3. To face (a person) again.

Reface, v. Add: 3. To face (a person) again.

Refer, v. 7. f. To call (a candidate) in an examination and direct (him) to sit again at a later date.

Referendal (referē·ndǎl), a. [f. REFERENDUM + -AL.] Of, pertaining to, or connected with giving decisions on matters about which reference is made.

Referent, sb. [Later example.]

Refiguration (rĭfĭgiurēi·ʃən), sb. A renewed arithmetical calculation. (In quot. *fig.*)

Refill (rī·fĭl), sb. [f. the vb.] Designed or appointed to refill a person.

Refill (rĭfĭ·l), v. [Later example.]

Refine, v. [Later example.]

Refiner, sb. Add: 1. c. A special form of beater employed in paper-making.

Refinery. Add: XX. 1. 497 By the care of the refiner the necessaries in the refining.

Refinished, ppl. a.

Reflection. Add: 1. c. *transf.* Of the atmosphere: To change the direction in which the incidence sound is propagated because of the increased velocity of the wind or lower temperature of the air at higher levels.

Refraction. Add: 3. c. The change in the direction of sound waves produced by different temperatures of the air at different velocities at different levels.

Refractive. Add: 5. Having power to refract.

REFRACTOMETRIC

Refractome·tric, a. [f. REFRACTOMETER + -IC.] Of or pertaining to a refractometer; made by means of refractometry. So **Refracto·metry,** the measurement of the refractive power of media.

Refracture, sb.

Refresher. Add: **c. attrib.**

Refrigerating, vbl. sb. Add: attrib.

Refrigerator. 2. b. (Earlier example.)

Refuge, v. 2. (Further fig. example.)

Refugee, sb. Add: 3. c. refugee camp.

Refund, v. 1. (Later example.)

Refusing, vbl. sb. (Later example.)

Refusive.

Regain. sb.

Regal. B. 1. 3. a. (Modern hist. example.)

Regalia 2. (Earlier example.)

Regard, v. 7.

Regardless, a. 1. b. ellipt. (passing into adv.) for regardless of expense.

Registered, ppl. a. Add: b. Of a rope.

Regrade, v.

Regress, v. 2. (Further examples.)

Regression. Add: **b.** *Psycho-analysis.*

Regime. Add: 3. transf.

Regimen. Add: b.

Regional, a. adj. Add: 3. b. Army slang.

Regionaliza·tion.

Regre·ntalous. [f. REGENTAL a. + -NESS.]

Begrou·pment.

Regrow, v.

Regular. C. regular-built (earlier example).

Regulator. 5. b. [f. Regulator lamp.

Rehabi·litating, vbl. sb.

Rehearsed, ppl. a. Add: b.

Reigner. (Recent example.)

Reimergence.

Reimpression. (Recent example.)

Reincarna·tionism. [f. REINCARNATION + -ISM.]

Reined, ppl. a. 1. Also rein·ed-back.

Reinfected, v. Also fig.

Reinforced concrete.

Reissue, v. b. (Further examples.)

Reject, v. 1. b. spec. A person rejected as unfit for military service.

Rejected, ppl. a. as sb. A rejected person or thing.

Rejection, sb. Add: [L.] ...

Rejector.

Rejuvenate, v. 1. b. transf.

Relativist. Add: 2. One who studies or holds the theory of relativity.

Relativistic, a. Connected with or based on relativity.

Relativity. Add: 3. That branch of physics which is concerned with the correlation of the descriptions of phenomena by observers using frames of reference in relative motion with respect to each other.

Relaxing, ppl. a.

Relegation. Add: 1. c. In Association Football Leagues.

Relent, sb. 1. (Recent example.)

Reliability. Also attrib.

Reliable, sb. as sb.

Relict, sb. Add: 2. c.

Relief, sb. Add: relief-carving; relief map.

Relay, v. Add: 4. trans. In ordinary and wireless telegraphy: To re-broadcast (signals, messages, music, etc.) by means of suitable apparatus.

Release, sb. Add: 6. c.

Release, v. Add: 7.

Releasing, ppl. a.

Relieve.

Religious. A. adj. Add: 5. Comb., religion-minded, -mindedness.

Reliever.

Relinquish, v. 2. Also absol.

Reliquary, a. Add: b. Residual.

Re-lished, ppl. a.

Relocate, v. 2. (Earlier example.)

Relucence.

Reluctant. Add: + -ISM.]

Remainder. 1. 6. remainder binding (recent example); also (sense 5) remainder binding, v.

Remainder·ed, ppl. a.

Relegation.

Relievo, sb.

Remember, v.

Remedy, v. 6.

Remeet, v.

Remembrance, sb. Add: 10. attrib.

Remembrance Day, the anniversary of the Armistice on 11th November 1918.

Remicle.

Remigratory, a.

Remigrant (re·migrant), sb. [f. L. remigrant- stem of remigrāre to remigrate + -ANT.] Pertaining to or connected with roving.

REMIND. 169 REPERTORY. REPETEND. 170 RESIDUARY.

Remind, v. 2. Also absol.

Reminiscing, vbl. sb. The action of the verb REMINISCE.

Remi·ttence. [as REMITTENT + -ENCE.]

Remnant. 2. d. as sb.

Remonetize.

Remove, sb. Add: c. attrib., as remove-master.

Removed, ppl. a. 3. (Further example.)

Remuda (remū·da). [Sp. remuda exchange.]

Remnant·al.

Renaissanci·st.

Render, v. Add: 10. c. To make (a decision).

Rendezvous, v.

Renegade. Also ruangue. 3. and 4 b.

Renege, v. Also ruangue. 3. and 4 b.

Reni·. Add: rent-portal (see PORTAL 2).

Renig. U.S. variant of RENEGUE.

Rent, sb.1 Add: 2. d. For rent: to be let for rent.

Repetend (re·ptend), a. [ad. L. repetendus, gerundive of repetere to REPEAT.] That is to be repeated.

Replace, v.

Replaceability replaced.

Repressed, ppl. a. *Psycho-analysis.*

Repression. 2. (Further examples.)

Replay, v. Also, to play (a gramophone record) a second time.

Replete, a. (rɪplē·t). *Path.*

Replication. 3. b. Add: *Obs.* in English courts since 1875.

Replotter.

Replumbing (rī-), vbl. sb. [f. RE- 5 a.]

Reply, sb. Add: 2. b. A pleading by the plaintiff after the delivery of the defence.

Reply-paid.

Reportorial, a. Of a reporter.

Repository.

Repertory. Add: 4. attrib., as repertory theatre.

Repo·sal.

Repose, sb. 5. b.

Repositional, a.

Representativity (reprezentātī·vĭti). Representative character; representativeness.

Repress, v.1 Add: 3. a. *Psych.* To check or refrain from exercising (a tendency, desire or instinct).

Re-roller. [f. RE-ROLL v.]

Re-rubber, v. [f. RE- 5 a.]

Reprobationary.

Reproduction. (Modern example.)

Reprobationary, a.

Reprobation, sb.

Reptilian.

Reptiliary.

Republican.

Repudiationist. (Later example.) Also attrib.

Republication.

Reportial.

Repute.

Reputed.

Required, ppl. a. 1. (Further example.)

Reputable.

Rescind.

Rescind.

Rescue, v. 1. b. rescue bid (see 3).

Research, sb. Add: 4. attrib. and Comb., research degree, doctorate, officer, scholar, station, student, worker.

Rescuing, vbl. sb. (Later example.)

Researchist (rĭsɔ·ɹtʃist).

Reserval.

Reservation. (Later examples.)

Reservationist.

Reserve, sb.

Reservoir.

Reserval.

Resettle.

Resident. B. sb.1 Add: c. An animal that does not migrate.

Residentially, adv.

Residuary. Add: 3. **c.** Applied to the Established Church of Scotland after the Disruption of 1843.

Residue, *sb.* 3. Delete *Obs.* and read: Now only in some special senses. a. In the theory of numbers: (see quot. 1890). b. In the theory of functions of a complex variable: (see quot. 1893).
1890 *Century Dict.* s.v. *Residue*, Any fourth power of an integer divided by 5 gives as remainder either 0 or 1. These are, therefore, the *biquadratic residues of* 5. 1893 A. R. Forsyth *Theory of Functions* ii. 42 Such a coefficient A, the coefficient of $\frac{1}{z-a}$ in the expansion of the function, is called by Cauchy the *residue* of the function relative to the point.

Resilient, *a.* Add: 3. b. as *sb.* A resilient person.
1913 *Chambers's Jrnl.* Feb. 99/1 The sailor is a resilient, with fewer cares ashore than landsmen.

Re-silver, *v.* Also, to coat (the glass of a mirror) anew with mercury amalgam.
1875 [in Dict.]. 1910 *Chambers's Jrnl.* Apr. 268/1 The inventor resilvered half the mirror-back by his process.

Resin, *sb.*³ 3. Add: resin-gnat (see quot.); resin-wash, a liquid insecticide containing resin.
1895 Comstock *Man. Insects.* 447 The *Resin-gnat, *Diplosis resinicola*. This species infests the branches of various species of pine. 1900 *Yearbk. U.S. Dept. Agric.* 260 The Kerosene and *resin washes formerly used in California have now given place, to a considerable extent, to a modification of kerosene wash known as 'distillate'.
b. *resin-gall.*
1896 W. R. Fisher in *Schlich's Man. Forestry* V. 71 Isolated trees are more subject to resin-galls than those grown in a dense wood.

Resined, *ppl. a.* Add: b. Of wood: From which resin has been extracted or collected.
1926 *Contemp. Rev.* May 640 Resined wood lasts better than wood not resined, or wood from the same tree above the limit of the cuts.

Resiner (re·zinəɹ). [f. Resin *sb.* + -er ¹ or ad. F. *résinier*.] A person who collects resin from pine trees.
1922 *Chambers's Jrnl.* July 429/2 The professional resiners ..usually receive one half of the raw material as their remuneration.

Re·sining, *vbl. sb.* [f. Resin *sb.* + -ing ¹.] The action of collecting resin from trees; in quot. *attrib.*
1926 *Contemp. Rev.* May 640 The resining process in some degree seasons the wood.

Resinized, *ppl. a.* Add: b. Containing resin.
1908 W. R. Fisher *Schlich's Man. Forestry* (ed. 2) V. 706 Resinised wood, owing to its easy combustibility, is excellent for kindling purposes, and in mountain districts abroad is still employed for torches.

Resinosis (rezinōᵘ·sis). [mod.L. f. L. *rēsina* Resin + -osis.] The formation of resin in trees and plants.
1902 *Encycl. Brit.* XXXI. 578/1 Outflows of resin—*Resinosis*—also come under this general heading. 1908 W. R. Fisher *Schlich's Man. Forestry* V. 83 When wood is wounded and exposed, resin instead of water passes into the cell-walls (resinosis).

Resinous, *a.* Add: 5. b. *Geol.* (See quot.)
1882 Geikie *Text-bk. Geol.* 87 *Resinous* is the term applied to vitreous rocks having the lustre of pitchstone and others which are still less vitreous.

Resistance. 1. (Further example.)
1931 F. L. Allen *Only Yesterday* vii. 169 To cajole, exhort, or intimidate the consumer into buying,—to 'break down consumer resistance'.
6. resistance-furnace, an electric furnace; resistance-welding (see quot.).
1904 *Elect. World & Engin.* 23 Jan. 176 (Cent. Suppl.) *Resistance-furnace. 1926 *Gloss. Electr. Terms.* (Brit. Engin. Stand.) 212 *Resistance welding*, the welding of metals by means of heat generated by passing a current between the two metals or the two portions of metal to be welded.

Resistant. A. *adj.* Add: b. That withstands adverse biological or climatic conditions, diseases, pests, etc.
1897 Muir & Ritchie *Man. Bacteriol.* 291 An animal is shedding into the air..myriads of bacilli which may rapidly spore, and thus arrive at a very resistant stage. 1898 *Yearbk. U.S. Dept. Agric.* 57 The introduction and cultivation of varieties of *Vitis vinifera* on resistant stocks in that region. 1925 *Scribner's Mag.* July 1/1 Genetics has made possible better strains of livestock...Disease is less to be feared because of resistant stocks.

Resistive, *a.* Add: b. as *sb.* A body which offers resistance to an electric current.
1903 *Elect. World & Engin.* 11 Apr. 607 (Cent. Suppl.) A non-inductive resistive in the shape of a barrel of water was connected between the common bus-bar and ground.

Resistor. [-or.] = Resister 2.
1905 *Sci. Amer.* Suppl. 27 May 24586/1 The resistance medium or 'resistor', when solid, usually consists of a core of carbon, coke, or graphite.

Resole, *v.* Add: b. *intr.* To admit of being resoled.
1922 *Daily Mail* 24 Nov. 11 Advt., You can get 'cheap' shoes which look worse every day you wear them, and won't re-sole once.

Resolvancy (rɪzǫ·lvănsi). [f. Resolve *v.* + -ancy.] An outcome or solution.
1930 Gwen. Greene *Two Witnesses* 84 The crowded confused days..have to reach their own resolvancies.

Resonance. 3. Add: *resonance vibration.*
1909 *Westm. Gaz.* 4 Sept. 10/1 If the period of vibration of the two parts is the same 'resonance vibrations' are set up.

Resonant. A. *adj.* Add: 2. b. Of colours: Emphasizing each other by contrast.
1887 W. Armstrong in *Portfolio* XVIII. 233/2 His painting has ever become slighter, higher in tone and less full and resonant in color.

Resonate, *v.* Add: b. *trans.* To act as a resonator for.
1904 *Phys. Rev.* Apr. 231 Having the radiating aërial resonating the primary circuit, it is now necessary to have a second primary circuit in tune with the first.

Resonator. 3. Also *attrib.*
1907 *Phys. Rev.* May 421 As Garbusso first showed, the resonator gratings here used possess selective properties for electric waves.

Resort, *sb.* Add: 7. (Further example.)
1893 Kate D. Wiggin *Polly Oliver* ii. (1894) 30 She would become the head of a summer resort, with a billiard-room and a bowling-alley.
b. *attrib.*
1928 *Publishers' Weekly* 3 Nov. 1866/2 On one occasion we drove fifty miles to one of the biggest resort hotels north of Portland. *Ibid.* 1868/1 The..delay involved when a package must change trains in a resort railroad station.

Resorter. (Recent example.)
1927 *Scribner's Mag.* Apr. 383/2 Take me along on a Southern trip to see what the rich resorters are wearin'?

Resound, *v.* 1. Also with *to.*
1861 F. O. Morris *Rec. Anim. Sagacity & Character* 121 He..lies buried..in those very shrubberies which had so often resounded to his joyous cries.

Respect, *sb.* Add: 18. *Comb.*, as *respect-worthy* adj.
1915 Quiller-Couch *Nicky-Nan* xxiii. 296 A neighbours' quarrel, and between folks I know to be so respectworthy.

Respirator. 2. b. Any form of protection against poison-gas; a gas-mask.
1916 'Ian Hay' *First Hundred Thous.* xvi. 215 In his breast-pocket he carries a respirator.

Responder. (Further example.) Also, an instrument that responds to stimuli.
1904 *Elect. Rev.* 3 Sept. 330 (Cent. Suppl.) The principle of this receiver or 'responder', is based upon the fact that the Hertzian oscillations produce sudden electrolytic action in a cell containing certain electrodes and solutions. 1932 *Daily Tel.* 8 Oct. 15/5 The partner of the opening bidder is known as the responder.

Responding, *ppl. a.* (Further example.)
1921 Gwen. Cecil *Life Ld. Salisbury* II. vi. 219 His action was generally attributed to the decision to call out the Reserves..and Lord Beaconsfield implied as much in his responding speech.

Response. Add: 6. *Comb.*, as *response-movement.*
1892 tr. *Ziehen's Introd. Physiol. Psychol.* i. 14 Goltz has termed the automatic movements 'response-movements'.

Responsivity. Delete *rare*⁻¹.
1900 *Smithsonian Rep.* i. 68 A principle of knowledge which may appropriately be styled the responsivity of mind.

Rest, *sb.*¹ 14. a. Add: *rest-room*; rest-gown, a gown used for evening wear at home.
1915 *Home Chat* 20 Nov. 326/1 Evening dress..has ceased to exist, its place being taken by smart little demi-toilettes for restaurant and theatre wear, and *rest-gowns that are really restful for home wear. 1925 Joan Sutherland *Circle of Stars* xxvi. 287 Gathering the folds of her rest-gown about her, Norma went up to the next story. 1929 *Daily Tel.* 8 Jan. 12/2 Boys' and girls' clubs, holiday camps, reading-rooms, *rest-rooms and institutes.

Rest, *v.*¹ Add: 2. f. *To rest up*: to recover one's strength by resting. *U.S.*
1911 H. S. Harrison *Queed* x. 125 She had been remanded to bed for a day or two to rest up. 1918 W. J. Locke *Rough Road* xix. 239 They packed me home for a fortnight to rest up—while the regiment, what there's left of it, went into reserve. 1922 Zane Grey *To Last Man* xiii. 284 Get rifle and ammunition, bake bread, and rest up before taking again the trail of the rustlers.

Restarter (rī-). [f. Restart *v.* + -er¹.] One who or that which restarts; a device for starting a phonograph or gramophone again.
1927 W. E. Collinson *Contemp. Eng.* 112.

Resta·ter (rī-). [f. Restate *v.*² + -er ¹.] A person who restates.
1925 G. O'Brien *Econ. Effects Reformation* ii. 125 Luther ..regarded Christ and the Apostles as merely the restaters and expositors of the Decalogue.

Restaurative (restǫ·rătiv), *a.*² [F. *restauratif*, L. *restaurāt-* ppl. stem of *restaurāre* to Restore; cf. -ive.] = Restaurant *attrib.*
1875 in G. J. Holyoake *Hist. Co-op.* (1906) I. 141 In a short time the restaurative omnibuses will circulate through Paris. ..These vehicles will contain broth and sauce for the whole city.

Rester ¹. Add: 2. A ledge for placing articles on in front of a balcony.
1921 *L.C.C. Rep. Theatres & Music Halls Com.* (in L.C.C. Proc. 1922) 158 In order to prevent trays..being pushed off the resters in the front of balconies at theatres, etc... we have ..decided to require..that the rester shall be sloped at, say, an angle of 30 deg.

Rest-house. Add: b. A boarding-house or inn for persons requiring rest and recreation.
1928 Galsworthy *Swan Song* iii. ii. 231, I feel I should be ever so much more interested if I ran a place of my own in the country—a sort of rest-house that I could make attractive for girls who wanted air and that.
c. *Comb.*, as *rest-house keeper.*
1909 R. Farrer in *Athenæum* 24 Apr. 492/1, I dislike the ramshackle rest-house, and its rude indifferent rest-house-keeper.

Resting, *ppl. a.* 1. b. Also *resting bud.*
1904 *Nature* 24 Nov. 76/2 Figures are given of resting-buds, twigs and their transverse sections [etc.].

Resto·ringly, *adv.* [-ly².] In a restoring manner.
1846 Lowell in *Hist. Amer. Lit.* II. (1919) 250 Falling gently and restoringly as the dew on the withered youth-flowers of the oppressor.

Restrainer. Add: 2. b. *Electr.* A chemical used to increase the life of the electrodes of an arc-lamp.
1904 *Elect. World & Engin.* 21 May 975 (Cent. Suppl.) A much better method of producing electrodes was found by not reducing the material but adding a restrainer.

Restraint, *sb.* Add: 6. *Comb.*, as *restraint summons.*
1910 *Daily Chron.* 11 Mar. 5/3 The restraint summons was served on the town clerk..yesterday forenoon.

Resu·rface (rī-), *v.* [Re- 5 a.] *trans.* To provide with a fresh surface.
1900 *Yearbk. U.S. Dept. Agric.* 352 When the road was resurfaced with limestone..it became excellent. 1929 *Daily Express* 11 Jan. 2/2 If these minor roads were..strengthened and resurfaced in accordance with modern road practice [etc].

Resurrectible (rezʊ̆re·ktib'l), *a.* [f. Resurrect *v.* + -ible.] Capable of being resurrected.
1924 *Countries of the World* II. 1197/1 The eighteenth century wisely saw that the founder, Henry VI., was dead, and his architect not resurrectible.

Resurre·cting, *vbl. sb.* [f. Resurrect *v.* + -ing ¹.] The action of the verb Resurrect.
1906 P. Lowell *Mars & its Canals* xii. 130 To call the lunar *maria* seas may..be..only a resurrecting in epitaph what was the truth in its day.

Resurrection, *sb.* 5. c. Add: *Resurrection fern* = Resurrection plant.
1924 J. A. Thomson *Science Old & New* v. 30 The 'resurrection fern',..curls up its fronds in drought, and uncurls them when the rains return.

Resuscitable. Delete *Obs. rare*⁻¹.
1842 Carlyle *New Lett.* (1904) I. 250 It lies buried under two centuries of quackeries, scepticisms, owleries,—*not* resuscitable. 1919 W. De Morgan *Old Madhouse* xvii. 274 Flinder's mill-pool yielded when dredged a resuscitable corpse.

Re·take (rī-), *sb.* [f. the vb.] The action of filming a scene over again in taking motion pictures; a film or picture obtained thus.
1918 Homer Croy *How Motion Pictures are Made* v. 126 Directly on finishing the scene it is filmed again, the second exposure being called a 'retake'. 1919 H. L. Wilson *Ma Pettengill* ii. 67 Only one little retake, where she's happy over her boy's promotion in the factory.

Retaliator. (Earlier example.)
1788 W. Gordon *Hist. Amer. Revol.* IV. 287 A set of vindictive rebels, known by the designation of *Monmouth retaliators.*

Retarder. (Further examples.)
1902 *Rep. Admir. Comm. on Naval Boilers* § 29. 15 The Committee..think it right to state that retarders will be found in many cases to render existing cylindrical boilers more efficient and economical than they are at present. 1905 *Chambers's Jrnl.* Mar. 237/2 The planting of trees, bushes, and sand-loving plants as retarders to sand-movement is of great effect.

Rete·ller. [Re- 5 a.] One who tells or relates anew.
1929 *Camb. Med. Hist.* VI. xxv. 827 It must be admitted that Chrétien himself does not claim to be an inventor, but rather a re-teller of tales.

Retention. Add: 3. d. Something that is kept back or retained.
1922 *Daily Mail* 15 Dec. 11 Major Doyle both rode and trained Ilderton, who looked a cheap retention at 100 gs.

Retentiveness. Add: b. *Electr.* = Retentivity.
1885 J. Hopkinson in *Phil. Trans.* CLXXVI. 465 If hard steel were bedded as small particles in a non-magnetic matrix, we should expect the mixture to have low retentiveness, but comparatively high coercive force. 1902 *Encycl. Brit.* XXX. 430/2 A metal which has great retentiveness may at the same time have small coercive force.

Retimber, *v.* (Further example.)
1924 *Countries of the World* III. 1928/1 The state..is responsible for the systematic retimbering of the Alps in the upper valley of the Durance.

Retinoscopist (retinǫ·skŏpist). [f. Retina + -scope + -ist.] An oculist who practises retinoscopy.
1904 *Optical Jrnl.* 2 June 938 (Cent. Suppl.) No matter what the defect, hyperopia, myopia, astigmatism, simple, compound or mixed, all give up the secrets to the skilled retinoscopist.

Retinule (re·tiniul). Anglicized form of Retinula.
1924 *Glasgow Herald* 31 May 4/2 The insect's compound eye..has its numerous lenses and retinules each wrapped up in a black mantle.

Retiracy. 1. (Earlier example.)
1835 *Louisville Public Advt.* 24 June, The pigmies are to be..pushed into..retiracy.

Retired, *sb.* [f. the ppl. adj.] A retired person.
1923 Una L. Silberrad *Lett. Jean Armiter* v. 126, I don't know what the other men were; retireds, I should think.

Retort, *sb.*² 5. Add: *retort furnace*; retort cell, a flask-shaped cell occurring in certain mosses.
1880 R. Braithwaite *Sphagnaceæ* 14 Flask-shaped or retort cells, more or less ventricose at base and gradually contracted upward into a more or less distinct..neck. 1896 H. N. Dixon *Student's Handbk. Brit. Mosses* 1 The articular sheath of the branches usually has in addition an outer series of flask-shaped cells. 1879 *Encycl. Brit.* X. 91/2 Retort furnaces are commonly fired or heated with a portion of the coke which forms one of the bye-products of the gas manufacture.

Retort, *v.*² (Earlier example.)
1850 N. Kingsley *Diary* 123 A warm [day]; the boys retorted the last week's work.
b. *intr.* To fall *off* or *away* in quantity when heated in a retort.
1850 N. Kingsley *Diary* 151 Got..1296 dollars amalgam and [this] ought not to retort off more than ¼. 1851 *Ibid.* 166 We had 3654 dollars in amalgam and it retorted away to 2546 dollars.

Retract, *v.*¹ Add: 1. e. *Phon.* To pronounce with the tongue drawn back.
1902 H. Sweet *Primer of Phonetics* 77 The first element of the diphthong in *high* is sometimes retracted towards 3.

Retract, *v.*² Add: 1. c. *Chess.* To take back (a piece) after making a move; to unmake (a move). So Retra·cting *vbl. sb.*
1871 *Dubuque Chess Jrnl.* 12 White retracts his last move and mates in 1 move. 1874 T. M. Brown *Bk. Chess Probl.* No. 20 The Dubuque Chess Journal Tourney..for retracting problems. 1881 F. C. Collins *Sel. Chess Probl.* No. 101 Retract White's last move, then White to play and mate in one move. 1907 [see *Retractor 4].

Retracted, *ppl. a.*¹ Also in sense *1 e of verb.
1908 H. Sweet *Sounds of Engl.* 37 The fully retracted back vowels.

Retractile, *a.*² (Further example.)
1919 H. G. Wells *Outl. Hist.* xxix. § 1. 327/2 Hadrian, his successor, was of a cautious and retractile disposition.

Retraction. 4. Also in sense *1 e of verb.
1890 H. Sweet *Primer of Spoken Engl.* 4 Each of the vowels formed by the different combinations of retraction and height is either *narrow* or *wide*.

Retractive. A. *adj.* Add: 3. *Chess.* (See quot. 1890.)
1890 B. G. Laws *Two-Move Chess Probl.* 16 These are called 'Retractive' problems. 1890 J. Rayner *Chess Probl.* 9 A retractive problem is one in which some move..has to be retracted, and then mate or sui-mate in a given number of moves.

Retractor. Add: 4. *Chess.* (See quot.)
1902 *Brit. Chess Mag.* 455 Two-move Retractors. 1907 S. S. Blackburn *Terms & Themes of Chess Probl.* 33 Retractors. Problems wherein the conditions require that the last move of one, or both, of the players shall be retracted, and that, when this is done, the problem shall be solved according to the usual conditions.

Retranslate, *v.* Add: 2. *Eccl.* To transfer (a bishop's see) back to the place from which it was originally removed.
1842 F. W. Faber *Foreign Churches* i. 54 Gregory XI. retranslated the Holy See to Rome.

Re-trea·d (rī-), *v.* [f. Re- 5 a + Tread *sb.*] To furnish (a tyre) with a fresh tread. So Re-trea·ding *vbl. sb.*
1908 *Daily Report* 7 Feb. 11/4 Advt., 10–12 h.p. Wolseley, in excellent condition, front pneumatics, just been retreaded. 1922 *Daily Mail* 11 Nov. 8 Advt., Send tyres for retreading to A—— M——.

Retreative (rɪtrī·tiv), *a.* [f. Retreat *sb.* + -ive.] Pertaining to or suggestive of retreat.
1899 Tarkington *Gentl. Indiana* xix. 376 As they neared the brick house Harkless made out, through the trees, a retreative flutter on the porch.

Retrieverish (rɪtrī·vəriʃ), *a.* [f. Retriever + -ish.] Resembling or suggestive of a retriever.
1909 H. G. Wells *Tono-Bungay* iii. ii. 243 There were two or three fox-terriers, a retrieverish mongrel, and an old, bloody-eyed, and very evil-smelling St. Bernard.

Re·troflexing, *a.* [f. as Retroflex *a.* + -ing ².] That bends or turns backwards.
1898 H. C. Porter tr. *Strasburger's Bot.* ii. § 1. 396 The male branches give rise..to spherical stalked antheridia, which open at the apices by means of retroflexing valves, and let free the spirally twisted spermatozoids.

Retrograde. B. *sb.* Add: 3. Backward spin given to a billiard ball.
1896 W. Broadfoot *Billiards* (1906) vi. 199 Backward rotation, retrograde, or screw, is obtained by striking the ball on CB below the centre.

Re·trospecti·vity. [f. Retrospective *a.* + -ity.] = Retrospectiveness.
1920 *Glasgow Herald* 23 Feb. 11/2 The adoption of the principle of the non-retrospectivity of financial law.

Retroversion. Add: 5. The state or condition of being retroverted or turned back.
1887 Sir J. D. Hooker *Life* (1918) II. xli. 297 The retroversion of the anthers in Gentiana was first described by myself in the Flora Antarctica as characteristic of the southern species.

Retrusible (rɪtrū·zib'l), *a.* [f. L. *retrūs-* ppl. stem of *retrūdĕre* to thrust back.] Capable of being thrust back.
1902 *Encycl. Brit.* XXVII. 301/1 The *Cydippidea* are generally spherical or ovoid, with two long retrusible pinnate tentacles.

Retune, *v.* (Further example.)
1909 M. Greenwood in *Further Adv. Physiol.* (ed. Hill) 410 'Retuning' with orange red and green both act like orange itself in inducing a negative image.

Return, *sb.* Add: 1. g. *ellipt.* (See quot.)
1898 Houston *Dict. Elect.* (ed. 4) 460/1 The word returns is sometimes used in a system of distribution by parallel circuits, to distinguish between the conductor by which the current goes back or returns from the receptive devices to the dynamo, and the conductor that leads it to the receptive devices.
h. *ellipt. pl.* Unsold newspapers returned to the publisher.
1897 *N. & Q.* 29 May 424/2 'Returns only' [on doors of newspaper office].
15. b. (See quot.)
1902 *Chambers's Jrnl.* Feb. 114/1 For every sample withdrawn from a package an equal quantity of approximately similar quality must be returned by the sampler; and this accounts for the bags of tea, known as 'returns' which the samplers who come to the warehouse bring from the establishments they represent.
16. return address, the address, put outside an envelope or other postal package, to which it is to be returned in case of non-delivery.
1928 *Publishers' Weekly* 30 June 2605 All envelopes must carry the name and *return address of the sender in the upper left hand corner.

Return (rɪtǝ̄·ɹn), *adv.* *U.S.* [f. the vb.] In phr. *and return*, and back again.
1887 C. B. George 40 *Years on Rail* v. 88 The train..ran from Waukegan to Chicago and return every day.

Reub (rūb). *U.S.* Also Reuben, Rube. A country bumpkin; a yokel. Also *attrib.*, rustic, uncultivated.
1896 G. Ade *Artie* i. 8 If I had time I'd go over to that church and make a lot o' them Reubs look like thirty-cent pieces. 1899 — *Fables in Slang* (1900) 10 Alas, the Rube Town in which she Hung Forth was given over to Croquet. 1911 H. Quick *Yellowstone N.* xii. 313 I took a basket of eggs an went in among 'em, feelin' like a animal trainer in a circus parade as the Reubens gathered around the train. 1923 Sadleir *Desolate Splendour* 33 A girl rube from the Canadian backwoods.

Reune (rī̩yū·n), *v. slang.* [f. Reunion.] *intr.* To hold a reunion.
1929 E. W. Springs *Above bright blue Sky* 237 She had seen in the paper where the 14th was going to reune at the banquet.

Reunion. 3. (Recent attrib. example.)
1929 E. W. Springs *Above bright blue Sky* 233 Are you going to the Aviators' Reunion Dinner to-night to celebrate the anniversary of the Armistice?

Reunionist. Also, one who favours reunion in other connections; in quot. of the divided Liberal party.
1923 *Glasgow Herald* 22 Mar. 9/1 One of the difficulties the 'Reunionists' are confronted with is that [etc.].

Rev (rev), *sb.* Abbreviation of Revolution. Also *Comb.*
1901 *Catal. Mech. Engin. Coll.* (Vict. Alb. Mus.) I. 35 The example has 3 in. cylinders, with 4 in. stroke, and is intended to run at 300 revs. per min. 1917 *Blackw. Mag.* May 803/2 The rev.-counter showed that the number of revolutions per minute had fallen off appreciably. 1918 *Chambers's Jrnl.* May 301/1 The revs dropped off.

Rev (rev), *v.* [f. the sb. or f. Revolve.]
1. *trans.* To cause (an internal-combustion engine) to run quickly, esp. before bringing it into use; to to speed *up*.
1920 *Blackw. Mag.* Oct. 449/1 A Bristol Fighter whose pilot was revving up his 250-horse-power Rolls Royce Falcon.
2. *intr.* To make or do revolutions; to revolve; also, with *up*, to increase in speed of revolutions.
1923 *Daily Mail* 9 Mar. 12 This little engine..cheats the taxation authorities by its long stroke and its capacity for 'revving' fast without vibration. 1928 *Daily Express* 29 Feb. 9/5 The engines' rev.' up to a roar. 1930 *Times* 29 Mar. 17/6 Advt., The oil..is specially refined for the fast-revving engines of to-day.

Revaloriza·tion (rī-). [Re- 5 a.] The action or process of establishing a fresh price or value for something; *esp.* a restoration of the value of a country's currency. So Reva·lorize *v. trans.*
1926 *Glasgow Herald* 6 Aug. 8 A preliminary revalorisation [of the franc] through a restoration of confidence should first be attempted. 1928 *Brit. Industr. Future* (Lib. Ind. Inq.) v. xxviii. 410 The desire to 'revalorise' the currency (i.e. to raise its exchange value) before 'stabilising' it. This process of revalorisation..is infallibly accompanied..by severe trade depression. 1928 *Daily Tel.* 27 Mar. 14/3 The leading banks..replied that they would not advance a pfennig until the war debts had been revalorised and admitted.

Revealing, *ppl. a.* (Recent example.)
1927 H. Belloc *Hist. Eng.* II. 210 The second rebellion against Henry II was a longer and much more revealing thing than the first.

Revelator. (Earlier examples.)
1801 *Massachusetts Spy* 20 May 1/2 They shall have their part (saith John the Revelator) in the lake which burneth. 1840 *Millenial Star* June 28 (Th.) The prophet Daniel and the revelator John.

Revenue. 7. a. Add: *revenue act* (earlier example), *boat*, *cutter* (earlier example), *department*, *man* (later example), *stamp*, *tariff*, *tax*.
1791 Washington *Diaries* IV. 196 The discontents which it was supposed the last *Revenue Act..would create subside as fast as the law is explained. 1846 *Knickerbocker Mag.* XXVIII. 244 The *revenue-boat from the *guarda-costa* came on board before our sails were furled. 1790 *Ann. 1st Congress* II. 2277 The officers of the *revenue cutters hereinafter mentioned. *Ibid.* I. 1040, I likewise nominate the following persons to fill offices in the *Revenue Department of the United States. 1895 *Century Mag.* July 378/2 I'm always skeered o' the *revenue men bein' about. 1870 Medbery *Men & Myst. Wall St.* 52 The acknowledgements are covered with *revenue stamps. 1820 *Ann. 16th Congress* 1 Sess. II. 1966 They enacted a *revenue tariff without the least regard to the situation of the country.

Reverend, *a.* Add: 6. *Reverend set*, an attitude or position adopted when poling a boat. *U.S.*
1833 J. K. Paulding *Banks of Ohio* I. 145 They placed their shoulders against the long poles, one end of which was loaded with iron, and making what was called a 'reverend set,' walked steadily to the stern of the broad-horn, propelling her forward at the same time.

Reverize (re·vəraiz), *v.* [f. Reverie + -ize.] *intr.* To indulge in reveries.
1910 Amy E. Tanner *Stud. Spiritism* 313 Sometimes merely lying back in a chair with intent to reverise, is sufficient.

Reverse, *a.* 5. (Further examples.)
1920 *Autocar Hdbk.* 132 To provide a reverse gear, it is necessary for the shaft H to be driven in the opposite direction to A. 1931 F. L. Allen *Only Yesterday* i. 7 He must remember to brake with the reverse pedal, or the low-speed pedal.

Reversing, *vbl. sb.* Add: b. The action of putting an automobile into the reverse gear.
1929 J. B. Priestley *Good Companions* i. ii. § 3. 67 Miss Trent discovered once again the terrors and dangers of reversing.

Reversion ¹. Add: 8. *attrib.*, as *reversion duty.*
1909 *Westm. Gaz.* 28 May 8/1 Clause 7 deals with reversion duty.

Reversional, *a.* Add: 2. = Reversionary *a.* 3.
1904 *Amer. Naturalist* Jan. 3 A curious reversional condition is seen in many high bred domestic dogs.

Review, *sb.* 3. *attrib.* (Earlier example.)
1815 W. Tomkinson *Diary Cavalry Officer* (1894) 326 The Prussians..assembled on the Boulevard..where the sovereigns stood to see them pass in review order.

Reviewery (rɪviū·əri). [f. Review *sb.* + -ery.] The sphere or domain of reviews; reviews considered collectively.
1876 R. L. Stevenson in *Lett.* (1911) I. 215, I was not a hundred miles from being miserably drowned, to the..permanent impoverishment of British Essayism and Reviewery.

Revisionism (rɪvi·ʒəniz'm). [f. Revision + -ism.] A scheme of revision; the policy of the Revisionists.
1921 *Glasgow Herald* 4 Apr. 10 The British Foreign Office has got over its momentary lapse into revisionism. 1929 *Encycl. Brit.* III. 459/1 Eduard Bernstein..was best known as the author of 'Revisionism', a changed conception of Marxism.

Revisionist. Add: 1. b. *spec.* One of a German political party favouring a gradual redistribution of capital.
1920 H. G. Wells *Outl. Hist.* 516 What are called 'Revisionists' in German Socialism incline in the same direction. 1929 *Encycl. Brit.* XX. 802/2 The revolutionary ideas of Marxism were challenged by 'revisionists' desirous of working less for a sudden overthrow than for a gradual transformation of capitalist society.

Revi·sitant, *sb.* [f. L. *revīsitant-*, *revīsitans* pres. pple. of *revīsitāre* to Revisit.] A person who revisits a place.
1923 *Times Lit. Suppl.* 21 June 417/1 The old lady was very solicitous after her baggage—as indeed some sixteen centuries earlier had been the revisitants of Pompeii.

Revolution, *sb.* Add: 6. c. *Geol.* (See quot.)
1925 J. Joly *Surface-Hist. of Earth* vi. 102 We have now traced the origin of the crust movements which culminate in the 'Revolution'. The latter name is applied by American geologists, not to the whole sequence of cyclical events, but to the great events attending the folding and elevation of the mountains.

Revolu·tionarily, *adv.* [f. Revolutionary + -ly ².] In a revolutionary manner.
1927 *Daily Express* 11 Feb. 1/1 Lisbon is traversed from north to south by wide avenues—splendid places for those who are revolutionarily inclined.

Revo·lvered, *a.* [f. Revolver + -ed ¹.] Provided with a revolver or with revolvers.
1901 *Pall Mall Gaz.* 6 Mar. 1 The revolvered footman.. is not quite so grotesque as the revolvered Protestant lecturer. 1922 *Blackw. Mag.* Jan. 123/1 Whom should he see but his American friend the casket king, still picturesque and revolvered, on his way to the station bar.

Revolving, *ppl. a.* c. (Further example.)
1911 Edna Ferber *Dawn O'Hara* xii. 170 The big man seated in the revolving chair up in front.
d. *Finance.* Applied to a credit, etc., which is automatically renewed on repayment.
1921 W. Thomson *Dict. Banking* 564/2 *Revolving credit*, a credit opened with a bank by an importer in order to enable an exporter to obtain payment for goods when ready for shipment. 1928 *Brit. Industr. Fut.* (Lib. Ind. Inq.) ii. ix. 101 The Local Loans Fund is a revolving fund vested in the National Debt Commissioners.

Revue (rɪviū·). [ad. F. *revue*: see Review.] A dramatic entertainment consisting of a series of more or less connected scenes depicting and often satirizing current events and topics.
1912 *Tatler* 30 Oct. 145 'Kill that Fly.' The New Revue which is Crowding the New Alhambra. 1913 *Punch* 9 July 41/3 The report that Mr. Lloyd George will shortly appear in a Revue at the National Liberal Club. 1920 Gardiner *Leaves in Wind* 71 One of those dismal things called revues, that are neither comedies nor farces, nor anything but shambling, hugger-mugger contraptions into which you fling anything that comes handy. 1929 Guedalla *Missing Muse* 192 Long years ago, when there were pantomimes at Christmas instead of second-rate revues.

Hence **Revu·ette**, a short revue; **Revu·ist**, a writer of revues.
1930 *Daily Express* 6 Oct. 5/3 Jane Renouardt in Rip's revuette gives a marvellous imitation of Yvonne Printemps. 1927 *Observer* 25 Sept. 11/1 Alfred Savoir, in collaboration with Rip, the revuist, has written 'Comme le temps passe'.

Re-winding, *vbl. sb.* Also *Comb.*
1930 *Daily Express* 6 Sept. 2/1 Fire broke out in the re-winding room of the Rialto Cinema..yesterday.

Re-wi·re (rī-), *v.* [Re- 5 a.] *trans.* 1. To provide with fresh wires, *esp.* for conducting electricity.
1903 *Motoring Ann.* 295 In cases of trouble from short circuits or broken wires, there is no remedy but to re-wire the car. 1910 *Installation News* IV. 64/2 They have decided to rewire the whole building.
2. To re-transmit (a telegraphic message).
1907 *Westm. Gaz.* 2 Dec. 13/1 News..is telegraphed to Madrid, to be forthwith re-'wired' to the capitals.

Rework, *v.* (Further example.)
1926 W. J. Locke *Old Bridge* iv. xii. 218 The frozen sap of ten years re-worked in her veins.

Rewrite, *v.* 2. Also *refl.*
1928 *Manch. Guard. Weekly* 5 Oct. 265/2 The events of the last four years in which the history of 1906 to 1914 was rewriting itself.

Rexine (re·ksīn). Trade name of a variety of artificial leather used in upholstery.
1911 Coutts & Stephen *Man. Libr. Bookbinding* iv. 56 There are several textile fabrics, known as Rexine,..and Pegamoid, etc., produced as substitutes for leather. 1922 *Daily Mail* 10 Nov. 15 Advt., Seats in red, brown, green or blue rexine, pegamoid or velvet. 1924 *Chambers's Jrnl.* Dec. 848/1 A cushion covered with rexine fits into the bottom of the box for baby to sit on.

Rhapsodical, *a.* Add: 2. b. *transf.* Applied to recurring volcanic explosions.
1903 Geikie *Text-bk. Geol.* (ed. 4) 33 Professor Suess.. arranged the evidence furnished by the moon in the following manner..3rd, formation of fissures with rhapsodical explosions.

Rhapsody (ræ·psŏdi), *v.* [f. the sb.] 1. = Rhapsodize *v.* 2.
1822 *Blackw. Mag.* Aug. 231/2 A conclusion, in which Sidney heartily joined, rhapsodying— 'O Paris, fatal was the hour' [etc.].
2. = Rhapsodize *v.* 3.
1899 *Westm. Gaz.* 13 June 2/3 Miss J.H.O...rhapsodies this morning on 'Our Guns'. 1909 W. J. Locke *Septimus* xxi. 321 His face beamed as it had beamed in the days when he had rhapsodied over the vision of an earth one scab to be healed by Sypher's Cure.

Rhenium (rī·niǝ̆m). *Chem.* [f. L. *Rhēn-us* Rhine + -ium.] An element resembling manganese in properties discovered spectroscopically in 1925 by Noddack and Tacke along with *Masurium in certain platinum ores, and now obtainable commercially. Symbol Re; atomic weight 186·31; atomic number 75.
1925, 1926 [see *Masurium].

Rheograph (rī·ogrɑf). [f. Rheo- + -graph.] An instrument for observing rapid variations in electric current or potential.
1900 *Nature* 6 Dec. 142/2 In the rheograph..M. Abraham uses a galvanometer with a period of about 1/10th of a second, and attempts to compensate errors due to the inertia of the moving part by utilising the effects of electromagnetic induction. 1904 E. Hospitalier in *Jrnl. Inst. Electr. Engin.* XXXIII. i. 75.

‖ **Rhexis** (re·ksis). [mod.L., a. Gr. ῥῆξις, f. ῥηγ- to break.] The breaking or bursting of the wall of a blood-vessel.
[1693 tr. *Blancard's Phys. Dict.* (ed. 2) *Rhexis*, the same that *Rhegma*. 1704 J. Harris *Lex. Techn.* I.] 1866 A. Flint *Princ. Med.* (1880) 27 When the extravasation is through the ruptured wall of a vessel, it is called hemorrhage by rhexis. 1899 *Allbutt's Syst. Med.* VI. 244 It cannot be doubted that the red corpuscles escape by diapedesis not by rhexis.

Rhi·nelander. [f. Rhineland + -er ¹.] A native or inhabitant of the Rhineland.
1861 *Times* 7 Oct. 6/3 What have the pious Belgians or the warm-hearted Rhinelanders..done in defence of the Pope's authority? 1873 Bryce *Holy Rom. Emp.* xvii. 308 The fall in A.D. 1477 of the great principality..was seen with pleasure by the Rhinelanders. 1928 *Daily Tel.* 27 Mar. 14/2 A parallel case..is the veto placed by the Coblenz High Commission on the singing by the Rhinelanders of the 'Wacht am Rhein'.

Rhinoceros. 3. Add: *rhinoceros-run*; *rhinoceros-like* adj.
1909 *Chambers's Jrnl.* Sept. 568/2 Elephant-tracks and rhinoceros-runs pierced the jungle here and there. 1915 E. R. Lankester *Diversions of Naturalist* xxviii. 260 The skulls and whole skeletons of great rhinoceros-like animals ..are dug up in early tertiary sands.

Rhitidome, variant of Rhytidome.

Rhizomatist (raizōᵘ·mătist). [f. Rhizoma + -ist.] One who studies or deals in rhizomata.
1904 *Field* 6 Feb. 236/3 One of the most enterprising and successful of all modern Dutch rhizomatists and collectors of new and rare bulbs.

Rhizomic (raizǫ·mik), *a.* *Bot.* [f. Rhizome + -ic.] Pertaining to or of the nature of a rhizome.
1902 *Nature* 21 Aug. 399/2 The examination of rhizomic material of the unique fern *Matonia pectinata.*

Rhizopodist (raizǫ·pŏdist). [f. Rhizopoda + -ist.] One who studies Rhizopoda.
1902 *Proc. Zool. Soc.* I. 231 This handsome species was for a long time..almost unknown to rhizopodists.

Rhodamine (rōᵘ·dămain). *Chem.* [f. Gr. ῥόδον rose + Amine.] Any one of a class of synthetic basic dyestuffs, chiefly yellows and reds, of great brilliancy and tinctorial power.
1888 *Jrnl. Soc. Chem. Industry* VII. 386/2 The Badische Anilin u. Soda Fabrik have introduced a new colour Rhodamine. *Ibid.* 560/2 Tannic acid produces in presence of sodium acetate a bright crimson precipitate (Rhodamine tannate). 1920 Cross & Bevan *Paper-Making* 270 To the phthalein group..belongs the important pink dyestuff Rhodamine.

Rhodesian (rodī·ʃən), *a.* and *sb.* [f. *Rhodesia*, a state in South Africa (named after C. J. *Rhodes*, 1853–1902) + -an.] a. *adj.* Of or belonging to Rhodesia. b. *sb.* A native or inhabitant of Rhodesia.
1901 G. Grey in *Geog. Jrnl.* XVIII. 64 No one could fail to be impressed by the magnificence of the mighty river, much less a Rhodesian. 1902 *Encycl. Brit.* XXXII. 232/1 In November 1897 the Rhodesian Railway,..had reached Bulawayo. 1920 *Glasgow Herald* 10 Apr. 4 The tobacco has become an entirely new type in colour and flavour, and must eventually be known as 'Rhodesian' tobacco. 1928 W. P. Pycraft etc. (*title*) Rhodesian Man and Associated Remains.

Rhodora (rodōᵊ·ră). [mod.L. *Rhodora*, f. L. *rhodōra*, the plant *Spiraea ulmaria*, f. Gr. ῥόδον rose.] A flowering shrub, *Rhodora canadensis*, growing in the north-eastern parts of North America.
1731 Bailey II. *Rhodora* [*Bot.*] a Plant that bears a leaf like a nettle, and a flower like a rose. 1786 Abercrombie *Gard. Daily Assist.* 32/2 *Rhodora* or Canada rosebay. 1845 S. Judd *Margaret* ii. i. 193 She transferred to her flower-beds a spring-beauty, a rhodora, a wintergreen. 1847 Emerson *Poems* (Rhodora) 59 In May, when sea-winds pierced our solitudes, I found the fresh Rhodora in the woods, Spreading its leafless blooms in a damp nook. *a* 1886 E. Dickinson *Poems* (1927) 82 Rhodora's cheek is crimson.

Rhone (rōᵘn). = Rouen. (Cf. Roan *sb.*³)
1854 Meall *Moubray's Poultry* 309 The Rouen variety [of duck] is known by several names—as *Rhone*,..*Rohan*,.. and *Roan.*

Rhumb. 3. Add: rhumb-track = *rhumb-line.*
1902 *Encycl. Brit.* XXXI. 110/1 The rhumb track, the great circle, and the polar track.

Rhy·melet. [f. Rhyme *sb.* + -let.] A short piece of rhyme or poetry.
1870 M. Collins in F. Collins *Lett. & Friendships* (1877) I. 66, I meant to say your rhymelets smell More of the country than Pall Mall. 1917 J. Adams *Student's Guide* 76 Many of us..have been grateful to the author of certain flagrant rhymelets.

Rhy·mingly, *adv.* [f. Rhyming *ppl. a.* + -ly ².] In a rhyming manner.
1880 Ruskin in *19th Cent.* Aug. 198 This necessity..of completing the nomenclature rhythmically and rhymingly.

Rhynchocephalic (riŋkosĭfæ·lik), *a.* [f. mod.L. *Rhynchocephala* + -ic.] = Rhynchocephalian.
1901 R. C. Punnett in *Proc. Zool. Soc.* II. 97 Rhynchocephalic diverticulum.

Rhynchocœlic (riŋkosī·lik), *a.* *Zool.* [f. Rhynchocœle + -ic.] Of or pertaining to the *Rhynchocœla.*
1902 *Encycl. Brit.* XXXI. 121 Rhynchocœlic blood-vessel.

Rhynchotal (riŋkǫ·tăl), *a.* *Ent.* [f. as Rhynchotous + -al.] = Rhynchotous.
1903 *Nature* 23 Oct. 616/1 Mr. W. L. Distant communicated additions to the rhynchotal fauna of Central America.

Rhythmal (ri·ðmăl, ri·þmăl), *a.* [f. Rhythm *sb.* + -al.] = Rhythmical.
1908 Hardy *Dynasts* iii. i. vi. 346 Whose emissaries knock at every door, In rhythmal rote.

Rhythmi·city. [f. Rhythmic + -ity.] Rhythmical quality or character. So **Rhy·thmicize** *v. trans.*, to make rhythmical.
190. *Buck's Handbk. Med. Sci.* III. 109 (Cent. Suppl.) The pulse rate presents more or less regular and extensive variations in the course of a day...They are hardly the expression of an inherent rhythmicity. 1907 R. Boughton *Bach* iii. 47 We must have before us the melody of Luther's noble hymn, rhythmicized according to Bach.

Rhythmizable (ri·ðm-, ri·þmaizăb'l), *a.* [f. Rhythmize *v.* + -able.] Capable of being made rhythmical. So **Rhythmiza·tion.**
1901 J. E. W. Wallin *Yale Psychol. Stud.* IX. 70 The limit of irregularity..may be determined by taking an easily rhythmisable series of intervals [etc.]. 1901 E. B. Titchener *Exper. Psychol.* I. ii. x. 339 The object of this experiment is to bring out the fact of subjective rhythmisation, or (as it is also termed) subjective accentuation. 1923 W. Thomson *Rhythm of Speech* 443.

Rhytidome. Also rhitidome.
1908 W. R. Fisher *Schlich's Man. Forestry* V. 631 The dead bark, or *rhitidome*, arises from the above cell-forms by the scale-like formation of cork.

Ria. Add: b. *Comb.*, as *ria(s)-coast.*
1902 *Encycl. Brit.* XXVIII. 623/1 A fjord-coast, ria-coast, or lagoon-coast. 1924 tr. *Wegener's Orig. Continents & Oceans* 53 These strongly planed-down chains..stretch.. westwards so as to form a wild jagged type of coast (the so-called rias-coast) in south-western Ireland and Brittany.

Riata. (Earlier examples.)
1848 E. Bryant *California* xxiii. 291 A *riata* (rope) was then made fast to the broken bone, and the jaw dragged out. 1850 L. H. Garrard *Wah-To-Yah* xvii. 231 We replied, not if there was any virtue in seventy minutes suspension with rawhide riatas.

Rib, *sb.*¹ 14. c. rib-riding, a method of ascending ridges in mountaineering; rib-stall, a set of wall-bars for physical exercises.
1920 G. W. Young *Mountain Craft* 169 *margin*, *Rib-riding. 1908 *Mosquito* Dec. 2 The heart of the Games' Mistress still yearns after some more *ribstalls, a Norwegian ladder, and a bench for remedial work.

Riband, *sb.* 5. a. Add: riband cane, development = *ribbon cane, development*: see *Ribbon *sb.* 10.
1834 *Visit to Texas* x. 92 The *riband cane requires to be planted every three years. 1836 Edward *Hist. Texas* ii. 43 The species called the violet, would have the advantage of the riband cane, by coming to maturity earlier in case of frost. 1928 *Observer* 18 Mar. 13/3 A district could have no worse advertisement than *riband development.

Ribbed, *ppl. a.* 2. b. (Earlier examples.)
1756 *Essex Inst. Hist. Coll.* XLIII. 277 Smith wore when he went away..blue ribb'd Stockings. 1782 *Ibid.* I. 13/1 A patton [= pattern] of white ribed stuff for a wescoat.

Ribbon, *sb.* Add: 5. d. (Further example.)
1899 A. Conan Doyle *Duet.* 68 Across their vision, from the end of Whitehall to Victoria Street, the black ribbon of traffic whirled and circled.
e. A streak or band of different colour in slates.
1898 *19th Ann. Rep. U.S. Geol. Surv.* vi. 257 The normal product of roofing slates is called No. 1 stock, and this is entirely free from ribbons.
f. A footpath on the Downs at Epsom.
1923 *Daily Mail* 26 May 8 The public are requested not to walk on the roadway, but either on the paths or the specially prepared ribbons on the Downs.
10. *ribbon rasp*; ribbon building, development, the building of houses along a main road, extending outwards from a town; ribbon cane, a variety of sugar cane.
1928 *Daily Express* 27 Sept. 10/6 *Ribbon-building should be abolished. 1929 *Times* 19 Jan. 8/1 Ribbon building is discouraged as far as possible. 1833 B. Silliman *Man. Sugar Cane* 10 The varieties of Cane cultivated in the United States, are the Creole,..the *Ribbon Cane [etc.]. 1849 *Rep. Comm. Patents, Agric.* (1850) 168, I did not succeed in getting the ribbon-cane, as I desired and ordered. 1929 L. F. Carr *America Challenged* 252 Some extra fine ribbon-cane molasses. 1929 *Times* 19 Jan. 8/1 Condemnation of *ribbon development. 1915 E. R. Lankester *Diversions of Naturalist* 147 Every one of the hundreds of univalve molluscs has this *ribbon-rasp.

Ribbon, *v.* Add: 3. Of a track or road: To stretch *out* like a ribbon.
1926 J. B. Ames *Valley of Missing Men* iv. 29 The trail ribboned endlessly through a rough, hill country that seemed utterly deserted. 1926 *Hutchinson's Best Story Mag.* Nov. 88/2 Where the great white road ribbons out eastward to the sea.

Ribbonism. (Earlier example.)
1828 Anglesey in *Peel's Mem.* (1856) I. 34 Ribbonism is extending.

Ribby, *a.* Add: 2. Suggestive of or resembling ribs.
1924 C. E. Montague *Right Place* ix. 122 All sorts of ribby ridges and intercostal hollows dropping down from that spine to the water-line on each side.

Rib-grass. 2. (Earlier example.)
1880 *Encycl. Brit.* XI. 53/2 The word [grass] is in common language, also used..for many plants of widely different affinities which possess some resemblance..to truly gramineous species; *e.g.*..rib-grass (*Plantago*).

Ribwork. (Earlier example.)
1848 E. Bryant *California* xxi. 271 These *rancherias* consist of a number of huts constructed of a rib-work or frame of small poles.

Rice ¹. Add: 4. (Modern example.)
1895 R. Marsden *Cotton Weaving* viii. 272 The hanks are placed upon light, collapsible hexagon reels termed rices.
5. rice creel, a frame for holding rices (sense 4).
1895 R. Marsden *Cotton Weaving* viii. 272 They are very light, and easily revolve with the pull of the thread. This is termed the *rice creel.

Rice ². Add: 5. b. *rice-clearing*, *-flat.*
1895 Conrad *Almayer's Folly* vi. 116 Finding shelter under that man's roof in the modest *rice-clearing. 1905 'Laurence Hope' *Indian Love* 57 The velvet *rice-flats lie so emerald green.
c. *rice-barn*, *-kettle*, *-pot.*
1901 *Chambers's Jrnl.* Aug. 538/1 Nearer the water a few small houses..and a higher two-storied *rice-barn. 1895 Conrad *Almayer's Folly* v. 86 The fire was burning in the cooking shed, with the *rice kettle swinging over it. *Ibid.* iv. 81 He eyed..the aged statesman sitting..by his domestic *rice-pot.
6. b. *rice-dressing* adj.
1901 *Chambers's Jrnl.* Feb. 125/1 An English firm.. erected a *rice-dressing mill on the shores of the Caspian.

Richardsonian. A. *adj.* (Later example.)
1930 A. Birrell *Et Cetera* ix. 161 Doddridge's love affairs are narrated by him at Richardsonian length.

Ri·chening, *ppl. a.* [f. Richen *v.* + -ing ².] That is becoming richer.
1930 A. L. Reys in *G. K.'s Weekly* 26 July 316/2 Each generation of mankind may be said to inherit an ever-richening treasure of synthetic wisdom from the total human past.

Ricinol-. Add: Ri·cinolein.
1876 *Encycl. Brit.* V. 200/2 Its purgative properties were supposed by Soubeiran to be due to the presence of an acrid oleoresin and to ricinolein.

Rick, *sb.*¹ 2. a. Add: *rick-lifter.*
1910 *Encycl. Brit.* XIII. 108/2 Various forms of rick-lifters are in use. 1924 *Glasgow Herald* 24 Dec. 6/7 Skiffs have been transported across the island on rick-lifters to augment the temporary fishing fleet.

Ri·ckety-ra·ckety, *a.* [redupl. f. Rickety.] Unsteady; shaky; tottering.
1895 *Punch* 21 Sept. 135 We're a rare old—fair old—rickety, rackety crew. 1931 Ramsay Macdonald in *Times* 5 Nov. 14/4 The whole world has got into what we in this corner of it would call a ricketty-racketty state.

Ricochet, *sb.* 2. b. Add: *ricochet mound.*
1902 *Kynoch Jrnl.* Apr.–May 80/2 At various points we have placed ricochet mounds, the first of which will catch any low or accidentally fired shot.

Rid, *v.* 1. c. (Later dial. and U.S. examples.)
1891 Hardy *Tess* lii, Are you house-ridding to-day? 1919 T. K. Holmes *Man fr. Tall Timber* xii. 144 I'll rid up the place and get our dinner.

Riddle, *sb.*² 4. Add: riddle-land (see quot.).
1818 *Massachusetts Spy* 14 Oct. (Th.) And what is riddle land? That which is of so open and loose a texture as to let the rain falling on it pass through it.

Riddle, *v.*² 2. (Further examples.)
1916 Boyd Cable *Action Front* 209 Machine-gunners riddling holes in a target or a row of posts. 1928 *Daily Mail* 3 Aug. 16/7 London is riddled through and through with receivers of textile goods.

Ride, *sb.*¹ Add: 1. f. *U.S.* (See quot.).
1931 F. L. Allen *Only Yesterday* x. 261 Another favourite method was to take the victim 'for a ride': in other words, to lure him into a supposedly friendly car, shoot him at leisure, [etc.].

Ride, *v.* Add: 6. c. (Further example.)
1931 *Daily Express* 21 Sept. 15/4 The course rode dead, and was not in favour of weight-carrying.
20. d. *To ride off*: To lead (a person) away from a subject *on* a side issue; to side-track.
1918 'Sapper' *Female of Species* x. 161 Look here, Peter—we've got to try and ride them off.
21. *To ride on a rail* (earlier examples.)
1855 *Jrnl. Disc.* II. 80/2, I guess they would give me a coat of tar and feathers, and ride me on a rail. 1866 Seba Smith *Way Down East* x. 251 Others..proposed..giving him a good coat of tar and feathers, and riding him out of town on a rail.
e. To bring *in* or introduce (a cinematographic picture) with an accompaniment of music.
1927 *Observer* 17 Apr. 3/3 The orchestral prelude is usually quite elaborate, and the picture is what is called 'ridden in'.

Rideable, *a.* Add: 3. Suitable for being hunted on horseback.
1910 *Blackw. Mag.* Apr. 557/1 We were a long time before we found a rideable pig.

Rider. Add: 6. b. Short for *circuit-rider* (*Circuit *sb.* 10).
1884 'C. E. Craddock' *In Tenn. Mts.* i. 15 The rider says ther's some holp in prayer. *Ibid.* iii. 143 All them Peels, the whole lay-out, war gone down ter the Settlemint ter hear the rider preach.

Rider (rai·dəɹ), *v.* *U.S.* [f. the sb.] *trans.* To strengthen (a fence) with riders.
1760 Washington *Diaries* I. 155 Good part of my new fencing was that was not ridered was leveld. 1787 *Ibid.* III. 208 Women staking and ridering fence of the said field. 1858 J. A. Warder *Hedges & Evergreens* 151 In Delaware.. worm-fences, not ridered, were to be five feet high.

Ridered, *a.* 2. (Earlier examples.)
1877 *Rep. Indian Affairs* 56 During the year the Indians have..built into good substantial staked and ridered fence 33,390 rails. 1885 'C. E. Craddock' *Prophet Gt. Smoky Mts.* xii. 231 The corn that Dordain had ploughed on the steep slope was high, and waved above the staked and ridered fence.

Ridge, *sb.*¹ 4. (Further example.)
1847 Tennyson *Princess* v. The storm Of galloping hoofs bare on the ridge of spears And riders front to front, until they closed.

Ridge-pole. 2. (Earlier example.)
1814 *Niles' Weekly Reg.* V. 322/2 At the time I left the boat the waters were about midway on the roofs of the houses generally, and quite to the ridge poles of several.

Ri·dge-tiling, *vbl. sb.* [f. Ridge-tile + -ing ¹.] The action of placing ridge-tiles; *concr.*, a set of ridge-tiles on a roof.
1876 *Encycl. Brit.* IV. 501/1 A common ridge tiling is necessary to prevent theft of the lead in some localities.

Ridibund (ri·dibǝnd), *a.* [ad. L. *rīdibund-us* laughing, f. *rīdēre* to laugh.] Inclined to laugh; laughing.
1909 *Engl. Rev.* Feb. 402 If Ischia could procure a well-regulated outlet after the manner of Stromboli, this danger might be averted and a more ridibund race of men gradually evolved.

Ridiculous, *a.* 2. b. As *adv.* (U.S. example.)
1834 C. F. Hoffman *Winter in Far West* I. (1835) 267 (Th.) Those Indians behaved most ridiculous. They dashed children's brains against the door-post.

Riding, *vbl. sb.* 5. c. Add: *riding-boat*, *-horse* (earlier examples).
1908 Sanger *Seventy Yrs. a Showman* xvi. 57 My father was able to add '*riding' or 'over and over' boats, as they were called, to his peep-show and roundabouts. 1641 *Boston Rec.* II. 61 Its ordered that all dry cattle shall be driven of the necke, and not be suffered to abide there, except *Riding horses. 1714 *Essex Inst. Hist. Coll.* XX. 179 Voated that the Neck of Land..be granted and reserved for the use of the Town of Salem for a pasture for Milch Cows and Riding Horses.

Riding, *ppl. a.* 3. (Further examples.)
1886 *Encycl. Brit.* XXI. 604/1 **Riding cable*, the cable bearing the strain. 1883 *Man. Seamanship for Boys* 27 Tops..are secured by placing two pieces of wood, called sleepers, or *riding crosstrees, on the top directly over the lower crosstree.

-rife, the adj. Rife used as a suffix, in Cauldrife (*a* 1662), Sailrife (1513), Wakerife (1480), etc.

Riff (rif), *sb.*⁶ and *a.* Also Rif. [f. *Rīf* the name of a district in Morocco.] a. *sb.* A Berber of the Rīf district of Morocco. b. *adj.* Of or belonging to the Riffs. So **Ri·ffian** *a.* and *sb.*
1902 *Encycl. Brit.* XXV. 5/1 The Sultan..made a vigorous campaign against the Riffians and others of his disaffected subjects. 1909 *Westm. Gaz.* 13 Aug. 5/4 The guns are now trained against the town, and are evidently being handled by Riffian merchants familiar with the main buildings. 1923 *Contemp. Rev.* Nov. 616 Representatives of the Riffs now demand the formal recognition of the Riff Republic. 1926 *Chambers's Jrnl.* Mar. 158/1 Hussein was a good Riff, and the killing lust was upon him.

Riffle, *sb.* Add: 3. b. *To make the riffle*: to be successful in an attempt or undertaking.
1859 Mrs. Duniway *Capt. Gray & his Company* 235 (Th.) I guess they'll make the riffle. 1873 'Mark Twain' & Warner *Gilded Age* xxxi. 279 There's old Balaam, was in the Interior—..he's made the riffle on the Injun; great Injun pacificator and land-dealer. 1883 J. Hay *Bread-winners* x. 151 He tried it oncet, and couldn't make the riffle. 1902 Harben *Abner Daniel* xxvi. 230 I don't want to kill a man fer jest tryin' to steal an' not makin the riffle. 1911 R. D. Saunders *Col. Todhunter* i. 19 I ain't got no business doin' that, but I'll try if I can make the riffle.
5. (Earlier example. Also 9 rifle.)
1850 N. Kingsley *Diary* 120 Finished the riffles to the machine to day. 1876 *Encycl. Brit.* IV. 702/1 The detritus ..leaves its auriferous particles in the 'rifles', which are chinks or cavities between the bars or blocks of wood or stone with which the bottom of the sluice is lined.

Riffle, *v.* Add: 2. d. To ruffle in a slight or rippling manner. *U.S.*
a 1904 S. E. White *Blazed Trail Stories* vii. 118 The breeze and sun played with the prairie grasses, the breeze riffling them over. 1926 *Ladies' Home Jrnl.* Nov. 228 Even the wail of music from the Palace of Dance barely riffled his preoccupation.
3. b. To turn over (the pages of a book).
1922 Titus *Timber* viii. 77 He riffled the pages slowly. Many of them were covered with just such notes.

Riffled (ri·f'ld), *a.* [f. Riffle *sb.* + -ed ¹.] Furnished with riffles (sense 5).
1927 *Chambers's Jrnl.* Feb. 109/2 In action the human dry-blower shovels some sand on to the top perforated riffled sheet: and then he shakes the entire machine.

Ri·ffler ³. = Riffle *sb.* 5.
1850 N. Kingsley *Diary* 122 Stoped down to day and made a panning trough to pour quicksilver from the riffler into.

Riffling (ri·fliŋ), *ppl. a.* [f. Riffle *v.* + ing ².] Of water: Moving in riffles; agitated.
1911 J. F. Wilson *Land Claimers* ix. 123 She..heaved her catch out of the grip of the riffling water.

Rifle, *sb.*³ Add: 3. c. *rifle battalion, company, corps* (earlier examples).
1775 *Jrnl. Cont. Congress* 25 Oct. III. 305 To John Biddle, ..Commissary of the rifle battalion. *Ibid.* 14 Sept. II. 250 The expences incurred for raising and arming the riffle companies. *Ibid.* III. 260 A captain of one of the rifle companies from Maryland. *Ibid.* 264 Money advanced for the riffle companies. 1777 J. Thatcher *Military Jrnl.* 121 The gallant Colonel Morgan, at the head of his famous rifle corps ..commenced the action.
e. rifle-coat = *rifle-frock*; rifle-frock (earlier examples); rifle-grenade, a grenade discharged from a rifle.
1877 *Rep. Indian Affairs* 5 The coats to be in shape like the old fringed *rifle-coat or blouse. 1782 Trumbull *M'Fingal* (1785) 132 While *rifle-frocks sent Gin'rals cap'ring. 1811 *Niles' Weekly Reg.* I. 45/2 In this valuable class of cotton goods are included rifle-frocks. 1915 B. Cable in *Cornhill Mag.* June 802 A storm of bombs, hand grenades, *rifle grenades, and every other fiendish device of high-explosives, preceded the attack. 1928 Gamble *Story N. Sea Air Station* v. 87 It was also intended that the Marten Hale rifle-grenade should be issued for use from aircraft.

Rifledom (rai·f'ldəm). [f. Rifle *sb.*³ + -dom.] The use of rifles.
1927 *Blackw. Mag.* Nov. 589/2 A hammered bullet sizzled overhead with that peculiar noise which is not often heard in these days of universal rifledom.

Riflery (rai·flǝri). [f. Rifle *sb.*³ + -ry.] Rifles collectively; firing from rifles.
1846 Sage *Scenes Rocky Mts.* (1859) 250 A volley of riflery was discharged among the promiscuous throng, with fatal effect. 1869 *Punch* 27 Mar. 119/1 When once before Shakespeare's cliff reverberated with the roar of riflery.

Rifle-shot. 1. (Earlier examples.)
1802 Ellicott *Jrnl.* 249 We anchored about rifle shot from the sloop. 1815–16 *Niles' Weekly Reg.* IX. Suppl. 190/2 The schooner now thought it prudent to claw off, and had just escaped out of rifle shot.
3. (Earlier examples.)
1837 Irving *Capt. Bonneville* (1895) I. 107 There were the remains of the rude fortress in the swamp, shattered by rifle shot. 1846 Sage *Scenes Rocky Mts.* (1859) 191 The sharp crack of a rifle-shot.

Rift, *sb.*² Add: 1. (Modern U.S. example.)
1889 *Coll. N. H. Hist. Soc.* IX. 144 Chestnut was a favorite timber [for morticed posts] on account of its easy rift and durability.
2. f. (See quot.)
1902 *Encycl. Brit.* XXXII. 102/1 In gneisses the parallel arrangement of the minerals usually coincides with a direction of easy cleavage, known to quarrymen as the 'rift'.

Rift, *v.*¹ 1. (Modern U.S. examples.)
a 1861 T. Winthrop *John Brent* xix. 209 A little pathway in the sage-bushes suddenly opened before me, as a lane rifts in the press of hurrying legions 'mid the crush of a city thoroughfare. 1898 H. S. Canfield *Maid of Frontier* 75 The mass of vapor overhead rifted for a moment.

Riftless, *a.* (Earlier example.)
1797 *Spirit Farmer's Museum* (1801) 71 From the gnarl'd oak..To the green vine, which twines its riftless sides.

Rig, *sb.*⁶ Add: 3. a. (Earlier example.)
1860 G. T. Clark *MS Diary* 14 Saw Coles rig which we bought after tea.
c. An outfit or plant.
1867 *Rep. Iowa Agric. Soc.* (1868) 174, I consider the Victor mill & Cook's evaporator the best rig for making sirup profitably from cane, that I have examined.

Rig, *sb.*⁷ *dial.* Also rigg. [Of obscure origin.] The tope, *Galeus vulgaris.*
1887 Parish & Shaw *Kentish Dial.* 128. 1927 *Glasgow Herald* 7 Sept. 11/7 On the south-east coasts of England a species of small shark, known locally as 'rigg', is caught on strong lines baited with mackerel.

Rig, *v.*⁶ Add: 1. b. To take to task; to rag or tease. *U.S.*
1899 A. H. Quinn *Pennsylv. Stories* 100, I rigged him about it once and he said he'd reform.

Rigg. [app. a misunderstanding of L. *regius* royal, as in *regii et grandes pisces.*] Regarded as the name of a particular royal fish.
1547 1 *Edw. VI* vii. m. 5 pisces regal viz sturgions balenas cetas porpec delphinos regges graspes. 1549 3 *Edw. VI* ii. m. 40 pisces regal videl' sturgiones balenas cetas porpec delphinos rigges graspes. 1764 *Commission of Vice Adm. in Prov. of Quebec* in G. O. Stuart *Cases in Vice-Adm. Court of Lower Canada* (1858) App. 372 And of royal fishes, namely sturgeons, whales, porpoises, dolphins, Riggs [*sic*] and grampusses. 1831 2 *Hagg* 442 Royal fish viz., sturgeons, grampuses, whales, porpoises, dolphins, riggs, and graspes.

Rigger ¹. Add: 1. b. A person attending to the rigging of aircraft.
1921 *Dict. Occup. Terms* (1927) § 278 *Rigger*, fixes wire stays on aeroplane or airship and is responsible for their proper tautness, alignment, and position. 1930 *Times* 13 Oct. 13/4 That young man was a rigger on R 101 and now sleeps with his fellow enthusiasts.

Rigging, (*vbl.*) *sb.*² 5. Add: rigging position *Aeron.* (see quot.).
1920 *19th Cent.* July 145 The angle at which the main planes are set relatively to an arbitrary datum plane of the whole machine is known as the angle of incidence, and, when this datum plane is horizontal, the aeroplane is said to be in the rigging position.

Ri·gging, *vbl. sb.*³ [f. Rig *v.*⁶ + -ing ¹.] The action of the verb Rig ⁶; ragging or teasing.
1913 H. Croly *Marcus A. Hanna* 460 He was constantly on the lookout for a chance to joke about the peccadilloes of his friends. There were few of them who escaped some kind of rigging.

Right, *sb.*¹ Add: 9. (Further example.)
1930 *Times* 28 Mar. 21/2 The buying of the last-named stock being stimulated by expectations of an early offering of new stock giving 'rights' to stockholders.
18. d. A game-bird (shot) on the right-hand side.
1908 R. H. Benson *Conventionalists* i. iii. 82 On Saturday he had killed three rights and lefts. 1910 *Blackw. Mag.* Jan. 140/1, I got a right and left with the big gun.

Right, *a.* Add: 5. b. *Comb.* as *right-hearted*, *-principled.*
1908 Mary & Jane Findlater *Crossriggs* xlvii. 363 Alex gave it the reverent attention that details of the kind will always command from right-hearted people. 1926 A. Conan Doyle *Firm of Girdlestone* 189, I believe you to be hard-working and right-principled.
7. e. *That's right*, that is so, I agree. *colloq.*
15. c. Also *right oh! righto! right-o!* etc., expressing agreement with, acquiescence in, or understanding of some opinion, arrangement, proposal, etc. *slang.*
1902 C. J. Cutcliffe Hyne *Mr. Horrocks, Purser* 52 Do it how you like, only anyway do it. 'Right-O', said the fourth officer. 1907 *Punch* 26 June 464/1 'He's really a hopeless person.'..'And how about her?'..'She's better. At any rate she does say Right-O!' 1912 H. Walpole *Prelude to Adv.* i, 'See you in Hall?' 'Right-o!' 1915 T. Burke *Nights in Town* 191 Righto, laddie, righto. I get you. 1916 B. Cable *Action Front* 134: 'Then if the shells pitch too near we can slip the cable and run for it.' 'Right-oh!' said the captain. 1920 Wodehouse *Damsel in Distress* viii. 110 'Give this note to Lady Maud.' 'Right ho.' 1921 Galsworthy *To Let* i. v. 53 Stable secret! Righto! 1922 A. A. Milne *Red House Myst.* xvi. 149 'Come and see me before you go down.' 'Righto.'
21. Parasynthetic combinations as *right-eared*, *-eyed*, *-footed* adjs.
1907 G. M. Gould in *Science* 1 Nov. 594/1.
22. *Comb.* as right bower, the knave of trumps at euchre; right-winger, a player in the right wing of a football or hockey team; right-wrong, applied *attrib.* to a system of marking examination papers.
1872 Bret Harte *Truthful James etc.* 135 Till at last he put down a *right bower, Which the same Nye had dealt unto me. 1878 *Encycl. Brit.* VIII. 654/2 In the trump suit the knave (called the *right bower*) is the highest trump. 1929 *Daily Express* 7 Nov. 19/2 *Right-winger. 1923 P. B. Ballard *New Examiner* xvii. 181 Once we depart from a rigid *right-wrong system of marking we open the floodgates of personal vagaries and lose the benefit of a scale which is objective and invariable.

Right-handed, *a.* 6. as *adv.* Delete *rare*.
1910 *Blackw. Mag.* July 24/1 A single stag has swung right-handed. 1929 *Morn. Post* 30 Dec. 13/1 He [a fox] ..left at the Toft end going straight..over the railway, leaving Kingston village right-handed.

Right of way. Add: 1. (Further example.)
1925 A. J. Toynbee in *Surv. Internat. Affairs* 1920–23 I. 41 The part played by the League in the problems of the right of way through the Kiel Canal, the Aaland Islands, East Karelia, [etc.]..is noticed in Part III.
2. (Further example.)
1919 T. K. Holmes *Man fr. Tall Timber* xxix. 365 The right-of-way of the railroad was not wide enough to halt the conflagration in any case.
3. *attrib.* as *right-of-way man.*
1904 F. Lynde *Grafters* xxviii. 361 Our right-of-way man has just sent a telegram to all agents.

Ri·ghtwise, *adv.* [f. Right *a.* + Wise.] In a right-hand direction.
1908 Hardy *Dynasts* III. II. ii. 369 Henceforward, masses of the foe Withdraw, and, firing as they go, Pass rightwise from the cockpit out of sight.

Rigid. A. *adj.* Add: 1. c. *spec.* Of airships: Belonging to the type whose shape is maintained by a framework of metal or other material and not (chiefly) by the pressure of gas in the envelope.
1909 A. Berget *Conquest of Air* ii. 26 There is obviously another way..; it is to make the balloon rigid. 1910 C. C. Turner *Aerial Navig. To-day* 62 One of the most famous airships of the rigid type was Zeppelin No. 4. 1920 [see *B 2.]
B. *sb.* 2. A rigid airship (see *A. 1 c).
1920 *Glasgow Herald* 3 Dec. 5 The lecturer said that after comparing non-rigids, semi-rigids, and rigids it was obvious that it would be the rigid airships which would be developed for commercial work. 1928 *Daily Tel.* 12 June 17/2 When the Mayfly, the first naval rigid, was being built [etc.].

Rigidify, *v.* a. (Further example.)
1911 Galsworthy *A Sheaf* (1916) 148 Which of us does not know the deflecting power of trusteeship, rigidified, as it is by law?

Rigidity. 1. (Further example.)
1900 *Strand Mag.* Sept. 313/2 The rigidity of the balloon—important in view of its great length—has also been established.

Rig-up. Add: b. Something that is rigged up or erected as a makeshift.
1931 B. Brown *Talking Pictures* 161 Al Jolson never seemed so good as when over that rig-up he sang his last song.

Rig-vedic (rig₁vē·dik), *a.* [f. Rig-veda + -ic.] Of or pertaining to the Rig-veda.
1895 E. W. Hopkins *Relig. India* iii. 74 The end of the Rig Vedic period. 1923 H. D. Griswold *Relig. of Rigveda* ii. 28 The primary source for the Rigvedic age is, of course, the *Rigveda*.

Rile, *v.* 2. Also with *up.* U.S.
1857 J. G. Holland *Bay Path* iii. 32 It only raises the devil in me, and riles me all up.

Riled, *ppl. a.* (Further example.) Also *riled-up.*
1856 Seba Smith *Major Jack Downing* lxxx. 452 I found the President..looking kind of riled and very resolute. 1872 W. A. Hickman *Brigham's Destroying Angel* iii. 72 Some of the boys began to get terribly riled up, and wanted to stop and hunt the Indians.

Rill, *sb.*[1] 3. (Earlier example.)
1876 E. Neison *Moon* iii. 71 There is one class of formations..which, from their unknown nature, cannot well be classified. These are the rills or clefts.

Rilling, *vbl. sb.* Add: 2. The action of the verb Rill (sense 1).
1929 Bridges *Test. Beauty* I. 313 Valleys vocal with angelic rilling of rocky streams.

Rim, *sb.*[1] 6. Add: rim-band, a driving belt or band passing round the rim of a wheel.
1892 J. Nasmith *Cotton Spinning* viii. 253 By means of the *rim band this movement is communicated to the spindles.

Rimal (rai·măl), *a.* [f. Rima + -al.] Of or belonging to a rima.
190. *Buck's Handbk. Med. Sci.* II. 174 (Cent. Suppl.).

Rime, *v.*[1] 3. (Later example.)
1915 *Hastings's Encycl. Relig. & Ethics* VIII. 258/1 'Riming' people to death—a practice used by the *filid* as well as by the druids—was connected with the power of the spoken word.

Rime, *v.*[2] (Later example.)
1907 Neil Munro *Daft Days* xxxii, Oh, London, London! ..The multitudinous monuments rimed by years.

Rimy, *a.* Add: b. *Comb.* as *rimy-white.*
1912 W. W. Gibson *Fires* 33 Her hair, as ruddy as the fern..Had shrivelled rimy-white In one short summer's night.

Rind, *sb.*[1] Add: 4. c. An upper layer of soft rock.
1849 *Presid. Mess. Congress* II. 609 The rock is 'rind', and can probably be penetrated to the depth of two or three hundred feet before striking a greenstone vein.
6. c. Impudence; 'cheek'. *slang.*
1915 Wodehouse *Something Fresh* v. You have the immortal rind to suppose that I will stand being nagged and bullied.

Rind, *v.*[1] Also, to rub the skin off (a part of a person's body).
1893 *Eng. Illustr. Mag.* Sept. 872/1 Tom Walker used to rub his bleeding fingers in the dust after being rinded by David Harris.

Rinder[3]. [f. Rind *v.*[1] + -er[1].] One who removes the rind or bark from trees; a barker.
1917 *Royal Cornwall Gaz.* 17 May 1/3 Rinders wanted for Oak Coppice at Brentor.

Ring, *sb.*[1] Add: 4. b. *pl.* A competitive game in which rings are thrown on to hooks.
1906 B. Kennedy *Wander Pict.* 245 Over yonder on the [inn] wall is the target with hooks at which they play the game of rings. They stand off and pitch rubber rings on to the hooks.

6. c. The boundary of a cricket field.
1903 H. G. Hutchinson *Cricket* iii. 67 It is a stroke that requires very accurate timing, but when timed well, the ball often goes to the ring like a flash of lightning.
9. i. (Earlier example.)
1836 Gardiner *Journ.* 100 (Pettman) Both man and woman shave their heads close, the former leaving only sufficient to attach the isigoko or ring.
10. d. A number of cattle arranged in a circle to keep them from straying.
1912 *Chambers's Jrnl.* June 364/2 The only alternative to tying up was to form what were called 'off-droves' or 'rings'—bunches of from fifteen to twenty cattle in a compact group, heads inward.
13. a. Also, *To keep* or *hold the ring*, to be a spectator while others fight with each other.
1905 *Spectator* 21 Jan. 79/1 There is a cynicism which nothing but conscious impotence could excuse in the thought of 'keeping a ring' while the Bulgarians of the Principality ..are drawn into a life-and-death struggle with the Turks. 1928 *Brit. Industr. Fut.* (Lib. Ind. Inq.) III. xv. 166 There are still many people who hold that the State ought not to meddle with industry,..but should confine itself to holding the ring while the disputants fight out their differences.
15. a. *ring-game, -plait.*
1916 A. S. Neill *Dominie Dismissed* viii, The *ring games down at the school there nearly all deal with love and matrimony. 1908 W. G. Collingwood *Scandinavian Brit.* 245 The ornament with *ring-plaits and a peculiar form of interrupted double-strand, interlacing, cannot be earlier than the tenth century.
c. *ring-sider.*
1901–2 *Rep. Kansas State Board Agric.* 173 (Cent. Suppl.) There may be a 'topper' of each type in the class, each having many friends among the *ringsiders for premier honors.
16. *ring-brooch, -foot, -mountain, -scissors, -spot.*
1894 W. Bateson *Study of Variation* I. xii. 305 The ring-spots of the upper or sub-dorsal row had, as a variation, a red centre or nucleus. 1902 W. M. Davis *Elem. Phys. Geog.* vii. 221 It sometimes happens that the upper part of a volcano is destroyed by a violent eruption..forming a greatly enlarged crater, or caldera. Volcanoes of this form are sometimes called ring mountains. 1908 *Practitioner* June 769 Later Mr. Jessop introduced his 'ring-scissors', which made this piecemeal removal of the gland an easier matter. 1927 Peake & Fleure *Priests & Kings* 162 Deep cups have been found..also bottles with lugs instead of handles and sometimes with hollow ring-feet. 1931 Joan Evans *Eng. Posies & Posy Rings* Introd. p. xii, Such inscriptions were commonly engraved in the thirteenth and fourteenth centuries on the ring-brooches that were used to fasten the dress at the neck.
18. **ring-around,** a ring of diseased tissue surrounding a vine stem; **ring beam,** a ring-shaped beam of yarn; **ring-keeper** (example); **ring-oiling** *a.*, automatically supplied with lubricating oil by means of oil-carrying rings; **ring-porey** *a.*, of timber, characterized by soft porous substance between harder (cylindrical) layers; **ring-road,** a circular road passing round a town; **ring-room,** a room in which spinning is done on ring-frames; **ring-shake,** a defect in timber (see quot.); **ring-spinner,** a spinner using a ring-frame; **ring velvet,** velvet so fine that it is capable of being drawn through a ring; **ring-winding,** a system for winding dynamos; **ring-yarn,** yarn produced by ring-spinning.
1896 E. G. Lodeman *Spraying of Plants* II. 295 It frequently occurs that a part is completely girdled, causing a '*ring-around', as it is commonly called. 1924 *Times Trade & Engin. Suppl.* 29 Nov. 247/1 'Ring beams are now worse off in margin by 1d. per lb. compared with a month or six weeks ago. 1912 *Chambers's Jrnl.* June 394/1 He organized a body of '*ring-keepers' to preserve order as far as possible. 1904 *Elect. Rev.* 10 Sept. 410 (Cent. Suppl.) The journal bearings are of the *ring-oiling, self-aligning type. 1895 Schlich *Man. Forestry* III. 73 To fell a tree and count the concentric rings on the stump..is easiest in the so-called *ring-porey broad-leaved species, and in conifers, which produce a darker coloured summer, or autumn, wood than that formed in spring. 1928 *Daily Express* 27 Aug. 8/6 London has no form, no symmetry. I suggest that we could give her this by cutting a broad *ring-road through the old nineteenth century suburbs. 1928 *Manch. Guard. Weekly* 21 Sept. 221/4 The maximum temperatures agreed upon as being 'reasonable' are rather startling—80 degrees for cardrooms and *ringrooms and 95 degrees for mulerooms. 1905 *Sci. Amer.* Suppl. 25 Mar. 24433/1 *Ringshake..consists in a partial or entire separation of two consecutive annual rings, and appears on a cross section as one or more splits running concentrically around the log. 1909 *Westm. Gaz.* 25 Aug. 8/3 *Ring-spinners..will not be able to compete with cops made on mule machinery. 1927 *Times* 20 Oct. 17/4 The bride.. wore a picture gown of white *ring velvet. 1931 *Daily Tel.* 21 May 6/3 A green satin beauté gown..lined with green ring velvet. 1902 *Encycl. Brit.* XXVII. 582/1 The simple *ring winding consisting of a continuous helix is in itself unaffected by the number of poles. 1892 J. Nasmith *Cotton Spinning* ix. 348 A method of winding *ring yarn on a cylindrical surface.

Ring, *v.*[1] Add: 2. e. Of a dog: 'To circle around (the game) in order to catch the scent' (Cent. Suppl.).
1903 *Forest & Stream* 24 Jan. 63 (Cent. Suppl.) Any dog that 'rings' game, or from any cause breaks his point to take up another, may be trained to report.
5. d. To enclose in a ring.
1909 *Daily Chron.* 18 Aug. 4/4 You never by any chance got your own table-napkin. Mark it as you would; be-ribbon it, ring it, your distinguishing mark was removed.

11. *Austr.* To beat (a shedful of men) at sheep-shearing.
1896 A. B. Paterson *Man fr. Snowy River* 136 The man that 'rung' the Tubbo shed is not the ringer here, That stripling from the Cooma side can teach him how to shear. 1910 Davis *Our Selection* xiv. 127 He shore at Welltown, and rung the shed by half a sheep.

Ring, *v.*[2] Add:
6. d. Phr. *To ring the bell*: to attain a complete success.
1925 E. Wallace *Strange Countess* x. 93 'You've certainly rung the bell this time, Lois.' 'It seems too good to be true, doesn't it?' 1930 *Times Lit. Suppl.* 23 Oct. 866/1 It looks very much to me as if Miss Theodora Benson and Miss Betty Askwith's 'Lobster Quadrille', is going to ring the bell.
10. (Later fig. example.)
1924 D. H. Lawrence *England, my England* 45 The clanging pain in his head rang out the rest of his consciousness.
c. Also *intr.*, of a curtain. (Chiefly *fig.*)
1916 Sheila Kaye Smith *John Galsworthy* 63 Thus the curtain rings down on Irene Forsyte, crushed under the heel of prosperity.
d. Of a telephone (with *off*): To be disconnected. (Cf. *Ring-off.)
1911 *Chambers's Jrnl.* Aug. 557/2 The telephone rang off.

Ringer[1]. Add: 6. *U.S.* A person accompanying or attaching himself to a party to which he does not belong; one voting in a district where he does not reside; an outsider.
1896 G. Ade *Artie* xi. 100 About a dozen ringers followed us in and stood around rubberin'. 1904 *N.Y. Tribune* 8 Nov. 3 The Democratic leaders to-day started to send a lot of alleged 'ringers' across the line into West Virginia to vote to-morrow. 1928 *Manch. Guard. Weekly* 26 Oct. 335/2 Perhaps seventy-five were really newspaper men and women, the others being what the American language calls 'ringers', 'gate-crashers', or 'dead-heads'.

Ringer[2]. Add: 3. *U.S.* A ringing cheer.
1901–2 *Rep. Kansas State Board Agric.* 360 (Cent. Suppl.) The air was rent with cheers. Auctioneer Judy called for a ..ringer for [the man] who had sold the highest-priced beef steer in the world.
4. *To be a ringer for*: to resemble closely; to be the image of.
1900 G. Ade *More Fables in Slang* (1902) 162 Bob..was a Ringer for a United States Senator, all except the White Coat. 1904 'O. Henry' *Cabbages & Kings* 180 The man was a ringer for the pictures of the fat Weary Willie in the funny papers. 1909 — *Options* (1916) 46, I saw once..an outlaw..who was a dead ringer for him.

Ringhals (ri·ŋhæls). [Du., f. *ring* Ring + *hals* neck.] A species of cobra, *Sepedon hæmachætes*, belonging to South Africa, characterized by a ring of colour round the neck.
1864 T. Baines *Explorations* xiv. 449, I think the species is called 'ring hals' (or ringed throat) in the Colony. 1906 *Westm. Gaz.* 16 Jan. 4/1 A Spurred Chameleon, a small Monitor, and a couple of Ring-hals snakes. 1925 *Other Lands* July 44/2 They pointed to the half-open door, where she saw uncoiling itself a large ringhals.

Ringing, *ppl. a.*[1] 2. Forming a ring: standing round.
1904 F. Lynde *Grafters* xxvi. 339 The waiting was a little awkward. The ringing idlers were good-natured but curious.

Ring-off. [f. *to ring off*: Ring *v.*[2] 10 d.] (The signal for) the severance of a telephonic connection.
1902 *Encycl. Brit.* XXXIII. 237/1 When the conversation is finished a ring upon the call-bell ('ring off') causes the drop to fall.

Ringster. Add: 2. A member of a price-ring.
1879 *Harper's Mag.* Oct. 717 The inopportune arrival of several cargoes of Texan beef broke the ring and ruined the ringsters.

Ringtail. Add: 4. **ringtail roarer** = *ring-tailed roarer* (Ring-tailed *a.* 4); so **ringtail ranger, snorter.**
1833 J. K. Paulding *Banks of Ohio* I. xiv. 219, I got tired of making fun of the ringtail roarer. 1861 J. R. Lowell *Biglow Papers* II. i. 259 My eldes' boy's so took up, wut with the Ringtail Rangers An' settin' in the Jestice-Court for welcomin' o' strangers. 1859 *Oregon Argus* 10 Dec. (Th.) Here lies James D. Porter, Who lived as he hadn't orter, But as a Methodist exhorter Was a regular ringtail snorter.

Ring-tailed, *a.* 4. *Ring-tailed roarer* (earlier examples); also *ring-tailed squealer.*
1830 *Massachusetts Spy* 25 Aug. (Th.) I'm a ringtailed roarer from Big Sandy River. I can outrun,..and outfight any man in Kentucky. 1836 Crockett *Yaller Flower Almanac* 9, I am a raal ringtailed roarer. 1837 R. M. Bird *Nick of Woods* I. iii. 56 Stranger, my name's Ralph Stackpole, and I'm a ring-tailed squealer.

Ring-up. [f. *to ring up*: Ring *v.*[2] 10 b.] The action or fact of endeavouring to communicate with a person by telephone.
1910 *Daily Chron.* 26 Feb. 6/2 That most modern of human summonings, a telephone 'ring up'.

Rink, *sb.*[2] Add: 4. A bowling-green.
1902 *Encycl. Brit.* XXVI. 328/2 The Scottish Association holds that the ditch within the limits of ther ink is part of the green so far as the jack and the touchers are concerned.

Rinkle (ri·ŋk'l). [Of obscure origin.] Calcined arsenical ore.
1923 *Discovery* Nov. 291/1 The strongly fuming mass [of mundic] is mechanically raked during the process, the ash or rinkle, as the workmen call it, falling off the edge of the furnace floor into the pit.

Rinse, *v.* Add: 2. c. With water or other liquid as the object.
1840 R. H. Dana *Bef. Mast* xxxv. (1841) 114/2 This be swallowed..and rinsed it about his gums and throat.
3. *intr.* Of soap: To admit of being washed off or removed with water.
1911 *Century Mag.* Christm. No. Advt. 128 It lathers freely, rinses easily and leaves the skin soft, sweet, smooth and exquisitely clean.

Riot, *sb.* Add. 2. e. Something that achieves great popularity or arouses much enthusiasm for a short time; a 'rage'.
1930 E. V. Lucas *Down the Sky* 235 I've got a peach of a new song. It's been a riot in Australia.
4. c. Also *transf.* in phr. *to read the Riot Act*: to announce or declare that some course of action or conduct must cease.
1916 H. L. Wilson *Somewhere in Red Gap* v. 185 When Henrietta declared herself, Alonzo read the riot act and declared marital law. 1920 A. E. W. Mason *Summons* xix. 193 'Have a whisky-and-soda.' 'Thanks.'..'Lucky man! The doctor's read the Riot Act to me.' 1928 *Sunday Express* 29 Apr. 13/3 Next Sunday evening..the famous cabaret singer will be seen in flowing Grecian robes, as Xantippe, 'reading the Riot Act' to her husband, Socrates.
5. *attrib.*, as **riot call** *U.S.*, a message for means to deal with a riot; **riot gun,** a gun used in quelling riots.
1905 *N. Y. Even. Post* 7 Nov. 2 Charges of illegal voting resulted in a disturbance which police were unable to subdue, and a riot call was sent in. 1930 *Morn. Post* 9 Apr. 12 Detectives in motor-cars equipped with 'riot guns' toured through the districts where violence was anticipated.

Riotously, *adv.* 2. Also *fig.*
1922 Bennett *Lilian* III. iii, The wild chants of the Marquesas or the Fiji Islands rang riotously through the correctness of the restaurant.

Rip, *sb.*[4] Add: 3. (Earlier example). Also, a burst *of* laughter. *U.S.*
1855 *Knickerbocker Mag.* XLV. 129 List to the rip and the roar of the song. 1867 T. Lackland *Homespun* II. 271 Sometimes he could not help giving a rip of laughter that drew the eyes of the whole school round to him in an instant.
4. *U.S. colloq.* *Like rips*: to an excessive degree; energetically, strongly, violently, or keenly.
1901 Harben *Westerfelt* iv. 42 An' she said Jasper Webb swore like rips when the administrator tol' him the trade was closed with Luke as yore agent. 1904 — *Georgians* 133 I've got girls of my own,..and I feel like rips for one when she has to stand up and sing or say anything in public.

Rip, *v.*[2] Add: 5. a. (Later example.)
1916 B. Cable *Action Front* 255 A shell cracked overhead, and the shrapnel ripped down along the trench behind them.
7. a. (Earlier examples.)
1853 *Daily Morning Herald* (St. Louis) 19 Jan. (Th.) We've got 'em on the hip, Letter Rip! Letter Rip! 1853 *Life Scenes* 209 (Th.) [Captain Muggs's] spirited 'let her rip' was an infinite improvement on the 'fire' of the old Steuben manual.
c. *trans.* To bring or drive *along* at a fast pace.
1876 *Fur, Fin & Feather* Sept. 89, I had my doubts about ripping her along when I found her sides only an inch above water.
9. *Comb.* as **rip valve,** a valve that can be ripped open in the envelope of a balloon.
1907 *Jrnl. Soc. Arts* 19 Apr. 602/2 By means of the rip valve they were able to come down pleasantly and easily.

Ripper. 3. a. Also of persons.
1905 *Pall Mall Mag.* July 111/1 He had found her a ripper as to looks. 1916 Boyd Cable *Action Front* 149 Wally had shown him her photograph once, 'and a real ripper she is too'.

Ripping, *vbl. sb.* 2. Add: *ripping-cord, -line, -panel, -rope.*
1907 *Strand Mag.* Feb. 149/1 The utility of the *ripping-cord was brought home to me. 1908 H. G. Wells *War in Air* ii. § 5 The ripping-cord failed, and the valve wouldn't act. 1907 *Strand Mag.* Feb. 149/1 The '*ripping-line'..—that comparatively new invention that has done so much for the safety of aeronauts. 1909 *Westm. Gaz.* 21 Aug. 11/2 The examination revealed a bullet hole made..on the right side of the balloon..near the *ripping panel. 1922 *Encycl. Brit.* XXX. 89/1 *note*, Moisture had condensed on the *ripping ropes and frozen there, until each cord was about as thick as a man's forearm.

Ripping, *ppl. a.* Add: 2. Also as a complement.
1894 A. Hope *Dolly Dial.* ix. 51 She did look ripping in that white frock.
b. Very fast or rapid.
1826 [see sense 2]. 1868 H. Woodruff *Trotting Horse* xi. 116 There is no occasion for the ripping spurts which intervene in the other training.

Ri·ppingness. [f. Ripping *ppl. a.* + -ness.] Splendid quality; excellence.
1927 C. E. Montague *Right off Map* xviii. 174 It's the doing the thing that..makes you half drunk with the rippingness of it.

Ripple, *sb.*[3] Add: 5. *attrib.* and *Comb.*, as **ripple cloth,** cloth having a rippled appearance; **ripple-flaking,** a method of flaking flint.
1922 *Westm. Gaz.* 27 Dec. 12 Advt., Ripple Cloth. An ideal washing fabric for Ladies' Dressing Jackets and Dressing gowns. 1928 *Daily Express* 23 June 5/1 Materials suitable for covering are velveteen, mohair plush, ripple cloth,..flannelette, and stockinette. 1921 *Chambers's Jrnl.* Mar. 145/1 Brierly Stratton and I were..discussing the intensive examination of ripple flaking.

Ripple, *v.*[3] 2. c. (Further example.)
1901 A. E. W. Mason *Clementina* xiii, The girl reading it drew a breath and rippled out a length of gladness.

Ripplet. (Earlier example.)
1820 Shelley *Orpheus* 60 Each riplet makes A many-sided mirror for the sun.

Rip-rap, *sb.* 1. b. Also, the sound of fireworks detonating.
1909 Hall Caine *White Prophet* I. I. 8 Once more the words rang like a rip-rap down the line. 1930 *Sea Breezes* 72 The..rip-rap of the fireworks.
3. (Earlier examples.)
1833 H. Barnard in *Maryland Hist. Mag.* XIII. 314 We passed in our way..Old Point Comfort, upon which you know Fortress Monroe is situated—the ripraps directly opposite, which two..will effectually secure the Bay.
attrib. 1838 J. Childs *Western Railroad* (1839) 25 To guard the embankments by rip-rap walls. *Ibid.* 29 Rip-rap slope.

Ri·p-roaring, *a.* U.S. [cf. Rip-roarious.] Full of vigour, spirit or excellence; first-rate; boisterous; full-blooded.
1834 Carruthers *Kentuckian in N. Y.* I. 62 There was a rip-roaring sight of slight o' hand and tumbling work there. 1845 J. J. Hooper *Adv. Simon Suggs* x. 127 And I seed the biggest, longest, rip-roarenest, blackest, scaliest..alligator. 1883 Nye *Baled Hay* 231 He thought..Kirke was there.. to give Laramie the grandest, riproaringest tempest of mirth that she had ever experienced. 1906 *N.Y. Even. Post* Sat. Suppl. 8 Sept. 1 When he was called upon to address the conference he got a rip-roaring welcome. *a* 1909 'O. Henry' *Roads of Destiny* xxii. 368 I'm feeling just like having one more rip-roaring razoo with you for the sake of old times. 1913 *Daily Mail* 28 Feb. 10 Advt., It's a rip-roaring, red-blooded yarn that no man or woman will be able to read unmoved. 1928 *Saturday Even. Post* 12 May 69/1 The Westerner had to pay a damage of more than $600..But he had had a riproaring time.

Riproarious, *a.* (Earlier example.)
1840 *Congress. Globe* 2 Apr. 376 (Th.) Here and there a gentleman from both political parties, who had been drawn out by curiosity to witness their riproarious proceedings.

Riproa·riously, *adv.* U.S. [f. Riproarious + -ly [2].] In a riproarious or boisterous manner.
1834 Crockett *Narr. Life* xi. 78 The next day it rained rip-roriously.

Ri·p-snorting, *a.* U.S. = *Rip-roaring. So **Ri·p-snorter; Ri·p-staver.**
1833 Crockett *Sk.* xi. 144 In ten minutes he yelled enough, and swore I was a ripstavur. 1846 *Yale Lit. Mag.* XI. 336 (Th.) What a rip-snorting red head you have got. 1904 *Topeka Capital* 2 June 4 It is now stated that Bryan will make a rip-snorting speech at the St. Louis convention. 1909 R. A. Wason *Happy Hawkins* 42, I was surprised at the way Brophy talked. I'd allus heard at he was a rip-snortin' screamer, an' here he was talkin low an' level like. 1925 R. Clements *Gipsy of Horn* 87 It came on to blow in a way that the packet-rats called a 'rip-snorter'. 1926 *Spectator* 10 July 44/1 It's a ripsnorting, red-blooded show —a wow.

Rise, *sb.* 15. c. (Earlier examples.) Also in respect of time.
1839 *Southern Lit. Messenger* V. 379/1 It is the rise of a week since I last shifted. 1845 *Congress. Globe* App. 154/1, I do not propose myself to number [the States yet to be admitted]; but..I set them down at twenty and the rise. 1845 J. J. Hooper *Adv. Simon Suggs* xii. 141 Bill..has been ded the rise of twenty year. *Ibid.* 157 'What *will* chickens be wuth this fall?' 'How many have you?' 'The rise of seventy, and three hens a-settin!'

Rise, *v.* Add: 22. c. *As they rise*, as they come to hand.
1910 W. De Morgan *Joseph Vance* 277 He sells you your stock brick back at a pound a thousand took as they rise, bats and all.
29. b. To exceed in number or amount. *U.S.*
1843 C. Matthews *Writ.* 82/1 Brother George counted the strokes of his arm upon the cushion, and thinks he rose a hundred in the course of the sermon.

Riser. Add: 7. b. The flat vertical side of the heel of a boot or shoe.
1928 *Daily Express* 18 Dec. 5/4 The captain took one of them to the window, and..studied the riser of the heel.
12. An electrical conductor or water-pipe passing from one floor of a building to another.
190. *Engin. Rec.* XXXVIII. 566 (Cent. Suppl.) The grouping of risers has been made, however, so that the average current demand on each pair of lighting bars will be about equal.

Rising, *vbl. sb.* 11. b. (Later U.S. example.)
1867 A. D. Richardson *Beyond Mississippi* xi. 133 He spoke of a swelling upon his knee as a 'rising'.

Rising, *ppl. a.* 6. Add: **rising box,** a movable shuttle-box; a drop-box.
1894 C. Vickerman *Woollen Spinning* i. 12 In 1769..Robert Kaye invented the rising-box, or, as it was then called, the *drop-box.*

Rising, *pr. pple.* Add: 3. a. (Earlier examples.)
1775 *Massachusetts Gaz.* 13 Feb. (Th.) To be sold, an elegant little black Mare, rising six years. 1802 *Lancaster* (Pa.) *Jrnl.* 13 Sept. (Th.) Strayed from the subscriber on Sunday the 7th instant, a red cow rising four years old. 1837 W. Jenkins *Ohio Gaz.* 64 It enjoys a yearly income of rising $4.500. 1845 in C. Cist *Cincinnati Misc.* 258 This..delegation..will probably be composed of rising 250 members.

Risk, *sb.* 3. Add: *Risk-rate* (see quot.).
1928 *Brit. Industr. Fut.* (Lib. Ind. Inq.) III. xvi. 187 Capital will not be forthcoming for any enterprise unless it can expect (*a*) a normal rate of interest..and (*b*) in addition to that a 'risk-rate' corresponding to the chance of loss in the particular business.

Ri·skfulness. [f. Riskful + -ness.] = Riskiness.
1925 *Glasgow Herald* 20 June 4/2 The most remarkable feature is the riskfulness of the life-history.

Risqué (riske), *a.* [F.] = Risky *a.* 3.
1924 P. Marks *Plastic Age* 228 The comic magazine, which coined money by publishing risqué jokes and pictures of slightly dressed women. 1924 *Brit. Weekly* 18 Dec. 301/3 In remote corners others are reading risqué novels with a sex interest.

Ritschlian (ri·tʃliăn), *a.* and *sb.* [f. the name of Albrecht *Ritschl*, German theologian (1822–1889).] a. *adj.* Of or pertaining to Ritschl or his doctrines. b. *sb.* A follower of Ritschl or a student of Ritschlianism. **Ri·tschlianism,** the theological or philosophical doctrines of Ritschl.
1891 *Chambers's Encycl.* VIII. 733/2 The distinguishing feature of the Ritschlian theology is perhaps the eminence it gives to the practical, ethical, social side of Christianity. *Ibid.* 734/1 The Ritschlians now form a large and important school in Germany. 1892 J. Orr in *Thinker* Aug. 148 Ritschlianism has a metaphysic, and a specially dangerous one. 1897 R. M. Wenley *Contemp. Theol.* 82 In approaching the Ritschlians, a preliminary warning must be issued. 1899 A. E. Garvie *Ritschlian Theol.* I. § vi. 20 It is in this spirit that the writer now invites the reader to study the Ritschlian Theology. 1904 *Athenæum* 6 Feb. 167/2 If Ritschlianism is so illusory a creed..the plain man..may well wonder [etc.]. 1917 Bartlet & Carlyle *Christianity in Hist.* v. v. 596 Ritschlianism and Catholic Modernism are the most marked movements in this direction.

Rived, *ppl. a.* (Later example.)
1853 *Trans. Mich. Agric. Soc.* IV. 156 Either the rived or sawed bolt may be used.

River, *sb.*[1] Add: 4. g. *river-borne, -caught, -fed.*
1928 *Daily Tel.* 4 Dec. 12/4 Splitting the market into two, for *river-borne and rail-borne supplies respectively. 1924 A. J. Small *Frozen Gold* xii. 248 Others sat round the braziers and held great slabs of *river-caught salmon against the red-hot grids. 1913 E. F. Benson *Thorley Weir* i, A strip of *river-fed grasses and herbs of the waterside.
5. **river-pearl** (see quot.); **river-scape,** a picture or prospect of a river.
1885 *Encycl. Brit.* XVIII. 447/2 *River-pearls are produced by the fresh-water mussels inhabiting the mountain-streams of temperate climates in the northern hemisphere. 1903 C. S. Smith *Barbizon Days* 17 Grez [has] a church more picturesque than that of Montigny, *riverscapes more alluring, and a ruined château. 1930 *Time & Tide* 9 May 606 Mr. Lamorna Birch and Sir H. Hughes Stanton show very capable riverscapes.

River-bottom. (Earlier example.)
1752 C. Gist *Jrnls.* 75 [We] continued our course..the last 5 [miles] thro the river bottoms, which were a mile wide and very rich.

Riverine. A. *adj.* 2. (Further example.)
1905 *Chambers's Jrnl.* Mar. 220/1 Its fishes are closely allied to riverine forms in some cases.

Rivet, *sb.*[1] 2. Add: *rivet-bar, -hearth.*
1890 D. K. Clark *Steam Engine* I. 657 The diameter of the ⅞-inch *rivet-bars was reduced ·03 inch. 1902 *Encycl. Brit.* XXXII. 597 The riveters also work in squads,..with sometimes a catcher, *i.e.*, a boy to pass on the heated rivets when the distance from the *rivet-hearth is great.

Riveting, *vbl. sb.* 1. (Further example.)
1902 *Encycl. Brit.* XXXII. 597 In shipbuilding the large proportion of the riveting is done by hand.
c. *spec.* The attaching of the soles of boots and shoes with metal rivets.
1886 *Encycl. Brit.* XXI. 831/1 Three principal methods of attaching soles to uppers are in use at present..The second is the system of 'riveting or clinching' with iron or brass nails.

Roach, *sb.*[1] 2. b. Add: *roach-swim.*
1902 *Chambers's Jrnl.* Nov. 699/1, I was preparing to fish a not unpromising roach-swim, and was trying the depth.

Roach, *sb.*[3] Add: 2. *attrib.* in sense of *Roached *a.* 2.
1781 *Royal Georgia Gaz.* 8 Mar. Advt. (Th.) A Black Horse, about 13 and an half hands high, half roach main [etc.]. 1835 J. T. Irving *Ind. Sketches* II. 4 She was mounted upon a little wall-eyed, cream-coloured pony, with a roach mane and a bobtail.

Roach, *v.* Add: 2. (Earlier example.)
1818 *Missouri Gaz.* 25 Dec. (Th.) His mane has been divided,..and that part that laid on the left side cut off as if to roach him.
b. Of persons: To cut (the hair) short except one ridge on the top of the head where it is allowed to stand on end. Also with *up.*
1833 Crockett *Sk.* ii. 38 His hair was roached, and he wore an air of much dignity. 1854 J. G. Baldwin *Flush Times Alabama* (1858) 108 His hair was roached up, and stood as erect and upright as his body. 1900 G. Ade *More Fables in Slang* 62 He would go to School with his Face scrubbed to a shiny pink and his Hair roached up on one side. 1916 H. L. Wilson *Somewhere in Red Gap* iv. 148 His hair was gray, and he was either shedding or had been roached. 1919 — *Ma Pettengill* iii. 84 She was..a kind of a slaty blonde with bobbed hair—she'd been roached fore and aft.

Roached, *a.* Add: (Earlier examples.)
1776 *N. Eng. Chron.* 25 Jan. Advt. (Th.) Strayed or stolen a sorrel horse—roach'd back, 3 white feet, [etc.]. 1844 *Scribblings & Sk.* 176 (Th.) The two [horses] with roatched backs, and ears glued to their necks, were scrambling.
2. Of hair (on a horse or person): Cut short so that it stands on end.
1836 *Southern Lit. Messenger* II. 303/1 The..fat, impudent pony, with roached main and bobtail. 1856 P. Cartwright *Autob.* xii. (1858) 76 This young man had a mighty bushy roached head of hair.

Roaching (rōu·tʃiŋ), *vbl. sb.*[2] [f. Roach *v.* + -ing [1].] (See quot.)
1903 *N. Y. Even. Post* 24 Oct., When brought to market

he [the mule] undergoes the process of 'roaching', which consists of removing all the hair of poor quality and scanty growth.

Road, *sb.* Add: 9. a. *road-racer.*
1908 H. G. Wells *War in Air* i. 14 Even a *road-racer, geared to a hundred and twenty, failed to satisfy him.
b. *road-bank* (earlier example).
1864 B. Taylor *H. Thurston* xxv. 332 As they drove homewards through the cool of the evening air, through.. the golden-rod on the *road-banks.
c. *road-fund, -locomotion, -system, -traffic, -web.*
1920 *Act* 10 & 11 *Geo. V* c. 72 § 3 There shall be established for the purposes of this Act,..a fund to be called the *Road Fund. 1927 W. E. Collinson *Contemp. Engl.* 88 The Chancellor of the Exchequer..is raiding the road-fund. 1912 *Chambers's Jrnl.* Sept. 613/2 The change which is taking place in *road-locomotion. 1904 W. M. Ramsay *Lett. Seven Ch.* xxix. 416 Laodicea was a knot on the *road-system. 1909 *Chambers's Jrnl.* June 340/1 A successful attempt was made to conduct *road-traffic without the use of animal-power. 1925 Deeping *Sorrell & Son* vi. 58 Then take the *road-web for the ordinary tourist. London some hundred miles. Salisbury thirty or so.
10. a. *road-board, -scout.*
1887 W. B. Withers *Hist. Ballarat* (ed. 2) 308 Ballarat history includes a record of the foundation of *road boards. 1915 *Pol. Quarterly* May 180 The Road Board..has restricted the grants to completing advances promised before the war. 1931 *Star* 8 May 16/1 While being chased by a *road scout on a motor-cycle..a car collided with a lamp post.
b. *road-breaker, -upper.*
1928 *Daily Mail* 31 July 13/3 One side of Kensington-road,..is also in the hands of the *road-breakers. 1928 *Daily Express* 12 June 3/4 The '*road-uppers' are busy in London again.
12. **road-bridge,** a bridge forming part of a road; **road-craft,** knowledge of or skill in matters pertaining to roads; **road-farer,** one who travels by road; so **road-faring** *ppl. a.*; **road-ferry,** a ferry serving a road; **road-life,** the life of those who are 'on the road'; **road-mobile** *a.*, suitable for transporting by road; **road-rail** *a.*, suitable for use on both road and railway; **road-sense,** capacity for intelligent handling of vehicles on the road.
1819 *Massachusetts Spy* 3 Nov. (Th.) A salute was fired from a *road-bridge by a detachment of artillery. 1868 Journeyman Engineer *Great Unwashed* 265 The old tramp..has a beneficial knowledge of what may be called *road-craft. 1897 H. S. Merriman *In Kedar's Tents* xii, Conyngham learnt much of that road-craft which had raised Concepcion Vara to such a proud eminence among the rascals of Andalusia. 1923 *Daily Mail* 22 May 4 Hotels,.. which set out to cater efficiently for the growing army of *roadfarers. 1925 *Chambers's Jrnl.* June 379/2 She would probably not average over 2 m.p.h., which seems almost incredible to a different section of the *road-faring fraternity. 1920 *Act* 10 & 11 *Geo. V* c. 72 Sched. 1, The definition of 'roads' shall be extended so as to include *road-ferries and footways. 1902 *N. Y. Times* 28 Dec. (Cent. Suppl.) A comedian who has seen so much of the unlovely side of '*road' life that he might well be the writer of tragedies. 1922 *Encycl. Brit.* XXX. 249/1 The French guns up to the 6 in., and howitzers up to the 9.45 in. inclusive will be *road-mobile...All heavier natures will be on railway mountings. 1927 *Times* 20 Dec. 11/3 The '*road-rail' truck represents in a modified form the upper part of a railway wagon which can be exchanged between road and rail vehicles. 1923 *Daily Mail* 10 Aug. 6/3 The good driver uses care instinctively because he has the imagination or '*road-sense' which tells him instantly what he can and what he cannot do. 1929 W. E. Collinson *Spoken Engl.* 84 It is easy to drive a car if you have road-sense.

Roadability (rōudăbi·lĭti). [f. Road *sb.* + -ability.] Suitability for travelling on the road; roadworthiness.
1928 *Sunday Dispatch* 16 Sept. 5 Advt., Wider track, lower centre of gravity, improved roadability.

Road hog, *sb.* (See Road *sb.* 12.)
1891 *Outing* Dec. 238/2 The 'road hog' curses him and the wayside brute calls out the dog. 1898 [see Road *sb.* 12]. 1909 *Q. Rev.* Jan. 143 The habitually reckless motorist.. commonly known as the 'road-hog'. 1925 *Public Opinion* 14 Aug. 151/3 Road-hogs who run down pedestrians.
Hence **Roa·d-hog** *v. intr.*, to be a road hog or act like a road hog; **Roa·d-hogging** *ppl. a.* and *vbl. sb.*; **Roa·d-hoggish** *a.*; **Roa·d-hoggism.**
1914 'Ian Hay' *Knight on Wheels* xviii. 174, I wouldn't go road-hogging if I were you...Road-hogging is rotten bad form. 1923 *Daily Mail* 28 May 5 In four days, without road-hogging, we have covered 646 miles of Britain. 1926 *Glasgow Herald* 12 July 6/3 The perfect Sunday—to hide at home while the rest of the world road hogged it out of town. 1927 *Scots Observer* 16 July 10/4 Avoiding excess of speed and other road-hoggisms. 1928 *Daily Express* 24 Apr. 10/2 The road-hogging motor-coach. 1930 *Time & Tide* 7 Feb. 172 No motorist, however road-hoggish he may be, deliberately slays a child or any other person.

Roadman. Add: 2. A person using the roads for any purpose; an itinerant canvasser or seller of goods; a tramp or vagrant.
1906 S. E. Sparling *Introd. Business Organiz.* 206 Another method of direct selling is found in the system of canvassers and road-men sent out by factories. 1912 A. S. M. Hutchinson *Happy Warrior* v. vi. 318 There cried to them 'Away! away!' all the instinct that, since first law came on the land, has bade roadmen, gipsies, outlaws, take immediate flight from trouble.

Roadster. Add: 2. c. A type of motor-car.
1922 Titus *Timber* xxix. 255 Rowe stood..a long interval, ..watching her roadster disappear into the jack pines. 1928 F. N. Hart *Bellamy Trial* ii. 30 We drove out from New York in my roadster. 1930 C. J. Dutton *Shadow of Evil* iv. 61 It was just ten o'clock when he ran the long blue roadster out of the garage.

Roa·dworthiness. [f. Roadworthy + -ness.] Roadworthy character; reliability on the road.
1923 *Daily Mail* 6 Aug. 4/4 One object was to demonstrate the roadworthiness or otherwise of these..family cars. 1928 *Daily Tel.* 16 Oct. 17 Advt., The low centre of gravity gives to the new Humber a road-worthiness unequalled.

Roam, *v.* Add: 4. To cause (the eyes) to look over a scene.
1900 Bloundelle-Burton *Seafarers* xii. 118 As he spoke he roamed his eye around the tranquil, glassy sea.

Roar, *sb.*[1] Add: 2. b. *To go with a roar*, to make uninterrupted progress or be a conspicuous success.
1907 *Punch* 1 May 308/2 Everything went with a roar.

Roar, *v.* Add: 3. e. To travel on a vehicle of which the engine is making a loud noise; to motor or fly rapidly.
1923 *Motor Cycling* 26 Sept. 658/3 Marsden roared through on his last lap. 1928 Gamble *Story N. Sea Air Station* xii. 171 On the approach of our cruisers, the Germans roared back.

Roarer[1]. Add: 1. (Further example.)
1903 W. S. Blunt *Seven Golden Odes* 33 Fled to the land of the lions, roarers importunate.
5. *U.S.* An oil-well from which the oil pours rapidly and noisily.
1887 B. T. Crew *Treat. on Petroleum* viii. 227 We have no right, perhaps, to expect a continuance of the 'roarers', or 'gushers' as they are termed.

Roasting, *vbl. sb.* 1. (Further example.)
1891 J. Wrightson *Farm Crops* iii. 31 Besides, the great object in working a fallow is the 'roasting' of the weeds by means of the midsummer sun.

Rob, *v.* 1. (Further fig. example.)
1926 *Publishers' Weekly* 19 June 1966/1 You may improve your golf game...Why not get rid of that disconcerting slice which robs your drive?

Robber. 2. b. Add: *robber baron.*
1905 D. G. Phillips *Plum Tree* 195 He was..about the greediest and cruelest 'robber baron' in the West.

Ro·bberism. [f. Robber + -ism.] The conduct or business of robbers; robbery.
1921 *Glasgow Herald* 18 Jan. 6 Communism in Russia is robberism.

Robin[1]. 3. (Earlier examples.)
1750 J. Birket *Voyage N. Amer.* (1916) 13 They have..a bird like our field fare with a red brest which they call a Robin that sings delightfully. 1774 P. V. Fithian *Jrnl.* (1900) 121 The finest morning we have yet had; the Robbins & blue Birds singing all around us.

Robot (rōu·bɒt). [Czech, f. *robota* statute labour, *robotnik* serf.] Applied by Karel Capek in his play *R.U.R.* to a mechanical apparatus doing the work of a man; hence, any such apparatus; a person whose work or activities are entirely mechanical; an automaton.
1923 Selver tr. *Capek's R.U.R.* (Rossum's Universal Robots) 28 You see..the Robots have no interest in life. They have no enjoyments. 1923 *Times* 9 June 10/5 If Almighty God had populated the world with Robots, legislation of this sort might have been reasonable. 1924 *Blackw. Mag.* Oct. 537/2 In his tirelessness there was something of a mechanism, something of a robot. 1926 Joad *Babbitt Warren* 82 Robots live by standardization. 1928 *Daily News & Westm. Gaz.* 20 Apr. 11/4 The latest..Rotary Press, a veritable Robot in the complicated work it performs night after night without hitch.
b. An automatic traffic-signal.
1931 *Even. Standard* 5 Aug. 2/1 (heading) Traffic 'Robots' in the City.
2. *attrib.* and *Comb.*, as *robot army, clerk, pilot*; *robot-like* adj.
1927 *Morn. Post* 20 Aug. 9 (heading) Robot army 'gassed'. 1928 *Daily Express* 8 June 3/2 A new automatic selling machine, described as the 'Robot clerk,' which will say 'Thank you' and give change, will replace the present automatic machines. *Ibid.* 11 Aug. 3/7 Yet the romance of past centuries and robot-like drama of modern times meet at Sandwich. 1930 *Aberdeen Press & Jrnl.* 31 Mar. 7/3 One of these robot pilots has been fitted to a big twin-engined Supermarine Napier flying boat.
Hence **Robote·sque** *a.*, resembling or suggestive of a robot. **Robo·tian** *a.*, of or belonging to robots. **Ro·botism,** mechanical behaviour or character. **Robotiza·tion,** the process of making or fact of being mechanical in behaviour. **Ro·botize** *v. trans.*, to subject to the operation of robots; to render mechanical. **Ro·botized** *ppl. a.* **Ro·botizing** *vbl. sb.* **Ro·botry,** the business, position, or condition of robots.
1927 C. M. Grieve *Albyn* 46 Dostoevsky's mistake was to imagine that Russia alone could prevent the robotization of Europe. 1927 *Daily Express* 11 Mar. 6/4 'Robotesque' movements..acquire a singular menace and significance in the screen medium. *Ibid.* 30 Aug. 3/4 The Girl in the Lift must on some occasions drop her magnificent Robotry. Perhaps she even marries. *Ibid.* 7 Nov. 10/2 Lacking a skilled class of artisans, it is only by Robotising industry ..that she can hope to fight her way back to prosperity. 1928 *Observer* 15 Jan. 11/2 These robotised people..are only employed and allowed to exist because no one has yet been sufficiently energetic to invent a machine to replace them. *Ibid.* 29 Jan. 9/3 (heading) The Robotism of Architecture. 1928 *Daily Express* 17 Mar. 4/2 A few have their wooden craniums transfixed by bodkins, and some have Robotian books instead of hands.

Rock, *sb.*[1] Add: 2. e. *A pocketful of rocks*, a large amount of money.
1847 J. S. Robb *Streaks of Squatter Life* 165 If I had a 'pocket full of rocks', you should share them. 1850 J. R. Lowell *Unhappy Lot of Mr. Knott* 30 A pocket-full of rocks 't would take To build a house of freestone.
6. a. *rock-house.*
1901 C. Mohr *Plant Life Alabama* 17 The..fern, *Trichomanes petersii*,..with others like it hidden in the dark recesses of rocky defiles and the so-called 'rock houses'.
b. *rock-painting.*
1908 *Hastings's Encycl. Relig. & Ethics* I. 822/2 The rock-paintings..are either stencilled..or painted in outline.
7. c. *rock-painter.*
1919 H. G. Wells *Outl. Hist.* xii. 77/2 The simplicity, directness, and detachment of a later Palæolithic *rock-painter appeal more to modern sympathies than does the state of mind of these Neolithic men.
8. c. *rock-steady.*
1928 *Outlook* 26 May 650/1 Consols were rock-steady at 112.
9. **rock-bottom** (further example); **rock-hog,** a labourer engaged in tunnelling through rock; **rocksman** = Rockman; **rock-wool,** a wool-like insulating substance prepared from limestone.
1904 Harben *Georgians* 200 Now cool off, an' let's git down to *rock bottom. 1909 *Chambers's Jrnl.* Dec. 828/2 The *rock-hogs had not proceeded far before they pierced a large pocket. 1852 Macgillivray *Hist. Brit. Birds* V. 434 The dexterity of these *rocksmen is truly astonishing. 1931 *Times Trade & Engin. Suppl.* 5 Sept. 535/3 Certain deposits of impure limestone outcropping in the Niagara district of Ontario are suitable for the production of *rock wool or mineral wool.

Rock, *v.*[1] Add: 6. e. In mountaineering: To work one's way *up* a chimney by a rocking movement.
1920 G. W. Young *Mountain Craft* 168 The body is kept upright in the middle on the spring of the bent knees and supported by the pressure of the hands, placed like the feet one against each wall. In this fashion we can 'rock' up satisfactorily.

Rock, *v.*[2] 2. (Earlier example.)
1836 *Public Ledger* (Philad.) 30 Aug. (Th.) Jacket over coat,—rock him! rock him! cried the boys of Marblehead, 'rock him round the corner.'
3. To remove the calcareous deposit or 'fur' from the inside of (a kettle).
1880 Hardy *Trumpet-Major* xvi, The broken clock-line was mended, the kettles rocked, the creeper nailed up, and a new handle put to the warming-pan.

Rocker[1]. Add: 2. c. *Off one's rocker* (later examples).
1923 Wodehouse *Inimit. Jeeves* vii. 78 The Duke is off his rocker. 1929 J. Buchan *Courts of Morning* II. iv. 199 The question is how long it will be till he goes clean off his rocker.
4. c. (Earlier example.)
1833 H. Barnard in *Maryland Hist. Mag.* XIII. 346 The top soil is removed—then the gravel is washed, by being thrown into what is called a rocker, or cradle, which is in fact little more than a large cradle.
f. A tanning-vat designed for moving backwards and forwards.
1897 C. T. Davis *Manuf. Leather* (ed. 2) 382 The hides are next suspended in 'rockers'...They remain in the 'rockers' from seven to ten days.
5. b. (Earlier example.)
1853 B. F. Taylor *Jan. & June* (1871) 155 Who says, the boys sha'n't skate? Who grudges them the 'rockers'?
c. = Rocking-turn (see *Rocking *vbl. sb.*).
1892 Witham etc. *Figure-skating* 109 In the rockers and counters (which figures used to be designated rocking turns and counter-rocking turns) although there is a change of direction, the nature of the edge is preserved.
g. A rock-shaft.
1926 *Gloss. Electr. Terms* (Brit. Engin. Stand.) 64 *Rocker gear*, the worm wheel or other gear by means of which the position of the brush-rocker may be adjusted. 1930 Field & Weill *Electro-Plating* 30 To allow for this setting they [*sc.* the brushes] are mounted on a rocker.
6. *rocker-arm, -box.*
1875 M. N. Forney *Catechism of Locomotive* xi. 195 The dotted lines *h a* and *h b* represent the two extreme positions into which the rocker-arm would be moved by the action of the link. 1931 J. W. Day *Speed* xi. 159 A rocker arm broke, the exhaust valve jammed, and a piston came up and hit it. 1892 J. G. A. Meyer *Mod. Locomotive Constr.* 199 The lifting-shaft bearing and rocker-box..are bolted to the front splice.

Rocket, *v.* 2. a. *transf.* Of lightning.
1924 W. J. Locke *Coming of Amos* xxiv. 312 A flash of lightning rocketed across the black gap of the open window.

Rocking, *vbl. sb.*[1] Add: 3. **rocking-turn,** a movement or figure in skating (see quot.).
1869 Vandervell & Witham *Figure-skating* 219 After having exhausted the Q, I began to consider the feasibility of making the change direct from the inside forwards to inside backwards and *vice versâ*..by the employment of a kind of turn, for which..I can find no more simple..name than the 'Rocking Turn'.

Rocking, *ppl. a.* 2. Add: *rocking shackle.*
1902 *Encycl. Brit.* XXVI. 464/1 The mooring cable..is secured to a 'rocking shackle' on the upper surface of the buoy.

Rocky, *a.*[1] Add: 1. c. (Earlier example.)
a 1861 T. Winthrop *John Brent* vi. 60 At the foot of those bare, bulky mounds of mountain by which the Wasatch range tones off into the great plains between it and the Rockys, we overtook the Salt Lake mail.
6. *colloq.* Destitute of means; = *on the rocks* (Rock *sb.* 2 d).
1923 Galsworthy *Captures* 152 Are you at all—er—er—rocky? I mean—if I can be of any service, don't hesitate!

Rococo. A. *adj.* 1. (Later example.)
1902 H. L. Wilson *Spenders* ix. 92 She is rather a beauty, you'll find;..a bit rococo in manner, I suspect.

Rod, *sb.*[1] Add: 11. b. *rod-stand.*
1902 *Chambers's Jrnl.* July 425/1 Any trout-rod, even after a brief life spent in such a manner, might have accepted its pensioner peg on the *rod-stand.
c. In sense 9 b as *rod-pigment, -vision, -white.*
1921 E. B. Titchener *Text-bk. Psychol.* 89 Animals whose eyes lack this *rod-pigment—fowls, pigeons—are strictly diurnal in their habits. *Ibid.*, Whether the visual purple is essentially concerned in *rod-vision. 1922 Woodworth *Psychol.* x. 226 Dim-light vision, or *twilight vision* as it is sometimes called, is *rod vision* and not cone vision. 1904 *Nature* 18 Feb. 379/1 The light red colour seen in gazing at the platinum plate changes in indirect vision into a peculiar colourless white, the '*rod-white'.

Rodeo. Add: 1. b. *transf.* An assembly or rally of other things.
1928 *Daily Express* 7 May 15/3 On Wednesday..a motor-cycle rodeo in the afternoon will be followed by a carnival procession through the town.

Rogation. Add: 4. *Comb.*, as *Rogationtide.*
1924 W. P. M. Kennedy *Eliz. Episc. Admin.* I. iv. p. ciii, The parson was to wear the surplice at least,..to go in procession at Rogationtide, to preach if licensed.

Rogue, *sb.* Add: 7. *rogue-eyed* adj.
1867 Meredith *Vittoria* I. ix. 133 She had, in tripping down the Piazza with her rogue-eyed cousin from Milan, looked away [etc.].

Roil, *v.*[3] 2. (Later example.)
1907 *Springfield Weekly Republ.* 17 Jan. 6 The publication of such a work naturally roiled the publishers of Webster's international dictionary.

Roll, *sb.*[1] Add: 6. e. A quantity of bills or notes rolled together; the money a person possesses. *U.S.*
1904 *N. Y. Times* 16 May 5 It was as easy to be separated from one's 'roll' at a shell game there a quarter of a century ago as it was ten years ago. *a* 1906 'O. Henry' *Trimmed Lamp* etc. 171 He drew out his 'roll' and slapped five tens upon the bar. 1919 H. L. Wilson *Ma Pettengill* ii. 62 [He] asked her how big her roll was, saying that he lived out there and it cost something to make a home. 1926 J. Black *You Can't Win* iv. 35 No Missouri dip would take his roll, extract two fifty dollar bills, and put the rest back in his pocket.
13. *roll-film, -shutter, -wave.*
1903 *Science Siftings* 23 May 88/2 A novel hand-camera for the exposure of roll films has just been brought to our notice. 1911 *Chambers's Jrnl.* Feb. 141/2 At the kerb end the front is provided with a roll-shutter. 1907 *Geog. Jrnl.* Jan. 23 In certain rivers..the 'first rise' of water in the lower reaches frequently takes the form of a steep-fronted wave, or bore, travelling down-stream. On the Tees the phenomenon is called a roll-wave.
17. **roll-scale,** oxide of iron falling in scales from iron in the process of rolling.
1887 Phillips & Bauerman *Elem. Metallurgy* 148 Roll- and hammer-scale are essentially magnetic oxides of iron; they are chiefly used in the forges.

Roll, *v.*[2] Add: 11. d. Of the foot: To slip upon a rolling object.
1882 Stevenson *New Arabian Nts.* II. 148 His foot rolled upon a pebble. 1904 L. Tracy *King of Diamonds* ix. 123 Philip..almost fell too, for his left foot rolled on the constable's staff.
12. b. *To roll up*: Also, to arrive; to appear on the scene.
1929 'Sapper' in *Legion Bk.* 214 The man hasn't rolled up yet, but he won't be long.
21. e. Of an aeroplane: To sway or turn on an axis parallel to the direction of flight.
1918 *War Birds* (1927) 69 He was looping and rolling between the church spires.

Roll-call. 1. (Earlier examples.)
1775 *Essex Inst. Hist. Coll.* XLVIII. 61 This morning we went to rol col & then got our Brefust. 1777 *Ibid.* XIII. 118 Ordered that the Hour for Roll Call be altered to Nine o'clock in the morning.

Ro·ll-call, *v.* [f. the sb.] *trans.* To call the roll for (a group or body of persons).
1928 *Daily Express* 19 Mar. 12/2 The German officers were counted or 'roll-called' in their rooms to save them the trouble of having to assemble or fall in with the other prisoners.

Roll-collar. (Recent example.)
1929 *Even. News* 18 Nov. 6/5 Advt., Below we show the D.B. Chester with long roll collar.

Rolled, *ppl. a.* 1. (Further example.)
1928 *Daily Mail* 3 Aug. 10/4 Members of the audience looked twice before they could..appreciate the fact that she had rolled stockings.
3. (Earlier example.)
1789 *Ann. 1st Congress* 17 Apr. 174 It was agreed to lay an impost of seven and a half per cent..on..slit or rolled iron.

Roller, *sb.*[1] Add: 1. b. A rubber-covered cylinder used for reducing one's weight.
1930 *London Mercury* Feb. 323 She makes the roller earn its keep, I can tell you!
15. b. A low rising or undulation on land. *U.S.*
1849 N. Kingsley *Diary* 88 The land on the left rises in rollers from 10 to 50 feet and the soil appears rich. 1850 W. Cotton *Three Years in Calif.* xxiii. 321 Our course, which was determined by a pocket-compass, now lay among mountain spurs, till we reached the rollers, which ridge the plain of the San Joaquin.
23. b. Also *roller-bearinged* adj.
1922 *Encycl. Brit.* XXX. 36/2 Connecting-rods of rotary and radial engines consist usually of one master-rod, ball or roller-bearinged [etc.].
24. **roller-box,** a box containing drawing-rolls in a cotton-spinning machine; **roller-cloth** = *roller towel*; **roller-race,** the channel in which the rollers of a roller-bearing move; **roller-towel** (earlier example).
1902 Thornley *Cotton-Combing Machines* iii. 85 In times past a good deal of trouble has arisen in connection with the quadrant and *roller box system. 1862 'Gail Hamilton' *Country Living* etc. 11, I become acquainted..with the *modus operandi* of '*roller-cloths'. 1877 Eliz. S. Phelps *Story of Avis* 224 A roller-cloth would do, dear. 1903 *Sci. Amer.* Suppl. 21 Feb. 22689/1 The rollers are made to fit the inner and outer treads of the *roller race. 1845 *Knickerbocker Mag.* XXV. 444 Beside the window was the linen *roller-towel.

Ro·ller-skate, *v.* [f. the sb.] *intr.* To use roller-skates; to travel on roller-skates.
1928 *Daily Tel.* 7 Feb. 4/7 Splendid and Partner can roller-skate as agilely on one table as Barrie Oliver can dance on another.

Rolling, *vbl. sb.*[2] Add: 1. b. Short for Log-rolling. *U.S.*
1847 in H. Howe *Hist. Coll. Ohio* 358 Many times were we called from six to eight miles to assist at a rolling or raising, and cheerfully lent our assistance to the task.
4. d. 'Taxying' in an aeroplane.
1915 Kipling *Mary Postgate* in *Div. of Creatures* (1917) 423 Wynn..had finished 'rolling'..and had gone on from a 'taxi' to a machine more or less his own.
6. b. A turning movement of aeroplanes or motor-cars about the direction of motion.
1922 *Encycl. Brit.* XXX. 18/1 French pilots again pointed the way in the art of 'rolling', a manoeuvre in which the aeroplane is rolled about its longitudinal axis. 1930 *Morn. Post* 21 July 4 Sideway or rolling occurs at right angles to the propeller shaft.
9. c. **rolling-hitch;** also **rolling chamber,** a compartment for water-ballast extending across the beam of a ship.
1900 *Geog. Jrnl.* Jan. 34 The ship has a rolling chamber to keep her steady. 1883 *Man. Seamanship for Boys* 87 Q. What is a rolling-hitch used for..? A. Bending a small rope to a large one, putting a tail jigger on a backstay.

Rolling, *ppl. a.* 6. a. Add: *rolling croquet, grass.*
1877 *Encycl. Brit.* VI. 609/2 *Rolling croquet*, in which the balls are sent together in nearly the same line, is made by trailing the mallet after the balls as soon as the stroke or tap is made. 1889 Maiden *Usef. Pl.* 108 *Spinifex hirsutus* ..'Spring *Rolling Grass.'

Rolling (rōu·liŋ), *pr. pple.* [f. Roll *v.*[2] 19.] Short for *rolling in wealth.*
1921 G. O'Donovan *Vocations* xiii. 193, I wish the dear nuns would share some of their poverty with us. They must be rolling. 1922 Mrs. Sidgwick *Victorian* xxi. 163 He isn't a bad old thing at all and he's simply rolling.

Roll stone. *U.S.* A stone rounded by friction or attrition on a beach or in the bed of a river.
1845 Fremont *Exped.* 124 A swift current, over a bed composed entirely of boulders or roll stones. 1872 *Rep. Vermont Board Agric.* I. 688 A fine specimen of gold from a rollstone he found, while digging a well.

Ro·ll-up, *a.* [f. *to roll up*: Roll *v.*[2] 8 b.] Suitable for rolling up.
1923 *Daily Mail* 12 Feb. 2 Advt., Roll-up felts at half price.

Roman, *sb.*[1] Add: 5. b. A Roman hyacinth.
1925 *Glasgow Herald* 26 Aug. 8/7 Early Romans are in, but at a very high price.

Ro·man Catholi·city. [f. Roman Catholic + -ity.] = Roman Catholicism.
1806 M. B. Pembridge *Rom. Cath. Ch. Vindicated* i. 40 These edifices still bear the external signature of Roman Catholicity.

Romance, *sb.* and *a.* 7. a. Also *romancewards* adv.
1920 Rose Macaulay *Potterism* vi. iii. 228 He was also leaning romancewards and departing from the realm of pure truth.

Romanesque, *a.* Add: 4. Romantic.
1869 K. H. Digby *Little Low Bushes* 260 All fair things, lovely, picturesque, Serene, or wild, or romanesque.

Romanian, *a.*[2] (Later example.)
1930 H. Belloc *Wolsey* i. 25 The road through the Romanian plain.

Romanist, *sb.* Add: 5. A Roman citizen.
1927 W. M. Ramsay *Asianic Elem. Gk. Civil.* xvii. 247 *note*, Iconium was made a Roman colony by Hadrian; but no Latins or Romanists were sent to it.

Romano-. Add: *Romano-Briton.*
1896 A. H. Keane *Ethnol.* II. xiv. 398 The Teutons merged everywhere in diverse proportions with the Romano-Britons.

Roma·nticalism. [f. Romantical + -ism.] = Romanticality.
1922 W. J. Locke *Tale of Triona* xiii. 142 She..was driven by she knew not what idiot romanticalism into the grey worries of wifehood and motherhood.

Roma·nticizing, *vbl. sb.* [f. Romanticize *v.* + -ing [1].] The action of the verb Romanticize.
1899 *Speaker* 15 Apr. 424 (Cent. Suppl.) Enlivened by champagne and some grotesque romanticising on the part of the amorous Duchess.

Romeward, *adv.* and *a.* Add: 3. b. Directed towards or facing the city of Rome.
1850 J. Miley *Hist. Papal State* I. Introd. 6 Not less so on the Adriatic side of the Apennines than on the Romeward side.

Ro·mewardness. [f. Romeward *adv.* + -ness.] Tendency towards Roman Catholicism.
1901 *Daily Chron.* 27 Aug. 5/1 The young Duchess was forgiven by her relatives for her Romewardness.

Romp, *sb.* Add: 2. b. *In a romp*, (to achieve something or win a contest) with the greatest ease.
a 1909 'O. Henry' *Roads of Destiny* xviii. 308 Rompiro will win in a romp... We'll carry the country by 10,000.

Romp, *v.* 2. Also *transf.*
1927 *Observer* 18 Sept. 17/2 It is a bad blow to official Labour that Mr. Larkin should have romped home in north Dublin. 1928 *Sunday Express* 22 July 1/2 The child of 1928 simply romps through papers which were 'teasers' for the child of 1914.

Romper. Add: 2. A garment for a child to wear at play; also (*U.S.*), a style of knickerbockers worn by men.
1922 *Westm. Gaz.* 20 Oct. 9 Advt., An attractive romper suit for a small child is made of white washing material. 1925 *Scribner's Mag.* July 13/1 Advt., Miss Walton will be glad to tell you where to go for rubies, rugs, or a sale in rompers. 1928 L. North *Parasites* 18 Many of them wore sweaters that would have put Joseph's coat to shame. And very long, very baggy knickers, Hollywood rompers.

Roneo (rōu·nio), *sb.* (The name of a company manufacturing) a special type of duplicating machine. Also *attrib.* and *Comb.* Hence **Ro·neo** *v. trans.*, to copy or reproduce with a Roneo.
1914 D. Fraser *Winning a Primitive People* III. xxvi. 272 A native clerk is there..turning on the Roneo hundreds of copies of some circular to the teachers. 1920 *Glasgow Herald* 3 Dec. 10 The staff of typists and Roneo operators required is very numerous and well paid. 1921 *Spectator* 7 May 584/1, I have had the memorandum 'Roneo'd' for circulation among near acquaintances. 1926 *Contemp. Rev.* June 682 Newspapers were re-appearing in weird type-written or roneo-ed form. 1926 *Socialist Rev.* June 10 No printed newspapers (a few roneo bulletins), no trains.

Röntgen. Add: b. *Comb.*, as *Röntgen-rayed* adj.
1908 *Practitioner* Mar. 392 An experiment made on the effect of injection of Roentgen-rayed spleen-substance.
Hence **Rö·ntgen,** *v. trans.*, to submit to the action of Röntgen rays; to X-ray; in quot. *fig.* **Röntge·nically** *adv.*, by means of Röntgen rays. **Röntgeniza·tion,** the process of röntgenizing. **Röntge·nogram,** a shadow-picture obtained with Röntgen rays; a radiograph. **Röntgeno·graphy,** radiography. **Röntgenolo·gically** *adv.* **Röntgeno·logist,** one who studies or is expert in the use of X rays. **Röntgeno·logy,** the study of Röntgen or X rays. **Röntgeno·scopy,** examination by means of Röntgen rays; radioscopy. **Röntgenothe·rapy,** the treatment of diseases with Röntgen or X rays.
Shorter forms, e.g. *Röntgram, Röntgraph, Rönt(o)graphy*, have occasionally been used.
1896 *Strand Mag.* July 111/2 The sock was visible optically, almost invisible Röntgenically. 1903 *Med. Record* 31 Jan. 168 (Cent. Suppl.) Röntgenotherapy. 1904 F. F. Moore *Original Woman* xii, Lady Evelyn felt that her inmost thoughts were being Röntgened. 1905 *Nature* 27 July 301/1 Among the results of the recent Röntgen congress at Berlin has been the authoritative adoption by a special committee of the following terminology:—Röntgenology = the study of Röntgen rays, Röntgenoscopy = observation by Röntgen rays, Röntgenography = photography by the rays. ..Röntgenotherapy and the verb to Röntgenise in their obvious meanings. 1907 *Med. Record.* 10 Aug. 246 (Cent. Suppl.) Röntgenogram. *Ibid.* 9 Nov. 760 (Cent. Suppl.) Röntgenization. 1911 *Archives Roentgen Ray* Jan. 308 Whether this Roentgen Qualimeter..has all the requisites.. so much sought for by every Roentgenologist is a question. 1914 Von Den (*title*) A Short Manual of Roentgenology. 1917 *Sei-i-Kwai Med. Jrnl.* 10 Nov. 110 The authors examined rontgenologically the morphology and motility of the normal stomach in about 50 Japanese.

Roof, *sb.* Add: 2. e. A high plateau or table-land.
1902 D. G. Hogarth *Nearer East* 31 The course of this ridge in the Anatolian roof..determines the parting of all the waters.
9. **roof-water,** rain-water collected off the roof of a house.
1910 W. De Morgan *Affair of Dishonour* iv. 55 To him who drinks no water, *roof-water and well-water are welcome alike.

Roofing, (*vbl.*) *sb.* 1. b. Add: *roofing bone, felt.*
1875 *Encycl. Brit.* III. 707/1 The roofing bones [of a skull] are now well seen; the largest of these are the frontals. 1929 *Morn. Post.* 2 Oct. 6/5 These industries include electrical engineering, paint and varnish making, roofing-felts, ..and the manufacture of linoleum.

Roofless, *a.* Add: 3. Applied to poker played with no limit to the raise.
1913 R. W. Service *Rhymes of Rolling Stone* 104 Your trouble was a roofless game of poker now and then.

Rooinek (rō₁inek). [Cape Du., f. Du. *rood* red + *nek* neck.] A term applied by Boers to Englishmen in South Africa.
1897 Schulz & Hammar *New Africa* xxix. 397 Rooi Nek, once a term of bantering endearment, has unfortunately lost its charm since it has been converted into a term of dislike by the Boers for the foreigner. 1921 *Chambers's Jrnl.* Jan. 32/1 I was thinking of the efforts that that infernal rooinek (red-neck) of a son of yours is making to deprive me of my only child. 1923 Kipling *Land & Sea Tales* 39 And you will see how we can shoot rooineks.

Rookus (ru·kəs), variant of *Ruckus.
a 1909 'O. Henry' *Roads of Destiny* ix. 156 He talks all spraddled out..'bout the rookuses he's been in. He claims to have saw the elephant and hearn the owl. 1924 W. M. Raine *Troubled Waters* vi. 60 Course there'll be a rookus between him and Joe Tait.

Rooky, *sb.* Also **rookie.** (Later examples.)
1909 R. A. Wason *Happy Hawkins* 142 'Why, you blame rookie,' sez I, 'You don't really think I was mad do you?' 1915 *Literary Digest* (N.Y.) 21 Aug. 336/2 A swarm of

other notables serving as rookies in the business and professional men's military-training camp at Pittsburg, N.Y.

b. A beginner at base-ball.

1917 Mathewson *Sec. Base Sloan* 271 Chris Farrel'll be sending another rookie along first thing anyone knows. 1929 *Daily Express* 15 Jan. 9/7 In 1915..he was a member of the Baltimore baseball team as a gawky 'rookie.'

Room, *sb.*1 Add: **9. e.** A set of brine vats used in salt-making.

1903 *Sci. Amer.* Suppl. 3 Oct. 23198/2 Of the three kinds of rooms belonging to a salt yard, about one-third are deep and lime rooms; the rest are salt rooms.

10. *room-fellow, -rent* (earlier examples); **room-temperature,** the normal temperature of a room, about 60° Fahrenheit.

1930 Rose Macaulay *Relations* ix. 122 Snakes might be her companions, wild cats her *room-fellows, but she..abandoned herself to these. 1835 Martin *Descr. Virginia* 82 Board,..during the session..$ 100; fuel and candles $ 15, *room-rent $ 8. 1851 C. Cist *Cincinnati* 65 The annual term bill for room rent..and incidental expenses is ten dollars. 1924 tr. *Wegener's Orig. Continents & Oceans* 128 They can prove that the earth is about two or three times as rigid at *room-temperature as steel.

Room, *adv.* **3.** (Modern example.)

1902 J. M. Barrie *Little White Bird* xv. 163 He was drifted towards the far shore, where are black shadows he knew not the dangers of, but suspected them, and so..went roomer of the shadows until he caught a favouring wind.

Room, *v.*2 **2. b.** (Earlier example.)

1860 *Blackw. Mag.* Jan. 112/2 A miserable public-house, where I was 'roomed', or in other words, put into the same room with a rising medical practitioner.

Rooming-house. (Later examples.)

1909 *Washington Times* 2 Mar. 1 Hundreds of persons who never slept in any but first-class hotels when away from home will tonight get their rest in rooming houses. 1923 E. F. Wyatt *Invis. Gods* III. ii. 105 Fairfax Avenue was now a nondescript street of rooming houses, apartments and carpet-cleaning establishments.

Roorback. (Earlier examples.)

[1844 *Congress. Globe* 22 Dec. XIV. App. 76/2 I shall next advert to the gold humbug, which originated also in the Roorback mint.] 1855 [Pray] *Mem. J. G. Bennet* 368 Among the efforts made to defeat the election of Mr. Polk was one to which allusion is frequently made in political discussion, politicians speaking of a political lie as a 'Roorback'.

Rooster. 1. (Earlier examples.)

1806 *Balance* (Hudson N. Y.) 22 July 227 (Th.) The New York Rooster—may he continue to crow! 1813 *Niles' Weekly Reg.* IV. 192/1 If ever he lived to see Baltimore, the rooster should be treated with *pound cake.*

Rooseveltian (rōᵘ·z-, rū·zěveltiǎn), *a.* [f. the name of Theodore *Roosevelt* (1858–1919), president of the U.S. 1901–1909.] Of, pertaining to, or characteristic of Roosevelt. So **Roo·seveltism.**

1915 *Fatherland* (N.Y) 20 Dec. 346 We do not believe that the German Americans will have to choose between the devil of Rooseveltism and the deep sea of Wilson. 1927 *Observer* 24 July 6 A thorough-going Rooseveltian book on the Philippines.

Root, *sb.*1 Add: **17.** *root-tubercle.*

1897 W. G. Smith tr. *Tubeuf's Dis. Plants* ix. 101 First-year alders without tubercles do not thrive in soil free from nitrogen..; when, however, provided with *root-tubercles they assimilate nitrogen.

c. *root-eaten.*

1915 *Proc. Soc. Antiq.* 11 Mar. 149 I have often picked up on the surface of the camp pieces of old *root-eaten human bones.

19. *root-treatment.*

1927 W. E. Collinson *Contemp. Engl.* 60 If a tooth is decaying or hollow we have it stopped or filled..or we have root-treatment (sterilization and withdrawal of nerve).

20. *root-cause, -reason.*

1915 E. Carpenter *Healing of Nations* i. 12 One might be on safer ground by trying to get at the *root-causes of this war. 1924 R. Hichens *After the Verdict* III. xiv. 491 I hated her then because I loved you. That was the *root reason.

22. root-ball = Nigger-head; **root-beer, -digger** (earlier examples).

1930 *Sat. Even. Post* 13 Dec. 11/2 Bogs of black muck dotted with devilish, rotating *root-balls that throw a man waist-deep. 1843 *Knickerbocker Mag.* XXII. 85 Let..the temperance halls and the *root-beer perambulatories make answer. 1837 Irving *Life Rocky Mts.* II. iv. 48 These are of that branch of the great Snake tribe called Shoshokoes, or *Root Diggers, from their subsisting, in a great measure, on the roots of the earth.

Root, *v.*2 Add: **1. c.** (Further example.)

1920 Rose Macaulay *Potterism* I. ii. 20 Watching Tane's ..hand with its short square fingers rooting in the sand for shells.

e. *Root hog or die,* used of or addressed to persons, implying the necessity of labour or exertion to maintain life or prosperity. So *root-hog-or-die policy, principle.*

1834 Crockett *Narr. Life* viii. 60 We therefore determined to go on the old saying, root hog or die. 1836 [W. T. Porter] *Q. Race in Kentucky* (1846) 18 (Th.) Go it with a looseness—root, little pig, or die. 1843 *Amer. Pioneer* II. 419 This letter exhibits his as well as my own hard case in that day; for it was 'root hog or die,' and hard times have come back again! 1853 J. Dow Junr. *Patent Sermons* III. 193 (Th.) Obliged to go upon the root-hog-or-die principle. 1872 *Rep. Vermont Board Agric.* I. 373 The soil is nearly exhausted, and we must 'root hog or die'. 1879 Tourgee *Fool's Errand* xxv. 150 The 'root-hog-or-die' policy. 1904 *N. Y. Even. Post* 20 Aug. 4 'The school and college', explains President Eliot, 'cannot use the method of Nature—root, hog, or die.'

Rootage. Add: **3.** A system of roots; a rootstock.

1927 H. E. Fosdick *Pilgr. to Palestine* 60 The very rootage from which came Aaron's rod that budded..the solemn monks still show to the visitor.

Roo·t-and-brancher. [f. *root and branch*: Branch *sb.* 6 b.] One who favours a root-and-branch policy.

1928 *Manch. Guard. Weekly* 5 Oct. 275/2 The Cardiff Conference consisted of 95 per cent. 'root-and-branchers'.

Rooty, *a.* Add: **b.** Belonging to or suggestive of roots.

1905 E. F. Benson *Image in Sand* xviii. 292 The warm wind bore with it..the good, moist, rooty smell of the dusky heather.

Rope, *sb.*1 Add: **2. f.** A rope or line suspended on posts marking the boundary of a cricket ground.

1904 A. A. Milne in *Later Poems fr. Punch* (1909) 144 Time was when I cared for cricket,..Cutting a ball to the ropes for four.

4. c. (Further examples.)

1850 D. G. Mitchell *Lorgnette* (1852) II. 186 (Th.) The belle of two weeks standing, who has 'learned the ropes'. 1854 *Congress. Globe* 20 May, App. 893/2 They are familiar with all the dodges of the season, understand the ropes about town [etc.].

8. e. *rope-soled.*

1920 *Blackw. Mag.* Apr. 507/2 He was dressed quaintly in well-washed dungarees,..a gaudy waist-cloth, rope-soled shoes [etc.].

9. rope-boring, the boring of wells with a drill suspended and worked by means of a rope; **rope-race,** the compartment or passage through which a driving-rope passes; **rope-rider** (see quot.)

1888 *Chambers's Encycl.* II. 331/2 The *rope-boring machinery of Mather and Platt of Salford..is in extensive use. 1902 *Encycl. Brit.* XXX. 763/2 In Europe rods, either of iron or wood, seem to be preferred, though rope boring is by no means unknown. 1892 Nasmith *Cotton Spinning* xii. 400 In arranging the blowing rooms it is now customary to separate them from the main building by the *rope race. 1903 *Sci. Amer.* 23 May 392/2 In soft-coal mines the man in charge of the cable train is called a '*rope rider'. In bringing his cars out of the mine he sits upon the ring which connects the cable with the train.

Rope, *v.*1 **1. d.** (Further example.)

1925 E. F. Norton *Fight for Everest, 1924* 115 It was one of our rules that any party of porters..must be met at the Col and escorted and roped over the intricate route into camp.

4. b. *To rope in* (further examples); also, to arrest.

1916 Boyd Cable *Action Front* 10 They..roped in my captain to identify me. 1925 *Strand Mag.* Sept. 254/2 I'm sorry for you, my man, but..another twenty-four hours, and we might have been roping you in, too. 1930 Mackail *How Amusing* 108 He remembered now; they'd roped him in as a godfather.

Rope-maker. Add: **b.** *Rope-maker's eye,* a special eye made on a rope.

1883 *Man. Seamanship for Boys* 127 A Rope-Maker's Eye is generally made in the end of a jibstay when fitted with a slip at the jib boom end, and has a thimble in it to receive the slip.

Rope-walk. (Earlier example.)

1671 *Boston Rec.* VII. 72 John Harrison's rope walk.

Roping, *vbl. sb.* **1.** (Further example.)

1883 *Man. Seamanship for Boys* 50 Q. What is the roping? A. The bolt rope round the edges of the sail to prevent it from rending.

Ro·rty, *adv. slang.* [f. the adj.] In a rorty manner.

1923 'Bartimeus' *Seaways* vii. 96 Isn't he a little man?.. Bettin' with bookies and actin' rorty.

Rose, *sb.* Add: **4. c.** (Further examples.)

1872 Dean Hole *Six of Spades* (1909) 166 It seems to say, with the perfumed earth in the Persian fable, 'I am not the rose; but cherish me, for we have dwelt together'. 1890 [see 7 b]. 1897 G. W. E. Russell *Collect. & Recollect.* xxiii. (1909) 215 That extraordinary child of Israel who, though he was not the Rose, lived uncommonly near it.

19. b. *rose-land.*

1929 Bridges *Test. Beauty* III. 666 In the New World far Pasadena's *roseland.

23. rose-fever (earlier example); **rose-gold** (*b*): see quot.; **rose-head,** (*c*) a spreading top on an upright rain-pipe; **Rose Sunday,** the fourth Sunday in Lent; **rose-wine** = Rosolio.

1851 Lady E. S. Wortley *Trav.* III. 22 This complaint [hay-asthma] is known in the U.S., and is called there, *rose-fever. 1926 *Gloss. Electr. Terms* (Brit. Engin. Stand.) 129 *Rose gold,* a gold deposit containing copper and having a reddish colour. 1883 *Specif. Alnwick & Cornhill Rly.* 51 Four-inch rain-pipes are to be provided, with proper *rose-heads. 1880 McClintock & Strong *Cycl. Bibl. & Eccl. Lit.* IX. 130 It is not known when the ceremony of consecrating the rose was introduced...The day is always the fourth Sunday in Lent, which is consequently known as '*Rose-Sunday'. 1891 tr. *Pastor's Hist. Popes* I. 220 Golden roses were bestowed each year on Laetare Sunday, hence called Rose Sunday. 1852 in *Venerabile* (1930) Apr. 357 A good dinner and caffe after with beautiful *rose-wine.

c. rose-bug (earlier example); **rose-hopper,** an insect of the genus *Thrips,* injurious to roses.

1800 *Massachusetts Spy* 1 Oct. (Th.) He suggests that the *Rose-bug is the pre-existing state of those worms. 1920 P. G. Wodehouse *Damsel in Distress* i, The small, yellowish-white insect..sometimes called a *rose-hopper and sometimes a thrip.

Roseness (rōᵘ·znės). [f. Rose *sb.* + -ness.] The quality or factor which makes the comb of a fowl a rose-comb.

1907 R. C. Punnett *Mendelism* (ed. 2) 42 Strip off 'roseness' from a rose and single remains.

Rosette. Add: **5. d.** (See quot.)

1926 *Gloss. Electr. Terms* (Brit. Engin. Stand.) 133 *Rosette,* a device for the attachment of an overhead suspension wire to a wall or structure.

Rosetted, *a.* (Further example.)

1909 W. Bateson *Mendel's Princ. Heredity* 33 The rough or rosetted condition of the coat in the Guinea-pig dominates over the normally smooth condition.

Rosettling (roze·tliŋ). [f. Rosette + -ling.] A small rosette.

1907 R. Fauer *My Rock-Garden* viii. 118 *Aretiacides* is.. a minute Pyrenean, with tiny ligulate leaves, grey with silver markings in dense hard rosettlings.

Roster. 2. (Further example.)

1930 *New Statesman* 3 May p. iii/1 One particular point is worth noting as to the names in this amazing roster of public enemies.

Roster (rǫ·stəɹ), *v.* [f. the sb.] *trans.* To include or exhibit (names) in a list of those selected for duty.

1922 *Glasgow Herald* 26 Jan. 8 The men can be rostered up to nine hours, with overtime paid after eight hours.

Rostrifacture (rǫ·strifæktiŭɹ). [f. L. *rostrum* beak: after Manufacture.] A structure made by a bird with its beak.

1884 Coues *Key N. Amer. Birds* 408 Distinguished as the orioles are for the dexterity and assiduity they display in their elaborate textile rostrifactures [etc.].

Rostro-. Add: *rostro-carinate;* also as *sb.* a rostro-carinate implement used by prehistoric man.

1919 H. G. Wells *Outl. Hist.* ix. § 2. 50/1 Three views of a rostro-carinate (earliest period) implement. *Ibid.,* The Mousterian Age implements, and all above it, are those of Neanderthal men or, possibly in the case of the rostro-carinates, of sub-men.

Rostrum. Add: **2. d.** A platform for policemen when superintending the traffic at a crossing.

1930 *Morn. Post* 16 July 12/5 There is the constable on the rostrum, a never-failing source of amusement to the small boy population.

Rot, *v.* Add: **1. d.** (Further example.)

1913 *Chambers's Jrnl.* Jan. 63/1 These [stumps] rot out after a few years' cultivation.

4. b. Also with *down.*

1912 Galsworthy *Inn Tranq.* 79 'They don't do a stroke more than they're obliged,' he ended;..'Yes,' he muttered, 'the nation is being rotted down.'

c. (Earlier example.)

1811 *Niles' Weekly Reg.* I. 5 Oct. 86/1 Process for rotting hemp.

d. *U.S.* To make (snow or ice) soft by melting or thawing.

1892 [implied in Rotting *vbl. sb.*]. 1905 *Pall Mall Mag.* Dec. 563/2 The Sun's beginning to rot the snow.

Rotang. Also rotan.

1927 H. M. Tomlinson *Gallion's Reach* xxxi, The climbing palms, the rotans, flourished about it.

Rotarian (rotē·riăn), *a.* and *sb.* [f. *Rotary + -ian.] **a.** *adj.* Of, belonging to, or characteristic of the Rotary or a Rotary Club. **b.** *sb.* A member of a Rotary club. Hence **Rota·rianism,** the Rotarian system or its aims.

1912 (*title of Mag.* Chicago, U.S.A.) The Rotarian. 1921 *Glasgow Herald* 10 Feb. 9/4 The President..said the Prince lived out consistently the motto of Rotarians, 'Service, not self'. *Ibid.* 15 June 11/1 An effective programme on education must produce a more intense study of Rotarian literature, a more liberal use of the Rotarian speakers available [etc.]. 1928 L. North *Parasites* 270 Rotarians and women's clubs wrote her letters applauding her patriotic stand for home-products. 1928 *Daily Express* 20 June 2/5 A pantomime symbolising the story of the spread of Rotarianism throughout the world.

Rotary. A. *adj.* Add: **2.** Also *Comb.* as *rotary-engined* adj.

1909 *Westm. Gaz.* 23 Oct. 9/1 Delagrange brought out his rotary-engined Bleriot.

4. *Zool.* Resembling a wheel; trochal.

1870 Rolleston *Anim. Life* Introd. p. cxxxviii, Their ciliated 'rotary' disk is in most [Rotifera] the main organ of locomotion.

5. Of or belonging to an international system of service clubs of which the first was formed by P. P. Harris of Chicago in 1905 and met at the premises of each member in turn. Each club requires to be in a town of not less than 5,000 inhabitants, and to have as its members no more than one person from any calling.

1921 *Glasgow Herald* 10 Feb. 9/4 Sir Harry Lauder was the guest of honour at a Rotary Club luncheon at the Hotel Cecil, London, yesterday afternoon. *Ibid.* 15 June 11/1 The subjects under consideration included Rotary education, publicity, and business methods.

B. *sb.* (Further example.)

1904 *Science* 24 June 945/2 A three-phase 120-cycle alternator driven by an inverted rotary.

2. The system of Rotary clubs (see *A 5) or the ideals or activities of these.

1921 *Glasgow Herald* 10 Feb. 9/4 Sir Harry Lauder..said Rotary was like the lamplighter who came into a dark street. 1922 *Westm. Gaz.* 8 Sept. 6/4 The beneficent influence that Rotary is exercising upon the world. 1927 *Daily Tel.* 10 Feb. 9/3 (heading) Rotary week by week.

Rotate, *v.* Add: **1. b.** *transf.* To be under a rotative system.

1917 G. Young *Portugal* vi. 264 There was no improvement in its international position and internal politics continued to 'rotate' as ineffectively as before.

3. (Earlier example.)

1861 *Trans. Ill. Agric. Soc.* IV. 318 We must rotate crops.

Rotativism (rōᵘ·tătiviz'm). [f. Rotative + -ism.] A system whereby different political parties hold office in turn according to a pre-arranged plan.

1908 *N. Y. Sun* 3 Feb. (Cent. Suppl.) Each party held office by arrangement alternately. This arrangement was known as rotativism. 1921 *Edin. Rev.* Jan. 158 The country must in effect sink back into the slough of 'rotativism'.

Rotativist (rōᵘ·tătivist). [f. Rotative + -ist.] One who favours or practises rotativism in politics; often *attrib.* or as *adj.*

1909 *Spectator* 12 June 918/2 The late King [of Portugal] yielded to the intrigues of the 'rotativist' parties. 1917 G. Young *Portugal* vi. 217 The collapse of the Portuguese colonial empire must come with the continuance of the struggle between rotativist Royalism and revolutionary Republicanism. 1926 *Glasgow Herald* 24 Dec. 4/7 They recalled the indifference of the electorate on the frequent occasions of general elections by order of the Rotativists.

Rotatorial (rōᵘtătōᵊ·riăl), *a.* [f. *Rotatoria* + -al.] Of, pertaining to, or consisting of *Rotatoria.* So **Rotato·rian** *a.*

1890 *Science Gossip* XXVI. 202/2 Rotatorial life and chlorine, and many of its compounds are incompatible. 1909 *Rep. Brit. Assoc.* 509 The Rotatorian fauna of the Dominion [of Canada] therefore remains quite unknown.

Ro·tograph, *v.* [f. the sb.] *trans.* To make a rotograph of.

1914 *Eng. Hist. Rev.* Oct. 727 The chancellor of the diocese..by whose permission the extract which follows was rotographed.

Rotogravure (rōᵘ:to,grăviūᵊ·ɹ). [f. L. *rota* wheel + ending of Photogravure.] Photogravure printed on a rotary machine.

1925 *Scribner's Mag.* July 13/2 It may be that those..read the rotogravure sections of the papers more attentively. 1926 C. N. Bennett *Photogravure* 117 (heading) The 'doctor' the secret of rotogravure.

Rotor. Add: **3.** A vertical rotating metal cylinder used as a means of obtaining greater power from wind.

1924 *Public Opinion* 14 Nov. 483/3 Very little electric power is required to work the rotors. 1924 *Glasgow Herald* 17 Nov. 4 The navigational importance of Herr Anton Flettner's 'rotor' as an auxiliary. 1925 *Ibid.* 6 Feb. 9 These towers—technically called rotors—are supported on strong internal masts.

b. One of the rotating planes which provide the lifting power in helicopters.

4. *attrib.,* as (sense 2) *rotor coil, tooth;* (sense *3) *rotor ship, turret,* etc.

1922 *Encycl. Brit.* XXXII. 1022/2 These induce currents of still greater frequency in the *rotor coils. 1924 *Glasgow Herald* 12 Dec. 8/2 The *Rotor ship is apparently a thing devoid of beauty. 1922 *Encycl. Brit.* XXXII. 1023/1 These *rotor teeth as they pass between the stator teeth decrease the reluctivity of the air gap and increase the magnetic flux passing. 1924 *Glasgow Herald* 23 Dec. 7/1 The principle of the new invention is different from that on which the *rotor turret is based.

Rottenly, *adv.* (Recent examples.)

1912 Hueffer *Panel* I. ii. 37 In those days he had been lonely, rottenly poor,..and more irresponsible. 1913 Rupert Brooke in *Mem.* (1918) p. cvi, When the *Times* begins saying that the employers are in the wrong, they must be very unpardonably and rottenly so indeed.

Rotting, *vbl. sb.* **1.** Also *rotting-down.*

1916 Galsworthy *A Sheaf* 269 Economically..such rotting-down of the boys is grievously short-sighted.

Rouge. B. *sb.*1 **1. c.** Add: *rouge compact.*

1931 F. L. Allen *Only Yesterday* v. 107 For every adult woman in the country there were being sold annually over a pound of face powder and no less than eight rouge compacts.

Rough, *sb.*1 Add: **9. c.** Applied to alum used as an adulterant in bread.

1855 *Second Rep. Comm. on Adulteration of Food* (Min. of Evid.) 47 There are several trade names for alum; one of them, being very characteristic of its effects on the mucous surface, is 'roughs', and another is 'seasoning'.

Rough, *a.* **21. rough-stuff,** also *transf.*; (*c*) unruliness, violent behaviour.

1915 H. L. Wilson *Ruggles of Red Gap* ii. (1917) 30 But you'll have to be firm, because he's full of tricks. And if he starts any *rough-stuff, just come to me. 1930 *Observer* 20 Apr. 11 Mistakes of acting..may..have falsified the beginning and given it an air of ordinary 'rough-stuff' which it never deserved.

23. b. (Further example.)

1901 *Nature* 19 Sept. 523/2 Seven *Rough-keeled snakes (*Dasypeltis scabra*).

Rough, *adv.* Add: **2. a.** *rough-school, -sketch.*

1909 *Country Life* 23 Oct. 577/1 One could see him rough-schooling younger brothers and companions. 1910 W. J. Locke *Simon the Jester* xxiv. 315 The story of his marriage is a little lunatic drama all to itself and I will tell it some day. But now I can only rough-sketch the facts.

b. *rough-plucked.*

1909 *Daily Chron.* 18 Oct. 4/5 Fowls are sold both dead and rough-plucked, and alive for fattening.

Rough, *v.*1 **2. c.** (Earlier and later examples.)

1845 W. G. Simms *Wigwam & Cabin* I. 58 She [the bear] roughed me once or twice more with her paws. 1904 *Baltimore Amer.* 1 Aug. 2 (headline) Bad man roughs a train, but is shot in the hand by a plucky trainman. 1928 *Daily Mail* 25 July 12/4 Tunney knows he will be roughed and bustled around for the first few rounds.

6. b. (Earlier example.)

1770 *Maryland Hist. Mag.* XII. 352, I think you are wrong to have the Capitalls &c. finished there; they may be defaced in the carriage, which danger would be avoided if only roughed out there.

7. (Earlier example.)

1770 *Maryland Hist. Mag.* XII. 351 The stone cutters wish to have a draft of the Bases & Capitalls; they could rough the stones to that draft, & save a great deal of carriage.

Roughage. Add: **2.** In general use: The indigestible fibrous matter or cellulose in vegetable food-stuffs. Also *fig.*

1927 *Lancet* 16 July 106/1 I suspect that the advocacy of this bread was begun on the ground that the extra cellulose which it contains, forming what has been termed 'roughage', is of advantage as a mechanical irritant to the mucous membrane of the colon. 1931 *Mus. Times* Jan. 74/1 This was another of the oddities that we have to accept as roughage to the Hallé [orchestra] fare.

Rough-and-tumble. A. *adj.* Add: **4.** Roughly constructed or improvised; makeshift.

1923 Kipling *Land & Sea Tales* 70 They heaved up their rough-and-tumble anchor, and made after a..sailing-ship.

Rough-dry, *v.* (Further example.)

1923 Kipling *Land & Sea Tales* 27 Sweating men rough-dried sweating horses with wisps of precious forage.

Rough house, *sb. Orig. U.S.* [Rough *a.* 21.] An uproar, disturbance, or row; quarrelling or rioting.

1887 M. Roberts *Western Avernus* 54 He called the bridgeman a very opprobrious name, and for a moment there was great danger of a 'rough house' out of hand. 1895 [see Rough *a.* 21]. 1902 G. H. Lorimer *Lett. Self-made Merchant* xvi. 238 [He] said he liked things lively, but there was altogether too much rough house on Beacon Hill for him. 1904 *Grand Rapids Even. Press* 2 June 2 John Jackson came home intoxicated last night and stirred up a 'rough house' at his home. 1911 R. D. Saunders *Col. Todhunter* iii. 49 But an ominous cry rose from his front. 'Rush 'em, boys! Make a rough-house.' 1923 H. L. Foster *Beachcomber in Orient* xi. 240, I..watched Singapore fade into the distance with its memories of vice, iniquity, and general rough-house. 1929 Conan Doyle *Maracot Deep* 166 There will be such a rough house as they never saw.

b. *attrib.* (Hyphened.)

1906 *N. Y. Globe* 22 Aug. 6 On that rough-house occasion more force than was necessary was used to eject the Bryanite faction. 1919 H. L. Wilson *Ma Pettengill* ii. 74 Two or three other directors..had put him into rough-house funny plays where he got thrown downstairs or had bricks fall on him.

Rou·gh-house, *v. Orig. U.S.* [f. the sb.] **1.** *trans.* To handle (a person) roughly; to assail violently; to maltreat by rough usage.

1902 H. L. Wilson *Spenders* xxxvi. 436 You rough-housed the boy considerable yesterday. 1903 *N. Y. Times* 6 Oct. 1 After the rush the classes adjourned to Massachusetts Avenue and began to 'rough house' the passing street cars. 1905 D. G. Phillips *Plum Tree* 353 His eyes glistened. Except his growing fortune, nothing delighted him so much as a chance to 'rough-house' his eminently respectable 'pals'. 1909 R. H. Barbour *Double Play* xvii. 202 The fellows went to the circus..and rough-housed the show. 1925 H. L. Foster *Trop. Tramp Tourists* 188 The S[ocial] M[anager] must not risk the loss of their future patronage by mauling or roughhousing such as might not enjoy it, or at least tolerate it. 1928 *Daily Express* 4 Sept. 9/5 Harvey as a boxer of exceptional skill should not have allowed West to rush into close quarters and 'rough-house' him.

2. *intr.* To make a disturbance or row; to behave or act violently. Also with *it.*

1920 'Sapper' *Bull-Dog Drummond* ix. § iv, Somebody has been rough-housing by the look of things. 1928 *Chambers's Jrnl.* Apr. 211/2 He had a veteran in combat to deal with, a man who had 'rough-housed' it all over the world.

Hence **Rou·gh-houser** (in quot. *fig.*); **Rou·gh-housing** *vbl. sb.*

1904 *N. Y. Even. Post* 2 Jan., In fiction whether it is historic society or the work of literary rough housers [etc.]. 1927 *Blackw. Mag.* June 843/2 It is more than mere rough-housing. 1929 *Saturday Even. Post* 7 Dec. 249/2 This explains much of his boisterousness, his rough housing.

Roughing, *vbl. sb.* **5.** Add: *roughing-filter, -shop;* also *roughing-out drill.*

1903 *Rep. Brit. Assoc.* 761 The other two original tanks were converted into six roughing filters containing 3 feet in depth of fine gravel. 1901 *Jrnl. Brit. Inst. Elect. Engin.* Nov. 312 Two drills should in all cases be provided, one a roughing-out drill, and the other a finishing drill. 1910 *Daily Chron.* 15 Jan 7/2 The cause of the fire was the fusing of an electric motor in the 'roughing' shop [of an opticians' factory].

Rough neck, rough-neck. *U.S.* [Rough *a.*] A rough or rowdy; a person of rough habits or quarrelsome disposition.

1836 Crockett *Col. Crocket in Texas* iv. 58 You may be called a drunken dog by some of the clean shirt and silk stocking gentry; but the real rough necks will style you a jovial fellow. 1903 *N. Y. Sun* 25 Nov. 2 The police were kept on the jump chasing away gangs of 'rough necks' (the pet name for the rowdies in Sam Park's late union) who went from building to building trying to intimidate members of the new union. 1917 *War Birds* (1927) 30 But there are a few rough-necks in every outfit that will cause trouble and get the whole bunch in wrong. 1922 H. L. Foster *Adv. Trop. Tramp.* 5 The host of swearing, fighting, drinking, sweating, working roughnecks who built the [Panama] canal. *transf.* 1916 H. L. Wilson *Somewhere in Red Gap* v. 208 And so the party moved on for an hour or two, with the roguish young roughnecks cutting up merrily at all times, pretending to be cowboys coming to town on pay day, [etc.].

b. *attrib.* Rough; uncultivated; rowdy.

1920 C. Sandburg *Smoke & Steel* 7 The others were rough-neck singers a long ways from home. 1928 L. North *Parasites* 37 Most of these rough-neck editors and things round here never get the hang of it.

Roughness. 1. d. (Earlier and later examples.)

1846 *Knickerbocker Mag.* XXVIII. 313 The truck's all soaked, and there can't nobody stay here to save souls without some kind of *roughness* to keep up natur'. 1868 *Putnam's Mag.* I. June 711/1 The 'black un' had sought to burn her 'roughness',..shucks, or corn-husks. 1891 *Fur, Fin & Feather* Mar. 185 The supplies need not include feed for the horses, for corn and 'roughness', which is the localism for fodder, are to be cheaply and conveniently obtained from the natives.

Rough-rider. 1. (Earlier example.)

1733 Bramston *Man of Taste* 17, I would with Jockies from Newmarket dine, And to Rough-riders give my choicest wine.

Roumanian. B. *adj.* (Earlier example.)

1860 *Universe* 8 Dec. 1/2 His projects extend to the formation of a great Roumanian State.

Roumelian (rumī·liăn), *a.* Also **Rumelian.** [f. *Roumelia* (see Roumeliote) + -an.] Of or belonging to Roumelia.

1888 *Encycl. Brit.* XXIII. 655/2 This is partly due to the Christian communities, notably the Maronites and others in Syria, the Anatolian and Roumelian Greeks, and the Armenians. 1902 D. G. Hogarth *Nearer East* 155 Most thinly peopled are the mountainous districts between the Vardar and the Rumelian plains.

Round, *sb.*1 Add: **2. e.** *pl. Comm.* Articles that naturally have or are made up in round shapes.

1911 *Chambers's Jrnl.* May 297/1 Formerly 'flats' and 'rounds' used to be spoken of to distinguish the imports of this drug [*sc.* rhubarb]. 1928 *Daily Mail* 25 July 19/3 Potatoes.—Spitalfields: English Kidneys 6s to 7s, rounds 5s to 5s 6d per cwt.

6. b. *spec.* In surveying: A complete circle (of measured angles).

1899 *Geog. Jrnl.* XIII. 411 Rounds of angles were taken from Pegi Hill, the hill on Kaweri island,..and a rock near Ngo.

Round, *a.* **15.** Add: round turn, also *fig.,* a sudden check, a 'jerk'; **round wood,** (*a*) timber in its natural shape, (*b*) short logs of small diameter from the tops of spruce and pine trees, used for box-making.

1920 Galsworthy *In Chancery* II. vi. 175 The end came swiftly on the 20th of January with a telegram...It brought him up with a *round turn. 1910 *Timber Trades Jrnl.* 8 Jan. 37/1 The wood shipped from Archangel is the now well-known *roundwood. 1930 *Aberdeen Press & Jrnl.* 3 Apr. 8 So far as the 'round wood' or 'pulp wood' is concerned, most of the Aberdeen contracts for the season are now fixed-up.

16. *round-lipped, -pollened, -sterned.*

1906 Hardy *Dynasts* II. iv. i. 230 The Archduchess, a fair, blue-eyed, full-figured, *round-lipped maiden. 1913 W. Bateson *Mendel's Princ. Heredity* I. v. 93 It was..more usual to find whites exclusively produced by the cross of two extracted F_2 whites, long-pollened and *round-pollened respectively. 1897 J. L. Allen *Choir Invis.* xiii, Where some *round-sterned packet from New England or New Amsterdam was unloading its cargo.

Round. A. *adv.* **1. e.** (Further example: cf. *Hog-round.) Also of a price: On the whole or average.

1770 *Maryland Hist. Mag.* XII. 362 Mr. Howard has nigh £12 round for eight Hgds., one of which was greatly damaged. 1831 Peck *Guide for Emigrants* 172 The price of bacon the last season and the present, taking the hog round, is six and seven cents.

B. *prep.* Add: **2. c.** *U.S.* Of time: About; approximately.

1928 F. N. Hart *Bellamy Trial* iii. 92 It must have been round quarter to nine.

Round, *v.*1 Add: **5. e.** (Earlier U.S. and recent transf. examples.)

1844 J. J. Webb *Mem.* 154 We saw the Indians busily engaged in 'rounding up' and driving off a herd of mules. 1923 *Manch. Guard. Weekly* 469/2 Examining what prospects, if any, there are of rounding-up German capital invested or deposited outside Germany. 1931 *Daily Express* 15 Oct. 6/3 The star-traders of the talkies have been out rounding up fresh material from which to carve the box-office idols of the future.

8. a. Also *refl.* In quot. *fig.*

1926 *Publishers' Weekly* 29 May 1789/2 Presently we came away. The inquiry was rounding itself out.

13. b. (Further example.)

1924 Galsworthy *White Monkey* I. xiii, He rounded-in from the Embankment towards home.

f. To turn round *on*; to attack or assail, *esp.* in words.

1909 *Blackw. Mag.* Sept. 413/1 On one occasion..she had rounded on him and scolded him for a full half-hour.

14. e. *To round out*: to expand and assume a rounded form; to become plump.

1912 *Red Mag.* Apr. 510/2, I guess she didn't know how she had rounded out in the mountain air.

Round about. A. *adv.* Add: **5.** About; approximately.

1926 W. R. Inge *Lay Thoughts of a Dean* 182 In the Middle Ages the births and deaths in the undrained towns were both round about 50 per thousand in each year.

Roundabout. A. *sb.* Add: **2. b.** (Earlier and later examples.)

1818 in *Trans. Ill. State Hist. Soc.* (1910) 177, I have twelve shirts six pair Pantaloons 6 vests..two roundabouts [etc.]. 1823 J. F. Cooper *Pilot* I. vi. 66 The young sailor..slipped his arms into the sleeves of a morning round-about, covered with the trappings of his profession. 1904 *N. Y. Even. Post* 7 Jan. 7 Only yesterday this young man was playing about the streets of Washington, a schoolboy in roundabouts.

c. (Earlier example.)

1844 *Lowell Offering* IV. 175 (Th.) [He sat] in a large flag-bottomed 'roundabout', on the opposite side of the fire-place.

7. A place where all traffic has to follow a circular course; a system of regulating traffic at crossings by a one-way circular route.

1927 *Glasgow Herald* 3 Jan. 7/2 There is only one drawback to the roundabout, and that is the inconvenience caused to pedestrians. 1928 *Daily Tel.* 10 Apr. 8/5 The City's first roundabout was opened yesterday. 1932 *19th Cent.* Feb. 208 Some temporary alleviation has been secured by the introduction of roundabouts and automatic signals.

B. *adj.* Add: **7.** Applied to a system or method of directing traffic (cf. *A. 7).

1927 *Rep. Commissioner Police Metropolis, 1926,* 18 During the past year round-about systems of traffic have been put into operation at Parliament Square, [etc.]. 1927 *Autocar* 18 Feb. 277/2 Experiments will be made for a month with one-way 'roundabout' traffic at the junction of Knightsbridge and Brompton Road.

Rounder. Add: **1. d.** (Earlier example.)

1854 *Congress. Globe* 17 Jan. App. 1220 (Th.), I have always found him a very kind and agreeable man—what the 'rounders' in New York would term a 'glover'.

e. *U.S.* (See quot.)

1903 *Charities* 3 Oct. 283 The class of persons known as 'rounders', people who go from one hospital to another seeking advice and treatment, a species of medical mendicants.

Roundhead. Add: **4.** (Further example.)

1908 A. Wyatt Tilly *Eng. People Overseas* I. ii. 72 The former was strongly cavalier and episcopal; the latter was as strongly roundhead and puritan.

5. A round-headed person; one of a race or type of man characterized by the roundness of the head.

1896 A. H. Keane *Ethnol.* I. v. 106 Mounds differing in type from those of the round-heads.

Round-headed, *a.* Add: **1. b.** The specific designation of a race or type of man.

1896 A. H. Keane *Ethnol.* I. v. 106 Mr. W. K. Moorehead, ..recognises two distinct mound-building races, the old long-headed, and the later round-headed intruders.

Round-house, *sb.* **4.** (Earlier example.)

1870 *Rail-Road Gaz.* (De Vere) Engineers and firemen often..have to spend considerable time about the round-house.

Round Table, *sb.* Add: **4.** Also ellipt. for **Round-table conference.*

1928 *Publishers' Weekly* 12 May 1962 The round-tables should be turned to even greater value. 1928 *Daily Express* 3 July 2/4 The Archbishop of Canterbury made a striking proposal yesterday for a 'round table' to discuss the future relations of Church and State.

b. *Round-table conference,* a conference at which the parties present are all on an equal footing.

1892 *Rev. Reviews* Feb. 148/1 The subject of the 'Round Table Conference'..is what part churches should take in labour problems. 1901 H. W. Paul *Life Gladstone* xxi. 245 The year 1887 opened with an attempt to reconcile the conflicting elements of the Liberal Party, which came to be known as the Round Table Conference. 1929 *Times* 31 Oct. 14/3 Mr. Benn himself proposed to visit India forthwith for ..a round-table conference.

Round trip. *U.S.* [Round *a.* 15.] A circular tour or trip; an outward and return journey.

1868 *Putnam's Mag.* I. Mar. 351/1 Time for the round trip..44 hours. *c* 1871 'Mark Twain' *Sketches* Wks. XIX. 78, I sailed round and round in it forty-four times..each round trip a half mile. 1911 J. F. Wilson *Land Claimers* xi. 151 Spencer..making the round trip between dawn and dark. 1921 R. D. Paine *Comr. Rolling Ocean* xiii. 223 We signed for the round trip in the Liberty Chimes, but we don't feel like taking her all the way home.

b. *attrib.*

1860 *Dinsmore's Railroad Guide* Sept. 142 Round trip tickets [issued by the Baltimore and Ohio R.]. 1874 'Mark Twain' *Sketches* Wks. XIX. 408 Complimentary round trip tickets have been tendered to General Butler. 1897 — *Following Equator* xiv. 152 The tickets were round-trip ones—to Melbourne, and clear to Adelaide in South Australia, and then all the way back to Sydney. 1910 *N. Y. Even. Post* 17 Dec. 7 The round-trip railroad fare will be $6. 80.

Round-up. Add: **2.** (Earlier and later examples.) Also *transf.*

1878 J. H. Beadle *Western Wilds* xxviii. 437 These cattle, having run wild upon the plains of western Texas, are collected by a grand 'round-up'. 1879 *Tinsley's Mag.* XXIV. 353 One's companions, when camping out on the 'round up' are often anything but desirable. 1898 H. S. Canfield *Maid of Frontier* 90 The inner mysteries of camp cookery, midnight round-ups, forays. 1907 S. E. White *Arizona Nights* iii. 60 We had our first round-up, found the natural increase much in excess of the loss by Indians. *transf.* 1903 *N. Y. Times* 23 Sept., Thirty-three alleged members of the East Side gangs were arrested by detectives in a round-up Monday night. 1927 Agatha Christie *Big Four* v. 54 A short time ago a round-up was made of certain crooks and gunmen. 1928 *Daily Mail* 2 Jan. 6/5 Some time ago the police organised a weekly round-up of all suspects.

b. (Earlier example.)

1880 *Harper's Mag.* Feb. 380/2 Why, we old fellows have a round up 'most every year in Denver.

4. *attrib.,* as *round-up camp, party, week.*

1923 R. Pocock in *Outward Bound* Mar. 410/2 Seventeen miles across the Mesa la Sal, in Utah, brought me to a round-up camp. 1891 *Fur, Fin & Feather* Mar. 188 Wolves naturally follow in the wake of round-up parties. 1924 W. M. Raine *Troubled Waters* iv. 40 A poster..announced Round-up Week,..roping, and other Western sports.

Rou·pily, *adv.* [f. Roupy *a.*2 + -ly 2.] As if affected with the roup.

1907 Neil Munro *Daft Days* xxxi, Discretion..forbids enumeration of the roasted hens. Chanticleers in the town crowed roupily and ruefully for months thereafter.

Rouse, *sb.*2 **3.** Also *rouse-out.*

1885 C. A. Stephens *Adv. Six Young Men* 122 The result was a most unwelcome rouse-out shortly after ten o'clock.

Rousedness (rau·zdnės). [f. Roused *ppl. a.*1 + -ness.] Roused condition; alertness.

1928 D. H. Lawrence *Rainbow* iv. 96 And there was a kind of bristling rousedness in the room.

Rouser. 2. (Earlier example.)

1839 C. F. Briggs *Harry Franco* I. xiv. 127 We never exchanged another word until we reached the fire, and then, says he to me, I tell you what, Smith, it is going to be a rouser.

Rousseauan, *a.* Add: **b.** as *sb.* = Rousseauist.

1928 C. Hollis *Dr. Johnson* iii. 68 Rousseauans had been responsible for the generalisation that man was good.

Rou·stabout, *v.* [f. the sb.] *intr.* To be or act as a roustabout.

a 1909 'O. Henry' *Roads of Destiny* vii. 107 I hurried the rest of the way up the river, roustabouting on a lower coast packet that made a landing for every fisherman that wanted a plug of tobacco.

Rou·sting, *vbl. sb.* [f. Roust *v.*1 + -ing 1.] The action of the verb Roust.

1916 Dennis *Digger Smith* 82 All me roustin' leaves 'em both serene.

Rout, *v.*8 **3. b.** (Later example.)

1909 Masefield *Hawbucks* 101 He went home to his cellar and routed out a bottle of port.

Route, *sb.* **4.** Add: *route-march.*

1909 *Blackw. Mag.* Sept. 396/1 They have all been called out to some absurd inspection, or route march, or manœuvres, or something.

Route, *v.* Add: **b.** *transf.*

1926 *N. Y. Times Mag.* 15 Aug. 6 Complaints were routed past the complaint department to the President's office.

Routi·ned, *a.* [f. Routine + -ed 1.] Subjected to or regulated by routine.

1913 E. F. Benson *Thorley Weir* i, The gleaming romance and glory that lie so close below the surface of the most routined and rutted life. 1928 *Manch. Guard. Weekly* 23 Nov. 407/2 Criticism will do well not to base on this routined output a judgment which leaves out of account the Schubert of the year of his death.

Routinely (ruti·nli), *adv.* [f. Routine + -ly 2.] In a regular or unvaried manner.

1924 *Scribner's Mag.* Aug. 216/1 Even now I think we take policemen, professors, conductors, etc., much too routinely.

Routing (rū·tiŋ), *vbl. sb.* Also *transf.*

1930 M. Clarke *Home Trade* 198 All waste of time in the passage of any piece of work through the factory, scientific management methods endeavour to eliminate by 'routeing'.

Rover 1. Add: **3. c.** A member of a senior branch of boy scouts. Also *rover scout.*

1922 Sir R. Baden-Powell *Rovering* 210 Rovers are a Brotherhood of the *Open Air* and *Service.* 1926 *Glasgow Her.* 26 Aug. 7 Rover, or senior Scout, movement in America.

Row, *v.*1 Add: **8. c.** *To row out*: to exhaust by rowing.

1928 *Daily Express* 7 Aug. 12/6 Both pairs finished in a distressed condition, Boardman being completely rowed-out.

Row, *v.*3 **2.** Also with const.

1908 *Smart Set* June 143/1 Most fathers would have rowed me out of the house.

Row-de-dow, variant of Rowdy-dowdy.

1823 *Ann. Congress* 13 Mar. 2128 The rub-a-dub and row-de-dow excitement.

Rowdy, *v.* (Earlier example.)

1825 Paulding *J. Bull in Amer.* xii. 209 Notwithstanding ..their being regulated and rowdied, and obliged to cut down trees as big round as a hogshead.

Rowdy-dowdy, *a.* (Earlier example.)

1854 Maria S. Cummins *Lamplighter* 260 To offer herself as a champion for that rowdy-dowdy child.

Rowel, *v.*1 **2.** Also *transf.*

1918 F. Hackett *Ireland* xii. 331 The indecency and indignity of personal subjection rowelled Parnell like a spur with teeth in it.

Rowing, *vbl. sb.*1 Add: **2. b.** *rowing-machine.*

1894 *Outing* Mar. 458/1 The exercises consist of hard work on rowing-machines or in the tank, vigorous dumb-bell exercise, and a run of two miles per day. 1911 H. S. Harrison *Queed* vii. 89 Introducing the beloved apparatus to the visitor under its true names and uses..a rowing-machine, the horizontal and parallel bars [etc.].

c. *rowing-tank.*

1898 *Outing* Jan. 277/2 In 1887 the rowing tank was first put into practical use in the Yale gymnasium.

Row·-off. [f. Row *v.*1 + Off *adv.*] A final contest to decide superiority in rowing, *esp.* after a dead heat.

1928 *Daily Tel.* 7 Aug. 12/1 Under the repechage system of rows-off between previous losers, J. Wright..and T. D. A. Collet..had another chance in the sculling event.

Royal. A. *adj.* **12. b.** Add: *royal yard* (see quot.).

1883 *Man. Seamanship for Boys* 31 Q. Which are the royal yards? A. Those next above the topgallant yards.

15. royal jelly, the jelly-like food prepared for a queen bee by her attendant bees.

1875 *Encycl. Brit.* III. 494/2 As a proof that any worker egg or young larva not more than three days old may be made to produce a queen, the experimenter has only to supply to such an one a portion of the *royal jelly. 1880 *Harper's Mag.* Oct. 780/2 This is the way the royal jelly is prepared. It has a very rich taste—'something between cream, quince jelly, and honey.'

B. *sb.* Add: **8.** Short for *royal blue.*

1922 *Daily Mail* 11 Dec. 1 Advt., Beautifully made in.. Black, Grey, or Royal.

Royally, *adv.* **2.** Also, by the king.

1923 *Times Lit. Suppl.* 30 Aug. 565/1 Byrd's..legal quarrels with a recusant family, who had been royally dispossessed in his favour, though he, too, was a recusant.

Royster, variant of Roister.

Rub, *sb.*1 **2. c.** Also *fig.*

1931 *Times Lit. Suppl.* 31 Dec. 1048/4 If he is unfortunate in having finished his task before his problem was knocked completely out of shape by England's suspension of the gold standard, that is just the 'rub of the green.'

Rub, *v.*1 **13.** *Rub up*: also, to make clean, clear, or bright (again) by rubbing.

1859 Mrs. Stowe *Minister's Wooing* xviii. 179 He rubbed up his optical instruments to see whether they were rising in right order. 1886 F. R. Stockton *Mrs. Licks & Mrs. Aleshire* III. 111 In the morning I'll rub up that floor till it's as bright as new.

Rubbed, *ppl. a.* Add: **b.** Irritated, annoyed. (Cf. Rub *v.* 13 e.)

1927 *Chambers's Jrnl.* Jan. 40/1 He could never be sure of not saying hasty things when he was in a 'rubbed' temper.

Rubber, *sb.*1 Add: **6.** Also, a brake acting by friction on the wheels of a vehicle.

1850 R. Glisan *Jrnl. Army Life* (1874) iv. 32 The third vehicle, having no rubbers, or brakes, to the wheels, went so fast, down a steep hill, that the driver was thrown from his seat.

7. (Later example.)

1897–98 *Rep. U.S. Geol. Surv.* VI. B. 407 A second kind, and one much used in London for fronts, is a large, light-red brick, so soft as to be readily scratched by the knife. These are called 'rubbers'.

11. b. (Earlier example.)

1857 Sara Robinson *Kansas* xii. 160 The snows..are fast melting, and mingling with the clayey soil. So, besides the burden of rubbers, one has to carry no little portion of the native earth.

12. a. (Earlier and later examples.) Also *rubber-stamp* adj.

1844 *Knickerbocker Mag.* XXIV. 287 Old rubber-shoes! old rubber-shoes! Humble theme for heavenly muse! 1849 N. Kingsley *Diary* 78 Some of the fellows went in swimming this afternoon by takeing rubber beds. 1850 *Ibid.* 157 I put on my Rubber Coat and built a chimney outside the tent. 1863 'Gail Hamilton' *Gala-Days* 271 The man who gave rubber-boots to woman did more to elevate woman than all theorizers, male or female that were ever born. 1907 *Sci. Amer.* 5 Oct. 240/2 Scrap rubber, or rubber 'shoddy' as it is called, is made up principally of worn-out boots and shoes. 1931 *Government of Oxford* 5 Others believe that..interest would be stimulated if Congregation could be relieved of its 'rubber stamp' duties.

13. b. Also with vbl. sbs., as *rubber-collecting.*

1910 *Blackw. Mag.* May 729/1 Rubber-collecting is less laborious, but takes you into dangerous parts.

c. *rubber-cored.*

1908 *Chambers's Jrnl.* Feb. 181/1 The undoubted improvement in golf-playing is due principally to the introduction of the rubber-cored ball. 1929 Deeping *Roper's Row* xxxv, Sillocks was a golf maniac, and went from Rye to Hoylake..smiting a rubber-cored ball.

d. rubber check *U.S. slang,* a cheque returned by the bank; **rubber-gum,** the sap or latex of rubber trees; **rubber-leather** *a.,* consisting of rubber and leather.

1928 *Sunday Express* 2 Dec. 2/6 After a while the club came to an unfortunate end, due to what Americans call '*rubber checks,' i.e., the type that comes bouncing back from the bank. 1910 *Chambers's Jrnl.* Mar. 153/2 In these forests grow the trees which yield the finest quality of *rubber-gum. 1923 *Daily Mail* 28 May 3 A new process for the manufacture of *rubber-leather compounds.

Rubber, *sb.*2 **2.** Also at bridge.

1886 *Biritch or Russian Whist* 3 After each rubber there is a fresh cut for partners. 1908 *Laws of Auction Bridge* § 11 At the end of the rubber the total scores..are added up.

b. *attrib.* and *Comb.*

1908 R. F. Foster *Auction Bridge* 32 It is very important not to let players make a declaration that will put them out, especially on the rubber game. 1928 A. E. Manning Foster *Auction Bridge for All* 201 Z's bid was a good and cheap rubber saver. 1912 Flor. Irwin *Fine Pts. Auction Bridge* 166 The rubber-value is 250 points above the line.

Rubber, *v.* Add: **1.** (Earlier and later examples.)

1896 G. Ade *Artie* xi. 100 About a dozen ringers followed us in and stood around rubberin. 1908 G. H. Lorimer *J. Spurlock* iv. 71 Oh, the fat little bachelor, who rubbers at the girls from a window of the Ascot Club every afternoon! 1916 H. L. Wilson *Somewhere in Red Gap* ii. 58 So I rubbered awhile,..and then I forgot 'em, looking at some other persons that come in.

3. *intr.* To collect rubber.

1924 *Chambers's Jrnl.* Mar. 190/2, I was a young man rubbering down on the border when I first heard of this valley.

Rubberized (rɒ·bəraizd), *a.* [f. Rubber + -ize + -ed 1.] Treated, coated, or impregnated with rubber.

1925 *Sunday at Home* Mar. 346/1 The balloon..is of rubberised fabric. 1927 *Glasgow Herald* 19 Oct. 11/2 Bright coloured silks proofed for wear in showery weather now seem to be giving way to rubberised garments.

Rubber-neck, *sb.* and *v.* (Earlier example.)

1896 G. Ade *Artie* iii. 23 I stood around there on one foot kind o' rubber-neckin to find an openin.

b. *sb.* (Later example.) Also *attrib.* as **rubber-neck car,** etc., a vehicle intended to convey tourists round the sights of a town or district.

1906 'O. Henry' *Four Million* xix. (1916) 192 The Rubberneck Auto was about ready to start. The merry top-riders had been assigned to their seats by the gentlemanly conductor. 1908 G. H. Lorimer *J. Spurlock* xi. 321 The Major inquired loudly of Horton, the Governor's secretary, whether he was 'runnin' a blank rubber-neck waggon'. 1910 G. B. McCutcheon *Truxton King* iii. 41 They are the nobility—the swells. They don't hang around the streets like tourists and rubbernecks. 1926 Galsworthy *A Sheaf* 276 There exists in America a vehicle called the 'rubber-neck car. 1925 H. L. Foster *Trop. Tramp Tourists* 326 The tourists go riding through town in rubberneck parties.

Hence **Rubber-necking** *ppl. a.*

1927 H. V. Morton *In Search of England* ix, Here's a great sight going on that hundreds of rubber-necking tourists would pay anything to see.

Rubbery (rɒ·bəri), *a.* [f. Rubber *sb.* + -y.] Suggestive of or resembling rubber.

1907 Galsworthy *Country House* II. v, He left his hand against the animal's warm, soft, rubbery mouth. 1910 *Practitioner* Apr. 467 Atrophic chronic mastitis..may reduce the gland to a firm, 'rubbery,' highly convex disc. 1928 *Collier's* 10 Nov. 20/2 He..wrapped a thick hairy arm about Dan's neck in a chancery hold and squeezed his face into the thick rubbery flesh of his side.

Rubbishry (rɒ·biʃri). [f. Rubbish + -ry.] Rubbish; a collection of rubbish.

1896 Kipling *Seven Seas* 35 Fillin' my bunk wi' rubbishry the Chief put overside.

Rubble, *sb.* **5. a.** Add: *rubble bed.*

1886 S. Baring-Gould *Germany* xxxiii. 196 Above Mannheim the river is too rapid and too full of shifting rubble-beds to be safely navigated.

Ru·b-down. [f. *to rub down*: Rub *v.*1 8.] The act of rubbing down in any sense.

1896 Susan Hale *Lett.* 299 We reached here reeking, just in time for a rubdown. 1903 [see Rub *sb.*1 1 c].

Rube, variant of *Reub.

1904 *Philadelphia Ledger* 1 Oct. 13 The 'country-man' promises to become extinct in the United States, says the Washington Evening Star. The 'rube' is to follow the mastodon, the Indian and the buffalo. 1927 *Scots Observer* 26 Feb. 3/4 They know a Rube when they see him, or a guy, or a crook, or a bonehead.

Rubenesque (rūběne·sk), *a.* [f. the name of Peter Paul *Rubens* (1577–1640), Flemish painter + -esque.] Suggestive or characteristic of the paintings of Rubens.

1925 Deeping *Sorrell & Son* xx, He had a view of her broad back, and her robust curves...A Rubenesque figure, sumptuous and solid. 1927 *Observer* 17 July 15/4 The models of his choice are of rather Rubenesque fullness.

Ruberoid (rū·bəroid). Also rubberoid. Trade name of a roofing material composed of felt impregnated with bitumen.

1916 *Cornhill Mag.* Apr. 504 Myself and a chum had just returned..laden with 3″ by 4″ timbers and ruberoid which we found. 1921 H. G. Ponting *Gt. White South* 123 The roof..was covered with a thicker layer of ruberoid, and was lined with a single thickness of boards. 1925 *Glasgow Herald* 3 Aug. 5 The hut..was timber-built and roofed with rubberoid.

Rubricize (rū·brisəiz), *v.* [f. Rubric *sb.* + -ize.] *trans.* To provide with a rubric or rubrics.

1920 R. Harris *Testimonies* II. vii. 65 There is no reason to alter the opinion that the *Testimony* material should be rubricized.

Ruby, *sb.* **10. b.** Add: *ruby-eyed.*

1919 R. C. Punnett *Mendelism* (ed. 5) ix. 95 In canaries, again, there are ruby-eyed cinnamon forms corresponding to the various green and yellow varieties.

Ruched, *ppl. a.* (Recent example.) So **Ru·ching** *vbl. sb.*

1932 *Woman's Weekly* 19 Mar. 467/1 The..skirt is cut in wide scallops and trimmed with ruching. Little ruched pieces..give the frock quaintness and charm.

Ru·cksacked, *a.* [f. Rucksack + -ed 1.] Provided with or carrying a rucksack.

1909 H. G. Wells *Ann Veronica* xvi, To walk beside him, dressed akin to him, rucksacked and companionable, was bliss in itself.

Ruckus (rɒ·kəs). *U.S.* Also **rucus.** [cf. Ruction and Rumpus.] An uproar, disturbance or row.

1907 *Dialect Notes* III. III. 226 *Rukus,* a violent altercation or personal encounter. (Northwest Arkansas). *a* 1909 'O. Henry' *Roads of Destiny* 210 There shall be no rucus in Salvador. *Ibid.* xxii. 372, I see the cause of the rucus. 1922 Mulford *Black Buttes* ii. 26 'Them two bummers [restless cattle] was raisin' more of a ruckus than usual to-night.' 1928 *Collier's* 29 Dec. 8/1 Back in the early days when Buffalo Bill and Old Man Beck started this town there was occasional ruckuses of course. 1929 *Ibid.* 5 Jan. 34/3 The goat..gazed around him as if inquiring what all the ruckus was about.

Rudbeckia (rɒdbe·kiă). [mod.L. *Rudbeckia* (f. *Rudbeck* surname of two professors at Upsala before Linnæus), the name of the genus.] A herbaceous flowering plant of the genus *Rudbeckia,* native to North America.

1921 G. Jekyll *Colour Schemes for Flower Garden* 88 The fine double Rudbeckia called Golden Glow is treated in the same way. 1931 *Daily Mirror* 27 Aug. 7/3 Among the best of autumn-flowering perennials for the mixed border, or the wild garden, are the rudbeckias.

Rudder, *sb.* **6. a.** Add: *rudder-bar.*

1912 *Q. Rev.* July 240 Machines like Dunne's, which have no separate rudder-bar allowing of foot-correction.

b. *rudder flutter.*

1928 *Daily Tel.* 13 Mar. 11/3 The machine dived into the sea from a height of about 100 ft. after developing what appeared to be rudder flutter.

Ruddy, *a.* Add: **2. e.** Substituted for Bloody.

1914 Ld. Chas. Beresford *Mem.* I. 119 All I've got to say, is to say you've got a ruddy good billet. 1918 C. Mackenzie *Sylvia Scarlett* iv, What ho, Bill, old cock! Lost your ruddy cab, old sporty? 1918 W. J. Locke *Rough Road* v. 51 You've got to be a ruddy soldier. 1924 Galsworthy *White Monkey* II. i, Only why didn't Mr. Elderson say: 'You ruddy liar!'? 1925 Belloc *Mr. Petre* 67 'They're ruddy well right,' said the Duke.

Ru·ffing, *ppl. a.*2 [f. Ruff *v.*1] That is becoming ruffled.

1866 Blackmore *Cradock Nowell* I. i. 3 The blackcocks.. swell their ruffing breasts, and crow for their rivals to come and spar with them.

Ruffle, *sb.*1 **7.** (Further Comb. example.)

1927 Deeping *Kitty* xxix, The ruffle-headed pianist bumping up and down in his chair.

Ruffled, *a.* **b.** (Further example.)

1849 *Rep. U.S. Comm. Patents, Agric.* (1850) 289 The ruffled oat is very much cultivated, and highly esteemed.

Ruffle shirt. *U.S.* A shirt adorned with ruffles; a ruffled shirt. So **Ru·ffle-shirted** *a.* **Ru·ffled-shirt, Ru·ffle-shirter,** a person wearing a ruffled shirt.

1838 Drake *Tales & Sk.* 64 The colonists presented, indeed, a curiously grotesque appearance, loitering about the station in ruffle shirts and coon-skin caps. 1840 Longstreet *Georgia Scenes* (1843) 81 The ruffle-shirted little darling of the present day. 1842 *Knickerbocker Mag.* XIX. 305 Many a taunt, hitherto repressed, was thrown at the ruffle-shirters, as the town boys called them. 1848 *Ibid.* XVIII. 520 It was asserted ..that he wore a ruffle-shirt and overshoes. 1856 Strickland *Peter Cartwright* ii. 132, I got clear of my ruffle-shirted dandy. 1860 O. W. Holmes *Professor at Breakf.-t.* ii. 19 Joe Warren, the first bloody ruffled-shirt of the Revolution, was as good as born here. 1864 [see Ruffle *sb.*1 7].

Rufous, *a.* **1. c.** Also *rufous bee.*

1928 *Observer* 17 June 24/3 That queen of burrowers,..the rufous bee, Andrena.

Rugose, *a.* Add: **c.** *Comb.* as *rugose-punctate.*

1903 *Proc. Zool. Soc.* 12 May 33 The disc sparingly punctured, the sides strongly rugose-punctate, the extreme lateral margins and the anterior angles testaceous.

Rule, *sb.* Add: **23. c. rule-box,** a rectangle of ruled or printed lines.

1928 *Publishers' Weekly* 30 June 2605 Above the stamp.. must be *printed* the words..enclosed in a rule box.

Rule, *v.* **6. b.** Also, to maintain a particular standard, level, value, etc.

1909 *Chambers's Jrnl.* June 409/1 During the past year the longest period when the wind velocity ruled below five miles per hour was only seven days.

8. d. (Further examples.)

1925 N. E. Odell in E. F. Norton *Fight for Everest, 1924* 335 The disadvantage of the North Col is the fact that the camp here must be pitched on snow, though under all but the worst conditions this need not rule it out. 1928 *Daily Tel.* 12 June 13/4 The possibility of a battle between the rival Southern commanders cannot be ruled out.

Ru·le-of-thumbite. A person who works by rule of thumb.

1916 H. G. Wells *Mr. Britling* I. § 6. 16 Ruskin and Morris..were as reactionary and anti-scientific as the dukes and the bishops. Machine haters. Science haters. Rule of Thumbites to the bone.

Rum, *sb.*1 Add: **2. a.** *rum-still.*

1914 F. C. Glass *With Bible in Brazil* iv. 45, I recalled the big *rum-still in the back-yard.

b. *rum-runner, -running* (Run *v.* 45 c).

1925 H. L. Foster *Trop. Tramp. Tourists* 7 Is that a rum-runner? 1928 *Publishers' Weekly* 26 May 2109 The Confessions of a Rum-runner. By James Barbican. 1926 *Scribner's Mag.* Aug. 166/2 Tully—an old friend of mine, in the rum-running game now—will get you over the line into Canada. 1930 *Times* 15 Mar. 11/4 The Bill..had as its objective the prevention of smuggling and rum-running.

3. rum baron *U.S.,* a magnate in the contraband liquor traffic; **rum-fleet** *U.S.,* a 'fleet' engaged in rum-running; **rum-jar** *slang,* a type of German trench-mortar shell; **rum-joint** *U.S.,* a place where illicit liquor is sold; **rum row** *U.S.* (see quot.); **rum-ship,** a ship engaged in rum-running.

1923 *Westm. Gaz.* 4 Apr. 8/5 Reminiscences are inevitable in any gathering of *rum barons. *Ibid.* Off-shore is the *rum fleet. 1917 *Chambers's Jrnl.* Mar. 175/2, I heard the horrid 'chuff-chuff' of a *Rumjar. 1928 *Sunday Express* 24 June 8/4 One of our men started a row with one of these birds...They fought in a *rum-joint and everyone joined in. 1927 *Scribner's Mag.* Feb. 205/2 It was.. reported that *Rum Row was about dried up. 1927 W. E. Collinson *Contemp. Engl.* 81 We all know..about..Rum Row (where the liquor ships gather outside the prohibited area). 1926 *Encycl. Brit.* I. 408/1 By 1924 as many as 336 *rum ships were known to be engaged in boot-legging.

Rumble (rɒ·mb'l), *v.*3 *slang.* [Of obscure origin.] *trans.* To get to the bottom of; to see through; to grasp, detect, discover, or understand.

1886–96 Marshall *Beautiful Dreamer* (Farmer & Henley), I rumbled the tip as a matter of course. 1898 A. M. Binstead *Pink 'Un & Pelican* ix. 209, I soon rumbled he was in it, when I heard Ball givin' him the 'me lord' for it. 1912 C. Mackenzie *Carnival* x, I've properly rumbled your friends. 1925 N. Venner *Imperfect Impostor* iii, He'd have rumbled me. He can't rumble me now. 1930 Philip Macdonald *Link* 74 If I hadn't had so many queer things happen to me in such a short time..I'd never have rumbled him.

Rumbu·stiousness. [f. prec. + -ness.] Rumbustious character; boisterous behaviour.

1926 C. L. Graves *Hubert Parry* II. 106 In spite of his occasional exuberance and 'rumbustiousness' (a favourite word of his) he could, when the need arose, assume a wonderful dignity of demeanour.

Rummager. 2. (Later example.)

1856 E. G. Parker *4 July Orat.* (Boston) 9 Layard, the great rummager of Nineveh.

Rummy, *sb.*2 Also *U.S.* rum. A card game played by three or more persons with two packs of cards, closely resembling *Coon-can.

1918 in F. A. Pottle *Stretchers* 285 Opposite the stove Capt. Summers..and Lt. Chambers of Wanston, Ill. are playing Rummy on Summers' cot. 1919 Sinclair Lewis *Free Air* xviii. (1924) 177 He takes some kind of dope, and he cheats at rummy. 1928 *Daily Express* 5 Nov. 1/3 When they are together they invariably play the card game 'rummy' before retiring. 1928 L. North *Parasites* 285 Sometimes they played écarté..or Rummy.

Rummy, *a.*2 (Earlier example.)

1843 *Amer. Pioneer* II. 372 He departed, muttering curses loud and deep, and in a voice peculiarly rummy.

Ru·mmy, *vb.* [f. Rummy *sb.*2] *intr.* To obtain a hand which can be laid down at rummy, *i.e.* one in which the cards not included in sequences or sets of one denomination count to not more than seven; to say 'rummy' signifying this.

1929 *Encycl. Brit.* XIX. 658/2 Directly a player rummies that deal is finished, and all the hands are exposed and added up.

Rumorous, *a.* **1.** (Recent example.)

1929 Galsworthy *Mod. Comedy* I. II. 443 The rumorous town still hummed: the sky was faintly coloured.

Rump, *sb.*1 **5. a.** Add: *rump-patch.*

1902 *Nature* 14 Aug. 375/2 The author states that the gaur and the gayal have a white rump-patch.

Ru·m-strum, *v.* [Echoic.] *intr.* To strum.

1872 T. Hardy *Under Greenw. Tree* II. II. viii. 23 [He'd] want to see her young figure sitting up at that quare instrument, and her young fingers rum-strumming upon the keys.

Rumti-. (Further examples.)

1906 Galsworthy *Man of Property* I. I. 22 Did you ever see such a collection of rumty-too people? 1912 *World* 7 May 690/2 Mr. Cyril Maude makes a rather rumtifootling bishop amusing and forgivable even in his most flagrant lapses from clerical circumspection. 1918 Galsworthy *Five Tales, A Stoic* ii. § 3. 123 This little house was a rumty-too affair.

Run, *sb.*1 Add: **1. e.** = Rush *sb.*2 4.

1930 *Publishers' Weekly* 8 Feb. 697 On April 22, 1889, this strip was opened up with the land rush known as the famous Oklahoma Run.

2. c. *Croquet.* The passage of a ball under a bridge or hoop.

1863 Mayne Reid *Croquet* 34 If a ball, after running a bridge, strike an obstacle, and recoil back through the bridge, the run remains good.

14. d. (Earlier example.)

1815 *Niles' Weekly Reg.* IX. 187/1 The whole expence in generating steam sufficient to drive two run of stones upon this principle will not exceed two hundred and twenty dollars.

19. Also, the amount of maple juice collected at one time.

1890–3 E. M. Tabor *Stowe Notes* 40 The early runs are not so sweet as the later; the trees being full of frost. 1896 *Rep. Vermont Board Agric.* XV. 33 Car loads of the last run of the Vermont maple orchards are sent to these cities each year.

c. (Further example.)

1920 *Discovery* Mar. 88/1 The 'colour' is..poured into the 'sow-box', or trough of the machine, giving the pieces [of burlap] two runs in opposite directions so as to secure shades.

22. (Earlier Amer. example.)

1658 *Brookhaven Rec.* 3 This land and the grass thereof for a range, or run, for to feed horses or cattle on..I have sold.

23. c. A rent or ladder in a garment.

1922 Marg. B. Houston *Witch-man* xii. 146 She looked the suit over, darned a tiny run in the tights, polished the sword hilt and helmet, [etc.].

32. b. Also *The run of one's knife.*

1927 *Daily Mirror* 10 Dec. 9/1 Sir Granville Ryrie..began work as a cattle driver at £30 a year and the 'run of his knife', which means his food.

Run, *v.* Add: **7. b.** (Earlier example.)

1851 Quitman in *Life & Corr.* (1860) II. xvi. 147 A majority of the people have declared against the course of policy.. upon which alone I had consented to run as a candidate.

8. b. (Earlier example.)

1881 *Amer. Naturalist* XV. 178 Of these species, the quinnat and blue-back salmon habitually 'run' in the spring, the others in the fall.

12. e. Of physical features: To extend.

1904 W. M. Ramsay *Lett. Seven Ch.* xxvii. 395 A long vale runs up south-east from the Hermus Valley into the flank of the central plateau.

13. d. Also, to have a history extending back *to.*

1889 R. W. Worth *Tourist's Guide Worcestershire* xi. 110 Some of the effigies and brasses, which run back to the 14th century, are exceptionally good.

16. b. Also, of a player at golf: (See quot.).

1902 *Encycl. Brit.* XXIX. 25/2 *Run-up,* to send the ball low and close to the ground in approaching the hole—opposite to lofting it up.

17. b. (Recent example.)

1931 F. L. Allen *Only Yesterday* i. 8 Plants which had been running overtime on war-work began to throw off men by the thousand.

21. (Earlier U.S. examples, of ice.)

1807 P. Gass *Jrnl.* 61 The ice began to run in the river. 1867 A. D. Richardson *Beyond Mississippi* xi. 145 Reaching

the Missouri again, I found the ice running so heavily, that it was impossible to cross.

35. e. *To run the water*: of hunted animals, to run through a river or stream.

1885 *Field* 7 Nov. 652/1 At the brook the deer had soiled, and probably ran the water; at any rate, hounds threw up just below the village.

35. f. To hunt (a ditch, etc.) for rats.

1911 *Chambers's Jrnl.* June 370/1 In 'running' a ditch or drain with a few good terriers, it is absolutely necessary that they work quietly.

41. b. To attach (a ribbon or similar ornament) to cloth by passing it through a series of holes.

44. e. (See quot.)

1919 *War Slang* in *Athenæum* 18 July 632/2 'Running a man' means bringing a charge against him for orderly room.

45. b. (Further example.)

1904 Harben *Georgians* 207 Don't bother. I have enough cash to run me.

51. b. (Further example.)

1924 *Discovery* June 98/1 Simple..apparatus of this kind can be run off an ordinary lighting circuit.

c. (Earlier examples.) Also, to display in print, to publish.

1827 *Massachusetts Spy* 3 Oct. (Th.) (heading) Running a Bank. 1861 O. J. Victor *Hist. S. Rebellion* I. 252/2, I suppose I will have to run the machine as I find it. 1930 *Publishers' Weekly* 8 Feb. 667/2 The full page advertisement we ran in the New York Times..brought in more business than any advertisement we have ever run.

52. b. (Earlier examples.)

1789 *Maryland Jrnl.* 2 Jan. (Th.) It was agreed to run the following ticket in their respective Districts. 1800 *Aurora* (Philad.) 5 Dec. (Th.) With regard to the person to be run [with Mr. Jefferson] as Vice President, there appears some difference of opinion. 1825 J. K. Paulding *J. Bull in Amer.* v. 85 [They] talk of running him for the next governor.

c. (Earlier example.)

1872 Marietta Holley *My Opinions* (1891) 411 'But', says I, not wantin' to run anybody to their backs, 'she thought it was her spear to marry'.

53. g. To play in succession (a number of cards) from one suit.

1929 M. C. Work *Compl. Contract Bridge* iv. 21 The bidder..is insured against having his adversaries open and 'run' that particular suit.

74. Run in. d. (Earlier example.)

1857 *Quinland* Introd. I. 1 Got an hour to spare—thought I'd just run in and see what you were all about.

k. To bring (new machinery) into proper condition by preliminary working.

1928 *Daily Tel.* 20 Mar. 17/1 To-day's run served the two-fold purpose of getting the competitors here and of 'running-in' the machines.

75. Run off. f. Also, to produce or turn out with a machine.

1901 Merwin & Webster *Calumet K* vi. 106 Now, we'll write to Mr. Brown—no,..I'll do that one myself. You might run off the other and I'll sign it.

77. Run out. l. (*c*). (Further example.)

1911 *Chambers's Jrnl.* Sept. 596/2 When you have read it over, I will run out another copy.

79. Run through. e. = sense 45 c.

1906 *Chambers's Jrnl.* Sept. 662/1 A chief promised a certain white man a quart of diamonds if he could succeed in 'running' through for him a Gatling gun.

Run, *ppl. a.* Add: **11. b.** Exhausted with running.

1876 *Coursing Calendar* 147 Troapham proved herself a rare stayer, for she was fearfully run in her first course.

14. *run-after*, sought after or popular.

1908 R. W. Chambers *Firing Line* vi. 75 I've heard that you are the most assiduously run-after girl at Palm Beach.

Run-about. 4. Also, a small aeroplane.

1922 *Westm. Gaz.* 14 Nov. 3/6 Arrangements are being made..to launch the first power-driven runabout of the air.

5. Applied *attrib.* to garments suitable for every-day use.

1932 *Mod. Weekly* 5 Mar. 997 Run-about Frocks. 1932 *Woman's Weekly* 19 Mar. 467 A runabout jumper-suit.

Run-around. Add: **2.** A channel for leading water past a dam.

1904 *Elect. World & Engin.* 13 Feb. 305 (Cent. Suppl.) A few hundred feet below the main dam the bed of the run-around again joins the river.

Runaway. Add: **4. b. runaway switch,** a switch designed to stop a mining bucket which runs away when being hauled up a slope.

1911 *Act* 1 & 2 *Geo. V* c. 50 § 46 (4) Runaway switches or other suitable contrivances shall be provided..to prevent accidents in the event of a tub running away.

Ru·n-back. [Run *sb.*[1] 8.] **1.** The action or fact of running backwards. (In quot. Comb.).

1926 *Gloss. Electr. Terms* (Brit. Engin. Stand.) 140 *Run-back preventer*, a system of connection in a tramcar controller such that, in the event of the car running backwards, the motors act as short-circuited generators and thus exert a braking action.

2. The additional space provided at either end of a tennis court.

1908 A. W. Myers *Compl. Lawn Tennis Player* 213 At Auteuil..the run-back is inadequate and the timbered roof too low. 1927 *Daily Express* 30 May 3/5 The proper run-back for a court should be 21 ft. from the base-line to the stop-netting.

Rune[2]. **3. b.** Add: *rune-tree.*

1899 A. H. Keane *Man, Past & Present* ix. 341 A great feature of the system were the 'rune-trees', made of pine or birch bark, inscribed with figures of gods, men, or animals, which were consulted on all important occasions.

Ru·nically, *adv.* [f. Runic + -al + -ly [2].] In a runic manner.

1920 *Times Lit. Suppl.* 28 Nov. 779/3 Runically inscribed objects contained in..better known public collections.

Runiform (rū·nifǫɹm), *a.* [f. Rune + -form.] Having the form of a rune; runic.

1900 J. Deniker *Races of Man* x. 363 The runiform inscriptions of Mongolia.

Ru·n-in. [Run *sb.*[1] 8.] **1.** (See Run *sb.*[1] 8.)

2. A quarrel or row.

1912 Mathewson *Pitching* viii. 180 Fred Tenny has said for a long time that Mr. Klem gives him a shade the worst of it on all close ones because he had a run in with that umpire one day when they came to blows. 1916 H. L. Wilson *Somewhere in Red Gap* viii. 346 On top of that, I had a run-in with the Swede for selling his rotten whiskey to them poor Injin boys. 1920 Is. Ostrander *How Many Cards?* xii. 145 The cook at the de Forests' two doors away had a run-in with that Sarah, the butler's wife, and she won't speak to any of them.

Runner. Add: **1. d.** (See quot.)

1905 E. Hussey *Miss Badsworth M.F.H.* xxvii. 209 An individual belonging to that race of intelligent and remarkable persons to be found amongst the retinue of most hunts, entitled 'runners', or 'the man with the terriers'.

3. e. (Earlier examples.)

1784 'Lælius' in *Maryland Jrnl.* 14 Dec. (Th.) Men who, by getting in with the runners of the Bank,..find out who is pressed for the day, and extort the most enormous discounts. 1800 *Mass. Mercury* 27 June (Th.) A couple of runners attended a numerous meeting, and made their usual display of eloquence upon the occasion. 1836 Sarah M. F. Ossoli *Life on Lakes* I. 31 (Th.) [At Oswego] a struggle began between the runners of the two boats.

6. b. An American species of black snake.

1838 R. M. Bird *Peter Pilgrim* I. 223, I approached..within twenty feet of a black snake..of the kind which the people there [in Connecticut] call *runners* or *choking-snakes*. 1855 W. G. Simms *Forayers* xxxix. 456 Push forward, quick as a *runner* (black snake) when I say [the word].

10. e. A wheel with an incised edged used in decorating pottery.

1893 E. A. Barber *Pottery & Porcelain of U.S.* i. 9 Incised ornamentation is sometimes added by the use of a small wheel, bearing an engraved device on the edge, called the 'runner', which is held in a frame.

13. e. A long narrow strip of (embroidered) cloth, esp. one placed along or across a table as a ornament.

1904 *Buffalo Commercial* 2 June 6 Two long linen runners, one each way of the table, are now used in preference to the whole cloth or doilies. 1922 *Daily Mail* 11 Dec. 14 The illustrated table runner..was decorated at each end with a simple design. 1923 *Ibid.* 13 Feb. 14 The strips of the embroidery extend at either side in the form of narrow runners.

f. A ladder in a knitted garment.

1928 L. North *Parasites* 42 His quick eye detected a neatly darned spot near the heel of one, and a laboriously-checked runner in the other.

Runner-up. Add: **1. c.** *transf.* or *fig.*

1932 *New Yorker* 11 June 24/3 Blyth Daly is the horsy young lady who serves as runner-up to the Brat in offensiveness.

Running, *vbl. sb.* Add: **11. c.** (Earlier and later examples.)

1832 D. J. Browne *Sylva Amer.* 232 The scraping is a coating of sap which becomes solid before it reaches the boxes, and which is taken off in the fall and added to the last runnings. 1872 *Trans. Dep. Agric. Illinois* 73, I have a plantation five or six years old, parts of which still grow fine fruit, with two runnings annually.

17. *running fence*; **running set,** a country dance.

1848 H. W. Haygarth *Bush Life in Australia* i. 8 Again the forest opens, and discovers the 'running fence' of a paddock, leading to a wayside inn. 1927 *Observer* 27 Nov. 14/5 He got..from elsewhere in that district, the 'running set'—a fine dance which has been received here with outspoken enthusiasm.

b. (Further example.)

1931 *Times* 16 Jan. 14/2 He acquired a large practice, esp. in running-down cases.

Running, *ppl. a.* Add: **9.** *running postman.*

1898 Morris *Austral. Engl.* 247/1 K[ennedya] *prostrata* is called the Coral Pea..or Running Postman. 1917 Richardson *R. Mahony* I. ix. 87 The short-lived grass was picked out into patterns by the scarlet of the Running Postman.

17. e. *Running commentary*, a continuous commentary accompanying or dealing with a text; a commentary, report or criticism extending over or made concurrently with events that are taking place; now usu. a broadcast report of a game or contest. (Cf. quot. 1822 in 17.)

1858 *Chambers's Jrnl.* 4 Dec. 359/1 (heading) Bill Fustian's Running Commentary on the doings of the Respectable Classes. 1859 *Guardian* 1 June 483/1 [This book] does not pretend to give a history of the art [of poetry], but rather, a running commentary illustrative of its close connection with ..the human soul. 1894 *Strand Mag.* VII. 189 He makes a running commentary on the speech that is going forward. 1928 *Times* 10 Aug. 10/2 There will be..a running commentary by Mr. Douglas H. Scott on the set reels and piping.

Ru·nning-board. *U.S.* [Running *vbl. sb.* 17.] **1. a.** A narrow gangway on either side of a keel-boat.

1817 *Essex Inst. Hist. Coll.* VIII. 240 Our boat being very deep..[we] were obliged to give up after being at the expense of putting on running boards. 1826 T. Flint *Recoll.* xix. 218 The waves came in on the running-boards, as they are called, of the boat. 1834 H. Brackenridge *Recoll.* iv. 37 One night..I..lay..on the running board (a plank at the edge of the boat, on which the men walk in pushing with the pole).

b. A foot-board extending along either side of a locomotive, a motor-car, or other vehicle.

1917 Mathewson *Sec. Base Sloan* 284 The cars that buzzed and clanged their way past Wayne were filled to the running-boards. 1920 Deeping *Second Youth* xxxiii, Laverack took a seat on the running board of the nearest car. 1927 *Saturday Even. Post* 24 Dec. 83/4 We tied her on the running board of the pilot car, and with..Manuel on a seat built on the other running board, we set out. 1929 *Daily Express* 14 Jan. 6/3 Heath, leaning over the running-board, shouted some unintelligible words.

2. A framework for holding reels of electric cables while they are being unwound.

1898 E. J. Houston *Dict. Elect. Words* (ed. 4) 911/1 *Running-Board*, a device employed in the construction of a heavy overhead line.

Ru·n-through. [Run *sb.*[1] 8.] A hasty perusal or rehearsal.

1929 *Even. News* 18 Nov. 5/3 Whenever that rehearsal ends I shall hurry over to Manchester—see a final run-through there—..and then rush back to Liverpool.

Run-up. 1. b. Also *attrib.*

1907 'Ian Hay' *Pip* xi, Anything in the shape of a run-up ball would be trapped. 1931 *Daily Express* 31 Jan. 9/5 Compston, playing a run-up shot to the first green, shouted after the ball, 'Hit the stick.'

Runway. 1. a. (Earlier examples.)

1840 Hoffman *Greyslaer* I. x. 116 That cliff commands the whole valley below, and there is a deer runway leading up from the water-side to its base. 1855 *Knickerbocker Mag.* XLV. 193 The sound of the rifle has by this time brought the other hunters from their run-ways.

2. (Earlier and later examples.)

1883 E. W. Howe *Country Town* (1926) 36 Pushing this into my wagon with the assistance of his wife, after we had first made a runway of boards, I hauled him to Fairview. 1901 Merwin & Webster *Calumet K* xiii. 246 A runway from the hoist to the end of the building. 1904 *N. Y. Sun* 9 Aug. 1 The women became hysterical and stampeded for the wagon runway in the middle of the [ferry] boat. 1908 *Chambers's Jrnl.* Feb. 207/1 The gangway, also, is of great value for the loading and unloading of live-stock, since it provides an excellent runway.

4. (Earlier example.)

1874 B. F. Taylor *World on Wheels* II. vii. 250 Like the dusty 'run-ways' of thy brooks, soft pulses have grown dry and dumb.

Rupestral, *a.* Add: **b.** as *sb.* A rupestral plant.

1926 *Nat. Hist. Oxford Distr.* 104 Many of these [*sc.* alpine species] are rupestrals.

Rush, *sb.*[1] **4.** (Further example.)

1902 W. T. Hannan *Textile Fibres Comm.* 64 The Hard rush, *Juncus glaucus*, has been utilised in the making of brooms and whisks...The hard rush generally grows in dry situations.

Rush, *sb.*[2] Add: **1. b.** (Further example.)

1916 Boyd Cable *Action Front* 113 At nine, sharp to the tick of the clock, the rush, rush, rush of a field battery's shells passed overhead.

3. c. (Earlier example.)

1860 *Yale Lit. Mag.* XXVI. 22 As a basis, a Rush tacitly assumes that it is promoting a rivalry that is proper and praiseworthy.

9. rush edition, an edition (of a paper) produced in a very short time; **rush job,** a job requiring to be performed in a hurry; **rush-joke** (see quot.); **rush line** (later examples); also *transf.*; **rush season,** a season of increased activity in a particular business; **rush telegram** *U.S.*, a telegram transmitted and delivered with the least possible delay; **rush-work,** work at an increased pace to meet an urgent demand.

1901 C. Moffett *Careers of Danger* 381 Already the mail clerks are swarming at the pouches, like printers on a *rush edition. 1901 Merwin & Webster *Calumet K* vii. 126 But if you ever try to put me on a *rush job, I'll quit and buy a small farm. 1904 *N. Y. Even. Post* 16 Aug. 3 The contractors kept the men at work, as it was a 'rush' job. 1930 *Daily Express* 6 Oct. 10/7 The *rush-joke, in which the goggle-eyed reader..is simply clapped on the back and buffeted in the dust before he knows where he is. 1887 *Century Mag.* XXXIV. 891/2 Across the field stretch the foot-ball infantry, the '*rush-line' or 'rushers'. 1906 *Life* 4 Oct. 366 We hear of a surprising prevalence among the young men..of the disposition to get into the political rush-line. 1921 R. D. Paine *Comr. Rolling Ocean* i. 3 The unlucky young men who were left in his wake when he tore through a rush-line. 1906 U. Sinclair *Jungle* x. 124 Liable to be thrown out of work..liable again to be kept overtime in *rush seasons. 1928 *Daily Express* 8 June 19 Advt., The best accommodation at between 'rush-season' rates. 1903 *N. Y. Times* 24 Aug., Out in the Yellowstone National Park, probably beyond the reach of a *rush telegram. 1904 *N. Y. Herald* 17 Sept. 1 He stated that six weeks' *rush work would be required to repair the boilers to make them serviceable and the ship seaworthy. 1920 B. Cronin *Timber Wolves* 115 He made mental note of each man's capability, ..his power of endurance under rush-work conditions.

b. With advs. as *rush-in.*

1884 J. M. Weylland *These Fifty Years* 101 When it [the door] was opened the rush-in commenced.

Rush, *v.*[2] **4. b.** (Further example.)

1902 Harben *Abner Daniel* 268 Wish I had more time at my disposal..but I really am rushed, to-day particularly.

5. d. To say or tell rapidly.

1901 *Chambers's Jrnl.* Apr. 210/1 Candida rushed her news.

e. To increase, raise, or put *up* (prices) quickly.

1930 *Daily Express* 6 Nov. 2/5 When they have driven the British manufacturer out of business they will rush up prices.

Rush-bottom, *a.* and *sb.* *U.S.*

1. a. *adj.* = *Rush-bottomed. **b.** *sb.* A rush-bottomed chair.

1809 Irving *Knickerb.* vi. 258 The young ladies seated themselves demurely in their rush-bottom chairs. 1874 B. F. Taylor *World on Wheels* II. iii. 209 There is a chair—a low rush-bottom chair. 1923 Deeping *Secret Sanctuary* xiii, He made a move to sit down, and she saw him take one of the straight-backed rushbottoms.

2. *sb.* A 'bottom' in which rushes grow.

1831 Peck *Guide for Emigrants* II. 105 In all the rush bottoms they [cattle] fatten during the severe weather on rushes.

Rush-bottomed, *a.* [Rush *sb.*[1] 6 b.] Having a bottom made of rushes.

1759 [see Rush *sb.*[1] 6 b]. 1840 Hoffman *Greyslaer* III. i. 96 The apartment..was large and rudely furnished, containing only..a small cherry-wood table and a few rush-bottomed chairs as its customary moveables. 1867 A. D. Richardson *Beyond Mississippi* xi. 131 The adjacent settlers came..in heavy ox-wagons sitting upon rush-bottomed chairs. 1884 'C. E. Craddock' *In Tenn. Mts.* III. 139 Jerry Shaw hastened to abdicate and offer one of the rush-bottomed chairs.

Rush hours. *U.S.* (See Rush *sb.*[2] 9.)

1898 [see Rush *sb.*[2] 9]. 1909 'O. Henry' *Options* (1916) 239 During rush hours a Mexican youth..aided him in waiting on guests.

b. *attrib.* (In form *rush-hour.*)

a 1906 'O. Henry' *Trimmed Lamp* etc. 233 As solid as granite in the 'rush-hour' tide of humanity, stood the Man from Nome. 1928 *Chambers's Jrnl.* 17 Mar. 246/2 American railroads have reduced this 'rush-hour' catering to an exact science. 1928 *Hearst's Internat.* Aug. 101/1 I'm makin' the rush-hour express uptown as usual. 1931 *Morn. Post* 18 Aug. 6/4 Rush-hour trains held up.

Rushing, *vbl. sb.* **c.** (Later example.)

1929 *Old Oregon* June 10 They went through rushing, pledging, moving, 'open house', freshman duties, in a cycle which at that time seemed to move ponderously over each event.

Rushing, *ppl. a.* Add: **b.** Of trade: Active; lively; 'roaring'.

1915 *World* in *Literary Digest* (N. Y.) 21 Aug. 338/2 All this time the soda-water stands were doing a rushing business.

Rushlight. 1. c. Also of persons.

1866 *Yale Lit. Mag.* XXXI. 229 (Th.) P. told him that good scholars were looked upon here as mere rush-lights.

Rushy (rʊ·ʃi), *adv.* [f. Rush *sb.*[2] + -y.] Hurriedly.

1908 H. G. Wells *War in Air* iv. § 7 Too soon, Bert, my boy—too soon and too rushy.

Rusk, *v.*[2] Delete *rare*—° and add: **b.** *refl.* To feed or diet (oneself) on rusks. In quot. const. with *into.*

1928 *Daily Express* 5 Sept. 8/2 Women..have dieted and reduced and starved and rusked..themselves into a fantastic aversion from the pleasures of the table.

Russian. A. *sb.* **1. c.** (Earlier example.)

1848 H. W. Haygarth *Bush Life in Australia* xii. 135 Though he had been among horses since he was a child, his present lot were a set of the veriest 'Russians' (Anglicè, wild things) *he* ever had anything to do with.

B. *adj.* **2. d.** *Russian boot.*

1931 *N. & Q.* 30 May 387/1 When did Russian boots come into use in Western countries?

Russic, *a.* (Later example.)

1757 Dyer *Fleece* IV. 399 Culder's woofs, and those of Exe and Frome,..Thither by Russic caravans are brought.

Rust, *sb.*[1] Add: **9. a.** *rust-proofed, -resisting.*

1925 *Morris Owner's Manual* 83 The K.L.G. is a detachable plug consisting of three parts—a rustproofed steel body and gland nut and an insulated central electrode. 1909 *Chambers's Jrnl.* Nov. 766/1 The steel used is a special light, thin, rust-resisting, seamless metal.

10. rust-disease = sense 6; **rust-hypha** = sense 6 b.

1913 W. Bateson *Mendel's Princ. Heredity* 25 Susceptibility to *rust-disease (*Puccinia glumarum*) and resistance to the same. *Ibid.*, Miss Marryat found that the *rust-hyphae are checked before entering the stomata of the resistant plants.

Rustle, *v.* Add: **4.** (Further example.)

1881 *N. Y. Times* 18 Dec. in *N. & Q.* Ser. VI. V. 65/2 Cattle, in winter, 'rustle' for food by nosing through the snow to the dried grass beneath.

b. (Later examples.)

1903 A. Adams *Log Cowboy* iv. 53 Our foreman..sent Honeyman to rustle in the horses. *Ibid.* xxi. 332 Honeyman being excused on agreeing to rustle the wood and water. 1907 S. E. White *Arizona Nights* xvi. 227 Tusky kep' the fire goin' and I rustled greasewood. 1924 A. J. Small *Frozen Gold* iii. 81 Why ain't you rustlin' a crowd of the boys up to corral the swabs? 1925 *Chambers's Jrnl.* Mar. 168/1 It is accustomed to rustle its living through the long severe winters of its habitat.

c. To steal (cattle); also *transf.*

1902 F. McElrath *Rustler* xii. 167 Then the cowpuncher who had used to go out and 'rustle' mavericks for his employer became on his own account a 'rustler'. 1902 A. H. Lewis *Wolfville Nights* xv. 234, I claims that this Bowlaig b'ar is guilty of rustlin' the mails an' must..be hanged. 1920 W. M. Raine *B. O'Connor* 219 We're after them for rustling a bunch of Circle 33 cows.

d. *absol.* or *intr.* To steal cattle.

1916 'B. M. Bower' *Phantom Herd* xiv. 243 You hold a grudge against your dad, and you rustle from him mostly.

Rustling, *vbl. sb.* Add: **3.** *U.S.* Stealing of cattle.

1924 Mulford *Rustler's Valley* x, There had been no sign of rustling for months.

Rutted, *ppl. a.* Also *fig.*

1913 E. F. Benson *Thorley Weir* i. 30 The gleaming romance and glory that lie so close beneath the surface of the most routined and rutted life.

Rye, *sb.*[1] Add: **3.** (Earlier and later examples.)

1836 Ingraham *South-West* II. 56 The painful effects of old rye' in the abstract upon the body. 1890 *Buckskin Mose* xvii. 248 But for the quantity of rye we had all of us been swallowing, the others must have seen through this imprudent operation as I had done. 1906 'O. Henry' *Four Million* iv. (1916) 45 'Gimme a rye-high,' he said to the servitor.

5. rye coffee *U.S.*, 'coffee' made from roasted rye.

1836 *Knickerbocker Mag.* VIII. 278 We had *rye coffee and hominy for breakfast. 1848 *Indiana Gen. Assoc. Doc.* II. 77 The food consists of, at breakfast, corn bread, boiled bacon and rye coffee.

S

S. Add: **2. c.** *S-rope, -sofa, -turn.*

1883 Gresley *Gloss. Coal-m.*, *S-rope*, the winding rope which passes round the under side of the drum from or to the pulley; so called because it takes the form of the letter S. 1906 W. De Morgan *Joseph Vance* xxvi, I found myself sitting beside Miss Spencer on a thing like an S in the back drawing-room. As I sat by Miss Spencer on the S-sofa. *Ibid.* xxvii, The S-sofa séance. 1920 A. J. L. Scott *Sixty Squad* 56 Putting in a couple of 'S' turns, he made a good slow landing. 1928 V. Page *Mod. Aircraft* 522 A series of wide S turns can be made to reduce speed as well as altitude.

4. a. S. = Society, as in S.J., Society of Jesus; S.P.C.K., Society for the Promotion of Christian Knowledge. S.A. = small-arms; sex appeal. S-A, sino-auricular. S.B. = (*a*) stretcher-bearer; (*b*) *U.S.* Bachelor of Science; (*c*) simultaneous broadcast. S.C.M. = Student Christian Movement. S.C.R. = in the University of Oxford, senior common room. S.G. = screened grid. S.H.P. = shaft horse power. S.M. = short metre. S.O. (*U.S.*) = seller's option. S.P. = (*a*) spark or sparking plug; (*b*) starting price. S.P.Q.R. (*jocular*), small profits quick returns. S.W.G. = standard wire gauge. See also *SOS.

1763 A. Williams *Universal Psalmodist* (ed. 4) 16 (Tune) Southwell. Psalm 90. Dr. W. S.M. 1879 *Man. Artill. Exerc.* II. 39 Metal-lined Cases..for..blank S.A cartridges. 1886 A. Wilmot *Hist. Soc. Jesus* 136 Father Christopher Clavius, S.J., of Bamberg in Bavaria. 1895 *Starting Price* 23 Mar. 2/4 We advise readers to bet 'S.P.' only on this race. 1902 *Encycl. Brit.* XXVIII. 345/2 Mrs. Ewing produced a number of charming children's stories...Many of these were published by the S.P.C.K. 1912 *Motor Manual* ii. (ed. 14) 24 'SP' on an English coil means 'spark plug'. *Ibid.* 47 The 'secondary' winding, composed of many turns of fine wire (42 or 44 s.w.g.). 1920 G. W. Deeping *Second Youth* xix, 'Ere, you blitherin' S.B.'s, get a move on. Gently, gently! 1923 *Pop. Wireless, Suppl.* 13 Oct. 1 A coil consisting of 380 turns of No. 24 S.W.G. wire. 1927 E. J. P. Benn *Trade* 52 Our grandfathers used to talk of small profits and quick returns. 'S.P.Q.R.', which most schoolboys of my time imagined had something to do with the early Romans, was a very favourite shop sign. 1928 C. F. S. Gamble *North Sea Air Station* xiii. 213 The S.P.G. bullet ..issued to the Services early in 1916. 1929 *Encycl. Brit.* XXII. 999/1 A club-shaped formation known as the sino-auricular or the S-A node. 1930 H. R. Wakefield in *London Merc.* Feb. 315 They possessed so much S.A., IT, and B.U., that males of all ages..immediately fell for them. 1930 *B.B.C. Year-Bk.* 310 One or two transmissions are, perhaps, being sent to the provinces via the S.B. lines...Tests are being taken of outside broadcasts or incoming S.B. 1931 *Times Trade & Engin. Suppl.* 24 Jan. p. iv/3 Six vessels, of 10,500 s.h.p. 1931 *Daily Express* 15 Oct. 7/6 Six valves (2 S-G., detector, push pull output stage and rectifier). 1932 P. Macdonald *Maze* 116 A Gallic young woman with apparently some looks and, let us say, 98 per cent. vigorous S.A.

c. (See quot.)

1931 B. Brown *Talking Pictures* x. 215 A complete sound wave is, however, expressed as a letter 'S' or 'sine wave.'

Sabadine (sæ·bădin, -in). *Chem.* Also -in. [f. Sabadilla + -ine [5].] An alkaloid, $C_{29}H_{51}NO_8$, obtained from sabadilla seeds. Hence **Sabadinine** (sæ·bădinin, -in), also -in, a crystalline principle, $C_{27}H_{45}NO_8$, obtained from sabadilla.

1891 *Jrnl. Chem. Soc.* LX. II. 844 Sabadine is best separated as the nitrate. *Ibid.*, Sabadinine, $C_{27}H_{45}NO_8$, the second alkaloid, does not melt at any definite temperature.

Sabbath. 4. Sabbath-school (earlier and later U.S. examples).

1822 Weems *Lett.* III. 334 The Sabbath school of this town. 1895 M. A. Jackson *Memoirs* v. 77 In the autumn he began his Sabbath school.

Sabbatic, *a.* Add: Also = *Sabbatical *a.* 2 c.

1907 *N. Y. Even. Post* 23 Sept. 8 Professors Wilcox and Kendall are spending their sabbatic year in Europe.

Sabbatical, *a.* Add: **2. c.** *Sabbatical year*, a year of absence from duty for the purposes of study and travel, granted to professors of American universities at certain intervals. So *sabbatical leave.*

1903 *Science* 7 Aug. 191/2 Sabbatical year. 1903 *N.Y. Even. Post* 23 Sept. 8 Professors Wilcox, Adams, Sears and Hill are absent during the year on sabbatical leave. 1909 Oona H. Ball *Their Oxford Year* 5 He was entitled to start on his Sabbatical Year.

Sabe (sæ·be), *sb.* = Savey *sb.*, q.v.

1892 [see Savey *sb.*]. 1907 S. E. White *Arizona Nights* II. iii. 256 I will have to give it up..and the sabe of the country enough to lead.

Sabe, *v.* = Savey *v.*, q.v. *trans.* and *intr.* To know, understand.

1884 B. Harte *On the Frontier* 41 'I don't think—I—quite sabe, boys,' he added. 1889 Munroe *Golden Days* vii. 69 I forgot you..don't sabe the lingo. 1903 A. Adams *Log Cowboy* vi. 37 Girls, you know, sabe each other that way. 1907 S. E. White *Arizona Nights* i. 9 I sabed that they'd seen the original exhibit your Uncle Jim was making of himself.

Sable, *a.* **2.** Add: *His sable excellency* or *majesty*: applied to a dark-complexioned potentate; *spec.* the Devil.

1875 J. D. Lang *Hist. Acc. N.S.W.* (ed. 4) I. 393 If Her Majesty could have commissioned the Prince of Darkness to represent her in the colony.., I doubt not but his sable Excellency would have received a Farewell Address of respect. 1861 [see Majesty 2.] 1895 *Photos* 8 June 10 His sable majesty..is a man of great force of character.

Sabotage (sæ·botāʒ, ‖ sabotāʒ), *sb.* [ad. F. *sabotage*, f. *saboter* to make a noise with sabots, to perform or execute badly, e.g. to 'murder' (a piece of music), to destroy wilfully (tools, machinery, etc.), f. *sabot*: see Sabot and -age.] Deliberate and organized destruction of plant, machinery, etc., by dissatisfied workmen; hence *gen.* any malicious or wanton destruction.

1910 *Church Times* 11 Nov. 631/2 We have lately been busy in deploring the *sabotage* of the French railway strikers. 1916 *Sydney Morning Herald* 18 Oct., A shearing rouse-about,..charged..with having written a letter to Senator Lynch, threatening him and certain other Labour politicians and employers of Australia with acts of sabotage. 1918 Farrow *Dict. Mil. Terms*, *Sabotage*, wanton destruction of property to embarrass or injure an enemy; such as the smashing of machinery, flooding of mines, burning of wheat and grain, destroying fruit and provisions, dynamiting reservoirs and aqueducts, tying up railroads, etc. 1920 *Glasgow Herald* 26 June 7 Forces are at work in Germany for the sabotage of the Treaty. 1923 Brewer *Dict. Phrase & Fable*, *Sabotage*, wilful and malicious destruction of tools, plant, machinery, materials, etc., by discontented workmen or strikers. The term came into use after the great French railway strike of 1912, when the strikers cut the shoes (*sabots*) holding the railway lines. 1930 *Times Lit. Suppl.* 20 Nov. 959/2 When the colliers meditated a strike he gave them sound, worldly wise advice concerning the danger to their own interests of destructive acts and sabotage. 1931 W. Martyn *Scarlett Murder* iv, He was in that mood of smouldering rage which only sabotage would slake.

Hence **Sa·botage** *v. trans.*, to ruin or destroy deliberately and maliciously. **Saboteu·r** [Fr.], one who engages in sabotage.

1918 *New Appeal* 7 Dec. 1/2 Testimony..that the companies are sabotaging the government. 1920 *Glasgow Herald* 20 Aug. 7 When the miners threaten to sabotage the commerce of the country struggling to get back to pre-war prosperity. 1921 *Contemp. Rev.* Sept. 335 The blockade by Czecho-Slovakia and other Succession States..has hindered essential materials from reaching Budapest, and so sabotaged Hungarian industries. 1921 tr. *W. Rathenau's New Soc.* 125 The *saboteurs* of labour. 1931 *Observer* 11 Jan. 20/2 Two managers of a dairy were dubbed saboteurs and sentenced to five and two years of imprisonment for letting two hundred tons of butter spoil.

Sabre, *sb.* **4.** Add: **sabre-rattler,** a reckless militarist, one who threatens violent action in a cause; so **sabre-rattling.**

1922 *Weekly Dispatch* 19 Nov. 8 A policy of adventure, sabre-rattling, and reckless expenditure. 1928 *Observer* 26 Feb. 16/4 A sabre-rattling gesture against a nation with whom we have been at peace for more than a hundred years. 1928 *Daily Express* 6 Dec. 5/2 There is no reason for supposing that the child Napoleon will grow up a sabre-rattler. 1932 *Bombay Chron.* 5 Aug. 6 Henceforward sabre-rattling in Prussia will be severely taboo.

Sabreur. Add: **b.** One who fences with a sabre.

1930 *Morning Post* 16 July 17/7 The school undoubtedly possess a natural sabreur in Woods.

Saccharilla (sækări·lă). *Disused.* [app. fancifully f. L. *saccharum* sugar.] A kind of muslin.

1851 *Illustr. Catal. Gt. Exhib.* III. 480/1 Saccharilla book muslin. 1858 Simmonds *Dict. Trade*, Saccharilla, a kind of muslin. 1875 Knight *Dict. Mech.* s.v. *Muslin*, Varieties are known as..lawn, saccharilla, harness. 1886 *Encycl. Brit.* XVII. 109/2 Plain, striped, and figured grenadines, and saccharilla.

Saccharomycetes (sækăromai·sītīz), *sb. pl.* [mod.L., f. Gr. σάκχαρ sugar + μύκητες Mycetes.] The yeast-fungi. Also occas. sing. **-myces.** Hence **Saccharomycete.**

1885 *Encycl. Brit.* XIX. 51/2 Certain Schizomycetes and Saccharomycetes. 1902 *Ibid.* XXVIII. 560/2 No satisfactory proof has as yet been given that Saccharomycetes are derivable by culture from any higher form. 1901 Dorland *Med. Dict.* (ed. 2), *Saccharomycetic*, due to the presence of yeast-fungi.

Sack, *sb.*[1] **3.** Add: *To hold the sack*: to be left in the lurch (cf. *Bag *sb.* 18). *U.S.*

1904 W. H. Smith *Promoters* xxiv. 343 They are the ones that are always left to hold the sack. 1928 Mulford *Bar-20 Three* xii. 169 ..left holding the sack. 1929 *Univ. Kansas Graduate Mag.* Apr., We will be holding the sack for an additional..deficit of nearly $1000.

Sack, *sb.*[4] **2.** (Earlier U.S. examples of *sack-coat.*)

1853 P. Kennedy *Blackwater Chron.* v. ii. 93 He wears an old brown sack-coat. 1869 S. Bowles *Our New West* v. 100 My last winter's thick pantaloons and heavy sack coat..completed my clothing.

Sa·cker[2]. *U.S.* [f. Sack *v.*[1] 6.] One engaged in sacking logs.

1902 S. E. White *Blazed Trail* lii. 360 It was noon. The sackers looked up in surprise.

Sacking, *sb.*[3] Add: **1.** Also *transf.* of other material used for the same purpose.

1843 R. Carlton *New Purchase* 163 Next was a sacking of clap-boards pinned down; and then a very thick straw bed.

3. (Earlier U.S. examples of *sacking-bottom.*)

1841 Catlin *N. Amer. Ind.* I. 191 A sacking-bottom, made of the buffalo's hide. 1868 G. G. Channing *Early Recoll. Newport, R.I.* 254 Sometimes it [*sc.* the bedstead] was furnished with a 'sacking bottom'.

Sacrament, *sb.* **1.** Add: *The last sacraments*, Holy Communion and Extreme Unction administered to the dying.

1760 in J. O. Payne *Old Engl. Cath. Missions* (1889) 29 Jan. 7, William Hornby died at Middleham. He had the last sacraments. 1893 E. Bellasis *Mem. Serjt. Bellasis* viii. 184 He left him,..to go and tell the Curé..that the Sergeant ought to have the last Sacraments without delay.

Sacred, *a.* and *sb.* **A.** *adj.* **3. b.** Add: *Sacred orders* [eccl. L. *ordines sacri*], the holy or major orders.

[1709 Bingham *Orig. Eccl.* III. i. II. 9 The Clergy of the Superior Orders are commonly called the ἱερώμενοι Holy and Sacred, as in Socrates and others.] 1726 Ayliffe *Parergon* 184 The first [*sc.* sub-deacons, deacons, and priests] the Canon Law..stiles Sacred Orders. 1884 Addis & Arnold *Cath. Dict.* 622/1 s.v. *Order*, The orders of bishop, priest, deacon, and (but only since the thirteenth century) subdeacon are called 'sacred' or 'greater'. 1901 Procter & Frere *Prayer Bk.* 650 *note*, The Sacramentary of Serapion gives forms of ordination only for the three sacred orders.

Sacred Heart. The heart of Jesus, regarded as an object of devotion. Similarly, *Sacred Heart of Mary.*

1813 (*title*) The Devotion to the Sacred Heart of our Lord Jesus Christ...And the Little Office of the Sacred Heart. c 1829 in *Cath. Rec. Soc. Publ.* (1911) IX. 412 Sister Lucy Magdalen Whitechurch of the Sacred Hearts of Jesus and Mary. 1853 J. B. Dalgairns *Dev. Hrt. Jesus* Introd. (1868) 45 They had distributed pictures of the Sacred Heart of Jesus among the peasantry. 1873 Manning (*title*) The Divine Glory of the Sacred Heart. 1884 Addis & Arnold *Cath. Dict.* 393/1 s.v. *Heart of Jesus*, On February 6, 1765, Clement XIII. permitted several churches to celebrate the feast of the Sacred Heart, which was extended in 1856 to the whole Church.

Sacrifice, *sb.* Add: **3. b.** *Sacrifice of praise (and thanksgiving)*: a biblical phr. (e.g. Lev. vii. 12, Ps. xlix [l]. 14, 23, Heb. xiii. 15) used gen. for an offering of praise to God, and liturgically in the Anglican Communion Service, tr. *sacrificium laudis* of the Latin Canon of the Mass.

1535 Coverdale *Heb.* xiii. 15 Let vs therfore by him offre allwayes vnto God the sacrifice of prayse. 1549 *Bk. Com. Prayer, Communion*, Entierely desiryng thy fatherly goodnes, mercifully to accepte this our Sacrifice of praise and thankes geuing. 1611 *Bible* Jer. xvii. 26 Bringing sacrifices of praise vnto the house of the Lord. 1864 F. S. Pierpoint *Hymn, 'For the Beauty of the Earth'*, Christ our God to thee we raise This our sacrifice of praise. 1872 H. Varley (*title*) The Sacrifice of Praise: Hymns for Congregational Use and Gospel Meetings. 1877 E. Daniel *Prayer Bk.* (1880) 296 That sacrament in which we offer our sacrifice of praise and thanksgiving for the redemption of the world. 1884 Addis & Arnold *Cath. Dict.* 564/1 s.v. *Mass*, The Mass is a sacrifice of adoration, of praise and thanksgiving.

5. (Later example.)

1915 *Yale Rev.* ..'Being convinced that his trade sacrifice' will result in increased business.

b. *Baseball.* = *sacrifice hit* (see 6 in Dict.).

1904 R. H. Barbour *Bk. Sch. & Coll. Sports* 173 When the batsman is looking for a sacrifice keep the ball high. 1912 C. Mathewson *Pitching* ..He was all set for the sacrifice.

6. (sense 5) *sacrifice sale.*

1904 G. H. Lorimer *Lett. Self-made Merchant* x. 129 ..the record-breaking, marked-down sacrifice sale of the year on good bases.

Sacrifice, *v.* Add:

3. c. To sell or get rid of at a sacrifice, esp. in commercial use. Also *absol.*

1900 Farmer & Henley *Slang*, *Sacrifice*...to sell regardless of cost. 1930 *San Anton. (Texas) Light* 31 Jan. 14/7 Owner Must Sacrifice..

d. *Baseball. trans.* and *intr.* To make a hit which advances another player, the batter being put out.

1912 C. Mathewson *Pitching* ix. 202 Brown sacrificed, sending Kling to second.

Saddle, *sb.* Add: **4. c.** In mining.

1872 *Rep. Vermont Board Agric.* 630 The miners were quarreling about false and true veins, horses of rock and saddles of ore.

9. *saddle-cover, -horn* (earlier U.S. example), *-seat*; *saddle-boil.*

1816 U. Brown *Jrnl.* in *Maryland Hist. Mag.* XI. 151 Cumberland's back is full of *saddle biles & in a full fever. 1884 'Mark Twain' *Huck. Finn* ii. 8 He said they rode him all over the world..and his back was all over saddle-boils. 1676 S. Sewall *Diary* (1878) I. 27 *Saddle Cover (was) lost. 1895 M. A. Jackson *Memoirs* xx. 403 A superb English saddle, bridle, holsters, saddle-cover. 1856 Alice Cary *Married* 184 The bridle rein was twisted around the *saddle horn. 1822 J. Fowler *Jrnl.* 135 Seven miles to the river and crossing over found the watter up to the *saddle seats. 1849 *Rep. U.S. Comm. Patents* (1850) 263 The bent tension springs CC, for supporting the saddle seat.

10. saddle-coloured *a.*, (of complexion) tanned; **saddle-feather, -hackle,** each of the long linear feathers that droop from the saddle of the domestic cock; hence **saddle-hackled** *a.*; **saddle gun,** a gun carried on the saddle of a horse; **saddle-stone,** (*b*) (example).

1900 Kipling *Land & Sea Tales* (1923) 39 The *saddle-coloured sons of the soil looked down their noses. 1854 Meall *Moubray's Poultry* 128 The hackle and *saddle feathers are straw colour. 1855 *Poultry Chron.* III. 44/1 A well-known Yorkshire amateur described them to me as 'bad hen-feathered | a little bit approaching to the saddle-feather, and yet neither one thing or other.' 1913 W. Bateson *Mendel's Princ. Hered.* 51 In the cocks the hackles and saddle-feathers are full black. 1886 *Outing* (U.S.) VIII. 7/1 I..had with me the little forty-sixty Winchester *saddle gun. 1854 Meall *Moubray's Poultry* 85 The *saddle hackle and back feathers. 1855 *Poultry Chron.* III. 209/1 Back and saddle-hackle evenly spangled. *Ibid.* 209/2, I consider the really perfect hen-feathered cocks vastly superior in plumage to the long-feathered *saddle-hackled. 1895 G. J. Manson *Sporting Dict.* 54 *Saddle Hackles*, long streamers growing on each side of a cock's rump. 1932 Boumphrey *Story of the Wheel* 42 The '*saddle-stone', which had a hollow face in which a smaller stone was rubbed backwards and forwards.

Saddle, *v.* Add: **1.** *To saddle off* = Off-saddle *v.* *S. Africa.*

1835 Moodie *Ten Years S. Africa* I. 65 He..asked us if we would 'saddle off' our horses.

6. c. To attach after the manner of a saddle.

1881 *Amer. Naturalist* XV. 217 One nest..was saddled to a horizontal limb after the fashion of our wood pewee.

Saddleback, *sb.* Add: **4. g.** A Wessex breed of pig.

1919 (*title*) The Wessex Saddleback Pig Society's Herd Book. 1923 R. E. Davies *Pigs & Bacon Curing* 11 The Wessex Saddleback and Gloucester Old Spot are breeds which have come to the front considerably of recent years. 1927 *Daily Tel.* 6 Dec. 9/2 Mr. Douglas Vickers' herd of Wessex saddlebacks at Temple Dinsley, Hitchin.

h. The Nilgiri ibex, *Capra hylocrius.*

1921 *Blackw. Mag.* July 30/2 The shootable male is termed a saddle-back, for he carries a whitish saddle-like stain on his back.

Saddle-backed, *a.* Add: **1. b.** Placed astride like a saddle.

1878 J. H. Beadle *Western Wilds* xxx. 487 Colorado is divided nearly down the center by the main chain of the Rocky Mountains—or, in miner's phrase, 'saddle-backed across the range'.

Saddle-bag. 1. (Earlier U.S. example.)

1780 W. Fleming in *Trav. Amer. Col.* 651 Capt. Pawling ..had gone back for my saddlebags.

Sa·ddlebag, *v.* *Logging.* *U.S.* [f. the sb.] *intr.* (see quot.).

1905 *Terms Forestry & Logging* 45 *Saddlebag*, as applied to a boom, to catch on an obstruction and double round it.

Sadhu (sā·dū). [Skr. साधु *sādhú* good, pious, holy man, saint, from *sādh* to succeed, attain.] In India, a holy man or sage.

1845 *Encycl. Metrop.* XXI. 672/2 When their [*sc.* spiritual guides'] sanctity is such, that they are believed to have the power of securing or withholding divine blessings, they are styled Sád'hú (saint). 1920 *Glasgow Herald* 25 May 9 He put on the saffron robe of the Sadhu. 1924 *Blackw. Mag.* Oct. 481/2 The temple's guest-chamber, kept for visiting *sadhus* and *sanyasis.*

Sad-iron. (Earlier U.S. examples.)

1787 *Maryland Gaz.* 1 June 1/2 Hardware, of all kinds.. Sad-Irons in casks of 2 cwt. 1815 *Niles' Weekly Register* IX. 91/2 Sad irons [were manufactured].

Sadism. Add: So **Sa·dic** *a.*; **Sa·dist** *attrib.* or *adj.*; **Sadi·stic** *a.* (examples); **Sadi·sticism** = Sadism.

1915 C. R. Payne tr. *O. Pfister's Psychoanal. Method* 78 The sadistic-masochistic instinctive tendency. *Ibid.* 187 *note*, Bloody sadisticism. 1919 H. Walpole *Secret City* I. x, There was something almost sadist..in the old gentleman's observation of Markovitch's labours. 1922 Joan Riviere tr. *Freud's Intr. Lect. Psycho-Anal.* 289 Regression of..the Libido to the antecedent stage of the sadistic-anal organization. 1928 *Daily Tel.* 6 Nov. 10/6 The oily warder..finds a Sadic pleasure in flogging the life out of his helpless charges.

Saeter (sē·tər). Also saetter, saeter, setter, soter, sotter. [Norw. *sæter* (ON. *sætr* seat, residence, mountain pastures, dairy lands: see Seat *sb.*).]

1. A meadow; a pasturage attached to a dwelling. *Shetland and Orkney.*

1795 *Statist. Acc. Scot.* XIV. 321 *note*, As to our meadows, they are also called Setters. 1809 A. Edmondston *View Zetland Isl.* I. 137 Many names of places..terminate in *seter*.] 1822 Hibbert *Descr. Shetland Isl.* 427 *note*, In the ancient Shetland language, the green pasturage attached to a dwelling was named a *Setter* or *Seater.*

2. In Scandinavia, a mountain pasture where cattle remain during the summer months. Also *attrib.*

1841 Ht. Martineau *Feats on the Fiord* vi, The mountain pasture belonging to a farm is called its saeter. 1882 J. A. Lees & Clutterbuck *Three in Norway* 56 This sæter is in a most beautiful situation, perched on a little flat bit of ground on the mountain side. 1929 J. Buchan *Crts. of Morning* II. i, The kind of thing by which in Norway the saeter hay is moved to the valley. 1930 Chas. Archer & J. S. Scott tr. *S. Undset's Kristin Lavransdatter, The Cross* I. ii, She busied herself with some milk-pans and troughs that stood by the sæter wall. *Ibid.*, *Garland* III. iii, You cannot rob folk's sæters in a year like this.

b. A mountain dairy or farm on a 'saeter'.

1923 G. F. Barbour *Life Alex. Whyte* xxii. 451 He and Dr. Sutherland Black..drove seventy miles up the Saetersdal..picnicked for several days in a fishing 'saeter'. 1925 *Countries of World* V. 3017/2 The 'saeters' or mountain dairies in the upland pastures. 1926 *Public Opinion* 25 June 585/2 Mountain farms were being turned into saeters. 1931 *Hardy's Anglers' Guide* 42 The angler taking up his quarters at a small farm or 'saeter'.

Safari (săfā·ri), *sb.* Also **sefari, suffari.** [Swahili, f. Arab. سفر *safar* journey, voyage.]

1. A journey; an expedition on foot, especially for hunting. Often in phr. *on safari.*

[1896 W. A. Chanler *Through Jungle & Desert* 35 The porters shouting joyfully to one another, 'Safari! Safari!' (Journey! Journey!).] 1907 J. H. Patterson *Man-Eaters of Tsavo* vi. 61 [He] had left me and gone on *safari* (a caravan journey) to Uganda. *Ibid.* xi. 119 They join another caravan and begin a new *safari* to the Great Lakes. 1922 H. B. Hermon-Hodge *Up against it in Nigeria* iv. 54, I am an indifferent marksman both at range and on safari. 1928 *Morning Post* 20 Oct. 9/6 The Prince..took ship across Lake Albert towards the Murchison Falls to start a week's 'safari'.

2. A sportsman's or traveller's caravan.

1892 *Daily News* 15 July 5/6 It would be a great thing if the next sefari (caravan) brought up a small Nordenfelt or Hotchkiss gun. 1900 *Smithsonian Rep.* 433 We collected our safari of one hundred and thirty Manyema carriers. 1909 W. S. Rainsford *Land of Lion* vi. 141 Be always careful to look for signs of crocodiles,..and warn your sefari to be careful. 1926 *Blackw. Mag.* Oct. 540/1 It is seldom indeed that a safari passes through the bush without some news of it being 'telegraphed' ahead by the natives.

3. *attrib.* and *Comb.*, as *safari horn, -kit, -path*; **safari ant,** the driver ant, *Anomma arcens.*

1926 D. Strickland *Through Belgian Congo* vi. 94 The driver or *safari ant. 1928 *Blackw. Mag.* Oct. 540/1 The sound of a *safari horn came drifting across the bush. 1928 *Daily Express* 29 Nov. 1/1 The Prince, dressed in *safari kit. 1920 *Blackw. Mag.* Feb. 205/1 A good *safari path winds through a deep valley in the Livingstone Mountains.

Hence **Safa·ri** *v. intr.*, to go on safari.

1908 *Times Lit. Suppl.* 19 Nov. 413/1 Mr. Chapman then has safaried twice for pleasure to British East Africa. 1927 *Chambers's Jrnl.* 693/1 Every hunter who has safaried through the vast Masai and Nandi reserves. 1928 M. Johnson *Safari* 29 We could safari out after game in trackless deserts on camels.

Safe, *sb.* Add: **1. b.** (Earlier U.S. example.)

1820 *Boston (Mass.) Selectmen* 4 Oct., A fire-proof safe in the Selectmen's room for the security of the records.

3. A lead tray laid under plumbing fixtures to receive any water that is spilled.

1852 *Catal. Internat. Exhib., Brit.* II. No. 6392 Patent Bath, sienna marbled inside, verdantique outside. Taps and safe fitted. 1905 *Technol. & Sci. Dict.* (ed. Goodchild & Tweney).

4. [f. Safe *a.*] *At safe*: having the safety slide set.

1920 G. Burrard *Notes on Sporting Rifles* 71 One may.. fail to stop a dangerous charge through the rifle being at 'safe'.

5. *attrib.* and *Comb.*, as *safe-robbery*; **safe-blower,** one who opens a safe by the use of a blowpipe; hence **safe-blowing** *vbl. sb.*

1910 *N. Y. Even. Post* 4 Apr. (Th.) He had already attained some fame...as a *safe-blower. 1927 *Scribner's Mag.* Feb. 180/1 The depredations of porch-climbers, safe-blowers, stick-up men. 1928 *Daily Express* 23 Jan. 2/7 Crooks, especially safe-blowers. *Ibid.* 16 Aug. 9/7 *Safe-blowing, pocket-picking, or purse-snatching. 1928 H. Asbury *Gangs of New York* x. § 2. 217 [Marm Mandelbaum] also offered advanced courses in burglary and safe-blowing. 1886 *Leslie's Pop. Monthly* XXI. 47/2 The Egerton *safe-robbery.. had baffled all the detectives in town.

Safe, *a.* Add: **9. e.** *Safe for*: without prospects or possibilities of danger to.

1917 Woodrow Wilson *Address to Congress* 2 Apr. in *Sel. Addresses* (1918) 195 The world must be made safe for democracy. Its peace must be planted upon the tested foundations of political liberty. 1932 A. P. Herbert in *Punch* 15 June 653/2 The last few years of the War were directed by the great brains up above to thinking out new ways of making the War safe for the infantry. 1932 Sir John Fortescue in *Eighteen-Sixties* 244 The pain of seeing the world made safe for that most unsafe and lowering of influences, vulgarity.

14. safe-hit *Baseball* (see quot. 1895); **safe-light,** transfer † to sense in Dict., and add (*b*) *Photog.* (see quot. 1918); **safe-tray** = *Safe *sb.* 3.

1895 G. J. Manson *Sporting Dict.* 58 *Safe Hits*, this term is applied to high hits sent from the bat when the ball..falls to the ground either over the heads of the infields, but not far enough out for the outfielders to catch. 1897 *Encycl. Sport* I. 77/1 Immediately the batsman hits a 'fair' ball he endeavours to get to first base...He may get there on a safe bit made by the succeeding batsman. 1903 A. Payne *Pract. Orthochrom. Photog.* 90 Red sensitive plates..may be used with a *safe light. 1918 *Photo-Miniature* XV. Mar. (Gloss.), *Safe-Light*, a screen used in the darkroom lamp to supply a yellow, red, or green light, according to the sensitiveness of the plate or paper. Of glass or (more usually of late years) of dyed gelatine films between glass plates. 1886 *Encycl. Brit.* XXI. 715/2 Under most plumbing fixtures it is usual to place a *safe-tray to receive any water accidentally spilt.

Safeguard, *v.* Add: **c.** To 'protect' (a native industry against foreign imports).

1928 *Manch. Guardian Weekly* 10 Aug. 105/1 By appointing a Royal Commission to inquire into the expediency of safeguarding the iron and steel industries. 1929 *Morning Post* 5 Feb. 14/4 Safeguarding Wool.

Safeguarder (sē^i·fgāɹdəɹ). [f. next: see -er [1].] One who favours safeguarding as a fiscal policy.

1928 *Daily Mail* 25 July 12/4 Mr. Churchill's answer to the safeguarders was: The Government will not agree to any fundamental change in their existing fiscal system. 1928 *Daily Express* 17 Dec. 10/7 Side by side we have the basic arguments of the safeguarder and the Free Trader.

Safeguarding (sē^i·fgāɹdiŋ), *vbl. sb.* [f. Safeguard *v.* + -ing [1].] The protection of native manufactures and industries against foreign imports. Also *attrib.*

1921 *Act* 11 & 12 *Geo. V* c. 47 Part I, Safeguarding of Key Industries. 1925 *Times* 10 Feb., The Safeguarding Scheme. ..The idea of introducing a general Safeguarding of Industry Bill has been abandoned. 1926 Sir H. Bell in F. W. Hirst *Safeguarding* Pref. p. vi, Protection is no longer called 'Tariff Reform'. It is called 'Safeguarding of Industries' or 'Buy British Goods' or 'Merchandise Marks'. 1928 *Daily Chron.* 3 Nov. 4 The 'Safeguarding' group meets to-day. 1928 *Britain's Industr. Future* I. v. 54 The Government has been quietly introducing small doses of protection under the euphemistic disguises of 'safeguarding', 'luxury taxes', etc. 1932 G. D. H. Cole *Brit. Trade & Industry* 366 The McKenna and Safeguarding duties.

Safety. Add: **1. g.** Hence in phr. (*To play*) *for safety*: to act in such a way as to avoid risks.

1911 *Concise Oxf. Dict.* s.v. 1931 C. K. Webster *For. Pol. Castlereagh* 15 How little he played the politician's trick of trying to ride for safety at the expense of others.

h. *Safety first*: a maxim or slogan inculcating the necessity of taking precautions for the avoidance of accident. Also *attrib.*, esp. applied to the safest kinds of investment.

1873-4 *Cassell's Mag.* (New Ser.) VIII. 71/2 A system that would go on the motto of safety first. 1914 G. M. Price *Mod. Factory* 138 Corporations which have within the last five years taken up the slogan of 'safety first' and have done great work in accident prevention. 1917 *Punch* 7 Mar. 161/1 'Safety first' was a creed with him. 1924 J. S. C. Bridge *Hist. France* II. 118 The so-called battles were conducted under the rules of a carefully framed code, of which 'safety first' was the unacknowledged watchword and inspiration. 1927 *Daily Mail* 5 Aug., Rising 'Safety First' Stocks. 1930 *Time & Tide* 30 Aug. 1088 All safety-first securities.. are at a premium. 1931 *Daily Mirror* 27 Aug. 4 These and other safety first signs are being introduced all over the Dominion.

9. b. = *safety-razor* (see *10 below).

1932 Dorothy L. Sayers *Have his Carcase* iv. 62 A young man who had so much difficulty with his razor would be more likely to change over to a safety and use a new blade every few days.

c. *attrib.* of a touch-down, hit, etc. made for safety (in various games); *sb.* a safe-hit. *U.S.*

1887 *Century Mag.* XXXIV. 889/2 A 'safety' touch-down counts two points against the side which makes it. 1931 *Randolph Enterprise* (W. Va.) 9 July 5/3 The locals hammered out 15 hits on the first contest while the visitors collected eight safeties.

10. *safety device*; **safety-catch,** (*a*) a catch or stop attached to a mechanical contrivance as a safeguard, especially in hoisting apparatus, e.g. in lifts; (*b*) *Electr.* a safety-fuse; (*c*) a device for securing jewellery, etc., to the clothing to afford protection against its loss; **safety-chain,** (*a*) a chain (as on jewellery) to provide additional security, or to hold railway-cars together in case of an accident to the main coupling; (*b*) see quot. 1875; **safety-curtain,** in theatres, a fire-proof curtain to safeguard the main body of the theatre in case of fire on or behind the stage; **safety-film,** a slow-burning film specially prepared for cinematograph work; **safety-fund,** a fund which private banks are compelled by law to establish and maintain to guarantee their circulating notes; also *attrib.*; **safety-fuse,** (*b*) *Electr.* = *Fuse *sb.*[5]; **safety-glass,** a patent glass composed of two sheets of glass with a layer of celluloid between them to prevent splintering; **safety-man,** an official whose work is to guard a temporarily disused pit in readiness for the resumption of work; **safety-paper,** paper specially prepared to guard against the tampering with or counterfeiting of documents; **safety-razor,** a razor in which the blade is prevented by a guard from cutting the skin; **safety-stop,** …; **safety-vault,** a strong room for the safe custody of valuables; **safety-zone,** an island or part of a road or square where pedestrians may wait in safety from traffic.

1875 Knight *Dict. Mech.* … 1884 Knight *Dict. Mech.* Suppl.

Supplement, p. 3873; Corrigenda, p. 4092; Spurious words, p. 4093; Books quoted, p. 4094

s.v. *Safety Catch*, Safety catches attached to the cage are held away from the guides while the weight of the cage hangs on the rope. 1909 *Chambers's Jrnl.* 61/2 The door can be opened a few inches and yet be held by the safety-catch. 1841 C. H. Gregory *Managem. Locom. Engine* 10 The draw-bar connecting the Engine and Tender must be secure, and the *safety-chains attached. 1851 *Illustr. Catal. Gt. Exhib.* III. iii. 674/1 Safety chain brooches, for effectually fastening a lady's dress. 1875 Knight *Dict. Mech.*, *Safety-chain*, a slack chain which attaches a truck to a car-body and limits the excursions of the former as it slues round. 1909 *Weekly Budget* 21 Aug. 4/6 The *safety curtain at the Lyceum went on strike one evening last week. 1912 *Theatreland* 11 Oct. 4/2 It was left to his successor, Richard Brinsley Sheridan, to stand sponsor for the iron 'safety' curtain. 1884 *Harper's Mag.* Dec. 118/1 If the elevator has a *safety device. 1928 *Daily Mail* 25 July 5/5 All the film used is *safety film. 1930 *Sel. Gloss. Motion Pict. Techn.*, *Safety Film* has a base of acetate which is slow-burning, and so is less inflammable than ordinary nitrate film. 1890 *Safety fuse [see *Fuse *sb.*[1]]. 1902 *Chambers's Jrnl.* 638/2 As a protection, safety-fuses are used,—thin strips of tin or other easily fusible lead alloy wires—which melt and volatilise when an excessive current is passed through. 1922 *Tatler* 4 Oct., Advts. p. xii, Another striking testimony for the Triplex *Safety Glass. 1929 *Daily Express* 7 Nov. 8/4 All the latest safety devices, such as four-wheel or six-wheel brakes, and safety glass. 1931 *Daily Tel.* 21 May 3/1 The safety glass department..has been a continual source of expenditure. 1928 *Sunday Dispatch* 23 Dec. 3/4 These officials, known as '*safety men', will eat their dinner in semi-darkness hundreds of feet below the surface of the earth. 1851 *Illustr. Catal. Gt. Exhib.* III. III. 540/1 White and coloured *safety paper for bankers' cheques. 1875 Knight *Dict. Mech.*, Safety-paper. *Safety-razor. 1893 *Graphic* 21 Jan. 54 Midget Patent Safety Razor. 1920 *Punch* 29 Sept. 255/1 Mr. James Milfly, who recently sustained a laceration of the finger while cleaning his safety razor after use. 1846 M'Kenney *Mem.* I. 26 One set [of vouchers was] for the Treasury Department, one for my office proper, and the third for a *safety vault. 1902 A. D. McFaul *Ike Glidden* xvii. 129 The safe suddenly became the people's depository and safety vault.

Sag, *sb.*[2] **3.** (Earlier U.S. example.)

1849 *Rep. U.S. Comm. Patents, Agric.* (1850) 443 Strawberries are met with..on the edges of 'sloughs' or 'saggs'.

Sagaciate (sǎgēⁱ·ʃiˌeⁱt), *v.* *U.S.* [App. jocularly f. Sagacious + -ate[3].] *intr.* Used as a fanciful substitute for: To get on, do, be, act, think, or the like.

1842 *Literary Gaz.* 1 Jan. 6/3 How does your copperosity sagaciate this morning? 1881 J. C. Harris *Uncle Remus* ii, 'How duz yo' sym'tums seem ter segashuate?' sez Brer Rabbit, seze. 1904 A. Morrison *Green Eye of Goona* v. ii, The police sagaciate that Pooley must ha' gone straight to London. 1909 'O. Henry' *Roads of Destiny* xxii. 366, I sagatiated in your associations once, if I am not mistaken.

Sage, *sb.*[1] Add: **5. b. sage-brush**; also *attrib.* (see quots.).

1904 *N.Y. Even. Post* 6 May 7 A senator from one of the 'sagebrush' States..Mr. Newlands of Nevada. 1917 *Boston Even. Globe* 11 Apr. 16/4 Nevada has been known for many years as the Sagebrush State.

c. sage chicken, fowl = *sage grouse*; **sage hen, rabbit** (earlier examples).

1873 Eliz. B. Custer *Boots & Saddles* App. 293 A pair of *sage-chickens, a pair of curlew, and a jack-rabbit complete my present collection. 1902 O. Wister *Virginian* iv. 53 We..shot some young sage chickens, which were good at supper, roasted at our camp-fire. 1870 *Amer. Naturalist* III. 82 *Sage Fowl (*Centrocercus Urophasianus*). I saw nothing of the Sage Fowl, which..is very rare there. 1848 E. Bryant *What I saw in California* ix. 135 An antelope and *sage-hen were killed during our march to-day. 1846 Sage *Scenes Rocky Mts.* (1859) 55 A large *sage rabbit... This animal is nearly three times the size of the common rabbit, and of a white color, slightly tinged with grey. It derives its name from being found principally in countries abounding with *absinthe* or wild sage.

Saggar, *sb.* Add: **3.** A metal box or crucible used in the preparation of malleable cast-iron; also, a fire-clay vessel used in case-hardening.

1884 W. H. Greenwood *Steel & Iron* 284 The castings are then packed in cast-iron boxes or crucibles known as 'saggers'. 1904 *Technol. & Sci. Dict.* (ed. Goodchild & Tweney), Sagger. 1921 *Dict. Occup. Terms* (1927) § 220 s.v. *Hardener*, Within an iron box, a sagger or other fire-clay vessel.

Sago. 3. Add: **sago-meal**, sago in the form of a meal or flour.

1851 *Illustr. Catal. Gt. Exhib.* IV. I. 874/2 The so-called sago meal is deposited in the cellular part of the stems of the sago palm. 1860 *Ure's Dict. Arts* III. 618. 1866 *Treas. Bot.* s.v. *Sagus*.

Sahara. Add: **2.** A fashion shade of brown: in full *sahara brown*.

1923 *Daily Mail* 9 Oct. 1/1 Colours: Lemon,..Fawn, Sahara, Mole. 1930 *Daily Express* 8 Sept. 11/5 The suit is stocked in shades of Sand, Sahara Brown and Grey.

Saice, variant of Syce.

Sail, *sb.*[1] **10.** Add: **sail-flying** *Aviation*, a form of gliding; **sail-plane** *Aviation*, a form of glider; hence **sail-planing**.

1931 Gymnich in *Henley's ABC of Gliding* 148 By *sail-flying we understand a flight without any kind of motor or other driving power in which the energy required for the flight without loss in altitude, is taken solely from the air currents. *Ibid.* 153 A good gliding and sailflying territory includes mountains or hills of the proper configuration and of suitable height. 1931 (*title*) Henley's ABC of Gliding and Sailflying. 1922 *Daily Mail* 28 Oct., New German '*Sail-plane'. 1931 *Henley's ABC of Gliding* 149 Flying with sail-planes is being differentiated by common acceptance into two types. 1930 *Daily Express* 8 Sept. 16 The first lesson in the art of *sail-planing.

Sail, *v.*[1] Add: **2. b.** Applied to an airship.

1910 *Daily Mail Year Bk.* 149/2 The Gross was compelled to descend, after sailing above the enemy's line.

5. b. (Earlier U.S. example.)

1836 Dunlap *Mem. Water Drinker* (1837) I. 22 Mrs. Epsom sailed majestically about the house.

c. (Earlier U.S. example.)

1883 'Mark Twain' *Life Mississippi* xliii, She sails in and goes the O'Shaughnessy about four hacks and an omnibus better.

Sailing, *vbl. sb.*[1] Add: **4. a. sailing line**, (*b*) a line (Line *sb.*[2] 22) of sailing vessels; **sailing master** (earlier U.S. examples).

1905 *Chambers's Jrnl.* May 366/1 *Sailing-lines to the West Indies..give Bermuda a wide berth. 1779 *Rec. N.H. Comm. Safety* 194 Appointed—Curtice *Sailing Master of the armed ship Hampden. 1799 *Essex Inst. Hist. Coll.* XIII. 39 The other two Lieutenants and the Purser are much wanted, as is a Sailing Master.

b. (Early U.S. examples.)

1748 Franklin *Electrical Exper.* (1751) 38 At the stern and in the wake of every sailing vessel. 1775 *Jrnls. Cont. Congress* III. 293 That a swift sailing vessel..be fitted..for a cruise of three months. 1785 *Maryland Hist. Mag.* XX. 51 He had been accustomed to go up and down Jones's falls in canoes, row boats, and sailing boats. *Ibid.* 52 Battaus, canoes, and sailing yawles.

Sail-maker. (See Sail *sb.*[1] 10.) Also in aeroplane construction.

1596, 1773 [see Sail *sb.*[1] 10]. 1839 *Knickerbocker Mag.* XIII. 43 The sail-maker..proceeded to sew him up in his hammock. 1886 *Outing* (U.S.) VIII. 169/2 A squall carried away our..flying jib—a good job for the sail maker. 1916 H. Barber *Aeroplane Speaks* 103 All is now ready for the sail-maker to cover the surface with fabric.

Sais, sais, variants of Syce.

1890 Kipling *Plain Tales, Miss Youghal's Sais* 30 He..deserved a V.C., if it were only for putting on a *sais's* blanket. 1924 L. Eckenstein *Tutankh-aten* ii. 24 The *saises* running on either side of the chariots as only outrunners in Egypt can run.

Saiva (sai·vă, ʃəi·vă). Also **Shaiva.** [a. Skr. शैव *śaiva* relating, belonging, or sacred to Śiva; a worshipper or follower of Śiva.] A member of one of the three great divisions of modern Hinduism exclusively devoted to the worship of the god Śiva as the Supreme Being. Also *attrib.*

1810 E. Moor *Hindu Pantheon* 15 *Saivas*, or worshippers of Siva. 1842 *Penny Cycl.* XXII. 65/2 The great Saiva reformer, Sankara Acharya. 1845 *Encycl. Metrop.* XXI. 672/2 The Saivas, or adherents of Mahádéó, in preference to Vishnu. 1876 *Encycl. Brit.* IV. 210/1 The *Śaiva*, *Vaishnava*, and *Sākta* sects.

Saivism (səi·viz'm, ʃəi·viz'm). Also **Shaivism.** [f. *Saiva + -ism.] = Sivaism.

1878 Monier-Williams *Hinduism* viii. 97 Saivism and Vaishnavism are not opposite or incompatible creeds. 1882 *Encycl. Brit.* XIV. 228/1 Saivism is supreme, and Buddhism is even nominally extinct. 1913 J. N. Farquhar *Crown of Hinduism* 384 From Saivism there sprang the two Sakta sects.

Saivite (səi·vəit, ʃəi·vəit). Also **Shaivite.** [f. *Saiva + -ite[1].] = Sivaite.

1867 Milman in F. M. Milman *Mem.* (1879) 48 This temple is reckoned..the holiest shrine in India..among the Shaivites. 1882 *Encycl. Brit.* XIV. 228/1 Saivite gods or devils.

Sakellaridis (sækĕlæ·ridis). Also abbreviated **Sakel** (sæ·kĕl). [Personal name.] A variety of Egyptian cotton.

1912 W. L. Balls *Cotton Plant in Egypt* 103 The main varieties at present cultivated on a commercially important scale are Yannovitch and Sakellaridis in the 'fine-spinning' group. *Ibid.* 106 Afifi was introduced commercially about 1887,..Sakel in 1909. *Ibid.* 107 The Sakel cotton contains at least two entirely distinct types of seed fuzz. 1915 J. A. Todd *World's Cotton Crops* 276 Sakellaridis, or Sakel, as it is commonly called,..is similar to Jannovitch, but superior in some respects, and lighter brown in colour. 1927 — *Cotton World* 45 In 1924,..owing to the very low premiums of Egyptian generally, and especially Sakel, Upper Egyptian types invaded the Delta. 1931 *Times* 17 Nov. 13/1 With Sakellaridis at 7d. per lb.

Sakta (sā·ktă, ʃā·ktă). Also **Sacta, Shakta.** [a. Skr. शाक्त *śākta* relating to power or to the Śakti; a worshipper of the Śakti.] A member of one of the principal sects of modern Hinduism which worships the Śakti or divine energy, especially as identified with Durgā, the wife of Śiva.

1810 E. Moor *Hindu Pantheon* 116 Those, of whatever sect, who worship exclusively the female power..are called Sactas. 1845 *Encycl. Metrop.* XXIV. 443/1 The Hindús are almost always either 1. Vaishnavas..; 2. Saivas..; or 3. Sáktas. 1931 Geo. MacMunn *Relig. India* 69 The Sakta groups have borrowed much from aboriginal practices and influence.

Sakti (sa·kti, ʃa·kti). Also **Sakti, Shakti.** [a. Skr. शक्ति *śakti* divine energy, f. शक् *śak* to be strong.] The female principle, especially when personified as the wife of a god, as Durgā is the Śakti of Śiva, etc. Also *attrib.*

1810 E. Moor *Hindu Pantheon* 10 All the principal, and several of the secondary deities..have wives assigned to them, who are called Sacti. 1842 *Penny Cycl.* XXII. 67/1 That thou, united with thy Sakti, dost in sport create the universe from thy own substance. 1871 J. Garrett *Class. Dict. India* 540 The Sakti is said to have originated in God, the Supreme Being... There are many special forms of Sakti-worship. 1913 J. N. Farquhar *Crown of Hinduism* 384 Hindu sects recognize every goddess as the sakti or energy of her husband. 1921 *Brit. Mus. Return* 68 Hindu stone sculptures from Java, representing Saktis of Bodhisattvas.

Saktism (sa·ktiz'm, ʃa·ktiz'm). Also **Shak-.** [f. *Sakti + -ism.] The worship of the Sakti.

1878 Monier-Williams *Hinduism* ix. 123 Tantrism, or Saktism, is Hinduism arrived at its last and worst stage of medieval development. 1902 *Census of India, 1901* I. 181. 1931 Geo. MacMunn *Relig. India* 160 The really secret cult of Saktism.

Salacetol (sælæ·sitǫl, -oul). *Chem.* [f. Salicylic + Acetone + -ol.] A colourless crystalline compound of acetone and salicylic acid, used as an antirheumatic and antiseptic.

1901 Dorland *Med. Dict.* (ed. 2). 1909 *Jrnl. Chem. Soc.* XCVI. I. 245 Santalyl salacetol carbonate, a yellow, syrupy liquid, is produced from santalol and salacetol chlorocarbonate.

Saladang, salandang, varr. of *Seladang.

Salagrama (sālăgrā·mă). Also **sal(a)gram, saligram, saligrama.** [a. Skr. सालग्राम *Sālagrāma*, a village situated on the river Gaṇḍakī, f. *sāla* sal-tree + *grāma* village (whence Hindi *sālgrām*, Hind. *sālagrām*).] A black schistose stone containing a fossil ammonite, especially abundant in the bed of the river Gaṇḍakī, and worshipped by the Hindus as a representation of Vishnu.

1801 H. T. Colebrooke in *Asiatic Researches* VII. 240 A Sálagráma stone ought to be placed near the dying man. 1833 R. Everest *Ibid.* XVIII. II. 111, I have several times looked for such among the Salagrams in the Hindoo temples. 1845 *Encycl. Metrop.* XV. 193/2 The schistose stones, (sálgráms) containing remains of the cornu ammonis. 1874 H. H. Cole *Catal. Ind. Art S. Kens. Mus.* App. 267 Ammonites, or Saligrams; holy stones sacred to Vishnu. 1895 E. W. Hopkins *Rel. India* 502 The black Çālagrāma pebble, an object of reverent awe. 1913 J. N. Farquhar *Crown of Hinduism* 267 If he recognizes Vishnu, he may possess a discus, a *salagrama* stone, a conch shell or a *tulsi* plant.

Salamander, *sb.* **3. a.** (Later U.S. example.)

1897 Moore *How to Build* ii. 19 A wooden house..with salamander, asbestos, or other fire-proof material between floors.

6. Salamander safe *U.S.* (earlier example).

1845 in C. Cist *Cincinnati Misc.* 194 These Salamander safes are made of stout, wrought bar and plate iron,..lined with a chemical preparation, which is a non-conductor of heat, and is indestructible by fire.

Salamander, *v.* Add: **c.** To brown by means of a salamander.

1878 *Amer. Home Cook Bk.* 65 When it is cooked, glaze the top and salamander it.

Salariat (sălē·riăt, ‖ salarya). [Fr.: see Salary *sb.* and -ate[1].] The salaried class.

1918 Reckitt & Bechhofer *Meaning Nat. Guilds* iv. 85 Hypnotized by the round 'O' in the figure of their pay, the salariat feel that they really are important members of the industry. 1922 *Q. Rev.* Apr. 288 The 'salariat' is almost as much enslaved as the proletariat. 1931 *Sat. Rev.* 19 Sept. 355/1 Glance at the Conservative ranks in the Commons—where are the manual workers, the lesser-paid salariat, the working class and lower middle classes generally?

Salary, *sb.* **3.** Add: *salary man, officer.*

1763 *Essex Inst. Hist. Coll.* XLIX. 139 Our provinces..who have greatly wronged many..generous creditors, and salary men, by means of their awful breaches of their public faith. 1822 *Ann. 17th Congress* 1st Sess. I. 168 To fix the compensation of a collector, so it would neither exceed nor fall short of a particular sum,..would be making them all salary officers.

Sale, *sb.*[2] Add:

1. d. *Bookselling.* The ordinary trade rate.

1900 *What will it cost?* 48 [Trade phrases] *Sale*, 30% discount off published price.

2. g. *Sale of work*, a sale of articles made by members of a congregation or association on behalf of some charitable or religious object.

1869 in J. A. Langford *Mod. Birmingham* (1877) II. ii. 469 [A] Sale of Work [took place in 1869, by which £1,188 were realised.] 1890 *New Road Chapel Monthly Visitor* Feb. 18 b/1 Sale of Work and Mothers' Meetings. 1917 Flora Klickmann *Betw. Larch-Woods & Weir* ii. 21 The vermilion satin cushion embroidered with yellow eschscholtzias, that had lain in a trunk in the attic since the last Sale of Work but two.

3. *sale catalogue, -goer, price* (sense 1 c), *week.*

1821 *Kaleidoscope* 1 May 346/3 *Sale catalogue. 1852 *Fraser's Mag.* June 723/2 When he [*sc.* wholesale bookseller] subscribes a book, or issues a sale catalogue. 1910 *Quaritch's Catal.* No. 286 Sale-Catalogue of the library of David Garrick. 1927 *Daily Express* 4 July 3/3 *Sale-goers are advised to remember the date. 1897 (*title*) The *Sale Prices of 1896. 1901 *Connoisseur* Dec. 280/1 On December 15th will be published the first issue of a supplement to *The Connoisseur* with the title *Sale Prices*. 1902 *To-Day* XXXV. 123/1 Some people, so long as they see '*Sale Price', written on a card pinned to some goods, are content to pay any price. 1912 *Sale Catal.*, Fleecy overcoat,..Usual Price 52/6, Sale Price 29/6..Owing to the great pressure of work during the *Sale Week..nothing can be sent on approval.

b. *sales-goer, -hand, -people, -person, -room.*

1925 *Glasgow Herald* 6 Jan. 7/2 The large number of men among the *sales-goers. 1927 *Daily Express* 17 Feb. 5/5 As mannequins and as *sales-hands. 1928 *Publishers' Weekly* 9 June 2370 Special lectures for groups of *sales people from the local stores. *Ibid.* 10 Nov. 1962/2 We shall be glad to send a complimentary copy of the novel on request to any retail *salesperson to read. *Ibid.* 1977/2, I have known a book-store where one sales person turned over more stock than any other four put together. 1840 *Knickerbocker Mag.* XVI. 226 Ejecting a crowded audience from his *sales-room because an unlucky wight had the temerity to bid six-pence for a tattered copy of Paradise Lost.

Sale, *v.* Add: **2.** *intr.* To hold a sale; to shop at the sales. Hence **Sa·ler**, one who frequents sales.

1901 *Sketch* 3 July 443/1 To go 'saleing' in Bond..Street. 1902 *To-Day* XXXV. 447/1 All London is 'saleing' at the present moment. 1928 *Daily Express* 19 June 3/2 Men went 'sale-ing' at lunch time. *Ibid.* 31 Dec. 5/3 'Saleing' has become a specialised art. 1929 *Ibid.* 8 Jan. 3/4 The great furniture houses are 'saling'. 1928 *Morning Post* 25 June 8 Many experienced 'salers' will tell you that it is an excellent plan to go to the sales with an open mind.

Saleratus. *U.S.* (Earlier example.)

1837 Sylv. Graham *Bread-making* 46 Pearl ash or saleratus is also used by them in considerable quantities.

Salesian (sălī·ʃăn), *a.* and *sb.* [ad. F. *Salésien*, f. the name of St. François de Sales + -ian.] **a.** *adj.* Of or pertaining to St. Francis of Sales, and to communities living according to his rule, as the order of the Visitation founded in 1610 under his direction, and a congregation founded by Dom Bosco (1815–1888) for the rescue of poor and neglected children. **b.** *sb.* A follower of St. Francis of Sales or a member of a Salesian order; a Salesian father or brother.

1884 *Month* Jan. 46 His [*sc.* Dom Bosco's] institution henceforth went by the name of 'The Oratory of St. Francis of Sales', and his co-labourers were called 'Salesians'. *Ibid.* 58 All his Salesian houses are managed on the same system. ..One word of sorrow, on the part of the Salesian Father, is enough to stop a boy who is about to do wrong. 1890 Lady Martin tr. *Villefranche's Life Dom Bosco* xx. (ed. 3) 196 His first missionary expedition..included ten priests and coadjutor Salesian Brothers. 1912 F. M. Capes *Gemma Galgani* 15 The Order of Salesian sisters in Lucca.

Salic (sæ·lik), *a.*[2] *Petrog.* [f. *sal* (coined by Suess from S(ilica and Al(umina, now superseded by *Sial) + -ic.] In the quantitative system of classification, designating one of the two principal groups of standard minerals, the members of which are chiefly characterized by silica or alumina. (Cf. *Femic.)

1903 W. Cross, Iddings, etc. *Quant. Classif. Igneous Rocks* 115 Salic Minerals. 1905 *Rep. Brit. Assoc.* 390 The alumo-alkaline (or salic) and ferro-magnesian (or femic) rocks. 1909 R. Fletcher *Introd. Study Rocks* (ed. 4) 146 The ten sets of standard molecules are regarded as belonging to one or other of two kinds, termed respectively salic and femic. 1920 A. Holmes *Nomencl. Petrol.* 203 *Salic*...A mnemonic term..applied to the group of standard normative minerals which includes quartz, felspars and felspathoids.

Salicetum (sælisī·tǫm). [Late L., f. L. *salic-*, *salix* willow + *-ētum*, after *quercētum*, etc.] A willow plantation.

1910 *Encycl. Brit.* III. 482/1 The most extensive English willow plantation or salicetum..of the present day. 1926 *Nat. Hist. Oxford Distr.* 73 Many interesting Willows which were formerly grown in the Salicetum in the Botanic Gardens.

Salicologist (sælikǫ·lŏdʒist). [f. L. *salic-*, *salix* willow + -(o)logist.] A student of or an authority on willows.

1925 *Jrnl. Bot.* LXIII. 293 Dr. Enander the eminent Swedish salicologist.

Salient, *a.* and *sb.* **A.** *adj.* Add

6. Electr. *Salient pole* (see quots.).

1904 *Technol. & Sci. Dict.* (ed. Goodchild & Tweney), *Salient Pole*, when the poles of a dynamo project inward towards the armature, from a closed ring of iron, and are each magnetised by one coil only, they are termed Salient Poles, as distinguished from Consequent Poles. 1910 *N. Hawkins' Electr. Dict.*, *Salient Poles*, the poles of a dynamo or motor field magnet occurring at the ends of the pole pieces, as distinguished from *consequent poles*.

B. *sb.* **b.** A projecting section of a line of offence or defence, e.g. in trench-warfare; *spec.* (with *the*) the salient at Ypres in the War of 1914–18.

1914 *War Illustrated* 5 Dec. 366/1 The British salient at Ypres fascinated the Kaiser. 1918 Farrow *Dict. Mil. Terms*, *Salient*..in map reading, a projection from the side of a hill or mountain, running out and down from the main feature. 1920 *Bairnsfather Case* 113 Ypres, which at that time to [*sic*] every soldier outside the salient, was regarded as the most fearful quarter on the whole of the Western Front. 1927 R. H. Mottram *Spanish Farm* 206 The trench line..became as fixed as the old line from the Ypres salient to La Bassée had been. 1927 'S. Rohmer' *Morn of Madness* iii, The last time I saw him—coming out of the salient with what was left of the Irish Guards. 1932 D. L. Sayers *Have his Carcase* iv. 62 The only young Endicott was killed in the Salient.

Salina[2] (sălai·nă). *Geol.* The name of a township and town in Onondaga county, New York, designating the saliferous deposits of New York of the Upper Silurian division. Hence **Sali·nan** *a.*

1879 *Encycl. Brit.* X. 339/2 Upper Silurian...Salina Formation. Onondago salt group, nearly barren of fossils. 1895 J. D. Dana *Man. Geol.* (ed. 4) 552 The Salina beds of shales and marlytes, or the Salt Group. 1924 C. Schuchert *Geol.* II. (ed. 2) 264 Cayugan or Upper Silurian..Salinan. 1925 Ries & Watson *Engin. Geol.* (ed. 3) 663 Salina beds.

Salinigrin (sælinai·grin). *Chem.* [f. L. *salix* willow + *nigr-*, *niger* black + -in[1].] A glucoside formed from the bark of the black willow.

1900 H. A. D. Jowett in *Jrnl. Chem. Soc.* LXXVII. 708 A new glucoside for which the name of salinigrin is provisionally proposed.

Sal-lal (sæˌlˌlæl). *Canadian.* (See quots.)

1884 Phillipps-Wolley *Trottings of a Tenderfoot* 140 In front lay in the river-bed a grove of cottonwood, and the bush I think British Columbians call 'sal lal'. 1927 *Blackwood's Mag.* Aug. 205/1 The last hen had scurried past him towards the safety of the thick sal-lal brush above the beach.

Salle. Add: **3.** In a paper-mill, a large room used for sorting and packing sheets of paper. Also *attrib.*

1888 C. F. Cross & E. J. Bevan *Paper-Making* 175 The sheets of paper are now ready to be examined before being finally sent away from the mill. This is done in the 'Finishing-house', or 'Salle' as it is sometimes called. 1894 G. Clapperton *Pract. Paper-making* 147 The different stages through which the paper passes in the salle are entirely dependent on the qualities produced in the mill. 1921 *Dict. Occup. Terms* (1927) § 518 s.v. *Finisher*, Salle finisher. *Ibid.* s.v. *Sorter*, Salle sorter.

Sallee (sæ·li). *Australia.* Also **sally.** [Native name.] (See quots.)

1889 J. H. Maiden *Usef. Pl. Australia* 149 *Acacia falcata*,..'Hickory'. 'Lignum-Vitæ'. 'Sally'. *Ibid.* 250 *Eucalyptus stellulata*,..'Sally' or 'Black Gum'. *Ibid.* 355 *Acacia falcata*...Called variously 'Hickory',..and 'Sally' or 'Sallee'. 1898 E. Morris *Austral Eng.* s.v. *Acacia*, The species are very numerous, and are called provincially by various names, e.g. 'Wattle', 'Mulga', 'Giddea', and 'Sally', an Anglicized form of the aboriginal name *Sallee*.

Sally, *v.*[2] Add: **4.** (See quots.)

1825 Brockett *N.C. Gloss.*, *Sally*, to move or run from side to side; as is customary with the persons on board of a ship after she is launched. 1887 *Jamieson's Sc. Dict.* Suppl. 210 To *Sally*, *Saully*, v. n., to move or run from side to side, as children do in certain games, and as workmen do on board a ship after it is launched; to rock or swing from side to side, like a small boat at anchor; also, to rise and fall, like a ship on a rough sea. 1894 Heslop *Northumb. Gloss.*, *Sally*, to sway a boat or ship, in play, from side to side...This was done by a rush or sally to one side, which caused a lurch. 1919 Shackleton *South* i. 33 The engines running full speed astern produced no effect until all hands joined in 'sallying' ship.

Sally-nixon (sæliˌni·ksən). Corruption of *salenixon*, Sal enixum. Also **salonix** and **sally.**

1882 Crookes *Dyeing & Tissue-printing* 81 The crystallized sulphate of soda, known..in many dye-houses as Sally Nixon ..a corruption for *sal enixum*. 1891 C. Lunge *Sulphuric Acid* (ed. 2) I. 96 'Nitre-cake' or, in the workmen's language, 'sally nixon'.

Salmine (sæ·lməin). *Chem.* [f. L. *salmo* Salmon + -ine[5].] A protamine derived from the spermatozoa of the salmon.

1896 *Jrnl. Chem. Soc.* LXX. I. 582 Protamine..from sturgeon sperm has rather different solubilities in sodium chloride solutions, and the names *salmine* and *sturine* are suggested by the two protamines. 1926 H. G. Rule tr. *J. Schmidt's Org. Chem.* 729 The individual protamines are named after the fish from whose testicles they are obtained, *e.g.* salmine from salmon, sturine from sturgeon.

Salmite (sæ·lməit). *Min.* [Named by E. Prost from the river Salm, Belgium + -ite[1].] A manganese variety of chloritoid.

1892 E. S. Dana *Dana's Syst. Min.* (ed. 6) 640. 1906 J. P. Iddings *Rock Minerals* 439 There are varieties containing MnO that have nearly the formula of chloritoid (salmite and masonite).

Salmon, *sb.*[1] **4. c.** Add: **salmon-bass** (see quot. and *Kabeljou); **salmon-disease**, an infectious fungoid disease, causing injury to the skin and flesh of salmon and ultimately the death of the fish; **salmon fungus**, a species of *Saprolegnia* causing ulcerations of the skin of the salmon.

1931 *Hardy's Anglers' Guide* 48 The Kabeljaauw, known in Natal as *Salmon Bass..runs to as much as 150 lbs. 1878–9 Stirling in *Proc. Roy. Soc. Edin.* X. 242 That the so-called *salmon disease does not depend upon a prediseased condition of the fish. 1882 T. H. Huxley in *Q. Jrnl. Microsc. Sci.* XXII. 328 The Saprolegnia is the cause of the salmon disease. *Ibid.* 317 The stem-hyphæ answer exactly in size and structure to the hyphæ of the *salmon fungus. 1886 *Encycl. Brit.* XXI. 227/1 The salmon fungus grows with great luxuriance on other animal substances.

Salmonella (sælmǫne·lă). *Bacteriology.* [mod. L., f. the name of Daniel E. Salmon (1850–1914), American pathologist + *-ella* L. fem. dim. suffix.] The bacillus of hog-cholera, *Bacillus choleræ suis*. Hence **Sa:lmonello·sis** *Path.*, infection with salmonella.

1913 H. J. Hutchens tr. *A. Besson's Pract. Bacteriol.* 422 Lignières proposed to designate all those organisms which had the morphological and cultural attributes of the bacillus of hog-cholera..by the name Salmonella after Salmon. 1913 Dorland *Med. Dict.* (ed. 7), *Salmonellosis*, infection with *Bacillus choleræ suis*. 1921 R. T. Hewlett *Man. Bacteriol.* (ed. 7) 444 The Gärtner group of organisms has been termed the Salmonella group.

Salmon-trout. 2. (Earlier examples.)

1726 Penhallow *Indian Wars* (1824) 113 Our men were well entertained with moose, bear, and deer, together with salmon-trout. 1807 P. Gass *Jrnl.* xxi. 228 In the evening one of the large fish was caught, which we found to be a salmon-trout. 1848 E. Bryant *What I saw in California* xi. 158 He had taken with his hook about a dozen salmon-trout.

Saloon. Add: **4. a.** Also, the cabin for the accommodation of passengers in an aeroplane.

1921 *Daily Mail Year Bk.* 27/1 Eight passengers..in armchair seats in a draught-proof saloon.

c. In full *saloon car*: a type of motor car with a closed body, and without a partition behind the driver. *Saloon landaulette*, a saloon with a folding head.

1912 *Motor Manual* (ed. 14) 99 Other forms of bodies fitted to more expensive cars include the brougham, landaulet, saloon, double phaeton, [etc.]. 1918 *Ibid.* (ed. 22) 128 Landaulets, cabriolets, and saloon cars. 1925 *Morris Owner's Man.* 62 Morris-Oxford (Saloon and Cabriolet). 1927 B. K. Seymour *Three Wives* I. x, He secured..the services of a Buick saloon. 1930 *Motor Body Building* May 105 Saloon landaulette.

6. (Earlier examples.)

1848 Lowell *Biglow P.* Ser. I. *Third Let. B. Sawin* 51 I've ben consid'ble round in bar-rooms an' saloons Agetherin' public sentiment. 1853 Brewerton *With Kit Carson* (1930) 184 As I reentered the bar-room labeled 'saloon', of mine inn.

Salopian, *a.* and *sb.* Add:

2. Belonging to (a member of) Shrewsbury School.

1866 *Blackw. Mag.* Apr. 432/2 He has left us specimens of Latin verses of which even modern Salopians might be proud. 1877 (*title*) The Salopian.

3. *Geol.* (See quots.)

1869 *Q. Jrnl. Geol. Soc.* XXV. I. 174 Nor do we find any representatives of the Permian beds referable to the Salopian type to the north of this part of England. 1905 *Technol. & Sci. Dict.* (ed. Goodchild & Tweney) s.v., In the Lake District and in Southern Scotland the rocks of Salopian age attain to a thickness of many thousand feet. The rocks above the Salopians are now classed as Downtonian and the remainder of the Silurian Rocks below as Valentian. 1912 Jukes-Browne *Stratigr. Geol.* 165 Salopian Series.—The succession of limestones and shales which form this series at Woolhope and Malvern.

Salpiglossis. Add: Also, any plant of this genus.

1841 Loudon *Encycl. Plants* Suppl. 1224. 1915 H. H. Thomas *Bk. Hardy Flowers* 392 The great improvement in the size and colour of the flowers..during recent years renders the Salpiglossis very desirable for beds and groups in the border. 1931 A. N. Scott tr. *Hans Carossa's Boyhood & Youth* v, A whole host of the most beautiful salpiglosses.

Salpingectomy (sælpindʒe·ktŏmi). *Surg.* [f. Gr. σαλπιγγ- (see Salpingo-) + ἐκτομία excision.] Excision of a Fallopian tube.

1889 *Buck's Handbk. Med. Sci.* VIII. 758/3. 1903 W. G. Spencer *Walsham's Surg.* 1082 In salpingectomy especial care is needed not to rupture a pyosalpinx when freeing it. 1910 *Practitioner* Apr. 517 An ovariotomy for a large cystic adenoma..and a bilateral salpingectomy with ventrifixation.

Salt, *sb.*[1] Add: **1. b.** *English salt* (see quot.).

1858 Simmonds *Dict. Trade* s.v. *Salts*, English salt is chloride of soda.

5. b. *Salt of lemon* (*salt of lemons, salts of lemon*), binoxalate of potash, potash combined with oxalic acid; also *occas.* oxalic acid alone; a highly poisonous white crystalline salt used to remove ink-stains and iron-mould from linen; *Carlsbad, Vichy salts*, salts prepared from the mineral springs in these places, or imitations thereof; *Everitt's s., Monsel's s.* (see quot. 1890), *Preston salts*, a variety of smelling-salts.

1815 *New Family Receipt-Book* (new ed.) Index 402 Essential Salt of Lemons. 1829 W. Henry *Elem. Chem.* (ed. 11) II. 223 Salt of sorrel, or essential salt of lemons. 1840 Barham *Ingol. Leg.* Ser. II. *Aunt Fanny*, Salt of Lemon Will make it, in no time, quite fit for the Gemman! 1858 Simmonds *Dict. Trade*, *Preston-salts*,..smelling-salts..containing carbonate of ammonia in small pieces, with a drachm of the following mixture added, viz. oils of bergamot, cloves, and lavender, and the strongest solution of ammonia. 1866 *Chambers's Encycl.* VIII. 453/2 The celebrated Preston smelling-salts are scented with oils of cloves and pimento. 1868 *Chambers's Encycl.* X. 75/2 Ink-stains..require to be taken out with..the essential salts of lemon. 1890 Billings *Med. Dict.*, *Everitt's salt*, a compound of cyanide of iron and potassium, formed when potassium ferrocyanide is decomposed by sulphuric acid. *Ibid.*, *Monsel's salt*, $Fe_4O(SO_4)_5$. Basic ferric sulphate. 1895 *Army & Navy Co-op. Soc. Price List* 15 Sept. 696/1 Carlsbad Salts. *Ibid.* 710/2 Vichy Salts, Effervescing. 1902 *Encycl. Brit.* XXXIII. 275/2 The powdered Carlsbad salts (*pulverförmig*).

6. *Ethereal salt*, an ester. *Metallic salt*, a salt of which the basic component is an oxide or hydroxide of a metallic element.

1876 *Encycl. Brit.* V. 553/2 The thio-acids also form ethereal salts. 1904 *Technol. & Sci. Dict.* (ed. Goodchild & Tweney) 180/1 After-treatment with a metallic salt, *e.g.* copper sulphate.

10. (Modern U.S. example.)

1901 S. E. White *Westerners* xviii. 156 When I get those Easte'n capitalists interested, and ready to put a little *salt* in.

12. c. salt-bath furnace, a type of hardening furnace; **salt lake**, a saline lake of which the chief chemical constituents are sodium and magnesium chlorides and magnesium and calcium sulphates.

1913 *Lockwood's Dict. Mech. Engin.* (ed. 4), *Salt Bath Furnace*, a type of hardening furnace in which the temperature is regulated by the employment of fused salts. 1836 *Penny Cycl.* VI. 343/2 A great number of smaller and larger *salt lakes. 1885 Geikie *Text-bk. Geol.* (ed. 2) 380 Saline lakes, considered chemically, may be grouped as *salt lakes*, where the chief constituents are sodium and magnesium chlorides with magnesium and calcium sulphates: and *bitter lakes*.

Salt, *v.*[1] Add: **1. b.** (Earlier U.S. example.)

1849 N. P. Willis *Rural Lett.* viii. 355 'Calm as the shadow of a rock across the foam of a cataract', would be a neat thing to 'salt down' for Calhoun or Van Buren.

d. Also *actively*, to render immune by inoculation.

1905 *Rep. Brit. Assoc.* 545 Dr. Edington..reports that..

by inoculating mules with Heart-water blood he has been able to salt them against Horse-sickness.

5. b. *To salt down*, to 'dress' down. *U.S. colloq.*

1904 *Springfield* (Mass.) *Weekly Republ.* 9 Sept. 6 Senator Depew salts down William Allen White, who has stated that the senator tried to bully the president into [etc.].

6. d. (Earlier U.S. examples.)

1819 E. Dana *Geog. Sk. Western Country* 234 It is rare in this country that cattle are either fed, salted, or sheltered. 1838 H. Colman *Rep. Agric. Mass.* (1839) 75 He is careful to salt them once a week, or oftener, if the season is wet.

9. Also *transf.*

1927 *Lond. Mercury* Oct. 563 Immediately after seeing the Glozel site and the objects recovered from it, [he] pronounced the whole thing to be a fake, and the site to have been 'salted' with spurious remains.

Salta (sæ·ltă). [f. L. *saltāre* to leap.] A game resembling halma.

1901 *Daily Express* 23 Mar. 8/7 Salta is played on a board of 100 squares, each player having fifteen pieces. *Ibid.*, Like in the first international salta tournament.., a chess master has again held his own against the draughts and salta experts who competed. 1904 Mrs. Alec-Tweedie *Behind Footlights* viii. 153 She [*sc.* Sarah Bernhardt]..plays Salta with her son. This game is a kind of draughts.

Saltation. Add: **1. d.** *Biol.* Mutation, or a result of this.

1870 [see 1 c in Dict.]. 1906 *Pop. Sci. Monthly* June 485 (Cent. D. Suppl.) The name 'saltation', or in recent years 'mutation', has been applied to extreme fluctuation, the immediate cause of which is unknown. The experiments of Dr. Hugo de Vries on the saltations of the descendants of an American form of evening primrose. 1930 R. A. Fisher *Genet. Theory Nat. Sel.* vii. 163 Unless such a resemblance formerly existed a gradual mimetic evolution is precluded, and we should be forced to admit that the mimetic females arose as sports or saltations totally unlike their mothers. *Ibid.* 164 A single saltation from a male of the same species.

Salt-cellar. Add: **c.** Each of the hollows at the base of the neck. *colloq.*

1913 *Queen* 17 May, Advt. 35 'Saltcellars' and thinness of the Neck and Shoulders. 1917 C. Dane *Regim. Women* xxvii, Her neck! You should see her neck—salt-cellars, literally. 1918 'O. Onions' *Story of Louie* i, The copper-haired girl with the long thin neck and the 'salt-cellars' showing through her white flannel blouse.

Salt grass. *U.S.* [Salt *a.*[1] 3 b.] **a.** Grass growing in salt meadows, largely species of *Spartina*. **b.** A pasture-grass of the arid plains of the western States.

1704 *Rec. of Providence, R.I.* V. 224 The which sd Cove is a place of Salt Grass called Thatch. 1800 B. Hawkins *Sk. Creek Country* 43 Such is the attachment of horses to this moss, or as the traders call it, salt grass. 1846 Sage *Scenes Rocky Mts.* (1859) 148 A blueish salt grass (herba salée) showed itself in plats uncropped by game. 1859 [see Salt *a.*[1] 3]. 1875 *Fur, Fin, & Feather* 119 [The wild fowl] very soon after feeding on the succulent salt-grasses..acquire a delicious flavor. 1910 Jer. Hart *Vigilante Girl* xxv. 350 The little stream which ran from the spring through bunches of salt grass.

Salt hay. *U.S.* [Salt *a.*[1] 3 b.] Hay made from salt grass. Also *attrib.*

1743 MacSparran *Diary* (1899) 10 Mr. Robinson has sent a load of salt Hay. 1763 [see Salt *a.*[1] 3]. 1837 H. Colman *Rep. Agric. Mass.* (1838) 18 A large amount of salt hay is cut in the county. 1859 [see Salt *a.*[1] 3]. 1863 'Gail Hamilton' *Gala-Days* 54, I,..a squalid, salt-hay gunlow, ..sank down in confusion.

Salt meadow. Chiefly *U.S.* [Salt *a.*[1] 1 c. Cf. F. *pré salé*.] A meadow liable to be flooded by salt water.

1279 [see Salt *a.*[1] 1 c]. 1670 *Rec. Providence, R.I.* III. 174 A certaine peece of meadow..being part of it salt meadow and part of it fresh meadow. 1722 *Ibid.* XVI. 204 The South side of the Channel neere against my salt meadow called four stack meadow. 1726 [see Salt *a.*[1] 1 c]. 1789 Morse *Amer. Geog.* 287 There are large bodies of salt meadow along the Delaware. 1839 *Knickerbocker Mag.* XIII. 503 He travelled very comfortably over the salt meadows. 1881 *Harper's Mag.* Jan. 254/2 The sluggish river winds through tracts of salt-meadow.

Saltoun (sǫ·ltǔn). [Proper name.] Angler's name of an artificial trout fly.

1926 *Chambers's Jrnl.* 165/1 There's a two-pounder at the stream-mouth that has risen twice to the saltoun. 1931 *Hardy's Anglers' Guide* 66 Lake and Sea Trout Flies... No. 44. Saltoun.

Sa·lt-ri·sing. *U.S.* [Salt *a.*[1] 1.] 'A leaven or yeast for raising bread, consisting of a salted batter of flour or meal' (Cent. Dict.).

1836 [see Rising *vbl. sb.* 15]. 1865 Mrs. Stowe *House & Home P.* 236 Salt-rising bread. 1880 *Scribner's Monthly* Jan. 426/1 A..discussion of the relative merits of salt-risin's, milk-emptin's, and potato yeast. 1907 *N.Y. Evening Post* (semi-weekly ed.) 20 June 4 Salt-rising biscuits.

Salt River. *U.S.* [Possibly from the name of a small winding stream in Kentucky.] 'An imaginary river, up which defeated politicians and political parties are supposed to be sent to oblivion' (Cent. Dict.). Usu. in the phr. *to row..up Salt River.*

1832 Frances Trollope *Dom. Mann. Amer.* II. xxviii. 117 This was one of those threats which in Georgia dialect would subject a man to 'a rowing up salt river'. 1834 W. G. Simms *Guy Rivers* I. 199 If the boys are only true..we can row this guard up Salt river in no time and less. 1910 *N.Y. Evening Post* 1 Oct., That imaginary stream called 'Salt River', up which defeated candidates are supposed to be rowed.

Salt spring. [Salt *sb.*[1] or *a.*[1] Cf. F. *source salée*, G. *salzbrunnen*, *-quelle*.] A flow of salt water or brine out of the earth; a brine-spring, brine-well.

1601 Holland *Pliny* xxxi. vii. II. 416 In some parts of Spaine there be salt springs. *a* 1647 [see Salt *a.*[1] 1]. 1683 Pettus *Fleta Min.* I. 321 Of Salt-Petre, Vitriol, Allum and Salt Springs. 1748 J. Hill *Hist. Fossils* 382 The Sea-water and Salt-springs sustain it [*sc.* alimentary salt]..in a liquid form. 1782 Pennant *Journ. Chester to London* 27 The Britons, who had, in several places, plenty of salt-springs. 1834 *Phil. Mag.* IV. 31 The comparative strength of the salt springs of that country at different depths. 1839 G. Roberts *Dict. Geol.*, *Salt springs*, which contain a large quantity of common salt, obtained from them by mere evaporation. 1852 J. Reynolds *Hist. Illinois* 86 They discovered in the present county of Galatin, salt springs.

attrib. 1853 *Trans. Mich. Agric. Soc.* IV. 9 The twenty-two sections of salt spring lands now unappropriated.

Saluki (sălū·ki). Also **salugi, selug(h)i.** [Arab. سلوقي *seluqī*, f. *Seluq*, a town in Greece famous for dogs.] A Persian greyhound.

1890 'Ouida' in *N. Amer. Rev.* Sept. 316 The Siberian and the Persian greyhounds are one and the same breed; called *sleughi* [sic] in Persia and Arabia. 1923 *Daily Mail* 6 Feb. 6 Every known breed, including some rarities like the Saluki, or Arabian greyhound. 1924 *Blackw. Mag.* Jan. 24/2 Among them..a few Selugis, Persian greyhounds of as ancient and pure a strain as our own. 1931 C. S. Jarvis *Yesterday & To-day in Sinai* 212 A Saluki hunt on camel-back.

Salung (sā·lǫŋ). [Siamese.] A Siamese silver coin.

1858 Simmonds *Dict. Trade*, *Salung*, a money of account in Siam, the fourth of a bat or tical, worth about 7½d. 1886 *Encycl. Brit.* XXI. 851/2.

Salutatory, *sb.* **2. b.** (Later example.)

1905 *N.Y. Evening Post* 12 June 12 The annual class day exercises of the University of Pennsylvania were held to-day. H. B. Taylor delivered the salutatory.

Salvarsan (sæ·lvāsæn). [Named by Paul Ehrlich (1910), German scientist, f. L. *salvāre* to save + G. *ars(enik* arsenic.] The proprietary name of a synthetic compound of arsenic, $C_{12}H_{12}O_2N_2As_2HCl$, used in the treatment of spirillic diseases, as syphilis and yaws. Also known as 606. *Salvarsan milk* (see quot. 1913).

1911 *Allbutt's Syst. Med.* IX. 515 The striking effects of hypodermic injection of dioxydiamido-arsenobenzol or salvarsan on the various cutaneous manifestations of syphilis. 1913 Dorland *Med. Dict.* (ed. 7) s.v. *Milk*, *Salvarsan milk*, the milk from a goat that has received injections of salvarsan: used in treating syphilis in children. 1926 *Spectator* 13 Mar. 479/1 The principle of chemico-therapy to which we owe such drugs as Salvarsan. 1926 S. Wright *App. Physiol.* 301 If salvarsan is injected together with glutathione in suitable doses.

Salvatorian (sælvătō·riăn), *a.* and *sb.* [f. L. *salvātor* (It. *salvatore*), Saviour + -ian.] Title of a Roman Catholic congregation.

1909 *Cath. Encycl.* V. 53/2 The Salvatorians have establishments in Italy, Sicily, Austria, Poland. 1929 *Cath. Times* 22 Feb., The Salvatorian Fathers. 1931 *Tablet* 22 Aug. 252/2 Father Melchior Geses, a German Salvatorian of the mission of Shaowu in the Vicariate of Foochow.

Salvatory, *a.* (Recent examples.)

1921 *Challenge* 18 Feb. 241/2 Salvatory and reconstructive work. 1922 J. Y. Simpson *Man & Attainm. Immortality* xiv. 334 The fact of Christ remains, solitary and salvatory.

Salvy, *a.* (Earlier U.S. example.)

1861 *Trans. Ill. Agric. Soc.* IV. 103 Care should be taken not to work it too much, as it will hurt the grain of the butter and make it salvy.

Samaderin (sæmădi·rin). *Pharm.* Also **-ine.** [f. mod.L. *Samadera*, a genus of trees of the family *Simarubaceæ* + -in[1].] A crystalline principle from the bark and seeds of *Samadera indica*.

1859 *Chem. Gaz.* XVII. 143. 1887 Bentley *Man. Bot.* (ed. 5) 505 Samaderine.

Samadh (sāmā·d). = next.

1828 *Asiatic Res.* XVI. 39 A temple, sacred to the deity whom they worship, or the *Samādh*, or shrine of the founder of the sect, or some eminent teacher. 1891 Monier-Williams *Brahmanism & Hinduism* 179 A native of Oudh, whose samadh or tomb is at Katwa. 1920 *Blackw. Mag.* Oct. 455/1 Thus was the samadh perfect, thus was the lesson plain.

Samadhi (sāmā·di). *Hinduism.* [Skr. समाधि *samādhi* a placing together, f. *sam* together + *ā* prefix + *dhā* to place (see Do *v.*).]

1. Profound or abstract meditation on the Supreme Being; the last stage of yoga, in which it is held that there is suspension of connexion between soul and body.

1853 R. S. Hardy *Man. Buddhism* 498 The five indrayas, or moral powers are:—1. Sardhawa, purity. 2. Wiraya, persevering exertion. 3. Sati, or smirti, the ascertainment of truth. 4. Samadhi, tranquility. 5. Pragnyawa, wisdom. 1913 E. F. Benson *Thorley Weir* v, He..lived a life of meditation that would have done credit to a student of Rāja Yoga attaining Samādhi. 1930 Dasgupta *Yoga Philos.* 336 Samādhi or trance contemplation results when by deep concentration mind becomes transformed in the form of the object of contemplation.

2. The tomb of a Hindu yogi, especially a place of self-immolation by burning or burying alive. Hence, the act of self-immolation.

1925 *Glasgow Herald* 24 Sept. 7 The Sadhu did not commit suicide, but performed the religious rite of Samadhi.

Samaj (sămā·dʒ). Also **Somaj.** [Skr. समाज *samāja* a meeting with, f. *sam* together + *aj* to drive.] An assembly or congregation; a church or religious body, as in *Brahmo Samaj* (see *Brahmoism).

1876 *Encycl. Brit.* IV. 201/1 He gave a printing-press to the Samāj. *Ibid.* 201/2 They encourage the establishment of branch Samājes in different parts of the country. 1913 J. N. Farquhar *Crown of Hinduism* 76 The truths of religion which they find there are the doctrines taught by the Samāj.

Saman (sā·măn). [Skr., = chant.] A sacred text or verse forming the third of the four kinds of Vedas; the name of the Veda thus formed. Also *attrib.* So **Sa·maveda**, the name of the third Veda.

1798 *Asiatic Res.* V. 364 Prayer..on beginning a lecture of the Samaveda. 1843 *Penny Cycl.* XXVI. 171/1 These are the Rich, Yajush, Sāman, and Atharvan's. *Ibid.*, The Sāmaveda contains songs of lyrical character to be recited with melody. 1886 *Encycl. Brit.* XXI. 277/1 The sāman-hymnal consists of two parts, viz., the *Sāmaveda-samhitā*, or collection of texts (rich) used for making up sāman-hymns, and the *Gāna*, or tune-books. *Ibid.* 278/1 The *Vamśa-brāhmaṇa*, a mere list of the Sāmaveda teachers. 1913 J. N. Farquhar *Crown of Hinduism* 77 The Saman, Yajus, and Athaswan exhibit the same polytheism.

Samang (sāmɑ·ŋ). Also **Semang.** A negrito of the nearly extinct tribes native to the interior of the Malay peninsula.

1860 Mayne Reid *Odd People* 415 The Samangs—a tribe inhabiting the mountainous parts of the Malayan peninsula—are also a negro or negrillo race. 1883 [see *Sakai]. 1907 *Rep. Brit. Assoc.* 642 Ethnological specimens of undoubted Semang origin. 1922 *Glasgow Herald* 30 Mar. 9 Yesterday to greet the Prince a bronzed group of Semangs ..rubbed shoulders with hardy British venturers.

Samara. (Later U.S. example.)

1881 *Harper's Mag.* Oct. 646 Others, like the samaras of the tulip-tree and elm, are launched from the tree-tops.

Samaritan, *sb.* **b.** Add: Often in full, *good Samaritan*, a kind and helpful person; hence (nonce-wds.) *good Samaritanism, good Samaritanship.*

1640 N. Rogers (*title*) The Good Samaritan, or an Exposition on that Parable Luke x. ver. xxx–xxxviii. 1840 Ruskin *Lett. Coll. Friend* ii. (1894) 11 You have sacrificed half a Good Samaritanship. 1846 [see Dict.] 1858 C. Reade *Jack of all Trades* viii, I..took leave of the good Samaritan, who appointed two of my niggers to see me out of the wood. 1871 Lowell *Study Windows* 44 It is seldom that debtors or good Samaritans waylay people under gas lamps in order to force money upon them. 1930 H. Redwood *God in Slums* 14 A co-opted partner in every kind of Good Samaritanism.

Sambal (sæ·mbăl). Also **sambel.** [Malay.] A Malay spiced condiment used as a relish with meat.

1817 Raffles *Hist. Java* I. 98 The most common seasoning..is the lombok; triturated with salt, it is called *sambel*. 1891 Duckitt *Hilda's 'Where is it?'* 199 Quince 'Sambal'.

Sam Browne (sæm braun). In full *Sam Browne belt*: an officers' field belt having a supporting strap over the right shoulder, which was invented by General *Sam J. Browne*.

1915 *Punch* 6 Oct. 288/3 Military Wedding Equipment. Sam Browne belt, single brace and frog, best bridal leather. *a* 1922 J. C. Squire *To a Bull-dog* iii, His bag and his thonged Sam Browne.

Sambunigrin (sæmbiuˌnai·grin). *Chem.* [f. the specific name *Sambucus nigra* (the common elder) + -in[1].] The glucoside $C_{14}H_{17}O_6N$. Hence **Sa:mbunigri·nic** *a.*

1905 *Jrnl. Chem. Soc.* LXXXVIII. I. 912 Sambunigrin, a new Cyanogenetic glucoside obtained from the leaves of Sambucus Nigra. 1917 *Ibid.* CXII. I. 657 Synthesis of Mandelonitrile-glucoside, Sambunigrin, and similar substances. 1919 *Ibid.* CXVI. I. 340, d-glucosido-d-mandelic acid, also called sambunigrinic acid.

Same, *a.* **B.** *absol.* Add: **2. d.** Phr. *Same here*: the same (thing) applies to me; my case is similar.

1915 *Punch* 13 Oct. 315/2 The Dawn of the No-treating Era. *First Reveller.* 'My health!' *Second Reveller.* 'Same here!'

Samhita (sa·mhitā). Also **sanhita.** [Skr. संहिता *saṃhitā* union, connexion, f. *sam* together + *dhā* to place.] A text treated according to sandhi; a version of the vedas which is the continuous text formed from the pada or separate words by the appropriate phonetic sound-changes. Also *attrib.*

1805 H. T. Colebrooke in *Asiatic Res.* VIII. 476 Tradition ..reckons sixteen Sanhitas of the Rigveda. 1843 *Penny Cycl.* XXVI. 171/1 The Rigveda is the first in order and its Sanhitā contains mantras..to the elemental deities. 1876 *Encycl. Brit.* IV. 201/2 The Hindū scriptures consist of four separate collections, or Sanhitās, of sacred texts. 1891 Monier-Williams *Brahmanism & Hinduism* 409 These Vedic texts may be recited according to any one or more of the five different Pāthas, or modes of recitation, called Samhita, Pada, Krama, Jaṭā, and Ghana.

Sammy (sæ·mi), *sb.* [Familiar dim. of the name *Samuel*: see -ie, -y[6].]

1. An American soldier in the war of 1914–18, so called from *Uncle Sam* (see Uncle *sb.* 2 c). *slang.*

1917 *Punch* 13 June 384/2 As a term of distinction and endearment [for the American 'Tommies'] Mr. Punch suggests 'Sammies'—after their uncle. 1917 *Nation* (N.Y.) 16 Aug. 164/1 The 'Sammies' whom the headlines are featuring. 1921 *Glasgow Herald* 8 July 7/2 While a French soldier costs on an average 13 francs 37 per day,..a 'Tommy costs 31 francs 69, and a 'Sammy' 59 francs 30.

2. A ninny, simpleton. *slang.*

[Cf. 1837 E. Howard *Old Commodore* xiv, You have been sammy-foozled by a rascally swindler.] 1837 R. B. Peake *Quarter to Nine* I. ii, What a Sammy, give me a shilling more than I axed him! [1843 Moncrieff *Scamps of London* II. i, I'm a ruined homo—a muff—a flat—a Sam—a regular ass.] 1897 Jane *Lordship* xv, Simple Sammy, as we called Mr. Pote, the new pastor.

Samoyed, *sb.* and *a.* Add: **2.** One of a breed of Arctic dogs extensively used by the Samoyeds for herding reindeer and as sledge-dogs; they are of medium size, characterized by erect ears, a long tail, and long hair, white to biscuit-colour.

1889 *Pall Mall Gaz.* 30 Apr. 6/2 A beautiful brown silky-haired sharp-eared Samoyed dog. 1923 *Westm. Gaz.* 28 Apr., The continued popularity of the Samoyeds, the white Arctic dogs.

Sampan[2] (sæ·mpăn). [Khoi-khoin *samban.*] = Tampan.

1898 Scully *Between Sun & Sand* i. 8 The ground beneath is full of the dreaded 'sampans', which bury themselves in the flesh and cause serious injury. 1920 *Glasgow Herald* 2 Sept. 4 The minor plagues of scorpions and 'sampans'.

Samsara (sæmsā·rā). *Hinduism.* Also **sansara.** [Skr. संसार *saṃsāra* a wandering through, f. *sam* prefix expressing completeness + *sṛ* to run, glide, move.] Metempsychosis.

1845 *Encycl. Metrop.* XV. 760/1 His [*sc.* the Brahman priest's] business is to assist in..the ten ceremonies called the sansára. 1886 *Encycl. Brit.* XXI. 289/1 The notion of samsāra has become an axiom, a universally conceded principle of Indian philosophy. 1930 Dasgupta *Yoga Philos.* 67 The metaphysics of the samsāra cycle in connection with sorrow, origination, disease, rebirth.

Samskara (sanskā·rā). Also **sanskara.** [Skr. संस्कार *saṃskāra* a making perfect, preparation, f. *sam* together + *kṛ* to make, perform.] An essential and sanctifying rite or ceremony among the Hindus, which purifies from the taint of sin contracted in the womb and leads to regeneration.

1845 *Encycl. Metrop.* XVI. 350/2 Ten ceremonies, called Sanscāra, must be duly performed before the child of a Bráhman can claim the honours inherited from his father. 1876 *Encycl. Brit.* IV. 204/1. 1876 Monier-Williams *Indian Wisdom* (ed. 3) 245 He is of course to go through all the twelve Sanskaras or purificatory rites.

Samson. Add: **5.** *Logging* (see quot.). Also *samson-post*. Hence **Sa·mson** *v.*

1905 *Terms Forestry & Logging* 45 *Sampson*, an appliance for loosening or starting logs by horsepower. It usually consists of a strong, heavy timber and a chain terminating in a heavy swamp hook. *Ibid.*, *Sampson a tree, to*, to direct the fall of a tree by means of a lever and pole.

Samsonite[1] (sæ·msənəit). [f. proper name Samson + -ite[1].] A variety of dynamite. Also *attrib.*

1909 *Jrnl. Soc. Chem. Industry* XXVI. 915. 1915 A. Marshall *Explosives* 213 A charge of undoubtedly hard frozen Samsonite exploded whilst being rammed home with a wooden rammer. 1921 *Glasgow Herald* 28 Feb. 11 Illegal possession..of 2980 gelignite cartridges, 10 samsonite cartridges.

Samsonite[2] (sæ·msənəit). *Min.* [f. name of *Samson* mine, Andreasberg, Harz, Germany: see -ite[1].] A manganiferous silver mineral.

1910 L. J. Spencer in *Min. Mag.* XV. 430. 1910 *Jrnl. Chem. Soc.* XCVIII. II. 620 Samsonite..was found..in association with pyrargyrite, galena, pyrolusite, quartz, calcite, apophyllite, etc.

San (sæn). Colloq. abbreviation of Sanatorium (esp. in sense *3).

1927 Anne MacDonald *Dorty Speaking* x, He said I must be put in the san at once, as I had whooping-cough.

Sanatorium. Add: **3.** A room in a school or college for the accommodation of the sick or the isolation of those who are under suspicion of infection.

1860 *Eton Gloss.* 30 Sanatorium. The Hospital—a modern improvement—where a boy seized with any infectious and dangerous illness is at once sent. 1901 *Eton Boy's Lett.* 98 They dont take measels to the Sanatorium as they arent dangerous.

Sancho[2] (sæ·nko). *U.S.* Nine of trumps in the game of **Sa·ncho-Pe·dro** (see quot. 1907).

1891 *Cent. Dict.* 1907 *Hoyle's Games* 12 Pedro Sancho. Eighteen points can be made in each deal; high, low, jack, game being worth 1 each; the five of trumps 5; the nine of trumps, 'sancho', 9.

Sand, *sb.*[2] Add: **1. h.** A fashion shade resembling the colour of sand.

1923 *Daily Mail* 13 Feb. 1 Artificial Silk Hose..in Black, White, Beaver, Nude, Cinnamon, Sand, Suede.

7. b. Chiefly *U.S.* (Earlier and later examples.)

1875 B. Harte *Tales of Argonauts* 71 Blank me if I didn't think he was losing his sand, till he walked to position. 1881 *N.Y. Times* 18 Dec. in *N. & Q.* 6th Ser. V. 65/2 *Sand.* To have 'sand in one's craw'; to be determined and plucky. Equivalent to 'grit'. 1924 Galsworthy *Forest* IV. ii. 120 By Jove, Mr. Farrell, there's sand in you. Tell me, isn't he ever ashamed of himself?

9. *sand-castle* (Castle *sb.* 3 b).

1886 *Chambers's Jrnl.* 6 Jan. 16/2 (*title*) Sand-Castles. 1915 H. G. Wells *Christina Alberta's Father* I. iv, They had..camped on the beach while Mr. Preemby and Christina Alberta had made sand-castles.

e. *sand-toned* adj.

1916 *Chambers's Jrnl.* Sept. 635/2 In the midst of the mass of sand-toned uniforms.

10. sand-club, (*b*) *U.S.*, a niblick; cf. *sand-iron* (b); **sand-devil**, in South Africa, a small whirlwind; **sand-draw** *U.S.*, a channel of a subterranean stream with sand overlying it; the stream itself; **sand-glacier**, a sand talus whose encroachment under prevalent wind action resembles that of a true glacier; **sand-hog** *U.S.*, a man who works underground, as in a caisson or in foundation-work; **sand-painting** (see quot. 1900); **sand-slow, -slue**, a barren, sandy area, usually depressed; **sand-sugar** = Lactose; **sand-table**, (*a*) a tray sprinkled with sand in which letters or designs may be traced and obliterated (cf. *sand-board*); (*b*) a sand-trap; **sand-tell box** (see quot.); **sand-trap**, a device for separating sand and other impurities from a stream of water or pulp passing through it, esp. in the manufacture of paper; **sand-tray**, a tray filled with sand, with which children play (cf. *sand-table, a*); **sand-wash** *U.S.*, a sloping surface of sand spread out by an intermittent stream; **sand-wind** = *sand-cloud*.

1912 *Punch* 15 May 380/2 Incidentally I am pleased to know that Americans call a niblick a *sand-club. 1901 *Lancet* 16 Mar. 771/1 A number of small whirlwinds, called '*sand-devils', which would pass slowly along sucking up quantities of sand and any light articles such as pieces of paper. *a* 1909 P. A. Rydberg *Contrib. U.S. Nat. Herb.* III. 470 (Cent. D. Suppl. s.v. *Draw*) A *sand draw is a subterranean stream. On the surface is seen only a broader or narrower band of pure sand, marking the channel. 1875 *Encycl. Brit.* III. 599/1 Among the less ordinary geological phenomena may be mentioned the '*sand glacier' at Elbow Bay. 1897 V. Cornish in *Geog. Jrnl.* Mar. 286 Wind blowing outwards from a deep sand tract forms a horizontal plateau terminated by a talus as steep as the sand can rest. Under these conditions the encroachment of sand recalls the manner of advance of a glacier, and to this formation I restrict the term 'sand glacier'. 1905 *N.Y. Even. Post* 11 Jan. 3 The men who are employed as '*sandhogs' or excavators in the caisson for the new Manhattan Bridge. 1907 *Sci. Amer.* 23 Mar. 250/1 Pressure-men, that remarkable class of men who make it their business to work in compressed air, and who are commonly known as 'sand-hogs'. 1900 W. Hough in *Smithsonian Rep.* (*Nat. Mus.*) 467 The ceremonial *sand painting of the Hopi and Navajo, where the most beautiful effects are secured by allowing sand in slender streams of different colors to fall from the hand guiding it over the surface to form designs. 1908 *Hastings's Encycl. Relig. & Ethics* I. 826/2 The sand-paintings..may be regarded as actual pictorial prayers. 1904 A. J. Walker tr. *A. F. Holleman's Lab. Man. Org. Chem.* 38 The taste of lactose is not so sweet as that of sucrose, and in the mouth it resembles sand, hence the name *sand-sugar. 1910 *Encycl. Brit.* XX. 728/2 To get rid of them [*sc.* impurities] the esparto pulp when washed and bleached is run from the potcher into storage chests, from which it is pumped over a long, narrow serpentine settling table or '*sand-table'. 1928 *Daily Tel.* 7 Aug. 4/4 A thorough groundwork of tactical knowledge has been formed by sand-table and week-end schemes during the winter. 1894 Maskelyne *Sharps & Flats* 194 The *sand-tell box is so called because it is used in conjunction with prepared cards, which have been 'sanded' or roughened on one side, or both sides...The cards which are intended to 'tell' are left smooth on their faces; all the others are slightly roughened on both sides. 1875 Knight *Dict. Mech.*, *Sand-trap*, a device for separating sand, etc., from water flowing through a pipe. 1885 *Encycl. Brit.* XVIII. 221/2 From them the pulp is pumped into the supply-box, which communicates with the sand-traps by means of a regulating cock. 1927 T. Woodhouse *Artif. Silk* 22 These sand traps are long, shallow, wooden troughs, the bottoms of which are covered by suitable rough-haired felt and baffle plates. 1899 *Geog. Jrnl.* June 625 The water-wave was really controlled by a submerged *sand-wave, the up-stream flank of which was exposed to a heavy shower of sand from the turbid water. 1877 *Encycl. Brit.* VII. 703/1 In the spring and summer..hot *sand-winds sometimes blow from the south, greatly raising the temperature.

c. sand-lily, a North American liliaceous plant, *Leucocrinum montanum*; **sand-oat** [Du. *zandhaver*], **-reed**, the sea-reed or marram, *Psamma arenaria*; **sand-verbena**, a plant of the genus *Abronia*, chiefly native to the dry sandy soils of N.W. America.

1929 *Encycl. Brit.* XIX. 939/1 *Sand Lily..native to plains and mountain valleys from South Dacota and Nebraska west to California. 1880 *Ibid.* XII. 60/1 The dunes show a tendency, except where the Dutch prevent it by planting wood or *sand-oats, to wear away on the side towards the sea. 1910 *Ibid.* XIII. 590/2 The most common plant here is the stiff *sand-reed (*Arundo arenaria*), called sand-oats in Drente and Overysel, where it is much used for making mats. 1929 *Ibid.* XIX. 940/1 The white *sand-verbena,..with very numerous fragrant flowers, occurs from Iowa to Idaho.

Sandbag, *v.* Add: **1. b.** *intr.* To attend to the sandbags.

1928 *Saturday Even. Post* (N.Y.) 4 Feb. 100/2 One of the chauffeurs had just finished fueling the plane. 'You fly her,' said Andy. 'I'll sandbag.'

2. Also *fig.*

1903 *N.Y. Times* 12 Sept., He has been sandbagged with stock from influential quarters where there still is antagonism to advancing market prices. *a* 1909 'O. Henry' *Roads of Destiny* vi. 93 About what figure had you and the calciminer agreed to sandbag the state for?

Sand-bar. (See Sand *sb.* 10, and add: Also, a sandbank in a river.)

1802 A. Ellicott *Jrnl.* 14 The fog was so thick that we could neither discover sand-bars nor logs. 1829 S. Cummings *Western Pilot* 7 There are..a great number of tow-heads and sand-bars. 1858 Teresa Vielé *Following the Drum* 76 The ship..went to pieces on a sand-bar. 1897 *Outing* (U.S.) XXX. 50/2 This one sheet of water formed a small harbor to the lee of a sand-bar.

Sand-beach. *U.S.* [Sand *sb.* 9 a.] A beach consisting of, or covered with, sand.

1728 J. Comer *Diary* (1923) 50 A schooner..was cast on shore on a sand beach at Westport. 1806 in *Ann. 9th Congress* 2 Sess. 1117 They passed a number of sand-beaches, and some rapids. 1821 T. Nuttall *Jrnl. Trav. Arkansa* xiv. 176 The sand-beaches, as hot and cheerless as the African deserts. 1878 [see Sand *sb.* 9 a]. 1879 *Harper's Mag.* June 70/1 The shores are generally bluff with narrow strips of sand beach along the water's edge.

Sand-burr. *U.S.* (See Sand *sb.* 10 c.)

1846 Sage *Scenes Rocky Mts.* (1859) 60 It is quite sterile, producing little other than sand-burrs. 1870 E. Eggleston *Queer Stories* vii. 53 It sticks to you like a sand burr. 1873 J. H. Beadle *Undevel. West* xxix. 639 Our horses were hungry enough to chew sand-burrs. 1904 *Topeka Daily Capital* 11 June 4 A sandbur will grapple on to a man's coat tail and stay there all day just to get a chance to fall into his bed at night.

Sandemanian, *sb.* and *a.* (Earlier examples.)

1773 *Publ. Col. Soc. Mass.* VI. 115 The Sandemanian Meeting House. *Ibid.* 116 Mr. Foster and Capen, two Persons of the Sect called Sandemanians.

Sand-fly. Add: **3. sand-fly fever**, a febrile disease associated with the bites of *Phlebotomus papatassii*, a dipterous insect native to India and the Mediterranean countries.

1913 Dorland *Med. Dict.* (ed. 7), *Phlebotomus papatassii*, ..is thought to convey by its bite an infection known as sandfly fever. 1921 *Manson's Trop. Dis.* (ed. 7) 230 Phlebotomus Fever...Three-day Fever; Sandfly Fever; 'Dog Disease'. 1927 *Daily Tel.* 23 Aug. 4/6 Thomas had three attacks of malaria before the war, and later sand-fly fever and pneumonia.

Sandhi (sa·ndi). *Philol.* [Skr. संधि *saṃdhi* junction, combination, f. *sam* together + *dhā* to place (see Do *v.*).] The term applied orig. by Sanskrit grammarians to assimilative changes occurring in Sanskrit in the final and initial sounds of words in a sentence (*external sandhi*), and in the final sounds of stems in word-formation (*internal sandhi*); extended by modern philologists to analogous phenomena in other languages.

1874 Sweet *Hist. Engl. Sounds* 13 Consonant influence on consonants..what is called *sandhi* in Sanskrit and *mutation* in the Celtic languages. *Ibid.* (1888) 15 As sandhi was of no use grammatically, it has been discarded in the modern Indian languages, as also generally in the other Arian languages, which in their earliest stages still show traces of it. But even in the present English we have such variations as *ðə mæn, ði ɪŋ, hiz ·ðei aa, hizr ·ij iz*. 1894 Lindsay *Lat. Lang.* ii. § 135 'Sandhi' in Latin. 1901 Macdonell *Skr. Gram.* ii, The rules of Sandhi are based chiefly on the avoidance of hiatus and on assimilation.

Sand-hill. b. (Earlier examples.)

1822 J. Fowler *Jrnl.* 128 Killed one sand hill crain and five gees[e]. 1849 *Rep. U.S. Comm. Patents, Agric.* (1850) 434 These broad prairies, which fifteen years ago were tenanted only..by the prairie-chicken and sand-hill crane.

Sandhya (sa·ndyā). [Skr. संध्या *saṃdhyā* a holding together, junction: cf. *Sandhi.] **a.** Twilight. **b.** The period which precedes a yuga or age of the world. **c.** Morning or evening prayers.

1868 *Chambers's Encycl.* X. 327/1 A long mundane period of years, which is preceded by a period called *Sandhyā*, 'twilight'. 1876 Monier-Williams *Indian Wisdom* (ed. 3) 248 The two Sandhyas of sunrise and sunset. 1891 — *Brahmanism & Hinduism* 401 The first act of the Morning Sandhyā Service..is sipping water. 1913 J. N. Farquhar *Crown of Hinduism* 164 The daily devotions (sandhya) are restricted to the three castes.

Sandy, *a.* **5. b.** Add: **sandy-oat**, a tall, early oat with small red and white grain; **sandy-pear**, the Chinese pear, *Pyrus sinensis*, native to Manchuria and Mongolia.

1865 *Chambers's Encycl.* VII. 21/2 The *Sandy Oat is..sown, more particularly when the climate is inferior and wet. 1884 A. de Candolle *Origin Cultiv. Plants* 233 *Sandy Pear, Chinese Pear.

Sang (sæŋ), *sb.*[1] Also 8 **sawng.** Colloq. U.S. abbreviation of Ginseng. Also *attrib.*

1843 R. Carlton *New Purchase* xxvii. 256 The storekeeper was obliged to book the nine and a quarter cents, to be paid in 'sang'. 1886 *Harper's Mag.* June 58/2 Formerly, digging 'sang', as they call ginseng, was a general occupation. *a* 1909 M. G. Kains *Ginseng* 31 (Cent. D. Suppl.) The average 'sang' digger has very little conscience.

Hence **Sang** *v. intr.*, to gather ginseng.

1877 *Field & Forest* III. 40 Why, I have sanged all over it [*sc.* the mountain].

Sang (sāŋ), *sb.*[2] Also **cheng, sheng, sing.** [Chinese *shēng*.] The Chinese organ: see quots.

1845 *Encycl. Metrop.* XVI. 579/2 The *Sheng* or *Sing*; the lower half of a gourd, in which a row of pipes is fixed, with a curved and lateral one on which the performer blows. 1848 S. W. Williams *Middle Kingdom* II. 170 The sāng is..the embryo of the organ; it is a hollow conical shaped box, which corresponds to a wind chest, having a mouthpiece on one side, and communicating with thirteen reeds of different lengths inserted in the top. 1876 Stainer & Barrett *Dict. Mus. Terms*, *Cheng*, the Chinese organ, which consists of a series of tubes having free reeds.

Sang (saŋ), *sb.*[3] [F. *sang* blood.] Anthrax.

Sanga (sæ·ŋgă). Also **sangu, sunga** (sɒ·ŋgă). [Abyssinian.] The Galla or Abyssinian ox, *Bos africanus*.

1814 H. Salt *Voy. Abyssinia* 258 I was gratified by the sight of the Galla oxen, or Sanga. 1862 *Chambers's Encycl.* IV. 383/1.

Sanhita, variant of *Samhita.

Sanidaster (sæ·nidæstəɹ). [mod.L., f. Gr. σανίς, σανιδ- board, tablet + ἀστήρ star.] A straight, rod-like microsclere, spinose throughout its length.
1887 *Encycl. Brit.* XXII. 417/2 The sigmaspire becoming spined produces the spiraster or spinispirula; this, by losing its curvature, becomes the sanidaster.

San(n)yasi, -asin, var. ff. Sunnyasee.
1876 Monier-Williams *Indian Wisdom* (ed. 3) 260 He is sometimes called a Sannyasin, 'one who has given up the world'. 1891 — *Brahmanism & Hinduism* 55 He was a Sannyāsī and an unmarried Smārta Brāhman. 1921 T. R. Glover *Jesus in Experience of Men* viii. 144 We sometimes see men with paralysed minds calling themselves Christians, as proud of the withered intellect as the Sannyasi of his ruined arm. 1921 B. H. Streeter & Appasamy *The Sadhu* v. 146 He hid the Hindi New Testament he had in his hand, thinking that I was a Hindu Sannyasi.

Sanochrysin (sæ̃nokrai·sin). Also erron. **-crysin**. *Pharm.* [irreg. f. L. *sānus* healthy, Sane *a.* + Gr. χρυσός gold + -in [1].] A gold-salt, sodium aurothiosulphate, used in the treatment of tuberculosis.
1924 *Brit. Med. Jrnl.* 8 Nov. 870/2 Arrangements have been made for producing it in bulk in Denmark under the name 'sanocrysin'. 1926 D. Masters *How to conquer Consumption* 103 Möllgaard's treatment is generally referred to ..as the 'gold treatment', because it consists of a metallic compound of gold, which the discoverer has named 'sanocrysin'. 1929 *Daily Express* 7 Jan. 4 In the treatment of consumption..by sanochrysin.

Sans, *prep.* **2. a. sans phrase**. Add:
1885 *Encycl. Brit.* XVIII. 793/2 This study gives us the science of empirical psychology, or, as it is now termed, psychology *sans phrase*.

Sansa (sæ·nsă). Also **sanse, zanza, zanze** (zæ·nză). [ad. Arab. زنج *zinj* cymbals.] An African musical instrument consisting of a wooden box having at the top tongues of bamboo or iron which the performer vibrates with his thumbs.
1864 Engel *Music most Anc. Nations* 14 Nos. 4, 5, and 6 show the notes of three *sanzes*. 1874 — *Catal. Mus. Instr. S. Kens. Mus.* (ed. 2) 297 The zanze, or sansa, is to be found principally among the Negro tribes of upper and lower Guinea. 1876 Stainer & Barrett *Dict. Mus. Terms*, *Zanze*...Known also by the names of mambira, ambira, marimba, ibeka, vissandschi, in different parts of Africa. 1905 *Rep. Brit. Assoc.* 529 A derivative from the African *sansa*.

Sansara, variant of *Samsara.

Sansevieria (sænsĭvi,ĭə·riă). [mod.L., f. the name of the Prince of *Sansevieria* (1710–1771) of Naples.] The bow-string hemp (see Bow-string 3, Hemp *sb.* 5). Also *attrib.*
1829 Loudon *Encycl. Plants* 268. 1851 *Illustr. Catal. Gt. Exhib.* iv. i. 882/2 Liliaceous plants, such as..the Sanseviera, the pine-apple, and even the plantain. 1899 F. V. Kirby *Sport E. C. Africa* xxiv. 268 Quantities of the sansevieria plants, which yield a valuable fibre.

Sanskara, variant of *Samskara.

Santal[2] (sæ·ntăl). Also **Santhal**. A member of one of the non-Aryan peoples of India, of Kolarian stock, dwelling chiefly in the hill-country of western Bengal. Hence **Sant(h)a·li**, the language spoken by the Santals, one of the principal dialects of the Kolarian group of non-Indo-European languages of India.
1876 Monier-Williams *Indian Wisdom* (ed. 3) 312 *note*, The Santhals and Kols of the hills to the west of Bengal. 1880 *Encycl. Brit.* XII. 777/2 'The Great Mountain' is the race-god of the Santāls. *Ibid.* 778/1 The Santāli verb..has twenty-three tenses. 1910 *Rep. Brit. Assoc.* 723 The group of forest tribes, from the Santāls and Pahārias on the east,.. to..the Bhils on the west.

Santonian (sæntōᵘ·niăn), *a.* *Geol.* [f. L. *Santones*, *-oni*, a people of Aquitania + -ian.] Designating a subdivision of the Upper Cretaceous system, characterized by species of *Micraster*.
1885 A. Geikie *Text-Bk. Geol.* (ed. 2) 833.

Saperda (săpɜ̄·ɹdă). *Ent.* [mod.L., f. Gr. σαπέρδης, a fish.] A beetle of the genus *Saperda* found in Europe and the United States.
1862 T. W. Harris *Ins. Injur. Veget.* (ed. 3) 114 In Europe one of these slender Saperdas attacks the hazel-bush, and another the twigs of the pear-tree.

Sap-head. (Earlier U.S. example.)
1796–1801 Fessenden *Orig. Poems* (1806) 44 The poet nimbly trips it back...And squibs each Jacobinick saphead.

Saphir d'eau (safīr dō). Also **sap(p)hire.** [Fr., lit. sapphire of water.] A translucent blue variety of iolite occurring in Ceylon.
1819 Bakewell *Introd. Min.* 368 *Sapphir d'Eau*.—A translucent variety of iolite from India is so called by the French jewellers. 1820 R. Jameson *Syst. Min.* (ed. 3) I. 174 The sapphire d'eau of collectors. 1883 *Encycl. Brit.* XVI. 418/2 The *Sapphire d'Eau* or *Luchssapphir* of the jewellers. 1897 L. Fletcher *Introd. Study Min.* 106 Cordierite is a silicate of magnesium, iron and aluminium; its transparent variety is the *Saphir d'eau* of jewellery.

Sapolan (sæ·polæn). *Pharm.* [f. L. *sāpō* Soap + *lan-* of Lanolin.] An ointment base used as an external application for eczema and other skin diseases.
1908 *Practitioner* Apr. 546 Sapolan ointment. 1910 *Ibid.* July 129 Obstinate pruritus is sometimes wonderfully improved by massage with camphorated sapolan.

Saponarin (săpǫ·nărin). *Chem.* Also **-ine.** [f. med. L. *sāpōnāria* soapwort + -in [1].] A glucoside found in *Saponaria officinalis*. Also **Saponaretin**, a substance formed from saponarin by hydrolysis.
1902 *Jrnl. Chem. Soc.* LXXXII. i. 387 Saponarin dissolves in about 1,000 parts of hot water and crystallises on cooling in minute, birefringent needles. 1906 *Ibid.* LXXXIX. ii. 1218 Saponaretin..is the chief product when saponarin is hydrolysed with dilute acids.

Sapotoxin (sæpotǫ·ksin). *Chem.* [f. Sapo(nin + Toxin.] A poisonous glucoside occurring in commercial saponin.
1892 *Jrnl. Chem. Soc.* LXII. i. 350 The sapotoxin of *Agrostemma* has the same composition as those of *radix saponariæ albæ* and of quillaja bark, but differs from them in its physiological properties. 1924 C. T. Kingzett *Chem. Encycl.* 486 Saponins from quillaya bark..are stated to consist of one-third quillajic acid and two-thirds of a body named sapotoxin. 1927 *Glasgow Herald* 11 June 4 The saponine and sapotoxine in effluents from beet-sugar factories.

Saprine (sæ·prin, -in). *Chem.* Also **-in.** [f. Gr. σαπρός foul, putrid + -ine [5].] A non-poisonous ptomaine formed in the decomposition of visceral substances.
1887 [see Cadaverine]. 1894 Morley & Muir *Watts' Dict. Chem.* IV. 430/2 Saprine $C_5H_{14}N_2$. 1910 *Practitioner* June 824.

Saprolite (sæ·prolait). *Geol.* [f. Gr. σαπρός rotten + -lite.] A name given by G. F. Becker (see below) to decomposed rock in situ. Hence **Saproli·tic** *a.*
1895 G. F. Becker in *16th Ann. Rep. U.S. Geol. Surv.* iii. 289, I propose the term *saprolite*. *Ibid.* 290 The deposits referred to..are gold-bearing saprolites. 1904 L. J. Spencer tr. *M. Bauer's Precious Stones* 361 Several crystals of rhodolite were found, during the summer of 1901, embedded in a decomposed saprolitic rock.

Sapropel (sæ·propel). *Geol.* [f. Gr. σαπρός putrid + πηλός mud, earth, clay.] A name given by Potonié to a mud or slime formed of more or less decomposed plankton matter, which constitutes the greater part of cannel coals; the mother substance of petroleum.
1906 *Rep. Brit. Assoc.* 748 The sapropel is formed from the excrements and bodies of completely aquatic animals and plants which have lived in stagnant water. 1929 H. B. Milner *Sedim. Petrog.* (ed. 2) 335 The coal-substance has been regarded by Potonié as 'sapropel', a solidified jelly-like carbonaceous slime.

Sarab, variant of *Serab.

Sarangi (sā·raŋgi). [Hind.; Hindi, Skr. सारङ्गी *sārangī*.] An Indian musical instrument resembling a violin.
1851 *Illustr. Catal. Gt. Exhib.* iv. i. 913/2 Sarungee and bow, or Hindoostanee fiddle. 1920 *Outward Bound* Oct. 74/1 The sārangi is really the Indian violin and is played with a bow. 1929 *Radio Times* 4 Jan. 38/3 The *sarangi* has a sweeter, slightly deeper tone than the violin; this is the first occasion on which it has been broadcast.

Saras, variant of Sarus.
1885 Hornaday *Two Yrs. in Jungle* iii. 35 We saw eight pairs of saras cranes stalking majestically over the open field.

Saratoga. (Earlier examples.)
1869 'Mark Twain' *New Pilgr. Progress* xxvii, This chute [in the pyramid] was not more than twice as wide and high as a Saratoga trunk. 1874 B. F. Taylor *World on Wheels* i. ix. 72 It is not a carpet-bag, nor a valise nor a Saratoga.

Sarc (sāɹk). *School colloq.* Short for Sarcasm. (Cf. *Sarky.)
1926 E. Wallace *Square Emerald* xv, She always knew when her young lady was indulging in what Lucretia described as 'sarc'.

Sardanapali·tic, *a.* = Sardanapalian *a.*
1860 W. H. Russell *Diary in India* II. iii. 39 After another Sardanapalitic breakfast, we lie on our charpoys all day.

Sardinian, *a.* and *sb.* **B.** *sb.* Add: **2.** The language of the Sardinians, a member of the Romanic group.
1841 *Penny Cycl.* XX. 427/1 A book was published at Cagliari, in both Sardinian and Italian, called 'Moriografia Sarda'. 1880 *Encycl. Brit.* XIII. 494/2 Corsican..unlike Sardinian,..treats ĭ and ŭ in the Italian fashion. 1894 Lindsay *Latin Lang.* ii. § 26 Short ŭ and ŏ of Latin are distinguished not only in Sardinian.., but also in Roumanian and in the Latin element of the Albanian language.

Sarge (sāɹdʒ). U.S. army abbrev. of Sergeant.
1930 Pottle *Stretchers* 238 But sarge, I've been out since five without a bite.

Sarky (sā·ɹki), *a.* *School colloq.* [f. *Sarc + -y [1].] Sarcastic.
1930 *Diary of Public School Girl* 76 Made some currant buns. Bob very sarky about them.

Sart[2] (sāɹt). [Turki.] A member of a Turkoman tribe, no longer nomadic, but town-dwellers and traders in Turkestan, and parts of Persia and Afghanistan. Hence **Sa·rtian** *a.*, designating a skin disease of Central Asia.
1879 *Encycl. Brit.* IX. 84/2 Tajiks..in the chief towns and central districts, who are known as Sarts, show a large infusion of Uzbeg and other Turki blood. 1890 Billings *Med. Dict.*, Sartian disease. 1920 *Blackw. Mag.* Jan. 89/1 The definite separation of the race into two, the Sarts or sedentary hordes, and the wandering hordes. 1920 *Glasgow Herald* 31 Aug. 8 It is among the highly intelligent Sarts and Tadjiks, speaking Persian and Arabic fluently and many of them conversant with Hindustani, that the Bolshevists find their cleverest agents.

Sartorially (saɹtō·riăli), *adv.* [f. Sartorial *a.* + -ly [2].] With regard to clothes.
1905 W. J. Locke *Morals of Marcus Ordeyne* xii, When she puts her foot upon my sartorially immaculate knee. 1916 — *Wonderful Year* xvii, Like a woman clothes-starved for years..Martin ran sartorially mad. 1928 *Daily Express* 16 Apr. 3/4 Sartorially magnificent in all-over woolly tights.

'Sarwan (sāɹwā·n). *Indian.* Also **serwan.** [Hind. ساربان *sārbān* camel-driver, f. Pers. *sār* camel + *bān* keeper.] A camel-driver.
1908 *Animal Managem.* (War Office) 280 When beginning to handle the animal the nose rope should be held by the attendant (*serwan*). 1920 *Blackw. Mag.* Nov. 569/2 Splashing men, sarwans, mule drabis, baggage-guard sepoys.

Sasanian, Sasanid, varr. Sassanian, Sassanid.
1904 F. C. Burkitt *Early East. Christ.* 25 The rise and decay of Christianity in the Sasanid Empire. 1908 Sasanian [see Dict.]. 1931 A. W. Seaby *Art in Life Mankind* 80 The Sasanians were as bitter enemies of the Christian eastern or Byzantine empire as they had been of pagan Rome. *Ibid.* 82 For sculpture the Sasanids used the cliff faces. 1931 *Times Lit. Suppl.* 8 Jan. 17/4 That the Sasanian builders made important contributions to arch, vault and dome construction is undoubtedly true.

Sasanqua (săsæ·nkwă). Also **sasankwa, sassanqua.** [Jap. *sasankwa*.] A theaceous plant, *Camellia Sasanqua*, native to China and Japan, yielding a sweet-smelling oil, which is used in the East for many domestic purposes.
1866 *Treas. Bot.* s.v. *Camellia*. 1876 *Encycl. Brit.* IV. 738/1. 1883 tr. *J. J. Rein's Japan* (1888) 441 In November and December Sasankwa and Cha..blossom.

Sass, Sassy, varr. Sauce, Saucy. (U.S. quots.)
1836 B. Tucker *Partisan Leader* (1861) 318 (Th.) [He] talked to me about living at home on codfish, and potatoes, and cider, and pies, and all sorts of sass. 1856 [G. H. Derby] *Phœnixiana* xvi. 125 While the squire..sasses all respectable persons With his talk of pills he's invented. 1860 *Knickerbocker Mag.* July 102 (Th. s.v. *Long sauce*) White turnip, yellow turnip, or any sort of sass, long sass or short sass. 1881 J. C. Harris *Uncle Remus* ii, Brer Rabbit pacin' down de road..dez ez sassy ez a jay-bird. *Ibid.* iv, You been runnin' roun' here sassin' atter me a mighty long time. *Ibid.*, Brer Rabbit wuz bleedzed for ter fling back some er his sass. 1883 Nye *Baled Hay* 134 It was a nuisance to..write..to Nicholson, telling him who to sass the next morning.

Sassatje (sæ·sätyĕ). *S. Africa.* Also **sarsartie, sasaitie.** [f. Malay *sisate* minced meat + Du. dim. suffix *-je*.] Veal or mutton cutlets curried slightly and cooked on a skewer over a fire (Pettman).
1883 Olive Schreiner *Story Afr. Farm* ii. iv. II. 67, I got the Hottentot girl to show me how to make 'sar-sar-ties' this morning. 1833 *Cape Gd. Hope Lit. Gaz.* 2 Sept. 138 (Pettman) *Sasaitie*, or cabobs, is really no despicable eating. 1894 *Cape Argus* 22 Dec. (Pettman) A Hittite..with a long spear and a very pronounced intention to spit you on it, like a sassatje.

Sastrugi (sæstrū·gi). Also **zastrugi.** [Russ. *zastruga* (pl. -*i*), furrow made on the shore by water.] As *pl.* Parallel snow ridges or furrows formed by the action of the wind and occurring on the open plains of Russia and in Arctic regions.
1900 *Rep. Brit. Assoc.* 817 The wind concentrating along the lines of the re-entrants, the general level of the surface here is lowered more quickly by abrasion than is the case along the intermediate lines of the salient angles. Thus is produced a well-marked form transitional between snow ripples and *sastrugi*. 1909 Shackleton *Hrt. Antarctic* I. 177. 1911 Scott *Jrnl. Last Exped.* (1913) I. 517 The hard surface gave place to regular sastrugi. 1921 H. G. Ponting *Gt. White South* 94 The going was easy enough, except when periodically we encountered heavy sastrugi.

Satellite. Add: **2. c.** *attrib.* passing into *adj.* Secondary, minor, satellitic.
1923 N. Shaw *Forecasting Weather* v. 115 Two detached secondary or satellite depressions. 1926 H. Macpherson *Mod. Astron.* 75 The satellite-systems of the outer planets are of a different order. 1929 *Times* 17 July 17/6 Since neither complete decentralization nor the proposal to 'departmentalize' the government of Greater Paris is found to give general satisfaction, the system of 'satellite towns' has been suggested as a way out.

Satin, *sb.* (and *a.*). Add: **8. a. satin-finish**, also any effect resembling satin in texture or surface produced on materials in various ways; **satin-leather**, leather finished with a bright black polish so as to resemble satin; so **satin oil (leather)**; **satin weave** (see quot.).
1865 Mrs. Stowe *House & Home P.* 157 For *satin finish, ..American papers equal any in the world. 1929 *Encycl. Brit.* XXIX. 7/2 Frequently the surface [of glass] had been dulled by acid so as to produce a 'satin' finish. 1903 Flemming *Pract. Tanning* 264 Wax calf and *satin leather are finished upon the flesh or inner side. 1897 C. T. Davis *Manuf. Leather* (ed. 2) 434 This blacking is for *satin oil, glove grain, plow grain, oil grain and dongola. *Ibid.* 431 Satin oil leather. 1897 Stephenson & Suddards *Text Bk. Ornam. Design Woven Fabrics* 104 What is known in textile manufacturing as a *satin weave, which is a construction of cloth where the weft comes to the surface in greater proportion than the warp, or *vice versa*, in a certain definite order.

b. satin-bush, a S. African shrub, *Podalyria sericea*, with a silky pubescence on the calyces and flower-stems; **satin-flower**, (*c*) a plant belonging to either of two N.-W. American genera, *Sisyrinchium* and *Brevoortia*; see also quot. 1884; **satin-leaf** (*a*) the N. American alum-root, *Heuchera americana*; (*b*) a small tree of the West Indies, *Chrysophyllum monopyrenum*, so called from the

golden pubescence on the underside of the leaves; **satin-wood**, (*b*) any of various trees having a hard light-coloured wood, as *Xanthoxylum brachyacanthum*, *Daphnandra micrantha* of Australia, *Xanthoxylum caribæum* of the West Indies, and *X. flavum*, *Fagara flava* of S. Florida, *Murraya paniculata* of India.
1884 Miller *Plant-n.*, *Podalyria sericea*, African *Satin-bush. *Ibid.*, *Brodiæa coccinea*, crimson-flowered Californian Hyacinth, Crimson *Satin-flower, Vegetable Fire-Cracker. *Ibid.*, *Sisyrinchium*, Pig-root, Rush-Lily, Satin flower. 1883 W. Robinson *Engl. Flower Garden* 53/1 *Brevoortia coccinea* (Crimson Satin flower). 1884 Miller *Plant-n.*, *Heuchera Richardsoni* (*H. americana*, *H. ribifolia*), *Satin-leaf. 1886 *Encycl. Brit.* XX. 174/1 *Satinwood, the *Xanthoxylum brachyacanthum*.

c. satin beauté, a soft finely woven material with a dull crêpe back and brilliant satin finish; **satin de chine**, 'a firm silk with dull satin finish' (Webster 1911); **satin de Lyon**, a variety of satin with a ribbed back.
1922 *Daily Mail* 18 Dec. 8 Her gown, in the Early Italian style, will be of cream *satin beauté. 1928 *Times* 9 May 10/5 Pink satin beauté. 1895 *Army & Navy Co-op. Soc. Price List* 15 Sept. 1095/1 *Satin de Lyon..*Satin de Chine, for dress linings. 1923 *Daily Mail* 19 Feb. 1 Our renowned guaranteed quality Satin de Chine.

Satrangi (sātrɒ·ndʒi). Also 7 **sitternegee, cittringe,** 9 **sattrangee, su-, satrunjee, su-, satringee,** etc. [Bengali, f. Skr. *caturanga* chess (played by four parties).] An Indian cotton carpet made in Bengal and northern India.
1621 in W. Foster *Eng. Factories India* (1906) 354 [With the help of skins] cittringes [&c., they saved most of them [*sc.* linens] from harm]. 1629 *Ibid.* (1909) 360 [Five] sitternegees. 1851 *Illustr. Catal. Gt. Exhib.* iv. i. 917/2 Cotton carpets (*Satrunjees*) of different sizes—from Bengal. 1858 Simmonds *Dict. Trade*, *Sattrangee*, *Satringee*, a kind of fibrous striped mat or carpet made in India. 1859 M. Thomson *Story of Cawnpore* 189 They provided us with straw to lie upon, and gave us a sutringee each (a piece of carpet) to cover our bodies. 1876 *Encycl. Brit.* V. 129/2 Cotton carpets or *Suttringees* are a cheap substitute for woollen fabrics in almost universal use throughout India.

Sats (säts). *Skiing.* [Sw., = jump, leap.] (See quots.)
1904 *E. C. Richardson's Ski-Running* 56 When within about a yard of the edge of the take-off make the '*sats*'... The '*sats*' is a downward pressure of the ski on the snow made by rising on the toes, and nearly straightening the knee and thigh joints, the arms at the same time being thrown upwards. 1913 Arnold Lunn *Ski-ing* 93 The beginner..until he has carefully mastered the 'sats'..should not attempt to jump. 1929 *Daily Express* 16 Jan. 8/3 He crouches low, in the position known as the 'sats'..knees almost touching the skis in front and arms hanging low at the sides.

Sat-upon (sæ·t,ǒpǫn), *ppl. a.* *colloq.* [See Sit *v.* 26 d.] Downtrodden, humiliated, 'squashed'.
1893 *Chambers's Jrnl.* 25 Feb. 128 With that sat-upon sort of man..you never know where he may break out. *Mod.* She had that sat-upon sort of look.

Saturated, *ppl. a.* Add: **3.** Read: *Physics* and transfer quot. 1888 to *6.

6. *Phys. Chem.* That has equal and opposite quantities of electricity in each molecule or atom; having all the valencies satisfied.
1888 [see 3 in Dict.]. 1892 Morley & Muir *Watts' Dict. Chem.* III. 417/1 But gases..such as NO, behave at these temperatures with respect to electricity like saturated gases. 1902 *Encycl. Brit.* XXVI. 717/1 Apparently the only saturated molecules known to us at present, *i.e.*, molecules destitute of all power of exercising an external influence, are those of gases such as helium and argon.

Saturation. 5. Add: **saturation current** *Electr.*, the maximum value of current that can be carried, as by a gas, etc.; **saturation factor** *Electr.* (see quot.); **saturation-point** *Phys.* = 'point of saturation' (see Saturation 3); also *fig.*; **saturation-pressure** *Phys.*, the pressure at which vapours begin to condense.
1896 *Phil. Mag.* Ser. v. XLII. 403 The *saturation current depends only on the number of conducting particles produced by the rays. 1902 *Encycl. Brit.* XXVIII. 26/1 There is thus, until the electric field ionizes the gas, a limiting value to the current which can be carried by the gas; this maximum value is often called the saturation current. 1930 *B.B.C. Year-Bk.* 450/2 As the anode voltage applied to a three-electrode valve is increased, the anode current also increases up to a point, when a further increase in anode voltage does not increase the anode current. This maximum value of current is called the 'saturation current'. 1916 *Standard. Rules Amer. Inst. Electr. Engin.* 17 *Saturation Factor*...The ratio of a small percentage increase in field excitation to the corresponding percentage increase in voltage thereby produced. Unless otherwise specified, the saturation factor of a machine refers to the no-load excitation required at normal rated speed and voltage. 1858 *saturation point [in Dict.]. 1902 *Encycl. Brit.* XXXIII. 631/2 It is a fair inference that similar behaviour would be observed up to the saturation-point if surface condensation could be avoided. 1927 *Sunday Times* 13 Feb. 2 Those controlling the industry realize that the world production of motor-cars has by no means reached saturation point. 1927 *Daily Express* 26 Mar. 11/1 The saturation point in linoleum would never be reached, so many new houses annually needed their floors covered, and ..old floors would require fresh covering. 1884 *saturation pressure [in Dict.]. 1902 *Encycl. Brit.* XXXIII. 631/1 The values of the saturation-pressure have been very accurately determined for the majority of stable substances.

Saturdaying (sæ·təɹdeⁱiŋ), *vbl. sb.* [f. Saturday + -ing [1], after Russ. *subbótnik* a Saturday worker.] In the Soviet Union, the performance of manual labour gratis. So **Sa·turdayi·te.**
1920 *Nation* (N.Y.) 13 Mar. 344/1 The voluntary labor, which goes by the name of 'Saturdaying', undertaken by Communists and non-Communists in Soviet Russia. 1920 *Contemp. Rev.* Oct. 504 For members of the Bolshevik party, 'Saturdaying' had become compulsory. 1932 C. T. Hogarth tr. *Kollontai's Free Love* 233 She will persuade you..that it is necessary..to deny oneself everything that gives joy, to live only for the 'Saturdayites'.

Saturnian (sătɜ̄·ɹniăn), *a.*[2] and *sb.*[3] [f. mod. L. *Saturnia*, generic name, fem. of L. *Sāturnius* pertaining to Saturn: see -an.] Of or pertaining to the genus *Saturnia* or the family *Saturniidæ* of bombycid moths; a moth of this genus or family. So **Satu·rniid** *a.* and *sb.*
1862 T. W. Harris *Insects injur. Veget.* (ed. 3) 382 The injuries committed by the caterpillars of the Saturnians. 1892 W. L. Distant *Natur. in Transvaal* 122 The fine Saturniid moth *Urota sinope*.

Satyagraha (satyă·graha). [Skr., f. सत्य *satya* true, sincere, faithful + आग्रह *āgraha* obstinacy.] Passive resistance. So **Satya·grahist.**
1921 *Daily Tel.* 1 Mar. 12/1 Satyagraha in its original form was mere continuation of policy which less advanced 'reformers' have always advocated. 1929 *Daily Express* 10 Jan. 1/5 The ex-soldiers expressed their intention of performing satyagraha until their leader was released. 1930 *Aberdeen Press & Jrnl.* 7 Apr. 7/1 The 'Untouchables', dissatisfied with his campaign, have threatened counter satyagraha. 1931 J. S. Hoyland *Cross Moves East* 91 The principle of *Satyagraha*, which has recently come into such prominence as the controlling force behind the movement for Indian independence led by Mr. Gandhi.

Sauce, *sb.* **1.** Add: *Hard sauce* (U.S.), sauce which is not liquid. *Sauce hollandaise*: see *Hollandaise.
1928 S. Lewis *Man who knew Coolidge* i. 103 A..Plum Pudding..with both hard and soft sauce.

Sauroderma (sǫrodɜ̄·ɹmă). *Path.* [mod.L., f. Gr. σαῦρος lizard + δέρμα skin.] A form of ichthyosis characterized by dry and warty knobs. Also (irreg.) **Sauride·rma.**
1901 Dorland *Med. Dict.* (ed. 2), *Sauriderma*, ichthyosis hystrix.

Sausage. Add: **2. c.** (*a*) Applied to a sausage-shaped gas-bag. (*b*) An observation balloon, so called from its sausage-like shape.
1874 *Belgravia* Aug. 170, I am not..quite certain.. whether the body of the 'sausage' balloon was provided with two valves. *Ibid.*, This sausage was encased in the ordinary net-work and dependent shrouds. 1916 Buchan *Battle of Somme* 20 Captive balloons, the so called 'sausages', glittered in the sunlight. 1916 Bean *Lett. from France* (1917) 74 The Germans have not a single 'sausage' in the air that I can see. 1917 'Sapper' *No Man's Land* 97 A row of sausage balloons like a barber's rash adorned the sky. 1928 C. F. S. Gamble *North Sea Air Station* xx. 356 While the first pilot brings the boat down to 1,000 feet and flies over the air station to have a careful look at the 'sausage' to confirm the wind direction.

4. d. sausage-finger, a finger which is of the same width from tip to base.
1910 *Practitioner* Jan. 33 The fingers..as large at their tips as at their base—the so-called sausage fingers.

Savage (sæ·vedʒ), *sb.*[2] The name of *Savage* used *attrib.* or *absol.* to designate a repeating rifle invented by him.
1902 *Encycl. Brit.* XXXII. 657/2 The Savage magazine rifle, model 1899, is a 'hammerless', lever-action repeating arm. 1903 *Kynoch Jrnl.* Feb.–Mar. 62/1, I had my ·301 Savage.

Savage, *v.* Add: **4. b.** *fig.*
1923 *Public Opinion* 2 Sept. 103/2 Human lust and hatred has first savaged them to death. 1926 *Bulletin* 9 June 13 He is much too severe on the form of novels—the Cogglesby comedy in 'Evan' is savaged, for example. 1926 *Glasgow Herald* 19 June, They savaged her with threats.

Savagerous (sæ·vedʒĕrəs), *a.* *U.S. slang.* Also **sevagerous, sawagerous, savig(e)rous** (cf. *Servigrous). [f. Savage *a.* + Dangerous *a.*] Fierce.
1831 Frances Trollope *Dom. Mann. Amer.* xiii. I. 182 The visitor took it [*sc.* a dagger] up, and examining it with much emotion, exclaimed, 'What! do you really jab this into yourself sevagerous?' 1843 *Philadelphia Spirit of Times* 25 Aug. (Th.) The Editor [of the *Age*] calls his savagerous enemy a remarkably pious and moral young man. 1847 Porter *Big Bear* 121 (Farmer) They war mighty savagerous arter likker. c 1852 *Traits of Amer. Humour* III. 53, I looked at him sorter savigerous like. a 1855 Dow Jun. *Patent Serm.* iv. 263 (Th.) A very sawagerous creature called the Youknowcan. 1866 C. H. Smith *Bill Arp* (1873) 56 Habeus Korpus..is..when suspended, the most savagerous beest that ever got after tories and trators. 1925 G. P. Krapp *Engl. Lang. in Amer.* I. 115 Fantastically coined or combined words, as..*savagerous*, *savigrous*.

Savanilla (sævăni·lă). *U.S.* [Name of a port of Columbia, S. America.] **a.** The tarpon. **b.** *Savanilla rhatany*: see Rhatany.
1884 Goode *Nat. Hist. Aquatic Anim.* 611 The 'Tarpum' or 'Tarpon ..is..the 'Savanilla' of Texas.

Save, *sb.*[2] Add: **3.** *Bridge.* (See quot. 1927.)
1927 *Observer* 31 July 14/5 Now consider the position if Z had doubled 'Six Hearts' instead of going on with Spades..which would have saved the game and rubber. A cheap save and well worth while! 1928 A. E. M. Foster *Auction Bridge* 200 A Good Save on Majority Bidding.

Save, *v.* **8. f.** Add: Hence *save-face*, the action of saving one's face.
1917 *Chambers's Jrnl.* Jan. 13/2 The civilian native staff had bolted at the first sign of trouble, 'going to report to the authorities' being their 'save face' for it!

Saving, *vbl. sb.* **4.** Add: (war) **savings certificate**, introduced February 1916, re-named 1920, (national) **savings certificate**, a certificate declaring that the holder has invested 15*s.* 6*d.* (later 16*s.*) in government funds, encashable at any time with accrued interest, and usually maturing at five or ten years.
1916 *Times* 19 Feb. 5/1 The new War Savings Certificates, which can be bought from to-day for 15*s.* 6*d.* each at any money-order office. *Ibid.*, No income-tax is payable in respect of the accumulated interest on War Savings Certificates. 1916 R. McKenna in *War Savings* Sept. 5/1 Post Office Exchequer Bonds and War Savings Certificates are our rifles and hand-grenades. 1919 *Saving* 3 Dec. 140/1 Leyton school children have bought Savings Certificates to the value of over £48,000. 1920 *Act* 10 & 11 *Geo. V* c. 12 (*title*), An Act..to extend to National Savings Certificates the enactments relating to War Savings Certificates. 1927 G. W. Deeping *Doomsday* xix. § 3 Seventy-five pounds in Savings Certificates.

Savorous, *a.* **1. b.** (Modern archaic example.)
1923 Sadleir *Desolate Splendour* 264 Were it not doubly savourous to wreak his revenge.

Savoy[2] (săvoi·). The name of the *Savoy* Theatre, London, used *attrib.* to designate the Gilbert and Sullivan operas originally produced there by the D'Oyly Carte company.
1902 *Encycl. Brit.* XXXIII. 56/2 The Savoy operas did not aim at intellectual or emotional grandeur. 1907 W. S. Gilbert in *Daily Mail Year Bk.* 99/1 Savoy opera..was snuffed out by the deplorable death of my distinguished collaborator, Sir Arthur Sullivan. 1930 *Times* 22 Mar. 13/4 Savoy Opera is a tree deeply rooted in our national fantasy.

Savoyard, *sb.* and *a.* **A.** *sb.* Add: **3.** A member of the company that played at the Savoy theatre in the original productions of the Gilbert and Sullivan operas.
1891 W. S. Gilbert (*title*) Songs of a Savoyard. 1908 R. Barrington *Rec. 35 Yrs. Eng. Stage* 265 To have been an 'old Savoyard', that is to say, one of the original company, seems to confer not only a great measure of dignity, but.. a greater natural activity in old age. 1922 H. A. Lytton *Secr. of a Savoyard* vi. 81 It is my melancholy distinction to be the last of the Savoyards.

Saw, *sb.*[1] Add: **1. c.** A flexible kind of saw which is used as a musical instrument, being played with a bow.
1931 *Daily Mail* 6 Oct. 16/3 Saw solos.

5. d. saw-buck, also *saw-buck saddle*; hence as *adj.* = having the form of x; (*b*) a ten dollar bill; **saw palmetto** (earlier example).
1855 M. Thompson *Doesticks* xxxv. 322 Macduff..stands over the conquered Macbeth in a grand *saw-buck attitude. 1857 *Quinland* II. 166, I know fifty fellows..that for one end of a saw-buck a-piece, would be on hand with a whole company of voters at their heels. 1907 S. E. White *Arizona Nts.* ii. 12 We skirmished around and found..a sawbuck saddle with kyacks. 1800 B. Hawkins *Sk. Creek Country* 20 There is some light pine barren, with *saw palmetto and winegrass.

Saw, *v.*[1] **1.** Add: *To saw wood* (fig.): to attend to one's own affairs. *U.S. slang.*
1909 *N.Y. Even. Post* 15 Apr. (Th.) Mr. Sullivan should take down his copy of Livy, and read what happened to Hannibal at Capua while the defeated Romans were busy sawing wood.

Sawahili, var. Swahili.
1845 *Encycl. Metrop.* XXV. 1392/2 Southward of the Pangani river are the Sawáhili tribes.

Sawed, *ppl. a.* Add: *sawed-off gun*, a gun of which the greater part of the barrel has been sawn off so that it can be handled more easily. *U.S. slang.*
1930 *Times* 25 Nov. 13/4 The bandits..aimed..sawed off shotguns at the entertainers and guests.

Saw-log. *U.S.* [Saw *sb.*[1] or *v.*[1]] A log suitable for sawing into planks.
1831 T. Buttrick *Trav.* 57 There were also many rafts of boards and shingles timber and saw logs. 1842 [see Saw *sb.*[1] 5 d]. 1866 *Rep. Indian Affairs* 83 Hauling saw-logs to the saw-mill. 1885 *Ibid.* 199 Other Indians had cut and hauled a large number of saw-logs. 1908 S. E. White *Riverman* iv. 40 A good riverman understands the correlation of forces represented by saw logs and water-pressure.

Saw-mill. *attrib.* (Earlier U.S. examples.)
1739 W. Stephens *Jrnl. Proc. Georgia* 402 Director of the Saw-Mill Work at Old Ebenezer. 1818 Fessenden *Ladies' Monitor* 35 His elbows, hoofs and paws That rip and rend and rive like saw mill-saws. 1843 *Yale Lit. Mag.* VIII. 406 What lots of saw-mill logs there are here.

Sawqui: see Sockeye.
1896 Jordan & Evermann *Fish N. & Middle Amer.* i. 481 *Oncorhynchus Nerka*. Saw-qui Salmon.

Saxe. Add: Also *absol.* = Saxe blue.
1922 *Daily Mail* 14 Nov. 1 Knitted Wool Cardigans... Colours: Fawn, Wine, Saxe, Putty. 1928 *Queen* 5 Sept. Advt. p. i, Silk bodice in..Almond, Rose, Fawn, Saxe, and Cherry.

Saxonian, *a.* and *sb.* Transfer † *Obs.* to senses in Dict. and add: **2.** *Geol.* Designating a division of the Permian system in Europe. *Saxonian epoch*, a subdivision of the glacial period in northern Europe; the second glacial epoch.
1903 A. Geikie *Text-Bk. Geol.* (ed. 4) 1069 The middle [Permian] includes the Red Sandstones, which in Saxony

and the north-west of England attain such development, and has been termed Saxonian. *Ibid.* 1313 Saxonian or 2nd Glacial Epoch, including the accumulations of the period of maximum glaciation. 1924 Schuchert *Hist. Geol.* 421 Middle Permian or Saxonian (Middle and Lower Zechstein).

Say, *sb.*[4] **2.** (Later Amer. example.)
1704 Sarah Knight *Jrnl.* 30 So I remembered the old say, and supposed I knew Sarah's case.

Say, *v.*[1] Add: **B. 2. c.** (Modern examples.)
1894 'R. Andom' *We Three & Troddles* xv, Giants are always wicked people. It says so in the children's books. 1900 B. Pain *Eliza* 54 'You told me it was port!' 'So it is.' 'It says tonic port on the label.'

1. Phr. *When all is said and done*: after all, in the long run.
c 1560 Tho. Ingelend *Disobedient Child* A iii, Whan all is saide and all is done, Concernynge all thynges both more and lesse. 1583 Melbancke *Philotimus* S iij, It must be as yᵉ woman will, when all is said & done. 1930 'Sapper' (H. C. McNeile) *Finger of Fate* 162 But when all is said and done, a prospective son-in-law is as important as any letter.

7. b. *To say a few words*: to make a short (extempore) speech.
1930 *B.B.C. Year-Bk.* 214 When I am suddenly called upon to 'say a few words'.

13. d. Say out. (*c*) To give plain utterance to. See Out *adv.* 11 and cf. Out-loud.
1853 Mrs. Gaskell *Ruth* xiii, Miss Benson said boldly out, 'The lady I named in my note, Sally'.

Scab, *sb.* **4. b.** (Earlier example.)
1806 in *Doc. Hist. Amer. Industr. Soc.* (1910) III. 74, I concluded at that time I would turn a Scab.

Scab, *v.* **3.** (Earlier U.S. example.)
1806 in *Doc. Hist. Amer. Industr. Soc.* (1910) III. 75 To watch the Jews that they did not scab it.

Scads (skædz), *sb. pl.* (*Western*) *U.S. colloq.* Also **skads.** [Origin unascertained.] **a.** Dollars, money.
1856 *Sacramento City Item* (Th. s.v. *Sardine*) So off he went with good three hundred 'scads'. 1869 *Overland Monthly* III. 65 Come out with the scads! 1883 Nye *Baled Hay* 59 We have mercenary motives...We desire the scads. 1902 Harben *Abner Daniel* ix. 70 Ef he kin possibly raise the scads to pay the tax.

b. A large amount, 'heaps'.
1869 *Overland Monthly* III. 131 A Texan never has a great quantity of anything, but he has 'scads' of it..or 'Scadoodles'. 1904 W. H. Smith *Promoters* ii. 52 What did England do when she found she could raise scads of opium in India, but had no market for it? 1931 E. Linklater *Juan in Amer.* ii. xvi. 176 And the pay? Skads of dough. Oodles and oodles of money.

Scaffold, *sb.* **7.** Add: Also, a framework upon which tobacco is dried. So **Scaffolding** (see quot. 1886).
1784 J. Smyth *Tour U.S.* II. 134 When the tobacco plants are cut and brought to the scaffolds. 1886 C. G. W. Lock *Tobacco* 75 Scaffolding is done by placing poles on forks, about 4 feet apart, and 4–5 feet from the ground; then hang the tobacco between the poles. *Ibid.*, Some prefer hanging the tobacco on scaffolds in the field until it is ready to be put in the barn and cured by the fire. 1888 *Encycl. Brit.* XXIII. 424/2 Red shipping qualities [*sc.* of tobacco] are prepared by leaving the cut stems either in the field or hung on scaffolds in the barns for a few days to wilt and wither in the air.

Sca·ffy boat. *Sc.* (See quot. 1879.)
1877 E. W. H. Holdsworth *Sea Fisheries* 168 The Buckie boats, known as 'Scaffs' or 'Scaffy boats'. 1879 *Encycl. Brit.* IX. 257/2 Buckie boats have long been remarkable for their peculiar build and rig, having a low and broad midship section with a flat or rather hollow floor; they are very fine at both ends, and have considerable rake of both stem and stern post. They are commonly known as 'scaffy' boats. 1927 *Glasgow Herald* 3 May 7 Scaffie boats gave way to Zulu and Fifie types.

Scag. *U.S.* [Cf. Skeg *sb.*[4]] A cleat.
1874 J. W. Long *Amer. Wild-Fowl Shooting* 90 A scag of inch oak is put on along the centre of this slant.

Scalawaggery. *U.S.* (See Scallywag 2.)
1911 H. S. Harrison *Queed* iv. 45 The morning *Post* was an old paper...It had crucified carpet-baggism and scalawaggery upon a cross of burning adjective.

Scald, *sb.*[2] Add: **2. b.** Scalded curd.
1859 *Trans. Mich. Agric. Soc.* (1860) X. 115 Do you observe a rule as to the age of the curd when you begin to heat up the scald?

4. (Later U.S. example.)
1882 *Econ. Geol. Illinois* II. 124 Where the soil becomes shallow, and the hard-pan reaches the surface there we find the so-called 'scalds', or barren spots, in the fields.

Scaldesian (skǫldī·ʃiăn). *Geol.* [ad. F. *Scaldisien*, f. L. *Scaldis*, the river Scheldt.] A division of the Pliocene Tertiary in Belgium and Holland.
1893 Geikie *Text-bk. Geol.* (ed. 3) 1015 Above the Diestian sands comes the group known as Scaldesian.

Scalding, *vbl. sb.* **1. d.** (Earlier U.S. example.)
1861–2 *Trans. Ill. Agric. Soc.* (1865) V. 208 Here is no swaying of trees to the east, no scalding of the west side of the trunks in the sun.

Scale, *sb.*[2] **12.** Add: **scale-blue**, also, china having a groundwork of scale-blue.
1909 *Chambers's Jrnl.* Nov. 750/2 A Chippendale cabinet ..stacked with old 'scale-blue'.

Scale, *v.*[3] **II. 4. b.** Add: Also with *up*. Also Comb. *scale-down* attrib.
1891 *Daily News* 17 Jan. 2/5 The scaling up instead of scaling down the London, Chatham, and Dover stock. 1931 *Times* 16 Mar. 19/6 There was some Continental scale-down buying which served to keep the decline in check.

Scallywag. 1. Add: Also *attrib.*
1925 C'tess von Arnim *Love* i. xviii. 181 You know how strongly I feel about motor-cycles, and the type of scallywag youth who uses them. 1926 *Glasgow Herald* 10 Sept. 11 Go back to your scallywag union.

Scalma (skæ·lmă). [mod.L. (Wilhelm Dieckerhoff of Berlin, 1885), f. OHG. *scalmo* pestilence.] A contagious disease affecting the pharynx, larynx, and bronchi of horses.
1890 Billings *Med. Dict.*

Scalp, *sb.* **6. c. scalp-dance** (earlier U.S. example); **scalp-ticket** *U.S.* (see Scalper [2] 2 a).
1837 W. Irving *Capt. Bonneville* I. iv. 56 They were now bound homewards, to appease the manes of their comrade.. and intended to have *scalp-dances and other triumphant rejoicings. 1882 Sala *Amer. Revis.* (1883) 365 There are 'round trip' tickets which are a great deal more than return tickets; and finally, there are *'scalp' tickets, which you can deal in and discount.

Scalp, *v.*[2] **2. a.** *U.S.* (Earlier example.)
1815 J. Lorain *Pract. Husb.* 335 The Yankee farmer first chops the fallen timber, then scalps off the grubs level with the ground.

Scalper. 3. (Earlier U.S. example.)
1837 R. M. Bird *Nick of Woods* II. xviii. 245 Captain Ralph Stacpole did..meet another Injun-savage in the woods ..with gun, axe, and scalper.

Scaly, *a.* **8.** Add: **scaly-bark hickory** (earlier example); **scaly-tail** (see quot.).
1786 Washington *Diaries* III. 30 Spaded up some of the ground in my botanical garden for the purpose of planting the *scaly bark hickory nut of Gloucester in. 1921 *Brit. Mus. Return* 97 A West African *Scaly-tail (*Anomalurus erythronotus*), and an Ituri Scaly-tail (*Anomalurus pusillus*).

Scan, *v.* Add: **8.** *Television.* To submit (a picture) to a device by which it is resolved into its elements of light and shade for purposes of transmission.
1930, 1931 [see *Scanning *vbl. sb.* 3].

Scandalize *v.*[1] **3.** Add:
1931 *Star* 8 May 16/2 It was submitted..that the article scandalised one of his Majesty's judges.

Scanian (skē̆ⁱ·niăn), *a.* (*sb.*). *Geol.* [f. L. *Scania* Scandinavia + -an.] Designating a subdivision of the Pleistocene or first glacial epoch of northern Europe; also as *sb.*
1909 *Cent. Dict.* Suppl. 1913 Jas. Geikie *Antiq. Man in Eur.* (1914) 248 The Scanian or First Glacial Epoch.

Scanning, *vbl. sb.* Add:
3. *Television.* (See *Scan *v.* 8, and quots. below.) Also *attrib.*
1928 *Science & Invention* (U.S.) Oct. 489/2 If..the scanning disc has 48 holes and spins at..600 revolutions per minute. 1930 *B.B.C. Year-Bk.* 450/2 *Scanning disc*, in *Television or Picture Transmission*, a rotating opaque disc perforated with a series of holes in the form of a spiral. A ray of light passing through the holes is thus caused to move over (scan) a picture or an object placed behind the holes on the farther side from the source of light. *Ibid.*, *Scanning frequency*, the rate at which the picture or object is scanned. 1931 *Daily Tel.* 6 Jan. 11/7 A selective apparatus that dissects each picture into its component elements of light and shade, a process known as 'scanning'. *Ibid.*, Below this speed the pictures flicker, and the intermittences of the scanning device obstruct the view.

Scape, *sb.*[1] Add: **4. b.** The steam from an escape pipe. *U.S.*
1878 J. H. Beadle *Western Wilds* xxiii. 373 Steamboat Spring, from which the water bursts forth at brief intervals with a loud 'cough' like the 'scape' of a slowly moving distant steam-boat.

7. scape-pipe *U.S.*, an escape pipe for steam.
1876 'Mark Twain' *Old Times* 132 Presently tall columns of steam burst from the 'scape-pipes of both steamers. 1882 *Harper's Mag.* Jan. 169/2 Aft of the pilot-house the twin ''scape-pipes' rise from the engine room.

Scar, *sb.*[1] Add: **4. b.** A lump or cake of imperfectly fused ferrous sulphide formed in the burning of iron pyrites for the manufacture of sulphuric acid.
1879 G. Lunge *Manuf. Sulphuric Acid* I. 155 It does not happen so often that fused masses, 'scars', are formed in the burner. 1905 *Technol. & Sci. Dict.* (ed. Goodchild & Tweney).

Scar, *sb.*[2] Add: **scar-tissue**, cicatricial tissue, formed after granulation.
1885 *Encycl. Brit.* XVIII. 366/2 The cells having (as a characteristic of scar-tissue after repeated healing) brown pigment-grains in their substance. 1910 *Practitioner* June 786 The application to the endometrium of agents so powerful as to replace the mucosa by a layer of scar-tissue.

Sca·re-head, *v.* [f. *scare-head* (see Scare *sb.*[2] 4).] *trans.* To furnish with a scare-head or sensational heading.
1903 F. Norris *Respons. Novelist* 300 The name of the leading lady or leading man is 'scare-headed' [on theatre bills]. 1911 H. S. Harrison *Queed* xviii, The..penny evening paper..scareheaded a jaundiced account of the affair.

Scarf, *sb.*[1] Add: **3. g.** (See quot.)
1910 *Encycl. Brit.* VII. 277/2 *Scarf* is a kind of dhootie made usually with a taped or corded border.

Scarily, *adv.* (Earlier U.S. example.)
1845 W. G. Simms *Wigwam & Cabin* Ser. i. 107 My heart as cold as ice, and jumping up and down as scarily as a rabbit's.

Scarlet, *a.* **4.** Add: **scarlet woman**, (*b*) a harlot.
1919 J. Huneker *Painted Veils* (1930) 293 The great singing harlot of modern Babylon, a vocal Scarlet Woman. 1924 H. Havelock Ellis *Stud. Psychol. Sex* I. 124, I sought out a scarlet woman in the streets of —— and went home with her.

Scarlet fever. Add: **c.** A passion for soldiers: with reference to their scarlet uniform. *jocular slang.*
1889 Barrère & Leland *Dict. Slang* s.v., Ladies who run after military society are said to have scarlet fever.

Scary, *a.*[1] **2.** (Earlier U.S. examples.)
1800 Weems *Lett.* II. 160, I have always been very scary about our monies. 1816 U. Brown *Jrnl.* in *Maryland Hist. Mag.* X. 358 Ferryed over on Cumberland (felt a little scary, when about half way the wind blew fresh down the river).

Scat, *int.* Add: Also in phr. *quicker than scat.*
1902 A. D. McFaul *Ike Glidden* iii. 20 'Bet you twenty dollars I'll beat you back.' I took him quicker'n scat. 1909 Gene Stratton-Porter *Girl of Limberlost* xvii. 325 And quicker'an scat there was her ma a-whirling.

Scatterer. Add: Also, a device for scattering seed.
1867 *Rep. Iowa Agric. Soc.* (1868) 227 The seed is scattered by a vibrating scatterer.

2. A stray person. *U.S.*
1840 W. G. Simms *Border Beagles* 31, I wouldn't advise a lad to go up into the Yazoo now while it's unsettled..and none but scatterers about.

Scatter-gun. *U.S.* (Earlier example.)
1845 J. J. Hooper *Daddy Biggs' Scrape* 197 This d—n scatter-gun crowd.

Scattery, *a.* Add: **b.** Scatter-brained. *colloq.*
1928 Galsworthy *Swan Song* iii. i. 227 So feather-pated and scattery.

Scavenge, *v.* Add: **3. b.** Of an internal-combustion engine: To expel from the cylinder the exhaust gases and waste products of combustion. Also *trans.* Chiefly in **Sca·venging** *vbl. sb.* and *ppl. a.* Hence **Sca·venge** *sb.*, the action or fact of scavenging.
1894 *Work* 17 Feb. 73/3 Questions such as late ignitions, scavenging, varying explosive charges [etc.]. 1896 B. Donkin *Gas, Oil, & Air Engines* i. xix. (ed. 2) 269 The increase in economy obtained with the new (1894) 'scavenging' Crossley-Atkinson engine. *Ibid.*, The success obtained in the new 'scavenging' motor. 1899 J. Perry *Steam Engine* 452 Scavenging is effected in the Wells (Premier) engine by pumping air into the cylinder. *Ibid.*, The shapes of the passages and piston end, &c., which facilitate this scavenging action. 1902 *Encycl. Brit.* XXVIII. 607/2 The removal or scavenging of all products of combustion from the compression space in the cylinder. *Ibid.*, Scavenging reduces the risk of the explosive mixture being fired prematurely. *Ibid.*, After a misfire in a non-scavenging engine of a large size the explosive force is excessive, and has to be provided for by specially strengthening the engine. With a scavenging engine this trouble is avoided. 1903 *Amer. Inventor* 15 Aug. 78 (Cent. D. Suppl.) In all engines employing the two-stroke cycle, scavenging must be accomplished either by special piston movement or by a blast of air from an auxiliary pump, directed in such a manner as to force out the remaining burned gases... The engine under description scavenges thoroughly and completely upon the return stroke of the pistons, which then draw in their charge of explosive mixture, undiluted either by products of combustion or by scavenging air. 1924 *Times Trade & Engin. Suppl.* 29 Nov. 250/3 As is usual with large Sulzer engines the scavenging air is supplied from electrically driven turbo blowers installed in the engine-room. 1925 *Glasgow Herald* 1 Apr. 7 This new type of engine, with its straight through scavenge and absence of air and exhaust valves.

Scavenger, *sb.* **4.** Add: **scavenger charge** (see quot. and cf. prec.).
1894 B. Donkin *Gas, Oil, & Air Engines* i. ii. 16 A third complete stroke is added, in order to cleanse the cylinder thoroughly of the products of previous combustion by what is called a 'scavenger' charge of pure air.

Sceau, erron. form of *Seau.

Sceaux (sōᵘ). The name of a French town near Paris used *attrib.* and *absol.* to denote tin-enamelled faience made there in the latter part of the eighteenth century, often painted with floral and figure subjects and modelled in the form of figures.
1884 P. Gasnault & Garnier *French Pottery* Index 182 Sceaux mark on faïence. 1903 Solon *Old French Faïence* 125 An anchor, in allusion to the dignity of the Duke de Penthièvre, High Admiral of France, or the stencilled name: 'Sceaux', are the marks of the productions.

Scenic, *a.* **3.** Add: *Scenic railway*, a railway on a very small scale running through artificial representations of beautiful scenery, forming an attraction at fairs, etc.
1901 *Pan-Amer. Exposition, Buffalo* folder, The Midway will have the choicest of the world's amusement novelties. There will be a Trip to the Moon,..Scenic Railway and Rivers. 1908 [see Dict.].

Scent, *sb.* **2. d.** Add: *On the right* or *wrong scent* (fig.): pursuing the right or wrong method.
1912 *Motor Manual* (ed. 14) 181 If he did it would prevent him getting on to wrong scents, even to the extent of pulling the engine to pieces.

Scentless, *a.* **3.** Add: Also of a day on which there is no scent for the hounds to follow.
1885 *Field* 4 Apr. 428/1 That dry, scentless cycle of days. 1921 *Ampleforth Jrnl.* Jan. 137 On October 16th we hunted the high country, after a scentless day at Tom Smith's Cross on the previous Wednesday.

Schaapsteker (ʃā·pstekəɹ). *S. Afr.* Also **scarpsticker, scha(a)pstikker.** [Afrikaans, f. Du. *schaap* sheep + *steken* to sting.] A snake of the family *Coronellidæ*, *Psammophylax rhombeatus*.
1856 F. Fleming *Southern Africa* 406 The 'Scarpsticker' of the Dutch, or Night-Adder; a small dingy-brown Adder, spotted with black, about eighteen inches long. 1887 *Encycl. Brit.* XXII. 197/1 The second African snake of this family is the 'schapsticker' (Sheep Stinger), *Causus rhombeatus*.

1912 Fitzsimons *Snakes S. Africa* 130 The farmer..comes along, finds the dying sheep, and seeing Schaapstekers about, immediately concludes they are the guilty parties.

Schabzieger (ʃa·pıtsīgər). Also **schapsziger, chapsager, -ziger.** = Sapsago, q.v.
1837 *Penny Cycl.* VII. 15/2 The green Swiss cheese, commonly called *Schabzieger*, which is made in the canton of Glarus. 1846 chapsager [see Sapsago]. 1866 *Treas. Bot.* s.v. *Melilotus*, Schabzieger or Chapziger. 1879 *Encycl. Brit.* X. 636/1. 1887 Bentley *Man. Bot.* (ed. 5) 534 They [*sc.* flowers and seeds of *Melilotus officinalis*] are used to give flavour to the 'Schabzieger'.

Schadenfreude (ʃā·dənfroidə). [G., f. *schade* damage + *freude* joy.] Malicious enjoyment of other people's difficulties or losses.
1922 *Glasgow Herald* 6 May 9 You may buy a hat for 500 marks to-day, and it may be worth 700 marks to-morrow. So you..perhaps, will feel a little of schadenfreude at the expense of the vendor who sold it to you a day too soon. 1926 *Spectator* 24 July 120/2 There is no English word for *Schadenfreude*, because there is no such feeling here. 1927 *Daily Tel.* 8 Feb. 12/2 The 'Schadenfreude' so openly exhibited by a large section of her Press over our difficulties in China.

Schal, variant of *Shal.

Schalstein (ʃā·lstain). *Petrol.* Also **schaalstein**, semi-Anglicized **schaalstone.** [G., f. *schale* layer, lamina (see Shale *sb.*) + *stein* Stone.] A variety of tufaceous rock.
1804 Jameson *Syst. Min.* I. 519 Schaalstone. 1836 T. Thomson *Min., Geol.* etc. I. 129 Bisilicate of Lime. Table spar, schaalstein, grammite, wollastonite, of Haüy. 1879 Rutley *Stud. Rocks* xiii. 248 Schalstein is, according to Gümbel, a tuff, or sedimentary deposit, the material for which has been derived from 'diabase-eruptions'.

Schappe (ʃæp, ‖ ʃa·pə). [G. *schappe* silk waste.] A fabric or yarn made from waste silk. Also *attrib.* Hence **Schappe** *v. trans.*, to ferment (silk) in order to remove the gum.
1885 *Harper's Mag.* July 246 Now they [*sc.* waste cocoons] are spun into yarn,..and made into *schappe* or 'spun silk' fabrics, not as lustrous as reeled silk goods, but stronger and cheaper. 1902 Hannan *Textile Fibres Commerce* 177 Schappe Silk—This is known also as spun silk. 1921 R. Beaumont & Hill *Dress, Blouse, & Costume Cloths* 94 The 'Schappe' or 'steeping practice' consists in placing the supply of waste silk in jacketed pans. 1932 *Sale Catal.*, Tailored Blouse, made of schappe silk.

Schedule, *sb.* **4.** *attrib.* Add: = provided for in the time-table, e.g. *schedule time*; hence *on schedule*, to schedule time. orig. *U.S.*
1881 A. A. Hayes *New Colorado* vii. 94 As he rounded the curves in about half of schedule time. 1884 on schedule time [in Dict.]. 1903 O. Wister *Philosophy* 4 2 As a delayed train makes the last few miles high above schedule speed. 1904 W. H. Smith *Promoters* vii. 123 Such things don't move on schedule time. 1909 *Springfield* (Mass.) *Weekly Republ.* 19 Aug. 10 The train was running exactly on schedule when the party left it. 1931 *Statesman* (Calcutta) 5 Dec., Throughout the flight, which was soon ahead of schedule time.

Schellingian (ʃeli·ŋgiăn), *a.* [f. *Schelling* (see below) + -ian.] Of or pertaining to the German philosopher, F. W. J. von Schelling (1775–1854), or to his doctrine. *Neo-Schellingian*, concerned with New Schellingism. Hence **Schellingism** (ʃe·liŋiz'm) [ad. G. *Schellingismus*], the system of philosophy taught by Schelling. *New Schellingism*, the philosophy of certain disciples of Schelling, particularly of F. J. Stahl. **Sche·llingist**, a disciple of Schelling.
1865 tr. *D. F. Strauss' New Life Jesus* I. 190 Similar instances may be brought forward from the history of the Schellingian philosophy. 1865 Pater *Appreciations* (1889) 75 Schellingism, the 'Philosophy of Nature', is indeed a constant tradition in the history of thought. 1874 tr. *Ueberweg's Hist. Philos.* II. 114 Kantism, the renewed Spinozism (Schellingism), and Herbartism lay conjoined and undeveloped in the doctrine of Leibnitz. *Ibid.* 226 Friedrich Julius Stahl..protesting against the designation of his philosophy..as 'New Schellingism'. *Ibid.* 231 To the Neo-Schellingian School belongs Wilh. Rosenkrantz. 1895 C. Garnett tr. *Turgenev's On the Eve* iv, My father was a learned man, a Schellingist.

Scheme, *sb.*[1] **7. b.** *Scheme of colour.* Add: Now chiefly = *colour scheme* (in both senses): see *Colour *sb.* 18. Often *ellipt.*
1925 R. W. G. Hingston in E. F. Norton *Fight for Everest, 1924* 265 Certain of the little birds are decidedly conspicuous, and in some cases we see the obvious reason why they do not require a protective scheme. *Ibid.* 267 Its scheme of colour [*sc.* of a locust] was grey and black with delicate transverse bands across its thighs.

Schick (ʃik). The name of Dr. *Schick* of Vienna, used *attrib.* to denote a test to determine the susceptibility of a subject to diphtheria.
1918 Webster Addenda. 1922 *Ashby & Wright's Dis. Children* (ed. 6) 230 The susceptibility to diphtheria can now be recognised by means of the Schick test. 1923 *Daily Mail* 15 Feb. 6 The 'Schick Test' method of preventing diphtheria.

Schistosomiasis (skistosomai·ăsis). *Path.* [f. mod.L. *Schistosoma*, a genus of trematode parasites, f. Gr. σχιστός divided + σῶμα body + -ίασις: see -asis.] The disease caused by *Schistosoma hæmatobium*.
1913 Dorland *Med. Dict.* (ed. 7). 1931 *Times* 10 Mar. 7/5 Malaria, sleeping sickness, kala azar, schistosomiasis.

Schizanthus (skai-, skizæ·nþəs). [mod.L., f. Schizo- + Gr. ἄνθος flower.] A solanaceous plant of the genus so named, a native of Chile.
1829 Loudon *Encycl. Plants* 16. 1915 H. H. Thomas *Bk. Hardy Flowers* 404 Although..better known as a greenhouse plant, the Schizanthus (Natural Order Solanaceae) is also a lovely annual for the garden. 1931 *Daily Tel.* 21 May 17/1 The pansy-flowered schizanthus.

Schlenter (ʃle·ntəɹ), *a.* and *sb.* *S. Afr. colloq.* or *slang.* Also **sh-.** [Du. *slenter* trick.]
a. *adj.* Of doubtful value, not genuine, untrustworthy, make-believe. **b.** *sb.* A counterfeit; *spec.* in *sing.*, imitation gold; in *pl.*, imitation diamonds.
1891 C'tesse de Brémont *Gent. Digger* viii, 'Of course,' whispers the seller who had pushed his way to the side of the buyer, 'this sale was only shlenter.' 1898 *Cape Argus* (weekly ed.) 16 Mar. 35 (Pettman) A small sack containing bars of gold or schlenter. 1899 G. Griffith *Knaves Diam.* ii. 35 Good Lord, man, can't you see they're all schlenters? 1925 *Chambers's Jrnl.* 239/2 All the police found in the trunk was *schlenter* (that is, counterfeit).

Schlich (ʃlixʸ). *Metallurgy.* [G.] = Slick *sb.*[2]
1677 slich [see Slick *sb.*[2]]. 1756–7 tr. *Keysler's Trav.* (1760) IV. 148 The ore is mixed with an equal quantity of quicklime, and this mixture, which is called *schlich*, is put into iron retorts. 1839 Ure *Dict. Arts* 814 Water..is made to flow with greater or less velocity and abundance over the schlich or pasty mud spread on a table of various inclination. 1855 Leifchild *Cornwall* 207 Should the product (called schlich) seem tolerably rich, the operative turns the table round its axis.

Schmelz (ʃme·lts). Also erron. **schmel(t)ze.** [G. *schmelz* enamel.] Any one of several varieties of decorative glass, *spec.* a variety coloured red with a metallic salt, used to flash white glass.
1851–4 *Cycl. Useful Arts* (ed. Tomlinson 1867) I. 784/1 Smetz [*read* Smelz] glass is formed by fusing lengths of coloured glass into each other, so that the section shall resemble carnelian and the agates. 1859 R. Hunt *Guide Mus. Pract. Geol.* (ed. 2) 111 The Bohemian ruby is thus prepared:—a preparation called schmelze is made; it is composed of silica 500, minium 800, nitre 100, calcined potash 100. 1866 *Christie's Sale Catal. Marryat Coll.* 65 A small vase, of variegated Schmeltze. 1879 *Encycl. Brit.* X. 652/1 That peculiar kind of glass usually called schmelz, an imperfect imitation of calcedony, was also made at Venice in the 15th century. 1882 *Hamilton Sale Catal.* No. 846 A Fluted Tumbler, of red and white schmelz.

Schnauzer (ʃnou·tsər). [G.] A dog of a German breed so named.
1930 *Observer* 9 Feb. 13/2 The German Schnauzers have sterling qualities, though they may not be particularly showy in their close wiry coats. 1931 *Woman's Jrnl.* Sept. 23/2 Notably good as house dogs, are the Keeshond, the Schnauzer,..and the Dandy Dinmont terriers.

Schnitzel (ʃni·tsəl). [G., = shaving, paring, cutlet.] A veal cutlet, *esp.* in *Wiener* (vī·nər) *schnitzel*, one garnished with lemon, capers, and sardines in the Vienna style.
1913 Pettman *Africanderisms* s.v. *Sassatjes*, They are quite as toothsome as a 'Wiener schnitzel'. 1926 E. Phillips Oppenheim *Golden Beast* i. x, My cook knows the sort of things you like—schnitzel and veal [*sic*], eh?

Schol. Colloq. abbreviation of Scholarship.
1899 *Captain* Nov. 115/2 Wardour had licked Eccles and forfeited the 'schol'.

Scholasticized (skǒlæ·stisaizd), *ppl. a.* [f. as Scholasticizing *ppl. a.*: see -ed [1].] Imbued with or influenced by scholasticism.
1923 C. Singer in *Edin. Rev.* Jan. 101 Dioscorides, the drug-monger, appealed to scholasticised minds for centuries. 1927 W. R. Inge *Protestantism* 12 This philosophy, already scholasticised by Proclus.

School, *sb.*[1] Add:
5. c. From the sense of 'body or set of persons following a particular doctrine or practice', in such expressions as *school of thought*, the word has acquired the sense of 'type or brand' of doctrine or practice (cf. branch III in Dict.).
Cf. *school of opinion* in 5, quot. 1864.
1892 *New Review* May 571 He is a 'gentleman and scholar',..'trained in a liberal school of thought'. 1909 A. Berget *Conquest of Air* ii. v. 230 We are confronted by two schools of aviating apparatus: the American school.. which demands everything of the aviator, and the French school..which requires..the minimum from the pilot. 1916 *Q. Rev.* Apr. 297 Systems of metaphysics of more than one type, and drawing their inspiration from more than one school. 1919 M. K. Bradby *Psycho-analysis* 223 It is..a point of view derived from the leaders of their own school of thought. 1925 N. E. Odell in E. F. Norton *Fight for Everest, 1924* 329 The results of the Second Expedition to Mount Everest in 1922 went to show that two schools of thought prevailed from the experiences of the high-climbing parties. 1927 *Public Opinion* 28 Feb. 179/1 There is in philosophy a school of thought christened by Professor William James with the name Pragmatism.

7. Also *U.S.*, a college or university.
1767 P. V. Fithian *Jrnl. & Lett.* (1900) 1 A letter to my Father, begging him to put me to School. 1904 *Delineator* Oct. 657 College pillows..of crimson, with 'Harvard' in white letters; of orange, with 'Princeton' in black, and similarly with the names and colours of other schools.

19. school-inspector, an inspector who examines and reports on the condition of schools and the teaching therein; hence **school-inspectorship**; **school-leaver**, a boy or girl who leaves school after having reached a certain age; **school-method**, the method which an intending teacher has to study; the method used in teaching; also *attrib.*; **school work**, (*a*) work done in, or under the direction of, a school; (*b*) the work of a particular school of painting, etc.
1838 F. B. Hawkins *Germany* xii. 201 A board of education which employs school-inspectors. 1883 *Edin. Rev.* LVII. 515 There is..at the principal place of the circle (*Kreis*) another inspector, whose sphere comprehends all the schools of the circle. He has the title of School-Inspector of the Circle. (Kreis-Schul-Inspector.) 1920 *Sat. Rev.* 23 Oct. 330 No Government School inspectors or systems of examination can compete with a method of..selection so infallible. 1911 H. Walpole *Mr. Perrin & Mr. Traill* iii. 47 He saw himself at Eton or Harrow, or a *school-inspectorship. 1925 *Contemp. Rev.* May 634 The problem of the unemployed '*school-leaver' complicates in many ways the problem of the boy at work. 1927 Carr-Saunders & Jones *Soc. Struct. Eng. & Wales* p. xv, We are led to ask..what kind of openings are available to school leavers. 1897 *Pract. Teacher* XVIII. 171/1 *School Method and the Education Department. 1917 J. D. Beresford & K. Richmond *W. E. Ford* ix. 194 A description of a typical staff-meeting discussion of school method. 1927 J. Adams *Errors in School* 35 School-method books. 1857 *school work [see 16 a in Dict.]. 1889 *Sonnenschein's Cycl. Educ.* (ed. 2) 407/1 Girls..have fewer games..than boys, and for this reason are much more apt to suffer in consequence of school-work. 1913 *Rep. Brit. Assoc.* 296 Proper and improper use of the eyes in school-work. 1923 G. Sturt *Wheelwright's Shop* iii. 12 Finishing my school work with the first term of 1884.

School-book. 1. (Earlier U.S. examples.)
1745 Franklin *Let. to W. Strahan* Wks. 1905 II. 296 So at present I only send for a few school books, and books of navigation. 1766 in G. E. Littlefield *Early Schools* (1904) 104 A catalogue of the school books now in general use.

School district. *U.S.* (See quot. 1903.)
1831 Peck *Guide for Emigrants* 245 A law was passed.. authorizing the people to form school districts. 1846 *Ind. Hist. Soc. Publ.* III. 417 It would call out thousands to the school district meetings, who have never attended one. 1878 J. H. Beadle *Western Wilds* i. 19 The citizens have the right to organize a school district as they will. 1903 A. B. Hart *Actual Govt.* 542 The smallest unit of school administration is the school district, which in many States has its own board, raises its own taxes, and appoints its own teachers.

School-keeping. (Earlier Amer. examples.)
1651 *Dedham* (Mass.) *Rec.* 191 The time of couenant in ye schoole keepeing being expired. 1827 A. Sherwood *Gazetteer Georgia* (1837) 267 Why is it that school-keeping is so disreputable an employment in our State? 1842 *Knickerbocker Mag.* XIX. 308 Considerations which give quite a new coloring to the employment of school-keeping.

School-land(s). *U.S.* Land set apart for the maintenance of a school. Also *attrib.*
1695 *Braintree Rec.* 30 The Towns lands and medows comonly caled the scool lands. 1775 in *Coll. New Hampsh. Hist. Soc.* IX. 89, I might..lay out for the clearing the School Lands to the amount of £500 Sterl^g. 1837 W. Jenkins *Ohio Gaz.* Introd. p. x, Laws were passed for leasing the school lands and salt reservations. 1885 *Rep. Indian Affairs* 147 Others claim they have purchased their lands from the State of Nevada under the school-land grant.

School-ma'am, -marm. *U.S.* (Earlier example of *-marm*.)
1872 *Trans. Dept. Agric. Illinois* 275 Their thoughtful, stiff, precise, school-marm mode of utterance always seems to say to you: 'I am a pedant'.

Schoolmistress. Add: **2.** *Comb.*: **schoolmistress fish**, a kind of fish of the West Indies (cf. Schoolmaster *sb.*[1] 2).
1929 R. Hughes *High Wind in Jamaica* 22 The black and yellow schoolmistress-fish.

Schopenhauer (ʃǫ·pənhauəɹ). The name of the German pessimistic philosopher, Arthur *Schopenhauer* (1788–1860), used allusively for a pessimist. Hence **Scho·penhau·erian** *a.*, characterized by Schopenhauerism, following the doctrines of Schopenhauer; *sb.*, a follower of Schopenhauer or his system of philosophy; **Scho·penhauerism**, **Scho·penhauereanism**, the pessimistic philosophy taught by Schopenhauer, according to which all existence is essentially evil, and release (through reason) from the tyranny of the radically evil will can be attained only by overcoming the insatiable lust for existence, e.g. in the possibilities of contemplation afforded by science and art.
1881 W. S. Lilly in *19th Cent.* 713 Schopenhauerism..is little more than Buddhism vulgarized. 1882 *Athenæum* 18 Nov. 659/2 A heroine whose life is unconscious Schopenhauerism. 1906 *Daily Chron.* 26 Sept. 4/4 You would say at one glance that he is a pessimistic ass, a Schopenhauer of donkeys. 1908 *Edin. Rev.* Apr. 423 He is a Schopenhauerian. 1928 Joad *Diogenes, or Future of Leisure* 96 We shall all be living Schopenhauerian lives.

Schottische. (Earlier U.S. example.)
1855 J. E. Cooke *Ellie* 151 This abominable German usage we have imported—the polka and the schottish too.

Schraufite (ʃrau·fait). *Min.* [ad. G. *schraufit* (1875), f. the name of A. *Schrauf*, Austrian mineralogist: see -ite [1].] A fossil resin of a blood-red colour, found in schistose sandstone.
1896 Chester *Dict. Min.*

Schreiner (ʃrai·nəɹ). The name of Ludwig *Schreiner*, used *attrib.* to denote a method (patented 1895) of finishing mercerized fabrics by passing between rollers engraved with a network of very fine lines; also the high lustre imparted by this method. Hence **Schrei·nered** *ppl. a.*, finished in this way. **Schrei·nering, Schrei·nerizing**, the method of finishing cloth in this way.
1904 *Dyer & Calico Printer* XXIV. 9 The Schreiner finish is daily growing in importance. 1905 Bean & McCleary *Chem. Finishing* 375 When the 'schreinering' process is combined with 'mercerising', it gives the nearest approach

Supplement, p. 3873; Corrigenda, p. 4092; Spurious words, p. 4093; Books quoted, p. 4094

to silk ever obtained. *Ibid.* 376 Plain woven calico goods may also be 'schreinered' with advantage. 1906 *Dyer & Calico Printer* XXVI. 17 Schreiner cylinder engraving. 1907 *Cotton Finishing* vii. 67 Certain effects such as schreinerizing..are produced by calenders of special form. 1910 A. F. Barker *Textiles* ix. 225 Schreinering. 1929 E. Midgley *Finishing of Woven Fabrics* xii. 152 The lustre possessed by mercerized cotton goods is greatly enhanced by the schreiner finish. *Ibid.*, Schreinered Venetian.

Schrötterite (ʃrö·tərait). *Min.* Also **schroetterite.** [ad. G. *schrötterit* (1839), f. the name of A. *Schrötter*: see -ITE[1].] A pale green hydrous silicate of aluminium, related to allophane.
1855 *Orr's Circle Sci., Inorg. Nat.* 516 Schrotterite. 1868 Dana *Min.* (ed. 5) 421.

Schubertian (ʃubɜ̄·rtiăn), *a.* [f. the name of Franz Peter *Schubert* (1797–1828), Austrian composer + -IAN.] Of, pertaining to, or characteristic of Schubert.
1927 *Observer* 2 Oct. 14 A truly Schubertian progression. 1928 *Daily Tel.* 27 Mar. 6 Their interpretation..had the Schubertian qualities of spontaneity and finish.

Schuchardtite (ʃū·χaɹtait). *Min.* [ad. G. *schuchardtit* (1882), f. the name of Th. *Schuchardt*, mineral dealer: see -ITE[1].] (See quot. 1896.)
1896 Chester *Dict. Min.*, *Schuchardtite*,..the so-called Chrysopraserde of Silesia. 1924 *Brit. Mus. Return* 225.

Schungite (ʃu·ŋəit). *Min.* [ad. G. *schungit* (1886), f. *Shunga*, Russia, its locality: see -ITE[1].] An amorphous form of carbon intermediate between graphite and anthracite.
1896 Chester *Dict. Min.*

Schwabacher (ʃvā·bāχər). *Typog.* [Ger., f. *Schwabach*, name of a town in Franconia.] A German fount used for printing in the vernacular.
[1910 *Encycl. Brit.* VII. 723/2 For these scanty writings the German so-called 'Schwabach' characters were used.] 1922 Updike *Printing Types* I. 62 The smaller type of the Indulgences, which is a rounder black-letter, has certain peculiarities later found in 'schwabacher' fonts. 1926 Morison *Type Designs* 11 (Gutenberg's) informal type is ..interesting..mainly as the ancestor of the *fraktur* and *schwabacher* later employed for vernacular and less important uses.

Schwärmerei (ʃvɛ̄·rmərai). [G., f. *schwärmen* to rave (Swarm *v.*[1]).] Extravagant enthusiasm; *esp.* schoolgirl attachment to another female.
1886 *Athenæum* 3 Apr. 451/3 A few hours' *schwärmerei* over what Joan [of Arc] must have felt under certain circumstances. 1927 F. B. Young *Portrait of Clare* I. vi. 63 The expression of liberty and exultant youth that her mother's mid-Victorian fantasias and Miss Boldmere's *Schwärmerei* denied her. 1927 Naomi Royde-Smith *J. Fanning's Legacy* xxix, All her old 'schwärmerei' for Paula Ochs revived. 1930 E. Scott *Forgotten Image* xiii, Her idiotic, schoolgirlish *schwärmerei* attachment.

Science. Add: **5. d.** = *Christian Science.
1915 E. B. Holt *Freudian Wish* 21 The 'Science' healer was immediately consulted.

Scilli- (si·li), combining form of Scilla b, used in the names of certain glucosides obtained therefrom, as **Scillipi·crin** [Gr. πικρός bitter], used as a diuretic; **Scillito·xin**, a cardiac poison similar in its action to digitalis.
1883 Martindale *Extra Pharmacop.* 239. *Ibid.* 240 Scillitoxin. Syn.—Scillain..A principle from *Scilla maritima*—the squill bulb. 1887 *Encycl. Brit.* XXII. 437/1 The activity of the drug appears to be due to the active principles, scillipicrin, scillitoxin, and scillin, which were first obtained by Merck in 1878.

Scintillantly (si·ntilăntli), *adv.* [-LY[2].] In a scintillating manner.
1900 H. Harland *Cardinal's Snuff-box* xix, The..buildings stood out..: the white marble, palely, scintillantly amethystine. 1928 A. L. Fleming *Dwellers in Arctic Nt.* 151 Flashes of light from the Aurora Borealis move scintillantly in the sky.

Scintillating, *ppl. a.* Add: *Scintillating scotoma* (Path.): the optical symptoms in teichopsia. *Scintillating screen* (see quot.).
1889 *Jrnl. Ophth., Otol. & Laryngol.* I. 326 Scintillating scotomata; a personal experience. 1905 *Jrnl. Amer. Med. Assoc.* XLIV. 1262 The scintillating scotoma or transient functional hemianopia. 1931 C. G. Darwin *New Concept. Matter* iv. 79 A scintillating screen is made by lightly powdering a sheet of glass with zinc sulphide crystals... When such a screen is exposed to a stream of electrons, scintillations appear irregularly all over it.

Scintillatingly (si·ntileitiŋli), *adv.* [-LY[2].] In a scintillating manner; sparklingly.
1927 *Sunday Express* 6 Feb. 4 A scintillatingly funny burlesque.

Sciot (sai·ǫt), *a.* and *sb.* Also **-ote.** [f. It. *Scio* Scio[2], a. Gr. Χίος Chios + -OT[2].] **a.** *adj.* Of or pertaining to Scio, the ancient Chios, an island of the Ægean Sea, or to its inhabitants. **b.** *sb.* A native or inhabitant of Scio. Hence **Scio·tic** *a.*
1860 Schoolcraft *Archives Aborig. Knowl.* IV. 127 The small Sciotic mounds of sacrifice. 1866 *Chambers's Encycl.* VIII. 549/1 A number of the Sciotes having, in 1822, joined the Samians,..the inhabitants..were indiscriminately massacred. ..Subsequently..many of the Sciote families returned.

Scissors. Add:
2. b. *Rugby Football.* (See quots.)
c 1915 R. A. Lloyd in E. B. Poulton *Life R. P.* (1919) 218 The 'Scissors' trick was this: when I had the ball, and Ronald was running beside me just as if he was going to take an ordinary pass, he would suddenly change his direction and come racing straight across at me and practically take the ball out of my hands, and breaking clean through would run right across to the opposite wing. 1927 Wakefield & Marshall *Rugger* 229 The two [sc. a centre and wing three-quarter] may also combine when the centre still has the ball, when, for example, they exploit the scissors movement...This movement takes place when there is a large gap between the opposing centre and wing. The attacking centre, seeing this, dashes in the direction shown and shouts a code word, so that his wing goes all out for the gap, taking the ball as the centre crosses his path. *Ibid.* 230 This scissors, and dummy scissors, attack may be tried also by two centres or by a centre and stand-off half.

c. *Swimming.* An alternate movement of the legs from the hips in parallel planes, in which knees and ankles are kept more or less straight, and the legs approach each other rapidly and are parted slowly.

5. scissor-bill, (*b*) *slang* (see quot.); **scissor cut** (see quots.); **scissors jump** (see quot.); **scissor-leg,** a deformity in which the legs are crossed.
1931 B. Starke *Touch & Go* xvi. 259 Dick praised me for not saying anything. 'You're not a *scissor-bill'. A scissor-bill was a woman who gossiped and nagged and was bad generally. 1931 *Times Lit. Suppl.* 25 June, Suppl. p. iii/2, While his many brilliant students have perhaps done more service to the book-jacket than to the page by some of their shadow, *scissor-cut and engraved letter-forms. *Ibid* iv/2, Professor D. P. Sterenberg portrays objects of daily life in flat lithographs that resemble scissor-cuts. 1897 *Encycl. Sport* I. 50/2 The methods of jumping are various, but two main types predominate—viz., the straight jump, and the side-way or *scissors jump. 1901 Dorland *Med. Dict.* (ed. 2), *Scissor-leg.

Sclaff (sklæf), *sb. Golf.* [See the vb.] A stroke in which the club scrapes the ground before hitting the ball. Hence **Scla·ffy** *a.*
1893 H. Hutchinson *Golfing* (ed. 2) 82 'Tops', and 'sclaffs' and misses. 1896 W. Park Jr. *Game of Golf* 91 The sight of bare earth..gives the impression that contact between it and the club-head, which might happen with a sclaffy shot, would inevitably result in damage to the club. 1903 W. J. Travis *Pract. Golf* 20 If..the head is allowed to move, the chances are that a sclaff or a top will result.

Scleroscope (sklīə·rǒskoup). [f. Sclero- + -scope.] An instrument for measuring the hardness of metals.
1908 *Patent Specif.* No. 10,752 An instrument [consisting of a hard pointed hammer allowed to fall from a predetermined height and means for measuring the rebound of the hammer] for testing the hardness of metals and other solid bodies..called the scleroscope. 1921 *Glasgow Herald* 23 Sept. 9 The use of the scleroscope on light specimens of metals. 1923 *Ibid.* 9 Mar. 7/1 A New Form of Magnified Hammer in the Scleroscope Hardness Test.

Scoff, *sb.*[2] Add: Also in English slang or colloq. use.
1899 Flynt *Tramping* II. iii. 234 Moochers were satisfied when they could beg a 'bob'..a day besides 'scoff'. 1928 *Daily Express* 14 May 10/6 While you've had me locked up, I've eaten your scoff!

Scoop, *sb.*[1] **7.** Add: **scoop-bonnet,** a woman's bonnet shaped like a scoop.
1897 J. L. Allen *Choir Invisible* I. 3 On her head she wore an enormous white scoop-bonnet.

Scoop, *sb.*[2] Add: **1.** Also, a quantity scooped up.
1829–32 J. P. Kennedy *Swallow Barn* I. iii. 34 Nine scoops of water in the hollow of the hand, from a sycamore spring.., will break an ague.

b. In singing (see quot.). *colloq.*
1911 W. K. Smith *Training Village Choirs* 8 The scoop is made on the commencing note of a tune or phrase. It consists in attacking it by way of a chromatic slide from the 'fourth' below.

Scoop, *v.*[1] Add: **5. a.** (Earlier examples.)
1850 W. Colton *Three Years in Calif.* xxxiii. 440 A faith that could scoop up whole tribes of savages,..impressing them with the conviction that submission to the padres was obedience to God. 1867 A. D. Richardson *Beyond Mississippi* xl. 134 'Scooped' was an importation from Wall Street. 'I am badly scooped' meant: 'I am used up' or defeated.

6. *trans.* To propel or take by or as by a scooping movement.
1910 *Blackw. Mag.* Feb. 269/1 A very dark-coloured little man, with his arms and legs cut off, short at the knees and elbows,..scooping himself along on his stumps. 1916 Boyd Cable *Action Front* 257 And he moved as if to scoop the German's head under his arm again.

Scooter. Add: **3.** *U.S.* (Earlier example.)
1854 *Florida Plant. Rec.* 104 Corn plowes 20, cotton shovels 22, Scuters 14.

4. A boat, propelled by sails, capable of being used both on ice and in water. *U.S.*
1903 *N. Y. Times* 13 Dec., The 'scooter'..is built with a bottom and a deck which are duplicates of each other. 1904 *Sci. Amer.* 5 Mar. 201/1 Incredible speed is attained by the larger and more completely equipped scooters. *Ibid.* 201/2 There are..few more interesting sights seen than those afforded by a scooter plunging at full speed from the ice into the water. 1909 *Cent. Dict.* Suppl. s.v. *Ice-scooter*, These scooters may be run alternately through water and over ice.

b. A fast motor-boat, used in the war of 1914–18.
1919 *Times* 21 Feb. 11/2 The war has produced 'P' boats and 'Q' boats and 'U' boats, but the wildest of all wild things is the 'scooter', professionally known as the coastal motor-boat. 1925 E. Fraser & Gibbons *Soldier & Sailor Words.*

5. A child's toy, which consists of a footboard running on two tandem wheels, on which he rests one foot while pushing with the other, and which is guided by means of a long handle; also, a similar machine propelled by a motor.
1917 *Little Folks* Nov. p. vi, The Free-Wheel Auto-Scooter propelled by Pedal. 1919 *Times* 21 Feb. 11/2 The 'scooter' we knew before the war was a new terror to the pavement. 1919 C. Orr *Glorious Thing* xix. 237 A brightly painted scooter. 1930 *Punch* 19 Mar. 331/1 A gutter-snipe negotiating Park Lane on his home-made scooter.

Scopol-. Add: **Scopo·leine,** an alkaloidal compound analogous with the tropeines; **Sco·poline,** a crystalline compound, $C_8H_{13}NO_2$, obtained from scopolamine by decomposition.
1901 Dorland *Med. Dict.* (ed. 2), *Scopolein*, a crystalline alkaloid, $C_{17}H_{21}NO_4$, from plants of the genera *Scopolia Duboisia*, and *Atropa*: a strong mydriatic and sedative. 1887 *Brit. Med. Jrnl.* 8 Jan. 62/1 In rheumatic iritis the use of *scopoline was obviously effective in reducing the pain and injection of the globe.

Scorching, *ppl. a.*[1] Add: **c.** quasi-*adv.*, as in *scorching-hot.*
1873 E. Hoorer *Nurseries & School Rooms* 197 The sand so scorching hot that one could not bear one's hand upon it. 1883 *Century Mag.* July 428/1 The sun was scorching hot and the shade chilly.

Score, *sb.* **21.** Add: **score-bid** *Contract Bridge* (see quot.); **score-game,** also in *Lawn Tennis.*
1928 Work *Contract Bridge* 76 Bidding to the Score. The following remarks upon bidding are premised on the assumption that there is no score on the game. For example: If my side has a contract score of 60, I must put a construction on my partner's minor two bid different from the construction put upon such a bid at no score. '*Score-bids' are exceptions to the general rules, but do not justify an original one bid without the prescribed minimum of two quick tricks. 1928 *Observer* 17 June 28/2 Moon only lost one *score game in the whole match.

Score, *v.* **5** *U.S.* (Earlier and later examples.)
1813 Paulding *J. Bull & Br. Jon.* xx. (ed. 2) 107 She.. fell upon Beau Nappery, and scored him at such a rate, that [etc.]. 1930 *Publishers' Weekly* 8 Mar. 1331/2 Smoot's Secret Session Scored.

Scoring, *vbl. sb.* Add: **1. b.** The action of recording the scores made in a game; the action of making a score or adding to the score; the amount of score or number of points made.
1850 'Bat' *Cricketer's Man.* 46 Printed forms for scoring are not procurable. *Ibid.* 47 Their scores..will serve to illustrate the principles of scoring. 1876 Geo. Eliot *Dan. Der.* II. xi, Shall we go now and hear what the scoring says? 1882 *Daily Tel.* 19 May, The scoring..was remarkably fast up to 67. 1896 *Sportsman* 10 July 4/8 Brown..made most of the scoring.

c. *Mus.* (*a*) The action of writing down in score. (*b*) The action of composing or arranging for orchestral performance.
1811 Busby *Dict. Music, Scoring*, the art of forming a score by collecting and properly arranging under each other the several detached parts of any composition. 1897 C. Vincent (*title*) Scoring for an Orchestra. 1903 A. W. Patterson *Schumann* 211 Facsimile of Scoring (From the B flat Symphony).

Scorzonera. b. Add: *scorzonera-fed* adj.; **scorzonera moth,** a moth fed on scorzonera leaves.
1914 *Rep. Brit. Assoc.* 406 Scorzonera-fed parents...The capacity of fertilization..of Scorzonera moths.

Scotch, *a.* and *sb.*[3] **A.** *adj.* **4.** Add: **Scotch (barley) broth,** a soup containing pearl barley and small pieces of vegetables; **Scotch eggs,** hard-boiled eggs cut in halves and surrounded by sausage-meat; **Scotch woodcock** (see Woodcock *sb.* 3 d).
1747 Mrs. Glasse *Cookery* vi. 65 To Make *Scotch Barley Broth. 1834 Hood *Tylney Hall* xv, We shall have an ounce of mutton swimming in a tureen of barley-water—I've heard of their Scotch broths. 1851 *Family Friend* IV. 338/1 Scotch Broth. Take four pounds of mutton [etc.]. 1877 *Cassell's Dict. Cookery* 842/2 Scotch Broth. c 1827 *Domestic Cookery* ix. 319 *Scotch Eggs.

Scotland Yard (skǫ·tlănd yā·ɹd). The name of the head-quarters of the metropolitan police, formerly situated in Great Scotland Yard, a short street off Whitehall, London, and in 1890 removed to New Scotland Yard on the Thames Embankment: used allusively to designate the detective department of the metropolitan police force. Also *attrib.*
1864 Miss Braddon *Henry Dunbar* xxxi, I have called again upon the Scotland-Yard people, and I gave them a minute description of the scene. *Ibid.* xxxvii, Detective officer Henry Carter, of Scotland Yard. 1881 *Punch* 9 July 6/2 As in all great crimes, they [sc. criminals] are too much for Scotland Yard and the Seldom-at-Home Secretary. 1885 *Encycl. Brit.* XIX. 338/2 This office [in Westminster], established in a room with a table and two chairs, in an outlet from Whitehall, is the origin..of the far-famed 'Scotland Yard'. 1888 (*title*) Scotland Yard Detective Series. 1906 D. C. Murray *Brangwyn Myst.* xxvi, He laid before the authorities at Scotland Yard the statement that he would never have revealed the real criminal if he had not himself been exposed to the risk of an ignominious ..death. 1926 E. Wallace *Ringer* i, Nobody knows, but Scotland Yard and—Henry Arthur Milton. 1927 P. Haworth (*title*) Before Scotland Yard. Classic tales of roguery and detection collected.

Scotometer (skotǫ·mǐtəɹ). [f. Scoto(ma + -meter.] An instrument for diagnosing and measuring scotomata.
1890 *Brit. Med. Jrnl.* 27 Sept. 741/1 Those who frequently meet with cases of toxic amblyopia..must have found the small coloured squares used in detecting scotomata both an inadequate and inconvenient test...To obviate these disadvantages, I [sc. G. Ferdinands] have had made for me a little instrument..which I propose to call a scotommeter. 1902 *Lancet* 12 July 83/2 A New Scotometer. Messrs. Weiss and Son, Limited, have made for me a little instrument which.. I have found very useful for the purpose of rapid determination of the condition of central colour disturbance common in toxic amblyopia. 1932 *Optician* LXXXIII. 397/1 I did not take the fields for white, relying on the evidence of the scotometer.

Scour, *sb.*[2] **5.** Add: Also *U.S.* in plural.
1847 *Rep. U.S. Comm. Patents* (1848) 507 They say the disease called the 'scours' is the principal one to which sheep are liable. 1863 D. G. Mitchell *My Farm* 223 His calves will very likely take the 'scours'. 1882 *Rep. Maine Board Agric.* XXVI. 25 Indigestion and scours, diseases which are very common among young calves.

Scour, *v.*[2] Add: **1.** With *up*: To give a polish to by scouring. *U.S.*
1833 Seba Smith *Life & Writ. Major Jack Downing* (1835) 190 He put on his regimentals and scoured up the old piece of a scythe that he used to have for a sword. 1870 Julie P. Smith *Widow Goldsmith's Dau.* vii, Being called back to scour up the pot-hooks, polish the crane, [etc.].

g. *intr.* To work without the soil adhering and thus become clean and bright by rubbing or friction, *spec.* of agricultural implements.
a 1909 *Amer. Encycl. Agric.* 742 (Cent. D. Suppl.) In the average soil there [sc. Eastern U.S.] the cast-iron plow would scour perfectly.

h. *trans.* To clean (metal) in tin-plate making or electroplating. (Cf. *Scouring *vbl. sb.*[2] 2 c.)
1888 *Lockwood's Dict. Mech. Engin.* s.v. *Scouring*, Plates of sheet iron used in the tinplate manufacture are scoured with sand and water to cleanse them, after preliminary immersion in dilute sulphuric acid. 1921 *Dict. Occup. Terms* (1927) § 250 *Scourer*; cleans or scours, by dipping in acid baths and rubbing with tow, sheet metal articles in preparation for enamelling or japanning.

6. b. Also with *out.*
1887 T. N. Page *In Ole Virginia* 163 The river..scoured out a new bed for itself.

11. f. To clean (wheat) from dust, etc., before milling. (Cf. *Scouring *vbl. sb.*[2] 2 b.)

12. To scrape (leather) in order to remove the flesh or the bloom.
1860 *Ure's Dict. Arts* (ed. 5) II. 687 In this apartment also is placed a large, flat, slate stone, called a scouring-stone, or, more consistently, the stone on which the leather is scoured. *Ibid.* 689 In respectable manufactories, it is usual first to scour on the flesh. 1882 *Encycl. Brit.* XIV. 387/2 These [sc. brushes and pieces of slate or thin stone], with a small jet of water, scour and brush the entire surface of the leather lying on the platform, effectually scouring out bloom and all soluble impurities.

Scouring, *vbl. sb.*[2] Add: **2. b.** The action of rubbing or brushing wheat in order to remove dust and other impurities; also, in *pl.*, the residue left after scouring.
1884 Knight *Dict. Mech.* Suppl. s.v. *Brushing Machine*, In the Becker brush the concave jacket is of punched iron and steel wire, between which and the brush the wheat passes, polishing and scouring and taking the dust out of the crease. *Ibid.*, *Scouring*, a process in which grain is rubbed and brushed to remove smut, dust, mildew, etc.

c. The cleaning of metal in tin-plate making or electroplating.
1888 [see *Scour *v.*[1] 2 h]. 1904 *Technol. & Sci. Dict.* (ed. Goodchild & Tweney), *Scouring*, cleaning by rubbing with sand and water or dilute acid; used in tin plate manufacture.

8. b. The method or process of treating hides by rubbing or brushing in order to remove the flesh or the bloom.
1860 *Ure's Dict. Arts* (ed. 5) II. 687 This stone..forms a table..so constructed, that the water, which is freely used in scouring, may drain off on the opposite side from that on which the workman is engaged. 1884 Knight *Dict. Mech.* Suppl. s.v., Scouring on the flesh...Scouring on the grain.

9. scouring-ball, a ball composed of cleansing materials for removing stains, grease, etc., from cloth; **scouring barrel, drum,** a barrel or cylinder in which castings, etc., are cleaned by friction against each other; **scouring brick,** a Bath brick (see quot.); **scouring-brush, -house** (*b*), **machine** (*b*), **stone** (*b*), **-table,** apparatus, etc. used in the scouring of leather.
1858 Simmonds *Dict. Trade, Bath Brick*, a *scouring brick of calcareous earth, used in cleaning knives, and for polishing purposes. 1860 *Ure's Dict. Arts* (ed. 5) II. 690 In harness leather..the pumice-stone is seldom used, the stock-stone and *scouring-brush being lustily applied until the bloom is sufficiently removed. 1888 *Lockwood's Dict. Mech. Engin.*, Scouring Drum. 1860 *Ure's Dict. Arts* (ed. 5) II. 686 The place or apartment thus used, is called the *scouring-house. *Ibid.* 687 The floor above the scouring-house..is what is specially designated the shop. 1882 *Encycl. Brit.* XIV. 387/2 Another machine now largely used by curriers is the *scouring machine. 1860 *Ure's Dict. Arts* (ed. 5) II. 689 The skin is taken out of the water, and laid on the *scouring-stone. 1884 Knight *Dict. Mech.* Suppl. s.v. *Scouring*, On being taken out of the water the skins are spread out and set on the *scouring table by passing a steel slicker over the flesh side.

Scouring, *ppl. a.* Add: **2.** (Later example.)
1858 C. L. Flint *Milch Cows* 288 Dysentery, or scouring rot.

4. Used for cleaning cultivated land.
1861 *Trans. Ill. Agric. Soc.* IV. 204 It is..plowed four times in its cultivation with shovel plows..the two last times with scouring plows.

Scout, *sb.*[4] Add: **2. d.** An official of the Automobile Association or the Royal Automobile Club employed to assist motorists on the road.
1909 *Q. Rev.* Jan. 143 The scouts have, beyond doubt, done a great deal to check reckless driving.

e. One of a small number of bees which go out in advance of a swarm to find a place for the swarm to establish itself.
1835 *Penny Cycl.* IV. 153/1 It is said that bees send out scouts before leaving the hive, to search for a convenient situation for their new abode. 1909 S. L. Bensusan *Children's Story of Bee* vii. 108 The scouts..might have been seen following their aërial roads to where the swarm was stationed. *Ibid.* 110 The last of the old queen's scouts had come bringing news of a hive—clean, sweet-scented and empty—in a garden across the valley.

f. A fellow, person. *slang.*
1922 J. A. Dunn *Man Trap* ix, She isn't such a bad old scout, after all. *Ibid.* xii, You didn't tell me your name, old scout. 1930 P. Macdonald *Link* vii. 113 That poor scout they've jailed.

3. (Later U.S. examples.)
1798 I. Allen *Hist. Vermont* 92 He sent a scout of about 300, mostly Indians. 1867 J. N. Edwards *Shelby*, etc. xxiii. 412 At Current River a scout of fifty were encountered.

5. Also, an airship or aeroplane so used; *spec.* a small, single-seated machine of very great speed, often called *speed-scout.* Also *attrib.*
1909 A. Berget *Conquest of Air* II. vii. 260 Airships or aeroplanes? As 'combatants' or 'scouts'? 1911 *Chambers's Jrnl.* July 461/1 Two diminutive dirigibles acting as scouts. 1914 *Daily Express* 31 Dec. 3/4 We have 'scouts' which can beat anything the enemy can bring against us. 1916 H. Barber *Aeroplane Speaks* Pl. 21, The little Gnome-engined scout biplanes. 1922 *Encycl. Brit.* XXX. 87/2 Torpedoing ships at anchor, by seaplanes, probably in pairs or escorted by 'scout' (*i.e.* air fighting) machines.

8. *scout-craft* (later examples).
1910 *Chambers's Jrnl.* Feb. 114/2 They are taught scout-craft, which includes the art of stalking wild creatures. 1917 *19th Cent.* Feb. 311 This, and much other scout-craft, had he learnt when on active service among the sand dunes of Africa.

Scout-boat. [Scout *sb.*[4]] A boat employed for the purpose of scouting.
1733 *Col. Rec. Georgia* III. 90 The Scout Boat at Port Royal attended the new Settlers as occasion requir'd. 1771 J. Habersham *Lett.* 159 I am to let him have the Scout Boat, in order to make an actual survey. 1837 A. Sherwood *Gaz. Georgia* (ed. 3) 16 The Scout-boat (which is an armed Bark, employed for the same purpose by water). 1902 [see Scout *sb.*[4] 8].

Scouter. (Later U.S. example.)
1867 J. N. Edwards *Shelby*, etc. xiv. 232 One of the truest scouters who ever fired a pistol.

Scouting, *vbl. sb.* **1.** *attrib.* (Earlier and later Amer. examples.)
1757 in *Lett. to Washington* II. 97 The Fireing of the Cannon..was occasion'd by a large Scouting Party leaving that Place to come this Way. 1790 D. Fanning *Narrative* 12 We kept scouting parties through the country, and had many skirmishes. 1880 Cable *Grandissimes* xxxv. 277 A small scouting-party of tears reappeared on the edge of her eyes.

Scow, *v.*[1] (Recent example.)
1929 W. Heyliger *Builder of Dam* 39 From this point I will scow the supplies over to the job.

Scraggly, *a.* (Earlier U.S. example.)
1869 Mrs. Stowe *Oldtown Folks* xlii. 534 That's all we scraggly old people are good for.

Scramble, *v.* Add: **1. d.** *trans.* with preps. To deal with in a hasty or ill-considered manner.
1869 *Punch* 3 July 270/2 One 'Lord Hamilton' who had been scrambling away his money, at a low public in Shadwell. 1911 *Q. Rev.* July 218 Amendments hastily scrambled through committee in a House of Commons. 1931 *Times* 18 Feb. 4 The putter scrambled the ball in from a foot away.

4. *Wireless Telegr.* (See quots.)
1929 *Times* 9 Nov. 12/2 An improved means for ensuring the secrecy of radio-telephonic conversations by 'scrambling' the words of the message—that is, by changing high frequencies to low frequencies and *vice versa*, so that the conversation is completely unintelligible until the 'inverted' conversation has been retranslated. 1930 *Daily Express* 6 Sept. 4/6 A series of mixed or 'scrambled' wave lengths, the key to which would only be in the possession of individual subscribers to the television service.

Scrap, *sb.*[1] Add: **2. a.** *Scrap of paper*: applied contemptuously to a document containing a treaty or pledge which one does not intend to honour: esp. with allusion to the phrase alleged to have been used of the Treaty of London of 1839 by the German Chancellor when Belgian neutrality was violated by Germany in August 1914.
1840 *Chambers's Jrnl.* 11 Apr. 94/1 He no more dreamt of ..honouring his scraps of paper..that of paying the national debt. 1914 Sir E. Goschen *Let.* 8 Aug. in *Coll. Diplomatic Documents* (1915) 111 The Chancellor said that..just for a word—'neutrality',—just for a scrap of paper Great Britain was going to make war on a kindred nation. 1919 *Daily Mail Year Bk.* 62 Those familiar with the 'scrap of paper' theory need hardly be told that the pledges given by the German Emperor..were not observed. 1932 K. Campbell *Sarah, Duchess of Marlb.* 83 James made it plainer every day..that, compared with his Church, the constitution of England and his own coronation oaths were mere scraps of paper.

d. *A scrap of a*: a small or diminutive.
1898 H. James *Two Magics, Turn of Screw* vii, 'Perhaps she likes it!' 'Likes *such* things—a scrap of an infant!' 1928 Oppenheim *Chron. Melhampton* v. 146, I wasn't here for long, and I was a scrap of a fellow those days.

3. c. *collect. sing.* A commercial name for the crude rubber allowed to dry on the bark of the trees and then peeled off. Often in *pl.*
1880 *Encycl. Brit.* XII. 837/1 The milk..is allowed to remain on the tree for several days, until it becomes dry and solid, when it is pulled off in strings, which are either rolled up into balls or put into bags in loose masses, in which form it enters commerce under the name of Ceara 'scrap'. *Ibid.* 838/2 Small 'negroheads' or 'balls' of scrap.

6. scrap-ground, a place where old motor vehicles are scrapped; **scrap man,** a man who removes such parts of old cars as are usable; **scrap paper,** paper for repulping, etc.
1927 *Observer* 21 Aug. 19/2 Six years is about the maximum age of the cars taken for scrapping in America. Some reach the *scrap-ground much earlier. *Ibid.*, The *scrap man's interest in these vehicles is purely that of a replacement part merchant. 1885 *Encycl. Brit.* XVIII. 228/2 The materials for the commoner classes of work are old waste and *scrap paper, repulped...For very delicate relief ornaments, a pulp of scrap paper is prepared.

Scrap, *sb.*[2] Add:
2. b. A row, quarrel, squabble, heated discussion.
1889 Barrère & Leland *Dict. Slang* s.v., Having a *scrap up* is having a quarrel, a row. 1903 *New York Tribune* 6 Sept., In directing the proceedings Mr. Hill was careful to sidetrack anything containing the germ of a scrap. 1928 Galsworthy *Swan Song* II. xi. 199 It was his impression that they'd been having a scrap.

Scrap, *v.*[2] Add: **c.** *intr.* To quarrel, squabble, engage in heated argument or angry dispute.
1909 *Cent. Dict.* Suppl. 1923 *Daily Mail* 28 June 5 Are you going on scrapping over this garden fence for the rest of your lives?

Scrape, *v.* Add: **2.** (U.S. examples.)
1772 *Carroll Papers* in *Maryland Hist. Mag.* XIV. 150 We want a good season much, most of our tob[acc]o ground being scraped. 1835 Ingraham *South-West* II. 283 The cotton..is thinned out, or as it is called, 'scraped'.

f. *To scrape out*: to clean or empty by scraping.
1894 'R. Andom' *We Three & Troddles* xxi, When you have done with that jam you might let me have the pot to scrape out. 1919 Shackleton *South* xii. 237 As the cook and his 'mate' had the privilege of scraping out the saucepans, there was some anxiety to secure the job. 1925 *Morris Owner's Man.* 14 Thoroughly scrape out and oil cams until they work quite freely.

g. To damage (growing plants, etc.).
1909 *Chambers's Jrnl.* 104/1 The Night Riders..have destroyed buildings in addition to 'scraping' or uprooting fields of young tobacco-plants.

h. To draw (one's hair) tightly *back* from the forehead.
1926 O. Douglas *Proper Place* xxxi, I couldn't have believed that she had such pretty, soft hair for she wore it scraped back.

9. *To scrape home*: to attain with difficulty the position or result at which one is aiming.
1927 *Observer* 18 Sept. 17/3 Mr. Blythe, who at the last election scraped home in Monaghan. 1928 *Sunday Express* 1 July 20/6 Smith fought out a grim battle with characteristic Scottish grit, but the little Sheffielder just scraped home.

Scratch, *sb.*[1] Add:
6. The sound produced by the friction of the needle in sound-recording apparatus and heard as an unwanted noise during reproduction of the record or film.
1930 *Sel. Gloss. Motion Pict. Techn.* (Acad. Techn. Bureau Hollywood), *Optical scratch*, defect on sound track, occurring as a line parallel to the edges of the film, due to a particle of dust or mechanical imperfection in the slit through which light was sent to the sound track. *Ibid.*, *Shadow scratch*, same as *Optical scratch.* 1931 B. Brown *Talking Pictures* vii. 174 Scratch and surface noise are defects belonging to disc and film methods of reproduction respectively. Scratch is due to the friction of the pick-up needle in the groove of the disc and occurs at the higher frequencies.

11. b. scratch-belt *Talking Pictures*, the belt in a cinema house or theatre where a considerable amount of unwanted noise or scratch is heard; **scratch dial,** a group of marks found on the walls of old churches, usually considered to be an ancient form of sundial; **scratch filter,** a filter to remove unwanted noise during the reproduction of a sound film or record; **scratch-paper,** scribbling paper.
1931 B. Brown *Talking Pictures* vii. 175 Horns of the exponential type give a more or less thin '*scratch belt' as it is called. With normal type of horn setting..scratch is likely to be noticed most at the back of the stalls. This may often be remedied by raising the horns a little, and thus throwing the scratch belt above the heads of the stalls yet below the balcony. 1913 *Proc. Somerset Archaeol. Soc.* 26 The name *scratch-dial has been given to this ancient form of sun-dial. 1927 *N. & Q.* 26 Nov. 393/2 Scratch dials.—Examples will be found outside the tower of either Redbourn or Flamstead Church, and East Shefford. It has been suggested that they are masons' setting-out marks, as they are not in suitable positions for sundials. 1930 *Sel. Gloss. Motion Pict. Techn.* (Acad. Techn. Bureau Hollywood), **Scratch filter*, a choke coil and condenser used to filter out very high frequency sounds or ground noises—usually the needle scratch in wax reproduction. 1931 B. Brown *Talking Pictures* 128 Usually, scratch filters are placed across the two pick-ups. 1899 Tarkington *Gentl. Indiana* xiii. 223 Sheets of blank *scratch-paper lay before them, and they relaxed not their knit brows.

Scratch, *v.* Add: **5. a.** *To scratch for oneself*, to look after oneself or one's own interests. *U.S.*
1850 H. C. Watson *Camp-fires Revol.* 30 Then each one had to scratch for himself. 1856 Alice Cary *Married* 304 Shaking off the other child, [she] told him to scratch for himself a time, while she began to prepare the supper.

c. To move, make off. *U.S.*
1876 'Mark Twain' *Old Times* 49 The moment it splits at the top..I know I've got to scratch to starboard in a hurry. 1887 *Outing* (U.S.) X. May 120/1 As I fired the gun and the horses scratched away from the mark. a 1904 S. E. White *Blazed Trail Stories* i. 5 This little town will scratch for th' tall timber..when the boys goes in to take her apart.

7. c. *U.S. Politics.* (Earlier and later examples.)
1847 *Knickerbocker Mag.* Apr. 382 (Th.) He never scratched the regular ticket. a 1859 *N.Y. Com. Advertiser* (Bartlett) Though all the other candidates upon the ticket were successful, so many had scratched the name of the alderman, that he was defeated by more than fifty votes. 1880 *Scribner's Monthly* Oct. 909/1 They sometimes take the liberty of scratching a name, but they prefer, when the nominations are not too bad, to vote the regular ticket. 1904 *N.Y. Tribune* 8 Nov. 6 Vote the straight Republican ticket, without scratching.

Scratcher. Add: **1. c.** *U.S. Politics.* (Earlier example.)
1880 *Scribner's Monthly* Feb. 621/2 Mr. Evarts will be obliged to look among the 'scratchers,'..for the indorsement of..Civil Service reform.

2. d. *Forestry.* (See quot.)
1905 *Terms Forestry & Logging* 19 *Scratcher*, an instrument used for marking trees.

e. A cider mill in which the apples are torn to pieces instead of being crushed.

f. A day-book. *U.S. colloq.*
1887 *Philad. Ledger* 30 Dec. (Cent. Dict.) He [sc. a bank-teller] would not enter deposits in his scratcher after a certain hour.

Scratchily (skræ·tʃili), *adv.* [-LY[2].] In a scratchy manner; *Sporting*, in an uneven, ragged manner.
1927 *Daily Express* 27 May 13/2 Wethered,..reaching the turn rather scratchily in forty-two, stood one down. *Mod.* This pen writes rather scratchily.

Scratchy, *a.* Add: **4. b.** Inclined to scratch (said of women).
1928 Joan Sutherland *The Knot* xvi. 210 Very well—but you are rather scratchy, and I'm feeling horrible.

Scrawled, *ppl. a.* Add: **2.** *transf.* or *fig.* Sprawling; stretched out in an awkward or ungainly manner.
1895 Mrs. H. Ward *Bessie Costrell* ii. 27 A wide plain travelled into the sunset, its level spaces cut by the scrawled elms and hedgerows of the nearer landscape. 1910 J. Buchan *Prester John* xxi, There..was the body of Henriques, lying scrawled on the sand.

Scream, *sb.* Add:
c. A person or thing that excites mirth or ridicule; a ludicrous occurrence; a person of comical appearance or habits. *slang* or *colloq.*
1915 *Home Chat* 9 Oct. 45/2 'He's married.'..'It's a fact. His bailiff told our chauffeur...Isn't it a scream?' 1918 *War Birds* (1927) 150 We left Hounslow about eleven and our take-off was a scream. 1919 T. K. Holmes *Man fr. Tall Timber* xxiv. 292 That Anabelle Whitman is a perfect scream. 1919 G. W. Deeping *Second Youth* xxv, Ain't it a wicked scream my gettin' all that, and Bill out there in the trenches on a bob or so a day. 1929 R. C. Sherriff *Journey's End* III. ii, Oh, skipper, you *are* a scream—and no mistake!

d. The giving of information or evidence, *spec.* against one's accomplices in crime.
1925 E. Wallace *Melody of Death* vii. 113 'Look here, George,..is it a scream?' 'A scream?' Mr. Wallis was puzzled innocence itself. 'Will you turn King's evidence?' said the other shortly.

e. An angry or excited message.
1929 'Seamark' *Down River* i, 'Smuggling?' queried the surgeon. 'That's the line, sir. Had a scream from Headquarters about it only this morning.'

Scream, *v.* Add: **1. e.** To turn King's evidence; to give evidence against one's accomplices.
1925 E. Wallace *Melody of Death* vii. 114, 'I don't want to hear any more about your conscience,' said the officer wearily. 'Do you scream or don't you?' 'I don't scream,' said Mr. Wallis emphatically.

2. b. *fig.*
1930 'Sapper' *Finger of Fate*, etc. 147 With every nerve in his body screaming for the stuff [sc. whisky].

Screamer. Add: **1. b.** (See quot.)
1896 W. Park *Game of Golf* 269 Screamer, a very long stroke, so called from the whistling noise made by the ball.

Screen, *sb.*[1] Add:
1. f. A flat, vertical, white surface or sheet, usually of canvas, on which may be displayed either shadowgraphs or images thrown by a magic lantern, cinematograph, or television apparatus; *spec.* (in full, *silver screen*) the screen on which moving pictures are projected; *transf.* (usually with definite article), moving pictures collectively; the cinema; the films.
1815 *New Family Receipt-Bk.* (new ed.) xx. 224 To make Transparent Screens for the Exhibition of the Phantasmagoria. 1819–23 [see 6 in Dict.]. 1846 *Penny Cycl.* Suppl. II. 234/2 Magic lantern is a species of lucernal microscope, its object being to obtain an enlarged representation of figures, on a screen in a darkened room, by means of the pencils of light issuing from a lamp or candle and passing through a convex lens. 1876 Tait *Rec. Adv. Phys. Sci.* ix. (ed. 2) 213 Showing the spectrum of light..on the screen. 1882 *Cassell's Family Mag.* Sept. 638/2 The light streaming through projects each figure of the illustrated disc in rapid succession on the screen, and the result is a changing picture which resembles a living moving creature. 1891 *Ibid.* 575/2 Instantaneous photographs..are projected on a screen by the calcium light in such a way as to give the impression of living action. 1897 [see Kinematograph]. 1902 *Encycl. Brit.* XXVII. 95/2 In its perfected form it [sc. the cinematograph] throws the successive images on a screen by means of a lantern so that an entire audience can see them. 1926 R. W. Hutchinson *Wireless* xiii. 255 Television..—the seeing of say a speaker on a screen at the same time as the hearing of him, say on the telephones—is..a much more complicated problem than picture transmission. 1928 E. Wallace *The Double* i, 'What is her name?' 'Mary Dane. ..Mary Dane—sounds like something off the screen, doesn't it?' 1931 B. Brown *Talking Pictures* i. 20 Showing talking pictures demanded skill and a degree of knowledge far in advance of what was adequate for the silent screen. *Ibid.* xii. 302 Stage and screen will have combined.

g. *Cricket.* An erection of canvas or wood placed, behind the bowler, near the boundary of the playing area, to provide a white background and a shield from moving objects behind the bowler's arm.
1895 *Army & Navy Co-op. Soc. Price List* 15 Sept. 1441 Cricket screens for bowlers. 1897 *Encycl. Sport* I. 211/1 Two white screens should be provided, to be set up behind the bowler's arm so as to give the batsman a good sight of the ball.

h. Any thin extended surface set up to intercept shot in gunnery trials.
1879 *Man. Artill. Exerc.* I. 17 The shot passes through two screens placed a certain distance apart...The velocity of the shot at the various screens [is] calculated from a comparison of the screen and time records. 1880 *Encycl. Brit.* XI. 300/1 The shot, after leaving the gun, cuts the wire of the first screen, and subsequently the wire of the second screen.

3. e. A wind-screen of a motor vehicle; also, (*a*) a secondary screen to shield the occupants of the back seat in an open car; (*b*) a screen of celluloid for protecting the sides of an open car.
1904 A. B. F. Young *Complete Motorist* vii. (ed. 2) 176 When a cover is used it should have a removable glass screen in front. 1912 *Motor Man.* iii. (ed. 14) 59 Most cars now have adjustable and detachable glass or celluloid wind-screens as a protection against the weather, dust, etc.; screens can also be made of wire gauze and waterproof material. 1925 *Morris Owner's Man.* p. xi, There are.. rear screens and rear screens.

f. *Meteorol.* A small chamber with louvred sides which admit air while excluding sunshine, etc., in which meteorological instruments are placed.
1895 *Army & Navy Co-op. Soc. Price List* 15 Sept. 1630 Thermometer screens. 1902 *Encycl. Brit.* XXX. 699/1 Various forms of open lattice work and louvre screens have been devised and used by Glaisher..and others, in all of which the wind is supposed to blow freely through the screens, while the latter cut off the greater part of the direct sunshine. 1923 F. Wild *Shackleton's Last Voy.* i. 12 One large screen, containing hair hygrograph, standard thermometer and thermograph.

g. A frame of brush, laths, etc., for the partial shading from light of a seed-bed.
1905 *Terms Forestry & Logging* 19.

6. b. *Wireless.* (*a*) See quots. 1923, 1926. (*b*) See quot. 1932 and *Screened *ppl. a.* 4.
1915 Hawkhead & Dowsett *Handbk. Wireless Telegr.* (ed. 2) 263 Some valves are fitted with an additional screen of copper gauze covering the outside of the glass bulb... This screen protects the valve from heavy spark discharges in the neighbourhood. 1923 E. W. Marchant *Radio Telegr. & Teleph.* iii. 25 If an 'L' type aerial is used, the 'earth screen' wires are arranged a short distance above the ground, immediately underneath the horizontal part of the 'L'. In the screen which has been set up at Carnarvon, sixty-four wires..have been used as the earth. 1926 R. W. Hutchinson *Wireless* ix. 164 Sometimes..they [sc. the wires] are not earthed at all, in which case they form the lower portion of a balanced aerial system (frequently referred to as an aerial screen). 1932 *B.B.C. Year-Bk.* 397 Screened grid valves require a lower voltage on the screen than on the anode, therefore either a separate H.T. battery must be used for the screen, or tappings arranged on the anode battery. *Ibid.* 398 Manufacturers are not all in agreement as to the values of anode voltage and screen voltage.

c. *Photog.* A transparent plate or sheet of glass, ruled with fine lines, used in photographing for half-tone reproduction.
1897 *Knowledge* 1 Nov. 254/1 Immediately in front of the sensitive plate..is placed a glass plate ruled with fine cross-lines, after the fashion of a micrometer grating. This is called the cross-line screen. 1901 *Ibid.* 1 Jan. 7/1 The three negatives are made upon one plate by the simple expedient of replacing the three successive light-filters by a 'screen' ruled with fine lines of transparent stained gelatine in successive rulings of red, green, blue, red, green, blue. 1902 *Encycl. Brit.* XXXII. 15/2 To produce a half-tone block from a picture..a negative is exposed in the camera..with this screen quite close to it..; and the subject is photographed..through the screen.

7. screen grid *Wireless* (see *Grid *sb.* 5); **screen-plate** *Photog.*, a plate in which colour filters are incorporated in the plate itself; **screen-wiper,** a device of metal and rubber attached to the outside of the wind-screen of a motor vehicle, which can be set in motion in order to wipe off moisture which obscures the driver's vision.
1928 G. E. Sterling *Radio Man.* 167 The connection to the *screen grid is made to the regular grid connection on a standard socket. 1930 *Sel. Gloss. Motion Pict. Techn.* (Acad. Techn. Bureau Hollywood), *Screen grid tube*, a modified type of vacuum tube with high amplification. A fourth electrode—the screen grid—is used to reduce the electrostatic effect between grid and plate. 1930 *B.B.C. Year-Bk.* 450/2 *Screen-grid valve*, a four-electrode valve having two grids, and designed to reduce the capacity between the anode and the control grid. 1930 *Manch. Guardian* 20 Sept. 15/7 The 'Osram Music Magnet Four', comprising two screen-grid stages, detector, and low frequency stages. 1911 Webster, *Screen-plate. 1918 *Photo-Miniature* XV. Mar. (Gloss.) *Screen-Plate*..., a plate coated with a minute irregular or regular pattern of color-patches (red, green, and blue-violet), with a coating of emulsion over it. 1928 E. Wallace *The Double* iii, With his *screen-wiper swinging madly, his mackintosh black with driving rain, Dick Staines came to Brighton.

b. In sense 1 f above, as *screen actor, beauty, fever, rights, world*; *screen-struck* [after *stage-struck*] adj.
1915 *Film Fun* Dec. 1 The screen actor has the best of it in holiday season. *Ibid.*, Screen-struck. Everybody wants to get into motion pictures. It is an epidemic of screen fever. 1915 *Film Flashes* 11 Dec. 4 Are we to live only for ourselves, forgetting our brothers and sisters of the screen world? 1919 H. L. Wilson *Ma Pettengill* ii. 38 It is the face of one of our famous screen beauties. *Ibid.* 39 That famous screen star, J. Harold Armytage. 1920 *Q. Rev.* July 185 The feverish haste exhibited at the present time to secure the screen-rights of classics in the world of fiction.

Screen, *v.* Add: **1. c.** *Wireless.* To furnish with a screen (see *Screen *sb.*[1] 6 b).
1913 *Work* XLV. 240/1 The waves are badly 'screened' in one direction. 1932 *B.B.C. Year-Bk.* 422 It will..be advisable to screen the coils L_1, L_2, the tuning condenser K_1, and the secondary circuit, L_3, K_2.

7. *trans.* To show (a picture) on a screen; to project on to a screen as with a magic lantern or cinematograph; to exhibit as a cinematographic production; also *intr.*, to be (well or ill) suited for reproducing on a cinema-screen.
1915 *Durham County Advert.* 18 June 8/7 'Tommy Atkins', a stirring patriotic picture, which will be screened at an early date. 1915 *Film Flashes* 13 Nov. 3 'Stingaree' to be screened. 1919 H. L. Wilson *Ma Pettengill* ii. 67 She'll screen well, and she's one of the few that can turn on the tears when she wants to.

Screenage (skrī·nĕdʒ). [f. Screen *sb.*[1] + -age.] The material of which screens are made; screens collectively; *spec.* applied to fluorescent screens.
1930 *Brit. Med. Jrnl.* 8 Feb. 234 Into these recesses can be inserted lead plugs..which to some extent control the dimensions of the 'radiant beam'...The screenage, amounting to the equivalent of just over 1 mm. of platinum, consists of monel metal, brass, aluminium, and wood.

Screened, *ppl. a.* Add: **1.** *spec.* in *Meteorol.*, placed in or occurring in a screen (see *Screen *sb.*[1] 3 f).
1894 [see Dict.]. 1920 *Westm. Gaz.* 2 Dec. 6/4 At Greenwich, a minimum screened temperature of 27 deg. was registered.

4. *Wireless.* Furnished with a screen (see *Screen *sb.*[1] 6 b).
1922 *Wireless World* X. 416/2 A screened oscillator. 1926 S. O. Pearson *Dict. Wireless Techn. Terms*, *Screened Aerial*, an aerial beneath which is spread a network of wires to act as a counterpoise. 1926 E. H. Chapman *Illustr. Wireless Dict.* s.v., A screened coil is a coil completely enclosed in a metal screening case. 1930 *B.B.C. Year-Bk.* 323 Great use is now being made of screened grid valves. *Ibid.* 381 A new type of screened grid valve has recently been developed in America. 1932 *News Chron.* 26 Feb. 3 To enjoy Radio programmes from Europe's best Broadcasting centres, you must have a Screened Grid Set.

5. Projected on a screen.
1917 C. N. Bennett *Kinematography* ix. 160 Distortion of the Screened Image. *Ibid.*, [It] shows the normal proportions of the screened picture.

Screening, *vbl sb.* Add: **1. b.** In technical usages, *spec.* in *Wireless.*
1909 *Cent. Dict.* Suppl., *Screening*, in *elect.* and *magnetism*: (*a*) The method of surrounding the apparatus inside of the screen with a shield of soft iron, so as to protect it from external magnetic influences. (*b*) The method of surrounding with a shield, cage, or netting made of good conducting material for protection against external electric forces. In large conductors carrying alternating currents, the outside part of the conductor may screen the inside so that less or no current flows in the interior, and the effective resistance of the conductor is thereby increased. 1914 *Work* XLVI. 501/1 This would not account for KAV not being heard, and this the writer fears must be due to the 'screening' alluded to. 1920 *Discovery* Apr. 116/1 Mountains..close to a wireless station may produce serious screening in that direction. 1930 *B.B.C. Year-Bk.* 339 A copper sheet shield may be fixed to the rear of the panel for screening purposes. *Ibid.* 450/2 *Screening*, an arrangement to prevent one circuit carrying alternating current from affecting another adjacent to it. It generally consists of a sheet of metal (usually copper) placed between the two circuits.

2. b. *spec.* in *pl.*, the second grade of wheat or polished rice. *U.S.*
1867 Simmonds *Dict. Trade Products* Suppl., *Screenings*, a name in the United States for the inferior wheat that is removed by the screens and fans. 1900 *Yearbk. U.S. Dept. Agric.* 135 (Cent. D. Suppl.), 9,400 pounds of screenings, and 3,500 pounds of brewer's rice.

Screening, *ppl. a.* Add: **b.** In technical usages.
1912 *Q. Rev.* July 234 Eighteen per cent. of the lift is lost by reason of the screening effect of one plane over the other. 1919 R. Stanley *Wireless Telegr.* I. 163 The importance of having the transmitter and receiver in the open and well away from screening effects. 1920 *Discovery* Apr. 116/1 Provided that there are no screening effects caused by opaque bodies intervening between their eyes and the lamp. 1926 R. W. Hutchinson *Wireless* ix. 154 An aerial passing along a passage between the gable ends of two houses..is not efficient owing to the screening effect of the houses.

Screwmatic (skrumæ·tik), *a.* and *sb.* Humorous perversion of Rheumatic *sb.* 1, after Screw. Also Screws.
1892 P. H. Emerson *Engl. Lagoons* 50, I had the screwmatic fever three times. 1895 — *Birds Norf. Broadland* 396 'Wiper's oil' is a reputed specific for 'screwmatics'. 1897 G. Bartram *People of Clopton* 51 In bed roarin' mad wi' the screws. 1916 E. V. Lucas *Vermilion Box* 209 Wet, and rats,..and dirt and screwmaticks.

Scrimshonging, early U.S. var. of Scrimshawing.
1850 N. Kingsley *Diary* 161 There is plenty of time to tinker or read or do any kind of 'Scrimshonging' any-one feels disposed to do.

Scrip, *v.*[3] [f. Scrip *sb.*[4]] *trans.* To issue scrip for.
1882 *Century Mag.* Sept. 769 They make a treaty with the rail-road company for a section of land...Then they 'scrip' the adjoining sections of Government land.

Scripee (skripī·). *U.S.* [f. Scrip *sb.*[4] + -ee.] In the Department of the Interior, one to whom land is allotted by scrip.
1911 Webster.

Script[1]. Add: **2. d.** A style of handwriting resembling printing, both in the shape of the characters and in their not being joined together. In full *script-writing, print-script.*
1920 *Child Study* Dec., These norms for cursive writing were obtained from London children with the same words and under the same conditions as those for script-writing. 1929 A. S. Osborn *Questioned Documents* (ed. 2) 105 Finger movement writing..and the later so-called printed 'script', is essentially a printing movement which permits the formation of but a few characters without a readjustment of the arm and a new start.

Scrooch, scrouch (skrūtʃ), *v. dial.* and *U.S. intr.* To crouch, cower.
1882 *Century Mag.* Apr. 888/2, I scrooch'd down in the bag. 1884 'Mark Twain' *Huck. Finn* ii. 6 We scrouched down and laid still. 1885 Helen M. F. Jackson *Zeph* ii. 71 Sittin' all scrouched into a heap. 1911 J. C. Lincoln *Cap'n Warren's Wards* i. 12 Scrooch down and see if you can't wriggle down underneath.
Hence **Scroo·chy** *a. U.S.*, cowering.
1844 'Jon. Slick' *High Life N.Y.* II. 220 The white finger at t'other eend the entry was..lookin kinder scroochy.

Scroop, *sb.*[1] Add: **b.** A crisp, crackling sound given out, when handled, by silk that has been treated with weak mineral acids; also, the feel of such silk. Also *attrib.*
1892 G. H. Hurst *Silk Dyeing* i. 9 Dilute mineral acids have no appreciable action on silk, but they have the property of imparting to it a peculiar 'scroop' or crackle. 1916 Knecht, Rawson & Lowenthal *Man. Dyeing* iv. 64 The silk acquires a peculiar feel, emitting when compressed in bulk a peculiar crackling sound (scroop silk; Fr. craquant). ..The scroop feel produced by acetic acid disappears after a time. 1921 C. Salter tr. *Ganswindt's Dyeing Silk* 32 The so-called 'scroop' of silk..is only observed in scoured silk that has been treated with weak acids.

Scrouge, *v.* Add: **3.** To draw together, contract.
1909 R. A. Wason *Happy Hawkins* 162 The old man looked at me with his little shiny eyes all scrouged up.

Scrou·ging, *ppl. a. U.S.* [Cf. Scrouger 1.] Thumping, huge.
1846 Sol. Smith *Theatrical Apprent.* 209 Away he goes to Cincinnati—plays a very successful engagement there—has a scrouging benefit.

Scrounge (skraundʒ), *v. colloq.* and *dial.* Also **scrunge.** [Altered f. the dialectal *scringe.*]
1. a. *intr.* To pry or search about for what one can find.
1927 [see *scrounging* below]. *Mod.* I must scrounge round and see if I can find anything that will do.
b. *trans.* To appropriate without leave; to annex; to acquire by doubtful means; to obtain surreptitiously; to 'pinch'.
1909 Ware *Passing Engl.*, *Scrunging* (Country Boys'), stealing unripe apples and pears—probably from the noise made in masticating. 1919 *War Slang* in *Athenæum* 11 July 582/2 Before the war..'scrounge', except in dialect, was unknown. 1923 *Chambers's Jrnl.* 291/1 He had scrounged some food and got into the hold. 1927 G. W. Deeping *Kitty* xii, Private Dipper went off to try and scrounge some cigarettes. 1928 Galsworthy *Swan Song* II. iv. 136 'How are you going to get the money?' 'Win, wangle and scrounge it.'
2. *intr.* To sponge (*on*); to live at the expense of others. orig. *U.S.*
1911 Webster, Scrunge. 1922 *Glasgow Herald* 1 May 6 I did not see anything in front of me except scrounging on my own people.
Hence **Scrounge** *sb.*, (*a*) the action of scrounging; (*b*) a scrounger. **Scrou·nger,** one who sponges on others; one who takes what belongs to others. **Scrou·nging** *vbl. sb.*
1911 Webster, Scrunger. 1918 E. S. Farrow *Dict. Mil. Terms, Scrounger*, a slang term for a soldier with plenty of resource in getting what he wants. 1919 tr. *A. L. Vischer's Barbed Wire Dis.* 44 The complaints about 'scrounging', which are nothing but outbreaks of loss of moral judgment. 1923 *Blackw. Mag.* Oct. 436/1 The mightiest hunter of the wilds, he becomes a scrounger in backyards. 1927 *Ibid.* Mar. 373/2 By dint of a little scrounging in the kitchen we managed to supply them. 1927 *Observer* 17 July 15/5 A stirring tale of diamond scrounging. 1927 *Daily Express* 17 Aug. 3 Suffolks on the Scrounge. Village Trek for Recruits.

Scrub, *sb.*[1] Add: **4. a.** (Earlier and later U.S. examples.)
1858 C. L. Flint *Milch Cows, etc.* 28 We meet with good milkers of all forms, from the round close-built Devon to the coarsest-boned scrub. 1861 *Trans. Ill. Agric. Soc.* IV. 255 It costs but little or no more to raise a valuable colt than a poor scrub. 1896 *Vermont Agric. Rep.* XV. 22 Good cows have taken the place of the unprofitable scrub.

6. scrub-rider *Austral.*, one who rides in search of cattle that have escaped into the scrub.
1881 A. C. Grant *Bush-Life in Queensland* xv. (1882) 150 A favourite plan amongst the bold scrub-riders.

Scrub, *sb.*[2] Add: **2.** *spec.* in *Glass-painting*, a brush used in the treatment of matting (see quot.). Cf. *Scrub *v.*[1] 4 b.
1927 *Daily Express* 27 May 5/5 An even coat of matt is put on, the detail of delicate light and shade being etched out again with brushes known as scrubbs and stipples.

3. b. *Sports.* A player not belonging to the regular team; a second or weaker team; one who takes part in a scrub-game or race; a game of baseball played with less than the usual number of players. *U.S.*
1903 *New York Even. Post* 28 Oct. 9 The halfback tries his mettle against the scrubs. 1910 *Ibid.* 15 Oct. Suppl. 1 The 'scrubs', or second team men. 1917 Mathewson *Sec. Base Sloan* 126 At the end of a week or so they were playing 'scrub' every noon hour. 1920 W. Camp *Football without a Coach* 62 Do not let the absence of a scrub disturb you in the least. Many a team is better off without a second eleven. 1930 M. Sullivan *Our Times* iii. 214 At the University of Wisconsin, as a 'scrub', an outsider, a non-fraternity man, he endured experiences of a sort that most boys ultimately forget.

5. scrub centre *U.S.*, one who plays centre in a scrub team; **scrub-eleven, team,** etc. *U.S.*, a second or weaker eleven or team; a scratch team; also *transf.*
1887 *Century Mag.* XXXIV. 895/1 The 'University team' is selected provisionally; it is pitted daily against a second, or 'scrub', team of somewhat larger numbers. 1888 T. Roosevelt *Ibid.* XXXVI. 200/2 With much difficulty we got together a scrub wagon team of four as unkempt, dejected, and vicious-looking broncos as ever stuck fast in a quicksand. 1892 J. L. Ford *Dr. Dodd's School* i. 5 The school eleven..were playing a practice game of foot-ball with a scrub eleven enrolled for the occasion. 1901 *Kynoch Jrnl.* Oct.–Nov. 7/2 It was practically a local scrub team of American marksmen which met the Ulster team at the long ranges. 1920 W. Camp *Football without a Coach* 63 You will have your regular center playing against a scrub center.

Scrub, *a.* Add: **1.** (Later U.S. examples.)
1840 J. P. Kennedy *Quodlibet* 158 If he..makes a little fortune, we can call him a..Scrub Aristocrat. 1881 *Harper's Mag.* June 88/2 Her little scrub-class in the Sunday-school. 1901 Marah E. Ryan *That Girl Montana* ix. 125 There are always a lot of scrub whites ready to take advantage of war signals.

3. Of vegetation: Low-growing, stunted. *U.S.*
1779 *Mass. Hist. Soc.* Ser. II. II. 465 Their breastwork was made of pine Logs cover'd with green scrub bushes. 1816 U. Brown *Jrnl.* in *Maryland Hist. Mag.* X. 266 Pines of a scrubby kind, Jack Oaks and other Scrub wood. 1872 *Rep. Vermont Board Agric.* I. 78 Men are as choice of a little scrub apple tree..as they would be were it classed among the favorite varieties of the day. 1904 Gene Stratton-Porter *Freckles* ix, There was a swarm of wild bees settled on a scrub-thorn only a few yards away.

4. Of cattle: Of inferior size or breed. *U.S.*
1839 *Indiana Ho. Repr. Jrnl.* 232 The half-blooded calves of the improved Durhams will sell, at weaning, for $20, while those of our scrub breed will only bring 3. 1867 *Rep. Iowa Agric. Soc.* (1868) 99 To raise and fatten a scrub steer and put him into market at four years old. *Ibid.* 130 The general idea pervades..that a larger animal of blooded stock can be produced by the same amount of feed than can be made with the same feed fed to scrub stock. 1872 *Trans. Dept. Agric. Illinois* 204 A common scrub hog can scarcely be found in the county. 1905 *Springfield* (Mass.) *Weekly Republ.* 28 July 5 The term 'scrub' is applied..to cattle that have no particular breeding, no matter how good or bad they may be.

Scrub, *v.*[1] Add: **3. c.** *absol.* Also with *away.*
1870 Julie P. Smith *Widow Goldsmith's Dau.* xxvi, She ..scrubbed for dear life. 1895 Gallichan *Like Stars that Fall* ii, I must scrub and clean for you the rest of my life. 1892 'J. S. Winter' *Mere Luck* ix, Scrubbing away at a flight of stone steps.
d. To 'scrape' *along.* *U.S.*
1901 S. Merwin & H. K. Webster *Calumet K* xi. 202 The rest of the road had to scrub along as best it could.
4. b. *Glass-painting.* To etch *out* (lights) with a scrub (see *Scrub *sb.*[2] 2).
1902 L. F. Day *Windows* vi. (ed. 2) 65 The practice in the sixteenth century was mainly, by a process of scrubbing lights out of matted or washed tints of brown, to get very considerable modelling.

Scrubbable (skrɒ·băb'l), *a.* [f. Scrub *v.*[1] + -able.] That may be scrubbed or will not be injured by scrubbing.
1923 *Daily Mail* 29 May 10 Matone's 'scrubbable' matt finish is fadeless. 1928 *Evening News* 28 Dec. 4/2 Unpolished, 'scrubbable' wood.

Scrubbed (skrɒbd), *ppl. a.* [f. Scrub *v.*[1] + -ed[1].] Cleaned by rubbing with a hard brush and water.
1870 Julie P. Smith *Widow Goldsmith's Dau.* ii, Both.. were kept scrubbed and combed, and 'cleaned up' within an inch of their lives. 1905 E. M. Albanesi *Brown Eyes of Mary* xvi, The sight of the old kitchen, with its scrubbed boards and red tiles.

Scru·bman. *U.S.* [Scrub *v.*[1] 5.] A man employed in scrubbing.
1905 *Cleveland Plain Dealer* 24 Jan. 3 Once a soldier in the army of the great white czar, now a scrubman in one of the large department stores.

Scrub-oak. *U.S.* (See Scrub *sb.*[1] 6 c.)
1779 *Mass. Hist. Soc.* Ser. II. II. 474 The land the Army came by this day is very poor, chiefly scrub-oak plains. 1796 B. Hawkins *Lett.* 16 The lands in this vale not rich, the timber small and mostly scruboak. 1815 *N. Amer. Rev.* I. 20 It brings to the fancy a flock of merino lambs in a field of scrub oaks. 1848 E. Bryant *What I saw in California* xi. 155 I noticed in one of the ravines to-day, the scrub-oak, or what is commonly called black-jack. 1861 O. W. Norton *Army Lett.* 26 The timber here is mostly small, scrub oaks, etc. 1897 *Outing* (U.S.) XXX. 68/2 Then getting into a dense pine woods we left the trail entirely, and found ourselves wandering around in a thicket of scrub oaks.

Scrub-pine. *U.S.* (See Scrub *sb.*[1] 6 c.)
1810 Michaux *Arbres* I. 16 Jersey pine,..dans New Jersey où elle abonde. Scrub pine, nom usité en Virginie. 1832 D. J. Browne *Sylva Amer.* 234 In the last mentioned state [sc. Pennsylvania] it is called Scrub Pine. 1872– [see Scrub *sb.*[1] 6 c].

Scruff, *v.*[1] (Recent U.S. example.)
1920 C. Sandburg *Smoke & Steel* 25 Wearing leather shoes scruffed with fire.

Scruff, *v.*[2] Add: **b.** To seize and hold (calves) while certain operations are performed. *Austral.*
1881 A. C. Grant *Bush-Life in Queensland* xvi, The smaller calves are scruffed. 1909 *Chambers's Jrnl.* Dec. 810/2 After the calves are separated from their mothers,.. the former are one by one 'scruffed'—that is, seized by a couple of men and held down while knife and branding-iron are applied.
c. To push roughly. *U.S.*
1926 J. Black *You Can't Win* ix. 121 After they got done scruffing me around, two of them took me by each arm.

Scruffy, *a.* Add: **b.** Despicable, mean, shabby.
1925 E. Fraser & Gibbons *Soldier & Sailor Words*, *Scruffy*, dirty: slovenly: untidy in appearance. 1931 *Star* 8 May 6/3 Anyone who has travelled through lottery countries and seen the hundreds of scruffy ticket-shops in the cities.

Scrum. Add: **scrum-half,** in Rugby football, the half-back who puts the ball into the scrum.
1922 *Somerset County Herald* 11 Feb. 4/3 As scrum-half [he] manfully overcame his disadvantage in weight.

Scrummy (skrɒ·mi), *a. slang.* [f. Scrum(ptious + -y[1].] Excellent, enjoyable, first rate.
1918 Galsworthy *Five Tales* 122 He's promised to take mother and me to the theatre and supper afterwards. Won't it be scrummy! 1922 Joad *Highbrows* iii. 105 Dorothy confided in a cheerfully subdued voice that her mother was away. 'Isn't that scrummy?' she said.

Scrumptiously (skrɒ·mᵖʃəsli), *adv.* [-LY[2].] Excellently, in a scrumptious manner. So **Scru·mptiousness,** the state or condition of being scrumptious.
1881 *Punch* 30 July 47/2 There is a certain exquisite scrumptiousness and goloptiousness about Real Turtle. 1927 *Observer* 1 May 8 He shows us 'Life' and 'High Life' simultaneously, so scrumptiously and yet with O such a touch of wanton wistful weariness!

Scrunch, *v.* **2. b.** (Later U.S. example.)
a 1906 'O. Henry' *Trimmed Lamp* etc. 181 You sit there with your shoulders scrunched up, giving an imitation of Reginald Vanderbilt driving his coach.

Scrunchy (skrɒ·nʃi), *a.* [f. Scrunch *v.* + -y[1].] That scrunches; that emits a crisp, crunching sound when crushed.
1905 *Eng. Dial. Dict.* Suppl., *Scrunchy*, of frozen grass: emitting a crisp, crunching sound when trodden on. 1907 W. De Morgan *Alice-for-short* xxvi, Of course you may have scrunchy toast if you like. 1927 *Daily Express* 6 Dec. 11 The delicious, scrunchy crispness of 'Ovaltine' Rusks.

Scuff, *v.* Add: **2. c.** *intr.* Of leather: To become rubbed or marked on the surface.
1930 *Publishers' Weekly* 21 June 2976 In some respects its wearing qualities are superior, particularly as regards scuffing.

Scuffle, *v.*[2] Add: **b.** *transf.* To scratch, mark with scratches.
1923 C. F. Jenkins *Tortola* xi. 67 Our two boys took off their shoes, so that the rough going over the sharp stones would not scuffle them, their feet being tougher than their Sunday shoes.

Scuffler[1]. Add: **b.** One who rakes out small coal and stone in a colliery. Also **Scu·ffer, Scu·ppler.**
1921 *Dict. Occup. Terms* (1927) § 042 *Cleaner*;..*scuffer, scuffler, scuppler*; rakes small coal or stone..out of groove cut by coal cutting machine, and loads into tubs or throws back into goaf.

Scug, *sb.*[3] Add: Also in extended use. Hence **Scu·ggish, Scu·ggy** *adjs.*
1916 E. F. Benson *David Blaize* v, These are all college houses, inboarders, and rather scuggy compared to outboarders. *Ibid.* viii, You were such a scug, you see, that you didn't do those things when it was scuggish not to. 1928 *Observer* 15 Apr. 29/4 A band of what I can only describe as 'Scugs' in bowler hats.

Sculduddery. 3. *U.S.* (Earlier example of form *sculduggery.*)
1867 A. D. Richardson *Beyond Mississippi* xi. 134 Do you see Smith and Brown whispering there in the corner? They are up to some scull-duggery.

Scull, *v.* Add: **4.** *intr.* To skate forward or back without lifting the feet from the ice.
1895 *Funk's Standard Dict.*

Sculp, *sb.*[2] Add: Also, in early U.S. use, a human scalp.

1758 *Essex Inst. Hist. Coll.* XVIII. 180 They obtained fifty-two Sculps and two Prisoners. 1845 W. G. SIMMS *Wigwam & Cabin* Ser. I. 53 A pretty fellow..at his time of life to be looking after sculps of women and children.

Sculp, *v.*[2] Add: Also *U.S.*, to scalp (a person).

1759 *Essex Inst. Hist. Coll.* XIX. 188 [He] retook one of ye Prisoners and killed and sculpt one of ye Indians. 1834 CARRUTHERS *Kentuckian in New York* I. 24 Shootin and sculpin Injuns. 1845 W. G. SIMMS *Wigwam & Cabin* Ser. I. 44 They'll be sculped, every human of them, in their beds. *Ibid.* 51 We heard of murders and sculpings on every side. 1884 A. E. SWEET & J. A. KNOX *On Mexican Mustang Thr. Texas* xviii. 246 I'm a scout from the Far West, whar ..the coyote sleeps in the deserted wigwams of the skulpt Indian.

Sculptured, *ppl. a.* 2. (Later U.S. example.)

1870 *Amer. Naturalist* IV. 53 How the Sculptured Turtle (*Glyptemys insculpta* Ag.) deposits her eggs.

Scum, *sb.* 4. Add: **scum-cock**, a cock in a steam-boiler for the removal of surface scum from the water without loss of pressure; **scum-pipe**, a pipe in a steam-boiler for the removal of scum; **scum-trough**, a trough in a steam-boiler provided for the reception of scum.

1891 W. S. HUTTON *Steam-Boiler Constr.* 318 When a scum-cock..is employed it is to blow off scum from the surface of the water in a steam-boiler. 1888 *Lockwood's Dict. Mech. Engin.*, *Scum Cock*, a cock placed in the side of a marine boiler for the purpose of getting rid of the dirt and scum which are carried to the surface of the water...*Scum Trough*, or *Scale Pan*, or *Sediment Collector*, a shallow trough provided in large marine and stationary boilers, for the collection of the fine sediment which is ballooned to the surface by the ebullition of the bubbles of steam.

Scuppernong. *U.S.* (Earlier examples.)

1847 *Rep. U.S. Comm. Patents* (1848) 470 Profits of a Scuppernong Vineyard. 1849 *Ibid., Agric.* (1850) 167 The incalculable value of the White Scuppernong to these Southern States.

Scuppler: see *SCUFFLER.[1]

Scurfer (skɜ̄·ɹfəɹ). [f. SCURF *v.* 3 + -ER[1].] An operative who removes incrustations of dirt from boilers, metal plates, etc.

1881 *Instr. Census Clerks* (1885) 36 Scurfer (Ships). 1921 *Dict. Occup. Terms* (1927) § 699 *Scurfer, retort scurfer* (gas works);..chips off deposited gas carbon from sides of retorts when it gets too thick. *Ibid.* § 952 *Boiler cleaner, boiler scaler, boiler scraper, boiler scurfer,..scurfer boy..*; removes 'scale' (incrusted deposit) from inner surface of boilers and from boiler tubes.

Scurry, *v.* Add: 3. b. To hurry over, get through quickly and slovenly.

1908 M. & J. FINDLATER *Crossriggs* v, The lad is willing enough to read to me,..but..he mumbles, or else he scurries, just those bits that are worth reading.

Scut, *sb.*[1] 2. b. Delete †*Obs.* and add examples.

1876 *Coursing Cal.* 21 Handling her hare in grand style, never left the scut until she killed. *Ibid.* 29. *Ibid.* 78 Keeping well to the scut, she never gave her opponent a chance. 1921 GALSWORTHY *To Let* III. xi, He sat..dreaming his career, faithful to the scut of his possessive instinct.

3. A contemptuous or playful appellation of a human being or number of human beings. *colloq.* or *dial.*

1895 M. E. FRANCIS *Frieze & Fustian* 63 I'll pinnance ye, ye little scut! 1901 *Longman's Mag.* Sept. 405 Moran, ye scut! don't be skirmishin'. 1923 SILBERRAD *Lett. Jean Armiter* iii, I'm not going to sit by and bear women called 'unproductive' because they don't happen to have a scut of children they couldn't have afforded to bring up. 1929 G. W. DEEPING *Roper's Row* ix. § 3 He always was a precocious little scut.

Scu·tchell. [f. SCUTCH *v.*[2]] = SCUTCHER[2] I.

1873 J. H. BEADLE *Undevel. West* xix. 352 The women with high-backed combs which looked like sections of a flax scutchell.

Scuttle, *sb.*[2] Add: 1. d. The section of a motor car which connects the bonnet with the body.

1924 *Chambers's Jrnl.* Mar. 206/1 The scuttle-dash protects his body and chest from the wind. 1922 *Autocar* 10 Nov. 967 The two-panel screen..is made to follow the curvature of the scuttle dash. *Ibid.* 973 The coachwork, which now tapers from bonnet to scuttle in an unbroken sweep. 1925 *Morris Owner's Man.* 71 Under the butterfly nut at the back of the bonnet hinge (on top of the scuttle).

Scuttle, *v.*[1] Add: 1. c. *trans.* To hurry *off.*

1924 W. J. LOCKE *Coming of Amos* iv, I scuttled him off to Nice in the car.

Sea, *sb.* Add: 18. n. *sea-trader, -trading.*

1899 CUTCLIFFE HYNE *Further Adv. Capt. Kettle* i, Kettle had come across many types of sea-trader in his time. 1921 *19th Cent.* July 150 She failed..to become a great sea-trading nation.

23. **sea-cloth**, (*b*) cloth used for sailors' clothes; **sea-end**, the end (of a road) at the sea; **sea-fever**, longing or desire for the sea; **sea-gulf**, (*b*) a deep place in the sea; **sea-impoldering** (*IMPOLDER *v.*); **sea-scout** (see quots.); so **sea-scouting**; **sea-silk**, a silky substance obtained from the sea-silk-worm; **sea-sled** (see quot.); **sea-stack**, an isolated rock mass rising abruptly from the floor of the sea; **sea-time**, (*c*) time spent at sea on a single journey.

1883 STEVENSON *Treas. Isl.* VI. xxxi, 'He was a seaman,' said George Merry, who..was examining the rags of clothing. 'Leastways, this is good *sea-cloth.' 1905 'Q' (Quiller Couch) *Shining Ferry* III. xviii, A bustious, big fellow, with a round hat like a missionary's, and all the rest of him in sea-cloth. 1904 W. M. RAMSAY *Lett. Seven Churches* xxii. 296 The *sea-ends of the two great roads. 1902 MASEFIELD (*title of poem*) *Sea-fever. 1931 *Daily Express* 23 Sept. 9/4 Men with the sea-fever on them pottered about among the débris of the docks. 1902 D. G. HOGARTH *Nearer East* 87 That profound *sea gulf, which compensates the abrupt incline of Crete. 1899 D. S. MELDRUM *Holland & Hollanders* 213, I cannot give a better idea of the practical work of *sea-impoldering. 1911 BADEN-POWELL *Sea Scouting for Boys* 8 *Sea Scouts are of two kinds, viz. (1) Coastguard Scouts; (2) Seamen Scouts. 1912 BERESFORD *ibid.* p. vi, The Sea Scouts were formed as an auxiliary to..the Boy Scouts. The object of the Sea Scouts is to teach lads at or near the sea seamanship, navigation, pilotage, knotting and splicing, how to handle boats under oars and sail [etc.]. 1902 HANNAN *Textile Fibres Commerce* 184 *Sea Silk. 1921 *Chambers's Jrnl.* 61/1 The United States naval authorities have lately experimented with land-aeroplanes carried on and flown from a very fast type of motor-boat. This boat, known as the '*sea-sled', is of unusual design. If a boat were cut in halves along the line of the keel, and the halves were placed side by side with the half-keels outermost, they would give a form of hull somewhat resembling the sea-sled. 1923 *Glasgow Herald* 4 May 9/1 Motor boats of the 'sea sled' type. 1899 *Geog. Jrnl.* Mar. 288 The isolated rock-masses and *sea-stacks, which we are enabled to trace by means of the soundings. 1930 *Times* 26 Mar. 17/4 Her *sea-time beat the Bremen's best..by eighteen minutes.

Seaboard. 4. (Earlier U.S. examples.)

1789 MORSE *Amer. Geog.* 447 The soil..after you leave the sea board..changes from a grey to a red colour. 1803 *Ann. Congress* 24 Feb. 192 The seaboard can send few if any troops beyond the mountains.

Sea-craft. Add: 3. Sea-vessels collectively.

1919 *Q. Rev.* Jan. 184 Vessels, whether sea-craft or air-craft. 1923 *Daily Mail* 24 Jan. 5 Certain types of surface naval craft should have sufficient power in their engine-rooms..to transform them from seacraft into machines which fly. 1928 *Daily Express* 18 Jan. 1 Our oldest craft, seacraft.

Sea-dog. 5. (Earlier U.S. example.)

1823 J. F. COOPER *Pilot* II. xi. 181 Ahead, heave ahead, seadogs!

Seadrome (sī·drōum). [f. SEA *sb.* + *-drome* of *AERODROME.] A floating construction moored in the sea for the landing of aeroplanes.

1923 *Daily Mail* 17 July 10 The feature of the project is that there should be eight 'seadromes'..moored permanently on the Atlantic air route. 1927 *Daily Express* 6 July 9/5 A seadrome which is to be moored about five hundred and fifty miles east of New York to provide a landing-place for Transatlantic airplanes.

Sea-food. *U.S.* [SEA *sb.* I.] Food obtained from the sea; fish or shell-fish, crabs, etc., used as food.

1836 *Knickerbocker Mag.* VIII. 423 She said that she had come to Scrammy Point to get 'sea-food'. 1906 *N. Y. Evening Post* 10 Mar. 5 Up State residents are among the best customers of the sea food, fruit and produce dealers.

Sea-going, *a.* Add:

1. b. Capable of being used or suitable for use on a sea-going vessel; carried on by sea.

1911 WEBSTER s.v., A seagoing chronometer. 1928 C. DAWSON *Age of Gods* viii. 182 The sea-going trade of the Ægean world.

Sea-island. (Earlier U.S. example.)

1807–8 W. IRVING *Salmag.* xvi. 362 The lady of a Southern planter will..trail a bale of sea-island cotton at her heels.

Seak (sīk, sīᵊk). *local.* [f. dial. *seak* vb., to ooze, leak, percolate.] 'The polluted liquid left after the scouring of wool or cloth; the process of scouring or washing' (Eng. Dial. Dict.).

[1858 SIMMONDS *Dict. Trade*, *Seak*, a preparation of the best mottled soap used in milling cloth.] 1921 *Dict. Occup. Terms* (1927) § 159 *Seak* (or *sceak*) *breaker*; receives hard cakes of wool grease from which oil has been squeezed out by seak (or sceak) maker and breaks them up for hop garden manure...*Seak* (or *sceak*) *maker*..; (i) runs sulphuric acid into soapy liquor (containing wool grease) that has been used to wash out fats from raw wool;..puts fat..into canvas bags [etc.].

Seal, *sb.*[1] 5. Add: **seal-rookery** = ROOKERY 2b.

1910 *Chambers's Jrnl.* Mar. 176/2 The value of the seal-rookeries on the shores.

Seal, *sb.*[2] Add: 7. d. The projection of the edge of a steam valve over the edge of an opening in order to make a steam-tight joint. e. (See quot.)

1884 KNIGHT *Dict. Mech.* Suppl., *Seal*, an automatic valve closing a pipe.

8. b. **seal-paper** (see quot.).

1848 J. S. SMITH *Handbk. Pract. Crt. Chancery* iv. 51 There are no fixed days for hearing the several kinds of business before the Court, but previously to the commencement of the sittings, the Court issues a seal paper, detailing the business for each day.

Sealed, *ppl. a.* Add: 2. d. Among the Irvingites (see *SEALING *vbl. sb.*[1] 6 b).

1914 *Hastings's Encycl. Relig. & Ethics* VII. 425/1 The 'sealed' were not necessarily required to withdraw from the communion of other Churches.

3. Of playing cards: Placed face downwards.

1908 M. W. JONES *A.B.C. of Patience* Gloss. 12 *Sealed*, cards or packets which are placed face down.

Sealer, *sb.*[1] Add: 2. (Later U.S. example.)

1906 *Springfield* (Mass.) *Weekly Republ.* 1 Mar. 16 P. J. Tetrault, sealer of weights and measures..found that every-one of them was selling butter that was one ounce short of a pound.

c. One who attaches a seal to meat which has been slaughtered in accordance with Jewish custom.

1881 *Instr. Census Clerks* (1885) 62 Sealer Jews' Meat Market. 1921 *Dict. Occup. Terms* (1927) § 448 *Sealer*..; supervises slaughtering and affixes seal to Kosher meat.

5. One who or that which seals (SEAL *v.*[1] 8); an instrument for sealing tins.

1881 *Instr. Census Clerks* (1885) 58 Blacking Manufacture: Liquid:..Sealer. 1921 *Dict. Occup. Terms* (1927) § 159 *Sealer, ink bottle*; seals filled bottles of ink with sealing wax or with paper seals. *Ibid.* § 318 *Sealer, sealer-in* (lamps). *Ibid.* § 949 Petrol can sealer. 1928 *Daily Express* 6 July 5/5 The machine seals the lids of special cans... Mr. A. Appleyard..and Mr. Hirst..have tested this British hand sealer scientifically.

Sealing, *vbl. sb.*[1] Add:

6. b. Among the Irvingites (see quot.).

1914 *Hastings's Encycl. Relig. & Ethics* VII. 425/1 A rite of 'sealing', or laying on of hands, by which those who received the witness of the last times were set apart against the final day of Redemption.

Sealing, *vbl. sb.*[2] (Earlier U.S. examples.)

1835 J. F. COOPER *Monikins* vii. 81 The sealing-business, which is my ra'al occupation. *Ibid.* xii. 179 The secret of new sealing grounds. 1839 *Southern Lit. Messenger* V. 3/1 In a few years [they] made Stonington famed for sealing.

Sealyham (sī·libæm, sī·li,ăm). Also **Sealy Ham.** [The name of the seat of the Edwardes family in Pembrokeshire.] A breed of wire-haired terrier (see quot. 1907). Also *attrib.*

1894 R. B. LEE *Mod. Dogs* (1896) 420 There is a strain of terrier much talked about of late known as the Sealy Ham. 1907 R. LEIGHTON *New Bk. Dog* 318/2 The Sealy Ham Terrier..is..an excellent worker...The Sealy Ham derives its breed name from the seat of the Edwardes family, near Haverfordwest...It is a long-bodied, short-legged terrier, with a hard, wiry coat, frequently whole white, but also white with black or brown markings. 1909 A. C. SMITH *Everyman's Bk. Dog* 171 The Sealyham Terrier.

Seam, *sb.*[1] Add: 1. *French seam*: a seam that is folded in to hide the stitches, then stitched on the under side. Hence *French seamer* as an occupational term.

1903 *Home Fashions* 12 Sept. 18/3 The sleeve is joined by French seam. 1921 *Dict. Occup. Terms* (1927) § 419 French seamer.

Seam, *v.*[2] Add: 5. In the manufacture of shoddy: To remove the seams from old garments. Hence (*rag*) *seamer* as an occupational term.

1904 in *Eng. Dial. Dict.*

Seaming, *vbl. sb.* b. *Seaming machine* (earlier U.S. example).

1846 *Rep. U.S. Comm. Patents* (1847) 214 My improved seaming machine for turning down and forming a seam of the flange surrounding the bottoms of the buckets.

Seamless, *a.* Add: b. In sense 6 of SEAM *sb.*[1]

1876 *Encycl. Brit.* IV. 218/2 Solid or seamless brass tubes ..are made by drawing down short thick cast cylinders of brass till they reach the desired gauge and thinness. 1895 *Army & Navy Co-op. Soc. Price List* 15 Sept. 251 Balmoral seamless Enamelled Basin and Stand. 1904 *Technol. & Sci. Dict.* (ed. Goodchild & Tweney) s.v. *Cycles*, The frame is generally formed of thin seamless steel tubing.

Seaplane (sī·plēⁱn). [f. SEA *sb.* + *PLANE *sb.*[5]] An aeroplane capable of rising from and descending on the sea: now usually one with floats, as distinct from a *flying-boat*. Also *attrib.*

1913 *Aeroplane* 25 Dec. 676/1 Our constructors did not know how bad the French sea-planes were. 1914 *Daily Express* 2 Nov. 5/2 The old cruiser Hermes..which had been recently used as a seaplane-carrying ship. 1928 C. F. S. GAMBLE *Story North Sea Air Station* i. 39 The Hermes continued to act as a seaplane-carrier till October 30, 1914.

Sear, *v.* Add: 5. (See quot.)

1888 *Lockwood's Dict. Mech. Engin.*, *Searing*, the practice of smoothing the surface of the rougher class of foundry patterns with a flat-faced red hot iron, as a substitute for paint or varnish.

Search, *sb.* Add: 2. d. (Earlier U.S. example.)

1798 *Ann. 5th Congress* II. 1907 Gentlemen appeared to confound the right of search with the right of capture.

6. **search-coil** *Physics*, a small coil of insulated wire for determining the strength of magnetic fields by means of the currents induced in the coil.

1909 in *Cent. Dict.* Suppl. 1926 R. W. HUTCHINSON *Wireless* xiii. 246 A small search coil is placed as indicated.

Search, *v.* Add:

3. c. *Search me*: used to imply that the speaker has absolutely no knowledge of some fact, or no idea what course to take. *slang* (chiefly *U.S.*).

1901 S. MERWIN & H. K. WEBSTER *Calumet K* iii. 37 'Search me', said Denis. 'They've tied us up for these two weeks.' 1904 'O. HENRY' *Cabbages & Kings* iii, 'Search me!' said Smith. 'I don't know what she weighs in at.' 1912 L. J. VANCE *Destroying Angel* vii, 'Where is he?' 'You can search me.' *Ibid.* xii, 'What'd he want?' 'Search me.' 1916 'B. M. BOWER' *Phantom Herd* xi. 191 What ails that darned thing?..You can search me.

Search-light. Add: 2. The beam of light thrown by such a lamp.

In recent Dicts.

Sea-road (sī·rōᵘd). *U.S.* [f. SEA *sb.* + ROAD *sb.*] A line of communication over the sea; the route taken by ships between two places.

The instance of *sea roade* in ed. 3 of Berners' *Huon of Bordeux* is an alteration of *sirode* of ed. 1 (see E.E.T.S. ch. cvii. 359), which is an error for *siroke* or *siroche* (Fr. orig. *siroh* south-east).

1893 *Columbus* (Ohio) *Dispatch* 9 Nov., If fish disappeared from the sea-roads and fiords. 1906 *Outlook* 19 May 677/1 We hold the great sea-roads to the East. 1907 T. C. MIDDLETON *Geogr. Knowl. Discov. Amer.* 25 The Vivaldi brothers of Genoa, who in 1291 essayed a sea-road to India.

Sea-service. Add. 3. *attrib.*

1880 *Encycl. Brit.* XI. 308 Sea Service Rifled Guns. 1884

H. BOND *Milit. Small Arms* vi. (1888) 106 A large number of percussion muskets, pattern 1842, were converted into rifles by being grooved, and were issued to the Royal Marines, and made available for sea-service, whence the term 'sea-service rifle'.

Sea-shell. *attrib.* (Earlier U.S. example.)

1871 MRS. STOWE *Pink & White Tyranny* i. 4 When he saw this distant vision of airy gauzes, of pearly whiteness, of sea-shell pink.

Sea-side. 4. (U.S. example.)

1879 *Harper's Mag.* July 163 Nowhere else in all sea-side resorts will he be likely to get so much..elbow-room.

b. (U.S. examples.)

1785 H. MARSHALL *Amer. Grove* 20 *Sea-side alder, *Betula-Alnus maritima*. 1808–13 A. WILSON *Amer. Ornith.* (1831) II. 261 *Fringilla maritima*, Wilson.—*Sea-side Finch...It inhabits the low, rush-covered sea-islands along our Atlantic coast. 1872 COUES *Key N. Amer. Birds* 137 *Ammodromus maritimus*...Sea-side Finch. Olive-gray, obscurely streaked on the back and crown with darker or paler. 1837 J. L. WILLIAMS *Terr. of Florida* 37 The *seaside grape, different kinds of plumbs, and custard apples are frequently found in the hammocks.

Sea-sider. *U.S.* [f. SEA-SIDE.] A frequenter of the sea-side.

1870 *Amer. Naturalist* III. 230 The Savannah Sparrow, though only occasionally found breeding so far south as Massachusetts, is evidently a sea-sider.

Season, *sb.* 21. Add: **season-check** *U.S.*, 'a longitudinal crack in timber caused by too rapid seasoning'; **season crack**, a longitudinal crack developed in brass or bronze rods; so **season-cracking**.

1837 J. KIRKLAND *Zury* 32 Ye see that *season-check in the butt-end [*sc.* of a black-walnut log]. 1911 WEBSTER, *Season cracks...*Season-cracking. 1930 *Nature* CV. 744/1 The phenomenon of 'season-cracking' in brass.

Seasonable, *a.* Add: 4. = SEASONAL *a.* 2. Hence **Seasonably** *adv.* (in same sense).

1923 *Glasgow Herald* 20 Mar. 9 Persons engaged in seasonable trades in which the duration of seasonable employment is too short to enable them to qualify for benefit. 1928 *Brit. Industr. Future* (*Lib. Ind. Inq.*) IV. xxvii. § 7. 388 The hours worked in all the jobs concerned (omitting those in which hours varied weekly or seasonably).

Seasonal, *a.* Add: 1. c. Occurring at or lasting for a certain season of the year.

1920 *Act 10 & 11 Geo. V* c. 76 § 10 (7) (*f*) Permanent pasture which the landlord has been in the habit of letting annually for seasonal grazing.

Seasoning, *vbl. sb.* Add: 1. g. In diamond-cutting, the charging of the lapidary's mill with diamond dust and oil; the charge itself.

1882 *Encycl. Brit.* XIV. 299/1 The charge of diamond dust or seasoning.

h. The application of a solution of blood and logwood to leather prior to blacking. Also *attrib.*

1897 C. T. DAVIS *Manuf. Leather* (ed. 2) 358 A seasoning mixture is applied to the surface after tanning and before coloring. Fig. 97 shows a form of seasoning machine which is largely used for all kinds of glazed kid. *Ibid.* 360 The quality of work that a machine will do depends so much on the condition of the skins and the seasoning.

Sea-swallow. Add: 3. b. The esculent swallow (see SWALLOW *sb.*[1] 2 b).

1902 [see 3 in Dict.].

Seat, *sb.* Add: 7. c. Phr. *The anxious seat*: see *ANXIOUS *a.*

22. b. The position of a horse-shoe with respect to the foot.

1851 STEPHENS *Bk. Farm* (ed. 2) I. 338 The transparent shoe, showing the usual seat given to the shoe upon the fore-foot.

29. **seat-board**, (*d*) a board forming a seat in a vehicle; **seat-stick**, a walking-stick which may be adapted to form a seat.

1873 J. H. BEADLE *Undevel. West* iii. 70 The wagon made fearful lurches, and our *seatboard rattled over it in every direction. 1931 *Sale Catal.*, A neat light weight *seat stick.

Seat, *v.* 4. a. Add: To place (a cartridge) in its correct position in a firearm.

1902 *Encycl. Brit.* XXXII. 655/1 Closing the bolt by a reverse motion..seats the cartridge in the chamber.

Seated, *ppl. a.* Add: 1. b. *Ordnance.* (See quot.)

1918 E. S. FARROW *Dict. Mil. Terms*, *Seated*, in artillery, a piece is said to be seated when the trail-spade has sunk into the ground sufficiently so that the gun carriage does not go further backwards when fired.

7. Of a horse shoe: Hollowed out so that the bearing surface rests on the wall of the hoof.

1831 YOUATT *Horse* xvii. 311 The Concave-Seated Shoe. *Ibid.* 319 It [*sc.* the expanding shoe] is either seated or concave like the common shoe. 1908 *Animal Managem.* (War Office) 227 Seating is the hollowing out of the bearing surface, opposed to the sole, so that a seated shoe bears on the wall alone. *Ibid.* 228 A seated foot surface cannot offer as solid and extensive bearing as a flat one.

Seater. Add: 1. *N. Amer.* (Earlier example.)

1693 *Braintree Rec.* 29 Seaters of the meeting hous. Voted that the present selectmen..are chosen to seat the meeting hous.

2. Also in other parasynthetic formations referring to vehicles of all kinds.

1906 [see Dict.]. 1912 *Motor Manual* iv. (ed. 14) 138 It is best to have a four-seater. 1916 H. BARBER *Aeroplane Speaks* Pl. xvi, The familiar biplanes with 80 h.p. Gnomes, and 5-seater with 100 h.p. Anzani. 1923 GALSWORTHY *Captures* 217 Hubert Marsland..had occasion to stay the progress of his two-seater about ten miles from London for a minor repair.

Seating, *vbl. sb.* Add: 5. b. Of a horse-shoe: (*a*) = *SEAT *sb.* 22 b; (*b*) the hollowing out of a shoe so that the outer part rests on the wall of the hoof (cf. *SEATED *ppl. a.* 7).

1831 YOUATT *Horse* xvii. 319 A strip of felt or leather is sometimes placed between the seating of the shoe and the crust. 1908 *Animal Managem.* (War Office) 228 The object of seating is to take pressure off the sole.

c. The placing of a cartridge in its correct position in a firearm.

1902 *Encycl. Brit.* XXXII. 655/2 The final seating of the cartridge.

6. a. *seating-face.*

1925 *Morris Owner's Manual* 77 These two photographs show a valve before..and after grinding-in. Note the different appearance of their seating faces.

Seau (sōᵘ). *Ceramics.* Pl. **seaux**. Also *erron.* **sceau.** [Fr., = bucket.] A dish in the shape of a pail or bucket, usually forming part of dinner services made in England in the eighteenth century.

1851 *Illustr. Catal. Gt. Exhib.* III. III. 710/1 Porcelain Inkstands, Seaux, Card Trays. 1862 *Catal. Internat. Exhib., Brit.* II. No. 6884, Pair of sceaux..painted wreath and pendants of passion flower and festoons. 1875 ELIZA METEYARD *Wedgwood Handbk.* Gloss. 409 Seaux formed a part of all costly dinner and dessert services, particularly if intended for foreign countries...A choice pair of seaux in sea-green jasper is in the Marjoribanks Collection.

Seborrhœid (sebori·id). *Path.* [f. SEBORRHŒA + -ID[2].] A seborrhœic affection.

1908 *Practitioner* June 858 The important group of Seborrhoeic Dermatitis and the Seborrhoeids.

Sec (sek), *a.* [Fr.] Of champagne and other wines: = DRY *a.* 8. Also *fig.*

1889 *Judge* (U.S.) XVI. 419/2 Berton 'sec' Champagne. 1895 *Army & Navy Co-op. Soc. Price List* 15 Sept. 167 Achille Morat, 1st quality. Sec..Irroy's Ernest, Carte d'Or, Extra Sec. 1931 *Morning Post* 10 Aug. 4/3 The Bayreuth Festival...Wagner Sec.

Secodont (se·kodǫnt), *a.* *Zool.* [f. L. *secāre* to cut + Gr. ὀδοντ-, ὀδούς tooth.] Of teeth: Adapted or suited for cutting. Of an animal: Having teeth that cut.

1891 FLOWER & LYDEKKER *Introd. Mammals* 32 Trituberculism differentiating into a secodont and a bunodont series, according as to whether the dentition becomes of a cutting or a crushing type. 1913 DORLAND *Med. Dict.* (ed 7), *Secodont*, having teeth in which the tubercles of the molars are provided with cutting edges.

Second, *sb.*[1] 3. Add: **second-foot** = *foot-second* (*FOOT *sb.* 35).

1902 WEBSTER Suppl. 1928 *Manch. Guardian Weekly* 31 Aug. 178/3 The assumption is made that the main river, suitably fortified with levees, can carry rather less than 2,000,000 cubic feet of water per second (or 2,000,000 second feet as it is briefly described).

Second, *a.* and *sb.*[2] Add: A. *adj.* 1. *Second gear*, the gear next above the lowest gear. Often ellipt., as *to go into second.*

1902 A. C. HARMSWORTH *Motors & Motor-Driving* x. 204 If the calculated speed of the second gear is, say, eighteen miles per hour. 1925 *Morris Owner's Manual* 10 When changing gear up from first to second, or second to top, the clutch pedal should be pressed down. *Ibid.* 12 When descending very long steep hills, slow down at the top and engage the second or first gear. 1932 *News Chron.* 10 Mar. 2/1 The Silent Second makes it pleasant to use your gears as you should.

7. **second ballot**, an electoral method in which a second or supplementary election is held when no candidate has secured a majority of the votes cast; also, the second poll itself; **second day**, in Quaker usage, Monday; **second division**, (*b*) (see *DIVISION *sb.* 10 f); **second finger**, the finger next to the forefinger, the middle finger; **second gear** (see sense 1 above); **second growth** (earlier U.S. example), (*b*) the second category of the classed growths or qualities into which wines are divided; **second Isaiah** = Deutero-Isaiah; **second motion shaft** = *secondary shaft* (*SECONDARY *a.* 3 l); **second nerve**, either of the second pair of cranial nerves; the optic nerve; **second-season**, used *attrib.* to denote an animal, etc., in its second season; **second shaft** = **second motion shaft*; **second speed**, the next to the lowest speed in the gearing of motor vehicles; also *attrib.*; **second string** (see STRING *sb.* 4 c); **second tap**, the tool used in the second stage of making internal screw threads; **second winding** = *secondary winding* (*SECONDARY *a.* 3 h).

1914 *Concise Oxf. Dict.* Addenda, *Second ballot. 1927 *Observer* 27 Nov. 13/1 The Second Ballot means..a second election held a week or a fortnight after the first, whenever at the first election no candidate has secured an absolute majority of the votes. 1932 *News Chron.* 15 Mar. 9/1 The electorate, at the second ballot, were left to choose between Hindenburg, Marx and Thaelmann. 1691 G. FOX *Jrnl.* (1911) II. 367 For the yearly *second days Meetting in London. 1898 *second division [see *DIVISION *sb.* 10 f]. 1860 *Man. Artill. Exerc.* 241 The cock resting against the knuckle-joint of the first finger; this and the *second finger only resting on the small of the stock. 1932 *News Chron.* 15 Mar. 8/6 Making the tips of his first and little fingers touch; then bringing the second finger smoothly under the arch thus formed. 1829 J. F. COOPER *Wish-ton-wish* ii. 27 Much of the surface of this opening, too, was now concealed by bushes, of what is termed *second growth. 1833 REDDING *Wines* 110 The best wines are from the *noirien* grape, and the best of the first growths fetch sixty-six francs, and of the second growths forty-four francs. 1843 *Penny Cycl.* XXVII. 463/1 To the second and third growths the red wines of Roussillon, Bene Carlo from Spain, and brandy are added. 1888 *Encycl. Brit.* XXIV. 605/2 If..a first growth is vintaged a little too late and does not succeed so well as some second growths. 1880 *Ibid.* XIII. 380/2 How unlike it is to the honied rhetoric of him whom we are accustomed to call the *Second Isaiah. 1904 A. B. F. YOUNG *Complete Motorist* iv. (ed. 2) 116 On the top speed the drive is direct, the *second-motion shaft then lying idle. 1823 C. BELL *Expos. Nerves Hum. Body* (1824) 373 The first nerve..is..called olfactory nerve. The *second [nerve] is the optic nerve. 1876 *Coursing Calendar* 315 Conster, a *second-season dog, went through the stake in good style. 1902 A. C. HARMSWORTH *Motors & Motor-Driving* x. 202 Immediately above this shaft is a *second shaft arranged parellel to it...This second shaft and its attached gear wheels are contained in the same metal gear-case in which the other gear wheels are enclosed. 1904 A. B. F. YOUNG *Complete Motorist* iv. (ed. 2) 132 With their well-cut and thoroughly hardened gear-teeth the second shaft runs noiselessly. 1902 A. C. HARMSWORTH *Motors & Motor-Driving* x. 205 To obtain the *second of the three speeds provided. 1912 *Motor Manual* iii. (ed. 14) 74 Second speed position. *Ibid.* 75 Moved to the left it [*sc.* the left-hand sleeve] gives the second speed. 1925 *Morris Owner's Manual* 10 When it [*sc.* the car] has gained some headway, change into second speed. To do this again depress the clutch pedal, bring the gear lever into the neutral position, then swing it to the right and push it forward, when the second-speed gear will be engaged. 1888 *Lockwood's Dict. Mech. Engin.*, **Second Tap*, a tap intermediate in size between a taper and a plug tap. 1904 *Technol. & Sci. Dict.* (ed. Goodchild & Tweney) s.v. *Tap*, After the tapering tap has roughed out the thread in the hole, a Second Tap with somewhat less taper may be passed through. 1932 *B.B.C. Year-Bk.* 435/1 When a varying direct current is passed through one winding of such a transformer an alternating current is induced in the *second winding.

B. *sb.*[2] 1. d. = *second base* (in baseball).

1899 G. ADE *Fables in Slang* (1900) 34 She believed that she could get away with any Topic that was batted up to her and then slam it over to Second in time to head off the Runner.

5. Also of other commodities.

1877 W. F. WOODS *Lett. Oyster Fisheries* 19 From this cause the loss of 'seconds'—*i.e.* oysters other than natives—..is very great. 1881 INGERSOLL *Oyster-Industr.* (Hist. Fish. Industr. U.S.) 248. 1932 *Sale Catal.*, Three knots selected seconds..artificial silk stockings.

Second, *v.*[2] Add: Also *transf.* of officials in other occupations and employments.

1920 *Westm. Gaz.* 22 May 10/1 It was finally agreed that Lord Moulton should be seconded to the service of the Corporation and of the dye industry for..one year. 1928 *Times* 21 July 13/3 They established an elaborate organization, under an important Minister, and manned by specially seconded Civil servants of high standing.

Secondary, *a.* Add:

1. c. *Secondary wife*: (delete † and add) also among modern polygamous peoples.

1924 LADY HOSIE *Two Gentl. China* ix. (ed. 2) 91 The ladies of the household..often wield a power that must be reckoned with, if they are fond of intrigue, like a certain secondary wife of an official of our acquaintance. 1931 W. F. SANDS *Undiplomatic Mem.* 69 From kitchenmaid she was raised to the first rank of secondary consorts..and in due course became the mother of the monarch's third son.

h. Law. *Secondary conveyance, use* (see quots.). *Secondary evidence*: evidence which is not primary or first-hand, but which may be allowed if better evidence is not forthcoming, as when witnesses testify to the contents of a document instead of producing the document itself.

1765 [see USE *sb.* 4 b]. 1821 ARCHBOLD *Digest Law Plead. & Evid.* 354 Before secondary evidence is offered, a foundation for it must first be laid, by proving that better evidence cannot be obtained. *Ibid.* 355 You will be permitted to give secondary evidence of the execution of the deed, that is, you may prove the deed by proving the hand-writing of the witness and party. 1835 *Tomlin's Law-Dict.* (ed. 4), *Secondary Conveyances*, those which presuppose some other conveyance precedent, and only serve to confirm, alter, restrain, restore, or transfer the interest granted by such original conveyance. 1848 WHARTON *Law Lex.*, *Secondary use*, a use limited to take effect in derogation of a preceding estate; otherwise called a shifting use, as a conveyance to the use of A. and his heirs, with a proviso that when B. returns from India, then to the use of C. and his heirs. 1885 RIGBY in *Law Rep.* 29 Chanc. Div. 290 A probate was not even secondary evidence of a lost will. 1902 ILBERT in *Encycl. Brit.* XXVIII. 336/1 The distinction between primary and secondary evidence relates only to documentary evidence.

3. h. *Secondary circuit*: one in which the current is induced. *Secondary winding*: the coil of the secondary circuit of an induction-coil.

1847 *Patent Jrnl.* 16 Oct. 476/1 Upon the primary circuit being completed through the primary coils, a secondary circuit is induced through the secondary coils, but in an opposite direction. 1881 S. P. THOMPSON *Elem. Less. Electr. & Magn.* 365 Causing the inductive action in the secondary circuit at 'make' to be comparatively feeble. 1905 *Proc. Roy. Soc.* LXXIV. 478 We have an alternating high frequency magnetic field produced, which affects the secondary circuit at a distance. 1912 *Motor Manual* ii. (ed. 14) 47 This winding [*sc.* the primary winding] is very carefully insulated, and then over it is wound the 'secondary' winding. 1916 *Standard. Rules Amer. Inst. Electr. Engin.* 25 The terms 'primary' and 'secondary' serve to distinguish the windings in regard to energy flow, the primary being that which receives the energy from the supply circuit, and the secondary that which receives the energy by induction from the primary. 1926 R. W. HUTCHINSON *Wireless* v. 72 In Fig. 56 AB diagrammatically represents a coil of wire joined to a galvanometer; it is referred to as the secondary circuit. 1932 *B.B.C. Year-Bk.* 436/2 The output of the secondary winding of the output transformer.

k. *Secondary compensation*: additional compensation to eliminate the slight error left uncorrected by the (primary) compensation; also, the mechanism used for this.

1850 DENISON *Clock & Watch-m.* ii. 162 Secondary Compensation. 1888 LD. GRIMTHORPE in *Encycl. Brit.* XXIV. 396/1 Molyneux took a patent for a secondary compensation. *Ibid.*, The action is here equally continuous with Dent's, and the adjustments for primary and secondary compensation are apparently more independent of each other.

l. *Secondary shaft*: a shaft which actuates the second and third gears and controls the second and third speeds of a motor vehicle.

1902 A. C. HARMSWORTH *Motors & Motor-Driving* x. 205 Causing the secondary shaft..to be rotated. 1904 A. B. F. YOUNG *Complete Motorist* iv. (ed. 2) 107 The secondary shaft drives to the differential shaft by means of a bevel gear.

4. a. (Additional *Bot.* examples.)

1861 BENTLEY *Man. Bot.* 122 Adventitious or Secondary Root.—This name is applied to all roots which are not produced by the direct elongation of the radicle of the embryo. 1880 BESSEY *Bot.* 147 Where the secondary leaves (leaflets) grow from an extremely short axis.

5. f. (Earlier U.S. examples.)

1835 *Southern Lit. Messenger* I. 275 Others classify them into 1st *primary* schools,..and *secondary* schools, for the rudiments of Arithmetic, Geography, English Grammar, and further progress in reading and writing. 1852 *Ind. Hist. Soc. Publ.* III. 615 Those engaged in studies of a more advanced character constitute another class, termed secondary.

Second hand. C. *sb.* (See quot.)

1928 *Daily Express* 4 Apr. 9/2 A new naval rating, termed 'Second hand,' is now established..to denote seamen petty officers of the Royal Naval Reserve belonging to the Patrol Service when called into actual service in any commissioned trawler, drifter, or other small vessel.

Second-ha·ndedness. [-NESS.] = SECOND-HANDNESS.

1920 ROSE MACAULAY *Potterism* II. iii. § 3 Once you are tied up with a party, you can only avoid second-handedness, taking over views ready made. 1929 WHITEHEAD *Aims Educ.* iv. 79 The second-handedness of the learned world is the secret of its mediocrity.

Secos, variant of *SEKOS.

Secret, *a.* 1. i. Add: *Secret dovetail* (*joint*): a joint in which the dovetailing is concealed.

1882 W. J. CHRISTY *Joints* 168 Mitred Dovetail Joint... It is also designated secret dovetail.

Secretary, *sb.*[1] 5. (Earlier U.S. example.)

1815 *Niles' Weekly Register* IX. 36/1 Sideboards, secretaries, bureaus, and other articles of cabinet furniture.

Secretin (sĭkrī·tin). *Org. Chem.* [f. mod.L. *secretum* secretion + -IN[1].] A substance derived from the mucous membrane of the intestine, which stimulates the pancreas to secrete its juice.

Secretin is supposed to occur in the epithelial cells of the mucous membrane of the intestines in an inactive form called *prosecretin.*

1902 BAYLISS & STARLING in *Proc. Roy. Soc.* LXIX. 352. 1927 HALDANE & HUXLEY *Anim. Biol.* i. 18.

-sect [ad. L. *sect-us* cut, pa. pple. of *secāre* to cut], a termination of adjs. in scientific use, denoting 'cut, divided'; *spec.* in *Bot.* denoting forms of leaves which are divided as far as the midrib without being articulated so as to form separate leaflets, as in *palmatisect, pinnatisect.*

Section, *sb.* Add: 2. e. (Examples of U.S. use.)

1805 in *Ann. 9th Congress* 2 Sess. 1032 If the said lands shall be surveyed in townships of six miles square each, and the same divided into sections of one mile square each. 1831 PECK *Guide for Emigrants* 257 A district of country is first divided into..square miles, or..sections, as they are called in the surveys. 1871 *Scribner's Monthly* II. 664 A thicket of pines on a hillside, a 'section' that had been left when the adjoining fields were cleared. 1903 *Indian Laws & Tr.* III. 8 Section sixteen shall become a part of the reservation heretofore set apart for the use..of the Torros band.

g. *Mil.* Now, the fourth part of a platoon. Also (with qualification), a number of men detailed for a special service.

1913 *Army Order 323* 1 Oct. 4 The non-commissioned officers and men of the machine-gun section..will be distributed for discipline and administration in peace amongst the four companies. 1914 *Infantry Training* I. i. § 2. 4 The section commander must know his men thoroughly. *Ibid.* iii. § 75. 64 Section drill. The section will be exercised in all the movements of squad drill. 1915 D. O. BARNETT *Lett.* 100 At first I thought the whole section was done in, as rifles and equipment flew in the air. 1919 G. K. ROSE *2/4th Oxf. & Bucks Lt. Infty.* 119 When all the sections—the Lewis-gunners, bombers, rifle-grenadiers, and riflemen—were finally complete.

n. (See quot.)

1924 H. J. SKELTON *Econ. Iron & Steel* 278 In Great Britain the product in bars or rods shaped in a rolling mill, when not round or square or flat in cross section, is called a 'section' or sectional material.

7. a. (Further U.S. examples in senses 2 e (*b*), 2 k.)

1884 A. E. SWEET & J. A. KNOX *On Mexican Mustang Thr. Texas* x. 121 Mr. O'Lafferty was *section-boss of No. —, on the G. H. and S. A. Railroad. 1817 *Niles' Weekly Register* XII. 97/2 At the distance of every mile..*section corners are established. 1845 CAROLINE M. KIRKLAND *Western Clearings* 6 Such ransacking of the woods (as there was) for section corners, ranges and base lines! 1887 C. B. GEORGE *40 Years on Rail* ix. 167 The men, from *section hands to conductor, would have gone to the ends of the earth to do him a good turn. 1903 *Congressional Directory* 116 As a common laborer or 'section hand' on the railroad. 1878 J. H. BEADLE *Western Wilds* iii. 51 A *section-house by the roadside..marks the site where sales to the amount of millions were made in two months. 1903 *N. Y. Evening Post* 29 Aug., Crowbars and tools were identified as having been taken from the railroad section house.

Sectional, *a.* Add: 1. (Earlier U.S. example.)

1806 in *Ann. 9th Congress* 1 Sess. 1042 Let a narrow, selfish, local, sectional policy prevail and struggles will commence.

3. *Sectional bookcase*, one composed of a stack or stacks of book sections, which may be expanded to any height and width by fitting together additional sections and stacks.

1901 *Furniture Record* 15 June, Suppl. 4 The Gunn K.D. Sectional Book Cases. a 1909 'O. HENRY' *Roads of Destiny* v. 74 A whole deckle-edged library..in sectional bookcases.

4. Of steel: Rolled in the form of sections (see *SECTION *sb.* 2 n).

1924 H. J. SKELTON *Econ. Iron & Steel* 279 Wherever practicable, it is desirable that rolled shapes or sectional material in mild steel should be ordered from the list of British Standard Sections. 1924 *Times Trade & Engin. Suppl.* 29 Nov. 242/3 Although there is a very slight increase in the demand for sectional material, steelmakers are scarce of specifications for ship and boiler plates.

Sectionalization (sekʃənəlaizēⁱ·ʃən). [See -ATION.] The action or result of dividing into sections.

1920 *Public Opinion* 17 Sept. 268/1 The very formula of 'nationalisation' was a sham, sectionalisation was the object. 1929 *Times* 22 July 15/2 Extreme individualism, unorganized competition, over-sectionalization, out-of-date methods of marketing..are some of the more general causes of the present distresses.

Sector, *sb.* Add: 1. b. Also *spherical sector.*

c. *Mil.* A portion or section of a front, corresponding generally to a sector of a circle the centre of which is a headquarters.

1916 BOYD CABLE *Action Front* 237 The Colonel was..vainly trying to recall any sap-head within his sector of line. 1917 W. J. LOCKE *Red Planet* xiv, Somewhere in this region —or sector, as we call it nowadays—there was a certain bit of ground that had been taken and retaken over and over again. 1918 E. S. FARROW *Dict. Mil. Terms* s.v., The combination of several supporting points under one commander forms a sector.

Secure, *v.* Add: 7. To obtain the services of (a person).

1854 *Punch* 29 Apr. 178/1 The great tragedian Mackean had been 'secured' to perform the highest possible tragedy at the lowest possible salary.

8. *Horticulture.* (See quot.)

1928 *Daily Express* 11 Aug. 4/2 The Japanese varieties of the chrysanthemum are now beginning to show their flower buds, and these should be 'secured', as it is called, at the earliest possible moment. This is done by pinching out with the thumb and finger the incipient side shoots or laterals that will be found in process of formation immediately beneath the buds and in the axils of the leaves.

Security. 11. Add:

1925 *Times* 2 Sept., The jurists who are discussing the technical details of the proposed *Security Pact at the Foreign Office. 1933 *Ibid.* 8 Mar. 13/3 Security Pact for Europe. 1932 *News Chron.* 23 Sept. 6/3 Only about six British engravers can produce satisfactory stamps. They count as '*security printing,' like banknotes.

Sedan. Add: 1. (Later U.S. example.)

1857–8 *Trans. Ill. Agric. Soc.* III. 362 All sorts of vehicles, from the single sedan of the physician..to the twenty and fifty horse power team.

c. A motor car having a single compartment for four or more persons including the driver. *U.S.*

1915 *Literary Digest* (N.Y.) 21 Aug. Cover advt., A touring car when the windows are down...With the windows raised, a luxurious sedan. 1922 *Short Stories* Feb. 98/1 The sedan had been equipped with an exhaust foot warmer or heater. 1928 WATKINS *Air Murders* xxii, The car was a dusty sedan.

Sedate, *a.* Add: 1. e. Of inanimate objects: Not unduly striking in colour or design; quiet and restful in tone.

1924 ANNA D. SEDGWICK *Little French Girl* I. vi, Sedate chairs with backs and seats embroidered in green and dove-colour were ranged along the wall. *Ibid.*, There was a sedate sofa to match the chairs.

Sedentary, *a.* Add: 5. *Geol.* Of soil or loose rock material: Remaining upon the rock of which it was formed by disintegration.

1870 S. W. JOHNSON *How Crops Feed* II. iii. 143 (Funk) Sedentary soils, or soils in place, are those which have not been transported by geological agencies. 1929 *Daily Tel.* 22 Jan. 4/7 The soil being considered 'sedentary' in character.

Seder (sēⁱ·dəɹ). [Aram.] The Ashkenazic name for the ritual of the first night of the Passover.

1865 *Chambers's Encycl.* VII. 312/1 At a later period, a certain number of cups of red wine were superadded to this meal, to which, as its special ceremonies and the order of its benedictions were fixed, the name *Seder* (arrangement) was given. 1909 *Cent. Dict.* Suppl. s.v., The seder table is very elaborately decorated...The celebrant, generally the head of the family, begins with the first of the thirteen functions in the seder service.

Sedge, *sb.*[1] 6. Add: **sedge-boat**, (*b*) *U.S.*, a boat for transporting sedge; **sedge-ground** *U.S.*, ground covered with sedge.

1839 *Knickerbocker Mag.* XIII. 503 The bridge..under which *sedge-boats could pass with their sails set. 1843 *Ibid.* XXII. 33 Here two negro boatmen..had consented to ..row us out in their new sedge-boat. 1667 *Plymouth Rec.* 95 All that parte of the pod or *sedge-ground which lyeth between a place there called the Gurnett and the bounds. 1740 in *Mayflower Desc.* XI. 5 Richard Mayo & Rebecca Mayo his wife..sold to Richard Sparrow..that lot of Medow or sedge ground lying in Eastham. 1910 C. HARRIS *Eve's Husband* 30 The poor brown sedge-ground of an old field.

Sediment, *v.* Add: b. To cause to deposit sediment.

1908 *Practitioner* Jan. 55 The urine should be sedimented and examined for gonococci.

Sedra (sēⁱ·dră). [Aram.; = Syriac *sedro* order, arrangement.] In Jewish sabbatical liturgy, one of the fifty-four sections of the Pentateuch read in the synagogue at the Sabbath morning service.

1909 *Cent. Dict.* Suppl. s.v., The sedras must be read at the morning Sabbath services during the year, but as a year has only 52 weeks, in order to finish the sedras two of them are read on two special sabbaths.

See, *v.* Add: 3. Also, to understand (a person). *U.S.*

1872 E. EGGLESTON *End of World* xxiii. 158 '[I] See yer,' said Bill, trying in vain to draw his coat. 1873 J. H. BEADLE *Undevel. West* xx. 369 'Marshal's got a good thing, though.' I see you; best place to make money in the United States.

h. To perceive (good qualities) *in* a person or thing; to perceive (a certain characteristic or type) *in* one who is usually regarded in another way.

1831 SCOTT *Ct. Robert* iv, Hereward, though flattered by the unusual degree of attention which the Princess bestowed upon him, saw in her only the daughter of his Emperor. 1835 BROWNING *Paracelsus* III. 419 A professorship At Basil! Since you see so much in it. 1864 BRYCE *Holy Rom. Emp.* ix. (1875) 146 He put to death the rebel Crescentius, in whom modern enthusiasm has seen a patriotic republican. 1891 'J. S. WINTER' *Lumley* iii, 'What on earth can be see in *her*?'..'It doesn't matter what you see or don't see. You are not wanted to marry her, so it is immaterial whether you can see anything in her or not!'

i. In negative or interrog. context: To see in one's mind's eye; to imagine or contemplate the possibility of.

1926 B. GILBERT *Lett. Amer.* 117 I can't see you doing the trick. *Mod.* I can't see myself bathing in the river before breakfast.

j. To forecast, prophesy. *U.S.*

1927 *Boston Herald* 19 Sept., 58 seats seen for Cosgrave.

7. b. *See* (*him, etc.*) *off*: a command to a dog to get rid of an intruder.

1929 *Times* 21 Feb. 11 When he and another detective went to arrest the men Hughes called to the Alsatian. 'See 'em off.'

10. *To have seen better days*: also, of a thing.

1806 [see DAY *sb.* 13 a]. *Mod.* He was dressed in an old coat that had seen better days.

12. b. (Earlier U.S. examples.)

1871 BARNUM *Struggles & Triumphs* 692 The New York Legislature having refused us a charter unless I would 'see' the 'ring' a thousand dollars' worth, which I declined. 1873 'MARK TWAIN' & WARNER *Gilded Age* xv. 141 'It will take a good deal of money to start the enterprise,' remarked Mr. Bolton, who knew very well what 'seeing a Pennsylvania legislature meant'.

24. d. Phrases. *To see through a brick wall, a millstone* (see MILLSTONE 2).

1861 H. KINGSLEY *Ravenshoe* xxxv, He could see through a brick wall as well as most men. 1896 FARMER & HENLEY *Slang* s.v. *Millstone*, To see (or look) through a mill-stone (or brick wall), to be well-informed; to judge with precision; to be quick of perception.

27. d. (Earlier U.S. example.)

1782 *Essex Inst. Hist. Coll.* I. 13/2, I am detarmend, as I have beene so long in the servis, to se it out.

28. (Later examples.)

1890 *Harper's Mag.* Oct. 715/2 Most of the college boys remained,..to get the worth of their tickets, and to 'see the thing through'. 1916 H. G. WELLS (*title*) Mr. Britling sees it through.

Seed, *sb.* Add: 5. c. The larvæ of the insect which produces lac.

1901 *Knowledge* Nov. 252/2 Propagation..is effected by tying small twigs, on which are crowded the eggs or larvæ of the insect, to the branches of the trees. These larvæ are technically called 'seed'.

6. b. A small seed-shaped tube to contain radium.

1923 *Glasgow Herald* 26 Mar. 9 To capture the gas emanating from radium, purify it, and bottle it in tiny tubes called from their shape seeds. *Ibid.*, Arrangements have now been made for the supply of these curative seeds to other hospitals.

c. *Sugar-manufacture.* Crystals of sugar placed in concentrated syrup to start fresh crystallization.

1915 H. C. P. GEERLIGS *Pract. White Sugar Manuf.* 80 White sugar destined for direct consumption should not only be white and brilliant, but should also possess a regular form and a rather large size; this latter desideratum makes it preferable to start the building up of the grain from a well-developed seed.

7. b. *seed-planter, -sower, -sowing.*

1852 *Trans. Mich. Agric. Soc.* III. 30 Best *seed planter, for hand or horse power, for hills and drills. 1849 *Rep. U.S. Comm. Patents, Agric.* (1850) 113 Their *seed-sowers and grain-crushers..do much to expedite the labors of the farm. 1873–4 *Rep. Vermont Board Agric.* II. 236 Then sow seed with a seed sower at the rate of four pounds per acre. 1865 *Rep. Maine Board Agric.* X. 65 The use of the drill for general *seed-sowing is at present considered too expensive.

8. **seed-feeder**, (*b*) a grub which lives in and feeds on seeds; **seed-leaf tobacco**, a kind of tobacco grown in the northern United States used chiefly for wrapping cigars, probably so called because it was first grown from imported seeds; **seed-station**, a place where seeds are tested; **seed-testing**, the examination of seeds in order to determine their purity, germinating power, etc.

1902 *Encycl. Brit.* XXVII. 633/1 These *seed-feeders may be killed in the seeds by subjecting them to the fumes of bisulphide of carbon. 1888 *Ibid.* XXIII. 425/2 The '*seed-leaf' tobacco of Pennsylvania, Connecticut, and Ohio, grown from Havana seed, is devoted to cigar-making in the United States. 1911 *Q. Rev.* Jan. 108 Almost every European country has *seed-stations. 1910 *Chambers's Jrnl.* Oct. 685/1 Next comes *seed-testing under the microscope, which shows the weed, seeds, and rubbish amongst them.

Seed, *v.* Add: 6. Also *absol.*

1888 *Vermont Agric. Rep.* X. 48, I..then seed broadcast with grass-seed.

7. (Earlier modern examples.)

1814 J. TAYLOR *Arator* 154 When the wheat was seeded on high and narrow ridges. 1851 C. CIST *Cincinnati* 317 The cotton crop is seeded in the spring.

11. *Sugar-manufacture.* To place sugar-crystals in (syrup) to promote crystallization. (Cf. *SEED *sb.* 6 c.)

1909 in *Cent. Dict.* Suppl.

b. *intr.* To form small grains of solid matter.

1887 *Col. & Indian Exhib.* 1886, *Rep. Col. Sect.* 272 The fatty acids 'seed' on cooling slowly, and yield a distinct solid and liquid on pressing.

12. *Sport*, esp. *Lawn Tennis.* To manage (the draw) so that certain players of the same nationality (orig. *U.S.* the best competitors) do not meet until the later rounds of a competition or tournament; also, to separate (players) in this way. Also in *ppl. a.*

1911 WEBSTER s.v., To seed the draw. 1924 *Times* 23 June, This year, for the first time, the draw has been 'seeded'. 1929 *Ibid.* 29 June 4/4 Three of the women who had been 'seeded' for the draw were defeated during the day...Miss Eileen Bennett, who was one of the 'seeded' players. 1929 *Star* 21 Aug. 16/3 Mrs. Michell meets Miss Gladman, one of the 'seeded' Americans, and two more of the 'seededs' will clash in the match between Miss Nuthall and Mrs. Bundy. 1930 *Times* 24 June 15/2 One of the seeded players was beaten by the American. 1931 *Daily Tel.* 21 May 17/6 The seeded pairs are drawing nearer together.

Seed-cake. (Later example.)

1871 MRS. STOWE *Pink & White Tyranny* ii. 23 A plate of seed-cakes covered with a hemstitched napkin.

2. Oil-cake. *U.S.*

1881 *Harper's Mag.* Oct. 726/2 The mass of kernels left after the hulls have been removed and the oil pressed out, is made into seed-cake, a most desirable food for stock.

Seed-corn. (Later U.S. example.)

1894 *Vermont Agric. Rep.* XIV. 47 Can common seed corn be raised at a profit?

Seeder. Add: 2. (Earlier U.S. example.)

1867 *Rep. Iowa Agric. Soc.* (1868) 226 The seeder can be adjusted in five minutes.

3. An apparatus for seeding fruit, etc.

1895 *Funk's Standard Dict.*

Seeing, *vbl. sb.* Add: 2. b. *Astr.* 'The state or quality of telescopic vision as affected by the condition of the atmosphere' (Funk's Standard Dict. 1928).

Seeker. Add: 1. d. A seeker after religion. *U.S.*

1838 CAROLINE GILMAN *Recoll. Southern Matron* 270 Persons of colour..become *seekers* in any church, and under any leader they prefer. 1880 *Scribner's Monthly* July 423/2 The crash seemed an electric summons to 'Brudder Brockus's' flock, and saints and 'seekers' came hurrying in.

Seep, *v.* Add: Also *fig.*

1925 H. L. FOSTER *Trop. Tramp Tourists* 121 Through the closed doors there seeped out a great babble of conversation. 1930 COOPER *Ship of Truth* ii. 216 Serenity had seeped into his very soul.

Hence **See·ping** *ppl. a.*

1927 M. EIKER *Over the Boat-Side* xi. § 2. 161 The nagging, monotonous, unessential, seeping harassments that sap a man of achievement.

Seer[3] (sīᵊɹ). [Corruption of the Pg. name *serra* lit. 'saw'.] = SEIR-FISH.

1931 *Hardy's Anglers' Guide* 54 The big-game fishing includes..'seer' or 'surmai' (Cybium Guttatum).

Seercraft. [SEER[1].] The prophetic art.

1883 R. C. JEBB *Sophocles* I. 139 Thus did the messages of seer-craft (*O. T.* 723 φῆμαι μαντικαί) map out the future. 1913 G. MURRAY tr. *Rhesus of Euripides* 6 Sage and prophet, learned in the way of seercraft.

Seerhand (sī·rhand). [Name of a town, Panjab, India.] A medium-weight muslin.

1858 SIMMONDS *Dict. Trade*, *Seerhand*, a kind of muslin between nainsook and mull, particularly adapted for dresses, retaining its clearness after washing. 1882 CAULFEILD & SAWARD *Dict. Needlework*, *Seerhand Muslin*, this is a description of cotton fabric somewhat resembling Nainsook and Mull, being a kind of intermediate quality, as compared to them.

Seersucker. (Earlier Amer. examples.)

1722 in *Maryland Hist. Mag.* XX. 64 To Corded Dimothy. To I Sea Sucker Do. 1725 *Boston News-Letter* 24 June, A Seersucker Jacket and Breeches. 1736 *Virginia Gazette* 15 Oct., A Seesucker Gown, one white Linen Ditto.

See-see (sī·sī). Also **seesee, sisi.** [? Imitative.] In full *see-see partridge*: A small sand-partridge, *Ammoperdix bonhami*, of western Asia and India.

1895 *Funk's Standard Dict.* 1922 *Blackw. Mag.* Dec. 816/2 There were see-see to be chased at odd moments in the ravines. 1923 *Ibid.* July 125/2 Game abounded—black

partridge and sisi, hare and pigeon. 1928 *Ibid.* Apr. 544/2 We had an exciting and noisy hunt after a see-see partridge...It is almost impossible to get see-sees to rise.

Segmented, *ppl. a.* Add: 1. c. In general sense: Divided into sections or segments.

1920 *Glasgow Herald* 9 Mar. 9 Vestiges of a segmented central gallery were disclosed.

Sego. *U.S.* (Earlier example.)

1875 *Amer. Naturalist* IX. 18 The general Indian name of 'Sego' is applied indiscriminately to all the edible bulbs of this region.

Segregable, *a.* Delete *rare*[−1] and add examples.

1905 BATESON & PUNNETT in *Rep. Evol. Com. Roy. Soc.* II. 124 (Cent. D. Suppl.) An extracted type..may carry on segregable determinants. 1909 BATESON tr. *Mendel's Princ. Heredity* 13 Until the properties and laws of interaction of the segregable units have been much more thoroughly examined. 1909 R. H. LOCK *Variation, Heredity, & Evol.* xi. 301 When the parent types differ in more than one pair of segregable characters.

Segregate, *v.* Add: 4. Of Mendelian hybrids: To separate into dominants, recessives, and hybrids, in conformity with a numerical law.

1905 R. C. PUNNETT *Mendelism* (1907) 23 The characters are said to segregate in the gametes. 1909 R. H. LOCK *Variation, Heredity, & Evol.* iii. 216 A considerable number of cases were formerly described in which the first cross or heterozygote of F1 bred true instead of segregating in F2. 1930 R. A. FISHER *Genet. Theory Nat. Selection* i. 9 Mendel also demonstrated what a theorist could scarcely have ventured to postulate, that the different factors examined by him in combination, segregated in the simplest possible manner, namely independently.

Segregation. Add: 1. e. *Biol.* The separation or isolation of a group of organisms from closely related groups by some reproductive or physical barrier.

1902 *Encycl. Brit.* XXVIII. 344/2 Wallace's studies of island life, and the work of many different observers on local races of animals and plants, marine, fluviatile, and terrestrial, have brought about a conception of segregation as apart from differences of environment as being one of the factors in the differentiation of living forms. The segregation may be geographical, or may be the result of preferential mating, or of seasonal mating.

f. In Mendelian inheritance: (*a*) the separation of the descendants of Mendelian inheritance into dominants, recessives, and hybrids; (*b*) the separation of allelomorphic characters in the gametes formed by a hybrid organism.

1905 R. C. PUNNETT *Mendelism* (1907) 23 *margin*, The Principles of Gametic Segregation. 1909 BATESON *Mendel's Princ. Heredity* 11 This phenomenon, the dissociation of characters from each other in the course of the formation of the germs, we speak of as *segregation*. 1909 R. H. LOCK *Variation, Heredity, & Evol.* viii. 202 Mendel's law of segregation. 1930 R. A. FISHER *Genet. Theory Nat. Selection* i. 8 The segregation of single pairs of genes, that is of single factors, was demonstrated by Mendel in his paper of 1865.

Segregator (se·grĭgēⁱtəɹ). [f. SEGREGATE *v.* + -OR.] An instrument for obtaining the urine from one kidney unmixed with that of the other.

1903 *Ann. Surg.* Jan. 30 The segregator could not possibly have attained the results given thus by catheterism and the strong aspiration. 1907 *Practitioner* Nov. 642 A slow secretion of dilute urine from the affected side is shown by the segregator. 1910 *Ibid.* Mar. 302 The ureteric catheterisation possesses advantages over the segregator.

Seivhal, sei whale: see *SEJHVAL.

Seize, *sb.* [f. SEIZE *v.* 11.] An act of 'seizing'.

1912 F. A. TALBOT *Motor-Cars* 35 The heat causes the cylinder and the piston rings to expand until at last they become jammed irremovably together, precipitating what is known in motoring parlance as a 'seize'.

Seize, *v.* 11. Add: Also with *up*. Hence **Sei·ze-up**, the state of bearings, etc., being seized up.

1912 *Motor Manual* vi. (ed. 14) 232 Unless one makes quite certain that every bearing and cylinder be properly relubricated before starting up again, a 'seize-up'..is not improbable. 1917 *Blackw. Mag.* May 807/1 Our engine recovered slightly now that its recovery was not so important, and it behaved well until it seized up for better or worse when we had landed. 1925 *Morris Owner's Manual* 29 Neglect of this results in harsh running and an overheated engine, loss of power, and finally 'seizing-up' of pistons or connecting rods.

Sejhval (sē·vāl). Also **seivhal**; semi-anglicized **sei whale.** [Norw.] One of the smaller rorqual whales, *Balænoptera borealis*, found in British seas.

1912 *Rep. Brit. Assoc.* 158 The Right whales and Sejhvals are said to appear only during the earlier part of the season. 1914 *Ibid.* 146 The only Sejhval which was captured was brought in on September 6, a fact which is to be noted in connection with the whalers' statement to Burfield, that the Sejhval disappears by the end of June. 1919 R. W. CLARK in Shackleton *South* I. App. 364 The sperm-whale and the sei-whale have shown a good deal of seasonal variation, though never numerous. 1923 *Chambers's Jrnl.* 112/1 The lesser rorqual, the seivhal, and the humpback.

Sekos (sī·kǫs). Also **secos.** [a. Gr. σηκός pen, enclosure.] A sacred enclosure in an ancient Egyptian temple, where none but those privileged may enter.

1820 BELZONI *Narr. Egypt & Nubia* III. 291 Having observed, that the part where the sekos and cella must be was not touched..the sekos or shrine containing the figure of the deity. 1887 *Archit. Publ. Soc. Dict.* s.v., In the Egyptian temples the *secos* was the same as the *adytum* of the Greeks and Romans.

Seladang (sĕlā·dæŋ). Also **saladang, salandang, sladang.** [Borneo *seladang*, Sumatra *saladang*.] a. Malay name for the gaur, *Bos gaurus*. b. The Indian tapir, *Tapirus indicus*.

1820 RAFFLES in *Trans. Linnean Soc.* XIII. 270 It [*sc.* Tapirus Malayanus] is known by different names in different parts of the country [*sc.* Sumatra]. By the people of Limun [in Sumatra] it is called Saladang. 1884 STERNDALE *Mammalia India & Ceylon* 481 *Gavæus gaurus. Salandang* in the Malay countries. 1898 RATHBORNE *Camping in Malaya* 68 Elephants and seladang (*bos sondaicus*). 1905 HUBBACK *Elephant & Seladang Hunting* 44 The seladang has no dew-lap and no hump. *Ibid.* 47 Seladang are only found in little-inhabited districts. 1910 *Chambers's Jrnl.* May 282/1 Larger game, such as the tiger, sladang, pig, and deer, abound. 1927 H. M. TOMLINSON *Gallion's Reach* xxxv. § 3 A likely corner for sladang.

Selamlik (sĕlā·mlik). [Turkish.] a. That part of a Mohammedan house reserved for the men. b. The official visit of the Sultan to the mosque every Friday.

1895 *Funk's Standard Dict.* 1905 *N.Y. Globe* 21 July (Cent. D. Suppl.) It is reported here officially from Constantinople that during to-day's *selamlik* an attempt was made to assassinate the sultan. 1922 *Glasgow Herald* 22 Nov. 9 The ordinary Selamlik at the Fatis Mosque. *Ibid.* 25 Nov. 9 The Selamlik completed, the new Khalif returned to the Seraglio.

Selbornian (selbǭ·ɹniăn), *a* and *sb.* [f. *Selborne*, a parish in Hampshire + -IAN.] a. *adj.* Of, pertaining to, or connected with Selborne, the residence of Gilbert White (1720–1793), natural historian; *spec.* in *Geol.*, denoting the Gault and Upper Greensand taken together (see quot. 1900). Also *absol.* b. *sb.* A lover of the writings of Gilbert White.

1869 LOWELL *Lit. Ess.*, *My Garden Acquaintance* Writ. 1890 III. 194 How pleasant is his innocent vanity in adding to the list of the British, and still more of the Selbornian, *fauna*! 1900 JUKES-BROWN *Cretaceous Rocks Brit.* I. 1 The Selbornian comprises the beds which are generally known as the Gault and the upper Greensand. *Ibid.* 31 It is not intended that the name Selbornian shall supersede those of Gault and Greensand...As a matter of fact gault clay and greensand are only two of the different kinds of deposits that make up the group for which the name Selbornian is now proposed...The group will be the Selbornian, and its subdivisions will be zones characterised by different assemblages of fossils. 1928 *Observer* 26 Feb. 8/5 Another book about 'Gilbert White',..a book full of pleasures for all Selbornians.

Seldomly, *adv.* (Modern U.S. example.)

a 1886 E. DICKINSON *Poems* (1927) 310 What distance far, So I the ships may see That touch how seldomly Thy shore?

Selectivity (sĭlekti·vĭti). *Wireless Telegr.* [f. SELECTIVE *a.* + -ITY.] The quality or condition of being selective; the power to select a particular wave-length or frequency and to exclude others.

1903 *Elect. World & Engin.* 1 Aug. 173 (Cent. D. Suppl.) The system of selectivity devised by Sir Oliver [Lodge]. 1921 *Discovery* Apr. 93/2 For a warship very selective apparatus is an absolute essential..but in the merchant service great selectivity may often be a distinct disadvantage. 1925 P. J. RISDON *Crystal Receivers & Circuits* 22 Fair selectivity can be obtained with such an arrangement of vario-coupler as that indicated.

Self, *pron., a.*, and *sb.* Add: B. *adj.* 3. b. Also in wider application.

1930 R. A. FISHER *Genet. Theory Nat. Selection* vii. 165 The hooded grandchildren would have received these equally from their self and from their hooded grand-parents. 1932 *Sale Catal.*, Little Boys' Shirt Blouses...Fast colour self poplins.

C. *sb.* 6. b. An animal of a uniform colour.

1930 R. A. FISHER *Genet. Theory Nat. Selection* vii. 165 Rats of both selected lines were bred back to unselected selfs.

Self (self), *v.* [f. the sb.] *trans.* in *pass.* To be fertilized by its own pollen, to be self-fertilized.

1905 PUNNETT *Mendelism* 61 When this, the normal mode of fertilisation, takes place, the flower is said to be selfed. 1924 E. W. MACBRIDE *Study of Heredity* vi. 143 When the recessive green peas are sown they give rise to plants which, when 'selfed', bear only green peas.

Self-. Add examples of obvious compounds in various senses. Also: 1. a. **self-affirmation** *Psychol.*, the recognition and assertion of the existence of the conscious self; **self-differentiation** *Embryol.*, that specialization or differentiation of structures which in their development are largely independent of adjacent structures.

1901 'LUCAS MALET' *Hist. Sir R. Calmady* I. ix, Her mother-love..had none of the sweet *self-abandon..which that earlier passion had. 1924 W. B. SELBIE *Psych. Relig.* 183 If there is any truth in our contention that religion is natural to man, then it should grow with his growth and become one of the normal factors in his development and in his *self-adjustment to the universe. *Ibid.* 53 The part which feeling plays in the religious consciousness generally points to the giving of a religious direction to that desire for self-realization, or *self-affirmation, which is so characteristic of man at all the stages of his development. 1900 *Science* 10 Jan. 62/1 The observations proved conclusively that the casting off of the rays [*sc.* of star-fish] is, in most cases at least, not accidental, but a true *self-amputation. 1904 KATH. C. THURSTON *John Chilcote* xi, He had..a feeling of bitter *self-commiseration that for the moment outweighed all other considerations. 1897 W. J. LOCKE *Derelicts* xxiii. The tragic futility of such *self-crucifixion. 1922 *Glasgow Observer* 18 Nov. 6 If Ireland was to be saved from *self-delusion. 1929 W. J. LOCKE *At Gate of Samaria* i.

Seven. B. *sb.* Add: **2. e.** Short for *seven-a-side (game, match)*, in Rugby football, one played with seven men on each side.

1931 *Daily Tel.* 4 May 9/1 Our sevens have been the means of raising nearly £8,000 for hospital charities.

Sevener. Add: **c.** A line of verse containing seven syllables.

1920 *Glasgow Herald* 15 June 5 The Italian sevener with normally three accents.

Seventeen, *a.* **4.** Add: **seventeen-year locust** (earlier U.S. examples).

1844 *Yale Lit. Mag.* IX. 335 The American Seventeen Year Locust. 1870 *Amer. Naturalist* III. 206 The eggs and young of the seventeen-year Cicada.

Seventh, *a.* and *sb.* Add: **A.** *adj.* **2. c.** *Seventh nerve*, each of the seventh pair of cranial nerves, a facial nerve.

1821 C. Bell *Expos. Nerves Hum. Body* (1824) 115 The *portio dura* of the seventh nerve. *Ibid.* 133 Although the fifth nerve was free, the pressure on the seventh nerve was sufficient to paralyze the muscles of the side of the face. *a* 1883 Fagge *Princ. & Pract. Med.* (1886) I. 486 It was formerly considered difficult to understand why the ninth and the seventh nerves..should..resemble the nerves of the limbs in showing impairment of function on the side opposite the lesion in the brain.

Seventy. **A.** *adj.* **2. b.** Add: *Seventy-five* (*b*), = F. *soixante-quinze*, a rapid-firing French gun of 75 mm. calibre.

1915 E. Wharton *Fighting France* 56 We began to come more and more frequently on big colonies of 'Seventy-fives'.

Severance. Add: **3.** *Comb.*: **severance cutting, felling** *Forestry*, the felling of a narrow strip of trees in order that the adjacent trees may become stronger.

1905 *Terms Forestry & Logging* 20 *Severance cuttings are made to strengthen the trees on the edge of a stand which will later be entirely exposed through the removal of the stand which now protects it. 1895 W. R. Fisher tr. *R. Hess' Forest Protection* 469 *Severance-fellings should be forty to fifty feet broad.

Severe, *a.* **9.** Add: In extended use (see quot.).

1881 *Sportsman's Year-bk.* 49 Twenty miles a day is often the work of a crack greyhound intended to run in a severe country.

Sewage, *sb.* **3.** Add: *sewage disposal* (also *attrib.*).

1902 *Encycl. Brit.* XXXII. 524/2. 1921 *Dict. Occup. Terms* (1927) § 970 Sewage disposal labourer. 1930 *Times* (weekly ed.) 9 Jan. 34 A large scale sewage disposal works.

Sewelling, variant of Shewelling.

Sewing, *vbl. sb.*[1] **4.** Add: *sewing bee, circle, room*; *sewing-bird* (earlier example).

1880 *Harper's Mag.* Aug. 354/2 There is church twice a month, *sewing bees, and apple-butter stirrings. 1885 Mrs. Eliz. B. Custer *Boots & Saddles* xii. 125 The ladies quietly arranged, as a surprise, a sewing-bee. 1868 in Hale *Ingham Papers* (1869) 224 What is the matter with New-Altona? Emily has a very good *sewing-bird that was made there. 1846 *Knickerbocker Mag.* XXVII. 373 As if I too belonged to a *sewing-circle, and read charity sermons. 1860 J. G. Holland *Miss Gilbert's Career* ii. 18 She managed the village sewing circle. 1880 *Harper's Mag.* Mar. 577/2 I've attended reg'lar to prayer meetin's and sewin' circle. 1852 E. E. Hale *If, Yes & Perhaps* (1868) 56 I always offered my services in the Sunday-schools and *sewing-rooms. 1881 *Rep. Indian Affairs* 189 In the sewing-room a number of the large girls cut and fit garments.

Sex, *sb.* Add: **5.** *sex-conflict, -disqualification, -equality.*

1909 *Daily Chron.* 3 Nov. 6/4 Once..introduce the lamentable *sex-conflict..and you introduce into the married problem a new and sordid element of discord. 1919 *Act* 9 & 10 *Geo. V* c. 71 § 4 This Act may be cited as the *Sex Disqualification (Removal) Act, 1919. 1921 *Daily Mail Year Bk.* 42/1 The organization of the League of Nations has from the outset been founded on the principle of *sex equality.

b. In many modern scientific terms relating to the origin, transmission, and functions of sex: **sex-chromosome**, a chromosome which transmits sex; **sex-control**, the control or modification of inherited characteristics by the sex of the inheritor; hence **sex-controlled** *a.*; **sex-determination**, the determination or influences which decide the sex of an individual; hence **sex-determiner**, that which determines sex; **sex-determining** *ppl. a.*; **sex-factor, -gene**, the factor or gene responsible for sex; **sex-intergrade**, an individual having characteristics of both sexes; **sex-limitation**, the limitation of certain characteristics to one sex; the occurrence of certain characteristics in one sex only; hence **sex-limited** *ppl. a.*, limited to one sex; **sex-linkage**, the state or condition of being sex-linked; **sex-linked** *a.*, denoting a character which is dependent on sex, so that it is dominant only in one or the other sex; also, denoting an individual possessing such a character; **sex ratio**, the ratio between the sexes under given circumstances; **sex-reversal**, a change in the sex of an organism.

1904 J. A. Thomson *Science Old & New* xxxii. 177 But our immediate point is simply that the *sex-antithesis may be but a special case of a still more widespread dichotomy. *Ibid.* xxiii. 128 The voice, primarily a *sex-call, becomes an instrument of reasonable discourse or a medium of purely aesthetic emotion. *Ibid.* xlii. 243 The suppression of the *sex-cell-bearing (gametophyte) generation. 1915 *Nature* 22 Apr. 197/1 Many facts point to the conclusion that a sex-determining factor sometimes resides in special *sex chromosomes. 1924 J. A. Thomson *Science Old & New* xxxii. 177 There are many indirect confirmations of this physiological theory of sex, which is not inconsistent with the view that the immediate index and trigger-puller of one sex or the other may be found in nuclear peculiarities (sex-chromosomes) in the germ-cells. 1931 E. B. Ford *Mendelism & Evol.* v. 96 This does not in the least mean that the stages in the development of *sex control have been arrived at by discontinuous variation. *Ibid.* 36 These two characters are *sex-controlled, that is to say they can only produce the characters for which they are responsible in the internal environment provided by one of the sexes. 1905 C. J. Bond in *Brit. Med. Jrnl.* 28 Oct. 1094/1 It is to this form of disease and *sex correlation that I wish to draw attention to-day. 1906 *Rep. Brit. Assoc.* 756 The segregation of *sex-determinants in a way analogous to the Mendelian segregation of inherited characters. 1905 T. H. Morgan in *Science* (N.S.) XXII. 839 Ziegler's Theory of *Sex Determination. 1909 R. H. Lock *Variation, Heredity, & Evol.* ix. 277 It is not necessarily to be supposed that the above description of the facts of sex-determination will hold good for every kind of organism. 1931 E. B. Ford *Mendelism & Evolution* v. 91 It has been established that sex determination is controlled quantitatively. 1913 W. Bateson *Mendel's Princ. Heredity* 321 Further suppose that N can only be borne by gametes containing a *sex-determiner. 1901 Geddes & Thomson *Evol. Sex* 31 In regard to Rotifers (*Hydatina*), Maupas maintains that temperature is the *sex-determining factor. 1915 *Nature* 22 Apr. 197/1 Many facts point to the conclusion that a sex-determining factor sometimes resides in special sex chromosomes. 1924 J. A. Thomson *Science Old & New* xxxii. 177 The *sex-divergence is primarily an illustration of a more wide-spread organismal dichotomy. *Ibid.* xv. 82 An expression and an evocation of *sex-excitement. 1919 R. C. Punnett *Mendelism* (ed. 5) 100 It is necessary to suppose that the male *Drosophila* is always heterozygous both for the *sex-factor and for the factor for red-eye. 1931 E. B. Ford *Mendelism & Evol.* i. 24 Sex is dependent upon genetic factors carried in a particular pair of chromosomes. They have a quantitative action; one dose of the sex factors producing one sex and two doses the other. 1930 R. A. Fisher *Genet. Theory Nat. Selection* vii. 164 In fishes it appears that we ought more properly to speak of the *sex-gene rather than the sex-chromosome as the agent of sex determination. 1919 R. C. Punnett *Mendelism* (ed. 5) 100 They have been able to correlate these peculiar differences in *sex-heredity with differences in the minute structure of the cells of which the bodies of the two sexes are composed. 1924 J. A. Thomson *Science Old & New* xxi. 114 The occurrence of '*sex-intergrades', such as very masculine females, is well known among pigeons. 1919 *Daily Mail Year Bk.* 10/1 The mysteries of life, and especially of *sex-life, should be unfolded to young people wholesomely, but clearly. 1924 J. A. Thomson *Science Old & New* xxii. 125 Disturbances in the sex-life are often registered in abnormalities of the antlers. 1913 W. Bateson *Mendel's Princ. Heredity* 229 Dr. C. J. Bond..calls attention to evidence suggesting *sex-limitation in certain deaf-mute families, sometimes the male, sometimes the female being the affected sex. 1909 *Darwin & Mod. Science* (ed. A. C. Seward) v. 94 A study of the *sex-limited descent of certain features in other animals. 1919 R. C. Punnett *Mendelism* (ed. 5) 95 Sex-limited inheritance or the type we have been discussing has been demonstrated in other birds besides poultry. 1930 R. A. Fisher *Genet. Theory Nat. Selection* vi. 132 The influence of mutual combats of the males in the evolution of sex-limited weapons. 1931 E. B. Ford *Mendelism & Evol.* i. 14 *Sex-linkage. 1914 *Rep. Brit. Assoc.* 419 Two other traits appear ..as *sex-linked characters. They are transmitted through mothers to some or all of their sons. 1930 R. A. Fisher *Genet. Theory Nat. Selection* iii. 65 Since the factor is sex-linked, dominance can only appear in the female. 1908 J. A. Thomson *Heredity* xiii. 505 The particular *sex-ratio now general has been long established. 1930 G. R. de Beer *Embryol. & Evol.* iii. 22 A series of degrees of intersexuality can be established from very slight to complete *sex-reversal.

c. Pertaining to or characterized by (excessive or morbid) consciousness of sex; pertaining to the reactions of a member of one sex to a member of the other, as *sex antagonism, feeling, life, repression*; sometimes = Sexual *a.* 3; **sex appeal**, the appeal exercised through sexual attraction; qualities which attract members of the opposite sex; hence **sex-appeal** *v.*, to exercise sex appeal (upon); **sex hatred**, hatred caused by or having its origin in feelings aroused by sex; **sex instinct**, the instinct which is held to govern the relations between the sexes; *esp.* the desire for the opposite sex; **sex urge**, desire for the gratification of the sexual impulse.

1923 *Q. Rev.* July 144 Doctrines calculated to foster *sex-antagonism. 1927 *Sunday Express* 14 Aug. 4 She has a large endowment of the 'plus' quality of femininity, the unexplainable but unmistakable flair called '*sex-appeal'. 1928 B. Nichols *Star-spangled Manner* xxi. 245 She is called The Evangelist with the Sex Appeal. 1930 Joanna Cannan *No Walls of Jasper* 138 Phyl did not get on with men. It wasn't only that she hadn't sex appeal. 1928 *Daily Express* 24 Nov. 4/1 *Sex-appealing women should cut out the hurt feelings, the dewy eyes, trembling lips, the 'Please, I'm just a woman' stuff. 1928 *Sunday Dispatch* 9 Dec. 12/3 A person not being 'sex-appealed' is simply inconceivable to them. 1932 R. Lynd in *News Chron.* 20 June 4/1 Both [stories] are glittering, glamorous, sex-appealing. 1932 P. K. Sen *From Punishment to Prevention* 137 Jealousy, hatred, *sex feeling..combine to cloud the judgement and stand in the way of the normal exercise of reason over a long period of time. 1914 Geddes & Thomson *Sex* i. (1925) 15 *Sex-festivals..with their strange mingling of religious emotion and sexual license. 1926 M. Leinster *Dew on Leaf* v. 60 It was the primitive *sex-hatred for the other woman. 1913 D. H. Lawrence *Sons & Lovers* ix. The *sex instinct that Miriam had over-refined for so long now grew particularly strong. 1922 W. S. Swisher *Relig. & New Psychol.* 17 Since the sex-instinct is the strongest of all instincts, the one upon which the perpetuation of the race depends, it is to be expected that religion should be full of idealized sex emotion. 1923 Rose Macaulay *Told by an Idiot* i. § 13. 49 She was..the type of mother whose strong sex instinct leads her to prefer boys to girls. 1925 J. C. Powys *Ducdame* x. 138 That first revelation of what the sex-instinct can sink into. 1922 S. Paton *Signs of Sanity* vi. 205 Some phases of our instinctive activities..we discuss frankly..; others, notably the *sex-life, we treat in a..furtive manner. 1927 B. K. Seymour *Three Wives* i. ix. There are lots of people who want a sex life but don't by any means want marriage. 1925 G. W. Deeping *Sorrell & Son* xii. § 1 It was not evident that the women wished to kiss Sorrell. He was more than a *sex-man. 1909 — *Roper's Row* vii. § 1 She saw in him a man-child who would need the mother in woman more than the *sex-mate. 1923 W. R. Inge *Lay Thoughts* (1926) 254 The pleasantest side of our civilisation—the ease with which innocent friendships are made between men and women—stands or falls with that Christian *sex-morality which is now being openly flouted. 1925 G. W. Deeping *Three Rooms* xxv. § 2 She was in a state of emotional confusion, rebel and lonely child, the victim of her unrealized *sex-pride. 1926 M. Leinster *Dew on Leaf* v. 59 He talked..about health, climate, and *sex-repression. 1925 G. W. Deeping *Sorrell & Son* xxxvii. § 2 Getting up in the morning and going to bed, catching trains, eating indifferent food, responding rather blindly to the *sex urge.

Sexed, *a.* Add: **3.** With prefixed adj. or adv.: Having the sexual desires and emotions (highly, etc.) developed.

1908- [see *Over-sexed *a.*]. 1921 *Outward Bound* Mar. 13/2 Had Elizabeth been as strongly sexed as she. 1925 G. W. Deeping *Sorrell & Son* xiii. § 2 She was not a bad woman, only a highly sexed one.

Sexology (seksǫ·lŏdʒi). [f. Sex *sb.* + -ology.] The scientific study of sex and of the relations between the sexes. Hence **Sexolo·gical** *a.*, of or pertaining to sexology; **Sexo·logist**, one who studies sexology.

1920 *Contemp. Rev.* July 93 *note*, A point of some sexological interest. 1927 *British Weekly* 15 Sept. 516/3 The section on Sexology is rather overshadowed by the fact that the doctor is a specialist in this subject. 1929 *19th Cent.* Oct. 459 When he leaves his province, as many so-called sexologists are in the habit of doing.

Sexual, *a.* Add: **2.** *Sexual selection*: see Selection 3 b.

e. *Sexual dimorphism*: (*a*) the condition in a species in which the two sexes have marked differences in form; (*b*) the condition of having one of the sexes existing in two forms, as in certain kinds of butterflies where the females are of two forms.

1888 [see Dimorphism b]. 1900 J. T. Cunningham (*title*) Sexual Dimorphism in the Animal Kingdom. 1902 *Encycl. Brit.* XXVII. 625/2 *Bonellia* and *Hamingia* are very interesting examples of sexual dimorphism.

Sexy (se·ksi), *a.* [f. Sex *sb.* + -y[1].] Engrossed in or concerned with sex. Hence **Se·xiness.**

1928 *Daily Express* 5 Nov. 10/3 But it is much more dangerous to enter into a conversation of this sexy sort with foolish, meddling people. 1928 *Sunday Dispatch* 2 Dec. 19/2 Australian audiences..like sex plays, but they mustn't be too sexy.

Seym (sǟm). [Pol.] The Polish parliament.

1920 C. R. Ballard *Russia* ii. 45 The worst curse of Poland was its aristocracy. The constitution was a limited monarchy, but all power was really in the Seym or House of Lords. 1921 *Blackw. Mag.* Jan. 77/2 Poland had set out to elect a provisional Seym or Parliament. 1928 *Spectator* 10 Mar. 346/2 When he seized political power the Seym was so divided as to be incapable of any good work.

Sh (ʃ), *v.* [f. Sh *int.* (Cf. Shshsh, *Shush.)] *trans.* To reduce to silence or tranquility with the (repeated) sound of 'sh!'; to hush.

1887 Augusta Wilson *Tiberius* vii, I patted and 'she-e-d' her [*sc.* a baby]. [1916 Boyd Cable *Action Front* 62 Ainsley 'sh-sh-shed' him to silence.]

Shab, *v.* Add: **4.** To stint, 'scrimp'.

1886 *Century Mag.* XXXI. Apr. 867/1 There ain't anything mean about this house,..they don't shab the measure.

Shabby, *v.* [f. the adj.] *intr.* To act shabbily.

1898 Marg. Deland *Old Chester Tales* 213 'They'll be shabbying on me', said Katy.

Shack, *v.*[2] Add: **1. b.** To move *along* with a slow ambling gait. *U.S.*

1916 H. Titus *I conquered* ii. 31 Yonder [was] a man shacking along on a rough little horse, head down, listless.

Shackling, *ppl. a.* **2.** *U.S.* (Earlier example.)

1853 F. W. Thomas *John Randolph*, etc. 216 Our host, Mr. Stetson, was the owner of an old, shabby, shackling gig.

Shackly, *a.* *U.S.* (Earlier example.)

1843 *Indiana Q. Mag. Hist.* III. 121, I stopped at a small poverty-stricken little town called Mt Meridian; shackly houses, huts and hovels..gave no great expectation of refinements.

Shad, *sb.* **4. b.** Add: **shad-blow** *U.S.* [Blow *sb.*[3]] = *shad-blossom, -bush*; **shad-bush** (earlier example; also *ellipt.*); **shad-spirit** *U.S.*, the shad-bird.

1869 Jane G. Fuller *Uncle John's Flower Gatherers* 30 This is what you children call '*Shadblow'. 1890 *Harper's Mag.* Apr. 710/2 Shadblow, with leaves of bluish green, white flowers or green berries waiting for the sun to make them red. 1837 Peck *Gaz. Illinois* I. 43 *Shadbush leaved out, April 12, 1834. 1886 *Harper's Mag.* June 149/1 Kites, tops, hoops..all appear in due season as regularly as..the blossoms of the 'shad'. *a* 1888 Grinnell in Trumbull *Names Birds* 157 (Cent. D. Suppl.) As the bird arrives about the same time as the shad..the fishermen..bear its sharp cry as it flies away through the darkness. They do not know

the cause of the sound, and from the association they dubbed its author the *shad spirit.

Shad-bellied, *a.* *U.S.* (Earlier example.)

1829-32 J. P. Kennedy *Swallow Barn* II. i. 5 A shad-bellied blue bobtail coat.

Shadchan (ʃā·dχan, ʃā·dtʃān). Also **schadchan, s(c)hatchen, shadkin.** [Yiddish, a. mod. Heb. *shadkhān*, f. Aram. *sh'dukh* to pacify.] A professional marriage-broker, esp. among the Russian and Eastern Jews.

a 1889 *American Paper* (Barrère & Leland) The shadkin business has received a bad set-back in Brooklyn. A shadkin is a marriage broker. He is a very useful man. He finds out spinsters who have money and then he makes a bargain with some fellow who wants a wife with money and gets the couple introduced. Ten per cent. of the dowry goes to the shadkin when the others become kin.

Shade, *sb.* Add: **11. a.** (U.S. examples.)

1863 O. W. Norton *Army Lett.* 174 A large force of men putting up booths or shades of poles and brush over the tents. 1867 *Amer. Naturalist* I. 145 This year I made a shade open on all sides, protected by a roof to keep out the hot rays of the sun. 1889 Mrs. Eliz. B. Custer *Tenting on Plains* vi. 185 The staff-officers had caused a long shade to be built, instead of shorter ones, which would have stood the storms better.

13. shade-bearing *a.* = Tolerant *a.* d; **shade-card**, a card illustrating the range of colours in which goods are supplied; **shade-glass**, a darkened or coloured glass screen placed between the eyepiece and object-glass of an astronomical instrument to diminish the brightness of the object under observation (cf. Sunshade 4).

1895 W. R. Fisher tr. *R. Hess' Forest Protection* 347 Plants are termed lightdemanding or *shadebearing according to their demands in the matter of light, or capacity for bearing shade. 1905 *Terms Forestry & Logging* 25 *Tolerant*, capable of enduring more or less heavy shade. Syn.: shade-bearing, shade-enduring. 1930 *Morning Post* 19 July 4/6 Pure silk washing Frocks in cream, colours, and checks..; *shade card. 1930 *Daily Express* 6 Nov. 6/3 Fingers treated with a different hue, so that they look like dressmakers' shade-cards.

Shade, *v.*[1] Add: **9. c.** To modify the pitch of (an open organ stop) by placing something near the top of the pipe.

1876 Stainer & Barrett *Dict. Mus. Terms*, *Shading of pipes*, the placing of anything so near the top of an organ pipe as to affect the vibrating column of air which it contains.

d. *Commerce.* To make a slight or gradual reduction in (prices).

1898 E. N. Westcott *David Harum* 17 'Don't you want the roan fer your own use?' I says. 'Mebbe we c'd shade the price a little.' 1903 *Boston Transcript* 24 Oct. 22 To spur his freight traffic manager to get business without shading rates. 1913 Gene Stratton-Porter *Laddie* ix, He said Mr. Pryor had shaded his price so that if the money had to go, he would be tempted to see if we couldn't manage it ourselves. 1928 *New Statesman* 28 July, Finance Suppl. p. x, The newsprint and pulp industry..has..been developed rather faster than the demand, with the result that prices have been shaded.

Shader. (U.S. example.)

1839 *Southern Lit. Messenger* V. 314/1 The people..have a mortal aversion to fine spreading trees; which under the horrible name of 'shaders' they extirpate in the most cruel manner.

Shading, *vbl. sb.* Add: **6.** The method or process of testing the truth of the interior of a gun barrel by a shadow thrown down the tube.

1880 *Encycl. Brit.* XI. 283/2 Two tests are employed,—the first being that by shading. 1902 *Kynoch Jrnl.* IV. Oct.–Nov. 21/1 Independently of its practical utility, the shading of a gun barrel is an interesting optical problem.

Shadow, *sb.* Add: **4.** Phr. *Under* or *in the shadow of*: within the purlieus of, close up against, in proximity to.

1853 C. Brontë *Villette* v, I lie in the shadow of St. Pauls. 1931 *Times Lit. Suppl.* 20 Aug. 625/4 The gradual rise of Innsbruck from a little village lying under the shadow of the great castle of the Dukes of Andechs to the..capital city of Tyrol.

16. shadow-boxing *gerund* and *pres. pple.*, boxing against an imaginary opponent, as a form of training; **shadow cabinet** (see quot. 1926[1]); **shadow-corpuscle** (see sense 5 c); **shadow-cretonne, -print, -tissue**, a reversible material having a woven-in pattern which gives a shadowy or blurred effect; **shadow embroidery** = *shadow work*; **shadow-grey** *a.* and *sb.*, dark grey; **shadow-photometer**, a kind of photometer invented by Rumford, in which light is measured by means of two shadows cast by a vertical rod upon a white screen; **shadow-proof** *a.*, designating materials which are impermeable to light; **shadow-stitch**, (*b*) a criss-cross embroidery stitch used on sheer materials for filling in spaces, and which, being worked on the wrong side, shows through on the right side in a shadowy way with an outline resembling a back-stitch; **shadow work**, embroidery done in shadow-stitch; also *attrib.*

1919 Corri *Refereeing 1,000 Fights* 69 The mascot stripped to the waist to do some *shadow boxing. 1924 S. Lewis *Free Air* i. 8 She fought the steering-wheel as though she were shadow-boxing. 1926 *Scribner's Mag.* Aug. 8/2 Cease shadow-boxing with these vague menaces to the Constitution. 1906 A. J. Balfour *Let.* in Newton *Ld. Lansdowne* (1929) 354 If we are to have, as you suggest, a Committee consisting of members selected from the Front Bench in both Houses, I think it would be very difficult to exclude any member of the late Cabinet who had a seat in the present Parliament, and, if that be so, what we should really have would be a *shadow Cabinet once a week. 1926 Earl of Oxford in *Daily News* 2 June 7/1 The 'Shadow' Cabinet is the substitute when the leaders of a Party are in opposition for the actual Cabinet when they are in office, and it has always been understood that membership of it involves similar obligations. 1926 Rose Macaulay *Crewe Train* ii. iv. § 1 The politician who was weighted with the cares of not being in office, and having only a shadow cabinet to mind. 1901 Dorland *Med. Dict.* (ed. 2), *Shadow-corpuscle. 1932 *Sale Catal.*, Made of good quality *Shadow Cretonne. 1920 J. Hergesheimer *Linda Condon* ii. 11 *Shadow embroidery and fine shell edges. 1918 W. Beebe *Jungle Peace* ii. (1919) 26 The *shadow-grey sea. 1932 *Sale Catal.*, A beautiful quality plain silk..Shades:..shadow grey and gunmetal. 1905 *Technol. & Sci. Dict.* (ed. Goodchild & Tweney) s.v. *Photometers*, A simpler arrangement, which possesses the advantage that it may be used in a room which is not quite dark, is Rumford's *Shadow Photometer. 1928 G. G. Denny *Fabrics* (ed. 3) 111 Warp print or *shadow print. Silks, ribbons and cretonnes woven with plain filling on a printed warp which gives a faint and shadowy design. 1923 *Daily Mail* 17 Feb. 10 *Shadowproof Silk Lustre. 1932 *Modern Woman* Feb. 56/1 This *shadow stitch is just like herring-boning worked rather closely together...It gives you the shape of the leaf outlined in back-stitch on the right side and padded with long, crossed stitches on the wrong. 1920 *Queen* 3 Apr., Advt. 17 *Shadow Tissue. 1932 *Sale Catal.*, Reversible Shadow Tissue in a delightful well-covered design of Tulips. 1932 *Modern Woman* Feb. 56 The *Shadow Work Tea Cloth and Cosy.

Shadowing, *vbl. sb.* **4.** (Modern U.S. example.)

1827 J. F. Cooper *Prairie* (1879) 5 The martin's fur..was of a fineness and shadowing that a queen might covet.

Shaft, *sb.*[3] **4. b. shaft-house** (U.S. example). Also *attrib.*

1882 Mrs. Mary Foote *Led-Horse Claim* 15 The lights which beckoned to each other across it shone from the shaft houses of Led-Horse and Shoshone mines. 1914 Gertrude Atherton *Perch of Devil* ii. 355 Not daring to summon the shaft-house man, he was sneaking down the ladder.

Shafter. Add: Also, any animal which goes in the shafts of a vehicle.

1865 Milton & Cheadle *N.-W. Passage* viii. (1867) 126 The..dogs [of the sleigh] were not equal to the emergency. ..The leader was willing, but young..: the middle one..was aged and asthmatic; and the shafter,..lame and lethargic.

Shagreen. Add: **1. d.** The fashion shade of dull green resembling the colour of shagreen.

1932 *Sale Catal.*, Colours: Maize, Sunrise, Shagreen, Parchment or Ivory.

Shake, *sb.*[1] Add: **2. i.** *A fair shake*: a fair deal. *U.S. slang.*

1834 S. Smith *Major Downing* 5 Says I, any way that will be a fair shake. 1845 [W. T. Thompson] *Chron. Pineville* 34 (Farmer) Give Bill Sweeny a fair shake, and he can whoop blue blazes out of ye. 1847 D. P. Thompson *Locke Amsden* 59 (Th.) Now you know, father, that wasn't a fair shake. 1902 S. E. White *Blazed Trail* xxxi. 218 'That ain't a fair shake,' cried the man excitedly.

Shake, *v.* Add: **5. b.** *To shake a stick at*: an expression indicating a considerable amount or number. *U.S. colloq.*

1818 *Lancaster* (Pa.) *Jrnl.* 5 Aug. (Th.) We have in Lancaster as many Taverns as you can shake a stick at. 1836 J. C. Neal *Peter Brush* (Bartlett) I've..got more black eyes..than you could shake a stick at. 1835 Crockett *Tour Down East* 87 (Bartlett) This was a temperance house, and there was nothing to treat a friend to that was worth shaking a stick at. 1843 R. Carlton *New Purchase* I. xii. 86 Our queen snake was..retiring, attended by more of her subjects than we even dared to shake a stick at. 1928 Sinclair Lewis *Man who knew Coolidge* ii. 131 There was more posters and banners..than you could shake a stick at.

12. c. *To shake on to*: to take to, accept. *U.S.*

1927 Vachell *Dew of the Sea* etc. 262 You Britishers.. don't shake on to the goods as quick as we do.

16. b. Also with *down*.

1927 J. Barbican *Confess. Rum-Runner* xiv. 148 For only last week they were shook down for five hundred by a stray fellow from the Department.

Shake-down. Add: **2. b.** A forced contribution; an exaction. (Cf. *Shake *v.* 16 b.) *U.S.*

1903 A. Hodder *Fight for City* 219 He [*sc.* a New York policeman] was fined 30 days' pay because he would not stand for a 'shake-down', which means that he had refused to give from time to time upon demand 5 or 10 dollars from his meagre salary to his superiors to be used for purposes unknown.

Shaker. **4. b.** *attrib.* (Examples of *shaker bonnet.*)

1863 *Trans. Ill. Agric. Soc.* (1865) V. 256 Your committee would..suggest that they put on their high heeled, thick soled shoes, shaker bonnet, [etc.]. 1881 *Harper's Mag.* May 854/2 Is that all the bonnet you have?..I will buy you a Shaker at the store.

Shake-up. [Shake *v.* 21.]

1. A roughly-made article. Also *attrib.*

1873 J. H. Beadle *Undevel. West* xxxiv. 728 A rather rough looking frontier town, consisting of rude frames and 'shake-ups' of pine lumber. *Ibid.* 823 A man with ten thousand cattle upon the range, is content to..sit on a hickory 'shake-up' chair.

2. An extensive or drastic re-arrangement or changing round.

1903 *N. Y. Evening Post* 16 Sept., Big Police Shake-up. Eight Captains Transferred by Greene. 1904 *N. Y. Sun* 7 Aug. 5 Looking wistfully across the street was a police captain who was in Commissioner McAdoo's recent shake-up. He had been transferred from a 'fat' to a 'lean' precinct. 1911 H. S. Harrison *Queed* xviii. 237, I see a kind of shake-up [in local politics] comin'.

Shaking, *vbl. sb.* **1. e.** Add: **Shaking-out** = *shake out* (Shake *sb.*[1] 8 a).

1928 *Daily Mail* 9 Aug. 12/4 The best opinion is that a thorough shaking-out will do much good, but there is no need for alarm.

Shaku (ʃæ·ku). Also 8 **saku, sackf, sak.** [Jap., ad. Chinese *chih* a foot.] **a.** A Japanese measure of length, equal to 11⅞ English inches. **b.** A wooden or ivory baton which was anciently used by Japanese court nobles for noting memoranda on, but later carried as a mark of honour in the presence of the emperor.

1727 Scheuchzer tr. *Kæmpfer's Hist. Japan* i. xi. 136 One *Sackf* and a half long. *Ibid.* ii. iv. 180 Snow..to the height of four *Sak* and five Suns, that is about four foot and a half. *Ibid.* iii. vi. 246 His Stature..of nine *Saku*, and nine *Suns*, proportionable to the greatness of his Genius. 1867 Simmonds *Dict. Trade* Suppl., *Shaku*, a Japanese long measure of ten tsun. 1875 F. V. Dickins tr. *Chiushingura* (1880) 197 'Twas the Emperor's whim That the tree should from him Have a *shaku* with Ta-iu writ on. 1878 *Trans. Asiatic Soc. Japan* VI. ii. 249 The seismograph consisted of a copper vessel, whose diameter was 8 *shaku* or feet. 1883 tr. *J. J. Rein's Japan* (1888) 415 The interval of three shaku (1 metre). 1894 C. M. Salwey *Fans of Japan* 6 The *shaku* ..was a stick in shape of the outside frame of a folding fan, about two feet in length, about an inch and a half to two inches at the top, decreasing at the base to about one inch. The *shaku* was made of wood or ivory, and had to be held in a certain manner, viz., right in front of the holder, pressing against the lower part of the chest, and slightly inclined outwards to give the body a dignified bearing in the presence of royalty.

Shal (ʃāl). Also **schal.** Applied to several fishes of Africa and India (see quots.).

[1845 *Encycl. Metrop.* XXIII. 380/1 It [*sc. Pimelodus Schilan*, Cuvier] is very common in Upper Egypt, where it is called both *Schal a raby* and *Schal beledy*.] 1867 Simmonds *Dict. Trade* Suppl., *Shal* (*Ophiocephalus marulius*), one of the most common fish in Lower Bengal, and largely eaten by the natives. 1887 *Encycl. Brit.* XXII. 68/2 *Synodontis* is an African genus and common in the Nile, where the various species are known by the name of 'Shal'.

Shallow, *a.*[1] and *sb.*[3] Add: **A.** *adj.* **1. e.** Designating wells which are sunk into a superficial permeable stratum and collect the surface waters only.

1888 *Encycl. Brit.* XXIV. 404/2 Shallow wells, sunk in the ordinary manner, have long been used for collecting moderate supplies of water. 1905 *Technol. & Sci. Dict.* (ed. Goodchild & Tweney) s.v. *Sanitation*, Shallow well water is always to be looked upon with suspicion.

8. a. shallow-waisted *a.* (see quot.).

1867 Smyth *Sailor's Word-bk.*, *Shallow-waisted*, flush-decked vessels are thus termed, in contradistinction to the deep-waisted.

Shalwar, variant of Shulwar.

1885 *Encycl. Brit.* XVIII. 630/2 With boots are worn 'shalwârs', or baggy riding breeches, very loose, and tied by a string at the ankle.

Shamash (ʃā·mæʃ). Also **shammash, shammas, -os.** [Aram. *shammāsh* (Yiddish *shammes*) servant, f. *shammēsh* to serve.] One of the officers of a synagogue.

1892 Zangwill *Childr. Ghetto* Proem 3 Many of the worshippers were tempted to give beyond their means for fear of losing the esteem of the *Shammos*, or beadle, a potent personage only next in influence to the President. 1896 I. Abrahams *Jewish Life Mid. Ages* 8 It was an ancient custom in several places for the Shamash or verger to announce every Saturday the result of law-suits, and to inform the congregation that certain properties were in the market. 1903 *Standard* 27 Apr. (Palmer) There is a 'shammas' acting as beadle, door-keeper, collector, cook, and utility-man in emergencies.

Shamateur (ʃæ·mătə̄ı, ʃæ·mătiū·ı). [f. Sham *a.* + Amateur.] In sports, a player who is classed as an amateur, while often making money out of his play like a professional. Hence **Sha·mateurism.**

1901 *Daily Chron.* 29 Apr. 1 (Cassell's Suppl.) The shamateur, who enjoys all the privileges of the amateur, together with all the emoluments of the professional. 1927 *Pictorial Weekly* 17 Sept. 178/1, I do not mean to suggest that every cricketer who poses as an amateur is in reality a Shamateur. 1928 *Sat. Rev.* 4 Feb. 126 Where the interests of amphitheatre and arena come first, 'shamateurism' must pass eventually into an honest professionalism.

Sha·mbler. [f. Shamble *v.*[2]] A shambling person or animal.

a 1861 T. Winthrop *Canoe & Saddle* xi. 219 Shabbiest led off on his shambler [*viz.* a horse] in quite another direction from mine.

Shammatha (ʃămā·pā). [Aramaic *sh'mattā* excommunication.] The third degree of excommunication among the ancient Jews.

1862 *Chambers's Encycl.* IV. 186/2. 1878 *Encycl. Brit.* VIII. 799/1.

Shampoo, *sb.* Add: *Dry shampoo*, a preparation of powdered starch, etc., used for cleansing the hair. Also as vb.

1913 *Queen* 24 May Advt., When you want your hair to look extra nice and bright..just treat it to a dry shampoo with..Hair Powder. 1928 *Ibid.* Feb. 271/2 Dry Shampoo. Carbonate of Potash 1 oz. Water 32 ozs. Saponine ½ oz. Industrial Spirit 32 oz. Perfume, as desired.

Shan (ʃān), *a.* and *sb.* Also **Sam, Sciam, Shaan, Sham.** [Burmese *rham.*] **a.** *adj.* Of or pertaining to the Shans or their language. **b.** *sb.* A member of a numerous and widely spread Mongoloid race of the Tai family, found throughout Indo-China and especially in the Shan States; also the race itself. Also the language of the Shans, of the Tai branch of the Indo-Chinese languages.

1800 M. Symes *Acc. Embassy Ava* 274 An intelligent man informed him that..the first Shaan town was called Thangdat. *Note*, Shaan, or Shan, is a very comprehensive term given to different nations, some independent, others the subjects of the greater states. 1833 W. Tandy tr. *Sangermano's Descr. Burmese Emp.* 57 Princes of the Sciam. 1903 Risley & Gait *Census India 1901* I. i. 109 The proportions for the principal indigenous races show an excess of females amongst the Burmans, Shans, Chins and Kachins. *Ibid.* ii. 1 Burma includes the Shan States, the Chin Hills and Karenni, enumerated for the first time in 1901. 1920 *Blackw. Mag.* June 839/1 You sell liquor and opium to Burmans and Shans. 1920 *Public Opinion* 26 Nov. 521/2 Instruction in the following tongues: Shan, Swahili, Telugu.

Shanghaier (ʃæŋhai·ə.ı). [f. Shanghai *v.* + -er[1].] One who shanghais a person.

1917 *Chambers's Jrnl.* Jan. 19/1 Once..a shanghaier had been shanghaied by a rival shanghaier. 1926 J. Black *You Can't Win* xii. 152 Here I learned to beware the crafty shanghaier with his knockout drops.

Shank, *sb.* Add: **12.** *Golf.* An act of shanking the ball.

1927 *Daily Express* 26 Oct. 3/4 It is difficult to see how a 'shank' could be avoided.

Shank, *v.* Add: **4.** *Golf.* To strike (the ball) with the heel of the club. Also *absol.*

1924 C. J. H. Tolley *Mod. Golfer* 247 Shanking is a fault which is frequently occurring. 1925 J. M. Barnes *Guide Good Golf* 109 To..strike the ball down on the heel of the club,.. with the result that it flies out to the right...This is called socketing or shanking the shot. 1927 *Daily Express* 26 Oct. 3/4 Of all the awful things a man may do to a golf ball the most demoralising and the most mystifying is to 'shank' it. *Ibid.*, I should describe the cause of 'shanking' as a failure to keep the left elbow close in to the body when the ball is being struck. 1928 *Times* 13 July 6/6 Mrs. Baker again shanked her run-up to the 17th.

Shantung. Add: **b.** The name of a fashion shade.

1914 *Queen* 5 July, Advt. 15 Sports Coat, in Navy, Saxe,.. Cerise and Shantung.

Shape, *sb.* **13.** Add: Also *gen.*

1903 N. S. Shaler *Citizen* 132 This branch of law is in such excellent shape that the citizen need not feel himself called on to do more than to accept the conditions as they are. 1908 F. J. Mather in *Atlantic Monthly* Nov. 653 At the first visit the picture was apparently in fair shape.

Shape (ʃā·pe), *sb.*[2] [Tibetan.] A privy councillor; one of the five ministers who advise the Tibetan nomokhan in state affairs.

1894 Sandberg *Handbk. Colloq. Tibetan* 189 Kâlön: official title of each of the five members of the Privy Council...Shá-pé, other and more popular title of a *Kâlön*. 1902 *Encycl. Brit.* XXXIII. 325/2 Under him are five ministers of state (*kalön* or *shapé*), who divide among themselves, under the immediate supervision of the two Imperial Chinese residents.., the management of all secular affairs of the country. 1921 *Public Opinion* 15 Apr. 357/2 He also visited the Tibetan Council, called the 'Council of Shapes'.

Shape, *v.* Add: **11. c.** *intr.* Of events, etc.: To take a certain 'shape'; to show a specified tendency. Also with *up*.

1865 O. W. Norton *Army Lett.* 278 As things are shaping I do not much think I shall try till after Congress meets. 1903 *N. Y. Times* 10 Sept., Matters are shaping for an effort on the part of the organized teamsters to reproduce in this city the..conditions which exist in Chicago. 1907 *Springfield* (Mass.) *Weekly Republ.* 2 May 3 It is not at all certain that matters will shape up so as to permit them to do this. 1921 R. D. Paine *Comr. Rolling Ocean* xvii. 293 Here is how it shapes up to me. We can stave off a riot for a week or so.

16. e. *intr.* To shape one's course *for*.

1848 J. F. Cooper *Oak Openings* I. iv. 49 Perhaps it would be best for me to shape at once for Ohio.

20. *To shape out* or *up*: to assume a fighting attitude.

1899 MacManus *In Chimney Corners* 12 'I'll fight you,' says Billy, shaping out and winding the bit of stick three times over his head. 1927 *Daily Express* 31 May 7 He shaped up to Murphy, when he punched the watchman on the jaw with his fist and knocked him insensible.

Share, *sb.*[3] Add: **5. d.** (Earlier Amer. example.)

1656 Bradford *Plymouth Plant.* 341 All her men were upon shares.

6. share bonus (see Bonus *sb.* b); **share crop** *U.S.* (see quot.); hence **share-cropper**; **share hand** *U.S.*, **share-man** (earlier Amer. example); **share-mart** *U.S.*, a stock exchange; **share premium**, the price at which shares are valued in excess of their par value; **share-pusher** (see quot. 1914); so **share-pushing** *vbl. sb.* and *ppl. a.*

1928 *Daily Chron.* 9 Aug. 8/4 A *share bonus of 50 per cent. was provided on account of the year 1917–18. 1907 *Springfield* (Mass.) *Weekly Republ.* 25 Apr. 1 The '*share crop' system is what its name implies, the immigrant being housed and fitted with all the necessaries and then sharing the proceeds of the harvest with the landowner. 1929 L. R. Gottschalk *Era French Revolution* 33 Most of them had become métoyers, who, like our *share-croppers, farmed a piece of land for a stipulated portion..of the harvest. 1911 Jenks & Lauck *Immigration Problem* 83 How much value careful cultivation, kitchen gardens and small store accounts may be to the cotton '*share hand' and tenant. 1687 *Connecticut Public Records* III. 425 Fishermen..shall not presume to break off their voyage..without the consent of the owner, master and *share-men. 1870 Medbery *Men & Myst. Wall Street* 19 In all the great European *share-marts there is a general executive organization. 1930 *Daily Express* 6 Oct. 14/2 The discount on this issue has been entirely written off from *share premium and capital reserve accounts. 1914 Halford *Dict. Stock Market Terms* 79 *Share pusher*, one who endeavours to dispose of Shares to the public by circular or advertisement, instead of selling them on the market. 1930 *Times* 27 Mar. 11/3 The Home Office issued directions that he was not to be allowed to enter as he was suspected of being a 'share-pusher'. 1928 *Daily Mail* 3 Aug. 19/3 The day on which the sections penalising *share-pushing shall come into force. 1929 *Daily Express* 21 Jan. 2/1 Share-pushing hawkers, literally pedlars of shares, who go from door to door in little villages and hamlets in the country.

Shareable (ʃē·răb'l), *a.* [f. Share *v.*[2] + -able.] Capable of being shared.

1920 *Q. Rev.* July 161 It must be shared or at least must be shareable; otherwise it were nothing at all.

Shared, *ppl. a.* (under Share *v.*[2]). Add: *Physics.* Of an electron: see quot. 1923.

1923 *Trans. Faraday Soc.* XIX. 461 In chemically stable molecules we have only to consider atoms sharing pairs of electrons. It is well known that such structures do not exhibit any signs of electrical polarity. One must therefore suppose that the net charge on both atoms is zero, *i.e.* that the two shared electrons are in general so distributed that when one is in one atom the other is in the other. 1927 Sidgwick *Electronic Theory of Valency* 98 Orbits of Shared Electrons.

Shariah, shariat (ʃārī·ā, -āt). Also **Sheriat.** [Arab. شريعة *sharīca'* law, justice, f. شرع *sharac* law, etc.] The sacred law of the Mohammedans, consisting of the teachings of the Koran and the traditional sayings of Mohammed.

1877 *Encycl. Brit.* VII. 113/2 Shi'at or Sher'iat, *i.e.*, legal religion under the supervision of a murshid. 1920 *19th Cent.* Sept. 500 Questions of divorce and inheritance are decided by the religious or Sharieh judge, from whom there is an appeal to the Sharieh Court of Appeal in Jerusalem. 1921 *Glasgow Herald* 16 July 7 A code based on the Shariat and prepared under his orders would come into force. 1927 *Ibid.* 21 Oct 11 The Sheriat (Moslem) canonical law has practically been abolished, a civil code borrowed from Switzerland being substituted for all questions of marriage and inheritance.

Shark, *sb.*[1] Add: **2. e.** *U.S.* (See quots.)

1909 *Springfield* (Mass.) *Weekly Republ.* 8 July 12 The 'shark' does well in his lessons, but recognises that study is the first thing in college. 'Sharks' play games. 1914 *N. Y. Evening Post* 5 Jan., The..'shark' known to the American college world; primarily, the student who devours and digests learning with ease..and, secondarily, one who excels in any line of activity.

Shark, *v.*[3] Transfer *U.S. local* to sense in Dict. and add: **2.** *intr.* To swim with the back fin above the surface of the water.

1923 *Chambers's Jrnl.* 674/1 Trout were 'sharking'—that is, progressing through the water with their back fin above it.

Sharp, *sb.*[1] Add: **12. b.** (See quot.)

1903 W. R. Cattelle *Precious Stones* 67 To cleave, the crystal is fastened to the end of a stick and a V-shaped incision made in the grain with a sharp piece of diamond, called a 'sharp'.

Sharp-shooter. Add: **2.** In marksmanship, a rifleman of a particular grade (see quot. 1918); in the U.S. army and navy one who makes 60 % of the possible maximum score under certain definite conditions (Funk).

1906 *Small Arms Firing Register* (Cent. D. Suppl.). 1918 Farrow *Dict. Mil. Terms*, *Sharpshooter*,..also in small-arms firing, a grade of rifleman just below that of expert rifleman.

3. Any of several hemipterous insects which puncture the cotton-boll: the cotton-boll weevil.

1901 *Yearbk. U.S. Dept. Agric.* 377 (Cent. D. Suppl.) Early cotton..avoids to a great extent damage to the plant by the boll-worm, cotton worm, and sharp-shooter, as well as by a large number of fungous diseases.

Sharry, vulgar var. *Chara[2].

1924 *Chambers's Jrnl.* 7/1 Many who travel by 'sharry' do so because they want the pleasures of the road.

Shasta (ʃæ·stă). A place-name in California used *attrib.* to designate various plants etc. native to California, as *shasta fir*; **shasta daisy**, the ox-eye daisy, *Chrysanthemum Leucanthemum.*

1916 E. C. Booth *Fondie* ii. viii, A large straw hat trimmed with shasta daisies.

Shat (ʃɒt), variant of Shott.

1898 *Geog. Jrnl.* (R.G.S.) June 604 The shats, or salt lakes, of the south of Tunis are rather a disappointment to the traveller. 1902 *Encycl. Brit.* XXXIII. 482/1 These shats ..are, strictly speaking, not lakes at all at the present day.

Shatriya, variant of Kshatriya.

Shavable (ʃē·văb'l), *a.* [f. Shave *v.* + -able.] Ready or able to be shaved.

1928 *Sunday Dispatch* 9 Dec. 10 When I was of a shavable age I was presented with a safety razor.

Shave, *sb.*[2] **3.** (Earlier U.S. example.)

1838 *Knickerbocker Mag.* XII. 317 They speak of the above transaction but seldom, and invariably as 'the dead shave!'.

Shave, *v.* Add: **12.** *trans.* To cut down in amount.

1898 *Boston Herald* 23 Jan. 14/3 There are indications that tariff sheets are being secretly shaved.

Shaved, *ppl. a.* **1. a.** (Later U.S. example.)

1907 M. C. Harris *Tents of Wickedness* iv. ii. 344 The maid had brought in the..omelette, and the crisp, shaved potatoes.

Shavian (ʃē·viăn), *a.* and *sb.* [f. *Shavius*, latinized f. *Shaw*, the surname of George Bernard Shaw (born in Dublin 1856), playwright and critic + -ian.] Of, pertaining to, or characteristic of G. B. Shaw or his works and opinions. Also *sb.*, an admirer or follower of G. B. S. Hence **Sha·vianism**, the tenets or a characteristic saying of G. B. Shaw.

1907 Archd. Cunningham in *Offic. Rep. Ch. Congress* 3 Oct. 310 The Fabians and the Shavians. 1908 *New Age* 26 Sept. 438/1 It was a little odd to suddenly get this kind of Shavian spicing at the end. 1921 *Spectator* 28 May 680/2 The poet Eugene Marchbanks is perhaps as near to primary emotion as any Shavian. 1923 *Westm. Gaz.* 3 July, A comedy, Shavian in character, occupied the attention of the Commons for half an hour. 1928 *Observer* 18 Mar. 16/3 The Quintessence of Shavianism. 1928 *Sunday Express* 3 June 11 A Sheaf of Shavianisms.

Similarly **Shawe·sque** *a.*, **Shaw·ish** *a.*, **Shawism.**

1897 Ellen Terry *Lett. to G. B. Shaw* 9 Jan. (1931), How comes it it's all put in a Shawesque manner? 1896 *Westm. Gaz.* 15 Jan. 8/1 Mr. Raymond Blathwayt's 'Talk' with Mr. George Bernard Shaw..is full of characteristic Shawisms. 1928 *Weekly Dispatch* 13 May 12/7 Here was a golden opportunity for an exhibition of Shawishness that was instantly forthcoming.

Shaving, *vbl. sb.* **4. b.** *U.S.* (Earlier example.)

1818 H. B. Fearon *Sk. Amer.* 12 He replied that the only business which was good for anything at this time in New York, was shaving—meaning the buying and selling of bank-notes.

5. shaving-horse, -knife (earlier and later examples).

1841 *Southern Lit. Messenger* VII. 527/2 A receptacle for spinning-wheels, wash-tubs, pitchforks, *shaving horses, and sundry other implements of domestic industry. 1843 *Knickerbocker Mag.* XXII. 386 The rub-a-dub of the cooper's mallet, the creak of his *shaving-knife were still.

Shawabti (shawæ·bti). *Egyptology.* [Egyptian.] An image made of stone, wood, etc., such as was placed in ancient Egyptian tombs to act as a slave to the deceased.

1922 Ld. Carnarvon in *Daily Mail* 18 Dec. 10 Propped against the wall is a most beautiful portrait shawabti of the King. 1923 Carter & Mace *Tomb of Tut-ankh-amen* I. 120 Beside this shrine there was a large *shawabti* statuette of the king.

Shawesque, etc.: see under *Shavian.

Sheaf, *sb.* **7.** Add: **sheaf oats.**

1765 G. Croghan *Jrnl.* 140 The young reeds being preferable to sheaf oats. 1867 *Rep. Iowa Agric. Soc.* (1868) 126 In the Winter they generally have an open shed with sheaf oats or nubbins of corn.

Shear, *sb.*[1] **6.** Add: *shear-blade* (earlier U.S. example), *shear-crane* (cf. G. *scherenkran*).

1822 *Niles' Weekly Register* I. 25 Jan. 390/1 The subscriber at short notice can furnish clothier's *shear blades. 1824 Stevenson *Bell Rock Lighthouse* (1931) 89, 13th August [1809]. All hands were employed at low-water to-day in refitting the *sheer-crane at the eastern landing-place.

Shear, *sb.*[2] Add: **5. shear-boom, -skid** *Logging* (see quots.).

1905 *Terms Forestry & Logging* 37 *Fender skid*, a skid placed on the lower side of a skidding trail on a slope to hold the log on the trail while being skidded. Syn.:..shear skid. *Ibid.* 46 *Shear boom*, a boom so secured that it guides floating logs in the desired direction.

7. shear-structure, a rock-structure resulting wholly or partly from shearing.

1885 Geikie *Text-bk. Geol.* (ed. 2) 578 Regional metamorphism..is usually most pronounced where, as shown by plication, puckering and shear-structure, the rocks have been subjected to the greatest mechanical movement.

Shear, *v.* **5. d.** (U.S. examples.)

1852 *Trans. Mich. Agric. Soc.* III. 139 An article upon Sheep, describing bucks that shear the big fleeces. 1878 *Trans. Ill. Dept. Agric.* XIV. 239 They do not shear more wool, and are harder to shear. Smooth sheep shear as good clips.

Sheared, *ppl. a.* Add: **2.** *Geol.* Strained or distorted by shearing stress.

1930 Peach & Horne *Geol. Scotl.* 56 Sheared Granite-Gneiss. This rock belongs to the group of muscovite-biotite-gneiss.

Sheath[1]. Add: **3. b.** *Wireless.* The anode of a thermionic valve.

1923 *Daily Mail* 21 June 10 *Sheath*, another name for the 'plate' or 'anode' of a valve.

c. *Physics.* The surrounding ring of electrons in an atom.

1923 G. H. Knibbs *Presid. Addr. Austral. Assoc.* 14 A neutral atom consists of K+N protons and K electrons in its nucleus and N electrons in its rings or sheaths.

Sheave, *sb.*[2] Add: **3.** The specks and spots appearing in finished paper due to woody knots and other impurities in the pulp.

1880 J. Dunbar *Pract. Papermaker* 15 All rags, even the finest cotton, contain sheive, which nothing but judicious boiling will remove. 1920 Cross & Bevan *Paper-Making* 137 [Women] carefully remove such impurities as weeds, root-ends, etc., which from their lignified nature are with great difficulty boiled and bleached, and which if not removed would be liable to appear in the finished paper as dark-coloured specks, technically known as 'sheave'.

Shebang. *U.S.* (Earlier example.)

1862 Whitman *Specimen Days* (1892) 27 Their shebang enclosures of bushes.

Shebbel (ʃe·bəl). [Arab. *shābal, -il.*] A species of shad, known also as *Barbary salmon.*

1867 Simmonds *Dict. Trade* Suppl. *a* 1883 in *Encycl. Brit.* XVI. 834/1 The catching of the *shebbel* or Barbary salmon ..is a great industry on all the principal rivers of the coast.

Shechitah (ʃe·χitā). Also **shecheta.** [Heb., f. שחט *shāhaṭ* to slaughter.] The Jewish method of killing animals.

1921 *Dict. Occup. Terms* (1927) § 448 *Slaughterer*, Jewish; ..*shecheta, shochet*;..is employed by Jewish Board of Shecheta.

Shed, *sb.*[2] Add: **1. c.** = *Hangar b.

1909 *Daily Chron.* 3 Nov. 1/6 They have been watching the great shed gradually nearing completion..., and have been eagerly awaiting the advent of the airship. 1916 H. Barber *Aeroplane Speaks* 27 The Aeroplane is wheeled out of its shed on to the greensward of the Military Aerodrome.

4. shed roof (earlier Amer. example); **shed-room** *U.S.*, a shed attached to a house and serving as a room.

1736 in *Maryland Hist. Mag.* III. 45 The *Shead-Ruff of Cap[t] Cressap's house. 1843 *Knickerbocker Mag.* XXI. 304, I had in the morning secured a bed in a *shed-room. 1877 *Rep. Indian Affairs* 40 A dwelling house for the sawyer.. with shed-room, box style. 1889 *Century Mag.* Apr. 913/2 There Nanky placed her eye to a crack and peeped through into a tiny shed-room adjoining. 1904 Tom Watson *Bethany* (1920) 8 Springing off from the main roof, other rafters reached downwards to rest upon outer plates—forming a shed-roof; the half of this, being closed in with planks, made a shed-room.

Shed, *v.*[1] Add: **11. c.** Of the young bolls of cotton-plants: To fall prematurely owing to a failure of fertilization or to infection by a disease known as 'shedding' (see next).

1909 in *Cent. Dict.* Suppl.

d. To cast off a shell, etc.

1879 *St. Nicholas* Nov., He still grows till he is called a 'Buster', and then sheds. Then he is called a 'Soft Crab'.

12. b. To slope like the roof of a shed. *U.S.*

1857-8 *Trans. Ill. Agric. Soc.* III. 538 The roof may pitch both ways, or shed at the ends, presenting a gable end in front.

Shedding, *vbl. sb.* Add: **3. d.** The premature falling of the young bolls of cotton-plants; also, the disease which causes this.

1899 *Yearbk. U.S. Dept. Agric.* 728 Over the eastern portion shedding was reported, with complaints of drought in portions of the Carolinas.

Sheelah (ʃī·lă). *Austral.* A young woman.

1930 Palmer *Men are Human* xxvii. 251 There was a sheelah he had working for him once, a lively piece with black eyes.

Sheen, *v.* Add: **1. c.** Of materials: To have a particular sheen.

1895 J. E. Davis *Elem. Mod. Dressmaking* (ed. 2) 62 One piece of the dress may sheen differently from the others.

Sheep, *sb.* Add: **8. sheep bands** (see quot.); **sheep-sorrel** (earlier U.S. examples).

1865 Hannett *Bibliopegia* i. 150 Bands, or raised cords, were..used for school books, which species of binding is now universally known as '*sheep bands.' 1807 P. Gass *Jrnl.* xviii. 188 A great quantity of *sheep-sorrel..of a very large size. 1829-32 J. P. Kennedy *Swallow Barn* I. xxvii. 284 That waterish, gravelly soil that you see sometimes around a spring where nothing grows but sheep-sorrel.

9. sheep's grey, material composed of a mixture of black and white wool.

1852 *Trans. Mich. Agric. Soc.* III. 483 Ten yards or over of sheep's gray cloth. 1877 *Rep. Vermont Board Agric.* IV. 99 The men and boys' garments, of the sheep's grey. 1889 *Century Mag.* Jan. 462/1 Coarse sheep's gray jacket and trousers.

Sheep, *v.* Add: **2.** To eat *off* with sheep.

1922 Zane Grey *To Last Man* i, I see no sense in a sheep-man goin' out of his way to surround a cattleman an' sheep off his range. *Ibid.* iv, But what if you throwed your sheep round my range an' sheeped off the grass so my cattle would hev to move or starve?

Sheet, *sb.*[1] Add: **3. c.** Phr. *As white as a sheet*: deathly pale. 1866 [see White *a.* 5 b].

13. d. sheet music, music published in sheet form as opposed to book form.

1881 [see Dict.]. 1930 Priestley *Good Companions* iii. iii. § 2 Performing rights, sheet music, gramophone records.

Sheeted, *ppl. a.* Add: **5.** *Geol.* (See next.)

Sheeting, *vbl. sb.* Add: **2. d.** *Geol.* 'The breaking up of a massive rock into relatively thin, parallel tabulæ united by closely spaced faults or joints' (*Cent. Dict.* Suppl. 1909).

1902 *Contrib. Econ. Geol.* (U.S. Geol. Survey, Bulletin 213) 99 The granite is sheeted near the veins, the planes of sheeting being parallel to the veins themselves.

Sheety, *a.* Add: **2.** *Geol.* Showing a tendency to break up into thin tabulæ.

1902 *Contrib. Econ. Geol.* (U.S. Geol. Survey, Bulletin 213) 287 This coal..is almost invariably overlain by black, sheety, bituminous shale.

Sheikh. Add: **1. b.** *transf.* A 'cave-man'; also (*vulgar*), a girl's 'young man'. *slang.*

1926 *Westm. Gaz.* 7 Aug., The 'cave man' cult..cannot be quite so unhealthy as we have considered it; and next year, perhaps, the British Association will have a good word to say for the Sheik of romance. 1927 *Amer. Speech* II. Jan. 202/1 The girl calls the young man..' my sheik'.

Sheitan, var. Shaitan.

Shelf, *sb.*[1] **6.** Add: **shelf-back** *U.S.* = *Spine *sb.*[1] 9 b; **shelf-furnace**, a continuous fine-ore furnace with inclined shelving for the reduction of mercury ores; **shelf furniture** (see *Furniture 7 b); **shelf-lister**, one who compiles shelf-lists; **shelf-warmer**, an article which is laid on the shelf instead of being put to some use.

1925 J. A. Holden *Bookman's Gloss.* 97 *Shelf-back*, the back of a book, on which the title is lettered. 1931 *Publishers' Weekly* 9 May 2322 It..is strongly bound and has the name of the periodical stamped in gold on cover and shel.back. 1887 Phillips & Bauerman *Elem. Metallurgy* 553 The Hasenclever-Helbig *shelf-furnace, in which a series of inclined shelves, placed on the opposite walls of a vertical shaft, retard the descent of a column of somewhat finely divided ore. 1922 M. Sadleir *Excurs. Vict. Bibliogr.* 4 The obtaining of *shelf furniture in original cloth is a matter of much seeking and of progress measured in fractions of an inch. 1927 W. W. Bishop *Pract. Handbk. Mod. Libr. Catal.* 21 The catalog room..should be..on the same floor with the order clerks, classifiers and *shelf-listers. 1927 *Daily Express* 24 Nov. 9 Thousands of women's shoes,.. which women do not take a fancy to, which therefore become '*shelf-warmers'.

Shell, *sb.* Add: **1. c.** A fashion shade of delicate pink, shell pink.

1923 *Daily Mail* 28 May 2 Shades: Ivory, Champ., Shell, Primrose. *Ibid.* 16 July 2 In Ivory, Biscuit, Shell, Coral.

19. In other technical uses; as, the comparatively small piece of horse-hide obtained from the rump (quot. 1903); see also quots. 1887, 1905.

1887 Phillips & Bauerman *Elem. Metallurgy* 449 This nucleus or 'kernel', which gives its name to the process, is enclosed in a somewhat porous 'shell', consisting, mainly, of ferric oxide, which can be easily detached by a hammer. 1903 Flemming *Pract. Tanning* xxiv. 398 Upon the fore part a liquor of twenty degrees Baumé may be used, and a twenty-four degree liquor on the shell. 1905 Staples Browne in *Proc. Zool. Soc.* 12 Dec. 552 The Nun [pigeon] exhibits a tuft of reversed feathers standing up at the back of the head forming the 'shell'.

35. c. *shell road* (additional examples).

1855 *Knickerbocker Mag.* XLVI. 600 The ride or drive in itself is really a delightful one, and it is indebted to its own individual merits as a shell-road for it. 1873 J. H. Beadle *Undevel. West* 798 The omnibus rolled along the shell road as smoothly as if upon glass. 1897 *Outing* (U.S.) XXX. 539/2 Across the white shell-roads ruffed grouse mince daintily out of the pedestrian's way.

36. a. *shell-burst, -crater, -hole, -trap.*

1919 *Daily Mail Year Bk.* 48/1 He has been lucky enough to escape any large *shell-bursts quite close to his machine. 1920 *Blackw. Mag.* Apr. 508/2 The appalling crash of the shell-burst. 1916 Boyd Cable *Action Front* 49 The neutral ground..was a sea of mud, broken by heaped earth and yawning *shell craters. *Ibid.* 141 The stretcher-bearers who lifted him from the *shell-hole. 1914 *Illustr. Lond. News* 17 Oct. 549/1 Men of the Naval Brigade making the trenches *shell-splinter-proof. 1879 *Encycl. Brit.* IX. 461/2 Such *shell-traps..are scrupulously avoided by modern [military] engineers.

39. shell-beach, a beach wholly composed of sea-shell; **shell-bound** *a.*, designating birds which are unable to break through the shell when hatching; **shell-button** (earlier U.S. example); **shell-opal** (see quot.); **shell-parrot**, the budgerigar, *Melopsittacus undulatus*; **shell pink**, a delicate shade of pink; **shell-shock**, a nervous disorder prevalent during the war of 1914–18, resulting primarily from exposure to shell-explosion at close quarters; **shell-shocked** *a.*, suffering from shell-shock; **shell-transformer**, a transformer in which the iron circuit encloses the copper circuits.

1838 *Penny Cycl.* XI. 472/2 What is called 'the *shell beach' extends from half to three-quarters of a mile along the shore, and is composed of small perfect shells and fragments of larger ones, without any intermixture..of pebbles or sand. 1915 E. R. Lankester *Divers. Naturalist* 144 The shells which are accumulated as shell-beaches. 1905 *Kynoch Jrnl.* Apr.–June 72 Reports from several estates complain of *shell-bound chicks. 1789 *Annals Congress* I. 29 Aug. 826 An exclusive patent..for manufacturing *shell buttons of different dimensions. 1851 Woodward *Mollusca* i. 16 One of the most beautiful substances in nature is the *shell opal, formed of the remains of the ammonite. 1890 'Lyth' *Golden South* xiv. 127 The tiny budgerigar, sometimes called the *shell parrot. 1887, 1893, 1900 *shell pink [see Shell *sb.* 34 d, Pink *sb.*[4] 5 b]. 1916 *Lancet* 18 Mar. 610/1 He appeared to be in a state of semi-stupor typical of the state following *shell-shock. 1918 E. A. Mackintosh *War, the Liberator* 148 The Corporal..collapsed suddenly with twitching hands and staring, frightened eyes, proclaiming the shell-shock be had held off while the work was to be done. 1922 Woodworth *Psychol.* xix. 504 Some of his [*sc.* Freud's] followers have endeavored to interpret these shell-shock nightmares as meaning a desire to be killed and so escape from the strain. 1925 E. Fraser & Gibbons *Sailor & Soldier Words*, *Shell shock*...Since the war, the term has been officially abolished, in favour of the technical term 'Psycho-neurosis'. 1918 E. A. Mackintosh *War, the Liberator* 146 The man rejected the offer with scorn, as badly *shell-shocked men will. 1920 *Discovery* Mar. 69/2 The shell-shocked soldier had to face terrors that were more than he could bear. 1902 *Encycl. Brit.* XXXIII. 418/1 Alternating currrent transformers are classified into (i) Core and (ii) *Shell transformers, depending upon the arrangements of the iron and copper circuits.

b. shell-bark hickory *U.S.* (earlier example).

1785 Washington *Diaries* II. 362, I planted..a row of the Shell bark hickory Nutt from New York.

Shell, *v.* Add: **1. b.** Also *intr.*, to admit of being extruded.

1910 *Practitioner* June 786 Sessile submucous myomata may be enucleated with ease in some cases. All myomata, however, do not readily shell out.

d. (Later U.S. example.)

1861–2 *Trans. Ill. Agric. Soc.* (1865) V. 197 Tea wheat.. has the fault of shelling badly if left standing too long before cutting.

Shelled, *ppl. a.* Add: *Shelled corn*, Indian corn removed from the cob. *U.S.*

1676 *Maryland Archives* II. 560 A Peck of Indian shell'd Corn or Oates. 1699 *Col. Rec. N. Carolina* I. 521 That y[e] Marshal deliver..soe Much Sheld Corn. 1714 J. Green *Diary* in *Essex Inst. Hist. Coll.* (1869) X. 104, I agreed to give Mr. Ganson five bushels of shelled corn at harvest, for ye damage my oxen did ye last night. 1828 Cobbett *Treat. Cobbett's Corn* § 136 The Americans call it, and..we must call it, 'shelled corn'.

Sheller. **1. b.** (Earlier U.S. example.)

1867 *Rep. Iowa Agric. Soc.* (1868) 221 [Corn sheller and feed grinder], $60 for mill without sheller.

Sheller.[2] *U.S.* [f. Shell *sb.* + -er[1].] A shell-fish, *esp.* a crab.

1886 S. W. Mitchell *R. Blake* xxiv. 261 We'll stay all day, and I'll cook the shellers for you myself.

Shelter, *sb.* **3.** Add: *shelter-house* (earlier U.S. example); **shelter-association**, parasitism or symbiosis for the purpose of obtaining shelter or protection; **shelter-belt**, a belt of trees serving as a protection from inclement weather; *spec.* in *Forestry* (see quot. 1905); **shelter-parasite**, a parasite which seeks a place of shelter in the host; **shelter-tent** (earlier U.S. example); **shelter-wood** *Forestry* = *shelter-belt.

1924 J. A. Thomson *Science Old & New* xxvi. 142 For such a case and for the little fishes that swim about under the umbrella of a large medusa the term *shelter-association will perhaps suffice. 1868, etc., *shelter belt [see Dict.]. 1891 Schlich *Man. Forestry* II. 143 It may even be necessary to provide beforehand a special shelter-belt. 1905 *Terms Forestry and Logging* 21 *Shelter-belt*, natural or artificial forest maintained as a protection from wind or snow. 1910 Mrs. H. Ward *Canadian Born* Epil. 335 The thin background of a few taller trees. The 'shelter-belt' of the farm ..rising brown and sharp against the blue. 1866 *Rep. Indian Affairs* 244 The construction of *shelter-houses for the Santees for the coming Winter. 1897 W. G. Smith tr. *Tubeuf's Dis. Plants* 541 The manner in which typical chlorophyllous plants gradually become *shelter-parasites, and pass from this into the condition of true parasites, is well demonstrated amongst the algae. 1862 O. W. Norton *Army Lett.* 88 Anyone who has lived in these *shelter tents any length of time can appreciate the difficulties of writing in a heavy shower. 1891 Schlich *Man. Forestry* II. 135 The old or *shelter-wood gradually makes way for, and is replaced by, the new crop.

Sheltered, *ppl. a.* Add: **b.** Designating trades and industries which are not exposed to competition.

1924 *Westm. Gaz.* 18 Aug., In the so-called sheltered trades real weekly wages have generally been maintained at at least their pre-war level. 1925 F. L. McDougall (*title*) Sheltered Markets. A study of the value of Empire trade. 1928 *Brit. Industr. Future* (*Lib. Indep. Inq.*) i. ii. § 2. 17 There is a great difference between the increase [in wages] in sheltered and unsheltered industries. 1930 *Times* 24 Mar. 22/3 Comparing..miner's earnings with those of men employed in the so-called 'sheltered' occupations.

Shema (ʃemā·). Also **shemah, shemang.** [Heb. שמע *shema'* hear, imper. of *shāma'* to hear.] The first word of the verse Deut. vi. 4 used as a name for three portions of the Scriptures, Deut. vi. 4–9, xi. 13–21, Numbers xv. 37–41, which are repeated twice daily as a confession of faith by all free males of the Jewish nation.

1864 *Chambers's Encycl.* VI. 155/1 The first additions to the *Shemah* formed the introductory thanksgiving for the renewed day. 1883 *Encycl. Brit.* XVI. 503/2 One is in duty bound to recite the *Shema'* twice a day. 1926 *Brit. Weekly* 5 Aug. 367/3 Esther..joins in that immemorial declaration of her people the Shemang or Confession of the Unity.

Shemmal, variant of Shamal.

1900 Zwemer *Arabia* 107 The prevailing wind at Bahrein, ..is the *Shemmâl* or Northwester.

Shemozzle (ʃemǫ·z'l). orig. *East End slang.* Also **shlemozzle**; **shimozzle, chimozzle.** [orig. *shlemozzle*; Yiddish, f. G. *schlimm* bad + Heb. מזל *mazzāl* luck.] A muddle or complication; a quarrel, 'row', mêlée.

1899 Binstead *Houndsditch Day by Day* 23 It was through no recklessness or extravagance that he was in this shlemozzle. 1900 *From the Front* xiv. 183 We might look upon this little chimozzle as a kind o' misunderstanding. 1901 J. M. Cobban *Golden Tooth* xvii. 170 If Will comes out of this shemozzle. 1916 'Peter' *Trench Yarns* ii. 16 In the ensuing shemmozle Samuel got laid out with the butt-end of a rifle. 1916 'Taffrail' (H. T. Dorling) *Pincher Martin O. D.* vii. § 3. 120 'We ain't the best o' friends, 'cos me an' 'im 'ad a bit of a shimozzle—' 'Shimozzle!' . . 'What on earth's that?' 'Bit o' a dust-up, sir.' 1928 *Sunday Dispatch* 29 July 15/2 Those..who saw so little of war that they still think it to be a gloriously romantic shlemozzle.

Hence **Shemo·zzle** *v. intr.*, to decamp, 'be off'.

1902 Farmer & Henley *Slang*, *Shemozzle*..Verb (East End). To be off; to decamp. 1925 E. Fraser & Gibbons *Soldier & Sailor Words*, *Shemozzle, to*, to make off: to get out of the way—*e.g.*, 'We saw the M.P.'s (Military Police) coming, so we shemozzled.'

Shenanigan (ʃĕnæ·nigăn), *sb.* *U.S.* Also **shi-, shenannigin, -an, shenannikin.** [? Fanciful.]

Chaff, nonsense, humbug, esp. when advanced to cover up some trickery. Hence **Shena·nigan** *v.*

1871 *Evening Post* (Chicago) Jan. (Schele de Vere 632) To go to work and try better next time, instead of fooling members of Congress by a pair of black eyes..No shenannigan, Vinnie! 1877 Bartlett *Dict. Amer.* (ed. 4), *Shenanigan.* 1. A trick in which there is cheating. California. 2. Chaff; foolery; nonsense, especially when advanced to cover some scheme or little game. Yale College. 1893 Milliken *'Arry Ballads* 80/2 Never mind their shenanigan, Charlie; it don't do much 'urt, anyhow. 1894 Mary J. Jaques *Texan Ranch Life* 115 He assured me he was not 'shenan-neganning' me, and that the dish would prove a delicacy. 1897 *Outing* (U.S.) XXIX. 483/1 A man who is firmly kind, but who will stand no shinanigan. 1901 W. S. Walker *In the Blood* xxxi. 332 We're mates all round, an' no more shenannikin. 1930 'Van Dine' *Scarab Murder* xv. 212 There's too much shenanigan going on around here to suit me. I want action.

Shenzi (ʃe·nzi). [Swahili.] In East and West Africa, an uncivilized tribesman.

1910 Roosevelt *Afr. Game Trails* x. 258 The 'shenzis'—wild natives called in Swahili..'wa-shenzi'. 1921 *Blackw. Mag.* Jan. 121/2 He, an askari of G company, ran away from a lot of miserable shouting shenzis! 1926 *Spectator* 3 July 10/2 Local *shenzis*..had gathered round the gramophone.

She-oak. 2. Add: *She-oak net*, a net placed on either side or under the gangway from wharf to ship to prevent drunken sailors from falling into the water.

1898 Morris *Austral Eng.* 1925 Rex Clements *Gipsy of Horn* 111 Old Australian traders used to spread a net under the gangway, called therefrom the sheoke net, whose office it was to save mariners who 'missed stays' when coming aboard from falling into the dock.

Shepherd, *sb.* 6. d. Add: **German shepherd dog** = *Alsatian B. 2. 1926 [see *Alsatian].

Shereef. Add: 3. A dignitary of high standing having both temporal and spiritual power among the Mohammedans of the Philippine Islands.

1898 D. C. Worcester *Philippine Isl.* 159 The spiritual welfare of the people is looked after by *panditas*, or priests, who are in turn subject to *cherifs*.

Hence **Sheree·fate**, the office of shereef. **Sheree·fial** *a.* = Shereefian.

1920 *19th Cent.* Aug. 233 It was to the British Government ..that the Sherifial family of Mecca addressed their communications during the war. 1924 *Glasgow Herald* 8 Mar. 9 He began his official career by assisting successive Sherifs, and in 1908..was appointed to the Sherifate by the Porte.

Sheriat, variant of *Shariah.

Sheridanic (ʃeridæ·nik), *a.* [f. the name of the dramatist, Richard Brinsley *Sheridan* (1751–1816) + -ic.] Of, pertaining to, or characteristic of Sheridan or his characters. So **She·ridanism.**

1833 Disraeli *Lett.* (1887) 80 Her sister Mrs. Blackwood was very handsome and very Sheridanic. 1920 *19th Cent.* Dec. 1030 This Sheridanism brings us to Byron's vivid presentments of his wit in the troubled sunset of his old age.

Sheriff. Add: 1. a. (*b*). Short for *sheriff's officer* (see 4); = Bailiff 2.

1928 *Daily Mail* 30 July 7/1 You have had the sheriff in your house? *Ibid.*, Who put the sheriff into your house?

Sherivaree. *U.S.* Variant of Charivari; cf. Shivaree.

1837 J. L. Williams *Terr. of Florida* 116 Sherivarees are parties of idle people, who dress themselves in grotesque masquerade, whenever a widow or widower are married.

Sherlock Holmes (ʃɜ·ɹlǫk hō^u·mz). The name of the amateur detective who is the chief figure in the detective stories of A. Conan Doyle (1859–1931) collected under the titles *Adventures of Sherlock Holmes*, etc; used typically for a person who indulges in investigating and solving mysteries. Hence **Sherlock (Holmes)** *v. intr.*, to play the detective.

1890 A. Hill *Introd. Science* i. 56 A coincidence..that would hardly be devised in the fertile brain of a Sherlock Holmes. 1903 G. B. Shaw *Man & Superman* iii. 140 Miss Whitefield tracked you at every stopping place: she is a regular Sherlock Holmes. 1913 *Manch. Guardian* 15 Jan., Any man with a bundle or package was suspicious, so we 'sherlocked' around for a bit and watched him go into a barber's shop to get disguised by having his hair cut. There we 'pinched' him. 1929 G. W. Deeping *Roper's Row* iv. § 1 Let's do a little Sherlock Holmesing. Soames, you'll be Watson. 1931 'G. P.' (W. B. Cosens) *Your Servant the Doctor* iii. 27 The intelligence of a Sherlock Holmes.

Sherry, *sb.*¹ 1. b. Add: A glass or drink of sherry.

1924 Galsworthy *White Monkey* ii. ix, Will you have a sherry?

Shibuichi (ʃibuī·tʃi). [Jap., f. Chinese (= four parts one).] An alloy consisting of four parts of copper to one of silver, extensively used by the Japanese on account of its beautiful silver-grey patina.

1902 *Encycl. Brit.* XXIX. 720/1 Neither metal, when it emerges from the furnace, has any beauty, *shakudo* being simply dark-coloured copper, and *shibuichi* pale gun-metal. 1931 *Illustr. London News* 15 Aug. 268/2 An *inro* of *shibuichi*, the copper and silver alloy.

Shice (ʃəis), *a.* and *sb. slang.* Also **shise.** [G. *scheiss*; cf. Shicer.] a. *adj.* Counterfeit, base, spurious. b. *sb.* Base money.

1877 *Five Years' Penal Servitude* iii. 240, I ascertained while at Dartmoor that a very large 'business' is done in 'shise'. *c* 1890 *Five Years of Prison Life* ii. 62 Seeing how the fellow was acting he sent him two 'shise' notes, which gave him a dose that 'corked him'. *Ibid.* iii. 93 A Welshman, convicted or lagged for passing 'shise coin'—bad money.

Shick (ʃik), *a. Austral. slang.* [Cf. She-oak 2.] Drunk. Also **Shi·cker, Shi·ckered** *adjs.*

1916 C. J. Dennis *Ginger Mick* 19 The toff's too shick or silly fer to 'eave 'is carkis out. *Ibid.*, There's a shickered toff slings Rosie goo-goo eyes. 1925 E. Fraser & Gibbons *Soldier & Sailor Words*, Shicker, drunk. 1930 Groom *Merry Christmas* xvi. 123 Every time I get shikkered I sober up after an' say 'Never again, Sandy'.

Shid (ʃid), *v.* [Arab. *shadd(a)* (Syrian *shid*) to bind tightly, strap.] *trans.* To load (a camel). Hence **Shid** *sb.*, the act of loading a camel.

1920 *Blackw. Mag.* Nov. 670/1 It..sent us outside to superintend the shidding (loading). *Ibid.* 673/1 It was not until after four in the afternoon that the camels were again shidded. *Ibid.* 679/2 An early shid took us into Dibbis.

Shield, *sb.* Add:

1. d. *The other side of the shield*: the other side of a question or consideration, the side which is less obvious or which has not been presented. (Cf. F. *le revers de la médaille.*)

8. b. A guard placed on various types of machines to safeguard the workmen or protect the machinery from dust, etc.

1888 *Lockwood's Dict. Mech. Engin.*

c. Any protective device in clothing, as a *dress-shield.*

15. d. A policeman's badge. *U.S.*

1903 *N. Y. Evening Post* 29 Oct. 3 The ex-policeman who turned in his shield in September. 1906 *Ibid.* 16 Feb. 2 [They] stated that they were detectives, both showing him shields in support of their claim.

16. b. Of a chair-back: A centre resembling a shield.

1897 K. W. Clouston *Chippendale Period Eng. Furniture* 65 In the 'shield back' chair, which is Hepplewhite's favourite shape, the shield and its interior ornament making the splat never touch the seat of the chair at all.

19. **shield-back**, having a shield-shaped back.

1897 (see *16 b). 1925 Penderel-Brodhurst & Layton *Gloss. Eng. Furniture, Shield-Back Chair*, one of the distinctive chair-backs of Hepplewhite, which became popular shortly before his death in 1786.

Shift, *sb.* Add: 4. c. Shifty action.

1924 Galsworthy *White Monkey* i. xii, He did not miss the shift and blink in the manager's eyes.

14. c. *Bell-ringing.* (See quot.)

1901 Bulwer *Gloss. Techn. Terms Ch. Bells* 40 *Shift*, an accidental, but fatal, fault in 'change-ringing' caused by two bells becoming displaced in the 'coursing order', or changing places. (The expressions 'change-course' and 'shift-course' mean the same thing as 'shift', but the latter is preferable. 'Twisted' is a synonym for 'shifted'.)

15. b. *Pianoforte.* The action or an act of shifting the keyboard action by using the soft pedal.

1896 Hipkins *Pianoforte* 41 Unless these are directly opposite the strings by a decided shift or return, a snarling quality of tone will be heard.

18. **shift-course** = *sense 14 c; **shift-joint**, in masonry and brickwork (see quot.); **shift-key**, a subsidiary key for adjusting the mechanism in a typewriter when capitals or other special characters are to be used; **shift-lock**, a device for holding the shift-key of a typewriter continuously depressed.

1901 *shift-course [see *14 c]. 1875 Knight *Mech. Dict.* s.v. *Joint*, *Shift-joint. 1882 Christy *Joints* 27 *Shift Joint* is a broken joint, or one that is not continued straight, but given a shift to one side to break joint. 1904 *Knowledge* Feb. 18/2 A *shift key serves to adjust the type-wheel either for letters or figures. 1920 R. T. Nicholson *Mech. Devices Typewriter* 32 Depression of the shift-key marked 'Caps', sets the platen in position for writing capitals, or 'upper-case' letters. 1907 *Jrnl. Soc. Arts* 1 Mar. 435/1 The *shift-lock for capitals. 1920 R. T. Nicholson *Mech. Devices Typewriter* 33 The shift-lock is used whenever it is desired to hold a shift-key continuously depressed.

Shift, *v.* 16. b. Add: Also, to get rid of (money).

1923 E. P. Oppenheim *Inevitable Millionaires* xiv, I should trip it to Monte. That's the place to shift the shekels.

Shifter. 6. Add: also *attrib.*

1920 R. T. Nicholson *Mech. Devices Typewriter* 47 The pawl can be swung into engagement with either spool at will by means of the shifter-knob.

b. A small engine employed in making up a railway train.

1904 *Atlantic Monthly* Oct. 499 The shifter..is a little but powerful locomotive..much given to snorting and panting.

Shifting, *vbl. sb.* Add: 2. e. *Philol.* [tr. G. *verschiebung*]: see *sound-shifting* (*Sound *sb.*³ 7).

1905 O. F. Emerson *Hist. Eng. Lang.* § 267. 238 There has been no consistent shifting of a considerable number of consonants as in High German.

Shifting, *ppl. a.* 1. b. Add: *shifting valve*; **shifting keyboard**, a keyboard action of a grand piano, etc., which is moved by the use of the soft pedal; so **shifting pedal**; **shifting movement** (see Shifting *vbl. sb.* 4); **shifting spanner**, an adjustable spanner.

1896 Hipkins *Pianoforte* 40 In many upright pianos, however, although some are made with *shifting keyboards..a soft pedal is contrived by mechanically dropping a strip of cloth..between the hammers and the strings. 1880 Grove *Dict. Mus.* II. 682/2 The *shifting pedal, first introduced by Stein in his Saitenharmonica. 1883 *Ibid.* III. 637/1 The 'Verschiebung', or shifting pedal. 1813 *Niles' Weekly Register* III. Add. 1/2 Boiling decomposes water slowly... Therefore the *shifting-valve is necessary.

Shiftsman (ʃi·ftsmæn). [f. *shift's*, gen. case of Shift *sb.* + Man *sb.*¹] = Shifter 5, *shift-man* (Shift *sb.* 18).

1921 *Dict. Occup. Terms* (1927) § 044 *Shifter*, shiftman, shiftsman..: general terms for labourers assisting repairers, timberers, etc., in building stoppings and clearing falls of stone. *Ibid.* § 054 *Shifter*, shiftman, shiftsman:..works at night, when mine workers are absent, repairing road-ways, etc. 1924 *Public Opinion* 8 Feb. 127/1 Machinery shall be in charge of a competent shiftsman.

Shifty, *a.* Add: 1. (Earlier U.S. example.)

1838 'Texian' *Mexico v. Texas* 217 Flambeau, who was extremely shifty, soon built up a nice little booth.

2. b. in comb. *shifty-eyed* adj.

1922 H. Jenkins *John Dene of Toronto* i. 11 A shifty-eyed little man.

Shikara, variant of Shikra.

1880 *Encycl. Brit.* XII. 741/1.

Shikimi (ʃikī·mi). Also **sikimi, skim(m)i.** [Jap.] A Japanese tree, the evergreen anise, *Illicium religiosum.* Hence **Shiki·mic** *a.*, designating an acid, $C_7H_{10}O_5$, contained in the fruit of this tree. **Shiki·min**, a crystalline glucoside occurring in shikimi-seeds. **Shiki·mol** = Safrol.

1727 Scheuchzer tr. *Kæmpfer's Hist. Japan* v. iii. 418 Often also they put a branch of the *Fanna Skimmi* Tree over their doors, which is in like manner believ'd to bring good luck into their houses. *Ibid.* xv. 598 He had..a large tub of water standing by him..and some Skimmi branches lying by it. 1845 *Encycl. Metrop.* XX. 482/1 Small furrows filled with powdered bark of the Skimmi-tree. 1881 *Jrnl. Chem. Soc.* XL. 918 To this substance..the author [sc. Eykman] gives the name of 'sikimine', from the Japanese name of the fruit 'shikimi'. 1886 *Ibid.* L. 95 Schikimic acid..which is present in large quantities, is a white, crystalline compound, insoluble in alcohol, ether, and chloroform. 1888 *Ibid.* LIV. 495 The recently discovered shikimole appears to be identical with safrole. Both are optically inactive. 1889 tr. *Rein's Industries of Japan* 136 The fruits of the Skimi, which is consecrated to Buddha and therefore much grown about Buddhist temples and cloisters, made a great stir some time ago. They came to market as a spice, instead of the Staranis, which they closely resemble, and turned out to be poisonous. 1899 Greenish *Introd. Materia Medica* s.v. *Star Anise Fruit*, The poisonous constituent is the crystalline principle sikimin.

Shilling. Add: 6. b. = Solidus¹ 2.

1904 Hart *Rules for Compositors* (ed. 18) 38 The diagonal sign / or 'shilling-mark'.

Shilluk (ʃilu·k). Also **Shillook.** An African negro tribe dwelling on the banks of the White Nile, neighbours of the Dinka. Also, a member of this tribe.

1832 Leake in *Jrnl. R. Geog. Soc.* II. 26 On the twelfth day they reached the first island of the Shilluks. 1873 Ellen E. Frewer tr. *Schweinfurth's Hrt. Africa* I. 261 The jet-black Shillooks, Nueir, and Dinka, natives of the dark alluvial flats, stand out in marked distinction to the dwellers upon the iron-red rocks. 1913 *Rep. Brit. Assoc.* 633 Dr. Seligmann's discoveries among the Shilluks of the Nile Valley. 1927 *World Domin. Internat. Rev.* Oct. 319 All travellers note the Shilluk style of hairdressing.

Shimming, *vbl. sb.* 2. *U.S.* (Earlier example.)

1872 Huntington *Road-Master's Assistant* 78 In winter, when ballast is frozen so that track can not be surfaced by tamping, it is done by *shimming.*

Shimmy (ʃi·mi), *sb.*² *U.S.* Also **shimi.** [? A use of Shimmy, chemise.] A modern dance which resembles a fox-trot accompanied by simulated shivering. Also phr. *to shake a shimmy.*

1919 *N. Y. Sun* 16 Jan., I was dancing the shimi shiver. 1919 *N. Y. World* 17 Jan. (*headline*) Shimmy dance is banned in greater New York. 1921 *Punch* CLX. 398/3 From a description of the 'shimmy': 'The Negro invited his partner to dance by beating his feet and a sideways movement which consisted of "shimmying" or shivering.' 1922 *Weekly Dispatch* 31 Dec. 9 'Shimmy' banned in New York...The Chicago, camel-walk, scandal, balconnades, and shimmy dances must cease. 1924 P. Marks *Plastic Age* 275 That music was enough to make a saint shed his halo and shake a shimmy.

Hence **Shi·mmy** *v. intr.*, to dance the shimmy; also *fig.*, to tremble, shiver (with some emotion).

1920 C. Sandburg *Smoke & Steel* 223 Shimmying the fast shimmy to the Livery Stable Blues. 1925 C. R. Cooper *Lions 'n' Tigers* vii. 175 Old Mom [sc. an elephant] shimmied with delight. 1927 *Daily Express* 14 Dec. 4 Eight most attractive little girls..shimmied and Charlestoned with all the polish and precision of so many Tallulah Bankheads. 1928 Galsworthy *Swan Song* ii. xiii. 217 He..watched the dancing on deck—funny business nowadays, shimmying, bunnyhugging, didn't they call it?

Shimose (ʃimō^u·se). [Said to be short for *Shimonose*, f. the name of the Japanese inventor Masashika *Shimonose* Kogakubachi.] A military explosive prepared from picric acid, which was invented and used by the Japanese in their war with Russia, 1904–5. So **Shi·mosite.**

1904 *Knowledge* July 158/1 Shimose does not explode on percussion, or by fire, and is not injured by wetting. 1915 A. Marshall *Explosives* 322 The first satisfactory solution of the problem was the adoption of picric acid by France. This was quickly followed by similar measures taken by practically all the other Powers, each of whom, however, gave the substance a different name; France..Mélinite, England ..Lyddite,..Japan..Shimosite. 1918 Farrow *Dict. Mil. Terms, Shimose*, one of the picric powders, most successful as a military explosive. It is of Japanese manufacture.

Shimyaan (ʃi·myān). A Natal name for a powerfully intoxicating beverage made of treacle and water fermented in the sun (Pettman).

1870 A. F. Lindley *After Ophir* 306 (Pettman) Shimyan and jwarlar were produced for our consumption, and we were invited to witness the usual dancing performances at the kraal after dark. 1900 Sir J. Robinson *Lifetime S. Africa* 307 'Shimyaan,' a concoction of treacle and water allowed to ferment in the sun. This beverage was maddening in its effects, and the parent of much crime.

Shin (ʃīn), *sb.*² One of the castes of the Dards of the Gilgit basin. So **Shi·na**, the language spoken by these people.

1879 *Encycl. Brit.* X. 598/1 The *Shina* [sc. language], spoken in the rest of the basin, is clearly Aryan, and kindred to the Sanskritic languages of India. *Ibid.*, The middle castes, Shin and Yashkun, form the body of the Dard people. The pure Shin looks more like a European than any high-caste Brahman of India. 1903 Risley & Gait *Census India 1901* I. i. 310 Shina, one of the non-Sanskrit Indo-Aryan forms of speech. 1919 Sir G. A. Grierson *Ling. Surv. India* VIII. ii. 150 In various dialects, Shina is the language of the Gurez Valley in Kashmir.

Shin (ʃin), *sb.*³ [Jap., a. Chinese *shin* god. Cf. Shinto.] A tutelary god or spirit, or the gods or spirits collectively.

1845 *Encycl. Metrop.* XVI. 565/2 Within that enclosure there were two smaller altars dedicated to the *shin* or Superior Spirits, the Genii and Manes.

Shin, *v.* 3. Add: Also, to shoot in the shins.

1819 E. Evans *Pedestrious Tour* 214 Soldiers are apt to fire too high. He was often heard to say to his troops in battle: 'Shin them, my brave boys!'

Shin (ʃin), accommodated pronunciation of *sinh* = hyperbolic sine.

Shindy. 3. (Earlier U.S. example.)

1829 B. Hall *Trav. N. Amer.* III. 325, I never saw a more complete row, or as a fellow near me called it, 'a more regular shindy'.

Shine, *v.* Add: 10. c. *To shine up to*: to try to please; to make oneself pleasant to. *U.S.*

1882 *Century Mag.* Oct. 827 It was then that David first set out to shine up to her. 1886 *Congregationalist* 4 Feb. (Farmer) Mother was always hecterin' me about getting married, and wantin' I should shine up to this likely girl and that. 1902 S. E. White *Blazed Trail* xlii. 294 You might shine up to Hilda Farrand and join the rest of the fortune-hunters.

Shiner. Add: 1. f. A diamond. *S. Afr. slang.*

1884 *Queenstown Free Press* 15 Jan. (Pettman) When they dug it up they at once came to the conclusion it was a real shiner.

4. A stone built into a mortarless wall with its thickest side outward. *S. Africa.*

1881 Douglass *Ostrich Farming* 39 The great thing to look out for is that the men do not put in shiners—that is, stones showing their longest face to the front.

Shingle, *sb.*¹ Add: 1. e. A modern style of cutting women's hair short, as in the bob, but with the back hair shingled (see *Shingle *v.*¹ 2 a). Also, hair cut in this way.

1924 *Hairdressing* Feb. Illustr., Based on the 'shingle'. 1927 F. E. Bailey *Golden Vanity* xvii, Dosir powdered her face, combed her dark shingle, lit a cigarette, and picked up her beef cubes.

attrib. 1926 *Vogue* Late Nov. 85 A charming little shingle cap for night wear. 1928 *Times* 19 Dec. 15/7 After bathing the shingle-wig was slipped over the dishevelled head.

Shingle, *v.*¹ Add: 2. a. Also in modern usage, to cut (women's hair) in a style in which it is made to taper from the back of the head to the nape of the neck; also *absol.*, to have the hair cut in this way.

1924 *Punch* 17 Sept. 319 It moves me not if Araminta shingles Her locks, or Evelina has them bobbed. 1926 Galsworthy *Silver Spoon* iv, Fully dressed for the evening, she had but little on, and her hair was shingled. *Ibid.*, She had been one of the first twelve to shingle.

3. In sheep-shearing: To make a second cut over a part of a sheep's body. *Austral.*

1896 *Chambers's Jrnl.* 12 Sept. 592/1 Bad or careless shearers, in order to give the sheep the appearance of being properly shorn, may either 'shingle' or 'feather' the fleeces they cut off. By 'shingling' is meant making a second cut over the same part of the body of the sheep..close to the skin.

Shingled, *ppl. a.*¹ Add: 3. Of hair: Cut in a shingle. Also *fig.*, curt, abrupt.

1925 *Punch* 20 May 553 *Critic.* 'Doris isn't bad, but her manners are rather shingled.' 1928 Galsworthy *Swan Song* i. v. 39 A fashionable young woman with a clear and, no doubt, shingled head—he felt a great curiosity to see her again.

Shingling, *vbl. sb.*¹ Add: 2. (See *Shingle *v.*¹ 2 a.)

1924 *Chambers's Jrnl.* 483/2 You do not care for the shingling and bobbed hair styles? 1928 Galsworthy *Swan Song* ii. v. 146 Everything now depended on the Basque cap. If women took to them, shingling would stay; if not, hair might come in again.

Shinner² (ʃi·nəɹ). Colloq. abbreviation of *Sinn Feiner (ʃin fēi·nəɹ).

1921 *Glasgow Herald* 9 Apr. 12 The sands are running out as Ireland will shortly be ruined. 'Shinners' may be killed daily. 1922 *Blackw. Mag.* Dec. 740/2 If they took vengeance on the Shinners they would be playing into the hands of the enemy.

Ship, *sb.*¹ 4. b. Add: Also = aeroplane or other form of aircraft.

1928 V. Page *Mod. Aircraft* 522 Always make a landing into the wind, as this will..bring the ship to a stop quicker. 1929 B. Hall & J. J. Niles *One Man's War* 69 At first, I couldn't see why I couldn't have taken a ship [sc. aeroplane] up to the front and gone to making the war the very first day.

8. a. *ship-canal* (earlier U.S. example).

1798 I. Allen *Hist. Vermont* 268 A ship canal would be the means of importing salt, and exporting the preceding articles cheap.

Ship, *v.* Add: 7. c. *U.S.* (Earlier and later examples.)

1872 *Trans. Ill. Dept. Agric.* 205 The remainder is shipped by rail to other parts of this State. 1903 A. Adams *Log Cowboy* xiii. 201 No, I'll not ship any more cattle to your town. 1926 D. L. Colvin *Prohibition in U.S.* 533 A case of brewers in Illinois having shipped beer in kegs..to their agent in Iowa.

e. *intr.* To admit of being sent or transported by ship.

1867–8 *Trans. Ill. Agric. Soc.* VII. 510 It ships well, and is a very good peach. 1927 *Daily Express* 9 Nov. 5/5 Persimmons..will probably be as plentiful and popular as the banana, because it ships well and grows so freely that it can be sold at a low price.

10. b. (Earlier U.S. example.)

1833 B. Silliman *Man. Sugar Cane* 80 [The pan] is made to ship and unship.

13. *To ship a stripe*: to gain promotion in the navy or air-force.

1915 H. Rosher *In R.N.A.S.* (1916) 38, I see in this morning's paper that I have shipped another stripe (Flight Lieutenant). 1924 *Blackw. Mag.* Mar. 333/2 For once his clothes were more interesting than mine for he had 'shipped' his half-stripe, and was a whole degree more important in the world!

Shippable, *a.* Transfer *rare* to sense in Dict. and add: 2. That can be shipped.

1920 *Glasgow Herald* 17 Nov. 11 The Southern Hemisphere promises for 1921 a shippable surplus of 40,000,000qr. 1924 *Ibid.* 30 July 4 The holders of shippable reserves in North America have combined.

Ship-load. (Earlier Amer. example.)

1639 *Portsmouth* (R. I.) *Rec.* 10 For men to gett a shipp lood of..pipe stauffes.

Shipper. 3. b. *U.S.* (Earlier example.)

1898 *Atlantic Monthly* Apr. 436/2 The railway industry employs between eight and nine hundred thousand men, not counting the shippers.

4. (Earlier U.S. example.)

1852 *Trans. Mich. Agric. Soc.* III. 160 By the shipper the logs may be geared deeper or shallower.

Shipping, *vbl. sb.* 6, 6. b. Add: *shipping company, house, lane, pool*; **Shipping Board** (see quot. 1922); **shipping leaf** (see quot.).

1919 *Daily Mail Year Bk.* 78/1 Help of another kind was given to the Allies at sea by the American *Shipping Board. 1922 *Encycl. Brit.* XXXI. 1031/2 The Shipping Board was the first of the new war boards to begin to function. *Ibid.* XXXII. 146/2 The U.S. Shipping Board which fixed ocean freight rates. 1924 *Times Trade & Engin. Suppl.* 29 Nov. 250/3 Orders have now been placed by the United States Shipping Board for 18 Diesel engines to be installed in vessels of about 8,000 tons deadweight. *Ibid.* 239/1 *Shipping companies are complaining that apple shipments are not as heavy as they desire. 1919 *Brit. Manuf.* Nov. 40/2 The attempt to do away with the *shipping house. 1931 W. G. Carr *By Guess & by God* 194 German submarines which.. lurked about the *shipping lanes waiting to attack the Allied merchantmen. 1863 *Trans. Ill. Agric. Soc.* V. 609 Those heavy descriptions of tobacco known in Virginia as heavy *shipping leaf. 1926 *Century Mag.* CXIII. 204 Dayton, Tennessee, that small village was actually the shipping point for two million words of telegraphic news. 1911 *Encycl. Brit.* XXIV. 906/2 Early in 1902 a *shipping pool or 'combine' was effected in the case of certain important British steam lines engaged in the North Atlantic trade.

Shippo (ʃi·pō^u). [Jap., = (*a*) the seven precious things, viz. gold, silver, emerald, mother-of-pearl, agate, amber (or crystal), coral (or tortoiseshell), (*b*) *shippō yaki*; f. Chin. *ts'ih* seven + *pao* jewel.] Cloisonné-enamel ware. Also *attrib.*

1881 *Trans. Asiatic Soc. Japan* X. 41 A broken piece of old Shippô ware. 1889 tr. *Rein's Industries of Japan* 430 The metal decorations of the Japanese by means of enamel (Shippô), *i.e.* opaque coloured glassy flux.

Shirk, *v.* Add: 1. c. To shift or fend *for* oneself. *U.S.*

1849 N. Kingsley *Diary* 76, I can shirk for myself pretty well after going through a campaign in the New Haven and California Joint Stock company. 1850 [see sense 1 in Dict.]. 1861 *Trans. Ill. Agric. Soc.* IV. 515 You might just as well turn out your stall-fed..short-horn cow, and expect her to shirk for herself. 1874 *Rep. Vermont Board Agric.* II. 422 They are then turned into the pasture to shirk for themselves.

Shirley (ʃɜ·ɹli). [f. the name of *Shirley* Vicarage, Croydon, where the variety was produced by the Rev. W. Wilks.] In full *Shirley poppy*: A variety produced from the Common Corn Poppy, *Papaver Rhœas*, under cultivation, bearing single and double flowers of various colours and delicate shades of colour.

1886 *Jrnl. Hort.* 21 Oct. 367/1 (*heading*) Shirley Poppies. 1889 *Ibid.* 15 Aug. 126/2, I sent a pinch of seed to a leading firm of London nurserymen last spring for comparison with the Shirley. 1893 Robinson *English Flower Garden* (ed. 3) 568/1 Of recent years pretty single forms of the Corn Poppy have become popular under the name of 'Shirley Poppies'.

Shirred, *a.* 2. Add: Also *fig.*

1929 S. Jameson in *Legion Bk.* 105 The waters..in sunshine ruffled and shirred with living light.

Shirt, *sb.* Add: 2. f. *To keep one's shirt on*: to keep calm. *U.S. slang.*

1904 W. H. Smith *Promoters* i. 15 I'll tell you how, if you'll keep your shirt on. 1911 R. D. Saunders *Col. Todhunter* v. 70 It don't make any difference..so you can just keep your shirt on.

5. a. *shirt-tail* (earlier U.S. example).

1846 J. W. Webb *Altowan* I. vi. 174 He..leaped into the river,..and made a shirt-tail across the prairie on the other side.

c. **shirt-bosom, -button, -waist** (earlier examples); **shirt-front wicket**, a wicket or cricket pitch fancifully compared to a shirt-front for smoothness.

1833 J. Neal *Down-Easters* I. 3 His collar turned back, and his *shirt-bosom all open to the waist. 1678 *New Castle Court Rec.* 352, 3 Payer of *shirt Buttons. 1742 in *Maryland Hist. Mag.* XX. 178 Three or four Papers good shirt buttons but not made on wire. 1925 Ld. Harris in *Westm. Gaz.* 16 Jan., I deprecate these '*shirt-front' wickets; they enhance the luck of the toss. 1928 *Sunday Express* 18 Nov. 3 Long discourses on what they are pleased to describe as the 'shirt-front' wicket at Sydney, which, according to them, resembles nothing so much as a slab of highly-polished marble. 1889 *Kansas City Times & Star* 15 Apr., She obtained work..at Haar's *shirtwaist and overall factory. 1895 in Appel *Business Biogr. To. Wanamaker* (1930) 110 Five carloads of shirtwaists placed on sale.

Shirt-sleeve. *attrib.* (later example).

1931 W. F. Sands *Undiplomatic Mem.* 22, I admit some pride in believing that they acted like gentlemen in the matter, though perhaps it was only shirt-sleeves diplomacy.

Shise, variant of *Shice.

Shivaree, *sb.* and *v. U.S.* (Earlier examples.)

1843 R. Carlton *New Purchase* lv. 231 The musicians.. letting off at each repetition of the demand peals of shiver-ree. 1872 E. Eggleston *End of World* xlv. 291 O Uncle Andrew! is it a shivaree? *Ibid.* xlvi. 294 Among the manly recreations which they have proposed to themselves is that of shivereeing 'that Dutchman, Gus Wilde'. 1876 'Mark Twain' *Old Times* 55, I started such a rattling 'shivaree' down below as never had astounded an engineer in this world before.

Shiver, *v.*² Add: 2. c. *trans.* To shake, rustle.

1928 E. W. Hendy *Lure of Bird Watching* 49 The hen, at the conclusion of a dustbath, gave a low call, and shivered her wings.

Shivering, *vbl. sb.*² Add: 2. *Path.* (See quot. 1913.)

1903 *U.S. Dept. Agric., Rep. Dis. Horse* 207 (Cent. D. Suppl.). 1913 Dorland *Med. Dict.* (ed. 7), *Shivering*, chorea affecting the muscles of the hip and thigh of a horse.

Shock, *sb.*¹ 3. Add: *shock corn.*

1925 R. R. Snapp *Beef Cattle* 179 Before the silo became common, corn fodder or shock corn was used extensively for wintering cattle.

Shock, *sb.*³ Add: 7. *shock-test*; **shock-absorber**, also, a device on aircraft to lessen the shock of contact with the earth or other surfaces on landing; **shock-proof** *a.*, proof against breakage or injury by shocks or blows; also *fig.*

1926 H. Barber *Aeroplane Speaks* 112 In the case of rubber *shock absorbers, both the number of turns and the lengths must be equal. 1931 *Henley's ABC Gliding & Sailflying* 193 If the landing gear is not provided with shock absorbers, it is desirable to pad the pilot's seat well. 1911 Dreiser *Jennie Gerhardt* xviii, He was..curiously elated beneath a sturdy, *shock-proof exterior. 1928 *Daily Express* 19 June 3 It is a splinterless shock-proof safety glass with visibility unimpaired by constant use. 1930 Rose Macaulay *Staying with Relations* xiv. § 3. 203 They needed a shock-proof screen between them, to deaden the assaults of each on the other's strained nerves. 1905 *Trans. Instit. Naval Archit.* XLVII. ii. 382 Fremont's *shock test.

b. In **shock-troops** [tr. G. *stosstruppen*], forces of selected and specially armed men designed for use in assault operations, especially against strong positions or large numbers.

1918 Farrow *Dict. Mil. Terms, Shock Troops*, troops especially selected for assault work. They usually wear steel breastplates and other protection strong enough to turn a bullet at 50 or 60 feet. 1927 *Daily Express* 14 July 9/4 The G.P.U. troops..in..a war against Poland and Britain..would be used as shock troops. 1928 *Dict. Amer. Biogr.* I. 382/2 A master of strategy usually stays behind the lines. Not so Bishop Asbury. He asked no more of his skirmishers and shock-troops than he was himself prepared to undergo. 1931 A. H. Dallas tr. E. Seeberg in *Relig. World* 400 The Society of Jesus..was organized with such..efficiency that it became the 'spear head' or 'shock troops' of the Papacy.

c. Hence, in the U.S.S.R., applied to workers who are used for accomplishing a specially arduous task, and to the system under which they work, etc.

1930 S. N. Harper *Making Bolsheviks* 52 The so-called 'shock-brigade movement' among workmen, which is interpreted by the Communists as an illustration of a new attitude and as a new and vital force produced by the Revolution. *Ibid.* 53 The shock-brigade of a given factory or mine is a voluntary organization of workmen who have come together to fulfil and, if possible, exceed the quota of production assigned to the factory under the Five-Year Plan of expansion. *Ibid.* 55 October first of this year was proclaimed 'Shock-Brigade Day'. 1930 *Observer* 16 Nov. 11/2 Checking currency inflation has loomed up as one of the urgent 'shock problems' which are so common under the strained conditions of Soviet economic life. 1931 *Times Lit. Suppl.* 9 July 536/4 And 'cultural work' is still in effect a kind of propagandist 'shock work'. 1931 *Morn. Post* 11 Aug. 11/7 Three hundred and fifty Russian 'shock workers' landed in London from the s.s. Ukraine yesterday for a two days' 'holiday'. 1932 *Times* 11 Mar. 13/7 By order of the Soviet Government

March is to be a 'shock month for mobilizing financial resources'.

Shockability (ʃǫkăbi·lĭti). [f. Shockable *a.* + -ity.] The capacity for being shocked.

1929 Gerald Gould *Democritus* 89 What we want is to preserve the precious gift of shockability while remaining too intelligent to be shocked.

Shocker². (Earlier U.S. example.)

1786 Washington *Diaries* III. 91 For every two Cradlers to allow 4 rakes, 1 shocker, and two Carriers.

Shodden, *a.* (Earlier U.S. example.)

1829 J. F. Cooper *Wish-ton-wish* vi, His beast hath a shodden hoof.

Shoe, *sb.* Add: 5.

q. A box for dealing the cards in chemin-de-fer.

1924 W. J. Locke *Coming of Amos* viii. 101 'Chemin de fer'..She..handed him shoe and cards and counters. 1930 Byrne *Golden Goat* i. 8 They were only interested in the passing of the 'shoe' as the chemin-de-fer box is called.

6. c. **shoe-bench** *U.S.*, a shoemaker's bench; **shoe-boil**, capped elbow in horses or cattle (Dorland 1913); **shoe-button**, (*a*) a button used for fastening boots and shoes; (*b*) a small black spider, *Latrodectus mactans*; **shoe-deep** *a.*, deep enough to cover the shoe; **shoe-lastcelt** [Celt²] *Archæology*, a polished stone hoe, flat on one side and curved on the other, found in the area of neolithic Danubian culture; **shoe-parlour** *U.S.*, a shoe-cleaning shop; **shoe-rail**, a rod for supporting shoes in a wardrobe or similar piece of furniture; **shoe-tree** (earlier U.S. example).

1841 *Knickerbocker Mag.* XVII. 362 A few weeks' rumination on the *shoe-bench, or cogitation on the tailors' board. 1891 *Harper's Mag.* June 57/1 An express wagon was.. loaded with the old shoe bench. 1927 *Daily Express* 21 July 2/7 A small black spider known to entomologists as 'latrodectus mactans', and commonly called the 'black widow' or '*shoebutton', which has been introduced from Oriental ports into North America concealed in fruit and lumber, and caused more than twenty deaths last month. 1773 P. V. Fithian *Jrnl.* (1900) 75 Last night there fell a Snow which is about half *Shoe-deep. 1891 Mary E. Wilkins *New England Nun* 174 There had been a light fall of snow..but it was not shoe deep. 1927 Peake & Fleure *Priests & Kings* 126 They had knives of obsidian..and stone celts or hoes, among which is a type, not unlike that found in the Danube basin, known as the *shoe-last celt. 1929 Childe *Danube in Prehist.* 40 The universal stone implement of the Danubian I culture is the polished adze or hoe. It may be termed a 'shoe-last' celt, though strictly that name should be confined to the narrow chisel-like specimens. 1906 *Washington Post* 29 Apr. 9 Dainty society women performed the menial task of shining men's shoes. The improvised *shoe parlor was in All Souls' Unitarian Church. 1928 *Daily Mail Year Bk.* p. lxxxvii, Fitted wardrobe..with..*shoe rails (with space for 6 pairs). 1827 B. Drake & Mansfield *Cincinnati* viii. 60 In the third story the manufacture of *shoe trees is carried on.

Shoeblack. (Earlier Amer. example.)

1778 J. Adams *Diary* 29 Dec., Wks. 1850 II. 306 A porter, a shoeblack, or chimney sweeper.

Shoeing, *vbl. sb.* 2. b. (Earlier U.S. example.)

1780 *Narragansett Hist. Reg.* I. 104 Made shoeing for Bowland's boat keel.

Shoepack, -pac (ʃū·pæk). *U.S.* [Of Lenape (Delaware) Indian origin.] (See Shoe *sb.* 6 c.)

1755 in *Lett. to Washington* I. 99 It would be a good thing to have Shoe-packs or Moccosons for the Scouts. 1824 [see Shoe *sb.* 6 c]. 1852 J. Reynolds *Pioneer Hist. Illinois* 52 The men out of doors wore a coarser and stronger article made out of thicker leather, which the Americans call 'shoe packs'. 1897 J. L. Allen *Choir Invisible* iii. 26 The small, sensitive feet,..covered with coarse shoe-packs tied with leather thongs. 1903 S. E. White *Forest* x. 120 He brought to light..oil-tanned shoepacs, with and without the flexible sole.

Shoe·-string. 1. See Shoe *sb.* 6 c, and add: b. *On a shoe-string*, with very little capital; on a small margin. *U.S. colloq.*

1904 *Cosmopolitan* May 89 They said he..speculated 'on a shoe-string'—an exceedingly slim margin. 1926 J. Black *You Can't Win* viii. 90 The new owners had no bankroll, just opened up on a shoestring. 1932 *Nation* (N.Y.) 9 Mar. 271 American universities have started department after department on financial shoe-strings.

c. *attrib.* Small or petty in a peculiary way.

1923 'B. M. Bower' *Parowan Bonanza* xi. 137 The little shoestring propositions that go broke and leave empty houses behind them. 1926 J. Black *You Can't Win* xiii. 185 The cheap cheaters and tinhorn, shoestring gamblers never got a footing there.

2. (*a*) A kind of tobacco; (*b*) a Julienne potato (chiefly *pl.*). *U.S.*

1784 J. F. D. Smyth *Tour U.S.* II. 129 There are seven different kinds of tobacco..each varying from the other. They are named Hudson, Frederick, Thick-joint, Shoe-string, [etc.]. 1931 B. Starke *Touch & Go* x. 156, I..found that the word 'shoe-strings' on the menu really meant Julienne potatoes. I ate every last shoe-string.

Shoey (ʃū·i). *slang.* [f. Shoe *v.* + -y⁶.] An army shoeing-smith.

1919 *War Terms* in *Athenæum* 1 Aug. 695/2. 1925 E. Fraser & Gibbons *Soldier & Sailor Words.*

Shofer, variant of *Chauffeur.

1918 'Q' *Foe-Farrell* 110, I got in [the car] and sat back in the cushions, waiting for the Shofer, if that's how you pronounce it.

Shoji (ʃō^u·dʒi). [Jap.] A sliding screen of semi-transparent paper used to compose the partitions, and in the daytime in winter the walls, of a Japanese house.

1880 Miss Bird *Japan* (1905) 40, I closed the sliding windows, with translucent paper for window panes, called *shōji.* 1881 Satow & Hawes *Handbk. Japan* (1884) 482/1 *Amado* (rain doors)..replace the ordinary *shō-ji* (sliding screens). 1886 J. La Farge *Artist's Lett. Japan* (1897) 217 To look out of the *shoji* screens into the garden. 1922 J. Street *Mysterious Japan* ii. (1923) 24 Children glimpsed through the open wood and paper *shoji* of their matchbox houses.

Shomio, variant of *Siomio.

Shonkinite (ʃǫ·ŋkinəit). *Petrog.* [f. *Shonkin*, the Indian name for the Highwood Mountains, Montana + -ite¹.] A phaneric igneous rock of granular texture, composed essentially of augite with subordinate orthoclase. Hence **Shonkini·tic** *a.*, consisting of shonkinite.

1895 Weed & Pirsson in *Bull. Geol. Soc. Amer.* VI. 415 For this type of rock, then, we propose the name of shonkinite,..and shonkinite we define as a granular plutonic rock consisting of essential augite and orthoclase. 1930 Peach & Horne *Geol. Scotl.* 112 A discontinuous zone of fine-grained shonkinite and pulaskite. *Ibid.* 113 The degree of alteration is less in the more shonkinitic patches.

Shoo, *v.* Add: 1. b. To cause to move or go in a desired direction by following up gently. *U.S.*

1903 *N. Y. Sun* 17 Nov. 12 The police shoo everybody to the south side of the loops. 1903 *N. Y. Evening Post* 28 Dec. 1 So far from being gently shoved off by the Administration and 'shooed' toward home, Gen. Reyes has been treated with distinguished consideration. 1923 'B. M. Bower' *Parowan Bonanza* xiii. 151 You're supposed to shoo a lady gently before you down the aisle.

Shoofly. *U.S.* [Of obscure origin.] A temporary railway-track constructed for use while the regular track is not available.

Also used in other unrelated senses.

1905 *Los Angeles Express* 18 Mar. 8 A freight train had left the track. The work of building a shoofly around the train was at once begun. 1905 *N. Y. Evening Post* 29 July 1 The Southern Pacific Company's 'shoo-fly' around the tracks now submerged will be completed in a few days.

Shoot, *sb.*¹ Add: 1. i. The action of shooting a film (see *Shoot *v.* 22 f).

1929 *Morn. Post* 24 May 12/7 A Wembly 'Shoot' Described...A 'talkie' sequence is being 'shot' in the studio.

6. c. *U.S.* (Earlier examples.)

1865–6 *Trans. Ill. Agric. Soc.* VI. 319 Each railroad has one thousand feet of platform which is provided with 'shoots', leading directly into the yards and pens. 1873 J. H. Beadle *Undevel. West* xxii. 432 About a quarter section of cattle-yards and 'shoots' extend around the depot.

Shoot, *v.*

4. e. Also, to urge (one's mount) swiftly forward.

1928 *Morn. Post* 20 Oct. 14/1 The latter was travelling like a winner as far as the Dip, where Richards shot his mount into the lead.

11. j. To discard, get rid of; orig. in *shoot that hat*, etc., as a rude retort or mild imprecation. Also with *up. U.S. slang.*

1876 E. Burton *Songs* (Bartlett) The slang the gang is using now You'll hear from every lip; It's shoot the hat! and get it boiled; And don't you lose your grip. *a* 1877 *New York Herald* (Bartlett) One lady..with derisive scorn ..observed in the language of the day, 'Oh, shoot that hat!' 1883 J. Hay *Bread-winners* xvi. 249 If I had all the cash he takes in to-night, I'd buy an island and shoot the machine business. 1902 Farmer & Henley *Slang* s.v., *Shoot that (hat, man—anything)!*..a mild imprecation, 'Bother!' 1926 J. Black *You Can't Win* xii. 161 They grew so despondent over their plight..they decided to 'shoot up' the small portion of white stuff they had left. 1928 *Sunday Express* 18 Mar. 9/2 'Tell him to shoot that song-and-dance outfit'.., and jump into some plain overalls.

12. Also, to cast (a line) in fishing.

1870 Kendall *God's Hand* 9 (E.D.D.) Has to return without shooting his lines. 1931 *Hardy's Anglers' Guide* 13 This [slack] line is released during the forward stroke [in casting]. This is termed 'shooting' line.

18. e. Of a crab, lobster, etc.: To cast off or drop (a leg or limb).

1884 Goode *Nat. Hist. Aquat. Anim.* 805 Lobsters have the power of dropping or 'shooting' one or both claws, which may be more or less completely replaced by a new growth.

22. d. Phr. *To shoot the corn off*: to celebrate the harvest-home with the shooting of guns. *S. Africa.*

1886 *Hist., Product., & Resources C.G.H.* (ed. J. Noble) 226 Powder is given them to enable them to carry out what is known in the vernacular as 'shooting the corn off'.

f. Also *trans.* to photograph with a cinematograph camera; to make a cinematographic film of. Also *absol.*

1916 'B. M. Bower' *Phantom Herd* ii. 22 He..debated whether it should be 'shot' with two cameras or three. 1919 *Conquest* Dec. 70/2 First, the camera man 'shoots' on the tank containing the fishes with one half of the lens open. 1923 *Publishers' Circular* 29 Sept., Miss May Edgington's new novel, 'Triumph', is at the present moment being 'shot' for film production. 1927 *Daily Tel.* 21 June 17/1 Mr. Fox sent the players specially to this country in order to 'shoot' as many scenes as possible in the appropriate places. 1928 L. North *Parasites* 26 He passed a group of people gathered round the camera that had just shot the abortion he had seen enacted. 1932 *News Chronicle* 23 Sept. 3/5 The film of Cervantes' book which is being 'shot' in the Alps near Nice.

23. h. To give vent or utterance to. Also *absol.* in imper. = 'fire away!' *slang.*

1930 H. R. Wakefield in *London Mercury* Feb. 317 'Surely he wouldn't tell us,' said Dandylion. 'He'd be on the other side.' 'Well, shoot some of your S.A.,' said the young person, 'He'll soon come across.' 1930 *Observer* 23 Mar. 15 At shooting the smart stuff, Miss Blakeney has the world well beaten.

28. b. (Later U.S. example.)

1924 G. Overton *Cargoes for Crusoes* 41 In his chamber Doomdorf lay shot to death.

30. e. *To shoot up*: to assail or master by shooting; *esp.* to rush through (a place) shooting wildly in all directions. *U.S.*

1901 S. E. White *Westerners* iv. 31 If you try to shoot us up any, we'll kill every hoof you have. 1909 *Chambers's Jrnl.* Feb. 104/1 Armed and masked men..took entire possession of it [sc. Princeton], 'shot it up' until opposition subsided.

Shooter. Add: 10. A black morning coat. *slang.*

1902 Farmer & Henley *Slang, Shooter*.., a black morning coat (Harrow) as distinguished from the tail coat worn by the Fifth and Sixth Forms. 1920 Galsworthy *In Chancery* ii. vii, 'I suppose I'd better change into a "shooter",' he muttered, escaping to his room. He put on the 'shooter', a higher collar, a pearl pin, and his neatest grey spats.

Shooting, *vbl. sb.* 8. b. Add: **shooting-ground** (earlier U.S. example); **shooting-match** (later U.S. examples); **shooting-seat, -stick,** (*b*) a walking-stick which may be adapted to form a seat, used chiefly by shooters.

1843 *Knickerbocker Mag.* XXI. 121 A gentleman who had asked his advice about the *shooting-ground. 1813 *Niles' Weekly Register* IV. 35/1, I..gained their applause for my activity at our *shooting matches. 1853 J. G. Baldwin *Flush Times Alabama* 127 Shooting-matches..and card-playing. 1906 *Springfield* (Mass.) *Weekly Republ.* 29 Mar. 4 You are not the whole shooting match, but a good share of it. 1895 *Army & Navy Co-op. Soc. Price List* 15 Sept. 954 Cane *shooting seats. *Ibid.*, Wood, folding Shooting Seat, can be used as a Walking Stick. 1926 Oppenheim *Golden Beast* i. xvii, Judith had already disappeared, swinging her *shooting stick in her hand. 1929 H. V. Morton *In Search Scotl.* v. § 6. 137 The Mayfair and Belgravia clans sit their shooting-sticks with renewed expectation.

Shop, *sb.* 9. c. Add: **shop assistant**, a shopkeeper's assistant; **shop-clerk** *U.S.*, a shop assistant; **shop committee** (see quot. 1923); **shop-drive**, the apparatus necessary for operating the machinery of a shop or factory by electric power; **shop-fittings** *pl.*, the equipment of a shop, as counters, shelves, etc.; so **shop-fitter**; **shop-hours** *pl.*, the hours during which a shop assistant is employed, or a shop is kept open; **shop kitchen**, a kitchen connected with a factory; **shopland**, the shopping centre of a town or city; **shop-sign**, a sign or device for indicating the ownership or type of a shop; **shop-steward**, the foreman of a workshop; **shop-walk** *v. intr.*, to act as a shop-walker; **shop-work**, work done in a shop or workshop; **shop-worn** *a.* (earlier U.S. example).

1896 H. G. Wells *Wheels of Chance* i, Thus even in a *shop assistant does the warmth of manhood assert itself. 1902 *Encycl. Brit.* XXX. 98/1 Only three kinds of protective requirement are binding on employers of shop assistants. 1921 *Dict. Occup. Terms* (1927) § 775 *Shop assistant*..: serves customers with goods in retail shop or store, makes out bill or docket. 1911 H. S. Harrison *Queed* xiii. 151 There is your public..*shop-clerks, stenographers [etc.]. 1908 *Modern Business* Aug. 69/1 With a good *shop committee the men will not be afraid to ventilate their grievances. 1923 J. D. Hackett *Labor Terms* in *Man. Engin.* May, *Shop Committee*, a committee appointed by members of a works committee for the consideration of some special labor problem. 1903 *Iron Age* 26 Mar. 22 (Cent. D. Suppl.) *Shop-drive. 1921 *Dict. Occup. Terms* (1927) § 483 *Shop fitter*: receives wooden parts or sections of counters, desks,..and other shop fittings. 1858 Simmonds *Dict. Trade.* *Shop-fittings*, the counters, desks, shelves, gas-burners, and other fixtures of a shop. 1911 *Rep. Labour & Soc. Cond. Germany* III. vi–vii. 29 The building and shopfitting trade. 1892 *Act* 55 & 56 *Vict.* c. 62 § 1 This Act may be cited as the *Shop Hours Act, 1892. 1908 *Modern Business* Aug. 69/1 *Shop kitchens. 1928 *Daily Express* 20 Nov. 3 The opening of the new Ponting's is the most exciting event in *shopland this week. 1927 *Daily Express* 7 Mar. 5/3 Shopland, whether its particular province be Oxford-street and Regent-street, Knightsbridge, Kensington, or on the other side of the park in Queen's Road, has become one vast fair ground. 1930 *Daily Express* 6 Oct. 3/5 A great flame which lit up the whole sky..and clearly illuminated the *shop signs. 1915 *Political Quarterly* No. 6. 92 The *Shop-stewards' Committee at one of the factories called a mass meeting. 1905 H. G. Wells *Kipps* i. vi, Buggins, whose place it was to *shopwalk while Carshot served, shopwalked with quite unparalleled dignity. 1925 C. Fox *Educat. Psychol.* 177 Geometry and *shop-work. 1871 Barnum *Struggles & Triumphs* 40 A large quantity of tin ware which had been in the shop for years and was considerably '*shop-worn'.

Shop, *v.* Add: 1. b. To dismiss (a person) from a situation or post. *U.S.*

1915 H. L. Wilson *Ruggles of Red Gap* iv. (1917) 76 It seemed probable that I should be shopped by Mrs. Effie for what she had been led to believe was my rowdyish behaviour. *Ibid.* xvii. 308, I would have shopped the fellow in an instant,..had it been at any other time. He was most impertinent.

6. intr. *To shop around*: to look round for a situation or work. *U.S.*

1922 J. D. Hackett in *Management Engineering* Feb., During the war, although orders greatly exceeded production, absentism increased. Men took days off to 'shop around', knowing that if unsuccessful they would be welcomed back.

Shopman. Add: 3. A workshop hand.

1925 *Westm. Gaz.* 13 Jan., Mr. Cramp asked the Court to say that there should be one award for the whole of the shopmen employed on the railways of Great Britain.

Shor (ʃǭɹ). [Turki *shōr*, f. Turkish *shōr* adj., saltish, brackish.] In Turkestan, an elongated saline depression in desert sand.

1888 *Encycl. Brit.* XXIII. 512/1 A feature distinctive of the Turcoman desert is seen in the very numerous *shors*, or elongated depressions. 1898 *Geog. Jrnl.* (R.G.S.) Sept. 308 The *shors*..are seen on the southern border of the Kara-kum sands.

Shore, *sb.*¹ Add: 5. **shore-based** *a.*, having the base of operations on land; **shore-hold** *Logging* (see quot.); **shore-platform** *Geol.*, the comparatively flat sea-bottom extending outward from most coastlines, which supports the sedentary marine life; **shore-wall** *Geol.*, 'accumulations of sand and gravel pushed up into mounds by the expansion and contraction of ice formed on rivers and lakes' (Cent. Dict. *Suppl.* 1909).

1927 *Daily Tel.* 22 Mar. 10/7 The limitation of air armaments shall be effected by limiting the number of *shore-based aircraft of service type maintained in commission. 1905 *Terms Forestry & Logging* 46 *Shore hold*, the attachment of the hawser of a raft of logs to an object on the shore. 1895 Dana *Man. Geol.* (ed. 4) 222 (Cent. D. Suppl.) *Shore-platform. 1885 *Fifth Ann. Rep. U. S. Geol. Survey* 109 The base of a *shore wall stands somewhat above and beyond the ordinary margin of water. 1893 Geikie *Text-bk. Geol.* (ed. 3) 415 When the ice melts, this embankment of displaced material is left as a memorial of the severity of the climate. Such 'shore-walls' are of common occurrence on the margins of many lakes in Canada and the United States.

b. **shore-bug** *U.S.* (see quots.).

1895 Comstock *Man. Study Insects* 134 Family Saldidæ, the Shore-bugs...Some of the Shore-bugs dig burrows, and live for a part of the time beneath the ground. 1902 Howard *Insect Bk.* 291 [They] have been dubbed 'shore bugs' by Comstock for the reason that they are always found upon the sea beach.

c. In obvious attrib. uses; = of or pertaining to the shore; sometimes adj., = littoral.

1862 E. Hodder *Mem. N. Z. Life* 24 Shore clothes were unpacked, the ship was made tidy. 1884 Howells *Silas Lapham* xxiii. 415 A young fellow in the shabby shore-suit of a sailor. 1886 Prestwich *Geol.* I. 122 A 'shore-deposit' extends for a distance of about 150 miles...Near volcanic islands the shore deposit..is less argillaceous. 1901 *Chambers's Jrnl.* Aug. 551/2 Four keepers are employed in connection with the lighthouse, three being in constant attendance while the fourth is on shore-duty. 1911 J. A. Thomson *Biol. Seasons* Introd. 4 In modern studies..of the shore-fauna or of the flora of lakes. *Ibid.* iv. 352 What a variety of biological impressions we gain from this walk among the shore-jetsam. 1921 *Chambers's Jrnl.* Jan. 1/1 Clement glanced at the umbrella and the obvious shore-rig of bounding little men.

Shore-going, *vbl. sb., attrib.* (Earlier U.S. examples.)

1846 *Knickerbocker Mag.* XXVIII. 64 He rigged himself in his 'shore-going togs' after supper. 1887 B. Harte *Crusade of 'Excelsior'* 63 Captain Bunker..wore a shore-going suit of black broadcloth.

Short, *a.*, *sb.*, and *adv.* Add: A. *adj.* 14. a. *Short drink*, a dram of spirits.

1883 *Daily Tel.* 2 July 5/3 (Farmer) All these are short drinks—that is to say, drams. 1885 *Punch* 4 July 4/1 To procure what he calls 'a snack and a short drink'.

26. **short-change** *v. trans. U.S.*, to rob by giving insufficient change; **short column**, a column whose length is not more than 3 to 5 times its diameter; **short course** *Bell-ringing* (see quot.); **short focus** *Photog.*, a focus where the rays converge at a short distance from the lens; chiefly attrib., esp. in *short focus* (*portrait*) *lens*; **short game** *Golf*, putting; **short head** (*b*) *Racing*, a distance less than the length of a horse's head; also *attrib.*; hence **short-head** *v. trans. Racing*, to beat by this distance; **short jenny** *Billiards* (see Jenny 7); **short list**, a list of selected candidates for a post from which it is intended to make the final selection; hence **short-list** *v. trans.*, to put on a short list; **short-paid** *a.*, designating mail which is insufficiently stamped; **short-period** *a.*, extending over or lasting for a brief period of time; recurring at short intervals; **short sauce** *U.S.* (see Sauce *sb.* 4 a); **short-six**, (*a*) a variety of short candles of the weight of six to a pound (cf. Six B. 3 h); (*b*) *U.S.*, a make of cigar (cf. *Long nine); **short sleeves** *pl.*, sleeves which do not reach below the elbow; hence **short-sleeved** *a.*, having short sleeves; **short-spent** *a.*, unexpended; **short-spoon** *Golf*, a baffy; **short-staple** (earlier U.S. example); **short story**, a story with a fully worked-out motive but of much smaller compass and less elaborate in form than a novel; **short suit** *Cards*, a suit of which one has less than four cards; also *attrib.*; **short-thread** *a.*, designating a sewing-machine in which the needle passes through the material as in hand sewing; **short time**, the state or condition of working less than the regular number of hours per day or of days per week; **short title**, an abbreviated form of the full title; **short wave**, a wave which has a relatively short wave-length; *spec.* in wireless, one having a wave-length of less than 100 metres (3,000 k/c per second); also *attrib.*; **short week**, a week in which a workman's wage is below the average owing to short time.

1923 H. L. Foster *Beachcomber in Orient* xii. 308 A tourist is cheated and *short-changed so often in the East [etc.]. 1928 L. North *Parasites* 304 The girl at the cash-register short-changed him. 1888 *Lockwood's Dict. Mech. Engin.*, *Short Columns*, a term applied to columns whose length exceeds their diameter by from three to five times that amount, and which yield to rupture by simple crushing only. 1904 Bulwer *Gloss. Techn. Terms Bells & Ringing* 13 The effect of other 'calls' is to curtail the 'course', by cutting out a part of the 'work'. It is then termed a '*short course'. 1862 *Catal. Internat. Exhib., Brit.* II. No. 3122 It forms a portrait lens of *short focus. *Ibid.* No. 3154 The same camera can be used for either short-focus portrait or long-focus landscape lenses. 1892 *Photogr. Ann.* II. 307 Back can be moved up to the front for short focus work. 1856 *Chambers's Jrnl.* 4 Sept. 157/2 The '*short game'—coming into play when the ball lies from a hundred to one hundred and fifty yards from the hole. 1879 *Encycl. Brit.* X. 767/1 They have hitherto confined themselves to the 'short game', as it is termed, or putting. 1897 *Encycl. Sport* I. 473/1 *Short Game*, approaching and putting. 1903 H. G. Hutchinson, etc. *Bk. Golf* 238 Treat the combination of mashies (sometimes irons) and putting together, calling it the short game. 1898 A. E. T. Watson *The Turf* 133 There are legends of judges having made mistakes in *short head verdicts. 1921 *Daily Mail Year Bk.* 79/1 His stable companion Comrade beat Embry by a short-head. 1928 *Daily Chron.* 9 Aug. 10/2 To get her home by as much as half a length, although you would have thought that there was only time for a short head victory. 1922 *Weekly Dispatch* 12 Nov. 7 Danny caught him napping and *shortheaded him on the post. 1929 *Daily Express* 7 Nov. 18/4 In a most luckless effort he was short-headed. 1899 *short jenny [see Jenny 7]. 1904 Mannock *Billiards* 106 Fig. 28 shows..a 'short jenny' in the adjacent centre pocket. 1927 W. E. Collinson *Contemp. Engl.* 124 Selection committees to University posts first familiarised me with the meaning of the *short list. 1908 *Chambers's Jrnl.* Jan. 101/2 Any [letters] suspected to be *short-paid are placed aside and afterwards surcharged if necessary. 1887 *Encycl. Brit.* XXII. 509/1 *Short-period fluctuations between a maximum and minimum, within the limits of each single stroke. 1895 *Knowledge* 1 May 111/2 There is no longer any reason to doubt that all 'short-period variables' are really close binaries. 1900 *Ibid.* 1 Dec. 285/2 Brorsen's Comet...This interesting short-period comet. 1905 *Technol. & Sci. Dict.* (ed. Goodchild & Tweney), *Short Period Comets*, comets which have periods from three to eight years in length. Spoken of sometimes as Jupiter's family of comets. 1923 P. B. Ballard *New Examiner* 107 For..an overwhelming majority, short-period testing, when properly carried out, is as sound and as valid as long-period testing. 1931 *Times Lit. Suppl.* 19 Feb. 124/2 It may therefore be regarded as an original study in short-period economics. *Mod.* Short-period excursions. 1822 J. Neal *Randolph* I. 279 (Krapp) 'Long and *short sarse', as it is said, they call vegetables. 1825 J. C. Neal *Bro. Jonathan* I. 76 A quantity of long, short, and round sauce, or 'sarse', *i.e.* carrots, turnips, and potatoes. 1865 'Artemus Ward' *Trav.* 57 Tom Slink, who used to smoke *short-sixes and get acquainted with the little circus-boys. 1895 *Army & Navy Co-op. Soc. Price List* 15 Sept. 1116/1 White Vests, *Short Sleeves. 18.. Dickens *Novels & Tales* (ed. Tauchn.) VI. 129 (Flügel) *Short-sleeved. 1924 Rose Macaulay *Orphan Island* xiii. 156 Flora slipped into the short-sleeved, low-necked white cotton frock. 1898 *Naval Annual* i. i. 1 The sum *short-spent on new construction amounts to £2,270,000. 1858 *Chambers's Jrnl.* 4 Sept. 157/1 The names of the wooden-headed clubs..*short-spoon. 1879 *Encycl. Brit.* X. 765/2 *note*, A driving club, a long, a middle, and a short 'spoon'. 1893 H. Hutchinson *Golfing* 17 Therefore, we would urge the beginner, if he finds the iron a puzzle, to add a short or baffy spoon to his wooden clubs. 1802 *Steele Papers* I. 341 *Short Staple, or Green seed Cotton if the best quality, 16 cents. 1887 *Harper's Mag.* Feb. 482/1 We are tempted to claim a national primacy in *short-story writing. *Ibid.* 483/2 A short-story motive or a long-story motive. 1884 'Cavendish' (H. Jones) *Whist* (ed. 14) 133 Treating long suits like *short ones. 1893 'Hoffmann' tr. *Hertefeld's Game of Skat* 8 As..a suit consists of seven cards only, three or more constitute a long suit; and two or less a short suit. 1910 Dalton *'Saturday' Bridge* 91 The original English method, now known as the Short-suit Convention. *Ibid.* 93 On the other hand the short-suit doubler is by no means certain to get his desired suit led to him. 1875 Knight *Dict. Mech.* 2099/1 *Short-thread machines. 1908 *Daily Chron.* 3 Aug., *Short time for all is suggested as preferable to no work for some. 1911 *Rep. Labour & Soc. Cond. Germany* III. vi–vii. 198 In the case of industries where fluctuations of unemployment occur 'short time' instead of dismissal is more common in Germany than in this country. 1927 Bowley & Stamp *Nat. Income 1924* 34 Both the 1924 and the 1926 accounts show the effect of overtime and short-time. 1896 in *Chester's Dict. Min.* Advt. 1 *Short-Title Catalogue of ..Publications...Arranged under subjects. 1902 *Encycl. Brit.* XXVIII. 68/2 With very fine wires the condition *na* small can be fulfilled with quite *short waves. 1907 Erskine-Murray *Handbk. Wireless Telegr.* 5 Short-wave Hertzian telegraphy has never been successful at distances beyond a mile or two. 1909 [see *Long *a.*¹ 15]. 1928 D. Brunt *Meteorology* 38 The term 'high temperature radiation' is frequently used to denote the short-wave radiation of very hot bodies. *Ibid.* 40 We have to picture a beam of short-wave light from the sun reaching the outer boundary of the earth's atmosphere. 1932 *B.B.C. Year-Bk.* 466 Key to the Map of Short-Wave Stations. 1909 Ware *Passing Engl.*, *Short week.

e. (Cf. Short *adv.* 11.)

1870 Medbery *Men & Myst. Wall St.* 175 With..realizations upon short sales, Jerome felt rich enough to dissolve partnership. *Ibid.* 202 A sale profit either in a 'long' or 'short' operation. 1920 A. D. McFaul *Ike Glidden* xviii. 139 He bought and sold on the short side for cash and sold on the long side on credit. 1928 *Daily Mail* 9 Aug. 12/4 As there is no short interest in Canada the Montreal market, unlike New York, has only willing buyers. 1930 *Daily Express* 23 May 2/6 Short-selling in Case Threshing Machine, which declined more than 18 points, was an unsettling factor. 1931 *Ibid.* 22 Sept. 2/1 Short selling in the present circumstances would demoralise the market. Consequently all short positions carried must be reported in detail each day.

B. *sb.* 4. h. A short film used for filling out a cinema programme.

1930 *Times* 26 Mar. 14/2 The production of several multilingual talking pictures and a series of talking comedy 'shorts'. 1930 *Observer* 11 May 20 We have 'shorts' and shorts in thousands..but the bulk of these pictures are small in every sense of the word.

i. In the Morse code, a dot.

1875 Sir W. Thomson *Pop. Lect. & Addr.* (1891) III. 128 [It] renders quick and sure Morse signalling by longs and shorts impracticable. 1904 Kipling *Traffics & Discov.*, *Steam Tactics* 191 The longs and shorts as laid down by.. Mr. Morse. 1916 [see *Buzz *v.*¹ 9]. 1926 R. W. Hutchinson *Wireless* 112 The key in the primary circuit enables the train of sparks to be continued for a long or a short period of time, thus producing the 'longs' and 'shorts', *i.e.* the 'dashes' and 'dots' of the Morse Code.

5. (Earlier U.S. example.)

1857 *Hunt's Merch. Mag.* (N.Y.) XXXVII. 135 The clique sell their cash stock to the bears or shorts.

6. a. (Earlier Amer. example.)

1742 in *Maryland Hist. Mag.* XX. 166, I desire you will send the Bran, Short, & Middleings.

g. (*b*) (Earlier U.S. example.)

1881 *Harper's Mag.* Apr. 734/2 'Spots', 'futures', 'longs' and 'shorts' were unknown terms.

h. Short-dated securities. *Stock Exch. colloq.*

1932 *Manchester Guardian* 28 Jan. 15/1 The 'shorts' are all due for repayment at par at various dates between 1933 and 1936.

C. *adv.* 8. f. To come short. (See quot.)

1889 F. M. Halford *Dry-Fly Fishing* vii. 155 This unfortunate propensity of rising at the fly, and either not taking it at all or else handling it (or rather mouthing it) so gingerly as to be insecurely hooked, is technically called among dry-fly fishermen *coming short.*

11. (Earlier U.S. example.)

1872 Talmage *Abom. Mod. Society* 116 He hears that a brother broker has sold 'short'.

Short (ʃǭɹt), *sb.*² Name of manufacturers used *attrib.* or *ellipt.* for a type of seaplane.

1913 *Aeroplane* 30 Oct. 478/1 The First Lord, piloted by Commander Samson, R.N., on the famous No. 3 Short. 1916 *Ibid.* 19 Jan. 128/2 Compare the performances of Admiralty-designed seaplanes..with the Shorts, Schneider-Sopwiths,..and so on. 1926 Cadbury in C. F. S. Gamble *North Sea Air Station* (1928) 194, I went off in a 225 h.p. Short. 1928 *Ibid.* 189 He had just left the water in a Short seaplane.

Short-circuit, *v.* Add: Hence **Short-ci·rcuitage, Short-ci·rcuiting** *vbl. sb.*

1900 *Westm. Gaz.* 18 Oct. 8/2 The motor set the machinery in motion without anyone touching it owing to short circuitage. 1902 *Encycl. Brit.* XXXIII. 233/1 In this manner.. long and short discharges [can be] made in accordance with the signals of the Morse alphabet by manipulating the short-circuiting key of one of the choking coils. 1919 H. E. Penrose *Wireless Telegr.* iv. 75 Examine the band of the magnetic detector, the magnets, and the short-circuiting contacts of the manipulating key. 1928 *Daily Express* 21 Mar. 1/5 A successful operation for duodenal ulcer...The operation..is popularly known as 'short circuiting'.

Sho·rt-date, *a.* Lasting for a short period; *spec.*, designating excursion railway tickets, etc., available for return within a specified short period. Hence **Sho·rt-dater**, a stock, bill, note of hand, etc., which is to fall due at an early date.

1909 *Q. Rev.* Oct. 358 British railways offer facilities for cheap, short-date bookings. 1931 *Daily Tel.* 21 Jan. 2/4 'Short-daters' especially were heavy, Treasury Bond Fives of 1933–35..falling 3–16.

Shorten, *v.* 6. (Earlier U.S. modern example.)

1832 *Louisville Directory* 98 [The flour] was shortened, as the housewife phrases it, with racoon fat.

Shorthand. c. Add: **shorthand typist** (see quot. 1921).

1901 *Phonetic Jrnl.* 24 Aug. 541 To a large extent the occupation of the shorthand-typist has hitherto been synonymous with the lady typist. 1921 *Dict. Occup. Terms* (1927) § 939 *Shorthand typist*; wholly engaged in taking down letters, statements, memoranda, etc., in shorthand from dictation of another, and in transcribing them on typewriter.

Short-handed, *a.*² Add: 3. Having short hands.

1892 Stevenson & Osbourne *Wrecker* xxii, The cabman, a gross, salt-looking man, red-faced, blue-eyed, short-handed and short-winded, perhaps nearing forty.

4. *Hunting.*

1923 *Daily Mail* 7 May 8 To avoid the risk of crossing the line which the fox has taken, should the quarry have turned short-handed and altered his point.

Shorthorn. Add: 2. A new arrival, greenhorn. *U.S. slang.*

1905 A. H. Lewis *Sunset Trail* ii, Don't let no shorthorn have my room. 1907 S. E. White *Arizona Nights* iii. ix. 321 Th' shorthorn landed head-first in..Charlie's horse-trough.

3. An Air Force nickname for a type of Maurice Farman biplane. Also *ellipt.*

1913 *Aeroplane* 30 Oct. 485/2 The new type is likely to meet with the approval of the Royal Flying Corps, who have a high regard for the Maurice Farman, despite their having nick-named it the 'Mechanical Cow'. Perhaps, owing to the absence of the long front skids, the new type will become known as the 'Shorthorn'. *Ibid.* 11 Dec. 631/2 The machine is..of the 'short-horn'-type, without any front elevator. 1928 C. F. S. Gamble *North Sea Air Station* 49 Maurice Farman 'Shorthorn' 70 b.p. Renault.

Sho·rting, *vbl. sb.*2 *Electr.* [f. SHORT *v.*2 + -ING 1.] Short-circuiting.

1912 *Motor Manual* Advt. facing p. iii, The separators allow the plates to be placed closer together and yet make 'shorting' impossible.

Sho·rt-leaf, *attrib.* [SHORT *a.* 23.] *Short-leaf pine*: see next.

1800 B. HAWKINS *Sk. Creek Country* 20 The growth of timber is oak, hickory, and the short leaf pine. 1883 P. M. HALE *Woods N. Carolina* 210 Short-leaf pine and some walnut. 1911 [see SHORT *a.* 23].

Sho·rt-leaved, *a.* [SHORT *a.* 24.] *Short-leaved pine*, a common yellow pine (*Pinus echinata* or *mitis*) of the United States.

1805 SIBLEY in *Ann. 9th Congress* 2 Sess. 1091 The soil a good second quality, clay; timber, large oak, hickory, some short leaved pine. 1832 D. J. BROWNE *Sylva Amer.* 235 In the Middle States..it is called Yellow Pine, in the Carolinas and Georgia,..Short-Leaved Pine. 1883 P. M. HALE *Woods N. Carolina* 36 This tree is..also called Short-leaved Pine and Spruce Pine. 1884 [see SHORT *a.* 24].

Short-order. a. An order à-la-carte. *U.S.*

1920 C. SANDBURG *Smoke & Steel* 51 Short order counter. 1928 SINCLAIR LEWIS *Man who knew Coolidge* i. 31 We plan to have a restaurant there serving short-orders twenty-four hours a day.

b. *In* (or *on*) *short order*: see *ORDER *sb.* 27 d.

Shoshone (ʃoʃōᵘ·ni). Also -ee, -i. One of a tribe of North American Indians of Wyoming, Idaho, and northern Nevada, from which the Shoshonean stock is named; an Indian of the Shoshonean stock. Hence **Shoshonean** (ʃoʃōᵘ·niăn, ʃoʃonī·ăn) *a.*, designating, or of or pertaining to a widely-extended North American linguistic stock. **Shoshonite** (ʃoʃōᵘ·nəit) *Petrog.*, a basaltic rock of phenocrysts of labradorite, augite, and olivine in a ground-mass of sanidine.

1830 *Western Monthly Rev.* III. 562 The Shoshonee are a numerous and powerful tribe of Indians. 1834 A. PIKE *Sketches* 200 The Shoshones are the snakes. 1860 MAYNE REID *Odd People* 331 In respect to his 'settled' mode of life, the Shoshokee offers a striking contrast to the Shoshonee. Many of the latter are Indians of noble type. 1868 WHITNEY *Lang.* ix. (ed. 2) 350 The Shoshonee and Comanche ranged from the shores of Texas north-westward. 1880 *Encycl. Brit.* XII. 827 *Wininasht*, or *Western Shoshones*. 1895 IDDINGS (Cent. D. Suppl.) Shoshonite. 1902 *Encycl. Brit.* XXIX. 466/2 Hopi or Moki. Shoshonean.

Shot, *sb.*1 Add: **3. c.** 'One piece or section of an extended seine or drift-net' (Funk's *Standard Dict.*). *U.S.*

1880 *Scribner's Mag.* Aug. 492/2 The ordinary gill or drift net used for shad fishing in the Hudson is..divided into 'shots'. If a passing sloop or schooner catches it with her center-board or her anchor, it gives way where two of these shots meet, and thus the whole net is not torn.

7. e. (*b*) Also, a photograph taken with a cinematograph camera.

1923 'B. M. BOWER' *Parowan Bonanza* xxvi. 303 Bill and Tommy were both below examining the effect of their 'shots' of the evening before. 1925 E. WALLACE *Fellowship of the Frog* xxiv, He..told me that the quality of the films is improving with every new 'shot'. 1927 *Weekly Dispatch* 23 Oct. 14 The actual 'shot' of the midnight sun is as good as the recent negative of the eclipse. 1930 *Times* 26 Mar. 14/2 The magnification of portions of the film in order to emphasize certain salient episodes or 'shots' in the picture.

g. An injection (of morphia, etc.).

1929 'SEAMARK' *Down River* ii, The fishy glitter that came from them [*sc.* his eyes] was the spurious flash of a recent 'shot' of his enslaving narcotic.

9. d. (Earlier U.S. example.)

1871 EGGLESTON *Hoosier Schoolm.* xv. 121 That's more'n I'd a done by a long shot.

10. b. *spec.* in *Racing*, a venture.

1854 WHYTE MELVILLE *Gen. Bounce* xiii, But here we are at Tattersall's;..so now for 'good information, long odds, a safe man, and a shot at the favourite!' 1931 *Daily Express* 23 Sept. 17/6 Mick..will be a neat shot for anybody when the St. Leger is run.

22. c. *Big shot*, a prominent member of an organization, e.g. a notorious gangster. Cf. 'big gun' (*BIG *a.* B), 'big noise' (*NOISE *sb.* 6 b). *U.S.*

1931 *Times Lit. Suppl.* 30 Apr. 340/2 The 'Big Shots' whom 'the cops' would love to have alone are protected by their criminal associates.

23. g. Of spirits: A dram.

1928 *Collier's* 18 Aug. 6/2 He poured me a shot of Scotch and I downed it. 1929 W. J. LOCKE *Jorico* xii, He drank his shot of brandy.

29. *shot-belt* (later U.S. examples); *shot-mould* (earlier Amer. examples).

1837 W. IRVING *Capt. Bonneville* (1895) II. 85 His rifle beside him, the *shot-belt and powder-flask on the stock. 1851 C. CIST *Cincinnati* 211 The manufacture of rifles, shot belts, etc. 1633 *Doc. & Rec. New-Hampshire* I. 79 *Shott moulds. 1643 *Essex Inst. Hist. Coll.* L. 318 Alsoe I give vnto him my pistill shot-mould.

30. shot-compressor (see quot.); **shot group**, the group of hits made by a series of shots fired at the target; **shot-line** (see quot.).

1884 KNIGHT *Dict. Mech.* Suppl., *Shot Compressor*, a forceps to fasten leaden shot upon the ends of a ligature as a substitute for tying. 1918 FARROW *Dict. Mil. Terms* s.v., In a series of shots fired at a target, no two shots will strike in the same spot, the hits being arranged in a certain diagram called the *shot group. 1884 KNIGHT *Dict. Mech.* Suppl., *Shot Line*, the cord attached to a projectile fired from a piece to fall over a wreck or stranded vessel and thus establish communication between ship and shore.

Sho·t-bag. [f. SHOT *sb.*1 + BAG *sb.*]

1. A bag or pouch for carrying shot.

1638 in *Maryland Archives* IV. 32 It. one fowling piece & shott bagge. 1684 *Essex Inst. Hist. Coll.* XXV. 154 A brasse powder horne with a shot bag and belt. 1756 *Lett. to Washington* I. 260 Going to Load he missed his Shot Bag which had been carried away by one of the Shots. 1784 J. F. D. SMYTH *Tour U.S.* I. xxiii. 181 The shot bags and powder-horn..over one shoulder. 1809 in Horry *Life F. Marion* (1833) 131 Belted round with their powderhorns and shotbags. 1845 J. J. HOOPER *Adv. Simon Suggs* ix. 112 A stake was set up..and from its top hung a huge shot bag of crimson cloth. 1856 MRS. STOWE *Dred* II. 294 He seized his rifle and shot-bag. 1928 *Daily Mail* 31 July 6/3 Their [*sc.* our Indian labourers'] spokesman..who had found the bead, produced it from his shot-bag.

2. The North American bufflehead duck, *Charitonetta albeola*.

Shot-gun. b. Add: **shot-gun marriage** *U.S.*, a forced marriage.

1929 E. W. HOWE *Plain People* 267 Two people cordially disliked me for years because I thought it best to mention very briefly and respectfully their shot gun marriage.

Shot-hole. Add: **4.** *attrib.* and *Comb.*, as **shot-hole borer**, a beetle of the genus *Scolytidæ* (see quot.); **shot-hole disease**, a disease of the leaves of fruit-trees caused by various leaf-spot fungi; **shot-hole fungus**, any of the leaf-spot fungi, *Cercospora*, *Septoria*, etc., which attack the leaves of fruit-trees causing them to look as if perforated by fine shot.

1927 *Sunday Times* 13 Feb. 20/4 The Scolytidæ, sometimes called bark-beetles, or shot-hole borers, are a group of tiny beetles with an average length of less than one-eighth of an inch, and most of them are addicted to boring into the trunks and branches of trees.

Hence **Sho·t-holer**, one who drills shot-holes (sense 3).

1921 *Dict. Occup. Terms* (1927) § 072 *Shot holer*, a driller who drills holes for blasting, by hand or machine.

Shot-pouch. 1. (Later U.S. examples.)

1852 H. C. WATSON *Nights in Block-house* 229 They had not taken either his watch or his shot-pouch. 1885 'C. E. CRADDOCK' *Prophet Gt. Smoky Mtn.* ix. 159 Many jagged ledges..showing here a jug, and here a shot-pouch.

Shoulder, *sb.* **2. f.** (Recent U.S. examples.)

1904 W. H. SMITH *Promoters* v. 103 Then you'll..be in a shape to talk business, right from the shoulder. 1912 R. D. SAUNDERS *Col. Todhunter* ix. 118 A man that talks old-fashioned American Democracy straight from the shoulder. 1922 H. JENKINS *John Dene of Toronto* ii. 36 We aren't so thin-skinned as not to be able to take it from the shoulder.

Shoulder, *v.* Add: **15.** *trans.* To cross the shoulder of (a mountain).

1891 *Harper's Mag.* Sept. 578/1 Jo struck across country to shoulder Ouse Mountain.

Shout, *v.* Add: **1. c.** Also, in recent use: To be loud in support of (a candidate). *U.S.*

1907 *N.Y. Evening Post* (semi-weekly ed.) 21 Nov. 4 Federal office-holders in various Southern States have been dutifully shouting for Roosevelt.

g. *U.S. slang.* (Earlier and later examples.)

1876 *Scribner's Monthly* Nov. 142/1 'Then why prevaricate?' Said he perversely. 'Now yer shoutin'!' 1911 P. D. SAUNDERS *Col. Todhunter* vii. 99 'You're shoutin' now, Colonel,' agreed Tim.

4. f. *To shout down*: to reduce to silence by shouts of disapproval; to howl down.

Shouter2. **1.** Add: Also, one who loudly supports a particular candidate. *U.S.*

1904 *Rochester Post-Express* 26 May 4 The canvass..was very thorough, Hearst shouters being busily engaged in every city.

Shouting, *vbl. sb.* Add: **1.** (U.S. example.)

1904 *Minneapolis Times* 29 May 6 Thus far most of the enthusiastic shouting for Gorman can be traced to the Gorman press bureau.

3. *attrib.*, as *shouting meeting*, *time*.

1839 *Knickerbocker Mag.* XIV. 213 He was sternly opposed to what are called 'shouting meetings'. 1845 A. WILEY in *Indiana Mag. Hist.* XXIII. 22 He says, they had shouting times, but he could not form a class.

Shouting, *ppl. a.* (U.S. example.)

1876 J. BURROUGHS *Winter Sunshine* i. 23 About the only genuine shouting Methodists that remain are to be found in the coloured churches.

Shove, *sb.*1 Add: **1. c.** (See quot.)

1891 H. G. HUTCHINSON *Golf* 32 If the ball lie fairly and be truly struck, there is no fear of making a 'shove', or foul stroke [in putting].

Shove, *v.* Add: **B. 4. e.** To put *down*, *up*, etc. *slang.*

1902 P. G. WODEHOUSE *Pothunters* v. 93 You might shove up the list to-night. 1904 W. H. SMITH *Promoters* vii. 123 You want to have your paper all ready to shove [= push on the market]. 1912 C. MATHEWSON *Pitching in a Pinch* v. 109 Mowrey shoved a long fly to right field, which soared away toward the stand. 1927 W. E. COLLINSON *Contemp. Engl.* 23 At Dulwich..we plunked things down, we shoved down notes or we shoved up lists.

Shovel, *v.*1 Add: **2. b.** To clear *out* with a shovel.

1886 *Leslie's Pop. Monthly* Feb. 242/1 The path had not been shoveled out.

Shover. b. (Earlier U.S. example.)

1677 HABBERTON *Jericho Road* 186 Your bosses..are the smartest shovers of counterfeit money in the whole West.

Shover2 (ʃʊ·vəɹ). Also **shuv(v)er**. Jocular alteration of *CHAUFFEUR. So **Sho·ving** *vbl. sb.*

1908 *Daily Chron.* 8 May 3/3 A motor-car and a gentleman 'shuvver'. 1912 *World* 5 Nov. 707/2 She can drive [*sc.* a motor-car] as well as any 'shuver'. 1913 *Daily News* 23 June 11 We were thrown out, and Dane, that's my shover, you know, has got a nasty knock on the head. 1925 *Chambers's Jrnl.* 146/1 Joseph—our 'shover'—was in the back of the car. 1932 E. M. KEATE *The Mimic* vi, 'Paulett come and shove for me on Monday... My shover's ill.' Timothy enjoyed 'shoving'.

Show, *sb.*1 Add: **3. c.** (Earlier modern U.S. examples.)

1865 A. D. RICHARDSON *Secret Service* xxix. 353 As long as there is any show for us, we shall fight you. 1871 *Trans. Ill. Agric. Soc.* VIII. 15 They all know that they will have 'no show'. 1880 *Harper's Mag.* Feb. 387/1 The proprietor ..listened..with a view of 'giving the Gospel a show'.

5. c. (Earlier example.)

1756 in *Lett. to Washington* I. 231 Prospect of great Wealth from his Share of a Copper Mine which has a Show of much rich Ore.

15. b. An engagement, battle, raid, etc.; a 'do'. *Army slang.*

1915 in W. Wood *In Line of Battle* (1916) 217 Had a warm reception with artillery, and owing to some 'show' in the vicinity had to stand-to for hours. 1915 D. O. BARNETT *Lett.* 219 Don't get excited if you hear of a show soon. 1916 BOYD CABLE *Action Front* 105 Said he was looking forward to a good feed that night after the show was over. And—and he was killed that day. 1918 E. A. MACKINTOSH *War, the Liberator* 129 'Oh, God,' he whispered, 'don't let us get casualties before we start the show.'

16. (Earlier U.S. examples.)

1802 *The Coquette* (Charleston, Mass.) 37 (Th.) The show is over, as we yankees say; and the girl is my own. 1851 N. KINGSLEY *Diary* 171 He got 500 dollars for this share, which takeing the show as we now have it I think was a plenty.

20. *show field*, *ring*.

1870 H. H. DIXON *Saddle & Sirloin* ii. 39 When he met his friends..on the show-field at Carlisle. *Ibid.* iv. 89 When they met in the show-ring.

22. show-boat, a steamboat in which theatrical performances are given; **show-book**, a fair-copy book; **show-breeder**, one who breeds animals or birds for show purposes; **show-girl**, a young woman member of a theatrical company who appears on the stage merely to add beauty to a scene; **show-ground**, a piece of ground on which a show is held; **show-poker** (see quot. 1930 2, and cf. *show-down*, SHOW *v.* 37); **show-window** (earlier U.S. examples).

1869 *Atlantic Monthly* July 85/1 The little steamer Banjo, a *show-boat belonging to Dr. Spaulding, the manager of the Floating Palace, was advertised to be at Cape Girardeau. 1926 EDNA FERBER (*title*) Show Boat. 1908 E. M. SNEYD-KYNNERSLEY *H.M.I.* xxvi, He wrote on the blackboard a jejune essay, which the class copied verbatim into their *show-books. 1931 *Books of Month* Jan. 7 Discussions with famous *show-breeders. 1923 A. TRAIN *Children's Children* xv. 191 He found it hard to believe that she was an actress, and a *show-girl at that. 1930 *Daily Express* 23 May 10/5 The 'show-girl' who had nothing to do but stand with her hands on her hips and ogle the 'stalls'. 1853 *Trans. Mich. Agric. Soc.* IV. 18 At 9 o'clock the executive committee met on the *show ground. 1867 'T. LACKLAND' *Homespun* II. 203 The scenes on the show-grounds are then extremely interesting. 1870 H. H. DIXON *Saddle & Sirloin* iv. 94 When the great unknown descended from his van on the show ground, in the shape of a three-year-old. 1930 'SAPPER' *Finger of Fate*, etc. 40 'I tell you what I will do, Mr. Blake,' said Jefferson thickly. 'I'll play you one hand of *show poker for a monkey.' *Ibid.*, Being show poker he dealt the cards face upwards from a new pack. 1855 M. M. THOMPSON *Doesticks* xiv. 118 Those..ladies who used to perform their perpetual gyrations in the *show-windows. 1876 J. S. INGRAM *Centen. Exposition* 179 A large aquarium intended for a show window.

Show, *v.* Add: **22. d.** (Modern U.S. examples.)

1889 *Kansas City Times & Star* 2 Apr., But wait till Frank Householder comes flying down on his new Visitor. He'll show them. 1916 'B. M. BOWER' *Phantom Herd* vii. 112 As to the break I made in getting those boys out here, you'll have to show me—that's all.

27. Show up. c. To hand in (work).

32*. Show down. See 2 k and *show down* in 37.

1902 G. H. LORIMER *Lett. Self-made Merchant* xvi. 234 They just had to throw up both hands and pass you the pot when you showed down.

34. Show out. c. *trans.* To disclose, make manifest. *U.S.*

1854 'O. OPTIC' (W. T. Adams) *In Doors & Out* (1876) 133 Then you think I have not shown out what I am yet. 1883 *Century Mag.* Aug. 598, I..never show out in any way that I know there are young ladies or literature in the world.

37. Show-down. (More recent examples in the sense: An exhibition or declaration of achievements or possibilities.)

1904 F. LYNDE *Grafters* ix. 131 'You don't mean to say there is any doubt about our ability to do it?' 'Oh, no; I suppose not, if it comes to a show-down.' 1907 R. W. SERVICE *Songs of Sourdough* (1908) 63 It's great... To know you're acting foolish, yet to go on fooling still, Till Nature calls a show-down, and you Pay the bill. 1926 BENNETT *Lord Raingo* I. xxv. 119 What a show-down he could stage the next time Secret Service money was wanted! 1927 *Glasgow Herald* 19 Aug. 10 An opportunity of 'forcing a show-down' concerning British flights in China.

39. Show-up. b. An exhibition of work. *colloq.*

1931 *Church Times* 20 Feb. 235/3 A students' 'show-up' at an art school.

Show-case. (See SHOW *sb.*1 22.)

1839 C. F. BRIGGS *Harry Franco* II. i. 2 Glass show cases on the side walk displaying..jewelry, and soaps, and penknives. 1864 *Ret. Agric. Soc. Maine* 15 His show case.. would have been an ornament in any of our State exhibitions. 1876 J. S. INGRAM *Centennial Exposition* v. 150 In a high glass show-case..were shown..the prismatic compass, transit, sextant and other instruments. 1897 R. M. STUART *Simpkinsville* 121 Old Dr. Jenkins stood behind the show-case in his drug store. 1923 L. J. VANCE *Baroque* vi. 32 Aniello Barocco..was leaning on one of the show cases that fenced apart the make shift office and the body of the shop. *attrib.* 1903 A. H. LEWIS *The Boss* 189 He's no show-case proposition!..To look at him folks might take him for a fool.

Shower, *sb.*1 Add: **2. c.** (Earlier U.S. example.)

1873 'MARK TWAIN' & WARNER *Gilded Age* xxxiii. 308 He has fell back on hot foot-baths at night and cold showers in the morning.

4. b. A large number of gifts of a similar kind made, esp. to a bride, by many people at the same time. Also *attrib.*, as *shower-party*. *U.S.*

1904 *Grand Rapids Even. Press* 22 June 4 The 'shower parties' that through mistaken hospitality the wedded couple are forced to attend. 1904 *N.Y. Tribune* 27 Oct. 7 The managers of the Home for the Friendless invite the public to a linen shower and reception. 1926 *Publishers' Weekly* 26 June 2031/1 First comes June, then the showers, the wedding and after the honeymoon the settling down to a home life. *Ibid.* 2032/1 A bride's book-shower, where each guest would bring a volume of a coveted set. 1928 *Daily Express* 5 Mar. 13 A shower-party is one in which each of the guests brings a 'shower' of some special kind of present. A shower may consist of linen, hosiery, gloves, handkerchiefs, or perfume.

Showing, *vbl. sb.* Add: **1. d.** = SHOW *sb.*1 3 c.

1845 J. J. HOOPER *Adv. Simon Suggs* xi. 135 The Captain whispered to his lawyer, and urged him to put him on the stand, and make a showing for a continuance. 1853 J. G. BALDWIN *Flush Times Alabama* 145 Again and yet again—the plate passed on: but the Squire couldn't get a showing. 1874 J. W. LONG *Wild-fowl Shooting* i. 22, I intend to give the claims of the breech-loader an equal showing.

Showmanship (ʃōᵘ·mænʃip). [-SHIP.] The art of being a showman; esp. *transf.* and *fig.*, the capacity for showing or exhibiting one's wares, produce, capabilities, or achievements to the best advantage.

1859 [see Dict. s.v. SHOWMAN]. 1926 A. BENNETT *Ld. Raingo* II. lxiv, He had made a fine display of courage and wit on the doctor's declaration of his malady, but it was only a display, a proud piece of showmanship perhaps unworthy of so solemn an occasion. 1927 *Observer* 20 Mar. 22/3 Showmanship still gets away with it. Tell the public you are going to make their flesh creep with horror and they will roll up in their thousands to gloat over bloodshed. 1927 *Daily Express* 12 Aug. 9/3 She held a great reception yesterday, sitting in her red caravan, and chatted of the olden times and the present conditions of showmanship. 1930 *John o' London's Weekly* 715 Showmanship, both on and off the stage, is half the battle to the ambitious illusionist.

Show-me, *attrib. phr.* *U.S.* [*SHOW *v.* 22 d.] Demanding demonstration; believing only on clear evidence.

1909 R. A. WASON *Happy Hawkins* 283 He belonged to the show-me club. 1909 *N.Y. Even. Post* (semi-weekly ed.) 19 Apr. 88 Everything indicative of the 'show-me' State of Missouri.

Shriek, *sb.* Add: **d.** Also, an outcry of alarm, surprise, or reproof. *colloq.*

1929 'SEAMARK' *Down River* i, 'Yet this man is getting through?' 'Yes—and with bags of it, too, judging from the shriek we got from the Yard.'

f. = *SCREAM *sb.* c. *colloq.*

1930 BRAHAM *Little Flutter* iii. 37 She is a shriek, isn't she?

Shrimp, *sb.* Add: **1. c.** A shrimp prepared for use as a bait in angling.

1924 *Blackw. Mag.* Apr. 489/1, I would not trust the most experienced salmon with Michael Lydon and a Galway 'shrimp'. 1931 *Hardy's Anglers' Guide* 31 The shrimp will wake the lazy dozer, and he'll take it or your fly with a rush. *Ibid.* 180 Prawn and Shrimp Tackles.

d. In full *shrimp-pink*: A fashion shade of bright pink.

1882 *Cassell's Fam. Mag.* 236/1 Shrimp-pink with white is one of the happiest and latest combinations. 1922 *Daily Mail* 20 Dec. 1 Lingerie Crepe...Pink, Sky, Jade, Flesh, Shrimp, Saxe. 1927 T. WOODHOUSE *Artificial Silk* 81 The particulars of the colours and patterns are as under—No. 1. A shrimp ordinary crochet pattern. 1931 *Daily Tel.* 22 May 9/5 Her pale shrimp-pink chiffon dress was adorned with vertical frills and sunray pleats on the skirt.

3. *shrimp-net.*

1877 HOLDSWORTH *Sea Fisheries* 130 The shrimp net used here for catching the brown or true shrimp, is peculiar to the Thames and its immediate neighbourhood, and is practically a beam-trawl.

Shrimp, *v.* [f. SHRIMP *sb.*] *trans.* To fish (a pool, etc.) with shrimp as a bait. Hence **Shri·mping** *vbl. sb.*2

1931 *Hardy's Anglers' Guide* 31 And remember too that you may shrimp a pool in this manner and revert to fly without any fear of your pool being disturbed. *Ibid.*, I have had splendid sport, owing to this way of shrimping.

Shrimpi (ʃri·mpi). *S. Afr.* Also **swempi.** [Zulu *swempe.*] The bush partridge, *Francolinus subtorquatus.*

1906 *Blackw. Mag.* Sept. 396/1 Partridges, namaquas, and 'shrimpies' (a little partridge—a great delicacy)..were to be found everywhere. 1909 *South African Field* 30 July 141 (Pettman) Coquifrancolin, generally known as the Swempi from the Zulu name, but corrupted into Shrimpi by some.

Shriner (ʃrəi·nəɹ). *U.S.* [f. SHRINE *sb.* + -ER 1.] A member of the Order of Nobles of the Mystic Shrine, established in the United States in 1872.

1904 *Pittsburgh Gazette* 14 July 10 Many bands were composed entirely of Shriners, robed in gaudy yet beautiful costumes of the lands of Mohammed.

Shrinkage. 4. Add: **shrinkage-crack**, also, a crack similarly formed in other materials.

1930 *New Statesman* 27 Dec. 357/2 And even as regards telegraph poles and the like a preference is given to those with long shrinkage cracks.

Shrinker. Add: **2.** An operative employed in shrinking materials in various manufacturing processes; also a contrivance for shrinking a metal tire (see SHRINK *v.* 10 c).

1921 *Dict. Occup. Terms* (1927) § 190 Tyre shrinker. *Ibid.* § 384 *Crabber; cloth shrinker, potter, shrinker*,..tends crabbing machine, which passes cloth, at a suitable tension, through weighted rollers in a succession of troughs of water, ..where it is expanded or reduced to a specified width.

Shtchee, shtshi, variants of SCHI.

1904 *Westm. Gaz.* 21 Apr. 7/1 The dish of shtchee—fermented cabbage and meat—with vodka, he greatly enjoyed.

Shuffly (ʃʊ·fli), *a.* [f. SHUFFLE *v.* + -Y 1.] Characterized by shuffling.

1926 *Blackw. Mag.* Oct. 539/2 The step slower and, if possible, more shuffly.

'Shun (ʃʊn). Abbreviation of ATTENTION (sense 5), in which the stress has been artificially transferred to the last syllable for the sake of audibility and to emphasize the moment at which the manœuvre is to be executed.

1887 KIPLING *Plain Tales fr. Hills, Madness of Private Ortheris*, Stan' at—*hease*; 'Shun. 1915 'IAN HAY' *First Hundred Thousand* i, Squoad — 'Shun! 1918 E. A. MACKINTOSH *War, the Liberator* 121 Party, 'shun! Left-turn! You will parade again at 2.15 in full equipment. Party dis—miss!

fig. 1922 JOANNA CANNAN *Misty Valley* 41 Claire's newly recruited loyalty sprang, metaphorically speaking, to the 'shun.

Shunt, *sb.* Add: **1. c.** *Bell-ringing.* (See quot.)

1901 BULWER *Gloss. Techn. Terms Bells & Ringing* 30 Shunt. In a composition arranged in regular 'parts', or 'divisions', produced by similar calling, the omission of a 'call', or the insertion of an additional one, in order to divert the track of the composition to a corresponding point in another 'part'; the omission and insertion being termed respectively a 'shunting omit', and a 'shunting call' ('bob' or 'single'), or simply 'omit' and 'extra'.

5. a. shunt-brush, a brush (BRUSH *sb.*2 6 b) for a shunt circuit; **shunt loaded line** (see quot.); **shunt machine**, a continuous-current machine in which current is derived by a shunt from the main circuit; **shunt-ratio** (see quot.); **shunt turn**, any one of the ampere-turns in the shunt circuit of a compound-wound dynamo.

1925 *Morris Owner's Man.* 50 The position of the *shunt brush is correctly set relative to the position of the other two brushes before the machine leaves the works. 1916 *Standard. Rules Amer. Inst. Electr. Engin.* 96 A *shunt loaded line is one in which the normal inductance of the circuit has been altered by inductance applied in shunt across the circuit. 1902 *Encycl. Brit.* XXVII. 587/1 The second and third classes, namely, series and *shunt machines. 1893 SLOANE *Electr. Dict.*, *Shunt Ratio*, the coefficient expressing the ratio existing between the current in a shunt and in the apparatus or conductor in parallel with it.

Shunt-, the stem of SHUNT *v.* in comb. with advs., as **shunt-off, -out** *Electr.*, a shunt or a device for introducing a shunt (cf. SHUNT *v.* 6).

1890 *Telegr. Jrnl.* 7 Feb. 143/1 At present we have to deal simply with the '*shunt-offs' and cut-outs. *Ibid.*, In most instances these '*shunt-outs' are self-restoring.

Shush (ʃʊʃ), *v.* [Echoic, representing a repetition of SH *int.* Cf. SHSHSH.] *intr.* To utter the sounds denoted by *sh-sh*; esp. to call for silence by doing this; also *trans.* to call or reduce to silence; hence *intr.* to be silent.

1924 'O. DOUGLAS' *Pink Sugar* v, I [a horse] stood patiently while Nellie 'shushed' under her breath as she brushed, directing me at intervals, 'Stand still, will ye!' 1925 SIR P. GIBBS *Unchanging Quest* xvii, She would..'shush' away any intruders who came to interrupt her private conversation. 1929 PRIESTLEY *Good Comp.* II. i. 273 He gets no further, being fiercely requested by several of his colleagues to 'shush'. *Ibid.* III. iv. 553 Some people laughed. The remainder indignantly shushed again and then clapped. 1930 EDNA FERBER *Cimarron* i. § 12 The women listened... They shushed their children when they moved or whimpered.

Shut, *sb.*1 Add: **4. b.** The line of junction of door and jamb.

1911 M. R. JAMES *More Ghost Stories, Martin's Close* (1920) 197 There was..an edge of a brown stuff dress..sticking out of the shut of the door.

Shut, *v.* **3.** Add: Also *U.S.* in pa.pple. with verbs, as *push*, *draw*, etc. = TO D 4.

1884 *Century Mag.* Nov. 13 He..pushed the ground-glass door shut. 1911 H. S. HARRISON *Queed* ii. 23 The last boarder rising drew shut the folding-doors into the parlor. 1924 C. E. MULFORD *Rustlers' Valley* xiv, He kicked shut the draught door of the stove.

Shut-down. Add:

1916 *Standard. Rules Amer. Inst. Electr. Engin.* 35 This method consists in the measurement of the temperature of windings by their increase in resistance, corrected to the instant of shut-down when necessary.

Shute2. Add: **2.** A variety of raw silk; tram-silk.

1839 URE *Dict. Arts*, etc. 1102 There are three denominations of raw silk; viz., organzine, *trame* (shute or tram), and floss. 1868 [see TRAM *sb.*2 1].

Shu·t-eye. *Tramps' slang.* [f. SHUT *v.* + EYE *sb.*1] Sleep.

1919 BOYD CABLE *Old Contempt.* 76 That shut-eye done me good. 1923 C. E. MONTAGUE *Fiery Particles* 174 'We'll go on to-morrow,' I said. 'A bit of shut-eye for me now.' 1926 KATH. S. PRICHARD *Working Bullocks* iv, Red rose from the fire and stretched, yawning...'How's it for a bit of shut eye?' 1929 PRIESTLEY *Good Comp.* I. iv. 113, I could do with a bit of shut-eye and a drink and a bite of something.

Shu·t-in, *sb.* and *a.* [f. verbal phr. *to shut in* (see SHUT *v.* 15).] (A person who is) shut in, as an invalid or a cripple.

1849, 1904 [see SHUT *ppl. a.* 2]. 1909 *Springfield* (Mass.) *Weekly Republican* 25 Feb. 10 Flowers for distribution among the sick and shut-ins in the hospitals and the homes. 1909 *Sunday School Times* (Philad.) 27 Feb. 110 She had brought a handful of flowers and a heart full of sunshine to the shut-in mother. 1932 *N.Y. Herald Tribune* 2 May 11/5 Benefit for Shut-in Society.

Shut-off. Add: **2.** A stoppage of any kind. **b.** The close season for game. 1891 *Century Dict.*

Shu·t-out, *a.* and *sb.* [f. verbal phr. *to shut out* (see SHUT *v.* 17).] **A.** *adj.* **1.** That is shut out or excluded.

1853 [see SHUT *ppl. a.* 2].

2. *Shut-out bid*, in Bridge, a high bid intended to prevent one's opponents from bidding.

1917 'BASCULE' *Adv. Auction Bridge* (ed. 4) 77 To what extent does it pay to make what are known as pre-emptive, or 'shut-out' bids? 1921 A. E. M. FOSTER *Auction Bridge* 52 Pre-emptive bids are, in my opinion, a mistake, unless they are of the nature of necessary shut-out bids. 1932 *Daily Tel.* 8 Oct. 15/5 In using the term 'pre-emptive' I am not in any way ascribing the meaning of 'shut-out' to that word.

B. *sb.* **a.** A lock-out.

1924 *Times Trade & Engin. Suppl.* 29 Nov. 245/1 A policy ..leading to shut-outs and extra dock charges.

b. *Baseball.* A game or innings in which one side does not score; prevention from scoring. *U.S.*

1897 [see SHUT *ppl. a.* 2]. 1904 *N.Y. World* 3 Aug. (Cent. D. Suppl.) On the pitching..was entitled to a shut-out. The Tigers scored their only run in the fifth.

Shutter, *sb.* **3.** Add: **shutter-armature**, a piece of iron on the shutter of a telephone indicator by the attraction or release of which the signal is given; **shutter-eye** (see quot.); **shutter-weir**, a form of movable dam consisting of a shutter or a series of independent shutters which can be raised or lowered to regulate the flow of the water.

1884 KNIGHT *Dict. Mech.* Suppl., *Shutter Eye*, an eye for hanging a shutter to, having a projecting flange or support, which is built into the wall. 1886 *Encycl. Brit.* XX. 574/2 The earliest form of *shutter weir consisted of a gate, or shutter, turning on a horizontal axis at the bottom, supported by a prop when raised against the stream, and falling flat on the apron of the weir when the prop was withdrawn. 1903 *Nature* 20 Aug. 363/1 The Chanoine shutter weir is composed of a series of shutters supported centrally on a trestle, and turning on a horizontal axis.

Shutting, *vbl. sb.* **4. b.** Add: **shutting-post** (see quot. 1875); **shutting-stile**, the stile of a hinged door on which the fastenings are placed.

1875 KNIGHT *Dict. Mech.*, *Shutting-post*, the post or joint against which a gate or door is closed. 1909 *Chambers's Jrnl.* Nov. 764/1 On the under side of the shutting-post is a small roller which runs on to a bracket on the shutting-post itself, thus taking up the whole weight of the gate when it is closed.

Shuttle, *sb.*1 **9. b.** Add: **shuttle armature** *Electr.*, an armature having a single coil wound upon an elongated iron bobbin or shuttle; **shuttle car**, a car running backwards and forwards on a short route; **shuttle-winder**, an attachment for winding thread upon the shuttle, esp. of a sewing machine; **shuttle-winding** *Electr.*, the type of winding used in a shuttle armature; hence **shuttle-wound** *ppl. a.*

1894 *Work* 20 Jan. 11/2 A laminated *shuttle armature. 1902 *Encycl. Brit.* XXVII. 579/1 The H-form 'shuttle' armature invented by Dr. Werner von Siemens. 1912 *Motor Manual* 46 The armature is, in practically every standard type, of the well-known 'shuttle' section. 1905 CALKINS & HOLDEN *Modern Advertising* 89 They also have many *shuttle cars, or cars that make short runs. 1875 KNIGHT *Dict. Mech.*, *Shuttle-winder*, a device for winding a shuttle, such as the round shuttle of the Wheeler and Wilson sewing-machine, or a tatting-shuttle. 1893 G. KAPP *Dynamos*, etc. ix. 209 The simplest example of an open-coil armature is the so-called *shuttle-wound armature represented in Fig. 48. 1902 *Encycl. Brit.* XXVII. 577/1 The second or drum method was used in the original 'shuttle-wound' armatures invented by Dr. Werner von Siemens in 1856.

Shuttling, *vbl. sb.* Add: **b.** The method of controlling the shuttles in weaving.

1904 *Technol. & Sci. Dict.* (ed. Goodchild & Tweney) s.v. *Loom*, Several forms of automatic shuttling or shuttle changing motions are now being tried for plain work.

Shuv(v)er, variant of *SHOVER 2.

Shy, *a.* Add: **2. b.** Hence, said of a river in which the fish are too shy to afford good fishing.

1897 *Encycl. Sport* I. 485/2 On all but the very 'shy' chalk streams, it [*sc.* the grayling] may be risen..against its will.

9. *shy-making.*

1930 W. S. MAUGHAM *Cakes & Ale* 23 Popular adjectives (like 'divine' or 'shy-making'). 1930 *Time & Tide* 18 Oct. 1300 It is very shy-making to have a real Galsworthy to review.

Sial (səi·ăl). *Geol.* [f. SI(LICON + AL(UMINIUM.] The top crust of the earth's surface. Also *Comb.*, as *sialsphere.*

[1909 SOLLAS tr. *Suess' Antlitz der Erde* IV. 544 Further we assume the existence of three zones or envelopes as determining the structure of the earth, namely the barysphere or the Nife (Ni-Fe), Sima (Si-Mg), and Sal (Si-Al).] 1924 SKERL tr. *A. Wegener's Orig. Continents & Oceans* 36, I should like to write 'Sial' instead of 'Sal' in order that there may be no confusion with the Latin word for Salt. *Ibid.* 146 In this chapter the sialsphere, which to-day occurs only in fragments—the continental blocks—on the earth's surface, will be considered, and be dealt with—in the first place as a whole. 1927 PEAKE & FLEURE *Apes & Men* ii. 17 Argand, Kober, and Wegener..look upon the continents as crustal fragments, collectively termed Sial, floating in a very dense magma, termed Sima.

Hence **Sia·lic** *a.*, of or pertaining to the sial.

1924 SKERL tr. *A. Wegener's Orig. Continents & Oceans* 59 Molten sialic masses (granite) from the under side of the South American block. 1930 *Nature* 15 Mar. 426 The outer sialic shell was absent from the part whence the moon was removed.

Sibbald (si·bŏld). The name of Sir Robert *Sibbald* (1641–1722), Scottish scientist, used in the genitive to designate a rorqual of the Pacific Ocean, *Balænoptera sulphurea*, the sulphur-bottom.

1897 LYDEKKER in *Concise Nat. Hist.* 173 The blue or Sibbald's rorqual. 1920 *Brit. Mus. Return* 101 Tympanic bone of a Sibbald's Rorqual (*Balaenoptera musculus*). 1921 [see *KILLER 2].

Siberian, *a.* and *sb.* **A.** *adj.* **2. b.** Add: *Siberian wallflower*, a cruciferous plant, *Cheiranthus allionii* (*Erysimum perowskianum*), introduced from the Caucasus and Afghanistan, bearing orange-coloured flowers.

1925 G. W. DEEPING *Sorrell & Son* xxxvii. § 2 Burning orange Siberian wallflowers.

Sibilate, *v.* Add: **2. c.** To make sibilant.

1879 LEWIS & SHORT *Lat. Dict.*, *Serum*,..prob. sibilated from ὀρός. 1880 KING & COOKSON *Sound & Infl. Gr. & Lat.* 212 Linus, English *slime* (but *lime*, Anglo-Saxon *lím*, shows the non-sibilated root).

Sibiriak (sibi·ryæk). [Russ. *Sibiryak* Siberian.] A descendant of the first Russian settlers in the western part of Siberia.

1911 in WEBSTER.

Sibiric (sibi·rik), *a.* Also **Siberic, Sibirik.** [Russ. *Sibiri* Siberia + -IC.] Of or pertaining to the branches of the Asiatic race that inhabit northern Asia; Ural-Altaic.

1890 D. G. BRINTON *Races & Peoples* 206 The Sibiric Branch. The branch of the Asian race which I have called the Sibiric, as geographically designating its prehistoric home, has also been called the Turanian, the Ural-Altaic, the Finno-Ugric, the Mongolic, etc.

Sibling. Transfer † *Obs.* to sense in Dict. and add: **b.** Each of two or more individuals born to the same parents but not at the same birth; *occas.*, each of two or more individuals having one parent in common.

1897 KARL PEARSON *Chances of Death* II. ii. 161. 1905 E. L. THORNDIKE in *Jrnl. Philos. Psychol. & Sci. Methods* 28 Sept. 547 (Cent. D. Suppl.) The resemblance of twins in mental traits is roughly twice that of ordinary siblings. 1922 ADA E. SHEFFIELD *Case Study Possibilities* (U.S.) 61. 1930 *Nature* 15 Nov. 766 A few were odd twins who had a brother or sister at school, and the remainder were either siblings of twins, or pairs of siblings unconnected with twins.

Sican (səi·kăn). Also **Sikan.** [ad. L. *Sĭcānus*: cf. next.] A member of a tribe which inhabited ancient Sicily at the time of the coming of the Sicels.

1887 [see *SICEL].

Sicanian (sikēⁱ·niăn), *a.* Add: **b.** *Archæol.* Denoting the Neolithic period in Sicily.

1909 T. E. PEET *Stone & Bronze Ages Italy & Sicily* v. 123 By Professor Orsi..the pre-Hellenic period in the island, excluding the palæolithic, is divided into five divisions. To the first of these he gives the name Sicanian; the other four are called respectively First, Second, Third and Fourth Siculan periods.

Sicel (si·sĕl), *sb.* and *a.* Also **Sikel** (si·kĕl). [ad. Gr. Σικελός: cf. next.] **a.** *sb.* One of an ancient race who settled in Sicily and gave their name to the island. **b.** *adj.* Of or pertaining to the Sicels. Hence **Sike·lian** *a.* and *sb.*, in same senses; also *Archæol.*, denoting the Chalcolithic and Bronze Ages in Sicily. Also **Si·culan, Sicu·lian** [f. L. *Siculus*].

1836 THIRLWALL *Greece* xii. II. 92 The Sicels and the Phœnicians gradually retreated before the Greeks. 1881 JOWETT tr. *Thucydides* I. 409 The Sicels were originally inhabitants of Italy,..there are Sicels still in Italy, and the country itself was so called from Italus a Sicel king. 1887 *Encycl. Brit.* XXII. 15/1 It is possible..that the Sikels belonged to the same branch of the Aryan family as the Italian, while Sikans, like Ligurians and Iberians and the surviving Basques, belonged to the earlier non-Aryan population of western Europe. *Ibid.*, Some Sikel elements made their way into the Greek life of Sicily. *Ibid.* 15/2 The legend that a native Sikel prince led the Greek settlers to the foundation of Megara. 1909 PEET *Stone & Bronze Ages Italy & Sicily* v. 123 [see *SICANIAN b]. *Ibid.* xvii. 483 We ought to find, at some period of pre-history in Sicily, a sudden change due to this immigration, and, what is more, the new material (Siculan) in Sicily ought to resemble that left behind in Italy by the emigrants.

Siceliot (sise·liŏt), *sb.* and *a.* Also **Sikeliot** (sike·liŏt), **-ote.** [ad. Gr. Σικελιώτης, f. Σικελία Sicily: see -OT 2, -OTE.] **a.** *sb.* One of the ancient Greeks who colonized Sicily, distinguished from the Sicels who had settled in Sicily before their coming; also, any inhabitant of Sicily of whatever race. **b.** *adj.* Of or pertaining to the Siceliots.

1836 THIRLWALL *Greece* xxii. III. 263 [They were] linked together by the common name of Siceliots. 1842 *Penny Cycl.* XXIV. 407/1 The intimate knowledge which he [*sc.* Thucydides] shows respecting the history of the Italiotes and Sicelites. 1892 *Athenæum* 7 May 597/3 In Syracuse then lay the last hopes of rescue for the Siceliot Greeks.

Sicilian, *a.* **2. a.** Add: Also *Sicilian defence* (Chess).

1900 *Knowledge* 1 Aug. 192/1 The success attending the Sicilian defence is especially noteworthy.

Sicilienne. Add: **2.** *Mus.* (See quots.)

1883 *Grove's Dict. Mus.* III. 491/2 Siciliana, Siciliano, Sicilienne, a dance rhythm closely allied to the Pastorale. 1927 *Daily Tel.* 12 Feb. 5/2 The Sicilienne was quiet and restful.

Sick, *a.* and *sb.* Add: **A.** *adj.* **1.** Phr. *To go sick*: to become ill; to fall into a bad state of health; in army use, to be reported as sick.

1879 [see *1 f]. 1915 D. O. BARNETT *Lett.* 53 He's lots better this morning,..and he is not 'going sick' at all. 1927 E. J. THOMPSON *These Men thy Friends* 12 Filthy climate. No fun. But she just carries on. Hasn't gone sick once in six months. 1927 W. E. COLLINSON *Contemp. Engl.* 95 To go sick under false pretences.

f. Of pigeons: Denoting the disorder supposed to result when the parent birds lose their young and cannot get rid of the soft meat or food secreted for them.

1854 MEALL *Moubray's Poultry* viii. 455 We have never observed the old birds 'sick' (as most books assert they are) when the young have died. 1879 L. WRIGHT *Pract. Pigeon Keeper* iii. 37 In order that another young one from some other pair..may be given the parents to feed off their soft meat, and save them from 'going sick' with it.

5. Also *sick and tired.* (Cf. *sick-tired*, sense 11.)

1883 NYE *Baled Hay* 124 We are sick and tired of pointing out different avenues of wealth to be laughed at and ridiculed.

7. (Examples of other uses.)

1684 EVELYN *Diary* 4 Feb., The oranges and mirtills very sick, the rosemary and laurells dead to all appearance. 1817 in *Trans. Ill. State Hist. Soc.* 1910, 147 Sick Milk, Sick Wheat, a plenty of Ague near the large streams. 1847 H. HOWE *Hist. Collect. Ohio* 274 Those lands were too rich for wheat, making 'sick wheat', so termed, because when made into bread, it had the effect of an emetic. 1914 *Rep. Brit. Assoc.* 672 The fertility of this 'sick' soil can be restored by merely heating it for an hour or two to a temperature approaching that of boiling water. 1921 *Brit. Museum Return* 74 The treatment and cleaning of sick and dirty coins. 1930 *N. & Q.* 16 Aug. 124/2 A cheese..is sick when it has been over soured or over acidulated, and in time 'weeps', gradually becoming soft inside.

9. sick headache, a headache accompanied by nausea: = MEGRIM 1 1.

1778 FOTHERGILL in *Med. Observ.* (1784) VI. 103 Remarks on that Complaint commonly known under the Name of the Sick Head-ach. 1799 [see Dict.]. 1884 [see HEADACHE 1]. 1915 D. O. BARNETT *Lett.* 153 Shrapnel is for defenders, to stop an advance of infantry, but no more use against prepared positions than a sick headache.

10. b. sick-benefit, an allowance made to those who are away from work on account of illness; **sick-call**, (*a*) a summons to a minister of religion to visit a sick person; (*b*) *Mil.*, a call sounded by bugle, trumpet, etc., as a signal to those who are sick to attend at the hospital or report to the medical officer; **sick communion**, an administration of Holy Communion to a sick person; **sick-feeder**, a vessel resembling a cup for feeding invalids; **sick parade**, an inspection of those who are ill; **sick visiting**, the visiting of the sick, esp. by a minister of religion.

1909 *Chambers's Jrnl.* 56/2 Members who..may have received *sick-benefit. 1883 LADY HERBERT tr. *Life St. John Baptist de Rossi* III. iv. 147 The servants never again dared to fail to warn him of any *sick call. 1908 E. C. BOOTH *Cliff End* v. 37 You can be almost sure of catching me,.. without there be sick calls. 1918 FARROW *Dict. Mil. Terms*, *Sick Call*, a signal on the bugle or drum and fife for the formation of the sick squads. 1930 F. A. POTTLE *Stretchers* 31 Sick call is blown before the dispensary door. 1930 S. KAYE-SMITH *Sheph. Sackcloth* vii. § 11 Will you tell me.. how many *sick Communions you have weekly? 1895 *Army & Navy Co-op. Soc. Price List* 15 Sept. 1316 *Sick Feeders. 1915 'IAN HAY' *First Hundred Thousand* xi, M'Splae departs, grumbling, and reappears on *sick parade a few days later. 1925 E. F. NORTON *Fight for Everest, 1924* 47 He took the daily sick parade, and had an equally unerring eye for a malingerer or for the stout heart that made light of a genuine ailment. 1927 R. H. MOTTRAM *Spanish Farm* 267 They heard the bugles go 'Sick parade'.

Sick, *v.*2 Add: **1.** (Earlier U.S. example.)

1845 J. J. HOOPER *Taking Census* i. 154 Sick him Pomp, ..sick, sick, si-c-k him Bull.

2. (Earlier U.S. example.) Also, to set (a dog) *on.*

1845 J. J. HOOPER *Taking Census* i. 151 If I was to sick them on your old hoss younder, they'd eat him up afore you could say Jack Robinson. 1899 TARKINGTON *Gentl. Indiana* viii. 131 'Seems some of the boys..sicked the dogs on him. 1904 *N.Y. Sun* 9 Aug. 9 Orders, threats and the sicking of small dogs upon the intruders are without result. 1907 JACK LONDON *White Fang* 286 One day they openly sicked the dogs on him.

Sicken, *v.* Add: **1. d.** *To sicken for*: to be in the early stages of (a disease, which is not yet manifest).

1883 FLORENCE MONTGOMERY *Blue Veil* II. vii. 218, I was sickening for the mumps.

Sickle, *sb.* **2.** Add:

f. *Embryol.* A sickle-shaped thickening at the hind end of the blastodisc of certain vertebrate embryos.

1903 *Proc. Zool. Soc.* II. 18 In birds, typical concrescence can occur only during the earliest stage of formation of the primitive streak, *i.e.* so long as the groove of the sickle and knob is open.

Sickness. 6. Add: *sickness-fund, -insurance.*

1910 *Chambers's Jrnl.* July 438/1 All workers..are compelled to contribute a weekly sum to the State sickness-fund. 1911 *Q. Rev.* July 209 Sickness-insurance.

Sicula (si·kiulă). *Palæont.* [L., = little dagger.] (See quot. 1895.)

1895 *Funk's Standard Dict.*, *Sicula*.., the earliest stage of a graptolite when it is a small triangular corneous body. 1910 *Encycl. Brit.* XII. 366/2 It is the general practice of palæontologists to regard each graptolite polypary (rhabdosome) developed from a single sicula as an individual.

Sicul(i)an: see under *SICEL.

Sicyonian (sisiōᵘ·niăn), *a.* and *sb.* Also **Sikyonian.** [f. L. *Sicyōnius*, a. Gr. Σικυώνιος, f. *Sicyōn*, a. Gr. Σικυών: see -IAN.] **a.** *adj.* Of or pertaining to Sicyon, an ancient Greek city in the north of the Peloponnesus, noted for art, or to Sicyonia, the surrounding district. **b.** *sb.* A native or inhabitant of Sicyon or Sicyonia. Also **Sicyo-**, combining form.

1841 *Penny Cycl.* XXI. 126/2 They [*sc.* Dipœnus and Scyllis] were employed by the Sicyonians to make for them certain statues of their gods. 1887 *Encycl. Brit.* XXII. 32/1 The early bronze work of the Sicyo-Argive workshops. *Ibid.* 32/2 The Olympian treasury of the Sicyonians...Clisthenes was the most powerful and famous of the Sicyonian despots.

Sid 2 (sid). [Arab. سيد *sīd, sayyid* lord. Cf. CID, SIDI.] Master, sir; a title of respect among Mohammedans.

1883 *Encycl. Brit.* XVI. 835/2, 1882. Expedition to subdue Sid Hosein of Iligh. 1887 S. LANE-POOLE *Moors in Spain* 191 A Mohammedan gentleman is still addressed in Egypt and elsewhere by the title *Sid.*

Side, *sb.*1 Add: **2. b.** *Side-by-side* attrib.

1908 *Daily Chron.* 29 Nov. 9/5 The side-car..has the advantages of ready convertibility, low cost, and high speed, which, together with the far greater sociability afforded by the side-by-side accommodation, have combined to establish it as a universal favourite. 1909 *Ibid.* 23 Oct. 9/1 Into the side-by-side training are apt to enter certain distractions, rivalries and attachments. 1921 *Discovery* Apr. 97/2 Each axle [of a monoplane] carries twin side-by-side wheels of large size, about 4 feet in diameter.

10. b. *On the* (so-and-so) *side*: tending towards the condition denoted by the adjective.

1923 A. J. ANDERSON *Soul Sisters* xxiv. § 3. 252 'Michelmore was always on the rough side!' he remarked aloud. 1932 *News Chron.* 28 May 4/4 It must be pointed out that prices are on the high side.

13. e. *This side, the other side*: ellipt. for this side or the other side of the Atlantic. *colloq.*, orig. *U.S.*

1884 *Naturalist's World* Sept. 155/2 Canadian Postal Science College..is a society which has grown up very rapidly 'on the other side'.

14. b. *On the side*: (*a*) (orig. *U.S.*) in addition to one's regular or ordinary duties; as a subordinate occupation; as an extra. (*b*) (*U.S. colloq.*) in addition to the main portion, e.g. a drink of whisky with water *on the side.*

1898 *N.Y. Jrnl.* 26 Aug. 9/3 Samuel..started an ice cream parlor, with cigars, tobacco and delicatessen on the side. 1904 *N.Y. Times* 22 June 3 To attend the big fair and receive the entertainment of St. Louis on the side. 1906 *N.Y. Evening Post* 18 Apr. 8 Novels have degenerated into tracts. As yet the tractarians are too much impressed by their duty to point their morals to furnish a really good story 'on the side'. 1906 *Atlantic Monthly* Oct. 492 They..count that year a bad year in which they do not make as much or more than their salaries 'on the side'. 1915 P. G. WODEHOUSE *Something Fresh* iv. § 1 'I'm not asking you to be a valet and nothing else.' 'You would want me to do some cooking and plain sewing on the side, perhaps?' 1927 *Daily News* 11 Mar. 2/2 Y'see, Bill's in the rag-and-bone trade and he does a bit [*sc.* of receiving] on the side. Just anything he can pick up. 1931 *Punch* 28 Oct. 450/2 Several journalists I know sell refrigerators and vacuum-cleaners on the side.

17. f. An aspect of something (denoted by an adj. or sb. attrib.).

1910 *Rep. Brit. Assoc.* 578 The disease leans strongly towards the physiological side. 1914 *Ibid.* 673 The amelioration of soils on their physical side.

20. c. Used *allusively.*

1925 E. F. NORTON *Fight for Everest, 1924* 102 In a year, when, to a conspicuous degree, all played for the side.

24. c. *side talk.*

1931 B. BROWN *Talking Pictures* x. 250 The need for silence in the studio is increased, since side talk, coughs, etc., are liable to be picked up.

27. side-boy (earlier U.S. example); **side-chain**, (*a*) a chain at the side of a vehicle, *spec.* each of two chains in some types of motor vehicles which transmit motion from the engine to the driving wheels; also, see quots. 1849–50, 1883; (*b*) *Bacteriology*, a chain of atoms which may be attached to the principal chain in the constitution of a molecule; also *attrib.* in **side-chain theory**,

a theory propounded by Ehrlich to explain the phenomena of immunity; **side circuit** *Electr.* (see quot. 1916); **side curtain**, a curtain at the side of something; in an open motor vehicle, a protective screen at the side; **side-entrance**, a subsidiary entrance at the side into a building, motor vehicle, etc.; **side-hold**, a hold in mountaineering (see quot.); **side-lamp**, each of the lamps on either side of the front of a motor vehicle, giving an indication of the width of the vehicle; **side-lever**, in a steam engine, a working beam or lever at the side of the cylinder instead of above it; also *attrib.*; **side-lock**, a lock of hair worn at the side of the head, sometimes used in art as a distinguishing sign of childhood; **side-partner** *U.S.*, = *SIDE-KICK; **side-path**, a by-path, an unfrequented path as distinguished from the main road; also *fig.*; **side-piece**, (*b*) in general sense, a piece at the side; **side-play** *Mech.*, freedom of movement from side to side; **side-screen**, one of the side curtains of an open motor vehicle; **side-seat**, a seat facing to or placed at the side, esp. in a vehicle; **side-skid** *v. intr.* = *SKID *v.*1 3 b; **side splitter** (examples); **side-splitting** (earlier U.S. example); **side-splittingly** *adv.*, in an extremely funny manner; **side-stroke**, (*a*) see Dict. 24 a; (*b*) *Swimming*, a stroke employed in swimming on the side; **side-sway**, a rolling motion sometimes perceptible in a moving vehicle; **side-swimming**, swimming on the side, whatever stroke is used; **side-tiller**, (*a*) cf. *tiller-steerage, -steering*, TILLER *sb.*2 4; (*b*) cf. TILLER *sb.*3; **side-valve**, a valve fitted to the side of a cylinder block in an internal-combustion engine; hence **side-valved** *a.*; **side-whisker**, usually in *pl.*, the whiskers which grow on the cheek or side of the face; *transf.* curl of hair which hangs over the cheek; hence **side-whiskered** *a.*; **side-wire**, 'a stout wire introduced by Helmholtz as a shunt to the primary coil in du Bois-Reymond's inductorium' (Cent. D. Suppl. 1909); **side-work**, (*c*) any work regarded as of lesser importance than other work.

1823 J. F. COOPER *Pilot* I. iii. 31 The shrill whistle of the boat-swains mate, as he recalled the *side-boys. 1849–50 WEALE *Dict. Terms*, *Side chains*, chains and hooks fixed to the sides of the tender and engine for safety, should the central drag-bar give way. 1883 GRESLEY *Gloss. Coal-m.*, *Side Chain*, a chain hooked on to the sides of tubs when running upon an engine-plane or jig, to keep all the tubs together in case a coupling breaks. 1886 *Encycl. Brit.* XX. 247/2 Some companies have gone further and placed the guard or side chains upon springs. 1902 *Ibid.* XXVI. 67/1 Ehrlich who, in his so-called 'side-chain' (*Seitenkette*) theory, explains antitoxin production as an instance of regeneration after loss... The side-chains constitute the means by which other molecules are added to the living molecule. 1905 *Rep. Brit. Assoc.* 560 Molecules may be linked on to a side-chain and re-arrangements occur without the nucleus being disturbed. 1916 *Standard. Rules Amer. Inst. Electr. Engin.* 95 A *side circuit is a two-wire circuit forming one side of a phantom circuit. 1923 E. W. MARCHANT *Radio Telegr. & Teleph.* iv. 38 Multiple Receiving Circuits... The side circuit or tuning circuit is coupled to the aerial circuit in just the same way as is the oscillator in the transmitter. 1821 *side-curtain [see Dict. 23 b]. 1912 *Motor Manual* vi. (ed. 14) 161 The only car for such weather conditions is a covered one, either one with a Cape cart hood with side curtains well down..or the more complete enclosure of limousine or landaulet. 1928 [see *SIDE-ON]. 1932 *Modern* 26 Mar. 1143/1 A crazy little car, with side curtains flapping like wings, bore down on them. 1907 *Daily Mail Year Bk.* 74/2 In turn the prevailing form of body has been the.. *side-entrance phaeton, and the landaulet and limousine. 1912 *Motor Manual* v. (ed. 14) 139 Access being gained..by a revolving or tilting front seat or a 'side-entrance'. 1926 W. W. JACOBS *Sea Whispers* v. 113 To leave by the side-entrance was the best way of avoiding trouble. 1920 G. W. YOUNG *Mountain Craft* iv. 162 '*Side'-holds, where the edge or point of rock projects and is grasped sideways. 1912 *Motor Manual* iii. (ed. 14) 124 It is possible now..to adapt electric lighting very successfully to any car, both for interior lighting of limousines and landaulets, and for head, *side and rear lamps. 1839 *side levers [see *sway-beam* s.v. SWAY-]. 1875 KNIGHT *Dict. Mech.*, *Side-lever* (Steam-engine), a heavy lever, working alongside the steam-cylinder and answering in its functions to the working-beam... *Side-lever Engine*,..a marine engine having side-levers instead of a working-beam to turn the wheel-shaft. 1901 *Chambers's Jrnl.* Sept. 598/1 We have had beam engines, side-lever engines, steeple-engines, and engines of a direct action. 1848 *side-locks [see Dict. 23 b]. 1889 *Century Mag.* Sept. 710/1 The monuments represent him as a prince and nothing more, still wearing the side-lock of juniority. 1910 *J. Hastings's Encycl. Relig. & Ethics* III. 538/1 The side-lock so often represented on the bas-reliefs and frescoes... The same side-lock expresses the idea of childhood in sculpture. 1899 T. HALL *Tales* 151 Luckily for you my *side partner nabbed your note out of her pocket at the same time. 1931 R. D. PAINE *Comr. Rolling Ocean* ix. 159 We shall have to consult my side-partner, Briscoe. 1897 *side-path [see Dict. 23]. 1924 R. HICHENS *After the Verdict* II. vii, No false steps into side-paths for her. 1931 *Times Lit. Suppl.* 20 Aug. 625/4 Those who love to wander down historical sidepaths. 1850 DICKENS *Dav. Copp.* xiii, I mean a cap, much more common then than now, with *side-pieces fastening under the chin. 1928 *Daily Express* 16 Aug. 5/2 A car (with a left-hand drive and a hood but no side-pieces). 1902 A. C. HARMSWORTH *Motors & Motor-Driving* x. 206 All bearings will wear and will require rebushing,..and this should be done when any very perceptible shake or *side play is detected in them. 1903 *Sci. Amer.* 7 Feb. 99/1 Side play of this spring is prevented by beads on the post. 1932 *News Chron.* 6 Aug. 3/5 The assailant thrust a six-chambered revolver through a *side-screen and fired. 1856 *side seat [see Dict.]. 1901 *Daily News* 5 July 4 In the stern with the side-seats out there is room for 3 or 4 drift-nets. 1926 H. BARBER *Aeroplane Speaks* 36 The Momentum..heavily resents this change of direction, and tries its level best to prevent it and to pull the machine sideways and outwards from its spiral course—that is, to make it '*side-skid' outwards. 1880 *Punch* 11 Dec. 268/1 The intended *side-splitter begins well—that is, Mr. Toole begins well, his make-up and manner being intensely absurd. 1892 MILLIKEN *'Arry Ballads* 36/1 But now the Stage licks arf the 'Alls, mate, for side splitters, spice, and bare pink. 1856 S. MORDECAI *Virginia* xiv. (1860) 188 These among other *side-splitting tales, which he told and acted with the skill of a Matthews. 1907 A. BENNETT *Grim Smile Five Towns* 7 Something *side-splittingly funny. 1923 *Daily Mail* 21 May 4 Mr. George Graves..has never gagged more side-splittingly..than he gags in the revival of 'The Merry Widow'. 1867 STEEDMAN *Man. Swimming* 105 The five movements—three for the legs and two for the arms—required for the performance of the *side stroke. 1871 'STONEHENGE' (J. H. Walsh) *Brit. Rural Sports* (ed. 9) 659 The sidestroke..will enable him to get through the water at a much greater speed. 1890 M. COBBETT *Swimming* 27 History has not handed down the name of the founder of the side stroke. 1930 *Morning Post* 21 July 4 *Sideway or rolling occurs at right angles to the propeller shaft. 1931 *Daily Express* 28 Apr. 2/1 Long vanadium-steel springs, rear springs splayed to prevent sidesway. 1861 'R. HARRINGTON' *Swimming* 11 In *side swimming the arms and legs are not moved alternately as in chest swimming. 1904 A. B. F. YOUNG *Complete Motorist* iv. 93 Different either from the wheel system of steering or the American *side-tiller system. 1931 *Ann. Applied Biol.* XVIII. 41 Those plants from which the side tillers were cut off, formed further side branches and new leaves. 1928 *Daily Mail Year Bk.* p. lxiv, 3.49 H.P. *Side Valve 'Sports' Model. 1928 *Correct Lubrication* 12 A 4-cylinder side valve engine. 1932 *Observer* 9 Oct. 21/3 This [car] has a *side-valved engine of about a litre and a half cubic capacity. 1867 *Amer. Naturalist* I. Aug. 287 Their ears are often tufted, and one species, at least, has '*side-whiskers' formed by the true fur, in addition to the labial bristles which ordinarily receive this name. 1888 [see Dict. 23 b]. 1932 *Evening Standard* 28 Jan. 17/3 Lady Ancaster's veil stops short at the tip of her nose, and is only long enough to keep her 'side whiskers' in order. 1926 *Spectator* 24 July 126/1 Hilmar Tönnesen, *side-whiskered chief of the grotesques. 1901 TITCHENER *Exper. Psychol.* I. II. 144 The Helmholtz *side-wire is removed, and the Wagner hammer (interrupter) is out of function. 1920 A. OLIVER *Life G. C. Hutton* xii. 117 The pulpit..was not neglected for the platform or other *side-work.

Side, *v.* Add: **9.** (Earlier and later U.S. examples.)

1827 J. F. COOPER *Red Rover* i, It is..cloth that would do to side a house with. 1874 B. F. TAYLOR *World on Wheels* I. xvi. 119 Then afternoon, wherein the morning's frame was put together..raised, roofed and sided. 1877 *Rep. Indian Affairs* 40 Two dwelling houses and one school-house have been sided up with weather-boards.

11. b. Also with *in.*

1928 *Daily Express* 10 Oct. 6 'What can I do?' protested the shivering man. 'I get it in the neck either way.' 'Not if you side in with us.'

c. *To side up with*: to compare *with. slang.*

1895 *Punch* 23 Feb. 87/2 There ain't ne'er a Cockney C.C. as can side-up with Joey the Brum.

15. To show or present a side (of the colour specified).

1903 W. R. CATTELLE *Precious Stones* 41 Some [diamonds] face up blue, and side yellow.

Sideband (səi·dbænd). *Wireless Telegr.* [f. SIDE *sb.*1 + BAND *sb.*2] Each of a group of waves having a frequency a little above or below that of the carrier wave. Also *attrib.*

1926 R. W. HUTCHINSON *Wireless* xiii. 252 Every broadcast transmission of speech, music, etc., is accompanied by 'side-bands', *i.e.* waves just a little above or a little below the normal wave-length of the station. 1928 *Observer* 1 July 4/4 The added selectivity is quite likely to operate in the direction of cutting down sidebands. 1930 *B.B.C. Year-Bk.* 451/2, *Side-band Telephony*, a system of telephony transmission in which the side-bands only are transmitted and not the carrier wave. 1932 *Ibid.* 318 At one time the carrier wave and one side-band might be very weak, there being apparently only one side-band receivable.

Side-car, sidecar (səi·dkāɹ), *sb.* Also as two words. [f. SIDE *sb.*1 + CAR *sb.*1]

1. a. A jaunting-car. ? *Obs.*

1881 [see SIDE *sb.*1 27].

b. A vehicle designed to be attached to the side of a motor-cycle to accommodate one or more passengers; also *attrib.*

1904 MERCREDY *Dict. Motoring* 199 Another ingenious arrangement is the 'side car', in which the passenger vehicle is placed beside the [motor-]bicycle instead of in front. 1908 *Motor Cycle* 8 Jan. 34/2 The sidecar..was an ancient contraption with compensating joints. 1909 *Chambers's Jrnl.* May 336/1 The cycle has a third wheel, as in the ordinary side-car attachment.

2. A kind of cocktail.

1928 SINCLAIR LEWIS *Man who Knew Coolidge* I. 61 Mame took a Bronx, and Delmerine took a side-car,..and I ordered a Martini. 1932 *Modern* 26 Mar. 1026/2 You can drink anything you like from 'Side Cars' down to weak China tea.

Hence **Si·decar** *v. intr.*, to drive a motor-cycle with a side-car attached; **Si·decar(r)ing** *vbl. sb.*; **Si·decarist**, one who drives a motor-cycle combination.

1911 *Motor Cycle* 19 Jan. 21 Advt., Best after tests for side-caring,..for economy. 1914 *Motor Cycling* 12 May 8, 3½ h.p. is insufficient for sidecarring at a satisfactory speed. 1920 *Motor Cycle* 29 Apr. 487/2, I make this request because of its importance to sidecarists. 1923 *Ibid.* 25 Oct. 665/2 No doubt she would feel small and lonely when sidecarring by herself in one of these ample-looking bodies. *Ibid.* 1 Nov. 708/1 It will be agreed, I am sure, that we sidecarists do adhere to the main routes rather than we need.

Si·de-comb. orig. *U.S.* [SIDE *sb.*1 23 b.] A comb used to secure the hair at the side of the head. Also *transf.*

1825 *Austin Papers* (1924) II. 1081, 1 Side Comb..$.25. 1853 B. F. TAYLOR *Jan. & June* (1871) 85 Hens with very delicate side-combs like our Sweet-hearts. 1870 'FANNY FERN' *Ginger-Snaps* 146 She don't shuffle round..with horn side-combs fastening six hairs to her temple. 1897 [see SIDE *sb.*1 23 b]. *a* 1909 'O. HENRY' *Roads of Destiny* iv. 60 When I'm hard at work I can see things through my side-combs.

Sided, *ppl. a.* **1.** (Recent U.S. example.)

1904 *N.Y. Sun* 7 Aug. 20 The yard is sided by cabins.

Side-door. Add: Also *fig.*

1930 *Times* 21 Mar. 15/5 We maintain that these 'side door' credits are endangering our chances of securing recognition of our bonds.

Side-hill. (Earlier U.S. examples.)

1674 *Groton Records* (1880) 178 Bounded on the north with the sidhill. 1685 *Plymouth Rec.* 184 A small red oake.. upon a side hill above Princes botom. *attrib.* 1837 H. COLMAN *Rep. Agric. Mass.* (1838) 68 In some parts of the county, the side hill plough with a changeable mould-board is used for ploughing.

Si·de-kick, -ki·cker. *U.S. slang.* A comrade or companion, or associate.

(*a*) 1904 'O. HENRY' *Cabbages & Kings* vi. 103 Billy was my side-kicker in New York. 1926 J. BLACK *You Can't Win* xiii. 189 At Seattle, almost broke..I cast about for a 'sidekicker'.

(*b*) 1922 R. PARRISH *Case & the Girl* 335 He's Hogan's side-kick. 1923 L. J. VANCE *Baroque* viii. 49 Him and me used to be side-kicks. 1928 F. N. HART *Bellamy Trial* i. 15 Mr. Lambert was a side kick of old Curtiss Thorne—handled his estate and everything.

Sidelangle, *v.* (Amer. examples.)

1660 *Rowley Rec.* 105 That there shall bee no horses left tethered in the night time..or..any way side-langled.. neither shall any person..side-langel..any horse or asse in the day time. 1669 *Watertown Rec.* 95 [Any] horse..that is not side langled with iron fetters.

Side-light. Add: **3. c.** The lamp on either side of a motor vehicle.

1912 *Motor Manual* iii. (ed. 14) 120 Much better side lights have been provided than ever existed before.

Side-line, *sb.* Add: **1.** (Earlier U.S. example.)

1694 *Col. Rec. N. Carolina* I. 410 The dividing line..shall run parallel with Cornelius Terrys side line.

c. In Colonial usage: see quots.

1848 H. W. HAYGARTH *Bush Life Australia* xii. 129 The road..shelved off very rapidly towards the precipice, so as to afford little foot-hold for the cattle, and formed, what, in colonial phrase, is called a 'side-line'. 1889 FARMER *Americanisms*, *Side-line*, (1) In Demerara, a canal. Every estate has several side-lines, communication being carried on by means of these water-ways. (2) In Canada, a by-road running at right angles to the main or concession roads.

2. (Later U.S. example.)

1867 *Outing* (U.S.) X. 11/1 'Side lines' is the army substitute for hobbles.

3. b. *fig.* Something subsidiary to the main subject, consideration, line of action, or the like.

1927 HALDANE & HUXLEY *Anim. Biol.* xii. 266 The sponges thus represent an early side-line in evolution, along which life never developed far. 1928 *Daily Express* 8 Sept. 2/7 One of the most interesting side lines of the Trade Union Congress at Swansea has been the conversations between Mr. Arthur Henderson, the secretary of the Political Socialist Party, and the leaders of the more important trade unions.

Hence **Side-line** *v.* (earlier U.S. example).

1837 W. IRVING *Capt. Bonneville* ii, The horses were 'side lined', as it is termed: that is to say, the fore and hind foot on the same side of the animal were tied together, so as to be within eighteen inches of each other.

Si·de-loo·king, *a.* [SIDE *sb.*1 24.] Looking sidewards.

1829 J. F. COOPER *Wish-ton-wish* iii, A demure, side-looking young woman.

Side meat. *U.S.* [SIDE *sb.*1 22.] Meat (esp. bacon or pork) from the side of an animal.

1873 J. H. BEADLE *Undevel. West* xxiv. 482 Two bright-eyed, graceful, copper-coloured señoritas bring me a supper of coffee, side meat, eggs [etc.]. 1890 *St. Nicholas* Nov. 39 Side-meat, in the South and West, is the thin flank of a porker, salted and smoked after the fashion of hams. 1891 *Harper's Mag.* Aug. 486/2 The Mayor..set a piece of side meat to sizzling in a skillet. 1931 *Randolph Enterprise* (W. Va.) 7 May 1/5 Nothing more than two pieces of side meat were taken.

Side-on, *a.* and *adv.* [f. SIDE *sb.*1 Cf. *HEAD-ON.] **a.** *adj.* (*si·de-on*). Of a collision: Involving the meeting of the sides of two vehicles, or of the side of a vehicle with an object. **b.** *adv.* (*si·de-o·n*). With the side coming into direct contact with something.

1928 *Daily Mail* 16 Aug. 13/7 Side-on collisions frequently occur owing to blurred side curtains.

Sider 1. Add: **2.** *U.S.* (See quot.)

1869 *Overland Monthly* III. 126 The mighty herd..has 'pointers', who ride abreast of the head of the column, and 'siders' who keep the stragglers out of the chaparral.

Side-show. (Earlier fig. example.)

1866 C. H. SMITH (*title*) Bill Arp, so called. A Side Show of the Southern Side of the War.

Hence **Side-showman.**

1886 E. W. HOWE *Moonlight Boy* 73 A side-showman at a circus.

Side-slip, *sb.* Add: **5. b.** Of an aeroplane (see next b).

1912 *Q. Rev.* July 237 Any such attitude may be attended by protracted side-slip of the aeroplane downwards in the direction of the lower wing. 1916 H. Barber *Aeroplane Speaks* 17 Before you could say Warp to the Ailerons over the Aeroplane would go—probable result a bad side-slip. 1928 *Observer* 1 July 17/3 With the greatest of ease they performed side-slips, vertical dives, and loops.

fig. 1916 H. Barber *Aeroplane Speaks* p. v, The dreadful haltings, the many side-slips, the irregular speed, and, in short, the altogether disconcerting ways of a pen. 1921 Galsworthy *To Let* II. vi, He therefore confined himself to discussing with Dumetrius whether Monticellis would come again..and the future of Johns, with a side-slip into Buxton Knights.

Side-slip, *v.* Add: **b.** Of an aeroplane: To slip sideways, *spec.* towards the centre of curvature while turning (as distinguished from *Skid *v.* 3 c).

1912 *Q. Rev.* July 241 The fin or Vee catches the air through which the machine is side-slipping. 1918 E. M. Roberts *Flying Fighter* 253, I noticed that he was trying to side-slip. 1929 B. Hall & J. J. Niles *One Man's War* 115 He tipped over on his left wing and side-slipped out of the way.

c. *transf.* or *fig.*

1921 Galsworthy *To Let* I. iii, His heart moved in a disconcerting manner, as if it had side-slipped within his chest. 1930 H. R. Wakefield in *London Mercury* Feb. 319 Here he was suddenly realising that they controlled another mode of clutching. Better to side-slip that too—if he could.

Side-step, *v.* Add: **b.** (See quot.)

1924 *Ski Terms* in *Tourist* Winter Sports No. 12/2 *Side Stepping*, climbing by lifting the skis horizontally.

c. To go aside from the direct route.

1927 *Ladies' Home Jrnl.* Jan. 62, I was glad I side stepped, for the journey..was worth a deviation.

d. *trans.* To avoid by or as by stepping sideways; *spec.* in *Football*. Also *intr.*

1906 'O. Henry' *Four Million* 115 I've lost two inches of my tail trying to sidestep those swinging doors. 1920 W. Camp *Football without a Coach* 93 The man who catches the ball will not be able to sidestep him or pass him. 1931 *Times* 16 Feb. 5/1 Once, Arigho..managed to side-step Reeve. *fig.* 1906 *Springfield* (Mass.) *Weekly Republ.* 27 Sept. 8 The Idaho republicans are deftly side-stepping the anti-Mormon issue. 1915 P. G. Wodehouse *Psmith, Journalist* xxiii. (1923) 173 If I can put him away, it gets me into line with Jimmy, and he can't side-step me. 1920 — *Damsel in Distress* ii. 30 The party after the show which you can't side-step. *Ibid.* viii. 106 What do you say, George,..if we side-step the Amber Drawing Room? I'm wild to get into that garden. 1926 *Scribner's Mag.* Aug. 154/2 Van Allen side-stepped the enquiries by declaring that, really, he had no news to tell.

intr. 1930 P. Macdonald *The Link* vii. 114 I've even asked Dinwater that flat out on two occasions. But he's always side-stepped.

Hence **Si·de-ste:pper,** one who avoids a direct course or issue.

1909 *N.Y. Evening Post* (semi-weekly ed.) 1 Mar. 1 Had not Mr. Fairbanks been a really wonderful side-stepper, their essential differences might have long ago become public property.

Side-track, *sb.* (Earlier examples.)

1862 F. N. Otis *Hist. Panama Railroad* 45. 1874 B. F. Taylor *World on Wheels* I. xxi. 152 The engineer is doing his best to get upon the side-track before the Express wants the road.

Side-track, *v.* **1.** *fig.* Add: *spec.* To divert (a person) from the main trend of action, subject of conversation, etc., into another track or channel; to turn (a subject or matter) aside so as to prevent its proper treatment or consideration.

1891 F. H. Smith *Col. Carter* 139 Yancey broke away again, but Fitz side-tracked him with a gesture, and asked the colonel to repeat Klutchem's exact words. 1893 'O. Thanet' *Stories Western Town* 204, I guess it is no use to side-track the subject. 1904 F. Lynde *Grafters* xxii. 275 We have been sitting here talking the vaguest trivialities ever since Penelope and Loring side-tracked us.

Sideways, *adv.* **3. b.** Add: *To look sideways*: to have a suspicious or shamefaced look.

1921 Bernard Gilbert *Old England* § 55. 70 But he was known to be paying to three different women for a child each, And his housekeeper beginning to look sideways. *Ibid.* § 138. 188 I'm afraid Susan's in trouble; She's looking all sideways and never touched her dinner.

Si·de-wheel, *attrib.* *U.S.* (See Side *sb.*[1] 27; later examples.) Also **Si·de-wheeled** *a.*

1857 [see Side *sb.*[1] 27]. 1857 W. Chandless *Visit Salt Lake* I. i. 2 Except during the 'June rise' side-wheel boats rarely go up [the Missouri]. 1869 C. L. Brace *New West* i. 27 To change its side-wheel steamers for propellers. 1886 *Harper's Mag.* June 4/1 Limiting steam to side-wheel vessels. 1890 *Ibid.* June 145/1 A wheezy side-wheel boat. 1906 *Ibid.* Feb. 425 An old side-wheeled excursion-boat.

Hence **Si·de-wheeler,** a side-wheel steamer.

1884 [see Side *sb.*[1] 27]. 1888 C. D. Ferguson *Exp. Forty-niner* ii. 18 Struggling out by the aft gangway near the wheel, it being a side-wheeler. 1904 *N.Y. Times* 16 May 5 It was there that the two side-wheelers landed their passengers. *fig.* 1926 *Amer. Speech* I. Apr. 369/2 They [sc. baseball players] are 'south-paws' or 'port-siders' or 'side-wheelers' when they are left-handed.

Side-winder[1]. Add: (Earlier example.)

1840 *Daily Pennant* (St. Louis) 14 May (Th.) Tim gives him a 'sockdoliger' and two side-winders, and leaves him for dead on the spot.

2. 'A tree knocked down unexpectedly by the falling of another' (*Terms Forestry & Logging* 1905).

Sidey: see Sidy *a.*[2]

Sidhe (ʃi), *sb. pl.* [Irish *sidhe*: see *folk of peace* s.v. *Folk 3 c.] Fairy folk, fairies.

1906 S. Gwynn *Fair Hills Irel.* ii. 34 The heroes of the mysterious Tuatha de Danann who after their defeat by the Milesians withdrew from daylight into the recesses of the earth—and who are still there, fairy folk, the people of the *Sidhe*. 1919 N. Hill *Story Scott. Ch.* i. 3 Forests, rivers, and wells were thought to be haunted by Sidhe, a sort of fairy or elve, not always unfriendly. 1922 Christine Orr *Kate Curlew* v. 105 You did not think, then, that I was a prince of the *sidhe*.

Siding, *vbl. sb.* **5. b.** *U.S.* (Earlier examples.)

1829 J. F. Cooper *Wish-ton-wish* xvii, [Dwellings] constructed of a firm frame-work, neatly covered with sidings of boards. 1831 Peck *Guide for Emigrants* 189 Putting on the siding, or enclosing buildings.

Siege, *sb.* **6.** *fig.* (U.S. example. Also common in recent use, of illness.)

1929 *Randolph Enterprise* (W. Va.) 11 Apr. 1/1 The..Literary Society had another heavy siege Tuesday night of this week.

Siemens (sī·mĕnz, ‖zī·mĕns). The name of E. Werner von *Siemens* (1816–1892), German inventor, engineer, and manufacturer, or his brother Sir William *Siemens* (1823–1883), German-English engineer, used attrib. or in the genitive to denote certain processes, appliances, inventions, or laws, discovered, invented, or formulated by one or other of them.

Sometimes combined with the name of another inventor, as in the *Siemens-Halske Battery, Siemens-Martin process.*

1866 *Chambers's Jrnl.* 25 Aug. 543/2 For..any..process in which an intense heat is required, the Siemens furnace is eminently suitable. 1867 R. Sabine *Electr. Telegraph* 226 Siemens and Halske's modification of Daniell's Battery. *Ibid.* 978 The Siemens and Whitwell stoves. 1880 *Encycl. Brit.* XIII. 295/1 The composition of the gas from a Siemens gas producer. *Ibid.* 316/1 The Siemens-Cowper and Whitwell stoves. 1884 W. H. Greenwood *Steel & Iron* xviii. (ed. 2) 406 The Siemens direct process for the production of steel in the Siemens regenerative rotating furnace. *Ibid.* xx. 452 The Siemens or Siemens-Martin process. 1884 Knight *Dict. Mech.* Suppl., Siemens-Halske Battery. 1900 *Knowledge* 1 Dec. 281/1 An ordinary Siemens telegraph relay. 1912 *Motor Manual* iii. (ed. 14) 125 The Siemens metallic tungsten lamps are practically unaffected by shock.

Sierra Leone (siˌe·rā lĭō·n). The name of a British colony and protectorate on the west coast of Africa used attrib. to designate certain diseases, plants, etc., characteristic of or occurring therein, as **Sierra Leone fever,** a form of remittent fever (*Cent. Dict.*); **Sierra Leone peach,** the Guinea peach. Hence **Sie·rra-Leo·nean, -Leo·nian** *a.*, of or pertaining to Sierra Leone.

1866 *Treas. Bot.* s.v. *Sarcocephalus, S. esculentus* has pink flowers and an edible fruit, of the size of a peach, whence it has been called the Sierra Leone Peach. 1926 A. R. Slater *Introd. Butt-Thompson's Sierra Leone* 5 The relations of the 'Sierra Leonean' and the European are less intimate than they used to be. 1926 Butt-Thompson *Ibid.* Pref. 8 The object of the publication of this book is to give Sierra Leoneans a History of their own. 1926 *Chambers's Jrnl.* Nov. 660 1 Sierra-Leonean solicitors were hurrying to final interviews with retained advocates.

Sieva (sī·vă). In full *Sieva bean*: A tropical American bean of erect or climbing habit, a variety of *Phaseolus lunatus*.

1891 *Century Dict.*

Sieve, *sb.* **5.** *sieve-bottom* (earlier Amer. examples).

1686 S. Sewall *Letter Bk.* 33 Six doz. of Lawn sive Bottoms. 1714 *Essex Inst. Hist. Coll.* XLIII. 225 Sieve Bottoms.

Sifac (sī·fæk). Also **sifaka** (sifæ·kă). [Malagasy.] Any of several lemurs of Madagascar; a variety of the Babacoote or Indri.

1845 *Encycl. Metrop.* XVI. 429/1 It [sc. *Cercopithecus Nemæus*, Cuv.] is a native of Cochin China and Madagascar, where it is called *Sifac*. 1920 *Brit. Museum Return* 88 A Sifaka (*Propithecus deckeni*).

Sifema (si·fēmă). *Geol.* [f. the chemical symbols *Si* silicon, *Fe* iron + first two letters of Magnesium.] A rock rich in silicon, iron, and magnesium.

1930 Joly *Surface-Hist. Earth* 211.

Siffleur (siflœ̄r). [Fr.] **a.** An animal that makes a whistling noise, *spec.* the whistling marmot, *Arctomys pruinosus*.

1703 tr. *La Hontan's Voy. N. Amer.* I. 62 Certain little Beasts, call'd Siffleurs or Whistlers. 1839 *Penny Cycl.* XV. 517/1, *Arctomys Empetra*...This is..the Siffleur of the French Canadians, who apply the same name to the other species of Marmot and to the Badger.

b. (with fem. *-euse*). A whistling artiste.

1923 *Glasgow Herald* 7 July, There could be no doubt about the fact that he [sc. a mouse] was at least something of a siffleur. 1933 *Daily Tel.* 31 May 15/6 The Bishop of Colombo..revealed himself as an accomplished siffleur.

Sig, *sb.* Add: **2.** A solution applied to the grain side of leather before it is stained black. Also *attrib.*

1897 C. T. Davis *Manuf. Leather* (ed. 2) 693 In the making of 'sig' stains, blacks and pastes for leather, borax is the currier's friend. 1903 L. A. Flemming *Pract. Tanning* 51 A good 'sig' is made of forty gallons of water, twelve pounds of salts of tartar, five pounds of bichromate of potash and one quart of ammonia.

Sigh, *v.* Add: **1. c.** Also of turtles.

1929 R. Hughes *High Wind in Jamaica* 81 Only the children's luggage was left untouched: and the turtles. Their melancholy sighing was the sole sound to be heard.

3. c. with cognate object.

1789 Blake *Songs Innoc.*, *On Another's Sorrow* viii, Think not thou canst sigh a sigh, And thy Maker is not by. 1847 C. Brontë *J. Eyre* xvii, She sighed a sigh of ineffable satisfaction, as if her cup of happiness were now full. 1888 Mrs. H. Ward *R. Elsmere* xli, Robert sighed a long sigh.

Sight, *sb.*[1] Add:

1. Sometimes with the addition of the infinitives *to behold, to see,* with an intensifying force.

1865 Mrs. Riddell *Maxwell Drewitt* vi. I. 116 The inn-yards were a sight to behold, crammed full of carriages.

(*b*) In pregnant use, something which calls forth contemptuous, horrified, or amused glances; a shocking, repulsive, or ridiculous thing to look upon.

[1694 Penn *Rise of Quakers* ii. 53 It was not very easie to our Primitive Friends, to make themselves Sights and Spectacles, and the Scorn and Derision of the World.] 1862 F. W. Robinson *Owen* v. iv, I'm getting better now,..I was a sight last week. 1902 Farmer & Henley *Slang, Sight*. 3. An oddity; a scarecrow: also contemptuously, 'Her new jacket was a perfect sight', or 'You've made yourself a regular sight' = 'Not fit to be seen'. 1924 D. H. Lawrence *England, my England* 220 'I don't like you in those clothes,' he said. 'Do I look a sight?' he answered.

d. *Sight unseen*; used by schoolboy bargainers and others with the meaning: Without seeing the object to be exchanged, without previous inspection. *U.S.* and *dial.*

For the earlier phr. *unsight unseen* see Unsight *ppl. a.*[1]

1892 *Dial. Notes* I. v. 231 To trade knives sight unseen is to swap without seeing each other's knife. 1897 *Yearbk. U.S. Dept. Agric.* 427 The intelligent farmer of to-day has got beyond trading 'sight unseen' or 'buying a cat in a bag'.

2. b. (U.S. example.)

1896 J. C. Harris *Sister Jane* 63 If you'll believe me, that ain't all by a long sight.

5. c. Also, an opportunity or chance. *colloq.*

1902 Farmer & Henley *Slang*.

8. c. Contrasted with *faith* (cf. 2 Cor. v. 7 'We walk by faith, not by sight').

1858 W. Brock *Sir H. Havelock* xiii. 216 He might well have doubted of success had he walked by sight. 1871 H. Alford *Hymn*, '*Onward Christian Soldiers*' iii, Till the veil be lifted, Till our faith be sight.

14. c. Any of various devices through which the progress of an operation may be observed; *spec.* (*a*) a pane of glass in a sulphuric acid plant for observing the colours of gases; (*b*) a glass tube or vessel showing the flow of oil in a lubricator.

1912 *Motor Manual* iii. (ed. 14) 125 One way [sc. of indicating whether the rear light is on or off] is to use two 4-volt lamps, one for the rear light and one for the dash or the near-side lamp, especially if this has a small 'sight' or window adapted. *Ibid.* vi. 230 If one notes that the oil drips from the sights steadily and there is no accumulation of oil in the sight-glasses, of course it follows that the oil must be passing down the tubes.

16. c. In the sense 'by sight', 'working by sight'.

1918 M. B. Owen *Typewriting Speed* 145 The constant shifting of the eyes in sight writing. *Ibid.* 147 The sight typist writes spasmodically. *Ibid.* 153 Many sight writers use all the fingers.

17. sight bill, cheque, draft, a bill or draft payable at sight, i.e., on presentation; **sight food,** a device in a lubricator through which the feeding of the oil may be seen; also, a lubricator having such a device; also *attrib.*; **sight-glass** (cf. *14 c (*b*)); **sight-player,** one who is able to play music at sight; so **sight-playing**; **sight-read** *v. intr.*, to read music at sight; **sight-rule** = Alidade; **sight-setter,** on a warship, a member of a gun's crew whose duty is to keep the gun-sight at the correct elevation as shown by the range indicator.

1863 'E. Kirke' *My Southern Friends* xxii. 232, I enclose you *sight check of Branch Bank of Cape Fear on Bank of Republic, for $10,820. 1890 *Florida Plant. Rec.* 60 Your favor of the 22d ult. enclosing *sight draft on Messrs Habersham for $200. 1863 'E. Kirke' *My Southern Friends* xxi. 214 Dawsey's 'account' is a good one. He never draws against shipments, but holds on, and sells sight drafts, thus making the exchange. 1904 'O. Henry' *Cabbages & Kings* xiv. 254 It's a gold mine. It's a sight-draft on your president man for twenty thousand dollars. 1888 *Lockwood's Dict. Mech. Engin.*, *Sight Feed Lubricator, a lubricator in which the flowing or non-flowing of the oil is always apparent at sight, being enclosed in, or having to pass through a glass vessel. 1904 A. B. F. Young *Complete Motorist* iv. (ed. 2) 83 In connection with the sight-feed lubricator an important improvement is arranged whereby hot water, which is connected up to the sight feed, circulates from the engine round the lubricating oil. 1928 *Daily Tel.* 16 Oct. 7 Non-crushable back-lamps and sight-feed fuel gauges on the dashboard are in demand for the new cars. 1912 *sight-glass [see *14 c]. 1909 *Chambers's Jrnl.* May 334/2 Ask an accomplished *sight-player how he is able to translate so readily the symbols he reads with the eye into their relative notes. *Ibid.* 334/1 He maintains that *sight-playing does not depend upon an accurate knowledge of the relationship between notes and keys. 1903 Annie W. Patterson *Schumann* 181 We want more than a facility to '*sight read' in order to fully comprehend. 1909 *Rep. Brit. Assoc.* 767 Through the central pivot passes a pin, carrying a *sight-rule or alidade on the front of the transparent disc. 1909 *Cent. Dict.* Suppl., *Sight-setter. 1920 *Blackw. Mag.* Mar. 332/2 Dully from the concealed gun positions echoed the calls of the sight-setters.

Sight, *v.*[1] **3.** (Earlier U.S. example.)

1787 in *Maryland Hist. Mag.* XIX. 265 The mother of the complainants wife sighted with a compass from the tree.

Sigillaria. Add: **2.** [L. *sigillaria*.] *Roman Antiq.* The last two days of the Saturnalia, when little images were given as presents, especially to children.

1738 *Chambers's Cycl.* s.v., The sigillaria followed immediately after the saturnalia, and held two days. 1841 *Penny Cycl.* XX. 453/1 Children generally received little figures, which were called oscilla, or sigilla, from which the last day of the Saturnalia derived the name 'sigillaria'. 1900 M. B. Huish *Greek Terra-Cotta Statuettes* 214 A part of the Saturnalia at Rome, called Sigillaria, consisted in masters giving their slaves statuettes in wax or clay, and they also offered them as New Year's gifts to their friends.

Sigmoid, *a.* and *sb.* Add: **Sigmoidi·tis,** inflammation of the sigmoid flexure of the colon. **Sigmoi·doscope,** a speculum used in examining the sigmoid flexure; hence **Sigmoidosco·pic** *a.*, of or pertaining to sigmoidoscopy; **Sigmoido·scopy,** examination of the sigmoid flexure by means of a speculum.

1901 Dorland *Med. Dict.* (ed. 2), Sigmoidoscopy. 1906 P. L. Mummery *Sigmoidoscope* 37 A sigmoidoscopic examination will give valuable information if there is any question of being able to remove the growth. *Ibid.* 55 In cases of acute proctitis or sigmoiditis an examination with the sigmoidoscope may afford useful information.

Sign, *sb.* Add: **7.** (*b*) *Theol.* In sacramental ordinances, the outward and visible part which symbolizes the inward and spiritual part.

After the Christian use of L. *signum*, Gr. σημεῖον.

1553 Bradford in Coverdale *Lett. Martyrs* (1564) 293 There is Idolatry in worshipping the outwarde signe of breade and wyne. 1604 *Bk. Com. Prayer, Catechism*, Q. How many parts be there in a Sacrament? *A.* Two: the Outward visible signe, and the Inward spirituall Grace. *c* 1816 J. Marriott *Hymn*, Grant to this child the inward grace, While we the outward sign impart. 1861 *Hymn*, '*O food that weary pilgrims love*', Lord Jesu, Whom, by power divine Now hid beneath the outward sign, We worship and adore. 1898 Mortimer *Cath. Faith & Practice* I. 124 The matter [of a sacrament] is the outward sign; the form that which determines the matter to its special use or purpose.

transf. 1905 [see *Tick *sb.*[3] 3 b]. 1931 V. Dixon *Sebastian Wile* II. ii. § 1 Her governess had said farewell, outward and visible sign that Martha's days of childish servitude were over. 1932 Joan Conquest *Village Pompadour* xi, His christening present, a..pewter tankard, had doubtlessly been the outward sign of his inner and invincible craving.

d. *U.S.* (Earlier examples.)

1692 *Cal. Virginia St. Papers* I. 44 We ranged about to see if we could find the tract of any Indians, but we could not see any fresh signe. 1758 *Ibid.* 255 They..could not discover any fresh sign of Enemy. 1821 J. Fowler *Jrnl.* 33 Heare we find the first fresh sign of bever. *Ibid.* 36 We see old sign of Indeans...We again see the sign of white men a head of us.

e. *Path.* An objective evidence or indication of disease; often with defining word, as of the name of the person who discovered the 'sign' or connected it with its disease (see the medical dicts.).

1885 *Encycl. Brit.* XIX. 223/1 These various physical signs render it impossible to mistake the disease for other maladies the symptoms of which may bear a resemblance to it. 1908 *Practitioner* Jan. 10 We do not obtain ankle clonus, or Babinsky's, or Oppenheim's sign. 1927 G. W. Deeping *Kitty* xv. § 2 Mr. St. George had an undoubted paraplegia. There was definite spasticity of the lower limbs. ..Babinski's sign was present.

12. *sign-language* (earlier U.S. example); *sign-mark* (also fig.), *sign-writer* (Writer 1 b).

1847 Parkman in *Knickerbocker Mag.* XXX. 234 Knowing nothing at that time of the *sign-language of the Indians. 1911 *Chambers's Jrnl.* June 368/1 In continental Europe the horrors of war are much more present in men's mind, since its awful *signmark is indelibly written even today on many a fair landscape. 1871 Callingham *Sign Writing* i. 1 It is curious that the term '*sign-writer' is not to be found in any encyclopædia or dictionary, ancient or modern... Even Kelly's ponderous 'Post Office London Directory' does not deem the sign-writer worthy of separate enumeration in its list of trades. *Ibid.* 17 The formation of alphabetic characters as at present practised by the sign-writer. 1881 *Instr. Census Clerks* (1885) 52. 1910 *Daily News* 7 Nov. 3 A sign-writer has stumbled over a much easier word.

Sign, *v.*[1] Add: **5. b.** Also with *up*.

1903 A. H. Lewis *The Boss* 186 You can tell by th' way they go to bat, whether th' Blackberry has signed up to them to kill our franchise. 1926 *Ladies' Home Jrnl.* Apr. 25 So she signed up for evening classes.

6. c. Also with *up*.

1932 *Radio Times* 1 Apr. 5/2 Seversky immediately signed the violinist up for his broadcast.

Signal, *sb.* Add: **5. a.** *signal-code*.

1877 Habberton *Jericho Road* 94 Between the societies of neighboring counties there often existed signal-codes, and unwritten extradition and reciprocity treaties.

c. *signal corps* (earlier U.S. example).

1881–5 G. B. McClellan *Own Story* 135 The weak point in the signal corps..was that its officers were not trained soldiers.

d. signal strength *Wireless*, the strength of signals in a receiver, expressed by means of R and numerical degrees from 0 to 10.

1912 *Marconigraph* II. 269/1 Observations..showed that during totality the signal strength was increased. 1923 E. W. Marchant *Radio Telegr. & Teleph.* xi. 117 It is unlikely that we shall ever be able to forecast 'signal strength' with any greater certainty than we can forecast the weather that we are likely to have on any particular day. 1926 R. W. Hutchinson *Wireless* x. 175 Increasing the Signal Strength of a Crystal Receiver.

Signary (si·gnări). [f. L. *signum* Sign *sb.* + -ary[1], after *syllabary*.] An arrangement of signs; the signs which constitute the syllabic or alphabetic symbols of a language.

1902 *Encycl. Brit.* XXVII. 730/2 Probably all the signs in the hieroglyphic signary can be employed in their primary sense. 1909 A. J. Evans *Scripta Minoa* I. p. v, I have endeavoured to supply a preliminary apparatus criticus in the form of tables and explanatory catalogues of the different signaries. 1924 L. Eckenstein *Tutankh-aten* v. 42 There were other scribes of other signaries and languages who inscribed soft clay tablets with a copper stilus.

Signature, *sb.* Add: **8.** (See quot.)

1901 Dorland *Med. Dict.* (ed. 2), *Signature*, that part of a prescription which gives direction as to the taking of the medicine.

9. In full *signature tune*: A special tune used in broadcast programmes to announce a particular band.

1932 *Daily Mail* 4 Mar., B.B.C. Band's 'Signature'. 'Just the Time for Dancing' and 'Till Next Time' are the titles of the 'signature' tunes selected by Mr. Henry Hall for his new B.B.C. Dance Band, to be used every time the band begins or concludes a broadcast.

Sign-board. Add: Also *U.S.*, a board on a guide-post to direct travellers.

1833 *Knickerbocker Mag.* I. 88 Independent of roads and sign-boards. 1835 *Southern Lit. Messenger* I. 580 The post of a sign-board where several roads meet.

Signer. Add: **1. b.** *spec.* in *U.S.* One of the signatories to the Declaration of Independence.

1928 W. A. White *Masks in Pageant* 67 The grandson of a President and the great-grandson of a Signer.

Signet, *sb.* Add: **1. b.** The ring-shaped form of an early stage of the plasmodium of malaria.

1903 *Jrnl. Tropical Med.* 15 July 222/2 While some of the stained signets were much larger than others, there was nothing else seen to suggest a mixed infection.

Signet-ring. Add: **b.** A form of the plasmodium of malaria in which the ring-shaped body is thickened on one side.

1901 J. Ewing in *Jrnl. Exper. Med.* V. 446.

Sign-post (səi·nˌpōᵘst), *v.* [f. the sb.] *trans.* To equip or provide with sign-posts.

1923 *Daily Mail* 19 May 5 Where the road is not so good and badly needs proper signposting. *Ibid.* 21 May 4 Dartmoor is moderately well sign-posted. 1930 *Aberdeen Press & Jrnl.* 8 May 5 The R.A.C. propose only to signpost the main arteries.

Sikelian, Sikimi: see *Sicel, *Shikimi.

Sikkim (si·kim). The name of a native state in the Himalayas used attrib. to designate certain trees, fruits, animals, etc., native to or occurring therein.

1866 *Treas. Bot.* s.v. *Oak*, A similar effect is produced in the Sikkim Himalaya [sc. oak]. 1877 *Encycl. Brit.* VI. 688/1 The Sikkim cucumber. 1905 E. Candler *Unveiling of Lhasa* iii. 56 The shao, or Sikkim stag.

Sikra (sī·krā). Also **sikhra, sikar, sikr.** [Skr. शिखर *śikhara* point, peak, spire.] A pyramidal tower on a Hindu temple, sometimes having convexly curved sides.

1829 J. Tod *Ann. & Antiq. Rajast'han* I. 670 The pinnacle or *sikra* rises, like the crown of the Hindú Cybele. 1838 *Penny Cycl.* XII. 238/1 The body of the temple, or sanctuary, ..over which rises a pyramidal *sikr*, or roof.

Siksika (si·ksikă). = Black foot 1.

1902 *Encycl. Brit.* XXIX. 466/1 Blackfeet (Siksika).

Silcot (si·lkɒt). Also **silcott.** [f. Silk *sb.* + first syllable of Cotton *sb.*[1]] A material made of cotton finished to resemble silk.

1894 Jeanette E. Davis *Elem. Mod. Dressmaking* (1895) 93 Varieties of silkette or silcot (cottons finished to look and feel like silk). 1923 *Daily Mail* 28 Feb. 5 Silcott Petticoat with small crystal frill.

Silence, *sb.* Add: **2. d.** *spec.* The Two Minutes' Silence observed at 11 a.m., on the anniversary of Armistice Day (11 Nov. 1918).

1919 *Times* 12 Nov. 15/6 The Great Silence...At 11 o'clock yesterday morning the nation, in response to the King's invitation, paid homage to the Glorious Dead by keeping a two minutes' silence for prayer and remembrance. *Ibid.* 16/1 On the Stock Exchange, after the silence, a gong was sounded. 1930 *B.B.C. Year-Bk.* 78 Broadcasting the Silence November 11th, 1928.

7. silence cabinet, a sound-proof booth or small room from which a person may speak or telephone.

1893 Preece & Stubbs *Man. Teleph.* 227 At most telephone exchanges a 'silence cabinet' is provided in the public office. 1930 *B.B.C. Year-Bk.* 309 In Savoy Hill there are nine studios, six of which are equipped with silence cabinets (these are small rooms adjacent to the studios from which the announcer can speak before switching over to the studio itself).

Silent, *a.* and *sb.* Add:

A. *adj.* **3. e.** *spec.* Given, performed, etc. without the accompaniment of vocal utterance.

a 1794 Gibbon *Autobiog.* (1900) 191, I..supported with many a sincere and silent vote the rights ..of the mother country. 1848 Sir R. Peel in *Times* 12 Feb. 3 It was with great reluctance..that I gave a silent vote on the first occasion when this matter was brought under our consideration. 1897 *Peel City Guardian & Chron.* 11 Sept., He did not intend to give a silent vote on this question. 1913 *Hastings's Encycl. Relig. & Ethics* VI. 206/2 This so-called 'silent trade' is, in its simplest form, a transaction by way of exchange between persons who are unseen by one another. 1925 H. J. R. Murray *Gen. Rep. Teaching Eng. Lond. Elem. Sch.* 16 The effectiveness of this type of silent reading, as compared with the more usual practice..is obvious. 1931 A. Manning Foster *Auction Bridge* 119 When the opponents are saying 'No bid' they are not necessarily void of high cards. They may be willing to leave the bidders alone while the contract is under the game line, but quite prepared to step in with a punishing double if the game is bid. This is known as the 'Silent Trap'.

f. Of a cinema film: Not accompanied by speech, as distinguished from a *talking* film. Of a cinema or the film industry: That exhibits or is concerned with silent films only.

1929 *Morning Post* 24 May 12/7 One theatre..in New York made £17,600 in one week out of 'The Letter'—more than double its silent-film record. 1930 *Times* 27 Mar. 19/4 The loss incurred in the enforced shelving of many silent films. 1930 *B.B.C. Year-Bk.* 41 The gramophone, the silent screen, the talking screen, the wireless. 1931 [see *Screen *sb.*[1] 1 f].

4. c. Of machinery, etc.: That runs with a comparative absence of noise; that operates with little or no noise.

1887 *Encycl. Brit.* XXII. 524/1 Dr. Otto's 'silent' engine. 1904 A. B. F. Young *Complete Motorist* iv. (ed. 2) 103 The silent working of the Lanchester car makes it also an extremely useful carriage for town use. 1931 *Illustr. London News* 29 Aug. 342/3 The third speed is a 'twin top', with easy silent engagement by dog-clutches. 1931 B. Brown *Talking Pictures* x. 246 It is evident that gears and such like parts will revolve at high speed with reasonable noise; when slowed down they will be very much more silent. 1932 *B.B.C. Year-Bk.* 429/2 It..produces no sound in a receiver, except possibly a very faint 'hiss'. It is, in fact, a 'silent' carrier wave.

B. *sb.* **3.** A silent film (A. *3 f).

1929 *Morning Post* 24 May 12/7 Every recognised tradition of the 'silents' seems to have gone by the board. 1931 B. Brown *Talking Pictures* xi. 289 Over-acting for silents was accepted as natural.

Silhouette, *sb.* Add: **2. b.** The contour of a garment.

1920 *Glasgow Herald* 27 Nov. 4 The silhouette of this season is..much more attractive than that last year approved by Dame Fashion. *Ibid.* 4 Dec. 4 See that you preserve the silhouette of the gown.

Silica. b. Add: *silica dust*; **silica-wool** = *slag wool* (see Slag *sb.* 5).

1906 *Chambers's Jrnl.* Aug. 599/1 Slag-wool, or silica-wool, is in appearance and properties similar to asbestos. 1918 *Act* 8 & 9 *Geo. V* c. 14 § 1 (3) Any industry..involving exposure to silica dust.

Silk, *sb.* and *a.* Add:

1. (*b*) With defining word, usually indicating silk at some process or stage of manufacture, or some particular kind of silk: see *Hard *a.* 1 f, Raw *a.* 2 a, Reeled *ppl. a.*, *Soft *a.* 27, Spun *ppl. a.* 1, Thrown *ppl. a.*; also *Jap 2, *Schappe, Tusser 1 b, etc. *Waste silk*, the inferior silk from the outside of the cocoons and from cocoons out of which the moths have been allowed to escape.

1797 *Encycl. Brit.* (ed. 3) XVII. 486/1 Before you begin to wind, you must prepare your cocoons..In stripping them of that waste silk that surrounds them, and which served to fasten them to the twigs. 1851 *Illustr. Catal. Gt. Exhib.* III. III. 505/2 Illustrations of the production of waste silk from the eggs [sc. cocoons] of the silk-worm. 1887 *Colonial & Indian Exhib. 1886, Rep. Col. Sect.* 352 Specimens of waste silk under the head of 'Punjam'.

e. Silk sold in the form of thread or twist for purposes of embroidery, mending, sewing, etc.; usually with defining word, as *embroidery silk*, *knitting silk, sewing silk*.

1480–1826 [see Sewing *vbl. sb.*[1] 4]. 1851 *Illustr. Catal. Gt. Exhib.* III. III. 506/1 Veil, vest, and shawl embroidering silk. 1887 *Colonial & Indian Exhib. 1886, Rep. Col. Sect.* 332 The other parts worked in wool and silk.

f. *Artificial silk* [F. *soie artificielle*], thread or yarn manufactured from collodion or wood pulp; also, a fabric resembling silk made from this (often abbreviated *art silk*, and (as one word) *artsilk*).

1885 *Jrnl. Soc. Chem. Ind.* IV. 34 Mr J. B. Payne exhibited..some samples of 'artificial silk', a new filament produced by pressure through a die, from pyroxylin, the invention of Mr. J. W. Swan. 1896 *Jrnl. Q. U. Junior Sci. Club* May 56 The artificial silk can be prepared at about one-third of the cost of natural silk. 1902 *Encycl. Brit.* XXVIII. 508/2 This artificial silk [manufactured from collodion] was utilized by De Mare in 1894 for making [gas] mantles..and in the next year Knofler and then Plaissetty patented the manufacture of mantles by a similar process to De Mare's. 1921 T. Woodhouse tr. *Foltzer's Art Silk* iii. 19 Count Hilaire de Chardonnet, the great pioneer of artificial silk-making. 1922 *Daily Mail* 2 Dec. 1 Advt., Three charming designs in silcot, cotton, satin and art silk stockinette. 1928 *Ibid.* 3 Aug. 18/2 Snias and British Enkas were firmer among Artsilks.

2. c. So *to wear silk*.

1898 A. E. T. Watson *The Turf* 189 A gentleman, when this misfortune happens to him..can cease to wear silk, or at any rate need not ride over hurdles or fences.

4. *U.S.* (Earlier example.) Phr. *In silk*: at that stage when the silk (of maize) is prominent.

1770 Washington *Diaries* I. 395 Many Stalks were putting out entire new Shoots with young and tender Silk. 1774 P. V. Fithian *Jrnl. Virginia* 19 July (1900) 212 The Corn is beginning pretty generally to tassel, & I saw one hill in Silk, and in Blossom. *Ibid.* 21 July 213 Now many of the Hills are in Silk. 1784 J. F. D. Smyth *Tour U.S.* I. xxxviii. 295 These tassels are as soft as silk...This state of it is denominated the Corn being in silk.

b. The staple of cotton.

1870 Yeats *Nat. Hist. Comm.* II. (1872) 200 The value of cotton in commerce depends on the length and strength of the silk or staple. Cottons may be divided into the long silk and short silk.

c. A silky lustre in some rubies and sapphires, due to microscopic crystals, and considered a defect.

1886 *Jrnl. Franklin Inst.* CXXII. 380 In many genuine rubies we find a silky structure (called *silk* by jewellers). 1903 W. R. Cattelle *Precious Stones* 47 Rubies generally contain clusters of light or dark-colored spots...White, glistening streaks in the grain of the stone, called silk, are of frequent occurrence...If silk shows plainly when the stone is faced up, it is one of the most serious defects.

6. e. Made of or produced by silk threads, embroidery silk, etc.

1837 *Penny Cycl.* VII. 77/1 A piece of silk embroidery. 1880 E. J. Reed *Japan* II. 101 A very large and particularly fine specimen of Kioto silk embroidery in a picture..crowded with detailed figures exquisitely worked. 1887 *Encycl. Brit.* XXII. 91/1 Among the chief manufactures may be mentioned the gold, silver, and silk embroideries.

10. silk-hatted *a.*, that wears a silk hat; **silk-surface** *a.*, that has a surface resembling silk; **silk waste,** waste silk (see *1 (*b*)); also *attrib.*; **silk-wool,** wool which has been so treated with an acidified solution of bleaching-powder that it takes on a silky appearance.

1903 W. Le Queux *Seven Secrets* xxii, The *silk-hatted, frock-coated existence of the fashionable physician. 1920 P. G. Wodehouse *Damsel in Distress* iv, The silk hatted young man. 1932 *Sale Catal.*, Pure *Silk Surface Stockings. 1842 *Encycl. Brit.* (ed. 7) XX. 350/2 To introduce such alterations in the spinning of *silk waste as will supersede the cutting, carding, and scutching processes...The art of silk waste spinning, we may observe, is still in its infancy. 1881 *Instr. Census Clerks* (1885) 67 Silk Waste Spinner. 1901 *Chambers's Jrnl.* Apr. 217/1 The silk-waste, plush, and velvet industries. 1859 L. Oliphant *Narr. Earl of Elgin's Mission China & Japan* (1860) II. 255 The Japanese wear in winter garments thickly padded either with cotton or *silk wool. 1908 *Practitioner* Nov. 760 Silcool is a form of vegetable silk-wool.

b. silk bark, a South African tree, *Gymnosporia acuminata*; **silk-wood,** (*b*) see quot.; (*c*) = Calabur tree.

1912 *Cape Times* 12 Oct. 9 (Pettman) In the gorge beneath the fall an indigenous thicket, yellow-wood, Hottentot cherry, *silk bark, has been allowed to remain. 1922 Schlich *Man. Forestry* (ed. 4) I. 229 *Silkwood (*Flindersia Mazlini*).

Silk (silk), *v.* [f. the sb.]

1. *trans.* To clothe in or cover with silk.

1864 Chr. Rossetti *Farm Walk* Poet. Wks. (1904) 367/2 I've seen grand ladies plumed and silked. 1909 Marg. B. Saunders *Litany Lane* I. iii, Gorgeously furred and laced and scented and silked. 1919 T. Hardy *Sunshade* Poems 460 Twenty years have gone..Since it [sc. a sunshade] was silked in its white or pink.

2. *intr.* Of maize: To produce the silk (see Silk *sb.* 4). *U.S.*

1878 J. H. Beadle *Western Wilds* xv. 245 The summers are short and the nights cool. Corn will not silk. 1902 *U.S. Monthly Weather Rev.* July 346 (Cent. D. Suppl.) Corn mostly silking or earing.

Silked, *a.* Add: **2.** In the silk stage of growth (see Silk *sb.* 4).

1879 *Scribner's Monthly* Nov. 134/1 Leagues of Kansas Corn, seen in..their glory of silked and tasselled..strength.

Silker (si·lkəɹ). [f. Silk *sb.* + -er[1].] One who works in or with silk; in various technical uses.

1881 *Instr. Census Clerks* (1885) 50 Piano Manufacturing. ..Silker. *Ibid.* 69 Cotton...Silker. 1903 *Sci. Amer. Suppl.* 24 Jan. 22629 (Cent. D. Suppl.) From the cutters' room the leather, which has assumed the shape of the glove, is sent to the 'silkers', who embroider the back. 1921 *Dict. Occup. Terms* (1927) § 414 *Taper*,..*silker*; stitches tape by machine, down seam, in closing upper of a boot or shoe. *Ibid.* § 419 *Silker*; (i) finishes cloth piece..by stitching folds together, by hand, with a silk thread to hold them in position.

Silk grass. Add: **4.** In Australia, the rough bent-grass, *Agrostis scabra*.

1930 Billis & Kenyon *Pastures New* viii. 124 The silk grass, brought over by sheep from Van Dieman's Land, was regarded as a noxious weed.

Sill, *sb.*[1] Add: **4. c.** *Geol.* (See quot.)

1925 J. Joly *Surface-Hist. Earth* Gloss. 192 *Sill*, a fissure in the surface crust extending more or less horizontally.

Siltation (siltē^i·ʃən). [f. Silt *v.* + -ation.] The action of silting.

1932 *Min. Proc. Inst. Civ. Engin.* CCXXXII. 70 Siltation Records.—As there is a considerable quantity of silt in circulation in Bombay harbour, a detailed investigation was carried out during a complete year 1921 to 1922. *Ibid.* 71 Special Siltation Records at Harbour-Mouth.

Silva: see Sylva.

Silver, *sb.* Add: **12. c.** Designating a type of cinematographic screen.

Silver screen, often = talking pictures collectively.

1931 B. Brown *Talking Pictures* i. 19 Somehow there had crept into this new field of endeavour the romance of the silver screen. *Ibid.* v. 128 The popular and highly reflecting 'silver' type [of screen]. 1931 *Recording Sound for Motion Pictures* (ed. L. Cowan) 2 The intent of the magic was merely to bring the two lovers, sound and silver screen, together.

21. silver-bronze (*b*), see quot.; **silver doctor** *Angling*, an artificial fly having a body of tinsel; **silver-fawn** *a.*, a fanciers' term denoting fur of a fawn colour tipped with silver; *sb.* an animal having such fur; **silver-lip** (see quot.); **silver polish,** a polish used for cleaning and brightening silver; **silver ring** *Racing* (see quot. 1921).

c 1930 *Catal. Delta Metal Co. Ltd.* (ed. 11) 20 'Delta' Bronze No. 11 ('Silver Bronze) is a high-class alloy of a silver-white colour; it is malleable and takes a beautiful polish, and is specially suitable..for all purposes where a strong non-rusting material of a silver colour is required. 1895 *Army & Navy Co-op. Soc. Price List* 15 Sept. 1435 Salmon Flies...*Silver Doctor. 1902 *Encycl. Brit.* XXV. 447/1 In tidal pools there are few better flies than a silver-doctor tied exceedingly small. 1931 *Hardy's Anglers' Guide* 31 Your fairy shrimp, just as pretty..as any Jock Scott or Silver Doctor. 1913 W. Bateson *Mendel's Princ. Heredity* 81 Similarly the chocolate colour when diluted gives what fanciers call '*silver-fawn'. 1914 *Rep. Brit. Assoc.* 173 Five matings between silver-fawns gave 28 silver-fawn young. 1901 *Knowledge* Sept. 209/1 The large Austro-Malayan oyster, the valuable '*silver-lip' and 'gold-lip' of commerce. 1925 *Morris Owner's Man.* 34 The Radiator Casing..should be polished frequently, using a good brand of metal or *silver polish. 1921 E. Wallace *Law Four Just Men* ix. 261, I found a poor little bookmaker in the silver ring—the *silver ring is the enclosure where smaller bets are made than in Tattersall's reservation. 1928 J. H. Thomas in *Hansard's Parl. Debates* CCXX. 500 If there are these advantages, it would give them to the silver ring, to Tattersall's, and to others. *Ibid.* 501 When the totalisator is in operation, you will have the totalisator for the silver ring and for Tattersall's.

b. silver jackal, either of two South African animals, *Canis mesomelas* and *Vulpes chama*; **silver moth,** any of various moths marked with silver.

1892 J. A. Nicolls & Eglington *Sportsman S. Afr.* 95 The '*Silver Jackal', which is the largest and most common of the South African Jackals. 1893 *Trans. S. Afr. Phil. Soc.* V. II. p. xlvi, Mr. R. Trimen exhibited specimens of the '*Silver Moth' (*Leto Venus*) from the Knysna district of the Cape Colony.

d. silver-sides *U.S.* (earlier example).

1851 R. Glisan *Jrnl. Army Life* viii. (1874) 88 The purer streams from the hills abound in silver-sides.

e. silver-sword, a Hawaiian composite plant, *Argyroxiphium sandwicense*, having silvery hairs on its leaves, and rose-purple flowers.

1898 Jean A. Owen *Hawaii* ii. 40 The peculiar Silver-sword growing in the snowy region. 1917 *Nature* C. 57/2 Among the peculiar plants of the island is the silversword.

Silver age. 1. b. Add: Also *attrib.*

1863 Conington *Virgil, Æn.* III. 184 *note* II. 205/1 The poets and silver-age prose authors. 1929 R. Hughes *High Wind Jamaica* 66 A silver-age conception.

Silver-leaf. 3. Read: In full *silver leaf disease*: A disease incident to trees belonging to the genus *Prunus*, especially plum-trees, which causes the leaves to assume an unhealthy silvery colour.

1890 [see Dict.]. 1902 Percival in *Jrnl. Linn. Soc.* XXXV. 390 The disease known as 'Silver-leaf' is..confined to the *Pruneæ*. *Ibid.* 391 Specimens of plum- and apricot-trees affected with 'silver-leaf' disease. 1910 F. T. Brooks in *Rep. Brit. Assoc.* 776 Some Observations on the Silver-Leaf Disease of Fruit Trees. 1921 *Discovery* May 131/2 One disease of plums, known, because it causes the leaves to become silvery, as 'Silver Leaf', propagates itself only on dead wood.

Silverling[2]. [f. Silver *sb.* and *a.* + -ling[1].] A fish of a silver colour, *spec.* the tarpon.

1763 [see Crucian].

Silver maple. *U.S.* A common species of maple (*Acer saccharinum* or *eriocarpum*), also called *white* and *soft maple*.

1846 D. J. Browne *Trees Amer.* 95 Silver Maple, Silver-leaved Maple, [in] New York. 1861 *Trans. Ill. Agric. Soc.* IV. 207 They are almost entirely silver maples, embracing 25,000 trees. 1880 *Harper's Mag.* June 69 The clustered buds upon the silver maples burst in their exuberance. 1897 G. B. Sudworth *Nomencl. Arbor. Flora U.S.* 288 Weeping Silver Maple..Variegated Maple, etc. 1929 E. W. Howe *Plain People* 20 The tree was called a silver maple, and we children believed that when it was old enough to bear, the fruit would be silver dollars.

Silver paper. 2. Add: Also, loosely, tinfoil used chiefly as a damp-proof wrapping for tobacco and confectionery. *colloq.*

1911 *Concise Oxf. Dict.* 1930 *B.B.C. Year-Bk.* 404 The balance of the subscriptions..is paid into the local Radio Circle Funds, which are further increased in various ways such as by the sale of 'silver paper'.

Silver poplar. *U.S.* The white poplar (*Populus alba*) or a variety of this, so called from the silvery under-surface of the leaves.

1853 B. F. Taylor *Jan. & June* (1871) 80 The leaves of the Silver poplar, in breaths of air the faintest, go all day like French clocks. 1861 *Trans. Ill. Agric. Soc.* IV. 448 The Silver Poplar is an abominable pest in loose soil, casting up suckers. 1880 *Harper's Mag.* June 21/2 The silver-poplars showed only their leaden side.

Silvic(s, Silviculture, etc.: see Sylvic, etc.

Sima (səi·mă). *Geol.* [f. Si(licon + Ma(gnesia.)] That part of the earth's crust which lies immediately underneath the sial. Also in *simasphere*.

1909 [see *Sial]. 1924 Skerl tr. *A. Wegener's Orig. Continents & Oceans* p. viii, Similar rocks or magmas of the same composition underlie the sial of the continents...They constitute the sima (silica plus magnesia), in contradistinction to the sial. *Ibid.* 131 The simasphere is about 10,000 times as rigid as sealing-wax at the temperature of a room. 1926 *Encycl. Brit.* II. 172.

Simbil (si·mbil). [Native name.] An African stork, *Ciconia* or *Sphenorhynchus abdimi*, with bronze or black upper parts and white belly. So **Si·mbere.**

1869–73 T. R. Jones *Cassell's Bk. Birds* IV. 70 The Simbil (*Sphenorhynchus Abdimii*) is an inhabitant of Southern Africa, and represents a division of..birds having the face bare...The flesh of the Simbil is regarded by the colonists as excellent food.

Simiid (si·miˌid). [ad. mod. L. *Simiidæ*, f. Simia: see -id[3].] A member of the family *Simiidæ* of anthropoid apes.

1915 E. R. Lankester *Divers. Naturalist* 285 It might quite well have been described as the jaw of a simiid—a large ape allied to the chimpanzee—with some unimportant resemblance to a human one.

Similative (si·milătiv), *a.* *Gram.* [f. L. *similis* like + -ative.] Denoting or expressing similarity or likeness. Also as *sb.*, a similative word, case, verbal element, or compound.

1883 *N.E.D.* s.v. *Air* B. 3. 1903 *Amer. Anthropologist* Jan.–Mar. 13 Besides these, comitatives, similatives, partitives, and suffixes expressing similar ideas, are found. 1911 H. Bradley in *Encycl. Brit.* XXV. 209/1 The many ocularly similative uses of ordinary words, such as 'tin' for money.

Simmer, *v.*[1] Add: **1. d.** *To simmer down*: to become quiet; to lose heat; to calm down from an angry or excited state.

1889 Barrère & Leland *Dict. Slang, Simmer down!* (American), an exclamation to exhort one to silence. 1897 W. Beatty *Secretar* xiii. 102 In a while..he simmered down. 1902 Cutcliffe Hyne *Mr. Horrocks, Purser* 42 First Class passengers..don't handicap matters by interference—once they have simmered down.

'Simmon, *sb.*[3] *U.S.* Colloquial abbreviation of Persimmon. Also *attrib.*

1834 *Knickerbocker Mag.* III. 36 They seemed to me to fall just as fast as if I was shakin down 'simmons. 1839 *Southern Lit. Messenger* V. 378/2, I ask you no odds—the longest pole, you know, takes the simmon. 1860 Bartlett *Dict. Amer.* ed. 3) s.v., 'The longest pole knocks down the 'simmons.' 1881 *Harper's Mag.* Apr. 729/2 An' pleased they wuz ter see it—pleased as boys in 'simmon-time. 1883 P. M. Hale *Woods & Timbers N. Carolina* 117 The basis of a beverage, by no means despicable, called 'Simmon Beer. *a* 1869 *Dixie Land* (Farmer *Amer.*) I wish I was in de land of cotton, 'Simmon seed and sandy bottom. *a* 1909 'O. Henry' *Roads of Destiny* xxi. 350 That's why you see me cake-walking with the ex-rebs to the illegitimate tune about 'simmon seeds and cotton.

Simoleon (simōᵘ·lĭən). *U.S. slang.* [Origin obscure; ? modelled on *napoleon*.] A dollar.

1903 *Kansas City Daily Times* 23 Dec. (Cent. D. Suppl.) She wears a dress—it cost no less Than ninety-five simoleons. 1907 Mulford *Bar-20* xxv. 245 'Cortez panatella—two for a simoleon.' 1913 — *Coming of Cassidy* vii. 112 Sixty-two bucks, three score an' two simoleons; all I've got, every cent. 1927 J. Barbican *Confess. Rum-Runner* xiv. 148 'Four hundred simoleons a week these fellows pay for protection.'

Simp (simp), U.S. colloq. abbreviation of Simpleton.

1916 'B. M. Bower' *Phantom Herd* vii. 112 You can set some simp at it that don't know any better. 1921 R. D. Paine *Comr. Rolling Ocean* vi. 104, I heard you call this big simp of a Maddigan every name you could lay tongue to. 1922 Titus *Timber* xxvii. 240 'What can I do?' 'Stall, you poor simp.'

Simpatico (simpæ·tiko), *a.* Also (fem.) **simpatica.** [It.] Characterized by tender feeling.

1876 *Times* 13 May 6/5 The charming and *simpatica* Princess Margherita was leaning on his arm. 1888 *Q. Rev.* Oct. 508 The most *simpatico* specimen by Bassano, 'The Good Samaritan'. 1918 Max Beerbohm *And Even Now* (1920) 151 Mrs. T—, a woman whom..the word *simpatica* described exactly. 1927 *Daily Tel.* 6 Dec. 15/2 'Windmills and Waterways' is a book best described by that felicitous and illuminating Italian expression 'simpatico.'

Simple, *a.* Add: **6. b.** *Simple-lifer*, one who lives 'the simple life'.

1913 *Punch* 23 July 81/1 To buy up Buckingham Palace with a view to its being used as a cottage-annexe for simple-lifers. 1921 *Glasgow Herald* 29 Jan. 8 Even the most enthusiastic of simple-lifers would object to a book of verses under any bough with the ground as sodden as a bog.

15. b. (*e*) Applied to those vows which are taken by religious in the early stage of their profession and from which they may be dispensed: opp. to *solemn*.

1756–9 A. Butler *Lives Saints* (1780) X. 102. 1868 *Chambers's Encycl.* X. 31/2 Bishops are held to possess the power of dispensing in simple vows generally. 1884 Addis & Arnold *Cath. Dict.* (1897) 934/1 According to the law enacted by Pope Pius IX in 1857, only simple vows are to be taken after the noviceship in all religious orders.

Simply, *adv.* **6. d.** Add: Often in phr. *simply and solely*.

1872 Calverley *Fly Leaves, Lovers & a Reflection*, Simply and solely to rhyme with 'world'. 1920 *Act* 10 & 11 *Geo. V* c. 48 Sch. II, Any loss or damage due simply and solely to the existence of a state of war.

Sims (simz). The name of J. M. *Sims* (1813–1883), New York gynæcologist, used attrib. or in the genitive to denote certain instruments invented by him, and the position for an operation devised by him.

1890 Billings *Med. Dict.* 1908 *Practitioner* Sept. 436 The patient..is placed in the Sims position.

Sin, *sb.* Add: **2. d.** *In sin*: in a state of free sexual union or adultery.

1912 Dolf Wyllarde *Career of Beauty Darling* xvii, 'It's twelve shillings if ye are truly married',..'and fourteen if ye are living in sin!' 1925 A. P. Herbert *Laughing Ann* 92 Don't tell my mother I'm living in sin. 1932 *Times Lit. Suppl.* 1 Oct. 758/3 Lady Brabant..invites Niedermann, the composer, and Olga Nicolai, the soprano, to stay with her ..finds that they are 'living in sin', then cancels the invitation only to find that they have since been married.

Sine[2]. **4.** Add: *sine-law, -shape*; **sine-wave,** 'a wave in which the vibrations of the particles of the transmitting medium are simple harmonic motions' (Cent. D. Suppl.).

1930 *B.B.C. Year-Bk.* 451 Sine wave, a wave form representing an alternating quantity which varies according to a *sine law. 1913 *Wireless World* I. 27/2 Continuous waves of perfect *sine-shape. 1893 D. E. Jones tr. *H. Hertz's Electric Waves* 17 The vibration of the primary conductor is, at any rate to a first approximation, a uniformly damped *sine-wave of determinate period. 1902 *Encycl. Brit.* XXXIII. 223/1 In Squier and Crehore's Synchronograph system 'sine waves' of current, instead of sharp 'makes and breaks', or sharp reversals, are employed for transmitting signals. 1923 E. W. Marchant *Radio Telegr. & Teleph.* viii. 99 One of the chief difficulties in using it [sc. a method of sending signals] is the fact that it does not usually give a pure sine wave.

Sinfonia (sinfonī·ă). *Mus.* [It., = Symphony.] In early Italian operas, the overture.

1884 *Encycl. Brit.* XVII. 87/1 The sinfonia or overture which is often associated with his [sc. Scarlatti's] name.

Sinful, *a.* Add: **2. b.** (Later U.S. example.) Also, unfairly or excessively large, etc.

1869 'Mark Twain' *Innoc. Abr.* ix, They take with them a quantity of food, and when the commissary department fails, they 'skirmish', as Jack terms it, in his sinful, slangy way. 1881 J. C. Harris *Uncle Remus* xxviii, De way he stir up dem bees wuz sinful. 1920 P. G. Wodehouse *Damsel in Distress* ii. 35 The money that boy makes is sinful.

Sing, *sb.* Add: **1.** In wider use: Any noise produced by an inanimate object having the quality of a musical note. *On the sing*: (of a kettle) singing.

1917 E. C. Middleton *Way of Air* 70 The familiar 'sing' of an approaching shell. 1927 G. W. Deeping *Kitty* xxx. § 2 'All the kettles—' 'Two are boiling, miss; the other's on the sing.' 1930 A. Agius in *Carmina* Oct. 45 The sing Of a stone from the sling. 1930 *Sel. Gloss. Motion Pict. Techn.* (Acad. Techn. Bureau Hollywood), *Sing*, undesirable high-frequency oscillations in the recording circuit.

2. b. A sing-song; a gathering for community singing. *U.S.*

1850 N. Kingsley *Diary* 140 We had a fine sing in the Evening which put me in mind of home. 1895 *Century Mag.* Aug. 570/2 There had been a 'sing' at the house of Deacon Pelew. 1924 P. Marks *Plastic Age* 137 Spring brought first rain and slush and then the 'sings'. There was a fine stretch of lawn in the center of the campus, and on clear nights the students gathered there for a sing.

Singer[1]. Add: **1. c.** *Singers' seat*, a seat occupied by a church-choir; a 'singing-seat'. *U.S.*

1861 Mrs. Stowe *Pearl Orr's Isl.* I. ix. 72 Aunt Ruey..had in her youth been one of the foremost leaders in the 'singers' seat'. 1878 — *Poganuc People* ix. 79 The great meeting-house on the green was *our* meeting-house, and the singers' seat therein was *our* singers' seat.

Singh (sing). [Hind., a. Skr. सिंह *sinhá* 'the powerful one', lion.] A great warrior; a title borne by several of the warrior castes of northern India, as Rajputs and Sikhs.

1623 in Foster *Eng. Factories India* (1908) 218 Beinge soe hottly persued by Abdala Chan and Rajae Sursinge. *c* 1792 *Encycl. Brit.* IX. 213/2 In 1770 the rajah died, and was succeeded by his son Cheit Sing. 1841 *Penny Cycl.* XIX. 276/2 The bravery and talents of the regent Zalim Singh. 1882 *Encycl. Brit.* XIV. 503/2 Our latest narrative of a visit to Lhasa is that of the late Pundit Nain Singh.

Singing, *vbl. sb.* **4.** Add: **singing-book** (later U.S. examples); **singing-point** (see quot.).

1793 *Essex Inst. Hist. Coll.* XXII. 148 Voted to obtain 6 Psalm Books and 6 Singing Books for the use of the Parish. 1871 Mrs. Stowe *Sam Lawson* 130 They tore out all the leaves of the hymn-books, and the singin'-books besides. 1930 *Terms Telegraphs & Telephones* (Brit. Engin. Standards Assoc.) 17 '*Singing point* (1) Of a two-wire repeater. A measurement of the stability of a repeater against oscillation and harmful effect on articulation due to back coupling brought about by inexact balance between the balancing network and line...(2) of a line. In the case of a long line, the attenuation corresponding to the ratio of the power transmitted to the line at some specified frequency and the power returned to the sending end by reflection from irregularities. The term 'Singing Point' has a number of other meanings including the loss corresponding to the reflection coefficient when, for example, two lines are joined together.

Singing, *ppl. a.* **4. b.** Add: *Singing arc, (arc) lamp* (see quot. 1883). *Singing sand* (see quot.).

1903 *Work* 2 May 203/1 A *singing arc lamp, invented by a German named Simon, of Frankfort. 1913 *Year-Bk. Wireless Telegr. & Teleph.* 399 Duddell's discovery of the singing arc in 1900. 1883 Gresley *Gloss. Coal-m.*, *Singing Lamp, a safety lamp which, when placed in an atmosphere of explosive gas, gives out a peculiar sound or note. 1930 Partington *Inorganic Chem.* 725 '*Singing sand', which emits a peculiar squeaking note when pressed, consists of rounded grains of nearly uniform size. It occurs..in various localities.

Si·nging-ma:ster. [Singing *vbl. sb.*] A teacher of singing. Also *U.S.*, a precentor in church.

1711 [see Singing *vbl. sb.* 4]. 1789 *Boston Town Records* X. 190 Kimball John, singing-master. 1846 Sol. Smith *Theatrical Apprenticeship* 48 Excuse me if I'm mistaken, but are you or are you not our singing-master? 1872 E. Eggleston *End of World* x. 71 The singing-master, Mr. Humphreys, went to singing-school and church with Julia. 1891 *Harper's Mag.* Oct. 813/1 The precenter, or singing-master, as he was called, was a tall young man in a black suit with white ruffles.

Si·nging-school. Chiefly *U.S.* [f. as prec.] A school in which singing is taught.

1736 [see Singing *vbl. sb.* 4]. 1779 E. Parkman *Diary* 86 Mr. Badcock keeps a singing-school at Mr. Barn. Newtons. 1829–32 J. P. Kennedy *Swallow Barn* II. iii. 55 Like the pupils of a singing-school practising the elements of psalmody. 1848 in D. Drake *Pioneer Life Kentucky* viii. 188 Singing-schools were likewise held at the same place. 1863 B. Taylor *H. Thurston* iv. 48 A melody which he had learned at the Singing-school. 1886 *Leslie's Pop. Monthly* Feb. 239/2 That night Susy went to singing-school. 1929 E. W. Howe *Plain People* 23 There was so much indignation that thereafter the occasional spelling and singing schools were given up.

Si·nging-seat. *U.S.* [f. as prec.] A choir seat. (Cf. *singers' seat*, *Singer[1] 1 c.)

1774 *Essex Inst. Hist. Coll.* XXI. 271 Voted Liberty to build a singing Seat in the front of the Gallerary Pues. 1847 *Knickerbocker Mag.* XXX. 527, I..have obtained some notoriety in our parish choir for playing the bass-viol and leading the singers in the First Congregational singing-seats. 1864 [see Singing *vbl. sb.* 4 b]. 1887 Mary E. Wilkins *Humble Romance* 60 David Ayres, in his place in the second row of the singing seats, watched them soberly.

Single, *sb.* **3.** Add:

f. Also applied to woollen yarn. **j.** A single piece of furniture, silver, etc., not forming part of a set. **k.** An animal which alone is born at a birth. **l.** *pl.* Single-screened coal.

f. 1888 *Encycl. Brit.* XXIV. 659/2 Yarn, as delivered from the mule in woollen-spinning, or from the throstle in the case of worsteds, is in the condition known as singles. **j.** 1904 R. S. Clouston in *Burlington Mag.* July 381/2 Fine specimens, even if 'singles', have been added wherever possible. **k.** 1913 *Rep. Brit. Assoc.* 670 The relative profitableness of a crop of twin lambs, compared with a fall of 'singles'. **l.** 1921 *Glasgow Herald* 7 Dec. 9 Coals used in smithwork, say 'pearls' and 'singles', varied from 15*s.* to 18*s.* per ton f.o.b. 1931 *Times* 16 Mar. 19/7 Lanarkshire [coal]..trebles..doubles..singles.

Single, *a.* Add: **15.** Also of a game or contest: With one person only on each side.

1890 C. G. Heathcote *Lawn Tennis* (Badm.) 248 The tactics of the single game have grown up with its development. 1895 H. W. W. Wilberforce *Lawn Tennis* xii. 41 The standard of play in the double game is much lower than in the single game.

17. Other collocations.

Single court, in lawn tennis, a court for two players only. *Single crown* (Naut.), a single crowning given to a knot (see Crown *v.* 14, Crowning *vbl. sb.* 4). *Single hair, horse-shoe* (see quots.). *Single oyster* (*a*) 'an oyster which becomes detached from the bunches after two years' growth; hence, a grown or merchantable oyster' (Cent. Dict.); (*b*) see quot. *Single premium*, a sum which covers the entire cost of insurance in a single payment. *Single preventer*, a device in a drawing-frame in cotton manufacture which automatically stops the machine on the breaking of or the failure to take up a single strand of sliver; also *attrib.* *Single strength*, in Billiards, denoting a low-speed stroke (cf. Strength *sb.* 1 q). *Single width*, the width of a piece of cloth which is not doubled on the roll.

1890 C. G. Heathcote *Lawn Tennis* (Badm.) 195 The *single court may be marked in the same way. 1897 *Encycl. Sport* I. 611/2 The double court should be 12 yards wide, thereby permitting the inclusion of the single court in it. 1883 *Man. Seamanship for Boys* 121 Form a double-wall, single-crowned, then lay the strands by the sides of those in the *single-crown. 1881 *Sportsman's Year-bk.* 71 *Single hair is greatly used in the trout streams in the north of England with the artificial fly. 1902 *Encycl. Brit.* XXVII. 584/1 For bipolar machines the *single horse-shoe, which is the lineal successor of the permanent magnet employed in the first magneto-electric machines, has been very largely used. 1881 Ingersoll *Oyster Industr.* (Hist. Fish. Industr. U.S.) 248 *Single Oysters.—In the south 'single oyster' means an edible oyster in contradistinction from the raccoon oyster. 1880 *Encycl. Brit.* XIII. 171/2 We conclude..that the *single premium at age 20 for a whole-term assurance of £1 according to the H[M] mortality table, reckoning interest at 3 per cent., is £·32886, or 6*s.* 7*d.* 1930 *Times* 27 Mar. 22/1 Single premium (with loan) business. 1897 W. S. Taggart *Cotton Spinning* II. 24 All draw-frames are now made with what is generally termed a 'single preventer' motion. 1904 Mannock *Billiards* I. vi. 264 As an easy plain ball angle is to be gained by the lower position of the first object-ball, '*single-strength' only is needed in the stroke.

b. *single-decker, -hander* (a single-handed run), *-phaser* (a single-phase machine), *-seater*.

1910 *Sphere* 20 Aug. 176/1 The first aeroplane illustrated is the Santos Dumont aeroplane or *single-decker. 1930 *Aberdeen Press & Jrnl.* 12 Feb. 6/3 I see that the L.C.C. has been selling off old single-decker tramcars at £5 apiece. 1876 *Coursing Calendar* 217 War Note never seeing the hare, Adventurer fell in for a *single-hander of great length, the first-named being drawn ultimately. 1900 *Jrnl. Brit. Inst. Electr. Engin.* XXIX. 246 The motor is being supplied with single-phase currents and will continue running as a *single-phaser. 1916 H. Barber *Aeroplane Speaks* Pl. xxvi, A 50 h.p. Gnome *single-seater. 1930 *Morning Post* 5 Aug. 9/2 Mr. A. T. Cunningham..arrived at Wyndham..in his single-seater Australian-built machine. 1931 *Statesman* (Calcutta) 5 Dec., A single-seater biplane.

18. (Further examples.)

1902 *Encycl. Brit.* XXVII. 579/1 Such is the form taken by the *single-phase alternator. 1907 *Daily Mail Year Bk.* 66/1 The single-phase alternating current. 1919 H. L. Mencken *Amer. Language* iii. 83 *Single-track mind. 1924 A. J. Small *Frozen Gold* iv. 108 Sitka Charley's was a single-track mind; dour and grim and devilishly dogged, but still, single-track.

19. *single-crowned, -jointed*.

1883 *single-crowned [see *single crown* in *17]. 1910 D. W. Thompson tr. *Aristotle's Hist. Anim.* I. 15 The big finger or thumb is *single-jointed...Toes are without exception single-jointed.

Single, *v.*[1] Add: **7. b.** In oyster-culture (see quot.).

1907 *Victoria Hist. Essex* II. 427/1 After the spatting season, the culch or the live oyster bearing the 'brood' is dredged up, and those young oysters..are detached and thrown back into the water. This process is called 'singling' the oysters.

8. c. *To single up*: to cast off all turns of rope except one.

1925 Rex Clements *Gipsy of Horn* 103 Our moorings had been singled up. 1927 *Chambers's Jrnl.* 392/2 The mooring wires were being 'singled-up.'

Sing-song, *sb.* **4.** Add: Now more usually a gathering for the purpose of community singing.

Singspiel (si·ŋspīl, ‖zi·ŋʃpīl). *Hist.* [G., f. *singen* to sing + *spiel* play.] A semi-dramatic performance in which song and dialogue alternate, with subordination of the musical accompaniment to the vocal parts, popular in Germany in the latter part of the eighteenth century.

1883 *Grove's Dict. Mus.* II. 519/1 That best and truest form of German Opera, the 'Singspiel'. 1884 *Encycl. Brit.* XVII. 99/1 The *singspiel* is the German parallel to the opéra comique. 1930 *Observer* 23 Mar. 25 Many [operettas] of the German 'singspiel' type could be done.

Singularism (si·ngiŭlăriz'm). [See -ism.] A philosophy which explains the phenomena of the universe from a single principle: opp. to Pluralism. (Cf. Monism.) Hence **Si·ngularist** 3, one who holds such a philosophy; also *attrib.*

1911 J. Ward *Realm of Ends* 24 If the difficulties of Pluralism point the way to Singularism they will at least serve to make the character of the One clearer than any 'cheap and easy monism'..can ever do. *Ibid.* 201 The pluralist's extremity will doubtless be regarded as the singularist's opportunity. *Ibid.* 271 Singularist philosophers are fond of speaking of the world as the differentiation of the Absolute. 1922 A. G. Hogg *Redemption fr. this World* 262 My own philosophical tendency is toward a theistic or non-Singularist type of monism.

Sinh (ʃin). *Math.* Abbreviation of hyperbolic sine (see Hyperbolic *a.* 2 b).

1880 *Encycl. Brit.* XIII. 50/2 The hyperbolic cosine and hyperbolic sine of *v*..are usually written cosh *v*, sinh *v*.

Sinico- (si·niko), used as combining form of mod.L. *Sinicus* Sinic *a.* with the meaning 'Chinese and'.

1875 F. V. Dickins tr. *Chiushingura* (1880) 147 A Sinico-Japanese compound. *Ibid.* 161 In the great Sinico-Japanese Encyclopaedia. 1883 tr. *J. J. Rein's Japan* (1888) 396 The Japanese Language... Yamato- and Sinico-Japanese. 1902 *Encycl. Brit.* XXIX. 729/1 The Sinico-Japanese school. 1905 *Athenæum* 1 Apr. 396/3 Nothing original of any importance has yet been found in the Sinico-Japanese literature of the last millennium.

Sink, *sb.*[1] Add: **8. b.** *Electr.* A point at which the current leaves the sheet.

1902 *Encycl. Brit.* XXVIII. 18/2 In the case of current flow in plane sheets, we have to consider certain points called sources at which the current flows into the sheet, and certain points called sinks at which it leaves.

Sink (sink), *sb.*[3] Also **sync.** Colloquial abbreviation of Synchronism.

1929 *Photoplay* Apr., *In sink*, in synchronism; picture and sound perfectly timed together. *Outa sink*, not in synchronism. [1931 B. Brown *Talking Pictures* v. 128 The 'nonsync' is a comparatively simple piece of apparatus consisting of double turntables with electrical pick-ups.]

Sink, *v.* Add: **17. d.** *To sink tooth into*: to eat. *U.S. colloq.*

1891 *Outing* (U.S.) Nov. 136/1 Only a favored few of the millions of feasters on Thanksgiving Day will sink tooth into genuine wild turkey meat.

20. d. *To sink the wind*: to go against the wind; see also quot. 1886.

1847 R. S. Surtees *Hawbuck Grange* v. 96 We..found a hare by Clipstone Clump, who went as straight as an arrow to Gatley Coppice, from whence, sinking the wind all the way, she ran to Silverspring. 1886 Salvin & Brodrick *Falconry Brit. Isles* Gloss. 153 *To sink the wind*, to skim near the earth..in order to catch the wind and rise up-wind with it.

Sinker. Add: **5. d.** A dough-nut, orig. a heavy, sodden, or doughy one. *U.S.*

1903 F. B. Smith *How Paris Amuses Itself* 48 The New York Dairy Lunch, with..its elevating Bible texts, and depressing 'sinkers',..would never make a success with Parisians. 1912 L. J. Vance *Destroying Angel* vi, If the production flivvers, I'll need that thirty cents for coffee and sinkers at Dennett's. 1926 E. Ferber *Show Boat* xiii. 268 The coffee was hot, strong, revivifying; the sinkers crisp and fresh. 1928 Sinclair Lewis *Man Who Knew Coolidge* II. 100 They can't afford more'n coffee and sinkers for breakfast!

III. Something which sinks. **a.** A mistletoe root, so called because it sinks below the bark of the tree on which it grows.

1895 F. W. Oliver tr. *Kerner's Nat. Hist. Plants* I. 207 A slender process now grows into the bark of the host-plant. ..This..has been termed a 'sinker', and must be looked upon as a specially modified root. 1900 B. D. Jackson *Gloss. Bot. Terms, Sinker*, the secondary roots of Mistleto..forming laterals which strike perpendicularly downward into the wood of the host.

b. A sunken or partly submerged log. *U.S.*

1905 *Terms Forestry & Logging* 46.

Sinn Fein (ʃin fē^i·n). [Ir., lit. 'we ourselves'.] An Irish society, founded in 1905 by Arthur Griffith, Irish politician, aiming at political independence

and a revival of Irish culture and language. Also *attrib.* or *adj.*, of, pertaining to, or resembling this society or its aims and methods.

1907 *Westm. Gaz.* 25 July 2/1 The Sinn Féin policy of resisting taxation by an alien government. 1920 *Public Opinion* 16 July 58/3 The intellectual leaders of Sinn Fein can by no means bind the extremists. 1921 *Punch* 12 Jan. 28/1 Remarkable that I detected no outward evidence of Sinn Fein. 1930 Hancock *Australia* x. 213 Labour politicians preached Australia for the Australians and a sort of Sinn Fein exclusiveness.

Hence **Sinn Fei·ner**, a member or adherent of Sinn Fein; **Sinn Fei·nism**, the methods, aims, or policy of Sinn Fein.

1907 *Daily Chron.* 13 Aug. 6/2 Sir Thomas Esmonde's action in adopting Sinn Feinism as against Parliamentary agitation. 1907 *Westm. Gaz.* 31 Aug. 7/1 Sinn Feiners further suggest that the Irish representatives, having withdrawn from Westminster, should assemble in Dublin. 1918 *49th Rep. Dep. Kpr. Publ. Rec. Ireland* 3 This Office was occupied by the Sinn Féiners during the Dublin Rebellion.

Sino-. Add: **Si·nophile** *sb.*, a lover of the Chinese; **Si·nophobe** *a.* and *sb.*, hating, one who hates, the Chinese.

1900 *Outlook* 21 July 693 (Cent. D. Suppl.) That the author is no sinophile will be gathered from the following. 1920 W. J. Locke *House of Baltazar* iii, Water-End became divided into two camps—Sinophile and Sinophobe.

b. Combined with another adjective of nationality, with the meaning 'Chinese and'.

1903 B. Berenson in *Burlington Mag.* Oct. 13/1 We must place to the front the fact that Sino-Japanese design is almost exclusively an art of contours. 1904 *Amer. Nat.* Sept. 676 The restriction of the Sino-Australian continent to a certain part of the Cretaceous times consequently would meet the postulates both of geology and zoögeography. 1926 *Glasgow Herald* 23 Jan. 9 The rift in the Sino-Russian lute. 1927 *Observer* 10 July 18 Colliery and other interests of Sino-Japanese ownership.

Sinter (si·ntəɹ), *v.* [f. the sb.] *intr.* To be converted into cinders; to adhere in a mass by partial fusion. Also *trans.*, to cause to be sintered. See Dict. for **Sintered** *ppl. a.*, **Sintering** *vbl. sb.*

1903 *Amer. Chem. Jrnl.* XXIX. 487 On heating, it sintered at about 225°.

Sinuous, *a.* 3. Add: Also of people. Hence **Si·nuousness** (*b*) in this sense.

1906 B. Vaughan *Sins of Society* 229 The lithesome, sinuous girl trips with it across the stage to her mother. 1924 Rose Macaulay *Orphan Island* xiii. § 4 Like a sturdy little boy without feminine elegances, or any of Flora's wild-animal sinuousness.

Sinusitis (səinŭsəi·tis). *Path.* Also **sinuitis**. [f. Sinus + -itis.] Inflammation of a sinus.

1901 Dorland *Med. Dict.* (ed. 2).

Siomio (ʃiə·mio). *Jap. Hist.* Also **shomio.** [a. Jap. *shō-miyō*, f. Chinese *hsiao* small + *ming* name, person, title.] One of the inferior warrior nobles of Japan, who were vassals of the Shogun.

1727 Scheuchzer tr. *Kæmpfer's Hist. Japan* I. I. v. 80 All the *Siomio* are so far subject to the Emperor, that they are allow'd but six Months stay in their hereditary dominions. 1839 *Penny Cycl.* XIII. 94/1 The nobility, or hereditary governors of the provinces and districts, are called *Daimio*, or High-named, and *Siomio*, or Well-named...The Siomio govern the districts.

Sioux (sū). [Fr. spelling of the Indian name.] The name of an important group of North American Indians and the linguistic group represented by them; *spec.* one of the Dakotas, a tribe of that group. Also *attrib.* Hence **Siouan** (sū·ăn) *a.*, of or pertaining to the Sioux.

1815 Lewis & Clarke *Trav. up Missouri* I. 71 Whimsical instance of superstition of the Sioux Indians. *Ibid.* 73 This has inspired all the neighbouring nations, Sioux, Mahas, and Ottoes, with such terror, that no consideration could tempt them to visit the hill. *Ibid.* 75 Above this bluff we set the prairie on fire, to invite the Sioux. 1842 *Penny Cycl.* XXII. 46/1 The Sioux claim the whole tract to the boundary-line of the United States. 1900 *Knowledge* 2 July 153/2 Among the other Atlantic stocks are..the Siouans, some of the most famous tribes of the latter being the Sioux or Dakotas, and the Crows. 1924 S. Lewis *Free Air* ix. (1930) 90 She fancied that on it the Sioux scout still sat sentinel. *fig.* 1892 *Harper's Mag.* Mar. 493/2 The 'bull-dog'..is the Sioux of the insect world, as pretty as a warrior in buckskin and beads.

Sirab, variant of *Serab.

Sirdab, var. Serdab.

Sirdar 2 (sɔ̄·ɹdaɹ). [Pushtu *sarda.*] In *sirdar melon*: The melon, *Cucumis Melo.*

1880 *Encycl. Brit.* XIII. 836/2 The pomegranates of Kandahar, with its 'sirdar' melons and grapes, being unequalled in quality by any in the East.

Sirgang (sɔ̄·ɹgæŋ). [E. Ind.] An Asiatic corvine bird, *Cissa chinensis.* 1891 *Century Dict.*

Siringa, var. Seringa.

1880 *Encycl. Brit.* XII. 837/1 In French Guiana [rubber is obtained] from *H[evea] Guayanensis*, Aubl., where it is known as 'heve', 'siringa', or 'caboutchou'.

Siryanian (siryǣ·niăn). Also **Sirian-, Syrian-, -jen-, -yen-, Zirian-, -yan-, Zyr(y)en-.** See also *Syrian. [f. mod.L. *Syriænus*, G. *sürjänisch*, Russ. *zyryansk*, etc. + -ian.] A member of a Finno-Ugrian tribe of the Permic division of the eastern Finns. **b.** The dialect spoken by these people. Also as *adj.*, pertaining to this race or the language spoken by them.

[1780 W. Tooke tr. *J. G. Georgi's Russia* I. 175 The Biarms, Bessarmians, or ancient Permiaks, as well as the Siryains, have a very near relationship to the Finns.] 1851 *Illustr. Catal. Gt. Exhib.* III. III. 552/1 Sirenian St. Matthew. 1878 *Encycl. Brit.* VIII. 700/1 Finnic or Ugrian represented by..Siryenian. 1879 *Ibid.* IX. 219/2 The Permian Finns comprise the Siryenians,..the Permian proper,..and the Votyak. 1888 *Ibid.* XXIV. 1/1 Permian, Votyak, and Siryenian, between the Vyatka and Petchora rivers. 1910 *Ibid.* X. 389 The Syryenian headquarters are at the town of Ishma on the Pechora. 1930 Liddell & Scott *Gr.-Engl. Lex.*, Κάνναβις..borrowed perh. fr. Ugro-Finnish, cf...Syrianian *pïš* 'hemp'.

Sisal. Add: **2. b.** (Also with spelling **sisol.**) A fancy straw used for making hats.

1928 *New York Daily Times* 11 Jan., Hats of Bakou, sisol, and the new natural color straws. 1928 *Millinery Trade Review* (U.S.) June 6 Bakus and Sisols from China.

Siserskite (si·səɹskəit). *Min.* Also **sisserskite.** [ad. G. *sisserskit* (W. Haidinger, 1845), f. *Sissersk* in the Ural Mountains: see -ite 1.] A variety of Iridosmine.

1868 Dana *Min.* (ed. 5) 13 At a high temperature the Sisserskite gives out osmium.

Sisham, var. Shisham.

1890 Kipling *Soldiers Three* (ed. 6) 31 We three were comfortably settled under the big *sisham* [ed. 1889 *shisham*].

Sisi 1 (sī·sī). [Native name.] A skirt made of fibre, worn by women and girls in the South Sea Islands.

1908 *Rep. Brit. Assoc.* 435 Women making sisis. 1910 *Contemp. Rev.* Jan. 89 Eight young Vavauan girls, naked but for a sisi (or short skirt) of fibre.

Sisi 2, var. *See-see.

Sisith (zī·ziþ). Also **zizith.** [Heb. ציצית *tsītsīth.*] One of the tassels of twisted or knotted cord worn by Jews formerly on the upper garment, but now on the tallith.

Translated 'fringes' in A.V. and R.V. (see Numbers xv. 38, Deut. xxii. 12).

1738 'Gamaliel ben Pedahzur' *Bk. Relig. Jews* 4 The Fringe on each Corner is of eight worsted Threads double twisted [*marg.* Called Zizith]. 1877 C. Geikie *Life of Christ* II. xlii. 169 She could only dare to touch the zizith, or tassel, that hung on the corner of his outer garment, as on those of all other Jews. 1885 *Encycl. Brit.* XIX. 1/1 The zizith is no longer placed on the outer garment as in New Testament times. 1920 J. A. Robertson *Hidden Romance N. T.* viii. 173, I see you are a Jew, like myself... But you don't wear the Zizith any more than I do.

Sisol: see *Sisal.

Siss, *sb.*1 *U.S.* (Examples.)

1835 *Knickerbocker Mag.* VI. 293 All the friends called her sister,..which, as the half was easier to be bandied about than the whole,..soon dwindled into 'sis'. 1902 Harben *Abner Daniel* 258, I tell you she's fixed 'im. Yore little sis has done the most complete job out o' tough material I ever inspected. 1903 *Century Mag.* May 134/1 I'm goin' to a newer country yet, sis.

Sissy (si·si). *U.S. colloq.* [f. Siss *sb.*1 + -y 6.] **1.** A (little) sister; a young girl; also used in addressing a woman or girl regarded as a sister.

1859 [see Siss *sb.*1]. 1865 K. H. Digby *Short Poems* 39 The little one grasping with such a tight hold, The frock of sweet sissy, herself not too bold. 1869 — *Little Low Bushes* 8 Those two poor sissys toddling still.

2. An effeminate man or boy. Also *attrib.* or *adj.* (Cf. *Cissy.)

1891 *Harper's Mag.* Aug. 485/2 He approached and sat near me, deep in conversation with a young gentleman with sissy whiskers. 1893 *N. Y. Mercury* May (Ware) Sissy men in Society.—Powdered, painted and laced. They swarm at afternoon teas. 1899 T. Hall *Tales* 125 Scotty was, in the newspaper vernacular, 'a sissy boy'. *Ibid.* 131 'Well you are a sissy,' said Blinks contemptuously. 1924 P. Marks *Plastic Age* 218 Wasn't he perhaps a prig, a sissy? 1926 *Harper's Mag.* Feb. 350/1 There was a smug little bandbox chap in my father's church...Men regarded him as a sissy. 1926 *Ladies' Home Jrnl.* May 203 Advt., Dress your boy in 'He-Boy' style. Don't set him apart from other lads by dressing him in 'sissy clothes'. 1926 *British Weekly* 2 Sept. 452/3 There was nothing 'sissy' about him. He was a born fighter.

Hence **Si·ssified** *a.*, effeminate; **Si·ssiness,** effeminateness.

1905 J. C. Lincoln *Partners of Tide* iv, To be seen with girls was not so 'sissified' in his mind as it used to be. 1921 R. D. Paine *Comr. Rolling Ocean* i. 10 The campus.. thought him a bit sissified. 1926 *Harper's Mag.* Feb. 350/2 In spite of his funny sissiness there was not a dog in town that did not love him.

Sistine (si·stīn), *a.* [ad. It. *Sistino* Sixtine.] Epithet of the chapel and bridge built by pope Sixtus IV (1471–1484); hence, of or belonging to the Sistine Chapel.

1877 *Encycl. Brit.* VI. 240/1 Every morning..they [*sc.* the cardinals] proceed to a scrutiny..in the Sistine or in the Paoline Chapel. 1885 *Ibid.* XIX. 64/1 San Sisto..lost its chief attraction when Raphael's Sistine Madonna (now in Dresden) was sold by the monks. 1902 *Grove's Dict. Mus.* IV. 182/1 The traditions of the Sistine Choir.

Sit, *v.* Add: **3. d.** *To sit on one's hands*: to applaud feebly. (Cf. *Hand *sb.* 15 b.) *U.S. colloq.*

1926 *Amer. Speech* I. May 437/1 *Sittin' on their hands*, a cold audience, stingy with applause. 1926 E. Ferber *Show Boat* vi. 106 Well, they were sitting on their hands to-night, all right. Seemed they never would warm up.

8. c. *Coal-mining.* (See quot.)

1883 Gresley *Gloss. Coal-m.* s.v., A coal face or buttock is said to sit when, after the sprags have been drawn, it will not fall over and break up, but merely cracks off and rests in that position until pulled over.

17. c. Also *poet.*

1878 J. J. Aubertin *Camoens' Lusiads* VIII. lxiv, With a proud confidence, that sat him well.

21. Sit down. a. (*e*) Of an aviator: To land. *colloq.*

1926 *National Geog. Mag.* (U.S.A.) XLIX. No. 1 After a while he guessed he'd better 'sit down'..he got down all right.

c. (*b*) Also occas. *trans.*: To cause (an army) to encamp *before* a town, etc.

1927 Belloc *Hist. Eng.* II. iv. 406 He sat his army down before it.

e. *To sit down hard on*: to snub or denounce severely.

1880 *Kansas City Times & Star* 17 Sept., Since Mrs. Grover Cleveland sat down so hard on the bustle, the demand has slackened perceptibly. 1904 *Boston Advertiser* 5 Nov. 4 He sat down hard on the proposition that Canada should meet a penny of the 'imperial' expenses.

22. Sit in. a. Also in modern *U.S.* use, to join a party.

1868 Susan Hale *Lett.* (1919) 44 Before we got to lunch two Englishmen *sot in.* 1889 *Kansas City Times & Star* 9 Dec., Kansas City baseball men sat in at a western ball magnates' conference at St. Louis yesterday. 1903 A. Adams *Log Cowboy* xii. 179 When one was frozen out another sat in and took his place. 1916 C. Sandburg *Chicago Poems* 63 He didn't sit in with the big thieves.

25. Sit up. a. Colloq. phr. *to sit up and take notice*: to have one's interest (suddenly) aroused. *To sit up and take nourishment*: to be convalescent.

1889 *Kansas City Times & Star* 28 May, Alex Butts, in 'Starbeams',..asks 'the effete East to sit up and take notice'. 1909 *N. Y. Even. Post* (semi-weekly ed.) 8 Mar. 2 The crowd that fell upon Washington was of such a size that the District authorities sat up and took serious notice. 1912 Mulford & Clay *Buck Peters* iii. 47 Time enough to sit up and take notice when the flourishing danger signal appeared. 1914 Gertrude Atherton *Perch of Devil* I. 175 When he does sit up and take notice he doesn't so much as wink. 1918 Lucas *'Twixt Eagle & Dove* 152 The well-worn phrase 'to sit up and take nourishment'. 1930 'Sapper' *Finger of Fate*, etc. 205 Not that she weren't worth having without anything at all except her sweet self; but with them two farms chucked in like, the boys were fairly sitting up. 1932 *Sunday Express* 3 July 22/6 Horse racing and those responsible have to sit up and take notice.

27. Sit over. b. *Bridge.* To be on the left hand of, and consequently in an advantageous position over.

1921 A. Manning Foster *Auction Bridge* 84 A good bid by second hand over a 'One no trumps' called by the dealer is—when his cards justify it—'Two no trumps', because he is sitting over the declared strength.

Sit-down, *sb.* **1.** (Earlier U.S. example.)

1861 Mrs. Stowe *Pearl Orr's Isl.* I. xii. 104, I am come here for a good sit-down by your kitchen-fire.

Site, *v.*2 **1, Siting,** *vbl. sb.* Add: Now in general use.

1918 *Cornhill Mag.* June 620 In towns schools are invariably badly sited in squalid districts near to noisy and dusty roads. *Ibid.* 621 The short-sighted policy adopted in the siting and construction of schools. 1920 *Discovery* Apr. 116/1 It is advisable to avoid siting a wireless station close to higher ground. 1931 *Times Lit. Suppl.* 16 Apr. 310/2 A practical handbook on the siting, construction and upkeep of garden pools.

Sitka (si·tkă). The name of a town in Alaska used *attrib.* to denote certain trees growing in its neighbourhood, as **Sitka cypress,** *Chamæcyparis Nutkaensis*; **Sitka spruce,** *Picea sitchensis*, a large tree yielding valuable timber; **Sitka willow,** *Salix sitchensis* (Webster 1911).

1889 *Cent. Dict.* s.v. *Cypress*, The yellow or Sitka cypress, *C. Nutkaensis.* 1895 *Funk's Stand. Dict.* s.v. *Spruce*, Sitka spruce. 1920 *Daily Mail Year Bk.* 227/1 Sitka spruce and Douglas fir. 1928 *Daily Mail* 9 Aug. 13/4 The Duchy estates on Dartmoor, where it is hoped to plant 5,000 acres with sitka, Norway spruce, and Douglas fir.

Sito-. Add: **Sitoto·xin,** poison occurring in vegetable foods.

1901 Dorland *Med. Dict.* (ed. 2), *Sitotoxin*, any basic poison generated in a cereal food by a plant microörganism.

Sitter 1. Add: **1. g.** One who has a sitting with a medium. (Cf. Sitting *vbl. sb.* 5 d.)

1911 Webster. 1928 *Daily Mail* 25 July 6/2 If media [*sic*] were unable to get into a trance the sitting was cancelled and the money returned to the sitter.

6. Anything easy or certain of performance; anything which a person can hardly bungle e.g. an easy catch, a stroke that can be easily returned, a target which it is almost impossible to miss; an easy winner.

1898 *Tit-Bits* 25 June 252/3 A 'sitter' is a catch which falls absolutely into the hands. 1903 G. L. Jessop in *Hutchinson's Cricket* v. 117 The missing of a 'sitter' by some lazy fieldsman whose thoughts were anywhere but on the game. 1908 A. S. M. Hutchinson *Once aboard the Lugger* I. iv. § 3 'You know I got ploughed?'..'Bad luck, I suppose? I thought it was a sitter for you this time.' 1921 A. Manning Foster *Auction Bridge* 107 Z bid 'Four spades' and was doubled by A. He had a 'sitter' and unwisely redoubled. 1928 C. F. S. Gamble *Story North Sea Air Station* xv. 251 Any Zeppelin that had shown itself would have been a sitter. 1929 Vachell *Virgin* viii. 137 His aunt would take her on; that was a 'sitter'.

Sitter 2. *Oxford University slang.* [See *-er 6.] A sitting-room.

1904 [see *-er 6]. 1925 *Glasgow Herald* 24 Oct. 6 If

lectures are to be broadcast, the temptation to listen to them in the quiet and comfort of one's own 'sitter' will be irresistible.

Sitting, *ppl. a.* Add:

6. That can hardly be bungled. Cf. *Sitter 1 6.

1932 *Evening Standard* 28 Jan. 11/2 They had a hand which contained a 'sitting' game in Spades—one of two had five to the four top honours.

Sitting-room. 1. (Earlier Amer. example.)

1771 H. Pelham in *Copley-Pelham Lett.* (1914) 147 The Arches at the sides of the Chimnie in the Sitting Room, I like.

Situational (sitiu,ēi·ʃənăl), *a.* [f. Situation + -al.] Of or pertaining to situations; denoting a novel or play containing many or striking situations.

1903 *Academy* 27 June 632/1 As situational drama (if we may coin the term) always is rhetorical. 1927 *Observer* 24 Apr. 14/5 The main defect of this book seems to lie in the way in which literary or dramatic or situational clues are allowed to dictate musical judgments.

Situla (si·tiulă). Pl. **situlæ.** *Archæol.* [L., = bucket.] Applied to various bucket-shaped vessels.

1897 *Knowledge* 1 Oct. 229/1 Situla (Bucket), of Apulian fabric, with scene representing Dionysos espousing Ariadne. 1900 C. D. Edmonds in *Jrnl. Hellenic Studies* XX. 23 A silver situla standing upon three feet. 1905 *Brit. Mus. Guide Early Iron Age* 14 The succeeding (iron-sword) period..is richly represented by articles decorated in the *situla* style. Such is the name given to a method of ornamenting vessels of the bucket-type..by means of horizontal bands. 1906 J. G. Duncan *Hyksos* 49/1 A bronze situla with a thick mud cake in the bottom. 1928 MacIver *Italy bef. Romans* 61 An early example of the situla or bronze bucket for which Bologna no less than Este was to become famous in future years.

Sit-up, *sb.* Add: **2.** An act of sitting up.

1843 R. Carlton *New Purchase* ix. 64 This sit-up we instantly performed—as well, at least, as we could.

Situtunga (situtʊ·ŋgă). [Swahili.] An antelope of the genus *Limnotragus* or genus *Tragelaphus* inhabiting the swamps of eastern and central Africa. Also *attrib.*

1881 Selous *Hunter's Wand. Africa* x. (1893) 158 These men told me that in some thick beds of reeds near their town were some *Situtunga* antelope. 1920 *Brit. Museum Return* 81 Prominent among the specimens are the following mounted heads:—6 Moose,..20 Gemsbuck, 3 Situtunga. 1920 G. D. H. Carpenter *Naturalist on Lake Victoria* 80 The muffled bark of the Situtunga. 1926 *Blackw. Mag.* Sept. 333/1 Clad in comfortable *situtunga* skins.

Sivan (səi·văn, sīvā·n). Also 4–5 **Ciban, Siban, Siwan.** [Heb. סיון *çīwān.*] The third month of the Jewish ecclesiastical year and the ninth of the civil year, corresponding to the latter part of May and the earlier part of June.

1382 Wyclif *Esther* viii. 9 The thridde moneth, that is clepid Ciban [*later text* Siban], that is June. 1535 Coverdale *Ibid.*, In the thirde moneth, that is the moneth Siuan. 1737 Whiston *Josephus, Jewish War* III. vii. § 29 This fight happened upon the twentieth day of the month Desius (Sivan). 1902 *Encycl. Brit.* XXVI. 43/2 He [*sc.* Esar-haddon] thereupon returned to Nineveh, and on the 8th of Sivan (May) formally ascended the throne.

Siwalik (siwā·lik), *a.* Also **Sivalik.** [Hind.] Of, pertaining to, characteristic of, or occurring in the Siwalik hills, the southern outlying range of the Himalayas. *Siwalik formation, group*, a division of the tertiary period, rich in fossils.

1880 *Encycl. Brit.* XI. 827/2 It is from the ranges in the vicinity of the Jumna river that the characteristic Siwâlik fossils have chiefly been obtained. *Ibid.* 828/2 This embryo Himalaya may have been of such moderate height as to have permitted the passage across it of the Siwâlik mammals. 1902 *Ibid.* XXV. 466/1 Dr. Dubois..excavated from a bed, considered by him to be of Sivalik formation (Pliocene), a thighbone which competent anatomists decide to be human.

Siwash (səi·wɒʃ). [Chinook Jargon.] An Indian, *spec.* of the North Pacific coast; sometimes used as a familiar form of address. Also *attrib.*

a 1861 T. Winthrop *Canoe & Saddle* ii. 23 The three unsavory..mat-haired, truculent siwashes. 1868 *All Year Round* 10 Oct. 432/1 The foreman then said: 'We find the siwash was worried by a dog.' *Note*, Siwash, corrupted from the voyageurs' Sauvage, a savage, universally applied to Indians on the North Pacific Coast. *a* 1904 S. E. White *Blazed Trail Stories* viii. 135 Come down here, you siwash. 1904 Eliz. Robins *Magnetic North* 293 You soon learn it is the Siwash custom. 1927 *Blackw. Mag.* Aug. 207/2 He could see when any siwash ducks were on a shallow part of the lagoon.

Hence **Siwa·sh** *v. intr.*, to live like an Indian.

1904 Bp. Moore in *Churchman* 21 May 626 I have a lame shoulder, the result of continuous 'siwashing' and sleeping in the snow.

Six, *a.* and *sb.* Add: **A.** *adj.* **1. d.** *Six Nations* (earlier examples).

1726 Penhallow *Indian Wars* (1824) 101 The delegates of the six nations of Iroquois. 1789 *Ann. Congress* I. 25 May 40 The sachems and warriors of the Six Nations.

B. *sb.* **3. k.** A six-cylinder motor car.

1920 *Motor Man.* (ed. 23) 19 The chief constructional difference between the six and the four is in the crankshaft. 1931 *Daily Express* 16 Oct. 11/1 Morris and Austin 'sixes' at under £200. 1932 *Oxford Times* 23 Sept. 22/3 In these days of small 'six' efficiency and popularity.

C. *Comb.* **1.** *six-ball* (over), *six-cylinder*, *six-inch* (gun).

1910 *Blackw. Mag.* Jan. 97/2 He covered something between 250 and 300 yards in the course of each *six-ball over. 1912 *Motor* 17 Dec. 52/3 Lanchester, 28 h.p., *six-cylinder. 1913 *Ibid.* 14 Jan. 1151/2 A six-cylinder Delage. 1922 S. Lewis *Babbitt* v. § 3 I've got a good house and a six-cylinder car. 1918 Boyd Cable *Front Lines* 242 Whole batteries of 60-pounders and 'six-inch' tucked away in corners of woods.

c. *six-in-hand.*

1849 De Quincey *Eng. Mail Coach* P 28 He was the man in all Europe that could (if *any* could) have driven six-in-hand full gallop over Al Sirat.

3. *six-footer* (*sc.* coffin).

1853 Dickens *Bleak Ho.* xxxiii, He has received orders to construct 'a six-footer'.

5. six-eight, -four, -sixteen, -two *Mus.* (see quot. 1902); **six o'clock** (see A. 2 c); also, denoting any position resembling that of the hands of a clock at six o'clock, as **six (o'clock) hour circle,** an hour circle the plane of which is at right angles to the meridian.

1684 *Phil. Trans.* XVII. 672 The Courses [i.e. veins of ore] usually lying from East to West, or at Six a Clock as their Term is. 1902 *Grove's Dict. Mus.* IV. 119/1 Six-two Time, $\frac{6}{2}$; with two beats in each Bar; each represented by a dotted Semibreve—or its equivalent, three Minims... Six-four Time,..with two Beats in the bar, each represented by a dotted Minim—or its equivalent, three Crochets...Six-eight Time..., with two Beats in the Bar, each represented by a dotted Crochet—or its equivalent, three Quavers...Six-sixteen Time, $\frac{6}{16}$, with two Beats in the Bar, each represented by a dotted Quaver—or its equivalent, three Semiquavers. 1927 W. E. Collinson *Contemp. Engl.* 92 Two or three expressions I learnt at Bisley in 1909 when doing target-practice in the London O.T.C. viz. the six o'clock aim (from position on target focussed).

Sixpence. 2. b. (Earlier U.S. example.)

1818 H. B. Fearon *Sk. Amer.* 13 A beggar came in, and was relieved with a Spanish silver piece called a sixpence.

Sixpenny, *a.* **2.** (Later U.S. example.)

1878 H. H. Jackson *Travel at Home* 11 She didn't never want to see any o' them sixpenny towns agin.

3. c. (Earlier U.S. example.)

1840 *Knickerbocker Mag.* XV. 138 The larger newspaper establishments, satirically termed by their Lilliputian rivals, 'the respectable sixpennies'.

Six-shooting, *ppl. a.* (Earlier U.S. example.)

1858 Teresa Viele *Following the Drum* 224 A belt full of pistols,..and a six-shooting rifle.

So **Six-shoo·tering,** the firing of a six-shooter.

a 1909 'O. Henry' *Roads of Destiny* xxii. 371 We heard a yelling and a six-shootering.

Sixteen, *a.* and *sb.* Add: **B.** *sb.* **5.** A flower-pot nine inches in width, of which there are sixteen in a 'cast'.

1852 G. W. Johnson *Cottage Gard. Dict.* 392/2 Nine-inch pot..16s [= sixteens].

Sixth, *a.* and *sb.* **A.** *adj.* **1.** Add: *Sixth day*, the name given to Friday by members of the Society of Friends. *Sixth nerve*, a nerve of the sixth cranial pair; cf. B. 4. *Sixth sense*, a supposed faculty by which a person or creature perceives facts and regulates action without the direct use of any of the five senses.

1823 C. Bell *Expos. Nerves Hum. Body* (1824) 360 The *sixth nerve is called *abducens*, and *motor externus.* 1875 *Encycl. Brit.* I. 881/1 The Abducent or sixth nerve springs out of the groove between the lower border of the pons and the anterior pyramid of the medulla oblongata. *a* 1883 Fagge *Princ. & Pract. Med.* (1886) I. 540 Afterwards she had paralysis of each sixth nerve. 1837 *sixth sense [see Dict.]. 1903 *Science Siftings* 31 Oct. 46/1 The 'sixth sense' by which blind persons perceive certain objects. 1926 *Music & Lett.* Apr. 98 That 'sixth sense'..which enables them to divine intuitively the needs of their clients.., in a word, the sense of 'showmanship'. 1929 R. Hughes *High Wind in Jamaica* 70 Henry was steering by that sixth sense which only comes into operation when the other five are asleep. 1932 *New Yorker* 9 Apr. 59/2 Long Practice in the making of itineraries, with a sixth sense that picks out fascinating ports.

Sixty, *a.* and *sb.* Add: **B.** *sb.* **4. c.** A small flower-pot three inches in width, of which there are sixty in a 'cast'.

1852 G. W. Johnson *Cottage Gard. Dict.* 392/2 Three-inch pot..60s [= sixties]. 1908 W. P. Wright *Perfect Garden* III. i. 245 The most useful sizes of pots is 'sixties', etc.

C. *Comb.* **d.** *Sixty-fours*, sixty-four leaves forming a sheet of a book.

1808 Stower *Printer's Gram.* 195 A Half Sheet of Sixty-fours. 1839 T. C. Hansard *Print. & Type-Founding* 168 Forty-eights to be paid 2*s.* per sheet extra, and sixty-fours 2*s.* 6*d.* per sheet extra.

Size, *sb.*1 Add: **10. f.** *The size of* (a thing), what it amounts to or signifies. *colloq.*

1886–7 F. R. Stockton *Hundredth Man* xxxv, This is about the size of this business as it appears to me. 1904 *Hartford Courant* 24 June 10 Another competent military reporter says that General Oku had to send in 'the whole Japanese reserves'. We fancy that that was exactly the size of it. 1914 Gertrude Atherton *Perch of Devil* I. 89 That's the size of it, only I couldn't ever say it like that.

Size, *v.*1 **4.** (Later U.S. examples.)

1862 *Trans. Ill. Agric. Soc.* (1865) V. 233 There is no provision made for 'sizing the gavels' [in reaping]. 1897 Moore *How to Build* vii. 90 The first-story beams are to be sized and leveled upon the sill and upon the foundation.

6. *U.S.* (Later examples.)

1853 J. G. Baldwin *Flush Times Alabama* 113 The jury shortly after returned into court with a verdict which 'sized their pile'. 1873 J. H. Beadle *Undevel. West* xii. 198 They are satisfied to 'size your pile' and take quarter of it.

8. c. With *up*: To turn out, on being examined or considered, or allowed to develop.

1883 Nye *Baled Hay* 126 Time, at least, makes all things size up in proper shape. 1905 *N. Y. Evening Post* 21 Nov. 1 If the President does not think that Mr. Halpin sizes up as chairman of the County Committee. 1910 Jer. Hart *Vigilante Girl* ii. 28 Burke isn't a bad sort—he sizes up about as well as most of them.

Sizzler (si·zləɹ). [f. Sizzle *v.* + -er 1.] A sizzling heat, day, etc.

1901 *Emporia* (Kans.) *Gazette* 1 July 9 The drought, which is a sizzler and frier and boiler, is a good thing for Kansas. 1904 G. H. Lorimer *Old Gorgon Graham* 31 Satan may be down in Arizona cooking up a sizzler for the corn belt.

Skate, *sb.*2 Add: **1.** Phrase. *Army slang.* (See quots.)

1919 *War Slang* in *Athenæum* 8 Aug. 727/2 To evade duty, or get clear, you 'put your skates on'. 1925 E. Fraser & Gibbons *Soldier & Sailor Words, Skates, to put on*: To Hurry Up. Also to evade duty. To desert.

3. b. *skate-iron* (earlier U.S. example); **skate-sailing,** the practice of skating with the aid of a skate-sail.

1838 J. H. Ingraham *Burton* I. x. 143 It was placed on runners sixteen inches high, shaped like skate-irons. 1927 *Daily Express* 7 Mar. 12 Skate-sailing races in Sweden.

Skate, *sb.*3 *U.S. slang.* **a.** *A cheap skate*, a miserable or contemptible person. **b.** A poor, worn-out, decrepit horse.

1896 G. Ade *Artie* xvii. 163 Do you think I'm goin' out ridin' with her and have a lot o' cheap skates stoppin' to play horse with her everywhere we go? 1904 *N. Y. Times* 11 June 2 Any one who smokes that kind of cigarette is a cheap skate. 1929 S. Anderson in *Mercury Story Bk.* 233, I could have made a faster record than most of the skates of horses they had there.

Skatosine (skæ·tosīn, skēi·-). *Chem.* Also -in. [f. Skat(ol + -ose 2 + -ine 5.] A basic compound, $C_{10}H_{16}N_2O_2$, resulting from the auto-digestion of the pancreas; probably related to skatol.

1913 Dorland *Med. Dict.* (ed. 7).

Skeeball (skī·bǭl). [f. Ski + Ball *sb.*] (See quot.)

1923 *Daily Mail* 11 June 3 The game of Skeeball is an American invention which has been in increasing operation in the United States for some six years. It is the latest development of the game of bowls, sharply distinguished from all similar games by a hump in the centre of the alley which causes the ball to leap high in the air and enter a target.

Skeeter. (Earlier example.)

1842 *Knickerbocker Mag.* XX. 87 She wouldn't hurt a 'sketer if she knowed it.

Skeezicks (skī·ziks). *U.S. colloq.* Also -zecks, **-zacks, -sicks.** [? Fanciful.] A good-for-nothing; a rascal; a rogue. (Also used playfully.)

1850 *Frontier Guardian* 2 Oct. (Thornton) Though Kister, that skeezecks, with Hall at his back Should come at his thieving. 1869 B. Harte *Luck of Roaring Camp, Miggles* 40 Thar ain't nobody but him within ten mile of the shanty, and that ar'.. old skee-icks knows it. 1875 J. G. Holland *Sevenoaks* iii. 40 If there's anything awful bad..in the word] Skeezacks—I should say that Tom Buffum was a Skeezacks. 1894 Stevenson & Osbourne *Ebb-Tide* I. vi, Nobody wants to lose a schooner; they want to lose her course, you skeericks [*sic*]! 1909 'O. Henry' *Options* (1916) 39 This is a poor skeezicks that's got nothing to eat but an onion. 1927 *Chambers's Jrnl.* 238/2 The old skee-sicks ain't calling our hand this deal.

Skein, *sb.*1 Add:

2. c. *Cytology.* [tr. G. *knäuel.*] In mitosis or indirect cell-division, that stage of the nucleus in which the chromatin takes the form of a thread, continuous or segmented.

1889 tr. Waldeyer in *Q. Jrnl. Microsc. Sci.* XXX. 164 The first stage of karyokinesis, the so-called 'dense skein' ('dichter Knäuel'). *Ibid.* 173 Rable says definitely that he has always found the longitudinal splitting of the chromatic threads to be completed at the end of the skein phase. 1904 *Science* 4 Mar. 393/1 No sign of chromatin thread (spireme or skein) is apparent.

Skeiner (skēi·nəɹ). [See -er 1.] One who skeins.

1921 *Dict. Occup. Terms* (1927) § 367 *Skeiner*..; reeler, skein or rand machine, which winds finished twine into skeins. *Ibid.* § 943 *Bundler* (flax and hemp); skeiner; puts together necessary number of banks of yarn to form a bundle.

Skeletin (ske·lĭtin). *Chem.* [f. Skeleton *sb.* + -in 1.] One of a group of complex, albuminoid, insoluble, nitrogenous substances, such as spongin, chitin, sericin, etc., found in the skeletal tissues of invertebrates.

1886 *Jrnl. Chem. Soc.* L. 481 The term skeletin includes a number of nitrogenous but sulphur-free substances found in the skeletal tissues of invertebrates.

Skeleton, *sb.* Add: **7. c.** Applied to a staff, company, or the like, of the minimum size for carrying on the work to be done.

1925 *Strand Mag.* Sept. 255/2 A skeleton staff were working nervously under the direction of a chartered accountant. 1928 *Daily Mail* 7 Aug. 2/5 The establishment of skeleton air defence formations on the northern coast.

d. *skeleton gig, wagon*; **skeleton brass,** a memorial brass representing a skeleton; **skeleton construction, flashing** (*vbl. sb.*2), **framework** (see quots.); **skeleton drill** *Mil.*, infantry drill for the instruction of officers in which a small number of men represent a battalion; also *fig.*; **skeleton girder, -pattern** (see quots.).

1913 Ward *Brasses* 143 *Skeleton Brasses. 1897 *Building Construction* I. (new ed.) 117 Among the most recent examples of the application of mild steel to building purposes may be noted the so-called '*skeleton construction' as exemplified in some of the principal cities of the United States. Numerous buildings have been erected upon this principle, of 15 to 20 stories, and sometimes exceeding 250 feet in height, which are mainly dependent for their stability upon the combination of columns and girders which form the '*skeleton' framework, the exterior walling being frequently merely a veneer of terra cotta, brickwork, or stonework, anchored to, and carried by, the metallic framework. 1876 Voyle & Stevenson *Military Dict.* s.v. *Skeleton*, *Skeleton drill, which is a method of instructing officers and non-commissioned officers in drill, when a sufficient number of men cannot be collected to form a battalion in single rank. 1897 Hardy *Well-Beloved* III. v, Pierson..could consider and practise thoroughly a species of skeleton drill in receiving visitors when the pair should announce themselves as married. 1875 *Building Construction* I. 159 Another plan is to form a side gutter along the wall,..securing the upturned lead in a stepped raglet, or covering it by an apron all in one piece cut to fit the steps. *Note*, Sometimes called a *Skeleton Flashing. 1867 'T. Lackland' *Homespun* II. 181 At all hours of the day..a fly, a sulky, or a *skeleton gig could be seen somewhere about the yard. 1888 *Lockwood's Dict. Mech. Engin.*, *Skeleton Girder*, an open-webbed girder, or lattice girder. *Ibid.*, *Skeleton Pattern*, an open frame pattern, that is, one which is not precisely like its casting, but whose outlines or bounding edges alone are given. 1868 H. Woodruff *Trotting Horse Amer.* x. 112 If the race is to be run in harness, it will be advisable to change the sulky for a *skeleton wagon occasionally.

Skelter, *sb. dial.* and *colloq.* [f. the vb.] A quick rush or run; a scamper.

1899 *Cumbld. Gloss.*, *Skelter*, an open, free, slashing gait; a hasty retreat. 1923 *Daily Mail* 21 June 9 Lord Penrhyn's filly..drove the Princess and the royal friends into a sudden short skelter from its hoofs.

Skene 2 (skīn). The name of A. J. C. *Skene* (1838–1900), American physician, used chiefly in the genitive to designate certain small canals which open into the female urethra.

1890 Billings *Med. Dict.*, Skene's tubules. 1901 Dorland *Med. Dict.* (ed. 2) s.v. *Gland*, Skene's glands, two glands just within the meatus of the female urethra: regarded as homologues of the seminal vesicles. 1910 *Practitioner* Mar. 393 Two of these spots..probably represent the opening of Skene's ducts. *Ibid.* Apr. 487 The ducts of the two small glands in the floor of the female urethra, known as 'Skene's tubules'.

Skerrick (ske·rik). *Austral. colloq.* A small fragment.

1931 I. L. Idriess *Lasseter's Last Ride* xxv. 205 Half a goanna's tail, the long thin end with not a skerrick of meat on it.

Sketch, *sb.* Add: **1. c.** = *Sight *sb.*1 1 (*b*).

1931 Priestley *Angel Pavement* xi. § 4 You do look a sight, Dad...I never saw such a sketch.

6. *sketch-box, -paper.*

1888 *Lockwood's Dict. Mech. Engin.*, *Sketch Paper*, foolscap paper having faint lines crossing at right angles, producing squares of 1 inch, each divided into eight equal parts. Used for proportional drawing or sketching. 1902 *Chambers's Jrnl.* Dec. 779/1 The girl lingered while the painter unpacked his sketch-box.

Skeuomorph (skiū·omǭɹf). [f. Gr. σκεῦος vessel, utensil + μορφή form.] An ornament or ornamental design due to structure; an ornament or design representing an implement or utensil. Hence **Skeuomo·rphic** *a.*, of, pertaining to, exhibiting, or decorated with skeuomorphs. Also **Skeuobi·omorph**, an ornament, design, or form which combines the characteristics of a skeuomorph and a biomorph.

1889 H. Colley March in *Trans. Lanc. & Cheshire Antiq. Soc.* VII. 166 The forms of ornament demonstrably due to structure require a name. If those taken from animals are called zoomorphs, and those from plants phyllomorphs, it will be convenient to call those derived from structure, skeuomorphs. *Ibid.*, As soon as man began to make things, to fasten a handle to a stone implement, to construct a wattled roof, to weave a mat, skeuomorphs became an inseparable part of his existence. *Ibid.* 168 The transfer of thong-work from the flint axe, where it was functional, to the bronze celt, where it was skeuomorphic. 1905 [see *Anthropomorphic *a.* 2].

Skew, *sb.*3 Add: **2. d.** *Geom.* = Regulus 5. (Cf. Skew *a.* 2 b.)

1902 *Encycl. Brit.* XXVIII. 660/1 A Ruled Surface, Regulus, or Skew is a configuration of lines which..depend on only one parameter...The simplest example, that of a quadric surface, is really two skews on the same surface.

Skew, *a.* **2.** Add: *skew gearing.*

1875 Knight *Dict. Mech.*, *Skew-gearing*, cog-wheels with teeth placed obliquely, so as to slide into each other and avoid clashing. 1902 A. C. Harmsworth *Motors & Motor-Driving* x. 191 Another plan..substitutes for the bevel gearing what is known as skew or screw gearing.

Skewer, *sb.* Add: **1. e.** (See quot.)

1888 *Lockwood's Dict. Mech. Engin.*, *Skewers*, or *Wires*, pieces of iron wire from 3 to 6 inches in length, pointed at one end, and turned round into a loop at the other, and employed for the temporary holding of loose pieces in the foundry sand.

Skewiness. [f. *skewy adj.] = Skewness.

1862 'Gail Hamilton' *Country Living & Th.* 62 Though freedom from foreign growth discovered an intention of straightness, the most casual observer could not but see that skewiness had usurped its place.

Skew-whiff (skiū,hwi·f), *a.* and *adv.* (*sb.*) *dial.* and *colloq.* In 8 **scew-.** [f. Skew *a.* and *adv.*, *v.*2 + Whiff *sb.*1, *v.*1] Askew, awry (*lit.* and *fig.*). Also *on the skew-whiff.*

1754 *Scots Mag.* July 337/2 Behind, with a coach-horse short dock, cut your hair; Stick a flower before, scew-whiff, with an air. 1896 *Warw. Word-Bk.*

Ski, *sb.* **2.** Add: *ski-joring, -jumper*; *ski stick*, etc.

1927 *Sunday Times* 13 Feb. 17/2 In the skijoring races on the Lake,..the well-known Swiss hockey player fell. 1927 *Observer* 18 Dec. 9/4 This fun may be taken to include skiing, luge-ing, skating, ski-joring, and trailing by day. *Ibid.*, The introduction of aluminium skisticks in the place of the older forms in bamboo and hazel. 1931 *Times Lit. Suppl.* 5 Nov. 868/4 Championship as a ski-jumper.

Skiamachy: see Sciamachy.

Skiascope (skəi·äskoᵘp). Also **scia-.** [f. Gr. σκιά shadow + -scope.] **a.** An optical instrument used to determine the refracting action of the eye by throwing light into it from a small mirror and observing the retinal lights and shadows. **b.** = *Fluoroscope. Hence **Skiasco·pic** *a.*, of, pertaining to, or used in skiascopy; **Skia·scopy,** the use of a skiascope.

1890 Billings *Med. Dict.*, *Skiascopy*, a method of determining the refraction of the eye by observing the direction and rapidity of motion of the shadowy edges of the images, real or virtual, of a flame, formed by the refracting media of the eye. 1903 *Optical Jrnl.* Dec. 782 (Cent. D. Suppl.) To make a skiascopic chimney for an argand burner. 1923 G. F. Alexander (*title*) Principles of Ophthalmoscopy and Skiascopy.

Skid, *sb.* Add: **2. f.** A runner attached to an aeroplane, *spec.* each of the two runners used to facilitate landing.

Tail skid, wing skid, one placed under the tail and wings as a protection from contact with the ground.

1909 A. Berget *Conquest of Air* II. iii. 194 The planes rest upon two skids which form a kind of sleigh. 1910 C. C. Turner *Aerial Navig.* xxiv. 284 The machine is mounted on skids. 1911 *Rep. Brit. Assoc.* 482 In connection with the under-carriages of aeroplanes, the advantage of landing direct on skids is urged. 1916 H. Barber *Aeroplane Speaks* 141 *Undercarriage Skid*, a spar, mounted in a fore and aft direction, and to which the wheels of the undercarriage are sometimes attached. Should a wheel give way the skid is then supposed to act like the runner of a sleigh and to support the aeroplane. *Tail Skid*, a piece of wood or other material, orientable, and fitted with shock absorbers, situated under the tail of an aeroplane in order to support it upon the ground and to absorb the shock of alighting.

4. (Example.) Also, in extended use, with reference to motor-boats and aeroplanes.

1908 *Isle of Man Weekly Times* 12 Sept. 4/1 All the cars out complain of some bad skids. 1916 H. Barber *Aeroplane Speaks* 83 The velocity of the 'skid', or sideways movement. 1928 *Daily Express* 3 Sept. 5/2 The breath-taking sprawling skids round the cornering buoys.

Skid, *v.*1 Add: **1. c.** To throw (something) so that it scatters or glides over a surface.

1897 J. Hammond *Cornish Parish* 339 Instead of spreading manure, we 'skid' or 'skate' dung. 1897 G. B. Shaw *Lett. to Ellen Terry* 1 Mar. (1931), Get ten sovereigns and skid them out from the beach into the sea. 1901 'L. Malet' *Hist. Sir R. Calmady* v. iii, Helen skidded the hand-glass down upon the dressing-table.

3. b. Also of the vehicle itself.

1912 *Motor Manual* iii. (ed. 14) 101 To minimise the risk of a car skidding on greasy roads numerous devices have been introduced. 1926 Spanner *Naviators* i. 13 A car that looks as though it is going straight can be dodged, but one that skids about like a demented dog chasing its tail is not to be faced with assurance.

c. Of an aeroplane: To slip sideways away from the centre of curvature while turning. Cf. *Side-slip *v.* b.

1916 H. Barber *Aeroplane Speaks* 22 *note*, When an aeroplane is turned to the left or the right the centrifugal force of its momentum causes it to skid sideways and outwards away from the centre of the turn.

d. *trans.* in causal sense. To cause (a vehicle, its wheels, or track) to skid; also, to turn (a corner, etc.) by means of a skidding movement.

1925 Joan Sutherland *Circle of Stars* xxiii, Carter skidded the Ford to a standstill. 1928 *Sunday Express* 19 Aug. 1/2 Viscount Curzon..was cheered as he skilfully skidded the corners. 1931 Martel *In Wake of Tank* 84 Even a small swing on to a new direction caused loss of speed, while a turn through a right angle absorbed so much power in skidding the track round that it was usually necessary to change down to first gear on the machine.

Skiddoo (skidū·), *v. slang.* Also **skidoo.** [app. based on Skedaddle.] *intr.* To be off, depart, vamose.

1907 N. Munro *Daft Days* xxiv, I'll skiddoo from the gang for a day or two. 1920 *Chambers's Jrnl.* July 436/2 Such words and expressions as..skiddoo..,and many others, which would be more or less meaningless in London, are common to everyday Canadian speech.

Skiddy (ski·di), *a.* [f. Skid *v.*1 + -y 1.] On which one is liable to skid.

1928 *Daily Express* 10 Dec. 19 Motorists drove with caution on skiddy roads.

Skiffling (ski·fliŋ). *local.* [Cf. *scabbling, scappling.*] The action or process of rough-dressing building stone by knocking off the rough projections.

1875 Knight *Dict. Mech.* 1901 *J. Black's Carp. & Build., Masonry* 23 For ragstone ashlar work, the stone, when quarried, has its rough projections knocked off with a heavy double-pointed hammer...This operation is locally [*sc.* Kent] called 'skiffling', and is the same as that known in the neighbourhood of London and other parts of the country by the term of 'knobbling'.

Skil (skil). [Alaska.] **a.** The black candle-fish, *Anoplopoma fimbria.* **b.** The coal-fish, *Pollachius carbonarius.* Also **Ski·lfish.**

1886 *Encycl. Brit.* XX. 170/1 Holibut, herring, salmon, cod, and coal-fish or 'skil' (this last also rich in oil and a valuable food-fish) are likewise abundant.

Skilip (ski·lip). [f. *Iskilip*, a town in Asia Minor.] Impure scammony.

1886 *Encycl. Brit.* XXI. 365/2 This adulterated article is known as 'skilip', and the pure article as 'virgin scammony'.

Skimi, variant of *Shikimi.

Skimmer, *sb.* Add: **7. c.** A hydroplane. (*temporary.*)

1909 *Chambers's Jrnl.* Oct. 636/1 Elaborate experiments with small models following the lines of skimmers or hydroplanes.

8. b. *Cricket.* A ball that travels with a low trajectory.

1897 Ranjitsinhji *Jubilee Bk. Cricket* [illegible] promptly drives it just as expected—a real 'skimmer' [illegible] over extra-cover's head. 1903 G. L. Jessop *Cricket* [illegible] majority of his drives were low 'skimmers'.

Skimmi, variant of *Shikimi.

Skimming, *ppl. a.* Add: **4.** That drives the ball with a low trajectory. (Cf. *Skimmer 8 b.)

1888 Steel & Lyttelton *Cricket* 165 The low skimming fast bowler is generally an easy man to play. [illegible] *Post* 9 Aug. 14/1 Woolley..made a low skimming drive over the ring at long-on for 6 off S. Staples.

Skin, *sb.* Add: **1. d.** A bird or mammal stuffed but not mounted in imitation of life.

1888 *Encycl. Brit.* XXIII. 90/1 Powders consisting of tannin, pepper, camphor, and burnt alum are sometimes used for 'making skins', but they dry them too rapidly for the purposes of 'mounting'...When 'skins' only are wanted for the cabinet, it is sufficient to fill the head and body with chopped tow.

7. c. In other usages (see quots.).

1885 *Encycl. Brit.* XVIII. 446/2 A pearl of the first water should possess, in jewellers' language, a perfect 'skin' and a fine 'orient'. 1909 P. A. Vaile *Modern Golf* [illegible] One quaint notion was that they [*sc.* pimples] [illegible] outer skin of the ball. 1920 A. D. Passmore in [illegible] 9 A part of the old brown skin of the stone.

f. *Electr.* The outer or surface layers of a conductor, serving to carry current at high frequencies.

1902 *Encycl. Brit.* XXXIII. 216/2 With Hertzian waves the resistance is largely multiplied (compared with steady resistance), for it is the resistance of a thin skin.

9. b. = *whisky skin* (*Whisky *sb.*1 [illegible]). *U.S. slang.*

1919 Mencken *Amer. Lang.* 85.

13. skin-beetle, a beetle of the genus [illegible], which feeds upon skins and hides; **skin conduction** *Electr.*, conduction of a current by means of the outer layer only of a conductor; **skin current** *Electr.*, a current carried by the outer layer only of a conductor; **skin diver,** a naked pearl-diver; **skin drying,** the drying of the skin, *spec.* the skin of a mould used in metal casting; **skin-drying** *ppl. a.*, that dries the skin; **skin effect** *Electr.*, the tendency of an alternating current to flow through the outer layer only of a conductor at high frequency; **skin friction,** *spec.* the friction between aeroplane surfaces and the air; **skin-heart,** the vessels of the skin, the peripheral vessels, with reference to the processes carried on through the skin; **skin-mesh,** the interlaced structure of the skin; **skin-moth,** any of several moths whose larvæ infest skins and furs; **skin-pack,** a lotion massaged into the skin; **skin reflex,** a reflex action aroused by stimulating the skin; **skin resistance,** (*a*) the resistance of the metal plating of a vessel; (*b*) = *skin friction; (*c*) *Electr.*, the resistance of a conductor to alternating currents of high frequency whereby the outer layer alone conducts the current; **skin-running,** the smuggling of [illegible].

1862 T. W. Harris *Insects injur. Veget.* (ed. 3) [illegible] beetles (*Dermestadæ*, *Byrrhidæ*, and *Trogidæ*), [illegible] ..act the useful part of scavengers. 1893 [illegible] *Electromagnetic Theory* II. Pref. p. iii, My old [illegible] relating to *skin conduction. 1902 *Encycl. Brit.* [illegible] 216/2 In skin conduction the resistance depends [illegible] area of the surface of the conductor...It follows [illegible] such very rapid alternations as lead to skin conduction the *skin current concentrates itself where the [illegible] ment is strongest. 1932 *Blackw. Mag.* Jan. [illegible] relied solely upon their *skin divers—the divers' [illegible] term for a naked man. 1888 *Lockwood's Dict. Mech. Engin.*, *Skin Drying*, the drying of the surface [illegible] sand mould previous to closing it for the pouring [illegible] metal. Skin drying effects the removal of a portion [illegible] moisture and diminishes the risk of a blown or [illegible] casting. 1927 in Kendrew *Climates of Continents* [illegible] the coast they [*sc.* the winds] are hot and are skin-drying, lip-cracking, unpleasant visitants. 1900 *Jrnl.* [illegible] XLVIII. 878 Electric Oscillations.—1. Influence [illegible] quency upon alternating current phenomena... [illegible] effect. 1906 *Technol. & Sci. Dict.* (ed. Goodchild & [illegible]) *Skin Effect*, the tendency of any current which [illegible] in amount to flow in the outer layers of a conductor. [illegible] H. S. Maxim in *Century Mag.* Oct. 833/2 It would [illegible] fore appear that the *skin friction between the air [illegible] polished surface is so small that it need not be taken into

consideration. 1911 *Rep. Brit. Assoc.* 482 In order to extend the premisses to cover a plausible expression for the resistance to flight and the power expended thereon, it is necessary to adopt a value for skin friction. 1916 H. Barber *Aeroplane Speaks* 15 *note*, Skin friction is that part of the drift due to the friction of the air with roughnesses upon the surface of the aeroplane. 1907 F. W. Lanchester *Aerodynamics* 251 *Skin frictional = ξCρAV². 1901 Dorland *Med. Dict.* (ed. 2), **Skin-heart*, a name for the peripheral vessels: so called for their importance in various metabolic processes. 1907 *Practitioner* Apr. 516 Restoring the pulsations of the great skin-heart. *Ibid.* 503 When the capillaries of the *skin-mesh and the lung-mesh are distended, and greater quantities of blood are pumped through them, not only is heat escaping, but poisonous excretory matters. 1928 *Daily Express* 9 Nov. 5/3 There are many kinds of *skin-packs, but perhaps the most useful is the almond oil pack for a skin that is inclined to dryness. 1924 Ogden tr. *Koffka's Growth of Mind* 83 *Skin-reflexes. 1875 *English Mechanic* 3 Sept. 634/3 We have sufficient data from which the *skin-resistance [*sc.* of a ship's hull] can be determined. 1902 *Encycl. Brit.* XXXIII. 217/1 The resistance of the sea to Hertzian waves in 'wireless telegraphy' comes under the same principles, and may be calculated by the same formula as the skin resistance of wires. 1904 *Jrnl. Franklin Inst.* Apr. 248 The skin resistance of copper bonds increases with time. 1920 B. Cronin *Timber Wolves* 77 My partner, Colvin, told me that Timber Bend had a reputation for sly-grog selling and *skin running.

Skin, *v.* Add:

4. d. *To skin the cat*: in gymnastic exercises, to raise the feet and legs between the arms while hanging by the hands from a horizontal bar and so draw the body up and over the bar; also, to get through a very narrow opening. *U.S.*

1845–51 S. Judd *Margaret* II. i. (1874) 181 The boys betaking themselves to their several diversions, snapping the whip, skinning the cat, racing round the Meeting-house, or what not. 1873 'Mark Twain' & Warner *Gilded Age* iv. 43 They ran races up and down the deck,..'Skinned the cat' on the hog-chains. 1887 'C. E. Craddock' *Keedon Bluffs* 88 He did not wait a second but 'skinned the cat' among the rafters. 1888 *Phil. Ev. Bulletin* 23 Feb. (Farmer) Another Presidential candidate..utilized a pole daily for skinning the cat. 1907 Mulford *Bar-20* viii. 80 Don't yu remember how I used to shinny up this here wall an' skin th' cat gettin' through that hole up there what yu said was a window?

fig. 1905 *N. Y. Evening Post* 14 Oct., We have learned how to hide behind the back log of 'environment' or to 'skin the cat' in morality on the score of 'heredity'.

e. To keep (the eyes) open. (Cf. Skinned *ppl. a.* 4 b.)

1875 J. G. Holland *Sevenoaks* x. 133 Skin yer eyes, now, Mr. Balfour, we're comin' to a lick.

f. To remove the top layer of.

1904 *N. Y. Eve. Amer.* 2 Aug. (Cent. D. Suppl.) The [race-] track..has been 'skinned' and generally rendered faster.

5. b. To remove as if by skinning.

1904 'O. Henry' *Cabbages & Kings* vi. 96 Henry skinned a twenty off his roll.

c. *Taxidermy.* To remove or take *out* from the skin.

1888 *Encycl. Brit.* XXIII. 90/2 The neck and head are skinned out down to the inner edges of the lips and nose... Fishes..are skinned out by removing 'cutlets'.

7. b. (Earlier U.S. examples.)

1839 C. F. Briggs *Harry Franco* II. vi. 76 I wish I may be blown into a gin shop if I warnt skinned clean O! The young woman had..picked my pockets of every cent. 1844 J. J. Webb *Memoirs* 146 Many Americans have been drawn into the toils of the rascals, and skinned.

9. b. *intr.* To slip *through.* *U.S.*

1902 G. H. Lorimer *Lett. Self-made Merchant* xi. 141 If you would make a downright failure or a clean-cut success once in a while, instead of always just skinning through this way. 1920 W. Camp *Football without a Coach* 57 The best a runner can hope for is a chance to skin through that opening before it ceases to exist.

c. (Earlier U.S. example.)

1873 Joaquin Miller *Unwritten Hist.* iv. (1876) 63 Four aces! and what else? Skin 'em out, skin 'em out!

e. To beat or overcome completely: esp. in *to have* (*got*) *a person skinned.* *U.S. colloq.*

1904 'O. Henry' *Cabbages & Kings* iii. 51 I guess you've got us skinned on the animal and vegetation question. 1908 'Yeslah' *Tenderfoot S. Calif.* ii. 22 When it rains in California, it's got all the rest of the country skinned to death. 1911 H. Quick *Yellowstone N.* iv. 110 'Purty good little places,' said he, 'but the home place skins 'em all.' 1913 in *R. Brooke's Coll. Poems* (1918) Mem. p. lxxxiv, Sir, I may tell you that in my opinion you have Mr. Noyes skinned.

Skin-coat. Add: **3.** (See quotation.)

1897 Moore *How to Build* viii. 119 Plaster should be applied in three coats..The third is called the 'hard' or 'white' or 'skin' coat.

Skinflinty, *a.* (Earlier U.S. example.)

1886 F. R. Stockton *Casting Away Mrs. Lecks* etc. II. 122 If he undertook to be skinflinty he'd better try it on somebody else besides us.

Skinned, *ppl. a.* Add:

4. b. *To keep one's eye skinned* (earlier and later U.S. examples).

1846 J. W. Webb *Altowan* I. vi. 167 I thought Parfin had kept his eyes skinned to wear his scalp so long in the Indian country. 1852 J. Weir *Simon Kenton* 12 It ain't so bad for one to keep his eye skinned, even in this 'ere civilized country. 1904 Lorimer *Old Gorgon Graham* 35 The exception is the thing that you always want to keep your eye skinned for in business.

c. Stripped of timber.

1907 *N. Y. Evening Post* (semi-weekly ed.) 18 July 6 Lands in the watershed of the Mohawk range cost a dollar an acre for 'skinned' wood-lots.

Skinner. Add: **2. b.** An implement used for skinning animals.

1872 *Amer. Naturalist* VI. 223 The specimen could have been used as a knife, or 'skinner,' although now its edge is too irregular and dull for skinning.

7. A teamster.

1925 C. R. Cooper *Lions 'n' Tigers* v. 137 Ragsy belonged to a 'skinner' or teamster.

8. (See quot.)

1930 *Terms Telegraphs & Telephones* (Brit. Engin. Standards Assoc.) 42 *Skinner*, the length of insulated wire between a laced cable form and the connecting point.

Skinning, *vbl. sb.* **2. c.** (Earlier example.)

1856 *Trans. Mich. Agric. Soc.* VII. 171 The old plan of constant cropping without manure, or 'skinning', will ruin the land.

Skip, *sb.*1 Add: **2. d.** *Poker.* Three or more cards of the same suit having consecutive even or odd numbers, as 2, 4, 6, etc.

1909 R. F. Foster *Complete Hoyle* 214 Skip or Dutch Straight, any sequence of alternate cards, of various suits. Beats two pairs and a blaze.

e. *Wireless.* A silent belt between the point where the direct ray from a transmitting station becomes inaudible and the point where the reflected or indirect ray becomes audible. Also *attrib.* in **skip distance,** the distance or extent of this belt.

1930 *B.B.C. Year-Bk.* 451/2 *Skip distance*, the distance between the point where the direct ray from a transmitting station becomes so attenuated as to be inaudible, and the point where the reflected or indirect ray strikes the earth's surface. The skip distance is a function of the wave-length employed and increases with a decrease in wave-length. 1931 *Observer* 8 Nov. 18/5 Because of 'skip' it [*sc.* the new station] will hardly ever be audible in this country...The shorter the wave, the greater the 'skip' distance as a rule.

Skip, *v.*1 **6. c.** Add: Also, to 'jump' (one's bail).

1931 Slosson *Great Crusade* 88 The I.W.W. leader who had 'skipped bail' and fled abroad.

Skipetar (ski·pətāɹ). Also **Skip(i)tar, Skypetar, Shkyipetar.** [Albanian, lit. mountaineer, f. *skipe* mountain.] = *Albanian *sb.* Also *attrib.*

1833 *Penny Cycl.* I. 256/2 The Albanian..calls himself Skipitar. 1902 *Encycl. Brit.* XXV. 246/2 The Albanians ..call themselves *Shkyipetar.* 1923 *19th Cent.* Jan. 17 The Skiptars greet all these innovations with a kindly tolerance.

Skirmish, *v.* Add: **1. c.** To make excursions in order to see what one can find; to scout round in search of something.

1894 'R. Andom' *We Three & Troddles* xxiii, He left the room to skirmish after a clean handkerchief. *Ibid.* xxiv, We had them downstairs and into the cab before they could skirmish after more substantial fare.

Skirt, *sb.* Add: **1. c.** An underskirt or petticoat.

1862 *Catal. Internat. Exhib., Brit.* II. No. 3674 Counterpanes, toilette-covers, skirts. *Ibid.* No. 4935 Spiral Crinoline Steel and Bronze for Ladies' Skirts. 1895 *Army & Navy Co-op. Soc. Price List* 1090 Ladies' Skirts, &c. Cream or Scarlet Flannel...Girls' and Children's Skirts. White Long Cloth, trimmed Embroidery.

8. c. *Mech.*

1913 W. E. Dommett *Motor Car Mech.* 12 For the sake of lightness and more particularly for use on racing cars, holes are drilled around the lower part or *skirt* of the piston and two rings only may be used.

Skirting, *vbl. sb.* Add: **4. b.** *Naut.*

1923 F. Wild *Shackleton's Last Voy.* ii. 43 The ports, skirtings and boats were painted black.

Skit, *sb.*4 [Cf. *Scad.] A number, a crowd; *pl.*, 'lots', 'heaps'.

1925 A. S. M. Hutchinson *One Increasing Purpose* III. ix, 'What was that little red rosette he had on his left arm? I see skits of people with it.' 'Been vaccinated, of course.' 1927 *Blackw. Mag.* Nov. 594/1 The Kachins were in the jungle, a skit of them, trying to stop us at the ford.

Skite, *sb.* Add: **4.** A motor-cycle. *slang.*

1929 'Seamark' *Down River* iv, She went out on a skite. And what's more, she planted me on the pillion.

Skite, *v.*2 Add: **3.** To boast or brag. *Austral. slang.*

1916 *Anzac Bk.* 99 If there's one thing I hate, it is skiting.

Skitter, *v.*2 Add: **2. b.** To throw, shy. *U.S.*

1907 *Harper's Mag.* Feb. 460 The younger boy skittered rocks at a chicken-hawk.

Skittle, *sb.* Add: **1. d.** Chess not played seriously. *colloq.*

1856 Tomlinson *Chess Player's Ann.* 61 Nor will our royal Game less royal sound, If shallow men play skittles on the ground, Where first-rate Chess sedately sits in state, And spends long hours accomplishing a mate. 1868 *Westminster Papers* I. 87 With a great many good people the fascinations ascribed to Chess are entirely derived from what we may call the skittle phase of it. 1894 S. Tinsley *Let.* in *Daily News* 30 May 3/6 There is, as every experienced chessist knows, all the difference in the world between what is known as off-hand play or 'skittles' and chess.

Skittle, *v.* Add: **2.** *Cricket.* With *out*: To get (batsmen) out rapidly in succession.

1926 *Westm. Gaz.* 1 Sept., Glamorgan skittled out on difficult wicket. 1928 *Daily Tel.* 7 Feb. 16/1 Nupen skittled out the remaining batsmen.

3. To knock down (the pins) in the game of skittles.

1928 *Daily Express* 31 Mar. 3/4 Mine host and Mr. Herbert swung their arms, flung the cheeses, and skittled the pins.

4. *intr.* (See next.)

1856 Tomlinson *Chess Player's Ann.* 54 If your opponent cannot appreciate fine play, nevertheless play your best; for by skittling as he skittles you degrade yourself without raising him.

Skittling, *vbl. sb.* Playing a skittle game of chess; also *attrib.* So **Ski·ttler.**

1856 [see prec. 4]. 1868 *Westminster Papers* I. 87 We consider it quite possible to diffuse the game [of chess] without affording encouragement to the mere 'skittler'. *Ibid.*, Skittling Chess is..much more sociable than its elder sister. 1911 *Daily News* 24 Apr. 4 The spread of chess literature, which has made every 'skittler' a book player.

Skive, *v.*2 Add: **b.** *Army slang.* To dodge a duty. **c.** *U.S.* To evade expenditure (*Funk's Standard Dict.* 1928).

1919 *War Terms* in *Athenæum* 1 Aug. 695/1. 1925 Fraser & Gibbons *Soldier & Sailor Words.*

Skiver, *sb.*2 **2.** (Earlier U.S. example.)

1849 *Rep. U.S. Comm. Patents* (1850) 313 I claim..the application of a gauge or gauges to a skiver.

Skivvy (ski·vi). *colloq.*, usually *derogatory.* [Obscure.] A female domestic servant, esp. a rough 'general'.

1922 *Glasgow Herald* 23 Feb. 4 The domestic servant need not worry herself a great deal about the ill-natured sneers of 'slavey' and 'skivvy' which are levelled at her. 1924 'O. Onions' *Ghosts in Daylight* 177 One little skivvy in a shabby black frock and re-soled shoes. 1927 A. Bennett *Woman who Stole Everything* etc. 189 Never keep more skivvies with all them floors unless ye have to save 'em running up and a-running down. 1929 G. W. De[illegible] *Roper's Row* xxii, § 4, I saw Old Blizzard out on Sunday walking with the skivvy.

Skoda (skǭ·dă). The name of Emil von Skoda (1839–1900), Austrian gun-maker, used *attrib.* or *ellipt.* to designate certain types of artillery or of breech mechanism for guns.

1902 *Encycl. Brit.* XXIX. 166/1 In the Hotchkiss and also in the Skoda systems the mechanism is of the vertical breech block type. 1918 E. S. Farrow *Dict. Mil. Terms*, Skoda Gun...Skoda Mortar. 1920 *Blackw. Mag.* May 591/1 The regular army..had a variety of guns,..Austrian Skodas, French 75's, German and Turkish pieces.

Skogbölite (skǭ·gbölait). *Min.* [f. *Skogböle*, Sweden + -ite 1.] A metallic black ferrous tantalate, differing from ordinary tantalite in crystalline form.

1892 E. S. Dana *Dana's Min.* (ed. 6) 736 Skogbölite.. associated with rose quartz and gigantolite.

Skoke, variant of Scoke, poke-weed.

1794 [see Scoke]. 1846 Mrs. Whitcher *Widow Bedott P.* v. 50 She said he must take skoke berries and rum right off. 1855 *Trans. Mich. Agric. Soc.* VI. 149 The plants on the uplands are calumbo,..skoke or garget root.

Skookum-house. *slang.* [Chinook Jargon (from Salish) *skookum* strong.] The guard-room.

1905 Rex Beach *Pardners* ii. (1912) 59 So I was dragged to the 'skookum-house', where I spent the night figuring out my finish. 1910 'O. Henry' *Whirligigs* xxi. 235 The idea..gives me hyperesthesia of the roopteetoop! The skookum house for yours!

Skrelling (skre·liŋ). Also **Skraelling.** [ad. Olcel. *Skrælingjar* pl., native inhabitants of Vinland, the Olcel. name of the N.E. coast of North America.] A member of one of the native races of North America; *esp.* an Eskimo or Greenlander.

1860 Mayne Reid *Odd People* 87 Whatever, therefore, may be said of a 'Schelling' [*sic*], or native Greenlander, will be equally applicable to an Esquimaux of Labrador. *Ibid.* 92 The Danish and Norwegian colonists of West Greenland, though backed by constant intercourse with their mother-land, are but little more civilized than the 'Skellings' [*sic*], who are their neighbours. 1885 *Encycl. Brit.* XIX. 316/1 The settlers were attacked by Skrellings or Eskimo, who overran the West Bygd in 1349.

Skuett. (Modern example with form *skuet.*)

1928 *Daily Express* 11 Oct. 5/2 Bits of chicken, meat, or game,..threaded on small skewers alternately with tiny rolls of bacon..made good skuets.

Skulduddery, -duggery: see Sculduddery.

1818– [see Dict.]. 1911 H. Quick *Yellowstone N.* ix. 239 It began to look to me like Hen was up to some skulduggery.

Skulk, *sb.* **1.** (Earlier modern example.)

1838 *Knickerbocker Mag.* XI. 448 Spotswood had told the middie that Tudor was a great 'skulk', and would probably be reluctant to turn out.

Skupshtina (sku·pʃtinā). Also **Soubsch'tina, Skoupschina, Skuptchina.** [Serbian скупштина, f. скупа together, скупити to assemble.] The national assembly of Jugoslavia; formerly, of Serbia or Montenegro.

1862 W. Denton *Servia & Servians* xii, Immediately after the Servians had succeeded in liberating themselves from the Turkish rule they set about forming political institutions for themselves. Among the earliest is the assembly called the Skoupschina. 1866 *Chambers's Encycl.* VIII. 627 Each circle..sends a deputy to the *Scubsch'tina.* 1883 *Encycl. Brit.* XVI. 781/2 In 1851, Danilo..prevailed on the 'skuptchina' to declare Montenegro a secular state with the hereditary government of a prince. 1928 *Daily Tel.* 14 Aug. 7/2 The Croat members will not return to the Skupshtina unless their demands are granted.

Skutterudite (sku·tərūdait). *Min.* [f. *Skutterud*, Norway + -ite 1.] A pale-grey cobalt arsenide occurring in isometric crystals.

1868 Dana *Min.* (ed. 5) 71.

Sky, *sb.*1 Add: **5. a.** (Examples illustrating use as a fashion shade.)

Supplement, p. 3873; Corrigenda, p. 4092; Spurious words, p. 4093; Books quoted, p. 4094

1851 *Illustr. Catal. Gt. Exhib.* III. III. 506/2 Pink, white, sky, and maize gros de Naples for ladies' bonnets. 1920 *Queen* 19 June, Advt. 6 Attractive blouse..in pink, lemon, sky, ivory, and black.

9. sky advertising, advertising by means of sky-shouting or sky-writing; **sky-shade** *Photog.*, a screen attached to the shutter or lens-tube for cutting off part of the light from the sky; **sky-shine,** the rays and light which come from the sky; **sky-shouting,** the sending of advertisements or messages from an aeroplane to those below by means of a loud speaker; so **sky-shouter**; **sky wave** *Wireless*, a wave which travels upwards until it reaches the Heaviside layer and is deflected downwards; also *attrib.*; **sky-writing,** the tracing of legible signs in the sky, esp. for advertising purposes, by means of smoke-trails made by aircraft or letters and devices projected by searchlight; so **sky-writer, -writing** *ppl. a.*

1932 *Children's Newspaper* 23 Jan. 6/1 The attempts to introduce *sky advertising. 1918 *Photo-Miniature* XV. Mar. (Gloss.), *Sky Shade. 1919 *Brit. Jrnl. Photogr. Almanac* 244 A lens-hood is a short funnel..used for shielding the lens from strong light. The simpler form (a single screen) is a sky-shade. 1928 *Daily Express* 20 Dec. 8/3 There is little *sky-shine in a cloudy sky. 1932 *Children's Newspaper* 23 Jan. 6/1 The inventor..can now quote terms for *Sky Shouting or Sky Advertising. Concerning the *sky-shouters a really alarming invention has been successfully tried. 1932 *Times* 23 Feb., 'Sky-shouting' seemed to threaten even worse possibilities. 1932 *B.B.C. Year-Bk.* 313 Transmission is only possible over long distances by means of the '*sky' wave. *Ibid.* 314 It would appear that there is no reflection by the Heaviside layer, which means that there is no 'sky' wave radiation which will descend in other countries. 1927 *Pictorial Weekly* 17 Sept. 198 A window sign which reproduces in miniature the work of the *sky-writer. 1922 *Daily Mail* 8 Aug. 5/3 The Daily Mail *sky-writing aeroplane was over Margate and Folkestone yesterday. 1923 *Westm. Gaz.* 16 May, Sky-writing..did not commend itself to the general body of advertisers. 1932 *New Statesman & Nation* 23 Jan. 91/2 Sky-writing will provide a spectacle and people will marvel at it.

Skyhoot, *v.* ? Fanciful perversion of Scoot *v.*

1888 *Boy's Own Paper* Summer No. 38/1 'Something's skyhooted in my shoulder...That brute threw me on my head.' 1928 E. Wallace *Double* i, Why I'm sky-hooting down to Brighton for two days, heaven knows!

Sky-line. Add: **b.** The outline or silhouette of a building or number of buildings or other objects seen against the sky; similarly, in painting and similar arts of representation, the outline or profile of hills, trees, etc.

1903 Watkins *Watkins Man.* 40 Where suitable clouds are present, and the exposure is made by hand, it is a great advantage to hold a piece of brown or opaque paper in front of the lens for three-quarters of the time of exposure...The edge of the paper can be roughly torn to suit the sky line. 1932 *News Chron.* 5 July 9/5 The city's skyline of roofs was silhouetted against a blaze of gold. 1932 *Times Lit. Suppl.* 22 Dec. 972 The new sky-line that lofty skyscrapers have given it [*sc.* New York].

c. 'The line of the top row of pictures in an exhibition. *colloq.*' (Webster 1911).

Skyphos (skəi·fǫs). *Gr. Antiq.* [Gr. σκύφος (see Scyphus).] A large drinking-cup or bowl, having two handles not extending above the rim, and no foot.

1858 Birch *Anc. Pottery* II. 103 The Heracleotan *scyphos* had its handle ornamented with the Heraclean knot. 1921 *Brit. Museum Return* 61 Attic black-figure skyphos.

Skyway (skəi·wē¹). [f. Sky *sb.*¹ + Way *sb.*¹] The sky as a medium of transport or a route used by aircraft; an Airway.

1919 *Pearson's Mag.* Dec. 547/1 The letters will tell..the nationality of the ship passing along the world's skyways. 1921 *Spectator* 26 Mar. 396/1 As exiles returned by long sky-ways and lonely: The Souls of dead hill-men come home to their hills. 1924 *Public Opinion* 9 May 441/1 The highways and seaways and skyways of the world. 1928 L. Thomas (*title*) European Skyways. The Story of a Tour of Europe by Aeroplane.

Slab, *sb.*¹ Add: **1.** *transf.* (Earlier U.S. example.)

1882 *Harper's Mag.* July 321/2 From one of our exchanges ..we chip off the following slab of scientific knowledge.

b. A large piece or mass of cake, chocolate, etc., as distinguished from the smaller portions into which these goods are divided. Chiefly *attrib.*, as *slab-cake, -chocolate*, etc.

c. A commercial name for crude rubber in pieces one to two inches thick (*Cent. Dict.* Suppl.).

1880 *Encycl. Brit.* XII. 839/1 The rubber is glossy, of a bright pink colour and mottled appearance, and occurs in the form either of small balls pressed together or of irregular masses called 'slabs' or 'loaf' rubber. 1903 *Imperial Inst. Techn. Rep.* (ed. Dunstan) 153 The 'slabs' of blackish rubber alone being worth 1*s.* 11*d.* per pound.

3. d. *Building.* (See quot.)

1876 *Encycl. Brit.* IV. 466/2 The slab is that part of the floor of a room which is immediately before the fire-place, and along the extent of its front. In basement rooms, this slab is supported by a brick wall brought up from the ground; but in upper rooms the slab is supported by a flat half brick arch called a brick trimmer.

4. c. slab coil, inductance *Wireless* (see quots.).

1921 *Wireless World* IX. 163 The tuning is done by slab inductances, which can be easily fitted to the Marconi panel. .. By using different slabs a range of wave-lengths from 600 to 24,000 metres is obtained. 1930 *B.B.C. Year Bk.* 451/2 *Slab coil*, an inductance coil wound in a flat shape having the disadvantage of high self-capacity.

Slabber, *sb.*² Add: **c.** A workman who cuts or forms materials into slabs, or works on a slab.

1921 *Dict. Occup. Terms* (1927) § 118 *Slabber*; cements together tiles and other shaped articles for hearths, kerbs, etc. *Ibid.* § 159 *Slabber*,..cuts blocks of gelatine..into slabs. *Ibid.* § 381 *Dyer's labourer; slabber (slang), slab dyer*;..transfers dyed textiles from machine to draining slabs.

Slack, *sb.*³ Add: **2.** Also, a drop in the strength of a wind; a light wind.

1642 *Maine Doc. Hist.* III. 308 Ready..to attend for a slack of wind to bring over the ship to the Ile of Shoulds.

6. (Earlier example.)

1825 J. Neal *Bro. Jonathan* I. 156 'None o' your slack,' says I..'none o' your pokin' fun at me.'

Slack, *a.* and *adv.* **A.** *adj.* Add: **7. e.** *spec.* Of vowels: Open (Open *a.* 11 d).

1909 H. C. Wyld *Elem. Less. Eng. Gram.* ii. 28 Vowels formed with the tongue tense we call Tense Vowels, those with the tongue soft we call Slack Vowels.

10. *Slack sail* (cf. Slack *sb.*³ 4).

1621 [see sense 7]. 1867 Smyth *Sailor's Word-bk.* s.v. *Slab-lines*, They are used to truss up the slack sail, after it has been 'disarmed' by the leech and bunt-lines. 1883 *Man. Seamanship for Boys* 129 If the slacksail was allowed to hang down abaft the yard in a gale, and beat about, it would chafe the sail through. 1886 *Encycl. Brit.* XXI. 154/2 Where slack sail has to be taken in, it is the practice to leave it to the judgement of the sailmaker.

Slack, *v.* **9.** Add: Also with *it*.

1906 *Punch* 20 June 437 After a heavy morning on the Pier, I always slack it in the afternoon.

Slackage (slæ·kėdʒ). [f. Slack *sb.*³ + -age.] The amount allowed for the droop or sag of a rope or cable when not fully strained.

1903 *Electr. World & Engin.* 25 July 145 (Cent. D. Suppl.) The Anglia laid exactly 1,315 knots of cable from Midway to this point, and with the additional eighteen miles of shore end the actual amount of cable laid is 1,333 knots. There was about eight per cent. of slackage.

Slacken, *v.* **10.** and **10. b.** Add: Also with *off, up*.

1903 Conrad *Romance* v. i. 402, I wanted rest, woman's love, slackening off.

Slackness. Add: **5.** The tendency of a vessel under sail to fall away from the wind when the helm is amidships.

1877 W. H. White *Man. Naval Arch.* 484 The contrary condition, where the resultant resistance acts abaft the resultant wind pressure, and makes the head of the ship fall off from the wind, is termed 'slackness', and can only be counteracted by keeping the helm a-lee.

Slack-water. 3. (Earlier U.S. example.)

1837 Peck *Gaz. Illinois* III. 264 Fox river is susceptible of improvement by slack water at small expense.

Sladang, variant of *Seladang.

Slagless (slæ·glės), *a.* [f. Slag *sb.* + -less.] Of iron, steel, etc.: Free from slag. Hence **Sla·glessness.**

1902 *Encycl. Brit.* XXIX. 571/1 Slagless or 'Ingot-metal' Series. *Ibid.* 571/2 But the former lack the essential quality —slaglessness—which makes the latter steel.

Slalom (slā·lǫm). A ski-race down a course defined by artificial obstacles, esp. flags. Also *attrib.*

1921 *British Ski Year Bk.* 274 Slalom race on Inner-Arosa practice slopes. 1924 *Ibid.* 235 A downhill race and a Slalom competition. 1927 A. Lunn *Hist. Skiing* 414 A Slalom race should be the supreme test of a man's power to ski at high speed among obstacles. 1928 *Morning Post* 16 Feb. 13/3 Slalom racing at Muerren.

Slam, *sb.*² Add: **2. c.** *attrib.* (in Bridge), as *slam-bid, -bidding, -bonus, -convention.*

1928 Work *Contract Bridge* 69 The adoption of the special slam conventions too often closes the mouth of a player who otherwise would be able to make a highly useful and enlightening declaration of the normal conventional variety. 1929 — *Compl. Contract Bridge* p. xi, The partner..must jump if his hand warrant it—either one step..or a vault toward a slam bid. *Ibid.*, They may even score a slam bonus. *Ibid.* i. 5 The reward for slams is so great that special slam-bidding conventions have been invented.

Slam, *v.*¹ Add: **4. slam-jam** *adv.*, slap-bang.

1925 J. Gregory *Bab of Backwoods* xx, Do you think it was just accident that he copped off that hundred and sixty acres, right slam-jam in the middle of old Mart Willoughby's fifty thousand acres?

5. *trans.* = Slang *v.* 4. *U.S. slang.*

1926 H. L. Wilson *Somewhere in Red Gap* ii. 57 Couldn't even agree on the same kind of cocktail. Both slamming the waiter.

Slam-bang, *adv.* (Earlier example.)

1840 R. M. Bird *Robin Day* 25 Five or six hundred field pieces blazing away slambang.

Slam-banging, *vbl. sb.* (Earlier example.)

1843 *Knickerbocker Mag.* XXII. 41 The creaking on its rusty hinges and slam-banging of the sign of the Devil-Tavern.

Sla·mmer ². [f. Slam *v.*² + -er¹.] One who wins a slam.

1928 Work *Contract Bridge* 63 To make the slam and earn the tremendous bonus that goes with it, causes the slammer to feel like a golfer who has made a hole in one.

Slangwhang, *sb. U.S.* [Cf. Slangwhang *v.*] Violent or abusive language.

1834 H. M. Brackenridge *Recollections* xvi. 183 The young lawyer..who has acquired nothing of the ordinary slang-whang.

Slant, *sb.*¹ Add: **4. c.** *Bacteriology.* A slanting surface (e.g. of agar) used as a medium; also in full *slant-culture*: a culture made by inoculating the surface of a medium solidified in a slanting test-tube.

1901 Dorland *Med. Dict.* (ed. 2), *Slant*, a sloping surface of agar in a test-tube; also a slant-culture. *Slant-culture*, bacterial culture in which the test-tube is placed in a slanting position for the agar to solidify. 1909 *Practitioner* Nov. 506 *note*, The stock culture of prodigiosus is kept upon agar slants. 1925 [see *Slope *sb.*¹ 3 c].

6. (Later example.)

1868 H. Woodruff *Trotting Horse Amer.* iii. 58, I have known many that will be always watching slants to get an extra quart of oats for their colts.

b. A way of regarding a thing, point of view, 'angle'. *U.S.*

1905 *N. Y. Evening Post* 28 Jan. 5 The titles of articles on this subject bear an extremely pessimistic slant. 1921 R. D. Paine *Comr. Rolling Ocean* viii. 128, I need to get your slant on the situation. 1926 *Publishers' Weekly* 16 Jan. 168/2 New Slant on Books as Prizes. 1929 Guedalla *Missing Muse* 280 He explained..that Russian novels had a Message or an Outlook, or something (if he happened to be an American, he called it a Slant).

c. A glance, look. *U.S.*

1911 E. Ferber *Dawn O'Hara* viii. 109 You're supposed t' take a slant at th' things an' make up your mind w'at you want. 1921 R. D. Paine *Comr. Rolling Ocean* iv. 67 He took just one slant at me and read the story of my life.

Slanted, *ppl. a.* Add: **b.** *Bacteriology.* (Cf. *Slant *sb.*¹ 4 c.)

1925 [see *Sloped *ppl. a.* b].

Slantindicular, *a.* (Earlier example.)

1835 P. H. Nicklin *Lett. Descr. Virginia Springs* 30 [He] makes his bivouac among the trees..under a slantindicular shed.

Slantingways (slɑ·ntiŋwēⁱz), *adv.* [f. Slanting *ppl. a.* + -ways.] Slantwise.

1899 H. G. Wells *When Sleeper Wakes* vi, He walked slantingways across the room. 1916 — *Mr. Britling* II. iv. § 13 We were busy..pushing our trench out from an angle slantingways forward.

Slap, *v.*¹ **1.** Add: *To slap on the back* (transf.): to treat in a hearty or jovial manner; to congratulate, approve of.

1931 Barbara Worsley-Gough *Public Affaires* x, 'Lord,' said Venetia, 'I had forgotten the Bishop. What is he like?' 'Jovial. Jolly. Slap-you-on-the-back-for-tuppence.'

Slapjack. 1. *U.S.* (Earlier examples.)

1809 W. Irving *Knickerb.* II. 187 To these..we are indebted for the invention of slap-jacks. 1810 Marg. Van Horn Dwight *Journ. Ohio* (1912) 35 Saturday morn...We have nothing to eat and can get nothing but some slapjacks at a baker's some distance off.

Slap-stick (slæ·pstik). orig. *U.S.* [f. Slap *v.*¹ + Stick *sb.*¹] The flexible lath used by the harlequin in a pantomime, etc. for making a great noise with a pretence of dealing a heavy blow. Chiefly *attrib.*, esp. *fig.* applied to boisterous or knockabout comedy.

1906 *N. Y. Evening Post* 25 Oct. 10 It required all the untiring efforts of an industrious 'slap-stick' coterie..to keep the enthusiasm up to a respectable degree. 1907 *Weekly Budget* 19 Oct. 1/2 The special officer in the gallery, armed with a 'slap-stick', the customary weapon in American theatre galleries, made himself very officious amongst the small boys. 1911 L. J. Vance *Cynthia* 270 The way I have to stand for all the slapstick work in this turn. 1919 T. K. Holmes *Man fr. Tall Timber* viii. 94 It was a musical show—one of those girl and slap-stick affairs which could never by any possibility satisfy a cultivated audience. 1925 M. W. Disher *Clowns & Pantomimes* 13 What has caused the playgoers' sudden callousness? The slapstick. Towards the end of the seventeenth century Arlequin had introduced into England the double-lath of castigation, which made the maximum amount of noise with the minimum of injury. 1925 *Chambers's Jrnl.* 124/2 French slapstick affairs, dealing with the amusing pranks of children. 1926 *Amer. Speech* I. May 437/2 *Slap-stick*, low comedy in its simplest form. 1927 *Sunday Express* 1 May 11/7, I did slapstick comedy and emotional drama.

Slash, *sb.*¹ Add: **4.** Débris resulting from the destruction of trees by fire or natural agencies, or by the felling and utilization of the trees. Chiefly *U.S.* and *Canada.*

1905 *Terms Forestry & Logging* 47 *Slash*, the débris left after logging, wind, or fire. 1928 J. E. C. Turner in *Indian Forest Rec.* XIII. vii. 3 Comprehensively defined, *chir* slash includes all débris resulting from operations involving the felling and utilization of *chir* trees, and also from the destruction of trees of this species by such agencies as wind, snow, fire, lightning, floods, landslips, insects and fungi. 1928 *Daily Tel.* 9 Oct. 9/7 (Canada's Forests) To require the disposal of logging slash in order to prevent the spread of forest fires. We are adding to our accumulation of dry forest fire-kindling slash the tops and branches of 150,000,000 trees per year.

b. A forest clearing resulting from the destruction of trees by fire, wind, or logging; forest-land strewn with débris.

1881 *Harper's Mag.* Oct. 688/2 They [*sc.* the dogs]..crawling through the densest slash of burned and fallen timber. 1886 S. W. Mitchell *R. Blake* ii. (1895) 16 Both sides were 'falling' trees to construct breastworks, abatis and slashes. 1905 *Terms Forestry & Logging* 47 *Slash*, forest land which has been logged off and upon which the limbs and tops remain, or which is deep in débris as the result of fire and wind.

Slash, *v.* Add: **1. c.** To fell timber on. *U.S.*

1857 *Quinland* I. ii. I. 33 We then..began cutting down the forest to make a clearing...During the summer we 'slashed' about forty acres.

d. To cut down or reduce severely. *U.S.*

1906 *Washington Post* 29 Apr. 6 A disposition was manifested in the Senate Committee to slash the salaries of members of the commission. 1910 *Springfield* (Mass.) *Weekly Republ.* 8 Dec. 8 It is not a pleasant thing to slash a presidential message to this extent.

9. *Comb.*: **slash-hook** = Slasher 2 b.

1920 B. Cronin *Timber Wolves* ix. 161 Salter picked up a slash-hook and beckoned to Heritage. 1927 *Blackw. Mag.* Oct. 466/1 Getting our axes and slash-hooks unlimbered, we cut out a route of our own as we went along.

Slashed, *ppl. a.* Add: **4.** Subjected to felling. *U.S.*

1843 *Yale Lit. Mag.* VIII. 332 His eye wandered far away over acres of slashed timber.

Slasher. Add: **1. c.** One who cuts down timber recklessly.

1886 *Leslie's Pop. Monthly* June 750/2 We..can say to the Eastern slashers, 'Go ahead and chop down your forests.'

2. b. (Earlier U.S. example.)

1858 J. A. Warder *Hedges & Evergreens* 98 The slasher with a wooden handle set at an angle with the edge of the blade.

Slashing, *vbl. sb.* Add: **4. b.** (Earlier example.) Also, a clearing in which the felled trees are allowed to lie as they fall; also = *Slash *sb.*¹ 4.

1857 *Quinland* I. ii. I. 34 When it came dry in the spring, we burned the 'slashing' we had made the previous summer. 1864 O. W. Norton *Army Lett.* 211 Imagine a slashing of five hundred acres with an impassable swamp on each side. 1920 Sir C. Phillipps-Wolley *Songs Young Man's Land* 91 Are you hiding from us, Springtime, hiding in the slashing?

5. The sizing of yarn. Also *attrib.*

1895 R. Marsden *Cotton Weaving* 514 Blackburn prices for Tape-sizeing or Slashing. 1921 *Dict. Occup. Terms* (1927) § 369 *Dresser*,..one who prepares delicate and fine yarns by passing them through sizing or slashing frame. 1927 T. Woodhouse *Artificial Silk* 112 Other machines.. differ essentially from the slashing and ordinary sizing machines.

Slat, *sb.*¹ Add: **4. c.** *pl.* The ribs. *slang.*

1900 G. Bonner *Hard Pan* vi. 191 She got you straight in the slats that time. a 1906 'O. Henry' *Trimmed Lamp*, etc. 162 What they need is a man to come home and kick their slats in once a week. 1916 C. J. Dennis *Ginger Mick* 28 Why don't ole England belt 'em in the slats?

Slat, *v.*¹ Add: **2. b.** *intr.* To place or fix slats.

1874 *Rep. Vermont Board Agric.* II. 511 After they are all laid in their proper place, continue to slat between them.

Slat, *v.*² **1. b.** (Earlier example.)

1828 A. Sherburne *Mem.* ii. (1831) 55 The women and girls take and very dextrously..slat off their heads and split them.

Slate, *sb.*¹ **7.** Add: **slate-writer,** a person who practises slate-writing; **slate-writing,** writing on the inside of either of two slates which have previously been tied or sealed together, attributed to mediumistic agency.

1898 *Sci. Amer.* 8 Oct. 229/2 There has probably been nothing that has made more converts to spiritualism than the much talked of 'Slate Writing Test'. 1902 F. Podmore *Mod. Spiritualism* II. iv. ii. 221 *note*, Professional slate-writers. 1904 I. K. Funk *Widow's Mite* 369 Slate-writing has given us a class of physical phenomena which is under special suspicion because of the great amount of fraud perpetrated through it. 1905 *Smart Set* Sept. 110/1 There is only one true magic. And it is not slate-writing, toe-joint snapping, fortune telling or the vending of charms.

Slate, *v.*¹ Add: **3.** To remove hair from (hides) by means of a tool called a **Sla·ter.** Also in *vbl. sb.* (and *attrib.*).

1897 C. T. Davis *Manuf. Leather* (ed. 2) 113 It will pay to select in the beam-house such skins as are wanted for fancy colors, and to work them out well on the slating table before tanning. *Ibid.* 335 Upon removal from the bate the skins are 'slated', which is the removal of the fine hair remaining upon the skins after the unhairing operation. *Ibid.* 336 The 'slater' is a tool closely resembling a 'slicker', but the edge of the 'slater' is ground sharp. 1903 Flemming *Pract. Tanning* 12 In some cases it is necessary to work the skins through the slating machine, or upon the beams.

Slath (slɑþ). Also **slarth.** See Slat *sb.*¹ 5 a.

Slather (slæ·ðəɹ), *sb. U.S. colloq.* [Of obscure origin.] Usually *pl.*: A large amount.

1876 'Mark Twain' *Tom Sawyer* vii. 68 They get slathers of money—most a dollar a day. 1891 *Fur, Fin & Feather* 169 A good many straggling bears and slathers of black-tailed deer. 1906 *N. Y. Globe* 20 Aug. 6 There is the same slather of indefinite charges. 1911 E. Ferber *Dawn O'Hara* x. 172 It's going to be slathers of fun.

Slaughter, *v.* Add: **2. b.** To destroy by excessive felling.

1896 *Vermont Agric. Rep.* XV. 85 Our lumber forests are being slaughtered.

c. To defeat or demolish completely. *U.S. colloq.*

1903 *N. Y. Evening Post* 5 Oct. 3 McLaughlin's lieutenants are openly declaring that they will 'slaughter' the McClellan-Grout-Fornes ticket. 1909 C. E. Merriman *Chicago* 280 He was hopelessly beaten..in the primaries of 1907; and again slaughtered..in the primaries of 1915.

Slaughtery (slǫ·təri). Delete † *Obs.* and add examples.

1903 Hardy *Dynasts* I. vi. iii, If it indeed must be That this day Austria smoke with slaughtery, Quicken the issue as Thou knowest how. 1917 G. J. Nicholls *Bacon & Hams* 26 The exporting slaughteries or factories. *Ibid.*, There is appointed to each slaughtery at least one veterinary officer who acts as inspector.

Slav, *sb.* and *a.* **A.** *sb.* Add: **b.** A Slavonic tongue, or the prehistoric ancestor of the Slavonic languages (cf. F. *slave*).

1924 G. G. Walsh *Emperor Charles IV* iii. 34 The right of the monks, in his presence, to recite the Offices in Slav.

Slave, *sb.* Add: **4.** Also *attrib.*, as *slave-ant, -nest.*

1867 J. Greenwood *Purgatory of Peter the Cruel* iv. 100 Many of the slave-ants were busy milking. 1895 Comstock *Manual Insects* 641 The Slave-ant, *Formica subsericea*..is usually a dark-brown or ash-colored ant with reddish legs. 1924 J. A. Thomson *Science Old & New* xiii. 73 When they utilise scouts who have discovered an underground slave-nest, the army sometimes loses its way.

9. slave-bangle, a bangle of metal, glass, bone, etc., worn by women above the elbow.

1923 Una L. Silberrad *Lett. Jean Armiter* ii. 33 A green-glass slave bangle.

Slaw. Add: Also in Canadian use.

1916 *Chambers's Jrnl.* Feb. 143/1 In Canada it [*sc.* celery cabbage] is used for cold slaw.

Slay, sley, *sb.*¹ **2.** Add: **slay-block,** the beam of the slay of a loom; **slay-cap,** the grooved strip of wood for holding the reed in position in the slay of a loom; **slay-sword,** each of the supports upon which the slay of a loom oscillates during the process of weaving.

1895 R. Marsden *Cotton Weaving* 166 At the top it is retained in position by the slay-cap, at the bottom by a similar groove in the slay-block. *Ibid.*, The shaft is cranked, and by means of arms from these cranks is attached to the 'slay' or lathe..which oscillates upon the 'slay-swords'.

Sled, *sb.*¹ Add: **1. c.** (See quot. 1893.)

1893 Sloane *Electr. Dict.*, *Sled*, a contact for electric cars of the conduit system. It is identical with the plow, but is drawn after the cars instead of being pushed along with them. 1910 *N. Hawkins' Electr. Dict.*

Sledding, *vbl. sb. U.S.* (Earlier example.)

1713 *Essex Inst. Hist. Coll.* X. 102 Cold. Brave sledding.

Sledge, *sb.*² Add: **2. d.** The skid or runner of an aeroplane.

1910 *Daily Mail Year Bk.* 149/2 Beneath the aeroplane are strong skids, or sledges, to take the shock when it alights.

Sle·dger ². [f. Sledge *v.*¹ + -er¹.] One who uses or works with a sledge-hammer.

Quot. 1661 in Dict. s.v. Sledger perhaps belongs here. 1921 *Dict. Occup. Terms* (1927) § 072 *Sledger*, a breaker (hand) who breaks up rock for crushing mills, with heavy sledge hammer.

Sleep, *v.* Add: **B. 1. g.** To the sense 'to oversleep', add 'to sleep late'. *dial* and *U.S.*

1931 *Amer. Speech* VII. Oct. 20 *Sleep in*, to sleep late. 'I'm going to sleep in to-morrow.'

Sleeper. Add: **1. c.** A sleeping partner. Also *transf.*

1892 *Outing* (U.S.) Mar. 454/2 Williams won the high and low hurdles in record time, Clarke the two-mile bicycle race, Elcock two seconds in the weights and Harmar a second in the mile, being beaten by Wells, a 'sleeper' from Amherst. 1901 *Edin. Rev.* Apr. 385 If, in a routine business, a director can be treated as a purely sleeping partner, it can do that company no harm that, for the sake of public policy, the sleeper, on becoming a Minister, should cease to be a director.

4. b. An article that has a poor sale. *U.S.*

1926 *Publishers' Weekly* 10 July 117 'Sleepers' or 'Fast Sellers'—the Cover Often Decides!

5. b. An unbranded calf having a notch cut in its ear. Hence **Slee·per** *v. trans.*, to mark (a calf) in this way. *U.S.*

1910 C. E. Mulford *Hopalong Cassidy* xii. 79 Either the H2 was sleepering Bar-20 calves for their irons later on, or rustlers were at work. *Ibid.* 80 'I saw a H2 sleeper, up just above th' Bend.'..'Lazy trick, that sleepering.' 1918 — *Man fr. Bar-20* xii. 117 Nope; it's a sleeper. Somebody's took th' trouble to cut th' notch [in its ear].

Sleeping, *vbl. sb.* Add: **2. a.** *sleeping porch.*

1926 *Scribner's Mag.* Sept., Advt. 48/1 A Vassar Preparatory School for Girls, 5-acre campus—supervised sports—sleeping porches.

d. sleeping sickness, (*b*) a disease of silk-worms; (*c*) = *sleepy sickness* (*Sleepy 2 b).

1904 *Jrnl. R. Microsc. Soc.* Apr. 179 Sleeping Sickness of Silk-worms..is in no wise due to the micro-organisms of the mulberry leaves. 1918 *Proc. R. Soc. Med.* XII. *Section of Med.* p. xvii, The term 'sleeping sickness'..would not be an inappropriate name for this epidemic [*sc.* encephalitis]. 1920 *Lancet* 13 Mar. 620/2 Some popular term for encephalitis lethargica less cumbrous than 'lethargic encephalitis' and free from the objection to 'sleeping sickness'. 1921 *Times* 3 Feb. 7/2 The Registrar-General's returns for the week..show that there were 21 cases of sleeping sickness (*encephalitis lethargica*) notified..in London alone.

Sleeping, *ppl. a.* **1.** Add: *Sleeping beauty* (Perrault's *La belle au bois dormant*), the heroine of a fairy tale who slept for a hundred years; also applied allusively and jocularly to any person found asleep.

†1729 R. S[amber] *Perrault's Tales* (1795, repr. 1892) 87 The Sleeping Beauty in the Wood. 1830 Tennyson (*title*) The Sleeping Beauty.

Sleeping-car. *U.S.* = Sleeper 5.

1839 [see Sleeping *vbl. sb.* 2 a]. 1872 *Trans. Dept. Agric. Illinois* 23 That the sleeping car for use of the Board be brought on the Grounds. 1904 *Indian Laws & Tr.* III. 36 For traveling expenses..exclusive of transportation and sleeping-car fare.

Slee·ping-room. Now *U.S.* A bedroom.

1727, 1789 [see Sleeping *vbl. sb.* 2 a]. 1845 *Knickerbocker Mag.* XXV. 506 His handsome hostess conducted him to his sleeping-room. 1887 Mary E. Wilkins *Humble Romance* 221 She never had a fire; one in a sleeping-room would have been sinful luxury.

Sleepy, *a.* **2. b.** Add: *Sleepy disease* (see Sleeping *vbl. sb.* 2 d (*b*), quot. 1899). *Sleepy sickness*, an epidemic disease, *Encephalitis lethargica*; also, earlier applied to *sleeping sickness* (see Sleeping *vbl. sb.* 2 d). *Sleepy staggers* (see quot. 1913).

1831 Youatt *Horse* 103 Some say that there is a yellowness of the eye..in the early stage of sleepy or stomach-staggers. 1913 Dorland *Med. Dict.* (ed. 7) s.v. *Staggers*, *Sleepy staggers, stomach staggers*, a disease of horses, of unknown causation, but usually associated with the eating of moldy hay and grain. 1922 *Times Lit. Suppl.* 3 Aug. 511/2 The tomato suffers from the so-called 'Sleepy Disease' manifested in a wilting of the plant. 1923 *Daily Mail* 26 Feb. 9 Sleepy sickness (encephalitis lethargica) is attacking prominent people in Winnipeg.

Sleeve, *sb.* Add:

7. b. Of a celt or prehistoric axe.

1929 Childe *Danube in Prehistory* 78 Possibly they were shafted with the aid of horn sleeves. *Ibid.* 107 Axes and adzes hafted in deer-horn sleeves.

c. (See quot.)

1877 E. W. H. Holdsworth *Sea Fisheries* 88 It [*sc.* a seine-net] is always deeper in the middle or 'bunt' than at the 'sleeves' or 'wings', as the ends are called.

8. b. sleeve-valve (see quot. 1928).

1912 *Motor Manual* (ed. 14) 69 The sliding sleeve valves. 1914 'Ian Hay' *Knight on Wheels* x, The latest mode in such things as sleeve-valves and detachable rims. 1927 C. Lenanton *Mrs. Newdigate's Window* I. ii, 'Fourteen years old, and almost as silent as ever.'..'Ah! a sleeve-valve engine every time.' 1927 *Daily Express* 16 Mar. 7 A six-cylinder Silent-Knight Sleeve-valve engine. 1928 *Motor Manual* (ed. 27) 217 Sleeve valve.—A valve in the form of a cylinder which has a sliding movement instead of the up-and-down movement of the poppet valve. c 1930 *Daimler Transmission System* (Prospectus) 3 The introduction of the Daimler silent sleeve-valve engine in 1908, and its remarkable development in 1925 by the successful substitution of light steel sleeves for the previous cast-iron ones.

Sleigh-bell. (Earlier examples.)

c 1780 in *Amer. Poems* (1793) I. 208 Mind and have the sleigh-bells sent. 1796–1801 Fessenden *Orig. Poems* (1806) 130 My verse like brass kettle shall ring, Or sleigh bells, which gingle so pretty.

Slenderize (sle·ndərəiz), *v.* [f. Slender *a.* + -ize.] *intr.* and *trans.* To perform or subject to 'slimming' operations. Chiefly in gerund and ppl. adj.

1923 *Weekly Dispatch* 4 Feb. 2 A slight figure will be more essential than ever. 'You must slenderise,' said one, coining a useful word. 1923 *Daily Mail* 21 Mar. 6 Corsets for slenderising full figures. 1927 *Observer* 16 Oct. 5 Here each mode is characterised, not only by authentic fashion-knowledge but by supreme regard for slenderizing line. 1928 *Sunday Express* 29 Apr. 15/4 Chefs are searching their brains for the slenderising sweet that will tempt both men and women diners.

Sleughi, variant of *Saluki.

Sleuth, *v.*² Add: **2.** *intr.* To play the detective.

1904 *N. Y. Sun* 8 Aug. 3 It is through his clever sleuthing that the arrest of members of the gang was made. 1912 L. J. Vance *Destroying Angel* xx, So I went sleuthing; traced you through the canal to Peconic. 1924 *Weekly Westm. Gaz.* 13 Sept. 580/2 One always knew all about his theories and his sleuthing. 1930 'Sapper' *Finger of Fate*, etc. 99 My poor friend..labours under the delusion that he is a detective. He goes about with magnifying glasses, and sleuths.

Slew, *v.* **2.** Add: Also with *over*.

1914 Kipling *Diversities of Creatures, Vortex* (1917) 389 'We overtake on the right as a rule in England.' 'Thanks!' Mr. Lingnam slued over.

Slewed, *ppl. a.* (Earlier U.S. example.)

1801 A. Ellicott in *Life & Lett.* (1908) 201 He was two thirds slewed (as the Rahway people call being in liquor).

Slewing ². *Basket-making* (see quots.).

1902 P. N. Hasluck *Basket Work* 50 Next fill in by working two rods together; this process is known by basket makers as slewing. *Ibid.* 53 Start slewing with one rod, add another a few stakes farther on...Point two thick pieces of stick and push down the slewing.

Slick, *a.* Add: **2. b.** In good order, neat, trim.

1860 Holland *Miss Gilbert's Career* viii. 131, I love to see a young man that keeps things slick around him. 1891 *Century Mag.* Mar. 658 All that was really done was to.. see that everything was slick. 1911 *Springfield* (Mass.) *Weekly Republ.* 3 Aug. 9 A bellboy, slight of stature, slick of attire.

4. b. Of actions, etc.: Smartly or cleverly done.

1838 B. Drake *Tales & Sketches* 30 Well, now, that's right down slick, anyhow. 1891 *Fur, Fin & Feather* Mar. 169 They reckons to make mighty slick work in cleaning everything up on the way back. 1904 W. H. Smith *Promoters* i. 19 I've seen the thing done a hundred times, with a slick word every time.

5. (Earlier U.S. example.)

1840 C. F. Hoffman *Greyslaer* II. xii. 58 Add the salt and pepper fixings, and the king himself hasn't a slicker supper.

Slick, *adv.* **2.** (Earlier example.)

1818 H. B. Fearon *Sk. Amer.* 123 Did she die slick right away?

Slick, *v.* Add: **1. d.** *intr.* with *up*. To make oneself or a place neat or tidy; also *fig.*, to brighten up.

1841 *Knickerbocker Mag.* XVII. 41 In a little while he recovered his self-possession, or, to make use of one of his own expressions 'he slicked up'. 1842 Caroline M. Kirkland *Forest Life* I. xxx. 240 The beaux..who could not

perceive why Car'lene Hay should 'slick up'. 1887 Mary E. Wilkins *Humble Romance* 395 I'm going to slick up here a little for you while I stay. 1898 A. Nicholas *Idyl of Wabash* 6 It's certainly a dreadful shame they don't slick up more when they go to meeting.

Slicker. Add: **1. a.** Also *attrib.*, as **slicker coat,** a coating of oil applied to leather in preparation for the use of the slicker.

1897 C. T. Davis *Manuf. Leather* (ed. 2) 446 The hide then receives a slicker coat, which is linseed oil boiled to about the consistency of New Orleans molasses...After the slicker coat is dry..it is rubbed with a flat piece of pumice stone.

3. *U.S.* = Silver-fish 2.

1902 L. O. Howard *Insect Bk.* 380 (Order *Thysanura.*) The insects of this order are usually of very small size... They comprise the little insects known as springtails, bristle-tails, fishmoths or slickers.

Hence **Sli·cker** *v. trans.*, to smooth (leather) with a slicker.

1897 C. T. Davis *Manuf. Leather* (ed. 2) 398 As soon as one-half of the hide is slickered it is immediately hung up in the drying loft.

Slicking, *vbl. sb.* **1.** Add: Also with *up*.

1855 *Trans. Mich. Agric. Soc.* VI. 495 The farm needs a good deal of slicking up to make the general appearance equal to what nature has done for the land. 1907 *Springfield* (Mass.) *Weekly Republ.* 9 May 1 Denver has been having her period of spring slicking up.

Slide, *sb.* Add: **1. d.** *Baseball.* (See quot. 1929.)

1912 C. Mathewson *Pitching* Illustr. facing p. 214 This picture illustrates how easily the base runner, with his deceptive slide, can get away from the catcher. 1929 *Encycl. Brit.* III. 167/1 *Slide*, plunge by base runner along the ground to make the next base or return to one held.

6. Now, a kind of clasp for keeping the hair tidy. (Cf. *hair-slide*, *Hair *sb.* 9 b.)

1932 L. Golding *Magnolia Street* III. ix, That slide which has just slid out of her hair on to the parquet floor.

10. d. (See quot.)

1879 *Harper's Mag.* Nov. 889/1 Some [corrals] have what are called 'slides', or passages gradually narrowing until but one animal can pass, and he, as he cannot turn around, can be easily branded.

Slide, *v.* **5. b.** (Earlier U.S. example.)

1847 *Streaks of Squatter Life* 122 (Th.) If you have the least hankerin' arter the mean varmint, in course I'll let him slide.

Slide-. Add: **a. slide back** *Wireless* (see quots.); **slide-box,** (*a*) (see quot. 1875); (*b*) *Electr.* a resistance box in which a slide-wire takes the place of a coil; **slide-bridge** *Electr.*, a Wheatstone's bridge; **slide-rock** = Talus ¹ 2; **slide-wheel,** a part of the oscillating tappet-motion of a loom by which the pattern chain is rotated so as to place the weft in the fabric in proper progression; **slide-wire** *Electr.*, a resistance wire used in a Wheatstone's bridge; **slide-wire bridge,** a slide-bridge.

1930 *B.B.C. Year-Bk.* 451/2 *Slide back*, an apparatus for indicating in the control room of a broadcasting station the presence of a grid current (and hence distortion) in the modulation system of the transmitter. 1932 *Ibid.* 356 The 'slide-back'..consisted of a valve or similar device so biassed that no indication occurred until there was present and superimposed upon the bias a voltage greater than, and opposing in phase, the biassing voltage. 1875 Knight *Dict. Mech.*, *Slide-box, a slide-valve chest. 1902 *Encycl. Brit.* XXVI. 501/1 In the rare cases in which it is necessary to employ a long slide-wire..the calibration is best effected by comparison with a standard, such as a Thomson-Varley slide-box. 1900 *Yearbk. U.S. Dept. Agric.* 195 (Cent. D. Suppl.) In the mountains we often find the hillside slopes covered with broken rock of various sizes. This we call *slide rock. 1894 T. W. Fox *Mech. Weaving* 54 The tappet is made to oscillate in the following manner:—Pinion 1 on the crank shaft drives carrier wheel 2 round stud *m*, and it gears with *slide wheel 3. 1902 *slide-wire [see *slide-box* above]. 1902 *Encycl. Brit.* XXVI. 501/1 In all work of precision the slide-wire is supplemented by auxiliary resistances by which the scale may be indefinitely extended. 1905 *Technol. & Sci. Dict.* (ed. Goodchild & Tweney), *Slide Wire*, the straight wire which furnishes the two variable resistances in a Wheatstone Bridge of the straight form known as a Slide Wire Bridge.

c. slide-culture, a growth of germs upon a glass slide for microscopical study.

1886 H. M. Biggs tr. *Hueppe's Meth. Bacteriol. Investig.* 139 In the slide-cultures not the entire mass of gelatin, but only the lines of inoculation and their immediate surroundings are used. 1891 J. H. Linsley tr. *C. Fraenkel's Bacteriology* (ed. 3) 94 At the present day the 'slide cultures' are employed in exceptional cases only, for it was soon observed that by this procedure one of the advantages of gelatin was lost.

Slideably (sləi·dăbli), *adv.* [f. Slideable + -ly ².] So as to slide.

1907 F. W. Lanchester *Aerodynamics* 348 A square plane of thin brass, mounted 'slidably' on anti-friction rollers.

Slider. Add: **2.** (Earlier modern example.)

1811 R. Sutcliff *Trav. N. Amer.* iv. (1815) 84 They make use of a boat that has two sliders, one on each side of the keel.

4. e. *Bell-ringing.* (See quot. 1901.)

1871 [see Stay *sb.*² 2 h]. 1901 Bulwer *Gloss. Techn. Terms Bells & Ringing* 4 *Slider*, usually a bar of wood pivoted at one end on one of the lower members of the 'frame', and extending across the bottom of the 'bell-pit' so that its free end may move to and fro on a bed provided for it on the opposite side of the 'pit'.

f. A sliding-contact device.

1902 *Encycl. Brit.* XXVIII. 56/1 By moving the slider F it is possible to find one position for it in which sparks pass from the inside to the outside of C [a Leyden jar] across the tin-foil.

7. b. Ice-cream sandwiched between wafers.

1915 J. J. Bell *Wee Macgregor Enlists* ii, Come on oot wi' me an' I'll stan' ye a dizzen sliders. 1915 A. S. Neill *Dominie's Log* xviii, 'You like a glass, sir, instead of a slider?'..'I haven't had the joy of licking an ice-cream glass dry for many a long day.' 1927 W. E. Collinson *Contemp. Engl.* 16 The youngsters still ask for wafers and tasters (small quantities of ice in a glass). *Note*, called sliders in Edinburgh. 1930 *Punch* 7 May 517 Won't you join me in a slider?

Sliding, *ppl. a.* **6.** Add: *sliding change gear, contact, gear, inductance, ring, valve.*

1907 *Daily Mail Year Bk.* 73/1 MM. de Kuyff and Gharron ..have not contributed much towards development, the *sliding change gear being their chief point. 1906 *Technol. & Sci. Dict.* (ed. Goodchild & Tweney) s.v. *Wheatstone's Bridge*, The other end terminates in a *sliding contact which can be moved along till a 'balance' is obtained. 1926 Hutchinson *Wireless* 77 Sliding contacts can be moved to and fro along two brass sliding rails. *Ibid.*, The *sliding inductance consists of a single layer of enamelled copper wire wound on an insulating tube. 1932 *Hardy's Anglers' Guide* 340 Hardy 'Suction' Joint and fixed metal housing for one end of reel seat and long *sliding ring for the other end. 1909 *Westm. Gaz.* 11 Nov. 5/1 The new Daimler engine may be said to have brought us to the end of the first stage of the *sliding-valve principle.

Slim, *v.* Add: **4.** *intr.* To practise slimming (see next).

1933 *Oxford Times* 3 Feb. 6/6 Women who have slimmed at great personal inconvenience, and in some cases..with disastrous results.

Slimming (sli·miŋ), *gerund* and *vbl. sb.* [f. Slim *a.* + -ing ¹.] The practice of using special means such as dieting and exercises, to produce slimness of body; often *attrib.* (passing into *adj.*) as in *slimming diet, slimming exercises.*

1927 *Daily Chron.* 29 Mar. 15/4 Orange juice with a dash of gin in it..is said to be slimming! 1930 *Punch* 2 Apr. 366 The hostess ate hardly any. She is slimming. 1931 Galsworthy *Maid-in-Waiting* xi, Perhaps the young of to-day will nevah grow fat. They do slimming—ah-ha! *Ibid.* xvi, Em's still slimming—but we can all dine at the Coffee House. 1932 *Times* 1 Feb. 9/3 She was a bit exercised about getting too stout and might have been going in for 'slimming' exercises as sometimes ladies did. 1932 *Woman & Beauty* Apr. 79/2 All my clients in need of slimming.

Slimming (sli·miŋ), *ppl. a.* [f. Slim *a.* + -ing ².] Producing an appearance of slimness. (See also prec.)

1925 *Daily Express* 18 Nov. 6/3 The Lord Chamberlain took out the words 'slimming over the hips', which is a phrase used every day by fashionable costumiers. 1927 *Sunday Times* 13 Feb. 4/1 The pipings inserted down the sides give a very slimming effect. 1927 *Observer* 27 Mar. 8 The slimming line of the Kayser 'Slipper Heel' gives your ankles new grace.

Sling, *sb.*² Add: **1. b.** A kind of harness for supporting a horse on shipboard during rough weather.

1908 *Animal Management* (War Office) 264 The use of slings is unnecessary, except for veterinary cases.

7. sling-jacket (see quot. 1900).

1900 Hardy *A Changed Man* i, In those days the Hussar regiments still wore over the left shoulder that attractive attachment, or frilled half-coat, hanging loosely behind like the wounded wing of a bird, which was called the pelisse, though it was known among the troopers themselves as a 'sling-jacket'. 1908 — *Dynasts* III. II. i, Will the gay sling-jacket glow again beside the muslin gown?

Sling, *sb.*⁵ **1.** (Earlier U.S. example.)

a 1793 Freneau *Poems* (1809) I. 35 Rum ne'er shall meet my lips..In shape of toddy, punch, grog, sling, or dram.

Sling, *v.*¹ **3.** (Modern U.S. examples.) Also in other colloquial uses.

1874 E. Eggleston *Circuit Rider* vii. 72 He was beginning to sling his rude metaphors to the right and left. 1899 B. Harte *Mr. Jack Hamlin's Mediation*, etc. 173 He jest slung yarns about his doin's thar to last the hull rainy season. 1901 S. Merwin & H. K. Webster *Calumet K* xii. 232 It's funny to hear him sling that Grady talk around. I don't think he more'n half knows what it means. 1876 *Scribner's Monthly* Nov. 142/1 'See here! my lively moke,' said he, 'you sling on too much style.' 1891 E. S. Ellis *Check No. 2134* v. 35 That fellow slings a good hand (= writes well). 1906 'O. Henry' *Four Million, Adjustm. Nature* 108 I'm going back there and ask her to marry me. I guess she won't want to sling hash any more when she sees the pile of dust I've got.

Sling-. sling-shot *U.S.* (earlier and later examples).

1849 N. Kingsley *Diary* 77 Many are getting up sling-shots...but I hope we shall never have occasion to use them. 1904 *N.Y. Evening Post* 24 June 2 The guards are authorized to carry slingshots...[They] are heavily loaded with lead, and are securely attached to the wrist.

Slinger, *sb.*¹ Add: **3.** *pl.* (See quots.) *slang.*

1889 Barrère & Leland *Dict. Slang*, *Slingers* (popular), bits of bread floating in tea. 1918 Farrow *Dict. Mil. Terms*, *Slingers*,..a slang term among soldiers signifying a meal of bread and tea. 1925 E. Fraser & Gibbons *Soldier & Sailor Words*, *Slingers*, tea or coffee with bread soaked in it.

Slink, *v.* Add: **2. d.** To withdraw from.

1853 J. G. Baldwin *Flush Times Alabama* 26 Many a witness..'slunk his pitch mightily' when old Kasm put him through on the cross-examination.

e. *trans.* To turn (the eyes) *round* in a slinking manner.

1923 Galsworthy *Captures* 162 Leaning down to our scoundrel and slinking her eyes round at the Countess, she murmured something malicious.

Slinker. Add: **2.** [f. Slink *v.* 1.] One who slinks about; a slacker, shirker. So **Sli·nker** *v. intr.*, to slack off, shirk.

1880 G. Smith *Gipsy Life* ii. 48 When the task-master perceived the 'gang' had begun to 'slinker' he would shout out [etc.]. 1920 G. W. Deeping *Second Youth* xxviii, It makes a man so mean, so sly, such a slinker round corners. 1923 — *Secret Sanctuary* x, He had seen the most inveterate slinker change into a creature of crude and bounding energy when a piece of leather was to be kicked about a field.

Slinky (sli·ŋki), *a.* [f. Slink *v.* + -y ¹.] Of a garment: Close-fitting, as if moulded to the figure.

1923 *Glasgow Herald* 21 July 6 Jessica was swathed in a slinky gown of flat crepe in a deep blue shade. 1926 *Brit. Weekly* 24 June 250/5 The short skirt of a black dress with a slinky looking top to it. 1932 Dorothy L. Sayers *Have his Carcase* xviii. 235 She now selected a slinky garment, composed of what male writers call 'some soft, clinging material'.

Slip, *sb.*¹ **4. c.** Add: *slip-decorated, -decorator, -painting.*

1902 *Encycl. Brit.* XXXI. 874/2 Turning to the decorative side of pottery work, we have in slip-painting a method as old as primitive pottery itself. 1907 A. Bennett *Grim Smile Five Towns, Death Simon Fuge* ii, Huge slip-decorated dishes. 1921 *Dict. Occup. Terms* (1927) § 105 *Slip decorator*, applies a pattern to pottery in the green state by blowing on coloured clay slips.

Slip, *sb.*³ Add: **4. b.** Read: Now *dial.* except as short for *gym-slip.

f. *pl.* In full *bathing slips*: bathing-drawers.

1904 *Times* 11 Aug. 10/3 He wore a pair of bathing slips and a broad-brimmed white linen cap. 1927 W. E. Collinson *Contemp. Engl.* 62 Bathing togs consisting of a bathing suit and slips, a reduced type of bathing-drawers.

9. Also in various technical uses (see quots.).

1880 *Encycl. Brit.* XIII. 305/2 A 'slip' (or sudden jerky motion downwards of a mass of material that had previously more or less 'scaffolded'). 1884 W. H. Greenwood *Steel & Iron* 142 Under these circumstances the obstruction at a certain point frequently suddenly gives way, and descends with considerable force to the hearth, constituting what is known as a 'slip'. 1888 *Lockwood's Dict. Mech. Engin.*, *Slip*, the sliding of riveted joints one over the other to such an extent as to be visible. 1902 A. C. Harmsworth *Motors & Motor-Driving* vi. 95 On the road also, if a clutch does not act, due to slip, a small dose of water puts matters right at once if the mechanical portions are in order. 1904 Reynolds in *Physical Rev.* XVIII. 423 Between the pressures of 6 and 20 millimeters of mercury the value of the coefficient of slip was found to be inversely proportional to the density of the gas and very nearly equal to the free path of the molecules. 1912 *Q. Rev.* Jan. 182 The danger attendant on the 'slipping' of a charge in a blast furnace—the descent of hunks of limestone and ore that are hurled into the air when such a 'slip' occurs. 1925 *Morris Owner's Manual* 22 The more pressure there is on the foot-board the less pressure is available in the clutch, and consequently there is a danger of slip starting. 1929 B. Hall & J. J. Niles *One Man's War* 114 Our slip was a slow one. It would be impossible to come out of a fast slip because that was done by putting on the rudder nearest to the direction of the slip.

c. Of an aeroplane propeller (see quots.).

1897 *Strand Mag.* June 719/1 After due allowance for slip ..the actual length of the flight..was slightly over 3,000 ft. 1907 F. W. Lanchester *Aerodynamics* 299 The present theory enables us to define the slip of the propeller as the difference between the ordinates *b d* and *a d*, the slip ratio being represented by $\frac{ab}{ad}$. 1910 C. C. Turner *Aerial Navigation* 315 *Slip*, the difference between the forward movement of the propellers if they were in a solid (as a bolt screws into a nut) and the actual forward motion of the air-craft driven by the propeller. 1916 Barber *Aeroplane Speaks* 117 If a propeller has a pitch of, say, 10 feet, but actually advances, say, only 8 feet owing to slip, then it will be said to possess 20 per cent. slip.

e. *Electr.* The ratio of the difference between the frequencies of rotor and stator currents.

1902 *Encycl. Brit.* XXVIII. 96/1 The frequency of this induced current is proportional to the 'slip' between the rotor and the revolving field of the stator. 1912 G. Kapp *Electricity* viii. 227 The speed at which the rotor winding is cut by the revolving field is only a few per cent. of the speed at starting. It is the difference between the speed of the revolving field and the speed of the rotor. This is technically termed the 'slip' of the motor.

f. The back-current generated by the propeller of an aeroplane.

1916 Barber *Aeroplane Speaks* 10 *note*, As the propeller screws through the air, the latter to a certain extent gives back to the thrust of the propeller blades...Such 'give-back' is known as 'slip', and anyone behind the propeller will feel the slip as a strong draught of air.

12. c. *Mech.* and *Physics.* = Shear *sb.*² 6 a.

1899 Ewing & Rosenhain in *Phil. Trans.* Ser. A. (1900) CXCIII. 362 When the metal is strained beyond its elastic limit, as say by a pull in the direction of the arrows, yielding takes place by finite amounts of slips at a limited number of places...They consequently show as dark lines or narrow bands extending over the polished surface in directions which depend on the intersection of the polished surface with the surfaces of slip. 1906 *Rep. Brit. Assoc.* 658 The occurrence of this shear or slip.

15. (sense 1 a) *slip-side*; (sense 3 e) *slip-toggle*; (sense 9 c) *slip angle, ratio*; (sense *9 f) *slip stream*; (sense *12 c) *slip-band, -line, -surface*; (sense 14 b) *slip-catch.*

1902 *Encycl. Brit.* XXXII. 587/1 The *slip angle (obliquity of surface to the line of its motion) ought always to have the same value (proportional to the square root of the coefficient of friction). 1899 Ewing & Rosenhain in *Phil. Trans.* Ser. A. (1900) CXCIII. 363 The lines due to *slip-bands on one or more grains will shine out brightly when the light has a particular angle of incidence. 1903 *Ibid.* CC. 242 The characteristic lines known as 'slip-lines' or 'slip-bands', which appear in ordinary testing when any portion of the material has passed its limit of elasticity under strain. 1906 *Rep. Brit. Assoc.* 666 Photo-micrographs of slip-bands in section. 1928 *Daily Chron.* 9 Aug. 11/4 He then fell foul of a ball from Ashton, which ran away to the off, giving Nichols the opportunity to effect a *slip catch. 1903 *slip-line [see *slip-band* above]. 1906 *Rep. Brit. Assoc.* 661 The slip lines in cast metal are straight and regular. 1897 *Trans. Inst. Naval Archit.* XXXVIII. 234 In all screws, of whatever *slip ratio. 1902 *Encycl. Brit.* XXXII. 587/2 The number of revolutions was varied throughout a sufficient range of experiments, the slip or slip-ratio was thus varied. 1906 N. Munro *Daft Days* xiii, He..chased..the boys from the *slip-side where they might fall in and drown themselves. 1916 Fane in Gamble *Story North Sea Air Station* xii. (1928) 198, I was right in the *slipstream of her 5 engines which made the machine very difficult to control. 1920 *Blackw. Mag.* Nov. 563/1 The roar of the Rolls-Royce deafened me, and the slip stream pushed me under the seat. 1928 V. Page *Mod. Aircraft* 484 *Slipstream*, the stream of air driven astern by the propeller. 1899 Ewing & Rosenhain in *Phil. Trans.* Ser. A. (1900) CXCIII. 363 The sloping surfaces which mark the boundaries between the grains have not the sharply-defined inclination of *slip-surfaces. 1883 *Man. Seamanship for Boys* 56 The main is..attached to the lower bowline-bridle with a *slip-toggle.

Slip, *v.*¹ Add:

8. e. To lose grip of things; to fail, 'go off'. *U.S.*

1930 *Publishers' Weekly* 22 Feb. 933/2 I must be slipping for I turned in a measly 78 on No. 4 in the Lenz-Rendel book.

15. *spec.* in *To slip (in) the clutch* (*Clutch *sb.*¹ 6 a).

1904 A. B. F. Young *Complete Motorist* 214 When the brake lever is in the 'on' position, it is impossible to start the car by slipping in the clutch until it has been released. 1912 *Motor Man.* 73 The metal clutch..can be 'slipped' to any extent without affecting the surface of the discs. 1925 *Morris Owner's Man.* 22 Persistent slipping of the clutch must not be resorted to.

22. (Recent example.)

1924 C. J. Tolley *Mod. Golfer* 7 When we went out for walks..we were allowed to slip our guards and go for all-day tramps in the pine woods.

26. g. To deliver, hand, or give to one.

1912 C. Mathewson *Pitching in a Pinch* iii. 63, I attempted to slip a fast one over on Cooley and got the ball a little too high. 1921 R. D. Paine *Comr. Rolling Ocean* xiv. 253 Bad medicine, son, believe me. They slipped us a Jonah this time. 1926 J. Black *You Can't Win* vi. 69 A woman had just slipped me a dime an' was standin' in the front door.

h. *To slip it over* (a person): to delude, hoodwink. *slang.*

1927 *Daily Tel.* 29 Mar. 10/7 If one only had the nerve and audacity one could 'slip it over' the German every time.

Slip-. 2. Add:

slip-over *a.*, made without opening at the front, and to be slipped on over the head; **slip-up,** the act of slipping up, a failure, mistake.

1923 *Daily Mail* 17 Feb. 4 Nainsook nightdress, *slip-over Magyar shape. 1909 *N. Y. Evening Post* (semi-weekly ed.) 30 Sept. 1 Should there be any *slip-up in the present plans. 1924 Isobel Jamieson *Ginger-Beer Standard* iv, That was rather a slip-up on Anglican Octavia's part. 1929 A. C. & C. Edington *Studio Murder Myst.* xvii. 228 My only worry is that if we start this thing, you know, we can't afford to have a slip up. 1929 *Star* 21 Aug. 12/1 Notts obviously hold a favourite's chance, but a slip-up may let in one of the other sides.

Slipper, *sb.* Add: **1. b.** *To take one's slipper to*: to give (a person) a beating.

1932 A. J. Worrall *Eng. Idioms* 18 He is very impudent in his manner, and I should dearly like to take my slipper to him.

4. d. A fitting in a type of lady's side saddle.

1921 *Dict. Occup. Terms* (1927) § 344 *Devonshire slipper maker*, a brown saddler who makes the fitting known as a slipper for one type of lady's side saddle.

e. A steam-engine cross-head which somewhat resembles a slipper in shape. Also, a slipper-shaped guide block.

1867–72 Burgh *Modern Marine Engin.* (1881) 40/1 The guide blocks for the piston rods are the slipper kind. *Ibid.* 72/1 The guide channels..are the ordinary kind, arranged to receive slipper blocks.

6. c. A skeiner (cf. Slip *sb.*³ 11, Slipping *vbl. sb.*³ 1).

1921 *Dict. Occup. Terms* (1927) § 367 *Skeiner* (twine), *rander, slipper*..., minds skein or rand machine, which winds finished twine into skeins.

Slippering, *vbl. sb.* [f. Slipper *v.*² + -ing ¹.] Beating with a slipper.

1919 H. Walpole *Jeremy* ii. 33 A slippering from his father or idiotic punishments from the Jampot.

Slippery, *a.* Add: **1. c.** *Slippery path* = Slip *sb.*³ 1 b. Also *fig.*, the road to disaster or destruction.

1846 Dodd *Brit. Manuf.* VI. 167 Two temporary 'slippery paths' down which the vessel may slide into the river.

2. d. (Earlier examples.)

1748 in D. Drake *Pioneer Life Kentucky* iv. 73 Red or slippery elm. 1780 W. Fleming in *Trav. Amer. Col.* 640 A bunch of the slippery Elm bark.

f. *Slippery iron*, a tough, moderately hard variety of iron capable of being polished to a great slipperiness of surface.

1888 *Lockwood's Dict. Mech. Engin.*, *Slippery Iron*, a mixture of cast iron specially prepared for engine cylinders, cylinder liners, slide blocks, and moving surfaces generally.

Slipping, *vbl. sb.*¹ **3.** Add: **slipping-box,**

the box from which greyhounds are slipped or released.

1927 *Daily Tel.* 21 June 14/3 Each [dog] is quickly examined and passed to the slipping-box...The hare passes the box, and as it does so the trap is lifted and the dogs are halfway round the track before the spectators have time to shout 'They're off.'

Slit, *sb.* Add: **1. b.** *spec.*, a narrow opening in an optical instrument through which a beam of light can be projected. Also *attrib.*, as *slit lamp, spectroscope.*

1832 *Nat. Philos.* II. II. iii. 25/1 (Libr. Usef. Knowl.) Instead of a row of holes, he formed one narrow slit in the shutter...By this means a spectrum of any required breadth may be formed. 1863 E. Atkinson *Ganot's Physics* § 465. 409 A telescope, the eyepiece of which is replaced by a slit which can be regulated by a micrometric screw...The slit is in the focus of the object-glass of the telescope. 1875 Knight *Dict. Mech.* s.v. *Spectroscope*, The light *l* is admitted to the tube *f* through an adjustable slit in the piece *d*, the upper part only of which is open. 1884 *Encycl. Brit.* XVII. 801/1 The slit of the collimator is backed by a sodium flame. 1895 *Pop. Sci. Monthly* Aug. 470 A most useful appliance for viewing pictures is the so-called stenopaic slit. 1897 *Knowledge* 1 Feb. 37/1 A slit spectroscope. 1925 C. Goulden & C. L. Harris tr. F. E. Koby (*title*) Slit-lamp Microscopy of the Living Eye. 1932 *Optician* LXXXIII. 402/1 The slit-lamp microscope.

5. slit-bar (see quot.); **slit-jaw,** each of the two pieces forming the sides of a spectroscope slit; **slit-pocket,** a side-pocket, generally in an overcoat, made with a vertical opening through which one can slip the hand into the pocket or to the pocket of the garment beneath.

1888 *Lockwood's Dict. Mech. Engin.*, *Slit Bar, a bar having an open slot or central clear space within which a stud is slid or tightened at pleasure. 1902 *Encycl. Brit.* XXXII. 783/1 Huggins's reflecting *slit-jaws permit the star image to be seen on the slit, and are preferred by many observers to other guiding devices.

Slit, *ppl. a.* **3. c.** Add: *slit-iron, work* (earlier Amer. examples); **slit skirt,** a woman's outer skirt which is open down the front or side, but which wraps over to avoid gaping open.

1789 *Ann. Congress* I. 17 Apr. 174 To lay an impost of seven and a half per cent..upon..*slit or rolled iron. 1913 *Punch* 30 July 101/2 Four young women who last week promenaded Fifth Avenue, New York, in *slit skirts, etc., were surrounded by an enraged mob. 1636 *Springfield* (Mass.) *Rec.* I. 160 For the sawinge of all the boards & *slit worke. 1709 *Essex Inst. Hist. Coll.* VIII. 19 To 7 thousands of slit woork or more.

Slither, *sb.* Add: **4. b.** A hurry, rush. *slang.*

1915 E. Wallace *Man who bought London* ii, So many people were following closely in that hurried slither to the platform.

5. Counterfeit money. *slang.*

1929 *Daily Express* 3 Jan. 9/5 He produced twenty-three counterfeit florins from his trousers pocket, remarking, 'It's no good searching. That's all the "slither" I have got.'

6. *Archery.* A minute longitudinal split in a bow (cf. *Slither *v.* 6).

1894 Longman & Walrond *Archery* (Badm.) 301 Damp is also liable to cause 'slithers', or the rising of a splinter on the back.

Slither, *v.* Add: **5.** *intr.* To hurry (away), hasten. *slang.*

a 1889 in Barrère & Leland *Dict. Slang* s.v., Slither, you and your brother, or they'll nab you both. 1901 W. S. Walker *In the Blood* xxiii, They might 'a' slithered with your goods if you 'adn't been so mighty sharp with your hands.

6. *Archery.* To suffer a minute longitudinal split (cf. *Slither *sb.* 6).

1894 Longman & Walrond *Archery* (Badm.) 297 Hickory is the best wood there is for a back..; it gives the required elasticity, and is not liable to 'slither', as the lifting of the grain is termed.

Sliver, *sb.*¹ **1. c.** *U.S.* (Earlier example.)

1871 *Game Laws* in *Fur, Fin & Feather* (1872) 160 Any pumice, scraps or other offal arising from the making of oil slivers for bait.

Slob, *sb.*¹ Add: **1. d.** Surface ice and snow; slob-ice. *Newfoundland.*

1920 W. T. Grenfell *Labrador Doctor* ix. 174 This ice is of very different qualities. Now it is 'slob' mixed with snow, born on the Newfoundland coast. 1924 F. Baird *Parson John* vi. 110 Ice..takes many forms..It may be nothing but 'a thin string o' slob.' *Ibid.*, The 'slob' [may] make the ship's log tell lies and upset the most careful reckoning.

4. slob-ice, (*a*) ice which prevents ordinary navigation; (*b*) 'surface-ice brought down by the Labrador current to the coasts of Labrador and Newfoundland' (Funk); **slob-trout,** the *Salmo orcadensis* of Loch Stenness.

1910 R. E. Peary *North Pole* xiii. 117 It took an hour to break up the '*slob' ice which had cemented about the ship. 1920 W. T. Grenfell *Labrador Doctor* vi. 132 The slob ice had already made ballicaters. 1930 G. H. Nall *Life Sea Trout* 84 Estuarine or *Slob Trout...are simply fresh water Trout which have taken to feeding in brackish or salt water.

Slogan. Add: **1. b.** (Examples of extended use.)

1916 *Lit. Digest* (N. Y.) 1 Jan. 3/1 The German-Americans, committed to the slogan 'Anything to beat Wilson', may have to vote for the Colonel or see the President reelected. 1922 *Times* 20 June 7/4 'Post early.' New P.O. slogan on letters. 1928 *Publishers' Weekly* 9 June 2386 As an advertising man, Mr. Calkins believes the slogan 'a cent a copy to sell the art of reading,' a great and revolutionary one. 1930 *Punch* 19 Feb. 204/1 'Look at the price of bacon' was his slogan.

Slogger, *sb.* Add: **2. c.** *transf.* A hard worker (cf. Slog *v.* 3).

1928 Shaw *Intell. Woman's Guide Socialism* xlix. (1929) 208 The employers..pick out an exceptionally quick and indefatigable man called a slogger.

Sloop, *sb.*¹ **3.** *sloop-man* (earlier Amer. examples).

1715 *Essex Inst. Hist. Coll.* XLIV. 146 To deliver two hogsheads of Fish to Joshua Wetherell sloopman or coaster. 1737 *Cal. Virginia St. Papers* I. 229 Paid a Sloop man for 2 gal. of rum.

Sloosh (slūʃ), *sb. dial.* or *slang.* [Echoic; cf. Slosh. But perh. partly a variant of Sluice.] A wash; a sound as of washing. Also **Sloosh, Sloo·shy** *vbs.*

1907 W. De Morgan *Alice-for-Short* xlix, But Cook was turning cataracts of water into her sink, to slooshy it well out after a real good wash-up. 1919 *Athenæum* 11 July 582/2 Among the brand-new slang one may discern some that had an onomatopœic or at any rate an imitative origin; for instance 'sloosh,' a wash. 1920 *Blackw. Mag.* Apr. 500/2 There was the sloosh of bilge-water. *Ibid.* 502/2 The slooshing bilge-water. 1925 E. Fraser & Gibbons *Soldier & Sailor Words*, *Sloosh*, a wash.

Slop, *sb.*² Add: **2. b.** *fig.* Weak sentiment, gush. (Cf. *Sloppy *a.* 6.)

1924 Galsworthy *White Monkey* I. xiii, Sentiment being 'slop', and championship mere condescension. 1927 *Sunday Express* 24 July 4 'Seventh Heaven,' the swamp of sentiment into which the critics were invited to plunge a few days ago. Personally I should describe it as the sublimity of slop.

6. *slop-barrel, -pail* (earlier U.S. examples); *slop-can.*

1831 Peck *Guide for Emigrants* 172 With..a dairy and *slop barrel..pork may be raised from the sow. 1926 *Scribner's Mag.* Aug. 204/1 A strange black dog..supporting himself by raiding the *slop-cans of Nigger Town. 1854 Shillaber *Mrs. Partington* 212 My boy knows very well how to manage it when the *slop-pail is within reach.

Slop, *v.*² Add: **3. c.** To swill. *U.S.*

1920 C. Russell *Story of Nonpartisan League* 63 An angry representative told them to 'go home and slop the hogs'.

Slope, *sb.*¹ Add:

3. Also with defining words.

1898 *Geog. Jrnl.* May 533 Mud travels persistently from the shore seawards, and..forms the bottom over vast tracts beneath deep-sea water, *e.g.* at the foot of the continental slope. 1903 Howe in *Amer. Jrnl. Sci.* Oct. 317 The Soufrière rises on all sides, with even, constructional slopes of rather low angle, to an altitude of a little over 4,000 feet. 1905 *Physical Review* XX. 174 The difference of temperature slope at different parts of the two bars was measured by means of thermoelectric couples.

c. *Bacteriol.* = *Slant *sb.*¹ 4 c.

1925 J. W. Bigger *Handbk. Bacteriol.* 38 'Slopes' or 'slants' are generally used for the growth of bacteria already isolated in pure culture. 1928 L. E. H. Whitby *Med. Bacteriol.* 44 The medium may be..allowed to solidify as a slope by laying the tubes in a slanting position with a tilt of about 10°. *Ibid.* 50 Slope cultures. Slopes are used mainly for subculturing the pure colonies that have developed on plates.

5. *Wireless.* Mutual conductance. Also *attrib.*

1918 *Wireless World* VI. 458 A Thermionic Valve Slope-meter. 1932 *B.B.C. Year-Bk.* 395 It is now the common practice of valve manufacturers to give a figure for the mutual conductance (or slope) of each of their products.

Slope-. a. Add: *slope-current, wind.*

1931 *Henley's ABC Gliding & Sailflying* 150 This ascending air current, which is defined as a slope current, forms the source of energy for sailing flight. *Ibid.* 151 The flight of a sailplane in a slope wind is shown...As long as the sailplane remains within the range of this ascending slope wind it cannot sink.

Sloped, *ppl. a.* Add: **b.** *Bacteriology.* = *Slanted *ppl. a.* b.

1897 Muir & Ritchie *Man. Bacteriol.* 54 'Sloped' agar and gelatine tubes are used...Less frequently gelatine is also 'sloped'. *Ibid.* Index 516/2 Sloped cultures. 1925 J. W. Bigger *Handbk. Bacteriol.* 51 Sloped or slanted media. 1930 J. W. H. Eyre *Bacteriol. Techn.* (ed. 3) 265 Oblique slant or sloped tube, in which the medium has been allowed to solidify whilst the tube was retained in an inclined position.

Sloppy, *a.* Add: **1.** (Earlier Amer. examples.)

1707 *Essex Inst. Hist. Coll.* X. 75 Nov. 3rd. Cool. 11. Snow. 12. Sloppy. 1715 *Ibid.* XXXVI. 328 Sloppy in the morn(ing).

6. Weakly sentimental. *colloq.*

1896 G. Ade *Artie* ix. 81 And last night when I was sloppy I thought she was the best ever. 1904 G. H. Lorimer *Old Gorgon Graham* 53 A nice sloppy letter of introduction. 1919 J. C. Snaith *Love Lane* xxxi, The Corporal stopped suddenly, took Melia in his arms and kissed her. It was a sloppy thing to do, unworthy of old married people.

Slosh, *v.*¹ Add: **2. b.** To talk loosely or irrelevantly. *U.S.*

1880 *Harper's Mag.* Sept. 648/1 The Court..let him slosh around for a minute, when matters sort o' regulated themselves.

4. *trans.* To pour or dash (liquid); to pour or dash liquid upon. *colloq.* or *slang.* Also *fig.*

1885 *Century Mag.* XXXI. Nov. 63/2 If mining records was ever kep' as they'd ought to be, and not sloshed round so public like. 1902 *Emporia* (Kans.) *Gazette* 29 July, It pours over it the same oleaginous language that it once sloshed on Governor Roosevelt of New York. 1926 G. W. Deeping *Sincerity* ii, I can't stand these counter-bouncing little beasts like Threadgold. He's only fit to slosh people with treacle and water. 1926 E. Ferber *Show Boat* x. 221 Often he sloshed down whole gallons of river water before she came. *Ibid.* xi. 239 She was, perhaps, setting the Thebes

Sloshy, a. ... (Earlier U.S. example.)

Slot, sb.² Add: **b.** slot-winding ...

Slot, v.² Add: **4.** To thread through a hole or slot, as a belt, etc. Also *intr.*, to admit of being so slotted. So Slo'tting vbl. sb.

Slotted, ppl. a. Add: **b.** Slotted armature ...

Slouch, sb. ... (Earlier U.S. example.)

Slouch-eared, a. ... (Later U.S. example.)

Slough² ... variants of **Slaloки.**

Sloughy, a.¹ (Earlier Amer. example.)

Slow, a. Add: **7. b.** Of an oven.

Slow-motion, motion of slower speed ...

Slub, sb.² Add: ...

Sludge, sb. Add: ...

Sludging (slɯ·dʒiŋ), vbl. sb. [f. Sludge v. + -ing¹.]

Slug, sb.¹ Add: ...

Sluggard, sb. and a. Add ...

Slirt, sb. **3.** (Earlier examples.)

Slugged (slɒgd), ppl. a. ... + -ED².]

Slumber, sb. Add: ...

Slump, sb.¹ Add: **3.** A slumping movement ...

Slush, sb.¹ Add: **4. b.** Forged paper money.

Small, a. Add: **A.** adj. **3.** (Earlier example of small boys.)

Smarge (smä·mɹ), a. [f. SMARM v.]

Smalt, sb. Add: **6.** And *v.* prepares small.

Sma'lter, one who prepares small.

Smalm. to Substitute collog. for slack and adds:

Smarl, a. Add: **10.** (Later U.S. example.)

Smash, sb.¹ Add: **1.** (Earlier U.S. example.)

Smash, v.¹ **8.** Add: Also with run.

Smith's shop. Chiefly U.S. examples.

Smash-and-grab, [SMASH sb.², GRAB v.]

Smasher, sb.¹ Add: **5.** Also short for *smasher-hat.* S. Africa.

Smasher², sb. Add: A receiver of stolen goods.

Smear, v. Add: **4. e.** To coat over (a pitch).

Smee, sb.¹ The name of Alfred Smee (1818-77), English inventor, etc.

smoke-bomb, a bomb which generates a dense cloud of smoke ...

smoke-laden, a.

Smelt, v.¹ Add: ...

Smelling, sb. (Later examples.)

Smeller, Add: **5.** Anything exceptionally remarkable for violence, severity, etc.

Smellie, (Later) ...

Smilacina (smai·lăsɪnă) [mod. L.]

Smile, v. Add: **1. c.** To come up smiling.

Smoke, v. Add: **4.** (Later U.S. examples.)

Smoker, sb.² **2. b.** (Later U.S. examples.)

Smoking, vbl. sb. **6. b.** Add: smoking-car.

Smote, v.

Smity, a.

Smoky, a. Add: **8. b.** smoke-laden.

Smooch. ... Bad-tempered.

Smooch, sb.¹ ... (Later examples.)

Smooth, a. Add: **6. c.** Excellent, first-rate.

Smooth-bore. **1.** (Earlier U.S. examples.)

Smoothen, v. Add: **2. c.** To diminish or even ...

Smooth-wark, side.

Smooth, v. Add: **2. c.** ...

Smudge, sb.² Add: ...

Smudger, Add: **2.** A smudge pot used in California.

Smur, sb. Add: ...

Smut, v. Add: **5.** *trans.* To rub over the blackest side of a hole in coal ...

Snaffle, v.² Add: **2.** To 'pick up', 'appropriate', a seat.

Snag, sb.¹ Add: ...

Snag, v.² Add: **2. c.** To make a rent in (a ship, aeroplane, etc.)

Snagged, ppl. a.² (Earlier U.S. example.)

Snaggy, a.³ (Earlier U.S. examples.)

Snake, sb. Add: Applied to American Indians ...

Snake-fence, U.S.

Snap, sb. Add: ...

Snapped, ppl. a. Add: Of maize: That has been picked without releasing from the husk. U.S.

Snick, sb. Add: **5. b.** (with adv.), to throw open ...

Snicker, sb.² (Later U.S. example.)

Snide, sb. Add: **3.** A mean or low fellow.

Snap-snatch, U.S.

Snappy, a. Add: **5.** Also used of electric sparks.

Snaps, U.S. [Pl. of SNAP.] (See quot.)

Snap-shot, v. Also fig.

Snipe, sb. Add: A bankrupt broker.

Snare, sb. **b.** Add: snare-drummer.

Snark, (snä·ɹk), a. orig. U.S. [f. SNARK v.]

Snipped, ppl. a. Add: **2.** Also with end.

Snitch, sb. (Recent U.S. examples.)

Snitch, v. Add: **1.** (Recent U.S. example.)

Snapped, U.S.

Snarly, a.¹ (Later U.S. examples.)

Snob, sb.³ Add: Also in American use.

Snollygoster (snɒˈligɒstər), U.S. slang.

Snapping-turtle, U.S. (earlier example).

Snook, sb.³ Variant of SNORE.

Snooker, sb. Add: **b.** trans. To 'do down', 'do in', 'suspect' chiefly in pool.

Sneaker, B. (Later examples of sneaker's.)

Sneakably, adv. In a sneaking or stealthy manner.

Snoop, sb. Add: With other adverbs.

Snowball, sb. Add: **5.** re. ½'s The system of 'Snowball': multiplication at a very rapid rate.

Snob, sb.³ **2.** Add: (with adv.), to snowball.

Snowball, v. Add: **b.** fig. To accumulate by degrees like a rolling snowball.

Snide, B. adj. A mean or low fellow.

Snifily, adv., **Sniffiness** (see note under SNIFF a.)

Snook-bank. Chiefly U.S. [SNOW 7 a.]

Snorting, ppl. a. Add: **2.** Exceptionally remarkable for excellence, etc.

Snot, sb. Add: snot-rag swigar, a pocket-handkerchief.

Snubbed, ppl. a. Add: **2. b.** Shortened.

Snuffy, a. Add: **3.** Inclined to 'sniff', disdainful.

Snubber, sb. Add: A shock-absorber on a motor-car.

Snuff, *sb.*³ Add: **4.** *snuff-bottle* (earlier U.S. example).
1851 J. J. Hooper *Widow Rugby's Husb.* 94 Did you see.. that old snuff-bottle?

5. snuff-dipper, -dipping *U.S.* (earlier examples); **snuff-gourd,** the snuff-box gourd or bottle-gourd, *Lagenaria vulgaris.*
1845 T. J. Green *Texian Exped.* x. 137 We believe the most filthy of all practices is that of your '*snuff-dippers'. 1871 Barnum *Struggles & Triumphs* 96 The technical term for the proceeding is '*snuff-dipping'. 1901 Kipling *Kim* iv, The lama dipped deep into his *snuff-gourd. 1921 *U. F. Ch. Missionary Rec.* 190/2 Her dress consists simply of a ragged apron of goatskin, and a snuff-gourd hung round her neck.

Snug, *v.* **1.** (Later U.S. example with *up.*)
1873 J. H. Beadle *Undevel. West* v. 106 He used to complain that I 'snugged up' altogether too much.

Snugger, *v. vulgar U.S.* In *I snuggers*: euphemistic substitute for *I swear* (cf. *Snum, and Swan *v.*², Swow *v.*²).
1844 'Jon. Slick' *High Life N.Y.* II. 202, I snuggers, it made me feel streaked all over, to think [etc.].

Snuggler (snʌ·glər). [f. Snuggle *v.* + -er¹.] One who snuggles.
1889 Eliz. B. Custer *Tenting on Plains* xii. 379 It finally dawned upon us that the little horse was a constitutional snuggler.

Snum (snʌm), *v. vulgar U.S.* In *I snum* = I swear. (Cf. *Snugger and Vum = *vow.*)
1839 *Yale Lit. Mag.* IV. 357 (Th. p. 468) I snum, 'taint the thing for me. 1902 L. E. Richards *Mrs. Tree* xiii, 'Well, I snum!' said old Anthony. 1908 H. L. Wilson *Spenders* xxxvi. 444 'They ratified the preliminary agreement for a merger.' 'Well, I snum!' 1909 J. C. Lincoln *Keziah Coffin* xv, I snum if she ain't comin' up the road this blessed minute.

So, *adv.* Add: **5. g.** Ellipt. for *is that so?* (also in imitation of G. *so*).
1886 *Liverpool Even. Express* 9 Jan. 3/4 'Oh, Mr. Blobbs, you can form no idea of the terrible dream I had last night.' ..'So?' remarked Mr. Blobbs, continuing the perusal of the morning paper. [1916 H. Rae *Maple Leaves* xiv. 239 'That is all part of our system.' 'Ah! So,' answered the German.]

Soak, *v.* Add: **7. e.** Also *fig.* (e.g. to 'slate' a book). *To soak it*, to 'give it hot', administer punishment *to.* *U.S.*
1908 G. H. Lorimer *J. Spurlock* iii. 44 Yes, he done it! Soak it to him good! *Ibid.* vi. 107 My troubles came at me from all sides, and soaked it to me till my conscience fairly ached. 1925 H. L. Foster *Trop. Tramp Tourists* iii. § 3. 21, I found that we had on board..the man whose newspaper soaked my last book.

f. To impose upon (a person) by an extortionate charge or price; to charge or tax heavily. *slang.*
1899 *New York Jrnl.* 19 Apr. 6/1 That's all right. Let's soak New York. She can stand it. 1904 *Newspaperdom* 21 Apr. 8 When a local merchant asks you to give his business a friendly notice, soak him ten or fifteen cents a line. 1911 J. F. Wilson *Land Claimers* xiii. 178, I know he feels pretty sore over his claim and the way you soaked him. 1915 P. G. Wodehouse *Something Fresh* ii. § 2. 37 Especially after poor old Percy has just got soaked for such a pile of money. 1931 W. Martyn *Scarlett Murder* vii, Maybe there's more money in mushrooms than I knew... Just buy a dish anywhere and see what they soak you.

Soakaway (sōu·kăwei). [f. Soak *v.* + Away *adv.*] A contrivance for collecting rainwater by percolation through the soil.
1916 H. G. Wells *Mr. Britling* ii. iv. § 13 Someone stumbles into a soakaway for rainwater. 1928 *Daily Express* 31 May 5/3 Be sure to find out if your kitchen sink drains to a 'soak-away'. If it does, you must not let much water go down it, but throw out washing-up water and suchlike on the garden.

Soap, *sb.* Add: **6. soap-fat, -lock** *U.S.* (earlier examples).
1839 *Knickerbocker Mag.* XIII. 316 He clambered up on the top, with a turning screw in one hand and a horn of *soap-fat in the other. 1855 *Ibid.* XLV. 361 The surly soap-fat man can talk of soap-fat only. 1842 'Uncle Sam' *Peculiarities* I. 119 You are an incendiary, a robber by profession, a *soap-lock, and a loafer.

b. *soap-bark*: hence as *v.trans.*, to clean (garments) with soap-bark.
1930 *Cambridge Daily News* 25 Sept. 3/4 Gym slips should not be washed... It is much better at the beginning of the season to soap-bark them.

Soap, *v.* Add: **1. b.** fig. phr. *To soap the ways*: to make things smooth and easy. [? With ref. to the nautical sense, Way *sb.*¹ 3 a.]
1929 Vachell *Virgin* ix. 156, I mean to say that Peggy, *qua* Peggy, has—how shall I put it?—soaped the ways.

Soap-box. [Soap *sb.* 4 c.] A wooden box in which soap is packed; used, esp. in U.S., as a makeshift stand by a speaker. Hence **Soap-box** *v.*, **Soapboxer.**
1660, 1862 [see Soap *sb.* 4 c]. 1926 *Scribner's Mag.* Sept. 274/1, I made 'soap-box' speeches, talked on street-corners. 1927 T. C. Pease *United States* 546 The choice of party candidates by manipulation of party conventions and soap-box primaries. 1931 L. Adamic *Dynamite* 161 When still in her 'teens, she soap-boxed on street corners in New York. *Ibid.* 434 Late in the spring of 1930 I happened to listen to a soapboxer off Madison Street.

Soar, *v.* Add: **1. f.** *Aeronautics.* To fly in a machine without motor power and without loss of altitude; applied to a flight more sustained than 'gliding' (see *Glide *v.* 1 c). See also *Soaring *vbl. sb.* 3.
1908 W. Wright in J. B. Weiss *Gliding & Soaring Flight* (1923) 102 It would be easy to soar in front of any kind of hill of suitable slope whenever the wind blew with sufficient force to furnish support, provided the wind were steady. 1911 Berriman *Princ. Flight* 21 Alternatively they [*sc.* gliders] may soar in a wind having an upward trend. 1931 V. W. Pagé *ABC of Gliding* vii. 159 An expert in Germany recently soared for a distance of 42 miles.

Soarer. Add: **2.** *Aeronautics.* A soaring machine (see *Soaring *vbl. sb.* 3).
1931 V. W. Pagé *ABC of Gliding* vi. 144 In making a soarer of the sailplane. *Ibid.* viii. 164 The primary training or school machines..are gliders rather than soarers.

Soaring, *vbl. sb.* Add: **3.** *Aeronautics.* A type of engineless flight more sustained than 'gliding'; flying in a machine without motor power and without loss of altitude. Also *attrib.*, as *soaring flight, machine, plane, ship.*
1897 P. S. Pilcher in *Aeronaut. Jrnl.* Apr. 2/1 One of the great dangers with a soaring machine is losing forward speed and slipping backwards. 1931 V. W. Pagé *ABC of Gliding* p. vii, Soaring calls for considerably more skill and machines that are much more efficient aërodynamically than gliders. Soaring machines or sailplanes are usually monoplanes with a higher aspect ratio than found in the training planes. *Ibid.* vi. 117 Soaring planes. *Ibid.* vii. 146 At best, gliding is but preparation for the more advanced type of flying known as soaring. A soaring flight may last for hours. *Ibid.*, The soaring ship or sailplane.

Soave (soa·ve), *adv. Mus.* [It.] As a direction to the performer: Softly, with delicacy and tenderness. Also (in the same sense) **Soavemente** (soavemeˈnte).
1876 Stainer & Barrett *Dict. Mus. Terms*, *Soave, Soavemente* (It.), agreeably, delicately, gently, softly, sweetly.

Sob, *sb.* Add: **3. b.** *attrib.* = dealing with sentimental appeal to the emotions (see *Sob-stuff), as *sob-raiser, -sister* (see quot. 1927), *-story.* *U.S.*
1917 S. Graham *Priest of Ideal* xxix. 278 Our great sob-raiser who persistently pleads in the *Primer* for all causes which obviously evoke pity and rage. 1920 C. Sandburg *Smoke & Steel* 28 How easy to make a sob story over who she was once and who she is now. 1927 *Daily Express* 18 Apr. 4/2 'Sob sisters'—corps of women reporters specially employed to write sentimental accounts to appeal to the emotions of feminine readers. 1927 *Saturday Even. Post* (N.Y.) 24 Dec., The sob sisters and the sob brothers..who didn't raise their boys to be soldiers. 1931 *Times Lit. Suppl.* 1 Oct. 752/3 Julia Peterkin in 'Green Thursday' comes perilously near the 'sob-story' and triumphantly avoids it.

So·berish, *a.* [f. Sober *a.*] Somewhat sober.
a 1861 T. Winthrop *Canoe & Saddle* (1862) 19, I was urging the soberish Duke to revolutionary acts.

Sober-sided, *a.* (Later U.S. examples.)
1880 Cable *Grandissimes* i. 4 Honoré in mask? he is too sober-sided to do such a thing. 1925 *Scribner's Mag.* Oct. 340/1 Robert E. Lee...was no more sober-sided than the average cadet of good morals and intellect.

Sobful (sǫ·bfŭl), *a.* [f. Sob *sb.* or *v.*¹ + -ful.] Full of sobs, given to sobbing; provocative of sobs.
1921 W. J. Turner *Music & Life* 8 The composer of the most sobful ballad that ever made a drunkard weep. 1924 *Blackw. Mag.* Nov. 692/2 He was not really in a very sobful mood.

Sobranje (sobrā·niye). Also **Sobran(i)ye.** [Bulg. сьбрание (Russ. собраніе) assembly.] The parliament or national assembly of Bulgaria, under the Constitution of 1879.
1894 E. Dicey *Peasant State* xv. 142 There are..three Estates in Bulgaria: the Crown, the Ministers, and the Sobranje. 1896 W. Miller *Balkans* ii. v. 217 The Parliament, or ordinary *Sobranje*, was to consist of a single chamber, elected by manhood suffrage. 1915 N. Forbes *Balkans, Bulgaria* 60 Stambulov..in 1884 became president of the Sobraniye (Parliament). 1920 *Contemp. Rev.* Dec. 786 The Sobranye was summoned on the eve of war with Turkey.

So·b-stuff. orig. *U.S.* [*Sob *sb.* 3 b.] Speech or writing which makes a sentimental appeal to the emotions. Often *attrib.*
1920 A. B. Baxter *Parts Men Play* xxi, [American loq.] You ain't a child, and I see that I can't put over any sob stuff with you. 1921 *Spectator* 9 Apr. 463/2 We cannot afford to be merciful to a bad or doubtful premise because of a 'sob-stuff' appeal to Charity. 1924 Galsworthy *White Monkey* ii. vi. 167 A condition or acquiescence, fatalism, 'Who dies if England live' sort of sob-stuff state. 1924 M. Newman *Consummation* ii. x. 121 Julius answered...that he was 'trying to live down the dreadful past'. Freddy replied telling him to cut out all that sob-stuff and not be a stupid ass. 1928 S. Vines *Humours Unreconciled* xxi. 266 Dickensian sob-stuff.

Sociable, *a.* and *sb.* **B.** *sb.* Add: **2. a.** (Later U.S. example.)
1929 Eldershaw *House is Built* i. v. § 10. 117 A sociable drew up at the gate and set down Mrs. Bill's sister.

c. (Earlier example.)
1851 C. Cist *Cincinnati* 202 Dressing bureaus, sociables.. are sure to catch the visitor's eye.

d. A motor cycle to carry two persons (side by side or one behind the other). Also, an aeroplane with two seats side by side.
1899 *Motor-Car World* I. 60/1 Another singularly neat little vehicle, known as the Humber 'M.D.' motor sociable. 1909 *Chambers's Jrnl.* 336/1 The 'new-departure' sociable rear-car..is the safest sociable that has yet been devised. 1913 *Aeroplane* 1 May 517/1 Mr. Busteed on 'sociable' to Upavon. *Ibid.* 20 Nov. 548/2 More than one aviator has been killed by slipping along the undivided seat of a 'sociable' aeroplane.

Social, *a.* Add: **7. e.** *Social service*: service devoted to one's fellow-men, esp. as exhibited in organized movements for social betterment, settlements among the poor, and the like.
1897 G. Hodges (*title*) Faith and Social Service. 1900 J. P. Smyth (*title*) Social Service Ideals. 1911 J. B. Haldane *Social Workers' Guide* 127/1 Diocesan Social Service Committees. 1913 J. C. Carlile (*title*), Christian Union in Social Service. 1928 *Daily Mail Year Bk.* 229/2 United action taken by representatives of..the National Council of Social Service. 1929 E. A. Hughes and F. Stuenkel (*title*), The Social Service Exchange in Chicago.

f. *Social secretary*: a secretary to a group or community of people, a factory, etc. whose function it is to make arrangements for their social activities.
1931 *Daily Express* 13 Oct. 5/2 When I got my job as social secretary..I got a large salary and lived in luxury.

Socialize, *v.* Add: **3.** *intr.* To be social or sociable; as, he refused to *socialize* with us. *U.S.*

Sociétaire (sosyetɛ̄r). [Fr., f. *société* Society.] An actor-member of the Comédie Française, Paris, who has a share in the government and profits.
1889 Vandam tr. *A. Houssaye's Behind Scenes* iii. 58 Besides, assuming the *sociétaires* to tender their resignation, had I not the *pensionnaires*? 1901 *Scotsman* 16 Apr. 8/7 The vexed question of the distribution of rôles among sociétaires and pensionnaires—full members of the company and salaried aspirants. 1923 Sir G. Arthur *Sarah Bernhardt* 66 To the Directors of the Français the *Sociétaires* ranked only by seniority.

Society. 12. b. Add: **society-queen,** a lady who makes a great figure in fashionable society.
1901 *Chambers's Jrnl.* 232/2 He now takes life as becomes a man of affluence, with a wife who is a society-queen and a favourite in many capitals.

Socius. Add: **3.** *Philos.* Applied to God, as the 'Great Companion' of man.
1890 W. James *Princ. Psychol.* I. x. 316 The impulse to pray is a necessary consequence of the fact that whilst the innermost of the empirical selves of a man is a Self of the *social* sort, it yet can find its only adequate *Socius* in an ideal world. 1917 A. S. Pringle-Pattison *Idea of God* xv. 297 The idea of a divine *Socius* has been one of the most abiding inspirations of religious experience.

4. The individual person, considered as the unit of human society.
1912 C. A. Ellwood *Sociol. in Psychol. Aspects* ii. 21 The *socius*, or associated individual...the unit out of which all the simpler social groups are composed.

Sock, *sb.*¹ **2.** Add: Slang phrases. *Put a sock in* (or *into*) *it*: be quiet, 'shut up'. *To pull up one's socks*: to brace oneself for an effort.
1919 *War Terms* in *Athenæum* 8 Aug. 729/2 The expression 'Put a sock in it', meaning 'Leave off talking, singing or shouting'. 1924 Vachell *Quinney's Adventures* 269 Metaphorically an Irish-American 'pulled up his socks'. 1925 Fraser & Gibbons *Soldier & Sailor Words* s.v., 'Shut up, put a sock into it.' 1932 R. C. Ashby *Plot agst. Widow* xxi. 172 'Oh, put a sock in it!' she invited him scornfully.

attrib. and *Comb.*, **sock-suspender,** a device attached to the top of a sock to keep it up in place on the leg.
1919 P. G. Wodehouse *Damsel in Distress* xiii, An earthy brute who wore sock-suspenders.

Sock, *v.*² Add: **1. c.** (Earlier U.S. examples.) Phr. *To sock* (a person) *one*: to give (him) a hard blow.
1845 T. J. Green *Texian Exped.* xvii. 321 The corporal 'socked' it [*sc.* a shoe-maker's awl] in the thick of his back. 1850 L. H. Garrard *Wah-To-Yah* xiii. (1927) 163, I..socks my big knife up to the Green River, first dig. 1878 J. H. Beadle *Western Wilds* ii. 37 The very next day they put me in jail—socked me right in with them two Hodges. 1883 'Mark Twain' *Life Mississippi* xliii. 438 A rich man won't have anything but your very best; and you can..pile it on and sock it to him. 1927 D. B. W. Lewis *On Straw* 61 Sock 'im on the ear, Sargint. 1931 F. Buck & E. Anthony *Bring 'em Back Alive* 231 More than once I was tempted to sock him one.

d. To drive or push *down.*
1929 'Seamark' *Down River* i, The Spindrift, travelling at speed, sent up a young hill of water that would have made even a fully laden barge cock up her heels and sock her old nose down till half her rudder showed clear.

Sockdolager. *U.S. slang.* **1.** (Earlier example.)
1830 *Virginia Literary Museum* I. 479 Sock dologer, 'A decisive blow'.

3. (Earlier example.)
1842 *Knickerbocker Mag.* XIX. 223 This seemed to be a 'socdoliger' (which translated into Latin, means a ne plus ultra).

So·cker². *slang.* [f. Sock *v.*² + -er¹.] A hard hitter.
1931 *Daily Express* 16 Oct. 19/3 That guy was sure a socker, and he had me nursing my bruises for days.

Socket, *sb.* Add: **2. e.** *Golf.* That part of the head of an iron club into which the shaft is fitted. Hence, a shot made off the socket (see *Socket *v.* 2).
1887 Sir W. G. Simpson *Art of Golf* i. iv. 22 Irons and cleeks..have sockets instead of necks. 1896 W. Park *Golf* 269. 1922 C. Leitch *Golf* 98 There is no bad shot in golf which flurries a player so much as a shot off the socket. 1927 *Daily Express* 12 Feb. 3/7 In the down stroke, the left hand and arm get ahead of the right, and that causes either a socket or a 'push out'.

Socket, *v.* Add: **2.** *Golf.* To strike (the ball) off the socket or heel of an iron club; to make (a shot) in this way. Also *absol.*
1911 C. Leitch *Golf for Girls* 87 If you socket and don't want to, here's the cure. Keep your left elbow close to your side. 1920 *Isis* 27 Oct. 9/1 He socketed a couple of iron shots into the gorse. 1923 *Chambers's Jrnl.* 775/1 The joys and sorrows of studying a long putt, or of socketing an approach. 1927 *Daily Express* 31 Jan. 8/2 A mashie that persists in socketing the ball.

Hence **So·cketed** *ppl. a.* **So·cketer. So·cketing** *vbl. sb.*
1911 C. Leitch *Golf for Girls* 86 No worse fault can fasten on to a player than socketting, that is, hitting the ball off the socket, or shank, as some call it, of the club. *Ibid.*, At the finish of a socketted shot. 1912 *New Bk. Golf* 164 Socketing may occasionally proceed from too free a use of the wrist. *Ibid.* 341 Even the most confirmed socketer will find that with such a club socketing is a sheer impossibility. 1922 C. Leitch *Golf* 98 The more socketed shots I see played, the more I am convinced that the cause is to be found in the arm action.

Socketless, *a.* (at the end of Socket *sb.*). Add: *Golf.* Of an iron club: Made without a socket (see *Socket *sb.* 2 e).
1911 C. Leitch *Golf for Girls* 86 In some cases recourse is had to socketless clubs. This is not a cure but a subterfuge. 1912 *New Bk. Golf* 340 A socketless club has no heel, the shaft rises straight from the head.

Socratean (sǫkrā·tiăn), *a.* [See -an.] Pertaining to or resembling Socrates.
1930 Belloc *Richelieu* i. vi. 114 Father Joseph was short, bullet-headed, of a vivacious Socratean ugliness.

Sod, *sb.*¹ **3.** Add: phr. *Under the sod*: dead and buried. *To put under the sod*: to (kill and) bury.
1847 A. Trollope *Macdermots* III. vii. 286 I've heard the boys say that he would be undher the sod that day six months. *Ibid.* 288 A lot of boys swore together..to put him undher the sod.

5. a. *sod-crop* (cf. *Sod-corn a), *ground.* U.S.
1847 *Rep. U.S. Comm. Patents* (1848) 539 This gave a *sod crop without tending of thirty to forty bushels per acre. 1878 *Scribner's Monthly* Nov. 133/2 The sod crop being often the settler's main or only reliance for the first year. 1871 *Trans. Ill. Agric. Soc.* VIII. 238 The *sod ground of our prairie State.

Sod (sǫd), *sb.*³ *vulgar.* [Short for Sodomite.] A term of abuse for a male person. Also used jocularly without any definite implication (= 'beggar', 'chap', etc.).
a 1880 [remembered]. 1903 Farmer & Henley *Slang.* 1931 K. O'Brien *Without my Cloak* iii. xi. § 1 That auld sod of a husband making her black and blue every night of his filthy life. 1931 Tilsley *Other Ranks* 12 Lucky sods, getting this far and then going back.

Soda¹. Add: **5. a. soda-acid extinguisher,** a fire-extinguisher composed of sulphuric acid mixed just before use with bicarbonate of soda.
1931 Dougherty & Kearney *Fire* 240 The Soda-Acid Extinguisher is the type frequently seen in public buildings.

6. *soda-biscuit, -bread* (earlier U.S. examples), *-cocktail.*
1867 *Rep. Iowa Agric. Soc.* (1868) 65 The..hot saleratus or *soda biscuit which they..bolt down at their meals. 1850 N. Kingsley *Diary* 134 They raised some bread with it, which he said was the best *soda bread he ever tasted. 1879 *Newburgh* (N.Y.) *Daily Jrnl.* 22 Aug. 1/5 Day said 'Well, give me a *soda cocktail.

7. soda-fountain (also formerly **-font, -fount**) *U.S.*, an apparatus for supplying soda-water, syrups, ices, etc.; a 'store' or restaurant of which this is a feature.
1848 *Knickerbocker Mag.* XXXI. 40 They had not a theatre, nor an oyster-saloon, nor a *soda-font. 1850 N. Kingsley *Diary* 134 It was pure soda and possessed all the qualities of a *soda fount. 1851 C. Cist *Cincinnati* 244 Soda-founts and stands, Pattens generator, for making soda water. 1839 *Southern Lit. Messenger* V. 9/1 Barnyards, cow-houses, *soda-fountains, ice-houses and the like, are indispensable to the packets now. 1872 *Harper's Mag.* Aug. 345/2 When some enterprising Yankees set up an 'American Soda Fountain' at the Exposition of 1867. 1877 Eliz. S. Phelps *Story of Avis* 137 They became the abject prey of the soda-fountain and the lemonade boy. 1904 *Minneapolis Times* 23 June 8 He warned his congregation that, next to the saloon, the soda fountain is perhaps the deadliest enemy of humanity. 1926 Rose Macaulay *Crewe Train* ii. xiii. § 4. 223 Her lunch had consisted of a doughnut and two mixed fruit sundaes at a Lyons soda fountain. 1930 J. O. Dahl (*title*), Soda Fountain and Luncheonette Management.

Sod-corn. *U.S.* [Sod *sb.*¹] **a.** Indian corn grown on land which has been lying in sod. **b.** Whisky made from sod-corn.
1857 *Lawrence* (Kansas) *Republican* 6 Aug. 2 Sod corn promises now for about a half crop. 1867 *Rep. Iowa Agric. Soc.* (1868) 162 Our late crops, such as sod-corn, were entirely destroyed by grasshoppers. 1878 J. H. Beadle *Western Wilds* xii. 183 Chew's store..was the only place that sold bourbon—tothers only sod corn. 1879 *Scribner's Monthly* Nov. 133/2, I passed field after field of sod-corn. 1886 *Leslie's Pop. Monthly* XXII. Oct. 503/1 Here are..scattered fields of sod corn.

Soddy, *a.* (Later U.S. example.)
1865 *Rep. Maine Board Agric.* X. 62 The partially decomposed sward dries up on the surface, making the ground 'soddy' and uneven.

Soft, *a.* Add: **20. b.** Also *soft furnishing.*
1925 *Daily Tel.* 13 May 20/6 Soft furnishing department. 1927 *Ibid.* 11 May 18/6 Manageress wanted... Must have thorough experience in the sale and scheme side of soft furnishings.

d. *Comm.* Of commodities: Tending to yield or go down in price; not hard or stiff.
1930 *Morning Post* 19 Aug. 3/4 Oils were generally soft, while Coppers were far from being buoyant.

23. b. *Soft meat*: (*a*) food prepared by pigeons and fed to their young, being either ordinary food digested by them and regurgitated or a special secretion; called also *soft food*; (*b*) see quot. 1889 in Dict.
1854 Meall *Moubray's Poultry* viii. 454 The squab thrusts its bill into the side of the mouth of one of the old birds, which forthwith pumps up the contents of its stomach (called 'soft meat,' technically) into its own mouth. 1876 R. Fulton *Bk. Pigeons* iv. 39 This 'soft food',..is pumped up by the old ones with a sort of vomiting action. 1879 [see *Sick *a.* 1 f].

e. Of rays: Of a low penetrating power. Of a thermionic valve: Containing some residual gas or air.
1902 *Encycl. Brit.* XXVIII. 52/2 The rays coming from different discharge tubes have very different penetrating power. If the pressure in the tube is fairly high, so that the potential difference between its electrodes is small and the velocity of the cathode rays low, the Röntgen rays will be very readily absorbed. Such rays are called 'soft rays'. 1903 *Science Siftings* 18 July 198/2 In applying the x-ray they use a very feeble current, and what are called 'soft' bulbs. 1912 *Rep. Brit. Assoc.* 396 Rays...of an exceedingly soft or absorbable character. 1912 Soddy *Matter & Energy* vi. 163 If the vacuum is poor or 'low', the rays are not very penetrating or 'soft'. 1919 Fleming *Thermionic Valve* 154 Valves of not very high vacua or so-called soft valves. 1921 *Wireless World* IX. 17/2 The first and three subsequent valves are amplifiers and the last, a soft valve, is the rectifier. 1921 L. B. Turner *Wireless* 87 The most sensitive single tubes have been low-vacuum or 'soft' tubes. 1931 Duncan & Drew *Radio* (ed. 2) 214 The degree of vacuum in the tube would change and some tubes became *soft* (having less vacuum) while others became *hard* (having a higher vacuum, with little or no gas present).

27. *Soft cancer*, an encephaloid or colloid cancer. *Soft chancre*, a chancroid. *Soft corn*, (*b*) a variety of maize (*amylacea*); (*c*) a soft thickening of the epidermis between the toes. *Soft hail*, a kind of frozen snow. *Soft-nosed a.*, (of a bullet) expanding. *Soft palate*: see Palate *sb.* 1 b. *Soft paste*: see Paste *sb.* 3 b. *Soft pedal*: see Pedal *sb.* 1 b (*b*); hence as *vb. intr.* to play with the soft pedal down; (*trans.*) to 'tone down' (in quots. *fig.*). *Soft porcelain*, porcelain made of soft paste. *Soft rays*: see *23 e. *Soft second*, in *Bowls*, the second player of a rink or quartet. *Soft silk*, silk from which the gum has been removed. *Soft sore* = *soft chancre. *Soft sugar*, any prepared sugar not in the loaf or lump form (the precise application varies). *Soft wheat*, any wheat having a soft grain rich in starch.
1860 T. Holmes *Syst. Surg.* I. 523 Medullary cancer... Often called 'encephaloid', or..contrasted in respect to density with scirrhus by the title of '*soft cancer'. 1859 C. F. Maunder tr. *Ricord's Lect. Chancre* 9 Numerous examples of the *soft chancre. 1770 *Carroll Papers* in *Maryland Hist. Mag.* XIII. 72, I have a great deal of *soft Corn at all the Plantations. 1843 'Medicus' (G. B. C. Watson) *Hints for Pedestrians* 18 *note*, Corns...classed into hard and soft. 1864 T. Holmes *Syst. Surg.* IV. 764 Soft corns are found generally between the toes. 1902 L. H. Bailey *Cycl. Amer. Hortic.* IV. 2004/2 s.v. *Zea*, Soft corn (*Z. amylacea*, Sturt.). Kernels without horny or corneous endosperm. 1894 *Soft hail [see Graupel]. 1910 *Encycl. Brit.* XII. 820/1 Hail must be distinguished from the frozen snow, 'soft-hail' or 'graupel', that often falls at the rear of a spring cyclone. 1918 *Meteorol. Gloss.* 343 On colliding with any hard substance, soft-hail breaks up with a splash, and may thus be distinguished from true hail. 1899 *Soft-nosed [see 29]. 1901 G. H. Makins *Surg. Exp. S. Africa* iii. 92 Soft-nosed bullets of the Mauser and Lee-Metford patterns. 1909 *Chambers's Jrnl.* 803/1 There has followed a tacit understanding among civilised nations not to use soft-nosed collapsible bullets that 'set-up' or 'mushroom'. 1926 R. H. Davis *Over My Left Shoulder* xxix. 204 'Captain Sam heap mad!' replied the Peacemaker, with no effort to *soft pedal the announcement. 1927 *Daily Express* 19 July 3/4 Both parties are at present 'soft pedalling' on the world-revolution thesis. 1931 F. F. Bond *Mr. Miller of 'The Times'* 170 The leading educational centres tended to stress the utilitarian studies and soft-pedal those courses which sought merely cultural ends. 1819 Rees *Cycl.* XXVIII. Dd. 4/2 The porcelain is made of these substances [*sc.* porcelain clay and felspar]..but other materials are employed to give the required transparency at a lower temperature. This has received the name of *soft porcelain. 1839 Ure *Dict. Arts* etc. II. 1025 The manufacture of soft porcelain is longer and more difficult than that of hard. 1859 [see 24 b]. 1909 *Chambers's Jrnl.* 585/1 It is..essential for the collector to be able to differentiate between 'hard' and 'soft' porcelain if he would avoid the traps laid to catch the unwary. 1910 J. A. Manson in *Encycl. Brit.* IV. 347/2 The weakest player in the four is invariably played in the second place (the '*soft second'). 1875 Knight *Dict. Mech.* 2180/2 *Soft silk. 1881 *Instr. Census Clerks* (1885) 67 Soft Silk Piercer. Soft Silk Steward. Soft Silk Winder. 1887 J. L. Milton *Syphilis* 109 *Soft sore. 1908 Power & Murphy *Syst. Syphilis* I. 238 The soft sore, or ulcus molle. 1818 *Soft sugar [in Dict.]. 1812, 1843 *Soft wheat [see *Hard *a.* 22a]. 1875 *Encycl. Brit.* III. 251/1 In commerce the grain is distinguished as white and red, or as hard and soft wheats.

b. *Soft maple* (earlier U.S. examples).
1778 J. Carver *Trav. N. Amer.* 496 The Maple. Of this tree there are two sorts, the hard and the soft. 1807 P. Gass *Jrnl.* 195 The timber is mostly of the fir kind, with some.. soft maple.

c. *Soft crab* (earlier example).
1805 R. Parkinson *Tour Amer.* 315 There are soft crabs, which are reckoned great dainties.

Softening, *vbl. sb.* Add: **1. c.** (See *Soft *a.* 23 e.)
1926 E. H. Chapman *Wireless Dict.* 123 The effect of 'softening' in a valve is noticeable in the increased amount of anode current passing.

Soft-head². (Earlier modern example.)
1854 W. G. Simms *Southward Ho!* xvii. 390 We have, in the South, a race of 'soft-heads'.

Softly, *a.* **1.** (Later U.S. example.)
1875 Mrs. Stowe *Deacon Pitkin's Farm* ii. 45 Mis' Pitkin she's sot on't too in her softly way.

Soft-shell. 1. (Earlier U.S. example.)
1847 *Knickerbocker Mag.* XXIX. 494 A battle between a soft-shell turtle..and a terrier puppy.

2. *U.S.* (Earlier example.)
1845 *Knickerbocker Mag.* XXVI. 285 The 'Hard and Soft Shell Baptists'.

3. *U.S.* (Earlier example.)
1845 *Knickerbocker Mag.* XXVI. 285 A 'Hard-Shell' recently turned a 'Soft Shell' out of church.

b. Also, a soft-shelled turtle.
1830 R. C. Sands *Writings* II. 230 The soft-shell of the Red River. 1846 T. B. Thorpe *Myst. Backwoods* 156 It is Turtle Lake from its abundance of 'green, amphibious soft-shells'.

Soft soap, *sb.* **2.** (Earlier U.S. examples.)
1830 *Ann. 21st Congress* 1 Sess. VI. ii. 774, I will not use the vulgar phrase, and say he has been pouring soft soap down the backs of the New York delegation. 1840 W. G. Simms *Border Beagles* 18 Tush, young man, soft soap don't tickle me at my time of life.

Soft-soaper. (Earlier U.S. example.)
1852 'Mark Twain' in *Hannibal Jrnl.* Sept. 16 He was narrowly watching this soft-soaper of Democratic rascality.

Soft wood. 1. Add: *spec.* Coniferous trees and their timber.
1905 *Terms Forestry & Logging* 48 *Softwood*, a needle-leafed, or coniferous, tree. 1914 F. F. Moon & N. C. Brown *Elem. Forestry* 218 Many of our hardwoods are much softer in their wood structure than certain conifers or so-called softwoods. 1929 W. Dawson in *Timber Trade Lect.* 137 The light-seeded coniferous trees which produce our softwoods.

So·fty, *a.* [f. Soft *a.*] Characterized by softness.
1884 'Mark Twain' *Huck. Finn* xxvii. 272 When the place was packed full, the undertaker he slid around in his black gloves with his softy soothering ways.

Sog, *sb.*³ (Earlier example.)
1839 *Knickerbocker Mag.* XIII. 379 He was a most extraordinary fish; or, in the vernacular of Nantucket, 'a genuine old sog', of the first water.

Sog, *v.* Add: **1. a.** (Later U.S. example.)
1846–52 Mrs. Whitcher *Widow Bedott P.* xxix. 373 Some folks let their potaters lie and sog in the water ever so long before it biles.

Hence **Sogged** *ppl. a.*
1860 [see Sog *v.* 2]. 1929 H. Williamson *Beautiful Yrs.* xxiii. 237 A weary, misty dawn dispelled the phantasms and presented a reality of sogged ground and wet drippings from the trees.

Sogdian (sǫ·gdiăn), *a.* and *sb.* Also **Sughdian.** [ad.L. *Sogdiānus*, a. Gr. Σογδιανός, f. OPersian *Sughuda*, later *Soghd.*] **A.** *adj.* Of or belonging to Sogdiana (ἡ Σογδιανή), an ancient Persian province, corresponding to the modern Samarkand and Bukhara. **B.** *sb.* **a.** A native of this country. **b.** The language of the country (a form of Middle Iranian).
1909 Jackson in *Indogerm. Forsch.* XXV. 181 The Sughdian rendering of the Syriac version of the Greek. 1920 H. G. Wells *Outl. Hist.* (1924) 295/2 A very considerable literature..in Sogdian and another Aryan language has been discovered. 1929 *Encycl. Brit.* XII. 587/1 The Sogdian language. *Ibid.*, Sogdian has particularly close affinities with the 'Scythic' group of the Iranian languages. *Ibid.*, XVII. 566/2 The Sogdians (Pers. *Sugudu*) in the mountainous district between the Oxus and Iaxartes.

Soggy, *a.* **2.** (Earlier U.S. example.)
1846–52 Mrs. Whitcher *Widow Bedott P.* xxix. 375 Oh yes, to be sure it needs sugar, the best o' sugar too, not this wet, soggy, brown sugar.

Soho (sōhōu·), *sb.*² The name of a district in the West End of London, bounded by Charing Cross Road, Oxford Street, Regent Street, and Coventry Street, noted for its foreign population and restaurants.
1913 W. Whitten *Londoner's London* vi. 140 He had always a nice Soho taste in wine. [1930 W. S. Maugham *Cakes & Ale* 12 You drive away wondering whether when he comes he will think you are swanking if you ask him to Claridge's or mean if you suggest Soho.]

Soie (swa). The French word for 'silk', used with defining addition, as *soie de Chine.*
1923 *Daily Mail* 13 Feb. 7 Soie de Chine. *Ibid.* 24 Feb. 11 The latest version of *soie cloky* is called cloquelle.

Soigné, *fem.* **soignée** (swanʸe), *a.* [Fr., pa. pple. of *soigner* to take care of, f. *soin* care.] Dressed or adorned with great care and finish.
1921 *Spectator* 28 May 683/1 Candida was, above all, a splendid housewife and would have made the room not only comfortable, but beautiful. It would have had a *soigné* air. 1925 Oppenheim *Wrath to Come* xxi, She was herself again, *soignée*, as perfect in the small details of her toilet as [etc.]. 1927 A. E. W. Mason *No Other Tiger* xi. 98 As she stood there in that flood of radiance, *soignée*, polished from head to foot.

Soilage (soi·lėdʒ). Transfer † *Obs.* to senses in Dict. and add: **3.** The fact of soiling or condition of being soiled. *U.S.*
1926 *Publishers' Weekly* (N.Y.) 22 May 1679/2 One of the practical problems of retail bookselling is the rapid depreciation of stock due to soilage.

Sôk, variant of *Soc.

Sokol (sǭ·kǫl). [Czech (lit. falcon).] In Czechoslovakia, a gymnastic society for people of both sexes, aiming at the cultivation of mind and body, and bearing a falcon as their ensign. Also, a member of one of these societies. Also *attrib.*
1910 W. S. Monroe *Bohemia* x. 189 The organization of the Sokols in 1862 has undoubtedly been the most forceful factor in the social unification of the Bohemian people. *Ibid.* 194 A great gathering of all the Sokol unions of the world was called at Prague in 1887. 1915 *Scotsman* 10 Feb. 10/1 The gymnastic volunteer organisations ('sokols') which are popular among all the Slav nationalities of Austria. 1921 S. Graham *Europe—whither bound?* xiv. 189 The Sokol movement in Czecho-Slovakia and the Boy Scout movement are much more promising. 1925 F. L. Robson *Wayfarer in Czecho-Slovakia* viii. 126 It is a fine sight to see a really big Sokol exhibition, hundreds of men or girls moving like one.

Sol (sǫl), *sb.*⁶ *Phys. Chem.* [Short for *solution*, as in *Alcosol and *Hydrosol: cf. *Gel.] A liquid solution or suspension of a colloid.
The invention of this word and of *gel* is ascribed by later authorities to T. Graham (died 1869).
1899 W. B. Hardy in *Jrnl. Physiol.* XXIV. 164 *note*, Graham's nomenclature is as follows: The fluid state, colloidal solution, is the 'sol', the solid state the 'gel'. The fluid constituent is indicated by a prefix. Thus an aqueous solution of gelatine is a 'hydrosol', and on setting it becomes a 'hydrogel'. 1918 *Nature* 28 Mar. 66/1 Colloidal solutions are systems in which the solute individuals or *sols*, though apparently soluble, have not broken down to the molecular limit. 1922 A. W. Stewart *Physico-Chem. Themes* 175 When a gel is produced from a sol, the process is termed coagulation.

Sola, *a.* **2.** (Earlier Amer. examples.)
1737 W. Stephens *Proc. Georgia* 9 He brought a small Box with Sola Bills for a large sum. 1790 *Col. Rec. Georgia* VI. 323 The last Issue of Sola Bills was not sufficient to defray the Estimate to Michaelmas.

Solation² (sǫlē·ʃən). *Phys. Chem.* [f. *Sol *sb.*⁶ + -ation.] The conversion of a gel into a sol. Also **Sola·te** *v. intr.*, to be transformed into a sol.
1915 W. W. Taylor *Chem. Colloids* 11 There seems no escape from the adoption of the following terms:—gel, to gelate, gelation, sol, to solate, solation. 1922 A. W. Stewart *Physico-Chem. Themes* 175 *note*, The terms 'solation' and 'gelation' have been proposed in order to distinguish the two processes of sol-production and gel-formation.

Soldier, *sb.* Add: **1. d.** *To play at soldiers*: said of children, also derisively of volunteers.
1911 *Concise Oxford Dict.*

2. c. *Naut. slang.* A man, esp. a sailor, who shirks his work; one who does no more work than is necessary to secure pay or escape being discharged. (Cf. Soldier *v.* 3 d.)
1840 R. H. Dana *Bef. Mast* xvii, The captain called him a 'soger'. [Note], *Soger* (soldier) is the worst term of reproach that can be applied to a sailor. It signifies a skulk, a sherk [etc.].

8. soldier-bug, a North American predaceous beetle, esp. *Podisus spinosus.*
1870 *Amer. Naturalist* III. 98 The very same..may be true..of the Spined Soldier bug. 1876 *Rep. Vermont Board Agric.* III. 576 The spined soldier bug and the banded robber bug also prey upon the larvae of the potato beetle.

9. soldier's breeze = *soldier's wind*; **soldiers' home** *U.S.*, a place of stay for soldiers.
1894 Stevenson & Ll. Osbourne *Ebb Tide* ii. vii, The *Farallone* made a *soldier's breeze of it. 1865 *Atlantic Monthly* XV. 233, I wandered..from *soldiers' home to soldiers' home. 1866 J. C. Gregg *Life in Army* xxvi. 224 The idea of a Soldiers' Home is, I believe, original with the American people... It is said to have been first instituted in the city of Baltimore in 1861. 1881 *Harper's Mag.* Apr. 715/2 The handsome grounds of the Soldiers' Home.

Soldiering, *vbl. sb.* **2.** (Earlier and later U.S. examples.)
1840 Dana *Bef. Mast* xii, 'Sogering' was the order of the day. 1850 N. Kingsley *Diary* 108 There seems to be less sojering than usual. 1875 J. G. Holland *Sevenoaks* ii. 25 Remember:—seven o'clock, sharp, and no soldiering. 1903 *Sunday Herald* (Boston) 17 May 4/1 These physicians were appointed..for the ostensible purpose of preventing 'soldiering' among employes.

Sole, *sb.*¹ Add: **8. d.** *Geol.* An inclined thrust-plane.
Apparently named from the 'sole' of a wooden box (or of wooden blocks) in which clay, etc. was placed for experiments.
1888 H. M. Cadell in *Trans. Roy. Soc. Edin.* XXXV. 347 This experiment shows that underneath a series of beds repeated and heaped together by small thrusts, inclined perhaps at considerable angles, there runs..a major thrust or 'sole', inclined at a lower angle, along which the whole mass may have travelled for considerable distances. 1896 — *Geol. & Scenery Sutherland* 76 The thrust masses tend to move forward in a lump along 'soles' or major thrust-planes. 1930 Peach & Horne *Geol. Scot.* 117 The inclined thrust-plane or 'sole' along which the heaped-up strata were driven.

9. *sole-bend* (*Bend *sb.*² 4 b), *crêpe* (*Crepe *sb.* 2).
1924 *Times Trade & Engin. Suppl.* 29 Nov. 243/2 Supplies of low-class *solebends and offal are now small. 1925 *Daily Tel.* 13 May 4/4 The manufacture of *sole crepe.

Solemncholy, *a.* (Earlier Amer. example.)
1772 in *F. V. Fithian's Jrnl. & Lett.* (1900) 27 Being very Solemncholy and somewhat tired, I concluded to stay there all night.

b. *sb.* In *pl.*, a solemn or serious mood.
1834 W. A. Carruthers *Kentuckian in New York* I. 214 It drives away the solemncholies, and makes a fellow feel so good-natured, and so comfortable.

Solfège (sǫlfɛ̄ʒ). *Mus.* [Fr.] = Solfeggio. Also *attrib.*
1912 E. Ingham in *Eurhythmics Jaques-Dalcroze* 52 The solfège lessons are chiefly for ear-training and practical harmony. 1921 H. F. Rubinstein tr. *Jaques-Dalcroze's Rhythm, Music & Educ.* v. 78 One of these groups confined itself to studying solfège, the other commenced pianoforte lessons... The solfège students were then initiated into the study of the piano.

Solicitor. Add: **7.** A person who is employed to solicit orders on behalf of a business firm. *U.S.*
1903 E. L. Shuman *Pract. Journalism* 200 Have as many good solicitors out as necessary and make your rates low enough to invite this form of advertising. 1918 *Nation* (N.Y.) 7 Feb. 161/2 Life insurance salesmen as a class are.. about the least ambitious..salesmen in the entire round of commercial solicitors. 1926 *Publishers' Weekly* (N.Y.) 15 May 1580 Why can't he leave it to the judgment of the printers? Or to the advertising solicitor?

Solid, *sb.*¹ Add: **5.** A solid rubber tyre.
1919 *Brit. Manufacturer* Nov. 38/1, 50,000 pneumatic tyres a week, in addition to solids. 1924 A. W. Judge *Mod. Motor Cars* II. 178 Both ordinary and Giant Solids.

Solid, *a.* Add: **1. e.** *Photogr.* (See quots.)
1918 *Photo-Min* XV. Mar., *Solid*, applied to prints or enlargements made to include the background existing in the negative as distinguished from vignetting. 1919 *Brit. Jrnl. Photographic Alm.* 250 *Solid* applied to prints and enlargements.., denoting that the negative is printed full up to the edges—i.e., not vignetted or masked during printing.

8. b. (Earlier example.)
1878 J. H. Beadle *Western Wilds* xxvi. 418 Now Texas is the most solid outpost of the 'Solid South'.

Solidus¹. 2. Add: Used also in writing fractions and for other separations of figures and letters.
1891– [in Dict.]. 1923 Sir N. Shaw *Forecasting Weather* i. 35 A solidus (/) such as occurs in the combination 'bc/r' separates weather at the time of observation from the preceding weather, bc/r thus indicating 'fine or fair after rain or drizzle'.

Solifluxion (sǭ·liflʌkʃən). *Geol.* Also -fluction. [f. L. *solum* ground, earth + Fluxion.] A gradual downward movement or slide of particles of the earth's surface: soil-flow. Hence **Solifluxional** *a.*
1916 T. G. Taylor *With Scott* 115 These symmetrical polygons are due to a slow movement of half-frozen soil, which has been noted in polar lands, and is called solifluxion or soil-creep. 1924 Huxley & Odell in *Geog. Jrnl.* LXIII. 224 It remains to mention the chief modifications of the stone-polygons due to 'solifluction' (or soil-flow) and other causes. *Ibid.* 225 On well-developed solifluctional slopes of mixed material, the different-sized stones move downwards at different rates. 1928 *Greenland* I. 437 The peculiar solifluction within the areas of the less resistant nepheline-syenites.

Solifugid (sǭlĭ·fiūdʒid). *Zool.* [f. L. *solifuga* Solifuge + -id³.] An arachnid of the order *Solifugæ.*
1925 R. W. G. Hingston *Nature at Desert's Edge* xi. 230 The solifugid... Scientifically it belongs to the order *Solifugæ*, and the one under discussion is the species *Galeodes arabs.* 1925 — in E. F. Norton *Fight for Everest*, 1924 iii. § 2. 286 Solifugids occur up to 15,000 feet.

Solipsist. Add: **B.** *adj.* Favouring or characterized by solipsism. So **Solipsi·stically** *adv.*
1923 *Times Lit. Suppl.* 23 Aug. 549/2 There are tracts of experience which almost all of us are accustomed to explain solipsistically—our dream-worlds. 1927 V. McNabb *Cath. Ch. & Philos.* iii. 101 His [*sc.* Kant's] own words are ingenuously solipsist!

Solitary, *sb.* Add: **5.** Solitary confinement. *Prison slang.*
1924 W. M. Raine *Troubled Waters* xxvi. 262 'He's been in solitary for a week,' explained the warden.

Solo, *sb.* and *a.* Add: **A.** *sb.* **7.** *Aviation.* A solo flight; flying solo.
1920 G. C. Bailey *Complete Airman* xxiv. 191 A dual lesson being given after every two or three hours' solo. 1929 F. A. Swoffer *Learning to Fly* ix. 84 When a pupil is ready for solo. *Ibid.*, On your subsequent solos practise what you have been taught. 1930 G. L. P. Henderson *Pract. Flying* xvi. 125 Condemning..these practices as dangerous on the first solo, and indeed for many hours afterwards.

B. *adj.* **4.** *Aviation.* Alone, i.e. without an instructor or a mechanic.
1914 Rosher *In R.N.A.S.* (1916) 15 Hope to be flying solo by Thursday or Friday. 1918 *Punch* 3 Apr. 222/2 Yes, he crashed a few days ago—on his first solo flip. 1920 G. C. Bailey *Complete Airman* xxiv. 190 After this, dual and solo flying are undertaken alternately. 1930 G. L. P. Henderson *Pract. Flying* xvi. 128 The pupil is now safely solo and well on his way towards his 'A' licence.

Solo (sǭ·lo), *v.* [f. Solo *sb.* and *a.*]
1. *trans.* To perform (a piece of music) as a solo. Also *intr.* or *absol.*
1856 *Punch* 8 May 184/2 The sweetness of his oratory would be completely wasted on the air of '*Keemo Kimo*' soloed by the ophicleide. 1886 W. Booth *Orders & Regul. Salvation Army* iii. ii. 96 All cannot solo or speak eloquently.

2. *Aviation. intr.* To fly solo.
1917 *War Birds* (1927) 57, 4 have been flying for three days and Capt. Harrison says I can solo to-morrow if it's calm. 1931 V. W. Pagé *ABC of Gliding* 164 In training glider pilots the student usually 'solos' from the very start.

Soloist. Add: **2.** *Aviation.* One who flies solo.
1930 G. L. P. Henderson *Pract. Flying* xvi. 125 Let us however..prescribe..for first soloists. 1931 C. D. Barnard *Learning to Fly* xii. 140 The soloist must..take advantage of the longest run available when taking off.

Solution, *sb.* Add: **6. b.** *Cycling*, etc. In full *rubber solution*: a liquid preparation of caoutchouc, chiefly used in repairing rubber tyres.
1894 *Cycling* (Badm.) App. 471 The hole [is] discovered.. and a small patch of rubber stuck over it with rubber solution. 1897 A. C. Pemberton *Complete Cyclist* vii. 188 When the tube is clean a little rubber solution has to be rubbed on. *Ibid.* 190 The edges of the cut must be well cleaned and coated with solution. 1898 G. Lacy Hillier *Wrinkles for Cyclists* 64 Then solution should be pressed in. 1930 F. Gardner *How to repair your Cycle* 20 Spread a thin layer of solution over the part that has been rubbed.

Solution, *v.* Add: *spec.* in *Cycling*, etc. To treat with rubber solution; to fasten (*to, down, together*) with this. Hence **Solu·tioned** *ppl. a.*
1898 [see Dict.]. 1898 G. Lacy Hillier *Wrinkles for Cyclists* 64 To..compress the solutioned cotton. 1898 — *Cycling for Everybody* 81 The solutioned surface should be left alone for some minutes, which allows of the evaporation of the naphtha. *Ibid.* 84 The internal hole should be closed by a patch carefully solutioned to the internal rubber walls. 1909 'R. Andom' *On Tour with Troddles* 263, I ripped off the [tyre] cover, and found the patch hadn't quite caught, so we solutioned it down firmly. *Ibid.* 264 We strengthened the cover with strips of rubber and solutioned canvas.

Solutionist (sǫliū·ʃənist). [See -ist.] One who finds the solution of a problem or difficulty; *esp.* an expert in solving cross-word puzzles.
1885 *Liverpool Mercury* 24 Oct. 5 Mr. Paul de Cassagnac calls them 'Solutionists'. 1926 *Weekly Dispatch* 29 Aug., The insertion of clues capable of alternative solutions..gives the ordinary reader an equal chance with the professional solutionist. 1928 *Daily Express* 15 June 2/4 A professional solutionist ordered 5,000 copies of a single issue of a newspaper.

Solvate (sǫ·lveit), *sb. Phys. Chem.* [f. Solve *v.* + -ate¹.] A solute or dissolved substance which enters into combination with the solvent.
1910 H. C. Jones *Introd. Phys. Chem.* 100 Solvates in general. 1913 — *New Era Chem.* ix. 163 The solvates existing in the solution. 1922 A. W. Stewart *Physico-Chem. Themes* 269 Another form of explanation is arrived at by assuming that solvates are formed on the addition of the salt.

Solvate (sǫ·lveit), *v. Phys. Chem.* [f. Solve *v.* + -ate³.] *intr.* Of a solute: To enter into combination with the solvent.
1913 H. C. Jones *New Era Chem.* 165 Non electrolytes solvate very slightly. The electrolytes combine with large amounts of the solvent. *Ibid.*, It is the ions which are the chief solvating agents. *Ibid.*, Some non electrolytes show slight solvating power. 1917 M. H. Fischer tr. *W. Ostwald's Introd. Colloid Chem.* 134 The solvated colloids.

Solvation (sǫlvē·ʃən). *Phys. Chem.* [f. Solve *v.* + -ation.] The combination of a solute with its solvent. Also, the degree to which this takes place.
1913 H. C. Jones *New Era Chem.* 155 There is good reason to believe that dissolved substances in general combine with more or less of the solvent—in a word, solvation in solution is a general phenomenon. 1917 M. H. Fisher tr. *W. Ostwald's Introd. Colloid Chem.* 51 These colloids are characterized by their great hydration or solvation. Their particles have taken up a large amount of the dispersion media.

Somal (somā·l), **Somali** (somā·li). Pl. with or without *s.*
A native of Somaliland or the 'Eastern Horn' of Africa; they are a Hamitic race and Mohammedans. Also, their language. Also *attrib.*
1856 R. F. Burton *E. Africa* p. xxii, The Somal at Aden. *Ibid.* p. xxv, In the Somali, as in other countries of Eastern Africa. *Ibid.* 29 In the Somali country. *Ibid.* 89 *note*, In the latter sense it is the polite address to a Somali. *Ibid.* 644/2 Tale of a Somal chief. *Ibid.*, Belief of the Somali. 1880 F. M. Hunter *Gramm. Somali Lang.* p. xx, The *Somal* are essentially nomadic in their habits. *Ibid.* p. xxi, A *Somali* possesses but few personal effects. *Ibid.* 6 There is only one article in Somali. 1888 F. L. James *Unknown Horn of Africa* 7 The northern Somalis. *Ibid.* 30 'Hubla' (Somal for 'virgin'). *Ibid.* 168 Like the Somal, the Adone have large herds of cattle. *Ibid.* 169 The Adone detest the Somals. 1897 Larajasse *Somali Dict.* p. viii, Some Somal pronounce this consonant [*sc.* cerebral *d*] nearly as *rd.* 1921 H. Rayne *Sun, Sand & Somals* 19 The Somal tribes. *Ibid.* 21 The Somals are the most nomadic of people.

Somaten (somatē·n, somā·ten). Pl. **somatenes.** [Catalan (and Sp.) *somatén.*] In Catalonia, and hence in Spain, a body of civilians armed for the protection of a town or district. Hence **Somate·nist** [= *somatenista*], a member of a somaten.
1845 R. Ford *Handbk. Spain* I. 493/1 Thus time was given for the *somaten*, or tocsin, to be rung, and the armed peasantry collected... The Catalan *guerrilleros* were called *Somatenes*, from this bell. 1928 *Daily Tel.* 29 May 9/5 A member of the 'Somaten' (Militia) to-day succeeded in finding the young man who ran amok with a rifle last Monday. ..As he refused to surrender the 'Somatenist' fired and killed him. 1929 A. F. G. Bell in E. Allison Peers *Spain* 275 A more efficient city-police, together with the Somatenes and the Civil Guard, maintained order throughout Spain.

Some, *indef. pron.*, *a.*¹ Add: **A.** *indef. pron.* **4. e.** A good deal, a lot. *U.S.*
1850 N. Kingsley *Diary* 159 [He] has taken out this afternoon 30 ounces of amalgam, which I think is some for this bar. *Ibid.* 163 He took out over 80 ounces in amalgam; this is some & no mistake.

f. *And (then) some*: and a good deal or a great many in addition. *U.S. slang.*
1914 D. O. Barnett *Lett.* (1915) 19, I picked them out with those glasses, and let them have it, and then some!

B. *adj.* **4. e.** *U.S.* (Earlier and later examples.)
1845 *Knickerbocker Mag.* XXV. 273 The way he put in the licks was some! 1860 Holland *Miss Gilbert's Career* xii. 218 Good boy!.. You're some, that's a fact. 1876 'Mark Twain' *Tom Sawyer* i. 8 Smarty! You think you're *some*, now, don't you. 1888 'C. E. Craddock' *Broomsedge Cove* xix. 346 The weather is getting to be 'some' if not more, aint it?

f. In attrib. use: Such in the fullest sense, 'something like a', worthy of the name, worth talking about. *U.S.* and *slang.*
1914 Gertrude Atherton *Perch of Devil* i. 80 They're some geologists, he added with unwilling admiration. *Ibid.* 108 Butte is some education, believe me. 1915 Rosher *In R.N.A.S.* (1916) 87, I have written up her raids inside the fuselage—(1) Friedrichshafen, (2) Zeebrugge, (3) Ostend, (4) Ostend again, and (5) Hoboken—some record! *Ibid.* 90 Windows were broken in the streets all round—'some' mess, I can tell you. 1915 *Even. News* 25 Jan. 3/2 A man whose cheery optimism will make him crack a joke in the small hours when things are bad and his best pals have gone..is 'some' soldier. 1922 A. A. Milne *Red House Myst.* vii. 60 She's an actress, some actress too. 1923 S. Donoghue *Just my Story* 270 Forty miles in fifty-five minutes! 'Some' driver, Lucien.

Somebody, *sb.* Add: **3. b.** Used, like *thingamy*, when a person's name is forgotten or is of no importance to the matter in hand.
1825 Cobbett *Rur. Rides* 31 Oct., I see..the Ogles succeeded by a general or a colonel somebody.

Something, *sb.* Add: **1. b.** Also used as a substitute for a number unknown or unspecified.
1918 *Aeroplane* 2 Jan. 36/1 There are holes to drill, some 'nth' of an inch, and another row 'something' millimetres.

3. c. *Something* (*good* or *special*), a good or special tip for a horse-race.
1907 *Racing Expert* 9 July 3 For the benefit of those who care to wait and act upon the best information. 'The Expert' will occasionally wire when he knows Something Special. 1908 *Racing Judge* 6 June 4 Owing to Bank Holiday this Letter will be sent out on Tuesday Evening... Something good at Manchester will be given. 1924 'Ian Hay' *Sport of Kings* i. ii, We found 'The Sporting Times' and 'The Jockey' in your overcoat pocket...So we thought you might know something.

Hence **Something** *v.* (example of ppl. a.).
1925 E. Wallace *Valley of Ghosts* xiii, You called me..a fool, and a somethinged fool, almost the first time we met.

Somewhere, *adv.* and *sb.* **A.** *adv.* **1.** Add: In the war of 1914–18, used in phr. such as 'Somewhere in France' to refer to without identifying (because of the restrictions of the censorship) some locality in the theatre of war.
1915 *Illustr. London News* 20 Feb. 241 For the moment 'Victoria' looks like 'Somewhere in France'. 1915 *Daily Sketch* 17 Aug. 12/1 None of these soldiers a year ago expected to be snapped one day...—somewhere in Egypt. *Ibid.* 18 Aug. 9/2 She had just passed through from canteen work 'somewhere'.

Sommelier (sǫmǝlye). [Fr.; ult. f. *somme* burden. Cf. Somler.] A butler.
1923 E. P. Oppenheim *Inevitable Millionaires* xiv. 146 Harold..making cryptic signs with his fingers which intimated to the sommelier his urgent need of a cocktail. 1930 *Time & Tide* 24 May 665 The *sommelier* who brings him his bottle of Haut Brion. 1930 *New Statesman* 28 June 366/1 The fastidious wine-bibber, terror of sommeliers and his timider hosts.

Somnal (sǫ·mnăl). *Pharm.* [f. L. *somnus* sleep + -al, as in Chloral.] A proprietary name for a solution of chloral hydrate and urethane in alcohol, used as a hypnotic and diuretic.
1890 *Jrnl. Soc. Chem. Industry* IX. 101/2. 1892 *Work* IV. 545/1.

Son, *sb.* **6. d.** Used in the names of various societies. *U.S.*
1766 J. Habersham *Lett.* 55 The Sons of Liberty. 1846 *Knickerbocker Mag.* XXVIII. 145 The Sons of Temperance. 1866 A. D. Richardson *Secret Service* xxxix. 429 A secret organization known as the Sons of America, instituted expressly to assist Union men. 1867 Dixon *New Amer.* I. ii. 21 A meeting of Sons of the South. 1888 M. Lane *Pol. Catch-Words* 8 Nov. 15 Sons of Liberty.—This organization, known by different names, developed in the West in 1862, about the time for the first draft.

Sonantal (sonæ·ntăl), *a.* *Phonetics.* [See -al.] Of a sonant character.
1891 A. L. Mayhew *Syn. O.E. Phonol.* 36 The Indg. sonantal liquid ļ.

Sonder (zǫ·ndər). *U.S.* In full **sonder-class.** [G. *sonderklasse* special class: see Sunder.] The designation of a class of small racing yachts.
1913 C. W. Ernst *Letter* (MS.), Our yachtsmen, since 1907, talk of 'sonder-boats', sonder class, sonder race,—meaning certain boats recognised by the International Yacht Racing Union.

Song, *sb.* **2. d.** *Mus.* Substitute the following def. and quots. A musical composition sung or intended to be sung, consisting of a melody set to words (see 2), with or without instrumental accompaniment.
Song without words, an instrumental composition in the style of a song (after Mendelssohn's title 'Lieder ohne Worte'); also *transf.*
c 897 Ælfred *Gregory's Past C.* lii. 409 Ða singað ðone sang be nan mon elles singan ne mæg buton ðæt hundteontig & feowertig & feower ðusendo. *a* 1300 *E. E. Psalter* cxxxvi[i]. 5 Hou sal we singe sange wiþ blisse Ofe lauerd in outen land þat isse? 1450–1530 *Myrr. Our Ladye* i. xxi. 56 The notes and songe serue to the wordes, and the wordes serue to the inwarde sentence. 1596 Shaks. *1 Hen. IV*, iii. i. 216 She will sing the Song that pleaseth you. 1599 — *Much Ado* ii. iii. 77 By my troth, a good song. *Balth.* And an ill singer. 1781 Cowper *Truth* 458 The soul..Weeps tears of joy, and bursts into a song. 1840 *Penny Cycl.* XVI. 22/1 Handel's song, 'Sweet Bird', from *Il Penseroso*, always has been, and most likely always will be, admired as music. 1871 Smiles *Charac.* viii. 219 Cheerfulness..gives harmony of soul, and is a perpetual song without words. 1883 R. Prentice *Musician* ii. 95 The second movement [of a Beethoven sonata] is a veritable Song without Words. 1893 C. H. H. Parry *Art of Music* 319 The use of such characteristic figures in the instrumental part of songs is a very conspicuous feature in Schubert's work and that of all other great song-writers.

7. Add: **song-form** *Mus.*, the simplest form of instrumental composition, consisting of one or more melodic themes as in a vocal song; **song-hit,** a song that has made a hit; **song-plug** *v. trans. U.S.*, to repeat (a song) in a musical comedy, etc.; also *transf.*
1884 R. Prentice *Musician* iii. 4 The simplest *song-form is constructed on two or three sentences only. 1902 H. C. Banister *Mus. Anal.* i. 2 There is a term now in vogue to designate the simplest of all plans or forms: 'Song-Form' or 'Aria-Form'. 1929 W. E. Collinson *Spoken Engl.* 82 Some of the latter's *song-hits are likely to catch on. 1929 'Seamark' *Down River* i, Humming a snatch of the latest musical comedy song-hit to himself. 1927 *Daily Express* 22 Sept. 9/3 'Clap Yo' Hands' must have been *song-plugged for ten minutes right off...'Do-Do-Do' is another song-plugged number. *Ibid.* 6 Oct. 8/5 Think of musical comedy without song-plugging! 1927 *Sunday Express* 6 Nov. 5/6 The Salvation Army certainly used to borrow music-hall songs for their hymn tunes, but not everybody likes references to 'Satan' song-plugged to knee drill.

Sonic (sǫ·nik), *a.* [f. L. *sonus* sound + -ic.] In *Echo-sounding*, the designation of an instrument or process which works by the reflexion of an audible noise.
1926 *Internat. Ice Observation* (U.S.) 45 Sonic depth finder. 1926 *Encycl. Brit.* Suppl. II. 1025/2 The apparatus consists of two microphones, one of which registers the emission of a sonic signal and the other the arrival of the echo reflected by the bottom of the sea. *Ibid.* III. 592/1 Sonic depth soundings. 1929 *Times* 12 Mar. 13/3 The audible or 'sonic' form of apparatus.

Sonnet, *sb.* **3.** Add: **sonnet-sequence,** a set of sonnets connected in theme.
1881 D. G. Rossetti *Ballads & Sonnets* 161 The House of Life: a sonnet-sequence. 1931 G. Cockerill (*title*), Love's Universe and The Calendar: Sonnet-Sequences.

Sonny. (Earlier U.S. example.)
1850 *Knickerbocker Mag.* XXXVI. 288 'Pa' returned towards the cars; when 'sonny', quickly drawing his pocket-pistol, took a drink.

Sont, variant of Sunt.
1901 *Knowledge* June 138/2 The timber forming a raft is generally of the 'sont' tree.

Sontag (sǫ·ntæg, zo·ntax). [Named after Mme Henriette *Sontag*, a German singer.] A knitted jacket or cape with two long tabs which are crossed over the bosom and fastened at the back.
1863 Mrs. Whitney *Faith Gartney's Girlh.* xviii, Faith brought quickly, sontag, jacket and cloak.

Sook, var. *Suq.

Sool (sūl), *v. Austral.* [var. of Sowl *v.*³]
1. *trans.* Of a dog: To worry (an animal).
1896 Mrs. L. Parker *Austral. Leg. Tales* 90 She went quickly towards her camp, calling softly, 'Birree gougou', which meant 'Sool 'em, sool 'em', and was the signal for the dogs to come out. Quickly they came and surrounded the black fellows,..bit and worried them to death.

2. To set on or excite (a dog) to attack. Also with *on.*
1911 *Chambers's Jrnl.* 222/2 Don't 'sool' the dogs to an unwise assault. 1916 C. J. Dennis *Ginger Mick* 39 The bugles East and West sooled on the dawgs o' war.

Soorkee (sūə·ki). *India.* Also -i, -y. [Hind., a. Pers. *surkhī* redness, brick-dust.] A mortar consisting of pulverized brick mixed with lime.
1899 Mrs. E. Cotes *Path of Star* i. 4 There came a light crunch of wheels on the red soorkee drive outside.

Soot, *v.* Add: **3.** With *up*: To fill or choke with a sooty deposit.
1903 [see *sooting* vbl. sb.]. 1925 *Morris Owner's Manual* 46 Bad plug insulation is sometimes caused through sooting. 1929 W. E. Collinson *Spoken English* 84 The engine is knocking. One of the [sparking] plugs is probably sooted up.

Soothing, *ppl. a.* **2. b.** (Earlier U.S. example of *soothing syrup*; hence *soothing-syrupy* adj.)
1872 'Mark Twain' *Roughing It* xv. 125 Soothing syrup! Teething-rings! 1902 G. H. Lorimer *Lett. Self-made Merchant* xviii. 261 A lady..in a soothing-sirupy way asked if I would lend it to her.

Soppy, *a.* Add: **5.** Full of mawkish sentiment. Also *to be soppy on*, to be spoony or 'sweet' on (a person). *colloq.*
1920 H. G. Hibbert *Playgoer's Mem.* 257 The soppy-sentimental heroine. 1930 Galsworthy *Roof* iii, Don't be soppy, Bryn. 1930 Braman *Little Flutter* xix. 218, I may as well make up my mind that I'm soppy on the blighter. 1930 *Punch* 9 Apr. 412/1 It was a soppy book and I ought never to have opened it.

Sorbitize (sǫ·rbitəiz), *v.* [f. Sorbite² + -ize.] To form sorbite in (steel) in the process of heating and cooling.
1918 D. K. Bullens *Steel* (ed. 2) viii. 167 It will be noted that it required four quenchings to entirely sorbitize the steel. 1928 C. J. Allen *Steel Highway* 97 Another popular means of toughening the steel is by heat treatment, the process known as 'sorbitising' adding considerably to the wearing capacity with but a moderate addition to the cost of the rails.

Sorbose (sǭ·ɹbōus). *Chem.* [f. Sorb¹ + -ose.] = Sorbinose.
1899 J. R. Green *Fermentation* viii. 104 Of those [sugars] with 6 carbon-atoms we knew glucose, fructose, galactose and sorbose.

Sore, *a.*¹ **12. a.** Add: Also with *on* (= in regard to, against). *U.S.*
1868 H. Woodruff *Trotting Horse Amer.* iii. 54 This is an indication that he has had too much work for his age, and has got sore on it. 1904 *N.Y. Evening Post* 13 June 1 Kelly denied the charges and said the patrolman was 'sore' on him. 1931 R. D. Paine *Comr. Rolling Ocean* xiv. 252 All hands were sore on him, but he couldn't take a hint.

Soroche (sorō·tʃi). [Quichua *sorochi* pyrites, mountain sickness.] Native name in the Peruvian Andes for mountain sickness. Cf. Puna 2.
1891 E. B. Clark *Twelve Months in Peru* 104 A headache with a weighty feeling on the brow, vomiting, and breathlessness are the usual symptoms of *sorroche.* 1895 S. I. Bailey in *Ann. Astr. Obs. Harvard* XXXIV. 12 One of the party..suffered quite severely from *soroche* or mountain-sickness. 1925 *Contemp. Rev.* Jan. 93 The air is so rarified that the newcomer finds a difficulty in breathing, even if he escapes an attack of *soroche* (mountain sickness). 1927 Kendrew *Climates Cont.* 322 The 'soroche', as the complaint is called locally, causes breathlessness and palpitation, loss of appetite, and sometimes nose-bleeding.

Sororate (sǫrō·rēt). [f. L. *soror* sister + -ate¹, after Levirate.] The custom among some primitive tribes which allows or requires a man to marry his living or deceased wife's younger sisters.
1910 J. G. Frazer *Totemism & Exogamy* IV. 140 The other [custom] is the rule which allows or requires a man to marry the younger sisters either of his living or of his deceased wife... The latter custom..has no distinctive name, but on analogy I propose to call it the *sororate.* 1918 — *Folk-lore in O.T.* II. 265. 1921 E. Westermarck *Human Marriage* (ed. 5) III. 263–5.

Sorption (sǫ·ɹpʃən). *Phys. Chem.* [The second element of *adsorption*, *absorption* used independently.] A name proposed to designate the joint effect of absorption and adsorption.
1909 J. W. McBain in *Phil. Mag.* Ser. vi. XVIII. 916 The non-committal name '*sorption*' may be coined to designate the sum of the phenomena, while '*absorption*' and '*adsorption*' should be restricted to proven cases of the solution and surface condensation respectively. 1922 A. W. Stewart *Physico-Chem. Themes* 232 Adopting McBain's nomenclature, we may speak of the surface effect as *adsorption* and the diffusion into the charcoal pores as *absorption*; whilst to the joint effect of the two the name *sorption* may be given.

Sorrel-top. *U.S.* [Sorrel *a.* A. b.] A red-haired person.
1863 'E. Kirke' *My Southern Friends* iv. 58 'Har, you lousy sorrel-top', said the trader to the red-faced and red-headed bar tender. *a* 1909 'O. Henry' *Roads of Destiny* xviii. 298, I guess they don't raise 74-inch sorrel-tops with romping ways down in his precinct.

Sort, *v.*¹ **12. a.** Add: Also of things (= to become sorted).
1925 E. F. Norton *Fight for Everest*, 1924 51 Nearly 300 yak-loads of provision boxes, rolls of bedding and stores of all sorts, dumped higgledy-piggledy off the yaks, began to sort themselves into orderly lines and piles.

Sortes (sǫ·ɹtīz), *sb. pl.* [L., pl. of *sors* lot, chance.] Short for *sortes Virgilianae, Biblicae, Homericae* (and the like): divination by chance selection of a passage in Virgil, etc.
1886 D. C. Murray *Cynic Fortune* xv. (1899) 183 In the practice of the *sortes* (which was a favourite occupation of his) [he] was elevated or depressed by the text he fell upon.

SOS (esōues). A wireless code-signal summoning assistance in extreme distress, used esp. by ships at sea. Also *transf.*
The letters are arbitrarily chosen as being easy to transmit and distinguish. The signal was recommended at the Radio Telegraph Conference in 1906, and officially adopted at the Radio Telegraph Convention in 1908. (See G. G. Blake *Hist. Radio Telegr.*, 1926, 111–12.)
1910 Fleming *Princ. Electr. Wave Telegr. & Teleph.* (ed. 2) 882 *note.* 1912 *Rep. 'Titanic' Inquiry* 63/1 The Attorney-General explained that the signal C.Q.D. meant 'Come quick, danger', and that this had now been substituted for S.O.S. 'Save our souls'. 1917 'Sapper' *No Man's Land* 71 A row of grey-painted rockets with a red top, which in case of emergency send up the coloured flares that give the S.O.S. signals to those behind. 1918 *Punch* 13 Mar. 176 S.O.S. at Suburban Pictures. (In cases of emergency affecting any of the audience messages are sometimes thrown on the screen by the courtesy of the management.) 1920 *Sat. Rev.* 3 July 3 Our hospitals are vainly sending out S.O.S. signals to save them from insolvency. 1924 Galsworthy *White Monkey* ii. iii, I've just been talking to a little Cockney whose S.O.S. is 'Central Austrylia'. 1927 H. A. Vachell *Dew of the Sea* etc. 257 He received a letter from the gentleman, regarded (and rightly) by the McCullough as an S.O.S. signal. 1928 Work *Contract Bridge* 144 S.O.S. (redouble). Redouble made to indicate weakness rather than strength.

Hence **SOS** *v. intr.*, to make this signal.
1923 Kipling *Land & Sea Tales* 114 Then..this Baxterman got busy with his wireless and SOS'ed like winkie.

Sosh² (sǫʃ). *U.S. slang.* [Short for Social (sōu·ʃăl).] A person having social polish and little else.
1900 H. L. Wilson *Spenders* xxxi. 367 That's right, son. I knew I could make something more than a polite sosh out of you.

Souk, variant of *Suq.

Soul, *sb.* Add: **4. f.** *To have no soul* (cf. 3 a, b): to be lacking in sensibility or right feeling; to be wanting in emotional power (as an artist or a work of art). *colloq.*

1704 Swift *T. Tub* 64 That Fellow, cries one, has no Soul; where is his Shoulder-knot? 1850 'Luke Limner' (J. Leighton) *Christmas Comes but once a Year* 9 He seeks refuge in his organ, much to the annoyance of a little tailor in the attic who has no soul in him.

g. *To have a soul above*: to be indifferent to, not to care about (something). *colloq.*

1899 G. B. Burgin *Bread of Tears* I. iii, Miss Mercy Tressock evidently wrote a very bad hand, and she hadn't a soul above blots; they were dotted copiously about on every page.

22. *soul-absorbing, -agonizing, -awakening, -blenching, -rocking, -vibrating* ppl. adjs.

1906 W. De Morgan *Joseph Vance* xiii, I have been assured by artists that one serious nuisance of their lives is the perfect stranger's *soul-absorbing interest in their work. 1898 H. Rider Haggard *Dr. Therne* x, No South African mines or other *soul-agonising speculations for me. 1926 C. Barry *Detective's Holiday* iv. 33 Suddenly a *soul-awakening boom behind him smote his ears. 1910 H. G. Wells *Mr. Polly* ix. § 8 He wasted breath in saying what was to happen shortly—sanguinary, oriental, *soul-blenching things—when the broom no longer separated them. 1926 W. J. Locke *Stories Near & Far* 32 The *soul-rocking wonders of this night. *Ibid.* 6 Officially, the witchery was a *soul-vibrating secret.

25. soul-case, -sleeper (later U.S. examples); **soul-substance** *Anthropol.*, an animistic principle supposed to reside both in living creatures and in inanimate things.

1835 A. B. Longstreet *Georgia Scenes* (1843) 156 When you come to the half mile of each heat, run his heart, liver, lights, and *soul-case out of him. 1869 Mrs. Stowe *Oldtown Folks* xxiv. 292 The beautiful little hoax had nothing for it but her attractive soul-case. 1896 J. C. Harris *Sister Jane* 277 The way that hoss flung around wi' you was enough to jolt your soul-case loose. 1879 B. F. Taylor *Summer-Savory* xvii. 141 An Episcopalian,..an Adventist, a *Soul-Sleeper, and a Baptist. 1887 J. Kirkland *Zury* 65 He and Peddicomb had both been connected with the little sect of Christians called 'Soul-sleepers'. 1924 *Hastings's Encycl. Relig. & Ethics* VII. 234/2 Primitive man was always bent on increasing his *soul-substance in order to make his life stronger. *Ibid.* 237/2 Soul-substance of plants. *Ibid.* 238/1 Soul-substance of objects. 1924 W. B. Selbie *Psychol. Relig.* 28 Anthropologists are now fairly generally agreed that underlying all religions is what they call animism, or belief in a soul substance discoverable not merely in men but in things.

Sou markee. *U.S.* [ad. F. *sou marqué*, an old copper coin worth about a sou and a quarter.] A coin of little value; little or nothing.

1896 G. Ade *Artie* xii. 109 When he was staked to the office he didn't have a sou markee. 1903 A. H. Lewis *The Boss* 181, I don't pony for a sou markee.

Sound, *sb.*³ Add: **6. b.** *sound-detector, -indicator, -locator, -sender.*

1878 *Chambers's Jrnl.* 29 June 413/1 An extremely delicate *sound detector. 1928 C. F. S. Gamble *North Sea Air Station* xii. 188 It was the want of an adequate ground organization—guns, searchlights, and *sound indicators—that handicapped pilots..in their anti-airship operations. 1929 *Nature* 30 Oct. 182/1 *Sound-locators were also used on board anti-submarine craft. 1922 *Encycl. Brit.* XXX. 88/2 The sound locator is an instrument which is intended to indicate the angle of elevation, and the bearing in azimuth, of aircraft audible but invisible from the ground. 1878 *Design & Work* 9 Mar. 298/1 A paragraph explaining the *sound-sender of Reis.

7. sound-shift, -shifting *Philol.*, a literal rendering of G. *lautverschiebung*.

1886 T. Le M. Douse *Introd. Goth. Ulfilas* 67 This relationship is designated by German scholars *Lautverschiebung*, or sound-shifting. 1892 [see Dict., 6 b].

b. Denoting instruments or processes for the recording of sound or the resulting record, as *sound camera, record*; **sound-film**, a cinema film with audible dialogue, music, etc.; hence in many combs. connected with this, as *sound gate, head, path, picture, scene, stage, studio, track.*

1903 *Science Siftings* 10 Oct. 5/1 A slide block..is provided with a stylus held by tension of the spring against the sound-record. 1904 *Ibid.* 26 Mar. 353/1 A wonderful camera that will photograph noises... With this sound camera, all noises..can be realistically reproduced. 1916 *Chambers's Jrnl.* Jan. 61/1 Expression has to be ignored to a very considerable extent during the task of producing or recording, because the sound-line, into which the effects of a full orchestra have to be compressed, is of microscopic proportions. 1921 *Nature* 27 Oct. 276/1 Photographic films bearing sound-records which are reproducible. 1922 *Radio News* (U.S.) Nov. 867/1 It is possible to photograph 10 consecutive 'sound paths' on one strip of film. 1923 *Mod. Wireless* I. 418/2 The successful production of such a sound record upon a separate film, the sound-film and the picture-film being run simultaneously. 1927 *Daily Mail* 2 July 8/2 The sound-film of the Walker-Milligan fight which was made by the British Phonofilm Co. 1929 *Photoplay* Apr., *Sound track*, the narrow band of space along the left side of picture film on which is printed the ribbon-like strip of light and dark lines which constitute the record from which sound is projected. 1929 *Morn. Post* 24 May 12/7 There are now 17 sound-studios in New York and Long Island. 1929 *Times* 30 July 13/2 Contrasting 'dialogue films', which, in imitation of the stage, depend principally on dialogue to tell their story, with 'sound films', which use sound as a supplement to silent technique. 1931 *Times* 3 Mar. 12/4 The 'editing' of the film in 'sound-cutting' rooms. 1931 G. F. Jones *Sound-Film Reprod.* 12 The film must pass through the sound gate at a uniform speed, in order that the pitch of the music or speech shall not vary. In some sound-heads the film is fed through the gate by means of an ordinary toothed sprocket. 1931 L. Cowan *Record. Sound Motion Pict.* 37 A strip along the side of the film, known as the sound track. *Ibid.* 72 The sound-camera consists of a light-tight box containing the film-driving mechanism. *Ibid.* 243 Special buildings—sound stages—had to be constructed in which recording could be carried on. *Ibid.* 386 *Sound Gate*, gate, similar to that used in picture projectors, through which the sound track is pulled past the reproducing light beam in gate-type machines. *Ibid.* 387 *Sound Head*, compartment on the projector which contains sound-reproducing systems and mechanism for guiding and driving film.

Soup, *sb.* **4.** Add: **soup-fin shark**, a shark whose fin is used by the Chinese for making soup.

1905 D. S. Jordan *Fishes* I. 541 The soup-fin shark (*Galeus zyopterus*) is found on the coast of California, where its fins are highly valued by the Chinese. 1923 *Nature* 6 Oct. 521/1 The soupfin shark (*Galeus zygopterus*).

Sour, *a.* and *sb.*¹ Add: **B. 4.** *pl.* Pickles. *U.S.* [After G. *sauer* pickled.]

Source, *sb.* **4 e.** *attrib.* Add: *source-criticism*, etc. (after G. combs. with *quellen-*, e.g. *quellenforschung, -kunde*); **source-book** [tr. G. *quellenbuch*] orig. *U.S.*, a book of 'sources' or original documents to serve as materials for the historical study of a subject.

1899 A. B. Hart (*title*), *Source-Book of American History. *Ibid.* p. xvii, The Source Book is meant to supplement, not to supplant the text-book. 1927 *Sunday Times* 13 Feb. 9 A new series of source-books for students of history and literature. 1928 *Observer* 4 Mar. 8/3 These volumes will be amongst the source-books for the history of our own time. 1911 J. Moffatt *Introd. Lit. N. T.* 488 These features..show that *source-criticism of some kind is necessary in order to account for the literary and psychological data.

Sourceful (sōᵊ·ɹsfŭl), *a.* [f. Source *sb.* + -ful.] Acting as a source, capable of origination. Hence **Sou·rcefulness.**

1901 G. H. Howison *Limits Evol.* 304 That spontaneous sourcefulness of self-consciousness from which everlastingness arises. *Ibid.*, These consequences of the ascertained sourceful and directive power of our individuality. 1917 A. S. Pringle-Pattison *Idea of God* xvi. 317 From the nature of the case, we cannot get behind the 'sourceful' Ego, and therefore none of us can imagine either a beginning or an end of his existence.

Sousaphone (sū·zăfōun). [Named from John Philip *Sousa*, American bandmaster and composer (1854–1932), after *saxophone*, etc.] A proprietary name for a bass wind-instrument resembling a French horn.

1925 *Punch* 27 May 561/3 An instrument called the Sousaphone weighs eighteen pounds and is twenty feet long. 1927 *Daily Express* 24 Nov. 12 Jazz music, which depends so much on the rhythm, created mainly by the bass notes of the drums, sousaphone and, sometimes, double bass.

Souse, *sb.*⁶ Add: **1. b.** An act of getting drunk. *slang.*

1930 E. Wallace *Calendar* xviii, If ever a man had an excuse for a souse, you've got it.

3. A soaker, drunkard. *U.S.*

1915 H. L. Wilson *Ruggles of Red Gap* iv. (1917) 80 You don't look like a periodical souse. 1930 Byrne *Golden Goat* ix. 71 Mrs. Trelawny-Hocking..was an '*alcoolique terrible*', a most notable souse, in the vulgate.

Souse, *v.*¹ Add: **6. c.** To soak, drink so as to become intoxicated. *slang.*

1923 Watts *Luther Nichol* 43 Just as they're middling honest and don't souse.

Soused, *ppl. a.* **2.** (Modern examples.)

1902 H. L. Wilson *Spenders* ix. 87, I could see then that he was good and soused. 1930 Maugham *Gent. in Parlour* xliii. 265 He got soused every night.

Sous-entendu (suzaⁿtaⁿdü). [Fr.] Something not expressed but left to be understood by the hearer or reader.

1907 W. De Morgan *Alice-for-Short* xxxii, She knew well enough that the unheard portions of the conversation were worse than what had reached her ears, and the *sous-entendus* probably still worse than they.

Souteneur (sūt'nör). [Fr., = protector, f. *soutenir* to Sustain.] A man who lives on the earnings of a prostitute or prostitutes under his protection.

1906 tr. *Weiniger's Sex & Character* II. x. 234 The souteneur is always a criminal, a thief, a fraudulent person, or sometimes even a murderer. 1922 Galsworthy *Windows* III. Plays (1929) 732 As *you* know, sir,..there's a law nowadays against sooteners. 1927 *Daily Tel.* 12 Mar. 10/7 In the white slave traffic report it is said that souteneurs or traffic agents are at the same time dealing in drugs.

South, *adv.* **1. b.** Add: (without *down*) = in or into the southern States. *U.S.*

1885 'Mark Twain' *Huck. Finn* xiv, Whoever saved him would send him back home so as to get the reward, and then Miss Watson would sell him South, sure.

South-¹. Add: *south-bound* (in quot. ellipt. = south-bound train).

1904 Harben *Georgians* xxi. 207, I will take the south-bound at four in the morning.

Southernish (sʊ·ðəɹniʃ), *a.* [f. Southern *a.* + -ish¹.] Of a southern character.

1925 *Blackw. Mag.* Feb. 205/1 An occupation which soothes his excitable, strange, southernish self.

Southpaw (sau·þpǭ), *a.* and *sb.* *U.S.* [? f. South *a.* + Paw *sb.*] **a.** *adj.* Of a baseball player: Using the left hand in pitching. **b.** *sb.* A left-handed pitcher.

1912 C. Mathewson *Pitching in a Pinch* ii. 43 Devore has always been very weak at the bat with a southpaw in the box. 1915 *Literary Digest* (N. Y.) 21 Aug. 361/1 In another inning or two McGraw called to the lanky southpaw. 1922 H. Broun *Boy Grew Older* vi, That there were definite exceptions to the accepted theory that lefthanded batters do badly against southpaws.

Souvenir. Add: **2. c.** A bullet or shell. *jocular War use.* Hence **Sou·venir** *v. trans.*, to hit with a bullet or shell.

1915 D. O. Barnett *Lett.* 140 They kept sending their big black souvenirs over. 1915 *Chambers's Jrnl.* Oct. 663/1 Our periscope was 'souvenired' later on with a rifle-bullet clean through the tin sides.

Soviet (sǫ·vyet, sǭ·vyet, ‖ savye·t). [Russ. совѣтъ council.] In revolutionary Russia, a council elected by the workers, peasants, and soldiers of a district as the governing body of that district; also, an all-Russian congress of delegates from the local councils, which rules the country at large. Also, with *the*, the system of government by soviets. (The present designation of Russia is *The Union of Socialist Soviet Republics*, abbrev. *U.S.S.R.*)

1917 *Times* 27 July 6/4 Hostile vote against the Soviet. *Ibid.* 8 Sept. 6/4 A meeting of the Central Committee of the Soviet. 1917 *Spectator* 15 Sept. 260/1 The Soviet (the Council of Workmen's and Soldiers' Delegates). 1920 W. T. Goode *Bolshevism at Work* 69 The Soviet came into power in November 1917. *Ibid.* 85 Peasant instructors, selected by local Soviets. 1930 *Times Lit. Suppl.* 30 Oct. 880/1 The chairman of the village soviet..may in theory be master in his own limited sphere; in practice he is the servant of a Communist 'cell'.

b. *attrib.* or *adj.*

1918 *Decrees issued by Revolut. Peoples Govt.* 11 The Soviet Government does not look backward, but forward. 1920 W. T. Goode *Bolshevism at Work* 33 The Working of a Factory in Soviet Russia. *Ibid.* 65 The Soviet Republic. 1920 *19th Cent.* Mar. 521 The Soviet Government is now probably the most highly centralised Bureaucracy in Europe. 1925 A. J. Toynbee *Surv. Internat. Affairs* 1920–3 369 The new 'Red' Army of Soviet Armenia. *Ibid.* 370 A Soviet Republic of Georgia was proclaimed. 1928 *Manch. Guardian Weekly* 21 Sept. 223/1 A few thousands of Armenians..will not harm the British people even though their form of government be Soviet.

Hence **Sovie·tic, Sovie·tish** *adjs.*, belonging to, of the nature of, the Soviets. **So·vietism**, the Soviet system. **So·vietist**, an adherent of the Soviets. **So·vietize** *v. trans.*, to convert to Sovietism; so **So·vietized** *ppl. a.*, **So·vietizing** *vbl. sb.*, **So:vietiza·tion.**

1920 W. T. Goode *Bolshevism at Work* 68 The order existing in *Sovietic Moscow. 1920 *Contemp. Rev.* May 754 The Government, whatever the name may be, monarchical, republican, socialistic, sovietic. 1926 *Spectator* 29 May 899/2 They [*sc.* trades unions] are in the hands of small bureaucratic or *Soviet-ish oligarchies. 1920 *Glasgow Herald* 9 Mar. 7 Roumania, as one of the outposts against *Sovietism. 1927 *Observer* 20 Nov. 10/6 The intolerance which is the common vice of Sovietism and Fascism. 1920 W. T. Goode *Bolshevism at Work* 67 Meetings of the *Sovietists are held every week. 1921 *Glasgow Herald* 17 Jan. 11 It remains to be seen how the Persian Court will take to the idea of *Sovietisation. 1930 *Time & Tide* 24 May 657 Mussolini..stopped the spreading rot of sovietization. 1920 *Glasgow Herald* 16 Aug. 9 In fact, the whole of Western Europe is to be *Sovietised to the cry of 'No more wars!' 1921 *Contemp. Rev.* May 579 The Bolsheviks have now overrun and 'Sovietised' Georgia. 1920 *Glasgow Herald* 12 Aug. 7 A *Sovietised Poland subject to the Moscow Government. 1922 *19th Cent.* Apr. 605 The strained atmosphere and Sovietised conversation of the only comfortable 'Soviet Home'. 1922 *Glasgow Herald* 29 July 8 The Amir..cannot but view the *Sovietising of this region with great disfavour. 1925 *Ibid.* 26 Mar. 8 The principal virtue of wireless is its sovietising power.

Sow, *sb.*¹ **8.** Add: **sow-belly** *Mil.* and *Naut. slang*, salt pork, junk.

1874 J. C. McCoy *Hist. Sk. Cattle Trade*, To fish up a piece of 'sow belly' and dine sumptuously. 1898 *Daily News* 12 July 5/3 Some of them are begging food from the soldiers, who can give nothing except 'sow belly and hard tack'. 1902 O. Wister *Virginian* vi. 65 The eternal 'sow-belly', beans, and coffee.

Sowkar, var. of Soucar.

1927 *Blackw. Mag.* May 745/1 A Sowkar is, generally speaking, a banker and moneylender.

Sox, commercial spelling of pl. of Sock *sb.*¹ (Cf. *Clox.)

1905 H. G. Wells *Kipps* I. ii. § 1 He abbreviated every word he could; he would have considered himself the laughing-stock of Wood Street if he had chanced to spell *socks* in any way but 'sox'.

Sozzle, *v.* Add: **3.** In pa. pple.: Intoxicated. *slang.*

1921 *Blackw. Mag.* Feb. 157/1, I wasn't what you'd call sozzled. I might have been lit up a bit, but sozzled—no.

Space, *sb.*¹ Add: **17. a.** *space-band, -bar, -gauge* (in a type-writing or printing machine).

1888 J. Harrison *Man. Type-Writer* 18 In front of the four banks of keys there is a narrow strip of wood which is called the 'space-bar'. *Ibid.* 25 The 'space-gauge' is a little thumb-piece at the extreme right of the carriage. 1895 E. Collyns *Typists' Manual* 17 The space between the lines is regulated by the 'Space Gauge'. 1919 B. De Bear *Typewriting* 22 You depress the space-bar whenever you want to leave a space in a line of the work. 1925 J. R. Rogers *Linotype Instr. Bk.* 2 This part of the Linotype

mechanism includes means for justifying the line of matrices by means of double wedges called 'spacebands'.

d. *space-writer* (later example); *space rate* (examples).

1908 Eliz. Banks *Autobiogr. Newspaper Girl* 193 The 'space-writers'..are paid according to the amount of space they fill up in the paper. 1906 *Springfield* (Mass.) *Weekly Republ.* 29 Nov. 3 Newspaper men..who colored their reports in order to command space rates. 1909 'O. Henry' *Options* (1916) 25 Among the Vallambrosa's roomers are stenographers, ..space-rate writers, art students.

18. b. So *space-filler.*

1911 H. S. Harrison *Queed* xviii. 232 There's a little squib about the college that may serve as a space-filler.

19. space-charge, the charge of the electrons situated in the space between the electrodes of a valve; **space-lattice**, (*b*) a series of points of which each is one of the intersections of three systems of parallel and equally spaced lines; **space wave** (see quot. 1912).

1913 *Physical Rev.* Ser. II. II. 450 The effect of *space charge and residual gases on thermionic currents in high vacuum. 1921 Scott-Taggart *Thermionic Tubes* 9 This cloud of electrons..is an actual negative charge in space and is therefore generally termed a space charge. 1929 Lindemann in *Encycl. Brit.* VIII. 232/1 In pure metals at extremely low temperature, it seems possible that the electron *space-lattice might move almost unimpeded through the atomic space-lattice. 1930 N. K. Adam *Phys. and Chem. Surfaces* 276 The possible space-lattice structures and orientations which the atoms can assume. 1912 *Rep. Brit. Assoc.* 403 His theory leads to the conclusion that there are not only *space-waves (*Raumwellen*) in these media, but also surface-waves (*Oberflächenwellen*) at the boundary surface. 1917 *Wireless World* V. 151 The invention of thoroughly valid methods of measuring the true space wave radiation from transmitting aerials.

Space, *v.* **3. a.** Delete †*Obs.* and add modern example.

1916 Boyd Cable *Action Front* 73 The trenches were narrow and very deep,..spaced at regular intervals with sunk traps for draining off rain-water.

Space-time. [tr. G. *raumzeit.*] In Einstein's theory of relativity, the four-dimensional manifold or continuum (*raum-zeit-kontinuum, raumzeitliches kontinuum*) resulting from the fusion of time and three-dimensional space. Also *attrib.* Called also *Time-space.

1915 E. Cunningham *Relativity* 9 The Space-Time Transformations. *Ibid.* 10 Space-time coordinates. 1920 H. L. Brose tr. *M. Schlick's Space & Time* 46 The Measure-Determinations of the Space-time Continuum. 1930 Silberstein *Size of Universe* 1 The four-dimensional manifold known to modern physicists, astronomers, and mathematicians as Spacetime or 'world'.

Spad¹ (spæd). *U.S. Mining.* [Variant of Spud.] A metal nail with an aperture or hook at the head, driven into a wooden plug in order to mark a roof-station in underground surveying. Otherwise *spud* (see Spud *sb.* 3 e, quot. 1871).

1918 R. Peele *Mining Engineers' Handbk.* (1927) 1421 A spad in the form of an open hook is better than one having an eye, because it facilitates the hanging and unhanging of the plumb-bob.

Spad² (spæd). [From the initials of *Société pour l'Aviation et Dérivés*, the designers.] A form of French aeroplane. Also *attrib.*

1918 W. E. Dommett *Dict. Aircraft* 42 S. P. A. D. Aeroplanes. 1918 *War Birds* (1927) 60 They have Pups and Spads and Avros. *Ibid.* 88 There were three Spads so Capt. Foggin asked for Spad pilots. 1920 A. J. L. Scott *60 Squad.* 15 Foot..was given a 'Spad,' on which he did great execution during the autumn. 1926 J. L. Pritchard *Bk. Aeroplane* xii. 230 Spad machines were recognised as among the fastest..used by the Allies during the war.

Spadaite (spā·dăˌəit). *Min.* [ad. G. *spadait* (1843), named after Signor Medici *Spada*: see -ite¹.] A hydrous magnesium silicate.

1862 Dana *Min.* (new ed.) 149. 1883 *Encycl. Brit.* XVI. 414/2.

Spadassin (spæ·dăsin, ‖ spadasæ̃n). [Fr., ad. It. *spadaccino*, f. *spada* sword.] A swordsman, duellist, bravo.

Spade, *sb.*¹ **4. b.** Add: *spade-footed* (earlier example).

1867 *Amer. Naturalist* I. 108 The Spade-footed Toads..are more uncertain in their appearance, being governed entirely by the dampness or dryness of the season.

Spade, *sb.*² **2.** Add: *attrib.* as *spade flush* (Flush *sb.*³ 1).

1904 'O. Henry' *Cabbages & Kings* vi. 105 The invitations to the musicale came sliding in by pairs and threes and spade flushes.

Spa·de-work. Work done with a spade for the preparation of ground. **b.** *fig.* or in fig. context (e.g. quot. 1901 in Dict.), pioneer labour; later (with allusion to the 'digging' of archæologists), labour expended in investigating or exploring a new field of inquiry, esp. in collecting materials and first-hand evidence; pioneer research on a special subject.

1778, 1837, 1901 [see Spade *sb.*¹ 4 a]. 1912 H. G. Aldis in *Cambr. Hist. Engl. Lit.* IX. xiii. 346 Brian Twyne, a diligent Oxford antiquary who had done much pioneer spade-work in the same field. 1927 *Daily Tel.* 12 July 9/1 The discovery of a helpful blood-test for cancer may be placed among the important advances the near future may give us as a result of spade-work already carried out. 1929 *Times Lit. Suppl.* 27 June 511 Many modern novelists of folk life, in their desire to be strong and 'primitive,' ignore all spade work and romantically stake Man against Nature.

Spadger. Add: **2.** A small boy. *colloq.*

1899 *Captain* II. 273/2 If we've got to take these three young spadgers..we shall want something bigger'n this here gig.

Spaghetti (spăge·ti). [It., pl. of *spaghetto* cord, twine.] An Italian paste made in cords intermediate in thickness between macaroni and vermicelli and served like these.

1888 Beeton *Bk. Househ. Managem.* § 2952 Maccheroni, or Spaghetti, a smaller kind of macaroni,..generally follows the soup. 1892 M. Gironci *Recipes Italian Cookery* 59 Stewed Steak and Spaghetti. 1931 B. Starke *Touch & Go* iv. 51 A..school-teacher took us to lunch in Avon and showed us how to manage yards of spaghetti by rolling it up on our forks.

Spalt (spǭlt), *sb.*³ *Lumbering.* [Related to Spalt *a.* and *v.*] **a.** A section of a log from which shingles are sawn. **b.** The waste part or refuse of a shingle-bolt.

1879 *Lumberman's Gaz.* 15 Oct., In this machine..is combined with the Spalt all the requisites of a first class Shingle Machine. 1922 R. C. Bryant *Lumber* 477 *Spalt*. The residue of a shingle bolt, after cutting off shingles, which is too narrow to be cut into shingles.

Spalter (spǭ·ltəɹ), *sb.* *U.S.* [f. Spalt *v.* + -er¹.] 'The mechanism on a rotary shingle-machine for automatically removing the spalt or waste piece' (*Funk's Stand. Dict.* 1895).

Span, *sb.*¹ Add: **5. c.** *Aviation.* The maximum lateral dimension of an aeroplane, or of a wing, from wing tip to wing tip.

1910 *Sphere* 20 Aug. 177/2 Its triple planes and short span render the Roe machine easily distinguishable. 1913 *Aeroplane* 30 Oct. 480/1 Its small span and carefully streamlined body. 1919 Pippard & Pritchard *Aeropl. Struct.* 136 When the total effective span or the effective area of each wing is known. 1927 C. L. M. Brown *Conquest of Air* 98 It was a biplane, the two main wings being 32 ft. in frontal width (span) and 5 ft. in depth (chord).

Spandau (spæ·ndau). A gun manufactured at the arsenal at Spandau in Brandenburg, Prussia.

1929 E. W. Springs *Above bright blue Sky* 221 He was suddenly cold as he awaited the crack of the spandaus.

Spanish, *a.* (*adv.*) Add: **A.** *adj.* **7. Spanish salad, sauce** *U.S.*, a salad composed of beans, peas, and tomatoes.

1911 Webster s.v., Spanish salad. 1928 S. Lewis *Man who knew Coolidge* 79 Hamburg steak and Spanish sauce.

C. *adv.* (Earlier example.)

1838 *Yale Lit. Mag.* III. 269 Here, Bill! begone! why don't you 'walk Spanish?' hence I say.

Spanner¹. **2.** *attrib.* and *comb.* Add: **spanner-tight** *a.*, screwed tight by a spanner.

1925 *Morris Owner's Man.* 53 The nuts should always be kept (small) spanner tight. 1931 *Daily Express* 31 Jan. 3/6 Even where the nut was absolutely spanner tight.

Spanners (spæ·nəɹz). [f. Span *sb.*¹ + -er¹ + -s.] (See quot.)

1881 *Cassell's Bk. Sports & Pastimes* 350 Spanners. This is a good simple game for two players. Player No. 1 shoots off his taw, player No. 2 following suit, it being his object either to hit his opponent's taw with his own, or to place his own within a span of it.

Spar, *sb.*¹ Add: **4. b.** Each of the two main beams of the wing of an aeroplane, running transversely to the body, usually made of wood or tubular steel. They carry the ribs.

1913 *Aeroplane* 10 Apr. 428/1 Small pieces of wood are fastened to the spars inside the wings and the fabric is nailed to these. 1919 Pippard & Pritchard *Aeropl. Struct.* 17 The front and rear spars are braced together by drag bracing. 1930 Navler & Ower *Aviation* 154 The modern steel spar of an aeroplane wing.

Sparagmite (spăræ·gməit). *Geol.* [f. Gr. σπάραγμα piece torn off, or σπαραγμός a rending, tearing + -ite¹.] A felspathic sandstone or arkose at the base of the Cambrian in Scandinavia.

1882 A. Geikie *Text-bk. Geol.* 657 In central and northern Norway the Archæan gneiss is overlaid by reddish and grey sandstones and conglomerates (Sparagmite), with schists, quartzites, and limestones. 1930 Peach & Horne *Geol. Scot.* 72 The Sparagmite of Scandinavia is an arkose resembling the dominant type of the Torridon Sandstone.

Sparassodont (spăræ·sodǫnt). *Palæont.* [ad. mod.L. *Sparassodonta* n. pl., f. Gr. σπαράσσειν to tear + ὀδοντ-, ὀδούς tooth.] One of a group of extinct mammals of the Miocene of Patagonia.

1907 *Nature* 21 Mar. 499/1 That creodonts, sparassodonts, and carnivorous marsupials are..related groups,..appears almost certain. *Ibid.*, These early creodonts have developed in one direction towards the sparassodont type.

Spare, *sb.*¹ **3.** Add: A spare man in a team of players.

1930 *Daily Express* 6 Sept. 9/5 Yesterday Barney Balding, the British 'spare', wrenched his arm while playing with a scratch team at Meadowbrook.

Spare, *a.* Add: **1. a.** (*a*) **spare part**, a duplicate of a part of a machine (esp. of a motor vehicle) kept in readiness to replace a loss or breakage. (Cf. Spare *sb.*¹ 3.)

1897 *Trans. Instit. Naval Archit.* XXXVIII. 207. 1902 A. C. Harmsworth *Motors & Motor-Driving* xix. 368 These were the days when it was thought practical, as Mr. Butler informs me, 'to turn out a car of one-and-a-half horse-power to carry two passengers, and luggage, spare parts and tools'. 1907 *Chambers's Jrnl.* 431/1 Most people are familiar with the fact that spare parts for bicycles, motor-cars, gas-engines, and similar machinery can always be obtained. 1913 *Aeroplane* 25 Sept. 353 The Gnôme Engine Company...To whom all applications for Gnôme engines and spare parts should be made. 1925 H. G. Wells *Christina Alberta's Father* I. v. § 3. 123 The next evening was wet again, and as his Spare Part hadn't come Mr. Fenton was able to join us once more.

(*d*) **spare room**, a room reserved for special occupation; in England, a bedroom kept for the accommodation of a guest; *U.S.* a parlour.

1837 *Southern Lit. Messenger* III. 333 One of the third-story rooms we must keep for a spare room. 1855 *Knickerbocker Mag.* XLVI. 380 They have stolen away into the spare-room, otherwise, parlor. 1880 *Harper's Mag.* Dec. 90 You've got to feed 'em, and like enough keep a big fire up in the spare room.

Spark, *sb.*¹ Add: **6. c.** Short for *spark telegraphy* etc. (see *7 b).

1921 *Wireless World* IX. 21/1 Various circuits for the reception of Spark, C.W. and Telephony. 1922 *Ibid.* X. 76/2 When one is receiving spark or telephony.

d. *pl.* A wireless operator on a ship. *colloq.*

1917 *Wireless World* V. 37 In the Service the regular nickname for wireless telegraphists is graphically expressed as 'Sparks'. 1922 P. F. Westerman *Wireless Officer* iii. 25 A burly, jovial-featured man..greeted Mostyn as he stepped off the gang-plank. 'Hello, you're our Sparks, aren't you?' 1922 *Westm. Gaz.* 29 Nov., Cunarder's 'Sparks'.

7. b. *spark ball, discharge, discharger, frequency, note, station, telegraphy, transmission, transmitter, voltage.*

1848 *Patent Jrnl.* 5 Aug. 266/1 In frictional spark discharges, the consequent shock, light, and other peculiarities are in part owing to waves of..polarization. 1863 Atkinson tr. *Ganot's Elem. Treat. Physics* ix. iv. 587 Spark and brush discharge. 1898 *The Ludgate* (New Ser.) VII. 78/1 Mr. Marconi, in July, 1897, came to England to introduce his new plan of 'Spark Telegraphy'. *Ibid.* 78/2 Nor is this the greatest distance over which these 'spark telegrams' have been sent. 1906 J. A. Fleming *Princ. Electric Wave Telegr.* 152 Spark Voltages for Various Spark Lengths and Spark Balls of Various Diameters. 1912 *Brit. Assoc. Dundee Rep.* (1913) 402 Prolonged gushes of electricity in one direction, which, coming at the rate of the much lower spark frequency,..create in the telephone a shrill sound. 1913 *Year-Bk. Wireless Telegr. & Teleph.* 401 It does not follow..that a continuous-wave station is immune from interference by a spark station. 1916 J. A. Fleming *Princ. Electric Wave Telegr.* (ed. 3) 671 Spark transmitters. 1920 Dowsett *Wireless Telegr. & Telephony* 44 The spark discharge. 1921 E. E. Bucher *Pract. Wireless Telegr.* 83 The term *spark frequency* is employed to designate the number of spark discharges bridging the gap per second of time. *Ibid.* 101 Spark Dischargers for Radio-Telegraphy. *Ibid.* 106 Blunt discharge electrodes give an irregular spark note. 1926 E. H. Chapman *Wireless Dict.* 124 *Spark Station*.—A wireless transmitting station employing the spark method of telegraphy.

c. spark-plug *U.S.*, a sparking-plug; **spark-prop** *Thieves' slang*, a tie-pin (cf. 4 a); **spark spectrum**, a spectrum produced by the electric spark; **spark-tester**, a device for testing the sparking-plugs of a motor vehicle.

1914 F. Strickland *Petrol Motors* (ed. 2) 55 The high-tension leads and *spark plug. 1921 R. D. Paine *Comr. Rolling Ocean* xvi. 284 Smashed the porcelains in both spark plugs. 1921 *Chambers's Jrnl.* 410/2 To steal a tie-pin, or '*spark-prop', as it is termed in the slang of thieves, a different plan is followed. 1879 J. N. Lockyer in *Proc. R. Soc.* XXX. 27 Flame Spectrum...*Spark Spectrum. 1905 Baly *Spectroscopy* 374 The induction coil is used..for the production of the so-called spark spectra of substances. 1925 *Morris Owner's Man.* 84 The motorist should try each plug in turn with the aid of a '*spark tester'.

Spark, *v.*¹ Add: **1. c.** *Electr.* To emit an electric spark or sparks. Of a dynamo: To arc at the brushes. Of an internal-combustion engine: To have the electric ignition working.

1884 S. P. Thompson *Dynamo-electr. Machinery* 60 Any dynamo in which the curve of potentials at the commutator presented such irregularities..would probably spark excessively at the collector. 1892 *Ibid.* (ed. 4) 361 Drum-wound armatures are less liable to spark. 1895 Mrs. Koosen in A. C. Harmsworth *Motors & Motor-Driving* xix. 364 Motor sparked at once and went well.

3. c. Also *intr.* To be crossed or connected by a spark.

1916 *Standard. Rules Amer. Inst. Electr. Engin.* 57 The voltage at which a given gap sparks over. 1926 R. W. Hutchinson *Wireless* 112 The spark gap consists of two small spheres sparking across the diameters of two larger ones.

Sparking, *vbl. sb.*¹ **b.** Add: **sparking plug**, in an internal-combustion engine, a device consisting of a metal shell or barrel which screws into the combustion chamber, used for igniting the charge by means of an electric current.

1902 [in Dict.]. 1907 F. Strickland *Petrol Motors* 40 Sparking plugs in cylinders. 1908 tr. *Lieckfeld's Oil Motors* 85 A further improvement in electric ignition was introduced by the French firm [de Dion et Bouton] when they brought out the sparking plug.

Sparking, *vbl. sb.*² *U.S.* (Earlier examples.)

1796–1801 Fessenden *Orig. Poems* (1806) 77 She's courted been, by many a lad, And knows how sparking's done. 1844 'Jon. Slick' *High Life N.Y.* I. 47, I don't mean to say that Judy had any thing agin sparking.

Sparkler. Add: **4. b.** Applied to a trout.

a 1861 T. Winthrop *Life in open Air* (1863) 91 As the spotted sparklers were rapidly translated from water to a lighter element.

Sparklet. Add: **3.** *pl.* A trade name for a capsule containing carbonic acid gas under pressure, used with a siphon for making aerated water. Also *sing.*

1904 Kipling *Traffics & Discov.*, *Captive* (1908) 16 Give me a cigar—a Henry Clay and a whisky-and-sparklet. 1906 Maugham *Portug. E. Africa* 221 A couple of large-sized 'Sparklets' syphons with a good supply of charges will be found an excellent substitute for soda-water. 1920 *Blackw. Mag.* Apr. 542/2 His particular fancy in drinks—usually whisky and sparklet.

Sparring, *vbl. sb.*³ **3.** Add: **sparring partner**, a pugilist employed to keep another in practice while training for a contest.

1908 *Captain* Sept. 530/2 Jack was the best sparring partner he could have. 1930 *Daily Express* 8 Sept. 2/3 Cal Barton (Birmingham), Jack Hood's sparring partner.

Spartacist (spā·ɹtăsist). Also **-akist.** [ad. G. *Spartakist*: see below and -ist.] A member of a party of German socialist extremists in the revolution of 1918, led by Karl Liebknecht, who had adopted the pseudonym *Spartakus* in his political tracts. (Spartacus, a Thracian, was the leader in the Servile War against Rome, 73–71 B.C.) Also *attrib.* or *adj.* So (less usually) **Spa·rtacan** (-kăn).

1919 W. R. Inge *Outspoken Ess.* i. 18 The 'Spartacist' scoundrels who have betrayed and ruined their country. 1919 *Nation* (N.Y.) 19 Apr. 632 The Programme of the Spartacans. 1920 *19th Cent.* Mar. 560 The rattle of Spartacist machine-guns. *Ibid.*, The extreme Left wing of the Independents, known as Spartacists. 1920 W. J. M. Starkie *Euripides the Politician* in *Studies* (Dublin) June 197 The heroes of Marathon were conservative 'die-hards': the modern Athenian was a Socialist or Spartacist, who despised the gods. 1925 *Contemp. Rev.* Dec. 715 The movement which a few Spartakists originated in the hope of establishing Soviet rule in Germany.

Hence **Spartacism** (spā·ɹtăsiz'm), the policy and principles of the Spartacists.

1919 J. M. Keynes *Econ. Conseq. Peace* 271 A victory of Spartacism in Germany might well be the prelude to Revolution everywhere. 1920 *Glasgow Herald* 9 Apr. 9 Spartacism in Germany is a domestic matter for the German Government to deal with.

Spartacus (spā·ɹtăkŏs). Used *attrib.* as in *Spartacus group, party*, the Spartacists.

1918 *Spectator* 30 Nov. 607/1 The Spartacus group—the wild adherents to Liebknecht and Rosa Luxemburg.

Sparterie (spā·ɹtəri). [Fr., ad. Sp. *espartería*, f. Esparto.] Articles made of esparto grass.

Spatialize (spē·ʃălaiz), *v.* [f. Spatial *a.* + -ize.] *trans.* To make spatial; to think of as spatial; to invest with spatial qualities or relations. Hence **Spa·tialized** *ppl. a.*

1917 A. S. Pringle-Pattison *Idea of God* xix. 367 The spatialized time of physical theory and of ordinary reflective thinking. 1925 A. N. Whitehead *Science & Mod. World* vii. 177 Thus a duration is spatialised; and by 'spatialised' is meant that the duration is the field for the realised pattern constituting the character of the event.

Spatio-temporal (spēˈʃioˌte·mpŏrăl), *a.* [f. *spatio-*, used as comb. form of L. *spatium* Space + Temporal *a.*] Belonging to both space and time.

1917 A. S. Pringle-Pattison *Idea of God* xiv. 267 Even if we make space and time the *principium individuationis* and try to reduce the formal distinctness of individuals to difference of position in the spatio-temporal series. 1920 A. N. Whitehead *Concept of Nature* viii. 173 The spatio-temporal structure of events. 1921 *Hastings's Encycl. Relig. & Ethics* XII. 341/2 Spatio-temporal co-ordinates. 1925 A. N. Whitehead *Science & Mod. World* v. 128 The whole spatio-temporal world.

Spattee (spætī·). [f. Spat *sb.*⁵, after *puttee*.] An outer stocking or legging worn by women for protection against wet and cold.

1926 *Bulletin* 17 Aug. 4/3 The invention is called the 'Highland spattee' and is a Highlander's stocking made spat-fashion to allow the wearer to slip it easily over her shoes and silk stocking. 1928 *Daily Tel.* 10 Jan. 6 The knitted spattee.

Spawn, *sb.* Add: **7. b.** The bulbils of gladiolus.

1895 T. W. Sanders *Encycl. Gardening* (1896) 144 *Gladiolus*...Propagate by seeds..; by bulbils (spawn) growing at base of corms.

Speak, *v.* Add: **1.** (So-and-so) *speaking*: used by a speaker on the telephone to announce his identity.

1927 Anne MacDonald (*title*), Dorty Speaking. 1933 'Sapper' *Knock-out* i. 9 Standish..took the receiver from the other's hand. 'Hullo! Sanderson,' he said. 'Yes—Standish speaking. What now?'

17. b. *To speak out in meeting.* U.S. (Examples.)

1830 *Mass. Spy* 23 June (Th.), O dear, I spoke out in meeting. 1906 Foraker in *Springfield* (Mass.) *Weekly Republ.* 13 Sept. 8, I do not think the president will think any the less of me for speaking right out in meeting and saying that I am not for it.

21. c. *To speak a piece* (see *Piece *sb.* 17 d): also *transf.* (with poss. pron.) to say what one is deputed or appointed to say.

1845 Caroline M. Kirkland *Western Clearings* 138 Some of the best speakers mount the platform, and 'speak a piece'. 1903 Kate D. Wiggin *Rebecca* viii. 87 Most of the children hated 'speaking pieces'. 1906 *N. Y. Evening Post* 5 Feb. 2 The governor 'spoke his piece' on the subject of the Banking Department investigation this morning. It was a typical declaration.

Speak-easy (spī·kˌīzi). *U.S. slang.* [f. Speak *v.* + Easy *adv.* = softly.] An illicit liquor shop. Also *attrib.*

1889 [see Speak *v.* 36]. 1895 L. Pendleton *Corona of Nantahalas* iv. 45 A sort of rural 'speak easy', where the colourless liquid was poured into the purchasers' bottles from a new and innocent-looking kerosene can. 1903 A. H. Lewis *The Boss* xiii. 162 That..no side-doors or speak-easy racket [should be] stood for. 1908 *Ann. Amer. Acad. Polit. & Social Sci.* Nov. 23 Twenty-four dry counties..in which the law was poorly enforced, with the 'speak-easy' and the 'C. O. D.' business everywhere. 1930 *Punch* 12 Feb. 172 Before we had been introduced to any 'speak-easy', that is, before we had been a couple of hours in New York.

Speakie (spī·ki). Usually *pl.* (*Disused.*) [f. Speak *v.* after *movie*. Cf. *Talkie.] **a.** A stage-play as distinguished from the 'movies'.

1927 *Observer* 24 Apr. 15/1 She prophesied the downfall of the 'speakies' and the triumphant survival of the 'movies'. 1927 *Daily Tel.* 11 Oct. 6 An innovation last night was the introduction of a real stage set in the middle of the film.. Whether this mixture of 'movie' and 'speakie' is desirable may be questioned.

b. A *Talkie.

1928 *Sunday Dispatch* 15 July 14 'Talkies' or 'speakies' as they are calling them in Hollywood, have very definitely arrived.

Speaking, *vbl. sb.* Add: **1. b.** (Later U.S. examples.)

1895 'C. E. Craddock' *Myst. Witch-Face Mt.*, etc. 206 Thar war a big crowd at the cross roads ter hear the speakin'. 1910 Corra Harris *Eve's Second Husband* 75 The 'speaking' itself was to be in a grove upon the Molly's-borough battle ground.

c. *At the* (or *this*) *present speaking*: at this moment. *U.S.*

1835 J. P. Kennedy *Horse-Shoe Robinson* I. vi. 78 If I suspicioned a bamboozlement, which I am not far from at this present speaking. 1891 Marah E. Ryan *Told in Hills* III. v. 205 At the present speaking the days are not picnic days.

5. *speaking trip.*

1931 F. L. Allen *Only Yesterday* ii. 32 He would win them to his cause, making a speaking trip through the West.

b. speaking-film = *Talkie.

1918 H. Croy *How Motion Pictures are Made* 360 Speaking films will shortly be achieved.

Speako (spī·ko). *U.S. slang.* = *Speak-easy.

1932 *Amer. Mercury* Jan. 11 A brewery which supplied every other speako between Fourteenth and Canal streets.

Spear, *v.*³ Add: **2.** Also, of a plant: To thrust *up* spear-like leaves.

1925 G. W. Deeping *Sorrell & Son* viii. § 5 The bulbs spearing up in the borders.

3. *trans.* To throw like a spear.

1920 W. Camp *Football without a Coach* 85 The ball should be held in the hand and speared through the air by giving the hand a twist as the ball leaves it.

Spear-head. Add: **1. b.** *fig.* A person or body of persons chosen to lead a thrust or attack.

1929 *Times* 12 Nov. 17/3 The Belfast members of the society..were made the spearhead of a thrust for an advance of wages for shipyard joiners alone. 1931 *Ibid.* 12 July 6/3 Afterwards they [*sc.* Yorkshire] broke down before the Nottinghamshire attack, with Larwood as its spearhead, and lost seven wickets for 53 runs.

Special, *a.* **4. c.** Add: *Special partner*, a partner who has capital in a business under special conditions or provisions. *U.S.*

1826–30 Jas. Kent *Comm. Amer. Law* (1858) III. 35 A limited partnership for the transaction of any mercantile, mechanical, or manufacturing business..may consist of..one or more persons who furnish certain funds to the common stock, and whose liability shall extend no further than the fund furnished, and who are called *special* partners. *Ibid.* 36 The special partners may receive an annual interest on the capital invested, provided there be no reduction of the original capital. 1839 Marryat *Diary Amer.* Ser. I. II. 251 In America, if a person wishes to become a special partner (a sleeping partner) in any concern, he may do so to any extent he pleases. 1859 Bartlett *Dict. Amer.* (ed. 2), *Special partner*, a member of a limited partnership, who furnishes certain funds to the common stock, and whose liability extends no further than the funds furnished.

Specialization. b. *Biol.* Add: (With *pl.*) A particular kind or instance of specialized characters.

1916 F. Wood Jones *Arboreal Man* 216 The particular arboreal specialization which culminated in the power of flight. 1918 — *Probl. Man's Ancestry* 30 Pithecoid specializations vary so much in their manifestations in the different groups of monkeys.

Speciation (spīʃiˌēi·ʃən). [f. Species + -ation.] The formation of species by evolutionary process.

1907 O. F. Cook in *Proc. Wash. Acad. Sci.* VIII. 278 (Funk) Speciation is the attainment of differential characters by segregated groups of organisms, that is, by subdivisions of older species. 1926 H. F. Osborn in *Nature* 21 Aug. 271/1 Thus *speciation* through continuity stands in contrast with *mutation* through discontinuity. *Ibid.* 272/1 Isolation is the most important factor in the speciation of birds.

Specie. 8. Add: **specie jar**, a name for the large china jars displayed in chemists' shops and supposed to contain drugs or preparations (see Species 11 a); **specie point**, either of two points in the variations of foreign exchange rates at which it becomes profitable to pay or receive payments in gold.

1914 C. C. B. in *N. & Q.* 11th Ser. IX. 127/1 The well-known 'specie jars' of chemists' shops. 1929 C. J. S. Thompson *Myst. Apothecary* xix. 257 The large cylindrical vessels called 'specie jars', with metal or gilded lids, that still decorate some of the chemists' shop-windows. 1891 Geo. Clare *Money-Market Primer* 78 The price of bills is now said to have reached '*Specie Point' and can go no higher... 'Specie Point'..is the rate of exchange produced by buying gold in one country, and selling it in another. 1897 J. S. Nicholson *Pol. Econ.* II. 279 Accordingly, the price of bills cannot rise above the point at which it would be just as cheap to send the gold itself. This is the specie point or, more precisely, the gold-export point from England into France. 1920 J. W. Kunkt *Counting-House Dict.* 129 The limits to such fluctuations are set by what are known as the gold (or specie) points.

Species. 14. Add: *species-continuing, -making, -mongering.*

1911 J. A. Thomson *Biol. Seasons* III. 239 Periods of hunger and self-increase are followed by periods of love and species-continuing. 1918 L. Huxley *Life Sir J. D. Hooker* I. viii. 175 Excessive or ignorant species-making. *Ibid.* 189 Detestation of mere species-mongering.

Specific, *a.* Add: **4. c.** Of a duty or tax: Assessed on an article according to its quantity or amount without reference to its value.

1845 Polk *Diary* (1929) 23, I had recommended..the abolition of the minimum principle and specific duties. 1901 J. S. Nicholson *Pol. Econ.* III. 348 If the tax is specific and not *ad valorem*. 1930 M. Clark *Home Trade* 187 Specific duties are those which are based on the quantity of the imported produce, i.e. they are so much per lb. or so much per gallon, etc.

Speck, *v.*¹ Add: **5.** *trans.* and *intr.* To search for gold on the surface of alluvial deposits; also *trans.* to spot (gold). *Austral.*

1903 R. Bedford *True Eyes* lviii. 304 Billy was for working on and continuing the operation of 'specking'. *Ibid.* 305 With little cries of delight he 'specked' a four-ounce slug of the red gold. *Ibid.* lx. 315 They had sieved and dry-blown and 'specked' the little tongue of auriferous soil. 1926 *Spectator* 14 Aug. 240/2 Went 'specking' in nearby creeks. Got colours of gold but no nuggets.

Specta·cularism. [See -ism.] Spectacular character or quality.

1924 Webster Addenda. 1931 *Aberdeen Press & Jrnl.* 14 Oct. 6/4 The spectacularism of Noel Coward.

Spectral, *a.* Add: **5. c.** *Spectral palette*, a painter's palette laid with six colours (besides white) to represent the chief colours of the spectrum.

1901 D. S. MacColl in *Sat. Rev.* 9 Feb. 170/1 The theory of the spectral palette seems to me unsound, and its practice dangerous. 1911 — in *Encycl. Brit.* XIV. 345/1.

Spectro-. Add: **Spectrohe·liogram**, a photograph obtained by the spectroheliograph. **Spectrohe·lioscope**, a spectroscope provided with a pair of oscillating slits which exclude from the observer's eye all light except that of the red hydrogen line.

1924 *Glasgow Herald* 13 June 5 Solar cyclonic motions have in recent years been clearly demonstrated by *spectroheliograms obtained at the Mount Wilson Observatory. 1929 G. E. Hale in *Encycl. Brit.* XXI. 179/2 The long dark flocculi..shown on hydrogen spectroheliograms. 1932 — *Signals fr. Stars* 56 Objects familiar for years on hydrogen spectroheliograms. 1929 — in *Encycl. Brit.* XXI. 179/2 The *spectrohelioscope renders visible to the eye many of the phenomena of the solar atmosphere photographed with the spectroheliograph and also permits their velocities in the line of sight to be measured. 1932 — *Signals fr. Stars* 48 The first spectrohelioscope (as I have named the instrument).

Speech, *sb.*¹ Add: **8. d.** *King's* or *Queen's speech, speech from the throne*, a brief statement of foreign and domestic affairs and of the chief measures to be considered by Parliament, drawn up by the ministry and read by the sovereign (in person or by commission) at the opening of Parliament.

[1771: see Dict.] 1825 Lingard *Hist. Eng.* VI. iv. 272 His speech from the throne was calculated more to irritate than to allay the jealousy of those who trembled for the liberties of their country. 1844 T. E. May *Parlt.* vii. 142 The session is opened at once by the Queen's speech. *Ibid.* xxi. 326 On the opening of Parliament, the Queen, in her speech from the throne, addresses the commons. 1897 [see Dict.].

13. speech-area (cf. *speech-centre*); **speech-fellows**, people who speak the same language; **speech-hall** (cf. *speech-room*); **speech-room** (later use).

1885 *Harper's Mag.* Mar. 638/2 *Speech Area. 1913 *Q. Rev.* Jan. 114 Over a large portion of the highest level of the brain the special work of each group of cells or 'area' is now known. If our speech-areas are diseased we cannot speak. 1920 *Ibid.* July 165 The tribe, understood as the group of *speech-fellows. 1921 *Spectator* 14 May 619/1 Messrs. Newton's *speech-hall for Marlborough. 1920 *Times* 3 Dec. 9/3 The competition for the Marlborough College War Memorial has been won by Lieutenant-Colonel W. G. Newton...The memorial is to take the form of a *speech-room.

Speed, *sb.* **11. c.** Add: In colloquial designations of motorists, aviators, etc. who specialize in speed, or of vehicles built specially for great speed, as *speed-bug, -hog, launch, -merchant*; **speed-cop** orig. *U.S.*, a policeman who is detailed to observe the speed of motorists; also *speed-law*; **speed-limit** (later examples); **speed-road**, a speedway.

1928 *Daily Express* 14 July 4 A women's aquaplane race and various other '*speedbug' activities. 1925 *Dollar Mag.* Dec. 205 *Speed-cops are posted on the highways with powerful motor-cycles to catch unwary speedsters. 1928 *Daily Express* 23 Aug. 9/4 The scheme to limit '*speed-hogs'. 1904 *Trans. Instit. Naval Archit.* XLVI. 161 The American *speed launches. 1926 *Scribner's Mag.* Aug. 152/1, I hear you break *speed-laws as recklessly as hearts. 1902 *To-Day* 13 Mar. 648 The Automobile Club urges that the existing *speed limit should be abolished. 1903 *Punch* 15 July 21 The Premier's *chauffeur* has been twice convicted of exceeding the legal speed-limit for Motor Cars. 1909 *Chambers's Jrnl.* 225/1 A speed-limit sometimes as low as ..four and three-quarter miles per hour. 1923 *Daily Mail* 15 Feb. 6 The goggled '*speed merchant' cannot see so well as usual. 1928 *Sunday Express* 8 Apr. 2/3 This adventurous speed-merchant also hopes to have a crack at the motor-boat record. 1928 *Weekly Disp.* 20 May 20 To have to bat always against the three West Indian speed merchants on a wicket that is 'kicking' a bit. 1928 *Daily Chron.* 9 Aug. 5/1 The 'autostrada', the famous motor *speed road between Milan and Como.

Speed, *v.* Add: **11. d.** *Speed up* (later examples). Also in extended use.

1909 *Chambers's Jrnl.* 6/2 As though the Eastern worker ..could be at the same time underfed yet 'speeded up' indefinitely. 1923 *Daily Mail* 12 June 6 The London and North-Eastern Railway are speeding up their services. 1931 *Times Lit. Suppl.* 3 Dec. 979/3 He brought youth to the theatre; he speeded it up.

13. a. Also with *up*.

1926 *Scribner's Mag.* Aug. 146/2 Speed up now on that bag or we shall be late.

e. To drive a motor vehicle at a high rate of speed. Chiefly in *vbl. sb.* Also *trans.*

1904 *N. Y. Times* 13 June 1 Three automobilists were arrested to-day for speeding their machines. 1908 *Evening Star* (Washington) in *Daily Chron.* 7 Oct. 4/6 Baby carriages are required to carry lights at night in Chicago. That rapid city may yet find it necessary to provide special police to keep the baby carriages from speeding. 1922 J. A. Dunn *Man Trap* ii, Driving a car about the countryside at the expense of many fines for speeding. 1931 Galsworthy *Maid-in-waiting* xiii, 'I'm going to speed,' said Jean, looking back. The speedometer rose rapidly.

Spee·d-boat. (More fully *high speed* (*motor*) *boat*.) A light boat propelled at high speed by a motor engine. Also *attrib.* Hence **Spee·d-boa:ting** *vbl. sb.*

1911 *New Fry's Mag.* May 224/1 The number of speed-boats, pure and simple, has grown greatly. 1928 *Daily Express* 25 May 6 The speedboat,..with its underwater exhausts muffled, had approached near enough to open fire. 1928 *Sunday Dispatch* 5 Aug. 11/3 The heavy demand for petrol, created by the new sport of 'speed' boating. 1929 'Seamark' *Down River* i, Hillary Kittredge..had fallen under the lure of speed-boat racing. 1930 Joanna Cannan *No Walls of Jasper* viii. 139 He bathed with his boys, treated them to rides in speed boats.

Speeder. 3. (Earlier U.S. example.)

1847 *Knickerbocker Mag.* XXX. 517 A few [girls] tend the warpers', the 'spoolers', and the 'speeders'.

Speeding, *vbl. sb.* **4.** *Speeding up* (later examples).

1911 *Chambers's Jrnl.* 218/2 No general speeding-up can be proved from statistics; indeed for some years the *per capita* output of coal has been declining. 1923 *Daily Mail* 12 June 6 Railway speed-up. Next month will see a general speeding-up of British railways.

Speedster (spī·dstəɹ). [f. Speed *sb.* + -ster, after *roadster*.] **a.** A person who drives, flies, etc. at high speed. **b.** A speed-boat, fast motor car, etc.

1918 Webster Addenda, *Speedster*,..a high-speed roadster, usually with low seats, accommodating two persons seated side by side. 1927 *Bulletin* 13 June 22/2 Women Air 'Speedsters'. 1929 'Seamark' *Down River* i, I'm not telling everyone who comes up in a swell speedster [*sc.* a speed-boat]. 1929 *Motor Boat Man.* (ed. 9) 281 Owing to the demand for high-powered engines a racing unit known as the Elto Speedster..was introduced. *Ibid.* 283 The twin-cylinder Speedster model.

Spee·d-up. [f. verbal phr. *speed up*: see Speed *v.* 11 d.] The act of speeding up or accelerating.

1923 *Daily Mail* 3 Mar. 7 Train Speed-up..The speeding up of all services. 1923 [see *Speeding *vbl. sb.* 4].

Spee·dway. a. *U.S.* A road reserved and prepared for fast horse-driving. **b.** A track for motor-racing. Also, a road intended to be used only by fast motor vehicles. Also *attrib.* Also *transf.* and *fig.*

1894 [see Speed *sb.* 11 c]. 1903 *N. Y. Times* 16 Aug., The owners of rapid roadsters are devoting no inconsiderable portion of their summer leisure to spirited brushes on the new speedway. 1909 *Manchester Guardian* 18 Apr. 5/7 It should be explained that a speedway is simply what in England we should call a good macadamised road. 1909 *The World To-Day* (U.S.) July 698 An Automobile Speedway. 1919 *Public Opinion* 14 Nov., The Speedway to Prosperity. 1927 *Universe* 2 Sept. 11/1 Saints of the Speedway [i.e. railway engines named after the Saints]. 1927 *Daily Tel.* 15 Nov. 7/1 A 'speedway' reserved for high-speed vehicles. ..It will be a 'speedway' pure and simple, somewhat on the lines of the Italian Autostrada. 1928 *Manchester Guardian Weekly* 26 Oct. 328/2 The proposal to construct a motor-road speed-way between London and Brighton. 1930 S. Elder *Rom. Speedway* i. 9 Now that Speedway Racing has taken its place as one of our national pastimes. *Ibid.* ii. 27 In the first rank among Speedway riders. *Ibid.* 33 Habitual frequenters of Speedway gatherings.

Speleology, etc.: see Spelæology.

Spell, *v.*² Add: **3. e.** To put to the test in spelling; to put (a person) *down* in spelling. *U.S.*

1853 B. F. Taylor *Jan. & June* (1871) 259 They all stand in solid phalanx by schools, and the struggle is, to spell each other down. 1866 C. H. Smith *Bill Arp* 171 He therefore proposed to put Mr. Fretman on the stand and spell him. 1878 Eggleston *Hoosier Schoolm.* iv. 47 Ralph dreaded the loss of influence..if he should be easily spelled down. 1932 *Randolph Enterprise* (Elkins, W. Va.) 18 Feb. 4/5 He was fairly spelled down at close of my school at Job, spring 1882, by a little girl not 7 years old.

4. c. *To spell able* (see quot.). *U.S. colloq.*

1909 *Cent. Dict.* Suppl. s.v. *Able*, *To spell able*, to be able; to have all the ability and strength needed (for some particular purpose).

6. To make (specified) progress in spelling. *U.S.*

1857 E. Stone *Life of Howland* i. 17 After many trials he succeeded in 'spelling up' next to the head [*sc.* of the class].

Spe·ller⁴. [f. Spell *v.*³] One who takes the place of another at some work or labour.

1920 *Glasgow Herald* 16 Apr. 7 A 'Speller's' compensation claim...The pursuer was acting as substitute for an employee of the defender in unloading a boat at Ayr.

Spe·lling, *vbl. sb.*⁴ [f. Spell *v.*³] **1.** Acting as substitute for another at some work or labour.

1920 *Glasgow Herald* 16 Apr. 7 The Sheriff finds that the custom known as 'spelling' is recognised in the West of Scotland, and in this case the defender's stevedore assented to the pursuer 'spelling' for the regular employee.

2. Resting from work. Also *attrib.* *Austral.*

1911 *Chambers's Jrnl.* 591/2 Old Davy..settled down on a selection near Grassmere which the Cornet Scrubber,..used as a spelling-place in his spare hours. 1926 B. Cronin *Red Dawson* ii, There was need for their spelling before they sat in on the game in real earnest.

Spelt, *sb.*³ *Metallurgy.* = Spelter. *U.S. colloq.*

Spencer, *sb.*² Add: **5.** An American repeating rifle or carbine, named after its inventor, C. M. Spencer.

1884 A. E. Sweet & Knox *On Mexican Mustang thr. Texas* iii. 38 Weapons of all sorts, from the murderous Spencer rifle to the soothing and medicinal pocket-flask. 1898 E. C. R. Marks *Mod. Small Arms* ix. 84 The American Spencer rifle of 1860 may be considered as the first successful breech-loading repeating rifle. 1901 T. F. Fremantle *Bk. Rifle* iv. 79 The Spencer rifle..had cartridges placed in a tube in the stock, and brought forward by a spring. 1904 *Kynoch Jrnl.* Apr.–June 96 The second repeater—and the one most prominent in the war—was the Spencer, having a magazine in the butt containing seven cartridges. 1915 Ommundsen & Robinson *Rifles & Ammun.* v. 93. 1923 J. H. Cook *Fifty Yrs. on Old Frontier* 5, I had traded a pistol..for a Spencer carbine.

Spencerite (spe·nsərəit). *Min.* [Named after L. J. *Spencer*, of the Mineralogical Dept., British Museum: see -ite¹.] A hydrated basic zinc phosphate. It forms large stalactites in a cavern near Salmo, British Columbia.

1916 *Geol. Mag.* July 336. 1921 *Brit. Museum Return* 159 A series..of zinc phosphate minerals..viz., two specimens of spencerite as crystals (a new species). 1922 Dana & Ford *Text-bk. Min.* 612. 1922 *Encycl. Brit.* XXXI. 949/2.

Sperrylite (spe·rilait). *Min.* [Named after F. L. *Sperry*, who discovered it: see -lite.] An arsenide of platinum, found near Sudbury, Ontario.

1910 L. J. Spencer in *Encycl. Brit.* VII. 338/2 In the Medicine Bow Mountains of Wyoming a platiniferous covellite is mined, the platinum being present as sperrylite (platinum arsenide). 1911 *Ibid.* XXI. 806/1. 1911 L. J. Spencer *World's Min.* 56 The tiny crystals of the rare mineral sperrylite.

Sphingid (sfi·ndʒid), *a.* and *sb.* [See -id ³.] Belonging to, a member of, the family *Sphingidæ* or hawk-moths.

1911 *Trans. Zool. Soc. London* XX. 85 Almost the entire surface is thinly coated with fine, short, white hair, an exceptional feature with Sphingid larvæ. *Ibid.* 95 Erinnyis ello,...The commonest Sphingid of tropical America. 1930 *Proc. Entomol. Soc.* V. 22 The S. American Sphingid larva of *Pholus labruscæ*. *Ibid.* 24 The caudal horn was movable in many Sphingid caterpillars.

Sphingometer (sfiŋgǫ·mitəɹ). [f. Gr. σφίγγειν to bind tight + -meter.] An instrument for measuring the bending of a strut, as by deflexion of beams of light.

Sphingosin (sfi·ŋgǫsin). *Physiol. Chem.* Also -ine. [f. Gr. Σφίγξ, genit. Σφιγγός Sphinx + -in¹, -ine⁵. See quot. 1884.] An alkaloidal base in the white matter of the brain. Associated with this are **Sphi·ngol, Sphingomy·elin, Sphingomye·lic** or **-myeli·nic** (*acid*), **Sphingostea·ric** (*acid*).

1884 Thudichum *Chem. Constit. Brain* 106 Sphingomyelin is the principal..phosphorised ingredient of the so-called cerebrin mixture, which remains when white matter is exhausted by ether. *Ibid.* 115 Sphingomyelic acid. *Ibid.* 216 Sphingostearic acid. *Ibid.*, Analysis of Sphingol, a new Alcohol, from Sphingomyelin by Chemolysis with Barita. *Ibid.* 149 A body remains insoluble, which is of an alkaloidal nature, and to which, in commemoration of the many enigmas which it presented to the inquirer, I have given the name of Sphingosin. 1916 A. P. Mathews *Physiol. Chem.* 575 Sphingomyelinic acid..yields sphingol, an alcohol,..sphingosin, a base..and sphingo-stearic acid. 1920 J. J. R. Macleod *Physiol. & Biochem.* (ed. 2) 689 Other phospholipins present in nervous tissue are cephalin, cuorin and sphingomyelin.

Spice, *sb.* Add: **2. e.** A specially medicated preparation to be added to cattle or poultry food.

1928 Oppenheim *Chron. Melhampton* 143 A retired dealer in cattle spices.

8. spice-bush *U.S.* (earlier example).

1770 Washington *Diaries* I. 409 The Soil...being as black as Coal and the Growth, Walnut, Cherry, Spice Bushes.

Spick-and-spanness. (Examples.)

1911 Mrs. H. Ward *Richard Meynell* viii, [He] was himself a model of spick-and-span-ness. 1931 *Times Lit. Suppl.* 21 May 407/1 The ancient houses..had a touch of mysterious romance that the bright spick-and-spanness of the new architecture misses.

Spider, *sb.* Add: **3.** (Earlier example.)

1807 *Austin Papers* (1924) I. 132, 2 Spiders with Covers.

7. b. A bicycle with steel wheels: cf. *spider-wheel*. (So called when steel wheels were being substituted for those of wood.)

1874 *Bicycling* 4 Had he lived in the days of the 'Coventry Spiders'. 1908 Sneyd-Kynnersley *H. M. I.* ix, Safety bicycles were not yet: the Boneshaker was not tempting, and the Spider was perilous.

8. d. A variety of the card game of patience.

1890 'Cavendish' *Patience Games* 186 But, the Spider..requires quite sufficient exercise of thought to render it very interesting. 1925 B. Dalton *Double-pack Patience* 5 Certain games, such as 'The British Blockade,'..or 'The Spider,' afford as much scope for foresight and ingenuity as any kind of card game. 1930 Maugham *Gent. in Parlour* xv, I knew seventeen varieties of patience. I tried the Spider and never by any chance got it out.

10. spider-wheel, (*c*) a steel bicycle wheel with wire spokes; **spider-wire** (see Spider-line).

1875 *English Mechanic* 23 Apr. 146/2 With the *spider-wheels I found that there was rather a tendency to get loose. 1882 *The Bicycle* 15 The Spider-Wheel, invented by the Coventry Machinists Company and now almost universal. 1906 *Chambers's Jrnl.* 735/1 The introduction of the free spider-wheel, pneumatic-tired cycle. 1928 W. M. Smart *Sun, Stars & Universe* xiv. 214 In the focal plane are two parallel fixed '*spider-wires'.

Spiel² (spīl). *U.S. slang.* [G., = play, game.] A game, play; a talk, speech, story. Hence as *v. intr.*, to talk, speak, orate; *trans.*, to speak, reel off.

1896 G. Ade *Artie* xi. 100 There was a long spiel by the high guy in the pulpit. 1904 'O. Henry' *Cabbages & Kings* iii. 58 I'll come right back and hear you spiel the rest before bedtime. 1905 *N. Y. Evening Post* 29 Dec. 4 He will spare no pains to reach one of them if he thinks he has a good 'spiel' or story to tell. 1910 'O. Henry' *Whirligigs* xxi. 239 Here's a couple of gents..that want to hear you spiel something about the Bowery. 1912 Canfield *Squirrel Cage* xxvii, I must have dropped off just as you began your spiel. 1926 J. Black *You Can't Win* ii. 9 [He] does not say 'please'. He rips off his spiel in such exact and precise language that he gets your dime without it.

Spieler. Add: **2.** A talker or voluble speaker; a lecturer; a crier stationed outside a place of amusement or a shop to attract patronage; also, an instructor or attendant at cheap dancing-halls. *U.S. slang.*

1920 C. Sandburg *Smoke & Steel* 245 Is there a spieler who has spoken the word? 1924 W. M. Raine *Troubled Waters* v. 55 Streamers stretched across from building to building, and 'spielers' for side shows bawled the merits of their attraction. 1926 *Ladies' Home Jrnl.* May 32, I suddenly became interested in astronomy, and every night I appeared to listen to the spieler.

Spig. *U.S.* A Spanish negro native of America.

1922 H. L. Foster *Adv. Trop. Tramp* ix. 133 You little knock-kneed,..fat-faced daughter of a spig. 1923 *19th Cent.* Jan. 122 The Spanish negro natives, now generally called 'Spigs', are slow to learn English. 1928 S. Lewis *Man Who Knew Coolidge* ii. 116 We need a supply of cheap labour, and where get it better than by encouraging these Wops and Hunks and Spigs and so on to raise as many brats as they can?

Hence **Spi·ggoty** *U.S.*, negro Spanish.

1922 H. L. Foster *Adv. Trop. Tramp* ix. 132 Just stood around the dock and jabbered a lot of spiggoty talk at me, like I could understand spiggoty! I don't know a word of this damned Spanish, and I'm glad of it!

Spike, *sb.*² Add: **2. d.** A bayonet. *War slang.*

1928 E. Blunden *Undertones of War* 270 The cowman now turned warrior measured out His up-and-down *sans* fierce 'bundook and spike'.

2. e. A young buffalo (see quot.). *U.S.*

1931 *Amer. Speech* VII. Oct. 7 A two-year-old 'bull' having short sharp horns was called a 'spike'.

Spike, *sb.*⁴ *colloq.* [Back-formation from *Spiky *a.*² 4.] A 'spiky' person.

1902 *Church Times* 14 Mar. 320/2 A priest is wanted for this parish A hard-working Catholic. Not a 'spike.' 1914 J. Wickham Legg *Engl. Ch. Life* 159 It would seem that there were spikes (as Dr. Bright of Christ-church used to call them) in 1768. 1930 Sayers & Eustace *Docs. in Case* i. 37 He turned out to be an earnest and cultivated middle-aged spike from Keble.

Spike, *v.*¹ **5.** (U.S. example.)

1837 J. L. Williams *Terr. Florida* 42 The inhabitants of the keys are generally adepts in the art of spiking them [*sc.* turtles].

Spike-bozzle, *v. slang.* [Obscure.] *trans.* To demolish; to do away with.

1915 Rosher *In R. N. A. S.* (1916) 123 Last night 'old man Zepp' came over here... Two machines went up to spike-bozzle him, but, of course, never even saw him. 1915 *War Illustrated* 19 June 422/2 'Spike-bozzle' is the latest Naval Air Service vernacular for complete demolition. 1923 *Blackw. Mag.* July 5/1 Piffers used to wear them..until the clothing department spike-bozzled them.

Spiky, *a.*² Add: **4.** An unfriendly epithet for a high-church or 'ritualistic' person of a hard and rigid type. *colloq.*

1893 W. Bright *Sel. Lett.* (1903) 348 The ultras, as they might be called, on the Catholic side, present Church ideas, too often, in a form altogether too hard to be attractive; I believe I am said to have called it 'spiky', in a letter to my friend the Principal of Ely College. 1921 *Ch. Times* 12 Aug. 147/3 We wonder what would be thought of some of his [*sc.* Father Stanton's] sayings if they were uttered by a spiky young curate to-day. 1929 S. L. Ollard in *N. & Q.* 8 June 408/2 'Spiky' meant a hard, unyielding, rather 'wooden' type of Anglo-Catholic dogmatist...The adherents of this 'spiky' method came, naturally, to be called 'spikes'.

Supplement, p. 3873; Corrigenda, p. 4092; Spurious words, p. 4093; Books quoted, p. 4094

Spile, *sb.*² **2. b.** *U.S.* (Earlier examples.)
1844 *Knickerbocker Mag.* XXIII. 444 The spiles you see sticking from sugar-holes in every maple. 1868 *Amer. Naturalist* II. Mar. 39 He remembers very distinctly making 'spiles' of its [sc. elder] stems when tapping sugar-trees.

Spilikin, var. Spillikin.
1926 M. Leinster *Dew on Leaf* iii. 40 Poles, oars, and planks were criss-crossed like pieces in a game of spilikins.

Spilitic (spəili·tik), *a.* *Geol.* [See -ic.] Of the nature of or typified by spilite.
1911 Dewey & Flett in *Geol. Mag.* 242 In Upper Silurian times no spilitic eruptions have yet been recorded in Britain. *Ibid.* 243 The spilitic suite of igneous rocks. 1930 Peach & Horne *Geol. Scot.* 136 Interbedded with spilitic lavas.

Spill, *v.*¹ Add: **16.** *trans.* To speak, utter, divulge. Also with *over*. Also *to spill the beans*. *U.S. slang.*
Cf. 10 b, quot. 1574.
1920 C. Sandburg *Smoke & Steel* 44 Men at tables spill Peloponnesian syllables. 1923 'B. M. Bower' *Parowan Bonanza* iv. 47 Maybe he taught the parrot that lingo just to have her spill it in town and start a rush. 1925 J. Gregory *Bab of Backwoods* xii. 156 I'm wise, Mr. Baron. You don't have to spill-over a word to me; I've never asked you a thing yet, have I? *Ibid.*, I'll spill her the word. Where'll she meet you and when? 1929 E. Linklater *Poet's Pub* vii. 91 'Tell me the truth,' she says. 'Spill the beans, Holly, old man!' 1930 E. V. Knox in *Punch* 26 Feb. 236/2 The usherette, previously interviewed, who, examined again, was induced to spill it, and confessed.

Spill, *v.*² [f. Spill *sb.*¹] *To spill up*: to fine-bore (a gun barrel) with a wooden spill put on one side of the bit.
1902 *Kynoch Jrnl.* Oct.–Nov. 21/2 Then it is spilled up, a process the same as rough boring only the revolutions are greater, a piece of oak wood being put on one side which causes it to cut much more evenly.

Spin, *sb.*¹ Add: **2. c.** Also *Comb.*, as *spin-bowler*, *-swerve*.
1927 *Observer* 24 Apr. 27/3 The true spin-swerve which operates late in flight, and is sometimes even combined with the reverse break, is the most deadly of all balls. 1930 *Morning Post* 16 July 11/5 The attack at the present moment lacks that variety and danger which a couple of spin bowlers would give it.
6. *Aviation.* A diving descent combined with a continued rotation of the aeroplane.
1915 *Aeroplane* 10 Nov. 578/2 Several times their aeroplane got into a 'spin'. 1918 *War Birds* (1927) 69, I spun down and came out of the spin in the clouds. *Ibid.* 87 All in Camels and all doing right hand spins. 1929 F. A. Swoffer *Learning to Fly* 91 To go into a spin, close the throttle and commence a gliding turn. 1930 Nayler & Ower *Aviation To-Day* 324 To come out of the spin the pilot pushes his stick forward so as to unstall the wings.
7. The continued revolution of the clutch of a motor after being disengaged.
1919 B. H. Davies *Motor Driving* 129 The disc A is pressed against the disc B, which damps out the 'spin'.

Spin, *v.* Add: **2. f.** To convert (a viscous solution or pulp) into artificial silk; to form (artificial silk filaments). Also *intr.*, to admit of being thus converted. (Cf. *Spinning *vbl. sb.* 1 c.)
1894 *Work* 7 July 391/3 Dr. Lehner's new process for the production of artificial silk..The machinery employed to spin the stuff is much like an ordinary spinning frame. 1899 *Jrnl. Soc. Arts* 8 Dec. 63/2 If too much water is present the collodion will not be tenacious and therefore will not spin. 1921 T. Woodhouse tr. *J. Foltzer's Artif. Silk* 21 From this pulp the silk is afterwards spun. *Ibid.* 23 This solution ..is conducted or spun through special capillary tubes. *Ibid.* 28 The collodion..does not spin so well as if the treatment with chlorine had been omitted. 1927 M. H. Avram *Rayon Industry* 185 The filament is not spun as is the case with spun silk or cotton. It is ejected.
10. c. Of a motor clutch: To continue to revolve after being disengaged.
1918 *Dyke's Automob. Encycl.* (ed. 7) 662/1 When a clutch spins, when thrown out of engagement, it is difficult to shift gears. 1928 *Motor Man.* (ed. 27) 57 The flange..is brought into contact with the stop, which acts as a brake and prevents the cone or plate spinning.
d. *Aviation.* (*a*) *intr.* To make a diving descent combined with a continued rotation of the aeroplane. Said of the airman or of the machine.
1915 *Aeroplane* 10 Nov. 578/2 It is always possible to avoid spinning or side-slipping in fog or cloud. 1918 *War Birds* (1927) 66 If to-morrow is a good day, I am going up to ten thousand [feet] and shut off and spin down and see what happens. I am quite good at spinning but it makes me a little sick. 1929 F. A. Swoffer *Learning to Fly* 94 Aeroplanes do not spin very easily, and they sometimes refuse to do so even when a deliberate spin is intended. 1931 C. D. Barnard *Learning to Fly* 151 Only a stalled aeroplane will spin—in other words when the machine is no longer airborne.
(*b*) *trans.* To make (the aeroplane) perform this evolution.
1918 *War Birds* (1927) 87 Then Ortmeyer..spun a Camel into the ground and killed himself. 1928 O. Stewart *Aerobatics* 13 Machines fitted with Handley-Page automatic slots are extremely difficult to spin. 1930 Nayler & Ower *Aviation To-Day* 326 It is said that some aeroplanes cannot be spun.

Spindle, *sb.* Add: **7. c.** A machine for recessing an aeroplane spar. (See *Spindle *v.* 5.)
1920 F. T. Hill *Pract. Aerop. Constr.* 108 This is known as a French spindle, and its cutting action, in order to form the recesses, is shown in the enlarged view on the right. *Ibid.* 110 The cutters..are clamped in the slot in the rotating spindle by the set screw.
9. (Later U.S. examples.)
1847 *Knickerbocker Mag.* XXX. 239 The tall corn, whose spindles were high above your head. 1871 *Amer. Naturalist* V. 245 The corn..sent forth a new tassel or spindle.
c. *Cytol.* A spindle-shaped sheaf of achromatic threads or fibres formed during mitosis; = G. *spindel*. Also *attrib.*, as *spindle-fibre*, *figure*.
1896 E. B. Wilson *Cell* 49 The amphiaster..consists of a fibrous spindle-shaped body, the *spindle*, at either pole of which is a star or *aster* formed of rays or astral fibres radiating into the surrounding cytoplasm. *Ibid.* 50 Spindle-fibres. 1905 H. Wager in *Rep. Brit. Assoc.* 565 The chromosomes..arrange themselves in regular order in the equatorial plane of the spindle figure, and some of the spindle fibres become attached to them. 1920 L. Doncaster *Introd. Cytol.* 29 The 'mitotic spindle' or mechanism by which the chromosomes after division are separated into the daughter nuclei. *Ibid.* 30 The spindle-fibres connecting the two centrosomes. *Ibid.* 42 The achromatic spindle with the centrosomes at its poles.
12. a. *U.S.* (Later example.)
1904 *Hartford Courant* 19 Aug. 13 What this man was really doing was simply placing a spindle on Magazine Rock.
17. spindle-berry, the bright red fruit of the spindle-tree; also the tree itself; **spindle hour, point,** with reference to the time at or during which the process of spinning goes on.
1921 *19th Cent.* June 1039 The dying glory of bracken, oak, birch, mountain-ash and *spindle-berry. 1923 *Daily Mail* 12 Sept. 15/4 Pink spindle berries are lovely in a pewter mug. 1930 *Times* 24 Mar. 23/5 Mill activity in the cotton growing states, measured by *spindle hours, established a high record. 1927 *Observer* 2 Oct. 19/5 The prices agreed upon had been calculated upon the basis of mule and ring mills rationally equipped and financed, and take into consideration production for forty-eight hours, percentage loss up to *spindle point [etc.].

Spindle, *v.* Add: **5.** To recess and taper (an aeroplane spar). Also, to cut *out* (a recess) in the spar.
1919 Pippard & Pritchard *Aeroplane Struct.* 201 By far the commonest form of spar is the timber one, usually spruce or an equally good wood, cut out of the solid and spindled to an I section for lightness. *Ibid.*, Questions of strength determine the amount which can safely be spindled out. 1920 T. H. Jones & Frier *Aeroplane Struct. Design* 204 Originally they [sc. spars] were almost invariably cut from long solid pieces of timber suitably spindled at points between spar fittings into the common *I* section. *Ibid.* 205 The ordinary *I* section spindled out from the solid rectangular section. 1920 F. T. Hill *Pract. Aeropl. Constr.* 106 Having drilled the spar, the next operation will be to spindle out the recesses.

Spindleage (spi·nd'lėdʒ). [See -age.] The total number of cotton spindles in use at a given time and in a specified area.
1921 A. S. Wade *Cotton Spinning* 15 If you added to the destruction and wear and tear of the war the loss of [*misprand*] spindleage due to the reduction of the working week. 1926 *Encycl. Brit.* Suppl. I. 751/1 The growth of the United States spindleage from 31,505,000 spindles in 1913 to 37,937,000 spindles in 1925. 1927 J. A. Todd *Cotton World* 160 The world's spindleage has been increasing steadily. *Ibid.* 168 The spindleage of each country.

Spindling, *vbl. sb.* Add: **4.** The process of recessing and tapering an aeroplane spar. Also *Comb.*, as *spindling jig*, *machine*.
1919 Pippard & Pritchard *Aeroplane Struct.* 201 Spindling should not start rapidly, but should be gradual from the solid to the fully lightened section... Fig. 165, A, shows the wrong, and Fig. 165, B, the correct method of doing the spindling. 1920 F. T. Hill *Pract. Aeropl. Constr.* 106 Some form of spindling jig is required for this. *Ibid.* 116 Flanges are grooved on the spindling machine with a jig.

Spine, *sb.*¹ Add: **6. d.** *fig.* The vital or essential part of a thing. (Cf. *marrow*.)
1912 Galsworthy *Inn Tranq.* 189 The vice of drawing these distorted morals has permeated the Drama to its spine.
9. b. The 'back' of a book, *i.e.* the part (whether rounded or flat) which bears the title, etc., and which is visible when the book is standing on a shelf. Also, the corresponding part of a dust jacket.
1922 M. Sadleir *Vict. Bibliogr.* 14 Be wary of books in cloth which bear no publisher's imprint on the spine. 1928 *Times Lit. Suppl.* 13 Dec. 985/3 The title of this book is misleading if given, as it is on the spine, without the limiting dates. 1931 *Publisher & Bookseller* 20 Feb. 345/2 The utility of having the selling price printed on the spine of a book jacket.

Spi·nelessness. Flabbiness of character or disposition.
1921 *Chambers's Jrnl.* 35/2 His spinelessness and low tastes.

Sping (spiŋ), *v.* = Ping *v.*² 1.
1909 R. A. Wason *Happy Hawkins* 266 The bullet tore through the slack o' Dick's vest an' spinged into the wall behind him.

Spinnable, *a.* Add later examples (in different sense).
1926 *Chambers's Jrnl.* 726/1 The cotton fibres of spinnable length are removed..by machines called 'gins'. 1927 M. H. Avram *Rayon Industry* 186 Not every solution which possesses sufficient viscosity and is capable of being drawn into filaments is spinnable. A solution is only spinnable when it has the property which leaves the filament in a solid state.

Spinner. Add: **4. c.** = *Spinneret 2.
1904 W. T. Brannt tr. *J. Bersh's Cellulose* ix. 215 To the lower end of the cylinder is secured a steel pipe furnished with glass spinners.
10. *Aircraft.* A metal fairing, conical or paraboloid in shape, which is attached to the propeller boss and revolves with it.
1924 Webster Addenda. 1927 *Daily Tel.* 27 Sept. 9/5 It appears that Flight-Lieut. Kinkead came down because the spinner, a metal fitting streamlining the propeller boss, came off. 1928 V. Page *Mod. Aircraft* 481 Spinner, a fairing of approximately conical or paraboloidal form, which is fixed coaxially with the propeller boss and revolves with the propeller.

Spinneret. Add: Also **spinnerette.**
1926 T. H. Savory *Brit. Spiders* 8 Now it raises its abdomen..and secretes a drop of silk from its spinnerettes.
2. *Artificial Silk Manuf.* A capillary tube, or a set of these, through which the viscous solution is pressed out to form filaments or threads. (Made of glass or metal. Otherwise called *nozzle*.)
1894 *Work* 7 July 391/2 The resultant..substance..is next forced..through minute holes in a glass spinneret. 1921 T. Woodhouse tr. *J. Foltzer's Artif. Silk* 49 The solution..is expelled by air pressure through capillary tubes or spinnerets. 1927 M. H. Avram *Rayon Industry* 197 The spinnerettes from which the solution exudes to form the filaments.

Spinning, *vbl. sb.* Add: **1. c.** The process of forming artificial silk threads or filaments from a viscous solution. Also *attrib.*, as *spinning machine*, *mill*, *nozzle*, *plate*, *room*, *solution*.
1899 *Jrnl. Soc. Arts* 8 Dec. 63/2 To eliminate every particle of suspended matter which may exist in the collodion before it arrives at the spinning machines. 1904 W. T. Brannt tr. *J. Bersh's Cellulose* xi. 250 In this spinning-plate are fixed a large number of extremely narrow glass tubes. 1921 T. Woodhouse tr. *J. Foltzer's Artif. Silk* 23 Spinning with the aid of water..has been replaced by a system of dry spinning. *Ibid.* 49 The Spinning Mill. *Ibid.* 52 An artificial silk spinning machine. 1927 M. H. Avram *Rayon Industry* 185 The pressing of this viscose mass in continuous filaments through a fine aperture is commonly known as spinning. 1927 T. Woodhouse *Artif. Silk* 31 The viscous solution is forced to the spinning-room, first passing through a filter and then through the multiple jets of the spinning nozzle. *Ibid.* 34 The viscous spinning solution. 1931 S. E. & E. R. Trotman *Artif. Silks* 49 The spinning nozzle consists of a head or rose containing a number of capillary apertures through which the spinning solution enters the coagulating bath or evaporating chamber.
4. b. Of a motor clutch: The fault of continuing to revolve after being disengaged.
1913 W. E. Dommett *Motor Car Mech.* 125 The clutch shaft has a coned brake which prevents 'spinning' when gear changing. 1918 *Dyke's Automob. Encycl.* (ed. 7) 662/1 Clutch spinning is often due to excessive friction in the spring thrust bearing.
c. *Aviation.* A diving descent combined with a continued rotation of the aeroplane. Also *spinning dive*. Cf. *Spin *v.* 10 d.
1915 Rosher *In R.N.A.S.* (1916) 137 He got into a spinning nose dive on a Morane parasol, and by the Grace of God got out again at 500 feet. 1919 W. B. Faraday *Gloss. Aeronaut. Terms* 52 Spinning Dive. 1930 G. L. P. Henderson *Pract. Flying* 171 Spinning is the result of the excessive abuse of the controls. 1930 Nayler & Ower *Aviation To-Day* 324 Spinning..was first started in the War as a means to bewilder, or escape from, the enemy.
6. b. *concr.*
1927 *Daily Tel.* 11 May 18/6 To place orders for general metal spinnings.

Spinning-jenny. Add: **3.** (See quot.)
1928 C. F. S. Gamble *North Sea Air Station* ix. 134 Sopwith two-seaters (familiarly known as 'Spinning Jennies', because of certain peculiarities aptly described by their name).

Spi·nningly, *adv.* [f. Spinning *ppl. a.* + -ly ².] In a spinning manner; with a spinning flight.
1923 *Daily Mail* 19 May 6 The ball is cracked spinningly through the gap between point and third man.

Spinozism, Spinozist: Add forms **Spinozaism, Spinozaist.**
1912 *Q. Rev.* Oct. 393 Modern Spinozaism is inclined to identify ethics with religion. *Ibid.* 398 He no longer speaks as a Spinozaist.

Spiral, *sb.* Add: **5.** *Aviation.* A flight in a spiral path; a spiral glide.
1910 *Sphere* 30 July 103/2 This descent..was composed of several high-speed dives and short spirals. 1913 *Aeroplane* 27 Mar. 374/2 Engine not pulling well, but pilot did usual fine spirals. 1918 E. M. Roberts *Flying Fighter* 272 When I came out of my spiral, at the height of about 500 feet, my engine would not start again. *Ibid.* 301 The Hun machine started upward in a spiral.

Spiral, *a.*¹ Add: **1. d.** *U.S. Football.* (See quot.)
1920 W. Camp *Football without a Coach* 85 Forward passes are of two kinds, the lob pass and the spiral... The spiral is thrown like a spear and goes more nearly on a line.

Spiral, *v.* Add: **3.** *intr.* To fly an aeroplane in a spiral path, usually in descending. Also with *down*, *downwards*.
1916 E. C. Middleton *Aircraft* 33 The pilot either 'spirals' or glides down. 1918 E. M. Roberts *Flying Fighter* 272 On getting over the station at which I was to land I shut off power and started to spiral down. 1918 *War Birds* (1927) 66, I also hear that Al Rothwell distinguished himself by spiralling into the ground. 1922 H. L. Foster *Adv. Trop. Tramp* xi. 173 As the aviator spiraled downwards towards his landing place.

Spiralization (spəi⁴rălәiz*ᵉ*·ʃən). [f. Spiralize *v.* + -ation.] The fact of making, or state of being made, spiral.
1910 J. A. Fleming *Princ. Electr. Wave Telegr.* (ed. 2) 127 The increase in resistance of a solenoid due to the spiralization. 1928 T. C. Chamberlin *Two Solar Families* 135 The Spiralization of the Solar Projectiles.

Spiralize, *v.* Add: To make spiral, give a spiral form to. Hence **Spi·ralized** *ppl. a.*, **Spi·ralizing** *vbl. sb.* or *ppl. a.*
1928 T. C. Chamberlin *Two Solar Families* 145 A group of bodies already separated may respond to the spiralizing whirl of two centers of gravity even more freely than an eruptive body from which the spiralized matter must be shot forth. *Ibid.*, The state of the material when spiralized.

Spirantize, *v.* (under Spirant *sb.* and *a.*) Add: Hence **Spi·rantizing** *vbl. sb.* and *ppl. a.*, **Spi·rantiza·tion.**
1911 *Amer. Jrnl. Philol.* XXXII. 36 The former [sc. Iranian] is a spirantizing language, like the old Germanic. *Ibid.*, The spirantizing of voiceless aspirates in Iranian. *Ibid.* 37 Breath stress was weaker here than in Germanic, where spirantization took place in spite of the escape of breath in a preceding nasal.

Spireme (spəi·rīm). *Cytology.* Also -em. [ad. G. *spirem*, ad. Gr. σπείρημα, Ionic f. σπείραμα coil.] The chromatin of a cell nucleus when in the form of a coiled thread. Also *attrib.*
[1889 tr. Waldeyer in *Q. Jrnl. Microsc. Sci.* XXX. 171 We call this stage, with Flemming, the 'Knäuel-Stadium' (skein stage), or 'spirem', or 'mother-skein'.] 1896 E. B. Wilson *Cell* 47 The chromatin resolves itself little by little into a more or less convoluted thread, known as the skein (Knäuel) or spireme. 1902 A. J. Cunningham *Anat.* 10 A convoluted cord of chromatin, the skein or spirem. 1905 H. Wager in *Rep. Brit. Assoc.* 570 The two spirems fuse together into a single thread in the sinaptic stage. *Ibid.*, The spireme thread first becomes longitudinally split. 1927 Haldane & Huxley *Animal Biol.* ii. 56 The chromosomes have begun to appear (spireme stage).

Spiritual. B. *sb.* **5.** Add: More fully, *negro spiritual* (which marks its origin).
1870 [in Dict.]. 1875 E. King *Southern St. N. Amer.* 617 One of the oarsmen, who was asked his theory of the origin of the spirituals, as the negroes call their songs, said, 'Dey start jist out of curiosity.' 1930 G. B. Johnson *Folk Culture St. Helena Isl.* 65 It is the spiritual that really gives the Negroes a chance to express themselves in song.

Spirochæte (under Spiro-). Add: Hence **Spirochæ·tal** *a.*, caused by a spirochæte.
1922 *Encycl. Brit.* XXXI. 906/1 It is best described as spirochætal jaundice rather than by the older name of Weil's disease. 1927 *Daily Express* 6 May 2/6 The germ which causes spirochætal jaundice has been found..largely prevalent in rats.

Spiroidal (spəiroi·dăl), *a.* [f. Spiroid *a.* + -al.] = Spiroid *a.*
1928 T. C. Chamberlin *Two Solar Families* 143 The train ..would obviously be curved in a spiroidal manner. *Ibid.* 144 The spiroidal deployments in the heavens.

Spirt, *v.*¹ Add: **1. b.** To flare *up* with sudden anger or excitement. *U.S.*
1854 Mary J. Holmes *Tempest & Sunshine* xvi. 205 What's the row now? What's happened to make little Sunshine spirt up so?

Spit, *sb.*¹ Add: **4. f.** An instrument used at the Customs for probing and examining goods. Hence the similar use of **Spit** *v.*¹
1925 *Chambers's Jrnl.* 666/1 A barbed 'spit' is used for examining cotton, wool, and various coarse goods, so that a portion of the interior may be drawn out. A flat, wooden 'spit' is used in the examination of rolls of carpet, cloth, linoleum... A short fine 'spit' is used for probing the stuffing and packing in and around furniture. *Ibid.*, The officer.. selects a number of bales for inspection. These he 'spits' —that is, he inserts a special iron instrument, which is capable of penetrating to the interior of a large bale and extracting a small piece of the commodity.

Spit, *v.*² **10.** Add: *Spit and polish*, a derogatory expression for parade smartness as opposed to utility.
1914 Ld. Chas. Beresford *Mem.* I. 120 From that day onwards I set myself steadily against bright-work and spit-and-polish. 1920 *Q. Rev.* Jan. 106 Gunnery had been neglected in pursuit of 'spit and polish'.

Spi·t-ball. *U.S.* **1.** Paper chewed and rolled into a ball, to be thrown as a missile.
1846 *Knickerbocker Mag.* XXVII. 410 They..crooked pins, made pop-guns, ejected spit-balls. 1873 'Mark Twain' & Warner *Gilded Age* liii, So awed were they..that during three minutes not a 'spit-ball' was thrown. 1888 *Judge* (U.S.) 10 Nov. 68/1 All statements to the opposite effect are spit-balls at the moon. 1897 Anna Fuller *Pratt Portraits* 237 'Why, how could he make a spot so high up?' 'He threw a spit-ball.' 1899 W. James *Talks & Teachers* 92 The spitballs that Tommy is ready to throw.
2. *Baseball.* A pitched ball moistened on one side with saliva, so that it slips readily from the pitcher's hand and acquires a break.
1912 C. Mathewson *Pitching in a Pinch* x. 222 When the spit ball was first discovered by Stricklett, a Brooklyn pitcher, several seasons ago. 1913 A. E. Crawley *Bk. of Ball* ii. 44 The Baseball pitcher moistens the horse-hide cover of the ball with saliva. The 'spit-ball', thus produced, may (it is said) reverse its curvature. 1917 C. Mathewson *Sec. Base Sloan* 293 The elongated spit-ball artist of the visiting club. 1928 G. H. Ruth *Baseball* vi. 75 All spit balls break down, but by turning the wet spot one way or the other the pitcher can make the ball break in or out as he desires.
3. (See quot.)
1925 E. Fraser & Gibbons *Soldier & Sailor Words & Phrases*, *Spit Ball*: Hand-grenade. (U.S. Army.)
Hence **Spi·t-baller,** a player who pitches spit-balls.

Spitcher (spi·tʃəɹ), *v.* *Naval slang.* *trans.* To sink (an enemy submarine).
1920 *Blackw. Mag.* Mar. 340/2 'Cease firing!' screamed the C.O. 'He's spitchered.'

Spite, *sb.* Add: **7.** Comb.: **spite fence** *U.S.* (see quots.).
1904 *Chicago Tribune* 21 Aug. 5 With no friendly judge to be found to hear a plea for an injunction a 'spite fence' was hurried into place last evening separating the Commerce building from the Traders', the Imperial, and the Western Union buildings. Instead of a wide court the tenants of the north side will find this morning a solid iron railing eight feet high and ninety feet long. 1928 *Hearst's International* Aug. 89/2 For the full depth of the boundary ran a tall fence of unpainted boards set upright. This fence was fully eighteen feet high. It was what is known as a spite-fence.

Spitter². Add: **3.** *Baseball.* A spit-ball.
1924 Webster Addenda. 1928 G. H. Ruth *Baseball* vi. 75 The theory of the spitter is simple enough. The ball is wet on one side. Naturally that makes a slippery spot which reduces friction and gives added speed to the opposite side where friction is applied.

Spitting, *ppl. a.* Add: **3.** *Spitting image*, alteration of dial. *spitten image* (for *spit an' image*: see Spit *sb.*² 3).
1929 H. Walpole *Hans Frost* III. v. 370 In another twenty years..she would be her mother's spitting image.

Spitz² (spits). *U.S.* = next.
1876 J. Burroughs *Winter Sunshine* vii. 163 [The spitzenberg apple] can stand the ordeal of cooking, and still remain a spitz.

Spitzenberg (spi·tsənbɜːg). Also -burg(h. In full *S. apple*: An American red and yellow apple.
1809 W. Irving *Knickerb.* v. i. 224 Mottled and streaked with dusky red, like a spitzenberg apple. 1845 *Knickerbocker Mag.* XXVI. 584 We went to steal some Spitzenberg apples from Dean Williams. *Ibid.*, The Deacon was a tart man, and stingy of his Spitzenbergs. 1876 J. Burroughs *Winter Sunshine* vii. 163 The apple of apples for the household is the spitzenberg. 1894 H. Frederic *Copperhead* etc. 71 He..picked out another apple—a spitzenberg this time.

Spitzflute (spi·tsˌflūt). [ad. G. *spitzflöte*, f. *spitz* pointed, acute + *flöte* flute.] An organ stop of the type of the gemshorn.
1855 E. J. Hopkins *Organ* 118 The pipes of the Spitz-flute are slightly conical. 1894 T. Elliston *Organs* (1924) 271 *Spitz flute*, 8 ft. pitch. An open pipe of light Gemshorn tone. 1923 N. A. Bonavia-Hunt *Mod. Organ Stops* 31 s.v. *Gemshorn*, The spitzflöte differs in having a more graduated taper.

Spitzkop (spi·tskɒp). *S. Africa.* Also in dim. form **-kopje.** [Du. *spitskop*.] A sharp-pointed hill.
1905 G. W. Stow *Native Races S. A.* 396 The head-quarters of 'Kousopp were at the two spitzkopjes to the left of 'Gumaap.

Splanchno-. Add: **Splanchnomegaly** [mod. L. *-megalia*, f. Gr. μέγας great, large], abnormal enlargement of any of the viscera.
1901 Dorland *Med. Dict.* (ed. 2), Splanchnomegalia. 1910 *Practitioner* Jan. 34 There is sometimes also a general increase in the size of the various internal organs, a condition of splanchnomegaly.

Splash, *sb.*¹ Add: **1. e.** A small quantity of soda-water (or other effervescent liquid) added to spirits.
1929 W. E. Collinson *Spoken Engl.* 52 Would you like a whisky and soda (whisky and 'splash')?
f. Pieces of the lead of a bullet melted by the force of impact on a metal plate (see quot.).
1931 Martel *In Wake of Tank* 45–6 The question of 'splash' was one which caused us much trouble and necessitated experimental work. When a bullet hits a steel plate, the heat generated fuses the lead and this squirts along the armour plate and enters the tank at any crevices that exist, such as the clearance between a revolving turret and the walls of the tank. This lead enters the tank as a bright flash, and is known as splash. It is curious that the Germans never realised the effect of splash on our crews.
4. b. *Med.* In full *splash sound*: A sound of moving liquid elicited in the stomach or other organ. (Cf. *Splashing *vbl. sb.*¹ 1 b.)
1890 F. Taylor *Pract. Med.* 435 The presence of air and liquid together in the pleural cavity may be demonstrated by the test known as *Hippocratic succussion*, or *splash sound*. 1908 Hutchison & Rainy *Clin. Methods* (ed. 4) 66 *note*, It should be remembered..that a splash may be elicited over even a normal stomach shortly after a meal containing much fluid,..and care should also be taken not to mistake a splash produced in the transverse colon for a stomach splash. 1910 *Practitioner* June 760 If the stomach be drained apparently dry a splash can still be obtained over the pyloric end.
5. c. A slight admixture *of* some other breed or stock.
1929 *Star* 21 Aug. 16/2 They have two or three crosses of St. Simon and a couple of splashes of Carbine.

Splash, *v.*¹ Add: **2. c.** To pour *out* with a splash (hastily or recklessly).
1908 E. F. Benson *Blotting Bk.* ii, Mills..splashed himself out a liberal allowance of brandy into his glass.
d. To make a 'splash' of, display ostentatiously or sensationally.
1930 H. R. Wakefield in *London Mercury* Feb. 317 All the evening papers have 'splashed' the story.

Splashing, *vbl. sb.*¹ Add: **1. b.** *Med.* A sound of moving liquid elicited (by means of palpation) in the stomach (or other organ), and indicative of dilatation.
1890 F. Taylor *Pract. Med.* 344 In cases of hydro- or pyo-pneumothorax, shaking the patient will elicit a splashing sound. 1897 Hutchison & Rainy *Clin. Methods* 62 If 'splashing' be elicited it will be partly heard and partly felt. Distinct splashing elicited three hours after a meal..is very suggestive of a dilated stomach. 1903 T. D. Savill *Clin. Med.* I. 350 Gastric succussion or splashing. 1907 H. L. McKisack *Dict. Med. Diagn.* 389 Splashing sounds may be elicited by placing the left hand flat over the epigastrium, and pressing suddenly or striking sharply with the right hand over the lower ribs on the left side.

Splat, *v.*² [Echoic.] *intr.* Of a bullet: To shatter with the impact of striking against a hard surface. Also as adv., *to go splat*.
1897 'H. S. Merriman' *In Kedar's Tents* v, A bullet went 'splat' against a rock. 1922 J. A. Dunn *Man Trap* xvi, A bullet whistled by Jimmy's head, *splatting* on the lava crust.

Splatter, *v.* Add: **1. b.** Also *transf.* (cf. prec.).
1931 W. G. Carr *By Guess & By God* 91 A salvo of shells splattered around the periscope.

Spleen, *v.* **1. c.** Add: Const. *at*, *against*. *U.S.*
1869 Rose T. Cooke *Steadfast* xviii. 198 [It] makes me spleen to think on't! 1902 H. L. Wilson *Spenders* x. 110 Well, I knew Dan'l J. purty well, and I spleened against some of his ways, but that's done fur.

Splendid, *a.* **6.** Add: *Splendid isolation*: phr. coined in 1896 (see quots. of that year s.v. Isolation) in reference to the isolation of Great Britain among the nations; also *transf.*
1898 [in Dict.]. 1909 *London Mag.* Feb. 634/2 Once cross the Channel by aeroplane, and England no longer remains an island enjoying 'splendid isolation'. 1918 *Review of Reviews* July 63/1 The abandonment by Great Britain of her splendid isolation. 1933 *Times* 21 Feb. 12/3 A Nazi band played in splendid isolation in the square.

Splenium (splī·niəm). *Anat.* [L.: see Splenial *a.*] The posterior rounded end of the corpus callosum.
1902 D. J. Cunningham *Anat.* 529 The massive posterior end..lies over the mesencephalon... It is called the splenium, and it consists of an upper and a lower part. 1910 *Practitioner* July 49 *Cisterna Venæ Magnæ* between the splenium of the corpus callosum and the cerebellum.

Spleno-. Add: **splenomega·lic** *a.*, pertaining to **splenome·galy** [Gr. μεγαλ-, μέγας great, large; also in L. form -ia], enlargement of the spleen; **sple·nopexy** [Gr. πῆξις fixation; also in L. ff. *-pexia*, *-pexis*], surgical fixation of a wandering spleen.
1900 F. Taylor in *Guy's Hosp. Rep.* LIV. 1 *Splenomegalic cirrhosis of the liver. 1908 *Practitioner* Apr. 456 Two typical cases of splenomegalic polycythæmia. 1901 Dorland *Med. Dict.* (ed. 2), *Splenomegalia, *Splenomegaly. 1903 T. K. Monro *Man. Med.* 316 Splenic Anæmia (Primary Splenomegaly). 1898 Rose & Carless *Man. Surg.* 900 *Splenopexy, as the operation is termed. 1903 Dorland *Med. Dict.* (ed. 3), *Splenopexia, *Splenopexis, Splenopexy. 1924 H. W. Carson *Mod. Operat. Surg.* I. 675 Wandering spleen cannot be cured by splenopexy, and removal is indicated.

Splice, *sb.* Add: **1. c.** *To sit on the splice*: to play a cautious defensive game. *Cricket slang.*
1926 *Westm. Gaz.* 29 Jan., Lord Hawke added the opinion that if there was the will to play the game and not to sit on the splice..we should see the matches brought to a conclusion. 1927 *Punch* 26 Jan. 108/1 'I don't think you're helping the score at all,' I protested. 'You're just sitting on your splice and leaving it all to me.' 1928 *Daily Tel.* 7 Feb. 16/1 Stevens played the correct game by sitting on the splice for the first few overs.

Splice, *v.* Add: **3. b.** *intr.* To get married.
1874 E. Eggleston *Circuit Rider* xxiii. 216, I heerd say as he was goin' to splice with a gal that could pray like a angel afire. 1875 J. G. Holland *Sevenoaks* xii. 155 Jim, be ye goin' to splice?

Splicer. Add: Also, a splicing implement.
1923 J. H. Cook *Fifty Yrs. on Old Frontier* 114 A wire cutter, splicer, and staple-puller combined.

Splint, *sb.* Add: **3. b.** A fragment or broken piece of diamond. *S. Africa.*
1872 C. Rhodes in Macdonald *Life* (1928) 20 The great proportion [of the diamonds] are nothing but splints. 1887 J. W. Matthews *Incwadi Yami* xxvii. 415 Faithfully carrying out their master's behests, and never robbing him of a single splint. 1903 W. R. Cattelle *Precious Stones* 79 Beyond the small pieces resulting from cleavages, other fragments are saved which cannot be cut to jewels. Some of these are called 'splints', and are used for mechanical purposes or ground to powder.
9. b. (*b*) (= made of interwoven strips of wood) *splint-bottom* (hence *-bottomed* adj.), *rocker*. *U.S.*
1850 *Knickerbocker Mag.* XXXVI. 73 She wiped out the seats of some splint-bottomed chairs with her calico apron. 1851 Mrs. Stowe *Pearl Orr's Isl.* I. iv. 19 Rows of old fashioned splint-bottomed chairs against the wall. 1876 'Mark Twain' *Tom Sawyer* vi, The master, throned on high in his great splint-bottom arm chair, was dozing. 1919 T. K. Holmes *Man fr. Tall Timber* iv. 36 A comfortable armchair with splint-bottom. *Ibid.* v. 46 Their splint-bottomed armchairs. 1922 Marg. B. Houston *Witchman* i. 17 Straight hickory chairs and a splint rocker were set at irregular angles about the room.

Splinter, *sb.* Add: **1. f.** *transf.* A long light narrow boat.
1929 'Seamark' *Down River* i, She was a beauty, that long splinter of a boat.

Splinterless (splintəɹlės), *a.* [f. Splinter *v.* + -less.] Of glass: Guaranteed not to break into splinters.
1928 *Sunday Express* 15 Jan. 6 The manufacture of splinterless glass. 1928 *Daily Express* 19 June 3 A splinterless shock-proof safety glass.

Split, *sb.*¹ Add: **2.** *Comb.* (Earlier and other quots.)
1838 *Southern Lit. Messenger* IV. 28/1, I took an inventory of all and singular..to wit: Beds, split-bottom Chairs. 1843 J. S. Williams *Our Cabin* in *American Pioneer* II. Oct. 444 Four split-bottomed chairs. 1880 *Scribner's Monthly* Mar. 676/2 It was a split-seated chair, painted green.

c. Also *centre splits* (see quots.).
1901 *Chambers's Jrnl.* 787/2 The uppers are made of what are known as 'centre splits', and the soles are an artificial compound of leather waste. *Ibid.* 788/1 The 'centre splits' are very ingenious forms of shoddy. Good honest skins are cunningly split into three thicknesses. The centre sheet is soft and spongy, and has no natural grain upon it; but this defect in its appearance is supplied by a process of printing which produces a surface 'grain' and makes it, to the inexperienced eye, just like ordinary leather.
4. d. *Croquet.* (See quot. and cf. Split *v.* 4 f.)
1896 *Cassell's Bk. Sports & Pastimes* 305 The Split is a stroke used when you desire in taking croquet to move both balls some distance.
e. A division of profits, etc. *slang.*
1919 *Detective Story Mag.* 25 Nov. 58 You put up a couple of hundred and draw down an even split when we cash in.
8. With adv., as *split-up*.
1930 *Daily Express* 23 May 2/6 American Machine Foundry was sold off following an announcement of a proposed five-for-one stock split-up.

Split, *v.* Add: **4. b.** *To split one's ticket, ballot*: to divide one's vote. Also *absol.* *U.S.*
1842 *Spirit of Times* (Philad.) 14 July (Th.), The cry is raised of 'Vote the whole ticket! Don't split your ticket!' 1848 *Knickerbocker Mag.* XVIII. 515 Didn't Squire Great ..split his ticket a couple of years since? 1851 J. J. Hooper *Widow Rugby's Husb.* 23 Never split in my life. 1905 *N. Y. Evening Post* 17 Oct. 1 Plenty of talk is heard about intentions to split ballots. 1906 *Ibid.* 6 Nov. 1 The time taken by the voters in the polling booths indicates that considerable splitting is being done.
g. *intr.* To divide profits, etc. *slang.*
1919 *Detective Story Mag.* 25 Nov. 59 You'll split even on anything we take.

Split, *ppl. a.* Add: **2. a.** *split second* (see quots. 1884, 1888 in Dict.) in *attrib.* use; also *transf.*, a very brief moment of time. Also *split minute*.
1912 Chesterton *Manalive* I. iv. 97 Mr. Moon stood for one split second astonished. 1916 H. L. Wilson *Somewhere in Red Gap* ix. 379 When I left 'em Jake was holding a split-second watch on the waiter he'd just given an order to. *Ibid.* 396 His split-second repeater. 1928 *Chambers's Jrnl.* 261/1 I'll be done in a split second. 1931 W. G. Carr *By Guess & By God* 27 Using his one periscope for split-minute looks.

Splitacer (spli·tˌĕɪsəɹ). *slang.* [See *Ace 2 b.] An aeroplane stunt flyer.
1919 C. P. Thomson *Cocktails* 226 Eddy, in addition to being a flight-commander, was the squadron splitacer, which is 'stunter' in the vernacular.

Splosh (splɒʃ), *sb.* *colloq.* and *dial.* [Imitative of the sound: cf. *splash*, *splodge*, *splotch*.] A sudden noisy drop or dash into water; a quantity of water suddenly dashed or dropped.
1919 G. W. Deeping *Second Youth* xii, The roof had dropped a splosh of water on Uncle Reginald's new hat. 1929 W. E. Collinson *Spoken Engl.* 92 If you want to see some splashing I'd better..go down the chute or try a 'bunny splosh'.
b. Money. *slang.*
1893 Gus Elen *Song*, '*E Dunno Where 'E Are* (Farmer) Since Jack Jones come into that little bit o' splosh. 1902 Boothby *My Strangest Case* III. iv. 266, I reckon we ain't a-goin' to see no splosh this 'ere trip. 1924 *Westm. Gaz.* (weekly ed.) 30 Aug. 526/3 The gentleman in the Old Kent Road who came into a little bit of splosh.
So **Splosh** *v.*
1904 *Eng. Dial. Dict.* (S. Not.), What are yer sploshin the watter about for? 1923 Wodehouse *Inimit. Jeeves* iii. 30 As I sploshed the sponge about.

Splosh, *adv.* [f. prec.] Used interjectionally to express a sudden noisy drop or dash or splash.
1901 J. Prior *Forest Folk* xi. 111 Nell continued to turn the handle of her old barrel churn. Splash! splosh! went the cream. 1924 Galsworthy *White Monkey* II. ix, Down came death—splosh! and a creature wiped out, like a fly on a wall.

Sploshy, *a.* (Earlier U.S. example.)
1851 *Knickerbocker Mag.* XXXVII. 377 The deep, 'sploshy' snow, through which he tramped.

Spludge (splɒdʒ). *U.S.* = Splurge *sb.* 1. *To cut a spludge*: to cut a dash.
1846–52 Mrs. Whitcher *Widow Bedott Papers* vi, Didn't she cut a spludge, tho? *Ibid.* ix, She tries to cut a spludge and make folk think she's a lady.

Splurge, *sb.* Add: **1. b.** An outburst of activity, emotion, or the like.
1895 *Punch* 1 June 258/2 My anti-gambling old Gaffer 'as spiled the whole splurge. 1928 *Publishers' Weekly* 16 June 2429 The Sales Force hadn't the courage to urge big splurges. 1929 G. W. Deeping *Roper's Row* xxx. § 3 He was not to be the slave of other people's animal appetites, their sex splurges.

Splurgy, *a.* *U.S.* (Earlier example.)
1856 Hall *College Words* (ed. 2) 440 *Splurgy*, showy... Applied to a lesson which is well rehearsed but little appreciated [etc.].

Spoil, *v.*¹ **10. d.** Add: *To spoil* (a person's) *beauty* or *face for him* (e.g. by giving him a black eye), etc.
1847 *Sporting Life* 16 Oct. 106/2 Hudson returned some heavy hitting; but Cannon would not be denied, although he met with a stopper that would have spoiled the upper works of the best-chancery lawyer in the kingdom. 1866 *Chambers's Jrnl.* 20 Jan. 33/1 Come on, you beggar!.. I'll spile your pretty face for you.

Spoky, *sb.* *Service slang.* Also -ey. [f. Spoke *sb.* + -y ⁶.] A wheelwright.
1925 E. Fraser & Gibbons *Soldier & Sailor Words* 266 *Spokey*: Wheelwright.

Spondaize (spɒ·ndeˌəiz), *v.* [f. Spondaic *a.* and *sb.* + -ize. Cf. Gr. σπονδαΐζειν, var. of -ειάζειν to consist of spondees.] *trans.* To make spondaic. Hence **Spo·ndaized** *ppl. a.*
1922 S. Grew *Art of Player-Piano* 149 Music 'spondaises' an iamb in triple-time, by bringing the short upon the middle count of the pulse. 1924 — *Engl. Prosody* 76 The Spondaized Iambus.

Spondylo-. Add: **Spondylolisthe·sis** [Gr. ὀλίσθησις a slipping and falling, dislocation] (see quots.); hence **Spo·ndylolisthe·tic** *a.*
1896 Dorland *Man. Obstet.* 536 The Spondylolisthetic Pelvis... By spondylolisthesis..is understood a forward dislocation of the last lumbar vertebra. 1898 Rose & Carless *Man. Surg.* 616 Spondylo-listhesis..a curious and somewhat uncommon deformity, in which the lumbar vertebræ are displaced downwards and forwards from the top of the sacrum. 1899 B. C. Hirst *Text-Bk. Obstet.* IV. i. 460 The name 'Spondylolisthesis' indicates the condition—a slipping down or dislocation of the vertebræ. *Ibid.*, The spondylolisthetic pelvis was first described in 1839 by Rokitansky.

Sponge, *sb.*¹ **13.** Add: **sponge cloth,** (*b*) a cotton fabric of loose texture for women's wear; also *sponge crêpe*; **sponge-painted** *pa. pple.*, **-painting** *vbl. sb.* (see quot.).
1919 *Queen* 26 July 138 White *sponge cloth is the thing for this new coat and skirt. 1923 *Daily Mail* 5 Feb. 13 For the opening of the Tennis Season, nothing looks nicer than plain Sponge Cloth. *Ibid.* 19 Feb. 7 *Sponge Crepe. This useful material is greatly in demand. 1921 *Spectator* 2 Apr. 421/1 The woodwork has all been '*sponge-painted' in blue and white.. Here I must add a word as to *sponge-painting. The paint is put on with sponges instead of with a brush.

Sponsor, *sb.* Add: **4.** An advertiser who pays the expense of a wireless broadcast programme which introduces advertisements of his wares.
1931 P. Dixon *Radio Writing* 18 The sponsor wants a dramatic type of program and is willing to spend one thousand dollars a week for the program. 1931 F. A. Arnold *Broadcast Advert.* x. 70 The sponsor or advertiser.

Sponsor, *v.* Add: **b.** To pay the expense of a wireless broadcast programme for advertising purposes. Hence **Spo·nsored** *ppl. a.*
1931 P. Dixon *Radio Writing* 10 The first sponsored program was broadcast in 1924. *Ibid.* 25 When an advertiser decides that the program is worth sponsoring. 1931 F. A. Arnold *Broadcast Advert.* x. 78 The travelogue type of program, sponsored by a tourist agency or a steamship company.

Sponsorship. Add: In reference to wireless broadcasts (see *Sponsor *sb.* 4).
1931 P. Dixon *Radio Writing* 25 The sponsorship of the Philadelphia Symphony Orchestra by Philco. *Ibid.* 26 The men who do 'Amos 'n' Andy'..worked for years without sponsorship and at very small salaries.

Spoof, *sb.* and *v.* Add: Hence **Spoo·fer,** a cheat, humbug. **Spoo·fery,** cheating, deceit.
1914 *Concise Oxford Dict.* Addenda, *Spoofer*. 1926 A. H. Godwin *Gilbert & Sullivan* 219 Bunthorne..is, in common language, a spoofer. 1925 K. Grahame *Sanger's Seventy Years a Showman* Introd. 20 And in fact the whole thing was unabashed 'spoofery'—clumsy fakes, dried fish, abortions in bottles,..and so on. 1928 *Sunday Express* 27 May 7/4 'I don't believe it, do you?' 'Of course not,' I replied, 'The fellow's a spoofer.'

Spoon, *sb.* **11.** Add: **spoon-bow,** a spoon-shaped overhanging bow; hence **spoon-bowed** *a.*
1927 A. R. Freeman *Certain Dr. Thorndyke* I. ix, She was a large yacht of the type that was fashionable when the America Cup was new; when spoon-bows and bulb keels were things as yet undreamed of. 1900 spoon-bowed [see 10 in Dict.].

Sporadism (spɒ·rădiz'm). [See -ism.] Sporadic activity (in opening up communications in a virgin forest).
1928 Haardt & Audouin-Dubreuil *Black Journey* 165 For the barter of produce it was logical that production must first be organized, and that is how the system of 'sporadism' began. Towns sprang up along the rivers to receive the supplies necessary for their development.

Sporeling (spōə·ɹliŋ). *Bot.* [See -ling.] **a.** A prothallus of a fern or other pteridophytic plant. **b.** A young sporophyte.
1924 *Glasgow Herald* Mar. 11 The simple structure in the sporeling.

Sporocyst. Add: Hence **Sporocy·stic, -cy·stid** *adjs.*
1926 C. M. Wenyon *Protozool.* II. 782 When the zygote divides directly into sporozoites, the oöcyst is known as asporocystid, while if sporocysts are present, it is termed sporocystid.

Sporont (spōə·rɒnt). [f. Spore + Gr. ὀντ-, ὤν, pr. pple. of εἶναι to be, exist.] In Sporozoa, a cell or zygote which forms spores by encystment and subsequent division.
1885 *Encycl. Brit.* XIX. 854 The epimerite serves to attach the parasite to its host, and may for that purpose carry booklets. It is always shed sooner or later. The phase in which it is present is called a 'cephalont', the phase after it has broken off a 'sporont'. 1918 E. A. Minchin *Introd. Study Protozoa* 166 Generations of individuals, 'sporonts', appear which do not multiply like the schizonts, but which as gametocytes, give rise to the gametes. 1924 Hegner & Taliaferro *Hum. Protozool.* 181 When the intracellular form breaks out into the digestive cavity (usually), body cavity or blood vessels, and when the extracellular forms become free from the epithelial cells to which they were attached, the parasites are known as sporonts. The sporonts are uninuclear but may be septate or polycystid.

Sport, *sb.*¹ Add: **8. d.** A good fellow; one who behaves in 'sportsmanlike' fashion. *Old sport*, often used jocularly for a person of any description. *Be a sport!* behave in a generous and sportsmanlike spirit.
1905 *Punch* 22 Mar. 199, I shouldn't mind, Old Sport. 1907 *Ibid.* 26 June 465 Toodle'oo, old sport. 1915 R. H. Davis *With the Allies* viii. 159 All that was asked of the stranded Americans was to keep cool and, like true sports, suffer inconvenience. 1918 C. Mackenzie *Sylvia Scarlett* I. ii, You're no sport, Maudie. You've got the chance of your life and you're turning it down. 1919 *Punch* 30 Apr. 336/3 The old sport just leaned forward in her seat. 1923 Galsworthy *Captures* 145 'Let me go, mister!' came the hoarse voice again. 'Be a sport!'
9. *sport-lover*.
1929 *Daily Express* 12 Jan. 3 To-day the thoughts of sport-lovers will be spread over thirty-two battle-grounds, where the third round of the F. A. Cup competition will be fought.
b. *sports-box*, *-field*, *-folk*.
1923 *Daily Mail* 12 May 12 True sportsfolk find an added delight in what may be called their 'gear'. 1925 G. W. Deeping *Sorrell & Son* xvi. § 4 To St. Benedict's he went, rigged out with a school-kit... He had his 'sports-box', and a pound in pocket-money. 1931 *What is Fascism & Why?* 274 You must give houses, schools, baths, gardens, and sports fields to the working Fascist people.
c. Of articles of attire: Suitable for outdoor sports; hence, suitable for informal outdoor wear; as *sports coat*, *jacket*, *suit*, *wear*. In plural; also *U.S.* in sing.
1912 *Sphere* 17 Aug. p. ii/1 The shirts I can also specially commend for holiday as well as for..sports wear. 1914 *Queen* 4 July Advt. p. 15 Smart fitting mercerised Sports Coat. *Ibid.* 18 July Advt. 8 Walking or Sports Skirt. *Ibid.*, Smart Tailor Skirt for sports wear. *Ibid.* 25 July 172/2 Styles in sports suits. 1916 H. L. Wilson *Somewhere in Red Gap* v. 188 Beryl Mae Macomber in her sport shirt. *Ibid.* 204 A blue-striped sport blouse. 1923 G. G. Denny *Fabrics* 90 Sports silk, a wide variety of novelties used for sports clothes. 1924 J. Sutherland *Circle of Stars* xviii, Norma merely put an old sports-coat of Nixie's over her bare arms. 1927 *Daily Express* 29 Sept. 9 Finest woollen sportswear.
d. Applied (usu. *pl.*) to open low-built fast motor-cars of the racing type.
1925 *Correct Lubrication* 52 Lea-Francis (Sports Models). 1927 *Scribner's Mag.* Feb. 159/1 Labap, furious, mounts his Sport-model Camel and takes after the elopers. 1932 G. Winn *Unequal Conflict* xviii, She nourished a wild hope that..she would find Derek's silver sports car standing outside.

Sporting, *vbl. sb.* **3. c.** Add: **sporting-editor** *U.S.*, a sports-editor.
1889 *Kansas City Times & Star* 25 Mar., The Times' sporting editor. 1899 T. Hall *Tales* 128 The somewhat intellectual-looking sporting editor of the aforesaid *Universe*.

Sporting, *ppl. a.* Add: **2. b.** Also *sporting parson*.
1837 T. Bacon *First Impr. Hindostan* I. 154 That we have upon our establishment a very long list of 'sporting parsons' is well known.
3. Also *transf.*
1923 Wodehouse *Inimit. Jeeves* ix. 91 Will you give me a sporting two to one..that [etc.]?

Sposhy, *a.* *U.S.* (Earlier example.)
1843 *Yale Lit. Mag.* VIII. 96, I can't always decipher quail tracks—specially in *sposhy* weather.

Spot, *sb.*¹ Add: **3. c.** fig. *Spots in the sun*, blemishes or imperfections in a character otherwise splendid.
1931 *Times Lit. Suppl.* 20 Aug. 630/4 He had his small tyrannies and pedantries... Mr. Nowell Smith..candidly acknowledges the spots in the sun.
4. c. Now usually without the def. article. (Earlier example.)
1861 *Atlantic Monthly* June 747/1, I wish I had control of chain-lightning for a few minutes;..I'd make it come thick and heavy and knock spots out of Secession.
5. d. Also, a card having a specified number of pips.
1844 [see *ten-spot*, *Ten D. 2]. 1873 J. H. Beadle *Undevel. West.* iv. 92 The ace is your winning card. The eight and ten spot win for me.
7. d. *transf.* and *fig.* examples. Also, *a spot* simply = a drink.
1915 H. Rosher *In R.N.A.S.* (1916) 117 Pity I'm not due for another spot of leave yet. 1924 D. B. W. Lewis *At Sign of Blue Moon* 272 What about a spot of lunch? 1929 Priestley *Good Comp.* I. iii. 79 Open your ears..and they shall drink in melody and harmony and what's its name—a spot or two of counterpoint. *Ibid.* III. v. 584, I suppose I must be thinking about a spot of food. 1930 E. V. Lucas *Down the Sky* 266 Sorry, old man, but come in and have a spot anyway. 1932 *Daily Tel.* 18 Jan. 9/1 What about a spot of sense of proportion?
9. d. *To put on the spot*: to determine the assassination of. *U.S. slang.*
1930 *Punch* 16 Apr. 442 You get rid of inconvenient subordinates..by 'putting them on the spot'—that is deliberately sending them to their death. 1931 E. Wallace *On the Spot* viii, They never gave you a chance, Shaun. They put you on the spot, didn't they?
10. b. *To touch the spot*: to hit the mark, be effective, produce the required result.
1868 *Putnam's Mag.* I. 670/1, I hope that last corjul set you right? Yes, Mr. Plunkitt, it went right to the spot. 1897 *Strand Mag.* May 500/2 Then percussion or detonation

was tried, and that 'touched the spot!' *Advt. of patent remedy*, —— touches the spot.
c. *Theatr.* = *Spot-light *sb.* 1.
1927 C. B. Kelland *Jahala* xii. 163 As she danced, as the spot followed her, the floodlights touched her with their magic glow. 1928 Fuerst & Hume *XXth Cent. Stage Decor.* I. 111/2 Flood-lights and bunches have been constructed with a lens which now makes it possible to utilize them either as spots or as flood lights. *Ibid.* We have seen a return to the use of the arc spot, which produces a pure white light of much greater intensity.
11. Attrib.: *spot cash*, cash down, ready money.
1907 *Chicago Tribune* 8 May 19 We always pay spot cash for improved or vacant city property. 1924 A. J. Small *Frozen Gold* vi. 137 The amount of spot cash the Skagway agent happened to have in his possession.
c. Short for *spot cotton*, *rubber*, etc. (see 12 d).
1928 *Daily Sketch* 10 Aug. 20/3 Courtaulds' shares remain a firm spot at 4½. 1930 *Sunday Times* 12 Oct. 2/4 Raw Rubber prices became easier, and spot was dealt in down to 3 11–16d.
12. b. *spot-development*, *-group*, *-zone*.
1909 G. Forbes *Hist. Astron.* 105 During the sun-spot maximum the corona seems most developed over the spot-zones—*i.e.*, neither at the equator nor the poles. 1926 H. Macpherson *Mod. Astron.* 41 The regions where the bombs are likely to appear are around and among active spot-groups. *Ibid.* 45 A relation between high-rotation speeds and spot-development.
14. spot-fish *U.S.*, a food fish, *Leiostomus xanthurus*.
1875 *Fur, Fin & Feather* 122 You are always welcome to a seat in his boat, if disposed for snipe or duck, or spot-fish.

Spot, *v.* Add: **3.** (Earlier U.S. example.)
1849 *Rep. U.S. Comm. Patents, Agric.* (1850) 456 These varieties spot better, and produce a finer leaf than any I have ever seen.
7. (Later example.) Also without *out*: To free (a cinema film) from defects or marks.
1915 B. E. Jones *Cinematograph Bk.* 175 Conspicuous transparent holes or scratches in the pictures themselves may as well be 'spotted' out. *Ibid.* 176 Having cleaned and spotted the film, attention may be given to any torn portions or broken perforations.
9. d. *Mil.* To locate (an enemy position). Also *intr.* Also **Spo·tting** *vbl. sb.* and *ppl. a.*
1914 *Aeroplane* 11 Nov. 425/2 He poised..for a spell to spot the lurking place of the battery. 1915 Rosher *In R.N.A.S.* (1916) 109, I wasn't going back on the chance of spotting the sheds, with anti-aircraft guns waiting for me below. 1915 D. O. Barnett *Lett.* 51, I had a man with a periscope spotting for me, and he registered some near things for the Bosch's face. 1916 Boyd Cable *Action Front* 135 'Stand by for trouble. That brute is spotting for his gun.' The aeroplane dropped a light, turned, and circled round to the left. 1921 *Daily Mail Yr. Bk.* 71/1 The United States Navy..employs aeroplanes, seaplanes, and kite-balloons for spotting and gunnery work. 1922 *Encycl. Brit.* XXX. 17/1 In 1915 the artillery on the ground came to rely almost entirely on aerial 'spotting'. 1925 E. Fraser & Gibbons *Soldier & Sailor Words*, *Fly-catchers*,..their duty is to protect reconnoitring or spotting aeroplanes. 1927 *Blackw. Mag.* Apr. 477/1 The resourcefulness of the spotting officer.

Spo·t-light, *sb.* **1.** *Theatr.* A spot or circle of light thrown on a particular person or object, leaving the rest of the stage more or less unilluminated. Also, the lamp or apparatus which throws this light. Contrasted with *Flood-light.
1922 C. Aiken *Jig of Forslin* 25 While in the warm dark seats, we watch the spot-light Dazzle upon the singer's hair and eyes. 1927 *Daily News* 3 Oct. 5/2 With a shaft of sun directed like the spotlight of a theatre on to his fine head. 1928 Fuerst & Hume *XXth Cent. Stage Decor.* I. 111/2 Spot-lights and projectors..fitted with lenses. *Ibid.*, Spot-lights are manufactured which carry lamps up to three thousand watts. 1929 P. Gibbs *Hidden City* xi, She..stood for a moment as though the spot light were on her. 1929 *Encycl. Brit.* XXI. 285/2 The spot-light..can be controlled and focussed accurately upon one particular spot.
b. *transf.* and *fig.* (Cf. *Limelight.)
1904 *Minneapolis Times* 1 Aug. 4 In the drama that was enacted Mr. Galvin was not in the spotlight at any time, but it cannot be denied that his was an important part. 1914 Gertrude Atherton *Perch of Devil* I. 159 We'll just thresh this question out, turn the spot-light on every side of it. 1926 *Lit. Digest* (N.Y.) 8 Jan. 89/1 It will put the magnates and the self-styled fighters..into the background and give the players the spot-light. 1930 *Daily Express* 30 July 8/2 The spotlight passes now from Ottawa to Westminster. 1931 *Time & Tide* 19 Sept. 1092/1 It conceives the consciousness as a kind of spotlight directed on the part of the soul that the whole regards as necessary to bring into play at the moment.
2. In a motor-vehicle (see first quot.).
1924 *Motor Man.* (ed. 25) 217 *Spotlight.*—An auxiliary electric lamp with a special reflector and mounted on a universal joint, useful for directing a beam of light on a sign-post. 1928 *Daily Express* 28 Sept. 9 Another alternative to ensure safe night driving is to make compulsory the adoption of dimmed headlights of universal power, with the concession of a spot light on the near side. 1931 E. Wallace *On the Spot* vii, A car passed him. Somebody switched a spotlight full in his face. He was momentarily blinded.
Hence **Spo·t-light** *v. trans.*, to illuminate with a spot-light, direct a spot-light upon. **Spo·t-lighted** *ppl. a.*
1923 B. Hecht *Florentine Dagger* v. 72 A crowd..stood watching officials and the spotlighted figures of mystery enter. 1926 H. T. Wilkins *Marvels Mod. Mechanics* 234 These panorama lamps can be swung round in a circle, and, along with flood lights, be concentrated in a beam of rays to 'spot-light' the stage stars. *Ibid.*, Should the stage controller wish to spotlight an actor or actress.

Spotted, *ppl. a.* **6.** *Spotted Dick*: also, a Dalmatian dog; = *Spotted dog 1.
1880 Hugh Dalziel *Brit. Dogs* 272 Dr. James's Spotted Dick. 1927 C. C. Sanderson *Pedigree Dogs* 261 He [the Dalmatian] is commonly known as the 'plum pudding' dog, or 'Spotted Dick'.

Spotted dog. **1.** A white or light-coloured dog with black or dark spots (esp. a Dalmatian). Found as a tavern sign, representing a talbot.
1910 F. W. Hackwood *Inns, Ales*, etc. 288 The 'Talbot' readily became known among the vulgar as the 'Spotted Dog'. 1930 E. C. Ash *Pract. Dog Bk.* 47 The Spotted Dog [sc. the Dalmatian] became the dog of the Circus.
2. A boiled pudding with currants showing outside; plum-duff.
c 1880 (remembered). 1928 *Daily Tel.* 24 Jan. 9/7 It was not till I went to live in London in 1866 that I heard these puddings, that were displayed in cookshop windows, called 'spotted dog'.

Spotter. Add: **3.** *Mil.* An aviator detailed to locate enemy positions.
1914 *Illustr. Lond. News* 29 Aug. 320/3 Electric contrivances for communicating messages between the 'spotter' aloft and the gun-layer below. 1918 E. M. Roberts *Flying Fighter* 108, I also learned that the fire was being directed from the ground from what the battery commander called the O. P., or observation post. He sent me up to that post with one of the spotters. 1932 *19th Cent.* Feb. 204 Spotters and reconnaissance aircraft.

Spotting, *vbl. sb.* and *ppl. a.*: see also s.v. *Spot *v.* 9.

Spout, *sb.* **11.** Add: **spout-bath,** a natural douche-bath (see quot.).
1929 C. C. Martindale *Risen Sun* 164 There are things in New Zealand that they call 'spout-baths'. A solid shining stream thuds on to your back from a height, and you feel as strong as it does.

Spouting, *ppl. a.* **2.** Add: *spouting well* = Spouter 3 b.
1898 *Knowledge* 1 June 124/2 This was followed by numerous other flowing or 'spouting' wells. *Ibid.*, The 'spouting' wells of Russia entirely eclipse those of America in output.

Spraddle, *v.* Add: **2.** *trans.* To spread or stretch (one's legs) wide apart. Also, to 'stretch' (one's legs) = walk or move on (in quot. *transf.*).
1913 Jack London *Son of Sun* vii. 87 He stood with legs spraddled over a large grass basket. 1929 'Seamark' *Down River* i, Let this decrepit tub of yours spraddle her old legs a little faster.

Spraddling, *ppl. a.* (Modern U.S. example.)
1898 H. S. Canfield *Maid of Frontier* 89 He rode with the spraddling seat of a man more accustomed to the plow than to the scout's saddle.

Sprag, *sb.*³ **2.** Add: In a motor vehicle (see quot. 1924).
1902 A. C. Harmsworth, etc. *Motor & Motor-driving* xv. 331 The Sprag..is an adjunct fitted to most cars... The sprag should be dropped before the car actually starts to run backwards. 1902 C. N. & A. M. Williamson *Lightning Conductor* 179, I seized the lever of the hand-brake and jammed it on. Next instant..I jumped out, ran to the front, and lowered the sprag. 1924 *Motor Manual* (ed. 25) 217 *Sprag.*—Usually a form of ratchet and pawl mechanism fitted so as to act on the transmission and prevent the car running back on a hill if the brakes fail.

Sprangly, *a.* *U.S.* (Earlier examples.)
1840 C. F. Hoffman *Greyslaer* III. i. 103 His great sprangly beard. 1886 *Leslie's Pop. Monthly* XXII. 503/1 We can command a view through their sprangly branches.

Sprawl, *v.* **3.** Add: Also *refl.* (in quot. *fig.*).
1929 B. Hall & J. J. Niles *One Man's War* 11 What war there was in 1913 sprawled itself out over the hills of Adrianople.

Spraw·lingly, *adv.* [f. Sprawling *ppl. a.* + -ly ².] In a sprawling manner.
1921 *Spectator* 7 May 585/2 Gauntly outlined, white and still, Three haystacks peer above the hill; Three aged rakes thrust sprawlingly Fantastic tendons to the sky. 1927 *Observer* 12 June 13/3 Building..so widely and sprawlingly distributed that it disfigures an area ten or twenty times greater than is needed.

Spread, *sb.* Add: **2. e.** *Aviation.* = *Span *sb.*¹ 5 c.
1894 *To-Day* II. 171/2 The wings have a spread of twenty yards square. 1909 A. Berget *Conquest of Air* 188 The spread of the wings is 10·20 metres. 1918 W. E. Dommett *Dict. Aircraft*, *Spread*, American term. See *Span*.
f. An expansion in a (middle-aged) person's girth.
1930 *Field* 29 Nov. 775/2 An older woman..middle-aged, with, possibly, a 'spread'.
g. *Diamond-cutting.* Surface in proportion to the depth of a stone.
1930 W. R. Cattelle *Precious Stones* 62 Since the trade have found how important it is to have a proper 'spread' to the stone..there has been a tendency to demand stones too shallow for the best results.
6. b. Jam, paste, or the like, spread on bread to make it tasty; e.g. *sandwich spread*. *U.S.*
1886 F. R. Stockton *Casting away of Mrs. Lecks* 40 There was some sort of jam left at the bottom, so that the one who gets the last biscuit will have somethin' of a little spread on it.
9. A space between two limits; the distance from one point to another. **a.** *Mech.* The distance between the centres of the cylinders of a duplex pump.
1911 Webster.
b. The difference between two rates or prices.
1919 A. C. Whitaker *Foreign Exchange* xii. § 86. 369 The spread between the local and the foreign money rates. *Ibid.* xxi. 597 There are three primary or true spreads.. These are (1) the spread between the cable and the sight rate, (2) that between the sixty-days' rate and the sight rate, and (3) that between the ninety-days' rate and the sight rate. 1928 W. F. Spalding *Foreign Exchange* vii. 69 This difference between the rate for telegraphic or cable transfers and that for demand bills is called the 'Spread' between the two rates. 1928 — *Dict. World's Currencies* 180/1 A 'spread' ..is usually defined as the variation between the demand rate of exchange on the one hand and the rates of exchange for telegraphic transfers and long bills on the other. 1928 *Britain's Industr. Future* (*Lib. Ind. Inq.*) IV. xxiv. § 7. 331 The Linlithgow Committee..came to the conclusion that 'the spread between the producer's and the consumer's prices is unjustifiably wide'. 1928 *Incomes & Living Costs Univ. Faculty* (Yale Univ.) 23 The associate professors..exhibit the least spread—from $3,000 to $6,000—with $4,500 as both the most frequent and the median salary.
10. *U.S. Stock Exchange.* = Straddle *sb.* 2.
1911 Webster. [app. short for *spread eagle*.]
11. *Contract Bridge.* (See quot.)
1929 Work *Compl. Contract Bridge* Gloss. 245 *Spread*, a hand which Declarer can show in proof of his ability to win all thirteen tricks.
12. *Advertising.* Short for *double-page spread*.
1924 Webster Addenda.

Spread, *v.* Add: **4. e.** To record, enter in a documentary record. *U.S.*
1858 D. K. Bennett *Chronol. N. Carolina* 67 Resolved, that the Governor of the State transmit a copy of these resolutions with the preamble to the family of the deceased, and that they be spread on the journals of both branches of the General Assembly. 1905 *N.Y. Even. Post* 24 Feb. 1 The law requires that the names of the members of the jury be spread on the records.
17. *Contract Bridge.* (See quot. and cf. *Spread *sb.* 11.)
1929 Work *Compl. Contract Bridge* Gloss. 245 *Spread*, to 'claim the rest'.

Spread eagle, *sb.* Add:
1. d. *U.S. Stock Exchange.* = Straddle *sb.* 2.
1857 *Merchants' Mag.* XXXVII. 136 The buyer can call when he pleases, which would compel the 'spread eagle' operator to deliver. 1870 Medbery *Men & Myst. Wall St.* 86 One modification of this is the Spread Eagle, formerly a highly popular style of speculation with capitalists who had plenty of money and a wide-awake broker. 1910 *Encycl. Brit.* V. 55/1 A combined option of either calling or putting is termed a 'straddle', and sometimes on the American stock exchange a 'spread-eagle'.
6. *quasi-adv.* Like a spread eagle, spread-eagle-wise.
1929 R. Hughes *High Wind in Jamaica* 45 Lying spread-eagle in their check-shirts.

Spreader. Add: **3. d.** A strip of cork for setting butterflies and moths with wings extended.
1916 G. W. Deeping *Sincerity* x, Cork spreaders for setting butterflies and moths.

Spreading-board. **1.** A board on which sheep are laid while being shorn.
1874 T. Hardy *Far fr. Mad. Crowd* xxii, The issue of their dialogue was the taking of her hand by the courteous farmer to help her over the spreading-board into the bright June sunlight outside.
2. A setting-board (for insect specimens).
1911 Webster.

Spread-over. [See Spread *v.* 4 c.] An elastic arrangement by which a fixed number of work-hours may be performed at varying times within a given period. Also *attrib.*, as *spread-over plan*, *system*.
1923 *Westm. Gaz.* 14 Apr., A 'spread-over' of 44 hours. 1924 *Ibid.* 7 Mar., The 'spread-over' system—the performance of eight hours' work any time within twelve hours. 1930 *Times* 15 Mar. 12/3 To make permissive a spread-over of the working hours within a fortnightly period, in substitution for a rigid 7½-hour day. *Ibid.* 27 Mar. 14/3 There is undoubtedly a disposition among the owners to give the 'spread-over' plan a full and fair trial. 1930 *New Statesman* 27 Dec. 350/2 The Lancashire miners resolved..to work the spreadover.

Spree, *v.* Add: *trans.* To spend (money) in reckless amusements.
1928 B. Shaw *Intell. Woman's Guide Socialism* lxiv. (1929) 296 They destroy the sense of security which induces the possessors of spare money to invest it instead of spreeing it.

Spring, *sb.*¹ Add:
7. c. spring salmon, in British Columbia, the quinnat and other species which enter the river in the spring.
1866 J. K. Lord *Naturalist Brit. Columbia* I. 53 *Salmo Gairdneri* and *S. quinnat* are the spring salmon. 1905 D. S. Jordan *Study of Fishes* II. 80 The economic value of any species depends in great part on its being a 'spring salmon'.
21. c. *Bootmaking.* The raising or rise of the toe of a last above the ground-line. Also, arch or curvature in the instep.
1902 F. Y. Golding *Boots & Shoes* 107 *Spring* is the term used to denote the elevation of the toe of the last... If the substance of the sole be light, very little spring is required. *Ibid.*, Sometimes the term 'spring' is used to describe the hollowness or arch of the waist. 1905 Swaysland *Boot & Shoe* 20 For light dress work the spring of the toe should be half an inch. 1916 F. Plucknett *Boot & Shoe Manuf.* ii. 17 It is advisable to put spring into the forepart of the last, equal to the amount which the boot would probably acquire in wear.
25. a. *spring-bows*, *-dividers* (see Bow-compass 1); *spring-gaiter*, *-washer* (in motor-vehicles).
1906 P. N. Hasluck *Cassell's Carpentry & Joinery* 4/1

5. A rest, cessation from work.
1930 C. R. Samson *Fights & Flights* 100 He told me..to give my cars a stand-off for the rest of the day.

6. *Rugby Football.* = *stand-off half.*
1922 *Daily Mail* 15 Nov. 11 Cassels at stand-off seeming to be able to take any sort of pass. 1927 W. W. Wakefield & Marshall *Rugger* 229 He will find this most difficult when the stand-off has cut inwards away from strength. 1931 *Times* 21 Feb. 5/1 A new stand-off player.

Stand out. Add: **2.** Something outstanding. *U.S.*
1928 *Collier's* 29 Dec. 26/2 When the show opened, this girl had improved in her dancing so amazingly that she was a distinct 'standout'.

Stand-still, *sb.* and *a.* Add: **A.** *sb.* **2.** (U.S. examples.)
1868 H. Woodruff *Trotting Horse Amer.* xxx. 254 The little bay mare beat him to what is called 'a standstill'. 1898 H. S. Canfield *Maid of Frontier* i. 16 She would..dance to a stand-still any five men within a hundred miles. 1921 R. D. Saunders *Col. Todhunter* vii. 101 His only play is to bluff the girl's mother to a standstill.

B. *adj.* **2.** Characterized by the absence or restriction of movement.
1852 J. Reynolds *Hist. Illinois* 266 The cotillons, or stand still dances, were not then known. 1927 *Daily Express* 27 Dec. 1 A 'standstill' order prohibiting all movements of cattle, sheep, pigs, or goats in thirteen counties. *Ibid.*, The Ministry has..declared a standstill area comprising the whole of the counties of Derby, Stafford, Leicester, Warwick.

Stand-up. A. *adj.* **2.** Add: Also, designating a counter or buffet where a stand-up meal may be obtained.
1920 H. G. Wells *Outline Hist.* xviii. 130/2 A stand-up buffet for light refreshments.

Staphylinic (stæfili·nik), *a.* [-ic.] = Staphyline *a.* 2.
1901 *Amer. Anthrop.* (N.S.) III. 38 Staphylinic [index], posterior breadth × 100 ÷ palatal length.

Star, *sb.*[1] Add: **3. b.** *To be through with one's star*: to have come to the end of one's good fortune; to have lost one's popularity or success.
1922 J. A. Dunn *Man Trap* xiv, As for this boob, Royce, he's through with his star as far as this town is concerned.

6. c. As a badge of rank or authority (cf. 14).
1908 W. H. Davies *Autob. Super-Tramp* 48 With that the marshal of the town stood before the open door, showing the star of his authority on his dark clothes. 1924 C. J. Tolley *Mod. Golfer* 6, I..passed on from there in '16 with a second lieutenant's star in that regiment.

15. c. *star-powdered, -scattered, -sown, -spattered, -strewn* adjs.
1891 'L. Malet' *Wages of Sin* iv. iii, The..star-scattered, blue-black, winter night. 1901 Kipling *Kim* v, The mango trees dark against the star-powdered sky. 1906 W. R. Inge *Truth & Falsehood in Relig.* 18 The star-sown abysses of space. 1918 Mrs. B. Lowndes *Out of the War!* xvi. 210 Outlined against the surging, luminous sea, and the star-powdered sky. 1920 J. Gregory *Man to Man* xxiv. 284 The field of star-strewn sky. 1924 A. J. Small *Frozen Gold* vi. 150 Black against the star spattered sky.

20. star-bill, a bill advertising a theatrical star; **star connexion** *Electr.*, in a polyphase system, an arrangement by which the coils or circuits have a common junction, forming a Y in a three-phase system and a + in a four-phase system; so **star-connected** *a.*; **star current,** a current flowing through a star connexion; **star image,** the image of a star as seen through a telescope or on a photographic plate; **star quad cable** (see quot.); **star-sight,** an observation of the stars made through an instrument for purposes of navigation; **star-stream** *Astr.*, either of two systematic drifts of stars one of which comprises the stars nearest to the solar system and moves towards Orion; so **star-streaming,** the movement of the stars in these two drifts; **star system,** (*a*) *Astr.*, a group of stars forming a system divided by a vast space from other groups; an island universe; (*b*) a system of having one or two brilliant actors or singers in a company and the rest of no particular merit; **star trap,** (*b*) a device for the registration of stars visible on certain occasions; **star turn,** the principal or most important item in an entertainment; also *fig.*; **star winding** *Electr.* = *star connexion; **star-wound** *a. Electr.*, denoting a polyphase alternating-current winding in which a star connexion occurs.
1898 A. Chevalier *Before I forget* (1901) 157 Just ordered fresh stock of special printing, *star bills, &c. 1902 *Encycl. Brit.* XXVII. 592/1 With the above *star connexion the voltage between the outer pair of wires *a* and *c* is $\sqrt{2}$. 1904 *Nature* 9 June 135/2 The error inherent in the *star-images. 1930 *Brit. Stand. List Terms Telegraphs & Telephones* 31 Quad cable. *Star quad cable. A cable containing a number of quads, each quad formed by twisting together four insulated conductors about a common axis. 1927 *Blackw. Mag.* Oct. 555/2 The Navigator had reported a reliable result of his *star-sights. 1894 *Knowledge* 1 June 133/1 The streams are in most cases accompanied by narrow black channels in the general nebulosity, which run parallel to and alongside of the *star streams. 1905 Kapteyn in *Rep. Brit. Assoc.* 263, I will call the points of the sphere towards which the star-streams seem to be directed the *vertices* of the stellar motion. 1921 *Discovery* Feb. 36/1 Kapteyn found..that the brighter and nearer stars belong to one or other of two vast interpenetrating star-streams. 1905 *Rep. Brit. Assoc.* 257 *Star Streaming. By Professor J. C. Kapteyn. 1873 Proctor *Expanse of Heaven* (1886) 275 Irregular masses of luminous gas, clinging..around stars, and *star systems. 1902 *Encycl. Brit.* XXXI. 43/1 Italian opera as such (*i.e.*, with Italian as the exclusive language employed and the old 'star' system in full swing) ceased to exist as a regular institution a few years after that. 1928 A. S. Eddington *Nature Phys. World* viii. (1930) 167 The star-systems such as our galactic system. 1901 *Knowledge* 1 Apr. 73/2 The wonderful photographic '*star traps' organised by Prof. Pickering at Harvard and Arequipa, by which all the principal stars visible every fine night are duly registered. 1909 *Flight* 3 July 378/1 M. Bleriot..is the '*star turn' at the Brayelle aerodrome at Douai just now.

Star, *v.* Add: **5. d.** *intr.* To disperse in different directions (likened to the rays of a star).
1916 Kipling *Sea Warfare* 165 When the German fleet ran for home, on the night of May 31, it seems to have scattered—'starred', I believe, is the word for the evolution—in a general *sauve qui peut*.

7. *spec.* To advertise as a theatrical star; to give a 'star part' to (a film actor or actress); also with reference to exemption from war service (cf. *Starred *ppl. a.* 2 c).
1898 A. Chevalier *Before I forget* (1901) 157 In defiance of your theories, I actually 'star' my own name. 1929 Edington *Studio Murder Myst.* viii. 102 And already we are going to star her! Already we baff bought a story, just for her. 1932 L. Golding *Magnolia Street* ii. ii. § 3 He thought for his part that his profession was as essential as his neighbour's, and was rather hurt that they did not 'star' him.

Starch, *sb.* **4.** (Additional examples.)
1902 O. Wister *Virginian* xix. 227 'It would certainly take the starch out of me,' he concluded. 'I couldn't be a serious mutineer after that.' 1912 C. Mathewson *Pitching in a Pinch* ii. 29 The pitching staff had lost all its starch.

Stardom. Delete *nonce-wd.* and add examples.
1911 'O. Henry' *Rolling Stones* (1915) 185 Besieging..the ultimate high walls of stardom. 1926 *Manchester Guardian Weekly* Aug. 175/4 After him..stardom will lose something of its supremacy. 1927 *Radio Times* 21 Oct. 143/2 From a clerkship in an insurance office to 'stardom' at a Royal Variety Performance is a long step. 1930 *Observer* 7 Sept. 13/3 Quite a number of young people..asserted the strongest claims to stardom.

Starred, *ppl. a.* **2. e.** Add: Denoting occupations exempted from war service.
1916 *Parl. Hist. Conscription Gt. Brit.* (1917) 183 Starred and badged men at Sheffield who have asked for exemption forms have been refused such forms on the ground that the applicants were starred and badged. 1917 'Ian Hay' *Carrying On* vii. 179 It was found that the single members of this noble army of martyrs were all 'starred', or 'reserved', or 'ear-marked'.

Starring, *vbl. sb.* Add:
1841 *Punch* 17 July 12/1 We consider Mr. Phelps' opposition to this ruinous system of 'starring' as commendable and manly. 1929 Edington *Studio Murder Myst.* xi. 153 Starting next month she gets fifteen hundred, and a starring contract.

Start, *v.* Add: **11. c.** Of a motor engine: To begin to operate.
1902 A. C. Harmsworth *Motors & Motor Driving* ix. 165 A petrol engine will generally start most easily with all the cold-air inlets closed. 1925 *Morris Owner's Man.* 76 Usually the engine starts perfectly easily after decarbonizing.

12. f. To begin to go. *U.S.*
1898 C. A. Bates *Clothing Bk.* No. 1270 That boy..will have to start to school soon. 1931 *Amer. Speech* VII. Oct. 20 *Start.* Begin to go. Used mainly in the one expression, start to school. 'I started to school when I was five'. (Widespread.)

23. g. *To start up*: to cause (an engine) to commence working. *To start (up) from cold*: to cause (an engine) to commence working when it is cold.
1912 *Motor Man.* iii. (ed. 14) 108 Cars having compressed air starting-up devices are always equipped for rapid tyre inflation from the air pressure cylinder. 1925 *Morris Owner's Man.* 8 Before starting up the engine make sure that the gear lever is in the central or neutral position. *Ibid.* 28 That faint blue smoke from the exhaust on first starting-up which assures the experienced motorist that 'All's well' with pistons and cylinders. *Ibid.* 37 Before the engine is started from cold. 1928 *Correct Lubrication* 27 Do not race the engine when starting up from cold.

28. start cold, denoting the position which must be given to the lever controlling the mixture of the carburetter when an engine is being started from cold.
1925 *Morris Owner's Man.* 9 See..that the carburetter mixture control is put over to 'start cold'. *Ibid.* 38 Not to keep this lever in the 'Start Cold' position longer than is necessary.

Starter. Add: **4. b.** (See quot.)
1876 J. Burroughs *Winter Sunshine* v. 116 In the lumber countries,..starters are at work with their pikes and books starting out the pine logs on the first spring freshet.

6. Also *attrib.*
1925 *Morris Owner's Man.* 9 The starter switch should immediately be released. 1928 *Correct Lubrication* 39 Starter motor spins without turning engine.

7. Something that starts or gives a start to an action or (technical) process. *As or for a starter* (colloq.): as a beginning, to begin with, for a start. *U.S.*
1873 J. H. Beadle *Undevel. West* xxii. 450 He gave me twenty drops of laudanum as a starter. 1876 'Mark Twain' *Tom Sawyer* vi. 61 He would begin to groan, as a 'starter', as he called it. 1880 *Harper's Mag.* Oct. 778/1 Into the large frame there may be set eight little one-pound frames, each with its foundation 'starter'. 1896 *Vermont Agric. Rep.* XV. 67 This may be done..by using a 'starter' made from cream. 1902 G. H. Lorimer *Lett. Self-made Merchant* v. 64 All that he ever needed was a few hundred for a starter. 1908 [in Dict.]. 1911 'O. Henry' *Rolling Stones* (1915) 194 If he don't..offer you fifty a week as a starter, I'll let you draw it from my own salary.

Starting, *vbl. sb.* Add: **2. a.** *spec.* relating to the starting of motor engines.
1902 A. C. Harmsworth *Motors & Motor-Driving* viii. 161 A sharp back-fire may be experienced on the starting-handle. 1925 *Morris Owner's Man.* 9 The engine starting switch is controlled by a round black knob on the left-hand side of the dashboard.

b. starting-box *Electr.*, an auto-transformer or rheostat.
1930 *Sel. Gloss. Motion Picture Techn.* (Acad. Techn. Bureau Hollywood), *Starting box*, rheostat used to control current supplied to a motor during starting, to prevent damage to the motor winding.

Starty, *a.* (Earlier U.S. example.)
1861 Mrs. Stowe *Pearl Orr's Isl.* I. ix. 70 The little feller was starty and fretful in his sleep last night.

Stasis. Add: Also *transf.*
1920 *Glasgow Herald* 30 Nov. 9 The prevailing mood of Labour is indefinite; a condition of stasis has been caused by the coal strike and the dread of unemployment.

Statal, *a. U.S.* (Additional example.)
1880 Tourgee *Invisible Empire* xi. 489 Public education flourished as a part of the statal economy.

State, *sb.* Add:
14. b. *Bibliography.* (See quots.)
1931 P. H. Muir *Points* 12 A word is still needed to describe changes made before any publication takes place. These changes may be made while the entire edition is still in the publisher's hands, they may take place at the printer's, at the binder's, or even at a stage intermediate between the issue of some of the review copies and the actual date of publication. Any differences that may arise before that time will be referred to as 'states'. *Ibid.* 13 It is probable that copies of the book in all three states will be issued on the same day. They will all be 'first issues'; but some will be first, some second, and others again third 'states' of the first edition. 1931 G. Worthington *Bibliogr. Waverley Novels* Pref. p. viii, I have..decided to use the word 'State' whenever between two copies of a first edition there are differences of sufficient importance to be noticed; and my 'First State' is the variety which I believe to be preferable to any other. *Ibid.* 37 Guy Mannering...There are four States of the first edition.

40. b. *state-owned, -paid, provided* adjs.
1901 *Edinb. Rev.* Apr. 453 In Germany we have seen a State-paid clergy help to create and keep on foot the great parliamentary party of the Centre. 1911 *Rep. Labour & Soc. Cond. Germany* III. vi–vii. 193, I found the land was mostly State-owned. 1927 Carr-Saunders & Jones *Soc. Struct. Eng. & Wales* 148 To complete the tale of State-provided benefits that school children may receive. 1931 *Times Lit. Suppl.* 22 Jan. 53/3 The largest area of State-owned and State-planted forests in any single State in the Empire.

41. state-department = *department of state* (see Department *sb.* 3 b); *spec.* in *U.S.*, an executive division of the government, presided over by the Secretary of State, charged with the conduct of foreign affairs; **state hospital** *U.S.*, a public asylum for the insane, owned and operated by the State in which it is located; **state socialism,** (*a*) in Germany (*staatsozialismus*), legislation introduced by Bismarck to improve the condition of the working-classes by pensions, insurance, and the provision of co-operative associations under state protection; (*b*) theoretically, a form of government in which the state regulates the means of production for the benefit of all, with the object of bringing about a more equitable distribution of wealth; in practice, a system of state control and ownership of industries, railways, etc. (distinguished from that form of socialism in which control and ownership is in the hands of the workers); hence **state-socialist, state-socialistic** *a.*; **state-wide** *a. U.S.*, extending over or comprehending a whole State.
1790 *Ann. 1st Congress* II. 1505 The resolution laid on the table yesterday, respecting the *State Department. 1836 *Diplom. Corr. Texas* (1908) I. 117 This morning..I went to the State Department, to have a conference with the present Acting Secretary of State. 1889 Donisthorpe *Individualism* xi. 368 Compare the success of a private firm of letter-carriers in America with that of the State department. 1893 *Souvenir World's Fair, Government Building*, The State Department exhibit extends from the rotunda to the east end. 1901 *Daily Mail Year Bk.* 81 The State Departments.—These offices include the great administrative Departments of State which do the work for Government whichever party is in power. 1930 *Times* (weekly ed.) 9 Jan. 35/1 On the eve of its meeting the State Department published the New Year greetings exchanged between King George and President Hoover. 1845 Dorothea L. Dix in *5th Rept. State Comm. Lunacy Pennsylvania* (1888) 7, I ask you to provide for the immediate establishment of a *State hospital for the insane. 1889 *Compend. Laws Pennsylvania* 98 State Hospital for the Insane, Danville. 1921 J. A. Goldberg *Social Aspects Treatm. Insane* 114 Overcrowding in the State Hospitals. 1879 G. J. Holyoake in *19th Cent.* June 1114 *State socialism is one of the diseases of despotism. *Ibid.*, State Socialism, so far as any taste for it exists in England, is a growth of Toryism. 1886 *Times Register Events 1885*, p. xix, The Housing of the Working Classes Bill..was found to include some provisions flavoured with the doctrine of 'State Socialism'. 1887 *Encycl. Brit.* XXII. 216/1 Little can here be said of the state socialism of Bismarck,—a very recent movement, which has not yet had time to pass into history. 1889 Donisthorpe *Individualism* iii. 69 The Conservative party have thrown in their lot with

State socialism. 1879 G. J. Holyoake in *19th Cent.* June 1116 True co-operators are no *State Socialists. 1888 J. Rae in *Contemp. Rev.* Sept. 383 The State-Socialists of Germany. 1927 *Church Times* 22 July 105/2 The State Socialists of the Snowden type. 1879 G. J. Holyoake in *19th Cent.* June 1115 The only persons in this country likely to be suspected of the *State Socialistic craze are the working class co-operators. 1913 La Follette *Autobiog.* 559 Such a resolution at a *state-wide conference. 1929 L. P. Stryker *Andrew Johnson* 11 Johnson's reputation as a capable political combatant was now statewide.

Stateship (stē^i·tʃip). *Irish Hist.* [f. State *sb.* + -ship.] = Tuath.
1917 D. Figgis *Gaelic State Past & Future* 11 To make more easy the general administration of the country, he [*sc.* Cormac] regrouped the administrative units of the country. Until then the nation had consisted of a number of separate stateships. *Ibid.* 12 The old stateships were known as Tuatha. 1918 in *Studies* June 259 For the unit of the Irish polity—sometimes spoken of as the Gaelic State—was the *Tuath*. It was at once a political and an economic unit; a stateship of a state. 1928 A. de Blacam *Towards the Republic* iii. 24 Along the western counties, where the Irish language still predominates, traces of the life of the stateships linger to this day.

Statesman[1]. **1.** Add: *Elder Statesman*: see *Elder *a.* 1 c.

Static, *a.* and *sb.* Add: **A.** *adj.* **3. c.** *Aeronautics.* Pertaining to one kind of motion considered in isolation from attendant motions and circumstances. So *static thrust*.
1928 C. F. S. Gamble *North Sea Air Station* ix. 141 When proceeding at full speed at an inclination of 10 degrees, the dynamic lift may be as much as one-tenth of the total static lift of the airship. *Ibid.* xix. 317 L.Z. attained a speed of 58 miles an hour,..and the ratio of net lift to gross lift was 37 per cent., while her static ceiling was in the neighbourhood of 9,000 feet.

d. *Static characteristic* (see quot. 1926).
1919 *Wireless World* VII. 77/2 From the static characteristic of a valve..it is clear that if the grid voltage varies ..the variation will be exactly reproduced in the anode circuit. 1926 S. O. Pearson *Dict. Wireless Terms* 211 The 'static' characteristics of a thermionic valve are the curves showing the relation between the various voltages and currents when these voltages and currents have steady values.

5. g. *Psychol.* Concerned with the perception of bodily position.
1895 E. B. Titchener tr. *O. Külpe's Outl. Psychol.* 149 We now pass to the consideration of another common sensation, giddiness, which has lately come to be regarded as the function of a particular sense organ, that of the static sense. 1902 J. M. Baldwin *Dict. Philos. & Psychol.* II. 600/2 Static sensation, sensation arising in connection with bodily position.

7. Distinguished or characterized by the absence of movement on a large scale; in quots. of trench warfare.
1930 Whyte & Atteridge *Hist. Queen's Bays* 296 With the entry of the Regiment into the now famous Ypres salient, our introduction to trench warfare took place: that static struggle..continued up to the fracture of the German line on August 8, 1918. 1930 *Times Lit. Suppl.* 28 Aug. 675/3 When the War turned 'static', it became for the cavalry one long series of hard trials and bitter disappointments.

B. *sb.* **4.** = *Statics d. *U.S.*
1913 *Wireless World* I. 508/1 Communication will also be had with New Orleans, which the static formerly prevented. 1916 *Electrician* LXXVI. 800/1 A slight change in the character of the static. 1928 *Saturday Even. Post* (N.Y.) 12 May 50/3 He had just paid $300 for a new radio and.. tried to get Dubuque, but there was much static.

5. = *Statics e.
1916 'B. M. Bower' *Phantom Herd* xiv. 233 All that negative I took to-day is chock full of 'static'. *Ibid.* 234 Static is a technical word used a good deal in motion picture photography.

Statical, *a.* Add: **4. d.** (Cf. Stationary *a.* 1 e.)
1902 *Encycl. Brit.* XXXII. 587/1 It may be noted that at 19 knots the ship's statical wave has approximately the same length as the wave which would travel freely at the same speed as the ship.

Statico- (stæ·tiko), combing form of Static *a.*, as in **Sta:tico-dyna·mic** *a.*, producing changes in the social order without wholly transforming or revolutionizing it; **Sta:tico-kine·tic** *a.*, pertaining to the sociological school of thought which differentiates potential and active social forces.
1905 Ross *Foundations Sociol.* viii. 204 Next to the *statico-dynamic processes come transmutations. 1898 L. F. Ward *Outl. Sociol.* 192 The *statico-kinetic school might also with considerable propriety be called the Spencerian school.

Statics. Add: **d.** *Wireless Telegr.* = *Atmospherics.
1918 Webster Addenda. 1926 *Glasgow Herald* 15 May 4 A wall of 'statics' may be responsible for the fact that no wireless messages have been received from the airship for some time. 1930 *B.B.C. Year-Bk.* 452/1.

e. *Cinematography.* (See quots.)
1923 F. A. Talbot *Moving Pictures* 84 Many exasperating troubles, one of the worst of which is generically known as 'statics'. It is common knowledge that if a celluloid comb be vigorously rubbed for a few seconds, it will become charged with static electricity and will attract small pieces of brown paper. A similar effect was produced in the cinematograph camera when the film was run at high speed, or cranking was continued for a long period through the ribbon making frictional contact with the various pressure and other devices introduced. *Ibid.*, Williamson and other pioneers did not wholly subjugate 'statics' because this phenomenon is influenced by meteorological and climatic conditions.

Station, *sb.* Add: **20. c.** The starting-place or terminus of a service of omnibuses, etc. (freq. with waiting-room, booking-office, etc.); (*air station*) the aerodrome, hangars, and other equipment for an aircraft service.

29. station agent *U.S.*, a person in charge of a stage, railway, or other station.
1857 *Trans. Ill. Agric. Soc.* II. 25 The active co-operation of this company, through its station agents,..in bringing forward an interesting show. 1910 Jer. Hart *Vigilante Girl* xv. 203 He stopped at the stage station... When the station agent looked to see what the man had written [etc.].

Stationary, *a.* **1. e.** Add: *Stationary wave* (Electr.).
1900 *Jrnl. Soc. Arts* 5 Nov. 878/2 Hertz's production of stationary electric waves in dielectrics. 1905 Tesla *British Patent* No. 8,200 In consequence of the interference of the impressed and reflected oscillations, the phenomenon of 'stationary waves'..is produced. 1923 E. W. Marchant *Radio Telegr. & Teleph.* i. 10 Hertz, in his experiments on stationary waves, used an oscillator similar to that which has been described previously.

Stator[2]. Add: **3.** *attrib.* **stator armature,** (*a*) an armature which remains stationary while the machine is operated; (*b*) an immovable part of a machine which is also its armature; **stator coil, field** (see quots.); **stator winding** = *stator coil*.
1906 '*Mechanical World' Pocket Diary & Year Bk. for 1907*, 226 The mutual action between the rotor field and the rotating field of the stator winding. 1910 *N. Hawkins' Electr. Dict.* 421/1 *Stator armature*, in an induction motor, an armature which, instead of rotating, is fixed, while the field revolves around it. *Stator coils*, the windings upon the stationary field of an induction motor, or, sometimes, the armature coils when the armature is fixed. *Stator field*, the stationary field of a dynamo or motor.

Statutory, *a.* **2.** Add: In certain specific uses. *Statutory company*, a company created by statute, as distinguished from a chartered company or a joint-stock company. *Statutory meeting* (see quot. 1900). *Statutory report*, a report of which a copy must be sent to all members of a public joint-stock company within seven days before the statutory meeting.
1900 *Act 63 & 64 Vict.* c. 48 § 12 Every company limited by shares and registered after the commencement of this Act shall, within a period of not less than one month nor more than three months from the date at which the company is entitled to commence business, hold a general meeting of the members of the company, which shall be called the statutory meeting. 1929 *Act 19 & 20 Geo. V*, c. 23 § 113 The directors shall, at least seven days before the day on which the meeting is held, forward a report (in this Act referred to as 'the statutory report') to every member of the company. The statutory report shall be certified by not less than two directors of the company. 1931 *Daily Express* 28 Apr. 2/4 Churchyards.., public parks,..and land owned by a statutory company were to be exempt [from land tax].

Steady, *sb.* Add: **3.** Ellipt. for 'steady company': A regular sweetheart (see next). *U.S. slang.*
1900 G. Ade *More Fables in Slang* (1902) 179 Lutie then selected for her Steady a Young Man with Hair who played the 'Cello. 1907 N. Munro *Daft Days* xx, She's got heaps of beaux, but he's her steady. 1929 Mazo de la Roche *Whiteoaks* vii, She's got her steady with her.

Steady, *a.* Add: **4. f.** *Steady beau, company*: a regular lover or admirer. *U.S. slang.*
1922 Stella Benson *Poor Man* v, She had just mislaid her last steady beau, so she was at the moment a little susceptible.

Steam, *sb.* Add: **7. d.** Also, *to let off steam*: to give vent to one's feelings.
1919 Mary K. Bradby *Psycho-analysis* 70 Commonsense says that it is better..'to let off steam' than to 'eat your heart out'. 1931 *Times Lit. Suppl.* 1 Oct. 737/3 She.. wrote sedate and quite readable novels to the prescribed pattern—but let off steam in stormy poems privately printed.

14. *steam-blower, -dredge, -dredger, -drier, -shovel, -trowel, -trumpet.*
1874 Knight *Dict. Mech.* s.v. *Dredging-machine*, In 1796, Watt made a steam dredger for deepening Sunderland Harbor. 1877 *Encycl. Brit.* VII. 464/1 The construction of large river steam dredges is now carried on by many engineering firms. 1892 *Lockwood's Dict. Mech. Engin.* Suppl., *Steam Blower*, a pipe and cock on a locomotive, employed to create a draught before the engine starts. 1902 *Encycl. Brit.* XXX. 763/2 The principal types of mechanical excavators are the steam navvy, or steam shovel, as it is commonly called in the United States. 1904 *Jrnl. Inst. Electr. Engin.* XXXIII. 965 Steam-dryers are fitted in the flues of two of the boilers. 1906 W. De Morgan *Joseph Vance* xli, He told how he and she were awakened by the sudden stoppage of the screw, followed by the roar of the steam-trumpet. 1928 *Observer* 15 Apr. 5/4 The people in the restaurants shovel food into their mouths as the steam-trowel takes up its load of earth.

15. *steam-hopper* (Hopper[1] 6), *-screw* (Screw *sb.*[1] 8), *-trade*.
1861 Mayhew *Lond. Labour* III. 186/1 He was..steward on board the Royal Hydaspes, a steam screw she is. 1877 *Encycl. Brit.* VII. 404/2 The steam hoppers employed to receive and remove the dredgings carry about 500 tons of excavations. 1899 *Westm. Gaz.* 25 Oct. 6/3 The steamer *Germanic* was run into last night in the Mersey by a steam hopper. 1902 *Encycl. Brit.* XXXII. 845/1 This was the pioneer of the steam-trade along the western coast of South America. 1923 *Blackw. Mag.* Nov. 681/1 In the harbour.. there were lying odd craft...The one romance of life for these steam-hoppers..had been quenched.

16. *steam-heated* (also *steam-heater, -heating*).
1884 Knight *Dict. Mech.* Suppl., *Steam Heater*,..a low pressure steam-heating apparatus...In Campbell & Pryor's method of steam heating for dwellings, the steam boiler and radiators are inclosed in a heating room in the cellar. 1890 *Harper's Mag.* Sept. 576/1 The Kents lived in a steam-heated flat. 1893 Kate D. Wiggin *Polly Oliver* xvi. (1894) 173 Who ever feels like telling a precious secret over a steam-heater? 1911 *Rep. Labour & Soc. Cond. Germany* III. vi–vii. 110 The rooms are steam-heated. 1917 S. Graham *Priest of Ideal* iv. 53 This mansion, with its good roof and closed windows and doors, and probably steam-heating to keep out the damp.

17. steam-car, -carriage, -doctor (earlier examples); **steam-drive,** the supplying of motive power by means of steam; **steam-eater** *colloq.*, an engine or apparatus which consumes a great amount of heated steam either on account of its size or through waste; **steam-kettle,** a kettle used in sick-rooms to create a moist warm atmosphere; **steam-owner,** an owner of steamships; **steam-pocket,** 'a place below the water-level of a boiler where steam accumulates or is formed and does not pass away quickly' (*Cent. D.* Suppl. 1909); so **steam-pocketing**; **steam-point** *Physics*, the point on a thermometric scale corresponding to the temperature of steam under a pressure of 76 centimetres of mercury; **steam-raiser,** a steam-engine; **steam-tent,** a tent used in the treatment of laryngeal and pulmonary disease; **steam-tug murmur** *Path.* (see quot.); **steam-turbine** (see Turbine 1 b).
1836 *Southern Lit. Messenger* II. 762 The canal and the rail road, the steam boat and *steam car, constitute in fact the great and characteristic powers of the age in which we live. 1789 in *Rep. U.S. Comm. Patents* (1850) 581 If any person..shall make..any elevator, hopper-boy, or any *steam carriage..without the consent of the said Oliver Evans. 1833 J. Neal *Down-Easters* I. 15 Never hearn tell o' the rain water doctor? some calls him the screw-augur doctor, and some the *steam-doctor. 1910 *Chambers's Jrnl.* 751/2 We had no steam-power available to drive the winding-rollers...A few days later we succeeded in rigging up an old, primitive system of *steam-drive which enabled us to get up a greater speed on the band. 1900 *Jrnl. Inst. Electr. Engin.* XXIX. 581 These pumps are the worst *steam-eaters in the ship. 1890 F. Taylor *Man. Pract. Med.* (1891) 356 In the intervals, the laryngitis is to be treated by a moist warm atmosphere (*steam-kettle) and mild opiates as in other cases. 1899 C. J. Cutcliffe Hyne *Further Adv. Captain Kettle* vi, Why, sir, you've been a *steam-owner in your time. 1910 *Chambers's Jrnl.* 60/2 The steam has the greatest facility for its escape from the tubes without any signs of *steam-pocketing, which is a serious evil in this class of *steam-raiser. 1903 *Phil. Trans.* Ser. A. CC. 122 The observed pressure at the *steam-point. 1892 Carmichael *Disease in Children* 238 The patient [is] put to bed in a *steam tent. 1901 Dorland *Med. Dict.* (ed. 2), *Steam-tug murmur, a murmur heard in aortic obstruction and insufficiency, and resembling the sound of the exhaust of a steam-tug.

Steamer. Add: **10.** A stroke in swimming (see quots.).
1861 'R. Harrington' *Swimming* 10 The 'steamer'..consists in striking the water violently with the foot, raising each leg alternately out of the water to do so. 1879 *Boy's Own Annual* I. 415/3 The Steamer... Lie on the back, point your feet as much as possible, and then strike them alternately into the water, the knees being kept quite stiff.

Steaming, *vbl. sb.* **4.** (Earlier example.)
1836 *Southern Lit. Messenger* II. 696 Steaming from Washington to Baltimore is an improvement upon that route at least.

Steam-mill. *U.S.* (See Steam *sb.* 14.)
1815 D. Drake *Cincinnati* iii. 137 The most capacious.. building in this place is the Steam Mill. 1857 D. Braman *Inform. Texas* iii. 79 There are three steam-mills in operation, sawing lumber, and grinding wheat and corn. 1880 *Harper's Mag.* Aug. 344/2 The grist from it [*sc.* the tide-mill] is said to be of a better quality than from the steam-mills, as being less heated in the process.

Steam-roller, *v.* [f. the sb.] *trans.* To crush or break down as if with a steam-roller.
1921 *Round Table* June 651 His block majority, with which, if necessary, he could steam-roller opposition. 1924 S. Baldwin *On England* 5 Let us see to it that we never allow our individuality as Englishmen to be steam-rollered.

Stedman (ste·dmăn). The name of Fabian Stedman (c 1670), used to designate a method of change-ringing invented by him.
1731 *Norwich Gaz.* 11 Sept. in E. Morris *Hist. & Art Change Ringing* (1931) 328 That most Noted and harmonious Peal on 7 Bells called Stedman's Triples. 1813 W. Shipway *Campanalogia* 1. 98 Let a ringer choose what method he will, it must still be on Stedman's principle. 1814 *Ibid.* II. 187 Doubles, or, as commonly called, a Stedman Grandsire, is completed by two singles. 1903 C. D. P. Davies *Stedman* 1 Throughout the whole province of Change Ringing, there is no more delightful method than Stedman. 1931 E. Morris *Hist. & Art Change Ringing* 78 The Norwich ringers performed a 'touch' of Stedman Cinques.

Stee, variant of Sty *sb.*[2]

Steel, *sb.*[1] Add: **1. c.** with defining attribute. *Pressed steel*, steel moulded under hydraulic pressure.
See also Basic (*a.* 2 c), Crucible (*sb.* 3), Granulated (*ppl. a.* 1), Gun (*sb.* 14), *High-speed (*a.*), *Ingot (3), Mild (*a.* 8 b), *Slagless (*a.*), Soft (*a.* 24 b), *Stainless (*a.* 2), Tungsten (3), Wolfram (3).
1902 *Encycl. Brit.* XXIX. 572/1 Alloy Steels and Cast Irons are those which owe their properties chiefly to the presence of one or more elements other than carbon. *Ibid.* 573/2 Self-hardening steels, such as manganese steel containing 7 per cent. of manganese. 1912 *Motor Manual* 83 The axle casing is held by the pressed steel distance or torque stay. 1932 *New Yorker* 9 Apr. 51/1 The hood is long and the radiator slightly V-nosed, with a rustless-steel grille.

e. The name of a cold shade of grey resembling the colour of steel; steel-grey.
1923 *Daily Mail* 6 Feb. 2 Luvisca shirts in plain shades of Ivory..Saxe, Grey, Rose and Steel. *Ibid.* 26 Mar. 1 In Tan, Black, Navy,..Mole, Steel, Silver.

17. *steel-fisted* (fig.), *-nerved* (cf. 15 b), *-rimmed, -studded.*
1909 *Westm. Gaz.* 11 Nov. 5/2 A new steel-studded tyre. 1912 *Motor Manual* 101 The most popular of these [non-skid devices] is the steel-studded leather band. 1915 *Pearson's Mag.* XXXIX. 136/1 That steel-fisted British fleet. 1924 W. J. Locke *Coming of Amos* xvi, What kind of a steel-nerved wisp of a woman are you? 1926 C. Barry *Detective's Holiday* vii, A pair of steel-rimmed spectacles.

18. steel alloy, steel which contains an appreciable quantity of a metal or metals other than iron; **Steelbacks** (see quots.); **steel-concrete,** ferro-concrete; **steel frame** (cf. *Concrete *sb.* 3); **steel road,** a railway.
1903 Farmer & Henley *Slang*, *Steelbacks (*The*)...1. The 1st Batt. Northamptonshire Regiment, the late 48th Foot; and 2) The 1st Batt. Middlesex Regiment, the late 57th Foot. 1925 E. Fraser & Gibbons *Soldier & Sailor Words* 204 *Steelbacks, The*: The Northamptonshire Regiment. Through the 1st Battalion, as the 48th Foot. In allusion to the stoical way in which, according to tradition, the men bore their punishment when flogged. (An 18th century nickname.) 1906 Atkinson & Bagenal *Theory & Elem. Archit.* I. 6 *Steel-frame or reinforced concrete construction. 1909 *Cent. Dict.* Suppl. 1145–6 *Steel road, roadway. 1929 Lady Hosie *Portrait Chinese Lady* xxxv. 381 A million Yunnanese labourers..died of fever for the making of that steel road to the coast.

Steel Helmet. [tr. G. *stahlhelm*.] The designation of an organization of German ex-service men drawn mainly from the Nationalist Party and having a strong conservative bias; also, a member of this.
1925 *Spectator* 28 Mar. 467/1 How could he really fail to stand for monarchy when he is championed by such societies as the 'Steel Helmet League' and the 'Front Fighters'? 1926 *Times* 25 May 14/3 The Nationalist 'Steel Helmet' organization. *Ibid.*, Most of the 'Steel Helmets' wore iron crosses. 1927 *Ibid.* 28 Apr. 13/2 The chief task of the Steel Helmet League was the preservation of the soldierly spirit in the nation and the preparedness to bear arms. 1932 Knickerbocker *Germany—Fascist or Soviet* 137 The four militant organizations are the Republican Reichsbanner, the National Socialist Storm Troops, the Conservative Steel Helmets, and the Communist Red Front. 1932 *J. H. Kraus' Crisis German Democr.* 7 'The National Opposition.'.. Its chief representatives are the National Socialists, the German National Party (Hugenberg party), and, thirdly, the Steelhelmets.

Steep, *sb.*[1] **4.** Add: A solution or bath in which metals are dipped in preparation for electro-plating.
1886 A. Watt *Electro-Deposition* 287 Dips, or Steeps. Besides the potash solution, certain other liquids are employed in nickel-plating after the work has been 'potashed' and scoured. 1891 G. E. Bonney *Electro-Plater's Handbk.* 107 The required condition of surface for plating may be imparted by dipping them in an acid solution...The acid solutions are known as 'dips' or 'steeps'.

Steer, *sb.*[1] **b.** Add: *steer-roping.*
1924 *Glasgow Herald* 17 June 9 The 'steer roping', which at Saturday's display met with some public disapproval, was withdrawn.

Steer, *sb.*[2] Add: **2. e.** *fig.* A suggested course of action or idea. *U.S.*
1902 H. L. Wilson *Spenders* xxxi. 363 He not only tried to hedge on what he told me..but he actually had the nerve to give me the opposite steer. 1919 T. K. Holmes *Man fr. Tall Timber* xxx. 374 That girl from New York gave me the right steer, I do believe.

Steering, *vbl. sb.* Add: **3. a.** *steering-arm, axle, -bridge, -chain, -circle, -knuckle, -lever, -light.*
1902 in A. C. Harmsworth *Motors & Motor-Driving* 216 With a broken *steering arm..a car..may be hurled into a ditch. 1909 *Westm. Gaz.* 2 Nov. 5/2 Two pronged forks,.. fitted..on the end of the steering-arm to connect the rod leading to the off-side steering knuckle. 1912 *Motor Manual* 87 Details of *steering axle with steering arms and connecting bar. 1902 *Chambers's Jrnl.* 739/1 He left the bridge, roused all hands, and arraigned them on the *steering-bridge. 1877 Habberton *Jericho Road* 189 A line fastened to one of the *steering-chains near the rudder. 1912 *Motor Manual* 88 Whichever wheel is on the inside of the *steering circle turns through a wider angle than the outer wheel does. 1904 *Sci. Amer. Suppl.* 27 Aug. 23953 (Cent. D. Suppl.) The front axle is provided with ball-bearing *steering knuckles. 1912 *Motor Manual* 214 Steering knuckle pins. 1928 *Correct Lubrication* 22 Steering Knuckles and Connections. 1900 Hiscox *Horseless Vehicles* 20 When you have the *steering-lever in your hand and can speed ahead at your own pleasure. 1910 *Blackw. Mag.* Aug. 171/1 Grahame had set his '*steering-light' for the guidance of the helmsman upon the barge.

b. steering-box, the gear-box of a motor car; **steering line** *Meteorol.* (see quot.); **steering-pillar,** the cylindrical shaft of a motor to which the steering wheel is attached; **steering-wheel,** (*c*) also, each of the front wheels of a motor-car.
1928 *Correct Lubrication* 16 The *steering box should be inspected every 1,000 miles and replenished with lubricant if found necessary. 1923 Sir N. Shaw *Forecasting Weather* v. 155 The dividing line of the cyclone from the centre towards the eastern or advancing side is called the *steering line or more recently, warm front. 1902 in A. C. Harmsworth *Motors & Motor-Driving* 218 Looseness between *steering wheel and end of *steering pillar can be found at any time. 1916 *Chambers's Jrnl.* Nov. 766/2 The handle of the control-cock is connected..to a sector set on the steering-pillar. 1912 *Motor Manual* 231 A weakened [tyre] cover will, as a general rule, give a considerable period of further service mounted on a steering wheel.

Steering (stiə·riŋ), *ppl. a.* [f. Steer *v.*[1] + -ing[2].] *Steering committee* U.S., a committee of management; also *spec.* (see quot.).
1903 A. B. Hart *Actual Government* 242 What is called the 'Steering Committee',—an unofficial conclave of members of the Senate and the House. As guides to the majority, the Steering Committee practically decides what measures to press to a vote and what measures to drop. 1929 C. E. Merriam *Chicago* 223, I had been appointed a member of the Chicago Charter Convention, and was a member of the Steering Committee of that body.

Steinberger (ʃtai·nbəːgəɹ). Also **Steinberg.** [G., f. *Steinberg*, a vineyard in the Rheingau, Germany.] A choice Rhenish wine.
1833 Redding *Wines* 205 The Steinberger..takes rank after the Schloss-Johannesberger among these wines. 1851 *Ibid.* (ed. 3) 223 In some years Steinberg has fetched a much higher price than Johannesberg. 1886 *Encycl. Brit.* XX. 14/2 Many of the choicest varieties, such as Steinberger, Johannisberger, and Rüdesheimer.

Stem, *sb.*[1] **8.** Add: **stem analysis, density** *U.S., Forestry* (see quots.); **stem-form** [G. *stammform*] *Biol.*, the ancestral form; **stem-mother,** a female plant-louse which, being hatched in the spring from a winter egg, is the foundress of a summer colony of *Aphididæ*; **stem-ware** *U.S.*, a general term for wine and liqueur glasses.
1905 *Terms Forestry & Logging* 25 *Tree analysis*, a series of measurements and observations upon a felled tree to determine its growth and life history. *Stem analysis. *Ibid.* 23 **Stem density*, the extent to which the total number of trees in a given forest approaches the total number which the index forest of the same age and composition contains. 1900 B. D. Jackson *Gloss. Bot. Terms* Suppl., *Stem-form. 1901 *Nature* 26 Sept. 545/1 Darwin was inclined to believe that articulate speech came at an early period in the history of the stem form of man. 1895 Comstock *Man. Insects* 159 From the winter egg there hatches, usually in the spring, an agamic female, which as she is the stock from which the summer generations spring, is often called the *stem-mother. 1900 *Proc. Assoc. Econ. Ent.* 68 (Cent. D. Suppl.) During the last week in April the stem mothers of an aphis..were found depositing young. 1930 *U. S. Catal.*, Czecho-Slovakian *stemware. 1932 *New Yorker* 9 Apr. 50/3 A new Fostoria design in stemware.

Stem, *v.*[4] Add: **3. a, b.** (Earlier examples.)
1724 H. Jones *Present St. Virginia* 40 It lies till they have Leisure or Occasion to *stem* it (that is pull the Leaves from the Stalk) or *strip* it (that is take out the great Fibres). 1797 Imlay *Descr. West. Terr. N. Amer.* (ed. 3) 248 This done, you stem the tobacco, or pull out the middle rib of the leaf. 1873 *Trans. Dept. Agric. Illinois* X. 61 The grapes were pressed without stemming.

4. To provide with a stem, as in the sewing on of buttons. Hence **Ste·mming** *vbl. sb.*[3]
1894 Jeanette E. Davis *Elem. Mod. Dressmaking* i. 50 Each button should be stemmed and the fastening-off done in the stemming.

Stemming, *vbl. sb.*[2] Add: **2.** (See quot.)
1924 *Ski Terms* in *Tourists' Winter Sports* No. 12/2 *Stemming.* Slowing down by making a point inward angle. Stemming turns are very useful on hard snow, though a variety of it, the Christiania, in which first the inner ski and then the outer are lifted, is often used in deep soft snow.

Stender (ste·ndəɹ). The name of Wilhelm P. Stender, a manufacturer of Leipzig, used attrib. to designate glass dishes used in microscopic work.
1901 Dorland *Med. Dict.* (ed. 2) *Stender-dish*, a dish of various forms and sizes used in preparing and staining histologic specimens. 1904 *Bot. Gaz.* Jan 12 (Cent. D. Suppl.), A simpler..method is to float a quantity of these spores on the surface of water half filling a stender dish.

Stengah (ste·ŋgä). Also **stingah.** [Malay, = half.] A small whisky and soda. Also, a person of mixed blood. (Cf. *Stinger 3.)
1903 W. Del Mar *Around World thr. Japan* vii. 64 A 'peg' of whiskey and tonic-water, followed by a *stengah* (the Malay word for half, usually pronounced *stinger*) or split drink. 1921 *Chambers's Jrnl.* 594/2 Come on, Crawford, and join me in a *stengah*. 1927 H. M. Tomlinson *Gallion's Reach* xxiv, A stengah..is a small whisky and soda. 1927 *Blackw. Mag.* June 726/1 At this establishment we learn all about gin-slings and 'Stingahs.'

Steno (ste·no). *U.S. colloq.* = *Stenog.
1928 L. North *Parasites* 34 Chapter Two. 'Stalls' and Stenos. *Ibid.* 89 That Whispering Slim guy seems to be falling for that steno' of his.

Steno-. Add: **Stenoba·thic** *a. Zool.*, (of an animal) capable of living in only a narrow range of depth of water. **Stenocho·ria** *Path.*, **Ste:nocompre·ssor,** etc. (see quots.).
1902 *Encycl. Brit.* XXXIII. 934/1 Similarly, in regard to depth, species have been classed as eurybathic and *stenobathic. 1848 Dunglison *Med. Lex.* (ed. 7), **Stenochoria*, ..contraction of the vagina. 1859 Mayne *Expos. Lex.*, *Stenocheria*..a diminution of the lachrymal passages. 1901 Dorland *Med. Dict.* (ed. 2), *Stenochoria*, stenosis, or narrowing. *Stenocompressor*, an instrument for closing the opening of Stenson's duct during dental operations. 1884 Knight *Dict. Mech.* Suppl., *Steno Compressor. 1859 Mayne *Expos. Lex.*, **Stenocoriasis*,..contraction of the pupil. *Ibid.*, **Stenothorax*,..one disposed to phthisis, having a strait, short chest. 1901 Dorland *Med. Dict.* (ed. 2), *Stenothorax*, abnormal narrowness of the chest.

Stenog (stenǫ·g). *U.S. colloq.* Short for Stenographer. Hence **Ste·nog** *v.*, to write in shorthand.
1906 'O. Henry' *Four Million* xiv. (1916) 130 Not being able to stenog, she could not enter that bright galaxy of office talent. 1919 Mencken *Amer. Lang.* 160 Some [clipped forms] linger on the edge of vulgarity:..*stenog* for *stenographer*. 1922 E. Wallace *Valley of Ghosts* xxix, It will look better if I put it into police-English than if you dig up the hotel stenog.

Stensen (ste·nsən). Also erron. -on. The name of the Danish anatomist Niels Stensen (1638–86), used in the genitive to designate certain organs and operations, as **Stensen's duct** = Stenonian *duct*; **Stensen's experiment, foramen** (see quots.).
1877 *Encycl. Brit.* VII. 222/2 The excretory duct of the gland, called Stenson's duct, passes forwards superficial to the masseter muscle. 1890 Billings *Med. Dict.*, *Stenson's experiment*, tying abdominal aorta of a dog above renal arteries, thus producing, by malnutrition, rigidity of muscles of posterior extremities, disappearing when the ligature is removed. 1901 *Proc. Zool. Soc.* I. i. 117 Hyrtl's figure of the relations between Stensen's duct and the buccal gland is misleading. 1901 Dorland *Med. Dict.* (ed. 2) s.v. *Foramen*, *Stenson's foramen*, the two foramina behind the outer incisor teeth: each transmits an artery.

Stentorphone (ste·ntǫ:əfōun). [f. Stentor[2] + *-phone.] An electrical device for reproducing sounds, esp. the human voice, with increased intensity.
1921 *Punch* 2 Feb. 86/1 At Oxford Circus I have known What townsmen call the 'stentorphone'. 1922 *Weekly Dispatch* 12 Nov. 9 A stentorphone is being used to give the results in one restaurant. 1925 G. W. Deeping *Three Rooms* xvi. § 1 An indefatigable concierge was functioning like a stentaphone [*sic*] that has been fitted with some sort of soft pedal. 1925 — *Sorrell & Son* xiii. § 3 To erect a huge stentophone [*sic*] somewhere, and set it shouting. 1927 *Dancing Times* June 357/1 *Al fresco* dancing under cover is provided, with stentorphone music.

Step, *sb.* Add: **12.** *Mind the step*, be careful not to trip over a step which is unexpectedly or obscurely situated: frequently used as a jocular or ironical valediction to a visitor. *colloq.*
1881 [see Mind *v.* 10 b].

f. In the Eton game of fives, the shallow step which divides the court into an inner and outer part.
1890 A. C. Ainger *Fives* (Badm.) 463 The vertical face of the 'step' does not reckon as part of the floor of the court. 1897 *Encycl. Sport* I. 398/2 From this ancient court, too, were derived the step and the hole which, with the 'pepper-box', have given the Eton game its special character.

15. c. *Aeronautics.* (See quot. 1915.)
1913 *Captain* Sept. 1075/1 The 'stepped' float..with one or more steps in the bottom, is becoming popular. 1915 Grahame-White & Harper *Aeroplane* 171 In the floats of the Avro will be noticed a notch, or cut-away section, which occurs at about the centre of the float upon its lower side. This is called the 'step', and is to help the float to lift from the water. 1922 *Encycl. Brit.* XXX. 52/1 The main 'step' under the centre of gravity was proved necessary, but the area of the planing surfaces forward of less importance.

18. step-chair, (*a*) a form of railway chair (Chair *sb.*[1] 12 b); (*b*) a chair which can be converted into a short step-ladder; **step-collar,** a collar with a V-shaped opening at the junction of the collar and lapel; **step-gable,** a gable with the sloping edge shaped like a series of steps, a corbie-gable; **step-pattern,** an ornamental pattern resembling the bit of a stepped key; **step-printer** (see quot.); **step-rail,** a tramway-rail with raised outside tread for flanged wheels; **step-roll collar,** *Tailoring*, a rolled step-collar (cf. Roll-collar).
1871 Huntington *Road-Master's Assistant* 96 In laying repaired iron, what are known as *step-chairs should be used. 1895 *Army & Navy Co-op. Soc. Price List* 15 Sept. 229/1 Folding Step Chairs, 4 Step. 1895 J. P. Thornton *Sectional Syst. Cutting* 104 Step collar vest. 1931 *Burberry's Catal.*, The Burberry (Step-Collar). 1921 *Glasgow Herald* 8 Jan. 6 It is a whitewashed house, with *step-gables. 1908 *Hastings's Encycl. Relig. & Ethics* I. 841/2 Geometrical ornament, consisting in: (*a*) *step- and key-patterns, (*b*) interlacing- or knot-work, and (*c*) spirals. *Ibid.* 842/1 'Step' patterns occur in the *cloisonné* settings of Teutonic jewels. 1930 *Sel. Gloss. Motion Pict. Techn.* (Acad. Techn. Bureau Hollywood), **Step printer*, machine which prints a positive, a frame at a time. 1888 *Encycl. Brit.* XXIII. 506/1 The '*step rail'.. consisting of a flat surface..and a raised tread on the outer side. 1881 *Record of Fashion* 27 July 178/2 *Step roll is the most suitable style for most of the goods now fashionable. 1901 *Tailoring* (ed. P. N. Hasluck) 99 Step-roll collar vest.

Step, *v.* Add:
3. e. *To step lively*: to hurry up. orig. *U.S. slang.*
1891 *Outing* (U.S.) Nov. 147/2 There was the usual rush; the guard's admonition to 'step lively'. 1906 Mary E. Wilkins Freeman *By Light of Soul* 41 When she was told to step lively on the trolley-cars.

15. Step on —. b. *To step on the gas* or *juice*: see *Gas *sb.*[2], *Juice *sb.* 4 c. Hence *To step on it*: to hurry. *slang.*
1930 F. L. Packard *Jimmie Dale & Blue Envelope Murder* xxii, Then for heaven's sake step on it, old man!

25. Step off. d. *intr.* To die. *slang.*
1926 E. Wallace *Man from Morocco* iii, There will only be the bit of money I have when I—er—step off.

26. Step out. e. To die. *U.S.*
1844 *Yale Lit. Mag.* IX. 381 Of the other pieces..some will be found in the present number,..and the remainder have '*stept out*'. 1845 *Knickerbocker Mag.* XXV. 91 No home to eat a dinner at; no friends..; they've all stepped out, or forgotten us. 1851 T. A. Burke *Polly Peabl. Wedding* 177 Ay, dead!—stepped out!—d-d-dead as Tecumseh! 1902 A. D. McFaul *Ike Glidden* xxx. 277 He is the cause of my ruin. Yes, that is why he stepped out when he did.

28. Step up. g. *transf.* To raise the status or standard of (as by 'steps' or degrees). *U.S.*
1930 *Glasgow Herald* 8 July 7 They would suggest that this increase..should be 'stepped up' over a period of years. 1932 *Amer. Speech* Oct. Advt. p. 4 of Cover, Can you 'step-up' education to meet the new requirements of society?

Stephanid (ste·fănid), *a.* and *sb.* [ad. mod.L. *Stephanidæ*: see -id[3].] Of or pertaining to, a member of, the *Stephanidæ*, a family of pupivorous hymenoptera. So **Ste·phanoid** *a.*
1895 Comstock *Man. Insects* Suppl. 624 Family Stephanidæ. The Stephanids.

Step-in. [f. phr. *to step in*: see Step *v.* 24.] A garment which one may put on by stepping into it and pulling it up over the body without the help of fastenings. Also *attrib.*, designating this type of garment.
1923 *Weekly Dispatch* 18 Feb. 12 Step-in Cami-Knickers. 1923 *Daily Mail* 30 May 1 Princess slips..in the popular 'step-in' style. 1928 *Sunday Dispatch* 15 July 16 The same *couturière* is all for 'step ins' for swimmers. 1929 E. L. Rice *Street Scene* ii. 118 Mae, about to slip out of her step-in, sees him.

Stepney (ste·pni). [Said to be from the name *Stepney* in Stepney-street, Llanelly, the place of manufacture.] A spare wheel with ready inflated tyre but no spokes, carried by motorists.
1907 *Westm. Gaz.* 3 Dec. 4/3 The popularity of the Stepney Wheel has never been more clearly demonstrated than at the Olympia Show. 1908 *Autocar Handbk.* (ed. 2) 113 The Stepney spare wheel. 1914 *Motor Cycle* 19 Mar. 10 Insure yourself now against punctures by equipping your car with a Stepney. 1925 *Chambers's Jrnl.* 148/2 The Stepney was fixed in ten minutes.
fig. 1926 E. Sutton tr. *A. Londres' Road to Buenos Ayres* ii. 18, I told her I had a woman already in Buenos Ayres, that she could only be my little sweetheart, as we say, or my 'stepney', if you like that better. 1929 E. Linklater *Poet's Pub* xxvi, Redemption being carried as a kind of stepney on the best of all possible worlds.

Stepping, *vbl. sb.* Add: **2. d.** The arrangement of the steps of a key (cf. Step *sb.* 15).
1911 *Chambers's Jrnl.* 529/1 The stepping of the key.. enables great variations to be secured.

Stereo-. Add: **Ste:reofluoro·scopy,** stereoscopic fluoroscopy; hence **Ste:reofluorosco·pic** *a.*, **Ste:reognosis,** **Ste:reogonio·meter, Ste:reo-photogra·mmetry** (see quots.). **Ste:reota·xis** = Thigmotaxis; so **Ste:reota·xic** *a.*
1928 F. H. Humphris in *Lancet* 3 Mar. 412/2 A note on the latest development in *stereofluoroscopic work. *Ibid.*, The law governing *stereofluoroscopy has not been fully recognised. The law stated simply is that angles of vision which the X rays make with the body should be identical with those made by the vision of the observer of the body... Early in the days of X rays the tubes were of a size which rendered stereofluoroscopy impossible. 1901 Dorland *Med. Dict.* (ed. 2), **Stereognosis*..1. The faculty of recognizing the nature of objects by handling them. 2. Perception by the senses of the solidity of objects. 1919 S. Paget *Sir V. Horsley* 194. 1928 *Times* 8 Sept. 15/7 The *stereogoniometer, an instrument for deducing reliable mapping data from aerial photographs. 1926 *Encycl. Brit.* Suppl. III. 697/2 Stereo-photo surveying, sometimes called *stereo-photogrammetry. 1919 S. Paget *Sir V. Horsley* 189 R. H. Clarke ..also devised a *stereotaxic apparatus, probably the most complex of all the mathematical instruments of physiology.

Sternutator (stɜ̄·rnĭutə^i tǫɹ). [Agent-n. f. L. *sternutāre*: see Sternutation.] A sternutatory.
1929 *Encycl. Brit.* V. 351 Sensory Irritants of Eyes, Nose and Chest (Sternutators).

Sterol (ste·rǫl). *Biol. Chem.* The ending of *Cholesterol, *Ergosterol, etc., used as a separate word to denote one of a group of allied complex solid alcohols of importance in the synthesis of vitamins.
1913 *Biochemical Jrnl.* VII. 617 It is now proposed to limit the terms zoo- and phyto-sterol to sterols which are found as tissue constituents of animals and plants respectively. 1915 *Jrnl. Chem. Soc.* CVIII. ii. 290 The substance left after the removal of the sterols from the unsaponifiable portion of the fats has also been investigated. 1926 *Rep. Med. Research Council* 15 The vitamin in which cod-liver oil is especially rich..is actually formed when cholesterol and certain other sterols are exposed to rays of ultra violet light.

Stetefeldt (ste·tafelt). The name of an American mining engineer, Charles A. Stetefeldt, used in the genitive to designate a type of shaft furnace invented by him (see quot.)
1879 *Encycl. Brit.* IX. 845/2 Stetefeld's furnace, used for the conversion of sulphuretted silver ores into chlorides.. in the silver mines of the western States of America.

Stethal (ste·þæl). *Chem.* [f. the first syllable of Stearic *a.* + Ethal.] = *Stethylic *alcohol*.
1868 Watts *Dict. Chem.* V. 431 Stearic acid [formed] from stethal.

Stethylic (steþi·lik), *a. Chem.* [f. prec. + -yl + -ic.] *Stethylic alcohol*, an octadecylic alcohol found as a stearate in spermaceti.
1868 Watts *Dict. Chem.* V. 430 Stethal, or Stethylic alcohol, $C^{18}H^{38}O = C^{18}H^{37}.H.O$. The alcohol of the series $C^nH^{2n+2}O$, corresponding to stearic acid.

Stetson (ste·tsən). [f. the maker's name.] A slouch hat worn by Anzac soldiers. Also *Stetson hat*.
1911 H. Quick *Yellowstone Nights* xi. 271 The Professor was evidently pleased when his name came from the Stetson for the second time. 1924 *Westm. Gaz.* 26 Aug., The modern coster wants to wear a Stetson hat. 1925 *Chambers's Jrnl.* 230/2 Dick galloped forward and touched his 'Stetson'. 1925 *Literary Digest* 27 June 46/2 Stray locks of hair streaming back under a rakish Stetson.

Stevensonian (stīvənsōu·niăn), *a.* and *sb.* [f. the name of Robert Louis *Stevenson* (1850–94), author + -ian.] **a.** *adj.* Of, pertaining to, or characteristic of the spirit or style of R. L. Stevenson. **b.** *sb.* An admirer of R. L. Stevenson or of his writings.
1900 *Fortn. Rev.* Jan. 97 But he did not underrate *Kidnapped* as a whole. 'By far the most human of my labours hitherto,' is his verdict, anticipating that of all the true Stevensonians. 1913 *Smart Set* No. 3. 45/1 That polished peasant style that passes for Stevensonian English in 'culture' clubs. 1928 *Observer* 22 Jan. 15/1 Bouvet Island is a Stevensonian treasure island, bare, uninhabited, bleak. 1929 W. J. Locke *Ancestor Jorico* iii. 39 If you like to start out as a romantic writer, here's something Stevensonian to your hand.

Stew, *v.* **2. b.** Add: Also (of an infusion of tea, etc.), to 'stand' on the leaves, etc.
1906 *Rep. Brit. Assoc.* 783 There is found in tea and coffee an astringent substance which gives the well-known bitter taste to the infusions when they are allowed to 'stew'.

Stewing, *vbl. sb.* **b.** Add: **stewing-meat,** meat which is suitable for stewing.

Stibianite (sti·biănəit). *Min.* [f. Stibium + -an + -ite[1].] A hydrated pentoxide of antimony occurring in Australia.
1878 E. Goldsmith in *Proc. Acad. Nat. Science* 154 Stibianite, a new mineral...The mineral is massive, having the general aspect of a piece of rough feldspar.

Stibio-. Add: **Sti:biodomey·kite,** an arsenide of copper containing a small proportion of antimony. **Sti:biota·ntalite,** a rare mineral occurring in Australia and California, containing tantalum, columbium, and antimony.
1900 G. A. Koenig in *Amer. Jrnl. Sci.* Ser. iv. X. 445 *Stibio-domeykite. With this name I propose to designate the domeykite from the Mohawk mine, Keweenaw Co. 1903 *Min. Mag.* XIII. 377 Stibio-domeykite...Massive domeykite containing a small amount of antimony. 1893 G. A. Goyder in *Jrnl. Chem. Soc.* LXIII. 1076 *Stibiotantalite. A New Mineral. 1901 *Ibid.* LXXX. ii. 454 The occurrence of native tin is noted in the stanniferous gravels at Greenbushes, and further information is given of stibiotantalite from the same locality.

Sticharion (stikeə·riŏn). *Eccl.* Pl. **-ia.** Also **stoicharion.** [Gr. στιχάριον, f. στίχος line, band.] In the Greek Church, a vestment corresponding to the alb of the Western Church.
1772 J. G. King *Rites Gr. Ch.* 277 The new ordained.. kisses the cross upon the stoicharion. 1868 W. B. Marriott *Vest. Christianum* 169 note, The Sticharion as being white set forth τὸ φωτοειδὲς Ἰησοῦ. 1870 *Holy Eastern Church* 61 The Sticharion used to be of linen, now it is made of silk or velvet. 1880 Smith & Cheetham *Dict. Chr. Antiq.* 1933/2 It is possible..that the *sticharion* may have received its name from the bands or lines [στίχοι] upon it. *Ibid.* 1934/1 In Lent..purple *sticharia* are worn.

Sticheron (stiki·rǫn). *Eccl.* Pl. **-a.** Also **stoicheron.** [Gr. στιχηρόν (sc. τροπάριον), f. στιχηρός in rows, in verse, f. στίχος line, verse.] = Troparion.
1862 J. M. Neale *Hymns Eastern Ch.* 59 The following Stichera, which are generally..attributed to S. John Damascene. 1880 *Encycl. Brit.* XII. 580/1 A hymn in irregular 'stichera' or stanzas.

Stick, *sb.*[1] Add: **4. f.** *Stick and groove*, a primitive method of producing fire by friction.
1865 Tylor *Early Hist. Man.* ix. 236 One of the simplest machines for producing fire is that which may be called the 'stick-and-groove'. A blunt-pointed stick is run along a groove of its own making in a piece of wood lying on the ground.

10. e. Also *pl.* A drummer. *slang.*
1909 Ware *Passing English*. 1926 [see *Snare *sb.* 3 b].

f. The controlling lever of an aeroplane: a joy-stick.
1914 Rosher *In R.N.A.S.* (1916) 13 Mr. Stutt, our instructor..controls the engine switch and covers your hand on the stick. 1929 B. Hall & J. J. Niles *One Man's War* 166 We wanted a ship that would dive as long as one was willing to hold the 'stick' forward. 1931 *Times* 19 Feb. 17/3 Instead of flattening out he pushed the stick (control) forward to approach nearer to the water.

12. *Crooked stick* (earlier U.S. example).
1834 S. Smith *Major Downing* (Bartlett 1859) The widow R— must have been dreadfully put to it for a husband, to take up with such a crooked stick as Elder B—.

16. stick-back chair = *Windsor chair* (b); **stick-bomb** (see quot. 1925); **stick-dice game,** a gambling game played by the North American Indians, in which sticks bearing different marks are tossed up; **stick grenade** (see quot.); **stick legs,** legs consisting of plain rods, as those of a Windsor chair.
1928 *Daily Express* 14 Dec. 4 'Stick-back chairs..are worth twenty to twenty-five shillings apiece in London. 1916 in Gamble *Story N. Sea Air Station* xiii. (1928) 212 The silent firing of projectiles varying in size from the Mills grenade to the 250-lb *stick bomb. 1925 E. Fraser & Gibbons *Soldier & Sailor Words*, *Stick-bomb*, a type of trench-mortar bomb attached to a hollow steel rod which passed down the bore of the projectile. 1930 Whyte & Atteridge *Hist. Queen's Bays* 302 The crash of exploding stick-bombs. 1903 S. Culin in *Amer. Anthrop.* Jan.–Mar. 60 A comparative study of the *stick-dice game. 1918 Farrow *Dict. Mil. Terms*, **Stick Grenade*, a grenade attached to a stick and thrown over short distances like a dart. 1912 A. Hayden *Chats Cottage & Farmhouse Furniture* 246 The *Stick Legs without Stretcher. Obviously this is the earliest type...[A chair] with a plain seat, but still having the stick legs set at an angle towards the centre of the chair.

Stick, *v.*[1] Add: **6. e.** *Cards.* To refuse to make a declaration.
1931 Tilsley *Other Ranks* 147 A little group in the centre of the room sprawled on their blankets playing pontoon. 'I'll stick!' 'Twist one!' 'Busted!' 1932 [see *Go *v.* 36 c].

7. c. With a thing as object.
1920 W. J. Locke *House of Baltazar* xxiii, She would go mad, cut off from every opportunity of hearing instant developments of this nerve-racking situation. She couldn't stick it. 1922 A. S. M. Hutchinson *This Freedom* iv. iii, I couldn't stick the place. *Ibid.*, 'Oh, Huggo, it was the name we loved you by.' 'Well, I can't stick it. My name's Hugh.' 1928 *Daily Tel.* 27 Mar. 9/1, I resigned...because I could stick the chief's bullying no longer. 1929 Vachell *Virgin* iv. 80 June wondered if she could 'stick' London. She had to stick it, so why not make the best of it?

32. Stick out. c. Also *trans.*
1916 Lo. E. W. Hamilton *First 7 Div.* 259 By this method, companies, and sometimes whole battalions, which had stuck out the shell-fire, were overwhelmed and annihilated.

e. (Example with personal obj.)
1916 Bennett *Lion's Share* vii. 53, I knew he was going to be ill when I left him in the cabin, but he stuck me out he wasn't.

34. Stick up. k. (U.S. examples.)
1904 'O. Henry' *Cabbages & Kings* xvii. 302, I couldn't take it with me, not knowing but what the monkeys might stick me up. *a* 1909 — *Roads of Destiny* ix. 158 Latch Ear Rodgers was to stick up the station agent. 1926 J. Black *You Can't Win* vii. 81 He may not miss that junk till he goes to close up... Anyway we'll sure be stuck up and frisked at Evanston.

n. To cook meat by spitting it and setting it to roast. *Austral.*
1852 Mrs. L. A. Meredith *My Home Tasmania* iv. I. 55 To men that are hungry, stuck-up kangaroo and bacon are very good eating.

35. stick-at-it *colloq.*, a plodding conscientious person; **stick-jaw,** (*b*) a variety of coco-nut toffee; also *gen.* any kind of sticky toffee; **stick-pin** *U.S.*, any (ornamental) pin that is merely stuck in (as distinguished from a safety-pin), esp. a tie-pin; hence **stick-pinned** *ppl. a.*; **stick-to-it-ive** *a. U.S.*, persistent, indomitable; hence **stick-to-it-iveness.**
1909 H. G. Wells *Tono-Bungay* ii. ii. § 1 I'm a boiler-over, not a simmering 'stick-at-it. 1894 R. Wells *Toffy & Sweets* 71 'Stick-jaw. 1894 E. Skuse *Compl. Confectioner* 26 Coconut toffee, or Stickjaw. 1903 *N. Y. Sun* 21 Nov. 2 Dr. Amador presented to the President a gold *stickpin containing the flag of the new republic. 1919 *Detective Story Mag.* 25 Nov. 45, I..ran my stickpin through the cork, making a small vent for the air to filter through. 1928 'S. S. Van Dine' *Greene Murder Case* v, I was only looking for that old emerald stick-pin you borrowed and never returned. 1909 'O. Henry' *Options* (1916) 77 They were..pearl *stick-pinned like other young New Yorkers. 1867 in Eliz. B. Custer *Tenting on Plains* xvi. (1889) 520 With the *stick-to-it-iveness of a fox-hound when once on a trail. 1887 C. B. George *40 Years on Rail* xi. 231 They devote their quick wit and their stick-to-ativeness to 'sponging' for a living. 1905 (*Amer.*) *Dialect Notes* III. 21 *Stick-to-it-iveness*, perseverance. 1922 J. A. Dunn *Man Trap* xiv, And there must have been some wonderful strain of inherited stick-to-it-iveness in him for him to have pulled through. 1928 *Daily Express* 15 May 1/4 Success ..is mostly hard work. It's work and it's stick-to-it-iveness. You've got to keep at it all the time.

c. stick-on *a.*, gummed ready for sticking.
1935 J. W. Bigger *Handbk. Bacteriol.* 60 Stick-on labels may be used, but these must never be licked in a bacteriological laboratory.

Stickability (sti:kăbi·lĭti). *colloq.* [f. *stickable + -ity.] Capacity for endurance.
1922 *Chambers's Jrnl.* 634/2 The foreigner has supplanted the middle and lower class Chilian in nearly every branch of industry in which the quality best described as 'stickability' is required. 1905 *British Weekly* 28 May 193/2 To be able to take rebuffs happily and still go on requires, to use a coined word, 'stickability'.

Stick-up, *a.* and *sb.* **B.** *sb.* Add: **c.** A thief armed with a revolver who orders his victims to put their hands up. Also, a job performed by this type of criminal; a hold-up. Also *attrib. U.S.*
1905 *N. Y. Times* 2 Jan. (Cent. D. Suppl.) The man..is declared to be a typical 'yeggman of the stick-up' class... The 'stick-up' is always a powerful man, whose duties are to intimidate intruders and kill them, if necessary, while the others are at work on a safe. 1927 *Scribner's Mag.* Feb. 180/1 The depredations of..safe-blowers, stick-up men, murderers. 1930 E. V. Knox in *Punch* 26 Feb. 236/1 He was reminded..that he had worked on the Babylon stick-up, and consented to come clean. 1930 *Daily News* (N.Y.) 6 Nov. 1 She foiled stickup.

Sticky, *a.*[2] Add: **1.** Also, covered or smeared with adhesive or 'tacky' foreign matter.
1870 [in Dict.].

4. Unpleasant, extremely disagreeable. *slang.*
1915 D. O. Barnett *Lett.* 86 We had rather a sticky time in the trenches..as the enemy's artillery and snipers showed 'a certain liveliness'. 1915 Rosher *In R.N.A.S.* (1916) 40, I wish we could get out to the front...I would much rather come to a sticky end out there than here. 1930 'Sapper' *Finger of Fate*, etc. 17 It seems to me you have the alternative of a sticky five minutes with three savage Alsatians.

5. *Comb.*: **sticky-back,** a small photograph with a gummed back; **sticky dog** *colloq.*, a sticky wicket.
1928 *Weekly Dispatch* 20 May 4/2 She..brought out a *sticky-back of a gentleman in his shirt-sleeves. 1925 D. J. Knight in *Country Life* 18 July 95/1 If you..get a chance

of bowling on one of these '*sticky dogs', as we call them. 1928 *Daily Express* 9 July 17/1 Should he bat first or should he put Somerset in and hope for a 'sticky dog' wicket?

Stictaurine (sti·ktǭrin). *Chem.* [f. mod.L. *Sticta aurata*: see -IN ¹.] A golden-coloured compound, $C_{36}H_{22}O_9$, contained in various lichens, esp. in *Sticta aurata*.

1899 *Jrnl. Chem. Soc.* LXXVI. I. 716 Stictaurin, the orange-red compound obtained from *Sticta aurata*. 1921 ANNIE L. SMITH *Lichens* 223 Stictaurin.

Stictic (sti·ktik), *a.*² *Chem.* [f. mod.L. *Sticta* + -IC.] Of or pertaining to *Sticta*, a genus of lichens. *Stictic acid*, an acid resembling cetraric acid in composition and properties, derived from *Sticta pulmonacea*. Hence **Sti·ctate**, a salt of stictic acid.

1868 WATTS *Dict. Chem.* V. 431 According to Knop and Schneedermann..the acid of *Sticta pulmonacea*, which they call stictic acid, is distinct from cetraric acid. *Ibid.*, Stictate of potassium is less soluble than the cetrarate.

Stiff, *a.*, *sb.*, and *adv.* Add: **A.** *adj.* **2. e.** orig. *Racing slang.* Said of a horse which is certain either not to run or, if it runs, not to win: chiefly in *stiff 'un* (cf. *CORPSE 2 f, *STUMER 2). Also, of a horse, athlete, etc.: Dead certain to win.

1871 'HAWK'S-EYE' *Turf Notes* 11 Most assuredly it is the bookmakers that profit by the 'safe uns', or 'stiff uns', as.. horses that have no chance of winning are called. *a* 1889 in Barrère & Leland *Dict. Slang* s.v., I backed a stiff 'un with it. 1897 in Farmer & Henley *Slang* s.v., Do not invest money Until you read The Rialto. Never on stiff 'uns, wrong 'uns, or dead 'uns. 1903 *Ibid.*, Grand Flaneur is stiff for any race for which he may enter. 1912 *Punch* 21 Aug. 168/3 He ought to have this event absolutely stiff at the next Olympic Games.

11. In predicative use. *To bore* (a person) *stiff*: to be excessively boring to, to bore to extinction. *To scare stiff*: to give a thorough fright to.

1905 REX BEACH *Pardners* i. (1912) 32 He was scared stiff to hear that Morrow was in town. 1928 W. J. LOCKE *Rough Road* ix, I think I ought to tell you that you're boring Durdlebury stiff. 1921 R. D. PAINE *Comr. Rolling Ocean* ix. 150 When that crazy fireman broke loose just now, I was scared perfectly stiff. 1928 F. B. YOUNG *My Bro. Jonathan* II. v. 284 She bores everybody she meets stiff with talking about him.

19. b. *Finance.* = TIGHT *a.* 10 c.

1845 *Punch* 11 Oct. 164/2 Money's stiff they say. 1912 *Q. Rev.* July 103 Money is in such keen demand all the world over that the rates tend to become high, whereupon it is called 'stiff' or 'tight'.

20. d. *stiff-jointedness* (fig.).

1921 *Public Opinion* 27 May 493/3 Half the stern, immutable principles that are so much admired, are mere stiff-jointedness. 1931 *Times Review of Year 1930* 1 Jan. p. i/1 The stiffjointedness of all too many of our national habits.

B. *sb.* **2. b.** Money. *slang.*

1930 BELLOC *New Cautionary Tales* 58 He wrang his hands, exclaiming, 'If I only had a bit of Stiff How different would be my life!'

3. b. *Racing.* = *CORPSE 2 f. (Cf. *STIFF *a.* 2 e.)

a 1889 *St. Louis Republican* (Barrère & L.) 'What do they mean by a stiff in the race?' 'That means generally a horse that on public form should win the race, and that either the jockey, trainer, or horse has been 'fixed' so that he will not win.'

4. b. An unskilled dock-labourer. *slang.*

1915 *Truth* 20 Jan. 90/2 A hopeless shortage of the best labour on the one hand, and an unusual proportion of 'stiffs' on the other.

c. (Freq., *big stiff*). A hopeless or incorrigible person. orig. *U.S.*

1896 G. ADE *Artie* ii. 17 There I set like a big stiff for five hours. *Ibid.* iv. 36, I do n't come in here to give coin to no such stiffs as you. 1905 D. G. PHILLIPS *Plum Tree* xvii. 218 This the more because they regarded Simpson as a 'stuff' and a 'stiff'. 1911 R. D. SAUNDERS *Col. Todhunter* ix. 138 Dere won't be enough left of youse in a minit for your frien's to bury, you damned stiff! 1916 H. L. WILSON *Somewhere in Red Gap* vi. 268 It's that big stiff Len Wales. 1925 E. FRASER & GIBBONS *Soldier & Sailor Words*, *Stiff*, an incorrigible or worthless fellow. An unlucky man: one always in trouble. 1930 *Punch* 26 Feb. 228/2 He said 'You big stiff!' in a very loud voice and went.

Stiffener. Add: **2.** A cigarette card.

1926 *Chambers's Jrnl.* 10 July 497/2 'Stiffener', the name by which the cigarette-card has always been, and still is, known in the trade.

3. A reviving drink. *slang.*

1928 D. L. SAYERS *Bellona Club* ii, Dick Challoner..took the gasping Fentiman away into the deserted library for a stiffener.

Stigmarian, *a.* Add: *sb.* A fossil plant of the genus *Stigmaria*.

1930 *Brit. Museum Return* 137 A plaster cast of the Stigmarian, *Dictyophloios minor*.

Still, *a.* and *sb.*² Add: **A.** *adj.* **1. d.** Used also of other beverages, as *still lemonade*.

e. *Bridge.* Designating the pack not in use in any particular round.

1927 in E. V. Shepard *Corr. Contract Bridge* (1930) 245 The next dealer deals in the regular way with the still pack. 1929 WORK *Compl. Contract Bridge* 188 The hand is abandoned and the next dealer deals the still pack.

B. *sb.*² **5.** An ordinary photograph, as distinguished from a motion picture. Also *attrib.*, as *still-man, photograph, photographer, photography*.

1918 E. V. LUCAS *'Twixt Eagle & Dove* 61 A 'still' (as it is called in the movie world—meaning a photograph in the ordinary sense of the term). 1925 B. BEETHAM in E. F. Norton *Fight for Everest, 1924* 324 His time was so fully taken up with cinema work that most of the still photography had to be done by other members of the party. 1928 *Manch. Guardian Weekly* 26 Oct. 335/1 There are four motion picture newsreel camera-men, and four 'still' photographers. 1929 *Penrose's Annual* XXXI. 41 In cases where small apertures are used, as in the reproduction of 'stills'. 1930 *New Statesman* 27 Dec. 362/1 The plates with which his book is packed are as striking as the stills of expert shots from a film.

Still, *adv.* **3. e.** Add: *still and all* (U.S.).

1928 F. N. HART *Bellamy Trial* iv. 104 Still and all, I believe that he was there precisely when he said he was.

Still-birth and **Still-born** are also applied to cases of suspended animation: see quots.

1880 *Brit. Med. Jrnl.* 9 Oct. 596/2 Stillbirth—Resuscitation after two hours and five minutes. 1890 BILLINGS *Med. Dict.*, *Stillborn*, term used vaguely to mean either born dead, or born with so little vitality as to die a few moments after birth. 1913 R. W. JOHNSTONE *Midwifery* 397 *Asphyxia Neonatorum*, Still Birth. In this condition the infant is born in a state of suspended animation..'Still birth' is therefore not the same thing as the child's being born dead, although death may supervene if prompt treatment is not applied. 1918 R. M. BARCLAY *Midwifery* 146 Apnœa neonatorum, or still-birth, occurs when respiration is delayed.

Still-house. (Modern U.S. examples.)

1834 A. PIKE *Sketches* 24 Our party reached the still house in the valley. 1865 *Atlantic Monthly* XV. 395 A low brick building called the still-house. 1884 'C. E. CRADDOCK' *In Tenn. Mts.* ii. 118 Josiah Tait had put his troubles in to soak at the still-house.

Still-hunt, -hunting. *U.S.* (Recent examples.)

1881 *Harper's Mag.* Oct. 690/2 That season of the year which intervenes between jack-hunting and still-hunting. 1903 *N.Y. Sun* 15 Nov., The typical titled foreigner supposed to be on a still hunt for the American heiress. 1916 'B. M. BOWER' *Phantom Herd* ii. 32 I'm out on a still hunt for some real boys. 1923 J. H. COOK *Fifty Yrs. on Old Frontier* 26, I found times that I could slip out of camp for a little still-hunting.

Still water. 2. (U.S. examples.)

1832 W. D. WILLIAMSON *Hist. Maine* I. 66 The Metawamkeag..has frequent falls and intervening still-waters. 1907 *N.Y. Evening Post* (semi-weekly ed.) 22 Apr. 6 The ice descends the stream. Now and then it stops, usually at the head of a stillwater.

Stimulus. Add: **3. c.** *Psychology.* A process of stimulation or excitement which affects the area of a sense-organ (*external stimulus*), or which originates within a sense-organ (*internal stimulus*). Also *attrib.*, as *stimulus-complex, -pattern, -threshold, -unit, -word*.

1894 CREIGHTON & TITCHENER tr. *Wundt's Human & Anim. Psychol.* 16 The processes of motion which, by their operation upon our senses, give rise to sensations, we commonly denominate *stimuli*, or more particularly *sense-stimuli*. .. Thus we regard the sound-waves of the air or the light-waves set up in surrounding space as stimuli, corresponding to our sensations of sound and light. In the same way, those motion-processes which are aroused, by the agency of such external stimuli, in our sense-organs and in the brain, may also be regarded as processes of stimulation or as constituents of the entire stimulation-process. For the sake of clearness, we will call these last *internal* stimuli. *Ibid.* 37 The way to determine this is obviously to set out, not from a definite stimulus-unit, but from the unit of sensation. 1897 C. H. JUDD tr. *Wundt's Outl. Psychol.* 254 The stimulus from which the resulting psychical process, for example, a sensation, can be just apperceived, is called the *stimulus-threshold*. 1920 T. P. NUNN *Educ.* 44 In this case ..it is impossible to foresee what kind of 'reaction' the 'stimulus-word' will provoke. 1924 R. M. OGDEN tr. *Koffka's Growth of Mind* 87 Fine differences in the stimulus-complex may lead to opposite reactions. *Ibid.* 137 The phenomenon corresponding to a given stimulus-pattern. 1924 JOAN RIVIERE tr. *Freud's Coll. Papers* II. 14 The very variable relation of the stimulus-word to the reaction-word.

Sting, *v.*¹ Add: **2. e.** *pass.* To be heavily charged, or involved in expense or loss of money. Less commonly *actively*, to involve in heavy expense or loss of money. *slang* (orig. *U.S.*).

1903 *Kansas City Daily Star* 21 Apr. (Cent. D. Suppl.), An undergraduate is no longer 'stuck' for a dinner, a seat at a play, a railroad ticket; he is 'stung'. 1911 W. J. LOCKE *Glory of Clementina Wing* xxi, They were left, they were done, they were stung—they were all things that slang has invented to describe the position of men deceived by those in whom they trusted. 1923 C. J. CUTCLIFFE HYNE in *Daily Mail* 22 Jan. 8 [He] told me..he stood to lose some enormous number of millions of marks if Germany went *phut*... He seemed hurt when I said I was very glad if he got stung for trading with the enemy. 1925 E. FRASER & GIBBONS *Soldier & Sailor Words* s.v., He stung me for one shilling. 1928 S. VINES *Humours Unreconciled* xix. 248 It was better to pay than to be suddenly deserted by the whole staff, so..Ditchling had to consent to be 'stung'. 1928 L. NORTH *Parasites* 69 She stung us on salary—eight hundred a week. 1929 MAZO DE LA ROCHE *Whiteoaks* v. 78, I was talking the other day to a young fellow who had paid a fancy price for one [*sc.* a horse]... But he'd got badly stung.

Stinger³ (sti·ŋəɹ). Corruption of *STENGAH.

1901 *Scribner's Mag.* Jan. 106 Two 'stingers' were brought... A 'stinger'..is a noggin of Scotch whiskey, enlivened by much or little, according to individual taste, of the local buzz-water. 1903 [see *STENGAH]. 1916 H. L. WILSON *Somewhere in Red Gap* ix. 376, I found 'em in the palm grill, or whatever it's called, drinking stingers.

Stingo. Add: **b.** *fig.* Vigour, energy, vim. *To give* (a person) *stingo*: to give it him hot.

1885 *Punch* 22 Aug. 86/3 It's rare fun, by Jingo! I give 'em hot stingo. 1927 *Daily Tel.* 19 July 15 To keep in good trim and add stingo to your efforts in sport. 1927 GALSWORTHY A. A. *Horn's Ivory Coast* Foreword 5 A gorgeous book..full of sheer stingo. 1928 *Observer* 18 Mar. 23/3 Some shanties, sung by Raymond Newell and a chorus, are full of stingo.

Stink, *sb.* Add: **3. b.** *Like stink*: with desperate speed, intensely hard, etc. *slang.*

1929 R. C. SHERRIFF *Journey's End* I. 40 If you see a Minnie coming..you have to judge it and run like stink sometimes.

5. **stink-bomb**, a gas-shell; also, a glass ball which when broken emits a nauseating smell.

1915 D. O. BARNETT *Lett.* 192 It seems that the tobacco stores had amalgamated with a stink-bomb dépôt. 1923 *Daily Mail* 12 Mar. 9 Stink-bombs and rubber rods were used last night by shocked schoolboys..in protest against the performance of an unclothed dancer [in Vienna]. 1928 *Daily Express* 26 Mar. 2/1 Hungarian anti-Semitic students bombarded the Budapest Opera House with stink-bombs.

Stink, *v.* **2. b.** Add: Also phr. *to stink of money*: to be 'offensively' rich. *slang.*

1929 *Concise Oxford Dict.* (new ed.). 1932 IVOR BROWN *Marine Parade* xii, We must do our best. He stinks of money. Will you fix up about rooms and for God's sake let's have a decent dinner.

Stinker. Add: **6.** Something rousing or offensive, as a pungent speech, letter, etc. *slang.*

1919 G. K. ROSE *2/4th Oxf. & Bucks Lt. Infty.* 207 A 'stinker' followed, to which we could only retaliate by posting sentries the next day to warn us of the General's approach.

Stink-pot. Add: **5.** A term of abuse for a person or thing. *vulgar.*

1932 *Everybody's Weekly* 31 Dec. 21/1 Stan back, Stinkpot, cancher?

Stipple, *sb.* Add: **2. c.** A brush which is used to produce a stippled effect.

1927 *Daily Express* 27 May 5/5 An even coat of matt is put on, the detail of delicate light and shade being etched out again with brushes known as scrubbs and stipples.

Stock, *sb.*¹ Add: **52. c.** *fig.* In expressions referring to the estimation in which a person or thing is held.

1930 *Times Lit. Suppl.* 17 Apr. 334/4 He found British stock very high in North Germany.

56. *To take* (*no*) *stock in*: to have (no) regard for. orig. *U.S.*

1874 *Rep. Vermont Board Agric.* II. 378 He..did not take stock in all the remarkable yields of butter reported on grass and hay. 1889 ROSE T. COOKE *Steadfast* vi. 76 'I don't take no stock in that feller!' she confided. 1898 'MARK TWAIN' *Myst. Stranger* (1916) 5 Father Peter took no stock in the astrologer. 1902 G. H. LORIMER *Lett. Self-made Merchant* v. 61 I've always taken a good deal of stock in what you call 'Blood-will-tell' if you're a Methodist. 1903 *N.Y. Evening Post* 17 Sept. 6 We take no stock whatever in the stories that the President was unaware of the effects of the rules which he signed.

62. **stock collateral** (see COLLATERAL *sb.* 6).

1929 *Observer* 17 Nov. 3/4 Time money on stock collateral is now quoted 5½ to 6 per cent.

65. **stock box**, a compartment of a bee-hive in which a 'stock' or swarm of bees is kept.

1875 *Encycl. Brit.* III. 501/1 There are also two supers or honey boxes, the same diameter as the stock boxes. 1888 F. R. CHESHIRE *Bees & Bee-Keeping* II. 50 Both of these hives may be extended, by the addition of stock-boxes and supers.

Stockholm (stǫ·khōᵘm). The name of the capital of Sweden used *attrib.* in **Stockholm pitch**, pitch yielded by **Stockholm tar**, a variety of tar, prepared from resinous pinewood, and used in ship-building.

1867 *Chambers's Encycl.* IX. 296/1 The Stockholm tar, which is so widely used in ship-building. 1888 *Encycl. Brit.* XXIII. 57/1 Wood tar, known also as Stockholm and as Archangel tar. 1929 R. HUGHES *High Wind in Jamaica* 50 He did envy the chap whose job it was to dip his hand in a great pot of aromatic Stockholm tar.

Stockist (stǫ·kist). [f. STOCK *sb.*¹ + -IST.] One who stocks (certain) goods for sale.

1922 *Autocar* 10 Nov. 52 We are Stockists of High grade Cars. 1923 *Daily Mail* 12 Feb. 16 Stockists for Yorkshire. *Ibid.* 12 June 5 Call at any 'Telemac' stockist and see for yourself. 1926 *Prospectus*, A Raleigh spare parts stockist has been appointed in nearly every town.

Stodge, *v.* Add: **5.** To walk or trudge through mud or slush. Also, to walk with short heavy steps. Also *trans.* To trample (mud). *dial.* or *colloq.*

1854 MISS BAKER *Northampt. Gloss.*, *Studging*, walking with short heavy steps; always used with the adjunct along. 'He goes studging along.' 1902 *Aberdeen Weekly Free Press* 7 June (E.D.D.) A polissman wha was comin' stodgin' doon the street. 1920 G. W. DEEPING *Second Youth* xxiii, The 'Old Man' and his orderly stodged back again up a water-logged communication trench. 1929 — *Roper's Row* viii, § 2 She had seen the feet of cattle stodging the mire in Melfont.

Stodger (stǫ·dʒəɹ). *colloq.* [f. STODGY *a.* + -ER ¹.] A stodgy person; one who is lacking in spirit or liveliness. Hence **Sto·dgery**, action characteristic of such a person.

1905 *Punch* 25 Jan. 62/1 The other regular old stodgers who go to all the parties within a radius of six miles. 1907 *Ibid.* 9 Jan. 20/2 Well, father's quite right, they are the most awful stodgers. You know they are. 1920 G. W. DEEPING *Second Youth* iv, If you were starving, Miles, I suppose you would walk down Oxford Street and say nothing. What stodgery! We middle-class people are hopeless!

Stole, *sb.*³ (Later U.S. example.)

1886 *Harper's Mag.* June 78/2 After the first cutting of the new plants the stole or stool left sends up another growth of cane.

Stolkjærre (stǭ·lkyerə, -χerə). [Norw., f. *stol* seat, STOOL *sb.* + *kjærre* cart.] A two-wheeled cart with seats for two persons. Hence **Sto·lkjærre** *v. intr.*, to ride in this.

1885 *One & a Half in Norway* 125 The court-yard of the station was quite busy with carrioles and stolkjærres. 1924 *Public Opinion* 9 May 454/2 The traveller in stolkjaerre or automobile ascends to snow-mantled plateaux. 1932 *New Yorker* 9 Apr. 59/2 Yachting on the Trollfjord, stolkjaerreing through the Naeroedal, automobiling in the Baltic Capitals.

Stomatograph (stǫ·mătǫgrɑf). *Bot.* [f. STOMATO- + -GRAPH.] An instrument for recording the action of the stomata or breathing-pores of leaves.

1911 W. L. BALLS in *Nature* 10 Aug. 180/1 The 'Stomatograph'..consists of an electrical air-pump... The..appliance is..composed of a box like a microscope case, which is placed on the ground under the plant to be examined; from this box issues the air-tube leading to the leaf and the telegraph wire to the recorder... The trace of five consecutive days recorded from the same leaf..shows the stomata slowly closing ..and remaining closed all night, opening slowly after sunrise. 1912 — *Cotton Plant in Egypt* 41.

Stone, *sb.* Add: **1. c.** A fashion shade of yellowish or brownish grey; stone-colour.

1923 *Daily Mail* 2 June 1 In delightful shades of Fawn,.. Dove Grey, Stone, Beaver.

7. b. A diamond. *S. Afr. slang.*

1887 A. B. ELLIS *S. Afr. Sketches* vii, Last night from my tent there was taken a small packet of stones. 1891 GLANVILLE *Fossiker* xxix, The cooling mud has closed around the 'stones', taking the impress of every angle and facet.

14. c. Phr. *To give a stone and a beating to*: to outrun or surpass easily. orig. *Racing slang.*

1885 *Daily News* 4 Feb. (Ware) *Canis vulpis* is, as a rule, able to give, intellectually speaking, and in language germane to the matter, 'a stone and a beating' to the majority of his pursuers. 1906 *Punch* 18 Apr. 286/3 Their Smokeroom is deliciously comfy, and can give a stone and a beating to ours at the Camellia.

20. **stone bag**, (*b*) a dungeon (cf. STONE JUG 2); **stone-craft**, the art of working in stone; sculpture; **stone-dust**, dust consisting of small particles of stone.

1889 G. KENNAN in *Century Mag.* Sept. 737/2 *note*, It [*sc.* the Russian Government] shrinks from allowing political convicts to die of self-starvation, and yet it puts them to a slow death in the '*stone bags' of the castle of Schlusselburg. 1903 J. R. HARRIS *Dioscuri in Chr. Legends* 37 We recognized *stonecraft amongst the arts of the Dioscuri. 1931 *Catholic Bulletin* (Dublin) June 578 Metal-work, stone-craft, and architecture. 1896 MARY E. WILKINS *Madelon* 362 The shattering of all the commandments into *stone-dust. 1920 *Chambers's Jrnl.* 266/2 This fact is taken advantage of to localise explosions in some American mines by mixing the first rush of air with stone-dust.

Stone, *v.* **4.** Add: Also with adv.

1897 C. T. DAVIS *Manuf. Leather* (ed. 2) 185 Previous to splitting, leather is usually 'stoned out' to remove the wrinkles in the sides. *Ibid.* 200 If you skive the leather it should be jacked or stoned down to take the wrinkles out of the neck. *Ibid.* 248 The machines shown in Figs. 39 and 83 are also used for stoning-out.

Stone-boat. 2. *U.S.* (Earlier example.)

1861–2 *Trans. Ill. Agric. Soc.* (1865) V. 207 These are drawn to the house on a *stone boat*.

Sto·ne-bruise. Injury to the feet caused by walking on stony ground. Hence **Stone-bruised** *a.*

1839 *Southern Lit. Messenger* V. 329/2 One of my toes.. had the worst kind of stone-bruise on it. 1850 W. H. FOOTE *Sk. Virginia* 526, I travelled the whole route barefooted; and had at one time three stone bruises on each foot. 1885 *Century Mag.* Nov. 29/1 Angy, who was complaining of a stone-bruise, got up. 1906 'O. HENRY' *Four Million* 133 I've seen Father Time get pretty bad stone bruises on his heels when he walked through the gold diggings. *a* 1909 — *Roads of Destiny* xxi. 354 Five of my best staff-officers fell, suffering extremely with stone-bruised heels.

Stonemason. (Earlier Amer. examples.)

1758 in *Lett. to Washington* II. 269 Our Stone Masons has been Sick, Ever Since you have been Away, and our Stone Work is much Behind hand. 1770 WASHINGTON *Diaries* I. 370 Joseph Gort a stone Mason came here to raise Stone.

Stonework. Add: **3.** *Printing.* Work done on the stone, such as the imposing of formes, etc.

a 1909 DE VINNE *Mod. Bk. Composition* 306 (Cent. D. Suppl.) Correct stone-work depends primarily on properly justified lines and exact make-up.

Stook, *sb.*² *slang.* Also **stoock**. [prob. Yiddish, a. G. *stück*.] A pocket-handkerchief.

1859 *Slang Dict.*, *Stook*, a pocket-handkerchief. A *stook-hauler*, or buzzer, a thief who takes pocket-handkerchiefs. 1889 E. SAMPSON *Tales of Fancy* 18 A dirty face, and a still more dirty 'stook'. 1893 P. H. EMERSON *Signor Lippo* xiv, All I get is my kip and a clean mill tog, a pair of pollies and a stoock.

Stool, *sb.* **19. b.** **stool-pigeon** *U.S.* (earlier example).

1841 J. F. COOPER *Deerslayer* xvi, Unless..the Mingos have..put her as a stool-pigeon to catch us.

Stool, *v.* **3.** (U.S. examples.)

1770 in *Maryland Hist. Mag.* XII. 360 Our Wheat particularly which cannot stool or Branch. 1886 *Harper's Mag.* Sept. 533/2 On light land strawberry plants..do not develop or 'stool out'.

Stoop, *sb.*³ *U.S.* (Earlier example.)

1755 *Essex Inst. Hist. Coll.* LII. 78 The Houses of one Story and a Stoop to each.

Stop, *sb.*² Add: **28. b.** *Bridge.* A card of such value that it can reasonably be counted on, in conjunction with other cards in the same suit, to take a trick in that suit. Usually *to have* (or *hold*) *a stop in* (hearts, diamonds, etc.). Cf. *STOPPED *ppl. a.* 2 d, *STOPPER *sb.* 1 g.

1920 E. V. SHEPARD *Correct Auction* 100 If that suit has already been bid by an opponent you can bid 2-No Trumps if you have safe stops in the suit with quick side tricks.

29. **stop-bead** *Carpentry*, (*a*) a moulding on a door-frame against which the door closes; (*b*) a moulding on the inner side of a window-frame along which the sash slides; **stop-butt**, the slope or bank behind a rifle-range, which stops the bullets; **stop-cylinder**, a printing press in which the cylinder is stopped to permit the return of the reciprocating carriage; **stop-light**, a light on the rear of a motor vehicle, which lights automatically when the brakes are applied; **stop-list**, a list of persons with whom members of an association are forbidden to do business; **stop-needle, -speculum** (see quots.).

1876 *Encycl. Brit.* IV. 496/1 An inner or *stop bead is mitred round on the inside to complete the groove or channel for the lower sash. 1864 A. WALKER *Rifle* (ed. 2) 114 If at a smaller angle it would, instead of acting as a *stop-butt [etc.]. 1923 KIPLING *Land & Sea T.* 177 The long shed of the Village Rifle Club reeked with the oniony smell of smokeless powder, machine-oil, and creosote from the stop-butt. 1887 R. R. BOWKER in *Harper's Mag.* July 174/2 The finest illustrated work..is mostly done with the '*stop cylinder'. 1902 *Encycl. Brit.* XXXII. 5/2 The stop-cylinder..is a little inferior to the two-revolution cylinder in performance. ..In this machine the cylinder stops after every impression and allows the feeder to place properly the sheet to be printed. 1930 D. MACKAIL *How Amusing!* 190 His *stop-light flickered almost ceaselessly as he crawled round the square. 1920 *Daily Tel.* 18 May 16/5 The association published his name on their *stop list, the object of which was to prevent all members of the association having any trade relations with the offending agent. 1928 *Daily Express* 27 Apr. 2/4 To restrain the..Association from publishing their names on a 'stop list' where are inserted the names of people to be boycotted. 1901 DORLAND *Med. Dict.* (ed. 2) s.v. *Needle*, **Stop-needle*, a needle with a shoulder that prevents it being plunged in more than a certain distance. *Ibid.* s.v. *Speculum*, **Stop-speculum*, an eye-speculum with an appliance for controlling the degree to which its branches spread.

Stop, *v.* Add: **15. c.** Also, to hit (game).

1845 *Punch* 25 Jan. 46/2 Out they [*sc.* the hares] rushed from every quarter—so many—that it was often impossible to 'stop' more than one out of half-a-dozen.

e. *To stop a bullet, to stop one*, etc.: to be killed or wounded. *To stop a blast*: to receive a reprimand. *Army slang.*

1916 E. V. LUCAS *Vermilion Box* clxxxiv. 213 Poor boy, I do so hope he manages not to 'stop one'. 1916 BOYD CABLE *Action Front* 151 It can't be his own chum, 'cause he 'stopped one'. 1925 E. FRASER & GIBBONS *Soldier & Sailor Words*, *Stop a blast*, to receive a rebuke or reprimand from a superior. *Stop a packet*, to be hit by a bullet: wounded: killed. 1927 *Observer* 8 May 20 The lieutenant who had just obtained leave for Blighty..and then contrived to 'stop one' from a 'sniper'.

35. b. *U.S.* (Earlier examples.)

1857 MARY J. HOLMES *Meadow-Brook* xvi, Wishing to see a friend of his who lives here, we have stopped over one train. 1873 'MARK TWAIN' & WARNER *Gilded Age* xxiv, Once when you renewed your ticket after stopping over in Baltimore.

c. *To stop over*: to remain on the side to which one has travelled; to settle down across the sea. *U.S.*

1909 *Daily Chron.* 20 Oct. 5/2 New industries will be created, and older ones will be developed as the wealthy men of the old country 'stop over'.

43. **stop-volley** *Lawn tennis* (see quots.).

1919 tr. *S. Lenglen's Lawn Tennis for Girls* 54 The 'stop' and 'draw' volleys are very useful to the net player... The 'stop' [must be played] by relaxing the grip, and..withdrawing the racket from the ball. 1927 *Daily Express* 25 May 17/7 Browne owed his victory to..the great variety of his game. Cut and chop and exquisite stop-volleys were mixed up in a most astute way. 1928 BETTY NUTHALL *Learning Lawn Tennis* 106 One of the most useful strokes in the game..is what is called the 'stop volley'... It is necessary to be quite close to the net to play it. The racket is just put in the way of the ball, which drops dead on the other side of the net.

b. In cinematography, involving the irregular stoppage of the camera for the production of bizarre effects.

1912 F. A. TALBOT *Moving Pictures* 201 When the 'stop' call was given the witch disappeared from the stage. *Ibid.*, The strange effects produced in the witch's cave were obtained both by double printing and the 'stop-motion'. 1915 J. B. RATHBUN *Motion Picture Making* 73 Trick street scenes, commonly known as 'stop' pictures.

44. **stop-over**, (*b*) permission given to a passenger to break his journey; (*c*) a place where a journey is broken. Also = *stop-over ticket*. *U.S.*

1881 *Harper's Mag.* Apr. 767/2 They are allowed stop-over tickets which give them the privilege of turning their stock out at any place for the winter, and then sending them on in the spring to market. 1885 *Outing* (U.S.) Nov. 150/2 There I took advantage of what, in railroad parlance, is called a 'stop-over'. 1905 *Chambers's Jrnl.* 87/1 At Vancouver I stepped on board a Canadian Pacific Railway steamer bound for Hong-kong, with a stop-over on my second-class ticket. 1925 *Scribner's Mag.* July 37 Advt., Optional stop-overs for visiting cultured Latin cities. 1928 *Blue Peter* July Advt. p. iv, A Convenient Stopover. Honolulu is a regular port of call for passenger steamers crossing to or from the Orient.

Stoppage. Add: **7. b.** *spec.* A cessation of work owing to disagreement between employer and employees; a strike or a lock-out.

1902 *Encycl. Brit.* XXV. 554/1 The adjustment of differences that might otherwise lead to stoppage. *Ibid.* XXXIII. 74/1 To distinguish stoppages as strikes or lock-outs according to the source of the original demand for a change of conditions would lead to a very arbitrary and misleading classification. 1926 *Publishers' Circular* 29 Dec. 895/3, 1926 ..The year of the General Stoppage.

Stopped, *ppl. a.* Add: **2. d.** *Bridge.* (See quots.)

1901 R. F. FOSTER *Foster's Bridge* 35 A Suit is Stopped when you can make one trick in it, or can compel the adversary to quit it and lead something else. *Ibid.* 52 If they have both the red suits surely stopped. 1929 WORK *Compl. Contract Bridge* iv. 20 A suit is stopped when the bidder holds such cards in it that he can be sure of taking at least one trick in that suit.

Stopper, *sb.* Add: **1. b.** Also, = STOP *sb.*² 26.

1927 *Chambers's Jrnl.* 125/1 Pheasants were running here and there as they were afraid to face the stoppers.

g. *Bridge.* = *STOP *sb.*² 28 b.

1901 R. F. FOSTER *Foster's Bridge* 112 When the make is original, a guarded king is very likely a stopper in the dealer's suit. 1924 SOLUS *Auction Bridge* 89 *Stopper*, a card fairly certain to make a trick in opponent's suit. An ace is a certain stopper, a K. x. x. or Q. x. x. x. are fairly safe stoppers.

7. d. (See quots.)

1897 J. JEFFERY *Rowing* 8 That part against which the oar is pressed in rowing is called the 'thowl', and the opposite, or after-thowl, is called the 'stop', or 'stopper'. 1904 G. RIXON *Rowing & Sculling* 2 In some stock gigs it will be found that there is not sufficient room between the thowl and stopper, causing the oar to stick or 'lock' on a full reach forward.

Storm, *sb.* **6. d.** Add: **storm-apron**, (*a*) *Naut.*, an apron-like protection for a steersman in stormy weather; (*b*) on the open top of an omnibus, a waterproof sheet covering a seat or the knees of persons sitting there; **storm-collar**, (*a*) [G. *sturmkragen*], the long low roll of cloud that accompanies a squall or thunder-storm (Funk); (*b*) a high coat-collar which may be turned up and fastened close round the neck; **storm-lantern**, a lantern in which the flame is protected from wind and rain; **storm-shoes**, strong shoes for use in stormy weather; **storm-troops** *Mil.* [G. *sturmtruppen*] = *shock-troops* (*SHOCK *sb.*³ 7 b); **storm-wind**, (*b*) a wind having the Beaufort number 11.

1928 E. C. VIVIAN *Nine Days* vi, A wooden-faced steersman's head showed from behind the *storm-apron. 1908 *Isle of Man Weekly Times* 12 Sept. 3/5 The high *storm collar almost enveloping the ears. 1928 *Daily Mail* 31 July 3/1 Adjustable straps on cuffs, storm collar. 1923 G. W. DEEPING *Secret Sanctuary* xx, He..lit the *storm-lantern he used at night, and extinguished the lamp. 1913 W. H. DOOLEY *Man. Shoemaking* 56 In the uppers of the best *storm shoes you will always find box calf. 1918 E. S. FARROW *Dict. Mil. Terms*, *Storm-troops.

Story, *sb.*¹ **6. e.** *U.S.* (Earlier examples.)

1889 *Kansas City Times & Star* 2 Dec., Henry Van Brunt has a splendid story on 'Western Architecture' in the Atlantic Monthly. 1903 E. L. SHUMAN *Practical Journalism* 59 A news article, or 'story' as it is called.

Stoss (stǫs, ‖ʃtōs), *a.* *Geol.* [G., = thrust, push, blow.] Of a hill, rock, etc.: Facing the direction from which a glacier moves or has moved; opposed to *lee*. Also *transf.*

1891 SALISBURY *Geol. Surv. New Jersey* 47 There was also more rapid erosion upon the north or stoss side of hills than upon the southern or lee side. 1905 CHAMBERLIN & SALISBURY *Geol.* I. 284 Erosion is greatest on the 'stoss' side of an obstruction (the side against which the ice advances), and deposition on the lee side. 1928 CHAMBERLIN *Two Solar Families* 180 Let us picture the accretions in evortical motion as running in convergently at one end of the axis of the core (the stoss end) and as running out divergently at the other (the lee end).

Stott, variant of STOT *v.*

1903 W. J. TRAVIS *Pract. Golf* 134 Generally speaking, if a ball stotts or bounces well it will fly well.

Stoush (staʊʃ), *v.* Also **stouch**. *Austral. slang. trans.* To strike, thrash; also *fig.*, to rate soundly. Hence **Stoush** *sb.*, a battering or beating.

1893 J. A. BARRY *S. Brown's Bunyip*, etc. 66 I'll get stoushed over this job yet. 1900 H. LAWSON *Over Sliprails* 10 One or two wanted to go back and 'stoush' that landlord. 1914 *Glasgow Even. Times* 30 Dec. 2 It took half an hour or so and a varied selection of stoush to disprove the allegation. 1925 E. FRASER & GIBBONS *Soldier & Sailor Words*, *Stouch*, to fight, to thrash.

Stove, *v.*¹ **8.** (Additional example.)

1880 HEALY *Lett. & Leaders* (1928) I. 87 The whole of the American houses are stoved in the same way.

Stover, *sb.*¹ Add: **2. c.** The stalks and leaves of maize. *U.S.*

1837 H. COLMAN *Rep. Agric. Mass.* (1838) 24 The stover of the Pennsylvania corn..would probably yield from a third to a half more than ours in weight. 1894 *Vermont Agric. Rep.* XIV. 42 There is more stock food in the stover or stalks of a corn crop, than in the ears.

Stowaway. Add: **2.** *gen.* Something stowed away. Also, a place where things may be stowed.

1913 E. F. BENSON *Thorley Weir* iii, For all these weeks Charles had never touched the cupboard except to insert some further stowaway. 1915 W. J. LOCKE *Jaffery* xx, Of all the stowaway places under my control..only one is locked. 1928 *Daily Express* 21 Mar. 5/3 The window-seat top lifts up, and this makes another good stowaway for toys.

Straddle, *sb.* Add: **3.** (Examples.)

1843 *Knickerbocker Mag.* XXII. 233 These are..subjects for the straddle. The fence..is our only..safety on these p'ints. 1903 A. B. HART *Actual Govt.* 97 The so-called straddle..that is, a declaration which means anything to anybody.

7. **straddle reversing** *Stock Exchange* (cf. sense 2 b in Dict.); **straddleways** *adv.* = *straddlewise*.

1927 *Daily Tel.* 11 May 4/7 In the afternoon the tendency of prices was downwards on liquidation by bull interests and *straddle reversing by American houses. 1919 H. WALPOLE *Secret City* I. iii, I can imagine Lawrence standing *straddleways on the deck of the *Jupiter*, his short thick legs wide apart.

Straddle, *v.* Add: **6.** *U.S. colloq.* (Later example.)

1904 *N.Y. Tribune* 27 Oct. 1 The Democratic platform dodges some questions and straddles others.

8. *Stock Exchange.* To be both long and short of (stock).

1900 S. A. NELSON *ABC Wall St.* 161 A speculator who has bought and is long of one stock, and sold and is short of another, has straddled the market.

Straddle, *adv.* (Earlier U.S. example.)

1857 *Quinland* I. 24 He found a crazy fellow sitting straddle of a grave, holding on to the tombstone.

Strafe, *v.* Add: Hence **Stra·fer**. **Stra·fing** *vbl. sb.*

1916 BOYD CABLE *Action Front* 135 One would expect the same old field will get a strafing this afternoon. 1917 *Chambers's Jrnl.* Jan. 45/1 If the fog clears the 'strafers' will spot us for a dead cert. 1918 E. A. MACKINTOSH *War, the Liberator* 86 To..place, obedient to my country's call, A deadlier strafer in their hands than all. *Ibid.* 96 We got such a strafing it whitened our hair. 1923 *Contemp. Rev.* Jan. 16 Mr. Bonar Law endured this moral strafing with dogged heroism. 1930 C. R. SAMSON *Fights & Flights* 98 We left a car to attend to the Zeppelin strafers and take their mechanics away.

Straff (strɑf), variant of STRAFE *v.* and *sb.*

1915 in *Naval Review* (1916) IV. 267 The usual daily straff. 1916 BOYD CABLE *Action Front* 45 Straff the Germans and all their works, particularly their mine works!

Straight, *a.*, *sb.*, and *adv.* Add: **A.** *adj.* **3. e.** Used as *int.* = Really and truly. *vulgar colloq.*

1890 CHEVALIER *Coster's Courtship* (Farmer) Straight! ses I, I'm on the job for better or for wuss.

9. d. Without ornamental additions.

1928 [see *HOT *a.* 8 h].

10. c. **straight betting** *Racing*, backing a horse to win; **straight-eight**, a motor vehicle having eight cylinders in line; **straight fight**, a direct contest between two candidates; **straight goods** *U.S.*, the truth; **straight paper**, negotiable paper bearing the name of one individual; **straight play**, a play in which there is plain dialogue without music, etc.; **straight-side** *a.*, having straight sides, as a pneumatic automobile tyre having a straight-sided bead reinforced by a wire or wires contained in the bead; hence *sb.*, a type of ski.

1928 *Daily Sketch* 10 Aug. 20/4 It..can be used either for *straight or place betting. 1927 *Observer* 16 Oct. 27 Sunbeam's enterprise in standardising eight-cylinder-in-line engined carriages is now..supported..by the 21–60-h.p. Wolseley *straight-eight. 1931 *Daily Express* 16 Oct. 3/2 There was a prospect at one time of three-cornered fights in four of Bristol's five divisions, but to-day the position is that there are to be *straight fights all round. 1903 A. H. LEWIS *The Boss* 275 Every word, however, was true. I but handed her th' *straight goods. 1911 H. QUICK *Yellowstone N.* v. 27 Some of this was straight goods, an' some stall. 1932 A. J. WORRALL *Engl. Idioms* 55, I like Godfrey Tearle best in *straight plays. 1928 WEBSTER Addenda, *Straight-side. 1923 E. JESSUP *Snow & Ice Sports* 22 The 'cross country' and 'straight side' are names by which one of these models is variously known. *Ibid.* 26 With the 'straight side' model, there is no disadvantage in wearin' a ski which is considerably longer than your reach.

B. *sb.* **1. e.** *The straight*: the truth. *U.S.*

1902 G. H. LORIMER *Lett. Self-made Merchant* xviii. 271 No one except the widow ever really got at the straight of Bud's conduct. 1909 R. A. WASON *Happy Hawkins* 198, I ain't heard the straight of it.

8. b. *ellipt.* for *straight flight, play*, etc.

1913 *Aeroplane* 9 Oct. 410/1 Mr. Hucks was gaining slightly on the straights, though losing at the sharp corners. 1914 H. ROSHER *In R.N.A.S.* (1916) 20 Yesterday I did five straights (straight flights) alone. 1928 *Punch* 23 May 12/3 The character-actors have no doubt an easier task than the 'straight' actors.

5. (Earlier examples.)

1866 C. H. SMITH *Bill Arp* 39 The Yankees had a strait, which would have taken Forrest and raked down the pile.

13. In trap-shooting, a perfect score. *U.S.*

1903 *Forest & Stream* 21 Feb. 160 (Cent. D. Suppl.) In the 20-bird event W...and C. each made a straight.

17. *U.S.* (See quot. 1928.)

a 1906 'O. HENRY' *Trimmed Lamp*, etc. 272 I managed to soak in a little straight. 1928 *Collier's* 29 Dec. 42/2 There is Juarez whisky, for intance. It is sometimes called 'American Straight'.

C. *adv.* **7. a.** *straight-flying* pres. pple. and ppl. adj.; **straight-bred** *a.*, descended from one particular breed without admixture; **straight-out**, i.e. cut in a straight line; *spec.* of tobacco, cut lengthwise of the leaf into long silky fibres; *sb.*, tobacco cut in this way; a cigarette made from straight-cut tobacco.

1901–2 *Rep. Kansas State Board Agric.* 57 (Cent. D. Suppl.) Certain so-called 'pure' or '*straight-bred' strains of pedigreed cattle. 1840 *straight-cut [see Dict.]. 1913 *Punch* 8 Jan. 24/1 A young gentleman of fashion who.. toyed with a priceless straight-cut. 1927 G. W. DEEPING *Kitty* ii. § 2, I want some cigarettes—straight-cuts—. 1925 J. GREGORY *Bab of Backwoods* ii, Whatever Dick Gale had done pointed the *straight-flying arrow for Bab's following. 1928 C. G. STEWART *Two Poems Airman, Loop* 1 Straightflying, I Drop downward rushing. *Ibid.* 14 Sudden another Land!..Above it I'm straightflying.

Straightaway (strē̆ᵗăwē·), *adv.* (*a.*) [= *straight away* (see STRAIGHT *adv.* 2 c) spelt as one word.] = STRAIGHTWAY *adv.*

1910 *Sphere* 20 Aug. p. vi/1 Radley flies a mile straightaway at a speed of 75 miles an hour. 1920 G. W. DEEPING *Second Youth* xxviii, She interested me straightaway. 1923 *Daily Mail* 26 May 9 It was so evident that Evander had been badly hurt that he was straightaway withdrawn.

b. as *adj.*

1913 *Captain* Sept. 1072/2 In straight-away flights even higher speeds have been established.

Straighten, *v.* **4.** Add: Also with *out, up*; *spec.* used of aircraft.

1911 GRAHAME-WHITE & HARPER *Aeroplane* 136 Instead of performing the evolution which is known as 'straightening up' a machine. 1914 [see *FLATTEN *v.* 2 b]. 1917 *Times* 5 July 6/5 Two machines..swerved and one started to fall for some hundreds of feet before it straightened out and regained flying speed. 1921 *Review of Reviews* Aug. 99/2 The..expectations..that the Silesian tangle was straightening out have proved quite illusory. 1931 *Daily Mirror* 27 Aug. 2/2 [The plane] straightened out and made terrific bursts of speed along the measured mile course.

Straight-out, *a.* *U.S.* (Earlier example.)

1848 W. ARMSTRONG *Stocks* 9 The Stock is to be delivered and paid for upon a certain day—these are sometimes termed straight out contracts.

Strain, *sb.*² Add: **9. c.** *To take the strain*, in a tug of war: see quot.

1912 *Games & Nav. Milit. Tournament* 3 The pulls will be started by the Referee by word of mouth as follows:— 'Take the strain', on which both teams will put a strain on the rope without pulling.

15. (sense 9) *strain-slip* (*cleavage*), *-twinning* (TWINNING *vbl. sb.*² 2).

1903 GEIKIE *Text-bk. Geol.* (ed. 4) 681 Frequently the puckerings have been ruptured and a fine cleavage or jointing has been produced (Ausweichungsclivage, *strain-slip cleavage). 1906 *Technol. & Sci. Dict.* (ed. Goodchild & Tweney), *Strain Slip Cleavage*, a structure developed in certain rocks by dynamic metamorphism. 1908 W. B. WRIGHT in *Q. Jrnl. Geol. Soc.* LXIV. 308 The folding and subsequent strain-slip would seem therefore to be the result of stresses acting on a decidedly heterogeneous rock. 1930 PEACH & HORNE *Geol. Scotl.* 53 *Strain-twinning then begins to develop in the oligoclase and albite.

Strainless (strē̆ⁱnlės), *a.* [f. STRAIN *sb.*² + -LESS.] Produced without strain; free from strain. Hence **Strai·nlessly** *adv.*

1927 SIDGWICK *Electronic The. Valency* 237 We are..not justified in assuming either that Ingold's simple calculation of the angles from the volume relationships of the attached groups is correct, or that the resulting angles are 'strainless'. 1927 *Daily Tel.* 10 Feb. 16/4 Eluding the volleying vigilance of the Australian by drives as supremely accurate as they were strainlessly produced. 1928 *Ibid.* 5 June 17/6 In the men's final..Cochet was his glorious little self. His was ..the imaginative brio and the strainless elegance of the born genius.

Strait, *a.*, *sb.*, and *adv.* **B.** *sb.* Add: **3. d.** *pl.* A middle grade of cod-liver oil, of a pale brown colour, produced by compressing the livers after the pale or shore oil has been run off. Also *Straits oil*. (? So called from the Strait of Belle Isle, between Newfoundland and Labrador.)

1849 *Rep. U.S. Comm. Patents* (1850) 165, I..claim..the combination of the straits oil with the magnesia. 1897 C. T. DAVIS *Manuf. Leather* (ed. 2) 229 The oil is clarified and bleached by boiling and filtering. Thus refined it is called 'straits'.

Stram, *v.* *U.S.* (Earlier example.)

1846–52 MRS. WHITCHER *Widow Bedott P.* xxv. 306 She ..strammed right across the room and sot down.

Strand, *v.*² **3.** Add: (See also quot.)

1894 JEANETTE E. DAVIS *Elem. Mod. Dressmaking* 116 In addition to running or overcasting, very careful workers strand their button-holes—*i.e.* carry a thread of silk across each edge over which to work the stitch. In stranding, a tiny upward stitch is taken at one end of the hole, and a tiny downward one at the other, and the two stitches being repeated, leave two strands of silk along each edge of the slit, below which the needle is to come at every stitch.

Strandveldt, -veld (strænd‑velt). *S. Africa.* [f. Du. *strand* STRAND *sb.*¹ + *veldt*, now *veld* field.] The coast lands south of Bredasdorp and Riversdale. Also *attrib.*

1875–84 R. B. SHARPE *Layard's Birds S. Afr.* 47 Mr. John Van der Byl's farm, Nacht-wacht in the Strandveldt. 1880 *Trans. S. Afr. Phil. Soc.* I. III. 196 The variety is usually termed the 'Strandveldt' (sea-coast) locust.

Strap, *sb.* **17.** Add: **strap-game** *U.S.* (earlier examples); **strap-hang** *v. intr.*, to be a straphanger (see Dict.); also in *vbl. sb.*; **strap-rail** *U.S.* (earlier examples).

1847 *Knickerbocker Mag.* XXIX. 281 He was accused of having 'come the *strap-game' over a native. 1873 J. H. BEADLE *Undevel. West* vii. 140 A score of 'smart Alecks' relieved of their surplus cash by betting on the 'strap game'. 1917 *Daily Mail* 28 Aug. 2/5, I think those weary girls look like tired little flowers as they *strap-hang for half an hour or more. 1919 *Electrician* LXXXII. 497/2 The somewhat elaborate provision made for 'strap hanging'. 1928 *Outlook* 26 May 646/2 Passengers need not 'strap-hang' if they did not wish, since all they had to do was to wait for a train with a vacant seat. 1928 *Daily Express* 22 Dec. 7/2 Straphanging rule dispute. 1874 B. F. TAYLOR *World on Wheels*, etc. I. xiii. 105 Years ago, he rode on a train of the old Toledo & Adrian Railway—*strap-rail at that. 1887 C. B. GEORGE *40 Years on Rail* 33 Some of the old strap-rails were in use on the Boston and Maine when I went on that road.

Strap, *v.*¹ Add: **1. e.** *intr.* for *pass.* To admit of being fastened by means of a strap.

1924 ANNE D. SEDGWICK *Little French Girl* I. v, Grey shoes strapping across the instep with a buckle.

Strapontin (strapontæ̃). [Fr.] A bracket seat, such as are used in carriages and cars; also, a similar kind of seat used in play-houses.

1926 W. J. LOCKE *Old Bridge* v. xviii, Perella insisted on sitting on the little seat, so that Silvester should be at the back with Beatrice. 'He loves it—hates *strapontins*.' 1927 *Observer* 29 May 12 As for the strapontins, which, at every performance of a successful play, block up all the gangways, actors and managers agree that they are dangerous.

Strapper¹. Add: **5.** A workman who furnishes or secures a thing with straps.

1881 *Instr. Census Clerks* (1885) 79 Leather Goods..Maker. Strapper. 1921 *Dict. Occup. Terms* (1927) § 044 *Strapper*, puts up straps of wood or steel in support of roof in machine cut coal face. *Ibid.* § 345 *Strapper*, attaches straps to bags, trunks, etc.

Strass². Delete *rare*⁻⁰ and add: **2.** A kind of waxed straw with a silky appearance, used for dress trimmings, etc.

1926 *Westm. Gaz.* 10 Mar., Raspberry red strasse (a sort of waxed straw) was made into rosettes for a trimming on one black frock. 1927 *Daily News* 8 Apr. 2/2 Beneath the large strass-trimmed finish to the belt in front fell a full panel of white georgette trimmed with strass.

Stratfordian (strætfō·ɹdiăn). [f. *Stratford-on-Avon* + -IAN.] A supporter of the view that William Shakespeare of Stratford-on-Avon was the author of the plays generally attributed to him. Also as *adj.*

1908 SIR G. GREENWOOD *Shakesp. Probl. Restated* 172 Really, really, there must be some limits even to Stratfordian demands on our credulity! *Ibid.* 226 The futilities which are gravely trotted out by enthusiastic Stratfordians as valuable evidence to illustrate the life of Shakspere. 1923 — *Lee, Shakesp. & a Tertium Quid* 36 Any work which happens to be published in support of the 'orthodox' Stratfordian tradition.

Stratosphere (stræ·tǫsfīᵊɹ). *Meteorol.* [f. *strato-*, irreg. comb. f. STRATUM + SPHERE *sb.*] The layer of atmospheric air lying above the troposphere, of unknown thickness, in which the temperature ceases to fall with height, and remains constant; the isothermal layer. Cf. *TROPOSPHERE.

1908 SOLLAS tr. *Suess's Face of the Earth* III. 2 So great is the part played by stratified deposits in the structure of the earth's crust that we might be tempted to speak of the *stratosphere* of the earth in contradistinction to the *scoriosphere* of the moon. 1914 C. J. P. CAVE in *Q. Jrnl. R. Meteorol. Soc.* App. 108 M. Teisserenc de Bort discovered that the atmosphere is divided into two parts, the troposphere, which extends from the surface to about 7 miles, and the stratosphere, which lies above; the troposphere is constantly churned up by convection currents; the stratosphere lies above the reach of these turbulent motions. 1928 BRUNT *Meteorology* 46 The stratosphere is colder over the equator than over the poles.

Stratum. 7. Add: **strata peat**, a class of combustible bioliths consisting of layers of peat and saprokoll.

1906 *Rep. Brit. Assoc.* 748 The strata peat comes from places where the peat is periodically under water.

Straw, *sb.*¹ Add: **1. d.** A fashion shade of yellow resembling the colour of straw.

1902 *Encycl. Brit.* XXIX. 730/1 Yellow (canary or straw). 1923 *Daily Mail* 19 Feb. 5 A full range of new colourings, including..Peach, Lemon, Straw, Rose.

14. **straw-basher** *slang*, a man's or boy's straw hat or boater; **straw-boss** *U.S.*, a sub-foreman (see quot. 1905); **straw-ciré** (see *CIRÉ *a.*).

1931 CRONIN *Hatter's Castle* II. xii. 421 A stiff, board-like *straw-basher. 1905 *Terms Forestry & Logging* 50 *Straw boss*, a subforeman in a logging camp. 1922 *Short Stories* Feb. 67/1 Josephine saw the straw-boss move with apparent carelessness toward the prisoner. 1928 *Daily Express* 15 June 5/5 Trimmings of coloured felt flowers on shapes of *straw-ciré.

Strawberry. Add: **1. b.** The fruit of certain marine plants, as those of the genus *Chara*, which in colour and shape resemble strawberries. Also *attrib.*: **strawberry bottom**, a sea-bottom covered with plants bearing this fruit.

1897 KIPLING *Capt. Cour.* iii. 53 The hook had fouled among a bunch of strawberries, red on one side and white on the other. *Ibid.* viii. 167 She acts as though she were on strawberry-bottom. It's all sand here, ain't it?

Stray, *a.* **3.** Add: Also, occurring or met with casually or unexpectedly; sporadic, occasional; as *a stray instance, a stray remark, a stray customer or two*.

Streak, *sb.* Add: **2. h.** The cut in a pine-tree from which the resin exudes for the manufacture of turpentine.

3. c. (Earlier U.S. examples.)

1839 *Knickerbocker Mag.* XIII. 298, I see him yesterday afternoon..starting off like a streak, to go to Norridgewock. 1849 C. LANMAN *Lett. Alleghany Mountains* xi. 89 The water wheeled my head round to the hole, and in I went quick as a streak. 1887 MARY E. WILKINS *Humble Romance* 376 He went past me like a streak when I was coming up the road.

d. A course of travel, esp. at a rapid rate. *To make a streak*: to make off in haste, to hurry. *U.S.*

a 1861 T. WINTHROP *John Brent* xxii. (1862) 243 She's got the old man to take care of and follow off on his next streak. 1875 J. G. HOLLAND *Sevenoaks* iv. 60 We'll wopse 'im up in some blankits, an' make a clean streak for the woods. 1909 R. A. WASON *Happy Hawkins* 280 She was in the habit of estimatin' just how little nourishment it would take to run her to the next feed, gettin' it into her in the shortest possible time, an' then makin' a streak for it.

6. b. (Earlier and later U.S. examples.)

1843 *Knickerbocker Mag.* XXI. 303, I had 'struck a streak of bad luck'. 1865 'MARK TWAIN' *Sketches* (1926) 203 There never was a bad James in the Sunday-school books that had such a streak of luck as this sinful Jim. 1871 B. HARTE *Luck of Roaring Camp*, etc. 34 We've had a streak of bad luck since we left Poker Flat. 1912 C. MATHEWSON *Pitching in a Pinch* xi. 233 But what's a new hat against a losing streak or a batting slump?

7. **streak-disease**, a disease in maize and sugar-cane caused by the **streak-virus** (see quots.); **streak-plate**, (*a*) *Bacteriol.* a plate or mass, e.g. of gelatine, which is infected by making streaks (sense 2 g) on it with the bacteria-covered point of a needle; (*b*) *Min.* a small tablet of unglazed pottery on which minerals are rubbed to ascertain the colour of the streak (sense 2 d).

1925 H. H. STOREY in *Rep. Proc. Imperial Bot. Confer.* (title), *Streak-disease: an infectious chlorosis of sugar cane. 1930 H. H. STOREY & MCCLEAN in *Ann. Applied Biol.* XVII. 691 The name of *Streak Disease* has been used to designate a characteristic chlorotic condition which has been observed in South Africa in a number of species of plants of the family Gramineæ. *Ibid.* 623 Our maize *streak virus was taken from a naturally streaked maize plant. 1895 *Buck's Handbk. Med. Sci.* Suppl. 83/1 '*Streak-plates' are made on gelatine and agar, after the medium has been poured in the plates and become solidified, by drawing an infected needle across them in four or five parallel courses. 1904 BRUSH & PENFIELD *Determ. Min. & Blowpipe Anal.* (ed. 16) 228 The streak of a mineral..may be quickly determined by rubbing it on a piece of white unglazed porcelain... Streak-plates, are made especially for this purpose.

Streak, *v.*² Add: **4. c.** For the sense 'To go quickly or at full speed', now often associated with this word, see *STREEK, STREAK *v.* 5.

Stream, *sb.* **9. c.** Add: **stream-jam** *Logging* (see quot.); **stream-sail**, short for *stream-line sail* (*STREAM-LINE 1 b).

1905 *Terms Forestry & Logging* 33 *Center jam*, a jam formed on an obstacle in the middle of a stream, and which does not reach either shore; *stream jam. 1920 *Glasgow Herald* 16 July 7 The three hours' trial of the *streamsail on the eve of the great race.

Streaming, *ppl. a.* Add: **1. b.** Of a cold: accompanied by copious running of the eyes and nose.

1923 W. R. INGE *Lay Thoughts* (1926) 229 Persons.. suffering from streaming colds, which are quite as infectious as..mumps or chicken-pox.

Stream-line. Add: **1.** Also in *Aerodynamics*, (*a*) the direction of an air current impinging upon a moving body, as a motor car or aeroplane; (*b*) designating the shape given to motor cars and aircraft to offer the minimum resistance to the air.

1907 F. W. LANCHESTER *Aerodynamics* 104 The lines of flow and..the stream lines, the latter term being employed in all cases where the primary flow is superposed on a motion of translation. 1909 C. C. TURNER *Aerial Navig. To-day* (1910) 112 In the case of a concavo-convex plane there is the additional advantage of reduced resistance to the air, the form of the plane more closely approaching 'streamline'. 1916 H. BARBER *Aeroplane Speaks* 142 *Stream-Line*, a form or shape of detrimental surface designed to produce minimum drift.

b. in various *attrib.* and *adj.* uses with meaning 'designed to decrease wind-resistance', 'having a stream-line form', as *stream-line body, coat, part, sail, shape, system, wire*; also **stream-line flow**, **motion**, the motion of a fluid or current of air past an obstacle when the paths of all the particles are smooth; **stream-line sail** (see quot. 1920).

1898 stream-line motion [in Dict.]. 1907 F. W. LANCHESTER *Aerodynamics* 11 The fluid in the vicinity of a streamline body is of necessity in a state of motion and contains energy. *Ibid.* 28 In order that streamline motion should be possible such motion must be a stable state. *Ibid.* 27 If..we assume continuity as hypothesis, then all bodies must be streamline. *Ibid.* 38 Streamline flow general. 1916 H. BARBER *Aeroplane Speaks* 60 The importance of adjusting all stream-line parts to be dead-on in the line of flight. 1918 CADBURY in C. F. S. Gamble *Story North Sea Air Station* xxii. (1928) 408, I..seized a scarf, goggles and helmet, tore off my streamline coat, and, semi-clothed.. took a running jump into the pilot's seat. 1929 G. WHALE *Brit. Airships* 160 The remaining two engines are carried in a small streamline car situated amidships. 1920 *Glasgow Herald* 16 July 7 The 'stream line sail'..is a stream-line strip of canvas, a lacing device extending from the boom to the gaff along the mast, and calculated to prevent a vacuum or back wind by plugging up the open space of six inches or so that always extends beneath the mainsail and the mast from top to bottom. It makes practically a solid sail from the mast to the outer edge, and..the result aimed at..is..the decreasing of the wind resistance. 1922 *Encycl. Brit.* XXX. 21/1 'Stream-line' wires were first designed for the British army dirigible 'Beta' in 1912. 1922 *Daily Mail* 3 Nov. 2 The body of the car is streamline according to British practice.

Hence **Strea·m-line** *v. trans.*, to give a stream-line form to. **Strea·m-lined** *ppl. a.* **Strea·m-lining** *vbl. sb.*

1913 *Aeroplane* 30 Oct. 480/1 Its [*sc.* an aeroplane's] small span and carefully streamlined body. 1916 H. BARBER *Aeroplane Speaks* 59 Even the wires bracing the aeroplane together are, in many cases, stream-lined. 1918 *Ibid.* (ed. 6) 61 The weight of the stream-lining is always paid for many times over by the greater velocity and consequent increase of lift due to the decreased drift. 1927 HALDANE & HUXLEY *Anim. Biol.* xiii. 316 The air-sacs..are used to stream-line the body. *Ibid.* 318 Most of the fuselage of an aeroplane only serves for stream-lining. 1928 C. F. S. GAMBLE *Story North Sea Air Station* Introd. 10 Her two stream-lined gondolas..were designed to be capable of sustaining severe impact loads when alighting on water. *Ibid.* i. 43 An apparatus..had to be fixed on a platform outside the fuselage and streamlined in. 1930 *Observer* 16 Feb. 17/5 She has oval, instead of stream-lined funnels.

Streek, streak, *v.* **5.** *intr.* Delete 'Now *dial.* and *U.S. colloq.*' and add: The form *streak* in modern use is often associated with '*streak* of lightning'. (Later examples in general use.)

1915 ROSHER *In R.N.A.S.* (1916) 50, I..climbed to 2,000 feet and streaked off over the Channel. 1927 A. E. W. MASON *No Other Tiger* xix, Her car started forward, circled round the Square and streaked out into Piccadilly. 1928 *Chambers's Jrnl.* 2/2 The hooked fish streaked across the pool and got the line it asked for. 1928 *Sunday Express* 6 May 19 The two 'blues'..galloped after Jack Massey, who was streaking for the house. 1928 *Daily Express* 10 May 10/3 The golf dog then streaked howling out of the bunker and vanished. 1932 *Ibid.* 2 July 1/5 At a sudden signal the dog will streak away from his master's side.

f. *trans.* To cause to go 'like lightning'. Also *to streek its way*.

1916 G. W. DEEPING *Sincerity* xviii, She shot well, very few of her arrows streaking their way through the sunlight to stand slantingly in the grass. 1928 *Daily Express* 19 June 17/2 He hit only three 4's, and..streaked one from Staples dangerously through the slips when 28. *Ibid.* 25 June 17 Chapman..'streaked' several shots through the slips.

Street, *sb.* Add: **2. f.** Also *the Street* = *Fleet Street* (*FLEET *sb.*² 2 b), *Wall Street* (example).

1903 *N.Y. Times* 30 Aug., The Street has never received any direct information as to the identity of those now in control. 1932 *News Chron.* 11 Feb. 6/3 A year ago he was coming back as Editor to the Street.

3. i. *To be in* or *up a person's street*: to be his concern or business, to be in his line. *colloq.* or *slang.*

1903 FARMER & HENLEY *Slang*, *Street*..., a capacity, a method; a line: *e.g.* 'That's not in my street' = 'I am not concerned' or 'That's not my way of doing', etc. 1929 *Publishers' Weekly* (N.Y.) 21 Dec. 2813/2 A great many of the books published today are, as the saying is, right up her street.

4. e. **street dealing**, a transaction conducted outside after the Stock Exchange has closed; so **street market**; **street-kerb** = KERB *sb.* 2; also *attrib.*; **street-yarn** *U.S.* (earlier example).

1930 M. CLARKE *Home Trade* 269 Dealings may then be carried on outside the Exchange itself. Such dealings are termed '*street dealings'. 1913 *Punch* 26 Mar. 237/2 The *street-kerb sellers. 1931 *Daily Express* 15 Oct. 14/4 Quiet conditions prevailed in the *street market last night. 1816 *Mass. Spy* 6 Mar. (Thornton), I guess the man is a horse-jockey, and the woman a spinner of *street-yarn.

Strength, *sb.* Add: **2. e.** *To get the strength of*: to understand fully; to obtain the actual facts of.

1916 C. J. DENNIS *Ginger Mick* 63 Then, bit be bit, Mick gits the strength uv it. 1925 E. FRASER & GIBBONS *Soldier & Sailor Words*, *Strength, to get the*, to obtain the actual facts about anything.

Strephotome (stre·fǫtōᵘm). *Surg.* [f. Gr. στρέφειν to twist + *-TOME.] An instrument resembling a corkscrew for invaginating the hernial sac.

1890 BILLINGS *Med. Dict.*

Strepto-. Add: **Streptospondylian, -spondyline, -spondylous** *adjs.*, also applied to those ophiuroids in which the arms are capable of being coiled round straight objects (opp. to *zygospondyline*).

Stress, *sb.* **10.** Add: **stress mark** *Photogr.* (see quot. 1918).

1918 *Photo-Miniature* XV. Mar., *Stress Marks*, scummy appearance or black lines on a bromide or D. O. P. print. 1919 *Brit. Jrnl. Photogr. Alm.* 251 Free from tendency to give rise to stress or abrasion marks.

Stretcher. 6. a. (Earlier U.S. example.)

1832 *U.S. Stat.* c. ccxxvii. (1856) IV. 587 [Duty] on square wire used for the manufacture of stretchers for umbrellas,.. twelve per centum ad valorem.

11. (Additional example.)

1885 *Outing* (U.S.) Oct. 77/1 The trout..were lusty, vigorous fellows, and with a 'Silver Doctor' as a stretcher, I managed to forget myself..completely.

Strewage (strū·ėdʒ). [f. STREW *v.* + -AGE.] = STREWING *vbl. sb.* b.

1902 J. H. SKRINE *Pastor Agnorum* 266 The waking of that Syrian refugee..after his sleep among the great strewage of rocks on a down of Canaan. 1929 BRIDGES *Test. Beauty* III. 894 Vestiges of his stony asceticism imbue all time, thick as the strewage of his flinty tools, disseminate wheresoe'er he hath dwelt.

Striated, *ppl. a.* Add: **1. d.** *Striated discharge*, a form of electric discharge characterized at various low pressures by successive light and dark bands or striæ.

1882 SIEMENS *Sci. Wks.* (1889) III. 355 That a stria, with its attendant dark space, forms a physical unit of a striated discharge; that a striated column is an aggregate of such units formed by means of a step-by-step process. 1902 *Encycl. Brit.* XXVIII. 48/1 In the striated discharge we see..that recombination is greater than ionization in the bright parts, and less in the dark parts.

Striation. Add: **1. b.** *pl.* *Electr.* The successive light and dark bands of an electric discharge (cf. prec.).

1902 *Encycl. Brit.* XXVIII. 47/2 When the pressure is within certain limits its luminosity often exhibits remarkable periodic alterations in intensity. .. These are called striations.

Striature. Add: Also *fig.*

1918 F. HACKETT *Ireland* xiii. 362 This striature of Catholics and Protestants, nationalists and anti-nationalists, Irish and Scotch-Ulstermen, is by no means so insufferable as the tenor of argument may indicate.

Strictish (stri·ktiʃ), *a.* [f. STRICT *a.* + -ISH ¹.] Somewhat or rather strict.

1886 STUBBS *Mediæval & Mod. Hist.* vii. 145 A monk in a strictish convent.

Stricturing (stri·ktiŭriŋ), *vbl. sb.* *Path.* [f. STRICTURE *sb.*¹ + -ING ¹.] Formation of a stricture; narrowing (e.g. of the urethra).

1908 *Practitioner* Jan. 40 The laceration of the urethra by foreign bodies, such as calculi, does not, as a rule, give rise to much stricturing.

Stride, *sb.* Add: **1.** *To lengthen* or *shorten one's stride*: to increase or diminish one's speed.

1925 E. F. NORTON *Fight for Everest, 1924* 32 On April 8 we lengthened our stride and covered 12 miles.

3. c. *fig.*, esp. in phr. *to get into one's stride*.

1919 *Punch* 12 Mar. 210/1 The operator won the first game before I could get into my stride. 1929 *Star* 21 Aug. 12/2 The latter, opening the innings with Cutmore, got into his stride in Hill-Wood's first over with an excellent leg glide to the boundary.

Strigovite (stri·gǫvəit). *Min.* [ad. G. *strigovit* (1869), f. mod.L. *Strigovia*, Striegau, a town in Silesia: see -ITE ¹.] A dark green silicate of aluminium and iron found in the district of Striegau.

1875 DANA *Min.* App. II. (1880) 53. 1896 CHESTER *Dict. Min.*

Strikable (strəi·kăb'l), *a.* [f. STRIKE *v.* + -ABLE.] That may be struck.

1904 J. P. MANNOCK *Billiards Expounded* I. i. 23 The various 'strikable faces' of a ball.

Strike, *sb.* Add: **9.** *General strike, sympathetic strike*: see *GENERAL *a.* 2, *SYMPATHETIC *a.* 3 b.

20. (sense 8) *strike-faulting*; **strike-breaking** *vbl. sb.*, the action of a strike-breaker.

1920 *Manch. Guardian News Bulletin* 10 Sept. 2/1 A direct incitement to *strike-breaking. 1931 *Times* 24 Sept. 11/2 He [*sc.* Devito] was also the 'biggest racketeer in the Strike-breaking business'. 1925 N. E. ODELL in E. F. Norton *Fight for Everest, 1924* 299 There is considerable evidence of *strike faulting which would explain this.

Strike, *v.* Add: **2. e.** *To strike back*: to light or flash back (*FLASH *v.*¹ 9 c).

1904 *Technol. & Sci. Dict.* (ed. Goodchild & Tweney) s.v. *Bunsen Burner*, Occasionally the burner 'strikes back'— *i.e.* the gas catches light and burns inside the tube.

18. d. *To strike over*: to turn over on its side. (Cf. *keel over*, KEEL *v.*² 3.)

1930 *Times* 31 Mar. 7/5 The old vessel has been standing at the side of the slipway in Cowes, up which she was hauled and 'struck over' in the autumn of 1928. She was protected with an over-all covering.

Strike-out. [f. verbal phr. *strike out*: see STRIKE *v.* 83.] In baseball, an act of striking unsuccessfully (see quot. 1874 s.v. STRIKE *v.* 83 i).

1910 W. M. RAINE *B. O'Connor* 226 He's bound to make a hit or strike out. 1917 C. MATHEWSON *Sec. Base Sloan* 293 Wayne's opportunities to distinguish himself were few, for strike-outs were numerous.

Striker. Add: **3. f.** *Tanning.* One who smooths and stretches skins either by hand or by means of a machine. Also *striker-out*.

1921 *Dict. Occup. Terms* (1927) § 338 *Striker, striker-out*, (i) lays wet hide or skin on a slate or marble slab or table, and rubs it with a hand 'slicker' tool, of stone or steel, to stretch it, drive out excess of moisture, smooth it, and to close grain; (ii) sets rollers of a machine..in motion..and passes skin or hide between revolving rollers.

6. b. *U.S.* (Later examples.)

1898 *Harper's Mag.* Apr. 700/2 My 'striker' had just left me, with instructions to have my horse fed. 1929 B. DAVIS *Truth About Geronimo* 107 Geronimo's son demanded the post of striker (servant) to me.

c. *U.S.* (Earlier and later examples.)

1836 W. T. PORTER *Quarter Race Kentucky* (1846) 19 An awkward-looking striker of old Thompson's holding her by the cheek of the bridle. 1853 'P. PAXTON' *Stray Yankee in Texas* 355 To a few he [*sc.* John Murel] confided the extent of his design, and to each of these gave the authority to enlist all the minor villains of their acquaintance. The latter were termed Strikers, and used but as tools. 1873 J. H. BEADLE *Undevel. West* xi. 184, I had published a

Supplement, p. 3873; Corrigenda, p. 4092; Spurious words, p. 4093; Books quoted, p. 4094

Striking, *vbl. sb.* Add: 1. a. *Tanning.* The process of smoothing and stretching skins. Also *striking-out, sb.*

Strip, *sb.* Add: 1. *Comic strip*, in journals, a series of humorous pictures arranged in a row, and usually portraying some incident or story. *orig. U.S.*

Stripped, *ppl. a.* Add: b. Designating cards which have been cut or pared, so as to be easily drawn out.

Stripping, *vbl. sb.* Add: stripping-knife, also, a knife used for any stripping process; stripping-table *Electrotyping*, a heated iron table on which the wax mould is melted away from the copper shell formed on it.

Stroh, (strō, ʃrɔ̄). [G.— straw] in *stroh-fiedel* (G. straw fiddle), a kind of violin.

Strongylid (strɒ̃ŋgilid). *Zool.* and *mod. L. Strongylidæ* (= STRONGYLUS), a thread-worm.

Strongyloidosis (strɒ̃ŋgil-oidō·sis). *Path.* [mod. L. *Strongyloides* (strongylus) +-OSIS.] Infection with intestinal worms of the species *Strongyloides intestinalis.*

Strongylosis (strɒ̃ŋgil-ō·sis). *Path.* [STRONGYLE + -OSIS.] Infection with diseases of the genus *Strongylus.*

Strophanthin (strɒfæ·nθin). *Chem.* [f. *Strophanthus* +-IN]. A bitter, white, crystalline, poisonous compound obtained from certain varieties of *Strophanthus*, as *S. hispidus*, and used as a heart-tonic.

Studentess. [see under STUDENT]; earlier U.S. example.

Studerite (stiū·dərait). *Min.* [ad. G. *studerit* (R. L. von Fellenberg, 1864), f. name of B. *Studer* (1794–1887), Swiss geologist: see -ITE[1].] A variety of tetrahedrite containing arsenic and zinc.

Studio. Add: 2. c. *Cinematography.* A room in which a cinema-play is staged; *collect. pl.* such a room together with the attendant workshops and laboratories. Also *attrib.*

Strue, (strū), schoolboy's abbreviation of Con-STRUE.

Strumitis (strumai·tis). *Path.* [f. STRUMA +-ITIS.] Inflammation of the thyroid gland.

'Struth (strūθ). *vulgar colloq.* Short for *God's truth* used as an oath.

Struty, *a.* [f. STRUT *sb.*[1]+ -Y[1].] Given to strutting; walking with an affected air of dignity.

Stub, *sb.* Add: 12. *trans.* To extinguish (a cigarette) by pressing the lighted end of the stub against a hard object. Also *with out.* Hence *Stubber*, something against which a cigarette is stubbed out.

Stubble, *sb.* Add: stubble-fed, a. fed in a stubble-field; stubble-quail, a species of quail, *Coturnix pectoralis*, native to Australia and Tasmania.

Stubby, *stuboy*: see STUBBY.

Studium generale (stiū·dism dʒenerā·li). *Hist.* [f. studia generalia (-ā·liə). [med. L.—] Latin STUDY sb., generale, neut. sing. of generalis GENERAL *a.*] An earlier equivalent of universitas UNIVERSITY.

Stuff. Add: 8. d. *U.S. slang.* Round the recording line.

Stumble. Add: 6. a. *attrib. and Comb.*

Stump, *v.*[1] 13. Add: c. *U.S.* stump the boy, a boy to drink.

Stumpage. Add: 2. *Forestry.*

Stuff, *sb.* Add. 11. *attrib. and Comb.*

Stuffed, *ppl. a.* Add: 2. Stuffed-over = prec.

Stuffing, *vbl. sb.* Add:

Stunsail (stun·s'l), a naut. corruption of STUDDING-SAIL.

Stunt, *v.*[2] Add: 8. d. *Apt to take offence at any freedom of contact or manner; easily offended or shocked; strait-laced. slang.*

Stutter, *v.* 1. b. (Additional example.)

Stévnsite (sté·vnɪt). *Min.* [f. the name of Enrique *Stéven*, mining engineer + -ITE[1].] A hydrous silicate of aluminium, sodium, and magnesium; a native alum of Chili.

Stumer (stiū·məɹ). *slang.* b. A race-horse which is fraudulently run in such a way that it cannot win.

Stump, *sb.* Add: b. On or up a stump: 'up a tree', perplexed, in difficulty. (See also *quot.* 1834.) *U.S. slang.*

Stylization (stəiləpizēi·ʃən). The process of rendering stylized; stylopized condition.

Stylotypite (stəilo·tipait, stəi-lot-). [f. von Kobell, 1865), f. Gr. στυλος pillar + τυπος form, in allusion to the columnar form of its crystals: see -ITE[1].] An iron-black sulphide of antimony, copper, silver, and iron.

Stypticin (sti·ptisin). *Pharm.* [f. STYPTIC + -IN.] Hydrochloride of cotarnine, $C_{12}H_{13}NO_3$.HCl, used in haemorrhage.

Styptol (sti·ptɒl). *Pharm.* [f. STYPTIC + -OL.]

Styrene (stəi·rīn). *Chem.* [f. STYR-AX + -ENE.]

Sub-calibre, -caliber. [SUB- 5.] Used with reference to a projectile which is smaller in diameter than the calibre of the gun from which it is fired, or to the firing of such a projectile.

Suberite (siū·bərait). *Min.* [ad. mod. L. *Suberites*, SUBER: see -ITE[1].]

Subirrigate, v. *U.S.* [SUB- 2.] *trans.* To irrigate (land) by underground irrigation. Hence **Subirriga·tion.**

Subject, *sb.* Add: 6. b. Add example of predicative use.

Sublimation. Add: 5. b. In *Psycho-analysis*, applied to modification and adaptation of primitive impulses. Hence **Sublimating** *ppl. adj.*

Sub-man. [SUB- 14.] A man of markedly inferior development or capacities.

Submarine, *n.* and *sb.* Add: 4. *attrib. and Comb.*, in many obvious uses; *submarine scout*, a blimp.

Submariner (sʌbmɑˈɹiːnəɹ). A member of the crew of a submarine.

Submarinism (sʌbˈmæɹɪnɪz'm). [SUBMARINE sb. 3 + -ISM[1].]

Sub-sheriff. Add:

Subsidist (sʌ·bidist). [f. SUBSIDY *sb.* + -IST.] An advocate of a subsidy.

Sub-title, *sb.* Add: b. *Cinematography.* A caption.

Subtonic, A. *adj.* Add: 2. Imperfectly healthy; below the standard of normal healthy growth.

Subtractive, *a.* Add: c. *Photography.*

Subulist (siū·biulist). *Theol.* Eccl. L. *sub una* specie under one kind + -IST[1].] One who upholds communion in one kind only.

Suburban. Add (at end): Subu·rbanized *ppl. a.*; Subu·rbanism sb., the act of suburbanizing, or condition of being suburbanized.

Subvent, *v.* Delete + *Obs. rare*[–1]. and add: 2. SUBVENTION.

Succès (siksɛ). [Fr.,— SUCCESS.] *Succès de scandale*, success, as of a work of art, depending upon its scandalous character. *Succès d'estime*, success of a work of art based on personal respect for its author.

Succession. Add: 14. f. *Psychol.* That form of association in which the relationship is a sequence in time.

15. *Succession States*, the states resulting from the dismemberment of Austria-Hungary under the Treaty of Versailles.

Sucrase (siū·krēs). *Chem.* [f. *sucre* SUGAR + -ASE.] = INVERTIN.

Suction. Add: 6. *attrib. and Comb.*

Suctorian, A. *adj.* Add: 2.

Sudan. Add: Also used *attrib.* to designate various dyes used for colouring oils and varnishes.

Sudd, *sb.* Add: 3. d. The waste liquors produced in the scouring of wool before bleaching.

Sudden. Add: 3. d. *Sudden death*.

Sudding (sʌ·dɪŋ), *vbl. sb.* [f. SUD(S + -ING[1].] = *sud-cutting* (see SUDD 1).

Sucker. Add: e. *U.S. slang.*

Sucking. Add: 2. d. *sucking reflex*, the instinct to suck as possessed by the young of all mammals; *sucking stomach*, the muscular first stomach of various invertebrates.

Sudoriparous, a. Add: Also *suda cloth* = SUEDETTE.

Sueded, *ppl. a.* [f. SUEDE + -ED[1].] A fabric woven to imitate suede.

Sudsonian (sʌdsou·nɪən), *a. Geol.* [f. L. *Sudsinati*, -initis, the name of a Cænlish tribe (whence the place-name *Sudsina*) + -IAN.] Designating Eocene strata in the northern Apennines.

Sufficient, *a.* Add: 2. *Sufficient unto the day:* see the day thereof' (Matt. vi. 34).

Suffolk, *sb.* Add: Also = Suffolk brick, horse, sheep, etc.

Sugar, *sb.* Add: 4. *sugar grease, land* U.S.

Sudbury (sʌ·dbri). The name of a town in the Nipissing district of Ontario, Canada, used *attrib.* to designate the rocks and mineral deposits found in that area.

Sugar-bush. 1. *U.S.* (Later examples.)

Sugar-camp. *U.S.* (See SUGAR *sb.* 5.)

Suggestio falsi (sʌdʒæ·stio fæl·sɑɪ). [mod. L.,— suggestion of what is false.] An indirect lie; a conscious misrepresentation of something whether by words, conduct, or artifice.

Suisse. Add: 2. A small white cheese resembling Neufchâtel.

Suit, *sb.* Add: 20. *Long suit*: see LONG *a.*[1]

24. b. In *Bridge* where *suit* is contrasted with 'No Trump', as *suit-bid*, -*call*, -*declaration*, -*double*, -*game*, -*signal*.

Suite. Add: 2. d. Add: c. A collection of songs by one composer on one main subject or in sequence at one time.

piling suites for independent performance from ballet music. *Ibid.*, The composer..accepts the term 'suite' as one which allows him a freer hand than symphony and one which indicates more definiteness of design than symphonic poem. 1930 *Radio Times Dict. Mus. Terms* 56 Often music originally written for a play is afterwards made into a suite.

Sulea (sū·liă). [Bengali.] A threadfish of India, *Polynemus sele*, from which isinglass is obtained.

1842 Royle *Prod. Isinglass Coasts India* 25 The species affording the isinglass, is the *Polynemus Sele* of Buchanan, *sele* or *sulea* of the Bengalese. 1858 Simmonds *Dict. Trade*.

Sulham, variant of *Selham.

Suliote (sū·liout). Also **Souliote, Suliot.** [ad. Gr. Σουλιώτης: see -ote.] An inhabitant of the Suli mountains in Epirus, of mixed Greek and Albanian origin.

1812 Byron *Ch. Har.* ii. lxxii, Oh! who is more brave than a dark Suliote? 1825 Halleck *Marco Bozzaris* Poet. Writ. (1869) 13 Bozzaris ranged his Suliote band. 1832 T. Gordon *Hist. Gr. Revol.* I. i. 76 The Souliotes, the flower of Albanian warriors, were driven from Epirus. 1852 G. F. Bowen *Mount Athos*, etc. viii. 214 The Suliote hamlet of Kiafa. 1875 *Encycl. Brit.* I. 573/2 The country of the Suliotes in the south-west of Epirus. 1897 W. A. Phillips *War Gr. Independence* vii. 127 Marko Botzares, the Suliot hero.

Sulky, *sb.* **4.** *sulky cultivator, plow* U.S. (earlier examples).

1867 *Rep. Iowa Agric. Soc.* (1868) 154 It is then plowed with double-shovel, or sulky cultivators. 1865–6 *Trans. Ill. Agric. Soc.* VI. 49 Driving a sulky plow, and plowing his one-fourth acre.

Sulphonium (sʌlfōu·niəm). *Chem.* [mod.L., f. Sulphur, after Ammonium.] A hypothetical univalent radical, SH_3, of which the derivatives, formed by hydrocarbon radicals replacing the hydrogen, resemble the corresponding ammonium compounds.

1906 *Jrnl. Chem. Soc.* LXXXIX. 696 Neither purely aromatic nor mixed fatty aromatic sulphonium bases can be obtained by the usual method which applies in the aliphatic series. 1921 *Ibid.* CXIX. ii. 1643 The molecular conductivity of some sulphonium compounds in acetone. 1927 Sidgwick *Electronic The. Valency* 283 There is less tendency to form oxonium or sulphonium than ammonium salts.

Summer, *sb.*[1] **6.** Add: **summer-board** *v. trans.*, to take as a summer-boarder; **summer-boarder** *U.S.*, one who lives during the summer months, at a boarding-house, in the country; so **summer-boarding**; **summer oil**, a thick kind of oil suitable for use in automobile engines during hot weather; **summer resort** (orig. *U.S.*), sojourn at a seaside or country residence during the summer months; a locality where summer holidays are spent; **summer-weight** *a.*, designating specially thin and light underwear and woollen goods suitable for wear during the summer months.

1903 Kate D. Wiggin *Rebecca* x. 107 Mother has 'summer-boarded' a lot o' the school-marms. 1879 *Harper's Mag.* July 164 A few quiet 'summer boarders took shelter for a season's rest. 1886 C. D. Warner *Their Pilgr.* iii. (1888) 59 The species of American known as the 'summer boarder'. 1880 *Harper's Mag.* Sept. 536/1 *Summer boarding here can be had for one dollar per week. 1918 C. A. Mitchell *Edible Oils & Fats* 1 In the case of olive oil, products which will solidify readily are sold under the name of '*summer oils'. 1857 *Appleton's Illustr. Hand-Bk. Amer. Trav.* 148/1 Charges at the Mountain House are, as in most of the fashionable *summer resorts in the United States, $2.50 per day. *Ibid.* 119/2 Saratoga has been for many years..the most famous place of summer resort. 1857 S. H. Hammond *Wild Northern Scenes* p. xi, I have come to regard these mountains..as my settled summer resort. 1873 J. H. Beadle *Undevel. West* xv. 257 For a summer resort one can spend weeks very pleasantly there. 1887 *Baedeker's Great Britain* 500 Pitlochry, a favourite summer-resort, in the midst of pretty scenery. 1890 H. C. Bunner *Short Sixes* (1891) 188 The old gossips of a Summer-resort. 1902 Eliz. Banks *Newspaper Girl* ii. 13 A summer-resort hotel. 1931 *Daily Tel.* 22 May 9/6 *Summer-weight weaves in hopsack, tweed, and knitted mixtures. 1932 *Sale Catal.*, Men's white Scotch make silk mixture summer weight.

Summer, *v.*[1] Add: **5.** *To summer over*: to hold over unused during the summer. *U.S.*

1871 *Rep. Vermont Board Agric.* I. 138 Do not be afraid of summering over a few tons of hay. 1896 *Vermont Agric. Rep.* XV. 39 In what way would you take care of the sugar that is intended to be summered over?

Sump, *sb.* Add: **2. c.** An oil-reservoir at the bottom of the crank-case of an internal combustion engine.

1912 *Motor Manual* 96 A well or 'sump' in the bottom of the crankcase. 1920 F. T. Hill *Pract. Aeroplane Constr.* 69 The sump..is made up either from sheet steel cut out and bent and welded up, or else 'spun' to the shape required. 1925 *Morris Owner's Manual* 8 Before starting out see that there is a plentiful supply of oil in the engine sump.

Sun, *sb.* Add: **11. c.** *sun-umbrella* (earlier U.S. examples).

1861 *Cincinnati Daily Commercial* 3 July, Advt., Great Bargains in..Parasols and Sun Umbrellas. 1887 Mary E. Wilkins *Humble Romance* 60 Armed with stout fans and sun-umbrellas.

12. b. *sun-kissed* (spec. of fruit).

In U.S. commercial use freq. written *sunkist*.

1893 *Jrnl. Soc. Arts* 16 June 738/1 Patinas, which give to silver, and its alloys a bloom as of a sun-kissed peach.

13. sun-arc (see *sun-lamp*); **sun-bather**, one who exposes the body, usually partly clad, to the direct rays of the sun, esp. as a form of medical treatment; **sun-bump** *Aeronautics* (see *Bump *sb.*[1] 1 c); **sun-dance** (earlier U.S. example); **sun-lamp** (see quot.); **sun-parlour, -porch, -room**, one so constructed or designed as to catch the maximum amount of sunshine; **sun-print** *Photogr.*, a print made from a negative by means of sun-light; a daylight print; so **sun-printed** *a.*, **-printing**; **sun-round** *U.S.*, a space of a day; **sun-scald**, (*a*) earlier U.S. example; **sun-tank**, a tank in which water or a liquid (as in the bleaching of castor-oil) is exposed to the sun's rays; **sun-valve**, a device by which the light of a beacon is automatically increased or diminished in power by the action of daylight.

1929 *Daily Express* 14 Jan. 19/3 The groups of Lido *sun-bathers. 1849 Mary H. Eastman *Dahcotah* xxii, The Sioux worship the sun. The *sun dance is performed by young warriors who dance, at intervals of five minutes, for several days. 1930 *Sel. Gloss. Motion Pict. Techn.* (Acad. Techn. Bureau Hollywood), *Sun lamps, a large lamp (*Sun Arc* or *Sun Spot*) reflecting its light by means of a parabolic mirror. 1917 Mathewson *Second Base Sloan* 114 The fourth house from the corner.., the one with the *sun-parlor on it. 1928 *Daily Express* 10 Aug. 3/7 There is no 'ocean' pavilion nor 'sun parlour' over the water. 1931 B. S. Aldrich *White Bird Flying* xix. 206 Through the sun-parlor they went, with its cathedral-glass skylight and its French doors. 1925 S. Lewis *Arrowsmith* xxii. § 4. 266 The two women spent afternoons sitting on the *sun-porch. 1928 *Daily Express* 16 June 13/5 Look kinda nice slung on the sunporch back home. 1928 E. Blunden *Undertones of War* viii, A large *sunprint on view at headquarters 'suspected' many enemy mine shafts. 1858 Lake Price *Man. Photogr. Manip.* 218 Such a negative would suffer considerably by being *sun-printed. *Ibid.*, Injured by *sun-printing. 1925 *Scribner's Mag.* Sept. 76/2 Advt., Living-rooms,..libraries, and *sun-rooms. 1928 *Daily Express* 14 June 12/5 The glass-walled 'sun-room' of the doctor's home in Detroit. 1924 A. J. Small *Frozen Gold* i. 39, I can generally get on their trail inside a *sunround. 1855 *Trans. Mich. Agric. Soc.* VI. 158 Where the tree has received a *sun scald, and the sap soured in sequence. 1903 *Sci. Amer. Suppl.* 21 Mar. 22756 (Cent. D. Suppl.) *Sun-tank. 1910 *Chambers's Jrnl.* Nov. 762/1 A sun-tank six hundred and fifty feet square is capable of producing over a thousand horse-power for seven hours a day throughout the year. *Ibid.* Sept. 620/2 One great feature of this beacon is the *sun-valve, whereby the light is ignited and extinguished automatically at varying periods, according to the time of year. 1926 *National Geogr. Mag.* Jan. 20/1 A Routing beacon equipped with a Sun Valve.

Sun-bonnet. (See Sun *sb.* 13.)

1837 *Southern Lit. Messenger* III. 332 She had on a deep sun-bonnet. 1860 [see Sun *sb.* 13]. 1865 *Atlantic Monthly* XV. 537 She pushed the wet yellow sun-bonnet back from the gray hair. 1884 'C. E. Craddock' *In Tenn. Mts.* i. 5 Her calico sun bonnet was thrust half off her head. 1910 Jer. Hart *Vigilante Girl* viii. 122 Rows of gaunt and sunburnt women in sun-bonnets sat in rocking chairs.

Hence **Su·n-bo·nnetted** *a.*

1839 *Southern Lit. Messenger* V. 113/2 The bevy of sun-bonnetted lasses, who gave us of their pies and apples. 1843 Carlton *New Purchase* xviii. 137 One beau, having two sun-bonnetted damsels behind.

Sunburn, *sb.* Add: **2.** The name of a fashion colour.

1923 *Daily Mail* 11 Sept. 11 Nude, Sunburn, Mulatto, and all shades.

Sunburn, *v.* **2.** (Examples.)

1873 J. H. Beadle *Undevel. West* xxix. 640 An Indian will 'sunburn' as much or even more than a white man. 1928 *Daily Mail* 6 Aug. 12/6 One girl tells me she 'doesn't sunburn easily'.

Sundae (sʌ·ndei). *U.S.* [Origin unascertained. Perhaps merely a respelling of *Sunday*.] A portion of ice-cream mixed with crushed fruits, syrups, nuts, etc. Also with defining word, as *fruit sundae*.

1904 *N.Y. Evening Post* 21 May, The Sundi, so popular at the confectioner's, can be prepared at home. Make a rich vanilla ice cream and over it pour the juice of your preserved fruits. 1904 *Minneapolis Times* 15 June 6 In one of the Jersey City churches fans and lemonade are distributed. Some brands of 'sundae' might be added with propriety. 1910 *Chambers's Jrnl.* July 431/1 A sundae—a mixture of ice-cream, soda-water, and raspberry juice. 1920 *Christian World* 19 Aug. 4/1 A strawberry sundae. 1928 *Observer* 15 July 18/1 Glacial drinks and sundaes.

Sunday, *sb.* **3.** Add: **Sunday best** (earlier U.S. example); **Sunday closing**, the closing of shops on Sundays except for the sale of certain commodities; also *attrib.*; **Sunday saint**, a person whose religion consists chiefly in the observance of Sunday.

1849 N. P. Willis *Rural Lett.* iii. 325 It was that kind of Sabbath weather in which Nature seems dressed and resting—every tree looking its '*Sunday best'. 1883 *Harper's Mag.* Sept. 639/1 The *Sunday Closing Bill for Cornwall. 1889 Donisthorpe *Individualism* vi. 179 Acts relating to ..Sunday Closing. 1889 *Kansas City Times & Star* 22 May, Some violent protests were made against the Sunday closing law. 1932 Upton Sinclair *Candid Remin.* ii. ix, He would join the church, sign pledges, vote for Sunday closing. 1888 *Cassell's Encycl. Dict.*, *Sunday-saint. 1903 Farmer & Henley *Slang*, *Sunday-saint*, one who roisters through the week and pulls a long face on Sunday.

Sundayfied, *a.* (Earlier U.S. example.)

1870 *Bazar Book of Decorum* (N.Y.) 164 We are apt to be, as the French say, *endimanchés*, which we may translate by the coined word *Sundayfied*.

Sundowner. Add: (*b*) A glass of spirit drunk at sunset. *S. Africa.*

1921 *Chambers's Jrnl.* Jan. 43/1 Surely you are not going to refuse a solitary sundowner. 1922 *Ibid.* 359/1 As a rule he did not even take the almost universal 'sundowner', for he felt that he could not afford to spend his very meagre profits on luxuries.

(*c*) (See quot.) *U.S.*

1904 *N.Y. Sun* 14 Aug. 17 The Washington sundowner is so called because he practises a profession, usually medicine or dentistry, after the close of Government office hours, or after sundown.

Su·nfi:sher. *U.S. colloq.* [f. Sunfish *v.* + -er[1].] A horse that 'bucks' (see quot. 1888 s.v. Sunfish *v.* in Dict.). So **Su·nfishing** *vbl. sb.*

1924 W. M. Raine *Troubled Waters* v. 47 Rocking chair [an outlaw horse]..was a noted fence rower, weaver, and sunfisher. *Ibid.* 52 Neither side-bucking nor pitching, sunfishing nor weaving could shake the lean-loined, broad-shouldered figure from his seat.

Sunflower. 4. Add: **sunflower oil** (earlier U.S. example); **Sunflower State** *U.S.*, Kansas.

1819 *Plough Boy* I. 43 The *sun-flower oil was a subject of conversation. 1888 *Harper's Mag.* June 39/1 Her citizens affectionately speak of Kansas as the '*Sunflower State'. 1904 *Minneapolis Times* 7 June 5 The floods in Kansas are subsiding. There was danger for a time that the Sunflower state would grow a crop of pond lilies.

Sunk, *ppl. a.* **4. b.** Add:

Sunk-band, *a.*, designating a method of sewing books by which the bands of thread are sunk into grooves sawn in the back of the book. *Sunk-enamel*, champlevé.

*a*1909 W. Matthews *Mod. Bookbinding* 27 (Cent. D. Suppl.) *Sunkband, 1929 *Times* 2 Nov. 10/4 The coral inlay, and red *sunk-enamel (champlevé) on the handle.

Sunlight, *sb.* Add: **1. c.** *Artificial sunlight*: see *Sun-ray 3.

1928 *Daily Express* 27 June 3/6 The Committee on Artificial Sunlight in Industrial Hygiene.

2. b. A sun-lamp (see *Sun *sb.* 13).

1928 *Daily Express* 28 Aug. 2/1 Thick gutta-percha tables for the seven great 'sunlights' were scattered about the floor.

Sun-lighted, *ppl. a.* (Earlier U.S. example.)

1787 in *Maryland Hist. Mag.* XXI. 220 The bright, Sun lighted Wedding proceedings.

Sunnism (sʌ·niz'm). [f. Sunna or Sunni + -ism.] The religion of the Sunnites.

1902 D. G. Hogarth *Nearer East* 174 Sunnism must cover under one name two groups, distinct at heart.

Sunny, *a.* Add: **2. c.** *Sunny side*, in phrases expressive of cheerfulness or optimism. Also *to be on the sunny side of*: to be on the 'right side' of, i.e. less than (a given age). (Cf. Shady *a.* 2 b.)

1831 Trelawny *Adv. Younger Son* xlix, Then, only looking at the sunny side of things, all was bright. 1837 [in Dict., sense 5]. 1865 *Atlantic Monthly* XV. 711 How many of us,..on the sunny side of thirty, have gone through the 'Paradise Lost'? 1889 W. S. Gilbert *Gondoliers* ii, Live to love and love to live—You will ripen at your ease, Growing on the sunny side—Fate has nothing more to give. 1926 E. Wallace *Ringer* 5 Alan Wembury was on the sunny side of thirty.

Sun-ray. Add: **3.** (Also *artificial sun-rays*.) Ultra-violet rays used for the prevention and cure of diseases, and as an aid to health during the months when natural sunlight is not available. Also *attrib.*

1928 *Daily Express* 27 June 3/6 The speedy development of sun-ray clinics all over the country. *Ibid.*, The adoption.. of sun-ray treatment as part of the national health programme. *Ibid.*, The treatment of disease by artificial sun-rays. *Ibid.*, The..pressing need for the sun-ray treatment to be brought within the reach of everybody by the speedy erection in all suitable places of sun-ray clinics. *Ibid.*, The benefits of sun-ray treatment of disease.

So **Su·n-rayed** *a.*, pleated in the sun-ray style. Also **Su·n-ray-plea·ted** *a.*

1930 *Daily Tel.* 1 Dec. 9/3 All sorts of sun-rayed circular skirts. 1931 *Ibid.* 21 May 6/2 A train of sunray pleated mousseline de soie and gold lace.

Sunrise. Add: **2.** The name of a fashion colour, a pinkish shade of apricot. Also *attrib.*, as *sunrise pink*.

1923 *Daily Mail* 19 Feb. 1 Crepe Georgette..in the latest French shades..Bosphorus-Blue, Sunrise pink. 1927 *Daily Express* 9 May 4 Colours Azure, Lupine, Sunrise, Lavender.

Sunshade. 2. (Earlier U.S. example.)

1842 *New York Daily Times* 22 Mar., Advt., Umbrellas, Parasols and Sun-shades..manufactured at Newark, N. J.

Sunshine, *sb.* Add: **5. d.** With reference to a (saloon) motor car with a top which can be opened to admit sunshine.

1929 *Daily Express* 12 Jan. 4/7 The royal coupé, with a sunshine roof. *Ibid.*, The sunshine saloon. 1931 *Ibid.* 2 Sept. 9/2 A new de luxe model of this type with sunshine roof.

Sun-spot. Add: **3.** An incandescent type of sun-lamp.

1930 *Sel. Gloss. Motion Pict. Techn.* (Acad. Techn. Bureau Hollywood).

Sun-under (sʌ·nʌndəɹ). *Colonial.* [f. Sun *sb.* + Under *adv.*, after *sundown*. Cf. Du. *zononder*.] Sunset.

1891 E. Glanville *Fossicker* xii. 94, I would..creep on after him from sun up to sun under.

Sun-up. Add: **2.** The east. Also *attrib.*

1927 M. M. Bennett *Christison* v. 60 The Dalleburra might camp on the far side of the waterhole, sun-up side.

Supe. Add example and cf. *Super *sb.* 3 a.

1915 J. B. Rathbun *Motion Picture Making* 72 'Westerns' are invariably taken in their proper locale, the 'supes' usually being drawn from the ranches and towns surrounding the studio.

Supe, *v.* [f. Supe *sb.*] *intr.* To act as a super.

1893 W. K. Post *Harvard Stories* 107 Do you remember the time..that we saw the old man suping in that spectacular play?

Super, *sb.* **3. a.** Add: (Earlier example.) Also used of film actors and actresses.

1845 Sol. Smith *Theatrical Apprent.* i. 15 That..class of individuals, indispensable in all theatres, called 'supers', or more politely speaking, 'auxiliaries'. 1928 *Daily Express* 1 May 12 Film supers in a crowd scene.

Super, *a.* Add: **3.** Of superlative or exceptional quality (cf. Superfine *a.* 5).

1895 *Army & Navy Co-op. Soc. Price List* 15 Sept. 1079 White or Black super Opera Bodice. 1926 *Glasgow Herald* 19 Oct. 9 It is probably in the best interests of these super cows..to have them milked three times per day. 1931 *Daily Express* 31 Jan. 5/3 The 1931 super de luxe model. 1932 *Ibid.* 25 June 7/4 We have race meetings here, and super bathing.

Super-. Add: **2.** (*b*) **Superinvest** *v.*, delete † and add example. **Su:perprona·tion** = Supination.

1922 *19th Cent.* Oct. 594 Even sordidness itself has put off all its vileness, and is seen *superinvested in beauty. 1907 *Practitioner* Apr. 486 The arms are fixed in a position of rigid extension, and frequently *superpronation, so that the palms looked outward.

4. a. *supercarnal, -fit, -formicine, -legal, -moral, -muscan, -physical.* **Super-audible** *a. Wireless*, of a frequency so high as to be inaudible; supersonic.

1926 R. W. Hutchinson *Wireless* 237 The resultant wave is anything from 2,000 metres to, say, 12,000 metres in length (*super-audible frequency). 1895 J. R. Harris *Union with God* viii. 133 The great *supercarnal, supersensual fact that is above observation of history. 1930 Sir G. MacMunn *Behind Scenes in many Wars* 259 The convalescent became *super-fit. 1918 W. Beebe *Jungle Peace* ix. (1919) 223 By *superformicine exertions a single small worker at last won a path to the rim at the top. 1920 H. G. Wells *Outline History* 478/2 He was a real monarch, *super-legal. 1922 W. R. Inge *Outspoken Ess.* Ser. ii. 131 It would be too absurd to suppose that our own State is the only specimen of these superhuman and *supermoral individualities. 1903 S. Butler *Way of all Flesh* lxxx, Almost *supermuscan effort [*sc.* of a fly]. 1924 W. B. Selbie *Psychol. Relig.* 277 Various forms of *super-physical life.

6. c. (Further examples of the unlimited extension of this use.)

1914 E. Barker *Nietzsche & Treitschke* 25 Treitschke looks to war as the expression of an exclusively national super-nation. 1915 *Chambers's Jrnl.* Oct. 661/2 The journalistic words 'superguns' and 'supermania'. 1916 *Blackw. Mag.* June 813/2 The German superbosses. 1917 *Observer* 21 Jan. 12/4 They do not regard their gigantic supersubmarines as merely commerce destroyers. 1917 'Contact' *Airman's Outings* 211 The super-heroes of the war. 1919 S. C. Carpenter *Chr. acc. S. Luke* They cannot survey all the facts, because there is one leading fact, the superfact, which they have passed over. 1920 Br. Temple in H. Begbie *Painted Windows* (1922) 168 The greatest political aim of humanity, in my opinion, is a super-state. 1921 T. R. Glover *Jesus in Exper. Men* i. 8 The early Christian..really used the Gospel as a sort of super-magic. 1926 *Spectator* 13 Mar. 478/2 The Westerners are a super-variety of the breed. 1927 *Weekly Times* 13 Jan. 46/1 To establish the claim of Christianity to be, as it were, the 'Super-myth'. 1927 *Glasgow Herald* 1 June 15 If we cleaved our way above the ocean at the super-speeds now contemplated. 1928 *Manchester Guardian Weekly* 31 Aug. 180/3 To enlarge their docks for the building of a super-liner. 1929 *Encycl. Brit.* III. 367/1 As fast as the Liège forts fell to the super-guns. 1930 *Daily Express* 8 Sept. 2/4 A patient imagines—quite seriously—that he is a kind of super-being.

9. a. *super-athletic, -conscientious, -exact, -famous, -fatted, -swift.* **Su:per-rege·nerative** *a. Wireless*, in which 'a powerful high audio-frequency oscillation is permanently established by some means or other, in order to check periodically the radio-frequency oscillations started by excessive reaction' (E. H. Chapman).

1921 Sir S. Colvin *Mem. & Notes* 175 The quite abnormal and *superathletic activities of his own brains. 1891 *Voice* (N.Y.) 31 Dec., The idea that there is anything 'immoral' and 'wicked' in asking a man to adopt your method of accomplishing a result he desires..is *superconscientious, to say the least. 1926 *Spectator* 19 June 1042/2 Their fussy officers took a brutal delight in making them *superexact. 1925 A. S. M. Hutchinson *One Increasing Purpose* i. xx, The *super-famous novelist man. 1908 Guthrie in *Brit. Med. Jrnl.* 17 Oct. 1161/1 A *superfatted liver, rendered so by various causes, toxic, and perhaps dietetic. 1922 *Wireless World* XI. 207/2 We might announce a prize for the most efficient Armstrong *Super-Regenerative Circuit. 1927 *Glasgow Herald* 1 June 15 The *super-swift transport of the human body over vast distances.

b. *super-satiate, -tuning.*

1915 *Chambers's Jrnl.* Mar. 150/2 Refined Englishman.. who has *supersatiated a cursed wanderlust by adventure.. in many lands. 1928 *Daily Sketch* 7 Aug. 2/4 *Super-tuning..has worked wonders.

10. *super-cautiousness, -conscientiousness, -enfranchisement, -martiality, -mastery.* **Su:per-regenera·tion** (see *super-regenerative*, *9 a).

1921 *Spectator* 30 Apr. 544/2 Even this *super-cautiousness is breaking down. 1887 F. R. Stockton *Borrowed Month* 227 My own *superconscientiousness. 1922 *Glasgow Herald* 7 Nov. 8 The *super-enfranchisement of the wage-earning class. 1918 W. J. Locke *Rough Road* xiv, To march with *super-martiality of tread. 1922 *Q. Rev.* Apr. 378 *Supermastery of sharp practice. 1927 *Mod. Wireless* VII. 613/2 *Super-Regeneration. Armstrong succeeded in utilising this effect for the reception of telephony. 1930 *B.B.C. Year-bk.* 452/2 Super-regeneration provides a method by which the oscillations generated in the receiver are interrupted at a frequency above the range of inaudibility.

Supercharged, *pa. pple.* and *ppl. a.* Add: **2.** Of the engine of a motor car or aeroplane: Having the cylinder charge increased above the normal by means of a **Su·percharger**, a mechanical device in the form of a pump which supplies the engine with air or an explosive mixture at a higher pressure than normal in order to increase its efficiency. So **Su·percharging** *vbl. sb.*

1922 *Encycl. Brit.* XXX. 41/1 Supercharging for high flying. 1924 *Glasgow Herald* 6 May 4 The proposition of super-charging engines for sea-going and for road, as well as for air service. *Ibid.*, The problem of super-chargers. 1927 *Observer* 16 Oct. 26 The super-charged six-cylinder-engined Mercédès. 1927 *Daily Tel.* 1 Nov. 10/7 In order to give 'Fighters' a better altitude performance, the engine is usually fitted with a supercharger. 1928 C. F. S. Gamble *Story North Sea Air Station* xix. 320 To equip the airships with supercharged engines.

Su·perconscious, *a. Psychol.* [Super- 4 a.] Transcending human consciousness. Also *absol.*

1884 Myers in *Proc. Soc. Psychical Research* vii. 219 We shall come, perhaps, to find *super-conscious* as necessary a term as *sub-conscious*. 1886 — *Phantasms of Living* II. 285, I believe that *super-conscious* operations also are going on within us; operations, that is to say, which transcend the limitations of ordinary faculties of cognition. 1903 T. Hardy *Dynasts* i. v. iv, In that immense unweeting Mind, is shown One far above fore-thinking; processive, Yet super-conscious. 1913 *Q. Rev.* Jan. 125 To put on a scientific rational basis the ideas of 'sub-conscious' and 'super-conscious' mind. 1921 *Public Opinion* 28 Jan. 90/2 What the world needs is a man whose genius will come from the superconscious, the divine. 1924 Sir O. Lodge *Making of Man* v. 113 In his total personality there is a great element of the subconscious and the super-conscious. 1931 Edith Lyttelton (*title*) Our Superconscious Mind.

Hence **Su·perconsciousness.**

1898 *Advance* (Chicago) 27 Jan. 107/2 [Jesus] had now reached the state of mind known to Hindus as samahdo or super-consciousness, and there was no pain for him on the cross. 1901 *Harper's Mag.* CII. 788/1 Since this unpleasant whirl of superconsciousness had swept over him.

Superheat, *v.* Def.: delete 'in order to increase its pressure'.

Superhet. Short for next. Also *attrib.*

1926 R. W. Hutchinson *Wireless* 236 The multivalve.. 'Super-Het' is scarcely a receiving set..for a beginner. 1926 *Glasgow Herald* 12 Jan. 10 The real heart of a superhet set is the first detector. 1927 *Observer* 6 Mar. 25 This receiver rivals the 'superhet.' in the number of distant stations it will bring in. 1931 *Daily Express* 16 Oct. 9/3 Band-pass tuning and a super-het circuit of advanced design.

Superheterodyne (st̄ūpəɹhe·terŏdain). *Wireless.* [f. *Super(sonic + *Heterodyne.] In full *superheterodyne receiver*: A form of short- or medium-wave wireless receiver in which, by means of a local oscillator, a beat-note is set up with the incoming signal and is amplified at the resulting intermediate frequency.

1922 *Wireless World* X. 11/1 The Armstrong super-heterodyne principle, in which the incoming signals are heterodyned before the first detector valve. 1927 *Observer* 13 Mar. 27 Since these tests I have had a superheterodyne receiver submitted.

Su:perindivi·dual, *a.* [Super- 4 a.] Of or pertaining to that which is above or greater than the individual. Also *sb.*

1916 F. von Hügel *German Soul* 92 The moral relation between the individual and the super-individual unity. 1924 W. B. Selbie *Psychol. Relig.* 150 The crowd will then act and feel, and express itself together. In so doing it becomes an entity or super-individual. 1930 W. R. Inge *Chr. Ethics & Mod. Problems* ii. 79 A sphere of existence strictly super-individual.

Superlative, *a.* and *sb.* **A.** *adj.* **2. b.** Add: *Superlative surprise*, the name given to an especially complicated method of change-ringing (cf. Surprise *sb.* 5 b).

1845 *Cambr. Chron.* 6 Dec. in E. Morris *Hist. Change Ringing* (1931) 144 A company of change-ringers of Saffron Walden, performing..upwards of 1,200 changes of Superlative Surprise. 1931 *Ibid.* 458 Harry Withers..once..conducted a peal of Superlative Surprise at Selly Oak, Birmingham.

Superman. Add: Hence **Su·permanhood.**

1910 *Dublin Rev.* Oct. 344 Human nature..is likely to remain still exactly the same. Those who believe it to be travelling towards moral supermanhood have obviously not studied it. 1924 W. J. Locke *Coming of Amos* xix, My vanity was pricked by what seemed to be her lack of confidence in my supermanhood.

Su·permari·ne. [Super- 6 c.] In full *Napier supermarine*: a seaplane constructed by Messrs. Napier; hence applied to other seaplanes using a similar engine. Also *attrib.*

1922 *Glasgow Herald* 25 Aug. 8 The Napier supermarine flying boat. 1925 *Ibid.* 9 Oct. 9 The new supermarine 'Southampton' flying boats. 1928 *Daily Mail* 25 July 9/7 A supermarine Napier racing seaplane.

Superna·tional, *a.* [Super- 4 a.] Transcending or independent of national limitations; supra-national. Hence **Superna·tionalism. Su:pernationa·lity.**

1915 Alice Gardner in Foakes-Jackson *Faith & the War* 36 The adoption of a supernational religion. 1916 E. Holmes *Nemesis of Docility* i. 16 Those nations cling tenaciously to their respective nationalities, as against the supernationality of Germany. 1917 G. L. Dickinson *Choice before Us* 218 The Council of Conciliation which we have proposed would be a standing committee of the 'Supernational Legislature'. 1918 C. Montefiore *Lib. Judaism & Hellenism* vi. 327 Judaism means something supernational, something larger than race. 1919 J. L. Garvin *Econ. Found. Peace* 544 Internationalism and super-nationalism are usually confused. 1920 E. Walker in F. S. Marvin *Rec. Developm. Europ. Th.* xi. 275 Music is the most specifically international, or supernational, of all the arts. 1931 *Times* 30 Sept. 13/3 That the best way to rebuild European economy was to create super-national groups.

Su:pernorma·lity. [f. Supernormal + -ity.] The quality of being supernormal or of exceeding what is normal. Also, an instance of the supernormal.

1916 Sir O. Lodge *Survival of Man* 2 Assertions concerning psychological supernormalities. 1922 *19th Cent.* Oct. 600 One of the first indications of potential genius in school children is unusual precocity or mental supernormality. 1927 P. B. Ballard *New Examiner* 60 The same degree of supernormality, the same superiority over the oldest of her schoolfellows.

Superpe·rsonal, *a. Philos.* [Super- 4 a.] Transcending the limits of what is personal. So **Su·perperson, Superpe·rsonalism, Su:perpersona·lity** (see quots.).

1901 *J. M. Baldwin's Dict. Philos. & Psychol.* I. 489/1 Thus hyperpersonal or superpersonal is that which is of the nature of personality, but to which the predicates of personality, some or all, do not apply. 1926 W. D. Lighthall (*title*) Superpersonalism. The Outer Consciousness. *Ibid.* 26 We can proceed a stage further, and call it the Person of Evolution. But its vast and complex personality requires a differentiating term. May we not apply to it the term 'Superperson'? and call its personality a 'superpersonality', its point of view the 'superpersonal', the system of its study, 'Superpersonalism'? *Ibid.* 88 The comprehensive superpersonal view would at once dispose of most of the confusion. *Ibid.* 111 Where Superpersonalism differs is in holding that the whole of that race is inspired by an indwelling independent, directive Superperson—the Person of Evolution. 1929 J. Huxley *Ess. Pop. Sci.* xii. 155 The idea of a God who is either personal or superpersonal.

Superso·nic, *a.* and *sb.* [f. Super- 4 a + L. *sonus* Sound *sb.* + -ic.] **a.** *adj.* Of or pertaining to sound-waves of such a high frequency as to be inaudible.

1919 *Electrician* LXXXII. 434/2 The French have experimented with a system in which a continuous wave signal is heterodyned to a *supersonic frequency. 1922 *Wireless World* IX. 647/1 A group of prominent U.S. Radio amateurs including E. H. Armstrong the inventor of the well known supersonic heterodyne receiver. 1926 *Glasgow Herald* 12 Jan. 10 If any readers have experience of the supersonic circuit in short wave reception. *Ibid.* 15 June 8 Supersonic signalling. 1926 R. W. Hutchinson *Wireless* 236 The Principle of the Super-sonic Heterodyne.

b. *sb. pl.* The science of inaudible sound.

1928 *Daily Express* 26 June 12/3 Supersonics is the science of inaudible sound, sound of such high frequency waves that it can kill instantly any living thing within range.

Supper, *sb.*[1] **1. c.** *U.S.* (Earlier example.)

1817 Fearon *Sk. Amer.* (1818) 44 Tea (called supper) in the evening.

4. *supper-bell* (earlier Amer. example).

1770 Fithian *Jrnl. & Lett.* (1900) 9 About seven the supper Bell rings.

Supper, *v.* **1. b.** (Earlier U.S. example.)

1805 R. Parkinson *Tour Amer.* 68 Going to look at the horses after what is called suppering them up at night.

Supplantal (sŏplæ·ntăl). (U.S. example.)

1891 *Harper's Mag.* June 69/1 The excitements of the day had..withdrawn his mind from..his fear of supplantal.

Supple-jack. Add: **3.** A toy representing the human figure, the limbs of which are manipulated by a string. Also *fig.* (Cf. *souple Tam*, Supple *a.* 2 c.) *U.S.*

1829–32 J. P. Kennedy *Swallow Barn* II. i. 19 Flinging out his arms and legs like a supple-jack. 1835 Longstreet *Georgia Scenes* 13 Bob Simons danced..like a 'Suple-Jack' ..when the string is pulled with varied force, at intervals of seconds. 1853 P. Kennedy *Blackwater Chron.* x. 147 His body spread out as usual in his favorite position of a supple-jack distorted to the utmost. 1871 Whitman *Democr. Vistas* (1892) 224 How the millions of sturdy farmers and mechanics are thus the helpless supple-jacks of comparatively few politicians. 1904 *N. Y. Times* 8 July 5 Those political supplejacks who go about with sanctimonious moan, saying: 'The President is wrong, but we must support the President'.

Supply, *sb.* **12.** *supply-boat, -train, wagon* (earlier U.S. examples); *supply-station*.

1840 J. F. Cooper *Pathfinder* II. ix, We shall lie in wait ..to intercept their *supply-boats. 1909 F. Ash *Trip to Mars* xxxiv. 262 Airships are of no use without a *supply-station. 1862 O. W. Norton *Army Lett.* 121 They followed up in our rear and cut off our *supply train. 1866 A. D. Richardson *Secret Service* xix. 241 Their retreat was a stampede, leaving behind great quantities of ammunition.. *supply-wagons and ambulances.

Supporter. Add: **5. b.** *Sport.* One who supports a particular form of sport or who makes a practice of following the fortunes of a particular team, by attending matches, etc.

1922 *Glasgow Herald* 30 June 8 An enthusiastic supporter of baseball. 1928 *Daily Mail Year-bk.* 84/2 The supporters of the Chelsea F.C.

Suppose, *v.* **9.** Add: *pass.* Used to express the fact that the subject is (not) expected by the conditions of his office, employment, etc. *to do* or *be* so-and-so.

1931 *Morning Post* 31 Jan. 6 Officers..were not 'supposed' to keep a scrap log.

Mod. He was in the kitchen. Well, he's not supposed to go into the kitchen. He's supposed to clean out the sty once a week.

Suppression. Add: **7.** *Psychol.* [G. *verdrängung.*] A phenomenon of binocular vision in which the image of one eye predominates, causing partial or total disappearance of the image of the other eye.

1894 Creighton & Titchener tr. *Wundt's Human & Anim. Psychol.* 206 It may sometimes be observed that these phenomena of suppression do not extend to the entire image.

Suppressio veri (sŏpre·ʃio vī·rai). [mod. L., = suppression of what is true.] Misrepresentation of the truth by concealing facts which ought to be made known. (Cf. *Suggestio falsi.)

1755 Chesterfield in *World* No. 105. III. 631 Here is not only the *suppressio veri*, which is highly penal, but the *crimen falsi* too. 1889 *Athenæum* 20 Apr. 500/3 There is an unintentional *suppressio veri* in his assertion. 1905 *Spectator* 25 Feb. 286/2 The English Church Union could hardly subscribe *ex animo* to an interpretation containing an important *suppressio veri*. 1906 W. De Morgan *Joseph Vance* l, I said to myself thank God for my well-intentioned *suppressio veri*.

Suq (sūk), *sb.* Also **souk, sook, sukh, sôk.** [Arab. سوق] A market-place.

1899 A. E. W. Mason *Miranda of Balcony* ii. 24 Every evening he comes down to the Sôk, buys milk and bread. 1911 J. F. Fraser *Land of Veiled Women* xvi. 191 Let us saunter through the *souks*, the market places of the natives. 1921 *Glasgow Herald* 20 Oct. 4 The suqs or covered streets, which, being screened from the glare of the sun, afford fine shelter for shops and markets. 1923 *Blackw. Mag.* July 128/2 Sheep, chickens, and eggs were..sold to his profit in the neighbouring 'suq'. 1926 D. Byrne *Brother Saul* v. § 4. 64 When Anna went abroad..to the sook of the perfumers. 1931 Sir S. Low in *Observer* 6 Sept. 13 [In the market-place of Tangier] The sun-smitten pavement of the *sukh*.

Suralimentation (sərælimentā·ʃən). [ad. Fr.: see Sur- and Alimentation.] Therapeutic treatment by feeding in excess of the requirements of the appetite.

1890 Billings *Med. Dict.* 1926 *Spectator* 3 Apr. 627/2 Many physicians do all they can to achieve 'suralimentation', as the French call it.

Surculus (sɔ̄·ɹkiŭlŏs). *Bot.* Pl. **surculi** (-ai). [L., = young twig, branch, shoot.] A shoot rising from an underground base, a sucker.

1775 Ash, *Surculus*, a shoot, a sucker, a slip; a middle branch between the larger and smaller ribs of a leaf. 1826 Kirby & Sp. *Entomol.* III. 227 The cocoon of *Donacia fasciata* (?) is fastened by one side to the roots or surculi of *Typha latifolia*. 1851 Balfour *Man. Bot.* (Index) *Surculus*, a sucker proceeding from the neck of a plant, and afterwards rooting, as in the Rose. 1900 Jackson *Gloss. Bot. Terms.*

Sure, *a.* and *adv.* Add: **A.** *adj.* **9. a.** *Sure thing* (orig. U.S.): a certainty, safe thing; often as an ejaculation of strong assent = Yes, indeed! Also *attrib.*

1896 G. Ade *Artie* ii. 9 You never see such a sure-thing crowd in your life. *Ibid.* xvi. 147 'Sure thing,' says he. 1904 *Daily Chron.* 28 Apr. 3/1 A 'sure-thing grafter' is a petty thief, who will take no large risks. 1904 *N. Y. Evening Jrnl.* 13 May 2 'Give us a box,' said Mr. Lehr.. 'Sure thing,' said the man behind the window. *a* 1906 'O. Henry' *Trimmed Lamp* etc. 214 But he ever will be present in my heart, that's a sure thing. 1911 J. C. Lincoln *Cap'n Warren's Wards* viii. 132 Sure thing! If you know who did it, he's your mark. 1931 Galsworthy *Maid-in-Waiting* xx, 'Shall you be at Jean's wedding to-morrow?' 'Sure thing! I give her away.'

10. a. *Sure-fire* adj., certain to come off, unfailing. *U.S.*

1918 V. O. Freeburg *Photoplay Making* 57 That photoplay included many 'sure fire' pictures, from the dashing waves to the coiling smoke over a burning village. 1930 D. Mackail *How Amusing* 68, I don't say it was new, but it was a sure-fire laugh. 1930 Dorothy Canfield *Deepening Stream* 61 Daily she heard Mrs. Whitlock sticking little pins of ironic comment into..the phrases which he had always counted as sure-fire.

B. *adv.* **3.** Read: Now *poet.*, exc. *dial.* (Irish) and *U.S.*

1861 *Trans. Ill. Agric. Soc.* IV. 460 Once successfully transplanted it will live sure. 1876 'Mark Twain' *Tom Sawyer* iv. 83 They're coming, sure. 1901 W. Churchill *Crisis* i. viii. 67 He'll win the handicap sure. 1908 'Yeslah' *Tenderfoot S. Calif.* i. 14 It sure was a cold night. 1913 Mulford *Coming of Cassidy* vii. 113, I shore lost a wad playin' faro-bank agin a tow-head.

C. sure-enough *a. U.S.* (earlier example).

1846 in *Life & Corr. J. A. Quitman* 288 They found out that the old ranchero was the sure-enough general.

Sures (sū·res). [pl. of Sp. *sur* south, south wind.] The southerly winds of the coasts of Chile, Mexico, and Peru. Also *sures pardos* (lit. 'grey south winds'), the sures accompanied by fogs.

1760–72 tr. *Juan & Ulloa's Voy.* (ed. 3) I. 148 At the period of the brisas, the sures or south winds begin to blow. *Ibid.* II. 210 These fogs the sailors call Sures pardos, and are fond of them, as they are a sure sign the wind will be fresh and constant. 1867 Smyth *Sailor's Word-bk.*

Sûreté (sürte). [Fr., = Surety.] In full, *Service de la Sûreté*, the criminal department of a prefecture of police, the equivalent of the English C.I.D.

1926 C. Barry *Detective's Holiday* i. 9 That he had successfully concealed his connection with the English *sûreté* he was practically certain. *Ibid.* v. 42 Me! I am now of the Toulon *sûreté*. 1928 E. Wallace *Again the Three Just Men* x. 204, I heard two gentlemen of the Sûreté discussing your future just before we left La Bourget.

Surf, *v.* Add: **b.** To go surf-riding. Hence **Su·rfer; Su·rfing** *vbl. sb.*, also *attrib.*

1917 *Chambers's Jrnl.* Apr. 280/2 The depth of the lagoon is trifling.., and this it is which makes surfing there so safe and enjoyable. *Ibid.* 281/2 The mass breaks on the beach; and the surfer presently emerges, dazed yet exhilarated. 1927 *Observer* 27 Nov. 29/5 When we grow tired of surfing ..we return to the hotel. 1931 *Times Lit. Suppl.* 1 Oct. 737/4 There were no surfing beaches then.

Surface, *sb.* Add: **1. c.** *Aeronautics.* In full, *bearing, carrying, lifting surface*: A plane or arched structure capable of sustaining bodies by its movement through the air; an aerofoil.

*c*1903 W. Wright in C. C. Turner *Rom. Aeronautics* (1912) 178 A smaller surface set at a negative angle in front of the main bearing surfaces or wings will largely counteract the effect of the fore-and-aft travel of the centre of travel. 1909 C. C. Turner *Aerial Navig.* (1910) 311 *Biplane.*—A flying apparatus with two main planes or 'carrying surfaces' one over the other. 1916 Barber *Aeroplane Speaks* 133 The term surface, which..is the term usually used to describe the cambered lifting surfaces.

6. a. (*d*) *Naut.*, designating ships which move on the surface of the water as opposed to submarine vessels, as *surface-craft, vessel, warship*; also Comb., as *surface-borne, -sailing* adjs.

1904 *Rapid Review* Feb. 84/2 The submarine offers commercial advantages that will render it a dangerous rival to the surface-sailing vessel in particular waters. 1905 *Trans. Inst. Naval Archit.* XLVII. ii. 407 Misconceptions exist ..as to the relative chances of accidents happening to boats compared with surface craft. 1914 C. W. Domville-Fife *Submarines* 10 The 1,500 surface warships engaged in this titanic struggle for the dominion of Europe. 1915 W. E. Dommett *Submarine Vessels* 5 The term 'submersible vessels' should, however, be reserved for those which, whilst mainly surface vessels, can be brought to an awash or submerged condition. 1925 F. Fraser & Gibbons *Soldier & Sailor Words* 71 Attempts to lay mines by enemy surface-craft. 1928 C. F. S. Gamble *Story North Sea Air Station* xiii. 224 A pilot might sight, and be in position to bomb a submarine and a surface-borne craft like a cruiser or destroyer.

d. surface-blow, a device by which the surface-water in the boiler of a steam-engine, etc., may be blown off; **surface blow-off**, the act of blowing off this surface-water; **surface chemistry**, chemistry of colloidal systems; **surface-drive** *Austral.*, a ditch or trench; **surface lines** *U.S.*, lines on which surface cars run; **surface noise**, unwanted noise such as is caused by defects in the sound-track of a sound-film or by the travelling of a gramophone needle over the disk; **surface road** *U.S.* (example); **surface-speed**, (*a*) the circumference speed of a revolving wheel; (*b*) the speed of which a submarine is capable when moving on the surface; **surface travel** *U.S.*, travelling on surface roads.

*a*1909 Thurston *Man. Steam-Boilers* 446 (Cent. Dict. Suppl.) *Surface-blow. 1909 *Cent. Dict.* Suppl. s.v., The surface-blow is usually a pipe from the top or side of the shell, ending inside in a trumpet-shaped mouthpiece, and leading outward through the shell to drainage connections. 1888 *Lockwood's Dict. Mech. Engin.*, *Surface Blow-off*, the blowing off of the scum which collects on the top of the water in a boiler. 1926 E. K. Rideal (*title*) An Introduction to *Surface Chemistry. 1902 J. H. M. Abbott *Tommy Cornstalk* iv. 57 There were from one hundred to one hundred and fifty Boers in a deep ditch—a '*surface drive' it would be in Australia—which lay just before the buildings. 1931 B. Brown *Talking Pictures* 173 Scratch and *surface noise are defects belonging to disc and film methods of reproduction respectively. 1932 *Wireless World* 16 Dec. 533/1 [With a gramophone 'pick-up'] When the cut-off frequency came below the resonance frequency of the pick-up, the sound at once became intolerably shrill and full of surface-noise. 1903 *N. Y. Evening Post* 3 Sept., The short-haul business is well provided for by the existing *surface roads. 1901 *Pearson's Mag.* XI. 659/1 Two giant rollers..whirl around with a *surface speed of something like a mile a minute. 1902 *Encycl. Brit.* XXXII. 576/2 With her original machinery the *Plunger* was to have had a surface speed of 15 knots. 1909 *N. Y. Evening Post* (semi-weekly ed.) 4 Mar. 1 On streets leading to these ferries *surface travel was blocked by heavily laden vehicles stalled.

Surficial (sɔ̄ɹfi·ʃăl), *a. Geol.* [f. Surface *sb.*, after *superficial*.] Pertaining or relating to the surface (of the earth); = Superficial *a.* 1. Hence **Surfi·cially** *adv.*

1892 J. D. Dana in *Amer. Jrnl. Sci.* Aug. 166 The outflow retains a thickness of 250 feet quite to its extreme western limit, which it could not have done if it had been a subaerial, or, using a much needed new word, a surficial, flow. 1895 *Man. Geol.* (ed. 4) 272 *Surficial*, that is, subaerial [eruptions]. *Ibid.* 806 In the case of the Connecticut valley area, the trap was poured out *surficially* from fissures along the eastern margin of the area. 1903 W. H. Hobbs in *Science* 23 Oct. 538/2 The term physiography..is inclusive of glacial geology; and..is sometimes referred to as superficial or surficial geology. 1920 *Nature* CVI. 89/2 The distribution of the drumlins of the Green Bay glacier..is a very striking feature of the large 'surficial' map.

Surgery. **1.** Add: *Surgery of access.*

1926 A. E. H. Pinch *Radium Therapy* Pref. p. viii, At the present date much more work is done with tubes than flat applicators, and a special 'surgery of access' has gradually developed,..necessitating the employment of general anæsthesia. 327 operations of 'surgery of access' were performed during 1925, the regions treated comprising the nose, mouth, pharynx, larynx, œsophagus, stomach, rectum [etc.].

Surging, *vbl. sb.* Add: **3.** *Physics.* A rapid oscillation of electric current, a cross-current. So **Su·rging** *ppl. a.*

1910 *N. Hawkins's Electr. Dict.* s.v., When two alternators are working in parallel, but with slight variations in speed, a condition arises which is known as *hunting*, in which the machines alternately lag and lead with respect to each other. The current variation due to this hunting is known as *surging*. *Ibid.*, *Surging circuit*, an electric circuit which is undergoing oscillations due to rapid charging and discharging. *Ibid.*, *Surging discharge*, an oscillatory discharge. 1913 W. E. Dommett *Motor Car Mech.* 83 The armature is made up of thin sheets which are insulated from one another to prevent cross-currents (or surgings) from existing. 1926 R. W. Hutchinson *Wireless* 105 The discharge consists, not of a steady flow, but of a number of rapid oscillations or surgings of electricity to and fro.

Surprise, *sb.* **4. b.** Add: phr. *the surprise of one's life(time)*.

1927 W. E. Collinson *Contemp. Engl.* 117 The surprise of his lifetime. 1931 *Daily Express* 15 Oct. 19/3 You will have the surprise of your life.

Surrealist (sɔri·ălist), *sb.* and *a.* Also in F. form **surréaliste** (sürrealist). [ad. Fr.: see Sur- and Realist.] An extreme realist. Also *attrib.* or *adj.*

1927 *Observer* 4 Sept. 5 She decided that her only chance was to adopt a surrealist technique. 1930 *Times Lit. Suppl.* 7 Aug. 639/1 So late as 1870 it [*sc.* the 'horror' school] strongly marked the 'Maldoror' of Lautréamont, which is so much admired by the Surréalistes of to-day. *Ibid.* 20 Nov. 963/1 Our only complaint is that M. Alexeïeff is not quite *surréaliste* enough.

Sursum corda (sɔ̄·ɹsŏm kǭ·ɹdă). [L., lit. 'up hearts': *sursum* from below, up + *corda*, pl. of *cor* Heart.] In the Latin Mass, one of the priest's exhortations to the people preceding the Preface; the corresponding versicle ('Lift up your hearts') in the Communion Office of the Book of Common Prayer. Also *transf.* and *attrib.*

1559 Becon *Displ. Popishe Masse* Wks. 1563 iii. 41 b, Before it was *Sursum Corda*, Lift vp your hertes vnto the Lord, but now is *Sursum Capita*, come in, Lift up your heads. 1856 *N. & Q.* 2nd Ser. II. 68/2 What is supposed to be the proper posture for the people during the comfortable words, the *Sursum corda* and the *Sanctus*? 1880 Mrs. Oliphant *Cervantes* ii. 29 A *Sursum corda* more genuine, perhaps, in its frivolity than a more serious service. 1892 C. Whitaker *Stud. Aid Prayer Bk.* 80 The Sursum Corda in the liturgy is as ancient as S. Cyprian. 1917 *Daily Chron.* 2 July 2/6 A fine speech ended finely on the sursum corda note.

Surtax, *sb.* Add: **2.** In the Irish Free State: see quots.

1930 C. H. Tolley *Income Tax*, etc., *Irish Free State* B, Super-Tax..is assessed on the income-tax assessments of the preceding year. Sur-Tax, which came into force for the first time for 1928–29, is deferred income-tax for the *same* year (1928–29) and is based upon the assessed income of that same year in respect of which it is charged. 1931 — *Handbk. Income Tax* 18 For 1928–29 and after, the Irish Free State have substituted sur-tax for super-tax, calculated on practically the same lines as adopted in Great Britain and Northern Ireland.

Surucucu (surukū·ku). *S. Amer.* Also **-cucu, curukuku** (ku-). [Native name.] The bush-master, *Lachesis mutus*, a South American snake.

1845 *Encycl. Metrop.* XXV. 775/2 *Surukuku*,..probably the *Boschmeester*, or *Coeniconssi*, of the inhabitants of Surinam. 1883 *List Anim. Zool. Soc.* 624 *Lachesis mutus* ..Surucucu or Bush-master.

Surveyor. Add: **6.** *pl.* Mountain boots.

1912 *Chambers's Jrnl.* Apr. 221/1 His high-laced 'surveyors' or mountain-boots.

Susceptance (sŏse·ptăns). *Electr.* [f. Suscept(ible *a.* + -ance.] In an alternating-current circuit, the wattless component of admittance, the energy component being conductance.

1910 *N. Hawkins's Electr. Dict.* 1916 *Standard Rules Amer. Inst. Electr. Engin.* 19.

Susian (sū·ziăn), *a.* and *sb.* Also **Susianian** (sūzi,æ·niăn). [ad. L. *Sūsiānus*, f. *Sūsa* or *Sūsiānē*, a. Gr. Σοῦσα (whence Σούσιοι), Σουσιανή, a. Egypt. *Sush* (cf. Syriac, etc. *Shôsh*, Pers. *Shūsh*, biblical *Shushan*): see -ian.] **A.** *adj.* Of or pertaining to Susa, the ancient capital of Khuzistan, a province of Persia, its natives or inhabitants, or their language. Also **Susia·nic** *a.* **B.** *sb.* A native or inhabitant of Susa. **b.** The language of the Susians or Susianians, which belongs to an agglutinative group akin to Accadian.

1567 W. Bercker tr. *Xenophon's Cyropædia* iv. Q i b, They had selected a moste goodly tente for Cyrus, and a Seusian woman. 1601 Holland tr. *Pliny's Nat. Hist.* vi. xxvii, It receiveth the river Hedypnus..and one more out of the Susianes country. 1857 W. K. Loftus *Trav. Chaldæa & Susiana* 372 The details of the Susian and Persepolitan structures. *Ibid.* 408 A much-defaced and weathered inscription, written in a language which M. Oppert terms 'late Susanian'. *Ibid.* 426 Pliny, referring to Susa, says that 'the Eulæus surrounded the citadel of the Susians'. 1874 Sayce in *Trans. Soc. Bibl. Archæol.* III. 466 The Susians, or Susianians proper, who had their seat at Shushan. *Ibid.* 474 This plural in *-ib* (or *-be* after a consonant) meets us again in Susian. *Ibid.* 476 Susian or southern Susianian. *Ibid.* 484 The Susian and Accadian genitive follows the substantive which governs it. 1875 *Encycl. Brit.* III. 187/2 A last attempt, made by the Susianians and the Chaldeans of Babylonia to oppose the power of Assyria. *Ibid.*, The revolt in his rear was stirred up by the Susianian king. 1898 A. J. Butler tr. *Ratzel's Hist. Man.* v. § 2. III. 166 In the Susianic texts.

Suspensoid (sŏspe·nsoid). *Chem.* [f. Suspension + -oid.] A colloid which is incapable of redissolving after desiccation at ordinary temperatures.

1925 J. Alexander *Colloid Chem.* 27 The reversible colloids are therefore called *emulsoids* and the irreversible colloids *suspensoids*.

Suspicion, *v. U.S.* (Earlier example.)

*a*1820 in Cist *Cincinnati Misc.* 127 Accusing me of suspicioning him of a wish to rob me.

Sussexite (sʌ·seksait). *Min.* [f. *Sussex*, a county in New Jersey + -ite[1].] A hydrous borate of manganese and magnesium.

1868 G. T. Brush in *Amer. Jrnl. Sci.* Ser. ii. XLVI. 242 Sussexite may be regarded an analogous compound in which ⅓ of the water is replaced by manganese and magnesia. 1883 *Encycl. Brit.* XVI. 396/2.

Sustain, *v.* **9. d.** Delete † *Obs.* and add example.

1884 *Encycl. Brit.* XVII. 88/1 It was in that very opera, *The Siege of Rhodes*, that Mrs. Colman, daughter-in-law of one of the composers, sustained the character of Ianthe.

Sustaining, *ppl. a.* Add: **c.** *Sustaining programme*, that part of a wireless programme which is produced and paid for by the broadcasting station. *U.S.*

1931 F. A. Arnold *Broadcast Advertising* 17 Offering two outlets for either sponsored or sustaining programs. *Ibid.* 31 Sustaining programs are those which are prepared and paid for exclusively by the broadcasting station and in which the advertiser has no participation whatever.

Svanbergite (svɒ·nbəɹgəit). *Min.* [ad. G. *svanbergit* (1854), f. the name of L. F. Svanberg, Swedish chemist: see -ite[1].] A pale-red mineral composed of sulphate and phosphate of aluminium and calcium.

1866 Brande & Cox *Dict. Sci.*, etc. 532/3 Pissophane. Svanbergite. Amblygonite. 1883 J. H. Collins *Min.* II. 166. 1892 E. S. Dana *Dana's Syst. Min.* (ed. 6) 868 Svanbergite...In rhombohedral crystals, resembling cubes... Color honey-yellow to yellowish brown, reddish brown, and rose-red.

Svarabhakti (svarabhɑ·kti). *Philol.* [Skr., = vowel-separation, f. *svára* vowel + *bhakti* separation.] The process by which a parasitic vowel is inserted between two consonants. Hence **Svarabha·ktic** *a.*

1880 Sayce *Sci. Lang.* I. 317 The insertion..of vowels.. goes under the technical name of *Swarabhakti*. This name was imported from the Hindu grammarians by Johannes Schmidt. *Ibid.* 318 Prosthesis, or prothesis..is another illustration of *Swarabhakti*. 1894 Lindsay *Latin Lang.* 145 The inserted or 'parasitic' vowel (sometimes styled in the terminology of the Sanskrit grammarians 'svarabhaktic' vowel..) is often seen in the older Latin loanwords from Greek. 1908 Michelson in *Indogerm. Forsch.* XXIII. 254 The *-i-* of *pulisa-* and the second *-u-* of *puruṣa* are svarabhakti-vowels.

Swab, *sb.*[1] Add: **1. d.** *transf.* A naval officer. *U.S.*

1850 H. Melville *White Jacket* II. xliii. 289 Touch your tile whenever a swob (officer) speaks to you.

3. swab-tail, a midshipman.

1925 *Blackw. Mag.* July 131/1 You bally swabtails have no *esprit de corps*.

Swag, *sb.* **7.** (Earlier U.S. example.)

1848 *Holden's Dollar Mag.* Aug. 475 'A Swag' is often met with in the Western country. It is a concave spot, sunk in below the level by nature.

Swager[2] (swē·dʒəɹ). [f. Swage *v.*[3] + -er[1].] One who swages metal.

1881 *Instr. Census Clerks* (1885) 91. 1921 *Dict. Occup. Terms* (1927) § 190 s.v., Agricultural machine knife swager.

Swale, *sb.*[3] *attrib.* Add: *swale-grass, hay* (earlier example), *-land.*

1873–4 *Rep. Vermont Board Agric.* II. 189, I would commence about the 20th of June,..cutting..the lightest last, unless the lightest were *swale grass. 1837 *Rep. Agric. Mass.* 19 Considerable quantities of fresh meadow or *swale hay is cut. 1893 H. Frederic *Copperhead*, etc. (1894) 176 The original Turnbulls had..drained the *swail-lands, and turned the entire place from a wilderness into a flourishing and fertile home for civilised people.

Swallow, *sb.*[1] **4.** Add: **swallow-dive**, a form of fancy dive in which the arms are extended to simulate the outline of a swallow; so **swallow-diving** *vbl. sb.*; **swallow-fork** *U.S.* = *Swallow-tail 7 c.

1897 *Encycl. Sport* II. 425/1 The most graceful is that termed 'swallow-diving', the body being shot out from the board [etc.]. 1898 *Swimming Mag.* Oct. 46/1 To Englishmen the term 'swallow' dive, not 'swan', would best convey the notion of this idealistic manner of reaching the water. 1902 *Encycl. Brit.* XXXIII. 121/2 The 'swallow' is one of the most thrilling dives. 1805 *Cabarrus* (N.C.) *Quarter Sess.* 22 Oct. (MS.) The mark of his cattle, sheep, and hogs is a *swallowfork in the right ear. 1869 *Overland Monthly* III. 126 An over-slope and a slit in the right, and a swallow-fork in the left. *a*1909 'O. Henry' *Roads of Destiny* xxii. 370 I'll make a swallow-fork in your other ear.

Swallow-tail. Add: **7. c.** A forked cut used in marking cattle on the ear.

1644 in *Maryland Archives* IV. 288 Swallow-taile in the left eare. 1845 *Portsmouth* (R.I.) *Rec.* 387 The Ear Mark of the Creatures..is a fork or Swallows tail on the Right Ear.

Swaly (swē·li), *a.*[2] *U.S.* [f. Swale *sb.*[3] + -y[1].] Of the nature of a swale or swamp.

1792 *Mass. Hist. Soc. Coll.* I. 272 Besides this flat meadow, there are pretty large tracts of swaily or swampy land. 1874 *Rep. Vermont Board Agric.* II. 420 The Cotswolds are just the kind to improve springy, swaly pastures.

Swamp, *sb.* Add:

3. *swamp-jungle, -man.*

1902 D. G. Hogarth *Nearer East* 108 Torrential floods, which..support a dense *swamp-jungle. 1908 *Chambers's Jrnl.* May 352/1 It [*sc.* a tree] may also topple over in the wrong direction and before the cutters and *swampmen can get out of the way.

c. swamp-fuchsia, *Eremophila maculata* of Queensland.

1928 D. Cottrell *Singing Gold* i. v. 42 Rabbits crouched at the roots of stunted crimson swamp-fuchsia.

Swamp, *v.* **5.** *U.S.* (Earlier example.)

1851 J. S. Springer *Forest Life* 84 This is done by an experienced hand, who 'spots' the trees where he wishes the road to be 'swamped'.

Swamper. 1. *U.S.* (Earlier example.)

1851 J. S. Springer *Forest Life* 92 The swampers, who cut and clear the roads through the forest to the fallen trees.

Swamp-land. *U.S.* (See Swamp *sb.* 3.)

1663 *Conn. Hist. Soc. Coll.* XIV. 433 One parcel of land.. being Swamp land. 1692 *Derby* (Conn.) *Rec.* 152 Another tract of Swamp land on the north side of the two mile brook. 1741 *Narr. Georgia* in *Force Tracts* (1836) I. 67 The land is of several sorts; pine barren, oak land, swamp land, marsh. 1765 R. Rogers *Acc. N. Amer.* 138 The swamp-lands are covered with cyprus, or reeds. 1791, 1856 [see Swamp *sb.* 3]. 1874 *Rep. Vermont Board Agric.* II. 550 Now one hundred acres of what was swamp land can be mowed with a machine. 1908 S. E. White *Riverman* v. 49 Thickets of overflowed swampland.

Swamp maple. *U.S.* (See Swamp *sb.* 3 c.)

1810 Michaux *Arbres* I. 28 *Swamp maple*, (érable des Swamps). 1832 D. J. Browne *Sylva Amer.* 106 East of the Alleghanies it is called Red-Flowering Maple, Swamp Maple. 1869 Mrs. Stowe *Oldtown Folks* xiv. 153 Here and there, a swamp-maple seemed all one crimson flame. 1890–3 E. M. Tabor *Stowe Notes* 39 The new shoots of the swamp maples are bright red upon the green foliage. 1907 *N. Y. Evening Post* (semi-weekly ed.) 4 Apr. 6 In the moist lowlands where the skunk cabbage has its home the swamp maple puts forth its flowers.

Swampy, *a.* (Earlier Amer. example.)

1662 *Providence* (R.I.) *Rec.* I. 62 Low Swampie Land.

Swan, *sb.* **4. b.** Add: **swan-dive** *sb. U.S.*, = *swallow dive* (*Swallow *sb.*[1] 4); hence **swan-dive** *v. intr.*; **swan-shot** (early Amer. examples).

1898 *Swimming Mag.* Oct. 45/2 The diving..included forward headers,..somersaults and the 'Swan' dive from twenty, thirty, and forty feet. 1912 Jack London *Son of Sun* ii. § 3. 53, I used to swan-dive a hundred and ten feet in the clear. 1639 *New Haven Col. Rec.* 26, 4 pound of pistol shott or *swan shott at least. 1675 *Essex Inst. Hist. Coll.* VIII. 40 One pistole..Loaded with Gunpowder and three swann Shot. 1700 *Cal. Virginia St. Papers* I. 70 They have made holes in ye Roof of ye House as bigg as Swann Shott. 1761 S. Niles *Indian Wars* ii. 343 The corporal of the troops..had five swan-shot in his body.

Swank (swæŋk), *a.*[2] *slang.* [f. Swank *sb.*[2] or *v.*] Stylish, 'swell'.

1919 G. W. Deeping *Second Youth* xvii, Look here, come for a ride. Had this new swank machine just a week. 1928 *Publishers' Weekly* (N.Y.) 30 June 2578 Advt., From honor and riches to poverty and shame—from the swankest hunting set of England to a garret in the Latin Quarter of Paris.

Swankiness (swæ·ŋkinės). [f. Swanky *a.*[2] + -ness.] The quality of being swanky; swagger.

1920 *Christian World* 2 Sept 4/2 The average American is free from swankiness.

Swaraj (swarā·dʒ). *India.* [Skr. स्वराज *svarāj* self-ruling, f. *sva* one's own + *rāj* to reign, rule.] Self-government (for India); the agitation in favour of this.

[1845 *Encycl. Metrop.* XXI. 679/2 The Swa-râj, or 'Own sovereignty', secured to him all the territory possessed by Sivâ-ji.] 1907 *Westm. Gaz.* 18 Dec. 1/3 The movement known as Swaraj. 1908 *Times* 27 Oct. 8/3 There is a good deal of talk going on in these days about 'swaraj', or the making of India a self-governing country. 1929 *19th Cent.* Oct. 435 The Swaraj party.

Hence **Swara·jist**, one who advocates swaraj for India; also *attrib.*; **Swara·jism.**

1908 *Westm. Gaz.* 24 June 5/1 The family lawyer..introduced him to two men..who were ardent Swarajists. 1925 *Times* 2 Sept., Swarajism in Burma. *Ibid.*, The Swarajist Programme. 1929 *19th Cent.* Oct. 435 Not the least important item..being unwittingly contributed by the Swarajists themselves in the Nehru Report.

Swarm, *v.*[1] Add: **7.** *Skat.* So **Swa·rming** *vbl. sb.* (See quots.)

1891 L. V. Diehl *Skat* 27 Swarming, giving as many points as possible on tricks taken by one's partner, or which he may be expected to take. 1893 'Hoffmann' tr. *Hertefeld's Game of Skat* 9 Swarming.—As tricks are valuable only for the scoring cards they contain, it is a frequent practice for one of the Opponents to play a high scoring card of another suit to a trick, in the hope that such trick be won by his partner. A card so played is said to be 'swarmed' upon the trick.

Swash, *int.* or *adv.* and *sb.*[1] **B.** *sb.* **9. swash-plate** (see quot. 1906); **swash-slope**, a sloping bank of shingle, etc. caused by dashing water.

1884 Knight *Dict. Mech.* Suppl., *Swash plate. 1906 *Techn. & Sci. Dict.* (ed. Goodchild & Tweeney), *Swash Plate*, a disc keyed on the end of a rotating shaft in such a way that its plane is not at right angles to the shaft; it is used to communicate a reciprocating motion to a rod which rests on it. 1913 W. E. Dommett *Motor Car Mech.* 158 The plungers are driven by a swash-plate mechanism. 1931 *Geogr. Jrnl.* LXXVIII. 134 The waves..were busily pushing forward shingle to the top of their *swash slope.

Swat (swāt), *a.* and *sb.*[3] *India.* Also **Swautee, Swatee, -i.** [Origin unknown.] (Of or pertaining to) a member of an Indo-European tribe of this name, originating in the North-West Frontier Province.

1815 Elphinstone *Acc. Caubul* (1842) I. 417 The Swautees ..appear to be of Indian origin. 1866 Sir T. Seaton *From Cadet to Colonel* II. 202 Afreedees and Swatees, Affghans and Maguls. 1897 *Westm. Gaz.* 8 Sept. 2/2 The Afridi rising ..was all a matter of wire-pulling on the part of..the Swat Fakirs. 1911 G. P. Gooch *Hist. our Time* vii. 170 A rising began in 1897 among the Swats, Mohmands, and Afridis.

Swatchel (swɒ·tʃəl). *slang.* Also **schwassle.** [? f. G. *schwätzeln*, iterative of *schwatzen* to chatter, tattle.] A name for Punch in a Punch and Judy show; *attrib.* in **Swatchel box, cove** (see quots.).

1854 *Household Words* 24 Sept. 76/1 A Punch's show [is] a schwassle-box. 1865 *Slang Dict.*, *Swatchel-cove*, the master of a Punch-and-Judy exhibition who 'fakes the slum', and does the necessary squeak for the amusement of the bystanders. 1887 Henley *Villon's Good Night* in Farmer *Musa Pedestris* (1896) 174 You swatchel-coves that pitch and slam.

Swatter (swɒ·təɹ). [f. Swat *v.*[1] + -er[1].] One who swats flies; an instrument used for this (also *swatting-stick*).

1917 *Blackw. Mag.* May 753/1 Fly-papers and fly-swatters proved illusive. 1921 *Dundee Telegraph* 21 July 3/3 We have tried fly-papers, swatters, formaline solution, and nets. 1925 G. W. Deeping *Sorrell & Son* xiii. § 1 In his attitude to the house-fly Mr. Porteous was a thorough pragmatist... The windows would be closed, and yesterday's paper folded into a swatting stick. 1926 *Glasgow Herald* 4 Oct. 8 Poultry food is made from the Mexican bluebottle, professional 'swatters' making a good living by catching them.

Sway-back, *sb.* (See under Sway-backed; earlier U.S. example.)

1874 *Rep. Vermont Board Agric.* II. 402 The buckskin McClellan was a regular hollow or sway back.

Swayless (swē·lės), *a. poet.* [f. Sway *sb.* + -less.] Not swayed or swaying.

1856 *Tait's Mag.* XXIII. 548/1 A gnarled tree, which..free and swayless in the fresh air grew. 1897 F. Thompson *New Poems, Mistress of Vision* xxii, And with her magic singing kept she..That garden of enchanting In visionary May; Swayless for my spirit's haunting.

Swear, *v.* **21. c.** (Earlier U.S. examples.)

1877 Habberton *Jericho Road* vi. 64 I'd told the fellers.. that I was goin' to swear off, so I was ashamed to go there and drink. 1885 *Outing* (U.S.) Oct. 55/1 As it's the fashion to 'swear-off' on New 'Years'.

Swear-off. *U.S. colloq.* [f. prec.] A resolve to forswear something.

1910 Jer. Hart *Vigilante Girl* ii. 30 'So I stopped drinking...' 'And have you stuck to your swear-off?'

Sweat, *sb.* Add: **3.** See also Night-sweat.

9. *fig.* Delete *arch.* and add: Now *slang*.

b. *Old sweat*, an old soldier.

1919 *War Slang* in *Athenæum* 8 Aug. 727/2 'Old sweat' an old soldier. 1924 A. J. Small *Frozen Gold* i. 38 You're a levelheaded old sweat, I know, or you wouldn't be carrying the button. 1929 E. Wallace in *Legion Bk.* 23 The familiar groan of the old sweat with twenty years' service.

11. sweat-box (*a*), also *U.S.*, a compartment in which a prisoner is interrogated by the police; **sweat-rag** (U.S. example).

1904 W. H. Smith *Promoters* x. 168 That's the philosophy of a police *sweat box. 1905 *N. Y. Evening Post* 9 June 6 All the tortures of the 'sweat box' could not make him implicate a principal. 1843 R. Carlton *New Purchase* xi. 73 This luxury..was used only as a '*sweat rag', and not 'as a nose-cloth'.

Sweat, *v.* Add: **5. e.** In the game of house, *to sweat on*, to await anxiously (the last number). Also *transf.*, to be within an ace of (a thing), esp. in phr. *to sweat on the top-line*.

1917 Empey *From Fire Step* xix. 127 Sometimes you have fourteen numbers on your card covered and you are waiting for the fifteenth to be called. In an imploring voice you call out, 'Come on, Watkins, chum, I'm sweating on "Kelly's Eye".' *Ibid.* 252 *Sweating on leave*. Impatiently waiting for your name to appear in orders for leave.

Sweater. Add: **9.** *attrib.* and *Comb.*, as (sense 5) *sweater-shop*; (sense 7 b) *sweater-jumper*.

1928 *Weekly Dispatch* 13 May 16 Now as to *sweater-jumpers. Sometimes they are woven with designs [etc.]. 1901 *Chambers's Jrnl.* Jan. 29/1 It is by no means certain that the workpeople..had not to suffer that these things should be, for there are plenty of *sweater-shops even in free America.

Sweatered (swe·təɹd), *ppl. a.* [f. Sweater 7 b + -ed[2].] Clothed in a sweater.

1901 S. E. White *Claim Jumpers* i. 11 Two sweatered and white-ducked individuals. 1915 P. G. Wodehouse *Something Fresh* i. § 1 Her bright blue eyes, fixed on his flannelled and sweatered person. 1923 *Blackw. Mag.* Jan. 84/2 The white-sweatered young man..turned out to be the owner.

Sweat-house. 3. (See quot.)

1882 *Harper's Mag.* Nov. 872/2 The grapes for raisin-making..are removed to an airy building known as a 'sweat-house', where they remain possibly a month, till the last vestiges of moisture are extracted.

Supplement, p. 3873; Corrigenda, p. 4092; Spurious words, p. 4093; Books quoted, p. 4094

Sweating, *vbl. sb.* Add: **5. b.** Extreme pressure (including torture) for the purpose of extorting confession. *U.S.*

1824 in Jas. Hall *Sketches* (1835) I. 222 The torture of sweating..that is, of suspension by the arms, pinioned behind the back, brought a confession. 1904 *Cincinnati Enquirer* 21 Oct. 4 He confessed, under sweating, that he broke into several offices.

Swedge, *v.* Add: Also *intr.* To go *off* or depart without paying. *U.S. Naut. slang.*

1897 Kipling *Capt. Cour.* 132 'Seems kinder unneighbourly to let 'em swedge off like this,' Salters suggested, feeling in his pockets.

Swedish, *a.* Also *Swedish exercises.*

1923 Wodehouse *Inimit. Jeeves* xi. 123 If she had knocked off starchy foods and done Swedish exercises for a bit.

Sweeny. *U.S.* (Earlier example.) Hence **Sweenied** (swīˑnid) *a.*

1829–32 J. P. Kennedy *Swallow Barn* II. i. 22 He professed to cure the colt's distemper, sweeny, and other maladies. 1871 *Rep. Indian Affairs* (1872) 554 The three mules were thin, and one of them lame in the right shoulder, 'sweenied'.

Sweep, *sb.* Add: **3. c.** *Aeronautics.* (See quots.)

1907 F. W. Lanchester *Aerodynamics* 228 Let us term the vertical cross-section of this stream or stratum the 'sweep' of the plane. 1908 *Rep. Brit. Assoc.* 828 A theory founded on the hypothesis of constant sweep—that is, upon the assumption of a layer of air of defined thickness uniformly handled by the aeroplane. 1911 *Ibid.* 482 Two dimensions of the mass of air deflected are plausibly functions of the span and chord of the plane; the third, which defines the depth of the stratum and is known as the 'sweep' is taken as an empirical function of the chord.

33. b. *U.S.* (Examples.)

1846 *Yale Banger* 10 Nov., A Freshman by the faithful sweep Was found half buried in soft sleep. 1851 B. H. Hall *College Words* 296.

34. (in sense 19) *sweep-ticket.*

1930 *Daily Express* 23 May 3/4 Who sent out the Mayfair Luncheon Club's £20,000 sweep tickets?

Sweep, *v.* Add: **14. b.** *Ent.* To drag a net over the surface of (herbage, etc.) in order to catch insects. (Cf. Sweep-net 2.) Also in *vbl. sb.*

1877 *Encycl. Brit.* VI. 134/2 'Sweeping' and 'beating' are the means mainly relied upon by the coleopterist for filling his cabinet. 1926 *Nat. Hist. Oxford Distr.* 263 *Hemerodromia precatoria* Fln. and *H. raptoria* Mg. have been captured by sweeping water plants in 'Mesopotamia'.

Sweet, *a.* and *adv.* Add: **A.** *adj.* **3. e.** *Coal-mining.* Of coal, free from sulphur.

1863 *Edin. Rev.* Apr. 411 The 'sweetest' kinds of coal (the freest from sulphur) are reserved for the smelting furnace. 1910 *Rep. Brit. Assoc.* 611 The Coal Measures include 'sweet', *i.e.*, non-sulphurous, coals at several horizons.

C. *Comb.* **1. a. sweet oil** *spec.*, also rape oil.

1886 *Encycl. Brit.* XX. 273/2 Rape oil,..known also as 'sweet oil,' is obtained from seeds of cultivated varieties of the cruciferous genus *Brassica.*

b. sweet-bough *U.S.*, an early variety of apple.

1849 *Rep. U.S. Comm. Patents, Agric.* (1850) 231 Of summer apples, the best..are the early-harvest and early sweet-bough. 1906 Alice Brown in *Harper's Mag.* Apr. 667 He halted under the sweet-bough and gave one branch a shake.

Sweetie. Add: **2.** A sweetheart. *U.S.*

1778 [see Yankee 1 a]. 1928 *Daily Tel.* 24 Apr. 9/2 One of the most amusing episodes shows the comedian visiting Coney Island with his 'sweetie.'

Sweet singer. Add: **2.** A religious poet.

1560, 1652 [see Singer[1] 2]. 1892 Julian *Dict. Hymnol.* 1284/2 William Williams, of Pantycelyn, was the Sweet Singer of Wales. 1933 *The Sign* July 92/2 The sweet singer, Christina Rossetti.

Swell-. swell-head *U.S.* (earlier examples).

1845 J. J. Hooper *Adv. Simon Suggs* iv. (1928) 36 As for the present directory, they're all a pack of d—d swell-heads. 1852 *Doc. Hist. Amer. Industr. Soc.* VIII. 72 The swell-head aristocracy of Virginia.

Swile (swail). *local.* [Origin unascertained.] The common seal, *Phoca vitulina.*

1877 Hallock *Sportsman's Gaz.* (Cent. D.). 1920 W. T. Grenfell *Labrador Doctor* vii. 145 The 'swiles' (seals) had struck in, and all hands were out on the ice. 1923 F. Baird *Parson John of Labrador* iii, It's t' good Lord as does it, ..as made t'harbours for we—an' sends t' fish, an' the swiles.

Swilkie (swiˑlki), var. Swelchie.

1905 *Eng. Dial. Dict.*, *Swilkie*,..Cai[thness]. A large whirlpool in the sea. 1910 *Blackw. Mag.* June 897/1 The swilkies of Stroma and Swona.

Swill, *sb.*[2] **3.** *swill-barrel, -milk, -pail* (earlier U.S. examples).

1869 Mrs. Stowe *Oldtown Folks* xxxvi. 469 The wasteful excesses she had seen in the minister's *swill-barrel. 1858 C. L. Flint *Milch Cows*, etc. 208 The nefarious traffic in '*swill-milk', or milk produced from cows fed entirely on 'still-slops'. 1892 *Vermont Agric. Rep.* XII. 150 A vile imitation, compounded of..swill milk and sugar. 1741 *Boston News-Let.* 12 Feb., Taken up by John Morey, Esq...a *Swill-Pale, otherwise called a Hog-Pale. 1857 *Lawrence* (Kan-as) *Republican* 11 June 4 [The dog] always had his nose first in the swill-pail.

Swimmer[2] (swiˑmər). *colloq.* [See *-er[6].] A swimming-costume.

1929 *Daily Tel.* 3 June, Two coloured swimmer with brassiere attached.

Swimming, *vbl. sb.* **6.** Add: *swimming-hole, -pool.*

1912 J. H. Moore *Ethics & Educ.* 128 The boy's love for the water, his affection for the old *swimming-hole. 1932 *Daily Tel.* 8 Oct. 19/1 Verity, the Yorkshire bowler, injured a toe in the *swimming pool aboard the s.s. Orontes.

Swinburnian (swinbɜ̄ˑmiǎn), *a.* Of, pertaining to, imitative or characteristic of the poet Algernon Charles *Swinburne* (1837–1909).

1867 E. B. Lytton in *Lett. R. Lytton* (1906) I. 207 The 'Gyges and Candaules' have some dangerous supersensual lines which I advise you to reconsider. It will not do for you to be 'Swinburnian'. 1892 W. B. Scott *Autobiogr. Notes* I. 300 When the Swinburnian passion for French things..had infected nearly all our young writers. 1930 *Times Lit. Suppl.* 25 Dec. 1099/1 The poem 'Ad Mariam' [by G. M. Hopkins] is..thoroughly Swinburnian.

Swine. 5. Add: **swine-dog, -hound,** tr. G. *schwein(e)hund*, in the sense 'beastly, filthy person'; **swine-measles,** an epidemic disease of pigs.

1916 Boyd Cable *Action Front* 261 *Swine dog was about the prettiest name he had any use for. *Ibid.* 245 'Sulky, eh, my *swine-hound!' said the officer. 1902 *Encycl. Brit.* XXXVIII. 360/1 The following tables..give the results of Pasteur's treatment..against *rouget* (*swine-measles).

Swing, *sb.*[2] Add: **5. b.** *Swing around the circle*: see *Swing *v.*[1] 11 c. *U.S.*

1905 *Springfield* (Mass.) *Weekly Republican* 6 Oct. 1 Will the appropriated money be available for campaigning swings around the circle? 1913 La Follette *Autobiog.* 537 Who had been with Taft on his 'swing around the circle'.

11. b. Phr. *What you lose on the swings you make up on the roundabouts*, etc.: losses in one direction will be compensated by gains in others.

(The allusion is to swings and roundabouts as prominent amusements at fairs, etc.)

1912 P. R. Chalmers *Green Days & Blue Days* 19 What's lost upon the roundabouts we pulls up on the swings! *Ibid.* 20 An' losses on the roundabouts means profits on the swings! 1928 *Observer* 1 Apr. 20/3 The loss on inland telegrams..is estimated at £1,600,000; but the telephones..have begun to show a substantial surplus, so that, in colloquial phrase, what the Government have lost on the swings they are gaining on the roundabouts. 1931 Galsworthy *Maid in Waiting* xiii. 120 What we lose on the swings we gain on the roundabouts. 1932 Joan Conquest *Village Pompadour* xxvi, What they missed on the swings of eavesdropping in Drowsy Lane they could make up on the roundabouts of gossip.

Swing, *v.*[1] Add: **11. c.** *To swing around the circle*: to make a tour of a constituency. *U.S.*

1887 *Chicago Tribune* 2 Oct., President Andrew Johnson originated the phrase 'swinging round the circle' on the occasion of his famous tour to Chicago..in September, 1866. 1904 *Cleveland Plain Dealer* 23 Aug. 6 If he cannot be induced to 'swing around the circle', the hope is that he will at least appear at some of the principal cities in states where there may be a fighting chance. 1910 *N. Y. Evening Post* 29 Oct. 2 To stem the rising tide against him, Col. Roosevelt is to swing around the circle in Brooklyn to-night.

14. *U.S.* (Examples.)

1873 'Mark Twain' & Warner *Gilded Age* xlv. 405 You will find we can swing a two-thirds vote. 1923 'B. M. Bower' *Parowan Bonanza* iii. 40, I want one that can swing something besides his tongue.

Swing-. 2. Add: **swing-back,** (*b*) a reversion (of opinion, etc.); (*c*) the backward swing of the body, a weapon, etc.; **swing-forward** *Rowing*, the forward swing of the body; **swing-light,** a light hung so as to swing to and fro; **swing-man, rider** *U.S.* (see Swing *sb.*[2] 12 c); **swing-over,** a change to an opposite side or opinion to another; **swing-sign,** a sign-board suspended so as to swing to and fro in the wind; **swing-trivet** (see quot.)

1890 H. G. Hutchinson, etc. *Golf* iv. (1895) 102 It is an effect of stretching after an artificially long *swing back. 1898 *Encycl. Sport* II. 272/1 The swing back is so combined with the slide that as the swing comes to its extreme point back, so does the slide arrive at its backstop. 1924 *Public Opinion* 4 July 16/2 The swing-back to bi-illicism appears as an accomplished fact. 1931 *Star* 8 May 6/4 In this age of increasing amusements, there is a real swing-back in the direction of sweepstake interests. 1898 *Encycl. Sport* II. 272/1 As the *swing forward stops, all weight is taken off the handle of the oar. 1901 'L. Malet' *Hist. Sir R. Calmady* II. iv, To right and left a range of stable doors, with round *swing-lights between each. 1903 A. Adams *Log Cowboy* iii. 20 The herd trailed along behind the leaders ..guarded by outriders, known as *swing men. 1927 *Daily Tel.* 1 Nov. 13/5 Harden was twitted with the violence of his *swing-over. 1932 *Evening Standard* 28 Jan. 11/2 The 'swing over' was 1420 to the English side. 1903 A. Adams *Log Cowboy* xx. 312 We *swing riders were never out of sight of each other. 1912 *Daily News* 15 Aug. 7 The extent to which the *swing-sign habit has caught on is well illustrated by the example of Fleet-street. 1920 *Chambers's Jrnl.* 26 5/1 A *swing-trivet is arranged at each side of the stove, and these can be used over the open fire or with the hot plate down.

Swinger[3]. Add. **2. c.** *Gunnery.* A battery which is able to produce a sweeping fire.

1922 *Encycl. Brit.* XXX. 252/1 The fourth battery is a 'swinger', and covers two units on each side of its own unit, making 5,000 yd. of front.

d. *Cricket.* Short for *Inswinger, *outswinger.*

1923 *Cricketer Ann.* 1922–3 69 At present he..is apt to bowl the 'swinger' too often.

e. A badly centred gramophone record which causes the sound-box to swing.

1924 *The Gramophone* Jan. 155 Wavy-tone Records or 'swingers'. 1929 P. Wilson & Webb *Mod. Gramophones* xi. § 8. 252 Only too often one finds that the hole is slightly eccentric, and then we get what is known as a 'swinger'.

Swinging, *ppl. a.* **4. swinging bridge** (earlier Amer. example).

1708 *Boston Town Rec.* VIII. 52 The way leading from Madam Butlers Corner..to the Swinging Bridg.

Swipe (swaip), *sb.*[3] *U.S.* [Of obscure origin.] A race-horse groom.

1929 S. Anderson in *Mercury Story Bk.* 221, I had taken a job as swipe with one of the two horses Harry was campaigning.

Swipe (swaip), *sb.*[4] *slang.* [Cf. Swipes.] A term of abuse or reproach.

Mod. Get up, you miserable little swipe.

Swish (swiʃ), *a. colloq.* [? f. Swish *int.* or *sb.*[1]] Smart, 'swell'.

1879 *N. & Q.* 5th Ser. XI. 116 Provincialisms..in the neighbourhood of Lydford...*Bain't you swish!* = How smart you are. 1928 M. Kennedy *Dewdrops* 46 She'd got on a perfectly ripping dress, black and silver, really most frightfully swish.

Swiss, *sb.* and *a.* **A.** *sb* Add: **3.** Short for *Swiss muslin.*

1909 *Public Ledger Philadelphia* 24 June 5/7, 50 c. for 75 c. to $1. Dressing Sacques: lawns and Swisses. 1910 *Daily Chron.* 12 Mar. 7/3 A short sash curtain of dotted swiss or dimity is easier to handle. 1924 Mulford *Rustler's Valley* vi. 68 He thought he could make out an oval face drawing back from the dotted Swiss.

Switch, *sb.* Add: **6. b.** *Bridge.* A change of call from one suit to another. (Cf. *Take-out.)

1921 A. M. Foster *Auction Bridge* 101 Don't double if there is a probability of a switch into some other call which you cannot possibly double. 1923 — in *Daily Mail* 5 May 8 The supporting bid, the assist, the pre-emptive raise, and 'the switch' assume a new value.

7. b. *Tactics.* A line of fortified positions.

1918 *Glasgow Herald* 4 Sept. 4 The brilliant thrust at the junction of the switch with the main Hindenburg Line. 1919 *Daily Mail Year Bk.* 98/2 By Aug. 30 the British south-east of Arras had carried their advance up to the Wotan line, or Hindenburg 'switch'.

8. switch-bid, -suit *Bridge* (cf. *6 b); **switch-over,** a change-over; **switch-tailed** *a. U.S.*, having a switch tail.

1921 A. M. Foster *Auction Bridge* 121 A *switch bid will be regarded by the partner as an encouragement. *Ibid.* 124 No tricks need be lost in the *switch suit. 1928 *Daily Express* 12 Nov. 10/2 The opening left by America's *switch-over to the 'talkies' can be brilliantly exploited. 1809 W. Irving *Knickerb.* v. ii. 190 A raw-boned, *switch-tailed charger. 1836 *Southern Lit. Messenger* II. 156 Mounted on his little switch tailed grey.

Switch, *v.* Add: **1. c.** *I'll be switched*, used to imply negation or surprise. *U.S. colloq.*

1849 J. B. Jones *Wild Western Scenes* xiv. 190 I'll be switched if many folks lives in higher houses than I does. *a* 1861 Winthrop *John Brent* xvii. 196 I'll be switched round creation if you do. 1904 Gene Stratton-Porter *Freckles* 50 Well, I'll be switched!..If that ain't both their nest!

6. *U.S.* (Earlier example.)

1861 in Putnam *Mem. Publisher* (1915) 421 Each car.. carried in white letters the caution:..Not to be switched under penalty of death.

7. b. *Bridge.* To change to another suit in bidding.

1921 A. M. Foster *Auction Bridge* 32 Your partner..can support your call or switch into another bid. *Ibid.* 107 Your opponents..switch back into their suit which you may not be able to double. 1932 *Daily Tel.* 8 Oct. 15/5 At Contract he has the additional and highly important duty of raising the opener's bid as far towards a game or slam contract as his hand permits, and, if he switches, of deciding whether to make a pre-emptive bid or not.

Switchback. Add: **A.** *adj.* **c.** *Aeronautics.* Resembling the undulation of a switchback railway.

1908 F. W. Lanchester *Aerodonetics* 30 A magnificent flight, remarkable 'switch-back' flight path, distance, relative to wind, probably over 600 yards.

B. *sb.* (Earlier U.S. examples.)

1873 'Mark Twain' & Warner *Gilded Age* xlix. 445 There will have to be a branch track built, and a 'switch-back' up the hill. 1880 *Harper's Mag.* July 194/2 The railroad first using a very bold and ingenious 'switch-back' now runs through a tunnel.

Hence **Switchback** *v. intr.* (*b*) *Aeronautics*, to make a switchback flight.

1917 E. C. Middleton *Way of the Air* ii. 21 To 'switch-back' is to fly up and down, up and down, as the name implies.

Switchel. *U.S.* (Earlier and later examples.)

a 1793 Freneau *Poems* (1809) II. 236 Not spiritless switchel and vile hogo drams. 1914 H. Garland *Son of Middle Border* iii, In summer Harriet and I..carried 'switchel' to the men in the hay-fields by means of a jug hung in the middle of a long stick.

Switcher. Add: **d.** *Draughts.* A form of opening game (see quot.).

1881 J. Wyllie *Draughts. The 'Switcher' Opening* Pref., The 'Switcher' was so named by my esteemed and dear old friend, Mr. George Wallace, of Glasgow, and it was not inappropriately titled, for, with that weak and apparently silly opening, I have 'switched' and perplexed many an eminent player. 1902 *Encycl. Brit.* XXVII. 527/1.

Swither, *sb.* **2.** (U.S. example.)

1836 D. Crockett *Col. Crockett in Texas* 75 (Th.), I laughed heartily to think what a swither I had left poor Job in, at not gratifying his curiosity.

Swivel, *sb.* **4.** Add: *swivel-knife, piece, -principle, -rowlock, -seat.*

1886 *Encycl. Brit.* XXI. 31/2 The Americans have also the credit of two other inventions, viz., the steering apparatus.. and the swivel rowlock. 1907 *Practitioner* Oct. 528 By means of..Ballenger's 'swivel-knife',..the cartilage..is completely excised. 1911 J. Ward *Roman Era Brit.* xi. 202 The swivel-piece was large and ornamented with a large ring on the summit. 1913 *Daily News* 2 July 2 Her propellers do not work on a swivel principle. 1916 *Blackw. Mag.* Oct. 475/1 He walked unsteadily across the room and sat down on a swivel-seat.

Swiz(z (swiz), *sb. colloq.* [Origin unascertained.] A swindle.

1932 G. Clark *Mistress* II. v. § 2 They want us to go to lunch. Just round the corner here...Bit of a swiz, isn't it? I did my best to get out of it.

Swizzle, *v.* **1.** (Earlier U.S. example.)

1843 *Knickerbocker Mag.* XXII. 366 We were never groggy, 'intoxicated',..'swizzled' or 'tight', but once.

Swollen, *ppl. a.* Add: **2. c.** *Swollen head* = swelled head (Swelled *ppl. a.* b); also a person with a 'swollen head'. Hence *swollen-headed* adj.

1928 *Sunday Express* 17 June 5/4 It [*sc.* charm] is a thing he will lose, if he ever gets swollen head. 1928 *Daily Express* 23 July 9/3–4 British film-producers..are..annoyed with me for saying that their swollen-headed outlook was the root-trouble...I feel certain that the swollen heads will bring about many crashes in British film-production.

Swollenness (swōᵘˑl'n,nės). [f. Swollen *ppl. a.* + -ness.] The state or appearance of being swollen.

1902 E. Selous *Th.-transfer. Birds* (1931) 14 In a very little while..this swollenness subsides and there is the same average appearance of the birds.

Swop, var. of Swelp.

1890 P. H. Emerson *Wild Life* 46 Swop my bob. 1916 G. W. Deeping *Sincerity* xxviii, Swop me bob, somebody else will be callin' for the police.

Sword, *sb.* **6. d.** Add: **sword-and-basket trick,** a conjuring trick by which a child shut in a basket survives apparent thrusts from a sword; **sword-rest,** a stand for swords.

1883 *Encycl. Brit.* XV. 210/2 The *sword-and-basket trick was common in India many years ago. 1909 Marg. B. Saunders *Litany Lane* I. ix, The determined little white face looked out from between two *sword-rests.

Swotter (swǫˑtəɹ). *slang.* [f. Swot *v.* + -er[1].] = Swot *sb.* 2. Also *attrib.*

1919 *Cassell's New Engl. Dict.* 1922 *Stationer's Advt.*, Swotter [writing] Pads. 1925 *Times Lit. Suppl.* 26 Mar. 219/1 If we allow contempt to confuse thought, the 'swotter', for all his dullness, will have us on the hip.

Sycon (saiˑkǫn). [mod.L., ad. Gr. σῦκον fig.] **1.** A type occurring as a stage in the development of certain sponges, in which the flagellated chambers take the form of radial tubes; a genus of sponges so named.

1887 *Encycl. Brit.* XXII. 421/1 *Myxospongiæ* in which the canal system is simple, with simple or branched Sycon or eurypylous Rhagon chambers. *Ibid.* 421/2 Canal system usually simple, with Sycon chambers.

2. = Syconium.

1845 *Encycl. Metrop.* VII. 51/1 A sycon is a fleshy, concave receptacle surrounding the fruits.., which are numerous, small, and distinct. 1900 Jackson *Gloss. Bot. Terms.*

Hence **Syˑconid, Syˑconoid** *a.* and *sb.*

1887 *Encycl. Brit.* XXII. 427 *Heterocœla*, a Syconid, in the Jurassic system. 1911 *Ibid.* XXV. 719 *Ute argentea*, part of transverse section, showing the Syconoid canal-system.

Syllabic. A. *adj.* Add: **1. d.** Based on or determined by the number of syllables.

1923 L. Abercrombie in *Times Lit. Suppl.* 12 Apr. 247/1 English metre, according to many theorists, is neither syllabic nor quantitative, but simply accentual.

Syllid (siˑlid), *a.* and *sb.* *Zool.* [ad. mod.L. *Syllidæ*, f. *Syllis*: see -id[3].] (Of, pertaining to, or resembling) one of the *Syllidæ*, a group of polychætous annelids. So **Syllīˑdian** *a.* and *sb.*

1888 Rolleston & Jackson *Anim. Life* 607 The parent-form in these Syllidians remains non-sexual. 1910 *Encycl. Brit.* V. 793/1 There are even dimorphic forms among the Syllids where the sexes are, as in many Polychaets, separate. 1930 *Q. Jrnl. Microsc. Sci.* LXXIII. 651 On a new Hermaphrodite Syllid.

Syllogism. 1. Add:

Inductive syllogism (Gr. ὁ ἐξ ἐπαγωγῆς συλλογισμός, Aristotle): one in which a conclusion is reached from particular premisses.

1867 Lewes *Hist. Philos.* (ed. 3) I. 295 The basis of Science is therefore an Inductive Syllogism. 1882 *Encycl. Brit.* XIV. 789/1 Aristotle's solution is remarkable, both in itself and in its bearing on the inductive syllogism.

Sym-. Add: **Symphilic** (simfiˑlik) *a.*, characterised by symphily.

1919 W. Osler *Old Humanities & New Science* ii. 12 This attention is what our symphilic community—to use a biological term—bestows on you.

Symbasis (siˑmbăsis). *Biol.* [ad. Gr. σύμβασις, f. συμβαίνειν to come together.] Extensive crossing of specifically related organisms. Hence **Symbaˑsic, Symbaˑsical** *adjs.*, **Symbaˑsically** *adv.*

1903 O. F. Cook in *Pop. Sci. Monthly* May 15 The more complex the organic structure the greater the necessity that it be supported, as it were, by many diverse, intergrafting lines of descent...The reason..may be ascribed to a special property or requirement called Symbasis.

Symbiogenesis (siːmbaioˌdʒeˑnėsis). *Biol.* [f. Symbiosis + Genesis.] The mutual production and symbiotic utilization of biological values by the united and correlated efforts of organisms of all descriptions (Reinheimer). Hence **Symbiogenetic** (siːmbaioˌdʒėneˑtik) *a.*, of or pertaining to symbiogenesis. **Symbiogeneˑtically** *adv.*, in a manner relating to symbiogenesis.

1912 *Index Catal. Libr. Surg. Gen. Off. U.S. Army* Ser. II. XVII. 329/2 The theory of two plasms, as a principle of symbiogenesis, the new teaching concerning symbiogenesis. [transl. of title of article by K. S. Merezhkovski]. 1915 H. Reinheimer (*title*) Symbiogenesis. The universal law of progressive evolution. *Ibid.* p. xvii, Love may be primarily viewed as a symbiogenetic power. *Ibid.* 144 They [*sc.* certain pairs of characters] are in reality quite different in constitution and bioeconomically (or symbiogenetically) speaking on widely divergent paths of evolution. 1916 *Contemp. Rev.* May 680 His [*sc.* Reinheimer's] symbiogenetic theory supports the Lamarckian doctrine or principle of orthogenesis.

Symbionticism (simbaiǫˑntisiz'm). [f. Symbiont + -ic + -ism.] The tendency to live in symbiosis.

1927 I. E. Wallin (*title*) Symbionticism and the origin of species.

Symbiosis. 1. Delete † *Obs. rare*[−1] and add examples.

1910 *Spectator* 30 July 173/2 The savage, with his emotional outlook, his sense of 'participation', of 'symbiosis'. 1912 *Hastings's Encycl. Relig. & Ethics* V. 426/2 Westermarck is quite right in making local contiguity the all-important bond of primitive life...This may be termed the principle of *symbiosis*. 1920 *Q. Rev.* July 164 So long as the people concerned can talk freely together, they form one spiritual symbiosis, and their culture will be the same.

2. *Antagonistic symbiosis*, symbiosis in which the symbionts are 'at war' with each other.

1900 B. D. Jackson *Gloss. Bot. Terms*, *Syntrophism*,..the antagonistic symbiosis of Lichen with Lichen. 1921 Annie L. Smith *Lichens* 262 The 'parasitism' of *Pertusaria globulifera* on *Parmelia perlata* and *P. physodes*, as described by Bitter, may also be included under antagonistic symbiosis.

Hence **Symbioˑtics** *sb. pl.* (see quots.).

1915 H. Reinheimer *Symbiogenesis* p. xx, I have coined the terms *symbiotics* and *antibiotics*, the former to denote those specific ancestral activities calculated to enrich the organic world and, concurrently, the species itself, the latter to denote the opposite (anti-social) activities. *Ibid.* 163 *note*, The cultivated apple has become somewhat surfeited at the expense of symbiotics, whilst the crab has not. *Ibid.* 337 It [*sc.* the kangaroo] presents the example of an animal wisely preservative of symbiotics.

Symbolic, *a.* **3.** Add: *Symbolic seizure* (cf. Symbolical *a.* 3 b).

1928 *Daily Express* 26 May 7/1 The claim 'in replevin' brought by the London County Council against the Hackney Borough Council owing to the 'symbolic seizure' of a tram-car was decided in favour of the borough council..yesterday in the King's Bench Division.

Symbolo-, combining form of Gr. σύμβολον Symbol *sb.*[1], as in **Symbolofideism** (siːmbǫlofaiˑdiˌiz'm) [F. *symbolofidéisme*], the theory that symbols are of the essence of religious dogma. **Symbolophoˑbia** *Path.*, a morbid dread of having one's actions interpreted symbolically.

1921 *Hastings's Encycl. Relig. & Ethics* XII. 151 *Symbolofideism is the name given to the theology taught in the second half of the 19th cent. at the Protestant Faculty of Paris by Professors Auguste Sabatier and Eugène Ménégoz. 1911 Dorland *Med. Dict.* (ed. 7), *Symbolophobia.

Symcentre, -center (siˑmsentəɹ). *Geom.* [f. Sym(metry + Centre.] A centre of symmetry: see Symmetry 3 b. So **Symceˑntral** *a.*, symmetrical about a centre; having relation to a symcentre. **Symceˑntry,** symmetry about a centre.

1893 Halsted *Elem. Synthetic Geom.* iv. 19 Two points are said to be symcentral with regard to the midpoint of their joining sect. *Ibid.*, Two figures are symcentral when they can be placed so as to have a symcenter.

Symmetallism (sim,meˑtăliz'm). *Economics.* [f. Sym- + -metallism of Bimetallism.] A proposed monetary system in which the standard metal is a silver-gold alloy. So **Symmetaˑllic** *a.* **Symmeˑtallist,** an advocate of symmetallism: also *attrib.*

1895 F. Y. Edgeworth *Papers rel. Pol. Econ.* (1925) I. 431 The arrangement that there should be a *joint demand* for gold and silver money might, perhaps, be called *symmetallism*, to distinguish it from the arrangement that there should be a *composite supply* which is called bimetallism. *Ibid.* 434 The value of the symmetallic compound is a mean of the values of its components. 1897 *Daily News* 30 Nov. 4/6 [A man] may be a Symmetallist, and believe that standard coins should be made from a mixture of silver with gold. *Ibid.*, Whether a symmetallist coinage be possible or not, it is certain that we have a symmetallist Administration. 1923 A. Marshall *Money, Credit & Commerce* 64 Although coinage of gold and silver at a fixed ratio causes movements of prices to be governed chiefly by the production of gold and silver alternately, a plan can be devised which would make the two metals work together: it may be called Symmetallism.

Sympathetic, *a.* **3. b.** Add: *Sympathetic strike*, a strike by workmen of a trade or trades to give support to others on strike.

1901 [in Dict.]. 1902 *Encycl. Brit.* XXXIII. 31/1 An unsuccessful attempt was made to induce all trades in Chicago to join in a great sympathetic strike. 1920 *Century Mag.* Sept. 791/2 The sympathetic strike and the 'logical' boycott when they lead, as they usually do, to interference with freedom of contract, are simply other names for civil disorder.

Symphonically (simfǫˑnikăli), *adv.* [f. Symphonic: see -ically.] In a symphonic manner.

1923 G. Saintsbury in *Times Lit. Suppl.* 4 Jan. 2/1 There undoubtedly is room for ametric and unrhymed but symphonically rhythmed verse. 1927 R. Vaughan Williams in *Radio Times* 3 June 440/3 The words as well as the music are treated symphonically.

Symphony. Add: **6.** *attrib.* and *Comb.* (in sense 5 b), as *symphony concert, -form, -orchestra.*

1881 in *Grove's Dict. Mus.* (1902) IV. 43/1 Orchestra to be permanent, and to be called The Boston Symphony Orchestra. 1884 *Art Amateur* (N. Y.) Nov. 118/3 Every patron of the symphony concerts and opera. 1899 *Who's Who* 999/2 Queen's Hall Symphony Concerts 1897. 1911 *Contemp. Rev.* May 615 The idea that the symphonic poem is a further development of the symphony form. 1932 *Daily Tel.* 8 Oct. 1/5 London Symphony Orchestra. *Ibid.*, B.B.C. Symphony Concerts.

Syn-. Add: **Syncephalus** (-seˑfălǝs) *Path.* [Gr. κεφαλή head], a double monster having the heads fused; hence **Syncephaˑlic** *a.* **Synecology** (-ėkǫˑlŏdʒi) [*Ecology], the ecology of (plant-) associations. **Syngonidium** (-goniˑdiǝm) *Bot.* [Gonidium], an aggregation of gonidia. **Syngonimium** (-goniˑmiǝm) *Bot.* [Gonimium], an aggregation of gonimia. **Synoptiscope** (-ǫˑptiskoᵘp) [Optic *a.* + -scope], an optical instrument used for fusion exercises. **Synrhaˑbdosome** *Zool.* [*Rhabdosome], an aggregation of rhabdosomes. **Syntaˑgmatite** *Geol.* [Tagmatic *a.*], a crystalline hornblende occurring on Vesuvius. **Syˑntopite** *Palæontol.* [Gr. τοπίτης dweller in a place], one of two or more species occurring in the same deposit.

a 1909 *Buck's Handbk. Med. Sci.* VII. 685 (Cent. D. Suppl.) *Syncephalic. 1889 *Ibid.* VII. 24/1 The *syncephali are not specially rare. The literature contains not less than seventy human cases. 1892–3 *Univ. Med. Mag. Philad.* V. 112 A syncephalus and an otocephalus recently presented to the Wistar and Horner Museum. 1927 T. F. Chipp (*title*) The Gold Coast Forest. A Study in *Synecology. 1882 *Encycl. Brit.* XIV. 556/2 Connated gonidia (*syngonidia), as in some foliicolous species. *Ibid.*, *Collema* (or *Nostoc*) itself, according to Nylander, is to be considered but as a single *syngonimium. 1928 *Daily Tel.* 28 Sept., The *synoptiscope.. has what resemble two movable arms in each of which is part of a picture, the two together making the whole picture. 1910 *Encycl. Brit.* XII. 367/1 The more complex umbrella-shaped colonies of colonies (*synrhabdosomes) described as provided with a common swimming bladder. *Ibid.* XIII. 708/1 Brilliant black crystals (*syntagmatite) with augite and mica [are met with] in the sanidine bombs of Monte Somma, Vesuvius. 1917 S. S. Buckman *Brachiopoda Namyau Beds* in *Palæont. Indica*, New Ser. III. II. 234 *Heimia protracta*..is congeneric and contemporary with both and a stable-companion (*syntopite) of the first.

Synantherin (sinæˑnþėrin). Also **-anthrin.** *Org. Chem.* [ad. G. *synantherin* (Marquart, 1834), f. mod.L. *Synantheræ* (see Synantherеous + -in[1].] A form of inulin obtained from the tubers of Composites. Hence **Synaˑnthrose,** a plant-sugar, $C_6H_{10}O_5$; lævulin.

1877 Watts *Dict. Chem.* V. 311 Inulin prepared from the [dahlia] roots by washing with cold water is called by Marquart *synantherin.* 1888 *Buck's Handbk. Med. Sci.* VI. 240/1 Rye consists of nearly sixty per cent. of starch,.. four of sugar (synanthrose) [etc.].

Synapse (sinæˑps), *v.* *Anat.* [f. the sb.] *intr.* To form a synapse.

1910 *Practitioner* July 98 The rubro-spinal portion (Monakow's bundle) connects the red nucleus with the opposite side of the spinal cord, probably terminating by synapsing round the anterior horn cells.

Synchronism. 3. Add: *spec.* of the audible and visible components in cinematography, television, etc. So **Synchronization, Synchronize** *v.*, **Synchronized** *ppl. a.*, **Synchronizer, Synchronizing** *vbl. sb.* and *ppl. a.*, etc. (see quots.).

1910 *Chambers's Jrnl.* Mar. 206/1 The movements of the mouths of the characters on the screen synchronise with the utterance of the phonograph. *Ibid.*, The general means of insuring synchrony between the two machines is by means of dials. 1912 *Ibid.* July 495/2 The synchronising attachment being extremely sensitive and rapid. 1922 *Radio News* (U.S.) Nov. 867/1 Mr. de Forest has solved the secret of the 'talkie movie' with perfect synchronization. 1928 *Television* Mar. 37 Thus ensuring synchronism between the transmitter and the receiver. 1928 *Sci. & Invention* (U.S.) Oct. 489/2 The greatest difficulty..in television is the synchronizing feature. 1931 B. Brown *Talking Pict.* 3 So that voice and picture were perfectly synchronized. *Ibid.*, The earliest practical attempts at synchronizing, i.e. keeping speech and gesture perfectly in phase. *Ibid.* 4 Since the film dial position corresponded to those of the phonograph, all that was necessary for synchronism was for both hands to revolve at the same rate, and always keep together. *Ibid.* 5 The synchronizer itself consisted of a box having a transparent disc, bearing an indicating spot, and coupled by gearing to the mechanism of the cinema projector. *Ibid.* 129 As in the regular R.C.A. synchronous system, volume controls are separate from the fader. *Ibid.* 287 A synchronized picture differs from a true talkie in that the scenes are first taken silent and then the accompaniment is added.

Synchronized, *ppl. a.* Add: *spec.* (see prec.); also, **synchronized gear-changing, -shifting,** a form of gear-changing on cars in which the action of the clutch is automatically synchronized with movement of the gear-lever. So **Synchronizing** *vbl. sb.* and *ppl. a. spec.* (see prec.); also, of gun-firing apparatus; **synchronizing gear,** a form of interrupter gear (see *Interrupter c) employed on aeroplanes.

1928 C. F. S. Gamble *Story North Sea Air Station* iv. 63 The 'synchronizing gear', enabling a machine-gun to fire through the tractor air-screw. 1932 *The New Yorker* 9 Apr. 51/1 The new Ford has synchronized gear shifting and a silent second-speed.

Syncopator (siˑnkǒpeˑtəɹ). [f. Syncopate *v.* + -or.] One who performs syncopated jazz music.

1927 *Daily Tel.* 22 Feb. 12/1 You may see (and hear) the first 'Lady Syncopators',..cutting rhythm into jazz patterns with the best of mere male 'syncopators'.

Syˑncro-mesh, abbrev. of *synchronized mesh*, used *attrib.* to designate a form of automatic gear-changing box.

1932 *Daily Tel.* 3 Aug. 10/7 Easy-change or syncromesh gear-box, which enables the lever to be pushed from notch to notch silently, with just a momentary pause in 'neutral'. 1932 *Oxford Times* 23 Sept. 22/3 Free-wheeling and syncro-mesh gears have for some time been almost universal on cars built in the United States.

Syndicalistic (siˑndikăliˑstik), *a.* [f. Syndicalist + -ic.] Of or pertaining to syndicalism or syndicalists.

1912 *Daily News* 20 Mar. 1 There was nothing particularly syndicalistic about a request for a minimum wage. 1915 *19th Cent.* Nov. 1062 He has played a prominent part in terminating two serious syndicalistic outbreaks.

Synechia. Add: **2.** An adhesion in either of the nasal fossæ.

1884 [see Dict.] 1900 *Jrnl. Laryngol.* XV 654 In the naso-pharynx the synechia is usually found connecting the lip of one or other of the Eustachian tubes to some part of the pharyngeal vault.

Synœcology (sinīkǫˑlŏdʒi). Also **syne-.** [f. Gr. συνοικία a community (see Synœcious) + -ology.] The study of plant communities.

1911 Tansley *Types Brit. Vegetation* 2 Synecology.

Synovial, *a.* Add: Also *ellipt.* for *synovial membrane.*

1910 *Practitioner* Feb. 206 Many septic infections of joints have but a feeble power of destroying their surfaces, while some others..appear terribly destructive both to the cartilages and the synovials.

Syntactic, *a.* Add: **2.** *Phys. Geog.*

1909 H. Sollas tr. *Suess' Face of the Earth* IV. 288 Near Worcester, in the midst of the region of syntaxis, Schwarz observed a great fault: it strikes in a horse-shoe, corresponding with the bend of the syntactic folds.

Syntaxis. Transfer *Obs.* to sense 1 and add: **2.** *Phys. Geog.*

1909 H. Sollas tr. *Suess' Face of the Earth* IV. 280 In the direction of the syntaxis, i.e. towards the west, their strike bends back in an arc. *Ibid.* 302 Linking and Syntaxis. The frequently recurring arcuate form of the mountain chains is the most striking feature of the Asiatic system. The manner in which the arcs encounter each other is two-fold, either they enter into syntaxis, or one arc cuts across the direction of the other.

Syntethein (sinteˑþīˌin). *Org. Chem.* [Irreg. f. mod.L. genus name *Syntethys* + -in[1].] A green pigment resembling chlorophyll and occurring in the marine ascidian, *Diazona* (*Syntethys*) *violacea.*

1913 *Rep. Brit. Assoc.* 509.

Synthesization (siːnþīsəizēˑʃən). [f. Synthesize *v.* + -ation.] The act or process of synthesizing.

1924 *Contemp. Rev.* Jan. 71 These two great ideas need synthesisation.

Synthesize, *v.* Add: **c.** *Biol.* To build up (a new species or form) by the mating of like mutants.

1921 *Conquest* Sept. 452/1 Only those [sports] which are not detrimental will continue, and will by combining and recombining with each other, synthesize new forms.

Synthetic, *a.* Add: **2. b.** Applied gen. to preparations simulating a natural product; hence, artificial.

1916 *Edin. Rev.* July 205 The principal raw materials requisite for the manufacture of synthetic dyes. 1917 *Chambers's Jrnl.* May 344/2 Synthetic indigo. 1930 *Daily Express* 6 Nov. 15/4 The bogey is 46...See if you can beat that. Synthetic turf, natural hazards, sand bunkers, plantations, plateau and undulating greens. 1932 Barbara Hedworth *Foolish Pelican* II. iv. § 1 She had discovered..that synthetic stockings were better than pure silk.

c. Hence redundantly qualifying a derogatory epithet. *colloq.*

1930 *Daily Express* 16 Oct. 10/5 With the synthetic idiot, Harpo, you must have a vein of the ridiculous in your laughter gland if boredom is to be kept at bay.

Syphilo-. Add: **Syphiloˑlogist,** a student of syphilis. **Syphiloˑlogy,** the study of syphilis.

1819 *Cent. Dict.*, Syphilologist, Syphilology. 1894 P. A. Morrow (*title*) A system of genito-urinary diseases, syphilology and dermatology: by various authors. 1910 *Practitioner* Feb. 231 Few..syphilologists..would now venture to to give an opinion on a..lesion without previously examining a scraping.

Syrian[2], **Zyrian** (siˑrian, ziˑriǎn). Also **Zirian.** = *Siryanian.

1910 *Encycl. Brit.* XXVI. 317/2 Syryenians (also Sirianian, Syrjenian, Zyrenian, Zirianian, Zyrian and Zirian). 1926 *Chambers's Encycl.* VIII. 101/1 The Syriǎn is spoken by a large population in the districts of Perm, Viatka, Archangel, and Vologda. *Ibid.* X. 819/2 Zyrians or Syriǎns. 1929 *Encycl. Brit.* IX. 258/2 Zyrian is spoken by about 250,000 people.

Systematy (siˑstėmăti). [f. Gr. σύστημα, -ατ-, System + -y[3].] Systematic classification.

1912 W. L. Balls *Cotton Plant Egypt* 5 In this brief summary of the few available historical facts, it has seemed advisable to evade systematy. 1920 *Discovery* Apr. 124/1 Drawing attention to the general rottenness of the foundation of systematy. 1929 E. M. Nicholson *Study of Birds* 20 Mechanical and unfruitful as systematy inevitably is, ornithologists ought to be grateful to those who have plodded through it.

Szekel (seˑk'l). [Native name.] A member of the subdivision of the Magyar race inhabiting Transylvania. Also *attrib.*

1869 A. J. Patterson *Magyars* II. 354, I started for the little hamlet..accompanied by a Székel. 1888 E. Gerard *Land Beyond Forest* II. 151 The Szekel villages, of a formal simplicity, are as far removed from the Roumanian poverty as from Saxon opulence. 1920 *Glasgow Herald* 23 Apr. 8 At the very most 1,900,000 Magyars are lost, of whom over 900,000 (including the Szekels) are in Transylvania.

Also in Ger. form **Szekler** (seˑklər).

1843 *Penny Cycl.* XXV. 264/2 (Transylvania)..three bodies or 'nations', the Hungarians, the Szeklers, and the Saxons, who have the collective name of the 'Uniti'. *Ibid.*, When a Hungarian or Szekler nobleman of Transylvania settles in Hungary. 1869 A. J. Patterson *Magyars* II. 304 We find in the latter town a preponderance of Wallachs over Székiers. 1910 *Encycl. Brit.* X. 392/2 The isolated groups of Hungarians now found in Transylvania and called Szeklers are considered the purest descendants of the invading Magyars.

T

T. 6. Add: In astronomy, = of temporary magnitude; = Turkish (pounds; **T.B.** = *tuberculosis*; **T.B.D.** = torpedo-boat-destroyer; **T.M.** = trench mortar; **T.N.T.** = *trinitrotoluene*; **T.U.** = transmission unit.

1875 *Encycl. Brit.* II. 810/2 The star T in Corona Borealis. 1902 *Ibid.* XXXVIII. 507/2 About 6,000,000 modern Turkish pounds (£T1 = about 18s. 2d. in sterling). 1904 Kipling *Traffics & Discov.*, *Steam Tactics* 182 The chief engineer o' the *Djinn*, 31-knot T.B.D. 1915 D. O. Barnett *Lett.* 4 July 203 The yellow muck doesn't choke you, though, like the black greasy smoke (T.N.T.) which they generally have in the 6 and 8-inch shells. 1917 J. P. Jones *German Spy in Amer.* 54 The project of acquiring a monopoly in toluol, a constituent of the deadly explosive T.N.T. 1919 J. B. Morton *Barber of Putney* ii, On each side of the boat a T.B.D. acting as convoy, ploughed the water into white furrows. 1919 C. P. Thompson *Cocktails* 249, I passed an enjoyable day giving a T.B.D. lieutenant a headache. 1921 *Daily Mail Year Bk.* 73/1 An explosive charge of 550 lb., of T.N.T. blended with a still more powerful substance, hexanitrodiphenylamine. 1925 E. Fraser & Gibbons *Soldier & Sailor Words* s.v. *T.M.*, T.M. batteries were created for trench warfare and T.M. schools of instruction were established. 1927 B. K. Seymour *Three Wives* II. vi, He's a bit of a weed, isn't he, with a tendency to T.B.? 1932 B. Brown *Talking Pictures* 96, 10 per cent corresponds to ½ T.U., and 3 T.U.'s are equivalent to a ratio of 100 per cent.

't[2], dial. or vulgar shortened form of *that.*

1878 Rose T. Cooke *Happy Dodd* xxvii. (Th. p. 171) I didn't feel real cherk this week, so 't I didn't go to sewin' s'ciety.

Taa (tā). [Chinese.] A tapering tower erected as a memorial.

1875 *Encycl. Brit.* II. 449/1 The *taa* is not a pagoda or temple, but a memorial of some event or of some great personage.

Tab, *sb.* Add: **2. d.** A coloured tab, *esp.* a red tab or gorget patch, worn by a staff officer; hence, in army slang, a staff officer.

1917 *B.E.F. Times* 20 Jan., Realising Men must laugh, Some wise Men devised the Staff: Dressed them up in little dabs Of rich variegated tabs. 1918 *The 'Better Times'* Nov. 4/1 Some who by prowess lately proved in war, May sport red 'tabs' and ribboned breasts galore. 1925 E. Fraser & Gibbons *Soldier & Sailor Words* s.v. *A Tab*, a Staff Officer. In allusion to a Staff Officer's gorget patch.

5. (Earlier U.S. example.)

1883 T. D. Price *MS. Diary* 27 Jan., Sent in 130 tabs [of sheep] to register in W. S. Merino Register.

6. Also *to keep tabs.*

1904 *Buffalo Commercial* 26 May 11 The health authorities have been keeping tabs on events of this character. 1911 H. S. Harrison *Queed* x. 118 He kept the most careful sort of tabs upon himself. 1916 H. L. Wilson *Somewhere in Red Gap* iii. 111, I..lay on the big lounge by an open window where..I could keep tabs on the little ones at their sports.

b. *To throw up a tab*: to run up an account, to obtain credit.

1926 E. Ferber *Show Boat* xiii. 268 Lacking even the modest sum required for this sustenance, he [*sc.* a gambler] knew that there he would be allowed to 'throw up a tab' until luck should turn.

Tab (tæb), *sb.*[2] [Short for Cantab.] A Cambridge man.

1914 C. Mackenzie *Sinister Street* III. iii, He will get his blue next term and show the Tabs that he's a jolly good fellow.

Tabac, *a.* Add: Also *sb.*

1914 *Queen* 10 Oct. Advt. 8 In lovely shades of light and dark green, rose, blue, tabac, fawn.

Tabardillo (tabardīˑlʸo). [Sp. *tabardillo* (cf. med.L. *tabardilii*, 13th cent.).] An asthenic fever resembling typhus, common in Mexico and South America.

[1598 W. Phillip tr. *Linschoten* I. i. 2/1 Hee fell sicke of a disease called *Tauardilha*.] 1624 Sir W. Aston in *Cabala* (1654) 166 He hath been held divers dayes with a terrible Calenture, which proved at last a *Tabardillo*. 1851 Herndon *Explor. Vall. Amazon* I. (1853) 113 The most common diseases are pleurisies, rheumatisms, and a putrid fever called *tabardillo.*

Tabber (tæˑbəɹ). [f. Tab *v.* + -er[1].] One who fixes tabs.

1921 *Dict. Occup. Terms* (1927) § 429.

Tabby, *sb.* and *a.* **A.** *sb.* Add: **3. b.** A woman, girl. *Austral. slang.*

1916 C. J. Dennis *Ginger Mick* 20 Then the tabbies took to screamin'. 1925 E. Fraser & Gibbons *Soldier & Sailor Words* s.v., *A Tabby*, a girl.

Table, *sb.* Add: **5. b.** *To lay* (papers, etc.) *on the table* (examples).

1857 *Blackw. Mag.* Sept. 373/2 The President of the India Board..promised to lay 'papers' on the table of Parliament. 1857 *Trans. Philol. Soc.* 3 Dec., That for the present this Report be received and laid on the table.

10. f. *Table of Kindred and Affinity*, a list of the degrees of consanguinity within which marriage may not take place according to church law. Also *Table of Affinity*, *Table of Prohibited* or *Forbidden Degrees.*

The list was set forth in the visitation articles (§ 24) of Archbishop Parker in 1563, and was appointed by the Canons of 1604 to be 'in euery Church publikely set vp and fixed at the charge of the Parish'.

1846 Hook *Ch. Dict.* (ed. 5) s.v. *Consanguinity.* 1892 C. Whitaker *Stud. Aid Prayer Bk.* 115 Impediments [to Holy Matrimony] 1. Relationship within the degrees in the table of kindred and affinity. 1919 M. K. Bradby *Psycho-analysis* 34 Her fleshly desires towards individuals inside the table of affinity may be the lurking devils of her unconscious.

22. table jelly, a flavoured jelly to be served at table as a sweet; **table lamp,** a lamp to light a table, esp. one to stand on it.

1895 *Army & Navy Co-op. Soc. Price List* 16 *Table Jelly Powder. 1859 G. Meason *Lanc. & Carlisle Railw.* 175 Advt., *Table-lamps from 10s. 6d. each. 1922 Bennett *Lilian* II. vii, It was the silver table-lamps that impressed her. 1923 Edith Wharton *Son at the Front* I. vi, A hanging table-lamp under a beaded shade.

Tableau, *sb.* Add: **2. d.** In the game of patience (see quot.).

1913 'Prof. Hoffmann' *Sel. Patience Games* 5 The first step, in the case of most Patience games, is to arrange a certain number of cards face upwards on the table. The cards thus arranged are known as the 'lay out', or tableau. 1917 E. Bergholt *New Bk. Patience Games* 61 The following *tableau* shows a position in which all the gaps have been filled up, until no further progress is possible.

Tabloid. Add: **b.** A small Sopwith biplane. (*Disused.*)

1915 *War Illustrated* 20 Feb. 22/2 The 'Tabloid's' supreme value lies in its speed and climbing power. 1915 *Aeroplane* 21 July 57/2 Tabloid scout. 1915 C. R. Samson *Fights & Flights* (1930) 193 Two Sopwith Tabloids under repair. 1928 C. F. S. Gamble *North Sea Air Station* x. 149 In addition to its maximum speed of 92 miles an hour the 'Tabloid' was remarkable in those days for its great speed range.

c. A newspaper which gives its news in a concentrated and easily assimilable form. Also *attrib.*

1926 *Encycl. Brit.* II. 1055/2 The introduction of tabloids may be explained..by the passing remark of Lord Northcliffe, 'If some American does not start one I shall have to come over to do it'. 1928 *Observer* 5 Feb. 18/1 The..chain now includes 26 papers, in most cases 'tabloids' or papers with a popular appeal. 1929 *Nation* (N.Y.) 4 Dec. 662 The city editor of Boston's only tabloid. 1931 W. Martyn *Scarlett Murder* i, For a special writer on a tabloid to be one of those present at a murder was luck she had not dreamed of. *Ibid.* ii, The tabloid girl, Foster, had her fascinations.

Taboot[1] (tāˑbut). Also **tabut.** [Arab.] A form of water-wheel employed in Egypt.

1836 Lane *Mod. Egypt.* II. 25 There is a third machine, called *taboot*, used for the irrigation of lands in the northern part of Egypt. 1844 Kitto *Phys. Hist. Palestine* vii. 297 Another machine used for the irrigation of lands, when it is only necessary to raise the water a few feet..is called the *Taboot.* 1877 *Encycl. Brit.* VII. 708/1 The tâboot.. differs from the sâkiyeh principally in having a hollow wheel instead of the wheel with pots. 1924 *Countries of World* III. 1757/1 The primitive but still effective apparatus known as the 'sakieh,' the 'shaduf', and the 'tabut'.

Taboot[2] (tăbūˑt). Also **tabut.** [Hind., a. Arab. تابوت coffin, box, ark of the covenant.] A sacred box or coffin; *spec.* in Mohammedan countries, a processional box carried through the streets during Muharram.

1622 in Foster *Eng. Factories India* (1908) II. 94 This daye is heere aryved Sultan (Khus) roues taboots [*sic*] from Brampore, (which to-) morrowe is to bee dispeeded to H(elobass?) there to bee intered by his mother. 1862 Mrs. Speid *Last Years India* 230 Taboots, or tazzias, the representation of Hosain's mausoleum at Kurbulla. 1891 *Daily News* 9 Sept. 5/4 Immense sums of money are spent upon the *taboots*..that, carried in these processions, are broken to pieces and buried at the end of the ceremony. 1923 *Blackw. Mag.* Aug. 256/2 It [*sc.* the Abyssinian Church] venerates an object called the *tabot*, which is the replica of the Ark of the Covenant.

Tabriz (tābrīˑz). Also **-eez.** The name of the capital of Azerbaidjan used *attrib.* or *ellipt.*: **Tabriz carpet,** a soft Persian carpet exported from Tabriz; **Tabriz marble,** a form of marble found near Tabriz and susceptible of a very high polish.

1859 Page *Handbk. Geol. Terms*, *Tabreez Marble*, a beautiful transparent limestone..formed by deposition from a celebrated calcareous spring near Maragha. 1875 *Encycl. Brit.* III. 168/1 A kind of beautiful transparent marble or jasper which..is used..under the name of Tabreez or Belghami marble. 1931 C. Tattersall *Carpets of Persia* 36 Tabriz. Cotton warp: cotton weft, often pink. *Ibid.* pl. v Tabriz Rug. 1931 *Times Lit. Suppl.* 12 Feb. 117/1 Such points as..the softness of Tabriz, and the way the pile lies in Khorasan rugs are not touched upon at all.

Tachinid (tæˑkinid), *a.* and *sb.* *Ent.* [f. mod.L. *Tachina* (a. Gr. ταχινή, fem. of ταχινός swift) + -id[3].] Resembling the genus *Tachina* of parasitic insects; *sb.* an insect of this genus.

1891 *Cent. Dict.* 1902 *Knowledge* Oct. 234/2 The ants.. protect the caterpillars from the attacks of Ichneumon and Tachinid flies. 1925 R. W. G. Hingston in E. F. Norton *Fight for Everest* 285 Tachinids were common at the edge of a torrent at 17,000 feet.

Tack, *sb.*[1] **2.** Add: Phr. *To come* (or *get*) *down to* (*brass*) *tacks*: see *Brass *sb.* 5 b.

1903 A. H. Lewis *The Boss* 119 Let's cut out th' polite prelim'naries,..an' come down to tacks.

Tacking, *vbl. sb.* Add: **e.** *Lacrosse.* (See quot.)

1892 *Lippincott's Monthly Mag.* XLIX. 748 Tacking', as it is called in La Crosse parlance,—otherwise, passing into each other's hands.

Tackle, *sb.* **9. a.** Add: Also in *Hockey.*

Tackle, *v.* Add: **4. c.** Also *transf.*

1920 *Blackw. Mag.* Jan. 105/2 The sort of road that even a Ford would hesitate to tackle.

5. (*c*) In *Hockey.*

1895 Battersby *Hockey* 98 In defence, they [*sc.* the halves] must tackle everything, and stick to it. 1897 *Encycl. Sport* I. 518/2 The goalkeeper should..attempt to tackle him before he can get within shooting range.

Tackling, *vbl. sb.* **5.** Add: Also *attrib.*, as **tackling-bag** *U.S.*, a stuffed bag suspended and used for indoor practice in tackling.

1892 *Outing* (U.S.) Jan. 279/2 Their one special piece of apparatus is..the tackling bag, and this is..necessary to the indoor practice of a football team.

Tacky, *sb.* *U.S.* **a.** (Earlier examples.)

1800 W. Tatham *Agric. & Commerce* 81 A horse, a cow, or a little *tackie*, &c. (which last term signifies a poney or little horse of low price). 1824 P. Horry *Life F. Marion* (1841) 47 The fences all strung along with starved tackies. 1839 C. F. Hoffman *Wild Scenes* 117 The land pirates had disappeared, without molesting my tackey.

Tactile, *a.* and *sb.* Add: **A.** *adj.* **1. b.** In painting and sculpture (see quot. 1907).

1907 Eugénie Strong *Roman Sculpture* 66 It is the *tactile* quality of the subject, rather than its illusionist possibilities, which has attracted the artist. *Note.* I use this word in the sense given to it by Riegl who uses *taktisch* (*tactilis*) = 'stofflich' to express material dimension as distinct from the *illusion* of dimension conveyed by æsthetic means. 1929 A. N. Whitehead *Princ. Nat. Knowl.* 88 This property of 'conveying' an object..is already well-known in the theory of art-criticism, as is evidenced in such phrases as 'tactile-values.'

B. *sb.* One in whom tactile images are predominant. 1917 [see *Audile B. *sb.*].

Tactilist (tæˑktilist). [f. *Tactile *a* + -ist.] An artist who aims at giving an impression of tactility to the represented objects in painting and sculpture.

1921 *Contemp. Rev.* May 621 I gather that experts deplore ..the eccentricity and anarchy of cubists, vorticists, symbolists, tactilists.

Tactism (tæˑktiz'm). *Biol.* [f. Gr. τακτός ordered, arranged + -ism.] The motile response of living organisms to external stimuli.

1902 *Fortn. Rev.* June 1013 By his revelations of the *rôle* of the 'trophisms' and 'tactisms' Dr. Loeb drove boldly into the domain of mental phenomena. 1907 S. Dewey tr. *Le Dantec's Orig. & Nat. Life* 163 An observer conversant with the results of all these experiments in tactisms knows that the movements he observes in living bodies through the microscope are due to the colloid and chemical reactions of the mobile beings and the medium. 1912 A. Tridon tr. *Delage & Goldsmith's Theories Evol.* 164 Others..attribute differentiation to the influence of the various tropisms and tactisms.

Tacuacine (taˑkwasīn). [S. Amer. and Mex. Sp. *tacuacin*, ad. Aztec *tlacuatzin.*] The crab-eating opossum, *Didelphys cancrivora*, of South America.

1880 *Encycl. Brit.* XI. 240/1 Much annoyance is caused to the agriculturist by the little marsupial called the tacuacine.

Tad (tæd). *U.S.* [Of obscure origin.] **a.** (See quots.). **b.** A human being; usually, a child (*little tad*).

a. 1845 in C. Cist *Cincinnati Misc.* 240 Among a certain class in the eastern cities,..the word *Tad*, is applied to one who don't nor won't pay. 1851 B. H. Hall *College Words* 297 At Centre College, Ky., there is a society..composed of the very best fellows of the College, calling themselves Tads. 1890 Eliz. B. Custer *Following Guidon* 213 These youths [*sc.* graduates from West Point] were called 'tads' and 'plebes'.

Tasty, *a.* Add: **2. b.** Fastidious.
1905 A. Adams *Outlet* 102 The two strangers were rather tasty, but Siringo ate ravenously.

Ta-ta, *int.* Add: Also with pron. (tæ·tā·). **b.** *sb.* In sing. or pl. **Tata(s** (tæ·tā(z), a walk, as in *to go for a tata* or *to go tatas*.

Tatami (tata·mi). [Jap.] A Japanese floor-mat made of rice straw.
1909 *Cent. Dict.* Suppl. 1924 *Public Opinion* 28 Nov. 527/2 It is a strict rule that tatamis must be kept clean.

Tatter, *sb.*[3] *slang.* Also **tatterer.** [f. Tat *v.*[3] + -er[1].] A refuse-gatherer.
1889 Barrère & Leland *Dict. Slang, Tatter* (tramps), a rag-gatherer. 1898 *Leeds Mercury* Suppl. 26 Nov. (E.D.D.). 1920 *Church Times* 15 July, Their occupations being largely that of 'Tatterers'—*i.e.*, rag and bone and bottle-gatherers, and casual labourers. 1921 *Dict. Occup. Terms* (1927) § 970 Tatter,..collects [waste] with a hand-pushed barrow or cart.

Taube (tau·bə). (*Disused.*) [G., = Dove *sb.*] A type of monoplane employed by Germany in the war of 1914–18, distinguished by its recurved wings.
1913 [see *Fokker]. 1914 P. Vaux *Sea-Salt & Cordite* 171 'A Taube, sure enough,' said Perwynne harshly. 'This confounded calm helps 'em.' 1915 *Scotsman* 20 June, A Taube dropped bombs on Ostend in September [1914]. 1915 Rosher *In R. N. A. S.* (1916) 99 A Taube came over this morning and dropped a bomb at the end of the aerodrome. 1918 E. S. Farrow *Dict. Milit. Terms, Taube*, a German 'pigeon' shape monoplane, the outstanding feature of which is a retreating wing shape combined with upturned wing tips of flexible construction. 1930 C. R. Samson *Fights & Flights* 119 On arriving at H. Q., I found that everybody had brought the Taube down.

Tauchnitz (tau·k-, tau·χnits). [Surname of Baron *Tauchnitz*, a publisher in Leipzig.] A book or volume of the Library of British and American Authors published by Tauchnitz.
1895 *Daily News* 15 Aug. 5/2 The excitement lest the Customs' officer were to find the Tauchnitz in the trunk. 1901 *Ibid.* 5 Jan. 7/4 Desolate dwellings, strewn with a few sixpenny magazines and smuggled Tauchnitzes.

Taula (tau·la). *Archæol.* [Sp.:—L. *tabula* Table *sb.*] A form of mesolithic stone structure occurring in the Balearic Islands.
1927 *Times* (Weekly ed.) 6 Jan. 18/3 A taula is a two-stone monument from 5 ft. to 12 ft. high. 1927 F. Chamberlin *Balearics* xvi. 179 The T-shaped altars now called taulas.

Taungya (tǭ·ŋgyā). Also **toungya.** [Burmese, f. *taung* hill + *ya* plot, garden.] Used *attrib.* to designate a Burmese system of cultivation called in India Joom.
1876 *Encycl. Brit.* IV. 560/2 The system of cultivation known in Bengal as the *jūm*, that is clearing virgin soil by burning, cultivating it for one or two years, and then leaving it again to the jungle, is here [*sc.* Burmah] extensively practised under the name of *toungya* cultivation. 1906 Sir J. G. Scott *Burma* III. (1911) 219 The nomadic cultivator, the Taungya cutter of Burma. *Ibid.* 227 Taungya System. 1912 *Rangoon Gaz.* 31 Oct. 19/2 The practice of migratory agriculture carried on by the taungya cultivators. 1921 *Times Lit. Suppl.* 8 Sept. 574/3 The best system of raising teak is in taungya plantations.

Taunton turkey (tǭ·ntən tɜ̄·ɹki). *U.S.* = Ale-wife[2], a fish abundant near Taunton, Mass.
1850 Mrs. A. A. Curtis *Home Ballads* (Farmer) Taunton turkeys are so thick, We sell them by the rod.

Taupe (tǭp). [Fr.:—L. *talpa* mole.] A fashion shade of grey resembling that of moleskin.
1921 *Glasgow Herald* 18 June 4 Pearl, smoke, taupe, mouse and other soft becoming shades of grey. 1926 *Amer. Speech* I. Feb. 258/2 Other French names for colors have been familiar for years: *écru, taupe, beige, bisque*.

Tauro-. Add: **Tauro·ctonous** *a.* [Gr. ταυροκτόνος bull-slaying, f. κτείνειν to kill], the specific epithet of Mithras. **Tau·rodont** *a.* [Gr. ὀδούς, ὀδοντ- tooth] (of teeth), having the roots or ridges fused.
1921 *Contemp. Rev.* Dec. 770 Their far-off predecessors made *tauroctonous Mithras. 1927 Peake & Fleure *Hunters & Artists* 18 This condition of the teeth, known as *taurodont, has been found among some representatives of Neanderthal man.

Tauto-. Add: **Tau·tosylla·bic** *a.*, belonging to the same syllable.
1888 Wright tr. *Brugmann's Comp. Gram. Indo-Germ. Lang.* I. 92 Before the Christian era tautosyllabic *ai* became *ī* in Latin...Tautosyllabic *aj* and *au* remained diphthongic in Oscan.

Tavarish (tăvā·riʃ). [Russ. товáрищъ.] Comrade.
1922 *Blackw. Mag.* Nov. 569/1 His secretary..formerly a count and now plain 'tavarish' (comrade)..spoke English perfectly. 1925 E. Fraser & Gibbons *Soldier & Sailor Words, Tavarish*,..a Russian word in everyday use in the War among our men serving in North Russia.

Taw, *sb.*[2] **c.** (Modern U.S. examples.)
1904 Harben *Georgians* xxxii. 292 His wife's a bully woman; she fetched 'im to taw. 1911 R. D. Saunders *Col. Todhunter* xiv. 212 I'll bring you all to taw.

Tawareg, var. *Tuareg.

Taxi, *sb.* Add: **b.** *Comb.*: **taxi-dancer,** a dance-partner whose services may be hired.
1931 *New Statesman* 26 Sept. 386/1 The professional dancing-partner (or taxi-dancer).

2. Short for *Taxiplane.
1923 *Daily Mail* 7 Aug. 8/2 Companies..which send 'taxis', or aerial tramps, to anywhere between Plymouth and Stockholm.

3. An act or spell of taxi-ing.
1913 *Aeroplane* 3 Apr. 404/2 Doing well at his first attempt on mono, getting off after a couple of taxi straights. 1931 *Daily Mirror* 27 Aug. 2/2 The machine..was lost in clouds of spray as it ploughed its way in a graceful 'taxi'.

Taxi (tæ·ksi), *v.* [f. the sb.]
1. *intr.* To travel in a taxi-cab.
1918 Quiller-Couch *Foe-Farrell* xxiv. 397 From Victoria that evening I taxi'd straight to Jermyn Street. 1929 Martindale *Risen Sun* 109 That I might have the minimum distance to taxi in order to reach the Congress.

2. Of an aeroplane or seaplane: To travel along the ground or on the water under its own power before taking off or after alighting. Said also of the pilot. Also *trans.* Inflected *taxied, taxying.*
1912 *Aeroplane* 26 Dec. 645/1 On Bréguet 213, Capt. Beor taxying for 20 mins. 1914 *Ibid.* 5 Feb. 140/1 He taxied out to leeward,..turned,..opened out his engine. *Ibid.* 2 July 21/2 The de Bolotoff triplane was 'taxying', but showed no signs of lifting. 1915 Rosher *In R. N. A. S.* (1916) 67, I was taxying my machine to the far end of the aerodrome, to start off into the wind. 1920 *Blackw. Mag.* May 602/1 He landed without being hit, but in 'taxying' crashed into one of the few remaining boulders. 1927 *Daily Tel.* 6 Sept. 8/6 The machine can be taxied back, and its load lightened for another attempt. 1929 B. Hall & J. J. Niles *One Man's War* 180, I taxied her [*sc.* flying machine] up to the hangars. *Ibid.* 189 We..taxied the ships into the hangars.

Taxiplane (tæ·ksi,plēn). [f. Taxi *sb.* + *Plane *sb.*[5]] A light aeroplane for public hire.
1920 *Daily Tel.* 13 Apr. 1/7 Taxiplanes for any journey. Per mile, 2s. 6d. 1922 *Westm. Gaz.* 18 Dec., Giant transport machines and small 'taxi-planes'. 1926 *Bulletin* 6 Aug. 3/1 He made a dash to Constantinople with a taxi-plane.

Taylorite (tē·lŏrəit). *Min.* [Named after W. J. *Taylor*, the discoverer: see -ite[1].] A compound sulphate of potassium and ammonium occurring in the guano beds of the Chincha Islands.
1868 Dana *Min.* (ed. 5) 614.

Tazia (tāzī·ā). [Arab. تعزية *ta'ziyat* consolation, condolence.] A model of the tombs of Husain and Hassan carried in the Muharram procession.
1809 T. D. Broughton *Lett.* (1892) 53 There were more than a hundred *Taziyas*, each followed by a long train of *Fuqeers*..beating their breasts. 1862 [see *Taboot[2]]. 1895 Kipling *Soldiers Three*, etc. 325 Gilt and painted paper presentations of their tombs are borne with shouting and wailing,..which fakements are called tazias.

Tchaush, tchawoosh, var. Chiaus.
1819 T. Hope *Anastasius* (1820) II. 377 A Tchawoosh..walked in, and summoned me before the Soo-bashee. 1902 *Encycl. Brit.* XXVII. 213/2 The Sultan's guard consists of..the 'Tufenkdjis'..the 'Tchaush', of whom there are between 50 and 60, and who are messengers as well as guards [etc.]. 1930 *Observer* 26 Jan. 11 In the last war a peasant's wife, Fatma Hanem, served in the Army as a tchaush, i.e. a sergeant.

Tchernozem (tʃɜ̄·rnozem). *Geol.* Also **chern-, tchorn-, tschern-.** [Russ., lit. 'black earth'.] (See quot. 1859.) Also *attrib.*
1859 Page *Handbk. Geol. Terms, Tchornozem*, a local name for the black earth of the south of Russia, which covers the whole of the Aralo-Caspian plain. 1914 G. A. J. Cole *Growth of Europe* xi. 207 The Black Earth district of central Russia, where the famous tchernozem soil prevails.

Tchervonetz, var. *Chervonetz.
1923 *Glasgow Herald* 4 Dec. 13 The introduction into circulation of tchervonetz banknotes, issued..against a reserve of metal.

Tchinovnik (tʃinǭ·vnik). [Russ.] A Russian minor official.
1877 D. M. Wallace *Russia* xiii. 305 It is necessary to have a large and well-drilled army of officials. These..form a peculiar social class called Tchinovniks. 1907 Morley in *Recoll.* (1917) II. 229 He has much more vitality of mind than any other of your Tchinovniks.

Tchouma (tʃū·ma). [Chinese.] The grass-cloth plant: = Ramie, Rhea[2].
1866 *Treas. Bot.* 152. *Ibid.* 1127 *Tchouma*, a Chinese name for the fibre of *Böhmeria nivea*.

Tea, *sb.* Add: **9. a.** *tea merchant* (earlier Amer. example).
1781 S. Peters *Hist. Connecticut* (1829) 293 [To] exert themselves..in favour of the Bostonian tea-merchants.

c. tea-ball, a ball of wire or perforated metal in which tea is placed for infusion; **tea-bell, -cake, -cloth** (earlier U.S. examples); **tea-chop,** a chop for the transport of tea (see Chop *sb.*[5] 5); **tea-paper,** the ornamental paper used as a wrapper for tea; **tea-shop,** (*a*) a shop where the commodity is sold; (*b*) a café where tea (sense 2 or 4) is served.
1929 *Nation* (N.Y.) 4 Dec. 666 The *tea ball enables one to pull the tea out before it has given off its tannin. 1836 *Knickerbocker Mag.* VIII. 418 It was nearly time for the *tea-bell to ring. 1829 Lydia M. Child *Frugal Housewife* (1832) 71 There is a kind of *tea cake still cheaper. 1886 R. Brown *Spunyarn & Spindrift* xxvii. 318 The river was so swollen by the rains that the *tea-chops could not get through Foo-chow bridge. 1770 *Carroll Papers* in *Maryland Hist. Mag.* XIII. 62 A Hierling..stole a napkin two Towels and a *Tea Cloath wch we Recovered. 1884 *Birmingham Daily Post* 23 Feb. 3/4 Lithographic-printers. Wanted, a man..well up in *Tea-paper and Commercial Work. *a* 1745 *tea shop [in Dict., sense 9 a]. 1856 A. M. Lang *Diary* (Meean Meer, Punjab) 17 Sept. (MS.) Went to Tea Shop and billiards..at Artillery Mess. 1860 J. R. Edkins *Chinese Scenes* (1863) 153 Drinking tea with about forty nondescript Chinamen...I shall try to give you a little picture of the tea-shop.

Teach, var. Tache *sb.*[3]
1835 in J. H. Ingraham *South-West* I. 240 In the last kettle—the *teach* as it is termed—the sugar is concentrated to the granulating point. 1862 *Catal. Internat. Exhib., Brit.* II. No. 6130, Stoves, ranges, sugar pans, teaches, or boilers to any pattern or make. 1887 *Encycl. Brit.* XXII. 626/1 The [cane sugar] juice..is passed from the one [pan] into the other till it reaches the last of the series, the striking teach.

Teaching, *ppl. a.* (Earlier Amer. example.)
1642 T. Lechford *Plain Dealing* 15 Some Churches have no ruling Elders, some but one, some but one teaching Elder, some have two ruling, and two teaching Elders.

Team, *sb.* Add: **5. c.** *fig.* Usually *a whole* (or *full*) *team.* *U.S.*
1833 J. K. Paulding *Westward Ho!* II. 7 [He] was not only a whole team, but a team and a half, good measure. 1836 Crockett *Exploits & Adv. Texas* (1837) 37 But the General is a whole team, and when fairly started, will be going ahead. 1840 Haliburton *Clockm.* Ser. III. ii. 16 Ain't he a whole team that, and a horse to spare? 1844 'Jon. Slick' *High Life N.Y.* II. 221 So I put on a leetle extra grin myself, for I'm a hull team at larfin, and a hoss to let, when I once begin. 1851 *Polly Peablossom's Wedding* 67 (Th.) Mike is a team and no mistake. 1854 *Knickerbocker Mag.* XLIV. 416 (Th.) Jump him up when you will, and you'll find him a 'full team' at anything. 1863 'E. Kirke' *My Southern Friends* v. 77 The Gin'rals 'ooman—she's a 'ooman fur me—a whole team. 1892 *Harper's Mag.* Feb. 439/1 She says I'm a team in myself, with a little dog under the wagon.

11. team honours, honours awarded to a team; **team race,** a relay race; **team spirit,** the spirit of subordination of personal interests to those of the team; **team-work,** (*d*) work done by persons working as a team, i.e. with concerted effort.
1928 *Daily Mail* 7 Aug. 15/5 Eagle Road Club secured *team honours. 1928 *Britain's Industr. Future* (*Liberal Ind. Inq.*) III. xvi. 195 The 'fellowship bonus' system..evokes the *team-spirit. 1909 *World To-day* (U.S.) Sept. 3 *Team Work in Municipal Progress. *Ibid.*, The basis of all team-work, as applied to wholesaling, is found in the strength of the market.

Teamer. (Earlier Amer. example.)
1778 E. Parkman *Diary* 81 May God extend pity to ye miserable poor,—to Sailors, to Soldiers, to Teamers abroad.

Teapoy. Add: **b.** A china tea-caddy.
1884 A. H. Church *Engl. Earthenware* 56 The sweetmeat tray..has been made in a brass mould; the tea-poy probably in one of plaster. 1909 A. Hayden *Chats Engl. Earthenware* 207 Among the most beautiful designs in this plain white ware [*sc.* salt glaze] are..teapoys or tea canisters, and teapots.

Tear, *sb.*[1] **6. e.** Add: **tear-gas,** lachrymatory gas employed to disable an opponent; **tear-glass,** a wine-glass having an air bubble resembling a tear at the junction of the stem and the body; **tear-mask,** a gas-mask employed as a protection against tear-gas; **tear-mist,** a mistiness of vision due to tears or weeping; **tear-shell,** a shell containing tear-gas.
1923 *Daily Mail* 6 Oct. 5/7 Rifles, machine guns, *tear gas, and dynamite were used. 1924 *Blackw. Mag.* Aug. 212/1 This tear-gas had just reached me. 1930 *Daily Express* 6 Nov. 3/7 Mounted and foot police, armed with rifles and tear-gas bombs. 1927 *Ibid.* 9 Aug. 4 Old English witch-balls and *tear-glasses..are among the curious collecting quests of the moment. 1916 *War Illustrated* 23 Dec. 451/2 *Tear-masks were to be kept handy. 1926 Leinster *Dew on Leaf* 246 Through a *tear-mist she looked at a myriad ghost-pale lights. 1916 *War Illustrated* 23 Dec. 451/3 Don't you know the scent of *tear-shells when you smell it?

Tear, *sb.*[2] Add: **4.** *Comb.* **tear-fault** *Geol.* (see quot. 1924).
1924 Skerl tr. *Wegener's Orig. Continents* 58 A lateral displacement of great dimensions, a so-called tear-fault. 1925 N. E. Odell in E. F. Norton *Fight for Everest, 1924* 314 That the ice..was undergoing severe stress was apparent..from the faults—'flaws' or 'tear-faults'—that had been extensively developed in this area.

Tear, *v.*[1] Add:
3. e. *To be torn between*: to be distracted by two opposite desires or interests.
1871 L. Lockhart *Fair to See* viii, Torn between her desire to underrate Eila and to preserve her own dignity. 1888 Mrs. H. Ward *R. Elsmere* xxxv, Agnes, torn between her interest in what was going on and her desire to get back to her mother, had at last hurriedly accepted this Mrs. Sherwood's offer.

f. *To tear it*: to spoil one's chances; to put an end to one's hopes, plans, etc. *slang.*
1909 'Ian Hay' *Man's Man* xvii, 'I've fairly torn it, this time,' he reflected morosely. 1919 *War Slang* in *Athenæum* 29 Aug. 822/2 A much more popular and pregnant expression than 'knock the end in' is 'that's torn it'. 1922 *Blackw. Mag.* May 623/2 'Good Lord, that's torn it,' she panted. 'I am ruined for ever.' 1929 Vachell *Virgin* viii. 130, I discovered that I bored her to tears, which tore it for me.

9. b. *trans.* with *way* as obj.
1853 Kingsley *Hypatia* xxix, Furiously..he burst up as if from the ground..tearing his way toward his idol. 1888 Mrs. H. Ward *R. Elsmere* x, A little gully deep in bracken, up which the blast was tearing its tempestuous way.

Tearer. 1. Add: Also applied to things (esp. a storm) of violent action or effect. *U.S.*
1835 *Southern Lit. Messenger* I. 357 Oh, no..a real tearer—a regular turnout—been preparing a fortnight. 1892 Susan Hale *Lett.* (1919) 275 The storm increased as day went on, and by noon was a regular tearer.

Tearing, *ppl. a.*[1] **5.** (Modern example.)
1886 E. L. Dorsey *Midshipman Bob* II. xi. 219 'Don't you get mad ever, eh?'..'Yes, I'm sorry to say I do—tearing mad sometimes.'

Tebet (te·bet). Forms: 4–7 -th, 4, 8 th-, 9 -t. The tenth Jewish month, corresponding to January.
1382 Wyclif *Esther* ii. 16 The tenthe moneth, that is cleped Thebeth, that is Januer [1535 Coverdale, 1611 Tebeth]. 1793 *Encycl. Brit.* (1797) XII. 257/2 Thebet. 1876 *Ibid.* IV. 678/2 The age of the moon of Tebet.

Tec, Tech (tek), *sb.*[2] *slang.* Abbreviation for *Technical Institute, Technical School.*
1911 H. Quick *Yellowstone N.* iii. 63 The insufferable breed of dubs—..who..called an Institute of Technology a 'Tech'. *Ibid.*, I shall have outlived the disgrace of my Tech. training. 1915 E. Wallace *Man who bought London* viii, 'I'm off to the "Tec",' he said.

Technical, *a.* (*sb.*) Add: **3. e.** So regarded according to a strict legal interpretation. Chiefly in *technical assault.*
1911 *Encycl. Brit.* XX. 769/1 Finding himself non-suited in a court of law he commits a technical assault upon..some high legal functionary. 1914 A. Harrison *Kaiser's War* 126 He [*sc.* an officer] may not accept an apology in the event of a technical assault. Thus a man who on leaving a café, for example, brushes against an officer, is technically liable to be cut down. 1920 P. G. Wodehouse *Damsel in Distress* vi. 84 'You ought to have had the scoundrel arrested,' he said vehemently. 'It was a technical assault.'

Technicolor (te·knikɒlə*ɹ*). *Cinematography.* Also -our. [f. Technical *a.* + Colour *sb.*] A subtractive process of colour photography in which, by means of filters, the colours are separately but simultaneously recorded and then transferred to a single positive print by imbibition.
1930 E. V. Lucas in *Punch* 2 Apr. 385 *Show of Shows* at the Tivoli, the latest and greatest of technicolour talkie revues.

Technocracy (teknǫ·krăsi). [f. Techno- + -cracy.] (See quots.) Hence **Technocrat** (te·knokræt), an advocate of technocracy; **Technocra·tic** *a.*
1932 *N. Y. Herald Trib.* 15 Dec. 21/1 Technocracy is a word which seems to have been coined in 1919 by William H. Smyth, an engineer and inventor, of Berkeley, Calif., as the name for a new system and philosophy of government, in which the nation's industrial resources should be organized and managed by technically competent persons for the good of every one instead of being left to the management of private interests for their own advantage...Exploited recently by Howard Scott 436 West Twentieth Street. *Ibid.* 21/2 The haunts of technocratic science were situated at numerous places about town, principally in cubbyhole restaurants in Greenwich village. *Ibid.*, Other forums for discussion are the apartments of the technocrats. 1933 F. Soddy in *Daily Mail* 7 Jan., Technocracy, the movement now reported as running wildfire through the United States as a new order of economic and commercial salvation, means ..literally government by the technician. 1933 *Daily Tel.* 13 Jan. 9/4 'Technocracy'—the mechanised state of society governed by engineers, in which gold is abolished and currency becomes heat units.

Tectonically (tektǫ·nikăli), *adv.* *Geol.* [f. Tectonic *a.*: see -ically.] In a tectonic relation.
1925 J. Joly *Surface-Hist. Earth* Gloss. 191 *Laccolith*, an intrusive mass of igneous rock..generally associated tectonically with a mountain range.

Teenty, *a.* *U.S. colloq.* (Earlier examples.) Also *teenty tointy.*
1844 'Jon. Slick' *High Life N.Y.* II. 227 A little teenty tointy handful of wood keeps 'em [*sc.* stoves] warm as blazes. *Ibid.* 230 Then she took up one teenty glove. 1863 Mrs. Whitney *F. Gartney's Girlhood* v, She would open the window a 'teenty little crack'.

Teeny, *a.*[2] Add: (Earlier U.S. example.) Also **teeny, teeny weeny** *sbs.*
1825 J. Neal *Bro. Jonathan* I. 342 A leetle—teeny, mischievous, good for nothin'. 1931 *Daily Express* 1 Sept. 5/1 But never cold ham and tongue for the tiny 'teenies'. 1931 E. V. Lucas *Visibility Good* 18 Model tea-sets, and all the other teeny weenies.

Teeter, *sb.* **1. teeter-board** (earlier U.S. example).
1855 *Knickerbocker Mag.* XLVI. 88 We were having a grand time with our 'teeter'-boards upon the highest fence.

Teeter, *v.* *U.S. colloq.* **1. a.** (Example.)
1849 Mrs. Stowe *Mayflower* 169 Then he was *tetering* with her on a long board.

b. (Earlier examples.)
1844 'Jon. Slick' *High Life N.Y.* II. 231, I teetered up to her a tiptoe. *Ibid.* 234 We cut along..as chipper as two birds teeterin on an appletree limb in spring time.

Hence **Teetering-board,** = *teeter-board.*
1845 Caroline M. Kirkland *Western Clearings* 213, I laid a teeterin' board over it, so that if you stepped on it, down you went.

Teetery (tī·təri), *a.* *U.S.* [f. Teeter *v.* + -y[1].] Tottery, unsteady.
1900 *N. Y. Jrnl.* 25 Nov. 59/2 An attendant was there to help you off if you felt teetery or uncertain. 1905 Rex Beach *Pardners* i. (1912) 34 The orchestra spieled some teetery music.

Teftadar, tefterdar, var. *Defterdar.

Tegipudenda (tedʒipiude·ndā). *Anthropol.* [f. L. *tegĕre* to cover + *pudenda*, pl. of Pudendum.] A covering used by native women for the pudenda.
1908 Sir H. Johnston *Geo. Grenfell & Congo* II. 592 A young woman wears a very minute piece of bark cloth as a tegipudenda.

Tehseel, variant of *Tahsil.

Teindable (tī·ndăb'l), *a.* [f. Teind *v.* + -able.] Tithable.
1920 *Glasgow Herald* 2 June 11 Rental, which is no guide to the teindable rental. 1921 *Ibid.* 7 Jan. 5 The view that woodlands were teindable subjects.

Tekkieh (teki·e). Also **tekke, -eh.** [Arab. تكية.] A Moslem monastery.
1877 *Encycl. Brit.* VII. 113/2 The regular dervishes live in tekkiehs, khanakahs, or convents. 1930 *Observer* 30 Mar. 21 In 1925, it will be remembered, hundreds of 'tekkes' (male monasteries) were closed. 1932 G. Kampffmeyer in *Whither Islam?* 167 The *tekkes* or monasteries of the religious orders and the *turbes* or the tombs of the saints are closed.

Tele-. Add: **Tele-a·rchics** *sb. pl.* [Gr. ἀρχικός], the art of wireless control (of aircraft) from a distance. **Tele,a·xial** *a.* [Axial *a.*], denoting a form of gear in which the axes of the guns and the aligning telescope (of an aeroplane) remain parallel. **Tele-ca·mera,** a telephotographic camera. **Tele-ca·rdiogram** [*Cardiogram] *Radiography*, a cardiogram registered electrically at a distance. **Telece·ntric** *sb.*, a telecentric lens. **Te·leflasher** *Radiography*, a device for timing the excitation of an X-ray tube. **Tele·gnomy, Telegno·sis** *Psychics*, psychic apprehension of events happening at a distant place. **Te·le-hood,** a hood employed to screen a lens when taking telephotographs. **Te·le-lens,** a telephotographic lens. **Telence·phalon** [Encephalon] *Anat.*, the end-brain. **Telephoto-micro·graphy,** photography by means of a telemicroscope. **Te·leplasm** *Psychics*, a substance psychically materialized: hence **Telepla·smic** *a.* **Telepsy·chic,** a medium whose psychical powers are exerted over a distance. **Teleradi,o·graphy** [Radiography], = next. **Telerö·ntgeno·graphy,** X-ray photography with the tube at a distance from the body. **Telesei·smic** *a.*, of or pertaining to a teleseism. **Te·leseismo·logy,** the science of the study of remote earth-tremors. **Teleste·reograph,** the apparatus designed by E. Belin to transmit drawings, photographs, etc. **Telethe·rapy,** the employment of therapeutics (as radium) at a distance from the body. **Te·letype** *v. trans.*, to transmit by teletype. **Telety·pewriter,** an instrument for typewriting by wireless.
1926 *Westm. Gaz.* 10 Dec., '*Tele-archics', or remote wireless control, has been applied so that aircraft may be directed by its means. 1920 *Blackw. Mag.* July 78/1 The *teleaxial gear enabled the gunner to aim his guns by the aligning of a small sighting telescope. 1910 O. Wheeler *Mod. Telephotography* 68 Messrs. Zeiss also make a special *tele-camera. 1912 *Index-Catal. Libr. Surg. Gen. Office U.S. Army* Ser. II. XVII. 707 *Telecardiograms. 1921 *Glasgow Herald* 15 June 7 It was fitted with..a 12 in. *Telecentric, and a variant of my 'Dodo' tele-lens. 1923 R. Knox *Radiog. & Radio-Therap.* I. 47 The Victor *Teleflasher. 1906 *Pall Mall Gaz.* 24 Mar. 4 Mr. Grier possesses the faculty of '*telegnomy', which enables him..to perceive..events which are taking place on the other side of the Atlantic. 1911 W. F. Barrett *Psychical Research* xi. 161 Dr. Heysinger..suggests the term *telegnosis, or knowing at a distance, instead of clairvoyance. 1921 *Glasgow Herald* 22 June 7 If a proper *tele-hood is not available a cardboard tube..will serve. 1921 *tele-lens [see *telecentric]. 1903 Dorland *Med. Dict.* (ed. 3), *Telencephalon. 1911 *Jrnl. Comp. Neurol.* XXI. 2 The line of demarcation between the diencephalon and telencephalon was indicated by the velum transversum dorsally and by the caudal border of the chiasma-ridge ventrally. 1921 *Glasgow Herald* 9 Mar. 7 *Telephoto-micrography. 1927 *Daily Express* 28 Sept. 9 *Teleplasm..was shown issuing from the face of the tranced woman. 1914 Teixeira de Mattos tr. *Maeterlinck's Unknown Guest* ii. § 4 There are seers, so-called '*telepsychics', who are not psychometers. 1909–10 *Arch. Roentgen Ray* XIV. 38 An instantaneous shutter for *teleradiography. 1912 *Index-Catal. Libr. Surg. Gen. Office U. S. Army* Ser. II. XVII. 712 *Telerontgenography. 1923 R. Knox *Radiog. & Radio-Therap.* I. 303 When it is possible to obtain full exposures of the thorax at a distance of 2 metres, then tele-röntgenography of the thorax is of decided advantage. 1912 *Rep. Brit. Assoc.* 88 The object was to measure the angular component of *teleseismic motion. 1922 *Encycl. Brit.* XXXII. 390 *Teleseismology..or the study of the long-distance records. 1909 *Jrnl. Soc. Arts* LVIII. 29 The means adopted by..M. Belin in his *telestereograph. 1920 *New York World* 14 Nov. 1/2. 1913 Dorland *Med. Dict.* (ed. 7), *Teletherapy. 1930 *Brit. Med. Jrnl.* 8 Feb. 232 Radium Teletherapy. 1924 *Daily News* 19 Dec. 5/4 We must *teletype as well as teletalk. 1922 *Glasgow Herald* 4 Sept. 11 Another great stride in the advance of civilization is demonstrated by the *tele-typewriter.

Teleferica (telefe·rikā). Also **teleferic.** [It., f. Gr. τῆλε Tele- + φέρειν to bear + -ικός -ic.] = Telpher *sb.*
1926 *Windsor Mag.* Oct. 498 We walk a little way and then go up by the teleferic. 1918 *Times Lit. Suppl.* 21 Mar. 136/4 The only woman to journey from Cortina to.. the Terza Tofana by teleferic. 1919 W. Hutchinson *Doctor in War* xviii. 262 The miniature cable-railway, or teleferica.

Telemark (te·lĕmāɹk). *Ski-ing.* [f. *Telemark*, Norway, where this originated.] A swing turn with the leading ski advanced and the knee bent, employed to change direction or stop short; also, a form of ski. Also *attrib.* and as *v. intr.*
1910 *Westm. Gaz.* 15 Jan. 2/2 I had just time to perform that sudden semi-circular operation known as a 'telemark' (by which the skier's impetus can be stopped in a second or two) and arrive breathless at his side. *Ibid.* 1 Feb. 14/3 Very neat Telemark curves. 1920 A. Lunn *Cross-Country Ski-ing* 88 In powder snow one can Telemark in various undefined ways. 1921 — *Alpine Ski-ing* 27 *Telemark Crust* is the name given to any form of hard, unbreakable crust sufficiently softened on the surface to render Telemarks possible. 1923 E. Jessup *Snow & Ice* 51 The Telemark swing is a one-foot turn; that is, practically the whole weight of the body is on the forward ski and it is this ski which does all the work, the other following amiably behind, hardly more than an appendage.

Telephone, *sb.* **3.** Add: **telephone booth,** a booth at which prepaid calls may be made. So *telephone box, kiosk.*
1924 Galsworthy *White Monkey* III. xiv, He made for his club, and closeted himself in the *telephone booth. 1923 Swinnerton *Young Felix* IV. xix. § 1 Felix replaced the receiver and shot out of the *telephone-box. 1933 *Times* 19 Jan. 14/5 Thefts from Telephone Boxes.

Telephoner. (Examples.)
1925 E. Wallace *Strange Countess* xxxv. 303 Presently the telephoner came out. 'All right,' he said. 1932 *New Statesman & Nation* 23 Jan. 87/1, I have often watched one of these fanatical telephoners sitting opposite the telephone with his hand on the receiver.

Telephoto[2], short for Telephotograph *sb.*[1]
1931 *Daily Express* 13 Oct. 1/6 Picture by telephoto.

Telescopic, *a.* Add: Hence *telescopic rifle*, a rifle with a telescopic sight.
1918 E. A. Mackintosh *War, the Liberator* 114 With a telescopic rifle he is looking for a Hun.

Televise (te·lĕvəiz), *v.* [Back-formation from *Television.] *trans.* To transmit by television; also *absol.*
1927 *Glasgow Herald* 14 Jan. 9/1 The distance over which pictures can be televised. *Ibid.* 9 Apr. 10 It will [then] be a short step to 'televise' over vast areas of land and sea. 1930 *Observer* 31 Aug. 15/5 It is probable that Lord Gorrell will 'televise' himself from the studio.

Television (te·lĕviʒən). [f. Tele- + Vision.] Vision of a distant (moving) object or scene electrically transmitted and reproduced; also, the process by which this is effected.
[1904 *Daily News* 3 June 7 Dr. Low talks very modestly of the 'televista' (the name he has given to his 'seeing by wire' invention).] 1909 [in Dict. s.v. Tele-]. 1930 Buckingham *Matter & Radiation* 122 We have heard so much about Television lately that we are apt to forget that no portion of the apparatus used is novel to scientists.
Hence **Televisionist** (televi·ʒənist), one who is interested in television.
1927 *British Weekly* 6 Jan. 378/5 Televisionists will expect their heroes to stay put.

Televisor (te·lĕvəizə*ɹ*). [f. *Television + -or.] The name of the television apparatus designed by J. L. Baird.
1926 *Glasgow Herald* 11 Jan. 7 The Televisor. *Ibid.* 8 Oct. 9/1 The scene in front of the transmitting televisor is turned into electrical impulses. 1927 *Ibid.* 2 Feb. 9 The cost of televisor equipment for practical use. 1928 *Television* Mar. 33/1 We have now a revolving disc suitably mounted, and this constitutes the first and most essential part of our televisor. 1930 *Daily Express* 30 July 6/2 He has found it possible to place the television driving and scanning mechanism as well as the light source within the valve, thus producing a televisor of an extremely light and compact character.

Tell, *v.*[1] Add: **17.** *To tell the tale*: to tell a marvellous or incredible tale, *spec.* to tell a tale of woe in order to evoke sympathy. *slang.*
1918 W. J. Locke *Rough Road* xi, The temptation to 'tell the tale' to the newcomer was too strong. 1928 *Daily Express* 15 Dec. 7/4 Moneylender at Bow County Court. What did you tell me when you borrowed the money? Debtor: Oh, we all tell the tale when we want money.

d. *To tell* (*a person*) *good-bye*: to say good-bye to. *U.S.*
1860 Bartlett *Dict. Amer.* (ed. 3). 1872 E. Eggleston *End of World* xviii. 128 You aren't going without telling me good-by? 1897 J. L. Allen *Choir Invis.* xix. (1918) 206 And now all of you must come and shake hands with me and tell me good-bye. 1904 F. Lynde *Grafters* xxv. 314 Did you go to tell the household good-by? 1905 Tarkington *In Arena* 253 She told me to tell you good-bye.

e. *To tell the bees*: see Eng. Dial. Dict. s.v. Bee *sb.*[1] I. 2 (8).

20. *To tell the world*, to announce openly; to assert emphatically. *U.S.*
1924 A. J. Small *Frozen Gold* i. 37 I'll tell the world that ..not all the Mounted Sergeants in the Territories would be able to make him talk.

23. d. *Tell off*: to reprimand, scold, reprove.
1919 *Cassell's New Eng. Dict.* s.v. *Tell, To tell off*,.. (colloq.) to scold. 1930 A. J. L. Scott *Sixty Squad. R.A.F.* 57 He got..a well-deserved and proper 'telling-off' from the Brigadier and Wing Commander. 1927 Agatha Christie *Big Four* xiv. 202 They don't like you to notice things—especially if it should seem you were telling them off about it.

Tellina (telǝi·nā). [mod.L. (Linnæus 1758), a. Gr. τελλίνη shell-fish.] A member of the genus of bivalve molluscs of the family *Tellinidæ.* Hence **Te·llinoid** *a.*, resembling the genus *Tellina.*
1900 Dall in *Proc. U. S. Nat. Mus.* XXIII. 287 The Tellinas are mostly inhabitants of moderate depths. *Ibid.* 291 Shell tellinoid, thin.

Telo-[1]. Add: **Telopha·sic** *a.*, of or pertaining to the telophase.
1906 *Rep. Brit. Assoc.* 757 It [*sc.* the nucleolus] lies in the centre of the telophasic figure.

Temp., abbrev. of L. **tempore** (also used) = in the time of.
1859 Allibone *Dict. Engl. Lit.* I. 27 As we have frequently occasion to refer to the reigns of different English sovereigns without specifying dates,—*temp.* Edward II., *temp.* Henry II., &c. 1885 *Athenæum* 24 Oct. 539/3 A chart pedigree commencing *temp.* Henry VIII. 1891 *N. & Q.* 7th Ser. XI. 80/1 The Cardinal of S. Praxedes, who made it [*sc.* the family of Bainbrigge] famous *temp.* Henry VIII. 1932 *Ibid.* 16 Jan. 46/1 Old registers *tempore* mid-seventeenth century.

Temperamental, *a.* Add: **2.** Having or giving way to an erratic or neurotic temperament. Hence **Te·mperame·ntalist,** one who is temperamental.
1924 *Blackw. Mag.* June 786/1, I was what you might call a temperamentalist, and very easily hypnotised. 1928 E. Wallace *Elegant Edward, Amateur Detective*, Elegant Edward was not ordinarily temperamental.

Temperance. 2. b. Add: **temperance hotel** (example), **house.**
1837 W. Jenkins *Ohio Gaz.* 69 Barnesville..has..2 taverns, and 1 temperance hotel. 1841 G. Combe *Notes U.S.* I. 34, I had a warm bath,..at the 'Temperance House'; that is, a hotel in which abstinence from spirituous and fermented liquors is the rule.

Temperish (te·mpəriʃ), *a.* [f. Temper *sb.* II + -ish[1].] Inclined to or showing an exhibition of temper.
1925 *Chambers's Jrnl.* Nov. 764/1 From these temperish folk arise strange quarrels. 1929 *Times* 16 Jan., His [*sc.* Lord Haig's] reply was more than emphatic; it was almost temperish.

Tempersome (te·mpəɹsəm), *a.* orig. *dial.* [f. Temper *sb.* + -some[1].] Quick-tempered. Hence **Te·mpersomeness.**
1875 Parish *Dict. Sussex Dial., Tempersome*, hasty-tempered. 1879–81 Miss Jackson *Shropsh. Word-bk., Tempersome*, hot tempered; passionate. 1906 W. De Morgan *Joseph Vance* xliii, He was very tempersome about it. 1909 — *It Never Can Happen Again* xxv, Marianne, for all her tempersomeness and jealousy, loved and reverenced Challis. 1927 Sadleir *Trollope* 256 All were tempersome; but he was large and rough and incoherent.

Temple, *sb.*[1] **6. c.** Add: **temple-state,** a state centred round a temple or other religious building; also *attrib.*
1920 H. G. Wells *Outline Hist.* 150/2 There is no temple-state stage, no stage of priest Kings, in the Greek record. 1930 A. J. Toynbee *Surv. Internat. Affairs* 454 The emergence of a 'temple-state' from the dust of a pulverized world-empire was not a unique historical phenomenon. 1931 *Times Lit. Suppl.* 1 Jan. 3/2 The Pope's temporal domain ..is not a city-state but a temple-state.

Templist, *a.* and *sb.* [f. Temple *sb.*[1] + -ist, after G. *Templer.*] The name of a (Unitarian) sect founded in Württemberg (1861) having their headquarters in Haifa.
1881 B. Walker *Future of Palestine* 21 The religious tenets of the Templists..are in the main perfectly orthodox. 1916 *Q. Rev.* Oct. 415 *note*, A number of Germans, not members of the Templist sect, live in the colony at Haifa.

Tempo. Add: **1.** Also (in full, **tempo giusto**) strict time.
1931 M. D. Calvocoressi tr. *Bartók's Hungarian Folk Music* 23 A few tunes in *tempo giusto*. *Ibid.* 80 In fairly old tunes..a liking for variable *tempo giusto* rhythm is evinced.

b. *transf.*
1918 A. Gray tr. *The Crime* II. 239 He describes..their readiness 'to retard the tempo of the construction of our warships'. 1925 C. Fox *Educat. Psychol.* 271 Each person is possessed of a vital tempo. 1930 G. R. de Beer *Embryol. & Evol.* iii. 25 When the balance of the different hormones is upset, the tempo of development may be very seriously affected. 1931 *Times Lit. Suppl.* 31 Dec. 1052/2 'Tempo' is reduced by the huge rise in the export of timber.

3. *Comb.*: **tempo-plate,** the plate on a player-piano indicating the speed at which the notes are played.
1922 S. Grew *Art Player-Piano* 60 Changes are indicated by figures referring to the tempo-plate.

Ten, *a.*, etc. Add: **B.** *sb.* **5.** (*c*) ten-acre lot; (*d*) ten-syllable line; (*e*) ten-dollar note; (*f*) set of ten (racing) strokes; (*g*) ten-horse-power motor car.
1642 *Watertown Rec.* 8 Divisions for Farmers being Lotted out by Tens. 1841 *Knickerbocker Mag.* XVII. 345 Let the big fellow utter his threatenings in long tens and alexandrines. 1874 B. F. Taylor *World on Wheels* II. ii. 196 When I give her a 'ten' sometimes, she will fold her arms. *a* 1906 'O. Henry' *Trimmed Lamp*, etc. 171 He drew out his 'roll' and slapped five tens upon the bar. 1927 *Field* 16 June 1025/1 The unsteadiness thus produced cost the home crew its lead and although it still went up in the 'tens' the Aberdonians drew away to win by a length and a quarter. 1931 *Daily Express* 16 Oct. 11/2 Cheap 'Tens'.

D. 1. *ten-cent, -dollar, -oared* (earlier U.S. examples).
1846 Corcoran *Pickings* 26 He only gave me thirteen of these [*ten cent pieces] in change. 1873 E. Eggleston *Myst. Metrop.* xviii. 158 The joyful keys and the cheerful ten-cent coins lay in his pocket. 1911 H. S. Harrison *Queed* xvii. 203, I bought them at a ten-cent store on Sixth Avenue. 1825 J. Neal *Bro. Jonathan* I. 221 For a '*ten dollar bill' ..Peters would have set fire to it. 1740 W. Stephens *Jrnl. Proc. Georgia* 565 Capt. Heron..arrived..at Port-Royal in a *ten-oar'd Boat.

2. ten-finger, (*b*) a thief; **ten-gallon hat,** a large conical broad-brimmed hat worn by cowboys; **ten-gun brig** *Austral.* (see quot.); **ten-lined potato beetle, ten-liner** *U.S.* (see quots.); **ten-percenter,** one receiving ten per cent. interest; **ten-spot** *sb.* *U.S.* (earlier example).
1881 Ingersoll *Oyster-Industr.* (Hist. Fish. Industr. U.S.) 249 *Ten-finger.—A thief. 1928 *Daily Express* 17 Oct. 3/7 She instinctively recognised that he was a cowboy, even though he did not wear a *ten-gallon hat and a jacket embroidered with Mexican dollars. 1903 R. Bedford *True Eyes* 365 He..caught many little white fish with five square port-hole marks on their sides—the fish the Northerners call '*ten gun brigs'. 1876 *Rep. Vermont Board Agric.* III. 574 The famous *ten-lined potato beetle (*Doryphora decemlineata*, Say). *Ibid.* 676 Jack Frost..must overtake many of the *ten liners that supposed themselves safe from cold. 1902 *Westm. Gaz.* 30 July 9/2 Anxious as he is to make every speculative investor in the mines a *ten-percenter. 1844 'Jon. Slick' *High Life N.Y.* II. 215 'Jest so,' sez I, a flingin' down the *ten spot o' clubs and the ace-o' diamonds.

Tenant, *sb.* **4.** *tenant-farming* (earlier U.S. example).
1861 *Trans. Ill. Agric. Soc.* IV. 203 On the greater part of this farm are the usual indices of tenant farming.

Tendentiously (tende·nʃəsli), *adv.* [f. Tendentious *a.* + -ly[2].] In a tendentious manner; with a purposed tendency or aim. So **Tende·ntiousness.**
1920 *Glasgow Herald* 9 Apr. 8 This was not due to any tendenciousness on the part of official reports. 1924 *History* Oct. 215 If we could..speak with our enemies in the gate, we should doubtless teach geography..tendenciously. 1928 *Observer* 1 July 17/5 A mixture of innocent greenness..and deliberate tendentiousness. 1931 *Times Lit. Suppl.* 21 May 404/2 Here is Tolstoy..pleading for art which is free from 'movements' and any sort of tendentiousness.

Tenderloin. *U.S.* **1.** (Example.)
1864 Sala in *Daily Tel.* 27 Sept., The 'tenderloin', the 'porter-house' steak of America, are infinitely superior to our much-vaunted rump steak.
2. (Earlier example.)
1887 *Harper's Mag.* Mar. 500/2 His precinct is known as the 'Tenderloin', because of its social characteristics.

Tenebroso (tenĕbrō·so), *a.* and *sb.* Pl. -osi. [It. *tenebroso* shadowy.] The name of a group of Italian painters of the naturalist school of Caravaggio.
1886 W. M. Rossetti in *Encycl. Brit.* XX. 532/1 The naturalist school, called also the school of the Tenebrosi. *Ibid.*, Ribera..had by this time acquired so much mastery over the tenebroso style that his performances were barely distinguishable from Caravaggio's own.
So **Te·nebrist,** a painter belonging to this group.
1927 D. S. MacColl in *19th Cent.* Jan. 83 If the epochs of painting were announced by music as are the Plagues of Egypt in Handel's *Israel* the theme for the late sixteenth century of the Tenebrists would be *He sent forth a great darkness.*

Tenement. 5. tenement house (earlier U.S. example).
1861 T. Winthrop *C. Dreeme* 78 To light the rear range of a tenement-house.

Tennesseean (tenesī·ăn), *a.* and *sb.* Also -ean. [-an.] Of or belonging to, a native or inhabitant of, Tennessee, one of the southern United States of America.
1817 Anne Royall *Lett. fr. Alabama* xvi. (1830) 42 The Tennesseean is cool and steady. 1835 Ingraham *South-West* I. xix. 202 A daring Tennessean, with a blanket tied round him, and a hat with a brim of enormous breadth. 1857 T. B. Gunn *N. Y. Boarding-Houses* 202 A big Tennesseean. 1869 'Mark Twain' *Sketches, Journalism in Tennessee* (1875), The fervent spirit of Tennessean journalism. 1884 A. E. Sweet & Knox *On Mexican Mustang thr. Texas* iii. 41 The old Tennessean came to the front again. 1931 T. S. Stribling *Forge* xxiii, Tennesseans, countrymen,..I come asking you to lift your sword to defend the sacred altar of your country's freedom!

Tenorino (tenŏrī·no). Pl. -ini (-ī·ni). [It., f. *tenore* tenor + -*ino* dim. suffix.] A high tenor, *spec.* a castrato alto.
1867 *Cornhill Mag.* Jan. 32 At present the signor is the pearl of tenorini, and no other artist can match his delivery of the embroidered melodies of the *Cenerentola*, or the *Italiana in Algieri.* 1898 *Harper's Mag.* XCVI. 512, I was ..to be the tenor, or rather the *tenorino.*

Ten-pins. b. *ten-pin alley* (earlier U.S. example).
1852 Bristed *Upper Ten Thousand* v. 117 Perhaps we shall find him at the ten-pin alley.

Tense, *v.* (Additional modern examples.)
1911 Jack London *Adventure* i, The tensed body relaxed. 1921 L. R. Freeman *In Tracks of Trades* 85 There was a sharp tensing of the powerful frame. 1929 P. Gibbs *Hidden City* I, Rage causes an increase of adrenal secretion, tensing up the nerve cells.

Tent, *sb.*[1] Add: **2. f.** A contrivance used in laryngeal and respiratory diseases for regulating the temperature and moistness of the air breathed by the patient. Also *tent-bed.*
1892 J. Carmichael *Dis. Children* 235 The child should be put into a tent bed with one or two steam kettles. *Ibid.* 237 The steam of the tent may be medicated by iodine.

5. b. tent-caterpillar, -fly *U.S.* (earlier examples).
1872 *Rep. Vermont Board Agric.* I. 57 The *tent caterpillar is easily managed if you only watch him and destroy his nest when it first appears. 1849 T. T. Johnson *Sights Gold Region* xviii. 169 The *tent-fly is a second roof usually erected over the tent. 1862 in Henderson *Life Stonewall Jackson* (1906) I. 311 Tent-flies without poles or tents cut down to that size.

Tentage. (Additional modern examples.)
1899 *Boston Med. & Surg. Jrnl.* 16 Nov. 487/2 Tentage for tropical service. 1905 'Laurence Hope' *Indian Love* 20 No more the rugged roads of Khorasan, The scanty food and tentage of the past! 1921 *Brit. Museum Return* 87 A Committee appointed by the Army Council to advise as to processes to improve the durability of Tentage. 1925 E. F. Norton *Fight for Everest, 1924* 126 The inadequate number of porters available to carry up sufficient tentage.

Tented, *a.* **1.** (Later U.S. example.)
1871 *Rep. Indian Affairs* (1872) 261 Urah..had collected some of the chiefs and herdmen of the tribe to receive me in their tented camp.
2. (Later U.S. example.)
1848 E. Bryant *What I saw in California* i. 14 Long trains of oxen..pulling huge tented-wagons.

Tenter, *sb.*[2] (Earlier U.S. example.)
1846 A. Wiley in *Indiana Mag. Hist.* XXIII. 409 The eating hours were the same as those of the tenters.

Tenth, *a.* and *sb.* Add: **B.** *sb.* **4.** The tenth day of the month.
1580 in *Jesuits in Conflict* (1873) 105 The 10th of September, 1580. 1868 Eliz. S. P. Ward in *Atlantic Monthly* Mar. (*title*) The Tenth of January.

C. tenth nerve, the pneumogastric nerve.
1821 C. Bell *Expos. Nerves Hum. Body* (1824) 82 The nerves of the spine, the tenth or sub-occipital nerve, and the fifth or trigeminus of the system of Willis. 1928 M. Coque *Introd. Study Anat. & Physiol. Eye* 101 In any case in which the moderating power of the vagus or pneumogastric nerve (10th nerve) is increased, there is a hypersecretion of the suprarenal capsules.

Tenting, *vbl. sb.*[6] [f. Tent *sb.*[1] + -ing[1].] The use of a tent (*Tent *sb.*[1] 2 f).
1907 F. Taylor in *Brit. Jrnl. Childr. Dis.* June 258 Open windows, free exposure of the patient to the air in any way, in marked contrast to the 'tenting' and steam-kettle of recent times.

Tepee. (Earlier examples.)
1849 Mary H. Eastman *Dahcotah* xxii, The wigwam (or *teepee*, as the houses of the Sioux are called). *a* 1861 Winthrop *John Brent* xxiv. 254 We rode through a camp of Sioux 'tepees' like so many great white foolscaps.

Tequila (tekī·lā). [Name of a district of Mexico.] = Pulque.
1895 *Funk's Stand. Dict.* 1927 *Blackw. Mag.* Nov. 655/2 Two peons..offered me tequila, which I declined.

Teraconic (terăkǫ·nik), *a.* *Chem.* [f. Ter(ebic + Citr)aconic.] Designating a crystalline acid, $C_7H_{10}O_4$, obtained by distilling terebic acid.
1882 *Jrnl. Chem. Soc.* XLII. 42 Teraconic acid..is soluble in cold water and ether.

Teracrylic (terăkri·lik), *a.* *Chem.* [f. Ter(penylic + Acrylic.] Designating an acid, $C_7H_{12}O_2$, obtained from the distillation of terpenylic acid.
1877 *Jrnl. Chem. Soc.* II. 432 On Teracrylic Acid, a new acid belonging to the Acrylic Series...Teracrylic acid may be obtained pure by dissolving the distillate in sodium carbonate or caustic soda.

Tercentesimal (tɜ̄ɹsente·simăl), *a.* [f. Ter- + Centesimal *a.*] (See quot.)
1923 Sir N. Shaw *Forecasting Weather* Introd. p. xxi, Professor Marvin..rightly called attention to the fact that the scale of centigrade degrees measured from −273° C. is not, in fact, the same thing as the absolute scale and that another name is required. We have accordingly used the expression *tercentesimal scale* to indicate the arbitrary scale so defined.

Teredinid (terī·dinid), *a.* (*sb.*) *Zool.* [f. mod.L. *Teredinidæ*, a family of boring molluscs: see Teredo and -id[3].] Of or pertaining to the family *Teredinidæ*; also *absol.* a ship-worm. Also **Tere·dinoid** *a.*, resembling a ship-worm.
1895 *Funk's Stand. Dict.* 1924 *Glasgow Herald* 6 Jan. 4/2 A link between the Teredinid family and that of the Pholads or piddocks.

Term, *sb.* **8. b.** Add: *Terms of reference*: the heads or points upon which a person or body of persons has to make a decision or a settlement; the terms which define the scope of an inquiry.
1912 *Rep. Brit. Assoc.* 549 The nature of the Inquiry of the Industrial Council is explained in the following 'terms of reference'. 1921 *Board Educ., Teaching English in Eng.* 3 Our terms of reference do not include Wales. 1927 W. E. Collinson *Contemp. Engl.* 123 Terms of reference (defining the scope of a committee's labours).

Terminalia (tɜ̄ɹminē·liă). *Bot.* [mod.L. (Linnæus, 1767), f. L. *terminālis* Terminal.] A member of the genus of combretaceous shrubs or trees so named, characterized by the crowding of the leaves at the end of the twigs. Also *attrib.*
1829 Loudon *Encycl. Plants* 864. 1926 *Chambers's Jrnl.* June 411/2 He halted the elephant under one of the Terminalia trees.

Termite. b. Add: **termite heap** = *termite-hill.*
1910 *Dundee Advertiser* 25 Nov. 6 The athletes had to..jump from a small termite heap. 1920 *Blackw. Mag.* Feb. 205/1 Several enormous termite heaps.

Terrazzo (teræ·tso). [It., = terrace, balcony.] A proprietary name for a kind of concrete used for paving and building. Chiefly *attrib.* and *Comb.*
1902 *Encycl. Brit.* XXIX. 340/1 Wood has been superseded by terrazzo...Cracks may be seen in terrazzo floors introduced into several of the recently erected modern hospitals. 1925 *Glasgow Herald* 27 Feb. 7 Terrazzo-faced concrete blocks. *Ibid.*, The outer walls being of the terrazzo block. 1927 *Ibid.* 12 Jan. 9 The houses..are constructed of terrazzo blocks.

Terre-à-terre (tęratę̄ɹ), *sb.* and *adj. phrase.* [Fr., lit. 'earth to earth'.] **A.** *sb.* A kind of dance (see Terra a terra 2, note and quot. 1797).
B. *adj. phr.* Matter-of-fact, unimaginative.
1888, 1898 [see Terra a terra 2]. 1930 *Time & Tide* 18 Apr. 500/2 He was too frank not to admit that his friend and chief was, intellectually, very *terre-à-terre.* 1930 J. G. Fletcher *Europe's Two Frontiers* 175 Their efforts.. lacking in the wholly technical qualities that sweep audiences off their feet, were masterpieces of close, realistic, *terre-à-terre* argument.

Terricolous, *a.* Add: **b.** = Terricole *a.* 1.
1921 Annie L. Smith *Handbk. Brit. Lichens* 142.

Territory[1]. Add: **1. e.** The area over which a commercial traveller operates.
1925 *Daily Tel.* 13 May 20/7 Traveller Wanted...Live men can earn £10 week. Territory given. 1927 C. L. Bolling *Sales Managem.* 93 The majority of agents will press for a large territory and for exclusive selling rights. 1928 F. W. Shrubsall *Train. Travelling Salesmen* v. 37 When a salesman is appointed to, or takes over, a territory, be it town, district, county, or group of counties, he should immediately commence to study such territory.

3. a. Phr. *To take in too much territory*: to go too far, make too sweeping an assertion, or the like.
1927 *Daily Express* 30 Nov. 3/1, I think it is a fine plan to refuse, if possible, to be affected by an opponent's play... But I am sure I took in entirely too much territory when I said that his work should be ignored.

Terror, *sb.* Add: **2.** *Novel* or *romance of terror*: a genre of romance in which an atmosphere of terror is produced by the relation of horrific events, esp. of a supernatural kind.
1931 R. L. Mégroz *Conrad's Mind & Method* 237 The 'Gothic'-terror-romance of the eighteenth century.

b. A person who tries the feelings or patience of others; an exasperating or tiresome person; a nuisance. *colloq.*
1889 *Harper's Mag.* May 933/1 That bright boy..who was a terror six months ago, will no doubt be in the City Council in a few years. 1893 holy terror [see *Holy *a.* 4 c]. 1900 little terrors [see 2 in Dict.].

Terry Alt (te·ri ǫlt). *Irish Hist.* [According to the diary cited in quot. 1831 below, *Terry Alts* was the name of an innocent bystander who was supected of an outrage on a man.] Usually *pl.* A body of rebels which appeared in co. Clare after the Union and was associated with many outrages.
1831 *MS. Diary* in *Times Lit. Suppl.* 29 Sept. (1932) 691/4 Father Lynch..told us the origin of the name 'Terry Alts'. 1842 J. C. Hall *Ireland* II. 122 The Terry Aits in Clare. 1880 W. J. Fitz-Patrick *Life Dr. Doyle* II. 333 He urged the 'Shanavests', the 'Terryalts', the 'Rockites' and the Ribbonmen to cast their evil combinations to the winds. 1898 *Westm. Gaz.* 14 Nov. 4/2 The man was suspected of being a 'Terry Alt', or a member of a local agrarian conspiracy. 1905 *Blackw. Mag.* Jan. 57/1 A more tragic reminder of the Terry-Alts and their doings. 1921 *Edin. Rev.* Jan. 186 These crimes, and those of the Carders, of Captain Rock and the Terry Alts, produced great demoralization.

Tesla (te·slă). The name of Nikola *Tesla* (born 1857), American electrician and physicist, used *attrib.* to designate certain apparatus invented by him and phenomena caused by this apparatus; as **Tesla coil, transformer,** a form of induction coil for producing high frequency alternating or oscillating currents; **Tesla current,** a current generated by the Tesla coil; **Tesla discharge,** an oscillatory discharge of high frequency obtained from a Tesla coil.
1902 *Encycl. Brit.* XXXIII. 426/2 The oscillatory discharges produced by discharging a large condenser through a low resistance can be transformed in potential, and we can construct an oscillation transformer. This is usually called a Tesla coil. 1904 *Knowledge* Apr. 56/2 By means of high frequency currents (Tesla currents), luminous radiations may be produced inside the tube. 1924 *Discovery* June 84/1 The apparatus is indeed very similar to an ordinary tesla coil.

Test, *sb.*[1] **7. b.** Add: **test cricket,** the cricket of test-matches; also *attrib.*; **test-flame,** a flame serving or used as a test; also *fig.*; **test-hole,** also, a hole dug to ascertain the mineral-bearing or other condition of the soil; **test load** (see quot.); **test-piece,** (*b*) (see 7 a in Dict.); (*c*) in a music or recitation contest, a piece of music, poetry, etc., performed by each of the competitors in order to decide which is the best singer, player, reciter, etc.; **test pressure** (see quot. 1892).
1931 J. Hobbs *Playing for England!* (title) My *Test-Cricket Story. 1892 J. R. Harris *Memoranda Sacra* 130 The Christian's *test-flame is the peace of God. 1913 V. B. Lewes *Oil Fuel* 102 The cup has a close-fitting lid, and carries the 'test-flame' and thermometer. 1909 *Chambers's Jrnl.* Mar. 160/1 He [*sc.* the prospector] digs here and there, making *test-holes. 1888 *Lockwood's Dict. Mech. Engin.*, *Proof Load*, or **Test Load*, a load imposed on a structure greater in amount than the working load, in order to test its capability or margin of safety. 1888 *Ibid.* s.v. *Boiler Testing*, The *test pressure is usually from one and a half to twice that of the actual pressure to which it is intended to work the boiler. 1892 *Ibid.* App., *Test Pressure*, the pressure put upon a steam boiler before delivery to purchaser.

Test, *v.*[2] **2.** Add: *To test out*: to try out; to put (a theory) to the test of practice.
1926 *Publishers' Weekly* 29 May 1794/2 To test out the value of radio publicity. *Ibid.* 10 July 119 The owner, rather than have his very capable manager resign, agreed to test out their separate theories.

Testimonial, *a.* and *sb.* Add: **A.** *adj.* Involving the giving of testimony or witness.
1889 *Kansas City Times & Star* 17 Sept., The Christian Scientists had a 'testimonial meeting' on the third floor of the Gibraltar building Wednesday night.

B. *sb.* **6.** (sense 5) = serving as a testimonial or token of esteem. Also **testimonial book,** a book in which testimonials are written.
1895 *Funk's Stand. Dict.* s.v., A testimonial certificate, benefit, or banquet. 1905 E. F. Benson *Image in Sand* ii. 36, I..told him [*sc.* a dragoman] that he had been quite satisfactory, and if he wished I would write in his testimonial-book. 1931 *Daily Express* 21 Sept. 11/5 A testimonial dinner was given to..the millionaire American capitalist.

Testudinal, *a.* (Modern example.)
1900 Tuckwell *Remin. Oxford* 37 When the idea flashed upon him that the Cheirotherium footsteps were testudinal.

Tetarto-. Add: **Teta·rtocone,** the posterior internal cusp of an upper premolar tooth.
1896 [see Tritocone].

Tête-bêche (tęt bęʃ). *Philately.* [Fr., f. *tête* head + *bêche*, reduced from *bechevet* lit. double bed-head, f. *bes-* (L. *bis-*) + *chevet* bed-head.] A term used to describe the printing of postage stamps upside down or sideways with reference to one another. Sometimes used as *sb.*, an instance of such printing, or stamps so printed.
1882 E. B. Evans *Catal. Collectors Postage Stamps* etc. 56 One or more stamps upside down,..forming the varieties termed *têtes-bêches.* *Ibid.*, Varieties 2 and 3 are the result of stamps placed *tête-bêche.* 1891 *Philatelic Jrnl.* I. 14 France...1853, 1 fr., pair Tête Bêche, 17/-. 1891 *S. Gibbons' Monthly Jrnl.* 30 Jan. 153/2 The sheets are composed of four horizontal rows of five stamps,..each row is placed *tête-bêche* to the one below it. 1893 Napier *Ibid.* Dec. 120 Balliol Coll...Instances of *tête-bêche* occur on all the strips. 1893 *S. Gibbons' Philat. Handbk., Portuguese India* 58 From the fact of the value being printed in at a second printing one might expect to find the tête-bêches with the value inverted. 1921 F. A. Bellamy *Oxf. & Camb. Coll. Messenger Postage Stamps* 14 Balliol, a number of impressions were made one way, then the paper strip was turned round; so a tête bêche pair can be found on each strip.

Tetel (tā·təl, te·təl). Also **tetl.** [Local name.] An antelope, *Bubalis mauritanica*, allied to the hartebeest, found in Africa, Arabia, and Syria.
1867 Baker *Nile Trib.* 308 We had hardly ridden half a mile, when I perceived a fine bull tétel (*Antelope Bubalis*) standing near a bush. 1894 Sclater & Thomas *Bk. Antelopes* I. 16 The Tora or Tétel was confounded by von Heuglin and Sir Samuel Baker, its first discoverers, with the Bubal. 1920 *Blackw. Mag.* Nov. 672/2 A great herd of tetl—big animals the size of a mule—sprang up.

Tethys (te·þis). [L. *Tēthys*, Gr. Τηθύς, a sea-goddess.]
1. *Geol.* The name given to a former inland sea of large extent of which the present Mediterranean area formed a part. Hence **Te·thyan** *a.*
1893 Suess in *Nat. Sci.* Mar. 183 A great ocean which once stretched across part of Eurasia. The folded and crumpled deposits of this ocean stand forth to heaven in Thibet, Himalaya, and the Alps. This ocean we designate by the name 'Tethys', after the sister and consort of Oceanus. The latest successor of the Tethyan Sea is the present Mediterranean. *Ibid.* 184 The later Tethyan history. 1908 Hertha Sollas tr. *Suess's Face of Earth* III. 19 The existing Mediterranean of Europe is a remnant of the Tethys. 1925 J. Joly *Surface-Hist. Earth* vii. 125 In the case of the Mediterranean (in former times expanded into a far larger inter-continental sea which geologists call the Tethys), the widely extended shallows along the shores of the Tethys appear to have received the sediments.

2. *Astr.* The third innermost satellite of Saturn.
1886 A. Hall in *Rep. Brit. Assoc.* 543.

Teton (tī·tǫn). *U.S.* [ad. F. *téton*, f. OF. *tete* (mod. *tette*) teat.] (See quot. 1855.)
1855 J. Mullan *Pac. R. R. Explor.* I. 331 The word 'Teton' is applied to high, towering and prominent peaks of a mountain range that rises above the remaining portion of the ranges. 1864 A. J. Dickson *Across Plains* (1929) 120 To the north, remote, a triad of mountain majesty, the grand tetons towered above the surrounding peaks.

Tetragonal, *a.* Add: **5. b.** *Geom. & Cryst.* Having a relation to four angles; as *tetragonal symmetry*, the symmetry of a figure or body which coincides with its original position after rotation about an axis through one or any number of right angles (i.e. ¼, etc. of the whole circle).
1878 [in Dict., sense 5].

Tetraploid (te·trăploid). *Biol.* [f. Tetra-, after *Diploid.] A cell having four times the number of chromosomes characteristic of germ cells. Hence **Tetraploi·dy,** the condition or occurrence of such a cell.
1924 E. W. MacBride *Study Heredity* viii. (1925) 216 Other examples of such 'tetraploidy' (i.e. doubling the ordinary 'diploid' number of chromosomes) are known to occur amongst the progeny of hybrids between different species. 1930 R. O. Whyte in *Jrnl. Genetics* Sept. 106 The plates with the tetraploid number of chromosomes are regular and more suitable for counting.

Tetrode. Add: **2.** *Wireless.* (See quot. 1930.)
1919 W. H. Eccles in *Electrician* LXXXII. 475/2 To be systematic I suggest 'tetrode' and 'pentode' for vacuum tubes with four or five electrodes. 1930 *B.B.C. Year-Bk.* 436/1 *Four-electrode valve*, a thermionic valve having a kathode (filament), two grids and an anode. Sometimes called a tetrode.

Tettigonian (tetigō·niăn), *a.* and *sb.* *Ent.* [f. mod.L. *Tettigonia* (Linnæus, 1748), name of genus + -an.] (Pertaining to or resembling) a leaf-hopper of the genus *Tettigonia* or related genus. So **Tettigo·niid** *a.* and *sb.*, (pertaining to) a member of the family *Tettigoniidæ* of leaf-hoppers, of which the family *Tettigonia* is typical.
1862 T. W. Harris *Insects Injur. Veget.* (ed. 3) 226 The Tettigonians, or leaf-hoppers, have the head and thorax somewhat like those of frog-hoppers. 1931 *Oxf. Univ. Gaz.* 17 June 704/2 A Fossorial wasp with Tettigoniid (Locustid) prey.

Teuf-teuf (tö̆f,tö̆f). Also *Tuff-tuff. [Fr.; echoic.] An imitation of the repeated sound of gases escaping from the exhaust of a petrol engine. Hence **Teuf-teuf** *v. intr.*, (of a motor) to make such sound; (of a person) to ride in a motor vehicle.
1902 *Daily Chron.* 22 Aug. 3/4 The 'teuf-teuf' of the rapid motor is everywhere on the splendid roads. 1904 G. B. Shaw *John Bull's other Island* III. 77 His ear catches an approaching teuf-teuf...The noise of the motor ceases. 1904 H. G. Wells *Food of Gods* I. iv. § 5. 114 People..used to see him ..teufteufing slowly about Hyde Park. 1905 *Westm. Gaz.* 9 Sept. 11/3 The teuf-teufing of the motor is drowned by the tinkle of marriage bells. 1914 T. A. Baggs *Back fr. Front* 121 Suddenly, piercing the night stillness, came the harsh teuf-teuf of a motor-car.

Teutonized, *ppl. a.* [f. Teuton + -ize + -ed[1].] Made Teutonic; Germanized.
1918 *Hist. Amer. Lit.* I. 357 The Teutonized rhapsodies of Coleridge. 1924 *Blackw. Mag.* Aug. 280/2 All Germans kept their eyes firmly fixed on a Teutonised Europe.

Texan. Add: *sb.* A person or animal native to or inhabiting Texas.
1843 *Penny Cycl.* XXIV. 270/2 The Texans now attached themselves to the Federalists. 1878 Isabella L. Bird *Lady's Life Rocky Mts.* x. (1910) 172 These pure Texans, the old Spanish breed, weigh from 900 to 1000 pounds. 1920 *Cornhill Mag.* Sept. 335 The work of the Texans was neat and expeditious.

Texas. 1. *U.S.* (Earlier example.)
1857 Olmsted *Journ. Texas* 27 To this Texas, inveterate card-players retire on Sundays.
2. Texas fever (earlier example).
1867–9 *Trans. Ill. Agric. Soc.* VII. 183 An exact description of the external and internal manifestations of Texas fever.

†**Texian,** *a.* and *sb.* = Texan *a.* and *sb.*
1836 D. B. Edward *Hist. Texas* 45 The Texian farmer of the Gulf coast. *Ibid.* 74 [It] adds to the variety of a Texian landscape. 1837 *Chambers's Edin. Jrnl.* 22 Apr. 102/1 The Texians might have a decent excuse to seek their independence. 1843 *Illustr. Lond. News* 11 Mar. 164/3 The eruption of the party of Texians into Mexico. 1845 (*title*) Journal of the Texian Expedition against Mier.

Text, *sb.*[1] **4.** Add: *Golden text*, a text embodying the main thought of a lesson, learnt by heart by Sunday School children.

Thalenite (tā·lenəit). *Min.* [f. the name of R. *Thalen* + -ite[1].] A flesh-red silicate of yttrium found in Sweden.
1900 *Min. Mag.* XII. 393. 1922 W. E. Ford *Dana's Min.* 529.

Thalleoquin (þæ·lĭ,okwin). *Chem.* Also **thalleio-.** [f. Gr. θαλλία foliage + Quin(ine.] A green resinous substance, a test for quinine.
1877 Watts *Dict. Chem.* V. 740 *Thalleiochin*, or *Dalleiochin*, a product of the action of chlorine-water on sulphate of quinine. 1886 *Encycl. Brit.* XX. 185/1 An emerald green colour, due to the formation of thalleoquin, is developed. 1886 *Buck's Handbk. Med. Sci.* II. 163/1 Thalleioquin is afforded by: Quinine, Quinidine, Homoquinine. Thalleioquin is not afforded by: Cinchonine, Cinchonidine, Quinamine.

Thamudic (þămū·dik), *a.* [f. *Thamúd*, name of a pre-historic Arab tribe + -ic.] Of or pertaining to the Thamúd; *spec.* designating inscriptions resembling the Sabæan, found in the country of the Thamúd. So **Thamu·dite** [-ite[1]].
1880 *Encycl. Brit.* XIII. 117/2 [The graffiti] are mostly the productions of Thamudite soldiers in the Roman army. 1886 *Ibid.* XXI. 651/1 These inscriptions have been called 'Thamudic', because they were found in the country of the Thamúd. 1888 Doughty *Trav. Arabia Deserta* I. 205 Twice every year stands this canvas city of a day, in the Thamudite plain, full of traffic.

Thanatomania (þænătomē·niă). *Psychol.* [f. Thanato- + -mania.] The condition of being susceptible to the hypnotic suggestion of approaching death.
1902 Webster Suppl., *Thanatomania*, suicidal mania. 1915 *Hastings's Encycl. Relig. & Ethics* VIII. 248/2 The tendency which W. E. Roth..calls *thanatomania*; namely, the suggestibility leading..to death on the part of one who satisfies himself that he is doomed.

Thank, *sb.* **5.** Add: *thanks very much.*
1919 Wodehouse *Damsel in Distress* i, Oh, no, thanks very much! 1921 Hichens *Spirit of Time* xii, Very good of you. Thanks very much.

Thanksgiving. 1. Add: *Harvest thanksgiving* = harvest festival (Harvest *sb.* 7).
1859 *Chron. Convocation* 11 Feb. 15 An Office of Thanksgiving for the Harvest. 1867 *Leisure Hour* 3 Aug. 559/1 The service was that specially prepared by Convocation for harvest thanksgivings.

Thao (tā·o). [Chinese.] A gelatinous substance obtained from seaweed in Eastern countries, Chinese or Japanese isinglass.

1863 HALDANE *Workshop Receipts* Ser. II. 357/1 *Thao* is a very interesting substance...It is a gelatinous preparation made in Cochin China,..from seaweed.

That, *dem. pron.* Add: **5. d.** *That's so*: that is as you say, that statement is correct. Also interrogatively, *(Is) that so? That's right* (vulgar), as a formula of assent or approval. *So that's that*: an expression indicating that a discussion is closed or a matter settled beyond dispute: = that is the end of the matter. Similarly *so that was that*.

1857 *Knickerbocker Mag.* Jan. 86 One of the quaintest, quietest, most musical, and most engaging forms of acquiescence is in the new and popular phrase of '*That's so*', which is working its way into common parlance. 1872 S. BUTLER *Erewhon* vi. 45 'So that's that,' said I to myself, as I watched them scampering. 1891 MARAH E. RYAN *Pagan Alleghanies* vi. 93 'That so?' she said. 1905 *N. Y. Evening Post* 7 Apr. 2 The President's address was frequently interrupted with applause and cries of 'That's right'. 1921 G. O'DONOVAN *Vocations* iv. 59 'I half promised mother to stay till you got your vocation...So that we could enter on the one day...But he didn't make much of it.'..'So that's that,' Kitty said, with a frown. 1924 P. MARKS *Plastic Age* 24 'Well,' he exclaimed, 'that's that. At last I know where I'm going.' 1930 *Times* 26 Mar. 7/2 Bray and Jackson never looked like holding Martin-Smith and Bond, who raced away with 4's, 3's, and 2's: so that was that.

That, *pron.* Add: **5. b.** *And all that* (modern examples); also, often used as a trivial addition to a formula of thanks, congratulation, or the like.

1925 OPPENHEIM *Wrath to Come* II. xvi, 'Glad to see you and all that, Slattery,' he said. 1929 R. GRAVES (*title*) Good bye to all that. 1930 W. C. SELLAR & YEATMAN (*title*) 1066 and all that. 1930 SAYERS & EUSTACE *Docts. in Case* I. 25 Not good-looking, but full of S.A. and all that. *Mod.* Very many happy returns of the day, and all that!

d. *Come out of that!*: clear out! get off with you! *dial.* and *slang*.

That-away, *adv. dial.* and *U.S.* Also **that-aways, that-a-way.** [f. THAT II + AWAY *adv.*] **1.** In that direction.

1839 *Southern Lit. Messenger* V. 378/2, I expect, Tommy, you're a sparking that a way. 1847 HALLIWELL, *That-a-way*, that way. *Yorksh.* 1866 H. JACKSON *Gilbert Rugge* xxxii, Down in the marsh lands, that-a-way. 1901 JAS. PRIOR *Forest Folk* iv. 41 It's out o' my road or I'd show yer; that-away.

2. In that manner or respect.

1847 *Paddiana* I. 139 It's very careless I hear they are that aways. 1887 *Scribner's Mag.* Sept. 366/1 Flandroe said: 'I hadn' 'a' thought ye'd 'a' evidenced agin me that-a-way.' 1898 J. C. HARRIS *Tales of Home Folks* 283 They'd..come an' snatch 'em up an' bundle 'em off that-away.

Thawing, *vbl. sb.* Add: **b.** *attrib.*

1915 *Kynoch Jrnl.* Oct.–Dec. 200 Many consumers..put frozen cartridges in thawing pans several hours before they are required.

Theatre, *sb.* Add: **3. e.** In *good theatre*, etc.: see *GOOD *a.* 1 f.

1927 *Sunday Times* 27 Feb. 6/4 'The Letter' is superb theatre throughout. 1928 [see *GOOD *a.* 1 f].

Theatregraph (þi·ǎtəɪgrɑf). *Disused.* [See -GRAPH.] = *ANIMATOGRAPH.

1897 [see *ANIMATOGRAPH].

Thé dansant (te dɑ̃sɑ̃). See *DANSANT.

Thelitis (þīlai·tis). *Path.* [mod.L., f. Gr. θηλή nipple + -ITIS. Cf. F. *thélite*.] Inflammation of a nipple.

1848 DUNGLISON *Med. Lex.* (ed. 7).

Thematic, *a.* Add: **4.** Of or pertaining to a (Byzantine) 'theme' or province.

1914 J. B. BURY in *Engl. Hist. Rev.* Jan. 130 The strategoi of the Thematic system.

Thenabouts, *adv.* (Recent example.)

1931 D. CORKERY *Synge* Introd. p. vii, Ireland in 1907—thereabouts and thenabouts.

Thenceafter, *adv.* (Recent example.)

1932 BELLOC *Napoleon* iii. 182 Thenceafter, for a week or more, it was intrigue upon intrigue.

Theo-. Add: **Theoce·ntricism, -ce·ntrism.** Theocentric doctrine, principles, or belief.

1925 E. UNDERHILL *Mystics of Ch.* x. 205 The best traditions of French spirituality, its lofty theocentricism. 1930 *Monument to St. Augustine* viii. 272 The apparent theocentrism of the Calvinist 'glory of God'.

Theocin (þī·osin). *Chem.* [irreg. f. mod.L. *thea* tea + -IN¹.] Synthetic theophyllin, used as a diuretic.

1910 *Practitioner* June 777 Evacuants..must be used..with or without theocin sodium acetate.

Theocrasia (þīokrē·ziǎ). Also **-krasia.** [a. Gr. θεοκρασία a mingling with God.] = THEOCRASY.

1913 *Hastings's Encycl. Relig. & Ethics* VI. 422/1 The working of the *theokrasia* in the domain of religion and religious art. 1920 H. G. WELLS *Outline Hist.* 496/2 We have noted how a sort of theocrasia went on between Christianity and Judaism..and other competing cults.

Theocritean (þīǫkritī·ǎn), *a.* [f. L. *Theocritus*, a. Gr. Θεόκριτος Theocritus, a Greek poet of Sicily, of the 3rd c. B.C. + -EAN.] Of, pertaining to, or characteristic of Theocritus or his writings, esp. his pastoral poetry; of the style or like that of Theocritus; hence, pastoral, idyllic. So **Theocritan** (þīǫ·kritǎn) *a.*

1846 KEIGHTLEY *Notes Virg., Bucol.* v. Observ., He [*sc.* Virgil] was thoroughly imbued with the Theocritean poetry. 1873 SYMONDS *Greek Poets* x. 316 To reconstruct the mode of life of the Theocritean *dramatis personæ*. 1896 *McClure's Mag.* VI. 467/2 With his [*sc.* Corot's] Theocritan spirit, he could see the fountain of Jouvence in the woods of Sèvres. 1897 F. T. PALGRAVE in *Mem. Tennyson* II. 495 Tennyson read over to me the little Theocritean Idyll 'Hylas'. 1927 *Observer* 24 July 13/2 This bucolic, but far from Theocritan, idyll.

Theophrastian (þīǫfræ·stiǎn), *a.* Also **-an, -ean.** [f. L. *Theophrastus*, a. Gr. Θεόφραστος, a Greek philosopher of Eresus in Lesbos (4th c. B.C.) + -IAN.] Of, pertaining to, or characteristic of Theophrastus or his writings, esp. his 'Characters'. So **Theophra·stic, † Theophra·stical** *adjs.*

1662 J. SPARROW tr. *Behme's Rem. Wks., Apol. conc. Perfection* 132 Not Tinctured, according to the Cabalisticall, Theophrasticall, Roso-Crucian kind. 1924 *Public Opinion* 18 Jan. 53/2 Some charming little essay or Theophrastan Study. 1926 *Glasgow Herald* 8 Apr. 4 One of the earliest [Characters] which has the true Theophrastian ring. 1928 *Observer* 12 Feb. 4 Some of these Theophrastic 'characters' are very charming.

Theotokion (þīǫtǫ·kiǫn). *Eastern Church.* [eccl. Gr., f. θεοτόκος: see THEOTOKOS.] The final troparion of an ode, forming an ascription of praise to the Mother of God.

1850 NEALE *Hist. East. Ch.* I. 832 *note*, The theotokion is simply a sticheron or troparion addressed to the Mother of God. 1880 *Encycl. Brit.* XII. 580/1 A 'theotokion', or ascription of praise to the mother of our Lord.

There, *adv.* Add: **7.** *So there!* That is my final word or decision, that's flat!

1894 [in Dict.]. 1919 PAPLEX *Health* ii. 15 This worker of welfare..I won't bear on my stair—so there! 1924 ROSE MACAULAY *Orphan Island* xxi. § 3, I suppose you think I'm in love with you. Well, I'm not, so there.

12. a. *To get there* (U.S.): see GET *v.* 31 c.

Theremophone (þe·rīmǫfōun). [f. name of *Theremin*, its Russian inventor + *-phone* after *gramophone*, etc.] A musical instrument by which musical sounds are produced from air-waves by means of wireless apparatus.

1928 *Musical Times* Jan., The theremophone (let us call it) is a first-hand medium, not a mere re-producer. 1930 *Ibid.* May 413 Mr. Stokowski uses the theremophone in certain arrangements of Bach's organ works.

Therevid (þī·revid), *a.* and *sb.* *Ent.* [ad. mod.L. *Therevidæ*, f. Gr. θηρεύειν to hunt: see -ID³.] Of or belonging to the *Therevidæ*, a family of brachycerous dipterous insects; an insect belonging to this family, a stiletto-fly.

1921 *Brit. Museum Return* 146 A Therevid Fly in Burmese Amber.

Theriomorph (þī·riǫmǫɹf). [f. Gr. θηριο- THERIO- + μορφή form.] A representation of an animal form in art.

1913 [see *ORNITHOMORPH]. 1928 V. G. CHILDE *Most Anc. East* iv. 84 Some theriomorphs are made of just those variegated stones.

Therm². Add: **2.** The unit of calorific value, equal to 100,000 British thermal units, generally adopted by gas undertakings in Great Britain and elsewhere as a basis of charge for gas supplied.

1920 *Act* 10 & 11 *Geo. V* c. 28 § 1 (2) (*Gas Regulation Act*), A standard or maximum price for each hundred thousand British thermal units (in this Act referred to as 'a therm'). 1922 *Westm. Gaz.* 18 Oct., The therm system of charging for gas.

Therm (þɜ̄ɹm), *v.* [Cf. THERM³.] *trans.* In 18th c. cabinet-making, to turn (a leg or foot of a chair, table, etc.) to a rectangular form; also *absol.* So **Therm** *sb.*, a leg or foot so turned; hence *therm foot, leg*, a tapering foot or leg.

1788 *Cabinet-makers' Lond. Bk. Prices* (1803) No. 7 If the plinth of the Therms is work'd hollow [price, extra, 1½d]. *Ibid.* No. 12 The Price of Therming Legs...The Price of Therming in the Neck...When the legs are therm'd at the top only, the tapering to be paid for extra. 1802–3 SHERATON *Cabinet Dict.* (Simon's Eng. Furniture) *Therm*. Tapering. 1925 J. PENDEREL-BRODHURST & LAYTON *Gloss. Engl. Furniture*, *Therm Foot*, a rectangular tapering foot to the legs of chairs and tables, also called a spade or taper foot, often used by the brothers Adam and Hepplewhite, and to a lesser degree by Sheraton. *Therm Leg*, the taper or therm leg was a favourite feature of Hepplewhite and later designers.

Thermal, *a.* Add: **2. b.** Designating a bath the temperature of which exceeds 98° Fahr.

1906 *Practitioner* Nov. 623 Baths below 93° F. are..known as hypo-thermal baths..while above 98° they are called thermal.

Thermion (þɜ̄·ɹmiǫn). *Physics.* [f. Gr. θερμός hot, or θέρμη heat + ION.] An *ELECTRON emitted from a highly heated body.

1922 J. MILLS *Within the Atom* vii. 73 An electron which is emitted in this way is sometimes called a 'thermion'.

Thermionic (þɜɹmiǫ·nik) *a.* *Physics & Electr.* [f. prec. + -IC.] Of, pertaining to, or consisting of thermions; *spec.* defining an appliance giving a copious flow of electrons when heated, as the *thermionic valve* (see quot. 1922).

1915 *Electrician* LXXV. 241/1 The thermionic current..increased at first. 1917 FLEMING in *Wireless World* V. 152 The invention by the writer of this article of the thermionic detector. 1920 *Chambers's Jrnl.* 365/1 In one of its simplest forms the thermionic valve has the appearance of an electric incandescent filament lamp. 1922 *Encycl. Brit.* XXXII. 1024/2 The third type of high frequency electric oscillation generator which has become of great importance in the last five years is the thermionic valve, which is a development of the Fleming valve. *Ibid.*, Those electrons are attracted to it, and this creates a movement of negative electricity called a thermionic current. 1928 *Daily Express* 13 Dec. 9 A thermionic reflexometer. 1930 *Times* 21 Mar. 10/2 The thermionic telephone repeater which grew out of the valve.

Hence **Thermio·nically** *adv.*, in thermionic form.

1922 J. MILLS *Within the Atom* vii. 74 When electrons are being thermionically emitted from a heated wire. *Ibid.* 75 The thermionic emission of electrons at a heated electrode.

Thermite. Add: Used as a composition for incendiary bombs. Also *attrib.* defining a process or method of welding or casting with molten metal produced by igniting thermite in a crucible.

1905 *Chambers's Jrnl.* 78/2 A perfectly successful joint..has been made by utilising the thermite process steel. 1915 *Ibid.* 558/1 The thermit reaction is used largely in the preparation of metals from their oxides. 1920 *Discovery* May 142/2 Iron alloys..are prepared by..the thermit process. 1922 *Encycl. Brit.* XXX. 86/1 Thermite [as a composition for incendiary bombs]..consists of 76 parts magnetic oxide of iron and 24 parts aluminium.

Thermo-. Add: **Thermocre·scent** *a.*, defining a graphically recorded curve indicating the change of rate of growth of a plant as influenced by changes of temperature. **Thermo-ge·nerator** *Electr.* (see quot. 1910). **Thermo-lumino·sity** (see quot.). **The·rmo-tank,** a tank containing pipes through which water, air, or the like circulates for heating or cooling, esp. as a heating or ventilating system; also *attrib.*

1929 SIR J. C. BOSE *Growth* 40 A *Thermocrescent Curve was thus obtained, the ordinate representing increment of growth, and the abscissa the time as well as the rise of temperature. 1910 *Practitioner* July 135 The *Thermo-Generator provides..a means by which electricity generated by the liberation of the elements of certain metals can be utilised. 1927 *Times* 6 July 21/5 A thermo-generator for use with wireless receiving sets. 1903 *Chem. News* LXXXVIII. 223/2 Production of *Thermo-luminosity. 1904 *Knowledge* Apr. 72/1 Those varieties of Fluorite..which possess..the property of 'thermo-luminosity', that is to say, of spontaneously emitting light when heated. 1920 *Glasgow Herald* 2 Oct. 7 The *thermo-tank system of heating and ventilating. 1928 *Observer* 15 July 9/4 A new Thermo-Tank heating system.

Thermo-electric, *a.* (*sb.*). **B.** *sb. pl.* Add: The science of thermo-electricity.

1896 *Phil. Mag.* Ser. v. XLI. 480 A contribution of much permanent value to the data on thermo-electrics has recently been made by Noll.

Thermo-siphon, *attrib.* Add: esp. in motor-construction. Hence **Thermo-sipho·nic** *a.*

1909 *Daily Chron.* 13 Nov. 9/6 Thermo-syphon radiators. 1922 *Times* 20 June 8/5 Thermo-siphon cooling is used. 1922 *Autocar* 10 Nov. 966 Cooling water is circulated by thermo-syphonic action.

Thessalian (þesē·liǎn), *a.* and *sb.* [f. L. *Thessalius, Thessalus*, a. Gr. Θεσσάλειος, Θεσσαλός, adjs. f. *Thessalia*, Θεσσαλία Thessaly: see -AN, -IAN.] **a.** *adj.* Of or pertaining to Thessaly, a district in northern Greece, its inhabitants, or speech. **b.** *sb.* An inhabitant of Thessaly.

1590 SHAKS. *Mids. N.* IV. i. 127 Crooke kneed, and dewlapt, like Thessalian Buls. 1594 KYD *Cornelia* IV. ii. 63 When the Thessalian fields were purpled ore With swifter Armies murdered souldiers gore. 1667 MILTON *P. L.* II. 544 As when Alcides..tore Through pain up by the roots Thessalian Pines. 1842 TENNYSON *Talking Oak* 292 Or that Thessalian growth, In which the swarthy ringdove sat, And mystic sentence spoke. 1842 *Penny Cycl.* XXIV. 359/1 The Thessalians..became very rich, and luxurious in their mode of life. 1888 *Encycl. Brit.* XXIII. 299/1 These Thessalian passes were of the utmost importance to southern Greece. *Ibid.* 299/2 In race, as in geographical position, the Thessalians held an intermediate place between the non-Hellenic Macedonians and the Greeks of pure blood.

Thetine (þī·tin). *Chem.* [app. f. *th-* of THIO- after *betaine*.] Any one of a series of sulphur compounds analogous to betaine.

1893 *Jrnl. Chem. Soc.* LXIV. I. 633 Isomeric Thetines. 1895 *Ibid.* LXVIII. II. 8 In the thetines, the four valencies of the sulphur atom are of different values.

Thick, *a.* **12. b.** Add: **thick-bill,** also, a S. African bird (see quot.); **thick-ear,** a swollen or thickened external ear resulting from a blow or blows, esp. in phr. *to give* (a person) *a thick ear*; **thick space** *Typog.*, a three to an em space used in separating words; hence **thick-spaced** *a.*, having thick spaces dividing the words.

1899 R. B. & J. D. S. WOODWARD *Natal Birds* 79 (Pettman) We usually call this bird [*Amblyospiza albifrons*] the Hawfinch...The boys call it *Thick-bill. 1909 WARE *Passing Engl.*, **Thick ear*, one swelled by a blow. 1915 *Truth* 4 Aug. 190/2 Tommy knew..that to ask his father for help was merely to ask for what his son would have called 'a thick ear'. 1922 'SAPPER' (H. C. MCNEILE) *Black Gang* xvii. 286 If you propose to take me and endeavour to make my head impinge on a stone wall, someone is going to get a thick ear. 1683 MOXON *Mech. Exerc., Printing* viii. 99 Some [letters] are Space thick; that is, one quarter so thick as the Body is high; though Spaces are seldom Cast so thick,..and therefore, for distinction sake, we shall call these Spaces, *Thick Spaces. 1808 C. STOWER *Printer's Gram.* iii. 90 Of Spaces...They are cast to various thicknesses...Three to an m—or three thick spaces. 1892 [see SPACE *sb.*¹ 15 b]. 1824 J. JOHNSON *Typogr.* II. 132 A *d* and an *h*..will admit an addition, but not more than a middle and thin space to a *thick spaced line. 1893 HART *Rules for Compositors* 22 When the last line but one of a paragraph is widely spaced and the first line of the following paragraph is also more than thick-spaced.

Thickety, *a.* (Earlier Amer. examples.)

1640 in *Maryland Hist. Mag.* V. 374 The Neck of Land..lyeing between thicketty Creek on the North, hog pen Creek on the South. 1740 in *Coll. S. Carolina Hist. Soc.* IV. 152 They got into such thickety ground that they [*sc.* the Indians] could not overtake them.

Thicknesser (þi·knesəɹ). [-ER¹.] A thicknessing machine.

1920 F. T. HILL *Pract. Aeroplane Constr.* 103 Another machine is the surfacer and thicknesser, in which one set of cutters is used for both operations, the top table for the truing-up process.., and the bottom table for thicknessing.

Thick 'un (þi·kǫn). *slang.* [THICK *a.*; *'un* = ONE.] A sovereign (the coin); formerly also, a five-shilling piece.

1859 *Slang Dict.*, *Thick un*, a sovereign; a crown piece, or five shillings. 1862 *Cornh. Mag.* Nov. 648 If you like..I will send a few thickuns. 1873 *Slang Dict.* 361 Since i saw you last i have not earned a thick un. 1886 P. CLARKE *New Chum* 143 If..he has a drought within him and a friend or a 'thick-un' to stand by him, he is a poor, weak..fool to refuse. 1897 HALL CAINE *Christian* IV. iv, A 'thick 'un'? Oh, that was a sovereign, half a thick 'un half a sovereign. 1904 E. NESBIT *Phœnix & Carpet* v. 94 'Half a what?' asked Anthea. 'Arf a shiner, quid, thick 'un—half a sov, then.'

Thief. 5. Add: **thief-ant,** the ant *Solenopsis molesta*, which steals its food from other insects; **thiefwise** *adv.*, like a thief.

1902 W. M. WHEELER in *Amer. Naturalist* Dec. 952 The walls of the galleries in some of the formicaries were tenanted by teeming colonies of the..*thief ant, *Solenopsis molesta*. 1924 J. A. THOMSON *Science Old & New* xiv. 79 A little thief-ant, Solenopsis, that..burgles the beetles' houses. 1898 W. J. LOCKE *Idols* vi, Creeping *thiefwise up the stairs. 1903 T. HARDY *Dynasts* I. IV. iii, Stealing up to us Thiefwise, by our back door.

Thigenol (þaidʒe·nǫl). [irreg. f. THIO- + -GEN + -OL.] 'A soluble sulphur compound containing ten per cent of organic sulphur' (Dorland).

1908 *Practitioner* Feb. 253 Its [*sc.* ichthyol's] ally, Thigenol, may be used in its stead.

Thin, *a.* Add: **3. c.** Of a spark (cf. *FAT *a.* 3 c).

1907 *Rep. Brit. Assoc.* 731 The long thin spark that occurs in this case is not very suitable for wireless telegraphy, as its resistance is too high.

4. d. Phr. *A thin time*: a wretched period of experience. *slang.*

1924 A. J. SMALL *Frozen Gold* iv. 108 Yes, sure, you go...If you don't, she will give me such a thin time. 1927 R. CLAY *By Night* iii. 27 Must have had a thin time of it. Let's hope he'll find a difference.

b. thin fount *Typog.* (see quot.); **thin space** *Typog.*, a space used for separating words, cast five to an em of its own body.

1906 *Technol. & Sci. Dict.* (ed. Goodchild & Tweney) s.v., Founts of type of which the lower case letters *a* to *z* measure in width less than twelve times the depth of their body are called *thin founts. 1683 *thin-space [see SPACE *sb.*¹ 15 b]. 1808 C. STOWER *Printer's Gram.* iii. 90 Of Spaces...Five to an m—or five thin spaces. 1892 [see SPACE *sb.*¹ 15 b].

Thing, *sb.*¹ **10. a.** *Dear old thing*: an expression of affection applied to an elderly person. *Old thing*: a jocular or very affectionate form of addressing an intimate, recently used esp. by young people. *colloq.*

1852 *Punch* 31 July 55/2 Aunt Ratchet and I had quietly sat down, I to read and she to listen to a new novel—the greatest pleasure the dear old thing can experience. 1858 *Ibid.* 23 Jan. 34/2 Give Mamma my love, and the ten pounds I enclose, and make the dear old thing buy herself a new shawl. 1905 *Ibid.* 26 Apr. 296/2 'You dear old thing!' she said sadly, 'its a comfort to have you, but you don't understand.' 1919 *Ibid.* 5 Mar. 180/2 So long, old thing. *Bien à vous*, Anne. *Ibid.* 25 June 496/2 'My present trouble is that I've got to find a wife.'..'Nothin' easier, old thing.' 1920 [see *OLD *a.* 8 a]. 1920 ROSE MACAULAY *Potterism* I. iii, Do you want the last walnut chocolate, old thing? 1928 GALSWORTHY *Swan Song* II. v. 147 You ought to keep up your water-colours, old thing.

14. f. Similarly *to be up to a thing or two*.

1816 *Sporting Mag.* XLVIII. 173 The training-groom was up to a thing or two. 1823 MRS. M. M. SHERWOOD *Henry Milner* III. xix, He knows I am up to a thing or two. 1859 *Slang Dict.* 113 'To be up to a thing or two', to be knowing, or understanding. 1870 *Routledge's Ev. Boy's Ann.* 87 The fact of his being 'up to a thing or two'.

17. *Any old thing*: any thing whatever. *slang.*

1900 [see *OLD *a.* 1 c]. 1911 [see *ANY 1 c].

Think, *sb.* **3. think-tank** *U.S. slang*, the brain.

1908 K. MCGAFFEY *Show-Girl* 189, I don't believe your think tank is feeding properly. 1931 *Randolph Enterprise* (Elkins, W. Va.) 24 Dec. 5/6 We try to give the facts as near as our think tank will permit us.

Think, *v.*² Add: **3.** *To think out loud*, variant of 'to think aloud'.

1870 JULIE P. SMITH *Widow Goldsmith's Dau.* vi. 90 The merry mischief in his eyes..made her feel her absurdity in thinking out loud. 1872 G. W. DASENT *Three to One* x, She was a girl who thought out loud.

17. *U.S.* (Earlier and later examples.)

1855 MRS. STOWE *Tales & Sk. New Eng. Life* 79 Christmas is coming..and I have got to think up presents for everybody. 1901 S. MERWIN & H. K. WEBSTER *Calumet K* vi. 108, I had him pretty busy there for a while thinking up lies. 1905 D. G. PHILLIPS *Plum Tree* xxiv. 287 My boy Ed used to think up and do mischief just for the pleasure of pleasing me by confessing. 1912 C. JOHNSTON *Why World Laughs* 132 The monk who originally thought up that artful scheme to swear off his taxes. 1930 *G. K.'s Weekly* 15 Nov. 146/1 If Mr. Lloyd George can think up a good ticket.

Thinner. Add: **1. b.** (See quot.)

1921 *Dict. Occup. Terms* (1927) § 486 *Thinner*: heel thinner; wood heel thinner; reduces thickness of lip, i.e. front edge of seat, of wooden heel.

2. A liquid used to thin oil paints to a suitable consistency.

1904 *Jrnl. Franklin Inst.* July 17 The painter then adds thinners until the paint will work under his brush. 1906 *Technol. & Sci. Dict.* (ed. Goodchild & Tweney) s.v., Linseed oil and turpentine form the usual thinners of the house painter.

Thinning, *vbl. sb.* Add: **1. b.** *spec.* in *Forestry*. Removal of a part of the trees in a stand. *Accretion thinning*, a thinning made to increase the rate of growth in diameter of the remaining trees. *Improvement* or *preliminary thinning*, the first thinning of a forest.

1905 *Terms Forestry & Logging* 24 The following kinds of thinnings are distinguished: cleaning, improvement thinning, accretion thinning. 1922 SIR W. SCHLICH *Man. Forestry* (ed. 4) I. 5 The strength of the thinnings and the time of their execution are the most important matters with which the forester has to deal.

Third, *a.* and *sb.* Add: **I.** *adj.* **5. third flute,** a flute sounding a third above the written notes; **third nerve,** the oculomotor nerve.

1876 STAINER & BARRETT *Dict. Mus. Terms*, *Third flute. 1906 *Technol. & Sci. Dict.* (ed. Goodchild & Tweney) 434/2 There is also a flute in E♭ (often spoken of as the third flute in F, but tuned to E♭), which transposes a minor third higher. 1823 C. BELL *Expos. Nerves Hum. Body* (1824) 35, The voluntary nerves of the eye are the *third and sixth. The third nerve arises from the crus cerebri. *a* 1883 FAGGE *Princ. & Pract. Med.* (1886) I. 487 Such an affection of the third or of the seventh nerve is associated with hemiplegia.

II. *sb.* **9. e.** = *third speed*.

1931 *Daily Express* 16 Oct. 2/1 Four-speed gear box, with silent third.

Third degree. [THIRD *a.* 5.]

1. *Freemasonry.* The degree of master mason, conferred with impressive ceremonial.

1865 J. HOW *Freemason's Man.* (ed. 2) 138 The Third Degree, or the Master Mason. *Ibid.*, The Fellow-Craft who is duly qualified by time, on presenting himself as a candidate for the Third Degree, has to submit himself to an examination of his qualifications as a Craftsman. 1901 [see THIRD *a.* 5].

2. A severe examination of a prisoner by the police in order to extort an admission or confession of guilt. Also *attrib.* *U.S.*

1904 *New York Times* 6 July 5 He was at first arrested merely as a suspicious person, but when put through the 'third degree' at the station admitted that he entered the house last night. 1906 *Springfield* (Mass.) *Weekly Republican* 22 Mar. 3 His confession was secured through the rigorous operation of 'the third degree'. 1913 *Punch* 26 Feb. 153/3 The Third Degree of the New York police. 1928 *Outlook* 26 May 643/1 What are known as 'third degree' methods.

Hence **Third-degree** *v. trans.*, to put through such an examination.

1928 W. GILLETTE *Astound. Crime Torrington Rd.* v. 260 They third-degreed Jimmy Dreek good and plenty. *Ibid.* 269 The fools in Boston had third-degreed an innocent man to his death. 1929 EDINGTON *Studio Murder Myst.* vii. 95 All we got to do is third degree them birds.

Third party. Add: *Third-party insurance*, insurance against injury done to a person other than the insured, e.g. a bystander, which the underwriter contracts to meet; so, *third-party risk*.

1901 in *Insurance Guide & Hand-bk.* (1912) II. 165 Third Party Indemnity.—Claims by the General Public for Personal Injuries or Damage to Property, up to £100 in any one year. 1912 *Ibid.* (ed. 5) 163 At the end of 1898 a premium of £10 was quoted for £100 third party indemnity. 1913 *Punch* 8 Oct. 304/2, I am merely a third party risk. 1931 *Star* 8 May 2/3 A third party insurance policy.

Thirler² (þɜ̄·ɹləɹ). Also **thurler.** [f. THIRL *sb.*¹ or *v.*¹ + -ER¹.] One who makes a thirl; *spec.* in *Coal-mining* (see quot. 1921).

1881 *Instr. Census Clerks* (1885) 84 Coal Miner...Thurler. 1921 *Dict. Occup. Terms* (1927) § 042 *Thirler, thurler*; a hewer who makes a narrow place, holing or thirl in the solid coal..for..ventilation.

Thirteen. Add: In reference to the original thirteen states of the U.S.A.

1789 in C. Cist *Cincinnati* (1841) 213 The chief..wished to be informed..whether the thirteen fires had sent me hither. I..spread before them the thirteen fires, which I had in a flag then in my camp. 1834 H. M. BRACKENRIDGE *Recollections* vii. 69 Fort Fayette, surmounted by the stripes and stars of the old thirteen. 1904 *Hartford Courant* 30 Aug. 10 We want to see the Old Thirteen draw closer and closer together.

Thirteener. Add: **2. b.** Also in the game of bridge. **c.** A child of thirteen years of age.

1929 WORK *Complete Contract Bridge* Gloss. 246 *Thirteener*, card remaining when twelve of the suit have been played. 1907 W. DE MORGAN *Alice-for-Short* x, Not a bad shot for a thirteener.

Thirty. Add: *Thirty days* (see *DAY *sb.* 6 d): a month. *Canada* and *U.S.*

1928 *Publishers' Weekly* 30 June 2596 The ideal turnover would be about every thirty days or twelve times a year.

C. a. *thirty-knotter*.

1918 *Chambers's Jrnl.* July 462/2 She..was an old 'thirty knotter'.

Thirtyish (þɜ̄·ɹti,iʃ), *a.* *colloq.* [f. THIRTY *a.* + -ISH¹ *4.] Of about thirty years of age.

1925 F. M. FORD *No More Parades* I. i, A very thin man; thirtyish. 1926 BENNETT *Lord Raingo* II. lxxi. 320 The..little thirtyish nurse.

This. B. Add: **I. 3.** *This, that, and the other*: every sort of thing, everything possible or imaginable. Also as *adj.* or *adv.*

1916 BOYD CABLE *Action Front* 98 Cursing the grinning and sheepish private for a this, that, and the other crazy, play-acting idiot. 1928 [see *THUS *adv.* 1 g].

II. 1. d. Also, the present or existing. *colloq.*

1785 BOSWELL *Tour Hebrides* 22 Aug. 86 We were told this [*ed.* 2 the present] Mr. Waller was a plain country gentleman. *Ibid.* 26 Sept. 319 This [*ed.* 2 the present] Talisker. 1788 H. WALPOLE *Let. to Dr. Lort* 26 July, Do you know the medals of gold belonged to this Lord Pembroke's grandfather? *Mod.* I knew the last doctor very well. I don't get on with this one.

III. *This-side* adj.

1917 *19th Cent.* Jan. 118 Those on the other side can only use this-side terms and similies and analogies.

Thi·s-worldly, *a.* [See THIS WORLD and -LY¹.] Concerned with this world or the present state of existence. So **Thi·swo·rldness.**

1883 'MARK TWAIN' *Life Mississippi* xlviii. 480 The guests were always this-worldly, and often profane. 1913 N. S. TALBOT in *Foundations* 14 Thought of to-day is this-worldly. 1927 W. R. INGE *Protestantism* 12 A materialistic and wholly this-worldly apocalyptism. 1930 G. GREENE *Two Witnesses* 92 His sensitively spiritual soul could make no truce with any thisworldness.

Thoko (þǭu·ke). [Fiji *coko* = thoko.] A skin disease prevalent among Fijian children.

1879 *Encycl. Brit.* IX. 156/1 The natives have a bad skin disease, thoko, affecting also the bones. 1908 B. THOMSON *Fijians* xviii. 270.

Thomisid (þǭu·misid), *a.* and *sb.* [f. mod.L. *Thomisidæ*: see -ID³.] **a.** *adj.* Belonging to the *Thomisidæ*, a family of spiders. **b.** *sb.* A member of this family, a crab-spider.

1931 *Oxf. Univ. Gaz.* 17 June 705/2 Thomisid spiders.

Thong, *sb.* Add: **1. d.** *spec.* A cutting (of horseradish or seakale).

1927 *Smallholder* 26 Mar. 105 Plant [horseradish] each year..fresh pieces..made from the side roots or thongs. *Ibid.*, It is now time to plant out thongs of seakale.

Thoraco-. Add: **Thora·cobroncho·tomy,** incision of the bronchus through the thoracic wall.

1908 *Practitioner* Sept. 437 Anterior thoracobronchotomy.

Thoriated (þǭ·riēted), *a.* [f. THORIUM + -ATE² + -ED¹.] Coated with thorium.

1922 *Encycl. Brit.* XXXII. 1025/1 A thermionic valve of the latter type comprises a highly exhausted glass bulb having in it a filament of tungsten, or thoriated tungsten.

Thoroughbrace. Add: **b.** A stage coach (*U.S.*); a thoroughbraced bush-wagon (*Austral.*).

1886 *Leslie's Pop. Monthly* Dec. 722/1 The mustangs looked worse than the thorough-brace itself. 1930 GROOM *Merry Christmas* xv. 111 The heavily laden thoroughbrace was hitched behind seven lively horses.

Thoroughgoingness. (Earlier U.S. quot.)

1838 CAROLINE GILMAN *Recoll. Southern Matron* xxviii. 194 The gentleman had even the thoroughgoingness to request that my brother's large, stout new slate might be exchanged for a recently-invented tablet.

Thortveitite (þǭɹtvei·tait). *Min.* [Named after its discoverer, Olaus *Thortveit*: see -ITE¹.] (See quot. 1922.)

1915 *Dana's Min.* 3rd App. 1920 *Nature* CVI. 134/2 Thortveitite. This mineral..was discovered in 1911 by J. Schetelig in Norway. 1922 *Encycl. Brit.* XXXI. 949/2 Thortveitite, silicate of scandium, yttrium, etc. $(Sc)Y_2O_3{\cdot}2SiO_2$; occurring as large orthorhombic crystals of prismatic habit in pegmatite in Southern Norway and Madagascar.

Thoth (þǫþ, tǭut). *Egyptology.* [a. Gr. Θώθ, ad. Egyptian *Tehuti*.] An ancient Egyptian deity represented in the human form with the head of an ibis, identified with the Greek god Hermes.

1854 SIR J. G. WILKINSON *Anc. Egyptians* I. 299 On the 19th of the first month was celebrated the fête of Thoth, from whom that month took its name. 1862 *Chambers's Encycl.* III. 788/1 Thoth, the Egyptian Logos. 1877 *Encycl. Brit.* VII. 718/1 Thoth, or Tauut, is the head of the second cycle in the two principal forms of the cycles. As the chief moon-god he thus takes an inferior place corresponding to that of Ra...He is the god of letters and of the reckoning of time, and thus sometimes has solar attributes.

Thracian (þrē·ʃǎn), *a.* and *sb.* [f. L. *Thrācius, Thrācus*, a. Gr. Θρᾴκιος, f. Θρᾴκη Thrace: see -AN, -IAN.] **A.** *adj.* Of or belonging to Thrace, anciently a region to the N.E. of Macedonia, in modern times composed of Bulgaria, Roumelia, and the vilayet of Adrianople, now ceded to Greece.

1588 SHAKS. *Tit. A.* I. i. 138 The selfe same Gods that arm'd the Queene of Troy With opportunitie of sharpe reuenge Vpon the Thracian Tyrant in his Tent. 1590 — *Mids. N.* V. i. 49 The riot of the tipsie Bachanals, Tearing the Thracian singer, in their rage. 1594 KYD *Cornelia* III. ii. 49 Stoute Thracian Mars. 1667 MILTON *P. L.* VII. 34 The Race Of that wilde Rout that tore the Thracian Bard In Rhodope. 1697 DRYDEN *Æneis* VI. 877 The Thracian bard...There stands conspicuous in his flowing vest. 1781 GIBBON *Decl. & F.* xxvi. (1787) I. 593 Orders were immediately dispatched to the civil and military governors of the Thracian diocese. 1788 COWPER *Death Bullfinch* 63 So, when by Bacchanalians torn, On Thracian Hebrus' side The tree-enchanter Orpheus fell. 1819 SHELLEY *Cyclops* 313 And when the Thracian wind pours down the snow, I wrap my body in the skins of beasts. 1920 *Glasgow Herald* 12 May 9 Several of the Thracian harbours now under Greek sovereignty..are to be free. *Ibid.* 27 July 7 To-day at dawn the Thracian Army launched its offensive.

B. *sb.* A native or inhabitant of ancient or modern Thrace; also, the language of the ancient

Thracians, an Indo-European language related to Illyrian.

1569 STOCKER tr. *Diod. Sic.* 105 Aboute two thousand Mercenarie Grekes, and so many Thracians. 1618 BOLTON *Florus* (1636) 176 The Sordiscans were of all the Thracians the most savage. 1653 H. COGAN tr. *Diod. Sic.* 251 Having subdued the Thracians and taken the City. 1875 *Encycl. Brit.* III. 854/1 In the earliest times of history Bœotia was inhabited by various tribes, such as the Aonians, Temmicians, Thracians, [etc.].

Thraco- (þrē·ko), also **Thrako-,** used as combining form of *THRACIAN as in *Thraco-Illyrian* adj.

1902 *Encycl. Brit.* XXV. 249/2 Albanian is peculiarly interesting as the only surviving representative of the so-called Thraco-Illyrian group of languages which formed the primitive speech of the peninsula. *Ibid.* XXVI. 452/1 The ancient Thraco-Illyrian race. 1931 *Times Lit. Suppl.* 12 Feb. 116/4 The Thrako-Illyrian stratum which underlies all the races of the Peninsular.

Thrasher¹. Add: **1. c.** An operative who feeds rags and other materials into a mechanical beater.

1921 *Dict. Occup. Terms* (1927) § 519.

Thread, *sb.* Add: **14. a.** *thread-coupler, -drawer*; *thread-forming* adj.; *thread-wise* adv. **b. thread-miller,** a machine for milling or cutting threads.

1921 *Dict. Occup. Terms* (1927) § 399 **Thread coupler*; assists harness-builder..in setting-up harness for jacquard looms. *Ibid.* § 428 *Drawer*, **thread drawer*;..takes piece of material..to form a handkerchief, and draws..certain warp and weft threads. 1927 T. WOODHOUSE *Artif. Silk* 34 The tanks which supply the solution to the *thread-forming apparatus. 1922 *Daily Tel.* 12 June 20/3 Tools, furnaces, pumps, *thread millers. 1928 MRS. B. LOWNDES *Out of War?* xx, The narrow winding road which ran *thread-wise on the cliffs.

Thread, *v.* Add: **10.** *trans.* To arrange and fix (the roll-film) in a cinematographic camera; so, *to thread the camera*. Hence **Threa·der,** the film end.

1917 C. N. BENNETT *Guide Kinematogr.* i. 17 The film end, otherwise known as leader, tag, or threader. *Ibid.* iv. 42 Threading the film. *Ibid.*, Immediately after threading, set the film footage indicator..to read zero. 1923 F. A. TALBOT *Moving Pictures* 81 Threading the camera, as it is called, completed, the door of the exposed magazine is closed.

Threader. Add: **c.** An operator who feeds a machine which cuts threads on screws, etc. **d.** One who threads pile-yarn into a machine in carpet-making. **e.** One who strings a number of articles together, as needles for filing or grinding, electrical fittings for dipping, clog irons for storing; also with *up*.

1881 *Instr. Census Clerks* (1885) 97 Screw Making:..Threader. 1921 *Dict. Occup. Terms* (1927) §§ 118, 200, 279, 399, 949.

Threa·dnee·dle Street. A street in the City of London, the locality of the Bank of England; phr. *the Old Lady of* (or *in*), *the Old Woman of Threadneedle Street*, the Bank, its directors, or its business.

1797 [see *LADY 4 e]. 1872 *Porcupine* XIV. 469/2 The old woman of Threadneedle-street..hurried home without having inflicted upon the commercial community that one-per-cent blow.

Three, *a.* Add: **III. 1. a.** *three-piece, -position, -reel*. **b.** *three-engined* adj.

1931 *19th Cent.* Feb. 159 The *three-engined types. 1913 *Queen* 26 July p. viii, The *Three Piece Coat-Frock. 1921 *Daily Mail Year Bk.* 112/2 The new..railway is..equipped with '*three-position' signals. *Ibid.*, 'Three-position signalling' has found considerable favour in America. 1912 F. A. TALBOT *Moving Pictures* 106 It was the first *three-reel film subject ever produced in the United States.

2. three-ball *a.* *Golf* (see quots.); **three branch** *a.*, designating a tradesman who works as a glazier, painter, and plumber; **three-cent** *a.*, costing or sold at three cents; **three days' sickness,** in S. Africa, a disease affecting cattle; **three-electrode** *Wireless Telegr.*, designating a form of valve having three electrodes, a triode; **three-figure** *a.*, consisting of three figures, i.e. one hundred or more (runs, etc.); **Three Hours** (or **Hours'**) **Service,** a devotional service lasting from 12 to 3 o'clock in the afternoon of Good Friday, designed to cover the three hours of our Lord's Passion, and usually consisting of discourses and meditations on the Seven Last Words from the Cross; also *ellipt.* as in *to preach* or *take the Three Hours*; **three-minute** *a.*, that occupies or is done in three minutes; *U.S.* applied to a horse which covers a mile in three minutes; **three nines** (see quot.); **three out** (see *OUT *sb.* 1); **three-phaser** *Electr.*, a three-phase motor or generator; **three-point** *a.*, at or by means of three points or by the *three point problem* of fixing a point (of observation, etc.) by trigonometrical calculation or by the station pointer; **three slider** *a.*, having three slides; spec. in *Wireless Telegr.*; **three star** *a.*, designating a high-quality French brandy; **three wire mooring,** a system of mooring used to keep an airship at a constant height from the ground; **three-wood** *a.*, made of three pieces of wood; *sb.*, a bow so made.

1890 H. G. HUTCHINSON, etc. *Golf* viii. (1895) 229 The *three-ball match...two kinds,..each..against each,..two..against a third. 1899 *Rules of Golf* (1901) 5 Three players may play against each other, each playing his own ball, when the match is called 'a three-ball match'. 1881 *Instr. Census Clerks* (1885) 52 Painter, Glazier...*Three Branch Hand. 1921 *Dict. Occup. Terms* (1927) §§ 252, 569, 592. 1898 P. L. FORD *Hon. Peter Stirling* 281 Because the *three-cent papers..abuse me. 1909 *C.G.H. Agric. Jrnl.* Aug. 145 (Pettman) The scientific term, Ephemeral fever, as well as the lay term *Three days' sickness, are both somewhat appropriate. 1918 *Wireless World* VI. 144 De Forest was experimenting with a *three-electrode valve. 1922 *Encycl. Brit.* XXXII. 1024/2 In 1907, Lee de Forest in the United States, after he had become acquainted with Fleming's invention of the valve..added to it..a grid or zig-zag of wire placed between the cylinder and the filament...He thus made a so-called three-electrode thermionic valve. 1929 *Star* 21 Aug. 12/1 In a *three-figure stand. 1898 (*title*) The *three hours' service for Good Friday. 1833 *Knickerbocker Mag.* I. 160 The present Mrs. S. admired his *three minute roan. *a* 1846 W. T. PORTER *Quarter Race Kentucky*, etc. 49 You would not think she was a three-minute nag, to look at her. 1868 H. WOODRUFF *Trotting Horse Amer.* i. 41 A three-minute trotter in England. 1873–4 *Rep. Vermont Board Agric.* II. 211 They are able to ride in grand carriages with their three minute blacks hitched thereto. 1927 W. E. COLLINSON *Contemp. Engl.* 89 The house-agent's..terminology e.g...a *three nines agreement (i.e. 999 years). 1902–3 *Jrnl. Inst. Elect. Engin.* June 751 A..*three-phaser. 1912 G. KAPP *Electricity* vii. 187 We may also provide the armature with three distinct phase windings. Such a machine is called a 'three-phaser' or 'three-phase machine'. 1909 *Westm. Gaz.* 11 Nov. 5/2 The idea of the *three-point suspension principle is carried throughout the whole design of the Ford cars. 1928 C. F. S. GAMBLE *North Sea Air Station* i. 33 If the sea were very rough, even the best 'three-point' alighting would sometimes end in disaster. 1925 P. J. RISDON *Crystal Receivers & Circuits* 17 *Three-slider tuners are also made which enable the amount of inductance common to the aerial and receiver circuits to be varied. 1879 ATCHERLEY *Trip to Boërland* 32 In the up-country towns of the Transvaal..common brandy is retailed at 1s., and '*Three Star' at 1s. 6d. per glass. 1893 J. G. WOOD *Through Matabeleland* 32 An Albany man..presented us with..a bottle of 'Three-Star' brandy. 1875 *Encycl. Brit.* II. 376/1 Bows..made of three pieces,..are called *three-woods...Three-wood bows, being made a little reflex, should retain their shape.

Three-colour, *a.* Designating a photomechanical process of printing in which a coloured picture or letterpress is produced by the superposition of the three primary colours or their complementaries. (Cf. PHOTO-TRICHROMATIC *a.*, TRICHROMATIC *a.* b, TRICHROMIC *a.*)

1893 *Jrnl. Soc. Arts* 19 May 669/1 This three-colour print, a reproduction, of a chromo-lithograph. 1898, 1902 [see THREE *a.* III. 1 a]. 1902 *Encycl. Brit.* XXXII. 16/2 It was in America that the first three-colour blocks for letter-press printing were made, Mr. Ives, at Philadelphia, being their maker in 1881. 1909 *Chambers's Jrnl.* 268/1 The process is three-colour. 1921 *Dict. Occup. Terms* (1927) § 526 Three colour operator. *Ibid.* § 529 Three colour worker.

Three-er (þrī·əɹ). *colloq.* [f. THREE + -ER¹.] Something which counts as three; *Cricket*, a hit from which three runs are scored.

1895 H. G. HUTCHINSON *P. Steele* i. 22 This was hard luck on the batsman, for it should have been a three-er at least.

Three-legged, *a.* Add: Also *fig.*

1917 GALSWORTHY *Beyond* i, That three-legged whist-bridge—had always offended his fastidiousness.

Three-ply, *a.* Composed of three strands, webs, or thicknesses (see PLY *sb.* 1); esp. *three-ply wood* (*plywood*), plywood composed of three layers of wood (see *PLYWOOD); also *three-ply* absol.

1868 [see THREE *a.* III. 1 a]. 1905 *Timber Trades Jrnl.* 21 Jan. 72/1 Date cases, made entirely of three-ply wood, a material that is growing in demand. 1907 *Ibid.* 13 Apr. 831/2 Three-ply alder. 1914 *Ibid.* 3 Jan. 18/2 Direct Importers of 3-ply. 1924 MALLORY in E. F. Norton *Fight for Everest, 1924* 215 Wooden tables with three-ply wooden tops.

Threesome, *sb.* Add: **b.** *Golf.* A game in which one person plays against two opponents.

1899 *Rules of Golf* (1901) 5 A single player may play against two, when the match is called 'a threesome'. 1918 *Jrnl. Educ.* Apr. 203 We came here for a 'good old threesome'.

Three-volumer (vǫ·lyūməɹ). [f. *three-volume* (THREE *a.* III. 1 a) + -ER¹.] A three-volume novel. So **Three-vo·lumize** *v.*, **Three-vo·lumist.**

1835 *Fraser's Mag.* XII. 166 Which of the thousandfold novels now three-volumising the face of the earth occasioned this disappointment? 1861 *Under the Spell* II. 95 We do not set her up as a heroine for three-'volumists' to reverence. 1864 G. MEREDITH *Lett.* (1912) I. 162 My 'plain story' is first to right me and then the 3 volumer will play trumpets. 1927 *Daily Tel.* 27 Sept. 5/1 When the 'three-volumer' went out it was thought we had ceased to ask for literary quantity.

Threshold. Add: **2. e.** *Biol.* (See quot.)

1927 HALDANE & HUXLEY *Animal Biol.* vii. 156 These substances are only excreted if the quantity of one of them contained in a given volume of plasma exceeds a certain limit, called the 'threshold'.

f. *Wireless Telegr.*, in *threshold of oscillation*; **threshold howl** (*HOWL *sb.* 1), a howl set up by a receiver on the threshold of oscillation.

1927 *Mod. Wireless* VII. 613/2 A valve, when 'trigged' or maintained on the threshold of oscillation, was capable of giving an abnormal degree of amplification when impulsed by an incoming signal. 1927 [see *self-oscillation*, *SELF- 3 b]. 1931 *Answers* 10 Oct. 36/3 'Threshold howl' in a short-wave set.

Thrift, *sb.*¹ **1. c.** (Modern U.S. examples.)

1837 H. COLMAN *Rep. Agric. Mass.* (1838) 49 Their shape..and good humor [would be] an essential to thrift. 1873–4 *Rep. Vermont Board Agric.* II. 196 Any unusual indications of thrift in the herbage. *Ibid.* 247 For the thrift and development of animals, it is necessary to change their feed.

Thrip, *sb.* Add: A coin between a nickel and a dime in value. *U.S.*

1834 W. G. SIMMS *Guy Rivers* II. 108 Whom he rewarded with a thrip, the smallest silver coin known in the Southern currency, the five cent issue excepted. 1848 MAJOR JONES *Sk. Travel* 79 (Th.) The manager charged a thrip extra for admittin people when they was feedin the animals. 1887 [in Dict.].

Throater. *U.S.* (Earlier example.)

1846 *Knickerbocker Mag.* XXVII. 511 The 'throater', the 'header', the 'splitter' take stations at the speedily-erected table.

Throat-latch. Add: **2.** (See quot.) *U.S.*

1892 *Outing* (U.S.) Feb. 395/1 After the first unfortunate smelt finds its way out of the water the eyes and the solid piece of flesh between the gills, called by the fishermen the 'throat latch', are used for bait.

Throb-throb, *sb.* [Imitative.] A repeated throbbing sound.

1929 PRIESTLEY *Good Companions* I. iv. 107 It was the sound of a lorry engine, an urgent throb-throb.

Thro·gmo·rton Street. A street in the City of London, leading from Lothbury to Old Broad Street, the locality of the Stock Exchange in Capel Court; hence, the Stock Exchange, its members, or its operations.

1900 A. CONAN DOYLE *Green Flag, Shadow Before* 243 What could Worlington Dodds know at Dunsloe which was not known in Throgmorton Street?

Thrombose (þrǫmbōu·s), *v.* *Path.* [Back-formation from THROMBOSIS.] *trans.* To cause thrombosis.

1910 *Practitioner* June 779 Acute endometritis...When sufficiently severe..to thrombose the endometrial capillaries. 1911 EHRLICH & MCDONAGH *606 in The. & Pract.* 48 Occasionally after an intravenous injection the vein injected may become thrombosed.

Through (þrū), *sb.*⁴ A grade of bituminous coal.

1919 *Brit. Manufacturer* Nov. 33/2 The lesser qualities [of bituminous coal are quoted at]..53s. to 58s. for Throughs.

Through, *prep.* and *adv.* Add: **I.** *prep.* **6. b.** (U.S. examples.)

1834 CROCKETT *Narr. Life* viii. 64, I am glad that I am now through war matters. 1904 F. LYNDE *Grafters* vi. 78 After we were all through laughing at him.

II. *adv.* **3. b.** (Later U.S. examples.)

1887 *Scribner's Mag.* May 622/2 He..then..scrawled a dash underneath. 'There! I'm through!' he said. 1897 J. L. ALLEN *Choir Invis.* ii. (1918) 15, I was through with the lessons. 1902 HARBEN *Abner Daniel* vii. 55, 'I don't understand you.' 'Well, you will before I'm through with you.' 1904 — *Georgians* vi. 58 'Wait till I'm through,' Eric went on, huskily.

Throughput (þrū·put), *sb.* [f. THROUGH *adv.*, after *output*.] Production and distribution (of oil); also, the quantity produced.

1922 *Daily Mail* 15 Nov. 3 Throughput of oil will necessarily be interfered with temporarily. 1930 *Times* 26 Mar. 23/6 Your company..will be handling practically the same quantity of throughput.

Throw, *v.*¹ Add: **19. c.** To lose (a contest, race, etc.) intentionally or by corrupt prearrangement. *U.S.*

1868 H. WOODRUFF *Trotting Horse Amer.* xxxi. 263 It was..very unjust to charge Mr. Nodine with throwing the race. 1889 *Kansas City Times & Star* 29 Nov., Kittleman arranged with Strong that he would 'throw the race'. 1929 *Saturday Even. Post* (N.Y.) 14 Dec. 13/1 This little rat is asking me to throw the fight.

32. d. *intr.* Of a solution: To produce a deposit.

1930 S. FIELD & WEILL *Electro-Plating* iv. 61 Throwing power in an electro-depositing solution may be defined as the ability of the solution to produce even deposits on irregular surfaces. *Ibid.* 64 With copper and zinc sulphate solutions..there is little tendency to 'throw'.

41. Throw in. g. *To throw in one's hand*: to give up the contest or struggle.

1923 *Daily Mail* 3 July 8 Our plucky farmers are not 'throwing in their hands'. 1927 *Daily Express* 17 May 8/2 A large percentage..have to throw in their hands after a few years of hopeless struggle.

43. Throw on. e. To put on or apply (a brake) quickly.

1931 B. STARKE *Touch & Go* iv. 58 A smart Studebaker roadster came roaring down the road behind us and threw on the brakes.

48. Throw up. k. Of a bird: To produce (new feathers).

1854 *Poultry Chron.* I. 536 A partridge-coloured hen moulted last year but one, and threw up a few white feathers; but on moulting last year she threw up all white.

Throw-. 2. Add: **throwabout,** a toy to be thrown here and there as an amusement; **throw-out,** (*b*) *Cricket*, an act of throwing out a batsman (see 44 n); (*c*) in an electrical apparatus, a device for automatically breaking the circuit in an emergency; (*d*) *Logging* (see quot. 1905); (*e*) an apparatus for throwing out.

1922 *Daily Mail* 19 Dec. 10 Fancy Hats and *Throwabouts and other Dance Novelties. 1905 *Terms Forestry & Logging* 37 *Frog*,..a timber placed at the mouth of a slide to direct the discharge of the logs. (Gen.) Syn: *throw out. 1907 J. V. WOODWORTH *Punches, Dies & Tools* 464 Automatic throw-out for misplaced shells. 1928 *Weekly Dispatch* 24 June 20/5 That 'throw-out' which has to be executed so quickly at cover-point. 1929 *World-Radio* 27 Sept. 443 The throw-out of my main switch.

Throwee (þrōuī·). [f. THROW *v.*¹ + -EE¹.] The person thrown at.

1850 L. HUNT *Autobiog.* I. iii. 92 He [*sc.* a monitor] used to throw it at this boy and that; [and] make the throwee bring it back to him. 1927 A. P. HERBERT *Misleading Cases* ix. 72 [A boomerang] is as likely as not to do as much injury to the thrower as to the throwee.

Thrump (þrʌmp). [Imitative.] The sound of the firing of heavy artillery, of heavy tread, etc. (Usually repeated.)

1871 A. FORBES in *Daily News* 25 Jan., The heavy thrump, thrump of the mitrailleuse. 1903 *Westm. Gaz.* 5 Oct. 2/1, I awoke with the music of marching men's feet in my ears—thrump, thrump, thrump, thrump.

Thrush¹. Add: **1. b. White's thrush,** a ground-thrush of Asia, *Oreocichla varia*.

1839 JARDINE *Brit. Birds* II. 81 The general color of White's Thrush (Merula whitei) on the upper surface, is ochraceous yellow. 1843 *Zoologist* I. 104 The so-called White's Thrush..is only an accidental straggler into Europe.

Thruster. Add: **2. b.** *fig.* One who pushes his way.

1927 *Morning Post* 28 Nov. 10/4 The 'road thruster', or the man with the 'passing' mania, is usually a nuisance. 1927 *Observer* 6 Nov. 13/1 Those who described their more successful fellows as 'thrusters' and 'climbers'.

Thucydidean (þiūsididī·ǎn), *a.* Also †-ian, -æan. [Partly f. L. *Thūcydidius* (Cicero); mainly f. L. *Thūcȳdidēs*, Θουκυδίδης, name of a Greek historian of the fifth century B.C. + -EAN.] Of, pertaining to, or characteristic of Thucydides or his writings.

1752 *Phil. Trans.* XLVII. 385 The European plagues are much more violent than the eastern; those being really the Thucydidian, which sweep all away. 1826–7 K. H. DIGBY *Broad Stone Hon., Morus* (1848) 133 Having..no Thucydidean dignity of style. 1834 — *Mores Cath.* V. vi. 183 The Thucydidæan expression. 1872 W. MINTO *Engl. Lit.* II. v. 372 He aims at Thucydidean compactness. 1888 JEBB in *Encycl. Brit.* XXIII. 326/2 Thucydidean bibliography. 1911 *19th Cent.* Apr. 697 He even heightens the pathos of the Thucydidean original.

Thuenite (þiū·ənait). *Min.* [f. the name of the *Thuensky* Mountains, Urals + -ITE¹.] A variety of ilmenite.

1892 DANA *Min.* 1131 (Index). 1923 *Nature* CXI. 252/2.

Thulium (þiū·liǝm). *Chem.* [mod.L., f. THULE.] A rare metallic element found in gadolinite. So **Thu·lia,** a rare earth, consisting mainly of thulium oxide.

1879 CLÈVE in *Chem. News* XL. 126 For the radical of the oxide placed between ytterbia and erbia..I propose the name of Thullium [*sic*] derived from Thulé, the ancient name of Scandinavia. 1907 ROSCOE & SCHORLEMMER *Treat. Chem.* II. 784 Erbia..has been shown..to consist of at least four earths, the true *erbia, holmia, thulia* and *dysprosia*. 1922 *Nature* CIX. 781/1 Three lines of thulium were found.

Thumb, *sb.* Add: **6. c.** *thumb-latch* (earlier Amer. example). **e. thumb-cutter, -puncher,** an operative who cuts out the thumb-pieces in glove-making; **thumb-mould, plane** (see quots.).

1881 *Instr. Census Clerks* (1885) 76 Glover...Leather Gloves:..*Thumb and Fourchette Cutter and Puncher. 1921 *Dict. Occup. Terms* (1927) § 429 Thumb puncher. 1761 *Essex Inst. Hist. Coll.* XLVIII. 96 Hinges, *thumb latches, hammers. 1906 *Technol. & Sci. Dict.* (ed. Goodchild & Tweney), **Thumb Mould* (Join.), a moulding used on the edge of tables. 1888 *Lockwood's Dict. Mech. Engin.*, **Thumb Plane*, a small plane about four or five inches long, ..used for small work in general.

Thumb, *v.* Add: **5.** *To thumb one's nose*: to put one's thumb to one's nose and extend the fingers as a gesture of derision; to 'make a long nose'. *U.S.*

1916 B. HALL *One Man's War* (1929) 218 He thumbed his nose with both thumbs at once and told me to climb the Tour d'Eiffel and stay there. 1929 EDINGTON *Studio Murder Myst.* iv. 37 Underlings in the studio thumbed their noses at his back.

Thumber (þʌ·məɹ). [f. THUMB *sb.* + -ER¹.] An operative who sews thumb-pieces into gloves.

1921 *Dict. Occup. Terms* (1927) § 429.

Thumb-mark, *sb.* Add:

1863 *Clarendon Press Delegates' Orders* 6 Nov., That the Partners be empowered to use, on books printed by them which are not the property of the Delegates, a thumb mark similar to that used on the Delegates' books.

Thumby (þʌ·mi), *a.* *colloq.* [f. THUMB *sb.* + -Y¹.] **1.** Soiled by thumb-marks.

1900 *Daily News* 11 Jan. 7/2 The report books look as prosaic as any ordinary account books, only very black and 'thumby'.

2. Clumsy, 'all thumbs'. (Cf. THUMB *sb.* 5 c.)

1909 R. A. WASON *Happy Hawkins* 103 One day we was kiddin' him about bein' so thumby. 1912 — *Friar Tuck* xxvii. 194 His own thumby left-handedness. 1915 *Pearson's Mag.* XXXIX. 28 You have no idea how thumby your fingers are when fixing a bike under shrapnel fire.

Thump, *v.* Add: **1. c.** To express by thumps.

1928 *Manchester Guardian Weekly* 26 Oct. 335/3 His tail [*sc.* of a dog]..thumped a welcome.

Thumper. Add: **4.** In an organ = *thumping-board*.

1906 *Technol. & Sci. Dict.* (ed. Goodchild & Tweney).

Thunder, *sb.* Add: **3. a.** fig. phr. *To steal* (a person's) *thunder*: to use his weapons or equipment so as to reduce or annul the effect of his words or actions.

Derived from the utterance of John Dennis (1657–1734), 'Damn them!..they will not let my play run, but they steal my thunder', on hearing the production of stage thunder designed for his own play of *Appius & Virginia* being used for a performance of *Macbeth*. (Spence quoted in W. S. Walsh *Lit. Curios.* (1893) 1052; cf. Pope's note on *Dunciad* II. 223.)

1900 E. E. PEAKE *Darlingtons* iii. 23 You must all remember that popa had stolen my thunder. 1930 *Punch* 8 May 521 An underhand scheme concocted by certain light-minded Conservatives to steal the thunder, or rather the questions, of the all-too-inquisitive Mr. Day. 1931 *Time & Tide* 12 Sept. 1049 Sir Oswald Mosley's exploit was to steal a little of the protectionist thunder temporarily abandoned by the Conservatives.

4. (U.S. examples.)

1854 MARY J. HOLMES *Tempest & Sunshine* xv. 204 Don't none on you step on my corns for thunder's sake. 1865 *Atlantic Monthly* XV. 670 What in thunder do you pester me so about that cow for?

Thunderation. *U.S.* (Earlier example.)

1845 [W. T. THOMPSON] *Chron. Pineville* 181 (Th. p. 704) I'll blow 'em all to everlastin' thunderation.

Thundering, *ppl. a.* (*adv.*) **4. b.** (Substitute for 1839 in Dict.:—).

1807–8 W. IRVING *Salmagundi* v. 112 He..prefers..telling his stories among cronies of his own gender..and thundering long stories they are. 1839 *Havana* (N.Y.) *Republican* Dec. 25 (Th.) He is thundering shy of me.

Thuringian (þiuri·ndʒiǎn), *a.* and *sb.* [f. the name *Thuringia* (see below) + -AN.] Of or pertaining to (a native or inhabitant of) Thuringia, a region (now a republic) of central Germany.

1839 J. F. STANFORD *Rambles & Researches* (1842) 158 In physical development the Thuringians..are..fine powerful men. *Ibid.* 159, I think you will be pleased with the collection I have made of Thuringian melodies. 1910 *Chambers's Jrnl.* 172/1 The great Thuringian forests. 1926 *Glasgow Herald* 20 Mar. 4 The Thuringian minnesinger.

Thurler, variant of THIRLER.

Thus, *adv.* Add: **1. g.** = So; esp. in *thus and so*, variant of *so and so* (cf. SO-AND-SO C. 2). *U.S.*

1873 J. H. BEADLE *Undevel. West* 788 Inquiring of a philosophical native why this was thus, he replied [etc.]. 1904 *New York Evening Post* 23 Apr., The statement that matters will result thus and so 'if the crops turn out all right'. 1928 *Nation* (N.Y.) 7 Feb. 161/1 They..offered us a contract in this, that, or the other company, whose dividend-paying record had been thus and so.

Thyatiran (þaiǎtai·rǎn), *a.* [f. L. *Thyatira* (see below), a. Gr. Θυάτειρα + -AN.] Of or belonging to Thyatira, the ancient name of Ak-hissar, a town N.E. of Smyrna, formerly a station on the Roman road from Pergamos to Laodicea.

1904 W. M. RAMSAY *Lett. Seven Churches* 319 The Thyatiran religion is obscure. *Ibid.* 353 It was..a serious thing for a Thyatiran to cut himself off from his guild.

Thyroxin (þairǫ·ksin). *Chem.* Also **-ine.** [f. THYRO- + *-oxin*, after *toxin*?] The active principle of the thyroid gland.

1922 *Encycl. Brit.* XXX. 862/1 Kendall believes that he has isolated the active principle of the thyroid gland, and to this he gives the name of *thyroxin*. 1930 *Biochem. Jrnl.* XXIV. II. 1185 The hypothesis that arginine and thyroxine are mutually antagonistic in respect to tumour growth.

Thyrsocephalic (þɜ̄ɹsosĭfæ·lik), *a.* *Anthrop.* [f. Gr. θύρσος stalk + κεφαλή head + -IC.] (See quot.)

1902 A. MACALISTER in *Encycl. Brit.* XXV. 398/2 When the union is of the coronal suture, the skull becomes short and high, or thyrsocephalic.

Ti² (tī). *Mus.* The name in Tonic Solfa for the seventh of the scale: arbitrarily substituted for the older name SI (see quot. 1889). In practice commonly spelt *te*.

c 1845 S. A. GLOVER *Norwich Sol-Fa System*. 1848 *J. Curwen's Gram. Vocal Music* 6 If the replicate of the key note be included (d'), Doh, Ray, Me, Fah will form the first tetrachord, and Soh, Lah, Te, Doh' the second. 1889 R. B. LITCHFIELD in Grove *Dict. Mus.* IV. 144/1 Tonic Sol-fa...The ancient sound-names do, re, mi, etc...are put before a class..in the form of a printed picture of the scale, called a 'Modulator'. For simplicity's sake they are spelt English-wise, and *si* is called *te* to avoid having two names with the same initial letter.

Tiang (tī·æŋ). An African antelope.

1915 *Chambers's Jrnl.* 700/2 Near allies of the hartebeest are the tsesseby..and its northern cousin the tapi or tiang. 1927 *Blackw. Mag.* Nov. 668/2 Herds of hartebeeste and tiang. 1930 *Brit. Mus. Return* 81.

Tiarella (tiǎre·lǎ). [mod.L., f. L. *tiara* tiara, turban + dim. suffix *-ella*.] A herbaceous perennial plant belonging to the saxifragaceous genus of that name.

1829 LOUDON *Encycl. Plants* 368. 1871 *Scribner's Monthly* II. 470 Tiarella leaves just tipped with claret color. 1887 *Harper's Mag.* July 303/1 The tiarella sent up feathery spikes of white. 1921 GERTRUDE JEKYLL *Colour Schemes* 27 Sheets of the foam-like Tiarella.

Tibbin (ti·bin). Also **tibben, tibn.** [Arab. تِبْن *tibn*.] Chaff.

1900 A. CONAN DOYLE *Green Flag, Three Corresp.* 271 Each camel provided with his own little heap of tibbin laid in the centre of the tablecloth. 1924 *Blackw. Mag.* Jan. 24/1 Over it all..whistles and whirls a pitiless wind, charged with tibn, sand, dust, [etc.].

Tibet. Add: *attrib.* = *TIBETAN *a.*

1845 YOUATT *Dog* (1858) 39 The colour of the Thibet dog is of a deep black, slightly clouded on the sides...He has the broad truncated muzzle of the mastiff, and the lips are still more deeply pendulous.

Tibetan (tibe·tǎn, ti·bĕtǎn), *a.* and *sb.* Also † **T(h)ibetian.** [f. TIBET + -AN.] **A.** *adj.* Of or pertaining to Tibet or its people; *spec.* in the names of animals native to Tibet.

1834 ALEX. CSOMA DE KÖRÖS (*title*) Grammar of the Tibetan Language in English. 1842 *Penny Cycl.* XXIV. 428/2 A fine specimen of Tibetan sculpture. 1880 *Encycl. Brit.* XII. 741/2 The Himálayan or Tibetan sun bear (*Ursus tibetanus*). 1888 *Ibid.* XXIII. 343/1 The centres for Tibetan trade. *Ibid.* 343/2 The Tibetan race is not thoroughly homogeneous. 1889 tr. *J. J. Rein's Industries of Japan* 517 Thibetian cats. 1891 ROCKHILL *Land of Lamas* 190 The Tibetan mastiff is rarely seen in eastern Tibet. 1902 *Encycl. Brit.* XXXIII. 327/1 Here are to be found..several varieties of deer, musk deer, and Tibetan antelope (*pantholops*)...The Tibetan sand-grouse is peculiar to the country. 1905 P. LANDON *Lhasa* I. xi. 387 The typical Tibetan terrier. *Ibid.* App. A. 403 The so-called Tibetan mastiff. *Ibid.*, The Tibetan spaniel..a small black dog..rather like a Pekinese spaniel. 1930 *Observer* 9 Feb. 13/2 Thibetan spaniels. 1931 *Times* 14 Mar. 9/3 Tibetan foxes are placed in a distinct species by most authorities.

B. *sb.* **a.** A native of Tibet. **b.** The language spoken by Tibetans.

1806 S. TURNER *Acc. Emb. Crt. Teshoo Lama* (ed. 2) 226 The Tibetians are great economists in their dress. 1842 *Penny Cycl.* XXIV. 429/1 The Tibetans belong to the Mongol race. 1849 *Ann. Propagation Faith* (Dublin) Jan. 54 Slips of paper, on which are printed sentences in Mongolian or in Thibetian. 1867 MISS M. JONES *Life & Trav. Tartary*, etc. vii. 104 He desired they should be translated; which was done into Thibetian, Chinese, and the Tartar language. 1888 *Encycl. Brit.* XXIII. 342/2 Every Tibetan is more or less of a trader. 1891 ROCKHILL *Land of Lamas* 97 It was with him..that I commenced studying Tibetan.

Tibeto- (tibe·to), used as comb. form = 'pertaining to Tibet and..'. **Tibeto-Burman** *a.*, comprising Tibet and Burma, their peoples, and languages; *spec.* applied to an Indo-Chinese group of languages spoken in central and south-eastern Asia; *sb.*, a non-Aryan linguistic stock of India including, among others, the Tibetan and Burmese dialects. So **Tibeto-Burmese; Tibeto-Himalayan** *a.*

1875 *Encycl. Brit.* II. 684/1 Tibeto-Himalayan mountains. 1878 R. N. CUST *Sk. Mod. Lang. E. Indies* 4 The great Tibeto-Burman sea. *Ibid.* 93 The Bhramu speak a purely Tibeto-Burman Language. 1880 *Encycl. Brit.* XII. 777/2 The early peoples of India belonged to three great stocks, known as the Tibeto-Burman, the Kolarian, and the Dravidian. 1894 T. DE LACOUPERIE *Begin. Writing Centr. & E. Asia* 143 The Corean *un-mun*..alphabet..was made..on a Tibeto-Indian base.

Tice, *sb.* (Earlier U.S. example.)

1869 LOUISA M. ALCOTT *Little Women* II. ix. 128 The phrases, 'caught off a tice', 'stumped off his ground',..were as intelligible to her as Sanscrit.

Tick, *sb.*¹ Add: **1. c.** Phr. *As full as a tick*: full to repletion.

1678 RAY *Prov.* 284 As full as a pipers bag; as a tick. 1822 *Yankee Phrases* in *New Jersey Alm. 1823*, Though of love I'm as full as a tick. 1889 J. NICHOLSON *Folk Sp. E. Yorksh.* 93 Ah's as full as a tick; Ah've had sike a jawtheram o' broth.

Tick, *sb.*³ Add: **3. b.** Of a bird: A feather or marking of another colour in the plumage. (Cf. TICKED *a.*)

1905 R. C. PUNNETT *Mendelism* 27 The presence of these 'ticks' is the outward and visible sign of the heterozygous nature of the bird on which they occur.

c. *attrib.*

1932 *Daily Tel.* 13 Sept. 8/7 Have you seen the new Tick-Weave? The tiny white dot is actually woven into the material.

4. Also, the precise moment of the tick of a watch or clock, in phr. *on* or *to the tick*, exactly at the appointed time, punctually.

1907 [in Dict.]. 1927 *Daily Express* 6 July 3/5, I am always here on the tick myself, and I do not see why jurors should not do the same.

Tick, *v.*¹ Add: **2.** (Later U.S. example.)

1904 'O. HENRY' *Cabbages & Kings* xvii. 299 'Three minutes gone,' I said. 'I'll tell you again while the other two tick off.'

d. *To tick over*: (of an internal combustion engine) to run or work slowly with the propeller or gears disconnected.

1916 H. BARBER *Aeroplane Speaks* 50 The engine is awake again and slowly ticking over. 1918 in C. F. S. Gamble *North Sea Air Station* xx. (1928) 352 The engines [were] started and allowed to 'tick over' for about 10 minutes or so, to warm up gradually.

4. *To tick off*: to reprimand (a person); to reprehend (a thing). orig. *Army slang*.

1919 *War Slang* in *Athenæum* 25 July 664/1 'To tick off'..to reprimand. 1928 *Observer* 3 June 8 She puts on, and ticks off, the fads and fashions of Society. 1929 G. D. H. & M. COLE *Poison in Garden Suburb* ix. 78 Cayley tried to tick me off, once; and I lost my temper. 1929 E. W. SPRINGS *Above bright blue Sky* 274, I don't think he ever did much in the way of ticking off.

Ticker³. b. Add: *attrib.*

1906 'O. HENRY' *Rolling Stones* (1913) 20 He..begins to pull something like ticker tape out of his pocket. 1911 *Chambers's Jrnl.* 336/2 At the end of the register-board are

Supplement, p. 3873; Corrigenda, p. 4092; Spurious words, p. 4093; Books quoted, p. 4094

reels of stock 'ticker' paper tape. *Ibid.*, The ticker-wheel stops, the total number of cards recorded being printed on the tape. 1922 Marg. B. Houston *Witch-man* xiv. 194 He has all the hilarious charm of a piece of ticker tape.

Ticket, *sb.*¹ Add: **4. c.** An airman's certificate as a qualified pilot.
1914 Rosher *In R.N.A.S.* (1916) 15, I shall take my ticket in a week or ten days. Hope to be flying solo by Thursday or Friday. 1916 W. A. Robson *Aircraft* 112 If the pupil's only desire is to secure his 'ticket' and announce himself a full-fledged aviator. 1917 E. C. Middleton *Way of Air* 32 His 'ticket' having been obtained, the 'quirk'..is given a little more practice in flying slow machines.

5. (Further specific uses.) *Coupon ticket*, a ticket with coupons or a coupon attached, as a through railroad ticket with a coupon for each of the lines traversed, or a theatre ticket with a reserved seat coupon *U.S.*; *meal ticket* (see *Meal sb.² 4); *mileage ticket*, one entitling the holder to travel a specified number of miles; *party ticket*, one enabling a party to travel at a reduced rate; *privilege ticket*, a half-price return ticket issued to railway employees.
1887 Coupon ticket [see *Coupon ¶].

6. *One's ticket*: one's certificate of discharge.
1869 *Temple Bar* Jan. 217 'Coiners'..as a rule returned to their profession as soon as they got their 'ticket'. 1919 *Punch* 16 Apr. 308/2 Yes, Sir, got my ticket last month—only been back on my old job a fortnight. 1925 E. Fraser & Gibbons *Soldier & Sailor Words* s.v., To work one's ticket.

10. (Further examples.)
1910 G. B. McCutcheon *Rose in Ring* i. 6 At the corner of the tented common stood the 'ticket wagon'. 1915 J. B. Rathbun *Motion Picture Making* 119 To prevent the tickets from being used a second time a 'ticket chopper' may be used that mutilates the ticket in such a way that it is impossible to present it without detection. 1924 D. H. Lawrence *England, my England* 52 They pounce on the youths who try to evade their ticket-machine. *Ibid.* 101 A great crowd of people was gathered round the ticket-caravan.

Ticketer. Add: An employee who affixes tickets or labels to goods.
1921 *Dict. Occup. Terms* (1927) § 949.

Tickle, *v.* **3.** (Earlier and later U.S. examples.)
1834 S. Smith *Major Downing* 200, I have just got it, and it has tickled me enymost to death. 1844 'Jon. Slick' *High Life N.Y.* I. 106 They stopped as if they were tickled to death to see her. *Ibid.* II. 169 They was so tickled tu git him among 'em. 1904 Harben *Georgians* xxii. 219 Tom seemed powerful tickled to see me. 1907 *New York Evening Post* (semi-weekly ed.) 4 Mar. 3 The President is vastly tickled over the prospect.

Tickler.¹ **2.** Add: U.S. uses (see quots.).
1905 E. E. Calkins & R. Holden *Art Mod. Advertising* 351 A tickler is any small piece of printed matter sent out to keep open a prospective sale on the part of the inquirer. 1922 *Wireless World* X. 430/2 The reaction coil (or 'tickler' as it is called over the water). 1925 *Scribner's Mag.* July 44/2 The intricate business of..whirling the tickler into place and moving the detector dial to the exact spot.

Tickler². *Army slang.* Jam (from the name of the maker). Also, a hand-grenade (a used jam-tin filled with an explosive substance).
1916 *B. E. F. Times* 1 Dec., A frugal meal of clorinated [*sic*] tea and Tickler. 1919 *War Slang* in *Athenæum* 8 Aug. 727/2 Hand-grenades were often referred to as 'Ticklers'. 1925 E. Fraser & Gibbons *Soldier & Sailor Words*, *Ticklers*, jam.

Tickly, *a.* **b.** Add: *U.S.* (Later example.)
1886 C. C. Abbott *Upland & Meadow* 52 (Funk) I have even seen them [*sc.* crows] play at 'tickley benders', but with the advantage over boys in that they can stay up always, even if the ice goes down.

Tick-tack (ti·k,tæ·k), *v.* Also tictac(k. [f. the sb.] **1.** *intr.* = *Tick-tock *v.*
1859 Mrs. H. B. Stowe *Minister's Wooing* ii, The solemn old clock that tick-tacked in the corner.
2. To signal by means of manual signs or waving the arms, esp. on a racecourse. Also *trans.* Hence as *sb.* (see quot. 1922).
1907 *Favourite* 30 Nov. 9/3 Kilbeg was 'tick-tacked' out at 4 to 1 by the private clerk of one particular firm. 1908 *Tatler* 3 June 247 The above system of signalling, which is known as tick-tacking, may be seen on any racecourse. 1922 *N. & Q.* 12th Ser. XI. 207/2 Tick-tack[s]. The agents of bookmakers who, by a code of manual signals, inform those who employ them of happenings in the betting rings which influence the odds offered. 1927 *Observer* 27 Mar. 18/6 A man in the body of the hall was detected tictacing to Labour supporters and guiding the uproar. 1929 *Times* 2 Nov. 5/1 The employment of runners will not be allowed, but apparently 'tictacking' will be permitted.

Tick-tock (ti·k,tǫ·k), *v.* [f. the sb.] *intr.* Of a clock: To make the alternating sounds of 'tick' and 'tock'.
1921 H. Walpole *Young Enchanted* III. iii, The gaudy clock..now tick-tocked along in amiable approval of them both. 1924 Anne D. Sedgwick *Little French Girl* II. iii, A tall clock tick-tocked on the stair.

Tiddle, *v.* Add: **2. b.** To move potteringly. *U.S.*
1881 Howells *Modern Instance* x. 130 Mr. Macallister, a slight little straight man..tiddled farcically forward on his toes.

Tiddley (ti·dli), *sb.* and *a.* *vulgar slang.* Also titley, tiddly. [See Tiddlywink.]
A. *sb.* Drink; a drink of alcoholic liquor. *On the tiddley*: 'in liquor', intoxicated.
1859 *Slang Dict.*, *Titley*, drink. 1865 *Ibid.*, *Titley*, drink, generally applied to intoxicating beverages. 1895 *Punch* 18 May 230/2 It took two 'ot tiddleys to warm 'er. *Ibid.* 12 Oct. 180/1 A helderly, hamorous gent, on the tiddley. 1898 *Daily News* 2 Apr. 6/6 You know she'd had a little drop of tiddley. 1923 Oppenheim *Inevitable Millionaires* xiv, Just a tiddly to drink success to the club. 1930 E. V. Lucas *Down the Sky* 222 If wasn't oysters that she really wanted, but, like hundreds of others, tiddley.
B. *adj.* Intoxicated.
1905 *To-Day* XLVI. 182/2 If ever you was tiddly in crossing the old 'un [*sc.* a bridge], it was as easy as anything to fall into that blarsted river. 1909 *Chambers's Jrnl.* 316/1 Mind you don't get tiddley and blow the gaff. 1931 *Observer* 6 Dec. 13 They both get 'tiddly'.

Tiddy (ti·di), *a.* *dial.* or *nursery word.* [Obscure. (The spelling *tidy* in 1781 is difficult; perh. an error.)] Small, very small, tiny. Also **Tiddy iddy** *a.*
1781 J. H[utton] *Tour to Caves* (E.D.S.), *Tidy*, small. 1868 W. S. Gilbert *Bab Ballads, Thos. Green & Harriet Hale* x, A tiddy iddy daughter, and a tiddy iddy son. 1870 Lady Verney *Lettice Lisle* xxii, Nought but a tiddy bit o' blue sky. 1895 *Daily News* 18 Dec. 3/5 Mr. J. Gregory, the spokesman, said theirs was a 'little tiddy village', forty miles off Oxford, where their stream joined the Thames. 1896 Kipling *Seven Seas, The Ladies* iv, An' I got me a tiddy live 'eathen..Funny an' yellow an' faithful—Doll in a teacup she were. 1907 *Daily News* 4 Feb. 2/5 Mrs. Gill..added it was only a 'tiddy' pup.

Tide, *sb.* Add: **16. a.** (*a*) *tide-roost* (Roost *sb.*², race); (*b*) *tide-flat, -rock* (example).
1859 Kingsley *Glaucus* (ed. 4) 146 The *tide-flats below are still unfinished, dry land in the process of creation. *Ibid.* 71 A cluster of barnacles..of the same family as those which stud the *tide-rocks in millions. 1912 *Chambers's Jrnl.* 757/2 Round the Shiant Isles there is often a strong *tide-roost.

Tide-mark. *fig.* (Examples.) (Cf. *high-water mark.)
1907 N. Munro *Daft Days* xxii, With a smut on your nose and tide-marks on your eyebrows. 1928 *Daily Express* 20 Dec. 5/3 Your fur collar leaves a horrid tide-mark after it has been worn for a time.

Tide-mill. (Earlier U.S. example.)
1755 *Mass. Prov. Laws* III. 810 Tide-mills that have or shall be set up on across the mouth of the rivers.

Tidesman. Add: **2. b.** (See quot.)
1921 *Dict. Occup. Terms* (1927) § 749 *Tidesman, tide waiter*, at each full tide, tows or warps vessels in and out of small slate shipping harbour or dock.

Tide-waiter. Add: **3.** = *Tidesman 2 b.

Tide-water. Add: **2.** *U.S.* (Earlier examples.)
1789 Morse *Amer. Geog.* 363 The distance from the Capes of Virginia to the termination of the tide-water..is above 300 miles. 1818 Fearon *Sk. Amer.* 49 Being banished to forty miles beyond tide-water. 1832 J. F. Watson *Hist. Tales N.Y.* 38 [Hudson City] is deemed at the head of tide water and ship navigation.
b. *attrib.* (quasi-*adj.*).
1829-32 J. P. Kennedy *Swallow Barn* I. xviii. 179 The tide-water country of Virginia. 1835 J. Martin *Descr. Virginia* 40 A tide water river, or more correctly a bay, the Chowan. 1873 J. H. Beadle *Undevel. West* xvii. 316 In the swamp and tide-water lands. 1895 *Century Mag.* Aug. 625/1 Just as the tide-water Virginians took the trail of the pioneers.

Tidingman, var. Tithingman ¹ c (*U.S.*).
1703 *Groton Rec.* (1880) 123 [Certain persons chosen] for Tiding men. 1846 *Knickerbocker Mag.* XXVIII. 466 He had been watched by a 'tiding-man' at church. 1878 Mrs. Stowe *Poganuc People* vi. 63 'They're goin' clean agin everything—Sunday laws and tiding man and all.

Tie, *sb.* Add: **4. b.** A small necklet of fur.
1919 *Queen* 4 Oct. 5 A..Mink Tie beautifully worked in three strands. 1930 *Daily Tel.* 8 Apr. 9/5 Wherever fashionable women may meet this Easter most assuredly will you mark the popularity of the Fur Tie. *Ibid.* 1 Dec. 7/4 A Fox Tie.
10. Also *tie game*.
1928 *Collier's* 29 Dec. 17/4 A tie game in football is certainly more thrilling..than a one-sided game.

Tie, *v.* Add: **1. f.** *intr.* for *pass.*
1924 Anne D. Sedgwick *Little French Girl* II. iii, A straightly falling dress,..tying at the breast with tassels and at the waist with a loosely knotted sash.
4. b. *U.S.* (Earlier example.)
1867 *Rep. Iowa Agric. Soc.* (1868) 212 [Concord grapes] will not do for the masses to tie to, in the West.
9. (Further examples.)
a 1904 S. E. White *Blazed Trail Stories* iv. 71 Just tie tight into her and keep her hustling. 1912 R. A. Wason *Friar Tuck* xiv. 99 They girded up their loins, an' tied into him a little harder.
11. Tie up, a. Also *intr.* for *pass.* of the thing.
1865 'L. Carroll' *Alice's Adv. Wonderland* xi. (1922) 172 A large canvas bag, which tied up at the mouth with strings.
c. Also, to delay. *U.S.*
1887 C. B. George *40 Years on Rail* vii. 140, I ran into a snow-storm that tied us up until we were six days making the run. 1901 S. Merwin & H. K. Webster *Calumet K* iii. 37 'Search me,' said Dennis. 'They've tied us up for these two weeks.' 1907 *Springfield* (Mass.) *Weekly Republican* 10 Oct. 16 Traffic west of Springfield was tied up until about midnight.
d. Also *fig.*
1876 *Fur, Fin & Feather* Sept. 107 They will find the Crossmon House a pleasant place to 'tie up to'.
i. *intr.* To associate or unite oneself or one's interests *with*. (Cf. *Tie-up *sb.* 7 b.) orig. *U.S.*
1903 *New York Evening Post* 5 Dec. 1 It becomes his first interest to make business for that yard. He can best do this by tying up with the other navy yard representatives on the committee. 1925 *Round Table* June 593 It is clearly to South Africa's interest to tie up definitely either with sterling ..or with gold. 1928 *Daily Express* 13 June 3/4 Registered readers..have..'tied up' with the newspaper which..offers the best..insurance benefits. 1928 *Publishers' Weekly* 30 June 2613 There are..well over one hundred booksellers.. who are tying-up with the national advertising campaign.

Tie-. 2. tie-back (U.S. example).
1927 *Ladies' Home Jrnl.* Dec. 35/3 Flat festoons of green used for tie-backs on the curtains.

Tied, *ppl. a.* Add: **1. c.** *Tied dyeing*, a method of pattern dyeing performed by winding cotton round a folded piece of material, which is then dipped in various dyes. Also called the *tie and dye process*.
1928 *Daily Express* 21 May 5/2 The 'tie and dye' process —an old craft which gives a charming hazed effect. *Ibid.* 29 June 5/2 'Tied Dyeing' is very similar to Batik work, though much simpler, being done entirely with string and dye.

Tienda (tie·nda). [Sp., = tent, awning, booth, shop: see Tent *sb.*¹] A shop, stall.
1844 G. W. Kendall *Santa Fé Exped.* II. ii. 38 Standing in front of a small tienda, or store. 1885 B. Harte *Maruja* 60, I met him outside the tienda on the highway. 1920 *Chambers's Jrnl.* 358/1 He followed him to a small *tienda*. 1921 *Blackw. Mag.* Nov. 658/2 Its *tienda* with long counter, handsome shelves, and fabulous profits.

Tier, *sb.*¹ **1.** Add: *spec.* A range or line of lots, townships, states, etc. *U.S.*
1693 *Conn. Hist. Soc. Coll.* XIV. 212 One lyeing in the Same Teere of lotts abutting on a Highway. 1720, 1722 [see Dict.]. 1730 *Waterbury Prop. Rec.* 139 Severall Lotts in the west teer. 1824 in S. C. Cox *Recoll. Early Settlem. Wabash V.* iii. (1860) 18 The land is sold in tiers of townships. 1860 *Congress. Globe* 19 Dec. 139/3 They constitute the first tier of the border slave States. 1872 *Trans. Dept. Agric. Illinois* 151 Edgar county is situated in the eastern tier of counties. 1887 *Harper's Mag.* Apr. 833/2 Mr. Van Buren's presence in the southern tier. 1904 *New York Evening Post* 7 Nov. 2 The big Republican majorities in the lower tier of counties.

Tiersman (tīə·zmæn). [f. Tier *sb.*¹ or *v.*¹ + Man *sb.*¹] A stower who arranges casks in tiers.
1921 *Dict. Occup. Terms* (1927) § 468.

Tie-up, *sb.* Add: **3. b.** The place where oxen are hitched for the night. *U.S.*
1851 J. S. Springer *Forest Life* 82 At the further end of the 'tie-up' he thinks he hears a little clattering noise. 1882 *Rep. Maine Board Agric.* XVI. 49 Those who have not the convenience for a barn cellar can save the manure very well by a tight floor in the tie-up.
6. (Further U.S. example.)
1904 *N.Y. Tribune* 29 Oct. 1 An accident to one of the motor cars caused a tie-up of the southbound trains.
7. b. An association or union (cf. *Tie *v.* 11 i).
1927 *Daily Express* 7 Mar. 11/5 There is a tie-up, too, over this firm with the gramophone records. Every record of the 'Happiness Boys' is an advertisement for Happiness Chocolates. 1930 *Publishers' Weekly* 4 Jan. 46, I consider general advertising without tie-up an absolute loss. *Ibid.* 15 Feb. 842/2 It represents an opportunity for a bookselling tie-up.

Tiffanyite (ti·fǎni,əit). *Min.* [f. the name of C. L. *Tiffany*, American jeweller + -ite ¹.] A hydrocarbon believed to exist in certain opalescent diamonds; also, a steel-blue possessing the property of emitting light in the dark, a phenomenon attributed to the presence of this hydrocarbon.
1895 Kunz in *Trans. N.Y. Acad. Sci.* XIV. 260. 1897 *Min. Mag.* XI. 241.

Tight, *a.* Add: **7.** (Earlier U.S. example.)
1843 *Knickerbocker Mag.* XXII. 366 We were never 'groggy', 'intoxicated', 'boozy'..or 'tight', but once.
10. c. Close *after* or *up to*. *dial.* and *U.S.*
1888 Elworthy *W. Somerset Word-Bk.* s.v., The bitch was tight arter'n. 1901 *Century Mag.* May 123/1 They was tight up t' me all the way.
13. b. A tight place; a position of difficulty. *U.S.*
1908 Harben *Abner Daniel* xxi. 182 It would tempt five men out of ten if they were inclined to go wrong, and were in a tight.
B. *adv.* **4.** (See quot.)
1930 *Times* 15 Mar. 4/4 You will never find..instructions are given to put white stones among the coloured ones.—There are instructions to sort 'finer', or 'better', or 'tighter', which mean the same thing.
5. *Tight on*: close on. *colloq.* or *dial.*
1919 Snaith *Love Lane* xxx, He lived to be tight on ninety.
C. tight back *Bookbinding*, a back that adheres to the sheets as distinguished from a loose back or spring back.

Tightish, *adv.* **1. b.** (Later example.)
1843 'Uncle Sam' *Peculiarities* I. 168 'I war fixed with a bull once,' said he, 'pretty considerable tightish.'

Tihore (tihore). *New Zealand.* [Maori.] A species of flax.
1845 E. J. Wakefield *Adv. N. Zealand* II. 124 The plants were all of the *tihore*, or best species of flax; with leaves ten to twelve feet long.

Tiki (ti·ki). *New Zealand.* [Maori *tiki* creator of man.] A large wooden image of the Maoris representing the creator of man or an ancestor; made also in miniature in greenstone as a charm or ornament. (Cf. *Hei-tiki.)
1878 Jas. Buller *Forty Years N. Z.* 199 *Tiki* is said to have been one of their first gods. 1889 Hocken *Catal. N. Z. Exhib.* 81 (Morris) Wooden Tikis, some of immense size, usually represented the ancestors. 1921 *Outward Bound* June 46/2 The beautiful and valuable greenstone from which the Maoris fashion all their..tikis. 1924 *British Weekly* 25 Dec. 329/3 The well-known Maori charm the Tiki.

Tilka (ti·lkă). [Skr. *tilaka* (f. *tila* sesamum seed), Hindi *tilak*.] In full *tilka-spot*: among Hindus, the caste mark impressed on the forehead.
1879 E. Arnold *Lt. Asia* II. 72 Slender hands and feet new-stained With crimson, and the tilka-spots stamped bright.

Tillite (ti·ləit). *Min.* [f. Till *sb.*² + -ite ¹.] A sedimentary rock composed of glacial till compacted into hard rock.
1918 *Nature* CII. 112/2 The first record of Silurian 'tillite'. 1924 Skerl tr. *A. Wegener's Orig. Continents* 47 Southern Brazilian tillite.

Tilloter (ti·lətəɹ). Also tillotter. [f. Tillot + -er ¹.] (See quots.)
1881 *Instr. Census Clerks* (1885) 83 Tilloter (a Ticketer). 1921 *Dict. Occup. Terms* (1927) § 949 *Tillotter*; wraps textile piece goods in tillot cloth (a special glazed waterproof cloth) for export.

Tilter, *sb.*¹ Add: **4.** A see-saw. *U.S.*
1727 J. Comer *Diary* (1923) 17 As I was playing a childish play on a tilter with one Power Merit..I fell.
5. A swaying motion. *U.S.*
1833 J. Neal *Down-Easters* I. 173 A lawyer..with..a tilter in his walk.

Tilter, *v.* (Earlier U.S. example.)
1825 J. Neal *Bro. Jonathan* III. 271 The..pistol,..it was tiltering too, as if it were just ready to go off, at every jump.

Timber, *sb.*¹ Add: **9.** *timber-boom, -carriage, value.*
1908 *Chambers's Jrnl.* May 352/1 To haul the bigger logs to the railroad or *timber-boom. 1901 'L. Malet' *Hist. Sir R. Calmady* II. iii, A miller's tented waggon,..a *timber-carriage, and a couple of spring-carts. 1917 *Chambers's Jrnl.* Jan. 9/2 What bearing has the presence, or the increase, of woodpeckers upon the problem of *timber-values?
10. timber-cruiser *Western U.S.* [*Cruiser 3], a timber prospector; timber-driver, one who is engaged in transporting timber from the forest; timber-drug, a carriage for timber, = Drug *sb.*² 1; timber wheels (see quot.).
1894 *Century Mag.* Mar. 671/2 The *timber-cruiser is a hero..The location of a choice tract of timber is a secret to be guarded with his life. 1920 *Blackw. Mag.* Nov. 616/1 *Timber-drivers. 1917 *Isle of Ely & Wisbech Adv.* 28 Nov. 6 Defendant..asked if he had a pair of *timber drugs he could hire. 1905 *Terms Forestry & Logging* 42 *Logging wheels*, a pair of wheels, usually about 10 feet in diameter, for transporting logs. Syn.:..*timber wheels.

Ti·mber-land. *U.S.* (Timber *sb.*¹ 9 a.)
1807 P. Gass *Jrnl.* 31 We..passed some timber land on the south side. 1836 J. Hall *Statistics of West* vii. 103 Timber lands, newly cleared. 1871 *Rep. Indian Affairs* (1872) 301 Funds were furnished to clear up timber-lands for their use. 1896 *Vermont Agric. Rep.* XV. 79 The owners of timberlands.

Timbo (tɪmbo·). [Tupi.] A mimosaceous tree of South America, *Enterolobium contortisiliquum*, from which a soft red wood is obtained.
1928 *Funk's Standard Dict.*

Time, *sb.* Add: **8. b.** (Earlier U.S. example.)
1842 *Congress. Globe* 2 Mar. App. 188/2 A single horse in a sulky would..be able to make..even better time, with the letter mail alone.
9. (U.S. examples of the sense 'time one has worked', or 'pay for that time'.)
1877 Habberton *Jericho Road* i. 10 Go below and tell the mate to take your time. 1902 S. E. White *Blazed Trail* viii. 56 So Pat and Henrys were not discharged—were not instructed to 'get their time'. 1902 O. Wister *Virginian* xvii. 205 Pay was due him—'time,' as it was called in cow-land.
b. *Time and lime*: in the shipbuilding trade, applied to a contract to build at cost plus an agreed percentage.
1920 *Glasgow Herald* 6 July 7/1 Shipowners will not listen to proposals on the basis of time and lime. *Ibid.*, The shipowners' reason for declining to make time and lime contracts. 1921 *Ibid.* 8 June 9/1 The new battleships..should be given out on the principle of time and lime, and not on a fixed contract price.
13. d. *Stock Exch.* The account.
1901 W. G. Cordingley *Dict. Stock Exch. Terms* 89 Time Bargains refer to those speculative transactions which are made for settlement on the next Account. They are made 'for time', and are 'Bought for the Account.' or 'Sold for the Account.' 1928 *Daily Mail* 13 Aug. 18/2 Dealing for 'new time,'..the new Stock Exchange account.
17. (So much) *a time*: on each occasion.
1718 R. Grosvenor in C. T. Gatty *Mary Davies* (1921) II. 205 One that is grown pretty rich by his attendance upon Patients in Garrets at Half-a-Crown a time.
18. b. *Every time* (see *Every *a.* 1 e). In modern use often trivially to emphasize a statement.
1928 S. Lewis *Man Who Knew Coolidge* i. 41 If he'd study his mother and me a little more..he'd be a lot better off! You bet! Every time!
24. b. *To kill time*: see Kill *v.* 5.
27. *Standard time*, the local mean time of each of the regions or zones extending 7° 30′ east and west of the twenty-four standard meridians at intervals of 15° east and west of Greenwich. In full *zone standard time*. *Summer time*: see Summer time 2.
1912 *Whitaker's Alm.* 98/1 By Standard Time is meant that the hour of each 15° of longitude becomes the local mean time for the zone or belt extending 7½° on each side of the central meridian. 1917 *Ibid.* 99/1 Since the year 1883 the system of Standard Time by Zones has been gradually accepted, and now the majority of the countries of the world use as Standard Time the time of some meridian which differs from that of Greenwich by a multiple of 15°, and the Standard therefore differs from Greenwich Mean Solar Time by an integral number of hours, either fast or slow.
42. d. *In time*: 'in the world', 'on earth'. *colloq.*
1883 *Harper's Mag.* Jan. 212/1 He..wondered what In time made 'em keep the cars so hot.
43. (Earlier U.S. examples.)
1848 *Stray Subjects* 30 (Th.) Spose you never heard of burying a man on time. 1867 A. D. Richardson *Beyond Mississippi* 384 (Th.), I am going to take this coach in to Carson City on time.
51. a. *time-allowance* (later example), *-cycle, -interval, -life, -programme, -sequence, -succession, -unit.*
1893 G. Clare *Money-Market Primer* (ed. 2) 21 *note*, The *time-allowance on gold taken to the Mint is said to be 20 days. 1903 Annie W. Patterson *Schumann* 7 That the mind should work in a regular *time-cycle, passing from one phase of sentiment to another with almost mathematical exactness. 1875 *Cornhill Mag.* June 707 Though the number of suns is enormously increased..the magnitude of the *time intervals concerned is correspondingly increased. 1890 *Rep. Brit. Assoc.* 499 A measurement of the time-interval between seeing a flash..and hearing the report. 1916 Sir O. Lodge *Survival of Man* 31 Perhaps some one may be able to detect a meaning in the time-interval, when a great number of similar instances are compared. 1906 W. R. Inge *Truth & Falsehood in Relig.* 167 Every incident in the *time-life of a moral being, has, in God's sight, two aspects. 1929 *Times* 2 Nov. 12/1 Had there been any suggestion of a *time-programme for the realization of Dominion status. 1924 K. M. Ogden tr. *Koffka's Growth of Mind* 82 Localization of a sound to the right or left depends upon the *time-sequence in which the sound-waves.. strike the right and left ear, respectively. 1922 Eddington *Theory of Relativity* 18 It [*sc.* the relativity theory] fully recognizes that the chain of events in such a *time-succession is a series of an entirely distinctive character from the succession of points along a line in space. 1925 Joly *Surface-Hist. Earth* v. 79 Our *time-units have become millions of years.
b. *time-saving*.
1865 *Atlantic Monthly* XV. 729 Time- and labor-saving agencies.
52. time bill, draft, a bill or draft payable at a specified future date or at a certain length of time after presentation or sight; time-fused *a.*, furnished with a time fuse; time-lag (example); time-money (see quot. 1914); time period *Wireless Telegr.* (see quot.); time process, the emergence of eternal being in time; time rush (see quot.); time-signal, (*b*) a wireless signal indicating the time of day; so time-signalling; time stamp, a clockwork device for stamping letters, etc. with the date and time of receipt; time study, the close observation of the movements involved in any industrial process with a view to time-saving alterations of the method of working; used *attrib.*; time switch *Electr.*, a switch that acts automatically at a set time; time-triangle (*a*) *Astr.*, the celestial spherical triangle formed by the pole, the zenith, and a heavenly body; (*b*) (see quot. 1922).
1851 C. Cist *Cincinnati* 90 This House deals extensively.. in *time bills on N. Orleans. 1863 'E. Kirke' *My Southern Friends* xxii. 224 Our banks requiring two home names on *time drafts, I have to beg you to honor a small bill at one day's sight. 1880 *Encycl. Brit.* XI. 306/2 The British 9-pounders, which threw with 200 f.s. more velocity a *time-fuzed shrapnel. 1928 *Britain's Industrial Future* (*Lib. Ind. Inq.*) iv. xxiv. 326 In a period of declining prices farming suffers with special severity by reason of the long *time-lag in its operations. 1914 H. Halford's *Dict. Stock Market Terms* 90 **Time Money*, loans granted for a fixed period, as opposed to 'Call Money'. 1929 *Observer* 17 Nov. 3/4 Time money on stock collateral is now quoted 5½ to 6 per cent. 1905 *Proc. Roy. Soc.* LXXIV. 488 The resulting *time-period when they are brought into inductive relation to each other. 1923 *Daily Mail* 21 June 10 Time Period. Time occupied by one cycle or complete alternation of A. C. or H. F. current. 1906 W. R. Inge *Truth & Falsehood in Relig.* 37 The *time-process is not an automatic ethical winnowing machine. *Ibid.* 145 By declaring the Logos fully Divine it gives reality and value to the time process, which is the spheres of the distinct activities of the Second Person in the Trinity. 1909 *Q. Rev.* Apr. 356 [Ethics] attempts to determine the ideal by which the time-process itself is to be judged. 1912 *Marconigraph* II. 104/2 A '*Time Rush' message was a preliminary telegram to inform a ship of the telegrams ready to be despatched for it. 1923 *Mod. Wireless* I. 72 *Time signals are sent out daily by the wireless stations at the Eiffel Tower, [etc.]. *Ibid.* 319 A..crystal-set for broadcast and *time-signal reception. 1915 *Wireless Time Signals* 39 The radio-telegraphic *time-signalling stations. 1892 *Work* IV. 73/3 The *time-stamp is altered every minute. 1928 *Britain's Industrial Future* (*Lib. Ind. Inq.*) III. xvi. 194 There should be means of revising rates..in consultation, with all the facts and the *time-study figures on the table. 1930 *John o' London's Weekly* 29 Mar. 1005 The principal function of a 'time-study' man is to sit beside a workman, stop-watch in hand, to time every movement. 1922 Eddington *Theory of Relativity* 22 The terrestrial observer can have a space-triangle..; he can also have a '*time-triangle', formed by three events on different dates, whose sides he must measure with *clocks*.

Timenoguy (ti·menǫgi). Delete † *Obs.* and add: Also timmey-noggy, timmynoggy.
1880 W. Bottrell *Tradit. W. Cornw.* 3rd Ser. 198/2 *Timmy-noggy*, a notched square piece of wood, used to support the lower end of the Vargord. 1886 R. Brown *Spunyarn & Spindrift* xxxi. 378 If the exact name of anything they [*sc.* sailors] want happens to slip from their memory, they call it a..timmey-noggy, or a wim-wom. 1925 E. Fraser & Gibbons *Soldier & Sailor Words*, *Timmynoggy*, a name given to various strop and toggle gadgets on board ship, used in connection with the upper yards to save time in sail drill. A device more or less makeshift, to enable something to be done more expeditiously than would be possible in the ordinary way.

Timer. Add: **3. d.** An instrument for measuring the mileage per hour of an automobile. **e.** An adjustable device for automatically timing the spark in an internal combustion engine.
1920 C. H. Stagg *High Speed* vi. 103 He adjusted a timer on one of the cars.

Tin, *sb.* Add: **2.** Phr. *Straight from the tin* (fig.): direct from the source; in a fresh and unspoilt condition.
1929 *Evening News* 18 Nov. 12/4 What they want here is Yankee twang straight from the tin.
c. *pl.* phr. *On the tins*: on the scoring-board. *Cricket colloq.*
1903 Jephson in *Cricket* (ed. H. G. Hutchinson) 97 The mouldy eight runs on the tins were only hoisted there by a mighty effort. *Ibid.* 115 The nervous batsman retired, having, however, before his departure credited himself with fifty or so on the sunburnt 'tins'.
4. a. *tin can, -ware* (earlier Amer. examples.)
1770 Washington *Diaries* I. 442 A Quart *Tinn Can. 1758 *Essex Inst. Hist. Coll.* XVIII. 104 Iron, Copper and *Tin ware. 1813 Paulding *J. Bull & Br. Jonathan* xviii. (ed. 2) 93 They sent among them dealers in tin-ware and wooden bowls.
(*b*) Applied disparagingly to buildings made of corrugated iron. *Tin tabernacle* (see Tabernacle *sb.* 6 b): a corrugated iron place of worship; an 'iron church'. *colloq.*
1898 Le Queux *Scribes & Pharisees* v. 54 Those galvanized-iron structures irreverently known as 'tin tabernacles'. 1919 Bassett *S. Barnabas' Oxford* 36 This was before the 'tin' church at Cowley S. John existed. 1930 Priestley *Good Companions* I. vi. § 3 That's the Station Refreshment Rooms, a tin place, just opposite.
c. *tin-pedlar* (earlier example).
1812 in [Paulding] *Beauties Bro. Bull-us* 33 Feather-merchants, rag-men, tin-pedlars, and horse-jockies.
5. tin fish *Navy slang*, a torpedo; tin-horn *a.*, of common or inferior type (cf. Tin-pot 4); also *absol.*; tin Lizzie, orig. *Army slang*, an automobile, esp. a Ford car (cf. *Lizzie); tin pan (earlier U.S. examples); tin wedding (day) *colloq.*, the tenth anniversary of a wedding.
1927 *Daily Express* 12 Oct. 3 'Hi!' comes the hail, 'we've got your *tin fish!' At the end of a rope is the shining, dripping, steel torpedo. 1931 W. G. Carr *By Guess & By God* 26 A try was made for a large one, but in the clear water the wake of the tin fish was too easily seen. 1887 F. Francis *Saddle & Mocassin* 173 The're a *tin-horn lot. 1902 W. J. Ghent *Our Benevolent Feudalism* 171 What is colloquially known as 'tin-horn' gambling has advanced by leaps and bounds. 1903 A. Adams *Log Cowboy* xii. 80 A tin horn lawyer. 1928 Vachell *Some Happenings* i. 2 Gamblers of the 'tin-horn' brand. 1908 S. E. White *Riverman* vi. 55 You ain't a tin-horn yourself? 1921 *Blackw. Mag.* Dec. 824/1 The Colonel and I set out in the one and only '*tin-Lizzie' that the force owned. 1927 *Daily Express* 7 Sept. 2/7 The present Ford model is no longer popular, because of its cheap appearance and association with the name 'Tin Lizzie'. 1806 *Austin Papers* (1924) I. 102, 1 doz. *Tin pans. 1843 *Knickerbocker Mag.* XXII. 50 With discordant fife and old tin-pans for drums. 1876 *Times* 27 Sept. 1/1 On the 25 inst. (*Tin Wedding-day). 1888 *Girl's Own Paper* 24 Mar. 407/3 The 'tin-wedding'..is the tenth anniversary of the happy day.

Tinaja (tinā·ha). [Sp.; see Tinage.] A large earthenware jar used in Spain for wine, oil and olives, etc.; also, a water-jar made by the Pueblo Indians.
1676, 1845 [see Tinage]. 1885 *Encycl. Brit.* XIX. 629/1 The earliest kinds now existing of Spanish pottery without either enamel or glaze are chiefly large wine-jars, 'tinajas', about 3 or 4 feet high, of graceful amphora-like shape, stamped with simple patterns in relief.

Tincalconite (tinkæ·lkǒnəit). *Min.* [f. Tincal + Conite.] 'A variety of borax in which the proportion of water is in excess of the normal' (Funk).
1892 Dana *Syst. Min.* (ed. 6) 887.

Tinfoiler (ti·nfoi·ləɹ). [f. Tinfoil *v.* + -er ¹.] An operative who wraps goods in tinfoil.
1921 *Dict. Occup. Terms* (1927) § 949.

Tinguaite (ti·ŋgwā,əit). *Min.* [f. the name of Serra de *Tingua*, Brazil, where it is found + -ite ¹.] An igneous rock consisting mainly of a dense green aggregate of alkalic feldspar.
1893 *Min. Mag.* X. 173 More markedly porphyritic types are a rock with porphyritic elæolite, an 'elæolite tinguaite' with porphyritic orthoclase. 1895 *Ibid.* XI. 116 Another type of dyke-rock in the district answers to the Tinguaite of Rosenbusch.

Tin hat. orig. *Army slang*.
1. A metal helmet (see quot. 1925). *To put a* or *the tin hat on it*: to finish it completely, to close a or the matter finally. (Cf. *to put the lid on*, *Lid *sb.* 1 c.)
1917 A. J. L. Scott *60 Squad.* (1920) 38 We managed to collect some tin hats, bombs,..and a few other odds and ends. 1919 *War Slang* in *Athenæum* 8 Aug. 727/2 The shrapnel helmet was invariably a 'tin hat', and 'to put the tin hat on it' is..'to ki-bosh it'. 1923 *Public Opinion* 23 Mar. 275/3 The army of occupation with all its paraphernalia of tin hats, bayonets, machine guns, tanks [etc.]. 1925 E. Fraser & Gibbons *Soldier & Sailor Words*, *Tin hat*: the steel shrapnel-helmet adopted in the spring of 1916 as the universal wear at the Front, and in London by Special Constables during air raids.
2. A general officer. (Cf. *brass hat*, *Brass *sb.* 7.)
1919 *Athenæum* 18 July 632/2.
3. Used predicatively: Drunk. *slang.*
1909 Ware *Passing Engl.*, *Tin hat* (Anglo-Port Said), drunk—two tin hats very drunk—three, incapable, and to be carried on board. 1925 E. Fraser & Gibbons *Soldier & Sailor Words*, *Tin hats*, drunk.

Tinned, *ppl. a.* Add: **4.** Of music: Produced by mechanical means, as in a cinema.
1929 *Evening News* 18 Nov. 12/4 This [film] has tinned music, but no dialogue. 1930 *Punch* 26 Feb. 248/3 Our orchestral performers shall not be supplanted by tinned music.

Tinniness. Add: **2.** The condition of being harsh and metallic in timbre.
1923 *Daily Mail* 1 Aug. 5/6 The 'tinniness', 'throatiness', and other distorting elements inherent in the majority [of loud-speakers]. 1930 *Punch* 23 Apr. 468/1 Tinniness and sibilance have been overcome.

Tin-tack. Add: **b.** Phr. *to come down to tin tacks*: to come to facts, realities, or essentials. (Cf. *Brass 5 b.)
1927 G. B. Shaw in *Sunday Express* 7 Aug. 7/2 As long as you avoid coming down to tin tacks. 1928 — *Intell. Woman's Guide Socialism* (1929) 104 So now let us come down to tin tacks.

Tinted (ti·ntėd), *ppl. a.* [See Dict. s.v. Tint *v.*] **a.** Coloured in a specified manner (denoted by a defining word in combination). **b.** Coloured, as for shading the light, e.g. *tinted glass(es, spectacles*.
1816 Southey *Poet's Pilgr.* I. iv. xxx, The autumnal-tinted groves. 1895 'C. Holland' *Japan. Wife* 1 My Mousmé! with Dresden-china-tinted cheeks. 1897 A. Page *Afternoon Ride* vi, The devilry..shining in her beryl-tinted eyes. 1901 'C. Holland' *Mousmé* xvii. 249 The stethoscope pressed against her olive-tinted skin. 1905 *Westm. Gaz.* 1 July 14/1 Frowning heights the outline of which stood out dark and desolate against the orange-tinted sky.

Tinter. Add: **d.** (See quot.)
1921 *Dict. Occup. Terms* (1927) § 920 *Tinter*;..washes and applies tint or colour to human hair on the head or in the manufacture of wigs.

Tip, *sb.* Add: **2. e.** *Aeronautics.* = *Aileron.
1913 *Aeroplane* 23 Oct. 461/2 The main spars are laminated and taper towards the tips, and there are no holes in them, as the ribs are attached with copper straps.

Tip, *v.*¹ **1. b.** Add: *tip-and-run raid* (see quots.).
1918 *Chambers's Jrnl.* 477 Any dark night might see one of the enemy's favourite 'tip-and-run' dashes to sea. 1925 E. Fraser & Gibbons *Soldier & Sailor Words*, *Tip and run raids*, a familiar expression for the German North Sea coast bombardment raids. 1927 *Rep. Commissioner Police Metropolis 1926* 16 Stolen cars are used in..'tip and run' raids on jewellers' shops.

Tip, *v.*² Add **2. b.** Similarly *to tip the beam*.
1895 *Funk's Stand. Dict.* 1927 *Observer* 11 Dec. 13/3 The view which will tip the beam is that of a member who said [etc.].
9. *To tip off*: (also) to put out of the way by a violent death, to kill. *slang.* (Cf. *to bump off*, Bump *v.*¹ 1 b.)
1928 *Evening News* 18 Aug. 11/5 Jake's sort o' done me a good turn, getting himself tipped off.

Tipiti (tipitī·). [Tupi.] A strainer used by Amazonian Indians for expressing the poisonous juice of the manioc root.
1860 Mayne Reid *Odd People* 52 A long elastic cylinder-shaped basket or net, of the bark of the 'jacitara' palm (*Desmoncus macroacanthus*). This is the tipiti. 1866 *Treas. Bot.* 396/1 Indians use strips of the stem [of the Jacitara palm] for platting the tipitis or strainers used for squeezing out the poisonous juice of the manioc root.

Tip-off. *U.S. slang.* [f. Tip *v.*⁶ + Off *adv.*] A hint.
1923 L. J. Vance *Baroque* xxvii. 176 I traced the tip-off back to him.

Tippable (ti·păb'l), *a.* [f. Tip *v.*⁴ + -able.] That may be tipped; that is amenable to tipping or the receiving of douceurs.
1907 *Sat. Rev.* 21 Dec. 752/1 The great aim of the tippable is to squeeze. 1921 S. Graham *Europe—Whither Bound?* 27 A tippable man was keeping a queue of all the rabble of the East.

Tippet, *sb.* **5.** Add: tippet-monkey.
1864 J. A. Grant *Walk Across Africa* 127 The tippet-monkey, who is said to believe his handsome skin so much coveted.

Tipping, *vbl. sb.*¹ Also tippen. Add: **2. b.** = Tippet *sb.* 4 a.
1881 W. Gregor *Folk-Lore N. E. Scotl.* 52 Lines, hair for tippens, hooks. 1924 *Chambers's Jrnl.* 710/1 Many of the books have been torn from their tippings.
4. *Tipping in* (see quot.).
1931 A. Esdaile *Man. Bibliogr.* 183 *Tipping-in.*—Pasting the edge of a single leaf to the next leaf.

Tipping, *vbl. sb.*² **3. d.** Add: *tipping machine*.
1877 *Scotsman* 1 Sept. 4/7 Tipping machine.

Tippy, *a.*¹ Add: **1. c.** *sb.* An exquisite; a fop. *U.S.*
a 1800 in *Spirit Farmers' Museum* (1801) 262 He is called the 'dandy', by one party, and the 'tippy' by another. 1804 *The Balance* (Hudson, N.Y.) 15 May 153 (Th.) A smirking race, called in fashion's vocabulary 'Tippies'. 1844 'Jon. Slick' *High Life N.Y.* II. 92 You wouldn't ketch one of our York tippies at that, let alone a genuine Lord.

Tippy, *a.*² *U.S.* (Later example.)
1923 E. F. Wyatt *Invis. Gods* III. i. 93 A tippy, wire-legged table.

Tip-tap, *adv.* [See the sb. and vb.]
1911 H. Walpole *Mr. Perrin & Mr. Traill* vi. i, He came tip-tap across the floor to him.

Tip-up, *sb.* **3.** *U.S.* (Examples.)
1880 *Harper's Mag.* Mar. 517 With baited lines and tip-ups set, we waited. 1892 *Outing* (U.S.) Mar. 439 The upper ends of the lines being..affixed to what are termed 'tip-ups'.

Tired, *ppl. a.*¹ Add: **1. a.** *To make* (a person) *tired*: to annoy and bore. orig. *U.S. slang.*
1896 G. Ade *Artie* iv. 35 'Oh, you make me tired,' said the intruder. *a* 1904 S. E. White *Blazed Trail Stories* iv. 65 Such talk made Daly tired, and he said so. 1907 M. C. Harris *Tents of Wickedness* II. vii. 200 'He makes me tired!' exclaimed Leonora, who had imbibed a little slang in these two months.
c. *Tired Tim* (or *Timothy*), usually associated with *Weary Willy*, both being taken as symbolical names for 'won't-works'.
1899 *Comic Cuts* 6 May 1 Two gents of the name of Weary Willy and Tired Tim. 1906 *Daily Chron.* 15 Feb. 3/5 Heroes of the Tired Timothy stamp. 1930 H. Herd *Diagnosis Mental Deficiency* 10 Mental defectives are the 'weary Willies and tired Tims' *par excellence*.

Tiriba (tirī·ba). [Brazilian.] A Brazilian wedge-tailed green parrakeet, *Conurus leucotis*.
1820 tr. *Wied-Neuwied's Trav. Brazil* vii. 97 Tiribas, Curicas, Camutangas, Mandayas and other kinds of parrots.

Tiring, *vbl. sb.*⁴ Add attrib. uses.
1932 Boumphrey *Story of Wheel* 27 This is a tiring-platform, and its purpose is to hold wheels firmly while their tires are being put on. *Ibid.*, The smith opens the door of the tiring-furnace. *Ibid.* 28 These others..by the aid of iron hooks (called tiring-dogs)..drop it [*sc.* the tire] on the rim of the wheel.

Tiringly (təi·riŋli), *adv.* [f. Tiring *ppl. a.* + -ly ².] In a tiring manner, to a tiring degree.
1894 E. Fawcett *New Nero* xx, 'It's a trifle tyrannical, is it not?' 'Yes; amusingly so.' 'Never tiringly so.'

Tirolese, var. Tyrolese.
1931 *Times Lit. Suppl.* 11 June 459/3 Tirolese civilization, with its feudal past and its long-standing autonomy.

Tirthankar (tɪəɹ·þaŋkāɹ). Also Tirthankara, Tirthanker. [Skr. *tīrthakara* making a passage (through life), head of a sect, f. *tīrthā* passage, place of pilgrimage, object of veneration, etc. + *karā* maker, causer.] In Jainism, any of the twenty-four prophets or early teachers, now revered as deities.
1835 J. Wilson in *Life* (1879) 117 There are the images of all the twenty-four Tirthankars. 1880 *Encycl. Brit.* XIII. 543/2 The Jains count twenty-four such prophets, whom they call Jinas, or Tirthankaras, that is, conquerors or leaders of schools of thought. 1901 Kipling *Kim* vi, I'd give a month's pay to hear how he explained it all at the Tirthankers' Temple at Benares. 1909 *Blackw. Mag.* Mar. 315/2 The images of their Tirthankaras preach disillusionment.

Tissue, *sb.* **9. a.** Add: (in sense 5).
1911 F. O. Bower *Plant-Life* 84 The large tissue-masses of the plant. 1912 J. A. Thomson *Biol. Seasons* III. 175 A sudden release of certain tissue-tensions. 1927 Haldane & Huxley *Animal Biol.* i. 33 The name [cell] was transferred to the living tissue-units of plants.

Tiswin. *U.S.* (Earlier example.)
1877 *Rep. Indian Affairs* 162 Addicted, also, to the use of intoxicating liquors, 'tiswin', which they manufacture from corn and whiskey obtained from traders.

Tit, *sb.*⁴ Add: **3.** *Comb.*: tit-drill, a flat drill used for levelling the bottom of a hole.

Tithonian (təiþǭ·niăn), *a.* *Geol.* [f. L. *Tīthōnus*, Gr. Τιθωνός + -ian.] = Portlandian *a.*
1914 *Brit. Mus. Return* 205 A new genus of Crinoidea from the Tithonian of Stramberg.

Titian. Add: A person with Titian hair and corresponding complexion.
1923 *Times* 3 May, Tecla pearls..are equally becoming whether worn by blondes, brunettes, or Titians.

Titler. Add: **3.** One who writes titles (of scenarios).
1928 *Daily Express* 20 Feb. 13/3 Editor and titler [of scenarios].

Titty³. Add: Also, a dummy teat, a comforter. *colloq.*
1927 W. E. Collinson *Contemporary Engl.* 8 Dummies, titties or comforters.

Titulus (ti·tiŭlǒs). [L.: see Title *sb.*] A superscription or the label bearing it. (Cf. Title *sb.* 1.)
1918 *By an Unknown Disciple* xx. 238 He ordered the centurion to have it so transcribed on the Titulus. 1927 A. H. McNeile *Introd. N.T.* 20 There was a deep irony in the mockery by the soldiers, and in the *titulus* on the Cross.

T.N.T. (tī,en,tī·): see *T 6.

To, *prep.* Add: **4.** *To home*: see also *Home *sb.*¹ 13.
8. Indicating the crop with which ground is planted. *local.*
1861 *Trans. Ill. Agric. Soc.* (1865) V. 154 The land..was ..mostly planted to potatoes. 1884 *Vermont Agric. Rep.* VIII. 355 Last year [I] planted an acre to Sanford corn. 1900 [see *Plant *v.* 6 a]. 1902 [in Dict.].
d. Included, contained, or involved in; chiefly in phr. *That is all there is to it*: it is that and nothing more. orig. *U.S.*
1886 E. L. Dorsey *Midshipman Bob* II. xii. 230 There's just this to it: if you'll go to any place [etc.]. 1895 Kipling *Day's Work, Ship that Found Herself* (1898) 83 'That's all there is to it,' seethed the white water roaring through the scuppers. 1898 Marg. Deland *Old Chester Tales* 243 Well, that was all there was to it. He saved me. 1903 A. H. Lewis *The Boss* 14 'Tell me what there is to this shindy.' 1914 Mr. & Mrs. V. Castle *Mod. Dancing* 44 Simply walk as softly and smoothly as possible...This is the One Step, and this is all there is to it.

Toa. Add: Also in reduplicated form toa toa.
1845 E. J. Wakefield *Adv. N. Zealand* II. 120 The *toa toa*..is much prized by the natives for walking-sticks. 1879 *Trans. Bot.* Suppl., Toa-toa.

Toad, *sb.* Add: **3. b.** Applied to children. (Cf. *Tad.) *U.S.*
1835 Haliburton *Clockmaker* Ser. I. xxvii, Two little orphan children, the prettiest little toads I ever beheld.

Toadless (tōᵘ·d,lės), *a.* [f. Toad *sb.* + -less.] Devoid of toads.
1911 *Chambers's Jrnl.* July 435/2 When the garden was dug..it was toadless. 1922 M. Temple *Shallowdale* iii. 39 No dog can be thoroughly happy in a toadless garden.

Toast, *sb.*¹ **2.** Add: *French toast*: (*a*) see quot. 1892; (*b*) thin bread-and-butter that has been toasted for a few seconds on the unbuttered side.
1892 *Encycl. Cookery* (ed. T. F. Garrett) I. 192/1 French Toast. Beat up one egg in a basin with a little salt and 1 teaspoonful of milk, and in this dip some thin slices of Bread ..; then plunge the Bread into a frying-pan of boiling fat, and fry to a light brown. Take them out, drain them... Spreading them over with stewed rhubarb, or other fruit in season, is a great improvement.

Tobacco. Add: **1. b.** A fashion shade; = *Tabac.
1923 *Daily Mail* 10 Jan. 1 Becoming Hat in good quality Petersham Ribbon...Colours: Grey, Cherry, Nigger, Tobacco, Peacock. *Ibid.* 5 June 6 In Pale and Mid Fawn,.. Sky, Tobacco, Lemon.
3. *tobacco-chewer, -planter; -tobacco-jar, -root, -worm* (U.S. examples).
1835 *Southern Lit. Messenger* I. 662 A solitary *tobacco chewer. 1775 *Essex Inst. Hist. Coll.* XIII. 186, 1 *Tobacco Jar; 1 Large Lead do. 1857 T. B. Gunn *N. Y. Boarding-Houses* 26 Hair-brush and tobacco-jar jumbled among your shirt-collars. 1791 Washington *Diaries* IV. 180 It bids fair to be a large Town..which is settling very fast by *Tobacco planters. 1838 *Southern Lit. Messenger* IV. 197 A fine old specimen of the real Virginia tobacco planter, a half domesticated son of France. 1845 Frémont *Exped.* 135 I ate here, for the first time, the kooyah, or *tobacco root, (*valeriana edulis*). 1847 *Rep. U.S. Comm. Patents* (1848) 168 The *tobacco worm was the subject of complaint. 1872 *Rep. Vermont Board Agric.* I. 319 The large night-flying moths, which come from, and in turn produce the large larvæ, as the potato-worm and tobacco-worm.

Toby, *sb.*¹ **4.** Add: Also *attrib.* (see quot. 1842).
1842 *Newton's Lond. Jrnl.* Conjoined Ser. XIX. 35 The printing [of the fabric] is to be done in an ordinary machine or press, the colours being furnished from what is called the 'toby tub'. 1881 *Instr. Census Clerks* (1885) 43 Toby and Rainbow Tub Maker.

Toccatella (tǫkāte·lā), **Toccatina** (-ī·nā). *Music.* [It.] A short toccata.
1873 Hiles *Dict. Mus. Terms* 260 Toccatina. 1889 *Grove's Dict. Music* IV. 130/1 Dupont has published a little pf. piece entitled Toccatella. *Ibid.*, The same composer [*sc.* Rheinberger] has used the diminutive term Toccatina for one of a set of short pieces; and another instance of the use of this term is the Toccatina in E♭ by Henselt.

Toc emma (tǫk e·mā). Also tock. [Representing T.M. (see *T 6) in telephonist's use: see *Emma.] A trench mortar.
1919 Tock Emma [see *Emma]. 1931 *Morning Post* 20 Aug. 8/5 And he was the only infantry officer..who had a good word for the Trench Mortar crowd. 'Are you Toc Emmas? You're just the men I want.'

Toc H (tǫk ēɪtʃ). [= T. H. (cf. prec.), initials of *Talbot House*, a rest-house and club for soldiers opened at Poperinghe, 15 Dec. 1915, in memory of Gilbert W. L. Talbot (died 1915).] An association of ex-service men founded by the Rev. P. B. Clayton to carry on comradeship from the war of 1914–18.
1918 in Clayton *Tales Talbot House* (1919) 138 Owing to the inconsiderate retirement of our old neighbours, the Boche, Toc. H. is in a pretty fix. 1923 Prince of Wales in *Times* 17 Dec. 7/3 The Toc H. spirit is one that is wanted very badly in this country to-day and will be wanted in the future. 1930 *Toc H Jrnl.* Jan. 3 Toc H will indeed begin ..to be..a power making for righteousness.

Tocharian (tǫkā·riăn, -ē·riăn), *a.* and *sb.* [ad. F. *tocharien*, f. Gr. Τοχάροι (Strabo) nomad Chinese tribes identified with the Yuechi: see -ian.] (Of or pertaining to) an extinct Indo-European language, of which remains have been discovered in Turkestan. Also **Tocharish** (tǫkā·riʃ, -ē·riʃ), after G. *tocharisch*.
1910 P. Giles in *Encycl. Brit.* II. 712/2 Up to 1909 only a preliminary account had been given of Tocharish, a hitherto unknown Indo-European language. 1927 Peake & Fleure *Peasants & Potters* 134 The Tocharian language of parts of Turkestan.

Tocht, variant of *Togt.

Tocusso (tǫku·so). Also -a. [Amharic.] An Abyssinian cereal, *Eleusine coracana* (Marna wheat).
1790 J. Bruce *Trav.* V. 79 In place of Teff, in these borders [the Kolla], there grows a black grain called Tocusso. 1866 *Treas. Bot.*, *Tocusso*, an Abyssinian corn-plant or millet, *Eleusine Tocusso*. 1875 *Encycl. Brit.* I. 63/1 The low grounds produce also a kind of corn known as *tocussa*, of which a black bread is made.

Toe, *sb.* **6.** Add: toe-board (earlier U.S. example); toe-dancing, the performance of a toe-dancer; toe-nail *sb.*, also (*b*) an iron nail employed for the toe in shoeing; toe parade *Army slang*, a foot inspection; toe-spin *Skating*, a spin performed on the toe.
1892 *Harper's Mag.* Jan. 271/1 The..bag..to put under his feet on the *toe-board. 1924 C. J. Sharp & Oppé *Dance* 47 *Toe-dancing is perhaps the most extreme instance of the virtuosity achieved by the ballet-dancers of the last century. The position *sur la pointe*..needs long and painful practice. 1908 *Animal Managem.* (W. O.) 138 The smith begins with the *toenails first. 1918 E. S. Farrow *Dict. Mil. Terms*, *Toe Parade,..inspection of the feet..with the surgeon or a medical assistant in attendance. 1928 *Daily Express* 19 Dec. 15/4 Her pirouettes, *toe-spins, and counter-rockers compel the awe and admiration of all beginners.

Toe, *v.* Add: **1.** Also with *off*.
1856 Mary J. Holmes *Rice Corner* iii, She..was toeing off the stocking only that morning commenced.
2. *To toe the mark* (earlier U.S. example). Also *to toe the trig* (Trig *sb.*²), *to toe up* (U.S.).
1813 Paulding *J. Bull & Br. Jonathan* xii. (ed. 2) 62 He began to think it was high time to toe the mark. 1817 *Ann. 14th Congress* 2 Sess. 792 The necessity appeared..of toeing the trig, and standing there at all hazards. 1901 S. Merwin & H. K. Webster *Calumet K* xii. 226 I'll give Brown one more warning..and then if he doesn't toe up, I'll get one and send him the bill.
4. Also, to turn the toes *in* or *out*.
1894 *Vermont Agric. Rep.* XIV. 120 Avoid a horse which toes in or toes out.

Toff, *v. slang.* [f. Toff *sb.*] To dress *up* like a 'toff', *esp.* in passive.
1928 *East End Star* Dec. 2/2 Notice the perfect stillness when the 'lovely lidy all toffed up' sings. 1932 L. Golding *Magnolia Street* II. ii. § 2 The fellows come in [*sc.* to a hair-dressing saloon] when they're on leave. They want to get toffed up for their girls.

Toffee. Add: Phr. *Not to be able* to do a thing *for toffee*: to be incompetent at it. *slang.*
1914 *Illustr. Lond. News* 12 Sept. 380/1 Their opponents cannot 'shoot for nuts' (or 'for toffee', as one Tommy more expressly put it). 1916 W. J. Locke *Far-away Stories* 9 He can't sell seeds for toffee.

Tofu (tǒfu·). [Jap.] The bean-curd or bean-cheese of China and Japan, made from soya beans.
1880 *Trans. Asiatic Soc. Japan* VIII. 390 *Tōfu* is made by pounding the soy beans after soaking in water. 1892 Simmonds *Dict. Trade* (new ed.) Suppl., *Tofu*, the oil-cake of beans and peas in Japan and China, used for soups and sauces. 1893 *Index-Catal. Libr. Surg. Gen. Office U. S. Army* XIV. 598/2 On 'tofu' (beancheese), its history, manufacture, analysis, and food value. 1923 J. Street *Mysterious Japan* iv. 46, I saw a bean-curd man jogging along the street with a long rod over his shoulder, at each end of which was suspended a box of *tofu*.

Togetherness. Delete *nonce-wd.* and add examples. Also **Toge·theriness.**
a 1902 S. Butler *Notebooks* (1912) 21 A piece of string is a thing that, in the main, makes for togetheriness. 1920 A. S. Pringle-Pattison *Idea of God* 354 Our primitive and basal experience of time is thus characterized by a togetherness of parts or elements. 1926 A. N. Whitehead *Science & Mod. World* 210 Cognition discloses an event as being an activity, organising a real togetherness of alien things. 1930 *Times Lit. Suppl.* 13 Nov. 925/3 The personages of Tourneur have..this togetherness.

Toggenburg (tǫ·gənbɔ̄ɹg), the name of a canton in Switzerland used *attrib.* or *ellipt.* to denote a goat of breed originating from this locality.
1891 *Goat-Keeper* 7 Champion Zampa, Swiss Toggenburg Goat, 5 years old, short-haired, hornless. 1921 *Blackw. Mag.* June 764/2 The white Nanny and her kid are Alpino goats, and the brown lot are Toggenburgs.

Toggle, *v.* **1.** *U.S.* (Earlier example.)
1836 *Knickerbocker Mag.* VIII. 207 'What,..has the devil toggled you at last, Jacky?'

Togt (tǫxt). *S. Africa.* Also tocht. [Du. *tocht* trading expedition.]
1. A trading venture.
[1818 Latrobe *Jrnl.* 265 The master..was about to set off..on a trip..to dispose of it [*sc.* arrack] in barter...They call this, going *op de tocht*.] 1860 *Queenstown Free Press* 8 Feb. (Pettman) Horses have been discovered amongst those of 'smouses' who were returning..after a somewhat successful *togt*.
2. Hired labour for a specified job.
1901 Turnbull *Tales from Natal* 120 The black devils.. so often put us about by deserting—without even the possibility of our being able to obtain togt even.
3. *attrib.* and *Comb.*, as togt boy, a native in Natal licensed to ply for hire for odd jobs; togt ganger, rider, a travelling trader; so togt-riding.
1898 *Port Elizabeth Telegr.* 2 Sept. (Pettman) A Chinaman refused to supply a small quantity of bread and sugar to a *togt boy on Saturday. 1895 *Funk's Standard Dict.*, *Tocht ganger. 1896 R. Wallace *Farming Industr. Cape Colony* 91 The plant [*sc.* prickly pear] was first spread in the Colony by transport riders or 'togt-gangers'. 1911 Webster, *Togt rider, *togt riding.

Tog-table (tǫ·g tā·b'l). [Of obscure origin.] A gambling board used at fairs.
1910 Sanger *Seventy Years a Showman* (1927) 155 These 'tog-tables' were..open-air gambling boards, twelve to fourteen feet long by about three wide.

Togue². *U.S.* (Earlier example.)
1864 *Ann. Rep. Agric. Maine* 132 The lake trout, or 'togue'.

Toile. 2 Add: Also with defining addition, as *toile de chine, toile de soie*.
1923 *Weekly Dispatch* 11 Feb. 14, 5,000 Yards of Toile de Chine. Made of the finest Spun Silk. 1923 *Daily Mail* 27 Aug. 1/3 Toile de Soie. 1927 *Observer* 13 Nov. 19/5 Dressing Gowns in Quilted Satin, Brocades, Toile-de-Soie.

Toilet, *sb.* **9. b.** Add: toilet cover (earlier U.S. example); toilet powder, a form of dusting powder employed in the toilet.
1838 Caroline Gilman *Recoll. Southern Matron* xxix. 207 The bride's chamber..neatly set off with white curtains and *toilet cover. 1895 *Army & Navy Co-op. Soc. Price List* 717/2 Cherry Blossom *Toilet Powder.

Toke (tōᵘk). *low colloq.* [Origin unascertained.] Food; *spec.* bread.
1859 *Slang Dict.*, *Toke*, dry bread. 1877 *Five Years' Penal Serv.* i, Some prisoner..had forgotten to eat what in prison slang is called his 'toke' or 'chuck'. 1899 Whiteing *No. 5 John St.* xxi, When the show was shut, I..sits down to my toke and pipe. 1905 H. G. Wells *Kipps* I. i. § 2 Toke and cold ground-rice puddin' with plums.

Token, *sb.* **16.** Add: token estimate, vote (see quots.).
1915 *Political Quarterly* May 147 For form's sake '*token' estimates were presented, on the basis of £1,000 for each vote and £100 for each appropriation in aid. 1923 *Times* 27 Feb. 18/3 On the Supplementary Vote of £10 for Diplomatic and Consular Services..the anticipated savings under various subheads were rather larger than £155,198, and would..be sufficient to cover the whole amount now asked for; but inasmuch as all but one of the subheads referred to new services, it had been thought right that a *token Vote of £10 should be put down in order to provide the opportunity for discussing these new services.

Toledan (tolī·dăn), *a.* [f. *Toledo* + -an.] Of or pertaining to Toledo (see Toledo and cf. Toletan *a.*).
1914 Masefield *Philip the King* 47 Till their Toledan armour was burnt black. 1931 *Times Lit. Suppl.* 16 Apr. 305/1 These Toledan Christians were bilingual.

Tolerable, *a.* (*adv.*). **5.** As *adv.* **a.** (Later U.S. examples.)
1850 E. C. Watson *Camp-fires Revol.* 63 We had got along thus far tolerable well. 1873 J. H. Beadle *Undevel. West* x. 178 If the 'later rain' has not put in an appearance, they are, in local phrase, 'tolerable dry'. 1884 'Mark Twain' *Huck. Finn* i. 3 Her sister, Miss Watson, a tolerable slim old maid, with goggles on.
b. (Later U.S. example.)
1856 [G. H. Derby] *Phœnixiana* ii. 33 If I..ask him.. 'How be does?' he infallibly replies—'Tolerable, thank you.'

Tolerance. 4. b. Add: Also *pl.*
1916 *Yorkshire Post* 28 Mar. 8/1 Permissible margins of error in workmanship are known as tolerances. 1920 *Conquest* Apr. 269/1 [In gauges] a very high accuracy was demanded, the tolerances being generally a few ten-thousandth parts of an inch.

Tolerant, *a.* (*sb.*) **A.** *adj.* Add: **e.** *Biol.* Able to endure a noxious influence.
1904 E. R. Lankester in *Q. Rev.* July 128 A more precise nomenclature would describe the attacked organism..as 'tolerant', for it tolerates the presence and multiplication of the parasite without suffering by it.

Toleration. 2. b. *U.S.* (Example.)
1881 Ingersoll *Oyster-Industr.* (Hist. Fish. Industr. U.S.) 249 Toleration.—License to gather oysters or operate beds...The money paid is called a Toleration fee.

Toll, *sb.*¹ Add:
2. g. esp. in phr. *the toll of the road*, etc.
1925 *Daily Mail*, The toll of the road. 1929 *Daily Express* 7 Nov. 2/3 Miners' members were artists in presenting the toll of the mines in its most impressive form.
i. A short distance telephone trunk call: freq. *attrib.*
[1890 *Century Mag.* June 260/2 The estimate for special despatches includes telegraph tolls and pay of the correspondents who furnish the news.] 1927 *Daily Tel.* 6 Dec. 11/2 It has been possible to include Southend-on-Sea,.. Chatham, Camberley, and Horsham in the toll area, and callers for these places should now ask for 'tolls' instead of 'trunks'. 1928 E. Wallace *Again the Three Just Men* x. 223 The telephone-bell rang. The voice of the porter informed him that a toll call had come through.

Toll-bait. *U.S.* (Earlier example.)
1870 *Amer. Naturalist* IV. 516 The 'toll-bait' consists chiefly of Menhaden (*Alausa menhaden*) ground very fine.

Tolly (tǫ·li), *sb.* *School slang.* [app. local f. Tallow *sb.*] A (tallow) candle.
1889 Barrère & Leland *Dict. Slang*, *Tolly* (public schools), a candle. 1905 Vachell *The Hill* xiii, An Olympian is privileged to work a little longer by the light of the useful 'tolly'. 1905 L. Portman *Hugh Rendal* xxxi, No tollies allowed after 10.30. 1924 E. Marsh tr. *Fables La Fontaine* 77 The luckless tolly..Ended as a pool of grease.

Tolly (tǫ·li), *v.* *Harrow School.* [Cf. prec.] *intr.* To work by candle-light after the lights have been extinguished; to 'burn the midnight oil'. Usually with *up*.
1889 Barrère & Leland *Dict. Slang*, *Tolly up*, (Harrow School), to keep a candle alight after the gas has been turned off. 1894 Welkins & Vivian *Green Bay Tree* I. 73 The process known as 'tollying-up', or working by candle-light after the legal hours.

Toltec (tǫ·ltek), *sb.* and *a.* **a.** *sb.* A member of a native race which ruled in Mexico *c* 700–1000 A.D.; the language of this people. **b.** *adj.* Of or pertaining to this race or its language. So **Toltecan** (tǫ·ltekān) *a.* and *sb.*
1814 [see *Aztec]. 1839 *Penny Cycl.* XV. 165/1 The older..monuments of Mexico are..the productions..of the Toltecans. *Ibid.* 165/2 The extraordinary vastness of..these ..Toltecan constructions. 1875 *Encycl. Brit.* I. 691/2 The Toltecan family embraced the civilised nations of Mexico, Peru, and Bogota. *Ibid.* 694/2 The Toltecs..left their original seat, far to the west, in 544. *Ibid.* 696/1 The Toltec and Aztec races. 1927 *Chambers's Jrnl.* Aug. 568/2, I sing the snake song the Toltec fathers sang.

Tolu-. Add: **Toluenyl** (tǫ·liu,ėni·l), the tolyl radical. **Tolusafranin** (tǫliusæ·frănin), a safranin dye-stuff derived from toluene. **Toluylene** (tǫ·liu,ilīn) = Stilbene, used *attrib.* to denote various dye-stuffs.
1868 Watts *Dict. Chem.* V. 861 *Toluenyl. 1888 Roscoe & Schorlemmer *Treat. Chem.* III. II. 412 Paraxylyl alcohol was obtained by Cannizzaro..,and was named toluenyl alcohol. *Ibid.* 80 *Tolusafranine, $C_{21}H_{20}N_4$..is simply known as 'safranine' in commerce. 1863 Fownes *Elem. Chem.* (ed. 9) 646 *Toluylene-diamine. 1872 *Chemical News* XXV. 22/1 Toluylen alcohol is a solid crystalline substance, having no constant melting-point. 1888 Roscoe & Schorlemmer *Treat. Chem.* III. II. 80 Toluylene-blue...Toluylene-red...Toluylene-violet forms red crystals.

Tom, *sb.*¹ **7. a.** Add: Tom Collins *U.S.*, a drink composed of lemon juice, gin, soda-water, and sugar. (Cf. *John Collins.)
1909 *Cent. Dict.* Suppl. 1919 Mencken *Amer. Lang.* 85. 1930 John van Druten *Woman on her Way* xiv, 'What can I have?' 'Anything. Scotch, gin, wine, liqueurs, Tom Collins. You've only got to say.'

Tom (tǫm), *sb.*² Gardener's and tradesman's abbrev. of Tomato.
1920 *Chambers's Jrnl.* 384/1 The acreage of 'outside toms' is increasing annually.

Tomato. Add: **1. b.** = *tomato-red*.
1920 *Queen* 22 May, Front Cover, Colours:..Apricot, Ivory, Mastic, Tomato, Suede, and Saxe.

Tombstone. 3. (U.S. example.)
1751 B. Lynde Jr. *Diary* 16 Oct. (1880) 176 Yesterday Cox and Stacey ½ day abo. Tombstone monument.

Tom-cod. *U.S.* (Earlier example.)
1769 *Mass. Gazette* 16 Feb. (Th. p. 772) Whether the ninety two tom-cod and seventeen scalpions are yet digested.

-tome¹ (tōᵘm), terminal element (= F. *-tome*) representing Gr. -τόμον, neut. of -τόμος -cutting, in designations of instruments used in the surgical operation expressed by the corresponding word in -tomy, e.g. Lithotome (1758), which is the earliest example; others are Cystotome, *Enterotome, Hysterotome, Laryngotome, Metrotome, Neurotome, Tonsillotome, Urethrotome.

-tome² (tōᵘm), terminal element representing Gr. τομή a cutting (cf. prec.) with the meaning 'section', 'segment', as in Myotome (1), Sclerotome.

Tommy, *v.* Add: **2.** *dial.* To rivet or fasten together; also with *on* (see quot. 1891). Hence **To·mmied** *ppl. a.*, made with a 'tommy' or forging stamp called an Oliver machine.
1891 *Sheffield Gloss.* Suppl., *Tommy*, *v.*, to rivet or fasten together; a term used by cutlers when they are fastening on the scales of the handles of knives...'Wanted a boy to tommy on'. 1909 *Act 9 Edw. VII* c. 22 Schedule, Hammered and dollied or tommied chain-making. 1921 *Dict. Occup. Terms* (1927) § 190 Tommied chain maker.

Tonal, *a.* and *sb.* **A.** *adj.* Add: **1. c.** Of or pertaining to music written in keys: opposed to *Atonal *a.* (q.v., quot. 1922).

Tonalist (tōᵘ·nălist). [f. Tonal *a.* + -ist.] **1.** A painter who aims at effect through colour harmonization rather than by contrasts.
1903 *N. Y. Times* 31 Jan. (Cent. D. Suppl.) The collection is one of colorists and tonalists without the aid of any of the more notable open-air landscape painters.
2. One who writes or approves of tonal music.

Tonalitive (tonæ·litiv), *a.* *Mus.* [f. Tonality + -ive.] Of or pertaining to tonality.
1918 *Mus. Assoc. Proc.* 1917–18, 162, I should expect the new tonalitive schemes of such composers as Debussy and Ravel to bring about great changes in composition. 1924 *Ibid.* 1923–4, 60 New harmonic progressions to suit the tonalitive, or it may be, the non-tonalitive scheme. 1924 Trotter *Music & Mind* 237 The old major and minor tonalitive schemes are giving way.

Tonbridge: see *Tunbridge.

Tondino. Add: **2.** *Ceramics.* A plate with a wide flat rim and deep centre usually made of majolica.
1885 *Encycl. Brit.* XIX. 627/2 The Faenza potteries produced..plates with wide flat rims and deep centres, called 'tondini'. *Ibid.*, Faenza plate (tondino), with border in deep ultramarine blues.

Tone, *sb.* **11.** Add: tone-arm, the tubular arm connecting the sound-box of a gramophone to the horn; tone-correction, the electrical control of the quality of a reproducing instrument: hence *tone-correction unit*; tone-painter (see *tone-painting*); tone-poem [G. *tondichtung*], (*a*) a form of musical composition for orchestra in which the thought is more poetical than musical; (*b*) a painting in which the tones are harmonized poetically; so tone-poet.

1913 G. F. Rowell Hints about Gramophones 19 If you get an instrument with a full-sized *tone-arm and horn..you can obtain a reproduction equal to any size or price made. 1903 Annie W. Patterson Schumann 49 How first the pianoforte, next the orchestra, and lastly the string quartet suggested sound pictures to the *tone-painter. 1908 To-Day 22 Oct. 402/2 The *tone-poems of Richard Strauss. 1903 Annie W. Patterson Schumann 152 His often veiled, if richly-coloured, tone-poems. 1906 Athenæum 6 Jan. 27/1 A symphonic tone-poem 'Lalla Rookh', by J. Jongen. 1922 Weekly Dispatch 3 Dec. 2 Arnold Bax..tackles the symphony only after having produced four of five tone-poems. 1927 Sunday Times 6 Mar. 7/4 Though his pictures are small they will..make a profound appeal..as gentle tone-poems. 1892 Review of Reviews Sept. 280/1 A most original *tone-poet. 1903 Annie W. Patterson Schumann Pref. p. viii, The writer..has endeavoured..to let the great tone poet speak through his own thoughts.

Tong (tɒŋ), sb.² [Chinese t'ang meeting-place.] A Chinese secret society.

1918 Webster Addenda. 1924 Glasgow Herald 29 Oct. 8 Rival Tongs, whose principal object seems to be mutual extermination. 1927 Daily Express 25 Mar. 2/1 Chinese Tong (secret society) warfare broke out at midnight throughout the United States. 1928 G. Burrard Myst. Mekong iii, I always feared that it might be but an offshoot of some far bigger Chinese tong.

Tongkang (tɒ·ŋ,kæ·ŋ). [Malay.] A junk of a type employed in the Malay archipelago.

1858 Simmonds Dict. Trade, Tongkang, a kind of boat or junk used in the seas of the Eastern archipelago. 1922 Chambers's Jrnl. 503/1 A string of big, heavy, tongkangs, towed by a puffing launch.

Tongue, sb. Add: **4. d.** Also, to stick (or thrust) one's tongue in one's cheek, as a gesture of contemptuous or sly humour. So with one's tongue in one's cheek, with sly humour.

1748 [see Cheek sb. 2]. 1849 Cupples Green Hand xi. (1856) 115 Hows'ever, I jist sticks my tongue in my cheek, ..watches my chance, an' off by a track-boat..to New Orleens. 1887 Sir R. H. Roberts In the Shires i. 10 [He] sticks his tongue in his cheek, and whispers to his neighbour. 1928 Observer 19 Feb. 5/1, I must confess my utter inability to grasp what Mr. B. Nicholson is after, though I am loath to believe that he painted his apparently flippant still life arrangements with his tongue in his cheek.

16. tongue ordeal, a form of ordeal in which torture is applied to the tongue; **tongue-speaker, -speech** (cf. sense 8 c and tongue-speaking in Dict.); **tongue traction**, rhythmic traction of the tongue applied in cases of asphyxia; **tongue tremor**, a tremor of the tongue used as a diagnostic in neurology.

1921 Hastings's Encycl. Relig. & Ethics XII. 384/2 Reference to the *tongue-ordeal among E. African natives was recently made in the British House of Commons. 1910 Ibid. III. 370/2 The *tongue-speaker' needed as his complement the 'interpreter'. Ibid. 371/1 The Pauline notices of '*tongue-speech' are concerned only with the Corinthian Church. 1901 Dorland Med. Dict. (ed. 2), *Tongue traction. 1902 Chambers's Jrnl. Oct. 682/2 The animal recovered after two and a half hours tongue-traction. 1907 Practitioner Apr. 521 Fine lip-tremor and coarse *tongue-tremor noted.

Tonguing, vbl. sb. **b.** Add: Also attrib., as tonguing plane.

1895 Army & Navy Co-op. Soc. Price List 992 Tongueing and grooving planes.

Tonk (tɒŋk), v. [Echoic.] trans. To strike vigorously. So **Tonk** sb.

1910 A. A. Milne Day's Play 114 Wanting four to win, I fairly tried to tonk the leather. 1922 Chambers's Jrnl. 801/2 Such a shot was, after all, merely a plain, straight, ordinary sort of tonk.

Tonnelle (tonɛ·l). [Fr., = Tunnel sb.] An arbour.

1861 Thackeray Round. Papers (1863) 219 Those who will sit down under my tonnelle, and have a half-hour's drink and gossip. a 1922 Sir H. Jones Old Memories (1923) 160, I can even yet see him sitting peaceably, sheltering from the heat in our vine tonnelle.

Tonner. (Earlier U.S. example.)

1851 A. O. Hall Manhattaner N. Orleans 177 A seven hundred tonner,..full of Dutch emigrants.

Tonsillectomy (tɒnsil,e·ktŏmi). Surg. [f. L. tonsilla Tonsil + Gr. ἐκτομή (f. ἐκ out + τέμνειν to cut) + -y ³.] Surgical excision of the tonsils. So **Tonsille·ctome**, an instrument for performing this.

1901 Dorland Med. Dict. (ed. 2). 1912 Medical Annual 539 The average tonsillectomy is attended by much more pain than tonsillotomy. 1913 Ibid. 636 Tonsillectome.—This instrument..has been designed by Dr. O'Malley as a modification of the instrument designed by Ballenge of Chicago. 1932 Oxford Times 23 Sept. 22/7 It would be a mistake to suppose that tonsilectomy [sic]..is indicated only where there is throat trouble.

Tony, a. Add: U.S. (Earlier example.)

1880 Harper's Mag. Jan. 209/2 He just put on heaps of style..you know—regular tony.

2. A fashion colour between red and brown; also as sb.

1922 Daily Mail 13 Dec. 1 All-Wool Brushed Hose..In these Heather tones: Green, Toney, Brown. 1923 Ibid. 4 July 14 In Black, White, Toney, Grey, Silver. 1927 W. E. Collinson Contemp. Engl. 61 Brogues..sometimes of ox-blood or tony red colour.

Too, adv. Add: **1.** (Mod. U.S. example of use at the beginning of a clause.)

1930 Publishers' Weekly 17 May 2514/2 Too, chain store merchandising tactics are the result..of the keenest, most skilful and most highly paid retailing brains in this country.

4. c. (Example of predicative use with a person.)

1881 Punch 26 Nov. 241/2 We are not prone to take offence. If people say we're not 'intense'—Or hint we're not 'too-too'!

Toodle-oo (tūd'l,ū·), int. [Apparently imitating the hoot of a motor-horn.] A jocular parting greeting.

1907 Punch 26 June 465 'Toodle-oo, old sport.' Mr. Punch turned round at the amazing word and gazed at his companion. 1919 P. G. Wodehouse My Man Jeeves 86 Toodle-oo, Bertie, old man. See you later. 1920—Damsel in Distress xv, Toodle-oo, laddie! We shall meet anon.

Tool, v. Add: **1. d.** trans. To manipulate. ? U.S.

1922 Titus Timber xvii. 158 The fish struck!..His left arm tooled the line carefully as he gave out.

e. To provide or equip with tools.

1927 Observer 25 Sept. 4 The work of tooling up the Manchester and Cork factories may result in production within the next two months.

2. c. intr. To take one's departure; to move off. slang.

1881 Punch 17 Dec. 285/2 Now we'll just tool off to some quiet sort of a place where we can divide this 'ere shining swag without fireworks.

Tooter.² Add: **3.** One who proclaims loudly.

1863 Rio Abajo Press 19 May 2 Although the nameless party's tooter speaks confidently of the success of its nominee.

4. = Touter 1.

1886 Harper's Mag. Aug. 417/2 The wharf..was alive with vehicles and tooters for the hotels.

Tooth, sb. Add: **8. h.** Long in the tooth: (orig. of horses) displaying the roots of the teeth owing to the recession of the gums with increasing age; hence gen. old.

1919 J. C. Snaith Love Lane xxi, One of the youngest R.A.s on record, but a bit long in the tooth for the army. 1932 Joan Conquest Village Pompadour xxv, Long in the tooth, he escaped the traps laid by widow, débutante and free-lance.

9. toothcomb v. trans., to go through minutely (cf. *Fine tooth a.); **tooth-glass, -mug**, a glass for use when cleaning the teeth; **tooth wash**, a liquid dentifrice.

1924 Glasgow Herald 28 Aug. 4/2 She was a strong woman, well accustomed to '*toothcomb' her husband's MS. 1858 Simmonds Dict. Trade, *Tooth-glass, a toilet water-glass for washing the mouth. 1926 C. Barry Detective's Holiday xii, Everything had been polished and cleaned..so that even the tooth-glass gave no results [sc. finger-prints]. 1891 Outing (U.S.) Dec. 244/2 Some drank their champagne out of *tooth mugs. 1895 Army & Navy Co-op. Soc. Price List 716/2 *Tooth Wash.

Tooth-brush. **b.** Add: tooth-brush glass.

1931 Mellersh Salt of the Earth vii. § 2 Put them [sc. flowers] in the toothbrush glass or something till May can see to them.

Toothpick. **4.** U.S. slang. (Earlier examples.)

1837 Act Alabama Legislature 30 June in Baltimore Comm. Transcr. 21 Sept. 2/4 Any knife or weapon, known as Bowie knives or Arkansaw toothpicks. 1840 Daily Pennant (St. Louis) 20 July (Thornton) The young gentleman who borrowed..an 'Arkansas toothpick' from our office.

Top, sb.¹ Add: **3. c.** (b) Billiards. Top-of-the-table game, play (see quot. 1902).

1902 Encycl. Brit. XXVI. 245/2 This method is known as top-of-the-table play, and may perhaps be best defined as an endeavour, after every cannon, to leave the opponent's ball near the spot and the red ball near a pocket, so that the next stroke may be an easy winning hazard, to be so played that either a spot-stroke or cannon may be left. 1927 Observer 20 Mar. 29 Prior..is essentially an all-round player with a tendency to make the top of the table game his chief scoring medium. Ibid. 27 Mar. 28 The top-of-the-table game..was usually his main scoring method.

d. The summit of the parapet of a trench. Phr. To go over the top (see *Go v. 62); also fig. to take a final or decisive step.

1916, 1917 [see *Go v. 62]. 1923 Publishers' Circular 24 Nov. 703/2 If Canada, metaphorically speaking, 'goes over the top,' it will be against the wishes of the rest of the Empire and against the wishes of her own authors and publishers. 1928 Galsworthy Swan Song III. i. 261 To-morrow she was going 'over the top'.

15. d. pl. (absol. use of top as adj.). Bridge. The two highest cards of a suit.

1929 Work Compl. Contract Bridge Gloss. 246 Tops, Aces and Kings.

26. top-buggy U.S. (earlier examples).

1849 Knickerbocker Mag. XXXIV. 266 An ordinary 'top-buggy' wagon. 1880 'Mark Twain' Tramp Abroad xxxiii. 358 A two-horse top-buggy.

32. top deck (see *Deck sb.¹ 4 b); **top drawer**, also, passing into adj.; **top fermentation** (Brewing), a process in which the yeast rises to the surface during fermentation; also attrib.; **top line**, (b) the headline of a newspaper, etc.; also attrib. and allusively; **top-liner**, one who or that which figures in the top line, at the head, or in the first or principal place; **top trail**, a trail at a higher elevation or higher up the country.

1920 Rose Macaulay Potterism I. i. § 4 The Potter family, however respectable now, wasn't really 'top-drawer'. 1905 J. L. Baker Brewing Industry 100 Brewers' yeast is divided into two classes, *top fermentation and bottom fermentation yeast. 1928 Boston Even. Transcript 30 Mar. 15/6 This big '*top line' caught my eye: 'The Pocasset filicide.' 1928 Daily Express 31 July 13/7 The top-line contest on Saturday next is that between Jack Stanley, of Deptford, and Gipsey Daniels, of Wales. 1930 Cambridge Daily News 25 Sept. 4/5 Two former working men are taking the 'top line' rôle at a West End music hall next week. 1904 'O. Henry' Cabbages & Kings vi. 101 You remember the old *top-liner in the copy book—'Honesty is the Best Policy'? 1904 N. Y. Evening Post 15 July 7 Juvenile 'comedians'.. who look forward eagerly to the time when they will be 'top liners' on some vaudeville stage. 1919 Performer XXIX. 20/1 The 'top-liner' at the Nelson Palace next week. 1927 Daily Express 9 June 9/1 Kelly's first fight as a top-liner at the Blackfriar's Hall. 1928 Ibid. 19 June 16/1 Every Ascot race is a top-liner. 1930 Sir G. MacMunn Behind Scenes in many Wars 319 Six top-liners, all with 'right of access', an impossible system to co-ordinate. 1924 A. J. Small Frozen Gold i. 30 He babbled..of the endless setbacks that had dogged him all the way down from the *top-trails. 1929 Chambers's Jrnl. Aug. 529/1 Talking is a short suit with mushers of the lonely top-trails, bar when they're riled.

Top, sb.² This word is prob. that used in the slang expression old top = old fellow, old girl.

1923 Wodehouse Inimit. Jeeves ix. 97 So you did, old top, so you did. 1932 A. J. Worrall Eng. Idioms 56, I say, old top! Do you like these?

Topchee (tōu·ptʃī). Also 7 topagee, toptchi, 9 tope-, topdji, topgey. [Hind. tōp-chī, f. Pers. توپ tōp cannon.] A term employed in the East for a gunner or artilleryman.

1683 in Foster Engl. Factories India (1908) 234 They delivered mee..into the hands of the Topagee. 1668 Rycaut Pres. State Ottoman Empire 200 The Toptchi. These are Gunners..; their quarters are at Tophana, or the place of Guns in the Suburbs of Constantinople. 1828 J. B. Fraser Kuzzilbash I. 337 The men..bore down like lightning on the topechees. 1867 Simmonds Dict. Trade Suppl., Topdjis, militia artillerymen in Turkey. 1918 E. S. Farrow Dict. Mil. Terms, Topgeys, the term for Turkish artillerymen or gunners.

Topical, a. (sb.) **B.** sb. Add: **2.** A film dealing with topical events.

1915 B. E. Jones Cinematograph Bk. 33 Something may here be said about topicals, or 'newsy' films. 1917 C. N. Bennett Guide to Kinematog. 123 Local Topicals..Generally speaking, fourpence or fivepence a foot will be the most a country showman will pay for a local topical. 1923 F. A. Talbot Moving Pictures 180 The topical..has been crushed out of existence by the thousand-foot standardisation of the reel.

Topkhana (tōu·pkānă). India. Also 7 tophana, 8 -conna, -khonnah, 9 tope-. [Hind. tōpkhāna, f. tōp (see *Topchee) + خانه khāna department.] An armoury or arsenal; spec. the Ordnance Department or Artillery.

1668 Tophana [see *Topchee]. 1765 Holwell Hist. Events (1766) I. 96 By the treachery of the Tope Khonnah Droger, the cannon were loaded with powder only. 1901 Kipling Kim iii. 67, I have known Him since he was a lieutenant in the top-khana (the Artillery).

Topmostly (tɒ·pmoustli), adv. U.S. [f. Topmost a. + -ly ².] Mainly, principally.

a 1861 T. Winthrop Life in Open Air (1863) 34 A Dish of Pork-and-beans. Topmostly this. There were lesser viands, buttresses to this towering triumph.

Topping, ppl. a. **4.** U.S. (Earlier examples.)

1815 D. Humphreys Yankey in Eng. 30 She's lofty—topping—has her highs—sometimes. 1852 Mrs. Stowe Uncle Tom's C. xxix, She'd..have me know..that I wasn't going to be so topping as I had been.

Toquilla (toki·lʲa). [Sp. toquilla small head-dress of gauze, f. toca Toque.] The palm-like screw-pine, Carludovica palmata, of Ecuador, the leaves of which are used to make Panama hats.

1876 Encycl. Brit. VII. 647/2 The leaves of the toquilla.. furnish material for the well-known hats. 1924 Countries of World III. 1713/1 The toquilla palm yields the leaf-fibre for the famous 'Panama' hats of Ecuador.

Torbanitic (tǫbăni·tik), a. [f. Torbanite + -ic.] Of, pertaining to, or resembling torbanite.

1925 Glasgow Herald 3 Aug. 4 It is to..the torbanitic cannels that we must look: their value as a source of oil is assured.

Torch, sb. **1. b.** Add: Phr. To hand on the torch: to pass on a tradition of duty or work, esp. with implication of continuing the work of enlightenment. Also in similar phr.

After L. lampada tradere, Gr. λαμπάδα παραδιδόναι, a metaphor from the Grecian torch-race, in which a lighted torch was held, and passed from each runner to the next. (Cf. Lamp sb.¹ 1 c.)

1887 Q. Rev. Oct. 276 Her [sc. Italy's] work has been done among the nations, and in their turn France, England and Germany hand on the torch. 1912 E. Gosse Portr. & Sk. p. viii, They were all..engaged in keeping bright, and in passing on unquenched, the torch of literary tradition. 1932 L. Golding Magnolia Street I. xi. § 1 He had sometimes hoped that in Max a son was born to him who would take the torch from his dying hand and jump on to the platform he had vacated. 1932 C. C. Abbott Early Med. Fr. Lyrics p. xxv, Those 'beaux Sonnetz'..handed on the torch of courtly love for good and ill to the Elizabethans.

Toric, a. Add: Toric lens, a spectacle lens characterized by having one of its surfaces a segment of an equilateral zone of a torus. Also ellipt. as sb.

Torii (tǫ·ri,i). [Jap.] A gateway in the enclosure of a Japanese temple consisting of two uprights and two cross-pieces, the lower straight and the upper curved and projecting.

1727 Scheuchzer tr. Kæmpfer's Hist. Japan III. ii. 208 At the entry of the walk, which leads to the temple, stands,

..a particular fashion'd gate, called Torij, and built either of stone or wood. 1874 Satow in Trans. Asiatic Soc. Japan II. 116 The torii gradually assumed the character of a general symbol of Shintô. 1877 W. E. Griffis Mikado's Empire I. x. 98 Before each temple stood a torii, or bird-rest. 1904 Sladen Playing the Game II. v, Tall torii, those mystic arches of Japan. 1910 Fergusson Ind. & Eastern Archit. I. iv. I. 118 The 'tori-is' in the latter [sc. Japan] are copies ..of these Sânchi gateways.

Tormentor. Add: **3. e.** (b) A screen employed in sound-recording: see quot.

1929 Photoplay Apr., Tormentor, a large portable wall draped with special material to prevent echo and resonance on the sound set.

Toroid (tǫ·roid), a. and sb. [f. Torus + -oid.] **a.** adj. Of or pertaining to a torus (Torus 4). **b.** sb. A figure of toroidal shape, spec. an astatic (fieldless) inductance coil of this shape.

1903 Astrophys. Jrnl. XVIII. 339 Each reflecting surface, according to this plan, would be part of a parabolic toroid. 1927 Glasgow Herald 3 Oct. 10 New coils, such as the.. 'Toroid.'

Torpedo, sb. Add: **2.** (Earlier U.S. example.)

1776 J. Thacher Milit. Jrnl. (1823) 75 Mr. Bushnell gave to his machine the name of American Turtle or Torpedo.

b. A similar missile discharged by aircraft. Also attrib.

1916 Boyd Cable Action Front 182 The terrific detonation of an aerial torpedo. 1922 Raleigh War in the Air I. 467 The hope of using the torpedo, launched from the air, against ships which are sheltered and protected from naval attack, was never long absent from the minds of those who directed the activities of the Royal Naval Air Service. 1932 19th Cent. Feb. 204 Twenty-six flights of torpedo bombers.

3. e. In gold-washing: see quot.

1882 A. G. Lock Gold iii. 862 The torpedo is a sloping (upwards) iron plate 4 ft. long, of the same width as the floor of the tom where it is joined to the latter, but narrowing considerably towards the end where it meets a riffle. There is a false bottom similarly perforated in the torpedo, and another in the launder leading away from the riffle...If the torpedo is properly arranged, no gold should be found beyond the riffle.

f. A type of car-body shaped like a torpedo.

1909 Daily Chron. 13 Nov. 9/6 There is a general tendency..to utilise the form of body known as the 'torpedo'. 1928 V. Palmer Passage III. i, Another car coming! They ..watched with strained eyes as the dusty torpedo shot into view.

4. in senses 2, *2 b, as torpedo-carrier, -carrying adj., -coxswain, -gunner, -releasing adj.; also **torpedo-aircraft**, aircraft able to discharge marine torpedoes; **torpedo-plane, -seaplane**, a torpedo-carrying seaplane; **torpedo-ship**, a ship designed to employ torpedoes; **torpedo-sight**, the apparatus used in aiming a torpedo.

1922 Raleigh War in the Air I. 469 In any future war.. *torpedo aircraft will prove to be a weapon of enormous power. 1928 C. F. S. Gamble North Sea Air Station v. 85 The two machines..were also intended to be *torpedo-carriers. 1922 Raleigh War in the Air I. 466 The *torpedo-carrying aeroplane or seaplane would outrival the submarine as a weapon of offence against enemy shipping. 1923 Kipling Land & Sea Tales 107 If his *torpedo-coxswain had ever allowed any one to look there. 1928 C. F. S. Gamble North Sea Air Station xiv. 234 The crew consisted of the pilot, the observer, the *torpedo-gunner, and a machine-gunner for the back seat. 1923 Daily Mail 26 June 9 Such 'slotted' wings ..have been incorporated in one of our new British *torpedo-planes. 1928 C. F. S. Gamble North Sea Air Station xiv. 234 A separate seaplane Command was formed..for the torpedo-plane flights for Zeebrugge and the eastern Baltic. Ibid., The *torpedo-releasing gear was also entirely satisfactory. 1922 Raleigh War in the Air I. 467 When H.M.S. Engadine was fitted out as a carrier..it was..stated..that her business was to carry *torpedo seaplanes to the scene of action. 1911 Q. Rev. Oct. 476 This gradual merging of the essential features of the gun-ship and the *torpedo-ship is now about to find expression in the submarine.

Torque ². Add: **c. torque brake**, a water-brake which works by means of a torque; **torque diagram**, a diagram showing a twisting force.

1922 Encycl. Brit. XXX. 35/1 Later the Escargot reaction *torque brake was evolved, corresponding in principle to the Heenan and Froude water brake. 1913 W. E. Dommett Motor Car Mech. 25 One diagram will do, yet..for future use in connexion with *torque diagrams [etc.]. Ibid. 35 We are now in a position to obtain a Torque or Crank Effort Diagram.

d. Optics. 'The twisting or rotatory effect of certain crystals and liquids upon the plane of polarization of light traversing them' (Webster 1911).

Torridonian (tɒridōu·niăn), a. and sb. Geol. [f. Loch Torridon in Ross-shire, Scotland.] (Of or pertaining to) the sedimentary pre-Cambrian sandstone occurring in N.W. Scotland. Also To·rridon attrib.

1885 Lyell Elem. Geol. (ed. 4) Index, Torridon Sandstone. 1893 Geikie Text-bk. Geol. (ed. 3) 699 Torridonian, dull red sandstones, shales and conglomerates attaining a thickness of at least 8,000 or 10,000 feet. Ibid. 706 The Torridon sandstone has been shorn from the mass of these formations below ground. 1902 Encycl. Brit. XXVIII. 655/2 This sedimentary accumulation is known as Torridonian from its large development in the district around Loch Torridon. 1930 Peach & Horne Geol. Scotl. 46 The old Archæan floor on which the Torridonian and Cambrian strata were deposited.

Torse (tǫɹs), a. Forestry. [f. as Torse ³.] Denoting wood having a natural spiral twist.

1908 W. R. Fisher tr. R. Gayer's Forest Utilization (ed. 2) 129 Twisted wood, or rather torse wood, for twisting implies an external force acting on the wood, may be left-inclined or right-inclined.

Tort (tǫɹt), v. Zool. [f. L. tort-, pa. ppl. stem of torquēre to twist.] intr. Of gasteropods: To undergo torsion in development.

1930 G. R. de Beer Embryol. & Evol. vii. 54 There is no possibility..of mistaking these detorting forms for the 'torting' forms for which we search in vain.

Tortillon (tǫrti·lʲɒn). [Fr., f. tortiller to screw up.] A stump made of paper rolled to a point for use in charcoal- or chalk-drawing.

a 1891 F. Fowler Charcoal Drawing 12 (Cent. Dict.). 1895 Army & Navy Co-op. Soc. Price List 674/2 Stumps for chalk drawing...Tortillons, White.

Tortoise. **4.** Add: **tortoise (-shaped) core** Archæol., a core (Core sb.¹ 5) resembling a tortoise in shape; **tortoise-tick**, a South African tick, Amblyomma hebræum, parasitic on sheep.

1919 R. A. Smith in Man July 101 *Tortoise-cores have been found on the bank of the ancient river to the south-east...Several hand-axes, but no tortoise-cores, have been found in the conglomerate. 1911 — in Archæologia LXII. II. 523 *Tortoise-shaped cores. This is perhaps the most striking group in the enormous series from Northfleet. 1905 Rep. Brit. Assoc. 553 Amblyomma hebræum, commonly known as the *tortoise tick.

Tortoise-shell. **5.** Add: **tortoiseshell worker**, one who makes articles in tortoiseshell.

1931 P. A. S. Phillips John Obrisset Title-p., Huguenot Carver, Medallist, Horn and Tortoiseshell Worker.

Tortula (tǫ·ɹtiulă). [mod.L. (Hedwig), f. L. tortus twisted + -ula, dim. suffix; in allusion to the twisted peristome.] A moss of the genus so named; a screw-moss.

1925 Public Opinion 6 Mar. 228/2 On each old roof or dyke will be the little bosses of tortula, the wall-screw. 1928 Bryologist XXXI. 124 The collection of Mosses, forty in number,..mostly comprised plants of dry exposed habitats, such as Grimmias, Weisias, Pottias, Tortulas [etc.].

Hence **Tortulaceous** (tǫɹtiulē·ʃəs) a., of, pertaining to, or resembling the genus Tortula or the Tortulaceæ.

1928 Bryologist XXXI. 125 Crossidium squamigerum (Viv.) Jur., a Tortulaceous moss having leaves with very long white hair points.

Torture, v. **3. b.** Add: Also with into.

1789 J. Moore Zeluco (1797) I. ix. 79 What he said was excusable; to endeavour to torture it into mutiny would be absurd. a 1849 Poe Tales of Mystery (1905) 365 An unredeemed dreariness of thought which no goading of the imagination could torture into aught of the sublime. 1857 J. Hyde, Jr. Mormonism iii. 65 A look,..a visit, above all when it is repeated, is tortured into 'Proof strong as holy writ'. 1866 Augusta Wilson St. Elmo xii, You torture my words into an interpretation of which I never dreamed.

Torulin (tǫ·riulin). Biol. Chem. [f. Torula + -in ¹.] The anti-neuritic vitamin of yeast.

1912 Biochem. Jrnl. VI. 234 A method of isolation of torulin, the anti-neuritic base of yeast. 1930 Ibid. XXIV. II. 1820 A quantitative comparison of the curative activity of torulin (vitamin B) upon the adult pigeon and the adult white rat.

Toss, sb.¹ Add: **3. b.** A throw from a horse, esp. in phr. to take a toss. Also transf. and fig.

1917 'Ian Hay' Petit-Jean, Golly! He took a toss and a half! 1923 Westm. Gaz. 14 Mar., The Prince of Wales took a toss in the second race. 1928 Byrne Destiny Bay vii. § 4. 335 The lad up seemed like taking a toss.

6. toss and catch = Pitch and toss. U.S.

1904 Atlantic Monthly Oct. 477 The smutty-handed Smoot playing at toss and catch with his conscience and honor.

Totalitarian (totælitē·riăn), a. Civics. [f. Totality + *-arian.] Of or pertaining to a polity which permits no rival loyalties or parties.

1928 Contemp. Rev. Apr. 453 Fascism renounces its function as a totalitarian régime, and enters the electoral field on equal footing with its adversaries. 1929 Times 2 Nov. 7/5 A reaction against parliamentarism..in favour of a 'totalitarian' or unitary state, whether Fascist or Communist.

Tote, sb.¹ **2.** Read: orig. Australian colloq. and add: attrib.: **tote club**, a club in which a totalisator machine or system is used; **tote double**, a double with totalisator odds; hence tote-double v.; **tote-house**, a house where a totalisator is in operation.

1913 Chambers's Jrnl. Feb. 155/1 There were gaming or 'tote' houses by the score [in Australia]. 1927 Times 28 Oct. (leading art.) Betting on the 'Tote'. 1928 Galsworthy Swan Song II. ii. 113 Jack Cardigan, from his front seat, had begun explaining a thing he called the 'tote'. It seemed to be a machine that did your betting for you. 1930 Cambridge Daily News 25 Sept. 5/7 In the Tote Double on the 2.30..the winning dividend was £10 13s. 9d. 1930 Daily Express 6 Nov. 10/3, I have any number of friends who think that the Tote double was their invention. Ibid., Every one is Tote doubling.

Tote, v. U.S. colloq. Add: To tote tales, to carry tales.

1901 Harben Westerfelt ii. 27, I never was much of a hand to tote tales.

Tother, pron. and a. Add: **A. 1.** Phr. To tell tother from which, jocular variant of to tell one from the other.

1914 Concise Oxf. Dict. Addenda.

Toto ¹ (tōu·to), hypocoristic f. Hippopotamus.

1916 Chambers's Jrnl. Nov. 719/2 The poor little 'toto', bereft of its mother.

Toto ² (tōu·to). War slang. [Fr. slang.] A louse.

[1918 E. S. Farrow Dict. Mil. Terms, Toto, a French slang term applied to the vermin in the trenches. 1925 E. Fraser & Gibbons Soldier & Sailor Words, Toto, vermin: lice. The universal French Army word..to some extent taken up by the British on the Western Front.] 1929 B. Hall & J. J. Niles One Man's War 46, I do not know who developed lice first, but I noticed them on that march. We called them 'totos'.

Tottlish, a. (See Tottle v.¹; earlier U.S. quot.)

1835 Knickerbocker Mag. VI. 6 Had she not been obliged ..to steady her tottleish bark with the paddle which now loitered behind the stern.

Totum ³. (Modern example.)

1927 A. H. McNeile Introd. N.T. 156 The influence of the epistle on the totum of Christian thought.

Touareg, -rick, variants of *Tuareg.

Touch-. Add: **1. a.** touch-organ, -paralysis, -spot. **b. touch-typist, -writer**, one who types solely by touch.

1924 R. M. Ogden tr. Koffka's Growth of Mind 251 The original *touch-organ of the suckling is not the hand, but the mouth. 1897 Brit. Med. Jrnl. II. 787/2 On '*touch paralysis', or the inability to recognise the nature of objects by tactile impressions. 1927 Haldane & Huxley Anim. Biol. v. 122 The fineness of discrimination for touch depends mainly on the closeness of *touch-spots. 1915 Literary Digest (N.Y.) 21 Aug. Advt. p. i, Great numbers were so-called *touch-writers—yet there has hardly been a single one who hasn't doubled or trebled his or her speed and accuracy.

2. touch-last, a game in which the player last touched is 'it'.

1927 Sunday Express 17 July 8/2 The younger and sprightlier guests..played 'touch last' on the lawn.

Toucher. Add: **1. d.** (Cf. Touch v. 16 b.)

1904 Chicago Tribune 30 Oct., The salaried clerk who keeps his wife and a pug dog at a fashionable hotel is, usually a toucher of the kind that makes a bold front.

Tough, a. **6.** Add: In mod. slang use.

1929 Wodehouse Mr. Mulliner Speaking i. 34, 'I suppose it's because I'm rather an out-size and modelled on the lines of Cleopatra.' 'Tough!' 'You bet it's tough. A girl can't help her appearance.'

Tough, v. U.S. slang. [f. Tough a.] With it: To rough it.

1830 Mass. Spy 27 Jan. (Th.), Judy with whom he had toughed it three years. 1834 S. Smith Major Jack Downing (1860) 26 (Th.), We little fellows had to tuff it out as well as we could. 1873 Celia Thaxter Isle of Shoals 64 (Th.), Our brave little schooner 'toughed it out' on the distant ledge.

Toungya, var. of *Taungya.

Tour, v. Add: **5.** intr. Of a car: To run at slow speed.

1908 Isle of Man Weekly Times 12 Sept. 4/1 All the cars simply toured along. 1927 Peel City Guardian 18 June 6/5 Bennett's engine had given out..and he came touring in, and retired. Ibid. 10 Sept., On this lap No. 26..retired ..while No. 21..toured in..with tyre trouble.

Tourer (tūə·rəɹ). [f. Tour v. + -er ¹.] **1.** A touring-car.

1927 Sunday Pictorial 28 Aug. 8/4 Two and five-seater tourers will be £495. 1929 Star 21 Aug. 13/3 Self-drive Sal[oon]s, tourers fr. 17/6 day.

2. One who tours or goes on tour.

1931 Times Lit. Suppl. 1 Oct. 746/3 Mürren..tends to breed racers, the other [sc. Maloja] tourers.

Touring, vbl. sb. **b.** Add: **touring-car** (earlier U.S. example); **touring-sedan** U.S., a touring-car with sedan body.

1903 Encycl. Amer. II. s.v. Automobile, Gasoline *Touring Cars. 1915 Literary Digest (N.Y.) 21 Aug. Cover advt., The *touring Sedan, for all seasons.

Tourmaliniferous (tūəɹmălini·fərəs), a. Geol. [f. Tourmaline + -iferous.] Containing tourmaline.

1905 F. W. Rudler Handbk. Coll. Min. Brit. Isl. 28 Rocks which are stanniferous, whether granite or killas, are almost invariably tourmaliniferous.

Tourmente (turmā̃nt). [Fr.:—L. tormenta, pl. of tormentum Torment.] A heavy (snow) storm: see Torment sb. 5.

1847, 1909 [see Torment sb. 5]. 1928 Blackw. Mag. May 601/1 Above the bowl of the tourmente came the crash of falling rocks.

Tournette (tūəɹne·t). Pottery. [Fr., f. tourner to Turn.] A rotating disk resembling a potter's wheel.

1927 Peake & Fleure Peasants & Potters 47 The pots were made on a tournette, a slow wheel turned by hand.

Tout, v.¹ Add: **3. b.** trans. **a.** To importune (a person) in a touting manner. **b.** To solicit custom for (a thing).

1928 Daily Tel. 5 May 9/6 It strikes one as..unfair for bankers to tout their clients for..investment business. 1930 Mottram Europa's Beast vii. 164 He was involved in the ghastly job of touting motor cars.

Tow, sb.¹ **4. a.** Add (Amer. uses): tow-cloth (earlier examples), -hat, linen, -shirt, string, -trousers (earlier example).

1706 Boston News-Letter 18 Nov., Ran-away..A Scotch Young man..hath with him..two Jackets..the uppermost ..lined with brown linen called western *Tow-cloth. 1746 Ibid. 17 July, A Negro Man Servant..had on..a good Tow cloth Shirt. 1838 Knickerbocker Mag. XII. 325 His serene head overshadowed by a vast canopy of a *tow-hat. 1792 Ann. 2nd Congress 1000 Great quantities of..counterpanes, *tow linens, coarse shirtings..are made in the household way. 1843 R. Carlton New Purchase xi. 79 His tow-linen trowsers. 1884 'Mark Twain' Huck. Finn xx, Some of the children didn't have on any clothes but just a tow-linen shirt. 1739

Boston News-Letter 18 Oct., An Indian Lad..had on..an old *tow Shirt. 1856 Mrs. Stowe Dred I. xiii. 186 She is one of the *tow-string order of women. 1881 J. W. Buel Border Outlaws 61 Rope and towstrings held many of the broken parts of the bridle together. 1767 Virginia Gaz. 11 June, Michael Murray, an Irishman..had on..*tow trousers.

Towable (tōu·ăb'l), a. [f. Tow v.¹ + -able.] That may be towed.

1927 Glasgow Herald Jan. 7 The dock..is towable to any part of Australia.

Towel, sb. Add: **1. b.** Phr. To throw (or toss) in the towel: to admit defeat. orig. Boxing.

1915 Corri 30 Yrs. Boxing Referee 223 In the nineteenth round Storbeck's seconds 'threw the towel' in literally. 1916 C. J. Dennis Ginger Mick 132 I've done me limit, an' tossed in the tow'l. 1921 Daily Tel. 13 Sept. 8/7 Joe Beckett defeated Boy McCormick in the 12th round, the latter's seconds throwing in the towel.

Tower, sb.¹ Add: **5. d.** A railway signal-box. U.S.

1904 N. Y. Times 5 May 1 A switch operated from the main tower at the terminal was so thrown as to shunt the outgoing train over toward the incoming. 1910 H. A. Franck Vagabond Journey 328 A man in the neighboring tower opened the block, and the diminutive freight screamed by us.

10. tower-man U.S., a man in charge of a signal-box on a railway; **tower-shell**, a gasteropod of the Turritellidæ.

1908 Atlantic Monthly Nov., Advt. 42 A practical railroad man, a tower man of long experience. 1888 Cassell's Encycl. Dict., *Tower-shell. 1927 Haldane & Huxley Anim. Biol. xii. 300 One fossil tower-shell stands nearly five feet high.

Tow-head. U.S. See Tow sb.¹ 4 c; also, a slight obstruction in a stream causing a white ripple or foam at the surface.

1829 S. Cummings Western Pilot 7 There are..a great number of tow-heads and sand-bars. 1830 Anne Royall Southern Tour I. 92 One insolent little tow-head. 1847 Indiana Mag. Hist. VIII. 273 [We] cut loose and run all islands and towheads to the right. 1868 Putnam's Mag. I. May 596/1 The snags, the sawyers, the bars, the 'tow-heads', ..phenomena of the Mississippi. 1883 'Mark Twain' Life Mississippi xxiii. 262 A large town which lay shut in behind a tow-head (i.e., new island).

So **Tow-headed** a.

1850 S. Judd R. Edney xlix. 450 Bronze-faced and tow-headed Wild Olive boys. 1880 'Mark Twain' Tramp Abroad xxiii. 224 A loose-jointed, long-legged, tow-headed, jeans-clad, countrified cub of about sixteen.

Towkay (tau·kei). A Chinese head man or mandarin.

1923 Weekly Dispatch 18 Mar. 8, I was invited by a Chinese 'Towkay' (i.e., 'a big pot') to a dinner to commemorate the marriage of his son. 1924 British Weekly 11 Sept. 511/5 In a comfortable lounge chair reclined the towkay smoking his opium pipe. 1928 Blackw. Mag. Apr. 469/2 If he had found anything good, he would have rushed into some Chinese towkay, and had him out..within twenty-four hours.

Town, sb. Add: **8. b.** Also, woman about town.

1927 Manch. Guardian Weekly Jan. 75/1 Another surrender to the woman-about-town who wants a different kind of entertainment.

10. town-plat U.S. (earlier examples); **town-platting** U.S., town-planning.

1656 Connecticut Colonial Rec. I. 282 Thos persons that cohabitt in the *towne platte. 1723 Waterbury Propr. Rec. 121 To settle the old Town platt Lotts. 1895 Century Mag. Aug. 638/2 The troop of boom-makers has actively given its perennial leisure to extravagant schemes of *town-platting.

Tow·n-plan, v. Add: Also trans.

1912 [in Dict.]. 1933 Morn. Post 27 Mar. 11 The most effective means of..protecting..the amenities of the district would be to town plan the area at once.

Townsman. Add: **4.** In various senses: see quots.

1881 Instr. Census Clerks (1885) 32 Merchants and Agents. ..Tourist Agent. Townsman. Turkey Broker. Ibid. 34 Other Railway Officials and Servants...Traffic Canvasser, Solicitor, or Townsman. 1921 Dict. Occup. Terms (1927) 700 Townsman, traffic solicitor. Ibid. § 719 Townsman, drives horse and van delivering goods from town shopkeepers to customers in countryside. Ibid. § 774 Townsman, canvasser who confines his selling to towns.

Towny, sb. **3.** (Earlier and later examples.)

1834 Knickerbocker Mag. IV. 279 Five or six fellows, whom I knew were friends and 'townies' of his. 1928 Chambers's Jrnl. Jan. 10/2 We're townies, ain't we?

Tow-path. (Earlier U.S. examples.)

1788 Washington Diaries III. 361 A tow path on the Maryland side. 1838 Indiana Ho. Repres. Jrnl. 74 To inquire into the expediency of constructing a tow-path from the St. Joseph Feeder Dam, along the pool of said Dam to Leedarville.

Toxi-. Add: **Toxi-infe·ction**, infection due to a toxin. **Toxi-tube·rculide**, a tuberculide caused by tubercular toxin.

1901 Dorland Med. Dict. (ed. 2), *Toxi-infection, infection by toxins or other poisonous agents. 1908 Practitioner Mar. 412 The influence of hypophysial opotherapy in toxi-infections. Ibid. Jan. 23 French dermatologists..have classified the disease [sc. lupus erythematosus] as a '*toxi-tuberculide'. 1913 Dorland Med. Dict. (ed. 7), Toxi-tuberculid.

Toxo-². Add: **Toxoge·nesis**, the production of a toxin. **Toxo·lysis**, the dissolution of a toxin.

1907 Practitioner Apr. 500 The vital problems are those of toxogenesis and toxolysis.

Toy, sb. Add: **9. b.** (Example.)

1855 [see *Hyacinth 3 b].

11. a, d. toy pistol; **toy-cap**, an explosive cap used in toy pistols; **toy drama**, drama for a toy-theatre; **toy-theatre**, a puppet theatre; also fig.

1897 Strand Mag. May 499/2 On the 14th of May, 1878, occurred a disastrous explosion of *toy-caps. 1931 N. & Q. 11 Apr. 253/2 Mr. Webb was the principal exhibitor at an exhibition of the *toy drama, held at the Faculty of Arts Gallery in August, 1926. 1883 *toy pistol cap; 1889 toy pistol [see *Amorce]. 1929 Johannesburg Sunday Times 12 May in N. & Q. (1931) 253/2 Since Stevenson wrote..his survey of the *toy theatre..articles have appeared ..on the juvenile drama. 1931 A. C. Ward Found. Engl. Prose 98–9 Stevenson loved to play with toy-theatres, and all his novels, with one exception, are reflected through the toy-theatre temperament; life is not in them.

Trace, sb.¹ Add: **6. d.** Meteorol. 'An amount of rainfall too small to be registered: abbreviated "T"'.

1928 Funk's Standard Dict.

Trace, sb.² **3.** Add: To break a trace, etc.

c 1845 W. T. Porter Big Bear Arkansas 101 You must marry that gal and no mistake, or brake a trace! 1871 Harper's Mag. Dec. 155/2, I do not feel that I ever was out of that party. I may have got one leg over the traces, but I was in the harness all the while.

Trace, v.¹ **6. b.** (Earlier U.S. example.)

1876 Rep. Vermont Board Agric. III. 107 The farmer loses sight of the fact that the character of the calf..may 'trace back', as it is termed, to a remote ancestor.

Trace, v.³ **1.** Add: Also with up.

1884 Vermont Agric. Rep. VIII. 285 The ears thus selected should be 'traced up' and hung away to dry.

Tracer ¹. Add: **4.** A bullet or shell emitting a trail of smoke by day and a flame or light by night, by which its flight may be traced in order to test correctness of range; used against aircraft: in full tracer bullet, shell. Also, the trail of smoke emitted.

1910 Blackw. Mag. July 6/2 The projectiles of airship guns may possibly give out a jet of flame and a smoke 'tracer' on discharge. 1916 Globe 23 Feb. 2/2 Both the tracer shells.. burst comparatively close to the airship. 1918 Boyd Cable Air Men o' War 22 note, Tracer bullets emit smoke and flame to allow the shooter to follow their flight. 1922 Encycl. Brit. XXX. 120/2 For night use the tracer shows a luminous spark, for day use the tracer gives a smoky trail.

Tracery. Add: **2.** Stump tracery: see Stump sb.¹ 18.

3. In lace-making, an added decorative pattern, used esp. in making pillow- or bobbin-lace.

1882 Caulfeild & Saward Dict. Needlework 498/2 Honiton Pillow Lace making is often enriched with Tracery, which is a kind of raised work, formed over a background of Cloth and Half Stitch.

Track, sb. Add: **4.** Also, the line of motion of the propeller-blades of an aircraft.

1928 V. Page Mod. Aircraft 442 In mounting propellers, great care should be taken that both blades rotate in the same plane. This is termed the 'track' of the propeller.

6. c. Each of the bands of a caterpillar tractor: see *Caterpillar 1 b. Also attrib.

1927 M. Terry Through Land of Promise 56 Gears were put in, tracks rattled quietly. 1927 Daily Tel. 10 May 4/5 Three flexible track machines were sent out to Nigeria, two of the metallic and one of the rubber type. 1931 Martel In Wake of Tank 83 The whole of the engine power could be transmitted to the track on the one or the other side of the tank as desired.

d. The transverse distance between a pair of wheels of a vehicle, esp. of an automobile.

1928 Webster Addenda.

13. track circuit, -circuiting, event (example), **-grading, -owner**; **track-layer**, also, one who lays the trail in training dogs to track criminals.

1931 MacDermot Hist. G.W.R. II. 498 *Track circuits, whereby the signals protecting an occupied section of line are electrically locked at Danger, were first introduced in August 1907. 1931 Times Lit. Suppl. 10 Dec. 999/1 *Track circuiting or automatic train control. 1928 Daily Sketch 10 Aug. 2/4 There are bound to be fine finishes in the international *track events. 1901 Chambers's Jrnl. Sept. 631/2 *Track-grading contracts. 1928 Daily Express 19 Sept. 2 Coastguards..acted as *track-layers for the open police dog trials. Ibid. 5 Oct. 2/6 *Track-owners are expected to confer with the National Greyhound Racing Club stewards.

Track, v.¹ Add: **1. c.** (See quot.)

1851 R. Glisan Jrnl. Army Life xxvii. (1874) 382, I observed..that he does not 'track' (step his hind foot straight after the fore one).

2. c. Also with up.

1838 Caroline Gilman Recoll. Southern Matron xviii. 127 Miss Neely, one buckra woman want for track up all de clean floor. 1901 S. Merwin & H. K. Webster Calumet K vi. 117 There's going to be a law passed about tracking mud inside the railing.

3. (U.S. examples.)

1843 R. Carlton New Purchase xxvii. 254 I'll track round a little—I wants any how to go over to the post-office. 1868 Putnam's Mag. I. June 670/1 We tracked through the dirty streets till we got to the house.

Tracked, ppl. a.¹ See after Track v.¹

Tracked (trækt), ppl. a.² [f. Track sb. + -ed ².] Of a vehicle: Furnished with caterpillar-wheels (see *Track sb. 6 c and *Caterpillar 5 b).

1926 Westm. Gaz. 26 Jan., 'Tracked' vehicles, or, as most people would say,..'caterpillar' or roadless tractors. 1928 Daily Tel. 20 Mar. 13/3 Tracked Transport.

Tract, sb.¹ Add: **3. b.** Tract for the times: also used gen. of any literary work put out to meet a particular need of the times.

1927 A. H. McNeile Introd. N.T. 95 The Tübingen conception of the book [of the Acts of Apostles] as a tract for the times mediating between the Judaic and the Pauline factions.

Tractite (træ·ktəit). [f. Tract sb.¹ + -ite ¹.] = Tractarian 2.

1843 Whately in Life & Corr. (1866) II. 45, I hope the 'learning' and the 'architecture' of the Tractites will not lead you any further. 1900 Tuckwell Remin. Oxford 174 He was warned by Whately against Manning..as an undoubted 'Tractite'—so Whately always called them.

Tractor. Add: **2. c.** Also, an automobile used for hauling or drawing; esp. a caterpillar tractor (see *Caterpillar 1 b).

1912 Philistine (U.S.) June 58 We find eight to eighteen plows hitched behind a tractor. 1917 Isle of Ely & Wisbech Adv. 28 Nov., This Tractor will operate on any land...It maintains a firm grip without injuring the lightest surfaces.

d. A screw acting as a tractor in an air-vessel; hence (in full tractor aeroplane, etc.) an aeroplane with one or more propellers or screws in front, as distinguished from a pusher. (Cf. *Pusher 3.)

1903 Work 18 Apr. 171/1 A screw,.., working in front and acting as a tractor. 1912 S. F. Walker Aviation iv. 28 In the later form of biplane, known as the tractor biplane, the engine and propeller are placed in front. 1913 Captain Sept. 1069/2 More biplanes than formerly use tractor screws in front, instead of propellers behind the main planes. 1914 Sphere 7 Mar. 302/3 The Short and Sopwith tractors. 1917 Daily Mail 19 July 4/5 A 'tractor' aeroplane is one in which the propeller is in front of the planes and the pilot. 1918 Blackw. Mag. Mar. 295 The 'tractor' in which you are now taken up is very different from the lumbering old 'pusher' Rumpety. 1919 Athenæum 23 May 360/2 Tractor-plane. 1922 [see *Pusher 3]. 1928 C. F. S. Gamble Story North Sea Air Station iv. 67 He was then of the opinion that 'pusher machines' were superior to 'tractor machines'.

4. attrib. and Comb.: tractor-driven adj.; **tractor-binder**, a mechanically driven binder or harvester; **tractor plough**, a mechanically driven plough; **tractor propeller, screw**, one fitted upon the front of an aeroplane.

1922 Ibid. 24 Nov. 8 He was driving a *tractor-binder through a crop of green wheat. 1921 Discovery Feb. 48/2 He can..use horse- or *tractor-driven machines..without damaging the crop. 1919 Athenæum 23 May 360/2 *Tractor-plough.

Trade, sb. Add: **6. c.** The Trade: the Submarine Service. Navy colloq.

1916 Kipling Sea Warfare 97 No one knows how the title of 'The Trade' came to be applied to the Submarine Service. 1930 W. G. Carr By Guess & by God i. 16 Keeping watch with me on the conning tower was an old-timer of the Trade.

9. (Earlier U.S. examples.)

1772 D. Taitt in Trav. Amer. Col. 533 He would not give them such a good Trade as the people of the Puckantallahassie did. 1802 Steele Papers I. 250, I could not make that trade with James Smith.

12. (Earlier U.S. examples.)

a 1656 Bradford Plymouth Plant. 277 This ship had store of English-beads (which were then good trade). 1802 Ellicott Jrnl. 15 They..made about 30 bushels of salt per day, which sold for 2 dollars cash per bushel, or 3 dollars in trade, as they term it.

14. a, 15. trade-association, -balance, -boom, -depression, -method, -trick; **trade benefit** (see quot. and *Benefit sb. 4 d); **trade calling** Comm. (cf. Call sb. 11); **trade-card**, a tradesman's card bearing his name, the designation of his trade, and place of business; **trade charge** (see quot.); **trade-cycle** (see quot. 1931); **trade discount** (see quot. 1930); also fig.; **trade-room**, a position or opening for trade; **trade show**, a private exhibition at which a new cinematograph film is shown to the trade; hence **trade-show** v.; **trade wastes** or **trades waste** (see quot.).

1928 Britain's Industr. Future (Lib. Ind. Inq.) II. viii. § 3. 98 *Trade Associations are Associations of Traders, Producers, or Employers. Ibid. I. iii. § 4. 26 The increased volume of imports, together with a diminished volume of exports, has made the visible *trade balance much less favourable. 1897 S. & B. Webb Indust. Democracy I. II. i. 153 It [sc. Mutual Insurance] includes also what are often termed *trade' benefits; grants for replacing tools lost [etc.]. 1925 Scribner's Mag. July 59 Nothing in the nature of a '*trade boom' could be discovered. 1930 J. Stephenson Princ. & Pract. Commercial Corr. 157 Some hedge selling and Continental liquidation being well absorbed by month-end *trade calling. 1931 N. & Q. 5 Sept. 173/1 Their two *trade-cards, except for the names, are practically identical. Ibid. 14 Nov. 354/1 An interesting engraved trade-card. Ibid. 19 Dec. 438/1 He issued a trade-card 'at the Seven Stars, over against Chancery Lane, Fleet Street'. 1929 Post Office Guide July 78 The amount to be collected under the Cash on Delivery System is called the '*Trade Charge'. 1928 Britain's Industr. Future (Lib. Ind. Inq.) v. xxviii. § 2. 411 The trade booms..and trade depressions..which were so prominent a feature of the pre-war '*trade cycle'. 1931 Times Lit. Suppl. 28 May 414/2 That alternate insufficiency and excess of world investment in comparison with saving which have become known as the trade cycle. 1928 *trade-depression [see *trade-cycle]. 1902 Windsor Mag. Dec. 199/2 Barclay is simply a surly brute, I never liked him, so you can take the usual *trade discount off my estimate. 1930 M. Clark Home Trade 103 Trade Discount,..an allowance made by one trader to another, usually in the same line of business. 1909 Chambers's Jrnl. July 423/2 Dishonest *trade-methods. 1892 Stevenson & Osbourne Wrecker xxii, Can't you give us a 'dead bird' for a good *trade-room? 1928 Daily Express 11 June 13 'Zero'..is awaiting *trade-show. 1928 Sunday Dispatch 5 Aug. 14 The trade show of

'The Red Dancer of Moscow'. 1928 Daily Express 11 June 13 Three hundred American films will have been *trade-shown in this country. 1911 J. A. Thomson Biol. Seasons II. 196 The *trade-tricks of the Phoenicians. 1902 Encycl. Brit. XXXII. 525/1 We may..enumerate some of the principal *trade wastes [sc. in sewage]; these are from dye-works, print-works, [etc.]. 1903 Sci. Amer. Suppl. 28 Feb. 22713 (Cent. D. Suppl.) In the majority of cases trades waste is likely to be strongly acid or strongly alkaline.

Trade, v. **9.** Add: (U.S. examples.) Also, To trade in: to give used articles in part payment for new ones. Hence **Tra·de-in** attrib. or as adj. U.S.

1793 Mass. Hist. Soc. Coll. III. 1 Good crops of corn and rye, which they trade off for spirituous liquors. 1796 B. Hawkins Lett. 50 He was glad I intended to increase the number, and trade them other useful things. 1927 Observer 21 Aug. 19/2 Americans..call him the 'junk' man because he buys what they call 'traded-in' cars for the purpose of scrapping them...Dealers..who have taken old cars in part purchase of new ones, which is called trading-in. 1929 Collier's 12 Jan. 9/2 If more than one third of his..transactions..is represented by trade-in cars.

Trader. Add: **3.** A horse for trading with. U.S.

1902 A. D. McFaul Ike Glidden viii. 66 All prosperous people there keep a 'driver' and a 'trader'.

Trading, vbl. sb. **b.** Add: trading-boat U.S., trading-place (later U.S. examples).

1738 W. Stephens Jrnl. Proc. Georgia 156 An Indian *Trading Boat. 1867 J. N. Edwards Shelby, etc. xx. 364 Marmaduke..hoped to capture a trading-boat, and thus put an immediate quietus on the cotton trade. 1755 L. Evans Anal. Map Colonies 10 The situation of Indian Villages, *trading Places, the Creeks [etc.]. 1883 E. W. Howe Country Town (1926) 154, I had never been to Twin Mounds, as there was a post-office and a small trading-place several miles nearer.

Tra·ding-house. U.S. (See Trading vbl. sb. b.)

1637 in Mass. Hist. Soc. Coll. Ser. IV. VI. 215 They say he came from a trading house which Plymouth men have at Qunnihticut. 1668 in Coll. New Hampsh. Hist. Soc. III. 217 The sayd Capt...did continue sending greate quantityes of Liquors..to ye sayde Trading Houses for the Indians. 1726 S. Penhallow Indian Wars (1824) 21 Trading-houses in several places were hereupon engaged. 1748 C. Weiser Jrnl. 27 We both lodged at this Town at George Croghan's Trading House. 1796 Act of Congress in Imlay Descr. Western Territory N. Amer. (1797) 546 That it shall be lawful for the president of the United States to establish trading-houses at such posts and places..as he shall judge most convenient. 1823 Long Exped. I. 91 There are no settlements on its banks, except at the mouth, where is a trading house, and a residence of a single family. 1849 President's Message to Congress II. 974 There is also another trading-house, to which I beg leave to call the attention of the department. 1899 H. B. Cushman Hist. Indians 478 A trading house for the accommodation of the Chickasaws has been established at the Bluffs.

Tra·ding post. U.S. (See Trading vbl. sb. b.)

1796 B. Hawkins Lett. 35 The land..has been recommended..as proper for a trading post. 1844 D. Lee & Frost Ten Yrs. in Oregon I. 16 To establish a line of trading posts along the Missouri and the Columbia. 1871 Rep. Indian Affairs (1872) 277 The Hudson Bay trading-post now belongs to the United States. 1899 H. B. Cushman Hist. Indians 539 He would establish a trading post among the Tunicas.

Traffic, sb. **6.** Add: **traffic constable, cop** U.S., policeman, a policeman engaged in the regulation of road traffic; **traffic (control) signal**, a signal used in controlling traffic; esp. in pl., the system of controlling traffic automatically at cross-roads by means of red ('stop'), amber, and green ('go') electric lamps operating alternately at definite intervals.

1927 Glasgow Herald 9 Mar. 10 An American traffic-cop held up a motorist who was in a hurry. 1929 Times 20 Sept. 10/5 Automatic Traffic Signals. 1930 Daily Express 8 Sept. 9/7 A traffic constable commandeered a passing car and gave chase. 1931 Parl. Deb. 5th Ser. CCLII. 385 Installations of automatic traffic control signals.

Tragico-. Add: **tragico-farcical** a., combining tragedy and farce.

1913 E. F. Benson Thorley Weir vi, Tragico-farcical situations.

Tragicose (træ·dʒikōus), a. [f. Tragic + -ose, after bellicose.] Imitating tragic style.

1901 R. A. Neil Knights Aristoph. 40 The rhythm is tragicose for the first three lines. Ibid. 200 Aristoph. [has it] here and Thesm. 973 in tragicose lyric.

Trail, sb.¹ **16.** Add: trail-cutter, -man U.S.; **trail-bridge** U.S., a ferry consisting of a boat controlled by a pulley running on a rope; **trail-fly, -hook** Angling, a fly or hook at the end of a fly-cast.

1903 A. Adams Log Cowboy vii. 88 Four..strange men.. representing themselves as *trail cutters. 1847 Stoddart Angler's Comp. 84, I recommend the use of a whitling hook, as the *trail-fly or stretcher. Ibid. 100 In the formation of the fly-cast, always commence at the stretcher or *trail-hook. 1891 Harper's Mag. Nov. 886/2 The *trail-men are sent out to cut what in general parlance would be called a path.

Trail, v.¹ Add: **1.** Phr. To trail one's coat or coat-tails: to be provocative in one's conduct.

Cf. Trailer 1 (1864), Tail sb.¹ 3 (1890).

1923 Daily Mail 7 Feb. 6 This risk [of war] is greatly increased by the presence of British troops at Constantinople and Chanak. Why should we thus be 'trailing our coats' before the Turks? Ibid. 3 Mar. 8 Mr. Gore appears to have been trailing his coat.

9. (Examples of more general use.) Also, to trail through U.S. (see quot.).

1906 N. Y. Even. Post Saturday Suppl. 27 Oct. 1, I determined to have the sheep 'trailed through' to Nebraska, which, in Western parlance, means driving them overland. 1915 H. L. Wilson Ruggles of Red Gap iv. (1917) 79 Those two poor fellows trailing you over Paris yesterday trying to save you from yourself. 1925 H. L. Foster Trop. Tramp Tourists 70 We trailed the other steamer. We trailed her through the Boca Chica...We trailed her past the little forts.

11. Also with in. U.S.

1875 Fur, Fin & Feather 112 Light and drink; drop off and trail in. 1907 S. E. White Arizona Nights xvi. 234 With exultant cackles of joy they'd trail in, reachin' out like quarter-horses.

15. (See quot.)

1907 Strand Mag. Feb. 147/1 As soon as the end of the rope [that hangs from the balloon] touches the ground you are 'trailing'.

16. Bowls. (Cf. *Trailing vbl. sb. 1 d.)

1908 J. M. Pretsell Game of Bowls 194 If a bowl trail the jack through between, and past the line square to the back of, the stationary bowls, it shall score 3. 1923 J. A. Manson Bowling 84 The Bowler is required to trail the jack, his own bowl accompanying or 'hugging' it, between the stationary bowls over both of the horizontal lines.

Trailer. Add: **4. b.** A supplementary motion picture (see quot.). U.S.

1931 Amer. Speech VII. Oct. 75 In the lingo of the motion pictures it designates something that goes in advance...For example,..'"Trailers" of New Films for the Week'.

Trailing, vbl. sb. Add: **1. d.** A form of bowling played on Scottish greens, the object being to trail or carry the jack into a semicircle drawn beyond two bowls placed three feet apart.

1902 Encycl. Brit. XXVI. 329/2 In trailing, two bowls are laid on the turf..and a jack is then deposited equidistant from each bowl...A semicircle is then drawn behind the bowls with a radius of nine feet from the jack. 1923 J. A. Manson Bowling 84 Trailing is the section of the Points game which is most worthy of attention.

Trailing, ppl. a. **1. b.** Add: Also in specific names of U.S. plants.

1813 Muhlenberg Catal. Plants N. Amer. 91 Trailing Willow. Ibid. 93 Trailing Juniper. 1861 Trans. Ill. Agric. Soc. IV. 462 We have on the lake shore a beautiful trailing evergreen—the Trailing Juniper. 1869 Jane G. Fuller Uncle John's Flower Gatherers 14 It comes forth with softly perfumed garments, and we call it Trailing Arbutus. 1878 Rose T. Cooke Happy Dodd 347 A profusion of trailing pine had been stored away in the barn cellar, before frost came.

Train, sb.¹ Add: **16.** Armoured train (Mil.), an armour-plated train used chiefly in transporting troops. Train de luxe: see Luxe 2.

1918 E. S. Farrow Dict. Mil. Terms s.v., From a tactical standpoint, the work of armored trains may be grouped into escort of work trains, escort of traffic trains, and independent operations.

22. b. train-boy, (b) (earlier example); **train-caller** (see quots.); **train-jumper** U.S., one who travels by train without paying the fare; **train-man** U.S.; **train porter**, a railway employee in charge of a train over a single-line section of railway; also attrib.; **train-staff**, (a) (earlier example); also attrib.; **train-ticket** (see quot. and cf. train-staff (a) in Dict.); also attrib.

1872 Harper's Mag. Mar. 638/2 He was going down to St. Paul to join the session, when a *train-boy passed through the car. 1921 Dict. Occup. Terms (1927) § 709 *Train caller; a porter whose only duty is to call out destination of a departing train...; also calls out name of own station on arrival of trains. 1927 Daily Express 10 Nov. 3/6 The loud speakers were installed on two platforms...Usually three 'train-callers' are occupied...Their whole time is spent in calling out the destinations of the trains. 1918 in F. A. Pottle Stretchers (1930) 289 The *train man said it would be 6 before the train left. 1859 Rept. Accid. Rlwys. 1858, 17 (P. P. Eng. XXV.) The system..of working by means of a *train porter. 1873 Returns Rlwy. Companies Connections etc. 11 Single Lines of Railway...Worked under the Train Porter System. 1859 Rept. Accid. Rlwys. 1858, 17 (P. P. Eng. XXV.) Regulations for the Use of the *Train Staff. Ibid., To make the train staff the means of opening the train-ticket box. Ibid., If another engine or train is intended to follow in succession, a *train ticket, stating 'staff following', will be given to the person in charge of the leading train, the staff itself being given to the last. Ibid., The engine-man is not to start..until the..person in charge has shown him the train staff or train ticket. 1873 Rept. Bd. Trade Rlwy. Accid. 1872, 175/2 (P. P. Eng. LVII.) This line is worked on the train staff ticket system, the stations at which the staffs and tickets are exchanged and issued being [etc.].

Trainante (trɛ̃nā̃nt), a. [F. traînante, fem. pres. pple. of traîner to drag.] Of vocal or musical sounds: Dragging, drawling.

1818 in Lady Morgan Autobiog. (1859) 104 The music.. possesses here and there fine strains of melody: per contra, it is trainante often too scientific and old-fashioned in its phrases. 1865 'Ouida' Strathmore I. x. 170 The tranquil trainante tones in which he always spoke his rudest things. 1899 Westm. Gaz. 5 Oct. 3/1 Talking in their pleasant, trainante tones to and of each other.

Trainer. Add: **5.** A member of a gun's crew who keeps a gun or the axis of its turret in line, laterally, on the target. U.S.

1904 Sci. Amer. 18 June 475/1 The turrets are trained by one man, the trainer.

Training, vbl. sb. **5.** Add: training-centre, department, ground (earlier U.S. examples).

1928 Britain's Industr. Future (Lib. Ind. Inq.) IV. xxv. § 4. 363 Experimental *training-centres established by the Ministry of Labour. 1906 Rep. Brit. Assoc. 271 To take a course of training in some existing training college or *training department. 1912 Training Women Teachers Secondary Sch. 10 The staff of the Training Department consists of the Organising Professor of Education, the Mistress of Method, and other Assistant Lecturers. 1644 Dedham (Mass.) Rec. 102 From the *Trayning ground to the Cart Bridge. 1845 Knickerbocker Mag. XXVI. 367, I was on the training-ground again.

Trai·ning-day. U.S. (See Training vbl. sb. 5.)

1633 Rec. Massachusetts Bay I. 109 If any trained solder shalbe absent from traineing, vpon their traineing dayes. 1676 [see Training vbl. sb. 5]. 1680 in Mass. Hist. Soc. Coll. Ser. IV. V. 208 Upon the receiving the new commissions, I.. had a training-day in our town. 1704 Sarah Knight Jrnl. 39 Their Diversions..are on Lecture days and Training days mostly. 1845 Knickerbocker Mag. XXVI. 367 It happened to be 'General Muster', or as we call it in New-Hampshire, 'Training-Day'. 1880 [see Training vbl. sb. 5]. 1871 Barnum Struggles & Triumphs 51 The first Monday in May—our 'general training' day. 1872 Eggleston Hoosier Schoolm. xvi. 130 In a public fight on election or training day.

Trajectory, a. Add: **3.** Aeronautics. (See quot.)

1918 W. E. Dommett Dict. Aircraft 48 Trajectory bands, a device used in Parseval type airships consisting of a number of fabric bands passed through loops attached to the envelope for distributing the weight of the car evenly over the envelope.

Tram, sb.² **8.** Add: tram-horn, -horse, -platform; **tram-bus** U.S., a vehicle combining the characteristics of a tram-car and omnibus.

1928 Daily Express 1 Feb. 16 A '*tram-bus' which will be introduced shortly in New York. 1922 Blackw. Mag. Apr. 447/1 The blowing of *tram-horns. 1901 Kipling Kim x, Truck-loads of *tram-horses. 1925 T. R. Glover Jesus Exper. Men xiii. 229 Jesus would not have pushed people off a *tram-platform.

Trammer ² (træ·məɹ). [f. Tram sb.¹ + -er ¹.] (See quot.)

1921 Dict. Occup. Terms (1927) § 372 Trammer; a thrower who minds frame on which..silk..is twisted into threads known as 'tram'.

Tramp, v.¹ Add: **5. c.** (See quot.)

1898 Science Siftings 8 Oct. 361/2 Trespassing on the railways is a misdemeanour [in Canada]...'Tramping the ties' (as such trespassing is commonly there called).

Trampoline ² (træ·mpəlin). [app. var. of *Tremplin.] (See quot. 1930.)

1928 Daily Express 13 June 13 A trampoline act, a wire act—formed, in fact, into a complete vaudeville programme. 1930 Observer 1 June 21 They perform on the apparatus resembling a spring mattress, which has been dubbed the 'trampoline'.

Trance, sb.¹ **4.** Add: trance-faculty, -utterance, -writing.

1911 W. James Mem. & Stud. viii. 190 All the resources of the automatist, including his or her trance-faculty of telepathy. 1911 W. F. Barrett Psych. Research xv. 228 The group of controls..manifested themselves also in the trance-writings. 1916 Sir O. Lodge Survival of Man 185 The.. question as to the origin of the trance-utterances.

Tranker (træ·ŋkəɹ). [f. Trank + -er ¹.] In glove-making, one who cuts the tranks.

1921 Dict. Occup. Terms (1927) § 411.

Transcriber. Add: **2.** A transcribing instrument.

1931 Times 16 Mar. 1/6 All-electric Dictaphone with Shaver and Transcriber: good condition.

Transduodenal (trɑːnsdiuˌodī·năl), a. [f. Trans- + Duodenal a.¹] Effected by cutting across the duodenum.

1908 Practitioner Dec. 826 Transduodenal or retro-duodenal operations.

Transfer, sb. Add: **2. c.** The transference of a worker or player from one sphere to another; also, one transferred. Cf. *transfer fee (below).

1911 Dalton Guardian 21 Jan. 11/6 (Football) The transfer of [A] and [B] was confirmed. 1923 J. D. Hackett Labor Terms in Management Engineering May, Transfer, the shifting of a worker from one occupation to another. 1929 Daily Express 7 Nov. 12/4 The prizes will hardly be glittering enough to attract the best 'transfers'.

4. b. U.S. (Examples.)

1892 Susan Hale Lett. (1919) 269, I mounted a cable, took a transfer, and went..out into the suburbs. 1903 A. B. Hart Actual Govt. 207 In most cities there is a system of free transfers, so that, starting from one suburb, one may often travel for a single fare 5, 10, or 15 miles to another suburb.

d. Comm. The instrument by which goods are transferred, a transfer order.

1924 Times Trade & Engin. Suppl. 29 Nov. 245/1 The buyer will retain this transfer until it suits him to collect the goods, or he may endorse and deliver it to some third party.

5. transfer fee, also Football, a sum of money paid by one club to another for the transfer of the services of a professional player; also **transfer money**; **transfer-man** (a) a railway porter who takes passengers' luggage from one station to another or one who transfers goods from one train to another; (b) U.S., = check-man (*Check sb.¹ 19); **transfer order** Comm., an instrument issued by an importer to a buyer for goods warehoused to

Supplement, p. 3873; Corrigenda, p. 4092; Spurious words, p. 4093; Books quoted, p. 4094

be held over to his order; **transfer porter** = transferman (*a*); **transfer value** (see quot.).

1921 *Dict. Occup. Terms* (1927) § 706 *Transfer man. *Ibid.* § 706, 759 *Transfer porter. 1932 L. Golding *Magnolia Street* I. iii. § 1 When Steve heard how much *transfer money had been paid for him. 1924 *Times Trade & Engin. Suppl.* 29 Nov. 245/1 Instead of a delivery order, an importer may issue a *transfer order. 1924 *Act 14 & 15 Geo. V* c. 38. § 43 (2) Where an insured person duly ceases to be a member of one approved society and becomes a member of another approved society, there shall, subject to the provisions of this Act, be transferred to that society in respect of that person a sum (called in this Act '*transfer value') representing the liability..of the first-mentioned society.

Transfer, *v.* 1. c. (U.S. example.)

1904 *N. Y. Herald* 13 Nov. 3 The man was transferring from the Queens car to the Jamaica car when be was struck.

Transference. Add: **1. b.** *Psycho-analysis.* [tr. G. *übertragung.*] See quot. 1920.

1916 C. E. Long tr. *Jung's Analyt. Psychol.* 245 It is clear that what has disgusted you in hypnotism is at bottom nothing but the so-called 'transference' to the doctor. 1920 E. Jones *Treatm. Neuroses* 40 What has happened..is that the patient has, usually unconsciously, been reminded by the physician of some person of significance in his past life, and that he has transferred to him various emotions which concerned the previous person..He is thus reacting not toward the physician, but rather toward the other person who has been brought together ('identified') with the latter in his mind, an occurrence technically known as 'transference'. 1924 Joan Riviere tr. *Freud's Coll. Papers* I. 32 In his treatment of her case, Breuer could make use of a very intense suggestible *rapport* on the part of the patient, which may serve us as a prototype of what we call 'transference' today. 1926 J. I. Suttie, etc. tr. *Ferenczi's Psycho-Anal.* 121 The remainder of the treatment progressed on the lines of the transference love.

Transhumance (tronshiū·māns). [a. Fr., f. *transhumer*, ad. Sp. *trashumar* (f. L. *trans* across, over + *humus* ground, soil).] (See quot. 1911.) Hence **Transhu·mant** *a.*, migrating between regions of differing climates; **Transhu·me** *v. intr.*

1911 Marion I. Newbigin *Mod. Geog.* vii. 179 Further, the summer drought makes it difficult for even these hardy animals to obtain food, and necessitates in many regions a curious form of nomadism, to which the name of transhumance is given. Transhumance, still well developed in Spain, is the periodic and alternating displacement of flocks and herds between two regions of different climate. 1931 C. F. Jones *South America* 366 Government concessions to permanent ranchers, who do not desire the migrating flocks, are reducing transhumance. 1932 E. H. Carrier *Water & Grass* 7 The merinos and metis (crossed breeds) transhume as do the native flocks. *Ibid.* 78 The transhumant flocks.

Transient, *a.* (*sb.*) Add: **1. b.** Of a newspaper advertisement: Appearing only once. *U.S.*

1857 *Lawrence* (Kansas) *Republican* 28 May 1 All transient advertisements must be paid for in advance. 1904 *Philadelphia Friends' Intelligencer* 15 Oct. p. ii, For transient advertisements, 5 cents per line.

4. (Later U.S. examples.) Also *transf.* of a hotel which caters for 'transients'.

1818 H. B. Fearon *Sk. Amer.* 44 Boarding..is 8 dollars a week, for what is termed 'a transient man'. 1851 *Knickerbocker Mag.* XXXVIII. 179 No wonder that it has been crowded by delighted boarders, permanent and transient. 1879 F. R. Stockton *Rudder Grange* xi. 121 We had no accommodations for them, neither had we any desire for even transient visitors. 1891 *Fur, Fin & Feather* Mar. 185 The transient rate for travelers at the Hilsabeck Hotel in Springfield is $1 a day. 1903 *N. Y. Evening Post* 19 Oct. 3 A 12-story transient hotel. 1906 *Springfield* (Mass.) *Weekly Republican* 9 Aug. 16 They will then rent apartments with or without board to transient and permanent guests.

Transition. **5.** *transition-state* (examples.)

1848 *Wesleyan Missionary Notices* VI. 174/1 They are now in a transition-state. 1862 *Leisure Hour* 11 Oct. 645/2 The night-cloud was in a transition state.

Transitive, *a.* **1.** (Later U.S. example.)

1906 *Springfield* (Mass.) *Weekly Republican* 8 Mar. 6 At present be is in a transitive state.

Trans-Jordan (-dʒǭ·rdăn), **Trans-Jordanic** (-dʒǭrdæ·nik), *adjs.* [Trans- 7.] Lying beyond Jordan, the largest river of Palestine; pertaining or relating to **Transjordania** (-dʒǭrdē·niă), the district east of the Jordan, under Arab administration and a British mandate (also called *Trans-Jordan*). Hence **Transjorda·nian** *a.*

1840 transjordanic, 1898 trans-Jordan *a.* [see Trans- 7]. 1865 H. B. Tristram *Land of Israel* xxii. 519 We mounted for our trans-Jordanic expedition. 1923 *Daily Mail* 30 Jan. 4 At present the number of Jews in Transjordania is only two. *Ibid.* 28 May 10 The Trans-Jordanian Government. 1927 *Daily Tel.* 19 July 5/1 The forces for the maintenance of security and the defence of Palestine and Trans-Jordan have been reorganised.

Translator. **2.** Add: Also *spec.* a mender and renovator of old garments and umbrellas.

1921 *Dict. Occup. Terms* (1927) § 404 *Repairer*, renovator; tailor's translator; alters and repairs garments. *Ibid.* § 416 *Mender*; renovator, repairer, translator;..mends umbrella or parasol covers;..etc.

Translatorese (trons,lĕitōrī·z). [f. Translator + -ese.] The style of language characteristic of translators in general.

1915 *Morning Post* 15 Apr. 2/4 The worst 'journalese is more English than schoolmasters' 'translatorese'. 1923 *Outline of Literature* I. i. 39/1 The curiously matter-of-fact translation in prose..is an excellent tonic against the conventional 'translatorese'.

Transmarginal (trons,mā·ɹdʒinăl), *a.* [f. Trans- + Marginal *a.*] Beyond the margin of normal consciousness.

1915 J. H. Tuckwell *Relig. & Reality* xi. 220 In the larger transmarginal or subliminal region of consciousness,..nothing is ever really forgotten.

Transmission. **b.** Add: *spec.* in *Wireless*; also, that which is transmitted. Hence **Transmi·ssional** *a.*

1907 *Rep. Brit. Assoc.* 731 To determine how many oscillations..take place in a certain wireless transmission. 1921 *Wireless World* IX. 52/2 In Surrey and Kent the transmissions were easily read. 1923 *Radio Times* 5 Oct. 51/2 Transmission from London of Dance Music by Savoy Orpheans. *Ibid.* 2 Nov. 173/3 Simultaneous transmissions have been practically perfect. 1930 *B.B.C. Year-Bk.* 310 It is not unusual for all these studios to be in use at the same time for either transmissions or rehearsals. *Ibid.*, One or two transmissions are, perhaps, being sent to the provinces via the S.B. lines. 1930 *Observer* 4 May 26 Churches are not often very good resonators..and sometimes the music sounded ghostly. There were a few transmissional hiccoughs, too.

Transmissi·vity. The quality of being transmissible.

1913 *Wireless World* I. 551/1 These instances of the connection between cloudiness and transmissivity.

Transmit, *v.* **3.** Add: *spec.* in *Wireless.*

1923 *Radio Times* 28 Sept. 2/1 The first occasion..on which the voice of a public man had been transmitted simultaneously through six wireless stations hundreds of miles apart. *Ibid.* 5 Oct. 40/2 An Indian, who had been taken to the transmitting station, gave orders to it [*sc.* an elephant] in the vernacular by wireless. 1930 *B.B.C. Year-Bk.* 314 Transmissions over the lines available occur without affecting in any way the quality of the programme being transmitted. *Ibid.* 394 These transmitters were capable of transmitting very long distances, having regard to their power and the type of receiver in use.

Transmitter. **b.** Add: Also, the transmitting apparatus used in wireless telegraphy; also *attrib.*

1898 *Ludgate* Nov. 79 The Marconi Transmitter. 1907 *Cornhill Mag.* Mar. 359 With the tuning-fork used as transmitter. 1912 *Chambers's Jrnl.* Jan. 60/1, I had got our receiver into 'tune' with the transmitter on board a steamer. 1931 *Times* 18 Feb. 16/3 A large wireless transmitter valve.

Transnational (trons,næ·ʃənăl), *a.* [f. Trans- + National *a.*] Extending beyond national bounds or frontiers. Hence **Transna·tionally** *adv.*, **Transna·tionalism.**

1921 N. Angell *Fruits of Victory* i. 14 Transport and credit, operating trans-nationally. *Ibid.* ii. 63 Much of Europe lives by virtue of an international, or more correctly, a trans-national economy. *Ibid.* 300 The old individualist 'trans-nationalism'. 1925 *Contemp. Rev.* Oct. 357 To accomplish necessary changes, not so much by altering frontiers as by 'transnational' arrangements.

Transparency. **2. c.** Add: (Later examples.) Also, used as an advertising sign.

1895 *Century Mag.* May 20/1 The Treasury had over its chief entrance a huge transparency which was a tolerable imitation of a ten-dollar..note. 1902 *Encycl. Brit.* XXV. 96/1 Advertising by posters, sign-boards.., transparencies, and similar devices.

Trans-parietal (trons,pārəi·ĕtăl), *a.* [f. Trans- + Parietal *a.*] Passing across the paries.

1910 H. D. Rolleston in *Practitioner* Apr. 440 Transparietal infection or the passage of micro-organisms from the colon to the kidney.

Transportee. Add: **2.** An animal that has been transported from its habitat and is not indigenous to the locality where it is found.

1920 Ritchie *Infl. Man Anim. Life Scotl.* viii. 469 No set of imported animals is more characteristic than the timber transportees.

Transverter (tronsvǭ·ɹtəɹ). *Electr.* [f. Trans(former + Con)verter.] (See quot.)

1924 *Glasgow Herald* 17 June 9 The machine..is called a transverter...It both transforms, by raising the pressure and converts into direct current.

Transylvanian (tron,silvē·niăn), *a.* and *sb.* [f. *Transylvania* (see below) + -an.] Of or belonging to, a native or inhabitant of, Transylvania, formerly the eastern portion of Austria-Hungary, now part of Roumania.

a 1773 A. Butler *Lives Saints* (1821) IX. 84 *note*, The vizier with one hundred and fifty thousand Turks (besides Hungarians, Transylvanians, and Tartars) sat down before Vienna. 1843 *Penny Cycl.* XXV. 165/1 The German universities are frequented by a considerable number of Transylvanian students, especially for divinity. 1875 *Encycl. Brit.* III. 116/1 The Transylvanian Highlands extend over Transylvania..into Moldavia and Wallachia. 1920 *Edin. Rev.* July 36 Hermannstadt (Sibiu) then the seat of the Transylvanian Government.

Trap, *sb.*[1] Add: **1. d.** A device at the entrance of a pigeon loft, which allows a pigeon to enter but not to escape from the loft.

1876 R. Fulton *Illustr. Bk. Pigeons* 274 Let the board, upon which the birds alight (when the trap is closed and admission only to be obtained through the bolting wires), be carried upon a pair of hinges. 1882 *Homing Fancier's Ann.* 8 On the lodger trying to make his escape the next morning, for another struggle through the air to reach his old cot, he finds the trap has been closed.

2. b. The mouth. *vulgar.*

[1785, 1860: see *potato-trap*, Potato *sb.* 7.] *c* 1860 in *Eng. Dial. Dict.* 1923 L. J. Vance *Baroque* xxvii. 178 You can count on Angelo's keepin' his trap tight.

4. b. In greyhound-racing, a compartment in which a greyhound is placed and from which it is automatically released at the starting of a race. Also *attrib.*

1928 A. R. D. Cardew *Greyhound Racing* 13 The owner ..is invited..to attend the draw for trap places 1 to 6, No 1 being the inside trap...The trap numbers are not given out to the Press. *Ibid.* 18 Plate, Leaving the Starting Trap. 1932 *Daily Tel.* 8 Oct. 19/1 Here are the runners in their trap order.

5. *Up to trap* (U.S. examples).

1837 W. Irving *Capt. Bonneville* II. i. 15 The beaver now being completely 'up to trap', approaches them cautiously. 1843 *Knickerbocker Mag.* XXI. 234 'I'm up to trap!' said the boy. 1877 Habberton *Jericho Road* xix. 170 You needn't come any of your..moral tricks on me. I'm up to trap.

9. d. The mould used in counterfeit coining. *slang.*

1929 *Daily Express* 3 Jan. 9/5 He said he had destroyed the 'trap', meaning the mould.

11. *trap-pool*; **trap crust** (see quot.); **trap-fish,** a fish caught in a trap-net, as distinguished from one caught by line-fishing; **trap nest** *sb.*, a nesting-box which a hen can enter but cannot leave until released; also as *vb.*; **trap-shy** *a.*, shy of approaching a trap; **trap-yard,** an enclosure used as a trap for animals.

1924 *Ski Terms* in *Tourist Winter Sports* No. 12/2 **Trap crust*, a horrible surface of friable crust which holds the ski and then lets it through. 1910 *Chambers's Jrnl.* 192/2 *Trap-fish were actually hawked on the Fraser at one halfpenny per fish! 1910 W. W. Broomhead *Poultry & Profit* 33, I asked Mr. Tapley if he had his fowls *trap-nested. 1917 — *Poultry for the Many* (ed. 10) 31 Much has been written about the trap nest, and..there can be little doubt that where pedigree layers are required, trap-nesting must be in vogue. 1920 *Chambers's Jrnl.* 232/1 The creatures [*sc.* crocodiles]..when muzzled and confined in *trap-pools soon become fairly manageable. 1922 *Contemp. Rev.* July 90 After a time the rat grows poison-shy and *trap-shy. 1906 *Chambers's Jrnl.* 380/1 There are..two means of capturing these horses. The first is to build a strong *trapyard on their line of retreat, and endeavour to run them into it.

Trap, *v.*[1] **2.** (Earlier U.S. examples.)

1834 A. Pike *Sketches* 36 Mr. John Harris..was collecting a party for the purpose of entering and trapping the Comanche country. 1837 W. Irving *Capt. Bonneville* II. xix. 192 A range of country is 'trapped', by small detachments from a main body.

4. b. *Baseball.* 'To stop (a ball) between the hand and something else, as the ground or the feet' (Funk 1928).

1906 *Spalding's Offic. Base Ball Guide* 126 *A Trapped Ball.*—A trapped ball play was made when runners were on bases, and a 'pop-up' fly ball was expected to be caught. Each runner holding a base was at once forced to leave on the hit and then became 'trapped', or thrown out, at the base to which they had to run...If a pop-up fly ball is made, if the fielder touches the ball before it reaches the ground it is regarded as a catch, and the trap ball play fails in consequence. 1912 C. Mathewson *Pitching in a Pinch* viii. 181 A Boston batter tapped one to Merkle which I thought he trapped, but Johnstone, the umpire, said he caught it on the fly.

Trattoria (tratorī·a). [It., f. *trattore* host, f. *trattare* to Treat.] In Italy, an eating-house and cook-shop.

1832 Gell *Pompeiana* I. iv. 49 A trattoria and coffee-house. 1873 'Ouida' *Pascarel* ii. iv. I. 169 Then he would pass methodically across the piazza to his favourite trattoriā. 1893 C. Booth in *Mem.* (1918) 72 I asked for any place where something to eat could be got. There was no trattoria, they said, and I passed on somewhat crushed. 1921 *Chambers's Jrnl.* 574/2, I..burst from that little *trattoria*, my pulses throbbing.

Trauma. Add: Also *Psycho-analysis.* (Pl. **traumata** (trǭ·mătă), also **traumas.**) An unpleasant or unusual experience which affects the mind or nerves of a person so as to induce hysteria or 'psychic' conditions. So **Trauma·tic** *a.*; whence **Trauma·tically** *adv.*; **Traumatism.**

1889 T. Savill tr. *J. M. Charcot's Clin. Lect. Dis. Nerv. Syst.* III. 304 In the case of our two male patients you have not forgotten that the cause was traumatic, a blow more or less violent on the shoulder. *Ibid.* 388 The existence of traumatic psychosis [*psychose traumatique*] adds still more to the gravity of the prognosis. 1910 A. A. Brill tr. *Freud's Sel. Papers Hysteria* i. (1912) 1 It is quite evident that in 'traumatic' hysteria it is the accident which evokes the syndrome. *Ibid.* ii. 29 The real traumatic moment is that in which the conflict thrusts itself upon the ego and the latter decides to banish it. *Ibid.* iii. 52 The reproduction of traumatically produced scenes. 1916 C. E. Long tr. *Jung's Analyt. Psychol.* xiv. 358 Hence arose the trauma-theory maintaining that the hysterical symptom..arises from some psychic injury (or trauma), the effect of which is retained in the unconscious indefinitely. 1917 C. R. Payne tr. *O. Pfister's Psych. Method* 61 Freud's assertion that the sexual traumas of early childhood were the cause of hysteria. 1920 E. Jones *Treatm. Neuroses* 104 More traumata (of all kinds, physical as well as psychical) than might be imagined are in this way half sought for, and persons of this sort are said to have a 'traumatophilic' disposition. *Ibid.* 202 Traumatic neuroses, including war shock. 1922 A. A. Brill *Psychoanalysis* i. 18 The psychic traumas which are supposed to be at the basis of hysterical symptoms. 1926 J. I. Suttie tr. *Ferenczi's The. & Techn. Psycho-analysis* 77 A certain amount of infantile sexual experience (that is to say, a little 'sexual traumatism'). 1929 *Times Lit. Suppl.* 4 July 528/2 The Freudian traumatic theory.

Travelled, *ppl. a.* **3.** *U.S.* (Earlier example.)

1874 *Rep. Vermont Board Agric.* II. 658 If the hill is

heavy clay, it may be much improved..by covering the traveled portion with gravel or sand.

Traveller. Add: **1. d.** An itinerant preacher. *U.S.*

1813 F. Asbury *Jrnl.* (1821) III. 346 Of these [preachers] there are only thirty-three travellers.

5. (Earlier U.S. example.)

1828 A. Sherburne *Mem.* iii. (1831) 63 He fixed a traveller on the rope, by which he first went on shore.

Travelling, *vbl. sb.* **b.** *Travelling bag, cap, trunk* (earlier or additional U.S. examples.)

1838 Caroline Gilman *Recoll. Southern Matron* ii. 18 He..called the little boy who held the *travelling bag a 'black-faced nigger'. 1889 *Century Mag.* Feb. 519/1 The hotel where he had left his traveling-bag. 1845 Sol. Smith *Theatrical Apprent.* 139 About half a mile from the starting place, we found John's *travelling cap. 1907 M. C. Harris *Tents of Wickedness* 1. i. 14 Her father, adjusting his traveling cap. 1854 *Penna. Agric. Rep.* 97 Their very handsome riding saddle and russet *traveling trunk.

Travelling, *ppl. a.* **b.** (Earlier and later U.S. examples.)

1775 F. Asbury *Jrnl.* 6 Nov. (1821) I. 124 At this meeting we admitted F. P. T. F. and J. H—y as travelling preachers. 1777 *Ibid.* 12 May 186 So greatly has the Lord increased the number of travelling preachers. 1848 *Indiana Mag. Hist.* XXIII. 2 More than 2,000 local preachers, besides the traveling ministers. 1874 E. Eggleston *Circuit Rider* xxvii. 252 The incessant activity of a traveling preacher's life.

Travelogue (træ·vəlǫg). orig. *U.S.* [irreg. f. Travel *sb.* + -logue.] A lecture or narrative descriptive of travel illustrated pictorially.

1903 *Daily Chron.* 16 Apr. 6/7 Mr. Burton Holmes, an American entertainer new to London, delivered last evening the first of a series of 'Travelogues'. 1921 *Glasgow Herald* 7 Nov. 10 The..Travelogue film, 'With Allenby in Palestine and Lawrence in Arabia.' 1922 H. L. Foster *Adv. Trop. Tramp* ix. 118 The several columns of travelogue that I turned out each week. 1927 H. E. Fosdick *Pilgr. Palestine* p. vii, Some [books] are simply travelogues in which the successive experiences of the traveler furnish the strand for the narrative.

Traverser. Add: **5.** (See quot. and cf. Traverse *v.* 6.)

1921 *Dict. Occup. Terms* (1927) § 200 *Traverser*; a turner engaged in shaping long shafts, rollers, or cylinders, mainly in the rough, *i.e.*, without putting a finished surface on them.

Travois. Also **travoi, -oy.** (Earlier and later examples.)

1847 Kit Carson in 'Buffalo Bill' *Wild West* (1888) 349 The Tlamaths..prevented his body from falling into our hands by drawing it away on a travoi. 1876 Bourke *Jrnl.* 28 July—8 Sept., [He] says he will stick with the column if he has to be hauled on a travois. 1902 S. E. White *Blazed Trail* ii. 10 The trails were perhaps three feet wide, and marvels of smoothness...They were called travoy roads.

Trawl, *sb.* **4.** Add: **trawl-fish,** fish caught in a trawl net; *spec.* (see quot.).

1636–1886 [in Dict.]. 1879 *Encycl. Brit.* IX. 248/2 Trawl-fish are separated for market purposes into two great classes, known respectively as 'prime' and 'offal'. Prime includes turbot, brill, soles, dories, and red mullet...Offal is the name given to plaice, haddocks, whiting, and other kinds of inferior fishes.

Tray, *sb.*[2] **4.** Add: **tray cell** *Electr.*, a battery in which the sulphate of copper crystals are contained in a copper-lined or copper tray; **tray stand,** a small stand used as a side table upon which to rest a tray.

1878 *Encycl. Brit.* VIII. 94/1 The *tray cell of Sir William Thomson, which consists of a large wooden tray lined with lead, the bottom of which is covered with copper by electrotyping. 1844 T. Webster *Encycl. Dom. Econ.* 241 A *tray-stand..formed of two frames and girth to fold up. 1895 *Army & Navy Co-op. Soc. Price List* 15 Sept. 311 Cairo Tray Stand.

Treacle, *v.* **2. b.** Add: Also *intr.*

1915 Wells *Boon* (1920) 115 Going round with the lantern when one is treacling for moths.

Tread, *v.* Add: **4. b.** *To tread on one's own tail* (fig.): to injure oneself in striking at others.

1901 *Kynoch Jrnl.* Oct.-Nov. 9/1 We consider any criticism..coming from the American side as rather of the nature of treading on your own tail.

7. b. intr. *To tread on the gas*: see *Gas *sb.*[2]

Treading, *vbl. sb.* Add: **1. c.** The action of treading water: see Tread *v.* 7.

1887 *Encycl. Brit.* XXII. 769/2 Of treading as a branch of swimming something should be known to every one.

Treadler (tre·dləɹ). [f. Treadle *v.* + -er[1].]

1. One who treadles (see Treadle *v.*).

2. An operative who guides fabric into and adjusts a treadling machine for brushing up the pile.

1921 *Dict. Occup. Terms* (1927) § 384.

Treasury, *sb.* Add: **3. c.** *pl.* Treasury bills.

1922 *Daily Tel.* 12 June 2/1 New secondhand Treasuries were dealt in at 2½ per cent. 1932 *Ibid.* 8 Oct. 2/6 This week's 'hot' Treasuries offered at ⅝ p.c. found buyers.

6. *treasury board* (earlier example). **treasury note,** earlier example in U.S. sense; also = *currency note* (*Currency 6).

1780 *Essex Inst. Hist. Coll.* LVI. 94, I wrote to the *Treasury board. 1756 in *Lett. to Washington* I. 202 Who is hereby required to pay the same in *Treasury Notes, to be emmitted by Virtue of the said Act of Assembly. 1843 *Illustr. London News* 11 Mar. 169/3 Authority should be given to the proper department to re-issue Treasury notes. 1926 *Whitaker's Almanack* 415 Treasury Notes of the value of £1 and 10s. are issued, and are legal tender to any amount.

Treater. Add: **4.** One who subjects a thing to treatment with a chemical or other agent.

1881 *Instr. Census Clerks* (1885) 61. 1921 *Dict. Occup. Terms* (1927) § 458 *Treater*; mixes 'finings' (isinglass, etc., used to clarify beer..) according to formula. *Ibid.* § 499 *Timber treater*..; seasons or treats timber with chemical substances.

Treatment. **4.** Add: Also, the chemical agent used.

1921 *Dict. Occup. Terms* (1927) § 148 *Treatment maker*..; mixes chemicals used for treating lye..in preparation for recovery of glycerine therefrom.

Treatyite (trī·ti,əit). [f. Treaty *sb.* + -ite[1].] One who approves and supports the acceptance of a particular treaty.

1922 *Glasgow Herald* 27 Apr. 7 The Treatyites are protected by the Ard Fheis agreement. 1927 *Observer* 25 Sept. 11/4 The existing cross-division of Treatyites and anti-Treatyites.

Treble, *sb.* Add: **2. h.** A total of three races won by the same horse (in a specified period).

1931 *Daily Express* 21 Sept. 15/4 Peacock wound up a fine week in Scotland, where Nevett landed a treble for him on Saturday.

Treble, *a.* **3.** Add: *Treble figures*, a sum or total of one hundred (pounds) or more, but less than one thousand. *Treble grip*, a series of three grips or hooked teeth which secure the barrel of a gun to the breech when closed. *Treble lines* (see quot. 1927).

1931 *Times Lit. Suppl.* 20 Aug. 636/3 Sixteen items were priced in *treble figures. 1880 *Encycl. Brit.* XI. 281/2 The *treble grip snap action is shown as specially devised for rifles firing heavy charges. 1927 *World's Paper Trade Rev.* 24 June, **Treble Lines*.—The ropes made of cow hair on which hand-made paper is still dried.

Tree, *sb.* **10.** Add: **a. tree-box,** (*a*) tall-growing boxwood; (*b*) a wooden casing used to protect a tree-trunk; **tree-jhow,** tree-like shrubby tamarisk; **tree mallow** (see Mallow 2); **b. tree lemur** = bush baby (see *Bush *sb.*[1] 11); **tree partridge** (*a*) an American partridge (see Partridge 2; (*b*) an Asiatic partridge of the genus *Arboricola*; (*c*) (see quot.); **tree squirrel,** the common squirrel, *Sciurus vulgaris*; **c. tree analysis** *Forestry* (see quot.); **tree bender** (see quot.); **tree-branch** *a.*, resembling the branch of a tree; **tree coral,** the red arborescent species of coral; **tree-divination,** divination by listening to the rustling of the leaves of a tree supposed to be the seat of a deity; **tree-feeder,** an animal that feeds on the leaves and branches of trees; **tree nest,** one attached to a branch or concealed within the bark of a tree, as distinguished from a ground nest; **tree-path, road,** the track of an arboreal animal; **tree scribe** = *Scratcher 2 d; **tree-tally** (see Tally *sb.*[1] 7 c); **tree turner** (see quot.).

1905 *Terms Forestry & Logging* 25 **Tree analysis*, a series of measurements and observations upon a felled tree to determine its growth and life history. 1921 *Dict. Occup. Terms* (1927) § 498 **Tree bender*; bends shafts or handles for scythes, shovels, etc., by placing in steam chamber [etc.] 1785 Washington *Diaries* II. 360, 12 Horse Chestnut Trees ..and an equal number of cuttings of the *Tree Box. 1858 J. A. Warder *Hedges & Evergreens* II. 240 Where a moderate or low hedge is needed,..nothing can be better than the Tree-box. 1876 'Mark Twain' *Tom Sawyer* ii. 27 [Tom] sat down on the tree-box discouraged. 1896 J. C. Harris *Sister Jane* 157 Whittling away with his pocket knife on the tree-box, against which he was leaning. 1908 *Practitioner* Dec. 861 The "Tree-branch" striations occasionally seen in skiagrams of tuberculous lungs. *Ibid.*, 'Tree-branch' arborescence only occurs in tuberculous patients. 1915 E. R. Lankester *Divers. Naturalist* 11 Great *tree-coral of these waters—the Paragorgia. 1921 *Hastings's Encycl. Relig. & Ethics* XII. 455/2 *Tree-divination was practised by the Ainus. 1914 *Chambers's Jrnl.* 75/1 A species of rhinoceros which was particularly a *tree-feeder. 1920 *Blackw. Mag.* Jan. 110/1 A patch of *tree-jhow. 1928 *Daily Express* 31 July 4 A *tree-lemur or 'bush-baby'. 1924 J. A. Thomson *Science Old & New* x. 55 A..Tineid caterpillar, found in the *tree-nest of one of the Termites. 1864 J. A. Grant *Walk Across Africa* 93 The..*tree-partridge, resembles the painted one of India, has yellow legs, beautiful plumage, and weighs about a pound. 1897 J. L. Allen *Choir Invisible* xv, The grass-path or the *tree-path of the cougar. 1895 Kipling *2nd Jungle Bk.* 218 When he tired of ground-going he threw up his hands monkey-fashion to the nearest creeper...he would follow a *tree-road till his mood changed. 1905 *Terms Forestry & Logging* 25 *Tree scribe. 1872 *Routledge's Ev. Boy's Ann.* 614/1 Dennis climbs like a *tree squirrel. 1910 *Chambers's Jrnl.* 143/1 The *tree-tallies are pierced at one end with a small hole for attachment to the tree. 1881 *Instr. Census Clerks* (1885) 173 *Tree Turner (Spade Handles). 1921 *Dict. Occup. Terms* (1927) § 486 *Treeturner*; a turner who shapes wooden handles of spades and shovels on a lathe.

Treer (trī·əɹ). [f. Tree *v.* + -er[1].] An operative who irons boots and shoes on a boot-tree.

1921 *Dict. Occup. Terms* (1927) § 414.

Trefoil, *sb.* Add: **3. c.** *Anat.* The triangular front of a molar tooth.

1904 *Ann. & Mag. Nat. Hist.* June 409 The tooth is very large.., high, and complicated, the anterior trefoil well developed.

Trehalase (trī·hălēs, trihā·lēs). *Chem.* [f. Trehala + *-ase.] A ferment which will effect the cleavage of trehalose into two molecules of dextrose.

1899 J. R. Green *Soluble Ferments* 132 Bourquelot states that the enzyme which effects the hydrolysis of trehalose is different from either invertase or glucase, though it co-exists with them in the mycelium of the fungi which he describes. He has given it the name *trehalase*.

Trek, *sb.* **2.** Add: **trek Boer** (*a*) a Boer who moved his family and stock from place to place; (*b*) one of those Boers who, esp. in the Great Trek of 1835–8, migrated from Cape Colony; **trek-farmer** = *trek Boer* (a); **trek-fever,** an insatiable longing for travelling or wandering in the veldt; **trek sheep,** sheep driven or carried a long distance for pasturage or to market.

1835 A. Steedman *Wand. S. Afr.* II. 53 The next day we met a *Trek Boor, with his cattle. 1912 *East London Dispatch* 14 Aug. 4 (Pettman) Long before the nomad trek Boers crossed the Drakensberg. *Ibid.* 1 May 5 (ibid.) The desirability of amending the railway tariff for *trek-sheep to enable *trek farmers to avail themselves of the railway. 1897 J. P. Fitzpatrick *Outspan* 3 When..this instinct.. awakens,..it becomes a madness, and they call it *trek-fever.

Trembling, *ppl. a.* **c.** *trembling prairie* (example.)

1868 *Putnam's Mag.* I. 592/1 The floating island will in time become a 'trembling prairie'—a marsh.

Tremolist (tre·mŏlist). [f. Tremolo + -ist.] One who uses the tremolo.

1926 *Mus. Assoc. Proc.* 1926-7, 18 The soprano tremolist is no longer tolerated.

Tremor (tre·mǫɹ), *v.* [f. Tremor *sb.*] *intr.* To be agitated by a tremor or tremors.

1921 *Chambers's Jrnl.* 858/1 The ship tremored, vibrated like mad. 1924 *Ibid.* 860/2 Her voice had tremor'd..with urgency. 1926 M. Walsh *Key above Door* x, His strong big jowl was..tremoring with the chill. 1928 — *While Rivers Run* vi, His car was purring and tremoring.

Trench, *sb.* **9.** Add: **trench artillery** *Mil.*, bomb-throwing machines and mortars used in the trenches; **trench-bomb** *Mil.*, a bomb to be thrown in or about enemy trenches; **trench candle,** a smokeless candle made from old newspapers and candle ends, used in the trenches; **trench coat,** a (thick) waterproofed coat worn by men in the trenches; also, a woman's coat in similar style; **trench dagger** *Mil.*, a dagger used by trench patrols; **trench fever,** an infectious disease incident to men engaged in trench warfare; **trench foot, feet,** a disease affecting the feet of soldiers exposed to extreme cold and wet in the trenches; **trench knife** = **trench dagger*; **trench mortar** *Mil.*, a small mortar designed to throw bombs from a front trench into enemy trenches; hence *trench-mortar* vb.; **trench sprayer** *Mil.*, an implement for clearing gas from trenches by spraying a neutralizing liquid; **trench strafing,** heavy bombardment of trenches; **trench waders,** thigh boots worn by a soldier while in the trenches; **trench warfare,** hostilities carried on by means of or in trenches.

1921 *Blackw. Mag.* Apr. 430/1 Every young man in Ireland nowadays wears a so-called *trench-coat. 1927 *Observer* 18 Dec. 9/4 ['Christmas in Switzerland', 'Sports Outfits'.] The tendency for women is also towards a costume consisting of a 'trench coat' in the new colour, with 'riding breeches'. 1915 *Lancet* 25 Sept. 734/1 The case of a twice-inoculated soldier suffering from *trench fever, whose case was diagnosed as pyrexia. 1924 C. E. Montague *Right Place* vii. § 3. 92 Restored for a season to his own friends in the line, be was presently sent travelling again, this time by trench fever. 1915 *Lancet* 17 Apr. 812/2 The term *trench-foot appears to us to be the most suitable for a condition which has practically only been met with in those who have had to remain for long periods in the trenches. *Ibid.* 2 Oct. 779/1 The problem of combating and preventing 'trench feet' is..of such importance that I venture to make the above suggestion. 1926 *Scribner's Mag.* Aug. 194/2 A Boche lad I killed with me *trench-knife. 1915 D. O. Barnett *Lett.* 107 The Germans are bombing our trenches with a *trench mortar. *Ibid.* 110 They..dropped trench-mortar bombs about on my trench. 1920 *Glasgow Herald* 28 Apr. 4 Trench-mortar fire. 1920 *Chambers's Jrnl.* 254/1 He shelled it; be *trench-mortared it, he raided it. 1931 *Times Lit. Suppl.* 22 Oct. 822/1 The squadron was required to assist the hard-pressed infantry by..'*trench strafing'. 1919 G. K. Rose 2/4th *Oxf. & Bucks Lt. Infty.* 15 After the operations of July 19 the former methods of *trench warfare were resumed. 1929 R. Graves *Good-Bye to All That* xii. 132 These were early days of trench-warfare.

Trencher[1]. **5.** Add:

1889 *Harper's Mag.* Jan. 238/2 He next binds his trap to a flat stone 'about the size of a tinkettle', opens the jaws, and arranges the 'trencher', as the pan is called, pressure on which springs the trap.

Trench-plough, *sb.* **1.** (See after Trench-plough *v.*) **2.** *Mil.* A machine used in trench-making.

1918 E. S. Farrow *Dict. Mil. Terms.*

Trenchscope (tre·n[t]ʃskoup). [f. Trench *sb.* + -scope.] A periscope designed for use in the trenches. So also **Tre·nchoscope.**

1915 *Morning Post* 11 Feb. 3/5 The Adams trenchoscope is the latest periscope for use in the trenches. 1918 E. S. Farrow *Dict. Mil. Terms*, Trenchscope.

Trepidation. Add: **3. b.** *Astr.* (See quot.)

1926 J. K. Fotheringham in *Monthly Notices Roy. Astron. Soc.* LXXXVII. 166, I therefore propose to use the term

'trepidation', which expresses the kind of movement we have in view, and which has the advantage of being the ancient term for one of the forms in which it manifests itself. The trepidation of the equinoxes..was a long-period forward and backward motion of the equinox..Such a motion of the equinox with a major period of 260 years is exactly one of the phenomena under discussion, and I propose therefore to give the name 'trepidation' to the whole of this group of phenomena.

Treponema (treponī·mă). Also **treponeme.** [mod.L., f. Gr. τρέπειν to turn + νῆμα thread.] A protozoan organism belonging to the genus of that name, having a slender corkscrew-like form with a flagellum at both ends.

1908 *Practitioner* Oct. 549 The treponema, or, as they are usually designated in this country, the spirochaetes. 1922 *Nature* CIX. 667/2 Existence of the treponeme in the cytoplasm of the nerve cells of the cerebral cortex.

Trestle, *sb.* **6. trestlework** (additional examples).

1853 *Survey Vicksburg & Texas R. R.* 9, 4500 lineal feet trestle-work at $4 a foot. 1891 E. S. Ellis *Check No. 2134* xiv. 94 The Express approached a piece of trestle work.

Triage. Add: **b.** (See quots.)

1930 F. A. Pottle *Stretchers* 141 The wounded were then carried back by ambulance to the *triage*, or sorting station, which was usually manned by a field hospital. *Ibid.* 222 A special triage officer at once surveys the patients to determine the urgency of their injuries.

Trial, *sb.*[1] Add: **10. c.** Short for *trial match.*

a 1914 J. E. Raphael *Mod. Rugby Football* (1918) 249 E. W. Baker played for the South and in other important trials. 1921 E. H. D. Sewell *Rugby Football* 337 He was nominated to play on the wing in the third Trial.

13. *trial flight, marriage* (example), *run*; **trial balance** (U.S. example); **trial-bed,** a nurseryman's bed for the trying-out of new plants; **trial eight** (example); also *attrib.*

1884 Cable *Dr. Sevier* viii. 59, I should begin to take a *trial-balance off the books. 1906 Quiller-Couch *From Cornish Window* 119 Messrs. Sutton's *trial-beds just outside Reading. 1873 C. C. Knollys *Oxford Univ. Chall. Races Pref.*, The crews of the *Trial and University Eights. 1900 W. E. Sherwood *Oxford Rowing* 63 In 1858..considerable alterations were made..the most important perhaps being the establishment of the Trial Eight race. 1909 F. Ash *Trip to Mars* xii. 89, I only took my trial-flight in it yesterday! 1930 *New Statesman* 27 Dec. 355/2 The Bishops of Miss Dunbar's Church recently gave an episcopal blessing to birth control, one prominent clergyman approving *trial marriage. 1931 *Times Lit. Suppl.* 12 Nov. 878/2 He is explicitly opposed to 'free love', 'trial marriage', and 'contract marriage'. 1903 *Trans. Inst. Naval Archit.* XLV. 295 Some twenty *trial runs..were made under various conditions as to speed. 1909 *Chambers's Jrnl.* 675/1 The first great trial-run of a number of motor-cars.

Trialist (trəi·ălist). An advocate or supporter of Trialism (sense 2).

1931 J. A. R. Marriott *Europe fr. 1815 to 1923* 429 On one detail of their programme the 'Trialists', as they began [1908–9] to be called, were not unanimous.

Triangle, *sb.* **2.** Add: *The wet triangle* [= G. *nasses dreieck*], the German part of the North Sea.

1927 W. E. Collinson *Contemp. Engl.* 84 The wet triangle.

Triatic, *a.* Add: Also as *sb.* = *triatic stay.*

1926 *Glasgow Herald* 7 Jan. 6/1 Vertical wires suspended from triatics attached to the arms of the masts.

Tribeswoman: see Tribe *sb.* 7 b.

Tri·bo-electri·city. [f. Gr. τρίβειν to rub: see -o-.] (See quot.) Hence **Tri·bo-ele·ctric** *a.*

1917 *Nature* C. 336/2 Tribo-electricity—that is, the subject which deals with the production of charges by rubbing together unlike materials. *Ibid.* 337/1 Tribo-electric effects.

Tribunal, *sb.* Add: **2. c.** A local board appointed to adjudicate upon claims for exemption from military service during the war of 1914–18.

1916 *Act 5 & 6 Geo. V* c. 104 § 2 An application may be made at any time before the appointed date to the Local Tribunal established under this Act..for the issue..of a certificate of exemption from the provisions of this Act... The Local Tribunal, if they consider the grounds of the application established, shall grant such a certificate. 1916 *Act 6 & 7 Geo. V* c. 15 § 4 Where a decision of a local tribunal has been varied on appeal to the appeal tribunal. 1932 L. Golding *Magnolia Street* II. iv. § 3 The Baritone, at least, managed to convince tribunal after tribunal that it would be a mistake to put him into khaki.

Tricarballylic (trəi·kaɹbăli·lik), *a.* *Chem.* [See Tri-.] A crystalline tribasic acid found in unripe beet-roots and produced synthetically.

1865 M. Simpson in *Jrnl. Chem. Soc.* XVIII. 334 This body has been named by Kekule carballylic acid...I propose..in order to avoid confusion, to call it *tri*-carballylic acid. *Ibid.* 335, I have prepared and analysed several of the salts and ethers of tri-carballylic acid. 1876 *Encycl. Brit.* V. 571/1 Tricarballylic acid $C_3H_5(CO_2H)_3$, [is obtained] from tricyanopropane.

Trichinopoli. Add: *Trichinopoli chain.*

1879 *Encycl. Brit.* IX. 163/2 Round plaited gold chains of fine wire,..made by the filigree workers of India, and known as Trichinopoly chains.

Trichomycetes (tri:kǫməisī·tīz), *sb. pl.* *Biol.* [mod. L., f. Tricho-[1] + Mycetes.] A group of filamentous organisms intermediate between fungi and the bacteria.

1910 *Practitioner* Apr. 531 Sometimes trichomycetes were also present.

Trichoplax (tri·kǫplæks). [mod.L., f. Tricho-[1] + Gr. πλάξ plate.] A minute marine animal belonging to the genus of that name, the body of which is composed of three layers of cells.

1902 *Encycl. Brit.* XXXI. 794/1 The Gastræadæ from which von Graff derives this Trichoplax..is an obscure group of heterogeneous and problematical members.

Trichorrhexis (trikore·ksis). *Path.* [mod.L., f. Tricho-[1] + Gr. ῥῆξις fracture.] The breaking off of the hair. Hence **Trichorrhe·xic** *a.*

1901 Dorland *Med. Dict.* (ed. 2), Trichorrhexis. 1910 *Practitioner* Apr. 528 The hair shafts were brittle and trichorrhexic.

Trick, *sb.* **13.** Add: *trick-flying, -shot*; **trick picture,** a faked moving picture presenting incidents of a weird, fantastic, or mystifying kind; so *trick film.*

1912 F. A. Talbot *Moving Pictures* xviii. 197 The *trick-film owes its inception to a well-known French prestidigitateur, Monsieur Méliès. 1914 *Chambers's Jrnl.* 429/2 A certain number of these craft [*sc.* aeroplanes] are kept..for ..*trick-flying, etc. 1912 F. A. Talbot *Moving Pictures* xix. 207 The achievements of Méliès and Paul set a very high standard of excellence in *trick pictures. Their popularity precipitated a 'trick film' fever. The market became inundated with so-called magic pictures. 1924 C. J. Tolley *Mod. Golfer* 229 He tried to recover by the aid of a *trick shot.

Trick, *v.* Add: **8.** *Trick and tie*: *orig.* app. to take one's turn at something with another; cf. *ride and tie* (Ride *v.* 22); in quots. as *adj.* (sometimes hyphened): Equal, even (*with* someone or something). *dial.*

1825 C. M. Westmacott *Engl. Spy* I. 241 Trick and tie you know is fair play. 1883 *Hampshire Gloss.*, *Trick-and-tie*, equal to each other. 1889 Barrère & Leland *Dict. Slang*, *Trick and tie* (sport), to be *trick and tie*, or touch and go, is to be equal in a race, or other athletic performance. 1903 Farmer & Henley *Slang* s.v., *To trick and tie* = (1) to be equal (sporting) and (2) to have something in reserve. 1905 *Engl. Dial. Dict.*, *Trick and tie*, (Berks.) At hay-carting and harvest. When one wagon comes up full just as the other is emptied, they are said to be 'trick and tie'. (Wiltshire) 'I'll keep trick-and-tie wi' un', will keep even or level with him.

Trickle, *sb.*[1] Add: **2.** Comb: **trickle charger** (see quot. 1930).

1927 *Observer* 24 July 4/5 A fool-proof set..is provided with a 'trickle charger' for keeping the filament battery up to strength. 1930 *B.B.C. Year-Bk.* 454 *Trickle charger*, an accumulator charger which is arranged to charge at a low rate, so that a battery which has been in use during the day can be left on charge all night, and thus be fully charged for subsequent use. The mechanical analogy is water trickling to fill a tank.

Trickle, *v.* Add: **1. c.** *intr.* Used facetiously for: To make one's way, go.

1920 P. G. Wodehouse *Damsel in Distress* i, I must trickle up to town and see it some time this week.

4. *trans.* To cause (a ball) to travel slowly over the surface of the ground, esp. in golf. Also *to trickle a putt.* Also *absol.*

1902 *Daily Chron.* 20 Aug. 7/3 He can..trickle the ball away to fine-leg with a delicate turn of the wrist. 1903 *Westm. Gaz.* 6 Feb. 3/2 If you bolt at the hole, you will not need to make the same allowance for incline as if you trickled. 1927 *Daily Tel.* 14 Mar. 13/1 'I will trickle the putt up to the hole'...It certainly was a trickle..for the ball stopped five feet short of the hole.

Trickless (tri·klĕs), *a.* [f. Trick *sb.* + -less.] Without a trick.

1927 *Observer* 29 May 25 If he finds his partner trickless, he must go down enormously. 1929 Work *Compl. Contract Bridge* iv. 50 The No-Trumper with a trickless dummy might fail to fulfil his contract.

Tricoline (tri·kǫlīn). [Trade name.] A fine cotton poplin resembling silk.

1923 *Daily Mail* 26 Feb. 14 Tricoline. A Charming Fabric in a complete range of stripes and plain colours.

Tricolour, *a.* Add: **3.** = *Three-colour.

1909 *Chambers's Jrnl.* 268/1 Tricolour painting.

Triennial, *sb.* Add: **3.** A publication that appears triennially.

1849 *Harvard Class Poem* 4 Our tale shall be told by a silent star, On the page of some future Triennial.

Trier. Add: **13.** *Trier-out*, in glove-making (see quot.).

1921 *Dict. Occup. Terms* (1927) § 429 *Tryer-out*; examines sewing of finished gloves by fitting on steel stretchers.

Trig. Colloq. abbrev. of *trigonometry.*

1924 P. Marks *Plastic Age* 36 Kane announced the textbook, and when Hugh caught the word 'trigonometry' he actually thrilled with joy. He had had trig in high school.

Trigger[1]. Add: **2.** *Quick on the trigger* (in literal sense).

1873 J. H. Beadle *Undevel. West* xx. 371 He is reported 'so quick on the trigger', that all the other 'shootists' in the country have an awe of him.

3. fig. *Quick on the trigger* (earlier U.S. examples). *To pull the trigger*, to set things in motion.

1808 Weems *Lett.* II. 377, I trust that all your Aids will be quick on the trigger. 1842 Caroline M. Kirkland *Forest Life* II. xlvii. 223 'Pretty quick upon the trigger!' muttered Uncle William. 1887 G. H. Darwin in *Leisure Hour* 354/2 The attraction of the moon or the variation in atmospheric pressure pulls the trigger.

4. *attrib.* Also freq. *fig.* 'operating like a trigger', as *trigger action, -pulling, question.*

1915 W. M. Bayliss *Princ. Gen. Physiol.* x. (1918) 304 The difference between what is sometimes called '*trigger action' and catalysis. *Ibid.*, Supersaturated solutions are cases of 'trigger action'. They remain indefinitely as such until infected with a crystal, and then the rate of crystallisation is independent of the amount of crystals added. 1928 A. S. Eddington *Nat. Physical World* ix. (1930) 200 This is not a trigger action releasing energy. 1924 J. A. Thomson *Science Old & New* xix. 105 A current of air is necessary as the *trigger-pulling stimulus. 1927 J. Adams *Errors in School* 213 In external written examinations, where..the clever pupil..is led astray by expecting a question, and then treating one of the questions actually set as the one he expected. These '*trigger questions', as they may be called, set off the candidate on the wrong track.

Trike (trəik). Colloq. abbreviation of Tricycle. Also **Trike** *v.*, **Tri·ker.**

1885 *N. & Q.* 6th Ser. XII. 386/1 Do you bike or trike? 1889 Barrère & Leland *Dict. Slang*, *Trike* (common), a tricycle; *triking*, cycling. Do you bike or trike? do you ride a bicycle or tricycle. 1901 *Pall Mall Gaz.* 5 Jan. 3 (Cassell's Suppl.) The automobile trike..must tend to develop a deal of self-reliant daring in the lady sitter. *Ibid.* 15 May 1 (Farmer) The commercial 'trike' is, perhaps, the least supportable of the various tyrannies on wheels. *Ibid.* (Cassell's Suppl.), I was further gratified with the intimation that the peccant triker had been discovered. 1904 Sir R. C. Jebb in *Life & Lett.* (1907) 403, I..'triked' round by Grantchester. 1912 A. S. M. Hutchinson *Happy Warrior* III. v. § 2 I'm all mixed up in this awful trike, you know.

Trilby (tri·lbi). *colloq.* [The title of a novel by George du Maurier (*Harper's Mag.* 1893, dramatized 1895), and the name of its heroine, an artist's model whose bare feet were an object of admiration.] **a.** A jocular term for the foot. (*temporary.*) **b.** In full *Trilby hat*: A soft felt hat, esp. one of the Homburg type with a narrow brim and indented crown.

1895 *People* 7 July (Ware) An American paper has spent its energy of psychological investigation on the foot (I beg pardon, the trilby). 1897 *Daily News* 6 Feb. 6/5 In the struggle Mr. Bennett lost his hat, a black 'Trilby'...Mr. Carr..was also wearing a black 'Trilby' hat. 1901 *Westm. Gaz.* 26 Feb. 6/3 A 'Trilby' hat—better known, perhaps, as a 'Homburg' hat to most people. 1902 *Daily Chron.* 1 Sept. 5/4 Botha wore a wide-brimmed 'trilby'. 1930 L. M. Cooper *Ship of Truth* i. 95 More than all else, he wanted a trilby hat. 1930 *Punch* 19 Mar. 322/3 He seized upon his hat—his dove-grey trilby.

Trim, *sb.* Add: **3. g.** A window display of goods. *U.S.*

1926 *Publishers' Weekly* 30 Jan. 328/1 A large red ribbon rosette, from which radiated white satin ribbons to a number of stands at each side of the trim. *Ibid.* 10 July 119/2 When Stone's trim was removed, Wheatly did his 'stuff'.

Trim, *v.* Add: **9. b.** *fig.* or in fig. context. To cheat (a person) out of money; to fleece. *slang.*

1600 [see 9 fig. in Dict.]. 1604 Dekker *News fr. Graves-End* Ep. Ded., Thou wouldst neuer haue gone to any Barbers in London..but haue bin trimd only there, for they are the true shauers, they haue the right Neapolitan polling. *a* 1700 B. E. *Dict. Cant. Crew*, *Trimming*, Cheating People of their Money. 1903 Farmer & Henley *Slang*, *Trim*, to cheat. 1928 E. Wallace *Again the Three Just Men* 217 Garry forgot his arrangement to trim the young guardsman that night in the thrill of confronting a bigger quarry.

13. Also *Aeronautics.*

1921 *Discovery* Apr. 95/2 When trimmed up by the bow, the airship will be found to ride satisfactorily.

Trimmed (trimd), *ppl. a.* [f. Trim *v.* + -ed[1].] See after Trim *v.* Also: spec. *trimmed joist*, each of the joists which are tenoned into the trimmer (see Trimmer 4), as distinguished from a 'trimming joist'.

1876 *Encycl. Brit.* IV. 482 Plate, Fig. 1 Trimmed Joists.

Trimmer. **4.** *attrib.* Add: *trimmer arch* (later U.S. example), *beam.*

1897 Moore *How to Build* iii. 32 'Trimmer'-beams enter the wall on each side of the chimney. *Ibid.* viii. 113 All hearths shall be constructed with trimmer-arches extending 20 inches from the chimney-breast to a 'skew back'.

Trimonthly, *a.* (Earlier U.S. example.)

1856 *Trans. Mich. Agric. Soc.* VII. 329 The Steamer Superior..made tri-monthly trips from Buffalo to Detroit.

Tri·-motor. [Tri- 4 c.] An aeroplane fitted with three motors. So **Tri-motored** *a.*

1923 *Glasgow Herald* 1 Jan. 8 The aeroplane which it is proposed to use will be a tri-motor. 1927 *Weekly Times* 9 June 632/3 Trimotored aeroplanes. 1929 *Saturday Even. Post* (N.Y.) 7 Dec. 63/1 The giant tri-motored Ford planes of this line.

Tringa (tri·ngă). [mod.L.: see Tring.] A bird belonging to the genus of that name; a sandpiper.

1752–1816 [see Tring]. 1844 [see Spoon-billed *a.*]

Trinil (trəi·nil). The name of a district in Java used attrib. with reference to a simian form of skull-cap excavated there in 1891–2.

1898 Du Bois in *Trans. Roy. Dublin Soc.* VI. 9 The human form of the Trinil femur is not sufficient to prove that it did not belong to the same individual as the skull-cap. *Ibid.* 12 The Trinil individual, if a human being, ought to have been a microcephalic idiot...The Trinil cranium..very much approaches the type of Anthropoid Apes. *Ibid.* 13 It may be that the Trinil skull is in other respects to be compared with the Neanderthal and Spy skulls. 1902 *Encycl. Brit.* XXV. 466/1 Classing the Trinil skull as human, it may be described as tending towards the simian type.

Trinitrotoluene (trəinəitrǫtǫ·liu,īn). Earlier **-toluol** (tǫ·liu,ǫl). [f. Trinitro- + Toluene, Toluol.] A high explosive consisting of a nitro-substitution compound of toluene; any of several isomeric compounds made by nitrating toluene, used as a filling for shells and as an ingredient

of various explosives. Abbreviated TNT, T.N.T. (see *T). Also *attrib.*

1916 *Yorkshire Post* 27 Mar. 5/1 Contact with tri-nitrotoluol may result in the occurrence of troublesome skin affections. 1917 *Causation & Prev. Tri-nitro-toluene (T.N.T.) Poisoning* (Nat. Health Insur.) 9 The material known commercially as T.N.T. is mainly composed of one of the three isomeric tri-nitro-toluenes. 1918 *Times* 17 Oct. 5/6 The trinitrotoluene plant of the British Chemical Works. 1919 *Athenæum* 23 May 360/1 'Trinitrotoluene', which the munitioneers shortened to T.N.T. 1928 C. F. S. Gamble *Story North Sea Air Station* v. 87 The Marten Hale rifle-grenade...The container holding a charge of about 6 ounces of tri-nitro-toluene.

Triode (trəi·oud). *Wireless Telegr.* [f. Tri- + Electr)ode.] In full *triode valve*: A three-electrode valve (see quot. 1926).

1919 *Nature* CIV. 178/2 Papers..on the internal action of a triode valve. 1922 *Encycl. Brit.* XXXII. 1024/2 A three-electrode thermionic valve, a name sometimes shortened into *triode*. 1926 R. W. Hutchinson *Wireless* viii. 140 The modern valve used in wireless and known as the triode consists of a tungsten filament and a plate, with a wire grid between them, the three being quite separate from each other.

Trip, *sb.*[1] **9.** Add: **trip shunter** (see quot.); **trip wire** (*a*) *Mil.* (see quot. 1918); (*b*) *Mech.*, a device for operating a flash-light.

1921 *Dict. Occup. Terms* (1927) § 704 **Trip shunter*; travels with goods train to do shunting work at a small yard or siding where no shunter is stationed. 1917 *Chambers's Jrnl.* Aug. 509/1 There was *trip-wire here, all unsuspected and uncut. 1918 E. S. Farrow *Dict. Mil. Terms*, *Trip Wires*,..wires placed in front of firing-points with the object of flinging individuals to the ground. 1928 *Daily Mail* 3 Aug. 8/3 Trip-wires to ensnare the enemy. 1928 *Daily Tel.* 16 Oct. 18 A flash-light operated by means of a 'trip wire'.

Trip (trip). Colloq. abbrev. of Tripos (in sense 2 d).

1925 G. W. Deeping *Sorrell & Son* xxiv. § 1, I want a first in the Science Trip.

Tri-pack (trəi·pæk). Also **-pak.** [f. Tri- 4 + Pack *sb.*[1]] In colour photography, a pack of three sensitive films designed to give three negatives of the same registration at one exposure, for printing in three separate colours. Also *attrib.*

1911 *Brit. Jrnl. Photogr.* 3 Mar., Suppl. 19 The Ives Tripak System of Colour Photography. 1924 *Ibid.* 5 Sept., Suppl. 36/1 It remains to be seen whether critical sharpness can be obtained by any bi- or tri-pack. 1927 *Ibid.* 1 July, Suppl. 26/2 The Tripak (polyfolium of two plates and one film). 1928 *Ibid.* 5 Oct. 39/2 The invention consists of a particular form of trifolium or tripack of three sensitive films or surfaces for the taking of the negatives at one exposure. 1928 *Times* 21 May 23/2 The well-known 'tri-pack' device in which three emulsions are used, sensitive respectively to three wave-length bands within the range of the visible spectrum.

Tripe[1]. **3.** Add: Now freq. of artistic productions, conversation, and the like: Inferior stuff, nonsensical rubbish, trash. *colloq.*

1892, 1895 [see Dict.] 1902 'T. Le Breton' (T. M. Ford) *Mod. Christian* viii, She puts in six or seven pages of her own tripe. 1925 *Love* I. ii. 19 Lewes would bring out views which Christopher..considered..as so much—the word was his—tripe. 1929 Priestley *Good Comp.* III. iii. 528 He.. glanced through about twenty of its newest songs, and most of them were so bad that he found himself gleefully whispering 'Tripe, tripe!'

Trip-hammer. (Earlier U.S. example.)

1781 S. Peters *Hist. Connecticut* (1829) 199 Anchor making is done by water and trip hammers.

Triping (trəi·piŋ). [f. Tripe[1] + -ing[1].] Coal as it is hewn and brought to the pit-head, mixed with dross and dirt, before it is cleaned and graded. Also *attrib.*

1901 *Scotsman* 29 May Advt. (E.D.D.) Estimates are wanted for supplying best Screened Climpy Triping. 1921 *Glasgow Herald* 21 Apr. 5 A 'triping' ton..represents about 55 per cent. of round coal, 40 per cent. of dross, and 5 per cent. of dirt. 1923 *Ibid.* 22 Dec. 5 The miner produces what is known in the trade as 'triping'. 1924 *Ibid.* 6 Oct. 8 The coals are filled in the hutches at the coal face as 'triping'—large and small mixed.

Triplane (trəi·plēn). [f. Tri- 4 + *Plane *sb.*[3]] An aeroplane or glider having three superimposed planes or main supporting surfaces. Also *attrib.*

1909 A. Berget *Conquest of Air* 141 Naturally we can make triplanes or quadriplanes, but one must not proceed too far in this direction. 1912 *Q. Rev.* July 234 A triplane has been successfully made. 1916 *Yorkshire Post* 24 Apr. 4/5 Mr. Wannaker, of the American Club, is building a triplane. 1920 *Glasgow Herald* 10 July 5 The Pullman triplanes of the British Company carry 18 people.

Triplet. Add: **2. j.** In the game of poker: see quot.

1885 *Encycl. Brit.* XIX. 283/1 Poker...Value of Hands... 6. Triplets (three cards of the same rank, with two other cards not a pair).

Triplice (tri·pliʃe). [It. *triplice* triple, Triplex.] The Triple Alliance between Germany, Austria, and Italy, formed in 1882–3 against Russia and France.

1896 *Daily News* 15 Dec. 5/3 The same demand has been made to the other members of the Triplice. 1897 *Ibid.* 6 Sept. 5/2 The Triplice desires peace at any cost. 1901 *Speaker* 20 Apr. 74/2 It would be misleading to call the *Triplice* a League of peace. 1909 *Q. Rev.* Oct. 581 The central pivot of the Triplice is in Berlin.

Hence **Tri·plicist,** a supporter of the Triplice. Also as *adj.*

1923 J. Buchan *Nations of To-day, Italy* 172 It was able to give a decidedly 'Triplicist' aspect to the enterprise. 1924 *Glasgow Herald* 15 Jan. 7 It is all to the credit of the Triplicists..and very little to that of the Allies.

Triploid (tri·ploid), *a.* *Biol.* [Formed as Triploid *sb.* (see Dict.).] Having the basic number of chromosome units trebled. Also as *sb.*

1930 *Jrnl. Genetics* XXII. 129 Earlier workers have shown that seventeen is the haploid number of chromosomes in the genus *Pyrus* (including *Malus*) and that cultivated forms are diploid and triploid. *Ibid.* 145 A second source of evidence is derived from the seedlings of the 'triploid' apple, Bramley's seedling. In selfing triploids or crossing them with diploids we find a resolution [etc.].

Tripoline (tri·pǫlīn), *a.*[2] [ad. It. *tripolino*, f. *Tripoli*: see -ine[1].] Of or belonging to Tripoli, a region, city, and port of North Africa. Also **Tripo·litan** *a.* [ad. It. *tripolitano*].

1819 Salamé *Narr. Exped. Algiers* 6 We found she was a Tripoline polacca, (I am sorry that she was not an Algerine). 1908 V. G. Childe *Most Anc. East* ii. 25 In the very heart of the Sahara at In-Ezzan, just south of the Tripolitan borders.

Trippery (tri·pəri), *a.* [f. Tripper + -y[1].] Of, pertaining to, or characteristic of trippers.

1926 W. J. Locke *Old Bridge* I. ii, 'But let us see all we can to-night'...'That wouldn't be fair to Florence. It's a bit trippery, isn't it?' 1928 *Daily Express* 11 Apr. 9/4 Venice,..the Queen of the Adriatic in its most trippery and least attractive garb.

Trippingly, *adv.* (Recent example.)

1910 'O. Henry' *Whirligigs* viii. 121 In ten minutes I shall..be legging it trippingly for the Canadian border.

Tritomite (tri·tǫməit). *Min.* [ad. G. *tritomit* (1850), f. Gr. τρίτομος thrice-cut: see -ite[1].] Fluosilicate of thorium, cerium, and other bases.

1868 Dana *Min.* (ed. 5) 412 Tritomite...Lustre submetallic, vitreous. Color dull brown. Streak dirty yellowish-gray. Subtranslucent.

Tri-weekly. **B.** *adv.* (Earlier U.S. examples.)

1837 Peck *Gaz. Illinois* III. 180 The mail..arrives here tri-weekly. 1857 *Annual Reps. U.S. P.M.G.* 980 Proposals to carry the mails tri-weekly in steamers between Cedar Key and New Orleans.

C. *sb.* A tri-weekly journal. *U.S.*

1851 C. Cist *Cincinnati* 74 These are all dailies, tri-weeklies and weekly reissues of dailies. 1884 *U.S. Census* VIII. 111 Three months only the *Spy* ran as a tri-weekly, and but three months longer as a semi-weekly.

Trochil (trǫ·kil). [Anglicized form of Trochilus[1].] = Trochilus[1] 1.

1925 *Blackw. Mag.* Aug. 197/2 The trochil, the bird that picks crocodiles' teeth.

Troglobiont (trǫg-, trǭu·globəiǫnt). Also **-bion.** [f. Gr. τρώγλη hole + βίων living, pres. pple. of βιοῦν to live.] An animal that lives in caves and dark waters. So **Tro·glophil** [Gr. φίλος friend], an animal that thrives but does not live entirely in dark places. **Tro·gloxene** [Gr. ξένος guest], an animal that is a casual visitor to dark places.

1924 *Glasgow Herald* 13 Dec. 4 Permanent cave-dwellers (the troglobions), like the Dalmatian Proteus newt. *Ibid.*, If we include many of the bats as troglophils. 1927 *Ibid.* 2 July 4 The three groups have received various names, such as troglobionts, troglophils, and trogloxenes.

Troller: see *Trolleyer.

Trolley, *sb.* **4.** Add: **trolley fittings,** sliding fittings (of a wardrobe, etc.) running on pulleys.

1930 *Daily Express* 30 July 4/6 Wardrobe Trunks..with trolley fittings.

Trolleyer (trǫ·liəɹ). [f. Trolley *sb.* or *v.* + -er[1].] **a.** A workman who conveys materials on a trolley or bogey in a foundry. **b.** (See quot.) Also **Troller** (trǫ·ləɹ).

1921 *Dict. Occup. Terms* (1927) § 043 *Drawer*,..trollier, truck lad,..; pushes coal or shale in tubs or corves from working face to pass-byes on main haulage road. *Ibid.* § 279 Troller. Trolleyer.

Trollop (trǫ·ləp), *v.* [f. Trollop *sb.*] **1.** *intr.* To walk in a slovenly way, to slouch. Cf. *lollop.*

1854 M. Dods *Early Lett.* (1910) 63, I felt deeply moved for her, thinking she would trollop away home. 1870 'Ouida' *Puck* vii, There's allus a lot of..bad wimmin a trolloping about. 1897 Crockett *Lochinvar* v, A lank hobbledehoy gooseherd who came trolloping along a path.., yawning. 1925 *Chambers's Jrnl.* 397/2 We'll go very slow and he can trollop behind.

2. (See Dict. s.v. Trollop *sb.*)

Trolloper (trǫ·ləpəɹ). *local.* [Obscure.] (See quots.)

1911 *Encycl. Brit.* XXVII. 218/2 Shank nets are sometimes worked from carts, when they are known as 'Trollopers'. 1921 *Dict. Occup. Terms* (1927) § 000 *Trolloper*; Wash district: a shrimper who catches shrimps with trawl dropped from boat or pulled by horse and cart.

Troop, *sb.* Add: **3. c.** A company of boy scouts consisting of not less than three patrols of six scouts.

1908 [see *Patrol 3 b].

5. troop-carrier (plane), **troop-plane,** a military aeroplane for transporting troops; **troop-siding,** a railway siding for the detrainment of troops.

1923 *Daily Mail* 23 June 5 Among landplanes there are huge new *troop-carriers capable of carrying 25 fully equipped soldiers. 1928 *Observer* 17 June 19/5 A twenty-one seater troop-carrier plane. 1923 *Daily Mail* 30 June 7 Our.. *troop-planes..will transport as many as 25 fully-equipped soldiers. 1911 *Chambers's Jrnl.* 47/2 The Blackshires leapt out of their trucks almost before the train had stopped at the *troop-siding.

Trooper, var. *Trouper.

Trooperess (trū·pərĕs). [f. Trooper + -ess.] A woman trooper.

1924 Galsworthy *White Monkey* II. iv. 152 When she was either torturing two men, or lying to them like a trooperess. 1927 *Daily Express* 2 Sept. 3 The stories related of the coarse, swearing 'trooperess' are astounding.

Tropacocaine (trǭu·păkǫkē·in). *Pharm.* [ad. G. *tropacocaïn*, irreg. f. *tropeïn* Tropeine + *cocaïn* Cocaine.] Benzoyl-pseudo-tropeine, an alkaloid resembling cocaine, first isolated from Javanese coca and employed as a local anæsthetic.

1902–3 *Calif. State Jrnl. Med.* I. 118–21 Spinal anesthesia with tropacocaine in genito-urinary surgery. 1909 *Practitioner* Feb. 231 He recommends tropa-cocaine in small doses.

Trophallaxis (trǫfălæ·ksis). [f. Gr. τροφή nourishment + ἄλλαξις exchange.] (See quot. 1924.) So **Trophalla·ctic** *a.*

1919 W. Osler *Old Humanities* ii. 13 The nursing function ..is really trophallactic..The larva is provided with..an ambrosia greedily lapped up by the nurse. 1922 W. M. Wheeler *Social Life among Insects* 45 We are able to observe in the social wasps more clearly than in other social insects the peculiar phenomenon which I have called 'trophallaxis', *i.e.*, the mutual exchange of food between adults and their larval young. 1924 J. A. Thomson *Science Old & New* x. 56 As this term does not bring out the fact that in the main the feeding of adults and larvæ is reciprocal, Professor Wheeler suggests the term 'trophallaxis.'

Tropopause (trǫ·pǫpǭz). *Meteorol.* [f. *Tropo(sphere + Pause *sb.*] The (imaginary) boundary between the troposphere and the stratosphere.

1919 W. H. Dines *Coll. Sci. Papers* (1931) 329 The terms 'tropopause' and 'lapse-limit' have been suggested to denote the plane of cessation of the vertical temperature gradient. 1922 *Encycl. Brit.* XXXI. 930 In a cyclone the tropopause is low, in an anticyclone high. 1923 Sir N. Shaw *Forecasting Weather* xv. 409 The name *tropopause* has been coined to indicate the boundary between the troposphere below and the stratosphere above.

Troposphere (trǫ·pǫsfīəɹ). *Meteorol.* [f. Gr. τρόπος turn + σφαῖρα ball, Sphere.] The layer of atmospheric air extending from the surface of the earth to the height of about seven miles, bounded by the stratosphere, and in which there is a fall of temperature with height. Cf. *Stratosphere.

1914 C. J. P. Cave in *Q. Jrnl. R. Meteorol. Soc.* Apr. 108 M. Teisserenc de Bort discovered that the atmosphere is divided into two parts, the troposphere, which extends from the surface to about 7 miles, and the stratosphere, which lies above. 1922 *Nature* CIX. 141/1 In..the troposphere, the atmospheric gases are kept well mixed up by winds and convection.

Trot, *sb.*[1] **5.** *U.S.* (Example.)

1924 P. Marks *Plastic Age* 299 I'm talking about the copying of math problems and the using of trots.

Trot, *v.* **3.** Add: With *step* as obj.

1927 D. H. Lawrence *England, my England* 202 [The horses] trotting a few sudden steps as they were led into the lane.

Trotskyism (trǫ·tski,iz'm). Also **Trotskyism.** [f. name of L. *Trotzky* (Bronstein), Russian Bolshevik minister of foreign affairs, 1917 + -ism.] The political principles or economic policy of Trotsky. So **Tro·tskyist.** (Cf. *Stalinism.)

1925 *Times* 30 Jan., Imperial News 4, I cannot..accept the accusation of trying to pursue my own line of policy (Trotskyism). 1927 *Daily Tel.* 22 Nov. 9/2 The adoption of the word 'Russia' by the Trotskyists. *Ibid.* 6 Dec. 11 The struggle between the Trotskists and the Stalinites. 1928 *Daily Express* 26 Nov. 11/4 Stalin..defended the Political Bureau's three fundamental decisions...That the party must fight both the Radical Trotskyists and the Conservative dissenters within the party's ranks. 1930 W. H. Chamberlin *Soviet Russia* iv. 74 The Party Congress..laid down the rule that adherence to the views of the Trotzkyist opposition was inconsistent with membership in the Communist Party. *Ibid.* 76 There would seem to be little political future in Russia for Trotzkyism.

Trottie (trǫ·ti). *dial.* or *colloq.* [dim. of Trot *sb.*[1]: see -ie.] A tiny toddling child; a toddler.

1914 *N.E.D.* s.v. Trot *sb.*[1] 4. 1924 'L. Malet' *Dogs of Want* vii. § 6 Darling girls, from the time when they were the tiniest trotties till now.

Trotty (trǫ·ti), *a. colloq.* Also **trottie.** [f. Trot *sb.*[1] + -y[1].] Of daintily small proportions.

1891 'L. Malet' *Wages of Sin* Epil., The son and heir is quite the trottiest of trots. *Ibid.* v. i, Some of the little silk shifties and night-i-gowns were simply too trottie for words. 1895 *Punch* 15 June 285/3 When countesses mount 'em at Chelsea, they're trotty and puffeck OK! *Ibid.* 17 Aug. 77/1 He..Looks perticularly fetchin' in a trotty yotting cap. 1928 Galsworthy *Swan Song* I. i. 4 Trotty little ladies with dresses tight blown about trotty little figures.

Trotyl (trǭu·til). [f. *Tri(ni)trot(oluene + -yl.] = *Trinitrotoluene.

1919 *Athenæum* 23 May 360/1 'Trinitrotoluene', which.. the expert called 'trotyl.' 1922 *Encycl. Brit.* XXXI. 50 Trinitrotoluene (TNT) which is known officially as Trotyl is..very similar in its action to picric acid and had been discovered by Wilbrand in 1863.

Trouble, *sb.* Add: **5.** Also, *to seek trouble.*

1905 *N. Y. Evening Post* 29 Aug. 2 In the possible chance of rounding up all who might be seeking trouble.

6. b. Faulty working of apparatus or machinery, esp. of the engine or motor of an aeroplane or other motor vehicle.

U

Twist, v. Add: **12.** d. *Insurance.* To induce (a person) to drop a policy in one company and take out a new one in another.

Twisted, *ppl. a.* Add: Of the stem of a wine-glass: Having a spiral ornament inside.

Twister, *sb.* Add: **4.** f. A dishonest person, a crook. *slang.*

Twistical, *a.* U.S. (Earlier example.)

Twistify (twistīfəi), v. [f. TWIST a. + -FY.] *trans.* To make twisty (*lit.* and *fig.*).

Twisty, *a.* Add: ... "TWISTED *ppl. a.* 3.

Twitch, *sb.*[2] Add: Said of a smile. Cf. next.

Twitchy, *a.*[1] Add: Said of a smile.

Two, *a.* and *sb.* Add: **B.** I. **4.** *I. No two ways about it:* see WAY 18. 1.
II. **b.** 2. h. A portrait group of two persons.

Two-bit, *a.* U.S., of the value of a quarter of a dollar; two-by-four, a post or batten measuring 2 by 4 inches; two-eyed stance, in Cricket (see quot. 1924); also one-eye stance.

Two-storied, *a.* [STORY *sb.*[2]] Having two storeys.

Two-story, *a.* (Earlier example.)

Tyburnia (təibə̄·mĭa). [mod.L., f. TYBURN.] A literary name for the residential district running along the Bayswater Road from Marble Arch to Lancaster Gate.

Tychism (təi·kĭz'm), sb. [f. Gr. τύχη chance + -ISM.] A theory that makes chance the operative principle in the universe.

Tyg. Also *tig.* (Earlier example.)

Type, *sb.* Add: **10.** type-casting, -founding, -setting (earlier U.S. examples).

Type, v. Add: **Med.** To compare (samples of blood for transfusion) in order to determine the compatibility of the blood of the donor for transfusion to that of the receptor.

Typological, *a.* Add: Now in wider use.

Typology. Add: **3.** *Archæol.* The classification of remains and specimens according to the type they exhibit and its evolution, etc.

Tyranness (ti·rănĕs). [f. TYRANT + -ESS.] Tyrannis. *Greek Hist.* = TYRANNY 2.

Tyrannosaurus (tĭrænŏsǭ·rŭs). [mod.L., f. Gr. τύραννος tyrant + σαῦρος lizard.] A very large dinosaur, discovered in Montana, U.S.A., in 1902.

U.2. c. (Earlier example.)

U.S.S.R. (Union of Socialist Soviet Republics.)

U-boat. (Examples.)

Ubiquist. (Earlier example.)

Ubiquity (ūbĭ·kwĭtĭ). (Earlier example.)

Udaller (ū·dălə̆r). Also uthaller. A person who holds land by udal tenure.

Ugro-. Ugro-Finn.

Ukulele (ūkŭlē·lĭ). Also oukulele, ukelele, ukalele. (Native name.) A four-stringed Hawaiian guitar.

Ule, ull: see *HULE.

Ulloon. Also uthoan.

Ulsterette (Earlier example.)

Ultima (ŭ·ltĭma). Add: *a.* Pertaining to typology or to archæological types.

Ultra-. Add: **B.** Denoting instruments adapted for very minute measurements, observations, etc. as *ultra-micrometer, -microscope.*

Ultra-violet, v. Also used in therapeutics and photography.

Ultramontane. A. *sb.* 1. b. (Earlier example.)

Ultrasonic (ŭltrasŏ·nĭk), a. and sb. [f. ULTRA- + SONIC.] *a. adj.* That is beyond the range of normal audibility. **b.** *sb.* Sound waves having too high frequencies to be audible.

Ultra-violet, a. b. Med.

Ulu. Also ul-lu.

Ulys (ū·lĭs). [Coined by W. de la Mare.] An imaginary flower.

Unco-nscient, a. [UN-[1] 7.] That is not conscient.

Unconsciously. (Later example; also *absol.*)

Unconsiderable, *a.* (Modern example.)

Uncoordinated. (Earlier and later examples.)

Uncurled, *ppl. a.* (Later example.)

Undenominational. (Earlier example.)

Under, *prep.* Add: **14.** f. Attended by or in respect of.

Under-arm, a. 3. *Lawn Tennis.*

Unalive, a. Add: **b.** Dead-looking; sluggish; lifeless.

Unbitted, *ppl. a.* (Earlier example.)

Unblocked, *ppl. a.* **c.** Not provided with books.

Unbloom (Earlier example.)

Unbrowning, *vbl. sb.* [-ING[1].] The action of the verb UNBROWN.

Untrunning, *vbl. sb.* (Earlier example.)

Uncared, *ppl. a.* (Later example.)

Uncharacter, *a.* Add: (Recent example.)

Unchildish, *a.* (Recent example.)

Uncivilised, *ppl. a.* Also *absol.*

Uncleared, *ppl. a.*

Uncoloured, *ppl. a.* (Later example.)

Unconsidered, *ppl. a.* Add: **2.** b. *Psych.* Of reflexes: inborn; not conditioned.

Unconditioned, *a.* Add: **2.** b. *Psych.*

Uncorrected, *ppl. a.* (Later example.)

Uncouth, a. (Later examples; also *absol.*)

Under-arm, a. 3.

Underbed. (U.S. example.)

Underbid, v. b. *Bridge.* To bid less (on a hand) than its strength warrants.

Underbidder. Add: **2.** *Bridge.*

Underbit. U.S. An earmark to indicate ownership.

Under-clerk. (Later example.)

Undercoat, v. II. b. *Haggard* under-clerks were opening shops or sweeping.

Undercut, v. Add: To fall under in cost.

Underdrain'n. Draining by means of underground drains.

Under-employment. [UNDER-[1] 10 b.] Insufficient employment.

Underfelt. (Earlier example.)

Underfoot, *adv.* All the ground that is walked upon.

Undergraduate, sb. collog. [UNDERGRADUATE + -ETTE.] A female undergraduate.

Underkeel. (Earlier example.)

Underkeeled, *ppl. a.* Marked with an under-keel.

Underlay, *sb.* Add: **4.** A layer of vegetation on the surface of the ground.

Under-nourished, *ppl. a.* [UNDER-[1] 10 a.] Not provided with sufficient nourishment.

Under-nourishment.

Underpass. [UNDER-[1] 6 c.] An underground or road-way providing passage under a railway, etc.

Under-pick, v. [UNDER-[1] 5 b.] Of a loom: Having the picking motion beneath the shuttle.

Under-planting, *vbl. sb.* [UNDERPLANT v.] The action of the verb UNDERPLANT.

Under-self. [UNDER-[1] 10 b.] The subconscious self.

Undershot, v. [UNDER-[1] 5 b.] At the moment she had been thinking of the under-hand.

Undership. [UNDER-[1] 8 c.] Fitted with inadequate springs.

Under-stain'dly, *adv.* [-LY[2].] In a manner that can be understood; conceivably.

Undertake, v. Add: b. *Jur.* 10/6 The members of the Fascist Militia...might understandably display an aggressive consciousness of their position and power.

Underthing.

Undertrick. *Bridge.* [UNDER-[1] 2 c.] A trick required to make up the number of the bid or contract, but not taken.

Undertype. v. *Electr.* [UNDER-[1] 5.] Of a dynamo: Having the armature below the yoke of the magnets.

Under-waist. See UNDER-[1] 5 and WAIST 2 d.

Underworld. Add: **4.** (Later fig. example.)

Undies (ə̆·ndĭz), *sb. pl.* [f. UNDER- in UNDER-GARMENT, UNDERWEAR, etc.] Articles of women's underclothing; occas. as *sing.* Undy.

Undulator (ə̆·ndŭlē̆tə̆r). [f. UNDULATE + -OR.] An instrument for recording morse signals in wire-less telegraphy.

Unemployable, *a.* and *sb.* Add: Also *absol.*

Unemployment. Also *unemployment benefit*.

Un-f·t, n. [f. the adj.] An unfit person.

Ungear, v. 1. (U.S. examples.)

Ungraded, *ppl. a.* 1. (Earlier example.)

Ungrateful, *a.* 2. (Later example.)

Ungranted, *ppl. a.* (Earlier examples, and of land.)

Unground, *v.* (Later example.)

Unguent, *sb.* [f. the adj.] Oily, smooth-tongued, unctuous.

Ungunnet, n. (Later example.)

Unhandling. (Later example.)

Unhearable, *a.* Add: **b.** Unable to hear.

Unheed'y, *a.*

Unhitch, v. 2.

Unhumanity. [UN-[1] 12.] Unhuman character.

Unhusbandly, *a.*

Unpegging, *vbl. sb.* [-ING[1].] The action of unpegging.

Unpin, v. Add: **5.** *trans. Chess.* To release a piece that has been pinned.

Unpleasantness. Add: The late or recent unpleasantnesses: the Civil War.

Unrip, v. b. (Modern example.)

Uncap, v. (Earlier example.)

Unsaleable, *a.* [UN-[1] 7 b.] That cannot be said.

Unscalped, *ppl. a.* (Earlier example.)

Unshingled, *ppl. a.* [UN-[1] 8.] That is not shingled.

Unshockable, *a.* [UN-[1] 7 b.] That cannot be shocked.

Unimproved, *a.* (Earlier example.)

Unsnarl, v. (Earlier intr. example.)

Unspan, v. (Recent example.)

Unspecific, *a.* [UN-[1] 7.]

Unspectacular, *a.* [UN-[1] 7 b.]

Unsplinterable, *a.* [UN-[1] 7 b.] That will not splinter.

Unsprung, *ppl. a.* [UN-[1] 8.] Not provided with springs.

Unstick, v. Add: **b.** *Aeronautics.* To rise from the water or the ground.

Unstressed, *ppl. a.* (Later example.)

Unstring, v. Add: b. A fit of nerves.

Untakeable, *a.* (Further example.)

Unthrift, *sb.* Add: **4.** Lack of thriving.

Untouchability. The quality or state of being an untouchable.

Untouchable, *a.* and *sb.* Add: A Hindoo belonging to one of the lowest castes.

Up-and-coming, a. [Up-[1] 3.]

Upanishadic, *a.* [f. UPANISHAD + -IC.] Of or pertaining to the Upanishads.

Upcast, *sb.* Add: **4.** b. (Further example.)

Upcli·mb, *sb.* [Up-[1] 3.] An upward climb.

Up-country, *sb.* Add: Also *adj.*

Upcountry, *a.* and *sb.*

Updraw, *sb.* (Later example.)

Upgrade, *sb.* (Earlier example.)

Upgrade, v. [Up-[1] 4.] To raise the grade of; to put on a higher grade.

Unwhitewashed, *ppl. a.* Also *fig.*

Umbrella. Add: **10.** *attrib.*: umbrella aerial, an aerial in which the wires are arranged like the ribs of an umbrella; umbrella-lamp, a lamp having an umbrella-like shade.

Umpteen (ə̆·mptīn), colloq. Also umteen.

Umpty (ə̆·mptĭ). colloq. An indefinite large number.

Unapt, *a.* (Modern example.)

Unloose, v. Add: To lead up to: see LEAD v.

Uncial. (Later example.)

Up and down. (Earlier example.)

Up and down, *adv.* Add: **7.** (Earlier example.)

Up-grade, v. (Later example.)

Upholding, *ppl. a.* Add: Also as a predicate.

Upholster, v. **2.** (Later example.)

Uplift, sb. **2.** Also *attrib.*

Unip. (Later example.)

Uplifted, *ppl. a.* 1. An uplifted manner.

Upon, *adv.* Add: To be *upon a man:* (slang) to set about him.

Upper, *sb.* **3.** c. *U.S.* Down on one's uppers.

Upper dog. (Further example.)

Upping, *vbl. sb.*[1]

Uppishly, *adv.* [UPPISH *a.* + -LY[2].]

Upright, *sb.* 2. Add: **3.** b. Also, one or other of the vertical posts of a goal.

Upright. Also *refl.*

Up and coming, a. [Up-[1] 3.]

Uprising, *ppl. a.* (Further example.)

Upriver, *ppl. a.* (Earlier example.)

Uproarious, *a.* (Further example.)

Upshut, *sb.* (Later example.)

Upsprang. Also *absol.*

Upspring, v. 1. b. (Further example.)

Upspring, *sb.*

Up-stage, v. 1. [UP-[1] 5.]

Upstairs.

Upstand, v. Add: **4.** *trans.* To set upright.

U·psurge, *sb.* [UP- 2.] An uprising.
1930 *Aberdeen Press & Jrnl.* 4 Feb. 7/5 The beginnings of a widespread revolutionary upsurge..are visualised in a proclamation issued by the Red International.

Upsurge, *v.* [UP- 4.] So **Upsurging** *vbl. sb.*
1925 DEEPING *Sorrell & Son* i, His own voice surprised him. It was resonant,..and it seemed to express the upsurging within him of some subconscious element.

Uptake, *sb.* **1.** (Later example.)
1927 VACHELL *Dew of the Sea* etc. 259 For a moment the chieftain was puzzled. But he was fairly quick at the uptake, replying after a pause [etc.].

Upthrust, *sb.* Also *fig.*
1930 D. B. WYNDHAM LEWIS *King Spider* ii. 52 It is an historical curiosity..that immediately after each apparent disaster there has followed a vigorous upthrust.

b. The upward force which a fluid exerts on a body immersed in it.
1916 ALLEN & MOORE *Text-bk. Pract. Physics* 54 The resultant supporting force may be termed the upthrust. 1923 H. MOORE *Text-bk. Int. Physics* 29 When a body is immersed in any fluid, it is subjected to a supporting force, or upthrust, equal to the weight of the fluid displaced.

U·p-to-dately, *adv.* [f. UP-TO-DATE B + -LY^2.] In an up-to-date manner.
1928 *Daily Express* 23 Mar. 5/4 Furnish and equip her studio charmingly..and above all 'up-to-dately'.

Up-town. 1. (Earlier examples.)
1836 *Q. Race Kentucky* (1846) 13 The muster at the stand was slim, it having been understood up town, that..the race would prove a water-haul. 1839 C. F. BRIGGS *Harry Franco* I. xiii. 96 The rain was pattering against the windows, and the house was far uptown. 1854 'O. OPTIC' *In Doors & Out* (1876) 120 Her husband engaged a room in a fashionable establishment 'up town'.

Upturn, *sb.* Add: **1. b.** A portion of the material of a garment turned up, esp. at the end of legs or sleeves.
1923 *Daily Mail* 11 Aug. 1 Advt., Shorts have good upturns for lengthening.

U·p-we·lling, *vbl. sb.* [UP- 7.] A pouring or welling upwards. Also *fig.*, esp. from the 'depths' of the mind.
1896 MRS. HUMPHRY WARD *Sir G. Tressady* II. xx. 462 Strange up-wellings of feelings long trampled on and suppressed. 1922 W. G. KENDREW *Climates of Continents* 11 This is a cool current..partly owing to the upwelling of cold water along the coast.

Uræus. Also *Comb.*
1924 LINA ECKSTEIN *Tutankh-aten* viii. 71 He playfully took from his head the golden uraeus-headed band, which he placed on the brow of the child.

Urbanism. (Later example.)
1929 *Times* 16 July 17/6 In all the opening speeches..the newly coined word 'urbanism' was prominent. It denotes town-planning [etc.].

Urbanist. 1. Also *attrib.*
1926 S. F. SMITH *Great Schism of West* 82 To say..that the urbanist succession was valid is by no means the same as [etc.].

U·rbanist^2. [f. URBAN + -IST.] A specialist in or advocate of town-planning.
1930 *Times Lit. Suppl.* 11 Sept. 708/4 To do so would be to entrust the fate of a city to the technical urbanist.

Urbanite (ɝ·ɹbǎnəit). [f. URBAN A + -ITE.] A dweller in a city.
1927 E. J. QUIGLEY in *Irish Rosary* July 508 And all comes from splendid organizing, bringing peasants, villagers, townsmen and urbanites to meet..and work with bishops, priests, university men.

Uruguayan (ūrūgwəi·ǎn, yūər-) *a.* and *sb.* [f. *Uruguay*, the name of a republic in S. America + -AN.] **a.** *adj.* Of or belonging to Uruguay. **b.** *sb.* A native or inhabitant of Uruguay.
1907 *Jrnl. Soc. Arts* 8 Feb. 361/2 In his review of Uruguayan affairs. 1912 *20th Cent. Impr. of Uruguay* 225/2 The Uruguayan soil contains the necessary chemical components for the general run of agricultural farming, without requiring artificial manure. 1927 *Glasgow Herald* 7 Mar. 12 The flying boat in which Uruguayan aviators were attempting to cross the Atlantic...His brother and two others, all Uruguayans, left Casablanca..on Wednesday last.

Us, *pron.* **2. b.** (Later U.S. examples.)
1861 O. W. NORTON *Army Lett.* 35 We..then took possession of a stack of wheat and made us good beds and slept well. 1907 S. E. WHITE *Arizona Nights* x. 166 We got us timbers and made a scow.

Use, *sb.* **21. b.** (Earlier example.)
1872 *Harper's Mag.* June 158/2 He was an obstinate fellow ..and moreover, he 'had no use for' the defendant any way.

Use, *v.* Add: **8. d.** To apply to oneself or make use of (a designation, title, etc.).
1921 *Act* 11 & 12 *Geo. V* c. 21 § 4 A person registered.. shall be entitled to take and use the description of dentist or dental practitioner.

Used-to-be. *U.S.* [cf. USE *v.* 20.] A person whose time of popularity or efficiency is past; a 'has-been'.
1853 B. F. TAYLOR *Jan. & June* (1871) 206 They..consign them [poets] to that grand receptacle of dilapidated 'has beens' and despised 'used-to-be's'—the old garret. 1911 J. C. LINCOLN *Cap'n Warren's Wards* xv. 237 One of 'em's a used-to-be, and the other's a never-was.

Useful, *a.* Add: **2. c.** *Useful lift*, lifting power possessed by an airship or aeroplane in excess of that required to sustain its own weight. *Useful weight*, the weight of the fuel, crew, etc. carried by an airship or aeroplane.
1928 GAMBLE *Story N. Sea Air Station* Introd. 10 She was warped into her shed for some alterations because she was found to be deficient in 'useful' lift. 1909 ALPHONSE BERGET *Conquest of Air* 205 A 'useful weight' in the form of fuel and oil to the extent of 80 kilogrammes.

User^2. Add: **b.** *transf.* Use or employment (of a term). *U.S.*
1926 *Publishers' Weekly* 18 Dec. 2284/1 My latinity revolts at the user of 'multos' and 'bonos'.

Ush, *v.*^{2} **2.** (Earlier example.)
1890 J. K. BANGS in *Harper's Mag.* Dec. 160/2 The six gentlemanly cow-boys..swore that whoever should prove to be the lucky man, the others would ush for him at the ceremony.

Utopographer (yūtopǫ·grǎfəɹ). [f. UTOPIA + -(O)GRAPHER.] One who describes a Utopia.
1927 *Punch* 27 July 110/1 *Mr. Sempack* is there to talk. He is a Utopographer.

Uttermost, *a.* **3.** (Recent example.)
1876 MORRIS *Sigurd* (1914) 121 And their hearts with doubt were shaken, as if with the Uttermost Horn.

V

V. Add: **2.** (Further examples.)
1920 G. BURRARD *Notes on Sporting Rifles* 49, V Backsights. There should be one standard V and no leaves. 1930 *Saturday Even. Post* 13 Dec. 11/3 Midway, the range was cleft from summit to base by a V more than 2000 feet deep. 1919 W. DE MORGAN *Old Madhouse* ii, Until you've seen her in a low neck, or at least a V, you really can't tell.

b. *V-blouse, -body, -girder, -neck.*
1915 *Contemp. Rev.* Sept. 370 Quaker maidens now wear tucks or V-blouses or anything else that is the fashion. 1885 'MRS. ALEXANDER' *Valerie's Fate* iv, That black satin and lace costume..with the clear sleeves and a V body. 1919 *Brit. Manufacturer* Nov. 24/1 The output of 'T,' 'V,' and lattice girders of all gauges. 1925 *Scribner's Mag.* Sept. 29 Advt., A two-piece knitted frock..has an overblouse with either V or round neck striped with Rayon silk.

c. *V-fronted; V-like* adjs.
1927 *Blackw. Mag.* Jan. 76/1 They stamp the snow from their V-fronted high-heeled jackboots.

Vacate, *v.* **2. b.** (Later example.)
1921 *Act* 11 & 12 *Geo. V* c. 21 Sched. 1. 4 As from the date next after the Order is made on which all the members of the Board vacate office.

3. c. *trans.* To make (a house) empty.
1904 *N. Y. Even. Post* 14 May 7 His system of vacating unlivable houses is less drastic. He does not summarily turn families out.

4. c. (Earlier example.)
1836 *Knickerbocker Mag.* VII. 15 Ned and I were vacating ..at his father's charming residence.

d. To leave or go away.
1872 EGGLESTON *Hoosier Schoolm.* xxxiv. 225 The Squire was a goin' to marry agin, and Marthy would ruther vacate. 1879 in Tourgee *Invis. Empire* (1880) v. 415 You must stop at once and vacate in 30 days.

Vacating (vǎkē^i·tiŋ), *ppl. a.* [f. VACATE *v.* + -ING^2.] That is retiring from office, etc.
1921 *Act* 11 & 12 *Geo. V* c. 21 Sched. 1. 6 Where the unexpired portion of the term of office of the vacating member is less than one year.

Vacation. 2. c. (Further example.)
1923 J. D. HACKETT *Labor Terms* in *Managem. Engineering* May, *Vacation*, a period of rest from work, of more than one day's duration, generally paid for and given at the instance of the employer.

5. (Modern example.)
1912 *Times* 19 Dec. 11/4 The vacation of Sir Stuart Samuel's seat.

Vaca·tioning, *ppl. a.* [-ING^2.] That is on holiday.
1926 *Scribner's Mag.* Aug. 7/2 Advice to vacationing young folks: In the dog days, don't be too Sirius.

Vaccine, *sb.* **2.** *attrib.* Also *vaccine-therapy*.
1913 SIR T. BARLOW in *Times* 7 Aug. 8/2 Two important methods of treatment, viz., serotherapy and vaccinetherapy.

Vacuum. 4. Add: **vacuum-bottle, flask,** a bottle or flask with a double wall enclosing a vacuum, designed originally to keep liquids cold but now widely used to keep liquids hot; **vacuum tube,** a tube from which the air has been exhausted, or in which the air pressure is less than normal esp. the bulb of an electric incandescent light or a wireless valve.
1910 *Chambers's Jrnl.* June 413/2 The *vacuum-bottle has entered so extensively into the domestic circle as to become regarded almost as indispensable. 1784 in *Pall Mall Mag.* (1896) Aug. 586 Grand *Vacuum Tube Company. Direct to Bengal. 1858 J. P. GASSIOT in *Phil. Trans.* CXLVIII. 15 If a vacuum tube..is placed on the induction coil in action..stratifications are discernible. 1870 *Chem. News* 9 Dec. 284/1 A long vacuum-tube with platinum poles. 1902 *Encycl. Brit.* XXVIII. 54/1 A longitudinal magnetic force applied to a vacuum tube at a very low pressure diminishes to a remarkable degree the difference of potential of the electrodes. 1912 R. A. HOUSTON *Stud. Light Production* x. 72 It supplies an occasion for a picturesque display of vacuum-tube pyrotechnics. *Ibid.* 73 In one sense at least, light from the vacuum tube is cold light.

Vacuumizing (væ·kiu,ǒməiziŋ), *vbl. sb.* [f. VACUUM + -IZE + -ING^1.] The process of making a vacuum.
1909 *Chambers's Jrnl.* July 478/1 Vacuumising is effected by means of a hand-wheel, or the machine can be worked by power if desired.

Vag, U.S. abbrev. of VAGABOND *sb.*
1895 *Denver Times* 5 Mar. 1/3 'Which are the vags and which is the jury?' asked Judge Cowell this morning. 1896 G. ADE *Artie* vi. 58 Say, Miller, am I a vag? 1925 *Lit. Digest* 11 July 50/1 A hobby for masquerading as a tramp and getting thrown into jail as a 'vag'.

Vagabonding, *vbl. sb.* (Later example.)
1925 H. L. FOSTER *Trop. Tramp Tourists* 148 In years of vagabonding about the far corners of the earth..I have never seen [etc.].

Vagary. Add: **1. c.** An irregular course or distribution.
1923 *World's Work* May 566/1 Huster's attention was arrested by the uniformity in the course and distribution of nerves in comparison with the vagary of blood-vessels.

Vaisya. (Later example.)
1919 H. G. WELLS *Outl. Hist.* 159/1 The four main castes seem to have been:..The Vaisyas—herdsmen, merchants, money lenders, and land-owners.

Vakeel. 2. (Earlier example.)
1849 *Dir. Rev. Off. N.W. Prov.* 230 He is allowed the assistance of the ablest Vakeel or pleader in the Court.

Valedictory. B. *sb.* (Earlier example.)
1838 *Southern Lit. Messenger* IV. 575/2 The valedictory of Doyle was very well written.

Valence. Add: **3. b.** *transf.* In Psychology.
1917 C. R. PAYNE tr. *Pfister's Psycho-Anal. Meth.* xi. 269 They are all representations of the cottage itself and more exactly the embodiment of inhibited endeavors of high valence, the so-called libido-symbols.

Valency. 3. Also *attrib.*
1922 F. W. ASTON *Isotopes* 98 The outermost shell of electrons..are therefore called valency electrons.

Valentinian (vælěnti·niǎn), *a.*^{2} [f. VALENTINE *sb.* + -IAN.] Of, belonging to, or appropriate to a valentine.
1928 *Daily Tel.* 14 Feb. 10/5 There are no valentines now. ..It is the chief of villains who in Mr. Shaw's world drops into Valentinian poetry.

Valeting, *vbl. sb.* (Recent example.)
1931 *Times* 16 Mar. 1/3 Advt., Clothes Valeting.

Valiance. 1. Also *fig.*
1929 BRIDGES *Test. Beauty* II. 402 They with the brave buds of March shall drink the valiance of his steepening rays.

Va·lidating, *ppl. a.* [f. VALIDATE *v.* + -ING^2.] That makes valid.
1923 *Contemp. Rev.* June 739 The necessary validating legislation in both countries will result in the fact that the restrictions will apply to every country in the world.

Valley, *sb.* **7.** Add: *valley-bottom* (earlier example), *-dweller*; **valley tan,** *U.S.* a kind of whisky.
1864 B. TAYLOR *H. Thurston* xxix. 373 The elms..had grown up since the *valley-bottom was cleared. 1927 PEAKE & FLEURE *Peasants & Potters* 37 It [the wild ass] was certainly tamed by the Libyans..from whom it reached the *valley-dwellers not long after 4000 B.C. 1868 *Life among Mormons* 59 Some of the stuff distilled in this country..and known as "Valley Tan". 1878 J. H. BEADLE *Western Wilds* xii. 182 Joe slowly filled his glass, seeing that the quart bottle of valley-tan already looked pretty sick.

Valorize (væ·lorəiz), *v.* [f. VALOR + -IZE.] *trans.* To raise or stabilize the value of (a commodity, etc.) by a centrally organized scheme.
1921 *Contemp. Rev.* July 53 It..attempted both to regulate the output and to stabilise and to 'valorise' the prices. 1927 in *Glasgow Herald* 27 Aug. 9/6 As our money has become valorised, the moment is propitious to give a solution of the problem of the stability of exchange.

Valorousness. (Recent example.)
1920 G. SANTAYANA *Char. & Opin. in U.S.A.* vii. 214 Their valorousness and morality consist in their indomitable egotism.

Valuational, *a.* (Later example.)
1924 W. B. SELBIE *Psychol. Relig.* 4 Americans are also inclined to lay undue stress on the merely functional and valuational aspect of psychology.

Value, *sb.* **7. c.** Add: *value-calling*, in bridge, the system of estimating calls or bids which takes into account the scoring values of the suits.
1927 *Daily Express* 8 Nov. 1/5 We do not consider that there is any general desire for the adoption of majority calling in place of value calling.

Valued, *ppl. a.* **2.** (Later example.)
1913 R. H. GRETTON *Mod. Hist. Engl. People* I. ii. 52 Rents were refused above the 'valued rent' scale.

Valuta (văliū·tă). [G. *valuta*, It. *valuta*, in same sense.] That kind of definitive money in which people can insist on state payments due to them being made. Also *attrib.* and *Comb.*
1924 LUCAS & BONAR tr. *Knapp's State Theory of Money* 106 Everywhere there is a valuta or standard money. *Ibid.* 165 If there is more than one kind of money in the country, the value in valuta money is always meant. 1924 *Contemp. Rev.* May 934 The uncertainty of Germany's position.. ('valuta-dumping' might most naturally be expected from her), has made her export..unstable. 1930 *New Statesman* 1 Nov. 106/1 A double purpose—that of obtaining foreign valuta, and that of intensifying the distress of the peasant.

Valve, *sb.*^{1} Add: **6. b.** *Wireless Telegr.* An apparatus consisting of an exhausted tube or bulb of glass containing a filament, a *PLATE, and (now usu.) a *GRID, designed to rectify a high-frequency alternating current or to amplify the direct current obtained through another valve or a crystal; a thermionic valve or vacuum tube.
1905 J. A. FLEMING in *Proc. Roy. Soc.* LXXIV. 479 This arrangement of a differential galvanometer and two valves transforms, of course, more of the alternating oscillation into direct current than when one valve alone is used. 1919 — *Thermionic Valve* ii. 59 The vacuum valve sifted out the alternating current flow and allowed the currents in one direction to pass, but nearly stopped those in the opposite direction. 1921 L. B. TURNER *Outl. Wireless* vi. 83 The unidirectional property illustrated in Fig. 54 is responsible for the application of the name 'valve' to such a vacuum tube. 1926 R. W. HUTCHINSON *Wireless* 188 Any general purpose or detector valve may be employed.

c. *Chess.* (See quot.)
1930 A. C. WHITE & G. HUME *Valves & Bi-Valves* 7 In chess problem terminology, the designation of a Valve has been given to any move which simultaneously opens one line while it closes another. In a broad sense, Valves include a large domain with many varied combinations of themes. There is a much narrower application of the term: Valve, and that is the particular case where not only is the move made by Black, but both of the lines affected are also Black.

7. a. In sense 6, *valve line, room*; in sense *6 b, as *valve circuit, detector, holder, noise, receiver, receiving set, set*, etc.
1915 HAWKHEAD & DOWSETT *Handbk. Wireless Telegraphists* 119 If an E.M.F. be applied to the *valve circuit a more sensitive condition is obtained. 1926 R. W. HUTCHINSON *Wireless* 190 In this valve circuit it is coupled to a secondary coil. 1915 HAWKHEAD & DOWSETT *Handbk. Wireless Telegraphists* 120 The *valve detector is used in connection with various circuits. 1926 R. W. HUTCHINSON *Wireless* 201 All these are also used in conjunction with a valve detector. 1928 *Daily Tel.* 28 Aug. 10/1 A royalty of 10 per cent. on the wholesale selling price, subject to a minimum charge of 5s on the first valve-holder and 2s 6d on each additional valve-holder fitted in the apparatus as sold. 1871 *Leisure Hour* 8 Apr. 222/2 The balloon had been gyrating, and the *valve-line become twisted. 1919 W. D. OWEN *Guide Ionic Valve* 13 It is seldom possible to use more than three or four in cascade efficiently on account of the many curious '*valve noises' that result. 1913 *Wireless World* I. 478/1 A *valve receiver of rather longer range than usual is used for receiving. 1909 *Westm. Gaz.* 8 Nov. 7/2 A quantity of gas and the under-side of the flooring in the *valve-room of the works were destroyed.

Valve, *v.* Add: **2. b.** *trans.* To discharge (gas) from a balloon by opening a valve.
1928 *Daily Tel.* 18 Sept. 9/6 The extra lifting effect of the expanding gas cannot be counteracted by allowing the gas to escape, or in other words by valving the gas.

Vamo·sing, *vbl. sb.* [f. VAMOSE *v.* + ING^1.] The action of the verb VAMOSE.
1862 LOWELL *Biglow P.* Ser. II. v. 75 Or, when the vamosin' come, ever to find [etc.].

Vamp (væmp), *sb.*^{3} [Abbrev. of VAMPIRE *sb.*] A woman who attracts and exploits men; an adventuress.
1918 *War Birds* (1927) 82 We walked into the vamp's house. We all got lit and had a hell of a time. 1922 *Observer* 1 Oct. 5/4 Her end was what a vamp's end ought to be. 1927 *Daily Express* 7 Mar. 1/4 Magda Lupescu, the red-headed vamp responsible for Rumania's dynastic troubles. 1926 *Spectator* 22 May 879/1 The most spectacular of whom she wins, after a running fight for his person with a 'vamp'. 1930 JOANNA CANNAN *No Walls of Jasper* 194 Though he knew that men did fall in love with women ten, twenty years their seniors, that was because the women were vamps.

Vamp (væmp), *v.*^{3} [f. the sb.] *trans.* To act as a vamp towards; to allure or attract (a man).
1922 MARG. B. HOUSTON *Witch-man* xii. 149 Look!.. Cinderella is trying to vamp him, as Marion says. 1924 A. J. SMALL *Frozen Gold* iii. 79 You jade; you're sitting there vamping me! 1929 *Daily Express* 7 Nov. 10/4 She exposes and derides the squire's lady. She also vamps the squire's son. 1927 *Observer* 20 Mar. 15/3 Her friend, Violet Usher, however, shamelessly vamped Randall, and he felt obliged to marry her.

b. *intr.* To act as a vamp; to be a vamp.
1922 *Observer* 1 Oct. 5/4 Trollope's Signora Neroni certainly vamped.

Va·mpiness. [f. *VAMP *sb.* + -Y + -NESS.] = *VAMPISHNESS.
1928 *Sunday Express* 29 July 4 The varnished vampiness of Greta Garbo.

Vamping, *ppl. a.*^{2} [f. VAMP *v.*^{3} + ING^2.] That acts as a vamp.
1927 *Daily News* 14 Mar. 3/4 Why censure as 'modern that made-up, cigarette-smoking, cocktail-absorbing, vamping, neo-Georgian nymph,' when one reads of the Restoration minx? 1929 *Randolph Enterprise* (Elkins, W. Va.) 26 Sept. 3/6 Beautiful girls, charming debutantes,..and vamping flappers.

Vampire, *sb.* **2.** (Further example: cf. *VAMP *sb.*^{3})
1928 BENNETT *Vanguard* vi. 38 She was plainly a vampire, an evil woman, and he was her dupe.

5. vampire trap (earlier example).
1845 SOL. SMITH *Theatr. Apprent.* viii. 63 Down I went through the trap-door (it was what actors call a Vampire trap) before any one was aware of my intentions.

Vampirish, *a.* Add: **b.** = *VAMPISH.
1929 *Sunday Dispatch* 13 Jan. 1/2 Among my own friends my reputation is notoriously the reverse of vampirish, money means nothing to me.

Vampish (væ·mpiʃ), *a.* [f. *VAMP *sb.*^{3} + -ISH.] Suggestive or characteristic of a vamp. Hence **Va·mpishness.**
1922 *Observer* 1 Oct. 5/4 'The Vavasour' in 'Strathmore' ..out of pure vampishness makes a conquest of the hero. 1928 *Observer* 15 July 12/4 Not international 'stars' of vampish wiles, but hundreds of Miss Betty Balfours should be sought and cherished.

Van, *sb.*^{3} **3.** Add: *van guard.*
1921 *Dict. Occup. Terms* (1927) 723 *Van guard*,..travels with and guards contents of mail vans. 1931 *Daily Express* 22 Sept. 7/3 A vanguard..was accused of being concerned with another man..in stealing a motor-car.

Van (væn), *sb.*^{5} *Lawn Tennis.* [Abbrev. of VANTAGE *sb.* 6.] Chiefly in phrases *van in, van out*, indicating that the first point after deuce has been gained by the server, or by the striker.
1929 W. E. COLLINSON *Spoken Engl.* 90.

Vane. 6. Add: *vane-wheel.*
1922 *Glasgow Herald* 28 June 9 The vane wheels may be placed side by side abaft the stern of the ship.

Vanette (vǣne·t). [f. VAN *sb.*^{3} + -ETTE.] A small motor van.
1921 *Glasgow Herald* 23 July 8 A company..were sent out from Jandola, followed..by Lewis guns in vanettes and an armoured motor car.

Vanish, *sb.* **1.** (Modern example.)
1872 'MARK TWAIN' *Roughing It* iii. 33 He..left for San Francisco at a speed which can only be described as a flash and a vanish.

Vanishing, *vbl. sb.* **2.** *Vanishing point*: also *fig.*
1913 SIR T. BARLOW in *Times* 7 Aug. 8/2 The danger of operation, *qua* operation, is retreating to a vanishing point.

Vanitous (væ·nĭtəs), *a.* [f. VANITY + -OUS.] = VAIN *a.* 4.
1905 MEREDITH *Lett.* (1912) II. 569 French criticism..instructs without wounding any but the vanitous person. 1930 *Mus. Times* 1 Mar. 210/2 It is only the very young, or the very vanitous, who think of making a world of themselves.

Vanity. 6. vanity-bag, -case (recent examples); also **vanity pocket.**
1922 *Weekly Disp.* 12 Nov. 3 She was wearing a navy blue costume and a long blue coat, and carried a..vanity-bag. 1928 GALSWORTHY *Swan Song* III. iv. 243 Fleur..accidentally left her vanity bag, behind her, in the studio. 1922 *Daily Mail* 2 Dec. 1 Advt., Lady's Vanity Case, in velvet calf, containing mirror and powder puff. 1923 *Ibid.* 12 June, Advt., Silk Handbag..Fitted captive mirror, vanity pocket.

Vantage, *sb.* **6.** (Further example.)
1904 J. P. PARET *Lawn Tennis* Gloss. 352 *Vantage-in* (or vantage-server). A term used to indicate that the server has won the 'vantage' point (opposite of 'vantage-out'). *Vantage-out* (or vantage-striker) [etc.].

Vaporization. Add: **b.** Treatment with vapour.
1905 *Smart Set* Sept. 28 A/2 Advt., For morning I..take a vaporisation with Rosée de Beauté.

Vapour, *sb.* **5. a.** Add: *vapour-capacity, -pipe.*
1922 KENDREW *Climates of Continents* 215 The sea is then coolest relatively to the land, so that the vapour-capacity of air blowing from the sea is increased over the land. 1913 V. B. LEWES *Oil Fuel* 79 A horizontal cylindrical boiler with a dome, from which a broad vapour-pipe leads the distilling vapours to the condensers.

Vara. (Later examples.)
1889 K. MUNROE *Golden Days* vi. 66, I..was..going him one better every time for a fifty vara lot. 1910 JEN. HART *Vigilante Girl* xi. 153 In the centre of the walled enclosure was a great plaza or rectangle of open ground some two hundred varas square.

Variate (vē^ə·riět), *sb. Statistics.* [f. L. *variāt-* ppl. stem of *variāre* to VARY.] The size or value of a particular character in one specimen.
1899 C. B. DAVENPORT *Stat. Meth.* iii. 17 Method A is used when integral variates are under consideration; method B when we deal with graduated variates. 1906 R. H. LOCK *Variation Heredity & Evolution* iv. 90 A *variate* is one of the separate numerical values from which a curve of variability can be constructed; the biometrician usually deals with some such number as 1,000 variates.

Variationist. Add: **b.** One who practises variation or introduces variety in anything.
1927 H. W. FOWLER *Mod. Engl. Usage* 132 The writers are confirmed variationists.

2. *Biol.* One who regards variation of species as the cause of new forms.
1859 SIR J. D. HOOKER in *Life* (1918) I. xxiv. 484 Thwaites was once a devoted variationist.

Variety. Add: **9. c.** *Variety theatre*, a theatre specializing in variety entertainments.
1901 *Referee* 29 Dec. 4 The chief variety theatres wisely got their fine holiday shows well in hand on Monday night. 1911 G. B. SHAW in *Daily Graphic* 2 Dec. 4/3 Do I mind having my play performed in a variety theatre?

Va·rihued, *a.* [f. L. *vari-us* VARIOUS.] = VARI-COLOURED.
1921 *Nat. Geog. Mag.* Sept. 274 The varihued deposits resemble brilliant mosaics.

Vario-coupler. [f. L. *vari-us* VARIOUS + -O- + COUPLER.] (See quots.)
1925 P. J. RISDON *Crystal Receivers & Circuits* 21 A vario-coupler is a sort of combination of a variometer and an ordinary tapped tuning inductance. 1926 R. W. HUTCHINSON *Wireless* 78 The vario-coupler inductance..consists of a variometer in which the rotor and stator are not joined in series, but are separate coils with separate terminals.

Variometer. *Electr.* [f. L. *vari-us* VARIOUS + -O(METER).] An apparatus consisting of a coil of insulated wire connected in series with and designed to turn inside a similar coil and so to vary the inductance of the two coils.
1921 *Wireless World* IX. 6/1 For amateur use the variometer has the advantage that it is cheap compared with a variable condenser. 1925 P. J. RISDON *Crystal Receivers & Circuits* 19 A variometer is another form of variable inductance.

Varmenty (vā·ɹmənti), *a.* [f. VARMENT^1 + -Y.] Suggestive of or like a varment.
1907 CONAN DOYLE *Thr. Magic Door* ii. 34 Louis, thin, ascetic, varminty.

Varsity. (Earlier attrib. example.)
1863 *Baily's Mag.* Jan. 360, I had conjured up all the most extravagant and erroneous ideas as to my 'Varsity career'.

Vartabed (vā·ɹtăbed). Also **vartabad, vartabet, vartabied, vertabiet.** [Armenian.] One of an order of clergy in the Armenian church (see quots.).
1718 OZELL tr. *Tournefort's Voy.* 2 303 These *Vertabiets*, who make such a noise among the Armenians, are not in reality great doctors. 1841 L. COLEMAN *Christian Antiq.* xxiii. § 2 The vartabeds live not among the people, but in convents. 1847 J. WILSON *Lands Bible* II. 482 The monkish clergy are denominated Vartabads or Doctors, and it is their peculiar office to teach and preach. 1875 *Encycl. Brit.* II. 549/2 The vartabed, or doctor of theology..has frequently charge of a diocese, with episcopal functions. 1923 *Blackw. Mag.* Aug. 252/1 The Patriarch and an Armenian *vartabed* ..are pushed inside.

Vary, *sb.* (Later example.)
1929 BRIDGES *Test. Beauty* I. 583 We should not in the field of Reason look to find less vary and veer than elsewhere in the flux of Life.

Va·selining, *vbl. sb.* [f. VASELINE *v.* + -ING^1.] The action of the verb VASELINE.
1921 *Librarian* Nov. 74 The combination of vaselining and varnishing is the best thing for the text books.

Vastidity. (Recent example.)
1929 BRIDGES *Test. Beauty* IV. 1385 The spiritual idea of Friendship, the huge vastidity of its essence.

Vaudeville. 2. (Later attrib. example.)
1911 G. B. SHAW in *Daily Graphic* 2 Dec. 4/3 There are vaudeville theatres in America and variety theatres in England.

Vaudevillian (voudvi·liăn), *a.* and *sb.* Also **-ean.** [f. VAUDEVILLE + -IAN.] **a.** *adj.* Of or pertaining to vaudevilles. **b.** *sb.* A writer or singer of vaudevilles.
1927 *Sunday Express* 1 May 4 German films are not believable unless they deal with 'vaudevillians' and 'metropolitans'. 1930 *Punch* 8 Oct. 415 The modish songs..serve pleasantly to exercise the vaudevillean gifts of Mr. Coward and Miss Lawrence.

Vector. Add: **3.** A carrier of disease or infection.
1926 *Encycl. Brit.* III. 153 Fleas as Vectors. The flea most commonly incriminated as a plague-vector is Xenopsylla cheopis. 1931 *Nature* 6 June 853 The insect vector of tobacco ringspot..does not appear to be known.

Vee. Also *Comb.* in sense 'V-shaped'.
1931 *London Illustr. News* 29 Aug. 342/1 The six-cylinder 19.8-h.p. Chrysler 'Six' has the new vee-radiator with wide rim.

Vegetable, *a.* **7.** Add: *Vegetable lard* (see quot.).
1918 C. A. MITCHELL *Edible Oils & Fats* iii. 33 Coconut oil is treated with alcohol and animal charcoal and the resulting product, which is practically tasteless, is sold as 'vegetable lard'.

Vegeta·tional, *a.* [f. VEGETATION + -AL.] Of, pertaining to, or characterized by vegetation.
1926 *Spectator* 4 Sept. 354/2 The dark areas observable on the surface of Mars are vegetational regions. 1927 *Observer* 20 Nov. 21/3 The vegetational phenomena shown by the photographs giving valuable information about the geology of the country.

Vegetatively, *adv.* (Later example.)
1926 *Jrnl. Bot.* LXIV. (Suppl.) 137, I have suspected for some time that *T[huidium] samoanum* Mitt. was doubtfully distinct from *T. glaucinoides* from which it is only separated, vegetatively, by the very slight papillosity of the leaves.

Vehicular, *a.* **1. c.** (Later example.)
1924 *Times Trade & Engin. Suppl.* 29 Nov. 248/2 The construction of the hulls of the two vehicular and passenger steamers.

Veil, *sb.*^{1} **8.** (Earlier U.S. example.)
1857 *Quinland* I. xiii. I. 186 Aunt Hepsa says he was born with a *veil* over his face, and says he can see things that we must not inquire about.

Veiling, *vbl. sb.* Add: **3. b.** The action of making or becoming a nun.
c 1890 I. GRANT *Popery in 1st Cent.* (C.T.S.) 2 Two events ..the veiling of Flavia Domitilla and the conversion of Theodora.

Veldt, veld. (Earlier example.)
1801 J. BARROW *Trav. S. Afr.* I. 378 Louw, the Veld Commandant, readily offered his services.

2. *veldt craft.*
1919 J. BUCHAN *Thirty-nine Steps* 42 My notion was to get off to some wild district, where my veldcraft would be of some use to me.

b. veldt-cornet (earlier example); **veldt-cornetship** = field-cornetcy FIELD *sb.* 21.
1801 CUYLER in G. E. CORY *Rise S. Afr.* (1910) I. viii. 173 All the Veld-Cornets on the East side of the Zondags River are hereby ordered [etc.]. *Ibid.* 229, I..request you to give us the same right over the inhabitants of your 'Veld-cornetship.

Veleta (velī·tă). A sequence dance for couples introduced by A. Morris in 1901.
1905 F. H. NORMAN *Compl. Dance Instructor* 29. 1920 *Glasgow Herald* 28 Dec. 5/2 They are reviewing the dances which our parents tripped—the petronellas, the valetas [*sic*], the quadrilles. 1929 *Daily Express* 18 Jan. 8/7 The saunter, the veleta,..the lancers, and the quadrilles.

Velocitous (vĭlǫ·sĭtəs), *a.* *nonce-wd.* [f. VELOCITY + -OUS.] Swift; speedy.
1907 E. V. LUCAS *Character & Comedy* 86 Would he still pin his faith to horses to convey most profoundly the impression of velocitous travel?

Velometer (velǫ·mĭtəɹ). [irreg. contr. of VELOCIMETER.] An instrument for measuring the speed with which an aeroplane passes through the air.
1921 *Dict. Brit. Sci. Instruments* 176.

Velvet, *sb.* Add: **1. f.** Profit, gain, winnings (cf. 1. d). *To the velvet*: to the good.
1901 S. E. WHITE *Westerners* xxiii. 228 'They's a good many ton of ore in four hundred foot of shaft.'..'Let that go for now... We can call that "velvet".' 1903 *N. Y. Times* 19 Sept. 1 The parties who own the new canal company got their stock for $15,000,000, and the rest of the $40,000,000 to be paid by the U.S. is all 'velvet'. 1908 K. MCGAFFEY *Show-Girl* 240 Before the whistle blew for dinner I was several hundred to the velvet. 1910 G. B. MCCUTCHEON *Rose in Ring* I. iii. 41 Five hundred dollars velvet, that's what this boy means to me. 1912 FLOR. IRWIN *Fine Pts. Auction Bridge* 56 Do your doubling early in the rubber (so as to pile up 'velvet' for yourself), and make a dash for game-points (below the line) towards the end.

7. b. velvet ant (example).
1862 T. W. HARRIS *Insects injur. Veget.* (ed. 3) 15 Stinging velvet-ants (*Mutilladæ*)..are predaceous in their habits.

Velvetiness. Also *fig.*
1906 GALSWORTHY *Man of Property* II. iv. 167 This was as near as he could get..to a description of the peculiar exasperation, velvetiness, and mockery, of which Bosinney's manner had been composed.

Venatical, *a.* (Later example.)
1880 A. TROLLOPE *Duke's Children* II. xii. 135 Reginald Dobbes..was..supposed to be capable of outwitting a deer by venatical wiles.

Vend, *sb.* Add: **3.** *attrib.*
1905–6 *Rep. Ind. Excise Comm.* (1907) vi. § 84. 33 While in most areas the still-head duty represents practically the whole of the taxation, vend fees..are added to it in Poona.

Veneerer (vĭnī^ə·rəɹ). [f. VENEER *v.* + -ER^1.] A workman who applies or fits veneer.
1862–3 E. E. HALE *If, Yes, & Perhaps* (1868) 14, I was at work as a veneerer in a piano-forte factory at Attica.

Venetian. A. *sb.* Add: **1. b.** The dialect used by Venetians.
1901 M. CARMICHAEL *In Tuscany* 99 Had Dante..written in Venetian..there would have been two classical languages in Italy to-day.

Venison, 4. b. Add: *venison ham, steak.*
1784 J. SMYTH *Tour U.S.* I. vi. 41 Very thin slices of Venison-ham, or hung beef. 1836 J. HALL *Stat. West* ix. 112 Venison hams and hides are important articles of export. 1833 J. HALL *Harpe's Head* 214 A little farther up were venison steaks, then fried ham. 1843 CARLTON *New Purchase* 164 Our supper tonight was of coffee, corn bread ..and venison steaks.

Venizelism (venize·liz'm). [f. the name of Eleutherios *Venizelos*, Greek statesman (1864–).] The principles or policy of Venizelos or support of these. So **Venize·list,** a supporter of Venizelos; also *attrib.*
1920 *Glasgow Herald* 4 May 7 Even the so-called Venizelist divisions were nothing more than a collection of supers. 1931 C. MACKENZIE *First Athen. Mem.* xv. 380 This result was not gained merely by abstentions in the Islands and the new territories where Venizelism was naturally predominant. *Ibid.* 384 It was they who by inventing revolutionary plots among Venizelists put it into the heads of the French that a revolution was possible.

Venta. Also *Comb.*
1927 *Blackw. Mag.* June 824/1 Two fig trees stood at the door of the little *venta*-shop.

Ventilate, *v.* **9.** (Modern example.)
1909 *Roy. Comm. Poor Law* App. XVI. 148 The houses, in themselves damp and dirty, are made worse by insanitary conveniences ventilating into them.

Verbal. A. *adj.* Add: **7.** *Comb.* in sense 'verbal and ..'.
1911 S. S. COLVIN *Learning Process* vii. 107 If I recall the name as written or printed on a page, I have a verbal-visual image; if I recall the name as spoken by some one, I have a verbal-acoustic image; if I recall the name in terms of the movements of my throat in speaking it, I have a verbal-motor image.

Verbality. 2. (Later example.)
1899 W. JAMES *Talks to Teachers* 257 We are stuffed with abstract conceptions, and glib with verbalities and verbosities.

Ver·berating, *vbl. sb.* [f. VERBERATE *v.* + -ING^1.] The action of the verb VERBERATE.
1927 H. M. TOMLINSON *Gallion's Reach* xxix, The humming of wires, the verberating of notes inaudible.

Verdin (vɜ̄·ɹdin). *U.S.* (See quot. 1881.)
1881 *Amer. Naturalist* Mar. 217, I will now describe the nest and eggs of another minute species of the titmouse family, the verdin or yellow-headed titmouse (*Parus flaviceps*). 1903 *Atlantic Monthly* July 103 The same fretting verdin was talking something with the old emphatic monotony.

Verge, *sb.* **16. a.** (Further example.)
1920 *Morn. Post* 12 June 10/5 He was within four feet of the grass verge and was unable to avoid the approaching motor cycle.

Verge (vɜ̄ɹdʒ), *v.*^{3} [Back-formation f. VERGER^2.] *intr.* To act as a verger; to be a verger.
1926 *Punch* 13 Oct. 400/2 I verges up the centre aisle; he verges up the sides. 1927 H. V. MORTON *In Search of Engl.* i, The profession of verging appears to induce mousy manners.

Verifiability. (Earlier example.)
1883 A. BARRATT *Phys. Metemp.* Note p. xxv, I cannot believe that the test of sensible verifiability will ever satisfy the higher longings..of humanity.

Veritableness. (Recent example.)
1926 R. CLEMENTS *Stately Southerner* 142 Whatever shape the apparition may have taken, a belief in its veritableness has persisted from of old.

Vermilionize, *v.* Also *fig.*
1924 W. J. LOCKE *Coming of Amos* iv. 43 If I had found myself at five-and-twenty with fifty thousand pounds lying at the bank, verily, I believe, I should have vermilionized the cosmos.

Vermin, *sb.* **5. c.** Add: *vermin-eaten.*
1901 'LUCAS MALET' *Hist. Sir R. Calmady* v. iii. 398 The removal of wailing, alms-demanding, vermin-eaten wrecks of humanity.

Verminicide (vɜ̄·ɹminisəid). [f. VERMIN *sb.* + -CIDE^1.] A preparation for killing vermin.
1925 *Blackw. Mag.* Sept. 313/2 During the summer verminicide became a necessary item in the 'bazar'.

Vermonteer (vɜ̄ɹmǫntī^ə·ɹ). [f. as next + -EER.] = next.
1798 I. ALLEN *Hist. Vermont* 57 So consequential were the Vermonteers, that an application for offensive operations came at the same time from different colonies.

Vermonter (vəɹmǫ·ntəɹ). Also **Varmounter.** [f. *Vermont* + -ER]. A native or inhabitant of the state of Vermont, U.S.A.
1825 J. NEAL *Bro. Jonathan* II. 280 A raw country boy..a downright Varmounter—'all but' is talking about his knowledge of women. 1837 *Knickerbocker Mag.* X. 380 A Vermonter is rarely a drunkard, away from his native state. 1866 A. D. RICHARDSON *Secret Service* xxx. 363 They told us that *The Confederate* was edited by two renegade Vermonters. 1897 SUSAN HALE *Lett.* 324 The party was six of us, two parsons,..two stray Vermonters.

Vermontese (vɜ̄ɹmǫntī·z), *sb.* and *a.* [f. as prec. + -ESE.] **a.** *sb.* = prec. Also as pl. **b.** *adj.* Of or belonging to Vermont.
a. 1798 I. ALLEN *Hist. Vermont* 262 You ask me if the Vermontese are good agriculturists? 1806 FESSENDEN *Orig. Poems*, 97 *note*, Hamilton was a Vermontese. 1845 *Knickerbocker Mag.* XXVI. 583 We should be pleased to hear these lines applauded by the Vermontese.
b. 1798 I. ALLEN *Hist. Vermont* 280 Our Vermontese housewives are not a little vain of their knowledge in making homemade wines. 1833 *Knickerbocker Mag.* II. 247 The Vermontese pronunciation of such words as *home* and *stone*.

Vernacularist (vəɹnæ·kiŭlărist). [f. VERNACULAR + -IST.] A vernacular writer.
1926 *Glasgow Herald* 27 Feb. 10 There was ample material ..which in the hands of a Vernacularist of genius could produce a play as striking as 'Strife'.

Vernacularity. 1. (Later example.)
a 1906 'O. HENRY' *Trimmed Lamp* etc. 87 Remsen touched his cap..and took refuge in vernacularity.

Verruga. *attrib.* (Further example.)
1918 *Chambers's Jrnl.* June 355/2 The toll that verruga-fever..took of the lives of the workmen.

Vers libre (vɛ̄ɹ libr). [F., free verse.] A form of composition in which the ordinary rules of prosody are or may be disregarded; verse consisting of an irregular alternation of long and short lines, often unrhymed, which is supposed to subordinate form to substance. So **Vers-li·brist,** a writer of vers libre.
1920 *Glasgow Herald* 8 July 4/2 Mr. Bunker..is most interesting in his vers-libres; unfortunately they are not poetry, though happily free of the pretentiousness of most vers-librists. 1921 HUGH WALPOLE *Young Enchanted* II. iv. 157 A beautiful *Vers-libre* flew like a coloured dove into Henry's brain just as he crossed the Circus. 1923 H. L. MENCKEN *Bk. of Burlesques* xi. 209 *Vers Libre*, a device for making poetry easier to write and harder to read. 1923 *Times Lit. Suppl.* 29 Nov. 815/2 The vers-librist experiment is recognized as providing no adequate support for a deliberate system.

Versal, *sb.* Transfer † *Obs.* to sense defined in Dict. and add: **2.** A special style of letter used at the beginning of a verse or paragraph.
1895 E. F. STRANGE *Alphabets* ix. 258 The versal is [a letter]..at the beginning of a chapter or section thereof. 1912 A. W. POLLARD *Fine Books* 84 The small red letters at the beginning of each verse of a psalm, sometimes called versals.

Vertical, *a.* Add: **3. f.** *Vertical combine, trust*, etc., a combination of firms engaged in all the stages in the production of goods of a particular kind.
1920 *Westm. Gaz.* 2 Dec. 6/1 The vertical Trusts constructed by Stumm, Thyssen and the other raw-material magnates. 1927 *Daily Tel.* 11 Oct. 15/4 He had created what is technically called a vertical combination, embracing every stage of the soap industry. 1930 M. CLARK *Home Trade* 304 'Vertical combines'..aim at securing for the manufacturing business adequate supplies of the essential raw materials.

Verticillary, *a.* Add: **2.** *Bot.* = VERTICILLATE 2.
1880 W. R. FISHER *Schlich's Man. Forestry* V. 703 There is connection between the vertical ducts of the cortex of different years' shoots, that is formed by cortex growing to the growth in thickness of the verticillary branches.

Vertimeter (vəɹti·mĭtəɹ). [f. as VERTICAL + -METER.] (See quot.)
1926 H. N. EATON *Aircraft Instruments* i. 46 Rate-of-Climb Meters (Vertimeters)..These instruments are used to measure the rate of climb or descent of aircraft.

Very (ve·ri). Also **verey.** [The name of the inventor S. W. *Very*.] Applied *attrib.* to lights or flares used by soldiers in night-signalling or for providing temporary illumination when fighting by night; also to the pistol from which these flares are fired.
1915 R. NICHOLS in *Muse in Arms* (1917) 49 The 'Verey' light had risen...On the air it hung glistening. 1915 D. O. BARNETT *Lett.* 95 When the 'Very' pistol came, I fired a rocket. 1917 *Chambers's Jrnl.* Oct. 695/2 The latter.. glances round to see that everything—ammunition-drums, verey pistol and flares, and revolver—is in its proper place. 1920 *Blackw. Mag.* June 747/2 Very flares were continually being fired into the air to light up dark corners.

Vespertilian, *a.* (Later example.)
1911 W. J. LOCKE *Glory of Clementina Wing* xxii. 277 But as the studio was rigorously closed to him during the daylight hours his visits were vespertilian.

Vest, *sb.* **3. e.** *vest-pocket*, also applied *attrib.* to articles of a small size, commodities made up in small packages, etc.
1912 *Brit. Jrnl. Photogr.* 5 July 525 The vest-pocket 'Tenax' camera. 1931 *Times* 16 Mar. 1/3 Advt., Unique vest-pocket treatment for Catarrh.

Vestee (vestī·). [f. VEST *sb.* + -EE.] = VEST *sb.* 3 d.
1930 *Ladies' Home Jrnl.* Dec. 36 With soft georgette vestee crossing diagonally to pass through a straight band of the material on the left.

Vestibular, *a.* Add: *spec.* Pertaining to or located in the vestibule of the ear.
1931 *Daily Tel.* 19 Jan. 10/7 The flier must have nervous stability, good muscle sense,..and vestibular stability.

Vestibule, *sb.* Add: **1. e.** *attrib.*, as *vestibule school* (see quot.).
1923 J. D. HACKETT *Labor Terms* in *Managem. Engineering* May, *Vestibule School*, a department in a plant whereby new workers are trained intensively to operate the same machines as the regular working force.

Vesting. *sb.* (Earlier examples.)
1813 *Niles' Weekly Reg.* IV. 295/1 For the best and handsomest fancy vesting, of cotton..a premium of a piece of plate or its value, forty dollars. 1822 *Ann. 17th Congress* 1st Sess. I. 319, [Purchased] 286 yards of Vestings.

Vestryman. Also *fig.*
1910 *Blackw. Mag.* Apr. 585/1 Mr. Shaw is the vestryman of dramatists. His work savours horribly of St. Pancras.

Vet. U.S. abbrev. of VETERAN.
1904 *Richmond Wkly. Times-Disp.* 22 June 4 All the old vets have returned from the reunion, some never to attend another, perhaps.

Vet, *v.* Add: **3.** *transf.* To subject (a person or apparatus) to careful examination; to cross-examine, scrutinize or test.
1904 KIPLING *Traffics & Disc.* 270 These are our crowd... They've been vetted, an' we're putting 'em through their paces. 1925 E. F. NORTON *Fight for Everest, 1924* 339 He should have all equipment..completely ready three or four months before shipment—only thus can everything be properly 'vetted' and criticised. 1926 BENNETT *Lord Raingo* I. xii. 57 He was there to be inspected, vetted, and probably put through his paces. 1927 VACHELL *Dew of the Sea* etc. 265 I understand. You want me to vet these sporting stunts.

Veteran. A. *sb.* Add: **3.** *U.S.* An ex-service man.
1906 *N. Y. Even. Post* 29 Jan. 1 A guard of honor selected from the ranks of the Spanish war veterans here. 1924 F. J. HASKIN *Amer. Government* 401 In the wake of the World War there came the problem of the treatment..of the disabled veterans of that great conflict.

Vetting (ve·tiŋ), *vbl. sb.* [f. VET *v.* + -ING^1.] The action of the verb VET.
1918 H. VACHELL *Some Happenings* iv. 42 He felt mildly interested in the vetting. 1927 *Observer* 24 July 12/4 This scheme..makes the local co-operative society responsible for the 'vetting' of borrowers.

Vexedness. (Recent example.)
1909 W. J. LOCKE *Septimus* xi. 160 Zora, regarding the egoist with mingled admiration and vexedness, could only say 'Oh'!

Viable, *a.*^{1} **b.** (Further example.)
1927 PEAKE & FLEURE *Apes & Men* 31 *note*, Viable, a term meaning 'capable of maintaining its life or the life of its kind', is used here in preference to the much controverted word 'fit.'

Vialled, *a.* (Later example.)
1906 HARDY *Dynasts* II. v. i. 188 The riskful blood of my previsioned line..To linger vialled in my veins alone.

Viatical, *a.* (Earlier example.)
1847 H. C. WATSON *Cybele Britannica* I. 66 Viatical. Plants of road-sides, rubbish heaps, and frequented places.

Vibratile, *a.* Add: **3.** as *sb.*, a vibratory consonant.
1899 E. J. PAYNE *New World called America* II. 151 Both vibratiles and sibilants..are generally employed throughout northern Asia and America.

Vibration. 4. Also *Comb.* as *vibration-proof* adj.
1917 C. C. TURNER *Aircraft of To-Day* vii. 114 The compass..must be carried in a vibration-proof box.

Vibro-. Add: *vibro-massage.*
1923 *Daily Mail* 10 Aug. 3/2 The owner-experts get their features in knots..and may be seen going off for vibro-massages in the evening.

Vicar. 4. c. Also *vicar apostolical.*
1731 in Odo Blundell *Catholic Highlands Scotland* (1917) II. 99 His Holiness..appoints him also Vicar Apostolical with singular powers. 1847 J. A. MANNING *Pius XI* I. 168 Differences broke out between the Vicar Apostolical and the Chilian government.

Vice, *sb.*^{2} **7.** Add: (sense 5) *vice-nip.*
1904 F. LYNDE *Grafters* xiv. 180 Elinor had said little about the vise-nip of hardship which the stock-smashing would impose upon three unguardianed women.

Vice-presidential, *a.* (Earlier example.)
1885 G. W. CABLE *Dr. Sevier* xlvi. 341 With a presidential candidate on one side and his vice-presidential man Friday on the other.

Vice-re·gency. [f. VICE-REGENT.] The position or office of a vice-regent.
1930 H. BELLOC *Wolsey* ix. 243 He drafted a form of Vice-regency, a delegation of Papal power to himself.

Vicinism (vi·siniz'm, visəi·niz'm). [f. L. *vicinus* + -ISM.] (See quot.) So **Vicinist,** a form resulting from vicinism.
1905 HUGO DE VRIES *Species & Varieties* 188 For this purpose I propose the word *vicinism*, derived from the Latin *vicinus* or neighbor, as indicating the sporting of a variety under the influence of others in its vicinity. *Ibid.* 201 Of two hundred seeds one became a blue atavist, or rather vicinist, while all others remained true to the white type.

Victimization. (Further example.)
1923 *Westm. Gaz.* 23 Apr. 3/5 The expression 'no victimisation' implied that a striker's place was not to be filled by an outsider.

Victorian, *a.*^{3} Add: **b.** *sb.*^{2} A native or inhabitant of Victoria in Australia.
1883 R. E. N. TWOPENY *Town Life Australia* 41 The Victorians have a much greater love of show than any of their fellow-Australians.

Victorianism. (Further examples.)
1913 MRS. H. WARD *Coryston Family* xi. 216 A heavy gold setting, whereof the Early Victorianism cried aloud. 1920 W. J. LOCKE *House of Baltazar* xvi. 193 Yes, Tennyson—a bit of a seer after all that Incarnation of Victorianism. 1932 *Sat. Rev.* 10 Jan. 114 His destruction..led to a reaction in favour of Victorianism today.

Victo·rianly, *adv.* [f. VICTORIAN + -LY^2.] In a Victorian fashion.
1924 *Chambers's Jrnl.* Aug. 546/2 The tone and manner, of this song were Victorianly simple.

Victrola (viktrou·lă). *U.S.* Trade name of a make of phonograph.
1919 MENCKEN *Amer. Lang.* 165. 1922 H. L. FOSTER *Adv. Trop. Tramp* v. 47 The camp victrola was broken and that I was the only man in camp that could rag the piano.

View, *sb.* **16. c.** *On view* (earlier example.)
1850 *Punch* 19 Oct. 164/1 The South Western Railway.. keeps a quantity of hissing, smoking, screaming engines always 'on view'.

18. b. *To take the long view*, to have regard for more than the present; to provide for the future.
1924 *Times Trade & Engin. Suppl.* 29 Nov. 247/2 Those who took the long view and ordered more than just to meet current needs are now reaping the benefit of such a policy.

19. *view day* (example).
1850 *Art Jrnl.* July 224 The rooms were crowded during the 'view' days with visitors.

Viewing, *vbl. sb.* Add: **b.** The action of expressing views on subjects.
1913 H. WALPOLE *Fortitude* III. iii. 291 He..started weekly viewing on *The Interpreter*.

Viewster (viū·stəɹ). *nonce-word.* [f. VIEW *sb.* + -STER.] A person expressing a view on something.
1922 W. DE MORGAN *Old Man's Youth* xxxvii. 410 Two views were expressed about it...The viewster hoped I should not be led away from the serious study of Art.

Vigent (vəi·dʒěnt), *a.* [ad. L. *vigent-*, *vigens*, pres. pple. of *vigēre* to thrive.] Flourishing; prosperous.
1930 J. WALL *Durham Cathedral* 183 Durham College.. after several changes of fortune is now vigent as Trinity College.

Vigilance. 1. (Further example; cf. 3.)
1851 *Harper's Mag.* Sept. 559/1 A large number of the most valuable citizens organized themselves into a Committee of Vigilance for the purpose of securing the punishment of criminals.

Vigintennial (vəidʒinte·niăl), *a.* [f. VIGINTI-: after BIENNIAL, TRIENNIAL, etc.] Occurring once in twenty years.
1921 *Glasgow Herald* 29 Jan. 13/3 Their [*sc.* the planets'] vigintennial conjunction is due a few months hence.

Vihara (vīhā·ră). [Skt.] A Buddhist temple or monastery.
1876 *Chambers's Encycl.* IX. 794/1 s.v., Such Vihāras are in Ceylon permanent structures. 1901 KIPLING *Kim* i. 8 There were hundreds of pieces,..fragments of statues and slabs crowded with figures that had encrusted the brick walls of the Buddhist *stupas* and *viharas*. 1924 RONALDSHAY *India* ii. 23 Temples, mosques, and viharas are the finger-posts directing one along a fascinating road.

Villagelet (vi·lédʒlet). [-LET.] A small village.
1920 *Blackw. Mag.* Nov. 572/2 The guns clamoured away in the villagelet of Asa Khan.

Vim. (Earlier example.)
1843 *Yale Lit. Mag.* VIII. 406 He would have acted out his vim and the ease and pathos which heroes always manifest in like circumstances.

Vimana (vīmā·nă). [Skt.] The central tower enclosing the shrine in an Indian temple.
1863 *Chambers's Encycl.* V. 552/1 The temples consist of the temple or vimana, in front of which is the pillared porch

Supplement, p. 3873; Corrigenda, p. 4092; Spurious words, p. 4093; Books quoted, p. 4094

or mantopa [etc.]. 1875 *Encycl. Brit.* I. 396/2 *note*, The Vimana or temple itself.

Vi·mful, *a.* [f. VIM + -FUL.] Full of vim or vigour.
1923 *Glasgow Herald* 7 Nov. 6/3 Valladolid..retains the vimful life of a capital.

Vine, *sb.* **4. c.** (Earlier examples.)
1708 E. COOK *Sot-weed Factor* 19 When sturdy Oaks, and lofty Pines Were level'd with Musmillion Vines. *Note*, Musmilleon Vines are what we call Musk milleon Plants. 1786 WASHINGTON *Diaries* III. 118, 2 girls began to gather Pease..nearly half of the vines appearing to be ripe. 1831 BRYANT *Marion's Men* 9 We know its walls of thorny vines, Its glades of reedy grass.
9. vine-chafer = VINE-FRETTER; **vine-hopper,** an insect, *Tettigonia vitis*, attacking vines.
1862 T. W. HARRIS *Insects injur. Veget.* (ed. 3) 34 One of our diurnal Melolonthians..resembles the vine-chafer of Europe in its habits. *Ibid.* 228 In the autumn the vine-hoppers desert the vines.

Vinegar, *sb.* **6.** Add: **vinegar-cherry,** a species of wild cherry; **vinegar-fly,** a species of fruit fly, *Drosophila melanogaster*.
1895 *Outing* XXVI. 394/1 Branches of reddening *vinegar cherries and sprays of sweet fern. 1926 *Nat. Hist. Oxford Distr.* 274 Nine species of *Drosophila* have occurred, including the well-known *vinegar-fly.

Vinegared, *ppl. a.* [f. VINEGAR *v.* + -ED [2].] Treated or flavoured with vinegar.
1892 CONAN DOYLE *Great Shadow* vi. 74 He set a dish of vinegared herrings before him.

Vineg(e)rone (vinīgərō·nə). *U.S.* Also **-garone.** [? Sp. *vinagrone*, f. *vinagre* vinegar.] The whip-tailed scorpion, *Mastigoproctus giganteus*, so called from the vinegary smell of the secretion of its stink-gland.
1891 *Century Dict.* 1914 *Blackw. Mag.* July 123/1 His late breaking-in, the lengthy vacation, [etc.]..keep the 'vinegarone' in his [a bronco's] composition. 1920 *Glasgow Herald* 8 July 4/2 His animal friends, the chief of whom seem to be vinegrones, some species of bug.

Viner [2]. **1.** (Modern example.)
1924 *Blackw. Mag.* Jan. 127/1 He is in reality farmer, gardener, viner, forester,..and tobacconist.

Vineyardist. (Earlier example.)
1847 *Rep. U.S. Comm. Patents* (1848) 199 A French wine maker and vineyardist..from Kentucky.

Vinology (vəinǫ·lǒdʒi). [f. L. *vin-um* wine + -(O)LOGY.] The scientific study of wines.
1846 FORD *Gather. Spain* xiv. 159 The Capataz..delivers an explanatory lecture on vinology.

Vint, *sb.*[2] Also **wint.** [Russ.] A Russian card-game resembling auction bridge.
1898 *Nat. Rev.* Aug. 809 At a game of *wint* or *bridge*. 1901 *Field* 2 Feb. 147 Recently the game of vint has been heard of as the parent of bridge. 1904 *To-Day* 17 Aug. 62/2 As Whist was to the Britisher so Vint is to the Russian. 1925 *Blackw. Mag.* Apr. 515/2 I too played at cards. Sometimes it was 'vint'.

Vintage. **1.** *fig.* (Recent example.)
1931 F. L. ALLEN *Only Yesterday* vi. 129 Harding had no sooner arrived at the White House than a swarm of practical politicians of the McKinley-Foraker vintage reappeared in Washington.

Violability (vəiolābi·līti). [f. VIOLABLE + -ITY.] Capacity for being violated.
1926 *Glasgow Herald* 1 Apr. 8/4 The suggestion..raises the whole question of the violability of contracts.

Violet, *a.* Add: **1. e.** Applied to days on which liturgical violet is used.
1931 E. C. TRENHOLME *Angl. Low Mass* 46 The Gloria is said on Sundays and all feasts and every day in octaves, except the violet Sundays in Advent and from Septuagesima to Easter.

Violinistic (vəiǝlini·stik), *a.* [f. VIOLINIST + -IC.] Belonging to or characteristic of a violin.
1821 A. RIVARDE *Violin & its Technique* 11 Many violinists ..are constantly blustering with long bows, very often spoiling the phrasing and making violinistic rather than musical effects.

Virgating (vɜ̄·ɹgetiŋ), *a.* *Geol.* [f. as VIRGATION + -ING [2].] (See quot.)
1899 *Q. Jrnl. Geol. Soc.* LV. 576 A divergent arrangement of fault-lines has been termed a 'virgating system' by American geologists.

Vir·gilism. [f. *Virgil* + -ISM.] = VIRGILIANISM.
1923 *Glasgow Herald* 9 Jan. 6/7 We praise the mellow Virgilisms in Tennyson.

Virgin. **17.** Add: *Virgin country*, country that has not yet been opened up for traffic, commerce, etc.; land in its natural state.
1929 *Daily Express* 7 Nov. 8/4 Great tractors that will take heavy loads over virgin country where there are no roads.

Virginia. **1. c.** Add: *Virginia rail.*
1914 *Chambers's Jrnl.* July 439/1 The Virginia rail, the larger cousin of the sora, is rare.
d. Virginia fence (earlier example.).
1671 *Portsmouth (R.I.) Rec.* 26 Apr., For a ffence called a Virginia ffence, It is ordered that it shall be fower foot and a halfe high, stakt with stakes halfe a foot above the fence.

Virginian. **A.** *sb.* **b.** (Earlier examples.)
1654 *Col. Rec. N. Carolina* I. 18 Sir, if you think good to acquaint the States with what is done by two Virginians born, you will honor our country. 1755 FRANKLIN *Wks.* (Sparks) VII. 97 The Virginians and Marylanders. 1770 WASHINGTON *Diaries* I. 416 By Virginians they mean all the People settled upon Red Stone, etc.

Virgular, *a.* Add: **3.** *Zool.* Characterized by virgulæ (sense 1).
1888 ROLLESTON & JACKSON *Anim. Life* 769 Two such organisms may be united back to back by their virgular aspects, as in the diprionid Graptolites.

Virility. Add: **3. c.** Virile persons considered collectively.
1921 *Edin. Rev.* Jan. 117 This eccentric and lovable being was the first of his breed to go adventuring on life's highway, as all the virility did of that period.

Viscoid (vi·skoid), *sb.* [f. the adj.] (See quot. 1908.)
1896 [see *VISCOSE]. 1908 FISHER *Schlich's Man. Forestry* V. 554 A watery solution of cellulose in combination with soda and carbon-bisulphide is named *viscose* and used as a substitute for glue; when this is heated a hard amorphous substance is produced, *viscoid*, which in various colours is used instead of celluloid.

Viscometry (viskǫ·mĭtri). [Irreg. f. L. *viscōsus* VISCOSE + -(O)METRY.] The measurement of the viscosity of fluids.
1931 G. BARR *Monogr. Viscometry* i. 5 The viscometry of gas provided one of the most brilliant verifications of the Kinetic Theory.

Viscontial (vəikǫ·ntiăl), *a.* [f. VISCOUNT + -IAL.] Belonging to or suggestive of a viscount.
1920 R. ASQUITH in *Autobiog. Margot Asquith* I. xiv. 276 You beat your tangled music out Lofty, aloof, viscontial.

Viscose. (Read:) Cellulose reduced to a viscous solution by special chemicals and processes, largely used in the manufacture of artificial silk; the sodium xanthogenite ester of cellulose. Also *attrib.*
1896 C. F. CROSS *Patent Specif.* 4713 Cellulose..requires a very much smaller proportion of alkali to convert it into alkali-cellulose suitable for use in other manufactures such ..as that of the substances now known as 'viscose' and 'viscoid'. 1901 CROSS & BEVAN *Researches on Cellulose* 174 Of the 'viscose' product we have a more intimate knowledge. 1925 *Good Housekeeping* Apr. 142/3 The remaining variety [of artificial silk], Viscose silk, is now being made in enormous quantities here, on the Continent, and in America. 1927 T. WOODHOUSE *Artificial Silk* 30 By far the greater percentage of artificial silk is made from Viscose.

Visibility. Add: **1. d.** *Comb.*, as *visibility-proof*.
1928 *Publishers' Weekly* 22 Sept. 1117/2 The lettering is visibility proof and can be read from every seat [of the bus].

Visible. **A.** *adj.* Add: **3. c.** *Finance.* Of imports or exports: Opposed to *INVISIBLE 1 d.
1917 J. A. TODD *Mech. Exchange* xiv. 184 Visible and invisible imports alike go to the debit side of the account. 1929 S. E. THOMAS *Elem. Econ.* (ed. 4) xxix. 520 These returns of our visible trade regularly disclose a large excess of imports over exports.

Visile (vi·zəil), *a.* and *sb.* [Irreg. f. first part of VISIBLE, VISION etc. + -ILE.] **a.** *adj.* Learning or recalling most readily in terms of visual presentations. **b.** *sb.* A visile person.
1909 *Daily Chron.* 22 Feb. 4/7 The three great classes of the Visile, Audile, and Motile. 1913 *Jrnl. Exper. Pedagogy* Dec. 175 Of the thirty boys tested, one was an exceptionally good visile. 1927 J. ADAMS *Errors in School* 74 This does not imply that the visiles get their knowledge entirely through the eye.

Visit, *sb.* Add: **1. f.** *U.S.* A chat or talk.
1890 *Harper's Mag.* Dec. 147/2 I've had a real nice visit with you. 1899 T. HALL *Tales* 226 Our visit together was quite uneventful but very delightful.
3. c. A turn of play at a billiard-table.
1927 *Times* 22 Feb. 16/3 At his second visit to the table he made a break of 111.

Visit, *v.* Add: **8. f.** *U.S.* To talk or chat.
1887 MARY E. WILKINS *Humble Romance* 319 'You an' Mis Wheat can visit a little while, while Becca an' I are out here,' said she. 1898 MARG. DELAND *Old Chester Tales* 75 You can eat it while I get out and visit with the minister. 1929 MILDRED ADAMS in *N.Y. Times Mag.* 20 Oct. 1 Having disposed of a batch of correspondence he was willing to visit in an informal..fashion. It was good talk.

Visitee. (Earlier example.)
1710 ARCHB. OF DUBLIN in *Swift's Wks.* XIV. 57 There are great men here as much out of humour, as you describe your great visitee to have been.

Visiting, *vbl. sb.* **4.** Add: **visiting book** (*b*) = *visitors' book* (see next).
1848 THACKERAY *Van. Fair* lv. 500 The Bishop went and wrote his name in the visiting-book at Gaunt House that very day.

Visitor. Add: **5.** *visitors' book*, a book in which visitors to a place enter their names.
1860 in J. A. Langford *Mod. Birmingham* (1877) II. i. 54 Their reports are signed in the visitors' book. 1870 *Punch* 1 Oct. 138/2 The Emperor Nicholas..'expressed himself much pleased', as the visitors' books have it. 1917 *Rangoon Gazette* 29 Jan. 29/1 His record of efficiency is written in the visitors' books.

Vita glass (vəi·tă glɑs). Trade name of variety of glass of a special composition which is transparent to or permits the passage of a large part of the ultra-violet rays of ordinary sunlight.
1925 *Spectator* 12 Dec. 1085/2 Only a very iconoclastic modernizer would tear out original Elizabethan leaded glass to replace it with 'Vitaglass'. 1927 *Observer* 9 Oct. 21/3 In order to secure the maximum benefit of these rays vita-glass has been placed in the south-facing windows of the rooms used by the boys.

Vitali·stically, *adv.* [f. VITALISTIC + -AL + -LY [2].] In a vitalistic manner.
1926 *Spectator* 27 Feb. 371/1 He was one of the first men to look consciously and vitalistically forward towards a higher type of man.

Vitamin (vəi·tămin, vi·t-). Orig. **vitamine** (-məin). [f. L. *vit-a* life + AMINE; named *vitamine* by Casimir Funk in the belief that an amino-acid was present, and later changed to *vitamin* to avoid suggesting this.] One of a number of 'accessory' food factors essential to health, of which the chemical nature is still unknown, present in most uncooked animal and vegetable foods, but largely destroyed by heating and oxidation. Different vitamins are distinguished as *Vitamin A, B, C, D, E*, etc., and specific diseases or incapacities are attributed to the absence of one or other of these.
1912 C. FUNK in *Jrnl. State Med.* 342 All these diseases.. can be prevented and cured by the addition of certain preventive substances; the deficient substances, which are of the nature of organic bases, we will call 'vitamines', and we will speak of a beri-beri or scurvy vitamine, which means a substance preventing the special disease. 1915 *Times Lit. Suppl.* 11 Nov. 400/3 The point about vitamines is that without them the animal ceases to grow or becomes diseased on a physiologically pure diet. 1916 *Med. Press & Circular* 9 Aug. 123/1 Much of the severity of the fever is due to the lack of vitamines. 1920 *Contemp. Rev.* Dec. 819 The boiling of vegetables has too often ruined some of the 'salts' and 'vitamines'. 1926 *Ibid.* Oct. 500 The plant alone knows how to manufacture vitamins. 1928 A. B. CALLOW *Food & Health* 39 Compared with the total daily ration of food, the amount of vitamin we need is almost negligible.
fig. 1921 *Spectator* 16 Apr. 492/2 A book..so full of the vitamines of literature. *Ibid.* 7 May 588/2 The vitamines of the spirit and..of true religion.
b. *attrib.* and *Comb.*
1921 *Conquest* Sept. 498/2 The only safe rule is this..eat vitamine-containing food on every possible occasion..and avoid, as far as practicable, vitamine-free foods. 1928 A. B. CALLOW *Food & Health* 22 The food value of different fats varies..according to the chemical constitution (to neglect for the moment the subject of vitamin content).
Hence **Vitami·nic** *a.*, **Vita·minous** *a.*, of or pertaining to vitamins; **Vi·taminize** *v. trans.*; **Vi·taminless** *a.*
1914 *Nature* 12 Mar. 42/1 Vitaminous foods are fresh milk .., whole grains, potatoes, carrots,..and apparently cod liver oil. *Ibid.*, Such vitamineless foods as sterilised milk, condensed milk, cornflours, starch, and sugar. 1926 *Chambers's Jrnl.* Apr. 291/2 The milk tends to become less and less valuable from the point of view of vitaminic value. 1930 *Observer* 13 Apr. 7 Adventure, we are told, is the 'vitaminizing element' in history. 1931 Sir C. J. HOLMES *Gram. Arts* iii. 27 Life..is the essential thing..and we must not starve ourselves of this vitaminous element.

Vitative (vəi·tătiv), *a.* *Phren.* [Irreg. f. L. *vita* life + -IVE.] Concerned with the preservation of life. So **Vi·tativeness.**
1913 *Funk's Standard Dict.* 1914 *19th Cent.* July 123 Man's merely vitative body may be considered, then, as a vegetative organism linking the psychical organism with environment.

Vitrain (vi·trein). [f. L. *vitrum* glass, and ending of *FUSAIN.] One of the four visibly distinct bands which together constitute bituminous coal.
1928 M. C. STOPES in *Proc. Royal Soc.* B. XC. 473 The fourth ingredient, the vitrain or brilliant bands, have been less considered in the past, but are..particularly interesting.

Vituperous, *a.* **1.** (Modern example.)
1914 R. M. JONES *Spiritual Reformers 16th & 17th Cent.* v. 69 Schwenckfeld was denounced in the most vituperous language of the period.

Vivid, *a.* Add: **7.** *Comb.*, as *vivid-skinned*.
1913 E. F. BENSON *Thorley Weir* i. 8 By the side of his daughter he looked like a dried Normandy pippin compared to a fresh apple, sun-tinted and vivid-skinned.

Vocal. **B.** *sb.* Add: **4.** Short for *vocal music*.
1928 SINCLAIR LEWIS *Man Who Knew Coolidge* i. 30 She felt more kind of called to the musical line, and she was taking vocal and piano.

Vocational, *a.* (Further example.)
1915 *Lit. Digest* 4 Sept. 473/1 The great menace of vocational training is that it might be used to confine the poor to an industrial education.
Hence (also) **Voca·tionalism**; **Voca·tionalize** *v. trans.*
1912 J. H. MOORE *Ethics & Education* 33 Schools should not be industrialized merely, nor commercialized, nor professionalized, but vocationalized. 1924 *Glasgow Herald* 1 May 8/6 The primary function of education is wider than mere vocationalism.

Voetsak (futsæ̆k), *int.* *S. Africa.* Also **footsek.** [Cape Du., f. Du. *voort zeg ik* be off, I say.] A command to leave (properly addressed to a dog).
1871 *Cape Monthly Mag.* III. 332 Cries of *foot-sek* with the slashing of a whip and the yelping of a defeated cur. 1899 A. WERNER *Capt. of Locusts* 194 Be off with you! How dare you annoy a lady like this? *Voetsak!*

Voguey (vōu·gi), *a.* [f. VOGUE + -Y.] That is in vogue or popular for the time being.
1928 *Observer* 22 July 9/2 An achievement..which steers a happy course between the 'arty' and the 'voguey'.

Voguish (vōu·giʃ), *a.* [f. VOGUE *sb.* + -ISH.] = prec.
1927 *Daily Express* 26 Mar. 8 Advt., Hundreds of the voguish Jumper Suits await your selection.

Voice, *sb.* **14. voice-hatch,** a hatch or opening for speaking through.
1899 CUTCLIFFE HYNE *Further Adv. Capt. Kettle* vi. 112 He bent down to the *voice hatch, and gave a bearing to the black quartermaster in the wheel-house below.

Void, *v.* **2. b.** (Modern example.)
1876 *Fur, Fin & Feather* Sept. 167 They [squirrels] should be voided..and kept several days in cold weather..

Voidless, *a.* Add: **b.** *Poet.* Unavoidable.
1908 HARDY *Dynasts* III. III. i. 382 All must prepare to grip with gory death In the now voidless battle.

Vol., abbrev. of VOLUME. Add: **b.** as *v. trans.*, to mark or number as volumes.
1930 *Blackwell's 277th Catal.* Oct. 45/2, 7 vols., uniform in size and 'volled' I.–VII. on back.

Volant. **B.** *sb.* **3.** (Earlier example.)
1851 *Harper's Mag.* Jan. 288/1 Five volants are set on full, each being trimmed at a little distance from the edge by a narrow guimpe.

Volcanic, *a.* Add: **4. c.** *fig.* as *sb. pl.*
1926 *Contemp. Rev.* Aug. 178 These politicians devoted themselves to editorial volcanics.

Vo·lcanolo·gical, *a.* [f. VOLCANO *sb.* + -(O)LOGICAL.] Of or pertaining to volcanology; vulcanological.
1902 *Cassell's Encycl. Dict.* Suppl. 1931 G. W. TYRRELL *Volcanoes* i. 12 With the establishment of volcanological observatories..the study of volcanoes has entered upon a new phase.

Volley, *v.* Add: **1. c.** To fire a volley or volleys at.
1908 HARDY *Dynasts* III. VII. ii. 489 (Stage direction) Kempt's brigade..volleys murderously Donzelot's columns..and repulses them.

Volsteadism (vǫ·lstèdiz'm). [f. the name of Andrew J. *Volstead* (1860–), originator of the *Volstead Act*, which was passed in 1919 by the U.S. Congress to enforce prohibition + -ISM.] The policy of the Volstead Act; prohibition (sense 4).
1923 H. L. FOSTER *Beachcomber in Orient* xi. 268 The Phillippines are not affected by Volsteadism and are wet enough to make up for the dryness of half a dozen States. 1927 *Observer* 24 July 18/4 Industry's own Volsteadism is supported by the overwhelming sentiment of management and men alike.

Volumetrically, *adv.* (Earlier example.)
1863 W. O. MARKHAM tr. *Anal. Urine* 305 The determination of the albumen volumetrically by means of ferrocyanide of potassium.

Voluminal (voliū·minăl), *a.* [f. L. *volūmin-* VOLUMEN + -AL.] Of or pertaining to volume.
1925 J. JOLY *Surface-Hist. of Earth* vii. 113 A small upward displacement must then be attended with voluminal expansion.

Volunteered, *ppl. a.* (Earlier example.)
1879 'GEO. ELIOT' *Theophrastus Such* i. 7 The fellow-feeling which should restrain us from turning our volunteered and picked confessions into an act of accusation against others.

Volve, *v.* **1.** (Modern example.)
1912 GALSWORTHY *Inn Tranq.* 9 If It did not volve and revolve on Itself It would peter out at one end or the other.

Vorticism (vǭ·ɹtisiz'm). [f. L. *vortic-*, *vortex*, (see VORTEX) + -ISM.] The principles of a modern school of art (see quots.).
1915 *Drawing* July 56/1 Vorticism..is in reality our old and amusing friend Cubism, but Cubism heavily charged with electricity. 1921 *Edin. Rev.* Apr. 313 Vorticism..was an ingenious British blend of Cubism, Futurism and Expressionism.

Vorticist. Add: **2.** An exponent of vorticism in art.
1915 *Observer* 1 Aug. 5/6 The reviled Post-Impressionists, ..Cubists, Futurists, Expressionists, Vorticists of to-day may be the honoured masters of to-morrow. 1919 'IAN HAY' *Last Million* 3 That school of unappreciated geniuses, the Futurists, or Cubists, or Vorticists, or whatever the malady is called.

Vote, *sb.* **10.** Add: **vote-proof** *a.*, not capable of being affected by voting.
1928 G. B. SHAW *Intel. Woman's Guide Socialism* 63. 291 Those who do understand it will never be unanimous in resisting it; consequently it is voteproof at the parliamentary elections.

Vote, *v.* **3.** (Further example.)
1926 *Socialist Rev.* Oct. 48 There are still hundreds of thousands of voters who cannot bring themselves to vote Conservative.
10. b. To present for voting; to record the votes of (electors).
1859 BARTLETT *Dict. Amer.* (ed. 2) s.v. *Cooping*, At a proper day [certain voters] are taken to the polls, and 'voted', as it is called, for the party. 1883 NYE *Baled Hay* 217, I believe they vote people there who have been dead for centuries. 1904 *N.Y. Even. Post* 8 Nov. 1, 25 men were in line in many places, and they were voted at a rate of nearly one a minute.

Voyage, *v.* **3. b.** (Further example.)
1909 *Chambers's Jrnl.* Oct. 659/1 In the same dirigible he voyaged into Switzerland and back.

Vulnerability. Add: **c.** *spec.* in *Contract Bridge*: (cf. *VULNERABLE *a.* 2 d).
1927 M. C. WORK *Contract Bridge* ii. 10 Trick values, the number of points to a game, game and rubber bonuses.. are not affected by vulnerability.

Vulnerable, *a.* Add: **2. d.** *Contract Bridge.* Applied to a side which has won one game towards rubber.
1927 A. E. MANNING-FOSTER in *Observer* 5 June 19/2 All over-trick bonuses gained by a vulnerable side count double, whether the opposing side is vulnerable or invulnerable.

Vulture, *sb.* **4. d.** Add: *vulture-wise* adv.
1892 STEVENSON & OSBOURNE *Wrecker* xiii. 206 Towards her the taut *Norah Creina*, vulture-wise, wriggled to windward: come from so far to pick her bones.

W

Waac (wæk). [f. the initials of Women's Army Auxiliary Corps.] A member of the Women's Army Auxiliary Corps, organized in 1917. Also *attrib.*
1917 *Times* 19 Nov. 11/3 The men call them 'the Waacs'. 1918 *War Birds* (1927) 85 He had a hundred and fifty Waacs of all sizes and contours and he was trying to line them up. *Ibid.*, A Waac officer can't walk out with a Tommy any more than an army officer can be seen with a Waac private.

Waahoo, variant of WAHOO.

Wade, *v.* Add: **3. e.** *To wade in*: to make a vigorous attack on one's opponent. *To wade into*: to assail with energy.
1872 EGGLESTON *Hoosier Schoolm.* i. 15 You can jist roll up and wade in. 1905 *N.Y. Even. Post* 2 Sept., When a herd of sheep wades in on a patch of bluebells, they stand still and eat all day. 1904 MRS. STRATTON-PORTER *Freckles* 365 You waded single-handed into a man almost twice your size. 1928 *Daily Express* 30 July 13/6 Though severely punished by Pattenden's lefts to the face he repeatedly waded in.

Wadi. Also *attrib.*
1902 D. G. HOGARTH *Nearer East* 139 The palm-lined wadi beds of Jebel Akhdar. *Ibid.* 143 Aromatic scrub and an occasional thorn is all that can be expected in the wadi bottoms.

Wading-place. [f. WADING *vbl. sb.*] A part of a river that can be crossed by wading; a ford. (In early Amer. use.)
1598 [see WADING *vbl. sb.* b]. 1650 *Providence* (R.I.) *Rec.* II. 9 The said land lying above the second wading-place above Pawtucket ffalls. 1675 *Connecticut Public Rec.* II. 256 From thence..runn a straight line till they meet with the line where the wading place is. 1733 *Maryland Hist. Mag.* XV. 218 From the lower wading place of the main falls of Potapsco to the second wadeing place of Gwinns Falls. 1781 *Narrag. Hist. Reg.* I. 281 Went in swimming at Robert's wadeing place.

Wafdist (wɑ·fdist), *a.* and *sb.* [f. *Wafd*, the name of the political organization supporting Zaghlul Pasha, the Egyptian Nationalist leader + -IST.] **a.** *adj.* Of or pertaining to the Wafd. **b.** *sb.* A member or supporter of the Wafd; an Egyptian Nationalist.
1926 *Glasgow Herald* 3 June 8 Doubts..were entertained of the prospect of the Wafdist leader taking such a moderate course. 1926 *Spectator* 19 June 1032/2 The Wafdists..are likely to be restrained by the knowledge that any too free indulgence in their characteristic tactics..would quickly make Adly throw up his office in disgust.

Waffle, *sb.*[1] **b.** Add: *waffle-frolic*, *-mould*, *-wagon*; **waffle-iron** (earlier examples).
1744 in *Mag. Amer. Hist.* (1878) II. 442 For my own part I was not a little grieved that so luxurious a feast should come under the name of a *wafel frolic. 1794 *S. Carolina State Gaz.* 30 Aug. 1/2 Woffle irons [advertised]. 1812 *Norfolk* (Va.) *Herald* 17 Feb. 1/4 Waffle Irons, Oil Cloths, etc. 1866 C. H. SMITH *Bill Arp* 115 Didn't the rebellion just close right up on the ground behind him, just like shutting up a pair of waffle-irons? 1864 'MARK TWAIN' *Sketches* Wks. XIX. 335 When he recovered from his illness his face was pitted like a *waffle-mould, and his comeliness gone forever. 1908 A. RUHL *Other Americans* vi. 90 Crowding round the pay-window just as boys at home might crowd round a *waffle-wagon or hokey-pokey ice-cream cart.

Wa·ffling, *vbl. sb.* [f. WAFFLE *sb.*[1]] The making of waffles.
1927 J. A. E. DUNN *Girl of Ghost Mountain* v. 87 Jackson had avowed his determination of learning the art of waffling.

Wage, *sb.* **4. a.** *wage-board*, *worker*; **b.** *wage-fixing*.
1925 *Scribner's Mag.* Oct. 415/2 The regulation of wages has been placed in the hands of *wage boards. 1928 *Brit. Industr. Future* (Lib. Ind. Inq.) III. xvi. 181 The practical considerations which ought to govern the process of *wage-fixing. 1904 *Boston Transcript* 11 June 18 The speaker went further than was necessary in his effort to do justice to the *wage-worker.

Wage, *v.* **6.** (Later examples.)
1825 J. NEAL *Bro. Jonathan* II. 55 Oh, my shins!—oh—oh!—they're pootely barked, I wage. 1876 [G. H. TRIPP] *Student Life* 18 Do something splendid on the mathematics and the 'orals', and I will wage anything you will pass clear.

Wagnerism. (Earlier example.)
1852 *Punch* 19 June 252/2 The infection called Wagnerism is spreading most rapidly throughout the musical profession.

Wagon, *sb.* Add: **9. b.** *slang.* Short for *water-wagon* (see WATER *sb.* 29).
1917 *War Birds* (1927) 23 Spriggs put him on the wagon for a week. 1924 P. MARKS *Plastic Age* 273 Carver was on the wagon and..had got as religious as holy hell.
11. a. *wagon-cover* (earlier example), *hire* (later examples).
1781 *Cal. Virginia St. Papers* I. 546 A number of *wagon-covers, for the protection of military stores. 1776 *Jrnls. Cont. Congress* IV. 118 To George Benner, for *waggon-hire. 1813 F. L. CLAIBORNE in *Sam Dale* (1860) v. 90 Already the two hundred dollars advanced by the quarter-master have been expended for wagon-hire.
b. *wagon builder* (earlier example.)
1786 WASHINGTON *Diaries* III. 137 A compleat Wheel right, *Waggon builder, and Plow and Hurdle maker.
12. wagon-bed (earlier example).
1863 *Rep. U.S. Comm. Agric.* 141 A larger portion of the top of the cane was cut off than usual in order to get it into the *wagon-bed.

Wagon, *v.* **1.** (Earlier U.S. example.)
1794 E. DENNY *Jrnl.* 199 The French had opened the Indian path..and wagoned considerable upon it.

Wagonable (wæ·gənăb'l), *a.* [f. WAGON *v.* + -ABLE.] Admitting of being traversed by a wagon.
1858 *Illust. News of World* 20 Feb. 35/1 The Po is now frozen over, and wagonable from Cremona to Ferrara and the sea.

Wagon box. *U.S.* The body of a wagon; a wagon-bed.
1810 *Austin Papers* (1924) I. 168, 13 Wagon Boxes. 1815 *Niles' Weekly Reg.* IX. 94/2 Waggon boxes and hollow ware of all kinds. 1850 L. SAWYER *Way Sketches* 30 We have found no wood since we struck the Platte, except fragments of wagon boxes..brought..by emigrants who have preceded us. 1878 J. H. BEADLE *Western Wilds* xx. 327 The boy climbed out of the rear of the wagon-box and begged to go on with them. 1888 C. D. FERGUSON *Exp. Forty-niner* 63 A wagon box, well corked and pitched so as to be water tight, was launched. *a* 1918 G. STUART *On Frontier* I. 39 In the wagon boxes we carried our supply of food and extra clothing.

Wagoning. (Earlier example.)
1837 *Southern Lit. Messenger* III. 87 There never was such a time for wagoning before.

Wagon-master. Latterly *U.S.* (See WAGON *sb.* 12.)
1645–1757 [see WAGON *sb.* 12]. 1775 *Jrnls. Cont. Congress* III. 329 There is due to Robert Erwin, waggon master, the sum of 169 pounds. 1847 in Emory *Military Reconn.* 546 Our successful passage over was entirely due to the perseverance and good management of the wagon-master. 1857 W. CHANDLESS *Visit Salt Lake* I. ii. 16, I believe the waggon-masters of one goods-train had strict orders not to travel on Sundays. 1875 *Fur, Fin & Feather* 106 Then you lazily..follow the train, listening to the wagon-master's many stories.

Wahoo. (Earlier examples.)
1810 MICHAUX *Arbres* I. 39 *Wahoo*, nom donné dans la partie maritime des Etats du midi. 1832 D. J. BROWNE *Sylva Amer.* 308 The Wahoo is a stranger to the Middle and Northern States.

Waif, *sb.*[2] **2.** (Earlier mod. examples.)
1839 *Knickerbocker Mag.* XIII. 382 Line-tubs, water-kegs, and wafe-poles, were thrown hurriedly into the boats. 1846 T. B. THORPE *Myst. Backwoods* 85 As the waiffe of the whaleman [marks] his victim on the sea.

Wain, *v.* **1.** (Modern example.)
1822 J. HOGG *Kilmeny* Poet. Wks. I. 184 But so swift they wained her through the light, 'Twas like the motion of sound or sight.

Wainage. **2.** (Earlier example.)
1910 G. CHALMERS *Caledonia* II. ii. 134 The waynage, or cultivable lands, and meadows of each district or manor, were possessed, and laboured, in separate portions, by the individuals of the manor.

Waist. **4.** (Further example.)
1902 D. G. HOGARTH *Nearer East* 2 The 'Medic' or 'Indian Isthmus', which is that Waist of Asia, reduced to 700 miles' breadth, which lies between the Caspian and the Indian Seas.
6. *waist-jacket*, *-sash*.
1901 'L. MALET' *Hist. Sir R. Calmady* II. viii. 155 A.. little stick of a man, arrayed in frayed and tarnished splendour of sky-blue *waist-jacket, silver lace, and jackboots. 1908 *Chambers's Jrnl.* Mar. 218/2 The men were armed with..long knives thrust through their red *waist-sashes.

Waistless, *a.* Add: **b.** (In sense 2 d of WAIST.)
1893 MRS. CUSTER *Tenting on Plains* iv. 85 It would have been rather serious joking if..I had not brought a jacket,.. for..I should have been huddled inside the closed ambulance, waistless and alone.

Wait, *v.*[1] **7. g.** (Further example.) Also *to wait till one sees*.
1905 *Smart Set* Oct. 11/1 You boys just wait till you see. I'll have you all jumpin' side-ways pretty soon. 1910 *Blackw. Mag.* May 747/1 Mr. Asquith has deemed it not incompatible with the gravity of his office to elude the curiosity of his opponents with the absurd formula, 'Wait and see'.
9. d. (Earlier example.)
1827 CARLYLE *Germ. Rom.*, *Tieck's Elves* (1871) 230 Andres waited supper.

Waiter. Add: **7. a.** (Later U.S. examples.)
1828 A. SHERBURNE *Mem.* (1831) i. 20, I was waiter to Mr. Charles Roberts the boatswain. *Ibid.* ii. 28 Part of our officers with five or six *waiters*..occupied an elegant house. 1861 *Army Regulations* 559, Non-commissioned officers not employed as waiters.
c. (Further U.S. examples.)
1838 CAROLINE GILMAN *Recoll. Southern Matron* i. 15 She followed the six negro female *waiters* dressed in white, with napkins pinned over their shoulders. 1846 *Knickerbocker Mag.* XXVII. 458 The next song shall be for the waiter in a private family.
12. A type of chess problem; a waiting problem (see next).
1906 A. C. WHITE *Tours de Force* Introd. p. xxxii, If a problem has no threat, it is called a 'waiter', and all the different continuations are variations.

Waiting, *vbl. sb.*[1] **2. c.** Add: **waiting problem,** *Chess.* (see quot.); **waiting race** (earlier example).
1907 S. S. BLACKBURNE *Chess Problems* 25 *Block problem.*—Otherwise called a "Waiting Problem", is one in which White's first move leads to mate after every reply of Black, in consequence of such reply. 1868 H. WOODRUFF *Trotting Horse* xxxvi. 297 Tallman made a *waiting-race of it, and pulled Flora back three lengths.

Waiting list. A list of persons waiting for appointments, selection for any purpose, or the next chance of obtaining something.
1897 *Outing* XXX. 347/2 The Michaux Club is composed of two hundred members, with a large 'waiting list'. 1913 LA FOLLETTE *Autobiog.* 227 It is certain that there were others on the waiting list who wanted the Senatorship.

Waiting-man. (Modern U.S. examples.)
1839 *Southern Lit. Messenger* V. 752/1 The door of the bachelor's hall was assaulted by a repetition of raps, which quickened the steps of Mr. Singlesides' sedate waiting-man. 1885 G. W. CABLE *Dr. Sevier* x. 69 The speaker ceased as the mulatto waiting-man appeared.

Wake-up. *U.S.* The golden-winged woodpecker, *Colaptes auratus*.
1866 *Game Laws Conn.* in *Fur, Fin & Feather* (1872) 31 No person shall wilfully shoot..the wake-up or high hole. 1867 *Amer. Naturalist* I. 109 The Golden-winged Woodpecker or Wakeup.

Waldensian. **B.** *sb.* (Earlier examples.)
1839 *Brit. Mag.* Apr. 377 A man could no more be a Leonist and a Catharist (or, in modern phrase, a Waldensian and an Albigensian) at the same time, than he could be both a Turk and a Dutchman. 1847 J. T. MULLOCK tr. *St. Alphonsus's Hist. Heresies* I. x. 260 Rainer..for seventeen years was a Waldensian.

Walk, *sb.*[1] Add: **4. e.** *To win in a walk*: To win a race or other contest without special exertion.
1903 A. H. LEWIS *The Boss* 138, I said that he won in a walk.
14. Also, the round or circuit of a postman.
1908 *Chambers's Jrnl.* Jan. 102/2 On arriving at the office of delivery letters are at once stamped and sorted to the 'walks' of the postmen.

Walk, *v.* **11.** Also *to walk guard*.
1930 F. A. POTTLE *Stretchers* 51 In France we always wore large automatics when we walked guard.
21. b. Of a ship: cf. sense 7 d.
1932 E. R. COOPER *Mardles fr. Suffolk* xx. 179 The *Lowestoft* took our towrope and walked us home at about ten knots.
24. d. To raise or draw *up* by walking and pulling a rope.
1886 R. BROWN *Spunyarn & Spindrift* xxviii. 338 With their assistance the topsail-yards were walked up to the mastheads in double quick time.
25. walk-along-Joe *U.S.*, a dance of American negroes; **walk-around** (earlier examples); also as *vb. intr.*, to dance the walk-around.
1862 'E. KIRKE' *Among Pines* xvii. 283 And then Jim danced breakdowns, "walk-along-Joes," and other darky dances. 1869 *Atlantic Monthly* July 72/2 In company with others [I] performed the Virginia *Walk-around. 1875 E. KING *Southern St. N. Amer.* 618 All the seats are cleared away, and the congregation begins the genuine 'walk-around' to the music of the 'spiritual'. 1888 *Century Mag.* Jan. 468 The dancer held her dress back and 'walked around', turning her toes in.

Walking, *vbl. sb.*[1] **4.** *walking boot*, *dress* (earlier examples).
1854 MARIA S. CUMMINS *Lamplighter* xxx, To change her slippers for thick *walking-boots occupied a few minutes only. 1753 WASHINGTON *Diaries* I. 63, I put myself in an Indian *walking Dress.
b. walking-beam (earlier examples).
1845 *Knickerbocker Mag.* XXV. 63 Some rushed to the upper deck, and climbed up the chain and up the machinery to the walking beam. 1850 C. MATHEWS *Moneypenny* 43 The walking-beam has broken in twain.

Walk-over. Add: **b.** *transf.* Anything that is easy to accomplish.
1902 G. H. LORIMER *Lett. Self-made Merchant* xv. 216 It wasn't any walk-over to hold the belt in those days. 1907 MRS. HARRIS *Tents of Wickedness* III. iv. 255 The first day ..Belinda whispered ecstatically that it was a walk-over. 1920 P. G. WODEHOUSE *Damsel in Distress* xiii. 164 The battle was a walk-over for the enemy. 1931 *Daily Tel.* 21 Jan. 8/4 This makes its acquisition by an American crook a walk-over.

Walk-round. *U.S.* A dance practised by American negroes; (cf. *walk-around*: WALK *v.* 25).
1861 *Temple Bar* May 199 The 'Jim Crow dance'..soon gave place to better tunes..and 'walk rounds'. 1862 'E. KIRKE' *Among Pines* vi. 147 Then about twenty 'gentleman and lady' darkies joined two at a time, in a half 'walk-round', half breakdown. 1892 *Harper's Mag.* Jan. 251/1 The darkies try to see which can put on the most style in a kind of walk-round.

Wa·lk-up, *a.* *U.S.* [f. *to walk up*: WALK *v.*[1] 5 g.] Applied to flats or apartments for which there is no lift.
1919 MENCKEN *Amer. Lang.* 111 *note*, In New York such apartments are commonly called *walk-up apartments*. 1928 F. N. HART *Bellamy Trial* vii. 302 She had to live in a little walk-up flat in the Bronx. 1929 ELMER L. RICE *Street Scene* I. 3 The exterior of a 'walk-up' apartment-house, in a mean quarter of New York.

Wa·lkway. *U.S.* = WALK *sb.*[1] 9 c.
1792 *Essex Inst. Hist. Coll.* (1865) VII. 37 We the Subscribers agree to pay to the Town Treasurer the Sums set against our respective Names, towards paving the Walk Way in the Main Street with Flatt Stones. 1816 W. BENTLEY *Diary* (1914) IV. 405 A walkway for the first time has been raised in the principal streets in the eastern part of the Town. 1904 *N.Y. Even. Post* 14 May 5 A space..sufficient to provide each house with a walkway to the rear. 1911 [see WALK *sb.*[1] 20].

Wall, *sb.*[1] **21. a.** Add: *wall clip, crane, fitting.*
1911 *Chambers's Jrnl.* 350/1 This [nailing trees to walls] is now rendered an absurdly simple task by a patent *wall-clip. 1902 *Cassell's Encycl. Dict.* Suppl. *Wall-crane. 1924 *Times Trade & Engin. Suppl.* 29 Nov. 252/2 Supply and erection of semi-portal, portal, and wall cranes. 1909 *Chambers's Jrnl.* Sept. 620/1 The current..can be drawn.. by the insertion of a plug and flexible connection in the lamp-holder or *wall-fitting.

Wallaby. Add: **1. b.** *pl.* Used for Australians.
1908 *Daily Chron.* 28 Sept. 4/6 The 'Wallabies', as the Australian football players..have christened themselves [etc.] 1916 *Glasgow Even. Times* 3 A big batch of Germans ..called upon the Wallabies to surrender.

Wallage (wǭ·lėdʒ). [f. WALL + -AGE.] Walls collectively; a piece of walling; wall-work.
1928 *Sunday News* 17 June 2/4 The..recorded test of.. cavity brick walls showed a crushing strength of some 48 tons in a wallage of the same area.

Wallah. **b.** (Further example.)
1926 *Chambers's Jrnl.* Christm. No. 879/1 A bag-wallah from India, or possibly a tea-planter from Ceylon.

Wall-and-crown knot. A wall-knot having a crown.
1924 R. CLEMENTS *Gipsy of Horn* iii. 57 An iron rod was passed down its whole length to stiffen it and a complicated wall-and-crown knot woven on top to serve as a handle.

Wall-paper. (Earlier examples.)
1827 DRAKE & MANSF. *Cincinnati* viii. 65 Two Wall Paper Factories, 9 hands. 1852 MRS. STOWE *Uncle Tom's C.* xxxv, The wall-paper was defaced in spots, by slops of beer and wine.

Walm, *v.* **1. c.** (Modern example.)
1908 HARDY *Dynasts* III. III. iii. 387 Throats shout 'advance' And forms walm, wallow, and slack suddenly.

Walnut [1]. **1. b.** Black Walnut (earlier example).
1714 J. LAWSON *Hist. Carolina* 99 The Walnut-Tree of America is call'd Black Walnut.
4. walnut comb, a type of comb in fowls whose shape is suggestive of a walnut; so **walnut-combed** *a.*
1905 R. C. PUNNETT *Mendelism* 35 From its resemblance in shape to the half of a walnut it may be called the 'walnut' comb. 1922 *Ibid.* (ed. 3) 33 The hybrid walnut-combed birds.

Walpolian (wǫlpōu·liăn), *a.* and *sb.* Also **-ean.** [f. the name of Horace *Walpole* (1717–97), politician and writer + -IAN.] **a.** *adj.* Pertaining to or suggestive of Walpole or his writings. **b.** *sb.* An admirer of Walpole.
1867 H. E. H. JERNINGHAM *Life in a Fr. Chateau* vi. 165 She had seen through the empty-heartedness and true Walpolian sense of the gratitude of those she had befriended. 1876 HARDY *Hand of Ethelberta* II. xl. 146 A tendency to talk Walpolean scandal about foreign courts was particularly manifest. 1927 *Observer* 24 Apr. 6/2 No Walpolian can be satisfied with anything less than the complete Toynbee edition of the Letters.

Waltz, *v.* Add: **d.** *trans.* To transport or convey (anything heavy or clumsy). *U.S.*
1884 'MARK TWAIN' *Huck. Finn* III. 22 They've got to waltz that palace around over the country wherever you want it. 1901 MERWIN & WEBSTER *Calumet K* xi. 197 He'd call the men off just the same, and leave us to waltz the timbers around all by ourselves.

Wambling, *ppl. a.* (Further example.)
1912 GALSWORTHY *Inn. Tranq.* 82 All the thin incapacity of that shadowy figure was pitilessly displayed; the desperate narrowness in that long pale face; the wambling look of those pale, well-kept hands.

Wan, *v.* Add: **3.** *trans.* To make pale.
1903 HARDY *Dynasts* I. I. iii. 16 The grey glooms of a ghost-eyed despondency Wanned as with winter the national mind.

Wandale [2]. Also **Wandal.** (Modern example.)
1908 W. G. COLLINGWOOD *Scandinavian Brit.* ii. 16 The tribal confederacies of the Baltic shores—Danes, Swedes, Wandals, Burgunds, Bards, Goths.

Wander, *v.* Add: **7.** *Comb.* as **wander-book** [G. *wanderbuch*], a passport in the form of a book; a guide-book; **wander-plug,** a plug which can be fitted into any of a number of sockets in a dry battery; **wander-soul** (see quot.); **wander-spirit** = *WANDERLUST.
1844 W. HOWITT tr. *Holthaus's Wanderings of a Journeyman Tailor* Introd. p. xiv, A fact..which was more than sufficiently shewn by his Wander-Book. 1860 W. WHITE *Wrekin* xxx. 358 And if haply Cotton be your wander-book, you may test his descriptive outpourings on the very scene of their inspiration. 1923 *Daily Mail* 5 June 13/5 A few high-tension batteries (50 volts, with wander-plugs). 1917 *Hastings's Encycl. Relig. & Ethics* IX. 281/2 With regard to the wander-soul, *i.e.* the immortal soul with a period of mundane existence remaining after the death of the body to which it belonged, [etc.]. 1927 *Observer* 19 June 22/4 There is a drive..which it is the first duty of every motor owner with the wander-spirit properly developed to explore.

Wanderer. Add: **2. b.** A species of dragon fly.
1926 *Nat. Hist. Oxford Distr.* 169 The 'wanderer', *Libellula quadrimaculata* Linn., has occurred at Shotover.

Wandering, *vbl. sb.* Add: **1. c.** In wireless telegraphy: (see quot.).
1926 *Gloss. Elect. Terms* (Brit. Engin. Stand.) 183 *Wandering*, the alteration of apparent direction of received signals due to changes not caused by either the transmitting or the receiving stations.

Wanderlust (va·ndərlust, wǫ·ndəɹlɒst). [G.] Eager desire or fondness for wandering or travelling. Hence **Wa·nderluster,** a person affected with wanderlust.
1902 *Athenæum* 4 Jan. 15 If the present reviewer knows anything of the wanderlust and the wallaby [etc.]. 1913 *Wireless World* I. 11/2 The Somali suffers from Wanderlust. 1927 *Glasgow Herald* 13 May 10/7 The wanderlust is on me and my blood is coursing free. 1928 *Daily Mail* 7 Aug. 12/5 For people who have the wanderlust there are some nice tours around these parts. 1927 *Sunday Express* 24 Apr. 3/4 The young wanderluster next turned up in Samoa, and went to Bombay to live in a harem.

Wangle (wæ·ŋg'l), *sb.* [f. WANGLE *v.*[2]] An act of wangling; an irregular or indirect method of working; something dishonestly contrived or manipulated.
1925 in *N. & Q.* Ser. XI. XI. 66 It's a wangle between this Office and the Inland Revenue. 1925 E. J. P. BENN *Conf. Capitalist* 12 Even his friends will entertain the suspicion that there is a 'wangle' somewhere. 1927 *Observer* 27 Mar. 16/5 Men who sought to achieve nothing by wangle or intrigue.

Wangle, *v.*[2] Also, to influence or induce (a person) to do something.
1926 COLE *Blatchington Tangle* xxi. 147 He was always on at me just lately to get Lady Blatchington to sell him the rubies. He said I could wangle her. 1928 *Daily Express* 27 Dec. 5/4 Aren't you glad..you wangled the old lady to relinquish the key.
b. With *constr.* Also, to work, move, etc., by some device or trick.
1922 *Sat. Rev.* 22 Dec. 953 President Wilson had to 'wangle' through Congress an act to restore the British treaty rights. 1931 S. H. GUEST tr. P. Poiret *My First Fifty Years* 222 The cellars were flooded one went about in a boat wangled by an oar.
c. *intr.* To obtain something or get somewhere by irregular means, scheming, etc.; to use irregular means to accomplish a purpose.
1920 DEEPING *Second Youth* xxii, He agitated for a transfer ..and to his joy he was wangled back to the Cockneys. *Ibid.* xxvi, He also knew that a man who has 'wangled'..may find himself..thrust rudely into the trenches. 1921 *Glasgow Herald* 16 June 9 We wangled in, an' we'll wangle oot.

Wangler. (Earlier example.)
1912 E. WALLACE *Private Selby* xxxi. 281 You're a bloomin' wangler, Short.

Want, *sb.*[2] **9.** Add: *want-ad, column* (earlier example).
1919 MENCKEN *Amer. Lang.* 160 *Ad-writer*, *want-ad,.. and *ad-man*, are already accepted in technical terminology. 1928 *Publisher's Weekly* 7 July 58/1 From the most economically condensed want-ad to the latest artistic appeal. 1883 NYE *Baled Hay* 239 The *want column of the Chicago *News* ..has the following: 'Twelve frightful examples wanted'.

Want, *v.* **5. e.** Const. *of*. (U.S. examples.)
1855 *Knickerbocker Mag.* XLV. 136 Salt, Miss? What do you want of salt? 1914 GERTR. ATHERTON *Perch of Devil* II. 246 But what does he want of two cottages?

War, *sb.*[1] Add: **1. b.** Also, a loud or confused demonstration.
1911 H. WALPOLE *Mr. Perrin & Mr. Traill* ix. 159 Everything shouted Mrs. Comber with a war of welcome.
8. *war-fever*, *-profiteer*, *-weariness*, *-wedding*.
1812 *Steele Papers* II. 668 The late report of the Secty. of the Treas[ur]y will probably cool the *war fever in some. 1845 T. J. GREEN *Texian Exped.* ii. 24 After the President had succeeded in lulling the popular war-fever. 1908 H. G. WELLS *War in Air* vi, To the normal high-strung energy of New York streets was added a touch of war-fever. 1920 — *Outl. Hist.* xl. 727/1 The rich and adventurous men, and particularly the new *war profiteers, were making their plans. 1922 *Encycl. Brit.* XXX. 342/2 On Sept. 15 ensued a violent attack against the Bulgarian army, in the ranks of which *war-weariness had for long past made serious inroads. 1915 *Truth* 4 Aug. 181/2 What do we hear from London about *war-weddings?
b. Also *war machine*.
1914 BRYAN in *Mem.* (1925) 390 While the allies see peace only in a success so signal as to crush the German war machine.
e. *war debt*, *tax* (attrib. example).
1869 C. C. ANDREWS *Recoll.* (1928) 220 He asked me if the Americans would repudiate their *war debt. 1898 *Boston Herald* 3 July 14/8 The Pullman method for affixing the *war tax stamps to parlor car seats.
11. war-baby, one born during a war, esp. that of 1914–18, whose father was on active service; **war bag** *U.S.*, a pack or kit of clothing, etc.; **war-bird,** also, a fighting airman; **war-book,** a book dealing with a war, esp. that of 1914–18; **war hatchet** (earlier examples); **war plane,** an aeroplane used for fighting; **war-talk,** also, talk about war in general; **war-work,** special work occasioned by war; **war-worker,** a person undertaking war-work; **war-worthy** *a.*, suitable for or befitting war; so **war-worthiness.**
1901 E. MORRISON *With Guns in S.A.* 239 Mrs. Jourdain's "war baby". 1915 *Truth* 4 Aug. 181/2 There could be no objection to their marrying..were it not for the thought of the consequent war babies. 1902 S. E. WHITE *Blazed Trail* iii. 26 'Where's that fellow's turkey?'..'That's the "turkey"—..his *war bag'. 1903 A. ADAMS *Log Cowboy* xiii. 190 The first and second guards..ransacked their war bags and donned their best toggery. *a* 1918 G. STUART *On Frontier* I. 233 Best suits packed in the bottom of our 'war bags'..were dragged out. 1916 *War Illustr.* 25 Nov. p. lx/1 (heading) Lord Northcliffe's *War Book. 1924 H. HOLT *Sixty Years a Publisher* v. 104 Another fashion was..in war books. 1760 G. CROGHAN *Jrnl.* 116 That you [chiefs and warriors] ..may..bury the *War Hatchet in the Bottomless Pitt. 1800 B. HAWKINS *Sk. Creek Country* 72 He lifts the war hatchet against the nation which has injured them. 1915 *Chambers's Jrnl.* Jan. 54/1 The steady daily tasks of the *war-plane men will continue on Christmas day. 1915 *Lit. Digest* 4 Sept. 475/1 The little pitchers with big ears have been taking in a good deal of *war talk. 1928 *N.Y. Even. World* in *Observer* 26 Feb. 16/4 Such war-talk is customary when large appropriations are pending for the War or Navy Department. 1915 *Let. to J. A. H. Murray* 19 July, We are rushed to death here just now with *war work. 1915 *Pol. Quarterly* May 108 It is not clear whether or no the special ..*war-workers..will be permanently shut out of the trades [etc.]. 1920 *Westm. Gaz.* 20 Nov. 5/3 The fate of the educated woman war-worker untrained in any peaceful profession. 1909 *Q. Rev.* Oct. 578 The aim must now be..to seize every opportunity to improve its *war-worthiness. 1908 HARDY *Dynasts* III. VII. viii. 510 Ney holds indignantly that such a feint Is not *war-worthy.

War, *v.*[1] Add: **1. d.** To reduce or beat *down* by warring.
1860 F. W. FABER *Precious Blood* ii. 50 Everywhere on the earth the Precious Blood is warring down this evil in detail. 1882 J. R. GREEN *Hist. Engl. People* III. 162 His pertinacity and severity warred it [resistance] down.

Warcraft. Add: **2. b.** A warship.
1918 *Chambers's Jrnl.* May 318/1 With a whisk of her stern, the warcraft stood off.

Ward, *sb.*[2] **25.** *ward-boss*, *-meeting* (earlier examples), *politician*, *politics* (example), *school*, *teacher*.
1904 F. LYNDE *Grafters* xxix. 374 Before his promotion.. Halkett had been a *ward boss in the metropolis of the State. 1809 IRVING *Knickerb.* III. vi. (1820) 198 *Ward-meetings, pot-house committees, and congressional deliberations. 1807–8 — *Salmagundi* iv. 84 He, however, maintained as mysterious a countenance as a Seventh *Ward politician. 1897 *Encycl. Soc. Reform* 541/2 The ward politician knows every voter in his precinct. 1898 P. L. FORD *Hon. Peter Stirling* 217 See! Here sits Peter Stirling, the ward politician, enthroned in Jeffersonian simplicity. *Ibid.* 187 'Don't you find *ward politics very hard?' she asked. 1870 *Scribner's Monthly* I. 46 The range of study is about the same as that in the *ward schools. 1904 MRS. STRATTON-PORTER *Freckles* 15 They sent me out to the nearest ward school as long as the law would let them. 1878 J. H. BEADLE *Western Wilds* xxi. 332 The *ward teachers had reported every case of real or supposed heresy.

Wardering (wǭ·ɹdəriŋ), *vbl. sb.* [f. WARDER *sb.*[1] + -ING [1].] The business of a warder.
1928 *Daily Express* 23 Nov. 10/3 He has also been a prison warder, and told me that wardering is by no means to be despised.

Wardless (wǭ·ɹdlės), *a.*[2] [f. WARD *sb.*[2] + -LESS.] Having no wards.
1927 R. A. FREEMAN *A Certain Dr. Thorndyke* II. xv, These wardless pin-keys are more subtle than they look.

Wardrobe. **7.** Add: **wardrobe trunk,** a trunk designed to stand on end and serve as a wardrobe.
1928 SINCLAIR LEWIS *Man Who Knew Coolidge* i. 39 My dress-suit..would'nt get wrinkled in a *wardrobe trunk.

Warfare, *sb.* **c.** (Further example.)
1902 *Chambers's Jrnl.* June 391/1 It is prepared to spend vast sums of money and to employ every tactic permitted in modern commercial 'warfare'.

Wa·rlessness. [f. WARLESS + -NESS.] Absence of war.
1928 E. BLUNDEN *Undert. War* xiv. 158 The sluggish weather and the general silence and warlessness encouraged us to take life easy.

Warning, *vbl. sb.*[1] **12.** Add: **warning district,** one of a number of districts into which a country is divided for the purpose of publishing warnings.
1922 *Encycl. Brit.* XXX. 92/1 It becomes necessary..to divide up the country into 'warning districts'.

Warp, *sb.*[1] Add: **7. b.** An inclination or set in growing trees or bushes caused by the wind.
1895 *Century Mag.* Sept. 677/2 When the wind beats up the peak, which it seldom does, as may be seen by the warp of the pines and tamaracks.

War-party. **2.** (Earlier example.)
1800 B. HAWKINS *Sk. Creek Country* 70 The war parties all march in Indian file, with a leader in front.

War-path. Add: *concr.* A path regularly used by an Indian tribe when going out to make war on another.
1768 *Maryland Hist. Mag.* II. 316 [At] 231 [miles], .. crossed a War path. 1784 J. Smyth *Tour U.S.* I. xli. 323, I descended the Ouasiatto mountains and in a short time fell into the great war path, which has been used by the Indians. 1821 J. Fowler *Jrnl.* 95 The chief.. still telling us to go to the mountains and out of the war path. 1841 C. Cist *Cincinnati* 16 The old Indian war-path.. crossed the Ohio at this point. 1876 Joaquin Miller *Unwritten Hist.* xx. 287 When.. the grass is growing in the last war-path of those people.

Warper. 3. (Earlier example.)
1847 *Knickerbocker Mag.* XXX. 517 A few tend the 'warpers'.. but these are generally young girls.

Warrantee. Add: 1. b. A person for whose arrest a warrant has been issued.
1921 *Daily Tel.* 27 Aug. 9/2 Only three men arrested out of those wanted... Twenty-five reserve men were left to continue the search for absconding warrantees.

Warrener. 2. Also *transf.*
1929 Bridges *Test. Beauty* IV. 284 Poor nomads.. warreners of the waste.

Warrigal. Also 9 warragle.
1848 H. W. Haygarth *Bush Life in Australia* v. 44 His 'coolie' dogs will awaken him on the approach of a 'warragle', or native dog.

Wartime. (Further attrib. example.)
1922 *Act* 10 & 11 *Geo. V* c. 74 The expression 'excess profits duty' includes any tax on war-time increases of wealth.

War-whoop. (Earlier example.)
1739 W. Stephens *Proc. Georgia* 474 In marching, our Indians set up the war whoop.

Was-bird. *slang.* A person who is no longer so able and efficient as he used to be; a 'has-been'.
1902 *Blackw. Mag.* Feb. 160/1 You are a fine lot of 'was-birds' with which to run a brigade.

Wash, *sb.* Add: 3. d. A special solution or liquid preparation with which plants are treated as a safeguard against disease or pests.
1921 *Discovery* May 130/1 The providing of suitable sprays and washes, and other material connected with the checking of plant pests.

6. d. Also, the action of rain and flowing water in wearing away or removing soil.
1857-8 *Trans. Ill. Agric. Soc.* III. (1859) 412 Land lying in such a position as to protect it from wash.. may be kept in constant cultivation.

21. **wash-book,** a scoring-book or tablet used at bridge.
1908 R. F. Foster *Auction Bridge* 38 The result of the rubber is usually transferred to a wash-book or flogger.

Wash, *v.* Add: 11. b. (Further example.)
1850 N. Kingsley *Diary* 156 They washed this forenoon and got over two ounces amalgam.

13. e. *trans.* To shuffle (the tiles) at Mah Jong.
1929 *Encycl. Brit.* XIV. 677/1 All the tiles are.. put face downward on the table and thoroughly shuffled or 'washed'.

15. Also, to form or hollow *out.*
1922 *Times Lit. Suppl.* 28 Sept. 613/3 The Thames washed out a new course through a belt of soft clays.
fig. 1929 *Times* 30 Oct. 14/1 Trans-America, which closed last night at 62½, opened to-day at 20¼.. —$840,000,000.. nominally washed away over-night.

d. (Later examples.)
1835 Ingraham *South-West* II. 87 The loose and friable nature of this soil, which renders it so liable to 'wash'. 1857-8 *Trans. Ill. Agric. Soc.* III. 452 Our black soil is several feet in depth, and not rolling enough to wash to any considerable extent. 1884 Sweet & Knox *Thr. Texas* ix. 119 On sloping ground, where the soil is light, the roads wash in wet weather, forming ravines.

20. b. **wash-bench** *U.S.,* a bench on which washing is done; **wash day,** the day on which the clothes of a household are washed; **wash-kettle,** a kettle in which water is heated for washing; **wash-kitchen** (earlier example); **wash-pan,** a pan for heating water for washing; **wash sale,** a washed sale (see Washed *ppl. a.* 1 f); **wash sink,** a sink used for washing.
1878 Rose T. Cooke *Happy Dodd* 35 Then they all sat down on the *wash-bench. 1885 G. W. Cable *Dr. Sevier* xxi. 145 She had reached down and taken from the wash-bench the lump of yellow soap. 1848 in Drake *Pion. Life Kentucky* v. 92, I have already spoken of.. going to the pond on *wash days. 1905 *Scribner's Mag.* Jan. 35 'You shouldn't dine with her on wash-days', said Selden. 1861 Whitman *Specimen Days* (1892) 23 They put *wash-kettles on the fire, for soup, for coffee. 1884 'C. E. Craddock' *In Tenn. Mts.* i. 7 The pine-knots flamed and glistened under the great wash-kettle. 1838 Caroline Gilman *Recoll. Southern Matron* xxix. 206 Preparations were made for the wedding which she chose to have performed in the *wash-kitchen instead of our parlour. 1884 'Mark Twain' *Huck. Finn* xxvii, We.. scratched around and found an old tin *washpan. 1848 W. Armstrong *Stocks* 10 These *wash sales are of course void between parties. They are of very frequent occurrence and very mischievous. 1900 S. A. Nelson *A B C Wall St.* 163 *Wash Sales,*.. where one broker arranges with another to pretend to buy a certain stock when he offers it for sale. 1857 *Lawrence* (Kansas) *Republ.* 2 July 4 'Here are all the conveniences for washing,' said the landlord, stepping to a mahogany *wash sink and raising the lid. 1876 'Mark Twain' & Warner *Gilded Age* xxix. 270 It was a small room, with a wash-sink in one corner.

Wash-board. 3. b. (Earlier example.)
1851 C. Cist *Cincinnati* 252 There are more zinc wash-boards made here than in any one state in the Union, or any city in the world.

Wash-bowl. 2. (Earlier example.)
1816 U. Brown *Jrnl.* in *Maryland Hist. Mag.* X. 369 His wash-bowl [is] the knot of a tree.

b. A vessel in which gold is washed.
1848 *Essex Inst. Hist. Coll.* XII. 106 With my wash bowl on my knee.

3. *transf.* A hat resembling a wash-hand basin in shape.
a 1861 T. Winthrop *John Brent* xix. 209 Men hatted with slouched hats, wash-bowls, and stove-pipes.

Wash-dish. 2. (Earlier and later examples.)
1805 *Austin Papers* (1924) I. 140, 1 Wash dish. 1857 *Quinland* II. i. I. 275 An iron kettle, which I and all the family used as a common wash-dish before breakfast. 1876 *Rep. Vermont Board Agric.* III. 628 The farmer.. was able to furnish a large maple block to set the wash-dish on.

Washed, *ppl. a.* 1. f. (Earlier and later examples.)
1886 *Harper's Mag.* July 205/1 Washed or fictitious sales, or false reports of sales, are also penal offences. 1900 S. A. Nelson *A B C Wall St.* 70 It will also be readily seen that the opportunity for washed sales is a very open one.

Wash-hands, *sb. pl.* [f. Wash *v.*] (See quot.)
1901 *Chambers's Jrnl.* Feb. 103/1 Jewellers.. sell all their waste products to them [*sc.* refiners]: sweepings, polishings, washings (or washhands, to use the more descriptive term), rags and so forth.

Wash-house. Add: 2. e. *Aeron. slang.* The region occupied by the clouds.
1928 Gamble *Story N. Sea Air Station* xix. 336, I.. preferred to avoid the so-called 'wash-house' and go above the clouds.

Wash-in. [After *Wash-out.] (See quot.)
1923 *R.A.F. Flying Training Man.* xxiii, *Wash in,* a colloquial expression used in reference to a wing to denote an increasing angle of incidence towards the wing tip.

Washing, *vbl. sb.* Add: 1. i. In sense 2 j of the vb.
1876 Trollope *Prime Minister* lxxii, The effects which causes will produce,.. the manner in which this or that proposition will come out in the washing, do not strike even Cabinet Ministers at a glance.

5. b. *Stockbroking.* (In sense 19 b of the verb.)
1870 Medbery *Men & Myst. Wall St.* 138 Washing is where one broker arranges with another to buy a certain stock when he offers it for sale. The bargain is fictitious. *Ibid.* 274 How much of this was due to 'washings' at Share Boards?

9. **washing-chest,** a chest for holding dirty clothes; **washing-machine** (*b*), a machine used in the manufacture of crêpe rubber, in which coagulated rubber is passed between rollers and subjected to a stream of water.
1928 *Sunday Express* 6 May 15/5 The washing-chest may serve as a toy or shoe cupboard. 1910 *Chambers's Jrnl.* May 283/2 The rubber is then turned out as 'crepe', 'block', &c., and washing-machines, vacuum-driers, and hydraulic-presses play their part.

Wash-out. Add: 3. (Earlier example.)
1879 *Harper's Mag.* Nov. 894/2 'Is it not a shame,' asked the writer,.. 'that the train should be so delayed by "wash outs"?'

5. *Aeron.* Decrease in the angle of incidence towards the wing tip of an aeroplane.
1923 *R.A.F. Flying Training Man.* xxiii, 'Wash out.' Used as above [*sc.* wash in] to denote a decreasing angle of incidence towards the wing tip.

Wa·sh-room. *U.S.* A room where facilities for washing are provided; a lavatory.
1806 *Mass. H.S. Coll.* X. 77 They have usually two good rooms in front, bedrooms, kitchen, wash-room, and other convenient apartments in the rear. 1838 Caroline Gilman *Recoll. Southern Matron* xxx. 207 As we left the threshold of the wash-room, the whole party shouted forth a Methodist hymn. 1855 'P. Paxton' *Capt. Priest* 160 Finally a long wash-room completed the odd assemblage. 1878 Rose T. Cooke *Happy Dodd* 293 He.. fairly went down on his knees to her in the wash-room. 1892, 1908 [see Wash *v.* 20 b].

Wash-up. Add: 1. c. The act of washing oneself.
1887 Bret Harte *Millionaire & Devil's Ford* 176 You boys can go there for a general wash-up.

Washwoman. (Later example.)
1912 H. S. Canfield *Squirrel Cage* I. iv. 36 She spoke of the 'washwoman' instead of the 'laundress'.

Waspily (wǫ·spili), *adv.* [f. Waspy *a.* + -ly [2].] = Waspishly.
1854 Shillaber *Mrs. Partington* 231 'Because she is a low, vile creature of the town,' said she, waspily. 1928 *Sunday Dispatch* 29 July 2/3 'That's what I'm doing. Turning over a new leaf—and I'm going to do well.' 'Yeah? And what comes after that?' snapped the P.C.M. waspily.

Waste, *sb.* 10. d. (Later example.)
1891 *Times* 3 Oct. 7/1 Little time was cut to waste at the post.

13. *waste-heap* (example in special sense).
1892 L. Hoffman *Illust. Bk. Patience Games* Introd. 4 If its [the card's] nature does not allow of its being so played, it is laid face upwards in front of the player, the cards so deposited being known as the 'waste-' or 'rubbish-heap'.

Wasty, *a.*[2] Add: 3. Wasteful.
1839 Townsend *Narr.* vii. 238 We have now abandoned the 'wasty ways' which so disgraced us when game was abundant.

Wat [4]. Also *wat-house.*
1930 S. Maugham *Gentl. in Parlour* iii. 10 No European any longer went into the wat-houses.

Watch, *v.* Add: 4. g. (Earlier example.)
1845 J. J. Hooper *Adv. Simon Suggs* ix. 115 He determined therefore to 'watch out' and keep himself 'whole' in a pecuniary point of view if possible.

h. *To watch in:* To use a wireless receiving-set adapted for television; to 'look in'.
1928 *Daily News* 17 Dec. 6/4 (heading) Pictures by Wireless. Where to 'watch-in' this week.

Watch-dog, *v.* [f. the sb.] *trans.* To attend or guard (a person) as a watch-dog.
1902 Cutcliffe Hyne *Mr. Horrocks, Purser* 70 There seems to be a whole regiment of ragamuffins on board here watchdogging her.

Watcher. Add: h. *Watcher-in:* (see *Watch *v.* 4 h).
1928 *Daily News* 17 Dec. 6/4 Watchers-in will be able to judge for themselves the value of picture transmissions during this week.

Water, *sb.* Add: 20. b. (Earlier example.)
1775 *Lond. Mag.* Nov. 556/2 She has an eye of that quick and brilliant water, that it penetrates and darts through the person it looks on.

24. a. *water-sack.*
1864 J. A. Grant *Walk Across Africa* 430 Here there is a bend in the Nile, and we were able to fill all our water-sacks afresh.

b. *water-tank.*
1869 *Overland Monthly* III. 78 The tender was provided with water-tanks. 1885 *Rep. Indian Affairs* 157 They are anxious to get them to build water-tanks. 1902 O. Wister *Virginian* iii. 41 There was a woman—the engineer's woman down by the water-tank—very sick.

e. *water-feed, -intake.*
1914 *Chambers's Jrnl.* May 334/2 The.. lamp.. works automatically, the *water-feed to the carbide being drop by drop. 1927 R. Rodd *Homer's Ithaca* 23 One [motor].. remained obstinately out of action; the *water-intake.. being choked with fine seaweed.

25. b. *water-lover.*
1862 T. W. Harris *Insects injur. Veget.* (ed. 3) 10 The water-lovers (*Hydrophilidæ*), rove-beetles.. act the useful part of scavengers.

26. a. *water-marrowed.*
1922 J. A. Dunn *Man Trap* iv. 49 Most of the young men nowadays are water-marrowed pups.

27. *water-living* adj.
1919 H. G. Wells *Outl. Hist.* 12/1 Water-living creatures which are always under water, wave the freely exposed gills by which they breathe in that water.

28. **water-cushion,** a cushion filled with water serving as a protection or buffer; **water-cycle** *sb.,* a vehicle resembling a cycle designed to travel over water; **water-cycle** *v. intr.,* to travel by means of a water-cycle; **water-guard** (*c*), a protection or defence in the form of water; **water jumper,** a horse trained for water jumps; **water-power, -privilege** (earlier examples); **water-rod,** a divining-rod; **water-silk** = watered silk; **water-soluble** *a.,* that is soluble in water; **water-wagon** (later examples).
1927 Haldane & Huxley *Animal Biol.* xiii. 304 This implied the evolution of a large-yolked egg, and the development of a protective *water-cushion or amnion over the embryo within the egg. 1901 *Referee* 14 Apr. 1 The.. *water-cycle trio made a record. 1930 *Daily Express* 6 Nov. 2/1 Reni Savard.. left Calais.. yesterday to *water-cycle across the Channel. 1930 *Times* 9 Jan. 15/5 Though manor house moats were not on the scale of those around castles, they served as a useful *waterguard. 1832 *Q. Rev.* XLVII. 239, I am on the best *water jumper in my stable. 1827 Drake & Mansf. *Cincinnati* i. 17 Much is anticipated from the *water power gained in the descent from the upper plain of Cincinnati. 1749 *N.H. Probate Rec.* III. 755 We set off to Deborah Shackford,.. the *Water Privilege belonging to said Estate. 1925 *Pearson's Mag.* XXXIX. 130 Like a diviner with a *water-rod. 1926 *Glasgow Herald* 1 Apr. 8/4 The copies.. are bound in magnificent leather volumes with sheets of *water-silk. 1922 *Times Lit. Suppl.* 27 Apr. 279/1 Chickens prove particularly susceptible to an insufficiency of the *water-soluble or B factor. 1908 'O. Henry' *Rolling Stones* (1915) 61 Wainwright was on the *water-wagon. 1910 *Century Mag.* Nov. 39 The advance of the water wagon. An apparent change of sentiment with regard to liquor drinking. 1912 C. Mathewson *Pitching* iv. 89 He was winning ball games for the Cardinals in 1911 until he fell off the water wagon.

30. **water-slater,** an isopodous crustacean of the genus *Asellus.*
1924 J. A. Thomson *Science Old & New* viii. 44 When small freshwater crustaceans, such as 'screws' (Gammarus) and *water-slaters' (Asellus), are kept for a long time in darkness, they become very pale.

31. **water maple** (earlier example).
1802 Ellicott *Jrnl.* 284 *Water maple, (acer negundo).

Water-binding. Binding of road metal with the use of water.
1912 *Chambers's Jrnl.* Sept. 612/1 What shall be substituted for the inefficient road-crust which consists of stones and water-binding?

Water-borne, *a.* 1. Add: Arising from, etc., water-carriage.
1922 *Encycl. Brit.* XXX. 14/2 The matter of stability when changing from waterborne to airborne conditions.

Water-boy. (See Water *sb.* 29). Also, a boy who supplies or takes round water. *U.S.*
1901 Merwin & Webster *Calumet K* xiv. 263, I wish you'd find a water boy and send him up to the hotel to get a couple of sandwiches and a bottle of coffee. 1903 *Congress. Directory* 116 He assisted himself in securing an education by working as a 'water boy' on the railroad. 1909 R. E. Wason *Happy Hawkins* 213 I'm water-boy to the E.Z. outfit.

Water-break. 3. Also, a structure designed to break the force of running water.
1848 *Indiana Gen. Assoc. Doc.* II. 297 The country through

which it passes is hilly, and the water following the wheel tracts does more injury than.. the travel. To remedy this evil, I was compelled to make water brakes on the slopes at considerable expense.

Water-carriage. Add: 2. c. = Water-cart.
1654 in Jeaffreson *Midsx. County Rec.* (1888) III. 227 That noe brewers [nor] water-carriers set their drayes or water-carriages in the streetes day or night as usually they have done.

Water-carrier. 2. (Earlier example.)
1654 [see *Water-carriage].

Wa·ter-cart, *v. slang.* [f. the sb.] *intr.* To weep.
1921 W. De Morgan *Old Man's Youth* xxix. 282 She makes believe she knew Gromp, and I know she didn't. She'd watercart.

Wa·tercoursed, *a.* [f. Watercourse + -ed [2].] Characterized by watercourses.
1925 *Blackw. Mag.* Apr. 466/1 To cross ten miles of unknown watercoursed country.. did not seem to us quite as simple.

Water-cracker. 3. (Earlier examples.)
1832 *Louisville Public Adv.* 10 Mar., J. Wolf.. keeps constantly on hand an extensive assortment of.. water crackers. 1851 C. Cist *Cincinnati* 171 Among other things produced was a tin can of water crackers.

Water-engine. (Later example.)
1864 Trollope *Small Ho. at Allington* xli, Calling for the police when there is a row in the house is like summoning the water-engines when the soot is on fire in the kitchen chimney.

Wa·ter-fence. Chiefly *U.S.* A boundary or barrier in the form of a ditch.
1654 *Warwick* (R.I.) *Rec.* 262 For the makinge and maintayninge of a water fence to secure Quinimicoke and Warwicke Necke. 1707 [see Water *sb.* 24 l]. 1760 *Smithtown Rec.* 428 We also lay out to him all the meadow edgings and creek thatch beds round his lands, beginning at the water fence. 1786 Washington *Diaries* III. 34 Finished the Land sides of my Paddock fencing, and as a temporary expedient, set about water fences at each end. 1852 [see Water *sb.* 24 l]. 1880 *Scribner's Monthly* Feb. 509/2 Of all fences, none is so simple as the water fence.

Water-finder. Add: b. An instrument for water-divining.
1908 *Chambers's Jrnl.* Mar. 269/1 The automatic water-finder, a scientific development of the divining-rod.

Waterily, *adv.* (Further example.)
1928 E. Blunden *Undert. War* iv. 45 Daylight was waterily spreading as we passed the cemetery and timber-yards of Béthune.

Waterish, *a.* 10. (Later example.)
1829-32 J. P. Kennedy *Swallow Barn* I. xxvii. 283 His constitution resembles that waterish gravelly soil you see sometimes around a spring.

Water moccasin. *U.S.* (See Moccasin 3.)
1821 T. Nuttall *Trav. Arkansa* ix. 216 The other frequents water, and is called the water-mockasin, and poisonous black-snake. 1842, 1853 [see Moccasin 3]. 1853 R. Glisan *Jrnl. Army Life* (1874) x. 128 When lo and behold a water moccasin began running furiously around my legs trying to make his escape. 1884 'Mark Twain' *Huck. Finn* xviii. 169 If you'll come down into de swamp I'll show you a whole stack of water-moccasins.

Water-plane. 3. (Earlier example.)
1912 *Q. Rev.* July 248 With this [float] Curtiss' waterplane was the first to quit the sea under its own power.

Water-ram, *v. trans.* [Water *sb.* 2 b + Ram *v.*[1] 1.] To ram (earth) using water.
1857 Moore *How to Build* vii, 109 He shall.. fill in the excavation and 'water-ram' the earth about the walls, using sufficient water to puddle and settle firmly.

Wa·ter-rot, *v.* Chiefly *U.S.* Variant of Water-ret. So **Water-rotted** *a.*; **Water-rotting** *vbl. sb.* **Water-rot** *sb.*
1794 [see Water-retting]. 1837 Colman *Rep. Agric. Mass.* (1838) 72 The superintendent states that the water-rotted flax of Scotland is much superior to ours, which is dew rotted. 1843 *Amer. Pioneer* II. 450 The manner of making ropes of linn bark, was to cut the bark in strips of convenient length, and water-rot it in the same manner as rotting flax or hemp. 1847 *Rep. U.S. Comm. Patents* (1848) 246 It is of great importance in raising flax.. that the water rot and dew rot must be used together to produce a fine white fibre. 1849 *Rep. U.S. Comm. Patents, Agric.* (1850) 330 The Navy of the United States will probably consume eight hundred tons of water-rotted hemp a year. 1863 *Rep. U.S. Comm. Agric.* 116 Water-rotting is essential for the finest fibre. 1872 *Trans. Dep. Agric. Illinois* 63 It should be shocked.. in the field till cured, and the first crop water-rotted the same as hemp.

Wa·tersider. [f. Waterside + -er [1].] A dockside labourer.
1925 *Glasgow Herald* 28 Oct. 12 The Entor is berthed at Fremantle under a police guard, with watersiders discharging her. 1929 *Daily Express* 15 Jan. 9/4 A mob of a thousand 'watersiders' rushed the McLaren Wharf at Port Adelaide to-day when the steamer Mareeba was being loaded by volunteers.

Water-wave. 3. (Examples.)
1882 *Harper's Mag.* Nov. 877/2 She is pasting down her wetted hair into a semblance of the 'water-waves' of fashionable society. 1923 E. F. Wyatt *Invis. Gods* I. i. 7 His grandmother.. bending over him her water waves and pearl powder.

Wa·ter-waving, *vbl. sb.* [f. Water-wave.] 1. The wavy or 'watered' appearance imparted to silk and other fabrics by pressing two pieces together.
1895 Jeanette E. Davis *Elem. Mod. Dressmaking* (ed. 2) 94 Beetled plain linings generally show a marking like a slight water-waving on the surface.

2. A method of waving hair with the use of water.
1925 *Daily Tel.* 13 May 20/5 Advt., Wanted, smart man... Must be thoroughly competent in perm. waving, Marcel and water waving. 1927 *Daily Express* 30 Nov. 13/3 She can give lessons in water waving, face massage, and chiropody.

Water-willow. 2. (Earlier example.)
1840 *Knickerbocker Mag.* XV. 295 The steam-boat broke through boughs of the water-willow in her progress.

Water-wings, *sb. pl.* Add: 4. Floats used by persons learning to swim.
1914 H. R. Austin *How to Swim* 19 Waterwings I do not like, as they are unstable and elusive. 1922 P. G. Wodehouse *Girl on Boat* v. 102 A little undersized shrimp of a fellow with a green face and ears like water-wings.

Water-witcher. [cf. Water-witch 3.] = Water-finder.
1917 *Chambers's Jrnl.* June 361/1 As an instance of the fallibility of the '"water-witcher', Mr. Ellis cites the experience of a land company.

Watteauesque (wǫtō,e·sk), *a.* [f. Watteau + -esque.] Suggestive of or in the style of Watteau.
1925 *Glasgow Herald* 25 Apr. 8/3 Opposite might hang a Watteauesque diversion representing an impossibly light and brilliantly fanciful landscape.

Wave, *sb.* 4. (Recent example.)
1930 Joanna Cannan *No Walls of Jasper* 162 She.. slept in a hair net to preserve the first glory of her wave.

9. b. *wave-subduer;* also for artificial waving of the hair as *wave-curler, -setter, -setting.*
1912 *Chambers's Jrnl.* Mar. 206/1 The 'wave-subduer' comprises a small cast-iron reservoir containing the oil. 1931 *Lady* 26 Feb. 300/1 Fix your wave-setting combs in place. 1932 *Even. Standard* 1 July 9 Advt., A.. wavesetter in your bag is almost as good as taking your hairdresser on holiday with you.

e. *wave-walled.*
1906 Hardy *Dynasts* II. I. vi, The Universal-empire plot Demands the rule of that wave-walled spot.

10. **wave-band,** a series of electro-magnetic waves of lengths that fall between two given limits; **wave-mechanics,** a system of mechanics, used esp. in small (atomic) regions, in which particles are regarded as centres of pulsations; (so **wave-mechanical** *a.*); **wave-meter,** also, an apparatus for determining the length of electro-magnetic waves; **wave-system** (*b*), a series of electro-magnetic waves; **wave-trap** (further examples).
1923 *Daily Mail* 28 Apr. 5 A receiver which will function efficiently over a *waveband stretching from 300 metres to 20,000 metres. 1927 H. F. Biggs *Wave Mechanics* 27 It was.. left to Schrödinger to bring out clearly how *wave-mechanics bears to the classical mechanics of particles exactly the same relation as wave-optics bears to ray-optics. 1928 E. Schrödinger *Four Lectures on Wave Mechanics* 6 In replacing the ordinary mechanical description by a *wave-mechanical description our object is to obtain a theory. 1913 *Year-Bk. Wireless Telegr. & Teleph.* 435 *Wave-meter. 1925 P. J. Risdon *Crystal Receivers & Circuits* 51 The aerial inductance may be found by the use of a spark coil and wave-meter. 1923 *Chambers's Jrnl.* Mar. 232/1 For such continuous *wave-systems.. arrangements are made. 1923 *Mod. Wireless* I. 247 The second frame aerial.. is stated.. to act as a '*wave-trap'. 1926 *Gloss. Electr. Terms* (Brit. Engin. Stand.) 193 *Wave-trap,* any form of receiving absorber primarily intended for the elimination of interference of one specific frequency.

Waved, *ppl. a.* 3. b. (Further example.)
1921 *Conquest* Sept. 495/2 Among the most conspicuous melanic moths is the Waved Umber (*Hemerophila abruptaria*).

Wa·ve-length. [f. Wave *sb.* 10.] The length of a wave. a. The distance from crest to crest or from hollow to hollow of a wave of water or other liquid. b. The distance between two successive points of maximum compression or maximum rarefaction in sound-waves. c. The distance between points in the same phase on two successive heat, light, electro-magnetic, or other waves; *esp.* the length of electro-magnetic wave employed by a broad-casting station; also *fig.*
1871-1907 [see Wave *sb.* 10]. 1905 J. A. Fleming in *Proc. Roy. Soc.* LXXIV. 491 The wave-length employed, reckoned in feet, is equal to 195·8 times the oscillation constant of the transmitter circuit. 1923 *Daily Mail* 21 June 10 Velocity (300,000,000 metres per second) divided by frequency gives wavelength. 1925 *Scribner's Mag.* July 47/2 He swung the dials round to where he could receive the commercial wave lengths. 1925 N. Venner *Imperfect Impostor* i, No. You're on the wrong wave length! Nothing doing. 1930 *Times Lit. Suppl.* 26 June 522/1 Bury's was not the only mind which used different wave-lengths on occasion.
attrib. 1921 *Conquest* Sept. 498/1 The question then arises, how short wavelength light can we use, as increased resolution is obtained by shortening the wavelength?

Wavelessly, *adv.* (Further example.)
1928 *Daily Express* 25 Aug. 3/1 Her black hair is parted in the middle and brushed, wavelessly, to a knot at the nape of her neck.

Waver, *v.* 1. (Modern example.)
1924 Galsworthy *White Monkey* I. viii, Michael watched him down the corridor, saw him waver into the dusky street.

Wavicle (wē·vik'l). [f. Wave *sb.,* after Particle.] An entity having characteristic properties both of waves and of particles.
1928 A. S. Eddington *Nat. Phys. World* x. 201 We can scarcely describe such an entity as a wave or as a particle; perhaps as a compromise we had better call it a 'wavicle'.

Wavy, *a.* 7. Add: *wavy-handled.*
1927 Peake & Fleure *Peasants & Potters* 72 The wavy-handled pots.

Wax, *sb.*[1] Add: 6. e. (See quot.)
1924 *Ski Terms* in *Tourist* Winter Sports No. 12/2 *Wax,* a paraffin preparation to prevent the snow balling under the ski.

11. c. *wax-bleacher, refiner.*
1881 *Instr. Census Clerks* (1885) 77 *Wax, Beeswax—Bleacher, Refiner [etc.]. 1908 *Westm. Gaz.* 29 Apr. 1/3 He.. became a wax-bleacher at Hoxton.

12. **wax-bath,** a bath in liquid wax.
1916 *Chambers's Jrnl.* Oct. 701/1 The wax-bath has not been found beneficial in chronic rheumatoid arthritis.

Waxy, *a.*[1] Add: 5. *Comb.* as *waxy-faced, -looking.*
1927 *Scots Observer* 1 Jan. 3/1 Barefoot women.. some with waxy-faced infants in their arms, gossiping at the close-mouths. 1915 E. R. Lankester *Diversions Naturalist* xviii. 166 We found.. whole banks covered with the waxy-looking flowers.. of the large milkwort.

Way, *sb.*[1] 8. d. *All the way from — to —*: expressing the lower and upper limits of value, number, etc., between which something varies or is estimated. *U.S.*
1878 J. H. Beadle *Western Wilds* xxxi. 493 The value of the booty taken has been estimated all the way from $150,000 to $300,000. 1883 *Ibid.* xxxv. 579 The population is estimated all the way from fifteen to forty thousand: take your choice.

40. **way freight** *U.S.,* freight that is picked up or set down at intermediate stations on a railway; **way-letter** (earlier example); **way train** *U.S.,* a train which stops at intermediate stations on a railway to pick up or set down passengers; **way-wisdom** *U.S.,* knowledge, experience.
1883 'Mark Twain' *Life Mississippi* xvi. 198 No way-freights and no way-passengers were allowed, for the racers would stop only at the largest towns. 1906 *Springfield Weekly Republ.* 28 June 16 A collision between an extra freight train and a way freight train. 1851 E. Bowen *U.S. Post-office Guide* 47 On the letters brought by a mail carrier to be mailed, called *way-letters,* one cent. is to be charged in addition to the usual postage. 1878 'Mark Twain' & Warner *Gilded Age* xxix. 269 Next morning.. he descended, sleepy and sore, from a way-train. 1903 *N.Y. Times* 15 Aug., To attempt to run way trains through the middle of the day while running express trains in the crowded hours would result in endless confusion. 1903 *Ibid.* 26 Aug., Her motives and her action, except for its lack of waywisdom, were above reproach.

Way, *adv.* 2. b. Earlier and additional examples with advs.
1851 E. S. Wortley *Trav. in U.S.* xiii. 138 The trading and wealthy cities of far off Alabama and Louisiana, 'way down south'. 1855 *Merry's Museum* XXIX. 58, I did not know that there was such a fine Magazine,.. for I live 'way back in the woods'. 1862 O. W. Norton *Army Lett.* 100 A minister of the gospel who was so wonderfully.. war-like way up in Erie. 1893 'E. Kirke' *Southern Friends* ix. 112 I'd make you feel way down in your pocket. 1887 F. Francis Jr. *Saddle & Mocassin* 81 A real way-up cook, who could make chile-con-carne, tamales, and all the best Mexican dishes. a 1909 'O. Henry' *Roads of Destiny* xviii. 299, I want to be manager of something way up—like a railroad or a diamond trust or an automobile factory. 1924 *Contemp. Rev.* Aug. 236 The well-known resourcefulness and sense of location of the present-day way-backs of Australia.. are due.. to lessons taught the pioneers by the natives.

Waying (wē·iŋ), *vbl. sb.* [f. Way *v.* + -ing [1].] A going away; departure.
1922 Hardy *Late Lyrics & Earlier* 120 So, with this saying, 'Good-bye, good-bye', We speed their waying.

Waylayment. [f. Waylay *v.*] The act or process of waylaying.
1863 Mrs. Whitney *F. Gartney's Girlh.* xiv, Dr. Wasgatt had.. a half a dozen more [patients].. to whom he was summoned by waylayment.

Way-leave. Also, permission to travel by air over a territory.
1928 H. G. Wells *Way World is Going* xi. 127 The exploitation of the air, as a means of.. available travel, is hopeless without the expenditure of.. fifty million pounds, plus secure wayleaves over Europe.

Weak, *a.* Add: 15. (Further example.)
1927 W. E. Collinson *Contemp. Engl.* 54 From tea-drinking we get our expressions weak tea for anything rather feeble and sloppy, and a storm in a tea cup.

22. *weak-middled.*
1915 H. de Sélincourt *Realms of Day* ix. 62 They laughed at him.. persisting that no one need be weak-middled, or out of condition.

Weak-kneed, *a.* (Earlier example.)
1863 *Rio Abajo Press* 24 Feb. 2 But we must forego these comforts and conveniences, because our legislators are too weak-kneed to enact a tax law.

Weald. 3. Add: **wealdsman,** an inhabitant of a weald.
1928 *Daily Tel.* 29 May 8/5 The flares signalled her triumph to the wealdsmen of Sussex.

Wear, *sb.* Add: 9. *Comb.* as *wear-proof* adj.
1928 *Daily Express* 27 Apr. 17 Advt., The cloth is made almost wearproof.

Wear, *v.*[1] 10. (Further example.)
1901 'L. Malet' *Hist. Sir R. Calmady* v. ii. 389, I have had a detestable winter... It wore upon me. It demoralised me.

Wear, *v.*[2] 2. Also with *round.*
1930 *Sea Breezes* 76, I had helped to wear the schooner partly round to drive her off.

Wearability (wē·rābi·liti). [f. Wearable + -ity.] Capacity for being worn, or for standing wear.
1927 *Daily Express* 5 Sept. 5/2 A series of distinctive models to demonstrate individuality with wearability.

Wea·r-out. [f. Wear *v.* 9.] = Wear *sb.* 5.
1897 C. T. Davis *Manuf. Leather* (ed. 2) 270 There is absolutely no wear-out to any of the working parts of the bed.

Weary, *a.* Add: 2. c. Exhausted or tired with waiting or longing *for.*
1902 'Laurence Hope' *Garden of Kama* 53 My arms are empty, and so weary for your beauty.

4. b. *Weary Willie:* a person of little strength or energy.
1926 Shaw *Intel. Woman's Guide Socialism* 72 Weary Willie may say that he hates work, and is quite willing to take less. 1931 H. Herd *Diagnosis Mental Deficiency* 10 Mental defectives are the 'weary Willies and tired Tims' *par excellence.*

Weasel. 5. (Earlier example.)
1845 in C. Cist *Cincinnati Misc.* 240 The inhabitants of.. S. Carolina [are called] Weasels.

6. *weasel-mind;* **weasel-word** *U.S.,* a word which takes away the force or meaning of the phrase or sentence in which it occurs; so *weasel-worded* adj.
1923 *Chambers's Jrnl.* Feb. 88/1 Simon would have dallied by the way, his weasel-mind alert to draw news of the hindering from this Heseltine. 1900 *Century Mag.* June 306/2 'The public should be protected—' 'Duly protected', said Gamage, 'That's always a good weasel word'. 1904 *Booklovers' Mag.* Jan. 7 Should there be a recurrence of the old custom of non-committal platforms, filled with 'weasel words', the identity of the Democratic nominee will still be a matter of great interest. 1923 Charnwood *Th. Roosevelt* x. 215 It is even comically reminiscent of the writer's own criticisms later of Mr. Wilson's 'weasel-worded' phrases.

Weasel (wī·z'l), *v.* [f. the sb.] 1. *trans.* To deprive (a word or phrase) of its force or meaning; also, to take away (its meaning) from a word or phrase. *U.S.*
1900 *Century Mag.* June 305/2 He's an expert on weaseling. I've seen him take his pen, and go through a proposed plank or resolution, and weasel every flat-footed word in it. Then the weasel word pleases one man, and the word that's been weaseled pleases another. 1919 Roosevelt in *Maine my State* 20 'His words weasel the meaning of the words in front of them,' said Dave, 'just like a weasel when he sucks the meat out of an egg and leaves nothing but the shell.'

2. *intr.* To extricate oneself from or get *out of* a place in the manner of a weasel.
1925 J. Bone *London Perambulator* 162 How to weasle out of London, north, south, east and west, with the fewest possible obstructions.

Weasing, variant of Wheezing.
1891 'L. Malet' *Wages of Sin* vii. v, Her breath coming irregularly in panting, weasing sobs.

Weather, *sb.* Add: 6. a. *weather-lorist, report* (example).
1905 *Westm. Gaz.* 21 Aug. 10/1 Which, according to the weather lorists, is a favourable augury for the coming year. 1863 R. Fitzroy *Weather Bk.* 349 Local changes should be indicated to observers.. by their own instruments, by signs of the weather,—and by due attention to the published Weather Reports.

7. **weather clerk** = *clerk of the weather:* Clerk *sb.* 6 c; **weather-coat,** a coat worn for protection in wet or stormy weather; **weather-dodger,** a screen on the bridge of a ship affording protection from the weather; **weather-fast** *a.,* secure against the weather; **weather-man** (mod. U.S. example); **weather-mark** (*a*), a mark made by the weather; (*b*) = *weather-sign;* (*c*), a mark on the weather side; **weather-strip** (earlier example).
1898 H. S. Canfield *Maid of Frontier* 111, I wouldn't have a *weather clerk inside of me for any thing. 1897 J. L. Allen *Choir Invis.* x. 132 He got up at last and wrapped his *weather-coat about him. 1925 R. Clements *Gipsy of Horn* 84 One was.. in comparative comfort under the lee of the *weather-dodger. 1910 J. Farnol *Broad Highway* I. xxiv, It was somewhat roughly put together, but still very strong, and seemed, save for the roof, *weather-fast. 1911 H. S. Harrison *Queed* xviii. 231 'Have you any friends here in the city?' asked he. 'Lord, no,' said the stranger, 'I'm the *weather man. 1693 *Weather-mark [see 6 a in Dict.]. 1849 Cupples *Green Hand* xiv. (1856) 139, I.. kept my eyes hard fixed upon the bank of cloud, as some new weather-mark stole out in it. 1894 *Outing* XXIV. 36/2 The 'Una' turned the weather-mark with a lead of nearly half an hour. 1846 *Rep. U.S. Comm. Patents* (1847) 94 One patent has been granted for improvements in fences, and another for a *weather strip for doors.

Weatherboard. Add: 1. c. A hut made of weatherboards.
1925 'H. H. Richardson' *Way Home* II. i. 123 Jerry and his bride had made ready their tiny weatherboard.

Weathercock, *sb.* Add: 1. b. The yellow balsam or Touch-me-not, a species of *Impatiens.*
1784 Cutler in *Mem. Amer. Acad.* (1785) I. 485 Weather-cock. Balsamine. Touch-me-not.

Weavement (wī·vmĕnt). [f. Weave *v.*[1] + -ment.] Something that is woven; a woven fabric. (In quot. *fig.*)
1904 *Academy* 23 Apr. 464/2 To work out the salvation of the play by joining up all the loose ends into a weavement which would astound and amuse the innocent author.

Web, *sb.* 18. Add: **web-nest,** the filmy tissue enclosing a group of caterpillars; **web-worm** (earlier example).
1895 *Schlich's Man. Forestry* IV. 279 The caterpillars, enclosed in their common *web-nest, first gnaw the upper side of the leaves. 1802 *Mass. Hist. Soc. Coll.* VIII. 190 The first [corn-pest] is the *web-worm, a small taper worm of a gray colour, about a half an inch in length.

Webby, *a.* 1. (Further example.)
1926 *Chambers's Jrnl.* June 384/1 She noticed a kind of momentary clogging of his movements as he passed through the canvas, as though there had been some little, 'webby' resistance to his passing.

Web-foot. 3. b. (Earlier example.)
1868 *All Yr. Round* 19 Sept. 354 Advt., We have changed the credit of one year and return to ready pay, without which no Webfoot need apply.

Webley (we·bli). [f. the name of the makers.] A type of revolver made by Messrs. F. Webley & Son.
1911 *Encycl. Brit.* XXI. 656/1 In the Webley the bolt is upon the standing breech and grips the extremity of the hinged barrel. 1913 Charl. Mansfield *Red Pearls* xxviii, The bullet from his Webley pierced through the heart of the gorilla. 1924 *Times* 7 Apr. 14/3 He was shot with a Webley Service revolver.

Wedge, *sb.* 10. Add: **wedge tent,** a ridge tent.
1862 O. W. Norton *Army Lett.* 49 We used to sleep on the ground or on pine boughs when we had the small wedge tents. 1891 *Fur, Fin & Feather* Mar. 169 One of the Englishmen bunked inside the wagon and the other two slept in a little wedge tent close to hand.

Wedge, *v.*[1] 5. b. Also, to come *out* as a wedge; to force one's way *through* a narrow place.
1839 Murchison *Silurian Syst.* 140 Limestone.. can be traced tapering away from a central mass to thin extremities, which really wedge out between the coal grits and the older deposits. 1914 Mary & Jane Findlater *Crossriggs* vii. 49 I've never been in quite such a tight place before, but I'll wedge through it in time.

Wedger (we·dʒəɹ). [f. Wedge *v.*[2] + -er.] A workman who cuts clay into lumps or wedges and beats it to expel air-bubbles.
1881 *Harper's Mag.* Feb. 361/2 The 'wedger' takes a lump of.. twenty pounds, lays it on the kneading block before him [etc.].

Weed, *sb.*[1] 2. (Further example.)
1918 *Peace of Mind* xiii. 95 Amiel.. lived, an unnatural life, to which he became as firmly addicted as an opium eater to his weed.

7. c. *weed-cutter* (earlier example).
1849 *Rep. U.S. Comm. Patents* (1850) 297, I likewise claim the combination of the adjustive weed cutter and leveler F.

Weed, *sb.*[2] 6. (Later U.S. examples.)
1873 Aldrich *Marj. Daw,* etc. 229 His hat had a weed on it, which struck me as being strange. 1893 Kate D. Wiggin *Polly Oliver* xi. (1894) 121 She had a coachman and a footman, both with weeds on their hats, and she seemed very sad and grave.

Weed, *v.* Add: 6. *intr.* Of a trout: To bury itself in weeds when hooked.
1889 F. M. Halford *Dry-Fly Fishing* ix. 211 Do not be afraid of weedy places. Trout.. seldom weed at night, probably because they do not see the angler. *Ibid.* 214 When a fish is once weeded, the following tactics are what I suggest.

Weeded (wī·dĕd), *a.*[2] [f. Weed *sb.*[2] + -ed [2].] Clothed in (widow's) weeds.
1895 Hardy *Jude the Obscure* v. vii. 369 Having ascertained thus much the immensely weeded widow retraced her steps.

Weedery [2] (wī·dəri). [f. Weed *sb.*[2] + -ery.] Mourning garments.
1908 Hardy *Dynasts* III. vi. ii. 459 Even as he For whom thou wear'st that filial weedery Was waylaid by my tipstaff nine years since [etc.].

Weediness (wī·dinĕs). [f. Weedy *a.*[1] + -ness.] Weedy character; lankiness; poorness of physique.
1925 Deeping *Sorrell & Son* viii, He realized that in spite of the other man's weediness he was a competitor who was to be respected.

Weeding hoe, prong. A hoe, or prong, used for removing weeds.
1639 *Maryland Archives* 80 A weeding hoe. 1703 *Col. Rec. N. Carolina* I. 579 Two weeding hoes, one hilling hoe. 1756 in *Lett. to Washington* I. 364 Bright Indian weeding Hoes. 1832 *Louisville Publ. Advt.* 1 Mar. Weeding Hoes—100 doz. of a superior quality, assorted sizes, are offered at low prices. 1841 *Gardener's Chron.* 5 June 366/1 A correspondent.. recommends the accompanying weeding prong, as being a most useful instrument. 1854 *Florida Plant. Rec.* 553. 39 Weeding hoes.

Wee·d-out. [f. *to weed out,* Weed *v.* 4 c.] An act or instance of weeding out or removing, esp. of inferior, weak, or undesirable members of any company, herd, etc.
1891 *Daily News* 19 Oct. 3/8 Four of the best yearlings and three of the best two-year-olds were bought in, and thus the sale was very much reduced in importance, being little more than a weed out.

Weedy, *a.* 3. (Earlier example.)
1865-6 *Trans. Ill. Agric. Soc.* VI. 638 Weedy—Flour made from wheat that has come in contact with a noxious weed imparting an unpleasant smell.

Week, *sb.* 7. **week-evening** = *week-night.*
1900 Ellen T. Fowler *Farringdons* viii. 141 It is our 'week-evening service.

Week-end, *v.* Also, to go *to* a place for a week-end holiday.
1928 *Daily Express* 17 Apr. 12/4 I have week-ended leisurely by airplane to Brunswick.

Wee·k-endy, *a.* [f. Week-end + -y.] Suggestive of the week-end.
1930 J. B. Priestley *Angel Pavement* xi. 567 The station was very crowded and weekendy.

Weekly. B. *sb.* (Earlier example.)
1833 *Knickerbocker Mag.* I. 185 We have articles on Political Economy in the monthlys, the weeklys, and the dailys.

Weep, *v.* 4. (Further example.)
1930 *N. & Q.* 16 Aug. 124/2 A cheese itself is sick when it has been over soured or over acidulated, and in time 'weeps', gradually becoming soft inside.

Weeper. 3. d. (Earlier example.)
1845 *Knickerbocker Mag.* XXVI. 585 The long black crape 'weeper', which it was the custom at that time to wear depending from the hat behind.

Weevil. 3. Add: *weevil-grub.*
1862 T. W. Harris *Ins. Injur. Veget.* (ed. 3) 74 In this country weevil-grubs are very common in hazel-nuts, chestnuts, and acorns.

Weft, *sb.*[1] 6. Add: **weft-feeler** = *Feeler 5; **weft-mixing,** a method of weaving (see quot.).
1927 T. Woodhouse *Artif. Silk* 130 A *weft feeler indicates when the weft in the active shuttle is nearly finished. *Ibid.* 130 In many cases.. two shuttles have to be employed, although one kind of weft is being used. The two shuttles insert two picks each alternately; the method is known as *weft-mixing, and is adopted to secure uniformity in thickness and shade of the weft.

Weigh, *v.* 9. Also of boxers before a fight, or in general use.
a 1909 'O. Henry' *Roads of Destiny* xviii. 307 He was six feet four and weighed in at 135. 1931 *Daily Express* 13 Oct. 1/7 Both boxers weighed in this afternoon.

o. *U.S. slang.* (See quot.)
1926 J. Black *You Can't Win* x. 135 We parted at Pocatello, agreeing to 'weigh in' (meet) at Ogden in the spring.

Weigher. 3. Also *weigher-in* (see quot.).
1928 *Daily Tel.* 25 Sept. 12/5 It is a rule that every fish caught must be kept alive, and after being weighed must be put back into the water by the official weigher-in.

Weight, *sb.*[1] 10. c. (Further examples.)
1917 Empey *From Fire Step* 31 And another piece of advice—don't chuck your weight about until you've been up the line and learnt something. 1928 *Sunday Express* 12 Feb. 9 Walcot thought I was throwing my weight about. So he belaboured me with his walking-stick.

12. d. *transf.* esp. in *light weight.*
1872 Lowell *Dante* Prose Wks. 1890 IV. 261 We feel profoundly that the latter [Euripides], though in some respects a better dramatist [than Æschylus], was an infinitely lighter weight.

15. b. (Later example.)
1927 Bowley & Stamp *Nat. Income 1924* 23 The 114 percentages for men form a 'normal' frequency group, and the average is little affected by choice of weights.

21. c. (U.S. examples, = pound.)
1759 *Essex Inst. Hist. Coll.* XIX. 190 He has got 150 weight of bread befoer hand. 1799 *Ibid.* XIII. 42 Six thousand weight of bread is yet to be baked. 1846 *Knickerbocker Mag.* XXVII. 276, I took out thirty weight of honey.

25. **weight-pole** *U.S.* (see quot. 1843).
1822 J. Woods *Engl. Prairie* 276 Short pieces of wood placed on the boards, to keep up the weight-poles. 1843 *Amer. Pioneer* III. 445 The weight poles [of a log cabin] are those small logs laid on the roof, which weigh down the course of clap-boards on which they lie, and against which the next course above is placed.

b. *weight-puller.*
1868 H. Woodruff *Trotting Horse* xxiii. 200 The weight-pullers.. are of medium weight.

Weight, *v.* Add: 2. e. To impart weight or force to.
1922 E. Bramah *Kai Lung's Golden Hours* viii. 188 So expertly was the thrust weighted that the point of the weapon protruded on the other side.

Weir, *sb.* 6. Add: *weir-side.*
1913 E. F. Benson *Thorley Weir* ii. 63 Only this morning by the weir-side he had found a gem of very pure ray.

Weir, *v.* Also, to dam *up* with a weir.
1920 *Nature* CV. 299/1 The restoration of the Kalahari and Ovamboland plains by weiring up the outlets on the north [etc.].

Weld, *sb.* 1. Also *fig.*
1895 B. Bosanquet *Comp. Plato's Republic* Introd. 35 Even if Plato's plan underwent discontinuous enlargement, the welds are now unbreakable, and, I incline to think, undiscoverable.

Welfare, *sb.* 4. Add: *welfare-centre.*
1917 *New Witness* 28 June 202/1 It is continually stated that Maternity Clinics and Infant Welfare Centres have met with the greatest success in France.

Welfare, *v.* [f. the sb.] *trans.* To do welfare work in.
1919 D. H. Pepler *Health* ii. 14 So she read Brieux on the Downs And turned to welfaring the towns.

Well, *sb.*[1] 13. Add: **well-fire, -grate** (see quot. 1910); **well-pipe** (modern example).
1906 *Studio* XXXVIII. 127/1 Well-fires are used in all the rooms. 1910 *Encycl. Brit.* XII. 378/2 In the closing years of the 19th century a 'well-grate' was invented, in which the fire burns upon the hearth, combustion being aided by an air-chamber below. 1929 *Camb. Med. Hist.* VI. xxii. 778 At Rochester the well-pipe is in the cross-wall, with an opening on each floor.

Well, *adv.* Add: 5. a. Also, *well-taken,* suitably selected for mention or comment. *U.S.*
1903 A. T. Hadley *Freedom & Responsibility* 165 To a certain extent this point is well taken. 1907 *Nation* (N.Y.) 14 Feb. 146 One of Mr. Heart's points seems to us well taken.

18. b. (Further example.)
1908 R. W. Chambers *Firing Line* xxiv. 407 'A man at your time of life—' 'My—what! Confound it, Louis I'm well this side of forty!'

e. *To be* (or *get*) *well away:* to have started or made considerable progress in something.
1910 *Glasgow Herald* 7 Feb. 13/2 From the drop out Andrew got well away but Henry pulled him up. 1922 *Ibid.* 20 Mar. 14/3 Stewart again seemed well away for the home side.

Well-fou·ndedness. [f. Well-founded + -ness.] The fact of being well-founded.
1920 *Glasgow Herald* 25 Feb. 9/3 There can be no discussion.. with regard to.. the well-foundedness of the charges.

Well-meant, *ppl. a.* Add: c. = Well-meaning *ppl. a.*
1849 Charlotte Brontë *Shirley* vii, A well-looked, well-meant, and, on the whole, well-dispositioned girl.

Well-natured, *a.* (Later example.)
1921 Galsworthy *To Let* II. i, He went as a well-natured dog goes for a walk with its mistress, leaving a choice mutton-bone on the lawn.

Well-possessed, *ppl. a.* [f. Well-possessed *pa. ppl.*] Having large possessions.
1912 A. S. M. Hutchinson *Happy Warrior* III. vi. 167 A nice little man, an indifferently-bred little man, but a most obviously well-possessed little man.

Wellsian (we·lziăn), *adj.* [f. the name of H. G. *Wells* (1866–) + -ian.] Of, pertaining to, or characteristic of the writings of H. G. Wells, esp. in the anticipation of future conditions.
1925 Deeping *Sorrell & Son* xvii, Winstonbury was still somewhat English, not Wellsian, or a snarling, love your brother sort of town, but love him with reservations. 1928 *Observer* 1 Apr. 11/4 And we hear stories, like Wellsian prophecies, of a garage that will accommodate motor-cars like books on a bookshelf and which is to be erected in the heart of Soho.

Well-thumbed, *ppl. a.* Also *fig.*
1929 *Daily Express* 7 Nov. 12/2 Some well-thumbed phrases have a queer sense of incongruity to the thinking mind.

Well-willing. A. *adj.* (Later example.)
1931 *Times Lit. Suppl.* 20 Aug. 631/1 Not even the most well-willing of critics can escape from its two main flaws.

Welshism (we·lʃiz'm). [f. Welsh + -ism.] An idiom or expression characteristic of the Welsh.
1761 L. Morris in *Cambrian Reg.* (1796) I. 368 Wonder not then, Sir, if you find many Welshisms in my letters: and pardon them as slips, which I do not see.

Wend, *v.* 15. (Example without possessive pron.)
1883 *Chambers's Jrnl.* Aug. 523 Clear water fareways, by which the fishermen wend a speedy course from point to point.

West. C. *sb.* Add: 3. b. (Earlier examples.)
1818 W. C. Bryant *Song* Poems (1832) 71 The hunter of the west must go In depth of woods to seek the deer. 1824 *Ann. Congress* XLII. 2024 Suppose the West procures the passage [of the protective tariff], do you suppose Brother Jonathan will not reap the advantage of it?

e. The characteristic speech of the western states of North America.
1926 J. Black *You Can't Win* vi. 66 If you're goin' west you better learn to talk west.

E. c. **west-central** *a.* (later example).
1929 W. Pett Ridge *Affect. Regards, Under Compulsion* 128 I posted the letter.. taking pains.. that it should bear a west-central postmark.

West-e·ndian, *a.* [f. West end + -ian.] = next.
1856 J. M. Ludlow in C. L. Graves *A. Macmillan* (1910) 91 A London shop 'more West-endian than Bell's or Nutt's'.

West-e·ndy, *a.* [f. West end + -y.] Suggestive of the West End; west-endish.
1912 J. Bone *Edin. Revisited* i. 12 A minister of the Gospel from the West Coast identified Edinburgh as an 'east-windy, west-endy city'. 1928 *Weekly Disp.* 15 Apr. 18/3 Surely that's West Endy enough for anybody!

Westering, *ppl. a.* Add: 3. Inclining towards or favouring the practice or policy of Western or European countries.
1920 H. G. Wells *Outl. Hist.* 555/1 These were but the outward and visible symbols of his westering tendencies.

Westerliness. (Recent example.)
1927 J. Adams *Errors in School* 222 Each of them has acquired an absolute quality, Edinburgh of easterliness and Liverpool of westerliness.

Western. A. *adj.* 5. (Earlier example.)
1803 *Ann. 7th Congress* 2 Sess. 135 Delaware.. who carries on little or no trade with the Western States.. has indeed lifted up her voice.

b. (Earlier examples.) Also, situated in or inhabiting the Western States.
1713 *Col. Rec. N. Carolina* II. 26 The Tuscaroroes have surprised and robbed our traders going to the Western Indians. 1784 Washington *Diaries* II. 326 The Western Settlers—from my own observation—stand as it were on a pivot. 1790 *Steele Papers* I. 67 My Western Lands had become so great an object to me that it had become absolutely necessary that I should go to the Western Country, to secure them. 1812 *Niles' Weekly Reg.* III. 13/1 The Western papers.. abound with the severest animadversions on General Hull.

B. *sb.* Add: 4. *U.S.* A western novel.
1930 *Publishers' Weekly* 8 Feb. 689 Advt., Here they are, five sure-shot Westerns.

Westernism. 1. (Earlier example.)
1838 *Knickerbocker Mag.* XI. 447, I now recollect but few specimens of Jack's *westernisms,* and these I think were not his best.

Westernize, *v.* Add: b. *intr.* To become western in character.
1903 L. F. Ward *Pure Sociol.* 33 Some of the nations of the East, notably Japan, are rapidly westernizing.

Westland. (Later example.)
1931 D. C. Cuthbertson (*title*) Highlands, Highways and Heroes, or Wanderings in the Westlands.

We·stness. [f. West + -ness.] The quality of being west; western character.
1930 C. C. Martindale in *Monument to St. Augustine* 88 Because of a radical South-ness and West-ness in his make-up, he never could find an affinity with Greek.

West Pointer. *U.S.* An officer trained in West Point (N.Y.) Military Academy.
1863 *Congress. Globe* 15 Jan. 327/3 There have been wounded since this war opened from thirty to forty general officers. Many of them were West Pointers... Hooker is a West Pointer, and has he not shown genius during this war? 1867 W. H. Dixon *New Amer.* I. xi. 135 He is also a soldier —a West Pointer—and of singular distinction in his craft. 1889 Mrs. Custer *Tenting on Plains* xiii. 434, I remember how every slip of a West Pointer was caught at by the others. 1903 A. B. Hart *Actual Government* 469 All the greatest commanders in the Civil War were West Pointers.

West-Ri·dinger. A native or inhabitant of the West Riding of Yorkshire.
1857 Mrs. Gaskell *C. Brontë* 28 The exceptional traits in the characteristics of these stalwart West-Ridingers, such as they were in the first quarter of this century.

West-sider. A resident of the West side of New York.
1903 *N.Y. Even. Post* 14 Nov. 4 The persistence with which the West Siders have followed up this question of the Broadway trees. 1914 Gertr. Atherton *Perch of Devil* I. 2 Ida, forced.. to accept employment with a fashionable dressmaker and consumed with envy of the 'West Siders' whose measurements she took.

Wet, *sb.*[2] Add: 2. *U.S.* A person who is opposed to prohibition.
1918 *Nation* (N.Y.) 11 Apr. 438/2 Massachusetts was counted upon by the 'wets' as one of the 'last-ditchers'. 1925 *Times* 30 Jan. 11/3 That at present they are effectively enforced nobody will contend seriously, neither 'drys' nor 'wets'. 1931 F. L. Allen *Only Yesterday* iv. 76 The growing company of the wets.

Wet, *a.* Add: 17. (Further example.)
1919 *Brit. Manufacturer* Nov. 27/1 The fibres are drawn out.. before passing through a trough of warm water—which dissolves the gummy connecting matter and enables finer yarns to be produced—to be tightly twisted into yarn or thread. This is known as 'wet-spinning'.

20. **wet-bobbing,** at Eton, boating; **wet day** (see quot.); **wet end,** that end of a drying machine into which the material to be dried is passed; **wet room** (see quot.); **wet spell** (see quot.).
1926 *Spectator* 3 July 11/1 Any alternative summer game or sport.. such as is provided by '*wet-bobbing' at a school like Eton. 1919 *British Rainfall* 15 A '*Wet Day* is a day ending at 9 h. (G. M. T.) on which 1 mm., or ·04 in., or more, of rain is recorded. 1906 R. W. Sindall *Paper Technol.* 33 *Wet end of machine. 1927 T. Woodhouse *Artif. Silk* 25 The wet pulp is now run on to the feed end, usually termed the 'wet-end', of the drying machine. 1901 *Chambers's Jrnl.* Oct. 670/1 My office is just under our '*wet room' (the usual term for the department where liquid pharmaceutical preparations are kept and prepared). 1919 *British Rainfall* 15 A '*Wet Spell* is a period of fifteen or more consecutive days, each one of which is a 'Wet Day'.

Wet, *v.* 7. e. (Earlier example.)
1783 J. Woodforde in J. Beresford *Diary Country Parson* II. 97 I walked to the Swan and there wetted with him, that is, drank a glass of wine together.

Wetness. Add: c. The fact of being opposed to prohibition.
1928 *Manch. Guardian Weekly* 19 Oct. 301/1 The Democratic candidate is assailed for his 'wetness' and for his Roman Catholicism.

Whack, *sb.* Add: 2. b. *Out of whack:* not in proper condition; disordered.
1899 G. Ade *Doc' Horne* viii. 79 My stomach seems to be out of whack. 1906 *McClure's Mag.* Feb. 34 Being able to get at any part of the mechanism which may be 'out of whack' is important. 1928 H. A. Vachell *Some Happenings* xii. 205 His liver is out of whack and no mistake. 1923 Watts *Luther Nichols* 85 There ain't nothing out o' whack with her.

Wha·ck-up. [f. Whack *v.* 3.] A sharing out or distribution.
1885 [see Whack *sb.* 2 b]. 1896 G. Ade *Artie* xii. 107 He hadn't been in on the whack-up six weeks till he was wearing one o' them bicycle lamps in his neck-tie. 1912 R. A. Wason *Friar Tuck* xi. 85 'What ya goin' to kill her with?' he asked, his eyes dancin' like an Injun's at the beef whack-up.

Whale, *sb.* 5. c. *A whale of* (later examples).
1929 M. C. Work *Compl. Contract Bridge* xi, All that dealer has to do is to bid one.. of his 'whale of a suit'. 1930 *Punch* 26 Feb. 236/1 The doctor, whom it had taken a whale of a time to arrive.

6. **whale-master,** the captain of a whaling-boat.
1924 *Chambers's Jrnl.* Feb. 95/2, I dine with the whale-masters and officers.

Whale, *v.*[2] 1. Also with *const.*
1928 M. Walsh *White Rivers Run* vi, 'Do you like porridge?' Aelec asked. 'I do. I was whaled into taking it as a boy.'

2. (Earlier examples.)
1846-52 Whitcher *Widow Bedott P.* vi. 67 You remember that one that come round a spell ago a whalin' away about human rights. 1886 *Harper's Mag.* July 322/1 In tones of wrath.. he whaled it at his opponent throughout the fifteen minutes alloted to him.

Whale-back. Add: 3. b. Any mass having the shape of the back of a whale.
1928 *Chambers's Jrnl.* Jan. 1/2 Behind all, a dim whale-back that might be Stroma, or Ultima Thule.

Whale-backed, *a.* (Earlier example.)
1869 'Mark Twain' *Innoc. Abroad* 441 We can see the long, whale-backed ridge of Mount Hermon projecting above the eastern hills.

Whale-boat. b. (Earlier examples.)
1682 *Connecticut Public Rec.* III. 318 How cam you up into these parts? In a whale boat, wth Ben Gaylord and one Perkins. 1721 *Mass. Province Laws* IX. 178 The flat botom'd Boats and whale Boats. 1781 *Essex Inst. Hist. Coll.* XXXV. 143 A sufficient Army.. provided with.. a sufficient number of whale-boats for passage by water.

Whaler. Add: 4. *attrib.* as *whaler-man.*
1888-90 Stevenson *South Seas* I. xiii. 115 Captain Chase, they called him, an old whaler-man.

Whaling, *vbl. sb.*[1] b. (Further example.)
1900 J. Nicholson in *Hist. Byways & Highways* 164 When Hull was the headquarters of the whaling fleet, whale oil was largely used.

Whang, *sb.*[2] Add: 2. *U.S.* A twang.
1883 'Mark Twain' *Life Mississippi* x. 130 An agonized voice, with the backwoods 'whang' to it, would wail out [etc.].

Whang, *v.*[1] 1. Also *intr.* with *at.*
1891 *Fur, Fin & Feather* Mar. 167 'Come on!' he yelled, and began whanging away at the bear with the club again.

Wha·ngable, *a.* [f. Whang *v.*[1] + -able.] That can be used for beating or lashing with.
1904 H. G. Wells *Food of Gods* I. ii, Almost all the available manhood of Hickleybrow.. were out with a remarkable assortment of flappish and whangable articles in hand—to commence the scooting of the giant hens.

Whangee. (Earlier example.)
1790 in W. Rougbead *Bad Companions* (1930) 6 He.. sometimes wears a cocked hat,.. and generally carries a Wangee cane in his hand.

Wharfer (hwǫ·ɹfəɹ). [f. Wharf + -er [1].] A dockside labourer.
1927 *Observer* 4 Dec. 16/5 The Australian wharfers' strike has paralysed oversea trade.

Wharf-master. Chiefly *U.S.* An official in charge of a wharf.
a 1618 [see Wharf *sb.*[1] 3]. 1851 C. Cist *Cincinnati* 87 A city treasurer, and marshal, a wharf and three market masters are elected. 1889 *Kansas City T. & Star* 4 May, Mayor Davenport rewarded one of his negro pre-election boosters.. with the office of wharfmaster. 1891 *Cent. Dict.* (Western U.S.).

Wharf-rat. (See Wharf *sb.*[1] 3.) Earlier examples.
1823 J. F. Cooper *Pilot* II. i. 13 To burrow like a rabbit, or jump from hole to hole, like a wharf-rat. 1848 W. E. Burton *Waggeries* 175 The old Dutchman.. soon became encircled by a crowd of.. wharf rats.

What. A. Add: 5. b. Also (U.S.), *what say?*
1825 J. Neal *Bro. Jonathan* I. 357 'Was he hurt, uncle Harwood?' 'What-say?' 1838 Caroline Gilman *Recoll. Southern Matron* v. 39 The common southern expression is Oh? or What say? pronounced almost like one word. 1841 *Knickerbocker Mag.* XVII. 50 I'll retire from business, Come, what say? 1886 *Harper's Mag.* Dec. 42/1, I say they are fools if they didn't. What say?

c. *What about it?:* an inquiry as to the course of action to be adopted.
1927 Vachell *Dew of the Sea* etc. 259 Your head keeper says we must have two guns apiece. Now—what about it?

Wheal(e, *sb.*[4] An error for 'whey' in some 1613 editions of the authorized version of the Bible, and in various later editions.
1613 *Bible, Translators' Pref.,* The imputation.. that our people had beene fed with gall of Dragons in stead of wine, with wheale [1611 whey] in stead of milk.

Wheal, *v.*[2] 1. (Later example.)
1921 *Chambers's Jrnl.* Apr. 268/2 He exposed his back all raw and whealed with blows.

Wheat, *sb.* 1. b. (Further example.)
1877 *N.Y. Tribune* Apr. (Bartlett p. 147) Surprised that he took it all for wheat, and in innocence of his heart was about to carry it into effect.

4. a. *wheat-belt, country; wheat-gold* adj. b. **wheat berry** (earlier example).
1910 *Chambers's Jrnl.* Mar. 205/2 The laying out of ready-made farms in the *wheat-belts of North-West Canada. 1847 *Rep. U.S. Comm. Patents* (1848) 373 Taking the outer coating or bran from the *wheat berry previous to grinding produces the following important results. *Ibid.* 101 The states of New York.. to Tennessee are properly the *wheat country of the union. 1915 Wodehouse *Something Fresh* ii, Jane Valentine was a tall girl, with *wheat-gold hair.

Wheel, *sb.* 3. h. (Further example.)
1929 J. B. Priestley *Good Comp.* I. ii. 67 For the next hour she sat at the wheel under his tuition.

8. b. *U.S.* A dollar; = Cartwheel 2.
1825 J. Neal *Bro. Jonathan* I. 160, I shows him a double handful o' the royal goold; the ginooine yeller stuff—wheels. 1902 Harben *Abner Daniel* 143 How will fifteen hundred round wheels strike you? 1907 Mulford *Bar-20* v. 47 An' would yu mind throwin' somebody else's hat? I paid twenty wheels for that eight years ago.

12. b. *On wheels* (recent example).
1914 Gertr. Atherton *Perch of Devil* I. 22 She was 'on the job' every minute until the cottage was 'on wheels'.

13. c. *To see the wheels go round:* To see how things are managed, how any business or organization works, etc.
[1876 J. Habberton *Helen's Babies* 11 'I want to see the wheels go round', said Budge.] 1889 *Kansas City T. & Star* 29 Mar., Hale Holden.. is in Washington seeing the wheels go 'round in that picturesque city. 1921 R. D. Paine *Comr. Rolling Ocean* ix. 160, I want to watch a supercargo and see his wheels go round.

15. A ride in or on a wheeled vehicle.
1880 *Scribner's Monthly* Feb. 483/1 A few possessors of the

Supplement, p. 3873; Corrigenda, p. 4092; Spurious words, p. 4093; Books quoted, p. 4094

birotate chariot, numbering some forty odd, enjoyed a 'wheel around the Hub'.

17. *wheel-spin, -wobble; wheel-pump, -table.*

1923 Deeping *Secret Sanctuary* ix, Stretton had seen the winch and bucket go, and a wheel pump under a pent-house had taken its place. 1928 *Daily Tel.* 11 Sept. 15/6 He took a grassy approach too wide, and had a wheel spin, from which he cleverly recovered. 1926 W. J. Locke *Stories Near & Far* 172 A probationer stood by serving the laden wheel-table.

18. wheel chair (earlier mod. examples); **wheel-dog**, a dog harnessed next to the wheels of a vehicle; **wheel-pit** (earlier examples).

1890 *Harper's Mag.* Mar. 613/1 Mrs. Aydler flitted backward and forward in her *wheel chair. 1891 *Century Mag.* Apr. 943 There is Mina..in a wheel-chair. 1924 A. J. Small *Frozen Gold* 296 The *wheel-dog somersaulted in his harness. 1850 S. Judd *R. Edney* iii. 43 The subordinate branches were carried on below, under the 'bed' or main floor of the mill, near the *wheel-pit. 1860 Holland *Miss Gilbert's Career* iv. 67 The constant plash of the water in the near wheel-pit.

Wheel, *v.* Add: **18.** To mark *out* with a wheel.

1895 Jeanette E. Davis *Elem. Mod. Dressmaking* (ed. 2) 5 Each piece should be pinned down previously to cutting-out, care being taken to put the pins between the fitting-lines, and not across them, that in the after wheeling-out they may not need removing.

Wheel-house. 1. (Earlier and later examples of sense 'pilot-house'.)

1835 Ingraham *South-West* I. xxiii. 247 The pilot (as the helms-man is here called) stands in his lonely wheel-house. 1849 *Rep. U.S. Comm. Patents* (1850) 624 Some boats have wheel-houses wide as their decks. 1866 *Rep. Indian Affairs* 167 It is said the firing was merely by boys throwing their arrows at the wheel-houses in sport. 1878 'Mark Twain' & Warner *Gilded Age* iv. 49 The Amaranth drew steadily up till her jack-staff breasted the Boreas's wheelhouse. 1922 R. Parrish *Case & Girl* 216 He noted..a bridge forward of the wheel-house, together with a decidedly commodious cabin aft.

Wheeling, *vbl. sb.* **e.** Earlier examples in sense 'travelling in a wheeled vehicle'; also, the possibility of this.

1850 L. Sawyer *Way Sketches* 81 Our road lay over deep barren sand, which rendered the wheeling very difficult. 1864 *Rel. Agric. Soc. Maine* 52 It happens..the January thaw ..gives us bare hills and wheeling. 1873 'Gail Hamilton' *Twelve Miles* ii. 25 He told her he would give her a sleigh-ride when it came wheeling.

Wheel-lock. Add: **3. b.** = Lock *sb.*² 15.

1927 *Observer* 20 Feb. 21/3 The majority of our fire-fighting appliances are not provided with adequate wheel-locks.

Wheelwrighting. (Earlier example.)

1883 *Rep. Indian Affairs* 253 Carpentry, harness-making, wheelwrighting.

Where, *adv.* Add: **5.** Also in various colloquial expressions; (see *At *prep.* 1 d, *Here *adv.* 5 b). *U.S.*

1904 W. H. Smith *Promoters* v. 95 Right there was where we got in our work.

12. c. = Whereas 2.

1929 R. A. Cram *Cath. Ch. & Art.* iv. 57 Where the pagan architecture had been an *exterior* art..and where Roman and Byzantine art had striven to achieve space in its simplest form, the North worked for interior space.

15. b. *whereamong, wherewithout* (recent examples).

1929 Bridges *Test. Beauty* i. 382 Whereamong hath the sceptic honourable place. 1899 M. Beerbohm *More* 95 Mere masses of colour, crude intensity of conception, wherewithout posters fail, were quite unnecessary.

Whereto, *adv.* **2.** (Recent example.)

1900 Alice Meynell *John Ruskin* vii. 119 Whereto, then, is the persuasion of this book directed?

Whereunder, *adv.* (Further example.)

1913 W. E. Cooper *Engl. Fatal Land Policy* i. 47 Thus establishing a freer system of international exchanges whereunder British trade and manufactures might pass to foreign countries.

Whew, *sb.*¹ Add: **1. b.** (See quot.)

1929 Priestley *Good Comp.* 118 Bruddersford has an elaborate system of factory buzzers—usually known as whews.

Whew, *sb.*² [f. Whew *v.*²] In phr. *all of a whew*, in a hurry; impatient or excited.

1922 Alice Brown *Old Crow* xi. 119 He wants me to go down in his river pastur', choppin'. All of a whew to git at it.

Whey, *v.* (Mod. U.S. example.) With *off*.

1877 *Rep. Vermont Board Agric.* IV. 37 When allowed to 'whey-off', as the separation is practically termed, the difference in structure and fluidity will readily appear in the amount of whey produced.

Whicker, *v.* Add: **1. b.** To make a hurtling sound.

1926 *Spectator* 28 Aug. 313/2 Bid Jove send down a thunderbolt to whicker through the sky.

Whiffet. 1. (Earlier example of *whiffet dog*.)

1848 *Ladies' Repository* VIII. 315 The best protection to a house, with a family in it that can be named—that is, a little, barking, noisy, cowardly, whiffet dog.

3. A small quantity of mist or cloud; a puff or wisp of smoke or vapour.

1910 Jer. Hart *Vigilante Girl* i. 14 At last, of the heavy fog-bank there remained but whiffets and rings and wreaths of mist.

Whiffle, *v.* Add: **2. c.** To cheat or swindle.

1902 A. D. McFaul *Ike Glidden* xxviii. 266, I am not trying to whiffle you out of your rights.

Whiffletree. (Earlier example.)

1846 *Rep. U.S. Comm. Patents* (1847) 289 What I claim as my invention..is, first, the connecting of the whiffletrees and eveners with the hames, in the manner above stated.

Whiffling, *vbl. sb.*² [f. Whiffle *v.*¹ + -ing ¹.] The action of Whiffle *v.*¹; vacillation or evasion.

1841 J. F. Cooper *Deerslayer* i, I would carry the gal off to the Mohawk by force, make her marry me in spite of her whiffling. 1906 *Springfield Weekly Republ.* 18 Oct. 3 This outcome of a week of doubt and whiffling will be viewed with mixed emotions.

Whim, *sb.*¹ **4.** Also, a four-wheeled vehicle used esp. for conveying large cast-iron pipes.

1922 *Metrop. Water Board, Contr. for Pipelaying* 3rd Sched., 1 horse, pipe whim and man.

Whimp, *v.* (Later example.)

1925 *Blackw. Mag.* Aug. 169/2 'Don't whimp', I said to Irene. 'I am not whimping, daddy.'

So **Whimp** *sb.* = Whimper *sb.*

1925 *Blackw. Mag.* 173/1 This was something beyond a whimp.

Whimsy-whamsy. Add: **b.** *attrib.*

1931 *Time & Tide* 26 Sept. 1118 Have we not enough whimsy-whamsy authors of our own without importing the too, too, quaint devices of foreign playwrights?

Whin¹. **4.** Add: **whin-mill,** a mill for crushing whin for horses' food.

1893 C. A. Mollyson *Parish of Fordoun* 188 With a plentiful supply of oilcake and other nutritious feeding stuffs there is no place now for the whin-mill.

Whine, *sb.* (Further example.)

1928 E. Wallace *Double* xx, They heard the whine of a car draw up on the ground below.

Whip, *sb.* Add: **10. c.** A whipping or springy action.

1923 *Cricketer Ann. 1922–3* 78 Kilner bowls left hand slow ..has a good action with a nice 'whip' in it.

Whip, *v.* **10.** (Further example.)

1886 R. Brown *Spunyarn & Spindrift* xxx. 355 The main-topgallant sail split right up the middle, and whipped itself into ribands when the halliards were let go.

Whip-. c. Add: **whip-room,** a room used by Parliamentary whips.

1922 *Glasgow Herald* 22 Nov. 11/2 This is a post which keeps its occupant more busily engaged in the Whip-room than in the House itself.

Whi·pper-snap, *v.* [Back-formation f. Whipper-snapper.] *intr.* To behave like a whipper-snapper; to be impertinent.

1908 W. De Morgan *Somehow Good.* xi. 100 The lines they might elect to whipper-snap on were not to be those of sentimental nonsense.

Whippiness (hwi·pinės). [f. Whippy *a.* + -ness.] Pliable quality; flexibility.

1881 *Sportman's Year-bk.* 70 Some successful anglers use the two extremes of whippiness and stiffness [in fly-rods]. 1913 W. E. Dommett *Motor Car Mech.* 130 This control has the objection..that the gear box has to be long with possible whippiness of the shafting. 1931 F. Greenslet in *Bk. Fly-rod* (ed. Sheringham & Moore) v. 44 A 12-foot four-piece fly-rod of a really delightful soft whippiness.

Whipping, *vbl. sb.* **4.** Add: **whipping-bee** *U.S.*, a gathering of persons for the purpose of whipping someone; **whipping-cart,** a cart to which a person sentenced to be whipped is tied; **whipping-house** *U.S.*, a building in which negroes were whipped.

1922 *Daily Mail* 29 Nov. 9 Members of this secret organization..in the last 18 months in Texas alone have conducted no fewer than 500 tar and feather parties and *whipping-bees. 1901 *Chambers's Jrnl.* Jan. 23/2 On the way we ran into a crowd following a *whipping-cart. 1852 Mrs. Stowe *Uncle Tom's C.* xxix, It was the universal custom to send women and young girls to the *whipping houses. 1865 *Atlantic Monthly* XV. 510 Without thought of nine o'clock, pass patrol, or whipping-house.

Whip-saw, *sb.* Add: **b.** *fig.* (Of something that 'cuts both ways'.)

1929 L. F. Carr *America Challenged* 79 The whip-saw of paying high prices for what they bought and being forced to receive low prices for what they sold.

Whip-saw, *v.* (Earlier example.) So **Whip-sawing** *vbl. sb.* (in quots. fig., cf. *Whip-saw b).

1842 *Amer. Pioneer* I. 83 Dwelling houses, made of wood, whip-sawed into timbers four inches thick, and of the requisite width and length. 1888 M. Lane *Pol. Catch-Words* 16 Whipsawing..The acceptance of bribes or fees from both sides in case of pending legislation or official action. The idea is taken from the action of the whipsaw, which cuts both ways. The term originated in the New York Assembly. 1903 *N. Y. Sun* 8 Nov. 10 These speculators have subjected themselves to the process known in Wall Street as whipsawing, that is, they have bought when the market was strong and sold when the market was weak, and found each time that they bought at the top and sold at the bottom.

Whipstalk. Also *U.S.* = Whipstock 5.

1861–2 *Trans. Ill. Agric. Soc.* V. (1865) 174 Never have we seen fifteen acres of apple tree nursery better cultivated.. nothing of the whip-stalk order.

Whip-stitch. 2. (Earlier examples.)

1824 P. Horry *Life of Marion* Pref. i, What can one do, When one's friends are..calling out at every whipstitch.. 'Well, but sir, where's Marion?' 1888 Stockton *Dusantes* 130 Every whip-stitch of his bag and baggage shall be trundled after him.

Whip-thong. *U.S.* The thong of a whip; a whip-lash.

1827 *Hallowell* (Maine) *Gaz.* 20 June 4/5 They have also received a large supply of..Whips and Whipthongs. 1897 *Outing* (U.S.) XXX. 252/2 If your whip thong gets caught in the harness drop your hand and push the stick forward, and the thong will, invariably, release itself.

Whirling, *vbl. sb.* Add: **4.** *Comb.* as *whirling-speed.*

1894 *Phil. Trans.* CLXXXV. i. 283 The whirling speed was taken to be at the commencement of whirl, that is to say, at the lowest speed at which the shaft definitely whirled.

Whirl-worm. 2. (Recent example.)

1927 *Daily Express* 31 Aug. 5/5 Dr. Kathleen Carpenter's paper is upon the survival of some ice-age relicts in fresh-water fauna of Cardiganshire, which relicts are whirl worms.

Whirly-. Add: **whirly-whirly,** a whirling cloud or eddy.

1930 Palmer *Men are Human* xiii. 112 A cool breeze that raised little whirly-whirlies of dust.

Whish, *v.*¹ **2.** (Further example.)

1929 R. Graves *Good-Bye to all That* xiii. 153, I heard one shell whish-whishing towards me.

Whisk, *v.* **1. b.** (Later examples.)

1919 H. Walpole *Secret City* ii. v. 353 A beautiful fruit just within his grasp...He's going to taste it, when whisk! it's gone. 1916 B. Cable *Action Front* 12, I heard..something else goin' *whisk* like a cane switched past your ear.

Whiskery, *a.* Add: **b.** Suggestive of whiskers.

1927 H. V. Morton *In Search Engl.* v, The dark room smelt of..that indefinite whiskery smell of old men.

Whiskified, *a.* (Later example.)

1918 W. J. Locke *Rough Road* xxi. 271 Bottles of the strongest old Burgundy, such as he thought would get a grip on Chipmunk's whiskyfied throat.

Whisky, *sb.*¹ **b.** Add: **whisky money,** the unappropriated residue of the beer and spirit duty which was allocated to technical education by the Local Taxation Act of 1890; **whisky-skin** *U.S. slang*, a drink containing whisky.

1911 *Encycl. Brit.* XXVI. 495/1 If the 'whisky' money.. were found to be well and carefully expended, no future Chancellor would be able to divert it to any other purpose. 1856 *Yale Lit. Mag.* XXI. 146 (Th.) Nine whiskey skins, and our spirits rushed together. 1871 Hay *Little Breeches*, etc. 24 Says he, 'Young man, the tribe of Phinns Knows their own whisky-skins!' 1889 Farmer *Amer.*, *Whiskey skin*, a concocted drink of whiskey, sugar, crushed ice, and mint.

Whiskyish (hwi·ski₁iʃ), *a.* [f. Whisky + -ish.] Inclined for whisky.

1929 Deeping *Roper's Row* ii, Don't be in a 'urry, my lad. Wait till they're warm. If they're whiskyish, wait till the whisky's got 'em.

Whisper, *sb.* **4.** Also *Comb.* as *whisper-proof*.

1876 *Gentl. Mag.* Sept. 339 To ascertain whether..our boasted right of asylum was really whisper-proof.

Whistle, *sb.* **1. b.** (*b*) *As clean as a whistle*: (further example).

1889 'R. Boldrewood' *Robbery under Arms* xlii, We've been sold as clean as a whistle.

Whistle, *v.* **10.** (Recent example.)

1917 H. A. Vachell *Fishpingle* xii, He hurried on, now doubly assured that Joyce had 'whistled'.

White, *sb.* Add: **19. b.** Also, a monarchist in Russia; a member of the White Army.

1924 E. G. Jellicoe *Playing the Game* xiii. 224 Expeditionary Armies of Britain and the United States, invaded Northern Russia..in order to link up with Russian Whites against Russian Bolsheviks.

White, *a.* Add: **1. e.** *transf.* (See quot.)

1927 N. V. Sidgwick *Electronic Th. Valency* 32 Hence, when atoms are struck by 'white' X-ray radiation (radiation having a continuous spectrum) absorption only begins when we reach a frequency great enough to expel the electron.

4. b. (Earlier example.)

1865 'Mark Twain' *Sk.* (1875) 74 The parson..was one among the whitest men I ever see.

6. a. (Further example.)

1877 J. Penderel-Brodhurst *Guide to Boscobel* v. 20 Whiteladies...The name is derived from the circumstance that the house was once a Priory of Cistercian or White Nuns.

11. c. white metal (hence *white-metalled, -metalling*).

1922 *Encycl. Brit.* XXX. 36/2 A hollow circular-sectioned shank carried an integral big-end, white-metalled internally and externally...The..thin and flexible section of the inner rod sleeve..enhanced the difficulty of white-metalling.

e. white dwarf, one of a class of small stars of great density radiating white light (see *Dwarf *sb.* 2 b); **white fuel,** water used as a source of power, in contrast to coal; **white plague,** tuberculosis; **White Russian** (*c*), a Russian monarchist; cf. sense 6 b; **white sale,** a sale of house- and body-linen at reduced prices; **white wear,** linen articles.

1927 A. S. Eddington *Stars & Atoms* 51 There can be little doubt that these '*white dwarfs', as they are called, are comparatively abundant in the stellar universe. 1913 Soddy *Matter & Energy* v. 135 The '*white fuel' of the Norwegian hill-sides. 1928 *Daily Tel.* 27 Mar. 10/7 Italy has..greater advantages for the development of 'white fuel', for Egypt has but one single river. 1909 *World To-Day* Sept. 924/1 The menace of the *White Plague is appalling. 1925 Deeping *Three Rooms* xxv, Influenza, apical pneumonia, and after that—the white plague. 1927 *Daily Tel.* 29 Mar. 11/6 The *White Russians in the Northern Army.. were purely soldiers, while the Reds were carrying on propaganda. 1923 *Daily Mail* 14 Feb. 5 Advt., Are you letting this most wonderful of *White Sales slip by without availing yourself of the..opportunities it affords? 1905 H. G. Wells *Kipps* i. ii. 39 Cretonnes, chintzes, and the like; serviettes, and all the bright, hard *whitewear of a well-ordered house.

12. c. white-piped (see quot.); **white-sighted,** of an eye, adapted for seeing white.

1896 Fisher *Schlich's Man. Forestry* V. 74 The wood may often be penetrated by repeated decaying stripes, as in

old oaks attacked by *Stereum hirsutum* (said to be *white-piped*.—Tr.). 1909 E. B. Titchener *Text-bk. Psychol.* i. 75 The white is thus seen with a white-sighted eye, and the black with a black-sighted eye.

e. white neb (see quot.).

1901 *Chambers's Jrnl.* Apr. 244/2 The scabrous part of the rook's beak comes on after the first moult. From this strong mark on the bill rooks are often called '*white-nebs'.

White-ant, *sb.*: see Ant *sb.* 3.

White-ant, *v.* [f. *white ant*: White *a.* 11.] *trans.* To destroy in the manner of termites or white ants.

1925 *Glasgow Herald* 14 Nov. 9/6 The extremists..have deliberately 'white-anted' the Labour movement..and squandered the funds of the wealthy unions.

White bear. 1. The Polar bear.

1860 Gosse *Rom. Nat. Hist.* 62 The white bear, seated on a solitary iceberg in the Polar Sea.

2. *U.S.* The grizzly bear.

1791 J. Long *Voyages* 95 The large white bear, commonly called the grizly bear, is a very dangerous animal. 1807 P. Gass *Jrnl.* vii. 82 Captain Lewis and some of the men travelled some distance by land and killed a white bear. 1837 Irving *Capt. Bonneville* II. v. 62 There you will find plenty of white bears and mountain sheep. 1852 J. Reynolds *Hist. Illinois* 172 He was destroyed there by a white bear.

White-bearded, *a.* **a.** (See White *a.* 12 c.)

b. Of wheat.

1788 Washington *Diaries* III. 417 Also sowing..one bushel of the White bearded Wheat sent me by Beale Boardly. 1849 *Rep. U.S. Comm. Patents, Agric.* (1850) 132 The white-bearded wheat, a valuable kind less liable to total failure than any other; not very popular with millers.

White birch. *U.S.* A North American species of birch (*Betula papyracea*), having light-coloured bark.

1789 Morse *Amer. Geogr.* 197 On the high lands are.. beech and white birch. 1832 D. J. Browne *Sylva Amer.* 123 The white birch is most frequently found..where the soil is dry and meagre. 1851 J. S. Springer *Forest Life* 188 On almost all sides of the mountain there is a short, tangled growth of alders and white birch coming up between the rocks. 1875 [see Birch *sb.* 1 b].

b. *attrib.*

1868 *Amer. Naturalist* June 178 After haunting..the white-birch swamps, it [a warbler] moves southward. 1871 Mrs. Stowe *Sam Lawson* 195 And she got her a little bit o' land, right alongside o' Old Black Hoss John's white-birch wood-lot.

Whitecap, *v.* *U.S.* [f. Whitecap *sb.*] *intr.* To be a whitecap (sense 4); to practise lynch law. Hence **Whi·tecapism; Whi·tecapper.**

1903 *N. Y. Even. Post* 22 Aug., A deputy marshal has arrested eleven prominent white planters on the charge of whitecapping. 1904 *Ibid.* 21 Dec. 3 The disgrace of whitecapism, which has retarded the development of the State of Mississippi. 1904 *Ibid.* 28 Jan. 9 The Mississippi has voted Gov. Vardaman a special appropriation to enable him to suppress the 'white cappers'.

Whi·te-capping, *a.* [f. Whitecap + -ing ².] Covering with or as with a white cap.

1912 J. London *Son of Sun* v. ii. 175 Their long slopes.. were broken by systems of smaller whitecapping waves.

White cedar. *U.S.* Used of varieties of cypress, juniper, etc., which resemble the cedar; (see Cedar 3).

1675 Josselyn *Two Voyages* 67 The white cedar is a stately tree, and is taken by some to be Tamarisk. 1807 P. Gass *Jrnl.* 165 The women have a kind of fringe petticoats, made of filaments or tassels of the white cedar bark. 1832 D. J. Browne *Sylva Amer.* 146 Among the resinous trees of the United States, the White Cedar is one of the most interesting for the varied utility of its wood. 1846 *Knickerbocker Mag.* XXVII. 283 The flexile white cedar bends over the rocks. 1879 *Scribner's Monthly* Nov. 20/1 White cedars.. invariably fringe the bank.

White-collar. *U.S.* Applied *attrib.* to persons engaged in non-manual work, or to the occupations of these.

1929 *Lit. Digest* 24 Aug. 10/2 No complete census..of our 'white-collar' army appears to be available. *Ibid.*, 'White-collar' occupations. 1928 *Collier's* 10 Nov. 49/2 The.. people at work in factories,..in white-collar jobs, and in the professions.

White elm. *U.S.* An American species of elm, *Ulmus americana.*

1770 [see White *a.* 11 b]. 1819 A. L. Hillhouse tr. *Michaux's Sylva* III. 83 This tree,..White Elm, is found over an extensive tract of the North American continent.

White frost. Frozen dew; hoar frost.

1382, 1563, 1739 [see Frost *sb.*²]. 1780 W. Fleming in *Trav. Amer. Col.* 634 Monday night there was a smart white frost. 1835 *Martin's Descr. Virginia* 66 Our white frost is generally harmless, it being simple dew slightly congealed.

Whitehall (hwai·thǭ·l). Any of the government offices situated in Whitehall, London.

1827 *Morn. Post* 24 Mar. 3/2 In consequence of that accommodation, an equal amount of Exchequer Bills before locked up at Whitehall are afterwards to be locked up in Threadneedle-street. 1850 *Daily News* 13 Mar. 5/2 The infection of..'Christian Socialism' is spreading to Whitehall. 1910 *Times Educ. Suppl.* 6 Sept. 13/2 The introductory remarks ..breathe a very different spirit from that of earlier official utterances of Whitehall. 1919 *Punch* 3 Sept. 202/1 The Passing of the Whitehall Flapper. 1931 Galsworthy *Maid in Waiting* xxii. 183 Without him, his flower, and his faint grin, Whitehall would have been shorn of something that made it almost human.

White line, *sb.* Add: **2. b.** *Engraving.* An engraved line which prints white.

1884 Dobson *Thos. Bewick & his Pupils* 145 The other difference, of which Bewick is said to be the inventor, consisted in the employment of what is known technically as 'whiteline'.

3. c. A narrow white (or yellow) strip painted on a road or street, esp. at a curve or corner, for the guidance of drivers of vehicles.

1925 *Glasgow Herald* 15 Oct. 9 The 'White Line'. The Minister of Transport is investigating the different methods ..of marking the road surfaces with white lines for the guidance of traffic.

White maple. The soft or silver maple, *Acer dasycarpum* or *eriocarpum.*

1810 Michaux *Arbres* i. 27 *White Maple* (érable blanc). seul dénomination sur les bords de l'Ohio. 1832 D. J. Browne *Sylva Amer.* 101 The white maple puts forth green and yellow flowers early in the spring. 1857–8 *Trans. Ill. Agric. Soc.* III. 479 Some trees, such as the red elm, and white and red maples ripen their fruit in May and June. 1882 *Rep. Vermont Board Agric.* VIII. 64 The rock maple makes the best sugar, while the white maple will make the whitest.

b. *attrib.*

1880 *Rep. Vermont Board Agric.* VI. 113 There seems to be a prevailing error..that clean white maple sugar is adulterated.

White monk. (Later example.)

1845 *Lives Eng. Saints, St. Robert* 52 A noble baron, called Ralph de Merlay, offered to endow a Cistercian house if they would send a colony of White monks into his lands.

White mulberry. A species of mulberry, *Morus alba*, obtained originally from China.

1610 *Estate of Virginia* 55 There are innumerable white Mulberry trees. 1737 John Wesley *Jrnl.* (1910) I. 402 The white mulberry is not good to eat. 1765 G. Croghan *Jrnl.* 16 The whole country abounds with great plenty of the white and red mulberry tree. 1804 J. Roberts *Penn. Farmer* 182 The leaves of both the black and white mulberry are used in raising silk-worms. 1846 D. J. Browne *Trees Amer.* 454 M. Pomier..recommends that the white mulberry be grafted on the Morus nigra.

White mule. *U.S.* Gin.

1928 *Collier's* 29 Dec. 8/1 What do you think about a bunch of boys and girls..stealin' a keg of white mule from a dealer? 1929 *Amer. Sp.* Aug. 440.

Whitening, *vbl. sb.* **1.** (Further example.)

1926 *Gloss. Electr. Terms* (Brit. Engin. Stand.) 129 *Whitening*, the deposition of a white film of silver on metals by simple immersion.

White oak. *U.S.* Any of various North American species of oak, esp. the Quebec oak, *Quercus alba*; also the wood of one or other of these.

1635 *Relat. Maryland* iii. 22 The White Oake is good for Pipe-staves, the red Oake for wainescot. 1662 *Groton Rec.* 7 Also that the meetinge house shall be sett upon the right hand of the path by a small whit Oak. 1746 *Baltimore Town Rec.* 19 One [gate] of five feet wide in the Clear within the posts White Oak framed and locust posts and sils. 1791 E. Denny *Jrnl.* 158 Upland thin, covered chiefly with white oak. 1819 E. Evans *Pedestrious Tour* 208 There are some rises of land, the soil of which is light, and the growth of timber upon them is principally white oak. 1852 D. G. Mitchell *Dream Life* 264 The few, lingering leaves of the white oaks rustle dismally. 1882 *Econ. Geol. Illinois* II. 21 In the breaks and bluffs of the creek, the white oak, a tree otherwise not common in this country, is quite abundant.

2. *attrib.* with *land*, etc.

1648 *Providence* (R.I.) *Rec.* XV. 21 The South-east corner is bounded with a gully and a white Oake tree. 1663 *Plymouth Rec.* 66 Lot..bounded..with two white oake stakes. 1703 *Conn. Col. Rec.* IV. 449 Running north from the sea to a white oak staddle on the bank with the top cutt off. 1754 *Col. Rec. Georgia* VI. 428 He prayed for five hundred Acres of Land, situated at a White Oak Swamp. 1770 Washington *Diaries* I. 428 You come..to a thin white Oak land, and poor. 1796–1801 Fessenden *Orig. Poems* 41 Simon dangling by a garter Hung on yonder white-oak tree. 1853 'P. Paxton' *Yankee in Texas* 79 Having chanced to light upon the price of white oak staves..he determined..he would engage a large gang. 1873 'Mark Twain' & Warner *Gilded Age* xvii. 163 You kin git all the rails you want outen my white-oak timber over thar. 1882 *Econ. Geol. Illinois* II. 21 These white oak lands are reckoned among the most fertile lands in the county.

White perch. *U.S.* (See Perch *sb.*¹ 2.)

1775 Burnaby *Trav.* 15 These waters are stored with incredible quantities of fish, such as sheeps-heads, rock-fish, drums, white perch. 1881 *Mass. Hist. Soc. Coll.* Ser. ii. X. 35 Vast quantities of sea or white perch are taken in the fall of the year. 1851 T. A. Burke *Polly Peaseblossom's Wedding* 129 The trout and white perch bit beautifully. 1863 *Game Laws* (Mass.) in *Fur, Fin & Feather* (1872) 75 Whoever takes or catches any smelts or white perch..shall forfeit..the sum of twenty-five cents.

White pine. 1. *U.S.* Any of various species of pine with light-coloured wood.

1682 *Providence* (R.I.) *Rec.* XIV. 113 From yͤ said heape of stones to range north and be west to a great white pine. 1765 R. Rogers *Concise Acc.* 43 The timber natural to this soil is chiefly oak, white pine, maple, walnut and chestnut. 1775 Burnaby *Trav.* 151 These [masts] are made of white pine, and are, I believe, the finest in the world. 1815 Drake *Cincinnati* iii. 134 The white pine..is annually floated down in immense quantities. 1835 *Southern Lit. Messenger* I. 644 The house..was decorated with a cluster of white pines. 1893 B. Torrey *Footpath-Way* 232, I cannot recollect the day when I did not regard the Weymouth pine (the *white pine* I was taught to call it:) with something like reverence.

b. *attrib.* with *board*, etc.

1708 *Boston Selectmen* 30 Aug., White-pine boards..and other lumber. 1769 in *Boston Even. Transcript* 28 Sept. 1911 III. 12, I have viewed the White pine Timber standing and growing on said Spaulding's land. 1789 Morse *Amer. Geog.* 197 The tract..is white pine land. 1815–16 *Niles' Weekly Reg.* IX. Suppl. 178/1, I observed hundreds—and I believe thousands of roads of strong substantial and durable fence, made of white pine stumps. 1844 *Knickerbocker Mag.* XXIII. 444 The clean white-pine buckets..into which the sap drips..are made expressly for this use. 1885 Cable *Dr. Sevier* xviii. 129 Shiny, sugary, and artificially crimson roasted apples, with neatly whittled white-pine stems to poise them on.

2. In Australia and New Zealand, any of various species of *Frenela* and *Podocarpus.*

1855, 1888, 1898 [see Pine *sb.*² 2].

White poplar. *U.S.* The abele; the tulip-tree.

1784 J. Smyth *Tour U.S.* I. xii. 93 The timber..consists of white and yellow poplars. 1831 Peck *Guide for Emigrants* ii. 123 In some sections of the State [Illinois] the white and yellow poplar prevails. 1837 *Southern Lit. Messenger* III. 738 The growth was principally white poplar—here called white wood—beach, birch, ash and hickory. 1893 *Amer. Folk-Lore* VI. 136 *Liriodendron tulipifera*, white, yellow, or hickory poplar. West Va.

Whitesmithery. (Earlier example.)

1812 *Niles' Weekly Reg.* 25 Jan. 390/2 Emery..is an article of the first consequence in the cotton and woolen manufactories, and in white smithery.

Whi·tesmithing, *vbl. sb.* [f. Whitesmith ¹ + -ing ¹.] = Whitesmithery.

1835 *Lexington Observer & Rep.* 10 June, Whitesmithing. Frederick Klaiber lately from Germany..has just commenced the above business. 1900 *Daily Chron.* 2 Jan. 3/1 Part of the bench at which the missionary-explorer learnt whitesmithing is exhibited.

White walnut. *U.S.* The North American Butternut, *Juglans alba* or *cinerea.*

1781–2 T. Jefferson *Notes on Virginia* (1787) 39 White walnut. Juglans alba. 1787 W. Sargent in *Mem. Amer. Acad.* IX. 157 White Walnut or Butternut, from 2 to 7 feet diameter. 1822 J. Woods *Engl. Prairie* 308 White-walnut, or butter-nut, and black-walnut, are not so good as the English walnut. 1832 D. J. Browne *Sylva Amer.* 173 In Pennsylvania and Maryland, and on the banks of the Ohio, it [Butternut] is generally known by..[the name] of White Walnut. 1857–8 *Trans. Ill. Agric. Soc.* III. 479 The black walnut and white walnut or butternut flourish finely upon our prairies.

Whiteweed. (Earlier examples.)

1803 *Mass. Hist. Soc. Coll.* IX. 200 On the upland and meadows grow burdens grass, ribwort, white weed, red top, clover, and herds grass. 1837 Colman *Rep. Agric. Mass.* 68 The principal weeds that infest the fields..are the ox-eyed daisy or white weed..and the charlock.

Whitleather. b. (Later example.)

1924 D. H. Lawrence *Boy in Bush* v. 76 Folks are tough in Australia: tough as whit-leather.

Whitley Council. [f. the name of J. H. *Whitley*, chairman of the committee of 1916 which recommended the setting up of such councils.] A council consisting usually of representatives of employers and workers for discussing and settling industrial relations and conditions. So *Whitley scheme*. **Whi·tleyism,** the use of Whitley Councils or similar methods for dealing with relations between employers and workers.

1923 *Daily Mail* 29 Jan. 7 Mistress and maid should be their own Whitley Council. *Ibid.* 29 May 9 The Industrial League and Council of Victoria-street, S.W., ..stands for an extension of 'Whitleyism'. 1924 *Glasgow Herald* 20 Sept. 11 He referred to the adoption of Whitleyism in Germany. 1925 *Contemp. Rev.* June 720 Statutory Whitleyism and Social Insurance are the keys of the future. 1928 *Brit. Industr. Future* (Lib. Ind. Inq.) iii. v. 174 It is important to understand the causes of the limited degree of success which has attended the Whitley scheme.

Whitmanese (hwitmănī·z). [f. the name of Walt *Whitman* (1819–92), American poet + -ese.] The characteristic style or diction of Whitman. **Whitmane·sque** *a.*, characteristic or suggestive of Whitman or his poetry. **Whi·tmanism,** Whitman's metrical or poetical style; a feature of this. **Whi·tmanize,** *v. intr.*, to write in the manner of Whitman.

1893 Le Gallienne *Retrosp. Rev.* (1896) I. 213, 'I see twenty-two young men from Foster's watching me, and the trousers of the twenty-two young men' is irresistible Whitmanese. 1882 *Good Lit.* Sept. 2 Clever persons can manufacture Whitmanesque verse quite equal to the average of the original. 1889 *Pall Mall Gaz.* 25 Jan. 3/2 Having thus ..settled upon what one might call the *technique* of Whitmanism, he began [etc.]. 1894 *Nation* 7 June 433/1 One of the worst of Whitmanisms, the interlarding of foreign words. 1902 *Academy* 16 Aug. 173/1 Mr. Moody does not Whitmanise on the one hand, or follow the outworn Tennysonian convention on the other. 1923 W. De La Mare in *Edin. Rev.* Jan. 193 Eloquence and facility are the danger of Whitmanesque verse of this nature.

Whi·tsuntide, *v.* [f. the sb.] *intr.* To take a holiday at Whitsuntide.

1928 *Sunday Express* 27 May 12/4 Let us go Whitsuntiding together.

Whizz, *v.* Add: **2. c.** *transf.* To move in a lively manner; to progress well; to 'go strong'.

1902 Harben *Abner Daniel* 139 But I really believe you have fallen on a better thing than any I ever struck. I could make it whiz.

4. To pass along or round rapidly or with a whizzing sound.

1911 H. S. Harrison *Queed* i. 6 Delivery wagons whizzed corners and bumped on among them.

Whizzer. Add: **c.** A long resounding word.

1886 E. L. Dorsey *Midshipman Bob* i. x. 93 'Foretopgallant studdingsail-boom-tricing-line-block strap-thimble.' Ain't that a whizzer?

Whizzing, *vbl. sb.* **b. whizzing-blade** = *whizzing-stick.*

1905 *Rep. Brit. Assoc.* 529 The 'whizzing-blade' or, to give it its popular name, the 'bull-roarer'.

Who, *pron.* **3.** (Further example.)

1922 G. M. Trevelyan *Brit. Hist. 19th Cent.* xxiii. 373 The British people, when left to themselves, neither knew nor cared who massacred whom between the Danube and the Ægean.

4. *Who's who* (further transf. example). Also as *v. trans.*, to look up in *Who's Who.*

1929 *Times Lit. Suppl.* 18 Apr. 308/2 First he [the biographer] gets out of the way the 'Who's Who' of Wallace Williamson's career in a terse opening chapter. 1930 *London Mercury* Feb. 318 He knew all about them by now, for Sister Anne had 'Who's Who'd' them for a full hour the night before.

Whole. D. whole-hog, also *attrib.*, thorough, out-and-out; *whole-hoggism* (earlier example).

1838 P. Hone *Diary* I. 308 Three other thorough whole-hog men..have no..notion of political honesty. 1840 *Kentucky Rifle* 31 Oct., They'd be whole-hog *Tippecanoe Boys.* 1840 J. P. Kennedy *Quodlibet* 51 [They were] thorough-bred, whole-hog democrats. 1855 [Pray] *Mem. J. G. Bennett* 141 James Gordon Bennett..is a thorough-going, 'whole-hog' Jackson man. 1848 *Blackw. Mag.* July 54 Purge the land of moderatism and anti-whole-hog-ism.

2. a. *whole-life.*

1845 *Williams's Directory of Leeds* 46 Advt., One-third of the 'Whole Life' Premium may remain unpaid..as a Debt upon the Policy. 1881 *Harper's Mag.* Jan. 79/1 Never take a whole-life policy to embarrass the declining and unproductive years of life. 1907 *Jrnl. Soc. Arts* 8 Feb. 346/1 The premium for..a whole-life policy..is [etc.].

Whole-or-none. Applied *attrib.* to a method of dealing with things which does not admit parts or fractions or intermediate stages.

1927 P. B. Ballard *New Examiner* 183 In the whole-or-none method of marking there is nothing wrong.

Wholesale, *sb.*, *a.*, *adv.* Add: **4. c.** As *sb.*, a wholesale business.

1928 *Daily Express* 29 May 7/4 The ability of the wholesales to adopt methods of mass production..must be lessened if [etc.].

Who·lesaling, *ppl. a.* [-ing ².] That sells goods by wholesale.

1926 N. S. B. Gras in *Legacy of Middle Ages* 440 Although many merchants might prefer the wholesale trade, they were not allowed to be exclusively wholesaling merchants.

Wholly. 1. (Later example of wholely.)

1915 D. H. Lawrence *Rainbow* xii. 327 Then, and then only..could he act wholely, without cynicism and unreality.

Whomp (hwǫmp). [Echoic.] A loud outburst of sound.

1926 *Blackw. Mag.* May 595/2 Ever think of Piccadilly in the evening, and the 'whomp' of an orchestra starting up in some theatre?

Whoop, *v.* Add: **1.** Also, to shout (in support of someone).

1905 *N. Y. Even. Post* 4 Nov. 10 Anybody who knows anything will tell you that Cassidy cares not a rap whether McClellan wins. Openly, of course, Cassidy whoops for McClellan.

e. (Later examples.)

1903 *N. Y. Sun* 18 Nov. 4 Three boys broke into the Garden and began to whoop things up. They rolled about, bumping into men and women. 1911 R. D. Saunders *Col. Todhunter* v. 64 I'm..primed for a campaign that'll..set 'em to whoopin' things up for you to beat the band. 1919 L. F. Cody *Buffalo Bill* 296, I went around and told the Indians to whoop it up as they never did before.

f. To increase or raise.

1896 G. Ade *Artie* xiv. 130 Since he went to the front for me and got my salary whooped I've got to be with him. 1904 *N. Y. Sun* 8 Sept. 10 The bail was reduced to $10,000, but was whooped up to $15,000 when Larry was re-arrested.

Whoopee (hŭpī·). *U.S.* [f. Whoop *sb.*] Esp. in phr. *to make whoopee*, to rejoice noisily or hilariously: to have a good time.

1928 Gus Kahn (song) *Makin' Whoopee*, Another bride, another June, Another sunny honeymoon, Another season, another reason for making whoopee! 1929 *Chicago Tribune* 25 Feb. 12/4 English newspapers are making whoopee about an endowed sermon that has been preached once every year for 448 years. 1930 *Saturday Even. Post* 13 Dec. 25/1 Novelists portray him as the gin-drinking patron saint of whoopee.

Whooper. a. Also *whooper-up* (in quot. attrib.).

1904 *N. Y. Times* 4 July 1 The only candidate who has back of him a boom which is not characterized by 'whooper-up' methods.

Whoo·p-up. *U.S.* [f. *whoop it up*: Whoop *v.* 1 e.] A disturbance caused by revellers; a time of revelry.

1927 *Daily Express* 5 Oct. 3/3 The Ward Room is—apart from the 'whoops up' natural to lonely men—noted for its air of sober responsibility.

Whooshle (hwū·ʃ'l), *v.* [Imitative; cf. Whoosh.] *intr.* = Whoosh *v.*

1900 J. H. M. Abbott *Tommy Cornstalk* 59 Bang! went a Horse Artillery gun, and the shell 'whooshled' over our heads to check the advancing Boers.

Whump (hwǫmp), *sb.* [Imitative: cf. next and *Wump.] A sound made by a falling body.

1926 Galsworthy *Escape* i. ii. 32 Still—up on the ladder and down with a whump—it hits 'em [gentlemen] harder than it does the others.

Whump (hwǫmp), *v.* [Imitative.] *intr.* To make a deep hollow ringing sound. So **Whu·mping** *vbl. sb.*

1928 *Blackw. Mag.* Jan. 2/1 The occasional whumping and booming of war-gongs calling from village to distant village. *Ibid.* 5/1 The look-out sentry..whumped twice, briskly, on his band-gong.

Wicked, *a.*¹ Add: **4. d.** That which is wicked.

1919 Mary K. Bradby *Psycho-analysis* v. 205 The wicked or diabolical goes in order to express the divine.

Wicking, *sb.* (Earlier example.)

1846 *Rep. U.S. Comm. Patents* (1847) 220 This is combined with a small tube within it, through which the wicking is introduced, to cause the tallow to unite around the wicking.

Wi·ckless, *a.* [f. Wick *sb.*¹ + -less.] Not having a wick.

1921 *Chambers's Jrnl.* Dec. 830/2 A wickless stove with a single burner, upon which every operation can be performed that is practicable with a large gas-cooker.

Wicopy. (Earlier example.)

1704 *Providence* (R.I.) *Rec.* V. 244 Two trees growing out of one Roote called Wickupp trees.

Wide, *sb.* Add: **3. b.** Short for *wide vowel*, Wide *a.* 7 b.

1881 H. Sweet in *Trans. Philol. Soc.* 232 The wides must be old in South German, for in some of the Swiss dialects their lengthenings are still wide.

4. *Broke to the wide*: completely broke.

1919 W. J. Locke *Jorico* 46 'You're broke'..'To the wide,' said Nicholas. 1930 S. Maugham *Gentl. in Parlour* xliii. 253 I was about broke to the wide when they took me on.

Wide, *a.* Add: **8. b.** *Stock Exch.* Of a quotation: Having a big difference between the buying and selling prices.

1912 *Q. Rev.* July 100 The broker protests that the price is too wide.

12. a. Add: *wide-mindedness, -ringed* adj.

1927 A. H. McNeile *Introd. to N. T.* 103 The former was interested in the wide-mindedness and kindly spirit shown by Gentile Christians in the young Church at Antioch. 1922 *Encycl. Brit.* XXX. 34/1 Defects peculiar to coniferous timbers, such as spiral grain,..alternating hard and soft grains, low density, wide-ringed timber and brittle or lifeless timber.

Wide-open, *a.* [Wide *adv.* 6.]

1. Open to a wide extent.

1852–77 [see Wide *adv.* 6].

2. Free from limitations or restrictions; clear.

1902 G. H. Lorimer *Lett. Self-made Merchant* xi. 143 You have had a wide open chance during the last few months to pick up a good deal about the practical end of the business.

3. In which no restrictions are observed; characterized by overt law-breaking.

1903 O. Kildare *My Mamie Rose* 71 A number of dance-halls completed the boast of the day that New York City was a 'wide-open town'. 1905 Tarkington *In Arena* 5 In fact, he had the reputation of running a disorderly town, and the truth is, it *was* too wide open. 1910 *N. Y. Even. Post* 27 Oct. 1 Never in all that time has the town been so wide open as now...There are violations of the excise law ..being flaunted that are degrading this city.

4. *Fencing, Boxing*, etc. Off one's guard.

1915 Corri *30 Yrs. Boxing Referee* 150 Johnny Summers ..in an unguarded moment, left himself wide open and encountered one of the most decisive knock-out punches I ever saw.

5. As *adv.* Without concealment; openly.

1923 J. H. Cook *Old Frontier* 90 As usual in such towns, gambling houses could be easily found and they were run 'wide open'.

Wi·de-sprea·dly, *adv.* [f. Wide-spread + -ly ².] In a wide-spread manner.

1927 *Glasgow Herald* 31 Oct. 12 To express publicly, wide-spreadly, and emphatically their repudiation of Dr. Barnes's ..teaching.

Wifie. (Earlier example.)

1819 Keats *Lett.* (1931) 439 I intend to write a letter to your wifie.

Wig, *sb.*³ **5.** Add: **wig-stand, -table,** a stand or small table at which wigs were adjusted and powdered.

1915 F. W. Burgess *Antique Furniture* 212 The so-called *wig-stands providing puff-box and powder, and a ewer of rose-water and a bowl, essentials to a gallant of that day, are extremely interesting. 1923 Deeping *Secret Sanctuary* xviii, A mahogany *wig table for a dressing-table.

Wiggle, *sb.* (Earlier examples.)

1816 Paulding *Lett. fr. South* I. 235 They suffered their hair to grow into a mighty bunch behind, and walked with the genuine *Rutland wiggle*; that is to say, on tiptoe, and with a most portentous extension of the hinder parts. 1869 Louisa M. Alcott *Lit. Women* II. xxiv. 355 Rob's footstool had a wiggle in its uneven legs.

2. A small wriggling creature found in water.

1831 Buttrick *Trav.* 78 The water was very bad...After straining it would still exhibit live insects, which they call wiggles.

Wiggle, *v.* Add: **1. b.** To extricate or get oneself *out of* something by wiggling.

1927 Vachell *Dew of the Sea* etc. 260, I must wiggle out of the mess.

Wiggle-waggle, *sb.* Also **-woggle.** Add: **b.** = *Cake-walk 2.

1910 *Penny Guide Japan-British Exhib.* 25 Fun on the Wiggle Waggle. 1925 Aldous Huxley *Those Barren Leaves* ii. iii. 106 Merry-go-round, wiggle-woggle, flip-flap and the like are beyond the power of my magic to conjure up.

Wiggly, *sb.* [f. the adj.] = *Wiggle *sb.* 2.

1910 *Chambers's Jrnl.* June 374/2 Travellers in warm climates may often have noticed small insects..which disport themselves in the water with a wriggling motion, whence the name 'wigglies' or 'wrigglies' applied to them in the United States.

Wig-wag, *sb.* (Further examples.)

1910 *Chambers's Jrnl.* June 368/1 Communication is by flags or 'wig-wag' by day and lanterns at night. 1925 *Blackw. Mag.* Feb. 202/1 We don't dance any wig-wag dances here.

Wild. A. *adj.* **15. b.** *To blow wild*: of an oil-well, to pour forth a stream of oil which cannot be regulated or controlled.

1931 *Times* 18 Feb. 15/6 When the wells 'blow wild' the city is enveloped in a dark spray of oil.

B. *sb.* **4.** *To play the wild*: To behave in a careless or reckless manner: to act without restraint. *U.S.*

1849 J. B. Jones *Wild West Scenes* i. 10 But love can play the 'wild' with any young man. 1911 R. D. Saunders *Col. Todhunter* ix. 143 I'm shorely glad to get home. I been playin' the wild in St. Louis.

Wild cat. Add: **4. c.** Applied to a train or engine running in addition to those on the time-table. *U.S.*

1885 *Good Words* July 452/1 Every now and then the newspapers allude to 'wild-cat' trains...The 'wild-cat' is the slowest of all trains. It is only used for freight, and reaches its destination when it can, running whenever the line is clear, and shunting when a passenger train is due on the same track. 1888 *Missouri Republ.* 23 Feb. (Farmer) The Montreal night express was thrown from the track..by a wild-cat engine that had been turned loose..by an evil-disposed person. 1891 E. S. Ellis *Check No. 2134* xiii. 88 There was just one chance in a hundred of a wild cat engine approaching.

Wi·lding, *ppl. a.* [f. Wild *v.* + -ing ².] Running wild; extravagant.

1903 Hardy *Dynasts* i. i. iii. 20 Must the House listen to such wilding words As this proposal?

Wild man. 1. c. (Earlier example, in sing.)

1905 D. G. Phillips *Plum Tree* 266 And I wished for a 'wild man' as the candidate for governor.

Wile, *sb.* Add: **4.** *Comb.* as *wile-weaving.*

1897 Hardy *Well-Beloved* i. ii, Sometimes at night he dreamt that she was 'the wile-weaving Daughter of high Zeus' in person.

Wi·leless, *a.* [f. Wile *sb.* + -less.] Free from wiles.

1873 K. H. Digby *Last Year's Leaves* 167 Bowers..where we can have the wileless feast Of conversation, tender, holy.

Will, *sb.*¹ Add: **5. c.** (Further examples.)

1926 Bennett *Lord Raingo* ii. lxiv. 287 Andrew Clyth would go ahead with his chicane and his will-to-win and his ruthless egotism. 1931 F. L. Allen *Only Yesterday* ii. 18 Further to strengthen the will to give, Charlie Brickley of Harvard drop-kicked a football across Wall Street into the arms of Jack Yates of Yale.

24. a. *will-gymnastics.* **c. will-form,** a form on which a will may be made out.

1924 D. H. Lawrence *England, my England* 150 Say I want to see Mr. Whittle as soon as he can, and will he bring a *will-form. 1908 *Practitioner* Apr. 520 The treatment is largely one of occupation, therapy and *will-gymnastics.

Will, *v.*¹ **3. b.** Also, to remove or take away by a will or testament.

1926 *Harper's Mag.* Feb. 367/2 It is also one of the few remaining states where it is possible to-day for a father to will away, or 'bequeathe', a child, born or unborn, from the mother.

Will, *v.*² **3. c.** (Further example.)

1922 J. Y. Simpson *Man and Attainm. Immortality* xiv. 332 He showed the reality of temptation for Himself in thus willing His own will into unison with that of God.

Willet. (Earlier example.)

1855 *Knickerbocker Mag.* XLVI. 222 In the marshes the black or dusky duck, willet,..and clapper-rail or mud-hen rear their young.

Willies, *sb. pl.* *U.S slang.* A nervous feeling of discomfort; 'the creeps'.

1900 G. Bonner *Hard Pan* iii. 99 But it just gives me the willies to think of your being down on your luck. 1911 H. Quick *Yellowstone N.* x. 216 He..began to get the Willies. 1914 Gert. Atherton *Perch of Devil.* i. 76 Not old masters, though. They give me the willys. 1927 Vachell *Dew of the Sea* etc. 261 But I sure got the willies at thought of meeting you.

Willie-ized, *pa. pple.* Made into a 'Weary Willie'.

a 1909 'O. Henry' *Roads of Destiny* xxii. 366 Great skyrockets! but I hated to see Perry all corrupted and Willie-ized like that.

Wi·lliness. [f. Willy *a.* + -ness.] Wilfulness.

1889 *Chambers's Jrnl.* 14 Sept. 579/1 This excessive independence, this unchecked 'williness' of our young folks.

Will-o'-the-wisp, *v.* (Modern example.)

1926 Priestley *G. Meredith* v. 129 Woman..is far less likely than man to be Will-o'-the-Wisped away by sheer unreason masquerading as reason.

Willow oak. *U.S.* (See Willow *sb.* 6 c.)

1717 [see Willow *sb.* 6 c]. 1737 Brickell *Nat. Hist. N. Carolina* (1911) 89 *Willow-Oak* is a kind of *Water-Oak*, so called from its leaves, which very much resemble those of the *Willow*. 1784 J. Smyth *Tour U.S.* I. xii. 94 In this part of America there are seven different species of oak, viz. black-oak, white-oak, red-oak, Spanish-oak, willow-oak. 1817 S. R. Brown *Western Gaz.* 24 [There are] three species of willow oak, upland, swamp, and shingle. 1832 D. J. Browne *Sylva Amer.* 279 The willow oak, in favorable situations, attains the height of 50 or 60 feet with a diameter of 20 or 24 inches. 1875 *Field & Forest* I. 36 The Willow oak (*Q. phellos*) is rather frequent.

Willow-ware. 1. Articles woven with osiers.

1851 C. Cist *Cincinnati* 172 Baskets, cradles, wagons, and other willow-ware. 1880 *Harper's Mag.* June 30/1 We

find women employed in making..willow-ware and cane chairs.

2. (See Willow *sb.* 6 c.)

c 1885 [see Willow *sb.* 6 c]. 1893 W. K. Post *Harvard Stories* 109 It was like the bridge in a blue willow-ware plate. 1904 Ellen Glasgow *Deliverance* 58 The china consisted of some odd, broken pieces of old willow-ware.

Wiltshire. (*b*) read: an undivided side of bacon.

Wimble, *sb.* Add: **2. b.** An implement for twisting ropes; a throw-crook.

1874 Hardy *Far fr. Madding Crowd* xxii, Gathering up the fleeces and twisting ropes of wool with a wimble for tying them round.

Wimble, *v.*¹ Add: **3.** *trans.* To make (ropes of hay) with a wimble.

1874 Hardy *Far fr. Madding Crowd* x, 'What have you been doing?' 'Tending thrashing-machine, and wimbling haybonds'.

Wimbrel, var. Whimbrel.

1898 J. A. Gibbs *Cotswold Village* 102 There are wimbrels and curlews that have been shot here..stuffed and hung up in glass cases.

Win, *v.*¹ Add: **4. b.** Now freq. with *out* (cf. 12 d). Orig. *U.S.*

1889 *Kansas City T. & Star* 30 Mar., He took charge..of a part of Governor France's campaign here last October and won through. 1898 *Boston Transcript* 27 Sept. 4/5 Why will the newsgatherer insist upon saying that such a horse or such a man 'won out' when the 'won' without the 'out' tells the story? 1902 A. D. McFaul *Ike Glidden* v. 35 As long as a fellow's got some good horse sense..he can win out in the law business. 1911 'O. Henry' *Rolling Stones* (1915) 194 I'd rather see one of the same gang win out before I would an East-sider. 1924 Galsworthy *Forest* iii. 78 You, Lockyer—a soldier! One spurt and we'll win out. Come!

12. (Further example.)

1927 *Daily Express* 14 Dec. 13/5 It is good to know that Wodehouse's clever humour has won through.

Wind, *sb.*¹ **3. b.** (Further example.)

1886 *Encycl. Brit.* XXI. 605/2 To take the wind out of another's sails, to pass close to windward, as yachts sometimes do.

31. wind-balanced *a.*, applied to rotary gun-mountings on aircraft having a device which automatically compensates for the turning moment caused by air pressure on the guns; so **wind-balancing** *a.* and *vbl. sb.*; **wind-channel** = *wind-tunnel*; **wind-divide,** a ridge of high-pressure from which wind blows outwards on either side; **wind-firm** *a.*, adapted to withstand wind; **wind-flag,** a flag on a shooting-range designed to indicate the direction and force of the wind; **wind-jammer** (*c*), a jumper or pull-over made of weather-proof material; **wind-pouch** = *Wind-bag 1 d; **wind-sight,** a special arrangement of the back-sight of a rifle capable of adjustment to compensate for the effect of the wind on the bullet; **wind-tunnel,** an enclosed chamber for testing aircraft models; **wind-turbine,** a turbine driven by the wind.

1928 *Daily Tel.* 6 Mar. 6/3 Royalties not exceeding £7,500 to Messrs. Vickers, Ltd., for *wind-balanced ring mountings. 1928 Gamble *Story N. Sea Air Station* xiii. 219 A *wind-balancing gear was provided which relieved the observer of much fatigue at high altitudes. 1918 Cowley & Levy *Aeronautics* iv. 98 A series of experiments are conducted in the *wind channel to test the lift and drag for different forms of sections. 1922 Kendrew *Climates of Continents* 203 A tongue of high pressure projects from the Atlantic over the centre of Europe towards Siberia. It is of only slight intensity, but sufficient to form a '*wind-divide'. 1895 Fisher *Schlich's Man. Forestry* IV. 300 They are used as severance cuttings to induce the edge trees of adjoining woods to form *wind-firm trees. 1923 Kipling *Land & Sea Tales* 181 He pointed towards the stiff-tailed *wind-flags. 1930 *Even. Standard* 20 Aug. 2 Advt., Thousands of golfers wear the Barker '*Windjammer' and report it to be a splendid garment. 1903 W. H. Pycraft in *Knowledge* Jan. 2/1 Finally the head is thrown back, and the *wind-pouch or air-sac as it is called, is inflated to an enormous size, almost burying the head therein. 1923 Kipling *Land & Sea Tales* 182 Give your *wind-sight another three degrees, Walters. 1919 A. Klemin *Text-bk. Aeronaut. Engin.* i. 7 From *wind-tunnel tests, the engineer may obtain data for the 'balancing' up of an aeroplane. 1922 *Encycl. Brit.* XXX. 19/1 Extensive wind-tunnel research has been carried out to find the best cross-section shape of wings. 1910 *Chambers's Jrnl.* Mar. 207/2 Should there be an excessive wind-velocity, the special tails fitted to the *wind-turbine tend to bring the wheel out of the wind.

Wind, *v.*¹ Add: **7. f.** To lead or cause to flow in a curved or sinuous course.

1921 *Times Lit. Suppl.* 8 Sept. 577/2 Who will, may have his *ferme ornée*, lay out his walks and wind his waters.

Wind, *v.*² Add: **5. b.** To put in good wind by training.

1870 *Pall Mall Gaz.* 12 Aug. 10 A pointer..requires to be both winded and hardened.

Windage. 3. Also *attrib.*

1922 *Encycl. Brit.* XXX. 35/2 'Windage loss', or the power absorbed by the engine itself.

4. The action or process of winding, or raising and lowering by winches, etc.

1911 *Chambers's Jrnl.* Apr. 219/1 Some of the managers have attempted to accelerate the haulage and windage.

Wind-bag. Add: **1. d.** A sac or cavity in the throat of certain birds that can be inflated.

1903 W. H. Pycraft in *Knowledge* Jan. 1/2 The development of purely ornamental wind-bags, used as adjuncts in courtship.

Wind-ball. (Later example.)

1883 Stallybrass tr. *Grimm's Teut. Myth.* III. 1000 It recalls to my mind the windball of the demons. *footn.* Witches confessed they had been converted into balls, and gone bobbing round stark naked on tables and benches.

Wind-break, *sb.* **1.** (Earlier example.)

1861 *Trans. Ill. Agric. Soc.* IV. 479 These trees, which are valuable as shade and as wind-breaks, should be planted.

Wind-breaker = Wind-break 1.

1873 J. H. Beadle *Undevel. West* xxxiv. 730 If there is any wind-breaker northwest, between there and Alaska, I had no evidence of it.

Wind-cutter. (Further examples.) Also *attrib.* So **Wind-cutting** *a.*

1894 *Daily News* 5 Mar. 5/3 These engines..are called wind-cutters, the fore-part, including the funnel, presenting a sharp blade like the stem of a ship. 1901 *Engineer* 26 Apr. 432/1 This [cab of an engine] is very spacious and convenient, well lighted, and has a wind-cutter, prow-shaped front. 1907 *Daily Chron.* 21 Nov. 7/4 It [a hat] is designed with wind-cutting peak and detachable dust protection.

Wind-drift. Add: **b.** The action of wind currents.

1898 *Geog. Jrnl.* June 662 The sand so produced is rounded by wind-drift in an unmistakable manner, the grains being entirely different from those of sea-sand.

Wind-gall ². (Earlier example.)

1823 J. F. Cooper *Pilot* I. ii. 19 There be streaked wind-galls in the offing, that speak..plainly..to shorten sail.

Windlet (wi·ndlėt). [f. Wind *sb.*¹ + -let.] A light puff of wind.

1914 H. D. Shawcross *Nature & Idealist* 52 A calm level sea, broken by zephyr-like windlets into a myriad wrinkled ripples.

Windmill, *sb.* **6.** Add: **windmill airplane, plane,** a type of flying machine supported by vanes revolving horizontally.

1928 *Daily Express* 10 Aug. 11/4 A 'windmill' airplane is to fly the channel. 1928 *Times* 24 Sept. 10/4 Known as the 'Windmill Plane', the Autogiro depends for its lift upon four vanes rotated..more or less horizontally.

Windmill, *v.* Add: **b.** *trans.* and *intr.* To move (one's arms or legs) in a manner suggestive of a windmill.

1927 W. E. Collinson *Contemp. Engl.* 18 At this school we had our first taste of fighting or rather windmilling with the arms. 1928 *Daily Express* 6 Nov. 8 They..set about their efforts again, windmilling his arms and legs until he gasped with unconscious exhaustion.

Window, *sb.* **4.** Also of newspapers.

1916 H. G. Wells *Mr. Britling* v. 160 A comparison of headlines..in the white windows of the newspapers through which those..looked out upon the world.

5. a. *window-card, weight.*

1910 *Blackw. Mag.* Apr. 575/2 In ill-lit little streets blue with John Burns's *window-cards. 1776 Mrs. Drinker *Jrnl.* (1889) 41 Two or three men called to look at our *window weights—found them to be of iron.

d. window-case (*b*), a show-case for use in a window; **window-casing** = *window-case* (in Dict.); **window-garden,** flower-pots or boxes on a window-ledge or sill; **window-trimmer** *U.S.* = *window-dresser*; **window-trimming** *U.S.* = *window-dressing.*

1898 L. Fletcher *Introd. Study Rocks* 113 The specimens ..are arranged in the *window-cases as follows. 1853 B. F. Taylor *Jan. & June* (1871) 205 Here are so-and-so's initials on the *window-casing. 1883 *Harper's Mag.* Dec. 32/1, I was knocking on the window-casing to make you hear, but you seemed preoccupied. 1885 Cable *Dr. Sevier* xii. 81 Where the asylumed widows of 'St. Anna's' could glance down into it over their poor little *window-gardens. 1910 *Chambers's Jrnl.* Aug. 512/1 Mr. W. W. Sawyer..was formerly a *window-trimmer in the cities of Chicago, Milwaukee, and Portland. 1926 *Publishers' Weekly* 22 May 1676/1 *Window-trimming.

Windowy, *a.* Add: **2.** Having many or large windows.

1863 'Gail Hamilton' *Gala-Days* 353 The homes of the students, which seem to have been built..solely to furnish shelter,—angular, formal, stiff, windowy. 1888 *Harper's Mag.* June 130/2 Several large, ugly, windowy wooden bulks grew up for shoe shops.

Wind-up (wi·nd₁ʊp), *sb.*² *slang.* [f. phr. *to get the wind up* Wind *sb.*¹ 10 b.] A state of nervous excitement.

1922 *Encycl. Brit.* XXX. 64/1 Many other pilots..have been through the same stages of 'wind-up'.

Windy, *a.* **9.** Add: **Windy City,** Chicago.

1890 *Congress. Rec.* 21 Apr. 3598/1 Descriptions of a 'Windy City' on the west shore of a lake which all know to be flat and low. 1908 K. McGaffey *Show-Girl* 58 Chicago is sure rightly named when they call it the Windy City.

Wine, *sb.*¹ Add: **2. b.** *U.S.* (See quot.)

1927 J. W. Johnson *Autobiog. Ex-Coloured Man* vii. 107 For his friends..he bought nothing but wine—in sporting circles 'wine' means champagne.

c. The name of a dark red colour. (cf. 7 c.)

1923 *Daily Mail* 30 Apr. 1 Advt., Colours include Cerise-Jade,..Navy, Wine and Grey.

Winful, *a.*² (Modern example.)

1844 Mrs. Browning *Child Asleep*, Poems II. 126 From his slumber, virtue winful Floweth outward with increase.

Wing, *sb.* **6. e.** (Further example.)

1928 *Daily Mail* 25 July 9/3 The force of the impact threw the car temporarily out of control, but with its front wings crumpled it continued its dash towards London.

Wing, *sb.* **19. Wing-and-wing** (earlier examples).

1781 *Maryland Hist. Mag.* V. 129 We were now wing and wing, that is right before the wind. 1828 J. F. Cooper *Red Rover* I. iii. 84 That..schooner would make more way going wing-and-wing than jammed up on a wind.

20. a. *wing-bone, -collar.*

1927 *Daily Express* 31 Aug. 8/3 It..is shaped like the wing-bone of a chicken. 1911 *Chambers's Jrnl.* Mar. 190/1 Wing-collars, brown shoes, and obtrusive socks..would destroy the prevailing scheme of colouring.

21. wing-dam *sb.* (earlier examples); **wing-flutter,** flutter or vibration of the wings of an aeroplane; **wing-loading,** the fact of having considerable load or weight in the wings of an aeroplane; **wing-over,** a lateral turning movement of an aeroplane; **wing-poke** (see quot.); **wing-spread** (*a*), the extent of a bird's wings when spread; (*b*), the surface or area of an aeroplane's wings; **wing-walking,** walking on the wings of an aeroplane in the air.

1808 in Fessenden *Pills Poetical* (1809) 36 All his rhetorick was directed toward election districts, and *wingdam bills, and seconding motions. 1850 N. Kingsley *Diary* 140 Five went down to work in the river and began a wing-dam. 1927 *Daily Tel.* 21 Jan. 10/7 *Wing-flutter is supposed to have disastrous results only when it leads to wing-breakage. 1912 *Q. Rev.* July 246 A range of this amount is obtained entirely by proportioning the position of the wing masses, the wing-curve and the *wing-loading. 1928 *Morn. Post* 20 Oct. 9/3 One of the passengers..got panicky when the pilot executed a '*wing-over'. 1910 H. G. Wells *Hist. Mr. Polly* i. 8 His collar was chosen from stock, and with projecting corners, technically a '*wing-poke'. 1898 'N. Blanchan' *Bird Neighbors* 143 Bank Swallow...About an inch shorter than the English sparrow, but apparently much larger because of its wide *wing-spread. 1912 *Q. Rev.* July 231 If the 1000 lb. aeroplane is to travel slower, it must have a larger wing-spread. 1928 *Even. News* 5 May 5/3 There will be *wing walking and a parachute drop by Miss June.

Wingedness. (Later example.)

1913 H. Bateson *Mendel's Prin. Heredity* 172 Here we see that the one 'dose' of wingedness—as we may call it—sufficed only to bring the wings to half the full size, and two 'doses' are needed to develop them properly.

Wingy, *a.* Add: **2. b.** (See quot.)

1912 C. Mathewson *Pitching* x. 218 The diamond at Marlin is skinned—that is, made of dirt, although it is billed as a grass infield, and the ball gets 'wingy'. Little pieces of the cover are torn loose by contact with the rough dirt.

Winner. 2. (Further example.)

1927 *Daily Express* 10 June 13/5 Miss Wills' point score must have included a record number of outright winners.

Winter, *sb.*¹ Add: **5. a. winter-fall,** the coming of winter; **winter-killed** *pa. pple.* (earlier example); also **winter-kill** *v. trans.*

1922 A. E. Housman *Last Poems* (1930) 32 And *winterfalls of old Are with me from the past. 1817 S. R. Brown *Western Gaz.* 49 That wheat..never gets *winter-killed or smutty. 1849 *Presid. Mess. Congress* II. 653 The..snow which lies upon the ground nearly six months in the year would be likely to '*winter-kill' it.

b. winter-gnat, a gnat appearing in winter; **winter-sleeper,** a hibernating animal.

1926 *Nat. Hist. Oxford Distr.* 257 Four species of '*Winter-Gnats' are always common from autumn to spring. 1911 J. A. Thomson *Biol. Seasons* iv. 333 A survey of the *Winter-sleepers seems to show that the life-saving reaction must have arisen by the natural selection of variants in the direction of the hibernating habit.

Winterer. Add: **1. c.** A hibernating animal.

1930 *Observer* 6 Apr. 24/2 Sudden warmth, such as may awake a winterer too precociously.

Wi·nterishly, *adv.* [f. Winterish + -ly ².] In a manner suggestive of winter.

1905 *Smart Set* Oct. 26/1 Though by good rights the day might have been winterishly cold it was of a balmy mildness.

Wi·ntersome, *a.* [f. Winter *sb.*¹ + -some.] = Wintry.

1864 Trollope *Small Ho. Allington* xlv, The fourteenth of February in London was quite as black, and cold, and as wintersome as it was at Allington.

Wipe, *v.* **9. e.** (Earlier example.)

1888 *Detroit Free Press* Aug. (Farmer) The Scroggin boy was as tough as a dogwood knot. He'd wipe up the ground with him; he'd walk all over him.

Wi·pe-out. [f. *to wipe out*: Wipe *v.* 6 d.] In wireless telegraphy or telephony: Obliteration of other signals by signals on a particular wave length. Used *attrib.* esp. of an area or zone round a transmitting station within which the strength of signals from that station is sufficient to obliterate extraneous interruptions.

1921 *Wireless World* IX. 13/1 With radiotelephony the case is worse, as the wipe out is continuous if it occurs at all. *Ibid.*, You get what is called a 'wipe out' effect. 1929 *Encycl. Brit.* IV. 218/2 Within a 'wipe-out' area uninterrupted service can be guaranteed, unless the interference is produced by listeners themselves. 1929 *Daily Express* 7 Nov. 14/3 The new types of constructors' sets..are free from trouble, and, except in the 'wipe out' zone, will give perfectly satisfactory results.

Wiper. 4. (Later example.)

1863 'E. Kirke' *Southern Friends* iv. 67 [He] planted what the 'profession' call a 'wiper' just behind Tom's left ear.

5. (Further example.)

1926 *Gloss. Electr. Terms* (Brit. Engin. Stand.) 274 *Wiper*, that portion of the moving member of a selector or other similar device which engages with the contacts of a bank.

Wire, *sb.* Add: **2. d.** A wire stretched across a race-course at the winning-post. Also *fig.*

1902 A. D. McFaul *The Gliddon* xxii. 202 Then came the decisive moment, when the conquering colt swept under the wire by a nose ahead of the trotter. *a* 1909 'O. Henry' *Roads of Destiny* xviii. 301 You remember how I brought Coughlin under the wire for leader of the nineteenth.

e. *To get under the wire of* (fig.), to fulfil the conditions for inclusion in (a particular category).

1929 M. C. Work *Compl. Contract Bridge* v. 75 There are some hands which may just 'get under the wire' of the above definitions.

15. c. *wire-milker* (see Milk *v.* 4 d), *-nippers.*

1899 Cutcliffe Hyne *Further Adv. Capt. Kettle* vi. 104 The *wire-milkers. 1916 Boyd Cable *Action Front* 119 The *wire nippers were in place.

16. *wire-walking* (example).

1898 *Pearson's Mag.* Sept. 332 *Wire-walking..must always retain a greater amount of fascination.

Wire, *v.* **2. c.** (Further example.)

1774 J. Wesley *Lett.* (1931) vi. 104 You must wire over the cupola.

Wired, *ppl. a.* Add: **2. b.** Provided with a telephone.

1930 E. E. Hunt *Audit Amer.* 20 In 1913 there were only 48 wired homes per 1,000 of the non-farm population.

Wireless. b. *attrib.* and *Comb.* (Further examples.)

1901 *Chambers's Jrnl.* May 345/2 A wireless telegraphic station has been established at the Lizard in Cornwall. 1909 *Ibid.* July 428/2 At Aldershot..there is a powerful wireless station. 1912 *Ibid.* Jan. 60/1 Ten or twelve years ago the only wireless telegraphists in existence were a few scientific experts and their assistants. 1929 W. J. Locke *Jorice* 66 He developed..a marvellous installation out of a cheap wireless set. 1929 W. E. Collinson *Spoken Engl.* 54 Please renew the dog-licence and the wireless-licence.

c. Short for *wireless set, wireless telegram.*

1926 Galsworthy in *Scribner's Mag.* Aug. 192/1 Going home to have a look at Kit and send Fleur a wireless, he passed four musicians.

Wirelessed, *ppl. a.* [f. Wireless *v.* + -ed [2].] Sent or received by wireless telegraphy or telephony.

1915 *Chambers's Jrnl.* Oct. 661/2. 1931 *Statesman* (Calcutta) 5 Dec., A practical demonstration of flying tuition was given by a pilot in the air obeying the wirelessed instructions of a lecturer on the ground.

Wirelessly, *adv.* (Further example.)

1922 *Daily Mail* 17 Nov. 8 The French are experimenting with an extraordinarily ingenious device for governing the ascent of a wirelessly controlled air-bomb.

Wire-puller. (Earlier example.)

1833 in *Doc. Hist. Amer. Ind. Soc.* VIII. (1910) 340 Wire-pullers..for the furtherance of..party interest.

Wirework. Add: **3.** Wire-walking.

1928 *Daily Express* 13 June 13/3, I learned acrobatics, wire work, dancing, and juggling.

Wi·rework, *v.* [f. Wire-worker 2 b.] *trans.* To influence by pulling wires.

1843 J. Q. Adams *Diary* (1929) 547 Mr. James Monroe was recalled by President Washington through Thomas Pickering wireworked by Alexander Hamilton.

Wire-worker. 2. b. (Later examples.)

1855 [Pray] *Mem. J. G. Bennet* 121 The wire-workers among the Anti-masons were visited with the severest inflictions of satire and ridicule. 1883 Shields *S.S. Prentiss* 199 The resemblance between this last beast [a baboon] and one of the noted wire-workers of the day was so striking that the bystanders recognized the hit.

Wise, *a.* **3. b.** (Earlier examples.)

1896 G. Ade *Artie* ii. 14, I told him that when he wanted to get wise to what was in my hand all he had to do was to dig up his bit and come in. 1904 *Bookman* May 248 In the favoured locution of the hour, he 'put them wise', and helped them to a clear understanding of the situation. 1907 Rex Beach *Barrier* viii. (1908) 113 But who put ye wise to this thing, in the first place? 1913 Bennett *Regent* x, The police have been put wise.

Wise, *v.*[2] (Earlier examples.)

1905 Rex Beach *Pardners* iv. (1912) 107, I cast the bad eye on the boys to wise 'em up. 1915 H. L. Wilson *Ruggles of Red Gap* ii. (1917) 25, I just thought I'd wise you up beforehand.

Wise crack. *U.S.* [*Crack *sb.* 5.] A smart sententious saying; a clever witticism. So **Wi·se-crack** *v. intr.*, to make 'wise cracks'; **Wi·se-cracker; Wi·se-cracking** *vbl. sb.*

1924 P. Marks *Plastic Age* 28 The lights flashed on and the crowd filed out, 'wise-cracking' about the picture. *Ibid.* 113 Carl the flippant, the voluble, the 'wise-cracker', lost his tongue. 1926 *Scribner's Mag.* Aug. 117/2 They have been makin' wise-cracks about His Majesty. 1928 *Daily Express* 15 Mar. 2/3 The audience had been amused by wise-crack dialogue of the wonderful American variety. 'That guy's so crooked the tears run down his back', was one remark. 1928 'Rebecca West' *Strange Necessity* 296 Miss Francis Newman's first novel, named with so sad an example of the higher wise cracking, *The Hard-Boiled Virgin.* 1930 *Publishers' Weekly* 8 Mar. 1267 The 1930 super-dreadnought wisecracker.

Wish, *v.* **1.** (*f*). (Further example.)

1926 *Publishers' Weekly* 22 May 1725/1 That is why we are able to wish that good job on him.

Wisp, *sb.*[1] **5. e.** (Further example.)

1927 Macpherson *Mod. Astron.* 74 Highly significant was the discovery [on Saturn] by Lowell of 'wisps' similar to the wisps of Jupiter—filamentous streaks between the belts, ..after the manner of the lacings of a sail.

Wisp, *v.* Add: **4. b.** To hang in wisps.

1922 A. S. M. Hutchinson *This Freedom* ii. ix. 164 Her face flushed; her hat awry; her hair escaped and wisped about her eyes and on her shoulders. She was drunk.

Witch, *sb.*[2] **5. a.** Add: *witch-proof* adj.; **b.** **witch-ball** (*b*), a ball of coloured glass formerly hung in a house to keep witches away; **witch-brooch,** a brooch worn as a charm against witches; **witch-top** = sense 4 d.

1927 *Daily Express* 4 Apr. 5/4 The old-fashioned, gleaming *witchball of brilliantly-coloured glass..is being copied as a lamp vase and fitted for electric light. 1913 *Hastings's Encycl. Relig. & Ethics* VI. 559/1 Such amulets..were also known in Scotland as '*witch-brooches'. 1929 *Sunday Express* 13 Jan. 3/4 Many a successful business man..will drive to his modern office in the most luxurious of up-to-date motor-cars which has first of all been made '*witch-proof' with small amulets nailed to the dashboard. 1898 Posselt *Rec. Impr. Textile Mach.* i. 19 Looms having *witch-tops, i.e. device for raising the harness.

Wi·tch-doctoring, *vbl. sb.* [f. Witch-doctor + -ing [1].] The business of witch-doctors.

1927 Shaw in *Sunday Express* 7 Aug. 7/7 The dismal survivals of augury and witch-doctoring.

Witcher (wi·tʃəɹ). [f. Witch *v.* + -er [1].] One who fascinates or bewitches.

1928 *Sunday Dispatch* 29 July 3/4 Miss Lily Elsie, the exotic foreign witcher.

Witch-hopple. *U.S.* The North American wayfaring tree or hobble-bush, *Viburnum lantanoides.*

1840 Hoffman *Greyslaer* ii. xi. 44 Tangled thickets of moosewood and wytch-hopple, gave now the springy footing the tired hunter loves. 1891 *Amer. Folk-Lore* IV. 148 Cornus Canadensis was *Pudding Berry*; Viburnum lantanoides, *Witch Hopple.* 1906 *N.Y. Even. Post* Sat. Suppl. 10 Nov. 1 The undergrowth consists chiefly of witchhopple and moosewood, with the broad, coarse leaves of the witch-hopple predominating.

Witcho·logist. [f. Witch *sb.* + -(o)logist.] One who studies witches or witchcraft.

1861 E. Lynn Linton *Witch Stories* 45 The doom dealt out to the witch who slew was equally allotted to the witch who saved. Yet the witchologists made a difference between the two.

Witful, *a.* **1.** (Modern example.)

1924 *Countries of World* I. 639/2 The women deck these stands with witful skill.

Withal. A. *adv.* Add: **3.** *Naut.* More or less; if anything.

1900 *Law Rep., Prob. & Adm.* 39 The Dalmatia had been navigating up the Thames on the south side of the river withal.

Withdraw·nness. [f. Withdrawn + -ness.] Withdrawn or retired character.

1927 *Public Opinion* Feb. 102/1 He has the curiosity and interest of a young man and has none of the settled habits and introspection and withdrawnness of an old man.

Witherer. (Further example.)

1927 *Daily Express* 12 Sept. 3/5 British engineers have devised machinery which embodies a new process of withering the green tea leaf. This 'witherer' will be erected on a tea-planting estate in Ceylon.

Wive, *v.* **5.** (Later example.)

1862 Lowell *Biglow P.* Ser. ii. iii. Let., Poems (1912) 318/2 Any drab would suffice to wive such pitiful adventurers.

Wiz, U.S. abbrev. of Wizard.

1924 W. M. Raine *Troubled Waters* xiii. 142 Millie done fixed my game laig up with that ointment good as new. I want to tell you-all that girl is a wiz. 1928 Sinclair Lewis *Man who Knew Coolidge* i. 36 Cousin Ed—he thinks he's such a wiz at cars, but Lord love you, he couldn't locate that squeak.

Woady (wōu·di), *a.* [f. Woad *sb.*[1] + -y.] Painted or smeared with woad.

1909 H. G. Wells *Ann Veronica* ii. 40 Ancestresses..must have danced through a brief and stirring life in the woady buff.

Wobbegong (wǫ·bĭgǫŋ). Also wobbygong, wobegong. [Native name.] The Australian carpet-shark, *Crossorhinus barbatus.*

1852 Mundy *Antipodes* (1857) 89 The most hideous to behold of the shark tribe is the wobegong, or woe-begone, as the fishermen call it. 1917 *Chambers's Jrnl.* Sept. 588/1 There is also the well-known wobbygong, a creature of extraordinary and beautiful colouring.

Wobble, *v.* **5.** Add: **wobble-energy** = *wobble-heat.*

1912 F. Soddy *Matter & Energy* v. 126 There must be continual readjustments, as the temperature is rising and falling, between the path-energy, spin-energy, and *wobble-energy.

Woe. B. *sb.* **6.** Add: *woe-monger.*

1927 *Daily Express* 1 June 8/2 We have no use for the pessimists, no patience with the woe-mongers.

Woffling, var. Waffling *ppl. a.*

1927 *Chambers's Jrnl.* Mar. 168/2 Almost immediately there was a woffling swell of hounds' cry.

Wolf, *sb.* **10. a.** *wolf trap* (earlier examples).

1642 *New Plymouth Laws* 70 All the Townes..shall make woolfe Trapps and bayte them and looke unto them dayly. 1684 *Plymouth Rec.* 179 Soe to a red oake tree neare the woolf trape.

Wolfer. 1. (Earlier example.)

1871 *Rep. Indian Affairs* (1872) 410 A regular stampede took place out of that section of the country of 'Wolfers' and whiskey traders.

Wolf-fish. (Later example.)

1871 *Amer. Naturalist* V. 400 The Wolf-fish (*Anarrhicas vomerinus*) is not at all particular as to its food.

Wolfian, *a.*[2] (Earlier example.)

1824 De Quincey *Rosicrucians & Free-masons* in *Lond. Mag.* Jan. 5/1 Was the Iliad the work of one mind, or (on the Wolfian hypothesis) of many?

Wolfish, *a.* Add: **2. b.** In sense 8 b of Wolf *sb.*

1902 *Grove's Dict. Mus.* IV. 89/1 Bad Tenors are worse than bad violins; they are unequal and 'wolfish.'

Wolf pen. *U.S.* A strong box made of logs used for trapping wolves.

1647 *Watertown Rec.* 12 The Towne gave: to John Witherel: there Right in the palisado that inclosed the woulfe pen. 1682 *Derby* (Conn.) *Rec.* 130, 20 acres of pastor land above Jonases woollf pin in yͤ Neck. 1847 H. Howe *Hist. Coll. Ohio* 275 Wolf pens were about 6 feet long, 4 wide and 3 high, formed like a huge square box, of small logs, and floored with puncheons. 1866 C. H. Smith *Bill Arp* 129 They marched me to the wolf pen and there I stayed till the fuss was over.

Wolfy (wu·lfi), *a.* [f. Wolf *sb.* + -y.] Resembling or suggestive of wolves.

1838 Drake *Tales & Sk.* 36, I say, Mr. Jack-of-knaves, it looks rather wolfy in these parts. 1839 J. Plumbe *Sk. Iowa* 59, I might find some of the law-makers of Wisconsin arrayed in wild cat caps and hunting shirts, some of them, also, rather 'wolfy about the head and shoulders'.

Woman, *sb.* **6. c.** Also *woman-proof* adj.

1926 C. Barry *Detective's Holiday* 94 He himself was woman-proof!

9. a and **b.** (Additional examples.)

1878 *Harper's Mag.* Mar. 602/2 The established physicians shook their heads. They never believed in 'women doctors'. 1849 F. Douglas *Life* 119 We have men-stealers for ministers, and women-whippers for missionaries.

Womera, var. Woomera.

Wonder, *sb.* **9.** Add: *wonder-dance, -gleam, -life, -song, -woman.*

1924 A. J. Small *Frozen Gold* 211 By the time the aurora ceased its *wonder dances. 1929 Bridges *Test. Beauty* iv. 1352 The shifting hues That sanctify the silent dawn with *wonder-gleams. *Ibid.* iii. 568 With what other numberless *wonder-lives of the Saints they wrote. 1924 A. J. Small *Frozen Gold* 223 All the *wonder-songs of the South. 1927 Conan Doyle *Case Bk. of Sher. Holmes* 15 A *wonder-woman in every way.

10. b. *wonder-fine.*

1929 Bridges *Test. Beauty* i. 647 Not to these look we with grateful pleasure or satisfaction of soul, wonderfine tho' they be.

Wo·nderlandish, *a.* [f. Wonderland + -ish.] Pertaining to, connected with, or suggestive of wonderland.

1929 J. B. Priestley *Good Comp.* 590 He was beginning to feel wonderlandish again, what with Mr. Memsworth and the champagne.

Wo·nder-working, *vbl. sb.* [f. Wonder *sb.* + Working *vbl. sb.*] Performance of wonders.

1900 Elworthy *Horns of Honour* iii. 180 There is some confusion about the several stories told of its [the hand of glory's] wonder-working.

Wonk (wǫŋk). [f. next.] In phr. *all of a wonk*, nervous, upset.

1918 *Chambers's Jrnl.* May 299/1, I feel all of a doo-dah, all of a wonk.

Wonky (wǫ·ŋki), *a. slang.* [Fanciful.] Shaky, trembling, unsound.

1925 E. Wallace *Strange Countess* ix. 83 Financial adviser to some heads of departments, whose accounts went a little wonky. 1929 P. Gibbs *Hidden City* xvi. 79 It had made his heart jump in a wonky sort of way.

Wood, *sb.*[1] **5. c.** (Further example.)

1906 *N.Y. Even. Post* 10 Feb., Many publishers as far back as five or six years ago were in the habit of saying, 'We'll give rag-time a few months more, and then to the woods for it. It's worn out'.

i. *To be in the wood*: to be a possible issue of a particular situation.

1904 *Hartford Courant* 24 June 10 Probably if it were in the wood for the Russians to defeat the Japanese where the two sides are fairly matched, he would have won it.

9. b. *wood-box* (earlier example).

1850 S. Judd *R. Edney* ix. 135 The Old Man romanced with the fire, making it seem how he could graduate it exactly to the necessities of the room, and the state of the *wood-box.

10. wood-corder *U.S.*, a person engaged in the cording of wood; **wood-flat** *U.S.*, a raft or flat-bottomed boat used for transporting wood; so **wood-float; wood-road,** a road or path through woods; **wood-saw** (examples); **wood-sawyer** (earlier and later examples).

1681 *Boston Town Rec.* VII. 143 Chosen..Overseers of *Wood Corders. 1781 *Baltimore Town Rec.* 43 The Commissers had it [the oath] administred to him and afterwards appointed him Wood-corder. 1850 *Knickerbocker Mag.* XXXVI. 205 When be has the long wand, he is a wood-corder. 1785 *Maryland Hist. Mag.* XX. 42 He hath gone up and down frequently in battans, scows and *wood-flats. 1883 'Mark Twain' *Life Miss.* xx. 237 The Pennsylvania was creeping along,..towing a wood-flat which was fast being emptied. 1847 H. Howe *Hist. Coll. Ohio* 224 There was no boats at hand, except a few large and unmanageable *wood-floats. 1821 J. F. Cooper *Spy* vii. (1831) 81 The English captain took the advice of this mysterious being and finding a *wood-road..turned down its direction. 1863 Susan Hale *Lett.* 14 For if you should wish a short description of the wood-road by Stillins's, I could give it to you in one word—viz.: *Raspberries.* 1891 *Century Mag.* Apr. 921, I moved camp, following the wood-road to the summit. 1816 *Austin Papers* (1924) I. 264, 1 *Wood Saw. 1849 *Knickerbocker Mag.* XXXIV. 537/1 With this he put down his wood-saw. 1884 'Mark Twain' *Huck. Finn* vi. 39, I found an old rusty wood-saw without any handle. 1815 *N. Amer. Rev.* II. 143 Deaths by Violence...In New York Mr. John Wood, killed in the street by Patrick Hart, a *wood-sawyer, with a stick of wood. 1891 Mary E. W. Freeman *N. Engl. Nun* 43 Matilda's antecedents had come of wood-sawyers and garden-laborers.

b. wood bee (later example); **wood buffalo** (earlier example); **wood cat** (earlier mod. example); **wood grouse** (later example); **wood-hog** *U.S.*, a variety of pig which feeds in the woods.

1836 *Southern Lit. Messenger* II. 96 The *wood-bee revels on their sweets, And 'neath their leaves the bright Fay sleeps. 1837 T. Simpson *Narr. Discoveries* (1843) 60 We saw three moose-deer on the top of one of the hills; and their tracks, and those of the *wood-buffalo, were numerous in every direction. 1791 J. Long *Voyages* 41 The country every where abounds with wild animals, particularly bears, moose and other deer,..otters, martins, minx, *wood cats, racoons, [etc.]. *a* 1861 T. Winthrop *John Brent* xxii. 245 The brace of *wood grouse he had shot that morning. 1805 Parkinson *Tour* 290 The real American hog is what is termed the *wood-hog: they are long in the leg, narrow on the back, short in the body, flat on the sides, with a long snout [etc.]. 1840 *Cultivator* VII. 81 The next fall, *mast* was plenty, and 'wood hogs' were fat.

c. wood betony (later example); **wood sanicle,** the common sanicle, *Sanicula europæa.*

1886 *Harper's Mag.* Dec. 99/1 The wood-betony, it is called—to select its worthier title—a common early flower of our woods. 1857 Anne Pratt *Flowering Plants & Ferns* III. 12 S[*anicula*] *Europæa* (Wood Sanicle).

Woodbine[2] (wu·dbəin). A cigarette of the *Wild Woodbine* brand.

1915 in A. G. Heath *Lett.* (1917) 134 [He] won't even send me a Woodbine. 1921 G. MacDonald in *Country Heart* Oct.–Dec. 127 We who consume these things—small-beer and woodbines—do rank..as souls pawned to pay for these things. 1924 H. de Sélincourt *Cricket Match* ii. 21 He picked a woodbine out of its paper on the mantelpiece.

Wooden, *a.* Add: **3. b.** = Wooded *ppl. a.*

1843 [see 3]. 1891 Marah E. Ryan *Pagan Allegh.* i. 12 And then there are others more seldom seen, the women from the 'wooden' country of the interior.

9. wooden nutmeg: see Nutmeg 1 b.

Woo·den-spoo·nist. [f. *wooden spoon*: Wooden *a.* 7.] A competitor or one of a group of competitors who are awarded the 'wooden spoon'.

1927 *Daily Express* 23 Mar. 13/3 Champions and wooden spoonists of the Isthmian League last season were opposed on the Civil Service ground at Chiswick.

Woodwork. Add: **3. c.** Work done in woods; forestry.

1904 G. A. B. Dewar *Glamour of Earth* x. 243 Making a good and sure living..and filling an honourable post in wood work, to our surprise he took one day a strange step: flung up his work and migrated..to the town.

Wool, *sb.* Add: **1. g.** (*g*) *Wool on the back*: money, assets.

1909 *London Mag.* Aug. 630/1 It is seldom that the clerk has a sufficiency of that commodity known as 'wool on the back' to go round amongst all the creditors.

2. d. Vague or slip-shod reasoning or thinking.

1920 *Round Table* Sept. 933 Intellectually impatient of 'wool', his kindness of heart made him tolerant of much that must have appeared to him to be vainness.

3. d. Also *fig.*, of a person.

1922 Galsworthy *Loyalties* ii. ii. 67 Mabel, you're pure wool, right through; everybody's sorry for you.

5. a. *wool hat* (earlier and later examples). **b.** *wool-carding* adj.

1812 *Niles' Weekly Reg.* II. 228/1 The fulling mills returned amount to 1630; and the *wool carding machines going by water to 1835. 1796 Morse *Geog.* I. 542, 300 hatters, distributed over the state, make annually above 54,000 fur, and 161,000 *wool hats. 1880 *Harper's Mag.* Dec. 159 An old 'wool-hat' came along with a cart drawn by a single ox.

d. wool alien, a plant introduced into a country by means of wool containing its seed; **wool-dyed** *a.* (earlier and later examples).

1919 Ida M. Hayward & G. C. Druce *Adventive Flora Tweedside* Introd. p. xxi, It must not, however, be assumed that all the *wool aliens will disappear. 1832 *Niles' Weekly Reg.* XLIII. 65/2 Messrs. *Randolf* and *Ritchie*, who are chiefs of the '*wool-dyed democrats' of the present day. 1904 *Charlotte Observer* 19 June 2 Higginson is one of the old abolition gang, is wool-dyed and blind.

Wool, *v.* **2.** (Earlier example.)

c 1831 A. Lincoln in H. Binns *Life Lincoln* (1927) 34, I never tussle and scuffle. I don't like this wooling and pulling.

Woo·lgathersome, *a.* [-some.] Suggestive of wool-gathering.

1929 C. E. Montague *Disenchantment* vii. 95 The average German soldier, the docile blond with yellow hair, long skull, and blue, woolgathersome eyes.

Woollenize (wu·lĕnəiz), *v.* [f. Woollen + -ize.] *trans.* To impart to (vegetable fibres) the appearance and texture of wool.

1890 *Times* 19 Aug. 10/4 The various processes to be carried out at the model fibre factory..comprise..cottonizing and woollenizing fibres to imitate fine cotton or wool. 1927 *Daily Tel.* 21 June 8 Advt., Successful fancy cloth effects have..been attained by the application of mercerising and woollenising processes to these yarns.

Woolleny (wu·lĕni), *a.* [f. Woollen + -y.] Made of or resembling woollen cloth.

1863 'Gail Hamilton' *Gala-Days* 41 I have a veil—none of your woolleny gruff fabrics.

Woolliness. (Further example.)

1927 *Glasgow Herald* 12 Oct. 11/1 Despite a certain amount of 'woolliness', however, songs and piano and violin solos are well reproduced.

Woolly, *a.* **2. b.** Also of the atmosphere in a place.

1894 Hall Caine *Manxman* 309 But no sooner had he breathed the soft, woolly, stagnant air within than a change came over him.

3. c. woolly sheep *U.S.*, a variety of the Rocky Mountain sheep; **woolly worm** *U.S.*, a hairy caterpillar.

1837 Irving *Capt. Bonneville* I. iii. 69 This animal is commonly called the mountain sheep, and is often confounded with another animal, the 'woolly sheep' found more to the northward. 1911 Edna Ferber *Dawn O'Hara* ii. 19, I do everything. I'd eat wooly worms if I thought they might benefit me.

d. Also simply *woolly.*

1891 Marah E. Ryan *Told in Hills* iii. iv. 191 Let us 'move our freight', 'hit the breeze', or any other term of the woolly West that means action. 1904 *N. Y. Even. Post* 22 June 7 A young woman who ropes steers with as much ease and expedition as the 'wooliest' cowboy. 1907 S. E. White *Arizona Nights* vii. 130 'Who's your woolly friend,' the shiny Jew asks of the girls.

7. *woolly-witted* adj.

1927 *Observer* 6 Nov. 15/1 The managerial attitude towards producers is at present woolly-witted.

Wop (wǫp). *U.S. slang.* A term of contempt for an Italian immigrant.

1915 Wodehouse *Psmith, Journalist* xix. 138 He's a wop, kid. 1916 H. L. Wilson *Somewhere in Red Gap* iii. 118 Anyway his was ordinary decent wops and not Blackhanders. 1927 P. Marks *Lord of Himself* 160 You wouldn't have called Caruso a dirty wop if you had known him. 1928 Sinclair Lewis *Man Who Knew Coolidge* i. 53 Too many foreigners—fellows with Wop names and Hunky names.

Wordable (wɔ̄·ɹdăb'l), *a.* [f. Word *v.* + -able.] Capable of being expressed in words.

1920 O. Elton *Engl. Lit. 1830–80* I. 356 The embodiment of hardly wordable feeling in 'Tears, idle tears'.

Wordage. (Further example.)

1926 *Glasgow Herald* 19 May 7/2 They have never placed upon the cables so large a wordage concerning any British domestic event.

Wo·rdlorist. [f. Wordlore + -ist.] One who studies words and their history.

1929 *N. & Q.* 15 June 419/2 No word-lorist who studies place-names.

Wordly, *a.* (Modern example.)

1927 M. Sadleir *Trollope* 370 This fact indicates..two of his personal qualities..his wordly proficiency and his good manners.

Work, *sb.* **34. work-shy** *a.*, also *absol.*

1928 *Daily Express* 2 Apr. 7/4 To make the lot of the work-shy as favourable as that of the worker. 1932 *Times* 10 Feb. 8/4 Bag-snatching from women has become a source of livelihood to the work-shy.

b. Combs. with *works*, as *works club, kitchen*; **works committee, council,** a committee of workers or their representatives; *esp.* one formed in accordance with the recommendations of the Whitley report; a Whitley council.

1908 *Mod. Business* Aug. 69/1 Any surplus is devoted to some charity or to some of the *works clubs. 1927 *Daily Tel.* 25 Oct. 9/3 The establishment of organised *works councils. *Ibid.* 15/4 He would seek industrial peace by some form of co-partnership, such as the *works committees instituted by Imperial Chemical Industries. 1908 *Mod. Business* Aug. 69/1 Another valuable outlet for its energies is in the management of a *Works Kitchen.

Work, *v.* **38.** Work out. **a.** Also *refl.*

1906 *Jrnl. Abnormal Psychol.* I. 37 We might properly say that the 'uncompleted emotion'..could be given an opportunity to work itself out.

Worker. 5. Add: **worker-major** (see quot.).

1924 J. A. Thomson *Science Old & New* xliv. 259 While the umbrella-ant workers are busy in the Brazilian forests cutting discs from the leaves, some of their fellows, with enormously large heads, simply walk about looking on; they have been called 'worker-majors'.

Working, *vbl. sb.* Add: **16. b. working order** (earlier example.) **c.** With adverbs as, *working-out, -up.*

1845 *Knickerbocker Mag.* XXVI. 410 The use of steam-pumps is requisite night and day, to keep them [mines] in working order. 1922 F. E. Penny *Swan's Curse* xiv. 128 Her actions were a preliminary working-up of evil passion by concentrating her thought on the contemplated crime.

Working-day. 2. (Earlier examples.)

1813 *Niles' Weekly Reg.* V. 78/1 She [a ship] was built in seventy-two 'working days' and is a complete piece of workmanship. 1853 in *Hogg's Instructor* X. 282/2 To grant the Saturday afternoon holiday, and to limit the duration of every other working day within a certain definite period of time, not exceeding twelve hours, including the proper interval for meals.

Working-man. (Earlier examples.)

1683 *Essex Inst. Hist. Coll.* IX. 67 Every working man [to mend the high-way] upon the 7th day of the moneth under the penaltie of 3s for evʳ one that is defective. 1789 Franklin *Paper Currency* Wks. (1905) 138 Working-men and their families are thereby induced to be more..extravagant.

Wo·rkmanize, *v.* [f. Workman + -ize.] *trans.* To make into or like workmen.

1930 S. N. Harper *Making Bolsheviks* 34 The leaders ordered the cleansing of the Soviet apparatus to eliminate harmful and hostile elements, and at the same time to 'workmanize' the governmental bodies.

Work-out. Also in general, a practice or test.

1909 R. A. Wason *Happy Hawkins* 161 I expect to give it a fair good work-out before I'm through with it. 1927 C. Mathewson *Sec. Base Sloan* 259 The morning's work-out ended with practice on the bases.

World, *sb.* Add: **23. a.** *world-construction, -government, -structure.*

1920 W. R. Inge *Truth & Falsehood in Relig.* 115 Science has no commission to produce an ideal *world-construction on a materialist basis. 1919 J. L. Garvin *Econ. Found. Peace* 10 The political and legal forms of any effort at *World-Government. 1922 A. S. Eddington *Theory of Relativity* 31 Einstein's law..is consistent with what we now know of the general plan of *world-structure.

b. *world-beating.* **c.** *world-forgotten, -read* adjs.

1928 *Sunday Express* 24 June 20/4 The way he flashed the passing shot wide of Higgs..was *world-beating stuff. 1896 Hardy *Jude the Obscure* iv. i. 250 Such is, and such was, the now *world-forgotten Shaston or Palladour. 1912 — *Postscript to Jude the Obscure*, An influential article..printed in a *world-read journal.

24. b. *world-cause, -market, -price, -war* (later examples).

1918 *Brit. Industr. Future* (Lib. Ind. Inq.) iv. xxiv. 331 This difference in price-level is largely the result of *world-causes. 1909 *World To-Day* Sept. 981/2 All that is required to make Chicago verily the *world-market is the same push and energy directed to foreign trade. 1928 *Brit. Industr. Future* (Lib. Ind. Inq.) i. v. 50 They showed that the practice of dumping demoralises the world-market to the ultimate disadvantage of all concerned. 1915 *Lit. Digest* 4 Sept. 477/2 It is only in the United States, which is as yet comparatively little affected by the great *world-war, that the remnants of the age of doubt still linger. 1927 V. McNabb *Cath. Ch. & Philos.* iii. 119 Those who are now engaged in the World War for Truth.

25. world-all [tr. G. *weltall*], the world considered as a unit; the universe; **world-point** (see quot.).

1925 R. M. Ogden tr. *Koffka's Growth of Mind* 347 For a child there is as yet no single world-all. 1926 R. G. Bury tr. *Plato's Laws* II. 363 All things are ordered systematically by Him who cares for the World-all with a view to the preservation and excellence of the whole. 1930 Silberstein *Size of Universe* 1 The event thus localized in space..and in time..is called a *worldpoint.

Worldlet (wɔ̄·ɹldlĕt). [f. World + -let.] A little world; a planetoid.

1926 *Spectator* 11 Sept. 375/1 So in turn we visit the asteroids, that belt of tiny worldlets flinging round the sun.

Worm, *sb.* **17. f. worm-cast,** also *transf.*; **worm-fence** (earlier example).

1913 E. F. Benson *Thorley Weir* iii, He squirted on to it [a palette] *worm-casts of colour. 1724 Jones *Virginia* 39 *Wormfences..are made of Rails supporting one another very firmly in a particular Manner.

Worm-eaten, *pa. pple.* **3.** *fig.* (Further example.)

1906 W. De Morgan *Joseph Vance* li. 519, I was worm-eaten with sad misgivings.

Wormhood. (Mod. example.)

1917 Ld. Braye *Lines in Verse & Fable* 63 Extinction of all influence and fame, And abject knowledge of my wormhood.

Worriedly (wʊ·ridli), *adv.* [f. Worried *ppl. a.* + -ly [2].] In a worried manner.

1926 'L. Malet' *Dogs of Want* v. 125 She worriedly wondered whether green isn't a more trying colour than blue when you get hot.

Worriment. (Earlier example.)

1834 Seba Smith *Major Downing* 90 I've had a good many head-flaws and worriments in my life time.

Worrisome, *a.* (Earlier example.)

1845 W. G. Simms *Wigwam & Cabin* 107 I...followed the old man into the house with my feelings getting more and more strange and worrisome at every moment.

Worriter (wʊ·ritəɹ). [f. Worrit *v.* + -er [1].] = Worrier 3.

1930 Sir G. MacMunn *Behind Scenes in many Wars* 263 Highly strung and a worriter, he took all be could out of himself.

Worse. B. *absol.* or as *sb.* **3. c.** (Recent example.)

1930 F. A. Pottle *Stretchers* 64 The weather was warm, and if worse came to worst, we could encamp in our pup tents where we were.

Wo·rsifica·tion. [f. Worse *a.* + -fication.] The fact or action of making something worse.

1849 J. R. Lowell in *Mass. Q. Rev.* Dec. 51 Since we have found fault with some of what we may be allowed to call the worsification, we should say that the prose work is done conscientiously and neatly. 1908 *Let. to Furnivall* 27 Nov., The worsification of the poetry written in younger days is far more complete and thorough in the Italian and French poets [Tasso and Ronsard] than the English one [Langland].

Worst. A. *adj.* **2. c.** (Later examples.) Also *the worst way.*

1887 F. Francis Jr. *Saddle & Mocassin* 107 He drove him off; but the old bull hated to quit—the worst kind. 1904 *N. Y. Tribune* 26 June, 'So you want to go to Cuba, do you?' asked Colonel Roosevelt. 'I do, worst kind', replied McShane. 1914 Gertr. Atherton *Perch of Devil* i. 55 I need new duds the worst way.

B. 3. d. (Further example.)

1899 Conan Doyle *Duet* 74, 'I feel a little chippy to-day.' 'That's the worst of those cheap champagnes.'

Worth, *a.* **3. c.** (Earlier example.)

1874 'Mark Twain' *Sk.* Wks. XIX. 409 We shall fly our comet for all it is worth.

Woven, *ppl. a.* **2.** (Further Comb. example.)

1903 Hardy *Dynasts* i. 5 O woven-winged squadrons of Toulon..draw westward Ere Nelson be near!

Wow (wau), *sb.*[2] *U.S. slang.* A 'great success'.

1927 E. Wallace in *Morn. Post* 20 Dec., I am told this [a melodrama] was a 'wow' in America; and a 'wow', as we all know, is American for sensational success.

Wraf (ræf). *slang.* [f. the initials.] A member of the Women's Royal Air Force.

1919 *Glasgow Herald* 19 Dec. 14/1. 1921 *Spectator* 4 June 719/2 Sketches with pen and pencil of the duties of the 'Wrafs'.

Wraith, *sb.* **4.** Add: *wraith-ship.*

1924 V. F. Boyson *Falkland Islands* viii. 181 Dimly as she came, so she passed away, as though in very truth the wraithship said to appear at every British naval fight.

Wraithly (rē¹·þli), *a.* [f. Wraith *sb.* + -ly [1].] Resembling a wraith; wraith-like.

1909 Marg. B. Saunders *Litany Lane* i. iv, The tinkle-tinkle of a wraithly Tom Moore singing flowery love-songs at fluted-silked pianos.

Wrap, *sb.* **2. b.** Also *attrib.*

1928 *Daily Mail* 9 Aug. 3/4 A..bathing dress worn under a well cut wrap-coat of..crêpe de Chine.

Wrapping, *vbl. sb.* **3. wrapping-paper** (earlier examples).

1791 *Ann. Congress.* II. App. 2130 The several duties shall be laid on the following goods...On all writing, printing and wrapping paper. 1809 Weems *Lett.* II. 435 Not wronging you even of a bundle of wrapping paper.

Wrathiness (rǭ·þinĕs). [f. Wrathy + -ness.] Wrathy or angry quality; wrathfulness.

1927 H. S. Buck *Smollett as Poet* 30 There breathes through *The Tears of Scotland* that 'wrathiness' of spirit so characteristic of Smollett.

Wrecker.[2] Add: **3.** (See quot.)

1904 *Booklovers' Mag.* May 663 This special train has been dubbed the 'Wrecker'. Really it is a relief train, ready to respond to any call for aid in case of accident.

4. A person employed to succour hunters who get into difficulties.

1932 Sir H. Maxwell *Even. Memories* 120 Neither during that or subsequent visits had I occasion for the services of a wrecker.

Wrecky (re·ki), *a.* [f. Wreck *sb.*[1] + -y.] Broken-down; debilitated.

1925 *Brit. Weekly* 17 Sept. 541/1 After which you are left a wreck and probably remain wrecky next day.

Wren.[2] [f. the initials.] A member of the Women's Royal Naval Service. (Orig. and chiefly in pl.)

1918 *Times* 15 Aug. 9/2 The much-needed 'Leave' Club for women in the different services, Waacs, Wrens, and Penguins. 1919 *Daily Mail Year Bk.* 49/1 The 'Wrens', of course, only work on land.

Wrenlet (re·nlĕt). [f. Wren + -let.] A young wren.

1858 *Chambers's Jrnl.* Aug. 82/2 It affords a cradle to near a score of wrenlets. 1927 *Observer* 22 May 23/2 In a knot in the rope was a wren's nest, with two or three wrenlets visible inside.

Write, *v.* Add: **3. h.** = Underwrite *v.* 2 b.

1882 'F. Anstey' *Vice Versa* xvi. 298 They talked of 'risks', of someone who had only been 'writing' a year and was doing seven thousand a week,..and of the uselessness of 'writing five hundred on everything'. 1931 *Times* 14 Mar. 12/6 Not all insurance companies have felt justified in writing the risks.

14. Write in. b. To send (a message) to headquarters, etc., in writing.

1928 *Publishers' Weekly* 14 July 183 The customers..were not slow about writing in their suggestions.

22. b. (*b*) Additional example.

1863 'E. Kirke' *My Southern Friends* xiv. 167, I do not write Hallet. You may give him as much or as little of this letter as you think will be good for him.

Wri·te-down. [f. *to write down*: Write *v.* 13 e.] A reduction in the amount of an account, capital, etc.

1932 *Daily Express* 28 Jan. 10/7 This has involved a write-down of securities.

Wri·te-off. [f. *to write off*: Write *v.* 15.] A cancellation; an amount written off or cancelled; a dead loss.

1905 [see Write *sb.*[2] 1 b]. 1918 *War Birds* (1927) 89 He wasn't hurt but the Spad [an aeroplane] was a write-off. 1927 E. W. Springs *Nocturne militaire* 250 Both machines were complete write-offs and the only things they salvaged were the magnetos.

Wri·te-up. *U.S.* [f. *to write up*: Write *v.* 18.] A written account or description of anything, *esp.* in an elaborate or journalistic style.

1887, 1902 [see Write *sb.*[2] 2]. 1905 Rex Beach *Pardners* i. (1927) 17 I'll..Feature it as a typical Klondyke card game. I'll give you a two-page write-up. 1910 *Chambers's Jrnl.* July 431/1 The 'write-up' and the interview are prominent features. 1922 Titus *Timber* xxi. 193 Ought to make a good write-up.

Writing, *vbl. sb.* **3. d.** (Further example.)

1927 *Daily Tel.* 14 June 3/2 Last year's realised profits, less writings off, was £12,343 higher.

Wrong. A. *adj.* Add: **6. d.** *wrong'un*: (in cricket) a googly. *slang.*

1926 Strudwick *25 Yrs. behind Stumps* 239 It is very difficult to detect his [*sc.* C. V. Grimmett's] 'wrong un'! 1931 *Daily Tel.* 31 July 17/2 Weir deserved better of fate than to be bowled by Peebles' wrong 'un in the last over of the day.

B. *adv.* Add: **2. g.** *To get a person in wrong*, to place in an unfavourable light; to bring into disfavour (*with* one). *U.S.*

1917 *War Birds* (1927) 30 There are a few rough-necks in every outfit that will cause trouble and get the whole bunch in wrong. 1925 Joan Sutherland *Circle of Stars* xxii, He's got you in wrong with the Governor while you were away.

Wronger. Add: **3.** An error or mistake.

1896 *African Critic* 24 Oct. 514/2, I am sorry to have to accuse Reuter of another 'wronger'.

Wrong-wise, *adv.* (Later example.)

1903 A. H. Lewis *The Boss* i. 6, I found such stimulus [beatings with hickory] to go much against the grain and to grievously rub wrong-wise the fur of my fancy.

Wry. C. *Comb.*, as *wry-formed.*

1906 Hardy *Dynasts* ii. v. vi. 281 What lewdness lip those wry-formed phantoms there?

Wuff, *v.* Add: **b.** *transf.* Of the sound of a shell in flight.

1919 C. P. Thompson *Cocktails* 110 As the first ranging shell 'wuffed' up two of the Gothas dropped away from the tail of the formation.

Wump (wʊmp), *sb.* [Echoic: cf. Dump, Thump.] The sound of a heavy body falling on a yielding surface, or any similar sound.

1915 *Blackw. Mag.* May 657/2 There were windsails..down which one shot..to end in a delicious 'Wump' at the bottom. 1917 *Ibid.* Apr. 472/1 Interest which is equalled by your relief when it [a shell] bursts clear or lands with a 'wump' in a neighbouring mud-hut. 1926 Galsworthy *Escape* Prol. 17 My God! That was a wump. I say!

Wump, *v.* [cf. prec. and Thump *v.*] *intr.* To throb.

1897 Ellen Terry *Lett.* 5 Feb. (1931) 126 Not a single speech do I know yet, and my head is thumping and wumping.

Wumph (wʊmf). = *Wump *sb.*

1913 *Daily News & Leader* 15 Aug. 5, I was ashamed of the heavy 'wumph' with which I landed on the other side amid the nettles. 1924 *Glasgow Herald* 20 Dec. 4/2 The female [bittern]..sometimes answers back with a subdued but exciting 'wumph'.

Wuzzy, var. Muzzy.

1924 Ida A. R. Wylie in *Sunday Times* 3 Feb. 7/3 Miss Sinclair is not for 'wuzzy' minds.

Wycliffian. A. *sb.* (Further example.)

1687 J. Mumford *Question of Questions* (ed. 2) iv. § 24. 520 You own the Wicleffians for Brethren.

Wycliffianism. (Modern example.)

1913 *Hastings's Encycl. Relig. & Ethics* VI. 621 Wyclifianism blended with the work of the Lollards from the Continent and passed into English life as a permanent influence.

Wykami·stically, *adv.* = Wykehamically.

1913 A. G. Bradley *Other Days* v. 156 The rector, being very Wykamistically connected, had some acquaintance with him [the headmaster of Winchester].

X

Xanthation (zænþē¹·ʃən). [f. Xanth(ate + -ation.] The process of forming cellulose xanthate.

1927 T. Woodhouse *Artif. Silk* 30 This mass is dissolved in water and weak caustic soda solution and agitated in a mixer until a perfect homogeneous solution is obtained. This process is termed xanthation, and the product was named 'Viscose' by its inventors.

Xanthogenic (zænþodʒe·nik), *a.* [f. Xanthogen + -ic.] = Xanthic *a.*

1905 *Rep. Brit. Assoc.* 154 On carefully heating the xanthogenic ether..a hydrocarbon is obtained.

Xeno-. Add: **Xe·nolith** *Geol.* [Gr. λίθος stone], a stone or rock occurring in a system of rocks to which it does not belong; hence **Xenoli·thic** *a.* **Xe·nophobe,** one who has a morbid fear or hatred of foreigners; so **Xenopho·bia, Xe·nophobism** = Xenophoby.

1926 T. Hannan *Isle of Mull* xix. 118 A '*xenolith' is simply a 'stranger'—one not belonging to the rock system of the district. 1930 Peach & Horne *Geol. Scotl.* 67 Grey igneous gneiss is interposed..and is *xenolithic. 1922 *Mail* 24 May 327/1 The Afghans are said to be suspicious of foreigners, even to be *xenophobes. 1919 *Nation* (N. Y.) 20 Dec. 800 Legitimate agitation for self government and democratic institutions is marred by *xenophobia. 1929 *Spectator* 26 Jan. 124/2 The [French] people's notorious and inescapable xenophobia. 1927 *Sunday Times* 13 Feb. 10/5 (heading) French '*Xenophobism.'

Xenophonic (zenǫfǫ·nik), *a.* [f. Gr. Ξενοφῶν + -ic.] = next.

1921 *Contemp. Rev.* Oct. 568 Platonic idealism, Aristotelian individualism, Xenophonic realism all go to the making of a liberal education.

Xenophontine (zenǫfǫ·ntəin), *a.* [f. as Xenophontean + -ine.] = Xenophontean.

1917 T. R. Glover *Pericles to Philip* vi. 178 The interrelations of the historic Socrates with the Platonic, the Xenophontine and the Aristotelian Socrates.

Xero-. Add: **Xerophile,** also *attrib.* **Xerophy·tically** *adv.*, in the manner of a xerophyte.

1926 *Nat. Hist. Oxford Distr.*, 305 Both xerophile and damp-loving species flourish, the former mainly on the high ground..the latter in hedgerows and woods. 1911 F. O. Bower *Plant Life on Land* 134 Xerophytically adapted, that is, that they shall be able to stand sudden conditions of extreme heat and drought.

X-ray·ing, *vbl. sb.* [f. X-ray *v.* + -ing [1].] The process of examining or treating with X-rays.

1920 *Glasgow Herald* 5 Oct. 7/2 Advantage is claimed for 'X-raying' over sterilization.

Xylo-. Add: **Xy·lolith** [Gr. λίθος stone], a composition made with sawdust. **Xylo·meter,** an instrument for measuring the volume of wood by the amount of water which it displaces; hence **Xylome·tric** *a.*, **Xylome·trically** *adv.*

1908 W. R. Fisher *Schlich's Man. Forestry* V. 616 With cement, soluble glass and gypsum, it [sawdust] is converted into xylolith or papyrolith. 1911 *Ibid.* III. 26 The instrument used is called a xylometer. *Ibid.* 33 In many cases it is desirable to ascertain the volume of the bark...This can be done stereometrically or xylometrically. *Ibid.* 48 The xylometric method has been explained.

Xylophonist (zəilǫ·fŏnist). [f. Xylophone + -ist.] A performer on the xylophone.

1927 *Daily Tel.* 10 May 12/1 Teddy Brown the xylophonist.

Supplement, p. 3873; Corrigenda, p. 4092; Spurious words, p. 4093; Books quoted, p. 4094

Y

Yachting, *vbl. sb.* (Further example.)
1928 *Daily Mail* 9 Aug. 10/3 Some wear full evening dress and others appear in jumper suits or yachting checks.

Ya·chtish, *a.* [f. Yacht + -ish.] Pertaining to or characteristic of a yacht.
1925 *Brit. Weekly* 16 July 354/1 A large roomy coasting vessel (its interior nicely fitted up..in a yachtish way).

Yager. b. (Earlier example.)
1835 J. T. Irving *Ind. Sketches* I. 97, I intend to make my yager speak to the first red skin what tries to take it.

Yakalo (yæ·kălo). [f. Yak + (Buff)alo.] A cross between the yak and the buffalo.
1926 *Bulletin* 5 Aug. 5/3 Canada, one hears, is evolving a true national beast, the Yakalo.

Yale lock. [f. the name of the inventor L. *Yale* (1821–68).] A type of lock having a revolving barrel, made first in America.
1882 *Encycl. Brit.* XIV. 751/1.

Yank, *sb.*[1] b. Also *fig.*
1906 *N.Y. Globe* 20 Aug. 6 Here is a fantastic proposition from Germany, which takes one back with an unpleasant yank into the middle ages.

Yank, *v.* 1. b. (Further examples.)
1883 Nye *Baled Hay* 64 Which the poet seems competent to yank loose from the history of the savage. 1886 *Harper's Mag.* Aug. 427/1 I don't see the fun in being yanked all over the United States territory in August. 1896 G. B. Shaw *Lett. to Ellen Terry* (1931) lxxvi. 114 She promptly went to that haunt, yanked Janet..out of it..and delivered her punctually..for the performance. 1902 Harben *Abner Daniel* xxxiii. 279 I don't think what you did to yank Wilson into line was nigh as bad. 1912 F. M. Hueffer *Panel* I. ii. 40 He had just sailed in to yank her out of it.

Yankee. C. b. Add: **Yankee fiddle,** a kind of bow-drill; **Yankee jib** (see quot.).
1892 Stevenson & Osbourne *The Wrecker* xv, Nares, sullenly but busily drilling sea-shells with the instrument called a *Yankee fiddle. 1928 *Daily Mail* 9 Aug. 19/6 There is a *Yankee jib which, as one sail, covers more than the combined area of jib and foresail.

Ya·nkeeness. [f. Yankee *sb.* + -ness.] Yankee character.
a 1909 'O. Henry' *Roads of Destiny* xxi. 352 Any Yankeeness I may have is geographical.

Yap, *sb.* Add: 1. b. Used contemptuously of persons. *U.S.*
1902 J. M. Forman *Journey's End* viii. 104 He [an actor] descended upon Calthrop in the evening, talking loudly of his triumph among the 'yaps'. 1915 W. Churchill *Far Country* xxiv. 452 The yaps that listen to him don't understand him, but somehow he gets under their skins. 1922 Titus *Timber* xvi. 149 These yaps haven't got anything to think with. 1929 S. Anderson in *Mercury Story Bk.* 237 There was a big gang of yaps.
2. b. *slang.* A chat.
1930 Dorothy L. Sayers & 'R. Eustace' *Documents in Case* 145 I'd like to have a yap with somebody who talks my language.

Yap, *v.* Add: 2. b. To chatter or talk idly.
1929 P. Gibbs *Hidden City* vii. 25 Their minds work too rapidly..they're always yapping about life. And they don't know the first thing about it.

Yapping, *vbl. sb.* and *ppl. a.* (Further examples.) Also **Ya·ppingly** *adv.*
1915 *Edin. Rev.* Apr. 225 Suddenly on every side of her broke out the yapping of guns. 1920 *Blackw. Mag.* Jan. 711/1 Long silences were variegated by bursts of frantic yappings and snappings. 1925 M. R. James *Warning to Curious* 52 A small man..gave directions in a rather yapping foreign accent to his chauffeur. 1924 *Chambers's Jrnl.* Feb. 128/1 Bob danced yappingly around him.

Yard, *sb.*[1] 3. Read: Now *dial.* and *U.S.*
1835 Ingraham *South-West* II. 88 Striped grass, cultivated in yards at the north. 1865 *Atlantic Monthly* XV. 492 The house..stood in its faultless green turfy yard, a perfect Pharisee among houses. 1869 C. L. Brace *New West* iii. 37 Every house, with bits of yards like ours in New York, makes the most splendid show of flowers. 1881 *Rep. Indian Affairs* 107 Their houses, with suitable space for yards, are all enclosed, generally with very neat fences. 1901 S. E. White *Westerners* iii. 16 He settled down into a little white house, in a little blossomy 'yard'. 1930 *Publishers' Weekly* 15 Feb. 859 Plant this spring and enjoy the yard this summer.

Yard, *v.*[1] 1. (Earlier and later examples.)
1758 *Essex Inst. Hist. Coll.* XII. 140 The Dutch here have a nasty practice of yarding their cows in ye street before their doors. 1930 Palmer *Men are Human* xxi. 192 The horses had already been yarded.

Yardage[1]. (Earlier example.) Also *attrib.*
1865–6 *Trans. Ill. Agric. Soc.* VI. 322 Net cash receipt for yardage, and profit on feed. 1903 A. Adams *Log Cowboy* xiii. 86 No. I'll not ship any more cattle to your town..until you adjust your yardage charges.

Yardland. 1. Also *Comb.*, as *yardland-holder.*
1890 E. W. Watson *Ashmore* 31 The two plough-oxen, the universal outfit of the English yardland-holder.

Ya·rdlander. [f. Yardland + -er[1].] A yardland-holder.
1891 *Athenæum* 16 May 632/3 The notes he gives as to the families of the yardlanders are most interesting.

Yarn, *sb.* 3. Add: *yarn-carrier.*
1927 T. Woodhouse *Artificial Silk* 100 The yarns now pass to their respective yarn carriers, the function of which is to place the yarn in the path of the single set of sinkers.

Yarn, *v.* Add: b. To recount or narrate.
1840 A. Russell *Tour Austral. Colonies* 40 One who can yarn the dangers of the deep so well.

Ya·rning, *vbl. sb.* [f. Yarn *v.* + -ing[1].] The action of 'spinning yarns'.
1916 *Blackw. Mag.* Apr. 493/1 Yarning seems to fill in the few leisure moments of the day.

Yatter (yæ·təɹ), *v.* *Sc.* [Echoic.] *intr.* To gabble or chatter.
1866 James Smith *Merry Bridal* 3 Wi' yatterin', an' clatterin', They made an unco din. 1896 P. A. Graham *Red Scaur* viii. 121 Grace likes to yatter about the days when she bondaged for him. 1910 S. R. Crockett *Dew of Youth* III. xxix. 236 They will be out talk-talking, yatter-yattering when the kye are being milked in the morning. 1919 J. Buchan *Mr. Standfast* I. vi. 122 No company but a wheen ignorant Hielanders that yatter Gawlic.

Yaw, *sb.*[1] b. Also *spec.* (See quot.)
1920 *Nature* 10 June 460/1 We must..determine experimentally the complete reaction of the air on the moving shell when the directions of its axis and the motion of its centre of gravity no longer coincide. In such a case the angle between these two directions is called the yaw.

Yaw, *v.*[2] Add: 2. To utter with the mouth gaping or yawning.
1917 S. Graham *Priest of Ideal* v. 67 The precentor in the box beneath the pulpit yawed out the tune.

Yawing, *ppl. a.* (Later example.)
1928 Galsworthy *Swan Song* II. xiii. 219 Soames' eyes tracked them through the shifting, yawing throng.

Yaw·nfully, *adv.* [f. Yawnful + -ly[2].] In a yawnful manner.
1914 W. De Morgan *When Ghost meets Ghost* I. xviii. 691 'On my way to Poynders,' said the Countess yawnfully.

Yawp, yaup, *sb.* b. (Earlier and later examples.)
1835 Ingraham *South-West* I. 29 'Hold your yaup, you youngster you,' roared the old man in reply. 1904 *Buffalo Commercial* 25 Aug. 6 When this contest is ended, the insincere and ridiculous yawp about the fierce belligerency of Theodore Roosevelt will be laid away with the other feeble fakes.

Yawp, yaup, *v.* Add: 1. b. To speak foolishly or noisily.
1872 Susan Hale *Lett.* 90 Perhaps it is just as well, however, not to yawp much about our going *alone*, as it may be considered loose in America. 1926 T. Beer *Mauve Decade* vi. 233 Where the boys who badgered Richard Harding Davis for autographs in 1890 will be yawping over 'Billy Baxter's Letters' in 1900.
So **Yawping, yauping** *vbl. sb.* (further example).
1904 *Brooklyn Eagle* 3 July, The Eagle is opposed to free trade nonsense and to anti-Imperialistic yawping because it believes they are wrong.

Yaw-yaw, *sb.* Cf. Yaw *int.* and Yaw-yaw *v.*
1931 G. Kitchin *Surv. Burlesque & Parody in Engl.* v. 143 We have witnessed the mere brutality of the Elizabethan parodists with their street urchin yaw-yaws against romantic excess or the use of cumbrous neologisms.

Yearman. Add: 2. A man selected to perform a yearly ceremony.
1913 J. G. Frazer *Golden Bough* (ed. 3) VI. iii. 144 Whether master or servant, the performer goes by the name of yearman (*toshi-otoko*), the rite being properly performed on the last day of the year.

Year-old. A. *adj.* (Earlier example.)
c 1670 in A. Bryant *K. Charles II* (1931) 95, I leve beare ..three big hefers and a boleke and seven which are yer old bes.

Yeast, *v.* 4. **yeast-bread,** bread made with yeast; **yeast-cake, -powder** (later examples).
1865 Mrs. Stowe *House & Home P.* x. 113 We earnestly entreat American housekeepers..to..return to the good *yeast-bread of their sainted grandmothers. 1898 A. Nicholas *Idyl of Wabash* 6 They don't know how to make yeast bread. 1897 R. M. Stuart *Simpkinsville* 136 Here, too, had passed pantalet patterns, bits of *yeast-cake and preserving-kettles. 1908 W. James in *McClure's Mag.* Feb. 421/2 We are to be the yeast-cake for democracy's dough. 1857 W. Chandless *Visit Salt Lake* I. vi. 95 Three boxes of *yeast-powder (at thirty cents each) to improve our bread. 1881 *Amer. Cyclop.* XVI. 777 Yeast powders, or baking powders, substitutes for yeast, used in making bread.

Yedda. A kind of straw grown in Italy, Japan, and the Philippine Islands and used for weaving hats. Hence *yedda braid, plait,* etc.
1918 Charlotte R. Aiken *Millinery Dept.* 28 Yedda braid was first produced in Italy, but the Japanese have made an imitation...Yedda is a tall grass grown in Italy, Japan, and the Philippines. 1927 *Daily News* 20 June 2/4 A smart little hat of varnished black yedda straw.

Yelky, var. Yolky *a.*[1] (Recent example.)
1918 W. J. Locke *Rough Road* ix. 104 With a hazardous plunge of his spoon he had made a yellow yelky horror of the egg-shell.

Yellow. A. *adj.* Add: 2. b. Craven, cowardly.
1896 G. Ade *Artie* i. 8 It was a yellow show. 1912 C. Mathewson *Pitching* ii. 36 When a new player breaks into the league, he is put to the most severe test by the other men to see if he is yellow. 1918 *War Birds* (1927) 264 One of our noblest he-men, a regular fire-eater to hear him tell it, has turned yellow at the front. 1925 *Scribner's Mag.* Oct. 375/1 You yellow? You a quitter?
c. (See quots.)
1920 *Glasgow Herald* 11 Sept. 7 The railwaymen..will be content to follow the lead of the General Confederation of labour and stick to the Amsterdam International, which the dictators of Russia have labelled 'yellow'—that is to say, 'blackleg'. 1920 *Ibid.* 24 Nov. 8/3 The Russian Soviet Republic has insolently rejected it as 'a Congress of yellow leaders who continually betray the fundamental interests of the Labour movement.'
B. 1. d. Cowardice; meanness; cf. *A 2 b.
1896 G. Ade *Artie* vi. 57 This is how I found that streak o' yellow in him.
2. c. *U.S.* Gold.
1901 Marah E. Ryan *That Girl Montana* xviii. 227 She would watch some strange miner dig and wash the soil in his search for the precious 'yellow'.
5. (Later example.)
1903 *N. Y. Times* Sat. Rev. 7 Nov. 796 A pretty southern widow who did newspaper work for the yellows.
C. 1. a. **yellow bear,** a yellow caterpillar of the genus *Euprepia* of bombycid moths; **yellow fly** (U.S. examples); **yellow snake,** a snake of a yellow or yellowish colour, esp. a species of boa, *Chilobothrus inornatus,* belonging to the West Indies. c. **yellow-cross gas,** mustard gas, the German shells containing this being distinguished by a yellow cross; **yellow jack** = *yellow jacket* b. e. **yellow streak,** cowardice or an indication of this; **yellow ware** (later example).
1867 *Amer. Naturalist* May 162 Many [insects] winter in the caterpiller or larva state, such as the larvae of several Noctuidae and the '*yellow-bear', and other caterpillars of Arctia and its allies. 1928 *Observer* 25 Mar. 17/5 The Germans..still possessed the advantage of their new methods of artillery and the new *yellow-cross gas, not yet adopted by the enemy. 1838 *Southern Lit. Messenger* IV. 25/1 The *yellow flies and moschetoes swarmed in myriads. 1850 L. Sawyer *Way Sketches* 73 We have been greatly annoyed by a species of yellow flies larger than the gnat. 1927 M. M. Bennett *Christison* iv. 49 These trees called *yellow-jacks are soft wood, so white ants enclose them with earth walls and eat the wood out. 1860 Mayne Reid *Odd People* 22 The '*Yellow Snake', or South African Cobra. 1868 J. G. Wood *Homes without Hands* iii. 85 Mr. Gosse gives a curious account of a burrow made by a Yellow Snake... This snake is very plentiful in Jamaica and is perfectly harmless to man. 1911 H. S. Harrison *Queed* v. 55 'A *yellow streak in him, and we didn't know it!' bellowed the Major. 1912 C. Mathewson *Pitching* ii. 36 Tennis players call it nervousness, and ball players, in the frankness of the game, call it a 'yellow streak'. 1929 C. Bush *Perfect Murder Case* xv. 195 There's a yellow streak in him somewhere and an absence of discipline. 1887 *Harper's Mag.* Dec. 31/1 Sometimes a cherry would fall upon her dark braids, and drop thence in among the verdant contents of the *yellow-ware bowl.
2. b. *yellow-robed* (earlier example).
1819 *Methodist Mag.* Oct. 723 We took leave of our *yellow-robed acquaintances.
c. **yellow-back** (*c*) *U.S.,* the yellow-backed warbler, *Compsothlypis americana*; (*a*) a U.S. currency note having the back coloured yellow; **yellow jacket** (earlier example); **yellow throat** (later examples).
1893 B. Torrey *Footpath-Way* 82 I wondered why this ..grove..should be the resort of so many birds,—robins and blue *yellow-backs. 1902 H. L. Wilson *Spenders* xiv. 150 She was dead in love with the nice long yellow-backs that I've piled up. 1906 'O Henry' *Rolling Stones* (1915) 16, I saw him tucking a yellow-back into his vest pocket. 1907 *Springfield Weekly Republ.* 4 July 6 The government has begun to pay out $10 gold certificates..and 'yellowbacks' will no longer enjoy the exclusive circulation of former times. 1811 in *Doc. Hist. Amer. Industr. Soc.* II. 199 In the months of July and August the insects are very troublesome, a large fly especially called the *yellow jacket. 1865 *Atlantic Monthly* XV. 521 I miss in the woods..the *Yellow Throat, the Yellow-Breasted Flycatcher. 1890 *Harper's Mag.* Apr. 710/1 The Maryland yellow-throat makes her little home at foot of tussock of sedge or tuft of tall fern.

Yellow-belly. Add: 5. The yellow-bellied flycatcher, *Empidonax flaviventris.*
1893 B. Torrey *Footpath-Way* 9 In his notes the yellow-belly may be said to take after both the least flycatcher and the wood pewee.

Yellow birch. *U.S.* A species of birch, *Betula lutea,* growing in North America.
1787 W. Sargent in *Mem. Amer. Acad.* IX. 158 Black and Yellow Birch, to 2 ft. dia. The bark of the latter is used by the Indians for making canoes. 1832 D. J. Browne *Sylva Amer.* 121 The wood of the yellow birch is inferior in quality and in appearance to that of the black birch. 1851 J. S. Springer *Forest Life* 23 The general outlines of the Yellow Birch often resemble the Elm, the root-spurs rise high up the trunk.

Yellow dog. *U.S.* [Yellow *a.* 1.] 1. A mongrel dog or cur, of a yellow or yellowish colour.
1840—[see Yellow C 1 a].
2. *fig.* A person or thing of no account or of a low type.
1903 *Everybody's Mag.* Oct. 562 In a cut-rate combination you are lucky if you get what you pay for. If there are five magazines in the combination, two of them are good. The rest are 'yellow-dogs'. 1924 A. J. Small *Frozen Gold* i. 44 Understand, I won't allow no yellow dog of a Siwash to step over me.
b. *attrib.*; applied *spec.* to organizations, etc., opposed to trade-unionism.
1902 *Mine Workers' Jrnl.* July 1 A yellow dog lease. 1903 *Outlook* 15 Aug. 931 In preference to a 'yellow dog' ticket his organization would support the Fusion candidate. 1905 D. G. Phillips *Plum Tree* 204 He could not carry a single state in the East where there are any large centerings of capital or enterprise—not even our yellow-dog states. 1920 *Motorman & Conductor* Oct. 34 A yellow dog contract. 1929 *Encycl. Brit.* XII. 300/1 It has been made illegal for a union to attempt to organize workers into unions if these workers have signed a so-called individual ('yellow-dog') contract with the employer agreeing not to do so.

Ye·llowism. [f. Yellow A 3 + -ism.] Unscrupulous or sensational character of news.
1906 *Springfield Weekly Republ.* 29 Nov. 3 The marketable value of alleged 'news' is found in the penny-a-liners to depend on its yellowism.

Yellow pine. *U.S.* Any of various species of pine with yellow wood, esp. *Pinus ponderosa.*
1789 Morse *Amer. Geog.* 247 There are..several kinds.. such as..yellow, spruce and pitch pines. 1817 S. Brown *Western Gaz.* 13 The uplands have yellow pine. 1822 [see Pine *sb.*[2] 2]. 1834 A. Pike *Sk.* 37, I observed that it was only one particular kind of pine which they used, viz. the rough yellow pine. 1857 D. Braman *Inform. Texas* iii. 50 There is also plenty of yellow pine, white oak, and timber of other kinds, necessary for ship building. 1869 *Amer. Naturalist* Oct. 409 The Yellow Pine is the prevailing species in most parts of the Rocky Mountains traversed. 1891 *Century Mag.* Feb. 527 Good yellow pine timber was abundant in the surrounding hills.

Yellow poplar. *U.S.* The tulip-tree of North America, *Liriodendron tulipiferum.*
1784 J. Smyth *Tour U.S.* I. xii. 93 The timber is of an immense bulk on the low grounds, and consists of white and yellow poplars. 1815 Drake *Cincinnati* ii. 82 The most valuable timber trees are the..yellow poplar, [etc.]. 1829 T. Flint *George Mason* 101 They took their dinner under a prodigious yellow poplar. 1865–6 *Trans. Ill. Agric. Soc.* VI. 390 The seedlings of our Yellow Poplar..are taken from beneath their native shelter. 1876 Whitman *Specimen Days* (1892) 89 Here is one of my favourites now before me, a fine yellow poplar, quite straight, perhaps 90 feet high, and four thick at the butt.

Yellow-wood. Also *attrib.*
1915 H. R. Haggard *Holy Flower* iv. 63 It..rolled under a great yellow-wood chest.

Yeoman. 6. Add: **yeoman wheat,** a variety of wheat originally grown in England.
1929 *Morn. Post* 2 Oct. 12/2 All-English [flour]..is made exclusively from English wheat other than yeoman wheat.

Yep, *v.* [f. prec.] *intr.* To say 'yep'.
1926 *Spectator* 6 Nov. 791/1 We shall presently find our people 'yepping' everywhere.

Yi·ddishist. [f. Yiddish + -ist.] = Yiddisher.
1917 *Edin. Rev.* Apr. 310 Russian Jewry rang for a time with the bitter controversy of the so-called Hebraists and Yiddishists.

Yielding, *vbl. sb.* 4. (Further example.)
1922 W. Schlich *Man. Forestry* I. 97 Timber fit for sawing would begin to be cut about 10 to 15 years later, and by the eightieth year the forests should be in full yielding.

Yielding, *ppl. a.* 2. (Later example.)
1849 C. Lanman *Lett. Alleghany Mts.* xx. 159 The yielding wells are somewhat over two hundred feet deep.

Yip (yip), *sb.* *U.S.* [Echoic.] A short high-pitched cry; a shout or exclamation.
1911 H. Quick *Yellowstone N.* xii. 303 They chase 'em, with wild whoops an' yips over the undulatin reservation. 1928 *Hearst's International* Aug. 74/1 At the first yip out of Babe or Cheeky he would yank two triggers.

Yip, *v.* Add: 2. *U.S.* To utter a sharp cry; to shout. So **Yipping** *vbl. sb.*
1907 Kate D. Wiggin *New Chron. Rebecca* 199 He would walk right up close and cuff 'em if they dared to yip. 1910 *N. Y. Even. Post* 14 Oct. 4 The applause was really deafening and continued for more than two minutes: not..yip-yipping..but steady volume of vocal uproar. 1927 P. Marks *Lord of Himself* 15, I love to hear you yip at him. 1927 *Sat. Even. Post* 24 Dec. 84/2 'Hey!' Jim yipped...'Get away from there!'

Yo·gic, *a.* [f. Yoga + -ic.] Of or pertaining to Yoga.
1921 Streeter & Appasamy *Sadhu* v. 136 The object of the Yogic trance is not to satisfy the heart but the head.

Yoke, *v.* 8. b. (Recent example.)
1920 Rose Macaulay *Potterism* II. i. 61 She is yoking together with an unbeliever.

Yoke-mate. (Further example.) So **Yo·ke-mated** *a.*
1914 *19th Cent.* July 111 In water, Oxygen is still further subjugated by its yoke-mate, Hydrogen. 1929 Bridges *Test. Beauty* IV. 325 Where lay the harness'd bones of the yoke-mated oxen.

Yoker. (Recent example.)
1913 R. Harris *Boanerges* xxxvii. 341 Since Jason is alone, another pair of twin yokers will come to his assistance.

Yo·nderness. [f. Yonder *adv.* + -ness.] The act or condition of being yonder.
1929 Deeping *Roper's Row* vi. 56 On Sisbury Hill she pondered over matters while feeling conscious of the yonderness of her son.

Yop, variant of Yawp, Yaup.

York, *v.* (Earlier example.)
1882 Pardon *Australians in Engl.* 42 Butler was 'yorked' the second ball he received.

Yorkshire. 1. b. Add: **Yorkshire fat** (see quot.).
1884 A. Watt *Soap-making* 28 Recovered grease, or Yorkshire fat, is obtained from the suds and washing waters of the fulling mills. It is of a brown colour, of disagreeable odour, and of a sticky consistence.

You-all. *U.S.* = You (as sing. or plur.).
1919 Mencken *Amer. Lang.* 215 In the South..the true plural is commonly indicated by you-all. 1922 Zane Grey *To Last Man* ii. 32 Aw, now, y'u-all cain't come thet on me. Ain't y'u an Injun. 1924 W. M. Raine *Troubled Waters* xix. 201 You-all are losing a better man than Missie ever had.

Young. C. 2. Add: *young-minded* adj.
1930 *Daily Express* 23 May 10/4 The Italians and Russians are *young-minded.

Youraballi, variant of *Juriballi.

Yugoslav, etc., variant of *Jugoslav.

Yup. *U.S.* Variant of Yep, yes.
1906 *Century Mag.* Jan. 410/2 'Will you go—if I swear?' 'Yup,' said Pinchas, airing his American. 1923 E. F. Wyatt *Invis. Gods* II. iv. 78 'Paul as mean as ever?' 'Yup,' replied Hancock..'and a little meaner.'

Z

Z. Add: 2. Also *Z-shaped.*
1903 J. R. Allen *Early Chr. Mon. Scotl.* 200 *Front.*—The double disc and Z-shaped rod symbol very rudely drawn. 1927 *Scot. N. & Q.* Ser. III. V. 2/1 Two plates of silver engraved with the double disc and Z-shaped rod symbol.
8. *Mil.* Abbrev. of Zero 6 b.
1930 S. Sassoon *Mem. Infantry Officer* IV. 61 Operation Orders..notified us that Thursday was 'Z' (or zero) day.

Zanyish (zē·niˌiʃ), *a.* [f. Zany *sb.* + -ish.] Like a zany; foolish.
1917 'H. H. Richardson' *R. Mahony* IV. x. 378 Mahony could not help feeling a trifle sore in advance..at the zanyish figure he was going to be obliged to cut.

Zanza, zanze, variants of *Sansa.

Zebra, *sb.* 3. Add: *zebra-marked, -striped* (example); **zebra suit** *U.S.,* a striped suit worn by convicts.
1924 J. A. Thomson *Science Old & New* v. 30 Butterflies like the unpalatable *zebra-marked Heliconius, which insectivorous birds leave unmolested. 1891 Hardy *Tess* xlvi, She moved off..across the *zebra-striped field. 1885 *Rep. Indian Affairs* 105 There are over twenty prisoners who are required to work and who wear the *zebra suit.

Zeeman effect. The effect which a strong magnetic field has on the spectrum from a luminous vapour of splitting up a spectrum line into a number of constituent lines, first observed by Zeeman in 1896.
1900 *Encycl. Brit.* XXX. 466/2 There are some interesting phenomena connected with the Zeeman effect which are more easily observed than the effect itself. 1928 E. Schrödinger *Four Lectures on Wave Mechanics* 16 The splitting up of the hydrogen lines in the Zeeman and Stark effects.

Zeitgeist. (Earlier and later examples.)
1884 *Macmillan's Mag.* Aug. 254 For realism in one form or another is the zeitgeist which will master us all. 1921 R. Hichens *Spirit of Time* iv. 74 It is not the Katyas who really influence us...It is the terrible Zeitgeist; it is the Spirit of the Time.

Zenithward, *adv.* (Earlier example.)
1868 Carlyle in Froude *Life* (1884) II. 371 It was as a ray of everlasting light and insight this, that had shot itself zenithward from the soul of a man.

Zephyr (ze·fəɹ), *v.* [f. the sb.] *intr.* To blow like a zephyr.
1922 Hardy *Late Lyrics & Earlier* 111 An aura zephyring round, That care infected not.

Zero. 6. (Further example.)
1916 Huneker *Ivory Apes & Peacocks* 35 We should soon reach a zero if we only registered the absence of 'necessary' traits in our poet.
b. *Hour of zero*: also simply *zero.*
1918 E. A. Mackintosh *War, the Liberator* We've got to be at Battalion Headquarters at 5, although I don't suppose we'll be for a good time after that.
7. a. **zero-hour** (*b*), the hour at which the lowest value of anything is reached or recorded.
1930 *Daily Express* 23 May 1/6 Psychologists have fixed 11 a.m. as the *zero hour of the worker.

Zero (zɪə·ro), *v.* [f. the sb.] *trans.* To fix the zero hour for the beginning of (a military operation).
1926 *Blackw. Mag.* Dec. 774/1 Plan no. 7 will be put in operation to-night. It will be zeroed as from 23.00 hours.

Zigsaw, zigzaw, variants of *Jig-saw.
1910 Sir H. Maxwell *Early Chron. rel. Scot.* I. 16 One of those zigzaw puzzles which had a fleeting vogue two or three years ago. 1919 D. Wyllarde *Holiday Husb.* xiii, As neatly as if she had found the right pieces of a zigsaw puzzle.

Zigzag, *v.* Add: 2. b. To traverse in a zigzag manner.
1930 F. L. Bird & F. M. Ryan *Recall Public Officers* 42 He literally zigzagged the whole tremendous territory, visiting almost every hamlet.

Zinc, *sb.* 2. b. Add: *zinc-covered, -lining.* c. **zinc-aluminium** *a.,* consisting of zinc and aluminium.
1911 *Daily News* 28 Sept. 3/1 The *zinc-aluminium alloys as used in the motor industry for gear-cases, etc., undergo a similar electrolytic or chemical change. 1890 Conan Doyle *Firm of Girdlestone* xxx. 238 A very seedy-looking individual who was leaning with his elbows upon the *zinc-covered counter. 1922 C. N. Moody *Saints of Formosa* vi. 132 Boxes had to be made or furnished with *zinc-lining.

Zip, *sb.* Add: 3. **zip-fastener, -fastening,** a form of fastener consisting of two flexible stringers which are made to engage or disengage by a sliding cam device which is pulled along between them.
1927 *Daily Express* 6 Sept. 3/4 The airwoman's costume of tango suede, complete from the zip fastening to the little hat..is attracting many admirers. *Ibid.* 22 Nov. 3/5 Many of the new sports suits have zip-fasteners.

Zip, *v.* Also, to move briskly or with a zip.
1907 Bennett *Grim Smile of Five Towns* 222 'Let her zip,' said Mr. Colclough. 1929 *Even. News* 3 Jan. 4/2 He ..hardly saw it [the ball] after it pitched, as it zipped off the ground and whipped round his bat to take the off stump.

Zipper (zi·pəɹ). [f. *Zip *sb.* 3 + -er.] A zip-fastener; a boot, bag, etc., fastening by this means. Also *zipper-fastener,* etc.
1925 *Scribner's Mag.* Oct. 22/2 Advt., No fastening is so quick, secure, or popular as the 'zipper'. 1928 *Daily Express* 13 Aug. 4/3 You will need five-eighths of a yard of material..and one 12-inch zipper fastener. *Ibid.* 11 Oct. 5/5 Boleros, zipper-fastened with 'zippers', press studs, or inset clips. *Ibid.*, Zipper-fastened. 1931 *Atlantic Monthly* Feb. 3/1 Advt. Both bags have zipper fastenings.

Zippy (zi·pi), *a.* [f. Zip + -y.] Bright; lively; energetic.
1923 P. G. Wodehouse *Inimit. Jeeves* xv. 195 I'm going to write..something zippy to brighten the thing up a bit. 1926 *Bulletin* 16 Oct. 18/2 A zippy show is 'Cheerio' at the Glasgow Empire this week.

Zi·ther, *v.* [f. the sb.] *intr.* To play the zither.
1908 W. J. Locke *Beloved Vagabond* ix. 114 We wandered and fiddled and zithered and tambourined through France till the chills and rains of Autumn rendered our vagabondage less merry.

Zizania. (Earlier example.)
1788 White *Jrnls.* (1931) 316 Linnaeus has given this plant the name of Zizania.

Zloty (zlɒ·ti). [Pol. *złoty,* f. *złoto* gold.] The Polish monetary unit having a par value of about 25 to the pound sterling.
1923 *Times* 13 Aug. 14/5 The zloty, or gold franc, the nominal unit of Poland. 1925 *Glasgow Herald* 31 July 14/1 After the collapse of the old Polish paper mark the zloty was introduced with a nominal gold value of one gold franc.

Zone, *sb.* 9. Add: **zone time,** the local time for any longitude as opposed to Greenwich time.
1908 H. B. Morse *Trade & Admin. Chinese Empire* viii. 203 The Eighteen Provinces roughly extend from..longitude 98° to 122° E., comprising the seventh and eighth hours of Zone time east of Greenwich. 1930 *Daily Express* 16 Aug. 1/3 The passengers wonder whether they should retire by Greenwich or zone time.

Zoning, *vbl. sb.* Add: b. *spec.* (See quots.)
1922 *World's Work* XLIV. 468/1 A zoning plan. This new idea of municipal growth had its origin in Boston in 1911. 1923 S. D. Adshead *Town Planning & Developm.* viii, In town planning in America, very great importance is attached to this question of zoning. 1927 F. E. Fremantle *Housing of Nation* 93 Laying down provisionally the 'zoning', as it is misnamed in the United States, meaning thereby the delimitation of residential, commercial and industrial areas respectively in the town.

Zoo-. Add: **Zoobe·nthos** [*Benthos], collective name for the various forms of animal life at or near the bottom of the sea. **Zooplankto·nic** *a.,* pertaining to or consisting of zooplankton.
1923 *Glasgow Herald* 19 Mar. 6 [He] continued his discussion of the animals of the ocean and dealt with the bottom-living fauna, or *zoobenthos. 1911 *Rep. Brit. Assoc.* 422 In the high Alpine lakes there exists an outstanding production of *zooplanktonic organisms.

Zooidiophilous (zōuˌoidiˌǫ·filəs), *a.* [f. as Zooid + -philous.] Adapted for pollination by animals.
1902 *Encycl. Brit.* XXV. 435/2 Many flowers..which are anemophilous may also be zooidiophilous.

Zoom, *sb.* (Example.)
1918 *Blackw. Mag.* June 762/1 The Hun's third repetition of the manœuvre was varied by a straight zoom instead of a climbing turn.

Zoom, *v.* 1. (Earlier and later examples.) Also to travel or move with a humming or buzzing sound.
1886 *Century Mag.* 426/1 The crystal went zooming into the fence-corner. 1924 *Brit. Weekly* 18 Dec. 270/1 Trams zoom along and buses rattle past. 1926 *Ladies' Home Jrnl.* Apr. 39 The little engine zoomed through space. 1929 W. Heyliger *Builder of Dam* 26 The wind was zooming down the lake.
2. *transf.* Of a bird.
1920 *Blackw. Mag.* July 71/2 The bird checked, swerved and dived and zoomed back into level flight again.
b. *trans.* To cause (an aeroplane) to zoom.
1918 V. Page *Mod. Aircraft* 521 A machine should never be 'zoomed' or made to jump into the air by a too rapid movement of the elevator flaps.

Zooming (zū·miŋ), *ppl. a.* [f. Zoom *v.* + -ing[2].] Making or accompanied by a humming or buzzing sound.
1923 *Blackw. Mag.* July 7/1 We settled into steady zooming flight. 1928 M. Walsh *White Rivers Run* xx. 280 There was a zooming patter, almost too quick for human feet, on the stairs outside.

ADDITIONS AND EMENDATIONS

ADDITIONS AND EMENDATIONS

A, *prep.*[2] 3. See further s.v. MANNER *sb.*[1] 9.

Acnode. Substitute for definition: = *conjugate point* (see CONJUGATE A. 6 a).

Angrom, Angromed should be deleted as erroneous forms depending on a misreading of derivatives of OE. *angsum*. See *Notes & Queries* 22 Sept. 1923, p. 228.

Annex, *sb.* Add the more recent pronunciation (æ·neks).

Atarned. Read ATREN *v.* for ATRUN *v.*

Autem. *Old Cant.* A church. Hence **autem mort,** a married woman, **autem cackler,** a Dissenting preacher. See Harman's *Caveat*, B.E. *Dict. Cant. Crew*, Grose, Farmer & Henley *Slang*.

Awl. The forms 1 **awel, awol,** 2 **owul,** 3 **eawl, eaule, owel, ouel,** 3–5 **oule,** belong to other words (OE. *áwel*, *ówel*, **ǽwel*) meaning 'flesh-hook'. See *Trans. Philological Society*, 1905–6, pp. 261–4.

Balance, *sb.* 8. First quot. for *c* 1384 CHAUCER read *c* 1410 HOCCLEVE.

Bane, *sb.*[1] *Etymology.* Delete 'also with Gr. φόνος . . . murderer'.

Bennet[1]. Delete form 3 **beneit,** and quot. *c* 1265, in which the form is Anglo-French.

Bison 2. Definition: for 'roams' read 'formerly roamed'.

Blunket B. First quot. read: *c* 1420 *Anturs Arth.* xxix, Here belle [= cloak] was of blunket.

Boodle[1] 1. Delete the form **buddle** and quot. 1625; the word is most probably HUDDLE *sb.* (q.v., 1 b).

Brang. Delete; error for CRANG or *Krang* (see KRENG).

Breath 4. Delete †.

Brisket 2. Quot. 1637 for 'shoon' read 'spoon'.

Broach, *v.*[1] For numbers of senses 6, 7, 8, read 5, 6, 7.

Bureaucracy. Earlier example:—1834 *Tait's Mag.* I. 180 bureauocracy.

Bye-bye[1]. Earlier example:—*a* 1500 *Carol* in *Rel. Ant.* II. 76–7 By, by, lulley . . . By and lulley.

Cent[2]. *Etymology.* The Romanic origin is established: *juego de los cientos*, i.e. 'hundred-game', is the Spanish name of piquet. Cf. CIENTO.

Chess-men. See MAN *sb.*[1] below.

Clead, cleed, *v.* *Etymology.* Omit the eighth line, and substitute: f. *klæði* sb.: see CLOTH.

Coincide and its derivatives are treated in a scholarly monograph by H. E. Shepherd, in the *American Journal of Philology*, vol. I. pp. 271–280, in which the history of the words in the mediæval Latin of Roger Bacon and the English writers of the 17th c. is traced with much fullness. For the verb, in sense 3, earlier instances are given from BERKELEY (1705) *Works* 1871 IV. 442, and W. WOLLASTON (1709) in Nichols *Illustr. Lit. Hist.* I. 201.

Corduroy. Earlier example of the form *corderoy*:—*Chadwick's Patent*, No. 1093, of 1774, specifies *inter alia*, 'cotton corderoys, cotton and linen corderoys'.

Cowl, *sb.*[2] Prof. Skeat points out the OE. form *cufel*, pl. *cuflas*, of date 963–84, in *Cartul. Saxon.* (ed. Birch) 367, 'ii cuflas & þry trogas' [two cowls and three troughs]. This makes certain its relationship to OHG. *chubil*, whether originally Teutonic, or of West German adoption from Latin.

Daver, *v. dial.* [In I. app. cognate with Du. *daveren* to shake, quake, MLG., LG. *dawern*, a word of frequentative form, of which the root is uncertain. In II. perh. transferred from the same.]

Davit. Early examples:—1485 *Naval Accts. Hen. VII* (1896) 40 Daviott for the bote. *Ibid.* 49 Daviottes in the ffore castell. 1495 *Ibid.* 193 Devettes with a shyver of yron. *Ibid.*, Dyvettes with a colke of brasse.

Dock, *sb.*[3] 4. Earlier examples:—1486 *Naval Accts. Hen. VII* (1896) 23 About the bringing of the same ship into her dokke. 1488 *Ibid.* 26 Keping the said Ship at Erith in her dokke. 1495 *Ibid.* 137 The Reparalyng, fortifying, and amendyng the dokke for the Kynges shippes at Portesmouth, makyng of the gates, & fortifying the bede of the same dokke. *Dock-head*: 1497 *Ibid.* 143 The dokke, the dokke hedde & gates of the same.

Dory, *sb.*[2] Earlier example:—1726 *Trav. Capt. N. Uring* 346 We launched the Dory over the reef.

Dunnage, *sb.* Earlier example:—1497 *Naval Accts. Hen. VII* (1896) 251 For xxxvj shegge Shevys layed alow in John Millers crayer for donage.

Each. The form **euych** should be deleted, with the quotation 1480–7 under A. ε, the correct reading being *eueryck* (see EVERY).

Egg-berry. (EGG *sb.* 7, p. 58/2.) This is a corrupt form of HAGBERRY, and ought not to have been given here.

Egromancy. The form *egremauncey* occurs *a* 1469 in *Gregory's Chron.* (Camden Soc. 1876) 183.

Eirant. Read:—Erroneous form of HAURIENT.

Enhendee. The word is, as stated in the text, a mistake for OF. *enheudee*; but the misreading occurs in Fr. writers, *e.g.* Palliot, 1664.

Eve-star. The quotation 1691 under this word should be deleted. The word *evester* occurring there is adapted from the mod.Lat. *evestrum*, which seems to have been arbitrarily invented by Paracelsus, and is explained in the *Onomasticon* of Toxites (1574) to mean, amongst other things, 'the astral body [*corpus sidereum*] of man, which foretells to us either death or any other evil'.

Eyelet-hole, *sb.* 1. Earlier example:—1497 *Naval Accts. Hen. VII* (1896) 334 Makyng of olyett-hooles with other necessaries for the seid sayles.

Faldstool. The explanation given of the OE. form *fyldestōl* is incorrect; cf. the gloss 'volumina, fyldas' in *Zeitschrift f. deutsches Alterthum*, IX. 494.

Fastgong, Fastingong. The ON. forms *fǫstugangr*, *fǫstu-inngangr*, should have been referred to. From the latter it appears that the correct analysis of *fastingong* is *fast* sb. + *ingang*.

For, *prep.* 7 c. The expression '*to name* (a child) *for* (= after) a person' is erroneously marked 'now only U.S.' It is still current in Sc.

Forayer. A reference should be given to the articles FOURRIER, FURRIER[1].

Fox, *sb.* 16. *Fox-whelp* b was app. a kind of cider. Cf. the following quot:—1664 EVELYN *Pomona* iv. 14 For the kinds then of Cider-Apples in being . . Some commend the Fox-Whelp.

Foy, *v.* Mr. G. H. Haswell informs us that on the north-east coast (esp. at Shields), a *foy-boat* was a small boat used (before the introduction of steam-tugs) to tow vessels in and out of harbour. The boat carried a small anchor or 'kedge', and was rowed a certain distance ahead of the vessel being towed; the kedge was then dropped, and the men on the ship 'hove upon' the kedge with a windlass until the vessel came over it, when the kedge was taken up and the process repeated. The operation was called *foying*, and the men employed *foy-men*. (See *The Maister: a Century of Tyneside Life*, p. 39.)

Gabion 2. The source of Scott's peculiar use of the word is found in the following quotations, but it does not appear what suggested the 'catachrestic' application:—1638 ADAMSON *Muses Threnodie* [no paging or signature] *note*, The ornaments of his Cabin, which by a Catachrestic name, he usually calleth *Gabions*. *Ibid.* (*title of piece*), Inventarie of the *Gabions*, in M. George his Cabinet.

Gable-end. Earlier example of the β form:—*a* 1380 *St. Bernard* 299 in Horstm. *Altengl. Leg.* (1878) 46 In þe gable end of þe churche Ben þreo wyndouwus.

Gadling[1]. The following passage is the original of the example quoted from Stow: *a* 1360 *Chronicon Galfridi le Baker* (1889) 113 Thomas quibusdam stimulis curtis et acutis quos manum dextram comprimendo digitorum nodi radicales e cirotecis laminatis expresserunt, et eos moderni vocant gadelinges, nudam Johannis faciem wlneravit.

Gage, *v.* Earlier example:—1474 CAXTON *Chesse* III. v. (1481) G vij, They began . . to axe and demande of her the besaunt that they had geuen to her. And she answerd That hit was holden and gaged vpon an ymage.

Gaid, gade. The word occurs also in the sense of 'goad':—1682 PEDEN in *Biogr. Presbyt.* (1838) I. 51 Their Theats will burn, and their Swingletrees will fall to the Ground . . and the Gade-men will throw away their Gades.

Game, *sb.* 7 ('prize contended for'). Earlier example:—*c* 1380 WYCLIF *Sel. Wks.* II. 258 Two men . . rennen a space for a priis, and he þat comeþ first to his ende shal have þe gamen þat is sett, wheþer it be spere . . or oþir þing þat is putt.

Gangrel 1. Earlier example:—*c* 1340 HAMPOLE *Perfect Living* viii. in Wks. 1895 I. 33 Gangrels, and langelers, & kepers of comers and gangars arely & late.

Gargoyle. Earlier example:—13 . . *S. Erkenwald* 48 in Horstm. *Altengl. Leg.* (1881) 267 Hit was a throghe of thykke stone . . With gargeles garnysht aboute, all of gray marbre.

Garter, *sb.* 6 a. Earlier example:—? 1504 in *Trevelyan Papers* (Camden Soc.) III. 7 The armys off Carminow, Garter seth . . came of

the iij brotherys. When ye ware made knytt ther wher but iiij cottes off recorde yn Garterys booke.

Gas, *sb.* In the Etymology, reference should have been made to the use of *chaos* by Paracelsus: see GNOME[2].

Gender, *sb.* 2. Earlier example:—*a* 1380 *St. Theodora* 109 in Horstm. *Altengl. Leg.* (1878) 36 Hire name, þat was femynyn Of gendre, heo turned in to masculyn.

Genitras (see GENITOR[1]). Add the following quotation:—13 . . *Minor Poems of Vernon MS.* xxxvii. 276 Men miȝte, ȝif his brech weore to-tore, seon his genitras [*rime* has].

Gentlemanly, *a.* Earlier example:—1433 LYDG. *S. Edmund* II. 128 This said Lothbrok was . . Riht gentilmanly in al his demenyng.

Gibbet, *sb.*[1] 5. The comb. *gibbet-tree* occurs many centuries earlier:—13 . . *St. Cristofer* 668 in Horstm. *Altengl. Leg.* (1881) 462 Myne eldirs . . sloughe hym on a gebete-tree.

Giesetrye. The OF. *giesiterie* is f. the med.L. *giesīta* (St. Bernard), which was anglicized as GYESITE, q. v.

Gist, *sb.*[3] See also JET *sb.*[4] The AF. law phrase (*cest*) *action gist*, '(this) action lies', which is the source of the Eng. sb., occurs 1502–3 in *Kelwey's Rep.* (1688) lf. 50 a, and is common in law-books. An earlier example of the sb. is:—1711 5 *Modern Reports* (1794) 305 (*Gatehouse* v. *Row*) Because it is the very gist of the action.

Gite[1], **gide.** Earlier example:—13 . . *Minor Poems of Vernon MS.* xxxvii. 281 Þis wymmen þat muchel haunteþ pride . . Heore reuersede gydes on hem are streyt drawe.

Glavering, *vbl. sb.* Earlier examples:—*c* 1425 *St. Mary of Oignies* II. v. in *Anglia* VIII. 165/26 Made proude wiþ glauerynge of prosperite. *Ibid.* 168/36 Pryde gaf me comforte . . wiþ brighte beemes of glauerynge.

Glooming, *vbl. sb.* 1. Earlier example:—13 . . *Peter & Paul* 74 in Horstm. *Altengl. Leg.* (1881) 77 Hetheli glowminge & wordes grete.

Glossary[1]. Earlier example:—*a* 1380 *S. Paula* 36 in Horstm. *Altengl. Leg.* (1878) 8 As seiþ þe bok, iclept Glosarie.

God-speed. Earlier examples:—*c* 1470 HENRYSON *Mor. Fab.* II. (*Town & C. Mouse*) xv, This burges brocht thame sone quhair thay suld be; Without god speid thair herberie was tane. *Ibid.* xxiv, Quhen in come gib hunter . . And bad god speid.

Golden, *a.* 4. Earlier example:—*c* 1400 *Rom. Rose* 5650 Pictagoras himsilf reherses In a book that the Golden Verses Is clepid.

Golden, *a.* 10, **Gold,** *a.* 10. Earlier examples of *golden rain*, *gold rain* (Fireworks) occur in 1672 VENN *Compleat Gunner* III. x. 19; this author also uses *golden* or *gold hair* in the same sense.

Go-summer. Earlier example:—1649 *Cupar Presb. Rec.* in Campbell *Balmerino* (1899) 381 In the last goesommer save one.

Goul maw. Delete the article. (See *gull maw*, GULL *sb.*[1])

Gourd[1]. Add to the Forms 6 gord, and insert the following earlier example in sense 4:—1596 RALEIGH *Disc. Guiana* 16 He . . called for his Calabaza or gords of the gold beades.

Gunpowder. Earlier example:—1411 *Indenture* in *Excheq. Accts.* Q. R. Bdle. 44, no. 17 (P.R.O.), Une petit barell' de gonpouder. [Misdated 1338 by Nicolas *Royal Navy* II. 476 App.]

Halfpennyworth. b. Earlier example of *halfpennyworth of tar*:—1631 CAPT. SMITH *Advt. Planters* 30 Rather . . to lose ten sheepe, than be at the charge of a halfe penny worth of Tarre.

Hander. *spec.* = HANDLER 2. 1746 *Acct. of Cock-fight* in *42nd Ann. Rep. Deputy Keeper P. R.* 166 In such manner as is usual for handers to account ten. 1794 *Sporting Mag.* III. 169 Called 'handers' or 'setters to'.

Hansard[1]. Early examples:—1449 *Rolls Parlt.* V. 144/2 Hanser. 1453 *Ibid.* V. 230/2 Another Subsidie . . of every Venecian, Esterlynge . . Lumbard, Hanszard, Prucier, and also other Straungers Merchauntz. *Ibid.*, Hansard.

Harrier[2], the dog. Earlier examples:—1408 *Privy Seal* (20 Aug.) 9 Hen. IV. (No. 5874) La garde de nos chiens appellez hayrers. 1413 *Rot. Pat.* 1 Hen. V. pt. 3, memb. 19, 12 June, Custodiam canum nostrorum vocatorum 'hayreres'. 1446 *Issues of Excheq.* (ed. Devon), [Hounds called] heireres.

†**Hask,** *a.* (used *adv.*) *c* 1440 *Pallad. on Husb.* VII. 124 Al hugely and haske [L. *rauce*].

†**Haskness.** *Obs.* [f. HASK *a.*] Hoarseness, huskiness. 1519 HORMAN *Vulg.* 28 He hath a great haskenes [*graui asthmate implicatur*]. 1540 EARL OF BATH in Ellis *Orig. Lett.* Ser. II. II. 158, I am . . sore aggreved with the agew myxte with a cough & haskenes. 16 . . in J. Thompson *Ann. Influenza* (1863) 9 A dry cough, pain of the breast, haskness and roughness of the throat.

Haversine. The name was introduced by Prof. Jas. Inman, D.D., in his *Navigation and Nautical Astronomy* ed. 3, 1835. Cf. *Dict. Nat. Biog.*

Haw, *sb.*[3] b. Earlier example:—*c* 1450 *ME. Med. Bk.* (Heinrich) 98 A charme for þe hawe in þe ye.

Headstock 1 f. (Of a bell.) Earlier example:—1688 R. HOLME *Armoury* III. 461/2 A Bell Azure hanging by its Headstock and Gugions in an Arch.

Hog-deer 1. Definition, read: The common name of a small Indian deer, *Axis porcinus*. (Sometimes also used to include *A. maculatus*.)

Hunch, *v.* 1. Earlier example:—1581 R. V. *Caluine on Gal.* iv. 30. 112 The heritage is saued for vs, howsoeuer bragly they hunche at vs for a time.

Husting 2 b. For a hustings court, *curia hustengorum*, in Oxford, see Wood's *Life & Times* (O. H. S.) IV. 183–4.

Hut, *sb.* 1 b. Earlier example, showing this to be the earlier use. 1545 *St. Papers, Hen. VIII*, X. 609 The French armey . . having broken up their campe and brent all their huittes, removed . . towardes Arde.

†**I-kepe,** *v. Obs.* The sense in the quots. is that of KEEP *v.* 5, 6 c, to watch for, wait for, intercept, ward off.

Immersion. Earlier example:—*c* 1450 *Mirour Saluacioun* 1407 Thas whilk in watire takes duwe inmersionne.

Imperial, *sb.* 8. Early example:—1839 WARREN *Ten Thousand a Year* i, An imperial—i.e. a dirt-coloured tuft of hair, permitted to grow perpendicularly down the under lip of puppies—poor Mr. Titmouse had been compelled to sacrifice some time before. [This makes the history of the word doubtful. Perh. it was merely revived in compliment to Napoleon III, to whom the French Dicts. refer it.] 1841 [see Supplement].

Inassuageable. Early example:—1654 GAYTON *Pleasant Notes* III. v. 96 Don Mariotto, Knight of the Inasswagable Panch.

Incitress. Literary example:—1654 GAYTON *Pleasant Notes* IV. vi, Bright Sun-beame, repairer and incitresse of my decaying heat.

Incluse, *a.* Later example:—1715 M. DAVIES *Athen. Brit.* I. Pref. 20 The Incluse Anchoret Peter, from the Confines of Spain.

Income, *v.* Delete quot. *c* 1565, the word being an error of the ed. cited.

Inconsutile, *a.* Early example in lit. sense:—*c* 1450 *Mirour Saluacioun* 3205 Marie didde onne hire sons cote inconsutyle with out semyng.

India paper. Cf. 1750 WALPOLE *Lett.* (1846) II. 351 Mrs. Frere . . screamed about Indian paper.

Indomable, *a.* Early example:—*c* 1450 *Mirour Saluacioun* 5062 The Egle indomable thow reclamed at the fulle.

Ingot. Anglo-Fr. example of sense 2:—1423 *Rolls Parlt.* IV. 22 Item, diverses Yngottes & kakes d'arg[ent], pois[auntz] xxxiii lb vii unc'. Item, vi Yngottes d'arg[ent], poisauntz vi lb ix unc' di.

Ingrain, *a.* 1 b (American use):—1836 *Penny Cycl.* VI. 314/1 Kidderminster . . carpets, or, as the Americans more descriptively term them, ingrain carpets.

Inscriber. Earlier example:—1674 SIR G. MACKENZIE *Laws & Customs Scotl. Matters Criminal* xix. § 8 (1699) The inscriber was according to the Civil Law, oblidged to find caution.

Insensible, *a.* 1. (Confirming this as earliest sense):—*c* 1380 WYCLIF *Wks.* (1880) 469 Bileue is insensible & more trewe þan siche signes; as þis treuþe is insensible þat two & þre maken fyue, & ȝit it is more certeyn þan ony sensible þing heere.

Instigatrix. Literary example:—1674 BREVINT *Saul at Endor* 109 The Woman should be the Instigatrix, or the first Sollicitress.

Interlace, *v.* 4. Earlier example:—1531 ELYOT *Gov.* III. xxv. (1880) II. 398 Admytte that some histories be interlaced with leasynges.

Invert, *v.*, sense 2, add: **g.** *Math.* To transform by inversion; to obtain the inverse of: see INVERSE *sb.* 2, INVERSION 3.

Irreclaimable, *a.* 2 b. Earlier example:—1812 BRACKENRIDGE *Views of Louisiana* (1814) 159 Of this portion, there is not more than a fourth which can be considered irreclaimable.

Irregular, *a.* Insert between senses 6 and 7:—*Math.* (see quots.). 1700 MOXON *Math. Dict.* s.v. *Regular*, Those [figures are] called Irregular, which have not the Equality of Sides and Angles, as are Prisms and Trapezia's. 1734 J. WARD *Introd. Math.* III. i. § 4 (ed. 6) 290 An Irregular Polygon is that Figure which hath many unequal Sides standing at unequal Angles.

Irrelevancy. Early example:—1592 *Sc. Acts Jas. VI* (1597) § 151 Seeing that diverse exceptiones and objectiones risis vpon criminall libelles . . be alleged irrelevancie thereof.

Ism, *quasi-sb.* Earlier example:—1680 E. PETTIT *Vis. Purgatory* 46 He was the great Hieroglyphick of Jesuitism, Puritanism, Quakerism, and all Isms from Schism.

Jasmine 1 β. Cf. 1548 TURNER *Names of Herbes* 44 Iasminum otherwise called Iasme.

Jaw, *sb.*[1] 7, *jaw-piece*. Read:— = JOWPY. See also Supplement.

Jerkin-head. Cf. KIRKIN-HEAD, the earlier existence of which suggests that *jerkin-head* originated in some error.

Jiboya. Early examples:—1613 PURCHAS *Pilgrimage* (1614) 842 [*Brasil*] Of Snakes without venome, he numbereth the *Giboya*, some of which are twentie foote long, and will swallow a Deere whole. *Ibid.* 839 *Iaboya*.

Lability. Earlier example:—1554 in *Maitl. Club Misc.* III. (1855) 65 The labilite and breuitie of tymes maneris and of men in this wale of teiris beand considerit.

Labyrinthine, *a.* Earlier example:—1632 LITHGOW *Trav.* III. 99 These Laborinthing Seas.

Lachrymous, *a.* Earlier example:—1490 CAXTON *Eneydos* viii. 35 Lacrymous and playnynge sorowes.

Lacquering, *vbl. sb.* For **lacquering-stone** read **lacquering-stove.**

Lake, *sb.*[3] The reference to LETCH *v.* in the etymology should be to LEACH *v.*[2]

Lamantin. Earlier example:—1666 J. DAVIES tr. *Rochefort's Caribby Isl.* I. xvii. 103 A certain fish by the French called Lamantin, by the Spaniards Namantin and Manaty. *Ibid.* 300 Their not eating of salt, Swines-flesh, Tortoises, and Lamantin.

Lamba. Earlier example:—1729 DRURY *Madagascar* 234 The Corps being . . wrapped up in a Lamber, or perhaps two Lambers.

Landaulet. Earlier example:—1771 *Patent Specif.* No. 997 The fore part of the head of a landawlet is constructed with a hinge [etc.].

Lantern, *v.*[2] Example:—1815 *Paris Chit-Chat* (1816) II. 184 He was himself very near being lanterned in the streets of Paris by a group of the *fauxbourg Saint Antoine*.

Lark, *sb.*[2] Phrase, *To make a lark of* = 'to make game of':—1850 THACKERAY *Pendennis* xxxix. (1885) 385 Don't make a lark of me, hang it!

Lathe, *sb.*[4] The Ger. *lade* is used in the same sense, and should have been cited as cognate.

Lawn, *sb.*[1] 3 b. For an explanation of the torture of the 'lawn', see 1569 JEWEL *Expos.* 1 *Thess.* Wks. 1848 VII. 42–3. (Cf. *linen-ball*, LINEN B 5.)

Ledger, *sb.* 1 b. Earlier examples:—1401 in Wylie *Hen. IV*, IV. 198 [Items of expenditure] 19 portos, 3 liggers. 1444 in *Dugdale's Mon.* VI. 1427 Duo portiphoria . . alias nuncupata lyggers.

Leetle, *a.* Earlier example:—1687 PHILLIPS *Don Quixote* 496 The Taylour . . held up five leetle Cloaks.

Legitimate, *a.* Earlier example of *legitimate drama*:—1821 BYRON *M. Faliero* Pref. 18 *note*, While I was in the sub-committee of Drury Lane Theatre . . we did our best to bring back the legitimate drama.

Let, *sb.*[1] 2. Earlier instance (*attrib.*):—1819 *Examiner* 7 Feb. in *Hazlitt's Table Talk* (1870) 118 His [Cavanagh the fives-player's] blows were not . . let balls like the Edinburgh Review.

Lettice. See also LITUIT.

Liberty 2 b. Earlier instance of *liberty of conscience*:—*a* 1572 KNOX *Hist. Ref.* Wks. 1846 I. 364 To suffer euerie man to leaf at libertie of conscience.

Lieutenant-general 2. Earlier example:—1589 [T. CATES] *Sir F. Drake's W. Ind. Voy.* 5 We descried another tall ship . . vpon whom Maister Carleill, the Lieutenant Generall, being in the Tiger, vndertooke the chase. [C. 'commanded the land forces against the Spanish West Indies' (Dict. Nat. Biog.).]

Lifehood. Delete quot. 1484: *lyuehode* is an error in the modern reprint for *lyuelode*.

Lift, *sb.*[2] 11. Add to the definition:—Also = LOCK *sb.*[2] 9 c. For the quotation read as follows:—1825 [see LOCK *sb.*[2] 9 c]. 1875 in KNIGHT *Dict. Mech.*

Lighthouse. Earlier example:—1622 BACON *Hist. Hen. VII* 142 They . . were executed . . at diuers places vpon the Sea-Coast . . for Sea-markes or Light-houses, to teach Perkins People to auoid the Coast.

Live, *a.* 3. Delete quot. 1865.

-lock, *suffix*, in mod. Eng. occurring only in *wedlock*, represents OE. *-lác*, the second element of numerous compounds (usually neuter: rarely masc.) in which the first element is a sb. OE. had about a dozen of these compounds (those in which *-lác* means 'offering', LAKE *sb.*[1], are not counted); in all these the second element may be rendered 'actions or proceedings, practice', as *brýdlác* nuptials, *beadolác*, *feohtlác*, *heaðolác* warfare, *hǽmedlác*, *wíflác* carnal intercourse, *réaflác* robbery, *wedlác* pledge-giving, also espousals, nuptials, *wíteláe* punishment, *wróhtlác* calumny. The *-lác* of these compounds should probably be identified with *lác* play, sport, LAKE *sb.*[2]; the words meaning 'warfare', which may have been the earliest examples of this use, may be compared with the synonymous compounds in *-plega* play. Of the OE. compounds of *lác* three (*brýdlác*, *feohtlác*, *réaflác*) survived into early ME., and *wedlác* still survives with altered meaning. In ME. the suffix was sometimes assimilated in form to the etymologically equivalent but functionally distinct Scandinavian -LAIK. A few examples, not recorded in OE., appear in early ME.: *dweomerlak* (DEMERLAYK), FERLAC, SHENDLAC, *treulac*, *wohlac* (cf. WOUHLECHE), the last from a vb.-stem, *woȝ-* to woo; but none of these survived later than the 14th century.

Long standing. The origin of this phrase seems to be illustrated by the following passage:—*a* 1568 ASCHAM *Scholem.* I. (Arb.) 34 Except a very fewe, to whom peraduenture blood and happie parentage, may perchance purchase a long standing vpon the stage.

Look, *v.* The synonymous MDu. *loeken* should have been cited as cognate.

Loot, *sb.*[1] See LUTE *sb.*[3], which is etymologically identical.

Machit, var. of MESQUITA[2].

Macute. The Rev. W. Holman Bentley, writing from the Congo Free State, informs us that *makuta* is the plural of **ekuta*, and denotes a bundle of ten mats of palm-fibre, still used as currency north of the Congo near the French frontier. Elsewhere the word survives only as the name of the Angola 'penny' piece or its value. Mr. Bentley says that it is derived from a Congo verb *kuta* to tie, now obsolete, but preserved in the reversing form *kutulula* to untie.

Mademoiselle. Earlier example:—*a* 1450 *Knt. de la Tour* (1868) 126 Madamoiselle! y praie you that ye ansuere not vnto this fole.

Maghoore, obs. variant of MOGUL.

Magnetician. Example:—1854 *Pereira's Polarized Light* (ed. 2) 65 The electrician and the magnetician have assumed, respectively, an electric and a magnetic fluid.

Mahone. Earlier example:—1572 MALIM in *Hakluyt's Voy.* (1599) II. I. 122 Great Hulkes called Maones.

Maidfeloun, obs. variant of MATFELLON.

Maim, *sb.* Earlier example:—*c* 1475 *Partenay* 6356 That mariage no mahyme to his kinred.

Main-brace[2]. Earlier example:—1680 SIR J. FOULIS *Acct. Bk.* 13 Aug. (Sc. Hist. Soc.) 487 To James Wilson, sadler, for . . helping yᵉ main braces.

Mainmort. Earlier example:—1387 TREVISA *Higden* (Rolls) VIII. 265.

Maiolica, var. form of MAJOLICA.

Man, *sb.*[1] 15. The view that CHESS-MEN originated as a corruption of *chess-meinie* is untenable, the word for '(chess-)man' in AF. being regularly *hom*. Earlier instances of *man* in this sense are:—*c* 1400 *Beryn* 1820 The Burgeyse seid: 'comyth nere! ye shul se þis man, How he shall be matid, with what man me list!' He drouȝe, & seyd 'chek mate!' *c* 1440 *Gesta Rom.* xxi. 71 (Harl. MS.) The first man, þat goth afore hath not but oo poynt, but whenne he goth aside, he takith anoþer . . . The secund, *scil.* alphyn, renneth iij poyntes both vpward and douneward.

Mandarin[1] 1 b. Earlier example:—1791 BOSWELL *Johnson* (ed. Hill) I. 31 From a man so still and so tame . . conversation could no more be expected, than from a Chinese mandarin on a chimney-piece.

Mandrague. Add etymology:—Corruptly a. F. *madrague*.

Mandrake 3. Earlier example:—1836 *Backwoods of Canada* 248 There is a plant in our woods, known by the names of man-drake, may-apple, and duck's-foot.

Mangy, *a.* 1. Earlier example:—1526 SKELTON *Magnyf.* (E.E.T.S.) 1123 *Fol.* In faythe, there is not a better dogge . . . *Fan.* Ye, but trowest thou that he be not maungey?

†**Mantist.** *Obs.* [f. Gr. μάντις + -IST.] A seer, prophet. 1588 J. HARVEY *Disc. Probl.* I. 84 Without which felicitie, neither Persian Magician . . nor Athenian Mantist . . shall euer passe with me for a prophet.

Manumotive. Earlier example:—1825 *Mech. Mag.* V. 97 (*heading*) Idea for a manumotive carriage.

Maracaibo. Earlier example:—1843 HOLTZAPFFEL *Turning* I. 94 Maracaybo is a furniture wood of moderate size, as hard as good mahogany, and in appearance between it and tulip-wood.

Marble, *sb.* 3. Earlier example:—1671 SALMON *Syn. Med.* III. 474 The reducing of any thing into a fine powder, by grynding it on a Marble.

Margent, *sb.* 2. Additional form and earlier example:—1432–50 tr. *Higden* (Rolls) I. 41 Y schalle purpulle the mariantes [TREVISA margyns] . . with a dowble ordre of yeres.

Mariner 1 b. See also MASTER *sb.*[1] 29. *Mariner portage* (in MARINER 4): Delete the explanation; see PORTAGE *sb.*[1]

Maritime. Add form 7 **maretine** and examples:—1652 EARL MONM. *Hist. Rel. Flanders* I. vii. 12 Of their Maretine Forces. 1654 — tr. *Bentivoglio's Wars Flanders* I. IV. 56 The City of Embden, . . one of the most considerable Towns of all the Maretine part.

Mark, *sb.*[1] 11 i. Earlier example:—1625 B. JONSON *Staple of News* IV. iv, Were he a learned Herald, I would tell him He can giue Armes, and markes.

Marriage 8. Earlier example of *marriage-rites*:—1621 BRATHWAIT *Natures Embass.*, *Sheph. Tales* Egl. ii. 198 For I your patience might wrong, To stand vpon these marriage rites too long.—According to modern editors *marriage rite* or *rites* should be read in SHAKS. *Pericles* IV. Gower 17, where the first Quarto (1608) has 'Euen right for marriage sight'.

Masse(n)ger(e, -inger(e, obs. forms of MESSENGER.

Massy, *a.* 5. The following quot. should have been given:—1632 MILTON *Penseroso* 158 With antick Pillars massy proof.

Master-hunt in MASTER *sb.*[1] 28. Read '**master-hunt** [see HUNT *sb.*[1]], a head huntsman' and transfer to 29, adding the following earlier instance:—*c* 1369 CHAUCER *Dethe Blaunche* 375 (Fairf. MS.) The mayster hunte anoon fote hote With a grete horne blewe thre mote.

Mere, *a.*[2] 1 c. Earlier example:—*c* 1400 MAUNDEV. (Roxb.) xxv. 116 Bringand cowpez of gold full of meere mylk.

Mesquita[1]. Earlier example:—1477 CAXTON *Dictes* 58 b, Somme men saye that legmon is buried in a toun called karanalle bitwene the mesquitte & the marche.

Mickle, *v.* Additional example:—*a* 1225 *Ancr. R.* 182 Sicnesse . . halt ine edmodnesse & mucheleð þe mede.

Minute, *sb.*[1] 7. To the definitions of *minute-bell*, *-gun*, add:—'used as a sign of mourning or distress'.

Montanous, *a.* Earlier example:—1658 ROWLAND tr. *Moufet's Theat. Ins.* 947 *Bombilophagus*, is a Fly, montanous, big, very black.

Moot, *v.*[1] 1. Quots. 1642–44 probably do not belong to this word: see MUTE *v.*[2]

Moquet. Delete this article, and substitute:—**Moquet,** obs. var. MUGGET[2].

Morhwell. The word (*morhuel*) is quoted as English by Rondelet *De Pisc. Mar.*, 1554, p. 280.

Motional, *a.* Earlier example:—1679 tr. *Willis's Pharmac. Rationalis* I. I. ii. 7 This Coat contains manifold orders of motional Fibres.

Motor, *sb.* 1 a. (*a*) The explanation given is erroneous; read:—'in mediæval astronomy, = PRIMUM MOBILE 1'.

Moustache 6. *Mustache monkey* occurs in Pennant *Syn. Quadrup.*, 1771, p. 114.

Myriad, Myrio-. Read: μυρίος countless, μύριοι ten thousand.

Obliterature. = OBLITERATION:—1711 G. HICKES *Two Treat. Christ. Priesth.* (1847) II. 50 A perfect obliterature of all injuries.

Obscure, *a.* 7 and *v.* 1. Earlier examples:—1432–50 tr. *Higden* (Rolls) II. 55 There be other names of cites founde in cronicles obscure to the intellecte. *Ibid.* VII. 411 That kynge dreamed that . . the bloode of hym obscurede and hidde the sonne.

Obstinative, *sb.* An obstinate tendency:—1561 T. HOBY tr. *Castiglione's Courtyer* (1577) I. D ij b, And of these errors there are diuers other causes and among other the obstinatiues of princes.

†**Obsu·rd,** *v. Obs. trans.* To make dull of hearing, deafen:—1639 J. WELLES *Soules Progr.* 109 Old age . . dimmed with blindness, obsurded with deafenes.

Occupable, *a. rare.* Capable of being occupied:—1851 WHEWELL *Grotius* I. 256 In things which are properly no-one's, two things are occupable; the lordship, and the ownership.

Octagonian, *a.* Earlier example:—1598 [see HEXAGONIAN].

Ogive. Early example:—1357–8 *Ely Sacr. Rolls* (1907) II. 180 In lvj pedibus de oggifs empt. per pede iijd. ob. 16ˢ. 4ᵈ.

†**Olyver currant,** *advb. phr. Obs.* [ad. OF. phr. *avoir l'olivier* or *son olivier courant* (in Cotgrave, *Il a tous ses oliviers courans*, hee hath his full swindge or libertie, he doth what he list); so med.L. *olivero currente* (Giraldus Cambrensis): origin unascertained. See Gaston Paris, *Romania* XVIII. 132 ff., Paul Meyer, *Ibid.* XXXII. 450–1, *Times Lit. Suppl.* 10 Aug. 1933, p. 537.] In accordance with one's plans or desires. 1470 SIR J. PASTON in *Paston Lett.* II. 415 If ye cowde fynde the meanes . . to cawse [the] Meyr in my Lordes ere to telle hym . . that the love of the contre and syte restyth on owr syde . . thys wolde do nonn harme, if it be soo that that [*sic*] all thynge go olyver currant.

Omnium 1, **Omnium gatherum** 3. Quot. 1775 should be 1761.

Oudemian. Earlier example:—*a* 1586 SIDNEY *Arcadia* III. (1598) 345 To meete as that night at Mantinea, in the Oudemian streete, at Charitas vncles house.

Out-be. To be beyond, excel:—1613 B. JONSON *To Earl of Somerset* (ed. Cunningham III. 465/2) May she . . Outbee that Wife in worth thy friend did make.

Out-dweller. Earlier example:—1594 NASHE *Unfort. Trav.* Wks. (Grosart) V. 40 Anie stranger or out-dweller.

Outputter[1]. Insert after sense 1:—b. A publisher. 1583 *Reg. Privy Council Scot.* Ser. I. III. 587 Sellaris and outputtaris of thair saidis buikis.

Pachyntic, *a.* Earlier example:—1704 J. HARRIS *Lex. Techn.* I, *Pachuntick* Medicines.

Package 1. Earlier example:—1540 in *Proc. Privy Council* (1837) VII. 48 Certain leade . . was stayed at London by the packer for lack of payment of package money.

Pagan. *Etymology.* The explanation of L. *pāgānus* in the sense 'non-Christian, heathen', as arising out of that of 'villager, rustic', given by Orosius (a Spaniard) *c* 417, has been shown to be chronologically and historically untenable, for this use of the word goes back to Tertullian *c* 202, when paganism was still the public and dominant religion, and even appears, according to Lanciani, in an epitaph of the 2nd cent. The explanation is now found in the L. use of *pāgānus* as = 'civilian, non-militant', opposed to *miles* 'soldier, one of the army'. The Christians called themselves *milites* 'enrolled soldiers' of Christ, members of his militant church, and applied to non-Christians the term applied by soldiers to all who were 'not enrolled in the army'. Cf. Tertullian *De Corona Militis* xi, 'Apud hunc [Christum] tam miles est paganus fidelis quam paganus est miles infidelis'. See also GIBBON xxi. *note*.

Pamp. For further evidence of this word see POMP *v.*[2]

Paper. Earlier (in Latin context) in *Ely Sacr. Rolls* 1341–2 papyr; 1359–60 paper.

Parabolic, *a.* 1. Early example:—*c* 1449 PECOCK *Repr.* (1860) II. 533 Signified bi likenes in parabolik speche.

Parapet 3. Earlier example:—1795 *Gen. Hist. Liverpool* 273 The foot paths here called parapets.

Parchmenter. Delete 'cf. PASSEMENTER'.

Parliament, *sb.* 5 b. Earlier example:—1583 *Cal. Inner Temple Recds.* (1896) I. 102 Parliament-house.

Particulate, *a.* In reference to organic matter, introduced 1871 by SIR J. BURDON SANDERSON (paper) *The Origin & Distribution of Microzymes* (*Bacteria*) *in Water* in *Q. Jrnl. Microsc. Sci.* XI. 325.

Pelfry. Quots. 1480, 1496, 1565 are removed to PILFER *sb.* In their place insert *c* 1460 *Promp. Parv.* 391/1 (MS. S) Pelfrey, *spolium*.

Petty, *a.* 1. *Obs.* add: exc. in special collocations (see 5).

Philosophic, *a.* 1 b. Add **Philosophic cotton:** see COTTON 7.

Pintle 2 a. Delete 'fixed erect . . small boats)', the ordinary practice in all cases being to have the pintles on the rudder.

Pleromorph, Plerophory. *Etymology.* Correct πληρής to πλήρης.

Plucky 2. Literary example:—1891 G. P. MERRILL *Stones for Build.* 39 Fine grained compact rocks . . break into concave and convex shell-like surfaces . . such stones are called *plucky* by the workmen.

Plump, *sb.*[2] Earlier example:—1477 NORTON in Ashm. *Theat. Chem.* 83 In Plomps . . Where heavie Water ariseth after Ayre.

Podike: see POWDIKE.

Port, *sb.*[6] Earlier example:—1543–4 (Jan. 11) *Adm. Ct. Exam.* 92 (Rypper's Depos.) The sayd [ship] mighte have layed his helme a porte.

Portitor. Later example:—1737 CHAMBERLAYNE *St. Gt. Brit.* Lists 213/2 Portitor and Taylor to the great Wardrobe, Mr. John Mills.

Postnares. Read: So **Postnarial** *a.* (*a*) situated behind the nostril: 1866 [see PRENARIAL[2]]; (*b*) belonging to the postnares.

Pourallee. For definition ¶, substitute: b. Subsequently used in the sense PURLIEU, as more fully shown under the form PURALÉ, q. v.

Prehalteres. Earlier:—1840 [see *pseudhalteres* s.v. PSEUDO- 2].

Previdence. In etym. read 'Late Latin'. Early example:—*c* 1374 CHAUCER *Boeth.* v. pr. vi. 83 (Sk.) For which it nis nat y-cleped previdence, but it sholde rather ben cleped purviaunce.

Principal, *sb.* Earlier examples:—[1 c] 1438 *Early Chan. Proc.* (P. R. O.) 75/11 One Roger Grey, Clerk, principalle of Brasenoce in Oxynforde. [2 d] 1709 STEELE *Tatler* No. 39 ¶ 24 The Principals put on their Pumps.

Procatalectic. Substitute for definition 'Catalectic in its former colon'. 1843 T. F. BARHAM tr. *Hephæstion* 195.

Provence. Delete the note following the definition, and quot. 1905; see next.

Provincial, *a.* 7 b. For definition read: Of, consisting of, or resembling a rose of Provence (= '*Rose de Provence*, the Prouince Rose, the double Damaske Rose', Cotgrave; *Rosa prouincialis*, Gerarde's Herbal, 1597).

Sabbatical, *a.* 2. Earlier example:—1599 PONT *Right Reckoning of Years* 2 These Sabbaticall yeares.

Sabbatine, *a.* Earlier example:—1674 BREVINT *Saul & Sam.* xiii. 281 Sabbatine bull.

Sagamite. Earlier example:—1698 *Hennepin's Contn. New Discov. Amer.* xxviii. 106 Sagamite, or Pap made of Indian Corn.

Salient, *a.* 3. The source of this use is Aristotle, *Hist. Anim.* VI. iii, Τοῦτο δὲ τὸ σημεῖον πηδᾷ καὶ κινεῖται ὥσπερ ἔμψυχον, 'this point [representing the heart in the egg] leaps and moves as alive'.

Saliva. Earlier example (in anglicized form):—*c* 1400 *Pety Job* 40 in *26 Pol. Poems* 122 Thow woldest suffer neuer more Me to swolowe my salyue?

Salsitude. Earlier example:—1623 COCKERAM I, *Salcitude*, brine liquor that is salt. *Ibid.* II, *Brine*, salsitude.

Saltation. Earlier example:—1623 COCKERAM I, *Saltation*, dancing.

Samcloth. Earlier example:—*a* 1450 *Glossary* (*MS. Harl.* 1002), *Hoc perzoma*, a samcloth.

Sanable, *a.* Earlier example:—1623 COCKERAM I, *Sanable*, which may be healed.

Sanguine, *a.* 5. Earlier example of *sanguine stone*:—1486 *Bk. St. Albans*, *Her.* a iii, The .v. stone is calde a Loys, a sanquine stone or sinamer hit is calde in armys. Also ellipt. as sb.:—*Ibid.*, Aloys is calde sinamer or sanquine in armys.

Sarrasin. Earlier example:—1621 LODGE *Summary Du Bartas* I. 135 That graine, which we call Sarazin Wheate, or Turky Wheate.

Saucer 4. Earlier example:—13 . . *Seuyn Sag.* (W.) 2784 With eghen that war ful bright and clere, And brade, ilkone, als a sawsere.

Sauciate, *v.* Earlier example:—1644 HAMMOND *Of Conscience* 27 Any such act of willfull sinne . . is a naturall meanes . . of sauciating and wounding the soule.

Scævity. Earlier example:—1623 COCKERAM I, *Scæuitie*, vnluckinesse.

Scale, *sb.*[2] 3. Earlier example:—*c* 1450 *ME. Med. Bk.* (Heinrich) 208 Þe scales of notes ant ryndes.

Scarlet, *sb.* 4 a. For quot. *a* 1683 substitute the following:—*c* 1610 BEAUM. & FL. *Philaster* v. i. (1622) 70 Doe the Lords bow, and the regarded scarlets, Kisse their gumd gols, and cry we are your seruants?

Scarlet, *a.* 4. Earlier example of *scarlet whore*:—1590 SPENSER *F. Q.* I. viii. 29 Forthwith he gaue in charge vnto his Squire, That scarlot whore to keepen carefully.

Scart, *sb.*[1] In list of Forms dele '9 scrath (? error)' and read 'See also SCRATH'.

Schiller. The Ger. word has been used by English entomologists in the literal sense: 1835 J. DUNCAN *Beetles* 87 The elegant tribe of *Cetonidæ* . . are generally of a fine green, often accompanied with a delicate schiller or play of colour.

School, *sb.*[1] 19. Additional example of *school-butter*:—1618 FLETCHER *Loyal Subj.* v. iv, *Anc.* He was whipt like a top, I never saw a whore so lac'd: Court schoole-butter? Is this their diet?

Screaling. Earlier example:—1594 BLUNDEVIL *Exercises* IV. (1597) 270, *Descr. of P. Plancius his Map*, This Countrey is inhabited of Dwarfes called in Latine *Pigmei*, being in height 4 foote as those be of Groynland, which are called Screlings [*printed* Serelings; *edd.* 1622, 1637 Sereelings].

Scuddle, *v.*[2] Earlier example:—1577 GRANGE *Golden Aphrod.* G iv, The Goddesses..skuddelyng and sekyng to defende themselues.

Sea-swallow 3. Delete quot. 1902 (where the word denotes a kind of swallow or swift).

Seed, *sb.* 5 a. Earlier example:—1620 *Observ. Making Fit Rooms Silkworms* 5 The Silk-wormes comming of ten ounces of seed [etc.].

Seeker 1 b. The date and authorship of the first quotation seem to be highly questionable. The passage quoted from Pagitt 1645 appears to contain the earliest known example of the use of the word as the designation of a sect, though the opinion there described was held by the three brothers Legate (*c* 1600), whose followers were called Legatine-Arians. (See C. Burrage, *The Early English Dissenters*, 1912, I. 214–6, 259–61, and App. A.)

Sentimentalize, *v.* 1. Earlier example:—1764 *Let. to W. C.* 5 Aug., Orig. Lett. (1788) 14. In the mean time we will philosophize and sentimentalize; the last word is a bright invention of the moment in which it was written, for yours or Dr. Johnson's service.

Sepal. The etymology should be as follows:—[ad. F. *sépale*, mod.L. *sepalum* (N. J. de Necker, *Phytologie philosophique*, 1790, p. 55, and *Corollarium ad Philosophiam botanicam Linnæi*, 1790, p. 18). Necker derives the word from Gr. σκέπη covering; as he refused to acknowledge the distinction between the calyx and the corolla (using the term *perigynanda* to comprise both), *sépale* (*sepalum*) in his use denotes the petals as well as what are now called 'sepals'.]

Servetist. Earlier example:—1621 LODGE *Summary Du Bartas* I. 9 The ancient and moderne Diuines, who haue disputed against the Arians, and Seruetists.

Shiner 1 b. The word in the quotation is perhaps a misprint for *shiver* (pulley).

-ship. At end of first paragraph delete 'and perhaps . . . region'. The alleged OE. *landsceap* is due to a misreading: see Napier *Contrib. OE. Lexicogr.* (1906) 41.

Shirley. For '*Obs.* or *spurious*' read '*Obs.*' The bird, a South American tanager, was named by G. Edwards (*Glean. Nat. Hist.*, 1764, III. 276) from *Shirley*, the family name of Earl Ferrers, to whom the specimen described belonged.

Shittle, *a.* The form *shuttle* survives *dial.*; see SHUTTLE *a.*, where additional quotations are given.

Shoe, *sb.* 6 c. The following examples of *shoe-thong* should have been given:—*c* 1000 *Ags. Gosp.* John i. 27 Ne eom ic wyrðe þæt ic unbinde his sceo-þwang. *c* 1200 ORMIN 10387 Þatt he ne wass nohht god inoh Cristess shoþwang tunnbindenn. *c* 1200 *Trin. Coll. Hom.* 137 Ac ich nam noht ne forðen wurðe þat ich un-cnutte his sho þuong.

Staddle, *sb.* Earlier example of sense 2: 1543 *Act* 35 *Hen. VIII*, c. 17 § 1 (1544) The same stathilles or storers [*elsewhere in the section* standilles or storers]. Earlier example of sense 3 a: *c* 1475 *Pict. Voc.* in Wr.-Wülcker 785/21 *Hic arcomus* [read *arconius*], a stathele.

Stanstickle. Earlier example:—*a* 1300 NECKAM *De Utensilibus* in Wright *Voc.* 98 *Gamarus*, *pinosche*, stanstikel.

Va·riolist. *rare*[—1]. [f. VARIOLA + -IST.] One who prefers small-pox to vaccination. 1799 *Gentl. Mag.* Aug. 665 A consciousness of propriety, which it seems that the Variolists have not had sufficient shame to acknowledge.

Ve·llumize, *v.* [f. VELLUM + -IZE.] *trans.* To convert into vellum. 1907 C. DAVENPORT *The Book* 173 The white 'vellumised' pigskin has always been the most favourite material for the covering of German books.

† **Vene·dic,** *a.* *Obs.* [f. med.L. *Venedi* (pl.): see WEND *sb.*] Wendish, Vendish. 1768 T. NUGENT *Trav. Germany* II. 178 Mirow is..supposed to have derived its name from the Sclavonic, or Venedic word *mir*, signifying peace. 1790 DORNFORD *Pütter's Hist. Developm. Ger. Emp.* I. 8 Except in Bohemia and Lusatia, the Venedic language has been under the necessity of yielding to the German.

Verger[2] 1. Earlier example:—*c* 1402 in *Peterborough Registry* (MS.), fol. 457, Officium hostiarii, alias dictum verger, in eodem [collegio de Wyndesore] vacans.

Vocabular, *sb.* Later example:—1659 W. JACOB in Somner *Dictionarium*, To list your names in this Vocabular.

†**Whene,** *v.* *Obs.* Also **wene, ȝwene.** [Aphetic f. ÁWHENE (OE. *áhwénan*).] *trans.* To afflict, trouble, offend. *a* 1310 in Wright *Lyric P.* 49 Lyare wes mi latymer, Sleuthe ant slep my bedyuer [= bed-fellow; *printed* bedyner], that weneth me unbe-while. Umbe-while y am to whene, when y shal murthes meten. *c* 1315 SHOREHAM I. 1908 And þaȝ þat lawe for-bede nauȝt Þat man and wyf ymene Toe-hebbe a child, ȝet scholdy nauȝt Honestete so ȝwene. *c* 1330 R. BRUNNE *Chron. Wace* (Rolls) 6887 'Lord,' he seyde, 'ȝow þar nought wene, Why y am comen ȝe may wel mene.'

Whistle, *v.* sense 9. *To go whistle.* Earlier example:—1453–4 PECOCK *Folewer to Donet* 106 If eny man pretende so greet a curiosite anentis þe persoon of crist þat he lackid þe passioun of angir, he may go whistle til he leerne bettir.

Y- *prefix* 3 c. The creation of new compounds falling under this heading began in the fifteenth century; examples are *ybete* (Kingis Quair), *ydrawe*, *yryve* (Lydgate), *ylipe*, *yminne*, *ypass*.

Yode. Earlier example:—*c* 1030 *Rule of S. Benet* xxvii. (ed. Logeman) 58 *Abiit*, se ðe ȝode. [How this spelling is to be interpreted in this instance is doubtful.]

LIST OF SPURIOUS WORDS

IN the following articles are treated in detail the more important spurious words (arising chiefly from misprints or misreadings) that have been current in English dictionaries or other books of some authority.

Dict. = New English Dictionary. Dicts. = (other) dictionaries.

Abishering, abishersing. App. error for MISKENNING: see Dict. and add: 1579 RASTELL *Expos. Termes Lawes*, *Abishersing* (and in some copyes Mishersing,) that is to be quite of amercementes before whom soeuer of transumption [ed. 1598 transgression] proued. 1610 FOLKINGHAM *Art of Survey* III. iv. 71 Abishersing, alias Mishersing, implies both forfaitures and Amerciaments of all transgressions within the Fee, and also the immunity from like penalties. 1696 PHILLIPS, Abishershing. 1706 PHILLIPS, Abisherifing.

Aristarchy. Erroneous alteration of *Aristarchi* 'severe critics' (= Gr. Ἀρίσταρχοι: see ARISTARCH) in some later edd. of the works cited below. Hence in WEBSTER (1828–32) and some later Dicts. (with erroneous definition). *a* 1612 HARINGTON *Brief View Ch. Eng.* in Park *Nugæ Antiquæ* (1804) II. 207 (from autograph copy) Some of the *Aristarchi* [ed. 1653 p. 153 Aristarchy] and sowr censurers of theise dayes. 1656 EARL MONM. tr. *Boccalini's Advts. fr. Parnass.* II. v. 205 The onely *Aristarchi* [ed. 1674 Aristarchy] of the world [*orig.* gli Arristarchi del Mondo].

Banket. Error for BANKER[4] a. 1846 W. M. BUCHANAN *Technol. Dict.*, *Banket*, in *bricklaying*, a piece of wood of about eight inches square, and nine feet in length, on which to cut the bricks. Hence in 1864 WEBSTER, 1889 *Century Dict.*

Censerie, misreading of TENSERIE in *O.E. Chron.* an. 1137 (Laud MS.).

Cherisance, -aunce. Error for CHEVISANCE[1], associated with *cherish*. 1658–62 PHILLIPS, *Cherisaunce* (old word), comfort. Hence in 1881 OGILVIE (Annandale) and some later Dicts.

Colophonian, *a.* The meaning 'relating to a colophon or the conclusion of a book' given in OGILVIE (Annandale, 1881, citing *Cudworth*) and some later dicts., is app. an error based on the following quot., in which the word means 'an inhabitant of Colophon', a town in Lydia. 1678 CUDWORTH *Intell. Syst.* 226 The same thing is .. intimated by Xenophanes the Colophonian.

Commonye. Explained as: Discourse, communing. Error in *Century Dict.* (1889) founded on *com'nye*, misreading of *comunye* (?). 16.. *Ballad of K. Arthur* xxxi. in Child *Eng. & Sc. Ballads* (1861) 237 To heere theire talke, and theire com'nye [ed. 1884 I. 285/2 comunye].

Compasture. Error for *composture* (Shaks. *Timon* IV. iii. 444). 1742–1800 BAILEY, *Compastures*, large Tracts of Pastures or Pasture Grounds, lying together. *Shakesp.*

Compearer. Form and meaning app. unauthorized. 1861 *W. Bell's Dict. Law Scot.*, *Compearer.* A party not called as a Defender in an action, but who conceives that he has an interest to oppose the action, may compear and claim leave to sist himself. If his claim is sustained, an interlocutor allowing him to sist himself is pronounced, and is designated as *Compearer*. [Not in earlier or later edd.] Hence in OGILVIE (Annandale) and *Century Dict.*

Conjoin, *a.* Explained as: Conjoined. App. some error for *conjoined* or *conjoint*, or a misunderstanding of *conjoin* used as a verb. 1864 WEBSTER, *Conjoin*, *a.* Conjoined. (*Obs.*) *Holland.* Hence in OGILVIE (Annandale) and *Century Dict.*

Corb. App. error for CORF, q.v., end of etymol. 1828–32 WEBSTER, *Corb*..1. A basket used in coaleries. Hence in *Century Dict.*

Corf. Explained as: A temporary building, a shed. Error founded on a misprint for *coif*, 16th c. Sc. form of COVE *sb.*[1] 1770 *Bannatyne Poems* 114 Intill a corf he crap [= Henryson's *Dog, Schiep, & Wolff* xxi, where the reading of the Bannatyne MS. is 'coif']. Hence in 1808 JAMIESON, 1864 WEBSTER, and some later Dicts.

Corfe. Erroneously inferred, with the sense 'a gap between hills', from *at Corfgeate* (F; Latin *Porta Corf*), *æt Corfes geate* (E) of *O.E. Chron.* an. 978, lit. 'at Corf's gate', the cleft in the chalk hills which was the site of the later Corfe Castle. 1882 *Cornhill Mag.* July 90 The great square castle that stands in the gap or 'corfe' from which it takes its name. 1883 *Good Words* July 464/1 That most lovely of all English ruins, Corfe Castle; the castle of the gap or *corfe* between the hills.

Cotgare. Erroneous compound of COT *sb.*[2] and GARE *sb.*[3] (AF. variant, if genuine, of OF. *gard*) due to misinterpretation of the formula *cot, gare, & vileine tuson* (31 Edw. III, Stat. i. c. 8), *cot, gard & vilein* (13 Rich. II, Stat. i. c. 9); cf. *sine cot, gard, et omni viti vellere* (1277 in J. M. Rigg *Sel. Pleas Rolls Exch. Jews* (1902) 93). 1706 PHILLIPS (ed. Kersey), *Cot, or Cotgare*, a kind of refuse Wooll, so clung, or clotted together, that it cannot be pull'd asunder. [Definition derived from Cowell's *Interpreter* s v. *Cot*.]

Cremett, -it(t. Error for EREMITE, inmate of a hospital. 1624 *Will* in *Ripon Ch. Acts* (Surtees) 363, I give sixteene cremets here, in Well, fower markes. *Note*, This word occurs occasionally in the older registers at Well, applied to the inmates of the hospital, 'eermits' once. 1709 in *Thoresby's Corr.* II. 221 The word Cremits in your old deed relating to the Hospital at Well, is doubtless, or should be, Eremits. 1736 DRAKE *Eboracum* 284 The Eremites, or Hermits, in the north were corruptly called Cremitts; and there is an annual rent..called Cremitt-money at this day.

Crepane. Error for CREPANCE. 1755 JOHNSON [citing *Farrier's Dict.*; but *The Farrier's and Horseman's Dictionary* by N.B., 1726, has *crepance*]. Hence in later Dicts.

Cresset. In *water cressets*, error for *water cresses* (WATER-CRESS). 1586 T. B. *La Primaud. Fr. Acad.* (1589) 669 A poore woman that sold Water cressets [so in ed. 1618]. 1730–6 BAILEY (folio), *Creset*, an Herb.

Crevet. App. an error for CRUSET, crucible. 1658 PHILLIPS, *Crevet*, or *Cruset*, from the French word *Creux*, hollow, a Goldsmiths melting pot. [So all edd. to 1706.] 1721 BAILEY, *Crevet*, *Cruset*, a Melting Pot used by Goldsmiths. 1823 CRABB *Technol. Dict.*, *Crevet*, a melting pot used by goldsmiths. [Hence in WORCESTER and some later Dicts.] 1881 RAYMOND *Mining Gloss.*, *Crevet*, a crucible.

Crinel. Error for CRINET 2, small hair-like feathers which grow about the cere of a hawk. 1730–6 BAILEY (folio), Crinels, Crinets [with definition of *Crinet* from 1721 Bailey]. Hence in 1775 ASH, 1823 CRABB *Technol. Dict.*, 1846 WORCESTER, 1864 WEBSTER, OGILVIE (Annandale), and *Century Dict.*

Cruyshage. Error for Du. *cruyshaye*, a species of shark (Marcgraf *Hist. Rer. Nat. Brasil.*, 1648, 181) = *kruis* cross + *haai* shark. 1753 CHAMBERS *Cycl. Supp.*, *Cruyshage*, ..the name of a fish of the shark kind, somewhat approaching to that strange fish the zygæna: but much less monstrous, its head being only triangular, or something like the figure of an heart... *Marggrave* p. 132. 1828–32 WEBSTER, *Cruyshage*, a fish of the shark kind, having a triangular head and mouth. *Dict. Nat. Hist.* [Hence in 1864 WEBSTER, and some later Dicts.]

Curriedew, -dow, curridow. Error based on a misreading of *curreiden* (see quot. *c* 1400 s. v. CURRY *v.*[1] 4 b). 1561 *Chaucer's Wks.* Ggg vi/2 Tho curreiden glosours. 1617 MINSHEU *Ductor*, *Curriedew*, in. Chaucer signifieth *Currie-fauour*, or *Flatter*. 1658 PHILLIPS, *Curriedow*, a curry-favour or flatterer. 1721 BAILEY, *Curridow*, a Curry-favour or Flatterer. *O[ld]*.

Cuvette. A spoon-like instrument used in extracting a cataract. Error for CURETTE. 1849 in CRAIG; hence in some later Dicts.

Dardy-line. Error for DANDY-LINE. 1889 in *Century Dict.* (citing Day *Brit. Fishes*).

David's staff. Originally an error of Pietro della Valle's, who gave *Dauidstoff* as the English name of an instrument for taking the altitude of the sun. This was reproduced by his translator, Havers, as *David's Staff*, which was copied by Blount and Phillips, and is repeated in some modern Dicts. So also *David's Quadrant* (= BACK-STAFF) in Phillips (ed. 1696), corrected in Kersey's ed. (1706) to *Davis's Quadrant*: see QUADRANT *sb.*[1], quot. 1696. 1623 PIETRO DELLA VALLE *Viaggi* Let. i. 22 Mar. (1663) IV. 16 Con diuersi altri strumenti: e con vno in particolare, che mi dissero, da poco tempo in quà, essere stato inventato da vn tal Dauid, che dal suo nome l'haueua chiamato *Dauidstoff*, che in lingua Inglese vale à dir legno di Dauid. 1664 G. HAVERS *translation*, One [instrument] invented by one *David*, and from his name call'd *David's Staff*. 1674 BLOUNT *Glossogr.*, *Davids-staff*, is an instrument in Navigation, consisting of two Triangles united together, one longer then the other, both having their base arched, and between them in the circle of their bases, containing an entire Quadrant of ninety degrees. *Valle's Travels.*

Declinous, *a.* Error for DECLIVOUS. 1864 in WEBSTER; hence in some later Dicts.

Declivant, *a.* Error for DECLINANT. 1830 ROBSON *Brit. Herald*, Declinant or Declivant. Hence 1881 OGILVIE (Annandale), Declinant, Declivant. 1890 in *Century Dict.*

Demoniasm. Error for DEMONIANISM: see note at end of article in Dict.

Dentise, -ize, *v.* To cut new teeth. Error due to misreading of L. *dentire*, inf. of *dentio* to cut teeth, in Bacon *Sylva*, 1626, § 755. 1773 JOHNSON (quoting *Bacon*). Hence in some later Dicts. [1626 BACON *Sylva* § 755 They tell a Tale of the old Countesse of Desmond,

who liued till she was seuen-score yeares old, that she did *Dentire*, twice, or thrice; Casting her old Teeth, and others Comming in their Place.]

Depectible, *a.* Error in Johnson's Dict. and some later Dicts. for DEPERTIBLE.

Deporture. Explained as: Carriage, bearing, deportment. Error for *departure*. [1611 SPEED *Hist. Gt. Brit.* IX. xxiv. § 285. 871/2 Her stately port and majesticall departure.] Quoted in 1775 *Gray's Poems* 34 *note*, Her stately port and majestical deporture. Hence in 1864 WEBSTER (citing *Speed*), and some later Dicts.

Desponsage. Explained as: Betrothal. Error for DESPOUSAGE. [*a* 1587 FOXE *A. & M.* (1596) 103/2 Despousage of Athilrid his daughter.] Quoted in 1836 RICHARDSON *Dict.* as desponsage. Hence in 1864 WEBSTER (citing *Foxe*).

Dialect, *v.* Explained as: To speak a dialect. [1599 NASHE *Lenten Stuffe* 41 By corruption of speech they false dialect and misse-sound it.] Here *false* is a vb. meaning to 'falsify', and *dialect* a sb. But 1881 DAVIES *Suppl. Eng. Gloss.* (quoting the above) has erron. entered *dialect* as a vb. Hence in some later Dicts.

Diffranchise, -ment. Errors for DISFRANCHISE, -MENT, due to reading ſ as f. 1755 JOHNSON. (No quotation.) 1828–32 WEBSTER, *Diffranchise*, *Diffranchisement*: see *Disfranchise*, which is the word in use. Hence in 1864 WEBSTER, and some later Dicts.

Disconsolancy. Explained as: Disconsolateness. Error for DISCONSOLACY. [1818 TODD Addenda, *Disconsolacy*, disconsolateness (quoting Barrow *On the Creed*, Penury, baseness, disconsolacy).] Entered in 1846 WORCESTER as *Disconsolancy* (citing *Barrow*); hence in some later Dicts. From this has been derived an erron. **Disconsolance** (1849 in CRAIG, and some later Dicts.).

Disjudication. Error for DIJUDICATION. [1664 BOYLE *On Colours* ii. 20 The Dijudications we make of Colours.] 1755 JOHNSON, *Disjudication*, judgment; determination; perhaps only mistaken for *dijudication*. *Boyle on Colours*. Hence in 1864 WEBSTER (citing Boyle), and some later Dicts.

Disquieture. Error for DISQUIETNESS. 1860 FROUDE *Hist. Eng.* V. 435 (quoting letter of 1552 of Sir J. Crofts to Cecil) Such disquietures of mind. [The original MS. reads *disquyetnes*.]

Dissoned. Explained as: Dissonant. Error for *distoned* in *Rom. Rose* 4248 (formerly ascribed to Chaucer). 1731 BAILEY, *Dissonid*, dissonant, disagreeing. *Chaucer*. 1881 OGILVIE (Annandale), *Dissoned*. Hence in some later Dicts.

Dog-ray, -reie. Explained in some mod. Dicts. as: Dog-fish. App. error arising from misreading *dorrey* (see quot.), var. of DORY. [1577 HARRISON *England* III. x. 110/1 in Holinshed *Chron.* I, Of the first [sort of fish, the flat] are the Plaice, the Butte, the Turbut, Dorrey, Dabbe, &c.]

Exidemic, -ical. Errors for EPIDEMIC, -ICAL, due to the similarity of *x* and *p* in 16th and 17th cent. hands. 1608 TOPSELL *Serpents* 76 A certaine token .. that some exidemicall [ed. 1658 epidemicall], generall pestilence or plague rageth amongst them. 1847–78 HALLIWELL, Exidemic (citing HALL).

Exiled, *a.* Explained as: Slender, weak. Error for EXILE *a.*, meagre, scanty. 1577 NORTHBROOKE *Dicing* Ded. 4 My exiled and slender learning. [So in the undated edition, supposed to be of 1577; but the much better edition of 1579 has 'exile'.] Hence in 1859 NARES (quoting the above), and in *Century Dict.*

Expediate, *v.* Error for EXPEDITE in an imperfect and unauthorized edition of Sandys' *Relation of the State of Religion*, reproduced by Cockeram, copied by Todd, 1818; hence in later Dicts. 1605 SANDYS *Rel. State Relig.* K3, Some great alterations in some kinde of marchandise .. which may serve for that present instant to expediate [*MS. correction by author and ed.* 1629 expedite] their businesse. 1623 COCKERAM, *Expediate*, to dispatch, or make ready.

Factable, Factabling. Errors for FRACTABLE, FRACTABLING. 1842 GWILT *Archit.* Gloss. 971 *Factabling*, the same as Coping. 1862 *Dict. Archit.* (Archit. Publ. Soc.), *Factabling* or *Coping*. A mistake in some books for *Fractable*. 1904 *Correspondent*, Factable is a word constantly used by architects, surveyors, and builders to denote the apex of a coping or the apex stone of the gable of a building.

Featherly. Error for FEATHERY. [1650 SIR T. BROWNE *Pseud. Ep.* II. i. (ed. 2) 55 Some feathery particle of snow.] 1773 JOHNSON, *Featherly*, resembling feather [quoting 'Brown' with the reading 'featherly']. Hence in 1828–32 WEBSTER, and some later Dicts.

Foupe, *v.* Error for *soupe* (see SWOOP *v.* 2 b), through misprint of ſ for f. 1605 CAMDEN *Rem.*, *Languages* 23 To soupe [edd. 1614–37 foupe; 1657, etc. soupe] their words out of the throat with fat and full spirits. Hence 1755 in JOHNSON [quoting the above with the reading 'foupe']. 1775 in ASH. Corrected by TODD, 1818.

Galverly, *adv.* Explained as: Cleverly, actively. Error for *galierdly*, GALLIARDLY. 1836 in RICHARDSON [quoting Wriothesley *To Sir T. Wyatt* Oct. 1537, A light gennet that is young and trotteth galverly; but the orig. MS. reads *galierdly*]. Hence in some later Dicts.

Garb-feathers. Error for *barb feathers* (see BARB *sb.*[1] 2). [1486 *Bk. St. Albans* bj, The federis vnder the beke be calde the barbe federis.] 1676–1732 COLES *Garbe feders*, the Feathers under a Hawk's beak. 1721–92 BAILEY, Garbe feeders [*sic*.]. 1848 HALLIWELL, *Garb feathers*, the feathers under the bill of a hawk (citing *Berners*, i.e. quot. 1486).

Gatchers. Error for *catchers*, the after-leavings of tin, originating in the glossary to Pryce's *Mineralogia Cornubiensis*. Also **Gatches** (*English Dialect Dictionary*). 1778 PRYCE *Min. Cornub.* 229 All dressers save the hinder stuff from the frame end, as it washes off in a pit by the name of Catchers. Gloss., *Gatchers*, the after leavings of Tin. 1849–50 WEALE *Dict. Terms*, *Gatchers*, the after-leavings of tin. [Hence 1890 in *Century Dict.*] 1882 JAGO *Anc. Lang. & Dial. Cornwall* 320 *Gatchers*, the after-leavings of tin ore. *Pryce.*

Geminal. Explained as: A pair. Error founded on *geminels*, misprint for *gemmels*: see GEMEL 1, quot. 1603. 1871 in LATHAM (quoting Drayton). Hence in some later Dicts. Also as *adj.* = geminate, in the following: 1657 TOMLINSON *Renou's Disp.* 344 Because its roots were frequently geminell [*read* Gemmell] resembling two Leggs.

Geotic, *a.* Error for GOETIC: see note in Dict. s. v. GOETY. 1755 JOHNSON, *Geotic*, belonging to the earth; terrestrial. *Dict.* [But 1727 BAILEY vol. II. (followed by 1730–6 folio) has '*Geotick*, a sort of Magick, performed by the assistance of a Dæmon, the same as Geomancy'.] Hence in 1864 WEBSTER, and some later Dicts.

Gofysshe, *a.* Error for *gosysshe* GOOSISH *a.*, silly, stupid, occurring in Thynne's ed. (1532) of Chaucer's *Troylus* (III. 584) and perpetuated in some modern editions. Hence the following dictionary entries: 1658–1706 PHILLIPS, *Gofish* (old word), sottish. 1864 WEBSTER, Goffish [citing *Chaucer*]; so in 1890 *Century Dict.*

Gosting. Explained in Johnson and some later Dicts. as 'madder', is taken from 1736 AINSWORTH *Thesaurus* I, '*Gosting* (herb), Rubia'. In the Eng.-Lat. part there is: '*Rubia*, Rubia tinctorum, an herb called gosling weed or clivers; madder'. Thus *gosting* in Ainsworth is a mistake for *gosling weed*, which does not mean, however, 'madder', but 'goose-grass' or 'cleavers'.

Graduction. Error for GRADUATION (sense 1 and 3 b). 1849 CRAIG. 1860 WORCESTER [citing *Brande*; but edd. 1842, 1853, and 1866 of *Dict. Sci.*, etc., read *Graduation*]. Hence in some later Dicts.

Grail. Error for BRAIL *sb.*[1] (sense 3). [1486 *Bk. St. Albans* a viij b, The same federis ye shall call the brayles or the brayle federis.] 1671 SKINNER *Etymol. Ling. Angl.* IV, *Grayll feders*, or *Graylles*, vox quæ apud solam Jul. Barns occurrit lib. de re Falconaria [*i.e.* quot. 1486], à Fr. G. *Gresle*, Gracilis. 1847 in HALLIWELL [citing *Blome*; but not found there]. Hence in some later Dicts.

Griefhead. Explained as: Sadness. Error for GREENHEAD[1], due to reading *grenehede* (Chaucer *Man of Law's T.* 65) as *greuehede* (taken to be f. *greue* GRIEF + *-hede* -HEAD). 1890 *Century Dict.*

Griefly, *a.* Explained as: Indicative of grief. Error for *griesly* GRISLY *a.* (through misreading ſ for f). [*a* 1586 SIDNEY *Arcadia* II. (1590) 165 b, Grisly [edd. 1629, 1633 griesly] Grones.] 1881 DAVIES *Suppl. Eng. Gloss.*, Griefly [quoting the above as 'griefly groans']. Hence in some later Dicts.

Grout. Explained as: A kind of wild apple. Error due to misinterpretation of *agromelum* (quasi *agriomelum*, Gr. ἀγριόμηλον wild apple), which occurs in glosses as a synonym of *idromelum*, etc. (see GROUT *sb.*[1] 2 b). 1755 JOHNSON, *Grout* .. 3. A kind of wild apple (*Agriomelum*, Latin.)

Guay. Originally in *cheval guay*, repr. F. *cheval gai*, a heraldic term for a horse without harness, misinterpreted as in quots. 1725 COATS *Dict. Her.* (1739), *Guay*, as *Cheval guay*, is a Horse rearing, and standing on his hinder Legs. 1730–6 in BAILEY (fol.). 1828–40 in BERRY *Encycl. Her.* I. 1830 ROBSON *Brit. Herald*, *Guay*, or *Cheval Guay*, a horse in the position of rearing, or standing on its hind legs.

Habenry. Inferred from: '*Habenries*, architectural decorations of some kind, but the exact meaning of the term does not appear to be known. It occurs in Chaucer, some copies reading *barbicans*' (Halliwell). The source is Chaucer's *House of Fame* 1189 (= III. 99), where Skeat, by emendation, reads 'Babewinnes' (see BABOON 1), MSS. and early printed edd. having various misreadings: *MS. Bodl.* Rabewynnes, *MS. Pepys* Babeweuries, edd. 1532 (Thynne), 1598 (Speght) babeuries, 1602 (Speght) habeuries, 1721 (Urry) Barbicans. 1882 OGILVIE, *Habenry*, a barbican; a corner turret. [So *Century Dict.*] 1888 *Cassell's Encycl. Dict.* [following Halliwell].

Herebode, Herebote. Spurious forms (due to 17th century antiquaries) compounded of OE. *here* army, HERE *sb.*, and *boda* messenger, BODE *sb.*[1], confused with *bót* compensation, BOTE, BOOT *sb.*[1] 1671 SKINNER *Etym. Ling. Angl.* Pppp 3 b, *Herebode*, vox ant. For. AS. olim Edictum Regis quo Cives seu subditi ad Militiam evocabantur, ab AS. *Here*, Exercitus, & *Bode*, Nuncius, *Bodian*, Denunciare, Indicere. 1727 *Cowell's Interpr.*, *Herebote*, the King's Edict, commanding his Subjects into the Field: From the Saxon *Here*, *exercitus*, and *Bode*, a Messenger. Hence *Herebote* in 1882 OGILVIE and *Cassell's Encycl. Dict.*, *Herebode* in *Century Dict.*

Icre. Error for *dicre* = DICKER *sb.*[1], the number ten, derived from a misinterpretation of quot. 1086 s.v. (xxxvi. dicras ferri), and reproduced in some mod. Dicts. 1610 HOLLAND *Camden's Brit.* I. 361 As we finde in the survey booke of England [*marg.* Doomesday-booke], the Kings demanded in maner no other tribute than certaine *Icres* of Iron [CAMDEN 1586 ferri Ieras; ed. 1607 ferri Icras], and Iron-barres.

Innuent, *a.* Explained as: Significant. First in Todd (1818), based on a misreading of *inuent* = *invent* in the following. 1628 BURTON *Anat. Mel.* II. ii. IV. 264 He may apply his minde .. to Heraldry, Antiquity, inuent Impreses, Emblems, make Epithalamiums [etc.].

Instinctly, *adv.* Error for INSTINCTIVELY. 1855 MRS. GASKELL *North & South* xxii, Margaret .. drew her ruffled, luxuriant hair instinctly [so in ed. 1855; ed. 1897 instinctively] over the cut. Hence in 1871 HOPPE *Engl.-Deutsches Suppl.-Lex.*, 1881 OGILVIE (Annandale), and some later Dicts.

Investive, *a.* Explained as: Encircling, enclosing. Error for INFESTIVE *a.*, troublesome, annoying. [1610 *Englands Eliza* in *Mirr. Mag.* 829 Th' horrid fire all mercilesse did choake The scorched wretches with infestiue smoake.] 1818 TODD [quoting this as 'investive']. Hence in some later Dicts.

Joves. Error for F. *joues* cheeks of a battery. 1883 WILHELM *Mil. Dict.*, *Joves* (Fr.), the two sides in the epaulment of a battery which form the embrasure are so called. [*Joves*, which is an error for F. *joues* (old-print spelling *IOVES*), is entered in *Century Dict.* (1890, citing *Wilhelm*) as an English word ('Origin not ascertained'). Hence in some later Dicts.]

Lolion. Error for LOTION (sense 1). [1549 LATIMER *6th Serm. bef. Edw. VI* Uj b, Their doctrine was vnsauery, it was but of Lotiones of decimacions of anets seade, and Cummyn and suche gere.] In ed. 1549 and later 16th c. editions 'Lotiones' is misprinted 'Loliones'. Hence in 1881 DAVIES *Suppl. Eng. Gloss.* [quoting this as 'lolions'], and in some later Dicts.

Lool. Error for LOOB (sense 1), a vessel to receive the washings of metallic ores. [1674 RAY *Collect. Words, Prepar. Tin* 121 The dross and earth .. is carried all along the trough to a pit or vessel, into which the trough delivers it, called a loob.] 1753 CHAMBERS *Cycl. Suppl.*, Lool (citing *Ray's English Words* p. 121). Hence in 1846 BUCHANAN *Technol. Dict.*, and some later Dicts.

Loudful, *a.* Error for *loud full*. [1606 MARSTON *Sophonisba* I. ii. B 4 b, The Cornets and Organs playing loud full Musicke for the Act.] 1864 WEBSTER, *Loudful*, full of sound; noisy; ringing. (*Obs.*) 'Loudful music' *Marston*. Hence in some later Dicts.

Mangering. Error for *mamering*, MAMMERING in Parker Society ed. of Philpot's *Exam. & Writ.* 315, where there is a note, 'A mangering: perplexing, throwing their faith into confusion, is the probable meaning, from *mang*, a word of Celtic origin, meaning to *stupify* or *confound*.' Hence in some mod. Dicts. [1559 PHILPOT *Jesus is God with us* C 3 b, Y[e] simple people might be brought in a mamering of their faith, & stande in doubte whome they myght beleue.]

Minutal. Explained as: A diminutive. Error due to misinterpreting L. *minutal* mincemeat. [1589 RIDER *Bibl. Schol.* 802 A Iussell, or meate made with diverse things, chopped together. 1 Minutal, n. 1656 BLOUNT *Glossogr.*, *Jussel* (*minutal*) meat made with divers things chopped together. *Rider*.] 1658–96 PHILLIPS, *Jussel*, a minutal from *jus*. [See JUSSEL in Dict.]

Misher(s)ing: see ABISHERING above.

Momblishness. Explained as: Muttering talk. Error for *moubliemies* in *ne moubliemies* forget-me-nots. [*a* 1500 *Assemb. Ladies* 61 (Addit. MS.) Ne moubliemies and souenez also.] 1532 *Chaucer's Wks.* 394 Ne momblysnesse and souenesse. 1721 BAILEY, *Momblishness*, talk, muttering. *O[ld word]*. 1837 RICHARDSON s.v. *Mumble*, 'Ne momblisnesse ne sonenesse.'—No *mumbling* talk nor noisy sound. *Chaucer*. 1890 *Century Dict.*, *Momblishness*, muttering talk. *Bailey*.

Munity. Explained as: Security, freedom. Error for MUTINY. [1648 W. MOUNTAGUE *Devout Ess.* I. 35 Devotion .. doth rather compose the mutiny [*misprinted* munity, *corrected in Errata*], then infringe the true liberty of our affections.] 1818 TODD [quoting this as 'munity']. Hence in 1864 WEBSTER, and some later Dicts.

Paddy, *a.* Explained as: Low in character or manners; mean; contemptible; poor. Error for *baddy*. [1585–6 T. DIGGES *Let. to Walsingham* 2/12 Jan. (P.R.O.) Such baddy persons as commonly, in voluntary procurements, men are glad to accept.] Quoted in 1860 MOTLEY *Netherl.* I. vii. 393 as 'paddy'. Hence in 1864 WEBSTER, and some later Dicts.

Parechasis, parecnasis, parecuasis. Errors for *parecbasis*, Gr. παρέκβασις deviation, digression. Also **Parectbaticall** *a.* 1584 SCOT *Disc. Witchcr.* XV. xxiii. 438 *marg.*, A parecuasis or transition of the author to matter further purposed. 1589 *Arte Eng. Poesie* III. 195 *marg.*, *Parecnasis*, or the Stragler. 1625 *A. Day's Eng. Secretary* II. 100 *Pareonasis* [sic], or *Digressio*, a speech beside the matter in present spoken on, as to say, But here let me remember vnto you something of the deserts and eternized memory of your worthy and most vertuous parents. 1659 *Quærees Prop. Officers Armie to Parlt.* 4 The first instrument together with a new fangled advice, have proved parectbaticall botcheries, or meer peccant forms of Polity, without any patterne or president in the Chequer Rolle of politicall Records. 1678 PHILLIPS (ed. 4), *Parechasis* [so 1696–1706], a digression, in Rhetorick, it is a wandering in discourse from the intended matter.

Pensible, *a.* Error for PENSILE. [1626 BACON *Sylva* § 15 The Water being made pensile.] Misprinted 'pensible' in ed. 1651. Hence in 1837 RICHARDSON; 1890 *Century Dict.*

Phantomnation. Explained as: Appearance as of a phantom; illusion. Error for *phantom nation*. [1725 POPE *Odyss.* X. 627 The Phantome-nations of the dead.] Entered as one word in 1820 JODRELL, in accordance with his method of writing compounds: *Phantomnation*, a multitude of spectres. Hence the following entries: 1860 WORCESTER, *Phantomnation*, illusion. *Pope*. 1864 WEBSTER, *Phantomnation*, appearance as of a phantom; illusion. (*Obs. and rare.*) *Pope*. So in OGILVIE (Annandale) and *Cassell's Encycl. Dict.*

Pisnet, puisnet. Errors for PINSNET. [1583 STUBBES *Anat. Abus.* I. (1879) 57 They haue corked shooes, pinsnets, and fine pantofles.] Quoted in 1834 PLANCHÉ *Hist. Brit. Costume* 261 as 'puisnets', and thence copied in 1860 FAIRHOLT *Costume* Gloss. s.v. *Boots*. 1860 *Ibid.* Gloss., *Pisnets*, a species of shoe, mentioned by Stubbes. Hence 1881 OGILVIE (Annandale), Pisnet, Puisnet. 1890 *Century Dict.*, Pisnet.

Quadrune. Error perhaps founded on a mistaken form of *Quadersandstein*, 'the German term for certain soft sandstones of the Chalk formation' (Page). 1832 WEBSTER, *Quadrune*, a gritstone with a calcarious cement. 1860 WORCESTER [citing MAUNDER]. Hence in *Cassell's Encycl. Dict.*, Funk's *Standard Dict.*

Sardel. Explained as: A precious stone. Error for *sardine* or *sardius*. [1721 BAILEY, *Sardel*, *Sardine*, a sort of Fish.] 1755 JOHNSON, *Sardel*, *Sardine Stone*, *Sardius*, a sort of precious stone. [Johnson omits Bailey's meaning 'a sort of Fish', but combines his *Sardel*, *Sardine* with *Sardius*.] Hence in 1828–32 WEBSTER, 1850–82 OGILVIE, and some later Dicts.

Sardonican, *a.* Error for SARDONIAN *a.* [1794 [T. TAYLOR] *Pausanias' Descr. Greece* III. 149 Homer first, and others after him, call laughter, which conceals some noxious design, Sardonian.] 1837 RICHARDSON, Sardonican [quoting this as 'Sardonican']. Hence in *Cassell's Encycl. Dict.*, *Century Dict.*, WEBSTER (1911).

Scise, *v.* Explained in 1864 WEBSTER, *Cassell's Encycl. Dict.*, etc. as: To cut, penetrate; and etymologized as from L. *scissus*, pa. pple. of *scindere* to cleave. Inferred from *scis'd*, misreading for *seiz'd* (early edd. *seaz'd*) in: 1600 FAIRFAX *Tasso* VII. xli. 125 The wicked steele seaz'd deepe in his right side. [See SEIZE *v.* 9 b, 'to penetrate deeply'.]

Sevant *a.*, **Sevantly,** *adv.* See note s.v. SUANTLY *adv.* in Dict.

Tendsome, *a.* Explained as: Requiring much attendance. Known only in the following Dict. entries. 1847 WEBSTER, *Tendsome*, requiring much attendance; as, a *tendsome* child. .. *Tensome*, see Tendsome. So 1850 OGILVIE, adding (*Obs.* or *fam.*). 1864 WEBSTER, adding (Written also *tensome*). 1891 *Century Dict.*

OTHER spurious forms (chiefly those having a more limited currency in dictionaries or in editions of texts) are entered in the main alphabet of the Dictionary; they are collected below for convenience of reference.

Abacot	Aneye	Bertying	Carlet	Cietezour	Collarage
Abarcy	Arerisement	Bewunus	Carnel, carnel-work	Civantick	Colligence
Abarstic	Arpentator	Bixwort	Cavilon	Claw-back *v.*	Comgage, com-habitant
Abatude	Arrid	Bord-halfpenny	Cesshery	Clinket	Commissionship
Abligurie	Arriont	Bouning	Chafter	Clolle	Commit
Abstable	At (for Ac *conj.*)	Brodeha(l)fpenny	Chare (after CHARE *v.*)	Cluttish	Commonance
Acherset	Barowe	Bronden	Chest-rope	Cocatrye	Cone and Key
Adventine	Beast (after BEAST *v.*)	Bullenger	Chirography	Cock *sb.*[8]	Confy
Agipe	Beneficience	Burgherisht	Chivancy	Cocket (after COCKET *sb.*[2])	Congrument
Aguiler	Beneficiency	Busyless	Chorl	Cockle (after COCKLE *sb.*[7])	Contrused, -sit
Ailingness	Beneficent	Buxion	Chukis	Coll	Convertile
Alienatory	Beneship	Caitisned			Conyne
Anagriph		Capriny			

Cook-mate
Coraage
Counterset
Cowdrife
Coysell
Crampland
Crathe
Creche
Cyne
Defray
Delapsation
Demple
Devastion
Devastitation
Devastor
Devoterer
Diplomatial
Dipsin
Disgore
Dishele
Disporting
Dissense, dis-ensse
Dooring
Drank
Duddels
Dulcerate, -ation
Dulciness
Eger
Emich, emych
Enanation
Enbreame
Encastic
Encortif
Enest
Enhendee
Ennation, ennea-tion
Ennoisies
Envyte
Eposculation
Eranc
Erynet
Evacate
Filour
Finiteless
Foreflow
Foreholding
Fortition
Frenchmore
Fructiculose
Furt
Gannok
Gingerness
Grimmer
Gryff
Guest-taker
Gurmie
Gyronnetty
Hamylone
Hanelon, -oune
Hastard
Hauselins
Heedlesshood
Heliospherical
Honorate
Hugesome
Humblehede
Impropriety
Incertain
Indoice
Indultif, -yf
Ingree
Inguilty
Insenseless
Instructess
Intervene *sb.*
Inveccyde
Inwood
Irrevalent
Irrevitable
Jimwhiskee
Journ-chopper
Jug (after Jug *sb.*[4])
Jumpish
Juter
Juventate
Kennet
Kerned
Kin-kind, ken-kind
Lastery
Leadman
Macegriefs
Maletent
Mandevi(l)le
Meine
Mestino
Microdermatous
Mightsome
Mightsomnes
Minovery
Moile
Mormal *a.*
Moveress
Moy (after Moy *sb.*[2])
Muggent
Obess(e
Obstruct *sb.*
Oilous
Onloðest
Onwhar, onwar
Opeagha
Ound
Ouster-le-mer
Out(-)bud
Outer
Out-joy
Outparter
Owser
Padar
Pailer
Pangetive
Pannell
Pantener
Pantoner
Papescent
Paramour *v.* (see Paramour *sb.* at end)
Pardelun
Parrett
Partel
Pavade, pauade
Pavon
Pentile
Pibling
Pickmire
Picy
Pile-worn
Pimprint
Planticle
Plenishing-nail
Pointel ¶
Ponk
Ponsondie
Pornial
Poteuere, pot-ewer
Poune
Preseeing
Prill
Quarteus
Rat (after Rat *v.*[3])
Ribaudred
Rip-towel
Sacratyle, -til
Sandaline
Scentingly
Scissible
Sea-bar
Segnotic
Semi-rife
Senacion
Serviant
Shairl
Silice
Snet(te
Strike
Strow
Take
Tantling
Terrosity
Tetrifolie, tetri-foil
Theaming
Therial
Thitling
Tidder
Tineman
Tip-cheese
Topinch
Tranect
Trefte
Trigen
Tumulate
Tyne
Wadage
Wafter
Wall-can
Waltron
Water-gauge, -gage
Wayward, -wards
Weasy
Winter-ground
Zimme

A LIST OF BOOKS QUOTED IN THE OXFORD ENGLISH DICTIONARY

NOTE

This List, which has been compiled by two members of the editorial staff of the *Oxford English Dictionary*, Mr. F. J. Sweatman and Mr. H. J. Bayliss, comprises the titles of such works as have been most commonly quoted in the Dictionary. While it has no claim to be regarded as a complete guide to English literature, it will be found to contain a large proportion of the more important works, together with many others less familiar; it includes a large number of titles of periodical publications.

The arrangement is according to the alphabetical order of authors' names or titles of works. Following each title is the date of the first edition, or of composition (ascertained or inferred), printed in thick type. Where it is possible or necessary to give only a limiting date, such as that of an author's death, or of a manuscript in which the work is extant, this is preceded by *a* (= *ante*), e. g. Bacon *Works* **a 1626**, *King Horn* **a 1300**. As occasion requires, the dates of editions used other than the first, or the names of editors or of series of publications, are added in ordinary type within round brackets. Where a title (e. g. Arnolde's *Chronicle*) is followed by a second title in brackets, the first is that by which the work is generally known, the second is its proper title. Round brackets are also occasionally used to indicate that works are questionably assigned to the authors under whom they are entered.

It is to be observed that the dates assigned (in the early years of the history of the Dictionary) to some Middle English texts and to a few books of later date (e. g. the plays of Shakespeare), as also certain ascriptions of authorship, have been modified by subsequent research (the resulting discrepancies rarely affect in any serious degree the chronology of words and senses).

SIGNS AND ABBREVIATIONS

a before a date = *ante* (before).
c „ „ „ = *circa* (about).
v.d. = various dates.
tr. = translated (by); translation of.
Ed., ed. = editor of; edited (by).

Cl. = Club.
Soc. = Society.
E.D.S. = English Dialect Society.
E.E.T.S. = Early English Text Society.
S.H.S. = Scottish History Society.
S.T.S. = Scottish Text Society.

A LIST OF BOOKS QUOTED IN THE OXFORD ENGLISH DICTIONARY

A. 1593: see Passionate Morrice
A., A. *Reply to Dr. Sanderson* 1650
A., D. *The art of converse* 1683
A., H. 1613, 1633: see Austin, Henry; Hawkins, Henry
A., W. *A speciall remedie against the furious force of lawlesse loue* 1579 (Roxb. Cl. 1844)
Abbay, Richard *The Castle of Knaresborough* 1887
Abbot, Charles *Jurisdiction and practice of the Court of Great Sessions of Wales on the Chester Circuit* 1795
Abbot, Abp. George *A briefe description of the whole worlde* (anon.) 1599 (1617, 1634)
An exposition upon the prophet Jonah 1600
A treatise of the perpetuall visibilitie and succession of the true church (anon.) 1624
Abbot, George *The whole book of Job paraphrased* 1640
Abbot, Robert *The old waye* 1610
Abbott, Charles C. *Waste-land wanderings* 1887
Abbott, Edwin A. *Francis Bacon: an account of his life and works* 1885
Abbott, Jacob *Wallace: a Franconia story* 1853
Abbott, John S. C. *Life of Napoleon* 1854 (1855)
Abdy, Edward S. *The water cure* 1842 (1843)
Aberbrothoc. Liber S. Thome de Aberbrothoc. Registrorum Abbacie de Aberbrothoc pars prior; pars altera v.d. (Bannatyne Cl. 1848, 1856)
Abercrombie, John *Every man his own gardener* 1767 (1803)
Abercromby, Hon. Ralph *Weather* 1887
Aberdeen, Extracts from the council register of the Burgh of 1398–1625 (Spalding Cl. 1844–48)
1625–1747 (Scott. Burgh Rec. Soc. 1871–72)
Aberdeen, Selections from the records of the Kirk session of 1562–1681 (Spalding Cl. 1846)
Abernethy, Bp. John *A christian and heavenly treatise containing physicke for the soule* 1615 (1622)
Abernethy, John *Diseases resembling syphilis* 1809 (1826)
Surgical observations 1804–06
Surgical works 1827
Abingdon. Accounts of the obedientiars of A. Abbey 1322–1479 (Camden Soc. 1892)
Abney, William de W. *Colour vision* 1895
A treatise on photography 1878 (1881)
Abridgment of the English military discipline 1685
Abridgments of specifications of patents relating to agriculture, artificial leather, etc. 1617–1866 (1876–77)
Academy, The: a monthly record of literature, learning, science, and art 1869–99
Account of the depredations committed on the Clan Campbell and their followers, during 1685–86 16.. (1816)
Account of the French Settlements in North America 1746
Account of the present persecution of the Church in Scotland 1690
Account of proceedings at the Guildhall 13 Sept. 1679 1679
Account of several late voyages and discoveries 1694 (1711)
Account of workhouses 1732
Account-book of Will. Wray c 1600 (in Antiquary XXXII)
Accounts of the Exchequer of the King's Remembrancer v.d. (MSS. in Public Record Office)
Accounts of the Lord High Treasurer of Scotland 1473– (Scott. Record series 1877–)
Accounts of the Revels at Court, Extracts from the, with an introduction and notes by Peter Cunningham 15.. (Shaks. Soc. 1842)
Accum, Friedrich C. A. *Chemical tests* 1816 (1818)
Acerbi, Giuseppe *Travels through Sweden, Finland, and Lapland, to the North Cape 1798–99* 1802
Acosta's (Joseph de) Naturall and morall historie of the East and West Indies tr. by E. G(rimstone) 1604
Act of Pennsylvania 1723
Acta Dominorum Auditorum (Acts of the Lords Auditors of Causes and Complaints) 1466–94 (Record Comm. 1839)
Acta Dominorum Concilii (Acts of the Lords of Council in civil causes) 1478–95 (Record Comm. 1839)
Acton, Eliza *English bread-book* 1857
Modern cookery 1845
Acton, Eugenia de *The nuns of the desert* 1805
A tale without a title 1804
Acts and ordinances made in the Parliament 1640–56 (ed. Henry Scobell 1658).
See also Statutes
Acts and proceedings of the general assemblies of the Kirk of Scotland (Booke of the universall Kirk of Scotland) 1560–1618 (Bannatyne Cl. 1839–45)
Acts of the Generall Assemblies of the Church of Scotland 1638–49 (1682)
Acts of the Parliaments of Scotland v.d. (1566, 1597, 1814–75)
Acts of the Privy Council of England 1542– (1890–)
Acts of Sederunt of the Lords of Council and Session 1553–1790 (1790)
Adair, James *The history of the American Indians* 1775
Adam, Alexander *Roman antiquities* 1791
Adam Bel, Clym of the Clough, and William of Cloudesly 15.. (Ritson 1791; Hazlitt 1864; Child 1888)
Adam Davy's five dreams about Edward II 13.. (E.E.T.S. 1878)
Adams, Andy *The log of a cowboy* 1903
Adams, Arthur, etc. *A manual of natural history* 1854
Adams, Francis W. L. *The new Egypt* 1893
Adams, George *Lectures on natural and experimental philosophy* 1794 (1806)
Micrographia illustrata; or the knowledge of the microscope explained 1746 (1747)
Adams, Henry *John Randolph* 1882
Adams, John *Works* a 1826 (1850–56)
A defence of the constitutions of government of the United States of America 1787–88
Familiar letters of J. A. and his wife, Abigail Adams, during the Revolution 17.. (1876)
Adams, Thomas *Works* v.d. (1629, 1861–62)
The barren tree 1623
The blacke devill or the apostate 1615
A commentary or exposition upon the second epistle by St. Peter 1633 (1865)
Diseases of the soule 1616
The divells banket described in sixe sermons 1614
Eirenopolis; the citie of peace 1622
Englands sicknes, comparatively conferred with Israels 1615
The gallants burden 1612
The happiness of the church considered in contemplations upon Hebrewes 1618
Heaven and earth reconcil'd 1613
The Holy Choice 1625
Lycanthropy, or the wolfe worrying the lambes 1615
The sacrifice of thankefulnesse 1616
The sinners passing-bell; or a complaint from heaven of mans sinnes 1614
The spirituall navigator 1615
The white devil, or the hypocrite uncased 1613
Adams, W. Bridges *English pleasure carriages* 1837
Adams, William H. D. *Great rivers of the world: The Amazon and its wonders* 1879 (1883)
Adamson, Henry *The muses threnodie, or mirthfull mournings on the death of master Gall* 1638 (1774)
Adamson, Robert *Fichte* 1881
Adanson's (Michel) Voyage to Senegal, the Isle of Goree and the River Gambia tr. 1759
Adderley, A. J. *The fisheries of the Bahamas* 1883 (Fisheries exhibition literature)
Addis, William E. and Arnold, Thomas *A Catholic dictionary containing some account of the doctrine, discipline, rites of the Catholic Church* 1884 (also 1897)
Addison, Alexander *Report of cases in the County Courts of the Fifth Circuit of Pennsylvania* 1800
Addison, Joseph *Works* v.d. (1721, 1726–27, 1758)
Cato 1712 (1721)
Count Tariff 1713
Dialogues upon the usefulness of ancient medals 1702 (1727)
The drummer, or the haunted house 1715 (1721)
Essay on 'Paradise Lost' 1719 (Arber)
The Freeholder 1716 (1751)
The Freethinker a 1719 (1722)
Poems 1705 (1726)
The present state of the war 1707 (1746)
Remarks on Italy 1705 (1733)
Rosamond 1707 (1726)
The Spectator 1711–14
The Tatler 1709–10
The Whig Examiner 1710–12
See also Garth, Sir S.
Addison, Lancelot *The first state of Mahumedism* 1678 (1679)
The life and death of Mahumed 1679
The present state of the Jews in Barbary 1675
West Barbary 1671
Addleshaw, W. P.: see Hemingway, Percy
Addy, Sidney O. *A glossary of words used in the neighbourhood of Sheffield* 1888. *Suppl.* 1891 (E.D.S.)
Adler, George J. *Fauriel's History of Provençal poetry* tr. 1860
Adlington, William *Apuleius: The XI bookes of the Golden asse, with the marriage of Cupido and Psiches* 1566 (1893)
Administration of affairs in Scotland under the Duke of Lauderdale 1679
Admonycion, A faythfull, of a certen trewe pastor (tr. from Luther) 1554
Adventurer, The (by Hawkesworth, Johnson, etc.) 1753–54
Adventures of Captain Robert Boyle 1726: see Chetwood, W. R.
Advice to a painter; being a satyr upon the French King, etc. 1692
Ady, Thomas *A candle in the dark; or, a treatise concerning the nature of witches and witchcraft* 1656
Ælfred *Boethius De consolatione philosophiae* tr. c 888 (Sedgefield 1899)
Gregory's Pastoral care tr. c 897 (E.E.T.S. 1871)
Orosius tr. c 893 (E.E.T.S. 1883)
Soliloquien des Augustinus (= *Blooms*) c 900 (1922)
Soliloquia Augustini selecta (Cockayne 1864–70)
Ælfric *De veteri et de novo testamento* c 1000 (Grein 1872; E.E.T.S. 1922)
Genesis, Exodus, etc. c 1000 (Grein 1872; E.E.T.S. 1922)
Grammar c 1000 (Zupitza 1880)
Homilies c 1000 (Thorpe 1844–46)
Lives of saints c 1000 (E.E.T.S. 1881–85)
See also Fragment
Æthelwold *Anglo-Saxon Benedictine rule* c 960 (Schröer 1885)
Affecting narrative of the catastrophe of his majesty's ship 'Wager' 1751
Agassiz, Louis J. R. *Scientific results of a journey in Brazil* 1871
Agiatis, Queen of Sparta, or the civil wars of the Lacedemonians tr. 1686
Aglionby, William *Painting illustrated in three dialogues* 1685
Agnel, H. R. *Chess for winter evenings* 1848
Agnew, David C. A. *Theology of consolation* 1881
Agricultural surveys of Great Britain and Ireland, and Scotland 1793–1815
Agrippa's Vanity of arts and sciences tr. 1684. See also Sanford, J.
Aikin, Arthur *A dictionary of chemistry and mineralogy* 1807–14
Ailesbury, Thomas *The passion sermon at Pauls-Crosse, April 7* 1626
A sermon preached at Paules-Crosse the second day of June, 1622 1623
Ailesbury, Thomas Bruce, 2nd Earl of *Memoirs* 17.. (Roxb. Cl. 1890)
Ainger, Arthur C.: see Heathcote, C. G.
Ainslie, Hew *A pilgrimage to the land of Burns: and poems* 1822, a 1878 (1892)
Ainsworth, Henry *Annotations upon Genesis* 1616; *Exodus* 1617; *Leviticus* 1618; *Numbers* 1619; *Deuteronomie* 1619; *the book of Psalms* 1617
Annotations upon the five bookes of Moses and the booke of Psalmes 1622; *and the Song of Songs* 1627 (1639)
Ainsworth, Robert *Thesaurus linguæ Latinæ compendiarius* 1736 (1773, etc.)
Ainsworth, William Harrison *Crichton* 1837
Jack Sheppard 1839
John Law 1864 (1881)
The Lancashire witches 1848
Merry England 1874
The miser's daughter 1842
Old St. Paul's 1841
Ovingdean Grange 1860
Rookwood 1834
Saint James's, or the court of Q. Anne 1844
Tower Hill 1871
The Tower of London 1840
Windsor Castle 1843
Aird, Thomas *Poetical works* 1848, 1856
Memoir of D. M. Moir 1852
Airy, George B. *Astronomy* 1851–59 (in Manual of scientific enquiry)
Undulatory theory of optics 1866
Aitchison, Charles U. *A collection of treaties, etc. relating to India and neighbouring countries* 1876–78
Aitken, William *The science and practice of medicine* 1863 (1866)
Aiton, John *Manual of domestic economy for clergymen* 1842 (1857)
Aiton, William *General view of the agriculture of the county of Ayr* 1811
Akenside, Mark *Poems* v.d. (1790)
The pleasures of imagination 1744
—— revised ed. (1788)
Akerman, John Y. *A glossary of provincial words and phrases in use in Wiltshire* 1842
Alabaster, Henry *The wheel of the law: Buddhism illustrated from Siamese sources* 1871
Albemarle, George Monk, 1st Duke of *Observations upon military and political affairs* 1671
Albin, Eleazar *A natural history of birds* 1731–38
A natural history of English insects 1720
Albion's triumph, a poem 1705
Alcilia 1613: see C., I. or J.
Alcock, Bp. John *Mons perfeccionis, the hyll of perfeccion* 1496 (1497)
Sermo pro episcopo puerorum c 1496 (W. de Worde)
Alcock, Sir Rutherford *The capital of the Tycoon: three years in Japan* 1863
Alcoran of Mahomet 1649: see Ross, A.
Alcott, Amos B. *Table-talk* 1877
Alcott, Louisa M. *Hospital sketches, and camp and fireside stories* 1863
Little women 1868 (1869)
Alday, John *Boaystuau's Theatrum mundi, the theatre or rule of the world* tr. 1566
Aldhelm glosses a 1100 (Napier 1900)
Aldrich, Thomas B. *Marjorie Daw, and other people* 1873
Prudence Palfrey 1874 (1885)
The story of a bad boy 1869
Alexander 1340–70 (Roxb. Cl. 1849, App.) (= *Alexander and Dindimus*, E.E.T.S. 1878)
Alexander, Alliterative romance of, a 1400–50 (Roxb. Cl. 1849) (= *The Wars of Alexander*, E.E.T.S. 1866)
Alexander, Prose life of c 1420 (E.E.T.S. 1913)
'Alexander, Mrs.' (Mrs. Annie F. Hector) *The admiral's ward* 1883
Stronger than love 1902
Alexander, Sir William a 1640: see Stirling, Earl of
Alexander, William *The history of women* 1779 (1782)
Alexander, William *Johnny Gibb of Gushetneuk* 1871
Alexander, Bp. William *St. Augustine's holiday, and other poems* 1886
Alexander, William L. *Dorner's (Isaac A.) Development of the doctrine of the person of Christ* tr. 1861–63 (1872)
Alexius, The legend or life of St. c 1400 (E.E.T.S. 1878)
Alford, Henry *Essays and addresses, chiefly on Church subjects* 1869
Alger, William R. *History of the doctrine of a future life* 1858
The solitudes of nature and of man 1866
Alick, Princess *Biographical sketch and letters* a 1878 (1884)
Alienist and neurologist 1880–
Alingham, William *Geometry epitomized* 1695
Alisaunder, King 13.. (Weber 1810; MS. Laud Misc. 622)
Alisaunder of Macedoine 1340–70 (E.E.T.S. 1867, App.)

B

BERNERS	8	BLUNT	BLYTH	9	BRAND

BRANDAN	10	BROWNING	BROWNING	11	BURNS

C

D

Eastlake, Elizabeth, Lady Life of John Gibson, R.A., sculptor 1870
Eastwick, Edward B. Dry leaves from young Egypt: being a glance at Sindh 1849 See also Lutfullah
Eastwood, Jonathan and Wright, William A. The Bible word-book: a glossary of old English Bible words 1866
Eaton, John The honey-combe of free justification by Christ alone 1642
Ebb and flow. A novel 1859 (1863)
Eccles, Arthur S. Sciatica 1893
Ecclesiologist, The 1843–61
Echard, Laurence A general ecclesiastical history 1702 (1710)
The history of England, from the first entrance of Julius Cæsar to the end of the reign of James II 1707–18
Plautus's comedies, Amphitryon, Epidicus, and Rudens tr. 1694
Echo, The (newspaper; various years) 1868–1905
Eclectic review 1805–68
Ecton, John A state of the proceedings of the corporation of the governours of the bounty of Queen Anne for the augmentation of the maintenance of the poor clergy, from 1704–18 1719
E.D.D. = English dialect dictionary
Eden, Charles H. My wife and I in Queensland 1872
Eden, F. A garden in Venice 1903
Eden, Richard Cortes' (Martin) Arte of nauigation tr. 1561
The decades of the newe worlde or west India tr. 1555 (Arber 1885)
A treatyse of the newe India tr. 1553 (Arber 1885)
Edersheim, Alfred The life and times of Jesus the Messiah 1883; new and revised ed. 1886
Edgar, Andrew Old Church life in Scotland 1885–86
Edgar, John G. Runnymede and Lincoln Fair 1866
Edgeworth, Maria Tales and novels v.d. (1832–33)
Belinda 1801
Castle Rackrent 1800
Early lessons 1801
Harrington 1817
Harry and Lucy concluded; being the last part of Early lessons 1825
Helen 1834
Leonora 1806
Letters for literary ladies 1795
Modern Griselda 1804
Moral tales 1801
Ormond 1817
The parent's assistant 1800
Patronage 1814
Popular tales 1804
Tales from fashionable life 1809–12
Life and letters ed. A. J. C. Hare (1894)
—— and Richard L. Essay on Irish bulls 1802
Practical education 1798 (1822)
Edgren, August H. Rydberg's (A. V.) Magic of the middle ages tr. 1879
Edinburgh, Charters and other documents relating to the city of 1143–1540 (Scott. Burgh Rec. Soc. 1871)
Edinburgh, Extracts from the records of the burgh of 1403–1589 (Scott. Burgh Rec. Soc. 1869–82)
Edinburgh, Medical essays and observations, revised and published by a Society in 1733–44
Edinburgh, Registrum cartarum ecclesie sancti Egidii de 1344–1567 (App. –1648) (Bannatyne Club 1859)
Edinburgh encyclopædia, The, conducted by D. Brewster a 1830
Edinburgh review, The 1802–
Editha, St. c 1420: see Chronicon Vilodunense
Edmondes, Clement Observations upon Cæsars Commentaries 1600 (1604)
Edmonds, Henry Botany for beginners 1896
Edmondson, Joseph A complete body of heraldry 1780
Edmondston, Arthur A view of the ancient and present state of the Zetland Islands 1809
Edmondston, Biot and Saxby, Jessie M. E. The home of a naturalist 1888
Edmondston, Eliza Sketches and tales of the Shetland Islands 1856
Edmondston, Thomas An etymological glossary of the Shetland and Orkney dialect 1866 (Philol. Soc.)
Edmundson, George The Church in Rome in the first century 1913
E.D.S.: see English Dialect Society
Educational review, The 1891–93
Edward I: see Elegy
Edward II, Household ordinances of tr. 1601: see Tate, F.
Edward II, A poem on the times of c 1325 (Percy Soc. 1849; in Political songs, Camden Soc. 1839)
Edward the third, The raigne of King 1596 (in Shakespeare Apocrypha, 1908)
Edward IV, Historie of the arrival of 1471 (Camden Soc. 1838)
Wardrobe accounts of a 1483 (Nicolas 1830)
See also Liber niger
Edward VI Iniunccions 1547
Journal a 1553 (1884)
Literary remains a 1553 (Roxb. Club 1857–58)
Edwardes, Charles Sardinia and the Sardes 1889
Edwards, Amelia B. Barbara's history 1864
Half a million of money 1865
Hand and glove 1858
Miss Carew 1865
A thousand miles up the Nile 1877
Edwards, Annie Archie Lovell 1866
Edwards, Bryan The history civil and commercial of the British colonies in the West Indies 1793–1801
Edwards, C. A. Organs and organ building 1881
Edwards, D. H. Historical guide to Edzell and Glenesk districts 1893
Ed. Modern Scottish poets, with biographical and critical notices v.d. (1880–97)
Edwards, Edward Life of Sir W. Raleigh 1868
Edwards, George A natural history of uncommon birds, and of some other rare and undescribed animals 1743–51
Gleanings of natural history 1758–64
Edwards, George The appropriate measures of true policy, competent to remove our burdens, grievances, etc. 1813
A plain practical plan, by which Great Britain may extricate herself from her present difficulties 1808
Edwards' (H. M.) Manual of zoology tr. R. Knox 1856

Edwards, John A demonstration of the existence and providence of God 1690
A discourse concerning the authority, stile and perfection of the books of the Old and New Testament 1693–95
A farther enquiry into several remarkable texts of the Old and New Testament 1692
Edwards, Jonathan Works v.d. (1804–47)
A careful and strict enquiry into the modern prevailing notions of that freedom of will, which is supposed to be essential to moral agency, etc. 1754
The doctrine of original sin as it was always held in the Catholick church 1711
A history of the work of redemption 1786
Edwards, Matilda Betham- Felicia 1875
John and I 1862 (1876)
Kitty 1869
Next of kin wanted 1887
Edwards, Richard The excellent comedie of two the moste faithfullest freendes, Damon and Pithias a 1566 (1571; Hazl. Dodsley)
The paradyse of dainty deuises a 1566 (1576, 1578)
Edwards, Thomas Gangræna; or, a catalogue and discovery of many of the errours, heresies, blasphemies and pernicious practices of the sectaries of this time 1646
Edwards, Thomas A supplement to Mr. Warburton's edition of Shakespear; being the canons of criticism, and glossary (anon.) 1748
Edwards, Thomas Strathearn lyrics and other poems 1889
Edwin 1803
Eedes, Richard Christ exalted and wisdom justified 1659
E.E.T.S.: see Early English Text Society
Egan, Pierce Book of sports and mirror of life 1832
Life in London; or, the day and night scenes of Jerry Hawthorn, etc. 1821
Real life in London 1821
See also Grose, F.
Eger. The history of sir Egeir, sir Gryme, and sir Gray-steill a 1650 (in Laing, Early metrical tales 1826; Percy MS., Hales and Furnivall, I)
'Egerton, George' Discords 1894
Egerton, John C. Sussex folk and Sussex ways 1884
Egerton papers, The. A collection of public and private documents, chiefly illustrative of the times of Elizabeth and James I 15.. (Camden Soc. 1840)
Eggleston, Edward The faith doctor 1891
The Graysons, a story of Illinois 1888
Roxy 1878
The transit of civilization from England to America in the seventeenth century 1901
Eglamour, The romance of Sir (Camden Soc. 1844)
'Eha' (E. H. Aitken) The tribes on my frontier 1881 (1883)
Εἰκὼν Βασιλική. The pourtraicture of his sacred maiestie in his solitudes and sufferings 1648
Εἰρηνικον, a poeme, wherein is perswaded the composing of the differences of all the faithfull in Christ Jesus 1656
'Eissler, Manuel The modern high explosives 1884
Elaboratory laid open, The; or the secrets of modern chemistry and pharmacy revealed 1750
Eland, William Hemerologium astronomicum, or an almanack for 1656 1656
A tutor to astrology. Whereunto is added an ephemeris for the years 1694, 1695, 1696 1694 (1704)
Elborowe, Thomas The famous epistles of Saint Polycarp and Saint Ignatius, with the epistle of Saint Barnabas tr. 1668
Elderfield, Christopher The civill right of tythes 1650
Elder's house, The; or the three converts 1850
Elderton, William The panges of loue and louers fittes 1559
Electricity in daily life; a popular account of the applications of electricity to every day uses by C. F. Brackett, F. L. Pope, etc. 1891
Elegy on the author of The true-born Englishman etc. 1704
Elegy on the death of Edward I 1307 (in Political songs, Camden Soc. 1839; Warton, Hist. Eng. poetry I. 1840)
Elene a 900: see Cynewulf
Elgin, James Bruce, 8th Earl of Letters and journals a 1863 (1872)
Elgin, The records of: see Cramond, W.
'Eliot, George' (Marian Evans) Adam Bede 1859
Amos Barton 1858
College breakfast party 1874
Daniel Deronda 1876
Essays v.d. (1884)
Felix Holt 1866
Impressions of Theophrastus Such 1879
Middlemarch 1872
The mill on the Floss 1860
Romola 1863
Scenes of clerical life 1858
Silas Marner 1861
The Spanish gypsy 1868
Life of, by J. W. Cross (1885)
Eliot, John Bertrand de Loque's Discourses of warre and single combat tr. 1591
Elisa Warwick, History of. By a lady 1778
Eliza's babes: or the Virgin's offering 1652
Elizabeth, Queen Copie of a letter to the Earle of Leycester 1586
Englishings of Boethius, De consolatione philosophiae 1593; Plutarch, De curiositate 1598; Horace, De arte poetica (part) 1598 (E.E.T.S. 1899)
See also Gilbert, Sir H.; Nichols, John
Elizabeth and her German garden 1898: see Arnim, Countess of
Elizabeth, Queen, and the Levant Company 1904
Elizabeth of York, Privy purse expenses of 14.. (Nicolas 1830)
Ellacombe, Henry T. The church bells of Devon: with a list of those in Cornwall. To which is added a Supplement on various matters relating to the 'Bells of the church' 1872
Practical remarks on belfries and ringers 1850 (1871)
Ellenborough, Edward Law, Earl of A political diary 1828–30 (1881)
Ellicott, Andrew Journal 1802 (1803)
Ellicott, Charles J. A commentary on St. Paul's Epistle to the Galatians 1854
The destiny of the creature: and other sermons 1858
Historical lectures on the life of Our Lord 1860
Elliot, Anne An old man's favour 1887
Elliot, Frances M. Roman gossip 1894

Elliot, George A very true report of the apprehension of that arch-Papist Edmund Campion 1581 (in Arber, Eng. Garner VIII)
Elliott, Charles W. The New England history, from the discovery of the continent by the Northmen, A.D. 986 to 1776 1857
Elliott, Ebenezer Poetical works 1840
—— new and revised ed. (1876)
The splendid village: corn law rhymes; and other poems 1832 (1904)
Ellis, Alexander J. On early English pronunciation, with especial reference to Shakspere and Chaucer 1869–89 (Philol. Soc., E.E.T.S., and Chaucer Soc.)
Ellis, Clement The vanity of scoffing 1674
Ellis, George Ed. Specimens of early English metrical romances v.d. (1805)
Ed. Specimens of the early English poets v.d. (1790)
Ellis, George V. Demonstrations of anatomy 1840
Ellis, Henry A voyage to Hudson's Bay in 1746–7, for discovering a north-west passage 1748
Ellis, Sir Henry The British Museum: Elgin and Phigaleian marbles 1833 (1846)
Ed. Original letters illustrative of English history v.d. (1824–46)
Ed. Original letters of eminent literary men of the sixteenth, seventeenth, and eighteenth centuries v.d. (Camden Soc. 1843)
Ellis, John S. Austin imitated; or retractations and repentings in reference to the late civil and ecclesiastical changes in this nation 1662
Ellis, John The knowledge of divine things from revelation 1743 (1811)
Ellis, Joseph Caesar in Egypt, Costanza and other poems 1876
Ellis, Philip Sermon preach'd before the King and Queen 1685 (1686)
Ellis, Robert The laws and practical regulations of the customs 1837–41
Ellis, Robinson The poems and fragments of Catullus tr. 1871
Ellis, Sarah Pique, a novel (anon.) 1850
Ellis, T. Mullett The three cat's-eye rings, a tale of the pursuit of the Khalifa 1899
Ellis, William A compleat system of experienced improvement, made in sheep, grass-lambs, and house-lambs 1749
Chiltern and Vale farming 1733
The country housewife's family companion 1750
Every farmer his own farrier a 1758 (1759)
The modern husbandman 1750
New experiments in husbandry for the month of April 1736
The practical farmer 1732 (1759)
The timber-tree improved 1738
Ellis, William A. Glasenapp's (C. F.) Life of R. Wagner tr. 1900–08
Ellis, William S. The antiquities of heraldry 1869
Ellistone, John The epistles of Jacob Behmen. Also, a warning from J. Beem to such as reade his writings tr. 1649 (1886)
Ellwanger, George H. The garden's story 1890
Ellwood, Thomas Davideis; the life of David, king of Israel, a sacred poem 1712
The history of the life of, written by his own hand a 1713 (1714)
Ellwood, Thomas Lakeland and Iceland, being a glossary of words in the dialect of Cumberland, Westmorland, and North Lancashire which seem allied to or identical with the Icelandic or Norse 1895 (E.D.S.)
Ellys, Bp. Anthony A plea for the sacramental test (anon.) 1736
Tracts on the liberty spiritual and temporal of Protestants in England a 1761 (1763–65)
Elmes, James A general and bibliographical dictionary of the fine arts 1824–26
Metropolitan improvements 1827
A practical treatise on the law of dilapidations 1823 (1829)
Elmhirst, Edward Pennell The cream of Leicestershire 1883
Elmore, H. M. The British mariner's directory and guide to the trade and navigation of the Indian and China seas 1802
Elphinston, James The epigrams of M. V. Martial tr. 1782
The principles of the English language digested 1765
Propriety ascertained in her picture 1786–87
Elphinstone, Howard W., Norton, R. F., and Clark, J. W. Rules for the interpretation of deeds 1885
Elphinstone, Mountstuart An account of the kingdom of Caubul 1815 (1842)
History of India 1841
Elsing, Henry Notes of the debates in the House of Lords 1621 (Camden Soc. 1870)
Elton, Charles I. Origins of English history 1882
Elton, Edward The complaint of a sanctified sinner answered; or an explanation of the seventh chapter of the epistle of St. Paul to the Romans 1618 (1622)
Elton, Romeo Life of Roger Williams 1852 (1853)
Elvin, Charles N. A dictionary of heraldry 1889
A synopsis of heraldry 1866
Elvina; a novel 1792
Elworthy, Frederick T. The evil eye 1895
The West Somerset word-book 1886 (E.D.S.)
Ely, Bishop of a 1707: see Patrick, S.; a 1723: see Fleetwood, W.
Ely, Richard T. French and German socialism in modern times 1883
An introduction to political economy 1891
Ely, Sacrist rolls of 1291–1360 (1907)
Elyot, Sir Thomas The boke named The gouernour 1531 (repr. 1880; 1537, 1580)
The castel of helth 1539 (1541)
Dictionary 1538, 1542, 1545
—— inriched by T. Cooper 1548, 1552
The defence of good women 1545
The doctrinal of princes tr. 1534
The image of gouernance 1540–41
Of the knowledge whiche maketh a wise man 153–
Pasquil the playne 1532 (1540)
Em 1592: see Faire Em
Emanuel, Henry Diamonds and precious stones 1865

Emare c 1400 (Ritson, Metr. rom. II; E.E.T.S. 1906)
Emerson, James Christianity in Ceylon 1850
Emerson, Peter H. Birds, beasts, and fishes of the Norfolk Broadland 1895
East coast yarns 1891
English idyls 1889
On English lagoons 1892
Marsh-leaves from the Norfolk Broad-land 1898
Signor Lippo, burnt-cork artist 1893
A son of the fens 1892
Wild life on a tidal water 1890
Emerson, Ralph W. Works v.d. (Bohn)
The conduct of life 1860
Correspondence with Carlyle v.d. (1883)
English traits 1856
Essays 1841–44
Lectures on the times 1841
Letters and social aims 1876
Miscellanies 1855
Nature 1836
New England reformers 1844
Poems v.d. (1847, 1857)
Representative men 1847
Society and solitude 1870
Emerson, William The doctrine of fluxions 1743
The method of increments 1763
The principles of mechanicks 1758
Emerton, James H. The common spiders of the United States 1902
Emillianne, G. D': see D'Emillianne, G.
Emmot, George A Northern blast, or the spiritual Quaker converted 1655
Encouragement to sea-faring people of Great Britain, Reasons for giving 1739
Encyclopædia Americana 1829–33, 1848; Suppl. 1883
Encyclopædia Britannica 1768–71; (ed. 2) 1777–84; (ed. 3) 1788–97; (ed. 4) 1801–10; (ed. 5) 1815–17; (ed. 6) 1823–24; (ed. 7) 1830–42; (ed. 8) 1853–60; (ed. 9) 1875–89; (ed. 10) 1902–03; (ed. 11) 1910–11; (ed. 12) 1922; (ed. 13) 1926
Encyclopædia metropolitana 1818–45
Encyclopædia of the laws of England 1897–1903
Encyclopædia of the laws of Scotland, Green's ed. John Chisholm 1897–1904
Encyclopædia of practical cookery ed. T. F. Garrett 1892–94
Encyclopædia of sport, The 1897–98
Encyclopædia Perthensis 1816
Encyclopedy, Select essays from the 1772
Enderbie, Percy Cambria triumphans; or Brittain in its perfect lustre 1661
Enfield, William The history of philosophy, drawn up from Brucker's Historia critica philosophiæ 1791
Engel, Carl Introduction to the study of national music 1866
Music of the most ancient nations 1864
Musical instruments 1875
Engineer, The 1865–
Engineering magazine 1898 (vol. XVI)
England and Germany, Letters and other documents illustrating the relations between 1618–19 (Camden Soc. 1865)
England's confession 1659
England's gazetteer 1751 (1778)
Englands Helicon (Poems collected and edited by John Bodenham) 1600 (1614; ed. Bullen 1887)
England's monarchy asserted, and proved to be the freest state, and the best common-wealth throughout the world 1659
Englands Parnassus 1600: see Allott, R.
Englands welcome to James, King of England 1603
Englische Studien. Herausgegeben von E. Kölbing 1877–
English chronicle c 1465: see Chronicle
English church furniture: see Peacock, E.
English conquest of Ireland, The, A.D. 1166–85 Mainly from the 'Expugnatio Hibernica' of Giraldus Cambrensis c 1425, c 1440 (E.E.T.S. 1896)
English dialect dictionary: see Wright, J.
English Dialect Society, Publications of the 1873–
English encyclopædia, The 1802–18
English garner: see Arber, E.
English gilds a 1400 (E.E.T.S. 1870)
English historical review 1886–
English home, Our 1861
English illustrated magazine, The 1883–
English life; or, manners at home 1825
Englishman, The (by R. Steele) 1713–14
English metrical homilies from MSS. of the fourteenth century c 1325 (ed. Small 1862)
English miscellanies, A volume of, illustrating the history and language of the northern counties of England 14.. (Surtees Soc. 1888)
English review, The 1905–
English Spanish pilgrime 1629: see Wadsworth, J.
English Theophrastus, The: or the manners of the age 1702
Englishwoman in India, The. By a lady resident 1864
Englishwoman in Russia, The; by a lady, ten years resident 1855
Enquiry concerning the election of the sheriffs of London, A modest 1682
Enquiry whether the tripe-wife etc. 1595: see Quest
Enterlude of youth 1557 (in Hazl. Dodsley)
Entertainer, The 1717–18
Entick, John History and survey of London and places adjacent 1766
Entomological Society of Washington, Proceedings 1886–
'Ephelia' Female poems on several occasions 1679
Ephesian matron 1659: see Charleton, W.
Epinal glossary, The. Latin and Old English c 825 (Sweet 1883; in Oldest English texts, E.E.T.S. 1885)
Epulario, or, the Italian banquet 1598
Epyphanye, The 14.. (in The Visions of Tundale, etc. 1843)
Erasmus' Playne and godly exposytion of the commune crede and of the x. commaundementes tr. 1533
See also various translators
Erceldoune, The romance and prophecies of Thomas of c 1425 (E.E.T.S. 1875)
Erckmann-Chatrian's Waterloo tr. 1865
Erfurt glossary c 875 (in Oldest English texts, E.E.T.S. 1885)
Erichsen, Sir John E. The science and art of surgery 1853 (1877)
Erkenwald, St. a 1400 (in Horstmann, Altengl. Leg. 1881)
Erl of Tolous c 1450 (Ritson, Metr. rom. III; Lüdtke 1881)
Erondelle, Pierre The French garden, being an instruction for attayning the French tongue 1605

Erskine, Ebenezer Sermons a 1754 (1755)
Erskine, John An institute of the law of Scotland a 1768 (1773)
Principles of the law of Scotland 1754 (1809)
Erskine, John F. General view of the agriculture of the county of Clackmannan 1795
Erskine, Thomas An essay on faith 1822 (1825)
Erthe upon erthe, The Middle English poem 13.. (E.E.T.S. 1911)
Escott, Thomas H. S. England: its people, polity, and pursuits 1879
Esquemeling's (J.) History of the Bucaniers of America tr. 1684
Esquiros, Alphonse Cornwall and its coasts 1865
Essay peace and truth in the church 1681: see Harley, Sir E.
Essay to revive the ancient education of gentlewomen in religion, etc. 1673
Essay to the memory of John lord Cutts 1707
Essay towards a method of speedily manning a fleet 1754
Essays and reviews 1860
Essays from the Batchelor 1771–72 (1773)
Essays on Christian union 1845
Essays on a liberal education 18.. (ed. F. W. Farrar 1867)
Essays on reform 1867
Essays on religion and literature 18.. (ed. H. E. Manning 1865, –67, –74)
Essays on social subjects, from the Saturday Review 1864–65
Essex, Arthur Capel, Earl of Letters 1675 (1770)
Essex papers 1672–79 (Camden Soc. 1890, 1913)
Essex's excellency; or, the gallantry of the freeholders of that county 1679
Essex freeholders, A faithful account of the behaviour of a party of 1679
Essex, Glossary of provincial words used in 1851
Established test, The, in order to the security of his majesties person, etc., against the malitious attempts of Rome 1679
Estcourt, Richard The fair example 1706
Esther, Queen (A new enterlude, drawen oute of the holy scripture, of godly queene Hester) 1561 (in J. P. Collier, Illustr. E. Eng. pop. lit. I, 1863; Grosart 1873)
Estwick, Nicolas Πνευματολογία, or a treatise of the Holy Ghost 1648
Etherege, Sir George Works a 1691 (1888)
The comical revenge, or love in a tub 1664
The man of mode 1676
She wou'd if she cou'd 1668
Etheridge, Robert Stratigraphical geology and palæontology 1885
Eton school days 1864: see Hemyng, B.
Etonian, The 1822
Etoniana ancient and modern 1865
Eugenius 1785: see Graves, R.
Europe, A brief description of the future history of, from 1650 to 1710 1650
European magazine, The 1804 (vol. XLV)
Eusden, Laurence Poems 1714, 1722
See also Garth, Sir S.
Eustace, John C. A tour through Italy 1813
—— ed. 2, entitled A classical tour through Italy 1814 (1815, 1821)
Evance, Daniel The noble order; or the honour which God conferr's on them that honour him 1646
Evangelium Nicodemi 13..: see Gospel of Nicodemus
Evans, Abel Vertumnus 1713
Evans, Arthur B. Leicestershire words, phrases, and proverbs 1848
— new ed. by Sebastian Evans 1881 (E.D.S.)
Evans, Sir Arthur J. Through Bosnia and the Herzegóvina on foot 1876
Evans, Edward P. Animal symbolism in ecclesiastical architecture 1896
Evans, Edward T. The history and topography of the parish of Hendon, Middlesex 1890
Evans, John A sketch of the denominations of the Christian world 1795 (1821)
Evans, John An excursion to Windsor 1817
Evans, Sir John The ancient stone implements, weapons, and ornaments of Great Britain 1872 (1897)
The coins of the ancient Britons 1864
Evans, Lewis 1574: see Withals, John
Evans, Lewis Geographical, historical, political, philosophical and mechanical essays; the first, containing an analysis of a general map of the middle British Colonies in America 1755
Evans, Maurice J. 1872: see Watson, John W.
Evans, Sebastian Brother Fabian's manuscripts; and other poems 1865
In quest of the Holy Graal 1898
See also Evans, Arthur B.
Evans, Thomas Ed. Old ballads, historical and narrative, with some of modern date v.d. (1777, 1784, 1810)
Evats, William The most excellent Hugo Grotius his three books treating of the rights of war and peace tr. 1682
Evelyn, John Acetaria, or a discourse of sallets 1699
De la Quintinie's Compleat gard'ner tr. 1693
Diary (a 1700) and correspondence v.d. (1850–52, 1879)
Fréart's Idea of the perfection of painting tr. 1668
Fréart's Parrallel of the antient architecture with the modern; to which is added an account of architects and architecture tr. 1664
The French gardener tr. 1658
Fumifugium; or, the inconveniencies of the aer and smoak of London dissipated 1661
The history of religion a 1706 (1850)
Kalendarium hortense 1664
The life of Mrs. Godolphin 1685
Memoirs v.d. (1818)
Miscellaneous writings v.d. (1825)
Mundus muliebris: see Evelyn, Mary
Navigation and commerce 1674
Numismata; a discourse of medals antient and modern 1697
Pomona 1664
Sculptura; or, the history and art of chalcography and engraving in copper 1662
The state of France as it stood in the ninth year of Lewis XIIII 1652
Sylva, or a discourse of forest-trees 1664 (1729, 1776)
Terra. A philosophical discourse of earth 1675 (1729, 1778)
Tyrannus, or the mode 1661

Evelyn, Mary Mundus muliebris: or, the ladies dressing-room unlock'd, and her toilette spread. Together with the fop-dictionary (ascribed to John or Mary Evelyn) 1690
Everard, Edmund Discourses on the present state of the Protestant princes of Europe 1679
The depositions and examinations of, concerning the horrid Popish plot 1679
Everett, Edward Orations and speeches, on various occasions 1836 (1850)
Everett, Joseph D. Illustrations of the centimetre-gramme-second system of units 1875
Ever green, The, being a collection of Scots poems, wrote by the ingenious before 1600, (ed.) by Allan Ramsay 1724
Everie woman in her humor 1609 (in Bullen, Old Plays IV, 1885)
Everyman c 1520 (in Eng. miracle plays, ed. Pollard 1890)
Every man his own mechanic (by F. Chilton-Young) 1881
Ewald, Alexander C. Stories from the State Papers 1882
Ewing, Juliana H. Dandelion clocks a 1885 (1887)
Mary's meadow a 1885 (1886)
Examination and refutation of a late pamphlet intituled Considerations on the Navy bill, An 1749
Examiner, The (ed. successively by W. King, J. Swift, Mrs. Manley, and W. Oldisworth) 1710–14
Examiner, The; a Sunday paper, on politics, domestic economy, and theatricals (ed. successively by Leigh Hunt, A. Fonblanque, and others) 1808–36
Examynatyons towcheynge Cokeye More 15.. (in Chetham Soc. Misc. II)
Exceptions of the presbyterian-brethren, against some passages in the present liturgy 1661
Excerpta historica: see Bentley, S.
Exchequer rolls of Scotland 1264– (Scott. Record series 1878–)
Execution for treason 1583 (1675): see Cecil, W.
Exercitation concerning usurped powers 1650: see Hollingworth, R.
Exeter book, The (Codex Exoniensis); an anthology of Anglo-Saxon poetry presented to Exeter Cathedral by Leofric (1050–71) a 1000 (Thorpe 1842; (Poems I–VIII) E.E.T.S. 1895)
Exhibition, Official descriptive and illustrated catalogue of the Great 1851
Exhibition, The International of 1862. The illustrated catalogue of the industrial department. British division 1862
Exhortation vnto prayer 1544
Exmoor courtship 1746 (in Gentleman's Mag. June)
Exmoor scolding 1746 (in Gentleman's Mag. July)
Exmoor scolding, also, an Exmoor courtship. (With) a vocabulary 1778 (E.D.S. 1879)
Explication, A short, of such foreign words as are made use of in the musick books 1724
Exposition of the doctrine of the Church of England, An (by Abp. W. Wake) 1686
Expositor, The 1875–
Expostulatory letter, A mild, from the plaindealing farmers of the neighbouring villages to the men of Buckingham c 1670
Eyton, Robert W. The antiquities of Shropshire 1854–60
Eyton, Thomas C. A history of the rarer of British birds 1836

F

F., A.: see Fleming, Abraham
F., E. The history of the life, reign, and death of Edward II 1627 (1680)
F., E. 1644–45: see Fisher, E.
F., I. or J. 1613: see Fletcher, Joseph
F., J. The merchant's warehouse laid open 1695
F., J.: see Freake, J.; French, John
F., N. The husbandmans fruitfull orchard 1608 (1609)
F., T. 1649: see Forde, Thomas
Faber, Frederick W. All for Jesus 1853
Growth in holiness 1854 (1872)
Hymns 1862
Spiritual conferences 1858 (1870)
The Styrian lake, and other poems 1842
Life and letters, edited by Father J. E. Bowden (1869)
Faber, George S. An account of Mr. Husenbeth's professed refutation of the argument of the difficulties of Romanism 1836
Christ's discourse at Capernaum fatal to the doctrine of transubstantiation 1840
The difficulties of infidelity 1824 (1833)
The difficulties of Romanism 1826 (1853)
A dissertation on the mysteries of the Cabiri 1803
A dissertation on the prophecies relative to the great period of 1260 years 1806
Eight dissertations upon the promise of a mighty deliverer 1817–44 (1845)
An enquiry into the history and theology of the Vallenses and Albigenses 1838
A general and connected view of the prophecies relative to the conversion of Judah and Israel 1808
Horæ Mosaicæ, or a view of the Mosaical records 1801 (1818)
Letters on Tractarian secession to Popery 1846
Many mansions in the home of the Father 1851
The origin of Pagan idolatry 1816
The predicted downfall of the Turkish power 1853
The primitive doctrine of election 1836 (1842)
The primitive doctrine of justification investigated 1837
The primitive doctrine of regeneration 1840
Provincial letters 1842 (1844)
Recapitulated apostasy the true rationale of the concealed apocalyptic name of the Roman empire 1833
The revival of the French emperorship 1853
The sacred calendar of prophecy 1827, 1843 (1844)
A treatise on the genius and object of the Patriarchal, the Levitical, and the Christian dispensations 1819 (1823)
A treatise on the origin of expiatory sacrifice 1827
Fabric rolls of York Minster v.d. (Surtees Soc. 1859)
Fabyan, Robert The newe cronycles of Englande and of Fraunce a 1513 (1516); continued to the death of Henry VII 1533, 1542; continued to the death of Q. Mary 1559 1811)

Faction display'd, a poem 1704
Fage, John Speculum aegrotorum, the sicke-mens glasse 1606
Fagge, Charles H. and Pye-Smith, Philip H. The principles and practice of medicine 1886 (1888)
Fahie, J. J. Historic notes on the telephone 1883
Fair trade cry, The: a letter to the rt. hon. sir Stafford Northcote 1881
Fairbairn, Andrew M. Catholicism; Roman and Anglican 1884–97 (1899)
The philosophy of the Christian religion 1902
The place of Christ in modern theology 1893
Studies in the life of Christ 1881
Studies in the philosophy of religion and history 1876
Fairbairn, Patrick Prophecy viewed in respect to its distinctive nature 1856
The typology of scripture 1845–47 (1857)
Fairbairn, William Iron, its history, properties, and processes of manufacture 1861
Faire Em, A pleasant commodie of 1592 (in Shakespeare Apocrypha 1908)
Fairfax, Edward Tasso's Godfrey of Bulloigne tr. 1600
Fairfax, Nathaniel A treatise of the bulk and selvedge of the world 1674
Fairfax, Thomas, 3rd Baron Short memorials a 1671 (1699; in Arber, Eng. Garner VIII)
Fairholt, Frederick W. Costume in England 1846 (1860)
—— ed. 3, enlarged and thoroughly revised by the Hon. H. A. Dillon 1885
A dictionary of terms in art 1854
Tobacco: its history and associations 1859 (1876)
Up the Nile, and home again 1862 (1863)
'Fairless, Michael' (Margaret F. Barber) The roadmender 1902
Falck, N. D. A philosophical dissertation on the diving vessel projected by Mr. Day 1775
Falconbridge, Alexander An account of the slave trade on the coast of Africa 1788
'Falconer, Lanoe' (Mary Eliz. Hawker) Mademoiselle Ixe 1890 (1891)
Falconer (Captain R.), Voyages of 1720: see Chetwood, W.R.
Falconer, William The shipwreck 1762
An universal dictionary of the marine 1769 (1776)
—— enlarged by W. Burney (1815)
Fale, Thomas Horologiographia; the art of dialling 1593
Falk, Hjalmar S. and Torp, Alf Etymologisk ordbog over det Norske og det Danske sprog 1901–06
Falkland, 2nd Viscount a 1643: see Cary, L.
Falkner, John M. Moonfleet 1898
Falkner, William Two treatises a 1682 (1684)
Falle, Philip An account of the isle of Jersey 1694
Fambresarius 1684: see La Framboisière, N. A. de
Family dictionary (Dictionaire oeconomique: or, the family dictionary. Tr. from M. Chomel. Revised and recommended by Mr. R. Bradley) 1725
Family in-compact, The, contrasted with the family compact 1778
Family of Rose of Kilravock, A genealogical deduction of the v.d. (Spalding Cl. 1848) See Rose, Hew
Fane, Julian C. H. and Lytton, Edward Robert Bulwer-Lytton, 1st Earl of Tannhäuser; or, the battle of the bards 1861
'Fan Kwae', The, at Canton before treaty days 1825–44: by an old resident 1882
Fanning, J. T. A practical treatise on water-supply engineering 1877
Fanshaw, Sir Thomas The practice of the Exchequer Court a 1601 (1658)
Fanshawe, Anne, Lady Memoirs, written by herself, to which are added extracts from the correspondence of Sir R. Fanshawe a 1680 (1829, 1905)
Fanshawe, Sir Richard Camoens' (Luis de) Lusiad tr. 1655
Guarini's (Baptista) Il Pastor fido; the faithfull shepheard tr. With an addition of divers other poems 1647–48
Faraday, Michael Chemical manipulation 1827
A course of six lectures on the chemical history of a candle 1861
Experimental researches in chemistry and physics 1821–57 (1859)
On the various forces of nature a 1867 (1874)
Fardle of facions 1555: see Watreman, W.
Farey, John General view of the agriculture and minerals of Derbyshire 1811
Faria's (F. de) Narrative; wherein is contained the several informations touching the popish plot 1680
Farindon, Anthony Forty sermons a 1658 (1663, 1672, 1849)
Thirty sermons 1657
Farjeon, Benjamin L. The betrayal of John Fordham 1896
Three times tried 1886
Farley, John The London art of cookery 1804
Farley, Robert Kalendarium humanæ vitæ 1638
Lychnocausia, sive moralia facum emblemata. Lights. Morall emblemes 1638
Farley's Exeter Journal 1725–28
Farlow, William G. Marine algæ of New England and adjacent coast 1881
Farmer, Edward Scrap book, being a selection of poems, songs, scraps, etc. 1846 (1869)
Farmer, John Forty several ways of two parts in one made upon a playn song 1591
Farmer, John S. Americanisms, old and new: a dictionary 1889
Ed. Musa pedestris: canting songs and slang rhymes 1536–1896 (1896)
The public school word-book 1900
—— and Henley, William E. Slang and its analogues, past and present 1890–1904
Farmer, Richard An essay on the learning of Shakespeare 1767
Farmer's complete guide through all the articles of his profession 1760
Farmer's magazine, The 1800–25
Farmer's Ha' 1776: see Keith, C.
Farquhar, George Works a 1707 (1742, 1892)
The beaux stratagem 1706–07
A constant couple 1700
The inconstant, or the way to win him 1702
Love and a bottle 1699
The recruiting officer 1706
Sir Harry Wildair 1701
Farquhar, William Poems on several occasions 1794

Farr, Edward Ed. Select poetry chiefly devotional of the reign of Queen Elizabeth a 1600 (Parker Soc. 1845)
Ed. Select poetry, chiefly sacred, of the reign of James I 16.. (1847)
Farragut, Loyall The life of D. G. Farragut 1879
Farrar, Frederic W. Chapters on language 1865
Darkness and dawn 1891
The early days of Christianity 1882
Eric; or, little by little 1858
Essay on the origin of language 1860
Families of speech 1869 (1873)
History of interpretation 1886
'In the days of my youth': sermons, Marlborough 1871–76 (1876)
Julian Home 1859
Life and work of St. Paul 1879
Life of Christ 1874
Lives of the Fathers 1889
Seekers after God 1868
The silence and the voices of God, with other sermons 1874
Witness of history to Christ 1871
Farrer, Reginald J. The garden of Asia: impressions from Japan 1904
Farrow, Edward S. Military encyclopedia 1885
Fary, John God's severity on man's sterility 1644 (1645)
Fasciculus florum: or, a nosegay of flowers 1636
Fashionable follies 1782: see Vaughan, T.
Fate of Sedley, The 1795
Fates of the Apostles a 1000 (Grein)
Father's instruction a 1000 (Grein)
Fathers of the desert 1867: see Hahn-Hahn
Faustus. The historie of the damnable life and deserued death of Dr. J. Faustus tr. by P. F. 1592 (in Thoms, Prose romances III, 1828)
The second report of Dr. John Faustus 1594 (ibid.)
Faux, W. Memorable days in America 1823
Favine's (André) Theater of honour and knighthood tr. 1623
Favour, John Antiquitie triumphing over noveltie 1619
Fawcet, Samuel A seasonable sermon for these troublesome times 1641
Fawcett, Henry Manual of political economy 1863 (1876)
Fawkes, Francis Poems a 1777 (1810)
Apollonius Rhodius tr. a 1777
The idylliums of Theocritus tr. 1767
Original poems and translations 1761
Fea, Allan Memoirs of the martyr King, being a detailed record of the last two years of the reign of Charles I 1905
Fearon, Henry B. Sketches of America 1818
Fearon, Samuel and Eyes, John A description of the sea coast of England and Wales 1738
Feathered world 1889–
Featley, Daniel Clavis mystica; a key opening divers texts of scripture 1636
The dippers dipt 1645 (1646)
Featley's Pelagius redivivus. Or, Pelagius raked out of the ashes. (Containing a transl. of 'Parallelismus nov-antiqui erroris Pelagiarminiani') 1626
The fisher catched in his owne net 1623
Roma ruens 1644
Stricturæ in Lyndomastigem 1638
Transubstantiation exploded 1638
Vertumnus Romanus 1642
Featley, John The honor of chastity 1632
Federalist, The 1788: see Hamilton, Alex.
Fell, Bp. John The life of Dr. H. Hammond 1661
Fellowes, Robert Milton's Second defence of the people of England tr. 1806 (in Milton's Works, VI, 1806)
Feltham, John The picture of London for 1802 1802
A tour through the Island of Mann in 1797–98 1798
Feltham, Owen Lusoria, or occasional pieces 1661 (in Resolves, ed. 8, 1661)
Resolves divine, morall, politicall ? 1623 (1628, 1661, 1677)
Three moneths observations of the Low Countries 1648 (1652)
Felton, Cornelius C. Familiar letters from Europe 1865
Greece, ancient and modern 1866 (1867)
Felton, Henry A dissertation on reading the classics, and forming a just style 1709 (1713)
Sermons on the creation, fall, and redemption of man a 1740 (1748)
Felton, William A treatise on carriages 1794 (1801)
Female foundling, The 1751
Female spectator, The 1744–45: see Haywood, Eliza
Female tatler, The 1709: see Baker, T.
Fenise 1651: see De-la-Coveras
Fenn, George Manville Dick o' the fens 1888
In an Alpine valley 1894
The master of the ceremonies 1886
Middy and ensign 1883
Patience wins 1886
Real gold 1894
Fenne, Thomas Frutes 1590
Hecubaes mishaps 1590 (in prec., lf. 91)
Fennell, Charles A. M. Michaelis' (A.) Ancient marbles in Great Britain tr. 1882
See also Stanford dictionary
Fenner, Dudley A defence of the godlie ministers, against the slaunders of D. Bridges 1587
Fenner, William Works a 1640 (1651–58)
Hidden manna, or the mystery of saving grace a 1640 (1652)
Fenton, Elijah Poems a 1730 (1790)
Mariamne, a tragedy 1723
Poems on several occasions 1717
Fenton, Sir Geoffrey Certaine tragicall discourses 1567
Golden epistles (sometimes erron. quoted in Dict. as Hellowes Guevara's Golden ep.) 1575, 1577 (1582)
The historie of Guicciardini, conteining the warres of Italie tr. 1579 (1599)
Fenton, Roger A treatise against the necessarie dependance upon that one head, and the present reconciliation to the church of Rome a 1615 (1617)
A treatise of usurie 1611
Fenton, Thomas Of speaking as the oracles of God. A sermon before the University of Oxford 1720
Ferguson, Adam The history of the progress and termination of the Roman republic 1783
Institutes of moral philosophy 1769
Principles of moral and political science 1792

Ferguson, David Scottish proverbs: gathered together a 1598 (1641, 1785; S.T.S. 1924)
Ferguson, Fergus A popular life of Christ 1878
Ferguson, James Ed. Papers illustrating the history of the Scots brigade in the service of the United Netherlands 1572–1782 (S.H.S. 1899–1901)
Ferguson, James Astronomy explained upon Sir Isaac Newton's principles 1756
Tables and tracts relative to several arts and sciences 1767
Ferguson, R. View of an ecclesiastick in his socks and buskins (anon.) 1698
Ferguson, Richard S. Carlisle 1889
A history of Cumberland 1890
—— and Nanson, W. Ed. Some municipal records of the city of Carlisle v.d. (1887)
Ferguson, Robert The dialect of Cumberland 1873
Ferguson, Robert M. Electricity 1866 (1870)
Ferguson, Samuel Lays of the Western Gael, and other poems 1865 (1888)
Poems 1880
Fergusson, David: see Ferguson, D.
Fergusson, James A brief exposition of the Epistles of Paul to the Galatians and Ephesians 1659
Fergusson, Sir James Decisions of the Court of Session from 1738 to 1752 1775
Fergusson, James History of architecture in all countries 1865–67 (1873–76)
The illustrated handbook of architecture 1855
Fergusson, Robert Works a 1774 (1807)
Poems 1773
Poems on various subjects a 1774 (1789)
Fergusson, Robert M. My village 1893
Rambling sketches in the Far North, and Orcadian musings 1883
A village poet 1897
Fergusson, William System of practical surgery 1842
Ferne (Henry), A fuller answer to a treatise written by 1642
Ferne, Sir John The blazon of gentrie 1586
Fernie, John A history of the town and parish of Dunfermline 1815
Ferrand's Melancholy 1640: see Chilmead, E.
Ferrar, Nicholas The hundred and ten considerations of Signior J. Valdesso tr. a 1637 (1638)
The story books of Little Gidding, being the religious dialogues recited in the great room 1631–32 (1899)
Ferriar, John Illustrations of Sterne; with other essays and verses 1798
Ferrier, Andrew Memoir and sermons 1841
Ferrier, David The functions of the brain 1876
Ferrier, James F. Institutes of metaphysic 1854 (1856)
Lectures on Greek philosophy and other philosophical remains a 1864 (1866)
Ferrier, Richard Journal while travelling in France 1687 (in Camden Misc. IX, No. 7, 1894)
Ferrier, Susan E. Destiny 1831
The inheritance 1824
Marriage 1818
Ferris, Richard The most dangerous and memorable adventure of R. F. 1590 (in Arber, Eng. Garner VI)
Ferumbras, Sir a 1380 (E.E.T.S. 1879)
Fessenden, Thomas G. Democracy unveiled 1805
Original poems 1804 (1806)
Terrible tractoration 1803
Festivall (John Mirk's Liber festivalis) 1483 (Caxton); 1493 (W. de Worde; 1515)
Festive songs: see Songs
Fetherstone, Christopher Calvin's Commentaries vpon the actes of the Apostles tr. 1585
Feuchterleben, E. von: see Lloyd, Hannibal E.
Feuillerat, Albert Ed. Documents relating to the office of the revels in the time of queen Elizabeth 1558–1602 (1908)
Ed. Documents relating to the revels at court in the time of king Edward VI and queen Mary 1547–1558 (1914)
Fiddes, Richard Fifty-two practical discourses on several subjects 1720
The life of cardinal Wolsey 1724 (1726)
Theologia speculativa, or the first part of a body of divinity 1718
Theologia practica, or the second part etc. 1720
Field, The, the farm, the garden: the country gentleman's newspaper 1853–
'Field, Michael' Attila, my Attila! 1896
Field, Nathaniel Amends for ladies 1618
A woman is a weathercocke 1612
Field, Nathaniel Some short memorials concerning the life of Dr. R. Field, dean of Glocester 1716–17
Field, Richard Of the Church. Five bookes 1606–10
Field, William Memoirs of the life, writings, and opinions of the rev. S. Parr 1828
Field exercises and evolutions of infantry 1877
Fielding, Henry Works a 1754 (1771, 1882)
Amelia 1751
The author's farce, and the pleasures of the town 1730
The coffee-house politician (= Rape upon rape) 1730
The Covent-garden journal 1752
The Covent Garden tragedy 1732
Don Quixote in England 1734
Eurydice 1737
The fathers, or the good-natured man a 1754
The Grub-street opera 1731
The historical register for the year 1736 1737
The history of the adventures of Joseph Andrews 1742
The history of Tom Jones 1749
The intriguing chambermaid 1734
Journal of a voyage to Lisbon 1754
The letter writers 1731
The life of Mr. Jonathan Wild the Great 1743
The lottery 1732
Love in several masques 1728
Miscellanies 1743
The miser 1733
Miss Lucy in town 1742
The mock doctor 1732
The modern husband 1732
The old debauchees 1732
An old man taught wisdom 1735
Pasquin 1736
The temple beau 1730
Tom Thumb 1730
Tumble-down Dick 1736
The universal gallant 1735
The wedding day 1743

Fielding, Sir John An account of the origin and effects of a police set on foot by the Duke of Newcastle in 1753 1758
Fielding, Sarah The adventures of David Simple in search of a faithful friend 1744–52
Familiar letters between the principal characters in David Simple and some others 1747
The history of the Countess of Dellwyn 1759
The history of Ophelia a 1768 (1785)
Field naturalist, The, and scientific student 1882–83
Fields, James T. Biographical notes and personal sketches; with unpublished fragments 1881
Fiennes, Celia Through England on a side saddle in the time of William and Mary; being the diary of C. Fiennes c 1710 (1888)
Fife-Cookson, John C. With the armies of the Balkans and at Gallipoli, 1877–78 1879
Fifteen oes (O Ihesu endles swetnes of louyng soules) 1491 (Caxton)
—— (The xv. oos in Englysshe with other prayers) 1529 (R. Copland)
Fight at Finnesburg, The Anglo-Saxon poem of the (in Beowulf, etc., ed. Thorpe 1855)
Figuier's (Louis) Human race tr. 1872
The insect world tr. by Y. D. 1868; new ed. by P. M. Duncan 1872
The ocean world tr. by W. S. O. 1868; new ed. by E. P. Wright 1872
Reptiles and birds tr. by P. Gillmore 1869 (1870)
The world before the deluge tr. by W. S. O. 1865; new ed. by H. W. Bristow 1867
Filmer, Sir Robert The necessity of the absolute power of all kings (anon.) 1648
Political discourses a 1653 (1679–80)
Finch, Sir Heneage An exact and most impartial account of the indictment, arraignment, etc. of twenty-nine regicides 1660 (1679)
Finch, Sir Henry Law, or, a discourse thereof, in foure bookes a 1625 (1636)
Finch-Hatton, Harold H. Advance Australia! 1885
Findlater, Charles General view of the agriculture of the county of Peebles 1802
Findlay, Alexander The phase rule and its applications 1904
Findlay, George Working and management of an English railway 1889
Fine arts quarterly review 1863–67
Finett, Sir John Philoxenis: some choice observations touching the reception and precedence, etc., of forren ambassadors in England a 1641 (1656)
Finlay, James Ed. Scottish historical and romantic ballads, chiefly ancient, with .. notes and a glossary (1808)
Finlayson, William Simple Scotish rhymes 1815
Firmin, Giles Πανουργία, a brief review of Mr. Davis's vindication 1693
A serious question stated 1651
A sober reply to the sober answer of Mr. Cawdrey 1653
First English book on America (Of the newe landes and of ye people founde by the messengers of the kynge of portyngale named Emanuel) c 1511 (Arber 1885)
Firth, Sir Charles H. Cromwell's army 1902
The last years of the Protectorate 1656–58 1909
Firth, John B. Highways and byways in Derbyshire 1905
Fish, Simon A supplicacyon for the beggers 1529 (E.E.T.S. 1871; Arber 1895)
Fisher, Edward The feast of feasts 1644
The marrow of modern divinity 1645 (1646)
Fisher, James Poems on various subjects 1790
Fisher, Jasper Fuimus Troes; Æneid. 2. The true Trojanes, being a story of the Britaines valour (anon.) 1633 (Hazl. Dodsley)
Fisher, Bp. John English works a 1535 (E.E.T.S. 1876)
Funeral sermon of Margaret Countess of Richmond (A mornynge remembraunce had at the moneth mynde of Margarete, countesse of Rychemonde) 1509 (1708)
Sermon made agayn ye pernicious doctryn of M. luther 1521
Sermon sayd in the cathedrall chyrche of saynt Poule the body beynge present of Kynge Henry the VII 1509
Treatise concernynge the fruytfull saynges of Dauyd in the seuen penytencyall psalmes 1508
Fisher's Godlie treatisse declaryng the benefites of prayer tr. 1560
See also Hall, R.
'Fisher, John' (John Percy) The answere unto the nine points of controversy prepared by our late soveraygne 1625–26
Fisher, Samuel Works (The testimony of truth exalted by the collected labours of S. Fisher) a 1665 (1679)
'Επίσκοπος ἀνεπίσκοπος. The bishop busied beside the businesse 1662
Rusticus ad academicos etc. The rustick's alarm to the Rabbies 1660
Fisheries (Great international) exhibition catalogue 1883
Fisheries of the United States 1884, –87: see Goode, G. B.
Fiske, John A century of science, and other essays 1899
Outlines of cosmic philosophy 1874
Fiske, Stephen Holiday stories (Jack's partner 1894) 1900
Fison, Lorimer and Howitt, Alfred W. Kamilaroi and Kurnai; group-marriage and relationship etc. 1880
Fitz, Sir John 1605: see Narrative
Fitz-Geffrey, Charles Poems a 1636 (Grosart 1881)
The blessed birth-day, celebrated in some pious meditations 1634 (1881)
Elisha his lamentation 1622
Sir Francis Drake his honorable lifes commendation 1596 (1881)
FitzGerald, Edward Euphranor, a dialogue on youth 1851 (1855)
Letters and literary remains a 1883 (1889)
Rubáiyát of Omar Khayyam tr. 1859
—— ed. 2 (enlarged) 1868; ed. 3, 1872
Fitzgerald, Percy H. Bella Donna: a romance 1864
Fatal zero 1869 (1888)
Recreations of a literary man 1882 (1883)
Fitzgerald, William Whitaker's (William) Disputation on holy scripture against the Papists especially Bellarmine and Stapleton tr. 1849 (Parker Soc.)
Fitzherbert, Sir Anthony The newe boke of Iustices of the peas 1538
Fitzherbert, John A newe tracte or treatyse moost profytable for all husbande men 1523
—— The boke of husbandry 1534 (E.D.S. 1882)

Fitzherbert, John (cont.)
A ryght frutefull mater: and hath to name the boke of surueyeng 1523
(Often attributed to Sir A. Fitzherbert)
Fitzherbert, Thomas A defence of the Catholyke cause. With an apology of his innocence in a fayned conspiracy 1602
Filsosborne's letters 1739: see Melmoth, W.
Fitzpatrick, William J. The life, times, and correspondence of the right rev. Dr. Doyle 1861
'The sham squire'; and the informers of 1798 1866
Fitzroy, Robert The weather book 1863
Five letters on inspiration 1690: see Le Clerc, J.
Five years' penal servitude 1877
Flagellum 1663: see Heath, J.
Flammarion's (Camille) L'inconnu: the unknown tr. 1900
Flamsteed, John The doctrine of the sphere 1680
Flandrau, Charles M. Harvard episodes 1897
Flatman, Thomas Heraclitus ridens: or a discourse between jest and earnest 1681–82 (1713)
Poems and songs 1674
Flaubert's (Gustave) Salammbô tr. by M. F. Sheldon 1886
Flavel, John Works a 1691 (1731)
The fountain of life opened 1672
Husbandry spiritualized 1669
The method of grace 1680
A practical treatise of fear 1682
The righteous man's refuge 1681
A saint indeed 1671
Flecknoe, Richard The damoiselles à la mode; a comedy 1667
Enigmaticall characters 1658
Love's kingdom 1664
A relation of ten years travels 1655
Fleetwood, Bp. William A complete collection of his sermons, tracts, and pieces of all kinds a 1723 (1737)
A charge delivered to the clergy of the diocese of Ely 1716
Chronicon preciosum; or, an account of English money 1707 (1745)
An essay upon miracles 1701
Fleming, Abraham Caius (Johannes): Of Englishe dogges, the diuersities and the properties tr. 1576 (1880; in Arber, Eng. Garner III)
A panoplie of epistles 1576
The schoole of skill 1581 (1598; Part III of The footepath to felicitie)
Virgil's Bucolikes tr. 1575; Bucoliks, Georgiks tr. 1589
See also Holinshed
Fleming, Sir Daniel Description of the county of Westmoreland 1671 (1882)
Fleming, David Hay Mary Queen of Scots 1897
The Reformation in Scotland 1910
Fleming, John A history of British animals 1828
The lithology of Edinburgh a 1857 (1859)
Fleming, Robert The fulfilling of the scripture 1669, 1677 (1726)
Fleming, William The vocabulary of philosophy 1857 (1876)
Fleming, William H. Slavery and the race problem in the South 1906
Fleta, seu commentarius juris Anglicani sic nuncupatus c 1290 (ed. Selden 1647)
Fletcher, Giles (the elder) Of the Russe common wealth 1591 (Hakluyt Soc. 1856)
Licia, or poemes of love. Whereunto is added The rising to the crowne of Richard the Third (anon.) 1593 (Grosart 1871; in Arber, Eng. Garner VIII)
Fletcher, Giles (the younger) Poems a 1623 (1868)
Brittain's Ida. Written by that renowned poet, Edmond Spencer (ascribed to Fletcher) a 1623 (1628)
Christs victorie, and triumph in heaven, and earth, over, and after death 1610
Fletcher, John The beggars bush 1622
The bloody brother a 1625
The chances 1620
The fair maid of the inn a 1625
The faithfull shepheardesse 1610
The humorous lieutenant 1619
The island princesse 1621
The knight of Malta 1619
The loyall subject 1618
The mad lover 1617
Monsieur Thomas 1619
The nice valour a 1625
The noble gentleman a 1625
The pilgrim 1621
Rule a wife and have a wife 1624
The sea-voyage 1622
The Spanish curate 1622
The tragedy of Thierry and Theodoret c 1616
Valentinian 1614
A wife for a month a 1625
The wild goose-chase 1621
Wit at severall weapons c 1614
The woman's prize a 1625
Women pleased c 1620
See also Beaumont, Francis
—— and others The Queene of Corinth a 1619
—— and Rowley, William The maide in the mill 1623
—— and Shirley, James The night-walker, or the little theife 1625
Fletcher, John W. (of Madeley) Works a 1785 (1800–04, 1826)
An appeal to matter of fact and common sense 1772
Checks to Antinomianism 1771–72
Logica Genevensis (Fourth and fifth check) 1772
Fletcher, Joseph Christes bloodie sweat. By I. F. 1613
Fletcher, Joseph S. The builders 1897
The wonderful wapentake 1895
Fletcher, Phineas Elisa: an elegie upon the unripe demise of Sr Antonie Irby 1633 (Pt. III of The purple island)
Locustae vel pietas Jesuitica. The Locusts or Appollyonists 1627
The purple island, or the isle of Man; together with piscatorie eclogs and other poeticall miscellanies 1633
Fletcher, R. Ex otio negotium. Or, Martiall his epigrams translated. With sundry poems and fancies 1656
Radius Heliconius; or, the revolution of a free state 1650
Fleury's (Claude) Ecclesiastical history tr. by H. Herbert 1727–30
Flint, Austin A treatise on the principles and practice of medicine 1866 (1880)

Flint, James Letters from America 1822
Flint, Timothy A condensed geography and history of the Western States, or the Mississippi valley 1828
George Mason, the young backwoodsman 1829
Flloyd, Thomas Gueullette's (T. S.) Tartarian tales tr. 1764 (1785)
Floddan field in nine fits, being an exact history of that famous memorable battle fought between the English and Scots on Floddan-Hill 1513 a 1600 (1664)
Flores, Jean de: see Aurelio and Isabell
Florice and Blauncheflour c 1330 (Abbotsford Cl. 1857)
See also Floriz
Florio, John Firste fruites. Also a perfect induction to the Italian, and English tongues 1578
Second frutes 1591
Montaigne's Essayes, or morall, politike and millitarie discourses tr. 1603 (1632)
A worlde of wordes, or most copious and exact dictionarie in Italian and English 1598 See also Torriano, G.
Queen Anna's new world of words 1611
Florist's journal 1845
Floris and Blauncheflur a 1300 (E.E.T.S. 1866, 1901; Hausknecht 1885)
Flower, Philip W. A history of the trade in tin 1880
Flower, William H. and Lydekker, Richard An introduction to the study of mammals 1891
Flower and the leaf, The a 1500 (in Chaucer's Works 1598; Chaucerian pieces, Skeat 1897)
Flower-garden display'd, The 1732
Floyer, Ernest A. Unexplored Baluchistan 1882
Floyer, Sir John The ancient ψυχρολουσία revived: or, an essay to prove cold bathing both safe and useful 1702 (1706)
Φαρμακο-βάσανος; or, the touch-stone of medicines 1687–90
The physician's pulse-watch 1707–10
The preternatural state of animal humours described by their sensible qualities 1696
The Sibylline Oracles tr. 1713
A treatise of the asthma 1698
Floyer, Mrs. L. S. Plain hints for examiners of needlework 1880
Flückiger, Friedrich A. and Hanbury, Daniel Pharmacographia; a history of the principal drugs of vegetable origin, met with in Great Britain and British India 1874
Fluff-hunters, The, by 'Marjoribanks' 1903
Fog's Weekly journal 1728–31: see Molloy, Charles
Foley, Henry Jesuits in conflict 1873
Records of the English Province of the Society of Jesus 1875–83
Folkard, Henry C. The wild fowler 1859
Folkingham, William Brachigraphy; or the art of short writing 1620
Feudigraphia. The synopsis or epitome of surveying methodized (Page-heading: The art of survey) 1610
Fonblanque, Albany England under seven administrations 1827–34 (1837)
Life and labours of (1874)
Fonseca, José N. da An historical and archæological sketch of the city of Goa 1878
Foot, James Penseroso, or the pensive philosopher in his solitudes, a poem 1771
Foot, Peter General view of the agriculture of the county of Middlesex 1794
Foote, Samuel Dramatic works a 1777 (1778, 1830)
The author 1757
The bankrupt 1773
Capuchin 1776
The commissary 1765
The cozeners 1774
The devil upon two sticks 1768
The Englishman in Paris 1753
The Englishman return'd from Paris 1756
The knights 1754
The lame lover 1770
The lyar 1762
The maid of Bath 1771
The mayor of Garret 1764
The minor 1760
The nabob 1772
The orators 1762
The patron 1764
Taste 1752
Trip to Calais 1776
Memoirs of (1778, 1805)
Forbes, Bp. Alexander P. An explanation of the Thirty-nine Articles 1867–68
A short explanation of the Nicene Creed 1852
Forbes, Archibald Chinese Gordon 1884
My experiences of the war between France and Germany 1871
Souvenirs of some continents 1885
Forbes, Duncan Reflexions on the sources of incredulity with regard to religion (anon.) a 1747 (1750)
Forbes, Edward A history of British starfishes, and other animals of the class echinodermata 1841
—— and Hanley, Sylvanus A history of British mollusca and their shells 1853
Forbes, Gordon S. Wild life in Canara and Ganjam 1885
Forbes, Henry O. A naturalist's wanderings in the Eastern Archipelago 1885
Forbes, James Oriental memoirs 1813–15
Forbes, John Certain records touching the estate of the Kirk in 1605 and 1606 16.. (Wodrow Soc. 1846)
Forbes, Sir John Laennec's (R. T. H.) Treatise on the diseases of the chest tr. 1821 (1834)
See also Cyclopædia
Forbes, Patrick A defence of the lawful calling of the ministers of reformed churches 1614
An exquisite commentarie upon the Revelation of Saint John 1613
Forbes, Peter Poems, chiefly in the Scottish dialect 1812
Forbes, Robert Ajax; his speech to the Grecian Knabbs, attempted in broad Buchans. To which is added a Journal to Portsmouth and a Shop-Bill in the same dialect, with a key 1742 (1755)
Select collection of Scots poems, A, chiefly in the broad Buchan dialect 1785
Forbes, William The dominie depos'd; or some reflections on his intrigue with a young lass ? 1746 (1785)

G

H

HAWES, STEPHEN (cont.)
The pastime of pleasure 1509 (1517)
—— another ed., entitled The historie of graunde Amoure and la bell Pucel, called The pastime of pleasure 1554 (1555; Percy Soc. 1845)
HAWKE, MICHAEL Killing is murder and no murder 1657
HAWKER, ESSEX The wedding 1729
HAWKER, LIEUT.-COL. PETER Diary 1802–53 (1893)
Instructions to young sportsmen in all that relates to guns and shooting 1824 (ed. 3)
HAWKER, ROBERT S. The Cornish ballads and other poems; including a second edition of 'The quest of the Sangraal' 1869
Footprints of former men in far Cornwall 1870
The quest of the Sangraal 1864
Life and letters a 1875 (1905)
HAWKESWORTH, JOHN An account of the voyages undertaken for making discoveries in the Southern Hemisphere and performed by Commodore Byron, Captain Wallis, Captain Carteret, and Captain Cook (from 1764–71) 1773
See also Adventurer
HAWKINS, EDWARD The silver coins of England arranged and described 1841
HAWKINS, FRANCIS Youth's behaviour: or, decency in conversation amongst men tr. 1646 (1663)
HAWKINS, HENRY Partheneia sacra. Or, the mysterious and delicious garden of the sacred Parthenes. By H. A. (i. e. Henry Hawkins) 1633
HAWKINS, SIR JOHN The first voyage made to the West Indies 1562
The (second) voyage made to the coast of Guinea and the Indies of Nova Spania, begun in 1564 (signed at end Iohn Sparke) c 1565
A true declaration of the (third) troublesome voyadge to the parties of Guynea and the west-Indies in 1567–68 1569 (in Hakluyt, Voy. 1589; Hakluyt Soc. 1878; partly repr. in Arber, Eng. Garner V)
HAWKINS, SIR JOHN A general history of the science and practice of music 1776
The life of Samuel Johnson 1787
See also Walton, I.
HAWKINS, LÆTITIA M. The Countess and Gertrude 1811
Memoirs, anecdotes, facts, and opinions 1824
HAWKINS, SIR RICHARD Observations in his voiage into the South Sea 1593 1622 (Hakluyt Soc. 1847, 1878)
HAWKINS, SUSANNA Poems and songs 1841
HAWKINS, SIR THOMAS Caussin's (N.) Holy court tr. 1626
Mansini's (G. B.) Political observations on the fall of Seianus tr. 1634
Matthieu's (P.) Unhappy prosperitie, expressed in the histories of Ælius Sejanus and Philippa tr. 1632 (1639)
The odes and epodes of Horace tr. 1625
HAWKINS, THOMAS The origin of the English drama 1773
Hawkstone 1845: see Sewell, W.
Hawkwood, History of Sir John (The honour of the taylors; or, the famous and renowned history of Sir J. Hawkwood) 1687
HAWTHORNE, JULIAN Dust 1883
Fortune's fool 1883
Garth 1877
The laughing mill and other stories 1879
Nathaniel Hawthorne and his wife 1885
HAWTHORNE, NATHANIEL The Blithedale romance 1852
Doctor Grimshawe's secret a 1864 (1883)
The house of the seven gables 1851
The marble faun (The original title of Transformation)
Mosses from an old manse 1846
Our old home 1863
Passages from the American note-books a 1864 (1868)
Passages from the English note-books 1853–58 (1870)
Passages from the French and Italian note-books a 1864 (1871)
The scarlet letter 1850
Septimius Felton; or the elixir of life a 1864 (1872)
The snow image, and other tales 1851
Tanglewood tales, for girls and boys: being a second Wonder-book 1853
Transformation; or the romance of Monte Beni 1860
Twice told tales 1837–42
A wonder-book for girls and boys 1851
HAY, ALEXANDER Saint Germain's (C. de) Royal physician tr. 1689
HAY, ANDREW Diary 1659–60 (S.H.S. 1901)
HAY, EDWARD History of the insurrection of the county of Wexford in 1798 1803
HAY, JOHN Pike county ballads, and other pieces 1871 (1880)
HAY, WILLIAM Deformity; an essay 1754
An essay on civil government 1728
Remarks on the laws relating to the poor 1735 (1751)
HAY, WILLIAM D. Elementary text-book of British fungi 1887
HAYDOCKE, RICHARD Lomazzo's (G. P.) Tracte containing the artes of curious paintinge tr. 1598
HAYDON, BENJAMIN R. Correspondence and table-talk a 1846. With a memoir by F. W. Haydon (1876)
HAYDON, G. H. The Australian emigrant 1854
Five years' experience in Australia Felix 1846
HAYE, SIR GILBERT The buke of the law of armys or buke of bataillis 1456 (S.T.S. 1901)
The buke of knychthede and the buke of the governaunce of princis 1456 (S.T.S. 1914)
HAYES, ALICE M. The horsewoman 1893
HAYES, CHARLES A treatise of fluxions 1704
HAYES, WILLIAM A natural history of British birds 1775
HAYES, WILLIAM A short introduction to conveyancing 1834 (1837, 1840)
HAYLEY, WILLIAM A philosophical, historical, and moral essay on old maids. By a friend to the sisterhood (i. e. W. Hayley) 1785
The triumphs of temper; a poem 1781
HAYMAN, ROBERT Owen's (J.) Epigrams tr. 1628
Quodlibets, lately come over from new Britaniola, old Newfoundland 1628
HAYNE, THOMAS The life and death of Dr. Martin Luther 1641
HAYWARD, ABRAHAM A selection from the correspondence of A. H., with an account of his early life 1834–84 (ed. H. E. Carlisle 1886)
HAYWARD, JAMES Biondi's (G. F.) Donzella desterrada; or the banish'd virgin tr. 1635
Biondi's (G. F.) Eromena; or love and revenge tr. 1632
HAYWARD, SIR JOHN Annals of the first four years of the reign of Queen Elizabeth a 1627 (Camden Soc. 1840)

HAYWARD, SIR JOHN (cont.)
An answer to the first part of a certaine conference concerning succession, published under the name of R. Dolman 1603
The first part of the life and raigne of King Henrie the IIII 1599
The life and raigne of King Edward the sixt a 1627 (1630)
The lives of the three Normans, kings of England 1613 (in Harl. Misc.)
A reporte of a discourse concerning supreme power in affaires of religion (anon.) 1606; another ed., entitled Of supremacie in affaires of religion 1624
The sanctuarie of a troubled soule 1604 (1616, 1620)
HAYWARD, SAMUEL Seventeen sermons on several important subjects 1758
HAYWARD, W. STEPHENS Love against the world 1875
HAYWOOD, MRS. A new present for a servant-maid: containing rules for her moral conduct, the whole art of cookery, etc. 1771
HAYWOOD, ELIZA The female spectator (anon.) 1744–45 (1748)
The history of Miss Betsy Thoughtless 1751
La belle assemblée by M. A. Poisson de Gomez tr. 1724–25 (1732)
HAZARD, SAMUEL Cuba with pen and pencil 1871
HAZLITT, WILLIAM Characters of Shakespear's plays 1817 (1818)
Lectures chiefly on the dramatic literature of the age of Elizabeth 1820
Lectures on the English poets 1818 (1869)
Political essays, with sketches of public characters 1819
The spirit of the age; or, contemporary portraits 1825
Table talk; or, original essays on men and manners 1821–22 (1824, 1869)
HAZLITT, WILLIAM C. English proverbs and proverbial phrases 1869
Four generations of a literary family 1897
The history of the origin and rise of the republic of Venice 1858
Offspring of thought in solitude: modern essays 1884
Ed. Remains of the early popular poetry of England v.d. (1864–66)
See also Dodsley, R.
HEAD, BARCLAY V. Historia numorum; a manual of Greek numismatics 1887
HEAD, SIR FRANCIS B. Bubbles from the Brunnens of Nassau 1834
Rough notes taken during some rapid journeys across the Pampas and among the Andes 1826
HEAD, SIR GEORGE Forest scenes and incidents in the wilds of North America 1829
A home tour through the manufacturing districts of England 1836
HEAD, PERCY R. and POYNTER, EDWARD J. Classic and Italian painting 1880
HEAD, RICHARD The canting academy, or, the devil's cabinet opened, with several new catches and songs 1673
The English rogue described in the life of Meriton Latroon 1665; Part II by F. Kirkman 1671; Parts III and IV by Head and Kirkman 1671 (1874)
Jackson's recantation, or, the life and death of the notorious highway-man now hanging in chains at Hampstead (anon.) 1674
Proteus redivivus: or the art of wheedling or insinuation 1675
HEADLEY, HENRY Poems and other pieces 1786
HEADRICK, JAMES General view of the agriculture of the county of Angus or Forfar 1813
View of the mineralogy, agriculture, manufactures and fisheries of the Island of Arran 1807
HEALEY, JOHN St. Augustine Of the citie of God with the learned comments of J. L. Vives tr. 1610 (1616)
Discovery of a new world, or a description of the South Indies, hitherto unknowne (a version in English of Bp. Jos. Hall's Mundus alter et idem) 1609
Epictetus his manuell. And Cebes his table tr. 1610
—— ed. 1616 adds (And) Theophrastus characters (1636)
Health. International health exhibition; official catalogue 1884
Health and longevity, Account of persons remarkable for their. By a physician 1829
HEARN, WILLIAM E. The Aryan household, its structure and its development 1878
HEARNE, SAMUEL A journey from Prince of Wales's fort in Hudson's Bay to the Northern ocean in 1769–72 1795
HEARNE, THOMAS Ductor historicus; or a short system of universal history 1698
—— ed. 2, augmented and improv'd 1704–05 (1714)
Reliquiæ Hearnianæ: the remains, being extracts from his MS. diaries 17.. (collected by P. Bliss 1857)
Remarks and collections 1705–12 (ed. C. E. Doble, O.H.S. 1885–89)
HEATH, FRANCIS G. The fern world 1877
The 'romance' of peasant life in the West of England 1872 (1880)
HEATH, JAMES A brief chronicle of the late intestine war in the three kingdoms of England, Scotland and Ireland 1663
England's chronicle: or, the lives and reigns of the kings and queens from the time of Julius Cæsar to K. William and Q. Mary 1689
Flagellum: or, the life and death, birth and burial of Oliver Cromwel. By S. T. gent. (i. e. James Heath) 1663 (1672)
HEATH, JAMES D. The complete croquet-player 1874
HEATH, JOHN B. Some account of the worshipful Company of Grocers of the city of London 1829 (1869)
HEATH, RICHARD The English peasant 1893
HEATH, ROBERT A natural and historical account of the islands of Scilly 1750
HEATH, THOMAS A manifest and apparent confutation of an astrological discourse (by R. Harvey) 1583
HEATH, SIR THOMAS L. Apollonius of Perga. Treatise on conic sections 1896
The works of Archimedes 1897
HEATHCOTE, CHARLES G. and JOHN M. Tennis: by J. M. Heathcote. Lawn tennis: by C. G. Heathcote. Rackets: by E. O. Pleydell-Bouverie. Fives: by A. C. Ainger. 1890 (Badminton Library)
HEATHCOTE, FREDERICK G.: see Claus, C.
HEATHCOTE, RALPH Sylva, or, the wood: being a collection of anecdotes, dissertations, characters, apophthegms, original letters, bons mots, and other little things (anon.) 1786

HEATON, MARY M. The history of the life of Albrecht Dürer 1870 (1881)
HEAVYSEGE, CHARLES Saul; a drama 1857 (1869)
HEBER, BP. REGINALD Hymns a 1826 (1827)
Life of Jeremy Taylor 1822
Narrative of a journey through the upper provinces of India, from Calcutta to Bombay 1824–25, with notes upon Ceylon; an account of a journey to Madras and the Southern provinces 1826, and letters written in India a 1826 (1828, 1844)
Palestine; a prize-poem 1803
Palestine and other poems v.d. (1843)
HEBERDEN, WILLIAM (the younger) Heberden's (W., the elder) Commentaries on the history and cure of diseases tr. 1803
HECTOR, MRS. ANNIE F.: see 'Alexander, Mrs.
HECTOR, JAMES Handbook of New Zealand 1883
HECTOR, WILLIAM Ed. Selections from the judicial records of Renfrewshire 16..–17.. (1876)
HEDDERWICK, PETER A treatise on marine architecture 1830
HEDGES, SIR WILLIAM Diary a 1701 (Hakluyt Soc. 1887–88)
HEDIN, SIR SVEN A. Through Asia 1898
HEILPRIN, ANGELO The geographical and geological distribution of animals 1887
Heister's (L.) General system of surgery tr. 1743
HELFENSTEIN, JACOB A comparative grammar of the Teutonic languages 1870
Heliconia; comprising a selection of English poetry 1575–1604 (ed. T. Park 1815)
Heliodorus' Triumphs of love and constancy: a romance, containing the heroick amours of Theagenes and Chariclea. In ten books. The first five rendered by a person of quality, the last five by N. Tate 1686
—— another ed., entitled Æthiopian adventures 1753
HELLOWES, EDWARD Guevara's (A. de) Chronicle, conteyning the lives of tenne emperours of Rome tr. 1577
Guevara's Familiar epistles tr. 1574 (1577, 1582, 1584)
(For Gueuara's Golden epistles see Fenton, Sir G.)
HELME, ELIZABETH St. Margaret's cave, or the nun's story 1801
HELPS, SIR ARTHUR Companions of my solitude 1851 (1874)
Essays written in the intervals of business 1841 (1875)
Friends in council 1847–49, 1859
Organization in daily life. An essay (anon.) 1862
Realmah 1868 (1876)
Social pressure 1875
Some talk about animals and their masters 1873 (1875)
Helps to the study of the Bible 1880 (1884; revised and enlarged edition 1893)
HELSHAM, RICHARD A course of lectures in natural philosophy a 1738 (1739)
Helvetius' (C. A.) Child of nature improved by chance tr. 1774
HELY, JAMES O'Flaherty's (R.) Ogygia, or, a chronological account of Irish events tr. 1793
Helyas, Knight of the Swanne 1512 (W. de Worde; in Thoms, Prose romances III. 1828)
HEMANS, FELICIA D. Works a 1835 (1839)
Poems 1808
Poetical works a 1835 (1875)
Early blossoms of spring, a collection of poems written between eight and fifteen years of age 1808 (1840)
England and Spain; or, valour and patriotism 1808
'HEMINGWAY, PERCY' (W. P. Addleshaw) Out of Egypt 1895
HEMYNG, BRACEBRIDGE Eton school days 1864
HENCHMAN, RICHARD A peace-offering in the temple; or, a seasonable plea for unity among dissenting brethren 1661
Henckel, J. F.: see Henkel, J. F.
HENDERSON, ALEXANDER The history of ancient and modern wines 1824
HENDERSON, ANDREW Scottish proverbs 1832 (1881)
HENDERSON, EBENEZER Iceland; or the journal of a residence in that island 1814–15 1818
HENDERSON, GEORGE The popular rhymes, sayings, and proverbs of the county of Berwick 1856
HENDERSON, JAMES Memorials 1867
HENDERSON, JOHN General view of the agriculture of the county of Caithness 1812
General view of the agriculture of the county of Sutherland 1812
HENDERSON, PETER Practical floriculture 1869
HENDERSON, WILLIAM Notes on the folk lore of the northern counties of England and the Borders 1866 (1878)
Hendyng, Proverbs of: see Proverbs of Hendyng
HENEY, THOMAS In middle harbour, and other verse, chiefly Australian 1890
HENFREY, ARTHUR An elementary course of botany 1857
The rudiments of botany 1849
The vegetation of Europe, its conditions and causes 1852
See also Griffith, John W.
Henkel's (J. F.) Pyritologia; or, a history of the pyrites tr. 1757
HENLEY, WILLIAM E. A book of verses 1888
For England's sake: verses and songs in time of war 1900
Poems 1898
—— and STEVENSON, ROBERT L. Three plays: Deacon Brodie, Beau Austin, Admiral Guinea 1892
See also Farmer, J. S.
HENNELL, MARY An outline of the various social systems and communities which have been founded on the principle of co-operation 1841 (1844)
Henry VII, Materials for a history: see Materials
Henry VII, Memorials of 15.. (Rolls series 1858)
HENRY VIII A declaration, conteynyng the iust causes and consyderations, of this present warre with the Scottis 1542 (in Complaint of Scotland, E.E.T.S. 1872)
The privy purse expences of 1529–32 (1827)
HENRY, ALEXANDER Travels and adventures in Canada and the Indian territories 1760–76 1809
HENRY, CALEB S. Doctor Oldham at Greystones, and his talk there 1860
HENRY, JOHN J. An accurate account of the hardships of that band of heroes who traversed the wilderness in the campaign against Quebec in 1775 1812
HENRY, MATTHEW Works a 1714 (1726, 1853)
Disputes reviewed; a sermon 1710
An exposition of the Old and New Testament 1710 (1737–38)
A sermon concerning the forgiveness of sin as a debt 1711
A short account of the life of lieutenant Illidge 1710
HENRY, PHILIP Diaries and letters 1631–96 (1882)

HENRY, ROBERT The history of Great Britain 1771–85; a 1790 (1793)
HENRY, THOMAS An account of a method of preserving water at sea from putrefaction 1781
HENRY, WILLIAM The elements of experimental chemistry 1810 (1826–40)
An epitome of chemistry 1800 (1808)
HENRY THE MINSTREL The actis and deidis of the illustere and vailȝeand campioun Schir William Wallace c 1470 (1570, 1820; S.T.S. 1889)
Henry and Isabella: a novel 1811
HENRYSON, ROBERT Poems c 1480 (S.T.S. 1906–14)
The morall fabillis of Esope c 1480 (1570; Maitland Cl. 1832; in Anglia IX. 1886)
Orpheus and Eurydice c 1480
The testament of Cresseid c 1480
HENSHALL, JAMES A. Camping and cruising in Florida 1884
HENSHALL, SAMUEL The Saxon and English languages reciprocally illustrative of each other 1798
HENSHAW, BP. JOSEPH Horæ succisivæ, or, spare-houres of meditations 1631 (ed. 2)
Meditations miscellaneous, holy and humane 1637; ed. 3, much enlarged, entitled Daily thoughts; or a miscelany of meditations, holy and humane 1651
HENSLOW, GEORGE The origin of floral structures through insect and other agencies 1888
HENSLOW, JOHN S. A dictionary of botanical terms 1856
The principles of descriptive and physiological botany 1835 (1836)
HENSLOWE, PHILIP Diary 1591–1609 (Shaks. Soc. 1845; 1904–08)
Henslowe papers, being documents supplementary to Henslowe's diary a 1616 (ed. W. R. Greg 1907)
HENTY, GEORGE A. The cornet of horse; a tale of Marlborough's wars 1881
With Lee in Virginia: a story of the American civil war 1890
Hentzner's (Paul) Journey into England in the year 1598 (being a part of the Itinerary of P. H. translated by R. Bentley; ed. H. Walpole, Earl of Oxford) 1757
HEPBURN, GEORGE B. General view of the agriculture and rural economy of East Lothian 1794
Heraclitus ridens 1681–82: see Flatman, T.
Herald, The. By Stentor Telltruth 1757–58
Herball, Grete: see Grete herball
HERBERT, EDWARD, 1ST BARON HERBERT OF CHERBURY The life and reigne of King Henry the eighth a 1648 (1649, 1682)
Life, written by himself a 1648 (1764, 1886)
Occasional verses a 1648 (1665)
HERBERT, SIR EDWARD A short account of the authorities in law, upon which judgement was given in Sir Edw. Hales his case 1688
HERBERT, GEORGE Poetical works a 1633 (Grosart 1876)
Outlandish proverbs a 1633 (1640)
—— another ed., entitled Jacula prudentum, or outlandish proverbs, sentences, etc. (1651)
A priest to the temple, or, The country parson his character, and rule of holy life a 1633 (1652)
The temple; sacred poems and private ejaculations 1633
HERBERT, GEORGE ROBERT C. (EARL OF PEMBROKE) and KINGSLEY, GEORGE H. South Sea bubbles 1872
HERBERT, H. 1727–30: see Fleury
HERBERT, HENRY, 10TH EARL OF PEMBROKE A method of breaking horses, and teaching soldiers to ride, designed for the use of the army 1761
—— ed. 3, entitled Military equitation 1778
HERBERT, HENRY W.: see 'Forester, Frank'
HERBERT, MARY E. Cradle lands 1867
Hübner's (J. A. von) Ramble round the world 1874 (1878)
Impressions of Spain in 1866 1867
HERBERT, SIR THOMAS A relation of some yeares travaile begunne anno 1626, into Afrique and the greater Asia 1634 (1638, 1665, 1677)
Threnodia Carolina 1678 (printed from original MS. in A. Fea, Memoirs of the martyr King 1905); repr. with additions under the title of Memoirs of the two last years of the reign of Charles I 1702
HERBERT, WILLIAM Ella Rosenberg, a romance 1808
HERBERT, WILLIAM The history of the twelve great Livery Companies of London 1834–37
HERD, DAVID Ed. Ancient and modern Scottish songs, heroic ballads, etc., v.d. (1776)
HERING, FRANCIS: see Herring, Francis
HÉRISTAL, ADAM D' Our discordant life 1894
HERKLESS, JOHN and HANNAY, ROBERT K. The archbishops of St. Andrews 1907–13
HERLE, CHARLES An answer to Dr. Ferne's Reply entituled: Conscience satisfied etc. 1643
David's song of three parts 1643
A fuller answer to a treatise written by Dr. Ferne, entituled, The resolving of conscience etc. 1642
HERMAN, HENRY His angel, a romance of the Far West 1891
See also Murray, D. C.
Hermann and Emilia 1805: see Lafontaine, A. H. J.
Hermann's (C. F.) Manual of the political antiquities of Greece historically considered tr. 1836
Hermeticall banquet drest by a spagiricall cook, for the better preservation of the microcosme 1652
Hermit in the country 1820–22; in Edinburgh 1824; in London 1819–20: see McDonogh, Felix
HERNE, SAMUEL Domus Carthusiana; or an account of the foundation of the Charter-House 1677
Hero and Leander 1651: see Loves of H. and L.
Herodian's History tr. 1629: see Maxwell, James
Herodotus, The famous hystory of, tr. by B. R(ich) 1584
Heroic epistle to an unfortunate monarch, by Peregrine the Elder 1778
Heroine of the Peninsula, The 1826: see McDonogh, Felix
HERON, ROBERT Information concerning the strength, views, and interests of the powers presently at war 1794
HERRICK, ROBERT The complete poems a 1674 (Grosart 1876)
Poetical works a 1674 (1869, 1915)
Hesperides: or, the works both humane and divine of R. H. 1648
The noble numbers: or, his pious pieces 1647
Herrig's Archiv: see Archiv
HERRING, FRANCIS A modest defence of the caveat given to the wearers of impoisoned amulets 1604
Oberndoerffer's (J.) Anatomyes of the true physition and counterfeit mounte-banke tr. 1602
HERRING, RICHARD Paper and paper-making, ancient and modern 1855

Herrings tayle 1598: see Carew, R.
HERSCHEL, SIR JOHN F. W. Essays from the Edinburgh and Quarterly Reviews, with addresses and other pieces v.d. (1857)
Familiar lectures on scientific subjects 1866
A manual of scientific enquiry, ed. by Sir J. F. W. Herschel 1849; ed. 3, superintended by Robert Main 1859
Meteorology 1859 (in Manual of scientific enquiry)
Outlines of astronomy 1849 (1853)
Physical geography 1861
A preliminary discourse on the study of natural philosophy 1830
Schiller's (J. C. F. von) Walk tr. 1847
A treatise on astronomy 1833
HERTFORD, FRANCES SEYMOUR, COUNTESS OF Correspondence between Frances, countess of Hartford (afterwards duchess of Somerset), and Henrietta Louisa, countess of Pomfret 1738–41 (1805)
HERVÉ, PETER Beauties of Paris 1818
How to enjoy Paris 1816
HERVET, GENTIAN Xenophon's Treatise of householde 1532 (1768)
HERVEY, MRS. The Mourtray family 1800
HERVEY, FREDERIC The naval history of Great Britain 1779
HERVEY, JAMES Meditations and contemplations. Vol. I. Meditations among the tombs, Reflections on a flower garden, A descant upon creation 1746; Vol. II. Contemplations on the night, Contemplations on the starry heavens, A winter piece 1747 (1767, 1818)
Theron and Aspasio: or, a series of dialogues and letters upon the most important and interesting subjects 1755
HERVEY, JOHN, BARON HERVEY OF ICKWORTH Memoirs of the reign of George the second a 1743 (ed. from the original MS. by J. W. Croker 1848)
Herzog's (J. J.) Religious encyclopædia: or, dictionary of Biblical, historical, doctrinal, and practical theology, ed. by P. Schaff 1882–83
HESLOP, RICHARD O. Northumberland words. A glossary of words used in the county of Northumberland and on the Tyneside 1892–94 (E.D.S.)
HESSEY, JAMES A. Sunday: its origin, history, and present obligation considered 1860
HESTER, JOHN A compendium of the rationall secretes of L. Phioravante tr. 1582
HETH, THOMAS 1583: see Heath, T.
HETLEY, SIR THOMAS Reports and cases in the third–seventh years of the late King Charles as they were argued at the Common-pleas barre 1657
HETT, CHARLES L. A glossary of popular, local, and old-fashioned names of British birds 1902
HEWETT, JOHN a 1658: see Hewit, J.
HEWETT, SARAH The peasant speech of Devon 1892
HEWETT, WILLIAM Glossary of Berkshire provincialisms 1847
HEWIT, JOHN Repentance and conversion the fabrick of salvation, or the saints joy in heaven for the sinners sorrow upon earth, being the last sermons preached by J. H. With other of his sermons a 1658 (1658)
HEWITSON, WILLIAM C. Coloured illustrations of the eggs of British birds 1846
HEWITT, JOHN a 1658: see Hewit, J.
HEWITT, JOHN Ancient armour and weapons in Europe 1855–60
HEWLETT, JOSEPH T. J. The parish clerk 1841
Parsons and widows 1844
Peter Priggins, the college scout (anon.) 1841
HEWLETT, MAURICE H. Earthwork out of Tuscany 1895
The forest lovers, a romance 1898
HEWYT, JOHN a 1658: see Hewit, J.
Hexameron of St. Basil: see Basil, St.
HEXHAM, HENRY A copious English and Netherduytch dictionarie 1647 (1660)
Groot-Woorden-Boeck; a large Netherdutch and English dictionarie 1648 (1658)
The principles of the art militarie 1637
A tongue-combat (anon. Preface signed H. Hexham) 1623: see Scott, Thomas
Hexham, The Priory of, its chroniclers, endowments and annals v.d.; its title deeds, black book, etc., v.d. (Surtees Soc. 1864–65)
HEY, JOHN Lectures in divinity, delivered in Cambridge 1780–85 1796–98
HEYDON, SIR CHRISTOPHER An astrological discourse in justification of the validity of astrology. Together with an astrological judgement upon the great conjunction of Saturn and Jupiter 1603 c 1610 (1650)
A defence of judiciall astrologie 1603
HEYLIN, PETER Κειμήλια ἐκκλησιαστικά. Historical and miscellaneous tracts a 1662 (1681)
Aerius redivivus; or, the history of the presbyterians from 1536 to 1647 a 1662 (1670)
Antidotum Lincolniense; or an answer to a book entituled, The Holy Table, name and thing 1637
A brief and moderate answer to the seditious and scandalous Challenge of H. Burton 1637
Certamen epistolare; or the letter-combate with Mr. Baxter, etc. 1659
A coale from the altar 1636
Cosmographie 1652: see Microcosmus, below
Cyprianus Anglicus; or the history of the life and death of William Laud a 1662 (1668, 1671)
Ecclesia restaurata; or, the history of the reformation of the Church of England 1661
Ecclesia vindicata; or, the Church of England justified 1657
Examen historicum, or a discovery and examination of the mistakes in some modern histories 1659
Extraneus vapulans; or, the observator rescued from the violent but vaine assaults of Hamon L'Estrange 1656
A full relation of two journeys: the one, into the main-land of France; the other, into some of the adjacent islands 1656
—— another ed., entitled A survey of the estate of France 1656
'Ηρωολογια Anglorum; or, an help to English history 1641
Historia quinqu-articularis; or a declaration of the judgement of the Western churches, particularly of the church of England, in the five controverted points reproached by the name of Arminianism 1660
The historie of episcopacie 1642
The history of St. George of Cappadocia 1631
The history of the Sabbath 1636

HEYLIN, PETER (cont.)
Microcosmus. A little description of the great world 1621 (–1639); enlarged and entitled Cosmographie in four books, containing the chorographie and historie of the whole world 1652 (1674)
(Relations and observations 1648–49: see C. Walker History of Independency)
The stumbling-block of disobedience and rebellion cunningly laid by Calvin in the subjects way, discovered, censured and removed 1658
Survey of the estate of France: see A full relation of two journeys, above
The undeceiving of the people in the point of tithes 1648
HEYNE, BENJAMIN Tracts, historical and statistical, on India 1814
HEYWOOD, ELIZA: see Haywood, Eliza
HEYWOOD, JASPER Seneca his tenne tragedies tr. by J. Heywood and others 1581
L. A. Senecæ Tragœdia prima quæ inscribitur Hercules Furens tr. 1561
The seconde tragedie of Seneca entituled Thyestes tr. 1560
The sixt tragedie of L. A. Seneca, entituled Troas tr. 1559
HEYWOOD, JOHN Dramatic writings 15.. (J. S. Farmer 1905–08)
Woorkes. A dialogue conteynyng prouerbes and epigrammes 1562 (Spenser Soc. 1867)
A dialogue conteinyng the nomber in effect of all the prouerbes in the Englishe tongue 1546 (1874)
A dialogue on wit and folly 15.. (Percy Soc. 1846)
Epigrammes 1555–60
A mery play betwene Iohan Iohan the husbande, Tyb his wyfe, and syr Jhan the preest 1533 (Brandl 1898)
A mery play betwene the pardoner and the frere, the curate and neybour Pratte 1533 (in Pollard, Eng. miracle plays 1890)
Of gentylnes & nobylyte: see Rastell, John
The playe called the foure PP. A newe and a very mery enterlude of a palmer, a pardoner, a potycary, a pedler ? 1545 (in Manly, Specim. pre-Shaks. drama I, 1897)
A play of love 1534 (Brandl 1898)
The play of the wether 1533 (Brandl 1898)
The spider and the flie, a parable 1556 (Spenser Soc. 1894)
HEYWOOD, OLIVER Works a 1702 (1825–27)
The best entail, or, dying parents living hopes for their surviving children 1693
Heart-treasure 1667–72
Autobiography, diaries, anecdote and event books, illustrating the general and family history of Yorkshire and Lancashire a 1702 (1881–85)
HEYWOOD, THOMAS Dramatic works a 1650 (1874)
An apology for actors 1612 (Shaks. Soc. 1841)
The brazen age 1613
The captives; or, the lost recovered 1624 (in Bullen, Old Plays IV)
A challenge for beautie 1636
England's Elizabeth, her life and troubles during her minoritie from the cradle to the crowne 1631 (1641; in Harl. Misc.)
The English traveller 1633
The exemplary lives and memorable acts of nine the most worthy women of the world 1640
The fayre mayde of the Exchange 1607 (Shaks. Soc. 1845)
The fair maid of the west 1631 (Shaks. Soc. 1850)
The foure prentices of London, with the conquest of Jerusalem 1615
A funerall elegie upon the death of Henry, Prince of Wales 1613
A funeral elegie upon the death of King James 1625
The golden age 1611 (Shaks. Soc. 1851)
Γυναικεῖον: or nine bookes of various history concerninge women 1624
The hierarchie of the blessed angells 1635
If you know not me, you know no bodie: or, the troubles of Queene Elizabeth 1605 (Shaks. Soc. 1851)
The second part of, If you know not me, you know no bodie. With the building of the Royall Exchange 1606 (Shaks. Soc. 1851)
The iron age 1632
The first and second partes of King Edward the fourth 1599 (Shaks. Soc. 1842)
Londini sinus salutis 1635
Londini speculum; or, Londons mirror 1637
Londini status pacatus; or, Londons peaceable estate 1639
London's jus honorarium exprest in sundry triumphs 1631
Loves maistresse: or the Queens masque 1636
A pleasant comedy called A mayden-head well lost 1634
A marriage triumphe 1613 (Percy Soc. 1842)
Philocothonista; or the drunkard opened, dissected, and anatomized 1635
Pleasant dialogues and dramma's 1637
Porta pietatis, or the port or harbour of piety 1638 (Percy Soc. 1844)
The rape of Lucrece 1608
The royall king and the loyall subject 1637 (Shaks. Soc. 1850)
Sallust's Two most worthy and notable histories tr. 1608–09
The silver age 1613 (Shaks. Soc. 1851)
Troia Britanica: or Great Britaines Troy 1609
A true description of his Majesties royall ship built at Wooll-witch 1637
The wise-woman of Hogsdon 1638
A woman kilde with kindnesse 1607 (Shaks. Soc. 1850)
See also Tourneur, C.
—— and BROME, RICHARD The late Lancashire witches 1634
—— and ROWLEY, WILLIAM Fortune by land and sea 16.. (1655; Shaks. Soc. 1845)
HIBBERT, HENRY Syntagma theologicum: or, a treatise wherein is concisely comprehended the body of divinity; whereunto are added certaine divine discourses 1662
HIBBERT(-WARE), SAMUEL A description of the Shetland Islands 1822
Hibbert journal, The; a quarterly review of religion, theology, and philosophy 1902–
HICHCOCK, ROBERT: see Hitchcock, R.
HICHENS, ROBERT S. The green carnation (anon.) 1894
The Londoners, an absurdity 1898
HICKERINGILL, EDMUND Works a 1708 (1709)
Miscellaneous tracts, essays, satyrs, etc. in prose and verse 1707

HICKERINGILL, EDMUND (cont.)
The black non-conformist discover'd in more naked truth 1682
The ceremony-monger, his character 1689
Curse ye Meroz, or the fatal doom 1680
Gregory, Father Greybeard, with his vizard off 1673
The history of whiggism 1682
The horrid sin of man-catching 1681
Jamaica view'd 1661
The lay-clergy; or, the lay-elder 1695
The naked truth 1680–82
—— A vindication of the naked truth. By Phil. (or rather Edmund) Hickeringill 1681
Priest-craft, its character and consequences 1705–07
—— The vindication of the character of priestcraft 1705
A speech without doors, or some modest inquiries humbly proposed to the Convention of Estates 1689
The Trimmer. Debate with the Observator 1683
HICKERINGILL, PHIL.: see Hickeringill, E.
HICKES, GEORGE The case of infant baptism 1683
The spirit of Popery 1680
Two treatises, one of the Christian priesthood; the other of the dignity of the episcopal order 1707 (1711, 1847)
—— and NELSON, ROBERT Memoirs of the life of John Kettlewell. Compiled (by F. Lee) from the collections of G. Hickes and R. Nelson 1718
HICKIE, WILLIAM J. The Comedies of Aristophanes tr. 1853 (1872)
HICKMAN, HENRY Historia quinq-articularis exarticulata; or, Animadversions on Doctor Heylin's Quinquarticular history 1673 (1674)
HICKOCK, THOMAS The voyage and travaile of M. C. Frederick into the East India tr. 1588
Hickscorner: see Hyckescorner
'HIEOVER, HARRY' (C. Brindley) Practical horsemanship 1850
The stud for practical purposes 1849
HIERON, SAMUEL Works a 1617 (1620)
Aarons bells a-sounding a 1617 (1623)
A defence of the ministers reasons for refusall of subscription to the Booke of Common Prayer 1607–08
A short dialogue proving that the ceremonyes now in question, are defended by arguments such as the papists have used (anon.) 1605
HIFFERNAN, PAUL: see H., P.
Higden's Polychronicon tr. 1432–50 (Rolls series 1865–86)
See also Trevisa
HIGGINS, GODFREY The Celtic Druids 1827
HIGGINS, JOHN The nomenclator, or remembrancer of Adrianus Junius tr. 1585
See also Huloet; Mirror for magistrates
HIGGINS, MATTHEW J. Essays on social subjects a 1868 (1875)
HIGGINSON, THOMAS W. Malbone: an Oldport romance 1869
Oldport days 1873
Young folks' history of the United States 1875
HIGGS, PAGET Ed. Magneto- and dynamo-electric machines ..From the German of Glaser de Cew 1885
High commission cases. Reports of cases in the Courts of Star Chamber and High Commission 1631–32 (Camden Soc. 1886)
Highland Society of Scotland, Prize essays and transactions of 1799–1843
—— Transactions 1843–
Highlanders, The 1824: see McDonogh, F.
Highlands of Scotland in 1750 17.. (From MS. in the British Museum. With introd. by A. Lang 1898)
HIGINS, JOHN: see Higgins, J.
Hildanus tr. 1643: see Steer, John
Hildebrand. The life of Hyldebrande, called Gregory, the seventh, pope of that name 1534 (W. de Worde)
HILDITCH, ANN Rosa de Montmorien. A novel 1787
HILDROP, JOHN Miscellaneous works 1754
A letter to a member of parliament, containing a proposal for bringing in a bill to revise, amend or repeal certain obsolete statutes, commonly called the Ten Commandments (anon.) 1738
HILES, JOHN Catechism of the organ 1876 (1878)
A complete dictionary of musical terms 1871
HILL, AARON Works a 1750 (1753)
Poems a 1750 (1822)
Advice to the poets. A poem 1731
HILL, ABRAHAM Familiar letters which passed between A. H. and several eminent and ingenious persons of the last century 16.. (1767)
Some account of the life of Dr. Isaac Barrow 1687 (in Barrow's Works, I. 1687)
HILL, DAVID J. American authors. W. C. Bryant, etc. 1879
HILL, JOHN The British herbal 1756
A general natural history: or, new and accurate descriptions of the animals, vegetables, and minerals of the different parts of the world. Vol. I. A history of fossils 1748; vol. II. An history of plants 1751; vol. III. An history of animals 1752
A history of the materia medica 1751
Pomet's (P.) Compleat history of drugs tr. 1748 (ed. 4)
The sleep of plants, and cause of motion in the sensitive plant, explain'd 1757
Theophrastus's History of stones tr. 1746 (1774)
The useful family herbal 1755 (1812)
HILL, ROBERT Christs prayer expounded, a christian directed and a communicant prepared 1606
—— another ed., entitled The pathway to prayer and pietie 1610 (1629, 1847)
HILL, THOMAS The arte of vulgar arithmeticke 1600
A briefe and pleasaunt treatise intituled: Naturall and artificiall conclusions tr. 1586
A most briefe and pleasaunt treatise, teachynge howe to dress, sowe, and set a garden 1563
—— another ed., entitled The profitable arte of gardening, now the third tyme set fourth. 2 pts. 1568
—— another ed. Whereunto is newly added a treatise of the arte of graffing and planting of trees 1574
A profitable instruction of the perfite ordering of bees 1579
HILL, THOMAS God's eternal preparations for his dying saints 1648
An olive branch of peace and accommodation budding 1648
The right separation incouraged 1644 (1645)
The spring of strengthning grace in the rock of ages, Christ Jesus 1648
The strength of the saints to make Jesus Christ their strength 1648
The trade of truth advanced 1642

HILL, THOMAS (cont.)
Truth and love happily married in the saints and in the churches of Christ 1648
HILLARY, WILLIAM Observations on the changes of the air and the concomitant epidemical diseases in the Island of Barbadoes 1766
HILLIARD, NICHOLAS A treatise concerning the arte of limning c 1600 (MS. in Edinb. Univ. Library; in Annual of Walpole Soc. I, 1912)
HILLS, RICHARD Proverbs from the common-place book of c 1530 (in Fraser's Mag., Aug. 1858)
See also Songs, carols, etc.
Hills of the Shatemuc 1856: see Warner, Susan
HILMAN, DANIEL Tusser redivivus. The calendar of the twelve months with notes, published by D. Hilman 1710
HINCHLIFF, THOMAS W. South American sketches 1863
HIND, HENRY Y. Explorations in the interior of the Labrador peninsula 1863
HIND, JOHN Eliosto libidinoso, described in two bookes 1606
HINDE, SIDNEY L. The fall of the Congo Arabs 1897
HINDE, WILLIAM A faithfull remonstrance of the holy life and happy death of John Bruen a 1629 (1641)
HINDLEY, CHARLES Ed. The life and adventures of a Cheap Jack 1876
Ed. The old book collector's miscellany 1871–73
'HINTON, BENEVENTURA' (Valentine Durrant) Until my lord's return. A romance of a river town 1892
HINTON, RICHARD J. English Radical leaders 1875
HIRD, FRANK The cry of the children: an exposure of certain British industries in which children are iniquitously exposed 1898
HIRST, HENRY B. The coming of the Mammoth, and other poems 1845
HISLOP, ALEXANDER The book of Scottish anecdote 1874
The proverbs of Scotland 1862 (1874)
HISSEY, JAMES J. A holiday on the road 1887
A tour in a phaeton through the eastern counties 1889
Historia litteraria; or, an exact and early account of the most valuable books published in the several parts of Europe. (Ed. by A. Bower) 1730–34
Historical collections of a citizen of London in the fifteenth century 14.. (Camden Soc. 1876)
Historical manuscripts, Reports of the royal commission on 1870–
Historical register, The, containing an impartial relation of all transactions foreign and domestic 1717 (1724)
Historical view of the Court of Exchequer 1738: see Gilbert, Sir G.
Historie of the arrival of Edward IV 1471 (Camden Soc. 1838)
History and antiquities of Rochester and its environs. (By W. Shrubsole and S. Denne) 1772
History and antiquities of the City of York (? By W. Combe) 1785
History of King Arthur (The story of the moste noble and worthy kynge Arthur newly imprynted) 1557 (W. Copland). See also Malory, Sir T.
History of Christina Allessandra of Swedland 1658: see Burbury, J.
History of Friar Gerund 1772: see Nugent, T.
History of the Holy Rood-tree 11.. (E.E.T.S. 1894)
History of independency: see Walker, C.
History of James VI 1582–88: see James VI
History of Jetzer 1679: see Waller, Sir W.
History of the mitre and purse, The 1714
History of modern Europe, The (by William Russell) 1779
History of Ned Evans 1796
History of Pelham, Mass., from 1738 to 1898. By C. O. Parmenter. (Chiefly from town and parish records) v.d. (1898)
History of Sir J. Hawkwood 1687: see Hawkwood, Sir J.
History of the troubles at Frankforth 1574: see Brieff discours
Histrio-mastix; or, the player whipt 1610 (in Simpson, School of Shakespeare II. 1878)
HITCHCOCK, EDWARD Ichnology of New England 1858
HITCHCOCK, ROBERT A general proportion and order of provision to victual a garrison of one thousand soldiers 1591 (App. to Garrard's Art of war 1591; in Arber, Eng. Garner II)
A pollitique platt for the honour of the prince 1580 (in Arber, Eng. Garner II)
Sansovino's (F.) Quintesence of wit tr. 1590
HITCHIN, CHARLES A true discovery of the conduct of receivers and thief-takers in and about the City of London 1718
HITCHINS, FORTESCUE and DREW, SAMUEL The history of Cornwall, from the earliest records and traditions, to the present time. Compiled by F. Hitchins and ed. by S. Drew 1824
HOADLEY, ABP. JOHN The abasement of pride; a sermon 1708
A sermon preach'd in the cathedral-church of Norwich 1704
HOADLY, BP. BENJAMIN Works a 1761 (1773)
HOADLY, BENJAMIN (son of the above) The suspicious husband; a comedy 1747 (1756)
HOADLY, JOHN Phoebe; a pastoral opera 1748
HOBBES, JOHN OLIVER: see Craigie, Pearl M. T.
HOBBES, STEPHEN C. S(c)hilander his chirurgerie tr. 1596
HOBBES, THOMAS English works a 1679 (1839–45)
Tracts a 1679 (1682)
The art of rhetoric, with a discourse of the laws of England a 1679 (1681)
Behemoth; or an epitome of the civil wars of England from 1640 to 1660 1679 (1680)
De corpore politico: or, the elements of law, moral and politick 1650
Decameron physiologicum: or, ten dialogues of natural philosophy 1678
Elements of philosophy tr.; to which are added Six lessons to the professors of mathematicks of the institution of Sir H. Savile, in the University of Oxford 1656
Mr. Hobbes considered in his loyalty, religion, reputation and manners. By way of a letter to Dr. Wallis 1662
—— another ed., entitled Considerations upon the reputation, loyalty, manners and religion of T. Hobbes. Written by himself 1680
Homer's Iliads tr. 1675
Homer's Odysses tr. 1674
Humane nature; or the fundamental elements of policie 1650
Leviathan, or the matter, forme, and power of a commonwealth, ecclesiasticall and civill 1651

HOBBES, THOMAS (cont.)
Of libertie and necessitie, a treatise, in answer to a treatise written by the Bishop of London-derry on the same subject 1654
The questions concerning liberty, necessity, and chance, clearly stated 1656
Philosophical rudiments concerning government and society 1651
Seven philosophical problems and two propositions of geometry a 1679 (in Tracts, 1682, Pt. IV)
Στιγμαὶ, or markes of the absurd geometry, rural language, Scottish church-politicks and barbarismes of John Wallis 1657
Thucydides' Eight bookes of the Peloponnesian warre tr. 1629
HOBHOUSE, JOHN C. (Baron Broughton) Historical illustrations of the fourth canto of Childe Harold 1818
Italy: remarks made in several visits 1816–54 (1859)
A journey through Albania, etc. 1813
The substance of some letters written by an Englishman resident at Paris (i. e. J. C. Hobhouse), during the last reign of the emperor Napoleon 1815–16 (1816)
HOBLYN, RICHARD D. A dictionary of the terms used in medicine and the collateral sciences 1835
—— ed. 2, 1844; ed. 8, enlarged 1858
HOBSON, JOHN Journal 1725–35 (in Yorkshire diaries, Surtees Soc. 1877)
HOBY, SIR EDWARD A counter-snarle for Ishmael Rabshacheh 1613
A curry-combe for a coxe-combe 1615
A letter to Mr. T(heophilus) H(iggons) in answere of his first Motive 1609
HOBY, SIR THOMAS Castiglione's (B.) Courtyer tr. 1561 (1577)
Travels and life, written by himself 1547–64 (Camden Soc., Misc. 1902)
HOCCLEVE, THOMAS De regimine principum (The regement of princes) c 1412 (Roxb. Cl. 1860; E.E.T.S. 1897)
Minor poems v.d. (E.E.T.S. 1892)
La male regle (The misrule) 1406
The mother of God c 1410
The tale of Jonathas 1422
Hochstetter's (F. von) New Zealand tr. 1867
HOCKIN, THOMAS A discourse of the nature of God's decrees 1684
HOCKLEY, WILLIAM B. Pandurang Hàri; or memoirs of a Hindoo (anon.) 1826
HODGES, JOHN A. Elementary photography 1893 (1907)
HODGES, RICHARD The plainest directions for the true-writing of English 1649
HODGES, THOMAS A glimpse of God's glory 1642
HODGES, THOMAS The hoary head crowned 1652
HODGES, WALTER The Christian plan exhibited in the interpretation of Elohim 1752 (1755)
Elihu; or an enquiry into the principal scope and design of the Book of Job 1750 (1755)
HODGES, WILLIAM Travels in India, during the years 1780–83 1793
HODGKIN, THOMAS Italy and her invaders 1880–99
HODGSON, CHRISTOPHER P. Reminiscences of Australia, with hints on the squatters' life 1846
A residence at Nagasaki and Hakodate in 1859–60 1861
HODGSON, FREDERICK T. Stair-building made easy 1884
HODGSON, JAMES T. Memoir of Francis Hodgson. With letters from Lord Byron and others 1878
HODGSON, JOHN A history of Northumberland 1820–40
HODGSON, SHADWORTH H. The philosophy of reflection 1878
Time and space; a metaphysical essay 1865
HODY, HUMPHREY A history of English councils and convocations 1701
Høffding's (H.) Outlines of psychology, tr. by Mary E. Lowndes 1891
HOFFMAN, CHARLES F. Greyslaer: a romance of the Mohawk 1840
HOFFMAN, WALTER J. The beginnings of writing 1895
Hoffman, Tragedy of: see Chettle, H.
Hoffmeister's (W.) Travels in Ceylon and Continental India tr. 1848
HOGARTH, GEORGE Musical history, biography, and criticism 1835
HOGARTH, WILLIAM The analysis of beauty 1753
'HOGG, CERVANTES': see Barrett, E. S.
HOGG, DAVID Life and times of the rev. John Wightman (1762–1847) 1873
HOGG, JABEZ The microscope 1854 (1861, 1867)
HOGG, JAMES Poetical works a 1835 (1838–40)
Tales and sketches 1818–35 (1836–37)
The Brownie of Bodsbeck, and other tales 1818
Dramatic tales 1817
The Jacobite relics of Scotland; being the songs, airs, and legends of the adherents of the House of Stuart. Collected by J. H. 1819–21 (1874)
The mountain bard 1807
Poems on different subjects 1806
Queen Hynde. A poem 1825
The queen's wake; a legendary poem 1813
Scottish pastorals, poems, and songs 1801
The shepherd's calendar 1829
The three perils of man; or war, women and witchcraft 1822
Winter evening tales 1820
HOGG, ROBERT The fruit manual 1860 (1862)
The vegetable kingdom and its products 1858
HOGG, THOMAS J. The life of Shelley 1858
HOLBROOK, JOHN E. North American herpetology 1836–42
HOLBROOK, M. L. Hygiene of the brain and nerves 1878
HOLCROFT, SIR HENRY Procopius' History of the warres of the Emperor Justinian tr. 1653
HOLCROFT, THOMAS Lavater's (J. C.) Essays on physiognomy tr. 1793
The life of Baron Frederic Trench tr. 1788 (1886)
Memoirs of Bryan Perdue 1805
Memoirs, written by himself, and continued to the time of his death, from his diary, notes, and other papers a 1809 (1816)
Stolberg's (F. L. zu) Travels through Germany, Switzerland, Italy, and Sicily tr. 1796–97
HOLDEN, LUTHER Human osteology 1855 (1878)
A manual of the dissection of the human body 1851
HOLDER, CHARLES F. Marvels of animal life 1885
HOLDER, WILLIAM A discourse concerning time 1694
Elements of speech 1669
A treatise on the natural grounds and principles of harmony 1694

Holderness glossary 1877: see Ross, Frederick
HOLDICH, BENJAMIN An essay on the weeds of agriculture 1825
HOLDSWORTH, EDWARD Remarks and dissertations on Virgil a 1746 (1768)
HOLDSWORTH, RICHARD The peoples happinesse; a sermon preached upon 27 of March, being the day of his Majesties inauguration 1642
HOLE, RICHARD Remarks on the Arabian Nights Entertainments 1797
HOLE, SAMUEL R. A book about roses, how to grow and show them 1869 (1870, 1891)
A little tour in America 1895
HOLINSHED, RAPHAEL The firste (laste) volume of the chronicles of England, Scotlande, and Irelande 1577
—— Continued to 1586 by John Hooker, alias Vowell (and Abraham Fleming) 1586–87 (1807–08)
The Scottish chronicle (1805)
'HOLLAND, CLIVE' (C. J. Hankinson) Mousmé 1901
My Japanese wife 1895
HOLLAND, SIR HENRY General view of the agriculture of Cheshire 1808
HOLLAND, SIR HENRY Essays on scientific and other subjects contributed to the Edinburgh and Quarterly Reviews v.d. (1862)
HOLLAND, HENRY SCOTT Christ or Ecclesiastes 1887 (1888)
Logic and life, with other sermons 1882 (1885)
Old and new 1900
HOLLAND, JOHN A treatise on the progressive improvement and present state of the manufactures in metal 1831–39
HOLLAND, JOSIAH G. Arthur Bonnicastle 1873
The bay-path 1857
Gold foil hammered from popular proverbs 1859
History of Western Massachusetts 1855
Kathrina 1868
Lessons in life 1862
Letters to the Joneses 1863
The life of Abraham Lincoln 1865
The marble prophecy 1872
Miss Gilbert's career 1860
The mistress of the manse 1874
Plain talk on familiar subjects 1865
The story of Sevenoaks 1875
Timothy Titcomb's letters to the young 1858
HOLLAND, PHILEMON Camden's (W.) Britain, or a chorographicall description of England, Scotland, and Ireland tr. 1610 (1637)
Livy's Romane historie tr. 1600
Pliny's Historie of the world, commonly called the Natural historie tr. 1601 (1634)
Marcellinus' (A.) Roman historie tr. 1609
Plutarch's Philosophie, commonlie called, the Morals tr. 1603 (1657)
Suetonius' Historie of twelve Cæsars tr. 1606
Xenophon's Cyrupædia tr. 1632
HOLLAND, SIR RICHARD The buke of the Howlat c 1450 (Bannatyne Cl. 1823; in Scott. allit. poems, S.T.S. 1891–92)
HOLLAND, ROBERT A glossary of words used in the county of Chester 1886 (E.D.S.)
HOLLAND, LADY SABA A memoir of the rev. Sydney Smith 1855
HOLLAND, SAMUEL Don Zara del Fogo; a mock-romance tr. 1656 (1719)
Hollands leaguer 1632: see Goodman, N.
HOLLEY, ALEXANDER L. A treatise on ordnance and armor 1865
HOLLINGSHEAD, JOHN My lifetime 1895
HOLLINGWORTH, RICHARD An exercitation concerning usurped powers 1650
HOLLINGWORTH, RICHARD A full and true account of the penitence of John Marketman 1680
A sermon preached before the Lord Mayor 1682
See also Vindiciæ Carolinæ
HOLLOWAY, WILLIAM A general dictionary of provincialisms 1838
HOLLYBAND, CLAUDIUS (C. Desainliens) Campo di Fior, or else the flourie field of foure languages 1583
A dictionarie French and English 1593
The treasurie of the French tong 1580
HOLLYBUSH, JOHN Braunschweig's (H.) Most excellent homish apothecarye tr. 1561
HOLMAN, JOSEPH G. Abroad and at home; a comic opera 1796
HOLMAN-HUNT, WILLIAM: see Hunt, W. Holman
HOLME, RANDLE The academy of armory, or a storehouse of armory and blazon 1688
—— 2nd vol. 1688 (ed. by I. H. Jeayes, Roxb. Cl. 1905)
HOLME, WILFRID The fall and euill successe of rebellion 1572 (repr. n.d.)
HOLMES, EDWARD The life of Mozart, including his correspondence 1845
HOLMES, OLIVER WENDELL Writings v.d. (1891–92)
Poetical works 1852 (1883, 1895)
The autocrat of the breakfast-table 1858
Elsie Venner; a romance of destiny 1860
The guardian angel 1867
John Lothrop Motley; a memoir 1878
Medical essays 1842–82 (1883)
Pages from an old volume of life. A collection of essays 1857–81 (1883)
The poet at the breakfast-table 1872
The professor at the breakfast-table 1860
Ralph Waldo Emerson 1885
HOLMES, TIMOTHY A treatise on surgery 1875
—— and HULKE, J. W. A system of surgery 1883 (ed. 3)
Holmesby (Capt. John), Voyages and travels, and wonderful discoveries of 1757
Holroyd (Maria J.), The girlhood of. Recorded in letters 1776–96 (1896)
HOLST, HERMAN VON John C. Calhoun 1882
Constitutional and political history of the United States tr. by J. J. Lalor and A. B. Mason 1876–85
HOLT, JOHN General view of the agriculture of the county of Lancaster 1794
HOLTZAPFFEL, CHARLES and JOHN J. Turning and mechanical manipulation 1843–50
HOLWELL, JOHN Z. Interesting historical events relative to the provinces of Bengal and the empire of Indostan 1765–71
HOLWELL, WILLIAM A mythological, etymological, and historical dictionary: extracted from (J. Bryant's) Analysis of ancient mythology 1793
Holy Land, The: being sketches of the Jews, and of the land of Palestine 1844

HOLYDAY, BARTEN A. Persius Flaccus his Satires tr. 1616 (1673)
D. J. Juvenalis and A. Persius Flaccus tr. a 1661 (1673)
Of the nature of faith: a sermon 1654
A sermon preached at Pauls Crosse, Aug. 5 1623 (1626)
A sermon preached at Pauls Crosse, March 24 1624 (1626)
A survey of the world 1661
Τεχνογαμία: or the marriages of the arts. A comedie 1618
HOLYOAKE, GEORGE J. The history of co-operation in England 1875–77
HOLYOKE, FRANCIS Dictionarie etymologicall 1606 (Pt. 2 of Rider's Dictionarie corrected 1606)
Dictionarium etymologicum Latinum 1633 (4th ed. of prec.)
HOLYOKE, THOMAS A large (Latin and English) dictionary, in three parts a 1675 (1677; an enlarged ed. of prec.)
HOMANS, ISAAC S. (senior and junior) A cyclopedia of commerce and commercial navigation 1858
HOME, SIR EVERARD Lectures on comparative anatomy 1814–28
HOME, HENRY: see Kames, Lord
HOME, JOHN Works a 1808 (1822)
Douglas: a tragedy 1756
'HOME, JULIAN' (E. R. Christie) Sketches of Cambridge, in verse 1879
Homer à la mode 1664: see Scudamore, J.
Homilies. Certayne sermons, or homilies, appoynted by the kynges maiestie, to be declared and redde by all persones vicars, or curates, euery Sondaye in their churches 1547; the seconde tome of homelyes 1563 (1859)
HONE, WILLIAM Ancient mysteries described 1823
The every-day book 1825–27
The table book of daily recreation and information 1827–28
The year book of daily recreation and information 1832
Honest cavalier, A sober discourse of the; also, a serious epistle to Hodge 1680
HONYMAN, BP. ANDREW A survey of the insolent..libel entituled Napthali (anon.) 1668 (1669)
HOOD, THOMAS Works a 1845 (1869–73)
Poems a 1845 (1875)
Complete poetical works a 1845 (1906)
Tylney hall 1834
Whims and oddities, in prose and verse 1824–27
Whimsicalities 1844
HOOD, THOMAS, Jr. Pen and pencil pictures 1857
HOOK, THEODORE E. Gilbert Gurney 1836
Jack Brag 1837
Love and pride (i.e. The widow and Snowdon) 1833; later edd. (1842–) The widow, and The marquess, or Love and pride
The parson's daughter 1833
Sayings and doings 1824–28
HOOK, WALTER F. A Church dictionary 1842 (1871)
Lives of the Archbishops of Canterbury 1860–76
HOOKE, ROBERT Posthumous works a 1703 (1705)
Micrographia, or some physiological descriptions of minute bodies made by magnifying glasses 1665
See also Philosophical collections
HOOKE, WILLIAM New Englands sence of Old England and Irelands sorrowes 1645
New Englands teares for Old Englands feares 1641
HOOKER, EDWARD 1683: see Pordage, John
HOOKER, FRANCES H. 1873: see Hooker, Sir J. D.
HOOKER, JOHN (J. Vowell) The description of the cittie of Excester ? 1575 (in Holinshed, Chron. 1587, III. p. 1007)
The Irish historie composed by Giraldus Cambrensis tr. 1586 (in Holinshed, Chron.) See also Holinshed, R.
The lyffe of Sir Peter Carew c 1575 (in Archaeologia XXVIII)
HOOKER, SIR JOSEPH D. Botany 1876
The botany of the Antarctic voyage of the Erebus and Terror in 1839–43 1844–60
A general system of botany by E. Le Maout and J. Decaisne, tr. by Frances H. Hooker and ed. by J. D. Hooker 1873
Himalayan journals 1854
The student's flora of the British Islands 1870
—— and BALL, JOHN Journal of a tour in Marocco and the Great Atlas 1878
HOOKER, RICHARD Works a 1600 (1888)
A learned discourse of justification 1586 (1612)
Of the lawes of ecclesiasticall politie Bks. I–IV 1594; Bk. V 1597 (1617); Bks. VI–VIII a 1600 (1648)
HOOKER, SIR WILLIAM J. Botany 1849 (in Manual of scientific enquiry 1859)
The British flora 1830–33
Journal of a tour in Iceland in 1809 1811 (1813)
See also Smith, Sir James E.
HOOLE, CHARLES M. Corderius's School-colloquies, English and Latine 1657 (1688)
See also Comenius
HOOLE, JOHN Ariosto's (L.) Orlando furioso tr. 1783
Tasso's (T.) Jerusalem delivered 1763
HOOLE, SAMUEL Discourses delivered in the parish church of All Saints, Poplar 1833
HOOPER, BP. GEORGE A discourse concerning Lent 1696
An inquiry into the state of the ancient measures (anon.) 1721
HOOPER, BP. JOHN Writings a 1555 (Parker Soc. 1843–52)
An answer unto my lord of wynchesters booke 1547
A declaracion of Christe and of his offyce 1547
A declaration of the ten holy commaundementes 1548
A godly confession and protestacion of the christian fayth ? 1551
An oversight and deliberacion upon the prophete Jonas 1550
HOOPER, ROBERT A compendious medical dictionary 1798
HOOPER, W. Sketches from academic life 1886
HOOSON, WILLIAM The miner's dictionary 1747
HOPE, ALEXANDER J. BERESFORD The Brandreths. A novel 1882
The English cathedral of the nineteenth century 1861
Essays 1844
'HOPE, ASCOTT R.' (A. R. H. Moncrieff) My schoolboy friends 1870
HOPE, FREDERICK W. The coleopterist's manual 1837–40
HOPE, SIR THOMAS Minor practicks; or, a treatise of the Scottish law a 1646 (1726)
HOPE, THOMAS Anastasius: or the memoirs of a Greek 1819
An essay on the origin and prospects of man 1831

HOPE, SIR WILLIAM The compleat fencing-master 1692 (ed. 2)
A new, short, and easy method of fencing 1707
See also Solleysel, J. de
HOPE, WILLIAM H. ST. JOHN Inventories of Christ Church, Canterbury. Ed. by J. Wickham Legg and W. H. St. John Hope 1902
Windsor Castle. An architectural history 1913
HOPKINS, CHARLES White-hall; or, the Court of England: a poem 1698
—— another ed., The court-prospect, a poem 1699
HOPKINS, EDWARD J. and RIMBAULT, EDWARD F. The organ; its history and construction 1855 (1877)
HOPKINS, ELLICE Rose Turquand 1876 (1880)
HOPKINS, BP. EZEKIEL Works a 1690 (1710, 1809)
Discourses or sermons on several scriptures a 1690 (1691–96)
An exposition of the Lord's Prayer 1692
A sermon preached at the funeralls of the Honourable A. Grevil 1663
The vanity of the world 1668
HOPKINS, JOHN: see Sternhold, T.
HOPKINS, MANLEY A handbook of average 1857
Hawaii; the past, present, and future of its island kingdom 1862
HOPKINS, MATTHEW The discovery of witches 1647
HOPKINS, WILLIAM The Book of Bertram, or Ratramnus, concerning the body and blood of the Lord tr. 1686
Seventeen sermons a 1700 (1708)
HOPLEY, CATHERINE C. Life in the South 1863
HOPPE, A. Englisch-Deutsches Supplement-Lexicon 1871
HOPPS, JOHN PAGE First principles of religion and morality 1875
The life of Jesus 1869
HOPTON, ARTHUR A concordancy of yeares 1612
Speculum topographicum; or the topographicall glasse 1611
Horæ subsecivæ 1777 (MS. Devonshire glossary)
HORBERY, MATTHEW Works a 1773 (1828)
HORE, J. P. The history of Newmarket, and the annals of the turf 1885–86
Hore beate marie virginis 1510 (1531)
HORLOCK, KNIGHTLEY W. ('Scrutator') The country gentleman 1862
HORMAN, WILLIAM Vulgaria 1519
HORN, THOMAS and ROBOTHAM, JOHN: see Comenius, J. A.
Horn, King a 1300, 13.. (in Ritson, Metrical Romances II. 1802; Horn et Rimenhild, Bannatyne Cl. 1845; E.E.T.S. 1866 (1901); ed. Jos. Hall 1901)
Horn childe and maiden Rimnild 1320–30 (in Ritson, Metrical Romances III. 1802; ed. Jos. Hall 1901)
HORNADAY, WILLIAM T. Two years in the jungle 1885
HORNBY, LADY EMELIA B. In and around Stamboul 1858
—— another ed., entitled Constantinople during the Crimean War 1863
HORNBY, WILLIAM The scourge of drunkennes 1618 (Halliwell 1859)
HORNE, BP. GEORGE Works a 1792 (1809, 1818)
A commentary on the Book of Psalms 1776
Discourses on several subjects and occasions a 1792 (1827)
Letters on infidelity 1784
HORNE, JOHN A year in Fiji 1881
HORNE, RICHARD H. Gregory VII; a tragedy 1840
HORNE, THOMAS H. An introduction to the critical study and knowledge of the Holy Scriptures 1818–21
HORNECK, ANTHONY The crucified Jesus 1686
The great law of consideration 1677 (1704)
The happy ascetick 1681
HORNER, SUSAN and JOANNA Walks in Florence 1873 (1884)
HORNUNG, ERNEST W. Mr. Justice Raffles 1909
Under two skies 1892
Hors, shepe, and ghoos c 1470 (Caxton 1479; Roxb. Cl. 1822)
See also Lydgate, J.
HORSEY, SIR JEROME Travels in Russia a 1627 (Hakluyt Soc. 1856)
HORSFIELD, THOMAS Zoological researches in Java, and the neighbouring islands 1824
HORSLEY, JOHN W. Jottings from jail 1887
HORSLEY, BP. SAMUEL Charges 1790–1806 (1813)
A sermon preached before the Lords, Jan. 30 1793
Sermons a 1806 (1816)
Speeches in parliament a 1806 (1813)
HORSLEY, WILLIAM The fool 1746–47 (1748)
HORSTMANN, CARL Ed. Altenglische Legenden (Childhood of Jesus; Birth of Jesus; Baarlaam and Josaphat; St. Patrick's purgatory) (1875)
—— 2nd series (1881)
Sammlung Altenglischer Legenden (1878)
HORT, FENTON J. A. Village sermons a 1892 (1897)
HORT, ABP. JOSIAH Instructions to the clergy of the diocese of Tuam, July 8 1742
Sermons on practical subjects a 1751 (1757)
HORTON, ROBERT F. The teaching of Jesus 1895
HORTON, THOMAS Wisdomes judgment of folly 1653
HORTOP, JOB The trauailes of an Englishman 1591 (in Hakluyt, Voy. III. 1600)
Hortus Anglicus 1822: see Clarke, Stephen
HOSIE, ALEXANDER Three years in Western China 1890
HOSKYNS, CHANDOS W. Talpa; or, the chronicles of a clay farm 1852 (1854)
HOSMER, JAMES K. A short history of Anglo-Saxon freedom 1890
Hospitalier's (E.) Modern applications of electricity tr. by J. Maier 1882
Hospitall of incurable fooles 1600: see Blount, E.
HOTTEN, JOHN C. A dictionary of modern slang, cant, and vulgar words 1859 (1860, 1864, 1874)
Houdin (R.) tr.: see Wraxall, Sir F. C. L.
HOUGHTON, R. M. MILNES, 1ST BARON A selection from his works 1867
Life, letters, and friendships, by T. W. Reid (1890)
Palm leaves; poems 1844
HOUGHTON, JOHN Ed. A collection of letters for the improvement of husbandry and trade 1681–83
A collection for improvement of husbandry and trade 1692–1703
HOUGHTON, THOMAS The laws of the miners in the Forrest of Dean 1687
The ancient laws of the miners in the King's Forrest of Mendipp 1687
Rara avis in terris; or the compleat miner; containing the liberties, laws and customs of the lead-mines in Derbyshire, the art of dialling and levelling grooves. With an explanation of the miners terms of art 1681 (E.D.S. 1874)

I

J

K

Supplement, p. 3873; Corrigenda, p. 4092; Spurious words, p. 4093; Books quoted, p. 4094

L

N

O

P

Q

R

Supplement, p. 3873; Corrigenda, p. 4092; Spurious words, p. 4093; Books quoted, p. 4094

Roberts, Orlando W. Narrative of voyages and excursions on the east coast and in the interiors of Central America 1827
Roberts, Peter The Cambrian popular antiquities 1815
Roberts, Sir Randal H. In the shires; a sporting novel 1887
Roberts, Thomas The English bowman, or tracts on archery 1801
Roberts, William An account of the first discovery and natural history of Florida 1763
Roberts, William The looker-on; a periodical publication by the rev. Simon Olive-Branch 1792–94
Roberts, William Memoirs of the life and correspondence of Mrs. Hannah More 1834 (1835)
Roberts, Sir William A practical treatise on urinary and renal diseases 1865 (1885)
Roberts, William H. Poems 1774
Roberts, William W. The pontifical decrees against the doctrine of the earth's movement, and the Ultramontane defence of them 1885
Roberts-Austen, Sir William C. Introductory lecture to the course of metallurgy at the Royal school of mines 1880
Robertson, Alexander Fra Paolo Sarpi 1893 (1894)
The Roman catholic church in Italy 1903
Robertson, Andrew Nuggets in the Devil's punch bowl and other Australian tales 1894
Robertson, E. William Historical essays in connexion with the land, the church etc. 1872
Robertson, Frederick W. Expository lectures on St. Paul's epistles to the Corinthians a 1853 (1859)
Lectures and addresses on literary and social topics a 1853 (1858)
Sermons 1848–53 (1855–63)
Robertson, George General view of the agriculture of Kincardineshire 1813
—— of Midlothian 1793
Robertson, Sir George S. Chitrál: the story of a minor siege 1898
Robertson, J. Drummond A glossary of dialect and archaic words used in the county of Gloucester 1889 (E.D.S. 1890)
Robertson, James General view of the agriculture in the county of Perth 1799
Robertson, James Old truths and modern speculations 1859 (1860)
Robertson, Joseph Lives of Scottish poets (anon.) 1821–22
Robertson, Muirhead A Lombard Street mystery 1888
Robertson, William Phraseologia generalis; a full large and general phrase book 1681 (1693)
Robertson, William Works a 1793 (1813, 1825, 1851)
An historical disquisition concerning the knowledge which the ancients had of India 1791
The history of America 1777 (1778)
The history of the reign of the emperor Charles V 1769 (1813)
The history of Scotland during the reigns of queen Mary and of king James VI etc. 1759 (1813)
Robin Goodfellow, The mad pranks and merry jests of 1628 (Percy Soc. 1841)
Robin Hood: see Ritson, J.
Robinson, C. Clough The dialect of Leeds and its neighbourhood (anon.) 1862
A glossary of words pertaining to the dialect of Mid-Yorkshire 1876 (E.D.S.)
Robinson, Charles New South Wales, the oldest and richest of Australian colonies 1873
Robinson, Charles Napier The British fleet 1894
Robinson, Clement, and others A handefull of pleasant delites 1584 (Heliconia II, 1815; Arber)
Robinson, Francis K. A glossary of Yorkshire words and phrases .. collected in Whitby and the neighbourhood (anon.) 1855
A glossary of words used in the neighbourhood of Whitby 1876 (E.D.S.)
Robinson, Frederick W. Coward conscience 1879
Female life in prison, by a prison matron (anon.) 1862
Grandmother's money (anon.) 1860
High church (anon.) 1860
Mattie:—a stray (anon.) 1864
No church (anon.) 1861
Owen:—a waif (anon.) 1862
Robinson, Harry P. Men born equal, a novel 1895
Robinson, Henry Crabb Diary, reminiscences and correspondence a 1867 (1869)
Robinson, Jane Whitefriars; or the days of Charles II (anon.) 1844
Whitehall; or the days of Charles I (anon.) 1845
Robinson, John Eudoxa or some probable inquiries into truth, .. together with A stone to the altar .. as also A calm ventilation of Pseudo-doxia epidemica 1658
Robinson, John Archæologia græca, or the antiquities of Greece 1807 (1827)
Robinson, Mrs. Mary Angelina; a novel 1796
Walsingham; or the pupil of nature 1797
Robinson, Matthew Autobiography a 1694 (1856)
Robinson, Nicholas A new theory of physick and diseases founded on the principles of the Newtonian philosophy 1725
Robinson, Philip Stewart ('Phil Robinson') In my Indian garden 1878
Under the punkah 1881
The valley of tee-totum trees: tales and sketches 1886
Robinson, Ralph A fruteful and pleasaunt worke of the beste state of a publyque weale, and of the newe yle called Utopia: written in Latine by Syr Thomas More knyght tr. 1551, 1556 (Arber; Lupton 1895)
Robinson, Ralph Christ all in all a 1655 (1656)
Robinson, Richard A golden mirrour, containing .. visions prognosticating good fortune to England 1589 (Chetham Soc. 1851)
Robinson, Sir Robert S. The nautical steam engine explained 1839
Robinson, Mrs. Sara T. L. Kansas; its interior and exterior life 1856 (ed. 2)
Robinson, Thomas The life and death of Mary Magdalene c 1620 (E.E.T.S. 1899)
Robinson, Thomas The anatomy of the English nunnery at Lisbon 1622
Robinson, Thomas An essay towards a natural history of Westmoreland and Cumberland .. To which is annexed A vindication of the philosophical and theological paraphrase of the Mosaick system of the creation 1709
Robinson, Thomas The common law of Kent; or the customs of gavelkind 1741
Robson, John Ed. Three early English metrical romances 1842 (Camden Soc.)
Robson, Joseph Philip Ed. Songs of the bards of the Tyne; or a choice collection of original songs, chiefly in the Newcastle dialect 1849 (1863)
Robson, Simon The choise of change, newly set foorth by S. R. 1585
A new yeares gift, The court of civill courtesie, out of Italian by S. R. 1582 (1591)
Robson, Stephen The British flora 1777
Robson, Thomas The British herald 1830
Roby, Henry J. A Latin grammar 1879 (1880)
Roby, John Traditions of Lancashire 1829–31 (1879)
Rochdale glossary 1886: see Cunliffe, H.
Rochester. The history and antiquities of Rochester and its environs (by W. Shrubsole and S. Denne) 1772
Rochester, Bishop of 1695: see Sprat, T.
Rochester, John Wilmot, 2nd Earl of Works a 1680 (1721, 1731)
Poems on several occasions (1701)
Valentinian, a tragedy as 'tis altered (from Fletcher) a 1680 (1685)
Rock, Daniel The church of our fathers 1849–53
Hierurgia; or the holy sacrifice of the mass 1833
Textile fabrics 1870
—— (South Kensington art handbook) 1876
Rock, William F. Jim an' Nell: a dramatic poem in the dialect of North Devon (anon.) 1867 (Nine specimens, E.D.S. 1896)
Rockhill, William W. The land of the lamas 1891
Rodger, Alexander Poems and songs 1838 (1897)
Rodriquez' (A.) Practice of christian perfection tr. 1697–99
Rodway, James In the Guiana forest 1894 (1897)
In Guiana wilds 1899
Rodwell, John M. The prophecies of Isaiah tr. 1881
Roe, Edward P. Nature's serial story 1884 (1885)
Roest, Theodore Noot's (Jan van der) Theatre, wherein be represented the miseries that follow the voluptuous worldlings tr. 1569
Rogers, Charles The modern Scottish minstrel 1855–57
Social life in Scotland 1884–86
Rogers, Daniel Naaman the Syrian, his disease and cure 1642
A treatise of the two sacraments of the gospell, baptisme and the supper of the Lord, by D. R. 1633
Rogers, Fairman A manual of coaching 1900
Rogers, Henry The eclipse of faith; or a visit to a religious sceptic 1852 (1863)
Essays selected from contributions to the Edinburgh review v.d. (1850–55)
The life and character of John Howe 1836 (1863)
The superhuman origin of the Bible inferred from itself 1873 (1874, 1893)
Rogers, Henry Darwin The geology of Pennsylvania 1858
Rogers, J. The new rush, and other poems and songs 1864
Rogers, James E. Thorold Ed. A complete collection of the protests of the Lords 1875
Historical gleanings: a series of sketches 1869–70
A history of agriculture and prices in England from 1259 to 1793 1866–87
A manual of political economy 1868
Six centuries of work and wages 1884
Rogers, John The glasse of godly love (anon.) 1569 (New Shaks. Soc. 1876)
Rogers, John A discourse of the visible and invisible church of Christ 1719 (1729)
The necessity of divine revelation 1727
A vindication of the civil establishment of religion 1728
Rogers, John Antipopopriestian; or an attempt to liberate and purify christianity from popery, etc. 1839
Rogers, Nehemiah A strange vineyard in Palæstina 1623
Rogers, Robert A concise account of North America 1765
Journals of major R. Rogers containing an account of the several excursions he made .. upon the continent of North America during the late war 1765 (1883)
Rogers, Samuel Poetical works a 1855
Human life, a poem 1819
Italy, a poem c 1820 (1822–28)
The pleasures of memory, a poem 1792
Recollections of the table talk of S. Rogers a 1855 (1856)
Rogers, Thomas Cæsar's (P.) General discourse against the damnable sect of usurers tr. 1578
The English creede consenting with the true auncient catholique and apostolique church in al the points and articles of religion 1585, 1587
The faith, doctrine and religion .. professed .. in .. England expressed in thirty-nine articles 1607 (1633; Parker Soc. 1854)
Geveren's (S. A.) Of the ende of this world and seconde comyng of Christ tr. 1575 (1578)
Of the imitation of Christ tr. 1580 (1629)
A right christian treatise entituled S. Augustines praiers tr. 1581 (1597)
Two dialogues .. concerning kneeling in the very act of receiving the sacramental bread and wine 1608
Rogers, Woodes A cruising voyage round the world 1712 (1718)
Roget, F. F. An introduction to Old French 1887
Roget, Peter Mark Animal and vegetable physiology considered with reference to natural theology (Bridgewater treatise) 1834 (1840)
Thesaurus of English words and phrases 1852 (1879)
Rokeby, Sir Thomas A brief memoir of Mr. Justice Rokeby (by J. Raine) comprising his religious journal (= Diary) 1688–99 and correspondence v.d. (Surtees Soc. 1861)
Roland. The romance of duke Rouland and Sir Otuell of Spayne, together with a fragment of The song of Roland c 1400 (Sege off Melayne, etc., E.E.T.S. 1880)
The romances of Rouland and Vernagu, and Otuel, from the Auchinleck manuscript a 1330 (Abbotsford Club 1836; with Rauf Coilȝear, E.E.T.S. 1882)
Roland, George An introductory course of modern gymnastic exercises 1854
A treatise on .. the art of fencing 1823
Roland, James The amateur of fencing; or, a treatise on the art of sword-defence 1809
Rolland, John The seuin seages tr. .. in Scottis meter 1560 (1578: Bannatyne Club 1837)
Ane treatise callit the court of Venus c 1550 (1575; S.T.S. 1884)
Rolle, Sir Henry Un abridgment des plusieurs cases et resolutions del common ley a 1656 (1668)
Rolle, Richard, of Hampole: see Hampole
Rolleston, George Forms of animal life 1870
—— (ed. 2) Revised and enlarged by W. H. Jackson 1888
Rolleston, Humphrey D. Diseases of the liver, gall-bladder and bile-ducts 1905
Rolliad. Criticisms on the Rolliad, a poem (by Joseph Richardson, R. Tickell, and others), being a more faithful portraiture of the present immaculate young minister (W. Pitt) and his friends than any extant 1784 (1785)
—— The Rolliad, in two parts; probationary odes for the laureatship; and political miscellanies (1795)
—— Probationary odes for the laureatship (pretended to be) by Sir John Hawkins (part of the Rolliad) 1785
Rollin's (C.) Ancient history of the Egyptians .. and Greeks tr. 1734–37 (1827, 1840–41)
—— Roman history tr. 1739 (1768)
Rollins, Mrs. Ellen C. New England bygones 1880
Rollock, Robert Select works a 1599 (Wodrow Soc. 1844–49)
Lectures upon the epistle .. to the Colossians a 1599 (1603)
Lectures upon the epistles .. to the Thessalonians a 1599 (1606)
Lectures upon the history of the passion, resurrection and ascension of our Lord Jesus Christ a 1599 (1616)
Rolls of parliament (Rotuli parliamentorum) 1278–1503 (1767–77)
Rolls series, The (The chronicles and memorials of Great Britain and Ireland during the Middle ages, published .. under the direction of the Master of the Rolls) 1858–96
Rollwyn, J. A. S. Astronomy simplified for general reading 1871
Rolt, Richard A new dictionary of trade and commerce 1756
Romance of a dull life, The (by Mrs. A. J. Penny) 1861
Romanes, George J. Animal intelligence 1882
Jelly-fish, star-fish and sea-urchins 1885
Thoughts on religion a 1894 (ed. C. Gore 1895)
Romans, Bernard A concise natural history of East and West Florida 1775
Romaunt of the rose, The lines 1–1705 (Chaucer) a 1366
—— lines 1706–end (anon.) c 1400 (Skeat, Chaucer I 1894; Kaluza 1891)
Romer, Mrs. Isabella F. The Rhone, the Darro, and the Guadalquivir 1843
Ronalds, Alfred The fly-fisher's entomology 1836
Ronalds, Edmund and Richardson T. Ed. Knapp's (Fr. C.) Chemical technology 1848–51 (1854)
Rood, The dream of the a 1000 (Grein 1888)
Rood, Ogden N. Modern chromatics, with applications to art and industry 1879
Roosa, Daniel B. St. J. A practical treatise on the diseases of the ear 1873
Roosevelt, Theodore Hunting trips of a ranchman 1885
—— and Grinnell, G. B. Ed. Hunting in many lands 1895
Root, Jesse Reports of cases adjudged in the Superior court and Supreme court of errors (of the state of Connecticut) 1789–93 1798
Roper, William The life and death of Sir T. More a 1578 (1729)
Ros, Sir Richard La belle dame sans merci tr. c 1460 (Political, religious and love poems, E.E.T.S. 1866, 1903; Skeat, Chaucerian pieces 1897)
Rosarian, The; a monthly organ of the Holy rosary fraternity 1871
Roscoe, Sir Henry E. Lessons in elementary chemistry 1866 (1871, 1874)
—— and Schorlemmer, C. A treatise on chemistry 1877–88
Roscoe, Thomas Cellini's (B.) Memoirs tr. 1822
Sismondi's (J. C. L. de) Historical view of the literature of the south of Europe tr. 1823 (1846)
Roscoe, William The life of Lorenzo de Medici 1795 (1806)
Roscommon, Wentworth Dillon, 4th Earl of Works a 1685 (1709, 1750)
An essay on translated verse 1684 (1709)
Horace's Art of poetry tr. 1680
Rose, Cooper Four years in southern Africa 1829
Rose, George The diaries and correspondence a 1818 (1860)
Rose, Hew A genealogical deduction of the family of Rose of Kilravock, with illustrative documents 1683–84 (Spalding Club 1848)
Rose, John The English vineyard vindicated ed. J. Evelyn 1666 (1675)
Rose, John B. The Æneis of Virgil tr. 1867
The Eclogues and Georgics of Virgil tr. 1866
The Fasti of Ovid tr. 1866
The Metamorphoses of Ovid tr. 1866
Rose, Joshua The complete practical machinist 1876
Rose, William S. Amadis de Gaule tr. 1803
Rosebery, Archibald P. Primrose, 5th Earl of Pitt 1891
'Rosemary' Under the Chilterns: a story of English village life 1895
Rosemary and Bayes: or animadversions upon .. The rehearsall trans-prosed (by H. Stubbe) 1672
Rosenberg, Justine, Countess Orsini Moral and sentimental essays by J. W., C-t-ss of R-s-g 1785
Rosenthal, Isidore General physiology of muscles and nerves 1881
Ross, family. Ane breve cronicle of the earlis of Ross, including notices of the abbots of Fearn, and of the family of Ross of Balnagown a 1615 (1850)
Ross, Alexander The Alcoran, translated from the French of the sieur du Ryer, with the life of Mahomet 1649
Arcana microcosmi: or the hid secrets of man's body discloſed 1651
The history of the world .. being a continuation of the famous history of Sir W. Raleigh 1652
Mel Heliconium, or poeticall honey gathered out of the weeds of Parnassus 1642 (1643)
Mystagogus poeticus, or the muses interpreter 1647 (1675)
Ross, Alexander The fortunate shepherdess, a pastoral tale .. in the Scotish dialect 1768
—— Third ed. corrected. Helenore, or the fortunate shepherdess (1789)
Ross, Frederick, and others A glossary of words used in Holderness in the East-riding of Yorkshire 1877 (E.D.S.)
Ross, James The fratricide (MS.) 1773

Ross, James Hobart Town almanack 1829–36
Ross, James A treatise on the diseases of the nervous system 1881
Ross, Sir James Clark A voyage of discovery and research in the southern and antarctic regions during 1839–43 1847
Ross, Janet Ann Three generations of Englishwomen 1888
Ross, Sir John Narrative of a second voyage in search of a north-west passage and of a residence in the arctic regions during the years 1829–33 1835
Ross, Thomas Silius Italicus' (C.) Second Punick war between Hannibal and the Romanes tr. 1661
Ross, Thomasina Humboldt's (Baron F. H. A. von) Personal narrative of travels to the equinoctial regions of America tr. 1852
Ross, William Aberdour and Inchcolme: being historical notices of the parish and monastery 1885
Busby and its neighbourhood 1883
Rosse, Irving C. Cruise of the revenue-steamer Corwin in Alaska and the N.W. Arctic ocean 1883
Rossetti, Christina G. Poems 1891 (Poetical works 1904)
Seek and find, a double series of short studies of the Benedicite 1879
Speaking likenesses 1874
Rossetti, Dante Gabriel Collected works a 1882 (1886)
Dante and his circle, .. a collection of lyrics, ed. and tr. a 1850 (1874)
Poems v.d. (1870)
Rossiter, William An elementary handbook of physics 1871
An illustrated dictionary of scientific terms 1878
Roth, Mathias Hand-book of the movement cure 1856
Rouen, Siege of: see Page, J.
Roughley, Thomas The Jamaica planter's guide 1823
Roule or Rowll, Sir John Heir followis the cursing of Sr Johine Rowlis vpoun the steilaris of his foulis 15.. (in Bannatyne MS., Hunterian Club, p. 298; D. Laing, Select remains of popular poetry of Scotland 1822; Maitland folio MS., S.T.S. 1919)
Rous or Rouse, Francis The balme of love, to heale divisions and the wounds made by them 1648
The bounds and bonds of publique obedience (anon.) 1649
The heavenly academie 1638
—— Academia cœlestis: the heavenly university (1702)
The mysticall marriage, or experimentall discoveries of the heavenly mariage betweene a soule and her saviour 1635 (1653)
The psalmes of David in English meeter 1643 (1646)
Thule, or vertues historie 1598
Rous, John Diary 1625–42 (Camden Soc. 1856)
Rousseau's (J. J.) Emilius; or a treatise of education tr. 1763
Routledge, Robert Discoveries and inventions of the nineteenth century 1876
A popular history of science 1881
Routledge's Every boy's annual 1866–89
Routledge's Young gentleman's magazine 1869–74
Rovinson or Rovenzon, John A treatise of metallica 1613 (1854)
Row, John The historie of the kirk of Scotland 1558–1637 a 1646; with a continuation to 1639 by his son J. Row, 1650 (Wodrow Soc. 1842)
Row, William Supplement to R. Blair's Autobiography 1676 (Wodrow Soc. 1848)
Rowbotham, James The pleasaunt and wittie playe of the cheastes renewed tr. 1562
Rowe, Eleanor Hints on chip-carving 1892 (1895)
Rowe, John Emmanuel, or the love of Christ explicated and applied a 1677 (1680)
Rowe, Nicholas Works a 1718 (1720, 1728)
The ambitious step-mother, a tragedy 1700
The biter, a comedy 1705
The fair penitent, a tragedy 1703
Lucan's Pharsalia tr. 1718
The royal convert, a tragedy 1707 (1708)
Tamerlane, a tragedy 1702
The tragedy of Jane Shore 1714
The tragedy of Lady Jane Gray 1715
Ulysses, a tragedy 1706
Rowe, Samuel A perambulation of the antient and royal forest of Dartmoor 1848 (1856)
Rowland: see Roland
Rowland, David Hurtado de Mendoza's (D.) Pleasaunt historie of Lazarillo de Tormes tr. 1586 (1672–77)
Rowland, John Topsell's (E.) History of four-footed beasts and serpents .. whereunto is now added, The theater of insects .. by T. Muffet, .. the whole revised .. and inlarged by J. R(owland) 1658
Rowlands, Henry Mona antiqua restaurata; an archæological discourse on the antiquities .. of the isle of Anglesey 1723
Rowlands, Samuel Works a 1630 (Hunterian Club 1880)
The betraying of Christ etc., by S. R. 1598
Diogines lanthorne (anon.) 1607
Doctor Merrie-man: or nothing but mirth, by S. R. 1609 (1627)
The famous history of Guy earle of Warwicke 1607
Good newes and bad newes, by S. R. 1622
Greenes ghost haunting conie-catchers (by S. R.) 1602 (1860)
Humors looking glasse (anon.) 1608
The knave of clubbes (by S. R.) 1600 (1609)
The knave of harts (anon.) 1612
—— More knaves yet? the knaves of spades and diamonds (by S. R.) 1613
—— The four knaves (Percy Soc. 1843)
The letting of humours blood in the head-vaine (anon.) 1600
Looke to it; for ile stabbe ye, by S. R. 1604
Martin Mark-all, beadle of Bridewell, his defence and answere to the (Dekker's) belman of London by S. R. (also attributed to S. Rid) 1610
The melancholie knight, by S. R. 1615
The night-raven, by S. R. 1620
A paire of spy-knaves? 1620
A sacred memorie of the miracles wrought by .. Jesus Christ 1618
A terrible battell betweene the two consumers of the whole world: time and death? 1606
Tis merrie when gossips meet (anon.) 1602 (1609)
A whole crew of kind gossips all met to be merry 1609
Rowlandson, James Gods blessing in blasting, and his mercy in mildew, two sermons suitable to these times of dearth 1623
Rowley, Samuel The noble souldier, a tragedy by S. R. 1634 (Bullen, Old plays I, 1882)
Rowley, William The birth of Merlin, or the childe hath found his father, by William Shakespear, and W. Rowley 16.. (1662; Shakespeare Apocrypha 1908)
A match at midnight, a comœdie 1633 (Dodsley)
A merrie and pleasant comedy .. called A shoo-maker a gentleman, by W. R. gentleman 1638
A new wonder, a woman never vext; a pleasant conceited comedy 1632 (Dodsley)
A search for money 1609 (Percy Soc. 1840)
See also Fletcher, John; Middleton, T.; Webster, J.
——, Dekker, T. and Ford, J. The witch of Edmonton, a known true story, composed into tragi-comedy by divers well-esteemed poets c 1623 (1658)
Rowll, Sir J.: see Roule
Rows, John Rol (the roll of the Warwick family) c 1485 (1845)
Rowzee, Lodowick The Queenes welles, that is, a treatise of the nature and vertues of Tunbridge water 1632 (Harl. Misc.)
Roxburgh, William Flora Indica or descriptions of Indian plants a 1815 (1820–24)
Hortus Bengalensis, or a catalogue of the plants growing in the .. East India Company's botanic garden at Calcutta 1813–14
Roxburghe ballads, The v.d. (Ballad Soc. 1869–99)
Roxburghe Club, Publications of the (1814–)
Roy, William, and Barlow, J. Rede me and be nott wrothe, For I saye no thinge but trothe (anon.) 1528 (Arber)
Royal Asiatic society, Journal 1834–
—— Transactions 1827–35
Royal Dublin society, Proceedings 1848–
Royal geographical society of London, Journal 1831– (Geographical journal 1893–)
Royal Irish Academy, Proceedings 1836–
—— Transactions 1787–
Royal Society. Philosophical transactions 1665–
—— abridged by J. Lowthorp and others (1716–56)
Proceedings 1830–
Royal society of Edinburgh, Transactions 1788–
Royal trade. Ἰχθυοθηρα, or the royal trade of fishing 1662
Royle, John Forbes The fibrous plants of India 1855
Illustrations of the botany and other branches of the natural history of the Himalayan mountains and of the flora of Cashmere 1839
A manual of materia medica and therapeutics 1847
—— Sixth ed. by J. Harley (1876)
Rudd, Thomas Euclides Elements .. the first IV books tr. 1651
Practical geometry (Arithmetick; Geometricall questions) 1650
Ruddiman, Jacob Tales and sketches 1828
—— Tales of a Scottish parish (1889)
Ruddiman, Thomas Ed. Virgil's Æneis tr. into Scottish verse by Bp. G. Douglas. To which is added a large glossary, explaining the difficult words: which may serve for a dictionary to the Old Scottish language 1710
Rudge, Thomas General view of the agriculture of the county of Gloucester 1807 (1813)
Rudim. navig. 1850: see Greenwood, James
Rudiments of ancient architecture 1794
Ruding, Rogers Annals of the coinage of Britain and its dependencies 1817 (1840)
Rudyerd, Sir Benjamin Speeches in the high court of parliament 1641
Rule of St. Benet, The: see Benedict, St.
Rules (and orders) of the Supreme court 1883 (1887)
Rules of civility, The 1671 (1673, 1703)
Rump: or an exact collection of the choycest poems and songs relating to the late times 1662 (1874)
Rumsey, Walter Organon salutis; an instrument to cleanse the stomach 1657
Runciman, James Skippers and shellbacks 1885
Runes a 1000 (Grein 1883)
Rush, Benjamin Essays, literary, moral and philosophical 1798 (1806)
Rushworth, John Historical collections of private passages of state, weighty matters in law, remarkable proceedings in five parliaments 1659–1701
Rushworth gospels, The c 975 (Skeat 1871–87)
Ruskin, John Arrows of the chace, being a collection of scattered letters 1840–80 (1880)
The Bible of Amiens: see Our fathers, below
The crown of wild olive, three lectures on work, traffic and war 1866 (1873)
Deucalion, collected studies of the lapse of waves and life of stones 1875–83
The eagle's nest 1872 (1887)
The elements of drawing 1857
The elements of perspective 1859
The ethics of the dust 1866
Fors clavigera: letters to the workmen and labourers of Great Britain 1871–84
Frondes agrestes: readings in 'Modern painters' 1875 (1879)
A joy for ever: see Political economy of art, below
Lectures on architecture and painting 1853 (1854)
Lectures on art 1870 (1875)
Love's meinie, lectures on Greek and English birds 1873–81
Modern painters 1843–60
Mornings in Florence 1875–77
Munera pulveris, six essays on the elements of political economy 1872
'Our fathers have told us.' Sketches of the history of christendom. Part I. The Bible of Amiens 1880–85
The political economy of art (later edd. A joy for ever) 1857
Præterita: outlines of scenes and thoughts .. in my past life 1885–89
Pre-Raphaelitism 1851
Proserpina, studies of wayside flowers 1875–86
The queen of the air: being a study of Greek myths of cloud and storm 1869 (1874)
St. Mark's rest: the history of Venice 1877–84
Sesame and lilies, two lectures. I. Of kings' treasuries, II. Of queens' gardens 1864 (1865)
The seven lamps of architecture 1849 (1855)
The stones of Venice 1851–53 (1874)
Time and tide, by Weare and Tyne 1867
The two paths: being lectures on art and its applications to decoration and manufacture 1858–59
'Unto this last', four essays on the first principles of political economy 1860 (1862)
Val d'Arno, ten lectures on .. Tuscan art 1873 (1874)
Russel, Richard The works of Geber (Jabir Ibn-Haiyan) the most famous Arabian prince and philosopher tr. 1678
Russel, William P. Verbotomy, or a classical improved vocabulary 1805
Russell, Alexander The natural history of Aleppo and parts adjacent 1756
—— ed. P. Russell (1794)
Russell, Dora The secret of the river 1891
Russell, E. Maitland of Lethington, the minister of Mary Stuart 1912
Russell, George W. E. Collections and recollections, by one who has kept a diary 1898
Russell, James Reminiscences of Yarrow a 1884 (1886)
Russell, John The boke of nurture, folowyng Englondis gise c 1460 (Babees book, E.E.T.S. 1868)
Russell, John, Earl Russell Ed. Memoirs, journal and correspondence of Thomas Moore 1853–56
Russell, John The Haigs of Bemersyde, a family history 1881
Russell, John Scott The wave of translation in the oceans of water, air and ether 1885
Russell, Rachel, Lady Russell Letters a 1723 (1819)
Russell, William The history of modern Europe (anon.) 1779
Russell, William Orthophony; or the cultivation of the voice, in elocution 1859 (1882)
Russell, William Clark Curatica, or leaves from a curate's note-book, by Sydney Mostyn 1891
The death ship, a strange story 1888
The good ship 'Mohock' 1894
Jack's courtship: a sailor's yarn 1884
John Holdsworth, chief mate 1875
Marooned 1889
A marriage at sea 1891
An ocean free-lance 1881
An ocean tragedy 1890
Sailors' language, a collection of sea-terms and their definitions 1883
A sailor's sweetheart, an account of the wreck of the 'Waldershare' 1880
A sea queen 1883
What cheer! 1896
The wreck of the 'Grosvenor' (anon.) 1877
Russell, Sir William Howard My diary in India in .. 1858–59 1860
My diary North and South 1863–65
The Prince of Wales' tour, a diary in India etc. 1877
The war (in the Crimea) 1855–56
Russia, The present state of, .. being the journal of a foreign minister tr. 1722–23
Rust, Bp. George A discourse of truth a 1670 (1682)
A letter of resolution concerning Origen and the chief of his opinions (anon.) 1661 (Phenix I, 1707, 1721)
Remains a 1670 (1686)
Rustamji Nasarvangi Khore: see Khory
'Rutherford, Mark': see White, William Hale
Rutherford, Samuel Joshua redivivus, or Mr. Rutherfoords letters a 1661 (1664)
—— Letters 1627–61 (1675; 1881; 1891)
The tryal and triumph of faith 1645
Rutland glossary 1891: see Wordsworth, Christopher
Rutland papers, original documents illustrative of the courts and times of Henry VII and Henry VIII (Camden Soc. 1842)
Rutledge (a novel, by Mrs. M. C. Harris) 1866
Rutley, Frank The study of rocks 1879
Rutter, John Delineations of Fonthill and its abbey 1823
Rutty, John An essay towards the natural history of the county of Dublin 1772
A spiritual diary (1753–75) and soliloquies a 1775 (1776, 1796)
Ruxton, George F. Adventures in Mexico and the Rocky mountains 1847
Life in the far west a 1848 (1849)
Rycaut, Sir Paul Continuation of Knolles' (R.) History of the Turks 1687
Gracian's (B.) Critick tr. 1681
The history of the Turkish empire 1679–80
The present state of the Greek and Armenian churches 1679
The present state of the Ottoman empire 1668 (1675)
Rydberg's (A. V.) Magic of the middle ages tr. A. H. Edgren 1879 See also Anderson, R. B.
Rye, Walter A glossary of words used in East Anglia founded on that of Forby 1895
A month on the Norfolk broads 1887
Ryland, Arthur The assay of gold and silver wares 1852
Ryland, Jonathan Edwards Hengstenberg's (C. F.) Dissertations on the genuineness of the Pentateuch tr. 1847
Ed. The life and correspondence of John Foster 1846
Neander's (J. A. W.) History of the planting .. of the christian church by the apostles tr. 1851
Rymer, Thomas Fœdera, conventiones, literæ, et cujuscunque generis acta publica, inter reges Angliæ et alios quosvis imperatores, reges, pontifices, principes, vel communitates .. ab anno 1101 ad nostra usque tempora, habita et tractata (1704–35; 1816–30)
A short view of tragedy 1693
The tragedies of the last age consider'd 1678
Ryves, Sir Thomas The poore vicars plea (for tithes) 1620

S

S., Mr. 1575: see Gammer Gurton
S., C. A briefe resolution of a right religion, touching the controversies that are nowe in England 1590
S., E. The discoverie of the knights of the poste 1597
S., E. Britaines busse: or a computation as well of the charge of a busse or herring-fishing ship as also of the gaine and profit thereby 1615 (Arber, Eng. Garner III)
S—, E—: see Smith, E.
S., F. 1557: see Seager, F.
S., G. Anglorum speculum or the worthies of England in church and state (an abridgement of Fuller's Worthies) 1684

S., J. Certaine worthye manuscript poems .. now first published by J. S. (The stately tragedy of Guistard and Sismond, The northern mothers blessing, The way to thrifte) 1597
S., J. Clidamas, or the Sicilian tale 1639
S., J. Bonarelli della Rovere's (G. U.) Filli di Sciro or Phillis of Scyros tr. 1655
S., J. Andromana, or the merchant's wife, by J. S. (? Shirley) 1660 (Dodsley)
S., J. 1661: see Stephens, John
S., J. 1665, 1700: see Sergeant, J.
S., J. (? John Smith) Horological dialogues .. shewing the nature, use and right managing of clocks and watches 1675
S., J. capt. Military discipline or the art of war? 1685
S., J. (? J. Sergeant) The history of monastical conventions and military institutions 1686
S., J. 1695: see Sage, J.
S., J. 1758: see Sparrow, J.
S., L. Natures dowrie: or, the peoples native liberty asserted 1652
S., N. Simon's (R.) Critical enquiries into the various editions of the Bible tr. 1684
S., R. 1591: see Southwell, R.
S., R. The phœnix nest built vp with the moste rare and refined workes of noblemen 1593 (in T. Park, Heliconia II, 1815)
S., R. 1623: see Speed, R.
S., S. Fortune's tennis-ball: or the .. history of Dorastus and Faunia rendred in .. English verse 1672
S., S. The loyal and impartial satyrist: containing eight miscellany poems (Dedication signed S. S.) 1694
S., T. 1583: see Stocker, T.
S., T. 1624: see Scott, T.
S., T. Arts improvement 1703
S., W. A compendious or briefe examination of certayne ordinary complaints of divers of our countrymen in these our dayes, by W. S. (? W. Stafford) 1581 (New Shaks. Soc. 1876)
— A discourse of the common weal of this realm of England c 1550 (1893)
S., W. The lamentable tragedie of Locrine 1595 (Shakespeare Apocrypha 1908)
S., W. The true chronicle historie of the whole life and death of Thomas Lord Cromwell 1602 (Shakespeare Apocrypha 1908)
S., W. The Puritaine or the widdow of Watling-streete 1607 (Shakespeare Apocrypha 1908)
Sabine, Sir Edward, and others Terrestrial magnetism 1851–59 (Manual of scientific enquiry, 1859)
Sacheverell, Henry The christian triumph, a sermon 1713
Sacheverell (Dr. H.), Tracts relating to the impeachment of 1710
Sackville, Thomas, 1st Earl of Dorset Works a 1608 (1859)
Induction to the Mirror for magistrates 1563 (see Mirror)
See also Norton, T. 1561
Sacrament, The play of the c 1460 (Philol. Soc. 1861; Noncycle mystery plays, E.E.T.S. 1909)
Sacred decretall, A, or hue and cry .. for the apprehension of .. Martin Mar-priest 1645
Sacrilege sacredly handled 1619: see Sempill, Sir J.
Sadler, Anthony The loyall mourner 1660
The subject's joy for the king's restoration 1660
Sadler, John Rights of the kingdom or customs of our ancestours (anon.) 1649 (1682)
Sadler, Sir Ralph State papers and letters a 1587 (1809)
Sage, Bp. John Works a 1711 (Spottiswoode Soc. 1844–46)
The fundamental charter of presbytery (The article) (anon.) 1695 (1697)
The principles of the Cyprianic age, by J. S. 1695
—— A vindication of the principles of the Cyprianic age 1701
St. Andrew. The Anglo-saxon legends of St. Andrew and St. Veronica. Ed. with English transl. by C. W. Goodwin (1851)
St. Barbe, Reginald In modern Spain: some sketches and impressions 1899 (1900)
St. Cuthbert. The life of St. Cuthbert in English verse c 1450 (Surtees Soc. 1891)
St. Foine improved: a discourse shewing the .. benefit which England .. may receive by the grasse called St. Foine .. Written by a person of honour 1671 (1674)
St. George's Hospital reports 1866–
Saint-German, C. tr. 1531: see Dialogue
St. James's gazette, The 1880–1905
St. John, Charles W. G. Short sketches of the wild sports and natural history of the highlands 1846
St. John, Henry a 1751: see Bolingbroke, Viscount
Saint John, Henry C. Notes and sketches from the wild coasts of Nipon 1880
Saint John, James A. History of the four conquests of England 1862
St. John, Percy B. Amy Moss, or the banks of the Ohio 1854 (1860)
The snow ship 1865
St. Johnstoun; or John, earl of Gowrie (by Mrs. Eliza Logan) 1823
St. Kathleen, or the rock of Dunnismoyle (by A. Sutherland) 1820
St. Leonards, Edward B. Sugden, 1st Baron A handy book on property law 1858
St. Nicholas: Scribner's illustrated magazine for girls and boys 1873–
Saint Patrick: a national tale of the 5th century, by an antiquary (Rennie) 1819
Saint Patrick's purgatory: see Patrick
St. Ursula. The lyf of saynt Ursula after the cronycles of englonde c 1480 (Roxb. Club 1818)
'Saint Victor, Helen' The ruins of Rigonda, a romance 1808
Saints' lives c 1290 (Early South-English legendary, E.E.T.S. 1887)
Saints' lives c 1305 (Early English poems, Philol. Soc. 1862)
See also Lives of saints
Saintsbury, George E. B. Dryden (English men of letters) 1881
A history of Elizabethan literature 1887 (1890)
A history of nineteenth century literature 1896
Saker, Austin Narbonus; the laberynth of libertie 1580
Sala, George Augustus Accepted addresses 1862
America revisited 1882
The Baddington peerage 1860
Dutch pictures 1861
Sala, George Augustus (cont.)
Gaslight and daylight 1859
Lady Chesterfield's letters to her daughter 1860
London up to date 1894
My diary in America in the midst of war 1865
Paris herself again 1879
Quite alone 1864
The seven sons of Mammon 1862
The ship chandler and other tales 1862
The strange adventures of Captain Dangerous 1863
A trip to Barbary 1866
Twice round the clock, or the hours of the day and night in London 1859 (1861)
Sale, George The Koran tr. 1734
Salernum: see Harington, Sir J.; Paynell, T. 1528
Salesbury, William A dictionary in Englyshe and Welsh 1547 (1877)
Salisbury, Jesse A glossary of words and phrases used in S.E. Worcestershire 1893 (E.D.S.)
Salkeld, John A treatise of angels 1613
A treatise of paradise 1617
Salkeld, William Reports of cases adjudg'd in the court of King's bench etc. a 1715 (1721–24, 1773)
Sallustius Crispus, Caius, All the works tr. 1687 (1692)
Salmagundi; a miscellaneous combination of original poetry etc. (by G. Huddesford and others) 1791 (1795)
Salmagundi 1807–08: see Irving, W.
Salmon, George The infallibility of the church 1888
Lessons introductory to the modern higher algebra 1859 (1885)
A treatise on the analytic geometry of three dimensions 1862 (1874)
A treatise on conic sections 1849 (1855)
A treatise on the higher plane curves 1852 (1879)
Salmon, Nathaniel A new survey of England 1728–30 (1731)
Salmon, Thomas A new abridgement and critical review of the state trials and impeachments for high treason 1737 (1738)
The universal traveller: or, a compleat description of the several nations of the world 1752–53
Salmon, William Diemerbroeck's (I. de) Anatomy of human bodies tr. 1689 (1694)
Doron medicum; or a supplement to the new London dispensatory 1683
The family dictionary or household companion 1696
Pharmacopœia Bateana, or Bate's (G.) Dispensatory tr. 1694 (1713)
Pharmacopœia Londinensis or the new London dispensatory tr. 1678
Polygraphice; or the art of drawing etc. 1672 (1675, 1701)
Seplasium .. The compleat English physician 1693
Synopsis medicinæ, or a compendium of .. physick 1671
Salmond, Stewart D. F. The christian doctrine of immortality 1895
Salomon and Saturnus, The dialogue of a 1000 (Ælfric Soc. 1848; Grein 1898)
—— (a later version) ? a 1300 (Ælfric Soc. 1848)
Salt, Henry S. The life of H. D. Thoreau 1890
Salter, James The triumphs of the holy Jesus, a divine poem 1692
Salter, Thomas F. The angler's guide 1815
Saltern, George Of the ancient lawes of Great Britaine 1605
Saltmarsh, John The practice of policie in a christian life 1639
Some drops of the viall powred out in a season when it is neither night nor day 1645–46
Sparkles of glory, or some beams of the morning-star 1647 (1847)
Saltonstall, Wye Eusebius (Pamphili) his life of Constantine tr. 1637
Picturæ loquentes, or pictures drawne forth in characters 1631
Saltus, Edgar E. Madame Sapphira: a Fifth Avenue story 1893
Salusbury, Sir John Poems a 1612 (E.E.T.S. 1914)
Samouelle, George The entomologist's useful compendium 1819
Sampson, George V. Statistical survey of the county of Londonderry 1802
Sanborn, Kate A truthful woman in southern California 1893
Sancroft, Abp. William Lex ignea: or the school of righteousness, a sermon 1666
Modern policies, taken from Macchiavel, Borgia, and other choise authors 1652 (1653)
Occasional sermons a 1693 (1694)
Sandars, Thomas C. Justinian's Institutes tr. 1859 (1874)
Sanday, William The criticism of the fourth gospel 1905
Inspiration (Bampton lectures) 1893
Sanders, Richard Physiognomie and chiromancie, metoposcopie, the symmetrical proportions and signal moles of the body, fully and accurately handled 1653
Sanderson, Bp. Robert Works a 1663 (1854)
De juramento, seven lectures concerning the obligation of promissory oathes tr. 1655
Episcopacy as established by law in England not prejudicial to royal power 1673
Five cases of conscience occasionally determined a 1663 (1666)
—— Two cases (1668); Eight (1674); Nine (1678)
A sermon 1648 (1653)
XII sermons 1632 (1635)
XXXIV sermons a 1663 (1674)
XXXV sermons (1681)
XXXVI sermons (1689)
Sanderson, Thomas Original poems 1800
Sanderson, Sir William A compleat history of the life and raigne of King Charles 1658
Graphice; or the use of pen and pensill, in designing, drawing and painting 1658
Sandford, Sir Daniel On the rise and progress of literature 1847
Sandford, Ernest G. Ed. Memoirs of Archbishop Temple 1906
Sandford, Mrs. Henry Thomas Poole and his friends 1888
Sandford, James: see Sanford
Sandivogius, M.: see French, J.
Sands, J. Sketches of Tranent in the olden time 1881
Sands, Robert C. Writings in prose and verse a 1832 (1834)
Sandys, Abp. Edwin Sermons 1575–85 (1585; Parker Soc. 1841)
Sandys, Sir Edwin Europæ speculum, or, a view or survey of the state of religion in the westerne parts of the world 1599 (1629, 1638)
—— A relation of the state of religion (1605)
Sandys, George Groot's (H. de) Christ's passion, a tragedy tr. 1640
Ovid's Metamorphosis tr. 1621–26 (1632)
A paraphrase upon the divine poems (Job, Psalms, Ecclesiastes, Lamentations etc.) 1638
A paraphrase upon the Psalmes of David 1636
A paraphrase upon the Song of Solomon 1641
A relation of a journey begun 1610 (Travels) 1615
Sandys, Sir Miles Prudence the first of the foure cardinall virtues (Essays) 1634
Sandys, William Ed. Christmas carols, ancient and modern 1833
Sanford, James Agrippa's (H. C.) Of the vanitie and uncertaintie of artes and sciences tr. 1569
Guicciardini's (L.) Houres of recreation tr. 1573 (1576)
The manuell of Epictetus tr. 1567
Sangster, Charles Hesperus and other poems 1860
Sanitary engineer, The; a monthly record of sanitary news 1880–
Sankey, William H. O. Lectures on mental diseases 1866
Sansone, Antonio Dyeing 1888
Sapskull, Sir Bartholomew: see Donaldson, W.
Sargent, Epes Peculiar, a tale of the great transition 1864
Sarpi, Pietro (Paolo Servita). The life of Father Paul (Sarpi) tr. by a person of quality 1651
—— with Sir N. Brent's History of the council of Trent (1676)
See also B., W.; Brent, Sir N.; Gentilis, R.; Potter, C.
Sarum primer (1557): see Primer
Satchell, Thomas Provisional index to a glossary of fish names 1879 (E.D.S.)
Satirical poems of the time of the Reformation 1565–84 (S.T.S. 1891–93)
Satirical songs and poems on costume, from the 13th to the 19th century (Percy Soc. 1849)
Saturday review of politics, literature, science and art, The 1855–
Satyr against the French, A 1691
Saul, Arthur The famous game of chesse-play truely discovered 1614 (1672)
Saunders, Howard An illustrated manual of British birds 1888
Saunders, John Abel Drake's wife 1862
The lion in the path, an historical romance 1875 (1876)
Saunders, Richard Plenary possession makes a lawfull power, a sermon 1651
Saunders, William Observations on the superior efficacy of the red Peruvian bark in the cure of agues 1782
A treatise on the chemical history of some of the most celebrated mineral waters 1805
Saunderson, R.: see Sanderson
Savage, James History of the hundred of Carhampton, in the county of Somerset 1830
Savage, John A compleat history of Germany 1702
A select collection of letters of the antients 1703
Savage, Marmion W. The bachelor of the Albany 1847 (1854)
The Falcon family, or young Ireland 1845 (1854)
Reuben Medlicott, or the coming man 1852 (1864)
Savage, Richard Works a 1743 (1775, 1777)
—— Poetical works (1807)
The bastard, a poem 1728
A collection of pieces in verse and prose 1732
The convocation: or a battle of pamphlets, a poem 1717
Love in a veil, a comedy 1718 (1719)
Miscellaneous poems and translations, by several hands. Publ. 1726
Of public spirit in regard to public works, an epistle 1737
The tragedy of Sir T. Overbury 1724
The wanderer, a poem 1729
Savage, Richard H. Brought to bay 1900
Savage, William A dictionary of the art of printing 1841
Savery, Thomas The miner's friend, or an engine to raise water by fire described etc. 1702
Savile, George: see Halifax, Marquis of
Savile, Sir Henry The ende of Nero and beginning of Galba, fower bookes of the histories of Tacitus. The life of Agricola tr. 1591 (1622)
Saville-Kent, William A manual of the infusoria 1880–82
Saviolo, Vincentio His practice, in two bookes, the first intreating of the use of the rapier and dagger, the second of honor and honorable quarrels 1594–95
Sawles warde a 1240 (Old English homilies I, E.E.T.S. 1868)
Saxe, John Godfrey Poems v.d. (1850, 1877)
'Saxon' (Mrs. M. Trotter) Galloway gossip sixty years ago 1877
Saxon and the Gael, The; or the northern metropolis (by Mrs. C. J. Johnstone) 1814
Saxon chronicle. Two of the Saxon chronicles parallel, with supplementary extracts from the others ed. J. Earle (1865) See also Anglo-Saxon chronicle
—— ed. C. Plummer (1892)
Saxon leechdoms: see Leechdoms
Say, Thomas American entomology, or descriptions of the insects of North America 1824–28
Say and Sele, William Fiennes, Viscount A speech in parliament 1642
Sayce, Archibald H. Introduction to the science of language 1880
The principles of comparative philology 1874 (1875)
Scammon, Charles M. The marine mammals of the north-western coast of North America described 1874
Scandal at Tunbridge-Wells, a fable 1760
Scanderbeg (George Castriota). The great Scanderbeg, a novel (by U. Chevreau) tr. 1690
Scanderbeg redivivus 1684: see G., H.
Scarburgh, Edmund The English Euclide tr. a 1696 (1705)
Scargill, William P. The puritan's grave 1833 (1846)
Scarlett, John The stile of exchanges tr. 1682
Scatcherd, Norrisson The history of Morley in .. Yorkshire 1830 (1874)
Schaefer, Edward A. Essentials of histology 1885 (1887)
Schaff, Philip Christ and christianity 1885
History of the christian church 1883–93
See also Herzog, J. J.
Scheele's (C. W.) Chemical essays tr. 1786
Scheffer's (J.) History of Lapland tr. 1674
Schele de Vere: see De Vere
Schellen's (H.) Spectrum analysis tr. Jane and C. Lassell, ed. W. Huggins 1871 (1872)

Scheme for equipping and maintaining sixteen men of war, A 1747
Scheuchzer, John G. Kæmpfer's (E.) History of Japan tr. 1727
Schiller, Ferdinand C. S. Riddles of the sphinx 1891
Schimmelpenninck, Mary Anne Narrative of the demolition of the monastery of Port Royal des champs 1815 (1816)
Schley, Winfield S. and Soley, J. R. The rescue of Greely 1885
Schliemann's (H.) Troja: results of the latest researches tr. 1884
Schmid, Reinhold Die Gesetze der Angelsachsen 1858
Schmidt, Alexander Shakespeare-lexicon 1874–75 (1886)
Schmidt's (E. O.) The doctrine of descent and Darwinism tr. 1875 (ed. 2)
Scholasticall discourse against symbolizing with Antichrist in ceremonies, A (by R. Parker) 1607
Scholehous of vngracious women, The vertuous (attrib. to E. Gosynhill) c 1550
Scholehouse of women, The, wherin every man may read a goodly praise of the conditions of women c 1541 (1572 in Hazl. Popular poetry IV)
Scholes, J. Tim Gamwattle's jaunt (to see the queen) 1857
Schomburgk, Sir Robert H. A description of British Guiana 1840
The history of Barbados 1848
School for good living, The; an essay on the European kitchen 1814
School of man, The; tr. from the French (of F. Génard) 1753
Schoolcraft, Henry Rowe Historical and statistical information respecting the history, conditions, and prospects of the Indian tribes of the United States 1851–60
Schreiner, Olive ('Ralph Iron') The story of an African farm 1883
Trooper Peter Halket of Mashonaland 1897
Schroeder, Henry The annals of Yorkshire 1851–52
Schützenberger's (P.) On fermentation tr. 1876
Science, an illustrated journal (Camb., Mass.) 1883–94, N.S. 1895–
Science-gossip, Hardwicke's 1865–93
—— continued as Science-gossip 1894–1903
Science lectures at South Kensington by Capt. Abney (and others) 1878
Science lectures for the people, delivered in Manchester 1866–80
Scientific American, The (a periodical) 1845–. Supplement 1881–
Scientific opinion: a weekly record of scientific progress 1869
Sclater, Philip L. Argentine ornithology 1888–89
Exotic ornithology 1869
See also Sclater, W. L.
Sclater, William A brief and plain commentary upon the prophecie of Malachy 1608 (1650)
The christians strength, a sermon 1612
An exposition with notes, on the whole fourth chapter to the Romanes a 1626 (1650)
An exposition with notes, upon the first epistle to the Thessalonians 1619 (1630)
—— the second epistle 1627 (1629)
A key to the key of scripture, or an exposition with notes, upon the three first chapters of the epistle to the Romanes 1611 (1629)
The ministers portion, a sermon 1612
The quæstion of tythes revised 1621 (1623)
Sermons experimentall on Psalms cxvi and cxvii a 1626 (1638)
The sick souls salve, a sermon 1612
A threefold preservative against three dangerous diseases of these latter times 1609 (1610)
Sclater, William Civil magistracy by divine authority 1652 (1653)
The crowne of righteousness (a funeral sermon) 1653 (1654)
The worthy communicant rewarded, a sermon 1639
Sclater, William L. and Sclater, P. L. The geography of mammals 1899
Scobell, Henry Ed. A collection of acts and ordinances .. made in the parliament 1640–56 (1658)
Scoffern, John Elementary chemistry of the imponderable agents and of inorganic bodies 1855
See also Orr's Circle of the sciences
Scogan, Scogin, or Scoggin, John His jestes 1613
Scoones, W. Baptiste Ed. Four centuries of English letters v.d. (1880)
Scoresby, William An account of the arctic regions, with a history and description of the northern whale-fishery 1820
Ed. Cheever's (H. T.) Whaleman's adventures in the southern ocean 1850 (1859)
Journal of a voyage to the northern whale-fishery 1823
Scot, Sir J.: see Scott
Scot, Reginald The discoverie of witchcraft 1584 (1886)
A perfite platforme of a hoppe garden 1574 (1578)
Scot, Walter A true history of several honourable families of the .. name of Scot in .. Roxburgh and Selkirk 1688 (1894)
Scot, William An apologeticall narration of the state of the kirk of Scotland since the reformation c 1630 (Wodrow Soc. 1846)
Scotch metrical version of the Psalms (1650): see Scottish psalter
Scotch paraphrases 1745: see Translations
Scotch presbyterian eloquence, The (by 'Jacob Curate') 1692 (1738)
Scotland. An account of the present persecution of the church of Scotland, in several letters 1690
An account of Scotland's grievances by reason of the duke of Lauderdal's ministry c 1674 (1693)
The actis and constitutiounis of the realme of Scotland (1566)
—— The lawes and actes of parliament (1597)
—— The acts of the parliaments of Scotland 1124–1707 (1814–75)
The acts of the Lords auditors of causes and complaints 1466–94 (1839)
The acts of the Lords of council in civil causes 1478–95 (1839)
Acts and proceedings of the general assemblies of the kirk of Scotland 1560–1618 (Bannatyne Club 1839–45)
—— The acts of the general assemblies of the church of Scotland 1638–49 (1682)
Scotland (cont.)
The acts of sederunt of the Lords of council and session 1553–1790 (1790)
The booke of common prayer .. for the use of the church of Scotland 1637
A brief and true account of the sufferings of the church of Scotland .. since the year 1660 1690
Calendar of the state papers relating to Scotland 1509–1603 (1858)
Compota thesaurariorum regum Scotorum, Accounts of the Lord high treasurer of Scotland 1473– (1877–)
A declaration .. from the generall assembly of the kingdome of Scotland 1642
A declaration of the lords of the secret councell and of the generall assembly of the kingdome and kirke of Scotland 1642
Miscellany of popular Scottish poems, chiefly of a humorous and descriptive character 1862
The new statistical account of Scotland, by the ministers of the respective parishes 1845. See also Sinclair, Sir J.
The petition of the commissioners of the generall assembly of the kirke of Scotland 1642
The register of the privy council of Scotland 1545– (1877–)
Registrum magni sigilli regum Scotorum, The register of the great seal of Scotland 1306– (1814, 1912; 1882–)
Registrum secreti sigilli regum Scotorum, The register of the privy seal of Scotland 1488–1529 (1908)
Rotuli scaccarii regum Scotorum, The exchequer rolls of Scotland 1264– (1878–)
The Scotts declaration in answer to the declaration sent unto them by their commissioners now at London 1642
Scotland's glory and her shame, being a brief historical account of her glory by presbytery etc. 1752 (1786)
Scots in Poland, Papers relating to the, 1576–1793 (S.H.S. 1915)
Scots magazine, The 1739–1817
Scots poems. A select collection of Scots poems, chiefly in the broad Buchan dialect 1785
Scots songs. A selection of the most favourite Scots songs, chiefly pastoral, adapted for the harpsichord 1790
Scott, Alexander Poems c 1560 (S.T.S. 1896; E.E.T.S. 1902)
Scott, Andrew Poems, chiefly in the Scottish dialect 1805 (1808)
Scott, Charles The practice of sheep-farming 1886
Scott, Sir G. Gilbert Gleanings from Westminster Abbey 1861 (1863)
Lectures on the rise and development of mediæval architecture a 1878 (1879)
Recollections personal and professional a 1878 (1879)
Scott, George Gilbert An essay on the history of English church architecture 1881
Scott, Hew Fasti ecclesiæ Scoticanæ, the succession of ministers in the parish churches of Scotland 1866–71
Scott, Sir James Sibbald D. To Jamaica and back 1876
Scott or Scot, Sir John The staggering state of the Scots statesmen (1550–1650) a 1670 (1754)
Scott, John Works a 1694 (1718)
The christian life 1681–86 (1730, 1747)
Practical discourses upon several subjects a 1694 (1697–98)
Scott, John 1773: see Observations
Scott, John Amwell; a descriptive poem 1776
Poetical works 1782
Scott, John A visit to Paris in 1814 1815 (1816)
—— Paris revisited in 1815 1816 (1817)
Scott, Jonathan Bahar-Danush; or, Garden of knowledge, an oriental romance tr. 1799
Ferishta's House of Dekhan tr. 1794
Scott, Joseph Nicol Bailey's (N.) New universal English dictionary Revised 1755 (1764)
'Scott, Leader' (Mrs. Lucy E. Baxter) Tuscan studies and sketches 1887 (1888)
Scott, Michael The cruise of the Midge 1834–35 (1863)
Tom Cringle's log 1829–33
Scott, Robert Forsyth A treatise on the theory of determinants 1880
Scott, Robert Henry Elementary meteorology 1883
Scott, Sarah Test of filial duty (anon.) 1772
Scott, Thomas The Belgicke pismire stinging the slothfull sleeper (anon.) 1622
The high-waies of God and the king (sermons) 1620 (1623)
Newes from Pernassus (anon.) 1622
A tongue-combat .. betweene two English souldiers 1623
Votivæ Angliæ; or the desires and wishes of England by S. R. N. I. 1624
Vox populi, or newes from Spayne 1620–24
Vox regis, by T. S. 1624
See also Raleigh's ghost
Scott, Thomas The holy Bible .. with original notes 1788–92
Scott, Thomas Poems; with Edwin and Catherine or the distressed lovers, a tragedy 1793
Scott, Sir Walter Miscellaneous prose works a 1832 (1834–71)
Poetical works a 1832
Waverley novels (1829–33)
The abbot 1820
Anne of Geierstein 1829
The antiquary 1816
Auchindrane, or the Ayrshire tragedy 1830
The betrothed 1825
The black dwarf 1816
The border antiquities of England and Scotland 1814–17
The bridal of Triermain 1813
The bride of Lammermoor 1818
Castle Dangerous 1831
Chronicles of the Canongate (The highland widow, The two drovers, The surgeon's daughter; Saint Valentine's day, or The fair maid of Perth) 1827–28
Count Robert of Paris 1831
The doom of Devorgoil 1830
Essays on chivalry, romance and the drama v.d.
The fair maid of Perth 1828
Familiar letters a 1832 (1894)
The fortunes of Nigel 1822
Guy Mannering; or the astrologer 1815
Halidon Hill: a metrical drama 1822
Harold the dauntless 1817
The heart of Midlothian 1818
The highland widow 1827
Ivanhoe, a romance 1819
Scott, Sir Walter (cont.)
Journal 1825–32 (1890)
Kenilworth 1821
The lady of the lake 1810
The lay of the last minstrel 1805
The legend of Montrose 1819
The letters of Malachi Malagrowther 1826 (see Thoughts, below)
Letters on demonology and witchcraft 1830
The life of Napoleon Buonaparte 1827
The lord of the isles 1814
Marmion 1808
The minstrelsy of the Scottish border 1802 (1803)
The monastery 1820
Old Mortality 1816
Paul's letters to his kinsfolk 1815 (1816, 1839)
Peveril of the Peak 1822
The pirate 1821
Provincial antiquities of Scotland 1826
Quentin Durward 1823
Redgauntlet 1824
Rob Roy 1818
Rokeby 1813
St. Ronan's well 1824
Ed. Sir Tristrem 1804 (1811)
The surgeon's daughter 1827
Tales of the crusaders (The betrothed, The talisman) 1825
Tales of my landlord (The black dwarf, Old Mortality, The heart of Midlothian, The bride of Lammermoor, A legend of Montrose, Count Robert of Paris, Castle Dangerous) 1817–32
The talisman 1825
Thoughts on the proposed change of currency by 'Malachi Malagrowther' 1826
The two drovers 1827
The vision of Don Roderick 1811
Waverley; or, 'tis sixty years since 1814
Woodstock, or the Cavalier 1826
See also Lockhart, J. G.
Scott, William An essay of drapery, or the compleate citizen trading justly 1635
Scottish alliterative poems a 1400–c 1475 (S.T.S. 1897)
Scottish Burgh Records Society, Publications of the (1868–1908)
Scottish field, The (a poem on the battle of Flodden) 1515 (Miscellanies II, Chetham Soc. 1856)
Scottish History Society, Publications of the (1887–)
Scottish legends. Legends of the saints in the Scottish dialect of the fourteenth century c 1375 (S.T.S. 1896)
Scottish pasquils. A book (a second, third book) of Scotish pasquils v.d. ed. J. Maidment (1827–28, 1868)
Scottish poems of the sixteenth century ed. J. G. Dalyell (1801)
Scottish psalter. The psalmes of David in metre, used in the kirk of Scotland 1596 (1615, 1633, 1635, 1650)
Scottish Text Society, Publications of the (1884–)
(Scottish) Trojan war, The c 1400 (Horstmann, Barbour's Legendensammlung 1881–82)
Scougal, Henry Works a 1678 (1765)
Discourses on important subjects a 1678 (1735)
Scourge of Venus, The: or the wanton lady, by H. A(ustin) 1613 (1614; Grosart 1876)
Scrafton, Luke Reflections on the government of Indostan 1763 (1770)
Scribbleomania; or the printer's devil's polichronicon, a poem (by W. H. Ireland) 1815
Scribner's Magazine 1887–
Scribner's Monthly, an illustrated magazine 1870–81
Scriven, John A practical treatise on copyhold tenure and court keeping 1816
—— A treatise on copyhold, customary freehold and ancient demesne tenure ed. H. Stalman (1846, 1867)
—— A treatise on the law of copyholds revised by A. Brown (1882)
Scrivener, Frederick H. A. Six lectures on the text of the New Testament 1874 (1875)
Scrivener, Scrivener C. Our fields and cities; or misdirected energy 1890 (1891)
Scroggs, Sir William Practice of courts-leet and courts-baron a 1683 (1701, 1714)
Scrope, George Poulett The geology and extinct volcanos of central France 1858 (ed. 2)
History of .. Castle Combe, in the county of Wilts 1852
Volcanos, the character of their phenomena 1862 (ed. 2)
Scrope, William Days and nights of salmon fishing in the Tweed 1843
'Scrutator' (K. W. Horlock) The country gentleman (a novel) 1862
Scrutton, Thomas E. Commons and common fields 1887
Scudamore, Sir Charles A medical visit to Gräfenberg 1843
Scudamore, Edward The nomenclator; a technological dictionary containing all the principal terms in use in the arts and sciences 1841
Scudamore, Frank Ives The day dreams of a sleepless man 1875
Scudamore, James Homer à la mode 1664
Scudder, Henry The christians daily walke in holy securitie and peace 1627 (1637)
A key of heaven: the Lord's prayer opened 1620
Scudder, Samuel Hubbard Butterflies: their structure .. and life-histories 1881
The butterflies of the eastern United States and Canada 1889
Scudery's (G. de) Curia politiæ: or the apologies of severall princes justifying to the world their most eminent actions tr. (by E. Wolley) 1654
Scully, William C. Kafir stories 1895
Sea-board 1860: see Warter, J. W.
Seafarer a 1000 (Grein)
Seager, F. The schoole of vertue and booke of good nourture for chyldren and youth to learne theyr dutie by, by F. S. 1557 (Babees book, E.E.T.S. 1868)
Seager, John Hermann's (J. G. J.) Elements of the doctrine of metres abridged and tr. 1830
A supplement to Dr. Johnson's Dictionary 1819
Seale, John Barlow An analysis of the Greek metres 1784 (1802)
Seaman, Sir Owen The battle of the bays 1897
In cap and bells 1899
'Search, Edward': see Tucker, A.

SOUTHWELL, ROBERT (cont.)
Marie Magdalens funerall teares, by S. W. 1591 (1594, 1602, 1823)
Saint Peters complaynt 1595
—— S. Peters complaint and Saint Mary Magdalens funerall teares, with sundry other selected and devout poems, by R. S. (1616)
The triumphs over death, by R. S. 1591 (1596; Archaica 1815)
Southwell minster, Visitations and memorials of v.d. (Camden Soc. 1891)
Sowdone of Babylone, The romaunce of the c 1400 (E.E.T.S. 1881)
SOWERBY, GEORGE B. A conchological manual 1839
Popular British conchology 1854
SOWERBY, JAMES English botany; or coloured figures of British plants (text from vol. IV by Sir J. E. Smith) 1790–1814 (1832–46)
SOYER, ALEXIS The gastronomic regenerator: a .. new system of cookery 1846
The pantropheon: or history of food and its preparation 1853
Spaewife, The 1823: see Galt, J.
SPALDING, JOHN The history of the troubles and memorable transactions in Scotland from 1624 to 1645 a 1670 (1792)
—— Memorialls of the trubles in Scotland and in England 1624–45 (Spalding Club 1850)
SPALDING, THOMAS A. Elizabethan demonology 1880
SPALDING, WILLIAM Italy and the Italian islands 1841
Spalding Club, Publications of the (1841–71)
—— Miscellany (1841–52)
Spallanzani's (L.) Dissertations relative to the natural history of animals and vegetables tr. 1784
—— Travels in the two Sicilies tr. 1798
Spanish history, The: or a relation of the differences that happened in the court of Spain between Don John of Austria and Cardinal Nitard; with other transactions of that kingdom (Running-title—Transactions of the court of Spain) tr. 1678
Spanish rivals, The; a musical farce, by M. Lonsdale 1784 (1785)
SPARKE, EDWARD Scintillula altaris, or a pious reflection on primitive devotion 1652 (1663)
SPARKE, MICHAEL Ed. Truth brought to light .. or a discourse .. of the first fourteen yeares of king James reigne 1651
SPARKE, THOMAS A brotherly perswasion to unitie and uniformitie in judgment and practise 1607
SPARKS, JARED Ed. Correspondence of the American revolution 1853
The library of American biography 1834–38
—— (Second series) 1844–47
Life of Gouverneur Morris, with selections from his correspondence and miscellaneous papers 1832
Sparrman's (A.) Voyage to the Cape of Good Hope tr. G. Forster 1785 (1786)
SPARROW, BP. ANTHONY A collection of articles, injunctions, canons etc. of the church of England v.d. (1684)
A rationale upon the Book of common prayer 1657 (1661)
SPARROW, JOHN Behmen's (J.) Mysterium magnum tr. 1654
Several treatises of J. Behme tr. 1661
The remainder of books written by J. Behme tr. 1662
SPARROW, JOHN Le Dran's (H. F.) Observations in surgery tr. J. S. 1758 (1771)
SPARROW, WILLIAM Select discourses 1877
SPARRY, FRANCIS Cattan's (C. de) Geomancie tr. 1591
Speaker, The; a review of politics etc. 1890–97
SPEARMAN, JAMES MORTON The British gunner 1828 (ed. 2)
Specimens of the British poets ed. T. Campbell (1819)
Specimens of lyric poetry a 1310 (Percy Soc. 1842)
Spectator, The (by J. Addison, Sir R. Steele, and others) 1711–14 (1868, 1891)
Spectator, The; a weekly review of politics etc. 1828–
Spectator, The new; with the sage opinions of John Bull 1784–86
Speculum Gy de Warewyke, an English poem c 1330 (E.E.T.S. 1898)
SPEDDING, JAMES Reviews and discussions, .. not relating to Bacon 1836–77 (1879)
—— and others Ed. Bacon's (F.) Works 1857–74
Speech for Mr. D—ss (Dundas) of Arnistoun, A (by D. De Foe) 1711
Speeches of the five jesuits (T. White, W. Harcourt, etc.) that were executed at Tyburn, 20th June 1679, The 1679
SPEED, ADOLPHUS Adam out of Eden, or an abstract of divers excellent experiments touching the advancement of husbandry c 1650 (1659)
SPEED, JOHN The history of Great Britaine 1611 (1623, 1632)
The theatre of the empire of Great Britaine 1611
—— England, Wales, Scotland and Ireland described and abridged c 1620 (1627)
SPEED, ROBERT The counter scuffle by R. S. 1623 (1628)
SPEEDY, THOMAS Sport in the highlands and lowlands of Scotland with rod and gun 1884
SPEID, MRS. JOHN B. Our last years in India 1862
SPEKE, JOHN HANNING Journal of the discovery of the source of the Nile 1863
SPELMAN, SIR HENRY The English works a 1641 (1723)
Archæologus. In modum glossarii ad rem antiquam posteriorem etc. 1626
—— Glossarium archaiologicum (1664)
De non temerandis ecclesiis, a tracte of the rights and respect due to churches 1613 (1646)
De sepultura (in English) 1630 (1641)
The history and fate of sacrilege, discover'd by examples a 1641 (1698)
—— and others Tithes too hot to be touched. Certain treatises wherein is shewen that tithes are due a 1641 (1646)
SPELMAN, SIR JOHN Case of our affairs 1643
The life of Ælfred the great a 1643 (1678, 1709)
Psalterium Davidis latino-saxonicum vetus (1640)
A view of a printed book (of Hen. Parker's) intituled Observations upon his Majesties late answers and expresses (anon.) 1642
SPENCE, CHARLES From the braes of the Carse, poems and songs a 1869 (1898)
SPENCE, FERRAND St. Euvremont's (Marguetel de St. Denis, C.) Miscellanea tr. 1686
Varillas' (A.) Secret history of the House of Medicis tr. 1686
SPENCE, JOHN Shetland folk-lore 1899
SPENCE, JOSEPH Anecdotes, observations and characters of books and men a 1768 (1820)
An essay on Pope's Odyssey 1726

SPENCER, BENJAMIN: see Spenser
SPENCER, HERBERT Ceremonial institutions (part of Principles of sociology) 1879
The data of ethics 1879
Education 1861 (1879)
Essays: scientific, political and speculative 1852–73 (1858, 1863, 1874)
First principles (a system of philosophy) 1862 (1875)
Illustrations of universal progress 1864
The man versus the state 1884
Political institutions (part of Principles of sociology) 1882
The principles of biology 1864–67
The principles of psychology 1855 (1870–72)
The principles of sociology 1876–82
Social statics 1851 (1854)
The study of sociology 1873
SPENCER, JOHN A discourse concerning prodigies 1663
—— Second ed. To which is added a short treatise concerning vulgar prophecies 1665
The righteous ruler, a sermon 1660
SPENCER, THOMAS The art of logick 1628
SPENCER, (WALTER) BALDWIN Horn scientific expedition. Through Larapinta Land 1896
SPENCER, WILLIAM ROBERT Poems 1811
SPENSER or SPENCER, BENJAMIN Vox civitatis, or London's complaint against her children in the country 1625 (Phenix 1732)
SPENSER, EDMUND Works a 1599 (Globe)
Amoretti 1594
Astrophel, a pastorall elegie upon the death of .. Sir Philip Sidney 1596 (in Arber, Eng. Garner I)
Colin Clouts come home again 1591–95
Complaints, containing sundrie small poemes of the worlds vanitie 1591
Daphnaïda, an elegie 1591
Epithalamion 1595
The faerie queene 1590–96
Fowre hymnes (in honour of love, in honour of beautie, of heavenly love, of heavenly beautie) 1596
Muiopotmos: or the fate of the butterflie 1590
Prosopopoia: or Mother Hubberds tale 1591
The shepheardes calender 1579
Three proper and wittie familiar letters, lately passed betwene two universitie men (E. Spenser and G. Harvey) 1580
—— Two other letters 1579 (1580)
A view of the present state of Ireland 1596 (1633; Globe)
Virgils gnat 1591
The visions of Bellay 1591
Brittains Ida: see Fletcher, G. (the younger)
SPILLING, JAMES Giles's trip to London (anon.) 1872
Molly Migg's trip to the seaside (anon.) 1873
SPINGARN, J. E. Ed. Critical essays of the seventeenth century 1908–09
Spinster, The; a defence of the woollen manufacture. Publ. J. Roberts 1719
Spirit of the metropolitan conservative press 1839 (1840)
Spirit of the nation, The; ballads and songs by the writers of 'The Nation' (Dubl.) 1845
Spirit of popery speaking out of the mouths of phanatical protestants, The (by G. Hickes) 1680
Spirit of the public journals, The 1797–1814, 1823–25 (1798–1826)
Spirituall counsayle, very necessarye for every persone to have c 1530
Splendid follies, a novel 1810
SPOFFORD, MRS. HARRIET E. P. The amber gods, and other stories 1863
Sir Rohan's ghost, a romance (anon.) 1859 (1863)
Spon's (E. and F. N.) Household manual 1887
SPON, ERNEST Spon's Encyclopædia of the industrial arts, manufactures and commercial products 1879–82
Workshop receipts 1873
—— (Second series, by R. Haldane 1883; third, fourth series by C. G. W. Lock 1884–85)
SPOONER, WILLIAM C. Veterinary art: a practical treatise on the diseases of the horse 1845 (1851)
Sporting magazine, The 1793–1870
Sports. A new book of sports, reprinted from the 'Saturday review' 1885
Sportsman's gazetteer and general guide, The (by C. Hallock) 1877 (also 1883)
SPOTTISWOOD, ABP. JOHN The history of the church of Scotland a 1639 (1677; Spottiswoode Soc. 1847–51)
SPOTTISWOODE, WILLIAM Polarisation of light 1874 (1879)
Spottiswoode Society, Publications of the (1844–51)
SPRAT, BP. THOMAS A discourse to the clergy of his diocese 1695 (1696)
The history of the Royal-society of London 1667
Poems a 1713 (1790; Chalmers 1810)
SPRIGGE, JOSHUA Anglia rediviva; Englands recovery 1647 (1854)
SPRIGGE, SAMUEL S. The life and times of Thomas Wakley 1897
Spring and summer in Lapland, A (by H. W. Wheelwright) 1863 (1864)
SPROULE, JOHN An essay on the growth and management of flax in Ireland 1844 (1846)
SPRY, WILLIAM J. J. The cruise of Her majesty's ship 'Challenger' 1876
SPURDENS, WILLIAM T. A supplementary volume to R. Forby's Vocabulary of East Anglia 1840 (1858)
See also Longinus, D. C.
SPURGEON, CHARLES HADDON John Ploughman's pictures 1880
The treasury of David; containing an original exposition of the Book of psalms 1870–86
SPURSTOWE, WILLIAM The spiritual chymist 1666 (1668)
The wels of salvation opened 1655
SQUIER, EPHRAIM G. Notes on Central America 1855
Peru: incidents of travel and exploration in the land of the Incas 1877
SQUIRE, JANE A proposal for discovering our longitude 1742
Squyr of lowe degre, The a 1400 (Ritson, Metrical romances III, 1802)
STABLES, W. GORDON The cruise of the land yacht 'Wanderer' 1886
Our friend the dog 1884
Stacions of Rome, The (verse) a 1400 (E.E.T.S. 1867; prologue only, Minor poems of the Vernon MS., E.E.T.S. 1901)
—— c 1440 (Polit., relig. and love poems, E.E.T.S. 1903)
—— (prose) c 1460–70 (E.E.T.S. 1867)

STACKHOUSE, THOMAS A new history of the holy Bible 1737 (1767)
Staehlin Storcksburg's (J. von) Account of the new Northern archipelago tr. 1774
STAFFORD, ANTHONY The femall glory, or the life and death of our blessed lady, the holy virgin Mary 1635 (1869)
Staffords heavenly dogge: or the life and death of .. Diogenes 1615
Staffords Niobe: or his age of teares 1611
STAFFORD, SIR THOMAS Pacata Hibernia. Ireland appeased and reduced 1633 (1821)
STAFFORD, WILLIAM 1581: see S., W.
STAGG, JOHN The minstrel of the north, or Cumbrian legends 1810 (1817)
Miscellaneous poems 1790 (1805)
—— another selection 1807 (1808)
STAINER, SIR JOHN Composition 1880
The music of the Bible 1879
The organ 1878
A theory of harmony 1871
—— and BARRETT, W. A. A dictionary of musical terms 1876
—— new and revised ed. (1898)
STAINTON, HENRY T. British butterflies and moths 1867
A manual of British butterflies and moths 1857–59
STAIR, SIR JAMES DALRYMPLE, 1ST VISCOUNT The institutions of the law of Scotland 1681 (also 1693)
STALKER, JOHN: see Parker, George
STALLYBRASS, JAMES S. Grimm's (J. L. C.) Teutonic mythology tr. 1880–88
Stamp collector's magazine, The 1863–74
STANBRIDGE, JOHN Vocabula 1510 (1525)
Vulgaria Stanbrigi 1510
Standard dictionary of the English language, A 1893–95 (Funk and Wagnalls)
Standard natural history, The: see Kingsley, J. S.
Standard of equalitie in subsidiary taxes and payments, The; or a just and strong preserver of publique liberty 1647 (Harl. Misc.)
STANDEN (—) A poem on the death of .. J. Weekes 1699
STANDISH, FRANK HALL The maid of Jaen 1830 (Poems 1838)
STANFORD, CHARLES Symbols of Christ 1865 (1878)
STANFORD or STAUNFORD, SIR WILLIAM An exposicion of the kinges prerogative, collected out of the great abridgement of Justice Fitzherbert a 1558 (1568)
Les plees del coron 1557 (1567)
Stanford dictionary of anglicised words and phrases, The ed. C. A. M. Fennell 1892
STANHOPE, GEORGE The christian's pattern, or a treatise of the imitation of Jesus Christ 1696 (1698)
A paraphrase and comment upon the epistles and gospels 1705–09
Pious breathings, being the meditations of St. Augustine made English 1701 (1704)
STANHOPE, LADY HESTER L. Memoirs, as related by herself in conversations with her physician a 1839 (1845)
STANHOPE, PHILIP DORMER, 4TH EARL OF CHESTERFIELD: see Chesterfield
STANHOPE, PHILIP H. STANHOPE, 5TH EARL History of England, comprising the reign of Queen Anne until the peace of Utrecht 1701–13 1870
STANLEY, ARTHUR PENRHYN Historical memorials of Westminster abbey 1867 (1868)
Lectures on the history of the Eastern church 1861 (1869)
Lectures on the history of the Jewish church 1863–65 (1877)
The life and correspondence of Dr. Arnold 1844 (1858)
Sinai and Palestine in connection with their history 1856 (1858)
STANLEY, HENRY MORTON The Congo and the founding of its free state 1885
In darkest Africa 1890
Through the dark continent 1878
STANLEY, THOMAS The history of philosophy 1655–61 (1687, 1701)
The history of the Chaldaick philosophy 1662 (1701)
Poems 1651
STANNARD, MRS. ARTHUR: see 'Winter, J. S.'
Stannaries of Cornwall, The. The case of the stannaries stated c 1650
The laws of the stannaries of Cornwall (1808)
Stans puer ad mensam c 1430 (Babees book, E.E.T.S. 1868)
—— c 1460 (ibid.)
STANYHURST, RICHARD Thee first foure bookes of Virgil his Æneis translated, .. wyth oother poetical diuises 1582 (1836; Arber)
The historie of Irelande .. continued 1577 (in Holinshed; also 1587)
A treatise contayning a playne and perfect description of Irelande 1577 (in Holinshed; also 1587)
STAPLETON, MRS. BRYAN Three Oxfordshire parishes 1893 (O.H.S.)
STAPLETON or STAPYLTON, SIR ROBERT Juvenal's sixteen satyrs tr. 1647
The slighted maid, a comedy 1663
Strada's (F.) De bello belgico, the history of the Low-countrey warres tr. 1650
STAPLETON, THOMAS Beda's History of the church of England tr. 1565
A fortresse of the faith 1565
A returne of untruthes vpon M. Jewelles replie 1566
STAPYLTON, C. B. Herodian his imperiall history tr. 1652
STAPYLTON, SIR R.: see Stapleton
Star (newspaper) 1888–
Star-chamber. Decree of the lords in the starre chambere touching printers, stationers, etc. 1584 (in J. P. Collier, Illustrations E.E. popular literature 1863)
A decree of Starre-chamber, concerning printing 1637 (Arber, Milton's Areopagitica)
Reports of cases in the courts of Star chamber and High commission 1631–32 (Camden Soc. 1886)
Select pleas of the court of Star chamber (Selden Soc. 1902–10)
STARK, JOHN Elements of natural history 1828
STARKEY, GEORGE Natures explication and Helmont's vindication 1657
Pyrotechny asserted and illustrated 1658
STARKEY, THOMAS England in the reign of Henry the eighth, a dialogue between Cardinal Pole and Thomas Lupset 1538 (E.E.T.S. 1878)
Life and letters a 1538 (ibid.)
State (= statement of legal case), Leslie of Powis etc. 1805 (cited by Jamieson)

State of the Philadelphian society or the grounds of their proceedings considered, The 1697
State papers: see also Calendar
State papers (during the reign of) Henry the eighth (1830–52)
State papers relating to Friends, Extracts from 1654–69 (1910–12)
State poems. Poems on affairs of state 1697–1707
State songs. A collection of state songs, poems &c. that have been published since the Rebellion (1716)
State trials. A complete collection of state trials (1730, 1776–81).
—— Cobbett's complete collection of state trials, with notes by T. B. Howell (1809–14; continued by T. J. Howell 1817–26)
—— new series, 1820– (1888–)
Statistical account of Scotland 1791–99: see Sinclair, Sir John
The new statistical account of Scotland, by the ministers of the respective parishes 1845
Statistical Society, Journal of the 1839–
STATON, JAMES T. Rays fro' th' loominary, a selection of comic Lancashire tales c 1860 (1866)
Statutes of the realm 1235–1713 (Record commission 1810–28)
—— The statutes, revised ed. 1235–1878 (1870–85)
The statutes at large from Magna carta to .. 1800 (ed. O. Ruffhead, D. Pickering, and others)
The statutes of the United Kingdom 1801–69
The public general statutes 1870–87
The public general acts 1888–
The statutes (in English) made and established from .. Henry III unto the fyrste yere of Henry VIII (Berthelet 1543; continued 1551–57)
A colleccion of all the statutes (ed. W. Rastell 1557, 1579)
A collection in English of the statutes now in force (1611)
A collection of all the statutes made in the reigns of Charles I and Charles II 1625–67 (ed. T. Manby 1667)
A collection of acts and ordinances .. made in parliament 1640–56 (ed. H. Scobell 1658)
Actis made 24 (etc.) yere Henry VIII 1532 (etc.)
The public general acts of 1 and 2 Vict. etc. 1837–67
A collection of public local and personal acts 1798– (1799–)
The private acts 1702–
The statutes of Ireland (ed. Sir R. Bolton 1621)
A collection of all the statutes now in use in the kingdom of Ireland (1678)
The statutes at large, passed in the parliaments held in Ireland 1310–1761 (1765)
—— another ed. 1310–1800 (1786–1801)
Statutes and ordynances for the warre 1544
STAUNFORD, SIR WILLIAM: see Stanford
STAUNTON, SIR GEORGE L. An authentic account of an embassy .. to the emperor of China 1797
STAUNTON, HOWARD The chess player's handbook 1847
STAVELEY, E. F. British insects 1871
STAVELEY, THOMAS The Romish horseleech 1674 (1769)
STAYNRED, PHILIP A compendium of fortification 1669 (with Sturmy's Mariners magazine)
STEBBING, THOMAS R. R. A history of crustacea 1893
STEDMAN, EDMUND C. Poets of America 1885
The prince's ball 1860
Victorian poets 1876
STEDMAN, JOHN G. Narrative of a five years' expedition against the revolted negroes of Surinam, .. elucidating the history of that country etc. 1796 (1813)
STEEDMAN, ANDREW Wanderings and adventures in the interior of southern Africa 1835
STEEL, ALLAN G. and LYTTELTON, R. H. Cricket (Badminton library) 1888 (1893)
STEELE, RICHARD The husbandmans calling, shewing the excellencies, .. duties etc. of the christian husbandman 1668 (1672)
STEELE, SIR RICHARD Dramatic works 1723, a 1729 (1777)
The christian hero 1701 (1711)
The conscious lovers, a comedy 1722 (1723, 1755)
The Englishman 1713–14
The funeral, or grief a-la-mode, a comedy 1701 (1702, 1734)
The guardian 1713: see Guardian
The lover 1714
The lying lover 1703 (1704, 1723)
The spectator: see Spectator
The tatler: see Tatler
The tender husband, or the accomplish'd fools, a comedy 1703 (1723)
STEELE, WILLIAM E. A hand book of field botany 1847
STEER, JOHN Gulielm. Fabricius Hildanus his experiments in chyrurgerie concerning combustions or burnings tr. 1643
STEGGALL, JOHN H. A real history of a Suffolk man .. narrated by himself. Ed. by the author of 'Mary Catchpole' (R. Cobbold) 1857 (1859)
Stegmann's (J.) Brevis disquisitio: or, a brief enquiry touching a better way then is commonly made use of, to refute Papists, and reduce Protestants to certainty and unity in religion (sometimes erron. ascribed to J. Hales) tr. 1653 (in Phenix 1708)
STEPHEN, SIR GEORGE Adventures of a gentleman in search of a horse, by Caveat emptor 1835 (1841)
STEPHEN, HENRY JOHN New commentaries on the laws of England 1841–45 (1874)
STEPHEN, SIR JAMES Essays in ecclesiastical biography 1849 (1850)
Lectures on the history of France 1851
STEPHEN, SIR JAMES FITZJAMES Defence of the rev. Rowland Williams 1862
Essays by a barrister (anon.) 1862
STEPHEN, JOHN The utterances of the cxix psalm 1861
STEPHEN, SIR LESLIE Alexander Pope (English men of letters) 1880
Essays on freethinking and plainspeaking 1873
History of English thought in the eighteenth century 1876
Hours in a library 1874, -76, -79 (1892)
The playground of Europe 1871 (1894)
Studies of a biographer 1898–1902
Swift (English men of letters) 1882
STEPHENS, GEORGE The old-northern runic monuments of Scandinavia and England 1866–68
STEPHENS, HENRY The book of the farm 1844
—— (another ed.) 1851 (1855)
—— and BURN, R. S. The book of farm-buildings 1861
STEPHENS, HENRY MORSE Albuquerque (Rulers of India) 1892
A history of the French revolution 1886–91

STEPHENS, JAMES BRUNTON Miscellaneous poems 1880
STEPHENS, JAMES F. Continuation of Shaw's (G.) General zoology 1815–26
STEPHENS, JOHN Satyrical essays, characters and others 1615
—— New essayes and characters 1631
STEPHENS, JOHN An historicall discourse briefly setting forth the nature of procurations, .. also of synodals and pentecostals 1661
STEPHENS, JOHN LLOYD Incidents of travel in Central America etc. 1841 (1854)
Incidents of travel in Greece, Turkey, Russia and Poland 1838
STEPHENS, WILLIAM R. W. The life and letters of E. A. Freeman 1895
STEPNEY, GEORGE Poems a 1707 (Chalmers 1810)
'STEPNIAK, SERGIUS' (S. M. Kravchinskii) Underground Russia 1885
STERLING, JOHN Essays and tales a 1844 (1848)
STERNBERG, GEORGE M. Magnin's (A.) The bacteria tr. 1881 (1883)
STERNBERG, THOMAS The dialect and folk-lore of Northamptonshire 1851
STERNE, LAURENCE Works a 1768 (1779)
The beauties of Sterne (1782, 1809)
Letters to his .. friends, with a fragment in the manner of Rabelais etc. a 1768 (1775)
The life and opinions of Tristram Shandy 1759–67
A sentimental journey through France and Italy 1768 (1778)
The sermons of Mr. Yorick c 1760 (1760–69, 1773)
STERNHOLD, THOMAS Certayne psalmes .. drawen into Englishe metre 1547
Al such psalmes of David as T. Sternhold did in his lyfe time drawe into English meter 1549
—— HOPKINS, J., and others The whole boke of psalmes (1562, 1564, 1638)
STERRY, JOSEPH ASHBY-: see Ashby-Sterry, J.
STERRY, PETER A discourse of the freedom of the will a 1672 (1675)
Englands deliverance from the northern presbytery 1652
The rise, race and royalty of the kingdom of God in the soul of man a 1672 (1683)
STEUART, SIR HENRY The planter's guide; or, a practical essay on the best method of giving immediate effect to wood, by the removal of larger trees etc. 1827 (1828)
STEUART, SIR JAMES, afterwards DENHAM, SIR J. S. An inquiry into the principles of political economy 1767
STEUART, WALTER Collections and observations methodiz'd, concerning the worship, discipline and government of the church of Scotland 1709
STEVENS, ABEL The history of methodism 1860–65
STEVENS, GEORGE ALEXANDER The adventures of a speculist, or a journey through London a 1784 (1788)
Songs, comic and satyrical 1772
STEVENS, JOHN Cieza's (Peter de) Seventeen years travel through Peru tr. 1709
Ed. A new collection of voyages and travels 1711
Quevedo's (F. de) Comical works tr. 1707 (1709)
Ed. Two additional volumes to Sir W. Dugdale's Monasticon Anglicanum 1722–23
STEVENSON, HENRY The birds of Norfolk 1866
STEVENSON, JOHN HALL- Works a 1785 (1795)
Crazy tales 1762
STEVENSON, MATTHEW The twelve moneths; or a pleasant .. discourse of every action .. proper to each particular moneth 1661
STEVENSON, ROBERT LOUIS Works a 1894
Across the plains 1879–88 (1892)
The black arrow: a tale of the two Roses 1888
Catriona: a sequel to 'Kidnapped' 1893
Familiar studies of men and books 1874–81 (1882)
In the south seas 1888–90 (1900)
An inland voyage 1878
Kidnapped: being memoirs of the adventures of David Balfour in 1751 1886
The master of Ballantrae, a winter's tale 1888
Memories and portraits 1882–87 (1887)
The merry men and other tales and fables 1878–85 (1887)
The misadventures of John Nicholson 1887 (1888)
New Arabian nights 1877–82 (1884)
Prince Otto, a romance 1885
St. Ives, being the adventures of a French prisoner in England a 1894 (1899)
The Silverado squatters 1883
Strange case of Dr. Jekyll and Mr. Hyde 1886
Travels with a donkey in the Cevennes 1879
Treasure Island 1883
Vailima letters 1890–94 (1895)
Virginibus puerisque and other papers 1874–79 (1881)
Weir of Hermiston, an unfinished romance a 1894 (1896)
—— and OSBOURNE, L. The wrecker 1892
The wrong box 1889
—— and STEVENSON, FANNY VAN DE G. More New Arabian nights, The dynamiter 1885
STEVENSON, THOMAS Lighthouse illumination 1859
STEVENSON, W. GRANT Puddin': an Edinburgh story 1894
STEVENSON, WILLIAM An hymn to the deity 1782
STEVENSON, WILLIAM General view of the agriculture of the county of Dorset 1812
—— of Surrey 1809
STEWART, ALEXANDER 'Twixt Ben Nevis and Glencoe: the natural history, legends and folk-lore of the west Highlands 1885
STEWART, BALFOUR The conservation of energy 1873
An elementary treatise on heat 1866 (1871)
—— and TAIT, P. G. The unseen universe (anon.) 1875 (1876)
STEWART, DUGALD Works a 1828 (1854–58)
Dissertation exhibiting a general view of the progress of .. philosophy 1816–21 (Encycl. Brit. Suppl.; 1858)
Elements of the philosophy of the human mind 1792–1827
Philosophical essays 1810
The philosophy of the active and moral powers of man 1828 (1854–58)
STEWART, GEORGE Shetland fireside tales 1877 (1892)
Stewart, James, The trial of, for the murder of Colin Campbell of Glenure 1753
STEWART, JOHN The tocsin of Britannia 1794
The tocsin of social life 1803
STEWART, W. C. The practical angler: or the art of trout-fishing 1857
STEWART, WILLIAM The buik of the croniclis of Scotland; or a metrical version of the history of Hector Boece tr. 1535 (Rolls series 1858)

STILL, JOHN: see Gammer Gurton
STILL, PETER The cottar's Sunday, and other poems, chiefly in the Scottish dialect 1845
STILLINGFLEET, BENJAMIN Biberg's Œconomy of nature tr. 1759 (Misc. tracts 1759)
The calendar of Flora (from the Swedish of A. M. Berger) 1761
Miscellaneous tracts relating to natural history, husbandry and physick 1759 (1762)
STILLINGFLEET, BP. EDWARD Works a 1699 (1710)
Charge begun at Worcester 11 Sept. 1690 1691
Irenicum, a weapon-salve for the churches wounds 1659 (1661)
Origines Britannicæ; or the antiquities of the British churches 1685
Origines sacræ; or a rational account of the grounds of the christian faith as to the truth and divine authority of the scriptures 1662 (1666)
Sermons preached on several occasions 1696–98
STIMSON, FREDERICK JESUP American statute law 1886
Stirling, Charters and other documents relating to the royal burgh of 1124–1705 (1884)
—— Extracts from the records of the royal burgh of 1519–1666, 1667–1752 (1884–89)
STIRLING, SIR WILLIAM ALEXANDER, EARL OF Poems a 1640 (Chalmers 1810)
The Alexandræan tragedie 1605
Aurora 1604
Doomesday; or the great day of the Lords judgment 1614
Recreations with the muses 1637
A supplement to Sir P. Sidney's Arcadia 1621 (1629)
The tragedie of Darius 1603
STIRLING, JAMES H. Jerrold, Tennyson and Macaulay, with other essays 1868
Philosophy and theology (Gifford lectures) 1890
Schwegler's (F. C. A.) Hand-book of the history of philosophy tr. 1867
The secret of Hegel: being the Hegelian system in origin, principle, form and matter 1865
STIRLING, afterwards STIRLING-MAXWELL, SIR WILLIAM The cloister life of the emperor Charles the fifth 1852 (1853)
STIRLING, WILLIAM 1885: see Landois, L.
STISTED, GEORGIANA M. The true life of Sir R. F. Burton 1896
Stitchill (Roxburghshire), Records of the baron court of 1655–1807 (S.H.S. 1905)
STOCK, RICHARD A learned .. commentary upon .. Malachy a 1626 (1641; 1865)
STOCKDALE, JOHN J. Sketches, civil and military, of the island of Java etc. 1811
STOCKER, THOMAS A righte noble .. history of the successors of Alexander, taken out of Diodorus Siculus tr. 1569
A tragicall historie of the .. civile warres of the Lowe countries, otherwise called Flanders, tr. by T. S. 1583
Viret's (P.) The worlde possessed with devils (Part II of The demoniacke worlde) tr. by T. S. 1583
Stockholm medical MS., Extracts from a, a 1400 (in Archaeologia XXX, 1844; Anglia XVIII, 1896)
STOCKTON, FRANK R. The Dusantes 1888
The lady or the tiger? 1884
Rudder Grange 1879
STOCKWOOD, JOHN A plaine and easie laying open of the meaning and understanding of the rules of construction in the English accidence 1590
A sermon preached at Paules Crosse 1578
STOCQUELER, JOACHIM H. The hand-book of (British) India 1844 (1854)
The military encyclopædia; a technical, biographical, and historical dictionary 1853
STODART, ROBERT R. Scottish arms, being a collection of armorial bearings 1370–1678 reproduced in facsimile 1881
STODDARD, CHARLES A. Cruising among the Caribbees 1895
STODDARD, FRANCIS H. The evolution of the English novel 1900
STODDARD, RICHARD H. Poems 1852, 1880
STODDART, ANNA M. John Stuart Blackie, a biography 1895
STODDART, SIR JOHN Grammar a 1845 (Encycl. metropolitana)
STODDART, THOMAS T. The angler's companion to the rivers and lochs of Scotland 1847
An angler's rambles, and angling songs 1866
—— Angling songs (1889)
Songs and poems 1839
STOKES, DAVID A paraphrasticall explication of the twelve minor prophets 1659
STOKES, SIR GEORGE GABRIEL Mathematical and physical papers 1880–1903
STOKES, WHITLEY The tripartite life of St. Patrick tr. 1887 (Rolls series)
STONE, JAMES K. The invitation heeded: reasons for a return to catholic unity 1870
STONE, SAMUEL Deceivers deceiv'd, a sermon 1661
STONE, SAMUEL The justices' pocket manual 1842
The justices' manual 1864 (1876)
STONE, THOMAS General view of the agriculture of the county of Lincoln 1794
'STONEHENGE' (J. H. Walsh) The dog, in health and disease 1859
Ed. The dogs of the British islands 1866–67
Manual of British rural sports 1856 (1875)
The shot-gun and sporting rifle 1859
STONEHOUSE, WILLIAM B. The history and topography of the isle of Axholme 1839
Stonor letters and papers, The 1290–1483 (Camden Soc. 1919)
S'too him Bayes: or some observations upon the humour of writing Rehearsals transpros'd 1673
STOPFORD, EDWARD A. The work and the counterwork; or the religious revival in Belfast 1859
STORER, DAVID H. Reports on the ichthyology and herpetology of Massachusetts 1839
STORER, THOMAS The life and death of T. Wolsey, cardinall 1599
STORK, WILLIAM A description of East Florida 1766 (with A journal kept by J. Bartram, 1769)
STORMONTH, JAMES Etymological and pronouncing dictionary of the English language 1871 (1884)
STORY, JOSEPH Commentaries on the constitution of the United States 1833
Miscellaneous writings a 1845 (1852)

STORY, JOSIAH An essay concerning the nature of the priesthood 1750
STORY, ROBERT H. The apostolic ministry in the Scottish church 1897
STORY, WILLIAM W. Roba di Roma 1863
STOUGHTON, JOHN A learned treatise in three parts. 1. The definition. 2. The distribution of divinity. 3. The happiness of man 1640
STOUGHTON THOMAS The christians sacrifice 1622
STOUT, WILLIAM Autobiography a 1744 (1851)
STOVEL, CHARLES Ed. Canne's (J.) A necessitie of separation from the church of England (1634), with introductory notice 1849
STOW, JOHN The annales of England 1592 (1605; continued by E. Howes 1615)
A summarie of Englyshe chronicles 1565
A survey of London 1598 (1603, enlarged 1633, 1842)
—— ed. J. Strype (1720, 1754–55)
STOWE, MRS. HARRIET ELIZABETH BEECHER Dred; a tale of the Great dismal swamp 1856
Little foxes 1865 (1866)
Oldtown fireside stories 1871
Oldtown folks 1869
The pearl of Orr's island 1861–62
Poganuc people, their loves and lives 1878
Uncle Tom's cabin; or life among the lowly 1852
STOWER, CHARLES The printer's grammar; or, introduction to the art of printing 1808
STRACHEY, WILLIAM The historie of travaile into Virginia Britannia c 1612 (Hakl. Soc. 1849)
STRAFFORD, THOMAS WENTWORTH, EARL OF Letters and dispatches a 1641 (1739)
STRAIN, MRS. EUPHANS H. Elmslie's dragnet 1900
Strand magazine, The 1891–
STRANG, JAMES A lass of Lennox 1899
STRANG, JOHN Glasgow and its clubs 1856
STRANGFORD, PERCY E. F. W. SMYTHE, 8TH VISCOUNT A selection from his writings a 1869 (1869)
Strasburger's (E.) Handbook of practical botany ed. W. Hillhouse 1887 (1889)
STRATFORD, BP. NICHOLAS Charge at Chester, May 5th 1691 1692
'STRATHESK, JOHN' (J. Tod) Bits from Blinkbonny 1882
More bits from Blinkbonny 1884 (1885)
STRATMANN, FRANZ H. A dictionary of the Old English language 1878 (ed. 3)
—— new ed. by H. Bradley (1891)
Strauss' (D. F.) New life of Jesus tr. 1865
STRAUSS, GUSTAVE L. M., and others England's workshops 1864
Straw, Jack. The life and death of Jack Straw, a notable rebell in England 1593
STREATFEILD, GEORGE S. Lincolnshire and the Danes 1884
STREET, GEORGE E. Brick and marble in the middle ages 1855 (1874)
Street robberies considered (by D. De Foe) 1728
STREETER, EDWIN W. Precious stones and gems 1877
STRETTON, CHARLES Memoirs of a chequered life 1862
'STRETTON, HESBA' ('Hannah', or rather Sarah, Smith) Through a needle's eye 1879
STRICKLAND, AGNES Lives of the queens of England 1840–48
Lives of the queens of Scotland, and English princesses connected with the regal succession of Great Britain 1850–59
STRINGER, ARTHUR The wire tappers 1906
STRODE, GEORGE The anatomie of mortalitie 1618
STRODE, WILLIAM The floating island; a tragi-comedy 1636 (1655)
STRUTHER, WILLIAM True happiness, or king Davids choice 1633
STRUTHERS, JOHN Poetical works 1850
STRUTT, JACOB G. Sylva Britannica; or portraits of forest trees 1822 (1830)
STRUTT, JOSEPH A compleat view of the manners, customs, arms, habits, etc. of the inhabitants of England 1775–76
A complete view of the dress and habits of the people of England 1796–99
The sports and pastimes of the people of England 1801 (1875)
STRYPE, JOHN Annals of the reformation and establishment of religion, and .. other occurrences in the church of England 1708–09, 1725–31 (1824)
Ecclesiastical memorials, relating chiefly to religion and the reformation of it .. under Henry VIII, Edward VI, and queen Mary the first 1721 (1822)
The history of the life and acts of .. E. Grindal, .. archbishop of Canterbury 1710
The life and acts of M. Parker .. archbishop of Canterbury 1711
The life and acts of .. J. Whitgift .. archbishop of Canterbury 1717–18
Memorials of T. Cranmer, sometime lord archbishop of Canterbury 1694
Stow's (J.) Survey of the cities of London and Westminster brought down .. to the present time 1720 (1754–55)
S.T.S. = Scottish Text Society
STUART, ARABELLA The life and letters a 1615 (ed. Elizabeth Cooper 1866)
STUART, GEORGE A joco-serious discourse, in two dialogues between a Northumberland gentleman and his tenant a Scotchman 1686
STUART, GILBERT The history of Scotland, from the establishment of the reformation till the death of queen Mary 1782
STUART, H. The novice's or young seaman's catechism 1860
STUART, HAMISH Lochs and loch fishing 1899
STUART, HENRY W. VILLIERS Egypt after the war 1883
STUART, MOSES A grammar of the Hebrew language 1828 (1831)
'STUART, ROBERT' (R. Meikleham) A descriptive history of the steam engine 1824
STUART, WILLIAM and MACPHERSON, J. Ebrard's (J. H. A.) Apologetics; or the scientific vindication of christianity tr. 1886–87
STUBBE, HENRY A censure upon certaine passages contained in The history of the Royal Society 1670–71
The Indian nectar, or a discourse concerning chocolata 1662
The miraculous conformist 1666
The Plus ultra reduced to a nonplus, or a specimen of some animadversions upon the Plus ultra of Mr. Glanvill 1670
Rosemary and Bayes: or, animadversions upon a treatise called The rehearsall trans-prosed (anon.) 1672

STUBBES, PHILIP The anatomie of abuses 1583 (New Shaks. Soc. 1877–79–82)
STUBBS or STUBS, JOHN The discoverie of a gaping gulf whereinto England is like to be swallowed by an other French mariage (anon.) 1579
STUBBS, BP. WILLIAM The constitutional history of England 1874–78
Ed. Select charters and other illustrations of English constitutional history 1870
Seventeen lectures on the study of mediaeval and modern history 1867–84 (1886)
STUCLEY, LEWIS A gospel glasse representing the miscarriages of English professors 1667 (1670)
Stucley, Play of. The famous historye of the life and death of Captaine T. Stukeley .. as it hath been acted 1605 (also Simpson, School of Shakspere 1878)
Student, The; or the Oxford and Cambridge monthly miscellany (by T. Warton and others) 1750
Student and intellectual observer, The (2nd series of The intellectual observer) 1868–71
STUDLEY, JOHN The fourth tragedy of L. A. Seneca entituled Hippolytus tr. 1567 (1581)
The seventh tragedie .. entituled Medea tr. 1566
The eyght tragedie .. entituled Agamemnon tr. 1566
The tenth tragedy .. entituled Hercules Œtæus tr. c 1566 (1581)
—— in Seneca his tenne tragedies (ed. T. Newton 1581)
Stukeley, Captain Thomas 1605: see Stucley
STUKELEY, WILLIAM Abury, a temple of the Druids 1743
The family memoirs of William Stukeley, and the antiquarian and other correspondence 17.. (Surtees Soc. 1882–87)
Itinerarium curiosum; or an account of the antiquitys and remarkable curiositys in nature and art observ'd in travels thro' Great Britain 1724 (1776)
Palæographia sacra, or discourses on sacred subjects 1763
Stonehenge, a temple restor'd to the British Druids 1740
STURMY, SAMUEL The mariners magazine, or Sturmy's mathematical and practical arts etc. 1669 (1683)
STURT, CHARLES Narrative of an expedition into central Australia 1849
Two expeditions into the interior of southern Australia 1833
STURTEVANT, SIMON Metallica; or the treatise of metallica 1612 (1855)
STYWARD, THOMAS The pathwaie to martiall discipline 1581
SUCKLING, SIR JOHN Aglaura 1638
Brennoralt, a tragedy 1639 (1646)
Fragmenta aurea, a collection of all the incomparable peeces written by Sir J. Suckling a 1642 (1646, 1648)
The goblins, a comedy 1638 (1646)
Poems, plays and other remains a 1642 (1874)
Sue's (M. J. Eugène) Mysteries of Paris tr. 1844
SUFFOLK, HENRIETTA HOWARD, COUNTESS OF Letters to and from Henrietta, Countess of Suffolk 1712–67 (1824)
Suffolk words, from Cullum's History of Hawsted 1813 (E.D.S. 1879)
Suicide, a poem 1773
SULIVAN, RICHARD J. A view of nature 1794
SULLIVAN, SIR EDWARD Woman the predominant partner 1894
SULLIVAN, JAMES The history of the district of Maine 1795
SULLY, JAMES Outlines of psychology 1884
Sensation and intuition; studies in psychology and æsthetics 1874
Summary of all the religious houses in England and Wales, A (by G. Duckett) 1717
Summary upon the famous poeme of William of Saluste, Lord of Bartas, A learned tr. (by T. Lodge) 1621
Summary view of the feudal law, A, with the differences of the Scots law from it (by J. Dundas) 1710
SUMNER, CHARLES Orations and speeches v.d. (1850)
Sunday magazine, The 1864–
Supernatural religion (by W. R. Cassels) 1874–77
Supplication of certaine masse priests falsely called catholikes directed to the kings maiestie, The 1604
Supplication of the poore commons, A 1546 (with Fish, Supplication, E.E.T.S. 1871)
A supplycacion to .. Kynge Henry the eyght 1544 (ibid.)
Suppression of monasteries, Three chapters of letters relating to the 1528–55 (Camden Soc. 1843)
SURFLET, RICHARD Estienne (C.) and Liébault's (J.) Maison rustique, or the countrie farme tr. 1600
—— augmented by G. Markham 1616
SURR, THOMAS S. Splendid misery (a novel) 1801
A winter in London; or sketches of fashion, a novel 1805 (1806)
SURREY, HENRY HOWARD, EARL OF Works a 1547 (Chalmers 1810; ed. Nott 1815; Anglia XXIX, 1906)
Certain bokes (II and IV) of Virgiles Æneis tr. a 1547 (1557; Roxb. Club 1814)
Five chapters from the Ecclesiastes of Solomon paraphrastically versified a 1547 (Park, Harington's Nugæ antiquæ II, 1804; Anglia XXIX)
Songes and sonettes, written by the .. Lorde Henry Haward late Earle of Surrey, and other (Tottel's miscellany) a 1547 (1557; Arber)
Surrey and Kent Sewer commission, Court minutes of the 1569–79 (L.C.C. 1909)
Surrey Archæological Society, Collections of the (1858–)
Surrey glossary 1876, 1893: see Gower, G. L.
SURTEES, ROBERT A memoir (with poems and letters) of R. Surtees (a 1834) by G. Taylor (Surtees Soc. 1852)
SURTEES, ROBERT S. Ask mamma 1858
Handley Cross; or the spa hunt 1843 (1854)
Mr. Facey Romford's hounds 1865
Mr. Sponge's sporting tour 1853
Surtees Society, Publications of the (1835–)
—— Miscellanea (1861)
—— A volume of English miscellanies (1890)
Survey of the affaires of the United Netherlands, An exact 1665
Survey of the insolent .. libel entituled Naphtali, A (by Bp. A. Honyman) 1668 (1669)
Susan: a novel (anon.) 1809
Sussex archæological collections, published by the Sussex Archæological Society (1848–)
SUTCLIFFE, HALLIWELL Mistress Barbara Cunliffe 1902
Shameless Wayne 1900
SUTCLIFFE, MATTHEW A briefe examination of a certaine .. petition presented .. to the kinges .. maiestie 1606
A briefe replie to a certaine .. libel lately published by a seditious Jesuite, calling himselfe N. D .. by O. E. (i.e. Sutcliffe) 1600

SUTHERLAND, ALEXANDER St. Kathleen, or the rock of Dunnismoyle (anon.) 1820
SUTHERLAND, ALEXANDER 1892: see Dawson, G. M.
SUTHERLAND, WILLIAM The ship builder's assistant 1711
SUTTON, EDWARD North Lincolnshire words 1881 (E.D.S.)
SUTTON, THOMAS A dictionary of photography 1858
SWAINSON, CHARLES A handbook of weather folk-lore 1873
Provincial names and folk lore of British birds 1885 (E.D.S.)
SWAINSON, WILLIAM On the natural history and classification of birds 1836–37
—— of fishes etc. 1838–39
—— of quadrupeds 1835
Zoological illustrations 1820–33
—— and SHUCKARD, W. E. On the history and natural arrangement of insects 1840
Swaledale glossary 1873: see Harland, J.
SWAN, ANNIE S. Aldersyde, a Border story 1883
Carlowrie; or, among Lothian folk 1884
Doris Cheyne, the story of a noble life 1888
The gates of Eden 1887
A victory won 1895
SWAN, JOHN Speculum mundi, or a glasse representing the face of the world 1635 (1643, 1670)
SWAYNE, HENRY J. F. Ed. Churchwardens' accounts of S. Edmund and S. Thomas, Sarum, 1443–1702 a 1892 (1896)
Sweden, A short survey of the kingdom of 1632
Swedenborg's (or Swedberg, Emanuel) The animal kingdom, considered anatomically, physically, and philosophically tr. J. J. G. Wilkinson 1843
The apocalypse revealed tr. 1791 (1876)
Heaven and its wonders, .. and hell tr. S. Noble 1839 (revised 1851)
The true christian religion tr. 1781 (1786, 1873)
SWEET, CHARLES A dictionary of English law 1882
SWEET, HENRY An Anglo-saxon reader 1876 (1908)
—— A second Anglo-saxon reader 1887
A handbook of phonetics 1877
A history of English sounds 1874 (1888)
A new English grammar 1892–98
Ed. The oldest English texts (E.E.T.S. 1885)
A primer of phonetics 1890
The student's dictionary of Anglo-saxon 1897
SWETE, HENRY B. Studies in the teaching of our Lord 1903
SWETNAM, JOSEPH The arraignment of lewd, idle, froward and unconstant women 1615
Swetnam the woman-hater arraigned by women 1620 (Grosart 1880)
SWETTENHAM, FRANK A. Malay sketches 1895
SWIFT, GILBERT Somerley: school-boy and undergraduate 1900
SWIFT, JONATHAN Works a 1745 (1735–38–46, 1751, 1755–68, 1814, 1841)
The battle of the books 1697 (with Tale of a tub 1704)
The bubble: a poem (Upon the South Sea project) 1721
Cadenus and Vanessa, a poem 1713 (1726)
A complete collection of genteel and ingenious conversation (Polite conversation) 1731–38 (1738; Wks. 1738 VI)
The conduct of the allies, and of the late ministry, in beginning and carrying on the present war 1711
Correspondence a 1745 (1841)
Directions to servants in general 1729 (1745)
A discourse concerning the mechanical operation of the spirit 1704 (with Tale of a tub)
A discourse of the contests and dissensions between the nobles and the commons in Athens and Rome 1701 (Misc. 1711)
The Drapier letters 1724, 1735
The history of the four last years of the queen a 1745 (1758)
The history of Martin 1720 (Misc. Works)
The journal to Stella 1710–13 (Wks., also 1901)
A letter .. concerning the sacramental test 1708 (Misc. 1711)
Letters by Dr. Swift and several of his friends 1703–40 (1767)
Letters to and from Dr. J. Swift 1714–38 (1741)
Miscellaneous works (The tale of a tub, Miscellanies in prose and verse) 1720
Miscellanies in prose and verse 1711, 1722
—— (with contributions by Pope, Arbuthnot, and Gay) 1727–35
A modest proposal for preventing the children of poor people from being a burthen to their parents, or the country 1729
Predictions for the year 1708, by I. Bickerstaff 1708 (Misc. 1711; Arber, Eng. Garner VI)
—— Vindication of I. Bickerstaff 1709 (ibid.)
A proposal for correcting, improving, and ascertaining the English tongue 1712
The publick spirit of the Whigs set forth 1714
Some free thoughts upon the present state of affairs 1714
The South Sea project: see Bubble, above
A tale of a tub, written for the universal improvement of mankind .. To which is added, An account of a battel between the antient and modern books in St. James's library 1704
Travels into several remote nations of the world, in four parts, by Lemuel Gulliver 1726
—— and others Memoirs of P. P. clerk of this parish c 1725 (Misc. 1727)
SWIFT, THEOPHILUS The gamblers, a poem 1777
SWINBOURNE, ALFRED Picture logic; or the grave made gay 1874 (1875)
SWINBURNE, ALGERNON CHARLES Atalanta in Calydon, a tragedy 1864 (1865, 1868)
Bothwell; a tragedy 1874
Chapman's (G.) Works, Poems and minor translations Ed. with an introduction by A. C. Swinburne 1875
Chastelard; a tragedy 1865
Erechtheus; a tragedy 1876
Locrine, a tragedy 1887
Miscellanies 1877 etc. (1886)
A note on Charlotte Brontë 1877
Note of an English republican on the Muscovite crusade 1876
Songs before sunrise 1871
Songs of the springtides 1880
Studies in prose and poetry 1883–93 (1894)
A study of Ben Jonson 1889
A study of Shakespeare 1879 (1880)

SWINBURNE, ALGERNON CHARLES (cont.)
A study of Victor Hugo 1886
Under the microscope 1872
William Blake, a critical essay 1867 (1868)
SWINBURNE, HENRY A briefe treatise of testaments and last willes 1590
A treatise of spousals or matrimonial contracts a 1623 (1686)
SWINBURNE, HENRY Travels through Spain 1779
SWINHOE, ROBERT Narrative of the North China campaign of 1860 1861
SWINNOCK, GEORGE The door of salvation opened by the key of regeneration 1660
SWITZER, STEPHEN Ichnographia, or the nobleman, gentleman, and gardener's recreation 1718
An introduction to a general system of hydrostaticks and hydraulicks 1729
The practical fruit gardener 1724
The practical kitchen gardener 1727
SYBTHORPE, ROBERT 1627: see Sibthorp
SYDENHAM, HUMPHREY Sermons upon solemne occasions v.d. (1637)
Sydenham Society, Publications of the New (1859–1901)
—— A biennial retrospect of medicine, surgery, and their allied sciences 1867–68 1869
—— Lexicon of medicine and allied sciences. By H. Power and L. W. Sedgwick 1879–99
Sydney papers: see Sidney state papers
Sylph, The; a novel (anon.) 1779
'SYLVANUS' The bye-lanes and downs of England, with turf scenes and characters 1850
SYLVESTER, JAMES JOSEPH Collected mathematical papers 1837–97 (1904–12)
SYLVESTER, JOSUAH Complete works a 1618 (Grosart 1880)
Bethulians rescue tr. 1614
A divine and true tragi-comedy; Job triumphant in his triall 1615
Du Bartas' (G. de S.) The batail of Yvry tr. 1614
Du Bartas his divine weekes and workes tr. 1591–1608 (1605, 1608, 1641)
Du Bartas' Triumph of faith, the sacrifice of Isaac, the ship-wracke of Jonas etc. tr. 1592
Lachrimæ lachrimarum; or the distillation of teares shede for the death of .. Panaretus 1612
Little Bartas, or brief meditations on the power .. and goodnes of God 1614
The maidens blush, or Joseph tr. a 1618
Micro-cosmo-graphia: the little-worlds description tr. (from H. Smith) 1613
Monodia 1594
The parliament of vertues royall (Panaretus) tr. 1614
—— The second session of the parliament of vertues royall 1616
The profit of imprisonment (A paradox against libertie) tr. 1593–94 (1605)
Tobacco battered and the pipes shattered c 1615 (1617)
Urania, or the heavenly muse 1605
SYLVESTER, MATTHEW Ed. Reliquiæ Baxterianæ: or Mr. R. Baxter's narrative of the most memorable passages of his life and times 1696
SYMES, MICHAEL An account of an embassy to the kingdom of Ava in 1795 1800
SYMMER, ARCHIBALD Rest for the weary 1630
A spirituall posie for Zion 1629
SYMMONS, CHARLES The life of John Milton 1806 (1810, 1822)
SYMMONS, EDWARD A loyall subjects beliefe, expressed in a letter to Master S. Marshall 1643
A vindication of king Charles 1648
SYMMONS, JOHN The Agamemnon of Æschylus tr. 1824
SYMONDS, JOHN ADDINGTON Italian byways 1883
The life of Michelangelo Buonarroti 1893
Renaissance in Italy 1875–86 (1898)
Shakespeare's predecessors in the English drama 1884
Shelley (English men of letters) 1878
Sketches in Italy and Greece 1874
Sketches and studies in Italy 1879
Sketches and studies in Italy and Greece (a new ed. of the two prec. and Italian byways 1898)
Studies of the Greek poets 1873–76
J. A. Symonds; a biography compiled from his papers and correspondence, by H. F. Brown (1895)
SYMONDS, JOSEPH A sermon before sundry of the House of Commons 1641
SYMONDS, RICHARD Diary of the marches of the royal army during the great civil war 1644–45 (Camden Soc. 1859)
SYMONDS, WILLIAM S. Records of the rocks; or, notes on the geology of Wales, Devon, Cornwall, etc. 1872
SYMONS, ARTHUR The symbolist movement in literature 1899
SYMSON, ANDREW A large description of Galloway 1684–92 (1823)
SYMSON, ARCHIBALD: see Simson
System of natural history, A. Botany, by E. Smith; Zoology, by W. S. Dallas 1855 (Orr's Circle of the sciences)

T

T., C. An advice how to plant tobacco in England 1615
T., D. 1608: see Tuvil, D.
T., D. Hieragonisticon; or, Corah's doom. Being an answer to (J. Eachard's) two letters of enquiry into the grounds and occasions of the contempt of the clergy and religion 1672
T., F. The case is altered. How? Aske Dalio and Millo 1604
T., F. 1712: see Tanner, F.
T., I. 1596: see Tanner, I.
T., I. Grim, the collier of Croydon: or the devil and his dame a 1600 (Gratiæ theatrales 1662; Dodsley, Old plays)
T., R. (= Christopher Carlile) A discourse, wherein is plainly proued .. that Peter was neuer at Rome etc. 1572
T., W. Nannini's (R.) Civill considerations upon many and sundrie histories tr. 1601
T., W. The compleat gunner 1672 (Book III of T. Venn's Military & maritime discipline)
T., W.: see Tomlinson, W.
TABOR, ELIZA Rachel's secret 1866
TAILOR, ROBERT The hogge hath lost his pearle 1614 (Dodsley)
TAIT, JAMES Mind in matter: a short argument on theism 1884; ed. 3, enlarged 1892

TAIT, PETER G. An elementary treatise on quaternions 1867 (1873)
Lectures on some recent advances in physical science 1876
See also Stewart, B.; Thomson, Abp. W.
Tait's Edinburgh magazine 1832–61
TALBOT, CATHERINE: see Carter, Elizabeth
TALBOT, CHARLES J. C., 19TH EARL OF SHREWSBURY Meliora, or better times to come ed. Viscount Ingestre 1852–53
TALBOT, CHRISTOPHER R. M. Newton's (I.) Enumeration of lines of the third order tr. 1861
TALBOT, BP. WILLIAM Charge to the clergy of his diocese (of Oxford) at his visitation 1712
Tales and quicke answeres, very mery, and pleasant to rede ? 1535 (in Shakspeare's Jest book 1814–15)
TALFOURD, SIR THOMAS N. The Athenian captive; a tragedy 1838
The Castilian; an historical tragedy 1853
Final memorials of Charles Lamb 1848
Glencoe; or the fate of the Macdonalds; a tragedy 1840
Ion: a tragedy 1835
The letters of Charles Lamb, with a sketch of his life 1837
Vacation rambles and thoughts 1845
TALLENTYRE, STEPHEN G. Life of Voltaire 1903
TALMAGE, THOMAS DE WITT Crumbs swept up 1871
The jewels of the soul 1877
Sermons delivered in the Brooklyn tabernacle 1872
Taming of a shrew, A pleasant conceited historie called 1594 (Shaks. Soc. 1844)
Tancred and Gismund: see Wilmot, R.
TANDY, WILLIAM Sangermano's (V.) Description of the Burmese empire tr. 1833
TANNAHILL, ROBERT Poetical works a 1810 (1825)
Poems and songs, chiefly in the Scottish dialect a 1810 (1815)
The soldier's return; a Scottish interlude in two acts, with other poems and songs 1807
TANNER, F. The plainest, easiest, and prettiest method of writing short-hand 1712
TANNER, I. A sermon preached at Paules Crosse, by I. T. 1596
TANNER, THOMAS H. A manual of the practice of medicine 1854 (1865, 1869, 1875)
On the signs and diseases of pregnancy 1860
Tannhäuser 1861: see Fane, J. C. H.
TAPPING, THOMAS The rhymed chronicle of Edward Manlove concerning the liberties and customs of the lead-mines within the wapentake of Wirksworth, Derbyshire, from the original ed. of 1653, to which is affixed a glossary 1851 (E.D.S. 1874)
TARLTON, RICHARD Newes out of purgatorie a 1588 (1590; Shaks. Soc. 1844)
Tarltons jests 1611 (1638; Shaks. Soc. 1844)
Tarquin and Tullia (a poem attributed to Dryden) c 1700 (in Poems on affairs of state III, 1704)
TARRAS, WILLIAM Poems, chiefly in the Scottish dialect 1804
TASISTRO, LOUIS F. Comte de Paris' History of the civil war in America tr. 1875
Tasso's Aminta tr. 1628
TATE, FRANCIS King Edward II's household and wardrobe ordinances tr. 1601 (Chaucer Soc. 1876)
TATE, GEORGE The geology of the district traversed by the Roman wall 1867 (in J. C. Bruce, Roman wall 1867)
TATE, JAMES An introduction to the principal Greek tragic and comic metres 1827
TATE, NAHUM Elegies 1699
Poems 1677
Portrait-royal; a poem upon her majesty's picture set up in Guildhall 1703
The triumph; or warriour's welcome 1705
See also Cowley, A.; Garth, Sir S.; and Heliodorus
—— and BRADY, NICHOLAS A new version of the Psalms of David, fitted to the tunes used in churches 1696 (1698, 1751)
—— and DRYDEN, JOHN The second part of Absalom and Achitophel 1682
TATE, RALPH A plain and easy account of the land and fresh-water mollusks of Great Britain 1866
TATHAM, JOHN Aqua triumphalis; being a relation of the city of London entertaining their Majesties upon the Thames 1662
The distracted state; a tragedy 1641 (1651)
London's tryumph 1659
The Scots figgaries: or, a knot of knaves; a comedy 1652
Tatler, The. By Isaac Bickerstaff (i.e. Sir R. Steele, J. Addison, and others) 1709–11
TAUBMAN, MATTHEW London's triumph, or the goldsmith's jubilee 1687
TAUNT, HENRY W. A new map of the river Thames from Oxford to London 1872
TAUNTON, ETHELRED L. The English Black Monks of St. Benedict 1897
TAUNTON, WILLIAM P. Reports of cases argued and determined in the Court of Common Pleas 1810–23
TAUTPHŒUS, BARONESS VON At odds; a novel 1863
Cyrilla; a tale 1853
The initials; a novel (anon.) 1850
Quits; a novel 1857
TAVERNER, JOHN Certaine experiments concerning fish and fruite 1600
TAVERNER, RICHARD The garden of wysdom 1539
Prouerbes or adagies with newe addicions, gathered out of the Chiliades of Erasmus 1539 (1545, 1552)
Tavernier's travels 1677–78: see Phillips, John
TAYLOR, ALFRED S. Poisons, in relation to medical jurisprudence and medicine 1848
TAYLOR, ANN (a 1866) and JANE (a 1824) Poetical works a 1866 (1878)
Original poems for infant minds 1808–14 (1843)
Rhymes for the nursery 1836
TAYLOR, BAYARD Critical essays and literary notes 1880
Eldorado; or, adventures in the path of empire 1850
Goethe's Faust tr. 1871 (1886)
Hannah Thurston: a story of American life 1863
Northern travel 1858
Pictures of Palestine, Asia Minor, Sicily, and Spain; or, the lands of the Saracen 1855
Poems 1856
Prince Deukalion 1878
Studies in German literature 1879
TAYLOR, CHARLES An introduction to the ancient and modern geometry of conics 1881

TAYLOR, EDWARD Behmen's theosophick philosophy unfolded 1691
TAYLOR, FRANCIS E. The folk-speech of South Lancashire 1901
TAYLOR, SIR HENRY Edwin the fair; an historical drama 1842
Isaac Comnenus: a play 1827
Philip van Artevelde; a dramatic romance 1834
St. Clement's Eve; a play 1862
The statesman 1836
Autobiography 1800–75 1885
TAYLOR, ISAAC (of Ongar) The ship; a description of different kinds of vessels a 1829 (1846)
TAYLOR, ISAAC (of Stanford Rivers) Ancient Christianity, and the doctrines of the Oxford tracts for the times 1839–42
Elements of thought; or, first lessons in the knowledge of the mind 1822 (1824)
Fanaticism 1833
Four lectures on spiritual Christianity 1841
History of the transmission of ancient books to modern times 1827
Home education (anon.) 1838
Logic in theology, and other essays 1830–31 (1859)
Loyola: and Jesuitism in its rudiments 1849
Natural history of enthusiasm (anon.) 1829
Physical theory of another life (anon.) 1836
The process of historical proof exemplified 1828
The restoration of belief (anon.) 1852 (1855)
Saturday evening (anon.) 1832
The spirit of the Hebrew poetry 1861
Spiritual despotism (anon.) 1835
Ultimate civilization, and other essays 1860
Wesley and Methodism 1851
TAYLOR, ISAAC (Canon of York) The alphabet; an account of the origin and development of letters 1883
Etruscan researches 1874
The origin of the Aryans 1889
Words and places: or etymological illustrations of history, ethnology, and geography 1864 (1873)
TAYLOR, JAMES The Scottish covenanters 1882
TAYLOR, JEREMY Works a 1667 (1822, 1828, 1831, 1847–54)
Clerus Domini: or, a discourse of the divine institution of the office ministeriall 1651
Contemplations of the state of man a 1667 (1684, 1699)
Deus justificatus; two discourses of original sin 1656
A discourse concerning prayer ex tempore, or by pretence of the Spirit, in justification of authorized and set formes of liturgie (anon.) 1646
— enlarged ed., entitled An apology for authorized and set forms of liturgie 1649
A dissuasive from Popery to the people of Ireland 1664, 1667 (1668)
Ductor dubitantium; or the rule of conscience in all her generall measures 1660
Ἐνιαυτός: a course of sermons for all the Sundaies of the year 1653–55
A funeral sermon (on 2 Sam. xiv. 14) preached at the obsequies of the Countesse of Carbery 1650
The golden grove; or a manuall of daily prayers and letanies 1655
The great exemplar of sanctity and holy life 1649
Of the sacred order and offices of episcopacy 1642
The real presence and spirituall of Christ in the blessed sacrament proved against the doctrine of transubstantiation 1654
The rule and exercises of holy living 1650 (1676)
The rule and exercises of holy dying 1651 (1686)
A sermon preached at the funeral of John (Bramhall) late Lord Archbishop of Armagh 1663
A sermon preached in Saint Maries Church in Oxford upon the anniversary of the Gunpowder-treason 1638
Θεολογία ἐκλεκτική. A discourse of the liberty of prophesying 1647
Unum necessarium: or, the doctrine and practice of repentance 1655
The worthy communicant 1660
See also Artificial handsomeness
TAYLOR, JOHN (Water poet) Works 1630
Works a 1653 (Hindley 1872; Spenser Soc. 1868–78)
An apology for private preaching 1642
An armado, or nauye of a hundred and three ships 1627
The carriers' cosmography 1637 (in Arber, Eng. Garner I)
Divers crabtree lectures 1639
The great eater of Kent, or part of the exploits of Nicholas Wood 1630
A kicksey winsey; or a lerry come-twang 1619
A new discovery by sea 1623
The nipping or snipping of abuses 1614
Odcombs complaint: or Coriats funerall epicedium 1613
The olde old very olde man: or the age and long life of T. Par 1635
Part of this summers travels, or news from Hell, Hull and Hallifax 1640
The pennyles pilgrimage 1618
The praise, antiquity and commodity of beggery, beggers and begging 1621
The praise of hemp-seed 1620
A short relation of a long journey .. encompassing the Principalitie of Wales 1652
Sir Gregory Nonsence his newes from no place 1622
The suddaine turne of Fortunes wheele 1631
Taylor's motto: Et habeo, et careo, et curo 1621
Three weekes, three daies, and three houres obseruation and travel from London to Hamburgh 1617
A verry merry wherry-ferry-voyage 1622
The whole life and progresse of Henry Walker the ironmonger 1642
The world runnes on wheeles 1623
TAYLOR, JOHN (of Liverpool) Poems and translations 1839
TAYLOR, LAURA W. Ballads and songs of Brittany 1865
TAYLOR, MEADOWS The story of my life 1877 (1878)
TAYLOR, SEDLEY Sound and music 1873 (1896)
TAYLOR, SILAS The history and antiquities of Harwich and Dovercourt. First collected by S. Taylor (a 1678) and now much enlarged by Samuel Dale (1730)
TAYLOR, THOMAS Beard's (T.) Theatre of God's judgements. Part II a 1633 (1642)
A commentarie upon the Epistle of St. Paul to Titus 1612 (1619)
TAYLOR, THOMAS The metamorphosis and philosophical works of Apuleius tr. 1822
Two orations of the emperor Julian tr. 1793

Taylor, Thomas (cont.)
Pausanias' Description of Greece tr. 1794
The works of Plato tr. (nine dialogues by F. Sydenham, the remainder by T. Taylor) 1804
The philosophical and mathematical commentaries of Proclus tr. 1788–89 (1792)
Taylor, Tom Leicester Square; its associations and its worthies 1874
Pictures in words 1863 (in B. Foster's Pictures of English landscape) See also Leslie, C. R.
Taylor, Mrs. Tom: see Taylor, Laura W.
Taylor, William Scots poems 1787
—— ed. 2, Poems chiefly in the Scottish dialect 1827
Taylor, William English synonyms discriminated 1813
Goethe's (J. W. von) Iphigenia in Tauris tr. 1793
Historic survey of German poetry 1828–30
A memoir of the life and writings of the late W. Taylor, containing his correspondence with R. Southey, etc. By J. W. Robberds (1843)
Teall, Jethro J. H. British petrography 1888
Techmer, F. Internationale Zeitschrift für allgemeine Sprachwissenschaft 1884–
Technological dictionary, English-German-French 1878 (ed. 3)
Teckely, Count 1693: see Memoirs
Tegetmeier, William B. The cottager's manual of poultry keeping 1893
The poultry book 1867 (1873)
Profitable poultry 1853 (1854)
Teignmouth, John Shore, Baron Memoirs of the life, writings and correspondence of Sir William Jones 1804 (1807)
Memoir of the life and correspondence of John Shore, baron Teignmouth (1843)
Teixeira's (P.) Travels tr. by William F. Sinclair 1902 (Hakluyt Soc.)
Telegraphic journal, The; and monthly illustrated review of electrical science 1872–
Tell-Trothes new-yeares gift; beeing Robin Good-fellowes newes 1593 (New Shaks. Soc. 1876)
Tempest, Sir Richard An entertainment of solitarinesse 1649
Temple, Frederick The relations between religion and science 1884 (1885)
Temple, Sir John The Irish rebellion 1646 (1746)
Temple, Josiah H. and Sheldon, George A history of the town of Northfield, Massachusetts 1875
Temple, Launcelot Sketches; or essays on various subjects 1758
Temple, Neville: see Fane, J. C. H.
Temple, Sir William Works a 1699 (1720, 1731, 1757, 1770)
An introduction to the history of England 1695
Letters written by Sir W. Temple and other ministers of state v.d. (1700–03)
Miscellanea 1680–90
Observations upon the United Provinces of the Netherlands 1673
Temple Bar; a London magazine 1861–
Templeton, William The locomotive engine popularly explained 1848 (ed. 2)
Ten Brink's (Bernhard) Early English literature tr. by H. M. Kennedy 1883
—— History of English literature Vol. II. tr. by W. C. Robinson 1893
—— Vol. III. tr. by L. Dora Schmitz 1896
Five lectures on Shakespeare tr. by Julia Franklin 1895
The language and metre of Chaucer tr. by M. Bentinck Smith 1901
Tender father, The 1775
Tenison-Woods, Julian E. Fish and fisheries of New South Wales 1882
Tennant, William Indian recreations 1803
Tennant, William Anster concert 1811
Anster fair; a poem 1812 (1827)
Anster fair and other poems 1838
Cardinal Beaton; a drama 1823
Papistry storm'd 1819 (1827)
The thane of Fife 1822
Tennent, Sir James Emerson Ceylon 1859
Sketches of the natural history of Ceylon 1861
The story of the guns 1864
Tenney, William J. The military and naval history of the rebellion in the United States 1865
Tennyson, Alfred, Lord Works a 1892 (1894)
Poems 1830, 1833, 1842
Becket 1884
The cup: a tragedy 1881
The falcon 1879
The foresters 1892
Harold: a drama 1876
Idylls of the king. Enid (renamed Geraint and Enid in 1870; divided into two parts, The marriage of Geraint and Geraint and Enid in 1886), Vivien (renamed Merlin and Vivien in 1870), Elaine (renamed Lancelot and Elaine in 1870), Guinevere 1859; Coming of Arthur, Holy Grail, Pelleas and Ettarre, Passing of Arthur 1870; Last tournament, Gareth and Lynette 1872; Balin and Balan 1885
In memoriam A. H. H. 1850
Maud, and other poems 1855
The princess; a medley 1847
The promise of May 1882
Queen Mary: a drama 1875
Tiresias, and other poems 1885
Tennyson, Hallam, 2nd Lord Alfred Lord Tennyson. A memoir by his son 1897
Teonge, Henry Diary 1675–79 (1825)
Terence tr. 1598: see Bernard, R.
Teresa, St., Life 1671: see Woodhead, A.
Termes de la ley, Les; or certaine difficult and obscure words and termes of the common lawes of this realme expounded (an enlarged ed. of W. Rastell's Exposicions of the termes of the lawes) 1624 (1641, 1708)
Terry, Edward A relation of Sir T. Roe's voyage into the Easte Indies (anon.) 1655. See also Havers, G.
Terton, Alice Lights and shadows in a hospital 1902
Test of filial duty (by Sarah Scott) 1772
Testament of love: see Usk, T.
Testamenta Eboracensia; or wills registered at York v.d. (Surtees Soc. 1836–1902)
Testamenta vetusta: see Nicolas, Sir N. H.
Testaments of the twelve Patriarchs 1575: see Gilby, A.
Tester, William H. L. Poems 1867

Thacher, James A military journal during the American war 1775–83 (1823)
Thacker, Thomas The courser's companion; to which is added the breeder's guide 1834–35
Rules for the decision of courses 1843
Thackeray, Anne Isabella: see Ritchie, A. I.
Thackeray, William Makepeace Works a 1863 (1869–86)
The adventures of Philip on his way through the world 1862
The book of snobs 1848
Catherine 1840
Denis Duval a 1863
Dr. Birch and his young friends 1848
The English humourists of the eighteenth century 1851–53
Essay on the genius of George Cruikshank 1840
Fitzboodle's professions 1842–43
The four Georges 1860
The history of the great Hoggarty diamond 1841
The history of Henry Esmond 1852
The history of Pendennis 1849–50
The history of Samuel Titmarsh 1849
The Irish sketch-book 1843
The Kickleburys on the Rhine 1850
Lovel the widower 1860
The luck of Barry Lyndon 1844
Men's wives 1843
Miscellanies, prose and verse 1855–57
Mrs. Perkins's ball 1847
The Newcomes; memoirs of a most respectable family 1854–55
The Paris sketch-book 1840
The professor 1837
Roundabout papers 1860–63
A shabby-genteel story 1840
The second funeral of Napoleon 1841
Some passages in the life of Major Gahagan 1838–39
Vanity fair 1848
The Virginians 1858–59
The Yellowplush papers 1838–40
Thanes of Cawdor, The book of the. A series of papers selected from the charter room at Cawdor 1236–1742 (Spalding Cl. 1859)
Thausing's (J. E.) Theory and practice of the preparation of malt and the fabrication of beer tr. by W. T. Brannt 1882
Theakston, Michael British angling flies 1883
Thearle, Samuel J. P. Naval architecture 1874
Theatre of worldlings 1569: see Roest, T.
Thelyphthora 1780–81: see Madan, M.
Theobald, Lewis The cave of poverty; a poem 1714
Double falshood; a play 1728
Shakespeare restored 1726
The works of Shakespeare. Collated with the oldest copies and corrected, with notes explanatory and critical 1733
Theologian, The 1844–47
Theophania: or, severall modern histories represented by way of romance 1655
Theophrastus. Characters: or, the manners of the age; with moral characters of Theophrastus tr. 1709
Thersites. A new enterlude called Thersytes 15.. (? 1560; in Pollard, Eng. miracle plays 1890; Hazl., Dodsley)
Thevet's (A.) New found worlde tr. 1568: see Hacket, T.
Thief-catcher, The; or, villainy detected 1753
Thierry's (J. N. A.) Formation and progress of the tiers état or the third estate in France tr. by F. B. Wells 1855
Thirlwall, Bp. Connop A history of Greece 1835–47
Letters to a friend a 1875 (1881)
Remains; literary and theological a 1875 (ed. J. J. S. Perowne 1877–78)
Schleiermacher's (F.) Critical essay on the gospel of St. Luke tr. 1825
Thiselton-Dyer, Thomas F. British popular customs 1875
English folk-lore 1878
Folk-lore of plants 1889
Thiselton-Dyer, Sir William T. Ed. Flora Capensis: being a systematic description of the plants of Cape Colony, Caffraria, and Port Natal (vols. IV–VII) 1897–1909
Ed. Flora of tropical Africa (vols. IV–VIII) 1899–1913
The needs of biology 1876
See also Bennett, A. W.; Trimen, H.
Thom, Walter The history of Aberdeen 1811
Thom, William Works 1799
Thom, William Rhymes and recollections of a hand-loom weaver 1844
Thomas, Annie (Mrs. Pender Cudlip) Denis Donne 1864
The modern housewife; or how we live now 1883
On guard 1865
Played out 1866
That other woman 1889
Walter Goring 1866
Thomas, Edward The chronicles of the Pathân Kings of Delhi 1871
Thomas, Ernest C. Lange's (F. A.) History of materialism tr. 1877
The Philobiblon of Richard de Bury tr. 1888 (1902)
Thomas, Gabriel An historical and geographical account of Pensilvania and of West-New-Jersey in America 1698 (1848)
Thomas, Henry S. The rod in India 1873
Thomas, J. J. Froudacity 1889
Thomas, Joseph A complete pronouncing medical dictionary 1886
A comprehensive medical dictionary 1864
Thomas, Pascoe A true and impartial journal of a voyage to the South-Seas and round the globe under the command of Commodore G. Anson 1745
Thomas, Ralph A few words on swimming; with practical hints 1868
Handbook of fictitious names 1868
Swimming 1904
Thomas, Theodore G. A practical treatise on the diseases of women 1868 (1872)
Thomas, Thomas Dictionarium linguæ Latinæ et Anglicanæ 1588 (1606)
Thomas, William The historie of Italie 1549 (1561)
The pilgrim: a dialogue of the life and actions of King Henry the eighth a 1554 (1861)
Principal rules of the Italian grammer, with a dictionarie 1550 (1567)
Thomas of Erceldoune: see Erceldoune, Thomas of

Thomason tracts. Pamphlets, books, newspapers, and manuscripts relating to the Civil War, the Commonwealth, and Restoration, collected by George Thomason 1640–61 (British Museum)
Thompson, Benjamin Kotzebue's (A. F. F. von) Stranger tr. 1802
Thompson, Charles W. Twelve months in the British legion 1836
Thompson, D'Arcy Wentworth Aristotle's Historia animalium tr. 1910
Thompson, Edith History of England 1873
Thompson, Edward The fair quaker: or, the humours of the navy. Formerly written by C. Shadwell, and now alter'd with great additions, and a new character, by E. Thompson 1773
The meretriciad (anon.) 1761 (1765)
Thompson, Edward Cullen's Nosologia methodica 1818–20
Thompson, Sir Edward Maunde Palaeography 1910
Thompson, Edward P. The passions of animals 1851
Thompson, Francis J. Poems 1893
New poems 1897
Thompson, Sir Henry The diseases of the prostate, their pathology and treatment 1860 (1868)
Thompson's (John) man 1829: see John Thompson's man
Thompson, John V. Zoological researches and illustrations 1828–30
Thompson, Maurice Witchery of archery 1879
Thompson, Pishey The history and antiquities of Boston 1856
Thompson, Robert The gardener's assistant 1859
Thompson, Robert J. The proofs of life after death 1907
Thompson, Silvanus P. Dynamo-electric machinery 1884
Elementary lessons in electricity and magnetism 1881
Philipp Reis: inventor of the telephone 1883
Thompson, Theophilus Annals of influenza or epidemic catarrhal fever in Great Britain from 1510 to 1837 1852
Thompson, Thomas The English rogue; a new comedy 1668
Thompson, Thomas Perronet Audi alteram partem 1857–61
Exercises, political and others 18.. (1842)
Thompson, William The royal navy-men's advocate 1757
Thompson, William Poems a 1766 (1810)
Poems on several occasions 1757
Thompson, William T. Major Jones's courtship (anon.) 1844
Thompson street poker club, The 1889
Thoms, William J. Ed. Anecdotes and traditions, illustrative of early English history and literature v.d. (Camden Soc. 1839)
The book of the court 1838 (1844)
Ed. A collection of early prose romances v.d. (1828, 1858)
Thomson, Anthony Todd The London dispensatory 1815 (1818)
Thomson, Sir Charles W. The depths of the sea 1873
The voyage of the 'Challenger' 1877
Thomson, David Musings among the heather: being poems chiefly in the Scottish dialect 1881
Thomson, David P. Introduction to meteorology 1849
Thomson, Henry J. 1921: see Lindsay, W. M.
Thomson, James Works a 1748 (1773)
The castle of indolence; an allegorical poem 1748
Edward and Eleanora; a tragedy 1739
Liberty; a poem 1735–36
The seasons (Autumn 1730; Spring 1728; Summer 1727; Winter 1726) 1746
Tancred and Sigismunda; a tragedy 1745
The tragedy of Sophonisba 1730
Thomson, James The city of dreadful night 1874
—— with some other poems 1880
Essays and phantasies 1881
Vane's story, Weddah and Om-el-Bonain, and other poems 1881
Thomson, John Lectures on inflammation 1813
Thomson, John Etymons of English words 1826
Thomson, John A treatise on hat-making and felting 1868
Thomson, John The Straits of Malacca, Indo-China, and China 1875
Thomson, John Arthur Outlines of zoology 1892
The science of life 1899
Thomson, John H. 1871: see Cloud of witnesses
Thomson, Joseph J.: see Poynting, John H.
Thomson, Mowbray The story of Cawnpore 1859
Thomson, Robert D. The British annual and epitome of the progress of science 1837–39
Cyclopædia of chemistry 1854
—— and Thomson, Thomas Records of general science 1835–36
Thomson, Spencer Wanderings among the wild flowers 1854 (1857)
Thomson, Thomas Annals of philosophy 1813–20
An attempt to establish the first principles of chemistry by experiment 1825
Chemistry of inorganic bodies 1831
Chemistry of organic bodies 1838
The history of chemistry 1830–31
Outlines of mineralogy, geology and mineral analysis 1836
A system of chemistry 1802 (1807)
See also Thomson, R. D.
Thomson, Thomas Western Himalaya and Tibet 1852
Thomson, William: see Watson, Robert
Thomson, Abp. William Outline of the laws of thought (anon.) 1842 (1860)
Thomson, Sir William, 1st Baron Kelvin Mathematical and physical papers 18.. (1882–1912)
—— and Tait, Peter G. A treatise on natural philosophy 1867 (1879–83)
Thomson, William Burns Reminiscences of medical missionary work a 1893 (1895)
Thomson, William M. The land and the book 1859 (1874)
Thoreau, Henry D. Early spring in Massachusetts. From the journal of H. D. Thoreau a 1862 (1881)
Excursions in field and forest a 1862 (1863)
Letters to various persons a 1862 (1865)
The Maine woods a 1862 (1864)
Walden; or life in the woods 1854
A week on the Concord and Merrimack rivers 1849
A Yankee in Canada; with anti-slavery and reform papers 1862 (1866)
Thoresby, Abp. John: see Lay folks' catechism
Thoresby, Ralph Diary 1677–1724 (1830)
Ducatus Leodiensis; or the topography of the town and parish of Leedes 1715
Glossary of Yorkshire words from Thoresby's Letter to Ray April 27, 1703 (Ray's Collection of words, E.D.S. 1874)

Thornbury, George Walter Greatheart 1866
The life of J. M. W. Turner 1861
A tour round England 1870
True as steel 1863
— and Walford, Edward Old and new London 1873–78
Thorndike, Herbert A discourse of the forbearance or the penalties which a due reformation requires 1670
A discourse of the right of the Church in a Christian state 1649
Of the government of churches 1641
Thornhill, Mark The personal adventures and experiences of a magistrate during the rise, progress, and suppression of the Indian mutiny 1884
Thornley, George Longus' Daphnis and Chloe tr. 1657 (1893)
Thornley, Thomas Cotton combing machines 1902
Thornthwaite, William H. Guide to photography 1845
Monckhoven's (D. van) Popular treatise on photography tr. 1863
Thornton, Alice Autobiography a 1669 (Surtees Soc. 1875)
Thornton, Bonnell Comedies of Plautus tr. 1767 (1769)
Thornton, Percy M. The Stuart dynasty 1890
Thornton, Richard H. An American glossary 1912
Thornton, Robert J. The philosophy of medicine 1799
Thornton, William Thomas On labour: its wrongful claims and rightful dues 1869
Thornton romances, The (Perceval, Isumbras, Eglamour, and Degrevant) a 1400 (Camden Soc. 1844)
Thoroton, Robert The antiquities of Nottinghamshire 1677; enlarged ed. by John Throsby (1797)
Thorpe, Benjamin Diplomatarium Anglicum aevi Saxonici. A collection of English charters, with a translation of the Anglo-Saxon by B. Thorpe v.d. (1865)
Yule-tide stories 1853
See also Anglo-Saxon laws; Exeter book; Psalter
Thorpe, John Registrum Roffense; or a collection of ancient records, charters, etc. necessary for illustrating the history and antiquities of the cathedral church of Rochester 1769
Thorpe, Thomas Bangs The mysteries of the backwoods 1846
Thorpe, Sir Thomas E. A dictionary of applied chemistry 1890–93
Thorpe, William, The examinacion of master ?1530 (in Arber, Eng. Garner VI)
Thrale, Mrs.: see Piozzi, Hester L.
Thre prestis of Peblis c 1500: see Peebles
Three early English metrical romances (The anturs of Arther, Sir Amadace, The avowynge of King Arther) 14.. (Camden Soc. 1842)
Three fifteenth-century chronicles 14.. (Camden Soc. 1880)
Three Germans tr. 1807
Three Gil Blas 1804: see La Martelière, J. H. F.
Three in Norway 1882: see Lees, J. A.
Three kings of Cologne, The c 1400 (E.E.T.S. 1886)
Three kings' sons, The c 1500 (E.E.T.S. 1895)
Three ladies of London 1584: see Wilson, R.
Threlkeld, Caleb Synopsis stirpium Hibernicarum alphabetice dispositarum 1726
Throsby, John 1797: see Thoroton, R.
Thrupp, George A. The history of coaches 1877
Thrush and nightingale a 1300 (in Reliquiæ ant. I, 1845; Hazlitt, Early pop. poetry I, 1864)
Thudichum, John L. W. A manual of chemical physiology 1872
A treatise on the pathology of the urine 1858
—— and Dupré, August A treatise on the origin, nature, and varieties of wine 1872
Thugs, Illustrations of the history and practices of the (by Edward Thornton) 1837
Thunberg's (C. P.) Travels in Europe, Africa, and Asia tr. 1795
Thurloe, John A collection of state papers 1638–59 (1742)
Thurston, Robert H. A history of the growth of the steam-engine 1878
Thwaites, Edward Ed. Heptateuchus, Liber Job, et Evangelium Nicodemi; Anglo-Saxonice (1698)
Thynne, Francis Animaduersions vppon the annotacions and corrections of some imperfections of impressiones of Chaucers workes 1599 (E.E.T.S. 1875)
Emblemes and epigrames 1600 (E.E.T.S. 1876)
See also Debate; T., F. 1604
Tibbits, Edward T. Medical fashions in the nineteenth century 1884
Tickell, Richard The camp, a musical entertainment 1778 (1795)
Tickell, Thomas Poetical works a 1740 (1807)
Poems a 1740 (1790)
An account of the life and writings of Joseph Addison 1721 (Addison's Works 1721; Arber, Eng. Garner VI)
'Ticklefoot, Tom' Some observations upon the late tryals of Sir George Wakeman, etc. 1679
Ticknor, George History of Spanish literature 1849
Life of William Hickling Prescott 1864
Life, letters, and journals a 1871 (ed. G. S. Hillard 1876)
Tidball, John C. Manual of heavy artillery service prepared for the use of the army and militia of the United States 1880
Tiele's History of religion tr. 1877: see Carpenter, J. E.
Tillotson, Abp. John Works a 1694 (1714–17, 1728)
The Protestant religion vindicated from the charge of singularity and novelty 1680
Tilney, Edmund A brief and pleasaunt discourse of duties in mariage (running title 'The flower of friendship') 1568
Timberlake, Henry Memoirs 1765
Timbs, John Club life of London 1866 (1872)
Times, The 1788–
—— weekly edition 1877–
Times storehouse: see Milles, T.
Time's telescope for 1814; or a complete guide to the almanack 1814
Times' whistle 1616: see C., R.
Timme, Thomas Commentarie of Iohn Caluine vpon Genesis tr. 1578
Du Chesne's (J.; Quersitanus) Practise of chymicall and hermeticall physicke tr. 1605
A plaine discouerie of ten English lepers 1592
Timon, a play c 1600 (Shaks. Soc. 1842)
Timperley, C. H. A dictionary of printers and printing 1839
Tindal, Matthew The rights of the Christian Church asserted 1706
—— A defence 1709

Tindal, Nicholas Rapin de Thoyras' History of England tr. 1725–31
—— Continued to the accession of King George II 1732–47
—— Continued to the present times 1757–63
Tindal, William The history and antiquities of the abbey and borough of Evesham 1794
Tindale, William Works a 1536 (1573; Parker Soc. 1848–50)
An answere vnto Sir Thomas Mores dialoge 1530
Erasmus's Enchiridion tr. 1533
An exposicion vpon the v. vi. vii. chapters of Mathew ? 1530
The exposition of the fyrste epistle of seynt Ihon 1531 (1537)
The exposition of the epistles of St. Ihon 1538
The fyrst (seconde–fifth) boke of Moses called Genesis, etc. tr. 1530 (1884)
The New Testament tr. 1526, 1534
The obedience of a christen man 1528
The parable of the wicked mammon 1528
A pathway to the holy scripture (anon.) 1533
The practyse of prelates (anon.) 1530
The prophete Jonas with an introduccion before teachinge to understonde him ? 1531
The souper of the Lorde (anon.) 1533
—— and Frith, John The testament of master William Tracie esquier 1535
Tinker of Turvey, The 1630: see Cobler
Tinsley's Magazine; conducted by Edmund Yates 1868–92
Tint quey 1796: see Twa cuckolds
Tiptoft, John, Earl of Worcester Iulius Cesars commentaryes tr. a 1470 (1530)
Tulle of olde age. Tullius de amicicia (also, two orations of Publius Cornelius and Gaius Flaminius, tr. from B. Magnomontanus (= Bonaccorso)) tr. a 1470 (Caxton 1481)
Tirwhyt, William The letters of Monsieur de Balzac tr. 1634
Titan. A monthly magazine 1856–59
Tit-bits 1881–
Titchener, Edward B. Experimental psychology 1901–05
See also Wundt, W.
Tithes into stipends, A brief discourse of changing ministers 1654
Titus, Silius Killing noe murder, by William Allen (i.e. Silas or Silius Titus and Edward Sexby) 1657
Tizard, William L. The theory and practice of brewing illustrated 1843 (1846)
Tobin, John The honey moon: a comedy 1805
Tod, James Annals and antiquities of Rajast'han, or the central and western Rajpoot states of India 1829–32
Todd, Henry J. A dictionary of the English language by Samuel Johnson. With numerous corrections and addition(s) by H. J. Todd 1818
Todd, James G. Strila; or, the palace of strife. With other poems and songs 1823
Todd, Robert B. Ed. The cyclopædia of anatomy and physiology 1835–59
—— and Bowman, William The physiological anatomy and physiology of man 1845–56
Todhunter, Isaac The elements of Euclid, with notes, an appendix, and exercises 1862
A history of the progress of the calculus of variations during the nineteenth century 1861
William Whewell, D.D.: an account of his writings, with selections from his .. correspondence 1876
Tofte, Robert Alba. The months minde of a melancholy louer 1598 (1880)
Laura. The toyes of a traueller. Or, the feast of fancie 1597 (in Arber, Eng. Garner VIII)
Montreux's (N. de) Honours academie, or the famous pastorall of the faire shepheardesse Julietta tr. 1610
Toland, John Clito, a poem on the force of eloquence 1700
A critical history of the Celtic religion and learning, containing an account of the Druids a 1722 (1726)
—— a new ed. by R. Huddleston (1814)
Reflections on Mr. Sacheverell's sermon preached at St. Pauls Nov. 5, 1709 1710
Toland's Pantheisticon tr. 1751
Toldervy, William The history of two orphans 1756
Toleration not to be abused 1672: see Fullwood, F.
Toller, Sir Samuel A treatise on the law of tithes 1808 (1816)
Toller, T. Northcote: see Bosworth, J.
Tolstoy, George The first forty years of intercourse between England and Russia, 1553–93; documents (in Russian and English) collected, copied, and edited by G. Tolstoy 1875
Tom Thumbe, his life and death 1630
Tom Thumb's folio; or, a new penny play-thing for little giants 1768 (1786)
Tom Tyler and his wife; an excellent old play 1598 (1661)
Tombes, John Anthropolatria; or the sinne of glorying in men 1645
Fermentum Pharisæorum; or the leaven of Pharisaicall wil-worship; declared in a sermon 1641 (1643)
Tomes, Sir John A system of dental surgery 1859
—— ed. 2, revised and enlarged by C. S. Tomes 1873
Tomes, Robert The Americans in Japan 1857
Tomkis, Thomas Albumazar (anon.) 1615 (Dodsley)
Lingua: or the combat of the tongue and the fiue senses for superiority (anon.) 1607 (Dodsley)
Tomlin, Jacob Missionary journals and letters 1844
Tomlins, Sir Thomas E. Jacob's (G.) Law-dictionary greatly enlarged and improved 1797 (1820)
Tomlinson, Charles Cyclopædia of useful arts 1852–54 (1866)
The useful arts and manufactures of Great Britain 1860
Tomlinson, John The level of Hatfield Chace, and parts adjacent 1882
Tomlinson, Matthew The Protestant's birth-right 1746
Tomlinson, Richard Renodæus' (J.) Medicinal dispensatory tr. 1657
Tomlinson, William An epistle to the flock, by W. T. 1674
Tomson, Laurence Calvin's Sermons on the Epistles to Timothie and Titus tr. 1579
Tonson, Jacob Poetical miscellanies 1709
Tonstall or Tunstall, Bp. Cuthbert A sermon made vpon Palme sondaye 1539 (1823)
Toogood, Mrs. Specimens of the Yorkshire dialect 1863 (MS.)
Tooke, George Annæ-dicata, or, a miscelaine of some different cansonets 1652 (1654)

Tooke, George (cont.)
The Belides, or eulogie and elegie of Lord Harrington 1647 (1659)
Tooke, John Horne The diversions of Purley 1786–1805 (1829, 1840)
Tooke, Thomas Considerations on the state of the currency 1826
Thoughts and details on the high and low prices of the last thirty years 1823 (1824)
Tooke, William Castera's Life of Catherine II tr. 1797
Lucian tr. 1820
Russia, or, a compleat historical account of all the nations which compose that empire 1780–83
View of the Russian empire during the reign of Catherine II 1799
Tooker, William Of the fabrique of the church and churchmens liuings 1604
Topham, Edward Letters from Edinburgh (anon.) 1774–75 (1776)
Topham, George Rome's tradition, the law and gospel's destruction 1682
Topinard's (P.) Anthropology tr. by R. T. H. Bartley 1878
Topsell, Edward The historie of foure-footed beastes 1607
The historie of serpents 1608
—— The history of four-footed beasts and serpents .. revised .. and inlarged by J. R(owland) (1658)
Times lamentation: or an exposition on the prophet Ioel 1599
Torkington, Sir Richard Ye oldest diarie of Englysshe travell: being the hitherto unpublished narrative of the pilgrimage of Sir R. Torkington to Jerusalem 1517 (1884)
Torments of hell 1658: see Richardson, S.
Torquemada's (A. de) Spanish Mandeuile of miracles (Prefatory epistles signed F. Walker, who attributes the translation to Lewes Lewkenor) 1600
Torrance, John Missions of the United Free Church of Scotland. Story of our Marâtha missions 1902
Torrens, Henry D'Oyley Travels in Ladak, Tartary, and Kashmir 1862
Torrens, Henry W. Remarks on the scope and uses of military literature and history 1846
Torrent of Portugal c 1435 (Halliwell 1842; E.E.T.S. 1887)
Torrey, Joseph Neander's (J. A. W.) General history of the Christian religion and Church tr. 1847–55
Torriano, Giovanni A dictionary Italian and English, formerly compiled by John Florio, now diligently revised 1659
Torriano, N. An historical dissertation on a particular species of gangrenous sore throat 1753
A tract on the formation of the fœtus, and the practice of midwifry 1753
Treatise on the nature of non-naturals 1753
Torshell, Samuel A designe about disposing the Bible into an harmony 1647 (Phenix 1707)
A helpe to Christian fellowship 1644
Total rout, or a brief discovery of a pack of knaves and drabs 1653
Tottel's miscellany (Songes and sonettes, written by the ryght honorable Lorde Henry Haward late Earle of Surrey, and other) 1557 (Arber 1870)
Totten, Benjamin J. Naval text-book 1841 (1862, 1864)
Touchstone, Timothy The trifler; a new periodical miscellany 1788
Tour of German Prince tr. 1832: see Austin, Sarah
Tourgee, Albion W. A fool's errand (anon.) 1879
Tournament. The turnament of Totenham a 1450 (ed. T. Wright 1836; in Hazlitt, Early pop. poetry III)
Tournefort, J. Pitton de Institutiones rei herbariæ 1700
Tournefort's Voyage into the Levant tr. 1718
Tourneur, Cyril Plays and poems a 1626 (1878)
The atheist's tragedie 1611
The revengers tragædie (anon.) 1607
Three elegies on the most lamented death of Prince Henrie by C. Tourneur, J. Webster, and T. Heywood 1613
The transformed metamorphosis 1600
Tout, Thomas F. History of England from William and Mary to the present time 1890
Towers, Joseph Memoirs of the life and reign of Frederick the third, King of Prussia 1788
Towerson, Gabriel An explication of the decalogue 1676
Of the sacrament of baptism 1687
Towler, John The silver sunbeam: a text-book on sun drawing and photographic printing 1864 (ed. 3)
Town and country magazine 1769–91
Towneley mysteries, The c 1460 (Surtees Soc. 1836)
—— The Towneley plays (E.E.T.S. 1897)
Townsend, George F. English hand-book of Malta 1869
Townsend, Joseph A journey through Spain in 1786–87 1791
Townsend, Richard Chapters on the modern geometry of the point, line, and circle 1863–65
Townsend, Thomas Solis's (A. de) History of the conquest of Mexico tr. 1724
Townshend, Chauncy H. Facts in mesmerism, with reasons for a dispassionate inquiry into it 1840
Townshend, Dorothea Life and letters of Mr. Endymion Porter 1897
Tozer, Henry F. Researches into the highlands of Turkey 1869
Tracts for the times. By members of the University of Oxford 1833–41
Trades increase, The (Epistle to the reader signed, I. R.) 1615 (in Harl. Misc.)
'Trafford, F. G.': see Riddell, Mrs. J. H.
Tragedy of Hoffman: see Chettle, H.
Tragedy of King Richard the second c 1590 (1870)
Tragedy of Nero: see Nero
Tragi-comicall history 1627: see D., W.
Traherne, Thomas Christian ethicks; or divine morality a 1674 (1675)
Poetical works a 1674 (1903)
Traheron, Bartholomew An exposition of a parte of S. Iohannes Gospel 1557
The most excellent workes of chirurgerye made by J. Vigon tr. 1543 (1550, 1586)
A warning to England to repente 1558
Traill, Catherine Parr The backwoods of Canada 1836
Traill, Henry Duff Ed. Social England 1893–97
Train, Joseph An historical and statistical account of the Isle of Man 1845
Poetical reveries 1806
Strains of the mountain muse 1814

Traits of American humour, by native authors (ed. T. C. Haliburton) 1852 (1866)
Transactioneer, The 1700: see King, William
Transactions at the court of Spain 1678: see Spanish history
Translations and paraphrases of several passages of sacred scripture, collected and prepared by a committee appointed by the General Assembly of the Church of Scotland 1745 (1781, 1786, 1793)
Trapham, Thomas A discourse of the state of health in the island of Jamaica 1679
Trapp, John Annotations upon the Old and New Testament 1646–62 (1654–62, 1867–68)
Vol. I. A commentary or exposition upon the five books of Moses 1650; together with the books of Joshua, Judges, Ruth, first and second of Samuel, first and second of Kings, and first and second of Chronicles 1656 (1662)
Vol. II. Ezra, Nehemiah, Esther, Job, and Psalms 1656 (1657)
Vol. III. Proverbs of Solomon, Ecclesiastes, the Song of Songs 1650; Isaiah, Jeremiah, Lamentations, Ezekiel and Daniel 1656 (1660)
Vol. IV. Twelve minor prophets (Hosea, Joel, Amos, Obadiah, Jonah, Micah, Nahum, Habakkuk, Zephaniah, Haggai, Zachariah, Malachy) 1654
Vol. V. New Testament 1646–47 (1656)
Mellificium theologicum, or the marrow of many good authors 1647 (1655, 1868)
Trapp, Joseph Abra-Mulé; or, love and empire 1704
Popery truly stated, and briefly confuted 1726
The Æneis of Virgil tr. 1718–20
The works of Virgil tr. 1731
Trappe, John Theologia theologiæ, the true treasure 1641
Travels of certain Englishmen 1609 (1612): see Biddulph, W.
Travestin (—) An account of the imperial proceedings against the Turks, with an exact diary of the siege of Newheusel 1685
Treasury of ancient and modern times: see Milles, T.
Treasury of botany: see Lindley, J.
Treasury of hidden secrets 1573: see Partridge, John
Treatise concerning the manner of fallowing of ground (by Rich. Bradley) 1724
Treatise of humane reason 1675: see Clifford, M.
Treatise of monarchy: see Hunton, P.
Treatise of scolding 1731
Treatise on domestic pigeons 1765
Treatise (Short) on harmony; containing the chief rules for composing in two, three, or four parts 1730
Treatyse of a galaunt: see Gallant
'Treddlehoyle, Tom' (Charles Rodgers) The Bairnsla foak's annual (various years) 1838–83
Tredgold, Thomas Elementary principles of carpentry 1820
A practical essay on the strength of cast iron 1822 (1824)
A practical treatise on rail-roads and carriages 1825
Tregellas, John T. Cornish tales, in prose and verse a 1863 (1868)
Tregelles, Samuel P. Remarks on the prophetic visions in the Book of Daniel 1847 (1864)
Trelawny, Edward J. Adventures of a younger son 1831 (1890)
Trench, Melesina Remains, being selections from her journals, letters, and other papers a 1827 (ed. R. C. Trench 1862)
Trench, Abp. Richard Chenevix Christ the desire of all nations 1846
Commentary on the epistles to the seven churches in Asia 1861
English, past and present 1855
Exposition of the sermon on the mount, drawn from the writings of St. Augustine 1844
The fitness of Holy Scripture for unfolding the spiritual life of men. Hulsean lectures 1845 1845
The Hulsean lectures for 1845 and 1846 1859 (ed. 4 revised)
Notes on the miracles of Our Lord 1846 (1856, 1862)
Notes on the parables of Our Lord 1841 (1844, 1855)
On some deficiencies in our English dictionaries 1857
—— ed. 2, revised and enlarged 1860
On the lessons in Proverbs 1853
On the study of words 1851 (1861)
Poems from Eastern sources 1842 (1851)
A select glossary of English words 1859 (1865)
Sermons preached in Westminster Abbey 1860
The story of Justin Martyr, and other poems 1835
Synonyms of the New Testament 1854
Trenchard, John Letter from a souldier to the Commons of England (anon.) 1702
The natural history of superstition (anon.) 1709
—— and Gordon, Thomas The independent Whig 1720
Trevelyan, Sir George O. Cawnpore 1865
The competition Wallah 1864 (1866)
The ladies in parliament, and other pieces 1869
The life and letters of Lord Macaulay 1876
Treves, Sir Frederick Highways and byways of Dorset 1906
The other side of the lantern 1905
Trevisa, John de Bartholomeus (de Glanvilla) De proprietatibus rerum tr. 1398 (Tollemache MS.; Add. MS. (B.M.) 27944; MS. e Museo (Bodl.) 16; W. de Worde 1495; 1535)
—— Batman vppon Bartholome (1582)
Polychronicon Ranulphi Higden tr. 1387 (Rolls series 1865–86)
'Trevor, Edward': see Lytton, E. R. Bulwer-
Trévoux. Dictionnaire universel françois et latin, vulgairement appellé Dictionnaire de Trévoux 1704, 1721, 1732, 1752, 1771
Trial. The proceedings and trial of the bishops in the Court of king's Bench, A.D. 1688 1689
The trial of Edward Coleman, for conspiring the death of the king 1678
The trials of Rob. Green, Henry Bury, and Lawrence Hill for the murder of Sir E. Godfrey 1679
The trials of W. Ireland, Tho. Pickering and John Grove, for conspiring to murder the king 1678
The trial of Richard Langhorn for conspiring the death of the king 1679
Trial of maha rajah Nundocomar, Bahader, for forgery 1776
An exact account of the trial between Sir W. Pritchard and Tho. Papillon Esq., in an action upon the case 6 Nov., 1684 1689

Trial (cont.)
Trial of the regicides (An exact and most impartial accompt of the indictment, arraignment, trial, and judgment of twenty nine regicides, the murtherers of his late sacred majesty) 1660
The trials of Sir G. Wakeman, W. Marshall, W. Rumley and James Corker for high treason 1679
The trials and condemnations of Tho. White, alias Whitebread, W. Harcourt, John Fenwick, (and other) Jesuits and priests, for high treason 1679
Triall of chevalry, The historie of the (? by W. Wager) 1605 (in Bullen, Old plays III, 1884)
Triall of treasure, A new and mery enterlude, called the 1567 (Percy Soc. 1850; in Hazl., Dodsley)
Triamoure: see Tryamoure
Tribes on my frontier 1881: see 'Eha'
Tricks of the town laid open 1747 (ed. 3)
Trifler, The 1788: see Touchstone, Timothy
Trimen, Henry and Thiselton-Dyer, Sir William T. Flora of Middlesex 1869
Trimmer, Joseph Practical geology and mineralogy 1841
Trimmer, Sarah The two farmers, an exemplary tale 1787
Trinity College homilies (Old English homilies of the twelfth century. From the MS. in the library of Trinity College, Cambridge. Second series) c 1200 (E.E.T.S. 1873)
Trinket, The 1774
'Tripe, Andrew' 1714: see Wagstaffe, William
Tristram, Henry B. The Great Sahara 1860
The land of Israel 1865
The land of Moab 1873
Tristrem, Sir: see Sir Tristrem
Triumphs of fortitude, The; a novel, in a series of letters 1789
'Troglodyte': see Schiller, F. C. S.
Troil's (Uno von) Letters on Iceland tr. 1780
Trojan war: see (Scottish) Trojan war
Trollope, Anthony Australia and New Zealand 1873
An autobiography a 1882 (1883)
Ayala's angel 1881
Barchester Towers 1857
The Belton estate 1865
The Bertrams 1859
Can you forgive her? 1864–65
Castle Richmond 1860
The Claverings 1867
Doctor Thorne 1858
Doctor Wortle's school 1881
The Eustace diamonds 1873
Framley Parsonage 1861
He knew he was right 1869
Lady Anna 1874
The last chronicle of Barset 1867
Linda Tressel 1868
Miss Mackenzie 1865
North America 1862
Orley farm 1862
The small house at Allington 1864
The three clerks 1858
The warden 1855
The West Indies and the Spanish main 1859
Trollope, Edward Sleaford, and the wapentakes of Flaxwell and Ashwardhurn 1872
Trollope, Frances Domestic manners of the Americans 1831
Life and adventures of Michael Armstrong, the factory boy 1840
A visit to Italy 1842
The widow married 1840
Trollope, Frances E. A charming fellow 1876
Trollope, Thomas A. Impressions of a wanderer in Italy, Switzerland, France, and Spain 1850
La Beata 1861
Marietta 1862
The story of the life of Pius the ninth 1877
A summer in Brittany 1840
A summer in Western France 1841
What I remember 1887–89
Tromholt's (S.) Under the rays of the Aurora borealis tr. 1885
Trotter, James General view of the agriculture of West Lothian 1794
Trotter, Mrs. M.: see Saxon
Trotter, Philip D. Our mission to the court of Marocco in 1880, under Sir J. D. Hay 1881
Trotter, Robert de Bruce Kirkcudbrightshire. Galloway gossip eighty years ago 1901
Trotter, Thomas An essay on drunkenness 1804
Troublesome raigne of John king of England 1591; the second part 1591 (1611)
Trowbridge, John T. Coupon bonds 1866 (1874)
A home idyl, and other poems 1881
True and perfect relation of the proceedings at the severall arraignments of (H. Garnet, etc.) 1606
True and sincere declaration of the purpose of the plantation begun in Virginia 1610 (1844)
True Briton, The (by Philip Wharton) 1723–24
True coppie of a discourse written by a gentleman employed in the late voyage of Spaine and Portingale 1589 (Grosart 1881)
True informer, The 1643
True non-conformist: see MacWard, R.
True notion of the worship of God, A; or a vindication of the service of the Church of England 1673
True patriot, The 1775
True spirit of popery, The 1688
True tragedie of Richard Duke of Yorke 1595
True tragedie of Richard the third 1594 (Shaks. Soc. 1844)
Trumbull, Gurdon Names and portraits of birds which interest gunners 1888
Trumbull, John Poetical works 1820
McFingal: a modern epic poem (anon.) 1776
Trusler, John Modern times; or, the adventures of Gabriel Outcast (anon.) 1785
Poetic endings; or, a dictionary of rhymes 1783
The principles of politeness and of knowing the world (extracted from Earl Chesterfield's Letters to his son), with additions by J. Trusler 1775 (1790)
Tryall of chevalry: see Triall
Tryamoure, The romance of syr c 1430 (Percy Soc. 1846)
Tryon, Thomas The good house-wife made a doctor 1692
Health's grand preservative; or the women's best doctor 1682; ed. 2, The way to health 1691
Miscellanea 1696
A treatise of dreams and visions 1695
Wisdom's dictates 1691

Tucker, Abraham Freewill, foreknowledge, and fate 1763
The light of nature pursued; vols. I–IV 1768; vols. V–VII a 1774 (1778; 1834, 1852)
Tucker, Josiah An apology for the present Church of England as by law established 1772
A letter to Edmund Burke 1775
Letters to Dr. Kippis 1773
Tucker, William J. Life and society in Eastern Europe 1886
Tuckerman, Edward An enumeration of North American lichenes 1845
A synopsis of the North American lichens 1882–88
Tuckerman, Henry T. The collector: essays on books newspapers, pictures 1868
Tuckey, James Hatschek's (B.) Amphioxus and its development tr. 1893
Tuckney, Anthony The balme of Gilead 1643
A good day well improved 1656
Θανατοκτασία: or, death disarmed, a sermon preached Dec. 22, 1653. To which are added two sermons more 1654
Tuckwell, William The ancient ways: Winchester fifty years ago 1893
Tudor proclamations. Facsimiles of proclamations of Henry VII, Henry VIII, Edward VI, and Philip and Mary 14..–15.. (1897)
Tuer, Andrew W. History of the horn-book 1896
Old London street cries and the cries of to-day 1885
Quads for authors, editors, and devils 1884
—— and Fagan, Charles E. The first year of a silken reign 1837–38 1887
Tuke, Daniel H. A dictionary of psychological medicine 1892
Tuke, John A general view of the agriculture of the North Riding of Yorkshire 1800
Tuke, Richard The divine comedian; or the right use of plays improved, in a sacred tragi-comedy 1672
Memoires of the life and death of Sir Edmondbury Godfrey 1682
Tuke, Sir Samuel The adventures of five hours: a tragi-comedy 1663
Tulk, Alfred Oken's (L.) Elements of physiophilosophy tr. 1847
Tull, Jethro The new horse-houghing husbandry (anon.) 1731, 1733 (1740, 1762, 1822)
Tullie, Isaac A narrative of the siege of Carlisle in 1644–45 c 1645 (1840)
Tulloch, John English Puritanism and its leaders 1861
Rational theology and Christian philosophy in England 1872
Tully (—) Narrative of a ten years' residence at Tripoli in Africa: from the original correspondence in the possession of the family of the late Richard Tully (written by Tully's sister-in-law) 1783–95 (1817)
Tully, Thomas A letter to Mr. Rich. Baxter 1675
Tunbridge-miscellany, The; consisting of poems, etc. written at Tunbridge Wells 1712
Tunbrigialia: or Tunbridge miscellanie 1719
Tundale, The visions of; together with metrical moralizations and other fragments of early poetry 14.. (Turnbull 1843; Wagner 1893)
Tunstall, Bp. Cuthbert: see Tonstall
Tupper, Martin F. Autobiography: my life as an author 1886
The crock of gold 1844
Heart 1844
Proverbial philosophy 1838–42 (1852)
The twins 1844
Turberville, George The booke of faulconrie or hauking 1575
The eglogs of Mantuan (= G. B. Spagnuoli) tr. 1567
Epitaphes, epigrams, songs and sonets 1567
The heroycall epistles of Pub. Ouidius Naso tr. 1567
The noble arte of venerie or hunting (anon.) 1575
Poems a 1610 (Chalmers 1810)
Tragical tales, (and other poems) 1587 (1837)
Turk, D. G. Treatise on teaching and practising the pianoforte 1804
Turkish spy: see Marana, J. P.
Turnbull, Gavin Justin's History of the world tr. 1746
Poetical essays 1788
Turnbull, Robert The pulpit orators of France and Switzerland 1848
Turner, Brandon A new English grammar 1840
Turner, Daniel De morbis cutaneis 1714 (1731)
Turner, Dawson Account of a tour in Normandy 1820
Turner, Edward Elements of chemistry 1827 (1847)
Turner, George J. Ed. Select pleas of the forest 1901 (Selden Soc.)
Turner, J. T. F. Slate quarries 1865
Turner, Sir James Memoirs of his own life and times 1632–70 a 1686 (Bannatyne Cl. 1829)
Pallas armata; or military essayes of the ancient Grecian, Roman and modern art of war 1670–71 (1683)
Turner, John A farther vindication of the soul's separate existence 1703
Turner, Richard An easy introduction to the arts and sciences 1783 (1821)
Turner, Robert Βοτανολόγια. The British physician; or the nature and vertues of English plants 1664
Paracelsus of the chymical transmutation tr. 1657
Turner, Samuel An account of an embassy to the court of the Teshoo Lama, in Tibet 1800
Turner, Sharon The history of the Anglo-Saxons 1799–1805 (1828)
The modern history of England 1826–29
The sacred history of the world 1832–37
Turner, Thomas H. Some account of domestic architecture in England 1851
—— Vols. 2 and 3 by J. H. Parker (1853–59)
Turner, William Avium præcipuarum, quarum apud Plinium et Aristotelem mentio est, brevis et succincta historia 1544
A booke of the natures and properties of the bathes in Englande 1562 (Also issued as pt. of 'The second part of Turners herball' 1562)
Libellus de re herbaria nouus 1538 (1877)
The names of herbes in Greke, Latin, Englishe, Duche and Frenche 1548 (E.D.S. 1881)
A new boke of the natures of all wines 1568
A new booke of spirituall physik 1555
A new herball 1551; the seconde parte 1562; the first and seconde partes lately ouersene, with the thirde parte, also a booke of the bath of Baeth 1568

Turner, William H. Ed. Selections from the records of the city of Oxford 1509–83 (1880)
Turnour, George The Mahâwanso, with the translation 1837
Turton, William A conchological dictionary of the British Islands 1819
Linnæus's General system of nature tr. 1802–06
A manual of the land and fresh-water shells of the British Islands 1831
A medical glossary 1797
Tusser, Thomas Fiue hundreth pointes of good husbandrie 1573 (1577, 1580; E.D.S. 1878)
A hundreth good pointes of husbandrie 1557 (E.D.S. 1878)
Tutchin, John A Pindarick ode in the praise of folly and knavery 1696
A search after honesty 1697
Tutin, John R. An index to the animal and vegetable kingdoms of Wordsworth 1892
Tuttle, Edmund B. Border tales around the camp fire in the Rocky Mountains 1878
Tuvil, Daniel Essaies politicke and morall 1608
Essayes, morall and theologicall 1609
Twa cuckolds, The, and the Tint Quey, or Thrawart Maggy. Two tales, in the Scottish dialect 1796
'Twain, Mark' (S. L. Clemens) The adventures of Huckleberry Finn 1884
The adventures of Tom Sawyer 1876
The innocents abroad 1869
The innocents at home 1872
Life on the Mississippi 1883
Roughing it 1872
Sketches 1872
A tramp abroad 1880
A Yankee at the court of King Arthur 1889
Twamley, Josiah Dairying exemplified, or the business of cheese-making 1784
Tweddell, John Remains a 1799 (1815–16)
Tweeddale, John Moff 1896
Tweedie, William K. The lakes and rivers of the Bible 1857 (1864)
Ed. Select biographies v.d. (Wodrow Soc. 1845–47)
Twelfth century homilies in MS. Bodley 343 11.. (E.E.T.S. 1909)
Twells, John Grammatica reformata, or, a general examination of the art of grammar 1683
Twin soul, The (by Charles Mackay) 1887
Twining (family of). Selections from papers of the Twining family: a sequel to 'The recreations and studies of a country clergyman' (see Twining, T.) 17..–18.. (1887)
Twining, Thomas Aristotle's Treatise on poetry tr. 1789 (1812)
Recreations and studies of a country clergyman of the eighteenth century; being selections from the correspondence of T. Twining 17.. (1882)
Travels in India a hundred years ago, with a visit to the United States c 1796 (1893)
—— Part IV reprinted with title Travels in America a hundred years ago (1894)
Twiss, Richard Chess (anon.) 1787–89
A tour in Ireland in 1775 (anon.) 1776
Travels through Portugal and Spain in 1772 and 1773 1775
Two Cosmos, The; a tale of fifty years ago 1861
Two fifteenth-century cookery-books c 1430, –50 (E.E.T.S. 1888)
Two noble kinsmen, The 1612 (1634; New Shaks. Soc. 1876; Shakespeare Apocrypha 1908)
Twyne, Thomas Petrarca's (F.) Phisicke against fortune tr. 1579
See also Phaer, T.
Twysden, Sir Roger The beginners of a monastick life a 1672 (1698)
Ed. Historiæ Anglicanæ scriptores decem 1652
Tyas, Robert Favourite field flowers; or, wild flowers of England popularly described 1848; second series 1850; third series, entitled Popular flowers; their propagation, cultivation, and general treatment in all seasons 1854
—— Large paper edition revised, entitled The wild flowers of England or favourite field flowers popularly described. First and second series 1859–60
Tyde taryeth no man 1576: see Wapull, G.
Tyers, Thomas An historical rhapsody on Mr. Pope (anon.) 1781 (1782)
Tyler, Moses C. Glimpses of England: social, political, literary 18.. (1898)
A history of American literature, 1607–1765 1879
Tylor, Edward B. Anahuac: or Mexico and the Mexicans 1861
Anthropology 1881
Primitive culture 1871
Researches into the early history of mankind and the development of civilization 1865
Tymme, Thomas: see Timme, T.
Tyndale, William: see Tindale, W.
Tyndall, John Essays on the floating-matter of the air in relation to putrefaction and infection 1881
The forms of water in clouds, rivers, ice and glaciers 1872
Fragments of science for unscientific people 1871 (1879)
The glaciers of the Alps 1860
Heat considered as a mode of motion 1863
Mountaineering in 1861: a vacation tour 1862
Notes of a course of nine lectures on light 1870
On radiation 1865
Sound: a course of eight lectures 1867
Tyrie, James The refutation of ane answer made be schir Iohne Knox 1573
Tyrrell, James The general history of England, as well ecclesiastical as civil 1696–1704
Tyrwhit, William: see Tirwhyt, W.
Tyrwhitt, Thomas The Canterbury tales of Chaucer. To which are added, an essay upon his language and versification; an introductory discourse; and notes (with a glossary) 1775–78
A vindication of the appendix to the poems, called Rowley's 1782
See also Chatterton, Thomas
Tyson, Edward Orang-outang, sive homo sylvestris; or the anatomy of a pygmie 1699
Phocæna, or, the anatomy of a porpess: with a preliminary discourse concerning anatomy 1680

Tytler, Ann Fraser Mary and Florence; or, grave and gay 1835
Mary and Florence at sixteen. A continuation of 'Grave and gay' 1838
Tytler, Patrick F. England under the reigns of Edward VI and Mary 1839
History of Scotland 1828–43 (1864)
'Tytler, Sarah' (Henrietta Keddie) The Blackhall ghosts 1888
The bride's pass 1882
Days of yore 1866
Lady Jean's son 1897
The Macdonald lass 1895
Phemie Millar 1854
The witch wife 1897

U

Ubaldini's (P.) Discourse concerninge the Spanish fleet invadinge Englande tr. 1590
Udall, Ephraim Funeral sermon 1643 (1645)
The good of peace and ill of warre; set forth in a sermon 1642
Noli me tangere, is a thinge to be thought on (anon.) 1642
Udall, John A demonstration of the trueth of that discipline which Christe hath prescribed (anon.) 1588 (Arber 1880)
The state of the Church of Englande, laide open in a conference betweene Diotrephes, a byshop, Tertullus, a papist, etc. (anon.) 1588 (Arber 1880)
Udall, Nicolas Apophthegmes, that is to saie, prompte saiynges. First gathered by Erasmus tr. 1542 (1564, 1877)
Floures for Latine spekynge. Selected and gathered out of Terence tr. 1533
Gemini's (T.) Compendiosa totius anatomie delineatio tr. 1553
The noble tryumphaunt coronation of quene Anne 1533 (in Arber, Eng. Garner II; Pollard 1903)
Ralph Roister Doister, a comedy a 1553 (Arber 1869; in Manly, Specim. pre-Shaks. drama II, 1898)
—— and others The first tome or volume of the paraphrase of Erasmus upon the Newe Testament tr. 1548
Ude, Louis E. The French cook 1813 (1822, 1827)
Udny, Alexander A golden bell and a pomgranate 1625
The voyce of the cryer 1628
Ueberweg's (F.) History of philosophy tr. by G. S. Morris 1872–74
Uhland's (W. H.) Corliss-engines and allied steam-motors tr. by A. Tolhausen 1879–82
U.K.S. = Useful Knowledge Society
Uncle Philip's conversations about the whale fishery and Polar seas 1836
Underdowne, Thomas The excellent historye of Theseus and Ariadne 1566
Ovid his invective against Ibis tr. 1569
Underhill, Edward A note off the examynacyon and impresonmentt off E. U. 1553 (in Narratives of the days of the Reformation, Camden Soc. 1859; Arber, Eng. Garner IV)
Underwood, Michael A treatise on the diseases of children 1784
—— ed. 3, entitled A treatise on the disorders of childhood 1797 (1799)
Unfortunate sensibility 1784
United Free Church magazine, The 1904–06
United service magazine, The 1890–
Universal magazine of knowledge and pleasure, The 1747–1803
—— continued as The universal magazine 1804–14
Universal review, The 1866
Unton inventories, relating to Wadley and Faringdon, Co. Berks 1596, 1620 (1841)
Unton, Sir Henry Correspondence 1591–92 (Roxb. Cl. 1847)
Upcott, Lewis E. An introduction to Greek sculpture 1887 (1899)
Upton, John Critical observations on Shakespeare 1746
Spenser's Faerie queene. A new ed. with a glossary, and notes explanatory and critical 1758
Upton, William Physioglyphics 1844
Upton-on-Severn glossary 1884: see Lawson, R.
Upward, Allen Songs in Ziklag 1888
Urban, Charles The cinematograph in science, education, and matters of state 1907
Ure, Andrew The cotton manufacture of Great Britain systematically investigated 1836 (1861)
A dictionary of arts, manufactures and mines 1839 (1843, 1853)
—— ed. 5, by R. Hunt (1860); ed. 7, by R. Hunt and F. W. Rudler (1875)
—— Supplement (1878)
A dictionary of chemistry 1821
A new system of geology 1829
The philosophy of manufactures 1835 (1861)
Ure, David General view of the agriculture of the county of Dumbarton 1794
General view of the agriculture of the county of Roxburgh 1794
The history of Rutherglen and East-Kilbride 1793
Ureisun a 1240 (in Old Eng. homilies, I, E.E.T.S. 1868)
Urie, The court book of the barony of 1604–1747 (S.H.S. 1892)
Urquhart, Sir Thomas Works a 1660 (Maitland Cl. 1834)
Εκσκυβαλαυρον; or, the discovery of a most exquisite jewel 1652
The first (second) book of the works of Mr. Francis Rabelais 1653 (1664)
—— The third book (1693, 1694) See also Motteux, P. A.
Urry, John Ed. The works of Geoffrey Chaucer, compared with the former editions, and many valuable MSS. Together with a glossary by (Timothy Thomas) 1721
Ursula, St., The life of c 1480 (Roxb. Cl. 1818)
Ushaw magazine, The 1891–
Usk, Thomas The testament of love 1387–88 (in Chaucer's Works, ed. Thynne 1532; Chaucerian pieces, Skeat 1897)

Ussher, James The annals of the world deduced from the origin of time a 1656 (1658)
An answer to a challenge made by a Jesuite in Ireland 1624 (1625)
A body of divinitie 1645 (1647)
Immanuel; or, the mystery of the incarnation of the son of God unfolded 1638 (1643)
The power communicated by God to the prince a 1656 (1661, 1683)
The reduction of episcopacie unto the form of synodical government received in the antient church 1656
A sermon preached before the Commons 18 Feb. 1620 (1621, 1624)
The life of James Ussher. With a collection of three hundred letters. Collected and published by Richard Parr (1686)
Utterson, Edward V. Ed. Select pieces of early popular poetry v.d. (1817)

V

Vacation tourists: see Galton, F.
Vachell, Horace A. The hill, a romance of friendship 1905
John Charity. A romance of yesterday 1900
Vacher, Francis On the transmission of disease by milk 1882
Valdesso's Considerations (1638): see Ferrar, N.
Valentia, George Annesley, 9th Viscount Voyages and travels to India, etc. 1802–06 1809
Valentine, Henry Foure sea-sermons 1635
Valentine, Thomas A dictionary of terms used in music 1824 (1833)
Valentinus' (B.) Of natural and supernatural things tr. by Dan. Cable 1670
Valiant Welshman 1615: see Armin, R.
Vallancey, Charles Collectanea de rebus Hibernicis 1770–1804
Memoir of the language, manners and customs of an Anglo-Saxon colony settled in the Baronies of Forth and Bargie (with a vocabulary of the language) 1788 (in Trans. R. Irish Academy, II, 1788)
Vallans, William The honourable prentice (anon.) a 1590 (1615)
Vámbéry's (H.) Travels in Central Asia tr. 1864
Van Beneden, P. J.: see Beneden, P. J. van
Vanbrugh, Sir John Works a 1726 (1734, 1840, 1893)
Æsop (anon.) 1697
The confederacy (anon.) 1705
The false friend (anon.) 1702
The mistake (anon.) 1706
The pilgrim 1700
The provok'd wife 1697
The relapse, or virtue in danger 1697
—— and Cibber, Colley The provok'd husband, or, a journey to London 1728
Van Buren, William H. and Keyes, Edward L. A practical treatise on the surgical diseases of the genito-urinary organs 1874
Vancouver, Charles General view of the agriculture in the county of Cambridge 1794
General view of the agriculture of the county of Devon 1808 (1813)
General view of the agriculture of the county of Essex 1795
General view of the agriculture of Hampshire, including the Isle of Wight 1813
'Vanderdecken' (W. Cooper) The yacht sailor; a treatise on practical yachtsmanship, cruising and racing 1862
Vanderstraeten's (F.) Improved agriculture tr. 1816
Vane's (Sir Harry) politicks, or his cases of conscience, lately found in his cabinet at Arabie 1661
Van Hare, G. Fifty years of a showman's life, or the life and travels of Van Hare by himself 1888
Vanity of the life of man, The 1688: see Burton, Richard
Vanity of scoffing, The 1674: see Ellis, C.
Van Oosterzee's (J. J.) Christian dogmatics tr. 1874: see Watson, John W.
Van Rensselaer, Mrs. M. King The devil's picture-books: a history of playing-cards 1890 (1892)
Van Rensselaer, Mrs. Schuyler English cathedrals 1892
Vansittart, Henry A narrative of the transactions in Bengal 1760–64 1766
Vattel's (E. de) Law of nations tr. 1759–60
Vaughan, Charles John Earnest words for earnest men 1870 (1878)
Memorials of Harrow Sundays 1859 (1863)
The young life equipping itself for God's service 1872 (1873)
Vaughan, Henry Works a 1695 (Grosart 1871)
Poems, with the tenth satyre of Juvenal Englished 1646
A fast sermon (on Matth. v. 20) 1644
Silex scintillans, or sacred poems and private ejaculations 1650
—— ed. 2, in two books 1655 (1858)
Thalia rediviva: the pass-times and diversions of a countrey-muse 1678
Vaughan, Sir John The reports and arguments of Sir J. V.; being all of them special cases a 1674 (1677)
Vaughan, Rice A discourse of coin and coinage a 1672 (1675)
Vaughan, Robert The age of great cities 1843
Vaughan, Robert A. Essays and remains a 1857 (1858)
Hours with the mystics 1856 (1860)
Vaughan, Thomas Anima magica abscondita; or a discourse of the universall spirit of nature 1650
Anthroposophia theomagica; or a discourse of the nature of man and his state after death 1650
Euphrates, or the waters of the East 1655
Vaughan, Thomas Fashionable follies 1782
Vaughan (W. O. G.), Voyages of 1736: see Chetwood, W. R.
Vaughan, William Boccalini's (T.) New-found politicke (Part III) tr. 1626
Vaughan (William), Examination of, in a committee of the House of Commons, April 22, 1796 1796
Vaus, John Rudimenta puerorum in artem grammaticalem 1522 (1531)
Vautrollier, Thomas Luther's Commentarie upon the epistle to the Galathians tr. 1575 (1577)

Supplement, p. 3873; Corrigenda, p. 4092; Spurious words, p. 4093; Books quoted, p. 4094

W

Wieland's (C. M.) History of Agathon tr. 1773
Wiener, Leo The history of Yiddish literature in the nineteenth century 1899
Wife: see Wyfe
Wife of Auchtermuchty, The a 1568 (in Ramsay's Evergreen 1724; Bannatyne MS., Hunterian Club)
Wiffen, Jeremiah H. Aonian hours, and other poems 1819 (1820)
Tasso's Jerusalem delivered 1824
Wiggin, Kate D. The diary of a goose girl 1902
New chronicles of Rebecca of Sunnybrook farm 1912
Wiggins, John The practice of embanking lands from the sea 1852
Wilberforce, Henry W. The Church and the empires a 1873 (1874)
Wilberforce, Reginald G. Life of the right rev. Samuel Wilberforce 1881–82
Wilberforce, Robert I. The doctrine of holy baptism 1849
The doctrine of the incarnation 1848 (1852)
Rutilius and Lucius; or stories of the third age 1842
Wilberforce, Bp. Samuel Addresses to the candidates for ordination 1860
Essays contributed to the 'Quarterly Review' a 1873 (1874)
A history of the protestant episcopal church in America 1844
Speeches on missions a 1873 (1874)
Wilbour, Charles E. The life of Victor Hugo 1887
Wilbraham, Frances M. The Cheshire pilgrims 1862
Wilbraham, Roger An attempt at a glossary of some words used in Cheshire 1818 (in Archaeologia XIX)
—— with additions 1820 (1826)
Wilbye, John The first set of English madrigals 1598 (in Arber, Eng. Garner VII)
Wilcocke, Samuel H. Stavorinus' (J. S.) Voyages to the East Indies tr. 1798
Wilcocks, James C. The sea-fisherman 1865 (1875)
Wilcocks or Wilcox, Thomas Works a 1608 (1624)
Wild or Wylde, Robert Iter boreale (anon.) 1660
A letter to his friend Mr. J. J. upon occasion of his majesty's declaration for liberty of conscience. Together with his Poetica licentia, and a friendly debate between a Conformist and a non-Conformist 1672
Oliver Cromwell's ghost 1679
Wild and tame. Pictures and pages of animal life 1892
Wild life in a southern county 1879: see Jefferies, R.
Wild sports of the west 1832: see Maxwell, W. H.
Wilde, Lady Jane F. S. Meinhold's (W.) Sidonia the sorceress tr. 1849 (1859)
Wilder, Burt G. and Gage, Simon H. Anatomical technology as applied to the domestic cat 1882
Wilhelm, Thomas A military dictionary and gazetteer 1881
Wilkes, Benjamin The English moths and butterflies 1749
Wilkes, John Correspondence a 1797 (1805)
The North Briton 1763
Wilkes, William Obedience or ecclesiasticall union 1605
—— another issue, entitled A second memento for magistrates 1608
Wilkie, William The epigoniad (anon.) 1757 (1759)
Wilkins, Sir Charles The Bhagvat-Geeta or dialogues of Kreeshna and Arjoon tr. 1785
Wilkins, David Concilia Magnae Britanniae et Hiberniae 1737
Ed. Leges Anglo-Saxonicae ecclesiasticae et civiles 1721
Wilkins, George The miseries of inforst mariage 1607 (Dodsley)
Wilkins, John The autobiography of an English gamekeeper 1892
Wilkins, Bp. John Mathematical and philosophical works a 1672 (1707–08)
A discourse concerning a new world and another planet 1640
A discourse concerning the gift of prayer 1651
The discovery of a world in the moone (anon.) 1638
Ecclesiastes; or, a discourse concerning the gift of preaching 1646
An essay towards a real character, and a philosophical language (with an alphabetical dictionary) 1668
Mathematicall magick; or, the wonders that may be performed by mechanicall geometry 1648
Mercury; or the secret and swift messenger 1641
Of the principles and duties of natural religion a 1672 (1675)
Wilkins, Mary E. A humble romance; and other stories 1887
The love of parson Lord 1900
Wilkins, William Songs of study 1881
Wilkins, William H. and Vivian, Herbert The green bay tree 1894
Wilkins, William W. Political ballads of the seventeenth and eighteenth centuries, anotated by W. W. W. (1860)
Wilkinson, James J. G. Swedenborg's Animal kingdom, considered anatomically, physically, and philosophically tr. 1843
Wilkinson, John A treatise collected out of the statutes concerning the office and authoritie of coroners and sherifes; together with an easie and plain method for the keeping of a court leet, court baron, and hundred court 1618
Wilkinson, Sir John G. Manners and customs of the ancient Egyptians 1837–41
Wilkinson, Robert Barwickbridge; or England and Scotland coupled 1617
The merchant royall 1607
A paire of sermons 1614
Wilkinson, William A confutation of certaine articles deliuered vnto the familye of loue 1579
Wilks, Mark Historical sketches of the south of India 1810–17
Will of deuyle: see Wyll
Willan, Leonard Astraea, or, true love's myrrour 1651
Willan, Robert A list of ancient words at present used in the mountainous district of the West Riding of Yorkshire 1811 (in Archaeologia XVII; E.D.S. 1873)
Willard, Samuel Mercy magnified on a penitent prodigal 1684
Willcock, John The great marquess; life and times of Archibald, 8th earl of Argyll (1607–61) 1903
Willdenow's (C. L.) Principles of botany, and of vegetable physiology tr. 1805 (1811)
Willet, Andrew An harmonie upon the first booke of Samuel 1607
Hexapla in Exodum 1608
Hexapla in Genesin 1605
Hexapla; or, a sixfold commentary on Daniel 1610
A treatise of Salomons mariage 1612

William of Normandy; an historic novel 1787
William of Palerne, The romance of: otherwise known as the romance of William and the Werwolf c 1350 (Roxb. Club 1832; E.E.T.S. 1867, 1881)
William of Shoreham: see Shoreham
Williams, Sir Charles H. Works a 1759 (1822)
Poems a 1759 (1763)
Odes a 1759 (1775)
Williams, David, and others Annals of the Empire; from the reign of Charlemagne. Translated from the French of Voltaire, constituting a part of a complete edition in English of the works of that writer 1781
Williams, Edward Poems, lyric and pastoral 1794
Williams, Frederick S. The Midland railway: its rise and progress 1876
Our iron roads; their history, construction, and social influences 1852
Williams, Helen Maria Letters containing a sketch of the politics of France 1795 (1796)
A narrative of the events which have taken place in France, from the landing of Napoleon Bonaparte, till the restoration of Louis XVIII. With an account of the present state of society and public opinion 1815
Personal narrative of travels to the equinoctial regions of the new continent during 1799–1804, by A. de Humboldt and Aimé Bonpland tr. 1814–29
Sketches of the state of manners and opinions in the French republic 1801
Williams, Isaac The Apocalypse, with notes and reflections 1852
The baptistery 1842–44
The Psalms interpreted of Christ 1864
Williams, Abp. John Great Britains Salomon: a sermon 1625
The holy table 1637
Perseverantia sanctorum: a sermon 1628
A sermon of apparell 1620
Williams, Bp. John The history of the gunpowder treason, collected from approved authors (anon.) 1678
Pulpit Popery, true Popery; being an answer to a book intitled Pulpit-sayings (by J. Gother) 1688
Williams, John ('Anthony Pasquin') Authentic memoirs of Warren Hastings 1793
A cabinet, etc. 1794
A calm examination 1793
The children of Thespis, a poem 1786–87
A crying epistle from Britannia to Col. Mack 1794
The life of the late Earl of Barrymore 1793
Shrove Tuesday, a satiric rhapsody (anon.) 1790 (1794)
Williams, John The ancient Welsh grammar compiled by Edeyrn tr. 1856
Williams, Joshua Principles of the law of real property 1845 (1877)
Rights of common and other prescriptive rights 1877 (1880)
Williams, Sir M. Monier-: see Monier-Williams
Williams, Nathaniel Imago sæculi: the image of the age represented in four characters 1676
Williams, Sir Roger The actions of the Lowe Countries a 1595 (1618)
A briefe discourse of warre 1590
Williams, Roger Experiments of spiritual life and health 1652 (1863)
A key into the language of America 1643
Williams, Samuel The natural and civil history of Vermont 1794 (1809)
Williams, Samuel Wells A Chinese commercial guide 1856
The Middle kingdom: a survey of the geography, etc. of the Chinese empire 1848
—— greatly enlarged and in part rewritten 1883
Williams, Wadham P. and Jones, William A. A glossary of provincial words and phrases in use in Somersetshire 1873
Williams, William The principles and practice of veterinary medicine 1874 (1888)
Williams, William Mattieu The fuel of the sun 1870
Through Norway with a knapsack 1859
Williams, William Meade Annals of the worshipful Company of Founders of the city of London 1867
Williams, William R. Religious progress: discourses on the development of the Christian character 1850 (1854)
Williamson, Benjamin An elementary treatise on the integral calculus 1875
Williamson, Thomas Goulart's (S.) Wise Vieillard, or old man tr. 1621
Williamson, Thomas The East India vade-mecum 1810
Oriental field sports 1807
Willis, Browne Notitia parliamentaria; or an history of the counties, cities, and boroughs in England and Wales 1715–16
Willis, John The art of stenographie (anon.) 1602
Willis, John C. A manual and dictionary of the flowering plants and ferns 1897
Willis, Nathaniel P. Lady Jane, and other poems 1844
Melanie, and other poems 1835
Pencillings by the way 1835
Poems, sacred, passionate and humourous 1846
Poems of early and after years 1848
Sketches 1827
Willis, Robert Architectural nomenclature of the middle ages 1844 (Cambr. Antiq. Soc.)
Remarks on the architecture of the middle ages 1835
—— and Clark, John W. The architectural history of the University of Cambridge, and of the colleges of Cambridge and Eton 1886
Willis' (T.) Remaining medical works tr. 1681
Willison, John The balm of Gilead for healing a diseased land 1742 (1800)
Willmott, Robert E. A. Pleasures, objects, and advantages of literature 1851 (1855)
Willobie, Henry Avisa; or, the true picture of a modest maid 1594 (1635, 1880)
Willock, John Voyages and adventures, (with) remarks on different countries in Europe, Africa and America 1798
Wills, Charles J. In the land of the Lion and the Sun; or modern Persia 1883
Wills, William G. Life's foreshadowings; a novel (anon.) 1859
Wills: see Earliest English wills; Lancashire and Cheshire wills
Wills and inventories from the registers of the Commissary of Bury St. Edmund's 13..–16.. (Camden Soc. 1850)

Wills and inventories, illustrative of the history, manners, language, etc. of the northern counties of England 13..–15.. (Surtees Soc. 1835)
—— Parts II and III entitled Wills and inventories from the Registry at Durham 15..–16.. (Surtees Soc. 1860, 1906)
Wills from Doctors' Commons 1495–1695 (Camden Soc. 1863)
Willsford, Thomas Nature's secrets 1658
The scales of commerce and trade; and Architectonice, or the art of building 1660
Willughby, Francis De historia piscium libri quatuor a 1672 (ed. J. Ray 1686; engraved title Icthyographia 1685)
Ornithologiæ libri tres a 1672 (ed. J. Ray 1676)
—— translated, and enlarged by J. Ray (1678)
Wilmot, Robert The tragedie of Tancred and Gismund 1591 (in Hazl., Dodsley)
Wilson, Alexander American ornithology 1808–13 (1831)
Poems 1790
—— ed. 2, Poems, humorous, satirical and serious 1791
Poems and literary prose a 1813 (ed. Grosart 1876)
Poems, chiefly in the Scottish dialect a 1813 (1816)
Poetical works a 1813 (1857)
Watty and Meg; or the wife reformed (anon.) 1792
Wilson, Andrew The abode of snow; observations on a journey from Chinese Tibet to the Indian Caucasus 1875
Facts and fictions of zoology 1882
Wilson, Arthur The history of Great Britain, being the life and reign of King James the first a 1652 (1653)
The Swisser 1631 (ed. Feuillerat, Paris 1904)
Wilson, Augusta J. Vashti; or, 'Until death us do part' 1867
Wilson, Charles Elements of Hebrew grammar 1782 (1794)
Wilson, Sir Daniel The archæology and prehistoric annals of Scotland 1851 (1863)
Prehistoric man 1862 (1865)
Wilson, Edward Spadacrene Dunelmensis: or a short treatise of an ancient medicinal fountain or vitrioline spaw near Durham 1675
Wilson, Frederick R. An architectural survey of the churches in the archdeaconry of Lindisfarne 1870
Wilson, Gavin A collection of Masonic songs 1787 (1788)
Wilson, George The five gateways of knowledge 1856 (1859)
—— and Geikie, Archibald Memoir of Edward Forbes 1861
Wilson, Henry Schütz Alpine ascents and adventures 1878
Studies in history, legend, and literature 1884
Wilson, Horace H. Works a 1860 (1861–71)
Essays on the religion of the Hindus a 1860 (1862)
A glossary of judicial and revenue terms, from the Arabic, Persian, Hindustani, etc. 1855
Mill's (J.) History of British India Ed. with continuation 1840–46
Wilson, James A complete dictionary of astrology 1819
Wilson, James Biography of the blind 1821 (1835)
Wilson, James Maurice Solid geometry and conic sections 1872
Wilson, John Andronicus Comnenius; a tragedy 1664
Belphegor: or the marriage of the devil. A tragi-comedy 1691
The cheats; a comedy (anon.) 1664 (1671, 1693)
The projectors; a comedy 1665
Wilson, John Synopsis of British plants; with a botanical dictionary 1744
Wilson, John General view of the agriculture of Renfrewshire 1812
Wilson, John Works a 1854 (1855–58)
The city of the plague, and other poems 1816
The Foresters 1825
The isle of palms, and other poems 1812
Lights and shadows of Scottish life (anon.) 1822
Noctes Ambrosianæ 1822–35 (from Blackwood's Mag.)
The recreations of Christopher North 1842
The trials of Margaret Lyndsay (anon.) 1823
Wilson, John British farming 1862
Wilson, John Cook Aristotelian studies 1879
On the traversing of geometrical figures 1905
Wilson, John Mackay Historical, traditionary, and imaginative tales of the Borders, and of Scotland a 1835 (1835–40, 1857–59)
Wilson, John Marius The rural cyclopedia 1847–49
Wilson, Robert A right excellent comedy called The three ladies of London 1584 (in Hazl., Dodsley)
The pleasant and stately morall of the three lordes and three ladies of London 1590 (ibid.)
Wilson, Robert The pleasures of piety, a poem 1837
Poems, chiefly in the Scottish dialect 1822
Wilson, Sir Robert T. Life, from autobiographical memoirs, journals a 1849 (ed. H. Randolph 1862)
Private diary of travels, personal services, and public events 1812–14 a 1849 (1861)
Wilson, Samuel An account of the province of Carolina in America 1682
Wilson, Thomas The arte of rhetorique 1553 (1567)
A discourse vppon vsurye 1572 (1584)
The rule of reason, conteinyng the arte of logique 1551 (1567, 1580)
Wilson, Thomas Jerichoes down-fall 1642 (1643)
Wilson, Bp. Thomas Works a 1755 (1781)
Wilson, Thomas The pitman's pay 1826–30
The pitman's pay, and other poems 1843 (1872)
Wilson, Thomas Woodrow Congressional government; a study in American politics 1885
Public papers, ed. by R. S. Baker and W. E. Dodd (1925)
The State 1893
Wilson, Walter The history and antiquities of dissenting churches and meeting houses in London 1808–14
Wilson, William Poems, chiefly in the Scottish dialect 1824
Wilson, Sir William J. E. The anatomist's vade mecum 1840 (1842)
On diseases of the skin 1847
Wilson, Woodrow: see Wilson, Thomas Woodrow
Wiltshire glossary 1893: see Dartnell, G. E.
Wily beguilde, A pleasant comedie, called 1606 (in Hazl., Dodsley)
Wimbledon, R. A sermon no lesse frutefull then famous (anon.) ? 1550 (1584)
Winchcombe (Gloucestershire). Landboc, sive registrum monasterii beatae Mariae Virginis et Sancti Cenhelmi de Winchelcumba v.d. (1892)

Winchell, Alexander Reconciliation of science and religion 1877
Walks and talks in the geological field 1886
World-life 1883 (1889)
Winchilsea, Anne Finch, Countess of Miscellany poems 1713
Windham, William Diary 1784–1810 (1866)
Speeches in parliament a 1810 (ed. Amyot 1812)
Windisch's (W. O. E.) Compendium of Irish grammar tr. by J. P. M'Swiney 1883
Windle, Sir Bertram C. A. Remains of the prehistoric age in England 1904
Windsor, Arthur L. Ethica; or characteristics of men, manners, and books 1860
Windsor Castle, History of 1749: see Pote, J.
Windsor magazine, The 1895–
Wing, John Abels offering: a sermon 1621
Wingate, Edmund Arithmetique made easie 1630
Λογαριθμοτεχνία, or the construction, and use of the logarithmeticall tables tr. 1635 (ed. 2)
Wingfield, Lewis S. Abigel Rowe, a chronicle of the regency 1883
Winȝet, Ninian Works (Certain tractates, etc.) 1562–63 (S.T.S. 1887–91)
The buke of four scoir thre questions, tueching doctrine etc. 1563
Certane tractatis for reformatioun of doctryne and maneris 1562
The last blast of the trompet of Godis worde aganis the vsurpit auctoritie of Iohne Knox 1562
Vincentius Lirinensis, for the antiquitie and veritie of the Catholik fayth tr. 1563
Winkworth, Susanna The history and life of J. Tauler, with twenty-five of his sermons tr. 1857
Winnere and wastoure 1352 (Roxb. Cl. 1897)
Winslow, Edward A briefe narration of the true grounds or cause of the first planting of New England 1646 (Appendix to next)
Hypocrisie unmasked 1646
A relation or journall of the beginning and proceedings of the English plantation setled at Plimoth in New England 1622
Winslow, Forbes B. On obscure diseases of the brain, and disorders of the mind 1860
Winslow's (J. B.) Anatomical exposition of the structure of the human body tr. G. Douglas 1733
Winslow, Octavius The inner life, its nature, relapse, and recovery 1850
Winsor, Justin Christopher Columbus and the spirit of discovery 1891
From Cartier to Frontenac 1894
The Mississippi Basin: the struggle between England and France, 1697–1763 1895
Winstanley, William England's worthies 1660 (1684)
The lives of the most famous English poets 1687
Winter, George New and compendious system of husbandry 1787 (1788)
'Winter, John Strange' (Mrs. Arthur Stannard) Bootles' baby; a story of the scarlet lancers 1885
In quarters; chronicles of the 25th (the Black Horse) dragoons 1885
Red coats 1894
Winter, William Shakespeare's England 1886
Winterbottom, Thomas M. An account of the native Africans in the neighbourhood of Sierra Leone 1803
Winthrop, John The history of New England a 1649 (1825–26, 1853)
Winthrop, Theodore The canoe and the saddle a 1861 (1862)
Winwood, Sir Ralph Memorials of affairs of state in the reigns of Q. Elizabeth and K. James I, collected (chiefly) from the original papers of Sir R. Winwood a 1617 (1725)
Wirt, William Sketches of the life and character of Patrick Henry 1817 (1818)
Wise, John The Churches quarrel espoused 1772
Wise, John R. The New Forest; its history and its scenery 1862
Wiseman, Nicholas P. S. Fabiola; or the Church of the Catacombs (anon.) 1855
Recollections of the last four Popes and of Rome in their times 1858
Twelve lectures on the connection between science and revealed religion 1836
Wiseman, Richard Severall chirurgical treatises 1676
A treatise of wounds 1672
Wit and science, Marriage of: see Marriage
Wit and science, Moral play of c 1530: see Redford, J.
Wit and wisdom, Marriage of: see Marriage
Wit restor'd, in severall select poems, not formerly publish't (by Sir J. Mennes and J. Smith) 1658
Wit's recreations: see Witts
Withals, John A shorte dictionarie (English and Latin) for yonge begynners 1553 (1556, 1568)
—— The seconde tyme corrected by Lewys Evans 1574 (1602)
Wither or Withers, Fabian Dariot's (C.) Breefe introduction to the astrologicall iudgement of the starres 1583 (1598)
Indagine's (J. ab) Briefe introductions vnto the art of chiromancy or manuel diuination, and physiognomy tr. 1558
—— ed. 1651, entitled The book of palmestry and physiognomy (1683)
Wither, George Workes 1620
Juvenilia 1622, 1633
Miscellaneous works a 1667 (Spenser Soc. 1872–78)
Abuses stript and whipt 1613
—— also the scourge. Epigrams 1613 (1614)
Britains remembrancer, containing a narration of the plague lately past 1628
Campo-Musæ, or the field-musings of Capt. G. W. 1643
A collection of emblemes, ancient and modern 1634–35
Epithalamia: or nuptiall poems 1612
Faire virtue, the mistresse of Philarete (anon.) 1622 (1633; in Arber, Eng. Garner IV)
Fidelia (anon.) 1615 (1617; in Arber, Eng. Garner VI)
Meditations upon the Lord's Prayer 1665
Prince Henries obsequies 1612
The shepherds hunting (anon.) 1615
Vox pacifica 1645
Withers motto. Nec habeo, nec careo, nec curo 1621

Withering, William A botanical arrangement of all the vegetables naturally growing in Great Britain 1776
—— ed. 2, entitled A botanical arrangement of British plants 1787–92; ed. 3, 1796
—— ed. 4, enlarged by W. Withering (the younger) (1801); ed. 5 (1812)
Witherings, John The orders, lawes, and ancient customes of swanns 1632 (1664; in Harl. Misc.)
Withers, Robert A description of the Grand Signour's seraglio. (ed. J. Greaves) 1650 (1653)
Wittie, Robert Primrose's (J.) Popular errors; or, the errours of the people in physick tr. 1651
Pyrologia mimica; or, an answer to Hydrologia chymica of W. Sympson 1669
Witts recreations (by Sir J. Mennes and J. Smith), with a thousand outlandish proverbs (selected by Mr. G. Herbert) 1640 (1663)
Wodenote, Theophilus Hermes theologus; or, a divine Mercurie despatcht with a grave message of new descants upon old records 1649
Wodroephe, John The spared houres of a souldier in his travels; or the true marrowe of the French tongue 1623 (1625)
Wodrow, Robert Collections upon the lives of the reformers and most eminent ministers of the Church of Scotland a 1734 (Maitland Cl. 1834–45)
Correspondence 1694–1732 (Wodrow Soc. 1842–43)
History of the sufferings of the Church of Scotland from the Restauration to the Revolution 1721–22 (1828–30)
The life of James Wodrow a 1734 (1828)
Wodrow Society, Publications of (1842–47)
—— Miscellany of (1844)
Woglom, Gilbert T. Parakites. A treatise on the making and flying of tailless kites for scientific purposes and for recreation 1896
Wohunge of ure lauerd, The a 1240 (in Old English homilies, I, E.E.T.S. 1868)
Wolcot, John ('Peter Pindar') Works 1794–1801, 1809, 1812, 1816, a 1819 (1824)
A benevolent epistle to Sylvanus Urban 1790
The Lousiad, an heroi-comic poem 1785–95
Lyric odes to the royal academicians 1782
More lyric odes to the royal academicians 1783
Subjects for painters 1789
Wolfenden, R. Norris Joal's Respiration in singing tr. 1895
Wollaston, William The religion of nature delineated (anon.) 1722 (1738)
Wolley, Charles A two years' journal in New York 1701 (1860)
Wolley, Edward: see Scudery, G. de
Wolley, Hannah: see Woolley, H.
Wollocombe, John B. From morn till eve: reminiscences 1898
Wollstonecraft (afterwards Godwin), Mary An historical and moral view of the origin and progress of the French Revolution 1794
Letters to Imlay a 1797 (1879)
Letters written during a short residence in Sweden, Norway and Denmark 1796
Posthumous works a 1797 (1798)
A vindication of the rights of woman 1792
Wolseley, Garnet J. W., Viscount The life of John Churchill, duke of Marlborough, to the accession of queen Anne 1894
The soldier's pocket-book for field service 1869
Woman of fashion, The 1767
Woman of honor, The 1768
Women saints. The lives of women saints of our contrie of England c 1610 (E.E.T.S. 1886)
Womock, Laurence Aron-bimnucha 1663
The examination of Tilenus before the triers 1658
Wonders of the physical world 1875
Wood, Alphonso The American botanist and florist 1866
A class-book of botany 1845 (1850)
Wood, Anthony Athenæ Oxonienses. An exact history of all the writers and bishops who have had their education in the university of Oxford from 1500 to 1690; to which are added, the fasti or annals of the said university 1691–92 (1721, 1813–20)
The history and antiquities of the colleges and halls in the university of Oxford; from the original MS. in the Bodleian Library; with continuation by John Gutch a 1695 (1786–90)
The history and antiquities of the university of Oxford; rom the original MS. in the Bodleian Library a 1695 (1792–96)
Life, from 1632 to 1672, written by himself; continued till 1695 a 1695 (1772, 1848, O.H.S. 1891–1900)
Survey of the antiquities of the city of Oxford 1661–66 (ed. Andrew Clark, O.H.S. 1889–99)
Wood, Ellen P.: see Wood, Mrs. Henry
Wood, George B. A treatise on therapeutics and pharmacology or materia medica 1856
Wood, H. Freeman The Englishman of the Rue Caîn 1889
The passenger from Scotland Yard 1888
Wood, Mrs. Henry The Channings 1862
East Lynne 1861
Elster's folly 1866
Lady Adelaide's oath 1867
A life's secret 1867
Lord Oakburn's daughters 1864
The master of Greylands 1873
Mildred Arkell 1865
Mrs. Halliburton's troubles 1862
Orville college 1867
Oswald Cray 1864
Parkwater 1876
Pomeroy Abbey 1878
The shadow of Ashlydyat 1863
St. Martin's eve 1866
Trevlyn Hold 1864
Verner's pride 1863
Wood, Horace G. A treatise on the limitation of actions at law and in equity 1883
Wood, Horatio C. A contribution to the history of the fresh-water algæ of North America 1872 (Smithsonian Contrib. knowl. XIX)
A treatise on therapeutics 1874 (1879)
Wood, James The elements of optics 1798 (1828)
The principles of mechanics 1796 (1803)
Wood, John G. The (boy's) modern playmate 1870 (1890)
The common objects of the sea shore 1858

Wood, John G. (cont.)
Homes without hands 1865 (1868)
The illustrated natural history 1853 (1855, 1859–63)
Out of doors: a selection of original articles on practical natural history 1874
The popular natural history 1867
Sketches and anecdotes of animal life 1854; second series 1855
Wood, Mary A. E.: see Green, M. A. E.
Wood, Michael Gardiner's (S.) De vera obedientia tr. 1553
Wood, Nicholas A practical treatise on rail-roads 1825 (1838)
Wood, Mrs. Nugent and Lapham, H. Waiting for the mail 1875 (Melbourne)
Wood, Owen An alphabetical book of physicall secrets, for all those diseases that are most predominant and dangerous in the body of man 1639
Wood, Robert An essay on the original genius of Homer (anon.) 1769
—— ed. 2, with a comparative view of the ancient and present state of the Troade a 1771 (1775)
Wood, Shakspere The new curiosum urbis: a guide to ancient and modern Rome 1875
Wood, Thomas An institute of the laws of England 1720 (1722)
Wood, William New Englands prospect 1634 (1865)
Wood, William A survey of trade 1718 (1719)
Wood, William The great advantages of our colonies and plantations to Great Britain 1775
Woodall, John The surgions mate 1617
—— with a treatise of yᵉ cure of yᵉ plague 1639
Viaticum, being the path-way to the surgions chest 1628
Woodbury, Walter E. The encyclopædia of photography 1892
Woodcocke, G. Justinus' (M. J.) Historie tr. G. W. 1606
Wooden world dissected, The 1706: see Ward, E.
Woodes, Nathaniel An excellent new comedie, intituled: The conflict of conscience 1581 (in Hazl., Dodsley)
Woodhead, Abraham The life of S. Teresa (anon.; tr. from Spanish) 1671
Motives to holy living a 1678 (1688)
Woodhouse, Robert An elementary treatise on astronomy 1812
Woods, Leonard Works 1851
Lectures on Church government 1844
Woods, Nicholas A. The Prince of Wales in Canada and the United States 1861
Woodward, Arthur S. Outlines of vertebrate palæontology 1898
Woodward, Horace B. The geology of England and Wales 1876
Woodward, John An account of some Roman urns 1713
—— ed. 3, entitled, Remarks upon the antient and present state of London, occasion'd by some Roman urns, coins, and other antiquities 1723
An attempt towards a natural history of the fossils of England a 1728 (1728–29)
An essay towards a natural history of the earth 1695 (1723)
Woodward, John and Burnett, George A treatise on heraldry 1892 (1896)
Woodward, Josiah An account of the rise and progress of religious societies in the city of London 1697 (1701)
Woodward, Samuel P. A manual of the mollusca; or, a rudimentary treatise of recent and fossil shells 1851–56
Woolley, Hannah The gentlewoman's companion 1675
The queen-like closet 1670
Woolman, John Journal of the life, gospel labours and Christian experiences of J. W. 1776
Woolner, Thomas My beautiful lady a 1861 (1863)
Woolsey, Theodore D. Communism and socialism in their history and theory 1880
Introduction to the study of international law 1860 (1864, 1875)
Woolson, Constance F. Anne; a novel 1883
Jupiter lights: a novel 1889
Woolton, Bp. John The christian manuell 1576 (Parker Soc. 1851)
Worboise, Emma J. Sissie 1882
Worcester, Bp. of 1690: see Stillingfleet, E.
Worcester, Earl of: see Tiptoft, J.
Worcester, Edward Somerset, 2nd Marquis of A century of.. inventions 1655 (1663, 1865)
An exact and true definition of the most stupendious water-commanding engine 1663
Worcester, Joseph E. A dictionary of the English language 1860
A universal and critical dictionary of the English language 1846
Worcester, William: see Botoner, W.
Worcestershire (West) glossary 1882: see Chamberlain, Mrs.
Words by an eyewitness 1901: see 'Linesman'
Wordsworth, Charles Annals of my early life, 1806–45 1891
Annals of my life, 1847–56 a 1892 (1893)
Wordsworth, Christopher (of Trinity College, Cambridge) Ecclesiastical biography 1810 (1853)
Who wrote Εἰκὼν Βασιλική? considered and answered in two letters, addressed to the Archbishop of Canterbury 1824
—— Documentary supplement 1825
King Charles the first, the author of Icôn Basilikè, further proved 1828
Wordsworth, Bp. Christopher Memoirs of William Wordsworth 1851
Miscellanies: literary and religious v.d. (1879)
Theophilus Anglicanus; or, instructions concerning the Church and the Anglican branch of it 1843 (1850)
Christopher Wordsworth, Bishop of Lincoln, 1807–1885. By J. H. Overton and Elizabeth Wordsworth (1888, 1890)
Wordsworth, Christopher Rutland words 1891 (E.D.S.)
Scholae academicae; some account of the studies at the English universities in the eighteenth century 1877
Social life at the English universities in the eighteenth century 1874
Wordsworth, William Poetical works v.d. (1849, 1888, 1895)
Poems (1807)
Prose works v.d. (Grosart 1876)
The Borderers; a tragedy 1795–96 (1842)
The excursion 1814
Peter Bell 1819

Wordsworth, William (cont.)
The prelude; or, growth of a poet's mind 1799–1805 (1850)
The white doe of Rylstone 1815
Worfat, William de: see Hutton, William
Worke for cutlers; or a merry dialogue betweene sword, rapier and dagger 1615
Workhouses. An account of several work-houses for employing and maintaining the poor 1725 (1732)
Workman, Fanny B. and William H. Algerian memories. A bicycle tour over the Atlas to the Sahara 1896
Workshop receipts 1873–85: see Spon, Ernest
World, The 1874–1921
World and the child. A propre new interlude of the worlde and the chylde, otherwyse called Mundus & infans c 1500 (Roxb. Club 1817; Hazl., Dodsley; Manly, Pre-Shaks. drama)
Worlidge, John Apiarium; or a discourse of bees 1676
Systema agriculturæ; the mystery of husbandry discovered 1669 (1681)
—— To which is added, Kalendarium rusticum and Dictionarium rusticum 1675 (1681)
Vinetum Britannicum; or a treatise of cider 1676 (1691)
Wornum, Ralph N. Analysis of ornament 1856
—— ed. 2, entitled The characteristics of styles 1861
Ed. Lectures on painting, by the Royal Academicians Barry, Opie, and Fuseli v.d. (1848)
Worsaae, Jens J. A. The industrial arts of Denmark from the earliest times to the Danish conquest of England 1882
Worthington, John Miscellanies a 1671 (1704)
Wotton, Anthony An answere to a popish pamphlet, entituled, Certaine articles discouering the absurdities of the Protestants religion 1605
Runne from Rome 1624
Wotton, Henry A courtlie controuersie of Cupids cautels tr. 1578
Wotton, Sir Henry Reliquiæ Wottonianæ; or a collection of lives, letters, poems, etc. a 1639 (1651, 1654, 1672, 1685)
The elements of architecture 1624
A short view of the life and death of George Villiers duke of Buckingham a 1639 (1642)
See also Smith, L. P.
Wotton, William The history of Rome from the death of Antoninus Pius to the death of Severus Alexander 1701
Reflections upon ancient and modern learning 1694 (1697)
Woty, William Poetical works 1770
Poems on several occasions 1780
Wrangham, Francis The Pleiad; or, a series of abridgements of seven distinguished writers, in opposition to the pernicious doctrine of deism 1820
Wraxall, Sir Frederick C. L. Hugo's (V. M.) Les misérables tr. 1862
Life in the sea; or the nature and habits of marine animals 1860
Memoirs of Robert-Houdin by himself tr. 1859
Wild oats 1858
Wraxall, Sir Nathaniel W. Historical memoirs of my own time, from 1772 to 1784 1815
Memoirs of the courts of Berlin, Dresden, Warsaw, and Vienna in the years 1777–79 1799
A tour through some of the northern parts of Europe 1775 (1776)
Wren, Christopher Parentalia; or memoirs of the family of the Wrens, compiled by Christopher Wren and published by Stephen Wren a 1747 (1750)
Wren, Bp. Matthew A sermon preached before the Kings Majestie 1627
Wren, Matthew Monarchy asserted 1659
Wright, Abraham Five sermons in five several styles or waies of preaching 1656
Wright, Edward Certaine errors in navigation 1599 (partly in Arber, Eng. Garner III)
Stevin's (S.) Haven finding art, by the latitude and variation tr. 1599
Wright, Edward P. Animal life 1879
Figuier's (L.) Ocean world tr. 1872
Wright, Frances Views of society and manners in America (anon.) 1821
Wright, Herbert E. A handy book for brewers 1892
Wright, Major J. Camus' (J. P.) Nature's paradox tr. 1652
Wright, James Historia histrionica 1699 (in Hazl., Dodsley; Arber, Eng. Garner II)
Wright, Joseph The English dialect dictionary 1896–1905
A grammar of the dialect of Windhill, in the West Riding of Yorkshire 1892 (E.D.S.)
—— and Wright, Elizabeth Mary Old English grammar 1908
Wright, Leonard The hunting of Antichrist 1589
Wright, Lewis The illustrated book of poultry: with practical schedules 1873
Wright, Thomas The passions of the minde 1601 (1621)
Wright, Thomas The Celt, the Roman, and the Saxon 1852
Dictionary of obsolete and provincial English 1857
Early travels in Palestine 1848
Essays on archæological subjects, and on various questions connected with the history of art, science and literature in the middle ages 1861
Essays on subjects connected with the literature, popular superstitions, and history of England in the middle ages 1846
A history of domestic manners and sentiments in England during the middle ages 1862
The homes of other days; a history of domestic manners and sentiments in England 1871
Ed. Political poems and songs v.d. (Rolls series 1859–61)
Ed. Political songs of England v.d. (Camden Soc. 1839)
Ed. Popular treatises on science v.d. (1841)
Ed. Specimens of lyric poetry a 1310 (Percy Soc. 1842)
Ed. A volume of vocabularies v.d. (1857); a second volume (1873)
Anglo-Saxon and Old English vocabularies. Second edition, ed. R. P. Wülcker (Wright-Wülcker) (1884)
—— and Halliwell, James O. Ed. Reliquiæ antiquæ v.d. (1841–43)
Wright, Walter R. Horæ Ionicæ: a poem descriptive of the Ionian Islands 1809
Wright, William Aldis: see Eastwood, J.
Wright's chaste wife, The c 1462 (E.E.T.S. 1865, 1869)

Wrighte, William Grotesque architecture 1767 (1790)
Wriglesworth, Captain W. MS. Log-book of the 'Lyell' 1730
Wriothesley, Charles A chronicle of England during the reigns of the Tudors 1485–1559 (Camden Soc. 1875–77)
Wroth or Wroath, Lady Mary The Countesse of Mountgomeries Urania 1621
Wülcker, R. P.: see Wright, T.
Wuertz' (F.) Surgeons guid tr. (and ed. by William Johnson) 1658
Wulfstan Homilies a 1023 (Napier 1883)
Wundt's (W.) Lectures on human and animal psychology tr. J. E. Creighton and E. B. Titchener 1894
Wurtz' (C. A.) Atomic theory tr. E. Cleminshaw 1880
Wyatt (Captain) The voyage of Robert Dudley, afterwards earl of Warwick and Leicester and duke of Northumberland, to the West Indies, 1594–95, narrated by capt. Wyatt, by himself, and by Abram Kendall, master c 1595 (Hakluyt Soc. 1899)
Wyatt, Sir Thomas Poetical works a 1542 (1810, 1816, 1821, 1913)
Wyche, Sir Peter A short relation of the river Nile tr. 1669 (1798)
Wycherley, William Posthumous works a 1716 (1728–29)
Dramatic works a 1716 (1840)
The country-wife 1675
The gentleman dancing-master 1673
Love in a wood 1672
The plain-dealer 1676
Wycket, Wycklyffes ? a 1500 (1546; ed. Pantin 1828)
Wyclif, John English works c 1380 (E.E.T.S. 1880)
Select English works c 1380 (1869–71)
Three treatises c 1380 (ed. Todd 1851)
The Holy Bible, made from the Latin Vulgate by John Wycliffe and his followers 1382, 1388 (ed. J. Forshall and Sir F. Madden 1850)
Wydeville, Anthony: see Rivers, Earl
Wyfe lapped in Morrelles skin, The c 1550 (in T. Amyot's Old taming of a shrew, Shaks. Soc. 1844; Hazlitt, Early pop. poetry, IV, 1866)
Wyl Bucke his testament: see Lacy, John
Wylde, James Ed. The circle of the sciences 1862–67
Wylde, Zachary The English master of defence 1711
Wylie, James H. History of England under Henry the fourth 1884–98
Wyll of the devill, The c 1550 (c 1825; Jyl of Brentford etc., Ballad Soc. 1871)
Wyllie, John W. S. Essays on the external policy of India a 1870 (1875)
Wylson, Thomas Demosthenes' Three orations in fauour of the Olynthians with fower orations against King Philip 1570
Wyndham, Anne Claustrum regale reseratum; or the King's concealment at Trent 1667 (1681)
Wyndham, Henry P. A gentleman's tour through Monmouthshire and Wales (anon.) 1775
Wynn, Sir John The history of the Gwedir family a 1600 (1878)
Wynter, Andrew Curiosities of civilization 1860
Our social bees; or pictures of town and country life 1861
Wyntoun, Andrew of Þe orygynale cronykil of Scotland c 1425 (1795, 1872–79, S.T.S. 1903–08)
Wyrley, William The true use of armorie 1592
Wyse, Sir Thomas An excursion in the Peloponnesus 1865
Wythe, George Decisions of cases in Virginia by the High Court of Chancery 1795
Wyvill, Sir Christopher The pretensions of the triple crown examined 1672

Y

Y., R.: see Younge, Richard
Yalden, Thomas Poems a 1736 (1790, 1810)
Yale. Studies from the Yale psychological laboratory ed. E. W. Scripture 1893–
Yarington, Robert Two lamentable tragedies 1601 (in Bullen, Old plays, IV, 1885)
Yarranton, Andrew England's improvement by sea and land 1677
Yarrell, William A history of British birds 1843
A history of British fishes 1835–39
—— ed. 3, ed. by Sir J. Richardson (1859)
Yate, William An account of New Zealand 1835
Yates, Edmund H. The black sheep 1867
Broken to harness; a story of English domestic life 1864
The forlorn hope 1867
Land at last 1866
The rock ahead 1868
Edmund Yates: his recollections and experiences 1884
Yates, John Ibis ad Cæsarem 1626
Year-book of facts in science and (the useful) art(s) 1839–80
Yearbook of medicine, surgery, and their allied sciences 1859–62 1860–63 (New Sydenham Soc.)
Year books of the reign of Edward I. Years 20–22, 30–35 1292–94, 1302–07 (ed. and tr. A. J. Horwood, Rolls series 1863–79)
—— of Edward II 1307–15 (ed. F. W. Maitland, etc., Selden Soc. 1903–27)
—— of Edward III. Years 11–20 1337–46 (ed. and tr. A. J. Horwood and L. O. Pike, Rolls series 1883–1911)
—— of Edward II to Henry VIII v.d. (15.., 16.., 1678–80)
Yeats, John The growth and vicissitudes of commerce 1872
The natural history of commerce 1870
The technical history of commerce 1871
Yeats, William B. The Celtic twilight: men and women, dhouls and faeries 1893
Fairy and folk tales of the Irish peasantry 1888
Yellow book, The, an illustrated quarterly 1894–97
Yeomans, John The Abecedarian, or, philosophic comment upon the English alphabet 1759
Yeowell, James Chronicles of the ancient British Church 1839 (1847)
Yong, Bartholomew: see Young, B.

Yonge, Charles D. Athenæus' Deipnosophists tr. 1854
Yonge, Charlotte M. Cameos from English history 1868–99
The clever woman of the family 1865
Countess Kate 1862
The daisy chain; or, aspirations 1856
The dove in the eagle's nest 1866
Dynevor Terrace; or, the clue of life 1857
The heir of Redclyffe 1853
History of Christian names 1863
Hopes and fears; or, scenes from the life of a spinster 1860
John Keble's parishes: a history of Hursley and Otterbourne 1898
Lads and lasses of Langley 1881
Landmarks of history; ancient history 1852
—— middle ages 1853
—— modern history 1857
Life of John Coleridge Patteson, missionary bishop of the Melanesian Islands 1874
The Stokesley secret 1861
A storehouse of stories 1870–72
The trial; more links of the daisy chain 1864
The young step-mother; or, a chronicle of mistakes 1861
See also Monthly packet
Yonge, James The gouernaunce of prynces 1422 (in Secreta secretorum, E.E.T.S. 1898)
Yonge, Nicholas Musica transalpina. Madrigales translated of foure, fiue and sixe partes 1588 (in Arber, Eng. Garner III)
Yonge, Walter Diary 1604–28 (Camden Soc. 1848)
York memorandum book 1376–1493 (Surtees Soc. 1912–15)
York Minster, Fabric rolls of v.d. (Surtees Soc. 1859)
York mysteries. (York plays. The plays performed by the crafts or mysteries of York on the day of Corpus Christi) c 1440 (1885)
York wills: see Testamenta Eboracensia
Yorke, James The union of honour 1640
Yorkshire archæological and topographical journal, The 1870–
Yorkshire chantry surveys (The certificates of the commissioners appointed to survey the chantries, guilds, hospitals, etc., in the county of York) 1546 (Surtees Soc. 1894–95)
Yorkshire dialogue in Yorkshire dialect; between an awd wife, a lass, and a butcher 1673 (in Nine specim. Eng. dialects, E.D.S. 1896)
See also Meriton, G.
Yorkshire glossary 1876: see Robinson, C. C.
Yorkshire tragedy, A 1608 (in Shakespeare Apocrypha 1908)
Yoshiwara episode: see Murdoch, A.
Youatt, William Cattle 1834
The dog 1845 (1858)
The horse (anon.) 1831 (1843)
Sheep (anon.) 1837
Youmans, Edward L. The hand-book of household science 1857
Young, Arthur An historical dissertation on idolatrous corruptions in religion 1734
Young, Arthur General view of the agriculture of the county of Essex 1807
—— of Hertfordshire 1804
—— of Lincoln 1799
—— of Norfolk 1804
—— of Oxfordshire 1809
—— of Suffolk 1794
The farmer's letters to the people of England, containing the sentiments of a practical husbandman (anon.) 1767
A tour in Ireland 1776–79 1780 (1887)
Travels 1787–89; undertaken with a view of ascertaining the cultivation, etc. of the kingdom of France 1792
Autobiography, with selections from his correspondence a 1820 (ed. M. Betham-Edwards 1898)
See also Annals of agriculture
Young, Arthur, the younger General view of the agriculture of the county of Sussex 1793 (1808)
Young, Arthur Nautical dictionary 1846 (1863)
Young or Yong, Bartholomew Boccaccio's (G.) Amorous Fiammetta tr. 1587
Montemayor's (J. de) Diana tr. 1598
See also Pettie, G.
Young, Charles A. The sun 1882
Young, David and Brown, John Memorials of Alexander Moncrieff and James Fisher 1849
Young, Edward Sermons on several occasions 1702–03
Young, Edward Works 1757
Poems a 1765 (1810)
The brothers; a tragedy 1753
Busiris, king of Egypt; a tragedy 1719
The Centaur not fabulous 1755
The complaint; or, night-thoughts on life, death and immortality (anon.) 1742–45
Conjectures on original composition 1759
The force of religion; or, vanquish'd love 1714
Love of fame 1728: see The universal passion
A paraphrase on part of the book of Job 1719
A poem on the last day 1713
Resignation 1762
The revenge; a tragedy 1721
The universal passion 1725–28
—— republished with title Love of fame, the universal passion 1728
A vindication of providence; or a true estimate of human life 1728
Life and letters by Henry C. Shelley (1914)
Young, Francis Chilton-: see Chilton-Young, F.
Young, George A geological survey of the Yorkshire coast 1822
Young, Jennie J. The ceramic art 1878 (1879)
Young, John The province of reason 1860
Young, John R. Mathematical dissertations 1841
The theory and practice of navigation and nautical astronomy 1856
Young, Thomas Englands bane, or, the description of drunkennesse 1617
Young, Thomas A course of lectures on natural philosophy and the mechanical arts 1807
—— new ed. by Prof. Kelland (1845)
Young gentleman's magazine, The 1869–73

Young man's calling, The, or the whole duty of youth (by Samuel Crossman) 1678
Younge, Richard The blemish of government, the shame of religion, the disgrace of mankind; or, a charge drawn up against drunkards 1655 (1863)
The drunkard's character, or, a true drunkard with such sinnes as raigne in him 1638
The victory of patience, and benefit of affliction 1636 (partly in Arber, Eng. Garner IV)
Younger, John Autobiography a 1860 (1881)
Younghusband, Ethel Glimpses of East Africa and Zanzibar 1910
Younghusband, Sir Francis E. The heart of a continent 1896
Yule, Sir Henry The book of ser Marco Polo tr. 1871
A narrative of the mission sent to the Court of Ava in 1855 1858
—— and Burnell, Arthur C. Hobson-Jobson: being a glossary of Anglo-Indian colloquial words and phrases 1886
Yule-tide stories 1853: see Thorpe, B.
Ywaine and Gawin c 1400 (in Ritson, Metrical romances I, 1802)

Z

'Zack' (Gwendoline Keats) On trial 1899
Tales of Dunstable weir 1901
The white cottage 1901
Zaehnsdorf, Joseph W. The art of bookbinding 1880
A short history of bookbinding 1895
Zangwill, Israel The Bachelor's club 1891
The big Bow mystery 1892
Children of the Ghetto 1892
The master 1895
Zeitschrift für deutsches Alterthum, herausgegeben von Moriz Haupt (und E. Steinmeyer) 1841–
Zeluca; or, educated and uneducated woman 1815
Zepheria (an amatory poem) 1594 (1842; in Arber, Eng. Garner V)
Zerffi, Gustavus G. Lectures delivered before the Sunday Lecture Society 1878

Ziegler's (E.) Text-book of pathological anatomy tr. by D. Mac Alister 1883–84
Ziemssen's (H. W. von) Cyclopædia of the practice of medicine tr. 1875–80 Suppl. 1881
Zimmermann's (J. G. von) Solitude tr. 1791 (1811, 1855)
Zimmern, Alice Blümner's (H.) Home life of the ancient Greeks tr. 1893
Zincke, Foster B. Wherstead, some materials for its history 1887 (1893)
Zittel's (K. A. von) History of geology and palæontology tr. by Maria M. Ogilvie-Gordon 1901
Zoflora, or, the generous negro girl (tr. from the French of J. B. Picquenard) 1804
Zoological journal, The 1825–26
Zoological Society of London, Proceedings of the 1833–
—— Transactions 1835–
—— List of the vertebrated animals now or lately living in the gardens 1883 (ed. 8)
Zoologist, The; a miscellany of natural history 1843–
Zosimus' New history tr. 1684
Zouch, Thomas Works a 1815 (1820)
Zouche, Richard The dove: or passages of cosmography 1613